German	Abbr	English
Meteorologie	*Met*	meteorology
Metallurgie, Hüttenkunde	*Metal*	metallurgy
militärisch	*Mil*	military
Bergbau	*Min*	mining
Mineralogie	*Miner*	mineralogy
Straßenverkehr	*Mot*	motoring and transport
Musik	*Mus*	music
Mythologie	*Myth*	mythology
Substantiv, Hauptwort	*n*	noun
nautisch, Seefahrt	*Naut*	nautical
verneint	*neg*	negative
nordenglisch	*N Engl*	Northern English
norddeutsch	*N Ger*	North German
Nationalsozialismus	*NS*	Nazism
Neutrum	*nt*	neuter
Zahlwort	*num*	numeral
Objekt	*obj*	object
obsolet, ausgestorben	*obs*	obsolete
veraltet	*old*	
Optik	*Opt*	optics
Ornithologie, Vogelkunde	*Orn*	ornithology
Parlament	*Parl*	parliament
Passiv	*pass*	passive
pejorativ, abschätzig	*pej*	pejorative

German	Abbr	English
regelmäßig	*reg*	regular
Relativ-	*rel*	relative
Religion	*Rel*	religion
jemand(em, -en)	*sb*	somebody
Schulwesen	*Sch*	school
Naturwissenschaften	*Sci*	science
schottisch	*Scot*	Scottish
Bildhauerei	*Sculpt*	sculpture
trennbar	*sep*	separable
Handarbeiten	*Sew*	sewing
süddeutsch	*S Ger*	South German
Singular, Einzahl	*sing*	singular
Skisport	*Ski*	skiing
Slang, Jargon	*sl*	slang
Sozialwissenschaften	*Sociol*	social sciences
Raumfahrt	*Space*	space flight
Fachausdruck	*spec*	specialist term
Börse	*St Ex*	Stock Exchange
etwas	*sth*	something
Konjunktiv	*subjunc*	subjunctive
Suffix, Nachsilbe	*suf*	suffix
Superlativ	*superl*	superlative
Landvermessung	*Surv*	surveying
schweizerisch	*Sw*	Swiss
Technik	*Tech*	technology
Nachrichtentechnik	*Telec*	telecommunications
Textilien	*Tex*	textiles
Theater	*Theat*	theatre, theater
Fernsehen	*TV*	television
Typografie, Buchdruck	*Typ*	typography and printing
Hochschule	*Univ*	university
(nord)amerikanisch	*US*	(North) American
gewöhnlich	*usu*	usually
Verb	*vb*	verb
Tiermedizin	*Vet*	veterinary medicine
intransitives Verb	*vi*	intransitive verb
reflexives Verb	*vr*	reflexive verb
transitives Verb	*vt*	transitive verb
transitives und intransitives Verb	*vti*	transitive and intransitive verb
transitives, intransitives und reflexives Verb	*vtir*	transitive, intransitive and reflexive verb

GROSSWÖRTERBUCH
DEUTSCH ▶ENGLISCH
ENGLISCH ▶DEUTSCH
GERMAN ▶ENGLISH
ENGLISH ▶GERMAN
DICTIONARY

German–English
English–German
Dictionary

UNABRIDGED

Fifth Edition

by
Peter Terrell
Veronika Schnorr Wendy V.A Smith
Roland Breitsprecher

Collins
An Imprint of HarperCollins*Publishers*

fifth edition 2004

© William Collins Sons & Co. Ltd. 1980
© HarperCollins Publishers 1991, 1997, 1999, 2004

HarperCollins Publishers
Westerhill Road, Bishopbriggs, Glasgow G64 2QT
Great Britain

www.collins.co.uk

Collins® and Bank of English® are registered trademarks of
HarperCollins Publishers Limited

ISBN 0-00-712630-1

This edition prepared by Collins in collaboration with
Langenscheidt editorial staff

HarperCollins Publishers, Inc.
10 East 53rd Street, New York, NY 10022

ISBN 0-06-073381-0

Library of Congress Cataloging-in-Publication Data has been applied for

www.harpercollins.com

First HarperCollins edition published 1991

HarperCollins books may be purchased for educational, business, or sales
promotional use. For information, please write to: Special Markets Department,
HarperCollins Publishers Inc., 10 East 53rd Street, New York, NY 10022

Acknowledgements
We would like to thank those authors and publishers who kindly gave
permission for copyright material to be used in the Bank of English. We
would also like to thank Times Newspapers Ltd for providing valuable data.

Note
Entered words that we have reason to believe constitute trademarks have
been designated as such. However, neither the presence nor absence of such
designation should be regarded as affecting the legal status of any trademark.

A catalogue record for this book is available from the British Library

Typeset by Druckhaus Thomas Münzer, Germany

Printed in Italy by Legoprint S.P.A.

FIFTH EDITION   FÜNFTE AUFLAGE

Publishing Director   **Gesamtleitung**

Lorna Sinclair Knight   Vincent Docherty

Project Management   **Projektleitung**

Michela Clari   Dorothée Ronge

Senior Editors   **Leitende Redakteure**

Maree Airlie   Joyce Littlejohn

Editors   **Redakteure**

Susie Beattie   Martin Fellermayer   Eveline Ohneis-Borzacchiello

Contributions from   **Mitarbeit**

Horst Kopleck   Sonia Brough

Data management   **Datenverarbeitung**

Oliver Schweiberer   Uli Stühlen

FOURTH EDITION VIERTE AUFLAGE

Publishing Director **Gesamtleitung**

Lorna Sinclair Knight

Project Management **Projektleitung**

Michela Clari

Senior Editors **Leitende Redakteure**

Horst Kopleck
Maree Airlie

Editors **Redakteure**

Veronika Schnorr   Christine Bahr
Susie Beattie   Stuart Fortey
Phyllis Gautier   Sigrid Janssen   Barbara Neeb
Robin Sawers   Eva Vennebusch
Sabine Citron
Daphne Day   Janet Gough

Contributions from **Mitarbeit**

Elspeth Anderson   Alexa Barnes   Bob Grossmith
Ulrike Seeberger   Claire Singer
Katerina Stein   Beate Wengel

Editorial Coordination **Koordination**

Joyce Littlejohn   Caitlin McMahon

Editorial staff **Redaktionelle Mitarbeit**

Jill Williams   Maggie Seaton
Sandra Harper   Anne Lindsay
Anne Marie Banks   Anne Convery   Alice Grandison
Irene Lakhani   Cindy Mitchell   Helga Panfil

Data management **Datenverarbeitung**

Ray Carrick   Paul Hassett   Sorcha Lenagh

SECOND AND THIRD EDITIONS   ZWEITE UND DRITTE AUFLAGE

Senior Editors   Leitende Redakteure

Peter Terrell
Horst Kopleck
Helga Holtkamp   John Whitlam

Publishing staff   Verlagsangestellte

Lorna Sinclair   Vivian Marr
Diana Feri   Stephen Clarke
Joyce Littlejohn   Diane Robinson   Christine Bahr

Contributions from   Mitarbeit

Veronika Schnorr
Michael Finn   Tim Connell
Roland Breitsprecher

FIRST EDITION   ERSTE AUSGABE

Senior Editors   Leitende Redakteure

Peter Terrell
Veronika Schnorr   Wendy V. A. Morris
Roland Breitsprecher

Editors   Redakteure

Dr Kathryn Rooney   Ingrid Schumacher   Dr Lorna A. Sinclair
Dorothee Ziegler   Ulrike Seeberger   Petra Schlupp

Compilers   Mitarbeiter

Dr Christine R. Barker   Angelika Moeller
Alexa H. Barnes   Günter Ohnemus
Michael Clark   Dr John Pheby
Francis J. Flaherty   Irmgard Rieder
Susanne Flatauer   Hanns Schumacher
Ian Graham   Olaf Thyen
Barbara Hellmann   Karin Wiese
Birgit Kahl   Renate Zenker-Callum
Christian Kay

Collins staff   Verlagsangestellte

Richard Thomas
Anne Dickinson   Irene Lakhani
Susan Dunsmore   Valerie McNulty   Alice Truten
Elspeth Anderson

CONTENTS

INHALT

INTRODUCTION

Since it was first published in 1980, the COLLINS GER-MAN DICTIONARY has become one of the standard reference works of its kind. The scale of its coverage as well as the clarity and accuracy of the information it provides have made it a recognized authority in both English- and German-speaking countries.

The scope and nature of the language treated

The emphasis is firmly placed on contemporary language. The range is wide: the headwords and compounds, phrases and idioms have been selected and arranged to present the user with the authentic language he or she will meet daily in newspapers, journals, books and in the street.

Particular attention has been paid to recent coinages and new meanings not found in existing bilingual dictionaries and even absent from some monolingual volumes, but essential if the dictionary is truly to reflect current, living language as it is spoken and written today.

Space has been found, too, for a considerable representation of the vocabulary of literature and science, and especially of those areas which have contributed notably to the modern consciousness – business, computing, education, the environment, medicine, politics, and so on.

One of our primary concerns has been to make the dictionary equally valid for German-speaking and English-speaking users. Our rigorous policy that every German word in the dictionary has been created and vetted by *German* lexicographers and every English word by *English* lexicographers, with constant discussion between them, means that German-speaking and English-speaking users can approach this dictionary with equal confidence. In addition, we have taken care that each side of the dictionary is equally helpful for translation from and into the foreign language.

The geographical spread of language is not neglected either. A wide coverage of American English is given. Swiss, Austrian and former East German usages are treated. And regionalisms from within the main body of British English and German are covered.

Layout and help

However well-chosen the content of a dictionary may be, much of its value is instantly lost if the user cannot easily and quickly find his or her way to the meaning that meets his needs. So we have put considerable effort into devising and implementing a comprehensive system of indicating material.

Not only are all complex entries clearly divided into separate areas of meaning, but the sense of each area is signposted by 'indicators' which immediately highlight the group of meanings in that category. In addition, variations of meaning within each category are precisely pinpointed by further indicating material. The *systematic* and consistent use throughout the dictionary of indicating material, which may take the form of field labels, synonyms, typical subjects or objects of verbs, and so on, is a feature of the dictionary to which we attach the greatest importance. This indicating material is a very effective way of helping the user to pinpoint the exact translation he or she is looking for.

One of the most insidious linguistic traps that besets the student of any foreign language is to use words or expressions inappropriate – occasionally grotesquely so – to the context. The complexities and subtleties of register, especially of social overtones, are impossible to acquire from the printed page, but we have created for this dictionary a range of 'style labels' that accurately characterize the stylistic restrictions that should be placed on any word or expression in the text – both in source language and in target language.

Words and expressions that are unmarked for style or register in source or target language are to be taken as standard language appropriate to any normal context or situation. Wherever this is not the case the nature of the restriction is indicated: formal, literary, school slang, humorous, pejorative, and so on.

A new, user-friendly style of presentation has been chosen for selected longer entries (for example, common verbs and prepositions) to make finding specific meanings or expressions easier.

Another feature of this dictionary is the wealth of phrases provided within many entries. These greatly expand the validity of the information provided by showing how translation and sometimes structure change in different contexts and by giving examples of the idioms and set expressions relating to the headword.

The pages that follow describe these and other features of the dictionary in greater detail.

Cultural Information

The fifth edition of this dictionary contains in-depth entries with information on important aspects of culture and everyday life in German- and English-speaking countries.

German Spelling Reform

This dictionary has fully implemented the German spelling reform. All headwords on the German-English side of the dictionary which have been affected by the spelling changes are marked accordingly in the text, while the supplement (pp 2087-2110) gives explanations on the extent of the spelling reform and the way it affects relevant entries in this dictionary.

Up-to-date usage

The aim of any new edition of a dictionary is usually to update the text to incorporate those words and phrases which have only recently come into the language – this dictionary does have several thousand new words and meanings on both sides of the text. However, to create a new edition fit for the 21st century we have moved beyond this and developed several other features which make this book more user-friendly and up-to-date than ever before.

The decisive factor in this was the determination to analyse the meaning and usage of existing entries and to expand or restructure them where appropriate. To achieve this, both traditional lexicographical methods and the latest electronic tools were used. The dictionaries we produce today benefit from use of the huge electronic corpora for English ("Bank of English") and German ("Deutsche Textbörse") developed through the groundbreaking research into computational linguistics carried out by COLLINS in partnership with the University of Birmingham since the 1970s. These corpora are collections of texts held on computer, which provide numerous examples of how words are actually used in the widest possible variety of contexts, be it in newspapers, in literature, in official reports or in ordinary spoken language. In much the same way as scientists who analyse objective data to confirm their hypotheses, dictionary editors now have access to vast databases of hard facts and evidence to back up their own linguistic intuition. The result is a degree of accuracy and depth of coverage that would be impossible to achieve using traditional methods alone. Here is an example of how authentic usage, as documented in our corpora, the Bank of English and the Deutsche Textbörse, is reflected in our dictionary entries.

turn will heat the air around it. The | heated | air will then rise, carrying the cloud
quickly and efficiently by circulating | heated | air through to every corner of your
own unique style. It's been a week of | heated | argument, stunning performances, and
say that Morgan had been involved in a | heated | argument with another man shortly
the abolition of the monarchy – and a | heated | debate on Christianity. And as far as
agency says the congress was marked by | heated | debates over the new party's rules,
That led to speculation that there were | heated | debates over whether to accept the
The council spent three hours in | heated | discussion of the century-old
More drafts were written and discarded. | Heated | discussions broke out over the wording
over these last 15 years. Those | heated | discussions with colleagues and
reported to have become involved in a | heated | dispute with the studio over the length
under the federal plan to end the | heated | dispute over forests, industry no-go
quickly after we arrived. In rather a | heated | exchange I told what looked to be a
tape failed to arrive in time. After a | heated | exchange with organisers, and having
they just went on the open bench in the | heated | greenhouse, but as the weather was
sown in the early part of the year in a | heated | greenhouse. The seedlings are grown on
harmonoius relationship. They had a | heated | meeting on Tuesday night which failed
railwayman to preside over us. I had a | heated | meeting with the Secretary of State,
proof locks, a rust-proofed body and | heated | rear window come as standard. Apart
armrest, automatic timer for the | heated | rear window and an interior light
or sleeping well wrapped up in a | heated | room. This ties in with the results of
last Christmas. Is it best kept in a | heated | room or does it prefer cool conditions?
we continue to breed them in cages and | heated | rooms we will never be able to enjoy
be financially worse off, has caused a | heated | row. Members of the 7th Armoured
The Tottenham MP became embroiled in a | heated | row with BR staff after they accused
and enjoy the amenities of a private | heated | swimming pool, from May to September.
acres of gardens with tennis courts and | heated | swimming pool screened by trees and
use of the leisure facilities, such as | heated | swimming pool, sauna, spa bath and
Different special offers every month on | heated | towel rails and selected suites.
in all type of radiators and | heated | towel rails, have several traditional
field when he allegedly exchanged | heated | words before landing his blow. All
irritation of his vice-captain, led to | heated | words in the dressing room. Other
did not agree, and things quickly grew | heated | between these two titans of ridicule
Families of deceased and accused grow | heated | and often irrational. It is common for
ministers became increasingly | heated | and the supporters of the democratic
star. Without exception each one became | heated | over the criticism or presumed
users post messages. Debate can become | heated, | and some messages, known as flames,
Internet debates can easily become | heated | to the point of mutual vilification.
worse than death. Things got pretty | heated | before he left them to it, Jeremy went
the tables. Before things got too | heated, | though, I made my excuses and left my

heated ['hi:tɪd] ADJ **a** (*lit*) *swimming pool, greenhouse etc* beheizt; *room* geheizt; *rear window, towel rail* heizbar; **~ air** Warmluft *f* **b** (*fig, = angry*) *debate, discussion, dispute, meeting* hitzig, erregt; *argument, exchange, row* heftig; *words* erregt; **to grow** *or* **become ~** (*person*) sich aufregen; (*debate*) hitzig *or* erregt werden; **things got very ~** die Gemüter erhitzten sich

EINLEITUNG

Seit seiner Erstveröffentlichung im Jahre 1980 ist das COLLINS GROSSWÖRTERBUCH zu einem Standardwerk geworden. Durch seine Materialfülle sowie die Klarheit und Genauigkeit der Informationsvermittlung stellt dieses Wörterbuch sowohl in deutsch- als auch englischsprachigen Ländern eine anerkannte Autorität dar.

Inhalt, Umfang und Methodik

Bei diesem Wörterbuch liegt das Schwergewicht eindeutig auf der englischen und deutschen Gegenwartssprache, wobei der Sprache des Alltags besondere Aufmerksamkeit gilt. Die Gesamtzahl der Stichwörter, Zusammensetzungen und Anwendungsbeispiele ist höher als 300.000. Schon ein kurzer Blick auf eine Auswahl von Stichwörtern und Wendungen zeigt deutlich, dass der Grund für diese Vollständigkeit nicht in der Aufnahme von seltenen Wörtern oder Redewendungen an der Peripherie der Sprache zu suchen ist. Ganz im Gegenteil ist in allen Arbeitsphasen bewusst Wert darauf gelegt worden, Abgelebtes und Ausgestorbenes aus diesem Wörterbuch zu verbannen. Auch ist die Vollständigkeit nicht einfach auf die Aufnahme von Neologismen zurückzuführen, obwohl freilich neue Wörter ebenso wie neu geprägte Redensarten einen breiten Raum in diesem Buch einnehmen.

Die Vollständigkeit beruht ganz einfach auf der Gründlichkeit und Ausführlichkeit, mit der die deutsche und englische Alltagssprache behandelt werden. Diesen eigentlichen Kern, den Baustoff der deutschen und englischen Sprache, der in anderen zweisprachigen (oder sogar einsprachigen) Wörterbüchern oft keinen Ausdruck findet, hat dieses Wörterbuch zu seinem Hauptanliegen gemacht. Es behandelt ein enormes Spektrum ganz gewöhnlicher Wörter und Redewendungen, die unentbehrlichen – oft recht schwierig zu übersetzenden – Elemente der sprachlichen Kommunikation in aller Gründlichkeit. Damit soll jedoch nicht gesagt sein, dass älteres oder sondersprachliches Wortgut schlechthin in diesem Wörterbuch unberücksichtigt bleibt. Ganz im Gegenteil. Wenn man den Umfang des Wörterverzeichnisses schlagwortartig als den „Wortschatz des gebildeten Laien" beschreibt, heißt das gleichzeitig, dass ältere und sondersprachliche Ausdrücke, die in diesen Wortschatz eingegangen sind, auch in das Wörterbuch aufgenommen wurden. So ist zum Beispiel die Sprache der Computertechnik ebenso wie die der traditionelleren Fachgebiete dokumentiert.

Auch die Verbreitung beider Sprachen in geografischer Hinsicht wird nicht vernachlässigt. Amerikanisches Englisch ist weitgehend berücksichtigt worden, und außer dem Sprachgebrauch in Deutschland wird dem in Österreich und der Schweiz gesprochenen Deutsch ausführlich Rechnung getragen. Das Gleiche gilt für den regionalen Sprachgebrauch in Deutschland und Großbritannien.

Für die Verfasser dieses Wörterbuches ist es von Anfang an eine Selbstverständlichkeit gewesen, dass der deutsche Text ausschließlich von Lexikografen mit Deutsch als Muttersprache und der englische Text ausschließlich von Lexikografen mit Englisch als Muttersprache verfasst werden musste. Damit ist die idiomatische Authentizität sowohl in der Ausgangssprache als auch in der Zielsprache gewährleistet.

Deutsche und englische Lexikografen haben im Team gearbeitet, und während der Redaktionsarbeit haben in allen Arbeitsphasen Diskussionen zwischen deutschen und englischen Muttersprachlern stattgefunden. Das heißt, dass der gesamte Text von Redakteuren ausschließlich in ihrer eigenen Sprache verfasst wurde und aus zweisprachiger Sicht geprüft worden ist. Dies ist die sicherste und zuverlässigste Methode, beide Sprachen miteinander zu verzahnen.

Artikelaufbau

Der Artikelaufbau in diesem Wörterbuch zeichnet sich vor allem durch die systematische Verwendung von Indikatoren und Kollokatoren (siehe Seite xiv) aus, die verschiedene Bedeutungs- und Anwendungsbereiche bezeichnen, sodass die angegebenen Übersetzungen sich immer auf den Kontext oder Kontextbereich beziehen, für den sie gelten. Der Benutzer wird nicht mit zwar möglichen, aber dennoch unterschiedlichen beziehungslosen Übersetzungen bombardiert. Statt dessen werden ihm kontextspezifische Übersetzungen geboten. Dies gilt sowohl für Übersetzungen, wo die unterschiedlichen Bedeutungen eines Wortes in der Ausgangssprache zu zeigen sind, als auch für Wörter, deren Gebrauch sich nach dem Kontext richtet, was z. B. bei der Verbindung (Kollokation) von Substantiv und Adjektiv der Fall ist.

Die Phraseologie bildet einen der wichtigsten Teile des Wörterbuchs und lässt sich grob in zwei Bereiche gliedern. Da sind zunächst die festen Wendungen im Deutschen und Englischen: die Sprichwörter, Redensarten und auch die Klischees; dann die Anwendungsbeispiele, mit denen die strukturelle Entsprechung beider Sprachen illustriert werden soll. So wird z. B. gezeigt, wie eine bestimmte allgemeine Übersetzung, sagen wir ein Substantiv, unter Umständen in einem bestimmten Kontext in eine Verbkonstruktion verwandelt werden muss, um die idiomatische Korrektheit – gelegentlich sogar die Verständlichkeit – zu wahren.

Für ausgewählte längere Einträge (z. B. gebräuchliche Verben und Präpositionen) wurde eine neue, benutzerfreundliche Darstellung gewählt, die das Auffinden gesuchter Bedeutungen oder Wendungen erleichtert.

Zur Vervollständigung dieses detaillierten Artikelaufbaus wird ein hoch entwickeltes System von Stilangaben verwendet, damit der Benutzer erkennt, ob eine bestimmte Übersetzung angemessen ist oder welchen Stellenwert ein Stichwort, das er nachschlagen möchte, aus stilistischer Sicht hat. Es wird dem Benutzer mitgeteilt, ja er wird gewarnt, wenn ein Wort umgangssprachlich, dichterisch, förmlich, veraltet, altmodisch, verhüllend o. Ä. ist, und es wird ihm gesagt, ob ein Ausdruck möglicherweise Anstoß erregt, Heiterkeit hervorruft, schwülstig, betulich, professoral oder abstoßend klingt. Weitere Erläuterungen zum Artikelaufbau werden auf den folgenden Seiten gegeben.

Landeskundliche Informationen

Die fünfte Auflage dieses Wörterbuchs enthält auch ausführliche Artikel zu Landeskunde und Kultur deutsch- und englischsprachiger Länder.

Deutsche Rechtschreibreform

Dieses Wörterbuch folgt der reformierten deutschen Rechtschreibung. Alle von der Rechtschreibreform betroffenen Wörter, die im deutsch-englischen Teil des Wörterbuchs als Stichwörter erscheinen, sind entsprechend gekennzeichnet. Erläuterungen zu Art und Umfang der deutschen Rechtschreibreform sowie zur Darstellung der neuen und alten Schreibweisen in diesem Wörterbuch sind ebenfalls im Anhang (S. 2087-2110) enthalten.

Aktualität

Jede Neuauflage eines Wörterbuchs zielt normalerweise zunächst auf eine Aktualisierung des Wortschatzes, um solche Wörter und Ausdrücke aufzunehmen, welche erst kürzlich Eingang in die Sprache gefunden haben – in diesem Fall mehrere Tausend neue Wörter und neue Bedeutungen auf beiden Seiten des Wörterbuchs. Für diese, auf das 21. Jahrhundert zielende Neuausgabe wurden jedoch darüber hinaus zahlreiche weitere Anstrengungen unternommen, die dieses Buch benutzerfreundlicher und aktueller machen als jemals zuvor.

Ausschlaggebend hierbei war das Bestreben, bestehende Wörterbuchartikel durch eine Analyse von Wortbedeutung und -gebrauch zu überprüfen und wo angebracht zu erweitern oder neu zu gliedern. Hierbei kamen sowohl traditionelle Methoden der Lexikografie als auch die neueste Computertechnik zur Anwendung. Dank der von COLLINS in Zusammenarbeit mit der Universität Birmingham seit den 70er Jahren durchgeführten Forschungsarbeiten auf dem Gebiet der Computerlinguistik profitieren unsere Wörterbücher heute von den seither aufgebauten riesigen elektronischen Textkorpora für Englisch („Bank of English") und Deutsch („Deutsche Textbörse"). Hierbei handelt es sich um auf Computer gehaltene Textsammlungen, welche Belege dafür enthalten, wie Wörter in den verschiedensten Kontexten gebraucht werden, sei es in der Presse, in der Literatur, in Berichten und Abhandlungen oder in der gesprochenen Sprache. In ähnlicher Weise wie Wissenschaftler Daten heranziehen, um ihre Hypothesen zu überprüfen, so können heute auch unsere Wörterbuchredakteure auf Datenbanken mit einer Fülle von Fakten und Belegen zurückgreifen, um ihr eigenes Sprachgefühl anhand dieser Daten zu verifizieren. Das Resultat ist ein Grad an Genauigkeit und Darstellungsbreite, der mit rein herkömmlichen Methoden unmöglich erreicht werden könnte. Im Folgenden ein Beispiel dafür, wie authentischer Sprachgebrauch, dokumentiert in Korpustexten, sich im entsprechenden Wörterbuchartikel widerspiegelt.

wenig scharlachrote Halsbinde ließ ihn	blühend	aussehen und schenkte ihm, besser
aus'', bedauert ein selbst nicht gerade	blühend	aussehender mittelalterlicher Herr
Lady Campers morgendlich frisches und	blühendes	Aussehen ein. Das kann kaum sichtbar
in ihren Sohn und behielt ihr	blühendes	Aussehen bei, auch das Schwarz der
ohne jede Langeweile unter einem	blühenden	Baum liegen, in Bibliotheken alte
Früher konnte ich mich vor einen	blühenden	Baum hinstellen und eine unglaubliche
laden zum Verweilen ein, die	blühenden	Bäume spenden Schatten, und vom nahen
beharrlich weiterfrisst, ist jede	blühende	Blume, jedes der Natur abgetrotzte
war ein kleiner grüner Fleck mit	blühenden	Blumen und Bäumen. Nach einem Zögern
Sie ist umgeben von Wiesen mit	blühenden	Blumen. Am Brunnen des Innenhofs kann
mehr hinter dieser Geschichte als die	blühende	Fantasie der Autorin. So viel braucht
herauszulesen vermag, hat eine	blühende	Fantasie und schießt über das Ziel hinaus
des Romanhelden, den wegen seiner	blühenden	Fantasie und erfindungsreichen
die unfruchtbares Land und Wüsten in	blühende	Felder und Gärten verwandeln, aus
Ende des Krieges glichen die einst	blühenden	Felder einer trichterübersäten
aus einer Steinwüste in einen	blühenden	Garten verwandelt. Sein Buch kommt
ist doch das: blühende Felder,	blühende	Gärten, blühende Wiesen, blühende
Dort kontrollieren sie nicht nur das	blühende	Geschäft mit der Prostitution, wofür
autonomer Gruppen, die mit dem Terror	blühende	Geschäfte machen. Und: Von einer
Plattenhersteller durch den weltweit	blühenden	Handel mit Raubkopien Einbußen von
beginnen sich langsam an dem	blühenden	Handel mit Rauschmitteln vor der
erreicht. Der Urlaub hat eine	blühende	Industrie geschaffen, die von einer
begründete damit vor 225 Jahren eine	blühende	Industrie. Die Goldstadt exportiert
zwischen Tang und Shilla hat der	blühenden	Kultur im damaligen China den Weg auf
Und wer nun, ganz undramatisch, der	blühenden	Kultur des Verbrauchs sich zuneigt,
ehemalige DDR in ein wirtschaftlich	blühendes	Land verwandeln, war der zweite
demokratischen und wirtschaftlich	blühenden	Landes zu danken. Österreich habe
Bürgern der DDR schnellen Wohlstand,	blühende	Landschaften zu versprechen und den
erfüllt. Die von ihm versprochenen	blühenden	Landschaften im Osten würden nicht in
festgestellt hatte, dass sie wie das	blühende	Leben aussehe, verfiel auch er in
sie positiv ist. Sie sah aus wie das	blühende	Leben. Valeries Leben hat 1965 in
Die Blumenhalle ist mit 60.000	blühenden	Pflanzen geschmückt. Wolfgang Müller,
Pracht, umgeben von Seerosen und	blühenden	Pflanzen, durch den naturgetreu
worden und hatte sich bald zu einer	blühenden	Stadt entwickelt. Die Gegend war
Assyriens Provinzen sollen mit ihren	blühenden	Städten und großartigen Bauwerken das
Glück, wies die Spekulationen als	blühenden	Unsinn zurück. Angeblich soll Glück
Seite. Dieser Vorwurf ist natürlich	blühender	Unsinn, sagte er mit Nachdruck, denn
der sich wie Raureif auf eine	blühende	Wiese senkte. Das Gelächter
aufwarf. An den Ufern begannen	blühende	Wiesen, die dieses Jahr noch niemand
Weite der Steppen, Berge und Seen,	blühende	Wiesen und weidende Tierherden,
der von Grundwerten faselt, eine	blühende	Zukunft verspricht und dazu noch
für Hongkong eine erfolgreiche und	blühende	Zukunft voraus. Die besondere Lage der

blü|hend ADJ *Baum* blossoming; *Blume, Pflanze* auch blooming; *Garten, Wiese, Feld* full of flowers; (*fig*) *Aussehen* radiant; *Geschäft, Handel, Industrie, Kultur, Stadt* flourishing, thriving; *Fantasie* vivid, lively; *Unsinn* absolute; *Zukunft* glowing; **~e Landschaften** green pastures; **ein wirtschaftlich ~es Land** a country with a thriving economy; **wie das ~e Leben aussehen, ~ aussehen** to look the very picture of health

Using the Dictionary

Hinweise zur Benutzung des Wörterbuchs

Layout and order

Aufbau und Anordnung der Einträge

1.1 Alphabetical order is followed throughout. Where a letter occurs in brackets in a headword, this letter is counted for the alphabetical order, eg **Beamte(r)** will be found in the place of **Beamter, vierte(r, s)** in the place of **vierter.**

1.1 Die alphabetische Anordnung der Einträge ist durchweg gewahrt. In Klammern stehende Buchstaben in einem Stichwort unterliegen ebenfalls der Alphabetisierung, so findet man z.B. **Beamte(r)** an der Stelle von **Beamter, vierte(r, s)** unter **vierter**.

1.2 Abbreviations, acronyms and **proper nouns** will be found in their alphabetical place in the word list.

1.2 Abkürzungen, Akronyme und **Eigennamen** sind in alphabetischer Ordnung im Wörterverzeichnis zu finden.

1.3 Superior numbers are used to differentiate between words spelt the same way.

1.3 Hochgestellte Ziffern werden verwendet, um zwischen Wörtern gleicher Schreibung zu unterscheiden.

rowing¹, rowing²; durchsetzen¹, durchsetzen²

1.4 Nouns which are always used in the plural are entered in the plural form.

1.4 Substantive, die stets im Plural verwendet werden, sind in der Pluralform angegeben.

trousers PL , **Ferien** PL

1.5 Compounds will be found in their alphabetical place in the word list. The term "compound" is taken to cover not only those written in one word or hyphenated (eg **Bettwäsche, large-scale**) but also attributive uses of English nouns (eg **defence mechanism**) and other set word combinations (eg **long jump**) which function in a similar way. Where possible a general translation has been given for the first element.

1.5 Zusammengesetzte Wörter stehen an ihrer Stelle im Alphabet. Der Begriff „zusammengesetzte Wörter" bezeichnet nicht nur zusammengeschriebene oder durch Bindestrich verbundene Komposita (z.B. **Bettwäsche, large-scale**) sondern auch die attributive Verwendung englischer Substantive (z. B. **defence mechanism**) und andere feste Verbindungen (z. B. **long jump**), die eine ähnliche Funktion haben. Wo immer möglich, ist für das erste Element eine allgemeine Übersetzung angegeben.

Mag|net- *in cpds* magnetic

From this the user can derive the translation for compounds not given in the word list.

Daraus kann der Benutzer die Übersetzung hier nicht angegebener Zusammensetzungen erschließen.

Where alphabetical order permits, compounds are run on in blocks with the first element printed in a large boldface type at the beginning of each block, and the headwords themselves in a slightly smaller typeface for easy identification. Illustrative phrases appear in a different typeface so that they can easily be distinguished from compounds.

Wo die alphabetische Ordnung es gestattet, werden die Zusammensetzungen in Blöcken angeordnet, wobei der erste Bestandteil am Anfang jedes Blocks fett und die Stichwörter selbst halbfett erscheinen. Für Wendungen wird eine andere Schrift verwendet, um dem Benutzer die schnelle Identifizierung von Wendungen und zusammengesetzten Wörtern zu erleichtern.

gum: gumtree N Gummibaum *m*; **to be up a ~** (*Brit, inf*) aufgeschmissen sein (*inf*)

1.6 Phrasal verbs (marked ▶) will be found immediately after the main headword entry.

1.6 *Phrasal verbs* (feste Verb-Partikel-Verbindungen im Englischen, durch ▶ bezeichnet) folgen unmittelbar auf das Hauptstichwort.

1.7 Idioms and set phrases will normally be found under the first meaningful element or the first word in the phrase which remains constant despite minor variations in the phrase itself. Thus, 'to breast the tape' is included under **breast** whereas 'to lend sb a hand' is treated under **'hand'** because it is equally possible to say 'to give sb a hand'.

1.7 Redensarten und feste Wendungen sind im Allgemeinen unter dem ersten bedeutungstragenden Element oder dem ersten Wort der Wendung, das trotz leichter Abwandlungen in der Wendung selbst unverändert bleibt, zu finden. So ist ,to breast the tape' unter ,**breast**' aufgenommen, ,to lend sb a hand' dagegen wird unter ,**hand**'

Certain very common English and German verbs such as 'be, get, have, make, put, bringen, haben, geben, machen, tun', which form the basis of a great many phrases e.g. 'to make sense', 'to make a mistake', 'etw in Ordnung bringen', 'etw in Gang bringen' have been considered as having a diminished meaning and in such cases the set phrase will be found under the most significant element in the phrase.

abgehandelt, weil es ebenfalls möglich ist, ‚to give sb a hand' zu sagen.

Bei als Funktionsverben gebrauchten Verben wie ‚be, get, have, make, put, bringen, haben, geben, machen, tun' werden die meisten festen Wendungen, wie z. B. ‚to make sense', ‚to make a mistake', ‚etw in Ordnung bringen', ‚etw in Gang bringen', unter dem bedeutungstragenden Bestandteil der Wendung behandelt.

Explanatory material

Erklärende Zusätze

General explanatory notes or 'signposts' in the dictionary are printed *in italics* and take the following forms:

Allgemeine erklärende Zusätze im Wörterbuch sind *kursiv* gedruckt und erscheinen in folgender Form:

2.1 Indicators in brackets ( ):

2.1 Indikatoren, in Klammern stehend ( ):

2.1.1 Explanations and Clarification

2.1.1 Erklärungen und Erläuterungen

lounge N (*in house*) Wohnzimmer *nt*; (*in hotel*) Gesellschaftsraum *m*

2.1.2 synonyms and partial definitions

2.1.2 Synonyme und Teildefinitionen

ge|fühl|voll ADJ a (= *empfindsam*) sensitive; (= *ausdrucksvoll*) expressive b (= *liebevoll*) loving

2.1.3 within verb entries, typical subjects of the headword

2.1.3 in Verb-Einträgen typische Substantiv-Ergänzungen

peel VI (*wallpaper*) sich lösen; (*paint*) abblättern; (*skin, person*) sich schälen *or* pellen (*inf*)

2.1.4 within noun entries, typical noun complements of the headword

2.1.4 typische Substantiv-Ergänzungen des Stichworts in Substantiv-Einträgen

Schar¹ [ʃaːɐ] F **-, -en** crowd, throng (*liter*); (*von Vögeln*) flock; (*von Insekten, Heuschrecken etc*) swarm

2.2 Collocators or typical complements, not in brackets:

2.2 Kollokatoren oder typische Ergänzungen, ohne Klammern stehend:

2.2.1 in transitive verb entries, typical objects of the headword

2.2.1 typische Objekte des Stichworts bei transitiven Verb-Einträgen

dent VT *hat, car, wing* einbeulen, verbeulen; *wood, table* eine Delle machen in (+*acc*); (*inf*) *pride, confidence* anknacksen (*inf*)

2.2.2 in adjective entries, typical nouns modified by the headword

2.2.2 typische, durch das Stichwort näher bestimmte Substantive in Adjektiv-Einträgen

neu [nɔy] ✪ 50.2 ADJ new; *Seite, Kräfte, Hoffnung, Truppen auch* fresh; (= *kürzlich entstanden auch*) recent; (= *frisch gewaschen*) *Hemd, Socken* clean; *Wein* young

2.2.3 in adverb entries, typical verbs or adjectives modified by the headword

2.2.3 typische, durch das Stichwort näher bestimmte Verben oder Adjektive bei Adverb-Einträgen

vaguely [ˈveɪglɪ] ADV vage; *remember also* dunkel; *speak also* unbestimmt; *understand* ungefähr, in etwa

2.3 Field labels are used:

2.3 Sachbereichsangaben werden verwendet:

2.3.1 to differentiate various meanings of the headword

2.3.1 um die verschiedenen Bedeutungen des Stichworts zu unterscheiden

Jung|frau F virgin; (*Astron, Astrol*) Virgo *no art*

2.3.2 when the meaning in the source language is clear but may be ambiguous in the target language

2.3.2 wenn die Bedeutung in der Ausgangssprache klar ist, jedoch in der Zielsprache mehrdeutig sein könnte

Virgo [ˈvɜːgəʊ] N (*Astrol*) Jungfrau *f*; **he's (a)** ~ er ist Jungfrau

A list of the field labels used in this dictionary is given inside the front and back covers.

Eine Liste dieser Sachbereichsangaben befindet sich auf den Umschlag-Innenseiten.

2.4 Style labels are used to mark all words and phrases which are not neutral in style level or which are no longer current in the language. This labelling is given for both source and target languages and serves primarily as an aid to the non-native speaker.

2.4 Stilangaben werden verwendet zur Kennzeichnung aller Wörter und Wendungen, die keiner neutralen Stilebene oder nicht mehr dem modernen Sprachgebrauch angehören. Die Angaben erfolgen sowohl in der Ausgangs- als auch in der Zielsprache und sollen in erster Linie dem Nichtmuttersprachler helfen.

When a style label is given at the beginning of an entry or category it covers all meanings and phrases in that entry or category.

Stilangaben zu Beginn eines Eintrages oder einer Kategorie beziehen sich auf alle Bedeutungen und Wendungen innerhalb dieses Eintrages oder dieser Kategorie.

(*inf*) denotes colloquial language typically used in an informal conversational context or a chatty letter, but which would be inappropriate in more formal speech or writing.

(*sl*) indicates that the word or phrase is highly informal and is only appropriate in very restricted contexts, for example among members of a particular age group. When combined with a field label eg (*Mil sl*), (*Sch sl*) it denotes that the expression belongs to the jargon of that group.

(*vulg*) denotes words generally regarded as taboo which are likely to cause offence.

(*geh*) denotes an elevated style of spoken or written German such as might be used by an educated speaker choosing his words with care.

(*form*) denotes formal language such as that used on official forms, for official communications and in formal speeches.

(*spec*) indicates that the expression is a technical term restricted to the vocabulary of specialists.

(*dated*) indicates that the word or phrase, while still occasionally being used especially by older speakers, now sounds somewhat old-fashioned.

(*old*) denotes language no longer in current use but which the user will find in reading.

(*obs*) denotes obsolete words which the user will normally only find in classical literature.

(*liter*) denotes language of a literary style level. It should not be confused with the field label (*Liter*) which indicates that the expression belongs to the field of literary studies, or with the abbreviation (*lit*) which indicates the literal as opposed to the figurative meaning of a word.

Style labels used in this dictionary are given inside the front and back covers.

2.5 *also, auch* used after explanatory material denotes that the translation(s) following it can be used in addition to the first translation given in the respective entry, category or phrase.

Grammatical Information

Gender
3.1 All German **nouns** are marked for gender in both sections of the dictionary.

3.2 Where a German translation consists of an adjective plus a noun, the adjective is given in the indefinite form which shows gender and therefore no gender is given for the noun.

(*inf*) bezeichnet umgangssprachlichen Gebrauch, wie er für eine formlose Unterhaltung oder einen zwanglosen Brief typisch ist, in förmlicherer Rede oder förmlicherem Schriftverkehr jedoch unangebracht wäre.

(*sl*) soll anzeigen, dass das Wort oder die Wendung äußerst salopp ist und nur unter ganz bestimmten Umständen, z. B. unter Mitgliedern einer besonderen Altersgruppe, verwendet wird. In Verbindung mit einer Sachbereichsangabe, z.B. (*Mil sl*), (*Sch sl*), wird auf die Zugehörigkeit des Ausdrucks zum Jargon dieser Gruppe hingewiesen.

(*vulg*) bezeichnet Wörter, die allgemein als tabu gelten und an denen vielfach Anstoß genommen wird.

(*geh*) bezeichnet einen gehobenen Stil sowohl im gesprochenen wie geschriebenen Deutsch, wie er von gebildeten, sich gewählt ausdrückenden Sprechern verwendet werden kann.

(*form*) bezeichnet förmlichen Sprachgebrauch, wie er uns auf Formularen, im amtlichen Schriftverkehr oder in förmlichen Ansprachen begegnet.

(*spec*) gibt an, dass es sich um einen Fachausdruck handelt, der ausschließlich dem Wortschatz von Fachleuten angehört.

(*dated*) weist darauf hin, dass das Wort bzw. die Wendung heute recht altmodisch klingen, obwohl sie besonders von älteren Sprechern noch gelegentlich benutzt werden.

(*old*) bezeichnet nicht mehr geläufiges Wortgut, das dem Benutzer jedoch noch beim Lesen begegnet.

(*obs*) bezeichnet veraltete Wörter, die der Benutzer im Allgemeinen nur in der klassischen Literatur antreffen wird.

(*liter*) bezeichnet literarischen Sprachgebrauch. Es sollte nicht mit der Sachbereichsangabe (*Liter*) verwechselt werden, die angibt, dass der betreffende Ausdruck dem Gebiet der Literaturwissenschaft angehört, und ebenso wenig mit der Abkürzung (*lit*), die die wörtliche im Gegensatz zur übertragenen Bedeutung eines Wortes bezeichnet.

In diesem Wörterbuch verwendete Stilangaben und ihre Bedeutungen befinden sich auf den Umschlag-Innenseiten.

2.5 *also, auch* nach erklärenden Zusätzen gibt an, dass die folgende(n) Übersetzung(en) zusätzlich zu der ersten Übersetzung, die in dem Eintrag oder der Kategorie angegeben ist, benutzt werden kann/können.

Grammatische Angaben

Geschlecht
3.1 Alle deutschen **Substantive** sind in beiden Teilen des Wörterbuchs mit der Geschlechtsangabe versehen.

3.2 Wenn eine deutsche Übersetzung aus einem Adjektiv und einem Substantiv besteht, wird das Adjektiv in der unbestimmten Form angegeben, die das Geschlecht erkennen lässt. Für das Substantiv erfolgt daher keine Geschlechtsangabe.

große Pause; zweites Frühstück

3.3 Nouns listed in the form **Rei|sen|de(r)** MF *decl as adj* can be either masculine or feminine and take the same endings as adjectives.

3.3 Substantive nach dem Muster **Rei|sen|de(r)** MF *decl as adj* können sowohl männlich wie weiblich sein und haben die gleichen Deklinationsendungen wie Adjektive.

m **der Reisende, ein Reisender, die Reisenden** *pl*
f **die Reisende, eine Reisende, die Reisenden** *pl*

3.4 Nouns listed in the form **Be|am|te(r)** M *decl as adj* take the same endings as adjectives.

3.4 Substantive nach dem Muster **Be|am|te(r)** M *decl as adj* haben die gleichen Deklinationsendungen wie Adjektive.

der Beamte, ein Beamter, die Beamten *pl*

3.5 Adjectives listed in the form **letzte(r, s)** do not exist in an undeclined form and are only used attributively.

3.5 Adjektive nach dem Muster **letzte(r, s)** haben keine unflektierte Form und werden nur attributiv verwendet.

**der letzte Mann, ein letzter Mann
die letzte Frau, eine letzte Frau
das letzte Kind, ein letztes Kind**

3.6 The **feminine forms** are shown, where relevant, for all German noun headwords; unless otherwise indicated, the English translation will be the same as for the masculine form.

Where the feminine form is separated alphabetically from the masculine form, it is given as a separate headword.

Where there is no distinction between the translations given for the masculine and feminine forms and yet the context calls for a distinction, the user should prefix the translation with "male/female *or* woman *or* lady ..."

3.6 Für alle deutschen Substantive, die ein natürliches Geschlecht haben, wird die **weibliche** neben der **männlichen Form** angegeben. Wenn nicht anders angegeben, lautet die englische Form für beide gleich.

Wo die weibliche Form in der alphabetischen Reihenfolge nicht unmittelbar auf die männliche folgt, wird sie in jedem Fall als eigenes Stichwort angegeben.

Wo die für die männliche und die für die weibliche Form angegebene Übersetzung dieselbe ist, im entsprechenden Zusammenhang aber betont werden soll, dass es sich um einen Mann bzw. eine Frau handelt, sollte der Benutzer der Übersetzung „male/female *or* woman *or* lady" voranstellen.

Lehrer = male teacher; Lehrerin = female *or* **woman** *or* **lady teacher**

Nouns

Substantive

4.1 Nouns marked *no pl* are not normally used in the plural or with an indefinite article or with numerals.

no pl is used:
  (a) to give warning to the non-native speaker who might otherwise use the word wrongly;
  (b) as an indicator to distinguish the uncountable meanings of a headword in the source language.

4.1 Substantive mit der Angabe *no pl* werden im Allgemeinen nicht im Plural, mit dem unbestimmten Artikel oder mit Zahlwörtern verwendet.

no pl dient:
  (a) als Warnung an den Nicht-Muttersprachler, der das Wort sonst falsch benutzen könnte;
  (b) zur Unterscheidung der unzählbaren und zählbaren Bedeutungen in der Ausgangssprache.

4.2 Nouns marked *no art* are not normally used with either a definite or an indefinite article except when followed by a relative clause.

4.2 Mit *no art* bezeichnete Substantive stehen im Allgemeinen weder mit dem unbestimmten noch mit dem bestimmten Artikel, außer wenn ein Relativsatz von ihnen abhängig ist.

4.3 The **genitive and plural endings** are given for all German noun headwords. The genitive and plural endings of German compound nouns are only given where the final element does not exist as a headword in its own right.

4.3 Bei allen deutschen Substantiv-Stichwörtern sind **Genitivendung und Plural** angegeben, bei zusammengesetzten Substantiven jedoch nur dann, wenn das letzte Element der Zusammensetzung nicht als eigenes Stichwort vorkommt.

4.4 Irregular plural forms of English nouns are given on the English-German side.

4.4 Unregelmäßige Pluralformen englischer Substantive sind im englisch-deutschen Teil angegeben.

4.4.1 Most English nouns take *-s* in the plural.

4.4.1 Die meisten englischen Substantive bilden den Plural durch Anhängen von *-s*.

bed -s, site -s, key -s, roof -s

4.4.2 Nouns ending in *-s, -z, -x, -sh, -ch* take *-es*

4.4.2 Substantive, die auf *-s, -z, -x, -sh, -ch* enden, erhalten die Endung *-es*.

gas -es, box -es, patch -es

4.4.3 Nouns ending in *-y* preceded by a consonant change the *-y* to *ie* and add *-s* in the plural, except in the case of proper nouns.

4.4.3 Substantive, die auf Konsonant + *-y* enden, verwandeln im Plural das auslautende *-y* in *-ie*, auf das die Pluralendung *-s* folgt. Ausnahmen bilden Eigennamen.

**lady — ladies, berry — berries
Henry — two Henrys**

Nouns ending in *-quy* also change the *-y* to *- ie* and add *-s* in the plural, except in the case of proper nouns.

Auf *-quy* auslautende Substantive verwandeln bei der Pluralbildung ihr *-y* ebenfalls in *-ie*, worauf *-s* folgt.

soliloquy — soliloquies

Adjectives and adverbs

5.1 As a general rule, adjective translations consisting of more than one word should be used postnominally or adverbially, but not before the noun.

Adjektive und Adverbien

5.1 Grundsätzlich sollten Übersetzungen von Adjektiven, die aus mehreren Wörtern bestehen, nur nachgestellt oder adverbial gebraucht und nicht dem Substantiv vorangestellt werden.

ọrd|nungs|ge|mäß ADJ according to *or* in accordance with the regulations, proper

5.2 On the German-English side of the dictionary adverbs have been treated as separate grammatical entries distinct from adjective entries whenever their use is purely adverbial (*e.g.* **höchst, wohl, sehr**) or when the adverbial use is also common.

5.2 Im deutsch-englischen Teil des Wörterbuchs sind Adverbien immer dann als selbstständige grammatische Einträge von Adjektiven unterschieden worden, wenn es sich um echte Adverbien handelt (*z. B.* **höchst, wohl, sehr**) oder wenn ein adverbialer Gebrauch wahrscheinlich ist.

Where no separate entry is given for the adverbial use of a German adjective, the user should form the English adverb from the translations given according to the rules given on page xxii.

Wo für den adverbialen Gebrauch eines deutschen Adjektivs kein gesonderter Eintrag vorliegt, ist es dem Benutzer selbst überlassen, aus den angegebenen Übersetzungen die englischen Adverbien nach den auf Seite xxii angeführten Regeln zu bilden.

5.3 On the English-German side of the dictionary adverbs have been accorded the status of headwords in their own right.

5.3 Im englisch-deutschen Teil des Wörterbuchs sind die Adverbien als selbstständige Stichwörter aufgeführt.

Verbs

6.1 With all German verbs which form the past participle without *ge-* the past participle form is shown.

Verben

6.1 Bei allen Verben im Deutschen, die das 2. Partizip ohne *ge-* bilden, wird die Partizipform angegeben.

um|ạr|men *ptp* **umạrmt** VT *insep*
ma|növ|rie|ren *ptp* **manövriẹrt** VTI

6.2 All German verbs beginning with a prefix which can be separable, but which are in this case inseparable verbs, are marked *insep*.

6.2 Alle deutschen Verben, die mit einer trennbaren Vorsilbe beginnen, jedoch untrennbar sind, werden durch *insep* bezeichnet.

ü|ber|rie|seln *ptp* **überriẹselt** VT *insep* **ein Schauer überrieselte ihn**

6.3 With all separable German verbs the hyphenation points are shown in the actual headword

6.3 Bei allen trennbaren deutschen Verben erfolgt die Trennungsangabe im Stichwort selbst.

ụm+schmei|ßen VT *sep irreg* **das schmeißt meine Pläne um**

Verbs beginning with the prefixes *be-, er-, ver-, zer-* are always inseparable.

Verben mit den Vorsilben *be-, er-, ver-, zer-* sind immer untrennbar.

6.4 All German verbs which form their perfect, pluperfect and future perfect tenses with "sein" as the auxiliary are marked *aux sein*.

6.4 Alle deutschen Verben, die die zusammengesetzten Zeiten mit dem Hilfsverb „sein" bilden, sind durch *aux sein* gekennzeichnet.

gehen *pret* **ging**, *ptp* **gegangen** *aux sein* **er ist gegangen** he went

Where the auxiliary is not stated, "haben" is used.

Erfolgt keine Angabe, ist „haben" zu verwenden.

6.5 German **irregular verbs** composed of prefix and verb are marked *irreg*, and the forms can be found under the simple verb. For example, the irregular forms of "eingehen" will be found under "gehen".

6.5 Zusammengesetzte **unregelmäßige** Verben im Deutschen sind durch *irreg* bezeichnet, ihre Stammformen sind beim Simplex angegeben. So sind beispielsweise die Stammformen von „eingehen" unter „gehen" zu finden.

6.5 If the present or past participle of a verb occurs simply as an adjective it is treated as a separate headword in its alphabetical place.

6.6 Wenn 1. oder 2. Partizip eines Verbs den Status eines Adjektivs haben, werden sie als eigenständige Stichwörter in alphabetischer Reihenfolge aufgeführt.

ge|reift ADJ (*fig*) mature
struggling ADJ *artist, musician, actor* am Hungertuch nagend

Phrasal verbs

7.1 Phrasal verbs are covered in separate entries marked ▶ following the main headword.

7.2 Verb + adverb and verb + preposition combinations have been treated as phrasal verbs:
(a) where either the meaning or the translation is not simply derivable from the individual constituents;
(b) for clarity in the case of the longer verb entries.

Where a combination consists simply of a verb plus an adverb or preposition of direction it will frequently be covered under the main headword.

dash ... VI a (= *rush*) ... **to ~ away/back/up** fort-/zurück-/hinaufstürzen

7.3 Irregular preterites and past participles are only given in phrasal verb entries in the rare cases where they differ from those given in the main entry.

7.4 Phrasal verbs are treated in four grammatical categories:

7.4.1 VI (intransitive verb)

▶ **grow apart** VI (*fig*) sich auseinander entwickeln

7.4.2 VI +*prep obj*
This indicates that the verbal element is intransitive but that the particle requires an object.

▶ **hold with** VI +*prep obj* (*inf*) **I don't hold with that** ich bin gegen so was (*inf*)

7.4.3 VT
This indicates that the verbal element is transitive. In most cases the object can be placed either before or after the particle; these cases are marked SEP.

▶ **hand in** VT *sep* abgeben; *forms, thesis also, resignation* einreichen

In some cases the object must precede the particle; these cases are marked *always separate*.

▶ **get over with** VT *always separate* hinter sich (*acc*) bringen
let's get it over with bringen wirs hinter uns

Occasionally the object must come after the particle, these cases are marked INSEP.

▶ **put forth** VI +*prep obj buds, shoots* hervorbringen

7.4.4 VT +*prep obj*
This indicates that both the verbal element and the particle require an object.

▶ **take upon** VT +*prep obj* **he took that job upon himself** er hat das völlig ungebeten getan

In cases where a prepositional object is optional its translation is covered under VI or VT.

▶ **get off** VI a (= *descend, from bus, train etc*) aussteigen (*prep obj* aus);
(*from bicycle, horse*) absteigen (*prep obj* von)
▶ **go down** VI hinuntergehen (*prep obj* +*acc*)

For example:

he got off er stieg aus/ab
he got off the bus er stieg aus dem Bus aus
he got off his bicycle er stieg von seinem Fahrrad ab
she went down sie ging hinunter
she went down the street sie ging die Straße hinunter

Phrasal verbs

7.1 *Phrasal verbs* (feste Verb-Partikel-Verbindungen) sind in eigenen Einträgen abgehandelt. Sie sind durch ▶ gekennzeichnet und folgen dem Stichworteintrag für das Verb.

7.2 Die Zusammensetzungen Verb + Adverb und Verb + Präposition werden als *phrasal verbs* abgehandelt:
(a) wo entweder die Bedeutung oder die Übersetzung sich nicht aus den Einzelbestandteilen ergibt;
(b) aus Gründen der Übersichtlichkeit bei längeren Verbeinträgen.

Bei einfachen Kombinationen von Verb + Adverb oder Präposition der Richtung ist unter dem Haupteintrag zu suchen.

7.3 Unregelmäßige Formen des Präteritums und des 2. Partizips werden in Einträgen, die *phrasal verbs* behandeln, nur in den seltenen Fällen angegeben, wo sie von den im Haupteintrag angegebenen abweichen.

7.4 *Phrasal verbs* werden unter vier grammatischen Kategorien abgehandelt:

7.4.1 VI (intransitives Verb)

7.4.2 VI +*prep obj*
Hiermit soll gezeigt werden, dass das Verbelement intransitiv ist, dass aber die Partikel ein Objekt erfordert.

7.4.3 VT
Dies gibt an, dass das Verbelement transitiv ist. In den meisten Fällen kann das Objekt vor oder hinter der Partikel stehen; diese Fälle sind mit SEP bezeichnet.

In einigen Fällen muss das Objekt der Partikel vorangehen; solche Fälle sind durch *always separate* bezeichnet.

Gelegentlich muss das Objekt der Partikel nachgestellt werden; solche Fälle sind durch INSEP bezeichnet.

7.4.4 VT +*prep obj*
Hiermit wird gezeigt, dass *sowohl* das Verbelement als auch die Partikel ein Objekt verlangen.

In Fällen, wo ein Präpositionalobjekt möglich, aber nicht nötig ist, findet man die entsprechende Übersetzung unter VI oder VT.

Zum Beispiel:

Cross references

8.1 Cross-references are used in the following instances:

8.1.1 to refer the user to the spelling variant treated in depth;

8.1.2 to refer the user to the headword where a particular construction or idiom has been treated;

8.1.3 to draw the user's attention to the full treatment of such words as numerals, languages, days of the week and months of the year under certain key words.

Punctuation and Symbols

, between translations indicates that the translations are interchangeable; between alternative phrases to be translated indicates that the phrases have the same meaning.

; between translations indicates a difference in meaning which is clarified by explanatory material unless:
- (a) the distinction has already been made within the same entry;
- (b) in the case of some compounds the distinction is made under the simple form;
- (c) the distinction is self-evident.

/ between translations indicates parallel structure but different meanings, e.g. **to feel good/bad**.
- (a) in a source language phrase it will normally be paralleled in the translation; where this is not the case, the translation covers both meanings
- (b) in a target language phrase where it is not paralleled by an oblique in the source language the distinction will either be made clear earlier in the entry or will be self-evident
- (c) in compounds it may be used to reflect a distinction made under the simple form.

~ is used within an entry to represent the headword whenever it occurs in an unchanged form.

In German headwords of the form **Reisende(r)** MF **decl as adj**, and **höchste(r, s)** ADJ it only replaces the element outside the brackets.

In blocks of German compounds it represents the whole compound, not just its first element.

— separates two speakers.

≈ indicates that the translation is approximate or the cultural equivalent of the term and may not have exactly the same sense; in the case of institutions, they are those of the country indicated and obviously not the same.

or is used to separate parts of a word or phrase which are semantically interchangeable.

also, auch used after indicating material denotes that the translation(s) following it can be used in addition to the first translation(s) given in the respective entry, category or phrase.

Querverweise

8.1 Querverweise sind gelegentlich verwendet worden:

8.1.1 um den Benutzer auf diejenige Schreibweise zu verweisen, wo die ausführliche Darstellung des Stichworts zu finden ist;

8.1.2 um den Benutzer auf das Stichwort zu verweisen, wo eine bestimmte Konstruktion oder Wendung abgehandelt wird;

8.1.3 um die Aufmerksamkeit des Benutzers auf die ausführliche Behandlung solcher Wortklassen wie Zahlwörter, Sprachbezeichnungen, Wochentage und Monate unter bestimmten Schlüsselwörtern zu lenken.

Satzzeichen und Symbole

, zwischen Übersetzungen zeigt an, dass die Übersetzungen gleichwertig sind; zwischen Wendungen in der Ausgangssprache zeigt an, dass die Wendungen die gleiche Bedeutung haben.

; zwischen Übersetzungen zeigt einen Bedeutungsunterschied an, der durch erklärende Zusätze erläutert ist, außer:
- (a) wenn die Unterscheidung innerhalb desselben Eintrags schon gemacht worden ist;
- (b) bei Komposita, wo die Unterscheidung schon unter dem Simplex getroffen wurde
- (c) wenn die Unterscheidung offensichtlich ist.

/ zwischen Übersetzungen zeigt an, dass es sich um analoge Strukturen aber verschiedene Übersetzungen handelt, z. B. **to feel good/bad**.
- (a) der Schrägstrich in einer ausgangssprachlichen Wendung wird im Allgemeinen seine Entsprechung in der Übersetzung finden; wo das nicht der Fall ist, gilt die Übersetzung für beide Bedeutungen;
- (b) hat ein Schrägstrich in der Zielsprache kein Äquivalent in der Ausgangssprache, geht die getroffene Unterscheidung entweder aus in dem Eintrag bereits Gesagtem hervor oder sie ist offensichtlich;
- (c) bei Zusammensetzungen kann der Schrägstrich verwendet werden, um an eine für das Simplex getroffene Unterscheidung anzuknüpfen.

~ wird innerhalb von Einträgen verwendet, um das unveränderte Stichwort zu ersetzen.

Bei deutschen Stichwörtern des Typs **Reisende(r)** MF **decl as adj** und **höchste(r, s)** ADJ ersetzt die Tilde den außerhalb der Klammer stehenden Teil des Wortes.

In deutschen Komposita-Blöcken ersetzt die Tilde das Stichwort selbst, also nicht nur das erste Element der Zusammensetzung.

— unterscheidet zwischen zwei Sprechern.

≈ weist darauf hin, dass die Übersetzung eine Entsprechung ist oder aufgrund kultureller Unterschiede nicht genau die gleiche Bedeutung hat. Bei Institutionen werden die des jeweiligen Landes angegeben, die natürlich nicht identisch sind.

or wird verwendet, um Bestandteile einer Wendung zu unterscheiden, die semantisch austauschbar sind.

also, auch nach erklärenden Zusätzen gibt an, dass die folgende(n) Übersetzung(en) zusätzlich zu der ersten Übersetzung oder Folge von austauschbaren Übersetzungen, die in dem Eintrag oder der Kategorie angegeben sind, benutzt werden kann/können.

in a phrase or translation indicate that the word is stressed.

CAPITALS GROSS- BUCHSTA- BEN

in Wendungen oder Übersetzungen geben an, dass das Wort betont ist.

(in German headwords) shows hyphenation points

|

(in deutschen Stichwörtern) zeigt die Worttrennung an

Adjectives and Adverbs

Declension of German adjectives

Adjectives ending in -abel, -ibel, -el drop the -e- when declined.

miserabel	ein miserabler Stil
	eine miserable Handschrift
	ein miserables Leben
heikel	ein heikler Fall
	eine heikle Frage
	ein heikles Problem

Adjectives ending in -er, -en usually keep the -e- when declined, except:

1 in language of an elevated style level

finster	seine finstren Züge

2 in adjectives of foreign origin

makaber	eine makabre Geschichte
integer	ein integrer Beamter

Adjectives ending in -auer, -euer usually drop the -e- when declined.

teuer	ein teures Geschenk
sauer	saure Gurken

German adverbs

German adverbs are in most cases identical in form to the adjective.

Comparison of German adjectives and adverbs

Irregular comparative and superlative forms are given in the text, including those of adjectives and adverbs with the vowels a, o, u which take an umlaut:

gut [guːt] **ADJ** *comp* **besser** [ˈbɛsɐ], *superl* **beste(r, s)** ...
ADV *comp* **besser**, *superl* **am besten**

Where no forms are given in the text, the comparative and superlative are formed according to the following rules:

1 Both adjectives and adverbs add -er for the comparative before the declensional endings:

schön — schöner
eine schöne Frau — eine schönere Frau

2 Most adjectives add -ste(r, s) for the superlative:

schön — schönste(r, s)
ein schöner Tag — der schönste Tag

3 Most adverbs form the superlative according to the following pattern:

schön — am schönsten
schnell — am schnellsten

4 Adjectives and adverbs of one syllable or with the stress on the final syllable add -e before the superlative ending:

(i)	always if they end in -s, -ß, -st, -tz, -x, -z
(ii)	usually if they end in -d, -t, -sch

spitz **ADJ** **spitzeste(r, s)**
ADV **am spitzesten**
gerecht **ADJ** **gerechteste(r, s)**
ADV **am gerechtesten**

The same applies if they are used with a prefix or in compounds, regardless of where the stress falls:

unsanft **ADJ** **unsanfteste(r, s)**
ADV **am unsanftesten**

Adjektive und Adverbien

Adverbialbildung im Englischen

1 Die meisten Adjektive bilden das Adverb durch Anhängen von -ly:

strange -ly, odd -ly, beautiful -ly

2 Adjektive, die auf Konsonant +y enden, wandeln das auslautende -y in -i um und erhalten dann die Endung -ly:

happy — happily
merry — merrily

3 Adjektive, die auf -ic enden, bilden normalerweise das Adverb durch Anhängen vom -ally:

scenic -ally
linguistic -ally

Steigerung der englischen Adjektive und Adverbien

Adjektive und Adverbien, deren Komparativ und Superlativ im Allgemeinen durch Flexionsendungen gebildet werden, sind im Text durch (+er) bezeichnet, z. B.

young ADJ *(+er)*

Komparativ und Superlativ aller nicht durch (+er) bezeichneten Adjektive und Adverbien sind mit *more* und *most* zu bilden. Das gilt auch für alle auf -ly endenden Adverbien, z. B.

grateful — more grateful — most grateful
fully — more fully — most fully

Unregelmäßige Formen des Komparativs und Superlativs sind im Text angegeben, z. B.

bad ADJ *comp* **worse**, *superl* **worst**

well ADV *comp* **better**, *superl* **best**

Die flektierten Formen des Komparativs und Superlativs werden nach folgenden Regeln gebildet:

1 Die meisten Adjektive und Adverbien fügen -er zur Bildung des Komparativs und -est zur Bildung des Superlativs an:

small — smaller — smallest

2 Bei auf Konsonant +y endenden Adjektiven und Adverbien wird das auslautende -y in -i umgewandelt, bevor die Endung -er bzw. -est angefügt wird:

happy — happier — happiest

3 Mehrsilbige Adjektive auf -ey wandeln diese Endsilbe in -ier, -iest um:

homey — homier — homiest

4 Bei Adjektiven und Adverbien, die auf stummes -e enden, entfällt dieser Auslaut:

brave — braver — bravest

5 Bei Adjektiven und Adverbien, die auf -ee enden, entfällt das zweite -e:

free — freer — freest

6 Adjektive und Adverbien, die auf einen Konsonant nach einfachem betontem Vokal enden, verdoppeln den Konsonant im Auslaut:

sad — sadder — saddest

Nach Doppelvokal wird der auslautende Konsonant nicht verdoppelt:

loud — louder — loudest

General rules for forming the genitive

Genitive endings

Genitive endings are formed for masculine and neuter nouns by adding **-s** or **-es**

> **der Mann:** *(gen)* **des Mann(e)s**
> **das Rad:** *(gen)* **des Rad(e)s**

for feminine nouns: no change

> **die Frau:** *(gen)* **der Frau**

Masculine or neuter nouns ending in **-s, -ss, -ß, -x** and **-z** always take the full form of **-es** for the genitive

> **das Glas:** *(gen)* **des Glases**
> **der Fluss:** *(gen)* **des Flusses**
> **das Maß:** *(gen)* **des Maßes**
> **der Komplex:** *(gen)* **des Komplexes**
> **der Geiz:** *(gen)* **des Geizes**

Masculine or neuter nouns ending in **-sch** or **-st** normally take the full form of **-es**, as do those ending in a double consonant

> **der Wunsch:** *(gen)* **des Wunsches**
> **der Gast:** *(gen)* **des Gastes**
> **das Feld:** *(gen)* **des Feldes**
> **der Kampf:** *(gen)* **des Kampfes**

Masculine or neuter nouns ending in **-en, -em, -el, -er** and **-ling** always take the short form of **-s**

> **der Regen:** *(gen)* **des Regens**
> **der Atem:** *(gen)* **des Atems**
> **der Mantel:** *(gen)* **des Mantels**
> **der Sänger:** *(gen)* **des Sängers**
> **der Flüchtling:** *(gen)* **des Flüchtlings**

If the genitive is not formed according to these patterns it will be shown in the entry after the gender and before the plural ending

> **Herz** -ens, -en SUBSTANTIV (NT)
> **Klerus** M -, *no pl*

Weak nouns

Weak nouns have the same **-en** ending in the accusative, genitive and dative cases in both singular and plural forms

> **der Mensch:** *(acc)* **den Menschen**
> *(gen)* **des Menschen**
> *(dat)* **dem Menschen**

The Pronunciation of German

A full list of IPA symbols used is given on page xxvi.

Stress and vowel length

1. The stress and the length of the stressed vowel are shown for every German headword, either by providing full or partial phonetics using IPA symbols or by showing stress marks in the headword itself. A full list of IPA symbols used is given on page xxvi.

2. When phonetics are given for the headword a long vowel is indicated in the transcription by the length mark after it:

Chemie [çe'miː]

3. Where no phonetics are given a short stressed vowel is marked with a dot in the headword:

Muttermal

and a long stressed vowel is marked with a dash:

Vatertag

4. Where phonetics are not given, vowel combinations which represent a stressed diphthong or a stressed long vowel are marked with an unbroken dash in the headword:

beiderlei, Haar, sieben

5. **ie**
Stressed **ie** pronounced [iː] is marked by an unbroken dash:

sieben

When the plural ending **-n** is added, the pronunciation changes to [-iːən]:

Allegorie, pl Allegorien [-iːən]

6. **ee** is pronounced [eː]
When the plural ending **-n** is added the change in pronunciation is shown:

Allee [a'leː] F -, -n [-'leːən]

Consonants

Where a consonant is capable of more than one pronunciation the following rules apply:

1. **v**
(i) Note that **v** is often pronounced [f]:

Vater ['faːtɐ]

(ii) Words ending in **-iv** are pronounced [iːf] when undeclined, but when an ending is added the pronunciation changes to [iːv]:

aktiv [ak'tiːf]
aktive (as in der aktive Sportler) [ak'tiːvə]

2. **ng**
(i) **ng** is generally pronounced [ŋ]:

Finger ['fɪŋɐ]

(ii) In compound words where the first element ends in **-n** and the second element begins with **g-** the two sounds are pronounced individually:

Eingang ['aingaŋ]
ungeheuer ['ʊngəhɔyɐ]

3. **tion** is always pronounced [-tsioːn] at the end of a word and [-tsion-] in the middle of a word:

Nation [na'tsioːn]
national [natsio'naːl]

4. **st, sp**
(i) Where **st** or **sp** occurs in the middle or at the end of a word the pronunciation is [st], [sp]:

Fest [fɛst], Wespe ['vɛspə]

(ii) At the beginning of a word or at the beginning of the second element of a compound word the standard pronunciation is [ʃt], [ʃp]:

Stand [ʃtant], sperren ['ʃpɛrən]
Abstand ['ap-ʃtant], absperren ['ap-ʃpɛrən]

5. **ch**
(i) **ch** is pronounced [ç] after ä-, e-, i-, ö-, ü-, y-, ai-, ei-, äu, eu- and after consonants:

ich [ɪç], Milch [mɪlç]

(ii) **ch** is pronounced [x] after a-, o-, u-, au-:

doch [dɔx], Bauch [baux]

6. **ig** is pronounced [ɪç] at the end of a word:

König ['køːnɪç]

When an ending beginning with a vowel is added, it is pronounced [ig]:

Könige ['køːnɪgə]

7. **h** is pronounced [h]:
(i) at the beginning of a word
(ii) between vowels in interjections:

oho [o'hoː]

(iii) in words such as Ahorn ['aːhɔrn] and Uhu ['uːhu].
It is mute in the middle and at the end of non-foreign words:

leihen ['laiən], weh [veː]

8. **th** is pronounced [t].

9. **qu** is pronounced [kv].

10. **z** is pronounced [ts].

Where the pronunciation of a compound or derivative can be deduced from the simplex no phonetics are given.

Glottal Stop

1. A glottal stop (*Knacklaut*) occurs at the beginning of any word starting with a vowel.
2. A glottal stop always occurs in compounds between the first and second elements when the second element begins with a vowel.

Ausspracheangaben zum Englischen

Die Zeichen der im Text verwendeten Lautschrift entsprechen denen der *International Phonetic Association.*

Die Lautschrift gibt die Aussprache für das in Südengland gesprochene britische Englisch (Received Pronunciation) an, das in der gesamten Englisch sprechenden Welt akzeptiert und verstanden wird. Nordamerikanische Formen werden angegeben, wenn die Aussprache des betreffenden Wortes im amerikanischen Englisch erheblich abweicht (z.B. **lever**), nicht aber, wenn die Abweichung nur im „Akzent" besteht, wenn also Verständigungsschwierigkeiten nicht zu befürchten sind.

Jedes Stichwort im englischen Teil ist mit der Lautschrift versehen. Ausnahmen dazu bilden folgende Fälle:

1. zusammengesetzte Stichwörter (*Komposita*), die getrennt geschrieben werden (z.B. **buffet car**, **buffalo grass**). Die Aussprache der einzelnen Teile ist unter dem entsprechenden Stichwort angegeben.

2. *phrasal verbs* (z.B. **bring back**, **bring down**, **bring round**), wo ebenfalls die Einzelbestandteile an anderer Stelle behandelt sind.

3. gleich lautende Stichwörter mit hochgestellten Ziffern (z.B. **bore²**, **bore³**, **bore⁴**), wo die Aussprache nur einmal beim ersten Eintrag in der Reihe (d.h. bei **bore¹**) angeführt ist.

4. wenn ein Stichwort auf eine andere Schreibweise verwiesen wird, die Aussprache aber gleich lautet (z.B. **checkered** ... = **chequered**). In diesem Falle wird die Aussprache nur unter dem Wort, auf das verwiesen wird (**chequered**) angegeben.

Sonstiges

1. Die Aussprache von Abkürzungen, die als Kurzwörter (*Akronyme*) gebraucht werden, ist angegeben (z.B. **NATO** ['neɪtəʊ], **ASLEF** ['æzlef]). Wenn jeder Buchstabe einzeln ausgesprochen wird (z.B. **PTA**, **RIP**) erfolgt keine Ausspracheangabe.

2. Endungen in **-less** und **-ness** sind in der Lautschrift als [-lɪs] bzw. [-nɪs] wiedergegeben. Die Aussprache [-ləs] bzw. [nəs] ist ebenso gebräuchlich.

3. Stammformen unregelmäßiger Verben: Präteritum und 1. Partizip sind gesondert an der entsprechenden Stelle in der alphabetischen Reihenfolge angeführt und dort mit der Lautschrift versehen. Die Ausspracheangabe wird bei der Grundform des Verbs nicht wiederholt. So findet man z.B. die phonetische Umschrift für **bought**, **sold** usw. unter diesen Einträgen, nicht aber unter **buy**, **sell** usw.

Phonetic Symbols

Zeichen der Lautschrift

Vowels/Vokale

matt	[a]
Fahne	[a:]
Vater	[ɐ]
	[ɑ:] calm, part
	[æ] sat
Chanson	[ã]
Chance	[ɑ̃]
	[ɑ̃:] double entendre
Etage	[e] egg
Seele, Mehl	[e:]
Wäsche, Bett	[ɛ]
zählen	[ɛ:]
Teint	[ɛ̃:]
mache	[ə] above
	[ɜ:] burn, earn
Kiste	[ɪ] pit, awfully
Vitamin	[i]
Ziel	[i:] peat
Oase	[o]
oben	[o:]
Fondue	[õ]
Chanson	[õ:]
Most	[ɔ]
	[ɒ] cot
	[ɔ:] born, jaw
ökonomisch	[ø]
blöd	[ø:]
Götter	[œ]
Parfum	[œ̃:]
	[ʌ] hut
zuletzt	[u]
Mut	[u:] pool
Mutter	[ʊ] put
Typ	[y]
Kübel	[y:]
Sünde	[ʏ]

Consonants/Konsonanten

Ball	[b]	ball
mich	[ç]	
	[tʃ]	child
fern	[f]	field
gern	[g]	good
Hand	[h]	hand
ja, Million	[j]	yet, million
	[dʒ]	just
Kind	[k]	kind, catch
links, Pult	[l]	left, little
matt	[m]	mat
Nest	[n]	nest
lang	[ŋ]	long
Paar	[p]	put
rennen	[r]	run
fast, fassen	[s]	sit
Chef, Stein, Schlag	[ʃ]	shall
Tafel	[t]	tab
	[θ]	thing
	[ð]	this
wer	[v]	very
	[w]	wet
Loch	[x]	loch
fix	[ks]	box
singen	[z]	pods, zip
Zahn	[ts]	
genieren	[ʒ]	measure

Other signs/Andere Zeichen

ǀ	glottal stop/Knacklaut
[ʳ]	[r] pronounced before a vowel/vor Vokal ausgesprochenes [r]
[ˈ]	main stress/Hauptton
[ˌ]	secondary stress/Nebenton

Diphthongs/Diphthonge

weit	[ai]
	[aɪ] buy, die, my
Haus	[au]
	[aʊ] house, now
	[eɪ] pay, mate
	[ɛə] pair, mare
	[əʊ] no, boat
	[ɪə] mere, shear
Heu, Häuser	[ɔy]
	[ɔɪ] boy, coin
	[ʊə] tour, poor

NB: Vowels and consonants which are frequently elided (not spoken) are given in *italics:*

Vokale und Konsonanten, die häufig elidiert (nicht ausgesprochen) werden, sind *kursiv* dargestellt:

convention [kənˈvenʃən]
attempt [əˈtempt]

ENGLISH~GERMAN DICTIONARY

WÖRTERBUCH ENGLISCH~DEUTSCH

A

A, a [eɪ] N A nt, a nt; (*Sch: as a mark*) Eins f, sehr gut; (*Mus*) A nt, a nt; **from A to Z** von A bis Z; **to get from A to B** von A nach B kommen; **A sharp** (*Mus*) Ais nt, ais nt; **A flat** (*Mus*) As nt, as nt → **major**

A **a** abbr of **answer** Antw. **b** (*dated Brit Film*) von der Filmkontrolle als nicht ganz jugendfrei gekennzeichneter Film **A certificate** Filmkennzeichnung, die Eltern vor dem nicht ganz jugendfreien Inhalt eines Films warnt

a [eɪ, ə] INDEF ART before vowel **an** **a** ein(e); **so large a school** so eine große or eine so große Schule; **a Mr X** ein Herr X; **a certain young man** ein gewisser junger Mann

b (*in negative constructions*) **not a** kein(e); **not a single man** kein einziger or nicht ein einziger Mann; **he didn't want a present** er wollte kein Geschenk

c (*with profession, nationality etc*) **he's a doctor/ Frenchman** er ist Arzt/Franzose; **he's a famous doctor/Frenchman** er ist ein berühmter Arzt/Franzose; **as a young girl** als junges Mädchen; **a Washington would have ...** ein Washington hätte ...

d (= *the same*) **to be of an age/a size** gleich alt/groß sein → **size**

e (= *per*) pro; **50p a kilo** 50 Pence das or pro Kilo; **twice a month** zweimal im or pro Monat; **50 km an hour** 50 Stundenkilometer, 50 Kilometer pro Stunde

f **in a good/bad mood** gut/schlecht gelaunt; **to come/to have come to an end** zu Ende gehen/sein; **in a loud voice** mit lauter Stimme, laut; **to have a headache/temperature** Kopfschmerzen/erhöhte Temperatur haben

a- PREF **a** (*privative*) **amoral** amoralisch; **atypical** atypisch **b** (*old, dial*) **they came a-running** sie kamen angerannt; **the bells were a-ringing** die Glocken läuteten

A-1 [ˈeɪˈwʌn] ADJ (*dated inf*) eins a (*inf*)

AA **a** abbr of **Automobile Association** Britischer Automobilclub **b** abbr of **Alcoholics Anonymous** **c** (*dated Brit Film*) für Jugendliche ab 14 freigegebener Film

AAA **a** abbr of **American Automobile Association** Amerikanischer Automobilclub **b** abbr of **Australian Automobile Association** Australischer Automobilclub

AAIB (*Brit*) abbr of **Air Accident Investigation Branch**

A & E abbr of **accident and emergency**

aardvark [ˈɑːdvɑːk] N Erdferkel nt

Aaron's beard [ˈeərnzˈbɪəd] N Hartheu nt

AB abbr **a** (*Naut*) of **able-bodied seaman** **b** (*US Univ*) = **BA**

ABA abbr **a** (*Brit*) of **Amateur Boxing Association** **b** (*US*) = **American Bar Association** **c** (*US*) = American Booksellers' Association

aback [əˈbæk] ADV **to be taken ~** erstaunt sein; (= *upset*) betroffen sein

abacus [ˈæbəkəs] N pl **abaci** [ˈæbəsiː] Abakus m

abaft [əˈbɑːft] ADV (*Naut*) achtern

abalone [æbəˈləʊnɪ] N Seeohr nt

abandon [əˈbændən] **VT** **a** (= *leave, forsake*) verlassen; *woman* verlassen, sitzen lassen; *baby* aussetzen; *car* (einfach) stehen lassen; **they ~ed the city to the enemy** sie flohen und überließen dem Feind die Stadt; **to ~ ship** das Schiff verlassen **b** (= *give up*) *project, hope, attempt* aufgeben; **to ~ play** das Spiel abbrechen **c** (*fig*) **to ~ oneself to sth** sich einer Sache (*dat*) hingeben **N** no pl Hingabe f, Selbstvergessenheit f; **with ~** mit ganzer Seele, mit Leib und Seele

abandoned [əˈbændənd] ADJ **a** (= *dissolute*) verkommen **b** (= *unrestrained*) *dancing* selbstvergessen, hingebungsvoll, hemmungslos (*pej*); *joy* unbändig

abandonment [əˈbændənmənt] N **a** (= *forsaking, desertion*) Verlassen nt **b** (= *giving-up*) Aufgabe f **c** (= *abandon*) Hingabe f, Selbstvergessenheit f, Hemmungslosigkeit f (*pej*)

abase [əˈbeɪs] VT *person* erniedrigen; *morals* verderben; **to ~ oneself** sich (selbst) erniedrigen

abasement [əˈbeɪsmənt] N Erniedrigung f; (*of concept of love etc*) Abwertung f; (= *lowering of standards*) Verfall m, Niedergang m; **~ of morality** Verfall der Moral

abashed [əˈbæʃt] ADJ beschämt; **to feel ~** sich schämen

abate [əˈbeɪt] **VI** nachlassen; (*storm, eagerness, interest, noise also*) abflauen; (*pain, fever also*) abklingen; (*flood*) zurückgehen **VT** (*form*) *noise, sb's interest* dämpfen; *fever* senken; *pain* lindern

abatement [əˈbeɪtmənt] N Nachlassen nt; (*of storm, eagerness, interest also*) Abflauen nt; (*of pain also*) Abklingen nt; (*of flood*) Rückgang m; (*of rent, tax*) Senkung f; **the noise ~ society** die Gesellschaft zur Bekämpfung von Lärm

abattoir [ˈæbətwɑː] N Schlachthof m

abbess [ˈæbɪs] N Äbtissin f

abbey [ˈæbɪ] N Abtei f; (= *church in abbey*) Klosterkirche f

abbot [ˈæbət] N Abt m

abbr., abbrev. **a** abbr of **abbreviation** Abk. **b** abbr of **abbreviated** abgek.

abbreviate [əˈbriːvɪeɪt] VT *word, title* abkürzen (*to* mit); *book, speech* verkürzen; **an ~d skirt** (*hum inf*) ein kurzes Röckchen

abbreviation [əˌbriːvɪˈeɪʃən] N (*of word, title*) Abkürzung f; (*of book, speech*) Verkürzung f

ABC¹ (*lit, fig*) Abc nt; **it's as easy as ~** das ist doch kinderleicht

ABC² abbr of **American Broadcasting Company** amerikanische Rundfunkgesellschaft

ABD (*US, Univ*) abbr of **all but dissertation** Status eines Doktoranden, der seine Dissertation noch schreiben muss **she was still ~ after four years** nach vier Jahren als Doktorandin hatte sie ihre Dissertation immer noch nicht geschrieben

abdicate [ˈæbdɪkeɪt] **VT** verzichten auf (+*acc*) **VI** (*monarch*) abdanken, abdizieren (*dated geh*); (*pope*) zurücktreten

abdication [æbdɪˈkeɪʃən] N (*of monarch*) Abdankung f, Abdikation f (*dated geh*); (*of pope*) Verzicht m; **his ~ of the throne** sein Verzicht auf den Thron

abdomen [ˈæbdəmən] N Abdomen nt (*form*); (*of man, mammals also*) Unterleib m; (*of insects also*) Hinterleib m

abdominal [æbˈdɒmɪnl] ADJ abdominal (*form*); (*in man, mammals also*) Unterleibs-; (*in insects also*) Hinterleibs-; **~ pain** Unterleibsschmerzen pl; **~ segments** Abdominalsegmente pl; **~ wall** Bauchdecke f

abduct [æbˈdʌkt] VT entführen

abduction [æbˈdʌkʃən] N Entführung f

abductor [æbˈdʌktə] N Entführer(in) m(f)

abeam [əˈbiːm] ADV (*Naut*) querab

abed [əˈbed] ADV (*old*) im Bett; **to be ~** (im Bette) ruhen (*geh*)

Aberdeen Angus [æbədiːnˈæŋgəs] N (*Zool*) Angusrind nt

Aberdonian [æbəˈdəʊnjən] **N** Aberdeener(in) m(f) **ADJ** Aberdeener inv

aberrant [əˈberənt] ADJ anomal

aberration [æbəˈreɪʃən] N Anomalie f; (*Astron, Opt*) Aberration f; (*in statistics, from course*) Abweichung f; (= *mistake*) Irrtum m; (*moral*) Verirrung f; **in a moment of (mental) ~** (*inf*) in einem Augenblick geistiger Verwirrung; **I must have had an ~** (*inf*) da war ich wohl (geistig) weggetreten (*inf*); **the housing scheme is something of an ~** (*inf*) die Wohnsiedlung ist (ja) eine Geschmacksverirrung (*inf*)

abet [əˈbet] **VT** *crime, criminal* begünstigen, Vorschub leisten (+*dat*); (*fig*) unterstützen **VI** → **aid VT**

abetment [əˈbetmənt] N **a** (= *support*) Hilfe f, Unterstützung f **b** (*Jur*) Beihilfe f, Vorschub m

abetter, abettor [əˈbetə] N Helfershelfer(in) m(f)

abeyance [əˈbeɪəns] N , no pl **to be in ~** (*law, rule, issue*) ruhen; (*custom, office*) nicht mehr ausgeübt werden; **to fall into ~** außer Gebrauch kommen, nicht mehr wirksam sein; **to hold/ leave sth in ~** etw ruhen lassen

abhor [əbˈhɔː] VT verabscheuen

abhorrence [əbˈhɒrəns] N Abscheu f (*of vor* +*dat*)

abhorrent [əbˈhɒrənt] ADJ abscheulich; **the very idea is ~ to me** schon der Gedanke daran ist mir zuwider; **the notion is ~ to the rational mind** der Verstand widersetzt sich einer solchen Idee

abidance [əˈbaɪdəns] N (*form*) **~ by the rules/ laws** die Einhaltung der Regeln/Gesetze

abide [əˈbaɪd] **VT** **a** (*usu neg, interrog*) (= *tolerate*) ausstehen; (= *endure*) aushalten; **I cannot ~ living here** ich kann es nicht aushalten, hier zu leben **b** (*liter:* = *wait for*) harren (+*gen*) (*liter*) **VI** (*old:* = *remain, live*) weilen (*geh*)

▶ **abide by** VI +prep obj *rule, law, decision, promise, results* sich halten an (+*acc*); *consequences* tragen; **I abide by what I said** ich bleibe bei dem, was ich gesagt habe

abiding [əˈbaɪdɪŋ] ADJ (*liter:* = *lasting*) unvergänglich; *desire also* bleibend

ability [əˈbɪlɪtɪ] N Fähigkeit f; **~ to pay/hear** Zahlungs-/Hörfähigkeit f; **to the best of my ~** nach (besten) Kräften; (*with mental activities*) so gut ich es kann; **a man of great ~** ein sehr fähiger Mann; **his ~ in German** seine Fähigkeiten im Deutschen; **she has great ~** sie ist ausgesprochen fähig

abiotic ADJ , **abiotically** ADV [ˌeɪbaɪˈɒtɪk, -lɪ] abiotisch (*spec*), unbelebt

abject [ˈæbdʒekt] ADJ **a** (= wretched) state, liar, thief elend, erbärmlich; poverty bitter; failure kläglich **b** (= servile) submission, apology demütig; person, gesture unterwürfig

abjectly [ˈæbdʒektlɪ] ADV submit, apologize demütig; fail kläglich; miserable, afraid erbärmlich

abjectness [ˈæbdʒektnɪs] N **a** (= wretchedness) Erbärmlichkeit f **b** (= servility) (of apology) Demut f; (of person, gesture also) Unterwürfigkeit f

abjuration [ˌæbdʒʊəˈreɪʃn] N Abschwören nt

abjure [əbˈdʒʊə] VT abschwören (+dat)

Abkhaz [æbˈkɑːz], **Abkhazi** [æbˈkɑːzɪ] ADJ abchasisch **N a** (a person) Abchase m, Abchasin f **b** (Ling) Abchasisch nt

Abkhazia [æbˈkɑːzɪə] N Abchasien nt

Abkhazian [æbˈkɑːzɪən] ADJ, N = **Abkhaz**

ablative [ˈæblətɪv] **N** Ablativ m; ~ **absolute** Ablativus absolutus **ADJ** Ablativ-; noun im Ablativ; ~ **ending** Ablativendung f

ablaut [ˈæblaʊt] N Ablaut m

ablaze [əˈbleɪz] ADV, ADJ pred **a** (lit) in Flammen; **to be ~** in Flammen stehen; **to set sth ~** etw in Brand stecken; **the paraffin really set the fire** – das Paraffin ließ das Feuer wirklich auflodern **b** (fig: = animated) **her eyes were ~** ihre Augen glühten; **his face was ~ with joy/anger** sein Gesicht glühte vor Freude/brannte vor Ärger; **to be ~ with light** hell erleuchtet sein; **to be ~ with colour** (Brit) or **color** (US) in leuchtenden Farben erstrahlen

able [ˈeɪbl] ADJ **a** (= skilled, talented) person fähig, kompetent; piece of work, exam paper, speech gekonnt **b** **to be ~ to do sth** etw tun können; **if you're not ~ to understand that** wenn Sie nicht fähig sind, das zu verstehen; **I'm afraid I am not ~ to give you that information** ich bin leider nicht in der Lage, Ihnen diese Informationen zu geben; **you are better ~ to do it than he is** Sie sind eher dazu in der Lage als er; **yes, if I'm ~** ja, wenn es mir möglich ist

-able [-əbl] ADJ suf -bar; **washable** waschbar; **to be doable** machbar sein

able-bodied [ˌeɪblˈbɒdɪd] ADJ (gesund und) kräftig; (Mil) tauglich

able(-bodied) seaman N Vollmatrose m

abled [ˈeɪbld] ADJ nicht behindert

abloom [əˈbluːm] ADJ pred (poet, liter) **to be ~** (flower) blühen (lit, fig); tree in Blüte stehen (liter)

ablution [əˈbluːʃən] N **a** Waschung f **b** **ablutions** PL (= lavatory) sanitäre Einrichtungen pl; **to perform one's ~s** (esp hum) seine Waschungen vornehmen; (= go to lavatory) seine Notdurft verrichten

ably [ˈeɪblɪ] ADV gekonnt, fähig

ABM abbr of **anti-ballistic missile**

abnegate [ˈæbnɪɡeɪt] VT entsagen (+dat)

abnegation [ˌæbnɪˈɡeɪʃən] N Verzicht m (of auf +acc), Entsagung f

abnormal [æbˈnɔːməl] ADJ anormal; (= deviant, Med) abnorm; ~ **psychology** Psychologie f des Abnormen

abnormality [ˌæbnɔːˈmælɪtɪ] N Anormale(s) nt; (= deviancy, Med) Abnormität f

abnormally [æbˈnɔːməlɪ] ADV grow, develop abnormal; high, low also abnorm

Abo [ˈæbəʊ] N (Austral, inf) = **aborigine**

aboard [əˈbɔːd] ADV (on plane, ship) an Bord; (on train) im Zug; (on bus) im Bus; **all ~!** alle an Bord!; (on train, bus) alles einsteigen!; **to go ~** an Bord gehen; **they were no sooner ~ than the train/bus moved off** sie waren kaum eingestiegen, als der Zug/Bus auch schon abfuhr **PREP ~ the ship/plane** an Bord des Schiffes/Flugzeugs; **~ the train/bus** im Zug/Bus

abode [əˈbəʊd] pret, ptp of **abide** **N** (liter. = dwelling place) Behausung f, Aufenthalt m (liter); (Jur: also **place of abode**) Wohnsitz m; **a humble ~** (iro) eine bescheidene Hütte (iro); **of no fixed ~** ohne festen Wohnsitz

abolish [əˈbɒlɪʃ] VT abschaffen; law also aufheben

abolishment [əˈbɒlɪʃmənt], **abolition** [ˌæbəʊˈlɪʃən] N Abschaffung f; (of law also) Aufhebung f

abolitionist [ˌæbəʊˈlɪʃənɪst] N Befürworter der Abschaffung eines Gesetzes etc, Abolitionist(in) m(f) (form)

A-bomb [ˈeɪbɒm] N Atombombe f

abominable [əˈbɒmɪnəbl] ADJ grässlich, abscheulich; spelling grässlich, entsetzlich; ~ **snowman** Schneemensch m

abominably [əˈbɒmɪnəblɪ] ADV grässlich, abscheulich; ~ **rude** furchtbar unhöflich

abominate [əˈbɒmɪneɪt] VT verabscheuen

abomination [əˌbɒmɪˈneɪʃən] N **a** no pl Verabscheuung f; **to be held in ~ by sb** von jdm verabscheut werden **b** (= loathsome act) Abscheulichkeit f; (= loathsome thing) Scheußlichkeit f

aboriginal [ˌæbəˈrɪdʒənl] **ADJ** der (australischen) Ureinwohner, australid; tribe also australisch **N** = **aborigine**

aborigine [ˌæbəˈrɪdʒɪnɪ] N Ureinwohner(in) m(f) (Australiens), Australide m, Australidin f

aborning [əˈbɔːnɪŋ] (US) **ADV to die ~** (project, idea) noch vor seiner/ihrer etc Durchführung scheitern **ADJ to be ~** im Entstehen begriffen sein

abort [əˈbɔːt] **VI** (Med) (mother) eine Fehlgeburt haben, abortieren (form); (foetus) abgehen; (= perform abortion) die Schwangerschaft abbrechen, einen Abort herbeiführen (form); (fig: = go wrong) scheitern; (Comput) abbrechen **VT** (Med) foetus (durch Abort) entfernen, abtreiben (pej); (Space) mission abbrechen; (Comput) abbrechen; **an ~ed coup/attempt** ein abgebrochener Coup/Versuch **N** (Space) Abort m (form)

abortion [əˈbɔːʃən] N Schwangerschaftsabbruch m, Abtreibung f (pej); (= miscarriage) Fehlgeburt f, Abort m (form); (fig: of plan, project etc) Fehlschlag m, Reinfall m (inf); (pej, = person) Missgeburt f (pej); **to get** or **have an ~** abtreiben lassen, eine Abtreibung vornehmen lassen

abortionist [əˈbɔːʃənɪst] N Abtreibungshelfer(in) m(f); (doctor also) Abtreibungsarzt m/-ärztin f → **back-street**

abortion pill N Abtreibungspille f

abortive [əˈbɔːtɪv] ADJ **a** (= unsuccessful) attempt, plan gescheitert, fehlgeschlagen; **to be ~** scheitern, fehlschlagen **b** (Med) drug abortiv (form), abtreibend

abortively [əˈbɔːtɪvlɪ] ADV end ergebnislos

abortuary [əˈbɔːtjʊərɪ] N (US pej) Abtreibungsklinik f

ABO system N (of blood groups) ABO System nt

abound [əˈbaʊnd] VI (= exist in great numbers) im Überfluss vorhanden sein; (persons) sehr zahlreich sein; (= have in great numbers) reich sein (in an +dat); **students/rabbits ~ in ...** es wimmelt von Studenten/Kaninchen in ...; **rumours** (Brit) or **rumors** (US) ~ **in this place** hier kursieren jede Menge Gerüchte

about [əˈbaʊt] **ADV a** (esp Brit) herum, umher; (= present) in der Nähe; **to run/walk ~** herum- or umherrennen/-gehen; **I looked (all) ~** ich sah ringsumher; **to leave things (lying) ~** Sachen herumliegen lassen; **to be (up and) ~** again wieder auf den Beinen sein; **we were ~ early** wir waren früh auf den Beinen; **there's a thief ~** ein Dieb geht um; **there's plenty of money ~** es ist Geld in Mengen vorhanden; **there was nobody ~ who could help** es war niemand in der Nähe, der hätte helfen können; **at night when there's nobody ~** nachts, wenn niemand unterwegs ist; **where is he/it?** – **he's/it's ~ somewhere** wo ist er/es? – (er/es ist) irgendwo in der Nähe; **it's the other way ~** es ist gerade umgekehrt; **day and day ~** (täglich) abwechselnd → **out, turn, up**

b to be ~ to im Begriff sein zu; (esp US inf: = intending) vorhaben, zu ...; **I was ~ to go out** ich wollte gerade ausgehen; **it's ~ to rain** es

regnet gleich or demnächst; **he's ~ to start school** er kommt demnächst in die Schule; **we are ~ to run out of coffee** uns geht demnächst der Kaffee aus, wir haben bald keinen Kaffee mehr; **are you ~ to tell me ...?** willst du mir etwa erzählen ...?

c (= approximately) ungefähr, (so) um ... (herum); **he's ~ 40** er ist ungefähr 40 or (so) um (die) 40 (herum); **~ 2 o'clock** ungefähr or so um 2 Uhr; **he is ~ the same, doctor** sein Zustand hat sich kaum geändert, Herr Doktor; **that's ~ it** das ist so ziemlich alles, das wärs (so ziemlich) (inf); **that's ~ right** das stimmt (so) ungefähr; **I've had ~ enough (of this nonsense)** jetzt reicht es mir aber allmählich (mit diesem Unsinn) (inf); **he was ~ dead from exhaustion** er war halb tot vor Erschöpfung → **just, round, time**

PREP a (esp Brit) um (... herum); (= in) in (+dat) (... herum); **the fields ~ the house** die Felder ums Haus (herum); **scattered ~ the room** im ganzen or über das ganze Zimmer verstreut; **somewhere ~ here** irgendwo hierherum; **all ~ the house** im ganzen Haus (herum); **to sit ~ the house** im Haus herumsitzen; **to do jobs ~ the house** sich im Haus (herum) nützlich machen; **he looked ~ him** er schaute sich um; **there's something ~ him/~ the way he speaks** er/seine Art zu reden hat so etwas an sich; **while you're ~ it** wenn du gerade or schon dabei bist; **you've been a long time ~ it** du hast lange dazu gebraucht; **and be quick ~ it!** und beeil dich damit!, aber ein bisschen dalli! (inf)

b (= concerning) über (+acc); **tell me all ~ it** erzähl doch mal; **he knows ~ it** er weiß darüber Bescheid, er weiß davon; **what's it all ~?** worum or um was (inf) handelt es sich or geht es (eigentlich)?; **he knows what it's all ~** er weiß Bescheid; **he's promised to do something ~ it** er hat versprochen, (in der Sache) etwas zu unternehmen; **they fell out ~ money** sie haben sich wegen Geld zerstritten; **how** or **what ~ me?** und ich, was ist mit mir? (inf); **how** or **what ~ it/going to the cinema?** wie wärs damit/mit (dem) Kino?; **what ~ that book? have you brought it back?** was ist mit dem Buch? hast du es zurückgebracht?; **(yes,) what ~ it/him?** ja or na und(, was ist damit/mit ihm)?; **he doesn't know what he's ~** er weiß nicht, was er (eigentlich) tut

about-face [əˌbaʊtˈfeɪs], **about-turn** [əˌbaʊtˈtɜːn] **N** (Mil) Kehrtwendung f; (fig also) Wendung f um hundertachtzig Grad; **to do an ~** kehrtmachen; (fig) sich um hundertachtzig Grad drehen **VI** (Mil) eine Kehrtwendung ausführen or machen **INTERJ about face** or **turn!** (und) kehrt!

above [əˈbʌv] **ADV a** (= overhead) oben; (= in a higher position) darüber; **from ~** von oben; **look ~** schau nach oben; **the apartment ~** die Wohnung oben or (above that one) darüber

b (in text) oben

PREP über (+dat); (with motion) über (+acc); (= upstream of) oberhalb (+gen); ~ **all** vor allem, vor allen Dingen; **I couldn't hear ~ the din** ich konnte bei dem Lärm nichts hören; **he valued money ~ his family** er schätzte Geld mehr als seine Familie; **to be ~ sb/sth** über jdm/etw stehen; **he's ~ that sort of thing** er ist über so etwas erhaben; **he's not ~ a bit of blackmail** er ist sich (dat) nicht zu gut für eine kleine Erpressung; **it's ~ my head** or **me** das ist mir zu hoch; **to get ~ oneself** (inf) größenwahnsinnig werden (inf)

ADJ attr **the ~ persons/figures** die oben genannten or oben erwähnten Personen/Zahlen; **the ~ paragraph** der vorangehende or obige Abschnitt

N the ~ (= statement etc) Obiges nt (form); (= person) der/die Obengenannte or oben Genannte; (several) die Obengenannten pl or oben Genannten pl

above: **above board** ADJ PRED, **above-board** ADJ ATTR korrekt; **open and ~** offen und ehrlich; **above-mentioned** ADJ obenerwähnt; **above-named** ADJ obengenannt

abracadabra [æbrəkə'dæbrə] N Abrakadabra *nt*

abrade [ə'breɪd] VT (*form*) *skin* aufschürfen, abschürfen; (*Geol*) abtragen

Abraham ['eɪbrəhæm] N Abraham *m*; **in ~'s bosom** in Abrahams Schoß

abrasion [ə'breɪʒən] N (*Med*) (Haut)abschürfung *f*; (*Geol*) Abtragung *f*

abrasive [ə'breɪsɪv] **ADJ** **a** *cleanser* scharf; *surface* rauh; **~ paper** Schmirgel- or Schleifpapier *nt* **b** (*fig*) *personality, person* aggressiv; *tongue, voice* scharf; *criticism, remarks* harsch **N** (= *cleanser*) Scheuermittel *nt*; (= *abrasive substance*) Schleifmittel *nt*

abrasively [ə'breɪsɪvlɪ] ADV *say* scharf; *criticize* harsch

abrasiveness [ə'breɪsɪvnɪs] N **a** (*of cleanser*) Schärfe *f*; (*of surface*) Rauheit *f* **b** (*fig*) (*of person*) Aggressivität *f*; (*of voice*) Schärfe *f*; (*of criticism*) Harschheit *f*

abreact [æbrɪ'ækt] VT (*Psych*) abreagieren

abreaction [æbrɪ'ækʃən] N (*Psych*) Abreaktion *f*

abreast [ə'brest] ADV Seite an Seite; (*Naut also*) Bug an Bug; **to march four ~** im Viererglied or zu viert nebeneinander marschieren; **~ of sb/ sth** neben jdm/etw, auf gleicher Höhe mit jdm/etw; **to come ~ (of sb/sth)** mit jdm/etw gleichziehen, auf gleiche Höhe mit jdm/etw kommen; **to keep ~ of the times/news** *etc* mit seiner Zeit/den Nachrichten *etc* auf dem Laufenden bleiben

abridge [ə'brɪdʒ] VT *book* kürzen

abridgement [ə'brɪdʒmənt] N (*act*) Kürzen *nt*; (= *abridged work*) gekürzte Ausgabe

abroad [ə'brɔːd] ADV **a** im Ausland; **to go/be sent ~** ins Ausland gehen/geschickt werden; **from ~** aus dem Ausland **b** (*esp liter.* = *out of doors*) draußen; **to venture ~** nach draußen or ins Freie wagen; **he was ~ very early** er war schon sehr früh unterwegs **c** **there is a rumour** (*Brit*) or **rumor** (*US*) **that ...** ein Gerücht geht um or kursiert, dass ...; **to get ~** an die Öffentlichkeit dringen → **publish d** (*liter.* = *far and wide*) *scatter* weit

abrogate ['æbrəʊgeɪt] VT *law, treaty* außer Kraft setzen; *responsibility* ablehnen

abrogation [æbrəʊ'geɪʃən] N (*of law, treaty*) Außerkraftsetzung *f*, Ungültigkeitserklärung *f*; (*of responsibility*) Ablehnung *f*

abrupt [ə'brʌpt] ADJ **a** abrupt; *descent, drop* unvermittelt, jäh; *bend* plötzlich; *manner, reply* schroff, brüsk; **to come to an ~ end** ein abruptes Ende nehmen; **to bring sth to an ~ halt** (*lit*) etw abrupt zum Stehen bringen; (*fig*) etw plötzlich stoppen **b** (= *brusque, curt*) *person* brüsk, schroff

abruptly [ə'brʌptlɪ] ADV *abrupt*; *descend, drop* unvermittelt, jäh; *bend* plötzlich; *reply, ask* schroff, brüsk; (= *steeply*) *rise* steil

abruptness [ə'brʌptnɪs] N abrupte Art; (*of person*) schroffe or brüske Art; (*of descent, drop, bend*) Plötzlichkeit *f*, Jäheit *f*; (*of reply*) Schroffheit *f*

ABS *abbr of* **anti-lock braking system** **~ brakes** ABS-Bremsen *pl*

abs [æbz] PL (*inf*) *abbr of* **abductors** Bauchmuskeln *pl*; **~ pl and pecs** *pl* Bauch- und Brustmuskeln *pl*

abscess ['æbsɪs] N Abszess *m*

abscond [əb'skɒnd] VI sich (heimlich) davonmachen, türmen (*inf*); (*schoolboys also*) durchbrennen

absconder [əb'skɒndə'] N Flüchtige(r) *mf*; (= *child*) Ausreißer(in) *m(f)* (*inf*)

abseil ['æbseɪl] (*Brit*) VI (*Mountaineering: also* **abseil down**) sich abseilen N Abstieg *m* (am Seil)

absence ['æbsəns] N **a** Abwesenheit *f*; (*esp from school, work etc*) Fehlen *nt*; **in the ~ of the chairman** in Abwesenheit des Vorsitzenden; **sentenced in one's ~** in Abwesenheit verurteilt; **it's not fair to criticize him in his ~** es ist nicht

fair, ihn in seiner Abwesenheit zu kritisieren; **her many ~s on business** ihre häufige Abwesenheit aus geschäftlichen Gründen; **~ makes the heart grow fonder** (*Prov*) die Liebe wächst mit der Entfernung (*Prov*) **b** (= *lack*) Fehlen *nt*; **~ of enthusiasm** Mangel *m* an Enthusiasmus; **in the ~ of further evidence/qualified staff** in Ermangelung weiterer Beweise/von Fachkräften **c** (= *person absent*) **he counted the ~s** er stellte die Zahl der Abwesenden fest; **how many ~s do we have today?** wie viele fehlen heute or sind heute nicht da or anwesend? **d** **~ of mind** Geistesabwesenheit *f*

absent ['æbsənt] **ADJ** **a** (= *not present*) *person* abwesend, nicht da; **to be ~ from school/work** in der Schule/am Arbeitsplatz fehlen; **~!** (*Sch*) fehlt!; **why were you ~ from class?** warum warst du in der Stunde?, warum hast du gefehlt?; **to be** or **go ~ without leave** (*Mil*) sich unerlaubt von der Truppe entfernen; **~ parent** nicht betreuender Elternteil; **to ~ friends!** auf unsere abwesenden Freunde! **b** (= *absent-minded*) *expression, look* (geistes)abwesend; **in an ~ moment** in einem Augenblick geistiger Abwesenheit **c** (= *lacking*) **to be ~** fehlen **VR** [æb'sent] **to ~ oneself (from)** (= *not go, not appear*) fernbleiben (+*dat*, von); (= *leave temporarily*) sich zurückziehen or absentieren (*hum, geh*) (von)

absentee [æbsən'tiː] N Abwesende(r) *mf*; **there were a lot of ~s** es fehlten viele; (*pej*) es haben viele krank gefeiert

absentee ballot N (*esp US*) ≈ Briefwahl *f*

absenteeism [æbsən'tiːɪzəm] N häufige Abwesenheit *f*; (*pej*) Krankfeiern *nt*; (*Sch*) Schwänzen *nt*; **the rate of ~ among workers** die Abwesenheitsquote bei Arbeitern

absentee: absentee landlord N nicht ortsansässiger Haus-/Grundbesitzer; **absentee voter** N (*esp US*) ≈ Briefwähler(in) *m(f)*

absently ['æbsəntlɪ] ADV (geistes)abwesend

absent-minded [æbsənt'maɪndɪd] ADJ (= *lost in thought*) geistesabwesend; (= *habitually forgetful*) zerstreut

absent-mindedly [æbsənt'maɪndɪdlɪ] ADV *behave* zerstreut; *look* (geistes)abwesend; **he ~ forgot it** in seiner Zerstreutheit hat er es vergessen

absent-mindedness [æbsənt'maɪndɪdnɪs] N (*momentary*) Geistesabwesenheit *f*; (*habitual*) Zerstreutheit *f*

absinth(e) ['æbsɪnθ] N Absinth *m*

absolute ['æbsəluːt] ADJ absolut; *power, monopoly, liberty, support also, command* uneingeschränkt; *monarch also* unumschränkt; *lie, idiot* ausgemacht; **the ~** das Absolute; **the divorce was made ~** die Scheidung wurde ausgesprochen

absolute altitude N (*Aviat*) absolute Höhe, Flughöhe *f* über Grund

absolutely [æbsə'luːtlɪ] ADV absolut; *agree, trust also, true* vollkommen, völlig; *amazing, fantastic* wirklich; *deny, refuse also* strikt; *forbidden also* streng; *stupid also* völlig; *necessary also* unbedingt; *prove* eindeutig; **~!** durchaus; (= *I agree*) genau!; **do you agree? – ~** sind Sie einverstanden? – vollkommen; **do you ~ insist?** muss das unbedingt or durchaus sein?; **he ~ refused to do that** er wollte das absolut or durchaus nicht tun; **it's ~ amazing** es ist wirklich erstaunlich; **you look ~ stunning/awful** du siehst wirklich großartig/schrecklich aus; **you're ~ right** Sie haben völlig Recht

absolute: absolute majority N absolute Mehrheit *f*; **absolute pitch** N absolute Tonhöhe; (*of person*) absolutes Gehör; **absolute zero** N absoluter Nullpunkt

absolution [æbsə'luːʃən] N (*Eccl*) Absolution *f*, Lossprechung *f*; **to say the ~** die Absolution erteilen

absolutism ['æbsəluːtɪzəm] N Absolutismus *m*

absolve [əb'zɒlv] VT *person* (*from responsibility*) entlassen (*from* aus); (*from sins*) lossprechen (*from* von); (*from blame*) freisprechen (*from* von); (*from vow, oath etc*) entbinden (*from* von, +*gen*)

absorb [əb'sɔːb] VT absorbieren, aufnehmen; *liquid also* aufsaugen; *knowledge, news also* in sich (*acc*) aufnehmen; *vibration* auffangen, absorbieren; *shock* dämpfen; *light, sound* absorbieren, schlucken; *people, firm* absorbieren, integrieren (*into* in +*acc*); *costs etc* tragen; *one's time* in Anspruch nehmen; **she ~s things quickly** sie hat eine rasche Auffassungsgabe; **to be ~ed in a book** *etc* in ein Buch *etc* vertieft or versunken sein; **to get ~ed in a book** *etc* sich in ein Buch *etc* vertiefen; **she was completely ~ed in her family/job** sie ging völlig in ihrer Familie/Arbeit auf

absorbency [əb'sɔːbənsɪ] N Saug- or Absorptionsfähigkeit *f*

absorbent [əb'sɔːbənt] ADJ saugfähig, absorbierend

absorbent cotton N (*US*) Watte *f*

absorbing [əb'sɔːbɪŋ] ADJ fesselnd

absorption [əb'sɔːpʃən] N Absorption *f*, Aufnahme *f*; (*of liquid also*) Aufsaugung *f*; (*of vibration*) Auffangen *nt*; (*of shock*) Dämpfung *f*; (*of people, firm*) Integration *f*; **her total ~ in her family/studies** ihr vollkommenes Aufgehen in ihrer Familie/ihrem Studium; **to watch with ~** gefesselt or gebannt beobachten

abstain [əb'steɪn] VI **a** (*from sex, smoking*) sich enthalten (*from* +*gen*); **to ~ from alcohol/drinking** sich des Alkohols/Trinkens enthalten (*geh*) **b** (*in voting*) sich der Stimme enthalten

abstainer [əb'steɪnə'] N **a** (*from alcohol*) Abstinenzler(in) *m(f)* **b** = **abstention b**

abstemious [əb'stiːmɪəs] ADJ *person, life* enthaltsam; *meal, diet* bescheiden

abstemiousness [əb'stiːmɪəsnɪs] N (*of person, life*) Enthaltsamkeit *f*; (*of meal, diet*) Bescheidenheit *f*

abstention [əb'stenʃən] N **a** *no pl* (*from sex, smoking etc*) Enthaltung *f*; (*from alcohol*) Enthaltung *f*, Abstinenz *f* **b** (*in voting*) (Stimm)enthaltung *f*; **were you one of the ~s?** waren Sie einer von denen, die sich der Stimme enthalten haben?

abstinence ['æbstɪnəns] N Abstinenz *f* (*from* von), Enthaltung *f* (*from* von); (= *self-restraint*) Enthaltsamkeit *f*; **total ~** völlige Abstinenz; **years of ~** jahrelange Abstinenz

abstinent ['æbstɪnənt] ADJ abstinent (*geh*), enthaltsam

abstract¹ ['æbstrækt] **ADJ** (*all senses*) abstrakt; **~ noun** Abstraktum *nt*, abstraktes Substantiv **N** (*kurze*) Zusammenfassung; **in the ~** abstrakt

abstract² [æb'strækt] VT abstrahieren; *information* entnehmen (*from* aus); *metal etc* trennen; (*inf.* = *steal*) entwenden

abstracted [æb'stræktɪd] ADJ abwesend, entrückt (*geh*)

abstractedly [æb'stræktɪdlɪ] ADV abwesend, entrückt (*geh*); *gaze* wie abwesend

abstraction [æb'strækʃən] N Abstraktion *f*; (= *abstract term also*) Abstraktum *nt*; (= *mental separation also*) Abstrahieren *nt*; (= *extraction: of information etc*) Entnahme *f*; (= *absent-mindedness*) Entrücktheit *f* (*geh*); **to argue in ~s** in abstrakten Begriffen or in Abstraktionen argumentieren

abstractness ['æbstræktnɪs] N Abstraktheit *f*

abstruse [æb'struːs] ADJ abstrus

abstruseness [əb'struːsnɪs] N abstruse Unklarheit

absurd [əb'sɜːd] ADJ absurd; **don't be ~!** sei nicht albern; **if you think that, you're just being ~** du bist ja nicht recht bei Trost, wenn du das glaubst; **what an ~ waste of time!** so eine blödsinnige Zeitverschwendung!; **the management is being ~ again** das Management spielt mal wieder verrückt (*inf*); **theatre of the ~** absurdes Theater

absurdist [əbˈsɜːdɪst] ADJ (Liter, Theat) absurd

absurdity [əbˈsɜːdɪtɪ] N Absurde(s) nt no pl (of an +dat); (thing etc also) Absurdität f

absurdly [əbˈsɜːdlɪ] ADV behave, react absurd; fast, rich, expensive etc unsinnig; **he suggested very ~ ...** er machte absurderweise den Vorschlag, ...

abundance [əˈbʌndəns] N (großer) Reichtum (of an +dat); (of hair, vegetation, details, illustrations, information, ideas, colours also, proof) Fülle f (of von, +gen); **in ~** in Hülle und Fülle; **to have an ~ of sth** etw im Überfluss haben; **a country with an ~ of oil/raw materials** ein Land mit reichen Ölvorkommen/großem Reichtum an Rohstoffen; **with his ~ of energy** mit seiner ungeheuren Energie; **such an ~ of open space** so unermesslich viel freies Land

abundant [əˈbʌndənt] ADJ reich; growth, hair üppig; time, proof reichlich; energy, self-confidence etc ungeheuer; **to be ~ in sth** reich an etw (dat) sein; **apples are in ~ supply** es gibt reichlich Äpfel, es gibt Äpfel in Hülle und Fülle

abundantly [əˈbʌndəntlɪ] ADV reichlich; grow in Hülle und Fülle, üppig; **to make it ~ clear that ...** mehr als deutlich zu verstehen geben, dass ...; **it was ~ clear (to me) that ...** es war (mir) mehr als klar, dass ...; **that is ~ obvious** das ist mehr als offensichtlich

abuse [əˈbjuːs] N a no pl (= insults) Beschimpfungen pl; **a term of ~** ein Schimpfwort nt; **to shout ~ at sb** jdm Beschimpfungen an den Kopf werfen; **to heap ~ on sb** jdn mit Beschimpfungen überschütten → shower, stream b (= misuse) Missbrauch m; (= unjust practice) Missstand m; **~ of confidence/authority** Vertrauens-/Amtsmissbrauch m; **~ of power** Machtmissbrauch m; **the system is open to ~** das System lässt sich leicht missbrauchen [əˈbjuːz] a (= revile) beschimpfen, schmähen (geh) b (= misuse) missbrauchen; one's health Raubbau treiben mit

abuser [əˈbjuːzə^r] N (of child, woman, man) Missbraucher(in) m(f)

abusive [əˈbjuːsɪv] ADJ beleidigend; (Psych) person, relationship abusiv; **~ language** Beschimpfungen pl, Beleidigungen pl; **children from an ~ home** Kinder pl, die zu Hause missbraucht werden/wurden; **to be/become ~ (towards sb)** (jdm gegenüber) beleidigend or ausfallend sein/werden; **he muttered something ~** er murmelte etwas Beleidigendes; **to get ~ (towards sb)** (jdm gegenüber) beleidigend or ausfallend werden

abusively [əˈbjuːsɪvlɪ] ADV refer to beleidigend; **to shout/scream ~ at sb** jdm Beleidigungen zurufen/entgegenschreien

abusiveness [əˈbjuːsɪvnɪs] N (of person) ausfallende Art; **a critic should not descend to mere ~** ein Kritiker sollte sich nicht in reinen Ausfälligkeiten ergehen

abut [əˈbʌt] VI stoßen (on/to an +acc); (land also) grenzen (on/to an +acc); (two houses, fields etc) aneinanderstoßen/-grenzen

abutment [əˈbʌtmənt] N (Archit) Flügel- or Wangenmauer f

abutter [əˈbʌtə^r] N (US) Anlieger(in) m(f); (to one's own land) (Grenz)nachbar(in) m(f)

abutting [əˈbʌtɪŋ] ADJ (daran) anstoßend attr; fields also (daran) angrenzend attr

ABV abbr of alcohol by volume Vol. %

abysmal [əˈbɪzməl] ADJ (fig) entsetzlich; performance, work, taste etc miserabel

abysmally [əˈbɪzməlɪ] ADV entsetzlich; perform, work etc also miserabel; **to fail ~** kläglich versagen; **our team did ~ in the competition** unsere Mannschaft schnitt bei dem Wettkampf miserabel ab

abyss [əˈbɪs] N (lit, fig) Abgrund m; **the ~ of war** der Abgrund des Krieges

Abyssinia [æbɪˈsɪnɪə] N Abessinien nt

Abyssinian [æbɪˈsɪnɪən] ADJ attr abessinisch N Abessinier(in) m(f)

AC a abbr of alternating current b abbr of aircraftman

A/C abbr of account Kto.

acacia [əˈkeɪʃə] N (also acacia tree) Akazie f

academe [ˈækədiːm] N (form) die akademische Welt; **the groves** pl **of ~** die akademischen Gefilde pl (form)

academic [ˌækəˈdemɪk] ADJ a akademisch; publisher, reputation wissenschaftlich; **~ advisor** (US) Studienberater(in) m(f); **~ dean** (US) Dekan(in) m(f); **~ officers** (US) akademisches Personal; **~ year** akademisches Jahr, Studienjahr nt b (= intellectual) approach, quality, interest wissenschaftlich; interests geistig; person, appearance intellektuell; style, book akademisch c (= theoretical) akademisch; **out of ~ interest** aus rein akademischem Interesse; **since the decision has already been made the discussion is purely ~** da die Entscheidung schon getroffen wurde, ist das eine (rein) akademische Diskussion N Akademiker(in) m(f); (Univ) Universitätslehrkraft f

academically [ˌækəˈdemɪkəlɪ] ADV a wissenschaftlich; **to be ~ inclined** geistige Interessen haben; **to be ~ minded** wissenschaftlich denken; **~ respectable** wissenschaftlich akzeptabel; **~ gifted** intellektuell begabt b **she is not doing well ~** (Sch) sie ist in der Schule nicht gut; (Univ) sie ist mit ihrem Studium nicht sehr erfolgreich; **she's good at handicraft but is not doing so well ~** im Werken ist sie gut, aber in den wissenschaftlichen Fächern hapert es

academicals [ˌækəˈdemɪkəlz] PL akademische Tracht

academician [əˌkædəˈmɪʃən] N Akademiemitglied nt

academy [əˈkædəmɪ] N Akademie f; **naval/military ~** Marine-/Militärakademie f; **~ for young ladies** ≈ höhere Töchterschule

Academy Award N (Film) Filmpreis der Academy of Motion Picture Arts and Sciences, Oscar m (inf)

Academy Awards ceremony N (Film) Oscarverleihung f (inf)

acanthus [əˈkænθəs] N (= plant) Bärenklau f, Akanthus m (also Archit)

a cappella [ˌækəˈpelə] (Mus) ADV sing a cappella ADJ A-cappella- attr inv

ACAS, Acas [ˈeɪkæs] abbr of Advisory Conciliation and Arbitration Service Schlichtungsstelle für Arbeitskonflikte

acc a abbr of account Kto. b abbr of accommodation Übern.

acc. (Banking) abbr of account Kto.

accede [ækˈsiːd] VI a **to ~ to the throne** den Thron besteigen; **to ~ to the Premiership/office of President** die Nachfolge als Premierminister/Präsident antreten b (= agree) zustimmen (to +dat); (= yield) einwilligen (to in +acc) c **to ~ to a treaty** einem Pakt beitreten

accelerate [əkˈseləreɪt] VT beschleunigen; speed also erhöhen VI beschleunigen; (driver also) Gas geben; (work-rate, speed, change) sich beschleunigen, zunehmen; (growth, inflation etc) zunehmen; **he ~d away** er gab Gas und fuhr davon; **he ~d out of the bend** er hat in der Kurve beschleunigt or Gas gegeben

acceleration [ækˌseləˈreɪʃən] N Beschleunigung f; (of speed also) Erhöhung f; **to have good/poor ~** eine gute/schlechte Beschleunigung haben, gut/schlecht beschleunigen

acceleration ratio N Beschleunigungswert m

accelerator [əkˈseləreɪtə^r] N a (also accelerator pedal) Gaspedal nt, Gas nt (inf); **to step on the ~** aufs Gas treten or drücken (inf) b (Phys) Beschleuniger m

accent [ˈæksənt] N (all senses) Akzent m; (= stress also) Betonung f; **~s** (liter. = tones) Töne pl, Tonfall m; **to speak without/with an ~** akzentfrei or ohne Akzent/mit Akzent sprechen; **to put the ~ on sth** (fig) den Akzent auf etw (acc) legen; **the ~ is on bright colours** der Akzent or die Betonung liegt auf leuchtenden Farben VT [ækˈsent] betonen

accentuate [ækˈsentjʊeɪt] VT betonen; (in speaking, Mus) akzentuieren; (Ling: = give accent to) mit einem Akzent versehen; **to ~ the need for sth** die Notwendigkeit einer Sache (gen) betonen or hervorheben

accentuation [ækˌsentjʊˈeɪʃən] N Betonung f; (in speaking, Mus) Akzentuierung f

accept [əkˈsept] ✪ 11.3, 12.1, 12.2, 19.5, 20.6, 25.1, 25.2, 26.3, 27.3 VT a akzeptieren; apology, offer, gift, invitation annehmen; responsibility übernehmen; (= believe) story glauben; **a photograph of the President ~ing the award** ein Bild von dem Präsidenten, wie er die Auszeichnung entgegennimmt; **we will not ~ anything but the best** wir werden nur das Allerbeste akzeptieren or annehmen; **to ~ sb into society** jdn in die Gesellschaft aufnehmen b (= recognize) need einsehen, anerkennen; person, duty akzeptieren, anerkennen; **it is generally or widely ~ed that ...** es ist allgemein anerkannt, dass ...; **we must ~ the fact that ...** wir müssen uns damit abfinden, dass ...; **I ~ that it might take a little longer** ich sehe ein, dass es etwas länger dauern könnte; **the government ~ed that the treaty would on occasions have to be infringed** die Regierung akzeptierte, dass der Vertrag gelegentlich verletzt werden würde; **to ~ that sth is one's responsibility/duty** etw als seine Verantwortung/Pflicht akzeptieren c (= allow, put up with) behaviour, fate, conditions hinnehmen; **we'll just have to ~ things as they are** wir müssen die Dinge eben so (hin)nehmen, wie sie sind d (Comm) cheque, orders annehmen; delivery annehmen, abnehmen VI annehmen; (with offers also) akzeptieren; (with invitations also) zusagen

acceptability [əkˌseptəˈbɪlɪtɪ] N Annehmbarkeit f, Akzeptierbarkeit f; (of behaviour) Zulässigkeit f; **social ~** (of person) gesellschaftliche Akzeptabilität; (of behaviour) gesellschaftliche Zulässigkeit

acceptable [əkˈseptəbl] ADJ annehmbar (to für), akzeptabel (to für); behaviour zulässig; (= suitable) gift passend; **that would be most ~** das wäre sehr or höchst willkommen; **any job would be ~ to him** ihm wäre jede Stelle recht; **only the best is ~** nur das Beste kann angenommen werden

acceptably [əkˈseptəblɪ] ADV a (= properly) behave, treat anständig, korrekt b (= sufficiently) **~ accurate/safe** ausreichend or hinlänglich genau/sicher; **noise levels were ~ low** der Lärmpegel war erträglich c (= adequately) akzeptabel, angemessen

acceptance [əkˈseptəns] ✪ 20.2 N a (of offer, gift, excuse) Annahme f; (of suggestion, work also, report, findings) Akzeptierung f; (of responsibility) Übernahme f; (of believing: of story) Glauben nt; (= receiving: of award) Entgegennahme f; **his ~ into the family** seine Aufnahme in der or die Familie; **to find or win or gain ~** (theories, people) anerkannt werden, Anerkennung finden; **to meet with general ~** allgemeine Anerkennung finden b (= recognition: of need, fact) Anerkennung f c (= toleration: of behaviour, fate, conditions) Hinnahme f d (Comm) (of cheque, orders) Annahme f; (of delivery also) Abnahme f

acceptance: acceptance house N (Fin) Akzept- or Wechselbank f; **acceptance trials** PL Abnahmeprüfung f

acceptation [ˌæksepˈteɪʃən] N (old, form, of word) Bedeutung f

accepted [əkˈseptɪd] ADJ truth, fact (allgemein) anerkannt; **it's the ~ thing** es ist üblich or der Brauch; **to do sth because it is the ~ thing** etw tun, weil es (eben) so üblich ist; **~ text** offizieller Text; **socially ~** gesellschaftsfähig

accepting [ək'septɪŋ] ADJ **to be ~ of sth/sb** für etw/jdn offen *or* zugänglich sein; (= *tolerant*) etw/jdm gegenüber tolerant sein

accepting house N (*Brit Fin*) Akzeptbank *f*

access ['ækses] **N** **a** Zugang *m* (*to* zu); (*esp to room, private grounds etc*) Zutritt *m* (*to* zu); **to be easy of** ~ leicht zugänglich sein; **to give sb ~** jdm Zugang gewähren (*to sb/sth* zu jdm/ etw), jdm Zutritt gewähren (*to sth* zu etw); **to refuse sb ~** jdm den Zugang verwehren (*to sb/ sth* zu jdm/etw), jdm den Zutritt verwehren (*to sth* zu etw); **this door gives ~ to the garden** diese Tür führt in den Garten; **this location offers easy ~ to shops and transport facilities** von hier sind Läden und Verkehrsmittel leicht zu erreichen; **to have ~ to sb/sth** Zugang zu jdm/etw haben; **to gain ~ to sb/sth** sich (*dat*) Zugang zu jdm/etw verschaffen; **the thieves gained ~ through the window** die Diebe gelangten durch das Fenster hinein; **"access only"** „nur für Anlieger", „Anlieger frei"; **right of ~ to one's children** Besuchsrecht für seine Kinder **b** (*Comput*) Zugriff *m* **c** (*liter: attack, fit*) Anfall *m* **VT** (*Comput*) file, data zugreifen auf (+*acc*)

accessary [æk'sesərɪ] N = **accessory c**

access code N Zugangskode *m*

access course N Brückenkurs *m*

accessibility [æk,sesɪ'bɪlɪtɪ] N (*of place, information*) Zugänglichkeit *f*

accessible [æk'sesəbl] ADJ *information, person* zugänglich (*to* +*dat*); *place also* (leicht) zu erreichen (*to* für)

accession [æk'seʃən] N **a** (*to an office*) Antritt *m* (*to* +*gen*); *also* **accession to the throne** Thronbesteigung *f*; (*to estate, power*) Übernahme *f* (*to* +*gen*); **since his ~ to power** seit seiner Machtübernahme **b** (= *consent: to treaty, demand*) Zustimmung *f* (*to* zu), Annahme *f* (*to* +*gen*) **c** (= *addition*) (*to property*) Zukauf *m*; (*to library*) (Neu)anschaffung *f*; **a sudden ~ of strength** (*liter*) eine plötzliche Anwandlung von Kraft

accessorize [æk'sesəraɪz] VT *dress* mit Accessoires versehen; *room* dekorieren

accessory [æk'sesərɪ] N **a** Extra *nt*; (*in fashion*) Accessoire *nt* **b** **accessories** PL Zubehör *nt*; **toilet accessories** Toilettenartikel *pl* **c** (*Jur*) Helfershelfer(in) *m(f)*; (*actively involved*) Mitschuldige(r) *mf* (*to an* +*dat*); **to be an ~ after the fact** (*Jur*) der Beihilfe schuldig machen; **this made him an ~ to the crime** dadurch wurde er an dem Verbrechen mitschuldig

access road N Zufahrt(sstraße) *f*

access time N Zugriffszeit *f*

accidence ['æksɪdəns] N (*Gram*) Formenlehre *f*

accident ['æksɪdənt] N (*Mot, in home, at work*) Unfall *m*; (*Rail, Aviat, = disaster*) Unglück *nt*; (= *mishap*) Missgeschick *nt*; (= *chance occurrence*) Zufall *m*; (*inf: = unplanned child*) (Verkehrs)unfall *m* (*inf*); **~ and emergency department/unit** Notfallstation *f*, Notaufnahme *f*; **she has had an ~** sie hat einen Unfall gehabt *or* (*caused it*) gebaut (*inf*); (*in car, train etc also*) sie ist verunglückt; (*in kitchen etc*) ihr ist etwas *or* ein Missgeschick *or* ein Malheur passiert; **little Jimmy has had an ~** (*euph*) dem kleinen Jimmy ist ein Malheur passiert (*inf*); **that was an ~ waiting to happen** das musste ja so kommen; **by ~** (= *by chance*) durch Zufall, zufällig; (= *unintentionally*) aus Versehen; **without ~** (*of driver, car*) unfallfrei; **who by an ~ of birth possessed riches** der zufälligerweise reich geboren wurde; **~s will happen** (*prov*) so was kann vorkommen, so was kommt in den besten Familien vor (*inf*); **it was an ~** es war ein Versehen; **it was pure ~ that ...** es war reiner Zufall, dass ...; **it's no ~ that ...** es ist kein Zufall, dass ...; (*not surprisingly*) es kommt nicht von ungefähr, dass ...

accidental [æksɪ'dentl] ADJ (= *unplanned*) *meeting, benefit* zufällig; (= *unintentional*) *blow, shooting* versehentlich; **one of the ~ effects of this scheme was ...** eine der Wirkungen, die

dieser Plan unbeabsichtigterweise mit sich brachte, war ... **b** (= *resulting from accident*) *injury, death* durch Unfall; **~ damage** (*Insur*) Unfallschaden *m* **N** (*Mus*) (= *sign*) Versetzungszeichen *nt*, Akzidentale *f* (*form*); (= *note*) erhöhter/erniedrigter Ton

accidentally [æksɪ'dentəlɪ] ADV (= *by chance*) zufällig; (= *unintentionally*) versehentlich; **~ on purpose** (*hum*) versehentlich-absichtlich (*hum*)

accident: accident insurance N Unfallversicherung *f*; **accident prevention** N Unfallverhütung *f*; **accident-prone** ADJ vom Pech verfolgt; **she is very ~** sie ist vom Pech verfolgt, sie ist ein richtiger Pechvogel; (*more serious*) ihr passieren ständig Unfälle

acclaim [ə'kleɪm] **VT** **a** (= *applaud*) feiern (*as* als); (*critics*) anerkennen **b** (= *proclaim*) **to ~ sb king/winner** jdn zum König/als Sieger ausrufen **N** Beifall *m*; (*of critics*) Anerkennung *f*

acclamation [æklə'meɪʃən] N Beifall *m no pl*; (*of audience etc also*) Beifallskundgebung *f*, Beifallsbezeigung *f*; (*of critics also*) Anerkennung *f*; **by ~** durch Akklamation

acclimate [ə'klaɪmeɪt] VT (*US*) = **acclimatize**

acclimatization [ə,klaɪmətaɪ'zeɪʃən], (*US*) **acclimation** [æklə'meɪʃən] N Akklimatisierung *f* (*to an* +*acc*), Akklimatisation *f* (*to an* +*acc*); (*to new surroundings etc also*) Gewöhnung *f* (*to an* +*acc*)

acclimatize [ə'klaɪmətaɪz], (*US*) **acclimate** [ə'klaɪmeɪt] **VT** gewöhnen (*to an* +*acc*); **to become ~d** sich akklimatisieren; (*person also*) sich eingewöhnen **VI** (*also vr*: **acclimatize oneself**) sich akklimatisieren (*to an* +*acc*, *to a country etc* in einem Land *etc*)

acclivity [ə'klɪvɪtɪ] N (*form*) Hang *m*

accolade ['ækəʊleɪd] N (= *award*) Auszeichnung *f*; (= *praise*) Lob *nt no pl*; (*Hist, Mus*) Akkolade *f*

accommodate [ə'kɒmədeɪt] **VT** **a** (= *provide lodging for*) unterbringen **b** (= *hold, have room for*) Platz haben für; (= *contain*) *machine part etc* enthalten; **the car can ~ five people** das Auto bietet fünf Personen Platz *or* hat Platz für fünf Personen **c** (= *be able to cope with: theory, plan, forecasts*) Rechnung *f* tragen (+*dat*) **d** (*form: = oblige*) dienen (+*dat*); *wishes* entgegenkommen (+*dat*); **I think we might be able to ~ you** ich glaube, wir können Ihnen entgegenkommen **VI** (*eye*) sich einstellen (*to auf* +*acc*) **to ~ oneself to sth** sich einer Sache (*dat*) anpassen

accommodating [ə'kɒmədeɪtɪŋ] ADJ entgegenkommend

accommodation [ə,kɒmə'deɪʃən] N **a** (= *lodging: US also* **accommodations**) Unterkunft *f*; (= *room*) Zimmer *nt*; (= *flat*) Wohnung *f*; **"accommodation"** „Fremdenzimmer"; **hotel ~ is scarce** Hotelzimmer sind knapp; **~ wanted** Zimmer/Wohnung gesucht; **they found ~ in a youth hostel** sie fanden in einer Jugendherberge Unterkunft, sie kamen in einer Jugendherberge unter **b** (= *space: US also* **accommodations**) Platz *m*; **seating ~** Sitzplätze *pl*; **there is ~ for twenty passengers in the plane** das Flugzeug bietet zwanzig Passagieren Platz *or* hat für zwanzig Passagiere Platz; **sleeping ~ for six** Schlafgelegenheit *f* für sechs Personen; **~ in the hospital is inadequate** die Unterbringungsmöglichkeiten im Krankenhaus sind unzureichend **c** (*form: = agreement*) **to reach an ~** eine Übereinkunft *or* ein Übereinkommen *nt* erzielen **d** (*of eye*) Einstellung *f* (*to auf* +*acc*)

accommodation: accommodation address N Briefkastenadresse *f*; **accommodation agency** N (*Brit*) *Agentur, die Mietobjekte vermittelt*; **accommodation bill** N Gefälligkeitswechsel *m*; **accommodation bureau** N Wohnungsvermittlung *f*; (*Univ*) Zimmervermittlung *f*; **accommodation ladder** N (*Naut*) Fallreep *nt*; **accommodation office** N (*Univ*) Zimmervermittlung *f*; **accommodation service** N Zimmernachweis *m*; **accommodation train** N (*US*) Personenzug *m*, Bummelzug *m* (*inf*)

accompaniment [ə'kʌmpənɪmənt] N Begleitung *f* (*also Mus*); **with piano** ~ mit Klavierbegleitung; **to the ~ of** begleitet von

accompanist [ə'kʌmpənɪst] N Begleiter(in) *m(f)*

accompany [ə'kʌmpənɪ] VT begleiten (*also Mus*); **pork is often accompanied by apple sauce** Schweinefleisch wird oft mit Apfelmus (als Beilage) serviert; **to ~ oneself** (*Mus*) sich selbst begleiten; **~ing letter** Begleitschreiben *nt*

accomplice [ə'kʌmplɪs] N Komplize *m*, Komplizin *f*, Mittäter(in) *m(f)*; **to be an ~ to a crime** Komplize bei einem Verbrechen sein, Mittäter eines Verbrechens sein

accomplish [ə'kʌmplɪʃ] VT schaffen; **he ~ed a great deal in his short career** er hat in der kurzen Zeit seines Wirkens Großes geleistet; **that didn't ~ anything** damit war nichts erreicht

accomplished [ə'kʌmplɪʃt] ADJ **a** (= *skilled*) *player, carpenter* fähig; *performance* vollendet; *liar* versiert; *young lady* vielseitig; **to be ~ in the art of ...** die Kunst ... (*gen*) beherrschen **b** *fact* vollendet

accomplishment [ə'kʌmplɪʃmənt] N **a** *no pl* (= *completion*) Bewältigung *f* **b** (= *skill*) Fertigkeit *f*; (= *achievement*) Leistung *f*; **social ~s** gesellschaftliche Gewandtheit

accord [ə'kɔːd] **N** **a** (= *agreement*) Übereinstimmung *f*, Einigkeit *f*; (*Pol*) Abkommen *nt*; **I'm not in ~ with him/his views** ich stimme mit ihm/seinen Ansichten nicht überein; **of one's/ its own ~** von selbst; (*of persons also*) aus freien Stücken; **with one ~** geschlossen; *sing, cheer, say etc* wie aus einem Mund(e); **to be in ~ with sth** mit etw in Einklang stehen **VT** (*sb sth* jdm etw) gewähren; *praise* erteilen; *courtesy* erweisen; *honorary title* verleihen; *welcome* bieten **VI** sich *or* einander entsprechen; **to ~ with sth** einer Sache (*dat*) entsprechen

accordance [ə'kɔːdəns] N **in ~ with** entsprechend (+*dat*), gemäß (+*dat*)

accordingly [ə'kɔːdɪŋlɪ] ADV (= *correspondingly*) (dem)entsprechend; (= *so, therefore*) (dem)entsprechend, folglich

according to [ə'kɔːdɪŋ'tuː] ✪ 26.2 PREP (= *as stated or shown by*) zufolge (+*dat*), nach; *person, book, letter also* laut; (= *in agreement with, in proportion to*) entsprechend (+*dat*), nach; **~ the map** der Karte nach *or* zufolge; **~ Peter** laut Peter, Peter zufolge; **we did it ~ the rules** wir haben uns an die Regeln gehalten

accordion [ə'kɔːdɪən] N Akkordeon *nt*, Ziehharmonika *f*

accordion file N (*US*) Ordnungsmappe *f*

accordionist [ə'kɔːdɪənɪst] N Akkordeonspieler(in) *m(f)*, Akkordeonist(in) *m(f)*

accost [ə'kɒst] VT ansprechen, anpöbeln (*pej*)

account [ə'kaʊnt] ✪ 20.7 **N** **a** Darstellung *f*; (= *report*) Bericht *m*; **to keep an ~ of one's expenses/experiences** über seine Ausgaben Buch führen/seine Erlebnisse schriftlich festhalten; **by *or* from all ~s** nach allem, was man hört; **by your own ~** nach Ihrer eigenen Darstellung, nach Ihren eigenen Angaben; **to give an ~ of sth** über etw (*acc*) Bericht erstatten; **to give an ~ of oneself** Rede und Antwort stehen; **to give a good ~ of oneself** sich gut schlagen; **to call *or* hold sb to ~** jdn zur Rechenschaft ziehen; **to be called *or* held to ~ for sth** über etw (*acc*) Rechenschaft ablegen müssen **b** (= *consideration*) **to take ~ of sb/sth, to take sb/sth into ~** jdn/etw in Betracht ziehen; **to take no ~ of sb/sth, to leave sb/sth out of ~** jdn/etw außer Betracht lassen; **on no ~, not on any ~** auf (gar) keinen Fall; **on this/that ~** deshalb, deswegen; **on ~ of him** seinetwegen; **on ~ of the weather** wegen *or* aufgrund *or* auf Grund des Wetters; **on my/his/their ~** meinet-/seinet-/ ihretwegen; **on one's own ~** für sich (selbst) **c** (= *benefit*) Nutzen *m*; **to turn sth to (good) ~** (guten) Gebrauch von etw machen, etw (gut) nützen **d** (= *importance*) **of little ~** von geringer Bedeutung; **of no ~** ohne Bedeutung

e (*Fin, Comm*) (*at bank, shop*) Konto *nt* (**with** bei); (= *client*) Kunde *m*, Kundin *f*; (= *bill*) Rechnung *f*; **to win sb's ~** jdn als Kunden gewinnen; **to buy sth on ~** etw auf (Kunden)kredit kaufen; **please charge it to my ~** stellen Sie es mir bitte in Rechnung; **£50 on ~** £ 50 als Anzahlung; **~(s) department** (*for customer accounts*) Kreditbüro *nt*; **to settle** or **square ~s** or **one's ~ with sb** (*fig*) mit jdm abrechnen; **the duel squared all ~s between them** das Duell bereinigte alles zwischen ihnen; **~ payee only** (*Brit*) nur zur Verrechnung

f PL (*of company, club*) (Geschäfts)bücher *pl*; (*of household*) Einnahmen und Ausgaben *pl*; **to keep the ~s** die Bücher führen, die Buchführung machen

VT (*form*: = *consider*) erachten als; **to ~ oneself lucky** sich glücklich schätzen

▶ **account for** VI +*prep obj* **a** (= *explain*) erklären; (= *give account of*) *actions, expenditure* Rechenschaft ablegen über (+*acc*); **how do you account for it?** wie erklären Sie sich (*dat*) das?; **he wasn't able to account for the missing money** er konnte den Verbleib des fehlenden Geldes nicht erklären; **all the children were/all the money was accounted for** der Verbleib aller Kinder/des (ganzen) Geldes war bekannt, man wusste, wo die Kinder alle waren/wo das Geld (geblieben) war; **there's no accounting for taste** über Geschmack lässt sich (nicht) streiten **b** (= *be the source of*) der Grund sein für; **this area accounts for most of the country's mineral wealth** aus dieser Gegend stammen die meisten Bodenschätze des Landes; **this area alone accounts for some 25% of the population** diese Gegend allein macht etwa 25% der Bevölkerung aus; **he accounts for most of the accidents** die meisten Unfälle gehen auf sein Konto (*inf*) **c** (= *be the cause of defeat, destruction etc of*) zur Strecke bringen; (*illness*) dahinraffen; *chances* zunichte machen; **Proctor accounted for five Australian batsmen** Proctor hat fünf australische Schlagmänner ausgeschlagen

accountability [əˌkaʊntə'bɪlɪtɪ] N Verantwortlichkeit *f* (*to sb* jdm gegenüber)

accountable [ə'kaʊntəbl] ADJ verantwortlich (*to sb* jdm); **to hold sb ~ (for sth)** jdn (für etw) verantwortlich machen

accountancy [ə'kaʊntənsɪ] N Buchführung *f*, Buchhaltung *f*; (= *tax accountancy*) Steuerberatung *f*

accountant [ə'kaʊntənt] N Buchhalter(in) *m(f)*; (= *external financial adviser*) Wirtschaftsprüfer(in) *m(f)*; (= *auditor*) Rechnungsprüfer(in) *m(f)*; (= *tax accountant*) Steuerberater(in) *m(f)*

account: account balance N Kontostand *m*; **account book** N Geschäftsbuch *nt*; **account card** N (*for a shop*) Kundenkreditkarte *f*; **account charge** N Konto(führungs)gebühr *f*; **account day** N (*Brit: St Ex*) Liquidationstag *m*; **account executive** N Kundenbetreuer(in) *m(f)*; **account holder** N (*Banking*) Kontoinhaber(in) *m(f)*

accounting [ə'kaʊntɪŋ] N Buchhaltung *f*, Buchführung *f*; **~ method** Buchhaltungsverfahren *nt*; **~ period** Abrechnungszeitraum *m*; **~ policy** Bilanzierungspolitik *f*

accounting department N (*US: of company*) Buchhaltung *f*

account number N Kontonummer *f*

accounts department N (*Brit: of company*) Buchhaltung *f*

accounts payable N (*Fin*) Verbindlichkeiten *pl*

accounts receivable N (*Fin*) Außenstände *pl*

accoutrements [ə'ku:trəmənts], (*US also*) **accouterments** [ə'ku:tərmənts] PL Ausrüstung *f*; **the ~ of the trade** das Handwerkszeug

accredit [ə'kredɪt] VT **a** *ambassador, representative* akkreditieren (*form*), beglaubigen **b** (= *approve officially*) zulassen, genehmigen; *herd* staatlich überwachen; *educational institution* anerkennen; (= *establish*) *belief, custom* anerkennen; **~ed**

agent bevollmächtigter Vertreter **c** (= *ascribe, attribute*) zuschreiben (*to sb* jdm)

accrete [ə'kri:t] **VI** zusammenwachsen; (= *increase*) zunehmen **VT** (= *enlarge*) anwachsen lassen

accretion [ə'kri:ʃən] N (*process*) Anlagerung *f*; (= *sth accumulated*) Ablagerung *f*

accrual [ə'kru:əl] N **a** (= *accumulation*) Ansammlung *f*; (*Fin: of interest*) Auflaufen *nt*; (= *addition*) Hinzukommen *nt* **b accruals** PL (*Fin:* = *liabilities*) Verbindlichkeiten *pl*

accrue [ə'kru:] VI **a** (= *accumulate*) sich ansammeln, zusammenkommen (*to* für); (*Fin: interest*) auflaufen; (= *be added to*) hinzukommen (*to* zu) **b to ~ to sb** (*honour, costs etc*) jdm erwachsen (*geh*) (*from* aus)

acculturation [əˌkʌltʃə'reɪʃən] N (*Sociol*) Akkulturation *f*

accumulate [ə'kju:mjʊleɪt] **VT** ansammeln, anhäufen; *accusation* (*form*); *evidence* sammeln; (*Fin*) *interest* akkumulieren or zusammenkommen lassen **VI** sich ansammeln or akkumulieren (*form*); (*possessions, wealth also*) sich anhäufen; (*evidence*) sich häufen

accumulation [əˌkju:mjʊ'leɪʃən] N Ansammlung *f*, Akkumulation *f* (*form*); (*of possessions, wealth also*) Anhäufung *f*; (*of evidence*) Häufung *f*

accumulative [ə'kju:mjʊlətɪv] ADJ = **cumulative**

accumulator [ə'kju:mjʊleɪtə'] N Akkumulator *m*

accuracy ['ækjʊrəsɪ] N Genauigkeit *f*; (*of missile*) Zielgenauigkeit *f*

accurate ['ækjʊrɪt] ADJ *worker, observation, translation, copy, instrument* genau, akkurat (*rare*); *missile* zielgenau; **the clock is ~** die Uhr geht genau; **his aim/shot was ~** er hat genau gezielt/getroffen; **the test is 90% ~** der Test ist 90%ig sicher; **her work is slow but ~** sie arbeitet langsam, aber genau; **to be (strictly) ~** um (ganz) genau zu sein

accurately ['ækjʊrɪtlɪ] ADV genau

accursed, accurst [ə'kɜ:st] ADJ **a** (*inf:* = *hateful*) verwünscht **b** (*old, liter:* = *under a curse*) **to be ~** unter einem Fluch or bösen Zauber stehen

accusation [ækjʊ'zeɪʃən] N Beschuldigung *f*, Anschuldigung *f*; (*Jur*) Anklage *f*; (= *reproach*) Vorwurf *m*; **he denied her ~ of dishonesty** er wehrte sich gegen ihren Vorwurf, dass er unehrlich sei; **a look of ~** ein anklagender Blick

accusative [ə'kju:zətɪv] **N** Akkusativ *m*; **in the ~** im Akkusativ **ADJ** Akkusativ-; **~ case** Akkusativ *m*; **~ ending** Akkusativendung *f*

accusatory [ə'kju:zətərɪ] ADJ anklagend

accuse [ə'kju:z] VT **a** (*Jur*) anklagen (*of* wegen, +*gen*); **he is** or **stands ~d of murder/theft** er ist des Mordes/Diebstahls angeklagt, er steht unter Anklage des Mordes/Diebstahls (*form*) **b** *person* beschuldigen, bezichtigen; **to ~ sb of doing** or **having done sth** jdn beschuldigen or bezichtigen, etw getan zu haben; **are you accusing me? I didn't take it!** beschuldigen Sie mich? Ich habe es nicht genommen; **are you accusing me of lying/not having checked the brakes?** willst du (damit) vielleicht sagen, dass ich lüge/die Bremsen nicht nachgesehen habe?; **to ~ sb of being untidy** jdm vorwerfen, unordentlich zu sein; **who are you accusing, the police or society?** wen klagen Sie an, die Polizei oder die Gesellschaft?; **I ~ the government of dishonesty** ich werfe der Regierung Unehrlichkeit vor; **a generation stands ~d of hypocrisy** eine Generation wird der Scheinheiligkeit beschuldigt or angeklagt or geziehen (*geh*); **we all stand ~d** uns alle trifft eine Schuld

accused [ə'kju:zd] N **the ~** der/die Angeklagte; (*several*) die Angeklagten *pl*

accuser [ə'kju:zə'] N Ankläger(in) *m(f)*

accusing [ə'kju:zɪŋ] ADJ anklagend; **he had an ~ look on his face** sein Blick klagte an

accusingly [ə'kju:zɪŋlɪ] ADV *say, look* anklagend

accustom [ə'kʌstəm] VT **to ~ sb/oneself to sth** jdn/sich an etw (*acc*) gewöhnen; **to ~ oneself to doing sth** sich daran gewöhnen, etw zu tun; **to be ~ed to sth** an etw (*acc*) gewöhnt sein; **to be ~ed to doing sth** gewöhnt sein, etw zu tun; **it is not what I am ~ed to** ich bin so etwas nicht gewöhnt; **to become** or **get ~ed to sth** sich an etw (*acc*) gewöhnen; **to become** or **get ~ed to doing sth** sich daran gewöhnen, etw zu tun

accustomed [ə'kʌstəmd] ADJ *attr* (= *usual*) gewohnt

AC/DC ADJ **a** *abbr of* **alternating current/direct current** Allstrom **b** **ac/dc** (*inf*) bi (*inf*)

ace [eɪs] N **a** (*Cards*) As *nt*; **the ~ of clubs** das Kreuz-As; **to have an ~ up one's sleeve** noch einen Trumpf in der Hand haben; **he was** or **came within an ~ of winning** er hätte um ein Haar gesiegt; **to hold all the ~s** (*fig*) alle Trümpfe in der Hand halten; **to be an ~ in the hole** eine Trumpfkarte sein **b** (*inf*: = *expert*) Ass *nt* (*at* in +*dat*); **tennis ~** Tennisass *nt* **c** (*Tennis*, = *serve*) Ass *nt*; **to serve an ~** ein Ass servieren **ADJ** *attr* (= *excellent*) Star-; **~ photographer** Starfotograf(in) *m(f)*; **he's an ~ striker** (*Ftbl*) er ist ein Stürmer-Ass

acerbic [ə'sɜ:bɪk] ADJ *person* gerissen; *wit* scharf; *remark, comment, style* bissig

acerbity [ə'sɜ:bɪtɪ] N Schärfe *f*

acetate ['æsɪteɪt] N Acetat *nt*, Azetat *nt*

acetic [ə'si:tɪk] ADJ essigsauer

acetic acid N Essigsäure *f*

acetone ['æsɪtəʊn] N Aceton *nt*, Azeton *nt*

acetylene [ə'setɪli:n] N Acetylen *nt*, Azetylen *nt*

ache [eɪk] N (*dumpfer*) Schmerz *m*; **I have an ~ in my side** ich habe Schmerzen in der Seite; **a few little ~s and pains** ein paar Wehwehchen (*inf*); **with an ~ in one's heart** (*fig*) mit wehem Herzen (*liter*)

VI **a** (= *hurt*) wehtun, schmerzen; **my head/stomach ~s** mir tut der Kopf/Magen weh; **it makes my head/arms ~** davon tut mir der Kopf/tun mir die Arme weh; **I'm aching all over** mir tut alles weh; **it makes my heart ~ to see him** (*fig*) es tut mir in der Seele weh, wenn ich ihn sehe; **my heart ~s for you** mir bricht fast das Herz (*also iro*)

b (*fig:* = *yearn*) **to ~ for sb/sth** sich nach jdm/etw sehnen; **to ~ to do sth** sich danach sehnen, etw zu tun; **I ~d to help him** es drängte mich, ihm zu helfen

achievable [ə'tʃi:vəbl] ADJ erreichbar

achieve [ə'tʃi:v] ✪ 8.1 **VT** erreichen, schaffen; *success* erzielen; *victory* erringen; *rank also, title* erlangen; **she ~d a great deal** (= *did a lot of work*) sie hat eine Menge geleistet; (= *was quite successful*) sie hat viel erreicht; **he will never ~ anything** er wird es nie zu etwas bringen **VI** (*Psych, Sociol*) leisten; **the achieving society** die Leistungsgesellschaft

achievement [ə'tʃi:vmənt] N **a** (*act*) Erreichen *nt*; (*of success*) Erzielen *nt*; (*of victory*) Erringen *nt*; (*of rank also, title*) Erlangen *nt*; **~-oriented** leistungsorientiert; **~-oriented society** Leistungsgesellschaft *f* **b** (= *thing achieved*) (*of individual*) Leistung *f*; (*of society, civilization, technology*) Errungenschaft *f*; **that's quite an ~!** das ist schon eine Leistung! (*also iro*); **for his many ~s** für seine zahlreichen Verdienste; **~ quotient/test** Leistungsquotient *m*/-test *m*

achiever [ə'tʃi:və'] N Leistungstyp *m* (*inf*); **to be an ~** leistungsorientiert sein; **high ~** (*Sch*) leistungsstarkes Kind

Achilles [ə'kɪli:z] N Achill(es) *m*; **~ heel** (*fig*) Achillesferse *f*; **~ tendon** Achillessehne *f*

aching ['eɪkɪŋ] ADJ *attr bones, head, muscles, limbs* schmerzend; (*fig*) *heart* wund, weh (*liter*)

achingly ['eɪkɪŋlɪ] ADV schmerzlich; **~ slow** quälend langsam

achy ['eɪkɪ] ADJ (*inf*) schmerzend; **I feel ~ all over** mir tut alles weh

acid ['æsɪd] **ADJ** **a** (= *sour, also Chem*) sauer **b** (*fig*) ätzend, beißend **N** **a** (*Chem*) Säure *f* **b** (*inf*: = *LSD*) Acid *nt* (*sl*)

acid drop N saurer *or* saures Drops

acidhead ['æsɪd‚hed] N (*inf*: = *LSD user*) Acidhead *m* (*sl*)

acidic [ə'sɪdɪk] ADJ sauer

acidity [ə'sɪdɪtɪ] N Säure *f*; (*Chem also*) Säuregehalt *m*; (*of stomach*) Magensäure *f*

acidly ['æsɪdlɪ] ADV (*fig*) ätzend, beißend

acid: acid-proof ['æsɪdpruːf] ADJ säurebeständig; **acid rain** N saurer Regen; **acid rock** N (*Mus*) Acid Rock *m*; **acid test** N Feuerprobe *f*; **acid-tongued** ADJ *person, remark* scharfzüngig

ack-ack ['æk'æk] N (= *fire*) Flakfeuer *nt*; (= *gun*) Flak *f*

acknowledge [ək'nɒlɪdʒ] ✪ 20.5 VT anerkennen; *quotation* angeben; (= *admit*) *truth, fault, defeat etc* eingestehen, zugeben; (= *note receipt of*) *letter, present etc* den Empfang bestätigen von; (= *respond to*) *greetings, cheers etc* erwidern; **to ~ oneself beaten** sich geschlagen geben; **to ~ sb's presence/existence** jds Anwesenheit/Existenz zur Kenntnis nehmen

acknowledged [ək'nɒlɪdʒd] ADJ *attr* anerkannt

acknowledgement [ək'nɒlɪdʒmənt] N Anerkennung *f*; (*of quotation*) Angabe *f*; (= *recognition*: *of truth, fault, defeat etc*) Eingeständnis *nt*; (*of letter, present*) Empfangsbestätigung *f*; (*of greetings, cheers etc*) Erwiderung *f*; **he waved in ~** er winkte zurück; **in ~ of** in Anerkennung (+*gen*); **to quote without ~** ohne Quellenangabe zitieren; **I received no ~** ich erhielt keine Antwort; **as an ~ of my gratitude** zum Zeichen meiner Dankbarkeit; **~s are due to …** ich habe/wir haben … zu danken; (*in book*) mein/unser Dank gilt …

acme ['ækmɪ] N Höhepunkt *m*, Gipfel *m*; (*of elegance etc*) Inbegriff *m*; **at the ~ of his powers** auf dem Gipfel seiner (Schaffens)kraft

acne ['æknɪ] N Akne *f*

acolyte ['ækəʊlaɪt] N (*Eccl*) (*Catholic*) Akoluth *m*; (*Protestant*: = *server*) Messdiener(in) *m(f)*, Ministrant(in) *m(f)*; (*fig*) Gefolgsmann *m*/-frau *f*

aconite ['ækənaɪt] N (*Bot*) Eisenhut *m*, Aconitum *nt*; (= *drug*) Aconitin *nt*

acorn ['eɪkɔːn] N Eichel *f*

acoustic [ə'kuːstɪk] ADJ akustisch; (= *soundproof*) *tiles, panel* schalldämpfend; **~ screen** Trennwand *f* (*zur Schalldämpfung*)

acoustically [ə'kuːstɪkəlɪ] ADV akustisch

acoustic coupler N (*Comput*) Akustikkoppler *m*

acoustic guitar N Akustikgitarre *f*

acoustics [ə'kuːstɪks] **a** *sing* (*subject*) Akustik *f* **b** *pl* (*of room etc*) Akustik *f*

acquaint [ə'kweɪnt] VT **a** (= *make familiar*) bekannt machen; **to be ~ed/thoroughly ~ed with sth** mit etw bekannt/vertraut sein; **to be ~ed with grief** mit Leid vertraut sein; **he's well ~ed with the situation** er ist mit der Situation vertraut; **to become ~ed with sth** etw kennen lernen; *facts, truth* etw erfahren; **to ~ oneself** *or* **make oneself ~ed with sth** sich mit etw vertraut machen **b** (*with person*) **to be ~ed with sb** mit jdm bekannt sein; **we're not ~ed** wir kennen einander *or* uns nicht; **to become** *or* **get ~ed** sich (näher) kennen lernen

acquaintance [ə'kweɪntəns] N **a** (= *person*) Bekannte(r) *mf*; **we're just ~s** wir kennen uns bloß flüchtig; **a wide circle of ~s** ein großer Bekanntenkreis **b** (*with person*) Bekanntschaft *f*; (*with subject etc*) Kenntnis *f* (*with* +*gen*); (*intimate, with sorrow etc*) Vertrautheit *f*; **to make sb's ~, to make the ~ of sb** jds Bekanntschaft machen; **a woman of our ~** eine uns bekannte Dame; **I have some ~ with Italian wines** ich kenne mich mit italienischen Weinen einigermaßen aus; **it improves on ~** man kommt mit der Zeit auf den Geschmack (davon); **perhaps he'll improve on ~** vielleicht gefällt er uns *etc* besser, wenn wir *etc*

ihn erst einmal näher kennen lernen → **nodding**

acquaintanceship [ə'kweɪntənsʃɪp] N Bekanntschaft *f* (*with* mit)

acquiesce [ækwɪ'es] VI einwilligen (*in* in +*acc*); (*submissively*) sich fügen (*in* +*dat*)

acquiescence [ækwɪ'esns] N Einwilligung *f* (*in* in +*acc*); (*submissive*) Fügung *f* (*in* in +*acc*); **with an air of ~** mit zustimmender Miene

acquiescent [ækwɪ'esnt] ADJ fügsam; *smile* ergeben; *attitude* zustimmend

acquire [ə'kwaɪə] VT erwerben; (*by dubious means*) sich (*dat*) aneignen; *habit* annehmen; **I see he has ~d a secretary/wife** wie ich sehe, hat er sich eine Sekretärin/Frau angeschafft (*inf*); **he ~d a fine tan** er hat eine gute Farbe bekommen; **where did you ~ that?** woher hast du das?; **to ~ a taste/liking for sth** Geschmack/Gefallen an etw (*dat*) finden; **once you've ~d a taste for it** wenn du erst mal auf den Geschmack gekommen bist; **caviar is an ~d taste** Kaviar ist (nur) für Kenner; **~d** (*Psych*) erworben; **~d characteristics** (*Biol*) erworbene Eigenschaften *pl*

acquirement [ə'kwaɪəmənt] N **a** (*act*) = **acquisition a** **b** (= *skill etc acquired*) Fertigkeit *f*

acquirer [ə'kwaɪərə] N (*Fin*) Erwerber(in) *m(f)*

acquisition [ækwɪ'zɪʃən] N **a** (*act*) Erwerb *m*; (*by dubious means*) Aneignung *f*; (*of habit*) Annahme *f* **b** (= *thing acquired*) Anschaffung *f*; (*hum*: = *secretary, girlfriend etc*) Errungenschaft *f*; **he's a useful ~ to the department** er ist ein Gewinn für die Abteilung

acquisitive [ə'kwɪzɪtɪv] ADJ auf Erwerb aus, habgierig (*pej*), raffgierig (*pej*); **the ~ society** die Erwerbsgesellschaft; **magpies are ~ birds** Elstern sind Vögel mit ausgeprägtem Sammeltrieb

acquisitiveness [ə'kwɪzɪtɪvnɪs] N Habgier *f* (*pej*)

acquit [ə'kwɪt] **VT** freisprechen; **to be ~ted of a crime/on a charge** von einem Verbrechen/einer Anklage freigesprochen werden **VR** (= *conduct oneself*) sich verhalten; (= *perform*) seine Sache machen; **he ~ted himself well** er hat seine Sache gut gemacht; (= *stood up well*) er hat sich gut aus der Affäre gezogen

acquittal [ə'kwɪtl] N Freispruch *m* (*on* von)

acre ['eɪkə] N ≈ Morgen *m*; **~s** (*old, liter, = land*) Fluren *pl* (*old, liter*); **~s (and ~s) of garden** hektarweise Garten

acreage ['eɪkərɪdʒ] N Land *nt*; (*Agr*) Anbaufläche *f*; **what ~ do they have?** wie viel Land *or* wie viele Morgen (*Agr*) haben sie?

acrid ['ækrɪd] ADJ *taste* bitter; (*of wine*) sauer; *smell* säuerlich; *comment, smoke* beißend

Acrilan® ['ækrɪlæn] N Acryl *nt*, Akryl *nt*

acrimonious [ækrɪ'məʊnɪəs] ADJ *discussion, argument* erbittert; *person, words* bissig; *divorce* verbittert ausgefochten

acrimoniously [ækrɪ'məʊnɪəslɪ] ADV *end, split, break up* verbittert

acrimony ['ækrɪmənɪ] N (*of discussion, argument*) erbitterte Schärfe *f*; (*of person, words*) Bissigkeit *f*

acrobat ['ækrəbæt] N Akrobat(in) *m(f)*

acrobatic [ækrəʊ'bætɪk] ADJ akrobatisch

acrobatics [ækrəʊ'bætɪks] PL Akrobatik *f*; **mental ~** (*fig*) Gedankenakrobatik *f*, geistige Klimmzüge *pl* (*inf*)

acronym ['ækrənɪm] N Akronym *nt*

acropolis [ə'krɒpəlɪs] N Akropolis *f*

across [ə'krɒs] **ADV** **a** (*direction*) (= *to the other side*) hinüber; (= *from the other side*) herüber; (= *crosswise*) (quer)durch; **shall I go ~ first?** soll ich zuerst hinüber(gehen/-schwimmen *etc*)?; **to throw sth ~** etw hinüberwerfen; **to row ~** hinüberrudern; **to help sb ~** jdm herüberhelfen; **to cut sth ~** etw (quer) durchschneiden; **he was already ~** er war schon drüben; **~ from your house** gegenüber von eurem Haus, eurem Haus gegenüber; **the stripes go ~** es ist quer gestreift; **draw a line ~** machen Sie einen

Strich; (*diagonal*) machen Sie einen Strich querdurch **b** (*measurement*) breit; (*of round object*) im Durchmesser **c** (*in crosswords*) waagerecht

PREP **a** (*direction*) über (+*acc*); (= *diagonally across*) quer durch (+*acc*); **to run ~ the road** über die Straße laufen; **to wade ~ a river** durch einen Fluss waten; **a tree fell ~ the path** ein Baum fiel quer über den Weg; **~ country** querfeldein; (*over long distance*) quer durch das Land; **to draw a line ~ the page** einen Strich durch die Seite machen; **the stripes go ~ the material** der Stoff ist quer gestreift **b** (*position*) über (+*dat*); **a tree lay ~ the path** ein Baum lag quer über dem Weg; **he was sprawled ~ the bed** er lag quer auf dem Bett; **with his arms (folded) ~ his chest** die Arme vor der Brust verschränkt; **from ~ the sea** (*geh*) von der anderen Seite des Meeres; **he lives ~ the street from us** er wohnt uns gegenüber; **you could hear him (from) ~ the hall** man konnte ihn von der anderen Seite der Halle hören; **~ the political spectrum** auf allen Seiten des politischen Spektrums

across-the-board [ə'krɒsðə'bɔːd] ADJ *attr* allgemein → *also* **board**

acrostic [ə'krɒstɪk] N Akrostichon *nt*

acrylic [ə'krɪlɪk] **N** Acryl *nt*, Akryl *nt* **ADJ** Acryl-, Akryl-; *dress* aus Acryl *or* Akryl; **~ paint** Acrylfarbe *f*, Akrylfarbe *f*

a/cs pay. (*Fin*) abbr of **accounts payable**

a/cs rec. (*Fin*) abbr of **accounts receivable**

ACT abbr of **Australian Capital Territory**

act [ækt] **N** **a** (= *deed, thing done*) Tat *f*; (*official, ceremonial*) Akt *m*; **my first ~ was to phone him** meine erste Tat *or* mein Erstes war, ihn anzurufen; **an ~ of mercy** ein Gnadenakt *m*; **an ~ of God** eine höhere Gewalt *no pl*; **an ~ of war** kriegerische Aktion *f*; **an ~ of folly/ madness** ein Akt *m* der Dummheit/des Wahnsinns; **a small ~ of kindness** eine Freundlichkeit; **Acts** (*Bibl*) **the Acts of the Apostles** (*Bibl*) die Apostelgeschichte → **faith a** **b** (= *process of doing*) **to be in the ~ of doing sth** (gerade) dabei sein, etw zu tun; **to catch sb in the ~** jdn auf frischer Tat (*sexually*) in flagranti ertappen; **to catch/watch sb in the ~ of doing sth** jdn dabei ertappen/beobachten, wie er etw tut **c** (*Parl*) Gesetz *nt*; **this was made illegal by an ~ of Parliament passed in 1976** nach einem 1976 vom Parlament verabschiedeten Gesetz ist das verboten **d** (*Theat*) (*of play, opera*) Akt *m*; (= *turn*) Nummer *f*; **a one-act play** ein Einakter *m*; **a one-act opera** eine Oper in einem Akt; **to get into** *or* **in on the ~** (*fig inf*) mit von der Partie sein; **how did he get in on the ~?** (*inf*) wie kommt es, dass er da mitmischt? (*inf*); **he's really got his ~ together** (*inf*) (= *is organized, efficient with sth*) er hat die Sache wirklich im Griff; (*in lifestyle etc*) er hat im Leben erreicht, was er wollte; **get your ~ together!** reiß dich doch mal zusammen!; **to clean up one's ~** (*inf*) sich zusammenreißen; **she'll be a hard** *or* **tough ~ to follow** man wird es ihr nur schwer gleichmachen; **to be a class ~** (*inf*) Spitze sein (*inf*) **e** (*fig*: = *pretence*) Theater *nt*, Schau *f* (*inf*); **it's all an ~** das ist alles nur Theater *or* Schau (*inf*); **to put on an ~** Theater spielen

VT *part* spielen; *play also* aufführen; **to ~ the innocent** die gekränkte Unschuld spielen

VI **a** (*Theat*: = *perform*) spielen; (= *to be an actor*) schauspielern, Theater spielen; (*fig*) Theater spielen, schauspielern, markieren; **to ~ on TV** im Fernsehen auftreten *or* spielen; **who's ~ing in it?** wer spielt darin?; **he learned to ~** er nahm Schauspielunterricht; **he should learn to ~!** er sollte erst mal richtig schauspielern lernen; **... but she can't ~** ... sie kann nicht spielen *or* ist keine Schauspielerin; **he's only ~ing** er tut (doch) nur so, er markiert *or* spielt (doch) nur; **to ~ stupid/innocent** *etc* sich dumm/unschuldig *etc* stellen, den Dummen/ Unschuldigen *etc* spielen

b (= *function*) (*brakes etc*) funktionieren; (*drug*) wirken; **to ~ as ...** wirken als ...; (= *have function*) fungieren als ...; (*person*) das Amt des/der ... übernehmen, fungieren als ...; **-ing in my capacity as chairman** in meiner Eigenschaft als Vorsitzender; **it ~s as a deterrent** das wirkt abschreckend; **to ~ for** or **on behalf of sb** jdn vertreten

c (= *behave*) sich verhalten; **~ like a man!** sei ein Mann!; **she ~ed as if** or **as though she was hurt/surprised** *etc* sie tat so, als ob sie verletzt/ überrascht *etc* wäre; **he ~s like** or **as though he owns the place** (*inf*) er tut so, als ob der Laden ihm gehört (*inf*)

d (= *take action*) handeln; **he ~ed to stop it** er unternahm etwas or Schritte, um dem ein Ende zu machen; **the police couldn't ~** die Polizei konnte nichts unternehmen

▶ **act on** VI +*prep obj* **a** (= *affect*) wirken auf (+*acc*); **the yeast acts on the sugar to produce alcohol** die Hefe wirkt auf den Zucker ein und führt zur Alkoholbildung **b** (= *take action on*) *warning, report, evidence* handeln auf (+*acc*); *hin*; *suggestion, advice* folgen (+*dat*); *orders* handeln aufgrund or auf Grund von; **acting on information received, the police ...** die Polizei handelte aufgrund or auf Grund der ihr zugegangenen Information und ...; **acting on an impulse** einer plötzlichen Eingebung gehorchend or folgend; **did you act on the letter?** haben Sie auf den Brief hin etwas unternommen?

▶ **act out** VT *sep fantasies, problems etc* durchspielen; **the drama/affair was acted out at ...** das Drama/die Affäre spielte sich in ... ab

▶ **act up** VI (*inf*) jdm Ärger machen; (*person also*) Theater machen (*inf*); (*to attract attention*) sich aufspielen; (*machine*) verrückt spielen (*inf*); **my back is acting up** mein Rücken macht mir Ärger

▶ **act upon** VI +*prep obj* = **act on**

actable ['æktəbl] ADJ *play* spielbar; **it is very ~** es lässt sich gut spielen or aufführen

acting ['æktɪŋ] **ADJ** **a** stellvertretend *attr*, in Stellvertretung *pred* **b** *attr* (*Theat*) schauspielerisch **N** (*Theat*) (= *performance*) Darstellung *f*; (= *activity*) Spielen *nt*; (= *profession*) Schauspielerei *f*; **what was the ~ like?** wie waren die Schauspieler?; **what was his ~ like?** wie hat er gespielt?; **I don't like his ~** ich mag seine Art zu spielen nicht; **he's done some ~** er hat schon Theater gespielt; (*professionally also*) er hat schon etwas Schauspielerfahrung

actinic ['æktɪnɪk] ADJ aktinisch

actinometer [æktɪ'nɒmɪtə'] N (*Met*) Aktinometer *nt*

action ['ækʃən] N **a** *no pl* (= *activity*) Handeln *nt*; (*of play, novel etc*) Handlung *f*; **now is the time for ~** die Zeit zum Handeln ist gekommen; **a man of ~** ein Mann der Tat; **to take ~** etwas or Schritte unternehmen; **have you taken any ~ on his letter?** haben Sie auf seinen Brief hin irgendetwas or irgendwelche Schritte unternommen?; **course of ~** Vorgehen *nt*; **"action"** (*on office tray*) „zur Bearbeitung"; **no further ~** keine weiteren Maßnahmen; (*label on file etc*) abgeschlossen; **the ~ of the play/novel takes place ...** das Stück/der Roman spielt ...; **~!** (*Film*) Achtung, Aufnahme!

b (= *deed*) Tat *f*; **his first ~ was to phone me** als Erstes rief er mich an; **to suit the ~ to the word** dem Wort die Tat folgen lassen, sein Wort in die Tat umsetzen; **~s speak louder than words** (*Prov*) die Tat wirkt mächtiger als das Wort (*prov*)

c (= *motion, operation*) **in/out of ~** in/nicht in Aktion; *machine* in/außer Betrieb; (= *operational*) einsatzfähig/nicht einsatzfähig; **to go into ~** in Aktion treten; **to put a plan into ~** einen Plan in die Tat umsetzen; **to put out of ~** außer Gefecht setzen; **he's been out of ~ since he broke his leg** er ist nicht mehr in Aktion gewesen or war nicht mehr einsatzfähig, seit er sich das Bein gebrochen hat; **he needs prod-**

ding into ~ man muss ihm immer erst einen Stoß geben

d (= *exciting events*) Action *f* (*sl*); **there's no ~ in this film** in dem Film passiert nichts, dem Film fehlt die Action (*inf*); **a novel full of ~** ein handlungsreicher Roman; **let's have some ~!** (*inf*) lass uns mal was unternehmen; **to go where the ~ is** (*inf*) hingehen, wo was los ist (*inf*); **that's where the ~ is** (*inf*) da ist was los (*inf*); **he was out looking for ~** (*inf*) er wollte was erleben (*inf*)

e (*Mil*) (= *fighting*) Aktionen *pl*; (= *battle*) Kampf *m*, Gefecht *nt*; **enemy ~** feindliche Handlungen or Aktionen *pl*; **killed in ~** gefallen; **he saw ~ in the desert** er war in der Wüste im Einsatz; **the first time they went into ~** bei ihrem ersten Einsatz; **they never once went into ~** sie kamen nie zum Einsatz

f (= *way of operating*) (*of machine*) Arbeitsweise *f*; (*of piano etc*) Mechanik *f*; (*of watch, gun*) Mechanismus *m*; (= *way of moving*) (*of athlete etc*) Bewegung *f*; (*of horse*) Aktion *f*; **to hit with a smooth ~** (*Sport*) ganz weich schlagen

g (*esp Chem, Phys: = effect*) Wirkung *f* (*on* auf +*acc*)

h (*Jur*) Klage *f*; **to bring an ~ (against sb)** eine Klage (gegen jdn) anstrengen

i (*Fin inf*) **a piece** or **slice of the ~** ein Stück *nt* aus dem Kuchen (*sl*)

actionable ['ækʃnəbl] ADJ verfolgbar; *statement* klagbar

action: action committee N Aktionskomitee *nt*; **action film** N Actionfilm *m*; **action group** N Aktionsgruppe *f*; **action man** N (*usu hum*) Actionmann *m* (*inf*); **action movie** N (*esp US*) Actionfilm *m*; **action-packed** ADJ *film, book* aktions- or handlungsgeladen; **action painting** N Aktion *f*; **action replay** N Wiederholung *f*; **action stations** PL Stellung *f*; **~!** Stellung!; (*fig*) an die Plätze!; **action woman** N (*usu hum*) Action-Frau *f* (*inf*)

activate ['æktɪveɪt] VT *mechanism* (*person*) betätigen; (*heat*) auslösen; (*switch, lever*) in Gang setzen; *alarm* auslösen; *bomb* zünden; (*Chem, Phys*) aktivieren; (*US Mil*) mobilisieren

activated sludge [ˌæktɪveɪtɪd'slʌdʒ] N Belebtschlamm *m*

activation [ˌæktɪ'veɪʃən] N Aktivierung *f*

active ['æktɪv] **ADJ** aktiv (*also Gram, Comput*); *mind, social life* rege; *volcano* aktiv, tätig; *dislike* offen, unverhohlen; *fire* im Gebrauch; (= *radioactive*) radioaktiv; **to be ~** (*terrorists, rebels*) operieren; (*lawyer, campaigner*) aktiv sein; **to be physically/actively/sexually ~** körperlich/politisch/sexuell aktiv sein; **to be ~ in politics** politisch aktiv or tätig sein; **they should be more ~ in improving safety standards** sie sollten die Verbesserung der Sicherheitsvorschriften etwas tatkräftiger vorantreiben; **to be under ~ consideration** ernsthaft erwogen werden; **on ~ service** (*Mil*) im Einsatz; **to see ~ service** (*Mil*) im Einsatz sein; **to be on the ~ list** (*Mil*) zur ständigen Verfügung stehen; **~ duty** (*esp US Mil*) aktiver Wehrdienst; **to be on ~ duty** (*esp US Mil*) aktiven Wehrdienst leisten; **he played an ~ part in it** er war aktiv daran beteiligt; **~ assets** (*Comm*) Aktiva *pl*; **~ partner** (*Comm*) persönlich haftender Gesellschafter; **~ ingredient** (*Chem*) aktiver Bestandteil; **~ suspension** (*Aut*) aktive Aufhängung **N** (*Gram*) Aktiv *nt*; **in the ~** im Aktiv

actively ['æktɪvlɪ] ADV aktiv; *dislike* offen, unverhohlen

activism ['æktɪvɪzm] N Aktivismus *m*

activist ['æktɪvɪst] N Aktivist(in) *m(f)*

activity [æk'tɪvɪtɪ] N **a** *no pl* Aktivität *f*; (*in market, town, office*) Geschäftigkeit *f*, geschäftiges Treiben; (*mental*) Betätigung *f*; **a scene of great ~** ein Bild geschäftigen Treibens; **a new sphere of ~** ein neues Betätigungsfeld, ein neuer Wirkungskreis

b (= *pastime*) Betätigung *f*; **classroom activities** schulische Tätigkeiten *pl*; **the church organizes many activities** die Kirche organisiert viele Veranstaltungen; **business/social activities** ge-

schäftliche/gesellschaftliche Unternehmungen *pl*; **criminal activities** kriminelle Tätigkeiten or Aktivitäten *pl*; **a programme of activities** ein Veranstaltungsprogramm *nt*

c (= *radioactivity*) Radioaktivität *f*

activity holiday N (*Brit*) Aktivurlaub *m*

actor ['æktə'] N (*lit, fig*) Schauspieler(in) *m(f)*

actress ['æktrɪs] N (*lit, fig*) Schauspielerin *f*

actressy ['æktrɪsɪ] ADJ (*pej*) theatralisch (*pej*)

actual ['æktjʊəl] ADJ **a** eigentlich; *reason, price also, result* tatsächlich; *case, example* konkret; **in ~ fact** eigentlich; **what were his ~ words?** was genau hat er gesagt?; **this is the ~ house** das ist hier das Haus; **there is no ~ contract** besteht kein eigentlicher Vertrag; **your ~ ...** (*inf*) ein echter/eine echte/ein echtes ..., der/die/ das echte ...; **~ size** wahre Größe **b** (= *precise*) genau; **I don't remember the ~ figures** ich erinnere mich nicht an die genauen Zahlen

actual bodily harm N (*Jur*) einfache Körperverletzung

actuality [ˌæktjʊ'ælɪtɪ] N (= *reality*) Wirklichkeit *f*, Realität *f*; (= *realism*) Aktualität *f*; **the actualities of the situation** die tatsächlichen Gegebenheiten

actualize ['æktjʊəlaɪz] VT verwirklichen

actually ['æktjʊəlɪ] ADV **a** (*used as a filler*) *usually not translated* **~ I haven't started yet** ich habe noch (gar) nicht damit angefangen; **~ we were just talking about you** wir haben eben von Ihnen geredet; **~ his name is Smith** er heißt (übrigens) Smith; **I'm going too ~** ich gehe (übrigens) auch; **~ what we could do is to ...** (wissen Sie,) wir könnten doch ...

b (= *to tell the truth, in actual fact*) eigentlich; (= *by the way*) übrigens; **as you said before, and ~ you were quite right** wie Sie schon sagten, und eigentlich hatten Sie völlig Recht; **~ you were quite right, it was a bad idea** Sie hatten übrigens völlig Recht, es war eine schlechte Idee; **I don't ~ feel like going there** ich habe eigentlich keine Lust, da hinzugehen; **do you want that/know him? – ~ I do/don't** möchten Sie das/kennen Sie ihn? – ja, durchaus or schon/ nein, eigentlich nicht; **you don't want that/ know him, do you? – ~ I do** Sie möchten das/ kennen ihn (doch) nicht, oder? – doch, eigentlich schon; **do you know her? – ~ I'm her husband** kennen Sie sie? – ja, ich bin nämlich ihr Mann; **I thought I could give you a lift but I won't ~ be going** ich dachte, ich könnte Sie mitnehmen, aber ich gehe nun doch nicht; **I bet you haven't done that! – ~ I have** Sie haben das bestimmt nicht gemacht! – doch; **I'm going soon, tomorrow ~** ich gehe bald, nämlich morgen; **it won't be easy, it'll ~ be very difficult** es wird nicht leicht, ja es wird sogar sehr schwierig sein

c (= *truly, in reality: showing surprise*) tatsächlich; **if you ~ own an apartment** wenn Sie tatsächlich eine Wohnung besitzen; **don't tell me you're ~ going now!** sag bloß, du gehst jetzt tatsächlich or wirklich!; **oh, you're ~ in/ dressed/ready!** oh, du bist sogar da/angezogen/fertig!; **... but ~ I could do it** ... aber ich konnte es doch; **I haven't ~ started/done it/met him yet** ich habe noch nicht angefangen/es noch nicht gemacht/ihn noch nicht kennen gelernt; **not ~ ..., but ...** zwar nicht ..., aber ...; **I wasn't ~ there, but ...** ich war zwar selbst nicht dabei, aber ...; **did he ~ say that?** hat er das tatsächlich or wirklich gesagt?; **what did he ~ say?** was genau hat er gesagt?, was hat er tatsächlich gesagt?; **what do you ~ want?** was möchten Sie eigentlich?; **does that ~ exist?** gibt es das denn überhaupt or tatsächlich?; **as for ~ working ...** was die Arbeit selbst betrifft ...; **as for ~ doing it** wenn es dann daran geht, es auch zu tun; **it's the first time that I've ~ seen him/that I've ~ been home in time for the news** das ist das erste Mal, dass ich ihn mal gesehen habe/dass ich mal rechtzeitig zu den Nachrichten zu Hause bin

d **it's ~ taking place this very moment** das findet genau in diesem Augenblick statt; **it was ~**

taking place when he ... es fand genau zu der Zeit statt, als er ...

actuarial [ˌæktjʊˈeərɪəl] ADJ (Insur) versicherungsmathematisch, versicherungsstatistisch

actuary [ˈæktjʊərɪ] N (Insur) Aktuar(in) m(f)

actuate [ˈæktjʊeɪt] VT (lit) auslösen; (fig) treiben

acuity [əˈkjuːɪtɪ] N Scharfsinn m, Klugheit f; (of mind) Schärfe f

acumen [ˈækjʊmen] N Scharfsinn m; **to show (considerable) ~** (großen) Scharfsinn beweisen; **business ~** Geschäftssinn m; **political ~** politische Klugheit

acupressure [ˈækjʊˌpreʃəʳ] N Akupressur f

acupuncture [ˈækjʊˌpʌŋktʃəʳ] N Akupunktur f

acute [əˈkjuːt] ADJ **a** (= intense, serious) pain, shortage, appendicitis akut; pleasure intensiv; **~ beds** (Med) Akutbetten pl **b** (= extreme) situation, problem, anxiety akut; embarrassment riesig **c** (= keen) eyesight scharf; hearing, sense of smell fein **d** (= shrewd) scharf; person scharfsinnig; child aufgeweckt **e** (Math) angle spitz **f** (Ling) ~ **accent** Akut m; **e** – e Akut **N** (Ling) Akut m

acutely [əˈkjuːtlɪ] ADV **a** (= intensely) akut; feel intensiv; embarrassed, sensitive, uncomfortable äußerst; ill akut; **to be ~ aware of sth** sich (dat) einer Sache (gen) genau or sehr bewusst sein; (= painfully) sich (dat) einer Sache (gen) schmerzlich bewusst sein **b** (= shrewdly) scharfsinnig; criticize, observe scharf

acuteness [əˈkjuːtnɪs] N **a** (= intensity: of pleasure) Intensität f **b** (= keenness: of eyesight) Schärfe f; (of hearing, sense of smell) Feinheit f **c** (= shrewdness) Schärfe f; (of person) Scharfsinn m; (of child) Aufgewecktheit f

acyclic [eɪˈsaɪklɪk] ADJ azyklisch

AD abbr of **Anno Domini** n. Chr., A.D.

ad [æd] N abbr of **advertisement** Anzeige f, Inserat nt

adage [ˈædɪdʒ] N Sprichwort nt

adagio [əˈdɑːdʒɪəʊ] ADV adagio **N** Adagio nt

Adam [ˈædəm] N Adam m; **~'s apple** Adamsapfel m; **I don't know him from ~** (inf) ich habe keine Ahnung, wer er ist (inf)

adamant [ˈædəmənt] ADJ hart; refusal also hartnäckig; **to be ~** unnachgiebig sein, darauf bestehen; **since you're ~** da Sie darauf bestehen; **he was ~ about going** er bestand hartnäckig darauf zu gehen; **he was ~ in his refusal** er weigerte sich hartnäckig

adamantine [ˌædəˈmæntaɪn] ADJ (liter, lit) diamanten (liter); (fig) hartnäckig

adamantly [ˈædəməntlɪ] ADV (= rigidly) hartnäckig; **to be ~ opposed to sth** etw scharf ablehnen

adapt [əˈdæpt] VT anpassen (to +dat); machine umstellen (to, for auf +acc); vehicle, building umbauen (to für); text, book adaptieren, bearbeiten (for für); **~ed to your requirements** nach Ihren Wünschen abgeändert; **~ed for Arctic conditions** arktischen Verhältnissen angepasst; **~ed for children/television** für Kinder/für Fernsehen adaptiert or bearbeitet; **~ed from the Spanish** aus dem Spanischen übertragen und bearbeitet **VI** sich anpassen (to +dat); (Sci also) sich adaptieren (to an +acc)

adaptability [əˌdæptəˈbɪlɪtɪ] N (of plant, animal, person) Anpassungsfähigkeit f; (of vehicle, hairstyle) Vielseitigkeit f; (of schedule) Flexibilität f

adaptable [əˈdæptəbl] ADJ plant, animal, person anpassungsfähig; vehicle, hairstyle vielseitig; schedule flexibel; **to be ~ to sth** (person, animal, plant) sich an etw (acc) anpassen können; (vehicle) sich in etw (dat) verwenden lassen

adaptation [ˌædæpˈteɪʃən] N **a** (of person, plant, animal) Anpassung f (to an +acc); (of machine) Umstellung f (to an +acc); (of vehicle, building) Umbau m; (of text) Bearbeitung f; **the ~ of space technology to medical ends** die Nutzung der Raumfahrttechnik für medizinische Zwecke **b** (of book, play etc) Adaption f, Bearbeitung f

adapter [əˈdæptəʳ] N **a** (of book etc) Bearbeiter(in) m(f) **b** (for connecting pipes etc) Verbindungs- or Zwischenstück nt; (to convert machine etc) Adapter m **c** (Elec) Adapter m; (for several plugs) Doppel-/Dreifachstecker m, Mehrfachstecker m; (on appliance) Zwischenstecker m

adapter card N (Comput) Adapterkarte f

adaption [əˈdæpʃən] N = **adaptation**

adaptive [əˈdæptɪv] ADJ ability, capacity anpassungsfähig; **~ response** Anpassungsreaktion f; **~ mechanism** Anpassungsmechanismus m

adaptor [əˈdæptəʳ] N = **adapter**

ADC abbr of **aide-de-camp**

ADD abbr of **attention deficit disorder** ADS

add [æd] **VT** **a** (Math) addieren; (= add on) hinzu- or dazuzählen (to zu); (= add up) addieren, zusammenzählen; **to ~ 8 and 5** 8 und 5 zusammenzählen or addieren; **to ~ 8 to 5** 8 zu 5 hinzuzählen **b** ingredients, money etc hinzufügen, dazugeben, dazutun (to zu); name hinzufügen (to zu), dazusetzen (to an +acc); (= say in addition) hinzufügen, dazusagen; (= build on) anbauen; **~ed to which ...** hinzu kommt, dass ...; **it ~s nothing to our knowledge** unser Wissen wird dadurch nicht erweitert; **transport ~s 10% to the cost** es kommen 10% Transportkosten hinzu; **they ~ 10% for service** sie rechnen or schlagen 10% für Bedienung dazu; **to ~ value to sth** den Wert einer Sache (gen) erhöhen; **~ed together the books weigh several tons** zusammengenommen wiegen die Bücher mehrere Tonnen; **if we ~ all the money together we can get them a really nice gift** wenn wir das ganze Geld zusammenlegen, können wir ihnen ein wirklich hübsches Geschenk besorgen → **insult** **N**

VI **a** (Math) zusammenzählen, addieren; **she just can't ~** sie kann einfach nicht rechnen **b** **to ~ to sth** dazu beitragen; **to ~ to one's income** sein Einkommen aufbessern; **it will ~ to the time the job takes** es wird die Arbeitszeit verlängern; **the house had been ~ed to** an das Haus war (etwas) angebaut worden

▶ **add on** VT sep number, amount dazurechnen; two weeks mehr rechnen; room anbauen; storey aufstocken; (= append) comments etc anfügen

▶ **add up** **VT** sep zusammenzählen or -rechnen **VI** **a** (figures etc) stimmen; (fig: = make sense) sich reimen; **it's beginning to add up** jetzt wird so manches klar; **it all adds up** (lit) es summiert sich; (fig) es passt alles zusammen **b** **to add up to** (figures) ergeben; (expenses also) sich belaufen auf (+acc); **that all adds up to a rather unusual state of affairs** alles in allem ergibt das eine recht ungewöhnliche Situation; **it doesn't add up to much** (fig) das ist nicht berühmt (inf)

added [ˈædɪd] ADJ attr zusätzlich; **~ value** Mehrwert m

addend [ˈædend] N (US) Summand m

addendum [əˈdendəm] N pl **addenda** [əˈdendə] Nachtrag m

adder [ˈædəʳ] N Viper f, Natter f

addict [ˈædɪkt] N (lit, fig) Süchtige(r) mf, Suchtkranke(r) mf; **he's a television/heroin/real ~** er ist fernseh-/heroinsüchtig/richtig süchtig; **to become an ~** süchtig werden

addicted [əˈdɪktɪd] ADJ süchtig; **to be/become ~ to heroin/drugs/drink** heroin-/rauschgift-/trunksüchtig sein/werden; **he's ~ to smoking** er ist nikotinsüchtig; **he is ~ to sport/films** Sport ist/Filme sind bei ihm zur Sucht geworden; **you might get ~ to it** das kann zur Sucht werden; (Med) davon kann man süchtig werden

addiction [əˈdɪkʃən] N Sucht f (to nach); (no pl: = state of dependence) Sucht f, Süchtigkeit f; **~ to drugs/alcohol** Rauschgift-/Trunksucht f; **~ to sport** übermäßige Sportbegeisterung; **to become an ~** zur Sucht werden

addictive [əˈdɪktɪv] ADJ **to be ~** (lit) süchtig machen; (fig) zu einer Sucht werden können; **these drugs/watching TV can become ~** diese

Drogen können/Fernsehen kann zur Sucht werden; **~ drug** Suchtdroge f; **to have an ~ personality** suchtanfällig sein, ein Suchttyp m sein (inf)

adding machine [ˈædɪŋməˌʃiːn] N Addiermaschine f

Addis Ababa [ˌædɪsˈæbəbə] N Addis Abeba nt

addition [əˈdɪʃən] ✪ 26.2 N **a** (Math) Addition f

b (= adding) Zusatz m; **the ~ of another person would make the team too large** eine zusätzliche or weitere Person würde das Team zu groß machen; **the ~ of one more country to the EU** die Erweiterung der EU um ein weiteres Land

c (= thing added) Zusatz m (to zu); (to list) Ergänzung f (to zu); (to building) Anbau m (to an +acc); (to income) Aufbesserung f (to +gen); (to bill) Zuschlag m (to zu), Aufschlag m (to auf +acc); **they are expecting an ~ to their family** (inf) sie erwarten (Familien)zuwachs (inf)

d in ~ außerdem, obendrein; **in ~ (to this) he said ...** und außerdem sagte er ...; **in ~ to sth** zusätzlich zu etw; **in ~ to her other hobbies** zusätzlich zu ihren anderen Hobbys; **in ~ to being unjustified his demand was also ...** seine Forderung war nicht nur ungerechtfertigt, sondern außerdem noch ...

additional [əˈdɪʃənl] ADJ zusätzlich; **~ charge** Aufpreis m; **any ~ expenditure over and above this** alle darüber hinausgehenden Ausgaben; **any ~ suggestions will have to be raised at the next meeting** irgendwelche weiteren Vorschläge müssen bei der nächsten Sitzung vorgebracht werden; **the author has inserted an ~ chapter** der Autor hat ein weiteres Kapitel eingefügt

additionally [əˈdɪʃənlɪ] ADV außerdem; say ergänzend; **~ there is ...** außerdem ist da noch ..., dazu kommt noch ...; **~ difficult/complicated** (nur) noch schwieriger/komplizierter

additive [ˈædɪtɪv] N Zusatz m

additive-free ADJ food ohne chemische Zusätze

addle [ˈædl] **VT** **a** brain benebeln **b** egg faul werden lassen, verderben lassen **VI** (egg) verderben, faul werden

addled [ˈædld] ADJ **a** brain, person benebelt; (permanently) verdummt **b** egg verdorben, faul

addle-headed [ˈædlˈhedɪd], **addle-pated** [ˈædlˈpeɪtɪd] ADJ (inf) trottelig (inf), dusslig (inf)

add-on [ˈædɒn] N (Comput) Zusatz m

address [əˈdres] **N** **a** (of person, on letter etc) Adresse f, Anschrift f; **home ~** Privatadresse f; (when travelling) Heimatanschrift f; **what's your ~?** wo wohnen Sie?; **I've come to the wrong ~** ich bin hier falsch or an der falschen Adresse; **at this ~** unter dieser Adresse; **who else lives at this ~?** wer wohnt noch in dem Haus?; **"not known at this ~"** „Empfänger unbekannt"

b (= speech) Ansprache f; **the Address** (Parl) die Adresse (die Erwiderung auf die Thronrede)

c form of ~ (Form f der) Anrede f

d (Comput) Adresse f

e (= bearing, way of behaving) Auftreten nt; (= way of speaking) Art f zu reden

f (form, = skill, tact) Gewandtheit f

g to pay one's ~es to a lady (liter) einer Dame die Cour machen (liter)

VT **a** letter, parcel adressieren (to an +acc)

b (= direct) speech, complaints, remarks richten (to an +acc)

c (= speak to) meeting sprechen zu; jury sich wenden an (+acc); person anreden; **don't ~ me as "Colonel"** nennen Sie mich nicht „Colonel"; **how should one ~ an earl?** wie redet man einen Grafen an?

d problem etc angehen

VR **a to ~ oneself to sb** (= speak to) jdn ansprechen; (= apply to) sich an jdn wenden

b (form) **to ~ oneself to a task** sich einer Aufgabe (dat) widmen

addressable [ə'drɛsəbl] ADJ (*Comput*) network, computer etc adressierbar

address: address book N Adressbuch nt; **address bus** N (*Comput*) Adressbus m

addressee [ædre'siː] N Empfänger(in) m(f), Adressat(in) m(f)

address label N Adressenaufkleber m

Addressograph ['ædrɛsəʊɡrɑːf] N Adressiermaschine f, Adrema® f

adduce [ə'djuːs] VT (*form*) anführen; evidence erbringen

adduction [æ'dʌkʃən] N (*form*) Anführung f; (of proof) Erbringung f

adductor [æ'dʌktə'] N , **adductor muscle** (*Anat*) Adduktor m (*spec*), Anziehmuskel m

ademption [ə'dɛmpʃən] N (*Jur*) Wegfall m (eines Vermächtnisses)

Aden ['eɪdn] N Aden nt; **Gulf of ~** Golf m von Aden

adenoidal [ædɪ'nɔɪdl] ADJ adenoid; voice, adolescent näselnd; **~ infection** Infektion f der Rachenmandeln

adenoids ['ædɪnɔɪdz] PL Rachenmandeln pl, Polypen pl (*inf*)

adenoma [ædɪ'nəʊmə] N pl **-s** or **adenomata** (*Med*) Adenom nt

adept ['ædɛpt] **N** (*form*) Meister(in) m(f), Experte m, Expertin f (*in, at* in +dat); she's quite ~ at that sort of thing sie hat ein Talent dafür

adequacy ['ædɪkwəsɪ] N Adäquatheit f, Angemessenheit f; **we doubt the ~ of his explanation/theory/this heating system** wir bezweifeln, dass seine Erklärung/Theorie/diese Heizung angemessen or adäquat or ausreichend ist; **he's beginning to doubt his ~ as a father** er zweifelt langsam an seinen Fähigkeiten als Vater

adequate ['ædɪkwɪt] ADJ adäquat; (= sufficient also) supply, heating system ausreichend; time genügend inv; excuse angemessen; **to be ~** (= sufficient) (aus)reichen, genug sein; (= good enough) zulänglich or adäquat sein; **this is just not ~** das ist einfach unzureichend or (not good enough also) nicht gut genug; **more than ~** mehr als genug; heating mehr als ausreichend; **there are no words ~ to express my gratitude** meine Dankbarkeit läßt sich in Worten gar nicht ausdrücken; **to be ~ to the task** der Aufgabe (dat) gewachsen sein

adequately ['ædɪkwɪtlɪ] ADV **a** (= sufficiently) prepared, trained, protected ausreichend; insured angemessen; **to be ~ supplied** genügend Vorräte haben **b** (= satisfactorily) function, respond, perform, explain angemessen; **I speak Turkish ~** ich spreche hinlänglich Türkisch

ADF (*Aviat*) abbr of **automatic direction finder**

adhere [əd'hɪə'] VI (*to an* +dat) (= stick) haften; (more firmly) kleben

▶**adhere to** VI +prep obj (= support, be faithful) bleiben bei; plan, belief, principle, determination also festhalten an (+dat); rule sich halten an (+acc)

adherence [əd'hɪərəns] N Festhalten nt (to an +dat); (to rule) Befolgung f (to +gen)

adherent [əd'hɪərənt] N Anhänger(in) m(f)

adhesion [əd'hiːʒən] N **a** (of particles etc) Adhäsion f, Haftfähigkeit f; (more firmly: of glue) Klebefestigkeit f **b** = **adherence**

adhesive [əd'hiːzɪv] **N** Klebstoff m **ADJ** haftend; (more firmly) klebend; **to be highly/not very ~** sehr/nicht gut haften/kleben; **~ label** Haftetikett nt; **~ plaster** Heftpflaster nt; **~ strength/powers** Adhäsionskraft f; (of glue) Klebekraft f

adhesive tape N Klebstreifen m

ad hoc [æd'hɒk] ADJ, ADV ad hoc inv

adhocracy [æd'hɒkrəsɪ] N , no pl Vertrauen nt auf Ad-hoc-Entscheidungen; (= organization) Adhokratie f

adieu [ə'djuː] (old, liter) **N** Adieu nt, Lebewohl nt (old); **to say one's ~s** adieu or Adieu sagen (old), Abschied nehmen; **INTERJ** adieu (old); **to**

bid sb ~ jdm adieu or Adieu or Lebewohl sagen (old)

ad inf. [æd'ɪnf] abbr of **ad infinitum**

ad infinitum [ædɪnfɪ'naɪtəm] ADV ad infinitum (geh), für immer

ad interim [æd'ɪntərɪm] (geh) **ADV** ad interim (geh), vorläufig **ADJ** interim (geh), vorläufig

adipose ['ædɪpəʊs] ADJ (*form*) adipös (*form*), Fett-; **~ tissue** Fettgewebe nt; (hum) Fettpölsterchen pl

adiposis [ædɪ'pəʊsɪs], **adiposity** [ædɪ'pɒsɪtɪ] N (*Med*) Adipositas f (*spec*), Fettsucht f

adjacent [ə'dʒeɪsənt] ADJ angrenzend; **to be ~ to sth** an etw (acc) angrenzen, neben etw (dat) liegen; **the ~ room** das Nebenzimmer, das Zimmer nebenan

adjectival ADJ , **adjectivally** ADV [ædʒek'taɪvəl, -ɪ] adjektivisch

adjective ['ædʒɪktɪv] N Adjektiv nt, Eigenschaftswort nt

adjoin [ə'dʒɔɪn] **VT** grenzen an (+acc) **VI** nebeneinander liegen, aneinander grenzen

adjoining [ə'dʒɔɪnɪŋ] ADJ benachbart, Nachbar-; (esp Archit etc) anstoßend; field angrenzend; (of two things) nebeneinander liegend; **~ province** Nachbarprovinz f; **the ~ room** das Nebenzimmer; **in the ~ office** im Büro daneben or nebenan

adjourn [ə'dʒɜːn] **VT a** (to another day) vertagen (until auf +acc); **he ~ed the meeting for three hours** er unterbrach die Konferenz für drei Stunden **b** (US, = end) beenden **VI a** (to another day) sich vertagen (until auf +acc); **to ~ for lunch/one hour** zur Mittagspause/für eine Stunde unterbrechen **b** (= go to another place) **to ~ to the living room** sich ins Wohnzimmer begeben

adjournment [ə'dʒɜːnmənt] N (to another day) Vertagung f (until auf +acc); (within a day) Unterbrechung f

adjudge [ə'dʒʌdʒ] VT **a** (*Jur*) **the court ~d that ...** das Gericht entschied or befand, dass ... **b** (= award) prize zuerkennen, zusprechen (to sb jdm); **he was ~d the winner** er wurde zum Sieger or Gewinner erklärt **c** (form, = consider) erachten für or als (geh)

adjudicate [ə'dʒuːdɪkeɪt] **VT a** (= judge) claim entscheiden; competition Preisrichter(in) sein bei **b** (*Jur*, = declare) **to ~ sb bankrupt** jdn für bankrott erklären **VI** entscheiden, urteilen (on, in bei); (in dispute) Schiedsrichter(in) sein (on bei, in +dat); (in competition, dog show etc) als Preisrichter(in) fungieren

adjudication [ədʒuːdɪ'keɪʃən] N Entscheidung f, Beurteilung f; (result also) Urteil nt; **~ of bankruptcy** Bankrotterklärung f

adjudicator [ə'dʒuːdɪkeɪtə'] N (in competition etc) Preisrichter(in) m(f); (in dispute) Schiedsrichter(in) m(f)

adjunct [ˈædʒʌŋkt] N Anhängsel nt; **a dictionary is an indispensable ~ to language learning** ein Wörterbuch ist unerlässlich fürs Sprachenlernen

adjuration [ædʒʊə'reɪʃən] N (liter) Beschwörung f

adjure [ə'dʒʊə'] VT (liter) beschwören

adjust [ə'dʒʌst] **VT a** (= set) machine, engine, carburettor, brakes, height, speed, flow etc einstellen; knob, lever (richtig) stellen; (= alter) height, speed verstellen; length of clothes ändern; (= correct, readjust) nachstellen; height, speed, flow regulieren; figures korrigieren, anpassen; formula, plan, production, exchange rates, terms (entsprechend) ändern; salaries angleichen (to an +acc); hat, tie zurechtrücken; **to ~ the lever upwards/downwards** den Hebel nach oben/unten stellen; **you have to ~ this knob to regulate the ventilation** Sie müssen an diesem Knopf drehen, um die Ventilation zu regulieren, die Ventilation lässt sich an diesem Knopf regulieren; **he ~ed the knobs on the TV set** er hat die Knöpfe am Fernsehapparat richtig gestellt; **do not ~ your set** ändern Sie nichts an der Ein-

stellung Ihres Geräts; **to ~ sth to new requirements/conditions** etc etw neuen Erfordernissen/Umständen etc anpassen; **because of increased demand production will have to be appropriately ~ed** die Produktion muss auf die verstärkte Nachfrage abgestimmt werden or muss der verstärkten Nachfrage angepasst werden; **the terms have been ~ed slightly in your favour** (Brit) or favor (US) die Bedingungen sind zu Ihren Gunsten leicht abgeändert worden; **the layout can be ~ed to meet different needs** die Anordnung lässt sich je nach Bedarf ändern; **we ~ed all salaries upwards/downwards** wir haben alle Gehälter nach oben/unten angeglichen; **would you please ~ your dress, sir** (euph) ich glaube, Sie haben vergessen, etwas or Ihre Hose zuzumachen; **if you could ~ the price slightly** (hum) wenn wir uns vielleicht noch über den Preis unterhalten könnten; **to ~ the seasoning (of sth)** (etw) nachwürzen

b **to ~ oneself to sth** (to new country, circumstances etc) sich einer Sache (dat) anpassen; to new requirements, demands etc sich auf etw (acc) einstellen

c (= settle) differences beilegen, schlichten; (Insur) claim regulieren

VI a (to new country, circumstances etc) sich anpassen (to +dat); (to new requirements, demands etc) sich einstellen (to auf +acc)

b (machine etc) sich einstellen lassen; **the chair ~s to various heights** der Stuhl lässt sich in der Höhe verstellen

adjustability [ədʒʌstə'bɪlɪtɪ] N (of tool, height, angle) Verstellbarkeit f; (of height also, speed, temperature) Regulierbarkeit f, Flexibilität f

adjustable [ə'dʒʌstəbl] ADJ tool, angle, strap, shelf, chair verstellbar; height verstellbar, regulierbar; shape veränderlich, variabel; speed, temperature regulierbar; tax, deadline, rate of production/repayment beweglich, flexibel; person, animal, plant anpassungsfähig; **partitions make the shape of the office ~** durch Trennwände lässt sich die Form des Büros verändern

adjustable-pitch propeller [ədʒʌstəblpɪtʃ-prə'pelə'] N Verstell-Luftschraube f, Verstellluftschraube f

adjustable spanner N Engländer m

adjuster [ə'dʒʌstə'] N (*Insur*) (Schadens)sachverständige(r) mf

adjustment [ə'dʒʌstmənt] N **a** (= setting, of machine, engine, carburettor, brakes, height, speed, flow etc) Einstellung f; (of knob, lever) (richtige) Stellung; (= alteration, of height, speed) Verstellung f; (of length of clothes) Änderung f; (= correction, readjustment) Nachstellung f; (of height, speed, flow) Regulierung f; (of formula, plan, production, exchange rate, terms) (entsprechende) Änderung; (of hat, tie) Zurechtrücken nt; **if you could make a slight ~ to my salary** (hum inf) wenn Sie eine leichte Korrektur meines Gehalts vornehmen könnten (hum); **a certain ~ of our traditional outlook** eine gewisse Änderung unserer traditionellen Haltung; **to make ~s** Änderungen vornehmen; **to make ~s to the manuscript/play** Änderungen am Manuskript/Stück vornehmen; **to make ~s to one's plans** seine Pläne ändern; **brakes require regular ~** Bremsen müssen regelmäßig nachgestellt werden

b (socially etc) Anpassung f

c (= settlement) Beilegung f, Schlichtung f; (Insur) Regulierung f

adjutant ['ædʒətənt] N **a** (*Mil*) Adjutant(in) m(f) **b** (*Orn*: also **adjutant bird**) Indischer Marabu

adjutant general N Generaladjutant(in) m(f)

ad lib[1] [æd'lɪb] ADV aus dem Stegreif

ad-lib[1] [æd'lɪb] ADJ attr, **ad lib[2]** ADJ pred improvisiert

ad-lib[2] **N** Improvisation f **VTI** improvisieren

ad libitum ADV (*Mus*) ad libitum, in freiem Tempo

Adm abbr of **admiral** Adm

adman ['ædmæn] N pl **-men** [-men] (inf) Werbefachmann m; **admen** Werbeleute pl

admass ['ædmæs] N durch Werbung leicht beeinflussbares Publikum

admin ['ædmɪn] abbr of **administration it involves a lot of ~** damit ist viel Verwaltung verbunden; **~ building** Verwaltungsgebäude nt

administer [əd'mɪnɪstə'] VT **a** institution, funds verwalten; business, affairs führen; (= run) company, department die Verwaltungsangelegenheiten regeln von; **the civil service ~s the country** die Beamtenschaft verwaltet das Land
b (= dispense) relief, alms gewähren; law ausführen, vollstrecken, vollziehen; punishment verhängen (to über +acc); **to ~ justice** Recht sprechen; **to ~ a severe blow to sb** (fig) jdm einen schweren Schlag versetzen
c (= cause to take) (to sb jdm) medicine, drugs verabreichen; sacraments spenden; last rites geben; **to ~ an oath to sb** jdm einen Eid abnehmen
VI a (= act as administrator) die Verwaltungsangelegenheiten regeln
b (form) **to ~ to the sick** sich der Kranken (gen) annehmen (geh); **to ~ to sb's needs** sich jds annehmen (geh)

administrate [æd'mɪnɪstreɪt] = **administer VT, VI a**

administration [əd,mɪnɪs'treɪʃən] N **a** no pl Verwaltung f; (of an election, a project etc) Organisation f; **to spend a lot of time on ~** viel Zeit auf Verwaltungsangelegenheiten or -sachen verwenden **b** (= government) Regierung f; **the Schmidt ~** die Regierung Schmidt **c** no pl (of remedy) Verabreichung f; (of sacrament) Spenden nt; **the ~ of an oath** die Vereidigung; **the ~ of justice** die Rechtsprechung

administrative [əd'mɪnɪstrətɪv] ADJ administrativ; **~ body** Verwaltungsbehörde f

administrative court N (US Jur) Verwaltungsgericht nt

administratively [əd'mɪnɪstrətɪvlɪ] ADV administrativ

administrator [əd'mɪnɪstreɪtə'] N Verwalter(in) m(f); (Jur) Verwaltungsbeamte(r) m/-beamtin f, Administrator(in) m(f)

administratrix [əd'mɪnɪstreɪtrɪks] N pl **administratrices** [-trisi:z] (Jur) Nachlassverwalterin f

admirable ADJ , **admirably** ADV ['ædmərəbl, -ı] (= praiseworthy, laudable) bewundernswert, erstaunlich; (= excellent) vortrefflich, ausgezeichnet

admiral ['ædmərəl] N Admiral(in) m(f); **Admiral of the Fleet** (Brit) Großadmiral(in) m(f) → **red admiral**

Admiralty ['ædmərəltɪ] N (Brit) Admiralität f; (= department, building) britisches Marineministerium; **First Lord of the ~** britischer Marineminister

admiration [,ædmə'reɪʃən] N **a** Bewunderung f; **in ~** bewundernd **b** (object) **to win the ~ of all/of the world** (person, object) von allen/von aller Welt bewundert werden

admire [əd'maɪə'] ❂ 13 VT bewundern

admirer [əd'maɪərə'] N Bewund(e)rer(in) m(f), Verehrer(in) m(f); (dated, hum, = suitor) Verehrer m (hum)

admiring ADJ , **admiringly** ADV [əd'maɪərɪŋ, -lı] bewundernd

admissibility [əd,mɪsɪ'bɪlɪtɪ] N Zulässigkeit f

admissible [əd'mɪsɪbl] ADJ zulässig; **~ as evidence** als Beweismittel zulässig

admission [əd'mɪʃən] N **a** (= entry) Zutritt m; (to university) Zulassung f; (to hospital) Einlieferung f (to in +acc); (= price) Eintritt m; **no ~ to minors** für Minderjährige verboten; **to gain ~ to a building** Zutritt zu einem Gebäude erhalten; **he had gained ~ to a whole new world** er hatte Zugang zu einer ganz neuen Welt gefunden; **a visa is necessary for ~ to the country** für die Einreise ist ein Visum nötig; **unrestricted ~ to a country** unbegrenzte Einreiseerlaubnis f; **~ fee** Eintrittspreis m

b (Jur, of evidence etc) Zulassung f
c (= confession) Eingeständnis nt; **on** or **by his own ~** nach eigenem Eingeständnis; **that would be an ~ of failure** das hieße, sein Versagen eingestehen

admissions officer [əd'mɪʃənz,ɒfɪsə'] N (Univ) für die Zulassung verantwortlicher Verwaltungsbeamter

admit [əd'mɪt] ❂ 11.1, 18.3, 26.3 VT **a** (= let in) hereinlassen; (= permit to join) zulassen (to zu), aufnehmen (to in +acc); **children not ~ted** kein Zutritt für Kinder; **he was not ~ted to the cinema/to college** er wurde nicht ins Kino hineingelassen/zur Universität zugelassen or in der Universität aufgenommen; **to be ~ted to hospital** ins Krankenhaus eingeliefert werden; **to be ~ted to the Bar** bei Gericht zugelassen werden; **this ticket ~s two** die Karte ist für zwei (Personen)
b (= have space for: halls, harbours etc) Platz bieten für
c (= acknowledge) zugeben; **do you ~ (to) stealing his hat?** geben Sie zu, seinen Hut gestohlen zu haben?; **he ~ted himself beaten** er gab sich geschlagen; **it is generally ~ted that ...** es wird allgemein zugegeben, dass ...; **to ~ the truth of sth** zugeben, dass etw wahr ist

▸ **admit of** VI +prep obj (form) zulassen (+acc)

▸ **admit to** VI +prep obj eingestehen; **I have to admit to a certain feeling of admiration** ich muss gestehen, dass mir das Bewundern abnötigt

admittance [əd'mɪtəns] N (to building) Zutritt m (to zu), Einlass m (to in +acc); (to club) Zulassung f (to zu), Aufnahme f (to in +acc); **I gained ~ to the hall** mir wurde der Zutritt zum Saal gestattet; **I was denied ~** mir wurde der Zutritt verwehrt or verweigert; **no ~ except on business** Zutritt für Unbefugte verboten

admittedly [əd'mɪtɪdlı] ADV zugegebenermaßen; **~ this is true** zugegeben, das stimmt

admixture [əd'mɪkstʃə'] N (= thing added) Zusatz m, Beigabe f

admonish [əd'mɒnɪʃ] VT ermahnen (for wegen)

admonishment [əd'mɒnɪʃmənt] N, **admonition** [ædmə'nɪʃən] N (form) **a** (= rebuke) Verweis m, Tadel m **b** no pl (= reproachfulness) Vorwurf m **c** (= warning) Ermahnung f

admonitory [əd'mɒnɪtərɪ] ADJ (er)mahnend

ad nauseam [,æd'nɔ:zıæm] ADV bis zum Überdruss, bis zum Geht-nicht-mehr (inf); **and so on ~** und so weiter, und so weiter

ado [ə'du:] N Aufheben nt, Trara nt (inf); **much ~ about nothing** viel Lärm um nichts; **without more** or **further ~** ohne weiteres

adobe [ə'dəubı] N (= brick) (ungebrannter) Lehmziegel, Adobe m; (= house) Haus aus Adobeziegeln; **~ wall** Mauer aus Adobeziegeln

adolescence [,ædəʊ'lesns] N (= puberty) Pubertät f, Adoleszenz f (form); **the problems of ~** Pubertätsprobleme pl; **in his late ~** in seiner späteren Jugend

adolescent [,ædəʊ'lesnt] N Jugendliche(r) mf; **he's still an ~** er ist noch im Heranwachsen/in der Pubertät ADJ Jugend-; (= in puberty) Pubertäts-, pubertär; (= immature) unreif; **his ~ years** seine Jugendjahre; **to be ~** er steckt noch in der Pubertät; **~ phase** Pubertätsphase f; **~ love** jugendliche Liebe

Adonis [ə'dəʊnɪs] N (Myth, fig) Adonis m

adopt [ə'dɒpt] VT **a** child adoptieren, an Kindes Statt annehmen (form); child in a different country, family, city die Patenschaft übernehmen für; **the orphan was ~ed into the family** das Waisenkind wurde in die Familie aufgenommen; **your cat has ~ed me** (inf) deine Katze hat sich mir angeschlossen **b** idea, suggestion, attitude, method übernehmen; mannerisms annehmen; ears schlagen, einschlagen; (dat) wählen **c** (Pol) motion annehmen; candidate nehmen

adopted [ə'dɒptɪd] ADJ Adoptiv-, adoptiert; **~ child** Adoptivkind nt; **her ~ country/home town** ihre Wahlheimat

adoptee [ə,dɒp'ti:] N (esp US) Adoptivkind nt

adoption [ə'dɒpʃən] N **a** (of child) Adoption f, Annahme f, an Kindes Statt (form); (of city, of child in other country) Übernahme f der Patenschaft; (into the family) Aufnahme f; **parents by ~** Adoptiveltern pl; **Japanese by ~** Japaner(in) m(f) durch Adoption **b** (of method, idea) Übernahme f; (of mannerisms) Annahme f; (of career) Wahl f; **his country of ~** seine Wahlheimat; **this custom is Japanese only by ~** dieser Brauch ist von den Japanern nur übernommen worden **c** (of motion, law, candidate) Annahme f

adoption agency N Adoptionsagentur f

adoptive [ə'dɒptɪv] ADJ Adoptiv-; **~ parents** Adoptiveltern pl; **~ home/country** Wahlheimat f

adorable [ə'dɔ:rəbl] ADJ bezaubernd, hinreißend; **she is ~** sie ist ein Schatz

adorably [ə'dɔ:rəblı] ADV bezaubernd, hinreißend

adoration [,ædə'reɪʃən] N **a** (of God) Anbetung f **b** (of family, wife) grenzenlose Liebe (of für) **c** (inf, of French, whisky etc) Liebe f (of für)

adore [ə'dɔ:'] VT **a** God anbeten **b** (= love very much) family, wife über alles lieben **c** (inf: = like very much) French, whisky etc (über alles) lieben; **to ~ attention** gern im Mittelpunkt stehen

adorer [ə'dɔ:rə'] N **a** (= worshipper) Anbeter(in) m(f) **b** (= admirer) Verehrer(in) m(f), Bewunderer m, Bewunderin f

adoring [ə'dɔ:rɪŋ] ADJ bewundernd; **his ~ fans** seine bewundernden or ihn anbetenden Fans

adoringly [ə'dɔ:rɪŋlı] ADV bewundernd, voller Verehrung

adorn [ə'dɔ:n] VT schmücken, zieren (geh); **to ~ oneself** sich schmücken

adornment [ə'dɔ:nmənt] N Schmuck m no pl; (act) Schmücken nt; (on dress, cake, design) Verzierung f; (on manuscript) Ornament nt; (in prose style) Ausschmückung f

ADP [eɪdı'pi:] abbr of **automatic data processing** automatische Datenverarbeitung

adrenal [ə'dri:nl] ADJ Nebennieren-; **~ glands** Nebennieren pl; **~ hormone** Nebennierenhormon nt

adrenalin(e) [ə'drenəlɪn] N **a** (Med) Adrenalin nt **b** (phrases) **I could feel the ~ rising** ich fühlte, wie mein Blutdruck stieg; **you burn up a lot of ~** Sie verbrauchen eine Menge Energie; **it's impossible to relax now the ~'s going** es ist unmöglich abzuschalten, wenn man so aufgedreht ist; **in a combat situation the ~ just takes over** in einer Kampfsituation leistet man einfach mehr; **working under pressure gets the ~ going** Arbeiten unter Druck weckt ungeahnte Kräfte

Adriatic (Sea) [,eɪdrɪ'ætɪk('si:)] N Adria f, Adriatisches Meer

adrift [ə'drɪft] ADV, ADJ pred **a** (Naut) treibend; **to be ~** treiben; **to go ~** (lit) sich losmachen or loslösen; (= go awry:) plan, scheme schief gehen; **to set** or **cut a boat ~** ein Boot losmachen **b** (fig) **to come ~** (wire, hair etc) sich lösen; (plans, scheme) fehlschlagen; (theory) zusammenbrechen; **we are ~ on the sea of life** wir treiben dahin auf dem Meer des Lebens; **he wandered through the city, lost and ~** (ziellos und) verloren irrte er in der Stadt umher; **you're all ~** (inf) da liegst du völlig verkehrt or falsch; **after a month's philosophy I felt all ~** nach einem Monat Philosophie war ich vollkommen durcheinander; **to cast** or **turn sb ~** jdn auf die Straße setzen **c** (Sport) **to be 15 points/seconds ~** 15 Punkte/Sekunden zurückliegen

adroit [ə'drɔɪt] ADJ lawyer, reply, reasoning gewandt, geschickt; mind scharf; **to be ~ at sth/doing sth** gewandt or geschickt in etw (dat) sein/darin sein, etw zu tun

adroitly [ə'drɔɪtlı] ADV gewandt, geschickt

adroitness [ə'drɔɪtnɪs] N (of lawyer, reply, reasoning) Gewandtheit f, Geschicklichkeit f; (of mind) Schärfe f

adsorb [æd'sɔːb] VT adsorbieren

adsorption [æd'sɔːpʃən] N Adsorption f

adulate ['ædjʊleɪt] VT **to ~ sb** jdn beweihräuchern, jdm lobhudeln

adulation [ædjʊ'leɪʃən] N Verherrlichung f

adulatory [ædjʊ'leɪtərɪ, (US) ˌædjʊ'leɪtərɪ] ADJ (= laudatory) comment bewundernd; (stronger) vergötternd

adult ['ædʌlt, (US) ə'dʌlt] N Erwachsene(r) mf; **~s only** nur für Erwachsene ADJ (= grown up) person erwachsen; animal ausgewachsen; **~ male** (Zool) ausgewachsenes Männchen; **he spent his ~ life in New York** er hat sein Leben als Erwachsener in New York verbracht **b** (= for adults) book, film für Erwachsene; **~ classes** Kurse pl für Erwachsene; **~ education** Erwachsenenbildung f **c** (= mature) decision reif; **we were very ~ about it** wir waren sehr ruhig und vernünftig

adulterate [ə'dʌltəreɪt] VT **a** wine, whisky etc panschen; food abwandeln; **some ~d Scottish version of Italian cooking** ein schottischer Abklatsch italienischer Küche **b** (fig) text, original version verfälschen, Gewalt antun (+dat); **an ~d version of the original** eine verhunzte Fassung des Originals (inf)

adulteration [əˌdʌltə'reɪʃən] N **a** (of wine) Pan(t)schen nt; (of food) Abwandlung f **b** (fig) Vergewaltigung f, Verhunzung f (inf)

adulterer [ə'dʌltərə'] N Ehebrecher m

adulteress [ə'dʌltərɪs] N Ehebrecherin f

adulterous [ə'dʌltərəs] ADJ ehebrecherisch

adultery [ə'dʌltərɪ] N Ehebruch m; **to commit ~** Ehebruch begehen; **because of his ~ with three actresses** weil er mit drei Schauspielerinnen Ehebruch begangen hatte

adulthood ['ædʌlthʊd, (US) ə'dʌlthʊd] N Erwachsenenalter nt; **to reach ~** erwachsen werden

adumbrate ['ædʌmbreɪt] VT (liter) **a** (= outline) theory umreißen **b** (= foreshadow) coming event ankündigen

adumbration [ˌædʌm'breɪʃən] N (liter) **a** (of theory) Umriss m **b** (of event) Ankündigung f, Anzeichen nt

advance [əd'vɑːns] N **a** (= progress) Fortschritt m
b (= movement forward, of old age) Voranschreiten nt; (of science) Weiterentwicklung f; (of sea, ideas) Vordringen nt; **with the ~ of old age** mit fortschreitendem Alter
c (Mil) Vormarsch m, Vorrücken nt
d (= money) Vorschuss m (on auf +acc)
e **advances** PL (amorous, fig) Annäherungsversuche pl
f **in ~** im Voraus; (temporal also) vorher; **to send sb sth in ~** jdn vorausschicken; **£10 in ~** £ 10 als Vorschuss; **thanking you in ~** mit bestem Dank im Voraus; **to arrive in ~ of the others** vor den anderen ankommen; **to be (well) in ~ of sb/one's time** jdm/seiner Zeit (weit) voraus sein
VT **a** (= move forward) date, time vorverlegen; **the dancer slowly ~s one foot** die Tänzerin setzt langsam einen Fuß vor
b (Mil) troops vorrücken lassen
c (= further) work, project voran- or weiterbringen, förderlich sein für; cause, interests, career fördern; knowledge vergrößern; (= accelerate) growth vorantreiben; (= promote) employee etc befördern
d (= put forward) reason, opinion, plan vorbringen
e (= pay beforehand) (sb jdm) (als) Vorschuss geben, vorschießen (inf); (= lend) als Kredit geben
f (= raise) prices anheben
VI **a** (Mil) vorrücken; **government troops are advancing against the rebels** die Regierungstruppen rücken weiter gegen die Rebellen vor
b (= move forward) vorankommen; **to ~ toward(s) sb/sth** auf jdn/etw zugehen; **to ~ upon**

sb drohend auf jdn zukommen; **as the sea ~s over the rocks** während die See über die Felsen vordringt; **old age is advancing on all of us** wir alle nähern uns dem Alter
c (fig, = progress) Fortschritte pl machen; **we've ~d a long way since those days** wir sind seither ein gutes Stück voran- or weitergekommen; **the work is advancing well** die Arbeit macht gute Fortschritte; **are we advancing toward(s) some kind of solution?** kommen wir irgend einer Lösung näher?; **as mankind ~s in knowledge** während die Menschheit an Wissen gewinnt
d (prices) anziehen; (costs) hoch gehen, ansteigen

advance: **advance booking** N Reservierung f; (Theat) Vorverkauf m; **~ opens on ...** der Vorverkauf beginnt am ...; **advance booking office** N (Theat) Vorverkaufsstelle f; **advance copy** N Vorausexemplar nt, Vorabdruck m

advanced [əd'vɑːnst] ADJ **a** student, level, age, technology fortgeschritten; studies, mathematics etc höher; ideas fortschrittlich; version, model anspruchsvoll, weiterentwickelt; level of civilization hoch; position, observation post etc vorgeschoben; society, country, economy hoch entwickelt; **~ work** anspruchsvolle Arbeit; **he is very ~ for his age** er ist für sein Alter sehr weit → **A level**
b (= developed) plan, programme ausgefeilt; **in the ~ stages of the disease** im fortgeschrittenen Stadium der Krankheit
c (form, = mature) **~ in years** in fortgeschrittenem Alter; **she is more/less ~ in years than ...** sie ist älter/jünger als ...
d (form) **the summer was well ~** der Sommer war schon weit vorangeschritten

advance: **advance guard** N Vorhut f; **advance man** N (US, Pol) Wahlhelfer m

advancement [əd'vɑːnsmənt] N **a** (= furtherance) Förderung f **b** (= promotion in rank) Vorwärtskommen nt, Aufstieg m

advance: **advance notice** N frühzeitiger Bescheid; (of sth bad) Vorwarnung f; **to be given ~** frühzeitig Bescheid/eine Vorwarnung erhalten; **advance party** N (Mil, fig) Vorhut f; **advance payment** N Vorauszahlung f; **advance publicity** N Vorabwerbung f; **advance warning** N = advance notice

advantage [əd'vɑːntɪdʒ] N **a** Vorteil m; **to have an ~ (over sb)** (jdm gegenüber) im Vorteil sein; **that gives you an ~ over me** damit sind Sie mir gegenüber im Vorteil, das verschafft Ihnen mir gegenüber einen Vorteil; **to have the ~ of sb** jdm überlegen sein; **you have the ~ of me** (form) ich kenne leider Ihren werten Namen nicht (form); **he had the ~ of youth** er hatte den Vorzug der Jugend; **she had the ~ of greater experience** sie war durch ihre größere Erfahrung im Vorteil; **to get the ~ of sb (by doing sth)** (dat) (durch etw) jdm gegenüber einen Vorteil verschaffen; **to have the ~ of numbers** zahlenmäßig überlegen sein
b (= use, profit) Vorteil m; **to take ~ of sb** (= exploit) jdn ausnutzen; (euph: sexually) jdn missbrauchen; **to take ~ of sth** etw ausnutzen, sich (dat) etw zunutze or zu Nutze machen; **he took ~ of her while she was drunk** er nutzte sich (dat) ihre Trunkenheit zunutze or zu Nutze; **to turn sth to ~** Nutzen aus etw ziehen; **he turned it to his own ~** er machte es sich (dat) zunutze or zu Nutze; **what ~ is that to us?** welchen Nutzen haben wir davon?; **it is to my ~ to ...** es ist vorteilhaft für mich ..., es ist für mich von Vorteil ...; **to use sth to best ~** das Beste aus etw machen; **to use sth to one's ~** etw für sich nutzen
c (Tennis) Vorteil m
VT (old, liter) zum Vorteil or Nutzen gereichen (+dat) (geh)

advantageous [ˌædvən'teɪdʒəs] ADJ von Vorteil, vorteilhaft; **to be ~ to sb** für jdn von Vorteil sein

advantageously [ˌædvən'teɪdʒəslɪ] ADV vorteilhaft

advent ['ædvənt] N **a** (of age, era) Beginn m, Anbruch m; (of jet plane etc) Aufkommen nt **b** (Eccl) **Advent** Advent m

Advent calendar N Adventskalender m

adventitious [ˌædvən'tɪʃəs] ADJ (form) zufällig

adventure [əd'ventʃə'] N **a** Abenteuer nt, Erlebnis nt; **an ~ into the unknown** ein Vorstoß m ins Unbekannte **b** no pl **love/spirit of ~** Abenteuerlust f; **to look for ~** (das) Abenteuer suchen; **a life of ~** ein abenteuerliches Leben
VI **~ venture** attr Abenteuer-; **~ holiday** (Brit) Abenteuerurlaub m

adventure playground N Abenteuerspielplatz m

adventurer [əd'ventʃərə'] N Abenteurer(in) m(f); (pej also) Windhund m

adventuresome [əd'ventʃəsəm] ADJ = adventurous

adventuress [əd'ventʃərɪs] N (pej) Abenteurerin f

adventurism [əd'ventʃərɪzəm] N Abenteurertum nt

adventurist [əd'ventʃərɪst] N Abenteurer(in) m(f) ADJ abenteuerlich

adventurous [əd'ventʃərəs] ADJ **a** person abenteuerlustig; journey abenteuerlich **b** (= bold) gewagt

adventurously [əd'ventʃərəslɪ] ADV (= boldly) gewagt; **we should be using the money more ~** wir sollten das Geld etwas riskanter einsetzen

adventurousness [əd'ventʃərəsnɪs] N **a** (of person) Abenteuerlust f; (of journey) Abenteuerlichkeit f **b** (= boldness) Gewagte(s) nt; **the ~ of his style** sein gewagter Stil

adverb ['ædvɜːb] N Adverb nt, Umstandswort nt

adverbial ADJ, **adverbially** ADV [əd'vɜːbɪəl, -ɪ] adverbial

adversary ['ædvəsərɪ] N Widersacher(in) m(f); (in contest) Gegner(in) m(f)

adverse ['ædvɜːs] ADJ criticism, comment ungünstig; criticism, comment also, reaction negativ, ablehnend; wind, conditions also widrig; effect also nachteilig

adversely [əd'vɜːslɪ] ADV comment, criticize, react negativ; affect also nachteilig

adversity [əd'vɜːsɪtɪ] N **a** no pl Not f; **a time of ~** eine Zeit der Not; **in ~** im Unglück, in der Not **b** (= misfortune) Widrigkeit f (geh); **the adversities of war** die Härten des Krieges

advert¹ [əd'vɜːt] VI (form) hinweisen, aufmerksam machen (to auf +acc)

advert² ['ædvɜːt] N (inf) abbr of **advertisement** Anzeige f, Annonce f, Inserat nt; (on TV, radio) Werbespot m

advertainment [ˌædvə'teɪnmənt] N unterhaltende Werbung, Advertainment nt

advertise ['ædvətaɪz] VT **a** (= publicize) Werbung or Reklame machen für, werben für; **I've seen that soap ~d on television** ich habe die Werbung or Reklame für diese Seife im Fernsehen gesehen; **as ~d on television** wie durch das Fernsehen bekannt
b (in paper etc) flat, table etc inserieren, annoncieren; job, post ausschreiben, inserieren; **to ~ sth in a shop window/on local radio** etw durch eine Schaufensteranzeige/im Regionalsender anbieten; **I saw it ~d in a shop window** ich habe die Anzeige dafür in einem Schaufenster gesehen
c (= make conspicuous) fact publik machen; ignorance offen zeigen
VI **a** (Comm) Werbung or Reklame machen, werben
b (in paper) inserieren, annoncieren (for für); **to ~ for sb/sth** jdn/etw (per Anzeige) suchen; **to ~ for sth on local radio/in a shop window** etw per Regionalsender/durch Anzeige im Schaufenster suchen

advertisement [əd'vɜːtɪsmənt, (US) ˌædvə'taɪzmənt] ✪ 19.1, 20.1 N **a** (Comm) Werbung f, Reklame f no pl; (esp in paper) Anzeige f; **TV ~s** die Werbung or Reklame im Fernsehen; **70% of the magazine is made up of ~s** die Zeitschrift besteht zu 70% aus Anzeigen *or* Werbung *or* Reklame; **he is not a good ~ for his school** er ist nicht gerade ein Aushängeschild für seine Schule **b** (= *announcement*) Anzeige *f*; **to put** *or* **place an ~ in the paper (for sb/sth)** eine Anzeige (für jdn/etw) in die Zeitung setzen, (für jdn/etw) in der Zeitung inserieren

advertisement column N Anzeigenspalte *f*

advertiser ['ædvətaɪzə'] N (*in paper*) Inserent(in) *m(f)*; **this company never was a very big ~** diese Firma hat nie viel Werbung *or* Reklame gemacht; **TV ~s** Firmen, die im Fernsehen werben

advertising ['ædvətaɪzɪŋ] N Werbung *f*, Reklame *f*; **he works in ~** er ist in der Werbung (tätig)

advertising *in cpds* Werbe-; **advertising agency** N Werbeagentur *f or* -büro *nt*; **advertising campaign** N Werbekampagne *f or* -feldzug *m*; **advertising rates** PL Anzeigenpreise *pl*; (*for TV, radio*) Preise *pl* für Werbespots; **advertising space** N Platz *m* für Anzeigen

advertorial [ædvə'tɔːrɪəl] N Anzeige *f* (*in Form eines Artikels*), Advertorial *nt*

advice [əd'vaɪs] **✪** 2.1, 2.2 N **a** *no pl* Rat *m no pl*; **a piece of ~** ein Rat(schlag) *m*; **let me give you a piece of ~** *or* **some ~** ich will Ihnen einen guten Rat geben; **you're a fine one to give ~** du hast gut raten, ausgerechnet du willst hier Ratschläge geben; **his ~ was always useful** er gab immer guten Rat *or* gute Ratschläge; **that's good ~** das ist ein guter Rat; **I didn't ask for your ~** ich habe dich nicht um (deinen) Rat gebeten *or* gefragt; **to take sb's ~** jds Rat (be)folgen; **take my ~** höre auf mich; **to seek (sb's) ~** (jdn) um Rat fragen; (*from doctor, lawyer etc*) Rat (bei jdm) einholen; **to take medical/legal ~** einen Arzt/Rechtsanwalt zu Rate ziehen; **my ~ to him would be ...** ich würde ihm raten ...; **it's not ~ we need** wir brauchen keine guten Ratschläge

    b (*Comm, = notification*) Mitteilung *f*, Avis *m or nt*

advice: advice column N = **agony column**; **advice columnist** N = **agony columnist**; **advice note** N Benachrichtigung *f*, Avis *m or nt*

advisability [ədvaɪzə'bɪlɪtɪ] N Ratsamkeit *f*; **he questioned the ~ of going on strike** er bezweifelte, ob es ratsam wäre zu streiken

advisable [əd'vaɪzəbl] **✪** 2.2 ADJ ratsam, empfehlenswert

advisably [əd'vaɪzəblɪ] ADV zu Recht

advise [əd'vaɪz] **✪** 1.1, 2.1, 2.2, 2.3 **VT a** (= *give advice to*) *person* raten (+*dat*); (*professionally*) beraten; **to ~ caution** zur Vorsicht raten, Vorsicht empfehlen; **I wouldn't ~ it** ich würde es nicht raten *or* empfehlen; **I would ~ you to do it/not to do it** ich würde dir zuraten/abraten; **to ~ sb against sth** jdm von etw abraten; **to ~ sb against doing sth** jdm abraten, etw zu tun; **what would you ~ me to do?** was *or* wozu würden Sie mir raten?

    b (*Comm, = inform*) verständigen, avisieren; **to ~ sb of sth** jdn von etw in Kenntnis setzen; **our agent keeps us ~d of developments** unser Vertreter unterrichtet uns ständig über neue Entwicklungen

    VI a (= *give advice*) raten; **I shall do as you ~** ich werde tun, was Sie mir raten; **his function is merely to ~** er hat nur beratende Funktion

    b (*US*) **to ~ with sb** sich mit jdm beraten

advisedly [əd'vaɪzɪdlɪ] ADV richtig; **and I use the word ~** ich verwende bewusst dieses Wort

advisedness [əd'vaɪzɪdnɪs] N Klugheit *f*, Ratsamkeit *f*

advisement [əd'vaɪzmənt] N (*US*) **to keep sth under ~** etw im Auge behalten; **to take sth under ~** (= *consider more carefully*) sich (*dat*) etw genauer überlegen; (= *consult experts*) Experten zu etw zu Rate ziehen

adviser [əd'vaɪzə'] N Ratgeber(in) *m(f)*; (*professional*) Berater(in) *m(f)*; **legal ~** Rechtsberater(in) *m(f)*; **spiritual ~** geistlicher Berater

advising bank [əd'vaɪzɪŋˌbæŋk] N (*Fin*) avisierende Bank

advisory [əd'vaɪzərɪ] ADJ beratend; **to act in a purely ~ capacity** rein beratende Funktion haben; **~ committee** beratendes Gremium

advocacy ['ædvəkəsɪ] N Eintreten *nt* (*of* für), Fürsprache *f* (*of* für); (*of plan*) Befürwortung *f*; **the skills of legal ~** juristische Wortgewandtheit

advocate ['ædvəkɪt] **N a** (= *upholder: of cause etc*) Verfechter(in) *m(f)*, Befürworter(in) *m(f)* **b** (*esp Scot: Jur*) (Rechts)anwalt *m*/-anwältin *f*, Advokat(in) *m(f)* ['ædvəkeɪt] **VT** eintreten für; *plan etc* befürworten; **those who ~ extending the licensing laws** die, die eine Verlängerung der Öffnungszeiten befürworten; **what course of action would you ~?** welche Maßnahmen würden Sie empfehlen

advocator ['ædvəkeɪtə'] N = **advocate** N

advowson [əd'vaʊzn] N (*Rel Brit*) Pfründenbesetzungsrecht *nt*

advt *abbr of* **advertisement**

adwoman ['ædwʊmən] N *pl* **-women** [-wɪmɪn] Werbefachfrau *f*

adz(e) [ædz] N Dechsel *f*

AEEU (*Brit*) *abbr of* **Amalgamated Engineering and Electrical Union** Vereinigte Techniker- und Elektrotechnikergewerkschaft

Aegean [iː'dʒiːən] ADJ ägäisch; **islands** in der Ägäis; **the ~ (Sea)** die Ägäis, das Ägäische Meer

aegis ['iːdʒɪs] N Ägide *f* (*geh*); **under the ~ of** unter der Ägide (*geh*) *or* Schirmherrschaft von

aegrotat ['aɪgrəʊˌtæt] N Examen, an dem der Prüfling aus Krankheitsgründen nicht teilnimmt und das bei Vorlage eines ärztlichen Attestes für bestanden erklärt wird

Aeneas [ɪ'niːəs] N Äneas *m*

Aeneid ['iːniːɪd] N Äneide *f*

Aeolian [iː'əʊlɪən] ADJ äolisch

Aeolian mode [iː'əʊlɪən-] N (*Mus*) äolische Tonart

aeon ['iːən] N Äon *m* (*geh*), Ewigkeit *f*; **through ~s of time** äonenlang (*geh*)

aerate ['ɛəreɪt] VT *liquid* mit Kohlensäure anreichern; *blood* Sauerstoff zuführen (+*dat*); *soil* auflockern; **~d water** kohlensaures Wasser

aerial ['ɛərɪəl] **N** (*esp Brit, = antenna*) Antenne *f* **ADJ** Luft-; **~ barrage** (*air to ground*) Bombardement *nt*; (*ground to air*) Flakfeuer *nt*; **~ combat** Luftkampf *m*; **~ map** Luftbildkarte *f*; **~ navigation** Luftfahrt *f*; **~ photograph** Luftbild *nt*, **~ photography** Luftaufnahmen *pl*; **~ reconnaissance** Luftaufklärung *f*; **~ view** Luftbild *nt*, Luftansicht *f*; **in order to obtain an ~ view of the site** um das Gelände von der Luft aus zu betrachten; **~ warfare** Luftkrieg *m*

aerial: aerial cableway N Seilbahn *f*; **aerial camera** N Luftbildkamera *f*; **aerial input** N (*TV*) Antennenanschluss *m*

aerialist ['ɛərɪəlɪst] N (*US, on trapeze*) Trapezkünstler(in) *m(f)*; (*on high wire*) Seiltänzer(in) *m(f)*

aerial: aerial ladder N Drehleiter *f*; **aerial mast** N Antennenmast *m*; **aerial railway** N Schwebebahn *f*; **aerial socket** N Antennenanschluss *m*; **aerial tram** N (*US*) Schwebebahn *f*

aero- ['ɛərəʊ] PREF aero- (*form*), Luft-

aerobatic [ɛərəʊ'bætɪk] ADJ kunstfliegerisch, Kunstflug-; **~ manoeuvre** (*Brit*) *or* **maneuver** (*US*) Kunstflugmanöver *nt*

aerobatics [ɛərəʊ'bætɪks] PL Kunstfliegen *nt*, Aerobatik *f* (*form*)

aerobic [ɛə'rəʊbɪk] ADJ **a** (*Biol*) aerob; **~ respiration** aerobe Atmung, Sauerstoffatmung *f* **b** (*Sport*) Aerobic-; **~ exercise** Aerobicübung *f*

aerobics [ɛə'rəʊbɪks] N *sing* Aerobic *nt*

aerodrome ['ɛərədrəʊm] N (*Brit*) Flugplatz *m*, Aerodrom *nt* (*old*)

aerodynamic [ˌɛərəʊdaɪ'næmɪk] ADJ aerodynamisch

aerodynamically [ˌɛərəʊdaɪ'næmɪkəlɪ] ADV *efficient, designed, built* aerodynamisch

aerodynamics [ˌɛərəʊdaɪ'næmɪks] N **a** *sing* (*subject*) Aerodynamik *f* **b** *pl* (*of plane etc*) Aerodynamik *f*

aero engine N Flugzeugmotor *m*

aerofoil ['ɛərəʊfɔɪl] N Tragflügel *m*; (*on racing cars*) Spoiler *m*

aerogramme ['ɛərəʊgræm] N Aerogramm *nt*, Luftpostbrief *m*

aeromodelling [ˌɛərəʊ'mɒdəlɪŋ] N Modellflugzeugbau *m*

aeronaut ['ɛərənɔːt] N Aeronaut(in) *m(f)*

aeronautic(al) [ˌɛərə'nɔːtɪk(əl)] ADJ aeronautisch

aeronautical engineering N Flugzeugbau *m*

aeronautics [ˌɛərə'nɔːtɪks] N *sing* Luftfahrt *f*, Aeronautik *f*

aeroplane ['ɛərəpleɪn] N (*Brit*) Flugzeug *nt*

aerosol ['ɛərəsɒl] N (= *can*) Spraydose *f*; (= *mixture*) Aerosol *nt*; **~ paint** Spray- *or* Sprühfarbe *f*; **~ spray** Aerosolspray *nt*

aerospace ['ɛərəʊspeɪs] *in cpds* Raumfahrt-; **aerospace industry** N Raumfahrtindustrie *f*; **aerospace research** N Raumforschung *f*

aerosphere ['ɛərəʊsfɪə'] N Erdatmosphäre *f*

Aertex® ['ɛəteks] N Aertex® *nt*, Baumwolltrikotstoff mit Lochmuster

Aeschylus ['iːskələs] N Aischylos *m*, Äschylus *m*

Aesculapian [ˌiːskjʊ'leɪpɪən] ADJ **a** Äskulap-; **~ staff** Äskulapstab *m* **b** (*Med*) ärztlich

Aesop ['iːsɒp] N Äsop *m*; **~'s fables** die äsopischen Fabeln

aesthete, (*US*) **esthete** ['iːsθiːt] N Ästhet(in) *m(f)*

aesthetic(al), (*US*) **esthetic(al)** [iːs'θetɪk(əl)] ADJ ästhetisch; **an aesthetical discussion** eine Diskussion über Ästhetik

aesthetically, (*US*) **esthetically** [iːs'θetɪkəlɪ] ADV in ästhetischer Hinsicht; **~ decorated** ästhetisch schön dekoriert; **~ pleasing** ästhetisch schön

aestheticism, (*US*) **estheticism** [iːs'θetɪsɪzəm] N Ästhetizismus *m*

aesthetics, (*US*) **esthetics** [iːs'θetɪks] N *sing* Ästhetik *f*

aestival, (*US*) **estival** [iː'staɪvəl] ADJ (*form*) sommerlich

aestivate, (*US*) **estivate** ['iːstɪveɪt] VI (*form, animals*) Sommerschlaf halten; (*person*) den Sommer verbringen

aetiological, (*US*) **etiological** [ˌiːtɪə'lɒdʒɪkəl] ADJ (*Med, fig*) ätiologisch

aetiology, (*US*) **etiology** [ˌiːtɪ'ɒlədʒɪ] N (*Med, fig*) Ätiologie *f*

afar [ə'fɑː'] ADV (*liter*) weit; **from ~** aus der Ferne, von weit her

affability [æfə'bɪlɪtɪ] N Umgänglichkeit *f*, Freundlichkeit *f*

affable ADJ , **affably** ADV ['æfəbl, -ɪ] umgänglich, freundlich

affair [ə'fɛə'] N **a** (= *event, concern, matter, business*) Sache *f*, Angelegenheit *f*; **the investigation was an odd ~ altogether** die Untersuchung war schon eine seltsame Sache *or* Angelegenheit; **a scandalous ~** ein Skandal *m*; **the Watergate/Profumo ~** die Watergate-/Profumo--Affäre; **the state of ~s with the economy** die Lage der Wirtschaft; **in the present state of ~s** bei *or* in der gegenwärtigen Lage *or* Situation, beim gegenwärtigen Stand der Dinge; **a state of ~s I don't approve of** ein Zustand, den ich nicht billige; **this is a sorry state of ~s!** das

sind ja schöne Zustände!; **your private ~s don't concern me** deine Privatangelegenheiten sind mir egal; **financial ~s have never interested me** Finanzfragen haben mich nie interessiert; **I never interfere with his business ~s** ich mische mich nie in seine geschäftlichen Angelegenheiten ein; **man of ~s** (*liter, form*) Geschäftsmann *m*; **~s of state** Staatsangelegenheiten *pl*; **~s of the heart** Herzensangelegenheiten *pl*; **it's not your ~ what I do in the evenings** was ich abends tue, geht dich nichts an; **that's my/his ~!** das ist meine/seine Sache! → *also* **current/ foreign affairs**
b (= *love affair*) Verhältnis *nt*, Affäre *f* (*dated*); **to have an ~ with sb** ein Verhältnis mit jdm haben
c (= *duel*) **~ of honour** Ehrenhandel *m*
d (*inf*: = *object, thing*) Ding *nt*; **what's this funny aerial ~?** was soll dieses komische Antennendings? (*inf*); **the committee was an odd ~** das Komitee war eine seltsame Sache

affect[1] [əˈfekt] VT **a** (= *have effect on*) sich auswirken auf (+*acc*); *decision, sb's life* beeinflussen, sich auswirken auf (+*acc*); (*detrimentally*) *nerves, material* angreifen; *health, person* schaden (+*dat*) **b** (= *concern*) betreffen **c** (*emotionally*: = *move*) berühren, treffen; **he was obviously ~ed by the news** er war von der Nachricht offensichtlich sehr betroffen, die Nachricht hatte ihn sichtlich mitgenommen **d** (*diseases*: = *attack*) befallen

affect[2] VT **a** (= *feign*) *indifference* vortäuschen, vorgeben **b** (*liter, = like to use etc*) *clothes, colours* eine Vorliebe *or* Schwäche haben für; *accent* sich befleißigen (+*gen*) (*geh*)

affectation [æfekˈteɪʃən] N **a** (= *pretence*) Vortäuschung *f*, Vorgabe *f* **b** (= *artificiality*) Affektiertheit *f no pl*; **her ~s annoy me** ihr affektiertes Benehmen ärgert mich; **an ~** eine affektierte Angewohnheit

affected [əˈfektɪd] ADJ *person, clothes* affektiert; *behaviour, style, accent also* gekünstelt

affectedly [əˈfektɪdlɪ] ADV *dress, speak, behave* affektiert; *simple, ironic* gewollt

affecting [əˈfektɪŋ] ADJ rührend

affection [əˈfekʃən] N **a** (= *fondness*) Zuneigung *f no pl* (*for, towards* zu); **to win sb's ~s** (*dated, hum*) jds Zuneigung gewinnen; **I have *or* feel a great ~ for her** ich mag sie sehr gerne; **don't you even feel any ~ for her at all?** fühlst du denn gar nichts für sie?; **you could show a little more ~ toward(s) me** du könntest mir gegenüber etwas mehr Gefühl zeigen; **children who lacked ~** Kinder, denen die Liebe fehlte; **everybody needs a little ~** jeder braucht ein bisschen Liebe; **he has a special place in her ~s** er nimmt einen besonderen Platz in ihrem Herzen ein; **display of ~** Ausdruck *m* von Zärtlichkeit
b (*Med*) Erkrankung *f*, Affektion *f* (*spec*)

affectionate [əˈfekʃənɪt] ADJ liebevoll, zärtlich; **your ~ daughter** (*letter-ending*) deine dich liebende Tochter; **to feel ~ toward(s) sb** jdm sehr zugetan sein, jdn sehr gern haben

affectionately [əˈfekʃənɪtlɪ] ADV liebevoll, zärtlich; **yours ~, Wendy** (*letter-ending*) in Liebe, deine Wendy

affective [əˈfektɪv] ADJ (*Psych*) affektiv

affidavit [æfɪˈdeɪvɪt] N (*Jur*) eidesstattliche Erklärung; (*to guarantee support of immigrant*) Affidavit *nt*; **to swear an ~ (that)** eine eidesstattliche Erklärung abgeben(, dass)

affiliate [əˈfɪlɪeɪt] VT angliedern (*to* +*dat*); **the two banks are ~d** die zwei Banken sind aneinander angeschlossen; **~d** angeschlossen, Schwester-; **~d company** Schwesterfirma *f* VI sich angliedern (*with an* +*acc*) N [əˈfɪlɪət] Schwestergesellschaft *f*; (= *union*) angegliederte Gewerkschaft

affiliation [əˌfɪlɪˈeɪʃən] N **a** Angliederung *f* (*to, with an* +*acc*); (*state*) Verbund *m*; **what are his political ~s?** was ist seine politische Zugehörigkeit? **b** (*Brit Jur*) **~ order** Verurteilung *f* zur Leistung des Regelunterhalts; **~ proceedings**

gerichtliche Feststellung der Vaterschaft, Vaterschaftsklage *f*

affinity [əˈfɪnɪtɪ] N **a** (= *liking*) Neigung *f* (*for, to* zu); (*for person*) Verbundenheit *f* (*for, to* mit) **b** (= *resemblance, connection*) Verwandtschaft *f*, Affinität *f* (*form*) **c** (*Chem*) Affinität *f*

affinity (credit) card N Kreditkarte, bei der bei jeder Zahlung ein Betrag an eine wohltätige Organisation abgeführt wird

affirm [əˈfɜːm] VT **a** (= *assert*) versichern; (*very forcefully*) beteuern; **he ~ed his innocence** er versicherte, dass er unschuldig sei, er beteuerte seine Unschuld **b** (= *ratify*) bestätigen VI (*Jur*) eidesstattlich *or* an Eidesstatt erklären

affirmation [æfəˈmeɪʃən] N **a** (= *assertion*) Versicherung *f*; (*very forceful*) Beteuerung *f* **b** (*Jur*) eidesstattliche Erklärung

affirmative [əˈfɜːmətɪv] N (*Gram*) Bejahung *f*; (*sentence*) bejahender *or* positiver Satz; **to answer in the ~** bejahend *or* mit Ja antworten; **put these sentences into the ~** drücken Sie diese Sätze bejahend aus ADJ bejahend, positiv; (*Gram*) affirmativ (*form*), bejahend; **the answer is ~** die Antwort ist bejahend *or* ja INTERJ richtig

---

AFFIRMATIVE ACTION

Affirmative action ist der in den USA übliche Ausdruck für die bevorzugte Behandlung ethnischer Minderheiten und Frauen bei der Besetzung von Arbeits- und Ausbildungsplätzen. Diese Politik wurde in den sechziger Jahren unter Präsident Kennedy begonnen, als erstmals Quoten festgesetzt wurden, um den unterrepräsentierten Bevölkerungsgruppen mehr Arbeits- und Studienplätze zu garantieren. Mit dem Equal Employment Opportunities Act von 1972 wurde eine Kommission geschaffen, die für die Durchsetzung der Garantien sorgen sollte. Allerdings führte **affirmative action** später zu Klagen über Diskriminierung bei Angehörigen der Mehrheiten (z.B. Weißen oder Männern), was als „reverse discrimination" – „Diskriminierung unter umgekehrtem Vorzeichen" – bekannt geworden ist. Daraufhin wurden die strengen Quotenreglementierungen etwas gelockert.

---

affirmatively [əˈfɜːmətɪvlɪ] ADV bejahend, positiv

affix[1] [əˈfɪks] VT anbringen (*to* auf +*dat*); *seal* setzen (*to* auf +*acc*); *signature* setzen (*to* unter +*acc*)

affix[2] [ˈæfɪks] N (*Gram*) Affix *nt*

afflatus [əˈfleɪtəs] N Inspiration *f*

afflict [əˈflɪkt] VT plagen, zusetzen (+*dat*); (*emotionally, mentally also*) belasten; (*troubles, inflation, injuries*) heimsuchen; **to be ~ed by a disease** an einer Krankheit leiden; **~ed with gout** von (der) Gicht geplagt; **to be ~ed by doubts** von Zweifeln gequält werden; **the ~ed** die Leidenden *pl*

affliction [əˈflɪkʃən] N **a** (= *distress*) Not *f*, Bedrängnis *f*; (= *pain*) Leiden *pl*, Schmerzen *pl* **b** (= *cause of suffering, blindness etc*) Gebrechen *nt*; (*illness*) Beschwerde *f*; (*worry*) Sorge *f*; **the ~s of old age** Altersbeschwerden *pl*; **the government is itself the nation's greatest ~** die Regierung ist selbst die größte Last für das Volk

affluence [ˈæfluəns] N Reichtum *m*, Wohlstand *m*; **to live in ~** im Wohlstand leben; **to rise to ~** zu großem Wohlstand kommen

affluent[1] [ˈæfluənt] ADJ reich, wohlhabend; **the ~ society** die Wohlstandsgesellschaft; **you ~ so-and-so!** du reicher Sack! (*inf*), du Großkapitalist!

affluent[2] N (*Geog spec*) Nebenfluss *m*

afford [əˈfɔːd] VT **a** sich (*dat*) leisten; **I can't ~ to buy both of them** ich kann es mir nicht leisten, beide zu kaufen; **he can't ~ to make a mistake** er kann es sich nicht leisten, einen Fehler zu machen; **you can't ~ to miss the chance** Sie können es sich nicht leisten, die Gelegenheit

zu verpassen; **I can't ~ the time (to do it)** ich habe einfach nicht die Zeit(, das zu tun); **an offer you can't ~ to miss** ein Angebot, das Sie sich (*dat*) nicht entgehen lassen können; **can you ~ to go? – I can't ~ not to!** können Sie gehen? – ich kann gar nicht anders
b (*liter, = provide*) (*sb sth*) jdm etw) gewähren, bieten; *shade* spenden, bieten; *pleasure* bereiten

affordable [əˈfɔːdəbl] ADJ , **affordably** ADV (= *inexpensive*) *price* erschwinglich; (= *reasonably priced*) finanziell möglich *or* tragbar

afforest [æˈfɒrɪst] VT aufforsten

afforestation [æˌfɒrɪsˈteɪʃən] N Aufforstung *f*

affranchise [æˈfræntʃaɪz] VT befreien

affray [əˈfreɪ] N (*esp Jur*) Schlägerei *f*

affricate [ˈæfrɪkət] N (*Ling*) Affrikata *f* (*spec*), Affrikate *f* (*spec*)

affright [əˈfraɪt] VT (*old, liter*) erschrecken

affront [əˈfrʌnt] VT beleidigen N Beleidigung *f* (*to sb* jds, *to sth* für etw), Affront *m* (*to* gegen); **such poverty is an ~ to our national pride** solche Armut verletzt unseren Nationalstolz

Afghan [ˈæfgæn] N **a** Afghane *m*, Afghanin *f* **b** (= *language*) Afghanisch *nt* **c** (*also* **Afghan hound**) Afghane *m*, Afghanischer Windhund **d** **afghan** (= *coat*) Afghan *m* ADJ afghanisch

Afghani [æfˈgænɪ] N (= *person*) Afghane *m*, Afghanin *f* ADJ afghanisch

Afghanistan [æfˈgænɪstæn] N Afghanistan *nt*

aficionado [əˌfɪʃəˈnɑːdəʊ] N *pl* **-s** Liebhaber(in) *m(f)*

afield [əˈfiːld] ADV **countries further ~** weiter entfernte Länder; **too/very far ~** zu/sehr weit weg *or* entfernt; **to venture further ~** (*lit, fig*) sich etwas weiter (vor)wagen; **to explore farther ~** die weitere Umgebung erforschen; **to go farther ~ for help** (*fig*) in der weiteren Umgebung Hilfe suchen; **his studies took him farther ~ into new areas of knowledge** seine Forschungen führten ihn immer weiter in neue Wissensbereiche

afire [əˈfaɪə] ADJ PRED, ADV in Brand; **to set sth ~** etw in Brand stecken, etw anzünden; (*fig*) etw entzünden; **~ with enthusiasm** hellauf begeistert; **this set his imagination ~** das entzündete seine Fantasie

aflame [əˈfleɪm] ADJ PRED, ADV in Flammen; **to set sth ~** etw in Brand stecken, etw anzünden; (*fig*) etw entzünden; **to be ~ with colour** (*Brit*) *or* **color** (*US*) in roter Glut leuchten; **~ with anger/passion** flammend *or* glühend vor Zorn/Leidenschaft

AFL-CIO *abbr of* **American Federation of Labor and Congress of Industrial Organizations** *amerikanischer Gewerkschafts-Dachverband*

afloat [əˈfləʊt] ADJ PRED, ADV **a** (*Naut*) **to be ~** schwimmen; **to stay ~** sich über Wasser halten; (*thing*) schwimmen, nicht untergehen; **to set a ship ~** ein Schiff zu Wasser lassen; **at last we were ~ again** endlich waren wir wieder flott; **cargo ~** schwimmende Ladung; **the largest navy ~** die größte Flotte auf See; **service ~** Dienst *m* auf See; **to serve ~** auf See dienen
b (= *awash*) überschwemmt, unter Wasser; **to be ~** unter Wasser stehen, überschwemmt sein
c (*fig*) **to get/keep a business ~** ein Geschäft *nt* auf die Beine stellen/über Wasser halten; **those who stayed ~ during the slump** die, die sich auch während der Krise über Wasser gehalten haben
d (*fig: rumour etc*) **there is a rumour ~ that ...** es geht das Gerücht um, dass ...

aflutter [əˈflʌtə] ADJ PRED, ADV aufgeregt; **her heart was all ~** ihr Herz flatterte

afoot [əˈfʊt] ADV im Gange; **there is something ~** da ist etwas im Gange; **what's ~?** was geht hier vor?

afore [əˈfɔː] (*obs, dial*) CONJ bevor ADV zuvor

aforementioned [əˌfɔːˈmenʃənd], **aforesaid** [əˈfɔːsed] ADJ *attr* (*form*) oben genannt, oben erwähnt

aforethought [əˈfɔːθɔːt] ADJ → **malice**

a fortiori [eɪˌfɔːtɪˈɔːraɪ] ADV aufgrund or auf Grund des Vorhergehenden

afoul [əˈfaʊl] ADJ PRED, ADV lines, ropes verheddert, verwirrt; **to run ~ of the law** mit dem Gesetz in Konflikt geraten

afraid [əˈfreɪd] ✪ 6.2, 12.3, 16.2, 21.4, 25.2 ADJ pred **a** (= frightened) **to be ~ (of sb/sth)** (vor jdm/etw) Angst haben, sich (vor jdm/etw) fürchten; **don't be ~!** keine Angst!; **it's quite safe, there's nothing to be ~ of** es ist ganz sicher, Sie brauchen keine Angst zu haben; **go and talk to him then, there's nothing to be ~ of** geh und sprich mit ihm, da ist doch nichts dabei; **I am ~ of hurting him** or **that I might hurt him** ich fürchte, ihm wehzutun or ich könnte ihm weh un; **I am ~ he will** or **might hurt me, I am ~ lest he (might) hurt me** (liter) ich fürchte, er könnte mir wehtun; **to make sb ~** jdm Angst machen or einjagen, jdn ängstigen; **I am ~ to leave her alone** ich habe Angst davor, sie allein zu lassen; **I was ~ of not being precise enough** ich fürchtete, dass ich mich nicht genau genug ausdrückte; **I was ~ of waking the children** ich wollte die Kinder nicht wecken; **to be ~ of work** arbeitsscheu sein; **he's not ~ of hard work** er scheut schwere Arbeit nicht, er hat keine Angst vor schwerer Arbeit; **he's not ~ to say what he thinks** er scheut sich nicht zu sagen, was er denkt; **that's what I was ~ of, I was ~ that would happen** das habe ich befürchtet; **go on, do it, what are you ~ of?** tus doch, wovor hast du denn Angst?; **I was ~ you'd ask that** ich habe diese Frage befürchtet; **to be ~ for sb/sth** (= worried) Angst um jdn/etw haben; **to be ~ for one's life** Angst um sein Leben haben

b (expressing polite regret) **I'm ~ I can't do it** leider kann ich es nicht machen; **there's nothing I can do, I'm ~** ich kann da leider gar nichts machen; **I'm ~ to say that ...** ich muss Ihnen leider sagen, dass ...; **I'm ~ you'll have to wait** Sie müssen leider warten; **are you going? – I'm ~ not/I'm ~ so** gehst du? – leider nicht/ja, leider; **well, I'm ~ you're wrong** so Leid es mir tut, aber Sie haben Unrecht; **can I go now? – no, I'm ~ you can't** kann ich jetzt gehen? – nein, tut mir Leid, noch nicht

afresh [əˈfreʃ] ADV noch einmal von vorn or neuem

Africa [ˈæfrɪkə] N Afrika nt

African [ˈæfrɪkən] **N** Afrikaner(in) m(f) **ADJ** afrikanisch

African-American [ˌæfrɪkənəˈmerɪkən] **ADJ** afroamerikanisch **N** Afroamerikaner(in) m(f)

African violet N Usambaraveilchen nt

Afrikaans [ˌæfrɪˈkɑːns] N Afrikaans nt

Afrikaner [ˌæfrɪˈkɑːnə'] N Afrika(a)nder(in) m(f)

Afro [ˈæfrəʊ] **PREF** afro- **N** (= hairstyle) Afrofrisur f, Afrolook m

Afro-: **Afro-American** **ADJ** afroamerikanisch **N** Afroamerikaner(in) m(f); **Afro-Asian** ADJ afroasiatisch; **Afro-Caribbean** ADJ afrokaribisch **N** Afrokaribe m, Afrokaribin f

aft [ɑːft] (Naut) **ADV** sit achtern; go nach achtern **ADJ** Achter-, achter-; **~ deck** Achterdeck nt

after[1] [ˈɑːftə'] ADJ attr (Naut) Achter-; **the ~ deck** das Achterdeck

after[2] **PREP** **a** (time) nach (+dat); **~ dinner** nach dem Essen; **~ that** danach; **the day ~ tomorrow** übermorgen; **the week ~ next** die übernächste Woche; **I'll be back the week ~ next** ich bin übernächste Woche wieder da; **it was ~ two o'clock** es war nach zwei; **ten ~ eight** (US) zehn nach acht

b (order) nach (+dat), hinter (+dat); (in priorities etc) nach (+dat); **the noun comes ~ the verb** das Substantiv steht nach or hinter dem Verb; **I would put Keats ~ Shelley** für mich rangiert Keats unter Shelley; **~ Germany, Japan is our biggest market** nach Deutschland ist Japan unser größter Markt; **~ you** nach Ihnen; **I was ~ him** (in queue etc) ich war nach ihm dran; **~ you with the salt** kann ich bitte das Salz nach dir haben?

c (place) hinter (+dat); **he shut the door ~ him**

er machte die Tür hinter ihm zu; **turn right about a mile ~ the village** biegen Sie etwa eine Meile nach dem Dorf rechts ab; **to shout ~ sb** hinter jdm herrufen or -schreien; **to shout sth ~ sb** jdm etw nachrufen

d (= as a result of) nach (+dat); **~ what has happened** nach allem, was geschehen ist; **~ this you might believe me** jetzt wirst du mir vielleicht endlich glauben

e (= in spite of) **to do sth ~ all** etw schließlich doch tun; **~ all our efforts!** und das, nachdem or wo (inf) wir uns so viel Mühe gegeben haben!; **~ all I've done for you!** und das nach allem, was ich für dich getan habe!; **~ all, he is your brother** er ist immerhin or schließlich dein Bruder; **and to do this ~ I had warned him** und das, nachdem ich ihn gewarnt hatte

f (succession) nach (+dat); **you tell me lie ~ lie** du erzählst mir eine Lüge nach der anderen, du belügst mich am laufenden Band; **it's just one thing ~ another** or **the other** es kommt eins nach dem anderen or eins zum anderen; **one ~ the other** eine(r, s) nach der/dem anderen; **one ~ the other she rejected all the offers** sie schlug ein Angebot nach dem anderen aus; **day ~ day** Tag für or um Tag; **we marched on for mile ~ mile** wir marschierten Meile um Meile weiter; **before us lay mile ~ mile of barren desert** vor uns erstreckte sich meilenweit trostlose Wüste

g (manner: = according to) nach (+dat); **~ El Greco** in der Art von El Greco, nach El Greco; **she takes ~ her mother** sie schlägt ihrer Mutter nach → **name**

h (pursuit, inquiry) **to be ~ sb/sth** hinter jdm/ etw her sein; **she asked** or **inquired ~ you** sie hat sich nach dir erkundigt; **what are you ~?** was willst du?; (= looking for) was suchst du?; **he's just ~ a free meal/a bit of excitement** er ist nur auf ein kostenloses Essen/ein bisschen Abwechslung aus

ADV (time, order) danach; (place, pursuit) hinterher; **for years/weeks ~** noch Jahre/Wochen or jahrelang/wochenlang danach; **the year/week ~** das Jahr/die Woche danach or darauf; **I'll be back some time the year ~** ich komme irgendwann im Jahr danach or im darauf folgenden Jahr wieder; **soon ~** kurz danach or darauf; **what comes ~?** was kommt danach or nachher?; **the car drove off with the dog running ~** das Auto fuhr los und der Hund rannte hinterher

CONJ nachdem; **~ he had closed the door he began to speak** nachdem er die Tür geschlossen hatte, begann er zu sprechen; **what will you do ~ he's gone?** was machst du, wenn er weg ist?; **~ finishing it I will ...** wenn ich das fertig habe, werde ich ...; **~ arriving they went ...** nachdem sie angekommen waren, gingen sie ...

ADJ **in ~ years** in späteren Jahren

N **afters** PL (Brit, inf) Nachtisch m; **what's for ~s?** was gibts hinterher or als or zum Nachtisch?

after: afterbirth N Nachgeburt f; **afterburner** N Nachbrenner m; **afterburning** N Nachverbrennung f; **aftercare** N (of convalescent) Nachbehandlung f, Nachsorge f; (of ex-prisoner) Resozialisierungshilfe f; **afterdeck** N Achterdeck nt; **after-dinner** ADJ coffee, conversation nach dem Essen; **~ walk/nap** Verdauungsspaziergang m/-schlaf m; **~ speech** Tischrede f; **aftereffect** N (of illness) (Psych) Nachwirkung f; (of events etc also) Folge f; **afterglow** N (of sun) Abendrot nt, Abendleuchten nt; (fig) angenehme Erinnerung; **after-hours** ADJ attr (in shops etc) nach Geschäftsschluss; (in pubs) nach der Polizeistunde; (in office etc) nach der Arbeit, nach Dienstschluss; **afterimage** N (Psych) Nachempfindung f, Nachbild nt; **afterlife** N Leben nt nach dem Tode; **after-lunch** ADJ **to have an ~ nap** ein Mittagsschläfchen halten; **aftermath** N Nachwirkungen pl; **in the ~ of sth** nach etw; **the country was still suffering the ~ of war** das Land litt immer noch an den Folgen or Auswirkungen des Krieges; **aftermost** ADJ (Naut) hinterste(r, s)

afternoon [ˌɑːftəˈnuːn] **N** Nachmittag m; **in the ~, ~s** (esp US) am Nachmittag, nachmittags; **at three o'clock in the ~** (um) drei Uhr nachmittags; **on Sunday ~** (am) Sonntag Nachmittag; **on Sunday ~s** Sonntag or sonntags nachmittags, am Sonntagnachmittag; **on the ~ of December 2nd** am Nachmittag des 2. Dezember, am 2. Dezember nachmittags; **this/tomorrow/yesterday ~** heute/morgen/gestern Nachmittag; **good ~!** Guten Tag!; **~! Tag!** (inf) **ADJ** attr Nachmittags-; **~ performance** Nachmittagsvorstellung f

afternoon tea N (Brit) (Nachmittags)tee m

after: afterpains PL Nachwehen pl; **after-sales service** N Kundendienst m; **aftershave (lotion)** N Aftershave nt, Rasierwasser nt; **aftershock** N (of earthquake) Nachbeben nt; **after-sun** **ADJ** After-Sun-; **~ lotion/cream** After-Sun-Lotion f/-Creme f **N** (= lotion) After-Sun-Lotion f; (= cream) After-Sun-Creme f; **aftertaste** N (lit, fig) Nachgeschmack m; **to leave an unpleasant ~** einen unangenehmen Nachgeschmack hinterlassen; **after-tax** ADJ profits etc nach Steuern, nach Steuerabzug; **afterthought** N nachträgliche or zusätzliche Idee; **if you have any ~s about ...** wenn Ihnen noch irgendetwas zu ... einfällt; **he added as an ~** fügte er hinzu, schickte er nach; **I just mentioned that as an ~** das fiel mir noch dazu or nachträglich ein; **the window was added as an ~** das Fenster kam erst später dazu; **after-treatment** N (Tech, Chem) Nachbehandlung f

afterward [ˈɑːftəwəd] ADV (US) = afterwards

afterwards [ˈɑːftəwədz] ADV nachher; (= after that, after some event etc) danach; **and ~ we could go to a disco** und anschließend or nachher or danach gehen wir in eine Disko; **can I have mine now? – no, ~** kann ich meins jetzt haben? – nein, nachher; **this was added ~** das kam nachträglich dazu

afterword [ˈɑːftəwɜːd] N Nachwort nt

afterworld [ˈɑːftəwɜːld] N Jenseits nt

Aga® [ˈɑːgə] N (Brit) eiserner, nach alter Vorlage gebauter Küchenherd

again [əˈgen] ADV **a** wieder; **~ and ~, time and ~** immer wieder; **to do sth ~** etw noch (ein-)mal tun; **I won't do that ~** das tue ich nie wieder; **I'll ring ~ tomorrow** ich rufe morgen noch einmal an; **never** or **not ever ~** nie wieder; **if that happens ~** wenn das noch einmal passiert; **all over ~** noch (ein)mal von vorn; **what's his name ~?** wie heißt er noch gleich?; **to begin ~** von neuem or noch einmal anfangen; **not ~!** (nicht) schon wieder!; **not mince ~!** (nicht) schon wieder Hackfleisch!; **it's me** (arriving) da bin ich wieder; (phoning) ich bins noch (ein)mal; (= my fault) wieder mal ich; **not you ~!** du schon wieder!?; **he was soon well ~** er war bald wieder gesund; **and these are different ~** und diese sind wieder anders; **here we are ~!** da wären wir wieder!; (finding another example etc) oh, schon wieder!; **~ we find that ...** und wieder einmal or wiederum stellen wir fest, dass ...

b (in quantity) **as much ~** doppelt so viel, noch (ein)mal so viel; **he's as old ~ as Mary** er ist doppelt so alt wie Mary

c (= on the other hand) wiederum; (= besides, moreover) außerdem; **but then** or **there ~, it may not be true** vielleicht ist es auch gar nicht wahr

against [əˈgenst] ✪ 26.1 **PREP** **a** (opposition, protest) gegen (+acc); **he's ~ her going** er ist dagegen, dass sie geht; **everybody's ~ me!** alle sind gegen mich!; **to have something/nothing ~ sb/sth** etwas/nichts gegen jdn/etw haben; **~ that you have to consider ...** Sie müssen aber auch bedenken ...; **~ my will, I decided ...** wider Willen habe ich beschlossen ...; **~ their wishes** entgegen ihrem Wunsch; **to fight ~ sb** gegen or wider (liter) jdn kämpfen

b (indicating impact, support, proximity) an (+acc), gegen (+acc); **to hit one's head ~ the mantelpiece** mit dem Kopf gegen or an das Kaminsims stoßen; **push all the chairs right back**

~ the wall stellen Sie alle Stühle direkt an die Wand; **c** (= *in the opposite direction to*) gegen (+*acc*); **d** (= *in front of, in juxtaposition to*) gegen (+*acc*); **~ the light** gegen das Licht; **e** (= *in preparation for*) sb's arrival, departure, one's old age für (+*acc*); misfortune, bad weather etc im Hinblick auf (+*acc*); **~ the possibility of a bad winter** für den Fall, dass es einen schlechten Winter gibt; **f** (= *compared with*) **(as) ~** gegenüber (+*dat*); **she had three prizes (as) ~ his six** sie hatte drei Preise, er hingegen sechs; **the advantages of flying (as) ~ going by boat** die Vorteile von Flugreisen gegenüber Schiffsreisen; **~ the euro** gegenüber dem Euro; **g** (*Fin*, = *in return for*) gegen; **the visa will be issued ~ payment of ...** das Visum wird gegen Zahlung von ... ausgestellt; **to draw money ~ security** gegen Sicherheit(sleistung) or Deckung Geld abheben; **ADJ PRED** (= *not in favour*) dagegen; **how many ~?** wie viele sind dagegen? → **for¹** ADJ

agape [ə'geɪp] ADJ *pred* person mit (vor Staunen) offenem Mund, bass erstaunt (*geh*)

agaric ['ægərɪk] N Blätterpilz m

agate ['ægət] N Achat m

agave [ə'geɪvɪ] N Agave f

age [eɪdʒ] **N** **a** (*of person, star, building etc*) Alter nt; **what is her ~?, what ~ is she?** wie alt ist sie?; **he is ten years of ~** er ist zehn Jahre alt; **trees of great ~** Bäume von hohem Alter; **~ doesn't matter** das Alter spielt keine Rolle; **at the ~ of 15** im Alter von 15 Jahren, mit 15 Jahren; **at your ~** in deinem Alter; **when I was your ~** als ich in deinem Alter war, als ich so alt war wie du; **when you're my ~** wenn du erst in mein Alter kommst, wenn du erst mal so alt bist wie ich; **I have a daughter your ~** ich habe eine Tochter in Ihrem Alter; **but he's twice your ~** aber er ist ja doppelt so alt wie du; **we're of an ~** wir sind gleichaltrig; **he is now of an ~ to understand these things** er ist jetzt alt genug, um das zu verstehen; **over ~** zu alt; **she doesn't look her ~** man sieht ihr ihr Alter nicht an, sie sieht jünger aus, als sie ist; **be or act your ~!** sei nicht kindisch!

b (= *length of life*) Lebensdauer f; (*of human*) Lebenserwartung f; **the ~ of a star can be millions of years** ein Stern kann viele Millionen Jahre existieren; **c** (*Jur*) **to be of ~** volljährig or mündig sein; **to come of ~** volljährig or mündig werden; (fig) die Kinderschuhe entwachsen; **under ~** minderjährig, unmündig; **~ of consent** (for marriage) Ehemündigkeitsalter nt; **intercourse with girls under the ~ of consent** Unzucht f mit Minderjährigen; **d** (= *old age*) Alter nt; **bowed with ~** vom Alter gebeugt; **~ before beauty** (hum) Alter vor Schönheit; **e** (= *period, epoch*) Zeit(alter nt) f; **the atomic ~** das Atomzeitalter; **the ~ of technology** das technologische Zeitalter; **in this ~ of inflation** in dieser inflationären Zeit; **the Stone ~** die Steinzeit; **the Edwardian ~** die Zeit or Ära Edwards VII; **the ~ of Socrates** das Zeitalter Sokrates; **down the ~s** durch alle Zeiten; **what will future ~s think of us?** was werden kommende Generationen von uns halten?; **f** (*inf*, = *long time*) **~s, an ~** eine Ewigkeit, Ewigkeiten pl, ewig (lang) (*all inf*); **I haven't seen him for ~s** or **for an ~** ich habe ihn eine Ewigkeit or Ewigkeiten or ewig (lang) nicht gesehen (*inf*); **it's been ~s since we met** wir haben uns ja eine Ewigkeit etc nicht mehr gesehen (*inf*); **to take ~s** eine Ewigkeit dauern (*inf*); (person) ewig brauchen (*inf*)

VI alt werden, altern; (wine, cheese) reifen; **you have ~d** du bist alt geworden; **she seems to have ~d ten years** sie scheint um zehn Jahre gealtert zu sein

VT **a** (dress, hairstyle etc) alt machen; (worry etc) alt werden lassen, altern lassen; **b** wine, cheese lagern, reifen lassen

age bracket N Altersklasse f, Altersstufe f

aged [eɪdʒd] **ADJ** **a** im Alter von, ... Jahre alt, -jährig; **a boy ~ ten** ein zehnjähriger Junge **b** ['eɪdʒɪd] person bejahrt, betagt; animal, car, building etc alt, betagt (hum) **PL** ['eɪdʒɪd] **the ~** die alten Menschen, die Alten pl

age: age difference, age gap N Altersunterschied m; **age group** N Altersgruppe f; **the forty to fifty ~** die (Alters)gruppe der Vierzig- bis Fünfzigjährigen

ag(e)ing ['eɪdʒɪŋ] **ADJ** person alternd attr; animal, thing, population älter werdend attr; **the ~ process** das Altern **N** Altern nt

ageism ['eɪdʒɪzəm] N Altersdiskriminierung f, Seniorenfeindlichkeit f

ageist ['eɪdʒɪst] ADJ altersdiskriminierend, seniorenfeindlich

age: ageless ADJ zeitlos; **she seems to be one of those ~ people** sie scheint zu den Menschen zu gehören, die nie alt werden; **age limit** N Altersgrenze f; **age-long** ADJ sehr lange, ewig (*inf*)

agency ['eɪdʒənsɪ] N **a** (*Comm*) Agentur f; (= *subsidiary of a company*) Geschäftsstelle f; **translation/tourist ~** Übersetzungs-/Reisebüro nt; **this garage is or has the Citroën ~** dies ist eine Citroën-Vertragswerkstätte, diese Werkstatt ist eine or hat die Citroën-Vertretung **b** (= *instrumentality*) **through the ~ of friends** durch die Vermittlung von Freunden, durch Freunde; **by the ~ of water** mithilfe or mit Hilfe von Wasser, durch Wasser; **to attribute sth to the ~ of Providence** etw der Vorsehung (*dat*) zuschreiben

agenda [ə'dʒendə] N Tagesordnung f; **a full ~** (lit) eine umfangreiche Tagesordnung; (fig) ein volles Programm; **to set the ~** (lit) die Tagesordnung festlegen; (fig) den Ton angeben; **they have their own ~** sie haben ihre eigenen Vorstellungen; **on the ~** auf dem Programm

agent ['eɪdʒənt] N **a** (*Comm*) (= *person*) Vertreter(in) m(f); (= *organization*) Vertretung f; **who is the ~ for this car in Scotland?** wer hat die schottische Vertretung für dieses Auto? **b** (= *literary agent, press agent etc*) Agent(in) m(f); (Pol) Wahlkampfleiter(in) m(f); **business ~** Agent(in) m(f) **c** (= *secret agent, FBI agent etc*) Agent(in) m(f); **~ in charge (of an/the investigation)** Untersuchungsbeamte(r) m/-beamtin f **d** (= *person having power to act*) **man must be regarded as a moral ~** der Mensch muss als moralisch verantwortlich handelndes Wesen angesehen werden; **determinism states that we are not free ~s** der Determinismus behauptet, dass wir nicht frei entscheiden können; **you're a free ~, do what you want** du bist dein eigener Herr, tu was du willst **e** (= *means by which sth is achieved*) Mittel nt; **she became the unwitting ~ of his wicked plot** unwissentlich wurde sie zum Werkzeug für seinen niederträchtigen Plan **f** (*Chem*) **cleansing ~** Reinigungsmittel nt; **special protective ~** Spezialschutzmittel nt

agent extraordinary N Spezialagent(in) m(f)

agent provocateur [æʒɒŋprɒvɒkæ'tɜː'] N pl **-s -s** Agent provocateur m, Lockspitzel m

age: age-old ADJ uralt; **age range** N Altersgruppe f; **age-related** ADJ altersspezifisch; **age spot** N Altersfleck m

agglomerate [ə'glɒməreɪt] **VI** agglomerieren **ADJ** [ə'glɒmərɪt] agglomeriert **N** [ə'glɒmərɪt] Agglomerat nt

agglomeration [ə،glɒmə'reɪʃən] N Anhäufung f, Konglomerat nt; (Sci) Agglomeration f

agglutinate [ə'gluːtɪneɪt] **VI** agglutinieren (also Ling), verklumpen, verkleben **ADJ** [ə'gluːtɪnɪt] agglutiniert (also Ling), verklumpt, verklebt

agglutinating [ə'gluːtɪneɪtɪŋ] ADJ (Ling) agglutinierend

agglutination [ə،gluːtɪ'neɪʃən] N Agglutination f (also Ling), Verklumpung f, Verklebung f

agglutinative [ə'gluːtɪnətɪv] ADJ agglutinierend

aggrandize [ə'grændaɪz] VT one's power, empire vergrößern, erweitern; person, one's family befördern; **to ~ oneself** sich befördern; (= *be self-important*) sich wichtig machen

aggrandizement [ə'grændɪzmənt] N (of power, empire) Vergrößerung f, Erweiterung f; (of person, one's family) Beförderung f

aggravate ['ægrəveɪt] VT **a** (= *make worse*) verschlimmern **b** (= *annoy*) aufregen; (deliberately) reizen; **don't get ~d** regen Sie sich nicht auf

aggravating ['ægrəveɪtɪŋ] ADJ ärgerlich, enervierend (geh); child lästig, enervierend (geh); **how ~ for you** wie ärgerlich für Sie!

aggravation [،ægrə'veɪʃən] N **a** (= *worsening*) Verschlimmerung f **b** (= *annoyance*) Ärger m; **she was a constant ~ to him** sie reizte ihn ständig

aggregate ['ægrɪgɪt] **N** **a** Gesamtmenge f, Summe f, Gesamtheit f; **considered in (the) ~** insgesamt betrachtet; **on ~** (Sport) in der Gesamtwertung **b** (Build) Zuschlagstoffe pl; (Geol) Gemenge nt **ADJ** gesamt, Gesamt-; **~ value** Gesamtwert m **VT** ['ægrɪgeɪt] **a** (= *gather together*) anhäufen, ansammeln **b** (= *amount to*) sich belaufen auf (+acc) **VI** ['ægrɪgeɪt] sich anhäufen, sich ansammeln

aggression [ə'greʃən] N **a** (= *attack*) Aggression f, Angriff m; **an act of ~** ein Angriff m, eine aggressive Handlung **b** no pl Aggression f; (= *aggressiveness*) Aggressivität f; **to get rid of one's ~** seine Aggressionen loswerden

aggressive [ə'gresɪv] ADJ **a** (= *belligerent*) aggressiv; lover draufgängerisch, ungestüm **b** (= *forceful*) salesman, businessman etc dynamisch, aufdringlich (pej); sales technique aggressiv

aggressively [ə'gresɪvlɪ] ADV (= *belligerently*) aggressiv; (= *forcefully*) energisch; sell aggressiv

aggressiveness [ə'gresɪvnɪs] N (= *belligerence*) Aggressivität f; (Sport: of play) Härte f, Aggressivität f; (of lover) Draufgängertum nt, Ungestüm nt **b** (= *forcefulness*) (of salesman etc) Dynamik f, Aufdringlichkeit f (pej); (of sales technique) Aggressivität f

aggressivity [،ægre'sɪvɪtɪ] N (= *belligerence*) Aggressivität f, Angriffslust f; (= *forcefulness*) Dynamik f

aggressor [ə'gresə'] N Angreifer(in) m(f), Aggressor(in) m(f)

aggrieved [ə'griːvd] ADJ betrübt (at, by über +acc); (= *offended*) verletzt (at, by durch); voice, look verletzt, gekränkt; **the ~ (party)** (Jur) der Beschwerte, die beschwerte Partei

aggro ['ægrəʊ] N (Brit inf) **a** (= *aggression, bother*) Aggressionen pl; **don't give me any ~** mach keinen Ärger (inf) or Stunk (inf); **I get ~ from my mother if ...** ich kriege Ärger mit meiner Mutter, wenn ... (inf); **she didn't want all the ~ of moving** sie wollte das ganze Theater mit dem Umziehen vermeiden; **motorways are too much ~** Autobahnen sind zu anstrengend **b** (= *fight*) Schlägerei f; **football fans looking for ~** Fußballfans, die auf Schlägereien aus sind

aghast [ə'gɑːst] ADJ pred entgeistert (at über +acc)

agile ['ædʒaɪl] ADJ person, thinker beweglich, wendig; body also, movements gelenkig, geschmeidig; animal flink, behände; **he has an ~ mind** er ist geistig sehr wendig or beweglich or flexibel

agilely ['ædʒaɪllɪ] ADV move, jump etc geschickt, behände; argue geschickt, gewandt; think flink, beweglich

agility [ə'dʒɪlɪtɪ] N (of person) Agilität f, Beweglichkeit f, Wendigkeit f; (of thinker) Beweglichkeit f, Wendigkeit f; (of body, movements) Gelenkigkeit f, Geschmeidigkeit f; (of animal) Flinkheit f, Behändigkeit f

aging ADJ, N = **ag(e)ing**

agio ['ædʒɪəʊ] N (Econ) Aufgeld nt, Agio nt

agiotage ['ædʒətɪdʒ] N (St Ex) Agiotage f

agitate ['ædʒɪteɪt] **VT** **a** (lit) liquid aufrühren; surface of water aufwühlen; washing hin und her bewegen **b** (fig, = *excite, upset*) aufregen, aus der Fassung bringen; **don't let him ~ you** lass dich von ihm nicht aufregen **VI** agitieren; **to ~ for sth** sich für etw stark machen

agitated ADJ , **agitatedly** ADV [ˈædʒɪteɪtɪd, -lɪ] aufgeregt, erregt

agitation [ædʒɪˈteɪʃən] N **a** (*lit, of liquid*) Aufrühren *nt*; (*of surface of water*) Aufwühlen *nt*; (*of clothes in washing machine*) Hin- und Herbewegung *f* **b** (*fig, = anxiety, worry*) Erregung *f*, Aufruhr *m*; (*on stock market*) Bewegung *f* **c** (*Pol, = incitement*) Agitation *f*

agitator [ˈædʒɪteɪtə'] N **a** (*= person*) Agitator(in) *m(f)* **b** (*= device*) Rührwerk *nt*, Rührapparat *m*

agleam [əˈgliːm] ADJ *pred* erleuchtet; **his eyes were ~ with mischief** seine Augen blitzten *or* funkelten schelmisch

aglitter [əˈglɪtə'] ADJ *pred* **to be ~** funkeln, glitzern

aglow [əˈgləʊ] ADJ *pred* **to be ~** (*sky, fire, face*) glühen; **the sun set the mountains/sky ~** die Sonne ließ die Berge/den Himmel erglühen *or* brachte die Berge/den Himmel zum Glühen; **to be ~ with happiness/health** vor Glück/Gesundheit strahlen

AGM *abbr of* **annual general meeting** JHV *f*

agnail [ˈægneɪl] N Niednagel *m*

agnostic [ægˈnɒstɪk] **ADJ** agnostisch **N** Agnostiker(in) *m(f)*

agnosticism [ægˈnɒstɪsɪzəm] N Agnostizismus *m*

ago [əˈgəʊ] ADV vor; **years/a week ~** vor Jahren/einer Woche; **a little while ~** vor kurzem; **that was years/a week ~** das ist schon Jahre/eine Woche her; **he was here a minute ~** er war noch vor einer Minute hier; **how long ~ is it since you last saw him?** wie lange haben Sie ihn schon nicht mehr gesehen?, wann haben Sie ihn das letzte Mal gesehen?; **how long ~ did it happen?** wie lange ist das her?; **he left 10 minutes ~** er ist vor 10 Minuten gegangen; **long, long ~** vor langer, langer Zeit; **how long ~?** wie lange ist das her?; **that was a long time** *or* **long ~** das ist schon lange her; **as long ~ as 1950** schon 1950

agog [əˈgɒg] ADJ *pred* gespannt; **the children sat there ~ with excitement** die Kinder sperrten Augen und Ohren auf; **the whole village was ~ (with curiosity)** das ganze Dorf platzte fast vor Neugierde; **~ for news** wild nach Neuigkeiten; **we're all ~ to hear your news** wir warten gespannt auf deine Nachrichten

agonize [ˈægənaɪz] VI sich (*dat*) den Kopf zermartern (*over* über +*acc*); **after weeks of agonizing he finally made a decision** nach wochenlangem Ringen traf er endlich eine Entscheidung

agonized [ˈægənaɪzd] ADJ gequält

agonizing [ˈægənaɪzɪŋ] ADJ qualvoll, quälend; *cry, experience* qualvoll

agonizingly [ˈægənaɪzɪŋlɪ] ADV qualvoll; **~ slow** aufreizend langsam

agony [ˈægənɪ] N **a** Qual *f*; **that's ~** das ist eine Qual; **it's ~ doing that** es ist eine Qual, das zu tun; **to be in ~** Schmerzen *or* Qualen leiden; **in an ~ of indecision/suspense** *etc* in qualvoller Unentschlossenheit/Ungewissheit *etc*; **put him out of his ~** (*lit*) mach seiner Qual ein Ende; (*fig*) nun spann ihn doch nicht länger auf die Folter; **to go through** *or* **suffer agonies** Qualen ausstehen **b** (*= death agony*) Todeskampf *m*, Agonie *f*; (*of Christ*) Todesangst *f*

agony (*Brit Press inf*): **agony aunt** N Briefkastentante *f* (*inf*); **agony column** N Kummerkasten *m*; **agony columnist** N Briefkastenonkel *m*/-tante *f* (*inf*); **agony uncle** N Briefkastenonkel *m* (*inf*)

agoraphobia [ægərəˈfəʊbɪə] N (*Med*) Agoraphobie *f* (*spec*), Platzangst *f*

agoraphobic [ægərəˈfəʊbɪk] (*Med*) **ADJ** agoraphobisch (*spec*) **N** an Agoraphobie (*spec*) *or* Platzangst Leidende(r) *mf*

agrarian [əˈgrɛərɪən] ADJ Agrar-; **~ reform** Agrarreform *f*; **~ society** Agrargesellschaft *f*

agree [əˈgriː] **⚙** 11, 12, 13, 26.1, 26.3 *pret, ptp* **a-greed** **VT** **a** *price, date etc* vereinbaren, abmachen **b** (*= consent*) **to ~ to do sth** sich einverstanden *or* bereit erklären, etw zu tun **c** (*= admit*) zugeben; **I ~ (that) I was wrong** ich gebe zu, dass ich mich geirrt habe **d** (*= come to or be in agreement about*) zustimmen (+*dat*); **we all ~ that ...** wir sind alle der Meinung, dass ...; **it was ~d that ...** man einigte sich darauf, dass ..., es wurde beschlossen, dass ...; **we ~d to do it** wir haben beschlossen, das zu tun; **to ~ to differ** *or* **disagree** sich (*dat*) verschiedene Meinungen zugestehen; **we ~ to differ** wir sind uns einig, dass wir uns uneinig sind; **is that ~d then, gentlemen?** sind alle einverstanden? → *also* **agreed**
VI **a** (*= hold same opinion, two or more people*) sich einig sein, übereinstimmen, einer Meinung sein; (*one person*) der gleichen Meinung sein; **to ~ with sb** jdm zustimmen; **I ~!** der Meinung bin ich auch; **we all ~, it's a silly suggestion** wir sind uns alle einig, das ist ein alberner Vorschlag; **I couldn't ~ more/less** ich bin völlig/überhaupt nicht dieser Meinung, ich stimme dem völlig/überhaupt nicht zu; **it's too late now, don't** *or* **wouldn't you ~?** finden *or* meinen Sie nicht auch, dass es jetzt zu spät ist? **b** **to ~ with a theory/the figures** *etc* (*accept*) eine Theorie/die Zahlen *etc* akzeptieren *or* für richtig halten **c** (*= come to an agreement*) sich einigen (*about* über +*acc*) **d** (*statements, figures etc*: *= tally*) übereinstimmen **e** **to ~ with sth** (*= approve of*) etw befürworten, mit etw einverstanden sein; **I don't ~ with children drinking wine** ich bin dagegen *or* ich bin nicht damit einverstanden, dass Kinder Wein trinken **f** (*food, climate etc*) **sth ~s with sb** jdm bekommt etw; **whisky doesn't ~ with me** ich vertrage Whisky nicht, Whisky bekommt mir nicht **g** (*Gram*) übereinstimmen **h** (*people*: *= get on together*) sich vertragen, miteinander auskommen

▶ **agree on** VI +*prep obj* *solution* sich einigen auf (+*acc*), Einigkeit erzielen über (+*acc*); *price, policy also* vereinbaren; **a price/policy/solution has been agreed on** man hat sich auf einen Preis/eine Linie/eine Lösung geeinigt; **we agreed on the need to save** wir waren uns darüber einig, dass gespart werden muss

▶ **agree to** 12.2 VI +*prep obj* zustimmen (+*dat*); *marriage also* einwilligen in (+*acc*), seine Einwilligung geben zu; *conditions, terms also* annehmen, akzeptieren; *increase, payment also* sich einverstanden erklären mit; **I cannot agree to your marrying her** ich kann einer Ehe nicht zustimmen

agreeable [əˈgriːəbl] ADJ **a** (*= pleasant*) angenehm; *decor, behaviour* nett **b** *pred* (*= willing to agree*) einverstanden; **are you ~ to that?, is that ~ to you?** sind Sie damit einverstanden?

agreeably [əˈgriːəblɪ] ADV angenehm; *decorated* nett; **to be ~ surprised** angenehm überrascht sein; **she behaved ~ for once** sie benahm sich ausnahmsweise nett

agreed [əˈgriːd] **⚙** 26.1 ADJ **a** *pred* (*= in agreement*) einig; **to be ~ on sth** sich über etw einig sein; **to be ~ on doing sth** sich darüber einig sein, etw zu tun; **are we all ~?** sind wir uns da einig?; (*on course of action*) sind alle einverstanden? **b** (*= arranged*) vereinbart; *time* verabredet, vereinbart; **it's all ~** es ist alles abgesprochen; **~?** einverstanden?; **~!** (*regarding price etc*) abgemacht, in Ordnung; (*= I agree*) stimmt, genau

agreement [əˈgriːmənt] **⚙** 11.2, 13 N **a** (*= understanding, arrangement*) Abmachung *f*, Übereinkunft *f*; (*= treaty, contract*) Abkommen *nt*, Vertrag *m*; **to break the terms of an ~** die Vertragsbestimmungen verletzen; **to enter into an ~ (with sb)** (mit jdm) einen Vertrag eingehen *or*

(ab)schließen; **to reach (an) ~ (with sb)** (mit jdm) zu einer Einigung kommen, (mit jdm) Übereinstimmung erzielen; **there's a tacit ~ in the office that ...** im Büro besteht die stillschweigende Übereinkunft, dass ...; **we have an ~ whereby if I'm home first ...** wir haben abgemacht, dass, wenn ich zuerst nach Hause komme, ... **b** (*= sharing of opinion*) Einigkeit *f*; **unanimous ~** Einmütigkeit *f*; **by mutual ~** in gegenseitigem Einverständnis *or* Einvernehmen; **to be in ~ with sb** mit jdm einer Meinung sein; **to be in ~ with sth** mit etw übereinstimmen; **to be in ~ about sth** über etw (*acc*) einig sein; **for once we were both in ~ on that point** ausnahmsweise waren wir uns in diesem Punkt einig *or* waren wir in diesem Punkt einer Meinung; **to find oneself in ~ with sb** mit jdm übereinstimmen *or* einig gehen **c** (*= consent*) Einwilligung *f* (*to* zu), Zustimmung *f* (*to* zu) **d** (*between figures, accounts etc*) Übereinstimmung *f* **e** (*Gram*) Übereinstimmung *f*

agribusiness [ˈægrɪbɪznɪs] N die Landwirtschaft

agricultural [ægrɪˈkʌltʃərəl] ADJ *produce, production, expert, tool etc* landwirtschaftlich; **the ~ country in the north** das landwirtschaftliche Gebiet im Norden; **~ ministry** Landwirtschaftsministerium *nt*; **~ nation** Agrarstaat *m*, Agrarland *nt*; **~ reform** Agrarreform *f*; **~ worker** Landarbeiter(in) *m(f)*

agricultural college N Landwirtschaftsschule *f*

agricultural engineer N Agrartechniker(in) *m(f)*

agricultur(al)ist [ægrɪˈkʌltʃər(əl)ɪst] N Landwirtschaftsexperte *m*/-expertin *f*; (*= farmer*) Landwirt(in) *m(f)*

agriculturally [ægrɪˈkʌltʃərəlɪ] ADV landwirtschaftlich

agricultural show N Landwirtschaftsausstellung *f*

agriculture [ˈægrɪkʌltʃə'] N Landwirtschaft *f*; **Minister of Agriculture** (*Brit*) Landwirtschaftsminister(in) *m(f)*

agrochemical [ægrəʊˈkemɪkəl] (*Agr*) **ADJ** agrochemisch **N** Agrochemikalie *f*

agronomist [əˈgrɒnəmɪst] N Agronom(in) *m(f)*

agronomy [əˈgrɒnəmɪ] N Agronomie *f*

aground [əˈgraʊnd] **ADJ** *pred ship* gestrandet, aufgelaufen, auf Grund gelaufen **ADV** **to go** *or* **run** ~ auflaufen, auf Grund laufen, stranden

ague [ˈeɪgjuː] N Schüttelfrost *m no art*

ah [ɑː] INTERJ ah; (*pain*) au, autsch; (*pity*) o, ach

aha [ɑːˈhɑː] INTERJ aha

ahead [əˈhed] ADV **a** **there's some thick cloud ~** vor uns *or* da vorne ist eine große Wolke; **the mountains lay ~** vor uns/ihnen *etc* lagen die Berge; **the German runner was/drew ~** der deutsche Läufer lag vorn/zog nach vorne; **he is ~ by about two minutes** er hat etwa zwei Minuten Vorsprung; **to stare straight ~** geradeaus starren; **keep straight ~** immer geradeaus; **full speed ~** (*Naut, fig*) volle Kraft voraus; **we sent him on ~** wir schickten ihn voraus; **in the months ~** in den bevorstehenden Monaten; **I see problems ~** ich sehe Probleme auf mich/uns *etc* zukommen; **we've a busy time ~** vor uns liegt eine Menge Arbeit; **to plan ~** vorausplanen **b** **~ of sb/sth** vor jdm/etw; **walk ~ of me** geh voran; **the leader is two laps ~ of the others** der Führende hat zwei Runden Vorsprung *or* liegt zwei Runden vor den anderen; **we arrived ten minutes ~ of time** wir kamen zehn Minuten vorher an; **to be/get ~ of schedule** schneller als geplant vorankommen; **the dollar is still ~ of the euro** der Dollar führt immer noch vor dem Euro; **to be ~ of one's time** (*fig*) seiner Zeit voraus sein

ahem [əˈhəm] INTERJ hm

ahold [ə'həʊld] N (esp US) **to get ~ of sb** jdn erreichen; **to get ~ of sth** (= procure) sich (dat) etw besorgen; **don't let him get ~ of this story** lass ihn diese Geschichte bloß nicht in die Finger kriegen (inf); **to get ~ of oneself** sich zusammenreißen

ahoy [ə'hɔɪ] INTERJ (Naut) ahoi; **ship ~!** Schiff ahoi!

AI abbr of **artificial intelligence** KI f

AIC abbr of **agent in charge (of investigation)**

aid [eɪd] **N a** no pl (= help) Hilfe f; **(foreign) ~** Entwicklungshilfe f; **with the ~ of his uncle/a screwdriver** mithilfe or mit Hilfe seines Onkels/ eines Schraubenziehers; **to come** or **go to sb's ~** jdm zu Hilfe kommen; **a sale in ~ of the blind** ein Verkauf zugunsten or zu Gunsten der Blinden; **what's all this wiring in ~ of?** (inf) wozu sind all diese Drähte da or gut?; **what's all this in ~ of?** (inf) wozu soll das gut sein? **b** (= useful person, thing) Hilfe f; (= piece of equipment, audio-visual aid etc) Hilfsmittel nt; (= hearing aid) Hörgerät nt; (= teaching aid) Lehrmittel nt **c** (esp US) = **aide** **VT** unterstützen, helfen (+dat); **to ~ sb's recovery** jds Heilung fördern; **~ed by** mit Unterstützung von; **to ~ and abet sb** (Jur) jdm Beihilfe leisten; (after crime) jdn begünstigen → **aiding and abetting**

aid agency N Hilfsorganisation f

aide [eɪd] N Helfer(in) m(f); (= adviser) (persönlicher) Berater

aide-de-camp ['eɪddə'kɒŋ] N pl **aides-de-camp** **a** (Mil) Adjutant(in) m(f) **b** = **aide**

aide-memoire ['eɪdmem'wɑ:'] N Gedächtnisstütze f; (= official memorandum) Aide-memoire nt

aiding and abetting ['eɪdɪŋəndə'betɪŋ] N (Jur) Beihilfe f; (after crime) Begünstigung f; **he was accused of ~** ihm wurde Beihilfe/Begünstigung vorgeworfen

aid programme, (US) **aid program** N Hilfsprogramm nt

AIDS, Aids [eɪdz] abbr of **acquired immune deficiency syndrome** Aids nt

AIDS: AIDS patient N Aids-Patient(in) m(f); **AIDS-related** ADJ illness, death aidsbedingt; **AIDS victim** N Aids-Kranke(r) mf

aigrette ['eɪgret] N Reiherfeder f, Reiherbusch m (old)

ail [eɪl] **VT** (old) plagen; **what's ~ing** or **what ~s you?** (inf) was hast du?, was ist mit dir? **VI** (inf) kränklich sein, kränkeln

aileron ['eɪlərɒn] N (Aviat) Querruder nt

ailing ['eɪlɪŋ] ADJ (lit) kränklich, kränkelnd; (fig) industry, economy etc krankend, krank

ailment ['eɪlmənt] N Gebrechen nt, Leiden nt; **minor ~s** leichte Beschwerden pl; **inflation, a national ~** die Inflation, eine nationale Krankheit; **all his little ~s** all seine Wehwehchen

aim [eɪm] **N a** Zielen nt; **to take ~** zielen (at auf +acc); **to miss one's ~** sein Ziel verfehlen; **his ~ was bad/good** er zielte schlecht/gut **b** (= purpose) Ziel nt, Absicht f; **with the ~ of doing sth** mit dem Ziel or der Absicht, etw zu tun; **what is your ~ in life?** was ist Ihr Lebensziel?; **to achieve one's ~** sein Ziel erreichen; **what is your ~ in saying that?** warum sagen Sie das?; **what is your ~ in doing that?** was wollen Sie damit bezwecken? **VT a** (= direct) guided missile, camera richten (at auf +acc); stone etc zielen mit (at auf +acc); **he ~ed a kick/punch at my stomach** sein Tritt/ Schlag zielte auf meinen Bauch; **to teach sb how to ~ a gun** jdm zeigen, wie man zielt; **to ~ a pistol at sb/sth** eine Pistole auf jdn/etw richten, mit einer Pistole auf jdn/etw zielen; **he ~ed his pistol at my heart** er zielte auf mein Herz; **the guns were ~ed directly at the city walls** die Kanonen waren direkt auf die Stadtmauer gerichtet; **you didn't ~ the camera properly** du hast die Kamera nicht richtig gehalten **b** (fig) remark, insult, criticism richten (at gegen);

this book/programme (Brit) or **program** (US) **is ~ed at the general public** dieses Buch/Programm wendet sich an die Öffentlichkeit; **to be ~ed at sth** (cuts, measure, new law etc) auf etw (acc) abgezielt sein; **I think that was ~ed at me** ich glaube, das war auf mich gemünzt or gegen mich gerichtet **VI a** (with gun, punch etc) zielen (at, for auf +acc) **b** (= try, strive for) **to ~ high** sich (dat) hohe Ziele setzen or stecken; **isn't that ~ing a bit high?** wollen Sie nicht etwas hoch hinaus?; **to ~ at** or **for sth** etw anstreben, auf etw (acc) abzielen; **with this TV programme** (Brit) or **program** (US) **we're ~ing at a much wider audience** mit diesem Fernsehprogramm wollen wir einen größeren Teilnehmerkreis ansprechen; **we ~ to please** bei uns ist der Kunde König; **he always ~s for perfection** er strebt immer nach Perfektion; **he ~s at only spending £10 per week** er hat sich zum Ziel gesetzt, mit £ 10 pro Woche auszukommen **c** (inf, = intend) **to ~ to do sth** vorhaben, etw zu tun, etw tun wollen

aiming point N (esp Mil) Zielpunkt m

aimless ADJ, **aimlessly** ADV ['eɪmlɪs, -lɪ] ziellos; talk, act planlos

aimlessness ['eɪmlɪsnɪs] N Ziellosigkeit f; (of talk, action) Planlosigkeit f

ain't [eɪnt] (incorrect) = **am not, is not, are not, has not, have not**

air [ɛə'] **N a** Luft f; **a change of ~** eine Luftveränderung; **war in the ~** Luftkrieg m; **perfumes drifting in on the ~** vom Windhauch hereingetragene Düfte; **to go out for a breath of (fresh) ~** frische Luft schnappen (gehen); **to take the ~** (Brit old) frische Luft schöpfen; **to take to the ~** sich in die Lüfte schwingen (geh); **by ~** per or mit dem Flugzeug; **to transport sth by ~** etw auf dem Luftweg transportieren; **to go by ~** (person) fliegen, mit dem Flugzeug reisen; (goods) per Flugzeug or auf dem Luftwege transportiert werden **b** (fig phrases) **there's something in the ~** es liegt etwas in der Luft; **it's still all up in the ~** (inf) es hängt noch alles in der Luft, es ist noch alles offen; **all her plans were up in the ~** (inf) all ihre Pläne hingen in der Luft; **to give sb the ~** (US, inf) jdn abblitzen or abfahren lassen (inf); **to clear the ~** die Atmosphäre reinigen; **to be walking** or **floating on ~** wie auf Wolken gehen; **to pull** or **pluck sth out of the ~** (fig) etw auf gut Glück nennen → **castle N a, thin ADJ d** **c** (Rad, TV) **to be on the ~** (programme) gesendet werden; (station) senden; **you're on the ~** Sie sind auf Sendung; **he's on the ~ every day** er ist jeden Tag im Radio zu hören; **the programme goes** or **is put on the ~ every week** das Programm wird jede Woche gesendet; **we come on the ~ at 6 o'clock** unsere Sendezeit beginnt um 6 Uhr; **to go off the ~** (broadcaster) die Sendung beenden; (station) das Programm beenden **d** (= demeanour, manner) Auftreten nt; (= facial expression) Miene f; (of building, town etc) Atmosphäre f; **with an ~ of bewilderment** mit bestürzter Miene; **an unpleasant ~ of self-satisfaction** ein unangenehm selbstzufriedenes Gehabe; **there was** or **she had an ~ of mystery about her** sie hatte etwas Geheimnisvolles an sich; **it gives** or **lends her an ~ of affluence** das gibt ihr einen wohlhabenden Anstrich; **she has a certain ~ about her** sie hat so etwas an sich **c** **airs** PL Getue nt, Gehabe nt; **to put on ~s**, **to give oneself ~s** sich zieren, vornehm tun; **~s and graces** Allüren pl; **to put on ~s and graces** den Vornehmen/die Vornehme herauskehren **f** (Mus) Weise f (old); (= tune) Melodie f **g** (liter, Naut: = breeze) leichte Brise, Lüftchen nt (liter) **VT a** clothes, bed, room (aus)lüften **b** anger, grievance Luft machen (+dat); opinion darlegen **c** (esp US Rad, TV) story, series senden **VI** (clothes etc) (after washing) nachtrocknen; (af-

ter storage) (aus)lüften; **to put clothes out to ~** Kleidung f zum Lüften raushängen

air in cpds Luft-; **air ambulance** N (= aeroplane) Rettungsflugzeug nt; (= helicopter) Rettungshubschrauber m; **air bag** N Airbag m; **air base** N Luftwaffenstützpunkt m; **air bed** N (Brit) Luftmatratze f; **airborne** ADJ (= flying) aircraft sich in der Luft befindend attr; **to be ~** sich in der Luft befinden; **~ freight** Luftfracht f **b** (Mil) **~ troops** Luftlandetruppen pl; **~ missile** Rakete f **c** (= floating) bacteria, virus in der Luft befindlich; **air brake** N (on truck) Druckluftbremse f; (Aviat) Brems- or Landeklappe f; **airbrick** N Entlüftungsziegel m; **air bridge** N Luftbrücke f; **airbrush** (Art) **N** Spritzpistole f, Airbrush f **VT** mit der Spritzpistole bearbeiten; **air bubble** N Luftblase f; **Airbus®** N Airbus m; **air cargo** N Luftfracht f; **Air Chief Marshal** N (Brit) General m; **air commodore** N (Brit) Brigadegeneral m; **air-conditioned** ADJ klimatisiert; **air conditioning** N (= process) Klimatisierung f; (= system) Klimaanlage f; **air-conditioning plant** N Klimaanlage f; **air-cooled** ADJ engine luftgekühlt; **air corridor** N Luftkorridor m; **air cover** N Luftunterstützung f; **aircraft** N pl **aircraft** Flugzeug nt, Maschine f; **various types of ~** verschiedene Luftfahrzeuge pl; **aircraft carrier** N Flugzeugträger m; **aircraft industry** N Flugzeugindustrie f; **aircraft(s)man** N Gefreite(r) m; **aircrew** N Flugpersonal nt; **air current** N Luftströmung f; **air cushion** N Luftkissen nt; **air display** N Flugschau f; **airdrome** N (US) Flugplatz m, Aerodrom nt (old); **airdrop** N Fallschirmabwurf m **VT** mit Fallschirmen abwerfen; **air-dry** VT lufttrocknen; **air duct** N Luftkanal m

Airedale ['ɛədeɪl] N Airedaleterrier m

airer ['ɛərə'] N Trockenständer m

air: airfare N Flugpreis m; **airfield** N Flugplatz m; **airflow** N Luftstrom m; (in air conditioning) Luftzufuhr f; **airfoil** N (US) Tragflügel m; (on racing cars) Spoiler m; **air force** N Luftwaffe f; **Air Force One** N Air Force One f, Dienstflugzeug des US-Präsidenten; **air force pilot** N Luftwaffenpilot(in) m(f); **airframe** N (Aviat) Flugwerk nt, Zelle f; **air freight** N Luftfracht f; (= charge) Luftfrachtgebühr f; **to send sth by ~** etw als Luftfracht verschicken; **air-freight** VT per Luftfracht senden; **air gun** N Luftgewehr nt; **airhead** N (inf pej) Hohlkopf m (inf pej); **air hole** N Luftloch nt; **air hostess** N Stewardess f

airily ['ɛərɪlɪ] ADV (= casually) say, reply etc leichthin, lässig; (= vaguely) vage; (= flippantly) blasiert, erhaben

airiness ['ɛərɪnɪs] N **a** **she liked the ~ of the rooms** ihr gefiel, dass die Zimmer so luftig waren **b** (= casualness: of manner, gesture) Lässigkeit f, Nonchalance f **c** (= vagueness) (of promise) Vagheit f; (of theory) Versponnenheit f **d** (= flippancy) Blasiertheit f, Erhabenheit f

airing ['ɛərɪŋ] N (of linen, room etc) (Aus- or Durch)lüften nt; **to give sth a good ~** etw gut durch- or auslüften lassen; **to give an idea an ~** (fig inf) eine Idee darlegen

airing cupboard N (Brit) (Wäsche)trockenschrank m

air: air-intake N Luftzufuhr f; (for engine) Luftansaugstutzen m; (= quantity) Luftmenge f; **air-lane** N Flugroute f; **airless** ADJ (lit) space luftleer; (= stuffy) room stickig; (= with no wind) day windstill; **air letter** N Luftpostbrief m, Aerogramm nt; **airlift** **N** Luftbrücke f **VT** **to ~ sth into a place** etw über eine Luftbrücke herein-/ hineinbringen; **airline** N **a** Fluggesellschaft f, Luftverkehrsgesellschaft f, Fluglinie f **b** (= diver's tube) Luftschlauch m; **airliner** N Verkehrsflugzeug nt; **airlock** N (in spacecraft etc) Luftschleuse f; (in pipe) Luftsack m

airmail ['ɛəmeɪl] N Luftpost f; **to send sth (by) ~** etw per or mit Luftpost schicken **VT** mit or per Luftpost schicken

airmail: airmail edition N (of newspaper) Luftpostausgabe f; **airmail letter** N Luftpostbrief *m*; **airmail stamp**, **airmail sticker** N Luftpostaufkleber *m*

air: airman N (= *flier*) Flieger *m*; (*US*: *in air force*) Gefreite(r) *m*; **air marshal** N (*Brit*) Generalleutnant *m*; **air mass** N Luftmasse *f*; **air mattress** N Luftmatratze *f*; **air mile** N Flugmeile *f*, ≈ Flugkilometer *m*; **Air Miles** Flugmeilen *pl*; **to collect Air Miles** Flugmeilen sammeln; **air miss** N (*Aviat*) Beinahezusammenstoß *m*; **air passenger** N Fluggast *m*; **airplane** N (*US*) Flugzeug *nt*; **airplay** N (*Rad*) Sendezeit *f*; **the song received extensive ~** das Lied wurde sehr oft im Radio gespielt; **air pocket** N Luftloch *nt*

airport ['ɛəpɔːt] N Flughafen *m*

airport: airport bus N Flughafenbus *m*; **airport tax** N Flughafengebühr *f*

air: air pressure N Luftdruck *m*; **airproof** ['ɛəpruːf] ADJ (= *airtight*) luftdicht; (= *unaffected by air*) luftbeständig; **air pump** N Luftpumpe *f*; **air rage** N aggressives Verhalten von Flugpassagieren, Flugkoller *m* (*inf*)

air raid N Luftangriff *m*

air-raid: air-raid shelter N Luftschutzkeller *m*; **air-raid warden** N Luftschutzwart *m*; **air-raid warning** N Fliegeralarm *m*

air: air rescue service N Luftrettungsdienst *m*; **air rifle** N Luftgewehr *nt*; **air route** N Flugroute *f*; **airscrew** N Luftschraube *f*; **air-sea rescue** N Rettung *f* durch Seenotflugzeuge; **air-sea rescue service** N Seenotrettungsdienst *m*; **air shaft** N (*Min*) Wetterschacht *m*; **airship** N Luftschiff *nt*; **airshow** N Luftfahrtausstellung *f* (*inf*) luftkrank; **airsickness** N Luftkrankheit *f*; **airside** ['ɛəsaɪd] N *Teil des Flughafens nach der Passkontrolle* ADV **to be located ~** (*restaurant, shop*) sich nach or hinter der Passkontrolle befinden ADJ **~ restaurant** Restaurant nach or hinter der Passkontrolle; **air sleeve**, **air sock** N Windsack *m*; **airspace** N Luftraum *m*; **airspeed** N Eigen- or Fluggeschwindigkeit *f*; **airstream** N (*of vehicle*) Luftsog *m*; (*Met*) Luftstrom *m*; **airstrike** N = **air raid**; **airstrip** N Start- und Lande-Bahn *f*; **air supply** N Luftüberlegenheit *f*; **air supremacy** N Luftüberlegenheit *f*; **air terminal** N (*Air*) Terminal *m* or *nt*; **air ticket** N Flugticket *nt*; **airtight** ADJ (*lit*) luftdicht; (*fig*) argument, case hieb- und stichfest; **airtime** N (*Rad, TV*) Sendezeit *f*; **air-to-air** ADJ (*Mil*) Luft-Luft-; **air-to-ground** ADJ (*Mil*) Luft-Boden-; **air-to-sea** ADJ (*Mil*) Luft-See-; **air-to-surface** ADJ (*Mil*) Luft-Boden-; **air traffic** N Flugverkehr *m*, Luftverkehr *m*; **air-traffic control** N Flugleitung *f*; **air-traffic controller** N Fluglotse *m*, Fluglotsin *f*; **air vent** N Ventilator *m*; (*shaft*) Belüftungsschacht *m*; **Air Vice Marshal** N (*Brit*) Generalmajor *m*; **airwaves** PL Radiowellen *pl*; **airway** N **a** (= *route*) Flugroute *f*; (= *airline company*) Fluggesellschaft *f*, Luftverkehrsgesellschaft *f* **b** (*Med*) Atemwege *pl*; **air waybill** N Luftfrachtbrief *m*; **airwoman** N Fliegerin *f*; **airworthiness** N Flugtüchtigkeit *f*; **airworthy** ADJ flugtüchtig

airy ['ɛərɪ] ADJ (+er) **a** room luftig; **to have an ~ feel (to it)** luftig wirken **b** (= *casual*) manner, gesture lässig, nonchalant; (= *vague*) promise vage; theory versponnen; (= *superior, flippant*) blasiert, erhaben **c** (*liter*: = *immaterial*) phantom körperlos

airy-fairy ['ɛərɪ'fɛərɪ] ADJ (*Brit inf*) versponnen; excuse windig; talk versponnen, larifari *inv* (*inf*); **your plans seem rather ~** deine Pläne scheinen ziemlich unausgegoren

aisle [aɪl] N Gang *m*; (*in church*) Seitenschiff *nt*; (*central aisle*) Mittelgang *m*; **~ seat** Sitz *m* am Gang; **to walk down the ~** vor den Altar treten; **to walk down the ~ with sb** jdn zum Altar führen; **he had them rolling in the ~s** (*inf*) er brachte sie so weit, dass sie sich vor Lachen kugelten (*inf*) or wälzten (*inf*)

aitch [eɪtʃ] N h *nt*, H *nt*; **to drop one's ~es** den Buchstaben „h" nicht aussprechen (= *be lower class*) ≈ „mir" und „mich" verwechseln

ajar [ə'dʒɑː] ADJ, ADV angelehnt

---

aka *abbr of* **also known as** alias, anderweitig bekannt als

akela [ɑː'keɪlə] N Wölflingsführer *m*

akimbo [ə'kɪmbəʊ] ADV **with arms ~** die Arme in die Hüften gestemmt

akin [ə'kɪn] ADJ pred ähnlich (*to* +*dat*), verwandt (*to* mit)

à la ['ɑːlɑː] PREP à la

alabaster ['æləbɑːstə] **N** Alabaster *m* ADJ (*lit*) alabastern, Alabaster-; (*fig liter*) Alabaster-, wie Alabaster; **~ skin** Alabasterhaut *f*

à la carte [ɑːlɑː'kɑːt] ADV eat à la carte, nach der (Speise)karte ADJ menu à la carte

alack [ə'læk] INTERJ (*obs*) wehe; **~ a day** wehe dem Tag

alacrity [ə'lækrɪtɪ] N (= *willingness*) Bereitwilligkeit *f*; (= *eagerness*) Eifer *m*, Eilfertigkeit *f*; **to accept with ~** ohne zu zögern annehmen

Aladdin [ə'lædɪn] N Aladin; **~'s cave** (*fig*, = *hoard*) Schatzhöhle *f*; **the shop was an ~'s cave of antiques** das Geschäft war eine Fundgrube für Antiquitäten; **~'s lamp** (*lit, fig*) Aladins Wunderlampe *f*

à la mode [ɑːlɑː'məʊd] ADJ (*US*) mit Eis

alarm [ə'lɑːm] **N** **a** no pl (= *fear*) Sorge *f*, Besorgnis *f*, Beunruhigung *f*; **to be in a state of ~** (= *worried*) besorgt or beunruhigt sein; (= *frightened*) erschreckt sein; **to cause a good deal of ~** große Unruhe auslösen; **to cause sb ~** jdn beunruhigen
b (= *warning*) Alarm *m*; **to raise** or **give** or **sound the ~** Alarm geben or (*fig*) schlagen
c (= *device*) Alarmanlage *f*; **~ (clock)** Wecker *m*; **car/house ~** Auto-/Hausalarmanlage *f*
VT **a** (= *worry*) beunruhigen; (= *frighten*) erschrecken; **don't be ~ed** erschrecken Sie nicht; **the news ~ed the whole country** die Nachricht alarmierte das ganze Land or versetzte das ganze Land in Aufregung
b (= *warn of danger*) warnen; fire brigade etc alarmieren

alarm *in cpds* Alarm-; **alarm bell** N Alarmglocke *f*; **to set ~s ringing** (*fig*) die Alarmglocken klingeln or läuten lassen; **alarm call** N (*Telec*) Weckruf *m*; **alarm call service** N Weckdienst *m*; **alarm clock** N Wecker *m*

alarming [ə'lɑːmɪŋ] ADJ (= *worrying*) beunruhigend; (= *frightening*) erschreckend; news alarmierend

alarmingly [ə'lɑːmɪŋlɪ] ADV erschreckend

alarmist [ə'lɑːmɪst] **N** Panikmacher(in) *m(f)*, Kassandra *f* (*geh*) ADJ speech Unheil prophezeiend attr; politician Panik machend attr

alarum [ə'lærəm] N (*old*) = **alarm**

alas [ə'læs] INTERJ (*old*) leider; **~, he didn't come** leider kam er nicht

Alaska [ə'læskə] N Alaska *nt*

Alaskan [ə'læskən] **N** Einwohner(in) *m(f)* von Alaska ADJ Alaska-; customs, winter in Alaska; fish, produce aus Alaska

alb [ælb] N (*Eccl*) Alba *f*

Albania [æl'beɪnɪə] N Albanien *nt*

Albanian [æl'beɪnɪən] ADJ albanisch **N** **a** Albaner(in) *m(f)* **b** (= *language*) Albanisch *nt*

albatross ['ælbətrɒs] N Albatros *m*; **to be an ~ around sb's neck** ein Mühlstein *m* um jds Hals sein

albeit [ɔːl'biːɪt] CONJ (*esp liter*) obgleich, wenn auch

albinism ['ælbɪnɪzəm] N Albinismus *m*

albino [æl'biːnəʊ] **N** Albino *m* ADJ Albino-; **~ rabbit** Albinokaninchen *nt*

Albion ['ælbɪən] N (*poet*) Albion *nt*

album ['ælbəm] N Album *nt*

album cover N Plattenhülle *f*, Cover *nt*

albumen ['ælbjʊmɪn] N Albumin *nt*

albuminous [æl'bjuːmɪnəs] ADJ albuminös

alchemical [æl'kemɪkəl] ADJ alchimistisch

alchemist ['ælkɪmɪst] N Alchemist(in) *m(f)*

alchemy ['ælkɪmɪ] N Alchemie *f*, Alchimie *f*

---

alcohol ['ælkəhɒl] N Alkohol *m*; **~ by volume** Alkoholgehalt *m*

alcohol-free ['ælkəhɒl'friː] ADJ alkoholfrei

alcoholic [ælkə'hɒlɪk] ADJ drink alkoholisch; person alkoholsüchtig, trunksüchtig **N** (*person*) Alkoholiker(in) *m(f)*, Trinker(in) *m(f)*; **to be an ~** Alkoholiker(in) or Trinker(in) sein; **Alcoholics Anonymous** Anonyme Alkoholiker *pl*

alcoholism ['ælkəhɒlɪzəm] N Alkoholismus *m*, Trunksucht *f*

alcopop ['ælkəpɒp] N alkoholisches kohlensäurehaltiges Getränk

alcove ['ælkəʊv] N Alkoven *m*, Nische *f*; (*in wall*) Nische *f*

aldehyde ['ældɪhaɪd] N Aldehyd *m*

al dente [æl'denteɪ, -tɪ] ADJ, ADV spaghetti al dente; rice körnig

alder ['ɔːldə] N Erle *f*

alder fly N Schlammfliege *f*

alderman ['ɔːldəmən] N pl **-men** [-mən] Alderman *m* (*Ratsherr*)

ale [eɪl] N (*old*) Ale *nt* → **real ale**

aleatory ['ælɪətərɪ] ADJ (*Jur*) aleatorisch, vom Zufall abhängig; **~ contract** aleatorischer Vertrag, Spekulationsvertrag *m*

aleck ['ælɪk] N → **smart aleck**

alehouse ['eɪlhaʊs] N (*old*) Wirtshaus *nt*, Schenke *f*, Schänke *f*

alert [ə'lɜːt] ADJ aufmerksam; (*as character trait*) aufgeweckt; mind scharf, hell; dog wachsam; **to be ~ to sth** vor etw (*dat*) auf der Hut sein **VT** warnen (*to* vor +*dat*); troops in Gefechtsbereitschaft versetzen; fire brigade etc alarmieren **N** Alarm *m*; **to give the ~** (*Mil*) Gefechtsbereitschaft befehlen; (*in the fire brigade etc*) den Alarm auslösen; (*fig*) warnen; **to put sb on the ~** jdn in Alarmbereitschaft versetzen; (*Mil*) jdn in Gefechtsbereitschaft versetzen; **to be on (the) ~** einsatzbereit sein; (= *be on lookout*) auf der Hut sein (*for* vor +*dat*)

alertly [ə'lɜːtlɪ] ADV aufmerksam

alertness [ə'lɜːtnɪs] N Aufmerksamkeit *f*; (*as character trait*) Aufgewecktheit *f*; (*of mind*) Schärfe *f*; (*of dog*) Wachsamkeit *f*

Aleutian Islands [ə'luːʃən'aɪləndz] PL Aleuten *pl*

A level ['eɪlevl] N (*Brit*) Abschluss *m* der Sekundarstufe 2; **to take one's ~s** ≈ das Abitur machen; **3 ~s** ≈ das Abitur in 3 Fächern

---

A LEVELS

A **levels** sind dem Abitur vergleichbare Hochschulqualifikationen. Zur Beendigung der höheren Schulbildung wählen Schülerinnen und Schüler in England, Wales und Nordirland zwei oder drei Fächer. Die Kurse schließen häufig an GCSE-Kurse der gleichen Fachbereiche an und dauern normalerweise zwei Jahre, die Abschlussprüfungen werden im Alter von 18 Jahren abgelegt. Zu den Universitäten werden Studenten im Allgemeinen nur dann zugelassen, wenn sie von den Universitäten festgelegte Notendurchschnitte in den **A levels** vorweisen können.
Das entsprechende schottische Pendant ist der **Higher Grade**, der auch oft einfach nur **Higher** genannt wird. Schüler belegen dafür bis zu fünf Fächer und nehmen nach einem Jahr an der Abschlussprüfung teil. → GCSE

Alexander [ælɪg'zɑːndə] N Alexander *m*; **~ the Great** Alexander der Große

alexandrine [ælɪg'zændraɪn] **N** Alexandriner *m* ADJ alexandrinisch

ALF N (*Brit*) abbr of **Animal Liberation Front** militante Tierschützerorganisation

alfalfa [æl'fælfə] N Luzerne *f*, Alfalfa *f*

alfresco [æl'freskəʊ] ADJ im Freien; **an ~ lunch** ein Mittagessen im Freien ADV im Freien

algae ['ælgiː] PL Algen *pl*

algal ['ælgəl] ADJ Algen-; **~ bloom** Algenblüte *f*

algebra ['ældʒɪbrə] N Algebra f
algebraic [ældʒɪ'breɪk] ADJ algebraisch
Algeria [æl'dʒɪərɪə] N Algerien nt
Algerian [æl'dʒɪərɪən] N Algerier(in) m(f) ADJ algerisch
Algiers [æl'dʒɪəz] N Algier nt
algorithm ['ælgərɪðəm] N Algorithmus m
algorithmic [ælgə'rɪθmɪk] ADJ algorithmisch
alias ['eɪlɪæs] ADV alias N Deckname m
alibi ['ælɪbaɪ] N Alibi nt VT ein Alibi liefern für
Alice band ['ælɪsˌbænd] N Haarreif m
alien ['eɪlɪən] N (esp Pol) Ausländer(in) m(f); (Sci-Fi) außerirdisches Wesen ADJ **a** (= foreign) ausländisch; (Sci-Fi) außerirdisch **b** (= different) fremd; **to be ~ to sb/sb's nature/sth** jdm/jds Wesen/einer Sache fremd sein **c** (Comput) fremd
alienable ['eɪlɪənəbl] ADJ (Jur) veräußerlich; landed property übertragbar
alienate ['eɪlɪəneɪt] VT **a** people befremden; affections zerstören, sich (dat) verscherzen; public opinion gegen sich aufbringen; **to ~ oneself from sb/sth** sich jdm/einer Sache entfremden; **Brecht set out to ~ his audience** Brecht wollte, dass sich die Zuschauer distanzieren **b** (Jur) property, money übertragen
alienation [eɪlɪə'neɪʃən] N **a** Entfremdung f (from von); (Theat) Distanzierung f; **~ effect** Verfremdungseffekt m; **~ of affections** (Jur) Entfremdung f **b** (Jur, of property) Übertragung f **c** (Psych) Alienation f
alight¹ [ə'laɪt] (form) VI **a** (person) aussteigen (from aus); (from horse) absitzen (from von) **b** (bird) sich niederlassen (on auf +dat); (aircraft etc) niedergehen (on auf +dat); **his eyes ~ed on the ring** sein Blick fiel auf den Ring **c to ~ on a fact/an idea** etc auf ein Faktum/eine Idee etc stoßen
alight² [ə'laɪt] ADJ pred **to be ~** (fire) brennen; (building also) in Flammen stehen; **to keep the fire ~** das Feuer in Gang halten; **to set sth ~** etw in Brand setzen or stecken; **her face was ~ with pleasure** ihr Gesicht or sie glühte vor Freude
align [ə'laɪn] VT **a** wheels of car, gun sights etc ausrichten; (= bring into line) in eine Linie bringen, ausrichten **b** (Fin, Pol) currencies, policies aufeinander ausrichten; **to ~ sth with sth** etw auf etw (acc) ausrichten; **to ~ oneself with a party** (= follow policy of) sich nach einer Partei ausrichten; (= join forces with) sich einer Partei anschließen; **they have ~ed themselves against him/it** sie haben sich gegen ihn/dagegen zusammengeschlossen VI **a** (lit) ausgerichtet sein (with nach); (= come into line) eine Linie bilden **b** (side, person, country) sich verbünden (with mit)
alignment [ə'laɪnmənt] N **a** (of car wheels, gun sights etc) Ausrichtung f; **to be out of ~** nicht richtig ausgerichtet sein (with nach) **b** (of currencies, policies etc) Ausrichtung f (with auf +acc), Orientierung f (with nach); **to be out of ~ with one another** nicht übereinstimmen, sich nicht aneinander orientieren; **to bring sb back into ~ with the party** jdn zurückschwenken, wieder auf die Parteilinie einzuschwenken; **his unexpected ~ with the Socialists** seine unerwartete Parteinahme für die Sozialisten; **he argued for a new ~ of the governing parties** er war für eine Neuordnung der Regierungsparteien; **the new ~ of world powers** die Neugruppierung der Weltmächte
alike [ə'laɪk] ⚙ 5.4 ADJ PRED, ADV gleich; **they're/they look very ~** sie sind/sehen sich (dat) sehr ähnlich; **they all look ~ to me** für mich sehen sie alle gleich aus; **you men are all ~!** ihr Männer seid doch alle gleich!; **it's all ~ to me** mir ist das gleich or einerlei; **they always think ~** sie sind immer einer Meinung; **winter and summer ~** Sommer wie Winter
alimentary [ælɪ'mentərɪ] ADJ (Anat) Verdauungs-; **~ canal** Verdauungskanal m
alimony ['ælɪmənɪ] N Unterhaltszahlung f; **to pay ~** Unterhalt zahlen
A list N Hautevolee f, Crème de la Crème f

aliterate [eɪ'lɪtərət] ADJ **to be ~** so gut wie nie lesen N Person, die so gut wie nie liest
alive [ə'laɪv] **a** pred (= living) lebendig, lebend attr; **dead or ~** tot oder lebendig; **to be ~** leben; **the greatest musician ~** der größte lebende Musiker; **the wickedest man ~** der schlechteste Mensch auf der ganzen Welt; **while ~ he was always ...** zu seinen Lebzeiten war er immer ...; **it's good to be ~** das Leben ist schön; **no man ~** niemand auf der ganzen Welt; **to stay** or **keep ~** am Leben bleiben; **to keep sb/sth ~** (lit, fig) jdn/etw am Leben erhalten; **to do sth as well as anyone ~** etw so gut wie jeder andere können; **to be ~ and kicking** (hum inf) gesund und munter sein; **he's been found ~ and well** er ist gesund und munter aufgefunden worden; **he's very much ~** er ist ausgesprochen lebendig; **to eat sb ~** (fig inf) jdn in der Luft zerreißen; (Press) über jdn herfallen; **we were eaten ~ by mosquitos** (inf) wir wurden von Moskitos halb tot gestochen (inf)
b (= lively) lebhaft; **to keep one's mind ~** geistig rege bleiben; **to come ~** (= liven up) lebendig werden; (= prick up ears etc) wach werden; **to bring sth ~** (story, character) etw lebendig werden lassen
c pred (= aware) **to be ~ to sth** sich (dat) einer Sache (gen) bewusst sein; **to be ~ to certain possibilities/sb's interests** gewisse Möglichkeiten/jds Interessen im Auge haben
d **~ with** (= full of) erfüllt von; **to be ~ with tourists/fish/insects** etc von Touristen/Fischen/Insekten etc wimmeln
alkali ['ælkəlaɪ] N pl **-(e)s** Base f, Lauge f; (metal, Agr) Alkali nt
alkaline ['ælkəlaɪn] ADJ basisch, alkalisch; **~ solution** Lauge f
alkalinity [ælkə'lɪnɪtɪ] N Alkalität f
alkaloid ['ælkəlɔɪd] N Alkaloid nt
alkie, (US) **alky** ['ælkɪ] N (inf) Alkie m (sl), Säufer(in) m(f) (inf)

---

all [ɔːl]
⚙ 26.1

1 ADJECTIVE	4 NOUN
2 PRONOUN	5 SET STRUCTURES
3 ADVERB	

1 – ADJECTIVE

a with nouns (plural) alle; (singular) ganze(r, s), alle(r, s)

> When **alle** is used to translate **all the** it is not followed by the German article.

we have considered all the possibilities wir haben alle Möglichkeiten in Betracht gezogen; **she brought all the children** sie brachte alle Kinder mit; **all the problems have been solved** alle or sämtliche Probleme wurden gelöst; **all kinds** or **sorts of people** alle möglichen Leute; **all the tobacco** der ganze Tabak, aller Tabak; **all the milk** die ganze Milch, alle Milch; **all the fruit** das ganze Obst, alles Obst; **all you boys can come with me** ihr Jungen könnt alle mit mir kommen; **the money was all there** alles Geld or das ganze Geld war da; **where's all that water coming from?** wo kommt das ganze or all das Wasser her?; **all the time** die ganze Zeit; **all day (long)** den ganzen Tag (lang); **all Spain** ganz Spanien; **to dislike all sport** jeglichen Sport ablehnen; **in all respects** in jeder Hinsicht
♦ + possessive **all my strength** meine ganze Kraft; **all my books/friends** alle meine Bücher/Freunde, meine ganzen Bücher/Freunde; **all my life** mein ganzes Leben (lang)
♦ pronoun + **all they all came** sie sind alle gekommen; **we all sat down** wir setzten uns alle; **I invited them all** ich habe sie alle eingeladen

> Note that **it all** is usually translated by **alles** alone:

he took/spent it all er hat alles genommen/ausgegeben; **it all happened so quickly** alles geschah so schnell, es geschah alles so schnell; **he's seen/done it all** für ihn gibt es

nichts Neues mehr, ihn kann nichts mehr erschüttern (inf)
♦ **all this/that I don't understand all that** ich verstehe das alles nicht; **what's all this/that about?** was soll das Ganze?; **what's all this/that?** was ist denn das?; (annoyed) was soll denn das!; **what's all this I hear about you leaving?** was höre ich da! Sie wollen gehen?
♦ **all possible/due with all possible speed** so schnell wie möglich; **with all due care** mit angemessener Sorgfalt; **with all due speed** in angemessenem Tempo; **they will take all possible precautions** sie werden alle möglichen Sicherheitsvorkehrungen treffen

2 – PRONOUN

a = everything alles; **all is well** alles ist gut; **I'm just curious, that's all** ich bin nur neugierig, das ist alles; **that's all that matters** darauf allein kommt es an; **that's all he said** das ist alles, was er gesagt hat, mehr hat er nicht gesagt; **that is all (that) I can tell you** mehr kann ich Ihnen nicht sagen; **it was all I could do not to laugh** ich musste an mich halten, um nicht zu lachen
♦ **all of all of Paris/of the house** ganz Paris/das ganze Haus; **all of it** alles; **I don't need all of it** ich brauche nicht alles; **all of 5 kms/£5** ganze 5 km/£ 5; **it took him all of three hours** er brauchte ganze drei Stunden
♦ **all or nothing** alles oder nichts
♦ **what all** (dial inf) **and I don't know what all** und was weiß ich noch alles
b = everybody alle pl; **all who knew him** alle, die ihn kannten; **all of them** (sie) alle; **the score was two all** es stand zwei zu zwei

3 – ADVERB

(= quite, entirely) ganz; **dressed all in white**, **all dressed in white** ganz in Weiß (gekleidet); **all woman** ganz Frau; **all dirty/excited** etc ganz schmutzig/aufgeregt etc; **that's all very fine** or **well** das ist alles ganz schön und gut; **all wool** reine Wolle; **an all wool carpet** ein reinwollener or rein wollener Teppich, ein Teppich aus reiner Wolle
♦ **all** + adverb/preposition **it was red all over** es war ganz rot; **all down the front of her dress** überall vorn auf ihrem Kleid; **all along the road** die ganze Straße entlang; **there were chairs all around the room** rundum im Zimmer standen Stühle; **he ordered whiskies/drinks all round** er hat für alle Whisky/Getränke bestellt; **what's the film all about?** wovon handelt der Film überhaupt?; **I'll tell you all about it** ich erzähl dir alles; **it was all about a little girl** es handelte von einem kleinen Mädchen

4 – NOUN

♦ **one's all** alles; **he staked his all on this race/deal** er setzte alles auf dieses Rennen/Unternehmen; **the horses were giving their all** die Pferde gaben ihr Letztes

5 – SET STRUCTURES

♦ **all along** (= from the start) von Anfang an, die ganze Zeit (über); **I feared that all along** das habe ich von Anfang an befürchtet, das habe ich schon die ganze Zeit (über) befürchtet
♦ **all but** fast; **he all but died** er wäre fast gestorben; **he all but lost it** er hätte es fast verloren; **the party won all but six of the seats** die Partei hat alle außer sechs Sitzen or alle bis auf sechs Sitze gewonnen
♦ **all for** (= in favour of) **I'm all for it!** ich bin ganz dafür
♦ **all found** insgesamt, alles in allem
♦ **all in** (inf: = exhausted) **to be** or **feel all in** total erledigt sein (inf)
♦ **all in all** alles in allem
♦ **all one** (= indifferent) **it's all one to me** das ist mir (ganz) egal or einerlei
♦ **all the** + comparative **all the hotter/prettier/happier** etc noch heißer/hübscher/glücklicher etc; **all the funnier because** ... umso lustiger, weil ...; **I feel all the better for my holiday** (esp Brit) or **vacation** (US) jetzt, wo ich Urlaub ge-

macht habe, gehts mir viel besser; **all the more so since ...** besonders weil ...; **all the better to see you with** damit ich dich besser sehen kann

♦ **all the same** trotzdem, trotz allem; **all the same, it's a pity** trotzdem ist es schade; **it's all the same to me** das ist mir (ganz) egal or einerlei; **if it's all the same to you** wenn es Ihnen egal ist

♦ **all there/not all there** (*inf: person*) **he's all there/not all there** er ist voll da/nicht ganz da (*inf*)

♦ **all too** + *adjective/adverb* viel zu, allzu; **all too soon/quickly** viel zu or allzu früh/schnell

♦ **... and all he ate the orange, peel and all** er hat die ganze Orange gegessen, samt der Schale; **the whole family came, children and all** die Familie kam mit Kind und Kegel; **what with the snow and all** (*inf*) mit dem ganzen Schnee und so (*inf*)

♦ **at all** (= *whatsoever*) überhaupt; **nothing at all** überhaupt or gar nichts; **did/didn't you say anything at all?** haben Sie überhaupt etwas gesagt/gar or überhaupt nichts gesagt?; (= *in the least*) **I'm not at all sure, I'm not sure at all** ich bin mir ganz und gar nicht sicher, ich bin gar nicht ganz sicher; **I'm not at all angry** *etc*, **I'm not angry** *etc* **at all** ich bin überhaupt nicht wütend *etc*, ich bin ganz und gar nicht wütend *etc*; **it's not bad at all** das ist gar nicht schlecht; **I don't know at all** ich weiß es überhaupt nicht; **if at all possible** wenn irgend möglich

♦ **for all** (= *despite*) trotz; **for all his wealth** trotz (all) seines Reichtums; **for all that** trotz allem, trotzdem

♦ **for all I know for all I know she could be ill** was weiß ich, vielleicht ist sie krank; **is he in Paris? – for all I know he could be** ist er in Paris? – schon möglich, was weiß ich!

♦ **in all** insgesamt; **ten people in all** insgesamt zehn Personen

♦ **all that** (*US inf*) einfach super (*inf*)

♦ **not all that it's not all that bad, it's not as bad as all that** so schlimm ist es nun auch wieder nicht; **it isn't all THAT expensive!** so teuer ist es nun wieder auch nicht

♦ **of all ...! of all the idiots!** so ein Idiot!; **of all the stupid things to do!** so was Dummes!; **why me of all people?** warum ausgerechnet ich?

♦ *superlative* + **of all of all happiest/earliest/clearest** *etc* **of all** am glücklichsten/frühsten/klarsten *etc*; **that would be best of all** das wäre am besten; **I like him best of all** von allen mag ich ihn am liebsten; **most of all** am meisten; **most of all I'd like to be ...** am liebsten wäre ich ...; **the best car of all** das allerbeste Auto

♦ **to be all things to all men** (*person*) sich mit jedem gut stellen; (*thing, invention, new software etc*) das Ideale sein; **a party which claims to be all things to all men** eine Partei, die behauptet, allen etwas zu bieten

♦ **you all** (*US inf*) ihr (alle); (*to two people*) ihr (beide)

Allah [ˈælə] N Allah *m*

all: all-American ADJ *team, player* uramerikanisch; **an ~ boy** ein durch und durch amerikanischer Junge; **all-around** ADJ (*US*) = **all-round**

ALL-AMERICAN

Der Begriff **all-American** wird für Sportlerinnen und Sportler aus College- und Universitätsmannschaften verwendet, die wegen ihrer herausragenden Fähigkeiten und Talente in ihrem Sportbereich in eine Ehrennationalmannschaft berufen wurden. Dabei treten die ausgewählten Spieler nicht als Team an – es ist eine reiner Ehrentitel. Das Football-Team umfasst die bekanntesten Sportler Amerikas, über die auch in den Medien am meisten berichtet wird.
Der Begriff wird außerdem für Menschen verwendet, die die amerikanischen Ansichten und die Ideale der Mittelklasse vortrefflich repräsentieren.

---

allay [əˈleɪ] VT verringern; *doubt, fears, suspicion* (weitgehend) zerstreuen

all: all clear N Entwarnung *f*; **to give/sound the ~** Entwarnung geben, entwarnen; **all-conquering** ADJ *hero, team* alle besiegend; **all-consuming** ADJ *passion, interest* überwältigend; **all-day** ADJ ganztägig; **it was an ~ meeting** die Sitzung dauerte den ganzen Tag; **all-dayer** [ˈɔːlˌdeɪəʳ] N (*inf*) ganztägige Veranstaltung

allegation [æliˈɡeɪʃən] N Behauptung *f*

allege [əˈledʒ] VT behaupten; **the remarks ~d to have been made by him** die Bemerkungen, die er gemacht haben soll or angeblich gemacht hat; **he is ~d to have said that ...** er soll angeblich gesagt haben, dass ...

alleged [əˈledʒd] ADJ , **allegedly** [əˈledʒɪdlɪ] ADV angeblich

allegiance [əˈliːdʒəns] N Treue *f* (*to* + *dat*); **oath of ~** Fahnen- or Treueeid *m*

allegoric(al) [æliˈɡɒrɪk(əl)] ADJ , **allegorically** [æliˈɡɒrɪkəli] ADV allegorisch

allegory [ˈæligəri] N Allegorie *f*

allegro [əˈleɡrəʊ] ADJ ADV allegro N Allegro *nt*

all-electric [ˌɔːlɪˈlektrɪk] ADJ **an ~ house** ein Haus, in dem alles elektrisch ist; **we're ~** bei uns ist alles elektrisch

alleluia [æliˈluːjə] INTERJ (h)alleluja N (H)alleluja *nt*

all-embracing [ˌɔːlɪmˈbreɪsɪŋ] ADJ (all)umfassend

Allen® [ˈælən]: **Allen key** N Inbusschlüssel® *m*; **Allen screw** N Inbusschraube® *f*; **Allen wrench** N (*US*) Inbusschlüssel® *m*

allergen [ˈælədʒən] N (*Med*) Allergen *nt*

allergenic [æləˈdʒenɪk] ADJ (*Med*) allergen

allergic [əˈlɜːdʒɪk] ADJ (*lit, fig*) allergisch (*to* gegen)

allergist [ˈælədʒɪst] N Allergologe *m*, Allergologin *f*

allergy [ˈælədʒɪ] N Allergie *f* (*to* gegen); **he seems to have an ~ to work** (*hum*) er scheint gegen Arbeit allergisch zu sein

alleviate [əˈliːvɪeɪt] VT lindern

alleviation [əˌliːvɪˈeɪʃən] N Linderung *f*

alley [ˈælɪ] N (*between buildings*) (enge) Gasse; (*between gardens*) Weg *m*, Pfad *m*; (*in garden*) Laubengang *m* (= *bowling alley, skittle alley*) Bahn *f*

alley: alley cat N streunende Katze; **to fight like ~s** sich in den Haaren liegen; **she's got the morals of an ~** (*inf*) sie treibts mit jedem; **alleyway** N Durchgang *m*

all: all-fired ADJ (*US inf*) furchtbar (*inf*), schrecklich (*inf*); **All Fools' Day** N der erste April; **All Hallows' (Day)** N (*Brit*) = **All Saints' Day**

alliance [əˈlaɪəns] N Verbindung *f*; (*of institutions also, of states*) Bündnis *nt*; (*in historical contexts*) Allianz *f*; **partners in an ~** Bündnispartner *pl*

allied [ˈælaɪd] (*Mil, Pol,* = *affiliated*) verbunden; (*for attack, defence etc*) verbündet, alliiert; **~ to** or **with/against sb/sth** mit/gegen jdn/etw verbündet; **the Allied forces** die Alliierten; **an Allied attack** eine Offensive der Alliierten (= *like, connected, associated*) **(closely) ~ to** or **with sth** (eng) mit etw verbunden (*Biol, fig*) verwandt

Allies [ˈælaɪz] PL N (*Hist*) **the ~** die Alliierten *pl*

alligator [ˈælɪɡeɪtəʳ] N Alligator *m*; **~(-skin) bag** Alligatorledertasche *f*

all: all-important ADJ außerordentlich wichtig; **the ~ question** die Frage, auf die es ankommt; **all-in** ADJ *attr*, **all in** ADJ (*inclusive*) Inklusiv-; **~ price** Inklusivpreis *m* → *also* **all 5**; **all-inclusive** ADJ Pauschal-; **all-in-one** N Einteiler *m* ADJ *sleepsuit, wetsuit* einteilig; **all-in wrestling** N (*Sport*) Freistilringen *nt*

alliterate [əˈlɪtəreɪt] VI einen Stabreim bilden, alliterieren

alliteration [əˌlɪtəˈreɪʃən] N Alliteration *f*, Stabreim *m*

alliterative [əˈlɪtərətɪv] ADJ alliterierend

all: all-knowing ADJ allwissend; **all-male** ADJ *attr* **an ~ household** ein reiner Männerhaushalt; **all-merciful** ADJ *God* allbarmherzig, allgütig; **all-night** ADJ *attr café* (die ganze Nacht) durchgehend geöffnet; *vigil* die ganze Nacht andauernd *attr*; **an ~ party** eine Party, die die ganze Nacht durchgeht; **we had an ~ party** wir haben die ganze Nacht durchgemacht; **it was an ~ journey** wir/sie etc sind die ganze Nacht durchgefahren; **we have ~ opening** wir haben (die ganze Nacht) durchgehend geöffnet; **~ opening is common in some countries** in manchen Ländern sind 24-stündige Öffnungszeiten üblich; **we have an ~ service** wir haben einen durchgehenden Nachtdienst; **there is an ~ bus service** die Busse verkehren die ganze Nacht über; **all-nighter** [ɔːlˈnaɪtəʳ] N (*inf*) *Veranstaltung etc, die die ganze Nacht hindurch andauert*

allocate [ˈæləʊkeɪt] VT (= *allot*) zuteilen, zuweisen (*to sb* jdm); (= *apportion*) verteilen (*to* auf +*acc*); *tasks* vergeben (*to an* +*acc*); **to ~ money to** or **for a project** Geld für ein Projekt bestimmen

allocation [æləʊˈkeɪʃən] N (= *allotting*) Zuteilung *f*, Zuweisung *f*; (= *apportioning*) Verteilung *f*; (= *sum allocated*) Zuwendung *f*

allopathy [əˈlɒpəθɪ] N (*Med*) Allopathie *f*

allophone [ˈæləfəʊn] N (*Ling*) Allophon *nt*

allot [əˈlɒt] VT zuteilen, zuweisen (*to sb/sth* jdm/etw); *time* vorsehen (*to* für); *money* bestimmen (*to* für)

allotment [əˈlɒtmənt] N (= *allocation*) Zuteilung *f*, Zuweisung *f*; (*of time*) Vorsehen *nt*; (*of money*) Bestimmung *f*; (= *amount of money allotted*) Zuwendung *f* (*Brit:* = *plot of ground*) Schrebergarten *m*

all: all out ADV mit aller Kraft; **to go ~** sein Letztes or Äußerstes geben; **to go ~ to do sth** alles daransetzen, etw zu tun; **to go ~ for victory** alles daransetzen, (um) zu siegen; **all-out** ADJ *strike, war* total; *attack* massiv; *effort, attempt* äußerste(r, s); *support* uneingeschränkt; **all-over** ADJ ganzflächig

allow [əˈlaʊ] ○ 3.1, 9.2, 10.4 VT (= *permit*) *sth* erlauben, gestatten; *behaviour etc* gestatten, zulassen; **to ~ sb sth** jdm etw erlauben or gestatten; **to ~ sb to do sth** jdm erlauben or gestatten, etw zu tun; **to be ~ed to do sth** etw tun dürfen; **smoking is not ~ed** Rauchen ist nicht gestattet; **"no dogs ~ed"** „Hunde müssen draußen bleiben"; **we were ~ed one drink** uns wurde ein Drink erlaubt or gestattet; **we're not ~ed much freedom** wir haben nicht viel Freiheit; **will you be ~ed to?** darfst du denn?; **will you ~ him to?** erlauben Sie es ihm?, lassen Sie ihn denn? (*inf*); **to ~ oneself sth** sich (*dat*) etw erlauben; (= *treat oneself*) sich (*dat*) etw gönnen; **to ~ oneself to be waited on/persuaded** *etc* sich bedienen/überreden *etc* lassen; **~ me!** gestatten Sie (*form*); **~ me to help you** gestatten Sie, dass ich Ihnen helfe (*form*); **to ~ sth to happen** etw zulassen, zulassen, dass etw geschieht; **to ~ sb in/out/past** *etc* jdn hinein-/hinaus-/vorbeilassen *etc*; **to be ~ed in/out/past** hinein-/hinaus-/vorbeidürfen (= *recognize, accept*) *claim, appeal, goal* anerkennen (= *allocate, grant*) *discount* geben; *space* lassen; *time* einplanen, einberechnen; *money* geben, zugestehen; (*in tax, Jur*) zugestehen; **~ (yourself) an hour to cross the city** rechnen Sie mit einer Stunde, um durch die Stadt zu kommen; **he ~ed me two hours for that** er gab mir zwei Stunden dafür; **~ 5 cms extra** geben Sie 5 cm zu (= *concede*) annehmen; **~ing** or **if we ~ that ...** angenommen, (dass) ...

VI **if time ~s** falls es zeitlich möglich ist

▶ **allow for** VI +*prep obj* berücksichtigen; *factor, cost, shrinkage, error also* einrechnen, einkalkulieren; **allowing for the fact that ...** unter Berücksichtigung der Tatsache, dass ...; **after allowing for** nach Berücksichtigung (+*gen*)

▶ **allow of** VI +prep obj zulassen

allowable [əˈlaʊəbl] ADJ zulässig; (Fin, in tax) absetzbar, abzugsfähig; ~ **expenses** (Fin) abzugsfähige Kosten

allowance [əˈlaʊəns] N **a** finanzielle Unterstützung; (paid by state) Beihilfe f; (parent to child) Unterhaltsgeld nt; (as compensation, for unsociable hours, overseas allowance etc) Zulage f; (on business trip) Spesen pl; (= spending money) Taschengeld nt; **clothing** ~ Kleidungsgeld nt; **petrol** ~ (Brit) Benzingeld nt; **his father still gives him an** ~ sein Vater unterstützt ihn noch immer finanziell; **he gives his wife a dress** ~ er gibt seiner Frau einen Zuschuss zu den Kleidungskosten; **he gave her an** ~ **of £100 a month** er stellte ihr monatlich £ 100 zur Verfügung **b** (Fin: = tax allowance) Freibetrag m **c** (Fin, Comm: = discount) (Preis)nachlass m (on für); (= quantity allowed: for shrinkage etc) Zugabe f **d** (= acceptance: of goal, claim, appeal) Anerkennung f **e** Zugeständnisse pl; **to make ~(s) for sth** etw berücksichtigen; **to make ~s for sb** bei jdm Zugeständnisse machen; **you have to make ~s** Sie müssen (gewisse) Zugeständnisse machen

allowedly [əˈlaʊɪdlɪ] ADV gewiss, zugegeben

alloy [ˈælɔɪ] N Legierung f VT legieren; (fig liter) (ver)mischen; **pleasure ~ed with suffering** von Leid getrübte Freude

all: all-party ADJ (Pol) Allparteien-; ~ **government** Allparteienregierung f; **all-pervading**, **all-pervasive** ADJ influence, presence alles durchdringend; **all-points bulletin** N Rundruf m an alle Streifen; **all-powerful** ADJ allmächtig; **all-purpose** ADJ Allzweck-; ~ **room** Allzweckraum m

all right [ˈɔːlˈraɪt] ADJ pred **a** (= satisfactory) in Ordnung, okay (inf); **it's** ~ (= not too bad) es geht; (= working properly) es ist in Ordnung; **that's** or **it's** ~ (after thanks) schon gut, gern geschehen; (after apology) schon gut, das macht nichts; **it's ~, you don't have to** schon gut, du musst nicht unbedingt; **to taste/look/smell** ~ ganz gut schmecken/aussehen/riechen; **is it ~ for me to leave early?** kann ich früher gehen?; **it's ~ by me** ich habe nichts dagegen, von mir aus gern; **it's ~ for you** du hast gut reden; **it's ~ for him to laugh** er hat gut lachen; **I made it ~ with him** ich habe das (mit ihm) wieder eingerenkt; **I saw him** ~ (inf, for petrol, money etc) ich hab ihn (dafür) entschädigt; **it'll be ~ on the night** es wird schon klappen, wenn es darauf ankommt; **he's** ~ (inf: = is a good guy) der ist in Ordnung (inf) **b** (= safe, unharmed) person, machine in Ordnung, okay (inf); object, building, tree etc heil, ganz, okay (inf); **are you ~?** (= healthy) geht es Ihnen gut?; (= unharmed) ist Ihnen etwas passiert?; **are you feeling ~?** fehlt Ihnen was?; (iro) sag mal, fehlt dir was?; **he's ~ again** es geht ihm wieder gut, er ist wieder in Ordnung (inf); **are you ~ (in there)?** ist alles in Ordnung (da drin)?; **the bomb damaged half the street but our house was ~** die Bombe hat die halbe Straße zerstört, aber unserem Haus ist nichts passiert; **is it ~ for us to come out now?** können wir jetzt rauskommen?; **it's ~ now, Susi's here** jetzt ist alles wieder gut, Susi ist ja da; **it's ~, don't worry** keine Angst, machen Sie sich keine Sorgen; **we're ~ for the rest of our lives** wir haben für den Rest des Lebens ausgesorgt ADV **a** (= satisfactorily) ganz gut, ganz ordentlich; (= safely) gut; **did I do it ~?** habe ich es recht gemacht?; **did you get home ~?** bist du gut nach Hause gekommen?; **did you get/find it ~?** haben Sie es denn bekommen/gefunden? **b** (= certainly) schon; **he'll come** ~ er wird schon kommen; **that's the boy** ~ das ist der Junge; **he's a clever man** ~ er ist schon intelligent; **oh yes, we heard you** ~ o ja, und ob wir dich gehört haben **INTERJ** gut, schön, okay (inf); (in agreement) gut,

in Ordnung; **may I leave early? – ~** kann ich früher gehen? – ja; ~ **that's enough!** okay or komm, jetzt reichts (aber)!; **~, ~!** I'm coming schon gut, schon gut, ich komme ja!

all: all-round ADJ (esp Brit) Allround-; student vielseitig begabt; improvement in jeder Beziehung or Hinsicht; ~ **artist** Allroundkünstler(in) m(f); **a good ~ performance** eine rundum gute Leistung; **all-rounder** N (Brit) Allroundmann m/-frau f; (Sport) Allroundsportler(in) m(f); **All Saints' Day** N Allerheiligen nt; **all-seater** ADJ (Brit Sport) stadium, stand ohne Stehplätze; **all-seater (stadium)** N (Brit Sport) (reines) Sitzplatzstadium; **all-singing, all-dancing** ADJ (Brit inf) alle Wünsche erfüllend attr; **All Souls' Day** N Allerseelen nt; **allspice** N Piment m; **all-star** ADJ Star-; ~ **cast** Starbesetzung f; **all-terrain bike** N Mountainbike nt; **all-terrain vehicle** N Geländefahrzeug nt; **all-ticket** ADJ sports match mit Vorverkauf; **all-time** ADV aller Zeiten; **the** ~ **record** der Rekord aller Zeiten; **an** ~ **high/low** der höchste/niedrigste Stand aller Zeiten; ~ **great** Unvergessliche(r) mf, Unvergessene(r) mf; **to be an** ~ **favourite** (Brit) or **favorite** (US) sehr eh und je beliebt sein ADV ~ **best/worst** beste(r, s)/schlechteste(r, s) aller Zeiten

allude [əˈluːd] VI +prep obj **to** ~ **to** anspielen auf (+acc)

allure [əˈljʊəʳ] VT locken, anziehen N Reiz m

allurement [əˈljʊərmənt] N Anziehungskraft f, Reiz m

alluring ADJ , **alluringly** ADV [əˈljʊərɪŋ, -lɪ] verführerisch

allusion [əˈluːʒən] N Anspielung f (to auf +acc)

allusive [əˈluːsɪv] ADJ voller Anspielungen

allusively [əˈluːsɪvlɪ] ADV indirekt

alluvial [əˈluːvɪəl] ADJ angeschwemmt

alluvium [əˈluːvɪəm] N Anschwemmung f

all: all-weather ADJ Allwetter-; ~ **jacket** Allwetterjacke f; ~ **pitch** Allwetterplatz m; ~ **surface** Allwetterbelag m; **all-wheel drive** N Allradantrieb m

ally [ˈælaɪ] N Verbündete(r) mf, Bundesgenosse m/-genossin f; (Hist) Alliierte(r) m VT [əˈlaɪ] verbinden (with, to mit); (for attack, defence etc) verbünden, alliieren (with, to mit); **to** ~ **oneself with** or **to sb** sich mit jdm zusammentun/verbünden or alliieren

alma mater [ˈælmɑːˈmeɪtəʳ] N Alma Mater f

almanac [ˈɔːlmənæk] N Almanach m → **nautical**

almighty [ɔːlˈmaɪtɪ] ADJ **a** god, person allmächtig; power unumschränkt; **Almighty God** (Eccl) **God Almighty** (Eccl) der Allmächtige; (address in prayer) allmächtiger Gott; **God** or **Christ Almighty!** (inf) Allmächtiger! (inf), allmächtiger Gott! (inf) **b** (inf) fool, idiot, row mordsmäßig (inf); blow mächtig (inf); **there was a** ~ **bang and ...** es gab einen Mordsknall und ... (inf) N **the Almighty** der Allmächtige

almond [ˈɑːmənd] N Mandel f; (= tree) Mandelbaum m

almond in cpds Mandel-; **almond-eyed** ADJ mandeläugig; **almond oil** N Mandelöl nt; **almond paste** N Marzipanmasse f; **almond-shaped** ADJ mandelförmig

almoner [ˈɑːmənəʳ] N **a** (dated Brit: in hospital) Krankenhausfürsorger(in) m(f) **b** (old: = distributor of alms) Almosenpfleger m

almost [ˈɔːlməʊst] ADV fast, beinahe; **he** ~ **fell** er wäre fast gefallen; **she'll** ~ **certainly come** sie kommt ziemlich sicher

alms [ɑːmz] PL Almosen pl

alms: alms box N Almosenstock m; **almshouse** N Armenhaus nt

aloe [ˈæləʊ] N (Bot, Med) Aloe f

aloe vera [ˈæləʊˈvɪərə] N Aloe Vera f

aloft [əˈlɒft] ADV **a** (= into the air) empor; (= in the air) hoch droben; (Naut) oben in der Takelung; **to go** ~ (Naut) in die Takelung hinaufklettern

alone [əˈləʊn] ADJ pred allein(e); **we're not** ~ **in thinking that** wir stehen mit dieser Meinung

nicht allein; **there is one man who, ~ in the world, knows ...** es gibt einen, der als Einziger auf der Welt weiß ... → **leave, let³** ADV allein(e); **to live on bread** ~ von Brot allein leben; **it's mine** ~ das gehört mir (ganz) allein(e); **that charm which is hers** ~ der ihr ganz eigene Charme; **the hotel** ~ **cost £95** das Hotel allein kostete (schon) £ 95, (allein) schon das Hotel kannte die Wahrheit nur Simon allein; **to stand** ~ (fig) einzig dastehen; **to go it** ~ (inf, = be independent) auf eigenen Beinen stehen; **I wanted to go it** ~ (inf) ich wollte es selbst und ohne fremde Hilfe machen

along [əˈlɒŋ] PREP (direction) entlang (+acc), lang (+acc) (inf); (position) entlang (+dat); **he walked** ~ **the river** er ging den or an dem Fluss entlang; **somewhere** ~ **the way** irgendwo unterwegs or auf dem Weg; (fig) irgendwann einmal; **somewhere** ~ **here/there** irgendwo hier(herum)/dort(herum); (= in this/that direction) irgendwo in dieser Richtung/der Richtung; **the Red Lion? isn't that somewhere** ~ **your way?** der Rote Löwe? ist der nicht irgendwo in Ihrer Nähe or Gegend? → **all 5** ADV **a** (= onwards) weiter-, vorwärts; **to move** ~ weitergehen; **he was just strolling** ~ er ist bloß so dahingeschlendert; **run** ~ nun lauf!; **he'll be** ~ **soon** er muss gleich da sein; **I'll be** ~ **about eight** ich komme ungefähr um acht; **are you coming? – yes, I'll be** ~ **in a minute** kommst du? – ja, (ich komme) gleich **b** (= together) with zusammen mit; **to come/sing** ~ **with sb** mit jdm mitkommen/mitsingen; **take an umbrella** ~ nimm einen Schirm mit

alongside [əˈlɒŋˈsaɪd] PREP neben (+dat); **he parked** ~ **the kerb** (Brit) or **curb** (US) er parkte am Bordstein; **we were moored** ~ **the pier/the other boats** wir lagen am Pier vor Anker/lagen Bord an Bord mit den anderen Schiffen; **the houses** ~ **the river** die Häuser am Fluss entlang; **he works** ~ **me** (= with me) er ist ein Kollege von mir; (= next to me) er arbeitet neben mir ADV daneben; **is the launch still** ~? liegt die Barkasse immer noch längsseits?; **a police car drew up** ~ ein Polizeiauto fuhr neben mich/ihn etc heran; **she was driving** ~ sie fuhr nebenher; **they brought their dinghy** ~ sie brachten ihr Dingi heran

aloof [əˈluːf] ADV (lit, fig) abseits; **to remain** ~ sich abseits halten; **to keep** or **stand** ~ **(from sth)** sich (von etw) distanzieren; **buyers held** ~ (Comm) die Käufer verhielten sich zurückhaltend ADV unnahbar

aloofness [əˈluːfnɪs] N Unnahbarkeit f

aloud [əˈlaʊd] ADV laut

alp [ælp] N Berg m in den Alpen

alpaca [ælˈpækə] N Alpaka nt attr Alpaka-; ~ **wool** Alpakawolle f

alpenhorn [ˈælpɪnhɔːn] N Alphorn nt

alpenstock [ˈælpɪnstɒk] N Bergstock m

alpha [ˈælfə] N **a** (= letter) Alpha nt **b** (Brit Sch, Univ) Eins f; ~ **plus** Eins (plus (hum)); (Sch also) Eins mit Stern (hum)

alphabet [ˈælfəbet] N Alphabet nt; **does he know the** or **his** ~? kann er schon das Abc?

alphabetic(al) [ˌælfəˈbetɪk(əl)] ADJ alphabetisch; **in alphabetical order** in alphabetischer Reihenfolge

alphabetically [ˌælfəˈbetɪkəlɪ] ADV alphabetisch, nach dem Alphabet

alphabetism [ˈælfəbetɪzəm] N (hum) Benachteiligung einer Person, weil der Anfangsbuchstabe ihres Nachnamens weit hinten im Alphabet steht

alphabetization [ˌælfəbətaɪˈzeɪʃən] N Alphabetisierung f

alphabetize [ˈælfəbətaɪz] VT alphabetisieren, alphabetisch ordnen

alphanumeric [ˌælfənjuːˈmerɪk] ADJ alphanumerisch

alpha: alpha particle N Alphateilchen *nt*; **alpha ray** N Alphastrahl *m*; **alpha rhythm**, **alpha wave** N (*Physiol*) Alpharhythmus *m*

alpine ['ælpaɪn] ADJ **a** **Alpine** alpin; *dialects* der Alpen **b** (*general*) alpin; (*Geol*) alpinisch; **~ flower** Alpenblume *f*; **~ hut** Berghütte *f*; **~ scenery** Gebirgs- *or* Berglandschaft *f*

alpinism ['ælpɪnɪzəm] N Alpinistik *f*, Alpinismus *m*

alpinist ['ælpɪnɪst] N Alpinist(in) *m(f)*

Alps [ælps] PL Alpen *pl*

already [ɔːl'redɪ] ADV schon; **I've ~ seen it, I've seen it ~** ich habe es schon gesehen

alright [ɔːl'raɪt] ADJ, ADV = **all right**

Alsace ['ælsæs] N das Elsass

Alsace-Lorraine ['ælsæslə'reɪn] N Elsass-Lothringen *nt*

Alsatian [æl'seɪʃən] ADJ elsässisch; **the ~ people** die Elsässer *pl* **N** (= *dialect*) Elsässisch *nt*

alsatian [æl'seɪʃən] N (*Brit: also* **alsatian dog**) (Deutscher) Schäferhund

also ['ɔːlsəʊ] ✪ 26 ADV **a** auch; **her cousin ~ came** *or* **came ~** ihre Kusine kam auch; **he has ~ been there** er ist auch (schon) dort gewesen; **not only ... but ~** nicht nur ... sondern auch; **~ present were ...** außerdem waren anwesend ... **b** (= *moreover*) außerdem, ferner; **~, I must explain that ...** außerdem muss ich erklären, dass ...

also-ran [ɔːlsəʊ'ræn] N **to be among the ~s, to be an ~** (*Sport, fig*) unter „ferner liefen" kommen

Alta *abbr of* **Alberta**

altar ['ɒltə'] N Altar *m*; **to lead sb to the ~** jdn zum Altar führen; **she was left standing at the ~** sie wurde in letzter Minute sitzen gelassen (*inf*); **to be sacrificed on the ~ of pride** *etc* auf dem Altar des Stolzes *etc* geopfert werden

altar: altar boy N Ministrant *m*; **altar cloth** N Altartuch *nt*, Altardecke *f*; **altarpiece** N Altarbild *nt*; **altar rail** N , **altar rails** PL Kommunionbank *f*

alter ['ɒltə'] **VT** **a** (= *change*) ändern; (= *modify*) (ab)ändern; **~ sth completely** etw vollkommen verändern; **that ~s things** das ändert die Sache; **it does not ~ the fact that ...** das ändert nichts an der Tatsache, dass ... **b** (*US: = castrate, spay*) kastrieren **VI** sich (ver)ändern; **to ~ for the better/worse** sich zu seinem Vorteil/Nachteil (ver)ändern; (*things, situation*) sich zum Besseren/Schlechteren wenden

alterable ['ɒltərəbl] ADJ veränderbar; **to be ~** sich ändern lassen

alteration [ɒltə'reɪʃən] N (= *change*) Änderung *f*; (= *modification*) (Ab)änderung *f*; (*of appearance*) Veränderung *f*; **a complete ~** eine vollständige Veränderung; **to make ~s in sth** Änderungen an etw (*dat*) vornehmen; (**this timetable is**) **subject to ~** Änderungen (im Fahrplan sind) vorbehalten; **closed for ~s** wegen Umbau geschlossen

altercation [ɒltə'keɪʃən] N Auseinandersetzung *f*

alter ego ['æltər'iːgəʊ] N Alter ego *nt*

alternate [ɒl'tɜːnɪt] ADJ **a** **I go there on ~ days** ich gehe jeden zweiten Tag *or* alle zwei Tage hin; **they do their shopping on ~ days** (= *every other day*) sie machen ihre Einkäufe jeden zweiten Tag; (= *taking turns*) sie wechseln sich täglich mit dem Einkaufen ab; **to go through ~ periods of happiness and despair** abwechselnd Zeiten des Glücks und der Verzweiflung durchmachen; **they put down ~ layers of brick and mortar** sie schichteten (immer) abwechselnd Ziegel und Mörtel aufeinander **b** (= *alternative*) alternativ; **~ route** Ausweichstrecke *f* **N** ['ɒltənɪt] (*US*) Vertreter(in) *m(f)*; (*Sport*) Ersatzspieler(in) *m(f)* **VT** ['ɒltəneɪt] abwechseln lassen; *crops* im Wechsel anbauen; **to ~ one thing with another** zwischen einer Sache und einer anderen (ab-)wechseln; **the chairs were ~d with benches** Stühle und Bänke waren abwechselnd aufgestellt **VI** ['ɒltəneɪt] (sich) abwechseln; (*Elec*) alternieren; **to ~ between one thing and another** zwischen einer Sache und einer anderen (ab-)wechseln; **the two actors ~d in the role** die beiden Schauspieler wechselten sich in der Rolle ab

alternately [ɒl'tɜːnɪtlɪ] ADV **a** (= *in turn*) im Wechsel, wechselweise, (immer) abwechselnd **b** = **alternatively**

alternating ['ɒltɜːneɪtɪŋ] ADJ wechselnd; **a pattern with ~ stripes of red and white** ein Muster mit abwechselnd roten und weißen Streifen; **~ current** Wechselstrom *m*

alternation [ɒltɜː'neɪʃən] N Wechsel *m*; **the ~ of crops** der Fruchtwechsel

alternative [ɒl'tɜːnətɪv] ADJ Alternativ-; **there is no ~ way** es gibt keine Alternative; **~ route** Ausweichstrecke *f*; **~ society** Alternativgesellschaft *f*; **for him, other than London, the only possible ~ place to live is ...** außer London kommt für ihn als Wohnort nur ... infrage *or* in Frage, ... ist für ihn als Wohnort die einzige Alternative zu London **N** Alternative *f*; **I had no ~ (but ...)** ich hatte keine andere Wahl *or* keine Alternative (als ...)

alternatively [ɒl'tɜːnətɪvlɪ] ✪ 26.2 ADV als Alternative, als andere Möglichkeit; **or ~, he could come with us** oder aber, er kommt mit uns mit; **a prison sentence of three months or ~ a fine of £500** eine Gefängnisstrafe von drei Monaten oder wahlweise eine Geldstrafe von £ 500

alternative medicine N Alternativmedizin *f*

alternative theatre, (*US*) **alternative theater** N Alternativtheater *nt*

alternator ['ɒltɜːneɪtə'] N (*Elec*) Wechselstromgenerator *m*; (*Aut*) Lichtmaschine *f*

althorn ['ælthɔːn] N B-Horn *nt*

although [ɔːl'ðəʊ] ✪ 26.2, 26.3 CONJ obwohl, obgleich; **the house, ~ small ...** wenn das Haus auch klein ist ..., obwohl das Haus klein ist ...

altimeter ['æltɪmiːtə'] N Höhenmesser *m*

altitude ['æltɪtjuːd] N Höhe *f*; **what is our ~?** in welcher Höhe befinden wir uns?; **we are flying at an ~ of ...** wir fliegen in einer Höhe von ...; **at this ~** in dieser Höhe

alt key ['ɒltkiː] N (*Comput*) Alt-Taste *f*

alto ['æltəʊ] N **a** (= *voice*) Alt *m*, Altstimme *f*; (= *person*) Alt *m* **b** (*also* **alto saxophone**) Altsaxophon *nt*, Altsaxofon *f*; **~ part** Altpartie *f* ADV **to sing ~** Alt singen

alto clef N Altschlüssel *m*, C-Schlüssel *m*

altogether [ɔːltə'geðə'] ADV **a** (= *including everything*) im ganzen, insgesamt; **taken ~**, *or* **~ it was very pleasant** alles in allem war es sehr nett, es war im Ganzen sehr nett **b** (= *wholly*) vollkommen, ganz und gar; **he wasn't ~ wrong** er hatte nicht ganz Unrecht; **he wasn't ~ pleased/surprised** er war nicht übermäßig *or* besonders zufrieden/überrascht; **it was ~ a waste of time** es war vollkommene Zeitverschwendung; **that is another matter ~** das ist etwas ganz anderes **N in the ~** (*hum inf*) hüllenlos, im Adams-/Evaskostüm; **the King is in the ~** der König hat ja gar nichts an

alto sax(ophone) N Altsaxophon *nt*, Altsaxofon *nt*

altricial bird [æl,trɪʃəl'bɜːd] N Nesthocker *m*

altruism ['æltruɪzəm] N Altruismus *m*

altruist ['æltruɪst] N Altruist(in) *m(f)*

altruistic ADJ , **altruistically** ADV [æltrʊ'ɪstɪk, -əlɪ] altruistisch

alum ['æləm] N Alaun *m*

aluminium [æljʊ'mɪnɪəm], (*US*) **aluminum** [ə'luːmɪnəm] N Aluminium *nt*; **~ foil** Alu(minium)folie *f*

alumna [ə'lʌmnə] N *pl* -**e** [ə'lʌmniː] (*US*) ehemalige Schülerin/Studentin, Ehemalige *f*

alumnus [ə'lʌmnəs] N *pl* **alumni** [ə'lʌmnaɪ] (*US*) ehemaliger Schüler/Student, Ehemalige(r) *m*

alveolar [æl'vɪələ'] ADJ alveolar N (*Phon*) Alveolar *m*

always ['ɔːlweɪz] ADV **a** immer; (= *constantly, repeatedly*) ständig, immer; **he is ~ forgetting** er vergisst das immer *or* ständig; **you can't ~ expect to be forgiven** du kannst nicht immer (wieder) erwarten, dass man dir vergibt **b** **we could ~ go by train/sell the house** wir könnten doch auch den Zug nehmen/könnten ja auch das Haus verkaufen; **there's ~ the possibility that ...** es besteht immer noch die Möglichkeit, dass ...; **there's ~ that to fall back on** wir können ja immer noch darauf zurückgreifen; **you can ~ come along later** Sie können ja auch noch später kommen

Alzheimer's (disease) ['ælts,haɪməz(dɪ,ziːz)] N Alzheimerkrankheit *f*

AM **a** (*Rad*) *abbr of* **amplitude modulation** AM **b** (*Brit, Pol*) *abbr of* **Assembly Member** Mitglied *nt* der walisischen Versammlung

am [æm] *1st pers sing present of* **be**

am, a.m. *abbr of* **ante meridiem 2 am** 2 Uhr morgens; **10 am** 10 Uhr morgens *or* vormittags; **12 am** 0 Uhr, Mitternacht; **do you mean 7 am or 7 pm?** meinen Sie 7 Uhr morgens oder abends?

amalgam [ə'mælgəm] N Amalgam *nt*; (*fig also*) Gemisch *nt*, Mischung *f*

amalgamate [ə'mælgəmeɪt] **VT** *companies, unions* fusionieren, verschmelzen; *departments* zusammenlegen; *metals* amalgamieren **VI** (*companies etc*) fusionieren; (*metals*) amalgamieren

amalgamation [ə,mælgə'meɪʃən] N (*of companies etc*) Fusion *f*; (*of metals*) Amalgamation *f*

amanuensis [ə,mænjʊ'ensɪs] N *pl* **amanuenses** [ə,mænjʊ'ensiːz] Sekretär(in) *m(f)*; (*Hist*) Amanuensis *m*

amaryllis [æmə'rɪlɪs] N Amaryllis *f*

amass [ə'mæs] VT anhäufen; *money also* scheffeln; *fortune, material, evidence also* zusammentragen

amateur ['æmətə'] **N** **a** Amateur(in) *m(f)* **b** (*pej*) Dilettant(in) *m(f)* ADJ **a** *attr* Amateur-; **~ boxing/competition** Amateurboxen *nt*/-wettkampf *m*; **~ painter** Hobbymaler(in) *m(f)*; **~ photographer** Hobby- *or* Amateurfotograf(in) *m(f)*; **~ video** Amateurvideo *nt* **b** (*pej*) = **amateurish**

amateur dramatics [æmətədrə'mætɪks] PL Laiendrama *nt*

amateurish ['æmətərɪʃ] ADJ (*pej*) dilettantisch; *performance, work also* laienhaft

amateurishly ['æmətərɪʃlɪ] ADV (*pej*) dilettantisch

amateurishness ['æmətərɪʃnɪs] N (*pej*) Dilettantismus *m*; (*of performance, work*) Laienhaftigkeit *f*

amateurism ['æmətərɪzəm] N **a** Amateursport *m* **b** (*pej*) Dilettantentum *nt*, Dilettantismus *m*

amatory ['æmətərɪ] ADJ Liebes-; *adventure also* amourös; *glance, remark, feelings* verliebt; **~ poem** Liebesgedicht *nt*

amaze [ə'meɪz] **VT** erstaunen, in Erstaunen (ver)setzen; **I was ~d to learn that ...** ich war erstaunt zu hören, dass ..., mit Erstaunen hörte ich, dass ...; **to be ~d at sth** über etw (*acc*) erstaunt *or* verblüfft sein, sich über etw (*acc*) wundern; **you don't know that, you ~ me!** Sie wissen das nicht, das wundert mich aber; **no, really? you ~ me** (*iro*) nein wirklich? da bin ich aber erstaunt *or* Sie setzen mich in Erstaunen; **it ~s me to think that only two years ago ...** es ist erstaunlich, wenn ich denke, dass erst vor zwei Jahren ...; **it ~s me that he doesn't fall** ich finde es erstaunlich, dass er nicht fällt **VI** **his generosity never fails** *or* **ceases to ~** seine Großzügigkeit versetzt einen immer wieder in Erstaunen

amazed [ə'meɪzd] ADJ *look, expression* erstaunt

amazement [ə'meɪzmənt] N Erstaunen *nt*, Verwunderung *f*; **much to my ~** zu meinem großen Erstaunen

amazing [əˈmeɪzɪŋ] ADJ erstaunlich; **he's the most ~ lawyer I've ever met** er ist der erstaunlichste Rechtsanwalt, den ich je gesehen habe; **darling, you're ~, what a fantastic meal** Schatz, du bist wirklich unschlagbar, so ein tolles Essen!

amazingly [əˈmeɪzɪŋlɪ] ADV erstaunlich; *simple, obvious also* verblüffend; **Sara has coped ~ (well)** Sara hat sich erstaunlich gut geschlagen; **~ (enough), he got it right first time** erstaunlicherweise hat er es gleich beim ersten Mal richtig gemacht

Amazon [ˈæməzən] N Amazonas *m*; (*Myth, fig*) Amazone *f*

ambassador [æmˈbæsədəʳ] N Botschafter(in) *m(f)*; (*fig*) Repräsentant(in) *m(f)*, Vertreter(in) *m(f)*

ambassador extraordinary, (*esp US*) **ambassador-at-large** [æmˈbæsədəɹətˌlɑːdʒ] N Sonderbotschafter(in) *m(f)*, Sonderbeauftragte(r) *mf*

ambassadorial [æmˌbæsəˈdɔːrɪəl] ADJ Botschafter-; *rank, dignity* eines Botschafters

ambassadress [æmˈbæsədrɪs] N Botschafterin *f*

amber [ˈæmbəʳ] N Bernstein *m*; (*colour*) Bernsteingelb *nt*; (*Brit: in traffic lights*) Gelb *nt* ▮ADJ aus Bernstein; (= *amber-coloured*) bernsteinfarben; (*Brit*) *traffic light* gelb; **the ~ nectar** (*Brit, Austral: inf*) das kühle Nass (*inf*), der Gerstensaft (*hum*)

ambergris [ˈæmbəɡriːs] N Amber *m*, Ambra *f*

ambidextrous [ˌæmbɪˈdekstrəs] ADJ mit beiden Händen gleich geschickt, beidhändig

ambidextrousness [ˌæmbɪˈdekstrəsnɪs] N Beidhändigkeit *f*

ambience [ˈæmbɪəns] N Atmosphäre *f*, Ambiente *nt* (*geh*)

ambient [ˈæmbɪənt] ADJ (*liter*) *air* umgebend; **~ temperature** (*Tech*) Umgebungstemperatur *f*; **~ music** Hintergrundmusik *f*

ambiguity [ˌæmbɪˈɡjuːɪtɪ] N Zwei- *or* Doppeldeutigkeit *f*; (*of joke, comment etc*) Zweideutigkeit *f*; (*with many possible meanings*) Mehr- *or* Vieldeutigkeit *f*

ambiguous [æmˈbɪɡjʊəs] ADJ zwei- *or* doppeldeutig; *joke, comment etc* zweideutig; (= *with many possible meanings*) mehr- *or* vieldeutig

ambiguously [æmˈbɪɡjʊəslɪ] ADV zweideutig; **~ worded** zweideutig formuliert

ambiguousness [æmˈbɪɡjʊəsnɪs] N Zwei- *or* Doppeldeutigkeit *f*; (= *with many possible meanings*) Mehr- *or* Vieldeutigkeit *f*

ambit [ˈæmbɪt] N Bereich *m*

ambition [æmˈbɪʃən] N ▮a (= *desire*) Ambition *f*; **she has ~s in that direction/for her son** sie hat Ambitionen in dieser Richtung/ehrgeizige Pläne für ihren Sohn; **my one *or* big ~ in life is ...** meine große Ambition ist es, ...; **my ~ is to become prime minister/to fly to the moon** es ist mein Ehrgeiz *or* Ziel *or* meine Ambition, Premierminister zu werden/zum Mond zu reisen; **it was never my ~ to take over your job** es war nie mein Bestreben *or* meine Absicht, Ihre Stelle zu übernehmen ▮b (= *ambitious nature*) Ehrgeiz *m*

ambitious [æmˈbɪʃəs] ADJ ehrgeizig, ambitiös (*pej*); *person also* ambitioniert (*geh*); *idea, undertaking* kühn; **he is ~ to ...** er setzt seinen ganzen Ehrgeiz daran, zu ...; **she is ~ for her husband** sie hat ehrgeizige Pläne für ihren Mann; **to be ~ for sth** etw anstreben

ambitiously [æmˈbɪʃəslɪ] ADV voll(er) Ehrgeiz, ehrgeizig; **rather ~, we set out to prove the following** wir hatten uns das ehrgeizige Ziel gesteckt, das Folgende zu beweisen

ambitiousness [æmˈbɪʃəsnɪs] N (*of person*) Ehrgeiz *m*; (*of idea, undertaking*) Kühnheit *f*

ambivalence [æmˈbɪvələns] N Ambivalenz *f*

ambivalent [æmˈbɪvələnt] ADJ ambivalent

amble [ˈæmbl] ▮VI (*person*) schlendern; (*horse*) im Passgang gehen ▮N Schlendern *nt*; (*of horse*) Passgang *m*; **he went for an ~ along the river**side er machte einen gemütlichen Spaziergang am Fluss entlang

ambrosia [æmˈbrəʊzɪə] N (*Myth, fig*) Ambrosia *f*

ambulance [ˈæmbjʊləns] N Krankenwagen *m*, Krankenauto *nt*, Ambulanz *f*

ambulance: ambulance driver N Krankenwagenfahrer(in) *m(f)*; **ambulanceman** N Sanitäter *m*; **ambulance service** N Rettungs- *or* Ambulanzdienst *m*; (*system*) Rettungswesen *nt*

ambulant [ˈæmbjʊlənt], **ambulatory** [ˈæmbjʊlətərɪ] (*US*) ADJ *patient* gehfähig

ambush [ˈæmbʊʃ] ▮N (= *place*) Hinterhalt *m*; (= *troops etc*) im Hinterhalt liegende Truppe/Guerillas *etc*; (= *attack*) Überfall *m* (aus dem Hinterhalt); **to lay an ~ (for sb)** (jdm) einen Hinterhalt legen; **to lie *or* wait in ~** (*Mil, fig*) im Hinterhalt liegen; **to lie in ~ for sb** (*Mil, fig*) jdm im Hinterhalt auflauern; **to fall into an ~** in einen Hinterhalt geraten ▮VT (aus dem Hinterhalt) überfallen

ameba N (*US*) = **amoeba**

ameliorate [əˈmiːlɪəreɪt] (*form*) ▮VT verbessern ▮VI sich verbessern, besser werden

amelioration [əˌmiːlɪəˈreɪʃən] N (*form*) Verbesserung *f*

amen [ˌɑːˈmen] INTERJ amen; **~ to that!** (*fig inf*) ja, wahrlich *or* fürwahr! (*hum*) ▮N Amen *nt*; **we'll all say ~ to that** (*fig inf*) wir befürworten das alle, wir sind alle dafür

amenability [əˌmiːnəˈbɪlɪtɪ] N (= *responsiveness: of people*) Zugänglichkeit *f*; **the ~ of these data to the theory** die Möglichkeit, diese Daten in die Theorie einzuordnen

amenable [əˈmiːnəbl] ADJ ▮a (= *responsive*) zugänglich (*to +dat*); **he is ~ to reasonable suggestions** er ist vernünftigen Vorschlägen zugänglich; **it is not ~ to this method of classification** es lässt sich in dieses Klassifikationssystem nicht einordnen ▮b (*Jur: = answerable*) verantwortlich; **~ to the law** dem Gesetz verantwortlich

amend [əˈmend] VT ▮a *law, bill, constitution, text* ändern, amendieren (*form*), ein Amendement einbringen zu (*form*); (*by addition*) ergänzen; **I'd better ~ that to "most people"** ich werde das lieber in „die meisten Leute" (ab)ändern ▮b (= *improve*) *habits, behaviour* bessern ▮c = **emend**

amendment [əˈmendmənt] N ▮a (*to bill, in text*) Änderung *f* (*to +gen*), Amendement *nt* (*form*) (*to +gen*); (= *addition*) Amendement *nt* (*to +gen*), Zusatz *m* (*to +gen*); **the First/Second** *etc* **Amendment** (*US Pol*) das Erste/Zweite *etc* Amendement, Zusatz *m* 1/2 *etc* ▮b (*in behaviour*) Besserung *f*

amends [əˈmendz] PL **to make ~ for sth** etw wiedergutmachen; **to make ~ to sb for sth** jdn für etw entschädigen; **I'll try to make ~** ich werde versuchen, das wieder gutzumachen

amenity [əˈmiːnɪtɪ] N ▮a (= *aid to pleasant living*) (**public**) **~** öffentliche Einrichtung; **the lack of amenities in many parts of the city** der Mangel an Einkaufs-, Unterhaltungs- und Transportmöglichkeiten in vielen Teilen der Stadt; **close to all amenities** in günstiger (Einkaufs- und Verkehrs)lage; **this house has every ~** dieses Haus bietet jeden Komfort; **a high/low ~ district** eine Gegend mit hoher/geringer Wohnqualität ▮b (= *pleasantness: of place*) angenehme Lage

amenorrhoea, (*US*) **amenorrhea** [æˌmenəˈriːə] N (*Med*) Amenorrhöe *f*

Amerasian [ˌæməˈreɪʃn] N Mensch amerikanisch-asiatischer Herkunft

America [əˈmerɪkə] N Amerika *nt*; **the ~s** Amerika *nt*, der amerikanische Kontinent

American [əˈmerɪkən] ADJ amerikanisch; **~ English** amerikanisches Englisch ▮N ▮a Amerikaner(in) *m(f)* ▮b (= *language*) Amerikanisch *nt*

American Indian N Indianer(in) *m(f)*

Americanism [əˈmerɪkənɪzm] N ▮a (*Ling*) Amerikanismus *m* ▮b (= *quality*) Amerikanertum *nt*

Americanization [əˌmerɪkənaɪˈzeɪʃən] N Amerikanisierung *f*

Americanize [əˈmerɪkənaɪz] VT amerikanisieren ▮VI sich amerikanisieren

American plan N Vollpension *f*

Amerindian [æməˈrɪndɪən] ▮N Indianer(in) *m(f)* ▮ADJ indianisch

amethyst [ˈæmɪθɪst] ▮N Amethyst *m*; (= *colour*) Amethystblau *nt*; (= *amethyst-coloured*) amethystfarben; **~ ring** Amethystring *m*

AmEx® [ˈæmeks] (*US*) ▮N *abbr of* **American Express** *no art* ▮ADJ **~ card** American Express-Karte *f*

Amex [ˈæmeks] N (*US*) *abbr of* **American Stock Exchange** Amex *f*

amiability [ˌeɪmɪəˈbɪlɪtɪ] N Liebenswürdigkeit *f*

amiable [ˈeɪmɪəbl] ADJ liebenswürdig

amiably [ˈeɪmɪəblɪ] ADV liebenswürdig; **he very ~ offered to help** er hat sich liebenswürdigerweise angeboten zu helfen

amicable [ˈæmɪkəbl] ADJ *person* freundlich; *relations* freundschaftlich; *discussion* friedlich; (*Jur*) *settlement, divorce, agreement* gütlich; **to be on ~ terms** freundschaftlich miteinander verkehren; **to part on ~ terms** sich friedlich trennen

amicably [ˈæmɪkəblɪ] ADV freundlich; *discuss* friedlich, in aller Freundschaft; (*Jur*) *settle* gütlich; **they got on quite ~** sie kamen ganz gut miteinander aus

amidships [əˈmɪdʃɪps] ADV (*Naut*) mittschiffs

amid(st) [əˈmɪd(st)] PREP inmitten (+*gen*)

amino acid [əˈmiːnəʊˈæsɪd] N Aminosäure *f*

Amish [ˈɑːmɪʃ] PL **the ~** die Amischen *pl* ▮ADJ amisch; **an ~ man** ein amischer Mann

amiss [əˈmɪs] ▮ADJ *pred* **there's something ~** da stimmt irgendetwas nicht; **what's ~ with you?** (*liter*) was fehlt Ihnen (denn)? ▮ADV **to take sth ~** (*Brit*) (jdm) etw übel nehmen; **to speak ~ of sb** schlecht über jdn sprechen; **to say something ~** etwas Falsches *or* Verkehrtes sagen; **a drink would not come *or* go ~** etwas zu trinken wäre gar nicht verkehrt

amity [ˈæmɪtɪ] N Freundschaftlichkeit *f*

ammeter [ˈæmɪtəʳ] N Amperemeter *nt*

ammo [ˈæməʊ] N (*inf*) Munition *f*

ammonia [əˈməʊnɪə] N Ammoniak *nt*

ammunition [ˌæmjʊˈnɪʃən] N (*lit, fig*) Munition *f*

ammunition: ammunition belt N Patronengurt *m*; **ammunition dump** N Munitionslager *nt*; **ammunition pouch** N Munitionsbeutel *m*

amnesia [æm'niːzɪə] N Amnesie *f*, Gedächtnisschwund *m*

amnesty ['æmnɪstɪ] N Amnestie *f*; **during** or **under the ~** unter der Amnestie; **a general ~** eine Generalamnestie; **Amnesty International** Amnesty International *no art*

amniocentesis [æmnɪəʊsen'tiːsɪs] N (*Med*) Fruchtwasseruntersuchung *f*, Amniozentese *f* (*spec*)

amoeba, (*US*) **ameba** [ə'miːbə] N Amöbe *f*

amoebic, (*US*) **amebic** [ə'miːbɪk] ADJ amöbisch; **~ dysentery** Amöbenruhr *f*

amok [ə'mɒk] ADV = **amuck**

among(st) [ə'mʌŋ(st)] PREP unter (+*acc* or *dat*); **~ other things** unter anderem; **she had sung with Madonna ~ others** sie hatte unter anderem mit Madonna gesungen; **to stand ~ the crowd** (mitten) in der Menge stehen; **they shared it out ~ themselves** sie teilten es unter sich or untereinander auf; **talk ~ yourselves** unterhaltet euch; **settle that ~ yourselves** macht das untereinander aus; **he's ~ our best players** er gehört zu unseren besten Spielern; **Manchester is ~ the largest of our cities** Manchester gehört zu unseren größten Städten; **to count sb ~ one's friends** jdn zu seinen Freunden zählen; **this habit is widespread ~ the French** diese Sitte ist bei den Franzosen weit verbreitet; **there were ferns ~ the trees** zwischen den Bäumen wuchs Farnkraut; **to hide ~ the bushes** sich in den Büschen verstecken

amoral [eɪ'mɒrəl] ADJ amoralisch

amorous ['æmərəs] ADJ amourös; *look also* verliebt; **to make ~ advances** Annäherungsversuche *pl* machen

amorously ['æmərəslɪ] ADV verliebt, voller Verliebtheit

amorphous [ə'mɔːfəs] ADJ amorph, strukturlos, formlos; *style, ideas, play, novel* strukturlos, ungegliedert; (*Geol*) amorph

amorphousness [ə'mɔːfəsnɪs] N Strukturlosigkeit *f*

amortization [ə͵mɔːtaɪ'zeɪʃən] N Amortisation *f*

amortize [ə'mɔːtaɪz] VT *debt* amortisieren, tilgen; *costs* amortisieren

amount [ə'maʊnt] ⚙ 20.7 **N** **a** (*of money*) Betrag *m*; **total ~** Gesamtsumme *f*, Endbetrag *m*; **debts to** (*Brit*) or **in** (*US*) **the ~ of £200** Schulden in Höhe von £ 200; **I was shocked at the ~ of the bill** ich war über die Höhe der Rechnung erschrocken; **in 12 equal ~s** in 12 gleichen Teilen, in 12 gleichen Beträgen; **an unlimited/a large/a small ~ of money** eine unbeschränkte or unbegrenzte/große/geringe Summe (Geldes); **a modest ~ of money** ein bescheidener Betrag; **any/quite an ~ of money** beliebig viel/ziemlich viel Geld; **large ~s of money** Unsummen *pl* (Geldes); **it's not the ~ of the donation that counts** nicht die Höhe der Spende ist maßgeblich; **if we increase the ~ of the loan** wenn wir die Darlehenssumme erhöhen

b (= *quantity*) Menge *f*; (*of luck, intelligence, skill etc*) Maß *nt* (*of an* +*dat*); **an enormous/a modest ~ of work/time** sehr viel/verhältnismäßig wenig Arbeit/Zeit; **any ~ of time/food** beliebig viel Zeit/Essen; **quite an ~ of time/food** ziemlich viel Zeit/Essen; **no ~ of talking would persuade him** kein Reden würde ihn überzeugen; **no ~ of paint can hide the rust** keine noch so dicke Farbschicht kann den Rost verdecken

VI **a** (= *total*) sich belaufen (*to auf* +*acc*) **b** (= *be equivalent*) gleichkommen (*to* +*dat*); **it ~s to the same thing** das läuft or kommt (doch) aufs Gleiche hinaus or raus (*inf*); **he will never ~ to much** aus ihm wird nie etwas or viel werden, der wird es nie zu etwas or zu viel bringen; **their promises don't ~ to very much** ihre Versprechungen sind recht nichts sagend; **so what this ~s to is that ...** worauf es also hinausläuft ist, dass ...

amour [ə'mʊə'] N (*dated, liter*) Liebschaft *f*; (= *person*) Liebe *f*

amour-propre [͵æmʊə'prɒprə] N Eigenliebe *f*

amperage ['æmpərɪdʒ] N elektrische Stromstärke (in Ampere)

amp(ère) ['æmp(εə')] N Ampere *nt*

ampersand ['æmpəsænd] N Et-Zeichen *f*, Und-Zeichen *nt*

amphetamine [æm'fetəmiːn] N Amphetamin *nt*

amphibian [æm'fɪbɪən] N (= *animal, plant*) Amphibie *f*; (= *vehicle*) Amphibienfahrzeug *nt*; (= *aircraft*) Amphibienflugzeug *nt*, Wasser-Land-Flugzeug *nt*; **~ tank** Amphibienpanzer *m*

amphibious [æm'fɪbɪəs] ADJ *animal, plant* amphibisch; (*Mil*) amphibisch; **~ vehicle/aircraft** Amphibienfahrzeug *nt*/-flugzeug *nt*

amphitheatre, (*US*) **amphitheater** ['æmfɪ͵θɪətə'] N **a** Amphitheater *nt*; (= *lecture hall*) Hörsaal *m* (*Halbrund mit ansteigenden Sitzreihen*) **b** (*Geog*) Halbkessel *m*; **a natural ~** ein natürliches Amphitheater

amphora ['æmfərə] N *pl* **-s** or **-e** [æm'fəriː] (*form*) Amphora *f*, Amphore *f*

ample ['æmpl] ADJ (+*er*) **a** (= *plentiful*) reichlich; **that will be ~** das ist reichlich; **more than ~** überreichlich; **to make ~ use of sth** etw reichlich benutzen **b** (= *large*) *figure, proportions* üppig; *boot of car etc* geräumig; *garden* weitläufig, ausgedehnt

amplification [͵æmplɪfɪ'keɪʃən] N weitere Ausführungen *pl*, Erläuterungen *pl*; (*Rad*) Verstärkung *f*; **in ~ of this ...** dies weiter ausführend ...

amplifier ['æmplɪfaɪə'] N (*Rad*) Verstärker *m*

amplify ['æmplɪfaɪ] **VT** **a** (*Rad*) verstärken **b** (= *expand*) *statement, idea* näher or ausführlicher erläutern, genauer ausführen **c** (*inf*: = *exaggerate*) übertreiben **VI** **would you care to ~ a little?** würden Sie das bitte näher or ausführlicher erläutern?, würden Sie bitte auf diesen Punkt näher eingehen?; **to ~ on sth** etw näher erläutern or ausführen

amplitude ['æmplɪtjuːd] N (*of knowledge*) Weite *f*, Breite *f*; (*of bosom*) Üppigkeit *f*, Fülle *f*; (*Phys*) Amplitude *f*

amply ['æmplɪ] ADV reichlich; *proportioned figure* üppig; *proportioned rooms* geräumig, großzügig

ampoule, (*US*) **ampule** ['æmpuːl] N Ampulle *f*

ampulla [æm'pʊlə] N *pl* **-e** [æm'pʊliː] (*Hist, Eccl*) Ampulla *f*

amputate ['æmpjʊteɪt] VTI amputieren

amputation [æmpjʊ'teɪʃən] N Amputation *f*

amputee [æmpjʊ'tiː] N Amputierte(r) *mf*

amuck [ə'mʌk] ADV **to run ~** (*lit, fig*) Amok laufen

amulet ['æmjʊlɪt] N Amulett *nt*

amuse [ə'mjuːz] **VT** **a** (= *cause mirth*) amüsieren, belustigen; **you ~ me, how can anyone ...?** dass ich nicht lache or da muss ich ja (mal) lachen, wie kann man nur ...?

b (= *entertain*) unterhalten; **let the children do it if it ~s them** lass die Kinder doch, wenn es ihnen Spaß macht

VR **the children can ~ themselves for a while** die Kinder können sich eine Zeit lang selbst beschäftigen; **could you ~ yourself with the magazines in the meantime?** könntest du dir derweil ein bisschen die Zeitschriften ansehen or dich derweil mit den Zeitschriften beschäftigen?; **to ~ oneself (by) doing sth** etw zu seinem Vergnügen or aus Spaß tun; **he ~s himself now you're retired?** wie vertreiben Sie sich (*dat*) die Zeit, wo Sie jetzt im Ruhestand sind?; **he ~s himself with crossword puzzles** er löst zum Zeitvertreib Kreuzworträtsel; **he's just amusing himself with her** er amüsiert sich nur mit ihr

amused [ə'mjuːzd] ADJ *person, look, smile, attitude* amüsiert; **she seemed ~ at my suggestion** sie schien über meinen Vorschlag amüsiert (zu sein); **I was ~ to see/hear that ...** es hat mich amüsiert zu sehen/hören, dass ...; **the teacher**

shouldn't appear to be ~ by the pupils' mistakes der Lehrer sollte es dich nicht anmerken lassen, dass ihn die Fehler der Schüler amüsieren; **to keep sb ~** jdn unterhalten, jdm die Zeit vertreiben; **give him his toys, that'll keep him ~** gib ihm sein Spielzeug, dann ist er friedlich; **to keep oneself ~** sich (*dat*) die Zeit vertreiben; **I have no problem keeping myself ~ now I'm retired** ich habe keinerlei Schwierigkeiten, mir die Zeit zu vertreiben, jetzt wo ich im Ruhestand bin; **he was anything but ~ to find the door locked** er fand es keineswegs or durchaus nicht komisch, dass die Tür verschlossen war; **we are not ~** (*hum*) das ist nicht besonders komisch

amusedly [ə'mjuːzɪdlɪ] ADV amüsiert

amusement [ə'mjuːzmənt] N **a** (= *enjoyment, fun*) Vergnügen *nt*; (= *state of being entertained*) Belustigung *f*, Amüsement *nt*; **the toys were a great source of ~** das Spielzeug bereitete großen Spaß; **he gets no ~ out of life** er kann dem Leben kein Vergnügen abgewinnen; **what do you do for ~?** was machst du als Freizeitbeschäftigung?; (*retired people*) was machen Sie zu Ihrer Unterhaltung or als Zeitvertreib?; **I see no cause for ~** ich sehe keinen Grund zur Heiterkeit; **to do sth for one's own ~** etw zu seinem Vergnügen or Amüsement tun; **to my great ~/to everyone's ~** zu meiner großen/zur allgemeinen Belustigung

b (= *entertainment: of guests*) Belustigung *f*, Unterhaltung *f*

c **amusements** PL (= *place of entertainment*) Vergnügungsstätte *f usu pl*; (*at fair*) Attraktionen *pl*; (= *stand, booth*) Buden *pl*; (*at the seaside*) Spielautomaten und Spiegelkabinett *etc* **what sort of ~s do you have around here?** was für Vergnügungs- und Unterhaltungsmöglichkeiten gibt es hier?

amusement: amusement arcade N (*Brit*) Spielhalle *f*; **amusement park** N Vergnügungspark *m*, Lunapark *m* (*dated*)

amusing [ə'mjuːzɪŋ] ADJ **a** amüsant; **how ~** wie lustig or witzig!, das ist aber lustig or witzig!; **I've just had an ~ thought** mir ist gerade etwas Lustiges or Amüsantes eingefallen; **I don't find that very ~** das finde ich nicht gerade or gar nicht lustig or zum Lachen **b** (*inf*) hat, *little dress etc* charmant, apart; **an ~ little wine** ein nettes Weinchen (*hum*)

amusingly [ə'mjuːzɪŋlɪ] ADV amüsant

an [æn, ən, n] **INDEF ART** → **a** **CONJ** (*obs*: = *if*) so (*old*)

Anabaptism [͵ænə'bæptɪzəm] N Anabaptismus *m*

Anabaptist [͵ænə'bæptɪst] N Anabaptist(in) *m(f)*, Wiedertäufer(in) *m(f)*

anabolic steroid [͵ænə'bɒlɪk'stɪərɔɪd] N Anabolikum *nt*

anachronism [ə'nækrənɪzəm] N Anachronismus *m*

anachronistic [ə͵nækrə'nɪstɪk] ADJ anachronistisch; (= *not fitting modern times*) nicht zeitgemäß, unzeitgemäß

anaconda [͵ænə'kɒndə] N Anakonda *f*

anaemia, (*US*) **anemia** [ə'niːmɪə] N Anämie *f*, Blutarmut *f*

anaemic, (*US*) **anemic** [ə'niːmɪk] ADJ **a** anämisch, blutarm **b** (*fig*) anämisch, saft- und kraftlos; *colour, appearance* bleichsüchtig, anämisch

anaerobic [͵ænə'rəʊbɪk] ADJ (*Biol, Chem*) anaerob; **~ reaction** anaerobe Reaktion

anaesthesia, (*US*) **anesthesia** [͵ænɪs'θiːzɪə] N Betäubung *f*

anaesthetic, (*US*) **anesthetic** [͵ænɪs'θetɪk] **N** Narkose *f*, Anästhesie *f* (*spec*); (= *substance*) Narkosemittel *nt*, Anästhetikum *nt* (*spec*); **general ~** Vollnarkose *f*; **local ~** örtliche Betäubung, Lokalanästhesie *f* (*spec*); **the nurse gave him a local ~** die Schwester gab ihm eine Spritze zur örtlichen Betäubung; **the patient is still under the ~** der Patient ist noch in der Narkose; **when he comes out of the ~** wenn er aus der Narkose aufwacht **ADJ** *effect* betäubend, anästhetisch; **~ drug** Betäubungsmittel *nt*

anaesthetist, *(US)* **anesthetist** [æ'ni:sθıtıst] N Anästhesist(in) *m(f)*, Narkose(fach)arzt *m/*-(fach)ärztin *f*

anaesthetize, *(US)* **anesthetize** [æ'ni:sθıtaız] VT *(Med)* betäuben; *(generally also)* narkotisieren

Anaglypta® [ˌænəˈglıptə] N Prägetapete *f*

anagram [ˈænəgræm] N Anagramm *nt*

anal [ˈeınəl] ADJ anal, Anal-; **~ intercourse** Analverkehr *m*; **you're so ~!** *(inf)* du bist ja so analfixiert!

anal eroticism N Analerotik *f*

analgesia [ˌænælˈdʒiːzıə] N Schmerzlosigkeit *f*, Analgesie *f* *(spec)*

analgesic [ˌænælˈdʒiːsık] N schmerzstillendes Mittel, Schmerzmittel *nt*, Analgetikum *nt* *(spec)* **ADJ** schmerzstillend

analog [ˈænəlɒg] ADJ *(Tech)* analog

analog computer N Analogrechner *m*

analogic(al) [ˌænəˈlɒdʒık(əl)] ADJ , **analogically** [ˌænəˈlɒdʒıkəlı] ADV analog

analogous ADJ , **analogously** ADV [əˈnæləgəs, -lı] analog *(to, with* zu)

analogue [ˈænəlɒg] N Gegenstück *nt*, Parallele *f*

analogy [əˈnælədʒı] N Analogie *f*; **arguing by ~ one could claim that ...** analog könnte man behaupten ...; **to draw an ~** eine Analogie herstellen, einen analogen Vergleich ziehen; **on the ~ of** analog zu, nach dem Muster (+*gen*); **it's an argument by ~** es ist ein Analogiebeweis, es ist eine analoge Argumentation

anal-retentive [ˌeınəlrı'tentıv] ADJ analfixiert

analyse, *(esp US)* **analyze** [ˈænəlaız] ✪ 26.1 VT **a** *(= examine)* analysieren; *(Gram)* *sentence* (zer)gliedern; **to ~ the situation** *(fig)* die Situation analysieren *or (to others)* erläutern; **to ~ sth into its parts** etw in seine Bestandteile zerlegen **b** *(= psychoanalyse)* psychoanalytisch behandeln, analysieren *(inf)*; **stop analysing me!** hör auf, mich zu analysieren! *(inf)*

analyser, *(US)* **analyzer** [ˈænəlaızə'] N Analysegerät *nt*

analysis [əˈnæləsıs] N *pl* **analyses** [əˈnæləsiːz] **a** *(= examination)* Analyse *f*; *(Gram, of sentence also)* (Zer)gliederung *f*; **what's your ~ of the situation?** wie beurteilen Sie die Situation?; **in the last** *or* **final ~** letzten Endes; **on (closer) ~** bei genauerer Untersuchung **b** *(= psychoanalysis)* Psychoanalyse *f*, Analyse *f* *(inf)*

analyst [ˈænəlıst] N Analytiker(in) *m(f)*; *(= psychoanalyst also)* Psychoanalytiker(in) *m(f)*; *(Chem)* Chemiker(in) *m(f)*; **food ~** Lebensmittelchemiker(in) *m(f)*; **he gave it to the ~ in the lab** er ließ im Labor eine Analyse davon machen

analytic [ˌænəˈlıtık] ADJ analytisch

analytical [ˌænəˈlıtıkəl] ADJ analytisch; **you should try to be more ~** Sie sollten versuchen, etwas analytischer vorzugehen; **he hasn't got a very ~ mind** er kann nicht analytisch denken

analytically [ˌænəˈlıtıkəlı] ADV analytisch

analyze [ˈænəlaız] VT *(US)* = **analyse**

analyzer [ˈænəlaızə'] N *(US)* = **analyser**

anapaest, *(US)* **anapest** [ˈænəpiːst] N *(Poet)* Anapäst *m*

anaphora [əˈnæfərə] N *(Liter, Gram)* Anapher *f*

anaphylactic [ˌænəfıˈlæktık] ADJ *(Med)* anaphylaktisch; **~ shock** anaphylaktischer Schock

anarchic(al) [æˈnɑːkık(əl)] ADJ anarchisch

anarchism [ˈænəkızəm] N Anarchismus *m*

anarchist [ˈænəkıst] N Anarchist(in) *m(f)*

anarchistic [ˌænəˈkıstık] ADJ anarchistisch

anarcho- [æˈnɑːkəʊ] PREF anarcho-, Anarcho-; **~syndicalism** Anarcho-Syndikalismus *m*

anarchy [ˈænəkı] N Anarchie *f*

anathema [əˈnæθımə] N *(Eccl)* Anathema *(form)* *nt*, Kirchenbann *m*; *(fig, no art)* ein Gräuel *m*; **voting Labour was ~ to them** der Gedanke, Labour zu wählen, war ihnen ein Gräuel

anathematize [əˈnæθımətaız] VT *(Eccl)* mit dem Bann belegen

anatomical ADJ , **anatomically** ADV [ˌænəˈtɒmıkəl, -ı] anatomisch

anatomist [əˈnætəmıst] N Anatom(in) *m(f)*

anatomy [əˈnætəmı] N Anatomie *f*; *(= structure also)* Körperbau *m*; *(fig)* Struktur *f* und Aufbau *m*; **on a certain part of her ~** *(euph)* an einer gewissen Stelle *(euph)*

ANC *abbr of* **African National Congress** ANC *m*, südafrikanische nationalistische Bewegung

ancestor [ˈænsıstə'] N Vorfahr *m*, Ahne *m*; *(= progenitor)* Stammvater *m*; **~ worship** Ahnenkult *m*

ancestral [ænˈsestrəl] ADJ seiner/ihrer Vorfahren; **~ home** Stammsitz *m*

ancestress [ˈænsıstrıs] N Vorfahrin *f*, Ahne *f*; *(= progenitor)* Ahnfrau *f*, Stammmutter *f*

ancestry [ˈænsıstrı] N *(= descent)* Abstammung *f*, Herkunft *f*; *(= ancestors)* Ahnenreihe *f*, Familie *f*; **to trace one's ~** seine Abstammung zurückverfolgen; **of royal ~** königlicher Abstammung *or* Herkunft

anchor [ˈæŋkə'] N **a** *(Naut)* Anker *m*; *(fig: hope, love, person etc)* Zuflucht *f*, Rettungsanker *m*; **to cast** *or* **drop ~** Anker werfen, vor Anker gehen; **to weigh** *or* **up ~** den Anker lichten; **to be** *or* **lie** *or* **ride at ~** vor Anker liegen; **to come to ~** vor Anker gehen; **the stone served as an ~ for the tent** der Stein diente dazu, das Zelt zu beschweren *or* am Boden festzuhalten **b** *(esp US TV: = presenter)* Anchorman *m*, Anchorwoman *m/*-frau *f* **VT** *(Naut, fig)* verankern; **we ~ed the tablecloth (down) with stones** wir beschwerten das Tischtuch mit Steinen; **to be ~ed in sth** *(fig)* in etw *(dat)* (fest) verankert sein **VI** *(Naut)* ankern, vor Anker gehen

anchorage [ˈæŋkərıdʒ] N *(Naut)* **a** Ankerplatz *m* **b** *(also* **anchorage dues)** Anker- *or* Liegegebühren *pl*

anchor buoy N Ankerboje *f*

anchorite [ˈæŋkəraıt] N Einsiedler *m*, Eremit *m*

anchorman [ˈæŋkəmæn] N *pl* **-men** [-mən] *(esp US TV)* Anchorman *m*, Ankermann *m*; *(Sport)* *(in relay race)* Letzte(r) *m*; *(in tug-of-war)* hinterster Mann; *(fig)* eiserne Stütze *f*, Eckpfeiler *m*

anchorwoman [ˈæŋkəwʊmən] N *pl* **-women** [-wımın] *(esp US TV)* Anchorwoman *f*, Ankerfrau *f*; *(Sport: in relay race)* Letzte *f*

anchovy [ˈæntʃəvı] N Sardelle *f*, An(s)chovis *f*; **~ paste** Sardellen- *or* An(s)chovispaste *f*

ancient [ˈeınʃənt] **ADJ a** alt; **in ~ times** im Altertum; *(Greek, Roman also)* in der Antike; **~ Rome** das alte Rom; **the ~ Romans** die alten Römer; **~ monument** *(Brit)* historisches Denkmal, historische Stätte **b** *(inf)* *person, clothes etc* uralt **N the ~s** die Völker *or* Menschen des Altertums *or* im Altertum; *(= writers)* die Schriftsteller des Altertums

ancient history N *(lit)* Alte Geschichte; *(fig)* graue Vorzeit; **that's ~** *(fig)* das ist schon längst Geschichte; **he's well-known in the field of ~** er ist ein sehr bekannter Altertumsforscher

anciently [ˈeınʃəntlı] ADV in (ur)alten Zeiten; **even as ~ as the times of ...** selbst vor so langer Zeit wie zu Zeiten von ...

ancillary [ænˈsılərı] ADJ *(= subordinate)* Neben-; *(= auxiliary)* Hilfs-; **~ course** *(Univ)* Begleitkurs *m*; **~ industry** Zulieferindustrie *f*; **~ staff/workers** Hilfskräfte *pl*; **~ subject** *(Univ)* Nebenfach *nt*; **~ troops** Hilfstruppen *pl*

and [ænd, ənd, nd, ən] CONJ **a** und; **nice ~ early/warm** schön früh/warm; **when I'm good ~ ready** wenn es mir passt, wenn so ich so weit bin; **you ~ you alone** du, nur du allein; **try ~ come** versuch zu kommen; **wait ~ see!** abwarten!, warts ab!; **don't go ~ spoil it!** nun verdirb nicht alles!; **come ~ get it!** komm und hols!;

one more ~ I'm finished noch eins, dann bin ich fertig; **there are dictionaries ~ dictionaries** es gibt Wörterbücher und Wörterbücher, es gibt sone Wörterbücher und solche *(inf)*; **~/or** und/oder; **~ so on, ~ so forth, ~ so on ~ so forth** und so weiter, und so fort, und so weiter und so fort

b *(in repetition, continuation)* und; **better ~ better** immer besser; **for hours ~ hours/days ~ days/weeks ~ weeks** stundenlang, Stunde um Stunde *(geh)*/tagelang/wochenlang; **for miles ~ miles** meilenweit; **I rang ~ rang** ich klingelte und klingelte, ich klingelte immer wieder; **I tried ~ tried** ich habe es immer wieder versucht; **~ he pulled ~ he pulled** und er zog und zog

c *(with numbers)* **three hundred ~ ten** dreihundert(und)zehn; **one ~ a half** anderthalb, eineinhalb; **two ~ twenty** *(old, form)* zweiundzwanzig

andante [ænˈdæntı] *(Mus)* **ADJ ADV** andante **N** Andante *nt*

Andean [ænˈdıən] ADJ Anden-; **~ country** Andenstaat *m*

Andes [ˈændiːz] PL Anden *pl*

andiron [ˈændaıən] N Kaminbock *m*

Andorra [ænˈdɔːrə] N Andorra *nt*

Andorran [ænˈdɔːrən] **N** Andorraner(in) *m(f)* **ADJ** andorranisch

Andrew [ˈændruː] N Andreas *m*

androgen [ˈændrədʒən] N Androgen *nt*

androgyne [ˈændrədʒaın] N Hermaphrodit *m*, Zwitter *m*

androgynous [ænˈdrɒdʒınəs] ADJ androgyn, zwitt(e)rig

androgyny [ænˈdrɒdʒını] N Androgynie *f*, Zwittrigkeit *f*

android [ˈændrɔıd] N Androide *m*

anecdotal [ˌænıkˈdəʊtəl] ADJ anekdotenhaft, anekdotisch

anecdote [ˈænıkdəʊt] N Anekdote *f*

anemia [əˈniːmıə] N *(US)* = **anaemia**

anemic [əˈniːmık] ADJ *(US)* = **anaemic**

anemometer [ˌænıˈmɒmıtə'] N Windmesser *m*

anemone [əˈnemənı] N *(Bot)* Anemone *f*, Buschwindröschen *nt*; *(= sea anemone)* Seeanemone *f*

aneroid barometer [ˌænərɔıdbəˈrɒmıtə'] N Aneroidbarometer *nt*

anesthesia *etc (US)* = **anaesthesia** *etc*

anew [əˈnjuː] ADV **a** *(= again)* aufs neue *or* Neue; **let's start ~** fangen wir wieder von vorn *or* von neuem an **b** *(= in a new way)* auf eine neue Art und Weise

angel [ˈeındʒəl] N *(lit, fig)* Engel *m*; *(Theat inf: = backer)* finanzkräftiger Hintermann; **on the side of the ~s** *(fig inf)* auf der Seite des Rechts

angel cake N ≈ Biskuitkuchen *m*

Angeleno [ˌændʒəˈliːnəʊ] N Einwohner(in) *m(f)* von Los Angeles

angel: angel face INTERJ *(hum inf)* mein Engel; **angel fish** N *(= shark)* Meerengel *m*, Engelhai *m*; *(= tropical fish)* Großer Segelflosser; **angel food cake** N *(US)* Biskuitkuchen *m*; **angel hair** N *(Christmas decoration)* Engelshaar *nt*

angelic [ænˈdʒelık] ADJ *(= of an angel)* Engels-; *hosts* himmlisch; *salutation* Englisch; *(= like an angel)* engelhaft, engelgleich *(liter)*; **~ appearance** Engelsgestalt *f*

angelica [ænˈdʒelıkə] N *(Bot)* Angelika *f*, Brustwurz *f*; *(Cook)* kandierte Angelika

angelically [ænˈdʒelıkə lı] ADV wie ein Engel, engelgleich

angels-on-horseback [ˌeındʒəlzɒnˈhɔːsbæk] PL *(Brit Cook)* in Schinkenscheiben eingewickelte Austern, auf Toast serviert

angelus [ˈændʒıləs] N Angelusläuten *nt*; *(= prayer)* Angelus *nt*

anger [ˈæŋgə'] **N** Ärger *m*; *(= wrath: of gods etc)* Zorn *m*; **a fit of ~** ein Wutanfall *m*, ein Zorn(es)ausbruch *m*; **red with ~** rot vor Wut; **public ~** öffentliche Entrüstung; **to speak/act**

in ~ im Zorn sprechen/handeln; **words spoken in ~** was man in seiner Wut or im Zorn sagt; **to do sth in ~** etw im Zorn tun; **to be filled with ~** zornig or wütend sein; **to provoke sb's ~** jdn reizen; **to rouse sb to ~** (liter) jdn in Wut or Rage bringen; **to make one's ~ clear** seinem Ärger or Unmut Luft machen

VT (stressing action) ärgern; (stressing result) verärgern; gods erzürnen (liter); **what ~s me is ...** was mich ärgert, ist ...; **to be easily ~ed** sich schnell or leicht ärgern; (= quick to take offence) schnell verärgert sein

angina (pectoris) N Angina pectoris f

angiogram ['ændʒɪəʊgræm] N (Med) Angiogramm nt

angiography [ændʒɪ'ɒgrəfɪ] N (Med) Angiographie f

angioplasty ['ændʒɪəʊplæstɪ] N (Med) Angioplastie f

angle¹ ['æŋgl] **N** **a** Winkel m; **at an ~ of 40°** in einem Winkel von 40°; **at an ~** schräg; **at an ~ to the street** schräg or im Winkel zur Straße; **he was wearing his hat at an ~** er hatte seinen Hut schief aufgesetzt; **~ of climb** (Aviat) Steigwinkel m; **~ of elevation** (Math) Höhenwinkel m; **~ of incidence** (Opt) Einfallswinkel m; **parking ~** Schrägparken nt **b** (= projecting corner) Ecke f; (= angular recess) Winkel m

c (= position) Winkel m; **if you take the photograph from this ~** wenn du die Aufnahme aus or von diesem (Blick)winkel machst **d** (of problem etc: = aspect) Seite f **e** (= point of view) Standpunkt m, Position f; **a journalist usually has an ~ on a story** ein Journalist schreibt seine Berichte gewöhnlich von einer gewissen Warte aus; **an inside ~ on the story** die Geschichte vom Standpunkt eines Insiders or eines Direktbeteiligten or eines direkt Beteiligten; **what's your ~?** (= what are you getting at?) worauf wollen Sie hinaus?

VT lamp etc (aus)richten, einstellen; (Sport) shot im Winkel schießen/schlagen; (fig) information, report färben; **the question was ~d at getting one particular answer** es war eine Suggestivfrage

angle² VI (esp Brit Fishing) angeln

▶ **angle for** VI +prep obj **a** (lit) trout angeln **b** (fig) compliments fischen nach; **to angle for sth** auf etw (acc) aus sein; **to angle for sb's sympathy** jds Mitleid erregen wollen

angle: angle bracket N **a** (for shelves) Winkelband nt, Winkelkonsole f **b** (Typ) spitze Klammer; **angle iron** N Winkeleisen nt; **Anglepoise (lamp)®** ['æŋglpɔɪz'læmp)] N Architekten- or Gelenkleuchte f

angler ['æŋglə'] N Angler(in) m(f)

Angles ['æŋglz] PL (Hist) Angeln pl

Anglican ['æŋglɪkən] **N** Anglikaner(in) m(f) **ADJ** anglikanisch

Anglicanism ['æŋglɪkənɪzəm] N Anglikanismus m

anglicism ['æŋglɪsɪzəm] N Anglizismus m

anglicist ['æŋglɪsɪst] N Anglist(in) m(f)

anglicize ['æŋglɪsaɪz] VT anglisieren

angling ['æŋglɪŋ] N (esp Brit) Angeln nt

Anglo- ['æŋgləʊ] PREF Anglo-; (between two countries) Englisch-; **Anglo-American** **N** Angloamerikaner(in) m(f) **ADJ** angloamerikanisch; **Anglo-Asian** **N** Anglo-Inder(in) m(f), Anglo-Asiat(in) m(f) **ADJ** angloindisch, angloasiatisch; **Anglo-Catholic** **N** Anglokatholik(in) m(f) **ADJ** hochkirchlich, anglokatholisch; **Anglo-German** ADJ englisch-deutsch; **Anglo-Indian** **N** (of British descent) in Indien lebender Engländer m/lebende Engländerin f; (= Eurasian) Angloinder(in) m(f) **ADJ** angloindisch; **Anglo-Irish** **PL** **the ~** die Angloiren pl **ADJ** angloirisch

Anglomania [æŋgləʊ'meɪnɪə] N Anglomanie f

Anglophile ['æŋgləʊfaɪl] **N** Anglophile(r) mf (form), Englandfreund(in) m(f) **ADJ** anglophil (form), englandfreundlich

Anglophobe ['æŋgləʊfəʊb] N Anglophobe(r) mf (form), Englandhasser(in) m(f), Englandfeind(in) m(f)

Anglophobia [æŋgləʊ'fəʊbɪə] N Anglophobie f (form), Englandhass m

Anglophobic [æŋgləʊ'fəʊbɪk] ADJ anglophob (form), anti-englisch, englandfeindlich

Anglo-Saxon ['æŋgləʊ'sæksən] **N** **a** (Hist: = person) Angelsachse m, Angelsächsin f **b** (= language) Angelsächsisch nt **ADJ** angelsächsisch

---

ANGLO-SAXON

Anglo-Saxon ist das Englisch, das ab ungefähr 400 n. Chr. bis zur normannischen Eroberung 1066 gesprochen wurde. Wichtige Bestandteile des heute gebräuchlichen, englischen Wortschatzes haben ihren Ursprung in der angelsächsischen Periode, zum Beispiel Wörter wie **man, child, cat, love** und **harvest**.

Angola [æŋ'gəʊlə] N Angola nt

Angolan [æŋ'gəʊlən] **N** Angolaner(in) m(f) **ADJ** angolanisch

angora [æŋ'gɔ:rə] **ADJ** Angora-; **~ wool** Angorawolle f **N** Angora(wolle f) nt; (Tex) Angoragewebe nt; (= angora rabbit, angora cat, angora goat) Angorakaninchen nt/-katze f/-ziege f

angostura [æŋgə'stjʊərə] N (= bark) Angosturarinde f; (also **angostura bitters**)® Angosturabitter m

angrily ['æŋgrɪlɪ] ADV wütend

angry ['æŋgrɪ] ADJ (+er) **a** zornig, ungehalten (geh); letter, look zornig, wütend; animal wütend; **to be ~** wütend or böse or verärgert sein; **to be ~ with** or **at sb** jdm or auf jdn or mit jdm böse sein, über jdn verärgert sein; **to be ~ at** or **about sth** sich über etw (acc) ärgern; **to get ~ (with** or **at sb/about sth)** (mit jdm/über etw acc) böse werden; **you're not ~ (with me), are you?** du bist (mir) doch nicht böse(, oder)?; **to be ~ with oneself** sich über sich (acc) selbst ärgern, sich (dat) selbst böse sein, über sich (acc) selbst verärgert sein; **to make sb ~** (stressing action) jdn ärgern; (stressing result) jdn verärgern; **it makes me so ~** es ärgert mich furchtbar, es macht mich so wütend or böse; **~ young man** Rebell m, Angry Young Man m (geh) **b** (fig) sea aufgewühlt; sky, clouds bedrohlich, finster; **the sky was an ~ purple** der Himmel war bedrohlich violett

c (= inflamed) wound entzündet, böse; **an ~ red** hochrot

angst [æŋst] N (Existenz)angst f

anguish ['æŋgwɪʃ] N Qual f; **to be in ~** Qualen leiden; **the look of ~ on the faces of the waiting wives** der angsterfüllte Blick in den Gesichtern der wartenden Frauen; **he wrung his hands in ~** er rang die Hände in Verzweiflung; **those who suffer the ~ of indecision** wer die Qual der Entschlusslosigkeit erleidet; **writhing in ~ on the ground** sich in Qualen auf dem Boden windend; **the news caused her great ~** die Nachricht bereitete ihr großen Schmerz; **the decision caused her great ~** die Entscheidung bereitete ihr große Qual(en)

anguished ['æŋgwɪʃt] ADJ qualvoll

angular ['æŋgjʊlə'] ADJ **a** shape eckig; face, features, prose kantig **b** (= bony) knochig **c** (= awkward) linkisch, steif

angularity [æŋgjʊ'lærɪtɪ] N **a** (of shape) Eckigkeit f; (of face, features) Kantigkeit f **b** (= boniness) Knochigkeit f

aniline ['ænɪli:n] N Anilin nt; **~ dye** Anilinfarbstoff m

anima ['ænɪmə] N (Psych) Anima f

animadversion [ænɪmæd'vɜ:ʃən] N (form) kritische Äußerung

animal ['ænɪməl] **N** Tier nt; (as opposed to insects etc) Vierbeiner m; (= brutal person) Bestie f, Tier nt; **man is a social ~** der Mensch ist ein soziales Wesen; **a political ~** ein politisches Wesen, ein Zoon politikon nt (geh); **there's no such ~**

(fig) so was gibt es nicht! (inf); **the ~ in him** das Tier(ische) or Animalische in ihm; **he's little better than an ~** er ist kaum besser als ein Tier **ADJ** attr Tier-; fat, products, cruelty, lust tierisch; **~ behaviour** (Brit) or **behavior** (US) (lit) das Verhalten der Tiere, tierhaftes Verhalten; (fig: = brutal) tierisches Verhalten; **~ experiments/testing** Tierversuche pl; **~ magnetism** rein körperliche Anziehungskraft; **~ needs** (fig) animalische Bedürfnisse pl; **~ spirits** Vitalität f; **full of ~ spirits** ausgelassen

animal cracker n (US) Keks m in Tierform

animalcule ['ænɪ'mælkju:l] N mikroskopisch kleines Tierchen

animal husbandry N Viehwirtschaft f

animality ['ænɪ'mælɪtɪ] N Tierhaftigkeit f

animal: animal kingdom N Tierreich nt, Tierwelt f; **Animal Liberation Front** N (Brit) militante Tierschützerorganisation; **animal liberationist** N militanter Tierschützer, militante Tierschützerin; **animal lover** N Tierfreund(in) m(f); **animal park** N (US) Wildpark m; **animal rights** PL der Tierschutz, Tierrechte pl; **~ activist/campaigner** Tierschützer(in) m(f), Tierrechtler(in) m(f); **animal sanctuary** N Tierschutzgebiet nt; **animal welfare** N Tierschutz m

animate ['ænɪmɪt] **ADJ** belebt; creation, creatures lebend **VT** ['ænɪmeɪt] (lit: God) mit Leben erfüllen; (fig) (= enliven) beleben; (= move to action) anregen, animieren; (Film) animieren; **Disney was the first to ~ cartoons** Disney machte als erster Zeichentrickfilme

animated ['ænɪmeɪtɪd] ADJ **a** (= lively) lebhaft, rege; discussion, talk lebhaft, angeregt **b** (Film) **~ cartoon/film** Zeichentrickfilm m

animatedly ['ænɪmeɪtɪdlɪ] ADV rege; talk angeregt, lebhaft

animation [ænɪ'meɪʃən] N Lebhaftigkeit f; (Film) Animation f; **she loved the ~ of Parisian life** sie liebte das Getriebe des Pariser Lebens

animator ['ænɪmeɪtə'] N Animator(in) m(f)

animatronics [ænɪmə'trɒnɪks] N SING (Film) Computer-Animation f

animism ['ænɪmɪzəm] N Animismus m

animosity [ænɪ'mɒsɪtɪ] N Animosität f (geh) (towards gegenüber), Feindseligkeit f (towards gegenüber)

animus ['ænɪməs] N , no pl **a** Feindseligkeit f **b** (Psych) Animus m

anise ['ænɪs] N Anis m

aniseed ['ænɪsi:d] N (= seed) Anis(samen) m; (= flavouring) Anis m; (= liqueur) Anislikör m

aniseed ball N Anisbonbon m or nt

ankle ['æŋkl] N Knöchel m

ankle: ankle biter N (Austral hum) Kind nt, Plage f (hum); **anklebone** N Sprungbein nt; **ankle boot** N Halbstiefel m; **ankle bracelet** N Fußkettchen nt; **ankle-deep** **ADJ** knöcheltief **ADV** **he was ~ in water** er stand bis an die Knöchel im Wasser; **the field was ~ in mud** auf dem Feld stand der Schlamm knöcheltief; **ankle joint** N Sprunggelenk nt; **ankle sock** N Söckchen nt; **ankle strap** N Schuhriemchen nt

anklet ['æŋklɪt] N **a** Fußring m, Fußspange f **b** (US: = sock) Söckchen nt

annalist ['ænəlɪst] N Chronist(in) m(f), Geschichtsschreiber(in) m(f)

annals ['ænəlz] PL Annalen pl; (of society etc) Bericht m; **in all the ~ of recorded history** in der gesamten bisherigen Geschichte

anneal [ə'ni:l] VT glass kühlen; metal ausglühen; earthenware brennen; (fig) stählen

annex [ə'neks] **VT** annektieren **N** ['æneks] **a** (to document etc) Anhang m, Nachtrag m **b** (= building) Nebengebäude nt, Annex m; (= extension) Anbau m

annexation [ænek'seɪʃən] N Annexion f

annexe ['æneks] N (Brit) = annex N b

annihilate [ə'naɪəleɪt] VT vernichten; army also aufreiben, auslöschen (geh); (fig) hope zerschlagen; *theory* vernichten, zerschlagen; (*inf*) *person, opponent, team* fertig machen (*inf*), in die Pfanne hauen (*inf*); **I felt completely ~d** ich war völlig am Boden zerstört (*inf*)

annihilation [ə,naɪə'leɪʃən] N Vernichtung *f*, Auslöschung *f* (*geh*); (*fig: of theory*) Vernichtung *f*, Zerschlagung *f*; **our team's** ~ die vollständige Niederlage unserer Mannschaft; **her ~ of her opponents** die Art, wie sie ihre Gegner fertig machte (*inf*)

anniversary [,ænɪ'vɜːsərɪ] N Jahrestag *m*; (= *wedding anniversary*) Hochzeitstag *m*; **~ celebrations** Feiern *pl* anlässlich eines Jahrestages/Hochzeitstages; **~ dinner/gift** (Fest)essen *nt*/Geschenk *nt* zum Jahrestag/Hochzeitstag; **the ~ of his death** sein Todestag *m*

anno Domini ['ænəʊ'dɒmɪnaɪ] N **a** (*abbr* **AD**) nach Christus, anno *or* Anno Domini; **in 53 ~** im Jahre 53 nach Christus **b** (*inf: of age*) Alter *nt*

annotate ['ænəʊteɪt] VT mit Anmerkungen versehen, kommentieren; **~d text** kommentierter Text

annotation [ænəʊ'teɪʃən] N (*no pl*: = *commentary, act*) Kommentar *m*; (= *comment*) Anmerkung *f*

annotator ['ænəʊteɪtəʳ] N Kommentator(in) *m(f)*

announce [ə'naʊns] ✪ 24 VT (*lit, fig: person*) bekannt geben, verkünden; *arrival, departure, radio programme* ansagen; (*over intercom*) durchsagen; (= *signal*) anzeigen; (*formally*) *birth, marriage etc* anzeigen; *coming of spring etc* ankündigen; **to ~ sb** jdn melden; **the arrival of flight BA 742 has just been ~d** soeben ist die Ankunft des Fluges BA 742 gemeldet worden

announcement [ə'naʊnsmənt] N (= *public declaration*) Bekanntgabe *f*, Bekanntmachung *f*; (*of impending event, speaker*) Ankündigung *f*; (*over intercom etc*) Durchsage *f*; (*giving information, on radio etc*) Ansage *f*; (*written: of birth, marriage etc*) Anzeige *f*; **after they had made the ~** nach der Bekanntgabe *etc*

announcer [ə'naʊnsəʳ] N (*Rad, TV*) Ansager(in) *m(f)*, Radio-/Fernsehsprecher(in) *m(f)*

annoy [ə'nɔɪ] VT (= *make angry, irritate*) ärgern; (= *upset: noise, questions etc*) aufregen; (= *pester*) belästigen; **to be ~ed that ...** ärgerlich *or* verärgert sein, weil ...; **to be ~ed with sb/about sth** sich über jdn/etw ärgern, (mit) jdm/über etw (*acc*) böse sein; **to get ~ed** sich ärgern, sich aufregen, böse werden; **don't get ~ed** reg dich nicht auf, nur keine Aufregung; **don't let it ~ you** ärgere dich nicht darüber

annoyance [ə'nɔɪəns] N **a** *no pl* (= *irritation*) Ärger *m*, Verdruss *m* (*geh*); **to cause (considerable) ~** (großes) Ärgernis erregen; **smoking can cause ~ to others** Rauchen kann eine Belästigung für andere sein; **to his ~** zu seinem Ärger *or* Verdruss **b** (= *nuisance*) Plage *f*, Belästigung *f*, Ärgernis *nt*

annoying [ə'nɔɪɪŋ] ADJ ärgerlich; *habit* lästig; **the ~ thing (about it) is that ...** das Ärgerliche (daran *or* bei der Sache) ist, dass ...; **it's so ~!** das kann einen ärgern, das ist derart ärgerlich; **he has an ~ way of speaking slowly** er hat eine Art, langsam zu sprechen, die einen ärgern *or* aufregen kann

annoyingly [ə'nɔɪɪŋlɪ] ADV aufreizend; **~, the bus didn't turn up** ärgerlicherweise kam der Bus nicht

annual ['ænjʊəl] N **a** (*Bot*) einjährige Pflanze **b** (= *book*) Jahresalbum *nt* ADJ (= *happening once a year*) jährlich; (= *of or for the year*) Jahres-; **~ accounts** Jahresbilanz *f*; **~ salary** Jahresgehalt *nt*

annual general meeting N Jahreshauptversammlung *f*

annualized ['ænjʊəlaɪzd] ADJ *figures* auf das Jahr hochgerechnet; **~ percentage** (*Econ*) effektiver Jahreszins

annually ['ænjʊəlɪ] ADV (= *once a year*) jährlich

annual report N Geschäftsbericht *m*

annual ring N (*of tree*) Jahresring *m*

annuitant [ə'njuːɪtənt] N (*form*) Rentenempfänger(in) *m(f)* (*einer Jahresrente*)

annuity [ə'njuːɪtɪ] N (Leib)rente *f*; **to buy an ~** eine Rentenversicherung abschließen

annuity bond N (*Econ*) Rentenbrief *m*, Rentenpapiere *pl*

annul [ə'nʌl] VT annullieren; *law, decree, judgement also* aufheben; *contract, marriage also* auflösen, für ungültig erklären; *will also* für ungültig erklären

annulment [ə'nʌlmənt] N Annullierung *f*; (*of law, decree, judgement also*) Aufhebung *f*; (*of contract, marriage also*) Auflösung *f*; (*of will also*) Ungültigkeitserklärung *f*

Annunciation [ə,nʌnsɪ'eɪʃən] N (*Bibl*) Mariä Verkündigung *f*; **the feast of the ~** das Fest Maria *or* Mariä Verkündigung

anode ['ænəʊd] N Anode *f*

anodize ['ænəʊdaɪz] VT anodisch behandeln, anodisieren

anodyne ['ænəʊdaɪn] N (*Med*) schmerzstillendes Mittel, Schmerzmittel *nt*; (*fig*) Wohltat *f* ADJ (*Med*) schmerzstillend; (*fig*) wohltuend, beruhigend

anoint [ə'nɔɪnt] VT salben; **to ~ sb king** jdn zum König salben; **to ~ sb as sth** (*fig*) jdn als etw auserwählen

anointment [ə'nɔɪntmənt] N Salbung *f*

anomalous [ə'nɒmələs] ADJ anomal, ungewöhnlich

anomaly [ə'nɒməlɪ] N Anomalie *f*; (*in law etc*) Besonderheit *f*

anomie, anomy ['ænəʊmɪ] N Anomie *f*, Gesetzlosigkeit *f*

anon¹ [ə'nɒn] ADV (*old*) alsbald (*dial, old*), bald; **ever and ~** (*old*) dann und wann; **see you ~** (*hum*) bis demnächst

anon² ADJ *abbr of* **anonymous** Anon (*at end of text*) Anonymus (*liter*), Verfasser unbekannt

anonymity [ænə'nɪmɪtɪ] N Anonymität *f*

anonymous ADJ , **anonymously** ADV [ə'nɒnɪməs, -lɪ] (*lit, fig*) anonym

anopheles [ə'nɒfiliːz] N *pl* **-les**, **anopheles mosquito** (*Zool*) Anopheles *f*, Malariamücke *f*

anorak ['ænəræk] N (*Brit*) Anorak *m*; (*pej inf*: = *nerd*) ungepflegter Fuzzi (*sl*)

anorectic [ænə'rektɪk] ADJ = **anorexic**

anorexia (nervosa) [ænə'reksɪə(nɜː'vəʊsə)] N Magersucht *f*, Anorexie *f* (*spec*)

anorexic [ænə'reksɪk] ADJ magersüchtig

another [ə'nʌðəʳ] ✪ 19.5, 26.1 ADJ **a** (= *additional*) noch eine(r, s); **~ one** noch eine(r, s); **take ~ ten** nehmen Sie noch (weitere) zehn; **I won't give you ~ chance** ich werde dir nicht noch eine *or* keine weitere Chance geben; **I don't want ~ drink!** ich möchte nichts mehr trinken; **in ~ 20 years he ...** noch 20 Jahre, und er ...; **without ~ word** ohne ein weiteres Wort; **and (there's) ~ thing** und noch eins, und (da ist) noch (et)was (anderes) **b** (= *similar, fig*: = *second*) ein zweiter, eine zweite, ein zweites; **there is not ~ man like him** so einen Mann gibt es nicht noch einmal *or* gibt es nur einmal; **~ Shakespeare** ein zweiter Shakespeare; **there will never be ~ you** für mich wird es nie jemand geben wie dich *or* du **c** (= *different*) ein anderer, eine andere, ein anderes; **that's quite ~ matter** das ist etwas ganz anderes; **~ time** ein andermal; **but maybe there won't be ~ time** aber vielleicht gibt es keine andere Gelegenheit *or* gibt es das nicht noch einmal PRON ein anderer, eine andere, ein anderes; **have ~!** nehmen Sie (doch) noch eine!; **he has found ~** (*dated, liter*) er hat eine andere gefunden; **many ~** manch anderer; **such ~** noch so einer; **they help one ~** sie helfen einander, sie helfen sich gegenseitig; **tell me ~!** (*inf*) Sie können mir sonst was erzählen (*inf*), das können Sie mir nicht weismachen; **at one time or ~** irgendwann; **what with one thing and ~** bei

all dem Trubel; **I assume this is ~ of your brilliant ideas!** ist das wieder so eine deiner Glanzideen? (*inf*); **she's ~ of his girlfriends** sie ist (auch) eine seiner Freundinnen; **yes, I'm ~ of his fans** ja, ich bin auch einer seiner Fans

Ansaphone® ['ɑːnsəfəʊn] N Anrufbeantworter *m*

ANSI *abbr of* **American National Standards Institute** *amerikanischer Normenausschuss*

answer ['ɑːnsəʳ] ✪ 19.4 **a** (= *response*) (*to* auf +*acc*) Antwort *f*, Entgegnung *f* (*geh*), Erwiderung *f* (*geh*); (*in exam*) Antwort *f*; **to get an/ no ~** Antwort/keine Antwort bekommen; **there was no ~** (*to telephone, doorbell*) es hat sich niemand gemeldet; **the ~ to our prayers** ein Geschenk *nt* des Himmels; **the ~ to a maiden's prayer** (*hum*) ein Traummann *m* (*inf*), der ideale Mann; **there's no ~ to that** (*inf*) was soll man da groß machen/sagen! (*inf*); **Germany's ~ to Concorde** Deutschlands Antwort auf die Concorde; **they had no ~ to the new striker** (*Ftbl*) sie hatten dem neuen Stürmer nichts *or* niemanden entgegenzusetzen; **in ~ to your letter/ my question** in Beantwortung Ihres Briefes (*form*)/auf meine Frage hin; **she's always got an ~** sie hat immer eine Antwort parat **b** (= *solution*) Lösung *f* (*to* +*gen*); **his ~ to any problem is to ignore it** seine Reaktion auf alle Schwierigkeiten ist, sie einfach nicht wahrhaben zu wollen; **there's no easy ~** es gibt dafür keine Patentlösung; **there's only one ~ for depression ...** es gibt nur ein Mittel gegen Depression ... **c** (*Jur*) Einlassung *f* (*form*), Stellungnahme *f*; **the defendant's ~ to the charge was ...** laut Einlassung des Beklagten ... (*form*); **what is your ~ to the charge?** was haben Sie dazu zu sagen? VT antworten auf (+*acc*); *person* antworten (+*dat*); *exam questions* beantworten, antworten auf (+*acc*); *objections, criticism* beantworten; **will you ~ that?** (*phone, door*) gehst du ran/hin?; **to ~ the telephone** das Telefon abnehmen, rangehen (*inf*); **to ~ the bell** *or* **door** die Tür öffnen *or* aufmachen, hingehen (*inf*); **who ~ed the phone?** wer war dran (*inf*) *or* am Apparat?; (*here at this end*) wer hat den Anruf entgegengenommen?; **shall I ~ it?** (*phone*) soll ich rangehen?; (*door*) soll ich hingehen?; **to ~ the call of nature** (*hum*) dem Ruf der Natur folgen; **5,000 men ~ed the call for volunteers** 5.000 Männer meldeten sich auf den Freiwilligenaufruf hin; **the fire brigade ~ed the alarm call** die Feuerwehr rückte auf den Alarm hin aus; **..., he ~ed ...**, antwortete er; **~ me this** sagen *or* beantworten Sie mir eins; **~ me!** antworte (mir)!, antworten Sie!; **to anyone who claims ... I would ~ this** jemandem, der ... behauptet, würde ich Folgendes erwidern *or* entgegen **b** (= *fulfil*) *description* entsprechen (+*dat*); *hope, expectation* erfüllen; *prayer* (*God*) erhören; *need* befriedigen; **people who ~ that description** Leute, auf die diese Beschreibung passt *or* zutrifft; **this ~ed our prayers** das war (wie) ein Geschenk des Himmels; **it ~s the/our purpose** es erfüllt seinen Zweck/es erfüllt für uns seinen Zweck **c** (*Jur*) *charge* sich verantworten wegen (+*gen*) VI antworten; **if the phone rings, don't ~** wenn das Telefon läutet, geh nicht ran *or* nimm nicht ab **b** (= *suffice*) geeignet *or* brauchbar sein, taugen

▶ **answer back** VI widersprechen; (*children also*) patzige *or* freche Antworten geben; **don't answer back!** keine Widerrede!; **it's not fair to criticize him because he can't answer back** es ist unfair, ihn zu kritisieren, weil er sich nicht verteidigen kann VT *sep* **to answer sb back** jdm widersprechen; (*children also*) jdm patzige *or* freche Antworten geben

▶ **answer for** VI +*prep obj* **a** (= *be responsible for*) verantwortlich sein für; **he has a lot to answer for** er hat eine Menge auf dem Gewissen; **I won't answer for the consequences** ich will für die Folgen nicht verantwortlich gemacht werden **b** (= *guarantee*) sich verbürgen für; (= *speak for also*) sprechen für

▶ **answer to** VI +*prep obj* **a** (= *be accountable to*) **to answer to sb for sth** jdm für etw *or* wegen einer Sache (*gen*) Rechenschaft schuldig sein; **if anything goes wrong you'll have me to answer to** wenn etwas nicht klappt, dann stehen Sie mir dafür ein *or* gerade *or* dann müssen Sie sich vor mir dafür verantworten **b** **to answer to a description** einer Beschreibung entsprechen **c** **to answer to the name of ...** auf den Namen ... hören **d** **to answer to the wheel/helm/controls** auf das Steuer/das Ruder/die Steuerung ansprechen

answerable ['ɑːnsərəbl] ADJ **a** *question* beantwortbar, zu beantworten *pred*; *charge, argument* widerlegbar **b** (= *responsible*) verantwortlich; **to be ~ to sb (for sth)** jdm gegenüber (für etw) verantwortlich sein; **to be made ~** verantwortlich gemacht werden; **parents are ~ for their children's conduct** Eltern haften für ihre Kinder

answer-back (code) ['ɑːnsəbæk(ˌkəʊd)] N (*for telex*) Kennung *f*

answerer ['ɑːnsərə'] N Antwortende(r) *mf*

answering machine ['ɑːnsərɪŋməˈʃiːn] N (automatischer) Anrufbeantworter

answerless ['ɑːnsəlɪs] ADJ ohne Antwort; *question* (= *not answered*) unbeantwortet; (= *not answerable*) unbeantwortbar

answer paper N (*in exam*) Lösung *f*, Antwortbogen *m*

answerphone ['ɑːnsəfəʊn] N (*Brit*) Anrufbeantworter *m*

ant [ænt] N Ameise *f*; **to have ~s in one's pants** (*inf*) Hummeln im Hintern haben (*inf*), kein Sitzfleisch haben

anta ['æntə] N *pl* **-ae** (*Archit*) Ante *f*, Pilaster *m*

antacid [ænt'æsɪd] N säurebindendes Mittel

antagonism [æn'tægənɪzəm] N (*between people, theories etc*) Antagonismus *m*; (*towards sb, ideas, a suggestion, change etc*) Feindseligkeit *f*, Feindlichkeit *f* (*to(wards)* gegenüber); **to arouse sb's ~** jdn gegen sich aufbringen

antagonist [æn'tægənɪst] N Kontrahent(in) *m(f)*, Gegner(in) *m(f)*, Antagonist(in) *m(f)*; (*esp Pol*) Gegenspieler(in) *m(f)*

antagonistic [æn,tægə'nɪstɪk] ADJ *reaction, attitude* feindselig; *force* gegnerisch, feindlich; *interests* widerstreitend, antagonistisch; **to be ~ to** *or* **toward(s) sb/sth** jdm/gegen etw feindselig gesinnt sein

antagonize [æn'tægənaɪz] VT *person* gegen sich aufbringen *or* stimmen; (= *annoy*) verärgern

Antarctic [ænt'ɑːktɪk] ADJ antarktisch, der Antarktis **N the ~** die Antarktis

Antarctica [ænt'ɑːktɪkə] N die Antarktis

Antarctic Circle N südlicher Polarkreis

Antarctic Ocean N Südpolarmeer *nt*

ant: ant bear N (*Zool*) Ameisenbär *m*; **ant bird**, **ant catcher** N (*Zool*) Ameisenvogel *m*; **ant colony** N Ameisenstaat *m*

ante ['ænti] **N** (*Cards*) Einsatz *m*; **to raise** *or* **up the ~** (*fig inf*) den Einsatz erhöhen **VT** (*also* **ante up**) einsetzen VI setzen, seinen Einsatz machen; **his father ~d up as usual** (*fig inf*) sein Vater blechte wie gewöhnlich (*inf*)

ante- PREF vor-

anteater ['ænt,iːtə'] N Ameisenbär *m*, Ameisenfresser *m*

antecedent [ænti'siːdənt] ADJ früher; **the crisis and its ~ events** die Krise und die ihr vorangehenden *or* vorausgehenden Ereignisse; **to be ~ to sth** einer Sache (*dat*) voran- *or* vorausgehen **N** **a** ~**s** (*of person,* = *past history*) Vorleben *nt*; (= *ancestry*) Abstammung *f*; (*of event*) Vorgeschichte *f* **b** (*Gram*) Bezugswort *nt*

ante: antechamber N Vorzimmer *nt*; **antedate** VT *document, cheque* vordatieren (*to auf* +*acc*); *event* vorausgehen (+*dat*) (*by* um); **antediluvian** [æntidɪ'luːvɪən] ADJ (*lit, fig inf*) vorsintflutlich

antelope ['æntɪləʊp] N Antilope *f*

ante meridiem [æntɪmə'rɪdɪəm] ADV (*abbr* **am**) vormittags

antenatal ['æntɪ'neɪtl] ADJ vor der Geburt, pränatal (*form*); ~ **care/exercises** Schwangerschaftsfürsorge *f*/-übungen *pl*; ~ **clinic** Sprechstunde *f* für Schwangere *or* für werdende Mütter

antenna [æn'tenə] N **a** *pl* **-e** [æn'teniː] (*Zool*) Fühler *m* **b** *pl* **-e** *or* **-s** (*Rad, TV*) Antenne *f*

antepenultimate ['æntɪpɪ'nʌltɪmɪt] ADJ vorvorletzte(r, s)

ante-post ['æntɪ'pəʊst] (*Brit Gambling*) ADJ ~ **bet** Vorwette *f*; ~ **favourite** Favorit(in) *m(f)* ADV **to bet ~** eine Vorwette machen

anterior [æn'tɪərɪə'] ADJ **a** (= *prior*) früher (*to* als); **to be ~ to** vorangehen (+*dat*), vorausgehen (+*dat*) **b** (*Anat etc*) vordere(r, s); ~ **brain** Vorderhirn *nt*

anteroom ['æntɪruːm] N Vorzimmer *nt*

anthem ['ænθəm] N Hymne *f*; (*by choir*) Chorgesang *m*

anther ['ænθə'] N (*Bot*) Staubbeutel *m*, Anthere *f* (*spec*)

ant hill N Ameisenhaufen *m*

anthologize [æn'θɒlədʒaɪz] VI eine Anthologie/Anthologien zusammenstellen VT in einer Anthologie zusammenfassen; (= *to include in an anthology*) in eine Anthologie aufnehmen

anthology [æn'θɒlədʒɪ] N Anthologie *f*

anthracite ['ænθrəsaɪt] N Anthrazit *m*

anthrax ['ænθræks] N (*Med, Vet*) Anthrax *m* (*spec*), Milzbrand *m*

anthropocentric [ænθrəpəʊ'sentrɪk] ADJ anthropozentrisch

anthropoid ['ænθrəʊpɔɪd] **N** Anthropoid *m* (*spec*); (= *ape*) Menschenaffe *m* ADJ anthropoid (*spec*)

anthropological [ænθrəpə'lɒdʒɪkəl] ADJ anthropologisch

anthropologist [ænθrə'pɒlədʒɪst] N Anthropologe *m*, Anthropologin *f*

anthropology [ænθrə'pɒlədʒɪ] N Anthropologie *f*

anthropomorphic [ænθrəʊpə'mɔːfɪk] ADJ anthropomorphisch

anthropomorphism [ænθrəʊpə'mɔːfɪzəm] N Anthropomorphismus *m*

anthropomorphize [ænθrəʊpə'mɔːfaɪz] VT *god, animal, object etc* anthropomorphisieren

anthroposophical [ænθrəpə'sɒfɪkəl] ADJ anthroposophisch

anthroposophy [ænθrə'pɒsəfɪ] N Anthroposophie *f*

anti ['æntɪ] (*inf*) ADJ *pred* in Opposition (*inf*); **are you in favour** (*Brit*) *or* **favor** (*US*)**? – no, I'm ~** bist du dafür? – nein, ich bin dagegen PREP gegen (+*acc*); ~ **everything** grundsätzlich gegen alles

anti *in cpds* Anti-, anti-; **anti-abortion** ADJ Antiabtreibungs-; ~ **campaign** Antiabtreibungskampagne *f*; **anti-abortionist** N Abtreibungsgegner(in) *m(f)*; **anti-ag(e)ing** ADJ ~ **cream** Creme *f* gegen Hautalterung; **anti-aircraft** ADJ Flugabwehr-; ~ **defence** (*Brit*) *or* **defense** (*US*) Luftverteidigung *f*; ~ **fire** Flakfeuer *nt*; ~ **gun** Flak(geschütz *nt*) *f*; ~ **missile** Flugabwehrrakete *f*; **anti-American** ADJ antiamerikanisch; **antiballistic missile** [ˌæntɪbə'lɪstɪk-] N Antiraketenrakete *f*; **antibiotic** [ˌæntɪbar'ɒtɪk] **N** Antibiotikum *nt* ADJ antibiotisch; **antibody** N Antikörper *m*

antic ['æntɪk] N → **antics**

antichoice ADJ abtreibungsfeindlich, gegen Abtreibung

Antichrist ['æntɪkraɪst] N Antichrist *m*

anticipate [æn'tɪsɪpeɪt] VT **a** (= *expect*) erwarten; **as ~d** wie vorausgesehen *or* erwartet **b** (= *see in advance*) vorausahnen, vorhersehen; (= *see in advance and cater for*) *objection, need etc* zuvorkommen (+*dat*); **he always has to ~ what his opponent will do next** er muss immer vorhersehen können *or* vorausahnen, was sein Gegner als Nächstes tun wird; **don't ~ what I'm going to say** nimm nicht vorweg, was ich noch sagen wollte

c (= *do before sb else*) zuvorkommen (+*dat*); **in his discovery he was ~d by others** bei seiner Entdeckung sind ihm andere zuvorgekommen; **a phrase which ~s a later theme** (*Mus*) eine Melodie, die auf ein späteres Thema vor(aus)greift **d** (= *do, use, act on prematurely*) *income* im Voraus ausgeben; *inheritance* im Voraus in Anspruch nehmen **VI** (*manager, driver, chess player etc*) vorauskalkulieren

anticipation [æn,tɪsɪ'peɪʃən] N **a** (= *expectation*) Erwartung *f*; **thanking you in ~** herzlichen Dank im Voraus; **to wait in ~** gespannt warten; **we took our umbrellas in ~ of rain** wir nahmen unsere Schirme mit, weil wir mit Regen rechneten

b (= *seeing in advance*) Vorausberechnung *f*; **we were impressed by the hotel's ~ of our wishes** beeindruckt, wie man im Hotel unsere Wünschen zuvorkam; **his uncanny ~ of every objection** die verblüffende Art, in der *or* wie er jedem Einwand zuvorkam; **the driver showed good ~** der Fahrer zeigte *or* bewies gute Voraussicht

c (*of discovery, discoverer*) Vorwegnahme *f*; (*Mus, of theme etc*) Vorgriff *m* (*of auf* +*acc*)

anticipatory [æn'tɪsɪ,peɪtərɪ] ADJ vorwegnehmend

anti: anticlerical ADJ antiklerikal, kirchenfeindlich; **anticlimactic** (*esp Brit*) ADJ nach links; **anticlimax** N Enttäuschung *f*; (*no pl, Liter*) Antiklimax *f*; **anticlockwise** (*esp Brit*) ADJ nach links; **in an ~ direction** entgegen dem Uhrzeigersinn ADV nach links, gegen den Uhrzeigersinn *or* die Uhrzeigerrichtung; **anticoagulant** [ˌæntɪkəʊ'ægjʊlənt] **N** Antikoagulans *nt* (*spec*) ADJ antikoagulierend (*spec*), blutgerinnungshemmend; **anticonvulsant** N Antikonvulsivum *nt* ADJ antikonvulsiv; **anticorrosive** ADJ Korrosionsschutz-; ~ **paint** Korrosionsschutzfarbe *f*

antics ['æntɪks] PL Eskapaden *pl*; (= *tricks*) Possen *pl*, Streiche *pl*; (= *irritating behaviour*) Mätzchen *pl* (*inf*); **he's up to his old ~ again** er macht wieder seine Mätzchen (*inf*); **the photocopier is up to its old ~ again** der Fotokopierer hat wieder seine Mucken (*inf*)

anti: anticyclical ADJ antizyklisch; ~ **policy** (*Econ*) Konjunkturpolitik *f*; **for ~ reasons** aus konjunkturpolitischen Gründen; **anticyclone** N Antizyklone *f*, Hoch(druckgebiet) *nt*; **antidandruff** ADJ *shampoo* gegen Schuppen; **antidazzle** ADJ (*Brit*) blendfrei; **antidepressant** N Antidepressivum *nt* ADJ antidepressiv; **antidote** ['æntɪdəʊt] N (*Med, fig*) Gegenmittel *nt* (*against, to, for* gegen); **antifemale** ADJ frauenfeindlich; **antifreeze** N Frostschutz(mittel *nt*) *m*

antigen ['æntɪdʒən] N Antigen *nt*

anti: antiglare ADJ (*US*) blendfrei; **anti-globalization** ADJ Antiglobalisierungs-; ~ **protester** Globalisierungsgegner(in) *m(f)*; **antihero** N Antiheld *m*; **antihistamine** N Antihistamin(ikum) *nt*; **anti-inflammatory** N Entzündungshemmer *m* ADJ *drug* entzündungshemmend; **antiknock agent** [ˌæntɪ'nɒk-] N Antiklopfmittel *nt*; **antilock** ADJ Blockierschutz-; ~ **brakes** Blockierschutzbremsen *pl*; ~ **braking system** Blockierschutzbremssystem *nt*; **antilog(arithm)** N Antilogarithmus *m*, Numerus *m*; **antimacassar** [æntɪmə'kæsə'] N (Sessel-/Sofa)schoner *m*; **antimalarial** ADJ gegen Malaria ADJ Malariamittel *nt*; **anti-marketeer** N EG-Gegner(in) *m(f)*; **antimatter** N Antimaterie *f*; **antimissile** ADJ Raketenabwehr-; ~ **system** Raketenabwehrsystem *nt*; **antimist** ADJ ~ **cloth** (*Mot*) Antibeschlagtuch *nt*

antimony ['æntɪmənɪ] N Antimon *nt*

anti: antinuclear ADJ (= *against nuclear energy*) Anti-Atom(kraft)-; (= *against nuclear weapons*) Anti-Atomwaffen-; **the ~ lobby/protesters** die

Atomkraftgegner pl, die Atomwaffengegner pl; **antinuclearist** [ˌæntɪˈnjuːklɪərɪst] N Atomkraftgegner(in) m(f), Kernkraftgegner(in) m(f); **antioxidant** N Antioxidans nt; **~s** Antioxidantien pl

antipasto [ˌæntɪˈpæstəʊ] N italienische Vorspeise

antipathetic [ˌæntɪpəˈθetɪk] ADJ **to be ~ to sb/sth** eine Antipathie or Abneigung gegen jdn/etw haben; **sb/sth is ~ to sb** (= arouses antipathy in) jd/etw ist jdm unsympathisch

antipathy [ænˈtɪpəθɪ] N Antipathie f (towards gegen), Abneigung f (towards gegen)

anti: antipersonnel ADJ gegen Menschen gerichtet; **~ bomb** Splitterbombe f; **~ mine** Antipersonenmine f; **antiperspirant** N Antitranspirant nt

antiphony [ænˈtɪfənɪ] N (Eccl, Mus) Antiphon f

antipodean [ænˌtɪpəˈdiːən], (US) **antipodal** [ænˈtɪpədəl] ADJ antipodisch; (Brit) australisch und neuseeländisch

antipodes [ænˈtɪpədiːz] PL (diametral) entgegengesetzte Teile der Erde; **Antipodes** (Brit) Australien und Neuseeland; (Geog) Antipodeninseln pl

antipope [ˈæntɪˌpəʊp] N Gegenpapst m

antiquarian [ˌæntɪˈkweərɪən] **ADJ** books antiquarisch; coins also alt; studies des Altertums, der Antike; **~ bookshop** Antiquariat nt **N** = **antiquary**

antiquary [ˈæntɪkwərɪ] N (= collector) Antiquitätensammler(in) m(f); (= seller) Antiquitätenhändler(in) m(f)

antiquated [ˈæntɪkweɪtɪd] ADJ antiquiert; machines, ideas also überholt; institutions also veraltet

antique [ænˈtiːk] **ADJ** antik; **~ pine** Kiefer f antik **N** Antiquität f

antiqued [ænˈtiːkt] ADJ auf antik gemacht

antique: antique dealer N Antiquitätenhändler(in) m(f); **antique(s) fair** N Antiquitätenmesse f; **antique shop** N Antiquitätengeschäft nt or -laden m

antiquity [ænˈtɪkwɪtɪ] N **a** (= ancient times) das Altertum; (= Roman, Greek antiquity) die Antike; **in ~** im Altertum/in der Antike **b** (= great age) großes Alter; **of great ~** uralt **c antiquities** PL (= old things) Altertümer pl

anti: antiriot ADJ **~ police** Bereitschaftspolizei f; **anti-roll bar** N (Brit Aut) Stabilisator m

antirrhinum [ˌæntɪˈraɪnəm] N Löwenmaul nt

anti: antirust ADJ Rostschutz-; **~ paint** Rostschutzfarbe f; **antiscorbutic** ADJ antiskorbutisch; **anti-Semite** N Antisemit(in) m(f); **anti-Semitic** ADJ antisemitisch; **anti-Semitism** N Antisemitismus m; **antiseptic** N Antiseptikum nt **ADJ** (lit, fig) antiseptisch; **antiskid** ADJ rutschsicher; **antislavery** ADJ speech etc gegen die Sklaverei; **antislip** ADJ floor rutschfest, rutschsicher; **anti-smoking** ADJ campaign, group Antiraucher-; **antisocial** ADJ person, behaviour etc unsozial; (Psych, Sociol) asozial; **to be in an ~ mood** nicht in Gesellschaftslaune sein; **don't be ~** (= don't be a spoilsport) sei kein Spielverderber; (= don't be aloof etc) mach doch mit; **may I smoke or would that be ~?** darf ich rauchen oder stört das?; **I work ~ hours** ich arbeite zu Zeiten, wo andere freihaben; **antistatic** ADJ antistatisch; **antitank** ADJ Panzerabwehr-; **~ gun** Panzerabwehrgeschütz nt; **ditch/obstacle** Panzersperre f; **antiterrorist** ADJ squad, measures zur Terrorismusbekämpfung; **antitheft device** N Diebstahlsicherung f

antithesis [ænˈtɪθɪsɪs] N pl **antitheses** [ænˈtɪθɪsiːz] (= direct opposite) genaues Gegenteil (to, of +gen); (of idea, in rhetoric) Antithese f (to, of zu) (form); (= contrast) Gegensatz m

antithetic(al) [ˌæntɪˈθetɪk(əl)] ADJ (= contrasting) gegensätzlich; phrases antithetisch (form); idea entgegengesetzt, antithetisch (form)

anti: antitoxin N Gegengift nt, Antitoxin nt; **antitrade (wind)** N Antipassat(wind) m; **an-**

titrust ADJ (US) **~ legislation** Kartellgesetzgebung f; **antivivisectionism** N Ablehnung f der Vivisektion; **antivivisectionist** **N** Gegner(in) m(f) der Vivisektion **ADJ his ~ views** seine ablehnende Haltung der Vivisektion gegenüber; **anti-wrinkle** ADJ Antifalten-; **~ cream** Antifaltencreme f

antler [ˈæntləʳ] N Geweihstange f; **(set** or **pair of) ~s** Geweih nt

antonym [ˈæntənɪm] N Antonym nt, Gegenwort nt (geh)

Antwerp [ˈæntwɜːp] N Antwerpen nt

anus [ˈeɪnəs] N After m, Anus m (spec)

anvil [ˈænvɪl] N Amboss m (also Anat)

anxiety [æŋˈzaɪətɪ] N **a** Sorge f; **to feel ~** sich (dat) Sorgen machen (about um, at wegen); **no cause for ~** kein Grund zur Sorge or Besorgnis; **to cause sb ~** jdm Sorgen machen **b** (= keen desire) Verlangen nt; **in his ~ to get away** weil er unbedingt wegkommen wollte

anxiety neurosis N (Psych) Angstneurose f

anxious [ˈæŋkʃəs] ADJ **a** (= worried) besorgt; person (as character trait) ängstlich; thoughts ängstlich; **to be ~ about sb/sth** sich (dat) um jdn/etw Sorgen machen, um jdn/etw besorgt sein; **to be ~ about doing sth** Angst haben, etw zu tun **b** (= worrying) moment, minutes der Angst, bang; wait bang; **it's been an ~ time for us all** wir alle haben uns (in dieser Zeit) große Sorgen gemacht; **he had an ~ time waiting for ...** war für ihn eine Zeit voll bangen Wartens auf (+acc) ... **c** (= strongly desirous) **to be ~ for sth** auf etw (acc) aus sein; **we are ~ for all the assistance we can get** uns geht es darum, jede nur mögliche Hilfe zu bekommen; **to be ~ to do sth** bestrebt sein or darauf aus sein, etw zu tun; **they were ~ to start/for his return** sie warteten sehr darauf abzufahren/auf seine Rückkehr; **I am ~ that he should do it** or **for him to do it** mir liegt viel daran, dass er es tut

anxious bench N (US Rel) → **anxious seat**

anxiously [ˈæŋkʃəslɪ] ADV **a** besorgt **b** (= keenly) gespannt

anxiousness [ˈæŋkʃəsnɪs] N , no pl Sorge f; (= keen desire) Verlangen nt

anxious seat N (US Rel) Sünderbank f; **to be on the ~** (fig) wie auf (glühenden) Kohlen sitzen, Blut und Wasser schwitzen

any [ˈenɪ] **ADJ a** (in interrog, conditional, neg sentences) not translated (emph: = at any at all) (with sing n) irgendein(e); (with pl n) irgendwelche; (with uncountable n) etwas; **not ~** kein/keine; **not ANY ... at all** überhaupt kein/keine ...; **if I had ~ plan/ideas/money** wenn ich einen Plan/Ideen/Geld hätte; **if I had ANY plan/ideas/money** wenn ich irgendeinen Plan/irgendwelche Ideen/(auch nur) etwas Geld hätte; **if you think it'll do ~ good/ANY good (at all)** wenn du glaubst, dass es etwas/irgendetwas nützt; **if it's ~ help (at all)** wenn das (irgendwie) hilft; **it won't do ~ good** es wird nichts nützen; **it wasn't ~ good** or **use (at all)** es nützte (überhaupt or gar) nichts; **you mustn't do that on ~ account** das darfst du auf gar keinen Fall tun; **without ~ difficulty (at all)** ohne jede Schwierigkeit **b** (= no matter which) jede(r, s) (beliebige ...); (with pl or uncountable n) alle; **~ one will do** es ist jede(r, s) recht; **~ excuse will do** jede Entschuldigung ist recht; **you can have ~ book/books you can find** du kannst jedes Buch/alle Bücher haben, das/die du finden kannst; **take ~ two dresses** nehmen Sie zwei beliebige Kleider; **~ one you like** was du willst; **~ one of us would have done the same** jeder von uns hätte dasselbe getan; **you can't just come at ~ time** du kannst nicht einfach zu jeder beliebigen Zeit kommen; **you can come at ~ time** du kannst jederzeit kommen; **thank you ~ time** danke! – bitte!; **~ time soon** irgendwann bald; **~ fool could do that** das kann jedes Kind; **~ old ...** (inf) jede(r, s) x-beliebige ... (inf) → **old**

PRON a (in interrog, conditional, neg sentences) (replacing sing n) ein(e), welche(r, s); (replacing pl n) einige, welche; (replacing uncountable n) etwas, welche; **I want to meet psychologists/a psychologist, do you know ~?** ich würde gerne Psychologen/einen Psychologen kennen lernen, kennen Sie welche/einen?; **I need some butter/stamps, do you have ~?** ich brauche Butter/Briefmarken, haben Sie welche?; **have you seen ~ of my ties?** haben Sie eine von meinen Krawatten gesehen?; **don't you have ~ (at all)?** haben Sie (denn) (gar or überhaupt) keinen/keine/keines?; **he wasn't having ~ (of it/that)** (inf) er wollte nichts davon hören; **the profits, if ~** die eventuellen Gewinne; **few, if ~, will come** wenn überhaupt, werden nur wenige kommen; **I'd like some tea/tomatoes if you have ~** ich hätte gerne Tee, wenn Sie welchen haben/Tomaten, wenn Sie welche haben; **if ~ of you can sing** wenn (irgend)jemand or (irgend)einer/-eine von euch singen kann **b** (= no matter which) alle; **~ who do come ...** alle, die kommen ...; **~ that I have ...** alle, die ich habe ...

ADV a colder, bigger etc noch; **not ~ colder/bigger** etc nicht kälter/größer etc; **it won't get ~ colder** es wird nicht mehr kälter; **we can't go ~ further** wir können nicht mehr weiter gehen; **should he grow ~ bigger he'll ...** wenn er noch mehr wächst, wird er ...; **are you feeling ~ better?** geht es dir etwas besser?; **he wasn't ~ too pleased** (Brit) er war nicht allzu begeistert; **do you want ~ more soup?** willst du noch etwas Suppe?; **don't you want ~ more tea?** willst du keinen Tee mehr?; **~ more offers?** noch weitere Angebote?; **I don't want ~ more (at all)** ich möchte (überhaupt or gar) nichts mehr **b** (esp US, inf: = at all) überhaupt; **you can't improve it ~** = du kannst es überhaupt nicht mehr verbessern; **it didn't help them ~** es hat ihnen gar or überhaupt nichts genützt

anybody [ˈenɪbɒdɪ] **PRON a** (irgend)jemand, (irgend)eine(r); **not ... ~** niemand, keine(r); **is ~ there?** ist (irgend)jemand da?; **(does) ~ want my book?** will jemand or einer mein Buch?; **I can't see ~** ich kann niemand(en) or keinen sehen; **don't tell ~** erzähl das niemand(em) or keinem **b** (= no matter who) jede(r); **~ will tell you the same** jeder wird dir dasselbe sagen; **~ with any sense** jeder halbwegs vernünftige Mensch; **it's ~'s game/race** das Spiel/Rennen kann von jedem gewonnen werden; **~ but him, ~ else** jeder außer ihm, jeder andere; **is there ~ else I can talk to?** gibt es sonst jemand(en), mit dem ich sprechen kann?; **I don't want to see ~ else** ich möchte niemand anderen sehen **N** (= person of importance) jemand, wer (inf); **she'll never be ~** sie wird nie wer sein (inf); **he's not just ~** er ist nicht einfach irgendwer or irgendjemand; **everybody who is ~ was there** alles, was Rang und Namen hat, war dort; **he wasn't ~ before she married him** er war niemand, bevor sie ihn geheiratet hat

anyhow [ˈenɪhaʊ] ADV **a** (= at any rate) jedenfalls; (= regardless) trotzdem; **~, that's what I think** das ist jedenfalls meine Meinung; **~, I went to see him** (also) jedenfalls, ich habe ihn besucht; **~, you're here now** jetzt bist du jedenfalls da; **I told him not to, but he did it ~** ich habe es ihm verboten, aber er hat es trotzdem gemacht; **he agrees ~, so it doesn't matter** er ist sowieso einverstanden, es spielt also keine Rolle; **it's no trouble, I'm going there ~** es ist keine Mühe, ich gehe sowieso hin; **who cares, ~?** überhaupt, wen kümmert es denn schon?; **~!** gut!, na ja! **b** (= carelessly) irgendwie; (= at random) aufs Geratewohl; **the papers were scattered ~ on his desk** die Papiere lagen bunt durcheinander auf seinem Schreibtisch; **things are all ~** alles ist durcheinander

anymore [ˌenɪˈmɔːʳ] ADV (+vb) nicht mehr; **I couldn't trust him ~** ich konnte ihm nicht mehr trauen → **any ADV a**

anyone [ˈenɪwʌn] PRON, N = **anybody**

anyplace ['enɪpleɪs] ADV (US, inf) = **anywhere**

anyroad ['enɪrəʊd] ADV (N Engl) = **anyhow a**

anything ['enɪθɪŋ] PRON **a** (irgend)etwas; **not ~** nichts; (emph) gar or überhaupt nichts; **is it/isn't it worth ~?** ist es etwas/gar nichts wert?; **it's worth ~ between £ 1,000 and £5,000** es ist irgendwas zwischen £ 1000 und £ 5000 wert; **did/didn't he say ~ else?** hat er (sonst) noch etwas/sonst (gar) nichts gesagt?; **did/didn't they give you ~ at all?** haben sie euch überhaupt etwas/überhaupt nichts gegeben?; **are you doing ~ tonight?** hast du heute Abend schon etwas vor?; **is there ~ more tiring than ...?** gibt es etwas Ermüdenderes als ...?; **hardly ~** kaum etwas; **he's as smart as ~** (inf) er ist clever wie noch was (inf) **b** (= no matter what) alles; **~ you like** (alles,) was du willst; **they eat ~** sie essen alles; **not just ~** nicht bloß irgendetwas; **I wouldn't do it for ~** ich würde es um keinen Preis tun; **~ else is impossible** alles andere ist unmöglich; **this is ~ but pleasant** das ist alles andere als angenehm; **~ but that!** alles, nur das nicht!; **~ but!** von wegen! → **if**, **go**, **like ¹ PREP**
ADV (inf) **it isn't ~ like him** das sieht ihm überhaupt nicht ähnlich or gleich; **if it looked ~ like him ...** wenn es ihm gleichsehen würde ...; **it didn't cost ~ like £100** es kostete bei weitem keine £ 100; **if it costs ~ like as much as before ...** wenn es auch nur annähernd so viel kostet wie früher ...; **~/not ~ like as wet as ...** auch nur annähernd/nicht annähernd so nass wie ...

anytime ['enɪtaɪm] ADV (esp US) jederzeit → **any**

anytime minutes PL (US: for mobile phone) Freiminuten pl (die ohne Zeitbindung vertelefoniert werden können)

anyway ['enɪweɪ] ADV = **anyhow a** → also **way**

anyways ['enɪweɪz] ADV (US dial) = **anyway**

anywhere ['enɪweə'] ADV **a** be, stay, live irgendwo; go, travel irgendwohin; **not ~** nirgends/nirgendwohin; **too late to go ~** zu spät, um (noch) irgendwohin zu gehen; **we never go ~** wir gehen nie (irgend)wohin; **he'll never get ~** er wird es zu nichts bringen; **I wasn't getting ~** ich kam (einfach) nicht weiter; **I haven't found ~ to live/to put my books yet** ich habe noch nichts gefunden, wo ich wohnen/meine Bücher unterbringen kann; **the cottage was miles from ~** das Häuschen lag jwd (inf); **they are the oldest caves ~ in the whole of North America** das sind die ältesten Höhlen in ganz Nordamerika; **there could be ~ between 50 and 100 people** es könnten (schätzungsweise) 50 bis 100 Leute sein **b** (= no matter where) be, stay, live überall; go, travel überallhin; **they could be ~** sie könnten überall sein; **~ you like** wo/wohin du willst, **ready to go ~** bereit, überallhin zu gehen

Anzac ['ænzæk] N australischer/neuseeländischer Soldat

AOB abbr of **any other business** Sonstiges

AOCB abbr of **any other competent business** Sonstiges

A-OK, A-okay ADJ, ADV (esp US inf) klasse (inf), prima (inf)

AONB abbr of **Area of Outstanding Natural Beauty**

A 1, A one ADJ **a** (Naut) erstklassig **b** (= sound) kerngesund; (= fit) gut in Form **c** (inf) super (inf), spitze (inf); **our holidays were ~** unsere Ferien waren super

aorist ['ɛɔərɪst] N Aorist m

aorta [eɪ'ɔːtə] N Aorta f

apace [ə'peɪs] ADV geschwind (geh)

Apache [ə'pætʃɪ] N **a** Apache m, Apachin f **b** (= language) Apache nt ADJ Apachen-, der Apachen; **~ leader** Apachenführer m

apart [ə'pɑːt] ADV **a** auseinander; **to stand/sit with one's legs ~** mit gespreizten Beinen dastehen/dasitzen; **I can't tell them ~** ich kann sie nicht auseinander halten; **to live ~** getrennt leben; **they're still far or miles ~** (fig) ihre Mei-

nungen klaffen or gehen immer noch weit auseinander; **to come** or **fall ~** entzweigehen, auseinander fallen; **the company is falling ~** die Firma geht vor die Hunde (inf); **her marriage is falling ~** ihre Ehe geht in die Brüche; **it came ~ in my hands** es fiel mir in der Hand auseinander; **to take sth ~** etw auseinander nehmen
b (= to one side) zur Seite, beiseite; (= on one side) abseits (from +gen); **he stood ~ from the group** er stand abseits von der Gruppe; **to hold oneself ~** sich abseits halten; **a class/thing ~** eine Klasse/Sache für sich
c (= excepted) abgesehen von, bis auf (+acc); **these problems ~** abgesehen von or außer diesen Problemen; **~ from that there's nothing else wrong** damit ist es abgesehen davon or bis auf das ist alles in Ordnung; **~ from that, the gearbox is also faulty** darüber hinaus or außerdem ist (auch) das Getriebe schadhaft

apartheid [ə'pɑːteɪt] N Apartheid f

apartment [ə'pɑːtmənt] N **a** (Brit: = room) Raum m **b apartments** PL (Brit: = suite of rooms) Appartement nt **c** (esp US: = flat) Wohnung f; **~ house** or **block** or **building** Wohnblock m

apathetic [æpə'θetɪk] ADJ apathisch, teilnahmslos; **they are completely ~ about politics** sie sind in politischen Dingen vollkommen apathisch; **they are completely ~ about their future** sie sind vollkommen apathisch, was ihre Zukunft angeht

apathetically [æpə'θetɪkəlɪ] ADV apathisch, teilnahmslos

apathy ['æpəθɪ] N Apathie f, Teilnahmslosigkeit f

APB (US) abbr of **all points bulletin to put out an ~ on sb** nach jdm eine Fahndung einleiten

ape [eɪp] N (lit, fig) Affe m; **to go ~** (inf) ausflippen (inf) VT nachäffen (pej), nachmachen

APEC ['eɪpek] N abbr of **Asia Pacific Economic Co-operation** APEC f

Apennines ['æpɪnaɪnz] PL Apennin m, Apenninen pl

aperient [ə'pɪərɪənt] N Abführmittel nt ADJ abführend

apéritif [ə,perɪ'tiːf], **aperitive** [ə'perɪtɪv] N Aperitif m

aperture ['æpətʃʊə'] N Öffnung f; (Phot) Blende f

apeshit ['eɪpʃɪt] ADJ to go ~ (sl) ausflippen (inf)

apex ['eɪpeks] N pl **-es** or **apices** Spitze f; (fig) Höhepunkt m

aphasia [ə'feɪzɪə] N Aphasie f

aphasic [ə'feɪzɪk] ADJ aphasisch N Aphasiker(in) m(f)

aphid ['eɪfɪd] N Blattlaus f

aphorism ['æfərɪzəm] N Aphorismus m

aphoristic [æfə'rɪstɪk] ADJ aphoristisch

aphrodisiac [æfrəʊ'dɪzɪæk] N Aphrodisiakum nt ADJ aphrodisisch

apiarist ['eɪpɪərɪst] N Bienenzüchter(in) m(f), Imker(in) m(f)

apiary ['eɪpɪərɪ] N Bienenhaus nt

apices ['eɪpɪsiːz] pl of **apex**

apiculture ['eɪpɪˌkʌltʃə'] N (form) Bienenzucht f, Imkerei f

apiece [ə'piːs] ADV pro Stück; (= per person) pro Person; **I gave them two ~** ich gab ihnen je zwei; **they had two cakes ~** sie hatten jeder zwei Kuchen

aplastic anaemia, (US) **aplastic anemia** [eɪˈplæstɪkəˈniːmɪə] N (Med) aplastische Anämie f

aplomb [ə'plɒm] N Gelassenheit f; **with ~** gelassen

Apocalypse [ə'pɒkəlɪps] N Apokalypse f

apocalyptic [ə,pɒkə'lɪptɪk] ADJ apokalyptisch

Apocrypha [ə'pɒkrɪfə] N **the ~** die Apokryphen pl

apocryphal [ə'pɒkrɪfəl] ADJ apokryph; (= of unknown authorship) anonym; **this story, which is almost certainly ~ ...** diese Geschichte, die

höchstwahrscheinlich jeder Wahrheit entbehrt ...

apogee ['æpəʊdʒiː] N (Astron) Apogäum nt, Erdferne f; (fig = apex) Höhepunkt m

apolitical [,eɪpə'lɪtɪkəl] ADJ apolitisch

Apollo [ə'pɒləʊ] N (Myth) Apollo m; (fig also) Apoll m

apologetic [ə,pɒlə'dʒetɪk] ADJ (= making an apology) gesture, look entschuldigend attr; (= sorry, regretful) bedauernd attr; **a very ~ Mr Smith rang back** Herr Smith rief zurück und entschuldigte sich sehr; **she wrote me an ~ letter** sie schrieb mir und entschuldigte sich vielmals; **I'm afraid you didn't win, he said with an ~ look** es tut mir Leid, aber Sie haben nicht gewonnen, sagte er mit bedauernder Miene; **he was most ~ (about it)** er entschuldigte sich vielmals (dafür); **his tone was very ~** sein Ton war sehr bedauernd; **his expression was very ~** seine Miene drückte deutlich sein Bedauern aus

apologetically [ə,pɒlə'dʒetɪkəlɪ] ADV say, smile entschuldigend

apologia [æpə'ləʊdʒɪə] N Rechtfertigung f, Apologie f (also Philos)

apologist [ə'pɒlədʒɪst] N Apologet(in) m(f)

apologize [ə'pɒlədʒaɪz] ❂ 18.1 VI sich entschuldigen (to bei); **to ~ for sb/sth** sich für jdn/etw entschuldigen

apology [ə'pɒlədʒɪ] N **a** (= expression of regret) Entschuldigung f; **to make** or **offer sb an ~** jdn um Verzeihung bitten; **to make** or **offer one's apologies** sich entschuldigen; **Mr Jones sends his apologies** Herr Jones lässt sich entschuldigen; **I owe you an ~** ich muss dich um Verzeihung bitten; **are there any apologies?** lässt sich jemand entschuldigen?; **I make no ~** or **apologies for the fact that ...** ich entschuldige mich nicht dafür, dass ... **b** (= poor substitute) trauriges or armseliges Exemplar (for +gen); **an ~ for a breakfast** ein armseliges Frühstück **c** (= defence) Rechtfertigung f, Apologie f

apoplectic [æpə'plektɪk] ADJ (Med) apoplektisch; person also zu Schlaganfällen neigend; (inf) cholerisch; **~ fit** (Med) Schlaganfall m; **he was ~ with rage** (inf) er platzte fast vor Wut (inf)

apoplexy ['æpəpleksɪ] N Apoplexie f (spec), Schlaganfall m

apostasy [ə'pɒstəsɪ] N Abfall m; (Rel also) Apostasie f (form)

apostate [ə'pɒstɪt] N Renegat(in) m(f), Abtrünnige(r) mf; (Rel also) Apostat m; **he's an ~ from the party** er ist ein Parteirenegat ADJ abtrünnig, abgefallen

apostatize [ə'pɒstətaɪz] VI (from church, faith, party) abfallen, sich lossagen (from von)

a posteriori ['eɪpɒs,terɪ'ɔːraɪ] ADV a posteriori

apostle [ə'pɒsl] N (lit, fig) Apostel m; **the Apostles' Creed** das Apostolische Glaubensbekenntnis

apostolic [,æpəs'tɒlɪk] ADJ apostolisch; **Apostolic succession** apostolische Nachfolge; **the Apostolic See** der Apostolische Stuhl

apostrophe [ə'pɒstrəfɪ] N **a** (Gram) Apostroph m **b** (Liter) Apostrophe f

apostrophize [ə'pɒstrəfaɪz] VT apostrophieren (form) VI sich in feierlichen Reden ergehen

apothecary [ə'pɒθɪkərɪ] N (old) Apotheker(in) m(f); **apothecaries' weights and measures** Apothekergewichte und -maße

apotheosis [ə,pɒθɪ'əʊsɪs] N Apotheose f (liter) (into zu)

appal, (US also) **appall** [ə'pɔːl] VT entsetzen; **to be ~led (at** or **by sth)** (über etw acc) entsetzt sein

Appalachian Mountains [æpə'leɪtʃɪən'maʊntɪnz], **Appalachians** [æpə'leɪtʃɪənz] PL Appalachen pl

appalling ADJ, **appallingly** ADV [ə'pɔːlɪŋ, -lɪ] entsetzlich

apparatus [æpə'reɪtəs] N (lit, fig) Apparat m; (= equipment also) Ausrüstung f; (in gym) Geräte *pl*; **a piece of** ~ ein Gerät *nt*; **the ~ of government** der Regierungsapparat

apparel [əˈpærəl] **N** , *no pl* (*liter, US Comm*) Gewand *nt* (*old, liter*), Kleidung *f* **VT** *usu pass* (*old*) gewanden (*old*)

apparent [əˈpærənt] ADJ **a** (= *clear, obvious*) offensichtlich, offenbar; **to be ~ to sb** jdm klar sein, für jdn offensichtlich sein; **it must be ~ to everyone** es muss jedem klar sein; **to become ~** sich (deutlich) zeigen; **for no ~ reason** aus keinem ersichtlichen Grund **b** (= *seeming*) scheinbar; **more ~ than real** mehr Schein als Wirklichkeit

apparently [əˈpærəntlɪ] ADV anscheinend

apparition [æpəˈrɪʃən] N **a** (= *ghost, hum,* = *person*) Erscheinung *f* **b** (= *appearance*) Erscheinen *nt*

appeal [əˈpiːl] **N** **a** (= *request*) (*for help, money etc*) Aufruf *m*, Appell *m*, (dringende) Bitte (*for* um); (*for mercy*) Gesuch *nt* (*for* um); **~ for funds** Spendenappell *or* -aufruf *m or* -aktion *f*; **to make an ~ to sb (to do sth)** an jdn appellieren(, etw zu tun); (*charity, organization etc*) einen Appell *or* Aufruf an jdn richten(, etw zu tun); **to make an ~ to sb for sth** jdn um etw bitten; (*charity, organization etc*) jdn zu etw aufrufen; **to make an ~ for mercy** (*officially*) ein Gnadengesuch einreichen

b (= *supplication*) Flehen *nt*

c (*against decision*) Einspruch *m*; (*Jur*) (*against sentence*) Berufung *f*; (*actual trial*) Revision *f*, Revisionsverfahren *nt*; **he lost his ~** er war in der Berufung *or* Revision unterlegen; **to lodge an ~** Einspruch erheben; (*Jur*) Berufung einlegen (*with* bei); **right of ~** Einspruchsrecht *nt*; (*Jur*) Berufungsrecht *nt*; **she lost the case on ~** sie hat in der Berufung verloren; **Court of Appeal** Berufungsgericht *nt*

d (*for decision, support*) Appell *m*, Aufruf *m*; **the captain made an ~ against the light** der Mannschaftskapitän erhob Einspruch *or* Beschwerde wegen der Lichtverhältnisse

e (= *power of attraction*) Reiz *m* (*to* für), Anziehungskraft *f* (*to* auf +*acc*); **his music has (a) wide ~** seine Musik spricht viele Leute *or* weite Kreise an *or* findet großen Anklang; **skiing has lost its ~ (for me)** Skifahren hat seinen Reiz (für mich) verloren; **I just don't understand the ~ of it** ich verstehe nicht, was daran so reizvoll sein soll

VI **a** (= *make request*) (dringend) bitten, ersuchen (*geh*); **to ~ to sb for sth** jdn um etw bitten *or* ersuchen (*geh*); **to ~ to the public to do sth** die Öffentlichkeit (dazu) aufrufen, etw zu tun

b (*against decision: to authority etc*) Einspruch erheben (*to* bei); (*Jur*) Berufung einlegen (*to* bei); **he was given leave to ~** (*Jur*) es wurde ihm anheim gestellt, Berufung einzulegen

c (= *apply: for support, decision*) sich wenden, appellieren (*to* an +*acc*); (*to sb's feelings etc*) appellieren (*to* an +*acc*); (*Sport*) Einspruch erheben (*from* bei), Beschwerde einlegen; **to ~ to sb's better nature** an jds besseres Ich appellieren

d (= *be attractive*) reizen (*to sb* jdn), zusagen (*to sb* jdm); (*plan, candidate, idea*) zusagen (*to sb* jdm); (*book, magazine*) ansprechen (*to sb* jdn); **it simply doesn't ~** es findet einfach keinen Anklang; **how does that ~?** wie gefällt Ihnen das?; **the story ~ed to his sense of humour** die Geschichte sprach seinen Sinn für Humor an

VT **to ~ a case/verdict** (*Jur*) mit einem Fall/gegen ein Urteil in die Berufung gehen; **to ~ a decision** Einspruch gegen eine Entscheidung einlegen *or* erheben

appealable [əˈpiːləbl] ADJ (*Jur*) berufungsfähig, revisionsfähig, beschwerdefähig; **the decision is ~** gegen die Entscheidung kann Berufung eingelegt werden

appeal fund N Hilfsfonds *m*, Spendenfonds *m*

appealing [əˈpiːlɪŋ] ADJ **a** (= *attractive*) attraktiv; *person, character* ansprechend, attraktiv; *smile, eyes* attraktiv, reizvoll; *kitten, child* süß,

niedlich; *cottage, house* reizvoll, reizend **b** (= *supplicating*) *look, voice* flehend

appealingly [əˈpiːlɪŋlɪ] ADV **a** (= *in supplication*) bittend; *look, speak* flehentlich, inbrünstig (*geh*) **b** (= *attractively*) reizvoll

appeal judge N Richter(in) *m(f)* am Berufungsgericht

appear [əˈpɪəʳ] VI **a** (= *emerge*) erscheinen, auftauchen; (*sun*) sich zeigen, erscheinen; **to ~ from behind sth** hinter etw (*dat*) hervorkommen *or* auftauchen; **to ~ through sth** sich zwischen *or* durch etw hindurch zeigen; **as will presently ~** (*fig*) wie sich gleich zeigen wird **b** (= *arrive*) erscheinen, auftauchen

c (*in public, Jur*) erscheinen; (*personality, ghost also*) sich zeigen; (*Theat*) auftreten; **to ~ in public** sich in der Öffentlichkeit zeigen; (*Theat*) vor Publikum auftreten; **to ~ in court** vor Gericht erscheinen; (*lawyer*) bei einer Gerichtsverhandlung (dabei)sein; **to ~ for sb** jdn vertreten; **to ~ as a witness** als Zeuge/Zeugin auftreten

d (= *be published*) erscheinen; **to ~ in print** gedruckt werden/sein

e (= *seem*) scheinen; **he ~ed (to be) tired/drunk** er wirkte müde/betrunken, er schien müde/betrunken zu sein; **it ~s that ...** es hat den Anschein, dass ..., anscheinend ...; **so it ~s, so it would ~** so will es scheinen, so hat es den Anschein; **it ~s not** anscheinend nicht, es sieht nicht so aus; **there ~s** *or* **there would ~ to be a mistake** anscheinend liegt (da) ein Irrtum vor, da scheint ein Irrtum vorzuliegen; **how does it ~ to you?** welchen Eindruck haben Sie?, wie wirkt das auf Sie?; **it ~s to me that ...** mir scheint, dass ...; **it ~s from his statement that ...** aus seiner Bemerkung geht hervor *or* ergibt sich, dass ...

appearance [əˈpɪərəns] ✪ 16.2 N **a** (= *emergence*) Erscheinen *nt*; (*unexpected*) Auftauchen *nt no pl*; (*Theat*) Auftritt *m*; **many court ~s** viele Auftritte vor Gericht; **to put in** *or* **make an ~** sich sehen lassen; **to make one's ~** sich zeigen; (*Theat*) seinen Auftritt haben; **cast in order of ~** Darsteller in der Reihenfolge ihres Auftritts *or* Auftretens

b (= *look, aspect*) Aussehen *nt*; (*esp of person*) Äußere(s) *nt*, äußere Erscheinung; **~s** (= *outward signs*) der äußere (An)schein; **good ~ essential** gepflegtes Äußeres *or* gepflegte Erscheinung wichtig; **in ~** dem Aussehen nach, vom Äußeren her; **at first ~** auf den ersten Blick; **he/it has the ~ of being ...** er/es erweckt den Anschein, ... zu sein; **for ~s' sake, for the sake of ~s** um den Schein zu wahren, um des Schein(e)s willen; (= *as good manners*) der Form halber; **to keep up ~s** den (äußeren) Schein wahren; **to give the ~ of being ...** den Anschein geben, ... zu sein; **~s are often deceptive** der Schein trügt oft; **~s were against him** der Schein sprach gegen ihn; **by** *or* **from** *or* **to all ~s** allem Anschein nach → **judge N c VI b**

appearance money N (*for TV show etc*) Honorar *nt*; (= *attendance fee*) Sitzungsgeld *nt*

appease [əˈpiːz] VT (= *calm*) *person, anger* beschwichtigen, besänftigen; (*Pol*) (durch Zugeständnisse) beschwichtigen; (= *satisfy*) *hunger, thirst* stillen; *curiosity* stillen, befriedigen

appeasement [əˈpiːzmənt] N (*of person, anger*) Beschwichtigung *f*, Besänftigung *f*; (*Pol*) Beschwichtigung *f* (durch Zugeständnisse); (*of curiosity*) Befriedigung *f*

appellant [əˈpelənt] N (*Jur*) Berufungskläger(in) *m(f)*

appellate [əˈpelət] ADJ (*Jur*) Berufungs-, Revisions-, Beschwerde-, zweiter Instanz (*nachgestellt*); **~ court** Berufungsgericht *nt*, Revisionsgericht *nt*; **~ jurisdiction** Zuständigkeit *f* in der Rechtsmittelinstanz

appellation [æpəˈleɪʃən] N Bezeichnung *f*, Benennung *f*

appellee [æpeˈliː] N (*Jur*) Revisionsbeklagte(r) *mf*, Revisionsgegner(in) *m(f)*

append [əˈpend] VT *notes etc* anhängen (*to* an +*acc*) (*also Comput*), hinzufügen; *seal* drücken (*to auf* +*acc*); *signature* setzen (*to unter* +*acc*); **the seal/signature ~ed to this document** das Siegel, mit dem/die Unterschrift, mit der das Dokument versehen ist

appendage [əˈpendɪdʒ] N (= *limb*) Gliedmaße *f*; (*fig*) Anhängsel *nt*

appendectomy [æpenˈdektəmɪ], **appendicectomy** [æpenˈsektəmɪ] N Blinddarmoperation *f*, Appendektomie *f* (*spec*)

appendices [əˈpendɪsiːz] *pl of* **appendix**

appendicitis [əpendɪˈsaɪtɪs] N Blinddarmentzündung *f*, Appendizitis *f* (*spec*)

appendix [əˈpendɪks] N *pl* **appendices** *or* **-es** **a** (*Anat*) Blinddarm *m*, Appendix *m* (*spec*); **to have one's ~ out** sich (*dat*) den Blinddarm herausnehmen lassen **b** (*to book etc*) Anhang *m*, Appendix *m*

apperception [æpəˈsepʃən] N (*Philos, Psych*) bewusste Wahrnehmung

appertain [æpəˈteɪn] VI (*form*) (= *belong*) gehören (*to* zu), eignen (+*dat*) (*geh*); (= *relate*) betreffen (*to sb/sth* jdn/etw); **this does not ~ to the argument** das gehört nicht zur Sache

appetite [ˈæpɪtaɪt] N (*for food etc*) Appetit *m*, (Ess)lust *f*; (*fig:* = *desire*) Verlangen *nt*, Bedürfnis *nt*, Lust *f*; (= *sexual appetite*) Lust *f*, Begierde *f*; **to have an/no ~ for sth** Appetit *or* Lust/keinen Appetit *or* keine Lust auf etw (*acc*) haben; (*fig*) Verlangen *or* Bedürfnis/kein Verlangen *or* Bedürfnis nach etw haben; **to have a good ~** einen guten *or* gesunden Appetit haben; **I hope you've got an ~** ich hoffe, ihr habt Appetit!; **to take away** *or* **spoil one's ~** sich (*dat*) den Appetit verderben

appetizer [ˈæpɪtaɪzəʳ] N (= *food*) Appetitanreger *m*; (= *hors d'oeuvre also*) Vorspeise *f*, Appetithappen *m*; (= *drink*) appetitanregendes Getränk

appetizing [ˈæpɪtaɪzɪŋ] ADJ appetitlich (*also fig*); *food also* appetitanregend, lecker; *smell* lecker; *description* verlockend

appetizingly [ˈæpɪtaɪzɪŋlɪ] ADV *present* appetitlich, appetitanregend; *describe* verlockend

Appian Way [ˈæpɪənˌweɪ] N Appische Straße

applaud [əˈplɔːd] **VT** (*lit, fig*) applaudieren, Beifall spenden *or* klatschen (+*dat*); (*fig*) *efforts, courage* loben; *decision* gutheißen, begrüßen; **the play was vigorously ~ed** das Stück erhielt stürmischen Beifall *or* wurde lebhaft beklatscht **VI** applaudieren, klatschen, Beifall spenden

applaudable [əˈplɔːdəbl] ADJ lobenswert

applause [əˈplɔːz] N , *no pl* Applaus *m*, Beifall *m* (*also fig*), Klatschen *nt*; **to be greeted with ~** mit Applaus *or* Beifall (*also fig*) begrüßt werden; **to win sb's ~** bei jdm Beifall finden

apple [ˈæpl] N Apfel *m*; **an ~ a day keeps the doctor away** (*Prov*) esst Obst und ihr bleibt gesund; **the ~ doesn't fall far from the tree** (*Prov*) der Apfel fällt nicht weit vom Stamm (*Prov*); **to be the ~ of sb's eye** jds Liebling sein

apple *in cpds* Apfel-; **apple brandy** N Apfelschnaps *m*; **apple butter** N (*US*) Apfelkonfitüre *f*; **applecart** N (*fig*) **to upset the ~** alles über den Haufen werfen (*inf*); **apple dumpling** N = Apfel *m* im Schlafrock; **apple fritters** PL in Teig ausgebackene Apfelringe; **apple green** N Apfelgrün *nt*; **apple-green** ADJ apfelgrün; **applejack** N (*US*) Apfelschnaps *m*; **apple juice** N Apfelsaft *m*; **apple pie** N = gedeckter Apfelkuchen, Apfelpastete *f*; **apple-pie bed** Bett, bei dem Laken und Decken aus Scherz so gefaltet sind, dass man sich nicht ausstrecken kann **in apple-pie order** (*inf*) pikobello (*inf*); **apple sauce** N **a** (*Cook*) Apfelmus *nt* **b** (*dated US, inf:* = *nonsense*) Schmus *m* (*inf*); **apple tree** N Apfelbaum *m*; **apple turnover** N Apfeltasche *f*

appliance [əˈplaɪəns] N **a** Vorrichtung *f*; (= *household appliance*) Gerät *nt*; (= *fire engine*) Feuerwehrwagen *m* **b** (*rare, of skill, knowledge*) Anwenden *nt*, Anwendung *f*; **the ~ of science** die

Anwendung wissenschaftlicher Methoden → application b

applicability [ˌæplɪkə'bɪlɪtɪ] N Anwendbarkeit f (to auf +acc)

applicable [ə'plɪkəbl] ADJ anwendbar (to auf +acc); (on forms) zutreffend (to für); **that isn't ~ to you** das trifft auf Sie nicht zu, das gilt nicht für Sie; **not ~** (on forms) entfällt, nicht zutreffend

applicant ['æplɪkənt] N (for job) Bewerber(in) m(f) (for um, für); (for grant, loan etc) Antragsteller(in) m(f) (for für, auf +acc); (for patent) Anmelder(in) m(f) (for +gen)

application [æplɪ'keɪʃən] ✪ 19.3 N **a** (for job etc) Bewerbung f (for um, für); (for grant, loan etc) Antrag m (for auf +acc), Gesuch nt (for für); (for patent) Anmeldung f (for +gen); **available on ~** auf Anforderung erhältlich; **to make ~ to sb for sth** (form) bei jdm etw anfordern; (written) einen Antrag auf etw (acc) an jdn richten
b (= act of applying, of paint, ointment, lotion) Auftragen nt; (of dressing, plaster) Anlegen nt; (of force, pressure, theory, rules) Anwenden nt, Anwendung f; (of skills, knowledge) Anwendung f, Verwendung f; (of funds) Verwendung f (to für), Gebrauch m (to für); (of embargo, sanctions) Verhängen nt, Verhängung f; **the ~ of a dressing to a head wound** das Anlegen eines Kopfverbandes; **"for external ~ only"** (Med) „nur zur äußerlichen Anwendung"
c (= diligence, effort) Fleiß m, Eifer m
d (form: esp Med) Mittel nt; (= ointment) Salbe f
e = applicability

application: application form N Antragsformular nt, Antrag m; (for job) Bewerbungsbogen m; **application program** N (Comput) Anwendungsprogramm nt; **application software** N (Comput) Anwendersoftware f

applicator ['æplɪkeɪtə] N Aufträger m; (for tampons, pessaries) Applikator m

applied [ə'plaɪd] ADJ attr maths, linguistics etc angewandt; **~ psychology** angewandte Psychologie

appliqué [æ'pliːkeɪ] (Sew) **N** Applikationen pl; **to do ~** applizieren **VT** applizieren **ADJ** attr **~ work** Stickerei f

apply [ə'plaɪ] ✪ 19.1 **VT** paint, ointment, lotion etc auftragen (to auf +acc), applizieren (spec); dressing, plaster anlegen, applizieren (spec); force, pressure, theory, rules anwenden (to auf +acc); knowledge, skills verwenden (to für), anwenden (to auf +acc); funds verwenden (to für), gebrauchen (to für); brakes betätigen; results, findings verwerten (to für); one's attention, efforts zuwenden (to +dat), richten (to auf +acc); embargo, sanctions verhängen (to über +acc); **to ~ oneself/one's mind (to sth)** sich/seinen Kopf (inf) (bei etw) anstrengen; **that term can be applied to many things** dieser Begriff kann auf viele Dinge angewendet werden or trifft auf viele Dinge zu
VI **a** (= make an application) sich bewerben (for um, für); **to ~ to sb for sth** sich an jdn wegen etw wenden; (for job, grant also) sich bei jdm für or um etw bewerben; (for loan, grant also) bei jdm etw beantragen; **no-one applied for the reward** keiner hat sich für die Belohnung gemeldet; **~ at the office/next door/within** Anfragen im Büro/nebenan/im Laden; **she has applied to college/university** sie hat sich um einen Studienplatz beworben
b (= be applicable) gelten (to für); (warning, threat, regulation) gelten (to für), betreffen (to +acc); (description) zutreffen (to auf +acc, für)

appoint [ə'pɔɪnt] VT **a** (to a job) einstellen; (to a post) ernennen; **to ~ sb to the office** jdn in ein Amt berufen; **to ~ sb sth** jdn zu etw ernennen or bestellen (geh) or als etw (acc) berufen; **to ~ sb to do sth** jdn dazu bestimmen, etw zu tun; **they ~ed him to the vacant position** sie gaben ihm die (freie) Stelle; (professorship) sie haben ihn auf den Lehrstuhl berufen **b** (= designate, ordain) bestimmen; (= agree) festlegen or -setzen, verabreden, ausmachen; **the date**

~ed for that meeting (form) der angesetzte Tagungstermin (form)

appointed [ə'pɔɪntɪd] ADJ hour, place festgesetzt, festgelegt, verabredet; task zugewiesen; representative, agent ernannt; **at the ~ time** or **the time** zur festgelegten or -gesetzten or verabredeten Zeit; **his ~ task** die ihm übertragene Aufgabe; **at the ~ time** zur festgesetzten or -gelegten or verabredeten Zeit

-appointed [-ə'pɔɪntɪd] ADJ suf well-/poorly-appointed gut/dürftig ausgestattet

appointee [əpɔɪn'tiː] N Ernannte(r) mf; **he was a Wilson/political ~** er war von Wilson/aus politischen Gründen ernannt worden; **the ~ to the ambassadorship** der neu bestellte Botschafter

appointment [ə'pɔɪntmənt] N **a** (= pre-arranged meeting) Verabredung f; (= business appointment, appointment with doctor, lawyer etc) Termin m (with bei); **to make** or **fix an ~ with sb** mit jdm eine Verabredung treffen/einen Termin mit jdm vereinbaren; **I made an ~ to see the doctor** ich habe mich beim Arzt angemeldet or mir beim Arzt einen Termin geben lassen; **do you have an ~?** sind Sie angemeldet?; **to keep an ~** einen Termin einhalten; **by ~** auf Verabredung; (on business, to see doctor, lawyer etc) mit (Vor)anmeldung, nach Vereinbarung
b (= act of appointing) (to a job) Einstellung f; (to a post) Ernennung f; (to an office) Berufung f (to zu); **his ~ to the position of treasurer** seine Bestellung zum Schatzmeister; **this office is not filled by ~ but by election** für dieses Amt wird man nicht bestellt or berufen, sondern gewählt; **"by ~ (to Her Majesty)"** (on goods) „königlicher Hoflieferant"
c (= post) Stelle f; **~s (vacant)** Stellenangebote pl
d **appointments** PL (= furniture etc) Ausstattung f, Einrichtung f

appointment(s) book N Terminkalender m
appointments bureau N Stellenvermittlung f

apportion [ə'pɔːʃən] VT money, food, land aufteilen; duties zuteilen; **to ~ sth to sb** jdm etw zuteilen; **to ~ sth among** or **between several people** etw zwischen mehreren Leuten aufteilen, etw unter mehrere Leute (gleichmäßig) verteilen; **the blame must be ~ed equally** die Schuld muss allen in gleicher Weise or zu gleichen Teilen angelastet werden

apposite ['æpəzɪt] ADJ comment, phrase treffend, passend; question angebracht

apposition [æpə'zɪʃən] N Apposition f, Beifügung f; **A is in ~ to B, A and B are in ~** A ist eine Apposition zu B

appraisal [ə'preɪzəl] N (of value, damage) Abschätzung f; (of character, ability) Beurteilung f; **to make an ~ of the situation** die Lage abschätzen; **his careful/accurate ~** seine sorgfältige/genaue Einschätzung

appraise [ə'preɪz] VT (= estimate) value, damage (ab)schätzen; (= weigh up) person einschätzen; character, ability (richtig) einschätzen, beurteilen; situation abschätzen; poem etc beurteilen; performance bewerten; **an appraising look** ein prüfender Blick; **he ~d the situation accurately/falsely** er hat die Lage genau/falsch eingeschätzt

appreciable [ə'priːʃəbl] ADJ beträchtlich, deutlich; difference, change also nennenswert, merklich

appreciably [ə'priːʃəblɪ] ADV beträchtlich, deutlich; differ, change also nennenswert, merklich

appreciate [ə'priːʃɪeɪt] ✪ 7.2, 13, 18.4 **VT** **a** (= be aware of) dangers, problems, value etc sich (dat) bewusst sein (+gen); (= understand) sb's wishes, reluctance etc Verständnis haben für; **I ~ that you cannot come** ich verstehe, dass ihr nicht kommen könnt
b (= value, be grateful for) zu schätzen wissen; **nobody ~s me!** niemand weiß mich zu schätzen!; **thank you, I ~ it** vielen Dank, sehr nett

von Ihnen; **my liver would ~ a rest** meine Leber könnte eine kleine Erholung gebrauchen; **I would really ~ that** das wäre mir wirklich sehr lieb; **I would ~ it if you could do this by tomorrow** könnten Sie das bitte bis morgen erledigen?; **I would ~ it if you could be a bit quieter** könnten Sie nicht vielleicht etwas leiser sein?; **we would really ~ it if you would pay what you owe** wir wären Ihnen sehr dankbar or verbunden, wenn Sie Ihre Schulden bezahlen würden
c (= enjoy) art, music, poetry schätzen
VI (Fin) **to ~ (in value)** im Wert steigen, an Wert gewinnen

appreciation [əˌpriːʃɪ'eɪʃən] N **a** (= awareness: of problems, dangers, advantages, value) Erkennen nt
b (= esteem, respect) Anerkennung f; (of abilities, efforts) Anerkennung f, Würdigung f; (of person) Wertschätzung f; **in ~ of sth** in Anerkennung einer Sache (gen), zum Dank für etw; **to show one's ~** seine Dankbarkeit (be)zeigen; **to smile one's ~** zum Dank lächeln
c (= enjoyment, understanding) Verständnis nt; (of art) Sinn m (of für); **to show (great) ~ of Mozart/art** großes Mozart-/Kunstverständnis zeigen; **to write an ~ of sb/sth** einen Bericht über jdn/etw schreiben
d (= comprehension) Verständnis nt
e (= increase) (Wert)steigerung f (in bei)

appreciative [ə'priːʃɪətɪv] ADJ anerkennend; audience dankbar; (= prepared to accept) bereitwillig; (= grateful) dankbar; **to be ~ of sth** etw zu schätzen wissen; (of music, art etc) Sinn für etw haben; (= aware of) sich (dat) einer Sache (gen) bewusst sein

appreciatively [ə'priːʃɪətɪvlɪ] ADV anerkennend; (= gratefully) dankbar

apprehend [æprɪ'hend] VT **a** (= arrest) festnehmen **b** (old, form: = understand) verstehen **c** (form: = anticipate) befürchten

apprehension [æprɪ'henʃən] N **a** (= fear) Besorgnis f, Befürchtung f; **a feeling of ~** eine dunkle Ahnung or Befürchtung; **she felt a moment of ~** sie war einen Moment lang beklommen or voller Befürchtungen **b** (= arrest) Festnahme f **c** (old, form: = understanding) Erkennen nt

apprehensive [æprɪ'hensɪv] ADJ ängstlich; **to be ~ of sth** etw befürchten; **to be ~ that ...** fürchten, dass ...; **he was ~ about the future** er schaute mit ängstlicher Sorge or verzagt in die Zukunft; **to be ~ for sb/about sb's safety** sich (dat) Sorgen um jdn/jds Sicherheit machen

apprehensively [æprɪ'hensɪvlɪ] ADV ängstlich

apprentice [ə'prentɪs] **N** Lehrling m, Lehrjunge m (dated), Auszubildende(r) m (form); **to be an ~** Lehrling sein, in der Lehre sein; **~ plumber/electrician** Klempner-/Elektrikerlehrling m; **~ jockey** angehender Jockey **VT** in die Lehre geben or schicken (to zu, bei); **to be ~d to sb** bei jdm in die Lehre gehen or in der Lehre sein

apprenticeship [ə'prentɪʃɪp] N Lehre f, Lehrzeit f; **to serve one's ~** seine Lehre or Lehrzeit absolvieren or machen

apprise [ə'praɪz] VT (form) in Kenntnis setzen (geh), Kenntnis geben (+dat) (geh); **I am ~d that ...** man hat mich davon in Kenntnis gesetzt or mir davon Kenntnis gegeben, dass ... (geh)

appro ['æprəʊ] N abbr of **approval on ~** (Comm) (to try out) zur Probe; (to look at) zur Ansicht

approach [ə'prəʊtʃ] **VI** (physically) sich nähern, näher kommen; (date, summer etc) nahen **VT** **a** (= come near) sich nähern (+dat); (Aviat) anfliegen; (in figures, temperature, time) zugehen auf (+acc), sich nähern (+dat); (in quality, stature) herankommen an (+acc); (fig) heranreichen an (+acc); **to ~ thirty** auf die dreißig zugehen; **to ~ adolescence/manhood** ins Pubertätsalter/Mannesalter kommen; **the train is now ~ing platform 3** der Zug hat Einfahrt auf Gleis 3; **something ~ing a festive atmosphere** eine annähernd festliche Stimmung

b (= *make an approach to*) *person, committee, organization* herantreten an (+*acc*) (*about* wegen), angehen (*about* um), ansprechen (*about* wegen, auf +*acc* hin); **I haven't ~ed him yet** ich habe ihn daraufhin noch nicht angesprochen, ich bin damit noch nicht an ihn herangetreten; **he is easy/difficult to ~** er ist leicht/nicht leicht ansprechbar **c** (= *tackle*) *question, problem, task* angehen, herangehen an (+*acc*), anpacken **N** **a** (= *drawing near*) (Heran)nahen *nt*; (*of troops*) Heranrücken *nt*; (*of night*) Einbruch *m*; (*Aviat*) Anflug *m* (*to an* +*acc*); **at the ~ of Easter** als das Osterfest nahte/wenn das Osterfest naht **b** (*to person, committee, organization*) Herantreten *nt*; **to make ~es/an ~ to sb** (*with request*) an jdn herantreten; (*man to woman*) Annäherungsversuche machen **c** (= *way of tackling, attitude*) Ansatz *m* (*to* zu); **a positive ~ to mathematics/teaching** eine positive Einstellung zu Mathematik/zum Unterrichten; **his ~ to the problem** seine Art *or* Methode, an das Problem heranzugehen, sein Problemansatz *m*; **you've chosen the wrong ~** du gehst die Sache falsch an; **try a different ~** versuchs doch mal anders; **new ~es in psychology** neue Ansätze in der Psychologie **d** (= *access*) Zugang *m*, Weg *m*; (= *road*) Zufahrt(sstraße) *f* **e** (= *approximation*) Annäherung *f* (*to an* +*acc*)

approachability [əˌprəʊtʃəˈbɪlɪtɪ] N (*of place*) Zugänglichkeit *f*; (*fig: of person*) Umgänglichkeit *f*

approachable [əˈprəʊtʃəbl] ADJ **a** *person* umgänglich, leicht zugänglich; **he's not ~ today** er ist heute nicht ansprechbar **b** *place* zugänglich; **it's ~ from above** man kommt von oben (heran) **c** *text, idea* verständlich

approaching [əˈprəʊtʃɪŋ] ADJ *attr* näher kommend; *date, occasion* herannahend, bevorstehend

approach: approach lights PL (*Aviat*) Lichter *pl* (*in* der Einflugschneise; **approach path** N (*Aviat*) Einflugschneise *f*; **approach road** N (*to city etc*) Zufahrtsstraße *f*; (*to motorway*) (Autobahn)zubringer *m*; (= *slip road*) Auf- *or* Einfahrt *f*; **approach shot** N (*Golf*) Schlag *m* zwischen Abschlag und Grün

approbation [ˌæprəˈbeɪʃən] N Zustimmung *f*; (*of decision also*) Billigung *f*; (*from critics*) Beifall *m*

appropriate¹ [əˈprəʊprɪɪt] ✪ 1.1, 26.1 ADJ **a** (= *suitable, fitting*) passend, geeignet (*for, to* für); angebracht (*for, to* für); (*to a situation, occasion*) angemessen (*to* +*dat*); *name, remark* treffend; **it was ~ that he came at that moment** es traf sich gut, dass er gerade kam; **clothing ~ for** *or* **to the weather conditions** wettergemäße Kleidung; **a style ~ to one's subject** ein dem Thema entsprechender *or* angemessener Stil; **to be ~ for doing sth** geeignet sein, etw zu tun **b** (= *relevant*) entsprechend; *body, authority* zuständig; **where ~** wo es angebracht ist/war, an gegebener Stelle; **put a tick where ~** Zutreffendes bitte ankreuzen; **delete as ~** Nichtzutreffendes *or* nicht Zutreffendes streichen; **it may be ~ (for you) to discuss this with your lawyer** sie sollten das vielleicht mit Ihrem Anwalt besprechen

appropriate² [əˈprəʊprɪeɪt] VT **a** (= *assume possession or control of*) beschlagnahmen; (= *take for oneself*) sich (*dat*) aneignen, mit Beschlag belegen; *sb's ideas* sich (*dat*) zu Eigen machen **b** (= *allocate*) *funds* zuteilen, zuweisen

appropriately [əˈprəʊprɪɪtlɪ] ADV treffend; *dressed* passend (*for, to* für), entsprechend (*for, to* +*dat*); (*to fit particular needs*) *designed, equipped* entsprechend (*for, to* +*dat*), zweckmäßig (*for, to* für); **~ enough the letter arrived at that very moment** passenderweise kam der Brief genau in dem Augenblick; **rather ~ she was called Goldilocks** der Name Goldköpfchen passte sehr gut zu ihr

appropriateness [əˈprəʊprɪɪtnɪs] N (= *suitability, fittingness*) Eignung *f*; (*of dress, remark, name, for a particular occasion*) Angemessenheit *f*

appropriation [əˌprəʊprɪˈeɪʃən] N **a** (*of land, property*) Beschlagnahme *f*, Beschlagnahmung *f*; (*of sb's ideas*) Aneignung *f* **b** (= *allocation: of funds*) Zuteilung *f*, Zuweisung *f*; **to make an ~ for sth** Mittel für etw zuteilen *or* zuweisen

approval [əˈpruːvəl] N **a** Beifall *m*, Anerkennung *f*; (= *consent*) Zustimmung *f* (*of* zu), Billigung *f* (*of* +*gen*), Einverständnis *nt* (*of* mit); **to win sb's ~ (for sth)** jds Zustimmung (für etw) gewinnen; **to give one's ~ for sth** seine Zustimmung zu etw geben; **to meet with sb's ~** jds Zustimmung *or* Beifall finden; **to seek sb's ~ for sth** jds Zustimmung zu etw suchen; **to have sb's ~** jds Zustimmung haben; **to show one's ~ of sth** zeigen, dass man einer Sache (*dat*) zustimmt *or* etw billigt; **submitted for the Queen's ~** der Königin zur Genehmigung vorgelegt **b** (*Comm*) **on ~** zur Probe; (*to look at*) zur Ansicht

approval rate N (*Pol*) **his ~ is 52 per cent** 52% der Bevölkerung sind mit seiner Politik einverstanden

approve [əˈpruːv] ✪ 14 VT (= *consent to*) *decision* billigen, gutheißen; *minutes, motion* annehmen; *project, sale, deal, plan* genehmigen; (= *recommend*) *hotel, campsite etc* empfehlen; **an ~d campsite** ein empfohlener Campingplatz VI **to ~ of sb/sth** von jdm/etw etwas halten, etw billigen *or* gutheißen; **I don't ~ of him/it** ich halte nichts von ihm/davon; **do you ~ of him/that?** hältst du etwas von ihm/davon?; **I don't ~ of children smoking** ich billige nicht *or* kann es nicht gutheißen, dass Kinder rauchen; **she doesn't ~ of it** sie missbilligt das; **how's this shirt, do you ~?** gefällt dir dies Hemd?

approved school [əˈpruːvdˈskuːl] N (*Brit dated*) Erziehungsheim *nt*

approving [əˈpruːvɪŋ] ADJ (= *satisfied, pleased*) anerkennend, beifällig; (= *consenting*) zustimmend

approvingly [əˈpruːvɪŋlɪ] ADV anerkennend, beifällig

approx. *abbr of* **approximately** ca.

approximate [əˈprɒksɪmɪt] ADJ ungefähr; **these figures are only ~** dies sind nur ungefähre Werte; **three hours is the ~ time needed** man braucht ungefähr drei Stunden VI [əˈprɒksɪmeɪt] **to ~ to sth** einer Sache (*dat*) in etwa entsprechen; **they ~ to one another** sie entsprechen einander in etwa VT [əˈprɒksɪmeɪt] **to ~ sth** einer Sache (*dat*) in etwa entsprechen

approximately [əˈprɒksɪmɪtlɪ] ADV ungefähr, etwa, circa; *correct* in etwa, annähernd

approximation [əˌprɒksɪˈmeɪʃən] N Annäherung *f* (*of, to an* +*acc*); (= *figure, sum etc*) (An)näherungswert *m*; **his story was an ~ of the truth** seine Geschichte entsprach in etwa *or* ungefähr der Wahrheit

appurtenances [əˈpɜːtɪnənsɪz] PL (= *equipment*) Zubehör *nt*; (= *accessories*) Attribute *pl*; (*Jur*: = *rights etc*) Rechte *pl*; **with all the ~ of affluence** mit allen Attributen des Wohlstands

APR *abbr of* **annual percentage rate** Jahreszinssatz *m*

après-ski [ˌæpreɪˈskiː] **N** Après-Ski *nt* **ADJ** *attr* Après-Ski-; **~ bar** Après-Ski-Lokal *nt*

apricot [ˈeɪprɪkɒt] **N** Aprikose *f* **ADJ** (*also* **apricot-coloured**) aprikosenfarben *attr* Aprikosen-; **~ jam** Aprikosenmarmelade *f*

April [ˈeɪprəl] N April *m*; **~ shower** Aprilschauer *m* → *also* **September**

April fool N Aprilnarr *m*; **~!** ≈ April, April!; **to play an ~ on sb** jdn in den April schicken

April Fools' Day N der erste April

a priori [eɪpraɪˈɔːraɪ] **ADV** a priori **ADJ** apriorisch

apron [ˈeɪprən] N Schürze *f*; (*Aviat*) Vorfeld *nt*; (*Theat*) Vorbühne *f*

apron: apron stage N Bühne *f* mit Vorbühne; **apron strings** PL Schürzenbänder *pl*; **to be**

tied to sb's ~ jdm am Schürzenzipfel hängen (*inf*)

apropos [ˌæprəˈpəʊ] PREP (*also* **apropos of**) apropos (+*nom*); **~ of nothing** ganz nebenbei ADJ *pred remark* passend, treffend

apse [æps] N Apsis *f*

APT *abbr of* **advanced passenger train** Hochgeschwindigkeitszug *m*

apt [æpt] ADJ (+*er*) **a** (= *suitable, fitting*) passend; *description, comparison, remark* passend, treffend **b** (= *able, intelligent*) begabt (*at* für) **c** (= *liable, likely*) **to be ~ to do sth** leicht etw tun, dazu neigen, etw zu tun; **he is ~ to be late** er neigt dazu, zu spät zu kommen; **I was ~ to believe him until ...** ich war geneigt, ihm zu glauben, bis ...; **it is ~ to rain in Glasgow** es regnet oft in Glasgow; **we are ~ to forget that ...** wir vergessen leicht *or* gern (*inf*), dass ...

Apt. *abbr of* **apartment** Z, Zi

aptitude [ˈæptɪtjuːd] N Begabung *f*; **she has a great ~ for saying the wrong thing** (*hum*) sie hat ein besonderes Talent dafür, immer das Falsche zu sagen

aptitude test N Eignungsprüfung *f*

aptly [ˈæptlɪ] ADV passend; **it did not fit ~ into the context** es passte nicht richtig in den Zusammenhang

aptness [ˈæptnɪs] N **a** (= *suitability*) **the ~ of the name was obvious** der Name war offensichtlich passend **b** (= *aptitude*) Begabung *f* **c** (= *liability, likelihood*) Neigung *f*

aquaculture [ˈækwəkʌltʃə] N Aquakultur *f*

aqualung [ˈækwəlʌŋ] N Tauchgerät *nt*

aquamarine [ˌækwəməˈriːn] **N** Aquamarin *m*; (= *colour*) Aquamarin *nt* **ADJ** aquamarin

aquanaut [ˈækwənɔːt] N Aquanaut(in) *m(f)*

aquanautics [ˌækwəˈnɔːtɪks] N *sing* Aquanautik *f*

aquaplane [ˈækwəpleɪn] **N** Monoski *m* **VI** (*Sport*) Wasserski laufen **b** (*car etc*) (auf nasser Straße) ins Rutschen geraten

aquaplaning [ˈækwəpleɪnɪŋ] N Aquaplaning *nt*; **in order to prevent the car from ~** um ein Aquaplaning zu verhindern

aquarium [əˈkwɛərɪəm] N Aquarium *nt*

Aquarius [əˈkwɛərɪəs] N Wassermann *m*

aquatic [əˈkwætɪk] ADJ Wasser-; *plants, animals, organisms etc also* im Wasser lebend, aquatisch (*spec*); **~ sports** Wassersport *m*

aquatint [ˈækwətɪnt] N Aquatinta *f*

aqueduct [ˈækwɪdʌkt] N Aquädukt *m or nt*

aqueous [ˈeɪkwɪəs] ADJ (*form*) *rocks* wasserhaltig; *solution* wässrig

aqueous humour N (*Med*) Kammerwasser *nt*, Humor aquosus *m* (*spec*)

aquiline [ˈækwɪlaɪn] ADJ gebogen; *profile* mit Adlernase, dinarisch (*geh*); **~ nose** Adlernase *f*

Aquinas [əˈkwaɪnəs] N Thomas von Aquin

Arab [ˈærəb] **N** Araber *m* (*also horse*), Araberin *f*; **the ~s** die Araber **ADJ** *attr* arabisch; *policies, ideas also* der Araber; **~ horse** Araber *m*

arabesque [ˌærəˈbesk] N Arabeske *f*

Arabia [əˈreɪbɪə] N Arabien *nt*

Arabian [əˈreɪbɪən] ADJ arabisch; **tales of the ~ Nights** Märchen aus Tausendundeiner Nacht

Arabic [ˈærəbɪk] **N** Arabisch *nt* **ADJ** arabisch; **~ numerals** arabische Ziffern *or* Zahlen; **~ studies** Arabistik *f*

arable [ˈærəbl] ADJ Acker-; **~ farming** Ackerbau *m*; **~ land** bebaubares Land; (*in use*) Ackerland *nt*

arachnid [əˈræknɪd] N Spinnentier *nt*

arachnology [ˌærækˈnɒlədʒɪ] N Arachnologie *f*, Spinnenkunde *f*

arachnophobia [əˌræknəʊˈfəʊbɪə] N Arachnophobie *f*, Angst *f* vor Spinnen

Aragon [ˈærəgən] N Aragon *nt*, Aragonien *nt*

arbiter [ˈɑːbɪtə] N **a** (*of fate etc*) Herr(in) *m(f)*, Gebieter(in) *m(f)* (*of* über +*acc*); **to be the ~ of** Herr(in) sein über (+*acc*); **they were the ~s**

of good taste/style sie waren die Päpste des guten Geschmacks/Stils **b** = **arbitrator**

arbitrarily [ˈɑːbɪtrərəlɪ] ADV willkürlich, arbiträr (geh)

arbitrariness [ˈɑːbɪtrərɪnɪs] N Willkürlichkeit f

arbitrary [ˈɑːbɪtrərɪ] ADJ willkürlich, arbiträr (geh)

arbitrate [ˈɑːbɪtreɪt] **VT** dispute schlichten **VI** **a** (in dispute) vermitteln **b** (= go to arbitration) vor eine Schlichtungskommission gehen

arbitration [ˌɑːbɪˈtreɪʃən] N Schlichtung f; **to submit a dispute to** = einen Streit vor ein Schiedsgericht or (esp Ind) eine Schlichtungskommission bringen; **to go to** ~ vor eine Schlichtungskommission gehen; (dispute) vor eine Schlichtungskommission gebracht werden

arbitrator [ˈɑːbɪtreɪtə] N Vermittler(in) m(f); (esp Ind) Schlichter(in) m(f)

arbor [ˈɑːbə] N (US) = **arbour**

arboreal [ɑːˈbɔːrɪəl] ADJ animal, bird auf Bäumen lebend; habitat auf Bäumen

arboretum [ˌɑːbəˈriːtəm] N Arboretum nt (spec), Baumschule f

arborist [ˈɑːbərɪst] N Baumzüchter(in) m(f)

arbour, (US) **arbor** [ˈɑːbə] N Laube f

arbutus [ɑːˈbjuːtəs] N Arbutus m

arc [ɑːk] N Bogen m

arcade [ɑːˈkeɪd] N (Archit) Arkade f; (= shopping arcade) Passage f

Arcadia [ɑːˈkeɪdɪə] N Arkadien nt

Arcadian [ɑːˈkeɪdɪən] ADJ (lit, fig) arkadisch

arcane [ɑːˈkeɪn] ADJ obskur

arch[1] [ɑːtʃ] **N** **a** Bogen m; ~ **of the heavens** Himmelsbogen m, Himmelsgewölbe nt **b** (Anat, of foot) Gewölbe nt (spec); **high/fallen** ~**es** hoher Spann/Senkfuß m; ~ **support** Senkfußeinlage f **VI** sich wölben; (arrow etc) einen Bogen machen **VT** back krümmen; eyebrows hochziehen; **the cat** ~**ed its back** die Katze machte einen Buckel

arch[2] ADJ attr Erz-; ~ **enemy** Erzfeind(in) m(f); ~ **rival** Erzrivale m, Erzrivalin f; ~ **traitor** Hochverräter(in) m(f)

arch[3] ADJ (= wicked, mischievous) neckisch, schelmisch

archaeological, (US) **archeological** [ˌɑːkɪəˈlɒdʒɪkəl] ADJ archäologisch

archaeologist, (US) **archeologist** [ˌɑːkɪˈɒlədʒɪst] N Archäologe m, Archäologin f

archaeology, (US) **archeology** [ˌɑːkɪˈɒlədʒɪ] N Archäologie f

archaic [ɑːˈkeɪɪk] ADJ word etc veraltet, archaisch (spec); (inf: = ancient) vorsintflutlich; **my car is getting rather** ~ mein Auto wird allmählich museumsreif

archaism [ˈɑːkeɪɪzəm] N veralteter Ausdruck, Archaismus m

arch: archangel [ˈɑːkˌeɪndʒl] N Erzengel m; **archbishop** N Erzbischof m; **archbishopric** N (= district) Erzbistum nt, Erzdiözese f; (= office) Amt nt des Erzbischofs; **archdeacon** N Archidiakon m, Erzdiakon m; **archdiocese** N Erzdiözese f, Erzbistum nt; **archducal** ADJ erzherzoglich; **archduchess** N Erzherzogin f; **archduchy** N Erzherzogtum nt; **archduke** N Erzherzog m

arched [ɑːtʃt] ADJ gewölbt; ~ **window** (Rund)bogenfenster nt; **the** ~ **curve of the temple roof** die Wölbung des Tempeldachs

archeological etc (US) = **archaeological** etc

archer [ˈɑːtʃə] N Bogenschütze m/-schützin f; (Astron, Astrol) Schütze m

archery [ˈɑːtʃərɪ] N Bogenschießen nt

archetypal [ˌɑːkɪˈtaɪpəl] ADJ archetypisch (geh); (= typical) typisch; **he is the** ~ **millionaire** er ist ein Millionär, wie er im Buche steht; **an** ~ **Scot** ein Urschotte (inf)

archetypally [ˌɑːkɪˈtaɪpəlɪ] ADV archetypisch

archetype [ˈɑːkɪtaɪp] N Archetyp(us) m (form); (= original, epitome also) Urbild nt, Urtyp m

archetypical [ˌɑːkɪˈtɪpɪkəl] ADJ = **archetypal**

archfiend [ɑːtʃˈfiːnd] N **the** ~ der Erzfeind

archiepiscopal [ˌɑːkɪˈpɪskəpəl] ADJ erzbischöflich

Archimedes [ˌɑːkɪˈmiːdiːz] N Archimedes m

Archimedes' principle [ˌɑːkɪˈmiːdiːz-] N das archimedische Prinzip

archipelago [ˌɑːkɪˈpelɪgəʊ] N pl **-(e)s** Archipel m; **the Archipelago** der Archipel(agos); (= sea) die Ägäis

architect [ˈɑːkɪtekt] N (lit, fig) Architekt(in) m(f); ~~**designed** von (einem) Architekten entworfen; **he was the** ~ **of his own downfall** er hat seinen Ruin selbst verursacht

architectural ADJ , **architecturally** ADV [ˌɑːkɪˈtektʃərəl, -ɪ] architektonisch

architecture [ˈɑːkɪtektʃə] N Architektur f (also Comput); (of building also) Baustil m

architrave [ˈɑːkɪtreɪv] N (Archit) Architrav m; (= frame) architravähnliche Einfassung (für Tür)

archival [ɑːˈkaɪvəl] ADJ archivalisch, Archiv-

archive [ˈɑːkaɪv] **N** Archiv nt (also Comput); ~ **file** Archivdatei f; ~ **material/film** Archivmaterial nt/-film m **VT** archivieren

archives [ˈɑːkaɪvz] PL Archiv nt

archivist [ˈɑːkɪvɪst] N Archivar(in) m(f)

archly [ˈɑːtʃlɪ] ADV neckisch, schelmisch

archness [ˈɑːtʃnɪs] N neckische or schelmische Art

archpriest [ɑːtʃˈpriːst] N (lit, fig) Hohepriester m

archway [ˈɑːtʃweɪ] N Torbogen m

arc lamp, arc light N Bogenlampe f, Bogenlicht nt

arctic [ˈɑːktɪk] **ADJ** (lit, fig) arktisch **N** **a** **the Arctic** die Arktis **b** (US: = shoe) gefütterter, wasserundurchlässiger Überschuh

arctic: Arctic Circle N nördlicher Polarkreis; **arctic fox** N Polarfuchs m; **Arctic Ocean** N Nordpolarmeer nt

arc welding N (Licht)bogenschweißung f

ardent [ˈɑːdənt] ADJ leidenschaftlich; supporter, admirer also begeistert; love also glühend; desire, longing also brennend, glühend; request, imprecations inständig

ardently [ˈɑːdəntlɪ] ADV leidenschaftlich; love heiß; desire, admire glühend

ardour, (US) **ardor** [ˈɑːdə] N (of person) Begeisterung f, Leidenschaft f; (in voice also) Überschwang m; (of feelings also) Heftigkeit f; (of passions) Glut f (liter), Feuer nt; (of poems, letters) Leidenschaftlichkeit f; **the** ~**s of youth** die Leidenschaft der Jugend

arduous [ˈɑːdjʊəs] ADJ beschwerlich, mühsam; course, work anstrengend; task mühselig

arduousness [ˈɑːdjʊəsnɪs] N Beschwerlichkeit f; (of task) Mühseligkeit f; **because of the** ~ **of the work** weil die Arbeit so anstrengend war/ist

are[1] [ɑː] N Ar nt

are[2] 2nd pers sing, 1st, 2nd, 3rd pers pl present of **be**

area [ˈɛərɪə] N **a** (measure) Fläche f; **20 sq metres** (Brit) or **meters** (US) **in** ~ eine Fläche von 20 Quadratmetern

b (= region, district) Gebiet nt; (= neighbourhood, vicinity) Gegend f; (separated off, piece of ground etc) Areal nt, Gelände nt; (on plan, diagram etc) Bereich m; (= slum area, residential area, commercial area) Viertel nt, Gebiet nt; **this is not a very nice** ~ **to live in** dies ist keine besonders gute Wohngegend; **in the** ~ in der Nähe; **do you live in the** ~? wohnen Sie hier (in der Gegend)?; **in the** ~ **of the station** im Bahnhofsgegend; **the thief is believed to be still in the** ~ man nimmt an, dass sich der Dieb noch in der Umgebung aufhält; **in the London** ~ im Raum London, im Londoner Raum; **protected/prohibited/industrial** ~ Schutz-/Sperr-/Industriegebiet nt; **drying/dispatch** ~ Trocken-/Verteilerzone f; **dining/sleeping** ~ Ess-/Schlafbereich or -platz m; **no smoking/recreation** ~ Nichtraucher-/Erholungszone f; **we use this corner as a discussion** ~ wir benutzen diese Ecke für Diskussionen; **the goal** ~ (Ftbl) der Torraum; **the (penalty)** ~ (esp Brit Ftbl) der Strafraum; **this** ~ **is for directors' cars** dieser Platz ist für Direktorenwagen vorgesehen; **you must keep out of this** ~ dies Gebiet darf nicht betreten werden; **this** ~ **must be kept clear** diesen Platz freihalten; **the public were told to keep well away from the** ~ die Öffentlichkeit wurde aufgefordert, das Gebiet unbedingt zu meiden; **a mountainous** ~ eine bergige Gegend; **mountainous** ~**s** Bergland nt; **a wooded** ~ ein Waldstück nt; (larger) ein Waldgebiet nt; **desert** ~**s** Wüstengebiete pl; **the infected** ~**s of the lungs** die befallenen Teile or (smaller) Stellen der Lunge; **the patchy** ~**s on the wall** die fleckigen Stellen an der Wand; **the additional message** ~ **on an air letter** der Raum für zusätzliche Mitteilungen auf einem Luftpostbrief; **the sterling** ~ die Sterlingzone

c (fig) Bereich m; ~**s of uncertainty/agreement** Bereiche, in denen Unklarheit/Übereinstimmung besteht; **his** ~ **of responsibility** sein Verantwortungsbereich m; ~ **of interest/study** Interessen-/Studiengebiet nt; **a sum in the** ~ **of £100** eine Summe um die £ 100

d (Brit: = basement courtyard) Vorplatz m

area: area bombing N Flächenbombardierungen pl; **area code** N (Telec) Vorwahl(nummer) f, Ortskennzahl f; **area command** N Gebiets- or Abschnittskommandantur f; **area manager** N Bezirks- or Gebietsleiter m; **area office** N Bezirksbüro nt; **areaway** N (US) **a** Vorplatz m **b** (= passage) Durchgang m, Passage f

arena [əˈriːnə] N (lit, fig) Arena f; ~ **of war** Kriegsschauplatz m; **to enter the** ~ (fig) die Arena betreten, auf den Plan treten

aren't [ɑːnt] = **are not, am not** → **be**

areola [əˈriːələ] N pl **areolae** (Anat: of nipple) Areola f (spec), Warzenhof m; (Med: of spot) entzündeter Hautring um einen Pickel

argent [ˈɑːdʒənt] (obs, poet, Her) **N** Silber nt **ADJ** silbern

Argentina [ˌɑːdʒənˈtiːnə] N Argentinien nt

Argentine [ˈɑːdʒəntaɪn] N **the** ~ Argentinien nt

Argentinian [ˌɑːdʒənˈtɪnɪən] **N** (= person) Argentinier(in) m(f) **ADJ** argentinisch

argon [ˈɑːgɒn] N Argon nt

Argonaut [ˈɑːgənɔːt] N Argonaut m

argot [ˈɑːgəʊ] N Argot nt or m; (criminal also) Rotwelsch nt

arguable [ˈɑːgjʊəbl] ADJ **a** (= capable of being maintained) vertretbar; **it is** ~ **that ...** es lässt sich der Standpunkt vertreten, dass ..., man kann behaupten, dass ... **b** (= open to discussion) **it is** ~ **whether ...** es ist (noch) die Frage, ob ...

arguably [ˈɑːgjʊəblɪ] ADV wohl; **this is** ~ **his best book** dies dürfte (wohl) sein bestes Buch sein

argue [ˈɑːgjuː] ✪ 26.1, 26.3 **VI** **a** (= dispute) streiten; (= quarrel) sich streiten; (about trivial things) sich zanken; **he is always arguing** er widerspricht ständig, er muss immer streiten; **there's no arguing with him** mit ihm kann man nicht reden; **don't** ~ **(with me)!** keine Widerrede!; **don't** ~ **with your mother!** du sollst deiner Mutter nicht widersprechen!; **I don't want to** ~, **if you don't want to** ich will mich nicht streiten, wenn Sie nicht wollen; **there is no point in arguing** da erübrigt sich jede (weitere) Diskussion; **you can't** ~ **with a line of tanks** mit Panzern kann man nicht diskutieren; **a 25% increase, you can't** ~ **with that** (inf) eine 25%ige Erhöhung, da kann man nichts sagen (inf) or nicht meckern (inf); **he wasn't used to employees arguing** Angestellte, die ihre Meinung sagten, war er nicht gewöhnt

b (= present reasons) **to** ~ **for** or **in favour** (Brit) or **favor** (US) **of sth** für etw sprechen; (in book) sich für etw aussprechen; **to** ~ **against sth** gegen etw sprechen; (in book) sich gegen etw aussprechen; **to ~ from a position of ...** von einem or dem Standpunkt ... (gen) aus argumentieren; **this ~s in his favour** (Brit) or **favor** (US) das spricht zu seinen Gunsten; **just one thing ~s against him/it** nur eins spricht gegen ihn/dagegen

VT **a** (= debate) case, matter diskutieren, erörtern; (Jur) vertreten; **a well ~d case** ein gut begründeter or dargelegter Fall; **to ~ a case for reform** die Sache der Reform vertreten; **to ~ one's way out of sth** sich aus etw herausreden **b** (= maintain) behaupten; **he ~s that ...** er vertritt den Standpunkt, dass ..., er behauptet, dass ...; **I'm not arguing that ...** ich will nicht behaupten, dass ... **c** (= persuade) **to ~ sb out of/into sth** jdm etw aus-/einreden **d** (= indicate) erkennen lassen, verraten

▶ **argue away** **VI** diskutieren **VT** sep facts wegdiskutieren

▶ **argue out** VT sep problem, issue ausdiskutieren; **to argue sth out with sb** etw mit jdm durchsprechen

arguer ['ɑːgjuːə'] N **a** (= quarreller) streitsüchtiger Mensch, Streithammel m (inf) **b** (= reasoner) logisch argumentierender Mensch; **to be a logical ~** logisch argumentieren (können)

argufy ['ɑːgjuːfaɪ] VI (esp hum) wegen jeder Kleinigkeit streiten

argument ['ɑːgjʊmənt] ✪ 26.1 N **a** (= discussion) Diskussion f; **to spend hours in ~ about how to do sth** stundenlang darüber diskutieren, wie man etw machen soll; **for the sake of ~** rein theoretisch; **he just said that for the sake of ~** das hat er nur gesagt, um etwas (dagegen) zu sagen; **it is beyond ~** das ist unbestreitbar; **he is open to ~** er lässt mit sich reden; **this is open to ~** darüber lässt sich streiten **b** (= quarrel) Auseinandersetzung f; **to have an ~** sich streiten; (over sth trivial) sich zanken; **without ~** widerspruchslos **c** (= reason) Beweis(grund) m, Argument nt; (= line of reasoning) Argumentation f, Beweisführung f; **first state your theory, then list the ~s for and against** stellen Sie erst Ihre These auf und nennen Sie dann die Gründe und Gegengründe; **one of the best ~s I have heard in favour** (Brit) or **favor** (US) **of private education** eines der besten Argumente zugunsten or zu Gunsten der Privatschule; **there's an even stronger ~ than that** es gibt ein noch stärkeres Argument; **that's not a rational ~, it's just a dogmatic assertion** das ist kein rationales Argument, das ist bloß eine dogmatische Behauptung **d** (= theme: of play, book etc) Aussage f, These f (esp Philos); (= claim) These f **e** (= statement of proof) Beweis m; **the two main types of ~** die beiden wichtigsten Beweisarten; **Professor Ayer's ~ is that ...** Professor Ayers These lautet, dass ...; **the Ontological/Teleological Argument** der ontologische/teleologische Gottesbeweis; **all the various ~s for the existence of a god** all die verschiedenen Gottesbeweise; **I don't think that's a valid ~** ich glaube, das ist kein gültiger Beweis; **an interesting ~** eine interessante These **f** (Math) Argument nt

argumentation [ˌɑːgjʊmənˈteɪʃən] N Argumentation f, Beweisführung f; (= discussion) Diskussion f; **an ingenious piece of ~** eine geniale Beweisführung

argumentative [ˌɑːgjʊˈmentətɪv] ADJ person streitsüchtig

argy-bargy ['ɑːdʒɪˈbɑːdʒɪ] (Brit inf) **N** Hin und Her nt (inf), Hickhack m or nt (inf) **VI** hin und her reden, endlos debattieren

aria ['ɑːrɪə] N Arie f

Arian[1] ['ɛərɪən] N, ADJ = Aryan

Arian[2] (Astrol) N Widder m; **to be an ~** Widder sein

ARIBA [əˈriːbə] abbr of **Associate of the Royal British Institute of Architects** Mitglied des britischen Architektenverbandes

arid ['ærɪd] ADJ (lit) countryside, soil dürr; climate trocken, arid (spec); (fig) subject trocken, nüchtern; existence freudlos, öd

aridity [əˈrɪdɪtɪ] N (of countryside, soil) Dürre f; (of climate) Trockenheit f, Aridität f (spec); (fig) (of subject) Trockenheit f, Nüchternheit f; (of existence) Freudlosigkeit f, Öde f

Aries ['ɛəriːz] N (Astrol) Widder m; **she is (an) ~** sie ist Widder

aright [əˈraɪt] ADV recht, wohl (old); **if I understand it ~** wenn ich das recht verstehe

arise [əˈraɪz] pret **arose** [əˈrəʊz] ptp **arisen** [əˈrɪzn] VI **a** (= occur) sich ergeben, entstehen; (misunderstanding, argument) aufkommen, entstehen; (problem) aufkommen, sich ergeben; (clouds of dust) entstehen, sich bilden; (protest, cry) sich erheben; (question) sich stellen, aufkommen, sich erheben (geh); (wind) aufkommen, sich erheben (geh); **should the need ~** falls sich die Notwendigkeit ergibt **b** (= result) **to ~ out of** or **from sth** sich aus etw ergeben **c** (old, liter: = get up) sich erheben (liter); **~ Sir Humphrey** erhebt Euch, Sir Humphrey!

aristocracy [ˌærɪsˈtɒkrəsɪ] N (system, state) Aristokratie f; (= class also) Adel m; **~ of wealth** Geldadel m, Geldaristokratie f

aristocrat ['ærɪstəkræt] N Aristokrat(in) m(f), Adlige(r) mf; **he is too much of an ~ to ~** (fig) er ist sich (dat) zu fein, um ... zu ...; **the ~ of the dog/cat family** der edelste Vertreter der Hunde-/Katzenfamilie

aristocratic [ˌærɪstəˈkrætɪk] ADJ (lit) aristokratisch, adlig; (fig also) vornehm

Aristotelian [ˌærɪstəˈtiːlɪən] ADJ aristotelisch **N** Aristoteliker m

Aristotle ['ærɪstɒtl] N Aristoteles m

arithmetic [əˈrɪθmətɪk] N Rechnen nt; (= calculation) Rechnung f; **could you check my ~?** kannst du mal gucken, ob ich richtig gerechnet habe?; **your ~ is wrong** du hast dich verrechnet; **~ book** Rechenfibel f or -buch nt; (= exercise book) Rechenheft nt

arithmetical [ˌærɪθˈmetɪkəl] ADJ rechnerisch; **~ genius** Rechenkünstler(in) m(f); **the basic ~ skills** Grundwissen nt im Rechnen; **~ progression** arithmetische Reihe

arithmetician [əˌrɪθməˈtɪʃən] N Rechner(in) m(f)

arithmetic mean N arithmetisches Mittel

ark [ɑːk] N **a** Arche f; **it looks as though it's come out of the ~** (inf) das sieht aus wie von anno Tobak (inf) → also **Noah's Ark** **b** Ark of the Covenant Bundeslade f

arm[1] [ɑːm] N **a** (Anat) Arm m; **in one's ~s** im Arm; **under one's ~** unter dem or unterm Arm; **he had a bandage on his ~** er hatte einen Verband am Arm or um den Arm; **to give sb one's ~** (Brit) jdm den Arm geben or reichen (geh); **with his ~s full of books** den Arm or die Arme voller Bücher; **to have sb/sth on one's ~** (Brit) jdn/etw am Arm haben; **to take sb in one's ~s** jdn in die Arme nehmen or schließen (geh); **to hold sb in one's ~s** jdn umarmen, jdn in den or seinen Armen halten (geh); **to put** or **throw one's ~s around sb** jdn umarmen, die Arme um jdn schlingen (geh); **to put an ~ around sb's shoulders** jdm den Arm um die Schulter legen; **~ in ~** Arm in Arm; (= arms linked) eingehakt, untergehakt; **at ~'s length** auf Armeslänge; **to keep sb at ~'s length** (fig) jdn auf Distanz halten; **to receive** or **welcome sb with open ~s** jdn mit offenen Armen empfangen; **to receive** or **welcome sth with open ~s** etw mit Kusshand nehmen (inf); **within ~'s reach** in Reichweite; **the long ~ of the law** der lange Arm des Gesetzes; **a list as long as your ~** eine ellenlange Liste; **a criminal with a record as long as your ~** ein Verbrecher mit einer langen Latte von Vorstrafen (inf); **it cost him an ~ and a leg** (inf) es kostete ihn ein Vermögen; **to put the ~ on sb** (dated US inf) jdn unter Druck setzen

b (= sleeve) Ärmel m, Arm m
c (of river) (Fluss)arm m; (of sea) Meeresarm

m; (of armchair) (Arm)lehne f; (of record player) Tonarm m; (of balance etc) Balken m; (of railway signal) (Signal)arm m; (Naut: = yard arm) Rahnock f

d (= branch) Zweig m; (Mil) Truppengattung f

arm[2] **VT** person, nation, ship etc bewaffnen; **to ~ sth with sth** etw mit etw ausrüsten; **to ~ oneself with sth** (lit, fig) sich mit etw bewaffnen; (fig: non-aggressively) sich mit etw wappnen; **he came ~ed with an excuse** er hatte eine Ausrede parat; **~ed only with her beauty, she ...** ihre Schönheit war die einzige Waffe, mit der sie ... **VI** aufrüsten; **to ~ for war** zum Krieg rüsten **N** (Mil, Her) = **arms**

armada [ɑːˈmɑːdə] N Armada f; **the Armada** die Armada; (= battle) die Armadaschlacht

armadillo [ˌɑːməˈdɪləʊ] N Gürteltier nt

Armageddon [ˌɑːməˈgedn] N (Bibl) Armageddon nt; (fig also) weltweite or globale Katastrophe

Armalite® ['ɑːməlaɪt] N automatisches, sehr leichtes Schnellfeuergewehr

armament ['ɑːməmənt] N **a** **armaments** PL (= weapons) Ausrüstung f **b** (= preparation) Aufrüstung f no pl; **much of the national budget is devoted to ~** ein großer Teil des Staatshaushalts geht in die Rüstung

armature ['ɑːmətjʊə'] N (Elec) Anker m

armband ['ɑːmbænd] N Armbinde f

armchair ['ɑːmtʃɛə'] **N** Sessel m, Lehnstuhl m **ADJ** **~ philosopher** Stubengelehrte(r) mf; **~ politician** Stammtischpolitiker(in) m(f); **~ strategist** Stammtisch- or Salonstratege m/-strategin f; **he is an ~ traveller** (Brit) or **traveler** (US) er reist nur mit dem Finger auf der Landkarte (inf)

armed [ɑːmd] ADJ bewaffnet

-armed [-ɑːmd] ADJ suf -armig; **one-armed** einarmig

armed: armed forces, armed services PL Streitkräfte pl; **armed robbery** N bewaffneter Raubüberfall

Armenia [ɑːˈmiːnɪə] N Armenien nt

Armenian [ɑːˈmiːnɪən] ADJ armenisch **N** **a** (= person) Armenier(in) m(f) **b** (= language) Armenisch nt

arm: armful N Arm m voll no pl, Ladung f (inf); **armhole** N Armloch nt

armistice ['ɑːmɪstɪs] N Waffenstillstand m

Armistice Day N 11.11., Tag des Waffenstillstands (1918)

arm: armlet N **a** = **armband** **b** (liter, of sea) kleiner Meeresarm; **arm-lock** ['ɑːmlɒk] N Armschlüssel m; (by police etc) Polizeigriff m

armor etc (US) = **armour** etc

armorial [ɑːˈmɔːrɪəl] ADJ Wappen-; **~ plate** Wappentier m **N** Wappenbuch nt

armour, (US) **armor** ['ɑːmə'] N **a** Rüstung f; (of animal) Panzer m; **suit of ~** Rüstung f; (fig) Panzer m, Rüstung f; **to wear ~** eine Rüstung tragen **b** (no pl: = steel plates) Panzerplatte(n) f(pl) **c** (= vehicles) Panzerfahrzeuge pl; (= forces) Panzertruppen pl **VT** panzern; (fig) wappnen

armour-clad, (US) **armor-clad** ['ɑːməˈklæd] ADJ (Mil, Naut) gepanzert

armoured, (US) **armored** ['ɑːməd] ADJ Panzer-, vehicle gepanzert; **~ car** Panzerwagen m; **~ personnel carrier** Schützenpanzer(wagen) m

armourer, (US) **armorer** ['ɑːmərə'] N (= maker) Waffenschmied(in) m(f); (= keeper) Waffenmeister(in) m(f)

armour, (US) **armor: armour-piercing** ADJ panzerbrechend; **armour-plated** ADJ gepanzert; **armour plating** N Panzerung f

armoury, (US) **armory** ['ɑːmərɪ] N **a** Arsenal nt, Waffenlager nt **b** (US: = factory) Munitionsfabrik f

arm: armpit N Achselhöhle f; (of garments) Achsel f; **armrest** N Armlehne f

arms [ɑːmz] PL **a** (= *weapons*) Waffen *pl*; **to ~!** zu den Waffen!; **to carry ~** Waffen tragen; **to be under ~** unter Waffen stehen; **to take up ~ (against sb/sth)** (gegen jdn/etw) zu den Waffen greifen; (*fig*) (gegen jdn/etw) zum Angriff übergehen; **to be up in ~ (about sth)** (*fig inf*) (über etw *acc*) empört sein; **~ limitation talks** Rüstungsbegrenzungsverhandlungen *pl* **b** (*Her*) Wappen *nt*

arms: arms control N Rüstungskontrolle *f*; **arms dealer** N Waffenhändler(in) *m(f)*; **arms race** N Wettrüsten *nt*, Rüstungswettlauf *m*

arm-twist [ˈɑːmtwɪst] VT (*inf*) jdm Daumenschrauben anlegen (*fig*); **to ~ sb into doing sth** jdn so lange unter Druck setzen, bis er/sie etw tut

arm-twisting [ˈɑːmtwɪstɪŋ] N (*inf*) Überredungskunst *f*; **with a bit of ~** … wenn man etwas nachhilft …; **it took a lot of/didn't take much ~ to get him to agree** er ließ sich nicht schnell/ schnell breitschlagen (*inf*)

arm wrestling N Armdrücken *nt*

army [ˈɑːmɪ] N **a** Armee *f*, Heer *nt*; **~ of occupation** Besatzungsarmee *f*; **to be in the ~** beim Militär sein; (*Ger also*) bei der Bundeswehr sein; (*Aus also*) beim Bundesheer sein; **to join the ~** zum Militär gehen **b** (*fig*) Heer *nt* **c** (= *division*) Armee(korps *nt*) *f attr* Militär-; *discipline* militärisch; **~ doctor** Militär- or Stabsarzt *m/* -ärztin *f*; **~ life** Soldatenleben *nt*; **~ officer** Offizier(in) *m(f)* in der Armee; **an ~ type** (*inf*) einer vom Barras (*inf*) or Bund (*Ger inf*)

army: army ant N Wanderameise *f*, Treiberameise *f*; **army-issue** ADJ Armee-; **~ rifle** Armeegewehr *nt*; **Army List** N (*Brit*) Rangliste *f*; **army-surplus** ADJ Armee-, Army-; **~ store** Armee- or Armyladen *m*

arnica [ˈɑːnɪkə] N (*Bot*) Arnika *f*

A-road [ˈeɪrəʊd] N (*Brit*) ≈ Bundesstraße *f*

aroma [əˈrəʊmə] N Duft *m*, Aroma *nt*

aromatherapist [əˈrəʊməˈθerəpɪst] N Aromatherapeut(in) *m(f)*

aromatherapy [əˌrəʊməˈθerəpɪ] N Aromatherapie *f*

aromatic [ˌærəʊˈmætɪk] ADJ aromatisch, wohlriechend

aromatize [əˈrəʊmətaɪz] VT aromatisieren

arose [əˈrəʊz] *pret of* **arise**

around [əˈraʊnd] **ADV** herum, rum (*inf*); **a house with gardens all ~** ein von Gärten umgebenes Haus, ein Haus mit Gärten ringsherum; **I looked all ~** ich sah mich nach allen Seiten um; **books lying all ~** überall herumliegende Bücher; **they came from all ~** sie kamen aus allen Richtungen or von überall her; **slowly, he turned ~** er drehte sich langsam um; **for miles ~** meilenweit im Umkreis; **to stroll/travel ~** herumschlendern/-reisen; **is he ~?** ist er da?; **if you want me I'll be ~** ich bin da, falls du mich brauchst; **he must be ~ somewhere** er muss hier irgendwo sein or stecken (*inf*); **I didn't know you were ~** ich wusste nicht, dass du hier bist; **he's been ~!** der kennt sich aus!; **it's been ~ for ages** das ist schon uralt; **he's been ~ for ages** (*inf*) der ist schon ewig hier (*inf*); **see you ~!** (*inf*) also, bis demnächst!, bis bald!; **where have you been? – (just) ~** wo warst du? – weg!

PREP **a** (= *right round*) (*movement, position*) um; (*in a circle*) um, … herum

b (= *in, through*) **to wander ~ the city** durch die Stadt spazieren; **to travel ~ Scotland** durch Schottland reisen; **to talk ~ a subject** um ein Thema herumreden; **to be** or **stay ~ the house** zu Hause bleiben; **I left it ~ your office somewhere** ich habe es irgendwo in deinem Büro gelassen; **the paper must be ~ here somewhere** die Zeitung muss hier irgendwo (he)rumliegen; **the church must be ~ here somewhere** die Kirche muss hier irgendwo sein

c (= *approximately*) (*with date*) um; (*with time of day*) gegen; (*with weight, price*) etwa, um die (*inf*) → *also* **round**

around the clock ADJ *pred*, **around-the- -clock** ADJ *attr* rund um die Uhr *pred*

arousal [əˈraʊsəl] N (*sexual*) Erregung *f*

arouse [əˈraʊz] VT **a** (*lit liter*) aufwecken, erwecken (*liter*) **b** (*fig*: = *excite*) erregen; *interest, suspicion etc* erregen, erwecken; **to ~ sb from his slumbers** (*fig*) jdn aus dem Schlaf wachrütteln

arpeggio [ɑːˈpedʒɪəʊ] N Arpeggio *nt*

arr *abbr of* **arrival** of **arrives** Ank.

arrack [ˈærək] N Arrak *m*

arraign [əˈreɪn] VT (*Jur*) *person* Anklage erheben gegen; (*liter*: = *denounce*) rügen; **to be ~ed on a charge** angeklagt werden

arraignment [əˈreɪnmənt] N (*Jur*) Anklageerhebung *f*

arrange [əˈreɪndʒ] VT **a** (= *order*) ordnen; *furniture, objects* aufstellen, hinstellen; *items in a collection, books in library etc* anordnen; *flowers* arrangieren; *room* einrichten; (*fig*) *thoughts* ordnen; **I don't want you arranging my life for me** ich will nicht, dass du mein Leben planst **b** (= *fix, see to*) vereinbaren, ausmachen; *details* regeln; *party* arrangieren; **to ~ a mortgage for sb** jdm eine Hypothek beschaffen; **I'll ~ for you to meet him** ich arrangiere für Sie ein Treffen mit ihm; **I have ~d for a car to pick you up** ich habe Ihnen einen Wagen besorgt, der Sie mitnimmt; **can you ~ an interview with the President for me?** können Sie mir ein Interview mit dem Präsidenten besorgen?; **we need some more glasses – I'll ~ that** es sind nicht genug Gläser da – das mache or reg(e)le (*inf*) ich; **his manager wants to ~ another fight next month** sein Manager will nächsten Monat noch einen Kampf ansetzen; **to ~ a sale/marriage** einen Verkauf/die Ehe vereinbaren; **an ~d marriage** eine arrangierte Ehe; **I'll ~ the drinks, you get the food** ich besorge die Getränke, und du kümmerst dich um das Essen; **if you could ~ to be ill that morning/there at five** wenn du es so einrichten kannst, dass du an dem Morgen krank/um fünf Uhr da bist; **I think I could ~ that** ich glaube, das lässt sich machen or arrangieren (*inf*); **that's easily ~d** das lässt sich leicht einrichten or arrangieren (*inf*); **how can we ~ it so it looks like an accident?** wie können wir es machen or drehen (*inf*), dass es wie ein Unfall aussieht?; **they'd obviously ~d things between themselves before the meeting started** sie hatten die Dinge offenbar vor Beginn des Treffens untereinander abgesprochen **c** (= *settle, decide on*) vereinbaren, abmachen; **nothing definite has been ~d yet** es ist noch nichts Verbindliches vereinbart worden; **a meeting has been ~d for next month** nächsten Monat ist ein Treffen abgemacht; **good, that's ~d then** gut, das ist abgemacht!; **I don't like having things ~d for me** ich habe es nicht gern, wenn man Dinge für mich entscheidet; **but you ~d to meet me!** aber du wolltest dich doch mit mir treffen!

d (*Mus*) bearbeiten, arrangieren

arrangement [əˈreɪndʒmənt] N **a** Anordnung *f*; (*of room*) Einrichtung *f*; (*inf*: = *contrivance*) Gerät *nt* (*inf*); **a floral** or **flower ~** ein Blumenarrangement *nt*; **the very unusual ~ of her hair** ihre sehr ungewöhnliche Haartracht **b** (= *agreement*) Vereinbarung *f*; (*to meet*) Verabredung *f*; (*esp shifty*) Arrangement *nt*; **by ~** laut or nach Vereinbarung or Absprache; **by ~ with** mit freundlicher Genehmigung (+*gen*); **salary by ~** Gehalt nach Vereinbarung; **a special ~** eine Sonderregelung; **to have an ~ with sb** eine Regelung mit jdm getroffen haben; **he has an ~ with his wife** er hat mit seiner Frau ein Arrangement …; **I've got a nice little ~ going** ich habe da so eine Abmachung or Absprache getroffen; **to make an ~ with sb** eine Vereinbarung or Absprache mit jdm treffen; **to come to an ~** eine Regelung finden; **to come to an ~ with sb** eine Regelung mit jdm treffen **c** (*usu pl*) (= *plans*) Pläne *pl*; (= *preparations*) Vorbereitungen *pl*; **to make ~s for sb/sth** für jdn/etw Vorbereitungen treffen; **to make ~s for sth to be done** veranlassen, dass etw getan wird; **to make one's own ~s** selber zusehen(,

wie …), es selber arrangieren(, dass …); **who's in charge of the transport ~s?** wer regelt die Transportfrage?; **seating ~s** Sitzordnung *f*; **"funeral ~s"** „Ausführung von Bestattungen"; **who will look after the funeral ~s?** wer kümmert sich um die Beerdigung?

d (*Mus*) Bearbeitung *f*; (*light music*) Arrangement *nt*

arranger [əˈreɪndʒə] N **a** (*Mus*) Arrangeur(in) *m(f)* **b** (= *organizer*) Organisator(in) *m(f)*

arrant [ˈærənt] ADJ Erz-; **~ coward** Erzfeigling *m*; **~ nonsense** barer Unsinn

arras [ˈærəs] N (*old*) (Arazzo)wandteppich *m*

array [əˈreɪ] **VT** **a** (= *line up*) aufstellen; (*Mil*) in Aufstellung bringen; **b** (= *dress*) schmücken (*geh*), herausputzen (*hum*) **N** **a** (*Mil*, = *arrangement*) Aufstellung *f*; **in battle ~** in Kampfaufstellung, in Schlachtordnung **b** (= *collection*) Ansammlung *f*, Aufgebot *nt* (*hum*); (*of objects*) stattliche or ansehnliche Reihe **c** (*Comput*) (Daten)feld *nt*, Array *nt* **d** (*liter*) Schmuck *m* (*geh*); (= *dress*) Staat *m*; **the trees in all their spring ~** die Bäume im Frühlingskleid (*poet*)

arrears [əˈrɪəz] PL Rückstände *pl*; **to be in ~ with sth** im Rückstand mit etw sein; **to get** or **fall into ~** in Rückstand kommen; **to have ~ of £5000** mit £ 5000 im Rückstand sein; **to be paid in ~** rückwirkend bezahlt werden

arrest [əˈrest] **VT** **a** (= *apprehend*) festnehmen; (*with warrant*) verhaften; *ship* aufbringen; (*fig*) *attention* erregen, erheischen (*liter*); **I am ~ing you** ich muss Sie festnehmen/verhaften **b** (= *check*) hemmen; *sth unwanted* (Ein)halt gebieten (+*dat*) (*geh*); **~ed development** Entwicklungshemmung *f* **N** (*of suspect*) Festnahme *f*; (*with warrant*) Verhaftung *f*; (*of ship*) Aufbringen *nt*; **to be under ~** festgenommen/verhaftet sein; **you are under ~** Sie sind festgenommen/verhaftet; **to put** or **place sb under ~** jdn festnehmen/verhaften; **to make an ~** eine Person festnehmen/verhaften; **they hope to make an ~ soon** man hofft, dass es bald zu einer Festnahme/Verhaftung kommt

arrestable [əˈrestəbl] ADJ **to be an ~ offence** (*Brit*) or **offense** (*US*) ein Grund zur Festnahme sein

arresting [əˈrestɪŋ] ADJ **a** (= *striking*) atemberaubend; *features* markant **b** **the ~ officer** der festnehmende Beamte

arrest warrant N Haftbefehl *m*

arrhythmia [əˈrɪðmɪə] N (*Med*) Arrhythmie *f*

arrival [əˈraɪvəl] N **a** Ankunft *f no pl*; (*of person*) Ankunft *f*, Eintreffen *nt no pl*; (*of goods, news*) Eintreffen *nt no pl*; **our eventual ~ at a decision** … dass wir endlich zu einer Entscheidung kamen …; **on ~** bei Ankunft; **he was dead on ~** bei seiner Einlieferung ins Krankenhaus wurde der Tod festgestellt; **~ time, time of ~** Ankunftszeit *f*; **~s and departures** (*Rail*) Ankunft/ Abfahrt *f*; (*Aviat*) Ankunft *f*/Abflug *m* **b** (= *person*) Ankömmling *m*; **new ~** Neuankömmling *m*; (*at school also*) Neue(r) *mf*; (*in hotel, boarding house*) neu angekommener Gast; (*in firm, office*) neuer Mitarbeiter, neue Mitarbeiterin; **a new ~ on the pop scene** ein neues Gesicht auf der Popszene; **when our firm was still a new ~ in the publishing world** als unsere Firma noch ein Neuling im Verlagswesen war; **the new ~ is a little girl** der neue Erdenbürger ist ein kleines Mädchen; **he was the latest ~** er kam als Letzter

arrivals board [əˈraɪvəlzbɔːd] N (*Rail*) Ankunftstafel *f*; (*Aviat*) Ankunftsanzeige *f*

arrivals lounge [əˈraɪvəlzlaʊndʒ] N Ankunftshalle *f*

arrive [əˈraɪv] ✿ 21.4, 25.2 VI **a** (= *come*) ankommen, eintreffen (*geh*); (= *be born*) ankommen; **to ~ home** nach Hause kommen; (*esp after journey etc*) zu Hause ankommen; **to ~ at a town/the airport** in einer Stadt/am Flughafen ankommen or eintreffen (*geh*); **the train will ~ at platform 10** der Zug läuft auf Gleis 10 ein;

the great day ~d der große Tag kam; **a new era has ~d!** ein neues Zeitalter ist angebrochen!; **the time has ~d for sth/to do sth** die Zeit für etw ist gekommen, die Zeit ist reif für etw/etw zu tun; **television has not ~d here yet** das Fernsehen ist noch nicht bis hier durchgedrungen; **to ~ at a decision** zu einer Entscheidung kommen or gelangen; **to ~ at the age of ...** das Alter von ... Jahren erreichen; **to ~ at an answer/a conclusion/result** zu einer Antwort/einem Schluss/Ergebnis kommen; **to ~ at a price** auf einen Preis kommen; (= agree on) sich auf einen Preis einigen
b (inf: = succeed) **then you know you've really ~d** dann weiß man, dass man es geschafft hat

arriviste [ˌæriˈviːst] N Emporkömmling m, Parvenü m (geh)

arrogance [ˈærəɡəns] N Arroganz f, Überheblichkeit f

arrogant [ˈærəɡənt] ADJ arrogant, überheblich

arrogantly [ˈærəɡəntlɪ] ADV arrogant; **the group had rather ~ assumed themselves to be in command** die Gruppe hatte arroganterweise or anmaßenderweise angenommen, dass sie das Kommando hätte

arrogate [ˈærəʊɡeɪt] VT **to ~ sth to oneself** etw für sich in Anspruch nehmen; title sich (dat) etw anmaßen

arrow [ˈærəʊ] N (= weapon, sign) Pfeil m VT way, direction durch Pfeile/einen Pfeil markieren
▸ **arrow in** VT sep (in text) durch Pfeil einzeichnen

arrow: arrow bracket N spitze Klammer; **arrowhead** N Pfeilspitze f; **arrow key** N (Comput) Pfeiltaste f; **arrowroot** N (= plant) Pfeilwurz f; (= flour) Arrowroot nt

arse [ɑːs] (Brit sl) N **a** (= move over) rutsch mal ein Stück (inf); (= hurry up) setz mal deinen Arsch in Bewegung! (sl); **get your ~ in gear!** setz mal deinen Arsch in Bewegung! (sl); **tell him to get his ~ into my office** sag ihm, er soll mal in meinem Büro antanzen (inf); **get your ~ out of here!** verpiss dich hier! (sl); **contribution? my ~!** Beitrag? das soll wohl ein Witz sein! (inf) **b** (= fool: also **silly arse**) Armleuchter m (inf) VT **I can't be ~d** ich hab keinen Bock (sl)
▸ **arse about** or **around** VI (Brit inf) rumblödeln (inf)

arse: arsehole N (Brit sl) Arschloch nt (vulg); **arse licker** N (Brit sl) Arschkriecher(in) m(f) (inf)

arsenal [ˈɑːsnl] N (Mil) (= store) Arsenal nt, Zeughaus nt (old); (= factory) Waffen-/Munitionsfabrik f; (fig) Waffenlager nt

arsenic [ˈɑːsnɪk] N Arsen nt, Arsenik nt; **~ poisoning** Arsenvergiftung f

arson [ˈɑːsn] N Brandstiftung f

arsonist [ˈɑːsənɪst] N Brandstifter(in) m(f)

art¹ [ɑːt] N **a** (= painting etc) Kunst f; **the ~s** die schönen Künste; **~ for ~'s sake** Kunst um der Kunst willen, Kunst als Selbstzweck; (slogan) L'art pour l'art → **work N c**
b (= skill) Kunst f; (= physical technique) Geschick nt, Kunst f; **there's an ~ to driving this car** es gehört ein gewisses Geschick dazu, mit diesem Auto zu fahren; **there's an ~ to it** das ist eine Kunst; **the ~ of war/government** die Kriegs-/Staatskunst; **the ~ of conversation/translation** die Kunst der Unterhaltung/Übersetzung; **~s and crafts** Kunsthandwerk nt, Kunstgewerbe nt
c (= human endeavour) Künstlichkeit f; **unspoiled by ~** unverbildet; **are they the products of ~ or nature?** sind sie natürlich oder von Menschenhand geschaffen?; **her beauty owes more to ~ than nature** sie verdankt ihre Schönheit mehr der Kunst als der Natur
d **~s** (Univ) Geisteswissenschaften pl; **~s minister** Kulturminister(in) m(f); **~s subject** geisteswissenschaftliches Fach → **bachelor, liberal**
e (usu pl: = trick) List f, Kunstgriff m
ADJ attr Kunst-; **~ critic** Kunstkritiker(in) m(f)

art² (old) 2nd pers sing present of **be**

art college N = **art school**

Art Deco [ˈɑːtˈdekəʊ] N Art déco f

Art-Deco [ˈɑːtˈdekəʊ] ADJ attr Art-déco-; **~ design** Art-déco-Design nt

artefact (Brit), **artifact** [ˈɑːtɪfækt] N Artefakt nt; **are these human ~s?** sind das Schöpfungen von Menschenhand?

arterial [ɑːˈtɪəriəl] ADJ **a** (Anat) arteriell **b** **~ road** (Aut) Fernverkehrsstraße f; **~ line** (Rail) Hauptstrecke f

arteriosclerosis [ɑːˌtɪəriəʊsklɪˈrəʊsɪs] N (Med) Arteriosklerose f, Arterienverkalkung f

artery [ˈɑːtəri] N **a** (Anat) Arterie f, Schlag- or Pulsader f **b** (also **traffic artery**) Verkehrsader f

artesian well [ɑːˈtiːziən'wel] N artesischer Brunnen

art form N (Kunst)gattung or -form f

artful [ˈɑːtfʊl] ADJ person, trick raffiniert, schlau; **~ dodger** Schlawiner m (inf)

artfully [ˈɑːtfəlɪ] ADV raffiniert

artfulness [ˈɑːtfʊlnɪs] N Raffinesse f

art: art gallery N Kunstgalerie f; **art-house** ADJ attr **~ film** Experimentalfilm m; **~ cinema** ≈ Programmkino nt

arthritic [ɑːˈθrɪtɪk] ADJ arthritisch; **she is ~** sie hat Arthritis

arthritis [ɑːˈθraɪtɪs] N Arthritis f, Gelenkentzündung f

arthropod [ˈɑːθrəpɒd] N Gliederfüßer m; **the ~s** die Arthropoden pl

arthrosis [ɑːˈθrəʊsɪs] N Arthrose f

Arthur [ˈɑːθəʳ] N Art(h)ur m; **King ~** König Artus

Arthurian [ɑːˈθjʊəriən] ADJ Artus-; **~ knight** Artusritter m

artic [ɑːˈtɪk] N (Brit inf) (Sattel)schlepper m

artichoke [ˈɑːtɪtʃəʊk] N Artischocke f → **Jerusalem artichoke**

article [ˈɑːtɪkl] N **a** (= item) Gegenstand m; (in list) Posten m; (Comm) Ware f, Artikel m; **~ of value** Wertgegenstand m; **~ of furniture** Möbelstück nt; **~s of clothing** Kleidungsstücke pl; **toilet ~s** Toilettenartikel pl (usu) **genuine**
b (in newspaper etc) Artikel m; (= encyclopedia entry) Eintrag m
c (of constitution) Artikel m; (of treaty, contract) Paragraph m; **~s of association** Gesellschaftsvertrag m; **~ of faith** Glaubensartikel m; (fig) Kredo nt; **~s of war** (Hist) Kriegsartikel pl
d (Gram) Artikel m, Geschlechtswort nt
e (of articled clerk) **to be under ~s** (Rechts)referendar sein; **to take one's ~s** seine Referendarprüfung machen
VT **apprentice** in die Lehre geben (to bei); **to be ~d to sb** bei jdm eine Lehre machen, bei jdm in die Lehre gehen; **to be ~d to sb/sth** an jdn/etw vertraglich gebunden sein; **~d clerk** (Brit Jur) ≈ Rechtsreferendar(in) m(f)

articulate [ɑːˈtɪkjʊlɪt] ADJ **a** sentence, book klar; **to be ~** sich gut or klar ausdrücken können; **clear and ~** klar und deutlich; **that is amazingly ~ for a five-year-old** das ist erstaunlich gut ausgedrückt für einen Fünfjährigen **b** (Anat) gegliedert VT [ɑːˈtɪkjʊleɪt] **a** (= pronounce) artikulieren **b** (state) reasons, views etc darlegen **c** (Anat) **to be ~d** zusammenhängen (to, with mit) VI [ɑːˈtɪkjʊleɪt] artikulieren

articulated bus [ɑːˈtɪkjʊleɪtɪdˈbʌs] N Gelenkbus m

articulated lorry (Brit), **articulated truck** [ɑːˈtɪkjʊleɪtɪd-] N Sattelschlepper m

articulately [ɑːˈtɪkjʊlɪtlɪ] ADV pronounce artikuliert; write, express oneself klar, flüssig; **an ~ presented argument** eine klar verständlich vorgetragene These

articulateness [ɑːˈtɪkjʊlɪtnɪs] N Fähigkeit f, sich gut auszudrücken

articulation [ɑːˌtɪkjʊˈleɪʃən] N **a** Artikulation f **b** (Anat) Gelenkverbindung f

artifact N = **artefact**

artifice [ˈɑːtɪfɪs] N **a** (= guile) List f no pl **b** (= stratagem) (Kriegs)list f

artificial [ˌɑːtɪˈfɪʃəl] ADJ **a** (= synthetic) künstlich; **~ light** künstliches Licht; **~ manure** Kunstdünger m; **~ hair/silk** Kunsthaar nt/-seide f; **~ limb** Prothese f, Kunstglied nt **b** (fig: = not genuine) künstlich; (pej: = not sincere) smile, manner gekünstelt, unecht; **you're so ~** du bist nicht echt; **if you say it that way it sounds ~** wenn du es so sagst, klingt das unecht

artificial: artificial horizon N künstlicher Horizont; **artificial insemination** N künstliche Befruchtung; **artificial intelligence** N künstliche Intelligenz

artificiality [ˌɑːtɪfɪʃɪˈælɪtɪ] N **a** Künstlichkeit f **b** (= insincerity, unnaturalness) Gekünsteltheit f

artificially [ˌɑːtɪˈfɪʃəlɪ] ADV künstlich; (= insincerely) gekünstelt

artificial respiration N künstliche Beatmung f

artillery [ɑːˈtɪləri] N (= weapons, troops) Artillerie f

artilleryman [ɑːˈtɪlərimən] N pl **-men** [-mən] Artillerist m

artisan [ˈɑːtɪzæn] N Handwerker(in) m(f)

artisanal [ɑːˈtɪzənəl] ADJ kunsthandwerklich

artist [ˈɑːtɪst] N Künstler(in) m(f); (fig also) Könner(in) m(f); **~'s impression** Zeichnung f; (of sth planned also) Entwurf m

artiste [ɑːˈtiːst] N Künstler(in) m(f); (= circus artiste) Artist(in) m(f); **~s' entrance** Bühneneingang m

artistic [ɑːˈtɪstɪk] ADJ künstlerisch; (= tasteful) arrangements kunstvoll; (= appreciative of art) person kunstverständig or -sinnig (geh); **the café has an ~ clientele** in dem Café verkehren Künstler; **~ temperament** Künstlertemperament nt; **an ~ life** ein Künstlerleben nt; **to look ~** wie ein Künstler aussehen; **she's very ~** sie ist künstlerisch veranlagt or begabt/sehr kunstverständig

artistically [ɑːˈtɪstɪkəlɪ] ADV künstlerisch; (= tastefully) kunstvoll

artistic director N künstlerischer Direktor, künstlerische Direktorin

artistry [ˈɑːtɪstrɪ] N (lit, fig) Kunst f

artless ADJ, **artlessly** ADV [ˈɑːtlɪs, -lɪ] unschuldig

artlessness [ˈɑːtlɪsnɪs] N Unschuld f

art lover N Kunstliebhaber(in) m(f) or -freund(in) m(f)

Art Nouveau [ˈɑːnuːˈvəʊ] N Jugendstil m; **~ movement** Jugendstilbewegung f

Art-Nouveau [ˈɑːnuːˈvəʊ] ADJ attr Jugendstil-; **~ building** Jugendstilbau m

art: art paper N Kunstdruckpapier nt; **art school** N Kunstakademie or -hochschule f

Arts [ɑːts] N **Arts Council** Kulturausschuss m (der britischen Regierung); **arts degree** N Abschlussexamen nt der philosophischen Fakultät; **Arts Faculty, Faculty of Arts** N philosophische Fakultät

art student N Kunststudent(in) m(f)

artsy [ˈɑːtsɪ] ADJ (US hum inf) = **arty**

artwork [ˈɑːtwɜːk] N **a** (in book) Bildmaterial nt; **this will have to be done as ~** das muss grafisch gestaltet werden **b** (for advert etc: = material ready for printing) Druckvorlage f **c** (= painting, sculpture) Kunstwerk nt

arty [ˈɑːtɪ] ADJ (+er) (inf) Künstler-; type also, tie, clothes verrückt (inf); person auf Künstler machend (pej); decoration, style auf Kunst gemacht (inf); film, novel geschmäcklerisch; **he was more of an ~ type than his brother** er war mehr ein Künstlertyp als sein Bruder; **she's in publishing/the theatre – oh yes, that was something ~** sie arbeitet im Verlag/Theater – ach ja, ich wusste doch, dass es etwas Künstlerisches war

arty-crafty ['ɑːtɪ'krɑːftɪ], (US) **artsy-craftsy** ['ɑːtsɪ'krɑːftsɪ] ADJ (inf) **a** = **arty b** object kunstgewerblerisch

arty-farty ['ɑːtɪ'fɑːtɪ] ADJ (hum inf) = **arty**

Aryan ['ɛərɪən] N Arier(in) m(f) ADJ arisch

as [æz, əz] ✪ 5.1, 5.4, 17.1, 26.2, 26.3 CONJ **a** (= when, while) als (two parallel actions) während, als, indem (geh); **he got deafer as he got older** mit zunehmendem Alter nahm seine Schwerhörigkeit zu; **as a child he would ...** als Kind er immer ...
b (= since) da
c (= although) **rich as he is I won't marry him** obwohl er reich ist, werde ich ihn nicht heiraten; **stupid as he is, he ...** so dumm er auch sein mag, ... er; **big as he is I'll ...** so groß, wie er ist, ich ...; **much as I admire her, ...** sosehr ich sie auch bewundere, ...; **be that as it may** wie dem auch sei or sein mag; **try as he might** sosehr er sich auch bemüht/bemühte
d (manner) wie; **do as you like** machen Sie, was Sie wollen; **leave it as it is** lass das so; **I did it as he did** ich habe es wie er gemacht; **the first door as you go upstairs/as you go in** die erste Tür oben/, wenn Sie hereinkommen; **knowing him as I do** so wie ich ihn kenne; **as you yourself said ...** wie Sie selbst gesagt haben ...; **he drinks enough as it is** er trinkt sowieso schon genug; **it is bad enough as it is** es ist schon schlimm genug; **as it is, I'm heavily in debt** ich bin schon tief verschuldet; **as it were** sozusagen, gleichsam; **as you were!** (Mil) weitermachen!; (fig) lassen Sie sich nicht stören; (in dictation, speaking) streichen Sie das; **my husband as was** (inf) mein verflossener or (late) verstorbener Mann
e (phrases) **as if** or **though** als ob, wie wenn; **he rose as if to go** er erhob sich, als wollte er gehen; **it isn't as if he didn't see me** schließlich hat er mich ja gesehen; **as for him/you** (und) was ihn/dich anbetrifft or angeht; **as from or of the 5th** vom Fünften an, ab dem Fünften; **as from now** von jetzt an, ab jetzt; **so as to** (= in order to) um zu +infin; (= in such a way) so, dass; **be so good as to ...** (form) hätten Sie die Freundlichkeit or Güte, ... zu ... (form); **he's not so silly as to do that** er ist nicht so dumm, das zu tun, so dumm ist er nicht

ADV **as ... as** so ... wie; **not as ... as** nicht so ... wie; **twice as old** doppelt so alt; **just as nice** genauso nett; **late as usual!** wie immer zu spät!; **is it as difficult as that?** ist das denn so schwierig?; **if he eats as quickly as that** wenn er so schnell isst; **it is not as good as all that** so gut ist es auch wieder nicht; **you hate it as much as I do** du magst das doch genauso wenig wie ich; **as recently as yesterday** erst gestern; **she is very clever, as is her brother** sie ist sehr intelligent, genau(so) wie ihr Bruder; **she was as nice as could be** (inf) sie war so freundlich wie nur was (inf); **as many/much as I could** so viele/so viel ich (nur) konnte; **there were as many as 100 people there** es waren bestimmt 100 Leute da; **this one is just as good** diese(r, s) ist genauso gut; **as often happens, he was ...** wie so oft, war er ...

REL PRON **a** (with same, such) der/die/das; (pl) die; **the same man as was here yesterday** derselbe Mann, der gestern hier war → **such**
b (dial) der/die/das; (pl) die; **those as knew him** die ihn kannten

PREP **a** (= in the capacity of) als; **to treat sb as a child** jdn als Kind or wie ein Kind behandeln; **he appeared as three different characters** er trat in drei verschiedenen Rollen auf
b (esp: = such as) wie (zum Beispiel); **animals such as cats and dogs** Tiere wie (zum Beispiel) Katzen und Hunde

asap ['eɪsæp] abbr of **as soon as possible** baldmöglichst, baldmögl.

asbestos [æz'bestəs] N Asbest m

asbestosis [ˌæzbes'təʊsɪs] N (Med) Asbestose f, Asbeststaublunge f

ascend [ə'send] VI (= rise) aufsteigen; (Christ) auffahren; (= slope upwards) ansteigen (to auf

+acc); **in ~ing order** in aufsteigender Reihenfolge VT stairs hinaufsteigen; mountain, heights of knowledge erklimmen (geh); throne besteigen; **to ~ the scale** (Mus) die Tonleiter aufwärts singen

ascendancy, ascendency [ə'sendənsɪ] N Vormachtstellung f; **to gain/have (the) ~ over sb** die Vorherrschaft über jdn gewinnen/haben; **to gain (the) ~ over one's fears** seine Ängste besiegen

ascendant, ascendent [ə'sendənt] N **to be in the ~** (Astrol) im Aszendenten stehen, aszendieren (spec); (fig) im Aufstieg begriffen sein; **his star is in the ~** (fig) sein Stern ist im Aufgehen

ascender [ə'sendəʳ] N (Typ) Oberlänge f

Ascension [ə'senʃən] N **the ~** (Christi) Himmelfahrt f

Ascension Day N Himmelfahrt(stag m) nt

ascent [ə'sent] N Aufstieg m; **the ~ of Ben Nevis** der Aufstieg auf den Ben Nevis; **it was his first ~ in an aeroplane** er ist das erste Mal in einem Flugzeug geflogen

ascertain [ˌæsə'teɪn] VT ermitteln, feststellen

ascertainable [ˌæsə'teɪnəbl] ADJ feststellbar

ascetic [ə'setɪk] ADJ asketisch N Asket m; **she's something of an ~** sie lebt ziemlich asketisch

asceticism [ə'setɪsɪzəm] N Askese f; **a life of ~** ein Leben in Askese

ASCII ['æskɪ] abbr of **American Standard Code for Information Interchange ~ file** ASCII-Datei f

ascorbic acid [ə'skɔːbɪk'æsɪd] N Askorbinsäure f

ascribable [ə'skraɪbəbl] ADJ **to be ~ to sth** einer Sache (dat) zuzuschreiben sein

ascribe [ə'skraɪb] VT zuschreiben (sth to sb jdm etw); importance, weight beimessen (to sth einer Sache dat)

ascription [ə'skrɪpʃən] N Zuschreibung f; **difficulties arising from the ~ of emotions to animals** Schwierigkeiten, die sich ergeben, wenn man Tieren Gefühle zuschreibt

asdic ['æzdɪk] N Echo(tiefen)lot nt

ASEAN ['æzɪən] abbr of **Association of South-East Asian Nations**

aseptic [eɪ'septɪk] ADJ aseptisch, keimfrei; (fig) atmosphere steril, klinisch

asexual [eɪ'seksjʊəl] ADJ ungeschlechtlich, geschlechtslos; person asexuell; reproduction ungeschlechtlich

asexually [eɪ'seksjʊəlɪ] ADV reproduce asexuell, ungeschlechtlich

ash¹ [æʃ] N (also **ash tree**) Esche f

ash² N **a** Asche f; **~es** Asche f; **to reduce sth to ~es** etw total or völlig niederbrennen; (in war etc) etw in Schutt und Asche legen; **to rise from the ~es** (fig) aus den Trümmern wieder auferstehen; **~es to ~es** Erde zu Erde → **sackcloth b ashes** PL (of the dead) Asche f **c** (Cricket) **the Ashes** Testmatch zwischen Australien und England

ashamed [ə'ʃeɪmd] ADJ beschämt; **to be** or **feel ~ (of sb/sth)** sich schämen (für jdn/etw, jds/einer Sache); **it's nothing to be ~ of** deswegen braucht man sich nicht zu genieren or schämen; **to be ~ that ...** sich schämen, dass ...; **I felt ~ for him** ich habe mich für ihn geschämt; **he is ~ to do it** es ist ihm peinlich, das zu tun, er schämt sich, das zu tun; **... I'm ~ to say ...**, muss ich leider zugeben; **to be ~ of oneself (for doing sth)** sich schämen(, etw getan zu haben); **you ought to be ~ (of yourself)** du solltest dich (was) schämen!, schäm dich!; **you may well look ~** schäm dich ruhig!

A shares ['eɪʃeəz] PL stimmrechtslose Aktien pl

ash: **ash bin** N Asch(en)eimer m, Aschentonne f; **ash blond** N Aschblonde(r); **ash blonde** N Aschblonde f; **ash-blond(e)** ADJ aschblond; **ashcan** N (US) = **ash bin**

ashen ['æʃn] ADJ colour aschgrau, aschfarben; face aschfahl (geh), kreidebleich

ashen-faced [ˌæʃn'feɪst] ADJ kreidebleich

ash-grey, (US) **ash-gray** ADJ colour aschgrau, aschfarben

ashlar ['æʃləʳ] N Quaderstein m

ashore [ə'ʃɔː'] ADV an Land; **to run ~** stranden, auf den Strand auflaufen; **to put ~** an Land gehen

ash: **ashpan** N Aschenkasten m; **ashtray** N Aschenbecher m; **Ash Wednesday** N Aschermittwoch m

ashy ['æʃɪ] ADJ **a** = **ashen b** (= covered with ashes) mit Asche bedeckt

Asia ['eɪʃə] N Asien nt

Asia Minor N Kleinasien nt

Asian ['eɪʃn], **Asiatic** [ˌeɪsɪˈætɪk] ADJ **a** asiatisch; (= from the Indian subcontinent) indisch-pakistanisch **b** (Brit: = from Indian subcontinent) indopakistanisch N **a** Asiat(in) m(f) **b** (Brit: = person from the Indian subcontinent) Indopakistaner(in) m(f)

Asian-American [ˌeɪʃnəˈmerɪkən] ADJ asiatisch-amerikanisch N Amerikaner(in) m(f) asiatischer Herkunft

Asian flu N asiatische Grippe

aside [ə'saɪd] ADV **a** (with verbal element) zur Seite, beiseite; **to set sth ~ for sb** für jdn etw beiseite legen; **to turn ~** sich zur Seite drehen, sich abwenden (esp fig)
b (Theat etc) beiseite
c (esp US) **~ from** außer; **~ from demanding an extra 10% ...** außer einer Zusatzforderung von 10% ...; **~ from being chairman of this committee he is ...** außer Vorsitzender dieses Ausschusses ist er auch ...; **this criticism, ~ from being wrong, is ...** diese Kritik ist nicht nur falsch, sondern ...
N (Theat) Aparte nt (rare); **to say sth in an ~** etw beiseite sprechen; **there are too many ~s to the audience** es wird zu viel zum Publikum gesprochen

A-side ['eɪsaɪd] N (of record) A-Seite f

asinine ['æsɪnaɪn] ADJ idiotisch; **what an ~ thing to do!** wie kann man bloß so ein Esel sein!

ask [ɑːsk] ✪ 4, 6.2, 21.1, 21.4, 26.1 VT **a** (= inquire) fragen; question stellen; **to ~ sb the way/the time/his opinion** jdn nach dem Weg/der Uhrzeit/seiner Meinung fragen; **to ~ if ...** (nach)fragen, ob ...; **he ~ed me where I'd been** er fragte mich, wo ich gewesen sei or wäre (inf) or bin (inf); **if you ~ me** wenn du mich fragst; **don't ~ me!** (inf) frag mich nicht, was weiß ich! (inf); **I ~ you!** (inf) ich muss schon sagen!
b (= invite) einladen; (in dancing) auffordern; **to ~ sb for or to lunch** jdn zum (Mittag)essen einladen
c (= request) bitten (sb for sth jdn um etw); (= require, demand) verlangen (sth of sb etw von jdm); **to ~ sb to do sth** jdn darum bitten, etw zu tun; **are you ~ing me to believe that?** und das soll ich glauben?; **all I ~ is ...** ich will ja nur ...; **you don't ~ for much, do you?** (iro) sonst noch was? (iro), sonst or weiter nichts? (iro); **could I ~ your advice?** darf ich Sie um Rat bitten?; **he ~ed to be excused** er bat, ihn zu entschuldigen, er entschuldigte sich; **that's ~ing the impossible** das ist ein Ding der Unmöglichkeit; **he ~s too much of me** er verlangt zu viel von mir; **that's ~ing too much** das ist zu viel verlangt
d (Comm) price verlangen, fordern
VI **a** (= inquire) fragen; **to ~ about sb/sth** sich nach jdm/etw erkundigen; **~ away!** frag nur!; **I only ~ed** ich habe doch nur gefragt; **and what does that mean, may I ~?** und was soll das bedeuten, wenn ich mal fragen darf?; **well may you ~** das fragt man sich mit Recht
b (= request) bitten (for sth um etw); **you just have to ~** du musst nur was sagen (inf), du brauchst nur zu fragen; **I'm not ~ing for sympathy** ich will kein Mitleid; **there's no harm in ~ing** Fragen kostet nichts!; **it's yours for the ~ing** du kannst es haben; **you are ~ing for trouble** du willst wohl Ärger haben; **if you do that you're ~ing for trouble** wenn du das tust, dann

kriegst du Ärger; **that's ~ing for trouble** das kann ja nicht gut gehen; **you ~ed for it** (inf) du hast es ja so gewollt; **he's ~ing for it** (inf) er will es ja so, er will es ja nicht anders; **to ~ for Mr X** Herrn X verlangen; **she was ~ing for you** (Scot) sie hat sich nach dir erkundigt; **to ~ for sth back** etw wiederhaben wollen

▶ **ask after** VI +prep obj sich erkundigen nach; **tell her I was asking after her** grüß sie schön von mir

▶ **ask around** VI herumfragen

▶ **ask back** VT sep **a** (= invite) zu sich einladen; **he asked us back for a drink** er lud uns zu sich auf einen Drink ein **b** **they never asked me back again** sie haben mich nie wieder eingeladen **c** **let me ask you something back** lassen Sie mich eine Gegenfrage stellen

▶ **ask in** VT sep (to house) hereinbitten; **she asked her boyfriend in** sie hat ihren Freund mit reingenommen

▶ **ask out** VT sep einladen

▶ **ask over** VT SEP zu sich (dat) einladen

▶ **ask round** VT SEP (esp Brit) = **ask over**

▶ **ask up** VT sep heraufbitten; **boyfriend** mit raufnehmen

askance [ə'skɑːns] ADV **to look ~ at sb** jdn entsetzt ansehen; **to look ~ at a suggestion/sb's methods** etc über einen Vorschlag/jds Methoden etc die Nase rümpfen

askew [ə'skjuː] ADJ, ADV schief

asking ['ɑːskɪŋ] N , no pl **to be had for the ~** umsonst or leicht or mühelos zu haben sein; **he could have had it for the ~** er hätte es leicht bekommen können; **she thought the world was hers for the ~** sie dachte, die Welt stehe ihr offen

asking price ['ɑːskɪŋˌpraɪs] N Verkaufspreis m; (for car, house etc also) Verhandlungsbasis f; **what's your ~?** was verlangen Sie (dafür)?

aslant [ə'slɑːnt] (liter) **ADV** quer, schräg **PREP** quer or schräg über

asleep [ə'sliːp] ADJ pred **a** (= sleeping) schlafend; **to be (fast** or **sound) ~** (fest) schlafen; **he was sitting there, ~** er saß da und schlief; **to fall ~** einschlafen (also euph); **to lie ~** schlafen; **he is not dead, only ~** er ist nicht tot, er schläft nur or liegt nur im Schlaf (geh) → **half** ADV a **b** (inf: = numb) eingeschlafen

ASLEF ['æzlef] (Brit) abbr of **Associated Society of Locomotive Engineers and Firemen** Eisenbahnergewerkschaft

ASM (Theat) abbr of **assistant stage manager** Assistent(in) m(f) des Inspizienten

asocial [eɪ'səʊʃəl] ADJ ungesellig

asp [æsp] N (Zool) Natter f

asparagus [əs'pærəgəs] N , no pl Spargel m

asparagus fern N Spargelkraut nt, Asparagus m

asparagus tips PL Spargelspitzen pl

aspect ['æspekt] N **a** (liter. = appearance) Anblick m, Erscheinung f; (of thing) Aussehen nt **b** (of question, subject etc) Aspekt m, Seite f; **the political ~ of his novel** der politische Aspekt seines Romans; **from the ~ of town planning** aus stadtplanerischer Sicht; **what about the security ~?** was ist mit der Sicherheit? **c** (of building) **to have a southerly ~** Südlage haben **d** (Gram) Aspekt m

aspectual [æ'spektjʊəl] ADJ (Gram) im Aspekt

aspen ['æspən] N (Bot) Espe f, Zitterpappel f; **to tremble like an ~** (liter) zittern wie Espenlaub

aspergillum [ˌæspə'dʒɪləm] N Weih(wasser)wedel m

asperity [æs'perɪtɪ] N Schroffheit f no pl, Schärfe f no pl; **the asperities of the winter** (liter) der raue Winter (geh)

aspersion [əs'pɜːʃən] N **to cast ~s on sb/sth** abfällige Bemerkungen über jdn/etw machen; **without wishing to cast any ~s** ohne mich abfällig äußern zu wollen

asphalt ['æsfælt] **N** Asphalt m **VT** asphaltieren **ADJ** attr Asphalt-, asphaltiert; **~ jungle** Asphaltdschungel m

asphodel ['æsfədel] N Asphodelus m, Affodill m

asphyxia [æs'fɪksɪə] N Erstickung f, Asphyxie f (spec)

asphyxiate [æs'fɪksɪeɪt] **VT** ersticken; **to be ~d** ersticken **VI** ersticken

asphyxiation [æsˌfɪksɪ'eɪʃən] N Erstickung f

aspic ['æspɪk] N (Cook) Aspik m or nt, Gelee nt

aspidistra [ˌæspɪ'dɪstrə] N Aspidistra f

aspirant ['æspɪrənt] N Anwärter(in) m(f) (to, for auf +acc); (for job) Kandidat(in) m(f) (for für), Aspirant(in) m(f) (hum); (for sb's hand in marriage) Bewerber m (for um)

aspirate ['æspɪrɪt] **N** Aspirata f (spec), Hauchlaut m **['æspəreɪt] VT** aspirieren, behauchen

aspiration [ˌæspə'reɪʃən] N **a** (hohes) Ziel, Aspiration f (geh); **his ~ towards** (Brit) or **toward** (US) **Lady Sarah's hand** (liter) seine Hoffnung auf Lady Sarahs Hand **b** (Phon) Aspiration f, Behauchung f

aspirational [ˌæspə'reɪʃənl] ADJ person auf sozialen Aufstieg bedacht; product den sozialen Aufstieg verkörpernd

aspire [ə'spaɪə] VI **to ~ to sth** nach etw streben, etw erstreben; **to ~ to do sth** danach streben, etw zu tun

aspirin ['æsprɪn] N Kopfschmerztablette f, Aspirin® nt

aspiring [ə'spaɪərɪŋ] ADJ aufstrebend

ass¹ [æs] N (lit, fig inf) Esel m; **silly ~!** blöder Esel!; **don't be an ~!** sei kein Esel!, sei nicht blöd!; **to make an ~ of oneself** sich lächerlich machen or blamieren

ass² N (US sl) Arsch m (vulg); **a nice piece of ~** eine geile Braut (sl); **he was looking for a piece of ~** er wollte eine Frau aufreißen (inf); **this place is just full of ~** hier laufen unwahrscheinlich viele Bräute rum (sl); **to kick ~** (= get tough) mit der Faust auf den Tisch hauen (inf); **to work one's ~ off** sich zu Tode schuften (inf); **to kiss ~** (esp US sl) ein Arschkriecher sein (inf); **to kiss sb's ~** (esp US sl) jdm in den Arsch kriechen (inf); **kiss my ~!** (esp US sl) du kannst mich mal am Arsch lecken! (vulg) → also **arse**

assagai N = **assegai**

assail [ə'seɪl] VT (lit, fig) angreifen; (fig: with questions etc) überschütten, bombardieren; **a harsh sound ~ed my ears** ein scharfes Geräusch drang an mein Ohr; **to be ~ed by doubts** von Zweifeln befallen sein or geplagt werden

assailable [ə'seɪləbl] ADJ (lit, fig) angreifbar

assailant [ə'seɪlənt] N Angreifer(in) m(f)

assassin [ə'sæsɪn] N Attentäter(in) m(f), Mörder(in) m(f)

assassinate [ə'sæsɪneɪt] VT ein Attentat or einen Mordanschlag verüben auf (+acc); **JFK was ~d in Dallas** JFK fiel in Dallas einem Attentat or Mordanschlag zum Opfer, JFK wurde in Dallas ermordet; **they ~d him** sie haben ihn ermordet

assassination [əˌsæsɪ'neɪʃən] N (geglücktes) Attentat, (geglückter) Mordanschlag (of auf +acc); **~ attempt** Attentat nt; **to plan an ~** ein Attentat planen; **before/after the ~** vor dem Attentat/nach dem (geglückten) Attentat

assault [ə'sɔːlt] **N a** (Mil) Sturm(angriff) m (on auf +acc); (fig) Angriff m (on gegen); **to make an ~ on sth** einen (Sturm)angriff gegen etw führen **b** (Jur) Körperverletzung f; **~ and battery** Körperverletzung f; **sexual ~** Notzucht f → also **indecent assault** **VT a** (Jur: = attack) tätlich werden gegen; (sexually) herfallen über (+acc); (= rape) sich vergehen an (+dat); **to ~ sb with a stick** jdn mit einem Stock angreifen **b** (Mil) stürmen

assault: assault course N Übungsgelände nt; **getting to the bathroom is like an ~** der Weg zum Badezimmer ist ein wahres Hindernisren-

nen; **assault craft** N Sturmlandefahrzeug nt; **assault rifle** N Maschinengewehr nt; **assault troops** PL Sturmtruppen pl

assay [ə'seɪ] **N** Prüfung f **VT a** mineral, ore, value, sb's worth prüfen **b** (liter) (= try) sich versuchen an (+dat); (= put to the test) troops prüfen

ass-backwards [ˌæs'bækwədz] (US sl) **ADJ** (= reversed) umgekehrt; (= confused) verdreht **ADV** (= in reverse) rückwärts; (= in confused manner) verdreht, verkehrt

assegai ['æsəgaɪ] N Assagai m

assemblage [ə'semblɪdʒ] N **a** (= assembling) Zusammensetzen nt, Zusammenbau m; (esp of car, machine) Montage f **b** (= collection) (of things) Sammlung f; (of facts) Anhäufung f; (of people) Versammlung f

assemble [ə'sembl] **VT** zusammensetzen, zusammenbauen; car, machine etc also montieren; facts zusammentragen; Parliament einberufen, versammeln; people zusammenrufen; team zusammenstellen **VI** sich versammeln; **we are ~d here today to ...** wir haben uns or sind heute versammelt, um ...

assembler [ə'semblə] N (Comput) Assembler m

assembly [ə'semblɪ] N **a** (= gathering of people, Parl) Versammlung f **b** (Sch) Morgenandacht f, tägliche Versammlung **c** (= putting together) Zusammensetzen nt, Zusammenbau m; (esp of machine, cars) Montage f; (of facts) Zusammentragen nt **d** (= thing assembled) Konstruktion f

assembly: assembly hall N (Sch) Aula f; **assembly language** N (Comput) Assemblersprache f; **assembly line** N Montageband nt; **assemblyman** [ə'semblɪmən] N (US) Abgeordnete(r) m; **Assembly Member** N Mitglied des walisischen Parlaments; **assembly plant** N Montagewerk nt; **assembly point** N Sammelplatz m; **assembly shop** N Montagehalle f; **assemblywoman** [ə'semblɪwʊmən] N (US) Abgeordnete f; **assembly worker** N Montagearbeiter(in) m(f)

assent [ə'sent] **N** Zustimmung f; **to give one's ~ to sth** seine Zustimmung zu etw geben; **by common ~** mit allgemeiner Zustimmung; **royal ~** königliche Genehmigung **VI** zustimmen; **to ~ to sth** einer Sache (dat) zustimmen

assert [ə'sɜːt] VT **a** (= declare) behaupten; one's innocence beteuern **b** (= insist on) **to ~ one's authority** seine Autorität geltend machen; **to ~ one's rights** sein Recht behaupten; **to ~ one's independence** seine Unabhängigkeit demonstrieren; **to ~ oneself** sich behaupten or durchsetzen (over gegenüber); **if you ~ yourself too much you will lose their support** wenn Sie zu bestimmt auftreten, verlieren Sie ihre Unterstützung

assertion [ə'sɜːʃən] ✪ 26.1 N **a** (= statement) Behauptung f; (of innocence) Beteuerung f; **to make ~s/an ~** Behauptungen/eine Behauptung aufstellen **b** no pl (= insistence) Behauptung f

assertive ADJ , **assertively** ADV [ə'sɜːtɪv, -lɪ] bestimmt

assertiveness [ə'sɜːtɪvnɪs] N Bestimmtheit f; **~ training course** Persönlichkeitstrainingskurs m

assess [ə'ses] VT **a** person, chances, abilities, needs einschätzen; problem, situation, prospects beurteilen, einschätzen; proposal abwägen; damage abschätzen **b** property schätzen, taxieren; person (for tax purposes) veranlagen (at mit); **to ~ sth at its true worth** einer Sache (dat) den richtigen Wert beimessen **c** fine, tax festsetzen, bemessen (at auf +acc); damages schätzen (at auf +acc)

assessable [ə'sesəbl] ADJ (Fin, Tax) steuer- or abgabenpflichtig; **~ income** steuerpflichtiges Einkommen

assessment [ə'sesmənt] N **a** (= evaluation) (of person, chances, abilities, needs) Einschätzung f; (of problem, situation, prospects also) Beurteilung f; (of proposal, advantages also) Abwägen nt; (of damage) Schätzung f; **in my ~** meines Erachtens; **what's your ~ of the situation?** wie sehen or beurteilen Sie die Lage? **b** (Fin, of property) Schätzung f, Taxierung f; (of person: for tax purposes) Veranlagung f **c** (Jur) (of fine, tax) Festsetzung, Bemessung f; (of damages) Schätzung f **d** (Sch, Univ: of student) Einstufung f; (Med: of patient) Beurteilung f

assessor [əˈsesə] N Schätzer(in) m(f), Taxator m (form); (Insur) (Schadens)gutachter(in) m(f); (Univ) Prüfer(in) m(f)

asset [ˈæset] N **a** (usu pl) Vermögenswert m; (on balance sheet) Aktivposten m; ~s Vermögen nt; (on balance sheet) Aktiva pl; **personal ~s** persönlicher Besitz **b** (fig) **it would be an ~ ...** es wäre von Vorteil ...; **he is one of our great ~s** er ist einer unserer besten Leute; **this player, the club's newest ~** dieser Spieler, die neueste Errungenschaft des Klubs; **he's hardly an ~ to the company** er ist nicht gerade ein Gewinn für die Firma; **good health is a real ~** Gesundheit ist ein großes Kapital; **his appearance is not his best ~** aus seinem Aussehen kann er kein Kapital schlagen

asset-stripping [ˈæsetstrɪpɪŋ] N Asset-Stripping nt, Aufkauf von finanziell gefährdeten Firmen und anschließender Verkauf ihrer Vermögenswerte

asseverate [əˈsevəreɪt] VT (form) beteuern

asseveration [əˌsevəˈreɪʃən] N (form) Beteuerung f

asshole [ˈæʃəʊl] N (US sl) Arschloch nt (vulg)

assiduity [ˌæsɪˈdjʊɪtɪ] N gewissenhafter Eifer

assiduous ADJ , **assiduously** ADV [əˈsɪdjʊəs, -lɪ] gewissenhaft

assiduousness [əˈsɪdjʊəsnɪs] N Gewissenhaftigkeit f

assign [əˈsaɪn] **VT a** (= allot) zuweisen, zuteilen (to sb jdm); (to a purpose) room bestimmen (to für); (to a word) meaning zuordnen (to +dat); (= fix) date, time bestimmen, festsetzen; (= attribute) cause, novel, play, music zuschreiben (to +dat); **at the time ~ed** zur festgesetzten Zeit; **which class have you been ~ed?** welche Klasse wurde Ihnen zugewiesen?

b (= appoint) berufen; (to a mission, case, task etc) betrauen (to mit), beauftragen (to mit); **she was ~ed to this school** sie wurde an diese Schule berufen; **he was ~ed to the post of ambassador** er wurde zum Botschafter berufen; **I was ~ed to speak to the boss** ich wurde damit beauftragt or betraut, mit dem Chef zu sprechen

c (Jur) übertragen, übereignen (to sb jdm) **N** (Jur: also **assignee**) Abtretungsempfänger(in) m(f)

assignable [əˈsaɪnəbl] ADJ **a** (= ascribable) bestimmbar **b** cause anführbar **c** (Jur) übertragbar

assignation [ˌæsɪɡˈneɪʃən] N **a** Stelldichein nt, Rendezvous nt **b** = **assignment b-d**

assignment [əˈsaɪnmənt] N **a** (= task) Aufgabe f; (= mission) Auftrag m, Mission f; **to be on (an) ~** einen Auftrag haben **b** (= appointment) Berufung f; (to case, task etc) Betrauung f (to mit), Beauftragung f (to mit); **his ~ to the post of ambassador/to this school** seine Berufung zum Botschafter/an diese Schule **c** (= allocation) Zuweisung f, Zuteilung f; (of room) Bestimmung f (to für); (of meaning) Zuordnung f (to zu) **d** (Jur) Übertragung f, Übereignung f

assignor [ˌæsɪˈnɔː, ˌæsɪˈnɔː] N (Jur) Abtretende(r) mf, Zedent(in) m(f) (spec)

assimilable [əˈsɪmɪləbl] ADJ **a** (Biol, Ling) assimilierbar **b** (= integrable) angleichbar

assimilate [əˈsɪmɪleɪt] VT food, information aufnehmen; (fig: into society etc also) integrieren; **newcomers are easily ~d** Neuankömmlinge können leicht integriert werden

assimilation [əˌsɪmɪˈleɪʃən] N (of food, knowledge) Aufnahme f; (fig: into society etc also) Integration f; **his powers of ~** seine geistige Aufnahmefähigkeit

assist [əˈsɪst] **VT** helfen (+dat); (= act as an assistant to) assistieren (+dat); growth, progress, development fördern, begünstigen; **to ~ sb with sth** jdm bei etw helfen or behilflich sein; **to ~ sb in**

doing or **to do sth** jdm helfen, etw zu tun; ... **who was ~ing the surgeon ...**, der dem Chirurgen assistierte; **in a wind ~ed time of 10.01 seconds** mit Rückenwind in einer Zeit von 10,01 Sekunden; **a man is ~ing the police (with their inquiries)** ein Mann wird von der Polizei vernommen

VI a (= help) helfen; **to ~ with sth** bei etw helfen; **to ~ in doing sth** helfen, etw zu tun **b** (= be present) (doctor) assistieren (at bei); (in church) ministrieren **N** (Sport) Vorlage f

assistance [əˈsɪstəns] N Hilfe f; **to give ~ to sb** (= come to aid of) jdm Hilfe leisten; **my secretary will give you every ~** meine Sekretärin wird Ihnen in jeder Hinsicht behilflich sein; **to come to sb's ~** jdm zu Hilfe kommen; **to be of ~ to sb** jdm helfen or behilflich sein; **can I be of any ~?** kann ich irgendwie helfen or behilflich sein?

assistant [əˈsɪstənt] **N** Assistent(in) m(f); (= shop assistant) Verkäufer(in) m(f); **are you in charge here? – no, I am just an ~** sind Sie hier der Chef? – nein, ich bin bloß Mitarbeiter **ADJ** attr manager etc stellvertretend

assistant: assistant master/mistress N Lehrer(in) m(f) (ohne besondere zusätzliche Verantwortung); **assistant priest** N Hilfspriester m; **assistant professor** N (US) Assistenz-Professor(in) m(f); **assistant referee** N (Ftbl) Schiedsrichterassistent(in) m(f)

assistantship [əˈsɪstəntʃɪp] N (Brit: at school) Stelle f als Fremdsprachenassistent(in); (US: at college) Assistentenstelle f

assisted [əˈsɪstɪd] **assisted place** N (Brit Sch) staatlich finanzierter Platz in einer Privatschule, der für einen Schüler aus bescheidenen Verhältnissen reserviert ist; **assisted suicide** N aktive Sterbehilfe

assizes [əˈsaɪzɪz] PL (Brit, dated) Gerichtstage pl, Assisen pl (old); **at the county ~** während der Bezirksgerichtstage

assn abbr of **association**

associate [əˈsəʊʃɪt] **N a** (= colleague) Kollege m, Kollegin f; (Comm: = partner) Partner m, Kompagnon m, Teilhaber(in) m(f); (= accomplice) Komplize m, Komplizin f **b** (of a society) außerordentliches or assoziiertes Mitglied **VT** [əˈsəʊʃɪeɪt] in Verbindung bringen, assoziieren (also Psych); **to ~ oneself with sb/sth** sich jdm/einer Sache anschließen, sich mit jdm/einer Sache assoziieren; **to be ~d with sb/sth** mit jdm/einer Sache in Verbindung gebracht or assoziiert werden; **it is ~d in their minds with ...** sie denken dabei gleich an (+acc) ...; **I don't ~ him with sport** ich assoziiere ihn nicht mit Sport, ich denke bei ihm nicht an Sport; **the Associated Union of ...** der Gewerkschaftsverband der ...; **~(d) company** Partnerfirma f **VI** [əˈsəʊʃɪeɪt] **to ~ with** verkehren mit

associate: associate director N Direktor einer Firma, der jedoch nicht offiziell als solcher ernannt wurde; **associate editor** N Mitherausgeber(in) m(f); **associate member** N außerordentliches or assoziiertes Mitglied; **associate partner** N (Geschäfts)partner(in) m(f); **associate professor** N (US) außerordentlicher Professor, außerordentliche Professorin

association [əˌsəʊsɪˈeɪʃən] **N a** no pl (= associating: with people) Verkehr m, Umgang m; (= cooperation) Zusammenarbeit f; **he has benefited from his ~ with us** er hat von seiner Beziehung zu uns profitiert; **he has had a long ~ with the party** er hat seit langem Verbindung mit der Partei **b** (= organization) Verband m **c** (= connection in the mind) Assoziation f (with an +acc) (also Psych); **~ of ideas** Gedankenassoziation f; **to have unpleasant ~s for sb** unangenehme Assoziationen bei jdm hervorrufen; **to be found in ~ with sth** zusammen mit etw vorkommen; **published in ~ with ...** in Zusammenarbeit mit ... veröffentlicht; **to be guilty/**

tainted by ~ indirekt schuldig/betroffen sein; **free ~** (Psych) freie Assoziation

association football N (Brit) Fußball m, Soccer nt

associative [əˈsəʊʃɪətɪv] ADJ assoziativ

assonance [ˈæsənəns] N Assonanz f

assort [əˈsɔːt] VI (form) **a** (= agree, match) passen (with zu) **b** (= consort) Umgang pflegen (with mit)

assorted [əˈsɔːtɪd] ADJ **a** (= mixed) gemischt **b** (= matched) zusammengestellt → **ill-assorted**

assortment [əˈsɔːtmənt] N Mischung f; (of goods) Auswahl f (of an +dat), Sortiment nt (of von); (of ideas) Sammlung f; **a whole ~ of boyfriends** ein ganzes Sortiment von Freunden

asst abbr of **assistant**

assuage [əˈsweɪdʒ] VT hunger, thirst, desire stillen, befriedigen; anger, fears etc beschwichtigen; pain, grief lindern; guilt vermindern; conscience erleichtern

assume [əˈsjuːm] ⊕ 20.3, 26.1 VT **a** (= take for granted, suppose) annehmen; (= presuppose) voraussetzen; **let us ~ that you are right** nehmen wir an or gehen wir davon aus, Sie hätten Recht; **assuming (that) ...** angenommen(, dass) ...; **assuming (that) this is true ...** angenommen or vorausgesetzt, (dass) das stimmt ...; **Professor X ~s as his basic premise that ...** Professor X geht von der Grundvoraussetzung aus, dass ... **b** power, control übernehmen; (forcefully) ergreifen **c** (= take on) name, title annehmen, sich (dat) zulegen; guise, shape, attitude annehmen; **to ~ office** sein Amt antreten; **to ~ a look of innocence/surprise** eine unschuldige/überraschte Miene aufsetzen; **the problem has ~d a new importance** das Problem hat neue Bedeutung gewonnen; **the sky ~d a reddish glow** (liter) der Himmel nahm rötliche Glut an (poet)

assumed [əˈsjuːmd] ADJ **a** ~ **name** angenommener Name; (for secrecy etc also) Deckname m **b** (= pretended) surprise, humility gespielt, vorgetäuscht; **in the ~ guise of a beggar** als Bettler verkleidet

assuming [əˈsjuːmɪŋ] ADJ anmaßend, überheblich

assumption [əˈsʌmpʃən] N **a** Annahme f; (= presupposition) Voraussetzung f; **to go on the ~ that ...** von der Voraussetzung ausgehen, dass ...; **the basic ~s of this theory are ...** diese Theorie geht grundsätzlich davon aus, dass ... **b** (of power, role, office etc) Übernahme f; (forcefully) Ergreifen nt **c** (of guise, false name etc) Annahme f; (insincere: of look of innocence etc) Vortäuschung f, Aufsetzen nt **d** (Eccl) **the Assumption** Mariä Himmelfahrt f

assurance [əˈʃʊərəns] N **a** Versicherung f; (= promise) Zusicherung f; **he gave me his ~ that it would be done** er versicherte mir, dass es getan (werden) würde; **do I have your ~ that ...?** garantieren Sie mir, dass ...?; **you have my ~ that ...** Sie können versichert sein, dass ... **b** (= self-confidence) Sicherheit f **c** (= confidence) Zuversicht f; **in the ~ of** (+acc), Vertrauen auf (in +acc); **in the ~ that ...** (liter) im Vertrauen darauf, dass ..., in der Zuversicht, dass ... **d** (Brit: = life assurance) Versicherung f

assure [əˈʃʊə] ⊕ 15.1 VT **a** (= say with confidence) versichern (+dat); (= promise) zusichern (+dat); **to ~ sb of sth** (of love, willingness etc) jdn einer Sache (gen) versichern; (of service, support, help) jdm etw zusichern; **to ~ sb that ...** jdm versichern/zusichern, dass ...; **I ~ you ...** versichere ich Ihnen **b** (= make certain of) success, happiness, future sichern; **to be ~d of a warm welcome wherever he goes** er kann sich überall eines herzlichen Empfanges sicher sein **c** (Brit: = insure) life versichern; **she ~d her life for £100,000** sie schloss eine Lebensversicherung über £ 100.000 ab

assured [əˈʃʊəd] **N** (Brit) Versicherte(r) mf **ADJ** sicher; income, future also gesichert; (= self-confident) sicher; **to rest ~ that ...** sicher sein, dass

...; **to rest ~ of sth** einer Sache (*gen*) sicher sein

assuredly [əˈʃʊərɪdlɪ] ADV mit Sicherheit; **yes, most ~** ganz sicher

Assyria [əˈsɪrɪə] N Assyrien *nt*

Assyrian [əˈsɪrɪən] **ADJ** assyrisch **N** **a** Assyrer(in) *m(f)* **b** (= *language*) Assyrisch *nt*

aster [ˈæstə'] N Aster *f*

asterisk [ˈæstərɪsk] **N** Sternchen *nt* **VT** mit Sternchen versehen

astern [əˈstɜːn] (*Naut*) **ADV** achtern; (= *towards the stern*) nach achtern; (= *backwards*) achteraus **PREP** **~ (of) the ship** achteraus

asteroid [ˈæstərɔɪd] N Asteroid *m*

asthma [ˈæsmə] N Asthma *nt*

asthmatic [æsˈmætɪk] **N** Asthmatiker(in) *m(f)* **ADJ** asthmatisch

asthmatically [æsˈmætɪkəlɪ] ADV asthmatisch

astigmatic [ˌæstɪɡˈmætɪk] ADJ astigmatisch

astigmatism [æsˈtɪɡmətɪzəm] N Astigmatismus *m*

astir [əˈstɜː'] ADJ *pred* **a** (= *in motion, excited*) voller *or* in Aufregung **b** (*old, liter.* = *up and about*) auf den Beinen, auf

ASTM (*US*) *abbr of* **American Society for Testing Materials** amerikanischer Normenausschuss, ≈ DNA *m*

ASTMS [ˈæstəmz] *abbr of* **Association of Scientific, Technical and Managerial Staffs** *Gewerkschaft der Wissenschaftler, Techniker und leitenden Angestellten*

astonish [əˈstɒnɪʃ] VT erstaunen, überraschen; **you ~ me!** (*iro*) das wundert mich aber! (*iro*), was du nicht sagst! (*iro*); **to be ~ed** erstaunt *or* überrascht sein; **I am ~ed** *or* **it ~es me that ...** ich bin erstaunt *or* es wundert mich, dass ...; **I am ~ed to learn that ...** ich höre mit Erstaunen *or* Befremden (*geh*), dass ...

astonishing [əˈstɒnɪʃɪŋ] ADJ erstaunlich

astonishingly [əˈstɒnɪʃɪŋlɪ] ADV erstaunlich; **~ (enough)** erstaunlicherweise

astonishment [əˈstɒnɪʃmənt] N Erstaunen *nt*, Überraschung *f* (*at* über +*acc*); **look of ~** erstaunter *or* überraschter Blick; **she looked at me in (complete) ~** sie sah mich (ganz) erstaunt *or* überrascht an; **to my ~** zu meinem Erstaunen

astound [əˈstaʊnd] VT sehr erstaunen, in Erstaunen (ver)setzen; **to be ~ed (at** *or* **by)** höchst erstaunt sein (über +*acc*)

astounding [əˈstaʊndɪŋ] ADJ erstaunlich

astoundingly [əˈstaʊndɪŋlɪ] ADV erstaunlich; **~, an American had won the Tour de France** erstaunlicherweise hatte ein Amerikaner die Tour de France gewonnen

astrakhan [ˌæstrəˈkæn] N Astrachan *m attr* Astrachan-; **~ coat** Astrachanmantel *m*

astral [ˈæstrəl] ADJ Stern-; (*in theosophy*) Astral-; **~ matter** Sternmaterie *f*; **~ projection** Astralreise *f*

astray [əˈstreɪ] ADJ verloren; **to go ~** (*person*) (*lit*) vom Weg abkommen; (*fig: morally*) vom rechten Weg abkommen, auf Abwege geraten; (*letter, object*) verloren gehen; (= *go wrong: in argument etc*) irregehen; **to lead sb ~** (*fig*) jdn vom rechten Weg abbringen; (= *mislead*) jdn irreführen

astride [əˈstraɪd] **PREP** rittlings auf (+*dat*) **ADV** rittlings; *ride* im Herrensitz

astringency [əsˈtrɪndʒənsɪ] N (*fig*) Ätzende(s) *nt*

astringent [əsˈtrɪndʒənt] **ADJ** adstringierend; (*fig*) *remark, humour* ätzend, beißend **N** Adstringens *nt*

astro- [ˈæstrəʊ-] PREF Astro-

astrolabe [ˈæstrəleɪb] N Astrolab(ium) *nt*

astrologer [əsˈtrɒlədʒə'] N Astrologe *m*, Astrologin *f*

astrological [ˌæstrəˈlɒdʒɪkəl] ADJ astrologisch; **~ sign** Tierkreiszeichen *nt*

astrologically [ˌæstrəˈlɒdʒɪkəl] ADV astrologisch

astrology [əsˈtrɒlədʒɪ] N Astrologie *f*

astronaut [ˈæstrənɔːt] N Astronaut(in) *m(f)*

astronautics [ˌæstrəʊˈnɔːtɪks] N *sing* Raumfahrt *f*, Astronautik *f*

astronomer [əsˈtrɒnəmə'] N Astronom(in) *m(f)*

astronomical [ˌæstrəˈnɒmɪkəl] ADJ (*lit, fig: also* **astronomic**) astronomisch

astronomical clock N astronomische Uhr

astronomically [ˌæstrəˈnɒmɪkəl] ADV (*lit, fig*) astronomisch

astronomical year N Sternjahr *nt*

astronomy [əsˈtrɒnəmɪ] N Astronomie *f*

astrophysics [ˌæstrəʊˈfɪzɪks] N *sing* Astrophysik *f*

astute [əˈstjuːt] ADJ schlau; *remark also* scharfsinnig; *businessman also* clever (*inf*); *child* aufgeweckt; *mind* scharf; **he's very ~ for one so old** er ist für sein Alter geistig sehr rege

astutely [əˈstjuːtlɪ] ADV *remark, observe* scharfsinnig

astuteness [əsˈtjuːtnɪs] N Schlauheit *f*; (*of remark also*) Scharfsinnigkeit *f*; (*of businessman also*) Cleverness *f* (*inf*); (*of child*) Aufgewecktheit *f*; (*of mind*) Schärfe *f*

asunder [əˈsʌndə'] ADV (*liter*) (= *apart*) auseinander; (= *in pieces*) entzwei, in Stücke; **to split ~** spalten; **her heart was rent ~** ihr brach das Herz; **... let no man put ~** ..., soll der Mensch nicht trennen *or* scheiden

asylum [əˈsaɪləm] N **a** Asyl *nt*; **to ask for (political) ~** um (politisches) Asyl bitten **b** (= *lunatic asylum*) (Irren)anstalt *f*

asylum-seeker N [əˈsaɪləmˌsiːkə'] Asylbewerber(in) *m(f)*

asymmetric(al) [ˌeɪsɪˈmetrɪk(əl)] ADJ asymmetrisch

asymmetric(al) bars PL Stufenbarren *m*

asymmetry [æˈsɪmɪtrɪ] N Asymmetrie *f*

asynchronous [æˈsɪŋkrənəs] ADJ (*also Comput*) asynchron

at [æt] PREP **a** (*position*) an (+*dat*), bei (+*dat*); (*with place*) in (+*dat*); **at a table** an einem Tisch; **at the window** am *or* beim Fenster; **at the corner** an der Ecke; **at the top** an der Spitze; **at home** zu Hause; **at the university** (*US*), **at university** an *or* auf der Universität; **at school** in der Schule; **at the hotel** im Hotel; **at the zoo** im Zoo; **at my brother's** bei meinem Bruder; **at a party** auf *or* bei einer Party; **to arrive at the station** am Bahnhof ankommen; **he came in at the window** er ist durch das Fenster hereingekommen; **the rain came in at the window** es hat durchs Fenster hineingeregnet; **where are you at with your work?** (*inf*) wie weit sind Sie mit Ihrer Arbeit?; **this is where it's at** (*esp US, inf*) da gehts ab (*sl*), da geht die Post ab (*inf*); **he doesn't know where he's at** (*inf*) der weiß ja nicht, was er tut (*inf*)

b (*direction*) **to aim/shoot/point** *etc* **at sb/sth** auf jdn/etw zielen/schießen/zeigen *etc*; **to look/growl/swear** *etc* **at sb/sth** jdn/etw ansehen/anknurren/beschimpfen *etc*; **at him!** auf ihn!

c (*time, frequency, order*) **at ten o'clock** um zehn Uhr; **at night/dawn** bei Nacht/beim *or* im Morgengrauen; **at Christmas/Easter** *etc* zu Weihnachten/Ostern *etc*; **at your age/16 (years of age)** in deinem Alter/mit 16 (Jahren); **three at a time** drei auf einmal; **at the start/end of sth** am Anfang/am Ende einer Sache (*gen*)

d (*activity*) **at play** beim Spiel; **at work** bei der Arbeit; **good/bad/an expert at sth** gut/schlecht/ein Experte in etw (*dat*); **his employees/creditors are at him** seine Angestellten/Gläubiger setzen ihm zu; **while we are at it** (*inf*) wenn wir schon mal dabei sind; **the couple in the next room were at it all night** (*inf*) die beiden im Zimmer nebenan haben es die ganze Nacht getrieben (*inf*); **the brakes are at it again** (*inf*) die Bremsen mucken schon wieder (*inf*)

e (*state, condition*) **to be at an advantage** im

Vorteil sein; **at a loss/profit** mit Verlust/Gewinn; **I'd leave it at that** ich würde es dabei belassen → **best, worst, that** [1]

f (= *as a result of, upon*) auf (+*acc*) ... (hin); **at his request** auf seine Bitte (hin); **at her death** bei ihrem Tod; **at that/this he left the room** daraufhin verließ er das Zimmer

g (*cause*: = *with*) *angry, annoyed, delighted etc* über (+*acc*)

h (*rate, value, degree*) **at full speed/50 km/h** mit voller Geschwindigkeit/50 km/h; **at 50p a pound** für *or* zu 50 Pence pro *or* das Pfund; **at 5% interest** zu 5% Zinsen; **at a high/low price** zu einem hohen/niedrigen Preis; **when the temperature is at 90** wenn die Temperatur bei *or* auf 90 ist; **with inflation at this level** bei so einer Inflationsrate → **all, cost, rate** [1]

atavism [ˈætəvɪzəm] N Atavismus *m*

atavistic [ˌætəˈvɪstɪk] ADJ atavistisch

ataxia [əˈtæksɪə] N Ataxie *f*

ataxic [əˈtæksɪk] ADJ ataktisch

ATB *abbr of* **all-terrain bike**

ate [eɪt, et] *pret of* **eat**

atheism [ˈeɪθɪzəm] N Atheismus *m*

atheist [ˈeɪθɪɪst] **N** Atheist(in) *m(f)* **ADJ** *attr* atheistisch

atheistic [ˌeɪθɪˈɪstɪk] ADJ atheistisch

Athenian [əˈθiːnɪən] **N** Athener(in) *m(f)* **ADJ** athenisch; (*esp modern*) Athener

Athens [ˈæθɪnz] N Athen *nt*

athirst [əˈθɜːst] ADJ (*fig liter*) **to be ~ for sth** nach etw (*dat*) dürsten (*liter*)

athlete [ˈæθliːt] N Athlet(in) *m(f)*; (= *specialist in track and field events*) Leichtathlet(in) *m(f)*; **he is a natural** ~ er ist der geborene Sportler

athlete's foot [ˌæθliːtsˈfʊt] N Fußpilz *m*

athlete's heart [ˌæθliːtsˈhɑːt] N Sportlerherz *nt*

athletic [æθˈletɪk] ADJ sportlich; (*referring to athletics*) *build* athletisch

athletically [æθˈletɪkəlɪ] ADV sportlich; *built* athletisch

athleticism [æθˈletɪsɪzəm] N Athletentum *nt*

athletics [æθˈletɪks] N *sing or pl* Leichtathletik *f*; **~ meeting** Leichtathletikwettkampf *m*; **~ coach** Leichtathletiktrainer(in) *m(f)*; **sexual ~** Sexualakrobatik *f*

at-home [ˈætˈhəʊm] N Empfang *m* bei sich (*dat*) zu Hause

athwart [əˈθwɔːt] **ADV** quer; (*Naut*) dwars **PREP** quer über; (*Naut*) dwars, quer

Atlantic [ətˈlæntɪk] N (*also* **Atlantic Ocean**) Atlantik *m*, Atlantischer Ozean **ADJ** *attr* atlantisch; **~ crossing** Atlantiküberquerung *f*; **~ liner** Ozeandampfer *m*

Atlantic Charter N Atlantik-Charta *f*

Atlantic wall N Atlantikwall *m*

atlas [ˈætləs] N Atlas *m*

Atlas Mountains PL Atlas(gebirge *nt*) *m*

ATM *abbr of* **automated telling machine**

atmosphere [ˈætməsfɪə'] N (*lit, fig*) Atmosphäre *f*; (*fig: of novel also*) Stimmung *f*

atmospheric [ˌætməsˈferɪk] ADJ atmosphärisch; (= *full of atmosphere*) *description* stimmungsvoll

atmospheric pressure N Luftdruck *m*

atmospherics [ˌætməsˈferɪks] PL (*Rad*) atmosphärische Störungen *pl*

atoll [ˈætɒl] N Atoll *nt*

atom [ˈætəm] N **a** Atom *nt* **b** (*fig*) **to powder sth into ~s** etw völlig zertrümmern; **not an ~ of truth** kein Körnchen Wahrheit

atom bomb N Atombombe *f*

atomic [əˈtɒmɪk] ADJ atomar

atomic *in cpds* Atom-; **atomic age** N Atomzeitalter *nt*; **atomic bomb** N Atombombe *f*; **atomic clock** N Atomuhr *f*; **atomic energy** N Atom- *or* Kernenergie *f*; **Atomic Energy Authority** (*Brit*), **Atomic Energy Commission** (*US*) N Atomkommission *f*; **atomic mass** N Atommasse *f*; **atomic number** N Ordnungszahl *f*; **atomic power** N Atomkraft *f*; (=

propulsion) Atomantrieb *m*; **atomic-powered** ADJ atomgetrieben; **atomic reactor** N Atomreaktor *m*; **atomic structure** N Atombau *m*; **atomic warfare** N atomare Kriegsführung; **atomic waste** N Atommüll *m*; **atomic weapon** N Atomwaffe *f*; **atomic weight** N Atomgewicht *nt*

atomism ['ætəmɪzəm] N (*Philos*) Atomismus *m*

atomistic [ˌætə'mɪstɪk] ADJ (*Philos*) atomistisch

atomize ['ætəmaɪz] VT *liquid* zerstäuben

atomizer ['ætəmaɪzə'] N Zerstäuber *m*

atom smasher N Teilchenbeschleuniger *m*

atonal [æ'təʊnl] ADJ atonal

atone [ə'təʊn] VI **to ~ for sth** (für) etw sühnen *or* büßen

atonement [ə'təʊnmənt] N Sühne *f*, Buße *f*; **to make ~ for sth** für etw Sühne *or* Buße tun; **in ~ for sth** als Sühne *or* Buße für etw; **the Atonement** (*Eccl*) das Sühneopfer (Christi)

atop [ə'tɒp] PREP (*liter*) (oben) auf (+*dat*)

A to Z® N Stadtplan *m* (*mit Straßenverzeichnis, meist in Buchform*)

at-risk ['æt,rɪsk] ADJ Risiko-; **~ group** Risikogruppe *f*; **~ register** (*Social Work*) Register *nt* gefährdeter Kinder

atrium ['eɪtrɪəm] N (*Archit*) Vorhof *m*, Atrium *nt* (*spec*); (*Roman*) Atrium *nt*

atrocious ADJ, **atrociously** ADV [ə'trəʊʃəs, -lɪ] grauenhaft

atrocity [ə'trɒsɪtɪ] N Grausamkeit *f*; (*act also*) Gräueltat *f*

atrophy ['ætrəfɪ] N Atrophie *f* (*geh*), Schwund *m* VT schwinden lassen VI verkümmern, schwinden

at sign N (*Comput*) at-Zeichen *nt*

att *abbr of* **attorney**

attaboy ['ætəbɔɪ] INTERJ (*esp US inf*) gut gemacht!

attach [ə'tætʃ] VT a (= *join*) festmachen, befestigen (to an +*dat*); *document to a letter etc* an- *or* beiheften; **please find ~ed ...** beigeheftet ...; **to ~ oneself to sb/a group** sich jdm/einer Gruppe anschließen; **is he/she ~ed?** ist er/sie schon vergeben?; **to ~ conditions to sth** Bedingungen mit etw verknüpfen *or* an etw (*acc*) knüpfen b **to be ~ed to sb/sth** (= *be fond of*) an jdm/etw hängen c (= *attribute*) *importance* beimessen, zuschreiben (to +*dat*) d (*Mil etc*) *personnel* angliedern, zuteilen (to +*dat*) VI **no blame ~es to him** ihm haftet keine Schuld an, ihn trifft keine Schuld; **responsibility ~ing *or* ~ed to this post** (*esp Brit*) *or* **position** Verantwortung, die dieser Posten mit sich bringt; **great importance ~es to this** dem haftet größte Bedeutung an

attachable [ə'tætʃəbl] ADJ **to be ~** sich befestigen lassen

attaché [ə'tæʃeɪ] N Attaché *m*

attaché case N Aktenkoffer *m*

attachment [ə'tætʃmənt] N a (= *act of attaching*) Festmachen *nt*, Befestigen *nt*; (*of document to a letter etc*)) An- *or* Beiheften *nt* b (= *accessory: for tool etc*) Zusatzteil, Zubehörteil *nt* c (*fig*: = *affection*) Zuneigung *f* (to zu) d (*Mil etc*: = *temporary transfer*) Zuordnung *f*, Angliederung *f*; **to be on ~** angegliedert *or* zugeteilt sein (to +*dat*) e (*Comput*) Anhang *m*, Attachment *nt*

attack [ə'tæk] N a (*Mil, Sport, fig*) Angriff *m* (on auf +*acc*); **there have been two ~s on his life** es wurden bereits zwei Anschläge auf sein Leben gemacht *or* verübt; **to be under ~** angegriffen werden; (*fig also*) unter Beschuss stehen; **to go on the ~** zum Angriff übergehen; **to return to the ~** wieder zum Angriff übergehen; **to launch an ~** einen Angriff vortragen *or* machen (on auf +*acc*); (*on sb's character*) angreifen (on +*acc*); **~ is the best form of defence** (*Brit*) *or* **defense** (*US*) Angriff ist die beste Verteidigung; **to leave oneself open to ~** Angriffsflächen bieten

b (*Med etc*) Anfall *m*; **an ~ of fever** ein Fieberanfall *m*; **to have an ~ of nerves** plötzlich Nerven bekommen

VT a (*Mil, Sport, fig*) angreifen; (*from ambush, in robbery etc*) überfallen b (= *tackle*) *task, problem, sonata* in Angriff nehmen c (*Med, illness*) befallen VI angreifen; **an ~ing side** eine angriffsfreudige *or* offensive Mannschaft; **ready to ~** zum Angriff bereit

attack dog N Kampfhund *m*

attacker [ə'tækə'] N Angreifer(in) *m(f)*

attagirl ['ætəgɜːl] INTERJ (*esp US inf*) gut gemacht!

attain [ə'teɪn] VT *aim, rank, age, perfection* erreichen; *knowledge, independence* erlangen; *happiness, prosperity, power* gelangen zu; **he has ~ed his ambitions** er hat sein Ziel erreicht VI **to ~ to sth** (to perfection) etw erreichen; to prosperity, power zu etw gelangen; **to ~ to man's estate** (*form*) das Mannesalter erreichen (*form*)

attainable [ə'teɪnəbl] ADJ erreichbar, zu erreichen; *knowledge, happiness, power* zu erlangen

attainder [ə'teɪndə'] N → **bill³ h**

attainment [ə'teɪnmənt] N a (= *act of attaining*) Erreichung *f*, Erreichen *nt*; (*of knowledge, happiness, prosperity, power*) Erlangen *nt*; **difficult/easy etc of ~** (*form*) schwierig/leicht zu erreichen *or* erlangen b (*usu pl*: = *accomplishment*) Fertigkeit *f*; **a low/high standard of ~** ein niedriger/hoher Leistungsstandard

attempt [ə'tempt] VT versuchen; *smile, conversation* den Versuch machen *or* unternehmen zu; *task, job* sich versuchen an (+*dat*); **~ed murder** Mordversuch *m*; **~ed suicide** Selbstmordversuch *m* N Versuch *m*; (on sb's life) (Mord)anschlag *m* (on auf +*acc*); **an ~ on Mount Everest/the record** ein Versuch, Mount Everest zu bezwingen/den Rekord zu brechen; **an ~ at a joke/at doing sth** ein Versuch, einen Witz zu machen/etw zu tun; **to make an ~ on sb's life** einen Anschlag auf jdn *or* jds Leben verüben; **to make an ~ at doing sth *or* to do sth** versuchen, etw zu tun; **he made no ~ to help us** er unternahm keinen Versuch, uns zu helfen; **at the first ~** auf Anhieb, beim ersten Versuch; **in the ~** dabei

attend [ə'tend] ✪ 19.3, 19.5, 25.1 VT a *classes, church, meeting, school etc* besuchen; *wedding, funeral* anwesend *or* zugegen sein bei, beiwohnen (+*dat*) (*geh*); **the wedding was well ~ed** die Hochzeit war gut besucht b (= *accompany*) begleiten; (= *wait on*) *queen etc* bedienen, aufwarten (+*dat*); **which doctor is ~ing you?** von welchem Arzt werden Sie behandelt?, wer ist Ihr behandelnder Arzt? VI a (= *be present*) anwesend sein; **are you going to ~?** gehen Sie hin?; **to ~ at a birth** bei einer Geburt helfen *or* assistieren; **to ~ (up)on sb** (*old*) jdm aufwarten (*old*) b (= *pay attention*) aufpassen

▶ **attend to** ✪ 20.7 VI +prep obj (= *see to*) sich kümmern um; (= *pay attention to*) *work etc* Aufmerksamkeit schenken *or* widmen (+*dat*); (= *listen to*) *teacher, sb's remark* zuhören (+*dat*); (= *heed*) *advice, warning* hören auf (+*acc*), Beachtung schenken (+*dat*); (= *serve*) *customers etc* bedienen; **are you being attended to?** werden Sie schon bedient?; **that's being attended to** das wird (bereits) erledigt

attendance [ə'tendəns] N a **to be in ~ at sth** bei etw anwesend sein; **to be in ~ on sb** jdm aufwarten, jdn bedienen; **she entered with her maids in ~** sie kam von ihren Hofdamen begleitet herein; **the police are in ~** (*form*) die Polizei ist vor Ort (*form*) b (= *being present*) Anwesenheit *f* (at bei); **regular ~ at school** regelmäßiger Schulbesuch c (= *number of people present*) Teilnehmerzahl *f*; **record ~** eine Rekordteilnehmerzahl, Rekordteilnehmerzahlen *pl*

attendance: attendance allowance N (*Brit*) Pflegegeld *nt*; **attendance centre** N (*Brit*)

Heim *nt* für jugendliche Straftäter; **attendance officer** N (*Brit*) *Beamter, der sich um Fälle häufigen unentschuldigten Fehlens in der Schule kümmert*; **attendance record** N (= *school register etc*) Anwesenheitsliste *f*; **he doesn't have a very good ~** er fehlt oft

attendant [ə'tendənt] N (*in retinue*) Begleiter(in) *m(f)*; (*in public toilets*) Toilettenwart *m*, Toilettenfrau *f*; (*in swimming baths*) Bademeister(in) *m(f)*; (*in art galleries, museums*) Aufseher(in) *m(f)*, Wärter(in) *m(f)*; (= *medical attendant*) Krankenpfleger(in) *m(f)*; (*of royalty*) Kammerherr *m*/-frau *f*; **her ~s** ihr Gefolge *nt* ADJ a *problems etc* (da)zugehörig, damit verbunden; **~ circumstances** Begleitumstände *pl*; **old age and its ~ ills** Alter und die damit verbundenen Beschwerden; **to be ~ (up)on sth** mit etw zusammenhängen, etw begleiten b (*form*: = *serving*) **to be ~ on sb** (*lady-in-waiting etc*) jdm aufwarten; **there were two ~ nurses** es waren zwei Krankenschwestern anwesend

attendee [ˌæten'diː] N (*esp US*) Teilnehmer(in) *m(f)*

attention [ə'tenʃən] ✪ 13, 20.6, 26 N a *no pl* (= *consideration, observation, notice*) Aufmerksamkeit *f*; **to call ~ to sth** (*acc*) aufmerksam machen; **to call *or* draw sb's ~ to sth, to call *or* draw sth to sb's ~** jds Aufmerksamkeit auf etw (*acc*) lenken, jdn auf etw (*acc*) aufmerksam machen; **to attract sb's ~** jds Aufmerksamkeit erregen, jdn auf sich (*acc*) aufmerksam machen; **to turn one's ~ to sb/sth** jdm/einer Sache seine Aufmerksamkeit zuwenden, seine Aufmerksamkeit auf jdn/etw richten; **to pay ~/no ~ to sb/sth** jdn/etw beachten/nicht beachten; **to pay ~ to the teacher** dem Lehrer zuhören; **to hold sb's ~** jdn fesseln; **can I have your ~ for a moment?** dürfte ich Sie einen Augenblick um (Ihre) Aufmerksamkeit bitten?; **~!** Achtung!; **your ~, please** ich bitte um Aufmerksamkeit; (*official announcement*) Achtung, Achtung!; **it has come to my ~ that ...** ich bin darauf aufmerksam geworden, dass ...; **it has been brought to my ~ that ...** es ist mir zu Ohren gekommen, dass ... b (*Comm*) **~ Miss Smith, for the ~ of Miss Smith** zu Händen von Frau Smith; **your letter will receive our earliest ~** Ihr Brief wird baldmöglichst *or* umgehend bearbeitet; **for your ~** zur gefälligen Beachtung c (*Mil*) **to stand to *or* at ~, to come to ~** stillstehen; **~!** stillgestanden! d **attentions** PL (= *kindnesses*) Aufmerksamkeiten *pl*; **to pay one's ~s to sb** (*dated*: = *court*) jdm den Hof machen

Attention Deficit Disorder N (*Med*) Aufmerksamkeits-Defizit-Störung *f*

attention-seeking [ə'tenʃənsiːkɪŋ] N Beachtungsbedürfnis *nt* ADJ **to show ~ behaviour** (*Brit*) *or* **behavior** (*US*) beachtet werden wollen

attention span N Konzentrationsvermögen *nt*; **to have a very short ~** sich nur sehr kurz konzentrieren können

attentive [ə'tentɪv] ADJ aufmerksam; **to be ~ to sb** sich jdm gegenüber aufmerksam verhalten; **to be ~ to sth** einer Sache (*dat*) Beachtung schenken; **to be ~ to sb's needs** sich um jds Bedürfnisse kümmern

attentively [ə'tentɪvlɪ] ADV aufmerksam

attentiveness [ə'tentɪvnɪs] N Aufmerksamkeit *f*

attenuate [ə'tenjʊeɪt] VT (= *weaken*) abschwächen; *statement also* abmildern; *gas* verdünnen; (= *make thinner*) dünn machen; **attenuating circumstances** mildernde Umstände VI (= *get weaker*) schwächer *or* abgeschwächt werden; (*gas*) sich verdünnen; (= *get thinner*) dünner werden ADJ (*Bot*) **~ leaf** lanzettförmiges Blatt

attenuation [əˌtenjʊ'eɪʃən] N (= *weakening*) Abschwächen *nt*, Abschwächung *f*; (*of statement also*) Abmildern, Abmilderung *f*; (= *making thinner*) Verdünnung *f*

attest [ə'test] VT a (= *certify, testify to*) *sb's innocence, authenticity* bestätigen, bescheinigen; *sig-*

nature beglaubigen; (*on oath*) beschwören; **~ed herd** (*Brit*) tuberkulosefreier Bestand **b** (= *be proof of*) beweisen, bezeugen

▶ **attest to** VI *+prep obj* bezeugen

attestation [ˌætesˈteɪʃən] N **a** (= *certifying*) Bestätigung *f*; (*of signature*) Beglaubigung *f*; (= *document*) Bescheinigung *f* **b** (= *proof: of ability etc*) Beweis *m*

attestor [əˈtestə] N Beglaubiger *m*

Attic [ˈætɪk] ADJ attisch

attic [ˈætɪk] N Dachboden *m*, Speicher *m*; (*lived-in*) Mansarde *f*; **~ room** Dachkammer *f*, Mansarden- or Dachzimmer *nt*; **in the ~** auf dem (Dach)boden *or* Speicher

Attica [ˈætɪkə] N Attika *nt*

Attila [ˈætɪlə] N Attila *m*; **~ the Hun** Attila, der Hunnenkönig

attire [əˈtaɪə] VT kleiden (*in* in +*acc*) N *no pl* Kleidung *f*; **ceremonial ~** Festtracht *f*, volles Ornat

attitude [ˈætɪtjuːd] ✪ 6.1 N **a** (= *way of thinking*) Einstellung *f* (*to, towards* zu); (= *way of acting, manner*) Haltung *f* (*to, towards* gegenüber); **~ of mind** Geisteshaltung *f*; **I don't like your ~** ich bin mit dieser Einstellung überhaupt nicht einverstanden; (= *manner*) ich bin mit Ihrem Benehmen überhaupt nicht einverstanden; **well, if that's your ~ ...** ja, wenn du SO denkst ...; **women with ~** kämpferische Frauen **b** (= *way of standing*) Haltung *f*; **to strike a defensive ~** in Verteidigungsstellung gehen **c** (*in ballet*) Attitüde *f* **d** (*Aviat, Space*) Lage *f*

attitudinal [ˌætɪˈtjuːdɪnəl] ADJ (*form*) die Einstellung betreffend *attr*; **~ change/difference** veränderte/unterschiedliche Einstellung; **social and ~ changes** Veränderungen in Gesellschaft und Einstellung

attitudinize [ˌætɪˈtjuːdɪnaɪz] VI so tun, als ob, posieren (*geh*)

attn *abbr of* **attention** z. Hd(n) von

attorney [əˈtɜːnɪ] N **a** (*Comm, Jur.* = *representative*) Bevollmächtigte(r) *mf*, Stellvertreter(in) *m(f)*; **letter of ~** (schriftliche) Vollmacht → **power b** (*US*: = *lawyer*) (Rechts)anwalt *m*/-anwältin *f*

Attorney General N *pl* **Attorneys General** *or* **Attorney Generals** (*US*: = *public prosecutor*) (*of state government*) ≈ Generalstaatsanwalt *m*/-anwältin *f*; (*of federal government*) ≈ Generalbundesanwalt *m*/-anwältin *f*; (*Brit*) ≈ Justizminister(in) *m(f)*

attract [əˈtrækt] VT **a** (*Phys, magnet etc*) anziehen **b** (*fig*: = *appeal to*) (*person*) anziehen; (*idea, music, place etc*) ansprechen; **she feels ~ed to him** sie fühlt sich von ihm angezogen *or* zu ihm hingezogen; **she feels ~ed to the idea** die Idee reizt sie; **I am not ~ed to her/by it** sie/es reizt mich nicht **c** (*fig*: = *win, gain*) *interest, attention etc* auf sich (*acc*) ziehen *or* lenken; *new members, investors etc* anziehen, anlocken; **to ~ publicity/notoriety** (öffentliches) Aufsehen erregen

attraction [əˈtrækʃən] N **a** (*Phys, fig*) Anziehungskraft *f*; (*esp of big city etc*) Reiz *m*; **to lose one's/its ~ toward(s) him** ich fühle mich noch immer von ihm angezogen; **to have an ~ for sb** Anziehungskraft *or* einen Reiz auf jdn ausüben; **what are the ~s of this subject?** was ist an diesem Fach reizvoll? **b** (= *attractive thing*) Attraktion *f*

attractive [əˈtræktɪv] ADJ **a** attraktiv; *personality, smile* anziehend; *house, view, furnishings, picture, dress, location* reizvoll; *story, music* nett, ansprechend; *price, idea, offer* reizvoll, verlockend **b** (*Phys*) Anziehungs-; **~ force** Anziehungskraft *f*

attractively [əˈtræktɪvlɪ] ADV attraktiv; *smile* anziehend; *dress, furnish, paint* reizvoll; **~ priced** zum attraktiven *or* verlockenden Preis (*at von*)

attractiveness [əˈtræktɪvnɪs] N Attraktivität *f*; (*of house, furnishing, view etc*) Reiz *m*; **the ~ of her appearance** ihr reizvolles *or* ansprechendes

or anziehendes Äußeres; **the ~ of the melody** die ansprechende Melodie

attributable [əˈtrɪbjʊtəbl] ADJ **to be ~ to sb/sth** jdm/einer Sache zuzuschreiben sein

attribute [əˈtrɪbjuːt] ✪ 17.2 VT **to ~ sth to sb** (*play, remark etc*) jdm etw zuschreiben; (= *credit sb with sth*) *intelligence, feelings etc also* jdm etw beimessen; **to ~ sth to sth** (*success, accident, problem, deaths etc*) etw auf etw (*acc*) zurückführen; (= *attach*) *importance etc* einer Sache (*dat*) etw beimessen N [ˈætrɪbjuːt] Attribut *nt*; (= *quality also*) Merkmal *nt*

attribution [ˌætrɪˈbjuːʃən] N **a** *no pl* **the ~ of this play to Shakespeare** (die Tatsache,) dass man Shakespeare dieses Schauspiel zuschreibt; **the ~ of the accident to mechanical failure** (die Tatsache,) dass man den Unfall auf mechanisches Versagen zurückführt **b** (= *attribute*) Attribut *nt*, Eigenschaft *f*

attributive [əˈtrɪbjʊtɪv] (*Gram*) ADJ attributiv N Attributiv *nt*

attributively [əˈtrɪbjʊtɪvlɪ] ADV attributiv

attrition [əˈtrɪʃən] N (*lit, form*) Abrieb *m*, Zerreibung *f*; (*fig*) Zermürbung *f*; (*Rel*) unvollkommene Reue, Attrition *f* (*spec*); **war of ~** (*Mil*) Zermürbungskrieg *m*

attune [əˈtjuːn] VT (*fig*) abstimmen (*to* auf +*acc*); **to ~ oneself to sth** sich auf etw (*acc*) einstellen; **to become ~d to sth** sich an etw (*acc*) gewöhnen; **the two of them are well ~d to each other** die beiden sind gut aufeinander eingespielt

atwitter [əˈtwɪtə] ADJ *pred* (*fig*) in heller Aufregung

atypical [eɪˈtɪpɪkəl] ADJ atypisch

atypically [eɪˈtɪpɪkəlɪ] ADV ungewöhnlich; **~, she is very young for this** atypischerweise *or* ungewöhnlicherweise ist sie sehr jung dafür

aubergine [ˈəʊbəʒiːn] N Aubergine *f*; (= *colour*) Aubergine *nt* ADJ aubergine(farben)

auburn [ˈɔːbən] ADJ *hair* rotbraun, rostrot

auction [ˈɔːkʃən] N Auktion *f*, Versteigerung *f*; **to sell sth by ~** etw versteigern; **to put sth up for ~** etw zum Versteigern *or* zur Versteigerung anbieten VT (*also* **auction off**) versteigern

auction bridge N (*Cards*) Auktionsbridge *nt*

auctioneer [ˌɔːkʃəˈnɪə] N Auktionator(in) *m(f)*

auction: auction house N Auktionshaus *nt*; **auction room** N Auktionshalle *f*, Auktionssaal *m*; **auction rooms** PL Auktionshalle *f*; **auction sale** N Auktion *f*, Versteigerung *f*

audacious ADJ , **audaciously** ADV [ɔːˈdeɪʃəs, -lɪ] **a** (= *impudent*) dreist, unverfroren **b** (= *bold*) kühn, wagemutig, verwegen

audacity [ɔːˈdæsɪtɪ], **audaciousness** [ɔːˈdeɪʃəsnɪs] N **a** (= *impudence*) Dreistigkeit *f*, Unverfrorenheit *f*; **to have the ~ to do sth** die Dreistigkeit *or* Unverfrorenheit besitzen, etw zu tun **b** (= *boldness*) Kühnheit, Verwegenheit *f*

audibility [ˌɔːdɪˈbɪlɪtɪ] N Hörbarkeit *f*, Vernehmbarkeit *f*

audible [ˈɔːdɪbl] ADJ hörbar, (deutlich) vernehmbar; **she was hardly ~** man konnte sie kaum hören

audibly [ˈɔːdɪblɪ] ADV hörbar, vernehmlich

audience [ˈɔːdɪəns] N **a** Publikum *nt no pl*; (*Theat, TV*) Zuschauer *pl*, Publikum *nt no pl*; (*of speaker*) Zuhörer *pl*, Publikum *nt no pl*; (*of writer, book*) Leserkreis *m*, Leserschaft *f*; (*Rad*) Zuhörerschaft *f*; **to have a large ~** ein großes Publikum haben *or* ansprechen (*also Rad, TV etc*); **to have ~ appeal** publikumswirksam sein; **I prefer London ~s** ich ziehe das Publikum in London vor **b** (= *formal interview*) Audienz *f* (*with* bei)

audio [ˈɔːdɪəʊ] *in cpds* Audio-; **audio book** N Hörbuch *nt*; **audio cassette** N Kassette *f*, Audiokassette *f*; **audio equipment** N (*in recording studio*) Tonaufzeichnungsgeräte *pl*, Audiogeräte *pl*; (= *hi-fi*) Stereoanlage *f*; **audio frequency** N Hörfrequenz *f*

audiometer [ˌɔːdɪˈɒmɪtə] N Audiometer *nt*, Gehörmesser *m*

audio: audio pollution N Lärmbelästigung *f*; **audio response** N (*Comput*) Sprachausgabe *f*; **audio typist** N Phonotypistin *f*; **audiovisual** ADJ audiovisuell

audit [ˈɔːdɪt] N Bücherrevision *f*, Buchprüfung *f* VT **a** *accounts, company* prüfen **b** (*US Univ*) belegen, ohne einen Schein zu machen, Gasthörer sein bei

audition [ɔːˈdɪʃən] N (*Theat*) Vorsprechprobe *f*; (*of musician*) Probespiel *nt*; (*of singer*) Vorsingen *nt*; **she was asked for ~** sie wurde zum Vorsprechen/Probespiel/Vorsingen eingeladen VT vorsprechen/vorspielen/vorsingen lassen VI vorsprechen/vorspielen/vorsingen

auditor [ˈɔːdɪtə] N **a** (*Comm*) Rechnungsprüfer(in) *m(f)*, Buchprüfer(in) *m(f)* **b** (*US Univ*) Gasthörer(in) *m(f)* **c** (= *listener*) Zuhörer(in) *m(f)*

auditorium [ˌɔːdɪˈtɔːrɪəm] N Auditorium *nt*; (*in theatre, cinema also*) Zuschauerraum *m*; (*in concert hall also*) Zuhörersaal *m*

auditory [ˈɔːdɪtərɪ] ADJ Hör-; **~ ability** Hörfähigkeit *f*; **~ nerve** Gehörnerv *m*

au fait [əʊˈfeɪ] ADJ vertraut; **to be ~ with sth** mit etw vertraut sein

Aug *abbr of* **August** Aug

Augean stables [ɔːˈdʒiːənˈsteɪblz] PL Augiasstall *m*; **to clean out the ~** (*Myth, fig*) den Augiasstall ausmisten

auger [ˈɔːgə] N Stangenbohrer *m*; (*Agr*) Schnecke *f*

aught [ɔːt] N (*old, liter*) irgendetwas; **he might have moved for ~ I know** was weiß ich, vielleicht ist er umgezogen

augment [ɔːgˈment] VT vermehren; *income also* vergrößern VI zunehmen; (*income etc also*) sich vergrößern

augmentation [ˌɔːgmənˈteɪʃən] N Vermehrung *f*; (*of income also*) Vergrößerung *f*; (*in numbers*) Zunahme *f*; (*Mus*) Augmentation *f*; **breast ~** Brustvergrößerung *f*

augmented [ɔːgˈmentɪd] ADJ (*Mus*) *fourth, fifth* übermäßig

au gratin [ˌəʊˈgrætæŋ] ADV überbacken, au gratin; **cauliflower ~** überbackener Blumenkohl, Blumenkohl *m* au gratin

augur [ˈɔːgə] VI **to ~ well/ill** etwas Gutes/nichts Gutes verheißen VT verheißen N (= *person*) Augur *m*

augury [ˈɔːgjʊrɪ] N (= *sign*) Anzeichen *nt*, Omen *nt*

August [ˈɔːgəst] N August *m* → *also* **September**

august [ɔːˈgʌst] ADJ illuster; *occasion, spectacle* erhaben

Augustan [ɔːˈgʌstən] ADJ augusteisch; **~ age** (*Hist, Art*) augusteisches Zeitalter *nt*; (*fig*) Blütezeit *f* (*einer nationalen Literatur*)

Augustine [ɔːˈgʌstɪn] N Augustinus *m*

Augustinian [ˌɔːgəsˈtɪnɪən] ADJ Augustiner-; **~ monk** Augustinermönch *m* N Augustiner *m*

auk [ɔːk] N (*Zool*) Alk *m*

auld [ɔːld] ADJ (+*er*) (*Scot*) alt; **Auld Lang Syne** (*song*) Nehmt Abschied, Brüder; **for ~ lang syne** um der alten Zeiten willen

aunt [ɑːnt] N Tante *f*

auntie, aunty [ˈɑːntɪ] N (*esp Brit inf*) Tante *f*; **~!** Tantchen!; **Auntie** (*Brit, hum*) die BBC (*britische Rundfunk- und Fernsehanstalt*)

Aunt Sally [ˌɑːntˈsælɪ] N (*Brit, WWWW, lit*) Schießbudenfigur *f*; (= *stall*) Schieß- *or* Wurfbude *f*; (*fig*) Zielscheibe *f*

au pair [ˌəʊˈpeə] N *pl* **-s** (*also* **au pair girl**) Aupair(mädchen *nt*) *nt* ADV au pair

aura [ˈɔːrə] N Aura *f* (*geh*), Fluidum *nt* (*geh*); **he has an ~ of saintliness about him** ihn umgibt eine Aura der Heiligkeit (*geh*), er steht im Nimbus der Heiligkeit; **she has an ~ of mystery about her** eine geheimnisvolle Aura (*geh*) *or* ein geheimnisvoller Nimbus umgibt sie; **an ~**

of sophistication ein Flair *nt* von Kultiviertheit; **he has an ~ of calm** er strömt *or* strahlt Ruhe aus; **it gives the hotel an ~ of respectability** es verleiht dem Hotel einen Anstrich von Seriosität

aural ['ɔːrəl] ADJ Gehör-, aural (*spec*); **~ sense** Gehörsinn *m*; **~ examination** Hörtest *m*

aureole ['ɔːrɪəʊl] N (*Astron*) Korona *f*; (*because of haze*) Hof *m*, Aureole *f*; (*Art*) Aureole *f*

auricle ['ɔːrɪkl] N (*Anat*) Ohrmuschel *f*, Auricula *f* (*spec*); (*of heart*) Vorhof *m*, Atrium *nt* (*spec*)

auricular [ɔːˈrɪkjʊlə'] ADJ (*Anat*) **a** (*of ear*) aurikular (*spec*), Ohren-, Hör-; **~ nerve** Hörnerv *m*; **~ confession** Ohrenbeichte *f*, geheime Beichte **b** (*of heart*) aurikular (*spec*), Aurikular- (*spec*); **~ flutter** (Herz)vorhofflattern *nt*

aurochs ['ɔːrɒks] N Auerochse *m*, Ur *m*

aurora australis [ɔːˌrɔːrəʊsˈtreɪlɪs] N (*Astron*) südliches Polarlicht, Südlicht *nt*

aurora borealis [ɔːˌrɔːrəbɔːˈreɪlɪs] N (*Astron*) nördliches Polarlicht, Nordlicht *nt*

auscultate ['ɔːskəlteɪt] VT abhören, auskultieren (*spec*)

auscultation [ˌɔːskəlˈteɪʃən] N Abhören *nt*

auspices ['ɔːspɪsɪz] PL **a** (= *sponsorship*) Schirmherrschaft *f*; **under the ~ of** unter der Schirmherrschaft (+*gen*), unter den Auspizien (+*gen*) (*geh*) **b** (= *auguries*) Vorzeichen *pl*, Auspizien *pl* (*geh*); **under favourable** (*Brit*) *or* **favorable** (*US*) **~** unter günstigen Vorzeichen *or* Auspizien (*geh*)

auspicious [ɔːsˈpɪʃəs] ADJ günstig; *start* viel verheißend, viel versprechend; **an ~ occasion** ein feierlicher Anlass

auspiciously [ɔːsˈpɪʃəslɪ] ADV verheißungsvoll, viel versprechend

Aussie ['ɒzɪ] (*inf*) **N a** (= *person*) Australier(in) *m(f)* **b** (*Austral*, = *country*) Australien *nt*; (= *dialect*) australisches Englisch **ADJ** australisch

austere [ɒsˈtɪə'] ADJ streng; *way of life also* asketisch, entsagend; *style also* schmucklos; *room* schmucklos, karg

austerely [ɒsˈtɪəlɪ] ADV streng; *furnish* karg, schmucklos; *live* asketisch, entsagend

austerity [ɒsˈterɪtɪ] N **a** (= *severity*) Strenge *f*; (= *simplicity*) strenge Einfachheit, Schmucklosigkeit *f*; (*of landscape*) Härte *f* **b** (= *hardship, shortage*) Entbehrung *f*; **after the ~ of the war years** nach den Entbehrungen der Kriegsjahre; **a life of ~** ein Leben der Entsagung; **~ budget** Sparhaushalt *m*; **~ measures** Sparmaßnahmen *pl*

Australasia [ˌɔːstrəˈleɪsjə] N Australien und Ozeanien *nt*

Australasian [ˌɔːstrəˈleɪsjən] **N** Ozeanier(in) *m(f)* **ADJ** ozeanisch, südwestpazifisch

Australia [ɒsˈtreɪlɪə] N Australien *nt*

Australian [ɒsˈtreɪlɪən] **N** Australier(in) *m(f)*; (= *accent*) australisches Englisch **ADJ** australisch

Austria ['ɒstrɪə] N Österreich *nt*

Austria-Hungary ['ɒstrɪə'hʌŋgərɪ] N Österreich-Ungarn *nt*

Austrian ['ɒstrɪən] **N** Österreicher(in) *m(f)*; (= *dialect*) Österreichisch *nt* **ADJ** österreichisch

Austro- ['ɒstrəʊ-] PREF österreichisch-; **~Hungarian** österreichisch-ungarisch

aut *abbr of* **automatic**

autarchy ['ɔːtɑːkɪ] N **a** Selbstregierung *f* **b** = **autarky**

autarky ['ɔːtɑːkɪ] N Autarkie *f*

authentic [ɔːˈθentɪk] ADJ *signature, manuscript* authentisch; *accent, antique, tears* echt; *claim to title etc* berechtigt

authentically [ɔːˈθentɪkəlɪ] ADV echt; *restored* authentisch

authenticate [ɔːˈθentɪkeɪt] VT bestätigen, authentifizieren (*geh*); *signature, document* beglaubigen; *manuscript, work of art* für echt befinden *or* erklären; *claim* bestätigen; **it was ~d as being ...** es wurde bestätigt, dass es ... war

authentication [ɔːˌθentɪˈkeɪʃən] N Bestätigung *f*, Authentifizierung *f* (*geh*); (*of signature, document*) Beglaubigung *f*; (*of manuscript, work of art*) Echtheitserklärung *f*

authenticity [ˌɔːθenˈtɪsɪtɪ] N Echtheit *f*, Authentizität *f* (*geh*); (*of claim to title etc*) Berechtigung *f*

author ['ɔːθə'] N (*profession*) Autor(in) *m(f)*, Schriftsteller(in) *m(f)*; (*of report, pamphlet*) Verfasser(in) *m(f)*; (*fig*) Urheber(in) *m(f)*; (*of plan*) Initiator(in) *m(f)*; **the ~ of the book** der Autor/die Autorin des Buches; **~'s copy** Autorenexemplar *nt*

authoress ['ɔːθərɪs] N Schriftstellerin *f*

authorial [ɔːˈθɔːrɪəl] ADJ (*liter*) eines/des Autors

authoritarian [ɔːˌθɒrɪˈtɛərɪən] **ADJ** autoritär **N** autoritärer Mensch/Vater/Politiker *etc*; **to be an ~** autoritär sein

authoritarianism [ɔːˌθɒrɪˈtɛərɪənɪzəm] N Autoritarismus *m*

authoritative [ɔːˈθɒrɪtətɪv] ADJ **a** (= *commanding*) bestimmt, entschieden; *manner* respekteinflößend; **to sound ~** Respekt einflößen, bestimmt auftreten **b** (= *reliable*) verlässlich, zuverlässig; (= *definitive*) maßgeblich, maßgebend; **I won't accept his opinion as ~** seine Meinung ist für mich nicht maßgeblich *or* maßgebend

authoritatively [ɔːˈθɒrɪtətɪvlɪ] ADV (= *with authority*) bestimmt, mit Autorität; (= *definitively*) maßgeblich *or* maßgebend; (= *reliably*) zuverlässig

authority [ɔːˈθɒrɪtɪ] N **a** (= *power*) Autorität *f*; (= *right, entitlement*) Befugnis *f*; (= *specifically delegated power*) Vollmacht *f*; (*Mil*) Befehlsgewalt *f*; **people who are in ~** Menschen, die Autorität haben; **the person in ~** der Zuständige *or* Verantwortliche; **who's in ~ here?** wer ist hier der Verantwortliche?; **I'm in ~ here!** hier bestimme ich!; **parental ~** Autorität der Eltern; (*Jur*) elterliche Gewalt; **to be in** *or* **have ~ over sb** Weisungsbefugnis gegenüber jdm haben (*form*); (*describing hierarchy*) jdm übergeordnet sein; **to put sb in ~ over sb** jdm die Verantwortung für jdn übertragen; **those who are put in ~ over us** diejenigen, deren Aufsicht wir unterstehen; **the Queen and those in ~ under her** die Königin und die ihr untergebenen Verantwortlichen; **to be under the ~ of sb** unter jds Aufsicht (*dat*) stehen; (*in hierarchy*) jdm unterstehen; (*Mil*) jds Befehlsgewalt (*dat*) unterstehen; **on one's own ~** auf eigene Verantwortung; **you'll have to ask a teacher for the ~** to take the key du brauchst die Erlaubnis *or* Genehmigung des Lehrers, wenn du den Schlüssel haben willst; **under** *or* **by what ~ do you claim the right to ...?** mit welcher Berechtigung verlangen Sie, dass ...?; **to have the ~ to do sth** berechtigt *or* befugt sein, etw zu tun; **to have no ~ to do sth** nicht befugt *or* berechtigt sein, etw zu tun; **he was exceeding his area of ~** er hat seinen Kompetenzbereich *or* seine Befugnisse überschritten; **to give sb the ~ to do sth** jdn ermächtigen (*form*) *or* jdm die Vollmacht erteilen, etw zu tun; **he had my ~ to do it** ich habe es ihm gestattet *or* erlaubt; **to have full ~ to act** volle Handlungsvollmacht haben; **to do sth on sb's ~** etw in jds Auftrag (*dat*) tun; **who gave you the ~ to do that?** wer hat Sie dazu berechtigt?; **who gave you the ~ to treat people like that?** mit welchem Recht glaubst du, Leute so behandeln zu können? **b** (*also pl*: = *ruling body*) Behörde *f*, Amt *nt*; (= *body of people*) Verwaltung *f*; (= *power of ruler*) (Staats)gewalt *f*, Obrigkeit *f*; **the university authorities** die Universitätsverwaltung; **the water ~** die Wasserbehörde; **the local ~** *or* **authorities** die Gemeindeverwaltung; **the Prussian respect for ~** das preußische Obrigkeitsdenken; **the concept of ~ in a state** der Autoritätsgedanke im Staat; **they appealed to the supreme ~ of the House of Lords** sie wandten sich an die höchste Autorität *or* Instanz, das Oberhaus; **this will have to be decided by a higher ~** das muss an höherer Stelle entschieden werden; **to represent ~** die Staatsgewalt verkör-

pern; **the father represents ~** der Vater verkörpert die Autorität; **you must have respect for ~** du musst Achtung gegenüber Respektspersonen haben

c (= *weight, influence*) Autorität *f*; **to have** *or* **carry (great) ~** viel gelten (*with bei*); (*person also*) (große *or* viel) Autorität haben (*with bei*); **to speak/write with ~** mit Sachkunde *or* mit der Autorität des Sachkundigen sprechen/schreiben; **I/he can speak with ~ on this matter** darüber kann ich mich/kann er sich kompetent äußern; **to give an order with ~** einen Befehl mit der nötigen Autorität geben; **to appeal to the ~ of precedent** auf einen Präzedenzfall zurückgreifen

d (= *expert*) Autorität *f*, Fachmann *m*/-frau *f*; **I'm no ~ but ...** ich bin kein Fachmann/keine Fachfrau, aber ...; **he is an ~ on art** er ist eine Autorität *or* ein Fachmann auf dem Gebiet der Kunst

e (= *definitive book etc*) (anerkannte) Autorität *f*; (= *source*) Quelle *f*; **to have sth on good ~** etw aus zuverlässiger Quelle wissen; **on the best ~** aus bester Quelle; **on whose ~ do you have that?** aus welcher Quelle haben Sie das?

authorization [ˌɔːθəraɪˈzeɪʃən] ⊙ 9.3 N Genehmigung *f*; (= *delegation of authority*) Bevollmächtigung *f*, Autorisation *f* (*geh*); (= *right*) Recht *nt*

authorize ['ɔːθəraɪz] ⊙ 9.4, 9.5 VT **a** (= *empower*) berechtigen, ermächtigen, autorisieren (*geh*); (= *delegate authority*) bevollmächtigen; **to be ~d to do sth** (= *have right*) berechtigt sein *or* das Recht haben, etw zu tun; **he was fully ~d to do it** er war voll und ganz befugt, das zu tun; **this licence** (*Brit*) *or* **license** (*US*) **~s you to drive ...** dieser Führerschein berechtigt Sie zum Fahren von ... **b** (= *permit*) genehmigen; *money, claim etc* genehmigen, bewilligen; *translation, biography etc* autorisieren

authorized ['ɔːθəraɪzd] ADJ *overdraft* bewilligt; *person, representative, bank* autorisiert, bevollmächtigt; *biography* autorisiert; **"authorized personnel only"** „Zutritt nur für Befugte"; **duly ~** (*Jur, Fin*) ordnungsgemäß bevollmächtigt; **~ dealer** Vertragshändler(in) *m(f)*; **~ signatory** Zeichnungsberechtigte(r) *mf*; **~ signature** Unterschrift *f* eines bevollmächtigten Vertreters

authorized capital N autorisiertes Kapital

Authorized Version N *die englische Bibelfassung von 1611*

authorship ['ɔːθəʃɪp] N **a** Autorschaft *f*, Verfasserschaft *f*; **of unknown ~** eines unbekannten Autors *or* Verfassers; **he claimed/denied ~ of the article** er bekannte/bestritt, den Artikel verfasst *or* geschrieben zu haben; **there are disagreements as to the ~ of the play** der Autor des Stückes ist umstritten **b** (= *occupation*) Schriftstellerberuf *m*

autism ['ɔːtɪzəm] N Autismus *m*

autist ['ɔːtɪst] N Autist(in) *m(f)*

autistic [ɔːˈtɪstɪk] ADJ autistisch

auto ['ɔːtəʊ] N (*US*) Auto *nt*, PKW *m*, Pkw *m*

auto- ['ɔːtəʊ-] PREF auto-, Auto-

autobank ['ɔːtəʊbæŋk] N Geldautomat *m*

autobiographer [ˌɔːtəʊbaɪˈɒgrəfə'] N Autobiograf(in) *m(f)*

autobiographical [ˌɔːtəʊbaɪəʊˈgræfɪkəl] ADJ autobiografisch

autobiography [ˌɔːtəʊbaɪˈɒgrəfɪ] N Autobiografie *f*

autocade ['ɔːtəʊkeɪd] N (*US*) Wagenkolonne *f* *or* -konvoi *m*

autochanger ['ɔːtəʊˌtʃeɪndʒə'] N (automatischer) Plattenwechsler

autocracy [ɔːˈtɒkrəsɪ] N Autokratie *f*

autocrat ['ɔːtəʊkræt] N Autokrat(in) *m(f)*

autocratic [ˌɔːtəʊˈkrætɪk] ADJ autokratisch

autocross ['ɔːtəʊkrɒs] N Autocross *nt*

Autocue® ['ɔːtəʊkjuː] N (*Brit TV*) Teleprompter *m*

auto-da-fé ['ɔːtəʊdɑːˈfeɪ] N *pl* **autos-da-fé** Autodafé *nt*

autodidact [ˈɔːtəʊˌdaɪdækt] N (form) Autodidakt(in) m(f)

autoerotic [ˌɔːtəʊɪˈrɒtɪk] ADJ autoerotisch

autoeroticism [ˌɔːtəʊˈrɒtɪˌsɪzəm] N Autoerotik f

autofocus [ˈɔːtəʊfəʊkəs] N (Phot) Autofokus m

autograph [ˈɔːtəgrɑːf] N (= signature) Autogramm nt; (= manuscript) Originalmanuskript nt VT signieren; **he ~ed my album** er hat mir ein Autogramm fürs Album gegeben

autograph: autograph album N Autogrammalbum nt; **autograph book** N Autogrammbuch nt; **autograph copy** N handgeschriebenes Manuskript

autohyphenation [ˈɔːtəʊˌhaɪfəˈneɪʃən] N (Comput) automatische Silbentrennung

autoimmune [ˌɔːtəʊɪˈmjuːn] ADJ autoimmun; ~ **disease** Autoimmunkrankheit f

autoinfection [ˌɔːtəʊɪnˈfekʃən] N (Med) Autoinfektion f

automat [ˈɔːtəmæt] N (US) Automatenrestaurant nt

automata [ɔːˈtɒmətə] pl of **automaton**

automate [ˈɔːtəmeɪt] VT automatisieren; **~d telling machine** Geldautomat m

automatic [ˌɔːtəˈmætɪk] ADJ (lit, fig) automatisch; **the refund is not ~** Rückerstattung erfolgt nicht automatisch; **he has the ~ right ...** er hat automatisch das Recht ...; **the film star's ~ smile** das Routinelächeln des Filmstars; **you shouldn't need telling, it should be ~** das sollte man dir nicht erst sagen müssen, das solltest du automatisch tun; ~ **camera** Automatikkamera f; ~ **choke** Startautomatik f; ~ **data processing** automatische Datenverarbeitung; ~ **defroster** Abtauautomatik f; ~ **exposure** (Phot) Belichtungsautomatik f; ~ **gearbox** or **transmission** (Aut) Automatikgetriebe nt; **the ~ model** das Modell mit Automatik; ~ **rifle** Schnellfeuergewehr nt; ~ **weapon** automatische Waffe, Schnellfeuerwaffe f N (= car) Automatikwagen m; (= gun) automatische Waffe, Maschinenwaffe f; (= washing machine) Waschautomat m

automatically [ˌɔːtəˈmætɪkəli] ADV automatisch

automatic writing N automatisches Schreiben

automation [ˌɔːtəˈmeɪʃən] N Automatisierung f

automaton [ɔːˈtɒmətən] N pl **-s** or **automata** [-ətə] (= robot) Roboter m; (fig also) Automat m

automobile [ˈɔːtəməbiːl] N Auto(mobil) nt, Kraftwagen m (form)

automotive [ˌɔːtəˈməʊtɪv] ADJ vehicle selbstfahrend, mit Selbstantrieb

automotive engineering N Kfz-Technik f

autonomous [ɔːˈtɒnəməs] ADJ, **autonomously** ADV [ɔːˈtɒnəməs, -lɪ] autonom

autonomy [ɔːˈtɒnəmi] N Autonomie f

autopilot [ˈɔːtəʊˈpaɪlət] N Autopilot m; **on ~** (lit) mit Autopilot; **to switch onto ~** (lit, fig inf) auf Autopilot umschalten; **he was on ~** (fig) er funktionierte wie automatisch or ferngesteuert; **I'm so shattered, I just do everything on ~** ich bin so geschafft, dass ich alles nur noch ganz automatisch mache

autopsy [ˈɔːtɒpsi] N Autopsie f, Leichenöffnung f

autoreverse [ˌɔːtəʊˈvɜːs] N Autoreversefunktion f

autosuggestion [ˌɔːtəʊsəˈdʒestʃən] N Autosuggestion f

autosuggestive [ˌɔːtəʊsəˈdʒestɪv] ADJ autosuggestiv

autotimer [ˈɔːtəʊtaɪmə] N (on cooker etc) Ein-/Abschaltautomatik f

autotrain N (US) Autoreisezug m

autumn [ˈɔːtəm] N (esp Brit) (lit, fig) Herbst m; **in (the) ~** im Herbst; **two ~s ago** im Herbst vor zwei Jahren ADJ attr Herbst-, herbstlich; ~ **leaves** bunte (Herbst)blätter pl

autumnal [ɔːˈtʌmnəl] ADJ herbstlich, Herbst-; ~ **weather** Herbstwetter nt

auxiliary [ɔːgˈzɪliəri] ADJ Hilfs- (also Comput); (= additional) engine, generator etc zusätzlich; ~ **note** (Mus) Nebennote f; ~ **nurse** Schwesternhelferin f; ~ **program** (Comput) Hilfsprogramm nt; ~ **verb** Hilfsverb nt N a (Mil, esp pl) Soldat(in) m(f) der Hilfstruppe; **auxiliaries** pl Hilfstruppe(n) f(pl) b (general: = assistant) Hilfskraft f, Helfer(in) m(f); **teaching ~** (Aus)hilfslehrer(in) m(f); **nursing ~** Schwesternhelferin f c (= auxiliary verb) Hilfsverb or -zeitwort nt

AV abbr of **Authorized Version**

Av abbr of **avenue**

av abbr of **average** Durchschn.

avail[1] abbr of **available**

avail[2] [əˈveɪl] VR **to ~ oneself of sth** von etw Gebrauch machen; **to ~ oneself of the opportunity of doing sth** die Gelegenheit wahrnehmen or nutzen, etw zu tun

VI (form) **nothing could ~ against their superior strength** gegen ihre Überlegenheit war nichts auszurichten

N **of no ~** erfolglos, ohne Erfolg, vergeblich; **of little ~** wenig erfolgreich, mit wenig or geringem Erfolg; **his advice was/his pleas were of no/little ~** seine Ratschläge/Bitten haben nicht(s)/wenig gefruchtet; **to no ~** vergebens, vergeblich; **to little ~** ohne großen Erfolg; **of what ~ is it to ...?** (liter) was nützt es, zu ...?; **and to what ~?** (liter) und zu welchem Behuf? (old form)

availability [əˌveɪləˈbɪlɪti] N (of object) Erhältlichkeit f; (Comm) (from supplier also) Lieferbarkeit f; (of stock) Vorrätigkeit f; (of worker, means, resources) Verfügbarkeit f; **the market price is determined by** der Marktpreis richtet sich nach dem vorhandenen Angebot; **because of the greater ~ of their product ...** weil ihr Produkt leichter erhältlich/lieferbar ist ...; **we'd like to sell you one, but it's a question of ~** wir würden Ihnen gern eines verkaufen, das hängt aber davon ab, ob es erhältlich/lieferbar ist; **offer subject to ~ while stocks last** (das Angebot gilt) nur solange der Vorrat reicht; **greater ~ of jobs** größeres Stellenangebot; **because of the limited ~ of seats** weil nur eine begrenzte Anzahl an Plätzen zur Verfügung steht; **to increase the ~ of culture to the masses** breiteren Bevölkerungsschichten den Zugang zu Kultur erleichtern; **his ~ for discussion is, I'm afraid, determined by ...** ob er Zeit für eine Besprechung hat, hängt leider von ... ab

available [əˈveɪləbl] ✪ 19.3 ADJ a object erhältlich; (Comm) (from supplier) lieferbar, erhältlich; (in stock) vorrätig; (= free) time, post frei; theatre seats etc frei, zu haben pred; (= at one's disposal) worker, means, resources etc verfügbar, zur Verfügung stehend; **to be ~** vorhanden sein; (= at one's disposal) zur Verfügung stehen; (person) (= not otherwise occupied) frei or abkömmlich (form) sein; (= can be reached) erreichbar sein; (for discussion) zu sprechen sein; **to make sth ~ to sb** jdm etw zur Verfügung stellen; (= accessible) culture, knowledge, information jdm etw zugänglich machen; **to make oneself ~ to sb** sich jdm zur Verfügung stellen; **could you make yourself ~ for discussion between 2 and 3?** könnten Sie sich zwischen 2 und 3 für eine Besprechung freihalten or zur Verfügung halten?; **the best dictionary ~, the best ~ dictionary** das beste Wörterbuch, das es gibt; **he caught the next ~ flight home** er nahm den nächsten or nächstmöglichen Flug nach Hause; **to try every ~ means (to achieve sth)** nichts unversucht lassen(, um etw zu erreichen); **reference books/consultants are ~** Nachschlagewerke/Berater stehen einem/Ihnen etc zur Verfügung; **all ~ staff were asked to help out** das abkömmliche or verfügbare or zur Verfügung stehende Personal wurde gebeten auszuhelfen; **are you ~ for tennis/a discussion tonight?** können Sie heute Abend Tennis spielen/an einer Diskussion teilnehmen?;

when will you be ~ to start in the new job? wann können Sie die Stelle antreten?; **I'm not ~ until October** ich bin vor Oktober nicht frei; **a professor should always be ~ to his students** ein Professor sollte stets für seine Studenten da sein or seinen Studenten stets zur Verfügung stehen; **he's ~ for consultation on Mondays** er hat montags Sprechzeit; **you shouldn't make yourself so ~ to him** du solltest es ihm nicht so leicht machen; **she's what is known as "available"** es ist bekannt, dass sie „leicht zu haben" ist b (form) ticket gültig

avalanche [ˈævəlɑːnʃ] N (lit, fig) Lawine f

avant-garde [ˌævɒŋˈgɑːd] N Avantgarde f ADJ avantgardistisch

avarice [ˈævərɪs] N Habgier f, Habsucht f

avaricious [ˌævəˈrɪʃəs] ADJ habgierig, habsüchtig

avariciously [ˌævəˈrɪʃəsli] ADV (hab)gierig

avatar [ˈævətɑː] N (Rel, fig) Inkarnation f

avdp abbr of **avoirdupois**

Ave abbr of **avenue**

Ave (Maria) [ˈɑːveɪ(məˈriə)] N Ave(-Maria) nt

avenge [əˈvendʒ] VT **to ~ oneself on sb (for sth)** sich an jdm (für etw) rächen; **an avenging angel** ein Racheengel m

avenger [əˈvendʒə] N Rächer(in) m(f)

avenue [ˈævənjuː] N a (tree-lined) Allee f; (= broad street) Boulevard m b (fig: = method) Weg m; **~s of approach** Verfahrensweisen; **an ~ of approach to the problem** ein Weg, das Problem anzugehen; **~ of escape** Ausweg m; **to explore every ~** alle sich bietenden Wege prüfen

aver [əˈvɜː] VT (form) mit Nachdruck betonen; love, innocence beteuern

average [ˈævərɪdʒ] N (Durch)schnitt m; (Math also) Mittelwert m; **to do an ~ of 50 miles a day/3% a week** durchschnittlich or im (Durch)schnitt 50 Meilen pro Tag fahren/3% pro Woche erledigen; **what's your ~ over the last six months?** was haben Sie im letzten halben Jahr durchschnittlich geleistet/verdient etc?; **on ~** durchschnittlich, im (Durch)schnitt; (= normally) normalerweise; **if you take the ~** (Math) wenn Sie den (Durch)schnitt or Mittelwert nehmen; (general) wenn Sie den durchschnittlichen Fall nehmen; **above ~** überdurchschnittlich, über dem Durchschnitt; **below ~** unterdurchschnittlich, unter dem Durchschnitt; **the law of ~s** das Gesetz der Serie; **by the law of ~s** aller Wahrscheinlichkeit nach

ADJ durchschnittlich; (= ordinary) Durchschnitts-; (= not good or bad) mittelmäßig; **above/below ~** über-/unterdurchschnittlich; **the ~ man, Mr Average** der Durchschnittsbürger; **the ~ Scot** der Durchschnittsschotte; **he's a man of ~ height** er ist von mittlerer Größe

VT a (= find the average of) den Durchschnitt ermitteln von

b (= do etc on average) auf einen Schnitt von ... kommen; **we ~d 80 km/h** wir kamen auf einen Schnitt von 80 km/h, wir sind durchschnittlich 80 km/h gefahren; **the factory ~s 500 cars a week** die Fabrik produziert durchschnittlich or im (Durch)schnitt 500 Autos pro Woche

c (= average out at) **sales are averaging 10,000 copies per day** der Absatz beläuft sich auf or beträgt durchschnittlich or im (Durch)schnitt 10.000 Exemplare pro Tag

▶ **average out** VT sep **if you average it out** im Durchschnitt; **it'll average itself out** es wird sich ausgleichen VI durchschnittlich ausmachen (at, to +acc); (= balance out) sich ausgleichen; **how does it average out on a weekly basis?** wie viel ist das durchschnittlich or im Schnitt pro Woche?

averagely [ˈævərɪdʒli] ADV durchschnittlich

averment [əˈvɜːmənt] N Beteuerung f

averse [əˈvɜːs] ADJ pred abgeneigt; **I am not ~ to a glass of wine** einem Glas Wein bin ich nicht abgeneigt; **I am rather ~ to doing that** es widerstrebt mir, das zu tun

aversion [ə'vɜ:ʃən] N a (= *strong dislike*) Abneigung f, Aversion f (*geh*, *Psych*) (*to* gegen); **he has an ~ to getting wet** er hat eine Abscheu davor, nass zu werden b (= *object of aversion*) Gräuel m; **smoking is his pet ~** Rauchen ist ihm ein besonderer Gräuel

aversion therapy N (*Psych*) Aversionstherapie f

avert [ə'vɜ:t] VT a (= *turn away*) eyes, gaze abwenden, abkehren (*geh*) b (= *prevent*) verhindern, abwenden; suspicion ablenken; blow etc abwehren; accident verhindern, verhüten

avgas ['ævɡæs] N (*inf*: *Aviat*) Flugbenzin nt

avian influenza ['eɪvɪən,ɪnflʊ'enzə], **avian flu** ['eɪvɪən,flu:] N Geflügel- or Hühnerpest f

aviary ['eɪvɪərɪ] N Vogelhaus nt, Voliere f

aviation [,eɪvɪ'eɪʃən] N die Luftfahrt; **the art of ~** die Kunst des Fliegens

aviator ['eɪvɪeɪtə'] N Flieger(in) m(f)

aviculture ['eɪvɪ,kʌltʃə'] N (*form*) Vogelzucht f

avid ['ævɪd] ADJ a (= *desirous*) gierig (*for* nach); (*esp for fame*, *praise*) süchtig (*for* nach); **~ for fame** ruhmsüchtig b (= *keen*) begeistert, passioniert; interest lebhaft, stark; **he is an ~ follower of this series** er verfolgt diese Serie mit lebhaftem Interesse; **as an ~ reader of your column** als eifriger Leser Ihrer Spalte; **I am an ~ reader** ich lese leidenschaftlich gern

avidity [ə'vɪdɪtɪ] N , no pl (*liter*) a (= *desire*, *eagerness*) Begierde f (*for* nach); (*pej*) Gier f (*for* nach); **with ~** begierig, gierig b (= *keenness*) Begeisterung f; (*of supporter*) Eifer m

avidly ['ævɪdlɪ] ADV a (= *eagerly*) begierig; (*pej*) gierig b (= *keenly*) eifrig; read leidenschaftlich gern

avionics [,eɪvɪ'ɒnɪks] N sing Avionik f

avocado [,ævə'kɑ:dəʊ] N pl -s (also **avocado pear**) Avocado(birne) f; (= *tree*) Avocadobaum m

avocation [,ævəʊ'keɪʃən] N (*form*: = *calling*) Berufung f

avoid [ə'vɔɪd] ⚙ 10.1 VT vermeiden; damage, accident also verhüten; person meiden, aus dem Weg gehen (+*dat*); obstacle ausweichen (+*dat*); difficulty, duty, truth umgehen; **to ~ danger** (*in general*) die Gefahr meiden; (*on a specific occasion*) der Gefahr (*dat*) entgehen; **in order to ~ being seen** um nicht gesehen zu werden; **he'd do anything to ~ washing the dishes** er würde alles tun, um nur nicht abwaschen zu müssen; **I'm not going if I can possibly ~ it** wenn es sich irgendwie vermeiden lässt, gehe ich nicht; **... you can hardly ~ visiting them** ... dann kommst du wohl kaum darum herum or kannst du es wohl schlecht vermeiden, sie zu besuchen; **to ~ sb's eye** jds Blick (*dat*) ausweichen, es vermeiden, jdn anzusehen; **to ~ being noticed** möglichst unbemerkt bleiben

avoidable [ə'vɔɪdəbl] ADJ vermeidbar; **if it's (at all) ~** wenn es sich (irgend) vermeiden lässt

avoidance [ə'vɔɪdəns] N Vermeidung f; **the ~ of inheritance tax** die Umgehung der Erbschaftssteuer; **his careful ~ of the truth** sein ständiges Umgehen der Wahrheit; **thanks only to her steady ~ of bad company** nur weil sie konsequent schlechte Gesellschaft mied

avoirdupois [,ævwɑ:dju:'pwɑ:] N Avoirdupois nt; (*hum*: = *excess weight*) Fülligkeit f, Üppigkeit f; **there's been an increase in her ~** (*hum*) sie ist ziemlich in die Breite gegangen

avow [ə'vaʊ] VT (*liter*) erklären; belief, faith bekennen; **to ~ one's love (to sb)** (jdm) seine Liebe erklären or gestehen, sich (jdm) erklären; **he ~ed himself to be a royalist** er bekannte (offen), Royalist zu sein

avowal [ə'vaʊəl] N Erklärung f; (*of faith*) Bekenntnis nt; (*of love*) Geständnis nt; (*of belief*, *interest*) Bekundung f

avowed [ə'vaʊd] ADJ erklärt

avowedly [ə'vaʊɪdlɪ] ADV erklärtermaßen

avuncular [ə'vʌŋkjʊlə'] ADJ onkelhaft

aw abbr of **atomic weight**

AWACS, Awacs ['eɪwæks] abbr of **airborne warning and control system** AWACS-Flugzeug nt, Awacs-Flugzeug nt, mit Frühwarnsystem ausgestattetes Aufklärungsflugzeug der US-Luftwaffe

await [ə'weɪt] ⚙ 20.5 VT a (= *wait for*) erwarten; future events, decision etc entgegensehen (+*dat*); **the long ~ed day** der lang ersehnte Tag; **parcels ~ing despatch** zum Versand bestimmte Pakete; **we ~ your reply with interest** wir sehen Ihrer Antwort mit Interesse entgegen; **to be ~ing trial** (*case*) zur Verhandlung anstehen; **he is ~ing trial** sein Fall steht noch zur Verhandlung an b (= *be in store for*) erwarten

awake [ə'weɪk] pret **awoke**, ptp **awoken** or **awaked** [ə'weɪkt] VI (*lit*, *fig*) erwachen; **to ~ from sleep/a dream** aus dem Schlaf/einem Traum erwachen; **to ~ to sth** (*fig*, = *realize*) sich (*dat*) einer Sache (*gen*) bewusst werden; (= *become interested*) beginnen, sich für etw zu interessieren; **to ~ to the joys of sth** (plötzlich) Vergnügen an etw (*dat*) finden; **his interest is only beginning to ~** sein Interesse ist erst neu erwacht

VT wecken; (*fig*) suspicion, interest etc also erwecken; **to ~ sb to sth** (= *make realize*) jdm etw bewusst machen; (= *make interested*) jds Interesse für etw wecken

ADJ pred (*lit*, *fig*) wach; (= *alert also*) aufmerksam; **to be/lie/stay ~** wach sein/liegen/bleiben; **to keep sb ~** jdn wach halten; **wide ~** (*lit*, *fig*) hellwach; **to be ~ to sth** (*fig*) sich (*dat*) einer Sache (*gen*) bewusst sein → **half** ADV a

awaken [ə'weɪkən] VTI = **awake**

awakening [ə'weɪknɪŋ] N (*lit*, *fig*) Erwachen nt; **a rude ~** (*lit*, *fig*) ein böses Erwachen ADJ (*fig*) erwachend

award [ə'wɔ:d] VT prize, penalty, free kick etc zusprechen (*to sb* jdm), zuerkennen (*to sb* jdm); (= *present*) prize, degree, medal etc verleihen (*to sb* jdm); **to be ~ed damages** Schadenersatz zugesprochen bekommen; **to ~ sb first prize** jdm den ersten Preis zuerkennen N a (= *prize*) Preis m; (*for bravery etc*) Auszeichnung f; (*Jur*) Zuerkennung f; **to make an ~ (to sb)** einen Preis (an jdn) vergeben b (*Univ*) Stipendium nt

award: award(s) ceremony N (*Film, Theat, TV*) Preisverleihung f; **award-winning** ADJ preisgekrönt

aware [ə'weə'] ADJ esp pred bewusst; **to be/become ~ of sb/sth** sich (*dat*) jds/einer Sache bewusst sein/werden; (= *notice also*) jdn bemerken/etw merken; **I was not ~ (of the fact) that ...** es war mir nicht klar or bewusst, dass ...; **you will be ~ of the importance of this** es muss Ihnen bewusst sein, wie wichtig das ist; **are you ~ that ...?** ist dir eigentlich klar, dass ...?; **not that I am ~ (of)** nicht dass ich wüsste; **as far as I am ~** so viel ich weiß; **we try to make ~ of what is going on in other companies/the world** wir versuchen uns auf dem Laufenden darüber zu halten, was in anderen Firmen/auf der Welt vor sich geht; **to make sb ~ of sth** jdm etw bewusst machen or zum Bewusstsein bringen; **to make sb more ~** jds Bewusstsein wecken; **for a three-year-old he's very ~** für einen Dreijährigen ist er sehr aufgeweckt; **she's very ~ of language** sie ist sehr sprachbewusst

awareness [ə'weənɪs] N Bewusstsein nt; **he showed no ~ of the urgency of the problem** er schien sich der Dringlichkeit des Problems nicht bewusst zu sein; **her tremendous ~ of the shades of meaning in the language/of other people's feelings** ihr außerordentlich waches Gespür für die Bedeutungsnuancen der Sprache/für die Empfindungen anderer; **to increase one's ~ of the outer world** seine Umwelt bewusster wahrnehmen

awash [ə'wɒʃ] ADJ pred decks, rocks etc überspült; cellar unter Wasser; **to be ~ with blood/money** im Blut/Geld schwimmen; **to be ~ with water** unter Wasser stehen; **Rome was ~ with rumours**

(*Brit*) or **rumors** (*US*) in Rom kursierten Tausende or tausende von Gerüchten

away [ə'weɪ] ADV a (= *to or at a distance*) weg; **three miles ~ (from here)** drei Meilen (entfernt) von hier; **lunch seemed a long time ~** es schien noch lange bis zum Mittagessen zu sein; **~ back in the distance/past** weit in der Ferne/vor sehr langer Zeit; **they're ~ behind/out in front/off course** sie sind weit zurück/voraus/ab vom Kurs b (*motion*) **~!** (*old, liter*) fort!, hinweg! (*old, liter*); **~ with the old philosophy, in with the new!** fort mit der alten Philosophie, her mit der neuen!; **come, let us ~!** (*liter*) kommt, lasst uns fort von hier (*old*); **~ with him!** fort mit ihm!; **but he was ~ before I could say a word** aber er war fort or weg, bevor ich den Mund auftun konnte; **to look ~** wegsehen; **~ we go!** los (gehts)!; **they're ~!** (*horses, runners etc*) sie sind gestartet; **they're ~ first time** gleich der erste Start hat geklappt c (= *absent*) fort, weg; **he's ~ from work (with a cold)** er fehlt (wegen einer Erkältung); **he's ~ in London** er ist in London; **when I have to be ~** wenn ich nicht da sein kann d (*Sport*) **to play ~** auswärts spielen; **they're ~ to Arsenal** sie haben ein Auswärtsspiel bei Arsenal e (= *out of existence, possession etc*) **to put/give ~** weglegen/weggeben; **to boil/gamble/die ~** verkochen/verspielen/verhallen; **we talked the evening ~** wir haben den Abend verplaudert f (= *continuously*) unablässig; **to work/knit etc ~** vor sich (*acc*) hin arbeiten/stricken etc g (= *forthwith*) **ask ~!** frag nur!, schieß los (*inf*); **pull/heave ~!** zieh los(, zieht/hebt an)!; **right or straight ~** sofort h (*inf*) **he's ~ again** (*talking, giggling, drunk etc*) es geht wieder los; **he's ~ with the idea that ...** er hat den Fimmel, dass ... (*inf*); **~ with you!** ach wo! ADJ attr (*Sport*) Auswärts-; **~ match** Auswärtsspiel nt; **~ win** Auswärtssieg m; **~ team** Gastmannschaft f N (*in football pools*: = *away win*) Auswärtssieg m

awe [ɔ:] N Ehrfurcht f, ehrfürchtige Scheu; **to be or stand in ~ of sb** Ehrfurcht vor jdm haben; (= *feel fear*) große Furcht vor jdm haben; **to hold sb in ~** Ehrfurcht or großen Respekt vor jdm haben; **to strike sb with ~** jdm Ehrfurcht einflößen; (= *make fearful*) jdm Furcht einflößen; **the sight filled me with (a sense of) ~** der Anblick erfüllte mich mit ehrfurchtsvoller Scheu VT Ehrfurcht or ehrfürchtige Scheu einflößen (+*dat*); **~ed by the beauty/silence** von der Schönheit/der Stille ergriffen; **in an ~d voice** mit ehrfürchtiger Stimme

awe-inspiring ['ɔ:ɪn,spaɪərɪŋ] ADJ Ehrfurcht gebietend

awesome ['ɔ:səm] ADJ (= *frightening*) beängstigend; (= *impressive*) beeindruckend; (*esp US inf*: = *excellent*) irre (*inf*)

awesomely ['ɔ:səmlɪ] ADV (= *frighteningly*) beängstigend; (= *impressively*) unwahrscheinlich, beeindruckend

awe-stricken ['ɔ:,strɪkən], **awe-struck** ['ɔ:,strʌk] ADJ von Ehrfurcht ergriffen; voice, expression also ehrfurchtsvoll; (= *frightened*) von Schrecken ergriffen; **I was quite ~ by its beauty** ich war von seiner Schönheit ergriffen

awful ['ɔ:fəl] ADJ a (*inf*) schrecklich, furchtbar; **how ~!** das ist wirklich schlimm!; **you are ~!** du bist wirklich schrecklich!; **the film was just too ~ for words** der Film war unbeschreiblich schlecht; **an ~ lot of time/money** furchtbar viel Zeit/Geld; **it's not an ~ lot better** das ist nicht arg viel besser b (*old*: = *awe-inspiring*) Ehrfurcht gebietend ADV (*strictly incorrect*) = **awfully** **he was crying something ~** er weinte ganz schrecklich or furchtbar

awfully ['ɔ:flɪ] ADV (*inf*) furchtbar (*inf*), schrecklich (*inf*); **it's not ~ important** es ist nicht so schrecklich or furchtbar wichtig (*inf*); **she is rather ~ ~** (*Brit, hum*) sie ist furchtbar vornehm (*inf*); **thanks ~** (*Brit*) vielen, vielen Dank!; **would**

you mind ~ (waiting for me)? (*Brit*) würde es Ihnen furchtbar viel ausmachen(, auf mich zu warten)? (*inf*)

awfulness ['ɔːfʊlnɪs] N (*of situation*) Schrecklichkeit *f*, Furchtbarkeit *f*; (*of person*) abscheuliche Art, Abscheulichkeit *f*; **we were shocked by the ~ of it all** wir waren von der Schrecklichkeit *or* Furchtbarkeit des Ganzen überwältigt

awhile [ə'waɪl] ADV (*liter*) eine Weile; **not yet ~!** noch eine ganze Weile nicht!

awkward ['ɔːkwəd] ADJ `a` (= *difficult*) schwierig; *time, moment, angle, shape* ungünstig; **4 o'clock is a bit ~ (for me)** 4 Uhr ist ein bisschen ungünstig *or* schlecht (*inf*) (für mich); **to make things ~ for sb** jdm Schwierigkeiten machen; **~ customer** übler Bursche (*inf*)
 `b` (= *embarrassing*) peinlich
 `c` (= *embarrassed*) verlegen; (= *shamefaced*) betreten; *silence* betreten; **I was at an ~ age** ich war in einem schwierigen Alter; **I feel ~ about that** das ist mir unangenehm; **I feel ~ about doing that** es ist mir unangenehm, das zu tun; **to feel ~ in sb's company** sich in jds Gesellschaft (*dat*) nicht wohl fühlen; **I felt ~ when I had to ...** es war mir unangenehm *or* peinlich, als ich ... musste
 `d` (= *clumsy*) *person, movement, style* unbeholfen

awkwardly ['ɔːkwədlɪ] ADV `a` (= *clumsily*) *fall, move, express oneself, translate* ungeschickt; *lie* unbequem; *hang* merkwürdig; **~ placed** an einem ungünstigen Ort; **~ timed** zu einer un-günstigen Zeit `b` (= *embarrassingly*) peinlich `c` (= *embarrassedly*) verlegen; (= *shamefacedly*) betreten `d` (= *clumsily*) unbeholfen

awkwardness ['ɔːkwədnɪs] N `a` (= *difficulty*) Schwierigkeit *f*; (*of time, angle, shape*) Ungünstigkeit *f* `b` (= *discomfort*) Peinlichkeit *f* `c` (= *embarrassment*) Verlegenheit *f*; (= *shamefacedness*) Betretenheit *f* `d` (= *clumsiness*) Unbeholfenheit *f*

awl [ɔːl] N Ahle *f*, Pfriem *m*

awning ['ɔːnɪŋ] N (*on window, of shop*) Markise *f*; (*on boat*) Sonnensegel *nt*; (*of wagon*) Plane *f*; (= *caravan awning*) Vordach *nt*

awoke [ə'wəʊk] *pret of* **awake**

awoken [ə'wəʊkən] *ptp of* **awake**

AWOL ['eɪwɒl] (*Mil*) *abbr of* **absent without leave**

awry [ə'raɪ] ADJ PRED, ADV (= *askew*) schief; **the picture/hat is ~** das Bild hängt/der Hut sitzt schief; **to go ~** (*plans etc*) schief gehen

axe, (*US*) **ax** [æks] **N** Axt *f*, Beil *nt*; (*fig*) (radikale) Kürzung; **to wield the ~ on sth** (*fig*) etw radikal kürzen; **to get** *or* **be given the ~** (*employee*) abgesägt werden; (*project*) eingestellt werden; **the ~ has fallen on the project** das Projekt ist dem Rotstift zum Opfer gefallen; **to have an/no ~ to grind** (*fig*) ein/kein persönliches Interesse haben; **~ murderer** Axtmörder(in) *m(f)* **VT** *plans, projects, jobs* streichen; *person* entlassen

axiom ['æksɪəm] N Axiom *nt*

axiomatic [ˌæksɪəʊ'mætɪk] ADJ axiomatisch; **we can take it as ~ that ...** wir können von dem Grundsatz ausgehen, dass ...

axis ['æksɪs] N *pl* **axes** ['æksiːz] Achse *f*; **the Axis (powers)** (*Hist*) die Achse, die Achsenmächte *pl*

axle ['æksl] N Achse *f*

axle: axle bearing N Achslager *nt*; **axle box** N Achsgehäuse *nt*; **axle grease** N Achs(en)fett *nt*; **axle housing** N Achsgehäuse *nt*; **axle load** N Achslast *f*; **axle pin** N Achs(en)nagel *m*; **axletree** N Achswelle *f*

ayatollah [ˌaɪə'tɒlə] N Ajatollah *m*

ay(e) [aɪ] **INTERJ** (*esp Scot, dial*) ja; **aye, aye, Sir** (*Naut*) jawohl, Herr Kapitänleutnant/Admiral *etc* **N** (*esp Parl*) Jastimme *f*, Ja *nt*; **the ayes** diejenigen, die dafür sind, die dafür; **the ayes have it** die Mehrheit ist dafür

aye [eɪ] ADV (*old, Scot*) immer

azalea [ə'zeɪlɪə] N Azalee *f*

Azerbaijani [ˌæzəbaɪ'dʒɑːnɪ] ADJ aserbaidschanisch **N** Aserbaidschaner(in) *m(f)*

Azeri [ə'zɛərɪ] ADJ, N = **Azerbaijani**

azimuth ['æzɪməθ] N (*Astron*) Azimut *nt or m*

Azores [ə'zɔːz] PL Azoren *pl*

AZT *abbr of* **azidothymidine** AZT *nt*

Aztec ['æztek] **N** Azteke *m*, Aztekin *f* **ADJ** aztekisch

azure ['æʒə'] **N** Azur(blau *nt*) *m* **ADJ** *sky* azurblau; *eyes also* tiefblau; **~ blue** azurblau

B

B, b [bi:] N B *nt*, b *nt*; (*Sch: as a mark*) zwei, gut; (*Mus*) H *nt*, h *nt*; **B flat** B *nt*, b *nt*; **B sharp** His *nt*, his *nt* → **natural**

B ADJ (*on pencil*) B

b *abbr of* **born** geb.

BA *abbr of* **Bachelor of Arts**

baa [bɑ:] N Mähen *nt no pl*; ~! mäh!; ~-**lamb** (*baby-talk*) Bählamm *nt* (*baby-talk*), Mähschäfchen *nt* (*baby-talk*) VI mähen, mäh machen (*baby-talk*)

babble ['bæbl] N a Gemurmel *nt*; (*of baby, excited person etc*) Geplapper *nt*; ~ (**of voices**) Stimmengewirr *nt* b (*of stream*) Murmeln *nt no pl* (*liter*), Plätschern *nt no pl* (*liter*) VI a (*person*) plappern, quasseln (*inf*); (*baby*) plappern, lallen; **don't** ~**, speak slowly** nicht so schnell, rede langsam; **the other actress tended to** ~ die andere Schauspielerin neigte dazu, ihren Text herunterzurasseln b (*stream*) murmeln (*liter*), plätschern

▶ **babble away** *or* **on** VI quatschen (*inf*) (*about* über +*acc*), quasseln (*inf*) (*about* von); **she babbled away** *or* **on excitedly** sie quasselte *or* plapperte aufgeregt drauflos (*inf*)

▶ **babble out** VT *sep* brabbeln; *secret* ausplaudern

babbler ['bæblə] N Plaudertasche *f* (*inf*)

babbling ['bæblɪŋ] ADJ *brook* murmelnd (*liter*), plätschernd

babe [beɪb] N a (*liter*) Kindlein *nt* (*liter*); ~ **in arms** (*esp Brit*) Säugling *m* b (*esp US, inf*) Baby *nt* (*inf*), Puppe *f* (*inf*); **hey Susie/Mike** ~! he du, Susie!/Mike! c (*inf: = girl*) Schnalle *f* (*sl*), Tussi *f* (*sl*), Braut *f* (*sl*) → *also* **baby e**

Babel ['beɪbl] N a **the Tower of** ~ (*story*) der Turmbau zu Babel *or* Babylon; (*edifice*) der Babylonische Turm b (*also* **babel**) (*= confusion*) Durcheinander *nt*; (*= several languages*) babylonisches Sprachengewirr

baboon [bə'bu:n] N Pavian *m*

babuschka [bə'bu:ʃkə] N Kopftuch *nt*

baby ['beɪbɪ] N a Kind *nt*, Baby *nt*; (*esp in weeks after birth*) Säugling *m*; (*of animal*) Junge(s) *nt*; **to have a** ~ ein Kind *or* Baby bekommen; **she's going to have a** ~ sie bekommt ein Kind *or* Baby; **I've known him since he was a** ~ ich kenne ihn von klein auf *or* von Kindesbeinen an; **the** ~ **of the family** der/die Kleinste *or* Jüngste, das Nesthäkchen; (*boy also*) der Benjamin; ~ **elephant** Elefantenjunge(s) *nt or* -baby *nt*; **he's a big** ~ er ist ein großes Kind; **don't be such a** ~! sei nicht so ein Baby! (*inf*), stell dich nicht so an! (*inf*); **to be left holding the** ~ (*Brit inf*) der Dumme sein (*inf*), die Sache ausbaden müssen (*inf*); **the bank cancelled the loan and I was left holding a very expensive** ~ (*Brit inf*) als die Bank das Darlehen rückgängig machte, hatte ich eine teure Suppe auszulöffeln; **to throw out the** ~ **with the bathwater** das Kind mit dem Bade ausschütten; **that encyclopedia is his first** ~ (*inf*) das Lexikon ist sein Erstling (*hum*) *or* erstes Kind; **this little** ~ **cost me a fortune** (*inf*) das (Ding) hat mich ein Vermögen gekostet b (*= small object of its type*) Pikkolo *m* (*hum*) c (*inf: = thing for which one is responsible*) **that's a costing problem, that's Harrison's** ~ das ist eine Kostenfrage, das ist Harrisons Problem; **I think this problem's your** ~ das ist wohl dein Bier (*inf*) d (*inf: = girlfriend, boyfriend*) Schatz *m*, Schätzchen *nt* e (*esp US inf, as address*) Schätzchen *nt* (*inf*); (*man to man*) mein Freund, mein Junge; **that's my** ~ jawohl, so ists prima (*inf*); **that's great,** ~ Mensch, das ist klasse (*inf*); **Mike/Susie** ~, **listen** du, Mike/Susie, hör mal her! VT (*inf*) wie einen Säugling behandeln

baby: baby barrier N Sicherheitstür *f*, Sicherheitsgitter *nt*; **baby-batterer** N jd, der Kleinkinder misshandelt; **baby-battering** N Kindesmisshandlung *f*; **baby blue** N Himmelblau *nt*; **baby-blue** ADJ (*inf*) *eyes, ribbon, car* himmelblau; **baby blues** PL (*inf*) Depressionen *pl* nach der Geburt; **baby bond** N (*US Fin*) Baby Bond *m*; **baby boom** N Babyboom *m*; **baby boomer** N Person, die während des Baby-booms geboren wurde; **baby bottle** N Saugflasche *f*; **Baby-bouncer**® N Babywippe *f*; **baby boy** N kleiner Junge; (*= son*) Sohn *m*; **baby break** N Babypause *f*; **baby brother** N kleiner Bruder; **baby buggy**® N (*Brit*) Sportwagen *m*; **baby bust** N drastischer Rückgang in der Geburtenziffer; **baby car** N Kleinwagen *m*, Autochen *nt* (*hum*); **baby carriage** N (*US*) Kinderwagen *m*; **baby clothes** PL Kindersachen *pl*, Babywäsche *f*; **baby-doll face** N Puppengesicht *nt*; **baby-doll pyjamas**, (*US*) **baby-doll pajamas** PL Babydoll *nt*; **baby-face** N Kindergesicht *nt*; (*of adult male*) Milchgesicht *nt*; **baby-faced** ADJ *person* milchgesichtig; **baby fat** N (*US*) Babyspeck *m* (*inf*); **baby food** N Babynahrung *f*; **baby girl** N kleines Mädchen; (*= daughter*) Tochter *f*, Töchterchen *nt*; **baby grand (piano)** N Stutzflügel *m*

babyhood ['beɪbɪhʊd] N frühe Kindheit, Säuglingsalter *nt*

babyish ['beɪbɪʃ] ADJ kindisch

baby linen N Babywäsche *f no pl*

Babylon ['bæbɪlən] N Babylon *nt*

Babylonian [ˌbæbɪ'ləʊnɪən] ADJ babylonisch N Babylonier(in) *m(f)*

baby: baby-minder N Tagesmutter *f*, Kinderpfleger(in) *m(f)*; **baby new potatoes** PL neue Kartöffelchen; **baby pool** N (*US*) Planschbecken *nt*; **baby-proof** ADJ kindersicher VT kindersicher machen

baby's breath N (*Bot*) Schleierkraut *nt*

baby: baby scales PL Baby- *or* Säuglingswaage *f*; **baby seat** N (*in car*) Baby(sicherheits)-sitz *m*; **baby sister** N kleine Schwester; **baby-sit** *pret, ptp* **baby-sat** VI babysitten; **she** ~**s for them** sie geht bei ihnen babysitten; **baby-sitter** N Babysitter(in) *m(f)*; **baby-sitting** N Babysitten *nt*, Babysitting *nt*; **baby snatcher** N Kindesentführer(in) *m(f)*; **baby-snatching** N Kindesentführung *f*; **baby stroller** N (*US*) Sportwagen *m*; **baby-talk** N Kindersprache *f*; **baby tooth** N Milchzahn *m*; **baby-walker** N Laufstuhl *m*

baccara(t) ['bækərɑ:] N Bakkarat *nt*

bacchanalia [ˌbækə'neɪlɪə] N (*Hist, fig*) Bacchanal *nt* (*geh*)

bacchanalian [ˌbækə'neɪlɪən] ADJ bacchantisch (*geh*)

Bacchus ['bækəs] N Bacchus *m*

baccy ['bækɪ] N (*inf*) Tabak *m*, Knaster *m* (*inf*)

bachelor ['bætʃələ] N a Junggeselle *m*; **still a** ~ immer noch Junggeselle b (*Univ*) **Bachelor of Arts/Science** ≈ Magister *m* (der philosophischen/naturwissenschaftlichen Fakultät)

bachelordom ['bætʃələdəm] N = **bachelorhood**

bachelor: bachelor flat N Junggesellenwohnung *f*; **bachelor girl** N Junggesellin *f*

bachelorhood ['bætʃələhʊd] N Junggesellentum *nt*

bacillary [bə'sɪlərɪ] ADJ (*Med*) bazillär (*spec*); *infection also* durch Bazillen; *form* stäbchenförmig

bacillus [bə'sɪləs] N *pl* **bacilli** [bə'sɪlaɪ] Bazillus *m*

back [bæk] N a (*of person, animal, book*) Rücken *m*; (*of chair*) (Rücken)lehne *f*; **with one's** ~ **to the engine** (*Brit*) mit dem Rücken zur Fahrtrichtung, rückwärts; **to be on one's** ~ (*= be ill*) auf der Nase liegen (*inf*), krank sein; **to wear one's hair down one's** ~ überschulterlange Haare haben; **to break one's** ~ (*lit*) sich (*dat*) das Rückgrat brechen; (*fig*) sich abrackern, sich abmühen; **we've broken the** ~ **of the job** (*Brit*) wir sind mit der Arbeit über den Berg (*inf*); **behind sb's** ~ (*fig*) hinter jds Rücken (*dat*); **to put one's** ~ **into sth** (*fig*) sich bei etw anstrengen, bei etw Einsatz zeigen; **to put** *or* **get sb's** ~ **up** jdn gegen sich aufbringen; **to turn one's** ~ **on sb** (*lit*) jdm den Rücken zuwenden; (*fig*) sich von jdm abwenden; **when I needed him he turned his** ~ **on me** als ich ihn brauchte, ließ er mich im Stich; **get these people off my** ~ (*inf*) schaff mir diese Leute vom Hals! (*inf*); **get off my** ~! (*inf*) lass mich endlich in Ruhe!; **he's got the boss on his** ~ **all the time** er hat dauernd seinen Chef auf dem Hals; **the rich have always lived off the** ~**s of the poor** die Reichen haben immer auf Kosten der Armen gelebt; **to have one's** ~ **to the wall** (*fig*) in die Enge getrieben sein/werden; **I was pleased to see the** ~ **of them** (*inf*) ich war froh, sie endlich los zu sein (*inf*) b (*as opposed to front*) Rück- *or* Hinterseite *f*; (*of hand, dress*) Rücken *m*; (*of house, page, coin, cheque*) Rückseite *f*; (*of material*) linke Seite; **I know London like the** ~ **of my hand** ich kenne London wie meine Westentasche; **the index is at the** ~ **of the book** das Verzeichnis ist hinten im Buch; **he drove into the** ~ **of me** er ist mir hinten reingefahren (*inf*); **on the** ~ **of his hand** auf dem Handrücken; **the** ~ **of one's head** der Hinterkopf; **at/on the** ~ **of the bus** hinten im/am Bus; **in the** ~ (*of a car*) hinten (im Auto); **one thing was at the** ~ **of my mind** ich hatte dabei eine Überlegung im Hinterkopf; **there's one other worry at the** ~ **of my mind** da ist noch etwas, das mich beschäftigt; **right at the** ~ **of the cupboard** ganz hinten im Schrank; **at the** ~ **of the stage** im Hintergrund der Bühne; **at the** ~ **of the garage** (*inside*) hinten in der Garage; (*outside*) hinter der Garage; **at the** ~ **of beyond** am Ende der Welt, jwd (*hum*); **in** ~ (*US*) hinten c (*Ftbl*) Verteidiger(in) *m(f)*; (*Rugby*) Hinterspieler(in) *m(f)*

ADJ Hinter-; *rent* ausstehend, rückständig; ~ **wheel** Hinterrad *nt*

ADV a (= *to the rear*) (**stand**) ~! zurück(treten)!, (treten Sie) zurück!; ~ **and forth** hin und her

b (= *in return*) zurück; **to pay sth** ~ etw zurückzahlen

c (= *returning*) zurück; **to come/go** ~ zurückkommen/-gehen; **to fly to London and** ~ nach London und zurück fliegen; **there and** ~ hin und zurück

d (= *again*) wieder; **he went** ~ **several times** er fuhr noch öfters wieder hin; **I'll never go** ~ da gehe ich nie wieder hin; **she is** ~ **at work** sie arbeitet wieder; ~ **in London** zurück in London

e (= *ago: in time phrases*) **a week** ~ vor einer Woche; **as far** ~ **as the 18th century** = *dating back*) bis ins 18. Jahrhundert zurück; (*point in time*) schon im 18. Jahrhundert; ~ **in March, 1987** im März 1987; **far** ~ **in the past** vor langer, langer Zeit, vor Urzeiten

PREP (*US*) ~ **of** hinter

VT a (= *support*) unterstützen; **I will** ~ **you whatever you do** egal was du tust, ich stehe hinter dir; **if the bank won't** ~ **us** wenn die Bank nicht mitmacht; **to** ~ **a bill** (*Fin*) einen Wechsel indossieren

b (*Betting*) setzen *or* wetten auf (+*acc*); **the horse was heavily ~ed** auf das Pferd wurden viele Wetten abgeschlossen

c (= *cause to move*) *car* zurückfahren *or* -setzen; *cart* zurückfahren; *horse* rückwärts gehen lassen; **he ~ed his car into the tree/garage** er fuhr rückwärts gegen den Baum/in die Garage; **to** ~ **water** (*Naut*) rückwärts rudern

d (*Mus*) *singer* begleiten

e (= *put sth behind*) *picture* mit einem Rücken versehen, unterlegen; (= *stick on*) aufziehen

VI a (= *move backwards: car, train*) zurücksetzen *or* -fahren; **the car ~ed into the garage** das Auto fuhr rückwärts in die Garage; **she ~ed into me** sie fuhr rückwärts in mein Auto

b (*Naut, wind*) drehen

▶**back away** VI zurückweichen (*from* vor +*dat*)

▶**back down** VI (*fig*) nachgeben, klein beigeben

▶**back off** VI **a** (*vehicle*) zurücksetzen **b** (= *step back*) zurückweichen; (*crowd*) zurücktreten; (= *withdraw from deal etc*) aussteigen (*inf*); (= *stop harassing*) sich zurückhalten; **back off!** (= *stop interfering*) verschwinde!

▶**back on to** VI +*prep obj* hinten angrenzen an (+*acc*)

▶**back out** VI **a** (*car etc*) rückwärts herausfahren *or* -setzen **b** (*fig: of contract, deal etc*) aussteigen (*of, from* aus) (*inf*) VT *sep vehicle* rückwärts herausfahren *or* -setzen

▶**back up** VI **a** (*car etc*) zurücksetzen; **to back up to sth** rückwärts an etw (*acc*) heranfahren **b** (*traffic*) sich stauen; (*US: drain*) verstopfen **c** (*Comput*) sichern VT *sep* **a** (= *support*) unterstützen; (= *confirm*) *story* bestätigen; *knowledge* fundieren; *claim, theory* untermauern; **he backed up the boy's story that ...** er bestätigte den Bericht des Jungen, wonach ...; **he can back me up in this** er kann das bestätigen **b** *car etc* zurückfahren **c** (*Comput*) sichern, sicherstellen

back: **backache** N Rückenschmerzen *pl*; **back alley** N Gasse *f*; **back bench** N (*esp Brit*) Abgeordnetensitz *m*; **the ~es** das Plenum; **backbencher** N (*esp Brit*) Abgeordnete(r) *mf* (*auf den hinteren Reihen im britischen Parlament*)

BACKBENCHER

Alle britischen Unterhausabgeordneten, die weder in der Regierung noch im Schattenkabinett der Opposition sind, werden als **backbenchers** bezeichnet, da sie nicht in den vorderen Rängen, den (**front benches**), des Unterhauses neben dem Premierminister bzw. dem Oppositionsführer sitzen. Da sie kein offizielles Amt innehaben, ist es für die **back-**

---

benchers oft einfacher, sich entgegen der offiziellen Parteilinie zu äußern oder gegen sie zu stimmen. Mit (**the back benches**) werden generell alle Abgeordneten beider Seiten im Unterhaus bezeichnet, die keine wichtige Stellung innehaben.

---

back: **back bend** N (*Sport*) Brücke *f*; **back-biting** N Lästern *nt*; **backboard** N (*Basketball*) Korbbrett *nt*; **back boiler** N Warmwasserboiler *m* (*hinter der Heizung angebracht*); **backbone** N (*lit, fig*) Rückgrat *nt*; **back-breaking** ['bækbreɪkɪŋ] ADJ erschöpfend, ermüdend; **back burner** N (*lit*) hintere Kochplatte; **to put sth on the** ~ (*fig inf*) etw zurückstellen; **this project's been on the** ~ **for years** an diesem Projekt wird seit Jahren nur so nebenbei gearbeitet; **back catalogue** N (*Mus*) ältere Aufnahmen *pl*, Back-Katalog *m*; **back-chat** N , *no pl* (*inf*) Widerrede *f*; **none of your** ~! keine Widerrede!; **backcloth** ['bækklɒθ] N Prospekt *m*, Hintergrund *m*; **backcomb** VT *hair* toupieren; **back copy** N alte Ausgabe *or* Nummer; **back country, backcountry** (*US*) **the** ~ das Hinterland, die tiefste Provinz ADJ *road* Land-; ~ **expedition** Expedition *f* ins Hinterland; **back cover** N (*of book, magazine*) Rückseite *f*; **backdate** VT (zu)rückdatieren; **salary increase ~d to May** Gehaltserhöhung rückwirkend ab Mai; **back door** N (*lit*) Hintertür *f*; (*fig*) Hintertürchen *nt*; **by the** ~ (*fig*) durch die Hintertür; **if you use the back-door means of doing it** wenn Sie das durchs Hintertürchen machen; **backdrop** N Prospekt *m*, Hintergrund *m* (*also fig*)

-backed [-bækt] ADJ SUF low/high-backed mit niedriger/hoher Rückenlehne; **a low-backed dress** ein Kleid mit tiefem Rückenausschnitt; **straight-backed** (*chair*) mit gerader Rückenlehne; *person* mit geradem Rücken

back end N (= *rear*) hinteres Ende; **at the** ~ **of the year** gegen Ende des Jahres, in den letzten Monaten des Jahres; **she looks like the** ~ **of a bus** (*inf*) sie ist potthässlich (*inf*)

backer ['bækə'] N **a** (= *supporter*) **his ~s** (diejenigen,) die ihn unterstützen **b** (*Betting*) Wettende(r) *mf* **c** (*Comm*) Geldgeber(in) *m(f)*

back: **backfile** N alte Akte; **backfire** N **a** (*Aut*) Fehlzündung *f* **b** (*US*) Gegenfeuer *nt* VI **a** (*Aut*) Fehlzündungen haben **b** (*inf, plan etc*) ins Auge gehen; **it ~d on us** der Schuss ging nach hinten los (*inf*); **back-flip** N Flickflack *m*; **back formation** N (*Ling*) Rückbildung *f*; **back four** N (+*pl vb*) (*Ftbl*) Viererkette *f*; **backgammon** N Backgammon *nt*; **back garden** N Garten *m* (*hinter Haus*)

background ['bækgraʊnd] N **a** (*of painting etc, fig*) Hintergrund *m*; **to stay in the** ~ im Hintergrund bleiben, im Hintergrund halten; **to keep sb in the** ~ jdn nicht in den Vordergrund treten lassen; **against a** ~ **of poverty and disease** vor dem Hintergrund von Armut und Krankheit

b (*of person*) (*educational etc*) Werdegang *m*; (*social*) Verhältnisse *pl*; (= *family background*) Herkunft *f no pl*; (*Sociol*) Background *m*; **he comes from a** ~ **of poverty** er kommt aus ärmlichen Verhältnissen; **comprehensive schools take children from all ~s** Gesamtschulen nehmen Kinder aus allen Schichten auf; **what do we know about the main character's ~?** was wissen wir über das Vorleben der Hauptperson?; **what's your educational ~?** was für eine Ausbildung haben Sie?

c (*of case, problem etc*) Zusammenhänge *pl*, Hintergründe *pl*, Hintergrund *m*; **he explained the** ~ **to the crisis** er erläuterte die Zusammenhänge *or* Hintergründe der Krise

ADJ *reading* vertiefend; ~ **music** Hintergrundmusik *f*, Musikuntermalung *f*; ~ **noises** *pl* Geräuschkulisse *f*, Geräusche *pl* im Hintergrund; ~ **information** Hintergrundinformationen *pl*; **what's the** ~ **information on this?** welche Hintergründe *or* Zusammenhänge bestehen hierfür?

---

background program N (*Comput*) Hintergrundprogramm *nt*

background radiation N (*Phys*) natürliche Strahlung *f*

back: **backhand** N (*Sport*) Rückhand *f no pl*, Backhand *f no pl*; (*one stroke*) Rückhandschlag *m* ADJ Rückhand-; ~ **stroke** Rückhandschlag *m* ADV mit der Rückhand; **backhanded** ADJ *compliment* zweifelhaft; *writing* nach links geneigt; ~ **shot** Rückhandschuss *m*; **backhander** N **a** (*Sport*) Rückhandschlag *m* **b** (*inf:* = *bribe*) Schmiergeld *nt*; **to give sb a** ~ jdn schmieren (*inf*); **back-heel** N Hackentrick *m*, Absatztrick *m* VT *ball* mit der Hacke *or* dem Absatz spielen

backing ['bækɪŋ] N **a** (= *support*) Unterstützung *f*; ~ **store** (*Comput*) Ergänzungsspeicher *m* **b** (*Mus*) Begleitung *f*; ~ **group** Begleitband *f*; ~ **singer** Begleitsänger(in) *m(f)*; ~ **vocals** Begleitung *f* **c** (*for picture frame, for strengthing*) Rücken(verstärkung *f*) *m*; (*for carpet, wallpaper etc*) Rücken(beschichtung *f*) *m*

back: **backlash** N (*Tech*) (= *jarring reaction*) Gegenschlag *m*; (*play*) zu viel Spiel **b** (*fig*) Gegenreaktion *f*; **backless** ADJ *dress* rückenfrei; **backlist** N (*in publishing*) Backlist *f*; **back-lit** ADJ *screen, photograph* hintergrundbeleuchtet; **backlog** N Rückstände *pl*; **I have a** ~ **of work** ich bin mit der Arbeit im Rückstand; **look at this** ~ **of typing** sieh dir diesen Berg unerledigter Schreibarbeiten an; **backlot** N (*Film*) *Hintergelände eines Filmstudios*; **back marker** N (*Sport*) Nachzügler(in) *m(f)*, Schlusslicht *nt*; **the ~s** die Nachhut; **backmost** ADJ hinterste(r, s); **back number** N (*of paper*) alte Ausgabe *or* Nummer; (*fig inf*) (= *person*) altmodischer Mensch; (= *thing*) veraltetes Ding; **he is a** ~ (*inf*) er ist altmodisch; **backpack** N Rucksack *m*; **backpacker** N Wanderer *m*, Wanderin *f*; (= *hitch-hiker*) Rucksacktourist(in) *m(f)*; **backpacking** N Wandern *nt*; (= *hitch-hiking*) Trampen *nt*; **to go** ~ auf (Berg)tour gehen; trampen; **back passage** N (*euph Anat*) Mastdarm *m*; **back pay** N Nachzahlung *f*; **back-pedal** VI (*lit*) rückwärts treten; (*fig inf*) einen Rückzieher machen (*inf*) (*on bei*); **back-pedal brake** N Rücktrittbremse *f*; **back pocket** N Gesäßtasche *f*; **back projection** N (*Film*) Rückprojektion *f*; **back rest** N Rückenstütze *f*; **back road** N kleine Landstraße; **back room** N Hinterzimmer *nt*; **back-room boy** N (*inf*) Experte *m* im Hintergrund; **backscratching** N , *no pl* gegenseitige Begünstigung, Vetternwirtschaft *f* (*pej*); **back seat** N Rücksitz *m*; **to take a** ~ (*fig*) sich zurückhalten *or* raushalten (*inf*); **back-seat driver** N Beifahrer, der dem Fahrer dazwischenredet; **she is a terrible** ~ sie redet beim Fahren immer rein; **back shift** N Spätschicht *f*; **backside** N (*Brit inf*) Hintern *m* (*inf*), Hinterteil *nt* (*inf*); **backsight** N (*on rifle*) Visier *nt*, Kimme *f*; **back-slapping** N (*inf*) Schulterklopfen *nt*; **backslash** N (*Comput*) Backslash *m*; **backslide** VI (*fig*) rückfällig werden; (*Eccl*) abtrünnig werden; **backslider** N Rückfällige(r) *mf*, Abtrünnige(r) *mf*; **backspace** VTI (*Typing*) zurücksetzen; **backspace key** N Rücktaste *f*; **backspacer** N (*Typing*) Rücktaste *f*; **backstage** ADV, ADJ hinter den Kulissen; (*in dressing room area*) in die/der Garderobe; ~ **crew** Leute *pl* hinter den Kulissen; (*at pop concert etc*) Backstagetruppe *f*; **backstairs** N *sing* Hintertreppe *f* ADJ ~ **deal** Hintertreppendeal *m*; **backstitch** N Steppstich *m*; **backstop** N (*Tennis*) Bande *f*; **back straight** N (*Sport*) Gegengerade *f*; **backstreet** N Seitensträßchen *nt*; **he comes from the ~s of Liverpool** er kommt aus dem ärmeren Teil von Liverpool; **backstreet abortion** N illegale Abtreibung; ~**s** Engelmacherei *f* (*inf*); **she had a** ~ sie war bei einem Engelmacher (*inf*); **backstreet abortionist** N Engelmacher(in) *m(f)* (*inf*); **backstretch** N (*Sport*) Gegengerade *f*; **back-stroke** N (*Swimming*) Rückenschwimmen *nt*; **can you do the ~?** können Sie rückenschwimmen?; **backswing** N (*Sport*) Durchschwung *m*; **backtalk** N Widerrede *f*; **back to back** ADV Rücken an Rücken; (*things*) mit den Rückseiten aneinander; **back-to-back** ADJ direkt aufeinander folgend *attr*; **back to front** ADV verkehrt herum; *read von hinten nach vorne*; **back tooth** N Backenzahn *m*; **backtrack** VI (*over ground*) denselben Weg zurückgehen *or* zurückverfolgen; (*on policy etc*) einen Rückzieher machen (*on* sth bei etw); **backup** N a Unterstützung *f* b (*Comput*) Sicherungskopie *f*, Backup *nt*, Back-up *nt* ADJ a *services* zur Unterstützung; ~ **troops** Unterstützungstruppen *pl*; ~ **train/plane** Entlastungszug *m*/-flugzeug *nt*; ~ **plan** Ausweichplan *m*; ~ **staff** Reservekräfte *pl*; ~ **service** (*for customer*) Kundendienst *m* b (*Comput*) Sicherungs-, Backup-; ~ **copy** Sicherungs- *or* Backupkopie *f*; **back-up light** ['bækʌp,laɪt] N (*US Aut*) Rückfahrscheinwerfer *m*; **back vowel** N (*Phon*) hinterer Vokal, Rachenvokal *m*

backward ['bækwəd] ADJ a ~ **and forward movement** Vor-und Zurückbewegung *f*; ~ **flow of information** Rückfluss *m* von Daten; **a ~ glance** ein Blick zurück; **a ~ step** (*fig*) ein Schritt *m* zurück b (*fig*) *economy, region* rückständig; (*pej: = retarded*) *child* zurückgeblieben; **to be socially/economically ~** gesellschaftlich/wirtschaftlich rückständig sein ADV = **backwards**

backward-compatible [,bækwədkəm'pætɪbl] ADJ = **backwards-compatible**

backwardness ['bækwədnɪs] N (*mental*) Zurückgebliebenheit *f*; (*of region*) Rückständigkeit *f*

backwards ['bækwədz] ADV a rückwärts; **to fall ~** nach hinten fallen; **to walk ~ and forwards** hin und her gehen; **to stroke a cat ~** eine Katze gegen den Strich streicheln; **to lean** *or* **bend over ~ to do sth** (*inf*) sich fast umbringen *or* sich (*dat*) ein Bein ausreißen, um etw zu tun (*inf*); **I know it ~** (*Brit*) *or* **and forwards** (*US*) das kenne ich in- und auswendig b (= *towards the past*) zurück; **to look ~** zurückblicken

backwards-compatible [,bækwədzkəm'pætɪbl] ADJ (*Comput, Hi-Fi etc*) abwärtskompatibel (*with* mit)

back: backwash N (*Naut*) Rückströmung *f*; (*fig*) Nachwirkung *f usu pl*; **those caught up in the ~ of the scandal** diejenigen, die in den Skandal mit hineingezogen wurden; **backwater** N (*lit*) Stauwasser *nt*, totes Wasser; (*fig*) rückständiges Nest; **this town is a cultural ~** kulturell (gesehen) ist diese Stadt tiefste Provinz; **backwoods** PL unterschlossene (Wald)gebiete *pl*; **backwoodsman** N Waldsiedler *m*; (*fig inf*) Hinterwäldler *m*; **back yard** N Hinterhof *m*; **in one's own ~** (*fig*) vor der eigenen Haustür

bacon ['beɪkən] N durchwachsener Speck; ~ **and eggs** Eier mit Speck; **to save sb's ~** (*inf*) jds Rettung sein; **to bring home the ~** (*inf: = earn a living*) die Brötchen verdienen (*inf*)

bacteria [bæk'tɪərɪə] *pl of* **bacterium**

bacterial [bæk'tɪərɪəl] ADJ bakteriell

bacteriological [bæk,tɪərɪə'lɒdʒɪkəl] ADJ bakteriologisch

bacteriologist [bæk,tɪərɪ'ɒlədʒɪst] N Bakteriologe *m*, Bakteriologin *f*

bacteriology [bæk,tɪərɪ'ɒlədʒɪ] N Bakteriologie *f*

bacterium [bæk'tɪərɪəm] N *pl* **bacteria** [bæk'tɪərɪə] Bakterie *f*, Bakterium *nt* (*old*)

bad[1] [bæd] *comp* **worse**, *superl* **worst** a schlecht; *smell* übel; *habit* schlecht, übel; *insurance risk* hoch; *word* unanständig, schlimm; (= *immoral, wicked*) böse; (= *naughty, misbehaved*) unartig, ungezogen; *dog* böse; **this thing to do** das hättest du nicht tun sollen; **it was ~ of you to treat her like that** das war gemein von dir, sie so zu behandeln; **he went through a ~ time** er hat eine schlimme Zeit durchgemacht; **I've had a really ~ day** ich hatte einen furchtbaren Tag; **you ~ boy!** du ungezogener Junge!, du Lümmel! (*also iro*); **he's been a ~**

---

boy er war unartig *or* böse; **I didn't mean that word in a ~ sense** ich habe mir bei dem Wort nichts Böses gedacht; **it's a ~ business** das ist eine üble Sache; **it's not so ~/not ~ at all** es ist nicht/gar nicht so schlecht; **things are going from ~ to worse** es wird immer schlimmer; **to go ~** schlecht werden, verderben; **he's gone ~** (*US*) er ist auf die schiefe Bahn geraten; **to be ~ for sb/sth** schlecht *or* nicht gut für jdn/etw sein; **he's ~ at French** er ist schlecht in Französisch; **he's ~ at sports** im Sport ist er schlecht *or* nicht gut, er ist unsportlich; **I'm very ~ at telling lies** ich kann schlecht *or* nicht gut lügen; **he speaks very ~ English, his English is very ~** er spricht sehr schlecht(es) Englisch; **to be ~ to sb** jdn schlecht behandeln; **there's nothing ~ about living together** es ist doch nichts dabei, wenn man zusammen lebt; **this is a ~ town for violence** in dieser Stadt ist es wirklich schlimm mit der Gewalttätigkeit; ~ **light stopped play** das Spiel wurde aufgrund des schlechten Lichts abgebrochen; **it would not be a ~ thing** das wäre nicht schlecht *or* keine schlechte Idee; **that's not a ~ idea!** das ist keine schlechte Idee!; **(that's) too ~!** (*indignant*) so was!; (= *bad luck!*) Pech!; **it's too ~ of you** das ist wirklich nicht nett von dir; **too ~ you couldn't make it** (es ist) wirklich schade, dass Sie nicht kommen konnten; **to have a ~ hair day** (*inf*) Probleme mit der Frisur haben; (*fig*) total durch den Wind sein (*inf*); **to feel ~ with sb** (*US*) bei jdm schlecht angeschrieben sein

b (= *serious*) *wound, sprain* schlimm; *accident, mistake, cold* schlimm, schwer; *headache* stark; **he's got it ~** (*inf*) ihn hats schwer erwischt (*inf*); **to have it ~ for sb** (*inf*) in jdn schwer *or* unheimlich verknallt sein (*inf*)

c (= *unfavourable*) *time, day* ungünstig, schlecht; **Thursday's ~, can you make it Friday?** Donnerstag ist ungünstig *or* schlecht, gehts nicht Freitag?

d (= *in poor health, sick*) *stomach* krank; *leg, knee, hand* schlimm; *tooth* (*generally*) schlecht; (*now*) schlimm; **he/the economy is in a ~ way** (*Brit*) es geht ihm schlecht/es steht schlecht um die *or* mit der Wirtschaft; **I've got a ~ head** (*Brit*) ich habe einen dicken Kopf (*inf*); **to feel ~** sich nicht wohl fühlen; **I feel ~** mir geht es nicht gut, mir ist nicht gut; **to be taken ~** (*Brit*) **to take a ~ turn** (*inf*) plötzlich krank werden; **how is he? – he's not so ~** wie geht es ihm? – nicht schlecht; **I didn't know she was so ~** ich wusste nicht, dass es ihr so schlecht geht *or* dass sie so schlimm dran ist (*inf*)

e (= *regretful*) **I feel really ~ about not having told him** es tut mir wirklich Leid *or* ich habe ein schlechtes Gewissen, dass ich ihm das nicht gesagt habe; **don't feel ~ about it** machen Sie sich (*dat*) keine Gedanken *or* Sorgen (darüber)

f *debt* uneinbringlich; *voting slip, coin* ungültig; (= *damaged*) *copies etc* beschädigt

N , *no pl* a **to take the good with the ~** (auch) die schlechten Seiten in Kauf nehmen; **there is good and ~ in everything/everybody** alles/jeder hat seine guten und schlechten Seiten

b **he's gone to the ~** (*Brit*) er ist auf die schiefe Bahn geraten

bad[2] *pret of* **bid**

bad: bad-ass ['bædæs] (*US sl*) N knallharter Typ (*inf*) ADJ *attitude* knallhart (*inf*); **a ~ kid** ein knallharter Bursche (*inf*); **bad blood** N böses Blut; **there is ~ between them** sie haben ein gestörtes Verhältnis; **bad cheque**, (*US*) **bad check** N (*containing a mistake*) ungültiger Scheck; (*not covered by funds*) ungedeckter Scheck

baddie ['bædɪ] N (*inf*) Schurke *m*, Bösewicht *m*

baddish ['bædɪʃ] ADJ (*inf*) ziemlich schlecht

bade [beɪd] *pret of* **bid**

badge [bædʒ] N a Abzeichen *nt*; (*made of metal*) Button *m*; (*on car etc*) Plakette *f*; (= *sticker*) Aufkleber *m*; ~ **of office** Dienstmarke *f* b (*fig: = symbol*) Merkmal *nt*

---

badger ['bædʒə'] N Dachs *m*; ~-**baiting** Dachshetzjagd *f* VT zusetzen (+*dat*), bearbeiten (*inf*), keine Ruhe lassen (+*dat*); **don't ~ me** lass mich in Ruhe *or* Frieden; **to ~ sb for sth** jdm mit etw in den Ohren liegen

badlands ['bædlændz] PL Ödland *nt*

badly ['bædlɪ] ADV a schlecht; **to do ~** (*in election, exam etc*) schlecht abschneiden; (*Fin*) schlecht stehen; (*Comm*) schlecht gehen; **to go ~** schlecht laufen; **to be ~ off** schlecht dran sein

b *wounded, mistaken* schwer; ~ **beaten** (*Sport*) vernichtend geschlagen; *person* schwer *or* schlimm verprügelt; **the ~ disabled** die Schwerstbeschädigten

c (= *very much*) sehr; *in debt, overdrawn* hoch; **to want sth ~** etw unbedingt wollen; **I need it ~** ich brauche es dringend; **he ~ needs** *or* **wants a haircut** er muss dringend zum Friseur

d (= *unfavourably*) **to reflect ~ on sb** ein schlechtes Licht auf jdn werfen; **to think ~ of sb** schlecht von jdm denken

bad-mannered [,bæd'mænəd] ADJ ungezogen, unhöflich

badminton ['bædmɪntən] N Federball *nt*; (*on court*) Badminton *nt*

bad-mouth ['bædmaʊθ] VT (*inf*) herziehen über (+*acc*) (*inf*)

badness ['bædnɪs] N , *no pl* a Schlechtheit *f*; (*moral*) Schlechtigkeit *f*; (= *naughtiness*) Unartigkeit *f*, Ungezogenheit *f* b (= *seriousness*) Schwere *f*; (*of headache*) Stärke *f*

bad-tempered [,bæd'tempəd] ADJ schlecht gelaunt *attr*, übellaunig; **to be ~** schlechte Laune haben; (*as characteristic*) ein übellauniger Mensch sein

baffle ['bæfl] VT a (= *confound, amaze*) verblüffen; (= *cause incomprehension*) vor ein Rätsel stellen; **a ~d look** ein verdutzter Blick; **the police are ~d** die Polizei steht vor einem Rätsel; **it really ~s me how …** es ist mir wirklich ein Rätsel, wie …; **a case that ~s all the experts** ein Fall, der den Experten Rätsel aufgab; **this one's got me ~d** ich stehe vor einem Rätsel b (*Tech*) *sound* dämpfen N (*also* **baffle plate**: *Aut*) Umlenkblech *nt*

bafflement ['bæflmənt] N (= *bewilderment*) Verblüffung *f*, Verwirrung *f*

baffling ['bæflɪŋ] ADJ *case* rätselhaft; *complexity* verwirrend; *mystery* unergründlich; *question* verblüffend; **I find it ~** es ist mir ein Rätsel

BAFTA ['bæftə] N (*Brit*) *abbr of* **British Academy of Film and Television Arts** britische Film- und Fernsehakademie

bag [bæg] N a Tasche *f*; (*with drawstrings, pouch*) Beutel *m*; (*for school*) Schultasche *f*; (*made of paper, plastic*) Tüte *f*; (= *sack*) Sack *m*; (= *suitcase*) Reisetasche *f*; ~**s** (Reise)gepäck *nt*; **to pack one's ~s** seine Sachen packen; **with ~ and ~gage** mit Sack und Pack; **to be a ~ of bones** (*inf*) nur Haut und Knochen sein (*inf*); **the whole ~ of tricks** (*inf*) die ganze Trickkiste (*inf*); **to be left holding the ~** (*US inf*) der Dumme sein (*inf*), die Sache ausbaden müssen (*inf*)

b (*Hunt*) **the ~** die (Jagd)beute; **to get a good ~** (eine) fette Beute machen *or* heimbringen; **it's in the ~** (*fig inf*) das habe ich *etc* schon in der Tasche (*inf*), das ist gelaufen (*inf*)

c ~**s under the eyes** (*black*) Ringe *pl* unter den Augen; (*of skin*) (hervortretende) Tränensäcke *pl*

d (*inf: = a lot*) ~**s of** jede Menge (*inf*)

e (*pej inf: = woman*) (**old**) ~ Schachtel *f* (*pej inf*); **ugly old ~** Schreckschraube *f* (*inf*)

f ~**s** PL (*Brit*) (= *Oxford bags*) weite Hose; (*dated inf: = trousers*) Buxe *f* (*dated inf*)

VT a in Tüten/Säcke verpacken

b (*Hunt*) erlegen, erbeuten

c (*Brit, sl*: = *get*) (sich *dat*) schnappen (*inf*); ~**s I have first go!** will anfangen!; **I ~s that ice cream!** will das Eis!

VI (*garment*) sich (aus)beulen

bagatelle [ˌbægəˈtel] N **a** (liter: = trifle) Bagatelle f **b** (= game) Tivoli nt

bagel [ˈbeɪgəl] N kleines, rundes Brötchen

bagful [ˈbægfʊl] N **a ~ of groceries** eine Tasche voll Lebensmittel

baggage [ˈbægɪdʒ] N **a** (= luggage) (Reise)gepäck nt **b** (Mil) Gepäck nt **c** (pej inf: = woman) Stück nt (inf) → **emotional a**

baggage (esp US): **baggage allowance** N Freigepäck nt; **baggage car** N Gepäckwagen m; **baggage check** N Gepäckkontrolle f; **baggage checkroom** N Gepäckaufbewahrung f; **baggage claim** N Gepäckausgabe f; **baggage handler** N Gepäckmann m; **baggage locker** N Gepäckschließfach nt; **baggage master** N Beamte(r) m am Gepäckschalter; **baggage rack** N (Rail) Gepäcknetz nt; **baggage reclaim** N Gepäckausgabe f; **baggage room** N Gepäckaufbewahrung f; **baggage wagon** N Gepäckwagen m

bagging [ˈbægɪŋ] N (material) Sack- or Packleinen nt

baggy [ˈbægɪ] ADJ (+er) (= ill-fitting) zu weit; dress sackartig; skin schlaff (hängend); (= out of shape) trousers, suit ausgebeult; jumper ausgeleiert; **~ trousers are fashionable again** weite (Flatter)hosen sind wieder modern

Baghdad [ˌbægˈdæd] N Bagdad nt

bag lady N Stadtstreicherin f (die ihre gesamte Habe in Einkaufstaschen mit sich führt)

bagpiper [ˈbægpaɪpə] N Dudelsackpfeifer(in) or -bläser(in) m(f)

bagpipe(s) [ˈbægpaɪp(s)] N(PL) Dudelsack m

bags [bægz] PL → **bag N d f**

bag-snatcher [ˈbægˌsnætʃə] N Handtaschendieb(in) m(f)

baguette [bæˈget] N Baguette f or nt, Stangenbrot nt

Bahamas [bəˈhɑːməz] PL **the ~** die Bahamas pl

Bahrain, Bahrein [bɑːreɪn] N Bahrain nt

bail¹ [beɪl] N (Jur) Kaution f, Sicherheitsleistung f (form); **to go** or **stand** or **put up ~ for sb** für jdn (die) Kaution stellen or leisten; **to grant/refuse ~** die Freilassung gegen Kaution bewilligen/verweigern; **he was refused ~** sein Antrag auf Freilassung gegen Kaution wurde abgelehnt; **to be (out) on ~** gegen Kaution freigelassen sein; **to let sb out on ~** jdn gegen Kaution freilassen

▶ **bail out** VT sep **a** (Jur) gegen Kaution or Sicherheitsleistung freibekommen, die Kaution stellen für **b** (fig) aus der Patsche helfen (+dat) (inf) **c** boat = **bale out**

bail² VI = **bale²**

bail³ N **a** (Cricket) Querholz nt **b** (in stable) Trennstange f

bailable [ˈbeɪləbl] ADJ (Jur) kautionsfähig

bail: bail bandit N (Brit, inf) jd, der eine Straftat begeht, während er gegen Kaution freigelassen ist; **bail bond** N (US Jur) (= document) Verpflichtungserklärung f; (= money) Kaution f; **bail bondsman** N (US Jur) Kautionsbürge m

bailee [beɪˈliː] N (Jur) Depositar(in) m(f) (einer beweglichen Sache), (treuhänderische(r)) Verwahrer(in) m(f)

Bailey bridge [ˈbeɪlɪˈbrɪdʒ] N Behelfsbrücke f

bailiff [ˈbeɪlɪf] N **a** (Jur) (Brit: also **sheriff's bailiff**) Amtsdiener(in) m(f); (Brit: for property) Gerichtsvollzieher(in) m(f); (US: in court) Gerichtsdiener(in) m(f) **b** (Brit: on estate) (Guts)verwalter(in) m(f), Landvogt(in) m(f) (obs)

bailor [beɪˈlɔː, ˈbeɪlə] N (Jur) Hinterleger(in) m(f) (einer beweglichen Sache), Deponent(in) m(f)

bailout [ˈbeɪlaʊt] N (Econ) Sanierung f; **~ plan** Sanierungsplan m

bairn [bɛən] N (Scot) Kind nt

bait [beɪt] N (lit, fig) Köder m; **to take** or **swallow the ~, to rise to the ~** (lit, fig) anbeißen; (fig: = be trapped) sich ködern lassen **VT a** hook, trap mit einem Köder versehen, beködern

b (= torment) animal (mit Hunden) hetzen; person quälen

baize [beɪz] N Fries m, Flaus m; **green ~** Billardtuch nt

bake [beɪk] **VT a** (Cook) backen; **~d apples** pl Bratäpfel pl; **~d potatoes** pl in der Schale gebackene Kartoffeln pl **b** pottery, bricks brennen; (sun) earth ausdörren **VI a** (Cook) backen; (cake) im (Back)ofen sein **b** (pottery etc) gebrannt werden, im (Brenn)ofen sein **c** (inf) **I just want to lie in the sun and ~** ich möchte mich in der Sonne braten lassen

bakehouse [ˈbeɪkhaʊs] N Backhaus nt

Bakelite® [ˈbeɪkəlaɪt] N Bakelit® nt

bake-off [ˈbeɪkɒf] N (US Cook) Backwettbewerb m

baker [ˈbeɪkə] N Bäcker(in) m(f); **~'s boy** Bäckerjunge m; **~'s (shop)** Bäckerei f, Bäckerladen m

baker's dozen [ˈbeɪkəzˈdʌzn] N 13 (Stück)

bakery [ˈbeɪkərɪ] N Bäckerei f

bakeware [ˈbeɪkwɛə] N Backformen und -bleche pl

Bakewell tart [ˈbeɪkwelˈtɑːt] N (Brit) Törtchen mit Mandel- und Marmeladenfüllung

baking [ˈbeɪkɪŋ] N **a** (act) Backen nt; (of earthenware) Brennen nt; **it's our own ~** das ist selbst gebacken **b** (batch: of bread, of bricks etc) Ofenladung f, Schub m **ADJ** (inf: = stifling, roasting) **I'm ~** mir ist vielmehr vor Hitze; **it's ~ (hot) today** es ist eine Affenhitze heute (inf)

baking: baking day N Backtag m; **baking dish** N Backform f; **baking mitt** N (US) Topfhandschuh m; **baking pan** N (US) Backblech nt; **baking powder** N Backpulver nt; **baking sheet** N Back- or Plätzchenblech nt; **baking soda** N ≈ Backpulver nt; **baking tin** N (Brit) Backform f; **baking tray** N (Brit) Kuchenblech nt

baksheesh [ˈbækʃiːʃ] N Bakschisch nt

Balaclava [ˌbæləˈklɑːvə] N (also **Balaclava helmet**) Kapuzenmütze f

balalaika [ˌbæləˈlaɪkə] N Balalaika f

balance [ˈbæləns] **N a** (= apparatus) Waage f; **to be** or **hang in the ~** (fig) in der Schwebe sein; **his life hung in the ~** sein Leben hing an einem dünnen or seidenen Faden; **to put sth in the ~** (= risk) etw in die Waagschale werfen **b** (= counterpoise) Gegengewicht nt (to zu); (fig) Ausgleich m (to für) **c** (fig: = equilibrium) Gleichgewicht nt; **sense of ~** Gleichgewichtssinn m; **to keep one's ~** das Gleichgewicht (be)halten; **to lose one's ~** aus dem Gleichgewicht kommen, das Gleichgewicht verlieren; **to recover one's ~** wieder ins Gleichgewicht kommen, das Gleichgewicht wiedererlangen; **off ~** aus dem Gleichgewicht; **to throw sb off (his) ~** jdn aus dem Gleichgewicht bringen; **the right ~ of personalities in the team** eine ausgewogene Mischung verschiedener Charaktere in der Mannschaft; **on the ~ of probabilities ...** wenn man die Möglichkeiten gegeneinander abwägt, ...; **the ~ of power** das Gleichgewicht der Kräfte; **~ of terror** Gleichgewicht nt des Schreckens; **to strike the right ~ between old and new/import and export** den goldenen Mittelweg zwischen Alt und Neu finden/das richtige Verhältnis von Import zu Export finden; **on ~** (fig) alles in allem

d (= preponderant weight) Hauptgewicht nt; **the ~ of advantage lies with you** der Hauptvorteil ist auf Ihrer Seite

e (Comm, Fin: = state of account) Saldo m; (with bank) Kontostand m, Saldo m; (of company) Bilanz f; **~ of trade** Handelsbilanz f; **~ in hand** (Comm) Kassen(be)stand m; **~ carried forward** Saldovortrag or -übertrag m; **~ due** (Banking) Debetsaldo m, Soll nt; (Comm) Rechnungsbetrag m; **~ in your favour** (Brit) or **favor** (US) Saldoguthaben nt; **~ of payments/trade** Zahlungs-/Handelsbilanz f

f (= remainder) Rest m; **to pay off the ~** den Rest bezahlen; (Banking) den Saldo begleichen;

my father has promised to make up the ~ mein Vater hat versprochen, die Differenz zu (be)zahlen

g (Art) Ausgewogenheit f

VT a (= keep level, in equilibrium) im Gleichgewicht halten; (= bring into equilibrium) ins Gleichgewicht bringen, ausbalancieren; **to ~ oneself on one foot** auf einem Bein balancieren; **the seal ~s a ball on its nose** der Seehund balanciert einen Ball auf der Nase

b (in the mind) two arguments (gegeneinander) abwägen; interests, needs, demands abwägen (against gegen); **to ~ sth against sth** etw einer Sache (dat) gegenüberstellen

c (= equal, make up for) ausgleichen

d (Comm, Fin) account (= add up) saldieren, abschließen; (= make equal) ausgleichen; (= pay off) begleichen; budget ausgleichen; **to ~ the books** die Bilanz ziehen or machen

e (Aut) wheel auswuchten

VI a (= be in equilibrium) Gleichgewicht halten; (scales) sich ausbalancieren; (painting) ausgewogen sein; **he ~d on one foot** er balancierte auf einem Bein; **with a ball balancing on its nose** mit einem Ball, den er auf der Nase balancierte

b (Comm, Fin, accounts) ausgeglichen sein; **the books don't ~** die Abrechnung stimmt nicht; **to make the books ~** die Abrechnung ausgleichen

▶ **balance out VT** sep aufwiegen, ausgleichen; **they balance each other out** sie wiegen sich auf, sie halten sich die Waage; (personalities) sie gleichen sich aus **VI** sich ausgleichen

balance account N (Fin) Ausgleichskonto nt

balanced [ˈbæltənst] ADJ **a** (= objective) report, account, assessment, picture ausgewogen **b** (= well-proportioned) diet, painting, photography, mixture ausgewogen; **nutritionally ~** vom Nährwert her ausgewogen; **~ budget** ausgeglichener Haushalt **c** (Psych) person, personality, life ausgeglichen; view vernünftig

balance: balance sheet N (Fin) Bilanz f; (= document) Bilanzaufstellung f; **balance wheel** N (in watch) Unruh f

balancing [ˈbælənsɪŋ]: **balancing act** N (lit, fig) Balanceakt m; **balancing trick** N Balancekunststück nt

balcony [ˈbælkənɪ] N **a** Balkon m **b** (Theat) oberster Rang

bald [bɔːld] ADJ (+er) **a** person kahl, glatzköpfig; head, tree kahl; bird federlos; **he is ~** er hat eine Glatze; **to go ~** eine Glatze bekommen, kahl werden; **he is going ~ at the temples** er hat Geheimratsecken; **~ patch** kahle Stelle **b** (Aut: = worn) tyre abgefahren **c** style, statement knapp **d** (liter: = bare, denuded) kahl

bald eagle N weißköpfiger Seeadler

balderdash [ˈbɔːldədæʃ] N (dated Brit inf) Kokolores m (dated inf)

bald: bald-faced ADJ (US) lie unverfroren, unverschämt, schamlos; **baldheaded** ADJ kahl- or glatzköpfig

balding [ˈbɔːldɪŋ] ADJ **his ~ head** sein schütter werdendes Haar; **a ~ gentleman** ein Herr mit schütterem Haar; **he is ~** er bekommt langsam eine Glatze **N** Haarausfall m

baldly [ˈbɔːldlɪ] ADV (fig) (= bluntly) unverblümt, unumwunden; (= roughly) grob, knapp

baldness [ˈbɔːldnɪs] N **a** Kahlheit f **b** (of style, statement) Knappheit f

baldy [ˈbɔːldɪ] N (inf) Glatzkopf m

bale¹ [beɪl] **N** (of hay etc) Bündel nt; (out of combine harvester, of cotton) Ballen m; (of paper etc) Pack m **VT** bündeln; zu Ballen verarbeiten

bale² VI (Naut) schöpfen

▶ **bale out VI a** (Aviat) abspringen, aussteigen (inf) (of aus) **b** (Naut) schöpfen **VT** sep (Naut) water schöpfen; ship ausschöpfen, leer schöpfen

Balearic [ˌbælɪˈærɪk] ADJ **the ~ Islands** die Balearen pl

baleful ['beɪlfʊl] ADJ **a** (= *evil*) böse; *look (of bull etc)* stier **b** (= *sad*) traurig

balefully ['beɪlfəlɪ] ADV (= *vindictively*) *watch* mit scheelem Blick; *scowl* böse; (= *sadly*) traurig

balk, baulk [bɔːk] **N a** (= *beam*) Balken *m* **b** (= *obstacle*) Hindernis *nt*, Hemmschuh *m* (*to für*) **VT** *person* hemmen; *plan* vereiteln **VI** (*person*) zurückschrecken (*at vor +dat*); (*horse*) scheuen, bocken (*at bei*)

Balkan ['bɔːlkən] ADJ Balkan-; **the ~ Mountains** der Balkan; **the ~ States** die Balkanländer *pl* **N the ~s** der Balkan, die Balkanländer *pl*

ball¹ [bɔːl] **N a** Ball *m*; (= *sphere*) Kugel *f*; (*of wool, string*) Knäuel *m*; **the cat lay curled up in a ~** die Katze hatte sich zusammengerollt; **~ and chain** Fußfessel *f* (mit Gewicht)
b (*Sport*) Ball *m*; (*Billiards, Croquet*) Kugel *f* **c** (= *delivery of a ball*) Ball *m*; (*Tennis, Golf*) Schlag *m*; (*Ftbl, Hockey*) Schuss *m*; (*Cricket*) Wurf *m*; **the backs were giving their strikers a lot of good ~(s)** die Verteidiger spielten den Stürmern gute Bälle zu; **no ~** (*Cricket*) falsch ausgeführter Wurf
d (= *game*) Ball *m*; (*US: = baseball*) Baseball *nt*; **to play ~** Ball/Baseball spielen
e (*fig phrases*) **to keep the ~ rolling** das Gespräch in Gang halten; **to start** *or* **set** *or* **get the ~ rolling** den Stein ins Rollen bringen; **to have the ~ at one's feet** seine große Chance haben; **the ~ is in your court** Sie sind am Ball (*inf*); **that puts the ~ back in his court** damit ist er wieder am Ball; **to be on the ~** (*inf*) am Ball sein (*inf*), auf Zack *or* Draht sein (*inf*); **to keep several ~s in the air** mehrere Eisen im Feuer haben; **to run with the ~** (*US, inf*) die Sache mit Volldampf vorantreiben (*inf*) → **play N b VT a**
f (*Anat*) **~ of the foot/thumb** Fuß-/Handballen *m*
g (*sl*) (= *testicle*) Ei *nt usu pl* (*sl*); (*pl*) Eier *pl* (*sl*), Sack *m* (*vulg*); **~s!** (= *nonsense*) red keinen Scheiß (*inf*); **~s to him** der kann mich am Arsch lecken (*vulg*); **~s to the regulations** ich scheiß doch auf die Bestimmungen (*sl*); **~s** (*inf: = courage*) Schneid *m* (*inf*), Mumm *m* (*inf*); **he's got us by the ~s** (*sl*) er hat uns in der Zange (*inf*)
h (*old, for gun*) Kugel *f* → **cannon ball**
i (*Cook, of meat, fish*) Klößchen *nt*, Klops *m* **VTI** (*dated US, vulg*) ficken (*vulg*)

ball² **N a** (= *dance*) Ball *m* **b** (*inf: = good time*) Spaß *m*; **to have a ~** sich prima amüsieren (*inf*)

ballad ['bæləd] N (*Mus, Liter*) Ballade *f*

ball-and-socket joint [bɔːlən'sɒkɪtdʒɔɪnt] N Kugelgelenk *nt*

ballast ['bæləst] **N a** (*Naut, Aviat, fig*) Ballast *m*; **to take in/discharge ~** Ballast aufnehmen/abwerfen **b** (= *stone, clinker*) Schotter *m*; (*Rail*) Bettung(sschotter *m*) *f* **VT** (*Naut, Aviat*) mit Ballast beladen

ball: ball bearing N Kugellager *nt*; (= *ball*) Kugellagerkugel *f*; **ball boy** N (*Tennis*) Balljunge *m*; **ball cock** N Schwimmerhahn *m*; **ball control** N Ballführung *f*

ballerina [bælə'riːnə] N Ballerina *f*; (*principal*) Primaballerina *f*

ballet ['bæleɪ] N Ballett *nt*

ballet dancer N Balletttänzer(in) *m(f)*, Balletteuse *f*

balletic [bæ'letɪk] ADJ ballettartig

ballet: ballet master N Ballettmeister(in) *m(f)*; **ballet pump, ballet shoe** N Ballettschuh *m*; **ballet skirt** N Ballettröckchen *nt*

ball: ball game N Ballspiel *nt*; **it's a whole new/different ~** (*fig inf*) das ist eine ganz andere Chose (*inf*); **ball girl** N (*Tennis*) Ballmädchen *nt*

ballistic [bə'lɪstɪk] ADJ ballistisch; **to go ~** (*inf*) ausrasten (*inf*), an die Decke gehen (*inf*)

ballistic missile N Raketengeschoss *nt*

ballistics [bə'lɪstɪks] N *sing* Ballistik *f*; **~ expert** Schusswaffenfachmann *m*

ball: ball joint N (*Tech*) Kugelgelenk *nt*; **ball loss** N (*Sport*) Ballverlust *m*

balloon [bə'luːn] **N a** (*Aviat*) (Frei)ballon *m*; (*toy*) (Luft)ballon *m*; (*Met*) (Wetter)ballon *m*; **the ~ went up** (*fig inf*) da ist die Bombe geplatzt; **that went down like a lead ~** (*inf*) das kam überhaupt nicht an **b** (*in cartoons*) Sprechblase *f* **c** (*Chem: also* **balloon flask**) (Rund)kolben *m* **VI a to go ~-ing** auf Ballonfahrt gehen **b** (= *swell out*) sich blähen

balloon glass N Kognakglas *nt or* -schwenker *m*

balloonist [bə'luːnɪst] N Ballonfahrer(in) *m(f)*

balloon tyre, (*US*) **balloon tire** [bə'luːn,taɪə'] N Ballonreifen *m*

ballot ['bælət] **N a** (= *method of voting*) (geheime) Abstimmung; (= *election*) Geheimwahl *f*; **voting is by ~** die Wahl/Abstimmung ist geheim; **to decide sth by ~** über etw (*acc*) (geheim) abstimmen **b** (= *vote*) Abstimmung *f*; (= *election*) Wahl *f*; **first/second ~** erster/zweiter Wahlgang; **to take** *or* **hold a ~** abstimmen, eine Wahl abhalten; **they demanded a ~** sie verlangten eine (geheime) Wahl **c** (*numbers*) abgegebene Stimmen; **a large ~** eine hohe Wahlbeteiligung **VI** abstimmen; (= *elect*) eine (geheime) Wahl abhalten **VT** *members* abstimmen lassen

ballot: ballot box N Wahlurne *f*; **ballot paper** N Stimm- *or* Wahlzettel *m*; **ballot rigging** N Wahlbetrug *m*, Wahlfälschung *f*

ball: ballpark N **a** (*US*) Baseballstadion *nt* **b** **~ figure** Richtzahl *f*; **in the ~** in dieser Größenordnung; **am I in the right ~?** bewege ich mich in der richtigen Größenordnung?; **ballplayer** N (*US*) Baseballspieler(in) *m(f)*; **ballpoint (pen)** N Kugelschreiber *m*; **ballroom** N Ball- *or* Tanzsaal *m*; **ballroom dancing** N klassische Tänze *pl*, Gesellschaftstänze *pl*

balls-up ['bɔːlzʌp], (*esp US*) **ball up** N (*inf*) Durcheinander *nt*; **he made a complete ~ of the job** er hat bei der Arbeit totale Scheiße gebaut (*sl*); **the repair was a ~!** das war vielleicht eine Scheißreparatur! (*inf*)

▶ **balls up**, (*esp US*) **ball up** VT *sep* (*inf*) verhunzen (*inf*)

ballsy ['bɔːlzɪ] ADJ (*inf*) tollkühn

ball winner N (*esp Ftbl*) zweikampfstarke(r) Spieler(in)

bally ['bælɪ] ADJ (*dated Brit inf*) verflixt (*inf*)

ballyhoo [,bælɪ'huː] (*inf*) **N a** Trara (*inf*), Tamtam (*inf*) *nt*; **to make a lot of ~ about sth** ein großes Trara *or* Tamtam um etw machen (*inf*) **VT** (*US*) marktschreierisch anpreisen

balm [bɑːm] **N a** (*lit, fig*) Balsam *m* **b** (*Bot*) Melisse *f*

balmy ['bɑːmɪ] ADJ (+*er*) (= *fragrant*) wohlriechend; (= *mild*) sanft, lind (*geh*); **~ breezes** sanfte Brisen, linde Lüfte (*geh*)

balneotherapy [,bælnɪə'θerəpɪ] N Balneotherapie *f*, *Behandlung mit Heilbädern und Badekuren*

baloney [bə'ləʊnɪ] **N a** (*inf*) Stuss *m* (*inf*), Quatsch *m* (*inf*); **she gave me some ~ about having had a difficult childhood** sie faselte was von einer schwierigen Kindheit (*inf*) **b** (*US*: = *sausage*) Mortadella *f*

balsa ['bɔːlsə] N (*also* **balsa wood**) Balsa(holz) *nt*

balsam ['bɔːlsəm] **N a** Balsam *m* **b** (*Bot*) Springkraut *nt*

balsam fir N Balsamtanne *f*

Baltic ['bɔːltɪk] ADJ Ostsee-; *language* (= *of Baltic States*) baltisch; **~ port** Ostseehafen *m*; **the ~ States** die baltischen Staaten, das Baltikum **N the ~** die Ostsee

Baltic Sea N Ostsee *f*

baluster ['bæləstə'] N Baluster *m*, Balustersäule *f*

balustrade [,bælə'streɪd] N Balustrade *f*

bamboo [bæm'buː] N Bambus *m attr* Bambus-; **~ shoots** *pl* Bambussprossen *pl*; **the Bamboo Curtain** (*Pol*) der Bambusvorhang

bamboozle [bæm'buːzl] VT (*inf*) (= *baffle*) verblüffen, baff machen (*inf*); (= *trick*) hereinlegen (*inf*); **he was ~d into signing the contract** sie haben es so getrickst *or* sie haben ihn mit Tricks dazu gebracht, dass er den Vertrag unterschrieben hat (*inf*)

ban [bæn] **N** Verbot *nt*; (*Eccl*) (Kirchen)bann *m*; (*Comm*) Embargo *nt*; **to put a ~ on sth** etw verbieten, etw mit einem Verbot/Embargo belegen (*form*); **to lift a ~ on sth** das Verbot einer Sache (*gen*)/das Embargo für etw aufheben; **a ~ on smoking** Rauchverbot *nt* **VT** (= *prohibit*) verbieten; (*Eccl*) auf den Index setzen; *footballer etc* sperren; **to ~ sb from doing sth** jdm verbieten, etw zu tun; **he is ~ned from this bar** er hat hier Lokalverbot; **she was ~ned from driving** ihr wurde Fahrverbot erteilt; **~ned substances** verbotene Substanzen

banal [bə'nɑːl] ADJ banal

banality [bə'nælɪtɪ] N Banalität *f*

banana [bə'nɑːnə] N Banane *f*

banana *in cpds* Bananen-; **banana plantation** N Bananenplantage *f*; **banana republic** N Bananenrepublik *f*

bananas [bə'nɑːnəz] ADJ *pred* (*inf*: = *crazy*) bekloppt (*inf*), bescheuert (*inf*), beknackt (*sl*); **this is driving me ~** das macht mich verrückt *or* ganz krank (*inf*); **he's ~ about her** er steht voll auf sie (*sl*); **the whole place went ~** der ganze Saal drehte durch (*inf*)

banana: banana skin N Bananenschale *f*; **to slip on a ~** (*fig*) über eine Kleinigkeit stolpern; **banana split** N (*Cook*) Bananensplit *nt*; **banana tree** N Bananenstaude *f*

band¹ [bænd] **N a** (*of cloth, iron*) Band *nt*; (*on barrel*) Fassband *nt*, Reifen *m*; (*over book jacket*) (Einband)streifen *m*; (*of leather*) Band *nt*, Riemen *m*; (= *waistband*) Bund *m*; (*on cigar*) Banderole *f*, Bauchbinde *f*; (= *ring: on bird; US: = wedding band*) Ring *m*; (*on machine*) Riemen *m* **b** (= *stripe*) Streifen *m* **c bands** PL (*Eccl, Univ: = collar*) Beffchen *pl* **d** (*Rad*) Band *nt* → **frequency band, waveband** **VT** *bird* beringen

band² **N a** Schar *f*; (*of robbers etc*) Bande *f*; (*of workers*) Trupp *m*, Kolonne *f* **b** (*Mus*) Band *f*; (= *dance band*) Tanzkapelle *f*; (*in circus, brass band, Mil etc*) (Musik)kapelle *f*

▶ **band together** VI sich zusammenschließen

bandage ['bændɪdʒ] **N** Verband *m*; (= *strip of cloth*) Binde *f* **VT** (*also* **bandage up**) *cut* verbinden; *broken limb* bandagieren; **with his heavily ~d wrist** mit einem dick verbundenen Handgelenk

Band-Aid® ['bændeɪd] (*US*) **N** Heftpflaster *nt* **ADJ** (*also* **band-aid**) (*inf*: = *makeshift*) *solution etc* behelfsmäßig

bandan(n)a [bæn'dænə] N großes Schnupftuch; (*round neck*) Halstuch *nt*

B & B [,biː ən'biː] N *abbr of* **bed and breakfast**

bandbox ['bændbɒks] N Hutschachtel *f*

banderol(e) ['bændərəʊl] N (*Naut*) Wimpel *m*, Fähnlein *nt*; (*Her*) Fähnchen *nt*; (*Archit*) Inschriftenband *nt*

bandit ['bændɪt] N Bandit(in) *m(f)*, Räuber(in) *m(f)*

banditry ['bændɪtrɪ] N Banditentum *or* -unwesen *nt*

band: band leader N Bandleader(in) *m(f)*; **bandmaster** N Kapellmeister *m*

bandolier [,bændə'lɪə'] N Schulterpatronengurt *m*

band saw N Bandsäge *f*

bandsman ['bændzmən] N *pl* **-men** [-mən] Musiker *m*, Musikant *m* (*old*); **military ~** Mitglied *nt* eines Musikkorps

band: bandstand N Musikpavillon *m or* -podium *nt*; **bandwagon** N (*US*) Musikwagen *m*, (Fest)wagen der Musikkapelle; **to jump** *or* **climb on the ~** (*also Brit: fig inf*) sich dranhängen, auf den fahrenden Zug aufspringen; **bandwidth** N (*Rad*) Bandbreite *f*

bandy[1] ['bændɪ] ADJ krumm; ~ **legs** (*of people*) O-Beine

bandy[2] VT *jokes* sich (*dat*) erzählen; (*old*) *ball* hin- und herspielen; **to ~ words (with sb)** sich (mit jdm) herumstreiten

▶ **bandy about** (*Brit*) or **around** VT *sep sb's name* immer wieder nennen; *story, secret* herumerzählen, herumtragen; *ideas* verbreiten; *figures, sum, words, technical expressions* um sich werfen mit; **the press have been bandying his name/ these words around a lot** die Presse hat seinen Namen/diese Wörter stark strapaziert; **I'd rather you didn't bandy my nickname around the office** es wäre mir lieber, wenn Sie meinen Spitznamen nicht im Büro herumposaunen würden (*inf*)

bandy-legged [,bændɪ'legd] ADJ (*Brit*) mit krummen Beinen; *person* krummbeinig, o-beinig, O-beinig

bane [beɪn] N **a** (= *cause of distress*) Fluch *m*; **he's/it's the ~ of my life** er/das ist noch mal mein Ende (*inf*) **b** (*old*: = *poison*) Gift *nt*

baneful ['beɪnfʊl] ADJ verhängnisvoll

bang[1] [bæŋ] **N a** (= *noise*) Knall *m*; (*of sth falling*) Plumps *m*; **there was a ~ outside** draußen hat es geknallt; **to go off with a ~** mit lautem Knall losgehen; (*inf*: = *be a success*) ein Bombenerfolg sein (*inf*); **to get more ~ for the buck** or **more ~s for your bucks** (*esp US*) etwas für sein Geld geboten kriegen (*inf*) **b** (= *violent blow*) Schlag *m*; **he gave himself a ~ on the shins** er hat sich (*dat*) die Schienbeine angeschlagen **c** (*Brit sl*: = *sex*) Nummer *f* (*inf*); **to have a ~ with sb** mit jdm bumsen (*inf*)

ADV **a** **to go ~** knallen; (*gun also*) peng machen (*inf*); (*balloon*) zerplatzen, peng machen (*inf*) **b** (*inf*: = *exactly, directly etc*) voll (*inf*), genau; **his answer was ~ on** seine Antwort war genau richtig; **is that right? – ~ on** stimmt das? – haargenau; **she came ~ on time** sie war auf die Sekunde pünktlich; **~ up to date** auf dem neuesten Stand; **they came ~ up against fierce opposition** sie stießen auf heftige Gegenwehr; **the whole ~ shoot** (*Brit*) das ganze Zeug (*inf*); (*people*) die ganze Bande (*inf*)

INTERJ peng; (*of hammer*) klopf; **~ goes my chance of promotion** (*inf*) und tschüs mit der Beförderung (*inf*), und das wars dann mit der Beförderung (*inf*); **~ go my dreams of fame and fortune** (*inf*) und das wars dann mit meinen Träumen von Ruhm und Reichtum (*inf*)

VT **a** (= *thump*) schlagen, knallen (*inf*); **he ~ed his fist on the table** er schlug or haute mit der Faust auf den Tisch; **I'll ~ your heads together if you don't shut up!** (*inf*) wenn ihr nicht ruhig seid, knallts (*inf*); **I felt like ~ing their heads together** (*inf*) ich hätte ihnen am liebsten ein paar links und rechts geknallt (*inf*) **b** (= *shut noisily*) door zuschlagen, zuknallen (*inf*); **you have to ~ the door to close it** Sie müssen die Tür richtig zuschlagen **c** (= *hit, knock*) head, shin sich (*dat*) anschlagen (*on an* +*dat*); **to ~ one's head etc on sth** sich (*dat*) den Kopf etc an etw (*dat*) anschlagen, mit dem Kopf etc gegen etw knallen (*inf*)

VI **a** (*door:* = *shut*) zuschlagen, zuknallen (*inf*); (*fireworks, gun*) knallen; (*engine*) schlagen, krachen; (*hammer*) klopfen; **the door was ~ing in the wind** die Tür schlug im Wind **b** **to ~ on** or **at sth** gegen or an etw (*acc*) schlagen

▶ **bang about** (*Brit*) or **around** VI Krach machen; (*heavy noise*) herumpoltern VT *sep* Krach machen mit; *chairs also* herumstoßen

▶ **bang away** VI **a** (*guns*) knallen; (*persons:* = *keep firing*) wild (drauflos)feuern (*at* auf +*acc*), wild (drauflos)ballern (*inf*) (*at* auf +*acc*); (*workman etc*) herumklopfen or -hämmern (*at* an +*dat*); **to bang away at the typewriter** auf der Schreibmaschine herumhauen or -hämmern (*inf*) **b** (*inf*: = *work industriously*) **to bang away**

(at sth) sich hinter etw (*acc*) klemmen (*inf*) **c** (*sl*: = *have sexual intercourse*) vögeln (*inf*)

▶ **bang down** VT *sep* (hin)knallen (*inf*); *nail* einschlagen; (= *flatten*) flach schlagen; *lid* zuschlagen, zuknallen (*inf*); **to bang down the receiver** den Hörer aufknallen (*inf*)

▶ **bang in** VT *sep nail* einschlagen

▶ **bang into** VI +*prep obj* **a** (= *collide with*) knallen (*inf*) or prallen auf (+*acc*) **b** (*inf*: = *meet*) zufällig treffen

▶ **bang on about** VI +*prep obj* (*Brit inf*) schwafeln von (*inf*)

▶ **bang out** VT *sep* **a** *nail* herausschlagen, heraushauen (*inf*) **b** **to bang out a tune on the piano** eine Melodie auf dem Klavier hämmern (*inf*); **to bang out a letter on the typewriter** einen Brief auf der Schreibmaschine herunterhauen (*inf*)

▶ **bang up** VT SEP (*sl*) *prisoner* einbuchten (*inf*)

bang[2] N (*US:* = *fringe*) Pony *m*, Ponyfransen *pl*; **~s** Ponyfrisur *f*

banger ['bæŋə] N **a** (*Brit inf:* = *sausage*) Wurst *f* **b** (*inf:* = *old car*) Klapperkiste *f* (*inf*) **c** (*Brit:* = *firework*) Knallkörper *m*

Bangladesh [,bæŋglə'deʃ] N Bangladesh *nt*

Bangladeshi [,bæŋglə'deʃɪ] **N** Einwohner(in) *m(f)* von Bangladesh, Bangladeshi *mf* ADJ aus Bangladesh

bangle ['bæŋgl] N Armreif(en) *m*; (*for ankle*) Fußreif or -ring *m*

bang-on [,bæŋ'ɒn] ADJ (*inf*) **to be ~** haargenau stimmen

bang-up ['bæŋʌp] ADJ (*US, sl*) klasse (*inf*), prima (*inf*)

banish ['bænɪʃ] VT *person* verbannen; *cares, fear* vertreiben

banishment ['bænɪʃmənt] N Verbannung *f*

banister, bannister ['bænɪstə] N (*also* **banisters**) Geländer *nt*

banjaxed ['bændʒækst] ADJ (*inf*) *machine* kaputt (*inf*)

banjo ['bændʒəʊ] N *pl* **-es** or (*US*) **-s** Banjo *nt*

bank[1] [bæŋk] **N a** (*of earth, sand*) Wall *m*, Damm *m*; (*Rail*) (Bahn)damm *m*; (= *slope*) Böschung *f*, Abhang *m*; (*of river, lake*) Kurvenüberhöhung *f*; **~ of snow** Schneeverwehung *f* **b** (*of river, lake*) Ufer *nt*; **we sat on the ~s of a river/ lake** wir saßen an einem Fluss/See or Fluss-/ Seeufer **c** (*in sea, river*) (Sand)bank *f* **d** (*of clouds*) Wand *f*, Bank *f* **e** (*Aviat*) Querlage *f*; **to go into a ~** in den Kurvenflug gehen VT **a** *road* überhöhen **b** *river* mit einer Böschung versehen, eindämmen **c** *plane* in die Querlage bringen VI (*Aviat*) den Kurvenflug einleiten, in die Querlage gehen

▶ **bank up** VI *sep earth etc* aufhäufen, aufschütten; (= *support*) mit einer Böschung stützen; *fire* mit Kohlestaub ab- or bedecken (*damit es langsam brennt*) VI (*snow etc*) sich anhäufen; (*clouds also*) sich zusammenballen

bank[2] N **a** **b** (*Gambling*) Bank *f*; **to keep** or **be the ~** die Bank halten or haben **c** (*Med*) Bank *f* **d** (*fig*) Vorrat *m* (*of an* +*dat*) VT *money* zur Bank bringen, einzahlen VI **where do you ~?** bei welcher Bank haben Sie Ihr Konto?; **I ~ with Lloyds** ich habe ein Konto or ich bin bei Lloyds

▶ **bank on** VI +*prep obj* sich verlassen auf (+*acc*), rechnen mit; *sb, sb's help also* zählen or bauen auf (+*acc*); **you mustn't bank on it** darauf würde ich mich nicht verlassen; **I was banking on your coming** ich hatte fest damit gerechnet, dass du kommst

bank[3] N **a** (*Naut:* = *rower's bench*) Ruderbank *f* **b** (= *row of objects, oars*) Reihe *f*; (*on organ, typewriter*) (Tasten)reihe *f*

bankable ['bæŋkəbl] ADJ *cheque etc* einzahlbar; **a very ~ film star** (*fig inf*) ein Filmstar, der viel Geld einbringt

bank: bank acceptance N Bankakzept *nt*; **bank account** N Bankkonto *nt*; **bank balance** N Kontostand *m*; **bank bill** N **a** (*Brit:*

Fin) Bankwechsel *m*, Banktratte *f* **b** (*US:* = *banknote*) Banknote *f*, Geldschein *m*; **bankbook** N Sparbuch *nt*; **bank card** N Scheckkarte *f*; **bank charge** N Kontoführungsgebühr *f*; **bank cheque**, **bank check** (*US*) N Bankscheck *m*; **bank clerk** N Bankangestellte(r) *mf*; **bank code number** N Bankleitzahl *f*; **bank deposit** N Bankeinlage *f*; **bank draft** N Bankwechsel *m*

banker ['bæŋkə] N (*Fin*) Bankier *m*, Bankfachmann *m*/-fachfrau *f*, Banker(in) *m(f)* (*inf*); (*gambling*) Bankhalter(in) *m(f)*

banker's: banker's card N Scheckkarte *f*; **banker's order** N (= *standing order*) Dauerauftrag *m*; **by ~** durch Dauerauftrag

bank: bank giro N Banküberweisung *f*; **bank holiday** N (*Brit*) öffentlicher Feiertag; (*US*) Bankfeiertag *m*

banking[1] ['bæŋkɪŋ] N **a** (*on road, racetrack*) Überhöhung *f* **b** (*Aviat*) Kurvenflug *m*

banking[2] N Bankwesen *nt*; **the world of ~** die Bankwelt; **he wants to go into ~** er will ins Bankfach or Bankgewerbe gehen *attr* Bank-; **the ~ business** das Bankgeschäft; **the ~ side of the business** die Bankangelegenheiten der Firma

banking: banking hours PL Schalterstunden *pl*; **banking house** N Bankhaus *nt*; **banking operation**, **banking transaction** N Bankgeschäft *nt*

bank: bank loan N Bankkredit *m*; **bank manager** N Filialleiter(in) *m(f)* (*einer Bank*); **my ~** der Filialleiter/die Filialleiterin meiner Bank; **banknote** N Banknote *f*, Geldschein *m*; **bank rate** N (*Brit*) Diskontsatz *m*; **bank reference** N (*for new customer etc*) Bankauskunft *f*; **bank robber** N Bankräuber(in) *m(f)*; **bank robbery** N Bankraub *m*; **bankroll** (*esp US*) **N** Bündel *nt* Geldscheine; (*fig*) Geld *nt*, Geldmittel *pl* VT **to ~ sb** jdn finanziell unterstützen; **to ~ sth** etw finanzieren

bankrupt ['bæŋkrʌpt] **N a** Gemein- or Konkursschuldner(in) *m(f)* (*Jur*), Bankrotteur(in) *m(f)* **b** (*fig*) **to be a moral ~** moralisch bankrott sein ADJ **a** (*Jur*) bankrott; **to go ~** Bankrott machen, in Konkurs gehen; **to be ~** bankrott or pleite (*inf*) sein **b** (*fig*) bankrott; **they are totally ~ of ideas** sie haben keinerlei Ideen VT *person, country* zugrunde or zu Grunde richten, ruinieren; *firm also* in den Konkurs treiben

bankruptcy ['bæŋkrʌptsɪ] N **a** (*Jur*) Bankrott *m*, Konkurs *m*; (*instance*) Konkurs *m*; **the possibility of ~** die Möglichkeit eines or des Bankrotts or Konkurses **b** (*fig*) Bankrott *m*

bankruptcy: Bankruptcy Court N Konkursgericht *nt*; **bankruptcy proceedings** PL Konkursverfahren *nt*

bankrupt's certificate ['bæŋkrʌpts-] N Eröffnungsbeschluss *m*

bankrupt's estate N Konkursmasse *f*

bank: bank sort code N Bankleitzahl *f*; **bank statement** N Kontoauszug *m*; **bank transfer** N Banküberweisung *f*

banner ['bænə] N Banner *nt* (*also fig*); (*in processions*) Transparent *nt*, Spruchband *nt*

banner headlines ['bænə'hedlaɪnz] N Schlagzeilen *pl*

banning ['bænɪŋ] N Verbot *nt*; **the ~ of cars from city centres** (*Brit*) or **centers** (*US*) das Fahrverbot in den Innenstädten; **the ~ of three athletes from the Olympic Games** der Ausschluss dreier Teilnehmer von den Olympischen Spielen

bannister ['bænɪstə] N = **banister**

banns [bænz] PL (*Eccl*) Aufgebot *nt*; **to read the ~** das Aufgebot verlesen; **where are you having your ~ called?** wo haben Sie das Aufgebot bestellt?

banquet ['bæŋkwɪt] **N** (= *lavish feast*) Festessen *nt*; (= *ceremonial dinner also*) Bankett *nt* VT üppig or festlich bewirten (*on* mit); (*ceremoniously*) ein Bankett abhalten für VI speisen, tafeln (*geh*); **to ~ on sth** etw speisen

banquet(ing)-hall [ˈbæŋkwɪt(ɪŋ)ˈhɔːl] N Festsaal m, Bankettsaal m

banquette [ˌbæŋˈket] N gepolsterte Bank

banshee [ˈbænʃiː] N (Ir, Myth) Banshee f, Todesfee f; **to scream like a ~** gespenstisch heulen

bantam [ˈbæntəm] N Bantamhuhn nt

bantamweight [ˈbæntəmweɪt] N Bantamgewicht nt

banter [ˈbæntə] N Geplänkel nt; **enough of this foolish ~** lassen wir das alberne Gerede! VT (old) verulken, necken

bantering [ˈbæntərɪŋ] ADJ (= joking) scherzhaft; (= teasing) neckend, flachsig (dial)

Bantu [ˌbænˈtuː] N (= language) Bantu nt; (pl: = tribes) Bantu pl; (= person) Bantu mf, Bantuneger(in) m(f) ADJ Bantu-; **~ tribe** Bantustamm m

banyan (tree) [ˈbænɪən(ˌtriː)] N Bengalische Feige, Banyan m

BAOR abbr of **British Army of the Rhine**

bap (bun) [ˈbæp(bʌn)] N (Brit) weiches Brötchen

baptism [ˈbæptɪzəm] N Taufe f; **~ of fire** (fig) Feuertaufe f

baptismal [bæpˈtɪzməl] ADJ Tauf-; **~ name** Taufname m

Baptist [ˈbæptɪst] N Baptist(in) m(f); **the ~ Church** (= people) die Baptistengemeinde; (= teaching) der Baptismus → **John**

baptize [bæpˈtaɪz] VT taufen

bar¹ [bɑː] N a (of metal, wood) Stange f; (of toffee etc) Riegel m; (of electric fire) Element nt; **~ of gold** Goldbarren m; **a ~ of chocolate, a chocolate ~** (= slab) eine Tafel Schokolade; (Mars® bar etc) ein Schokoladenriegel m; **a ~ of soap** ein Stück nt Seife; **a two-bar electric fire** ein Heizgerät nt mit zwei Heizstäben
b (of window, grate, cage) (Gitter)stab m; (of door) Stange f; **the window has ~s** das Fenster ist vergittert; **behind ~s** hinter Gittern; **to put sb behind ~s** jdn hinter Gitter or hinter Schloss und Riegel bringen
c (Sport) (horizontal) Reck nt; (for high jump etc) Latte f; (= one of parallel bars) Holm m; **~s pl** (parallel) Barren m; (wall) **~s** Sprossenwand f; **to exercise on the ~s** am Barren turnen
d (Ballet) Stange f; **at the ~** an der Stange
e (fig: = obstacle) Hindernis nt (to für), Hemmnis nt (to für); **to be a ~ to sth** einer Sache (dat) im Wege stehen
f (of colour) Streifen m; (of light) Strahl m, Streifen m
g (Jur) **the Bar** die Anwaltschaft; **to be a member of the Bar** Anwalt vor Gericht sein; **to be called** or (US) **admitted to the Bar** als Anwalt (vor Gericht) or Verteidiger zugelassen werden; **to read for the Bar** Jura studieren; **at the ~ of public opinion** (fig) vor dem Forum der Öffentlichkeit
h (for prisoners) Anklagebank f; **to stand at the ~** auf der Anklagebank sitzen; **prisoner at the ~** „Angeklagter!"
i (for drinks) Lokal nt; (esp expensive) Bar f; (part of pub) Gaststube f; (= counter) Theke f, Tresen m; (at railway station) Ausschank m
j (Mus) Takt m; (= bar line) Taktstrich m
k (Brit: on medal) **DSO and ~** zweimal verliehener DSO
l (Her) Balken m
m (Met) Bar nt
n (in river, harbour) Barre f
VT a (= obstruct) road blockieren, versperren; **to ~ sb's way** jdm den Weg versperren or verstellen; **to ~ the way to progress** dem Fortschritt im Wege stehen
b (= fasten) window, door versperren; **to ~ the door against sb** jdm die Tür versperren
c (= exclude, prohibit) person, possibility ausschließen; action, thing untersagen, verbieten; **to ~ sb from a competition** jdn von (der Teilnahme an) einem Wettbewerb ausschließen; **to ~ sb from a career** jdm eine Karriere unmöglich machen; **they've been ~red (from the club)** sie haben Klubverbot; **minors are ~red from**

this club Minderjährige haben keinen Zutritt zu diesem Klub

bar² PREP **~ none** ohne Ausnahme, ausnahmslos; **~ one** außer einem

barb [bɑːb] N a (of hook, arrow) Widerhaken m; (of barbed wire) Stachel m, Spitze f; (of feather) Fahne f; (Bot, Zool) Bart m b (of wit etc) Spitze f; (liter, of remorse) Stachel m VT (lit) mit Widerhaken versehen

Barbados [bɑːˈbeɪdɒs] N Barbados nt

barbarian [bɑːˈbɛərɪən] N (Hist, fig) Barbar(in) m(f) ADJ (Hist, fig) barbarisch

barbaric [bɑːˈbærɪk] ADJ barbarisch; guard etc grausam, roh; (fig inf) conditions grauenhaft

barbarically [bɑːˈbærɪkəlɪ] ADV barbarisch

barbarism [ˈbɑːbərɪzəm] N a (Hist, fig) Barbarei f b (Ling) Barbarismus m

barbarity [bɑːˈbærɪtɪ] N Barbarei f; (fig) Primitivität f; (= cruelty: of guard etc) Grausamkeit f, Rohheit f; **the barbarities of modern warfare** die Barbarei or die Gräuel pl des modernen Krieges

barbarous [ˈbɑːbərəs] ADJ (Hist, fig) barbarisch; (= cruel) grausam; guard etc roh; accent grauenhaft

barbarously [ˈbɑːbərəslɪ] ADV (= cruelly) grausam; speak also grauenhaft (inf)

Barbary [ˈbɑːbərɪ] N Berberei f

Barbary in cpds Berber-; **Barbary ape** N Berberaffe m; **Barbary Coast** N Barbareskenküste f; **Barbary States** PL Barbareskenstaaten pl

barbecue [ˈbɑːbɪkjuː] N a (Cook, = grid) Grill m b (= occasion) Grillparty f, Barbecue nt c (= meat) Grillfleisch nt/-wurst f etc VT steak etc grillen, auf dem Rost braten; animal am Spieß braten

barbed [bɑːbd] ADJ a arrow mit Widerhaken b (fig) wit beißend; remark spitz, bissig

barbed: barbed wire N Stacheldraht m; **barbed-wire fence** N Stacheldrahtzaun m

barbel [ˈbɑːbəl] N (fish) Barbe f; (= filament on fish) Bartel f, Bartfaden m

barbell [ˈbɑːbel] N Hantel f

barber [ˈbɑːbə] N (Herren)friseur m, Barbier m (old); **the ~'s** der Friseur(laden), das (Herren)friseurgeschäft; **at/to the ~'s** beim/zum Friseur

barbershop [ˈbɑːbəʃɒp] N (US) (Herren)friseurgeschäft nt or -laden m ADJ **~ quartet** Barbershop-Quartett nt

barber's pole [ˌbɑːbəzˈpəʊl] N Ladenzeichen der Friseure: Stange mit rot-weißer Spirale

barbican [ˈbɑːbɪkən] N Außen- or Vorwerk nt; (= tower) Wachtturm m

barbie [ˈbɑːbɪ] N (esp Austral inf) → **barbecue N b**

Barbie (doll)® [ˈbɑːbɪ(ˌdɒl)] N Barbie-Puppe® f

bar billiards N (esp Brit) eine Art Billard, das in Pubs gespielt wird

barbitone [ˈbɑːbɪtəʊn] N (Med) barbiturathaltiges Mittel

barbiturate [bɑːˈbɪtjʊrɪt] N Schlafmittel nt, Barbiturat nt; **a ~ overdose** eine Überdosis an Schlafmitteln

barbs [bɑːbz] PL (inf) abbr of **barbiturates**

bar: bar chart N Balkendiagramm nt, Säulendiagramm nt; **bar code** N Strichkode m, Bar-Code m; **bar-coded** ADJ mit Strichkodierung; **bar code reader** N Strichkodeleser m

bard [bɑːd] N a (= minstrel) (esp Celtic) Barde m; (in Ancient Greece) (Helden)sänger m b (old Liter, hum: = poet) Barde m, Bardin f; **the Bard of Avon** Shakespeare

bardic [ˈbɑːdɪk] ADJ poetry etc bardisch

bare [bɛə] ADJ (+er) a (= naked, uncovered) skin, boards, floor nackt, bloß; summit, tree, countryside kahl, nackt; earth, rock nackt; room, garden leer; sword blank; wire blank; style nüchtern; **he stood there ~ to the waist** er stand mit nacktem Oberkörper da; **~ patch** kahle Stelle; **to sleep on ~ boards** auf blanken Brettern schla-

fen; **to lay ~ one's heart** sein Innerstes bloßlegen; **the ~ facts** die nackten Tatsachen; **the ~ fact that he ...** allein die Tatsache, dass er ...; **with his ~ hands** mit bloßen Händen; **she told him the ~ bones of the story** sie erzählte ihm die Geschichte in groben Zügen
b (= scanty, mere) knapp; **a ~ majority** eine knappe Mehrheit; **a ~ subsistence wage** gerade das Existenzminimum; **a ~ ten centimeters** (Brit) or **centimeters** (US) knappe or kaum zehn Zentimeter; **with just the ~st hint of garlic** nur mit einer winzigen Spur Knoblauch; **the ~ minimum** das absolute Minimum
VT breast, leg entblößen; (at doctor's) freimachen; teeth (in anger) fletschen; end of a wire freilegen; **she ~d her teeth in a forced smile** sie grinste gezwungen; **to ~ one's head** den Hut etc ziehen, das Haupt entblößen (liter); **to ~ one's soul** seine Seele entblößen; **to ~ one's heart to sb** jdm sein Herz ausschütten

bare: bareback ADV, ADJ ohne Sattel; **a ~ rider** ein Reiter, der/eine Reiterin, die ohne Sattel reitet; **barefaced** ADJ (fig: = shameless) liar unverfroren, unverschämt, schamlos; cheek unverschämt; **it is ~ robbery** das ist der reine Wucher (inf); **barefoot** ADV barfuß ADJ barfüßig, barfuß pred; **barefooted** ADJ barfüßig, barfuß pred ADV barfuß; **bareheaded** ADJ barhäuptig (geh), ohne Kopfbedeckung ADV ohne Kopfbedeckung, barhaupt (geh); **barelegged** ADJ mit bloßen Beinen

barely [ˈbɛəlɪ] ADV a (= scarcely) kaum; (with figures) knapp, kaum; **we ~ know him** wir kennen ihn kaum; **~ had he started when ...** kaum hatte er angefangen, als ...; **~ concealed horror** kaum verhohlene Entsetzen; **she was ~ ten years old** sie war kaum or knapp zehn Jahre alt b furnished dürftig, spärlich

bareness [ˈbɛənɪs] N Nacktheit f; (of person also) Blöße f; (of trees, countryside) Kahlheit f; (of room, garden) Leere f; (of style) Nüchternheit f

Barents Sea [ˈbærənts siː] N Barentssee f

barf [bɑːf] (esp US inf) VI kotzen (inf) N Kotze f (inf)

barf bag N (esp US inf: Aviat) Kotztüte f (inf), Spucktüte f

barfly [ˈbɑːflaɪ] N (inf) Kneipenhocker(in) m(f) (inf)

bargain [ˈbɑːgɪn] N a (= transaction) Handel m, Geschäft nt; **to make** or **strike a ~** sich einigen; **they are not prepared to make a ~** sie wollen nicht mit sich handeln lassen; **I'll make a ~ with you, if you ...** ich mache Ihnen ein Angebot, wenn Sie ...; **to keep one's side of the ~** sich an die Abmachung halten; **it's a ~!** abgemacht!, einverstanden!; **you drive a hard ~** Sie stellen ja harte Forderungen!; **to offer sb a good ~** jdm ein gutes Angebot machen; **then it started raining into the ~** dann hat es (obendrein) auch noch angefangen zu regnen; **and she was rich into the ~** und außerdem war sie reich; **to get the worst/best of the ~** den schlechteren/besseren Teil erwischen
b (= cheap offer) günstiges Angebot, Sonderangebot nt; (= thing bought) Gelegenheitskauf m; **this jacket is a good ~** diese Jacke ist wirklich günstig; **what a ~!** das ist aber günstig!
VI handeln (for um); (in negotiations) verhandeln; **the traders are not prepared to ~** die Ladenbesitzer lassen nicht mit sich handeln

▶ **bargain away** VT sep rights, advantage etc sich (dat) abhandeln lassen; freedom, independence also veräußern

▶ **bargain for** VI +prep obj (inf, = expect) rechnen mit, erwarten; **I hadn't bargained for that** damit hatte ich nicht gerechnet; **I got more than I bargained for** ich habe vielleicht mein blaues Wunder erlebt! (inf); (in argument also) ich habe vielleicht eins draufbekommen! (inf)

▶ **bargain on** VI +prep obj zählen to on (+acc), sich verlassen auf (+acc)

bargain: bargain basement N Untergeschoss eines Kaufhauses mit Sonderangeboten; **bargain buy** N Preisschlager m (inf); **that's a real**

~ das ist wirklich günstig; **bargain counter** N Sonder(angebots)tisch *m*

bargainer ['bɑːɡɪnə] N **to be a good/bad ~** handeln/nicht handeln können; (*in negotiations*) gut/nicht gut verhandeln können; **to be a hard ~** hart handeln *or* (*in negotiations*) verhandeln

bargain: bargain hunter N the **~s** Leute *pl* auf der Jagd nach Sonderangeboten; **bargain-hunting** N Jagd *f* nach Sonderangeboten; **to go ~** auf Jagd nach Sonderangeboten gehen

bargaining ['bɑːɡɪnɪŋ] N Handeln *nt*; (= *negotiating*) Verhandeln *nt*; **~ position** Verhandlungsposition *f*; **~ table** Verhandlungstisch *m*

bargain: bargain offer N Sonderangebot *nt*, günstiges Angebot; **bargain price** N Sonderpreis *m*; **at a ~** zum Sonderpreis; **bargain rates** PL Sonderpreise *pl*; **bargain sale** N Ausverkauf *m*

barge [bɑːdʒ] **N a** (*for freight*) Last- *or* Frachtkahn *m*; (*unpowered*) Schleppkahn *m*; (= *lighter*) Leichter *m*; (= *ship's boat*) Barkasse *f*; (= *houseboat*) Hausboot *nt*; **the Royal/state ~** die königliche Barkasse/die Staatsbarkasse; (*unpowered*) das königliche Boot/das Staatsboot **b** (= *shove*) Stoß *m*, Rempler *m* (*inf*)
VT a he ~d me out of the way er hat mich weggestoßen; **he ~d his way into the room** er ist (ins Zimmer) hereingeplatzt (*inf*); **he ~d his way through the crowd** er hat sich durch die Menge geboxt (*inf*) **b** (*Sport*) rempeln; **he ~d him off the ball** er hat ihn vom Ball weggestoßen
VI a to ~ into a room (in ein Zimmer) herein-/hineinplatzen (*inf*); **to ~ out of a room** aus einem Zimmer heraus-/hinausstürmen; **he ~d through the crowd** er drängte *or* boxte (*inf*) sich durch die Menge **b** (*Sport*) rempeln

▶ **barge about** (*Brit*) *or* **around** VI (*inf*) herumpoltern (*inf*)

▶ **barge in** VI (*inf*) **a** (= *enter suddenly*) hinein-/hereinplatzen (*inf*) *or* -stürzen **b** (= *interrupt*) dazwischenplatzen (*inf*) (*on* bei); (= *interfere also*) sich einmischen (*on* in +*acc*)

▶ **barge into** VI +*prep obj* **a** (= *knock against*) *person* (hinein)rennen in (+*acc*) (*inf*); (= *shove*) (an)rempeln; *thing* rennen gegen (*inf*) **b** (*inf*) *room, party, conversation* (hinein-/herein)platzen in (+*acc*) (*inf*)

bargee [bɑːˈdʒiː] N Lastschiffer *m*; (= *master*) Kahnführer *m*

bargepole ['bɑːdʒpəʊl] N Bootsstange *f*; **I wouldn't touch it/him with a ~** (*Brit inf*) von so etwas/so jemandem lasse ich die Finger (*inf*); (*out of disgust, distaste*) das/den würde ich noch nicht mal mit der Kneifzange anfassen (*inf*)

bar graph N Balkendiagramm *nt*

baritone ['bærɪtəʊn] N Bariton *m* **ADJ** Bariton-

barium ['bɛərɪəm] N Barium *nt*

barium meal N Bariumbrei *m*

bark[1] [bɑːk] **N a** (*of tree*) Rinde *f*, Borke *f*; **to strip the ~ from** *or* **off a tree** einen Baumstamm schälen **VT** (= *rub off*) *skin* aufschürfen; (= *knock against*) anstoßen, anschlagen; **to ~ one's shin against the table** sich (*dat*) das Schienbein am Tisch anschlagen

bark[2] **N** (*of dog, seal, gun, cough*) Bellen *nt*; **his ~ is worse than his bite** (*Prov*) Hunde, die bellen, beißen nicht (*Prov*) **VI** bellen; **to ~ at sb** jdn anbellen; (*person also*) jdn anfahren; **to be ~ing up the wrong tree** (*fig inf*) auf dem Holzweg sein (*inf*)

▶ **bark out** VT *sep orders* bellen

bark[3], **barque** N **a** (*poet*) Barke *f* (*liter*) **b** (*Naut*) Bark *f*

barkeep(er) ['bɑːkiːp(ə')] N (*US*) Barbesitzer(in) *m(f)*, Gastwirt *m*; (= *bartender*) Barkeeper *m*, Barmann *m*

barker ['bɑːkə'] N (*outside shop, club*) Anreißer *m* (*inf*); (*at fair*) Marktschreier *m* (*inf*)

barking (mad) ['bɑːkɪŋ('mæd)] ADJ (*inf*) total verrückt *or* übergeschnappt (*inf*), völlig durchgeknallt (*sl*)

barley ['bɑːlɪ] N Gerste *f*

barley: barleycorn N Gerstenkorn *nt* → **John**; **barley sugar** N Gersten- *or* Malzzucker *m*; (*sweet*) hartes Zuckerbonbon; **barley water** N Art Gerstenextrakt **lemon/orange ~** konzentriertes Zitronen-/Orangegetränk; **barley wine** N (*Brit*) Art Starkbier

bar line N (*Mus*) Taktstrich *m*

barm [bɑːm] N (Bier)hefe *f*, Bärme *f*

bar: barmaid N Bardame *f*; **barman** N Barkeeper *m*, Barmann *m*

Bar Mitzvah [bɑːˈmɪtsvə] N (= *ceremony*) Bar Mizwa *nt* (= *boy*) Junge, der Bar Mizwa feiert

barmy ['bɑːmɪ] ADJ (+*er*) (*Brit, inf*) bekloppt (*inf*); *idea etc* blödsinnig (*inf*)

barn [bɑːn] N **a** Scheune *f*, Scheuer *f*; (*in field*) Schober *m* (*S Ger, Aus*); **a great ~ of a house** eine große Scheune (*inf*) **b** (*US, for streetcars, trucks*) Depot *nt*, Hof *m*

barnacle ['bɑːnəkl] N **a** (= *shellfish*) (Rankenfuß)krebs *m*, Rankenfüßer *m* **b** (*fig, = person*) Klette *f* (*inf*)

barnacle goose N Nonnengans *f*

barn dance N Bauerntanz *m*

barn door N Scheunentor *nt*; **(as) big as a ~** (*inf*) nicht zu verfehlen

barney ['bɑːnɪ] N (*esp Brit inf, = noisy quarrel*) Krach *m* (*inf*); (= *punch-up*) Schlägerei *f*, Keilerei *f* (*inf*)

barn: barn owl N Schleiereule *f*; **barnstorm** VI (*esp US, Theat*) in der Provinz spielen; (*Pol*) in der Provinz Wahlreden halten; **barnstormer** N (*US Pol*) Wahlredner(in) *m(f)* in der Provinz; (*Theat*) Wanderschauspieler(in) *m(f)*; **barnstorming** ADJ (*Brit*) *performance* hinreißend; **barnyard** N (Bauern)hof *m*; **~ fowl(s)** *pl* (Haus)geflügel *nt*

barometer [bəˈrɒmɪtə'] N (*lit, fig*) Barometer *nt*

barometric [ˌbærəʊˈmetrɪk] ADJ barometrisch, Barometer-

barometric pressure N Atmosphären- *or* Luftdruck *m*

baron ['bærən] N **a** Baron *m* **b** (*fig*) Baron *m*, Magnat *m*; **industrial ~** Industriebaron *m*; **oil ~** Ölmagnat *m*; **press ~** Pressezar *m* **c** (*of beef*) doppeltes Lendenstück

baroness ['bærənɪs] N **a** (*unmarried*) Baronin *f*; (*unmarried*) Baronesse *f*

baronet ['bærənɪt] N Baronet *m*

baronetcy ['bærənɪtsɪ] N (= *rank*) Baronetstand *m*; (= *title*) Baronetswürde *f*

baronial [bəˈrəʊnɪəl] ADJ (*lit*) Barons-; (*fig*) fürstlich, feudal

barony ['bærənɪ] N Baronie *f*

baroque [bəˈrɒk] **ADJ** barock, Barock- **N** (= *style*) Barock *m or nt*; **the ~ period** das *or* der Barock, die Barockzeit

barouche [bəˈruːʃ] N Landauer *m*

barque [bɑːk] N = **bark**[3]

barrack[1] ['bærək] VT *soldiers* kasernieren

barrack[2] **VT** *actor etc* auspfeifen, auszischen **VI** pfeifen

barracking[1] ['bærəkɪŋ] N (*Mil*) Kasernierung *f*

barracking[2] N Pfeifen *nt*, Zischen *nt*, Buhrufe *pl*; **to get a ~** ausgepfiffen werden

barrack-room ['bærəkˌruːm] ADJ *attr* rau, roh; **~ language** Landsersprache *f*

barrack-room lawyer N (*pej*) Paragraphenreiter *m* (*inf*)

barracks ['bærəks] **PL** (*often with sing vb, Mil*) Kaserne *f*; (*fig pej also*) Mietskaserne *f*; **to live in ~** in der Kaserne wohnen **ATTR ~ life** Kasernenleben *nt*; **barrack(s) square** Kasernenhof *m*

barracuda [ˌbærəˈkjuːdə] N Barrakuda *m*, Pfeilhecht *m*

barrage ['bærɑːʒ] N **a** (*across river*) Wehr *nt*; (*larger*) Staustufe *f* **b** (*Mil*) Sperrfeuer *nt*; **under**

this **~ of stones ...** unter diesem Steinhagel ...; **they kept up a ~ of stones** sie bedeckten die Polizei/uns *etc* mit einem Steinhagel **c** (*fig, of words, questions etc*) Hagel *m*; **he faced a ~ of questions** er wurde mit Fragen beschossen

barrage balloon N Sperrballon *m*

barre [bɑː'] N (*Ballet*) Stange *f*; **at the ~** an der Stange

barred [bɑːd] ADJ **a** *suf* **five-barred gate** Weidengatter *nt* (mit fünf Querbalken) **b** **~ window** Gitterfenster *nt*

barrel ['bærəl] **N a** Fass *nt*; (*for oil, tar, rainwater etc*) Tonne *f*; (= *measure: of oil*) Barrel *nt*; **they've got us over a ~** (*inf*) sie haben uns in der Zange (*inf*); **it wasn't exactly a ~ of laughs** (*inf*) es war nicht gerade komisch; **she wasn't exactly a ~ of laughs** (*inf*) sie war nicht gerade in bester Stimmung; **to pay cash on the ~** (*US*) bar auf den Tisch *or* die Kralle (*inf*) zahlen → **biscuit, scrape**
b (*of handgun*) Lauf *m*; (*of cannon etc*) Rohr *nt*; **to give sb both ~s** auf jdn aus beiden Läufen feuern; **I found myself looking down the ~ of a gun** ich hatte plötzlich eine Kanone vor der Nase (*sl*) → **lock**[2]
c (*of fountain pen*) Tank *m*
VT *wine etc* (in Fässer) (ab)füllen; *herring* (in Fässer) einlegen; **~led beer** Fassbier *nt*

▶ **barrel along** VI (*inf*) entlangbrausen (*inf*)

barrel: barrel-chested ADJ breitbrüstig, mit gewölbter Brust; **to be ~** einen gewölbten Brustkasten haben; **barrelful** N Fass *nt*; (*of oil*) Barrel *nt*; **barrelhead** N **to pay cash on the ~** (*US*) bar auf den Tisch *or* die Kralle (*inf*) zahlen; **barrelhouse** (*US*) **N** Kneipe *f*; (= *jazz*) Kneipenjazz *m* **ADJ** **~ blues** alte, in Kneipen gespielte Form des Blues; **barrel organ** N Drehorgel *f*, Leierkasten *m*; **barrel roll** N (*Aviat*) Rolle *f* (*im Kunstflug*); **barrel-shaped** ADJ fass- *or* tonnenförmig; **~ man/woman** Fass *nt* (*inf*)/Tonne *f* (*inf*); **barrel vault** N Tonnengewölbe *nt*

barren ['bærən] **ADJ** **a** unfruchtbar; *land also* karg **b** (*fig*) unfruchtbar, unproduktiv; *discussion also* fruchtlos; *atmosphere also* steril; *style, subject* trocken; *topic* unergiebig; **the house looks ~ without any furniture** das Haus wirkt ohne Möbel leer; **a government ~ of new ideas** eine Regierung, der neue Ideen fehlen *or* die keinerlei neue Ideen hat **N** **barrens** PL (*esp US*) Ödland *nt*

barrenness ['bærənnɪs] N **a** Unfruchtbarkeit *f*; (*of land also*) Kargheit *f* **b** (*fig*) Unfruchtbarkeit *f*, Unproduktivität *f*; (*of discussion also*) Fruchtlosigkeit *f*; (*of atmosphere also*) Sterilität *f*; (*of style, subject, study*) Trockenheit *f*; (*of topic*) Unergiebigkeit *f*

barrette [bəˈret] N (*US*) (Haar)spange *f*

barricade [ˌbærɪˈkeɪd] **N** Barrikade *f* **VT** verbarrikadieren

▶ **barricade in** VT *sep* verbarrikadieren

▶ **barricade off** VT *sep* (mit Barrikaden) absperren

barrier ['bærɪə'] N **a** (*natural*) Barriere *f*; (*man-made, erected also*) Sperre *f*; (= *railing etc*) Schranke *f*; (= *crash barrier*) (Leit)planke *f* **b** (*fig, = obstacle*) Hindernis *nt*, Barriere *f* (*to* für); (*of class, background, education, between people*) Schranke *f*, Barriere *f*; **trade ~s** Handelsschranken *pl*; **~ of language, language ~** Sprachbarriere *f*; **a ~ to success/progress** ein Hindernis für den Erfolg/Fortschritt *etc*; **because of the ~ of her shyness** aufgrund *or* auf Grund ihrer Schüchternheit, die ein Hemmnis ist/war *etc*; **to put up/break down ~s** Zäune errichten/niederreißen

barrier: barrier contraceptive N mechanisches Verhütungsmittel; **barrier cream** N Haut(schutz)creme *f*; **barrier reef** N Barriere-, Wallriff *nt*; **the Great Barrier Reef** das Große Barriereriff

barring ['bɑːrɪŋ] PREP **~ accidents** falls nichts passiert; **~ one** außer einem

barrister [ˈbærɪstə] N (Brit) Rechtsanwalt m/ -anwältin f (bei Gericht), Barrister m

barrow¹ [ˈbærəʊ] N Karre(n m) f; (= wheel barrow) Schubkarre(n m) f; (Rail: luggage barrow) Gepäckkarre(n m) f; (esp Brit: costermonger's) (handgezogener) Obst-/Gemüse-/Fischkarren etc m

barrow² N (Archeol) Hügelgrab nt

barrow boy N Straßenhändler m (mit Karren)

bar sinister N (Her) Bastardfaden m

bar stool N Barhocker m

Bart. abbr of **baronet**

bartender [ˈbɑːtendə] N (US) Barkeeper m; ~! hallo!

barter [ˈbɑːtə] VT tauschen (for gegen) VI tauschen; (as general practice also) Tauschhandel treiben; **to ~ for sth** um etw handeln; **to ~ for peace** über einen Frieden verhandeln N (Tausch)handel m

▶ **barter away** VT sep one's rights verspielen; **to barter sth away for sth** etw für etw verschachern

barter: barter economy N Tauschwirtschaft f; **barter society** N Tauschgesellschaft f

basal [ˈbeɪsl] ADJ **a** (lit, fig) Grund-, fundamental **b** (Med)

basal metabolism N Grundumsatz m

basalt [ˈbæsɔːlt] N Basalt m

bascule [ˈbæskjuːl] N Brückenklappe f; **~ bridge** Klappbrücke f

base¹ [beɪs] N **a** (= lowest part) Basis f; (= that on which sth stands also) Unterlage f; (Archit, of column also) Fuß m; (= support for statue etc) Sockel m; (of lamp, tree, mountain) Fuß m; (= undercoat also) Grundierung f; **at the ~ (of)** unten (an +dat)
b (= main ingredient) Basis f, Haupt- or Grundbestandteil m
c (of theory) Basis f; (= starting point also) Ausgangspunkt m; (= foundation also) Grundlage f
d (Mil etc, fig, for holidays, climbing etc) Standort m, Stützpunkt m; **to return to ~** zur Basis or zum Stützpunkt zurückkehren; **~ of operations** Operationsbasis f
e (Baseball) Mal nt, Base nt; **at** or **on second ~** auf Mal or Base 2, auf dem zweiten Mal or Base; **to get to first ~** (fig) die ersten Erfolge erzielen; **to touch ~** (US, inf) sich melden (with bei); **to touch** or **cover all the ~s** (US fig) an alles denken
f (Gram) Wortstamm m, Wortwurzel f
g (Math) Basis f, Grundzahl f
h (Chem) Lauge f, Base f
i (Geometry) Basis f; (of plane figure also) Grundlinie f; (of solid also) Grundfläche f
VT **a** (lit) stellen; **to be ~d on** ruhen auf (+dat); (statue) stehen auf (+dat); **the supports are firmly ~d in concrete** die Stützen sind fest in Beton eingelassen; **you need something to ~ it on** Sie brauchen dafür eine feste or stabile Unterlage
b (fig) opinion, theory gründen, basieren (on auf +acc); hopes, theory also setzen (on auf +acc); relationship also bauen (on auf +acc); **to be ~d on sb/sth** auf jdm/etw basieren; (hopes, theory also) sich auf jdn/etw stützen; **to ~ one's technique on sb/sth** in seiner Technik von jdm/etw ausgehen; **he tried to ~ his life on this theory** er versuchte, nach dieser Theorie zu leben
c (Mil) stationieren; **the company is ~d in London** die Firma hat ihren Sitz in London; **my job is ~d in Glasgow** ich arbeite in Glasgow; **I am ~d in Glasgow but cover all of Scotland** mein Büro ist in Glasgow, aber ich bereise ganz Schottland; **basing country** (Mil) Stationierungsland nt

base² ADJ (+er) **a** motive, character niedrig; person, thoughts, action, lie, slander gemein, niederträchtig **b** (= inferior) task, level niedrig; coin falsch, unecht; metal unedel **c** (obs) birth (= low) niedrig (old); (= illegitimate) unehelich

baseball [ˈbeɪsbɔːl] N Baseball m or nt

baseball cap N Baseballmütze f

baseboard [ˈbeɪsbɔːd] N (US) Fußleiste f, Lambrie f (S Ger)

base camp N Basislager nt, Versorgungslager nt

-based [-beɪst] ADJ suf **London-based** mit Sitz in London; **to be computer-based** auf Computerbasis arbeiten

base: base form N (Ling) Stammform f; **base hit** N (Baseball) Treffer, durch den der Schlagmann sicher das Mal erreichen kann; **base jumping** N Basejumping nt

baseless [ˈbeɪslɪs] ADJ accusations etc ohne Grundlage, aus der Luft gegriffen; fears, suspicion also unbegründet, grundlos

baseline [ˈbeɪslaɪn] N (Baseball) Verbindungslinie zwischen zwei Malen (Surv) Basis f, Grundlinie f; (of a diagram, Tennis) Grundlinie f (Art) Schnittlinie f von Grundebene und Bildebene

base load N (Elec) Grundlast f, Grundbelastung f

basely [ˈbeɪslɪ] ADV gemein, niederträchtig; act also niedrig

baseman [ˈbeɪsmən] N pl **-men** [-mən] (Baseball) Spieler m an einem Mal

basement [ˈbeɪsmənt] N **a** (in building) Untergeschoss nt, Untergeschoß nt (Aus), Souterrain nt; (in house also) Keller m, Kellergeschoss nt, Kellergeschoß nt (Aus); **~ flat** (Brit) or **apartment** Souterrainwohnung f **b** (Archit, = foundations) Fundament nt

base metal N unedles Metall

baseness [ˈbeɪsnɪs] N **a** (of motive, character) Niedrigkeit f; (of person, thoughts, action, lie, slander) Gemeinheit f, Niederträchtigkeit f **b** (of task) Niedrigkeit f; (of coin) Falschheit f **c** (obs: of birth) (= humbleness) Niedrigkeit f (old); (= illegitimacy) Unehelichkeit f

base: base price N Grundpreis m; **base rate** N Leitzins m, Basiszins m; **base unit** N (Phys) Grundeinheit f; **base wallah** N (Mil sl) Etappenhengst m (Mil sl)

bash [bæʃ] (inf) N **a** Schlag m; **to give sb a ~ on the nose** jdm (eine) auf die Nase hauen (inf); **he gave himself a ~ on the shin** er hat sich (dat) das Schienbein angeschlagen; **the door has had a ~** die Tür hat eine Delle abgekriegt (inf)
b I'll have a ~ (at it) ich probiers mal (inf); **have a ~** probier mal! (inf)
c (dated inf, = party) Party f
VT person (ver)hauen (inf), verprügeln; ball

knallen (inf), dreschen (inf); car, wing eindellen (inf); **to ~ one's head/shin (against** or **on sth)** sich (dat) den Kopf/das Schienbein (an etw (dat)) anschlagen; **I ~ed my shin against the table** ich bin mit dem Schienbein gegen den Tisch geknallt (inf); **to ~ sb on** or **over the head with sth** jdm mit etw auf den Kopf hauen

▶ **bash about** VT sep (esp Brit inf) person durchprügeln (inf), verdreschen (inf); objects demolieren (inf); **he/his luggage got rather bashed about in the accident** er/sein Gepäck ist bei dem Unfall ziemlich lädiert worden (inf)

▶ **bash down** VT sep (inf) door einschlagen

▶ **bash in** VT sep (inf) door einschlagen; hat, car eindellen (inf); **to bash sb's head in** jdm den Schädel einschlagen (inf)

▶ **bash up** VT sep (esp Brit, inf) person vermöbeln (inf), verkloppen (inf); car demolieren (inf), kaputtfahren (inf)

-basher [-bæʃə] suf (inf) **Paki-/queer-basher** Pakistaner-/Schwulenklatscher(in) m(f) (inf)

bashful [ˈbæʃfʊl] ADJ schüchtern; (on particular occasion) verlegen; **give us a song! ah, he's ~** sing was! ach, er geniert sich!

bashfully [ˈbæʃfəlɪ] ADV schüchtern; (on particular occasion) verlegen

bashfulness [ˈbæʃfʊlnɪs] N Schüchternheit f; (on particular occasion) Verlegenheit f

bashing [ˈbæʃɪŋ] N (inf) Prügel pl; **he got a nasty ~** er hat ganz schön was abgekriegt (inf)

-bashing suf (inf) **Paki-/queer-bashing** (physical) Überfälle pl auf Pakistaner/Schwule, Pakistaner-/Schwulenklatschen nt (inf); **Tory-bashing** (verbal) das Schlechtmachen or Heruntermachen (inf) der Konservativen → **Bible-bashing**

Basic [ˈbeɪsɪk] (Comput) abbr of **beginner's all-purpose symbolic instruction code** BASIC nt

basic [ˈbeɪsɪk] ADJ **a** (= fundamental) Grund-; problem also, reason, issue Haupt-; points, issues wesentlich; (= rudimentary) knowledge, necessities, equipment also elementar; character, intention, purpose also eigentlich; (= incompatibility, misconception, indifference, problem grundsätzlich; **to be ~ to sth** Voraussetzung sein für etw; **there's no ~ difference** es besteht kein grundlegender Unterschied; **he has a ~ mistrust of women** er misstraut Frauen grundsätzlich; **a certain ~ innocence** eine gewisse elementare Unschuld; **he is, in a very ~ sense, ...** er ist, im wahrsten Sinne des Wortes, ...; **the ~ thing to remember is ...** woran man vor allem denken muss, ist ...; **must you be so ~!** müssen Sie sich denn so direkt ausdrücken?; **his knowledge is rather ~** er hat nur ziemlich elementare Kenntnisse; **the furniture is rather ~** die Möbel sind ziemlich primitiv; **the room is rather ~** es ist ein recht einfaches Zimmer; **you should know that, that's ~** das müssten Sie aber wissen, das ist doch elementar; **this is ~ to the whole subject** das liegt dem Fach zugrunde or zu Grunde; **~ salary/working hours** Grundgehalt nt/-arbeitszeit f; **the four ~ operations** (Math) die vier Grundrechenarten; **~ vocabulary** Grundwortschatz m
b (= original) zugrunde or zu Grunde liegend; theory also, assumption ursprünglich
c (= essential) notwendig; **knowledge of French is/good boots are absolutely ~** Französischkenntnisse/gute Stiefel sind unbedingt nötig or sind eine Voraussetzung
d (Chem) basisch
PL **~s** das Wesentliche; **to get down to (the) ~s** zum Kern der Sache or zum Wesentlichen kommen; **to get back to ~s** sich auf das Wesentliche besinnen

basically [ˈbeɪsɪkəlɪ] ☻ 26.3 ADV im Grunde; (= mainly) im wesentlichen, hauptsächlich; **is that correct? – ~ yes** stimmt das? – im Prinzip, ja or im Grunde schon; **it's ~ finished** es ist praktisch or im Grunde fertig; **that's ~ it** das wärs im Wesentlichen

basic: basic English N englischer Grundwortschatz, Basic English nt; **basic food** N , **basic foodstuffs** PL Grundnahrungsmittel pl;

basic industry N Schlüsselindustrie f; **basic rate** N (of wage) Grundgehalt nt; (of tax) Eingangssteuersatz m; **the ~ of income tax** der Eingangssteuersatz bei Lohn- und Einkommensteuer; **basic salary** N Grundgehalt nt, Fixum nt; **basic slag** (Chem) N Thomasschlacke f; **basic wage** N usu pl Grundlohn m

basil ['bæzl] N (Bot) Basilikum nt, Basilienkraut nt

basilica [bə'zɪlɪkə] N Basilika f

basilisk ['bæzɪlɪsk] N (Myth, Zool) Basilisk m

basin ['beɪsn] N [a] (= vessel) Schüssel f; (= wash basin) (Wasch)becken nt; (of fountain) Becken nt [b] (Geog) Becken nt; (= harbour basin) Hafenbecken nt; (= yacht basin) Jachthafen m; (= hollow between mountains also) Kessel m

basinful ['beɪsnfʊl] N Schüssel f (voll)

basis ['beɪsɪs] N pl **bases** [a] (of food, mixture etc) Basis f, Grundlage f [b] (fig, = foundation) Basis f; (for assumption) Grund m; **we're working on the ~ that ...** wir gehen von der Annahme aus, dass ...; **to be on a sound ~** (business) auf festen Füßen stehen; (theory) auf einer soliden Basis ruhen; **to put sth on a sounder ~** einer Sache (dat) eine solidere Basis geben, etw auf eine solidere Basis stellen; **on the ~ of this evidence** aufgrund or auf Grund dieses Beweismaterials; **to approach a problem on a scientific ~** ein Problem wissenschaftlich herangehen

basis point N (Fin) Basispunkt m

bask [baːsk] VI (in sun) sich aalen (in in +dat); (in sb's favour etc) sich sonnen (in in +dat)

basket ['baːskɪt] N [a] Korb m; (for rolls, fruit etc) Körbchen nt; **a ~ of eggs** ein Korb/Körbchen (voll) Eier; **a ~ of currencies** ein Währungskorb m [b] (Basketball) Korb m [c] (euph sl, = bastard) Idiot m, Blödmann m

basket: basketball N Basketball m; **basket case** N (sl) hoffnungsloser Fall; **basket chair** N Korbsessel m; **basket clause** N (Jur) Generalklausel f; **basketful** ['baːskɪtfʊl] ADJ **a ~ of food** ein Korb voll(er) Essen; **basket-maker** N Korbmacher(in) m(f), Korbflechter(in) m(f)

basketry ['baːskɪtrɪ] N Korbflechterei f

basket: basket weave N Leinenbindung f; **basketwork** N Korbflechterei f; (= articles) Korbarbeiten pl; **a ~ chair** ein Korbstuhl m

basking shark ['baːskɪŋˌʃaːk] N Riesenhai m

Basle [baːl] N Basel nt

Basque [bæsk] N [a] (= person) Baske m, Baskin f [b] (= language) Baskisch nt ADJ baskisch

basque [bæsk] N Bustier nt

bas-relief ['bæsrɪˌliːf] N Basrelief nt

bass[1] [beɪs] (Mus) N Bass m ADJ Bass-

bass[2] [bæs] N pl **-(es)** (= fish) (Wolfs)barsch m

bass [beɪs]: **bass clef** N Bassschlüssel m; **bass drum** N große Trommel

basset hound ['bæsɪthaʊnd] N Basset m

bassinet [ˌbæsɪ'net] N Babykorb m; (old, = pram) Kinderwagen m

bassoon [bə'suːn] N Fagott nt

bassoonist [bə'suːnɪst] N Fagottbläser(in) m(f), Fagottist(in) m(f)

basso profundo [ˌbæsəʊprə'fʊndəʊ] N tiefer Bass

bass viol [beɪs-] N Gambe f

bastard ['baːstəd] N [a] (lit) uneheliches Kind, Bastard m (old); (fig, = hybrid) Bastard m, Kreuzung f [b] (sl, = person) Scheißkerl m (inf); **stupid ~** Arschloch nt (vulg); **poor ~** armes Schwein (inf), armer Hund (inf) [c] (sl, = difficult job etc) **this question is a real ~** diese Frage ist wirklich hundsgemein (inf); **a ~ of a job** etc eine Scheißarbeit etc (inf) ADJ [a] (lit) child unehelich [b] (fig, = hybrid) dog, plant Bastard-; language Misch-

bastard file N (Tech) Bastardfeile f

bastardize ['baːstədaɪz] VT (fig) verfälschen

bastard title N (Typ) Schmutztitel m

bastardy ['baːstədɪ] N (form) Unehelichkeit f; **~ proceedings** pl (US Jur) Vaterschaftsprozess m

---

baste[1] [beɪst] VT (Sew) heften

baste[2] VT (Cook) (mit Fett) beträufeln or begießen

basting[1] ['beɪstɪŋ] N (Sew, = act) Heften nt; (= stitches) Heftnaht f; **to take out the ~** die Heftfäden herausziehen

basting[2] N (inf, = beating) Prügel pl; **to give sb a ~** (team, critics) jdn fertig machen (inf)

bastion ['bæstɪən] N (lit, fig) Bastion f; (= person) Stütze f, Säule f

bat[1] [bæt] N (Zool) Fledermaus f; **to have ~s in the belfry** eine Meise or einen Sparren haben (inf); **he ran/drove like a ~ out of hell** er lief/fuhr, wie wenn der Teufel hinter ihm her wäre; **(as) blind as a ~** stockblind (inf); **silly old ~** (pej inf) alte Schrulle (pej inf)

bat[2] (Sport) N [a] (Baseball, Cricket) Schlagholz nt, Keule f; (Table-tennis) Schläger m; **off one's own ~** (Brit inf) auf eigene Faust (inf); **right off the ~** (US) prompt [b] (= batsman) he is a good ~ er schlägt gut [c] (inf, = blow) Schlag m VT (Baseball, Cricket) schlagen; **to ~ sth around** (US, inf, = discuss) etw bekakeln (inf) VI (Baseball, Cricket) schlagen; **to go (in) to ~ for sb** (fig) sich für jdn einsetzen

bat[3] VT **not to ~ an eyelid** (Brit) or **eye** (US) nicht mal mit der Wimper zucken

bat[4] N [a] (dated Brit, inf, = speed) **at a fair old ~** mit 'nem ganz schönen Zahn drauf (inf) [b] (US, sl, = binge) Sauftour f (inf); **to go on a ~** auf Sauftour gehen (inf)

batch [bætʃ] N (of people) Schwung m (inf); (of loaves) Schub m; (of prisoners, recruits also) Trupp m; (of things dispatched also) Sendung f, Ladung f; (of letters, books, work also) Stoß m, Stapel m; (of dough, concrete etc) Ladung f

batch (Comput): **batch command** N Batchbefehl m; **batch file** N Stapeldatei f, Batchdatei f; **batch job** N Stapelverarbeitung f; **batch processing** N Stapelverarbeitung f, Batchbetrieb m

bated ['beɪtɪd] ADJ **with ~ breath** mit angehaltenem Atem

bath [baːθ] N [a] Bad nt; **to have** or **take a ~** baden, ein Bad nehmen (geh); **to give sb a ~** jdn baden → **blood bath, Turkish** etc [b] (= bathtub) (Bade)wanne f; **to empty the ~** das Badewasser ablassen; **I was just in my** or **the ~** ich war or saß gerade im Bad or in der Wanne (inf); **a room** with **~** ein Zimmer mit Bad → **eyebath, foot bath** etc [c] **~s** pl (Hist) Bäder pl, Badeanlagen pl; **(swimming) ~s** pl (Schwimm-) bad nt; **(public) ~s** pl Badeanstalt f, öffentliches Bad nt; (Tech, Chem, Phot) Bad nt; (= container) Behälter m [e] (Brit) **the Order of the Bath** der Orden vom Bade VT (Brit) baden VI (Brit) (sich) baden

bath bun N Hefebrötchen mit Zitronat und Orangeat

Bath chair N Kranken- or Rollstuhl m

bath cube N Würfel m Badesalz

bathe [beɪð] VT [a] person, feet, eyes, wound etc baden; (with cotton wool etc) waschen; **to ~ one's eyes** ein Augenbad machen; **~d in tears** tränenüberströmt; **to be ~d in light** in Licht gebadet sein; **to be ~d in sweat** in Schweiß gebadet sein, schweißgebadet sein [b] (US) = **bath** VT VI baden N Bad nt; **to have** or **take a ~** baden

bather ['beɪðə'] N Badende(r) mf

bathhouse ['baːθhaʊs] N (old) Bad(e)haus nt (old)

bathing ['beɪðɪŋ] N Baden nt

bathing: bathing beach N Badestrand m; **bathing beauty** N Badeschönheit f; **bathing belle** N Badeschönheit f; **bathing cap** N Bademütze f, Badekappe f; **bathing costume** N Badeanzug m; **bathing hut** N Badehäuschen nt; **bathing machine** N transportable Umkleidekabine; **bathing suit** N (dated esp US) = **bathing costume**; **bathing trunks** PL Badehose f; **bathing waters** PL Badegewässer pl

---

bathmat ['baːθmæt] N Badematte f or -vorleger m

bathos ['beɪθɒs] N (= anticlimax) Abfall or Umschlag m ins Lächerliche; (= sentimentality) falsches Pathos

bathrobe ['baːθrəʊb] N Bademantel m

bathroom ['baːθruːm] N Bad(ezimmer) nt; (euph, = lavatory) Toilette f

bathroom: bathroom cabinet N Toilettenschrank m; **bathroom fittings** PL Badezimmerausstattung f; **bathroom scales** PL Personenwaage f

bath: bath salts PL Badesalz nt; **bath sheet** N großes Badetuch; **bathtowel** N Badetuch nt; **bathtub** N Badewanne f

bathysphere ['bæθɪsfɪə'] N Tauchkugel f, Bathysphäre f

batik ['bætɪk] N Batik m; (= cloth) Batikdruck m

batiste [bæ'tiːst] N Batist m

batman ['bætmən] N pl **-men** [-mən] (Mil) (Offiziers)bursche m

baton ['bætən, (US) 'bætən] N [a] (Mus) Taktstock m, Stab m; (Mil) (Kommando)stab m; **under the ~ of** (Mus) unter der Stabführung von [b] (of policeman) Schlagstock m; (for directing traffic) Stab m [c] (in relay race) Staffelholz nt, Stab m; **to hand on** or **pass the ~ to sb** (fig) die Verantwortung an jdn abgeben

baton: baton charge N Schlagstockeinsatz m; **to make a ~** Schlagstöcke einsetzen; **baton round** N (Mil) Plastikgeschosse pl; **baton twirler** N Tambourmajor(in) m(f)

bats [bæts] ADJ pred (inf) bekloppt (inf); **you must be ~** du spinnst wohl! (inf)

batsman ['bætsmən] N pl **-men** [-mən] (Sport) Schlagmann m

battalion [bə'tælɪən] N (Mil, fig) Bataillon nt

batten ['bætn] N [a] Leiste f, Latte f; (for roofing) Dachlatte f; (for flooring) (Trag)latte f [b] (Naut, for sail) Segellatte f; (for hatch) Schalklatte f VT [a] roof, floor mit Latten versehen [b] (Naut) sail mit Latten verstärken; hatch (ver-) schalken

▶ **batten down** VT sep **to batten down the hatches** die Luken schalken (spec) or dichtmachen; (fig, = close doors, windows) alles dicht machen; (= prepare oneself) sich auf etwas gefasst machen

▶ **batten on** VI +prep obj schmarotzen bei

▶ **batten onto** VI +prep obj idea sich (dat) aneignen

batter[1] ['bætə'] N (Cook, for frying) (Ausback)teig m; (for pancakes, waffles etc) Teig m

batter[2] N (Sport) Schlagmann m

batter[3] VT [a] (= hit) einschlagen auf (+acc); (= strike repeatedly) wife, baby schlagen, (ver)prügeln; (with battering ram) berennen; **he ~ed him about the head with an iron bar** er schlug ihm mit einer Eisenstange auf seinen Kopf ein; **the ship was ~ed by the waves** die Wellen krachten unentwegt gegen das Schiff; **the house was ~ed by the wind** der Wind rüttelte unentwegt am Haus [b] (= damage) böse or übel zurichten; car also, metal zer- or verbeulen; **the town was badly ~ed during the war** die Stadt wurde während des Krieges schwer zerbombt [c] (inf) opponent eins or eine draufgeben (+dat) (inf); **to get ~ed** eins or eine draufbekommen (inf) VI schlagen, trommeln (inf); **to ~ at the door** an die Tür hämmern or trommeln (inf)

▶ **batter about** VT sep (esp Brit) sb schlagen, verprügeln; sth grob umgehen mit, ramponieren (inf)

▶ **batter down** VT sep wall zertrümmern; door also einschlagen; resistance zerschlagen

▶ **batter in** VT sep door einschlagen; (with ram) einrennen

battered ['bætəd] ADJ böse or übel zugerichtet, lädiert (inf); wife, baby misshandelt; hat, car, teapot also verbeult; city zerbombt; house, furniture mitgenommen, ramponiert (*inf*); *nerves* zerrüttet; *image, reputation* ramponiert (*inf*); **~ baby syndrome** Phänomen *nt* der Kindesmisshandlung

batterer ['bætərə] N **wife-batterer** prügelnder Ehemann; **child-batterer** prügelnder Vater, prügelnde Mutter; **treatment programmes for ~s** Behandlungsprogramme für prügelnde Ehepartner und Eltern

battering ['bætərɪŋ] N (*lit*) Schläge *pl*, Prügel *pl*; (*of baby, wife*) Misshandlung *f*; **he/it got** *or* **took a real ~** er/es hat ganz schön was abgekriegt (*inf*), es hat schwer gelitten; **to give sb a ~** jdn verprügeln; **to give sth a ~** etw ramponieren (*inf*) *or* demolieren (*inf*); **he'll give his opponent a ~** er wird es seinem Gegner geben (*inf*)

battering ram N Rammbock *m*, Sturmbock *m*

battery ['bætərɪ] N (*all senses*) Batterie *f*; (*fig, of arguments etc*) Reihe *f* → **assault**

battery: battery acid N Batteriesäure *f*; **battery charger** N Ladegerät *nt*; **battery compartment** N Batteriefach *nt*; **battery farm** N Legebatterie *f*; **battery farming** N Legebatterien *pl*; **battery fire** N (*Mil*) Geschützfeuer *nt*; **battery hen** N (*Agr*) Batteriehuhn *nt*; **battery-powered** ADJ batteriebetrieben; **battery set** N (= *radio*) Batteriegerät *nt*

battle ['bætl] N (*lit*) Schlacht *f*; (*fig*) Kampf *m*; **to give/offer/refuse ~** sich zum Kampf *or* zur Schlacht stellen/bereit erklären/den Kampf *or* die Schlacht verweigern; **to fight a ~** eine Schlacht schlagen (*also fig*), einen Kampf führen; **I don't need you to fight my ~s for me** ich kann mich schon alleine durchsetzen; **to do ~ for sb/sth** sich für jdn/etw schlagen, sich für jdn/etw einsetzen; **to win the ~ but lose the war** (*fig*) die Schlacht gewinnen, aber den Krieg verlieren; **killed in ~** (im Kampf) gefallen; **~ of wits** Machtkampf *m*; **~ of words** Wortgefecht *nt*; **~ of wills** geistiger Wettstreit; **to have a ~ of wits** sich geistig messen; **we are fighting the same ~** wir ziehen am selben Strang; **that's half the ~** damit ist schon viel gewonnen; **getting an interview is only half the ~** damit, dass man ein Interview bekommt, ist es noch nicht getan; **~ of the giants** Kampf *m* der Giganten; **~ of the sexes** Geschlechterkampf *m* ◾ VI sich schlagen; (*fig also*) kämpfen, streiten; **to ~ for breath** um Atem ringen; **to ~ through a book** *etc* sich durch ein Buch *etc* (durch-) kämpfen ◾ VT (*fig*) **to ~ one's way through difficulties/four qualifying matches** sich (durch Schwierigkeiten)/durch vier Qualifikationsspiele durchschlagen

▶ **battle on** VI (*fig*) weiterkämpfen

▶ **battle out** VT *sep* **to battle it out** sich einen harten Kampf liefern

battle: battle-axe, (*US*) **battle-ax** N (= *weapon*) Streitaxt *f*; (*inf*, = *woman*) Drachen *m* (*inf*); **battle cruiser** N Schlachtkreuzer *m*; **battle cry** N Schlachtruf *m*

battledore ['bætldɔː'] N (Federball)schläger *m*; **~ and shuttlecock** Federball *m*

battle: battledress N Kampfanzug *m*; **battle fatigue** N Kriegsmüdigkeit *f*; **battlefield** N Schlachtfeld *nt*; **battle fleet** N Schlachtflotte *f*; **battleground** N Schlachtfeld *nt*; **battle lines** PL Kampflinien *pl*; **the ~ are drawn** (*fig*) die Fronten sind abgesteckt

battlements ['bætlmənts] PL Zinnen *pl*

battle: battle order N Schlachtordnung *f*; **battle plan** N (*lit, fig*) Schlachtplan *m*; **battle royal** N (*fig*, = *quarrel*) heftige Auseinandersetzung; **battle-scarred** ADJ (*lit*) *person, country* vom Krieg gezeichnet; (*fig*) *furniture* schwer mitgenommen, ramponiert (*inf*); (*inf*) *person* schwer mitgenommen, angeschlagen; **battleship** N Kriegs- *or* Schlachtschiff *nt*; **~s** (= *game*) Schiffeversenken *nt*; **battle song** N Kampf- *or* Kriegslied *nt*; **battle zone** N Kriegs- *or* Kampfgebiet *nt*

batty ['bætɪ] ADJ (*+er*) (*Brit inf*) verrückt; *person also* plemplem *pred* (*inf*); **to go ~** überschnappen (*inf*)

bauble ['bɔːbl] N Flitter *m no pl*; **~s** Flitterzeug *nt*

baud [bɔːd] N (*Comput*) Baud *nt*; **at 1200 ~** bei 1200 Baud; **~ rate** Baudrate *f*

baulk [bɔːk] N = **balk**

bauxite ['bɔːksaɪt] N Bauxit *m*

Bavaria [bə'vɛərɪə] N Bayern *nt*

Bavarian [bə'vɛərɪən] N *a* (= *person*) Bayer(in) *m(f)* *b* (= *dialect*) Bayrisch *nt* ADJ bay(e)risch

bawd [bɔːd] N (= *brothel keeper*) Bordellwirtin *f*, Puffmutter *f* (*inf*)

bawdiness ['bɔːdɪnɪs] N Derbheit *f*

bawdy ['bɔːdɪ] ADJ (*+er*) derb; **~ talk** derbes Gerede

bawl [bɔːl] VI *a* (= *shout*) brüllen, schreien; (= *sing*) grölen (*inf*); **to ~ for help** um Hilfe schreien *b* (*inf*, = *weep*) plärren (*inf*), heulen (*inf*) VT *order* brüllen, schreien; *song* grölen (*pej inf*)

▶ **bawl out** VT *sep* *a* *order* brüllen; *song* schmettern, grölen (*pej inf*) *b* (*inf*, = *scold*) ausschimpfen

bawling-out ['bɔːlɪŋ'aʊt] N (*inf*) Schimpfkanonade *f* (*inf*); **to give sb a ~** jdn zur Schnecke machen (*inf*)

bay[1] [beɪ] N Bucht *f*; (*of sea also*) Bai *f*; **Hudson Bay** die Hudsonbai

bay[2] N (*Bot*) Lorbeer(baum) *m*

bay[3] N *a* (*Archit*) Erker *m* *b* (= *loading bay*) Ladeplatz *m*; (= *parking bay*) Parkbucht *f*; (*Rail*) Abstellgleis *nt* *c* (*Aviat*, = *bomb bay*) Bombenschacht *m* *d* (= *sick bay*) (Kranken)revier *nt*

bay[4] N (*of dogs*) Bellen *nt no pl*; (*Hunt*) Melden *nt no pl*; **to bring to/be at ~** (*Hunt*) stellen/gestellt sein; (*fig*) in die Enge treiben/getrieben sein; **to have sb at ~** (*fig*) jdn in der Zange haben (*inf*); **to keep sb/sth at ~** jdn/etw in Schach halten VI bellen; (*Hunt also*) melden; **to ~ at the moon** den Mond anbellen *or* anheulen; **to ~ for blood** Vergeltung fordern; **to ~ for sb's blood** jds Kopf fordern

bay[5] ADJ *horse* (kastanien)braun N (= *horse*) Braune(r) *m*; **red ~** rötlicher Brauner

bay leaf N Lorbeerblatt *nt*

bayonet ['beɪənɪt] N Bajonett *nt*, Seitengewehr *nt*; **with ~s fixed/at the ready** mit aufgepflanzten/gefällten Bajonetten VT mit dem Bajonett *or* Seitengewehr aufspießen

bayonet fitting N (*Elec*) Bajonettfassung *f*

bayou ['baɪuː] N (*US, of river*) sumpfiger Flussarm; (*of lake*) sumpfiger Ausfluss (*aus einem See*)

bay: bay rum N Pimentöl *nt*; **bay tree** N Lorbeerbaum *m*; **bay window** N Erkerfenster *nt*

bazaar [bə'zɑː'] N Basar *m*

bazooka [bə'zuːkə] N Bazooka *f*, Panzerfaust *f*, Panzerschreck *m*

BB N (*Brit*) abbr of **Boys' Brigade** ADJ (*on pencil*) 2B

BBC abbr of **British Broadcasting Corporation** BBC *f*

BBFC abbr of **British Board of Film Classification**

BBQ abbr of **barbecue**

BBS (*Comput*) abbr of **bulletin board system** BBS *nt*

BC[1] abbr of **before Christ** v. Chr

BC[2] abbr of **British Columbia**

BCG abbr of **Bacille Calmette Guérin** BCG

BD abbr of **Bachelor of Divinity**

be [biː]	
pres **am, is, are**, *pret* **was, were**, *ptp* **been**	
1 COPULATIVE VERB	3 INTRANSITIVE VERB
2 AUXILIARY VERB	4 IMPERSONAL VERB

1 – COPULATIVE VERB

a with adjective, noun, pronoun sein; **to be critical of** kritisch sein *or* sich kritisch äußern über

(+*acc*); **be sensible!** sei vernünftig!; **who's that? – it's me/that's Mary** wer ist das? – ich bins/das ist Mary; **if I were you** wenn ich Sie *or* an Ihrer Stelle wäre; **he is a soldier/a German** er ist Soldat/Deutscher; **he wants to be a doctor** er möchte Arzt werden

> Note that the article is used in German only when the noun is qualified by an adjective.

he's a good student/a true Englishman er ist ein guter Student/ein echter Engländer

b referring to physical, mental state **how are you?** wie gehts?; **I'm better now** es geht mir jetzt besser; **she's not at all well** es geht ihr gar nicht gut; **to be hungry/thirsty** Hunger/Durst haben, hungrig/durstig sein; **I am hot/cold/frozen** mir ist heiß/kalt/eiskalt; **they were horrified** sie waren entsetzt

c age sein; **he's five** er ist fünf; **how old is she?** wie alt ist sie?; **he'll be three next month** er wird nächsten Monat drei (Jahre alt)

d = cost kosten; **how much is that?** wie viel *or* was kostet das?

e Math sein; **two times two is** *or* **are four** zwei mal zwei ist *or* sind *or* gibt vier

f with possessive gehören (+*dat*); **that book is your brother's/his** das Buch gehört Ihrem Bruder/ihm, das ist das Buch Ihres Bruders/das ist sein Buch

g in exclamations **was he pleased to hear it!** er war vielleicht froh, das zu hören!; **but wasn't she glad when ...** hat sie sich vielleicht gefreut, als ...

2 – AUXILIARY VERB

a in continuous tenses

> Note how German uses the simple tense:

what are you doing? was machst du da?; **she's always complaining** sie beklagt sich dauernd; **they're coming tomorrow** sie kommen morgen

> Note how German uses the present tense:

I have been waiting for you for half an hour ich warte schon seit einer halben Stunde auf Sie; **will you be seeing her tomorrow?** sehen *or* treffen Sie sie morgen?; **you will be hearing from us** Sie hören von uns, Sie werden von uns hören

> Note the use of bei + infinitive:

we're just drinking coffee wir sind (gerade) beim Kaffeetrinken; **I've just been packing my case** ich war gerade beim Kofferpacken; **I was packing my case when ...** ich war gerade beim Kofferpacken, als ...

b in passive constructions werden; **he was run over** er ist überfahren worden, er wurde überfahren; **the box had been opened** die Schachtel war geöffnet worden; **it is/was being repaired** es wird/wurde gerade repariert; **I will not be intimidated** ich lasse mich nicht einschüchtern

♦ **to be/not to be ...**

intention **they are shortly to be married** sie werden bald heiraten; **they were to have been married last week** sie hätten letzte Woche heiraten sollen; **the car is to be sold** das Auto soll verkauft werden; **she was/he was to have been dismissed but ...** sie sollte entlassen werden, aber .../sie hätte entlassen werden sollen, aber ...

◆ ought to **he is to be pitied/not to be envied** er ist zu bedauern/nicht zu beneiden; **not to be confused with** nicht zu verwechseln mit; **what is to be done?** was ist zu tun?, was soll geschehen?

obligation, command **I am to look after her** ich soll mich um sie kümmern; **I am not to be disturbed** ich möchte nicht gestört werden; **he is not to open it** er soll es nicht öffnen; **I wasn't to tell you his name** ich sollte *or* durfte Ihnen nicht sagen, wie er heißt; (*but I did*) ich hätte Ihnen eigentlich nicht sagen sollen *or* dürfen, wie er heißt

= be destined **she was never to return** sie sollte nie zurückkehren

possibility **he was not to be persuaded** er war

nicht zu überreden, er ließ sich nicht überreden; **if it were** or **was to snow** falls or wenn es schneien sollte; **and were I** or **if I were to tell him?** und wenn ich es ihm sagen würde?

c [in tag questions/short answers] **he's always late, isn't he? – yes he is** er kommt doch immer zu spät, nicht? – ja, das stimmt; **he's never late, is he? – yes he is** er kommt nie zu spät, oder? – oh, doch; **you're not ill, are you? – yes I am/no I'm not** Sie sind doch nicht (etwa) krank? – doch!/nein; **it's all done, is it? – yes it is/no it isn't** es ist also alles erledigt? – ja/nein

3 – INTRANSITIVE VERB

a sein; (= *remain*) bleiben; **I'm going to Berlin – how long will you be there?** ich gehe nach Berlin – wie lange wirst du dort bleiben?; **he is there at the moment but he won't be much longer** im Augenblick ist er dort, aber nicht mehr lange; **we've been here a long time** wir sind schon lange hier; **the powers that be** die zuständigen Stellen; **let me/him be** lass mich/ihn (in Ruhe); **be that as it may** wie dem auch sei; **to be or not to be** Sein oder Nichtsein

b = *be situated* sein; (*town, forest, papers*) liegen, sein; (*car, tower, chair*) stehen, sein

c = *visit, call* **I've been to Paris** ich war schon (ein)mal in Paris; **the milkman has already been** der Milchmann war schon da; **he has been and gone** er war da und ist wieder gegangen; **now you've been and done it** (*inf*) **!** jetzt hast du aber was angerichtet! (*inf*); **I've just been and (gone and) broken it!** jetzt hab ichs tatsächlich kaputtgemacht (*inf*)

♦ **here/there is... here is a book/are two books** hier ist ein Buch/sind zwei Bücher; **here/there you are** (= *you've arrived*) da sind Sie ja; (= *take this*) hier/da, bitte; (= *here/there it is*) hier/da ist es/sind sie doch; **there he was sitting at the table** da saß er nun am Tisch; **nearby there are two churches** in der Nähe sind or stehen zwei Kirchen

4 – IMPERSONAL VERB

sein; **it is dark/morning** es ist dunkel/Morgen; **tomorrow is Friday/the 14th of June** morgen ist Freitag/der 14. Juni, morgen haben wir Freitag/den 14. Juni; **it is 5 km to the nearest town** es sind 5 km bis zur nächsten Stadt

♦ **it was us/you** *etc* **who... it was us** or **we** (*form*) **who found it** WIR haben das gefunden, wir waren diejenigen, die das gefunden haben; **it was me** or **I** (*form*) **who said it first** ICH habe es zuerst gesagt, ich war derjenige, der zuerst gesagt hat

♦ **were it not ... were it not for the fact that I am a teacher, I would ...** wenn ich nicht Lehrer wäre, dann würde ich ...; **were it not for my friendship with him** wenn ich nicht mit ihm befreundet wäre; **were it not for him, if it weren't** or **wasn't for him** wenn er nicht wäre; **and even if it were not so** und selbst wenn das or dem nicht so wäre

♦ **had it not been for... had it not been** or **if it hadn't been for him** wenn er nicht gewesen wäre

B/E *abbr of* **bill of exchange**

beach [biːtʃ] **N** Strand *m*; **on the ~** am Strand **VT** *boat* auf Strand setzen

beach: beach ball N Wasserball *m*; **beach buggy** N Strandbuggy *m*; **beach chair** N Liegestuhl *m*; **beachcomber** N Strandgutsammler *m*; (*living rough*) am Strand lebender Einsiedler; **beachhead** N (*Mil*) Landkopf *m*; **beach hut** N Strandhäuschen *nt*; **beach umbrella** N Sonnenschirm *m*; **beach volleyball** N Beachvolleyball *m*; **beachwear** N Badesachen *pl*, Badezeug *nt* (*inf*); (*Fashion*) Strandmode *f*

beacon [biːkən] N (= *fire, light*) Leuchtfeuer *nt*; (= *radio beacon*) Funkfeuer *nt*; (= *one of a series of lights, radio beacons*) Bake *f*

bead [biːd] N **a** Perle *f*; (**string of**) **~s** Perlenschnur *f*; (= *necklace*) Perlenkette *f*; **to tell one's ~s** den Rosenkranz beten **b** (= *drop: of dew,*

---

sweat) Perle *f*, Tropfen *m* **c** (*of gun*) Korn *nt*; **to draw a ~ on sb** auf jdn zielen

beaded [biːdɪd] **ADJ** (= *decorated with pearls*) perlenverziert; **to be ~ with sweat** (*face, forehead*) schweißüberströmt sein

beading [biːdɪŋ] **N** Perlstab *m*, Perlschnur *f*

beadle [biːdl] **N** (*old Eccl*) Kirchendiener *m*; (*Univ*) Angestellter, der bei Prozessionen den Amtsstab trägt

beady [biːdɪ] **ADJ ~ eye** waches Auge; **I've got my ~ eye on you** (*inf*) ich beobachte Sie genau!

beagle [biːgl] **N** Beagle *m* (*englischer Spürhund*)

beak [biːk] N **a** (*of bird, turtle*) Schnabel *m* **b** (*inf, of person*) Zinken *m*, Rüssel *m* (*inf*) **c** (*Brit inf:* = *judge etc*) Kadi *m* (*inf*); (*Brit, Sch sl*) (Di)rex *m* (*sl*)

beaker [biːkə] **N** Becher *m*; (*Chem etc*) Becherglas *nt*

be-all and end-all [biːɔːlənd'endɔːl] **N the ~** das A und O; **it's not the ~** das ist auch nicht alles

beam [biːm] **N** **a** (*Build, of scales*) Balken *m* **b** (*of light etc*) Strahl *m*; **to drive on full** or **high ~** mit Fernlicht fahren; **to be on full** or **high ~** das Fernlicht eingeschaltet haben

c (= *radio beam*) Leitstrahl *m*; **to be on/off ~** auf Kurs sein/vom Kurs abgekommen sein; (*fig inf*) (*person*) richtig liegen (*inf*)/danebenliegen (*inf*); (*figures*) stimmen/nicht stimmen; **you're/ your guess is way off ~** (*fig inf*) Sie haben total danebengehauen (*inf*)/danebengeraten

d (= *smile*) Strahlen *nt*; **a ~ of delight** ein freudiges Strahlen

e (*Naut*, = *side*) Seite *f*; (= *width*) Breite *f*; **on the ~** querschiffs; **on the port ~** backbords; **the ~ of a ship** die Schiffsbreite; **to be broad in the ~** (*ship*) sehr breit sein; (*person*) breit gebaut sein

VI **a** (*light*) strahlen; **to ~ down** (*sun*) niederstrahlen

b (*fig, person, face*) strahlen; **she was ~ing with joy** sie strahlte übers ganze Gesicht

VT (*Rad, TV*) ausstrahlen, senden (*to* in, an +*acc*)

beam-ends [biːm'endz] **PL to be on one's ~** (*Naut*) stark Schlagseite haben; (*Brit fig*) auf dem letzten Loch pfeifen (*inf*)

beaming [biːmɪŋ] **ADJ** *sun* strahlend; *smile, face* (freude)strahlend

bean [biːn] N **a** Bohne *f*; **the proposals don't amount to a hill** or **row of ~s** (*inf*) die Vorschläge sind nicht überwältigend (*inf*); **he hasn't (got) a ~** (*Brit, inf*) er hat keinen roten or lumpigen Heller (*inf*); **hallo, old ~!** (*dated Brit, inf*) hallo, altes Haus! (*dated inf*) **b** (*fig*) **to be full of ~s** (*inf*) putzmunter sein (*inf*)

bean: beanbag N **a** (= *seat*) Sitzsack *m* **b** (= *toy*) mit Bohnen gefülltes Säckchen, das zum Spielen verwendet wird; **beanburger** N vegetarischer Hamburger (*mit Bohnen*); **bean-counter** N (*pej inf*) Erbsenzähler(in) *m(f)* (*inf*); **bean curd** N Tofu *nt*

beaner [biːnə] **N** (*pej sl*) Latino aus Kalifornien

beanery [biːnərɪ] **N** (*US, inf*) billiges Speiselokal

beanfeast [biːnfiːst] **N** (*inf*) Schmaus *m* (*inf*)

beano [biːnəʊ] **N** (*dated inf*) Schmaus *m* (*inf*)

bean: beanpole N (*lit, fig*) Bohnenstange *f*; **bean sprout** N Sojabohnensprosse *f*; **beanstalk** N Bohnenstängel *m*

bear¹ [bɛə] ○ 5.3 *pret* **bore**, *ptp* **borne** **VT** **a** (= *carry*) *burden, arms* tragen; *gift, message* bei sich tragen, mit sich führen; **to ~ away/back** mitnehmen/mit (sich) zurücknehmen; (*through the air*) fort- or wegtragen/zurücktragen; **the music was borne/borne away on the wind** (*liter*) die Musik wurde vom Wind weiter-/weggetragen; **he was borne along by the crowd** die Menge trug ihn mit (sich)

b (= *show*) *inscription, signature* tragen; *mark, traces also, likeness, relation* aufweisen, zeigen → **witness**

---

c (= *be known by*) *name, title* tragen, führen

d (= *have in heart or mind*) *love* empfinden, in sich (*dat*) tragen; *hatred, grudge also* hegen (*geh*); **the love/hatred he bore her** die Liebe, die er für sie empfand/der Hass, den er gegen sie hegte (*geh*) or empfand → **mind**

e (*lit, fig*, = *support, sustain*) *weight, expense, responsibility* tragen; (= *examination/comparison*) einer Prüfung/einem Vergleich standhalten; **it doesn't ~ thinking about** man darf gar nicht daran denken; **his language doesn't ~ repeating** seine Ausdrucksweise lässt sich nicht wiederholen

f (= *endure, tolerate*) ertragen; (*with neg also*) ausstehen, leiden; *pain* aushalten; *criticism, joking* vertragen; *smell, noise etc* aushalten, vertragen; **she can't ~ flying** sie kann einfach nicht fliegen; **she can't ~ doing nothing** sie kann einfach nicht untätig sein; **she can't ~ being laughed at** sie kann es nicht vertragen, wenn man über sie lacht; **could you ~ to stay a little longer?** können Sie es noch ein bisschen länger hier aushalten?

g (= *produce, yield fruit etc*) tragen → **interest**

h (= *give birth to*) gebären → **born**

VI **a** (= *move*) **to ~ right/left/north** sich rechts/links/nach Norden halten; **to ~ away** or **off** (*Naut*) abdrehen

b (*fruit tree etc*) tragen

c **to bring one's energies/powers of persuasion to ~** seine Energie/Überzeugungskraft aufwenden (*on* für); **to bring one's mind to ~ on sth** seinen Verstand or Geist für etw anstrengen; **to bring pressure to ~ on sb/sth** Druck auf jdn/etw ausüben

VR sich halten; **he bore himself with dignity** er hat Würde gezeigt

▶ **bear down** **VI** **a** (= *approach quickly*) sich nahen (*geh*); (*hawk etc*) herabstoßen; **to bear down on sb/sth** (*driver etc*) auf jdn/etw zuhalten

b (*woman in labour*) drücken **VT** *sep* niederdrücken; **he was borne down by poverty** seine Armut lastete schwer auf ihm; **to be borne down by the weight of ...** von der Last ... (*gen*) gebeugt sein

▶ **bear in (up)on** VT +*prep obj* **to be borne in (up)on sb** jdm zu(m) Bewusstsein kommen

▶ **bear on** VI +*prep obj* = **bear (up)on**

▶ **bear out** VT *sep* bestätigen; **to bear sb out in sth** jdn in etw bestätigen; **you will bear me out that ...** Sie werden bestätigen, dass ...

▶ **bear up** VI sich halten; **he bore up well under the death of his father** er trug den Tod seines Vaters mit Fassung; **bear up!** Kopf hoch!; **how are you? – bearing up!** wie gehts? – man lebt!

▶ **bear (up)on** VI +*prep obj* **a** (= *relate to*) betreffen; **does this bear (up)on what you were saying?** hat das einen Bezug zu dem, was Sie sagten? **b** (= *bear hard (up)on sb** sich hart auf jdn auswirken

▶ **bear with** VI +*prep obj* tolerieren; **if you would just bear with me for a couple of minutes** wenn Sie sich vielleicht zwei Minuten gedulden wollen

bear² **N** **a** Bär *m*; (*fig*, = *person*) Brummbär *m* (*inf*); **he is like a ~ with a sore head** er ist ein richtiger Brummbär (*inf*) **b** (*Astron*) **the Great/ Little Bear** der Große/Kleine Bär or Wagen **c** (*St Ex*) Baissespekulant *m*, Baissier *m* **VI** (*St Ex*) auf Baisse spekulieren

bearable [bɛərəbl] **ADJ** erträglich, zum Aushalten

bear: bear-baiting N Bärenhatz *f*; **bear cub** N Bärenjunge(s) *nt*

beard [bɪəd] **N** **a** Bart *m*; (*full-face*) Vollbart *m*; **a man with a ~** ein Mann mit Bart; **a week's (growth of) ~** ein eine Woche alter Bart; **small pointed ~** Spitzbart *m* **b** (*of goat, bird*) Bart *m*; (*of fish also*) Barthaare *pl*; (*of grain*) Grannen *pl* **VT** (= *confront*) ansprechen; **to ~ sb about sth** jdn auf etw (*acc*) hin ansprechen; **to ~ the lion in his den** (*Brit fig*) sich in die Höhle des Löwen wagen

bearded ['bɪədɪd] ADJ *man, animal, face* bärtig; **the ~ lady** die Dame mit dem Bart

beardless ['bɪədlɪs] ADJ bartlos; **~ youth** Milchbart *m* (*pej inf*), Milchgesicht *nt* (*pej inf*)

bearer ['bɛərə] N **a** (= *carrier*) Träger(in) *m(f)*; (*of news, letter, cheque, banknote*) Überbringer *m*; (*of name, title*) Träger(in) *m(f)*, Inhaber(in) *m(f)*; (*of passport*) Inhaber(in) *m(f)*; **~ bond** Inhaberschuldverschreibung *f*; **~ cheque**, **~ check** (US) Inhaberscheck *m*; **~ securities** pl Inhaberpapiere pl; **~ share**, **~ stock** (US) Inhaberaktie *f* **b** (= *tree etc*) **a good ~** ein Baum/Busch *etc*, der gut trägt

bear: bear garden N (*Brit*) Tollhaus *nt*; **bear hug** N ungestüme Umarmung; (*Wrestling*) Klammer *f*, Umklammerung *f*

bearing ['bɛərɪŋ] N **a** (= *posture*) Haltung *f*; (= *behaviour*) Verhalten *nt*, Auftreten *nt*, Gebaren *nt* **b** (= *relevance, influence*) Auswirkung *f* (*on auf* +*acc*); (= *connection*) Bezug *m* (*on zu*); **to have some/no ~ on sth** von Belang/belanglos für etw sein; (= *be/not be connected with*) einen gewissen/keinen Bezug zu etw haben **c** (= *endurance*) **to be beyond (all) ~** unerträglich *or* nicht zum Aushalten sein **d** (= *direction*) **to take a ~** sich orientieren; **to get a ~ on sth** sich an etw (*dat*) orientieren; **to take a compass ~** den Kompasskurs feststellen; **to get** *or* **find one's ~s** sich zurechtfinden, sich orientieren; **to lose one's ~s** die Orientierung verlieren **e** (*Tech*) Lager *nt*

bearish ['bɛərɪʃ] ADJ (*St Ex*) zur Baisse neigend *attr*; **to be ~ on sth** bei etw auf Baisse spekulieren

bear: bear market N (*St Ex*) Baisse *f*; **bear paw** N (*US inf: Mot*) Park-, Radkralle *f*; **bear-pit** N Bärengehege *nt*; **bearskin** ['bɛəskɪn] N (*Mil*) Bärenfellmütze *f*

beast [biːst] N **a** Tier *nt* → **burden, prey** **b** (*inf, = person*) Biest *nt*, Ekel *nt*; **don't be a ~!** sei nicht so eklig! (*inf*); **that ~ of a brother-in-law** dieser fiese Schwager (*inf*); **this (problem) is a ~, ~ (of a problem)** das (Problem) hats in sich (*inf*); **a good thriller is a rare ~ indeed** ein guter Krimi ist wirklich eine Seltenheit; **TV films are a different ~ (from movies)** Fernsehfilme sind etwas ganz anderes (als Kinofilme)

beastliness ['biːstlɪnɪs] N (*inf*) Scheußlichkeit *f*, Garstigkeit *f*; (*of person, conduct also*) Gemeinheit *f*, Ekligkeit *f* (*inf*)

beastly ['biːstlɪ] (*inf*) ADJ scheußlich, garstig (*inf*); *person, conduct also* gemein, eklig (*inf*); **what ~ weather** so ein Hundewetter; **it's a ~ business** das ist eine üble Angelegenheit; **what a ~ shame!** (*dated*) so ein Jammer! ADV (*dated*) scheußlich; **it's ~ difficult** es ist verteufelt schwierig (*inf*)

beat [biːt] **VB** *pret* **beat**, *ptp* **beaten** **N a** (*of heart, pulse, drum*, = *single beat*) Schlag *m*; (= *repeated beating*) Schlagen *nt*; **the ~ of her heart grew weaker** ihr Herzschlag wurde schwächer; **to the ~ of the drum** zum Schlag der Trommel; **he answered without missing a ~** er antwortete ohne sich aus der Ruhe *or* Fassung bringen zu lassen **b** (*of policeman, sentry*) Runde *f*, Rundgang *m*; (= *district*) Revier *nt*; **to be on** *or* **to patrol the ~** seine Runde machen **c** (*Mus, Poet*) Takt *m*; (*of metronome, baton*) Taktschlag *m*; **to have a heavy ~** einen ausgeprägten Rhythmus haben; **on/off the ~** auf dem betonten/unbetonten Taktteil **d** (= *beat music*) Beat(musik *f*) *m* **e** (*Hunt*) Treibjagd *f* **VT a** (= *hit*) schlagen; *person, animal also* (ver-) prügeln, hauen (*inf*); *carpet* klopfen; (= *search*) *countryside, woods* absuchen, abkämmen; **the crocodile ~ the ground with its tail** das Krokodil schlug mit dem Schwanz auf den Boden; **to ~ a/one's way through sth** einen/sich (*dat*) einen Weg durch etw bahnen; **to ~ a path to sb's door** (*fig*) jdm die Bude einrennen (*inf*); **to**

~ a/the drum trommeln, die Trommel schlagen; **to ~ the air** um sich schlagen, herumfuchteln; **to ~ one's breast** (*lit, fig*) sich (*dat*) an die Brust schlagen; (*ape*) sich (*dat*) gegen die Brust trommeln; **~ it!** (*fig inf*) hau ab! (*inf*), verschwinde! **b** (= *hammer*) *metal* hämmern; (= *shape also*) treiben; **to ~ sth flat** etw flach *or* platt hämmern **c** (= *defeat*) schlagen; *record* brechen; *inflation* in den Griff bekommen; *disease* erfolgreich bekämpfen; **to ~ sb at chess/tennis** jdn im Schach/Tennis schlagen; **his shot/forehand ~ me** ich war dem Schuss/Vorhandschlag nicht gewachsen; **to ~ sb into second place** jdn auf den zweiten Platz verweisen; **you can't ~ these prices** diese Preise sind nicht zu unterbieten; **you can't ~ central heating/real wool** es geht doch nichts über Zentralheizung/reine Wolle; **he ~s the rest of them any day** er steckt sie alle (jederzeit) in die Tasche (*inf*); **if you can't ~ them, join them** (*inf*) wenn dus nicht besser machen kannst, dann mach es genauso; **coffee ~s tea any day** Kaffee ist allemal besser als Tee; **that ~s everything** das ist doch wirklich der Gipfel *or* die Höhe (*inf*), das schlägt dem Fass den Boden aus (*inf*); (= *is very good*) darüber geht nichts; **it ~s me (how/why ...)** (*inf*) es ist mir ein Rätsel(, wie/warum ...) (*inf*); **well, can you ~ it!** (*inf*) ist das denn zu fassen? (*inf*); **he managed to ~ the charge** (*inf*) er wurde (von der Anklage) freigesprochen **d** (= *be before*) *budget, crowds* zuvorkommen (+*dat*); **to ~ sb to the top of a hill** vor jdm oben auf dem Berg sein *or* ankommen; **I'll ~ you down to the beach** ich bin vor dir am Strand; **to ~ sb home** vor jdm zu Hause sein; **to ~ the deadline** vor Ablauf der Frist fertig sein; **to ~ sb to the draw** schneller ziehen als jd; **to ~ sb to it** jdm zuvorkommen **e** (= *move up and down regularly*) schlagen; **the bird ~s its wings** der Vogel schlägt mit den Flügeln **f** (*Mus*) **to ~ time (to the music)** den Takt schlagen **g** (*Cook*) *cream, eggs* schlagen **VI a** (*heart, pulse, drum*) schlagen; **to ~ on the door (with one's fists)** (mit den Fäusten) gegen die Tür hämmern *or* schlagen; **with ~ing heart** mit pochendem *or* klopfendem Herzen; **her heart was ~ing with excitement** ihr Herz schlug vor Aufregung schneller → **bush**[1] **b** (*wind, waves*) schlagen; (*rain also*) trommeln; (*sun*) brennen **c** (*cream*) sich schlagen lassen **ADJ a** (*inf*, = *exhausted*) **to be (dead) ~** total kaputt *or* geschafft *or* erledigt sein (*inf*) **b** (*inf, = defeated*) **to be ~-(en)** aufgeben müssen (*inf*), sich geschlagen geben müssen; **I'm ~** ich gebe mich geschlagen; **he doesn't know when he's ~(-en)** er gibt nicht auf (*inf*); **we've got him ~** wir haben ihn schachmatt gesetzt; **this problem's got me ~** mit dem Problem komme ich nicht klar (*inf*)

▶ **beat back** VT *sep flames, enemy* zurückschlagen

▶ **beat down VI** (*rain*) herunterprasseln; (*sun*) herunterbrennen **VT** *sep* **a** (= *reduce*) *prices* herunterhandeln; *opposition* kleinkriegen (*inf*); **I managed to beat him down (on the price)** ich konnte den Preis herunterhandeln; **I beat him down to £20 for the chair** ich habe den Stuhl auf £ 20 heruntergehandelt **b** (= *flatten*) *door* einrennen; *wheat, crop* niederwerfen

▶ **beat in** VT *sep* **a** *door* einschlagen; **to beat sb's brains in** (*inf*) jdm den Schädel einschlagen (*inf*) **b** (*Cook*) *eggs etc* unterrühren

▶ **beat off** VT *sep* abwehren

▶ **beat out** VT *sep fire* ausschlagen; *metal, dent, wing* aushämmern; *tune, rhythm* schlagen; (*on drum*) trommeln; *plan* ausarbeiten, ausklamüsern (*inf*), austüfteln (*inf*); **to beat sb's brains out** (*inf*, = *kill*) jdm den Schädel einschlagen (*inf*)

▶ **beat up** VT *sep* **a** *person* zusammenschlagen **b** (*Cook*) *eggs, cream* schlagen

▶ **beat up on** VI +*prep obj* (*US inf*) (= *hit*) verhauen (*inf*), schlagen; (= *bully*) einschüchtern; (= *criticize*) auseinander nehmen (*inf*)

beat bobby N (*Brit inf*) Streifenpolizist(in) *m(f)*

beaten ['biːtn] *ptp of* **beat** ADJ **a** *metal* gehämmert; *egg* geschlagen **b** *earth* festgetreten; *path* ausgetreten; **a well-beaten path** ein Trampelpfad *m*; **to be off the ~ track** (*fig*) abgelegen sein **c** (= *defeated*) **a ~ man** ein geschlagener Mann

beater ['biːtə] N **a** (= *carpet beater*) Klopfer *m*; (= *egg beater*) Schneebesen *m* **b** (*Hunt*) Treiber(in) *m(f)*

beat *in cpds* Beat-; **Beat Generation** N Beatgeneration *f*; **beat group** N Beatgruppe *or* -band *f*

beatific [ˌbiːə'tɪfɪk] ADJ glückselig; *vision* himmlisch

beatification [biːˌætɪfɪ'keɪʃən] N Seligsprechung *f*

beatify [biː'ætɪfaɪ] VT selig sprechen, beatifizieren (*spec*)

beating ['biːtɪŋ] N **a** (= *series of blows*) Schläge pl, Prügel pl; **to give sb a ~** jdn verprügeln; (*as punishment also*) jdm eine Tracht Prügel verabreichen (*inf*); **to get a ~** verprügelt werden; (*as punishment also*) Schläge *or* Prügel bekommen **b** (*of drums, heart, wings*) Schlagen *nt* **c** (= *defeat*) Niederlage *f*; **to take a ~** eine Schlappe einstecken (*inf*); **to take a ~ (at the hands of sb)** (von jdm) nach allen Regeln der Kunst geschlagen werden **d** **to take some ~** nicht leicht zu übertreffen sein; (*idea, insolence etc*) seines-/ihresgleichen suchen **e** (*Hunt*) Treiben *nt*

beating-up [ˌbiːtɪŋ'ʌp] N Abreibung *f* (*inf*); **to give sb a ~** jdn zusammenschlagen; **to get a ~** zusammengeschlagen werden

beatitude [biː'ætɪtjuːd] N Glückseligkeit *f*; **the Beatitudes** (*Bibl*) die Seligpreisungen pl

beatnik ['biːtnɪk] N Beatnik *m*

beat poetry N Beatlyrik *f*

beat-up ['biːt'ʌp] ADJ (*inf*) zerbeult, ramponiert (*inf*)

beau [bəʊ] N (*old*) **a** (= *dandy*) Beau *m* (*dated*) **b** (= *suitor*) Galan *m* (*dated*), Kavalier *m*

Beaufort scale ['bəʊfət‚skeɪl] N Beaufortskala *f*

beaut [bjuːt] N (*esp Austral, inf*, = *thing*) Prachtexemplar *nt*; **to be a (real) ~** einsame Klasse sein (*inf*)

beauteous ['bjuːtɪəs] ADJ (*poet*) wunderschön, prachtvoll

beautician [bjuː'tɪʃən] N Kosmetiker(in) *m(f)*

beautiful ['bjuːtɪfʊl] ADJ schön; *weather, morning also, idea, meal* herrlich, wunderbar; (= *good*) *swimmer, swimming, organization, piece of work* hervorragend, wunderbar; **that's a ~ specimen** das ist ein Prachtexemplar; **the ~ people** die Schickeria; **~!** prima! (*inf*), toll! (*inf*) N **a** **the ~** das Schöne **b** (*inf*) **hello, ~** hallo, schönes Kind

beautifully ['bjuːtɪfəlɪ] ADV schön; *warm, prepared, shine, simple* herrlich, wunderbar; (= *well*) *sew, cook, sing, swim* hervorragend, sehr gut, prima (*inf*); **that will do ~** das ist ganz ausgezeichnet

beautify ['bjuːtɪfaɪ] VT verschönern; **to ~ oneself** (*hum*) sich schönmachen (*hum*)

beauty ['bjuːtɪ] N **a** Schönheit *f*; **~ is only skin-deep** (*prov*) der äußere Schein kann trügen; **~ is in the eye of the beholder** (*Prov*) schön ist, was (einem) gefällt **b** (= *beautiful person*) Schönheit *f*; **Beauty and the Beast** die Schöne und das Tier **c** (= *good example*) Prachtexemplar *nt*; **isn't it a ~!** ist das nicht ein Prachtstück *or* Prachtexemplar? **d** (= *pleasing feature*) **the ~ of it is that ...** das Schöne *or* Schönste daran ist, dass ...; **that's the ~ of it** das ist das Schöne daran; **one of the beauties of this job is ...** eine der schönen Seiten dieser Arbeit ist ...

beauty in cpds Schönheits-; **beauty care** N Kosmetik f no pl, Schönheitspflege f; **beauty competition**, **beauty contest** N Schönheitswettbewerb m; **beauty mark** N → **beauty spot**; **beauty parlour**, (US) **beauty parlor** N Schönheits- or Kosmetiksalon m; **beauty queen** N Schönheitskönigin f; **beauty salon**, **beauty shop** N Schönheits- or Kosmetiksalon m; **beauty sleep** N (hum) Schlaf m; **beauty specialist** N Kosmetiker(in) m(f); **beauty spot** N **a** Schönheitsfleck m; (= patch also) Schönheitspflästerchen nt **b** (= place) schönes or hübsches Fleckchen (Erde), schöner or hübscher Fleck; **beauty treatment** N kosmetische Behandlung

beaver¹ ['biːvə] N **a** Biber m; **to work like a ~** wie ein Wilder/eine Wilde arbeiten → **eager beaver b** (= fur) Biber(pelz) m **c** (= hat) Biber- or Kastorhut m

▶ **beaver away** VI (inf) schuften (inf) (at an +dat)

beaver² N (of helmet) Kinnreff nt

beaverboard N Hartfaserplatte f

becalm [bɪˈkɑːm] VT **to be ~ed** (Naut) in eine Flaute geraten; (fig) eine Flaute haben; **the ship lay** or **was ~ed for three weeks** das Schiff war or befand sich drei Wochen lang in einer Flaute

became [bɪˈkeɪm] pret of **become**

because [bɪˈkɒz] **☼** 17.1, 20.4, 26.3 **CONJ** weil; (= since also) da; **it was the more surprising ~ we were not expecting it** es war umso überraschender, als wir es nicht erwartet hatten; **if I did it, it was ~ it had to be done** ich habe es nur getan, weil es getan werden musste; **why did you do it? – just ~** (inf) warum or weshalb hast du das getan? – darum or deshalb **PREP ~ of** wegen (+gen or (inf) +dat); **I only did it ~ of you** ich habe es nur deinetwegen/Ihretwegen getan

beck [bek] N **to be (completely) at sb's ~ and call** jdm voll und ganz zur Verfügung stehen; **I'm not at your ~ and call** du kannst doch nicht so einfach über mich verfügen; **his wife is completely at his ~ and call** seine Frau muss nach seiner Pfeife tanzen; **to have sb at one's ~ and call** jdn zur ständigen Verfügung haben, ganz über jdn verfügen können

beckon ['bekən] **VI** winken; **he ~ed to her to follow (him)** er gab ihr ein Zeichen or winkte ihr, ihm zu folgen; **opportunities ~ for talented young players** jungen begabten Spielern stehen viele Möglichkeiten offen; **fame/Hollywood ~ed** der Ruhm/Hollywood lockte **VT** winken; (fig: name lockte) **he ~ed her to follow (him)** er gab ihr ein Zeichen or winkte ihr, ihm zu folgen; **he ~ed me in/back/over** er winkte mich herein/zurück/herüber

become [bɪˈkʌm] pret **became**, ptp **become VI a** (= grow to be) werden; **it has ~ a rule** es ist jetzt Vorschrift; **it has ~ a habit** es ist zur Gewohnheit geworden; **it has ~ a custom/nuisance** es ist üblich/lästig geworden; **he's becoming a problem** er wird zum Problem; **to ~ interested in sb/sth** anfangen, sich für jdn/ etw zu interessieren **b** (= acquire position of) werden; **to ~ king/a doctor** König/Arzt werden **c what has ~ of him?** was ist aus ihm geworden?; **what's to ~ of him?** was soll aus ihm werden?; **I don't know what will ~ of him** ich weiß nicht, was aus ihm noch werden soll **VT a** (= suit) stehen (+dat) **b** (= befit) sich schicken für, sich ziemen für (geh)

becoming [bɪˈkʌmɪŋ] ADJ **a** (= suitable, fitting) schicklich; **it's not ~ (for a lady) to sit like that** es schickt sich (für eine Dame) nicht, so zu sitzen **b** (= flattering) vorteilhaft, kleidsam; **that dress is very ~** das Kleid steht ihr/dir etc sehr gut

becomingly [bɪˈkʌmɪŋlɪ] ADV **a** (= suitably) passend **b** (= fetchingly) entzückend

becquerel [ˌbekəˈrel] N Becquerel nt

B Ed abbr of **Bachelor of Education**

bed [bed] N **a** Bett nt; **to go to ~** zu or ins Bett gehen; **to put** or **get sb to ~** jdn ins or zu Bett bringen; **to get into ~** sich ins Bett legen; **to get into ~ with sb** (lit, fig) mit jdm ins Bett gehen or steigen (inf); **he couldn't get her into ~ with him** er hat sie nicht ins Bett gekriegt (inf); **to get in** or **jump into ~ with sb** (inf) mit jdm ins Bett gehen or steigen (inf); **to be good in ~** gut im Bett sein; **he must have got out of ~ on the wrong side** (inf) er ist wohl mit dem linken Fuß zuerst aufgestanden; **to be in ~** im Bett sein; (through illness also) das Bett hüten müssen; **a ~ of rice** (Cook) ein Reisbett nt; **a ~ of nails** ein Nagelbrett nt; **life isn't always a ~ of roses** (prov) man ist im Leben nicht immer auf Rosen gebettet; **his life is not exactly a ~ of roses** er ist nicht gerade auf Rosen gebettet; **to make the ~** das Bett machen; **as you make your ~ so you must lie on it** (Brit Prov) **you make the ~ you lie in** (US Prov) wie man sich bettet, so liegt man (Prov); **a ~ for the night** eine Übernachtungsmöglichkeit; **can I have a ~ for the night?** kann ich hier/bei euch etc übernachten?; **to put a newspaper to ~** (Press) eine Zeitung in Druck geben; **the paper has gone to ~** (Press) die Zeitung ist im Druck; **to put sth to ~** (fig) bei etw zu einem Abschluss kommen **b** (of ore) Lager nt; (of coal also) Flöz nt; (of building, road etc) Unterbau m; **a ~ of clay** Lehmboden m **c** (= bottom) (= sea bed) Grund m, Boden m; (= river bed) Bett nt **d** (= oyster bed, coral bed) Bank f **e** (= flower bed, vegetable bed) Beet nt **f** (= base: of engine, lathe, machine) Bett nt **VT a** plant setzen, pflanzen **b** (old, hum, = have sex with) beschlafen (old, hum)

▶ **bed down VI** sein Lager aufschlagen; **to bed down for the night** sein Nachtlager aufschlagen **VT** sep **a** person das Bett machen (+dat); child schlafen legen; **the soldiers were bedded down in the shed** die Soldaten hatten ihr (Nacht)quartier im Schuppen **b** animals einstreuen (+dat)

▶ **bed in VT** sep foundations einlassen; machine betten; brakes einfahren **VI** (brakes) eingefahren werden

bed and breakfast N Übernachtung f mit Frühstück; (= house also **bed and breakfast place**) Frühstückspension f; **"bed and breakfast"** „Fremdenzimmer"

bedaub [bɪˈdɔːb] VT beschmieren; face anmalen, anschmieren

bedazzle [bɪˈdæzl] VT blenden

bed in cpds Bett-; **bed bath** N (Kranken)wäsche f im Bett; **to give sb a ~** jdn im Bett waschen; **bedbug** N Wanze f; **bedchamber** N (old) Schlafgemach nt (old); **bedclothes** PL (Brit) Bettzeug nt; **bedcover** N (= bedspread) Tagesdecke f; **~s** pl (= bedclothes) Bettzeug nt

bedding ['bedɪŋ] N **a** Bettzeug nt **b** (for horses) Streu f

bedding plant N Setzling m

beddy-byes ['bedɪbaɪz] PL (US baby-talk) **to go ~** Heia machen (baby-talk), in die Heia gehen (baby-talk)

bedeck [bɪˈdek] VT schmücken

bedevil [bɪˈdevl] VT komplizieren, erschweren; **~led** (Brit) or **~ed** (US) **by misfortune** vom Schicksal verfolgt; **~led** (Brit) or **~ed** (US) **by injuries** von Verletzungen heimgesucht

bed: bedfellow N **to be** or **make strange ~s** (fig) eine eigenartige Kombination or ein merkwürdiges Gespann sein; **bedframe** N Bettgestell nt; **bedhead** N Kopfteil m des Bettes; **bed jacket** N Bettjäckchen nt

bedlam ['bedləm] N (fig, = uproar) Chaos nt; **in the classroom it was absolute ~** in der Klasse ging es zu wie im Irrenhaus

bed linen N Bettwäsche f

Bedouin ['beduɪn] **N** Beduine m, Beduinin f **ADJ** beduinisch

bed: bedpan N Bettpfanne or -schüssel f; **bedplate** N (Mech) Grund- or Fundamentplatte f; **bedpost** N Bettpfosten m

bedraggled [bɪˈdrægld] ADJ (= wet) trief- or tropfnass; (= dirty) verdreckt; (= untidy) person, appearance ungepflegt, schlampig

bedridden ['bedrɪdn] ADJ bettlägerig

bedrock ['bedrɒk] N **a** (Geol) Grundgebirge or -gestein nt **b** (fig) **to get down to** or **to reach ~** zum Kern der Sache kommen

bedroom ['bedruːm] N Schlafzimmer nt

bedroom in cpds Schlafzimmer-; **bedroom slipper** N Hausschuh m

Beds abbr of **Bedfordshire**

beds abbr of **bedrooms** Zi.

bed: bed-settee ['bedseˈtiː] N (Brit) Sofabett nt; **bed sheet** N Bettlaken nt

bedside ['bedsaɪd] N **to be/sit at sb's ~** an jds Bett (dat) sein/sitzen

bedside: bedside lamp N Nachttischlampe f; **bedside manner** N Art f mit Kranken umzugehen; **he has a good/bad ~** er kann gut/nicht gut mit den Kranken umgehen; **bedside rug** N Bettvorleger m; **bedside table** N Nachttisch m

bedsit(ter) ['bedsɪt(ə')] (inf), **bedsitting room** ['bedˈsɪtɪŋruːm] (geh) N (Brit) **a** (one-room flat) Einzimmerappartement nt **b** (rented room) möbliertes Zimmer **c** (Wohnschlafzimmer nt; (for teenager etc) Jugendzimmer nt

bed: bedsock N Bettschuh m; **bedsore** N aufgelegene or wund gelegene Stelle; **to get ~s** sich wund liegen or aufliegen; **bed space** N (in hospital, hotel etc) Bettenzahl f, Bettenkapazität f; **bedspread** N Tagesdecke f; **bedstead** N Bettgestell nt; **bedstraw** N (Bot) Labkraut nt; **bedtime** N Schlafenszeit f; **it's ~** es ist Schlafenszeit; **his ~ is 10 o'clock** um 10 Uhr schlafen; **it's past your ~** du müsstest schon lange im Bett sein; **bedtime story** N Gutenachtgeschichte f; **bed-wetter** N Bettnässer(in) m(f); **bed-wetting** N Bettnässen nt

bee [biː] N **a** Biene f; **like ~s round a honeypot** wie die Motten ums Licht; **to have a ~ in one's bonnet** (inf) einen Fimmel or Tick haben (inf); **he's got a ~ in his bonnet about cleanliness** (inf) er hat einen Sauberkeitsfimmel or -tick (inf) **b** (= sewing bee) Kränzchen nt; (= competition) Wettbewerb m

Beeb [biːb] N the ~ (Brit, inf) die BBC

beech [biːtʃ] N **a** (= tree) Buche f **b** (= wood) Buche(nholz nt) f

beech: beech mast N Bucheckern pl; **beechnut** N Buchecker f; **beech tree** N Buche f; **beechwood** N **a** (= material) Buchenholz nt **b** (= trees) Buchenwald m

bee-eater ['biːiːtə'] N (Orn) Bienenfresser m

beef [biːf] N **a** (= meat) Rindfleisch nt **b** (inf, = flesh) Speck m (pej); (= muscles) Muskeln pl; **to have plenty of ~** jede Menge Bizeps haben (inf); **you'd better get rid of some of this ~** du musst ein bisschen abspecken (inf) **c what's his ~?** (inf) was hat er zu meckern? (inf) **VI** (inf, = complain) meckern (inf) (about über +acc); **what are you ~ing about?** was hast du zu meckern? (inf)

▶ **beef up** VT sep (= make more powerful etc) aufmotzen (inf)

beef: beefburger N Hamburger m; **beefcake** N , no pl (inf, = male photos) Männerfleisch nt (hum), Muskelprotze pl; **beef cattle** PL Schlachtrinder pl; **beefeater** N **a** Beefeater m **b** (US, inf) Engländer(in) m(f); **beef extract** N Fleischextrakt m; **beef olive** N Rinderroulade f; **beef sausage** N Rindswürstchen nt; **beefsteak** N Beefsteak nt; **beef tea** N Kraft- or Fleischbrühe f

beefy ['biːfɪ] ADJ (+er) fleischig

bee: beehive N a Bienenstock m; (dome-shaped) Bienenkorb m **b** (= hairstyle) toupierte Hochfrisur **ADJ ~ hairdo** toupierte Hochfrisur; **beekeeper** N Bienenzüchter(in) m(f), Imker(in) *m(f)*; **beeline** N **to make a ~ for sb/sth** schnurstracks auf jdn/etw zugehen

been [biːn] *ptp of* **be**

beep [biːp] (*inf*) **N** Tut(tut) *nt* (*inf*); **leave your name and number after the ~** hinterlassen Sie Ihren Namen und Ihre Nummer nach dem Signalton *or* Pfeifton **VT** **to ~ one's horn** hupen **VI** tuten (*inf*); **~ ~!** tut, tut (*inf*)

beer [bɪə] N Bier *nt*; **two ~s, please** zwei Bier, bitte; **life is not all ~ and skittles** das Leben ist nicht nur eitel Sonnenschein

---

BEER

In England und Wales ist das am weitesten verbreitete Fassbier (**draught beer**) ein **bitter**, das so heißt wegen seines vollen, leicht bitteren Geschmacks. Das schottische **heavy** ähnelt dem englischen **bitter**. Außerdem werden in Großbritannien andere Biersorten gerne getrunken, so z. B. das **stout**, das stark und sehr dunkel ist, das **mild**, das ähnlich wie ein **bitter** schmeckt, aber mit weniger Hopfen gebraut wird, und das **lager**, ein leichtes Bier, das am ehesten einem deutschen Export entspricht.
Der Begriff **ale** bezeichnete ursprünglich ein Bier, das ohne Hopfen gebraut wurde, wird aber heutzutage auch für **beer** im Allgemeinen benutzt. Beliebte Sorten sind hierbei **light ale** oder auch **pale ale** und **brown ale**, das dunkler, stärker und kräftiger im Geschmack ist.

---

beer *in cpds* Bier-; **beer belly** N (*inf*) Bierbauch *m* (*inf*); **beer bottle** N Bierflasche *f*; **beer bust** N (*US Univ sl*, = *party*) Bierfete *f* (*inf*), Biersause *f* (*sl*); (= *drinking spree*) Saufgelage *nt* (*pej inf*); **beer can** N Bierdose *f*; **beer cellar** N Bierkeller *m*; **beer garden** N (*Brit*) Biergarten *m*; **beer glass** N Bierglas *nt*; **beer gut** N (*inf*) Bierbauch *m* (*inf*); **beer mat** N (*Brit*) Bierdeckel *m*; **beer money** N (*inf*) Geld *nt* für Getränke; **to keep sb in ~** ein nettes Taschengeld für jdn sein; (*extra income*) ein nettes Zubrot für jdn sein; **beer-pull** N Bierpumpengriff *m*; **beer-swilling** ADJ (*pej inf*) Bier saufend (*inf*)

beery [ˈbɪərɪ] ADJ Bier-; *person* mit einer Bierfahne (*inf*); (= *tipsy*) bierselig; *face* biergerötet; **to have ~ breath, to smell ~** eine Bierfahne haben (*inf*), nach Bier riechen

bee sting N Bienenstich *m*

beeswax [ˈbiːzwæks] N Bienenwachs *nt*

beet [biːt] N Rübe *f* (*form*)

beetle¹ [ˈbiːtl] N Käfer *m*

▶ **beetle along** VI (*inf*) entlangpesen (*inf*); (*on foot also*) entlanghasten (*inf*)

▶ **beetle off** VI (*inf*) abschwirren (*inf*)

beetle² N (= *tool*) Stampfer *m*; (*for paving, pile-driving also*) Ramme *f*

beetle: beetle-browed [ˈbiːtlˈbraʊd] ADJ mit buschigen, zusammengewachsenen Augenbrauen; **beetle brows** PL buschige, zusammengewachsene Augenbrauen *pl*; **beetle-crushers** PL (*inf*) Elbkähne *pl* (*inf*), Kindersärge *pl* (*inf*)

beetling [ˈbiːtlɪŋ] ADJ *cliffs* überhängend; *brow* vorspringend

beet: beetroot N Rote Bete *or* Rübe; **beet sugar** N Rübenzucker *m*

befall [bɪˈfɔːl] *pret* **befell** [bɪˈfel] *ptp* **befallen** [bɪˈfɔːlən] (*old, liter*) **VI** sich zutragen **VT** widerfahren (+*dat*) (*geh*)

befit [bɪˈfɪt] VT (*form*) *sb* anstehen (+*dat*) (*geh*), sich ziemen für (*geh*); *occasion* angemessen sein (+*dat*), entsprechen (+*dat*); **it ill ~s him to speak thus** es steht ihm schlecht an *or* ziemt sich nicht für ihn, so zu reden (*geh*)

befitting [bɪˈfɪtɪŋ] ADJ gebührend, geziemend (*dated*)

befog [bɪˈfɒɡ] VT (*fig*) *issue* vernebeln; *person, mind* verwirren; (*alcohol, blow*) benebeln; **to be ~ged** (*person*) benebelt sein; (*issue*) verwirrt sein

---

before [bɪˈfɔː] **PREP** **a** (= *earlier than*) vor (+*dat*); **the year ~ last/this** vorletztes/letztes Jahr, das vorletzte/letzte Jahr; **the day ~ yesterday** vorgestern; **the day/time ~** that der Tag/die Zeit davor; **~ Christ** (*abbr* **BC**) vor Christi Geburt (*abbr v. Chr.*); **I got/was here ~ you** ich war vor dir da; **that was ~ my time** das war vor meiner Zeit; **to be ~ sb/sth** vor jdm/etw liegen; **~ then** vorher; **~ now** früher, eher, vorher; **you should have done it ~ now** das hättest du schon (eher) gemacht haben sollen; **~ long** bald; **~ everything else** zuallererst

b (*in order, rank*) vor (+*dat*); **to come ~ sb/sth** vor jdm/etw kommen; **I believe in honour** (*Brit*) *or* **honor** (*US*) **~ everything** die Ehre geht mir über alles, für mich ist die Ehre das Wichtigste; **ladies ~ gentlemen** Damen haben den Vortritt

c (*in position*) vor (+*dat*); (*with movement*) vor (+*acc*); **~ my (very) eyes** vor meinen Augen; **the task ~ us** (= *with which we are dealing*) die uns vorliegende Aufgabe; (= *with which we are confronted*) die Aufgabe, vor der wir stehen; (= *which lies ahead of us*) die uns bevorstehende Aufgabe; **to sail ~ the wind** (*Naut*) vor dem Wind segeln

d (*in the presence of*) vor (+*dat*); **he said it ~ us all** er sagte das vor uns allen; **~ God/a lawyer** vor Gott/einem Anwalt; **to appear ~ a court/judge** vor Gericht/einem Richter erscheinen

e (= *rather than*) **death ~ surrender** eher *or* lieber tot als sich ergeben; **he would die ~ betraying his country** er würde eher sterben als sein Land verraten

ADV **a** (*in time*, = *before that*) davor; (= *at an earlier time, before now*) vorher; **have you been to Scotland ~?** waren Sie schon einmal in Schottland?; **I have seen/read** *etc* **this ~** ich habe das schon einmal gesehen/gelesen *etc*; **never ~** noch nie; **(on) the evening/day ~** am Abend/Tag davor *or* zuvor *or* vorher; **(in) the month/year ~** im Monat/Jahr davor; **two hours ~** zwei Stunden vorher, **two days ~** zwei Tage davor *or* zuvor; **to continue as ~** (*person*) (so) wie vorher weitermachen; **things continued as ~** alles war wie gehabt; **life went on as ~** das Leben ging seinen gewohnten Gang

b (= *ahead*) **to march on ~** vorausmarschieren

c (*indicating order*) davor; **that chapter and the one ~** dieses Kapitel und das davor

CONJ **a** (*in time*) bevor; **~ doing sth** bevor man etw tut; **you can't go ~ this is done** du kannst erst gehen, wenn das gemacht ist; **it will be six weeks ~ the boat comes again** das Boot wird erst in sechs Wochen wieder kommen; **it will be a long time ~ he comes back** es wird lange dauern, bis er zurückkommt

b (= *rather than*) **he will die ~ he surrenders** eher will er sterben als sich geschlagen geben

beforehand [bɪˈfɔːhænd] ADV im Voraus; **you must tell me ~** Sie müssen mir vorher Bescheid sagen

before-tax [bɪˈfɔːtæks] ADJ *income, profits* vor Steuern

befoul [bɪˈfaʊl] VT (*liter: lit, fig*) besudeln; *atmosphere* verpesten

befriend [bɪˈfrend] VT (= *help*) sich annehmen (+*gen*); (= *be friend to*) Umgang pflegen mit; **she seems to have ~ed them** sie scheint sich mit ihnen angefreundet zu haben

befuddle [bɪˈfʌdl] VT **a** (= *make tipsy*) benebeln **b** (= *confuse*) durcheinander bringen; **he is rather ~d** er ist ziemlich durcheinander (*inf*) *or* verwirrt

beg [beɡ] **VT** **a** *money, alms* betteln um **b** (= *crave, ask for*) *forgiveness, mercy, a favour* bitten um; **to ~ sth of sb** etw von jdm erbitten; **he ~ged to be allowed to ...** er bat darum, ... zu dürfen; **the children ~ged me to let them go to the circus** die Kinder bettelten, ich solle sie in den Zirkus gehen lassen; **to ~ leave to do sth** um Erlaubnis bitten, etw tun zu dürfen; **I ~ leave to be dismissed** (*form*) gestatten Sie, dass ich mich entferne? (*form*); **I ~ to inform you ...** (*form*) ich erlaube mir, Sie davon in Kenntnis

---

zu setzen ...; **I ~ to differ** ich erlaube mir, anderer Meinung zu sein → **pardon**

c (= *entreat*) *sb* anflehen, inständig bitten; **I ~ you!** ich flehe dich an!

d **to ~ the question** an der eigentlichen Frage vorbeigehen

VI **a** (*beggar*) betteln; (*dog*) Männchen machen

b (*for help, time etc*) bitten (*for* um)

c (= *entreat*) **to ~ of sb to do sth** jdn anflehen *or* inständig bitten, etw zu tun; **I ~ of you** ich bitte Sie

d **to go ~ging** (*inf*) noch zu haben sein; (= *be unwanted*) keine Abnehmer finden

began [bɪˈɡæn] *pret of* **begin**

beget [bɪˈɡet] *pret* **begot** *or* (*obs*) **begat** [bɪˈɡæt] *ptp* **begotten** *or* **begot** VT **a** (*obs, Bibl*) zeugen → **begotten b** (*fig*) *difficulties etc* zeugen (*geh*); **violence ~s violence** Gewalt erzeugt Gewalt

begetter [bɪˈɡetə] N (*form*) Begründer(in) *m(f)*

beggar [ˈbeɡə] **N** **a** Bettler(in) *m(f)*; **~s can't be choosers** (*prov*) in der Not frisst der Teufel Fliegen (*prov*), wer arm dran ist, kann nicht wählerisch sein **b** (*Brit inf*) Kerl *m* (*inf*); **poor ~!** armer Kerl! (*inf*), armes Schwein! (*inf*); **a lucky ~** ein Glückspilz *m*; **a funny little ~** ein drolliges Kerlchen; (= *girl*) ein drolliger Fratz **VT** **a** (= *make poor*) an den Bettelstab bringen **b** (*fig*) **to ~ description** jeder Beschreibung (*gen*) spotten; **to ~ belief** nicht zu fassen sein

beggarly [ˈbeɡəlɪ] ADJ kümmerlich

beggar: beggarman N (*old*) Bettler *m*, Bettelmann *m* (*old*); **beggar-my-neighbour, beggar-your-neighbour** N (*Cards*) Kartenspiel, bei dem der gewinnt, der zum Schluss alle Karten hat; **beggarwoman** N (*old*) Bettlerin *f*, Bettelfrau *f* (*old*)

beggary [ˈbeɡərɪ] N Bettelarmut *f*; (= *beggars*) Bettler *pl*, Bettelvolk *nt*; **to have been reduced to ~** bettelarm sein

begging [ˈbeɡɪŋ]: **begging bowl** N Bettlerschale *f*; **to hold out a ~ (to sb)** (*fig*) (bei jdm) betteln gehen; **begging letter** N Bittbrief *m*

begin [bɪˈɡɪn] ✪ 26.1 *pret* **began**, *ptp* **begun** **VT** **a** (= *start*) beginnen, anfangen; *conversation also* anknüpfen; *song also* anstimmen; *bottle* anbrechen, anfangen; *book, letter, new cheque book, new page* anfangen; *rehearsals, work* anfangen mit; *task* in Angriff nehmen, sich machen an (+*acc*); **to ~ to do sth** *or* **doing sth** anfangen *or* beginnen, etw zu tun; **to ~ working** *or* **to work on sth** mit der Arbeit an etw (*dat*) anfangen *or* beginnen; **to ~ an attack** zum Angriff schreiten; **when did you ~ (learning** *or* **to learn) English?** wann haben Sie angefangen, Englisch zu lernen?; **she ~s the job next week** sie fängt nächste Woche (bei der Stelle) an; **he began his speech by saying that ...** er leitete seine Rede damit *or* mit den Worten ein, dass ...; **to ~ school** eingeschult werden, in die Schule kommen; **to ~ life as a ...** als ... anfangen *or* beginnen; **she began to feel tired** sie wurde allmählich *or* langsam müde; **she's ~ning to understand** sie fängt langsam an zu verstehen, sie versteht so langsam; **his mother began to fear the worst** seine Mutter befürchtete schon das Schlimmste; **I'd begun to think you weren't coming** ich habe schon gedacht, du kommst nicht mehr; **that doesn't even ~ to compare with ...** das lässt sich mal annähernd mit ... vergleichen; **they didn't even ~ to solve the problem** sie haben das Problem nicht mal annähernd gelöst; **I couldn't even ~ to count the mistakes** ich konnte die Fehler überhaupt nicht zählen; **I can't ~ to thank you for what you've done** ich kann Ihnen gar nicht genug dafür danken, was Sie getan haben

b (= *initiate, originate*) anfangen; *fashion, custom, policy* einführen; *society, firm, movement* gründen; (= *cause*) *war* auslösen; **he began the rumour** (*Brit*) *or* **rumor** (*US*) er hat das Gerücht in die Welt gesetzt

c (= *start to speak*) beginnen, anfangen; **it's late, he began** es ist spät, begann *or* fing *or* hub (*old*) er an

VI a (= *start*) anfangen, beginnen; (*new play etc*) anlaufen; **to ~ by doing sth** etw zuerst (einmal) tun; **he began by saying that ...** er sagte eingangs *or* einleitend, dass ...; **where the hair ~s** am Haaransatz; **before school ~s** vor Schulanfang; **to ~ in business** ins Geschäftsleben eintreten; (*as self-employed*) ein Geschäft aufmachen; **~ning from Monday** ab Montag, von Montag an; **~ning from page 10** von Seite 10 an; **say your names ~ning from the back** nennen Sie Ihre Namen von hinten nach vorn; **it all/the trouble began when ...** es fing alles/der Ärger fing damit an, dass ...; **to ~ with sb/sth** mit jdm/etw anfangen; **~ with me** fangen Sie bei *or* mit mir an; **he began with the intention of writing a thesis** anfänglich wollte er eine Doktorarbeit schreiben; **to ~ with there were only three** anfänglich waren es nur drei; **this is wrong to ~ with** das ist schon einmal falsch; **to ~ with, this is wrong, and ...** erstens einmal ist das falsch, dann ...; **to ~ on sth** mit etw anfangen *or* beginnen; **to ~ on a new venture/project** ein neues Unternehmen/Projekt in Angriff nehmen

  b (= *come into being*) beginnen, anfangen; (*custom*) entstehen; (*river*) entspringen; **since the world began** seit (An)beginn *or* Anfang der Welt; **when did this movement ~?** seit wann gibt es diese Bewegung?

beginner [bɪˈɡɪnəʳ] N Anfänger(in) *m(f)*; **~'s luck** Anfängerglück *nt*

beginning [bɪˈɡɪnɪŋ] N **a** (= *act of starting*) Anfang *m*; **to make a ~** einen Anfang machen **b** (= *place, of book etc*) Anfang *m*; (*temporal also*) Beginn *m*; (*of river*) Ursprung *m*; **at the ~** anfänglich, zuerst; **at the ~ of sth** am Anfang *or* (*temporal also*) zu Beginn einer Sache (*gen*); **the wedding will be at the ~ of July** die Hochzeit findet Anfang Juli statt; **the ~ of time/the world** der Anbeginn *or* Anfang der Welt; **in the ~** (*Bibl*) am Anfang; **from the ~** von Anfang an; **from the ~ of the week/poem** seit Anfang *or* Beginn der Woche/vom Anfang des Gedichtes an; **read the paragraph from the ~** lesen Sie den Paragraphen von (ganz) vorne; **from ~ to end** von vorn bis hinten; (*temporal*) von Anfang bis Ende; **to start again at or from the ~** noch einmal von vorn anfangen; **to begin at the ~** ganz vorn anfangen; **the ~ of negotiations** der Beginn der Verhandlungen, der Verhandlungsbeginn

  c (= *origin*) Anfang *m*; (*of custom, movement*) Entstehen *nt no pl*; **the shooting was the ~ of the rebellion** die Schießerei bedeutete den Beginn *or* Anfang der Rebellion; **it was the ~ of the end for him** das war der Anfang vom Ende für ihn; **his humble ~s** seine einfachen Anfänge; **from humble ~s** aus einfachen Verhältnissen; **Nazism had its ~s in Germany** der Nazismus hatte seine Anfänge *or* seinen Ursprung in Deutschland; **the ~s of science** die Anfangsgründe der Naturwissenschaft

begone [bɪˈɡɒn] VI *imper and infin only* (*old*) **~!** fort (mit dir/Ihnen); (*esp Rel*) weiche; **they bade him ~** sie befahlen ihm, sich fortzuscheren

begonia [bɪˈɡəʊnɪə] N Begonie *f*

begot [bɪˈɡɒt] *pret, ptp of* **beget**

begotten [bɪˈɡɒtn] *ptp of* **beget the only ~ son** der eingeborene Sohn

begrime [bɪˈɡraɪm] VT beschmutzen

begrudge [bɪˈɡrʌdʒ] VT **a** (= *be reluctant*) **to ~ doing sth** etw widerwillig tun **b** (= *envy*) missgönnen (*sb sth* jdm etw); **no one ~s you your good fortune** wir gönnen dir ja dein Glück; **he ~s him the air he breathes** er gönnt ihm das Salz in der Suppe nicht **c** (= *give unwillingly*) nicht gönnen (*sb sth* jdm etw); **I wouldn't ~ you the money** ich würde dir das Geld ja gönnen; **I won't ~ you £5** du sollst die £ 5 haben

begrudging [bɪˈɡrʌdʒɪŋ] ADJ widerwillig

begrudgingly [bɪˈɡrʌdʒɪŋlɪ] ADV widerwillig

beguile [bɪˈɡaɪl] VT **a** (= *deceive*) betören (*geh*); **to ~ sb into doing sth** jdn dazu verführen, etw

zu tun **b** (= *charm*) person betören; (*liter*) time sich (*dat*) angenehm vertreiben

beguiling [bɪˈɡaɪlɪŋ] ADJ betörend, verführerisch

begun [bɪˈɡʌn] *ptp of* **begin**

behalf [bɪˈhɑːf] ⊘ 22 N **on** *or* **in** (*US*) **~ of** für, im Interesse von; (*as spokesman*) im Namen von; (*as authorized representative*) im Auftrag von; **I'm not asking on my own ~** ich bitte nicht für mich selbst *or* in meinem eigenen Interesse darum

behave [bɪˈheɪv] VI sich verhalten; (*people also*) sich benehmen; (*children also*) sich betragen, sich benehmen; (= *be good*) sich benehmen; **to ~ well/badly** sich gut/schlecht benehmen; **what a way to ~!** was für ein Benehmen!; **to ~ badly/well toward(s) sb** jdn schlecht/gut behandeln; **to ~ irresponsibly toward(s) sb** sich jdm gegenüber verantwortungslos verhalten; **to ~ like an honest man** wie ein ehrlicher Mensch handeln; **to ~ very wisely** sich sehr klug verhalten; **~!** benimm dich!; **can't you make your son/dog ~!** kannst du deinem Sohn/Hund keine Manieren beibringen?; **he knows how to ~ at a cocktail party** er weiß sich bei Cocktailpartys zu benehmen; **how is your car behaving these days?** wie fährt dein Auto zurzeit?

  VR to ~ oneself sich benehmen; **~ yourself!** benimm dich!; **can't you make your son/dog ~ himself/itself?** kannst du deinem Sohn/Hund keine Manieren beibringen?

behaviour, (*US*) **behavior** [bɪˈheɪvjəʳ] N **a** (= *manner, bearing*) Benehmen *nt*; (*esp of children also*) Betragen *nt*; **to be on one's best ~** sich von seiner besten Seite zeigen, sich bestes Benehmen an den Tag legen **b** (*towards others*) Verhalten *nt* (*to(wards)* gegenüber) **c** (*of car, machine*) Verhalten *nt*

behavioural, (*US*) **behavioral** [bɪˈheɪvjərəl] ADJ *in cpds* Verhaltens-; **behavioural science** N Verhaltensforschung *f*; **behavioural scientist** N Verhaltensforscher(in) *m(f)*

behaviourism, (*US*) **behaviorism** [bɪˈheɪvjərɪzəm] N Behaviorismus *m*

behaviourist, (*US*) **behaviorist** [bɪˈheɪvjərɪst] N Behaviorist *m* ADJ behavioristisch

behaviour pattern, (*US*) **behavior pattern** N Verhaltensmuster *nt*

behead [bɪˈhed] VT enthaupten, köpfen

beheld [bɪˈheld] *pret, ptp of* **behold**

behemoth [bɪˈhiːmɒθ] N (*liter*, = *monster*) Moloch *m* (*geh*)

behest [bɪˈhest] N (*liter*) Geheiß *nt* (*liter*); **at his ~/the ~ of his uncle** auf sein Geheiß (*liter*)/auf Geheiß seines Onkels (*liter*)

behind [bɪˈhaɪnd] PREP **a** (= *in or at the rear of, stationary*) hinter (+*dat*); (*with motion*) hinter (+*acc*); **come out from ~ the door** komm hinter der Tür (her)vor; **he came up ~ me** er trat von hinten an mich heran; **walk close ~ me** gehen Sie dicht hinter mir; **close the door ~ you** mach die Tür hinter dir zu; **put it ~ the books** stellen Sie es hinter die Bücher; **he has the Communists ~ him** er hat die Kommunisten hinter sich (*dat*); **to be ~ an idea** eine Idee unterstützen; **what is ~ this/this incident?** was steckt dahinter/steckt hinter diesem Vorfall?; **she has years of experience ~ her** sie hat viele Jahre der Erfahrung hinter sich (*dat*)

  b (= *more backward than*) **to be ~ sb** hinter jdm zurück sein

  c (*in time*) **to be ~ time** (*train etc*) Verspätung haben; (*with work etc*) im Rückstand sein; **to be ~ schedule** im Verzug sein; **to be three hours ~ time** drei Stunden Verspätung haben; **to be ~ the times** (*fig*) hinter seiner Zeit zurück(geblieben) sein; **you must put the past ~ you** Sie müssen Vergangenes vergangen sein lassen, Sie müssen die Vergangenheit begraben; **their youth is far ~ them** ihre Jugend liegt weit zurück

  ADV a (= *in or at rear*) hinten; (= *behind this, sb etc*) dahinter; **the runner was (lying) a long**

way ~ der Läufer lag weit hinten *or* zurück; **from ~** von hinten; **to look ~** zurückblicken; **to stand ~** (= *be standing*) dahinter stehen; (= *position oneself*) sich dahinter stellen

  b (= *late*) **to be ~ with one's studies/payments** mit seinen Studien/Zahlungen im Rückstand sein; **we are three days ~ with the schedule** wir sind drei Tage im Rückstand *or* Verzug

  N (*inf*) Hinterteil *nt* (*inf*), Hintern *m* (*inf*)

behindhand [bɪˈhaɪndhænd] ADV ADJ **a** (= *late*) **to be ~** Verspätung haben **b** (= *in arrears*) **to be ~ with sth** mit etw im Rückstand *or* Verzug sein

behold [bɪˈhəʊld] *pret, ptp* **beheld** VT (*liter*) sehen, erblicken (*liter*); **~!** und siehe (da); (*Rel*) siehe; **~ thy servant** siehe deinen Diener

beholden [bɪˈhəʊldən] ADJ (*liter*) **to be ~ to sb for sth** jdm für etw verpflichtet sein (*geh*)

behove [bɪˈhəʊv], (*US*) **behoove** [bɪˈhuːv] VT IMPERS (*form*) sich geziemen (*geh*) (*sb to do sth* für jdn, etw zu tun)

beige [beɪʒ] ADJ beige N Beige *nt*

being [ˈbiːɪŋ] N **a** (= *existence*) Dasein *nt*, Leben *nt*; **to come into ~** entstehen; (*club etc also*) ins Leben gerufen werden; **to bring into ~** ins Leben rufen, (er)schaffen; **then in ~** damals bestehend **b** (= *that which exists*) (Lebe)wesen *nt*, Geschöpf *nt*; **~s from outer space** Wesen *pl* aus dem All **c** (= *essence*) Wesen *nt*; **with all or every fibre** (*Brit*) *or* **fiber** (*US*) **of my ~** mit jeder Faser meines Herzens

Beirut [beɪˈruːt] N Beirut *nt*

bejewelled, (*US*) **bejeweled** [bɪˈdʒuːəld] ADJ mit Edelsteinen geschmückt; **~ with sequins** mit Pailletten besetzt; **~ with dew/stars** (*poet*) mit glitzernden Tautropfen besät/sternenbesät (*poet*)

belabour, (*US*) **belabor** [bɪˈleɪbəʳ] VT **a** (= *hit*) einschlagen auf (+*acc*) **b** (*fig, with insults etc*) überhäufen; (*with questions*) beschießen, bearbeiten

belated ADJ , **belatedly** ADV [bɪˈleɪtɪd, -lɪ] verspätet

belay [bɪˈleɪ] VT (*Naut*) belegen, festmachen; (*Mountaineering*) sichern INTERJ (*Naut*) **~ there** aufhören

belaying pin [bɪˈleɪɪŋpɪn] N (*Naut*) Belegklampe *f*; (*Mountaineering*) (Kletter)haken *m*

belch [beltʃ] VI (*person*) rülpsen, aufstoßen; (*volcano*) Lava speien *or* ausstoßen; (*smoke, fire*) herausquellen VT (*also* **belch forth** *or* **out**) smoke, flames (aus)speien, ausstoßen N **a** (= *burp*) Rülpser *m* (*inf*) **b** (*of smoke etc*) Stoß *m*

beleaguer [bɪˈliːɡəʳ] VT belagern; (*fig*) umgeben

belfry [ˈbelfrɪ] N Glockenstube *f* → **bat**[1]

Belgian [ˈbeldʒən] N Belgier(in) *m(f)* ADJ belgisch

Belgium [ˈbeldʒəm] N Belgien *nt*

Belgrade [belˈɡreɪd] N Belgrad *nt*

belie [bɪˈlaɪ] VT **a** (= *prove false*) words, proverb Lügen strafen, widerlegen **b** (= *give false impression of*) hinwegtäuschen über (+*acc*) **c** (= *fail to justify*) hopes enttäuschen

belief [bɪˈliːf] N **a** Glaube *m* (*in an* +*acc*); **it is beyond ~** es ist unglaublich *or* nicht zu glauben; **a statement unworthy of your ~** (*form*) eine Aussage, der Sie keinen Glauben schenken sollten

  b (*Rel*, = *faith*) Glaube *m*; (= *doctrine*) (Glaubens)lehre *f*

  c (= *convinced opinion*) Überzeugung *f*, Glaube *m no pl*; **what are the ~s of the average citizen today?** woran glaubt der heutige Durchschnittsbürger?; **in the ~ that ...** im Glauben, dass ...; **acting in this ~** in gutem Glauben, im guten Glauben; **it is my ~ that ...** ich bin der Überzeugung, dass ...; **it is one of my ~s that ...** es ist meine Überzeugung, dass ...; **yes, that is my ~** ich glaube schon; **to the best of my ~** meines Wissens

  d *no pl* (= *trust*) Glaube *m* (*in an* +*acc*); **to have ~ in** glauben an (+*acc*)

believability [bɪˌliːvəˈbɪlɪtɪ] N Glaubhaftigkeit f, Glaubwürdigkeit f

believable [brˈliːvəbl] ADJ glaubhaft, glaubwürdig; **hardly ~** wenig glaubhaft

believe [brˈliːv] ❷ 26.2 **VT** **a** sth glauben; sb glauben (+dat); **I don't ~ you** das glaube ich (Ihnen) nicht; **don't you ~ it** wers glaubt, wird selig (inf); **it's true, please ~ me** es stimmt, bitte glauben Sie mir das; **~ me, I mean it** glauben Sie mir, es ist mir ernst or Ernst; **~ you me!** (inf) das können Sie mir glauben!; **~ it or not** ob Sies glauben oder nicht; **would you ~ it!** (inf) ist das (denn) die Möglichkeit (inf); **I would never have ~d it of him** das hätte ich nie von ihm geglaubt; **he could hardly ~ his eyes/ears** er traute seinen Augen/Ohren nicht; **if he is to be ~d** wenn man ihm glauben darf or Glauben schenken kann

b (= think) glauben; **he is ~d to be ill** es heißt, dass er krank ist; **I ~ so/not** ich glaube schon/nicht → **make-believe**

VI (= have a religious faith) an Gott glauben; **you must ~!** Sie müssen glauben!

▶ **believe in** VI +prep obj **a** God, ghosts glauben an (+acc)

b (= have trust in) promises glauben an (+acc); method also Vertrauen haben zu; **to believe in oneself** an sich selbst glauben; **the boss/his mother still believes in him** der Chef/seine Mutter glaubt immer noch an ihn; **please believe in me** bitte haben Sie Vertrauen zu mir; **he doesn't believe in medicine/doctors** er hält nicht viel von Medikamenten/Ärzten

c (= support idea of) **to believe in sth** (prinzipiell) für etw sein; **he believes in getting up early** er ist überzeugter Frühaufsteher; **he believes in giving people a second chance** er gibt prinzipiell jedem noch einmal eine Chance; **I don't believe in compromises** ich halte nichts von Kompromissen, ich bin gegen Kompromisse

believer [brˈliːvə] N **a** (Rel) Gläubige(r) mf **b** **to be a (firm) ~ in sth** (grundsätzlich) für etw sein; **I'm a ~ in doing things properly** ich bin grundsätzlich der Meinung, dass man, was man macht, richtig machen sollte; **he's a (firm) ~ in getting up early** er ist überzeugter Frühaufsteher; **he's not much of a ~ in getting up early** er hält nicht viel vom Frühaufstehen

Belisha beacon [bɪˌliːʃəˈbiːkən] N (Brit) gelbes Blinklicht an Zebrastreifen

belittle [brˈlɪtl] ❷ 26.3 VT herabsetzen, heruntermachen (inf); achievement also schmälern; **to ~ oneself** sich schlechter machen, als man ist

belittlement [brˈlɪtlmənt] N Herabsetzung f; (of achievement also) Schmälerung f

Belize [beˈliːz] N Belize nt

bell¹ [bel] **N** **a** Glocke f; (small: on toys, pet's collar etc) Glöckchen nt, Schelle f; (= school bell, doorbell, of bicycle) Klingel f, Glocke f (dated); (= handbell also) Schelle f; (of typewriter, Telec) Klingel f; **as clear as a ~** (voice) glasklar; picture gestochen scharf; hear, sound laut und deutlich; **as sound as a ~** kerngesund

b (= sound of bell) Läuten nt; (of doorbell, school bell, telephone etc) Klingeln nt; (in athletics) Glocke f zur letzten Runde; **there's the ~** es hat gelingt or läutet; **was that the ~?** hat es gerade geklingelt or geläutet?; **the teacher came in on the ~** der Lehrer kam mit dem Klingeln or Läuten herein; **he's coming up to the ~** er geht nun in die letzte Runde; **it was 3.02 at the ~** zu Beginn der letzten Runde hatte er eine Zeit von 3.02; **to give sb a ~** (Brit inf) jdn anrufen

c (Naut) Schiffsglocke f; (= ringing) Läuten nt (der Schiffsglocke); (for time also) Glasen nt (spec); **it is eight ~s** es ist acht Glas (spec); **to ring one ~** einmal glasen (spec)

d (of flower) Glocke f, Kelch m; (of trumpet) Stürze f; (of loudspeaker) (Schall)trichter m

VT eine Glocke/ein Glöckchen umhängen (+dat); **to ~ the cat** (fig) der Katze die Schelle umhängen

bell² **N** (of stag) Röhren nt **VI** röhren

belladonna [ˌbeləˈdɒnə] N (Bot) Tollkirsche f, Belladonna f; (Med) Belladonin nt

bell: bell-bottomed trousers (esp Brit), **bell--bottoms** PL ausgestellte Hosen; **bellboy** N (esp US) Page m, Hoteljunge m; **bell captain** N (US) Chef(in) m(f) der Hotelpagen

belle [bel] N Schöne f, Schönheit f; **the ~ of the ball** die Ballkönigin

bell: bellflower N (Bot) Glockenblume f; **bell heather** N Glockenheide f; **bellhop** N (US) = **bellboy**

bellicose [ˈbelɪkəʊs] ADJ nation, mood kriegerisch, kriegslustig; (= pugnacious) kampflustig, streitsüchtig

bellicosity [ˌbelɪˈkɒsɪtɪ] N (of nation, mood) Kriegslust f; (= pugnacity) Kampf(es)lust f, Streitsüchtigkeit f

belligerence, belligerency [brˈlɪdʒərəns, -sɪ] N (of nation) Kriegslust f, Kampf(es)lust f; (of person, attitude) Streitlust f; (of speech) Aggressivität f

belligerent [brˈlɪdʒərənt] **ADJ** **a** nation kriegslustig, kampflustig, kriegerisch; person, attitude streitlustig, kampflustig; mood streitlustig, kämpferisch; speech aggressiv **b** (= waging war) Krieg führend, streitend; **~ power** Streitmacht f **N** (= nation) Krieg führendes Land; (= person) Streitende(r) mf

belligerently [brˈlɪdʒərəntlɪ] ADV say, act, behave streitlustig

bell jar N (Glas)glocke f

bellow [ˈbeləʊ] **VI** (animal, person) brüllen; (singing also) grölen (inf); **to ~ at sb** jdn anbrüllen **VT** (also **bellow out**) brüllen; song also grölen (inf) **N** Brüllen nt

bellows [ˈbeləʊz] PL Blasebalg m; **a pair of ~** ein Blasebalg

bell: bell pull N Klingelzug m; **bell push** N Klingel f; **bell-ringer** N Glöckner m; **bell--ringing** N Glockenläuten nt; **bell rope** N (in church) Glockenstrang m; (in house) Klingelzug m; **bells and whistles** [ˌbelzənˈwɪslz] PL (esp Comput inf, = additional features) Extras pl; **bell--shaped** ADJ glockenförmig, kelchförmig

Bell's palsy [ˌbelzˈpɔːlzɪ] N (Med) bellsche Lähmung

bell: bell tent N Rundzelt nt; **bell tower** N Glockenturm m; **bellwether** [ˈbelˌweðə] N Leithammel m

belly [ˈbelɪ] N (general) Bauch m; (of violin etc) Decke f

▶ **belly out** **VT** sep sails blähen, schwellen lassen **VI** (sails) sich blähen, schwellen

belly: bellyache (inf) **N** Bauchweh nt (inf), Bauchschmerzen pl **VI** (= complain) murren (about über +acc); **bellyaching** N (inf) Murren nt, Gemurre f; **bellybutton** N (inf) Bauchnabel m; **belly dance** N Bauchtanz m; **belly-dance** VI bauchtanzen; **belly dancer** N Bauchtänzerin f; **bellyflop** N Bauchklatscher m (inf); **to do a ~** einen Bauchklatscher machen (inf)

bellyful [ˈbelɪfʊl] N **a** (inf: = more than enough) **I've had a ~ of him/writing these letters** ich habe die Nase voll von ihm/davon, immer diese Briefe zu schreiben (inf) **b** (inf, of food) **after a good ~ of beans** nachdem ich mir/er sich etc den Bauch mit Bohnen voll geschlagen hatte (inf)

belly: belly-land VI bauchlanden; **belly landing** N Bauchlandung f; **belly laugh** N dröhnendes Lachen; **he gave a great ~** er lachte lauthals los; **belly up** ADV **to go ~** (inf, company) Pleite gehen (inf); **his plans went ~** er ging mit seinen Plänen baden (inf)

belong [brˈlɒŋ] VI **a** (= be the property of) gehören (to sb jdm); **who does it ~ to?** wem gehört es?; **the parks ~ to everybody** die Parkanlagen sind für alle da

b (= be part of) gehören (to zu); (to town: person) gehören (to nach), sich zu Hause fühlen (to in +dat); (to club) angehören (to +dat); **to ~ together** zusammengehören; **the lid ~s to this box** der Deckel gehört zu dieser Schachtel; **to ~ to a club** einem Klub angehören; **why don't you ~?** warum sind Sie

nicht Mitglied?; **concepts that ~ to physics** Begriffe, die in die Physik gehören

c (= be in right place) gehören; **I don't ~ here** ich gehöre nicht hierher, ich bin hier fehl am Platze; **to feel that one doesn't ~** das Gefühl haben, dass man fehl am Platze ist or dass man nicht dazugehört; **you don't ~ here, so scram** Sie haben hier nichts zu suchen, also verschwinden Sie; **the vase ~s on the mantelpiece** die Vase gehört auf den Sims; **where does this one ~?** wo gehört das hin?; **that doesn't ~ to my area of responsibility** das gehört nicht in meinen Verantwortungsbereich; **this case ~s in the Appeal Court** dieser Fall gehört vor das Berufungsgericht; **that doesn't ~ to this department** das gehört nicht in diese Abteilung; **it ~s under the heading of ...** das gehört or fällt in die Rubrik der ...

belongings [brˈlɒŋɪŋz] PL Sachen pl, Besitz m, Habe f (geh); **personal ~** persönliches Eigentum, persönlicher Besitz; **all his ~** sein ganzes Hab und Gut

beloved [brˈlʌvɪd] **ADJ** geliebt; memory lieb, teuer **N** Geliebte(r) mf; **dearly ~** (Rel) liebe Brüder und Schwestern im Herrn

below [brˈləʊ] **PREP** **a** (= under) unterhalb (+gen); (with line, level etc also) unter (+dat or with motion +acc); **on it and ~ it** darauf und darunter; **her skirt comes well ~ her knees** or **the knee** ihr Rock geht bis weit unters Knie; **Naples is ~ Rome** (on the map) Neapel liegt unterhalb Roms; **the sun disappeared ~ the horizon** die Sonne verschwand hinter dem Horizont; **to be ~ sb** (in rank) (rangmäßig) unter jdm stehen

b (= downstream from) unterhalb (+gen), nach

c (= unworthy of) **or is that ~ you?** oder ist das unter Ihrer Würde?

ADV **a** (= lower down) unten; **the cows in the valley ~** die Kühe drunten im Tal; **they live one floor ~** sie wohnen ein Stockwerk tiefer; **the tenants/apartment ~** die Mieter/die Wohnung darunter; (below us) die Mieter/Wohnung unter uns; **write the name here with the address ~** schreiben Sie den Namen hierher und die Adresse darunter; **in the class ~** in der Klasse darunter; (below me) in der Klasse unter mir; **what's the next rank ~?** was ist der nächstniedere Rang?; **down ~** unten

b (Naut) unter Deck; **to go ~** unter Deck gehen

c (in documents) (weiter) unten; **see ~** siehe unten

d **15 degrees ~** 15 Grad unter null, 15 Grad minus

e **here ~** (= on earth) hier unten; **and on earth ~** (Bibl) und unten auf der Erde; **down ~** (= in hell) dort drunten

below strength ADJ pred, **below-strength** ADJ attr (Sport) ersatzgeschwächt

Belshazzar [belˈʃæzə] N **~'s Feast** Belsazars Gastmahl nt

belt [belt] **N** **a** (on clothes) Gürtel m; (for holding, carrying etc, seat belt) Gurt m; (Mil etc, on uniform) Koppel nt; (for cartridges) Patronengurt m; (= rifle sling) (Gewehr)riemen m; **a blow below the ~** (lit, fig) ein Schlag unterhalb der Gürtellinie, ein Tiefschlag m; **to hit sb below the ~** (lit, fig: person) jdm einen Schlag unter die Gürtellinie versetzen; **that was below the ~** das war ein Schlag unter die Gürtellinie; **to be a black ~** den schwarzen Gürtel haben; **to get the ~** (mit dem Lederriemen) eine auf die Finger bekommen; **to tighten one's ~** (fig) den Gürtel or Riemen enger schnallen; **under one's ~** (fig inf) auf dem Rücken (inf)

b (Tech) (Treib)riemen m; (= conveyor belt) Band nt

c (= tract of land) Gürtel m; **~ of trees** Waldstreifen m; (around house etc) Baumgürtel m; **industrial ~** Industriegürtel m → **commuter**

d (inf, = hit) Schlag m; **to give sb/the ball a ~** jdm eine knallen (inf)/den Ball knallen (inf)

e (US, = ring road) Umgehungsstraße f

f (US, inf, = drink) Schluck m aus der Pulle (inf)

VT **a** (= *fasten*) den Gürtel zumachen (*sth +gen*)
b (*Sch etc*, = *thrash*) (mit dem Lederriemen) schlagen
c (*inf*, = *hit*) knallen (*inf*); **she ~ed him one in the eye** sie verpasste *or* haute *or* knallte ihm eins aufs Auge (*inf*)
VI (*inf*, = *rush*) rasen (*inf*); **to ~ out** hinaus-/herausrasen (*inf*); **to ~ across** hinüber-/herüberrasen (*inf*); **we were really ~ing along** wir sind wirklich gerast (*inf*); **he ~ed off down the street** er raste davon die Straße hinunter (*inf*); **this novel really ~s along** dieser Roman ist wirklich tempogeladen (*inf*)

▶ **belt down** VT *sep* (*inf*, = *drink quickly*) hinunterschütten, hinunterkippen (*inf*)

▶ **belt on** VT *sep* sword umschnallen, sich umgürten mit (*geh*); *raincoat* anziehen

▶ **belt out** VT *sep* (*inf*) *tune* schmettern (*inf*); *rhythm* voll herausbringen (*inf*); (*on piano*) hämmern (*inf*)

▶ **belt up** **VT** *sep* jacket den Gürtel (+*gen*) zumachen **VI** **a** (*inf*) die Klappe *or* Schnauze halten (*inf*); (= *stop making noise*) mit dem Krach aufhören (*inf*) **b** (*esp hum*, = *put seat belt on*) sich anschnallen

belt bag N Gürteltasche *f*

belt buckle N Gürtelschnalle *f*

belt drive N Riemenantrieb *m*

belter ['beltə'] N (*inf*, = *singer*) toller Sänger (*inf*), tolle Sängerin (*inf*); (= *song*) Hit *m*; (= *party*) tolle Fete

belting ['beltɪŋ] N (*inf*) Dresche *f* (*inf*); **to give sb a good ~** jdn ganz schön verdreschen (*inf*)

belt loop N Gürtelschlaufe *f*

beltway ['beltweɪ] N (*US*) Umgehungsstraße *f*

bemoan [bɪ'məʊn] VT beklagen

bemused [bɪ'mjuːzd] ADJ ratlos; **to be ~ by sth** einer Sache (*dat*) ratlos gegenüberstehen

bemusedly [bɪ'mjuːzɪdlɪ] ADV ratlos

bench [bentʃ] **N** **a** (= *seat*) Bank *f*; **laughter from the government ~es** (*Brit*) Gelächter von der Regierungsbank
b (*Jur*, = *office of a judge*) Richteramt *nt*; (= *judges generally*) Richter *pl*; (= *court*) Gericht *nt*; **member of the ~** Richter *m*; **to be raised to the ~** zum Richter bestellt werden; **to be on the ~** (*permanent office*) Richter sein; (*when in court*) der Richter sein, auf dem Richterstuhl sitzen (*geh*)
c (= *workbench*) Werkbank *f*; (*in lab*) Experimentiertisch *m*
d (*Sport*: = *selected as substitute*) **on the ~** auf der Reservebank
VT (*US, Sport*) auf die Strafbank schicken; (= *keep as substitute*) auf die Reservebank setzen

bencher ['bentʃə'] N (*Brit Jur*) Vorstandsmitglied eines der Inns of Court

benchmark ['bentʃmɑːk] **N** (*Surv*) Höhenfestpunkt *m*; (*fig*) Maßstab *m* **ADJ** *attr* ~ **price** Richtpreis *m*; ~ **rate** Benchmark *f*; **the ~ machine** die Maschine, die Maßstäbe setzt

benchmarking ['bentʃmɑːkɪŋ] N (*Econ*) Benchmarking *nt*

bench: bench penalty N (*Ice hockey*) Bankstrafe *f*; **bench press** N (*Sport*) Bankdrücken *nt*; **bench seat** N (*in the car*) Sitzbank *f*; **bench test** N (*Tech*) Test *m* auf dem Prüfstand, Prüfstandtest *m*; **bench warmer** N (*Sport inf*) Ersatzspieler(in) *m(f)* (*der/die nur selten zum Einsatz kommt*)

bend [bend] *vb*: pret, ptp **bent** **N** **a** (*in river, tube, etc*) Krümmung *f*, Biegung *f*; (*90°*) Knie *nt*; (*in road also*) Kurve *f*; **there is a ~ in the road** die Straße hat (da) eine Kurve; **~s for 3 miles** 3 Meilen kurvenreiche Strecke; **don't park on the ~** parken Sie nicht in der Kurve; **to go/be round the ~** (*Brit inf*) durchdrehen (*inf*), verrückt werden/sein (*inf*); **to drive sb round the ~** (*Brit inf*) jdn verrückt *or* wahnsinnig machen (*inf*)
b (= *knot*) Stek *m*
VT **a** (= *curve, make angular*) biegen; *rod, rail,*

pipe also krümmen; *bow* spannen; *arm, knee also* beugen; *leg, arm also* anwinkeln; (*forwards*) *back also* beugen, krümmen; *head* beugen, neigen; **he can ~ an iron bar with his teeth** er kann mit den Zähnen eine Eisenstange verbiegen; **to ~ sth at right angles** etw rechtwinklig abbiegen *or* abknicken; **to ~ sth out of shape** etw verbiegen; **the bumper got bent in the crash** die Stoßstange hat sich bei dem Zusammenstoß verbogen; **on ~ed knees** auf Knien; (*fig also*) kniefällig; **to go down on ~ed knees** auf die Knie fallen; (*fig also*) einen Kniefall machen
b (*fig*) *rules, truth* es nicht so genau nehmen mit; **to ~ the law** das Gesetz beugen; **to ~ sb to one's will** (*dat*) jdn gefügig machen
c (= *direct*) *one's steps, efforts* lenken, richten
d (*Naut*) *sail* befestigen
VI **a** sich biegen; (*pipe, rail also*) sich krümmen; (*forwards also, tree, corn etc*) sich neigen; (*person*) sich beugen; **this metal ~s easily** (*a bad thing*) dieses Metall verbiegt sich leicht; (*a good thing*) dieses Metall lässt sich leicht biegen; **my arm won't ~** ich kann den Arm nicht biegen; **~ing strain** Biegespannung *f*
b (*river*) eine Biegung machen; (*at right angles*) ein Knie machen; (*road also*) eine Kurve machen; **the road/river ~s to the left** die Straße/der Fluss macht eine Linkskurve/-biegung
c (*fig*, = *submit*) sich beugen, sich fügen (*to +dat*)

▶ **bend back** **VI** sich zurückbiegen; (*over backwards*) sich nach hinten biegen; (*road, river*) in einer Schleife zurückkommen **VT** *sep* zurückbiegen

▶ **bend down** **VI** (*person*) sich bücken; (*branch, tree*) sich neigen, sich nach unten biegen; **she bent down to look at the baby** sie beugte sich hinunter, um das Baby anzusehen **VT** *sep edges* nach unten biegen

▶ **bend over** **VI** (*person*) sich bücken; **to bend over to look at sth** sich nach vorn beugen, um etw anzusehen → **backwards** **VT** *sep* umbiegen

bender ['bendə'] N (*Brit inf*) Kneipkur *f* (*hum inf*); **to go on a ~** (*Brit inf*) sich besaufen (*inf*); (= *go on pub-crawl*) auf eine Sauftour gehen (*inf*)

bends [bendz] N **the ~** die Taucherkrankheit

bend sinister N (*Her*) Schräglinksbalken *m*

bendy ['bendɪ] ADJ (*inf*) **a** (= *flexible*) biegsam **b** *road* kurvenreich, kurvig

beneath [bɪ'niːθ] **PREP** **a** unter (+*dat or with motion +acc*); (*with line, level etc also*) unterhalb (+*gen*); **to marry ~ one** unter seinem Stand heiraten → *also* **below PREP a** **b** (= *unworthy of*) **it is ~ him** das ist unter seiner Würde; **he regarded the critics as ~ his notice** er fand es unter seiner Würde, von den Kritikern überhaupt Notiz zu nehmen **ADV** unten → *also* **below ADV a**

Benedictine [,benɪ'dɪktɪn] **N** **a** (*Eccl*) Benediktiner(in) *m(f)* **b** (= *liqueur*) Benediktiner *m* **ADJ** Benediktiner-

benediction [,benɪ'dɪkʃən] N **a** (= *blessing*) Segen *m*; (= *act of blessing*) Segnung *f* **b** (= *consecration*) Einsegnung *f*

benefaction [,benɪ'fækʃən] N **a** (= *good deed*) Wohltat *f*, gute Tat **b** (= *gift*) Spende *f*

benefactor ['benɪfæktə'] N Wohltäter *m*; (= *giver of money also*) Gönner *m*

benefactress ['benɪfæktrɪs] N Wohltäterin *f*; (= *giver of money also*) Gönnerin *f*

benefice ['benɪfɪs] N Pfründe *f*, kirchliches Benefizium (*spec*)

beneficence [bɪ'nefɪsəns] N (*liter*) Wohltätigkeit *f*

beneficent [bɪ'nefɪsənt] ADJ (*liter*) wohltätig

beneficial [,benɪ'fɪʃəl] ADJ **a** gut (*to* für); *climate also* zuträglich (*geh*) (*to +dat*); *influence also* vorteilhaft; *advice, lesson* nützlich (*to* für); (= *advantageous*) günstig, von Vorteil; **the change will be ~ to you** die Veränderung wird Ihnen gut tun **b** (*Jur*) ~ **owner** Nutznießer(in) *m(f)*

beneficiary [,benɪ'fɪʃərɪ] **N** **a** Nutznießer(in) *m(f)*; (*of will, insurance etc*) Begünstigte(r) *mf* **b** (*Eccl*) Pfründner *m*

benefit ['benɪfɪt] **N** **a** (= *advantage*) Vorteil *m*; (= *profit*) Nutzen *m*, Gewinn *m*; **to derive** *or* **get ~ from sth** aus etw Nutzen ziehen; **for the ~ of his family/the poor** zum Wohl *or* für das Wohl seiner Familie/der Armen; **for the ~ of your health** Ihrer Gesundheit zuliebe, um Ihrer Gesundheit willen; **for your ~** Ihretwegen, um Ihretwillen (*geh*); **this money is for the ~ of the blind** dieses Geld kommt den Blinden zugute; **it is for his ~ that this was done** das ist seinetwegen geschehen; **to give sb the ~ of the doubt** im Zweifelsfall zu jds Gunsten entscheiden; **we should give him the ~ of the doubt** wir sollten das zu seinen Gunsten auslegen
b (= *allowance*) Unterstützung *f*; (= *sickness benefit*) Krankengeld *nt*; (*Brit*: = *child benefit*) Kindergeld *nt*; (= *social security benefit*) Sozialhilfe *f*; (*Brit*: = *maternity benefit*) Wochengeld *nt*; (= *insurance benefit*) Versicherungsleistung *f*; **old age ~** Altersrente *f* → **fringe benefits**
c (= *special performance*) Benefizveranstaltung *f*; (*Theat also*) Benefiz(vorstellung *f*) *nt*; (*Sport also*) Benefizspiel *nt*; **it's his ~** es ist eine Benefizvorstellung für ihn
d **without ~ of clergy** ohne kirchlichen Segen **VT** gut tun (+*dat*), nützen (+*dat*), zugute kommen (+*dat*); (*healthwise*) gut tun (+*dat*)
VI profitieren (*from, by* von); (*from experience also*) Nutzen ziehen (*from* aus); **who will ~ from that?** wem wird das nützen?; **but how do we ~?** aber was nützt es uns?; **he would ~ from a week off** eine Woche Urlaub würde ihm gut tun; **I think you'll ~ from the experience** ich glaube, diese Erfahrung wird Ihnen nützlich sein *or* von Nutzen sein; **a cure from which many have ~ed** eine Behandlung, die schon manchem geholfen hat

benefit: benefit concert N Benefizkonzert *nt*; **benefit match** N Benefizspiel *nt*; **benefit performance** N Benefizveranstaltung *f*

Benelux ['benɪlʌks] N Benelux-Wirtschaftsunion *f*; ~ **countries** Beneluxstaaten *or* -länder *pl*

benevolence [bɪ'nevələns] N Wohlwollen *nt*; (*of smile, gesture*) Gutmütigkeit *f*; (*as character trait*) Güte *f*; (*of emperor, judge*) Milde *f*

benevolent [bɪ'nevələnt] ADJ **a** wohlwollend; *pat, smile, twinkle* gutmütig; (*as character trait*) gütig; *emperor, judge* mild; **Benevolent Despotism** der aufgeklärte Absolutismus **b** (= *charitable*) ~ **fund** Unterstützungsfonds *m*, Unterstützungskasse *f*; ~ **institution** Wohltätigkeitseinrichtung *f*; ~ **society** Wohltätigkeitsverein *m*

benevolently [bɪ'nevələntlɪ] ADV *look, say* wohlwollend; *smile* gutmütig; (= *leniently*) milde

Bengal [beŋ'gɔːl] N Bengalen *nt*

Bengalese [,beŋgə'liːz] **N** Bengale *m*, Bengalin *f* **ADJ** bengalisch

Bengali [beŋ'gɔːlɪ] **N** (= *language*) Bengali *nt*; (= *person*) Bengale *m*, Bengalin *f* **ADJ** bengalisch

Bengal light, **Bengal match** N bengalisches Feuer *or* Hölzchen *nt*

Bengal tiger N Bengalischer Tiger, Königstiger *m*

benighted [bɪ'naɪtɪd] ADJ **a** (*fig*) *person* unbedarft; *country* gottverlassen; *policy etc* hirnrissig **b** (*lit*) von der Dunkelheit *or* Nacht überfallen *or* überrascht

benign [bɪ'naɪn], **benignant** [bɪ'nɪgnənt] (*rare*) ADJ **a** gütig; *planet, influence* günstig; *climate* mild; (= *harmless*) *substance, process, research* harmlos **b** (*Med*) *tumour* gutartig

benny ['benɪ] N (*sl*) *dim of* **Benzedrine**

bent [bent] pret, ptp *of* **bend** **a** *metal etc* gebogen; (= *out of shape*) verbogen
b (*Brit, inf*, = *dishonest*) *person* korrupt; *affair* unsauber (*inf*); **he's ~** er ist ein krummer Hund (*inf*)
c (*Brit pej inf*, = *homosexual*) andersrum *pred* (*inf*)
d **to be ~ on sth/doing sth** etw unbedingt *or* partout wollen/tun wollen; **he seemed ~ on**

self-destruction er schien von einem Selbstzerstörungstrieb besessen zu sein **N** (= *aptitude*) Neigung *f* (*for* zu); (= *type of mind, character*) Schlag *m*; **to follow one's ~** seiner Neigung folgen; **people with** *or* **of a musical ~** Menschen mit einer musikalischen Veranlagung; **people of his ~** Leute seines Schlags

benumb [bɪ'nʌm] VT **a** *limb* gefühllos machen; *person* betäuben; (*with cold also*) erstarren lassen; **he was/his fingers were ~ed with cold** er war/seine Finger waren starr vor Kälte **b** (*fig*) *mind* betäuben; (*panic, experience etc*) lähmen; **~ed by alcohol** vom Alkohol benommen

Benzedrine® ['benzɪdriːn] N Benzedrin *nt*

benzene ['benziːn] N Benzol *nt*

benzine ['benziːn] N Leichtbenzin *nt*

bequeath [bɪ'kwiːð] VT **a** (*in will*) vermachen, hinterlassen (*to sb* jdm) **b** (*fig*) *tradition* hinterlassen, vererben (*to sb* jdm)

bequest [bɪ'kwest] N (= *act of bequeathing*) Vermachen *nt* (*to an* +*acc*); (= *legacy*) Nachlass *m*

berate [bɪ'reɪt] VT (*liter*) schelten, auszanken

Berber ['bɜːbə'] **N a** Berber *m*, Berberfrau *f* **b** (= *language*) die Berbersprache **ADJ** berberisch

bereave [bɪ'riːv] VT **a** *pret, ptp* **bereft** (*liter*, = *deprive*) berauben (*geh*) (*of* +*gen*) **b** *pret, ptp* **bereaved** (= *cause loss by death: illness*) (*sb of sb* jdm jdn) rauben (*geh*), nehmen; **he was ~d of his son** sein Sohn ist ihm genommen worden (*geh*)

bereaved [bɪ'riːvd] ADJ leidtragend; **the ~** die Hinterbliebenen *pl*

bereavement [bɪ'riːvmənt] N **a** (= *death in family*) Trauerfall *m*; **owing to a/his recent ~** wegen *or* aufgrund *or* auf Grund eines Trauerfalls/dieses für ihn so schmerzlichen Verlusts; **to sympathize with sb in his ~** jds Leid teilen **b** (= *feeling of loss*) schmerzlicher Verlust; **to feel a sense of ~ at sth** etw als schmerzlichen Verlust empfinden

bereft [bɪ'reft] *ptp* of **bereave** ADJ **to be ~ of sth** einer Sache (*gen*) bar sein (*geh*); **his life was ~ of happiness** seinem Leben fehlte jegliches Glück

beret ['bereɪ] N Baskenmütze *f*

berg [bɜːg] N = **iceberg**

beribboned [bɪ'rɪbənd] ADJ mit Bändern geschmückt, bebändert; *general* mit Ordensbändern geschmückt

beriberi ['berɪ'berɪ] N Beriberi *f*

Bering ['berɪŋ]: **Bering Sea** N Beringmeer *nt*; **Bering Strait** N Beringstraße *f*

berk [bɜːk] N (*Brit, inf*) Dussel *m* (*inf*)

Berks [bɑːks] *abbr* of **Berkshire**

Berlin [bɜː'lɪn] N Berlin *nt*; **the ~ Wall** die Mauer

Bermuda [bɜː'mjuːdə] N Bermuda *nt* (*form rare*); **the ~s** die Bermudas *pl*, die Bermudainseln *pl*; **to go to ~** auf die Bermudas fahren

Bermuda shorts PL Bermudashorts *pl*

Bermuda Triangle N Bermudadreieck *nt*

Bernard ['bɜːnəd] N Bernhard *m*

Berne [bɜːn] N Bern *nt*

Bernese [bɜː'niːz] ADJ Berner; *village* im Berner Oberland

berry ['berɪ] **N a** (= *fruit*) Beere *f*; **as brown as a ~** (*Brit*) ganz braun gebrannt **b** (*Bot*) Beerenfrucht *f*

berrying ['berɪŋ] N Beerensammeln *nt*; **to go ~** Beeren sammeln gehen

berserk [bə'sɜːk] ADJ wild; **to go ~** wild werden; (*audience*) aus dem Häuschen geraten (*inf*), zu toben anfangen; (= *go mad*) überschnappen (*inf*), verrückt werden

berth [bɜːθ] **N a** (*on ship*) Koje *f*; (*on train*) Schlafwagenplatz *m* **b** (*Naut, for ship*) Liegeplatz *m* **c** (*Naut, = sea-room*) Raum *m*; **to give a wide ~ to** jdm Abstand zu einem Schiff halten; **to give sb/sth a wide ~** (*fig*) einen (weiten) Bogen um jdn/etw machen **VI** anlegen **VT to ~ a ship** mit einem Schiff (am Kai) anlegen; (= *assign berth to*) einem Schiff einen Lie-

geplatz zuweisen; **where is she ~ed?** wo liegt es?, wo hat es angelegt?

beryl ['berɪl] N Beryll *m*

beseech [bɪ'siːtʃ] *pret, ptp* **beseeched** *or* (*liter*) **besought** (*liter*) VT *person* anflehen, beschwören; *forgiveness* flehen um, erflehen (*geh*)

beseeching ADJ , **beseechingly** ADV [bɪ'siːtʃɪŋ, -lɪ] flehentlich (*geh*), flehend

beset [bɪ'set] *pret, ptp* **beset** VT (*difficulties, dangers*) (von allen Seiten) bedrängen; (*doubts*) befallen; (*temptations, trials*) heimsuchen; **to be ~ with difficulties/danger** (*problem, journey etc*) reich an *or* voller Schwierigkeiten/Gefahren sein; **he was ~ with difficulties** er wurde von Schwierigkeiten heimgesucht; **~ by doubts** von Zweifeln befallen

besetting [bɪ'setɪŋ] ADJ **his ~ sin** eine ständige Untugend von ihm; **his one ~ worry** die Sorge, die ihn nicht loslässt

beside [bɪ'saɪd] PREP **a** (= *at the side of*) neben (+*dat or with motion* +*acc*); (= *at the edge of*) *road, river* an (+*dat or with motion* +*acc*); **~ the road** am Straßenrand **b** (= *compared with*) neben (+*dat*); **if you put it ~ the original** wenn man es neben dem Original sieht **c** (= *irrelevant to*) **to be ~ the point** damit nichts zu tun haben **d** **to be ~ oneself** (*with anger*) außer sich sein (*with* vor); (*with joy also*) sich nicht mehr zu lassen wissen (*with* vor)

besides [bɪ'saɪdz] ADV **a** (= *in addition*) außerdem, obendrein; **he wrote a novel and several short stories** ~ er hat einen Roman und außerdem noch mehrere Kurzgeschichten geschrieben; **many more** ~ noch viele mehr; **have you got any others** ~**?** haben Sie noch andere *or* noch welche? **b** (= *anyway, moreover*) außerdem PREP **a** (= *in addition to*) außer; **others ~ ourselves** außer uns noch andere; **there were three of us ~ Mary** Mary nicht mitgerechnet, waren wir zu dritt; **~ which he was unwell** überdies *or* außerdem fühlte er sich nicht wohl **b** (= *except*) außer, abgesehen von

besiege [bɪ'siːdʒ] VT **a** (*Mil*) *town* belagern **b** (*fig*) belagern; (*with information, offers*) überschütten, überhäufen; (= *pester: with letters, questions*) bestürmen, bedrängen

besieger [bɪ'siːdʒə'] N (*Mil*) Belagerer *m*

besmirch [bɪ'smɜːtʃ] VT (*lit, fig*) beschmutzen, besudeln

besom ['biːzəm] **N a** (Reisig)besen *m* **b** (*pej inf*, = *woman*) Besen *m* (*pej inf*)

besotted [bɪ'sɒtɪd] ADJ **a** (= *drunk*) berauscht (*with* von) **b** (= *infatuated*) völlig vernarrt (*with* in +*acc*); (*with idea*) berauscht (*with* von)

besought [bɪ'sɔːt] (*liter*) *pret, ptp* of **beseech**

bespake [bɪ'speɪk] (*old*) *pret* of **bespeak**

bespangle [bɪ'spæŋgl] VT besetzen; **~d costume** mit Pailletten besetztes Kostüm; **the sky ~d with ...** (*liter*) der mit ... übersäte Himmel

bespatter [bɪ'spætə'] VT bespritzen

bespeak [bɪ'spiːk] *pret* **bespoke** *or* (*old*) **bespake**, *ptp* **bespoken** *or* **bespoke** VT **a** (= *indicate*) verraten, erkennen lassen **b** (*old*, = *reserve*) reservieren lassen, bestellen

bespectacled [bɪ'spektɪkld] ADJ bebrillt

bespoke [bɪ'spəʊk] *pret, ptp* of **bespeak** ADJ *goods* nach Maß; *garment also* Maß-; *service, software* maßgeschneidert, den Kundenbedürfnissen angepasst; **a ~ tailor** ein Maßschneider *m*

bespoken [bɪ'spəʊkən] *ptp* of **bespeak**

besprinkle [bɪ'sprɪŋkl] VT (*with liquid*) besprengen, bespritzen; (*with powder*) bestäuben

Bess [bes] N *dim* of **Elizabeth good Queen ~** Elisabeth I

Bessemer ['besɪmə'] *in cpds* Bessemer-; **~ converter** Bessemerbirne *f*

best [best] ♦ 1.1, 2.2, 7.1, 21.3, 23.1, 23.3, 23.5, 24.2, 24.3 **ADJ** *superl* of **good** beste(r, s) *attr*; (= *most favourable*) *route, price* also günstigste(r, s) *attr* **to be ~** am besten/günstigsten sein; **to be ~ of all** am allerbesten/allergünstigsten sein; **that was the ~ thing about her/**

that could happen das war das Beste an ihr/, was geschehen konnte; **that would be ~** *or* **the ~ thing for everybody** das wäre für alle das Beste; **the ~ thing to do is to wait, it's ~ to wait** das Beste ist zu warten; **may the ~ man win!** dem Besten der Sieg!; **to put one's ~ foot forward** (= *hurry*) seinen schnellsten Gang anschlagen; (*fig*) sein Bestes geben *or* tun; **the ~ part of the year/my money** fast das ganze Jahr/all mein Geld

ADV *superl* of **well** **a** am besten; **like** am liebsten *or* meisten; *enjoy* am meisten; **the ~ fitting dress** das am besten passende Kleid; **her ~ known novel** ihr bekanntester Roman; **he was ~ known for ...** er war vor allem bekannt für ...; **~ of all** am allerbesten/-liebsten/-meisten; **I helped him as ~ I could** ich half ihm, so gut ich konnte; **I thought it ~ to go** ich hielt es für das Beste zu gehen; **do as you think ~** tun Sie, was Sie für richtig halten; **you know ~** Sie müssen es (am besten) wissen

b (= *better*) **you had ~ go now** am besten gehen Sie jetzt

N a (= *person, thing*) **the ~** der/die/das Beste; **the ~ of the bunch** (*inf*) (noch) der/die/das Beste; **his last book was his ~** sein letztes Buch war sein bestes; **with the ~ of intentions** mit den besten Absichten; **they are the ~ of friends** sie sind enge Freunde; **he can sing with the ~ of them** er kann sich im Singen mit den Besten messen

b (= *clothes*) beste Sachen *pl*, Sonntagskleider *pl* (*inf*); **to be in one's (Sunday) ~** in Schale sein (*inf*), im Sonntagsstaat sein

c **to do one's ~** (= *level*) sein Bestes *or* Möglichstes tun; **that's the ~ you can expect** Sie können nichts Besseres erwarten; **do the ~ you can!** machen Sie es so gut Sie können!; **it's not perfect but it's the ~ I can do** es ist nicht perfekt, aber mehr kann ich nicht tun; **what a lame excuse, is that the ~ you can do?** so eine lahme Ausrede, fällt Ihnen nichts Besseres ein?; **to get the ~ of sb** jdn unterkriegen; **to get the ~ out of sb/sth** das Beste aus jdm/etw herausholen; **to get the ~ of the bargain** *or* **of it** am besten dabei wegkommen; **to play the ~ of three/five** nur so lange spielen, bis eine Partei zweimal/dreimal gewonnen hat; **to make the ~ of it/a bad job** das Beste daraus machen; **to make the ~ of one's opportunities** seine Chancen voll nützen; **the ~ of it is that ...** das Beste daran ist, dass ...; **we've had the ~ of the day** der Tag ist so gut wie vorbei; (= *the weather's getting worse*) das schöne Wetter wäre für heute vorbei; **it's all for the ~** es ist nur zum Guten; **I meant it for the ~** ich habe es doch nur gut gemeint; **to do sth for the ~** etw in bester Absicht tun; **to the ~ of my ability** so gut ich kann/konnte; **to the ~ of my knowledge** meines Wissens; **to the ~ of my recollection** *or* **memory** soviel ich mich erinnern kann; **to look one's ~** besonders gut aussehen; **to be at one's ~** (= *on form*) in Hochform sein; **he is at his ~ at about 8 in the evening** so gegen 8 abends ist seine beste Zeit; **roses are at their just now** jetzt ist die beste Zeit für Rosen; **that is Goethe at his ~** das ist Goethe, wie er besser nicht sein könnte; **it's not enough (even) at the ~ of times** es ist schon normalerweise nicht genug; **at ~** bestenfalls; **to wish sb all the ~** jdm alles Gute wünschen; **all the ~ (to you)** alles Gute!

VT schlagen

best: best-before date N Haltbarkeitsdatum *nt*; **best boy** N (*Film*) Assistent *m* des Elektromeisters; **best-dressed** ADJ bestgekleidet *attr*

bestial ['bestɪəl] ADJ *acts, cruelty* bestialisch, tierisch; *person, look, appearance* (= *cruel*) brutal; (= *carnal*) tierisch

bestiality [,bestɪ'ælɪtɪ] N **a** (*of behaviour*) Bestialität *f*; (*of person*) Brutalität *f* **b** (= *act*) Gräueltat *f* **c** (= *sex with animals*) Sodomie *f*

bestiary ['bestɪərɪ] N Bestiaire *nt*, Bestiarium *nt*

bestir [bɪ'stɜː'] VR (*hum, liter*) sich regen, sich rühren; **to ~ oneself to do sth** sich dazu aufraffen, etw zu tun

best: best-laid ADJ the ~ **plans (of mice and men)** noch so wohl bedachte Pläne; **best man** N Trauzeuge m (des Bräutigams)

BEST MAN

Bei einer traditionellen Hochzeit ist der **best man** der Trauzeuge des Bräutigams, normalerweise ein enger Freund oder Verwandter, zum Beispiel ein Bruder oder ein Cousin. Der **best man** ist dafür verantwortlich, dass am Hochzeitstag alles glatt läuft. Seine Pflichten umfassen so wichtige Aufgaben wie den Bräutigam pünktlich zur Kirche zu bringen, Hochzeitsgäste zu empfangen und sich um die Trauringe zu kümmern. Auf dem Hochzeitsempfang übermittelt er normalerweise die Glückwünsche all derer, die nicht kommen konnten, sagt die Redner an, hält selbst eine humorvolle Rede und bringt einen Toast auf das Brautpaar aus.

---

bestow [bɪˈstəʊ] VT **a** ((up)on sb jdm) (= grant, give) gift, attention schenken; favour, friendship, kiss also gewähren (geh); honour erweisen, zuteil werden lassen (geh); title, medal verleihen **b** (old, = place) verstauen, unterbringen

bestowal [bɪˈstəʊəl] N ((up)on an +acc) (of gift) Schenken nt; (of favour, friendship, kiss) Gewähren nt; (of honour) Erweisen f; (of title, medal) Verleihung f

bestraddle [bɪˈstrædl] VT = **bestride**

bestride [bɪˈstraɪd] pret **bestrode** or **bestrid** [bɪˈstrəʊd, bɪˈstrɪd] ptp **bestridden** [bɪˈstrɪdn] VT (= sit astride) rittlings sitzen auf (+dat); (= stand astride) (mit gespreizten Beinen) stehen über (+dat); (= mount) sich schwingen auf (+acc); (fig: = dominate) beherrschen; **to ~ the world like a Colossus** die Welt beherrschen

best: bestseller N Verkaufs- or Kassenschlager m; (= book) Bestseller m; (= author) Erfolgsautor(in) m(f); **bestselling** ADJ article absatzstark, der/die/das am besten geht; author Erfolgs-; **a ~ novel** ein Bestseller m; **this month's ~ books** die Bestsellerliste dieses Monats

bet [bet] vb: pret, ptp **bet** N Wette f (on auf +acc); (= money etc staked) Wetteinsatz m; **to make** or **have a ~ with sb** mit jdm wetten, mit jdm eine Wette eingehen; **I have a ~ (on) with him that ...** ich habe mit ihm gewettet, dass ...; **it's a good** or **safe/bad** ~ das ist ein sicherer/ schlechter Tip; **it's a good** or **safe ~ he'll be in the bar** er ist bestimmt or garantiert in der Kneipe; **Liverpool look a good** or **safe ~ for the championship** Liverpool hat gute Aussichten auf den Meistertitel; **he's a bad ~ for the job** er ist nichts für diese Arbeit (inf); **all ~s are off** (fig) es ist unmöglich vorauszusagen, was passieren wird

▪ VT **a** (Gambling) wetten, setzen (against gegen/on auf +acc); **I ~ him £5** ich habe mit ihm (um) £ 5 gewettet; **to ~ ten to one** zehn gegen eins wetten

b (inf: = wager) wetten; **I ~ he'll come!** wetten, dass er kommt! (inf); **I'll ~ you anything (you like)** ich gehe mit dir jede Wette (darauf) ein; **~ you!** wetten! (inf); **you can ~ your boots** or **your bottom dollar that ...** Sie können Gift darauf nehmen, dass ... (inf); **~ you I can!** (inf) wetten, dass ich das kann! (inf)

▪ VI wetten; **to ~ on a horse/horses** auf ein Pferd/Pferde setzen or wetten, Pferdewetten abschließen; **don't ~ on it** darauf würde ich nicht wetten; **you ~!** (inf) und ob! (inf); **(do you) want to ~?** (wollen wir) wetten?

beta [ˈbiːtə] N Beta nt; (Brit, Sch) gut

beta-blocker [ˈbiːtəˌblɒkə] N Betablocker m

betake [bɪˈteɪk] pret **betook**, ptp **betaken** [bɪˈteɪkn] VR (old, hum) sich begeben

beta ray N Betastrahl m

betcha [ˈbetʃə] INTERJ (inf) wetten(, dass) (inf)

betel [ˈbiːtəl] N Betel m

betel nut N Betelnuss f

bête noire [bet'nwɑːr] N **to be sb's** ~ jdm ein Gräuel sein

bethink [bɪˈθɪŋk] pret, ptp **bethought** VR (liter, obs) **to ~ oneself of sth/that ...** etw bedenken/ bedenken, dass ...

Bethlehem [ˈbeθlɪhem] N Bethlehem nt

bethought [bɪˈθɔːt] pret, ptp of **bethink**

betide [bɪˈtaɪd] VI geschehen; **whatever (may) ~** was immer auch geschehen mag (geh) ▪ VT geschehen (+dat) → **woe**

betimes [bɪˈtaɪmz] ADV (old, liter) beizeiten (geh)

betoken [bɪˈtəʊkən] VT (old) bedeuten, hindeuten auf (+acc)

betook [bɪˈtʊk] pret of **betake**

betray [bɪˈtreɪ] VT verraten (to +dat); trust enttäuschen, brechen; (= be disloyal to also) im Stich lassen; (= be unfaithful to) untreu werden (+dat); ideals, principles untreu werden (+dat), verraten; (Pol) verraten (to an +acc); **to ~ oneself** sich verraten; **his accent ~ed him as a foreigner** sein Akzent verriet, dass er Ausländer war

betrayal [bɪˈtreɪəl] N (= act) Verrat m (of +gen); (= instance) Verrat m (of an +dat); (of trust) Enttäuschung f; (of friends) Verrat m (of an +dat), Untreue f (of gegenüber); (of ideals, principles) Verrat m (of +gen); **the ~ of Christ** der Verrat an Christus; **a ~ of trust** ein Vertrauensbruch m

betrayer [bɪˈtreɪə] N Verräter(in) m(f) (of an +dat); (Pol) Verräter(in) m(f) (an +dat)

betroth [bɪˈtrəʊð] VT (obs, liter) angeloben (obs, liter) (to sb jdm), versprechen (liter) (to sb jdm), verloben (to sb mit jdm)

betrothal [bɪˈtrəʊðəl] N (obs, liter, hum) Verlobung f

betrothed [bɪˈtrəʊðd] N (obs, liter, hum) Anverlobte(r) mf (obs)

better[1] [ˈbetə] N Wetter(in) m(f)

better[2] ✿ 1.1, 2.3, 5.2, 7.2, 7.4, 13, 26.3 ADJ comp of good besser; route, way also günstiger; **he's ~** (= recovered) es geht ihm wieder besser; **he's much ~** es geht ihm viel besser; **the patient/his foot is getting ~** dem Patienten/seinem Fuß geht es schon viel besser; **I hope you get ~ soon** hoffentlich sind Sie bald wieder gesund; **~ and ~** immer besser; **that's ~!** (approval) so ist es besser!; (relief etc) so!; **to be ~ than one's word** mehr tun, als man versprochen hat; **it couldn't be ~** es könnte gar nicht besser sein; **I couldn't be ~** es könnte mir gar nicht besser gehen; **I am none the ~ for it** das hilft mir auch nicht; **she is no ~ than she ought to be** sie ist auch keine Heilige; **the ~ part of an hour/my money/our trip** fast eine Stunde/fast mein ganzes Geld/fast die ganze Reise; **it would be ~ to go early** es wäre besser, früh zu gehen; **you would be ~ to go early** Sie gehen besser früh; **to go one ~** einen Schritt weiter gehen; (in offer) höher gehen; **this hat has seen ~ days** dieser Hut hat auch schon bessere Tage gesehen (inf)

▪ ADV comp of well **a** besser; like lieber, mehr; enjoy mehr; **they are ~ off than we are** sie sind besser dran als wir; **he is ~ off where he is** für ihn ist es besser, da zu sein, wo er ist, er ist besser dran, wo er ist (inf); **you would do ~ or be ~ advised to go early** Sie sollten lieber früh gehen; **to think ~ of it** es sich (dat) noch einmal überlegen; **I didn't think any ~ of him for that** deswegen hielt ich ihn auch nicht mehr von ihm → **know, late**

b **I had ~ go** ich gehe jetzt wohl besser; **you'd ~ do what he says** tun Sie lieber, was er sagt; **I'd ~ answer that letter soon** ich beantworte den Brief lieber or besser bald; **I won't touch it – you'd ~ not!** ich fasse es nicht an – das will ich dir auch geraten haben

▪ N **a** one's ~s Leute, die über einem stehen; (socially also) Höhergestellte pl, höher Gestellte pl; **has no way to talk to your ~s** man muss immer wissen, wen man vor sich (dat) hat; **respect for one's ~s** Achtung f Respektspersonen gegenüber

b (= person, object) **the ~** der/die/das Bessere

c **it's a change for the ~** es ist eine Wendung zum Guten; **to think (all) the ~ of sb** (um so) mehr von jdm halten; **all the ~, so much the ~** umso besser; **it would be all the ~ for a drop of paint** ein bisschen Farbe würde Wunder wirken; **the bigger/sooner the ~** je größer/eher, desto besser; **it's done now, for ~ or worse** so oder so, es ist geschehen; **for ~, for worse** (in marriage ceremony) in Freud und Leid; **to get the ~ of sb** (person) jdn unterkriegen (inf); (illness) jdn erwischen (inf); (problem etc) jdm schwer zu schaffen machen

▪ VT (= improve on) verbessern; (= surpass) übertreffen

▪ VR (= increase one's knowledge) sich weiterbilden; (in social scale) sich verbessern

better half N (inf) bessere Hälfte (inf)

betterment [ˈbetəmənt] N **a** Verbesserung f; (educational) Weiterbildung f **b** (Jur) Wertsteigerung f; (of land) Melioration f

betting [ˈbetɪŋ] N Wetten nt; **the ~ was brisk** das Wettgeschäft war rege; **what is the ~ on his horse?** wie stehen die Wetten auf sein Pferd?

betting: betting man N (regelmäßiger) Wetter; **I'm not a ~** ich wette eigentlich nicht; **if I were a ~ I'd say ...** wenn ich ja wetten würde, würde ich sagen ...; **betting news** N Wettnachrichten pl; **betting shop** N Wettannahme f; **betting slip** N Wettschein m; **betting tax** N Wettsteuer f

Betty [ˈbetɪ] N dim of **Elizabeth**

between [bɪˈtwiːn] PREP **a** zwischen (+dat); (with movement) zwischen (+acc); **I was sitting ~ them** ich saß zwischen ihnen; **sit down ~ those two boys** setzen Sie sich zwischen diese beiden Jungen; **in ~** zwischen (+dat/acc); **~ now and next week we must ...** bis nächste Woche müssen wir ...; **there's nothing ~ them** (= they're equal) sie sind gleich gut; (no feelings, relationship) zwischen ihnen ist nichts

b (= amongst) unter (+dat/acc); **share the sweets ~ the two children** teilen Sie die Süßigkeiten zwischen den beiden Kindern auf; **divide the sweets ~ the children** verteilen Sie die Süßigkeiten unter die Kinder; **we shared an apple ~ us** wir teilten uns (dat) einen Apfel; **~ ourselves** or **~ you and me is not very clever unter uns** (dat) gesagt, er ist nicht besonders gescheit; **that's just ~ ourselves** das bleibt aber unter uns

c (= jointly, showing combined effort) **~ us/them** zusammen; **we have a car ~ the two/three of us** wir haben zu zweit/dritt ein Auto, wir zwei/ drei haben zusammen ein Auto; **~ the two/ three of us we have enough** zusammen haben wir (zwei/drei) genug; **we got the letter written ~ us** wir haben den Brief zusammen or gemeinsam or mit vereinten Kräften geschrieben

d (= what with, showing combined effect) neben (+dat); **~ housework and study I have no time for that** neben or zwischen Haushalt und Studium bleibt mir keine Zeit dazu

▪ ADV (place) dazwischen; (time also) zwischendurch; **in ~** dazwischen; **the space/time ~** der Zwischenraum/die Zwischenzeit, der Raum/ die Zeit dazwischen

betweentimes [bɪˈtwiːntaɪmz], **betweenwhiles** [bɪˈtwiːnwaɪlz] ADV in der Zwischenzeit

betwixt [bɪˈtwɪkst] PREP (obs, liter, dial) = **between** ADV = **and between** dazwischen

bevel [ˈbevəl] N Schräge f, Schrägfläche f, Abschrägung f; (also **bevel edge**) abgeschrägte Kante, Schrägkante f; (= tool: also **bevel square**) Schrägmaß f, Stellwinkel m VT abschrägen, schräg abflachen; **~led** (Brit) or **~ed** (US) **edge** Schrägkante f, abgeschrägte Kante; **~led** (Brit) or **~ed** (US) **mirror** Spiegel m mit schräg geschliffenen Kanten

bevel gear N Kegelradgetriebe nt

beverage [ˈbevərɪdʒ] N Getränk nt

bevvy [ˈbevɪ] N (Brit inf) N **a** (= drink) alkoholisches Getränk; **he fancied a few bevvies** er hatte Lust, einen trinken zu gehen; **to go for a ~** einen trinken gehen **b** (= drinking session) **we**

had a major ~ **after the match** nach dem Spiel haben wir ordentlich einen draufgemacht (*inf*); **c to go out on the ~** auf Sauftour gehen (*inf*); **VT to get bevvied** sich voll laufen lassen (*inf*)

bevy ['bevɪ] N (*of birds*) Schwarm *m*; (*of girls also*) Schar *f*

bewail [bɪ'weɪl] VT (= *deplore*) beklagen; (= *lament also*) bejammern; *sb's death also* betrauern

beware [bɪ'weə'] **☼** 2.3 **VI** *imper and infin only* **to ~ of sb/sth** sich vor jdm/etw hüten, sich vor jdm/etw in Acht nehmen; **to ~ of doing sth** sich davor hüten, etw zu tun; **~ of falling** passen Sie auf *or* sehen Sie sich vor, dass Sie nicht fallen; **~ of being deceived, lest you are deceived** (*old*) geben Sie Acht *or* sehen Sie sich vor, dass Sie nicht betrogen werden; **~ of how you speak** geben Sie Acht *or* sehen Sie sich vor, was Sie sagen; **~!** (*old, liter*) gib Acht!; **"beware of the dog"** „Vorsicht, bissiger Hund"; **"beware of pickpockets"** „vor Taschendieben wird gewarnt"
VT *imper and infin only* **to ~ sb/sth** sich vor jdm/etw hüten, sich vor jdm/etw in Acht nehmen; **to ~ doing sth** sich davor hüten, etw zu tun

bewigged [bɪ'wɪɡd] ADJ mit Perücke, Perücke tragend *attr*

bewilder [bɪ'wɪldə'] VT (= *confuse*) verwirren, irremachen; (= *baffle*) verblüffen, verwundern

bewildered [bɪ'wɪldəd] ADJ (= *confused*) verwirrt, durcheinander *pred* (*inf*); (= *baffled*) verblüfft, perplex (*inf*)

bewildering [bɪ'wɪldərɪŋ] ADJ (= *confusing*) verwirrend; (= *baffling*) verblüffend

bewilderingly [bɪ'wɪldərɪŋlɪ] ADV (= *confusingly*) verwirrend; (= *bafflingly*) verblüffend

bewilderment [bɪ'wɪldəmənt] N (= *confusion*) Verwirrung *f*; (= *bafflement*) Verblüffung *f*, Erstaunen *nt*; **in ~** verwundert; **his ~ was obvious** er war offensichtlich verwirrt/verblüfft

bewitch [bɪ'wɪtʃ] VT verhexen, verzaubern; (*fig*) bezaubern

bewitching ADJ, **bewitchingly** ADV [bɪ'wɪtʃɪŋ, -lɪ] bezaubernd, hinreißend

beyond [bɪ'jɒnd] **PREP a** (*in space, = on the other side of*) über (+*dat*), jenseits (+*gen*) (*geh*); (= *further than*) über (+*acc*) ... hinaus, weiter als; **~ the Alps** jenseits der Alpen; **I saw peak ~ snow-capped peak** ich sah schneebedeckte Gipfel bis weit in die Ferne; **the convent walls** außerhalb der Klostermauern
b (*in time*) **~ 6 o'clock/next week/the 17th century** nach 6 Uhr/nächster Woche/dem 17. Jahrhundert; **until ~ 6 o'clock** bis nach 6 Uhr; **until ~ next week/the 17th century** bis über nächste Woche/das 17. Jahrhundert hinaus; **~ the middle of June/the week** über Mitte Juni/der Woche hinaus
c (= *surpassing, exceeding*) **a task ~ her abilities** eine Aufgabe, die über ihre Fähigkeiten geht; **it's ~ your authority** das liegt außerhalb Ihrer Befugnis; **that is ~ human understanding** das übersteigt menschliches Verständnis; **~ repair** nicht mehr zu reparieren; **it was ~ her to pass the exam** sie schaffte es nicht, das Examen zu bestehen; **that's ~ me** (= *I don't understand*) das geht über meinen Verstand, das kapiere ich nicht (*inf*) → **compare, grave ¹, help** *etc*
d (*with neg, interrog*) außer; **have you any money – ~ what you have in the bank?** haben Sie außer dem, was Sie auf der Bank haben, noch Geld?; **~ this/that** sonst; **I've got nothing to suggest – this** sonst habe ich keine Vorschläge
ADV (= *on the other side of*) jenseits davon (*geh*); (= *after that*) danach; (= *further than that*) darüber hinaus, weiter; **India and the lands ~** Indien und die Gegenden jenseits davon; **... a river, and ~ is a small field** ... ein Fluss, und danach kommt ein kleines Feld; **the world ~** das Jenseits
N the great Beyond das Jenseits; (= *space*) der weite Raum

BF (*euph*) *abbr of* **bloody fool**

B/F, b/f *abbr of* **brought forward** Übertrag

BFPO *abbr of* **British Forces Post Office**

bhangra ['bæŋɡrə] N Bhangra *m*

bhp *abbr of* **brake horsepower**

bi- [baɪ] PREF bi, Bi-

Biafra [bɪ'æfrə] N (*Hist*) Biafra *nt*

Biafran [bɪ'æfrən] (*Hist*) **N** Biafraner(in) *m(f)* **ADJ** Biafra-; **~ war** Biafrakrieg *m*

biannual ADJ, **biannually** ADV [baɪ'ænjʊəl, -lɪ] zweimal jährlich; (= *half-yearly*) halbjährlich

bias ['baɪəs] *vb: pret, ptp* **biased** *or* (*US*) **biassed**
N a (= *inclination, of course, newspaper etc*) (einseitige) Ausrichtung *f* (*towards* auf +*acc*); (*of person*) Vorliebe *f* (*towards* für); **to have a ~ against sth** (*course, newspaper etc*) gegen etw eingestellt sein; (*person*) eine Abneigung gegen etw haben; **to have a left-/right-wing ~** *or* **a ~ to the left/right** nach links/rechts ausgerichtet sein, einen Links-/Rechtsdrall haben (*inf*); **to be without ~** unvoreingenommen sein, ohne Vorurteile sein
b (*Sew*) **on the ~** schräg zum Fadenlauf
c (*Sport, = shape of bowl*) Überhang *m*
VT *report, article etc* (einseitig) färben; (*towards sth*) ausrichten (*towards* auf +*acc*); *person* beeinflussen; **he ~ed** (*Brit*) *or* **~sed** (*US*) **his article in favour of a historical approach to the problem** in seinem Artikel ging er das Problem eher aus historischer Sicht an; **to ~ sb toward(s)/against sth** jdn für/gegen etw einnehmen

bias: bias attack N (*US*) = **bias incident**; **bias binding** N Schrägband *nt or* -streifen *m*

biased, (*US*) **biassed** ['baɪəst] ADJ voreingenommen, befangen; **... but then I'm ~** ... aber ich bin natürlich voreingenommen *or* befangen; **~ toward(s) sb/sth** gegenüber jdm/einer Sache voreingenommen; **~ in favour** (*Brit*) *or* **favor** (*US*) **of/against** voreingenommen für/gegen

bias incident N (*US*) rassistisch motivierter Vor- *or* Zwischenfall

biathlon [baɪ'æθlən] N Biathlon *nt*

bib [bɪb] N **a** (*for baby*) Latz *m*, Lätzchen *nt* **b** (*on garment*) Latz *m* **c** (*Brit inf*) **in one's best ~ and tucker** in Schale (*inf*); **she put on her best ~ and tucker** sie warf sich in Schale (*inf*)

Bible ['baɪbl] N Bibel *f*; (*fig also*) Evangelium *nt*

Bible: Bible-basher N (*inf*) aufdringlicher Bibelfritze (*sl*); **Bible-bashing** ADJ (*inf*) **~ father** ihr Vater, der fanatisch an die Bibel schwört/schwörte; **Bible class** N Bibelstunde *f*; **Bible school** N (*US*) Bibelschule *f*; **Bible story** N lange biblische Geschichte; **Bible-thumper** N (*inf*) aufdringlicher Bibelfritze (*sl*)

biblical ['bɪblɪkəl] ADJ biblisch, Bibel-

bibliographer [ˌbɪblɪ'ɒɡrəfə'] N Bibliograf *m*

bibliographic(al) [ˌbɪblɪəʊ'ɡræfɪk(əl)] ADJ bibliografisch

bibliography [ˌbɪblɪ'ɒɡrəfɪ] N Bibliografie *f*

bibliomania [ˌbɪblɪəʊ'meɪnɪə] N Bibliomanie *f*

bibliophile ['bɪblɪəʊfaɪl] N Bibliophile(r) *mf*, Büchernarr *m*

bibulous ['bɪbjʊləs] ADJ (*form*) *person* trunksüchtig

bicameral [baɪ'kæmərəl] ADJ (*Pol*) Zweikammer-

bicarb ['baɪkɑːb] N (*inf*) Natron *nt*

bicarbonate of soda [baɪˌkɑːbənɪtəv'səʊdə] N (*Cook*) ≈ Backpulver *nt*; (*Chem*) doppelt kohlensaures Natron *nt*

bicentenary [ˌbaɪsen'tiːnərɪ], (*US*) **bicentennial** [ˌbaɪsen'tenɪəl] **N** zweihundertjähriges Jubiläum, Zweihundertjahrfeier *f* (*of* +*gen*); **the ~ of Beethoven's birth/death** Beethovens zweihundertster Geburts-/Todestag **ADJ** Zweihundertjahr-, zweihundertjährig; *celebrations* Zweihundertjahr-

bicephalous [baɪ'sefələs] ADJ (*spec*) dizephal (*spec*), bikephalisch (*spec*)

biceps ['baɪseps] PL **Bizeps** *m*

bichromate [baɪ'krəʊmɪt] N Bichromat *nt*

bicker ['bɪkə'] VI (= *quarrel*) sich zanken, aneinander geraten; **they are always ~ing** sie liegen sich dauernd in den Haaren

bickering ['bɪkərɪŋ] N Gezänk *nt*

bickie ['bɪkɪ] N (*Brit, inf*) Keks *m*

bicuspid [baɪ'kʌspɪd] **ADJ** mit zwei Spitzen, zweihöckrig, bikuspidal (*spec*) **N** (*Anat*) vorderer Backenzahn

bicycle ['baɪsɪkl] **N** Fahrrad *nt*; **to ride a ~** Fahrrad fahren, Rad fahren **VI** mit dem (Fahr)rad fahren

bicycle *in cpds* → **cycle**

bicycle kick N (*Ftbl*) Fallrückzieher *m*

bicyclist ['baɪsɪklɪst] N (*dated*) Radfahrer(in) *m(f)*

bid [bɪd] **VT a** *pret, ptp* **bid** (*at auction*) bieten (*for* auf +*acc*)
b *pret, ptp* **bid** (*Cards*) reizen, bieten
c *pret* **bade** *or* **bad**, *ptp* **bidden** (= *say*) **to ~ sb good morning** jdm einen guten Morgen wünschen; **to ~ farewell to sb, to ~ sb farewell** von jdm Abschied nehmen, jdm Lebewohl sagen (*geh*); **to ~ sb welcome** jdn willkommen heißen
d *pret* **bade** *or* **bad**, *ptp* **bidden** **to ~ sb (to) do sth** (*old, liter*) jdn etw tun heißen (*old*)
VI a *pret, ptp* **bid** (*at auction*) bieten
b *pret, ptp* **bid** (*Cards*) bieten, reizen
c *pret* **bad**, *ptp* **bidden** **to ~ fair to ...** versprechen zu ...; **everything ~s fair to be successful** es sieht alles recht erfolgversprechend aus
N a (*at auction*) Gebot *nt* (*for* auf +*acc*); (*Comm*) Angebot *nt* (*for* für); **any more ~s?** (*at auction*) wer bietet mehr?
b (*Cards*) Ansage *f*, Gebot *nt*; **to raise the ~** höher bieten *or* reizen, überrufen; **to make no ~** passen; **no ~!** passe!
c (= *attempt*) Versuch *m*; **to make a ~ for power** nach der Macht greifen; **to make a ~ for fame/freedom** versuchen, Ruhm/die Freiheit zu erlangen; **his ~ for fame/freedom failed** sein Versuch, Ruhm/die Freiheit zu erlangen, scheiterte; **rescue ~ fails** Rettungsversuch erfolglos; **the ~ for the summit** der Griff nach dem Gipfel; **she tried acupuncture in a ~ to stop smoking** sie versuchte es mit Akupunktur, um das Rauchen aufzugeben

biddable ['bɪdəbl] ADJ (*liter*) fügsam, willfährig (*geh*)

bidden ['bɪdn] *ptp of* **bid**

bidder ['bɪdə'] N Bietende(r) *mf*, Steigerer *m*; **to sell to the highest ~** an den Höchst- *or* Meistbietenden verkaufen; **there were no ~s** niemand hat geboten *or* ein Gebot gemacht

bidding ['bɪdɪŋ] N **a** (*at auction*) Steigern *nt*, Bieten *nt*; **how high did the ~ go?** wie hoch wurde gesteigert?; **to raise the ~** den Preis in die Höhe treiben; **the ~ is closed** es werden keine Gebote mehr angenommen, keine Gebote mehr **b** (*Cards*) Bieten *nt*, Reizen *nt* **c** (= *order*) Geheiß *nt* (*old*), Gebot *nt*; **at whose ~?** auf wessen Geheiß? (*old*); **the slave does his master's ~** der Sklave tut, was sein Herr ihn heißt (*old*) *or* ihm befiehlt; **he needed no second ~** man musste es ihm nicht zweimal sagen

bidding war N (*Fin*) Übernahmeschlacht *f*

biddy ['bɪdɪ] N (*inf, = hen*) Huhn *nt*, Henne *f*; (= *old lady*) Muttchen *nt* (*inf*), Tantchen *nt* (*inf*)

bide [baɪd] **VT to ~ one's time** den rechten Augenblick abwarten *or* abpassen; **to ~ awhile** (*old*) verweilen (*geh*)

bidet ['biːdeɪ] N Bidet *nt*

bidirectional [ˌbaɪdɪ'rekʃənəl] ADJ (*Comput*) *printing* bidirektional

bid price N (*St Ex*) Geldkurs *m*

biennial [baɪ'enɪəl] **ADJ** (= *every two years*) zweijährlich; (*rare, = lasting two years*) zweijährig **N** (*Bot*) zweijährige Pflanze

biennially [baɪ'enɪəlɪ] ADV zweijährlich, alle zwei Jahre; (*Bot*) bienn

bier [bɪə'] N Bahre *f*

biff [bɪf] **N** (*inf*) Stoß *m*, Puff *m* (*inf*); **a ~ on the nose** eins auf die Nase (*inf*) **INTERJ** bums **VT** (*esp Brit inf*) *person* boxen; *car* eine Beule fahren in (+*acc*); *door* anschlagen; *lamppost* bumsen an

(+*acc*) or gegen (*inf*); **to ~ sb on the nose** jdm eins auf die Nase geben (*inf*)

bifocal [baɪˈfəʊkəl] ADJ Bifokal- N **bifocals** PL Bifokalbrille *f*

bifurcate [ˈbaɪfɜːkeɪt] VI (*form*) sich gabeln ADJ gegabelt

bifurcation [ˌbaɪfɜːˈkeɪʃən] N Gabelung *f*

big [bɪg] ADJ (+*er*) a (*in size, amount*) groß; *lie also* faustdick (*inf*); **a ~ man** ein großer, schwerer Mann; **she's a ~ girl** (*inf*) sie hat einen ganz schönen Vorbau (*inf*); **you ~ girl's blouse!** (*Brit inf*) du Angsthase! (*inf*); **5 ~ ones** (*inf*) 5 Riesen (*sl*); **~ with child/young** hochschwanger/trächtig

b (*of age*) groß; **my ~ brother** mein großer Bruder; **you're ~ enough to know better** du bist groß or alt genug und solltest es besser wissen

c (= *important*) groß, wichtig; **the Big Four/Five** die Großen Vier/Fünf; **Mr Big** (*inf*) der große Boss; **to look ~** (*inf*) ein bedeutendes Gesicht machen; **to be ~ in publishing/plastics** (*inf*) eine Größe im Verlagswesen/der Plastikproduktion sein; **to be onto something ~** (*inf*) einer großen Sache auf der Spur sein

d (= *great*) cheat, bully, liar groß

e (= *conceited*) ~ **talk** Angeberei *f* (*inf*), Großspurigkeit *f*; ~ **talker** Angeber *m* (*inf*), Maulheld *m* (*inf*), eingebildeter Schwätzer; **he's getting too ~ for his boots** (*inf, child*) er wird ein bisschen so aufmüpfig (*inf*); (*employee*) er wird langsam größenwahnsinnig; **to have a ~ head** (*inf*) eingebildet sein

f (= *generous, iro*) großzügig, nobel (*inf*); (= *forgiving*) großmütig, nobel (*inf*); **heart** groß; **few people have a heart as ~ as his** es sind nur wenige so großzügig/großmütig wie er; **he was ~ enough to admit he was wrong** er hatte die Größe zuzugeben, dass er Unrecht hatte; **that's really ~ of you** (*iro*) wirklich nobel von dir (*iro*)

g (*inf, = fashionable*) in (*inf*)

h (*fig phrases*) **to earn ~ money** das große Geld verdienen (*inf*); **to have ~ ideas** große Pläne haben, Rosinen im Kopf haben (*pej inf*); **to have a ~ mouth** (*inf*) eine große Klappe haben (*inf*); **to do things in a ~ way** alles im großen (Stil) tun or betreiben; **to live in a ~ way** auf großem Fuß or in großem Stil leben; **it's no ~ deal** (*inf, = nothing special*) das ist nichts Besonderes; (= *quite all right*) (das ist) schon in Ordnung; ~ **deal!** (*iro inf*) na und? (*inf*); (= *that's not much etc*) das ist ja ergreifend! (*iro*); **what's the ~ idea?** (*inf*) was soll denn das? (*inf*); **what's the ~ hurry?** warum denn so eilig?; **our company is ~ on service** (*inf*) unsere Firma ist ganz groß in puncto Kundendienst

ADV **to talk ~** groß daherreden (*inf*), große Töne spucken (*inf*); **to act ~** sich aufspielen, großtun; **to think ~** im großen (Maßstab) planen; **to go over** or **down ~** (*inf*) ganz groß ankommen (*inf*), großen Anklang finden (*with* bei); **to make it ~** (*as a singer/actor*) (als Sänger(in)/Schauspieler(in)) ganz groß rauskommen (*inf*)

bigamist [ˈbɪgəmɪst] N Bigamist *m*

bigamous [ˈbɪgəməs] ADJ bigamistisch

bigamy [ˈbɪgəmɪ] N Bigamie *f*

big: Big Apple N **the ~** (*inf*) New York *nt*; **big band** N Big Band *f* ADJ *attr* Bigband-; **Big Bang** N (*Brit, St Ex*) Big Bang *m* (*Tag der Umstellung der Londoner Börse auf Computerbetrieb*); **big bang** N (*Astron*) Urknall *m*; **big bang theory** N (*Astron*) Urknalltheorie *f*; **Big Ben** N Big Ben *m*; **Big Bertha** N die Dicke Berta; **big-boned** ADJ breit- or grobknochig; **Big Brother** N der große Bruder; **big bug** N (*inf*) hohes Tier (*inf*); **big business** N a (= *high finance*) Großkapital *nt*, Hochfinanz *f*; **to be ~** das große Geschäft sein b (*baby-talk*) großes Geschäft (*baby-talk*); **big cat** N Großkatze *f*; **big cheese** N (*inf*) hohes Tier (*inf*); **big dipper** N a (*Brit, at fair*) Achterbahn *f*, Berg-und-Talbahn *f* b (*US, Astron*) **Big Dipper** Großer Bär or Wagen; **big end** N (*Tech*) Pleuelfuß *m*, Schubstangenkopf *m*; **big-eyed** ADJ

(*pej*) gefräßig, unersättlich; **big game** N (*Hunt*) Großwild *nt*; **big game hunter** N Großwildjäger *m*

biggie [ˈbɪgɪ] N (*inf*) Hit *m* (*inf*), Knüller *m* (*inf*)

biggish [ˈbɪgɪʃ] ADJ ziemlich groß

big: bighead N (*inf, = person*) Angeber(in) *m(f)* (*inf*), eingebildeter Fatzke (*sl*); **bigheaded** ADJ (*inf*) eingebildet, angeberisch (*inf*); **bighearted** ADJ großherzig, großmütig; (= *forgiving*) weitherzig

bight [baɪt] N (*Geog*) Bucht *f*

big: Big Issue N *Obdachlosenzeitschrift in Großbritannien mit Ablegern in den USA, Südafrika, Namibia und Australien;* **bigmouth** N (*inf*) Großmaul *nt* (*inf*), Angeber(in) *m(f)* (*inf*); (= *blabbermouth*) Schwätzer(in) *m(f)* (*pej*); **big name** N (*inf, = person*) Größe *f* (*in* +*gen*); **all the ~s were there** alles, was Rang und Namen hat, war da; **big noise** N (*inf*) hohes Tier (*inf*)

bigot [ˈbɪgət] N Eiferer *m*; (*Rel also*) bigotter Mensch

bigoted ADJ , **bigotedly** ADV [ˈbɪgətɪd, -lɪ] eifernd; (*Rel*) bigott

bigotry [ˈbɪgətrɪ] N eifernde Borniertheit; (*Rel*) Bigotterie *f*

big: big point N (*Tennis*) wichtiger or entscheidender Punkt; **big shot** N hohes Tier (*inf*); **he thinks he is a ~ in his new Jag** (*inf*) er hält sich mit seinem neuen Jaguar für den Größten (*inf*); **big-ticket** ADJ (*US*) ~ **item** teure Anschaffung; **big time** N (*inf*) **to make** or **hit the ~** groß einsteigen (*inf*); **once he'd had a taste of the ~** nachdem er einmal ganz oben or groß gewesen war; **big-time** (*inf*) ADJ **one of the ~ boys** eine ganz große Nummer (*inf*); **a ~ politician** eine große Nummer (*inf*) in der Politik ADV **they lost ~** sie haben gewaltig verloren; **big toe** N große Zehe; **big top** N (= *circus*) Zirkus *m*; (= *main tent*) Hauptzelt *nt*; **big wheel** N a (*US, inf*) hohes Tier (*inf*); b (*Brit, at fair*) Riesenrad *nt*; **bigwig** N (*inf*) hohes Tier (*inf*); **the local ~s** die Honoratioren des Ortes

bijou [ˈbiːʒuː] ADJ (*esp in advertising*) ~ **residence** nettes kleines Haus/nette kleine Wohnung

bike [baɪk] (*inf*) N (Fahr)rad *nt*; (= *motorbike*) Motorrad *nt*, Maschine *f* (*inf*); **on your ~!** (*Brit, inf, = clear off*) verschwinde! (*inf*), zieh Leine! (*inf*) VI radeln (*inf*)

bike in *cpds* → **cycle: bike lane** N Fahrradspur *f*

biker [ˈbaɪkə] N (*inf*) Motorradfahrer *m*; (= *gang member*) Rocker *m*

bikini [bɪˈkiːnɪ] N Bikini *m*; ~ **line** Bikinilinie *f*

bi: bilabial N Bilabial *m* ADJ bilabial; **bilateral** ADJ , **bilaterally** ADV bilateral

bilberry [ˈbɪlbərɪ] N Heidelbeere *f*, Blaubeere *f*

bile [baɪl] N a (*Med*) Galle *f* b (*fig, = anger*) Übellaunigkeit *f*; **a man full of ~** ein Griesgram *m*

bilestone [ˈbaɪlstəʊn] N Gallenstein *m*

bilge [bɪldʒ] N a (*Naut*) Bilge *f* b (*also* **bilge water**) Leckwasser *nt* c (*of cask*) (Fass)bauch *m* d (*Brit, inf, = nonsense*) Quatsch *m* (*inf*), Mumpitz *m* (*dated inf*); **to talk ~** Unsinn verzapfen (*inf*) e (*Sch sl, = biology*) Bio *no art* (*Sch inf*)

bilharzia [bɪlˈhɑːzɪə] N Bilharziose *f*

bi: bilinear ADJ bilinear; **bilingual** ADJ , **bilingually** ADV zweisprachig; ~ **secretary** Fremdsprachensekretärin *f*; **bilingualism** N Zweisprachigkeit *f*

bilious [ˈbɪlɪəs] ADJ a (*Med*) Gallen-; ~ **attack** Gallenkolik *f* b (= *irritable*) reizbar; **he is very ~** ihm läuft immer gleich die Galle über (*inf*) c (= *sickly*) colour widerlich; **you're looking a bit ~** Sie sehen ein bisschen grün um die Nase (*inf*)

biliousness [ˈbɪlɪəsnɪs] N (*Med*) Gallenkrankheit *f*, Gallenleiden *nt*; (= *irritability*) Reizbarkeit *f*; (= *sickliness: of colour*) Widerlichkeit *f*

---

bilk [bɪlk] VT (*esp US*) creditor prellen (*of* um); debt nicht bezahlen

Bill [bɪl] N *dim of* **William**

bill[1] [bɪl] N a (*of bird, turtle*) Schnabel *m* b (*Geog*) Landzunge *f* VI (*bird*) schnäbeln; **to ~ and coo** (*birds*) schnäbeln und gurren; (*fig, people*) (miteinander) turteln

bill[2] N a (= *statement of charges*) Rechnung *f*; **could we have the ~ please?** (*esp Brit*) zahlen bitte!, wir möchten bitte zahlen

b (*US, = banknote*) Banknote *f*, Schein *m*; **five-dollar ~** Fünfdollarschein *m* or -note *f*

c (= *poster*) Plakat *nt*; (*on notice board*) Anschlag *m*; (= *public announcement*) Aushang *m*; **"post no ~s"** (*Brit*) „Plakate ankleben verboten"

d (*Theat, = programme*) Programm *nt*; **to head** or **top the ~, to be top of the ~** Star *m* des Abends/der Saison sein; (*act*) die Hauptattraktion sein

e ~ **of fare** Speisekarte *f*

f (*Parl*) (Gesetz)entwurf *m*, (Gesetzes)vorlage *f*; **the ~ was passed** das Gesetz wurde verabschiedet

g (*esp Comm, Fin, = certificate, statement*) ~ **of lading** (*Naut*) Seefrachtbrief *m*, Konnossement *nt*; ~ **of exchange** Wechsel *m*, Tratte *f*; ~ **of sale** Verkaufsurkunde *f*; ~ **of health** (*Naut*) Gesundheitsattest *nt*; **to give sb a clean ~ of health** (*lit, fig*) jdm (gute) Gesundheit bescheinigen; **to fit** or **fill the ~** (*fig*) der/die/das Richtige sein, passen

h (*Jur*) ~ **of attainder** (*Brit Hist*) *Anklage und Urteil gegen politische Persönlichkeiten in Form eines Gesetzes* (*US*) *unmittelbare Bestrafung einer Person durch den Gesetzgeber* ~ **of indictment** Anklageschrift *f*

VT a customers eine Rechnung ausstellen (+*dat*); **we won't ~ you for that, sir** (= *not charge*) wir werden Ihnen das nicht berechnen or in Rechnung stellen (*form*)

b play, actor ankündigen; (*fig: = advertise*) anpreisen; **he's ~ed at the King's Theatre** er soll im King's Theatre auftreten; **to ~ oneself as ...** sich anpreisen als ...

bill[3] N (= *tool*) = billhook

billabong [ˈbɪləbɒŋ] N (*Austral*) (*of river*) Seitenarm *m* eines Flusses; (= *pool*) stehendes Wasser

billboard [ˈbɪlbɔːd] N Reklametafel *f*

bill broker N (*Fin*) Wechselmakler(in) *m(f)*

billet [ˈbɪlɪt] N a (*Mil, = document*) Quartierschein *m*; (= *accommodation*) Quartier *nt*, Unterkunft *f* b (*fig inf*) **to have a cushy ~** einen schlauen Posten haben VT (*Mil*) soldier einquartieren (*on sb* bei jdm); **troops were ~ed on** or **in our town** in unserer Stadt wurden/waren Truppen einquartiert

billet-doux [bɪleˈduː] N Liebesbrief *m*, Billetdoux *nt* (*old*)

billeting [ˈbɪlɪtɪŋ] N (*Mil*) Einquartierung *f*; ~ **officer** Quartiermeister *m*

bill: billfold N (*US*) Brieftasche *f*; **billhead** N (= *heading*) Rechnungskopf *m*; (= *sheet*) Rechnungsformular *nt*; **billhook** N Hippe *f*

billiard [ˈbɪljəd] ADJ *attr* Billard-

billiard ball N Billardkugel *f*

billiard cue N Queue *nt*, Billardstock *m*

billiards [ˈbɪljədz] N Billard *nt*; **to have a game of ~** Billard spielen

billiard table N Billardtisch *m*

billing [ˈbɪlɪŋ] N (*Theat*) **to get top/second ~** an erster/zweiter Stelle auf dem Programm stehen

billion [ˈbɪljən] N Milliarde *f*; (*dated Brit*) Billion *f*; **~s of ...** (*inf*) tausende or Tausende von ...

billionaire [bɪljəˈnɛə] N (*esp US*) Milliardär(in) *m(f)*

billionth [ˈbɪljənθ] ADJ milliardste(r, s); (*dated Brit*) billionste(r, s) N Milliardstel *nt*; (*dated Brit*) Billionstel *nt*

Bill of Rights N ≈ Grundgesetz *nt*

BILL OF RIGHTS

Die **Bill of Rights** besteht aus den zehn ursprünglichen **Amendments** (Änderungen oder Zusätzen) zur Verfassung der Vereinigten Staaten von Amerika, die 1791 in Kraft traten. In einer Reihe von durchnummerierten Artikeln listet die **Bill of Rights** die Rechte auf, die jedem amerikanischen Bürger garantiert werden und definiert die verschiedenen Zuständigkeitsbereiche von Staat und Bundesregierung. In der **Bill of Rights** sind Religions-, Versammlungs- und Pressefreiheit (**First Amendment**), das Recht, eine Waffe zu tragen (**Second Amendment**), und das Recht auf eine faire Gerichtsverhandlung (**Sixth Amendment**) festgelegt. Zusatzartikel nach 1791 betreffen das Recht auf gleichen Schutz durch das Gesetz für alle Staatsbürger (**Fourteenth Amendment**) und das allgemeine Wahlrecht (**Fifteenth Amendment**) → FIFTH AMENDMENT

---

billow ['bɪləʊ] **N** **a** (liter, of sea) Woge f (geh) **b** (fig, of dress etc) Bauschen nt no pl; (of sail) Blähen nt no pl; (of smoke) Schwaden m **VI** **a** (liter, sea) wogen (geh) **b** (fig, sail) sich blähen; (dress etc) sich bauschen; (smoke) in Schwaden vorüberziehen

▶ **billow out** VI (sail etc) sich blähen; (dress etc) sich bauschen; (smoke) sich zu Schwaden formieren

billowy ['bɪləʊɪ] **ADJ** **a** (liter) sea wogend (geh) **b** sails, curtains etc gebläht; smoke in Schwaden ziehend

billposter ['bɪlpəʊstə], **billsticker** ['bɪlstɪkə] **N** Plakat(an)kleber m

Billy ['bɪlɪ] **N** dim of **William**

billy ['bɪlɪ] **N** (also **billycan**) Kochgeschirr nt

billy goat **N** Ziegenbock m

billyo(h) ['bɪlɪəʊ] **N** (esp Brit inf) **like ~** wie verrückt (inf)

bimbo ['bɪmbəʊ] **N** (pej inf: = attractive brainless female) Puppe f (inf), Häschen nt (inf)

bi: bimetallic **ADJ** **a** rod, bar Bimetall- **b** (Fin) **~ currency** Doppelwährung f; **bimetallism** N (Fin) Doppelwährung f; **bimonthly** **ADJ** **a** (= twice a month) vierzehntäglich **b** (= every two months) zweimonatlich **ADV** **a** (= twice a month) zweimal monatlich or im Monat **b** (= every two months) alle zwei Monate, jeden zweiten Monat

bin [bɪn] **N** **a** (esp Brit, for bread) Brotkasten m; (for coal) (Kohlen)kasten m; (= rubbish bin) Mülleimer m; (= dustbin) Mülltonne f; (= litter bin) Abfallbehälter m **b** (for grain) Tonne f

binary ['baɪnərɪ] **ADJ** binär; (Mus) form zweiteilig

binary: binary code N (Comput) Binärkode m; **binary fission** N Zellteilung f; **binary notation** N (Comput) Binärdarstellung f, binäre Schreibweise; **binary number** N (Math) Dualzahl f, binäre Zahl; **binary star** N (Astron) Doppelstern m; **binary star system** N (Astron) Doppelsternsystem nt; **binary system** N (Math) Dualsystem nt, binäres System

bind [baɪnd] pret, ptp **bound** **VT** **a** (= make fast, tie together) binden (to an +acc); person fesseln; (fig) verbinden (to mit); **bound hand and foot** an Händen und Füßen gefesselt or gebunden; **the emotions which ~ her to him** ihre emotionale Bindung an ihn

b (= tie round) wound, arm etc verbinden; bandage wickeln, binden; artery abbinden; (for beauty) waist einschnüren; feet einbinden or -schnüren; hair binden

c (= secure edge of) material, hem einfassen

d book binden

e (= oblige: by contract, promise) **to ~ sb to sth** jdn an etw (acc) binden, jdn zu etw verpflichten; **to ~ sb to do sth** jdn verpflichten, etw zu tun; **to ~ sb as an apprentice** jdn in die Lehre geben (to zu) → **bound³**

f (Med) bowels verstopfen

g (= make cohere, Cook) binden

VI **a** (= cohere: cement etc) binden; **stop the soil ~ing by adding some compost** lockern Sie den Boden mit Kompost; **the clay soil tended to ~** der Lehmboden war ziemlich schwer or klebte ziemlich; **the grass should help the soil ~** das Gras sollte den Boden festigen

b (Med, food) stopfen

c (= stick: brake, sliding part etc) blockieren **N** (inf) **a** **in a ~** in der Klemme (inf) **b** **to be (a bit of) a ~** (Brit) recht lästig sein

▶ **bind on** VT sep anbinden (+prep obj, -to an +acc); **to bind sth on(to) sth** (= on top of) etw auf etw (acc) binden

▶ **bind over** VT sep (Jur) **to bind sb over (to keep the peace)** jdn verwarnen; **he was bound over for six months** er bekam eine sechsmonatige Bewährungsfrist

▶ **bind together** VT sep (lit) zusammenbinden; (fig) verbinden

▶ **bind up** VT sep **a** wound verbinden; hair hochbinden **b** prisoner fesseln **c** (fig) verknüpfen, verbinden; **to be bound up** (with one another) verbunden or verknüpft sein; **to be bound up with** or **in sth** eng mit etw verknüpft sein

binder ['baɪndə] **N** **a** (Agr, = machine) (Mäh-)binder m, Bindemäher m; (= person) (Garben-)binder(in) m(f); (Typ, = person) Buchbinder(in) m(f); (= machine) Bindemaschine f **b** (for papers) Hefter m; (for magazines also) Mappe f

bindery ['baɪndərɪ] **N** Buchbinderei f

binding ['baɪndɪŋ] **N** **a** (of book) Einband m; (= act) Binden nt **b** (Sew) Band nt **c** (on skis) Bindung f **ADJ** **a** agreement, promise bindend, verbindlich (on für) **b** (Tech) bindend, Binde- **c** (Med) food etc stopfend

bindweed ['baɪndwiːd] **N** Winde f

binge [bɪndʒ] (inf) **N** (drinking) (Sauf)gelage nt (inf); (eating) (Fress)gelage nt (inf); (= spending spree) Großeinkauf m; **to go on a ~** auf eine Sauftour gehen (inf); eine Fresstour machen (inf); groß einkaufen gehen (inf) **VI** auf eine Sauf-/Fresstour gehen (inf); **you'll have to stop ~ing** du musst mit diesen Sauf-/Fressgelagen aufhören (inf)

bingo ['bɪŋgəʊ] **N** Bingo nt

bin liner **N** (Brit) Mülltüte f

binman **N** pl **-men** (Brit) Müllmann m

binnacle ['bɪnəkl] **N** Kompasshaus nt

binoculars [bɪ'nɒkjʊləz] **PL** Fernglas nt; **a pair of ~** ein Fernglas nt

bi: binomial **ADJ** (Math) binomisch **N** Binom nt; **binuclear** [baɪ'njuːklɪə] **ADJ** binuklear, zweikernig

bio [baɪəʊ]: **biochemical** **ADJ** biochemisch; **biochemist** N Biochemiker(in) m(f); **biochemistry** N Biochemie f; **biodegradable** **ADJ** biologisch abbaubar; **biodiversity** N Artenvielfalt f; **biodynamic** **ADJ** biodynamisch; **bioengineering** N Biotechnik f; **bioethics** N sing Bioethik f; **biofeedback** N Biofeedback nt; **biogenesis** N Biogenese f

biographer [baɪ'ɒgrəfə] **N** Biograf(in) m(f)

biographic(al) [‚baɪəʊ'græfɪk(əl)] **ADJ** biografisch

biography [baɪ'ɒgrəfɪ] **N** Biografie f, Lebensbeschreibung f

biological [‚baɪə'lɒdʒɪkəl] **ADJ** biologisch; **~ detergent** Biowaschmittel nt; **~ diversity** Artenvielfalt f; **~ weapons** biologische Waffen pl

biological clock **N** biologische Uhr

biologically [‚baɪə'lɒdʒɪkəlɪ] **ADV** biologisch

biologist [baɪ'ɒlədʒɪst] **N** Biologe m, Biologin f

biology [baɪ'ɒlədʒɪ] **N** Biologie f

bio: biomass N Biomasse f; **biomechanics** N sing Biomechanik f; **biomedical** **ADJ** biomedizinisch

biometrics [baɪə'metrɪks], **biometry** [baɪ'ɒmətrɪ] **N** Biometrie f

bionic [baɪ'ɒnɪk] **ADJ** bionisch

bio: biophysical **ADJ** biophysikalisch; **biophysics** N sing Biophysik f

biopic ['baɪəʊpɪk] **N** (inf) Filmbiografie f

biopsy ['baɪɒpsɪ] **N** Biopsie f

bio: biorhythm N usu pl Biorhythmus m usu sing; **biosphere** N Biosphäre f; **biosynthesis** N Biosynthese f; **biotechnology** N Biotechnik f; **bioterrorism** N Bioterrorismus m; **biotope** ['baɪətəʊp] N Biotop nt

bi: bipartisan **ADJ** Zweiparteien-; **bipartite** **ADJ** zweiteilig; (= affecting two parties) zweiseitig; **biped** **N** Zweifüßer m; (hum, = human) Zweibeiner m **ADJ** zweifüßig; **biplane** N Doppeldecker m; **bipolar** **ADJ** zwei- or doppelpolig

birch [bɜːtʃ] **N** **a** Birke f **b** (for whipping) Rute f **ATTR** Birken- **VT** (mit Ruten) schlagen

birching ['bɜːtʃɪŋ] **N** (= act) Prügeln nt; (Jur) Prügelstrafe f; **to get a ~** mit der Rute geschlagen werden

bird [bɜːd] **N** **a** Vogel m; **~ of paradise/passage** (lit, fig) Paradies-/Zugvogel m; **the ~ has flown** (fig) der Vogel ist ausgeflogen; **a little ~ told me** (inf) das sagt mir mein kleiner Finger; **that's strictly for the ~s** (inf) das ist geschenkt (inf); **a ~ in the hand is worth two in the bush** (Prov) der Spatz in der Hand ist besser als die Taube auf dem Dach (Prov); **to tell sb about the ~s and the bees** jdm erzählen, wo die kleinen Kinder herkommen → **feather, kill**

b (Cook) Vogel m (hum inf)

c (Brit, inf, = girl) Tussi f (sl)

d (inf, = person) Vogel m (inf); **he's a cunning old ~** er ist ein alter Fuchs

e **to give sb the ~** (esp Brit inf: = boo) jdn auspfeifen; (US sl: = show the finger) jdm den Stinkefinger zeigen; **to get the ~** (esp Brit inf) ausgepfiffen werden; (US sl) den Stinkefinger gezeigt bekommen

f (Brit, inf, = prison term) Knast m (inf); **to do ~** sitzen (inf)

bird: birdbath N Vogelbad nt; **bird box** N Vogelhäuschen nt; **bird brain** N (inf) **to be a ~** ein Spatzenhirn haben (inf); **birdcage** N Vogelbauer m or -käfig nt; **bird call** N Vogelruf m; **bird dog** (US) **N** (lit, fig) Spürhund m **VT** (inf) beschatten (inf)

birder ['bɜːdə] **N** Vogelbeobachter(in) m(f)

bird: bird fancier N Vogelzüchter m; **birdhouse** N Vogelhäuschen nt

birdie ['bɜːdɪ] **N** **a** (inf) Vögelchen nt; **watch the ~** gleich kommts Vögelchen raus! **b** (Golf) Birdie nt **VT** (Golf) **to ~ a hole** ein Birdie spielen

bird: bird-like **ADJ** vogelartig; **birdlime** N Vogelleim m; **bird of passage** N (lit, fig) Zugvogel m; **bird of prey** N Raubvogel m; **bird plague** N Geflügel- or Hühnerpest f; **bird sanctuary** N Vogelschutzgebiet nt; **birdseed** N Vogelfutter nt

bird's: bird's-eye view N Vogelperspektive f; **to get a ~ of the town** die Stadt aus der Vogelperspektive sehen; **bird's-foot** N Vogelfuß m

birdshot ['bɜːdʃɒt] **N** feiner Schrot

bird's: bird's nest N Vogelnest nt; **bird's-nest** VI **to go ~ing** Vogelnester ausnehmen; **bird's-nest soup** N Schwalben- or Vogelnestersuppe f

bird: birdsong N Vogelgesang m; **bird table** N Futterplatz m (für Vögel); **bird-watcher** N Vogelbeobachter(in) m(f)

biretta [bɪ'retə] **N** Birett nt

Biro® ['baɪərəʊ] **N** (Brit) Kugelschreiber m, Kuli m (inf)

birth [bɜːθ] ✪ 24.1 **N** **a** Geburt f; **the town/country of his ~** seine Geburtsstadt/sein Geburtsland nt; **blind/deaf from** or **since ~** von Geburt an blind/taub; **within a few minutes of ~** einige Minuten nach der Geburt; **the rights which are ours by ~** unsere angeborenen Rechte; **to give ~** gebären; (woman also) entbinden; **to give ~ to** entbinden; (animal) jungen; **she's going to give ~!** sie bekommt ihr Kind!

b (= *parentage*) Abstammung f, Herkunft f; **Scottish by ~** Schotte von Geburt, gebürtiger Schotte; **of good ~** aus gutem Hause or guter Familie; **of low** or **humble ~** von niedriger Geburt

c (*fig*) Geburt f; (*of movement, fashion etc*) Aufkommen nt; (*of nation, party, company also*) Gründung f, Entstehen nt; (*of new era*) Anbruch m, Geburt f (*geh*); (*of star*) Entstehung f; **to give ~ to sth** etw schaffen/aufkommen lassen/gründen/anbrechen lassen

birth: birth canal N (*Med*) Geburtskanal m; **birth certificate** N Geburtsurkunde f; **birth control** N Geburtenkontrolle or -regelung f; **birth-control clinic** N Familienberatungsstelle f; **birthdate** N Geburtsdatum nt

birthday ['bɜːðdeɪ] ✪ 23.3 N Geburtstag m; **what did you get for your ~?** was hast du zum Geburtstag bekommen?; **~ celebrations** Geburtstagsfeierlichkeiten pl; **on my ~** an meinem Geburtstag → **happy**

birthday: birthday cake N Geburtstagskuchen m or -torte f; **birthday card** N Geburtstagskarte f; **Birthday honours** PL (*Brit*) Titel- und Ordensverleihungen pl (*am offiziellen Geburtstag des britischen Monarchen*); **birthday party** N Geburtstagsfeier f; (*with dancing etc*) Geburtstagsparty f; (*for child*) Kindergeburtstag m; **birthday present** N Geburtstagsgeschenk nt; **birthday suit** N (*inf*) Adams-/Evaskostüm nt (*inf*); **in one's ~** im Adams-/Evaskostüm (*inf*)

birth father N (= *biological father*) leiblicher Vater

birthing ['bɜːθɪŋ] in cpds Geburts-; **birthing centre**, (*US*) **birthing center** N Geburtshaus nt; **birthing pool** N Entbindungsbadewanne f; **birthing room** N Entbindungsraum m, Kreißsaal m; **birthing stool** N Gebärstuhl m

birth: birthmark N Muttermal nt; **birth mother** N (= *biological mother*) biologische Mutter; (= *surrogate mother*) Leihmutter f; **birth name** N Geburtsname m; **birthplace** N Geburtsort m; **birth plan** N Geburtsplan m; **birthrate** N Geburtenrate or -ziffer f; **birthright** N Geburtsrecht nt **b** (= *right of first-born*) Erstgeburtsrecht nt; **birthstone** N Monatsstein m; **birth trauma** N Geburtstrauma nt

biryani [bɪrɪ'ɑːnɪ] N indisches Reisgericht

Biscay ['bɪskeɪ] N **the Bay of ~** der Golf von Biskaya or Biscaya

biscuit ['bɪskɪt] N **a** (*Brit*) Keks m; (= *dog biscuit*) Hundekuchen m; **that takes/you take the ~!** (*Brit inf*) das übertrifft alles or (*negatively*) schlägt dem Fass den Boden aus **b** (*US*) Brötchen nt **c** (= *porcelain: also* **biscuit-ware**) Biskuitporzellan nt **d** (= *colour*) Beige nt ADJ (*colour*) beige

biscuit barrel N Keksdose f

biscuity ['bɪskətɪ] ADJ *texture* keksartig; *colour* beige

bisect [baɪ'sekt] VT in zwei Teile or (*equal parts*) Hälften teilen; (*Math*) halbieren VI sich teilen

bisection [baɪ'sekʃən] N (*Math*) Halbierung f

bisector [baɪ'sektə'] N (*Math*) Halbierende f

bisexual [ˌbaɪ'seksjʊəl] ADJ bisexuell; (*Biol*) zwittrig, doppelgeschlechtig N (= *person*) Bisexuelle(r) mf

bisexuality [ˌbaɪseksjʊ'ælɪtɪ] N Bisexualität f; (*Biol*) Zwittrigkeit f, Doppelgeschlechtigkeit f

bishop ['bɪʃəp] N **a** (*Eccl*) Bischof m; **thank you, ~** vielen Dank, Herr Bischof **b** (*Chess*) Läufer m

bishopric ['bɪʃəprɪk] N (= *diocese*) Bistum nt; (= *function*) Bischofsamt nt

bismuth ['bɪzməθ] N Wismut nt

bison ['baɪsn] N (*American*) Bison m; (*European*) Wisent m

bisque [bɪsk] N **a** (= *pottery*) Biskuitporzellan nt **b** (= *soup*) Fischcremesuppe f

bissextile [bɪ'sekstaɪl] (*form*) N Schaltjahr nt ADJ Schalt-

bistable [baɪ'steɪbl] ADJ (*Tech*) bistabil

bistro ['biːstrəʊ] N Bistro nt

bit[1] [bɪt] N **a** (*for horse*) Gebiss(stange f) nt; **to take the ~ between one's teeth** (*fig*) sich ins Zeug legen → **champ**[1] **b** (*of drill*) (Bohr)einsatz m, Bohrer m; (*of plane*) (Hobel)messer nt **c** (*of key*) (Schlüssel)bart m

bit[2] N **a** (= *piece*) Stück nt; (*smaller*) Stückchen nt; (*of glass also*) Scherbe f; (= *section: of book, film, symphony*) Teil m; (*part or place in book, drama, text, symphony also*) Stelle f; **a few ~s of furniture** ein paar Möbelstücke; **a ~ of bread** ein Stück Brot; **I gave my ~ to my sister** ich habe meiner Schwester meinen Teil gegeben; **this is the ~ I hate, he said, taking out his wallet** das tue ich gar nicht gern, sagte er und zückte seine Brieftasche; **a ~** (= *not much, small amount*) ein bisschen, etwas; **would you like a ~ of ice cream?** möchten Sie etwas or ein bisschen Eis?; **there's a ~ of truth in what he says** daran ist schon etwas Wahres; **a ~ of advice/luck/ news** ein Rat m/ein Glück nt/eine Neuigkeit; **we had a ~ of trouble/excitement** wir hatten ein wenig Ärger/Aufregung; **I only read a ~ of the novel** ich habe nur ein bisschen or Stückchen von dem Roman gelesen; **don't you feel the slightest ~ of remorse?** hast du denn nicht die geringsten Gewissensbisse?; **it did me a ~ of good** das hat mir geholfen; **this is quite a ~ of help** das könnte eine kleine Hilfe sein; **it wasn't a ~ of help** das war überhaupt keine Hilfe; **quite a ~** einiges; **I've experienced quite a ~ in my life** ich habe in meinem Leben schon (so) einiges erlebt; **there's quite a ~ of work left to do/bread left** es ist noch eine ganze Menge Arbeit zu erledigen/Brot da; **in ~s and pieces** (= *broken*) in tausend Stücken; (*lit, fig, =come apart*) in die Brüche gegangen; **to do the work in ~s and pieces** die Arbeit stückchenweise machen; **the ~s and pieces** die einzelnen Teile; (= *broken bits*) die Scherben pl; **bring all your ~s and pieces** bring deine Siebensachen; **to pick up the ~s and pieces** (*fig*) retten, was zu retten ist; **to come** or **fall to ~s** kaputtgehen, aus dem Leim gehen; **to pull** or **tear sth to ~s** (*lit*) etw in (tausend) Stücke reißen; (*fig*) keinen guten Faden an etw (*dat*) lassen; **to go to ~s** (*fig inf*) durchdrehen (*inf*) → **bob**[3] N e

b (*with time*) **a ~** ein Weilchen nt; **he's gone out for a ~** er ist ein Weilchen or mal kurz weggegangen

c (*with cost*) **a ~** eine ganze Menge; **it cost quite a ~** das hat ganz schön (viel) gekostet (*inf*)

d to do one's ~ sein(en) Teil tun; (= *fair share also*) das seine or Seine tun; **look, you're not doing your ~** hör mal zu, du setzt dich nicht genügend ein

e ~ of a crack/bruise etc ein kleiner Riss/Fleck etc; **he's a ~ of a rogue/an expert** er ist ein ziemlicher Schlingel/ein Fachmann; **he's a ~ of a musician** er ist gar kein schlechter Musiker; **she's a ~ of a connoisseur** sie versteht einiges davon; **you're a ~ of an idiot, aren't you?** du bist ganz schön dumm; **he's got a ~ of a nerve!** der hat vielleicht Nerven!; **it's a ~ of a nuisance** das ist schon etwas ärgerlich; **now that's a ~ of an improvement** das ist schon besser

f ~ by ~ Stück für Stück; (= *gradually*) nach und nach; **he's every ~ a soldier/Frenchman** er ist durch und durch Soldat/Franzose; **it/he is every ~ as good as ...** es/er ist genauso gut, wie ...; **not a ~ of it** keineswegs, keine Spur (*inf*)

g when it comes to the ~ wenn es drauf ankommt

h (= *coin*) (*Brit*) Münze f; **2/4/6 ~s** (*US*) 25/ 50/75 Cent(s)

i (*Brit, inf*) Tussi f (*sl*)

ADV **a ~** ein bisschen, etwas; **were you angry? – a ~** haben Sie sich geärgert? – ja, schon etwas or ein bisschen; **wasn't she a little ~ surprised?** war sie nicht etwas erstaunt?; **I'm not**

a (little) ~ surprised das wundert mich überhaupt nicht or kein bisschen (*inf*) or keineswegs; **he wasn't a ~ the wiser for it** danach war er auch nicht viel klüger or schlauer; **quite a ~** ziemlich viel; **that's quite a ~ better** das ist schon besser; **he's improved quite a ~** er hat sich ziemlich gebessert

bit[3] N (*Comput*) Bit nt

bit[4] pret of **bite**

bitch [bɪtʃ] N **a** (*of dog*) Hündin f; (*of canines generally*) Weibchen nt; (*of fox*) Füchsin f; (*of wolf*) Wölfin f; **terrier ~** (*sl*, = *woman*) Miststück nt (*inf*); (*spiteful*) Hexe f; **silly ~** doofe Ziege (*inf*); **don't be a ~** sei nicht so gemein or gehässig; **she's a mean ~** sie ist ein gemeines Stück (*inf*); **life's a ~** das Leben kann ganz schön beschissen sein (*inf*) **c** (*inf, = complaint*) **to have a ~ (about sb/sth)** (über jdn/etw) meckern (*inf*); **what's your ~ this time?** was hast du diesmal zu meckern? (*inf*) VI (*inf, = complain*) meckern (*inf*) (*about* über +acc)

▶ **bitch up** VT sep (*sl*) versauen (*inf*)

bitchiness ['bɪtʃɪnɪs] N Gehässigkeit f, Gemeinheit f; (*of remark also*) Bissigkeit f

bitchy ['bɪtʃɪ] ADJ (+er) (*inf*) woman gehässig, gemein; *remark also* bissig; **that was a ~ thing to do/say** das war gehässig or gemein; **he started getting ~ (about her)** er fing an, bissige or gehässige Bemerkungen (über sie) zu machen

bite [baɪt] vb: pret **bit**, ptp **bitten** N **a** Biss m; **in two ~s** mit zwei Bissen; **he took a ~ (out) of the apple** er biss in den Apfel; **to get a second** or **another ~ at the cherry** (*fig*) eine zweite Chance bekommen

b (= *wound etc*) (= *dog, snake, flea bite etc*) Biss m; (= *insect bite*) Stich m; (= *love bite*) (Knutsch)fleck m (*inf*)

c (*Fishing*) **I think I've got a ~** ich glaube, es hat einer angebissen

d (*of food*) Happen m; **there's not a ~ to eat** es ist überhaupt nichts zu essen da; **come and have a ~** komm und iss 'ne Kleinigkeit; **do you fancy a ~ (to eat)?** möchten Sie etwas essen?

e there's a ~ in the air es ist beißend kalt; **the ~ of the wind** der beißende kalte Wind

f (*of file, saw*) **the file has lost its ~** die Feile ist stumpf geworden; **these screws don't have enough ~** diese Schrauben greifen or fassen nicht richtig

g (*of sauce etc*) Schärfe f

VT **a** (*person, dog*) beißen; (*insect*) stechen; **to ~ one's nails** an den Nägeln kauen; **to ~ one's tongue/lip** (*lit, fig*) sich (*dat*) auf die Zunge/Lippen beißen; **the trapeze artist ~s the rope between her teeth** die Trapezkünstlerin hält das Seil mit den Zähnen fest; **don't worry, he won't ~ you** (*fig inf*) keine Angst, er wird dich schon nicht beißen (*inf*); **to ~ the dust** (*inf*) dran glauben müssen (*inf*); **he had been bitten by the travel/music bug** ihn hatte das Reisefieber/das Musikfieber erwischt (*inf*); **once bitten twice shy** (*Prov*) (ein) gebranntes Kind scheut das Feuer (*Prov*); **to ~ the hand that feeds you** (*prov*) sich (*dat*) ins eigene Fleisch schneiden; **what's biting you?** (*fig inf*) was ist mit dir los? (*inf*), was hast du denn?

b (*cold, frost, wind*) schneiden in (+dat)

c (*file, saw*) schneiden in (+acc); (*acid*) ätzen

d (*inf, = swindle*) **I've been bitten** ich bin reingelegt worden (*inf*)

VI **a** (*dog etc*) beißen; (*insects*) stechen

b (*fish, fig inf*) anbeißen

c (*cold, frost, wind*) beißen, schneiden

d (*wheels*) fassen, greifen; (*saw, anchor*) fassen; (*screw*) greifen

▶ **bite into** VI +prep obj (*person*) (hinein)beißen in (+acc); (*teeth*) (tief) eindringen in (+acc); (*acid, saw*) sich hineinfressen in (+acc); (*screw, drill*) sich hineinbohren in (+acc)

▶ **bite off** VT sep abbeißen; **he won't bite your head off** (*inf*) er wird dir schon nicht den Kopf abreißen; **to bite off more than one can chew** (*prov*) sich (*dat*) zu viel zumuten

▶**bite on** VI +prep obj beißen auf (+acc); **give the baby something to bite on** gib dem Kind etwas zum Beißen

▶**bite through** VT insep durchbeißen

biter [ˈbaɪtəʳ] N **the ~ bitten!** mit den eigenen Waffen geschlagen!; (in deception also) der betrogene Betrüger!

bite-size(d) [ˈbaɪtsaɪz(d)] ADJ **a** food, piece mundgerecht **b** (fig) information etc leicht verdaulich

biting [ˈbaɪtɪŋ] ADJ beißend; cold, wind also schneidend

bit: bitmap N (Comput) **a** no pl (= mode) Bitmap nt **b** (also **bitmapped image**) Bitmap-Abbildung f; **bitmapped** (Comput) Bitmap-, bit-mapped pred; ~ **graphics** Bitmapgrafik f; **bit part** N kleine Nebenrolle; **bit(-part) player** N Schauspieler(in) m(f) in kleinen Nebenrollen

bitten [ˈbɪtn] ptp of **bite**

bitter [ˈbɪtəʳ] ADJ (+er) **a** taste bitter; **it was a ~ pill to swallow** (fig) es war eine bittere Pille **b** cold, winter bitter; weather, wind bitterkalt, eisig; **it's ~ today** es ist heute bitterkalt **c** enemy, struggle, opposition erbittert **d** disappointment, hatred, reproach, remorse, tears bitter; criticism scharf, heftig; **to the ~ end** bis zum bitteren Ende **e** (= embittered) bitter; person also verbittert; **to be** or **feel ~ at sth** über etw (acc) bitter or verbittert sein ADV **~ cold** bitterkalt N **a** (Brit, = beer) halbdunkles obergäriges Bier **b** **bitters** PL Magenbitter m; **gin and ~s** Gin m mit Bitterlikör

bitter lemon N Bitter Lemon nt

bitterly [ˈbɪtəlɪ] ADV **a** reproach, disappointed bitter; complain also, weep bitterlich; oppose erbittert; criticize scharf; jealous sehr **b** cold bitter **c** (= showing embitteredness) verbittert; criticize erbittert

bittern [ˈbɪtɜːn] N Rohrdommel f

bitterness [ˈbɪtənɪs] N **a** (of taste) Bitterkeit f **b** (of cold, winter) Bitterkeit f; (of weather, wind) bittere Kälte **c** (of struggle, opposition) Erbittertheit f **d** (of disappointment, hatred, reproach, remorse) Bitterkeit f; (of criticism) Schärfe f, Heftigkeit f; **such was the ~ of his disappointment/ jealousy** er war so bitter enttäuscht/derart eifersüchtig **e** (= anger) Bitterkeit f; (of person also) Verbitterung f

bittersweet [ˈbɪtəˌswiːt] ADJ (lit, fig) bittersüß, bitter süß N (Bot) Kletternder Baumwürger; (= nightshade) Bittersüßer Nachtschatten

bitty [ˈbɪtɪ] ADJ (+er) (Brit, inf, = scrappy) zusammengestoppelt (pej inf) or -gestückelt (inf)

bitumen [ˈbɪtjʊmɪn] N Bitumen nt

bituminous [bɪˈtjuːmɪnəs] ADJ ~ **coal** Stein- or Fettkohle f

bivalent [baɪˈveɪlənt] ADJ bivalent, zweiwertig

bivalve [ˈbaɪvælv] (Zool) N zweischalige Muschel ADJ zweischalig

bivouac [ˈbɪvʊæk] vb: pret, ptp **bivouacked** N Biwak nt VI biwakieren

bivvy [ˈbɪvɪ] N (inf) Biwakzelt nt VI **to ~ up** biwakieren

biweekly [baɪˈwiːklɪ] ADJ **a** (= twice a week) ~ **meetings/editions** Konferenzen/Ausgaben, die zweimal wöchentlich or in der Woche stattfinden/erscheinen **b** (= fortnightly) zweiwöchentlich, vierzehntäglich ADV **a** (= twice a week) zweimal wöchentlich, zweimal in der Woche **b** (= fortnightly) alle vierzehn Tage, vierzehntäglich

biz [bɪz] (inf) abbr of **business**

bizarre [bɪˈzɑːʳ] ADJ bizarr

BL abbr of **Bachelor of Law**

blab [blæb] VI quatschen (inf); (= talk fast, tell secret) plappern; (criminal) singen (sl) VT (also **blab out**) secret ausplaudern

blabbermouth [ˈblæbəˌmaʊθ] N (inf) Klatschmaul nt (inf)

black [blæk] ADJ (+er) **a** (colour) schwarz; ~ **man/woman** Schwarze(r) mf; ~ **and blue** grün

und blau; ~ **and white photography/film** Schwarzweißfotografie f/-film m; **the situation isn't so ~ and white as that** die Situation ist nicht so eindeutig schwarz-weiß or schwarzweiß **b** (= dirty) schwarz **c** (= wicked) thought, plan, deed schwarz; **he's not so ~ as he's painted** (prov) er ist nicht so schlecht wie sein Ruf **d** future, prospects, mood düster, finster; **he painted the future in the ~est colours** er malte die Zukunft in den schwärzesten Farben; **things are looking ~ for our project** es sieht für unser Vorhaben ziemlich schwarz or düster aus; **maybe things aren't as ~ as they seem** vielleicht ist alles gar nicht so schlimm, wie es aussieht; **in ~ despair** in tiefster Verzweiflung; **this was a ~ day for ...** das war ein schwarzer Tag für ... **e** (fig, = angry) looks böse; **he looked as ~ as thunder** er machte ein bitterböses Gesicht; **his face went ~** er wurde rot vor Zorn; **to be in a ~ mood** schlechte Laune haben **f** (Brit: during strike) **to declare a cargo** etc ~ eine Ladung etc für bestreikt erklären; ~ **goods** bestreikte Waren N **a** (= colour) Schwarz nt; **he's dressed in ~** er trägt Schwarz; **to wear ~** (in mourning) Trauer or Schwarz tragen; **it's written down in ~ and white** es steht schwarz auf weiß geschrieben; **a ~ and white** (Art) ein Schwarzweißzeichnung; (= film) ein Schwarzweißfilm m; **a film which oversimplifies and presents everything in ~ and white** ein Film, der durch seine Schwarzweißmalerei alles vereinfacht darstellt; **to swear that ~ is white** schwören, dass zwei mal zwei fünf ist **b** (= negro) Schwarze(r) mf **c** **in the ~** (Fin) in den schwarzen Zahlen **d** (Chess etc) Schwarz nt; (Billiards) schwarzer Ball; (Roulette) Schwarz nt, Noir nt **e** (of night) Schwärze f VT **a** (= blacken) schwärzen; **to ~ one's face** sich (dat) das Gesicht schwarz machen; **to ~ sb's eye** jdm ein blaues Auge schlagen or verpassen (inf) **b** shoes wichsen **c** (Brit: trade union) bestreiken; goods boykottieren

▶**black out** VI das Bewusstsein verlieren, ohnmächtig werden VT sep **a** building, stage, window verdunkeln **b** (= not broadcast) **the technicians have blacked out tonight's programmes** (Brit) or **programs** (US) durch einen Streik des technischen Personals kann das heutige Abendprogramm nicht ausgestrahlt werden **c** (with ink, paint) schwärzen

▶**black up** VI (Theat inf) sich schwarz anmalen

Black Africa N Schwarzafrika nt

blackamoor [ˈblækəmʊəʳ] N (obs) Mohr m (obs)

black: blackball VT (= vote against) stimmen gegen; (inf, = exclude) ausschließen; **black beetle** N Küchenschabe f; **blackberry** N Brombeere f; **to go ~ing** (Brit) Brombeeren pflücken gehen, in die Brombeeren gehen (inf); **blackbird** N Amsel f; **blackboard** N Tafel f; **to write sth on the ~** etw an die Tafel schreiben; **black book** N **to be in sb's ~s** bei jdm schlecht angeschrieben sein (inf); **little ~** Notizbuch nt (mit Adressen der Mädchenbekanntschaften); **black box** N (Aviat) Flugschreiber m; (= mysterious device) Blackbox f; **black bread** N Schwarzbrot nt; **black cab** N (Brit) britisches Taxi; **blackcap** N **a** (= bird) Mönchsgrasmücke f **b** (US, = berry) Barett nt; (Jur) schwarze Kappe (des Richters bei Todesurteilen); **black comedy** N schwarze Komödie; **Black Country** N Industriegebiet in den englischen Midlands; **blackcurrant** N schwarze Johannisbeere; **Black Death** N (Hist) schwarzer Tod; **black economy** N Schattenwirtschaft f

blacken [ˈblækən] VT **a** (= make black) schwarz machen; one's face schwarz anmalen; **the walls**

were ~ed **by the fire** die Wände waren vom Feuer schwarz **b** (fig) character verunglimpfen; **to ~ sb's name** or **reputation** jdn schlecht machen VI schwarz werden

black: Black English N Englisch nt der Schwarzen; **black eye** N blaues Auge; **to give sb a ~** jdm ein blaues Auge schlagen or verpassen (inf); **black-eyed** ADJ schwarzäugig; **blackfly** N Schwarze Blattlaus; **Black Forest** N Schwarzwald m; **Black Forest gateau** N (esp Brit) Schwarzwälder Kirschtorte f; **black frost** N strenge, aber trockene Kälte; **black grouse** N Birkhuhn nt

blackguard [ˈblægɑːd] N (old) Bösewicht m, (Spitz)bube m (old)

blackguardly [ˈblægɑːdlɪ] ADJ deed, person niederträchtig

black: blackhead N Mitesser m; **black-headed gull** N Schwarzkopfmöwe f; **black-hearted** ADJ böse; **black hole** N (Astron, fig) schwarzes Loch; **Black Hole of Calcutta** N (cramped) Affenstall m; (dirty, dark) scheußliches Verlies; **black humour**, (US) **black humor** N schwarzer Humor; **black ice** N Glatteis nt

blacking [ˈblækɪŋ] N **a** (for shoes) schwarze (Schuh)wichse; (for stoves) Ofenschwärze f **b** (Brit) (by trade union) Bestreikung f; (of goods) Boykottierung f

blackish [ˈblækɪʃ] ADJ schwärzlich

black: blackjack N **a** (= flag) schwarze (Piraten)flagge **b** (Cards, = pontoon) Siebzehnundvier nt **c** (US, = weapon) Totschläger m **d** (Hist, = drinking vessel) (lederner) Becher VT (US, = hit) prügeln; **black lead** N Graphit m, Grafit m; (for stoves) Schwärze f; **black-lead** VT stove schwärzen; **blackleg** (Brit, Ind) N Streikbrecher(in) m(f) VI Streikbrecher(in) sein, sich als Streikbrecher(in) betätigen VT one's fellow workers sich unsolidarisch verhalten gegen; **blacklist** N schwarze Liste VT auf die schwarze Liste setzen; **black lung** N Staublunge f

blackly [ˈblæklɪ] ADV (= gloomily) düster, finster

black: black magic N schwarze Kunst or Magie f; **blackmail** N Erpressung f; **to use emotional ~ on sb** jds Gefühle brutal ausnutzen; **that's emotional ~!** das ist die reinste Erpressung! erpressen; **to ~ sb into doing sth** jdn durch Erpressung dazu zwingen, etw zu tun; **he had ~ed £500 out of her** er hatte £ 500 von ihr erpresst; **blackmailer** N Erpresser(in) m(f); **Black Maria** [ˌblækməˈraɪə] N grüne Minna (inf); **black mark** N Tadel m; (in school register also) Eintrag m; **that's a ~ for against him** das ist ein Minuspunkt für ihn; **black market** N Schwarzmarkt m ADJ attr Schwarzmarkt-; **black marketeer** N Schwarzhändler(in) m(f); **black mass** N Schwarze Messe; **Black Muslim** N Black Moslem m; **Black Nationalism** N (US) schwarzer Nationalismus

blackness [ˈblæknɪs] N Schwärze f; **the ~ of his mood** seine düstere Laune

black: blackout N **a** (Med) Ohnmacht(sanfall m) f no pl; **I must have had a ~** ich muss wohl in Ohnmacht gefallen sein; **he had a ~** ihm wurde schwarz vor Augen **b** (= light failure) Stromausfall m; (Theat) Blackout nt; (during war) Verdunkelung f; (TV) Ausfall m **c** (= news blackout) (Nachrichten)sperre f; **Black Panther** N Black Panther m; **black pepper** N schwarzer Pfeffer; **Black Power** N Blackpower f, Black Power f; **black pudding** N = Blutwurst f; **Black Rod** N Zeremonienmeister des britischen Oberhauses; **Black Sea** N Schwarzes Meer; **black sheep** N (fig) schwarzes Schaf; **Blackshirt** N Schwarzhemd nt; **blacksmith** N (Grob- or Huf)schmied m; **at/to the ~'s (shop)** beim/zum Schmied; **black spot** N (also **accident black spot**) Gefahrenstelle f; **blackthorn** N (Bot) Schwarzdorn m; **black tie** N (on invitation) Abendanzug m ADJ dinner, function mit Smokingzwang; **is it ~?** ist da Smokingzwang?; **blacktop** N (US, = substance) schwarzer Straßenbelag; (= road) geteerte Straße; (paved with asphalt) Asphaltstraße f; **black velvet** N Sekt mit Starkbier; **black widow** N Schwarze Witwe f

bladder ['blædə'] N **a** (Anat, Bot) Blase f; **with all that beer in your ~** mit dem vielen Bier im Bauch **b** (Ftbl) Blase f

bladdered ['blædəd] ADJ (inf: = drunk) voll (inf), blau (inf); **to get ~** sich voll laufen lassen

bladderwrack ['blædəræk] N Blasentang m

blade [bleɪd] N **a** (of knife, tool, weapon, razor) Klinge f; (of pencil sharpener) Messerchen nt; (of guillotine) Beil nt **b** (of tongue) vorderer Zungenrücken; (of oar, spade, saw, windscreen wiper) Blatt nt; (of plough) Schar f; (of turbine, paddle wheel) Schaufel f; (of propeller) Blatt nt, Flügel m **c** (of leaf) Blatt nt, Spreite f (spec); (of grass, corn) Halm m, Spreite f (spec) **d** (liter, = sword) Klinge f (liter) **e** (old, = dashing fellow) schmucker Bursch (old) **f** (Anat) = **shoulder blade**

-bladed [-bleɪdɪd] ADJ suf **a twin-bladed propeller** ein Zweiblattpropeller m; **a two-bladed knife** ein Messer nt mit zwei Klingen

blaeberry ['bleɪbəri] N (Scot, N Engl) = **bilberry**

blag [blæg] VT (Brit inf) schnorren (inf); **to ~ one's way into a club** sich in einen Klub hineinmogeln (inf)

blah [blɑː] (inf) **N** (dated, = nonsense) Blabla (inf), Geschwafel (inf) nt **INTERJ ~, ~, ~** blabla (inf)

blame [bleɪm] **VT** **a** (= hold responsible) die Schuld geben (+dat), beschuldigen; **to ~ sb for sth/sth on sb** jdm die Schuld an etw (dat) geben, die Schuld an etw (dat) auf jdn schieben; **to ~ sth on sth** die Schuld an etw (dat) auf etw (acc) schieben, einer Sache (dat) die Schuld an etw (dat) geben; **you only have yourself or you have no-one but yourself to ~** das hast du dir selbst zuzuschreiben; **I'm to ~ for this** daran bin ich schuld; **who/what is to ~ for this accident?** wer/was ist schuld an diesem Unfall?; **I ~ him for leaving the door open** er ist schuld, dass die Tür aufblieb; **to ~ oneself for sth** sich (dat) etw selbst zuzuschreiben haben, selbst an etw (dat) schuld sein; (= feel responsible) sich für etw verantwortlich fühlen, sich selbst bezichtigen; **he ~s himself for starting the fire** er gibt sich selbst die Schuld daran, dass das Feuer ausgebrochen ist

b (= reproach) Vorwürfe machen (sb for jdm für or wegen); **nobody is blaming you** es macht Ihnen ja niemand einen Vorwurf

c **he decided to turn down the offer – well, I can't say I ~ him** er entschloss sich, das Angebot abzulehnen – das kann man ihm wahrhaftig nicht verdenken; **so I told her to get lost – (I) don't ~ you** da habe ich ihr gesagt, sie soll zum Teufel gehen – da hattest du ganz Recht; **so I told him what I really thought, do you ~ me?** da habe ich ihm gründlich meine Meinung gesagt, und doch wohl nicht zu Unrecht, oder?

N **a** (= responsibility) Schuld f; **to put the ~ for sth on sb** jdm die Schuld an etw (dat) geben; **to take the ~** die Schuld auf sich (acc) nehmen; (for sb's mistakes also) den Kopf hinhalten; **why do I always have to take the ~?** warum muss denn immer ich an allem schuld sein?; **parents must take the ~ for their children's failings** Eltern haben die Verantwortung für die Fehler ihrer Kinder zu tragen; **we share the ~** wir haben beide/alle Schuld; **the ~ lies with him** er hat Schuld or ist schuld (daran)

b (= censure) Tadel m; **without ~** ohne Schuld; (= irreproachable) life etc untadelig

blameable, **blamable** (US) ['bleɪməbl] ADJ tadelnswert, tadelnswürdig

blameless ['bleɪmlɪs] ADJ schuldlos; life untadelig

blamelessly ['bleɪmlɪslɪ] ADV unschuldig

blameworthy ['bleɪmwɜːðɪ] ADJ person schuldig; behaviour, action tadelnswert

blanch [blɑːntʃ] **VT** (Hort) bleichen; (illness) face bleich machen; (fear) erbleichen lassen; (Cook)

vegetables blanchieren; almonds brühen **VI** (with vor +dat) (person) blass werden; (with fear also) bleich werden, erbleichen (geh)

blancmange [blə'mɒnʒ] N Pudding m

bland [blænd] ADJ (+er) taste, food, diet fad; book, film, statement nichts sagend; person, character langweilig, farblos; expression, look, smile leer

blandish ['blændɪʃ] VT schönreden (+dat)

blandishment ['blændɪʃmənt] N Schmeichelei f

blandly ['blændlɪ] ADV say, reply regungslos; smile vage

blandness ['blændnɪs] N (of taste, food, diet) Fadheit f; (of book, film, statement) Inhaltslosigkeit f; (of person, character) Farblosigkeit f; (of expression, look, smile) Leere f

blank [blæŋk] **ADJ** (+er) **a** piece of paper, page, wall leer; silence, darkness tief; coin ungeprägt; **a ~ space** eine Lücke, ein freier Platz; (on form) ein freies Feld; **~ form** Formular(blatt) nt, Vordruck m; **please leave ~** (on form) bitte frei lassen or nicht ausfüllen

b (= expressionless) face, look ausdruckslos; (= stupid) verständnislos; (= puzzled) verdutzt, verblüfft; **he looked at me with ~ incomprehension** er sah mich völlig verständnislos an; **to look ~** (= expressionless) eine ausdruckslose Miene aufsetzen; (= stupid) verständnislos dreinschauen; (= puzzled) ein verdutztes Gesicht machen; **he just looked ~** or **gave me a ~ look** er guckte mich nur groß an (inf); **my mind** or **I went ~** ich hatte Mattscheibe (inf), ich hatte ein Brett vor dem Kopf (inf); **sorry, I've gone ~** (inf) tut mir Leid, aber ich habe totale Mattscheibe (inf)

c (= empty) life etc unausgefüllt, leer; **these ~ and characterless house fronts** diese nackten, charakterlosen Fassaden

N **a** (in document) freier Raum, leere Stelle; (= blank document) Vordruck m, Formular nt; (= gap) Lücke f

b (= void) Leere f; **I** or **my mind was/went a complete ~** ich hatte totale Mattscheibe (inf)

c (in lottery) Niete f; **to draw a ~** (fig) kein Glück haben

d (in a target) Scheibenmittelpunkt m

e (= cartridge) Platzpatrone f → also **blank cartridge**

f (= domino) Blank nt

g (= coin) Schrötling m (spec); (= key) Rohling m

VT (= ignore) person ignorieren

▶ **blank out** VT sep feeling, thought etc ausschalten

blank: **blank book** N Notizbuch nt; **blank cartridge** N Platzpatrone f; **blank CD** N (Comput) Rohling m; **blank cheque**, (US) **blank check** N Blankoscheck m; (fig) Freibrief m; **to give sb a ~** (fig) jdm Carte blanche geben (geh), jdm freie Hand geben

blanket ['blæŋkɪt] **N** (lit, fig) Decke f; **a ~ of snow/fog** eine Schnee-/Nebeldecke; **born on the wrong side of the ~** (hum inf) unehelich (geboren) **ADJ** attr statement pauschal; insurance, coverage umfassend; ban generell; bombing flächendeckend **VT** **a** (snow, smoke) zudecken; **fog ~ed the town** Nebel hüllte die Stadt ein **b** (Naut) ship den Wind abhalten von

blanket: **blanket bath** N Waschen nt im Bett; **to give sb a ~** jdn im Bett waschen; **blanket insurance** N Kollektivversicherung f; **blanket mortgage** N Gesamthypothek f; **blanket stitch** N Langettenstich m

blank line N (Typ) Leerzeile f

blankly ['blæŋklɪ] ADV (= expressionlessly) ausdruckslos; (= uncomprehendingly) verständnislos; **she just looked at me ~** sie sah mich nur groß an (inf)

blankness ['blæŋknɪs] N (= emptiness) Leere f; (of expression) Ausdruckslosigkeit f; (= not understanding) Verständnislosigkeit f; (= puzzlement) Verdutztheit f, Verblüffung f

blank verse N Blankvers m

blare [bleə'] **N** Plärren nt, Geplärr nt; (of car horn) lautes Hupen; (of trumpets) Schmettern nt **VI** plärren; (car horn) laut hupen; (trumpets) schmettern; **the music/his voice ~d through the hall** die Musik/seine Stimme schallte durch den Saal **VT** **be quiet!, he ~d** Ruhe!, brüllte er

▶ **blare out** **VI** (loud voice, music) schallen; (trumpets) schmettern; (radio, music also) plärren; (car horn) laut hupen; (person) brüllen **VT** sep (trumpets) tune schmettern; (radio) music plärren; (person) order, warning etc brüllen

blarney ['blɑːnɪ] **N** Schmeichelei f, Schmus m (inf); **he has kissed the Blarney Stone** (fig) der kann einen beschwatzen (inf) **VT** sb schmeicheln (+dat); **he could ~ his way out of trouble** er könnte sich aus allem herausreden **VI** schmeicheln

blaspheme [blæs'fiːm] **VT** lästern, schmähen (geh) **VI** Gott lästern; **to ~ against sb/sth** (lit, fig) jdn/etw schmähen (geh)

blasphemer [blæs'fiːmə'] N Gotteslästerer m

blasphemous ['blæsfɪməs] ADJ (lit, fig) blasphemisch; words also lästerlich, frevelhaft

blasphemously ['blæsfɪməslɪ] ADV blasphemisch; speak also lästerlich, frevlerisch

blasphemy ['blæsfɪmɪ] N Blasphemie f; (Rel also) (Gottes)lästerung f; (= words also) Schmähung f (geh)

blast [blɑːst] **N** **a** Windstoß m; (of hot air) Schwall m; **a ~ of wind** ein Windstoß; **an icy ~** ein eisiger Wind; **a ~ from the past** (inf) eine Erinnerung an vergangene Zeiten

b (= sound, of trumpets) Geschmetter nt, Schmettern nt; (of foghorn) Tuten nt; **the ship gave a long ~ on its foghorn** das Schiff ließ sein Nebelhorn ertönen; **to blow a ~ on the bugle** auf dem Horn blasen

c (= noise, explosion) Explosion f; (= shock wave) Druckwelle f; **to get the full ~ of sb's anger** jds Wut in voller Wucht abkriegen

d (in quarrying etc) Sprengladung f

e (of furnace) (Blas)wind m; **with the radio/ heating on (at) full ~** mit dem Radio/der Heizung voll aufgedreht

f (inf: = enjoyable experience) **it was a ~** das war echt Spitze (inf); **to have a ~** sich blendend amüsieren

VT **a** (lightning) schlagen in (+acc); (with powder) sprengen

b (= send) rocket schießen; ball mit Wucht schießen; air blasen

c (= shoot with gun) schießen auf (+acc); (= shoot dead) erschießen; **the police ~ed their way in** die Polizei hat sich den Weg ins Haus freigeschossen or (with explosives) freigebombt

d (inf, = criticize) verreißen; person herunterputzen (inf)

e (= blight) plant vernichten, zerstören; reputation also, future ruinieren

VI (in quarry) sprengen

INTERJ (inf) **~ (it)!** verdammt! (inf), so ein Mist! (inf); **~ what he wants!** das ist doch wurscht, was der will! (inf); **~ him for coming so late** Herrgott, dass er aber auch so spät kommen muss! (inf); **~ this car!** dieses verdammte Auto! (inf)

▶ **blast away** **VI** (with gun) drauflosschießen or -ballern (inf); (radio, rock band etc) dröhnen

▶ **blast off** **VI** (rocket, astronaut) abheben, starten

▶ **blast out** **VI** (music) dröhnen

blasted ['blɑːstɪd] **ADJ** **a** öde **b** (inf) verdammt (inf), Mist- (inf); **he was talking all the ~ time** verdammt, er hat die ganze Zeit geredet (inf) **ADV** (inf) verdammt (inf)

blast furnace N Hochofen m

blasting ['blɑːstɪŋ] N (Tech) Sprengen nt; **"danger ~ in progress"** „Achtung! Sprengarbeiten!" → **sandblasting**

blastoff ['blɑːstɒf] N Abschuss m

blat [blæt] (inf esp US) **VI** (sheep) blöken **VT** (= give away) ausposaunen (pej)

　　　　　　　　　　　　　　　　　　　　　　　　　blatancy – blind

blatancy ['bleɪtənsɪ] N (= obviousness) Offensichtlichkeit f; (of injustice, lie also) Eklatanz f; (of error) Krassheit f, Eklatanz f; **the ~ of their disregard for ...** ihre unverhohlene or offene Missachtung der ...

blatant ['bleɪtənt] ADJ (= very obvious) offensichtlich; injustice, lie, lack also eklatant; error krass, eklatant; liar, social climber unverfroren; colour schreiend; disregard offen, unverhohlen; **there's no need (for you) to be quite so ~ about it** (in talking) Sie brauchen das nicht so herumzuposaunen (inf); (in doing sth) Sie brauchen das nicht so deutlich zu tun

blatantly ['bleɪtəntlɪ] ADV offensichtlich; (= openly) offen; (= without respect) unverfroren; **you don't have to make it quite so ~ obvious** Sie brauchen es nicht so überdeutlich zu zeigen; **she ~ ignored it** sie hat das schlicht und einfach ignoriert

blather ['blæðə] N, VI (inf) = **blether**

blaze[1] [bleɪz] N **a** (= fire) Feuer nt; (of building etc also) Brand m; **"blaze at factory"** „Brand in Fabrik"; **six people died in the ~** sechs Menschen kamen in den Flammen um **b** (of guns etc) Feuer nt, Funkeln nt; **a ~ of lights** ein Lichtermeer nt; **a ~ of colour** (Brit) or **color** (US) ein Meer nt von Farben; **a sudden ~ of light from the watchtower** ein plötzlicher Lichtstrahl vom Wachturm; **he went out in a ~ of glory** er trat mit Glanz und Gloria ab **c** (of fire, sun) Glut f; (fig, of rage) Anfall m **d** (inf) **go to ~s** scher dich zum Teufel! (inf); **it can go to ~s** das kann mir gestohlen bleiben (inf); **what/how the ~s ...?** was/wie zum Teufel ...? (inf); **like ~s** wie verrückt (inf) VI **a** (sun) brennen; (fire also) lodern; **to ~ with anger** vor Zorn glühen **b** (guns) feuern; **with all guns blazing** aus allen Rohren feuernd

▶ **blaze abroad** VT sep (liter) verbreiten (throughout in +dat)

▶ **blaze away** VI **a** (soldiers, guns) drauflos feuern (at auf +acc) **b** (fire etc) lodern

▶ **blaze down** VI (sun) niederbrennen (on auf +acc)

▶ **blaze up** VI aufflammen, auflodern

blaze[2] N (of horse etc) Blesse f; (on tree) Anreißung f VT tree anreißen; **to ~ a trail** (lit) einen Weg markieren; (fig) den Weg bahnen

blazer ['bleɪzə] N Blazer m (also Sch), Klubjacke f

blazing ['bleɪzɪŋ] ADJ **a** building etc brennend; fire, torch lodernd; sun, light grell; sun (= hot) brennend **b** (fig) eyes funkelnd (with vor +dat); row furchtbar; **he is ~** (inf) er kocht vor Wut (inf), er ist fuchsteufelswild (inf)

blazon ['bleɪzn] N (Her) Wappen nt VT (liter: also **blazon abroad**) news verbreiten (throughout in +dat)

bldg abbr of **building**

bleach [bliːtʃ] N **a** Bleichmittel nt; (= household bleach) Reinigungsmittel nt **b** (act) Bleichen nt; **to ~ sth** etw bleichen VT **a** linen, bones, hair, skin bleichen; (sun) colour, fabric verbleichen lassen, ausbleichen VI (bones) (ver-)bleichen; (Phot: image) verblassen

▶ **bleach out** VT sep ausbleichen

bleachers ['bliːtʃəz] PL (US) unüberdachte Zuschauertribüne

bleaching ['bliːtʃɪŋ] N Bleichen nt; **they need a good ~** sie müssten richtig gebleicht werden

bleaching agent N Bleichmittel nt

bleaching powder N Bleichkalk m

bleak [bliːk] ADJ (+er) **a** landscape, place öde, trostlos **b** weather, wind rau, kalt **c** (fig) trostlos; prospects also trüb; smile, look, tone of voice niedergeschlagen; **his face was ~** er sah niedergeschlagen aus; **things look rather ~ for him** es sieht ziemlich trostlos für ihn aus

bleakly ['bliːklɪ] ADV look, say, smile niedergeschlagen

bleakness ['bliːknɪs] N (of landscape) Öde f, Trostlosigkeit f **b** (of weather) Rauheit f, Kälte

f **c** (fig) Trostlosigkeit f; (of prospects also) Trübheit f

blearily ['blɪərɪlɪ] ADV look mit trüben Augen

bleary ['blɪərɪ] ADJ (+er) **a** eyes trübe; (after sleep) verschlafen **b** (= blurred) verschwommen

bleary-eyed ['blɪərɪˌaɪd] ADJ (after sleep) verschlafen; **~ after proofreading** mit ganz trüben Augen nach dem Korrekturlesen

bleat [bliːt] VI **a** (sheep, calf) blöken; (goat) meckern **b** (fig inf, = complain, moan) meckern (inf) N **a** (of sheep, calf) Blöken nt, Geblök nt; (of goat) Meckern nt **b** (inf, = moan) Meckern nt (inf), Gemecker nt (inf)

bleed [bliːd] pret, ptp **bled** [bled] VI **a** (= lose blood) bluten; **to ~ to death** verbluten; **my heart ~s for you** (iro) ich fang gleich an zu weinen; **our hearts ~ for the oppressed** (liter) wir leiden mit den Unterdrückten (geh) **b** (plant) bluten, schwitzen; (wall) schwitzen VT **a** person zur Ader lassen **b** (fig inf) schröpfen (inf) (for um), bluten lassen (inf); **to ~ sb dry** or **white** jdn total ausnehmen (inf) **c** radiator (ent)lüften; (Aut) brakes lüften

▶ **bleed away** VI (lit, fig) ausströmen, verströmen (geh)

bleeder ['bliːdə] N **a** (Med inf) Bluter m **b** (Brit inf) (= person) Arschloch nt (vulg); (= thing) Scheißding nt (inf); **you're a cheeky little ~** du bist ein frecher Hund (inf)

bleeding ['bliːdɪŋ] N **a** (= loss of blood) Blutung f; internal ~ innere Blutungen pl **b** (= taking blood) Aderlass m **c** (of plant) Blutung f, Schwitzen nt **d** (of brakes) Lüftung f ADJ **a** wound, nose, gums blutend; (fig) heart gebrochen **b** (Brit inf) verdammt (inf), Scheiß- (inf); (in positive sense) miracle etc verdammt (inf); **get your ~ hands off** nimm deine Dreckpfoten weg (inf) ADV (Brit inf) verdammt (inf); **that's ~ marvellous** das ist ja wieder toll! (inf), na klasse! (inf); **who does he/she think he/she ~ well is?** für was hält sich der Kerl/die Kuh eigentlich? (inf); **not ~ likely** wohl kaum (inf)

bleeding heart N (pej: = person) Sensibelchen nt (inf)

bleeding-heart ['bliːdɪŋˌhɑːt] ADJ sentimental; **~ Liberal** sentimentaler Liberaler, sentimentale Liberale

bleep [bliːp] N (Rad, TV) Piepton m VI (transmitter) piepen VT (in hospital) doctor rufen

bleeper ['bliːpə] N Funkrufempfänger m, Piepser m (inf)

blemish ['blemɪʃ] N (lit, fig) Makel m; **without (a) ~** makellos, ohne Makel VT object beschädigen; work, beauty beeinträchtigen; reputation, honour beflecken; **~ed skin** unreine Haut; **~ed complexion** unreiner Teint

blench [blentʃ] VI bleich werden, erbleichen (geh)

blend [blend] N Mischung f; (of whiskies also) Blend m; **a ~ of tea** eine Teemischung VT **a** teas, colours etc (ver)mischen; cultures vermischen, miteinander verbinden; **to ~ a building (in) with its surroundings** ein Gebäude seiner Umgebung anpassen **b** (Cook, = stir) einrühren; (in blender) liquids mixen; semisolids pürieren VI **a** (= mix together, teas, whiskies) sich vermischen, sich mischen lassen; (voices, colours) verschmelzen; **sea and sky seemed to ~ into one another** Meer und Himmel schienen ineinander überzugehen or miteinander zu verschmelzen **b** (also **blend in**: = go together, harmonize) harmonieren (with mit), passen (with zu)

▶ **blend in** VT sep flavouring einrühren; colour, tea darunter mischen; building anpassen (with +dat) VI **b**

blended ['blendɪd] ADJ **~ whisky** Blended m

blender ['blendə] N Mixer m, Mixgerät nt

bless [bles] VT **a** (God, priest) segnen; **God ~ (you)** behüt dich/euch Gott; **God ~ America** Gott schütze Amerika; **~ you, my son** Gott segne dich, mein Sohn; **did you buy that for me,**

~ you? (inf) hast du das für mich gekauft? das ist aber lieb von dir! (inf); **~ you, darling, you're an angel** (inf) du bist wirklich lieb, du bist ein Engel (inf); **~ your little cotton socks** (inf) du bist ja ein Schatz (inf); **~ you!** (to sneezer) Gesundheit!; **~ me!** (inf) **~ my soul!** (inf) du meine Güte! (inf); **he's lost it again, ~ him** (iro) prima, er hat es wieder mal verloren! (iro); **I'll be ~ed** or **blest if I'm going to do that!** (inf) das fällt mir ja nicht im Traum ein! (inf); **well, I'll be ~ed!** (inf) so was! **b** **to ~ sb with sth** jdn mit etw segnen; **to be ~ed with** gesegnet sein mit **c** (Eccl, = adore) preisen

blessed ['blesɪd] ADJ **a** (Rel) heilig; **the Blessed X** der selige X; **~ be God!** gepriesen sei Gott!; **of ~ memory** seligen Angedenkens **b** (= fortunate) selig; **~ are the pure in heart** (Bibl) selig sind, die reinen Herzens sind **c** (liter, = giving joy) willkommen **d** (euph inf, = cursed) verflixt (inf); **I couldn't remember a ~ thing** ich konnte mich an rein gar nichts mehr erinnern (inf); **the whole ~ day** den lieben langen Tag (inf); **every ~ evening** aber auch JEDEN Abend ADV verflixt (inf); **he's too ~ lazy** er ist einfach zu faul N **the Blessed, the Blest** die Seligen pl

blessedly ['blesɪdlɪ] ADV zum Glück

Blessed Virgin N Heilige Jungfrau (Maria)

blessing ['blesɪŋ] N (Rel, fig) Segen m; **he can count his ~s** da kann er von Glück sagen; **you can count your ~s you didn't get caught** du kannst von Glück sagen, dass du nicht geschnappt worden bist; **the ~s of civilization** die Segnungen der Zivilisation; **it was a ~ in disguise** es war schließlich doch ein Segen

blest [blest] ADJ (liter) = **blessed** ADJ b, c N = **blessed 3**

blether ['bleðə] (Scot inf) VI quatschen (inf), schwätzen (S Ger inf) N **a** **to have a good ~** einen ordentlichen Schwatz halten (inf) **b** (= person) Quasselstrippe f (inf)

blethering ['bleðərɪŋ] N (inf) Gequatsche nt (inf)

blew [bluː] pret of **blow[2]**

blight [blaɪt] N **a** (on plants) Braunfäule f **b** (fig) **to be a ~ on** or **upon sb's life/happiness** jdm das Leben/jds Glück vergällen; **these slums are a ~ upon the city** diese Slums sind ein Schandfleck für die Stadt; **scenes of urban ~** verfallene Stadtteile; **this poverty which is a ~ upon our nation** die Armut, mit der unser Volk geschlagen ist VT **a** plants zerstören **b** (fig) hopes vereiteln; sb's career, future also verderben; **to ~ sb's life** jdm das Leben verderben

blighter ['blaɪtə] N (Brit inf) Kerl m (inf); (= boy) ungezogener Bengel; (= girl) Luder nt (inf); **a poor ~** ein armer Hund (inf); **you ~** du Idiot! (inf); **what a lucky ~!** so ein Glückspilz!

Blighty ['blaɪtɪ] N (Brit Mil sl) (= leave) Heimaturlaub m; (= England) die Heimat; **he's going back to ~** er geht nach Hause; **a blighty one** (= wound) ein Heimatschuss m

blimey ['blaɪmɪ] INTERJ (Brit, inf) verflucht (inf), Mensch (inf)

blimp [blɪmp] N **a** (Brit, inf) **(Colonel) Blimp** Stockkonservative(r) m, alter Oberst (inf) **b** (Aviat) Kleinluftschiff nt **c** (Film) Blimp m, Schallschutzgehäuse nt

blind [blaɪnd] ADJ (+er) **a** (= sightless) blind; **to go ~** erblinden, blind werden; **a ~ man/woman** ein Blinder/eine Blinde; **~ in one eye** auf einem Auge blind **b** (fig, to beauty, charm etc) blind (to für, gegen); **love is ~** Liebe macht blind; **to be ~ to sb's faults** jds Fehler nicht sehen; **to be ~ to the possibilities** die Möglichkeiten nicht sehen; **to turn a ~ eye to sth** bei etw ein Auge zudrücken; **she remained ~ to the fact that ...** sie sah einfach nicht, dass ... **c** (fig, = lacking judgement) obedience, passion blind; fury, panic also hell; **in a ~ fury** in heller Wut; **~ with passion/rage** blind vor Leidenschaft/Wut; **he came home in a ~ stupor** er kam sinnlos betrunken nach Hause; **~ faith (in**

sth) blindes Vertrauen (in etw *acc*); **~ forces** blinde Kräfte

d (= *vision obscured*) corner unübersichtlich → **blind spot**

e (*Brit inf*) **it's not a ~ bit of use trying to persuade him** es hat überhaupt keinen Zweck, ihn überreden zu wollen; **he hasn't done a ~ bit of work** er hat keinen Strich *or* Schlag getan (*inf*); **but he didn't take a ~ bit of notice** aber er hat sich nicht die Spur darum gekümmert (*inf*)

f (= *false*) *door, window* blind

g (= *without exit*) *passage* ohne Ausgang, blind endend *attr*; (= *without windows and doors*) *wall* ohne Fenster und Türen

VT a (= *make blind*: *light, sun*) blenden; **the explosion ~ed him** er ist durch die Explosion blind geworden; **he was ~ed in the war** er ist kriegsblind; **the war-blinded** die Kriegsblinden *pl*

b (*sun, light*) blenden

c (*fig, love, hate etc*) blind machen (*to* für, gegen); (*wealth, beauty*) blenden; **to ~ sb with science** jdn mit Fachjargon beeindrucken (wollen)

N a the ~ die Blinden *pl*; **it's the ~ leading the ~** (*fig*) das hieße, einen Lahmen einen Blinden führen lassen

b (= *window shade, cloth*) Rollo *nt*, Rouleau *nt*; (*slats*) Jalousie *f*; (*outside*) Rollladen *m*

c (= *cover*) Tarnung *f*; **to be a ~** zur Tarnung dienen

d (*fig sl*, = *booze-up*) Sauferei *f* (*inf*)

e (*US*, = *hide*) Versteck *nt*

ADV a (*Aviat*) fly blind

b (*Cook*) **to bake sth ~** etw vorbacken

c ~ drunk (*inf*) sinnlos betrunken

blind: blind alley N (*lit, fig*) Sackgasse *f*; **to be up a ~** (*fig*) in einer Sackgasse stecken; **blind date** N Rendezvous *nt* mit einem/einer Unbekannten; (= *person*) unbekannter (Rendezvous)partner, unbekannte (Rendezvous)partnerin

blinder ['blaɪndə] N **a** (*US*, = *blinker*) Scheuklappe *f* **b** (*Brit inf*, = *drinking spree*) Kneipkur *f* (*inf*) **c** (*Brit inf*) **to play a ~** (*Sport*) spitzenmäßig spielen (*inf*)

blind flying N (*Aviat*) Blindflug *m*

blindfold ['blaɪndfəʊld] **VT** die Augen verbinden (+*dat*) **N** Augenbinde *f* **ADJ** mit verbundenen Augen; **I could do it ~** (*inf*) das mach ich mit links (*inf*)

blinding ['blaɪndɪŋ] ADJ *light* blendend; *truth* ins Auge stechend; *headache, pain* furchtbar; **as ~ tears filled her eyes** von Tränen geblendet

blindingly ['blaɪndɪŋlɪ] ADV *bright* blendend; **it is ~ obvious** das sieht doch ein Blinder (*inf*)

blind landing N (*Aviat*) Blindlandung *f*

blindly ['blaɪndlɪ] ADV (*lit, fig*) blind(lings)

blind man's buff N Blindekuh *no art*, Blindekuhspiel *nt*

blindness ['blaɪndnɪs] N (*lit, fig*) Blindheit *f* (*to* gegenüber)

blind: blind side N (*Sport*) ungedeckte Seite; **blind spot** N (*Med*) blinder Fleck; (*Aut, Aviat*) toter Winkel; (*Rad*) tote Zone; **to have a ~ about sth** einen blinden Fleck in Bezug auf etw (*acc*) haben; **he has a ~ where she's concerned** er ist ihr gegenüber absolut blind; **trigonometry was his ~** Trigonometrie war sein schwacher Punkt; **blind staggers** N *sing* Taumelsucht *f*; **blind test** N Blindversuch *m*; **blind trust** N (*Fin*) Blind Trust *m*; **blindworm** N Blindschleiche *f*

blink [blɪŋk] **N** Blinzeln *nt*; **in the ~ of an eye** im Nu; **to be on the ~** (*inf*) kaputt sein (*inf*) **VI a** (*person*) blinzeln, zwinkern **b** (*light*) blinken **VT to ~ one's eyes** mit den Augen zwinkern

▶**blink at** VI +*prep obj* (= *ignore*) hinwegsehen über (+*acc*)

▶**blink away** VT *sep tears* wegblinzeln (*inf*)

blinker ['blɪŋkə] N **a** (*US inf*: = *light*) Blinker *m* **b blinkers** PL Scheuklappen *pl*

blinkered ['blɪŋkəd] ADJ **a** (*fig*) engstirnig; **they are all so ~** sie laufen alle mit Scheuklappen herum **b** *horse* mit Scheuklappen

blinking ['blɪŋkɪŋ] ADJ (*Brit, inf*) verflixt (*inf*), blöd (*inf*); **what a ~ cheek!** so eine bodenlose Frechheit! (*inf*); **it's about ~ time too!** das wird aber auch Zeit! (*inf*) ADV verflixt (*inf*) **N a** (*of eyes*) Blinzeln *nt*, Zwinkern *nt* **b** (*of light*) Blinken *nt*

blintz(e) [blɪnts] N (*US, Cook*) dünner Pfannkuchen, Crêpe *f*

blip [blɪp] N leuchtender Punkt (auf dem Radarschirm); (*fig*) kurzzeitiger Tiefpunkt

bliss [blɪs] N Glück *nt*; (*Rel*) (Glück)seligkeit *f*; **a feeling of ~** ein Gefühl *nt* der Wonne; **this is ~!** das ist herrlich *or* eine Wohltat!; **sun, sea, sand, ah sheer ~** Sonne, Meer und Strand, einfach paradiesisch; **ah ~, she sighed** herrlich, seufzte sie; **ignorance is ~** (*prov*) Unwissenheit ist ein Geschenk des Himmels → **marital, domestic ADJ a**

blissful ['blɪsfʊl] ADJ *time* herrlich, paradiesisch; *respite also* wohltuend; *feeling also* wonnig; *happiness* höchste(s); *state, look, smile* (glück)selig; *moments* selig; **in ~ ignorance of the facts** (*iro*) in herrlicher Ahnungslosigkeit; **in ~ ignorance of the fact that ...** (*iro*) in keinster Weise ahnend, dass ...

blissfully ['blɪsfəlɪ] ADV *stretch* wohlig; *peaceful* paradiesisch, herrlich; *smile* selig; **~ happy** überglücklich; **to be ~ ignorant/unaware** so herrlich ahnungslos/arglos sein; **he remained ~ ignorant of what was going on** er ahnte in keinster Weise, was eigentlich vor sich ging

blister ['blɪstə] **N** (*on skin, paint*) Blase *f*; (*Aviat, for gun*) Bordwaffenstand *m* **VI** (*skin*) Blasen bekommen; (*paintwork, metal*) Blasen werfen **VT** *skin, paint* Blasen hervorrufen auf (+*dat*)

blistered ['blɪstəd] ADJ **to have ~ skin/feet/ hands** Blasen auf der Haut/an den Füßen/an den Händen haben; **to be ~** Blasen haben; **~ paint** Blasen werfende Farbe

blistering ['blɪstərɪŋ] ADJ **a** *heat, sun* glühend; *pace* mörderisch **b** (= *scathing*) *attack, criticism* vernichtend, ätzend

blister pack N (Klar)sichtpackung *f*

blister-packed ['blɪstə‚pækt] ADJ klarsichtverpackt

blithe [blaɪð] ADJ (+*er*) (*pej*: = *casual*) unbekümmert, ungeniert; (*liter*: = *cheerful*) fröhlich, munter

blithely ['blaɪðlɪ] ADV *carry on* munter; *say, announce* unbekümmert; *unaware* erstaunlich; **he ~ ignored the problem** er setzte sich ungeniert *or* unbekümmert über das Problem hinweg

blithering ['blɪðərɪŋ] ADJ (*inf*) **a ~ idiot** ein Trottel *m* (*inf*); **don't be such a ~ idiot** du bist ja total bescheuert (*inf*)

B Litt *abbr* **of Bachelor of Letters**

blitz [blɪts] **N a** Blitzkrieg *m*; (*aerial*) Luftangriff *m*; **the Blitz** *deutscher Luftangriff auf britische Städte 1940-41* **b** (*fig inf*) Blitzaktion *f*; **he had a ~ on his room** er machte gründlich in seinem Zimmer sauber **VT** heftig bombardieren

blitzed [blɪtst] ADJ **a** *area* zerbombt **b** (*inf*, = *drunk*) voll (*inf*), zu (*inf*)

blizzard ['blɪzəd] N Schneesturm *m*, Blizzard *m*; (*fig*: *of products, letters, lawsuits*) Flut *f* (*of* von)

bloated ['bləʊtɪd] ADJ **a** aufgedunsen; **I feel absolutely ~** (*inf*) ich bin zum Platzen voll (*inf*) **b** (*fig, with pride, self-importance*) aufgeblasen (*with* vor +*dat*)

bloater ['bləʊtə] N Räucherhering *m*

blob [blɒb] N (*of water, honey, wax*) Tropfen *m*; (*of ink*) Klecks *m*; (*of paint*) Tupfer *m*; (*of ice cream, mashed potato*) Klacks *m*

bloc [blɒk] N (*Pol*) Block *m*

block [blɒk] **N a** Block *m*, Klotz *m*; (= *executioner's block*) Richtblock *m*; (= *engine block*) Motorblock *m*; **~s** (= *toys*) (Bau)klötze *pl*; **huge ugly ~s of concrete** riesige, hässliche Betonklötze; **to be sent to/to go to the ~** dem Henker überantwortet werden/vor den Henker treten; **to put** *or* **lay one's head on the ~** (*fig*) Kopf und Kragen riskieren

b (= *building*) Block *m*; **~ of flats** (*Brit*) Wohnblock *m*; **to take a stroll round the ~** einen Spaziergang um den Block machen; **she lived in the next ~/three ~s from us** (*esp US*) sie wohnte im nächsten Block/drei Blocks *or* Straßen weiter

c (= *division of seats*) Block *m*

d (= *obstruction, in pipe, Med*) Verstopfung *f*; (*mental*) geistige Sperre (*about* in Bezug auf +*acc*), Mattscheibe *f* (*inf*); **I've a mental ~ about it** da habe ich totale Mattscheibe (*inf*)

e (*Comput*) Block *m*

f (*of tickets, shares*) Block *m*

g (*inf*, = *head*) **to knock sb's ~ off** jdm eins überziehen (*inf*)

h (*usu pl*: *also* **starting block**) Startblock *m*; **to be first off the (starting) ~s** (*fig*) als Erster aus den Startlöchern kommen

i (*in ballet shoe*) Spitzenverstärkung *f*; (= *ballet shoe*) spitzenverstärkter Ballettschuh

j (*Typ*) Druckstock *m*

VT a *road, harbour, wheel, deal, move, sale* blockieren; *plans also* im Wege stehen (+*dat*); *traffic also, progress* aufhalten; *pipe* verstopfen; (*Ftbl*) *one's opponent* blocken; *ball* stoppen; **to ~ sb's way/view** jdm den Weg/die Sicht versperren

b *credit* sperren

c (*Comput*) blocken

VI (*Sport*) blocken

▶**block in** VT *sep* **a** (*Art*) andeuten **b** (= *hem in*) einkeilen

▶**block off** VT *sep street* absperren; *fireplace* abdecken

▶**block out** VT *sep* **a** (= *obscure*) *light* nicht durchlassen; *sun also* verdecken; **the trees are blocking out all the light** die Bäume nehmen das ganze Licht weg **b** (= *obliterate*) *part of picture, photograph* wegretuschieren **c** (= *ignore*) *pain, fact, past* verdrängen; *noise* (*double glazing etc*) unterdrücken; (*person*) ausblenden **d** (= *sketch roughly*) andeuten

▶**block up** VT *sep* **a** (= *obstruct*) *gangway* blockieren, versperren; *pipe* verstopfen; **my nose is** *or* **I'm all blocked up** meine Nase ist völlig verstopft **b** (= *close, fill in*) *window, entrance* zumauern; *hole* zustopfen

blockade [blɒ'keɪd] **N a** (*Mil*) Blockade *f*; **under ~** im Blockadezustand; **to break** *or* **run the ~** die Blockade brechen **b** (= *barrier, obstruction*) Sperre *f*, Barrikade *f* **VT** blockieren, sperren

blockade runner N Blockadebrecher *m*

blockage ['blɒkɪdʒ] N Verstopfung *f*; (*in windpipe etc*) Blockade *f*; (= *act*) Blockierung *f*

block: block and tackle N Flaschenzug *m*; **block booking** N (= *travel booking*) Gruppenbuchung *f*; (*Theat*) Gruppenbestellung *f*; **block brake** N (*Tech*) Backenbremse *f*; **blockbuster** N **a** (*inf*) Knüller *m* (*inf*); (= *film also*) Kinohit *m* (*inf*) **b** (*Mil*) große Bombe; **block grant** N Pauschalsubvention *f*; **blockhead** N Dummkopf *m*; **blockhouse** N Blockhaus *nt*

blockish ['blɒkɪʃ] ADJ (*inf*) dumm, doof (*inf*)

block: block letters PL Blockschrift *f*; **block vote** N Stimmenblock *m*

blog [blɒg] N persönliches Tagebuch im Internet

bloke [bləʊk] N (*Brit, inf*) Kerl *m* (*inf*), Typ *m* (*inf*)

blokey ['bləʊkɪ], **blok(e)ish** ['bləʊkɪʃ] ADJ (*Brit inf*) kumpelhaft

blond [blɒnd] ADJ *man, hair, beard* blond

blonde [blɒnd] ADJ blond; *skin* hell **N** (= *woman*) Blondine *f*

blonde bombshell N (*inf*) Superblondine *f* (*inf*)

blood [blʌd] **N a** Blut *nt*; **to give ~** Blut spenden; **to spill** *or* **shed ~** (*in conflict, war*) Blut vergießen; **it makes my ~ boil** das macht mich rasend; **his ~ is up** er ist wütend; **she's out for** or **after his ~** sie will ihm an den Kragen (*inf*); **his ~ ran cold** es lief ihm eiskalt über den Rücken; **this firm needs new ~** diese Firma braucht frisches Blut; **it is like trying to get ~ from a stone** (*prov*) das ist verlorene Liebesmüh; **~, sweat and tears** Blut, Schweiß und Tränen; **he has (their) ~ on his hands** an seinen Händen klebt (ihr) Blut → **bad blood**

b (*fig, = lineage*) Blut *nt*, Geblüt *nt* (*geh*), Abstammung *f*; **a prince of the ~** ein Prinz von edlem Geblüt (*geh*); **it's in his ~** das liegt ihm im Blut; **~ is thicker than water** (*prov*) Blut ist dicker als Wasser (*prov*)

c (*old, = dandy*) Geck *m* (*old*), Stutzer *m* (*dated*)

ATTR (*= purebred*) reinrassig

VT *hounds* an Blut gewöhnen

blood *in cpds* Blut-; **blood alcohol** N Blutalkohol *m*; **blood and thunder** N Mord und Totschlag *m*; **blood-and-thunder** ADJ **~ novel** Reißer *m*; **~ speech** melodramatische *or* donnernde Rede; **blood bank** N Blutbank *f*; **blood bath** N Blutbad *nt*; **blood blister** N Blutblase *f*; **blood brother** N Blutsbruder *m*; **blood cell** N Blutkörperchen *nt*; **blood clot** N Blutgerinnsel *nt*; **blood count** N (*Med*) Blutbild *nt*; **bloodcurdling** ADJ Grauen erregend; **they heard a ~ cry** sie hörten einen Schrei, der ihnen das Blut in den Adern erstarren ließ (*geh*); **blood donor** N Blutspender(in) *m(f)*; **blood feud** N Blutfehde *f*; **blood group** N Blutgruppe *f*; **blood guilt, blood guiltiness** N Blutschuld *f*; **blood heat** N Körpertemperatur *f*; **bloodhound** N **a** (*Zool*) Bluthund *m* **b** (*fig, = detective*) Schnüffler *m* (*inf*), Detektiv *m*

bloodily ['blʌdɪlɪ] ADV *defeat, repress, kill* blutig

bloodiness ['blʌdɪnɪs] N **a** (*of sight, war etc*) Blutigkeit *f* **b** (*inf, = horribleness*) Grässlichkeit *f*, Abscheulichkeit *f*

bloodless ['blʌdlɪs] ADJ (*rare, = without blood*) blutlos; (*= without bloodshed*) *victory, coup* unblutig; (*= pallid*) blutleer, bleich

bloodlessly ['blʌdlɪslɪ] ADV unblutig

bloodlessness ['blʌdlɪsnɪs] N (*of victory, coup*) Unblutigkeit *f*; (*= pallidness*) Blutleere *f*, Bleichheit *f*

blood: blood-letting N Aderlass *m*; **blood lust** N Blutrünstigkeit *f*; **bloodmobile** N (*US*) Blutspendewagen *m*; **blood money** N Mordgeld *nt*; **blood orange** N Blutorange *f*; **blood plasma** N Blutplasma *nt*; **blood poisoning** N Blutvergiftung *f*; **blood pressure** N Blutdruck *m*; **to have high ~** hohen Blutdruck haben; **blood pudding** N ≈ Blutwurst *f*; **blood-red** ADJ blutrot; **blood relation** N Blutsverwandte(r) *mf*; **blood sample** N (*Med*) Blutprobe *f*; **bloodshed** N Blutvergießen *nt*; **bloodshot** ADJ blutunterlaufen; **blood sport** PL *Jagdsport, Hahnenkampf etc*; **bloodstain** N Blutfleck *m*; **bloodstained** ADJ blutig, blutbefleckt; **bloodstock** N reinrassige Zucht; **bloodstone** N Blutjaspis *m*, Heliotrop *m*; **bloodstream** N Blut *nt*, Blutkreislauf *m*; **bloodsucker** N (*Zool, also*) Blutsauger *m*; **blood sugar** N Blutzucker *m*; **~ level** Blutzuckerspiegel *m*; **blood test** N Blutprobe *f*; **bloodthirstiness** N (*of tale, regime*) Blutrünstigkeit *f*; (*of person, animal, disposition also*) Blutgier *f*; **bloodthirsty** ADJ *tale, regime* blutrünstig; *person, animal, disposition also* blutgierig; **blood ties** PL Blutsbande *pl* (*geh*); **blood transfusion** N Blutübertragung *f*, (Blut)transfusion *f*; **blood type** N Blutgruppe *f*; **blood vessel** N Blutgefäß *nt*; **he almost burst a ~** (*lit*) ihm wäre beinahe eine Ader geplatzt; (*fig inf*) ihn traf fast der Schlag

bloody ['blʌdɪ] ADJ (+*er*) **a** (*lit*) *nose, bandage, battle* blutig; **to give sb a ~ nose** (*fig*) (*in contest*) jdm einen Denkzettel verpassen; (*in war*) jdm eine Niederlage beibringen

b (*Brit inf: = damned*) verdammt (*inf*), Scheiß- (*inf*); (*in positive sense*) *genius, wonder* echt (*inf*),

verdammt (*inf*); **it was a ~ nuisance/waste of time** Mann *or* Mensch, das war vielleicht ein Quatsch (*inf*) *or* Scheiß (*inf*)/das war reine Zeitverschwendung; **it was there all the ~ time** Mann (*inf*) *or* Mensch (*inf*) *or* Scheiße (*inf*), das war schon die ganze Zeit da; **I haven't got any ~ time** verdammt noch mal, ich hab keine Zeit (*inf*); **he hasn't got a ~ hope** Mensch *or* Mann, der hat doch überhaupt keine Chance (*inf*); **~ hell!** verdammt! (*inf*), Scheiße! (*inf*); (*in indignation*) verdammt noch mal! (*inf*); (*in amazement*) Menschenskind! (*inf*), meine Fresse! (*sl*); **he is a ~ marvel** er ist echt *or* verdammt gut (*inf*)

c (*inf, = awful*) gräulich (*inf*); *person, behaviour* abscheulich

ADV (*Brit, inf*) verdammt (*inf*), saumäßig (*inf*); *hot, cold, stupid* sau- (*inf*); (*in positive sense*) *good, brilliant* echt (*inf*), verdammt (*inf*); **that's ~ useless, that's no ~ good** das ist doch Scheiße (*inf*); **not ~ likely** da ist überhaupt nichts drin (*inf*); **he can ~ well do it himself** das soll er schön alleine machen, verdammt noch mal!

VT blutig machen

Bloody Mary N *Cocktail aus Tomatensaft und Wodka*

bloody-minded ['blʌdɪ'maɪndɪd] ADJ (*Brit, inf*) stur (*inf*)

blooey ['bluːɪ] ADJ, ADV (*US inf*) kaputt; **to go ~** (*thing*) kaputtgehen; (*= come apart*) zusammenbrechen; (*plan, = not succeed*) daneben gehen (*inf*)

bloom [bluːm] **N a** Blüte *f*; **to be in (full) ~** in (voller) Blüte stehen; **to come/burst into ~** aufblühen/plötzlich erblühen **b** (*fig*) **her skin has lost its ~** ihre Haut ist welk geworden; **in the ~ of youth** in der Blüte der Jugend; **in the first ~ of love** in der ersten Begeisterung ihrer Liebe **c** (*on fruit*) satter Schimmer; (*on peaches*) Flaum *m* **VI** (*lit, fig*) blühen

bloomer ['bluːmə] N (*Brit inf*) grober Fehler; **to make a ~** einen Bock schießen (*inf*)

bloomers ['bluːməz] PL Pumphose *f*

blooming ['bluːmɪŋ] *prp of* **bloom** ADJ (*inf*) verflixt (*inf*); **it was there all the ~ time** verflixt, das war schon die ganze Zeit da! (*inf*) ADV verflixt (*inf*)

blooper ['bluːpə] N (*US, inf*) Schnitzer *m* (*inf*)

blossom ['blɒsəm] **N a** Blüte *f*; **in ~** in Blüte **VI a** (*tree, plant*) blühen **b** (*fig, relationship*) blühen; (*person, trade etc also*) aufblühen; **to ~ into sth** zu etw aufblühen; (*person also*) zu etw erblühen (*geh*); (*relationship*) zu etw wachsen

▶ **blossom out** VI (*fig*) aufblühen (*into* zu)

blot [blɒt] **N a** (*of ink*) (Tinten)klecks *m* **b** (*fig, on honour, reputation*) Fleck *m* (*on* auf +*dat*); **a ~ on his career** ein schwarzer Fleck in seiner Karriere; **a ~ on the landscape** ein Schandfleck *m* in der Landschaft **VT a** (*= make ink spots on*) beklecksen; **to ~ one's copybook** (*fig*) sich unmöglich machen; (*with sb*) sich (*dat*) verderben **b** (*= dry*) *ink, page* ablöschen; *skin, face etc* abtupfen

▶ **blot out** VT *sep* **a** (*lit*) *words* unleserlich machen, verschmieren **b** (*fig, = hide from view*) *landscape, view* verdecken; (*= obliterate*) *memories* auslöschen; *pain* betäuben

blotch [blɒtʃ] **N** (*on skin*) Fleck *m*; (*of ink, colour also*) Klecks *m* **VT** *paper, written work* beklecksen, Flecken machen auf (+*acc*); *skin* fleckig werden lassen

blotchy ['blɒtʃɪ] ADJ (+*er*) *skin* fleckig; *drawing, paint* klecksig; **a rather ~ drawing** ein richtiges Klecksbild

blotter ['blɒtə] N **a** (Tinten)löscher *m* **b** (*US, = record book*) Kladde *f*; (*= police blotter*) Polizeiregister *nt*

blotting ['blɒtɪŋ]: **blotting pad** N Schreibunterlage *f*; **blotting paper** N Löschpapier *nt*

blotto ['blɒtəʊ] ADJ *pred* (*Brit inf: = drunk*) stockbesoffen (*inf*)

blouse [blaʊz] **N a** Bluse *f* **b** (*US, Mil*) (Feld-)bluse *f*

bloused [blaʊzd] ADJ blusig, wie eine Bluse

blouson ['bluːzɒn] N (*Brit*) Blouson *m or nt*

blow¹ [bləʊ] N (*lit, fig*) Schlag *m*; (*fig, = sudden misfortune also*) Schicksalsschlag *m* (*for, to* für); **to come to ~s** handgreiflich werden; **it came to ~s** es gab Handgreiflichkeiten; **at a (single) or one ~** (*fig*) mit einem Schlag (*inf*); **to give sb/sth a ~** jdn/etw schlagen; **to deal sb/sth a ~** (*fig*) jdm/einer Sache einen Schlag versetzen; **to strike a ~ for sth** (*fig*) einer Sache (*dat*) einen großen Dienst erweisen; **without striking a ~** ohne jede Gewalt; **to match sth ~ for ~** etw Schlag auf Schlag kontern; **they matched us ~ for ~** sie haben Schlag auf Schlag gekontert

blow² *vb: pret* **blew**, *ptp* **blown** **VI a** (*wind*) wehen, blasen; **there was a draught** (*Brit*) *or* **draft** (*US*) **~ing in from the window** es zog vom Fenster her; **the wind was ~ing hard** es wehte ein starker Wind

b (*person*) blasen, pusten (*on* auf +*acc*); **to ~ on one's soup** auf die Suppe pusten

c (*= move with the wind*) fliegen; (*leaves, hat, papers also*) geweht werden; **the door blew open/shut** die Tür flog auf/zu

d (*= make sound, bugle, horn*) blasen; (*whistle*) pfeifen; **then the whistle blew** (*Sport*) da kam der Pfiff

e (*fuse, light bulb*) durchbrennen; (*gasket*) platzen

f (*whale*) spritzen; **there she ~s!** Wal in Sicht!

g (*= pant*) pusten (*inf*), schnaufen (*inf*); (*animal*) schnaufen

h (*inf, = leave*) abhauen (*inf*)

VT a (*= move by blowing, breeze*) wehen; (*strong wind, draught*) blasen; (*gale etc*) treiben; (*person*) blasen, pusten (*inf*); **the wind blew the ship off course** der Wind trieb das Schiff vom Kurs ab; **to ~ sb a kiss** jdm eine Kusshand zuwerfen

b (*= drive air into*) *fire* anblasen; *eggs* ausblasen; **to ~ one's nose** sich (*dat*) die Nase putzen

c (*= make by blowing*) *glass, smoke rings* blasen; *bubbles* machen

d *trumpet* blasen; (*Hunt, Mil*) *horn* blasen in (+*acc*); **the referee blew his whistle** der Schiedsrichter pfiff; **to ~ one's own trumpet** (*Brit*) *or* **horn** (*US*) (*fig*) sein eigenes Lob singen

e (*= burn out, blow up*) *safe, bridge etc* sprengen; *valve, gasket* platzen lassen; *transistor* zerstören; **I've ~n a fuse/light bulb** mir ist eine Sicherung/Birne durchgebrannt; **the car blew a tyre** (*Brit*) *or* **tire** (*US*) an dem Auto ist ein Reifen geplatzt; **to be ~n to pieces** (*bridge, car*) in die Luft gesprengt werden; (*person*) zerfetzt werden

f (*inf, = spend extravagantly*) *money* verpulvern (*inf*)

g (*inf, = reveal*) *secret* verraten → **gaff²**

h (*Brit inf, = damn*) **~!** Mist! (*inf*); **~ this rain!** dieser mistige Regen! (*inf*); **~ the expense/what he likes!** das ist doch wurscht, was es kostet/was er will (*inf*); **well, I'll be ~ed** Mensch(enskind)! (*inf*); **I'll be ~ed if** I'll do it ich denke nicht im Traum dran(, das zu tun) (*inf*); **... and ~ me if he still didn't forget** ... und er hat es trotzdem glatt vergessen (*inf*)

i (*inf*) **to ~ one's chances of doing sth** es sich (*dat*) verscherzen, etw zu tun; **I think I've ~n it** ich glaube, ich habs versaut (*inf*)

j (*inf*) → **mind 1**

k (*esp US sl: = fellate*) **to ~ sb** jdm einen blasen (*sl*)

N a (*= expulsion of breath*) Blasen *nt*, Pusten *nt* (*inf*); **to give a ~** blasen, pusten (*inf*); (*when blowing nose*) sich schnäuzen

b (*Brit: = breath of air*) **to go for a ~** sich durchlüften lassen

▶ **blow away** VI (*hat, paper etc*) wegfliegen **VT** *sep* **a** wegblasen; (*breeze also*) wehen **b** (*inf: = kill*) abknallen (*inf*); (*inf: = defeat*) fertig machen (*inf*), in die Pfanne hauen (*inf*)

▶ **blow down** VI (*tree etc*) umfallen, umgeweht werden **VT** *sep* (*lit*) umwehen; **blow me down!** (*inf*) Mensch(enskind)! (*inf*)

▶ **blow in** VI a (*lit*, = *be blown down, window etc*) eingedrückt werden; (= *be blown inside, dust etc*) hinein-/hereinfliegen, hinein-/hereingeweht *or* -geblasen werden; (*wind*) hereinwehen, hereinblasen; **there was a draught blowing in** es zog herein b (*inf*, = *arrive unexpectedly*) hereinschneien (*inf*) (+*prep obj*, -*to* in +*acc*) VT *sep window, door etc* eindrücken; *dust etc* hinein-/ hereinblasen *or* -wehen (+*prep obj*, -*to* in +*acc*)

▶ **blow off** VI wegfliegen VT *sep* wegblasen; (+*prep obj*) blasen von; (*breeze also*) wegwehen; (+*prep obj*) wehen von; **to blow one's/sb's head off** (= *kill*) jdm/jds mit einer Kugel den Kopf jagen (*inf*) VT *insep* (*fig*) steam ablassen (*inf*)

▶ **blow out** VI a (*candle etc*) ausgehen b (*Aut: tyre*) platzen; (*Elec, fuse*) durchbrennen c (*gas, oil*) ausbrechen; (*oil well*) einen Ausbruch haben VT *sep* a *candle* ausblasen, löschen b (= *fill with air*) one's *cheeks* aufblasen c **to blow one's/sb's brains out** sich/jdm eine Kugel durch den Kopf jagen (*inf*) VR (*wind, storm*) sich legen; (*fig, passion*) verpuffen (*inf*)

▶ **blow over** VI a (*tree etc*) umfallen b (*lit, fig, storm, dispute*) sich legen VT *sep tree etc* umstürzen

▶ **blow up** VI a (= *be exploded*) in die Luft fliegen; (*bomb*) explodieren b (*lit, fig, gale, crisis, row*) ausbrechen; **his allegations could blow up in his face** seine Behauptungen könnten nach hinten losgehen c (*fig inf, person*) explodieren (*inf*) VT *sep* a *mine, bridge, person* in die Luft jagen, hochjagen b *tyre, balloon* aufblasen c *photo* vergrößern d (*fig*, = *magnify, exaggerate*) *event* aufbauschen (*into zu*)

blow: blowback N (*Tech, Mil*) Rückstoß *m*; **blow-by-blow** ADJ *account* detailliert; **blow-dry** N **to have a cut and ~** sich (*dat*) die Haare schneiden und föhnen lassen VT föhnen

blower ['bləʊə'] N a (= *device*) Gebläse *nt* b (= *glass blower*) Glasbläser *m* c (*Brit, inf*, = *telephone*) Telefon *nt*; **to be on the ~** an der Strippe hängen (*inf*); **to get on the ~ to sb** jdn anrufen

blow: blowfly N Schmeißfliege *f*; **blowgun** N (= *weapon*) Blasrohr *nt*; **blowhole** N a (*of whale*) Atemloch *nt* b (*Min*) Abzugsloch *nt*; **blow job** N (*sl*) **to give sb a ~** jdm einen blasen (*sl*); **blowlamp** N Lötlampe *f*

blown [bləʊn] *ptp of* **blow²** ADJ *flower* voll aufgeblüht; *glass* mundgeblasen

blow: blowout N a (*inf*, = *meal*) Schlemmerei *f*; **to have a ~** schlemmen (*inf*) b (= *burst tyre*) **he had a ~** ihm ist ein Reifen geplatzt; **in the case of a ~** wenn ein Reifen platzt c (*Elec*) **there's been a ~** die Sicherung ist durchgebrannt d (*Min*) Ausbruch *m*; (*on oil rig*) Ölausbruch *m*; **blowpipe** N a (= *weapon*) Blasrohr *nt* b (*Tech*) Gebläsebrenner *m*, Lötrohr *nt* c (*for glassmaking*) Glasbläserpfeife *f*

blowsy ['blaʊzɪ] ADJ = **blowzy**

blow: blowtorch N Lötlampe *f*; **blow-up** N a (*inf*, = *outburst of temper*) Wutausbruch *m* b (*inf*, = *row*) Krach *m*; **they've had a ~** sie hatten Krach c (*Phot*) Vergrößerung *f*

blowy ['bləʊɪ] ADJ (+*er*) windig

blowzy ['blaʊzɪ] ADJ (+*er*) *woman* schlampig

BLT [ˌbiːɛl'tiː] (*US inf*) *abbr of* **bacon, lettuce, and tomato sandwich**

blub [blʌb] VI (*inf*) heulen (*inf*), flennen (*inf*, *pej*)

blubber ['blʌbə'] N a Walfischspeck *m*; (*inf, on person*) Wabbelspeck *m* (*inf*) b (*inf*, = *weep*) **to have a ~** flennen (*inf*), heulen (*inf*) VTI (*inf*) flennen (*inf*), heulen (*inf*)

▶ **blubber out** VT *sep* (*inf*) flennen (*inf*), heulen (*inf*)

blubberer ['blʌbərə'] N (*inf*) Heulsuse *f* (*inf*)

blubbery ['blʌbərɪ] ADJ a wabb(e)lig (*inf*) b (*inf, = weepy*) verheult (*inf*)

bludgeon ['blʌdʒən] N Knüppel *m*, Keule *f* VT a (= *hit*) verprügeln; **to ~ sb to death** jdn zu Tode prügeln b (*fig*) bearbeiten (*inf*); **he ~ed me into doing it** er hat mich so lange bearbeitet, bis ich es getan habe (*inf*); **I don't want to ~ you into it** ich möchte dich nicht dazu zwingen

blue [bluː] ADJ (+*er*) a blau; **~ with cold** blau vor Kälte; **until you're ~ in the face** (*inf*) bis zur Vergasung (*inf*), bis zum Gehtnichtmehr (*inf*); **once in a ~ moon** alle Jubeljahre (einmal); **like a ~ streak** (*inf*) wie ein geölter Blitz (*inf*); **into the wide** *or* **wild ~ yonder** weit weit weg b (*inf*, = *miserable*) melancholisch, trübsinnig; **to feel ~** den Moralischen haben (*inf*); **to look ~** traurig aussehen c (*inf*, = *obscene*) *language* derb, nicht salonfähig; *joke* schlüpfrig; *film* Porno-, Sex-; **the air was ~ (with oaths)** da habe ich/hat er *etc* vielleicht geflucht (*inf*) d (*Pol*) konservativ N a Blau *nt*; **the boys in ~** (*inf*, = *police*) die Polizei *pl*, die Grünen *pl* (*dated inf*) b (*liter*, = *sky*) Himmel *m*; **out of the ~** (*fig inf*) aus heiterem Himmel (*inf*) c (*Pol*) Konservative(r) *mf* d (*inf*) **the blues** PL (= *depression*) der Moralische (*inf*); **to have the ~s** den Moralischen haben (*inf*) e (*Mus*) **the blues** PL der Blues; **a ~s** *sing* ein Blues f (*Univ Sport*) Student von Oxford oder Cambridge, der bei Wettkämpfen seine Universität vertritt (*oder* vertreten hat); (= *colours*) blaue Mütze, Symbol dafür, dass man seine Universität in Wettkämpfen vertreten hat VT (*inf*, = *spend*) auf den Kopf hauen (*inf*) (*on* für)

blue: blue baby N Baby *nt* mit angeborenem Herzfehler; **Bluebeard** N Ritter Blaubart *m*; **bluebell** N Sternhyazinthe *f*; (*Scot*, = *harebell*) Glockenblume *f*; **blue beret** N Blauhelm *m*; **blueberry** N Blau- *or* Heidelbeere *f*; **bluebird** N Rotkehlhüttensänger *m*; **blue blood** N blaues Blut; **blue-blooded** ADJ blaublütig; **bluebook** N a (*Brit Parl*) Blaubuch *nt* b (*US*: = *list of prominent people*) ≈ Who's Who *nt* c (*US*: = *used-car price list*) Gebrauchtwagenpreisliste *f*, ≈ Schwacke-Liste *f*; **bluebottle** N a Schmeißfliege *f*; **blue cheese** N Blauschimmelkäse *m*; **blue-chip** ADJ *company* erstklassig; *shares also* Blauchip-; *investment* sicher; **blue-collar** ADJ **~ worker/union/jobs** Arbeiter *m*/Arbeitergewerkschaft *f*/Stellen *pl* für Arbeiter; **blue-eyed** ADJ blauäugig; **sb's ~ boy** (*fig*) jds Liebling(sjunge) *m*; **blue helmet** N Blauhelm *m*; **bluejacket** N (*dated inf*) Matrose *m*; **to join the ~s** zu den blauen Jungs gehen (*dated inf*); **blue jeans** PL Bluejeans *pl*, Blue Jeans *pl*; **blue line** N (*US: Typ*) Blaupause *f*

blueness ['bluːnɪs] N a (*lit*) Bläue *f* b (*inf*: = *obscenity, of language*) Derbheit *f*; (*of joke*) Schlüpfrigkeit *f*; (*of film*) Sexgeladenheit *f* (*inf*)

blue: Blue Nile N Blauer Nil; **blue-pencil** VT (= *edit, revise*) korrigieren; (= *delete*) ausstreichen; **blue peter** N (*Naut*) Blauer Peter; **blueprint** N Blaupause *f*; (*fig*) Plan *m*, Entwurf *m*; **to have to draw you a ~?** (*inf*) muss ich dir erst 'ne Zeichnung machen? (*inf*); **blue rib(b)and** N Blaues Band; **blue rinse** N **with her ~** mit ihrem silberblau getönten Haar; **bluestocking** N (*fig*) Blaustrumpf *m*

bluesy ['bluːzɪ] ADJ (*Mus*) bluesartig

blue: bluetit N Blaumeise *f*; **blue-water** ADJ (*Navy*) **~ fleet/ship** Hochseeflotte *f*/-schiff *nt*; **blue whale** N Blauwal *m*

bluff¹ [blʌf] N (= *headland*) Kliff *nt*; (*inland*) Felsvorsprung *m* ADJ rau aber herzlich (*inf*); *honesty, answer* aufrichtig

bluff² VT bluffen; **he ~ed his way through it** er hat sich durchgeschummelt (*inf*) VI bluffen N Bluff *m*; **to call sb's ~** es darauf ankommen lassen; (= *make prove*) jdn auf die Probe stellen

▶ **bluff out** VT *sep* **to bluff it out** sich rausreden (*inf*); **to bluff one's way out of sth** sich aus etw rausreden (*inf*)

bluffer ['blʌfə'] N Bluffer *m*

bluish ['bluːɪʃ] ADJ bläulich

blunder ['blʌndə'] N (dummer) Fehler, Schnitzer *m* (*inf*); (*socially also*) Fauxpas *m*; **to make a ~** einen Bock schießen (*inf*); (*socially*) einen Fauxpas begehen VI a (= *make a blunder*) einen Bock schießen (*inf*), Mist bauen (*inf*); (*socially*) sich blamieren b (= *move clumsily*) tappen (*into* gegen); **to ~ in/out** hinein-/herein-/ hinaus-/heraustappen; **to ~ into a trap** (*lit, fig*) in eine Falle tappen; **to ~ into war/a life of crime** in einen Krieg/ein kriminelles Leben hineinschlittern; **he ~ed through the poem** er kämpfte sich mühsam durch das Gedicht

blunderbuss ['blʌndəbʌs] N Donnerbüchse *f*

blunderer ['blʌndərə'] N Schussel *m* (*inf*); (*socially*) Elefant *m* (*inf*)

blundering ['blʌndərɪŋ] ADJ a *person* (= *making mistakes*) schusselig (*inf*); (*socially*) ohne jedes Feingefühl; **~ idiot** Erztrottel *m* (*inf*) b (= *clumsy*) tollpatschig; *reading* holp(e)rig N Schussligkeit *f* (*inf*); (*socially*) gesellschaftliche Schnitzer *pl*

blunt [blʌnt] ADJ (+*er*) a stumpf; **with a ~ instrument** mit einem stumpfen Gegenstand b (= *outspoken*) *person* geradeheraus *pred*; *speech, warning, message, language* unverblümt; *fact* nackt, unbeschönigt; **he's rather a ~ person** er drückt sich ziemlich unverblümt *or* deutlich aus; **to be ~ about sth** sich unverblümt zu etw äußern; **he was very ~ about it** er hat sich sehr deutlich ausgedrückt; **let me be ~ about this** lassen Sie mich das ganz ohne Umschweife sagen VT *knife etc* stumpf machen; (*fig*) *palate, senses* abstumpfen; **his wits had been ~ed** er war geistig abgestumpft

bluntly ['blʌntlɪ] ADV *speak* freiheraus, geradeheraus; **he told us quite ~ what he thought** er sagte uns ganz unverblümt seine Meinung

bluntness ['blʌntnɪs] N a (*of blade, needle*) Stumpfheit *f* b (= *outspokenness*) Unverblümtheit *f*

blur [blɜː'] N verschwommener Fleck; **the ~ of their faces** ihre verschwommenen Gesichter; **the trees became a ~** man konnte die Bäume nur noch verschwommen erkennen; **a ~ of colours** (*Brit*) *or* **colors** (*US*) ein buntes Durcheinander von Farben VT a *inscription* verwischen; *writing also* verschmieren; *view* verschleiern; *outline, photograph* unscharf *or* verschwommen machen; *sound* verzerren; **to have ~red vision** nur noch verschwommen sehen; **to be/become ~red** undeutlich sein/werden; (*image etc also*) verschwommen sein/verschwimmen; **her eyes were ~red with tears** vor Tränen schwammen ihr die Augen; **the tape is ~red here** an dieser Stelle ist die Aufnahme verzerrt b (*fig*) *senses, mind, judgement* trüben; *memory also, meaning* verwischen; *intention* in den Hintergrund drängen VI (*vision, image*) verschwommen werden, verschwimmen

blurb [blɜːb] N Material *nt*, Informationen *pl*; (*on book cover*) Klappentext *m*, Waschzettel *m*

blurry ['blɜːrɪ] ADJ (+*er*) *outline, photograph* verschwommen, unscharf; *vision* verschwommen; *view* verschleiert

blurt (out) [blɜːt('aʊt)] VT *sep* herausplatzen mit (*inf*)

blush [blʌʃ] VI a (= *go red*) rot werden, erröten (*with* vor +*dat*) b (*fig*, = *be ashamed*) sich schämen (*for* für); **I ~ to say so** es ist mir peinlich, das zu sagen N Erröten *nt no pl*; **with a ~** errötend; **without a ~** ohne rot zu werden; **to spare** *or* **save sb's ~es** jdn nicht in Verlegenheit bringen; **to put sb to the ~** (*dated*) jdn in Verlegenheit bringen; **the first ~ of dawn** (*fig*) der zarte Schimmer der Morgenröte; **at first ~** auf den ersten Blick

blusher ['blʌʃə'] N Rouge *nt*

blushing ['blʌʃɪŋ] ADJ errötend; **the ~ bride** die sittsame Braut

bluster ['blʌstə'] VI a (*wind*) tosen, toben b (*fig: person*) ein großes Geschrei machen; (*angrily also*) toben VT **to ~ one's way out of it/sth**

es/etw lautstark abstreiten **N** (*of person*) großes Geschrei; (*angry also*) Toben *nt*

blustering ['blʌstərɪŋ] **⊃** person polternd; *manner* stürmisch

blustery ['blʌstərɪ] ADJ *wind, day* stürmisch

Blu-Tack® ['bluːtæk] N Klebmasse *f*

Blvd. *abbr of* boul**c**

BM **a** *abbr of* British **.** **br of Bachelor of Medicine**

BMA *abbr of* British Medical Association *britischer Ärzteverband*

B-movie ['biːmuːvɪ] N *als Beiprogramm gezeigter Kinofilm*, B-Movie *nt* (*spec*)

B Mus *abbr of* Bachelor of Music

BMX *abbr of* bicycle motocross (= *sport*) BMX--Radsport *m*, BMX-biking *nt*; (= *bicycle*) BMX--Rad *nt*

BO (*inf*) *abbr of* body odour Körpergeruch *m*

boa ['bəʊə] N Boa *f*; ~ **constrictor** Boa constrictor *f*

boar [bɔː] N (= *male pig*) Eber *m*; (*wild*) Keiler *m*; ~'s **head** Schweinskopf *m*

board [bɔːd] N **a** Brett *nt*; (= *blackboard*) Tafel *f*; (= *notice board*) schwarzes Brett; (= *signboard*) Schild *nt*; (= *floorboard*) Diele(nbrett *nt*) *f*; **the ~s** (*Theat*) die Bretter

b (= *provision of meals*) Kost *f*, Verpflegung *f*; ~ **and lodging** Kost und Logis; **full/half** ~ Voll-/Halbpension *f*

c (= *group of officials*) Ausschuss *m*; (= *board of inquiry, examiners also*) Kommission *f*; (*with advisory function*, = *board of trustees*) Beirat *m*; (= *permanent official institution*: = *gas board, harbour board etc*) Behörde *f*; (*of company*: *also* **board of directors**) Vorstand *m*; (*of British/American company*) Verwaltungsrat *m*; (*including shareholders, advisers*) Aufsichtsrat *m*; **to be on the ~, to have a seat on the ~** im Vorstand/Aufsichtsrat sein *or* sitzen; ~ **of governors** (*Brit, Sch*) Verwaltungsrat *m*; **Board of Trade** (*Brit*) Handelsministerium *nt*; (*US*) Handelskammer *f*

d (*Naut, Aviat*) **on** ~ an Bord; **to go on** ~ **the ship/plane** an Bord gehen; **on** ~ **the bus** im Bus; **he held a party on** ~ **his yacht** er veranstaltete eine Party auf seiner Jacht

e (= *cardboard*) Pappe *f*; (*Typ*) Deckel *m*

f (= *board of interviewers*) Gremium *nt* (zur Auswahl von Bewerbern); (= *interview*) Vorstellungsgespräch *nt* (vor einem Gremium); **to be on a** ~ einem Gremium zur Auswahl von Bewerbern angehören

g (*US St Ex*) Notierung *f*; (*inf*, = *stock exchange*) Börse *f*

h (*fig phrases*) **across the** ~ allgemein, generell; *criticize, agree, reject* pauschal; **a wage increase of £10 per week across the** ~ eine allgemeine *or* generelle Lohnerhöhung von £ 10 pro Woche; **to go by the** ~ (*work, plans, ideas*) unter den Tisch fallen; (*dreams, hopes*) zunichte werden; (*principles*) über Bord geworfen werden; (*business*) zugrunde *or* zu Grunde gehen; **that's all gone by the** ~ daraus ist nichts geworden; **to take sth on** ~ (= *understand*) etw begreifen; (= *deal with*) sich einer Sache (*gen*) annehmen

VT **a** (= *cover with boards*) mit Brettern verkleiden

b *ship, plane* besteigen, an Bord (+*gen*) gehen/kommen; *train, bus* einsteigen in (+*acc*); (*Naut, in attack*) entern

VI **a** in Pension sein (*with* bei)

b (= *lodger*) Internatsschüler(in) *m(f)* sein

c (*Aviat*) die Maschine besteigen; **flight ZA173 now ~ing at gate 13** Passagiere des Fluges ZA173, bitte zum Flugsteig 13

▶ **board out** **VT** *sep person* in Pension schicken (*with* bei) **VI** in Pension wohnen (*with* bei)

▶ **board up** VT *sep door, window* mit Brettern vernageln

boarder ['bɔːdə] N **a** Pensionsgast *m*; **to take in ~s** Leute in Pension nehmen **b** (*Sch*) Internatsschüler(in) *m(f)*; (= *weekly boarder*) *während der Woche im Internat wohnender Schüler* (*dated*, = *day boarder*) *Tagesschüler, der in der Schule zu Mittag isst* **c** (*Naut*) Mitglied *nt* eines Enterkommandos

board game N Brettspiel *nt*

boarding ['bɔːdɪŋ]: **boarding card** N Bordkarte *f*; **boarding house** N **a** Pension *f* **b** (*Sch*) Wohngebäude *nt* eines Internats; **boarding party** N (*Naut*) Enterkommando *nt*; **boarding pass** N Bordkarte *f*; **boarding school** N Internat *nt*

board: **board meeting** N Vorstandssitzung *f*; **boardroom** N Sitzungssaal *m* (*des Vorstands*); **he's** ~ **material** er hat Führungspotenzial *or*-potential; **boardroom floor** N Vorstandsetage *f*; **boardroom politics** PL Firmenklüngel *m* (*inf*); **board school** N (*Brit, Hist*) staatliche Schule; **boardwalk** N (*US*) Holzsteg *m*; (*on beach*) hölzerne Uferpromenade

boast [bəʊst] **N a** Prahlerei *f* **b** (= *source of pride*) Stolz *m*; **it is their** ~ **that ...** sie rühmen sich, dass ... **VI** prahlen (*about, of* mit *to sb* jdm gegenüber); **without ~ing, without wishing to** ~ ohne zu prahlen **VT a** (= *possess*) sich rühmen (+*gen*) (*geh*) **b** (= *say boastfully*) prahlen

boaster ['bəʊstə] N Aufschneider(in) *m(f)*, Prahlhans *m* (*inf*)

boastful ['bəʊstfʊl] ADJ , **boastfully** ['bəʊstfəlɪ] ADV prahlerisch

boastfulness ['bəʊstfʊlnɪs] N Prahlerei *f*

boasting ['bəʊstɪŋ] N Prahlerei *f* (*about, of* mit)

boat [bəʊt] **N a** (= *small vessel*) Boot *nt*; (*wooden: on lake, river etc also*) Kahn *m*; (*seagoing*: = *passenger boat*) Schiff *nt*; (= *pleasure steamer etc*) Dampfer *m*; **by** ~ mit dem Schiff; **to miss the** ~ (*fig inf*) den Anschluss verpassen; **to push the** ~ **out** (*fig inf*: = *celebrate*) auf den Putz hauen (*inf*); **we're all in the same** ~ (*fig inf*) wir sitzen alle in einem *or* im gleichen Boot **b** (= *gravy boat*) Sauciere *f*

boat: **boatbuilder** N Bootsbauer *m*; **boatbuilding** N Bootsbau *m*; **boat deck** N Bootsdeck *nt*

boater ['bəʊtə] N **a** (= *hat*) steifer Strohhut, Kreissäge *f* (*inf*) **b** (= *person*) Bootsfahrer(in) *m(f)*, Kahnfahrer(in) *m(f)*

boat: **boatful** N Schiffs-/Bootsladung *f*; **boat hire** N Bootsverleih *m*; (= *company*) Bootsverleiher *m*; **boathook** N Bootshaken *m*; **boathouse** N Bootshaus *nt* *or* -schuppen *m*

boating ['bəʊtɪŋ] N Bootfahren *nt*; **to go** ~ Bootsfahrten/eine Bootsfahrt machen; ~ **holiday/trip** Bootsferien *pl*/-fahrt *f*

boat: **boatload** N Bootsladung *f*; **boatman** N (*handling boat*) Segler *m*; Ruderer *m*; Paddler *m*; (*working with boats*) Bootsbauer *m*; (= *hirer*) Bootsverleiher *m*; **boat people** PL Bootsflüchtlinge *pl*; **boat race** N Regatta *f*; **boat-shaped** ADJ kahnförmig

boatswain, bosun, bo's'n ['bəʊsn] N Bootsmann *m*; ~'s **mate** Bootsmannsgehilfe *m*

boat: **boat train** N Zug *m* mit Fährenanschluss; **boatyard** N Bootshandlung *f*; (*as dry dock*) Liegeplatz *m*

Bob [bɒb] N *dim of* Robert ... and ~'s your uncle! (*inf*) ... und fertig ist der Lack! (*inf*)

bob¹ [bɒb] **VI a** (= *move up and down*) sich auf und ab bewegen; (*rabbit*) hoppeln; (*bird's tail*) wippen; (*boxer*) tänzeln; **to** ~ **(up and down) in** *or* **on the water** auf dem Wasser schaukeln; (*cork, piece of wood etc*) sich im Wasser auf und ab bewegen; **he** ~**bed out of sight** er duckte sich **b** (= *curtsey*) knicksen (*to sb* vor jdm) **VT a** (= *move jerkily*) *head* nicken mit; (*bird*) *tail* wippen mit **b** *curtsey* machen; **to** ~ **a greeting** zum Gruß kurz nicken **N a** (= *curtsey*) Knicks(chen *nt*) *m* **b** (*of head*) Nicken *nt no pl*; (*of bird's tail*) Wippen *nt no pl*

▶ **bob down** **VI** sich ducken **VT** *sep one's head* ducken

▶ **bob up** **VI** (*lit, fig*) auftauchen **VT** *sep* he bobbed his head up sein Kopf schnellte hoch

bob² N *pl* bob (*dated Brit, inf*) Shilling *m*; **that must have cost a** ~ **or two** das muss schon ein paar Euro gekostet haben (*inf*); **that must be worth a few** ~ das muss eine Stange Geld wert sein (*inf*); **he must be worth a few** ~ er muss eine Stange Geld haben (*inf*)

bob³ **N a** (= *haircut*) Bubikopf *m* **b** (= *horse's tail*) gestutzter Schwanz *m* **c** (= *weight: on pendulum, plumb line*) Gewicht *nt* **d** (*Fishing*, = *float*) Schwimmer *m* **e** a few/various bits and ~s so ein paar/verschiedene Dinge; **my personal bits and ~s** meine Siebensachen; **the usual plastic bits and ~s** die sonst üblichen Plastikdinger (*inf*); **to sell bits and ~s** Trödel verkaufen **VT** **to have one's hair ~bed** sich (*dat*) einen Bubikopf schneiden lassen; ~**bed** kurz geschnitten, gestutzt

bob⁴ N (= *sleigh*) Bob *m*; (= *runner*) Kufe *f*; **two-/four-man** ~ Zweier-/Viererbob *m*

bob-a-job [ˌbɒbə'dʒɒb] (*Brit*) *leichte, von Pfadfindern verrichtete Haus- und Gartenarbeit für ein geringes Entgelt* ~ **week** Woche, *in der Pfadfinder leichte Haus- und Gartenarbeiten für ein geringes Entgelt verrichten*

bobbin ['bɒbɪn] N Spule *f*; (= *cotton reel*) Rolle *f*

bobble ['bɒbl] N **a** Bommel *f*, Pompon *m* **b** (*US, inf*, = *mistake*) Schnitzer *m* (*inf*)

bobble hat N (*Brit*) Pudelmütze *f*

Bobby ['bɒbɪ] N *dim of* Robert

bobby ['bɒbɪ] N (*dated Brit inf*) Bobby *m*, Schupo *m* (*dated*)

bobby: **bobby-dazzler** N (*dated Brit inf*) (= *object*) Knüller *m* (*inf*), Sensation *f*; (= *girl*) Augenweide *f*; **bobby pin** N (*US*) Haarklemme *f*; **bobby sox** PL (*dated US*) kurze Söckchen *pl*; **bobbysoxer** N (*dated US, inf*) Teenager *m*, junges Mädchen

bob: **bob cap** N Pudelmütze *f*; **bobcat** N (*US*) Luchs *m*; **bobsleigh**, (*US*) **bobsled** **N** Bob *m* **VI** Bob fahren; **bobtail** N gestutzter Schwanz; **bobtail cap, bobtail hat** N Bommelmütze *f*; **bobtailed** ADJ *horse, dog* mit gestutztem Schwanz

Boche [bɒʃ] N (*pej inf*) Boche *m*

bod [bɒd] N **a** (*Brit, inf*: = *person*) Mensch *m*; **odd** ~ komischer Kerl **b** (*sl*: = *body*) Body *m* (*sl*)

bodacious [bəʊ'deɪʃəs] ADJ (*US inf*) toll

bode [bəʊd] **VI** **to** ~ **well/ill** ein gutes/schlechtes Zeichen sein **VT** bedeuten, ahnen lassen; **that** ~**s no good** das bedeutet nichts Gutes, das lässt Böses ahnen

bodge [bɒdʒ] N, VT = **botch**

bodice ['bɒdɪs] N **a** Mieder *nt*; (*of dress also*) Oberteil *nt* **b** (= *vest*) Leibchen *nt*

bodice: **bodice ripper** N (*inf*) schwülstiger historischer Film/Roman; **bodice-ripping** ADJ *attr* (*inf*) ~ **film/novel** schwülstiger historischer Film/Roman

-bodied [-'bɒdɪd] ADJ *suf* -gebaut, von ... Körperbau

bodiless ['bɒdɪlɪs] ADJ körperlos

bodily ['bɒdɪlɪ] ADJ (= *physical*) körperlich; ~ **illness** Krankheit *f* des Körpers; ~ **needs/wants** leibliche Bedürfnisse *pl*; ~ **harm** Körperverletzung *f*; ~ **functions/fluids** Körperfunktionen/-flüssigkeiten *pl*; ~ **injury** Körperverletzungen *pl* **ADV a** (= *forcibly*) gewaltsam **b** (= *in person*) leibhaftig **c** (= *all together*) geschlossen; (= *in one piece*) ganz

bodkin ['bɒdkɪn] N **a** (*Sew*) Durchziehnadel *f* **b** (*Hist*: = *hairpin*) lange Haarnadel; (*obs*, = *dagger*) Dolch *m*

body ['bɒdɪ] N **a** (*of man, animal*) Körper *m*; (*of human also*) Leib *m* (*geh*); **the** ~ **of Christ** der Leib des Herrn; **just enough to keep** ~ **and soul together** gerade genug, um Leib und Seele zusammenzuhalten; **she was committed,** ~ **and soul** sie war mit Leib und Seele bei der Sache **b** (= *corpse*) Leiche *f*, Leichnam *m* (*geh*) → **dead** **c** (= *main part of structure, of plane, ship*) Rumpf *m*, Körper *m*; (*of string instrument*) Korpus *m*, Schallkörper *m*; (*of church, speech, army: also* main body) Hauptteil *m*; **the main ~ of his readers/the students** das Gros seiner Leser/der Studenten; **in the ~ of the House** (*Brit, Parl*) im Plenum

d (= *coachwork: of car*) Karosserie *f*

e (= *group of people*) Gruppe *f*; **the student ~** die Studentenschaft; **a ~ of troops** ein Truppenverband *m*; **a great ~ of followers/readers** eine große Anhängerschaft/Leserschaft; **a large ~ of people** eine große Menschenmenge; **in a ~** geschlossen

f (= *organization*) Organ *nt*; (= *committee*) Gremium *nt*; (= *corporation*) Körperschaft *f* → **corporate, politic**

g (= *quantity*) **a ~ of facts/evidence/data** Tatsachen-/Beweis-/Datenmaterial *nt*; **a ~ of laws/legislation** ein Gesetzeskomplex *m*; **a large ~ of water** eine große Wassermasse

h (*inf*, = *person*) Mensch *m*

i (*Math, Phys, Chem*) Körper *m*

j (= *substance, thickness, of wine*) Körper *m*; (*of soup*) Substanz *f*; (*of paper, cloth*) Festigkeit *f*, Stärke *f*; **this conditioner will add ~ to your hair** diese Pflegespülung gibt Ihrem Haar mehr Volumen

k (*also* **body stocking**) Body *m*

body: body armour, (*US*) **body armor** N Schutzkleidung *f*; **body bag** N Leichensack *m*; **body blow** N Körperschlag *m*; (*fig*) Schlag *m* ins Kontor (*to, for* für); **body builder** N **a** (= *food*) Kraftnahrung *f* **b** (= *apparatus*) Heimtrainer *m* **c** (= *person*) Bodybuilder(in) *m(f)*; **body building** N Bodybuilding *nt* **ADJ** *exercise* muskelkräftigend; *food* stärkend, kräftigend; **bodycheck** N Bodycheck *m*; **body clock** N innere Uhr; **body control** N Körperbeherrschung *f*; **body count** N (*Mil*) Zählung *f* der Toten; **body double** N (*Film, TV*) Körperdouble *nt*; **body drop** N (*Judo*) Körperwurf *m*; **body fascism** N *Diskriminierung aufgrund körperlicher Merkmale*; **body fluids** PL (*Physiol*) Körpersäfte *pl*; **body growth** N körperliches Wachstum; **bodyguard** N (= *one person*) Leibwächter *m*; (= *group*) Leibwache *f*; **body heat** N Körperwärme *f*; **body language** N Körpersprache *f*; **body lotion** N Körperlotion *f*; **body mike** N Umhängemikrofon *nt*; **body odour** N, **body odor** (*US*) N Körpergeruch *m*; **body piercing** N Piercing *nt*; **body popping** N Breakdance *m*; **body (repair) shop** N Karosseriewerkstatt *f*; **body scanner** N Scanner *m*; **body scissors** N *sing* (*Wrestling*) über den Körper angelegte Schere; **body search** N Leibesvisitation *f*; **bodyshell** N (*Aut*) Karosserie *f*; **body shop** N **a** = **body (repair) shop** **b** (*in factory*) Karosseriewerk *nt*; **body slam** N (*Wrestling*) Wurf *m*; **body snatcher** N Leichenräuber(in) *m(f)*; **body stocking** N Body(stocking) *m*; **body-surf** VI bodysurfen; **body-surfing** N, *no pl* Bodysurfing *nt*; **body swerve** N **to give sb/sth a ~** (*fig inf*) einen weiten Bogen um jdn/etw machen; **body temperature** N Körpertemperatur *f*; **body warmer** N Thermoweste *f*; **bodywork** N (*Aut*) Karosserie *f*

Boer [ˈbəʊə] **N** Bure *m*, Burin *f* **ADJ** burisch; **the ~ War** der Burenkrieg

B of E *abbr of* **Bank of England**

boffin [ˈbɒfɪn] N (*Brit, inf*) Eierkopf *m* (*inf*), Egghead *m* (*inf*)

boffo [ˈbɒfəʊ] ADJ (*US inf*) klasse (*inf*), super (*inf*)

bog [bɒɡ] N **a** Sumpf *m*; (= *peat bog*) (Torf-)moor *nt* **b** (*Brit inf: = toilet*) Lokus *m* (*inf*), Klo *nt* (*inf*)

▸ **bog down** VT *sep* **to be bogged down** (*lit*) stecken bleiben; (*fig*) stecken geblieben sein, sich festgefahren haben; (*in details*) sich verzettelt haben; **to get bogged down** (*lit*) stecken bleiben; (*fig also*) sich festfahren; (*in details*) sich verzetteln

bogey¹, bogy [ˈbəʊɡɪ] N *pl* **bogeys, bogies** **a** (= *spectre, goblin*) Kobold *m*, Butzemann *m* **b** (*fig, = bugbear*) Popanz *m*, Schreckgespenst *nt* **c** (*Brit inf*) Popel *m* (*inf*)

bogey² (*Golf*) **N** Bogey *nt* **VT** **to ~ a hole** ein Bogey spielen or machen

bogeyman [ˈbəʊɡɪmæn] *pl* **bogeymen** [-men] Butzemann *m*, schwarzer Mann

boggle [ˈbɒɡl] VI (*inf*) glotzen (*inf*), völlig sprachlos sein; **the mind ~s** das ist nicht or kaum auszumalen (*inf*); **stories that make the mind ~** unglaubliche Geschichten

boggy [ˈbɒɡɪ] ADJ (*+er*) *ground* sumpfig, morastig

bogie [ˈbəʊɡɪ] N (*Rail*) Drehgestell *nt*; (= *trolley*) Draisine *f*, Dräsine *f*

bog paper, bog roll N (*Brit inf*) Klopapier *nt* (*inf*)

bog-standard [ˌbɒɡˈstændəd] ADJ (*Brit, inf*) stinknormal (*inf*)

bogus [ˈbəʊɡəs] ADJ *doctor, lawyer, name* falsch; *pearls also, document* gefälscht; *company, transaction* Schwindel-; *claim* erfunden; **~ asylum seekers** Scheinasylanten *pl*

bogy [ˈbəʊɡɪ] N = **bogey¹**

Bohemia [bəʊˈhiːmɪə] N (*Geog*) Böhmen *nt*; (*fig*) Boheme *f*

Bohemian [bəʊˈhiːmɪən] **N** **a** Böhme *m*, Böhmin *f* **b** (*fig*) **bohemian** Bohemien *m* **ADJ** **a** böhmisch **b** (*fig*) **bohemian** (*lifestyle*) unkonventionell, unbürgerlich; *circles, quarter* Künstler-

bohemianism [bəʊˈhiːmɪənɪzəm] N unkonventionelle *or* unbürgerliche Lebensweise

boho [ˈbəʊhəʊ] (*inf*) **N** unkonventioneller Künstler, unkonventionelle Künstlerin **ADJ** unkonventionell

boil¹ [bɔɪl] N (*Med*) Furunkel *m*

boil² **VI** **a** (*lit*) kochen; (*water also, Phys*) sieden; **the kettle was ~ing** das Wasser im Kessel kochte; **~ing oil** siedendes Öl; **allow to ~ gently** (*Cook*) langsam kochen; **to let the kettle ~ dry** das Wasser im Kessel verkochen lassen

b (*fig inf, = be hot*) **~ing hot water** kochend heißes Wasser; **it was ~ing (hot) in the office** es war eine Affenhitze im Büro (*inf*); **I was ~ing (hot)** mir war fürchterlich heiß; **you'll ~ in that sweater** in dem Pullover schwitzt du dich ja tot (*inf*)

c (*fig inf, = be angry*) kochen, schäumen (*with* vor +*dat*)

d (*fig, sea, river*) brodeln, tosen

VT kochen; **~ed/hard ~ed egg** weich/hart gekochtes Ei; **~ed potatoes** Salzkartoffeln *pl*

N **to bring sth to the** (*Brit*) or **a** (*US*) **~** etw aufkochen lassen; **to keep sth on the ~** etw kochen or sieden lassen; **to be on/come to/go off the ~** kochen/zu kochen anfangen/aufhören

▸ **boil away** VI **a** (= *go on boiling*) weiterkochen **b** (= *evaporate completely*) verdampfen

▸ **boil down** *sep* **a** einkochen **VI** **a** (*jam etc*) dickflüssig werden **b** (*fig*) **to boil down to sth** auf etw (*acc*) hinauslaufen; **what it boils down to is that ...** das läuft darauf hinaus, dass ...

▸ **boil over** VI **a** (*lit*) überkochen **b** (*fig, situation, quarrel*) den Siedepunkt erreichen; **he just boiled over** ihm platzte der Kragen (*inf*)

▸ **boil up** VI **a** (*lit*) aufkochen **b** (*fig*) **he could feel the anger boiling up in him** er fühlte, wie die Wut in ihm aufstieg

boiled shirt N (*inf*) weißes Hemd

boiled sweet N Bonbon *nt*

boiler [ˈbɔɪlə] N **a** (*domestic*) Boiler *m*, Warmwasserbereiter *m*; (*in ship, engine*) (Dampf)kessel *m*; (*old, for washing*) Waschkessel *m* **b** (= *chicken*) Suppenhuhn *nt*

boiler: boiler house N Kesselhaus *nt*; **boilermaker** N Kesselschmied *m*; **boilermaking** N Kesselschmieden *nt*; **boilerman** N Heizer *m*; **boilerplate letter** N (*US*) (Brief)rumpf *m*; **boiler room** N Kesselraum *m*; **boiler suit** N (*Brit*) Overall *m*, blauer Anton (*inf*), Blaumann *m* (*inf*)

boiling [ˈbɔɪlɪŋ]: **boiling fowl** N Suppenhuhn *nt*; **boiling point** N (*lit, fig*) Siedepunkt *m*; **at ~** (*lit, fig*) auf dem Siedepunkt; **to reach ~** (*lit, fig*) den Siedepunkt erreichen; (*feelings also, per-*

son) auf dem Siedepunkt anlangen; **boiling pot** N (*fig, = tumultuous situation*) Tohuwabohu *nt*

boisterous [ˈbɔɪstərəs] ADJ **a** (= *exuberant, noisy*) *person* ausgelassen; *game, party, dance also* wild **b** (= *rough*) *wind* tosend; *sea also* aufgewühlt

boisterously [ˈbɔɪstərəslɪ] ADV *shout, sing, laugh* ausgelassen; *play* wild, übermütig

bold [bəʊld] ADJ (*+er*) **a** (= *brave*) kühn (*geh*), mutig; *deed, plan also* verwegen

b (= *impudent, forward*) unverfroren, dreist; **to be** or **make so ~ as to ...** sich (*dat*) erlauben, zu ..., sich erkühnen, zu ... (*geh*); **might I be so ~ as to ...?** wenn ich es mir erlauben darf, zu ...?; **might I make so ~ as to help myself?** darf ich so frei sein und mich bedienen?; **to make ~ with sth** (*dat*) die Freiheit herausnehmen, sich bei etw einfach zu bedienen; **as ~ as brass** (*inf*) rotzfrech (*inf*)

c (= *striking*) *colours, pattern, stripes* kräftig; *checks also* grob; *strokes also* kühn (*geh*); *handwriting* kraftvoll, kühn (*geh*); *style* kraftvoll, ausdrucksvoll; **to bring out in ~ relief** stark hervortreten lassen

d (*Typ*) fett; (= *secondary bold*) halbfett; **~ type** Fettdruck *m*; **to set sth in ~ (type)** etw fett/halbfett drucken

boldface [ˈbəʊldfeɪs] (*Typ*) **N** (halb)fette Schrift **ADJ** (halb)fett; **in ~ type** (halb)fett, in (halb)fetter Schrift

boldly [ˈbəʊldlɪ] ADV **a** (= *bravely*) mutig, kühn (*geh*) **b** (= *forthrightly*) unverfroren, dreist **c** (= *strikingly*) auffallend

boldness [ˈbəʊldnɪs] N **a** (= *bravery*) Kühnheit *f* (*geh*), Mut *m*; (*of deed, plan also*) Verwegenheit *f* **b** (= *impudence, forwardness*) Unverfrorenheit *f*, Dreistigkeit *f* **c** (*of colours, pattern, stripes*) Kräftigkeit *f*; (*of checks also*) Grobheit *f*; (*of strokes also*) Kühnheit *f* (*geh*); (*of style*) Ausdruckskraft *f*

bole [bəʊl] N Baumstamm *m*

bolero [bəˈlɛərəʊ] N (*all senses*) Bolero *m*

Bolivia [bəˈlɪvɪə] N Bolivien *nt*

Bolivian [bəˈlɪvɪən] **N** Bolivianer(in) *m(f)*, Bolivier(in) *m(f)* **ADJ** bolivianisch, bolivisch

boll [bəʊl] N Samenkapsel *f*

bollard [ˈbɒləd] N (*on quay, road*) Poller *m*

bollocking [ˈbɒləkɪŋ] N (*Brit, sl*) Schimpfkanonade *f* (*inf*); **to give sb a ~** jdn zur Sau machen (*inf*)

bollocks [ˈbɒləks] PL (*sl*) **a** Eier *pl* (*sl*) **b** (= *nonsense*) **(that's) ~!** Quatsch mit Soße! (*inf*); **he was talking ~** der hat einen Scheiß geredet (*inf*)

boll weevil N Baumwollkapselkäfer *m*

Bollywood [ˈbɒlɪwʊd] N (*inf*) Bollywood *nt* (*inf, die indische Filmindustrie*)

bologna [bəˈləʊnɪ], **bologna sausage** [bəˌləʊnɪˈsɒsɪdʒ] N (*Cook*) Mortadella *f*

boloney [bəˈləʊnɪ] N = **baloney**

Bolshevik [ˈbɒlʃəvɪk] **N** Bolschewik *m* **ADJ** bolschewistisch

Bolshevism [ˈbɒlʃəvɪzəm] N Bolschewismus *m*

Bolshevist [ˈbɒlʃəvɪst] N, ADJ = **Bolshevik**

bolshie, bolshy [ˈbɒlʃɪ] (*inf*) **N** Bolschewik *m* **ADJ** (*+er*) **a** (*Brit fig, = uncooperative*) stur; (= *aggressive*) pampig (*inf*), rotzig (*inf*) **b** (*pej*) bolschewistisch

bolster [ˈbəʊlstə] **N** (*on bed*) Nackenrolle *f* **VT** (*also* **bolster up**) *person* Mut machen (+*dat*); *status* aufbessern; *currency* stützen; *economy, confidence* Auftrieb geben (+*dat*); *profits, power* erhöhen; *case* untermauern; *support* verstärken; **it ~s my ego** das gibt mir Auftrieb, das baut mich auf; **to ~ (up) sb's morale** jdm Mut machen

bolt [bəʊlt] **N** **a** (*on door etc*) Riegel *m* **b** (*Tech*) Schraube *f* (*ohne Spitze*), Bolzen *m* **c** (*of lightning*) Blitzstrahl *m*; **it came/was like a ~ from the blue** (*fig*) das schlug ein/war wie ein Blitz aus heiterem Himmel

d (*of cloth*) Ballen *m*
e (*of crossbow*) Bolzen *m* → **shoot**
f (*of rifle*) Kammer *f*
g (= *sudden dash*) Satz *m* (*inf*); **his ~ for freedom** sein Fluchtversuch *m*; **he made a ~ for the door** er machte einen Satz zur Tür; **to make a ~ for it** losrennen

ADV **~ upright** kerzengerade

VI **a** (*horse*) durchgehen; (*person*) Reißaus nehmen (*inf*); **too late now, the horse has ~ed** (*fig*) zu spät, der Zug ist schon abgefahren
b (= *move quickly*) sausen, rasen, pesen (*inf*)

VT **a** *door, window* zu- or verriegeln
b (*Tech*) *parts* verschrauben (*to* mit), mit Schraubenbolzen befestigen (*to an* +*dat*); **to ~ together** verschrauben
c (*also* **bolt down**) *one's food* hinunterschlingen

▶ **bolt in** **VI** (= *rush in*) herein-/hineinplatzen or -stürzen **VT** *sep* (= *lock in*) einsperren

▶ **bolt on** VT *sep* (*Tech*) festschrauben (*prep obj, -to an* +*dat*)

▶ **bolt out** **VI** (= *rush out*) hinaus-/herausstürzen **VT** *sep* (= *lock out*) aussperren

bolt hole N Schlupfloch *nt*

bolus ['bəʊləs] N *pl* **-es** (*Med*) große Pille

bomb [bɒm] **N** **a** (= *device*) Bombe *f*; **to put a ~ under sb/sth** (*Brit fig inf*) jdn/etw radikal verändern
b (*Brit inf*) **his party went like a ~** seine Party war ein Bombenerfolg (*inf*); **the car goes like a ~** das ist die reinste Rakete von Wagen (*inf*); **the car cost a ~** das Auto hat ein Bombengeld gekostet (*inf*); **to make a ~** eine Stange Geld verdienen (*inf*); **to go down a ~** Riesenanklang finden (*with* bei) (*inf*)
c (*US inf*) **the play was a real ~** das Stück war ein totaler Reinfall

VT **a** (*lit*) bombardieren; (*not from the air*) ein Bombenattentat verüben auf (+*acc*)
b (*US, inf, = fail*) durchfallen bei

VI **a** (*inf, = go fast*) fegen (*inf*), zischen (*inf*)
b (*US, inf, = fail*) durchfallen (*inf*)

▶ **bomb along** VI (*inf, = drive fast*) dahinrasen (*inf*)

▶ **bomb out** VT *sep* ausbomben

bomb alert N Bombenwarnung *f*

bombard [bɒm'bɑːd] VT (*Mil, fig*) bombardieren (*with* mit); (*Phys*) beschießen

bombardier [ˌbɒmbə'dɪə'] N (*Mil*) Artillerieunteroffizier *m*; (*Aviat*) Bombenschütze *m*

bombardment [bɒm'bɑːdmənt] N (*Mil*) Bombardierung *f* (*also fig*), Bombardement *nt*; (*Phys*) Beschießen *nt*

bombast ['bɒmbæst] N Schwulst *m*, Bombast *m*

bombastic ADJ , **bombastically** ADV [bɒm'bæstɪk, -əlɪ] schwülstig, bombastisch

bomb attack N Bombenangriff *m*

Bombay [bɒm'beɪ] N

Bombay duck N *kleiner getrockneter Fisch als Beigabe zur indischen Reistafel*

bomb: bomb bay N Bombenschacht *m*; **bomb carpet** N Bombenteppich *m*; **bomb crater** N Bombentrichter *m*; **bomb disposal** N Bombenräumung *f*; **bomb disposal expert** N Bombenräumexperte *m*; **bomb disposal squad**, **bomb disposal unit** N Bombenräumtrupp *m* or -kommando *nt*

bombed [bɒmd] ADJ (*inf*) total zu (*inf*)

bombed out [ˌbɒm'daʊt] ADJ (*inf*) **a** (= *exhausted*) völlig fertig (*inf*), fix und foxi (*sl*) **b** (= *drunk, on drugs*) zu (*inf*) **c** **our team's ~** (= *has no chance*) unsere Mannschaft hat keine Chance **d** (= *very busy*) *pub etc* gerammelt voll (*inf*)

bomber ['bɒmə'] N **a** (= *aircraft*) Bomber *m*, Bombenflugzeug *nt* **b** (= *person, Aviat*) Bombenschütze *m*; (= *terrorist*) Bombenattentäter(in) *m(f)*

bomber: bomber command N Bombenverband *m* or -geschwader *nt*; **bomber jacket** N

Fliegerjacke *f*; **bomber pilot** N Bomberpilot *m*

bomb factory N Bombenfabrik *f*

bombing ['bɒmɪŋ] **N** Bombenangriff *m* (*of* auf +*acc*); (*of target also*) Bombardierung *f* **ADJ** *raid, mission* Bomben-

bomb: bombproof ADJ bombensicher; **bomb scare** N Bombenalarm *m*; **bombshell** N **a** (*Mil*) Bombe *f* **b** (*fig*) Bombe *f*, plötzliche Überraschung; **this news was a ~** die Nachricht schlug wie eine Bombe ein; **to drop a** or **the** or **one's ~** die Bombe platzen lassen; **bomb shelter** N Luftschutzkeller *m*; (*specially built*) (Luftschutz)bunker *m*; **bombsight** N Fliegerbombenzielgerät *nt*; **bomb site** N Trümmergrundstück *nt*

bona fide ['bəʊnə'faɪdɪ] ADJ bona fide; *traveller, word, antique* echt; **it's a ~ offer** es ist ein Angebot auf Treu und Glauben

bona fides ['bəʊnə'faɪdiːz] N *sing* (*form, = trustworthiness*) Vertrauenswürdigkeit *f*

bonanza [bə'nænzə] **N** **a** (*US, Min*) reiche Erzader **b** (*fig*) Goldgrube *f*; **the oil ~** der Ölboom **ADJ** *attr year* Boom-

bonbon ['bɒnbɒn] N Bonbon *m* or *nt*

bonce [bɒns] N (*Brit inf, = head*) Birne *f* (*inf*); **curly ~** Krauskopf *m* (*inf*)

bond [bɒnd] **N** **a** (= *agreement*) Übereinkommen *nt*
b (*fig, = link*) Band *nt* (*geh*), Bindung *f*
c **bonds** PL (*lit, = chains*) Fesseln *pl*, Bande *pl* (*liter*); (*fig, = ties*) Bande *pl* (*geh*); (*burdensome*) Fesseln *pl*; **marriage ~s** das Band/die Fesseln der Ehe
d (*Comm, Fin*) Obligation *f*, Pfandbrief *m*, festverzinsliches Wertpapier, Bond *m*; **government ~** Staatsanleihe *f* or -papiere *pl*
e (*Comm, = custody of goods*) Zollverschluss *m*; **to put sth into ~** etw unter Zollverschluss geben; **goods in ~** Zollgut *nt*
f (= *adhesion between surfaces*) Haftfestigkeit *f*, Haftwirkung *f*; **nothing can break the ~ between the two surfaces** die beiden Flächen haften or kleben fest und unlösbar aneinander
g (*Build*) Verband *m*
h (*Chem*) Bindung *f*

VT **a** (*Comm*) *goods* unter Zollverschluss legen or nehmen
b (*Build*) *bricks* im Verband verlegen

VI **a** (*glue*) binden; (*bricks*) einen Verband bilden
b **to ~ with one's baby** Liebe zu seinem Kind entwickeln; **we ~ed immediately** wir haben uns auf Anhieb gut verstanden, wir waren uns auf Anhieb sympathisch

bondage ['bɒndɪdʒ] **N** **a** (*lit*) Sklaverei *f*; (*in Middle Ages*) Leibeigenschaft *f*; **in ~ to sb** in Sklaverei/Leibeigenschaft bei jdm, jdm hörig **b** (*fig liter*) vollständige Unterjochung; **in ~ to sth** einer Sache (*dat*) unterworfen; **her stronger will kept him in ~** ihr stärkerer Wille hielt ihn vollständig unterdrückt **c** (*sexual*) Fesseln *nt*; **~ gear/magazine** Sadomasoausrüstung *f*/-heft *nt*

bonded ['bɒndɪd] ADJ *goods* unter Zollverschluss

bonded labour, (*US*) **bonded labor** N Leibeigenschaft *f*

bonded warehouse N Zolllager *nt*, Zolldepot *nt*

bond: bondholder N Pfandbrief- or Obligationsinhaber(in) *m(f)*; **bondman**, **bondsman** N Sklave *m* (*medieval*) Leibeigene(r) *mf*

bone [bəʊn] **N** Knochen *m*; (*of fish*) Gräte *f*; **~s** *pl* (*of the dead*) Gebeine *pl*; **ham off the ~** Schinken *m* vom Knochen; **meat on the ~** Fleisch *nt* am Knochen; **chilled to the ~** völlig durchgefroren; **that was a bit close** or **near to the ~** (*fig*) das war hart an der Schmerzgrenze; **to work one's fingers to the ~** sich (*dat*) die Finger abarbeiten; **to cut costs to the ~** Kosten drastisch reduzieren; **~ of contention** Zankapfel *m*; **to have a ~ to pick with sb** (*inf*) mit jdm ein Hühnchen zu rupfen haben (*inf*); **I'll make**

no ~s about it, you're/this is ... (*inf*) du bist/das ist, offen gestanden or ehrlich gesagt, ...; **he made no ~s about saying what he thought** (*inf*) er hat mit seiner Meinung nicht hinterm Berg gehalten; **I can feel it in my ~s** das spüre ich in den Knochen; **my old ~s** (*inf*) meine alten Knochen (*inf*)
b (= *substance*) Knochen *m*
c (*of corset*) Stange *f*; (*smaller*) Stäbchen *nt*
d (*Mus*) **bones** PL Klangstäbe *pl*
e (= *dice*) **bones** PL (*inf*) Würfel *pl*, Knöchel *pl* (*old*)

ADJ *attr* (= *made of bone*) Bein-, beinern

VT die Knochen lösen aus, ausbeinen (*dial*); *fish* entgräten

▶ **bone up on** VI +*prep obj* (*inf*) *subject* pauken (*inf*)

bone china N feines Porzellan

boned [bəʊnd] ADJ **a** *meat* ohne Knochen; *fish* entgrätet **b** *bodice etc* mit Fischbeinstäbchen

-boned ADJ *suf* -knochig; **to be big-boned** starke Knochen haben

bone: bone dry ADJ *pred*, **bone-dry** ADJ *attr* (*inf*) knochentrocken; **bonehead** N (*inf*) Dummkopf *m*, Armleuchter *m* (*inf*); **boneheaded** ADJ (*inf*) blöd(e) (*inf*), doof (*inf*); **bone idle** ADJ (*Brit inf*) stinkfaul (*inf*); **boneless** ADJ *meat* ohne Knochen; *fish* ohne Gräten; **bone marrow** N Knochenmark *nt*; **bone meal** N Knochenmehl *nt*

boner ['bəʊnə'] N **a** (*US, sl*) Schnitzer *m* (*inf*), Hammer *m* (*inf*)

bone: boneshaker N **a** (*inf*) Klapperkiste *f* (*inf*), Mühle *f* (*inf*) **b** (*old, = cycle*) Fahrrad *nt* ohne Gummireifen; **bone structure** N (*of face*) Gesichtszüge *pl*; **boneyard** N (*inf*) Friedhof *m*

bonfire ['bɒnfaɪə'] N (*for burning rubbish*) Feuer *nt*; (*as beacon*) Leucht- or Signalfeuer *nt*; (*Guy Fawkes*) Guy-Fawkes-Feuer *nt*; (*for celebration*) Freudenfeuer *nt*

bonfire night N 5. November (*Jahrestag der Pulververschwörung*)

bongo ['bɒŋgəʊ] N Bongo *nt* or *f*

bonhomie ['bɒnɒmiː] N Bonhomie *f* (*geh*), Jovialität *f*

bonhomous ADJ , **bonhomously** ADV ['bɒnəməs, -lɪ] jovial

boniness ['bəʊnɪnɪs] N Knochigkeit *f*

bonk [bɒŋk] (*inf*) **VT** **a** (= *have sex with*) bumsen (*inf*) **b** (= *knock*) **he ~ed his head against the doorframe** er knallte mit dem Kopf gegen den Türrahmen (*inf*) **VI** bumsen (*inf*) **N** (= *sex*) **to have a ~** bumsen (*inf*)

bonkers ['bɒŋkəz] ADJ (*esp Brit, inf*) meschugge (*inf*); **to be ~** spinnen (*inf*); **to go ~** überschnappen (*inf*); **he's ~ about her** er ist völlig verrückt nach ihr (*inf*)

bonking ['bɒŋkɪŋ] N (*inf*) Bumsen *nt* (*inf*)

bon mot ['bɒn'məʊ] N Bonmot *nt* (*geh*)

Bonn [bɒn] **N** Bonn *nt* **ADJ** Bonner

bonnet ['bɒnɪt] N **a** (*woman's*) Haube *f*; (*baby's*) Häubchen *nt*; (*esp Scot, man's*) Mütze *f* **b** (*Brit, Aut*) Motor- or Kühlerhaube *f* **c** (*of chimney*) Schornsteinkappe *f*

bonnie, **bonny** ['bɒnɪ] ADJ (*esp Scot*) schön; *lassie also* hübsch; *baby* prächtig

bonsai ['bɒnsaɪ] N *pl* **-** Bonsai *nt*

bonus ['bəʊnəs] N **a** Prämie *f*; (*for output, production also*) Zulage *f*; (= *cost-of-living bonus*) Zuschlag *m*; (= *Christmas bonus*) Gratifikation *f*; **~ scheme** Prämiensystem *nt*; **~ point** (*in game, quiz etc*) Bonuspunkt *m* **b** (*Fin, on shares*) Extradividende *f*, Sonderausschüttung *f* **c** (*inf, = sth extra*) Zugabe *f*

bony ['bəʊnɪ] ADJ (+*er*) (= *of bone*) knöchern; (= *like bone*) knochenartig; *person, knee, hips* knochig; *fish* grätig, mit viel Gräten; *meat* mit viel Knochen

bonze [bɒnz] N Bonze *m*

bonzer ['bɒnzə'] ADJ (*Austral, inf*) klasse (*inf*)

boo [buː] **INTERJ** buh; **he wouldn't say ~ to a goose** (*inf*) er ist ein schüchternes Pflänzchen

VT *actor, play, speaker, referee* auspfeifen, ausbuhen; **to ~ed off the stage** ausgepfiffen *or* ausgebuht werden **VI** buhen **N** Buhruf *m*

boob [buːb] **N** **a** (*Brit, inf,* = *mistake*) Schnitzer *m* (*inf*); **a common ~** ein häufig gemachter Fehler **b** (*inf,* = *woman's breast*) Brust *f*; **big ~s** große Titten *pl or* Möpse *pl* (*sl*) **VI** (*Brit inf*) einen Schnitzer machen (*inf*); (= *fail*) Mist bauen (*inf*); **somebody ~ed, I didn't get the letter** da hat jemand was verbockt (*inf*), ich habe den Brief überhaupt nicht gekriegt

boob job **N** (*inf*) Brustkorrektur *f*

boo-boo ['buːbuː] **N** (*inf*) Schnitzer *m* (*inf*)

boob tube **N** **a** (*Brit Tex*) Bustier *nt* **b** (*esp US, inf,* = *television*) Röhre *f* (*inf*), Glotze *f* (*inf*)

booby ['buːbɪ] **N** (*inf*) **a** (= *fool*) Trottel *m* **b** = **boob** **N** **b**

booby: booby hatch **N** (*dated US, sl*) Klapsmühle *f* (*inf*); **booby prize** **N** Scherzpreis *für den schlechtesten Teilnehmer*; **booby trap** **N** **a** Falle *f* (*als Schabernack versteckt angebracht*) **b** (*Mil etc*) versteckte Bombe; **don't open that box, it's a ~** machen Sie die Schachtel nicht auf, da ist eine Bombe drin **VT** **the suitcase was booby-trapped** in dem Koffer war eine Bombe versteckt

booger ['buːgə] **N** (*US inf*) (Nasen)popel *m* (*inf*)

boogie-woogie ['buːgɪˌwuːgɪ] **N** Boogie-Woogie *m*

boohoo ['buːˈhuː] **INTERJ** (*to indicate crying*) huh-huh; (*to mock crying*) schluchz-schluchz

booing ['buːɪŋ] **N** Buhrufen *nt*

book [bʊk] ☉ 21.3 **N** **a** Buch *nt*; (= *exercise book*) Heft *nt*; (= *division: in Bible, poem etc*) Buch *nt*; **the (good) Book** das Buch der Bücher; **the Book of Genesis** die Genesis, das 1. Buch Mose; **to bring sb to ~** jdn zur Rechenschaft ziehen; **to throw the ~ at sb** (*inf*) jdn nach allen Regeln der Kunst fertig machen (*inf*); **by *or* according to the ~** nach dem Buchstaben; **he does everything by *or* according to the ~** er hält sich bei allem strikt an die Vorschriften; **to go by the ~** sich an die Vorschriften halten; **to be in sb's good/bad ~s** bei jdm gut/schlecht angeschrieben sein (*inf*); **I can read him like a ~** ich kann in ihm lesen wie in einem Buch; **to close the ~ on sth** das Kapitel einer Sache (*gen*) abschließen; **it's a closed ~ to me** das ist ein Buch mit sieben Siegeln für mich; **he/my life is an open ~** er/mein Leben ist ein offenes Buch; **he knows/used every trick in the ~** (*inf*) er ist/war mit allen Wassern gewaschen (*inf*); **he'll use every trick in the ~ to get what he wants** (*inf*) er wird alles und jedes versuchen, um zu erreichen, was er will; **that counts as cheating in my ~** (*inf*) für mich ist das Betrug; **I'm in the ~** (*Telec*) ich stehe im Telefonbuch **b** (*of tickets*) Heft *nt*; (*thicker*) Block *m*; **~ of stamps/matches** Briefmarken-/Streichholzheftchen *nt* **c** **books** PL (*Comm, Fin*) Bücher *pl*; **to keep the ~s of a firm** die Bücher einer Firma führen; **to do the ~s for sb** jdm die Bücher führen; **I've been doing the ~s** ich habe die Abrechnung gemacht **d** (*of club, society*) (Mitglieder)verzeichnis *nt*, Mitgliedsliste *f*; **to be on the ~s of an organization** im Mitgliederverzeichnis *or* auf der Mitgliedsliste einer Organisation stehen **e** (*Gambling*) Wettbuch *nt*; **to make *or* keep a ~** (*Horseracing*) Buch machen; (*generally*) Wetten abschließen **f** (= *libretto: of opera etc*) Textbuch *nt* **g** (*Comm*) **~ of samples, sample ~** Musterbuch *nt* **VT** **a** (= *reserve*) bestellen; *seat, room also* buchen, reservieren lassen; *artiste* engagieren, verpflichten; *cabaret act* nehmen; (*privately*) sorgen für; **this performance/flight/hotel is fully ~ed** diese Vorstellung ist ausverkauft/dieser Flug ist ausgebucht/das Hotel ist voll belegt; **can I ~ a time to see him?** kann ich einen Termin bei ihm bekommen?; **to ~ sb through to Hull** (*Rail*) jdn bis Hull durchbuchen **b** (*Fin, Comm*) order aufnehmen; **to ~ goods to**

sb's account jdm Waren in Rechnung stellen **c** (*inf*) *driver etc* aufschreiben (*inf*), einen Strafzettel verpassen (+*dat*) (*inf*); *footballer* verwarnen; **to be ~ed for speeding** wegen zu schnellen Fahrens aufgeschrieben werden; **let's ~ him** (*said by policeman etc*) den schnappen wir uns (*inf*) **VI** bestellen; (= *reserve seat, room also*) buchen; **to ~ through to Hull** bis Hull durchlösen

▸ **book in** **VI** (*in hotel etc*) sich eintragen; **we booked in at *or* into the Hilton** wir sind im Hilton abgestiegen **VT** *sep* **a** (= *register*) eintragen **b** (= *make reservation for*) **to book sb into a hotel** jdm ein Hotelzimmer reservieren lassen; **we're booked in at *or* into the Hilton** unsere Zimmer sind im Hilton bestellt *or* reserviert

▸ **book up** **VI** buchen **VT** *sep* (*usu pass*) reservieren lassen; **to be (fully) booked up** (ganz) ausgebucht sein; (*evening performance, theatre*) (bis auf den letzten Platz) ausverkauft sein

bookable ['bʊkəbl] **ADJ** **a** im Vorverkauf erhältlich **b** (*Sport*) **a ~ offence** (*Brit*) *or* **offense** (*US*) ein Verstoß *m*, für den es eine Verwarnung gibt

book: bookbinder **N** Buchbinder *m*; **bookbinding** **N** Buchbinderei *f*; **bookcase** **N** Bücherregal *nt*; (*with doors*) Bücherschrank *m*; **book claim** **N** (*Fin*) Buchforderung *f*, buchmäßige Forderung; **book club** **N** Buchgemeinschaft *f*; **book debt** **N** (*Fin*) Buchschuld *f*, buchmäßige Schuld; **book end** **N** Bücherstütze *f*

BOOKER PRIZE

Der **Booker Prize** ist ein Preis, der seit 1969 jährlich für ein Werk der Belletristik aus Großbritannien, Irland oder dem Commonwealth vergeben wird. Es handelt sich dabei um eine hohe Geldprämie, die von der Booker McConnell Maschinenbaugesellschaft ausgesetzt wird. Die Preisverleihung wird in den Medien mit großem Interesse verfolgt und sogar live im Fernsehen übertragen. Die Jury setzt sich normalerweise aus Schriftstellern, Universitätsdozenten und Kritikern zusammen, und ihr Urteil ist manchmal heftig umstritten.

---

book fair **N** Buchmesse *f*

bookie ['bʊkɪ] **N** (*inf*) Buchmacher(in) *m(f)*

booking ['bʊkɪŋ] ☉ 21.4 **N** Buchung *f*, Bestellung *f*, Reservierung *f*; (*of artiste, performer*) Engagement *nt*, Verpflichtung *f*; **to make a ~** buchen; **to cancel a ~** den Tisch/die Karte *etc* abbestellen, die Reise/den Flug *etc* stornieren; **to change one's ~** umbuchen; **have you got a ~ for *or* in the name of Higgins?** ist bei Ihnen etwas auf den Namen Higgins gebucht?

booking: booking clerk **N** Fahrkartenverkäufer(in) *m(f)*; (*in ticket booth also*) Schalterbeamte(r) *m*, Schalterbeamtin *f*; **booking fee** **N** Buchungsgebühr *f*, Reservierungsgebühr *f*; **booking office** **N** (*Rail*) Fahrkartenschalter *m*; (*Theat*) Vorverkaufsstelle *or* -kasse *f*

bookish ['bʊkɪʃ] **ADJ** gelehrt (*pej, hum*); (= *given to reading*) lesewütig; (= *not worldly*) lebensfremd; *language, expression* buchsprachlich; (*pej*) trocken, papieren; **a ~ word** ein Wort *nt* der Schriftsprache; **he is a very ~ person** er hat die Nase dauernd in einem Buch; (= *not worldly*) er ist ein richtiger Stubengelehrter (*pej*); **~ style** Buchstil *m*; (*pej*) papierener Stil

book: book jacket **N** Schutzumschlag *m*, Buchhülle *f*; **book-keeper** **N** Buchhalter(in) *m(f)*; **book-keeping** **N** Buchhaltung *f*, Buchführung *f*; **book knowledge, book-learning** **N** Bücherweisheit *f*

booklet ['bʊklɪt] **N** Broschüre *f*

book: book lover **N** Bücherfreund *m*; **bookmaker** **N** Buchmacher(in) *m(f)*; **bookmaking** **N** Buchmacherei *f*, **~ firm** Buchmacherfirma *f*; **bookmark** **N** Lesezeichen *nt*; (*Comput*) Lesezeichen *nt*, Bookmark *nt*; **bookmobile** **N** (*US*) Fahrbücherei *f*; **bookplate** **N**

Exlibris *nt*; **book post** **N** Büchersendung *f*; **to send sth by ~** etw als Büchersendung schicken; **~ is ...** Büchersendungen sind ...; **bookrest** **N** Lesepult *nt*; **book review** **N** Buchbesprechung *f*, Rezension *f*; **bookseller** **N** Buchhändler *m*; **bookselling** **N** der Buchhandel; **bookshelf** **N** Bücherbord *or* -brett *nt*; **bookshelves** PL (= *bookcase*) Bücherregal *nt*; **bookshop** (*esp Brit*), **bookstore** (*US*) **N** Buchhandlung *f or* -laden *m*; **bookstall** **N** Bücherstand *m*; **bookstand** (*US*) **a** (= *bookrest*) Lesepult *nt* **b** (= *bookcase*) Bücherregal *nt* **c** (= *bookstall: in station, airport*) Bücherstand *m*; **to hit the ~s** in die Buchläden kommen

booksy ['bʊksɪ] **ADJ** (*inf, pej*) hochgestochen (*pej*), intellektuell

book

book token **N** Buchgutschein *m*

book trade **N** Buchhandel *m*

book value **N** (*Fin*) Buchwert *m*, Bilanzwert *m*

bookworm **N** (*fig*) Bücherwurm *m*

Boolean ['buːlɪən] **ADJ** *algebra, logic* boolesch *attr*

boom[1] [buːm] **N** **a** (= *barrier, across river etc*) Sperre *f*; (*at factory gate etc*) Schranke *f* **b** (*Naut*) Baum *m* **c** (*Tech, also* **derrick boom**) Ladebaum *m*; (= *jib of crane*) Ausleger *m* **d** (*for microphone*) Galgen *m*

boom[2] **N** (*of sea, waves, wind*) Brausen *nt*; (*of thunder*) Hallen *nt*; (*of guns*) Donnern *nt*; (*of organ, voice*) Dröhnen *nt* **VI** **a** (*sea, wind*) brausen; (*thunder*) hallen **b** (*organ, person, voice: also* **boom out**) dröhnen; (*guns*) donnern **INTERJ** bum

▸ **boom out** **VI** = **boom**[2] **VI** **b** **VT** *sep* (*person*) order brüllen; **to boom out a command to sb** jdm mit Donnerstimme einen Befehl zubrüllen; **the bass booms out the chorus** der Bass singt den Refrain mit dröhnender Stimme

boom[3] **VI** (*trade, sales*) einen Aufschwung nehmen, boomen (*inf*); (*prices*) anziehen, in die Höhe schnellen; **business is ~ing** das Geschäft blüht *or* floriert **N** (*of business, fig*) Boom *m*, Aufschwung *m*; (= *period of economic growth*) Hochkonjunktur *f*; (*of prices*) Preissteigerung *f*; **to undergo a sudden ~** einen plötzlichen Aufschwung nehmen *or* erfahren

boom: boom box **N** (*US inf*) Ghettoblaster *m* (*inf*); **boom-bust** **ADJ** (*Econ*) Konjunktur-; **the ~ pattern of the economy in recent years** der Konjunkturzyklus der Wirtschaft in den letzten Jahren; **property is a ~ business** Immobilien sind ein Konjunkturgeschäft; **~ cycle** Kreislauf *m* von Hochkonjunktur und Rezession, Konjunkturzyklus *m*

boomerang ['buːməræŋ] **N** (*lit, fig*) Bumerang *m*; **to have a ~ effect** einen Bumerangeffekt haben **VI** (*fig inf, words, actions*) wie ein Bumerang zurückkommen (*inf*)

booming ['buːmɪŋ] **ADJ** *sound* dröhnend; *surf* brausend

boom: boom microphone **N** Mikrofon *nt or* Mikrophon *nt* an einem Galgen; **boom-slump ~ cycle** Konjunktur-Zyklus *m*; **boom town** **N** Goldgräberstadt *f*

boon[1] [buːn] **N** **a** (= *blessing, advantage*) Segen *m*; **it's such a ~** es ist ein wahrer Segen **b** (*obs,* = *favour, wish*) Gunst *f*, Gnade *f*

boon[2] **ADJ** **~ companion** (*old, liter*) lustiger Geselle *m* (*old*)

boondockers ['buːndɒkəz] PL (*US, inf,* = *heavy boots*) (schwere) Stiefel *pl*

boondocks ['buːndɒks] PL (*US, inf,* = *backwoods*) Wildnis *f*; **in the ~** irgendwo, jwd (*inf*)

boondoggle ['buːndɒgl] (*US, inf*) **VI** auf Staatskosten Zeit und Geld verplempern (*inf*) **N** Zeitverschwendung *f or* Kleinkrämerei *f* auf Staatskosten

boondoggler ['buːndɒglə] **N** (*US, inf*) staatlich angestellte Niete, kleinkarierte Beamtenseele, beamteter Kleinkrämer

boor [bʊə] **N** Rüpel *m*, Flegel *m*

boorish ADJ , **boorishly** ADV [ˈbʊərɪʃ, -lɪ] rüpelhaft, flegelhaft

boorishness [ˈbʊərɪʃnɪs] N Rüpelhaftigkeit f, Flegelhaftigkeit f

boost [buːst] **N** Auftrieb m no pl; (Elec, Aut) Verstärkung f; (= booster rocket) Zusatzantrieb m; **to give sb/sth a** ~ jdm/einer Sache Auftrieb geben, jdn aufmöbeln (inf)/etw ankurbeln or in Schwung bringen; (by advertising) für jdn/ etw die Werbetrommel rühren; **to give my bank account a** ~ um meinem Bankkonto eine Finanzspritze zu verabreichen; **this device gives the heart a** ~ dieser Apparat verstärkt den Herzschlag; **to give a** ~ **to sb's morale** jdm Auftrieb geben or Mut machen; **to give a** ~ **to sb's confidence** jds Selbstvertrauen stärken ◀ VT production, output, sales, economy ankurbeln; profits, prices, income, chances erhöhen; electric charge, engine, heart beat etc verstärken; immune system, confidence, sb's ego stärken; morale heben; **that's** ~**ed my ego** das hat mich aufgebaut, das hat mir Auftrieb gegeben

booster [ˈbuːstə] N ◀ **a** (Elec) Puffersatz m; (Rad) Zusatzverstärker m; (TV) Zusatzgleichrichter m; (Comput: on cable) Zwischengenerator m; (Aut, = supercharger) Kompressor m; (for heating) Gebläse nt; (= booster rocket) Booster m; (for launching) Booster m, Startrakete f; (Aviat) Hilfstriebwerk nt; (Space) Booster m, Zusatztriebwerk nt; **to act as a** ~ zur Verstärkung dienen ◀ **b** (Med: also **booster shot**) Wiederholungsimpfung f; ~ **dose** zusätzliche Dosis

booster: booster cables PL (US Aut) Starthilfekabel pl; **booster cushion** N , **booster seat** N (Aut) Kindersitz m; **booster shot** N (Med) Auffrischungsimpfung f

boot¹ [buːt] **N** ◀ **a** Stiefel m; **the** ~ **is on the other foot** (fig) es ist genau umgekehrt; **to give sb the (order of the (hum))** ~ (inf) jdn rausschmeißen (inf), jdn an die Luft setzen (inf); **to get the** ~ (inf) rausgeschmissen werden (inf); **it's the** ~ **for him** (inf) der fliegt (inf); **to die with one's** ~**s on** (inf) über der Arbeit or in den Sielen sterben; **to quake** or **shake** or **tremble in one's** ~**s** vor Angst fast umkommen; **to put the** ~ **in** (Brit inf) kräftig zutreten; (fig) zuschlagen; **to put the** ~ **into sb/sth** (Brit fig inf) jdn/etw niedermachen ◀ **b** (Brit, of car etc) Kofferraum m ◀ **c** (inf, = kick) **to give sb/sth a** ~ jdm/einer Sache einen Tritt geben or versetzen ◀ **d** (Brit, pej inf, = woman) Schreckschraube f (inf) ◀ VT ◀ **a** (inf, = kick) einen (Fuß)tritt geben (+dat); ball kicken ◀ **b** (Comput) laden, urladen ◀ VI (Comput) laden

▶ **boot out** VT sep (inf: lit, fig) rausschmeißen (inf)

▶ **boot up** (Comput) VT sep booten VI booten

boot² ADV (hum, form) **to** ~ obendrein, noch dazu

boot: bootblack N Schuhputzer m; **boot boy** N (Brit inf) Skinhead m; **boot camp** N (US Mil inf) Armee-Ausbildungslager nt

bootee [buːˈtiː] N (baby's) gestrickter Babyschuh

booth [buːð] N ◀ **a** (at fair) (Markt)bude f or -stand m; (at show) (Messe)stand m ◀ **b** (= telephone booth) (offene) Zelle f; (= polling booth, in cinema, language laboratory) Kabine f; (in restaurant) Nische f, Séparée nt (geh), Separee nt (geh)

boot: bootjack N Stiefelknecht m; **bootlace** N Schnürsenkel m; **to pull oneself up by one's (own)** ~**s** (inf) sich aus eigener Kraft hocharbeiten; **bootleg** VT ◀ **a** (= make) liquor schwarzbrennen (inf); (= sell) schwarz verkaufen; (= transport) schmuggeln ◀ **b** (inf, = produce illegally) schwarz herstellen; cassettes etc schwarz mitschneiden ◀ ADJ whisky etc schwarzgebrannt; goods schwarz hergestellt; cassettes etc schwarz mitgeschnitten ◀ N (= product, cassette etc) Raub

kopie f; **bootlegger** N Bootlegger m; (= seller also) Schwarzhändler m

bootless [ˈbuːtlɪs] ADJ (liter) nutzlos, eitel (liter)

boot: bootlicker N (pej inf) Speichellecker m (pej inf); **bootmaker** N Schuhmacher m; **boot polish** N Schuhcreme f

boots [buːts] N sing (Brit) Hausbursche or -diener m

bootstrap [ˈbuːtstræp] N Stiefelschlaufe f; **to pull oneself up by one's (own)** ~**s** (inf) sich aus eigener Kraft hocharbeiten; **he's British/a Tory to his** ~**s** er ist durch und durch ein Brite/Tory

booty [ˈbuːtɪ] N (lit, fig) Beute f

booze [buːz] (inf) **N** (= alcoholic drink) Alkohol m; (= spirits also) Schnaps m; (= drinking bout) Sauftour f (inf); **keep off the** ~ lass das Saufen sein (inf); **bring some** ~ bring was zu schlucken mit (inf); **he's gone back on the** ~ **again** er säuft wieder (inf); **all this boozing** diese Sauferei (inf); **boozing party** Besäufnis nt (inf); **to go out boozing** saufen gehen (inf)

boozed(-up) [ˈbuːzd(ʌp)] ADJ (inf) blau (inf), alkoholisiert (inf)

boozer [ˈbuːzə] N ◀ **a** (pej inf, = drinker) Säufer(in) m(f) (pej inf), Schluckspecht m (inf) ◀ **b** (Brit, inf, = pub) Kneipe f (inf)

booze-up [ˈbuːzʌp] N (inf) Besäufnis nt (inf)

boozy [ˈbuːzɪ] ADJ (+er) (inf) look, face versoffen (inf); **a** ~ **person** ein Schluckspecht m (inf); (stronger) ein versoffenes Loch (sl); **to have** ~ **breath** eine Fahne haben (inf); ~ **party** Sauferei f (inf); ~ **lunch** Essen nt mit reichlich zu trinken

bop [bɒp] **N** ◀ **a** (Mus) Bebop m ◀ **b** (inf, = dance) Schwof m (inf) ◀ **c** (inf, = blow) Knuff (inf), Puff (inf) m; **to give sb a** ~ **on the nose** jdm eins auf die Nase geben ◀ VI (inf, = dance) schwofen (inf) VT (inf) **to** ~ **sb on the head** jdm eins auf den Kopf geben

boracic [bəˈræsɪk] ADJ (Chem) Bor-, borhaltig

borage [ˈbɒrɪdʒ] N Borretsch m

borax [ˈbɔːræks] N Borax m

border [ˈbɔːdə] **N** ◀ **a** (= edge, side: of woods, field) Rand m ◀ **b** (= boundary, frontier) Grenze f; **on the French** ~ an der französischen Grenze; **on the** ~**s of France** an der französischen Grenze; **on the** ~**s of France and Switzerland** an der Grenze zwischen Frankreich und der Schweiz, an der französisch-schweizerischen Grenze; **the Borders** (Brit, Geog) das Grenzgebiet zwischen England und Schottland **north/south of the** ~ (Brit) in/nach Schottland/England ◀ **c** (in garden) Rabatte f → **herbaceous border** ◀ **d** (= edging, on dress) Bordüre f; (of carpet) Einfassung f; (of picture) Umrahmung f; **black** ~ (on notepaper) schwarzer Rand, Trauerrand m ◀ VT ◀ **a** (= line edges of) road, path säumen; garden, estate etc begrenzen; (on all sides) umschließen ◀ **b** (land etc: = lie on edge of) grenzen an (+acc)

▶ **border on** or **upon** VI +prep obj (lit, fig) grenzen an (+acc); **it was bordering on being rude** das grenzte an Unhöflichkeit

border dispute N Grenzstreitigkeit f; (= fighting) Grenzzwischenfall m

borderer [ˈbɔːdərə] N Grenzbewohner(in) m(f); (Brit) Bewohner des Grenzgebiets zwischen England und Schottland

border: border guard N Grenzsoldat m; **border incident** N Grenzzwischenfall m

bordering [ˈbɔːdərɪŋ] ADJ country angrenzend

border: borderland N (lit) Grenzgebiet nt; (fig) Grenzbereich m; **borderline** **N** ◀ **a** (between states, districts) Grenzlinie f, Grenze f ◀ **b** (fig, between categories, classes etc) Grenze f; **to be on the** ~ an der Grenze liegen, ein Grenzfall sein; **his marks were on the** ~ **between a pass and a fail** er stand mit seinen Noten auf der Kippe ◀ ADJ (fig) **a** ~ **case** ein Grenzfall m; **it was a** ~ **pass/fail** er etc ist ganz knapp durchgekommen/durchgefallen; **he/it is** ~ er/es ist ein

Grenzfall; **it's too** ~ das liegt zu sehr an der Grenze; **border raid** N Grenzüberfall m; **border state** N Grenzstaat m; **border town** N Grenzstadt f

bore¹ [bɔː] **VT** hole, well, tunnel bohren; rock durchbohren **VI** bohren **N** (= hole) Bohrloch nt; (of tube, pipe) lichte Weite, Durchmesser m; (of shotgun, cannon) Kaliber nt; **a 12** ~ **shotgun** eine Flinte vom Kaliber 12

bore² **N** ◀ **a** (= person) Langweiler m; **what a** ~ **he is!** das ist ein Langweiler!, der kann einen langweilen or anöden (inf); **the club/office** ~ der Langweiler vom Dienst ◀ **b** (= thing, profession, situation etc) **to be a** ~ langweilig sein ◀ **c** (= nuisance) **don't be a** ~ nun sei doch nicht so (schwierig)!; **he's a** ~, **he never wants ...** er ist eine Plage, er will nie ...; **it's such a** ~ **having to go** es ist wirklich zu dumm or lästig, dass ich etc gehen muss; **oh what a** ~! das ist aber auch zu dumm or lästig! ◀ VT langweilen; **to** ~ **sb stiff** or **to death** or **to tears, to** ~ **the pants off sb** (inf) jdn zu Tode langweilen; **to be/get** ~**d** sich langweilen; **I'm** ~**d** mir ist es langweilig, ich langweile mich; **he is** ~**d with his job/her** seine Arbeit/sie langweilt ihn; **he was** ~**d with reading/life** er war des Lesens/Lebens überdrüssig (geh), er hatte das Lesen/Leben über

bore³ pret of **bear¹**

bore⁴ N (= tidal wave) Flutwelle f

boredom [ˈbɔːdəm] N Lang(e)weile f; (= boringness) Stumpfsinn m, Langweiligkeit f; **with a look of utter** ~ **on his face** mit einem völlig gelangweilten Gesichtsausdruck

borehole [ˈbɔːhəʊl] N Bohrloch nt

borer [ˈbɔːrə] N (Tech) Bohrer m; (= insect) Bohrkäfer m

boric acid [ˈbɔːrɪkˈæsɪd] N (Chem) Borsäure f

boring¹ [ˈbɔːrɪŋ] **N** (Tech, = act) Bohren nt; (= hole) Bohrloch nt ADJ ~ **machine** Bohrmaschine f

boring² ADJ langweilig

boringly [ˈbɔːrɪŋlɪ] ADV langweilig

born [bɔːn] **PTP** of **bear¹** VT **h to be** ~ (person, fig: idea) geboren werden; (fig: organization) entstehen; **I was** ~ **in 1948** ich bin or wurde 1948 geboren; **when were you** ~? wann sind Sie geboren?; **he was** ~ **Harry Webb** er wurde als Harry Webb geboren; **to be** ~ **again** wieder geboren werden; **every baby** ~ **into the world** jedes Kind, das auf die Welt kommt; **he was** ~ **to a life of hardship/into a rich family** er wurde in ein schweres Leben/eine reiche Familie hineingeboren; **to be** ~ **deaf** von Geburt an taub sein; **the baby was** ~ **dead** das Baby wurde tot geboren or war eine Totgeburt; **he was just** ~ **to be Prime Minister** er war zum Premierminister geboren; **I wasn't** ~ **yesterday** (inf) ich bin nicht von gestern (inf); **there's one** ~ **every minute!** (fig inf) die Dummen werden nicht alle!; **the characteristics which are** ~ **in us** die uns angeborenen Eigenschaften; **he was** ~ **of poor parents** er war das Kind armer Eltern; **with that confidence** ~ **of experience** mit dem aus Erfahrung hervorgegangenen Selbstvertrauen ◀ ADJ suf (= native of) **he is Chicago-** ~ er ist ein geborener or geborener Chicagoer; **his foreign-/ French-born wife** seine Frau, die Ausländerin/ gebürtige Französin ist ◀ ADJ geboren; **he is a** ~ **poet/teacher** er ist ein geborener Dichter/Lehrer; **an Englishman** ~ **and bred** ein echter or waschechter (inf) Engländer; **in all my** ~ **days** (inf) mein Lebtag (dated), in meinem ganzen Leben

born-again [ˈbɔːnəgen] ADJ Christian etc wieder geboren

borne [bɔːn] ptp of **bear¹**

Borneo [ˈbɔːnɪəʊ] N Borneo nt

borough [ˈbʌrə] N ◀ **a** (also **municipal borough**) Bezirk m, Stadtgemeinde f ◀ **b** (Parl) städtischer Wahlbezirk

borrow ['bɒrəʊ] **VT** **a** (sich *dat*) borgen, sich (*dat*) leihen (*from* von); £5000 (*from bank*), car sich (*dat*) leihen; *library book* ausleihen; *word* entlehnen; (*fig*) *idea, methodology* borgen (*inf*), übernehmen (*from* von); **to ~ money from the bank/another country** Kredit bei der Bank/eine Anleihe bei einem anderen Land aufnehmen; **~ed word** Lehnwort *nt*; **he is living on ~ed time** seine Uhr ist abgelaufen **b** (*Math, in subtraction*) borgen (*inf*) **VI** borgen; (*from bank*) Kredit *m* aufnehmen; **~ing country** kreditnehmendes Land

borrower ['bɒrəʊə] N Entleiher(in) *m(f)*; (*of capital, loan etc*) Kreditnehmer(in) *m(f)*

borrowing ['bɒrəʊɪŋ] N Borgen *nt*, Leihen *nt*; (*of library book*) Ausleihen *nt*; (*of word*) Entlehnung *f*; (*fig, of idea, methodology*) Übernahme *f*; **~ of money from the bank** Kreditaufnahme *f* or (*short-term*) Geldaufnahme *f* bei der Bank; **government ~** staatliche Kreditaufnahme; **consumer ~** Verbraucherkredit *m*; **~s** (*Fin*) aufgenommene Schulden *pl*; (*of country also*) Anleihen *pl*; **~ requirements** Kreditbedarf *m*

borsch(t) [bɔːʃ(t)] N Borschtsch *m*

borstal ['bɔːstl] N (*Brit old*) Jugendheim *nt*, Besserungsanstalt *f*

borzoi ['bɔːzɔɪ] N Barsoi *m*

bosh [bɒʃ] N (*dated inf*) Quatsch *m* (*inf*), Quark *m* (*dated inf*)

bo's'n ['bəʊsn] N = **boatswain**

Bosnia ['bɒznɪə] N Bosnien *nt*

Bosnia-Herzegovina ['bɒznɪəˌhɜːtsəgəʊ'viːnə] N Bosnien-Herzegowina *nt*

Bosnian ['bɒznɪən] **ADJ** bosnisch **N** Bosnier(in) *m(f)*

bosom ['bʊzəm] **N** **a** (*lit, fig, of person*) Busen *m*; **to lay bare one's ~ to sb** (*fig liter*) jdm sein Herz erschließen (*liter*), jdm sein Innerstes offenbaren (*liter*) **b** (*of dress*) Brustteil *m* **c** (*fig*) **in the ~ of his family** im Schoß der Familie **ADJ** *attr friend etc* Busen-

bosomy ['bʊzəmɪ] ADJ (*inf*) vollbusig

Bosp(h)orus ['bɒsfərəs, 'bɒspərəs] N **the ~** der Bosporus

boss[1] [bɒs] N Chef *m*, Boss *m* (*inf*); **industrial/union ~es** Industrie-/Gewerkschaftsbosse *pl* (*inf*); **his wife is the ~** seine Frau hat das Sagen, bei ihm zu Hause bestimmt die Frau; **OK, you're the ~** in Ordnung, du hast zu bestimmen

▶ **boss about** (*Brit*) or **around** VT *sep* (*inf*) rumkommandieren (*inf*)

boss[2] N (= *knob on shield*) Buckel *m*; (*Archit*) Schlussstein *m*

bossa nova [ˌbɒsə'nəʊvə] N Bossa Nova *m*

boss-eyed [bɒs'aɪd] ADJ (*Brit inf*) schielend *attr*; **to be ~** schielen, einen Knick in der Optik haben (*inf*)

bossiness ['bɒsɪnɪs] N Herrschsucht *f*, herrische Art

boss man N (*inf*) Boss *m* (*inf*)

bossy ['bɒsɪ] ADJ (+*er*) herrisch; **don't be ~ with me!** kommandier mich nicht so rum (*inf*); **he tends to be rather ~** er kommandiert einen gern rum (*inf*)

Boston ['bɒstən]: **Boston baked beans** PL (*US*) weiße Bohnen mit gepökeltem Schweinefleisch und Melasse oder braunem Zucker; **Boston crab** N (*Wrestling*) Beinschraube *f*

bosun ['bəʊsn] N = **boatswain**

BOT (*Brit*) abbr of **Board of Trade**

botanic(al) [bə'tænɪk(əl)] ADJ botanisch, Pflanzen-

botanic(al) gardens [bəˌtænɪk(əl)'gɑːdnz] PL botanischer Garten

botanist ['bɒtənɪst] N Botaniker(in) *m(f)*

botany ['bɒtənɪ] N Botanik *f*, Pflanzenkunde *f*

botch [bɒtʃ] (*inf*) VT (*also* **botch up**) verpfuschen, vermurksen (*inf*); *plans etc* vermasseln (*inf*); **a ~ed job** ein Pfusch *m* (*inf*) N Murks *m*

(*inf*), Pfusch *m* (*inf*); **to make a ~ of sth** etw verpfuschen/vermasseln (*inf*)

botcher ['bɒtʃə'] N (*inf*) Murkser *m* (*inf*), Pfuscher *m* (*inf*)

botch-up ['bɒtʃʌp] (*inf*) N Murks *m* (*inf*), Pfusch *m* (*inf*)

botchy ['bɒtʃɪ] ADJ (*inf*) verpfuscht, vermurkst (*inf*)

botel [bəʊ'tel] N Botel *nt* (*als Hotel ausgebautes Schiff*)

botfly ['bɒtflaɪ] N (*Zool*) Pferdebremse *f*

both [bəʊθ] ❖ 26.2 **ADJ** beide; **~ (the) boys** beide Jungen
PRON beide; (*two different things*) beides; **~ of them were there, they were ~ there** sie waren (alle) beide da; **two pencils/a pencil and a picture - he took ~** zwei Bleistifte/ein Bleistift und ein Bild - er hat beide/beides genommen; **~ of these answers are wrong** beide Antworten sind falsch; **~ of you are wrong** ihr habt (alle) beide Unrecht; **come in ~ of you** kommt beide herein; **I meant ~ of you** ich habe euch beide gemeint
ADV **~ ... and ...** sowohl ..., als auch ...; **~ you and I** wir beide; **John and I ~ came** John und ich sind beide gekommen; **she was ~ laughing and crying** sie lachte und weinte zugleich or gleichzeitig; **I'm ~ pleased and not pleased** ich freue mich und auch wieder nicht; **is it black or white? - ~** ist es schwarz oder weiß? - beides; **you and me ~** (*inf*) wir zwei beide (*inf*)

bother ['bɒðə'] ❖ 7.5 **VT** **a** (= *annoy, trouble, person, noise*) belästigen; (*sb's behaviour, tight garment, hat, long hair*) ärgern, stören; (= *cause disturbance to, light, noise, sb's presence, mistakes etc*) stören; (= *give trouble, back, teeth etc*) zu schaffen machen (+*dat*); (= *worry*) Sorgen machen (+*dat*); (*matter, problem, question*) beschäftigen, keine Ruhe lassen (+*dat*); **I'm sorry to ~ you but ...** es tut mir Leid, dass ich Sie damit belästigen muss, aber ...; **well I'm sorry I ~ed you** entschuldigen Sie, dass ich (überhaupt) gefragt habe; **don't ~ your head about that** zerbrechen Sie sich nicht den Kopf; **don't ~ yourself about that** machen Sie sich (*dat*) darüber mal keine Gedanken or Sorgen; **I wouldn't let it ~ me** darüber würde ich mir keine Sorgen or Gedanken machen; **I shouldn't let it ~ you** machen Sie sich mal keine Sorgen; **don't ~ me!** lass mich in Frieden!; **he was always ~ing me to lend him money** er hat mich dauernd um Geld angegangen; **could I ~ you for a light?** dürfte ich Sie vielleicht um Feuer bitten?; **one thing is still ~ing him** eins stört ihn noch; **what's ~ing you?** was haben Sie denn?; **is something ~ing you?** haben Sie etwas? → **hot**
b **I/he can't be ~ed** ich habe/er hat keine Lust; **I can't be ~ed with people like him/with opera** für solche Leute/für Opern habe ich nichts übrig; **I can't be ~ed to do** or **with doing that** ich habe einfach keine Lust, das zu machen; **he can't be ~ed about** or **with small matters like that** mit solchen Kleinigkeiten gibt er sich nicht ab; **do you want to stay or go? – I'm not ~ed** ob ihr du bleiben oder gehen? – das ist mir egal; **I'm not ~ed about him/the money** seinetwegen/wegen des Geldes mache ich mir keine Gedanken
c (= *take trouble to do*) **don't ~ to do it again** das brauchen Sie nicht nochmals zu tun; **don't ~ to ask** Sie brauchen nicht (zu) fragen; **I won't ~ asking YOU again!** DICH werde ich bestimmt nicht mehr fragen!; **she didn't even ~ to ask/check first** sie hat gar nicht erst gefragt/nachgesehen; **please don't ~ getting up** or **to get up** bitte, bleiben Sie doch sitzen; **you needn't ~ to come** Sie brauchen wirklich nicht (zu) kommen
VI sich kümmern (*about* um); (= *get worried*) sich (*dat*) Sorgen machen (*about* um); **don't ~ about me!** machen Sie sich meinetwegen keine Sorgen; (*sarcastic*) ist ja egal, was ich will; **to ~ with sb** sich mit jdm abgeben; **he/it is not worth ~ing about** über ihn/darüber brauchen

wir gar nicht zu reden, er/das ist nicht der Mühe wert; **I'm not going to ~ with that** das lasse ich; **I didn't ~ about lunch** ich habe das Mittagessen ausgelassen; **don't ~!** nicht nötig!; **really you needn't have ~ed!** das wäre aber wirklich nicht nötig gewesen!; **don't ~!** nicht nötig!; **really you needn't have ~ed!** das wäre aber wirklich nicht nötig gewesen!
N **a** (= *nuisance*) Plage *f*; **it's such a ~** das ist wirklich lästig or eine Plage; **I've forgotten it, what a ~** ich habe es vergessen, wie ärgerlich or so was Ärgerliches; **he/the car can be a bit of a ~** er/das Auto kann einem wirklich Schwierigkeiten machen; **I know it's an awful ~ for you but ...** ich weiß, dass Ihnen das fürchterliche Umstände macht, aber ...
b (= *trouble, contretemps etc*) Ärger *m*; (= *difficulties*) Schwierigkeiten *pl*; **she's in a spot of ~** sie hat Schwierigkeiten; **we had a bit ~** or **bit of ~ with the car** wir hatten Ärger mit dem Auto; **I didn't have any ~ getting the visa** es war kein Problem, das Visum zu bekommen; **I'll do it tonight, no ~** (*inf*) kein Problem, das mache ich heute Abend; **that's all right, it's no ~** bitte schön, das tue ich doch gern; **it wasn't any ~** (= *don't mention it*) das ist gern geschehen; (= *not difficult*) das war ganz einfach; **the children were no ~ at all** wir hatten mit den Kindern überhaupt keine Probleme; **to go to a lot of ~ to do sth** sich (*dat*) mit etw viel Mühe geben; **please don't put yourself to any ~ on my account** machen Sie meinetwegen keine Umstände
INTERJ Mist (*inf*); **~ that man!** zum Kuckuck mit ihm! (*inf*); **oh ~ this lock!** das ist ein doofes Schloss! (*inf*)

botheration [ˌbɒðə'reɪʃən] INTERJ verflixt und zugenäht (*inf*)

bothersome ['bɒðəsəm] ADJ lästig; *child* unleidlich; **the cooker has been rather ~ lately** mit dem Herd hatte ich *etc* in letzter Zeit viel Ärger

bothie ['bɒθɪ] N = **bothy**

Bothnia ['bɒθnɪə] N **Gulf of ~** Bottnischer Meerbusen

bothy ['bɒθɪ] N (*Scot*) Schutzhütte *f*

Botswana [ˌbɒt'swɑːnə] N Botswana *nt*

bottle ['bɒtl] **N** **a** Flasche *f*; **a ~ of wine** eine Flasche Wein **b** (*Brit, inf*) Mumm *m* (in den Knochen) (*inf*) **c** (*fig inf, = drink*) Flasche *f* (*inf*); **to be off the ~** nicht mehr trinken; **to take to the ~** zur Flasche greifen; **he's too fond of the ~** er trinkt zu gern **VT** **a** in Flaschen abfüllen; **~d in ...** abgefüllt in ... **b** (*Brit inf*) **to ~ it** die Nerven verlieren

▶ **bottle out** VI (*Brit inf: = lose nerve*) die Nerven verlieren

▶ **bottle up** VT *sep emotion* in sich (*dat*) aufstauen, in sich (*acc*) hineinfressen (*inf*); **there's a lot of hate bottled up inside her** es ist viel aufgestauter Hass in ihr

bottle: bottle bank N Altglascontainer *m*; **bottle blonde** N (*inf*) Wasserstoffblondine *f* (*inf*)

bottled ['bɒtld] ADJ *wine* in Flaschen (abgefüllt); *gas* in Flaschen; *beer* Flaschen-; *fruit* eingemacht

bottle: bottle-fed ADJ **he is ~** er wird aus der Flasche ernährt; **a ~ baby** ein Flaschenkind *nt*; **bottle-feed** VT *baby* aus der Flasche ernähren; **bottle-green** ADJ flaschengrün; **bottleneck** N (*lit, fig*) Engpass *m*; **bottle-opener** N Flaschenöffner *m*; **bottle party** N Bottleparty *f*

bottler ['bɒtlə'] N (= *company*) Abfüllbetrieb *m*; (= *person*) Abfüller(in) *m(f)*; (= *machine*) Abfüllmaschine *f*

bottle: bottle rack N Flaschengestell *nt*; **bottle top** N Flaschenverschluss *m*; **bottle-washer** N Flaschenreiniger *m*

bottling ['bɒtlɪŋ] N Abfüllen *nt*; (*of fruit*) Einmachen *nt*; **~ plant** Abfüllanlage *f*

bottom ['bɒtəm] **N** **a** (= *lowest part, of receptacle, box, glass*) Boden *m*; (*of mountain, pillar, spire, printed character*) Fuß *m*; (*of well, canyon*) Grund *m*; (*of page, screen, wall*) unteres Ende; (*of list, road*) Ende *nt*; (*of trousers*) unteres Beinteil; (*of dress*) Saum *m*; **the ~ of the league** das Tabellenende, der Tabellenschluss; **which end is the ~?** wo ist unten?; **the ~ of the tree/wall** *etc* **is ...** der Baum/Wand *etc* ist unten ...; **at the ~ of the page/list/league/hill/wall/tree** *etc* unten auf der Seite/Liste/in der Tabelle/am Berg/an der Wand/am Baum *etc*; **at the ~ of the canyon** unten in der Schlucht; **at the ~ of the mountain/cliff** am Fuß des Berges/Felsens; **to be (at the) ~ of the class** der/die Letzte in der Klasse sein; **he's near the ~ in English** in Englisch gehört er zu den Schlechtesten; **at the ~ of the garden** hinten im Garten; **at the ~ of the table/ road** am unteren Ende des Tisches/am Ende der Straße; **~s up!** hoch die Tassen (*inf*); **from the ~ of my heart** aus tiefstem Herzen; **he took a card from the ~ of the pack** er nahm eine Karte unten aus dem Stapel; **at ~** (*fig*) im Grunde; **the ~ fell out of his world** (*inf*) für ihn brach alles zusammen; **the ~ dropped** *or* **fell out of the market** die Marktlage hat einen Tiefstand erreicht

b (= *underneath, underside*) Unterseite *f*, untere Seite; **on the ~ of the tin/ashtray** unten an der Dose/am Aschenbecher

c (*of sea, lake, river*) Grund *m*, Boden *m*; **at the ~ of the sea** auf dem Meeresboden *or* -grund (*geh*); **to send a ship to the ~** ein Schiff versenken; **the ship went to the ~** das Schiff sank auf den Grund

d (*of chair*) Sitz *m*, Sitzfläche *f*

e (*of person*) Hintern *m* (*inf*), Po *m* (*inf*); (*of trousers etc*) Hosenboden *m*

f (*fig, causally*) **to be at the ~ of sth** (*person*) hinter etw (*dat*) stecken; (*thing*) einer Sache (*dat*) zugrunde *or* zu Grunde liegen; **to get to the ~ of sth** einer Sache (*dat*) auf den Grund kommen, hinter etw (*acc*) kommen; **let's get to the ~ of the matter** wir wollen der Sache auf den Grund gehen

g (*Naut, of ship*) Boden *m*; **the ship floated ~ up** das Schiff trieb kieloben

h (*Brit, Aut*) **~ (gear)** erster Gang; **in ~ (gear)** im ersten Gang; **we're still in ~ gear** (*inf*) wir sind immer noch nicht richtig auf Touren gekommen (*inf*)

i bottoms PL (*US, = low land*) Ebene *f*

j tracksuit/pyjama (*Brit*) *or* **pajama** (*US*) **~s** Trainings-/Schlafanzughose *f*; **bikini ~(s)** Bikiniunterteil *nt*

ADJ *attr* (= *lower*) untere(r, s); (= *lowest*) unterste(r, s); *price* niedrigste(r, s); (*Fin*) Tiefst-; *pupil* schlechteste(r, s); **~ half** (*of box*) untere Hälfte; (*of list, class*) zweite Hälfte

▶ **bottom out** VI (= *reach lowest point*) die Talsohle erreichen (*at bei*); (= *pass lowest point*) die Talsohle verlassen *or* überwinden

bottom: bottom drawer N (*Brit*) **to put sth away in one's ~** etw für die Aussteuer beiseite legen; **bottom-fermented** ['bɒtəmfə'mentɪd] ADJ *beer* untergärig; **bottomless** ADJ (*lit*) bodenlos; (*fig*) *funds* unerschöpflich; *despair* tiefste(r, s); **a ~ pit** (*fig*) ein Fass ohne Boden; **she is a ~ pit** sie frisst wie ein Scheunendrescher (*inf*); **bottom line** N **a** (*of accounts etc*) Saldo *m*; **if the balance sheet shows a healthy ~** wenn die Bilanz einen gesunden Saldo aufweist **b** (*fig*) **that's the ~ (of it)** (= *decisive factor*) das ist das Entscheidende (dabei); (= *what it amounts to*) darauf läuft es im Endeffekt hinaus; **bottom-line** ADJ *attr management, publishing* gewinnorientiert; **bottommost** ADJ allerunterste(r, s); **bottom-up** ADJ *approach, view, analysis* von unten nach oben

botulism ['bɒtjʊlɪzəm] N Nahrungsmittelvergiftung *f*, Botulismus *m*

bouclé [buˈkleɪ] N Bouclé *nt*

boudoir ['buːdwɑːʳ] N Boudoir *nt* (*old*)

bouffant ['buːfɒŋ] ADJ *hairstyle* aufgebauscht

bougainvillea [ˌbuːgənˈvɪlɪə] N Bougainvillea *f*

bough [baʊ] N Ast *m*

bought [bɔːt] *pret, ptp of* buy

bouillon ['buːjɒŋ] N Bouillon *f*, klare Fleischbrühe

bouillon cube N (*US*) Brühwürfel *m*

boulder ['bəʊldəʳ] N Felsblock *m*, Felsbrocken *m*

boulder clay N (*Geol*) Geschiebelehm *m*

boulevard ['buːləvɑːʳ] N Boulevard *m*

bounce [baʊns] **VI a** (*ball etc*) springen; (*Sport: ball*) aufspringen; (*chins, breasts etc*) wackeln; **rubber ~s** Gummi federt; **the child ~d up and down on the bed** das Kind hüpfte auf dem Bett herum; **the car ~d along the bumpy road** das Auto holperte die schlechte Straße entlang; **he came bouncing into the room** er kam munter ins Zimmer

b (*inf, cheque*) platzen (*inf*)

VT a *ball* aufprallen lassen, prellen (*Sport*); *laser beams, light, radio waves* reflektieren; **he ~d the ball against the wall** er warf den Ball gegen die Wand; **he ~d the baby on his knee** er ließ das Kind auf den Knien reiten

b (*inf*) *cheque* platzen lassen

c (*inf, = throw out*) rausschmeißen (*inf*)

d (= *coerce*) **to ~ sb into doing sth** jdn dazu bringen, etw zu tun

N a (*of ball*: = *rebound*) Aufprall *m*; **to hit a ball on the ~** den Ball beim Aufprall nehmen; **count the number of ~s** zählen Sie, wie oft der Ball *etc* aufspringt

b *no pl* (*of ball*) Sprungkraft *f*; (*of hair also, rubber*) Elastizität *f*; (*inf, of person*) Schwung *m* (*inf*)

▶ **bounce back** VT *sep ball* zurückprallen lassen **VI** abprallen, zurückprallen; (*fig inf: person*) sich nicht unterkriegen lassen (*inf*); (*to boyfriend*) zurückkommen

▶ **bounce off** VT *always separate* **to bounce sth off sth** etw von etw abprallen lassen; *radio waves etc* etw an etw (*dat*) reflektieren; **to bounce an idea off sb** (*fig inf*) eine Idee an jdm testen (*inf*) **VI** abprallen; (*radio waves*) reflektieren

bounce pass N (*Basketball*) Bodenpass *m*

bouncer ['baʊnsəʳ] N (*inf*) Rausschmeißer(in) *m(f)* (*inf*)

bouncing ['baʊnsɪŋ] ADJ **~ baby** strammer Säugling

bouncy ['baʊnsɪ] ADJ (+*er*) **a** *ball* gut springend; *mattress, step* federnd; *springs, hair* elastisch; *ride* holpernd **b** (*fig inf*, = *exuberant*) vergnügt und munter, quietschvergnügt (*inf*)

bouncy castle® N Hüpfburg *f*

bound¹ [baʊnd] N *usu pl* (*lit, fig*) Grenze *f*; **to keep within ~s** innerhalb der Grenzen bleiben; **to keep within the ~s of propriety** den Anstand wahren, im Rahmen bleiben; **within the ~s of probability** im Bereich des Wahrscheinlichen; **his ambition knows no ~s** sein Ehrgeiz kennt keine Grenzen; **the bar is out of ~s** das Betreten des Lokals ist verboten; **this part of town is out of ~s** dieser Stadtteil ist Sperrzone **VT** *usu pass country* begrenzen; *area also* abgrenzen

bound² N Sprung *m*, Satz *m* → **leap VI** springen; (*rabbit*) hoppeln; **to ~ in/away/back** herein-/weg-/zurückspringen; **the dog came ~ing up** der Hund kam angesprungen

bound³ *pret, ptp of* bind ADJ **a** gebunden; **~ hand and foot** an Händen und Füßen gebunden

b *book* gebunden; **~ in board** kartoniert

c (= *sure*) **to be ~ to do sth** etw bestimmt tun; **but then of course he's ~ to say that** das muss er ja sagen; **it's ~ to happen** das muss so kommen

d (= *obliged*) *person* verpflichtet; (*by contract, word, promise*) gebunden; **but I'm ~ to say ...** (*inf*) aber ich muss schon sagen ...; **if you say X then you're ~ to say that ...** wenn Sie X behaupten, müssen Sie zwangsläufig sagen, dass ...; **I'm not ~ to agree** ich muss nicht zwangsläufig zustimmen → **honour**

e ~ variable (*Math*) abhängige Variable; **~ form** (*Chem*) gebundene Form

bound⁴ ADJ *pred* **to be ~ for London** (= *heading for*) auf dem Weg nach London sein, nach London unterwegs sein; (= *about to start, ship, plane, lorry etc*) nach London gehen; (*person*) nach London reisen wollen; **the plane/all passengers ~ for London will ...** das Flugzeug/alle Passagiere nach London wird/werden ...; **where are you ~ for?** wohin geht die Reise?, wohin wollen Sie?; **we were northward-/California-bound** wir waren nach Norden/Kalifornien unterwegs → **homeward**

boundary ['baʊndərɪ] N Grenze *f*; (*Cricket*) Spielfeldgrenze *f*; **to hit/score a ~** den Ball über die Spielfeldgrenze schlagen/4 oder 6 Punkte für einen Schlag über die Spielfeldgrenze erzielen

boundary: Boundary Commission N (*Brit, Pol*) Kommission *f* zur Festlegung der Wahlbezirke; **boundary line** N Grenzlinie *f*; (*Sport*) Spielfeldgrenze *f*; **boundary mark** N Grenzmal *nt*; **boundary rider** N (*Austral*) Arbeiter, *der die Grenzen des Weidelandes abreitet*; **boundary stone** N Grenzstein *m*; **boundary value** N (*Math*) Randwert *m*

bounden ['baʊndən] ADJ **~ duty** (*old, liter*) Pflicht und Schuldigkeit *f* (*geh*)

bounder ['baʊndəʳ] N (*dated Brit, inf*) Lump *m* (*dated inf*)

boundless ['baʊndlɪs] ADJ (*lit, fig*) grenzenlos

bounteous ['baʊntɪəs], **bountiful** ['baʊntɪfʊl] ADJ großzügig; *sovereign, god* gütig; *harvest, gifts* (über)reich

bounteousness ['baʊntɪəsnɪs], **bountifulness** ['baʊntɪfʊlnɪs] N Großzügigkeit *f*; (*of sovereign, god*) Güte *f*; (*of harvest, gifts*) reiche Fülle (*geh*)

bounty ['baʊntɪ] N **a** (= *generosity*) Freigebigkeit *f*; (*of nature*) reiche Fülle (*geh*) **b** (= *gift*) großzügige *or* reiche Gabe (*geh*) **c** (= *reward money*) Kopfgeld *nt*; **~ hunter** Kopfgeldjäger *m*

bounty: bounty-fed ['baʊntɪfed] ADJ (*Econ*) subventioniert; **bounty hunter** N Kopfgeldjäger(in) *m(f)*

bouquet ['bʊkeɪ] N **a** Strauß *m*, Bukett *nt* (*geh*) **b** (*of wine*) Bukett *nt*, Blume *f*

bouquet garni ['bʊkeɪgɑːˈniː] N (*Cook*) Kräutermischung *f*

Bourbon ['bʊəbən] N (*Hist*) Bourbone *m*, Bourbonin *f*

bourbon ['bɜːbən] N (*also* **bourbon whiskey**) Bourbon *m*

bourgeois ['bʊəʒwɑː] N Bürger(in) *m(f)*, Bourgeois *m* (*esp Sociol*); (*pej*) Spießbürger(in) *m(f)*, Spießer *m* ADJ bürgerlich; (*pej*) spießbürgerlich, spießig

bourgeoisie [ˌbʊəʒwɑːˈziː] N Bürgertum *nt*, Bourgeoisie *f*

bout [baʊt] N **a** (*of flu etc*) Anfall *m*; (*of negotiations*) Runde *f*; **a ~ of fever/rheumatism** ein Fieber-/Rheumaanfall *m*; **a drinking ~** eine Zecherei; **I did another final ~ of revision before the exam** ich habe vor dem Examen noch einmal alles wiederholt **b** (*Boxing, Wrestling, Fencing*) Kampf *m*; **to have a ~ with sb** einen Kampf mit jdm austragen

boutique [buːˈtiːk] N Boutique *f*

bovine ['bəʊvaɪn] ADJ (*lit*) Rinder-; *appearance* rinderartig; (*fig*) stupide, einfältig N Rind *nt*

bovver boots ['bɒvəˈbuːts] PL (*dated Brit, sl*) Rockerstiefel *pl*

bow¹ [bəʊ] N **a** (*for shooting arrows*) Bogen *m*; **~ and arrow** Pfeil und Bogen *pl* **b** (*Mus*) Bogen *m*; **up/down ~ stroke** Auf-/Abstrich *m* **c** (= *knot: of ribbon etc*) Schleife *f* **VI** (*Mus*) den Bogen führen **VT** (*Mus*) streichen

bow² N (*with head, body*) Verbeugung *f*; (*by young boy*) Diener *m*; **to make one's ~ to sb** sich vor jdm verbeugen *or* verneigen (*geh*), jdm seine Reverenz erweisen (*form*); **to take a ~** sich verbeugen *or* verneigen; **take a ~** (*fig*: = *take the credit*) das haben wir Ihnen zu verdanken

VI a (*person: with body*) sich verbeugen, sich

verneigen (geh) (to sb vor jdm); (young boy) einen Diener machen; **to ~ and scrape** katzbuckeln (pej), liebedienern (pej)
b (= bend: branches etc) sich biegen or beugen **c** (fig, = defer, submit) sich beugen (before vor +dat, under unter +dat, to +dat); **to ~ to the majority** sich der Mehrheit beugen; **to ~ to the inevitable** sich in das Unvermeidliche fügen
VT **a** **to ~ one's head** den Kopf senken; (in prayer) sich verneigen
b (= bend) branches beugen; **old age had not ~ed him** er war vom Alter ungebeugt (geh)
c (= defeat) **to be ~ed by sth** von etw schwer getroffen sein

▶ **bow down** **VI** (lit) sich beugen or neigen; **to bow down to or before sb** (fig) sich jdm beugen **VT** sep **bowed down with snow/cares** schneebeladen/mit Sorgen beladen

▶ **bow out** **VI** (fig) sich verabschieden; **to bow out of sth** sich aus etw zurückziehen

bow³ [baʊ] N often pl Bug m; **in the ~s** im Bug; **on the port/starboard ~** backbord(s)/steuerbord(s) voraus; **~ doors** Bugtor nt

Bow Bells [ˌbaʊ'belz] PL **he was born within the sound of ~** er ist ein waschechter Cockney (Londoner)

bowdlerize ['baʊdləraɪz] VT book von anstößigen Stellen säubern, reinigen; **a ~d version** eine zensierte Ausgabe

bowed¹ [baʊd] ADJ legs krumm

bowed² [baʊd] ADJ person gebeugt; shoulders hängend

bowel ['baʊəl] N usu pl **a** (Anat, of person) Eingeweide nt usu pl, Gedärm nt usu pl; (of animal also) Innereien pl; **a ~ movement** Stuhl(-gang) m; **to move one's ~s** Stuhl(gang) haben; **to control one's ~s** seine Darmentleerung kontrollieren; **he had something wrong with his ~s** mit seiner Verdauung stimmte etwas nicht **b** (fig) **the ~s of the earth/ship** etc das Erdinnere/Schiffsinnere etc, das Innere der Erde/der Schiffsbauch etc

bower ['baʊə] N Laube f

bowing ['baʊɪŋ] N (Mus) Bogenführung f

bowl¹ [baʊl] N **a** Schüssel f; (smaller, shallow also, fingerbowl) Schale f; (for sugar etc) Schälchen nt; (for animals, prisoners also) Napf m; (= punch bowl) Bowle f; (= washbowl also) Becken nt; **a ~ of milk** eine Schale/ein Napf Milch **b** (of pipe) Kopf m; (of spoon) Schöpfteil m; (of lavatory) Becken nt; (of lamp) Schale f; (of wineglass) Kelch m; (of retort) Bauch m **c** (Geog) Becken nt **d** (US, = stadium) Stadion nt

bowl² **N** (Sport, = ball) Kugel f → also **bowls** **VI** **a** (Bowls) Bowling/Boccia/Boule spielen; (tenpin) bowlen, Bowling spielen; (skittles) kegeln **b** (Cricket) werfen **c** (= travel: car, cycle etc) brausen (inf); **he came ~ing down the street** er kam auf der Straße angerauscht (inf) **VT** **a** (= roll) ball rollen; hoop also treiben **b** (Cricket) ball werfen; batsman ausschlagen

▶ **bowl along** **VI** dahergerauscht kommen/dahinrauschen (prep obj auf +dat) (inf)

▶ **bowl out** **VT** sep (Cricket) ausschlagen

▶ **bowl over** **VT** sep **a** (lit, with ball etc) umwerfen; (in car etc) umfahren, über den Haufen fahren (inf) **b** (fig) umwerfen, umhauen (inf); **to be bowled over** sprachlos or platt (inf) sein; **he was bowled over by the news/her/the idea** die Nachricht/sie/die Idee hat ihn (einfach) überwältigt or umgehauen (inf)

bow [baʊ]: **bow-legged** ADJ o-beinig, O-beinig; **bowlegs** PL O-Beine pl

bowler¹ [baʊlə] N **a** (Sport) Bowlingspieler(in) m(f); (of bowls also) Boccia-/Boulespieler(in) m(f) **b** (Cricket) Werfer m

bowler² N (Brit: also **bowler hat**) Melone f; **~ hat brigade** (hum) Bürohengste pl (inf)

bowline ['baʊlɪn] N Palstek m; (= rope) Bulin(e) f

bowling ['baʊlɪŋ] N **a** (Cricket) Werfen nt; **renowned for his fast ~** für seine schnelle Bälle berühmt **b** (= tenpin bowling) Bowling nt; (=

skittles) Kegeln nt; **to go ~** bowlen/kegeln gehen

bowling: bowling alley N Bowlingbahn f; **bowling green** N Spiel- or Rasenfläche f für Bowling/Boccia/Boule

bowls [baʊlz] N Bowling nt; (Italian, German) Boccia nt; (French) Boule nt

bowman ['baʊmən] N pl **-men** [-mən] Bogenschütze m

bows [baʊz] PL → **bow³**

bowsprit ['baʊsprɪt] N Bugspriet nt or m

Bow Street runner [baʊ-] N (Brit, Hist) Büttel m (der offiziellen Detektei in der Londoner Bow Street)

bow [baʊ]: **bowstring** N (Mus) (Bogen)bezug m; (in archery) (Bogen)sehne f; **bow tie** N Fliege f

bow wave [baʊ-] N Bugwelle f

bow window [baʊ-] N Erkerfenster nt

bow-wow ['baʊ'waʊ] (baby-talk) **INTERJ** wauwau (baby-talk) **N** ['baʊwaʊ] (= dog) Wauwau m (baby-talk)

box¹ [bɒks] **VI** (Sport) boxen **VT** (Sport) boxen; **to ~ sb's ears** or **sb on the ears** jdn ohrfeigen, jdm eine Ohrfeige geben **N** **a ~ on the ear** or **round the ears** eine Ohrfeige, eine Backpfeife (inf)

box² N (Bot) Buchsbaum m

box³ **N** **a** (made of wood or strong cardboard) Kiste f; (= cardboard box) Karton m; (made of light cardboard, = matchbox) Schachtel f; (= snuffbox, cigarette box etc, biscuit tin) Dose f; (of crackers, chocolates etc) Packung f, Schachtel f; (= jewellery box) Schatulle f, Kasten m; (= tool box) (Werkzeug)kasten m; (= ballot box) Urne f; (= money box, with lid and lock) Kassette f; (for saving) Sparbüchse or -dose f; (= collection box) (Sammel)büchse f; (in church) Opferbüchse f; (fixed to wall etc) Opferstock m; (Brit, old, = trunk) (Schrank)koffer m; **to be out of one's ~** (Brit inf: = drunk, drugged) total zu sein (inf)
b (on form) Kästchen nt; (on newspaper page) Kasten m; (Baseball) Box f; (Football) Strafraum m; (in road junction) gelb schraffierter Kreuzungsbereich **draw a ~ (a)round it** umranden Sie es; **tick the appropriate ~** das entsprechende Kästchen ankreuzen
c (Theat) Loge f; (= jury box) Geschworenenbank f; (= witness box) Zeugenstand m; (= press box) Pressekabine f; (outside) Pressetribüne f; (in court) Pressebank f
d (Tech, = housing) Gehäuse nt
e (building, = sentry box) Schilderhaus f; (= signal box) Häuschen nt; (= hunting box) (Jagd-) hütte f
f (= horse box) Box f
g (Brit, = pillar box) (Brief)kasten m
h (Brit, = phone box) Zelle f
i (esp Brit, inf, = TV) Glotze f (inf), Glotzkasten m (inf); **what's on the ~?** was gibts im Fernsehen?; **I was watching the ~** ich habe geglotzt (inf)
j (Brit, = gift of money) Geldgeschenk nt
k (on stagecoach) (Kutsch)bock m
VT **a** goods etc (in eine(r) Schachtel etc) verpacken
b **to ~ the compass** (Naut) alle Kompasspunkte der Reihe nach aufzählen

▶ **box in** **VT** sep **a** player in die Zange nehmen; parked car einklemmen; (fig) einengen, keinen or zu wenig Spielraum lassen (+dat) **b** bath etc verkleiden; (with wood also) verschalen

▶ **box off** **VT** sep abteilen, abtrennen

▶ **box up** **VT** sep **a** (= confine) einsperren **b** (= put in boxes) (in Kartons) einpacken

box: box bed N Klappbett nt; **box calf** N Boxkalf nt; **box camera** N Box f; **boxcar** N (US, Rail) (geschlossener) Güterwagen

boxer ['bɒksə] N **a** (Sport) Boxer m **b** (= dog) Boxer m

boxer shorts PL Boxershorts pl

box: box file N Flachordner m; **box girder** N Kastenträger m; **box hedge** N streng geschnittene Hecke

boxing ['bɒksɪŋ] N Boxen nt

boxing in cpds Box-; **Boxing Day** N (Brit) zweiter Weihnachts(feier)tag; **boxing match** N Boxkampf m; **boxing ring** N Boxring m

---

BOXING DAY

Der **Boxing Day** ist in Großbritannien der zweite Weihnachtsfeiertag. Traditionellerweise finden an diesem Tag auch eine ganze Reihe sportlicher Veranstaltungen statt. Der Name geht auf einen Brauch aus dem 19. Jahrhundert zurück, an dem Händler und Lieferanten an diesem Tag ein Trinkgeld oder ein Weihnachtsgeschenk, die so genannte **Christmas box**, erhielten.

---

box: box junction N (Mot) gelb schraffierte Kreuzung (in die bei Stau nicht eingefahren werden darf); **box kite** N Kastendrachen m; **box lunch** N (US) Lunchpaket nt; **box number** N Chiffre f; (at post office) Postfach nt; **box office** **N** Kasse f, Theater-/Kinokasse f; **to be good ~** ein Kassenschlager sein **ATTR** **~ success/hit/attraction** Kassenschlager m; **box pleat** N Kellerfalte f; **boxroom** N (Brit) Abstellraum m; **box seat** N (Theat) Logenplatz m; **to be in the ~** (Austral) in der besten Position sein; **box spanner** N Steckschlüssel m; **box tree** N Buchsbaum m; **boxwood** N Buchsbaum(holz nt) m

boxy ['bɒksɪ] ADJ (usu pej) building, car kastenförmig

boy [bɔɪ] N **a** (= male child) Junge m, Bub m (dial); **bad** or **naughty ~!** du frecher Bengel; (to animal) böser Hund! etc; **sit, ~!** (to dog) sitz!; **the Jones ~** der Junge von Jones; **~s will be ~s** Jungen sind nun mal so; **a school for ~s** eine Jungenschule; **good morning, ~s** guten Morgen(, Jungs)! → **old boy**
b (inf, = fellow) Knabe m (inf); **the old ~** (= boss) der Alte (inf); (= father) mein etc alter Herr
c (= friend) **the ~s** meine/seine Kumpels; **our ~s** (= team) unsere Jungs; **jobs for the ~s** Vetternwirtschaft f
d (= native servant, liftboy) Boy m; (= messenger boy, ship's boy) Junge m; (= butcher's etc boy) (Lauf)junge m; (= pageboy) (Hotel)boy m; (= stable boy) Stalljunge or (older) -bursche m
e **oh ~!** (inf) Junge, Junge! (inf)

boy band N (Mus) Boygroup f

boycott ['bɔɪkɒt] **N** Boykott m; **to impose a ~ on sth** einen Boykott über etw (acc) verhängen **VT** boykottieren

boy: boyfriend N Freund m; **boyhood** N Kindheit f; (as teenager) Jugend(zeit) f

boyish ['bɔɪɪʃ] ADJ jungenhaft; woman knabenhaft

boyishly ['bɔɪɪʃlɪ] ADV jungenhaft

boyo ['bɔɪəʊ] INTERJ (Welsh) Junge m

Boys' Brigade N Jugendorganisation, ≈ Junge Pioniere pl (DDR)

boy: boy scout N Pfadfinder m; **Boy Scouts** N sing Pfadfinder pl; **boy toy** N (inf, pej) **a** (= woman) junge, sexuell anziehende Frau **b** (= man) junger, besonders für ältere Frauen attraktiver Mann; **boy wonder** N (inf) Wunderkind nt, Wunderknabe m

bozo ['bəʊzəʊ] N (US) (primitiver) Kerl (inf)

bpi (Comput) abbr of **bits per inch** Bits pro Zoll

B-picture N → **B-movie**

BR abbr of **British Rail** die britischen Eisenbahnen

bra [brɑː] N abbr of **brassière** BH m

brace¹ [breɪs] N pl **- (** = pair: of pheasants etc) Paar nt

brace² **N** **a** (Build) Strebe f **b** (= tool) (= wheel brace) Radschlüssel m; (to hold bit) Bohrwinde f; **~ and bit** Bohrer m (mit Einsatz) **c** (on teeth) Klammer f, Spange f; (Med) Stützapparat

m **d** (*Typ*) geschweifte Klammer, Akkolade *f*
VT a (= *support*) (ab)stützen; (*horizontally*) verstreben; (*in vice etc*) verklammern **b** (*climate etc*: = *invigorate*) stärken, kräftigen **VR** sich bereithalten; (*fig*) sich wappnen (*geh*), sich bereitmachen; **to ~ oneself for sth** sich auf etw (*acc*) gefasst machen; **~ yourself, I've got bad news for you** mach dich auf eine schlechte Nachricht gefasst

bracelet ['breɪslɪt] N Armband *nt*; (= *bangle*) Armreif(en) *m*; (= *ankle bracelet*) Fußreif(en) *m*; **~s** (*inf*, = *handcuffs*) Handschellen *pl*

bracer ['breɪsə'] N *a* (*inf*, = *drink*) kleine Stärkung, Schnäpschen *nt* **b** (*Sport*) Armschutz *m*

braces ['breɪsɪz] PL (*Brit*) Hosenträger *pl*; **a pair of ~** (ein Paar) Hosenträger

bracing ['breɪsɪŋ] ADJ belebend, anregend; *climate* Reiz-

bracken ['brækən] N Adlerfarn *m*

bracket ['brækɪt] **N a** (= *angle bracket*) Winkelträger *m*; (*for shelf*) (Regal)träger *m*; (*Archit*) Konsole *f*; (*of stone*) Kragstein *m* **b** (*Typ, Mus*) Klammer *f*; **in ~s** in Klammern **c** (= *gas bracket*) Anschluss *m*; (*for electric light*) (Wand)arm *m* **d** (= *group*) Gruppe *f*, Klasse *f*; **the lower income ~** die untere Einkommensgruppe **VT a** (= *put in brackets*) einklammern **b** (*also* **bracket together**, = *join by brackets*) mit einer Klammer verbinden; (*Mus also*) mit einer Akkolade verbinden; (*fig*, = *group together*) zusammenfassen

brackish ['brækɪʃ] ADJ *water* brackig

bract [brækt] N Tragblatt *nt*

brad [bræd] N Stift *m*

bradawl ['brædɔ:l] N Ahle *f*, Pfriem *m*

brae [breɪ] N (*Scot*) Berg *m*

brag [bræg] **VI** prahlen, angeben (*about, of* mit) **VT** prahlen; **to ~ that** prahlen, dass, damit angeben, dass **N a** (= *boast*) Prahlerei *f*, Angeberei *f* **b** (*inf*) = **braggart**

braggart ['brægət] N Prahler *m*, Angeber *m*

bragging ['brægɪŋ] N Prahlerei *f*, Angeberei *f*

braid [breɪd] **N a** (*of hair*) Flechte *f* (*geh*), Zopf *m* **b** (= *trimming*) Borte *f*; (*self-coloured*) Litze *f* **c** (*Mil*) Tressen *pl*; **gold ~** Goldtressen *pl* **d** (*to tie hair*) (Haar)band *nt* **VT a** (= *plait*) *hair, straw etc* flechten **b** (= *trim*) mit einer Borte besetzen **c** (= *tie up with braid*) *hair* binden

Braille [breɪl] **N** Blinden- or Brailleschrift *f* **ADJ** Blindenschrift-; **~ library** Blindenbücherei *f*; **~ books** Bücher *pl* in Blindenschrift

brain [breɪn] **N** (*Anat, of machine*) Gehirn *nt*; **he's got sex/cars on the ~** (*inf*) er hat nur Sex/Autos im Kopf; **I've got that tune on the ~** (*inf*) das Lied geht or will mir nicht aus dem Kopf **b** **brains** PL (*Anat*) Gehirn *nt*; (*Cook*) Hirn *nt* **c** (= *mind*) Verstand *m*; **~s** *pl* (= *intelligence*) Intelligenz *f*, Grips *m* (*inf*), Köpfchen *nt* (*inf*); **to have a good ~** einen klaren or guten Verstand haben; **he has ~s** er ist intelligent, er hat Grips (*inf*) or Köpfchen (*inf*); **she's the ~s of the family** sie ist das Familiengenie (*hum*), sie ist die Schlauste in der Familie; **you're the one with the ~s** du bist doch der Schlaue or Intelligente hier; **use your ~s** streng mal deinen Kopf or Grips (*inf*) an; **he didn't have the ~s to ...** er ist nicht einmal darauf gekommen, zu ... **VT** den Schädel einschlagen (*sb* jdm)

brain: **brain activity** N (Ge)hirntätigkeit *f*; **brainbox** N (*hum inf*) Schlauberger *m* (*inf*); **brainchild** N Erfindung *f*; (= *idea*) Geistesprodukt *nt*; **brain damage** N (Ge)hirnschaden *m*; **brain-damaged** ADJ (*lit*) hirngeschädigt; (*fig inf*) (ge)hirnamputiert (*hum inf*); **brain-dead** ADJ (*lit*) hirntot; **brain death** N (Ge-)hirntod *m*; **brain drain** N Abwanderung *f* von Wissenschaftlern, Braindrain *m*; **brainfag** N geistige Erschöpfung; **brain failure** N (*inf*) Aussetzer *m* (*inf*); **brain fever** N Hirnhautentzündung *f*; **brain fog** N (*inf*) Gehirnnebel *m* (*inf*), *eingeschränkte geistige Leistungsfähigkeit*; **brain haemorrhage**, **brain hemorrhage** (*US*) N (Ge)hirnblutung *f*; **brainless**

ADJ *plan, idea* hirnlos, dumm; *person also* unbedarft; **brainpower** N Intelligenz *f*; **brain scan** N Computertomografie *f* des Schädels; **brain scanner** N Computertomograf *m* (*zur Untersuchung des Gehirns*); **brainstorm** N *a* (*Brit*) **to have a ~** geistig weggetreten sein (*inf*) **b** (*US*, = *brainwave*) Geistesblitz *m* **VI** ein Brainstorming machen **VT** gemeinsam erarbeiten; **brainstorming** N gemeinsame Problembewältigung, Brainstorming *nt*; **to have a ~ session** ein Brainstorming veranstalten or abhalten

brains trust N (= *discussion*) Podiumsdiskussion *f*; (= *panel*) Gruppe *f* von Sachverständigen or Experten

brain: **brain surgeon** N Neurochirurg(in) *m(f)*, Hirnchirurg(in) *m(f)*; **brain-teaser** N Denksportaufgabe *f*; **brain trust** N (*US*) Braintrust *m*, Expertenausschuss *m*; **brain tumour**, (*US*) **brain tumor** N Gehirntumor *m*; **brainwash** VT einer Gehirnwäsche (*dat*) unterziehen; **to ~ sb into believing/accepting** *etc* **that ...** jdm (ständig) einreden, dass ...; **brainwashing** N Gehirnwäsche *f*; **brainwave** N *a* (*Brit*) Geistesblitz *m* **b** **brainwaves** PL (*Physiol*) Gehirnströme *pl*; **brainwork** N Kopfarbeit *f*

brainy ['breɪnɪ] ADJ (+*er*) (*inf*) gescheit, helle (*inf*)

braise [breɪz] VT (*Cook*) schmoren

brake[1] [breɪk] **N** (*Tech*) Bremse *f*; **to put the ~s on** (*lit, fig*) bremsen; **to put the ~s on sth** (*fig*) etw bremsen; **to act as a ~** (*lit*) als Bremse wirken (*on* auf +*acc*); (*fig*) dämpfend wirken (*on* auf +*acc*), bremsen (*on* +*acc*) **VI** bremsen

brake[2] N (= *shooting brake*) Kombi(wagen) *m*

brake[3] N (*Bot*) (Adler)farn *m*

brake[4] N (= *thicket*) Unterholz *nt*

brake in *cpds* Brems-; **brake block** N Bremsbacke *f*; **brake disc** N Bremsscheibe *f*; **brake drum** N Bremstrommel *f*; **brake fluid** N Bremsflüssigkeit *f*; **brake horsepower** N Bremsleistung *f*; **brake light** N Bremslicht *nt*; **brake lining** N Bremsbelag *m*; **brakeman** N (*US, Rail*) Bremser *m*; **brake pad** N Bremsklotz *m*; **brake shoe** N Bremsbacke *f*; **brake van** N Bremswagen *m*

braking ['breɪkɪŋ] N Bremsen *nt*

braking: **braking distance** N Bremsweg *m*; **braking power** N Bremskraft *f*

bramble ['bræmbl] N *a* (= *thorny shoot*) dorniger Zweig, Dornenzweig *m* **b** (= *blackberry*) Brombeere *f*; (= *bush also*) Brombeerstrauch *m*; **~ jam** Brombeermarmelade *f*

bran [bræn] N Kleie *f*

branch [brɑ:ntʃ] **N a** (*Bot*) Zweig *m*; (*growing straight from trunk*) Ast *m* **b** (*of river, pipe, duct*) Arm *m*; (*of road*) Abzweigung *f*; (*of family, race, language*) Zweig *m*; (*of railway*) Abzweig *m*; (*of antler*) Sprosse *f*, Ende *nt* **c** (*in river, road, railway, pipe, duct*) Gabelung *f* **d** (*Comm*) Filiale *f*, Zweigstelle *f*; **main ~** Haupt(geschäfts)stelle *f*; (*of store*) Hauptgeschäft *nt*; (*of bank*) Hauptgeschäftsstelle *f*, Zentrale *f* **e** (= *field: of subject etc*) Zweig *m* **VI** (= *divide, river, road etc*) sich gabeln; (*in more than two*) sich verzweigen

▶ **branch off** VI (*road*) abzweigen; (*driver*) abbiegen

▶ **branch out** VI (*fig, person, company*) sein Geschäft erweitern or ausdehnen (*into* auf +*acc*); **the firm is branching out into cosmetics** die Firma erweitert ihren (Geschäfts)bereich jetzt auf Kosmetika; **to branch out on one's own** sich selbstständig machen

branch: **branch line** N (*Rail*) Zweiglinie *f*, Nebenlinie *f*; **branch manager** N Filialleiter *m*; **branch office** N Filiale *f*, Zweigstelle *f*; **branch road** N (*US*) Nebenstraße *f*

brand [brænd] **N a** (= *make*) Marke *f* **b** (= *mark, on cattle*) Brandzeichen *nt* **c** (*on criminal, prisoner, fig*) Brandmal *nt* **d** (*obs, poet*, = *sword*) Klinge *f* (*liter*) **VT a** (= *mark with brand*) *goods* mit seinem Warenzeichen versehen; **~ed goods** Markenartikel *pl* **b** *cattle, property* mit

einem Brandzeichen kennzeichen **c** (= *stigmatize*) *person* brandmarken

brand: **brand awareness** N Markenbewusstsein *nt*; **brand image** N Markenimage *nt*

branding iron ['brændɪŋaɪən] N Brandeisen *nt*

brandish ['brændɪʃ] VT schwingen, fuchteln mit (*inf*)

brand: **brand leader** N führende Marke; **brand loyalty** N Markentreue *f*; **brand manager** N Brandmanager(in) *m(f)*, Markenbetreuer(in) *m(f)*; **brand name** N Markenname *m*; **brand-new** ADJ nagelneu, brandneu (*inf*)

brandy ['brændɪ] N Weinbrand *m*, Brandy *m*

brandy: **brandy butter** N Weinbrandbutter *f*; **brandysnap** N *Gebäckröllchen aus dünnem, mit Ingwer gewürztem Teig*

brash [bræʃ] ADJ (*+er*) nassforsch, dreist; (= *tasteless*) *colour etc* laut, aufdringlich

brashly ['bræʃlɪ] ADV dreist

brashness ['bræʃnɪs] N nassforsche Art, Dreistigkeit *f*; (*of colour etc*) Aufdringlichkeit *f*

brasier N = **brazier**

brass [brɑ:s] **N a** Messing *nt* **b** **the ~** (*Mus*) die Blechbläser *pl*, das Blech (*inf*) **c** (= *thing made of brass*) (= *plaque*) Messingtafel *f* or -schild *nt*; (*in church: on tomb*) Grabplatte *f* aus Messing; (*no pl*: = *brass articles*) Messing *nt*; **to do** or **clean the ~(es)** das Messing putzen **d** (*inf*) **the top ~** die hohen Tiere (*inf*) **e** (*inf*, = *impudence*) Frechheit *f* **f** (*inf*, = *money*) Kohle *f* (*inf*) **ADJ** (= *made of brass*) Messing-, messingen (*rare*); (*Mus*) Blech-; **~ instrument** Blechblasinstrument *nt*; **~ player** Blechbläser *m*; **~ section** Blech(bläser *pl*) *nt*

brass band N Blaskapelle *f*

brassed off [,brɑ:st'ɒf] ADJ **to be ~** (*Brit sl*) die Schnauze voll haben (*inf*) (*with* von)

brass: **brass farthing** N **he hasn't got a ~** (*Brit inf*) er besitzt keinen Cent; **not to get a ~** (*Brit inf*) keinen Cent bekommen; **it doesn't matter a ~** (*Brit inf*) es ist völlig egal; **brass foundry** N Messinggießerei *f*; **brass hat** N (*Brit Mil sl*) hohes Tier (*inf*)

brassière ['bræsɪə] N (*dated, form*) Büstenhalter *m*

brass: **brass knuckles** PL (*inf*) Schlagring *m*; **brass monkey** N **it's cold enough to freeze the balls off a ~** (*Brit hum sl*) es ist arschkalt (*sl*); **real ~ weather, eh?** (*Brit hum inf*) arschkalt, was? (*sl*); **brass neck** N **to have a ~** Nerven haben (*inf*); **brass plaque**, **brass plate** N Messingschild *nt*; (*in church*) Messinggedenktafel *f* **brass rubbing** N (= *activity*) Durchpausen or -zeichnen *nt* (*des Bildes auf einer Messinggrabtafel*); (= *result*) Pauszeichnung *f* (*des Bildes auf einer Messinggrabtafel*); **brass tacks** PL **to get down to ~** (*inf*) zur Sache kommen

brassy ['brɑ:sɪ] ADJ (*+er*) **a** *metal* messingartig; *hair, blonde* messingfarben; *sound* blechern **b** (*inf*, = *impudent*) frech, dreist **c** (*pej*, = *flashy*) *woman* aufgedonnert (*pej inf*)

brat [bræt] N (*pej inf*) Balg *m* or *nt* (*inf*), Gör *nt* (*inf*); (*esp girl*) Göre *f* (*inf*)

bravado [brə'vɑ:dəʊ] N (= *showy bravery*) Draufgängertum *nt*, Wagemut *m*; (*hiding fear*) gespielte Tapferkeit; **this is just military ~** da lässt das Militär die Muskeln spielen

brave [breɪv] **ADJ** (*+er*) **a** *person, act* mutig, unerschrocken (*geh*); (= *showing courage, suffering pain*) tapfer; *attack* mutig; *smile* tapfer; **be ~!** nur Mut!; (*more seriously*) sei tapfer! **b** (*obs, liter*, = *fine*) schmuck (*dated*), ansehnlich; **~ new world** schöne neue Welt **N** (= *Indian*) Krieger *m* **VT** die Stirn bieten (+*dat*); *weather, elements* trotzen (+*dat*); *death* tapfer ins Auge sehen (+*dat*)

▶ **brave out** VT *sep* **to brave it out** es or das durchstehen

bravely ['breɪvlɪ] ADV tapfer

braveness ['breɪvnɪs], **bravery** ['breɪvərɪ] N (*of person, act*) Mut *m*; (*of attempt, smile*) Tapferkeit *f*

bravo [brɑːˈvəʊ] **INTERJ** bravo! **N** *pl* **-es** Bravoruf *m*

bravura [brəˈvʊərə] N Bravour *f*; (*Mus*) Bravourstück *nt*

brawl [brɔːl] **VI** sich schlagen **N** Schlägerei *f*

brawling [ˈbrɔːlɪŋ] N Schlägereien *pl*

brawn [brɔːn] N **a** (*Cook*) Presskopf *m*, Sülze *f* **b** Muskeln *pl*, Muskelkraft *f*; **to have plenty of ~** starke Muskeln haben, ein Muskelpaket *or* Muskelprotz sein (*inf*); **he's all ~ and no brains** (er hat) Muskeln, aber kein Gehirn

brawny [ˈbrɔːnɪ] ADJ (+*er*) muskulös, kräftig

bray [breɪ] **N** (*of ass*) (Esels)schrei *m*; (*inf, = laugh*) Wiehern *nt*, Gewieher *nt* **VI** (*ass*) schreien; (*inf, person*) wiehern

brazen [ˈbreɪzn] ADJ **a** (= *impudent*) unverschämt, dreist; *lie* schamlos; **to be ~ about sth** klar zu etw stehen; **to be ~ about doing sth** etw ganz dreist tun **b** (*obs*, = *of brass*) messingen (*rare*)

▶ **brazen out** VT *sep* **to brazen it out** durchhalten; (*by lying*) sich durchmogeln (*inf*)

brazen-faced [ˈbreɪznˌfeɪst] ADJ schamlos, unverschämt

brazenly [ˈbreɪznlɪ] ADV unverschämt, dreist; *lie* schamlos

brazenness [ˈbreɪznnɪs] N Unverschämtheit *f*, Dreistigkeit *f*; (*of lie*) Schamlosigkeit *f*

brazier [ˈbreɪzɪə] N (Kohlen)feuer *nt* (im Freien); (= *container*) Kohlenbecken *nt*

Brazil [brəˈzɪl] N Brasilien *nt*

brazil [brəˈzɪl] N (*also* **brazil nut**) Paranuss *f*

Brazilian [brəˈzɪlɪən] **N** Brasilianer(in) *m(f)* **ADJ** brasilianisch

breach [briːtʃ] **N a** Verletzung *f* (*of* +*gen*), Verstoß *m* (*of* gegen); (*of law*) Übertretung *f* (*of* +*gen*), Verstoß *m*; **a ~ of confidence/contract/faith** ein Vertrauens-/Vertrags-/Vertrauensbruch *m*; **a ~ of law** ein Rechtsbruch *m*; **a ~ of rule** eine Regelwidrigkeit *f*; (*Sport*) eine Regelverletzung *f*; **a ~ of security** ein Verstoß *m* gegen die Sicherheitsbestimmungen; **~ of the peace** (*Jur*) öffentliche Ruhestörung; **~ of privilege** Privilegienmissbrauch *m*; **~ of promise** (*Jur*) Bruch *m* des Eheversprechens
b (= *estrangement: in friendship etc*) Bruch *m*
c (= *gap, in wall etc*) Bresche *f*, Lücke *f*; (*in security*) Lücke *f*; **to make a ~ in the enemy's lines** (*Mil*) eine Bresche in die feindlichen Linien schlagen; **to step into the ~** (*fig*) in die Bresche springen
VT a *wall* eine Bresche schlagen in (+*acc*); *defences, security* durchbrechen
b *contract, treaty* verletzen

bread [bred] **N a** Brot *nt*; **a piece of ~ and butter** ein Butterbrot *nt*; **we just had ~ and butter** wir aßen nur Brot mit Butter; **he was put on (dry) ~ and water** er saß bei Wasser und (trocken) Brot; **he knows which side his ~ is buttered (on)** er weiß, wo was zu holen ist; **~ and circuses** Brot und Spiele *pl*
b (= *food, livelihood*) **writing is his ~ and butter** er verdient sich seinen Lebensunterhalt mit Schreiben; **to take the ~ out of sb's mouth** (*fig*) jdn seiner Existenzgrundlage (*gen*) berauben; **to break ~ with sb** (*old*) sein Brot mit jdm teilen, das Brot mit jdm brechen (*old*)
c (*inf*, = *money*) Kohle *f* (*inf*)
VT panieren

bread: bread-and-butter letter, bread-and-butter note N Bedankemichbrief *m*; **bread-and-butter pudding** N Brotauflauf *m*; **breadbasket** N **a** Brotkorb *m* **b** (*inf*) Wampe *f* (*inf*); **breadbin** N (*Brit*) Brotkasten *m*; **breadboard** N Brot(schneide)brett *nt*; **breadbox** N (*US*) = **breadbin**; **breadcrumb** N Brotkrume *f* *or* -krümel *m*; **breadcrumbs** PL (*Cook*) Paniermehl *nt*; **~ed** = paniert; **breadfruit** N Brotfrucht *f*; **breadknife** N Brotmesser *nt*; **breadline** N *Schlange vor einer Nahrungsmittelausgabestelle* **to be on the ~** (*fig*) nur das Allernotwendigste zum Leben haben

bread roll N Brötchen *nt*; **bread sauce** N Brottunke *f*; **breadstick** N Knabberstange *f*

breadth [bretθ] N Breite *f*; (*of ideas, theory*) (Band)breite *f*; **a hundred metres** (*Brit*) *or* **meters** (*US*) **in ~** hundert Meter breit; **his ~ of outlook** (= *open-mindedness*) seine große Aufgeschlossenheit; (= *variety of interests*) seine große Vielseitigkeit; **the ~ of his comprehension** sein umfassendes Verständnis

breadthways [ˈbretθweɪz], **breadthwise** [ˈbretθwaɪz] ADV in der Breite, der Breite nach

breadwinner [ˈbredwɪnə] N Ernährer(in) *m(f)*, Brotverdiener(in) *m(f)*

---

break [breɪk]
vb: pret **broke**, *ptp* **broken**

1 NOUN	3 INTRANSITIVE VERB
2 TRANSITIVE VERB	4 PHRASAL VERBS

1 – NOUN

a = fracture (*in bone, pipe*) Bruch *m*; (*Gram, Typ*, = *word break*) (Silben)trennung *f*; **... he said with a break in his voice** ... sagte er mit stockender Stimme; **break in the circuit** (*Elec*) Stromkreisunterbrechung *f*

b = gap Lücke *f*; (*in rock*) Spalte *f*, Riss *m*; (*in drawn line*) Unterbrechung *f*; **row upon row of houses without a break** Häuserzeile auf Häuserzeile, ohne Lücke *or* lückenlos

c = pause (*also Brit Sch*) Pause *f*; (*in journey*) Pause *f*, Unterbrechung *f*; **without a break** ohne Unterbrechung *or* Pause, ununterbrochen; **to take** *or* **have a break** (eine) Pause machen; **at break** (*Sch*) in der Pause; **after the break** (*Rad, TV*) nach der Pause; **give me a break!** (*inf, expressing annoyance*) nun mach mal halblang! (*inf*)

d = end of relations Bruch *m*

e = change Abwechslung *f*; **break in the weather** Wetterumschwung *m*

f = respite Erholung *f*; **the playgroup gives parents a break** die Spielgruppe verschafft den Eltern etwas Erholung

g = holiday Urlaub *m*; **I'm looking forward to a good break** ich freue mich auf einen schönen Urlaub

h **at break of day** bei Tagesanbruch

i = escape (*inf*) Ausbruch *m*; **they made a break for it** sie versuchten zu entkommen

j = opportunity (*inf*) **to have a good/bad break** Glück *or* Schwein (*inf*) *nt*/Pech *nt* haben; **we had a few lucky breaks** wir haben ein paar Mal Glück *or* Schwein (*inf*) gehabt; **she had her first big break in a Broadway play** sie bekam ihre erste große Chance in einem Broadwaystück

k Billiards Break *nt or* *m*, Serie *f*

2 – TRANSITIVE VERB

a in pieces (= *fracture*) *bone* sich (*dat*) brechen; *stick* zerbrechen; *rope* zerreißen; (= *smash*) kaputtschlagen, kaputtmachen; *glass, cup* zerbrechen; *window* einschlagen; *egg* aufbrechen; **to break sth from sth** etw von etw abbrechen; **to break one's leg** sich (*dat*) das Bein brechen → **heart**

b = make unusable *toy, chair* kaputtmachen

c = violate *promise, treaty, vow* brechen; *law, rule, commandment* verletzen; *appointment* nicht einhalten; **to break bail** die Haftverschonung brechen

d = interrupt *journey, silence, fast* unterbrechen; *spell* brechen; *monotony, routine* unterbrechen, auflockern; **to break a holiday short** (*Brit*) einen Urlaub abbrechen

♦ **to break + habit** **to break a habit** mit einer Gewohnheit brechen, sich (*dat*) etw abgewöhnen; **he couldn't break the habit of smoking** er konnte sich das Rauchen nicht abgewöhnen; **to break sb of a habit** jdm etw abgewöhnen

e = penetrate *skin* ritzen; *surface, shell* durchbrechen; **his skin is bruised but not broken** seine Haut ist zwar abgeschürft, aber nicht aufge-

platzt; **to break surface** (*submarine, fig*) auftauchen

f = surpass *record* brechen; *sound barrier* durchbrechen

g = open up → **ground**

h = tame *horse* zureiten; *person* brechen

i = destroy *person* kleinkriegen (*inf*), mürbe machen; *sb's health* ruinieren; *resistance, strike* brechen; *code* entziffern; (*Tennis*) *serve* durchbrechen; **his spirit was broken by the spell in solitary confinement** die Zeit in Einzelhaft hatte ihn seelisch gebrochen; **this betrayal nearly broke him** dieser Verrat hätte ihn fast zum Wahnsinn getrieben; **to break sb (financially)** jdn ruinieren, jdn bankrott machen; **to break the bank** (*Gambling*) die Bank sprengen; **37p, well that won't exactly break the bank** 37 Pence, na, davon gehe ich/gehen wir so noch nicht Bankrott; **his service was broken** (*Tennis*) er hat das Aufschlagspiel abgegeben

j = soften *fall* dämpfen, abfangen; **the wall breaks the force of the wind** der Wind bricht sich an der Mauer

k = get out of *jail, one's bonds* ausbrechen aus; **to break step** (*Mil*) aus dem Schritt fallen → **camp, cover, rank**

l = disclose *news* mitteilen; **how can I break it to her?** wie soll ich es ihr sagen?

3 – INTRANSITIVE VERB

a in pieces (= *snap*) (*twig, bone*) brechen; (*rope*) zerreißen; (= *smash, window*) kaputtgehen; (*cup, glass*) zerbrechen; **breaking strain** Belastbarkeit *f*

b = become useless (*watch, toy, chair*) kaputtgehen

c = become detached **to break from sth** von etw abbrechen

d = pause (eine) Pause machen, unterbrechen; **to break for lunch** Mittagspause machen

e = change *weather, luck* umschlagen

f = disperse (*clouds*) aufreißen; (*crowd*) sich teilen

g = give way *health* leiden, Schaden nehmen; (*stamina*) gebrochen werden; (*under interrogation etc*) zusammenbrechen; **his spirit broke** sein Mut verließ ihn

h wave sich brechen

i day, dawn anbrechen; (*suddenly: storm*) losbrechen

j voice (*with emotion*) brechen; **his voice is beginning to break** (*boy*) er kommt in den Stimmbruch

k = become known (*story, news, scandal*) bekannt werden, an den Tag *or* ans Licht kommen; **the news broke on Wall Street yesterday** gestern platzte diese Nachricht in der Wall Street

l = escape (*from jail*) ausbrechen (*from* aus) → **loose**

m company **to break even** seine (Un)kosten decken

n Billiards anstoßen

o ball **to break to the right/left** nach rechts/links wegspringen

p = let go (*Boxing etc*) sich trennen; **break! break!**

q = end relations brechen

4 – PHRASAL VERBS

▶ **break away** **VI a** (*chair leg, handle etc*) abbrechen (*from* von); (*railway coaches, boats*) sich losreißen (*from* von)
b (= *dash away*) weglaufen (*from* von); (*prisoner*) sich losreißen (*from* von); (*Ftbl*) sich absetzen; **he broke away from the rest of the field** er hängte das ganze Feld ab
c (= *cut ties*) sich trennen *or* lossagen (*from* von); (*US, Sport*, = *start too soon*) fehlstarten, zu früh starten; **to break away from a group** sich von einer Gruppe trennen; **to break away from the everyday routine** aus der täglichen Routine ausbrechen
VT *sep* abbrechen (*from* von)

▶ **break down** **VI a** (*vehicle*) eine Panne haben; (*machine*) versagen

b (= *fail, negotiations, plan, marriage*) scheitern; (*communications, law and order, theory*) zusammenbrechen

c (= *give way: resistance*) zusammenbrechen **d** (= *start crying, have a breakdown*) zusammenbrechen

e (= *be analysed, expenditure*) sich aufschlüsseln or -gliedern; (*theory*) sich unter- or aufgliedern; (*Chem: substance*) sich zerlegen (lassen); (= *change its composition: substance*) sich aufspalten (*into* in +*acc*)

VT *sep* **a** (= *smash down*) *door* einrennen; *wall* niederreißen

b (= *overcome*) *opposition* brechen; *hostility, reserve, shyness, suspicion* überwinden

c (*to constituent parts*) *expenditure* aufschlüsseln, aufgliedern; *argument* auf- or untergliedern, aufspalten; (= *change composition of*) umsetzen

▸ **break forth** **VI** (*liter, light, water*) hervorbrechen; (*storm*) losbrechen

▸ **break in** **VI** **a** (= *interrupt*) unterbrechen (*on sb/sth* jdn/etw) **b** (= *enter illegally*) einbrechen **VT** *sep* **a** *door* aufbrechen **b** (= *train*) *new employee* einarbeiten **c** *shoes* einlaufen

▸ **break into** **VT** +*prep obj* **a** *house* einbrechen in (+*acc*); *safe, car* aufbrechen; **his house has been broken into** bei ihm ist eingebrochen worden; **his car has been broken into** sein Auto ist aufgebrochen worden

b (= *use part of*) *savings, £20 note, rations* anbrechen

c (= *begin suddenly*) **to break into song/a run/a trot** zu singen/laufen/traben anfangen, in Laufschritt/Trab (ver)fallen; **to break into a smile** zu lächeln beginnen

d (*professionally*) **she finally broke into films** schließlich machte sie sich einen Namen beim Film

▸ **break off** **VI** **a** (*branch, piece*) abbrechen (*from* von) **b** (= *stop*) abbrechen, aufhören; (= *stop speaking*) abbrechen; (*temporarily*) unterbrechen; **to break off from work** die Arbeit abbrechen **VT** *sep* **a** *twig, piece of chocolate etc* abbrechen **b** *negotiations, relations* abbrechen; *engagement* lösen; **she's broken it off** sie hat die Verlobung gelöst

▸ **break open** **VI** aufspringen **VT** *sep* aufbrechen

▸ **break out** **VI** **a** (*epidemic, fire, war*) ausbrechen **b** **to break out in a rash/in spots** einen Ausschlag/Pickel bekommen; **he broke out in a sweat** er kam ins Schwitzen, ihm brach der Schweiß aus; **he broke out in a cold sweat** ihm brach der Angstschweiß aus **c** (= *escape*) ausbrechen (*from, of* aus) **d** (= *speak suddenly*) herausplatzen, losplatzen

▸ **break through** **VI** (*Mil, sun*) durchbrechen **VI** +*prep obj* *defences, barrier, crowd* durchbrechen; **to break through sb's reserve** jdn aus der Reserve locken

▸ **break up** **VI** **a** (*road, ice*) aufbrechen; (*ship*) (*in storm*) zerbersten; (*on rocks*) zerschellen **b** (*clouds*) sich lichten; (*crowd, group*) auseinander laufen; (*meeting, partnership*) sich auflösen; (*marriage, relationship*) in die Brüche gehen; (*party*) zum Ende kommen; (*political party*) sich auflösen, auseinander gehen; (*friends, partners*) sich trennen; (*empire*) auseinander fallen; (*inf, with laughter*) sich totlachen (*inf*); **to break up with sb** sich von jdm trennen; **when did the party break up last night?** wie lange ging die Party gestern Abend?

c (*Brit Sch, school, pupils*) aufhören; **when do you break up?** wann hört bei euch die Schule auf?, wann habt ihr Ferien?

d (*on mobile phone*) **you're breaking up** ich kann Sie nicht verstehen

VT *sep* **a** *ground, road* aufbrechen; *oil slick* auflösen; *ship* auseinander brechen lassen; (*in breaker's yard*) abwracken

b *estate, country, room* aufteilen; *paragraph, sentence* unterteilen; *empire* auflösen; *lines, expanse of colour* unterbrechen; (= *make more interesting*) auflockern

c (= *bring to an end, disperse*) *marriage, home* zerstören; *meeting (police etc*) auflösen; (*trouble-*

-makers) sprengen; *crowd (police*) zerstreuen, auseinander treiben; **he broke up the fight** er trennte die Kämpfer; **break it up!** auseinander!

breakable ['breɪkəbl] **ADJ** zerbrechlich **N** **breakables** PL zerbrechliche Ware

breakage ['breɪkɪdʒ] **N a** (*in chain, link*) Bruch *m* **b** (*of glass, china*) Bruch *m*; **to pay for ~s** für zerbrochene Ware or Bruch bezahlen; **were there any ~s?** hat es Bruch gegeben?, ist irgendetwas kaputtgegangen or zu Bruch gegangen?

breakaway ['breɪkəweɪ] **N a** (*Pol*) Abfall *m*; (*of state also*) Loslösung *f* **b** (*Sport*) Aus- or Durchbruch *m* **c** (*US, Sport, = false start*) Fehlstart *m* **ADJ** *group* Splitter-

break: break command N (*Comput*) Unterbrechungsbefehl *m*; **break dance** VI Breakdance tanzen; **break dancer** N Breakdancetänzer(in) *m(f)*; **break dancing** N Breakdance *m*

breakdown ['breɪkdaʊn] **N a** (*of machine*) Betriebsschaden *m*; (*of vehicle*) Panne *f*, Motorschaden *m* **b** (*of communications, system*) Zusammenbruch *m* **c** (*Med, physical, mental*) Zusammenbruch *m* **d** (*of figures, expenditure etc*) Aufschlüsselung *f*; (*of thesis, theory etc*) Auf- or Untergliederung *f* **e** (*Chem*) Aufspaltung *f*; (= *change in composition*) Umsetzung *f*

breakdown: breakdown service N Pannendienst *m*; **breakdown truck, breakdown van** N Abschleppwagen *m*

breaker ['breɪkə'] **N a** (= *wave*) Brecher *m* **b** (*also* **breaker's (yard)**) **to send a ship/vehicle to the ~'s (yard)** ein Schiff/Fahrzeug abwracken

breakeven point [breɪk'iːvən,pɔɪnt] N Gewinnschwelle *f*, Break-even-Punkt *m* (*spec*)

breakfast ['brekfəst] **N** Frühstück *nt*; **to have ~** frühstücken, Frühstück essen; **for ~** zum Frühstück **VI** frühstücken; **he ~ed on bacon and eggs** er frühstückte Eier mit Speck

breakfast *in cpds* Frühstücks-; **breakfast bar** N Frühstücksbar *f*; **breakfast cereal** N Cornflakes *pl*, Getreideflakes *pl*; **breakfast meeting** N Arbeitsfrühstück *nt*; **breakfast set** N Frühstücksservice *nt*; **breakfast television** N Frühstücksfernsehen *nt*; **breakfast time** N Frühstückszeit *f*

break-in ['breɪkɪn] N Einbruch *m*; **we've had a ~** bei uns ist eingebrochen worden

breaking ['breɪkɪŋ] N **~ and entering** (*Jur*) Einbruch *m*

breaking point N **a** (*Tech*) Festigkeitsgrenze *f* **b** (*fig*) **she is at** or **has reached ~** sie ist nervlich völlig am Ende (ihrer Kräfte)

break: breakneck ADJ **at ~ speed** (*Brit*) mit halsbrecherischer Geschwindigkeit; **break-out** N Ausbruch *m*; **break point** N (*Tennis*) Breakpunkt *m*; **breakthrough** N (*Mil, fig*) Durchbruch *m*; **break-up** N **a** (*lit, of ship*) Zerbersten *nt*; (*on rocks*) Zerschellen *nt*; (*of ice*) Bersten *nt* **b** (*fig, of friendship*) Bruch *m*; (*of marriage*) Zerrüttung *f*; (*of empire*) Zerfall *m*; (*of political party*) Zersplitterung *f*; (*of partnership, meeting*) Auflösung *f*; (*by trouble-makers*) Sprengung *f*; **break-up value** N (*Fin*) Liquidationswert *m*; **breakwater** N Wellenbrecher *m*

bream [briːm] N Brasse *f*, Brachsen *m*

breast [brest] **N a** (= *chest*) Brust *f*; (*Cook, of chicken, lamb*) Brust(stück *nt*) *f* **b** (*of woman*) Brust *f*; **a child/baby at the ~** ein Kind/Säugling an der Brust **c** (*fig liter*) Brust *f*, Busen *m* (*liter*) **VI** **to ~ the waves/the storm** gegen die Wellen/den Sturm ankämpfen **b** **to ~ the tape** (*Sport*) durchs Ziel gehen

breastbone ['brestbəʊn] N Brustbein *nt*; (*of bird*) Brustknochen *m*

breast cancer N Brustkrebs *m*

-breasted [-'brestɪd] ADJ *suf woman* -brüstig; **a double-/single-breasted jacket** ein Einreiher *m*/Zweireiher *m*

breast: breast-fed ADJ **to be ~** gestillt werden; **~ child** Brustkind *nt*; **breast-feed** VTI

stillen; **breast-feeding** N Stillen *nt*; **breast milk** N Muttermilch *f*; **breastplate** N (*on armour*) Brustharnisch *m*; (*of high priest*) Brustplatte *f* or -gehänge *nt*; **breast pocket** N Brusttasche *f*; **breaststroke** N Brustschwimmen *nt*; **to swim** or **do the ~** brustschwimmen; **breastwork** N (*Mil*) Brustwehr *f*

breath [breθ] **N a** Atem *m*; **to take a deep ~** einmal tief Luft holen; (*before diving, singing etc*) einmal tief einatmen; **bad ~** Mundgeruch *m*; **to have bad ~** aus dem Mund riechen, Mundgeruch haben; **with one's dying ~** mit dem letzten Atemzug; **to draw one's last ~** (*liter*) seinen letzten Atemzug tun; **out of ~** außer Atem, atemlos; **short of ~** kurzatmig; **to stop for ~** sich verschnaufen, eine Pause zum Luftholen machen; **to get one's ~ back** wieder zu Atem kommen; **in the same ~** im selben Atemzug; **to say sth all in one ~** etw in einem Atemzug sagen; **to take sb's ~ away** jdm den Atem verschlagen; **to say sth under one's ~** etw vor sich (*acc*) hin murmeln; **save your ~** spar dir die Spucke (*inf*); **you're wasting your ~** du redest umsonst → **fresh air**

b (= *slight stirring*) **~ of wind** Lüftchen *nt*; **there wasn't a ~ of air** es regte sich or wehte kein Lüftchen

c (*fig, = whisper*) Hauch *m*, Sterbenswörtchen *nt*

breathable ['briːðəbl] ADJ *fabric, garment* atmungsaktiv

breathalyze ['breθəlaɪz] VT blasen lassen; **he refused to be ~d** er weigerte sich, (ins Röhrchen) zu blasen

Breathalyzer® ['breθəlaɪzə'] N Atem(luft)messgerät *nt*, Promillemesser *m* (*inf*); **to blow into the ~** ins Röhrchen blasen

breathe [briːð] **VI** (*person, fabric, garment*) atmen; (*inf: = rest*) verschnaufen, Luft holen or schöpfen; (*liter, = live*) leben; **now we can ~ again** jetzt können wir wieder frei atmen; (= *have more space*) jetzt haben wir wieder Luft; **to ~ down sb's neck** jdm die Hölle heiß machen (*inf*); **I don't want him breathing down my neck** ich will nicht, dass er mir die Hölle heiß macht (*inf*); **red wine should be allowed to ~ before drinking** Rotwein muss atmen, bevor man ihn trinkt

VT **a** *air* einatmen; **to ~ one's last** seinen letzten Atemzug tun; **to ~ the air of one's own country again** wieder auf heimatlichem Boden sein or stehen

b (= *exhale*) atmen (*into* in +*acc*); **he ~d alcohol all over me** er hauchte mich solche Fahne; **he ~d garlic all over me** er verströmte einen solchen Knoblauchgeruch; **to ~ fire** Feuer spucken; **he ~d new life into the firm** er brachte neues Leben in die Firma

c (= *utter*) *prayer* flüstern, hauchen; **to ~ a sigh of relief** erleichtert aufatmen; **don't ~ a word of it!** sag kein Sterbenswörtchen darüber!

▸ **breathe in** VI, VT *sep* einatmen

▸ **breathe out** VI, VT *sep* ausatmen

breather ['briːðə'] N (= *short rest*) Atempause *f*, Verschnaufpause *f*; **to give sb a ~** jdn verschnaufen lassen; **to take** or **have a ~** sich verschnaufen

breathing ['briːðɪŋ] N (= *respiration*) Atmung *f*; **the child's peaceful ~** die ruhigen Atemzüge des Kindes

breathing: breathing apparatus N Sauerstoffgerät *nt*; **breathing mask** N Atemmaske *f*; **breathing space** N (*fig*) Atempause *f*, Ruhepause *f*

breathless ['breθlɪs] ADJ atemlos; (*with exertion also*) außer Atem; **he said in a ~ voice** sagte er, nach Luft ringend; **he is rather ~** (*through illness*) er leidet an Atemnot; **~ with excitement/anticipation** ganz atemlos vor Aufregung/Spannung; **it left me ~** (*lit, fig*) es verschlug mir den Atem; **at a ~ pace** atemberaubend schnell

breathlessly ['breθlɪslɪ] ADV atemlos; (*from exertion also*) außer Atem

breathlessness ['breθlɪsnɪs] N (*due to exertion*) Atemlosigkeit *f*; (*due to illness*) Kurzatmigkeit *f*

breathtaking ADJ , **breathtakingly** ADV ['breθteɪkɪŋ, -lɪ] atemberaubend

breath test N Atemalkoholtest *m*

breath testing N Atemalkoholkontrolle *f*

breathy ['breθɪ] ADJ (+er) rauchig; (*through shyness*) hauchig

bred [bred] *pret, ptp of* **breed**

-bred ADJ *suf* -erzogen

breech[1] [briːtʃ] N (*of gun*) Verschluss *m*

breech[2] ADJ *attr* (Med) birth, delivery Steiß-; **~ presentation** Steißlage *f*; **to be a ~ baby** eine Steißlage sein

breeches ['brɪtʃɪz] PL Kniehose *f*; (= *riding breeches*) Reithose *f*; (*for hiking*) (Knie)bundhose *f*

breeches buoy ['brɪtʃɪzbɔɪ] N Hosenboje *f*

breech-loader ['briːtʃləʊdə'] N (Mil) Hinterlader *m*

breed [briːd] *vb: pret, ptp* **bred** N (*lit, fig, = species*) Art *f*, Sorte *f*; **they produced a new** ~ sie haben eine neue Züchtung hervorgebracht; **a ~ apart** (*fig*) eine besondere *or* spezielle Sorte *or* Gattung VT a (= *raise, rear*) *animals, flowers* züchten → **born** b (*fig, = give rise to*) erzeugen; **dirt ~s disease** Schmutz verursacht Krankheit, Schmutz zieht Krankheit nach sich VI (*animals*) Junge haben; (*birds*) brüten; (*pej, hum, people*) sich vermehren

breeder ['briːdə'] N a (= *person*) Züchter(in) *m(f)* b (Phys: *also* **breeder reactor**) Brutreaktor *m*, Brüter *m*

breeding ['briːdɪŋ] N a (= *reproduction*) Fortpflanzung und Aufzucht *f* der Jungen b (= *rearing*) Zucht *f* c (= *upbringing, good manners: also* **good breeding**) gute Erziehung, Kinderstube *f*

breeding: breeding ground, breeding place N (*lit, fig*) Brutstätte *f*; **breeding season** N (*of birds*) Brutzeit *f*; (*of animal*) Zeit *f* der Fortpflanzung und Aufzucht der Jungen

breeze [briːz] N a (*esp US inf*) das ist kinderleicht

▶ **breeze in** VI fröhlich angetrabt kommen *or* hereinschneien; **he breezed into the room** er kam fröhlich ins Zimmer geschneit

▶ **breeze out** VI vergnügt abziehen (*of aus*)

▶ **breeze through** VI +prep obj (*inf, = do easily*) spielend *or* mit Leichtigkeit schaffen

breeze: breeze block N (*Brit Build*) Ytong® *m*; **breezeway** N (*US*) überdachter Durchgang

breezily ['briːzɪlɪ] ADV (*fig*) frisch-fröhlich

breeziness ['briːzɪnɪs] N (*fig*) frisch-fröhliche Art

breezy ['briːzɪ] ADJ (+er) a *weather, day* windig; *corner, spot also* luftig b *manner, person* frisch-fröhlich; *melody* locker-leicht

brekkie, brekky ['brekɪ] N (*Austral inf*) Frühstück *nt*

Bren gun ['brengʌn] N (Mil) leichtes Maschinengewehr; **~ carrier, Bren carrier** kleines leichtes Panzerfahrzeug

brer, br'er [breə'] N (*old*) Gevatter *m* (*old*)

brethren ['breðrɪn] PL (*obs, Eccl*) Brüder *pl*

Breton ['bretən] ADJ bretonisch N a Bretone *m*, Bretonin *f* b (*Ling*) Bretonisch *nt*

breve [briːv] N (*Brit, Mus*) Brevis *f*

breviary ['briːvɪərɪ] N Brevier *nt*

brevity ['brevɪtɪ] N a (= *shortness*) Kürze *f* b (= *conciseness*) Kürze *f*, Bündigkeit *f*, Knappheit *f*; **~ is the soul of wit** (*Prov*) in der Kürze liegt die Würze (*Prov*)

brew [bruː] N a (= *beer*) Bräu *nt* b (*of tea*) Tee *m*, Gebräu *nt* (*iro*); (*of herbs*) Kräutermischung *f* → **witches' brew** VT a *beer, ale* brauen; *tea* aufbrühen, aufgießen, kochen b (*fig*) *scheme, mischief, plot* ausbrüten, aushecken; **to ~ a plot** ein Komplott schmieden VI a (*beer*) gären; (*tea*) ziehen b (= *make beer*) brauen c (*fig*) **there's trouble/a storm ~ing (up)** da braut sich

ein Konflikt/ein Sturm zusammen; **there's something ~ing** da braut sich etwas zusammen

▶ **brew up** VI a (*inf, = make tea*) sich (*dat*) einen Tee machen b (*fig*) = **brew** VI c

brewer ['bruːə'] N Brauer *m*

brewer's droop N (*Brit hum inf*) alkoholbedingte vorübergehende Impotenz; **to get ~** (*Brit hum inf*) alkoholbedingt keinen hochkriegen (*inf*)

brewer's yeast N Bierhefe *f*

brewery ['bruːərɪ] N Brauerei *f*

brew-up ['bruːʌp] N (*inf*) **to have a ~** Tee kochen

briar ['braɪə'] N a (*also* **briarwood**) Bruyère (-holz) *nt*; (*also* **briar pipe**) Bruyère(pfeife) *f* b = **brier a**

bribable ['braɪbəbl] ADJ bestechlich

bribe [braɪb] N Bestechung *f*; (= *money also*) Bestechungsgeld *nt*; **as a ~** als Bestechung; **to take a ~** sich bestechen lassen, Bestechungsgeld nehmen; **to offer sb a ~** jdn bestechen wollen, jdm Bestechungsgeld anbieten VT bestechen; **to ~ sb to do sth** jdn bestechen, damit er etw tut

bribery ['braɪbərɪ] N Bestechung *f*; **open to ~** bestechlich

bric-a-brac ['brɪkəbræk] N Nippes *m*, Nippsachen *pl*

brick [brɪk] N a (*Build*) Ziegel- *or* Backstein *m*; **~s and mortar** (= *property*) Immobilien *pl*; **you can't make ~s without straw** (*Prov*) wo nichts ist, kann auch nichts werden; **he came** *or* **was down on me like a ton of ~s** (*inf*) er hat mich unheimlich fertig gemacht (*inf*); **to drop a ~** (*Brit fig inf*) ins Fettnäpfchen treten; **to drop sb/ sth like a hot ~** (*inf*) jdn/etw wie eine heiße Kartoffel fallen lassen b (= *toy*) (Bau)klotz *m*; **box of (building) ~s** Baukasten *m* c (*of ice cream*) Block *m* d (*dated inf*) feiner Kerl (*inf*); **be a ~!** sei ein Kumpel! e **~s** (*Brit sl:* = *money*) Kohle *f* (*inf*)

▶ **brick in** *or* **up** VT sep *door, window* zumauern

brick in cpds Backstein-; **brickbat** N (= *missile*) Backsteinbrocken *m*; (*fig*) Beschimpfung *f*; **brick building** N Backsteinbau *m*

brickie ['brɪkɪ] N (*Brit, inf*) Maurer *m*

brick: brick kiln N Ziegelofen *m*; **bricklayer** N Maurer *m*; **bricklaying** N Maurerarbeit *f*; (= *trade*) Maurerhandwerk *nt*; **brick-red** ADJ ziegelrot; **brick wall** N (*fig inf*) **I might as well be talking to a ~** ich könnte genauso gut gegen eine Wand reden; **it's like beating** *or* **banging one's head against a ~** es ist, wie wenn man mit dem Kopf gegen die Wand rennt; **to come up against** *or* **hit a ~** plötzlich vor einer Mauer stehen; **brickwork** N Backsteinmauerwerk *nt*; **brickworks** PL , **brickyard** N Ziegelei *f*

bridal ['braɪdl] ADJ Braut-; *procession also, feast* Hochzeits-; **~ gown/wear** Hochzeitskleid *nt*/ -bekleidung *f*; **~ vow** Eheversprechen *nt* der Braut

bridal party N Angehörige *pl* und Freunde *pl* der Braut

bridal suite N Hochzeitssuite *f*

bride [braɪd] N Braut *f*; **the ~ and (~)groom** Braut und Bräutigam, das Hochzeitspaar; **~ of Christ** Braut Christi

bridegroom ['braɪdgruːm] N Bräutigam *m*

bridesmaid ['braɪdzmeɪd] N Brautjungfer *f*

bridge[1] [brɪdʒ] N a (*lit, fig*) Brücke *f*; **to build ~s** Brücken schlagen; **that's all water under the ~** (*fig*) das ist alles Schnee von gestern; **don't cross your ~s before you come to them** (*fig*) lass die Dinge einfach auf dich zukommen b (*Naut*) (Kommando)brücke *f* c (*of nose*) Sattel *m*; (*of spectacles, violin*) Steg *m* d (*Dentistry*) Brücke *f* e (*Billiards*) Steg *m* VT *river, railway* eine Brücke schlagen *or* bauen über (+*acc*); (*fig*) überbrücken; **to ~ the gap** (*fig*) die Zeit überbrücken; (*between people*) die Kluft überbrücken

bridge[2] N (*Cards*) Bridge *nt*

bridge: bridge bond N (*Chem*) Brückenbindung *f*; **bridge-building** N Brückenbau *m*; **bridgehead** N Brückenkopf *m*; **to establish a ~** einen Brückenkopf errichten; **bridgehouse** N Brückenhaus *nt*; **bridge roll** N längliches Brötchen; **bridgework** N (*Dentistry*) Zahnbrücken *pl*; (*of individual*) Zahnbrücke *f*

bridging finance ['brɪdʒɪŋ'faɪnæns] N Zwischenfinanzierung *f*

bridging loan ['brɪdʒɪŋləʊn] N Überbrückungskredit *m*

bridle ['braɪdl] N (*of horse*) Zaum *m* VT a *horse* aufzäumen b (*fig*) *one's tongue, emotions* im Zaume halten VI sich entrüstet wehren (*at gegen*)

bridle path N Reitweg *m*

brief [briːf] ADJ (+er) kurz; (= *curt also*) *manner* kurz angebunden; **in ~** kurz; **the news in ~** Kurznachrichten *pl*; **to be ~** um es kurz zu machen; **could you give me a ~ idea ...** könnten Sie mir kurz erzählen ... N a (*Jur*) Auftrag *m* (*an einen Anwalt*); (= *document*) Unterlagen *pl* zu dem/einem Fall; (= *instructions*) Instruktionen *pl*; **to take a ~** (*Jur*) einen Fall annehmen; **to hold a ~ for sb** (*Jur*) jds Sache vor Gericht vertreten; **I hold no ~ for him** (*fig*) ich will nicht für ihn plädieren b (= *instructions*) Auftrag *m* c (*Brit sl:* = *lawyer*) Rechtsverdreher *m* VT a (*Jur*) *lawyer* instruieren; (= *employ*) beauftragen b (= *give instructions, information to*) instruieren (*on über* +*acc*); **the pilots were ~ed on what they had to do** die Piloten wurden instruiert, was sie tun sollten

briefcase ['briːfkeɪs] N (Akten)tasche *f*, (Akten)mappe *f*

briefing ['briːfɪŋ] N (= *instructions*) Instruktionen *pl*, Anweisungen *pl*; (*also* **briefing session**) Einsatzbesprechung *f*

briefly ['briːflɪ] ADV kurz

briefness ['briːfnɪs] N Kürze *f*

briefs [briːfs] PL Slip *m*; **a pair of ~** ein Slip

brier ['braɪə'] N a (= *wild rose*) wilde Rose; (= *bramble runner*) Ranke *f*; (= *thorny bush*) Dornbusch *m* b = **briar a**

brig [brɪg] N a (= *ship*) Brigg *f* b (*US, = cell on ship*) Arrestzelle *f* (*auf einem Schiff*); (*Mil sl*) Bunker *m* (*sl*)

Brig. abbr of **brigadier**

brigade [brɪ'geɪd] N (*Mil*) Brigade *f*

brigadier [,brɪgə'dɪə'] N (*Brit*) Brigadegeneral *m*

brigadier (general) N (*Brit, Hist, US*) Brigadegeneral *m*

brigand ['brɪgənd] N (*old*) Räuber *m*, Bandit *m*

bright [braɪt] ADJ (+er) a *light, fire* hell; *colour* leuchtend; *sunshine, star also, eyes, gem* strahlend; *day, weather* heiter; *reflection* stark; *metal* glänzend; **~ red** knallrot; **it was really ~ outside** es war wirklich sehr hell draußen; **~ with lights** hell erleuchtet; **~ intervals** *or* **periods** (*Met*) Aufheiterungen *pl*; **the outlook is ~er** (*Met*) die Aussichten sind etwas freundlicher; (*fig*) es sieht etwas besser aus; **the ~ lights** (*inf*) der Glanz der Großstadt b (= *cheerful*) *person, smile* fröhlich, heiter; **I wasn't feeling too ~** es ging mir nicht besonders gut; **~ and early** in aller Frühe → **side** c (= *intelligent*) *person* intelligent, schlau; *child* aufgeweckt; *idea* glänzend; (*iro*) intelligent; **I'm not very ~ this morning** ich habe heute Morgen Mattscheibe (*inf*); **I forgot to tell him – that's ~** (*inf*) ich habe vergessen, ihm das zu sagen – toll! (*inf*) d (= *favourable*) *future* glänzend; *prospects also* freundlich; **things aren't looking too ~** es sieht nicht gerade rosig aus

brighten (up) ['braɪtn(ʌp)] VT sep a (= *make cheerful*) *spirits, person* aufmuntern, aufheitern; *room, atmosphere* aufhellen, aufheitern; *conversation* beleben; *prospects, situation* verbessern b (= *make bright*) *colour, hair* aufhellen; *metal* aufpolieren VI a (*weather, sky*) sich aufklären *or* aufheitern **b** (*person*) fröhlicher werden; (*face*) sich aufhellen *or* aufheitern; (*eyes*) aufleuchten; (*prospects*) sich verbessern, freundlicher werden; (*future*) freundlicher aussehen

bright-eyed ['braɪtaɪd] ADJ mit strahlenden Augen; **~ and bushy-tailed** (*hum inf*) putzmunter (*inf*)

brightly ['braɪtlɪ] ADV **a** *shine, burn* hell; *reflected* stark; **~ lit** hell erleuchtet **b** (= *cheerfully*) *say, smile* fröhlich, heiter

brightness ['braɪtnɪs] N **a** (*of light, fire*) Helligkeit *f*; (*of colour*) Leuchten *nt*; (*of sunshine, star also, eyes, gem*) Strahlen *nt*; (*of day, weather*) Heiterkeit *f*; (*of reflection*) Stärke *f*; (*of metal*) Glanz *m*; **~ control** Helligkeitsregler *m* **b** (= *cheerfulness: of person, smile*) Fröhlichkeit *f*, Heiterkeit *f* **c** (= *intelligence, of person*) Intelligenz *f*; (*of child*) Aufgewecktheit *f* **d** (*of prospects*) Freundlichkeit *f*; **the ~ of the future** die glänzende Zukunft

Bright's disease ['braɪtsdɪˌzi:z] N brightsche Krankheit

bright young thing N (*fashionable*) junger Schicki (*inf*), junge Schicki (*inf*); (*male also*) Sonnyboy *m*; (*talented*) hoffnungsvolles Talent; **~s** (*recalling the 1920s*) die Jeunesse dorée

brill¹ [brɪl] N Glattbutt *m*

brill² ADJ (*Brit, inf*) toll (*inf*)

brilliance ['brɪljəns] N **a** (= *brightness*) heller Glanz, Strahlen *nt*; (*of colour*) Strahlen *nt* **b** (*fig, = intelligence*) Großartigkeit *f*; (*of scientist, artist, wit, achievement also*) Brillanz *f*; **a man of such ~** ein Mann von so hervorragender Intelligenz

brilliant ['brɪljənt] ADJ **a** (*fig*) großartig (*also iro*); *scientist, artist, wit, achievement also* glänzend, brillant; *student* hervorragend; **she is a ~ woman** sie ist eine sehr intelligente Frau; **he is ~ with my children** er versteht sich großartig mit meinen Kindern; **to be ~ at sth/doing sth** etw hervorragend können/tun können **b** *sunshine, light, eyes, colour* strahlend EXCL (*inf, = great*) super (*inf*)

brilliantine ['brɪljənˌti:n] N Brillantine *f*, Haarpomade *f*

brilliantly ['brɪljəntlɪ] ADV **a** *shine, lit, illuminated* hell; *sunny* strahlend; **~ coloured** (*Brit*) *or* **colored** (*US*) in kräftigen Farben **b** (= *very well, superbly*) großartig; *talented* glänzend; *play, perform* brillant; *funny, witty, simple* herrlich; **a ~ original idea** eine Idee von glänzender Originalität

Brillo pad® ['brɪləʊˌpæd] N Scheuertuch *nt* (*aus Stahlwolle*)

brim [brɪm] N (*of cup*) Rand *m*; (*of hat also*) Krempe *f*; **full to the ~ (with sth)** (*lit*) randvoll (mit etw); **she is full to the ~ with joy** sie strömt über vor Freude VI strotzen (*with von or vor +dat*); **her eyes were ~ming with tears** ihre Augen schwammen in Tränen

▶**brim over** VI (*lit, fig*) überfließen (*with vor +dat*)

brimful ['brɪm'fʊl] ADJ (*lit*) randvoll; (*fig*) voll (*of, with von*); **he is ~ of energy** er sprüht vor Energie; **she is ~ of health** sie strotzt vor Gesundheit

-brimmed [-brɪmd] ADJ *suf hat* -krempig

brimstone ['brɪmstəʊn] N (= *sulphur*) Schwefel *m*

brindled ['brɪndld] ADJ gestreift

brine [braɪn] N **a** (= *salt water*) Sole *f*; (*for pickling*) Lake *f* **b** (= *sea water*) Salzwasser *nt*; (*liter, = sea*) See *f*

bring [brɪŋ] *pret, ptp* **brought** VT **a** bringen; (*also bring with one*) mitbringen; **did you ~ the car/your guitar etc?** haben Sie den Wagen/die Gitarre etc mitgebracht?; **to ~ sb across/inside etc** jdn herüber-/hereinbringen *etc* **b** (= *result in, be accompanied by*) *snow, rain, luck* bringen; **to ~ a blush/tears to sb's cheeks/eyes** jdm die Röte ins Gesicht/die Tränen in die Augen treiben **c** (*+infin: = persuade*) **I cannot ~ myself to speak to him** ich kann es nicht über mich

bringen, mit ihm zu sprechen **d** (*esp Jur, = present for trial, discussion*) *case, matter* bringen (*before vor +acc*); **the trial will be brought next week** der Prozess findet nächste Woche statt → **action, charge** **e** (= *sell for, earn*) *price, income* (ein)bringen **f** (*in phrases, see also relevant nouns*) **to ~ sth to a close** *or* **an end** etw zu Ende bringen; **to ~ sb low** jdn auf null bringen (*inf*); **to ~ sth to sb's knowledge** jdm etw zur Kenntnis bringen; **to ~ sth to sb's attention** jdn auf etw (*acc*) aufmerksam machen; **to ~ ~ to perfection** perfektionieren, vervollkommnen

▶**bring about** VT *sep* **a** (= *cause*) herbeiführen, verursachen **b** (*Naut*) wenden; **he brought us about** er wendete

▶**bring along** VT *sep* **a** (= *bring with one*) mitbringen **b** = **bring on b**

▶**bring around** VT *sep* = **bring round a, d**

▶**bring away** VT *sep person* wegbringen; *memories, impression* mitnehmen

▶**bring back** VT *sep* **a** (*lit*) *person, object* zurückbringen **b** (= *restore*) *custom, hanging* wieder einführen; *government* wieder wählen; **a rest will bring him back to normal** ein wenig Ruhe wird ihn wiederherstellen; **to bring sb back to life/health** jdn wieder lebendig/gesund machen; **to bring a government back to power** eine Regierung wieder an die Macht bringen **c** (= *recall*) *memories* zurückbringen, wecken; *events* erinnern an (*+acc*)

▶**bring down** VT *sep* **a** (*out of air*) (= *shoot down*) *bird, plane* herunterholen; (= *land*) *plane, kite* herunterbringen; **to bring sb's wrath down (up)on one** sich (*dat*) jds Zorn zuziehen; **you'll bring the boss down on us** da werden wir es mit dem Chef zu tun bekommen **b** *opponent, footballer* zu Fall bringen; (*by shooting*) *animal* zur Strecke bringen; *person* niederschießen → **house** **c** *government etc* zu Fall bringen **d** (= *reduce*) *temperature, prices, cost of living* senken; *swelling* reduzieren, zurückgehen lassen

▶**bring forth** VT *sep* (*old, liter*) **a** *fruit* hervorbringen (*geh*); *child, young* zur Welt bringen (*geh*) **b** (*fig*) *ideas* hervorbringen; *suggestions* vorbringen; *protests* auslösen

▶**bring forward** VT *sep* **a** (*lit*) *person, chair* nach vorne bringen **b** (*fig, = present*) *witness* vorführen; *evidence, argument, proposal* vorbringen, unterbreiten **c** (= *advance time of*) *meeting* vorverlegen; *clock* vorstellen **d** (*Comm*) *figure, amount* übertragen; **amount brought forward** Übertrag *m*

▶**bring in** VT *sep* **a** (*lit*) *person, object* hereinbringen (*prep obj, -to in +acc*); *harvest* einbringen, bergen (*old DDR*); *sails* einziehen; **to bring in the New Year** das neue Jahr begrüßen **b** (*fig, = introduce*) *fashion, custom* einführen; (*Parl*) *bill* einbringen; **to bring sth into fashion** etw in Mode bringen **c** (= *involve, call in*) *police, consultant etc* einschalten (*on bei*); **don't bring him into it** lass ihn aus der Sache raus; **she's bound to bring Freud in** sie wird bestimmt Freud mit hereinbringen; **why bring Freud/that in?** was hat Freud/das damit zu tun? **d** (*Fin*) *income, money, interest* (ein)bringen (*-to sb* jdm); (*Comm*) *business* bringen **e** (*Jur, jury*) *verdict* fällen

▶**bring into** VT *always separate* **to bring sth into action/blossom/view** etw zum Einsatz bringen/blühen lassen/sichtbar werden lassen

▶**bring off** VT *sep* **a** *people from wreck* retten, wegbringen (*prep obj* von) **b** (= *succeed with*) *plan* zustande *or* zu Stande bringen, zuwege *or* zu Wege bringen; **to bring off a coup** ein Ding drehen (*inf*); **he brought it off!** er hat es geschafft! (*inf*) **c** (*sl, = bring to orgasm*) **to bring sb off** es jdm besorgen (*sl*)

▶**bring on** VT *sep* **a** (= *cause*) *illness, quarrel* herbeiführen, verursachen; *attack also* auslösen **b** (= *help develop*) *pupil, young athlete* weiterbringen; *crops, flowers* herausbringen **c** (*Theat*) *person* auftreten lassen; *thing* auf die Bühne brin-

gen; (*Sport*) *player* einsetzen; **to bring sb on the scene** (*fig*) jdn auf die Szene rufen **d** **to bring sth (up)on oneself** sich (*dat*) etw selbst aufladen; **you brought it (up)on yourself** das hast du dir selbst zuzuschreiben

▶**bring out** VT *sep* **a** (*lit*) (heraus)bringen (*of* aus); (*of pocket*) herausholen (*of* aus) **b** (= *draw out*) *person* die Hemmungen nehmen (*+dat*); **can't you bring him out (of his shell) a bit?** können Sie nicht tun, damit er ein bisschen aus sich herausgeht? **c** (= *elicit*) *greed, bravery* zum Vorschein bringen; *best qualities also* herausbringen; **to bring out the best/worst in sb** das Beste/Schlimmste in jdm zum Vorschein bringen **d** (*also* **bring out on strike**) *workers* auf die Straße schicken **e** (= *make blossom*) *flowers* herausbringen **f** (*to society*) *debutante* in die Gesellschaft einführen **g** (= *bring on the market*) *new product, book* herausbringen **h** (= *emphasize, show up*) herausbringen, hervorheben **i** (= *utter*) *few words* herausbringen; *cry* ausstoßen **j** **to bring sb out in spots/a rash** bei jdm Pickel/einen Ausschlag verursachen

▶**bring over** VT *sep* **a** (*lit*) herüberbringen **b** (*fig, to ideas*) überzeugen (*to* von); (*to other side*) bringen (*to auf +acc*)

▶**bring round** (*esp Brit*) VT *sep* **a** (*to one's house etc*) vorbeibringen **b** (= *steer*) *discussion, conversation* bringen (*to auf +acc*) **c** *unconscious person* wieder zu Bewusstsein bringen **d** (= *convert*) herumkriegen (*inf*)

▶**bring through** VT *always separate patient, business* durchbringen; **to bring sb through a crisis** jdn durch eine Krise bringen; **to bring sb through an illness** jdm helfen, eine Krankheit zu überstehen

▶**bring to** VT *always separate* **a** (*Naut*) stoppen **b** *unconscious person* wieder zu Bewusstsein bringen **c** **to bring sb to himself/herself** jdn wieder zu sich bringen

▶**bring together** VT *sep* zusammenbringen

▶**bring under** VT *always separate* (= *subdue*) unterwerfen VT +*prep obj* (= *categorize*) bringen unter (*+dat*); **this can be brought under four main headings** dies lässt sich in vier Kategorien gliedern → **control**

▶**bring up** VT *sep* **a** (*to a higher place*) heraufbringen; (*to the front*) her-/hinbringen → **rear** **b** (= *raise, increase*) *amount, reserves* erhöhen (*to auf +acc*); *level, standards* anheben; **to bring sb up to a certain standard** jdn auf ein gewisses Niveau bringen **c** (= *rear*) *child, animal* groß- *or* aufziehen; (= *educate*) erziehen; **a well/badly brought-up child** ein gut/schlecht erzogenes Kind; **to bring sb up to do sth** jdn dazu erziehen, etw zu tun; **he was brought up to believe that …** man hatte ihm beigebracht, dass … **d** (= *vomit up*) brechen; (*esp baby, patient*) spucken (*inf*) **e** (= *mention*) *fact, problem* zur Sprache bringen, erwähnen; **do you have to bring that up?** müssen Sie davon anfangen? **f** (*Jur*) **to bring sb up (before a judge)** jdn (einem Richter) vorführen **g** (*Mil*) *battalion* heranbringen → **rear** **h** **to bring sb up short** jdn innehalten lassen **i** **to bring sb up against sth** jdn mit etw konfrontieren

▶**bring upon** VT *sep* +*prep obj* = **bring on d**

bring-and-buy (sale) ['brɪŋən'baɪ(ˌseɪl)] N (*Brit*) Basar *m* (*wo mitgebrachte Sachen angeboten und verkauft werden*)

brink [brɪŋk] N (*lit, fig*) Rand *m*; **on the ~ of sth** (*lit, fig*) am Rande von etw; **on the ~ of doing sth** (*lit, fig*) nahe daran, etw zu tun

brinkmanship ['brɪŋkmənʃɪp] N (*inf*) Spiel *nt* mit dem Feuer

briny ['braɪnɪ] ADJ salzhaltig, salzig N (*inf*) See *f*

Bri-nylon® [ˌbraɪˈnaɪlən] N (Brit) britische Kunstfaser

brio [ˈbriːəʊ] N (= vigour) Feuer nt, Schwung m

briquet(te) [brɪˈket] N Brikett nt

brisk [brɪsk] ADJ (+er) **a** person, way of speaking forsch; sales assistant, service flott, flink; walk, pace flott; **to go for a ~ walk** einen ordentlichen Spaziergang machen **b** (fig) trade, betting, bidding lebhaft, rege; **business etc was ~** das Geschäft etc ging lebhaft or war rege; **voting got off to a ~ start** die Wahl begann mit einer lebhaften Beteiligung **c** wind, weather frisch

brisket [ˈbrɪskɪt] N (Cook) Bruststück nt

briskly [ˈbrɪsklɪ] ADV **a** speak, act forsch; walk flott **b** (Comm etc) trade, sell, bid lebhaft, rege

briskness [ˈbrɪsknɪs] N **a** (of person, way of speaking) Forschheit f; (of sales assistant, service) Flottheit f, Flinkheit f; (of walk, pace) flottes Tempo; **feeling warmed by the ~ of their walk, they ...** durch den flotten Spaziergang erwärmt, ... sie ... **b** (Comm etc, of trade, sales, bidding) Lebhaftigkeit f **c** (of wind, weather) Frische f

brisling [ˈbrɪzlɪŋ] N Brisling m, Sprotte f

bristle [ˈbrɪsl] N (of brush, boar etc) Borste f; (of beard) Stoppel f VI **a** (animal's hair) sich sträuben; **the dog ~d** dem Hund sträubte sich das Fell **b** (fig, person) zornig werden; **to ~ with anger** vor Wut schnauben **c** (fig) **to be bristling with people** von or vor Leuten wimmeln; **bristling with difficulties** mit Schwierigkeiten gespickt; **the dress was bristling with pins** das Kleid steckte voller Nadeln; **the soldiers ~d with weapons** die Soldaten waren bis an die Zähne bewaffnet

bristly [ˈbrɪslɪ] ADJ (+er) animal borstig; chin Stoppel-, stoppelig; hair, beard borstig

Bristol fashion [ˈbrɪstəlˌfæʃn] ADJ → shipshape

bristols [ˈbrɪstəlz] PL (Brit, inf) Titten pl (sl)

Brit [brɪt] N (inf) Engländer m, Tommy m (inf)

Britain [ˈbrɪtən] N Großbritannien nt; (in ancient history) Britannien nt

---

BRITAIN, GREAT BRITAIN, UNITED KINGDOM

Auch wenn man es häufig hören kann, dass fälschlicherweise von England gesprochen wird, wenn eigentlich ganz Großbritannien gemeint ist, sollte man diesen Fehler nicht nachmachen, da man dadurch Schotten, Waliser und einen Teil der Iren ankreidet. **Britain**, **Great Britain**, **the United Kingdom** und **the British Isles** sind Bezeichnungen, die man leicht verwechseln kann, und sogar englische Muttersprachler verwenden sie oft nach Gutdünken.

Great Britain, Großbritannien, ist der Name der britischen Hauptinsel mit England, Schottland und Wales. In der Amtssprache sind dabei auch alle Inseln vor der Küste mit eingeschlossen, mit Ausnahme der Isle of Man und der Kanalinseln.

The British Isles, die Britischen Inseln, ist die geografische Bezeichnung für Großbritannien, die Isle of Man, und die Insel Irland. Politisch gesehen umfassen sie zwei souveräne Staaten, nämlich the **United Kingdom of Great Britain and Northern Ireland** und die Republik Irland.

The United Kingdom of Great Britain and Northern Ireland oder auch **UK**, das Vereinigte Königreich, ist eine politische Einheit, die aus Großbritannien und Nordirland besteht. Es ist eine parlamentarische Demokratie mit einer konstitutionellen Monarchie und Mitglied der Europäischen Union.

Um die Verwirrung komplett zu machen, wird **Britain** sowohl als Synonym für **United Kingdom** als auch für **Great Britain** verwendet. Alle Angehörigen des Vereinigten Königreichs haben die britische Staatsbürgerschaft.

Britannia [brɪˈtænɪə] N (poet, = country) Britannien nt; (= personification) Britannia f

---

Britannic [brɪˈtænɪk] ADJ **Her/His ~ Majesty** Ihre/Seine Britannische Majestät

britches [ˈbrɪtʃəz] PL (US) = **breeches**

briticism [ˈbrɪtɪsɪzəm] N Britizismus m

briticize [ˈbrɪtɪsaɪz] VT anglisieren, britifizieren

British [ˈbrɪtɪʃ] ADJ britisch; **I'm ~** ich bin Brite/Britin; **~ English** britisches Englisch; **and the best of ~ (luck)!** (inf) na, dann mal viel Glück! → **luck** N **the ~** pl die Briten pl

British Council N British Council m, Organisation zu Förderung britischer Kultur im Ausland

British Empire N **the ~** das Britische Weltreich

Britisher [ˈbrɪtɪʃəʳ] N (dated US) Brite m, Britin f

British: British Honduras N Britisch-Honduras nt; **British Isles** PL **the ~** die Britischen Inseln; **British Telecom** N British Telecom f

Briton [ˈbrɪtən] N Brite m, Britin f

Britpop [ˈbrɪtpɒp] N (Brit, Mus) Britpop m

Brittany [ˈbrɪtənɪ] N die Bretagne

brittle [ˈbrɪtl] ADJ **a** spröde, zerbrechlich; old paper bröcklig; biscuit mürbe; **~ bones** schwache Knochen **b** (fig) nerves schwach; person empfindlich; voice, laugh schrill; **to have a ~ temper** aufbrausend sein

brittle bone disease N (= osteoporosis) Osteoporose f; (= osteogenesis) abnorme Knochenbrüchigkeit, mangelhafte Knochenbildung

brittleness [ˈbrɪtlnɪs] N **a** Sprödigkeit f, Zerbrechlichkeit f; (of old paper) Bröckligkeit f; (of biscuit) Mürbheit f; (of bones) Schwäche f **b** (fig, of nerves) Schwäche f; (of person) Empfindlichkeit f; (of voice, laugh) Schrillheit f

bro [brəʊ] N (US inf) **a** (= friend) Kumpel m; **hi, ~!** hallo, Kumpel! **b** (= brother) Bruder m

broach [brəʊtʃ] VT **a** barrel anstechen, anzapfen **b** subject, topic anschneiden

B-road [ˈbiːrəʊd] N (Brit) ≈ Landstraße f

broad [brɔːd] ADJ (+er) **a** (= wide) breit; **to grow ~er** breiter werden; (road, river also) sich verbreitern; **to make ~er** verbreitern; **it's as ~ as it is long** (fig) es ist Jacke wie Hose (inf) **b** (= widely applicable) theory umfassend; (= general) allgemein **c** (= not detailed) distinction, idea, outline grob; instructions vague; sense weit; **as a very ~ rule** als Faustregel; **to draw or paint sth in ~ strokes** (fig) etw in groben Zügen umreißen **d** (= liberal) mind, attitude, ideas großzügig, tolerant; **a man of ~ sympathies** ein aufgeschlossener Geist; **a ~ church** ein Sammelbecken nt verschiedenster Strömungen or Richtungen **e** wink, hint deutlich; (= indelicate) humour derb **f** (= strongly marked) accent stark; (= with long vowel sounds also) breit; **he speaks ~ Scots** er spricht breit(est)es Schottisch or starken schottischen Dialekt N **a** (= widest part) **the ~ of the back** die Schultergegend **b** **the (Norfolk) Broads** pl die Norfolk Broads **c** (sl: = woman) Tussi f (sl)

broad: broadband (Telec) N Breitband nt ADJ Breitband-; **broad-based** ADJ support breit; government auf breiter Basis; **broad bean** N dicke Bohne, Saubohne f; **broadbrush** ADJ (= general) grob, allgemein

broadcast [ˈbrɔːdkɑːst] vb: pret, ptp **broadcast** N (Rad, TV) Sendung f; (of match etc) Übertragung f; **~s** pl Programm nt, Sendungen pl VT **a** (Rad, TV) senden, ausstrahlen; football match, event übertragen **b** (fig) news, rumour etc verbreiten **c** (Agr) seed aussäen VI (Rad, TV, station) senden; (person) im Rundfunk/Fernsehen sprechen; **we're not ~ing tonight** heute Abend strahlen wir kein Programm aus

broadcaster [ˈbrɔːdkɑːstəʳ] N (Rad, TV, = announcer) Rundfunk-/Fernsehsprecher(in) m(f); (= personality) Rundfunk-/Fernsehpersönlichkeit f; **he's not a very good ~** er ist nicht besonders gut im Fernsehen/Rundfunk; **a famous ~** eine vom Rundfunk/Fernsehen bekannte Persönlichkeit

---

broadcasting [ˈbrɔːdkɑːstɪŋ] N (Rad, TV) Sendung f; (of event) Übertragung f; **end of ~** Ende des Programms; **to work in ~** beim Rundfunk/Fernsehen arbeiten; **the early days of ~** die Anfänge des Rundfunks/Fernsehens ATTR (Rad) Rundfunk-; (TV) Fernseh-

Broadcasting Standards Council N (Brit) Rundfunk- und Fernsehkontrollorgan

broadcasting station N (Rad) Rundfunkstation f; (TV) Fernsehstation f

broadcloth [ˈbrɔːdklɒθ] N merzerisierter Baumwollstoff

broaden (out) [ˈbrɔːdn(aʊt)] VT sep road etc verbreitern; (fig) person, attitudes aufgeschlossener machen; **to broaden one's mind/one's horizons** (fig) seinen Horizont erweitern VI breiter werden, sich verbreitern; (fig, person, attitudes) aufgeschlossener werden; (horizon) sich erweitern

broad: broad gauge N Breitspur f; **broad jump** N (US Sport) Weitsprung m; **broadloom** ADJ carpet überbreit

broadly [ˈbrɔːdlɪ] ADV **a** (= in general terms) allgemein, in großen Zügen; outline, describe grob; agree, accept weitgehend; welcome, support, applicable allgemein; differ beträchtlich; **~ speaking** ganz allgemein gesprochen; **~-based** breit gefächert **b** grin, smile, laugh breit; hint, wink deutlich

broad: broad-minded ADJ großzügig, tolerant; **broad-mindedness** N Großzügigkeit f, Toleranz f; **broadness** N = **breadth**; **broadsheet** N (Press) großformatige Zeitung → also **tabloid**; **broad-shouldered** ADJ breitschult(e)rig; **broadside** (Naut) N Breitseite f; (fig also) Attacke f; **to fire a ~** eine Breitseite abgeben or abfeuern; **he fired a ~ at the manager** (fig) er attackierte den Manager scharf ADV **~ on** mit der Breitseite (to nach); **broadsword** N breites Schwert

brocade [brəˈkeɪd] N Brokat m ATTR Brokat-, brokaten

brocaded [brəˈkeɪdɪd] ADJ (wie Brokat) verziert or bestickt

broccoli [ˈbrɒkəlɪ] N Brokkoli pl, Spargelkohl m

brochure [ˈbrəʊʃʊəʳ] N Broschüre f, Prospekt m

brodie [ˈbrəʊdɪ] N (US sl) **a** (= jump) Todessprung m; **to do a ~** sich in die Tiefe stürzen (in selbstmörderischer Absicht); **to do a ~ from a bridge** sich von einer Brücke stürzen **b** (= failure) Pleite f (inf), Reinfall m (inf)

brogue¹ [brəʊg] N (= shoe) ≈ Haferlschuh m (Aus), Budapester m

brogue² N (= Irish accent) irischer Akzent

broil [brɔɪl] VTI (Cook) grillen

broiler [ˈbrɔɪləʳ] N **a** (= chicken) Brathähnchen nt, (Gold)broiler m (dial) **b** (= grill) Grill m

broiling [ˈbrɔɪlɪŋ] ADJ (esp US) sun, summer brütend heiß

broke [brəʊk] pret of **break** ADJ pred **a** (inf) abgebrannt (inf), pleite (inf); **to go ~** Pleite machen (inf); **to go for ~** alles riskieren **b** **if it ain't ~, don't fix it** (fig inf) man sollte ohne Not nichts ändern

broken [ˈbrəʊkən] ptp of **break** ADJ **a** kaputt (inf); twig geknickt; bone gebrochen; rope also gerissen; (= smashed) cup, glass etc zerbrochen, kaputt **b** (fig) voice brüchig; chord gebrochen; heart, spirit, man gebrochen; health, marriage zerrüttet; **surely his voice has ~ by now** er muss den Stimmbruch schon hinter sich (dat) haben; **from a ~ home** aus zerrütteten Familienverhältnissen **c** promise gebrochen; appointment nicht (ein)gehalten **d** road, surface, ground uneben; coastline zerklüftet; water, sea aufgewühlt, bewegt; set unvollständig **e** (= interrupted) journey unterbrochen; line also gestrichelt; *sleep also* gestört **f** *English, German etc* gebrochen

broken: broken-down ADJ *machine, car, furniture* kaputt (*inf*); *building* heruntergekommen; **brokenhearted** ADJ untröstlich; **broken white** N gebrochenes Weiß; **broken-winded** ADJ kurzatmig, dämpfig (*spec*)

broker ['brəʊkə'] **N** (*St Ex, Fin, real estate*) Makler *m*; **yachting ~** Bootshändler *m* **VT** *deal, agreement* aushandeln

brokerage ['brəʊkərɪdʒ] N **a** (= *commission*) Maklergebühr *f*; (*of insurance broker also*) Maklerlohn *m* **b** (= *trade*) Maklergeschäft *nt*

broking ['brəʊkɪŋ] N Geschäft *nt* eines Maklers

brolly ['brɒlɪ] N (*Brit, inf*) (Regen)schirm *m*

bromide ['brəʊmaɪd] N **a** (*Chem*) Bromid *nt*; (*Typ*) Bromsilberdruck *m*; (*Med inf*) Beruhigungsmittel *nt* **b** (*fig, = platitude*) Plattitüde *f*, Allgemeinplatz *m*

bromide paper N (*Phot*) Bromsilberpapier *nt*

bronchia ['brɒŋkɪə] PL Bronchien *pl*

bronchial ['brɒŋkɪəl] ADJ bronchial

bronchial tubes PL Bronchien *pl*

bronchitis [brɒŋ'kaɪtɪs] N Bronchitis *f*

bronchus ['brɒŋkəs] N *pl* **bronchi** ['brɒŋkiː] Bronchus *m*

bronco ['brɒŋkəʊ] N *wildes oder halbwildes Pferd in den USA*

broncobuster ['brɒŋkəʊˌbʌstə'] N (*inf*) *Zureiter wilder oder halbwilder Pferde*

brontosaurus [ˌbrɒntə'sɔːrəs] N Brontosaurus *m*

Bronx cheer [brɒŋks'tʃɪə'] N (*US, inf*) **to get a ~** ausgelacht werden; **to give sb a ~** jdn auslachen

bronze [brɒnz] **N** (*all senses*) Bronze *f* **VI** (*person*) braun werden, bräunen **VT** **a** *metal* bronzieren **b** *face, skin* bräunen **b** Bronze-

Bronze: Bronze Age N Bronzezeit *f*; **Bronze Age man** N der Mensch der Bronzezeit

bronzed [brɒnzd] ADJ *face, person* braun, (sonnen)gebräunt

bronze medallist, (*US*) **bronze medalist** N (*Sport*) Bronzemedaillengewinner(in) *m(f)*

bronzer ['brɒnzə'] N Bräunungsmittel *nt*

bronzing ['brɒnzɪŋ] ADJ Bräunungs-; **~ powder** Bräunungspuder *m*; **~ gel** Bräunungsgel *nt*

brooch [brəʊtʃ] N Brosche *f*

brood [bruːd] **N** (*lit, fig*) Brut *f* **VI** **a** (*bird*) brüten **b** (*fig, person*) grübeln; (*despondently also*) brüten

▶ **brood over** *or* **(up)on** VI +*prep obj* nachgrübeln über (+*acc*); (*despondently also*) brüten über (+*dat*)

brooder ['bruːdə'] N **a** (*for breeding*) Brutapparat *m*, Brutkasten *m* **b** (*fig: = thinker*) Grübler(in) *m(f)*

brood mare N Zuchtstute *f*

broody ['bruːdɪ] ADJ **a** *hen* brütig; **the hen is ~** die Henne gluckt; **to be feeling ~** (*hum inf*) den Wunsch nach einem Kind haben **b** *person* grüblerisch; (= *sad, moody*) schwerblütig

brook¹ [brʊk] N Bach *m*

brook² VT (*liter, = tolerate*) dulden; **to ~ no delay** keinen Aufschub dulden

brooklet ['brʊklɪt] N Bächlein *nt*

broom [bruːm] N **a** Besen *m*; **a new ~ sweeps clean** (*Prov*) neue Besen kehren gut (*Prov*) **b** (*Bot*) Ginster *m*

broom: broom cupboard N Besenschrank *m*; **broomstick** N Besenstiel *m*; **a witch on her ~** eine Hexe auf ihrem Besen

Bros PL (*Comm*) *abbr of* **Brothers** Gebr.

broth [brɒθ] N Fleischbrühe *f*; (= *thickened soup*) Suppe *f*

brothel ['brɒθl] N Bordell *nt*, Puff *m* (*inf*)

brothel: brothel creepers PL (*hum*) Leisetreter *pl* (*hum*); **brothel-keeper** N Bordellwirt(in) *m(f)*

brother ['brʌðə'] N *pl* **-s** *or* (*obs, Eccl*) **brethren a** (*also Eccl*) Bruder *m*; **they are ~ and sister** sie sind Geschwister, sie sind Bruder und Schwester; **my/his ~s and sisters** meine/seine Geschwister; **the Clarke ~s** die Brüder Clarke; (*Comm*) die Gebrüder Clarke; **oh ~!** (*esp US, inf*) Junge, Junge! (*inf*) **b** (*in trade unions*) Kollege *m* **c** (= *fellow man, DDR, Pol*) Bruder *m*; **his ~ officers** seine Offizierskameraden; **our ~s** unsere Mitmenschen *or* Brüder (*geh, Eccl*)

brother: brotherhood N **a** brüderliches Einvernehmen, Brüderlichkeit *f*; **sense of ~** (*lit*) Brudersinn *m*; (*fig*) Gefühl *nt* der Brüderlichkeit **b** (= *organization*) Bruderschaft *f*; **~ of man** Gemeinschaft *f* der Menschen; **brother-in-arms** N Waffenbruder *m*; **brother-in-law** N *pl* **brothers-in-law** Schwager *m*

brotherliness ['brʌðəlɪnɪs] N Brüderlichkeit *f*

brotherly ['brʌðəlɪ] ADJ brüderlich

brougham ['bruːəm] N Brougham *m*

brought [brɔːt] *pret, ptp of* **bring**

brouhaha ['bruːhɑːhɑː] N *usu sing* Wirbel *m*, Tumult *m*

brow [braʊ] N **a** (= *eyebrow*) Braue *f* **b** (= *forehead*) Stirn *f* **c** (*of hill*) (Berg)kuppe *f*

browbeat ['braʊbiːt] *pret* **browbeat**, *ptp* **browbeaten** VT unter (moralischen) Druck setzen; **to ~ sb into doing sth** jdn so unter Druck setzen, dass er etw tut; **I can't ~ you into accepting it** ich kann euch natürlich nicht (dazu) zwingen, es anzunehmen; **I won't be ~en** ich lasse mich nicht tyrannisieren *or* unter Druck setzen

brown [braʊn] **ADJ** (+*er*) braun; (*Cook*) *roast etc also* braun gebraten **N** Braun *nt* **VT** (*sun*) *skin, person* bräunen; (*Cook*) (an)bräunen; *meat also* anbraten **VI** braun werden

▶ **brown off** VT **to be browned off with sb/sth** (*esp Brit, inf*) jdn/etw satt haben (*inf*); **I was pretty browned off at the time** ich hatte es damals ziemlich satt; **you're looking a bit browned off** du siehst so aus, als hättest du alles ziemlich satt

brown: brown ale N Malzbier *nt*; **brown-bag** VI (*US*) **to ~ lunch** sein Mittagessen mit zur Arbeit bringen; **brown bear** N Braunbär *m*; **brown bread** N Grau- *or* Mischbrot *nt*; (*from wholemeal*) Vollkornbrot *nt*; (*darker*) Schwarzbrot *nt*; **brown coal** N Braunkohle *f*; **brown-eyed** ADJ braunäugig; **brown goods** PL hochwertige Konsumgüter *pl* (*Fernsehgerät, Videorekorder etc*); **brown-haired** ADJ braunhaarig

brownie ['braʊnɪ] N **a** (= *chocolate cake*) *kleiner Schokoladenkuchen* **b** (= *fairy*) Heinzelmännchen *nt* **c** **Brownie** (*in Guide Movement*) Wichtel *m*

Brownie points PL Pluspunkte *pl*; **let's give him ~ for trying** dass er es versucht hat, können wir ihm ja anrechnen; **to score ~ with sb** sich bei jdm beliebt machen

browning ['braʊnɪŋ] N (*Cook, = act*) Anbraten *nt*; (= *substance*) Bratensoße *f*, Bratenpulver *nt*

brownish ['braʊnɪʃ] ADJ bräunlich

brown: brown-nose (*US inf*) **VI** arschkriechen (*inf, pej*) **N** Arschkriecher(in) *m(f)* (*inf, pej*); **brownout** N (*esp US, = blackout*) teilweiser Stromausfall; (*during war*) teilweise Verdunkelung; **brown owl** N (*Orn*) Waldkauz *m*; **Brown Owl** (*in Brownies*) die weise Eule; **brown paper** N Packpapier *nt*; **brown rat** N Hausratte *f*; **brown rice** N geschälter Reis; **brown sauce** N (*Brit Cook*) braune Soße; **Brown Shirt** N Braunhemd *nt*; **brownstone** N (*US, = material*) rötlich brauner Sandstein; (= *house*) (rotes) Sandsteinhaus *nt*; **brown study** N **to be in a ~** (*liter*) geistesabwesend sein, in Gedanken verloren sein; **brown sugar** N brauner Zucker

browse [braʊz] **VI a** **to ~ among the books** in den Büchern schmökern; **to ~ through a book** in einem Buch schmökern **b** (*Comput*) browsen, surfen **c** (*cattle*) weiden; (*deer*) äsen **N** **to have a ~ (around)**

sich umsehen; **to have a ~ through the books** in den Büchern schmökern; **to have a ~ around the bookshops** sich in den Buchläden umsehen

browser ['braʊzə'] N (*Comput*) Browser *m*

Bruges [bruːʒ] N Brügge *nt*

bruin ['bruːɪn] N (*Meister*) Petz *m*

bruise [bruːz] **N** (*on person*) blauer Fleck; (*more serious*) Prellung *f*, Bluterguss *m* (*esp Med*); (*on fruit*) Druckstelle *f* **VT** *person* einen blauen Fleck/blaue Flecke(n) schlagen (+*dat*) *or* beibringen (+*dat*); (*more seriously*) eine Prellung/Prellungen beibringen (+*dat*); *fruit* beschädigen; (*fig*) *person, spirit, feelings* verletzen; **to ~ oneself** sich stoßen, sich (*dat*) einen blauen Fleck holen; **to ~ one's elbow** sich (*dat*) einen blauen Fleck am Ellbogen holen **VI** (*person, part of body*) einen blauen Fleck/blaue Flecke(n) bekommen; (*fruit*) eine Druckstelle/Druckstellen bekommen; (*fig, person, feelings*) verletzt werden; **he ~s easily** er bekommt leicht blaue Flecken; (*fig*) er ist sehr empfindlich

bruised [bruːzd] ADJ **a** **to be ~** (*person*) einen blauen Fleck/blaue Flecke haben; (= *have severe bruising*) Prellungen haben; (*fruit, vegetable*) eine Druckstelle/Druckstellen haben; **she has a ~ shoulder, her shoulder is ~** sie hat einen blauen Fleck/blaue Flecke auf der Schulter; **I feel ~ all over** mir tuts am ganzen Körper weh **b** (*fig*) *ego, feelings, pride* verletzt; **to feel ~** sich verletzt fühlen

bruiser ['bruːzə'] N (*inf*) Rabauke *m*, Räuber *m* (*hum*)

bruising ['bruːzɪŋ] N Prellungen *pl*

brumal ['bruːməl] ADJ winterlich, Winter-

brunch [brʌntʃ] N Brunch *m*, Frühstück und Mittagessen in einem

Brunei ['bruːnaɪ] N Brunei *nt*

brunette [bruː'net] **N** Brünette *f* **ADJ** brünett

brunt [brʌnt] N **to bear the (main) ~ of the attack** die volle Wucht des Angriffs tragen; **to bear the (main) ~ of the work/costs** die Hauptlast der Arbeit/Kosten tragen; **to bear the ~** das meiste abkriegen

brush [brʌʃ] **N a** (= *object*) Bürste *f*; (= *artist's brush, paintbrush, shaving brush, pastry brush*) Pinsel *m*; (= *hearth brush*) Besen *m*; (*with dustpan*) Handbesen *or* -feger *m*; (= *flue brush*) Stoßbesen *m*; (= *flue brush with weight*) Sonne *f*; **to be as daft as a ~** (*inf*) total meschugge sein (*inf*) **b** (= *action*) **to give sth a ~** etw bürsten; *jacket, shoes etc* abbürsten; **to give one's hair a ~** sich die Haare bürsten; **your jacket/hair/teeth could do with a ~** du solltest deine Jacke/dein Haar/deine Zähne mal wieder bürsten **c** (= *light touch*) leichte, flüchtige Berührung, Streifen *nt*; **I felt the ~ of his lips against my neck** ich fühlte, wie seine Lippen meinen Nacken leicht berührten **d** (*of fox*) Lunte *f* **e** (= *undergrowth*) Unterholz *nt* **f** (*Mil: = skirmish*) Zusammenstoß *m*, Scharmützel *nt*; (= *quarrel, incident*) Zusammenstoß *m*; **to have a ~ with sb** mit jdm aneinander geraten **g** (*Elec, of commutator*) Bürste *f* **VT a** (= *clean, tidy*) bürsten; (*with hand*) wischen; **to ~ one's teeth** sich (*dat*) die Zähne putzen; **to ~ one's hair** sich (*dat*) das Haar bürsten **b** (= *sweep*) *dirt* fegen, kehren; (*with hand, cloth*) wischen; **to ~ sth into a pile** etw zu einem Haufen zusammenfegen **c** (= *touch lightly*) streifen **d** *fabric* bürsten, aufrauen

▶ **brush against** VI +*prep obj* streifen

▶ **brush aside** VT *sep obstacle, person* (einfach) zur Seite schieben; *objections* (einfach) abtun; *ideas* verwerfen

▶ **brush away** VT *sep* (*with brush*) abbürsten; (*with hand, cloth*) ab- *or* wegwischen; *insects* verscheuchen

▶ **brush down** VT *sep* abbürsten; *horse* striegeln

▶ **brush off** VT *sep* **a** *mud, snow* abbürsten; *insect* verscheuchen **b** (*inf*, = *reject*) *person* abblitzen lassen (*inf*); *suggestion, criticism* zurückweisen VI (*mud etc*) sich abbürsten *or* (*with hand, cloth*) abwischen lassen

▶ **brush past** VI streifen (*prep obj +acc*); **as he brushed past** als er mich/ihn *etc* streifte

▶ **brush up** VT *sep* **a** *crumbs, dirt* auffegen, aufkehren **b** *wool, nap* aufrauen, rauen (*form*) **c** (*fig:* also **brush up on**) *subject, one's German* auffrischen

brushed nylon [ˌbrʌʃtˈnaɪlən] N Nylon-Velours *m*

brush fire N **a** (= *fire*) Buschfeuer *nt* **b** (= *crisis*) begrenzter *or* lokaler Konflikt

brushings [ˈbrʌʃɪŋz] PL Kehricht *m no pl*

brush: brushoff N (*inf*) Abfuhr *f*; **to give sb the ~** jdn abblitzen lassen (*inf*), jdm einen Korb geben (*inf*); **to get the ~** abblitzen (*inf*), einen Korb kriegen (*inf*); **brushstroke** N Pinselstrich *m*; (= *way of painting*) Pinselführung *f*; **brush-up** N (*inf*) **I must give my Italian a ~** ich muss meine Italienischkenntnisse auffrischen; **brushwood** N **a** (= *undergrowth*) Unterholz *nt* **b** (= *cut twigs*) Reisig *nt*; **brushwork** N (*Art*) Pinselführung *f*

brusque [bruːsk] ADJ (+er) *person, tone, manner* brüsk, schroff; *reply* schroff

brusquely [ˈbruːsklɪ] ADV *behave* brüsk, schroff; *speak* brüsk, in schroffem Ton; *reply* schroff

brusqueness [ˈbruːsknɪs] N Schroffheit *f*

Brussels [ˈbrʌslz] N Brüssel *nt*

Brussels: Brussels lace N Brüsseler Spitze(n) *f(pl)*; **Brussels sprouts** PL Rosenkohl *m*

brutal [ˈbruːtl] ADJ brutal

brutalism [ˈbruːtəlɪzəm] N (*Archit*) Brutalismus *m*

brutality [bruːˈtælɪtɪ] N Brutalität *f*

brutalize [ˈbruːtəlaɪz] VT brutalisieren, verrohen lassen

brutally [ˈbruːtəlɪ] ADV brutal; **I'll be ~ frank** ich werde schonungslos offen sein

brute [bruːt] N **a** Tier *nt*, Vieh *nt* (*pej*) **b** (= *person*) brutaler Kerl; (= *savage*) Bestie *f*; **drink brings out the ~ in him** Alkohol bringt das Tier in ihm zum Vorschein **c** (*inf*, = *thing*) **it's a ~ of a problem** es ist ein höllisches Problem (*inf*); **this nail's a real ~ (to get out)** dieser Nagel geht höllisch schwer raus (*inf*) ADJ *attr strength* roh; *passion* tierisch, viehisch (*pej*); **by ~ force** mit roher Gewalt

brutish [ˈbruːtɪʃ] ADJ *person, behaviour* viehisch, brutal

BS (*US inf*) abbr of **bullshit**

BSc abbr of **Bachelor of Science**

BSc Econ abbr of **Bachelor of Economic Science**

BSE abbr of **bovine spongiform encephalopathy** BSE *f*, Rinderwahn *m*

BSI abbr of **British Standards Institution** *britischer Normenausschuss*

B-side [ˈbiːsaɪd] N (*of record*) B-Seite *f*

BST abbr of **British Summer Time** *or* **British Standard Time**

BT abbr of **British Telecom** *britisches Telekommunikationsunternehmen*

Bt. abbr of **baronet**

BTA abbr of **British Tourist Authority**

BTEC [ˈbiːtek] (*Brit*) abbr of **Business and Technology Education Council** **a** (= *organization*) *Fachschule für Betriebswirtschaften, Naturwissenschaften und Technologie* **b** (= *diploma*) *Diplom in Betriebswirtschaft, Naturwissenschaften und Technologie*

BTW (*inf*) abbr of **by the way**

bub [bʌb] N (*US inf*) Alte(r) *m* (*inf*), Mann *m* (*inf*)

bubble [ˈbʌbl] N Blase *f*; (*on plane etc*) (Glas-)kuppel *f*; **to blow ~s** Blasen machen; **to burst sb's ~** (*fig*) jdn auf den Boden der Tatsachen

zurückbringen; **the ~ has burst** (*fig*) alles ist wie eine Seifenblase zerplatzt VI **a** (*liquid*) sprudeln; (*heated also*) strudeln; (*wine*) perlen; (*gas*) Blasen/Bläschen machen *or* bilden **b** (= *make bubbling noise*) blubbern (*inf*); (*cooking liquid, geyser etc*) brodeln; (*stream*) plätschern **c** (*fig*) **to ~ with excitement/enthusiasm/confidence** fast platzen vor Aufregung/Begeisterung/Selbstvertrauen

▶ **bubble out** VI (*liquid*) heraussprudeln

▶ **bubble over** VI (*lit*) überschäumen; (*fig*) übersprudeln (*with* vor +*dat*)

▶ **bubble up** VI (*liquid*) aufsprudeln; (*gas*) in Blasen/Bläschen hochsteigen; (*excitement, emotions*) aufsteigen, hochkommen

bubble: bubble and squeak N (*Brit*) *zusammen gebratene Fleischreste und Gemüse*; **bubble bath** N Schaumbad *nt*; **bubble car** N (*Brit, opening at the top*) Kabinenroller *m*; (*opening at the front*) Isetta® *f*; **bubble chamber** N Blasenkammer *f*; **bubble gum** N Bubblegum *m*; **bubblehead** N (*esp US, pej inf*) Schwachkopf *m* (*inf*); **bubble-jet printer** N (*Comput*) Bubblejet-Drucker *m*; **bubble memory** N (*Comput*) Blasenspeicher *m*; **bubble pack** N (Klar)sichtpackung *f*

bubbler [ˈbʌblə] N (*US, Austral*) Trinkbrunnen *m*

bubbly [ˈbʌblɪ] ADJ (+er) **a** (*lit*) sprudelnd **b** (*fig inf*) *person, personality* temperamentvoll, lebendig; *mood* übersprudelnd N (*inf*) Schampus *m* (*inf*)

bubonic plague [bjuːˈbɒnɪkˈpleɪg] N Beulenpest *f*

buccaneer [ˌbʌkəˈnɪə] N Seeräuber *m*; (= *ship*) Piratenschiff *nt*

Bucharest [ˌbjuːkəˈrest] N Bukarest *nt*

buck [bʌk] N **a** (= *male deer*) Bock *m*; (= *male rabbit, hare*) Rammler *m* **b** (*US, inf*, = *dollar*) Dollar *m*; **20 ~s** 20 Dollar; **to make a ~** Geld verdienen; **to make a fast** *or* **quick ~** (*also Brit*) schnell Kohle machen (*inf*); **to get more bang for the ~** mehr für sein Geld kriegen **c to pass the ~** (*difficulty, unpleasant task*) den schwarzen Peter weitergeben; (*responsibility also*) die Verantwortung abschieben; **to pass the ~ to sb** jdm den schwarzen Peter zuschieben/die Verantwortung aufhalsen; **the ~ stops here** der schwarze Peter landet bei mir/uns; **the ~ stops with her** der schwarze Peter landet bei ihr **d** (*old, hum*, = *dandy*) Stutzer *m*, Geck *m* (*old*) **e** (*leap by horse*) Bocken *nt* **f** (*in gymnastics*) Bock *m* VI **a** (*horse*) bocken **b** (= *resist, object*) sich sträuben (*at* gegen) VT **a** **you can't ~ the market** gegen den Markt kommt man nicht an; **to ~ the trend** sich dem Trend widersetzen → **system b** (*horse*) *rider* abwerfen

▶ **buck for** VI +*prep obj* (*US, inf*) **to buck for promotion** mit aller Gewalt *or* auf Teufel komm raus (*inf*) befördert werden wollen

▶ **buck off** VT *sep rider* abwerfen

▶ **buck up** (*inf*) VI **a** (= *hurry up*) sich ranhalten (*inf*), rasch *or* fix machen (*inf*); **buck up!** halt dich ran! (*inf*) **b** (= *cheer up*) aufleben; **buck up!** Kopf hoch! VT **a** (= *make hurry*) Dampf machen (+*dat*) (*inf*) **b** (= *make cheerful*) aufmuntern **c to buck one's ideas up** sich zusammenreißen (*inf*)

buckaroo [ˌbʌkəˈruː] N (*US inf hum*) Cowboy *m*

buckboard [ˈbʌkbɔːd] N (*US*) (einfache, offene) Kutsche

bucket [ˈbʌkɪt] N **a** (*also of dredger, grain elevator*) Eimer *m*; (*of excavator, water wheel*) Schaufel *f*; **a ~ of water** ein Eimer *m* Wasser; **to weep** *or* **cry ~s** (*inf*) wie ein Schlosshund heulen (*inf*); **it's coming down in ~s** (*US inf*) es gießt *or* schüttet wie aus *or* mit Kübeln (*inf*) → **kick, drop** VI (*Brit, inf*) **it's ~ing!, the rain is ~ing (down)!** es gießt *or* schüttet wie aus *or* mit Kübeln (*inf*)

▶ **bucket about** VT *sep usu pass* (*Brit inf*) durchrütteln

▶ **bucket along** VI (*dated inf*) mit einem Affenzahn dahin-/entlangkutschen (*inf*) *or* -karriolen (*inf*)

▶ **bucket down** VI (*Brit inf*) = **bucket** VI

bucket brigade N Eimerkette *f*

bucketful [ˈbʌkɪtful] N Eimer *m*; **by the ~** (*fig inf*) tonnenweise (*inf*)

bucket: bucket seat N Schalensitz *m*; **bucket shop** N (*Fin*) unreelle Maklerfirma, Schwindelmakler *m*; (= *travel agency*) Agentur *f* für Billigreisen; **bucketwheel** N (*Tech*) Schöpfrad *nt*

buckeye [ˈbʌkaɪ] N (*US*) Rosskastanie *f*; (= *seed*) Kastanie *f*

Buck House [ˈbʌkˌhaʊs] N (*Brit, inf*) = **Buckingham Palace**

Buckingham Palace [ˈbʌkɪŋəmˈpælɪs] N Buckingham Palace *m*, der Buckingham-Palast

buckle [ˈbʌkl] N **a** (*on belt, shoe*) Schnalle *f*, Spange *f* **b** (*in metal etc*) Beule *f*; (*concave also*) Delle *f*; **there's a nasty ~ in this girder** dieser Träger ist übel eingebeult *or* (*twisted*) verbogen; **there's a nasty ~ in this wheel** diese Rad ist übel verbogen VT **a** *belt, shoes* zuschnallen **b** *wheel, girder etc* verbiegen; (= *dent*) verbeulen VI **a** (*belt, shoe*) mit einer Schnalle *or* Spange geschlossen werden **b** (*wheel, metal*) sich verbiegen

▶ **buckle down** VI (*inf*) sich dahinter klemmen (*inf*), sich dranmachen (*inf*); **to buckle down to a task** sich hinter einer Aufgabe klemmen (*inf*), sich an eine Aufgabe machen

▶ **buckle on** VT *sep armour* anlegen; *sword, belt* umschnallen

▶ **buckle to** VI sich am Riemen reißen (*inf*)

buck-passing [ˈbʌkˌpɑːsɪŋ] N , *no pl* (*inf*) *Abwälzen der Verantwortung auf eine andere Person*

buckram [ˈbʌkrəm] N Buckram *m* ADJ *attr* Buckram-

Bucks [bʌks] abbr of **Buckinghamshire**

bucksaw [ˈbʌksɔː] N Handsäge *f*

buck's fizz [ˌbʌksˈfɪz] N Sekt *m* mit Orangensaft

buckshee [bʌkˈʃiː] ADJ (*Brit, inf*) gratis, umsonst

buck: buckshot N grober Schrot, Rehposten *m* (*spec*); **buckskin** N Wildleder *nt*, Buckskin *m* **b buckskins** PL Lederhose(n) *f(pl)*; **bucktooth** N vorstehender Zahn; **bucktoothed** ADJ mit vorstehenden Zähnen; **buckwheat** N Buchweizen *m*

bucolic [bjuːˈkɒlɪk] ADJ (*liter*) bukolisch (*liter*)

bud¹ [bʌd] N **a** Knospe *f*; **to be in ~** knospen, Knospen treiben **b** (*Anat*) → **taste bud** VI (*plant, flower*) knospen, Knospen treiben; (*tree also*) ausschlagen; (*horns*) wachsen

bud² INTERJ (*US, inf*) = **buddy**

Budapest [ˌbjuːdəˈpest] N Budapest *nt*

Buddha [ˈbʊdə] N Buddha *m*

Buddhism [ˈbʊdɪzəm] N Buddhismus *m*

Buddhist [ˈbʊdɪst] N Buddhist(in) *m(f)* ADJ buddhistisch

budding [ˈbʌdɪŋ] ADJ knospend; (*fig*) *poet etc* angehend

buddy [ˈbʌdɪ] N (*US, inf*) Kumpel *m*; **hey, ~!** he, Kumpel, hör mal zu!; (*threatening*) hör mal zu, Kumpel *or* Freundchen (*inf*)

buddy-buddy [ˈbʌdɪbʌdɪ] ADJ (*US, inf*) **to be ~ with sb** mit jdm dick befreundet sein (*inf*); **to try to get ~ with sb** sich bei jdm anbiedern

buddy system N **to employ** *or* **use the ~** aus Sicherheitsgründen Zweiergruppen bilden (*um sich ggf. gegenseitig zu helfen*)

budge [bʌdʒ] VI **a** (= *move*) sich rühren, sich bewegen; **~ up** *or* **over!** mach Platz!, rück mal ein Stückchen! **b** (*fig*, = *give way*) nachgeben, weichen; **I will not ~ an inch** ich werde keinen Fingerbreit nachgeben *or* weichen; **he is not going to ~** er gibt nicht nach, der bleibt stur (*inf*) **VT** **a** (= *move*) (von der Stelle) bewegen **b** (= *force to give way*) zum Nachgeben bewegen; **we can't ~ him** er lässt sich durch nichts erweichen

budgerigar ['bʌdʒərɪɡɑː'] N Wellensittich *m*

budget ['bʌdʒɪt] **N** Etat *m*, Budget *nt*; (*Parl also*) Haushalt(splan) *m* **VI** haushalten, Haus halten, wirtschaften; **responsible for ~ing** für das Budget or den Etat or (*Parl also*) den Haushalt verantwortlich **VT** **a** (*money, time* ver-planen **b** (*also* **budget for**) *item* kostenmäßig einplanen; *costs* einplanen; **~ed costs** Vorgabekosten *pl*, vorgesehene Kosten *pl*; **~ed revenue** Sollertrag *m*

▶ **budget for** VI +*prep obj* (im Etat) einplanen

BUDGET

Das **Budget** ist die jährliche Verlautbarung der geschätzten Einnahmen und Ausgaben der Regierung, die der britische Finanzminister normalerweise im März im Parlament in Form einer Rede abgibt. Das **Budget** beinhaltet auch Änderungen an der Besteuerung und den Sozialausgaben. Daher wird die Rede in ihrer gesamten Länge im Fernsehen übertragen, damit die Bürgerinnen und Bürger aus erster Hand erfahren, welche Auswirkungen das **Budget** für sie persönlich bei den Steuern für beispielsweise Benzin, Alkohol und Zigaretten haben wird → TREASURY

-budget *suf* **low-budget** mit bescheidenen Mitteln finanziert; **big-budget** aufwändig (finanziert), groß angelegt; **a low-/big-budget film** ein mit bescheidenen Mitteln/aufwändig finanzierter Film, ein Low-Budget-/Big-Budget-Film *m*

budget account N Kundenkonto *nt*

budgetary ['bʌdʒɪtrɪ] ADJ Etat-, Budget-, Haushalts-; **~ problems** Etat- or Budget- or Haushaltsprobleme *pl*; **~ constraints** finanzielle Zwänge; **~ policy** Haushaltspolitik *f*

budget: budget day N (*Parl*) ≈ Haushaltsdebatte *f*; **budget deficit** N Haushaltsdefizit *nt*

budgeting ['bʌdʒɪtɪŋ] N Kalkulation *f*, Budgetierung *f*

budget speech N (*Parl*) Etatrede *f*

budgie ['bʌdʒɪ] N (*inf*) *abbr of* **budgerigar** Wellensittich *m*

Buenos Aires [,bweɪnɒs'aɪrɪz] N Buenos Aires *nt*

buff¹ [bʌf] **N** **a** (= *leather*) (kräftiges, weiches) Leder **b in the ~** nackt, im Adams-/Evaskostüm (*hum*) **c** (= *polishing disc*) Schwabbelscheibe *f* (*spec*), Polierscheibe *f*; (= *cylinder*) Schwabbelwalze *f* (*spec*) **d** (= *colour*) Gelbbraun *nt* **ADJ** **a** ledern, Leder- **b** (*colour*) gelbbraun **VT** *metal* polieren

buff² N (*inf, = movie/theatre etc buff*) Fan *m* (*inf*)

buffalo ['bʌfələʊ] N *pl* **-es**, *collective pl* **-** Büffel *m*

buffalo grass N (*US*) Büffelgras *nt*

buffer¹ ['bʌfə'] N (*lit, fig, Comput*) Puffer *m*; (*Rail, at terminus*) Prellbock *m*; **to hit the ~s** (*Brit: plan, project*) am Ende sein

buffer² N (*Brit, inf*) Heini *m* (*inf*)

buffering ['bʌfərɪŋ] N (*Comput*) Pufferung *f*

buffer: buffer solution N (*Chem*) Puffer *m*, Pufferlösung *f*; **buffer state** N (*Pol*) Pufferstaat *m*; **buffer zone** N Pufferzone *f*

buffet¹ ['bʌfɪt] N (= *blow*) Schlag *m* **VT** hin und her werfen; **~ed by the wind** vom Wind gerüttelt; **~ing wind** böiger Wind

buffet² ['bʊfeɪ] N Büffet *nt*; (*Brit Rail*) Speisewagen *m*; (= *meal*) Stehimbiss *m*; (= *cold buffet*) kaltes Büffett *nt*; **~ lunch/meal/supper** Stehimbiss *m*

buffet car ['bʊfeɪ-] N (*Brit, Rail*) Speisewagen *m*

buffeting ['bʌfɪtɪŋ] N heftiges Schaukeln; (*Aviat*) Rütteln *nt*; **to get** or **take a ~** hin und her geworfen or (*Aviat*) gerüttelt werden

buffoon [bə'fuːn] N Clown *m*; (*stupid*) Blödmann *m* (*pej inf*); **to act** or **play the ~** den Clown or Hanswurst spielen

buffoonery [bə'fuːnərɪ] N Clownerie *f*

bug [bʌg] **N** **a** Wanze *f*; (*inf, = any insect*) Käfer *m*; **~s** *pl* Ungeziefer *nt* **b** (= *bugging device*) Wanze *f* **c** (*inf, = germ, virus*) Bazillus *f*; **I might get your ~** du könntest mich anstecken; **he picked up a ~ while on holiday** (*esp Brit*) or **vacation** (*US*) er hat sich (*dat*) im Urlaub eine Krankheit geholt; **there must be a ~ going about** das geht zur Zeit um **d** (*inf, = obsession*) **now he's got the ~** jetzt hats ihn gepackt (*inf*); **she's got the travel ~** die Reiselust hat sie gepackt **e** (*inf, = snag, defect*) Fehler *m*; **~s** *pl* Mucken *pl* (*inf*) **f** (*Comput*) Programmfehler *m*, Wanze *f* **VT** **a** *room, building* verwanzen (*inf*), Wanzen *pl* installieren in (+*dat*) or einbauen in (+*acc*) (*inf*); *conversation, telephone lines* abhören; **this room is ~ged** hier sind Wanzen (*inf*), das Zimmer ist verwanzt (*inf*) **b** (*inf, = worry*) stören; (= *annoy*) nerven (*inf*), den Nerv töten (+*dat*) (*inf*); **don't let it ~ you** mach dir nichts daraus (*inf*)

bugaboo ['bʌɡəbuː] N Schreckgespenst *nt*

bug: bugbear N Schreckgespenst *nt*; **bugbite** N Wanzenstich *m*; (*of other insect*) Insektenstich *m*; **bug-eyed** ADJ mit vorstehenden or vorquellenden Augen; **bug-free** ADJ (*Comput*) fehlerfrei

bugger ['bʌɡə'] **N** (*inf*) Scheißkerl *m* (*inf*), Arschloch *nt* (*vulg*); (*when not contemptible*) Kerl *m* (*inf*); (= *thing*) Bazillus *f*; **this nail's a ~, it won't come out** dieser Scheißnagel geht einfach nicht raus (*inf*); **you lucky ~!** du hast vielleicht ein Schwein! (*inf*); **to play silly ~s** (*Brit inf*) Scheiß machen (*sl*) **INTERJ** (*Brit inf*) Scheiße (*inf*); **~ (it)!** Scheiße! (*inf*); **~ this car!** dieses Scheißauto (*inf*); **~ the cost!** ich scheiß auf die Kosten! (*sl*); **~ him** dieser Scheißkerl (*inf*); (= *he can get lost*) der kann mich mal (*inf*); **~ me!** (*surprise*) (du) meine Fresse! (*sl*); (*annoyance*) so'n Scheiß! (*inf*) **VT** **a** (*lit*) anal verkehren mit **b** (*Brit, sl*) versauen (*sl*)

▶ **bugger about** or **around** (*Brit, inf*) **VI** (= *laze about etc*) rumgammeln (*inf*); (= *be ineffective*) blöd rummachen (*inf*); **stop buggering about** or **around and get on with it** nun mach mal Nägel mit Köpfen (*inf*); **to bugger about** or **around with sth** an etw (*dat*) rumpfuschen (*inf*) **VT** *sep* verarschen (*inf*)

▶ **bugger off** VI (*Brit, inf*) abhauen (*inf*), Leine ziehen (*inf*)

▶ **bugger up** VT *sep* (*Brit, inf*) versauen (*inf*); **I'm sorry if I've buggered you up** tut mir Leid, dass ich dich in eine solche Scheißlage gebracht habe (*inf*)

bugger all [,bʌɡər'ɔːl] N (*Brit, inf, = nothing*) rein gar nichts

buggered ['bʌɡəd] ADJ (*Brit inf*) (= *broken, ruined*) *machine, car, pen etc* im Arsch (*sl*); (= *exhausted*) *person* fix und fertig (*inf*); **I couldn't be ~** (= *bothered*) es war mir scheißegal (*inf*); **I'm ~ if I'll do it** ich denke nicht im Traum daran, es zu tun; **well, I'll be ~!** ich glaub, ich krieg mich nicht mehr! (*sl*)

buggery ['bʌɡərɪ] N Analverkehr *m*; (*with animals*) Sodomie *f*

bugging ['bʌɡɪŋ] N Abhören *nt*; **the use of ~** der Gebrauch von Abhörgeräten; **elaborate ~** raffiniertes Abhörsystem

bugging device N Abhörgerät *nt*, Wanze *f* (*inf*)

buggy ['bʌɡɪ] N (*with horse*) Buggy *m*, leichter Einspänner *m*; (**baby**) ~ (*Brit*) Sportwagen *m*; (*US*) Kinderwagen *m*

bugle ['bjuːɡl] N Bügelhorn *nt*; **~ call** Hornsignal *nt*

bugler ['bjuːɡlə'] N Hornist *m*

bug: bug-proof ADJ *room, telephone* abhörsicher; **bug-ridden** ADJ **a** *hotel, mattress* von Wanzen befallen, verwanzt (*inf*) **b** (*Comput*) *software etc* voller Fehler

build [bɪld] vb: pret, ptp **built** **N** Körperbau *m* **VT** **a** (*generally*) bauen; **the house is being built** das Haus ist im Bau or befindet sich im Bau **b** (*fig*) *new nation, relationship, career, system etc* aufbauen; *a better future* schaffen **VI** bauen; **to ~ on a piece of land** auf einem Grundstück bauen; (= *cover with houses etc*) ein Grundstück bebauen

▶ **build in** VT *sep* (*lit, fig*) *wardrobe, proviso etc* einbauen; (*fig*) *extra time* einplanen → **built-in**

▶ **build on** **VT** *sep* anbauen; **to build sth onto sth** etw an etw (*acc*) anbauen **VI** +*prep obj* bauen auf (+*acc*)

▶ **build up** **VI** **a** (*business*) wachsen; (*anticyclone, atmosphere*) entstehen, sich aufbauen; (*residue*) sich ablagern; (= *increase*) zunehmen; (*Tech, pressure*) sich erhöhen; **the music builds up to a huge crescendo** die Musik steigert sich zu einem gewaltigen Crescendo **b** (*traffic*) sich verdichten; (*queue, line of cars*) sich bilden **c the parts build up into a complete …** die Teile bilden zusammen ein vollständiges … **VT** *sep* **a** *business* aufbauen (*into* zu); *finances* aufbessern; **to build up a reputation** sich (*dat*) einen Namen machen **b** (= *increase*) *ego, muscles, forces* aufbauen; *production, pressure* steigern, erhöhen; *forces* (= *mass*) zusammenziehen; *health* kräftigen; *sb's confidence* stärken; **porridge builds you up** von Porridge wirst du groß und stark; **growing children need lots of vitamins to build them up** Kinder im Wachstumsalter brauchen viele Vitamine als Aufbaustoffe; **to build up sb's hopes** jdm Hoffnung(en) machen **c** (= *cover with houses*) *area, land* (ganz) bebauen **d** (= *publicize*) *person* aufbauen; **he wasn't as good as he had been built up to be** er war nicht so gut, wie die Werbung erwarten ließ

builder ['bɪldə'] N (= *worker*) Bauarbeiter(in) *m(f)*; (*of ships*) Schiffsbauer *m*; (= *contractor*) Bauunternehmer *m*; (= *future owner*) Bauherr *m*; (*fig, of state*) Baumeister *m* (*geh*), Erbauer *m*; **John Higgins, Builders** Bauunternehmen John Higgins; **~'s labourer** (*Brit*) or **laborer** (*US*) Bauarbeiter *m*; **~'s merchant** Baustoffhändler *m*

building ['bɪldɪŋ] N **a** Gebäude *nt*; (*usually big or in some way special also*) Bau *m*; **it's the next ~ but one** das ist zwei Häuser weiter; **the ~s in the old town** die Häuser or Gebäude in der Altstadt **b** (= *act of constructing*) Bau *m*, Bauen *nt*; (*of new nation etc*) Aufbau *m*

building: building block N (*in toy set*) Bauklotz *m*; (*fig*) Baustein *m*; **building contractor** N Bauunternehmer *m*; (= *Bauunternehmen* *m*; **building costs** PL Baukosten *pl*; **building estimate** N Baukosten(vor)anschlag *m*; **building firm** N Baufirma *f*; **building freeze** N Baustopp *m*; **building industry** N Bauindustrie *f*; **building land** N Bauland *nt*; **building materials** PL Baumaterial *nt*, Baustoffe *pl*; **building site** N Baustelle *f*; **building society** N (*Brit*) Bausparkasse *f*; **building trade** N Baugewerbe *nt*; **building worker** N Bauarbeiter *m*

build-up ['bɪldʌp] N **a** (*inf*) Werbung *f*; **publicity** ~ Werbekampagne *f*, **they gave the play a good** ~ sie haben das Stück ganz groß herausgebracht (*inf*); **the chairman gave the speaker a tremendous** ~ der Vorsitzende hat den Redner ganz groß angekündigt **b** (*of pressure*) Steigerung *f*; (*Tech also*) Verdichtung *f*; **~ of troops** Truppenmassierungen *pl*; **a traffic ~, a ~ of traffic** eine Verkehrsverdichtung

built [bɪlt] pret, ptp of **build** ADJ **heavily/slightly** ~ (*person*) kräftig/zierlich gebaut; **to be ~ like a tank** (*inf*) (*person*) wie ein Schrank gebaut sein; (*object*) grundsolide gebaut sein

built: built-in ADJ *cupboard etc* eingebaut, Einbau-; (*fig, = instinctive*) instinktmäßig; **a camera with ~ flash** eine Kamera mit eingebautem Blitzlicht; **built-in obsolescence** N geplanter Verschleiß; **built-up** ADJ **a** ~ **area** (=

urbanized) bebautes Gebiet; (Mot) geschlossene Ortschaft **b** shoulders gepolstert; **~ shoes** Schuhe pl mit überhoher Sohle; (Med) orthopädische Schuhe pl

bulb [bʌlb] N **a** Zwiebel f; (of garlic) Knolle f **b** (Elec) (Glüh)birne f **c** (of thermometer etc) Kolben m

bulbous ['bʌlbəs] ADJ plant knollig, Knollen-; (= bulb-shaped) growth etc knotig, Knoten-; **~ nose** Knollennase f

Bulgaria [bʌl'geərɪə] N Bulgarien nt

Bulgarian [bʌl'geərɪən] N **a** bulgarisch **N a** Bulgare m, Bulgarin f **b** (Ling) Bulgarisch nt

bulge [bʌldʒ] **N a** (in surface) Wölbung f; (irregular) Unebenheit f; (in jug, glass etc also) Bauch m; (in plaster, metal: accidental) Beule f; (in line) Bogen m; (in tyre) Wulst m; **the Battle of the Bulge** die Ardennenoffensive; **what's that ~ in your pocket?** was steht denn in deiner Tasche so vor?
b (in birth rate etc) Zunahme f, Anschwellen nt (in +gen); **the post-war ~** der Babyboom der Nachkriegsjahre
VI a (also **bulge out**, = swell) (an)schwellen; (metal, sides of box) sich wölben; (plaster) uneben sein; (= stick out) vorstehen; **his eyes were bulging out of his head** (lit) die Augen traten ihm aus dem Kopf; (fig) er bekam Stieläugen (inf)
b (pocket, sack) prall gefüllt sein, gestopft voll sein (inf) (with mit); (cheek) voll sein (with mit); **his notebooks were absolutely bulging with ideas** seine Notizbücher waren berstend or zum Bersten voll mit Ideen

bulging ['bʌldʒɪŋ] ADJ stomach prall, vorstehend; pockets, suitcase prall gefüllt, gestopft voll (inf); **~ muscles** Muskelpakete pl; **~ eyes** Glotzaugen pl

bulimia [bə'lɪmɪə] N Bulimie f

bulimic [bə'lɪmɪk] ADJ bulimisch **N** Bulimiker(in) m(f)

bulk [bʌlk] **N a** (= size) Größe f; (of task) Ausmaß nt; (= large shape, of thing) massige Form; (of person, animal) massige Gestalt; **of great ~** massig **b** (also **great bulk**) größter Teil; (of debt, loan also) Hauptteil m; (of work, mineral deposits also) Großteil m; (of people, votes also) Gros nt; (of property, legacy etc also) Masse f **c** (Comm) **in ~** im Großen, en gros **VI to ~ large** eine wichtige Rolle spielen

bulkhead ['bʌlkhed] N Schott nt; (in tunnel) Spundwand f

bulkiness ['bʌlkɪnɪs] N **a** (of object) Sperrigkeit f; (of book) Dicke f; (of sweater, spacesuit) Unförmigkeit f **b** (of person) Massigkeit f, Wuchtigkeit f

bulk: bulk purchase N Mengen- or Großeinkauf m; **bulk sale** N Massenverkauf m

bulky ['bʌlkɪ] ADJ (+er) object sperrig; book dick; sweater, spacesuit unförmig; **~ goods** Sperrgut nt **b** person massig, wuchtig

bull¹ [bʊl] **N a** Stier m; (for breeding) Bulle m; **to take** or **seize the ~ by the horns** (fig) den Stier bei den Hörnern packen; **like a ~ in a china shop** (inf) wie ein Elefant im Porzellanladen (inf); **with a neck like a ~** stiernackig **b** (= male of elephant, whale etc) Bulle m; **a ~ elephant** ein Elefantenbulle m; **~ calf** Bullenkalb nt **c** (St Ex) Haussier m, Haussespekulant(in) m(f) **d** (Brit Mil sl) Drill m und Routine f **e** (inf, = nonsense) Unsinn m, Quatsch m (inf) **VI** (St Ex) auf Hausse spekulieren **VT** (St Ex) stocks, shares hochtreiben; **to ~ the market** die Kurse hochtreiben

bull² N (Eccl) Bulle f

bull bars PL (Aut) Kuhfänger m

bulldog ['bʊldɒg] N **a** Bulldogge f; **he has the tenacity of a ~** er hat eine zähe Ausdauer **b** (Brit, Univ) Helfer m des Proctors

bulldog: bulldog breed N he is one of the ~ er ist ein zäher Mensch; **bulldog clip** N (Brit) Papierklammer f; **bulldog edition** N Frühausgabe f (einer Zeitung)

bulldoze ['bʊldəʊz] VT **a** (fig, = force) **to ~ sb into doing sth** jdn zwingen, etw zu tun, jdn so unter Druck setzen, dass er etc etw tut; **to ~ a bill through parliament** eine Maßnahme im Parlament durchpeitschen; **she ~d her way through the crowd** sie boxte sich durch die Menge **b** they ~d the rubble out of the way sie räumten den Schutt mit Bulldozern weg

bulldozer ['bʊldəʊzə'] **N** Planierraupe f, Bulldozer m **ADJ** attr (fig) tactics etc Holzhammer- (inf)

bull dyke N (pej sl) kesser Vater (sl)

bullet ['bʊlɪt] N Kugel f; **to bite the ~** in den sauren Apfel beißen (inf); **to get** or **be given the ~** (inf) gefeuert werden (inf)

bullet: bullet head N (pej) Dickkopf m; **bullet-headed** ADJ rundköpfig; **bullet hole** N Einschuss(loch nt) m

bulletin ['bʊlɪtɪn] N **a** Bulletin nt, amtliche Bekanntmachung; **health ~** Krankenbericht m, Bulletin nt; **a ~ to the media** ein Pressekommuniqué nt, ein Pressekommunikee nt **b** (of club, society) Bulletin nt

bulletin board N (US, = notice board, Comput) schwarzes Brett

bullet: bulletproof ADJ kugelsicher **VT** kugelsicher machen; **bullet train** N (japanischer) Superexpress; **bullet wound** N Schusswunde or -verletzung f

bull: bullfight N Stierkampf m; **bullfighter** N Stierkämpfer m; **bullfighting** N Stierkampf m; **~ is ...** der Stierkampf ist ...; **bullfinch** N Dompfaff m, Gimpel m; **bullfrog** N Ochsenfrosch m; **bullheaded** ['bʊl'hedɪd] ADJ person dickköpfig; **bullhorn** N (US) Megaphon nt, Megafon nt

bullion ['bʊljən] N , no pl Gold-/Silberbarren pl

bullish ['bʊlɪʃ] ADJ **a** personality selbstsicher; **to be ~ about sth** in Bezug auf etw (acc) zuversichtlich sein **b** (St Ex) **the market was ~** der Markt war in Haussestimmung

bull market N (St Ex) Hausse f

bull-necked ['bʊlnekt] ADJ stiernackig

bullock ['bʊlək] N Ochse m

bull: bullpen N (US inf) **a** (Baseball) (= area) Bereich in dem sich Einwechsel-Werfer aufwärmen (= players) Einwechsel-Werfer pl, Einwechsel-Pitcher pl **b** (= office) Großraumbüro nt **c** = cell) Sammelzelle f; **bullring** N Stierkampfarena f; **bull's-eye** N **a** (of target) Scheibenmittelpunkt m or -zentrum nt; (= hit) Schuss m ins Schwarze or Zentrum; (in darts) Bull's eye nt; (in archery) Mouche f; **to get a** or **hit the ~** (lit, fig) ins Schwarze treffen; **~!** (lit, fig) genau getroffen!, ein Schuss ins Schwarze! **b** (= sweet) hartes Pfefferminzbonbon; **bullshit** (sl) **N** (lit) Kuhscheiße f (vulg); (fig) Scheiß m (inf) **INTERJ** ach Quatsch (inf); **~, of course you can** red keinen Scheiß, klar kannst du das (inf) **VI** Scheiß erzählen (inf); **to ~ sb** jdm Scheiß erzählen (inf); **he ~ted his way out of trouble** er hat sich ganz großkotzig aus der Affäre gezogen (inf); **bullshitter** N (sl) Dummschwätzer(in) m(f) (inf); **bull terrier** N Bullterrier m; **bullwhip N** Lederpeitsche f **VT** auspeitschen

bully¹ ['bʊlɪ] **N a** Tyrann m; (esp Sch) Rabauke m; **you great big ~** du Rüpel m; **to be a bit of a ~** den starken Mann markieren (inf); **don't be a ~ with your little sister** schikaniere or tyrannisiere deine kleine Schwester nicht **b** (Hockey) Bully nt **VT** tyrannisieren, schikanieren; (using violence) drangsalieren; (into doing sth) unter Druck setzen; **to ~ sb into doing sth** jdn so unter Druck setzen, dass er etc etw tut

▶ **bully about** VT sep (Brit) = bully around

▶ **bully around** VT sep herumkommandieren, tyrannisieren

▶ **bully off** VI (Hockey) das Bully machen

bully² INTERJ (dated) prima (inf), hervorragend; **~ for you!** (dated, iro) gratuliere!

bully: bully beef N (Mil inf) Cornedbeef nt, Corned Beef nt; **bullyboy** N Schlägertyp m (inf); **bully-boy** ADJ attr Einschüchterungs-; **~ tactics** Einschüchterungstaktik f

bullying ['bʊlɪɪŋ] **ADJ** person, manner tyrannisch; boss, wife also herrisch **N** Tyrannisieren nt, Schikanieren nt; (with violence) Drangsalieren nt; (= coercion) Anwendung f von Druck (of auf +acc)

bully-off ['bʊlɪ'ɒf] N (Hockey) Bully nt

bulrush ['bʊlrʌʃ] N Rohrkolben m; **in the ~es** im Schilfrohr

bulwark ['bʊlwək] N **a** (lit, fig) Bollwerk nt **b** (Naut) Schanzkleid nt

bum¹ [bʌm] N (esp Brit, inf) Hintern m (inf), Popo m (inf); **to put ~s on seats** (pop star etc) ein Publikumsmagnet sein

bum² (inf) **N a** (esp US) **a** (= good-for-nothing) Rumtreiber m (inf); (young) Gammler m; (= down-and-out) Penner m (inf), Pennbruder m (inf)
b (= despicable person) Saukerl m (inf)
c **to be on the ~** schnorren (inf); **he's always on the ~ for cigarettes** er schnorrt immer Zigaretten (inf)
ADJ (= bad) beschissen (inf); trick hundsgemein (inf); **~ rap** (US, inf) falsche Anklage; **to give sb a ~ steer** (US, inf) jdn auf die falsche Fährte locken
VT a money, food schnorren (inf) (off sb bei jdm); **could I ~ a lift into town?** kannst du mich in die Stadt mitnehmen?; **could I ~ a smoke?** kann ich 'ne Kippe abstauben (inf) or schnorren (inf)?
b **to ~med (his way) around Europe** er ist durch Europa gezogen (inf)
VI (= scrounge) schnorren (inf) (off sb bei jdm)

▶ **bum about** (Brit) or **around** (inf) **VI** rumgammeln (inf) **VI** +prep obj ziehen durch (inf)

bum bag N (Ski) Gürteltasche f

bumbershoot ['bʌmbəʃuːt] N (US, inf) Musspritze f (hum inf)

bumblebee ['bʌmblbiː] N Hummel f

bumbledom ['bʌmbldəm] N (inf) kleinlicher Bürokratismus

bumbler ['bʌmblə'] N Stümper(in) m(f) (pej), Pfuscher(in) m(f) (pej)

▶ **bumble through** ['bʌmbl'θruː] VI sich durchwursteln (inf) or -mogeln (inf) (+prep obj durch)

bumbling ['bʌmblɪŋ] ADJ (= clumsy) schusselig (inf); **some ~ idiot** irgend so ein Vollidiot (inf)

bumboat ['bʌmbəʊt] N Proviantboot nt

bum boy N (Brit, pej sl) Sexgespiele m

bumf [bʌmf] N = bumph

bum-fluff ['bʌmflʌf] N (inf) Flaumbart m

bummer ['bʌmə'] N (inf, = person) Niete f; **what a ~** (= nuisance etc) so 'ne Scheiße (inf); **this one's a real ~** das kannst du vergessen; **I had a ~ of a day** ich habe einen total beschissenen Tag gehabt (inf)

bump [bʌmp] **N a** (= blow, noise, jolt) Bums m (inf); (of sth falling also) Plumps m (inf); **to get a ~ on the head** sich (dat) den Kopf anschlagen; **I accidentally gave her a ~ on the chin** ich habe sie aus Versehen ans Kinn geboxt or gestoßen; **he sat down with a ~** er ließ sich plumpsen (inf); **the car has had a few ~s** mit dem Auto hat es ein paar Mal gebumst (inf); **each ~ was agony as the ambulance ...** jede Erschütterung war eine Qual, als der Krankenwagen ...; **~ and grind** (inf) erotische Zuckungen pl; (= sex) Bumserei f (inf)
b (on any surface) Unebenheit f, Hubbel m (inf); (on head, knee etc) Beule f; (on car) Delle f
c (Aviat, = rising air current) Bö f
VT a stoßen (obj gegen); car wing etc, one's

own car eine Delle fahren in (+acc); *another car* auffahren auf (+acc); **to ~ one's head/knee** sich (*dat*) den Kopf/das Knie anstoßen *or* anschlagen (*on, against an* +*dat*); **her father ~ed her up and down on his knee** ihr Vater ließ sie auf den Knien reiten **b** (*Sch inf*) hochwerfen **VI** (= *move joltingly*) holpern; **he fell and went ~ing down the stairs** er stürzte und fiel polternd die Treppe hinunter; **the economy is continuing to ~ along the bottom** (*Brit*) die Wirtschaft befindet sich noch immer auf der Talsohle **ADV to go ~** bumsen (*inf*); **things that go ~ in the night** Geräusche *pl* im Dunkeln *or* in der Nacht

▶ **bump about** (*Brit*) *or* **around VI** herumpoltern

▶ **bump into VI** +*prep obj* **a** (= *knock into*) stoßen *or* bumsen (*inf*) gegen; (*driver, car*) fahren gegen; *another car* fahren auf (+*acc*) **b** (*inf, = meet*) begegnen (+*dat*), treffen

▶ **bump off VT** *sep* (*inf*) abmurksen (*inf*), kaltmachen (*inf*)

▶ **bump up VT** *sep* (*inf*) (*to* auf +*acc*) *prices, total* erhöhen; *salary* aufbessern

▶ **bump up against VI** +*prep obj* treffen

bumper ['bʌmpə'] **N** (*of car*) Stoßstange *f* **ADJ** ~ **crop** Rekordernte *f*; **a special ~ edition** eine Riesensonderausgabe; **~ offer** großes Sonderangebot

bumper: bumper car N Boxauto *nt* (*dial*), Autoscooter *m*; **bumper sticker N** (*Aut*) Aufkleber *m*; **bumper-to-bumper ADJ ~ traffic** Stop-and-go-Verkehr *m*

bumph [bʌmf] **N** (*Brit, inf*) **a** (= *forms*) Papierkram *m* (*inf*) **b** (= *toilet paper*) Klopapier *nt* (*inf*)

bumpiness ['bʌmpɪnɪs] **N** (*of surface*) Unebenheit *f*, Hubbeligkeit *f* (*inf*); (*of road, drive*) Holp(e)rigkeit *f*; (*of flight*) Böigkeit *f*

bumpkin ['bʌmpkɪn] **N** (*also* **country bumpkin**, = *man*) (Bauern)tölpel *m*; (= *woman*) Trampel *f* vom Land

bump-start VT *car* anschieben **N** **to give a car a ~** ein Auto anschieben

bumptious ['bʌmpʃəs] **ADJ** aufgeblasen, wichtigtuerisch

bumptiousness ['bʌmpʃəsnɪs] **N** Aufgeblasenheit *f*, Wichtigtuerei *f*

bumpy ['bʌmpɪ] **ADJ** (+*er*) *surface* uneben, hubbelig (*inf*); *road, drive* holp(e)rig; *flight* böig, unruhig; **we had a very ~ drive** auf der Fahrt wurden wir tüchtig durchgerüttelt

bum's rush N (*inf*) **to give sb the ~** jdn abblitzen lassen (*inf*); **to get** *or* **be given the ~** abblitzen (*inf*)

bun [bʌn] **N** **a** (= *bread*) Brötchen *nt*; (= *iced bun etc*) süßes Stückchen *or* Teilchen; (*N Engl, = small cake*) Biskuittörtchen *nt*; **to have a ~ in the oven** (*sl*) einen Braten in der Röhre haben (*sl*) **b** (= *hairstyle*) Knoten *m*; **she wears her hair in a ~** sie trägt einen Knoten

bunch [bʌntʃ] **N** **a** (*of flowers*) Strauß *m*; (*of bananas*) Büschel *nt*; (*of radishes, asparagus*) Bund *nt*; (*of hair*) (Ratten)schwanz *m*, Zöpfchen *nt*; **a ~ of roses** ein Strauß *m* Rosen, **a ~ of flowers** ein Blumenstrauß *m*; **~ of grapes** Weintraube *f*; **~ of keys** Schlüsselbund *m*; **to wear one's hair in ~es** (Ratten)schwänze *pl or* Zöpfchen *pl* haben, **the pick** *or* **best of the ~** die Allerbesten, *things* das Beste vom Besten; **to pick the best of the ~** sich (*dat*) die Allerbesten/das Beste aussuchen; **a ~ of fives** (*inf*, = *fist*) 'ne Faust ins Gesicht (*inf*) **b** (*inf, of people*) Haufen *m* (*inf*); **a small ~ of tourists** ein Häufchen *nt or* eine kleine Gruppe Touristen **c** (*inf, = a lot*) **thanks a ~** (*esp iro*) schönen Dank; **there's still a whole ~ of things to do** es sind noch jede Menge Sachen zu erledigen (*inf*)

VI (*dress*) sich bauschen → **bunch together VI ~ up VI**

▶ **bunch together VT** *sep* zusammenfassen; (*at random*) zusammenwürfeln; **the girls/prisoners were sitting all bunched together** die Mädchen/Gefangenen saßen alle auf einem Haufen **VI** (*people*) Grüppchen *or* einen Haufen bilden; (*atoms*) Cluster bilden; **they bunched together for warmth** sie kauerten sich aneinander, um sich zu wärmen; **don't bunch together, spread out!** bleibt nicht alle auf einem Haufen, verteilt euch!

▶ **bunch up VT** *sep* **a** *dress, skirt* bauschen **b** (= *put together*) *objects* auf einen Haufen legen **VI** **a** (= *bunch together*) Grüppchen *or* Haufen bilden; **don't bunch up so much, spread out!** bleibt nicht alle auf einem Haufen, verteilt euch! **b** (*material*) sich bauschen

bunco ['bʌŋkəʊ] **N** *pl* **buncos** (*US inf*) (= *trick*) Bauernfängerei *f*; (= *swindle*) Betrug *m*, Schwindel *m*

bundle ['bʌndl] **N** **a** (= *pile*) Bündel *nt*; **to tie sth in a ~** etw bündeln **b** (*fig*) **a ~ of** (= *large number of*) eine ganze Menge; **he is a ~ of nerves** er ist ein Nervenbündel; **that child is a ~ of mischief** das Kind hat nichts als Unfug im Kopf; **her little ~ of joy** (*inf*) ihr kleiner Wonneproppen (*inf*); **a ~ of fun** das reinste Vergnügen; **it cost a ~** (*inf*) das hat eine Stange Geld gekostet (*inf*); **he didn't go a ~ on clubbing** (*inf*) er stand nicht so auf Nachtklubs (*inf*) **VT** **a** (*= in a bundle*) bündeln; **~d software** (*Comput*) Softwarepaket *nt*; **it comes ~d with ...** (*Comput*) ... ist im Softwarepaket enthalten → **bundle up**

b (= *put, send hastily*) *things* stopfen; *people* verfrachten, schaffen; (*into vehicle*) packen (*inf*), schaffen

▶ **bundle off VT** *sep person* schaffen; **he was bundled off to Australia** er wurde nach Australien verfrachtet

▶ **bundle up VT** *sep* (= *tie into bundles*) bündeln; (= *collect hastily*) zusammenraffen; **bundled up in his overcoat** in seinen Mantel eingehüllt *or* gemummelt (*inf*)

bun fight N (*dated inf*) Festivitäten *pl* (*dated*)

bung [bʌŋ] (*Brit*) **N** **a** (*of cask*) Spund(zapfen) *m* **b** (*inf: = bribe*) Schmiergeld *nt* (*inf*) **VT a** *cask* spunden, verschließen **b** (*inf, = throw*) schmeißen (*inf*) **c** (*inf: = bribe*) schmieren (*inf*)

▶ **bung in VT** *sep* (*Brit, inf, = include*) dazutun

▶ **bung out VT** *sep* (*Brit, inf*) rauswerfen (*inf*)

▶ **bung up VT** *sep* (*inf*) *pipe* verstopfen; **I'm all bunged up** meine Nase ist verstopft

bungalow ['bʌŋgələʊ] **N** Bungalow *m*

bungee jumping ['bʌndʒiː'dʒʌmpɪŋ] **N** Bungeespringen *nt*, Bungeejumping *nt*

bung-ho [bʌŋ'həʊ] **INTERJ** (*dated inf*) famos (*dated inf*)

bunghole ['bʌŋhəʊl] **N** (*Brit*) Spundloch *nt*

bungle ['bʌŋgl] **VT** verpfuschen, vermasseln (*inf*); **it was a ~d job** die Sache war vermasselt (*inf*) *or* verpfuscht **VI** **I see you've ~d again, Higgins** wie ich sehe, haben Sie wieder einmal alles verpfuscht *or* vermasselt (*inf*), Higgins **N** verpfuschte Sache, Stümperei *f*

bungler ['bʌŋglə'] **N** Nichtskönner *m*, Stümper *m*

bungling ['bʌŋglɪŋ] **ADJ** *person* unfähig, trottelhaft, dusselig (*inf*); *attempt* stümperhaft; **some ~ idiot has ...** irgendein Trottel hat ... (*inf*) **N** Stümperei *f*, Dusseligkeit *f* (*inf*)

bungy jumping ['bʌndʒiː'dʒʌmpɪŋ] **N** = **bungee jumping**

bunion ['bʌnjən] **N** Ballen *m*

bunk¹ [bʌŋk] **N to do a ~** (*Brit inf*) türmen (*inf*)

▶ **bunk off VI** (*Brit Sch inf*) schwänzen

bunk² **N** (*inf*) Quatsch *m* (*inf*)

bunk³ **N** (*in ship*) Koje *f*; (*in train, dormitory*) Bett *nt*

▶ **bunk down VI** (*inf*) kampieren (*inf*)

bunk beds PL Etagenbett *nt*

bunker ['bʌŋkə'] **N** (*Naut, Golf, Mil*) Bunker *m* **VT** (*Golf*) *shot* in den Bunker schlagen; **he was ~ed** er hatte den Ball in den Bunker geschlagen

bunk: bunkhouse ['bʌŋkhaʊs] **N** Schlafbaracke *f*; **bunkmate N** (*inf*) Bettnachbar(in) *m(f)* (*im Etagenbett*)

bunkum ['bʌŋkəm] **N** (*inf*) Blödsinn *m*, Quatsch *m* (*inf*)

bunny ['bʌnɪ] **N** (*also* **bunny rabbit**) Hase *m*, Häschen *nt*

bunny girl N Häschen *nt*

Bunsen (burner) ['bʌnsn('bɜːnə')] **N** Bunsenbrenner *m*

bunting¹ ['bʌntɪŋ] **N** (*Orn*) Ammer *f* → **corn bunting, reed bunting**

bunting² **N** (= *material*) Fahnentuch *nt*; (= *flags*) bunte Fähnchen *pl*, Wimpel *pl*

buoy [bɔɪ] **N** Boje *f*; **to put down a ~** eine Boje verankern

▶ **buoy up VT** *sep* **a** (*lit*) über Wasser halten **b** (*fig*) *person* Auftrieb geben (+*dat*); *sb's hopes* beleben; **buoyed up by new hope** von neuer Hoffnung beseelt **c** (*Fin*) *market, prices* Auftrieb geben (+*dat*)

buoyancy ['bɔɪənsɪ] **N** **a** (*of ship, object*) Schwimmfähigkeit *f*; (*of liquid*) Auftrieb *m*; **~ aid** Schwimmhilfe *f*; (*for canoeing*) Kajakweste *f* **b** (*fig, = cheerfulness*) Schwung *m*, Elan *m* **c** (*Fin: of market, prices*) Festigkeit *f*; (= *resilience*) Erholungsfähigkeit *f*

buoyancy chamber N (*Naut*) Trimmtank *m*

buoyancy tank N Luftkammer *f*

buoyant ['bɔɪənt] **ADJ a** *ship, object* schwimmend; *liquid* tragend; **fresh water is not so ~ as salt water** Süßwasser trägt nicht so gut wie Salzwasser **b** (*fig*) *person, mood* heiter; (= *energetic*) *step* federnd, elastisch **c** (*Fin*) *market, prices* fest; (= *resilient*) erholungsfähig; *trading* rege

buoyantly ['bɔɪəntlɪ] **ADV** (*fig, = optimistically*) guten Mutes

BUPA ['buːpə] **abbr of** **British United Provident Association** *private Krankenversicherung*

BUPA

Die **BUPA (British United Provident Association)** ist der größte Anbieter privater Gesundheitsfürsorge in Großbritannien und dabei der einzige mit eigenen Krankenhäusern und Kliniken. Obschon alle britischen Staatsbürger ein Anrecht auf kostenlose Gesundheitsfürsorge durch den National Health Service (NHS) haben, lässt sich ein zunehmender Trend zur Privatvorsorge feststellen → NHS

---

buppie, buppy ['bʌpɪ] **N** (*inf*) *abbr of* **black upwardly mobile professional** schwarzer Yuppie, schwarze Yuppie

bur, burr [bɜː'] **N** (*Bot, fig inf*) Klette *f*; **chestnut ~** Kastanienschale *f*

Burberry® ['bɜːbərɪ] **N** Burberry® *m*, Regenmantel aus hochwertigem Gabardine

burble ['bɜːbl] **VI a** *stream* plätschern, gurgeln **b** (*fig, person*) plappern; (*baby*) gurgeln; **what's he burbling (on) about?** (*inf*) worüber quasselt er eigentlich? (*inf*) **N** (*of stream*) Plätschern *nt*, Gurgeln *nt*; (*on tape etc*) Gemurmel *nt*

burbot ['bɜːbət] **N** Quappe *f*

burbs, 'burbs [bɜːbz] **PL** (*US inf*) = **suburbs**

burden¹ ['bɜːdn] **N a** (*lit*) Last *f*; **it puts too much of a ~ on him/the engine** das überlastet ihn/den Motor; **beast of ~** Lasttier *nt* **b** (*fig*) Belastung *f* (*on, to* für); **he has such a ~ of responsibility** er hat eine schwere Last an Verantwortung zu tragen; **~ of taxation** steuerliche Belastung, Steuerlast *f*; **the ~ of debts** die Schuldenlast; **I don't want to be a ~ to you** ich möchte Ihnen nicht zur Last fallen; **the ~**

of proof is on him er muss den Beweis dafür erbringen or liefern; (Jur) er trägt die Beweislast **c** (Naut) Tragfähigkeit f, Tragkraft f **VT** belasten; **to be ~ed by guilt/regret** von Schuldgefühlen/Bedauern geplagt sein

burden² **N** **a** (of song) Refrain m, Kehrreim m **b** (of speech, essay etc) Grundgedanke m

burdensome ['bɜːdnsəm] **ADJ** load schwer; condition lästig; task mühsam; **to be ~** eine Belastung darstellen

burdock ['bɜːdɒk] **N** Klette f

bureau [bjʊəˈrəʊ] **N** **a** (Brit, = desk) Sekretär m **b** (US, = chest of drawers) Kommode f **c** (= office) Büro nt **d** (= government department) Amt nt, Behörde f

---

BUREAU OF INDIAN AFFAIRS

Das **Bureau of Indian Affairs** ist eine Regierungsbehörde der USA, die sich um alle Belange der Nachkommen der amerikanischen Urbevölkerung kümmert. 1824 wurde sie als Teil des Kriegsministeriums eingerichtet und war ursprünglich für die Verwaltung der Indianerreservate verantwortlich. Heute ist sie dem Innenministerium unterstellt, sieht ihre Hauptaufgabe im Schutz des indianischen Landes und seiner Ressourcen und arbeitet mit der Urbevölkerung zusammen, um deren Lebensbedingungen zu verbessern. Dabei werden zum Beispiel Gesundheits- und Sozialämter erstellt sowie Ausbildungs- und Arbeitsplätze geschaffen. Seit 1960 stellt das Büro für indianische Angelegenheiten auch technische Hilfsmittel und Schulungsmöglichkeiten an dem Gebiet der Landwirtschaft und der Ressourcengewinnung → NATIVE A-MERICAN

---

bureaucracy [bjʊəˈrɒkrəsɪ] **N** Bürokratie f
bureaucrat ['bjʊərəʊkræt] **N** Bürokrat m
bureaucratic **ADJ** , **bureaucratically** **ADV** [ˌbjʊərəʊˈkrætɪk, -əlɪ] bürokratisch
bureau de change [ˌbjʊərəʊdɪˈʃɒndʒ] **N** pl **bureaux de change** Wechselstube f

burgeon ['bɜːdʒən] **VI** (liter: also **burgeon forth**, flower) knospen (liter); (plant) sprießen (liter); (fig) hervorsprießen (geh); **when young love first ~s** wenn die junge Liebe erblüht (liter)

burgeoning ['bɜːdʒənɪŋ] **ADJ** industry, market boomend; movement expandierend; career Erfolg versprechend, hoffnungsvoll; demand wachsend; population ständig wachsend

burger ['bɜːgə'] **N** (inf) Hamburger m
burger bar **N** Imbissstube f, Schnellimbiss m

burgess ['bɜːdʒɪs] **N** **a** (freier) Bürger, (freie) Bürgerin **b** (Hist) Abgeordnete(r) mf **c** (US) Abgeordneter der Volksvertretung der Kolonien Maryland und Virginia

burgh ['bʌrə] **N** (Scot) freie Stadt
burgher ['bɜːgə'] **N** (old) Bürger(in) m(f)
burglar ['bɜːglə'] **N** Einbrecher(in) m(f)
burglar alarm **N** Alarmanlage f

burglarize ['bɜːgləraɪz] **VT** (US) einbrechen in (+acc); **the place/he was ~d** in dem Gebäude/bei ihm wurde eingebrochen

burglarproof ['bɜːgləpruːf] **ADJ** einbruchsicher

burglary ['bɜːglərɪ] **N** Einbruch m; (= offence) (Einbruchs)diebstahl m

burgle ['bɜːgl] **VT** (Brit) einbrechen in (+acc); **the place/he was ~d** in dem Gebäude/bei ihm wurde eingebrochen

Burgundy ['bɜːgəndɪ] **N** Burgund nt; (= wine) Burgunder m

burial ['berɪəl] **N** Beerdigung f, Bestattung f; (= burial ceremony also) Begräbnis nt; (in cemetery also) Beisetzung f (form); **Christian ~** christliches Begräbnis; **~ at sea** Seebestattung f

burial: burial chamber **N** Grabkammer f; **burial ground** **N** Begräbnisstätte f; **burial mound** **N** Grabhügel m; **burial object** **N** (Ar-

cheol) Grabbeigabe f; **burial place** **N** Grabstätte f; **burial service** **N** Trauerfeier f

burin ['bjʊərɪn] **N** (Art) Stichel m
burk [bɜːk] **N** (Brit inf) = **berk**
burlap ['bɜːlæp] **N** Sackleinen nt

burlesque [bɜːˈlesk] **N** **a** (= parody) Parodie f; (Theat) Burleske f **b** (Liter) Persiflage f **c** (US Theat) Varietee nt, Varieté nt; (= show) Varieteevorstellung f **ADJ** **a** (= parodic) parodistisch; (Theat) burlesk; (Liter) persiflierend **b** (US, Theat) Varietee-; ~ **show** Varieteevorstellung f **VT** parodieren; book, author, style persiflieren

burly ['bɜːlɪ] **ADJ** (+er) kräftig, stramm
Burma ['bɜːmə] **N** Birma nt, Burma nt
Burmese [bɜːˈmiːz] **ADJ** birmanisch, burmesisch **N** **a** Birmane m, Burmese m, Birmanin f, Burmesin f **b** (Ling) Birmanisch nt, Burmesisch nt

burn¹ [bɜːn] **N** (Scot) Bach m

burn² vb: pret, ptp **burnt** (Brit) or **burned** **N** **a** (on skin) Brandwunde f; (on material) verbrannte Stelle, Brandfleck m; **severe ~s** schwere Verbrennungen pl; **second degree ~s** Verbrennungen zweiten Grades; **cigarette ~** Brandfleck m or (hole) Brandloch nt or (on skin) Brandwunde f von einer Zigarette **b** (Space, of rocket) Zündung f **c** (Sport inf) **to go for the ~** sich total verausgaben (inf) **VT** **a** verbrennen; incense abbrennen; village, building niederbrennen; **he ~ed me with his cigarette** er hat mich mit der Zigarette gebrannt; **to ~ oneself** sich verbrennen; **to be ~ed to death** verbrannt werden; (in accident) verbrennen; **to be ~ed alive** bei lebendigem Leibe verbrannt werden or (in accident) verbrennen; **to ~ a hole in sth** ein Loch in etw (acc) brennen; **to ~ one's fingers** (lit, fig) sich (dat) die Finger verbrennen; **he's got money to ~** (fig) er hat Geld wie Heu; **to ~ one's boats** or **bridges** (Brit fig) alle Brücken hinter sich (dat) abbrechen; **to ~ the midnight oil** (fig) bis tief in die Nacht arbeiten **b** meat, sauce, toast, cakes verbrennen lassen; (slightly) anbrennen lassen; (sun) person, skin verbrennen **c** (acid) ätzen; **the curry ~ed his throat** das Currygericht brannte ihm im Hals **d** (= use as fuel, ship etc) befeuert werden mit; (= use up) petrol, electricity verbrauchen **VI** **a** (wood, fire etc) brennen; **you will ~ in hell** du wirst in der Hölle schmoren; **to ~ to death** verbrennen → **ear¹** **b** (meat, pastry etc) verbrennen; (slightly) anbrennen; **she/her skin ~s easily** sie bekommt leicht einen Sonnenbrand **c** (ointment, curry, sun) brennen; (acid) ätzen; **the acid ~ed into the metal** die Säure fraß sich ins Metall **d** (= feel hot: wound, eyes, skin) brennen; **his face was ~ing (with heat/shame)** sein Gesicht glühte or war rot (vor Hitze/Scham); **it's so hot, I'm ~ing** es ist so heiß, ich komm bald um vor Hitze **e** **to be ~ing to do sth** darauf brennen, etw zu tun; **he was ~ing to get his revenge** er brannte auf Rache; **he was ~ing with anger** er war wutentbrannt; **he was ~ing with ambition** er war glühend ehrgeizig; **to ~ (with love/desire) for sb** (liter) von glühender Liebe/glühendem Verlangen nach jdm verzehrt werden (liter) **f** (Space, rockets) zünden

▶ **burn away** **VI** **a** (= go on burning) vor sich hin brennen **b** (wick, candle, oil) herunterbrennen; (part of roof etc) abbrennen **VT** sep abbrennen; (Med) wegbrennen

▶ **burn down** **VI** **a** (house etc) abbrennen **b** (fire, candle, wick) herunterbrennen **VT** sep abbrennen

▶ **burn off** **VT** sep paint etc abbrennen

▶ **burn out** **VI** (fire, candle) ausbrennen, ausgehen; (fuse, dynamo etc) durchbrennen; (rocket) den Treibstoff verbraucht haben

VR **a** (candle, lamp) herunterbrennen; (fire) ab- or ausbrennen **b** (fig inf) **to burn oneself out** sich kaputtmachen (inf), sich völlig verausgaben **VT** sep **a** enemy troops etc ausräuchern; **they were burned out of house and home** ihr Haus und Hof war abgebrannt **b** usu pass **burned out cars/houses** ausgebrannte Autos/Häuser; **he/his talent is burned out** (inf) mit ihm/seinem Talent ists vorbei (inf), er hat sich völlig verausgabt; **he looked completely burned out** (inf) er sah völlig kaputt (inf) or verbraucht aus

▶ **burn up** **VI** **a** (fire etc) auflodern **b** (rocket etc in atmosphere) verglühen **VI** +prep obj **to burn up the road** die Straße entlangbrettern (inf) **VT** sep **a** rubbish verbrennen; fuel, energy verbrauchen; excess fat also abbauen **b** he was burned up with envy er verzehrte sich vor Neid (geh) **c** (US, inf, = make angry) zur Weißglut bringen (inf)

burner ['bɜːnə'] **N** (of gas cooker, lamp) Brenner m

burning ['bɜːnɪŋ] **ADJ** **a** candle, town brennend; coals also, face glühend; **I still have this ~ sensation in my mouth/on my skin** mein Mund/meine Haut brennt immer noch; **the ~ bush** (Bibl) der brennende Dornbusch **b** (fig) thirst, question, topic brennend; desire also, fever, hate, passion, ambition glühend; ~ **issue** brandaktuelles Problem **N** there is a smell of ~, I can smell ~ es riecht verbrannt or (Cook also) angebrannt

burning: burning glass **N** Brennglas nt; **burning life** **N** Brenndauer f

burnish ['bɜːnɪʃ] **VT** metal polieren; (fig) image aufpolieren

---

BURNS' NIGHT

Mit der **Burns' Night** wird am 25. Januar der Geburtstag des schottischen Nationaldichters Robert Burns begangen. Auf der ganzen Welt treffen sich Schotten bei einem festlichen Abendessen, dem **Burns' Supper**, um das Leben und Werk Robert Burns' zu feiern. Der Hauptgang, der traditionellerweise feierlich unter Dudelsackbegleitung aufgetragen wird, besteht aus **haggis** (gefülltem Schafsmagen) mit „neeps" und „tatties" (Steckrüben- und Kartoffelpüree). Trinksprüche werden ausgebracht, und nach dem Essen werden Gedichte von Burns aufgesagt und seine Lieder gesungen.

---

burns unit ['bɜːnzˌjuːnɪt] **N** (Med) Verbrennungsintensivstation f

burnt [bɜːnt] **ADJ** (Brit) verbrannt; **there's a ~ smell** es riecht verbrannt or brenzlig or (Cook also) angebrannt; **the coffee has a slightly ~ taste** der Kaffee schmeckt wie frisch geröstet

burnt offering **N** (Rel) Brandopfer nt; (hum, = food) angebranntes Essen

burn-up ['bɜːnʌp] **N** (Brit, inf) Rennfahrt f; **to go for a ~** eine Rennfahrt machen

burp [bɜːp] (inf) **VI** rülpsen (inf); (baby) aufstoßen **VT** baby aufstoßen lassen **N** Rülpser m (inf)

burp gun **N** (inf) MG nt (inf)

burr¹ [bɜː'] **N** = **bur**

burr² **N** (Ling) breiige Aussprache (von R) **to speak with a ~** breiig sprechen

burrow ['bʌrəʊ] **N** (of rabbit etc) Bau m **VI** (rabbits, dogs etc) graben, buddeln (inf); (= make a burrow) einen Bau graben; **they had ~ed under the fence** sie hatten sich (dat) ein Loch or (below ground) einen Gang unterm Zaun gegraben or gebuddelt (inf) **VT** hole graben, buddeln (inf); **to ~ one's way into sth** (fig) sich in etw (acc) einschleichen

bursar ['bɜːsə'] **N** Schatzmeister(in) m(f), Finanzverwalter(in) m(f)

bursary ['bɜːsərɪ] **N** **a** (Brit: = grant) Stipendium nt **b** (= office) Schatzamt nt; (Univ) Quästur f

burst [bɜːst] *vb: pret, ptp* **burst** N a (*of shell etc*) Explosion *f*
b (*in pipe etc*) Bruch *m*
c (*of anger, enthusiasm, activity etc*) Ausbruch *m*; (*of flames*) (plötzliches) Auflodern; ~ **of laughter** Lachsalve *f*; ~ **of applause** Beifallssturm *m*; ~ **of speed** Spurt *m*; (*of cars etc*) Riesenbeschleunigung *f* (*inf*); **a** ~ **of automatic gunfire** eine Maschinengewehrsalve; **give them another** ~ verpass ihnen noch eine Salve
VI a (*balloon, bubble, tyre*) platzen; **to** ~ **open** (*box, door etc*) aufspringen; (*buds*) aufbrechen; (*abscess*) aufplatzen; (*wound*) aufbrechen, aufplatzen
b (= *be full to overflowing: sack etc*) platzen, bersten; **to fill sth to ~ing point** etw bis zum Platzen *or* Bersten füllen; **to be full to ~ing** zum Platzen *or* Bersten voll sein; **to be ~ing with health** vor Gesundheit strotzen; **to be ~ing with a desire to do sth** vor Begierde brennen, etw zu tun; **to be ~ing with pride** vor Stolz platzen; **if I eat any more, I'll ~** (*inf*) wenn ich noch mehr esse, platze ich (*inf*); **I'm ~ing** (*inf, = need the toilet*) ich muss ganz dringend (*inf*); **he was ~ing to tell us** (*inf*) er brannte darauf, uns das zu sagen → **seam**
c (= *start, go suddenly*) **to ~ into tears** in Tränen ausbrechen; **to ~ into flames** in Flammen aufgehen; **he ~ past me** er schoss an mir vorbei; **he ~ into the room** er platzte ins Zimmer; **we ~ through the enemy lines** wir durchbrachen die feindlichen Linien; **the sun ~ through the clouds** die Sonne brach durch die Wolken; **sunlight ~ into the room** Sonnenlicht fiel plötzlich ins Zimmer; **the oil ~ from the well** das Öl brach aus der Quelle; **to ~ into view** plötzlich in Sicht kommen; **to ~ into song** lossingen; **to ~ into bloom** plötzlich aufblühen
VT balloon, bubble, tyre zum Platzen bringen; platzen lassen; (*person*) kaputtmachen (*inf*); boiler, pipe, dyke sprengen; **the river has ~ its banks** der Fluss ist über die Ufer getreten → **blood vessel**

▶ **burst forth** VI (*liter, blood, sun*) hervorbrechen; (*blossoms*) ausbrechen

▶ **burst in** VI hinein-/hereinstürzen; (*on conversation*) dazwischenplatzen (*on bei*); **he burst in on us** er platzte bei uns herein

▶ **burst out** VI a (*emotions*) hervorbrechen, herausbrechen; (*lava*) ausbrechen; **she's bursting out of that dress** sie sprengt das Kleid fast
b **to burst out of a room** aus einem Zimmer stürzen *or* stürmen c (*in speech*) losplatzen; **he burst out in fury** er zog plötzlich vom Leder d **to burst out laughing/crying** in Gelächter/Tränen ausbrechen, loslachen/losheulen

burthen ['bɜːðən] N, VT (*old, liter*) = **burden**[1]

burton ['bɜːtn] N (*dated Brit, sl*) **to have gone for a** ~ im Eimer sein (*inf*)

bury ['berɪ] VT a *person, animal, possessions, differences* begraben; (*with ceremony also*) beerdigen, bestatten (*geh*); (= *hide in earth*) *treasure, bones* vergraben; (= *put in earth*) *end of post, roots* eingraben; **where is he buried?** wo liegt *or* ist er begraben?; (*in cemetery also*) wo liegt er?; **to ~ sb at sea** jdn auf See bestatten (*geh*), jdm ein Seemannsgrab geben; **he is dead and buried** er ist schon lange tot; **that's all dead and buried** (*fig*) das ist schon lange passé (*inf*); **she has buried three husbands** (*fig*) sie hat schon drei Männer begraben (*inf*); **buried by an avalanche** von einer Lawine verschüttet *or* begraben; **to be buried in work** (*fig*) bis zum Hals in Arbeit stecken; **to ~ one's head in the sand** (*fig*) den Kopf in den Sand stecken
b (= *conceal*) *one's face* verbergen; **to ~ one's face in one's hands** das Gesicht in den Händen vergraben; **to ~ oneself under the blankets/ (away) in the country** sich unter den Decken/ auf dem Land vergraben; **a village buried in the heart of the country** ein im Landesinnern versteckt gelegenes Dorf
c (= *put, plunge*) *hands, fingers* vergraben (*in in* +*dat*); *claws, teeth* schlagen (*in in* +*acc*); *dagger* stoßen (*in in* +*acc*)

d (= *engross*) **to ~ oneself in one's books** sich in seinen Büchern vergraben

burying ground N Begräbnisstätte *f*

bus[1] [bʌs] N *pl* **-es** *or* (*US*) **-ses** a Bus *m*; **by** ~ mit dem Bus → **miss**[1] b (*inf, = car, plane*) Kiste *f* (*inf*) VI (*inf*) mit dem Bus fahren VT (*esp US*) mit dem Bus befördern *or* fahren

bus[2] N (*Elec: also* **busbar**) Sammelschiene *f*, Stromschiene *f*; (*Comput*) (Daten)bus *m*

bus boy N (*US*) Bedienungshilfe *f*

busby ['bʌzbɪ] N hohe Pelzmütze

bus: bus conductor N (Omni)busschaffner *m*; **bus conductress** N (Omni)busschaffnerin *f*; **bus depot** N (Omni)busdepot *nt*; **bus driver** N (Omni)busfahrer(in) *m(f)*; **bus garage** N (Omni)bushalle *f*

bush[1] [bʊʃ] N a (= *shrub*) Busch *m*, Strauch *m*; (= *thicket: also* **bushes**) Gebüsch *nt*; **to beat about** (*Brit*) *or* **around the** ~ (*fig*) um den heißen Brei herumreden; (= *not act, take decision etc*) wie die Katze um den heißen Brei herumschleichen b (*in Africa, Australia*) Busch *m*; (*Austral, = the country*) freies *or* offenes Land c (*fig*) **of hair** Haarschopf *m*

▶ **bush out** VI (*hair, tail*) buschig sein

bush[2] N (*Tech*) Buchse *f*

bushbaby ['bʊʃbeɪbɪ] N Buschbaby *nt*

bushed [bʊʃt] ADJ (*inf, = exhausted*) groggy (*inf*)

bushel ['bʊʃl] N Scheffel *m*; **to hide one's light under a** ~ (*prov*) sein Licht unter den Scheffel stellen (*prov*)

bushfire ['bʊʃfaɪə[r]] N Buschfeuer *nt*

bushiness ['bʊʃɪnɪs] N Buschigkeit *f*

bushing ['bʊʃɪŋ] N (*US*) = **bush**[2]

bush: bush league N (*US*) Provinzliga *f*; **bush leaguer** N (*US*) Provinzspieler *m*; (*fig*) Dilettant *m*; **bushman** N (*Austral*) jd, der im Busch lebt und arbeitet; **Bushman** N (*in S Africa*) Buschmann *m*; **bushranger** N a (*Austral*) Bandit *m*, Strauchdieb *m* (*dated*) b (*US, Canada*) jd, der in der Wildnis lebt; **bush telegraph** N (*lit*) Urwaldtelefon *nt*; **I heard it on the** ~ (*fig inf*) ich habe da so was läuten gehört (*inf*), das ist mir zu Ohren gekommen (*inf*); **bushwhack** VI in den Wäldern hausen VT (= *ambush*) (aus dem Hinterhalt) überfallen; **bushwhacker** N (= *frontiersman*) jd, der in den Wäldern haust (= *bandit*) Bandit *m*; (= *guerilla*) Guerila(kämpfer) *m*

bushy ['bʊʃɪ] ADJ (+*er*) buschig

busily ['bɪzɪlɪ] ADV (= *actively, eagerly*) eifrig

business ['bɪznɪs] N a *no pl* (= *commerce*) Geschäft *nt*; (= *line of business*) Branche *f*; **to be in** ~ Geschäftsmann sein; **I am in** ~ **with him** ich habe geschäftlich mit ihm zu tun; **to go into** ~ Geschäftsmann werden; **to go into** ~ **with sb** mit jdm ein Geschäft gründen; **what line of** ~ **is she in?** was macht sie beruflich?; **to be in the publishing/insurance** ~ im Verlagswesen/ der Versicherungsbranche tätig sein; **to set up in** ~ ein Geschäft gründen; **to set up in** ~ **as a butcher/lawyer** *etc* sich als Fleischer/Rechtsanwalt *etc* niederlassen; **to go out of** ~ zumachen; **to do** ~ **with sb** Geschäfte *pl* mit jdm machen; ~ **is** ~ Geschäft ist Geschäft; **"business as usual"** (*during renovation etc*) das Geschäft bleibt geöffnet; **it's** ~ **as usual** alles geht wie gewohnt weiter; **how's** ~? wie gehen die Geschäfte?; ~ **is good** die Geschäfte gehen gut; **to look for** ~ sich nach Aufträgen umsehen; **to go to Paris on** ~ geschäftlich nach Paris fahren; **he is here/away on** ~ er ist geschäftlich hier/unterwegs; **to know one's** ~ seine Sache verstehen; **to get down to** ~ zur Sache kommen; **to combine** *or* **mix** ~ **with pleasure** das Angenehme mit dem Nützlichen verbinden; **you shouldn't mix** ~ **with pleasure** man sollte Geschäftliches und Vergnügen trennen; **looking for** ~? (*asked by prostitute*) na, Süßer, wie wärs?
b (*fig inf*) **now we're in** ~ jetzt kanns losgehen (*inf*); **to mean** ~ es ernst meinen; **it's/she's the** ~ das/sie ist spitze (*inf*)

c (= *commercial enterprise*) Geschäft *nt*, Betrieb *m*; **a small** ~ ein kleines Unternehmen; **a family** ~ ein Familienunternehmen *nt*
d (= *concern*) Sache *f*, Angelegenheit *f*; (= *task, duty also*) Aufgabe *f*; **that's my** ~ das ist meine Sache *or* Angelegenheit; **that's no** ~ **of mine/ yours, that's none of my/your** ~ das geht mich/ dich nichts an; **to make it your** ~ **to do sth** es sich (*dat*) zur Aufgabe machen, etw zu tun; **you should make it your** ~ **to see that all the products ...** Sie sollten sich darum kümmern, dass alle Produkte ...; **you've no** ~ **doing that** du hast kein Recht, das zu tun; **we are not in the** ~ **of doing that** es ist nicht unsere Aufgabe, das zu tun; **to send sb about his** ~ jdn in seine Schranken weisen; **I must be about my** ~ (*form*) ich muss (jetzt) meinen Geschäften nachgehen → **mind**
e (= *difficult job*) Problem *nt*
f (*inf, = affair*) Sache *f*; **I am tired of this protest** ~ ich hab genug von dieser Protestiererei (*inf*); **moving house can be a costly/stressful** ~ ein Umzug kann ganz schön teuer/stressig sein → **funny**
g (*Theat*) dargestellte Handlung
h (*inf, = defecation: of dog, child*) Geschäft *nt* (*inf*); **to do one's** ~ sein Geschäft machen *or* verrichten (*inf*)

business: business acumen N Geschäftstüchtigkeit *f*, Geschäftssinn *m*; **business address** N Geschäftsadresse *f*; **business associate** N Geschäftspartner(in) *m(f)*; **business card** N (Visiten)karte *f*; **business centre**, (*US*) **business center** N Geschäftszentrum *nt*; **business class** N Businessclass *f*, Businessklasse *f*; **business college** N Wirtschaftshochschule *f*; **business consultant** N Betriebsberater(in) *m(f)*; **business development loan** N Investitionskredit *m*; **business end** N (*inf, of knife, chisel etc*) scharfes Ende; (*of rifle etc*) Lauf *m*; **business expenses** PL Spesen *pl*; **business hours** PL Geschäftsstunden *pl*, Geschäftszeit *f*; **business letter** N Geschäftsbrief *m*

businesslike ['bɪznɪslaɪk] ADJ *person, firm* (= *good at doing business*) geschäftstüchtig; *person, manner* geschäftsmäßig; *transaction* geschäftlich; (= *efficient*) *person, prose* kühl und sachlich, nüchtern

business: business lunch N Geschäftsessen *nt*; **businessman** N Geschäftsmann *m*; **business management** N Betriebswirtschaft(slehre) *f*; **business manager** N (*for theatre*) Verwaltungsdirektor(in) *m(f)*; (*of pop star etc*) Manager(in) *m(f)*; **business park** N Industriegelände *nt*; **business people** PL Geschäftsleute *pl*; **business plan** N Geschäftsplan *m*; **business practices** PL Geschäftsgebaren *nt no pl*; **business proposition** N (= *proposal*) Geschäftsangebot *nt*; (= *idea*) Geschäftsvorhaben *nt*; **business school** N Wirtschaftsschule *f*; **business sense** N Geschäftssinn *m*; **business studies** PL Wirtschaftslehre *f*; **business suit** N Straßenanzug *m*; **business trip** N Geschäftsreise *f*; **businesswoman** N Geschäftsfrau *f*; **business year** N Geschäftsjahr *nt*

busing ['bʌsɪŋ] N = **bussing**

busk [bʌsk] VI *als Straßenmusikant vor Kinos, Theatern etc spielen*

busker ['bʌskə[r]] N Straßenmusikant *m*

bus: bus lane N Busspur *f*; **busload** N a ~ **of children** eine Busladung Kinder; **by the** ~ (*inf*) **in ~s** (*inf*) busweise (*inf*); **busman** N a ~'**s holiday** (*fig*) praktisch eine Fortsetzung der Arbeit im Urlaub; **bus pass** N Seniorenkarte *f* für Busse; (*for the disabled*) Behindertenkarte *f* für Busse; **bus route** N Buslinie *f*; **we're not on a** ~ wir haben keine Busverbindung; **bus service** N Busverbindung *f*; (= *network*) Busverbindungen *pl*; **bus shelter** N Wartehäuschen *nt*

bussing ['bʌsɪŋ] N (*esp US*) Busbeförderung *von Schulkindern in andere Bezirke, um Rassentrennung zu verhindern*

bus: bus station N Busbahnhof m; **bus stop** N Bushaltestelle f

bust[1] [bʌst] N Büste f; (Anat also) Busen m; ~ **measurement** Brustumfang m, Oberweite f

bust[2] vb: pret, ptp **bust** (inf) **ADJ a** (= broken) kaputt (inf)
b (= bankrupt) pleite (inf)
ADV (= bankrupt) **to go** ~ pleite gehen or machen (inf)
N (US, = failure) Pleite f (inf)
VT a (= break) kaputtmachen (inf); **the case ~ its sides** der Koffer ist an den Seiten kaputtgegangen (inf); **they ~ed their way in** sie haben die Tür/das Fenster eingeschlagen; (to a meeting) sie haben sich hineingedrängt; **to ~ sth open** etw aufbrechen; **to ~ a gut** sich (dat) den Arsch aufreißen (sl); **he just about ~ a gut doing it** er hat sich (dat) dabei fast einen abgebrochen (inf)
b (= catch, convict) hinter Schloss und Riegel bringen; drugs ring, syndicate auffliegen lassen (inf)
c (US Mil: = demote) degradieren (to zu)
VI (= break) kaputtgehen (inf)
▶ **bust out** (inf) **VI** ausbrechen **VT** sep herausholen (inf)
▶ **bust up** VT sep (inf) box, marriage kaputtmachen (inf); meeting auffliegen lassen (inf); (by starting fights) stören; **I hate to bust up the party** tut mir Leid, dass ich die traute Runde stören muss

bustard [ˈbʌstəd] N Trappe f

buster [ˈbʌstə] N (esp US inf, as address) Meister m (inf); (threatening) Freundchen nt (inf)

-buster suf (inf) -brecher; **sanctions-buster** Sanktionsbrecher(in) m(f); **crime-buster** Verbrechensbekämpfer(in) m(f)

bus ticket N Busfahrschein m

bustle[1] [ˈbʌsl] **N** Betrieb m (of in +dat); (of fair, streets also) geschäftiges or reges Treiben (of auf or in +dat) **VI to ~ about** geschäftig hin und her eilen or sausen (inf); **to ~ in** geschäftig hinein-/hereineilen or -sausen (inf); **to ~ out** geschäftig hinaus-/herauseilen or -sausen (inf); **the marketplace was bustling with activity** auf dem Markt herrschte großer Betrieb or ein reges Treiben

bustle[2] N (Fashion) Turnüre f

bustling [ˈbʌslɪŋ] ADJ person geschäftig; place, scene belebt, voller Leben

bust-up [ˈbʌstʌp] N (inf) Krach m (inf); **they had a ~** sie haben Krach gehabt (inf); (= split up) sie haben sich verkracht (inf)

busty [ˈbʌstɪ] ADJ (+er) (inf) woman vollbusig

busway [ˈbʌsweɪ] N (US) Busspur f

busy [ˈbɪzɪ] ✪ 27.3 ADJ (+er) **a** (= occupied) person beschäftigt; **a very ~ man** ein viel beschäftigter Mann; **are you ~?** haben Sie gerade Zeit?; (in business) haben Sie viel zu tun?; **not now, I'm ~** jetzt nicht, ich bin gerade beschäftigt; **the boss is always ~** der Chef hat immer viel zu tun; (= never available) der Chef hat nie Zeit; **I'll come back when you're less ~** ich komme wieder, wenn Sie mehr Zeit haben; **to keep sb/oneself ~** jdn/sich selbst beschäftigen; **I was ~ studying when you called** ich war gerade beim Lernen, als Sie kamen; **I was ~ studying all evening** ich war den ganzen Abend mit Lernen beschäftigt; **she's always too ~ thinking about herself** sie ist immer zu sehr mit sich selbst beschäftigt; **they were ~ plotting against him** sie haben eifrig Pläne gegen ihn geschmiedet; **let's get ~** an die Arbeit!
b (= active) life, time bewegt; place, street, town belebt; (with traffic) verkehrsreich; street stark befahren; **it's been a ~ day/week** gestern/diese Woche war viel los; **have you had a ~ day?** hast du heute viel zu tun gehabt?; **he leads a very ~ life** bei ihm ist immer etwas los; **the shop was ~ all day** im Geschäft war den ganzen Tag viel los
c (esp US) telephone line besetzt
d (= officious) person, manner (über)eifrig
e pattern, design, print unruhig

VR to ~ oneself doing sth sich damit beschäftigen, etw zu tun; **to ~ oneself with sth** sich mit etw beschäftigen

busybody [ˈbɪzɪˌbɒdɪ] N Wichtigtuer m, Gschaftlhuber m (S Ger); **don't be such a ~** misch dich nicht überall ein

busy signal N (esp US Telec) Besetztzeichen nt

but [bʌt] **CONJ a** aber; ~ **you must know that ...** Sie müssen aber wissen, dass ..., aber Sie müssen wissen, dass ...; ~ **HE didn't know that** aber er hat das nicht gewusst, er hat das aber nicht gewusst; ~ **he didn't know that** er aber hat das nicht gewusst; **they all went ~ I didn't** sie sind alle gegangen, nur ich nicht
b not X ~ Y nicht X sondern Y
c (subordinating) ohne dass; **never a week passes ~ she is ill** keine Woche vergeht, ohne dass sie krank ist; **I would have helped ~ that I was ill** (old, liter) ich hätte geholfen, wäre ich nicht krank gewesen (old)
d ~ **then he couldn't have known that** aber er hat das ja gar nicht wissen können; ~ **then you must be my brother!** dann müssen Sie ja mein Bruder sein!; ~ **then do you mean to say ...** wollen Sie denn etwa sagen ...; ~ **then it is well paid** aber dafür wird es gut bezahlt
ADV she's ~ a child sie ist doch noch ein Kind; **I cannot (help) ~ think that ...** ich kann nicht umhin zu denken, dass ...; **one cannot ~ admire him/suspect that ...** man kann ihn nur bewundern/nur annehmen, dass ...; **you can ~ try** du kannst es immerhin versuchen; **I had no alternative ~ to leave** mir blieb keine andere Wahl als zu gehen; **she left ~ a few minutes ago** sie ist erst vor ein paar Minuten gegangen; **Napoleon, to name ~ one, lived here** Napoleon, um nur einen zu nennen, hat hier gelebt
PREP no one ~ me could do it niemand außer mir or nur ich konnte es tun; **who ~ Fred would ...?** wer außer Fred würde ...?; **anything ~ that!** (alles,) nur das nicht!; **it was anything ~ simple** das war alles andere als einfach; **he/it was nothing ~ trouble** er/das hat nichts als or nur Schwierigkeiten gemacht; **the last house ~ one/two/three** das vorletzte/vorvorletzte/drittletzte Haus; **the first ~ one** der/die/das Zweite; **the next street ~ one/two/three** die übernächste/überübernächste Straße/vier Straßen weiter; ~ **for you I would be dead** ohne Sie wäre ich tot, wenn Sie nicht gewesen wären, wäre ich tot; **I could definitely live in Scotland, ~ for the weather** ich könnte ganz bestimmt in Schottland leben, wenn nur das Wetter nicht wäre
N no ~s about it kein Aber nt

but and ben N (Scot) Hütte bestehend aus Küche und kleiner Schlafkammer

butane [ˈbjuːteɪn] N Butan nt

butch [bʊtʃ] ADJ (inf) clothes, hairstyle, manner maskulin

butcher [ˈbʊtʃə] **N a** Fleischer m, Metzger m (dial), Schlachter m (N Ger); ~**'s (shop)** Fleischerei f, Metzgerei f (dial), Schlachterei f (N Ger); **at the ~'s** beim Fleischer etc; ~**'s boy** Fleischerjunge etc m; ~**'s wife** Fleischersfrau etc f **b** (fig, = murderer) Schlächter m **c butchers** PL (Brit inf: = look) **give us a ~s** lass mal gucken (inf); **take** or **have a ~s (at that)** guck mal (das an) (inf); **do you want a ~s?** willste mal gucken? (inf) **VT** animals schlachten; people abschlachten, niedermetzeln; (fig) play, piece of music, language vergewaltigen; **his ~ed body** seine schrecklich zugerichtete Leiche

butchery [ˈbʊtʃərɪ] N (= slaughter) Gemetzel nt, Metzelei f; **the ~ of millions** das Abschlachten or Niedermetzeln von Millionen; **stop the fight, this is ~!** brechen Sie den Kampf ab, das ist ja das reinste Gemetzel!

butler [ˈbʌtlə] N Butler m

BUTLINS

Butlins ist eine britische Ferienklubkette, die Rundum-Urlaub für die ganze Familie anbietet, wobei Wert auf ein gutes Preis-Leistungs-Verhältnis gelegt wird. Auf einem einzigen Gelände findet man Unterkünfte, Restaurants, Bars und ein breites Freizeitangebot. Für jedes Alter wird etwas geboten, zum Beispiel Sportwettkämpfe, Rummelplätze und Musikkonzerte für die Kinder und Jugendlichen oder Bingo und Tanzveranstaltungen für die älteren Semester. Die Animateure von Butlins werden **redcoats** (Rotröcke) genannt, weil das rote Jacken das dominierende Element ihres Outfits sind.

---

butt[1] [bʌt] N (for wine) großes Fass; (for rainwater) Tonne f

butt[2] N (also **butt end**) dickes Ende; (of rifle) (Gewehr)kolben m; (of cigar, cigarette) Stummel m

butt[3] N (US, inf, = cigarette) Kippe f (inf)

butt[4] **N a** (= target) Schießscheibe f **b** usu pl (on shooting range, behind targets) Kugelfang m; (in front of targets) Schutzwall m; (= range itself) Schießstand m **c** (fig, = person) Zielscheibe f; **she's always the ~ of his jokes** sie ist immer (die) Zielscheibe seines Spottes

butt[5] **N** (Kopf)stoß m; **to give sb a ~** jdn mit dem Kopf stoßen; (goat also) jdn mit den Hörnern stoßen **VT** mit dem Kopf stoßen; (goat also) mit den Hörnern stoßen
▶ **butt at** VI +prep obj (goat) stoßen gegen
▶ **butt in** VI sich einmischen (on in +acc), dazwischenfunken or -platzen (inf) (on bei)
▶ **butt into** VI +prep obj sich einmischen in (+acc), dazwischenfunken or dazwischenplatzen bei (inf)

butt[6] N (US, inf, = backside) Arsch m (vulg); **get up off your ~** setz mal deinen Arsch in Bewegung (sl)

butter [ˈbʌtə] **N** Butter f; **she looks as if ~ wouldn't melt in her mouth** sie sieht aus, als ob sie kein Wässerchen trüben könnte **VT** bread etc mit Butter bestreichen, buttern
▶ **butter up** VT sep (inf) schöntun (+dat), um den Bart gehen (+dat) (inf)

butter: butterball N (US, inf, = fat person) Fettkloß m (inf); **butter bean** N Mondbohne f; **buttercup** N Butterblume f, Hahnenfuß m; **butter dish** N Butterdose f; **butterfingers** N sing (inf) Schussel m (inf); ~**!** du Schussel! (inf)

butterfly [ˈbʌtəflaɪ] **N a** Schmetterling m; **I've got/I get butterflies (in my stomach)** mir ist/wird ganz flau im Magen (inf), mir ist/wird ganz mulmig zumute or zu Mute (inf) **b** (Swimming) Schmetterlingsstil m, Butterfly m; **can you do the ~?** können Sie Butterfly or den Schmetterlingsstil?

butterfly: butterfly bandage N Pflasterzugverband m; **butterfly kiss** N Schmetterlingskuss m; **butterfly net** N Schmetterlingsnetz nt; **butterfly nut** N Flügelmutter f; **butterfly stroke** N Schmetterlingsstil m, Butterfly m

butter: butter icing N ≈ Buttercreme f; **butter knife** N Buttermesser nt; **buttermilk** N Buttermilch f; **butterscotch N** ≈ Karamellbonbon m **ADJ** Karamell-; **butterwort** N (Bot) Fettkraut nt

buttery [ˈbʌtərɪ] N Vorratskammer f; (Univ) Cafeteria f

buttock [ˈbʌtək] N (Hinter)backe f, Gesäßhälfte f (form); ~**s** pl Gesäß nt, Hintern m (inf)

button [ˈbʌtn] **N a** Knopf m; **not worth a ~** (inf) keinen Pfifferling wert (inf); **his answer was right on the ~** (inf) seine Antwort hat voll ins Schwarze getroffen (inf); **he arrived right on the ~** (inf) er kam auf den Glockenschlag (inf); **to push** or **press the right ~s** (fig inf) es richtig anstellen (inf); **she knew which ~s to press to get what she wanted** (fig inf) sie wusste, wie sie es anstellen musste, um zu bekommen, was sie wollte (inf)
b (= mushroom) junger Champignon
c ~**s** sing (inf, = pageboy) (Hotel)page m
VT garment zuknöpfen; ~ **your lip** (inf) halt den Mund (inf)
VI (garment) geknöpft werden

▶**button up** VT sep zuknöpfen; **to have a deal all buttoned up** ein Geschäft unter Dach und Fach haben

button-down ['bʌtndaʊn] ADJ ~ **collar** Button-down-Kragen m

buttoned-up ['bʌtnd,ʌp] ADJ (inf: = reserved) zugeknöpft (inf)

button: buttonhole N **a** (in garment) Knopfloch nt **b** (= flower) Blume f im Knopfloch; **to sell ~s** Blumen fürs Knopfloch verkaufen ◆ VT (fig) zu fassen bekommen, sich (dat) schnappen (inf); **buttonhole stitch** N Knopflochstich m; **buttonhook** N (for boots) Stiefelknöpfer m; **button mushroom** N junger Champignon

buttress ['bʌtrɪs] N (Archit) Strebepfeiler m; (fig) Pfeiler m ◆ VT (Archit) wall (durch Strebepfeiler) stützen; (fig) stützen

butty ['bʊtɪ] N (esp N Engl, inf) Stulle f (dial)

buxom ['bʌksəm] ADJ drall

buy [baɪ] vb: pret, ptp **bought** ◆ VT **a** (= purchase) kaufen; (Rail) ticket also lösen; **there are some things that money can't ~** es gibt Dinge, die man nicht kaufen kann; **all that money can ~** alles, was man mit Geld kaufen kann; **to ~ and sell goods** Waren an- und verkaufen **b** (fig) victory, fame sich (dat) erkaufen; time gewinnen; (= bribe) bestechen, kaufen; **the victory was dearly bought** der Sieg war teuer erkauft **c** **to ~ sth** (inf, = accept) etw akzeptieren; **I'll ~ that** das ist o.k. (inf); (= believe) ja, das glaube ich **d** (inf, = be killed) **he bought it** den hats erwischt (inf) ◆ VI kaufen ◆ N (inf) Kauf m; **to be a good ~** ein guter Kauf sein; (clothes also, food) preiswert sein

▶**buy back** VT sep zurückkaufen

▶**buy forward** VT (Fin) auf Termin kaufen

▶**buy in** VT sep (= acquire supply of) goods einkaufen

▶**buy into** VI +prep obj **a** (Comm) business, organization, industry sich einkaufen in (+acc) **b** (fig) schlucken (inf), akzeptieren

▶**buy off** VT sep (inf, = bribe) kaufen (inf)

▶**buy out** VT sep **a** shareholders etc auszahlen; firm aufkaufen **b** (from army) los- or freikaufen (of von)

▶**buy over** VT sep kaufen; (= get on one's side) für sich gewinnen

▶**buy up** VT sep aufkaufen

buy-back ['baɪˌbæk] ADJ ~ **option** Rückkaufoption f; ~ **price** Rückkaufpreis m

buyer ['baɪə] N Käufer m; (= agent) Einkäufer m; ~'**s market** Käufermarkt m

buyout ['baɪaʊt] N Aufkauf m

buzz [bʌz] ◆ VI **a** (insect) summen, brummen; (smaller or agitated insects) schwirren; (device) summen; **did you ~, sir?** haben Sie nach mir verlangt?; **Miss Jones, I've been ~ing for 10 minutes** Fräulein Jones, ich versuche schon seit 10 Minuten, Sie zu erreichen **b** my ears are ~ing mir dröhnen die Ohren; **my head is ~ing** (with ideas etc) mir schwirrt der Kopf; (from noise) mir dröhnt der Kopf **c** the town is ~ing in der Stadt ist was los (inf) or herrscht reges Leben; **the city was ~ing with excitement** die Stadt war in heller Aufregung; **the news set the town ~ing** die Nachricht versetzte die Stadt in helle Aufregung ◆ VT **a** (= call) secretary (mit dem Summer) rufen **b** (US, inf, = telephone) anrufen **c** (plane, building dicht vorbeifliegen an (+dat); **we were ~ed** Flugzeuge flogen dicht an uns heran ◆ N **a** (of insect) Summen nt, Brummen nt; (of smaller or agitated insects) Schwirren nt; (of device) Summen nt **b** (of conversation) Stimmengewirr nt, Gemurmel nt; ~ **of excitement/anticipation** aufgeregtes/erwartungsvolles Gemurmel **c** (inf, = telephone call) Anruf m; **to give sb a ~**

▶**buzz about** (Brit) or **around** VI (inf) herumschwirren

▶**buzz off** VI (Brit, inf) abzischen (inf)

buzzard ['bʌzəd] N Bussard m

buzz bomb N Fernrakete f

buzzer ['bʌzə] N Summer m

buzz: buzz phrase N Modeausdruck m; **buzz topic** N Modethema nt; **buzz word** N Modewort nt

b/w abbr of **black and white** S/W

by [baɪ] PREP **a** (= close to) bei, an (+dat); (with movement) an (+acc); (= next to) neben (+dat); (with movement) neben (+acc); **by the window/fire/river** am or beim Fenster/Feuer/Fluss; **by the church** an or bei der Kirche; **a holiday** (esp Brit) or **vacation** (US) **by the sea** Ferien pl an der See; **come and sit by me** komm, setz dich neben mich; **she sat by me** sie saß neben mir; **to keep sth by one** etw bei sich haben **b** (= via) über (+acc) **c** (= past) **to go/rush** etc **by sb/sth** an jdm/etw vorbeigehen/-eilen etc **d** (time: = during) **by day/night** bei Tag/Nacht **e** (time: = not later than) bis; **can you do it by tomorrow?** kannst du es bis morgen machen?; **by tomorrow I'll be in France** morgen werde ich in Frankreich sein; **by the time I got there, he had gone** bis ich dorthin kam, war er gegangen; **but by that time** or **by then I had realized that ...** aber bis dahin war mir klar geworden, dass ...; **but by that time** or **by then it will be too late** aber dann ist es schon zu spät; **but by that time** or **by then he will have forgotten** aber bis dann or dahin hat er es schon vergessen; **by now** inzwischen **f** (indicating amount) **by the inch/kilo/hour/month** zoll-/kilo-/stunden-/monatsweise; **one by one** einer nach dem anderen; **they came in two by two** sie kamen paarweise herein; **letters came in by the hundred** hunderte or Hunderte von Briefen kamen **g** (indicating agent, cause) von; **killed by a bullet** durch eine or von einer Kugel getötet; **indicated by an asterisk** durch Sternchen gekennzeichnet; **a painting by Picasso** ein Bild von Picasso; **surrounded by** umgeben von **h** (indicating method, means, manner: see also nouns) **by bus/car/bicycle** mit dem or per Bus/Auto/Fahrrad; **by land and (by) sea** zu Land und zu Wasser; **to pay by cheque** (Brit) or **check** (US) mit Scheck bezahlen; **made by hand** handgearbeitet; **made by machine** maschinell hergestellt; **by daylight/moonlight** bei Tag(es)licht/im Mondschein; **to know sb by name/sight** jdn dem Namen nach/vom Sehen her kennen; **to be known by the name of ...** unter dem Namen ... bekannt sein; **to lead sb by the hand** jdn an der Hand führen; **to grab sb by the collar** jdn am Kragen packen; **he had a daughter by his first wife** von seiner ersten Frau hatte er eine Tochter; **by myself/himself** etc allein **i** by saving hard he managed to ... durch eisernes Sparen or dadurch, dass er eisern sparte, gelang es ihm ...; **by turning this knob** durch Drehen dieses Knopfes, wenn Sie an diesem Knopf drehen; **by saying that I didn't mean ...** ich habe damit nicht gemeint ...; **animals which move by wriggling** Tiere, die sich schlängelnd fortbewegen; **he could walk by supporting himself on ...** gestützt auf ... könnte er gehen **j** (according to: see also nouns) nach; **to judge by appearances** nach dem Äußern urteilen; **by my watch it is nine o'clock** nach meiner Uhr ist es neun; **if you play by the rules** (fig) wenn du dich an die Regel hältst; **by the terms of Article I** gemäß or nach (den Bestimmungen von) Artikel I; **to call sb/sth by his/its proper name** jdn/etw beim richtigen Namen nennen; **if it's OK by you/him** etc wenn es Ihnen/ihm etc recht ist; **it's all right by me** von mir aus gern or schon **k** (measuring difference) um; **broader by a foot** um einen Fuß breiter; **it missed me by inches** es verfehlte mich um Zentimeter **l** (Math, Measure) **to divide/multiply by** dividieren durch/multiplizieren mit; **a room 20 feet by 30** ein Zimmer 20 auf or mal 30 Fuß **m** (points of compass) **South by South West** Südsüdwest **n** (in oaths) bei; **I swear by Almighty God** ich schwöre beim allmächtigen Gott; **by heaven, I'll get you for this** das sollst or wirst du mir, bei Gott, büßen! **o** **by the right!** (Mil) rechts, links ...! **p** **by the way** or **by(e)** übrigens; **all this is by the way** or **by(e)** (= irrelevant) das ist alles Nebensache or zweitrangig ◆ ADV **a** (= past) **to pass/wander/rush** etc **by** vorbei- or vorüberkommen/-wandern/-eilen etc **b** (= in reserve) **to put** or **lay by** beiseite legen **c** (phrases) **by and by** irgendwann; (with past tense) nach einiger Zeit; **by and large** im Großen und Ganzen

by(e) [baɪ] N **a** (Cricket) Lauf bei Bällen, die nicht vom Schlagmann geschlagen worden sind **b** bye (Sport) **to get a bye into the second round** spielfrei in die zweite Runde kommen

bye [baɪ] INTERJ (inf) tschüs(s); ~ **for now!** bis bald!

bye-bye ['baɪ'baɪ] INTERJ (inf) Wiedersehen (inf); **that's ~ £200** (da sind) £ 200 futsch! (inf) ◆ **to go (to) ~s** (Brit baby-talk) or ~ (US baby-talk) in die Heia gehen (baby-talk)

by(e): by(e)-election ['baɪɪlekʃən] N Nachwahl f; **by(e)-law** ['baɪlɔː] N **a** (Brit: of community) Gemeindeverordnung f; (of town) städtische Verordnung **b** (of company, society etc) Satzung f

Byelorussia [ˌbjeləʊ'rʌʃə] N Weißrussland nt

Byelorussian [ˌbjeləʊ'rʌʃən] ADJ weißrussisch ◆ N **a** Weißrusse m, Weißrussin f **b** (Ling) Weißrussisch nt

bygone ['baɪgɒn] ADJ längst vergangen; **in ~ days** in früheren Zeiten ◆ N **to let ~s be ~s** die Vergangenheit ruhen lassen

by: bylaw, bye-law N Verordnung f; **by-line** N **a** (Press) Zeile mit dem Namen des Autors **b** (Ftbl) Seitenlinie f; (at goal) Tor(aus)linie f; **byname** N Inbegriff m (for von); **X is a ~ for tractors** X ist der Name für Traktoren

BYO abbr of **bring your own** Restaurant ohne Schankerlaubnis, in dem mitgebrachte alkoholische Getränke verzehrt werden dürfen

BYOB abbr of **bring your own bottle** or **beer** or (inf) **booze** alkoholische Getränke sind mitzubringen

bypass ['baɪpɑːs] N **a** (= road) Umgehungsstraße f; (Med, Tech: = pipe etc) Bypass m; **he's had a charisma/humour** (Brit) or **humor** (US) **~** (inf) als Charisma/Humor verteilt wurde, haben sie ihn vergessen ◆ VT town, village umgehen; (Med) umgehen; (Tech) fluid, gas umleiten; (fig) person übergehen; intermediate stage also überspringen; difficulties umgehen

bypass: bypass operation N Bypassoperation f; **bypass surgery** N Bypasschirurgie f; **to have ~** sich einer Bypassoperation unterziehen

by: by-play N (Theat) Nebenhandlung f; **by-product** N (lit, fig) Nebenprodukt nt

byre ['baɪə] N (Kuh)stall m

by: byroad N Neben- or Seitenstraße f; **bystander** N Umstehende(r) mf, Zuschauer m; **innocent ~** unbeteiligter Zuschauer

byte [baɪt] N (Comput) Byte nt

by: byway N Seitenweg m → **highway**; **byword** N **to become a ~ for sth** gleichbedeutend mit etw werden

Byzantine [baɪ'zæntaɪn] ADJ byzantinisch ◆ N Byzantiner(in) m(f)

Byzantium [baɪ'zæntɪəm] N Byzanz nt

C

C, c [si:] C, c *nt*; **C sharp** Cis *nt*, cis *nt*; **C flat** Ces *nt*, ces *nt* → also **major, minor, natural**

C *abbr of* **centigrade** C

c **a** *abbr of* **cent** c, ct **b** *abbr of* **circa** ca

C4 (*Brit TV*) *abbr of* **Channel Four**

CA **a** *abbr of* **chartered accountant** **b** *abbr of* **Central America**

c/a *abbr of* **current account**

cab [kæb] N **a** (*horsedrawn*) Droschke *f*; (= *taxi*) Taxi *nt*, Taxe *f* (*inf*), Droschke *f* (*form*) **b** (*of railway engine, lorry, crane*) Führerhaus *nt*

cabal [kə'bæl] N **a** (= *intrigue*) Intrige *f*, Komplott *nt*, Kabale *f* (*old liter*) **b** (= *group*) Clique *f*, Kamarilla *f* (*geh*)

cabaret ['kæbəreɪ] N Varietee *nt*, Varieté *nt*; (*satirical*) Kabarett *nt*

cabbage ['kæbɪdʒ] N **a** Kohl *m*, Kraut *nt* (*esp S Ger*); **a head of ~** ein Kohlkopf *m* **b** (*inf*: = *person*) geistiger Krüppel (*inf*); **to become a ~** verblöden (*inf*); (*sick person*) dahinvegetieren

cabbage: cabbage lettuce N Kopfsalat *m*; **cabbage rose** N Zentifolie *f*; **cabbage white (butterfly)** N Kohlweißling *m*

cab(b)alistic [ˌkæbə'lɪstɪk] ADJ kabbalistisch

cabby ['kæbɪ] N (*inf, of taxi*) Taxifahrer(in) *m(f)*; (*of horsedrawn vehicle*) Kutscher(in) *m(f)*

cab driver N Taxifahrer(in) *m(f)*

caber ['keɪbə'] N (*Scot*) Pfahl *m*, Stamm *m* → **toss**

cabin ['kæbɪn] N **a** (= *hut*) Hütte *f* **b** (*Naut*) Kabine *f*, Kajüte *f*; (= *stateroom*) Kabine *f* **c** (*of lorries, buses etc*) Führerhaus *nt* **d** (*Aviat, for passengers*) Passagierraum *m*; (*for pilot*) Cockpit *nt*, (*Flug*)kanzel *f*

cabin: cabin attendant N (*Aviat*) Flugbegleiter(in) *m(f)*; **cabin boy** N Schiffsjunge *m*; (= *steward*) Kabinensteward *m*; **cabin class** N zweite Klasse; **cabin crew** N (*Aviat*) Flugbegleitpersonal *nt*; **cabin cruiser** N Kajütboot *nt*

cabinet ['kæbɪnɪt] N **a** Schränkchen *nt*; (*for display*) Vitrine *f*; (*for TV etc*) Schrank *m*, Truhe *f*; (= *loudspeaker cabinet*) Box *f* **b** (*Parl*) Kabinett *nt*, Regierungsmannschaft *f* (*inf*)

CABINET

In Großbritannien besteht das **Cabinet** aus ungefähr zwanzig Ministern, die vom Premierminister berufen werden. Das Kabinett plant die wichtigsten Gesetze und legt sie dem Parlament vor. In den Debatten verteidigt es die Regierungspolitik.

Das US-**Cabinet** ist ein Organ, dessen einzige Aufgabe die Beratung des Präsidenten ist. Daher kann es keine politischen Richtlinien festlegen oder Gesetze einbringen. Die Mitglieder des Kabinetts sind entweder Leiter der Ministerien oder andere Regierungsbeamte, müssen aber nicht zwangsläufig Politiker sein. Sie werden vom Präsidenten ausgewählt und mit der Zustimmung des Senats ernannt. Weitere, allerdings inoffizielle Berater des Präsidenten gelten als „kitchen cabinet", als Küchenkabinett.

---

cabinet: cabinet edition N (= *book*) bibliophile Ausgabe; **cabinet-maker** N (Möbel-)tischler(in) *m(f)*, (Möbel)schreiner(in) *m(f)*; **cabinet-making** N Tischlern *nt*, Tischlerei *f*; **cabinet meeting** N Kabinettssitzung *f*; **cabinet minister** N ≈ Mitglied *nt* des Kabinetts, Minister(in) *m(f)*; **cabinet reshuffle** N (*Brit Pol*) Kabinettsumbildung *f*; **cabinet-size** ADJ (*Phot*) im Kabinettformat

cabin: cabin luggage N Kabinengepäck *nt*; **cabin staff** N Kabinenpersonal *nt*; **cabin trunk** N Schrank- or Überseekoffer *m*

cable ['keɪbl] N **a** Tau *nt*; (*of wire*) Kabel *nt*, Trosse *f* (*Naut*) **b** (*Elec*) Kabel *nt*, Leitung *f* **c** (= *cablegram*) Telegramm *nt*; (*from abroad*) (Übersee)telegramm *nt*, Kabel *nt*; **by ~** per Telegramm/Kabel **d** (= *cable television*) Kabelfernsehen *nt* VT *information* telegrafisch durchgeben; (*overseas*) kabeln; **to ~ sb** jdm telegrafieren/kabeln VI telegrafieren, ein Telegramm/Kabel schicken

cable: cable car N (*hanging*) Drahtseilbahn *f*; (= *streetcar*) (gezogene) Straßenbahn *f*; (= *funicular*) Standseilbahn *f*; **cablegram** N = **cable c**; **cable-knit** ADJ Zopfmuster-; **~ sweater** Zopfmusterpullover *m*; **cable-laying** N Kabelverlegung *f*, Kabellegen *nt*; **cable length** N (*Naut*) Kabellänge *f*; **cable railway** N Bergbahn *f*; **cable stitch** N (*Knitting*) Zopfmuster *nt*; **cable television** N Kabelfernsehen *nt*

cabling ['keɪblɪŋ] N (= *cables*) Kabel *pl*; (= *process*) Verkabelung *f*

caboodle [kə'bu:dl] N (*inf*) **the whole (kit and) ~** das ganze Zeug(s) (*inf*), der ganze Kram (*inf*)

caboose [kə'bu:s] N **a** (*Naut*) Kombüse *f* **b** (*US, Rail*) Dienstwagen *m*

cab rank N (*Brit*) Taxistand *m*, Droschkenplatz *m* (*form*)

cabrio ['kæbrɪəʊ] N (*inf*) Cabrio *nt*, Kabrio *nt*

cabriole ['kæbrɪəʊl] N (*of table etc*) geschwungenes or geschweiftes Bein

cabriolet [ˌkæbrɪəʊ'leɪ] N Kabriolett *nt*

cab stand N (*esp US*) = **cab rank**

cacao [kə'ka:əʊ] N (= *tree, bean*) Kakao *m*

cache [kæʃ] N **a** Versteck *nt*, geheimes (Waffen-/Proviant)lager *nt* **b** (*Comput: also* **cache memory**) Zwischenspeicher *m*, Cachespeicher *m* VT verstecken

cachepot ['kæʃpəʊ, -pɒt] N Übertopf *m*

cachet ['kæʃeɪ] N Gütesiegel *nt*, Gütezeichen *nt*; **the name has a certain ~ on the French market** der Name gilt auf dem französischen Markt als Gütezeichen; **it had given me a certain ~ in her parents' eyes** dadurch hatte ich bei ihren Eltern ein gewisses Ansehen

cachou ['kæʃu:] N Cachou(bonbon) *m or nt*

cack [kæk] N (*Brit sl: lit, fig*) Kacke *f* (*vulg*)

cack-handed ['kæk'hændəd] ADJ (*Brit, inf*) tollpatschig (*inf*)

cackle ['kækl] N (*of hens*) Gackern *nt*; (= *laughter*) (meckerndes) Lachen; (*inf, = chatter*) Geblödel *nt* (*inf*) VI (*hens*) gackern; (= *laugh*) meckernd lachen; (*inf: = talk*) schwatzen

cacophonous [kæ'kɒfənəs] ADJ misstönend, kakophon (*geh*)

cacophony [kæ'kɒfənɪ] N Kakophonie *f* (*geh*), Missklang *m*

cactus ['kæktəs] N Kaktus *m*

CAD [kæd] *abbr of* **computer-aided design** CAD

cad [kæd] N (*dated*) Schurke *m* (*old*), Schuft *m*

cadaver [kə'dævə'] N Kadaver *m*; (*of humans*) Leiche *f*

cadaverous [kə'dævərəs] ADJ (= *corpse-like*) Kadaver-, Leichen-; (= *gaunt*) ausgezehrt, ausgemergelt; (= *pale*) leichenblass

CAD/CAM ['kæd'kæm] *abbr of* **computer-aided design/computer-aided manufacture** CAD/CAM

caddie ['kædɪ] N (*Golf*) Caddie *m* VI Caddie sein *or* spielen (*inf*)

caddie car, caddie cart N (*Golf*) Caddywagen *m*

caddis fly ['kædɪs'flaɪ] N Köcherfliege *f*, Frühlingsfliege *f*

caddish ['kædɪʃ] ADJ (*dated*) schurkisch (*old*), niederträchtig

caddy ['kædɪ] N **a** (= *tea caddy*) Behälter *m*, Büchse *f* **b** (*US, = shopping trolley*) Einkaufswagen *m* **c** = **caddie b**

cadence ['keɪdəns] N (*Mus*) Kadenz *f*; (*of voice*) Tonfall *m*, Melodie *f*; (= *rhythm*) Rhythmus *m*, Melodie *f*; **the ~s of his prose** der Duktus seiner Prosa

cadenza [kə'denzə] N (*Mus*) Kadenz *f*

cadet [kə'det] N **a** (*Mil etc*) Kadett *m*; **~ school** Kadettenanstalt *f* **b** (*old*) jüngerer Sohn/Bruder

cadet corps M (*Mil etc*) Kadettenkorps *nt*

cadge [kædʒ] (*Brit inf*) VT (er)betteln, abstauben (*inf*), schnorren (*inf*); (*from sb* bei *or* von jdm); **could I ~ a lift with you?** könnten Sie mich vielleicht (ein Stück) mitnehmen? VI schnorren (*inf*)

cadger ['kædʒə'] N (*inf*) Schnorrer(in) *m(f)* (*inf*), Abstauber(in) *m(f)* (*inf*)

cadmium ['kædmɪəm] N Kadmium *nt*, Cadmium *nt*

cadre ['kædrɪ] N (*Mil, fig*) Kader *m*

caecum, (*US*) **cecum** ['si:kəm] N (*Anat*) Blinddarm *m*

Caesar ['si:zə'] N Cäsar *m*, Caesar *m*

Caesarean, (*US*) **Cesarean** [si:'zɛərɪən] ADJ cäsarisch, Cäsaren-; (= *of Caesar*) cäsarisch N (*Med: also* **Caesarean section**) Kaiserschnitt *m*; **he was a ~** er wurde mit Kaiserschnitt entbunden; **she had a (baby by) ~** sie hatte einen Kaiserschnitt

Caesarian, (*US*) **Cesarian** [si:'zɛərɪən] N = **Caesarean**

caesium, (*US*) **cesium** ['si:zɪəm] N (*Chem*) Cäsium *nt*, Zäsium *nt*

caesura, (*US*) **cesura** [sɪ'zjʊərə] N Zäsur *f*

café ['kæfeɪ] N Café *nt*

café society N , *no pl* Schickeria *f*

cafeteria [ˌkæfɪ'tɪərɪə] N Cafeteria *f*

cafetière [ˌkæfə'tjɛə'] N Kaffeebereiter *m*

caff [kæf] N (*Brit, inf*) Café *nt*

caffein(e) ['kæfi:n] N Koffein *nt*

caftan ['kæftæn] N Kaftan *m*

cag [kæg] N (*Brit inf*) → **cagoule**

cage [keɪdʒ] **N** **a** Käfig *m*; (= *small birdcage*) Bauer *nt or m*; **~ bird** Käfigvogel *m* **b** (*of lift*) Aufzug *m*; (*Min*) Förderkorb *m* **VT** (*also* **cage up**) in einen Käfig sperren, einsperren

cagey ['keɪdʒɪ] ADJ (*inf*) vorsichtig; *behaviour, answer also* zugeknöpft (*inf*); (= *evasive*) ausweichend; **what are you being so ~ about?** warum tust du so geheimnisvoll?; **she was very ~ about her age** sie hat aus ihrem Alter ein großes Geheimnis gemacht; **he was very ~ about his plans** er hat mit seinen Absichten hinterm Berg gehalten

cagily ['keɪdʒɪlɪ] ADV (*inf*) vorsichtig; (= *evasively*) ausweichend

caginess ['keɪdʒɪnɪs] N (*inf*) Vorsicht *f*, Zugeknöpftheit *f* (*inf*); (= *evasiveness*) ausweichende Art

cagoule [kə'guːl] N Windhemd *nt*

cahoots [kə'huːts] N (*inf*) **to be in ~ with sb** mit jdm unter einer Decke stecken

caiman ['keɪmən] N Kaiman *m*

Cain [keɪn] N Kain *m*; **to raise ~** (*inf,* = *be noisy*) Radau machen (*inf*), lärmen; (= *protest*) Krach schlagen (*inf*)

cairn [keən] **N** **a** Steinpyramide *f*, Steinhügel *m* **b** (*also* **cairn terrier**) Cairnterrier *m*

Cairo ['kaɪərəʊ] N Kairo *nt*

caisson ['keɪsən] **N** **a** (*Mil*) Munitionskiste *f*; (= *wagon*) Munitionswagen *m* **b** (*Tech,* = *underwater caisson*) Senkkasten *m*, Caisson *m*

cajole [kə'dʒəʊl] VT gut zureden (+*dat*), beschwatzen (*inf*); **to ~ sb into doing sth** jdn dazu bringen *or* jdn beschwatzen (*inf*), etw zu tun; **to ~ sb out of doing sth** jdm etw ausreden; **he would not be ~d** er ließ sich nicht beschwatzen (*inf*)

cajolery [kə'dʒəʊlərɪ] N Überredung *f*, Beschwatzen *nt* (*inf*)

cake [keɪk] **N** **a** Kuchen *m*; (= *gateau*) Torte *f*; (= *bun, individual cake*) Gebäckstück *nt*, Teilchen *nt* (*dial*); **~s and pastries** Gebäck *nt*; **a piece of ~** (*fig inf*) ein Kinderspiel *nt*, ein Klacks *m* (*inf*); **he/that takes the ~** (*inf*) das ist das Schärfste (*inf*); (*negatively also*) das schlägt dem Fass den Boden aus; **to sell like hot ~s** weggehen wie warme Semmeln (*inf*); **you can't have your ~ and eat it** (*prov*) beides auf einmal geht nicht; **he wants to have his ~ and eat it** (*prov*) er will das eine, ohne das andere zu lassen
b (*of soap*) Stück *nt*, Riegel *m*; (*of chocolate*) Tafel *f*
VT dick einschmieren; **my shoes are ~d with** *or* **in mud** meine Schuhe sind völlig verdreckt *or* dreckverkrustet
VI festtrocknen, eine Kruste bilden

cake: cake mix N Backmischung *f*; **cake mixture** N Kuchenteig *m*; **cake pan** N (*US*) Kuchenform *f*; **cake shop** N Konditorei *f*; **cake tin** N (*Brit, for baking*) Kuchenform *f*; (*for storage*) Kuchenbüchse *f*

cakey, caky ['keɪkɪ] ADJ klumpend; (= *lumpy*) klumpig

calabash ['kæləbæʃ] N Kalebasse *f*; **~ tree** Kalebassenbaum *m*

calaboose ['kæləbuːs] N (*US inf*) Kittchen *nt* (*inf*)

calamine ['kæləmaɪn] N Galmei *m*

calamine lotion N Galmeilotion *f*

calamitous [kə'læmɪtəs] ADJ katastrophal

calamity [kə'læmɪtɪ] N Katastrophe *f*

Calamity Jane N Pechmarie *f*

calcification [ˌkælsɪfɪ'keɪʃən] N Kalkablagerung *f*; (*Med*) Verkalkung *f*

calcify ['kælsɪfaɪ] **VT** Kalk *m* ablagern auf/in (+*dat*), verkalken lassen **VI** verkalken

calcium ['kælsɪəm] N Kalzium *nt*, Calcium *nt*

calcium carbonate N Kalziumkarbonat *nt*, kohlensaurer Kalk

calculable ['kælkjʊləbl] ADJ berechenbar, kalkulierbar

calculate ['kælkjʊleɪt] **VT** **a** (*mathematically, scientifically*) berechnen; *costs also* ermitteln **b** (*fig,* = *estimate critically*) kalkulieren, schätzen **c** **to be ~d to do sth** (= *be intended*) auf etw (*acc*) abzielen; (= *have the effect*) zu etw angetan sein **d** (*US, inf,* = *suppose*) schätzen, annehmen, meinen **VI** (*Math*) rechnen

▶ **calculate on** VI +*prep obj* rechnen mit; **I had calculated on finishing by this week** ich hatte damit gerechnet, diese Woche fertig zu werden

calculated ['kælkjʊleɪtɪd] ADJ (= *deliberate*) berechnet; **a ~ insult** ein bewusster Affront; **a ~ risk** ein kalkuliertes Risiko

calculating ADJ , **calculatingly** ADV ['kælkjʊleɪtɪŋ, -lɪ] berechnend

calculating machine N Rechenmaschine *f*

calculation [ˌkælkjʊ'leɪʃən] N **a** Berechnung *f*, Kalkulation *f*; (= *critical estimation*) Schätzung *f*; **to do a quick ~** die Sache schnell überschlagen; **with cold ~** eiskalt berechnend; **you're out in your ~s** du hast dich verrechnet; **by my ~s he will arrive on Sunday** nach meiner Schätzung müsste er Sonntag ankommen

calculator ['kælkjʊleɪtə] **N** **a** (= *machine*) Rechner *m* **b** (= *person*) Kalkulator(in) *m(f)*, Rechnungsbeamte(r) *m*/-beamtin *f* **c** (= *table of figures*) Rechentabelle *f*

calculus ['kælkjʊləs] **N** **a** (*Math*) Infinitesimalrechnung *f*, Differenzialrechnung *f*, Differentialrechnung *f* **b** (*Med*) Stein *m*

Calcutta [kæl'kʌtə] N Kalkutta *nt*

Caledonia [ˌkælə'dəʊnɪə] N Kaledonien *nt*

Caledonian [ˌkælə'dəʊnɪən] ADJ kaledonisch

calefactory [ˌkælə'fæktərɪ] ADJ (*form*) Wärme-

calendar ['kælɪndə] N (= *schedule*) Terminkalender *m*; (*Jur*) Prozessregister *nt*; **~ of events** Veranstaltungskalender *m*

calendar month N Kalendermonat *m*

calender ['kælɪndə] **N** Kalander *m* **VT** kalandern

calf[1] [kɑːf] N *pl* **calves** **a** Kalb *nt*; **a cow in** *or* **with ~** eine trächtige Kuh **b** (= *young elephant, seal etc*) Junge(s) *nt*, -junge(s) *nt* **c** (= *leather*) Kalb(s)leder *nt*

calf[2] N *pl* **calves** (*Anat*) Wade *f*

calf: calf love N (jugendliche) Schwärmerei *f*; **calfskin** N Kalb(s)leder *nt*

caliber N (*US*) = **calibre**

calibrate ['kælɪbreɪt] VT *gun* kalibrieren; *meter, instrument also* eichen

calibration [ˌkælɪ'breɪʃən] N **a** (*of gun*) Kalibrieren *nt*; (*of meter, instrument also*) Eichen *nt* **b** (= *mark, on gun*) Kalibrierung *f*; (*on meter, instrument also*) Eichung *f*

calibre, (*US*) **caliber** ['kælɪbə] N (*lit*) Kaliber *nt*; (*fig also*) Format *nt*; **a man of his ~** ein Mann seines Kalibers, ein Mann von seinem Format

calico ['kælɪkəʊ] N Kattun *m*

California [kælɪ'fɔːnɪə] N (*abbr* **Cal(if)**) Kalifornien *nt*

Californian [kælɪ'fɔːnɪən] **ADJ** kalifornisch **N** Kalifornier(in) *m(f)*

calipers ['kælɪpəz] PL (*US*) = **callipers**

caliph ['keɪlɪf] N Kalif *m*

calisthenics [ˌkælɪs'θenɪks] N (*US*) = **callisthenics**

calk[1] [kɔːk] **VT** mit Stollen versehen; *shoe also* mit Nägeln beschlagen **N** Stollen *m*; (*on shoe also*) Nagel *m*

calk[2] VT *drawing, design* durchpausen

calk[3] VT = **caulk**

call [kɔːl] ⊘ 27 **N** **a** (= *shout, cry, of person, bird etc*) Ruf *m*; (*of bugle*) Signal *nt*; **to give sb a ~** jdn (herbei)rufen; (= *inform sb*) jdm Bescheid sagen; (= *wake sb*) jdn wecken; **they came at my ~** sie kamen auf meinen Ruf hin, als ich rief, kamen sie; **within ~** in Rufweite *f*; **a ~ for help** (*lit, fig*) ein Hilferuf *m*
b (= *telephone call*) Gespräch *nt*, Anruf *m*; **to be on ~** telefonisch erreichbar sein; **to give sb a ~** jdn anrufen; **I'll give you a ~** ich rufe Sie an; **to take a ~** ein Gespräch entgegennehmen; **will you take the ~?** nehmen Sie das Gespräch an?
c (= *summons*) (*for flight, meal*) Aufruf *m*; (*of religion*) Berufung *f*; (*Theat: to actors*) Aufruf *m*; (*fig* = *lure*) Ruf *m*, Verlockung *f*; **to be on ~** Bereitschaftsdienst haben; **the doctor had a ~ at midnight** der Arzt wurde um Mitternacht zu einem Patienten gerufen; **that's your ~!** (*Theat*) Ihr Auftritt!; **the ~ of nature** die Stimme der Natur; **to answer a ~ of nature** (*euph*) mal kurz verschwinden gehen (*inf*); **the Call** *or* **~ came when he was 17** mit 17 Jahren spürte er die Berufung; **the ~ of duty** der Ruf der Pflicht; **he acted above and beyond the ~ of duty** er handelte über die bloße Pflichterfüllung hinaus; **to issue a ~ for unity** zur Einigkeit aufrufen
d (= *visit*) Besuch *m*; **to pay a ~ on sb** jdn besuchen, jdm einen Besuch abstatten (*form*); **I have several ~s to make** ich muss noch einige Besuche machen; **port of ~** Anlaufhafen *m*; (*fig*) Station *f*; **to pay a ~** (*euph*) mal verschwinden (*inf*)
e (= *demand, claim*) Inanspruchnahme *f*, Beanspruchung *f*; (*Comm*) Nachfrage *f* (*for nach*); **to have many ~s on one's purse/time** finanziell/zeitlich sehr in Anspruch genommen sein; **the sudden rain made for heavy ~s on the emergency services** die plötzlichen Regenfälle bedeuteten eine starke Belastung der Notdienste; **to have first ~ on sth** ein Vorrecht *nt* auf etw (*acc*) haben
f **at** *or* **on ~** (*Fin*) auf Abruf
g (= *need, occasion*) Anlass *m*, Grund *m*, Veranlassung *f*; **there is no ~ for you to worry** es besteht kein Grund zur Sorge, Sie brauchen sich (*dat*) keine Sorgen zu machen
h (*Cards*) Ansage *f*; **to make a ~ of three diamonds** drei Karo ansagen; **whose ~ is it?** wer sagt an?
i (*Tennis*) Entscheidung *f*
VT **a** (= *shout out*) rufen; **the landlord ~ed time** der Wirt rief „Feierabend"; **to ~ spades** (*Cards*) Pik reizen; **the ball was ~ed out** der Ball wurde für „aus" erklärt → **halt**
b (= *name, consider*) nennen; **to be ~ed** heißen; **what's he ~ed?** wie heißt er?; **what do you ~ your cat?** wie nennst du deine Katze?, wie heißt deine Katze?; **she ~s me lazy and selfish** sie nennt mich faul und selbstsüchtig; **to ~ sth by its proper name** etw richtig bezeichnen; **what's this ~ed in German?** wie heißt das auf Deutsch?; **let's ~ it a day** machen wir Schluss *or* Feierabend für heute; **~ it £5** sagen wir £ 5
c (= *summon*) *person, doctor* rufen; *meeting* einberufen; *elections* ausschreiben; *strike* ausrufen; (*Jur*) *witness* aufrufen; (= *subpoena*) vorladen; (= *waken*) wecken; **he was ~ed home** (*US*) *or* **to his maker** (*liter*) er ist in die Ewigkeit abberufen worden → **mind, question, bluff**[2]
d (= *telephone*) anrufen; (= *contact by radio*) rufen
e (*Fin*) *bond* aufrufen; *loan* abrufen
f (*US, Sport,* = *call off*) abbrechen
VI **a** (= *shout: person, animal*) rufen; **to ~ for help** um Hilfe rufen; **to ~ to sb** jdm zurufen
b (= *visit*) vorbeigehen/-kommen; **she ~ed to see her mother** sie machte einen Besuch bei ihrer Mutter; **the gasman ~ed to read the meter** der Gasmann kam, um die Gasuhr abzulesen
c (*Telec*) anrufen; (*by radio*) rufen; **who's ~ing, please?** wer spricht da bitte?; **London ~ing!** (*Rad*) hier ist London; **thanks for ~ing** vielen Dank für den Anruf

▶ **call (a)round** VI (*inf*) vorbeikommen

▶ **call aside** VT *sep person* beiseite rufen

▶ **call at** VI +*prep obj* (*person*) vorbeigehen bei; (*Rail*) halten in (+*dat*); (*Naut*) anlaufen; **a train for Lisbon calling at ...** ein Zug nach Lissabon über ...

▶ **call away** VT sep weg- or abrufen; **I was called away on business** ich wurde geschäftlich abgerufen; **he was called away from the meeting** er wurde aus der Sitzung gerufen

▶ **call back** ✿ 27.4, 27.6 VT sep zurückrufen VI zurückrufen

▶ **call down** VT sep **a** (= invoke) **to call down blessings on sb's head** jdn segnen **b** **to call sb down** (lit) jdn herunterrufen; (US, = reprimand) jdn ausschimpfen, jdn herunterputzen (inf)

▶ **call for** VI +prep obj **a** (= send for) person rufen; food, drink kommen lassen; (= ask for) verlangen (nach), fordern; **to call for sb's resignation** jds Rücktritt fordern or verlangen **b** (= need) courage, endurance verlangen, erfordern; **that calls for a drink!** darauf muss ich/müssen wir einen trinken!, das muss begossen werden!; **that calls for a celebration!** das muss gefeiert werden! **c** (= collect) person, goods abholen; (= come to see) fragen nach; **"to be called for"** (goods) (sent by rail) „bahnlagernd"; (sent by post) „postlagernd"; (in shop) „wird abgeholt"

▶ **call forth** VI +prep obj protests hervorrufen; abilities etc wachrufen, wecken

▶ **call in** VT sep **a** doctor zurate or zu Rate ziehen **b** (= withdraw) faulty goods etc aus dem Verkehr ziehen; currency also aufrufen (form); hire boats zurück- or aufrufen; books an- or zurückfordern VI (= visit) vorbeigehen or -schauen (at, on bei)

▶ **call off** VT sep **a** (= cancel) appointment, holiday absagen; deal rückgängig machen; strike absagen, abblasen (inf); (= end) abbrechen; engagement lösen; **let's call the whole thing off** blasen wir die ganze Sache ab (inf) **b** dog zurückrufen; **to call off the dogs** (fig) die Angriffe einstellen, die Hetzhunde zurückpfeifen (inf) VI absagen

▶ **call on** VI +prep obj **a** (= visit) besuchen **b** = call upon

▶ **call out** VI rufen, schreien VT sep **a** names aufrufen; (= announce) ansagen **b** doctor rufen; troops, fire brigade alarmieren **c** (= order to strike) zum Streik aufrufen

▶ **call out for** VI +prep obj food verlangen; help rufen um

▶ **call up** VT sep **a** (Brit Mil) reservist einberufen; reinforcements mobilisieren; **called up to go to Vietnam** nach Vietnam einberufen **b** (Sport) berufen (to in +acc) **c** (Telec) anrufen **d** (fig) (herauf)beschwören; images, thoughts also erwecken; memories also wachrufen; **to call up the Devil** den Teufel beschwören VI (Telec) anrufen

▶ **call upon** VI +prep obj **a** (= ask) **to call upon sb to do sth** jdn bitten or auffordern, etw zu tun; **I now call upon the vicar to say a few words** ich möchte nun den Herrn Pfarrer um ein paar Worte bitten **b** (= invoke) **to call upon sb's generosity** an jds Großzügigkeit (acc) appellieren; **to call upon God** Gott anrufen

callable ['kɔːləbl] ADJ (Fin) money abrufbar; security kündbar

call: call alarm N Notrufgerät nt (eines Kranken); **callback** N (Comm, = action) Rückrufaktion f; **there were 1,000 ~s** 1.000 wurden zurückbeordert; **call box** N (Brit) Telefonzelle f, öffentlicher Fernsprecher; **callboy** N (Theat) Inspizientengehilfe m (der die Schauspieler zu ihrem Auftritt ruft); **call centre** N (Brit) Telefoncenter nt, Callcenter nt

caller ['kɔːləʳ] ✿ 27.3 N **a** (= visitor) Besuch m, Besucher(in) m(f); **b** (Telec) Anrufer(in) m(f); **hold the line please ~!** bitte bleiben Sie am Apparat!

call forwarding N (Telec) Anrufweiterschaltung f

callgirl ['kɔːlgɜːl] N Callgirl nt

calligraphic [ˌkælɪˈɡræfɪk] ADJ kalligrafisch, Schönschreib-

calligraphy [kəˈlɪɡrəfɪ] N Kalligrafie f

calling ['kɔːlɪŋ] N Berufung f

calling card N Visitenkarte f; **to leave one's ~** (euph, cats or dogs) seine Visitenkarte hinterlassen (hum)

calliper brake, (US) **caliper brake** ['kælɪpə-, breɪk] N Felgenbremse f

callipers, (US) **calipers** ['kælɪpəz] PL Tastzirkel m

callisthenics, (US) **calisthenics** [ˌkælɪsˈθenɪks] N sing or pl Gymnastik f, Fitnessübungen pl, Kallisthenie f (dated)

call: call loan N (Fin) täglich kündbares Darlehen; **call money** N (Fin) Tagesgeld nt, tägliches Geld

callous ['kæləs] ADJ **a** (= cruel) gefühllos, herzlos **b** (Med) schwielig, kallös

calloused ['kæləst] ADJ schwielig, kallös

callously ['kæləslɪ] ADV herzlos

callousness ['kæləsnɪs] N Gefühllosigkeit f, Herzlosigkeit f

call-out charge, call-out fee ['kɔːlaʊt-] N Anfahrtkosten pl

callow ['kæləʊ] ADJ unreif; ideas etc unausgegoren; **a ~ youth** ein grüner Junge (inf)

call: call sign N (Rad) Sendezeichen nt; **call-up** N (Brit Mil) Einberufung f; (Sport) Berufung f (to in +acc); **call-up papers** PL (Brit Mil) Einberufungsbescheid m

callus ['kæləs] N **a** (Med) Schwiele f; (of bone) Kallus m, Knochenschwiele f; (Bot) Wundholz nt, Kallus m

callused ['kæləst] ADJ = calloused

calm [kɑːm] ADJ (+er) ruhig; weather also windstill; **keep ~!** bleib ruhig!; **the weather grew ~ again after the storm** nach dem Sturm beruhigte sich das Wetter wieder; **(cool,) ~ and collected** ruhig und gelassen; **~er waters** (lit, fig) ruhigere Gewässer pl N **a** Ruhe f, Stille f; (at sea) Flaute f; (of wind) Windstille f; **a dead ~** absolute Stille, Totenstille f; **the ~ before the storm** (lit, fig) die Ruhe vor dem Sturm **b** (= composure) Ruhe, Gelassenheit f VT beruhigen; pain, itch lindern; protests mildern; **to ~ sb's fears** jds Ängste abbauen, jdn beruhigen VI (sea) sich beruhigen; (wind) sich legen

▶ **calm down** VT sep beruhigen, beschwichtigen VI sich beruhigen; (wind) abflauen; **calm down!** beruhigen Sie sich!

calming ['kɑːmɪŋ] ADJ beruhigend

calmly ['kɑːmlɪ] ADV speak, act ruhig, gelassen; **he spoke ~** er redete mit ruhiger Stimme; **she ~ told me that she'd crashed the car** sie erzählte mir seelenruhig, dass sie das Auto kaputtgefahren hatte

calmness ['kɑːmnɪs] N (of person) Ruhe f, Gelassenheit f; (of wind, sea) Stille f

Calor Gas® ['kæləɡæs] N Butangas nt

caloric ['kælərɪk] ADJ kalorisch, Wärme-

calorie ['kælərɪ] N Kalorie f; **low on ~s** kalorienarm

calorie in cpds Kalorien-, kalorien-; **calorie-conscious** ADJ kalorienbewusst

calorific [ˌkæləˈrɪfɪk] ADJ wärmeerzeugend

calorific value N Heizwert m

calumniate [kəˈlʌmnɪeɪt] VT (liter) schmähen (geh), verunglimpfen

calumny ['kæləmnɪ] N (liter) Schmähung f (geh), Verunglimpfung f

Calvary ['kælvərɪ] N **a** Golgatha nt, Kalvarienberg m **b** **calvary** Bildstock m, Marterl nt (S Ger, Aus)

calve [kɑːv] VI kalben

calves [kɑːvz] pl of **calf**[1] of **calf**[2]

Calvin ['kælvɪn] N Calvin m

Calvinism ['kælvɪnɪzəm] N Kalvinismus m

Calvinist ['kælvɪnɪst] N Kalvinist(in) m(f) ADJ kalvinistisch

Calvinistic [ˌkælvɪˈnɪstɪk] ADJ kalvinistisch

calypso [kəˈlɪpsəʊ] N Calypso m

calyx ['keɪlɪks] N pl **calyces** or **-es** [ˈkeɪlɪsiːz, ˈkeɪlɪksəz] Blütenkelch m

CAM [kæm] abbr of **computer-aided manufacture** CAM

cam[1] [kæm] N Nocken m

cam[2] (inf) abbr of **camera**[1]

camaraderie [ˌkæməˈrɑːdərɪ] N Kameradschaft f

camber ['kæmbə] N (of ship, aircraft wing) Wölbung f; (of road also) Überhöhung f; (of wheels) Radsturz m VT road, deck wölben; **a ~ed wheel** ein Rad nt mit Sturz

Cambodia [kæmˈbəʊdɪə] N Kambodscha nt

Cambodian [kæmˈbəʊdɪən] ADJ kambodschanisch N **a** Kambodschaner(in) m(f) **b** (Ling) Kambodschanisch nt

cambric ['keɪmbrɪk] N (Tex) Kambrik m, Cambrai m, Kammertuch nt

Cambridge ['keɪmbrɪdʒ] N Cambridge nt

Cambs [kæmz] abbr of **Cambridgeshire**

camcorder ['kæmkɔːdə] N Camcorder m, Kamerarekorder m

came [keɪm] pret of **come**

camel ['kæməl] N Kamel m ATTR (= colour) coat kamelhaarfarben

camel driver N Kameltreiber m

camel hair, (US) **camel's hair** N Kamelhaar nt

camelhair [ˈkæməlhɛə] ADJ attr Kamelhaar-; **~ coat** Kamelhaarmantel m

camellia [kəˈmiːlɪə] N Kamelie f

cameo ['kæmɪəʊ] N **a** (= jewellery) Kamee f **b** (Liter) Miniatur f **c** (also **cameo part**) Miniaturrolle f

camera[1] ['kæmərə] N Kamera f; (for stills also) Fotoapparat m

camera[2] [ˈkæmərə] in (Jur) **in ~** unter Ausschluss der Öffentlichkeit; (fig) hinter verschlossenen Türen, in geschlossener Gesellschaft

camera: camera crane N Kamerakran m; **camera crew** N Kamerateam nt; **cameraman** N Kameramann m; **camera obscura** [ˈkæmərəɒbˈskjʊərə] N (Opt) Camera obscura f, Lochkamera f; **camera operator** N Kameramann m/-frau f; **camera-ready copy** N Druckvorlage f; **camera-shy** ADJ kamerascheu; **camerawoman** N Kamerafrau f; **camerawork** N Kameraführung f

Cameroons [ˌkæməˈruːnz] PL **the ~** Kamerun nt

camiknickers ['kæmɪˌnɪkəz] PL Spitzenhemdhöschen nt

camisole ['kæmɪsəʊl] N Mieder nt, Leibchen nt

camomile ['kæməʊmaɪl] N Kamille f; **~ tea** Kamillentee m

camouflage ['kæməflɑːʒ] N (Mil) Tarnung f; (fig) Tarnung f, Camouflage f (geh); **for ~** zur Tarnung; **~ nets** Tarnnetze pl VT (Mil, fig) tarnen; **she smiled but it didn't ~ her despair** ihr Lächeln konnte nicht über ihre Verzweiflung hinwegtäuschen

camouflage in cpds Tarn-

camp[1] [kæmp] N **a** Lager nt; (Mil) (Feld)lager nt; **to be in ~** im Lager leben or sein; (Mil) im Felde leben; **to pitch ~** Zelte or ein Lager aufschlagen; **to strike** or **break ~** die Zelte abbauen, das Lager or die Zelte abbrechen **b** (fig) Lager nt; **to have a foot in both ~s** mit beiden Seiten zu tun haben; **the socialist ~** das sozialistische Lager VI zelten, kampieren; **to go ~ing** zelten (gehen)

▶ **camp out** VI zelten

camp[2] ADJ (= theatrical, stagey) übertrieben, extrem (inf); performance manieriert, geschmäcklerisch; person's appearance aufgedonnert, aufgemotzt (inf); (= effeminate) tuntenhaft (inf); (= homosexual) schwul (inf); **to be as ~ as a row of tents** (inf) mächtig schwul sein (inf)

▶ **camp up** VT sep **to camp sth up** (= vamp up) etw aufmöbeln (inf), etw aufmotzen (inf); (= overact) etw überziehen, in or bei etw zu dick auftragen; **to camp it up** (= overact, exaggerate) es zu weit treiben; (Theat) es überziehen, zu dick auftragen; (= act homosexually) sich tuntenhaft (inf) or wie eine Schwuchtel (inf) benehmen

campaign [kæm'peɪn] **[N] [a]** (Mil) Feldzug m, Kampagne f (old); **Hitler's Russian ~** Hitlers Russlandfeldzug m **[b]** (fig) Kampagne f, Aktion f; (= election campaign) Feldzug m, Kampagne f; **~ headquarters** (Pol) Wahlkampfzentrale f **[VI] [a]** kämpfen, Krieg führen; **~ing in Ruritania** im Einsatz in Ruritanien **[b]** (fig) (for für) (against gegen) sich einsetzen, sich stark machen (inf), agitieren; (outdoors also) auf die Straße gehen; (politician, candidate) im Wahlkampf stehen, den Wahlkampf führen; (supporters) Wahlwerbung treiben; **we were out on the streets ~ing** wir waren auf der Straße im Einsatz

campaigner [kæm'peɪnə] N **[a]** (Mil) Krieger m; **old ~** alter Kämpe **[b]** (fig, for sth) Befürworter(in) m(f) (for +gen); (against sth) Gegner(in) m(f) (against +gen); (for politician) Wahlwerber(in) m(f)

campanology [ˌkæmpə'nɒlədʒɪ] N Kunst f des Glockenspiels

camp: camp bed N (Brit) Campingliege f; **camp chair** N Campingstuhl m

camper ['kæmpə] N **[a]** Camper(in) m(f) **[b]** (= vehicle: also **camper van**) Wohnmobil nt

camp: campfire N Lagerfeuer nt; **camp follower** N Marketender(in) m(f) **[b]** (fig) Anhänger(in) m(f), Mitläufer(in) m(f) (pej); **campground** N (US) Campingplatz m, Zeltplatz m

camphor ['kæmfə] N Kampfer m

camphorated ['kæmfəreɪtɪd] ADJ mit Kampfer präpariert

camphorated oil N Kampferöl nt

camping ['kæmpɪŋ] N Zelten nt, Camping nt; **no ~** Zelten verboten!

camping in cpds Camping-; **camping gas** N (US) Campinggas nt; **camping ground** N Zeltplatz m; **camping site** N Campingplatz m, Zeltplatz m; **camping van** N Wohnmobil nt

camp: camp meeting N (US, Rel) Campmeeting nt; **camp site** N = **camping site**; **camp stool** N Campinghocker m

campus ['kæmpəs] N Campus m, Universitätsgelände nt

campy ['kæmpɪ] ADJ (inf) = **camp²**

camshaft ['kæmʃɑːft] N Nockenwelle f

can¹ [kæn] **⚙** 3.3, 6.2, 9.2, 9.3, 9.4, 10.4, 12.1, 12.3, 15.4, 16.3, 16.4 pret **could** MODAL AUX VB (defective parts supplied by to be able to) **[a]** (= be able to) können; **~ you come tomorrow?** kannst du morgen kommen?; **I ~'t** or **~not go to the theatre tomorrow** ich kann morgen nicht ins Theater (gehen); **I'll do it if I ~** wenn ich kann(, tue ich es); **he'll help you all he ~** er wird sein Möglichstes tun, er wird tun, was in seinen Kräften steht; **as soon as it ~ be arranged** sobald es sich machen lässt; **could you tell me ...** können or könnten Sie mir sagen, ...; **~ you speak German?** können or sprechen Sie Deutsch?; **we ~ but hope that...**, **we ~ only hope that ...** wir können nur hoffen, dass ...; **they could not (help) but condemn it** sie konnten nicht anders, als das zu verurteilen **[b]** (= may) dürfen, können; **~ I come too?** kann ich mitkommen?; **~** or **could I take some more?** darf or kann ich mir noch etwas or noch einmal nehmen?; **you ~ go now** Sie können jetzt gehen; **~ I help you?** darf or kann ich Ihnen helfen?; **could I possibly go with you?** könnte or dürfte ich vielleicht mitkommen?; **I'd like to go, ~ I? – no, you ~'t** ich würde gerne gehen, darf ich? – nein, du darfst nicht; **I use your car? – no, you ~'t** kann or darf ich dein Auto nehmen? – nein **[c]** (expressing surprise etc) können; **how ~/could you say such a thing!** wie können/konnten Sie nur or bloß so etwas sagen!; **where ~ it be?** wo kann das bloß sein?; **where ~ they have gone?** wo können sie denn nur hingegangen sein?; **you ~'t be serious** das kann doch wohl nicht dein Ernst sein **[d]** (expressing possibility) können; **it could be**

that he's got lost vielleicht hat er sich verlaufen, (es ist) möglich, dass er sich verlaufen hat; **could he have got lost?** ob er sich wohl or vielleicht verlaufen hat?; **he could be on the next train** er könnte im nächsten Zug sein; **and it could have been such a good party!** und es hätte so eine gute Party sein können!; **to think he could have become a doctor** wenn man bedenkt, dass er hätte Arzt werden können **[e]** (with verbs of perception) können; **~ you hear me?** hören Sie mich?, können Sie mich hören? **[f]** (= be capable of occasionally) können; **she ~ be very nice when she wants to** wenn sie will, kann sie sehr nett sein **[g]** (indicating suggestion) können; **you could try telephoning him** Sie könnten ihn ja mal anrufen; **you could have been a little more polite** Sie hätten etwas höflicher sein können; **you could have told me** das hätten Sie mir auch sagen können **[h]** (= feel inclined to) können; **I could have murdered her** ich hätte sie umbringen können **[i]** **we could do with some new furniture** wir könnten neue Möbel gebrauchen; **I could do with a drink now** ich könnte jetzt etwas zu trinken vertragen; **this room could do with a coat of paint** das Zimmer könnte mal wieder gestrichen werden; **he looks as though he could do with a wash/haircut** ich glaube, er müsste sich mal waschen/er müsste sich (dat) mal wieder die Haare schneiden lassen

can² **[N] [a]** (= container) Kanister m; (= milk can) Kanne f; (esp US: = garbage can) (Müll)eimer m; **in the ~** (Film) im Kasten; **the contract's in the ~** (inf) wir haben den Vertrag in der Tasche (inf); **to carry the ~** (Brit fig inf) die Sache ausbaden (inf) **[b]** (= tin) Dose f; (of food also) Büchse f; **a ~ of beer** eine Dose Bier; **a beer ~** eine Bierdose; **a ~ of paint** eine Dose Farbe; (with handle) ein Eimer m Farbe → **worm** N **a [c]** (US, inf, = prison) Knast m (inf) **[d]** (US, inf, = lavatory) Klo nt (inf), Scheißhaus nt (sl) **[VT] [a]** foodstuffs einmachen, eindosen → **canned [b]** (inf) **~ it!** Klappe! (inf)

can in cpds Büchsen-, Dosen-

Canaan ['keɪnən] N Kanaan nt

Canaanite ['keɪnənaɪt] N Kanaaniter(in) m(f)

Canada ['kænədə] N Kanada nt

Canadian [kə'neɪdɪən] **ADJ** kanadisch **[N]** Kanadier(in) m(f)

Canadian elk N Wapiti(hirsch) m

canal [kə'næl] N **[a]** Kanal m; **~ barge** Schleppkahn m **[b]** (Anat) Gang m, Kanal m

canalization [ˌkænəlaɪ'zeɪʃən] N (lit) Kanalisation f; (fig) Kanalisierung f

canalize ['kænəlaɪz] VT (lit, fig) kanalisieren

canapé ['kænəpeɪ] N Cocktail- or Appetithappen m

canard [kæ'nɑːd] N (Zeitungs)ente f

Canaries [kə'nɛərɪz] PL = **Canary Isles**

canary [kə'nɛərɪ] N **[a]** Kanarienvogel m **[b]** (old, = wine) Kanarienwein m (old) **[c]** (dated US, sl, = female singer) Sängerin f **ATTR** (colour: also **canary yellow**) kanariengelb

Canary Isles [kə'nɛərɪ'aɪlz] PL Kanarische Inseln pl

canasta [kə'næstə] N Canasta nt

can bank N Altblech- or Dosencontainer m

cancan ['kænkæn] N Cancan m

cancel ['kænsəl] **⚙** 20.5, 21.4 **VT [a]** (= call off) absagen; (officially) stornieren; plans aufgeben, fallen lassen; train, bus streichen; **the last train has been ~led** (Brit) or **~ed** (US) der letzte Zug fällt aus **[b]** (= revoke, annul) rückgängig machen; command, invitation also zurücknehmen; contract also (auf)lösen; debt streichen; order for goods stornieren; magazine subscription kündigen; decree aufheben; (Aut) indicator ausschalten; **no, ~ that** (in dictation etc) nein, streichen Sie das **[c]** (= frank) stamp, ticket, cheque entwerten, ungültig machen

[d] (Math) kürzen; **this X ~s that one** dieses X hebt das X auf **[VI]** (= revoke commercial order, contract) stornieren; (= call off appointment, holiday) absagen

▶ **cancel out** **[VT]** sep (Math) aufheben; (fig) zunichte machen; **to cancel each other out** (Math) sich aufheben, sich kürzen lassen; (fig) einander aufheben, sich gegenseitig aufheben **[VI]** (Math) sich aufheben, sich wegkürzen lassen (inf)

cancellation [ˌkænsə'leɪʃən] N **[a]** (= calling off) Absage f; (official) Stornierung f; (of plans) Aufgabe f; (of train, bus) Streichung f, Ausfall m; **your appointment may be brought forward in the event of a ~** wir werden möglicherweise im Falle einer Absage auf Sie zurückkommen **[b]** (= annulment) Rückgängigmachung f; (of command, invitation also) Zurücknahme f; (of contract also) Auflösung f; (of debt) Streichung f; (of order for goods) Stornierung f; (of magazine subscription) Kündigung f; (of decree) Aufhebung f **[c]** (= franking: of stamp, ticket, cheque) Entwertung f **[d]** (Math) Kürzung f

cancellation clause N Rücktrittsklausel f

cancer ['kænsə] N (Med) Krebs m; (fig) Krebsgeschwür nt; **~ of the throat** Kehlkopfkrebs m; **Cancer** (Astrol) Krebs m; **he's (a) Cancer** er ist Krebs

cancerous ['kænsərəs] ADJ krebsartig; **~ growth** (lit, fig) krebsartige Wucherung

cancer: cancer relief N Krebshilfe f; **cancer research** N Krebsforschung f; **cancer screening** N Krebsvorsorgeuntersuchung f; **cancer stick** N (inf, = cigarette) Sargnagel m (inf)

candelabra [ˌkændɪ'lɑːbrə] N Kandelaber m, Leuchter m

candid ['kændɪd] ADJ offen, ehrlich; **he was quite ~ about it** er war ganz offen, er sprach ganz offen darüber; **my ~ opinion is that he ...** ich bin offen gesagt der Meinung, dass er ...

candida ['kændɪdə] N (Med) Candidose f

candidacy ['kændɪdəsɪ] N Kandidatur f

candidate ['kændɪdeɪt] N (Pol) Kandidat(in) m(f); (= exam candidate also) Prüfling m; **to stand as (a) ~** kandidieren; **they are ~s for relegation** (Sport) sie sind Abstiegskandidaten; **the obese are prime ~s for heart disease** Fettleibige stehen auf der Liste der Herzinfarktkandidaten ganz oben

candidature ['kændɪdətʃə] N (Brit) = **candidacy**

candidly ['kændɪdlɪ] ADV offen, ehrlich; **quite ~, ...** offen gestanden, ...; **to speak ~** offen or ehrlich sein

candidness ['kændɪdnɪs] N Offenheit f, Ehrlichkeit f

candied ['kændɪd] ADJ (Cook) kandiert, gezuckert; **~ peel** (of lemon) Zitronat nt; (of orange) Orangeat nt

candle ['kændl] N Kerze f; **to burn the ~ at both ends** mit seinen Kräften Raubbau treiben; **he can't hold a ~ to his brother** er kann seinem Bruder nicht das Wasser reichen; **the game is not worth the ~** es ist nicht der Mühe wert

candle in cpds Kerzen-; **candle end** N Kerzenstummel m; **candle grease** N Kerzenwachs nt; **candlelight** N Kerzenlicht nt, Kerzenschein m; **by ~** im Kerzenschein, bei Kerzenlicht; **a ~ dinner** ein Candlelight-Dinner nt, ein Essen nt bei Kerzenlicht

Candlemas ['kændlməs] N Mariä Lichtmess nt

candle: candlepower N (old Elec) Lichtstärke f; **candlestick** N Kerzenhalter m; **candlewick** **[N]** Kerzendocht m **[b]** (Tex) Frottierplüschmuster nt **ATTR** bedspread im Frottierplüschmuster

candour, (US) **candor** ['kændə] N Offenheit f, Ehrlichkeit f

candy ['kændɪ] **[N]** (US, = sweet) Bonbon m or nt; (= sweets) Süßigkeiten pl, Bonbons pl; (= bar of chocolate) (Tafel f) Schokolade f; (= individual chocolate) Praline f; **it's like taking ~ from a ba-**

by das ist kinderleicht **VT** *sugar* kristallisieren lassen; *fruit etc* kandieren

candy: candy apple N (*US*) kandierter Apfel; **candy-ass** N (*US sl*) Weichei *nt* (*pej inf*), Memme *f* (*pej*), Waschlappen *m* (*pej inf*); **candy bar** N (*US*) Schokoladenriegel *m*, Schokoriegel *m*; **candyfloss** N (*Brit*) Zuckerwatte *f*; **candy store** N (*US*) Süßwarenhandlung *f*, Bonbonladen *m* (*inf*); **candy-striped** ADJ bunt gestreift (*auf weißem Hintergrund*)

cane [keɪn] **N** **a** (= *stem of bamboo, sugar etc*) Rohr *nt*; (*of raspberry*) Zweig *m*; (*for supporting plants*) Stock *m*; **~ chair** Rohrstuhl *m* **b** (= *walking stick*) (Spazier)stock *m*; (= *instrument of punishment*) (Rohr)stock *m*; **to use the ~** den Rohrstock benutzen; **to get the ~** Prügel bekommen; (*on hand*) eine auf die Finger bekommen, eine Tatze bekommen (*S Ger*) **VT** *schoolboy* mit dem Stock schlagen

cane *in cpds* Rohr-; **canebrake** N (*US*) Röhricht *nt*, Rohrdickicht *nt*; **cane sugar** N Rohrzucker *m*

canicular: canicular days [kəˈnɪkjʊləˌdeɪz] PL Hundstage *pl*; **canicular heat** [kəˌnɪkjʊləˈhiːt] N Hundstagshitze *f*

canine [ˈkeɪnaɪn] **N** **a** (= *animal*) Hund *m* **b** (*also* **canine tooth**) Eckzahn *m* ADJ Hunde-

caning [ˈkeɪnɪŋ] N (= *beating with cane*) Schläge *pl* mit dem Stock, Prügeln *nt* (*inf*); **to give sb a ~** jdm eine Tracht Prügel verabreichen; **to get a ~** (*Sport*) haushoch geschlagen werden; (*new play etc*) verrissen werden

canister [ˈkænɪstə'] N Behälter *m*; (*for tea, coffee etc also*) Dose *f*; **~ shot** (*Mil*) Kartätsche *f*

canker [ˈkæŋkə'] N (*Med*) Mund- or Lippengeschwür *nt*; (*Vet*) Hufkrebs *m*, Strahlfäule *f*; (*Bot*) Brand *m*; (*fig*) (Krebs)geschwür *nt*

cankerous [ˈkæŋkərəs] ADJ (*Med*) entzündet; (*Vet, Bot*) brandig; (*fig*) krebsartig

cannabis [ˈkænəbɪs] N Cannabis *m*

cannabis resin N Cannabisharz *nt*

canned [kænd] ADJ **a** (*US*) Dosen-, in Dosen; **~ beer** Dosenbier *nt*; **~ goods** Konserven *pl* **b** (*inf*) **~ music** Musikberieselung *f* (*inf*); **~ laughter/applause** Gelächter *nt*/Applaus *m* vom Band; **~ heat** Brennspiritus *m* **c** (*inf, = drunk*) blau (*inf*), voll (*sl*)

cannery [ˈkænəri] N (*US*) Konservenfabrik *f*

cannibal [ˈkænɪbəl] **N** (= *person*) Kannibale *m*, Kannibalin *f*, Menschenfresser(in) *m(f)*; **these insects are ~s** diese Insekten fressen sich gegenseitig **ADJ** kannibalisch; *animals* sich gegenseitig auffressend

cannibalism [ˈkænɪbəlɪzəm] N (*of people*) Kannibalismus *m*, Menschenfresserei *f*

cannibalistic [ˌkænɪbəˈlɪstɪk] ADJ kannibalisch; *people also* Menschen fressend

cannibalize [ˈkænɪbəlaɪz] VT *old car etc* ausschlachten

cannily [ˈkænɪli] ADV clever, raffiniert; (*involving money also*) geschäftstüchtig; (*with plans also*) gewieft

canning [ˈkænɪŋ] N Konservenabfüllung *f*; (= *preserving*) Konservierung *f*; **the ~ of meat** die Herstellung von Fleischkonserven

cannon [ˈkænən] **N** **a** (*Mil*) Kanone *f* **b** (*Brit, Billiards*) Karambolage *f* **VI** (*Brit, Billiards*) karambolieren

▶ **cannon into** VI +*prep obj* zusammenprallen mit

cannonade [ˌkænəˈneɪd] N Kanonade *f*

cannon: cannonball N Kanonenkugel *f*; **cannon fodder** N Kanonenfutter *nt*

cannot [ˈkænɒt] **☉** 5.3, 10.4, 12.3, 16.3 NEG of **can**¹

cannula [ˈkænjʊlə] N *pl* **cannulae, cannuli** Kanüle *f*

canny [ˈkænɪ] ADJ (+*er*) (= *cautious*) vorsichtig; (= *shrewd also*) schlau, clever; (= *careful with money also*) sparsam

canoe [kəˈnuː] **N** Kanu *nt*; **to paddle one's own ~** (*fig*) auf eigenen Füßen or Beinen stehen **VI** Kanu fahren, paddeln

canoeing [kəˈnuːɪŋ] N Kanusport *m*, Kanufahren *nt*

canoeist [kəˈnuːɪst] N Kanufahrer(in) *m(f)*, Kanute *m*, Kanutin *f*

canon¹ [ˈkænən] N (*all senses*) Kanon *m*

canon² N (= *priest*) Kanoniker *m*, Kanonikus *m*

cañon N (*US*) = **canyon**

canonical [kəˈnɒnɪkəl] ADJ **a** (*Eccl*) kanonisch; **~ dress** Priestergewand *nt* **b** (*fig, = accepted*) anerkannt, rechtmäßig

canonization [ˌkænənaɪˈzeɪʃən] N (*Eccl*) Heiligsprechung *f*, Kanonisation *f*, Kanonisierung *f*

canonize [ˈkænənaɪz] VT (*Eccl*) heilig sprechen, kanonisieren

canon law N (*Eccl*) Kanon *m*, kanonisches Recht

canoodle [kəˈnuːdl] VI (*Brit inf*) rumschmusen (*inf*)

can-opener N Dosen- or Büchsenöffner *m*

canopy [ˈkænəpi] **N** **a** (= *awning*) Markise *f*, Überdachung *f*; (*over entrance*) Vordach *nt*, Pergola *f*; (*of bed, throne*) Baldachin *m*; (*of aircraft*) Kanzeldach *nt*; (*of parachute*) Fallschirmkappe *f* **b** (*fig liter, of sky, foliage*) Baldachin *m* (*liter*); **the ~ of the heavens** das Himmelszelt (*liter*)

canst [kænst] (*obs*) *2nd pers sing of* **can**¹

cant¹ [kænt] **N** **a** (= *hypocrisy*) Heuchelei *f*, scheinheiliges or leeres Gerede **b** (= *jargon*) Jargon *m*, Kauderwelsch *nt*; (*of thieves, gipsies*) Rotwelsch *nt*

cant² **N** (= *tilt*) Schräge *f* **VT** schräg stellen, kanten; **the wind ~ed the boat** der Wind brachte das Boot zum Kippen **VI** schräg or schief sein, sich neigen; (*boat*) kippen

can't [kɑːnt] *contr of* **can not**

Cantab [ˈkæntæb] *abbr of* **Cantabrigiensis** von der Universität Cambridge

cantaloup(e) [ˈkæntəluːp] N Honigmelone *f*, Buttermelone *f*

cantankerous [kænˈtæŋkərəs] ADJ mürrisch, knurrig

cantata [kænˈtɑːtə] N Kantate *f*

canteen [kænˈtiːn] **N** **a** (= *restaurant*) Kantine *f*; (*in university*) Mensa *f* **b** (*Mil, = flask*) Feldflasche *f*; (= *mess tin*) Kochgeschirr *nt* **c** (*Brit: of cutlery*) Besteckkasten *m*

canter [ˈkæntə'] **N** Handgalopp *m*, Kanter *m*; **to go for a ~** einen Ausritt machen **VI** langsam galoppieren

canticle [ˈkæntɪkl] N (*Eccl*) Lobgesang *m*; (= *song*) Volksweise *f*; **Canticles** Hohelied *nt*, Hohes Lied

cantilever [ˈkæntɪliːvə'] N Ausleger *m*

cantilever *in cpds* Ausleger-; **cantilever bridge** N Auslegerbrücke *f*; **cantilever roof** N (*Archit*) Krag- or Auslegerdach *nt*

canto [ˈkæntəʊ] N (*Liter*) Canto *m*, Gesang *m*

canton [ˈkæntɒn] N Kanton *m*

Cantonese [ˌkæntəˈniːz] **ADJ** kantonesisch **N** **a** Kantonese *m*, Kantonesin *f* **b** (*Ling*) Kantonesisch *nt*

cantonment [kənˈtuːnmənt] N Truppenunterkunft *f*, Kantonnement *nt* (*old*)

cantor [ˈkæntɔː'] N Kantor *m*

Canuck [kəˈnʌk] N (*US, pej inf*) (Franko)kanadier(in) *m(f)*

Canute [kəˈnjuːt] N Knut *m*

canvas [ˈkænvəs] N Leinwand *f*, Segeltuch *nt*; (= *set of sails*) Segel *pl*; (*for tent*) Zeltbahn *f*; (*Art, = material*) Leinwand *f*; (= *painting*) Gemälde *nt*; **under ~** (= *in a tent*) im Zelt; (*Naut*) mit gehisstem Segel; **~ chair** Liegestuhl *m*, Klappstuhl *m*; **~ shoes** Segeltuchschuhe *pl*

canvass [ˈkænvəs] **VT** **a** (*Pol*) *district* Wahlwerbung machen in (+*dat*); *person* für seine Partei zu gewinnen suchen; **to ~ the local electorate** in seinem Wahlkreis Stimmen werben or auf

Stimmenfang gehen (*inf*) **b** *customers, citizens etc* ansprechen, werben; *issue* unter die Leute bringen; *district* bereisen; (= *sound out*) *opinions* erforschen **VI** **a** (*Pol*) um Stimmen werben (*for sb* für jdn) **b** (*Comm*) werben, eine Werbekampagne durchführen, Klinken putzen (*inf*) **N** (*Pol, Comm*) Aktion *f*, Kampagne *f*

canvasser [ˈkænvəsə'] N **a** (*Pol*) Wahlhelfer(in) *m(f)* **b** (*Comm*) Vertreter(in) *m(f)*, Klinkenputzer(in) *m(f)* (*inf*)

canvassing [ˈkænvəsɪŋ] N **a** (*Pol*) Durchführung *f* des Wahlkampfs, Wahlwerbung *f* **b** (*Comm*) Von-Haus-zu-Haus-Gehen *nt*, Klinkenputzen *nt* (*inf*); (= *sounding-out: of opinions*) Meinungsforschung *f*; **~ by applicants is not allowed** es ist den Bewerbern nicht gestattet, mit Firmenangehörigen Kontakt aufzunehmen, um den Bewerbungsvorgang zu beeinflussen

canyon, (*US*) **cañon** [ˈkænjən] N Cañon *m*

cap¹ [kæp] **N** **a** (= *hat*) Mütze *f*; (= *soldier's cap also*) Käppi *nt*; (= *nurse's cap*) Haube *f*; (*Jur, Univ*) Barett *nt*; (*for swimming*) Bademütze or -kappe *f*; (*of jester*) Kappe *f*; (*of cardinal*) Hut *m*; (= *skullcap*) Käppchen *nt*; **~ in hand** kleinlaut; **if the ~ fits(, wear it)** (*Brit prov*) wem die Jacke passt(, der soll sie sich (*dat*) anziehen); **to set one's ~ at sb** (*dated*) es auf jdn abgesehen haben; **~ and bells** Schellenkappe *f*; **in ~ and gown** mit Doktorhut und Talar

b (*Brit Sport*) **he has won 50 ~s for Scotland** er ist 50 Mal mit der schottischen Mannschaft angetreten; **Owen is the team's only new ~** Owen ist der einzige Neuzugang in der Mannschaft

c (= *lid, cover, of bottle*) Verschluss *m*, Deckel *m*; (*of fountain pen*) (Verschluss)kappe *f*; (*of valve*) Kappe *f*; (*Mil: of shell, fuse*) Kapsel *f*; (*Aut, = petrol cap, radiator cap*) Verschluss *m*

d (= *contraceptive*) Pessar *nt*

e (= *explosive*) Platzpatrone *f*; (*for toy gun*) Zündplättchen *nt*

f (*of mushroom*) Hut *m*

g (*of shoe*) Kappe *f*

VT **a** (= *put cap on*) *bottle etc* verschließen, zumachen; (*fig, = cover top of*) *peaks* bedecken; **to have one's teeth ~ped** sich (*dat*) die Zähne überkronen lassen

b (*Sport*) **he was ~ped four times for England** er wurde viermal für die englische Nationalmannschaft aufgestellt

c (= *do or say better*) überbieten; **and then to ~ it all ...** und, um dem Ganzen die Krone aufzusetzen ...

d (*Scot, Univ*) einen akademischen Grad verleihen (+*dat*)

e (*in spending etc*) **they ~ped spending at £50,000** die Ausgaben wurden bei £ 50.000 gedeckelt; **the council was ~ped** (*Brit*) dem Stadtrat wurde von der Regierung ein Höchstsatz für die Kommunalsteuer *etc* auferlegt; **~ped rate mortgage** (*Brit*) Hypothek *f* mit Zinsobergrenze

cap² **N** (*Typ inf*) großer Buchstabe; **in ~s** in Großbuchstaben → *also* **capital N b**

CAP *abbr of* **Common Agricultural Policy** *gemeinsame Agrarpolitik der EG*, GAP *f*

capability [ˌkeɪpəˈbɪlɪti] N **a** (= *potential ability*) Fähigkeit *f*; (*no pl: = capableness also*) Kompetenz *f*; **sth is within sb's capabilities** jd ist zu etw fähig; **sth is beyond sb's capabilities** etw übersteigt jds Fähigkeiten **b** (*Mil*) Potenzial *nt*, Potential *nt*

capable [ˈkeɪpəbl] ADJ **a** (= *skilful, competent*) fähig, kompetent; *mother* gut

b **to be ~ of doing sth** etw tun können; (*person: = have physical, mental ability also*) fähig sein, etw zu tun; **to be ~ of sth** etw können, zu etw fähig sein; **it's ~ of exploding any minute** es kann jede Minute explodieren; **it's ~ of speeds of up to ...** es erreicht Geschwindigkeiten bis zu ...; **he's ~ of better** er ist zu Besserem fähig; **the poem is ~ of several interpretations** das Gedicht lässt mehrere Interpretationsmöglichkeiten zu; **~ of improvement** verbesserungsfähig; **he's quite ~ of changing his mind at the**

last minute er bringt es fertig und ändert seine Meinung in der letzten Minute; **thank you but I'm quite ~ of doing that myself** danke, ich kann das durchaus allein

capably ['keɪpəblɪ] ADV kompetent, geschickt

capacious [kə'peɪʃəs] ADJ geräumig; *dress* weit

capacitance [kə'pæsɪtəns] N (*Elec*) Speicherkapazität *f*

capacitor [kə'pæsɪtə] N Kondensator *m*

capacity [kə'pæsɪtɪ] ✪ 19.1 N **a** (= *cubic content etc*) Fassungsvermögen *nt*, (Raum)inhalt *m*; (= *maximum output*) Kapazität *f*; (= *maximum weight*) Höchstlast *f*; (*Aut*, = *engine capacity*) Hubraum *m*; **filled to ~** randvoll; (*hall*) bis auf den letzten Platz besetzt; **seating ~ of 400** 400 Sitzplätze; **to work to ~** voll ausgelastet sein; **working at full ~** voll ausgelastet; **the Stones played to ~ audiences** die Stones spielten vor ausverkauften Sälen **b** (= *ability*) Fähigkeit *f*; **his ~ for learning** seine Lern- or Aufnahmefähigkeit; **he has a great ~ for work** er kann sehr gut arbeiten; **this work is within/beyond his ~** er ist zu dieser Arbeit fähig/nicht fähig **c** (= *role, position*) Eigenschaft *f*, Funktion *f*; **in my ~ as a doctor** (in meiner Eigenschaft) als Arzt; **speaking in his official ~ as mayor, he said ...** er sagte in seiner Eigenschaft als Bürgermeister ...; **in a personal ~** als Privatperson; **they refused to employ him in any ~ whatsoever** sie lehnten es ab, ihn in irgendeiner Form zu beschäftigen **d** (= *legal power*) Befugnis *f*

caparison [kə'pærɪsn] (*liter*) N Schabracke *f* (*old*) VT mit einer Schabracke bedecken (*old*)

cape¹ [keɪp] N Cape *nt*, Umhang *m*, Pelerine *f* (*old*)

cape² N (*Geog*) Kap *nt*

Cape: Cape Canaveral N Kap Canaveral *nt*; **Cape Cod** N Cape Cod *nt*; **Cape Coloured** N Farbige(r) *mf*, Gemischtrassige(r) *mf*; **Cape Horn** N Kap *nt* Hoorn; **Cape of Good Hope** N Kap *nt* der guten Hoffnung

caper¹ ['keɪpə] VI herumtollen N **a** (= *skip*) Luft- or Freudensprung *m* **b** (= *prank*) Eskapade *f*, Kapriole *f* (*inf*, = *crime*) Ding *nt* (*sl*)

caper² N (*Bot, Cook*) Kaper *f*; (= *shrub*) Kapernstrauch *m*

capercaillie, capercailzie [kæpə'keɪlɪ] N Auerhahn *m*

Cape: Cape Town N Kapstadt *nt*; **Cape Verde Islands** PL Kapverdische Inseln *pl*, Kapverden *pl*

capful ['kæpfʊl] N **one ~ to one litre of water** eine Verschlusskappe auf einen Liter Wasser

capillary [kə'pɪlərɪ] ADJ kapillar, Kapillar-; **~ attraction** or **action** Kapillarwirkung *f* N Kapillare *f*, Kapillargefäß *nt*

capital ['kæpɪtl] N **a** (*also* **capital city**) Hauptstadt *f*; (*fig*: = *centre*) Zentrum *nt* **b** (*also* **capital letter**) Großbuchstabe *m*; **large ~s** Großbuchstaben *pl*, Versalien *pl* (*spec*); **small ~s** Kapitälchen *pl* (*spec*); **please write in ~s** bitte in Blockschrift schreiben! **c** *no pl* (*Fin, fig,* = *knowledge, skill*) Kapital *nt*; **to make ~ out of sth** (*fig*) aus etw Kapital schlagen; **~ and labour** Kapital und Arbeit **d** (*Archit*) Kapitell *nt* ADJ **a** *letter* Groß-; **love with a ~ L** die große Liebe; **a car with a ~ C** ein richtiges Auto; **unity with a ~ U** hundertprozentige Einheit **b** (= *major*) **of ~ importance** von größter Bedeutung **c** (*Jur*) Kapital-; **~ crime** Kapitalverbrechen *nt*; **they will be tried on a ~ charge of instigating the riots** sie werden des Kapitalverbrechens der Anstiftung zum Aufruhr angeklagt werden **d** (*dated inf*: = *excellent*) prächtig (*dated*), famos (*dated*)

capital *in cpds* Kapital-; **capital account** N Kapitalbilanz *f*; **capital allowance** N Abschreibung *f*; **capital assets** PL Kapitalvermögen *nt*; **capital base** N Kapitalbasis *f*;

capital costs PL Kapitalkosten *pl*; **capital employed** N Betriebskapital *nt*; **capital equipment** N (Betriebs)anlagen *pl*; **capital expenditure** N Kapitalaufwendungen *pl*; **capital gains** N Kapitalgewinn *m*; **capital gains tax** N Kapitalertragssteuer *f*; **capital goods** PL Investitionsgüter *pl*; **capital growth** N Kapitalzuwachs *m*; **capital-intensive** ADJ kapitalintensiv; **capital investment** N Kapitalanlage *f*

capitalism ['kæpɪtəlɪzəm] N Kapitalismus *m*

capitalist ['kæpɪtəlɪst] N Kapitalist(in) *m(f)* ADJ kapitalistisch

capitalistic [ˌkæpɪtə'lɪstɪk] ADJ kapitalistisch

capitalization [ˌkæpɪtəlaɪ'zeɪʃən] N **a** (*Fin*) Kapitalisierung *f*, Kapitalisation *f* **b** (*Typ*) Großschreibung *f*

capitalize ['kæpɪtəlaɪz] VT **a** (*Fin*) kapitalisieren **b** (*Typ*) *word* großschreiben

▶ **capitalize on** VI *+prep* (*fig*) Kapital schlagen aus

capital: capital levy N Vermögens- or Kapitalsteuer *f*; **capital loss** N (Kapital)veräußerungsverlust *m*; **capital market** N Kapitalmarkt *m*; **capital offence** N Kapitalverbrechen *nt*; **capital punishment** N die Todesstrafe; **capital reserves** PL Kapitalreserven *pl*; **capital returns tax** N Kapitalertrag(s)-steuer *f*; **capital spending** N = **capital expenditure**; **capital stock** N Gesellschaftskapital *nt*; **capital sum** N Kapitalbetrag *m*, Kapital *nt*; **capital transfer tax** N Kapitalverkehrssteuer *f*; (*for inheritance*) Erbschaftssteuer *f*

capitation [ˌkæpɪ'teɪʃən] N Kopfsteuer *f*

Capitol ['kæpɪtl] N Kapitol *nt*

capitulate [kə'pɪtjʊleɪt] VI kapitulieren (*also Mil*) (*to* vor *+dat*), aufgeben (*to* gegenüber)

capitulation [kəˌpɪtjʊ'leɪʃən] N Kapitulation *f*

capo ['kæpəʊ] N Kapodaster *m*

capon ['keɪpən] N Kapaun *m*

cappuccino [ˌkæpʊ'tʃiːnəʊ] N Cappuccino *m*

Capri [kə'priː] N Capri *nt*

caprice [kə'priːs] N **a** Laune(nhaftigkeit) *f*, Kaprice *f* (*geh*) **b** (*Mus*) Capriccio *nt*

capricious [kə'prɪʃəs] ADJ launisch, kapriziös (*geh*)

capriciously [kə'prɪʃəslɪ] ADV *act, behave* launenhaft; *decide, do sth* einer Laune gehorchend (*geh*)

capriciousness [kə'prɪʃəsnɪs] N Launenhaftigkeit *f*

Capricorn ['kæprɪkɔːn] N Steinbock *m*; **I'm (a) ~** ich bin Steinbock

capsicum ['kæpsɪkəm] N (*Bot*, = *plant, fruit*) Pfefferschote *f*, Peperoni *pl*

capsize [kæp'saɪz] VI kentern VT zum Kentern bringen

capstan ['kæpstən] N Poller *m*

capstone ['kæpstəʊn] N (*Archit*) (*lit, fig*) Schlussstein *m*; (*of wall*) Mauerkappe *f*

capsular ['kæpsjʊlə] ADJ Kapsel-

capsule [kæp'sjuːl] N Kapsel *f*

captain ['kæptɪn] (*abbr* **Capt**) N (*Mil*) Hauptmann *m*; (*Naut, Aviat, Sport*) Kapitän *m*; (*US, in restaurant*) Oberkellner *m*; **yes, ~!** jawohl, Herr Hauptmann/Kapitän!; **~ of industry** Industriekapitän *m* VT (*Sport*) *team* anführen; (*Naut*) *ship* befehligen; **he ~ed the team for years** er war jahrelang Kapitän der Mannschaft

captaincy ['kæptənsɪ] N Befehligung *f*, Befehl *m*; (*Sport*) Führung *f*; **to get the ~** (*Sport*) zum Mannschaftskapitän ernannt werden; **under his ~** mit ihm als Kapitän

caption ['kæpʃən] N Überschrift *f*, Titel *m*; (*under cartoon*) Bildunterschrift *f*; (*Film*, = *subtitle*) Untertitel *m* VT betiteln, mit einer Überschrift or einem Titel *etc* versehen

captious ['kæpʃəs] ADJ *person* überkritisch, pedantisch; *remark* spitzfindig

captivate ['kæptɪveɪt] VT faszinieren, entzücken

captivating ['kæptɪveɪtɪŋ] ADJ bezaubernd; *personality* einnehmend

captive ['kæptɪv] N Gefangene(r) *mf*; **to take sb ~** jdn gefangen nehmen; **to hold sb ~** jdn gefangen halten; (*fig*) jdn fesseln, jdn gefangen nehmen ADJ *person* gefangen; *animal, bird* in Gefangenschaft; **in a ~ state** in Gefangenschaft *f*; **a ~ audience** ein unfreiwilliges Publikum; **~ breeding** Zucht *f* (von artbedrohten Tieren) in Gefangenschaft

captive balloon N Fesselballon *m*

captive market N Monopol-Absatzmarkt *m*

captivity [kæp'tɪvɪtɪ] N Gefangenschaft *f*

captor ['kæptə] N derjenige, der jdn gefangen nimmt; **his ~s treated him kindly** er wurde nach seiner Gefangennahme gut behandelt; **his ~s were Ruritanian** er wurde von Ruritaniern gefangen genommen; **his ~s later freed him** man ließ ihn später wieder frei

capture ['kæptʃə] VT **a** *town* einnehmen, erobern; *treasure* erobern; *person* gefangennehmen; *animal* (ein)fangen; *ship* kapern, aufbringen (*spec*); **they ~d the town from the enemy** sie eroberten die vom Feind beherrschte Stadt **b** (*fig*) *votes* erringen, auf sich (*acc*) vereinigen; *prizes* erringen; (*painter etc*) *atmosphere* einfangen; *attention, sb's interest* erregen **c** (*Comput*) *data* erfassen N **a** Eroberung *f*; (*thing captured also*) Fang *m*; (*of escapee*) Gefangennahme *f*; (*of animal*) Einfangen *nt*; (*Comput, of data*) Erfassung *f*

capuchin ['kæpjʊtʃɪn] N **a** (= *hooded cloak*) Kapuzencape *nt* **b** (*Zool*) Kapuziner(affe) *m* **c** (*Eccl*) **Capuchin** Kapuziner(mönch) *m*

car [kɑː] N **a** Auto *nt*, Wagen *m*; **by ~** mit dem Auto or Wagen; **~ ride** Autofahrt *f*, Fahrt *f* mit dem Auto **b** (*esp US, Rail*, = *tram car*) Wagen *m* **c** (*of airship, balloon, cablecar*) Gondel *f*; (*US, of elevator*) Fahrkorb *m*

carafe [kə'ræf] N Karaffe *f*

car alarm N Auto-Alarmanlage *f*

caramel ['kærəməl] N (= *substance*) Karamell *m*; (= *sweet*) Karamelle *f*

caramel *in cpds* Karamell-; **caramel-coloured** ADJ hellbraun; **caramel-flavoured** ADJ mit Karamellgeschmack

carapace ['kærəpeɪs] N Schale *f*; (*of tortoise etc*) (Rücken)panzer *m*

carat ['kærət] N Karat *nt*; **nine ~ gold** neunkarätiges Gold

caravan ['kærəvæn] N **a** (*Brit, Aut*) Wohnwagen *m*, Caravan *m*; **~ holiday** Ferien *pl* im Wohnwagen **b** (= *gipsy caravan*) Zigeunerwagen *m* **c** (= *desert caravan*) Karawane *f*

caravanning ['kærəvænɪŋ] N Caravaning *nt*, Urlaub *m* im Wohnwagen; **to go ~** Urlaub im Wohnwagen machen

caravanserai [ˌkærə'vænsəˌraɪ] N Karawanserei *f*

caravan site N Campingplatz *m* für Wohnwagen

caravel ['kærəvel] N Karavelle *f*

caraway ['kærəweɪ] N Kümmel *m*

caraway seeds PL Kümmel(körner *pl*) *m*

carbide ['kɑːbaɪd] N Karbid *nt*

carbine ['kɑːbaɪn] N Karabiner *m*

car body N (Auto)karosserie *f*

carbohydrate ['kɑːbəʊ'haɪdreɪt] N Kohle(n)hydrat *nt*

carbolic [kɑː'bɒlɪk] ADJ Karbol- (*also* **carbolic soap**) Karbolseife *f*

carbolic acid N Karbolsäure *f*

car bomb N Autobombe *f*

carbon ['kɑːbən] N (*Chem*) Kohlenstoff *m*; (*Elec*) Kohle *f*

carbonaceous [ˌkɑːbə'neɪʃəs] ADJ Kohlenstoff-, kohlenstoffhaltig

carbonate ['kɑːbənɪt] N Karbonat *nt*

carbonated ['kɑːbəˌneɪtɪd] ADJ mit Kohlensäure (versetzt)

carbon: carbon copy N Durchschlag *m*; **to be a ~ of sth** das genaue Ebenbild einer Sache (*gen*) sein; **she's a ~ of her sister** sie sieht ihrer Schwester zum Verwechseln ähnlich; **carbon dating** N Radiokarbonmethode *f*, Kohlenstoffdatierung *f*; **carbon dioxide** N Kohlendioxid *nt*; **carbon fibre** N Kohlenstoffaser *f*

carbonic [kɑːˈbɒnɪk] ADJ Kohlen-

carbonic: carbonic acid N Kohlensäure *f*; **carbonic oxide** N Kohlenmonoxid *nt*

carboniferous [ˌkɑːbəˈnɪfərəs] ADJ (*Geol*) kohlehaltig

carbonization [ˌkɑːbənaɪˈzeɪʃən] N Karbonisation *f*, Verkohlung *f*

carbonize [ˈkɑːbənaɪz] VT karbonisieren, verkohlen (lassen)

carbon: carbonless paper N selbstdurchschreibendes Papier; **carbon monoxide** N Kohlenmonoxid *nt*; **carbon paper** N Kohlepapier *nt*; **carbon ribbon** N Kohlefarbband *nt*

CAR-BOOT SALE, GARAGE SALE

Car-boot sales sind in Großbritannien recht beliebte Flohmärkte, bei denen die Leute Dinge, die sie nicht mehr länger benötigen, wie Kleider, Möbel und andere Haushaltsgegenstände, aus den Kofferräumen ihrer Autos heraus verkaufen. Normalerweise werden solche Märkte auf Parkplätzen oder anderen Plätzen im Freien abgehalten, wobei die Autobesitzer eine kleine Gebühr für den Standplatz entrichten müssen.

In den USA verkaufen Hausbesitzer überflüssigen Hausrat und Kleider, indem sie einen **garage sale** oder auch **yard sale** abhalten und alles, von dem sie sich trennen wollen, im Garten oder in der Garage zum Verkauf anbieten. Manchmal schließen sich auch mehrere Nachbarn zusammen und veranstalten einen gemeinsamen **garage sale**.

---

carboy [ˈkɑːbɔɪ] N Korbflasche *f*

carbuncle [ˈkɑːbʌŋkl] N **a** (*Med*) Karbunkel *m* **b** (= *jewel*) Karfunkel(stein) *m*

carburettor, (*US*) **carburetor** [ˌkɑːbəˈretə'] N Vergaser *m*

carcass [ˈkɑːkəs] N **a** (= *corpse*) Leiche *f*; (*of animal*) Kadaver *m*, (Tier)leiche *f*; (*at butcher's*) Rumpf *m*; **move your fat ~!** (*inf*) schwing deinen Arsch weg! (*sl*) **b** (*of ship, house*) Skelett *nt*; (= *remains*) Überbleibsel *pl*, Trümmer *pl*

car chase N Verfolgungsjagd *f* (*mit dem Auto*)

carcinogen [kɑːˈsɪnədʒen] N Krebserreger *m*, Karzinogen *nt*

carcinogenic [ˌkɑːsɪnəˈdʒenɪk] ADJ karzinogen, Krebs erregend, krebserregend

carcinoma [ˌkɑːsɪˈnəʊmə] N Karzinom *nt*

car: car coat N Dreivierteljacke *f*; **car crash** N (Auto)unfall *m*

card¹ [kɑːd] N **a** *no pl* (= *cardboard*) Pappe *f* **b** (= *greetings, business card etc*) Karte *f*; (= *cheque/credit card*) (Scheck-/Kredit)karte *f* **c** **cards** PL (= *employment cards*) Papiere *pl*; **he asked for his ~s** (*inf*) er wollte sich (*dat*) seine Papiere geben lassen (*inf*) **d** (= *playing card*) (Spiel)karte *f*; **to play ~s** Karten spielen; **to lose money at ~s** Geld beim Kartenspiel verlieren; **pack of ~s** Karten *pl*, Kartenspiel *nt*; **game of ~s** Kartenspiel *nt*; **house of ~s** (*lit, fig*) Kartenhaus *nt* **e** (*Sport*, = *programme*) Programm *nt* **f** (*fig*) **to put** or **lay one's ~s on the table** seine Karten aufdecken or (offen) auf den Tisch legen; **to play one's ~s right/badly** geschickt/ungeschickt taktieren, taktisch geschickt/unklug vorgehen; **to hold all the ~s** alle Trümpfe in der Hand haben; **to play one's last/trump ~** seinen letzten/höchsten Trumpf ausspielen; **to play** or **keep one's ~s close to one's chest** or (*US*) **close to the vest** sich (*dat*) nicht in die Karten sehen lassen; **it's on the ~s** das ist zu

erwarten

g (*dated inf*, = *person*) ulkiger Vogel (*inf*)

card² (*Tex*) N Wollkamm *m*, Krempel *f*, Karde *f* VT wool, cotton kämmen, krempeln, karden

cardamom [ˈkɑːdəməm] N Kardamom *m or nt*

card: cardboard N Karton *m*, Pappe *f* ATTR Papp-; (*fig*) *character* stereotyp, klischeehaft, schablonenhaft; **cardboard box** N (Papp-)karton *m*, Pappschachtel *f*; **card-carrying** ADJ **a ~ member** ein eingetragenes Mitglied; **~ communist** Mitglied *nt* der Kommunistischen Partei; **card catalogue**, **card file** N Zettelkatalog *m*; (*in library*) Katalog(karten *pl*); **card game** N Kartenspiel *nt*; **card holder** N (*of credit card*) Karteninhaber(in) *m(f)*

cardiac [ˈkɑːdɪæk] ADJ Herz-

cardiac arrest N Herzstillstand *m*

cardigan [ˈkɑːdɪgən] N Strickjacke *f*

cardinal [ˈkɑːdɪnl] N **a** (*Eccl*) Kardinal *m* **b** → **cardinal number** ADJ (= *chief*) Haupt-; (= *utmost*) äußerste(r, s) *attr*

cardinal: cardinal number N Kardinalzahl *f*; **cardinal points** PL Himmelsrichtungen *pl*; **cardinal red** N Purpurrot *nt*; **cardinal sin** N Todsünde *f*; **cardinal virtue** N Kardinaltugend *f*

card index N Kartei *f*; (*in library*) Katalog *m*

cardio- [ˈkɑːdɪəʊ-] PREF Kardio-; **cardiogram** Kardiogramm *nt*

cardiologist [ˌkɑːdɪˈɒlədʒɪst] N Kardiologe *m*, Kardiologin *f*

cardiology [ˌkɑːdɪˈɒlədʒɪ] N Kardiologie *f*

cardiopulmonary [ˌkɑːdɪəʊˈpʌlmənərɪ] ADJ Herz-Lungen-; **~ resuscitation** Herz-Lungen-Wiederbelebung *f*

cardiovascular [ˌkɑːdɪəʊˈvæskjʊlə'] ADJ kardiovaskulär

card: cardphone N Kartentelefon *nt*; **card player** N Kartenspieler(in) *m(f)*; **card punch** N Lochkartenmaschine *f*; **card reader** N Lesemaschine *f*; **cardsharp(er)** N Falschspieler(in) *m(f)*, Zinker(in) *m(f)* (*inf*); **card table** N Spieltisch *m*; **card trick** N Kartenkunststück *nt*; **card vote** N (*Brit*) ≈ Abstimmung *f* durch Wahlmänner

CARE [keə'] *abbr of* **Cooperative for American Relief Everywhere ~ packet** Carepaket *nt*

---

care [keə']

⚙ 7.5

1 NOUN	3 TRANSITIVE VERB
2 INTRANSITIVE VERB	4 PHRASAL VERB

1 – NOUN

a = worry Sorge *f* (*of* um); **free of care(s)** ohne Sorgen, frei von Sorge; **he hasn't a care in the world** er hat keinerlei Sorgen; **the cares of the world** die Sorgen des Alltags; **the cares of state** die Staatsgeschäfte *pl*

b = carefulness Sorgfalt *f*; **this word should be used with care** dieses Wort sollte sorgfältig or mit Sorgfalt gebraucht werden; **paint strippers need to be used with care** Abbeizmittel müssen vorsichtig or mit Vorsicht angewandt werden; **driving without due care and attention** fahrlässiges Verhalten im Straßenverkehr; **to drive with due care and attention** sich umsichtig im Straßenverkehr verhalten; **"fragile, with care"**, **"handle with care"** „Vorsicht, zerbrechlich"; **it got broken despite all the care we took** es ist trotz aller Vorsicht kaputtgegangen; **have a care** (*old*: = *be careful*) gib Acht or Obacht! (*old*); (*inf*: = *be considerate*) nun mach mal einen Punkt! (*inf*)

♦ **to take care** (= *be careful*) aufpassen, vorsichtig sein; **take care when using weedkillers** beim Gebrauch von Unkrautbekämpfungsmitteln sollte man aufpassen or vorsichtig sein; **take care he doesn't cheat you** sehen Sie sich vor or nehmen Sie sich in Acht, dass er Sie nicht betrügt; **bye-bye, take care** tschüs(s), machs gut

♦ **to take care to do sth/not to do sth** sich bemühen or sich (*dat*) Mühe geben, etw zu tun/etw nicht zu tun; **I'll take care not to upset him** ich werde mich bemühen or ich werde mir Mühe geben, ihn nicht zu verärgern

♦ **to take care over** or **with sth/in doing sth** etw sorgfältig tun; **you should take more care with** or **over the details** Sie sollten sich sorgfältiger mit den Einzelheiten befassen

c = maintenance (*of teeth, skin, car, furniture etc*) Pflege *f*; **to take care of sth** (= *maintain*) auf etw (*acc*) aufpassen; *one's appearance, hair, car, furniture* etw pflegen; (= *not treat roughly*) *car, furniture, health* etw schonen; **to take care of oneself** sich um sich selbst kümmern; (*as regards health*) sich schonen, auf sich (*acc*) aufpassen; (*as regards appearance*) etwas für sich tun, sich pflegen

d of old people, children Versorgung *f*, Fürsorge *f*; *medical care* ärztliche Versorgung; **he needs medical care** er muss ärztlich behandelt werden; **he is in the care of Dr Smith** er ist bei Dr. Smith in Behandlung; **to take care of sb** sich um jdn kümmern; *patients* jdn versorgen; *one's family* für jdn sorgen; **they took good care of her in hospital** sie wurde im Krankenhaus gut versorgt

e = protection Obhut *f*; **care of** (*abbr* **c/o**) bei; **in** or **under sb's care** in jds (*dat*) Obhut; **to take a child into care** ein Kind in Pflege nehmen; **to be taken into care** (*of child*) in Pflege gegeben werden; **children placed in the care of the council** Kinder *pl* in der Obhut des Sozialamtes; **the children/valuables in my care** die mir anvertrauten Kinder/Wertsachen; **to take care of sth** (*valuables etc*) auf etw (*acc*) aufpassen; *plants, animals etc* sich um etw kümmern; (*over longer period*) etw versorgen

♦ **to take care of sb/sth** (= *see to*) sich um jdn/etw kümmern; *of arrangements, affairs etc* also etw erledigen; **that takes care of him/it** er/das wäre abgehakt (*inf*), das wäre erledigt; **let me take care of that** lassen Sie mich das mal machen, überlassen Sie das mir; **that can take care of itself** das wird sich schon irgendwie geben; **let the housewife take care of itself for a while** nun lass doch mal eine Zeit lang die Hausarbeit (sein)

f = concern (*of person*) Anteilnahme *f*, Fürsorglichkeit *f*; (*of state, council*) Interesse *nt* am Mitmenschen; **if the town planners showed more care** wenn die Städteplaner etwas mehr Menschenfreundlichkeit zeigen würden; **if only she showed a little care** wenn sie nur nicht so gleichgültig wäre; **the party has a genuine care for senior citizens** der Partei liegt das Wohl der älteren Mitbürger am Herzen

2 – INTRANSITIVE VERB

(= *feel concern*) **I don't care** das ist mir egal or gleichgültig; **as if I cared** als ob das etwas ausmachen würde; **for all I care** meinetwegen, von mir aus; **who cares?** na und?, und wennschon?; **he just doesn't care** das ist ihm so egal; **I didn't know you cared** (*hum*) ich wusste gar nicht, dass ich dir was bedeute; **the company that cares** die Firma mit Herz; **I wish you'd care a bit more** ich wünschte, das wäre dir nicht alles egal or gleichgültig

♦ **to care about sth** Wert auf etw (*acc*) legen; **we care about our image** wir legen Wert auf unser Image; **a company that cares about its staff** eine Firma, die sich um ihr Personal kümmert or für ihr Personal sorgt; **money is all he cares about** er interessiert sich nur fürs Geld, ihm liegt nur etwas am Geld; **that's all he cares about** alles andere ist ihm egal; **he cares deeply about her/this** sie/das liegt ihm sehr am Herzen; **he doesn't care about her** sie ist ihm gleichgültig; **I know you don't care about me/such things** ich weiß, dass ich dir gleichgültig bin/dass dir so etwas gleichgültig or egal ist

3 – TRANSITIVE VERB

a = mind **I don't care what people say** es ist mir egal or es kümmert mich nicht, was die

Leute sagen; **don't you care that half the world is starving?** berührt es Sie überhaupt nicht, dass die halbe Welt hungert?; **what do I care?** was geht mich das an?; **I couldn't care less what people say**, **I could care less** (*US*) es ist mir doch völlig egal or gleich(gültig), was die Leute sagen; **you don't care what happens to me – but I do care** dir ist es ja egal, was mir passiert – nein, das ist mir überhaupt nicht egal; **I didn't think you cared what I do** ich habe gedacht, das ist dir egal, was ich mache

b = **like** **to care to do sth** etw gerne tun mögen or wollen; **would you care to take off your coat?**, wollen or möchten Sie nicht (Ihren Mantel) ablegen?; **I wouldn't care to meet him/try** ich würde keinen gesteigerten Wert darauf legen, ihn kennen zu lernen/das zu probieren; **but I don't care to** ich will aber nicht

4 – PHRASAL VERB

▶ **care for** ⚙ +prep obj **a** (= *look after*) sich kümmern um; *hands, furniture etc* pflegen; **well cared-for** (*person*) gut versorgt; *hands, garden, hair, house* gepflegt; **the children are being cared for by their grandmother** die Großmutter kümmert sich um die Kinder

b (= *like*) **I don't care for that suggestion/picture/him** dieser Vorschlag/das Bild/er sagt mir nicht zu; **I don't care for your tone of voice** wie reden Sie denn mit mir?; **would you care for a cup of tea?** hätten Sie gerne eine Tasse Tee?; **care for a drink?** wie wärs mit einem Drink?, etwas zu trinken?; **care for another?** noch einen?; **I've never much cared for his films** ich habe mir noch nie viel aus seinen Filmen gemacht; **I didn't care for the hotel we stayed in** ich fand das Hotel, in dem wir waren, nicht nach meinem Geschmack; **but you know I do care for you** aber du weißt doch, dass du mir viel bedeutest or dass du mir nicht egal or gleichgültig bist

career [kə'rɪə] **N** Karriere *f*; (= *profession, job*) Beruf *m*; (= *working life*) Laufbahn *f*; **journalism is his new** ~ er hat jetzt die Laufbahn des Journalisten eingeschlagen; **to make a** ~ **for oneself** Karriere machen **ATTR** Karriere-; *soldier, diplomat* Berufs-; **a good/bad** ~ **move** ein karrierefördernder/karriereschädlicher Schritt ⚙ rasen; **to** ~ **along** rasen; **the car** ~**ed out of control** das Auto geriet außer Kontrolle

career break N Unterbrechung *f* der Berufstätigkeit

career girl, **career woman** N Karrierefrau *f*

careerist [kə'rɪərɪst] N Karrierist(in) *m(f)*, Karrieremacher(in) *m(f)*

careers guidance N Berufsberatung *f*

Careers Officer, **Careers Adviser** N Berufsberater(in) *m(f)*

carefree ['kɛəfriː] ADJ sorglos, unbekümmert; *song* heiter

careful ['kɛəfʊl] ❂ 2.3 ADJ sorgfältig, (= *cautious, circumspect*) sorgsam, vorsichtig; (*with money etc*) sparsam; **I gave the matter some** ~ **thought** ich habe die Sache gründlich überlegt; ~**!** Vorsicht!, passen Sie auf!; **to be** ~ aufpassen (*of* auf +*acc*); **be** ~ **with the glasses** sei mit den Gläsern vorsichtig; **be** ~ **what you do** sieh dich vor, nimm dich in Acht; **she's very** ~ **about what she eats** sie achtet genau darauf, was sie isst; **to be** ~ **about doing sth** es sich gut überlegen, ob man etw tun soll; **be** ~ **(that) they don't hear you** gib Acht or sei vorsichtig, damit or dass sie dich nicht hören; **be** ~ **not to drop it** pass auf, dass du das nicht fallen lässt; **he is very** ~ **with his money** er hält sein Geld gut zusammen; **you can't be too** ~ **these days** man kann heutzutage nicht vorsichtig genug sein

carefully ['kɛəfəlɪ] ADV sorgfältig; (= *cautiously*) sorgsam, vorsichtig; *consider* gründlich; *listen* gut; *read* sorgfältig, vorsichtig; *drive* vorsichtig; *explain* genau

carefulness ['kɛəfʊlnɪs] N Sorgfalt *f*; (= *caution*) Sorgsamkeit *f*, Vorsicht *f*; (*with money etc*) Sparsamkeit *f*

caregiver ['kɛə‚gɪvə'] N (*esp US*) → **carer**

care label N Pflegeetikett *nt*

careless ['kɛəlɪs] ADJ **a** (= *negligent, heedless*) *person, worker, work* nachlässig; *driver* unvorsichtig; *driving* leichtsinnig; *remark* gedankenlos; ~ **mistake** Flüchtigkeitsfehler *m*; **how** ~ **of me!** wie dumm von mir!; (= *clumsy*) wie ungeschickt von mir; **to be** ~ **of one's health** nicht auf seine Gesundheit achten; **to be** ~ **of sb's feelings** nicht an jds Gefühle (*acc*) denken; **to be** ~ **in one's remarks** gedankenlos daherreden; **to be** ~ **in one's behaviour** leichtsinnig handeln **b** (= *carefree*) sorglos, unbekümmert **c** *dress, elegance* lässig

carelessly ['kɛəlɪslɪ] ADV **a** (= *negligently, heedlessly*) *leave, discard, place, handle, allow* leichtsinnigerweise, unvorsichtigerweise **b** (= *casually*) *say* gedankenlos; *throw, toss* achtlos

carelessness ['kɛəlɪsnɪs] N **a** (= *negligence, heedlessness, of person, worker, work*) Nachlässigkeit *f*; (*of driver*) Unvorsicht(igkeit) *f*; (*of driving*) Leichtsinn *m*; (*of remark*) Gedankenlosigkeit *f* **b** (= *carefreeness*) Sorglosigkeit *f*, Unbekümmertheit *f*

care order N (*Brit: Jur, Sociol*) Fürsorgeanordnung *f*

carer ['kɛərə'] N im Sozialbereich Tätige(r) *mf*; **the elderly and their** ~**s** Senioren und ihre Fürsorgenden

caress [kə'res] **N** Liebkosung *f*, Zärtlichkeit *f* *usu pl*, Streicheln *nt no pl* **VT** streicheln, liebkosen

caressing [kə'resɪŋ] ADJ zärtlich, sanft, streichelnd

caret ['kærət] N (*Typ*) Einschaltungszeichen *nt*; (*on ruler*) Caret-Zeichen *nt*

care: caretaker N Hausmeister(in) *m(f)*; **caretaker government** N geschäftsführende Regierung; **care worker** N Heimbetreuer(in) für Kinder, Geisteskranke oder alte Menschen **health** ~ im Gesundheitswesen Tätige(r) *mf*; **child** ~ in der Jugendhilfe Tätige(r) *m(f)*; **careworn** ADJ von Sorgen gezeichnet

car: carfare N (*US*) Fahrpreis *m*; **car ferry** N Autofähre *f*

cargo ['kɑːgəʊ] N (Schiffs)fracht or -ladung *f*, Kargo *m* (*spec*); ~ **boat** Frachter *m*, Frachtdampfer *m*, Frachtschiff *nt*

car hire N Autovermietung *f*

carhop ['kɑːhɒp] N (*dated US*) Bedienung *f* in einem Drive-in-Restaurant

Caribbean [‚kærɪ'biːən, (*US*) kæ'rɪbɪən] ADJ karibisch; ~ **Sea** Karibisches Meer; **a** ~ **island** eine Insel in der Karibik **N** Karibik *f*

caribou ['kærɪbuː] N Karibu *m*

caricature ['kærɪkətjʊə'] **N** Karikatur *f* **VT** karikieren

caricaturist [‚kærɪkə'tjʊərɪst] N Karikaturist(in) *m(f)*

caries ['kɛəriːz] N Karies *f*

carillon [kə'rɪljən] N Glockenspiel *nt*

caring ['kɛərɪŋ] ADJ *person, attitude* warmherzig, mitfühlend, einfühlsam; *parent, husband* liebevoll; *teacher* engagiert; *government, society* sozial, mitmenschlich; **a child needs a** ~ **environment** ein Kind braucht Zuwendung or braucht eine Umgebung, die sich um es kümmert; ~ **profession** Sozialberuf *m*

car insurance N Kfz-Versicherung *f*, Kraftfahrzeugversicherung *f*

carious ['kɛərɪəs] ADJ (*Med*) *teeth* kariös, von Karies befallen *pred*

car: carjacker ['kɑːdʒækə'] N Autoräuber(in) *m(f)*, Carjacker(in) *m(f)*; **carjacking** ['kɑːdʒækɪŋ] N Autoraub *m*, Carjacking *nt*; **car keys** PL Autoschlüssel *pl*; **carload** N **a** (*Aut*) Wagenladung *f* **b** (*US Rail*) Waggonladung *f*

Carmelite ['kɑːməlaɪt] N Karmelit(in) *m(f)*, Karmeliter(in) *m(f)*

carmine ['kɑːmaɪn] ADJ karm(es)inrot **N** Karmesin *nt*, Karmin *nt*

carnage ['kɑːnɪdʒ] N Blutbad *nt*, Gemetzel *nt*; **a scene of** ~ ein blutiges Schauspiel; **fields covered with the** ~ **of war** mit Toten or Leichen übersäte Schlachtfelder

carnal ['kɑːnl] ADJ fleischlich, körperlich; ~ **desires** sinnliche Begierden *pl*; ~ **lusts** Fleischeslust *f* (*liter*); **to have** ~ **knowledge of sb** mit jdm (Geschlechts)verkehr haben

carnation [kɑː'neɪʃən] N Nelke *f*

carnival ['kɑːnɪvəl] **N** Volksfest *nt*; (= *village carnival etc*) Schützenfest *nt*; (*based on religion*) Karneval *m* **ATTR** Fest-, Karnevals-; ~ **procession** Fest-/Karnevalszug *m*

carnivore ['kɑːnɪvɔː'] N pl **carnivora** [kɑː'nɪvərə] (= *animal*) Fleischfresser *m*; (= *plant*) Fleisch fressende Pflanze

carnivorous [kɑː'nɪvərəs] ADJ Fleisch fressend, karnivor

carob ['kærəb] N Johannisbrotbaum *m*; (= *fruit*) Johannisbrot *nt*

carol ['kærəl] **N** Lied *nt* **VI** (*old, liter*) (fröhlich) singen, jubilieren (*old, liter*); (*bird*) tirilieren (*old, liter*)

carol: carol singers PL ≈ Sternsinger *pl*; **carol singing** N Weihnachtssingen *nt*

carom ['kærəm] (*US*) **N** Karambolage *f* **VI** (*billiards*) karambolieren; (= *rebound*) abprallen

carotene ['kærətiːn] N Karotin *nt*

carotid (artery) [kə'rɒtɪd('ɑːtərɪ)] N Halsschlagader *f*, Karotide *f* (*spec*)

carousal [kə'raʊzəl] N (*old*) (Zech)gelage *nt*, Schmaus *m*

carouse [kə'raʊz] VI (*old*) zechen, Gelage feiern

carousel [‚kæruː'sel] N **a** Karussell *nt* **b** (*for slides*) Rundmagazin *nt*

car owner N Autohalter(in) *m(f)*

carp¹ [kɑːp] N (= *fish*) Karpfen *m*

carp² VI etwas auszusetzen haben, nörgeln; **to** ~ **at sb** an jdm etwas auszusetzen haben, an jdm herummeckern (*inf*); **to** ~ **at sth** an etw was auszusetzen haben, über etw (*acc*) meckern (*inf*)

carpal bone ['kɑːpl'bəʊn] N Handwurzelknochen *m*

carpal tunnel syndrome [‚kɑːpl'tʌnlsɪndrəʊm] N (*Med*) Karpaltunnelsyndrom *nt*

car: car park N (*Brit, open-air*) Parkplatz *m*; (*covered*) Parkhaus *nt*; **car parking** N ~ **facilities are available** Parkplatz or Parkmöglichkeit(en) vorhanden; **car park ticket** N Parkschein *m*

Carpathians [kɑː'peɪθɪənz] PL (*Geog*) Karpaten *pl*

carpel ['kɑːpl] N Fruchtblatt *nt*

carpenter ['kɑːpɪntə'] N Zimmermann *m*, Zimmerfrau *f*; (*for furniture*) Tischler(in) *m(f)*

carpentry ['kɑːpɪntrɪ] N Zimmerhandwerk *nt*, (Bau)tischlerei *f*; (*as hobby*) Tischlern *nt*

carpet ['kɑːpɪt] **N** (*lit, fig*) Teppich *m*; (*fitted*) Teppichboden *m*; **the subject on the** ~ das Thema, das zur Zeit diskutiert wird; **to be on the** ~ (*inf*) zur Schnecke or Minna gemacht werden (*inf*) **VT** **a** *floor* mit Teppich(en)/Teppichboden auslegen; **the wood** ~**ed with flowers** der blumenbedeckte Waldboden **b** (*Brit inf*: = *reprimand*) zur Minna machen (*inf*)

carpet: carpetbag N Reisetasche *f*; **carpetbagger** N **a** (*US Pol inf*) politischer Abenteurer, politische Abenteurerin; (*Hist*) politischer Ämterjäger, der mit nichts als einer Reisetasche nach dem Sezessionskrieg in die besetzten Südstaaten kam **b** (*Fin*) Spekulant(in) *m(f)* (*der/die Geld bei vielen verschiedenen Hypothekenbanken investiert in der Hoffnung, bei Änderung der Statuten einen Gewinn zu machen*); **carpet-beater** N Teppich- or Ausklopfer *m*; **carpet bombing** N (*Mil*) Flächenbombardierung *f*

carpeting ['kɑːpɪtɪŋ] N Teppiche *pl*

carpet: carpet slippers PL Pantoffeln pl, Hausschuhe pl; **carpet-sweeper** N Teppichkehrer m, Teppichkehrmaschine f; **carpet tile** N Teppichfliese f

car phone N Autotelefon nt

carping ['kɑːpɪŋ] **ADJ** a ~ **old woman** eine alte Meckerziege (inf); **she grew weary of his ~ criticism** sie wurde sein ständiges Nörgeln leid N Nörgelei(en) f(pl), Gemecker nt (inf)

carpool ['kɑːpuːl] N a (= people) Fahrgemeinschaft f b (= vehicles) Fuhrpark m VI eine Fahrgemeinschaft bilden (with mit)

carport ['kɑːpɔːt] N Einstellplatz m

car radio N Autoradio nt

carrel ['kærəl] N (in library etc) Arbeitsnische f, Arbeitsplatz m

car rental N (US) Autovermietung f

carriage ['kærɪdʒ] N a (= horse-drawn vehicle) Kutsche f; (US, = baby carriage) Kinderwagen m; ~ **and pair** Zweispänner m b (Brit, Rail) Wagen m c (Comm, = conveyance) Beförderung f; (= cost of carriage also) Beförderungskosten pl; ~ **forward** Fracht zahlt Empfänger; ~ **free** frachtfrei; ~ **paid** frei Haus d (Typ) Wagen m; (Comput) Return nt e (Mil, = gun-carriage) Lafette f f (of person: = bearing) Haltung f

carriage: carriage clock N ≈ Stiluhr f; **carriage return** N Wagenrücklauf m; **carriageway** N (Brit) Fahrbahn f

carrier ['kærɪə] N a (= goods haulier) Spediteur m, Transportunternehmer m; (= passenger airline) Fluggesellschaft f b (of disease) Überträger m c (= aircraft carrier) Flugzeugträger m; (= troop carrier) Transportflugzeug nt/-schiff nt d (= luggage rack) Gepäckträger m e (Brit: also **carrier bag**) Tragetasche f, Tragetüte f f (also **carrier pigeon**) Brieftaube f; **by ~ (pigeon)** mit der Taubenpost g (Chem) Träger(substanz f) m; (= catalyst) Katalysator m

carrion ['kærɪən] N Aas nt

carrion crow N Rabenkrähe f

carrot ['kærət] N Mohrrübe f, Karotte f, Möhre f; (fig) Köder m; **to dangle a ~ before sb** or **in front of sb** jdm einen Köder unter die Nase halten; **the stick and the ~** Zuckerbrot und Peitsche

carrot: carrot-and-stick ADJ ~ **policy** Politik f von Zuckerbrot und Peitsche; **carrot cake** N Karottenkuchen m; **carrot top** N (hum inf) Rotkopf m, Kupferdach nt (hum inf)

carroty ['kærətɪ] ADJ hair kupferrot

carrousel [ˌkæruːˈsel] N = carousel

carry ['kærɪ] VI a load, person, object tragen; message (über)bringen b (vehicle: = convey) befördern; goods also transportieren; **this coach carries 30 people** dieser Bus kann 30 Personen befördern; **a boat ~ing missiles to Cuba** ein Schiff mit Raketen für Kuba; **the boat was carried along by the wind** der Wind trieb das Boot dahin; **the current carried them along** die Strömung trieb sie mit sich; **the wind carried the sound to him** der Wind trug die Laute zu ihm hin or an sein Ohr c (= have on person) documents, money bei sich haben or führen (form); gun, sword tragen; **to ~ sth about** or **around with one** etw mit sich herumtragen; **to ~ money on one** Geld bei sich haben; **to ~ the facts in one's head** die Fakten im Kopf haben; (= remember) die Fakten (im Kopf) behalten; **the ship was ~ing too much sail** das Schiff hatte zu viele Segel gesetzt d (fig) **his denial did not ~ conviction** sein Leugnen klang nicht überzeugend; **he carried his audience (along) with him** er riss das Publikum mit, er begeisterte das Publikum; **to ~ interest** (Fin) Zinsen tragen or abwerfen; **the loan carries 5% interest** das Darlehen wird mit 5% verzinst; **this job carries extra pay/a lot of responsibility** dieser Posten bringt eine höhere Bezahlung/viel Verantwortung mit sich; **the offence carries a penalty of £50** auf dies Vergehen or darauf steht eine Geldstrafe von £ 50 e (bridge etc: = support) tragen, stützen

f (Comm) goods, stock führen, (auf Lager) haben g (Tech, pipe) water, oil, electricity führen; (wire) sound (weiter)leiten, übertragen h (= extend) führen, (ver)legen; **they carried the pipes under the street** sie verlegten die Rohre unter der Straße; **to ~ sth too far** (fig) etw zu weit treiben; **they carried the war into the enemy's territory** sie trugen den Krieg in feindliches Gebiet; **this theme is carried through the whole book** dies Thema zieht sich durch das ganze Buch i (= win) einnehmen, erobern; **to ~ the day** siegreich sein, den Sieg davontragen; **to ~ all before one** freie Bahn haben; (hum, woman) viel Holz vor der Tür haben (inf); **the motion was carried unanimously** der Antrag wurde einstimmig angenommen; **he carried his point** er ist mit diesem Punkt durchgekommen; **he carried all seven states** er hat die Wahl in allen sieben Staaten gewonnen j **he carries himself well/like a soldier** er hat eine gute/soldatische Haltung; **he carries himself with dignity** er tritt würdig auf; **she carries her head very erect** sie trägt den Kopf sehr aufrecht k (Press) story, photo bringen l (Med) **people ~ing the AIDS virus** Menschen, die das Aidsvirus in sich (dat) tragen m (= be pregnant with) erwarten, schwanger gehen mit (geh); **to be ~ing a child** schwanger sein, ein Kind erwarten m (Math) ... and ~ **2** ... übertrage or behalte 2, ... und 2 im Sinn (inf) VI a (voice, sound) tragen; **the sound of the alphorn carried for miles** der Klang des Alphorns war meilenweit zu hören b (ball, arrow) fliegen

▶ **carry away** VT sep a (lit) (hin)wegtragen; (torrent, flood) (hin)wegspülen; (whirlwind, tornado) hinwegfegen b (fig) **to get carried away** sich nicht mehr bremsen können (inf); **don't get carried away!** übertreibs nicht!, brems dich (inf); **to get carried away by sth** bei etw in Fahrt kommen; **to be carried away by one's feelings** sich in seine Gefühle hineinsteigern; **don't get carried away by your success** dass dir dein Erfolg nicht in den Kopf steigt!; **she got carried away by all the excitement** sie wurde von all der Aufregung mitgerissen; **she got carried away with excitement** sie war vor Aufregung ganz aus dem Häuschen (inf)

▶ **carry back** VT sep (fig) person zurückversetzen (to in +acc)

▶ **carry forward** VT sep (Fin) vortragen

▶ **carry off** VT sep a (= seize, carry away) wegtragen b (= win) prizes, medals gewinnen, mit nach Hause nehmen (inf) c **to carry it off** es hinkriegen (inf) d (= kill) (hin)wegraffen (geh)

▶ **carry on** VI a (= continue) weitermachen; (life) weitergehen b (inf, = talk) reden und reden; (= make a scene) ein Theater machen (inf); **to carry on about sth** sich über etw (acc) auslassen; **they just kept carrying on about it until somebody did something** sie haben so lange weitergeredet, bis jemand etwas gemacht hat c (= have an affair) etwas haben (inf) (with sb mit jdm) VT sep a (= continue) tradition, family business fortführen b (= conduct) conversation, correspondence, business führen; profession, trade ausüben

▶ **carry out** VT sep a (lit) heraustragen b (fig) order, rules, job ausführen; promises, obligations erfüllen; plan, reform, search, experiment durchführen; threats wahrmachen

▶ **carry over** VT sep a (Fin) vortragen b (to next meeting etc) vertagen

▶ **carry through** VT sep a (= carry out) zu Ende führen b (= sustain) überstehen lassen

▶ **carry up** VT sep hinauftragen, hochtragen

carry: carryall N (US) (Einkaufs-/Reise)tasche f; **carrycot** N (Brit) Babytragetasche f

carrying: carrying agent ['kærɪŋˌeɪdʒənt] N Spediteur(in) m(f); **carrying capacity**

['kærɪŋkəˌpæsɪtɪ] N a (of load) Tragfähigkeit f; (of vehicle) Ladefähigkeit f b (Elec) Belastbarkeit f; **carrying charge** N (US) (Fin) Nebenkosten pl; (Mot) Speditionskosten pl, Transportkosten pl; **carryings-on** ['kærɪŋzˈɒn] (inf) übles Treiben (inf); **all these ~ next door** was die da nebenan alles so treiben (inf), was sich da nebenan alles so abspielt

carry: carry-on N (inf) Theater nt (inf); **carry-out** (US, Scot) N a (= restaurant) Imbissstube f/Restaurant nt für Außer-Haus-Verkauf; (= bar) Schalter m für Außer-Haus-Verkauf, Gassenschenke f (S Ger) b (= meal, drink) Speisen pl/Getränke pl zum Mitnehmen; **let's get a ~** kaufen wir uns etwas zum Mitnehmen; **~s aren't allowed in the grounds** auf das Gelände dürfen keine Getränke mitgebracht werden ADJ attr Außer-Haus-; **the ~ menu is quite different** für Gerichte zum Mitnehmen gibt es eine ganz andere Speisekarte; **carry-over** N Überbleibsel nt; (Fin) Saldovortrag m, Übertrag m; (Math) Rest m

car: carsick ADJ I used to get ~ früher wurde mir beim Autofahren immer übel or schlecht; **carsickness** N Übelkeit f beim Autofahren

cart [kɑːt] N Wagen m, Karren m; **to put the ~ before the horse** (prov) das Pferd beim Schwanz aufzäumen (prov) VT (fig inf) mit sich schleppen

▶ **cart away** or **off** VT sep abtransportieren, wegbringen

cartage ['kɑːtɪdʒ] N (= act, cost) Transport m

carte blanche ['kɑːtˈblɑːnʃ] N , no pl Blankovollmacht f; **to give sb ~** jdm Carte blanche f (geh) or eine Blankovollmacht geben

cartel [kɑːˈtel] N Kartell n

carter ['kɑːtə] N Fuhrmann m

Cartesian [kɑːˈtiːzɪən] ADJ kartesianisch, kartesisch N Kartesianer(in) m(f)

Carthage ['kɑːθɪdʒ] N Karthago nt

Carthaginian [ˌkɑːθəˈdʒɪnɪən] ADJ karthagisch N Karthager(in) m(f)

carthorse ['kɑːθɔːs] N Zugpferd nt

cartilage ['kɑːtɪlɪdʒ] N Knorpel m

cartload ['kɑːtləʊd] N Wagenladung f

cartographer [kɑːˈtɒɡrəfə] N Kartograf(in) m(f)

cartographic(al) [ˌkɑːtəʊˈɡræfɪk(əl)] ADJ kartografisch

cartography [kɑːˈtɒɡrəfɪ] N Kartografie f

cartomancy ['kɑːtəˌmænsɪ] N Kartenlegen nt, Kartomantie f (spec)

carton ['kɑːtən] N (Papp)karton m; (of cigarettes) Stange f; (of milk) Tüte f

cartoon [kɑːˈtuːn] N a Cartoon m or nt; (= single picture) Karikatur f b (Film, TV) (Zeichen-)trickfilm m; **Mickey Mouse ~** Mickymausfilm m c (Art, = sketch) Karton m

cartoon character N Comicfigur f

cartoonist [ˌkɑːˈtuːnɪst] N a Karikaturist(in) m(f) b (Film, TV) Trickzeichner(in) m(f)

cartoon strip N Cartoon m or nt, Comic m, Zeichengeschichte f

cartouche [kɑːˈtuːʃ] N Kartusche f

cartridge ['kɑːtrɪdʒ] N (for rifle, pen) Patrone f; (Phot, for tape recorder) Kassette f; (for record player) Tonabnehmer m

cartridge in cpds Patronen-; **cartridge belt** N Patronengurt or -gürtel m; **cartridge case** N Patronenhülse f; **cartridge clip** N Magazin nt; **cartridge paper** N Zeichenpapier nt

cart: carttrack N Feldweg m; **cartwheel** N (lit) Wagenrad nt; (Sport) Rad nt; **to turn** or **do ~s** Rad schlagen

carve [kɑːv] VT a (Art, = cut) wood schnitzen; stone etc (be)hauen; ~**d out of** or **in wood** aus Holz geschnitzt; ~**d out of** or **in marble** aus Marmor gehauen; ~**d in(to) the wood** in das Holz geschnitzt; ~**d in(to) the stone** in den Stein gehauen or gemeißelt; **to ~ sth on a stone** etw in einen Stein einmeißeln; **to ~**

one's initials on a tree seine Initialen in einen Baum einritzen *or* schnitzen; **a frieze ~d with flowers** ein geschnitzter *or* (*in stone*) gemeißelter Blumenfries; **the sculptor was still carving the face** der Bildhauer schnitzte *or* (*in stone*) meißelte noch das Gesicht

b (*Cook*) aufschneiden, zerteilen, tranchieren **c** (*fig*) **to ~ a road through the jungle** eine Straße durch den Dschungel schlagen; **to ~ one's way through the crowd** sich (*dat*) seinen Weg durch die Menge bahnen; **to ~ a niche for oneself (as), to ~ oneself a niche (as)** sich (*dat*) seine Sporen verdienen (als) **VI** (*Cook*) tranchieren

▶ **carve out** VT *sep* **a** (*in wood*) schnitzen; (*in stone*) meißeln **b** (*fig*) *piece of land* abtrennen, loslösen **c** **to carve out a career for oneself** sich (*dat*) eine Karriere aufbauen

▶ **carve up** VT *sep* **a** *meat* aufschneiden; (*surgeon*) aufschneiden; *body* zerstückeln **b** (*fig*) *inheritance* verteilen; *country* aufteilen, zerstückeln; *area of land etc* zerreißen, auseinander reißen **c** (*inf, with knife*) *person* (mit dem Messer) böse zurichten (*inf*); **to carve up sb's face** jdm das Gesicht zerfetzen (*inf*) **d** (*inf, driver*) schneiden

carver ['kɑːvə'] N (= *knife*) Tranchiermesser *nt*; **a set of ~s** ein Tranchierbesteck *nt*

carvery ['kɑːvərɪ] N Buffet *nt*

carve-up ['kɑːvʌp] N (*inf, of inheritance*) Verteilung *f*; (*of estate, country*) Zerstückelung *f*

carving ['kɑːvɪŋ] N (*Art*, = *thing carved*) Skulptur *f*; (*in wood also*) (Holz)schnitzerei *f*; (= *relief*) Relief *nt*; (*in wood*) Holzschnitt *m*

carving knife N Tranchiermesser *nt*

carwash ['kɑːwɒʃ] N (= *place*) Autowaschanlage *f*, Waschstraße *f*; (= *wash*) Autowäsche *f*

caryatid [ˌkærɪˈætɪd] N Karyatide *f*

casanova [ˌkæsəˈnəʊvə] N (*hum*) Casanova *m* (*inf*)

cascade [kæˈskeɪd] **N** Kaskade *f*; (*fig, of lace etc*) (Spitzen)besatz *m*; (*of sparks*) Regen *m*; **a ~ of green sparks** ein grüner Funkenregen **VI** (*also* **cascade down**) (*onto* auf +*acc*) (in Kaskaden) herabfallen; (*sparks*) herabsprühen, herabregnen; (*hair*) wallend herabfallen; (*boxes etc*) herunterpurzeln (*inf*)

cascading menu [kæˈskeɪdɪŋˌmenjuː] N (*Comput*) Untermenü *nt*

case¹ [keɪs] ✪ 26.1 N **a** (= *situation*) Fall *m*; **if that's the ~** wenn das der Fall ist, wenn das zutrifft *or* stimmt; **is that the ~ with you?** ist das bei Ihnen der Fall?, trifft das auf Sie zu?; **if it is the ~ that you're right ...** sollten Sie wirklich *or* tatsächlich Recht haben ..., im Fall(e), dass Sie tatsächlich Recht haben ...; **if it is a ~ of his not having been informed** wenn er nicht benachrichtigt worden ist; **such being the ~** da das der Fall ist, da dem so ist (*geh*); **as the ~ may be** je nachdem

b (= *instance, police case, Med etc*) Fall *m*; **in most ~s** meist(ens), in den meisten Fällen; **a typical ~ (of)** ein typischer Fall (von); **it's a clear ~ of double standards** das ist ein klarer Fall von Doppelmoral; **in ~** falls; **(just) in ~** für alle Fälle; **in ~ of emergency** im Notfall *m*, bei Gefahr *f*; **in any ~** sowieso; **in this/that ~** in dem Fall; **in no ~** unter keinen Umständen, auf keinen Fall; **in such a ~** in einem solchen Fall; **five ~s of smallpox/pneumonia** fünf Pockenfälle/Fälle von Lungenentzündung *f*

c (*Jur*) Fall *m*; **to win one's ~** seinen Prozess gewinnen; **the ~ for the defence/prosecution** die Verteidigung/Anklage; **what's the ~ for the prosecution?** worauf stützt sich die Anklage?; **could we hear the ~ for the defence?** das Wort hat die Verteidigung; **the ~ Keeler** der Fall Keeler; **in the ~ Higgins v Schwarz** in der Sache Higgins gegen Schwarz; **to take a ~ to the High Court** einen Fall vors oberste Gericht bringen; **to make out a good ~ for sth** überzeugende Argumente für etw liefern; **the ~ for/against the abolition of capital punishment** die Argumente für/gegen die Abschaffung der To-

desstrafe; **you haven't got a ~** das Belastungsmaterial reicht nicht für ein Verfahren; (*fig*) Sie haben keine Handhabe; **to have a good ~** (*Jur*) gute Chancen haben durchzukommen; **you/they have a good ~** es ist durchaus gerechtfertigt, was Sie/sie sagen; **there's a very good ~ for adopting this method** es spricht sehr viel dafür, diese Methode zu übernehmen; **they do not have a very good ~** sie haben nicht viel Chancen, damit durchzukommen; **to put one's ~** seinen Fall darlegen; **to put the ~ for sth** etw vertreten; **there's a strong ~ for legalizing pot** es spricht viel für die Legalisierung von Hasch; **there's a good ~ for voting Labour** es gibt viele Gründe, Labour zu wählen; **the court decided that there was no ~ against him** das Gericht entschied, dass nichts gegen ihn vorlag; **a ~ of conscience** eine Gewissensfrage *or* -entscheidung

d (*Gram*) Fall *m*, Kasus *m*; **in the genitive ~** im Genitiv

e (*inf*. = *person*) Witzbold *m*, Type *f* (*inf*); **a hopeless/sad ~** ein hoffnungsloser/trauriger Fall; **a hard ~** ein schwieriger Fall **f** (*inf*) **to be on sb's ~ (about sth)** jdn (wegen etw) nerven (*inf*); **to get on sb's ~ (about sth)** an jdm (wegen etw) herummeckern (*inf*); **get off my ~!** lass mich in Ruhe! (*inf*)

case² **N a** (= *suitcase*) Koffer *m*; (= *crate, packing case*) Kiste *f*; (= *display case*) Vitrine *f*, Schau- *or* Glaskasten *m*; **a ~ of champagne** eine Kiste Champagner **b** (= *box*) Schachtel *f*; (*for jewels*) Schatulle *f*, Kästchen *nt*; (*for spectacles*) Etui *nt*, Futteral *nt*; (= *seed case*) Hülse *f*, Hülle *f*; (*for CD, umbrella*) Hülle *f*; (= *pillowcase*) Bezug *m*; (*for musical instrument*) Kasten *m*; (*of watch*) Gehäuse *nt* **c** (*Typ*) (Setz)kasten *m*; (*of book*) Schuber *m*; **upper/lower ~** groß-/kleingeschrieben **VT** (*inf*) *bank, house* inspizieren; **to ~ the joint** sich (*dat*) den Laden ansehen (*inf*)

casement ['keɪsmənt] N (= *window*) Flügelfenster *nt*; (= *frame*) Fensterflügel *m*

case: case-sensitive ADJ case-sensitive, Groß-/Kleinschreibung beachtend; **case squad** N Sonderkommission *f*; **case study** N Fallstudie *f*; **casework** N (*Sociol*) ≈ Sozialarbeit *f*; **caseworker** N (*Sociol*) ≈ Sozialarbeiter(in) *m(f)*

cash [kæʃ] **N a** Bargeld *nt*; (= *change also*) Kleingeld *nt*; **~ in hand** Barbestand *m*, Kassenbestand *m*; **to pay (in) ~** bar bezahlen; **ready ~** verfügbares Geld; **how much do you have in ready ~?** wie viel Geld haben Sie verfügbar? **b** (= *immediate payment*) Barzahlung *f*; (= *not credit*) Sofortzahlung *f*, **~ down** Barzahlung *f*, Sofortzahlung *f*; **£250 ~ down and the rest over ...** £ 250 sofort (zu bezahlen), und der Rest über ...; **to pay ~** (in) bar/sofort bezahlen; **~ or charge?** zahlen Sie bar oder mit Karte?; **~ with order** zahlbar bei Bestellung; **~ on delivery** per Nachnahme

c (= *money*) Geld *nt*; **to be short of ~** knapp bei Kasse sein (*inf*); **I'm out of ~** ich bin blank (*inf*), ich habe kein Geld **VT** *cheque* einlösen

▶ **cash in** **VT** *sep* einlösen **VI** **to cash in on sth** aus etw Kapital schlagen, sich (*dat*) etw zunutze *or* zu Nutze machen; **we want to stop others cashing in (on the act)** (*inf*) wir wollen verhindern, dass andere aus der Sache Kapital schlagen

▶ **cash up** VI (*Brit*) Kasse machen

cash: cash advance N Vorschuss *m*; **cash-and-carry** **ADJ** Cash-and-carry-; **~ price** Mit-

nahmepreis *m* **N** (*for retailers*) Cash and Carry *m*, Abholmarkt *m*; (*for public*) Verbrauchermarkt *m*; **cashback** N **a** (*with purchases*) Rückerstattung *f*; (*with mortgage*) Barerstattung *f* (*bei Abschluss bestimmter Hypotheken*); **"get £5 ~!"** „Sie bekommen £ 5 zurück!" **b** (*at supermarket*) Barauszahlung *f* (*zusätzlich zu dem Preis der gekauften Ware, wenn man mit Kundenkarte bezahlt*); **I'd like £10 ~, please** und ich hätte gern zusätzlich £ 10 in bar; **cash balance** N Kassenbestand *m*, Kassensaldo *nt*, Barguthaben; **cash-book** N Kassenbuch *nt*; **cash box** N (Geld)kassette *f*; **cash business** N Bar(zahlungs)geschäft *nt*, Kassageschäft *nt*; **cash card** N (Geld)automatenkarte *f*; **cash cow** N (*fig inf*) Milchkuh *f* (*fig*), Cashcow *f*; **cash crop** N zum Verkauf bestimmte Ernte; **cash desk** N (*Brit*) Kasse *f*; **cash discount** N Skonto *m or nt*, Rabatt *m* bei Barzahlung; **cash dispenser** N (*Brit*) Geldautomat *m*

cashew ['kæʃuː] N (= *tree*) Nierenbaum *m*; (= *nut*) Cashewnuss *f*

cash: cash expenditure N Barausgaben *pl*, Barauslagen *pl*; **cash flow** ['kæʃfləʊ] **N** Cashflow *m* **ATTR** **cash-flow analysis** Cashflowanalyse *f*; **cash-flow forecast** Cashflowprognose *f*; **cash-flow position** Bruttoertragslage *f*; **cash-flow problems** Liquiditätsprobleme *pl*; **I've got cash-flow problems** (*personal*) ich bin in Geldschwierigkeiten

cashier¹ [kæˈʃɪə'] N Kassierer(in) *m(f)*

cashier² VT (*Mil*) (unehrenhaft) entlassen, kassieren (*old*)

cashier's check [kæˈʃɪəztʃek] N (*US*) Bankscheck *m*, Banktratte *f*

cashless ['kæʃləs] ADJ bargeldlos

cash machine N (*esp US*) Geldautomat *m*

cashmere ['kæʃmɪə'] N Kaschmir *m*; **~ (wool)** Kaschmirwolle *f*

cash: cash offer N Bar(zahlungs)angebot *nt*; **cash office** N Kasse *f*, Kassenbüro *nt*; **cash payment** N Barzahlung *f*; **cash point** N (*Brit: = ATM*) Geldautomat *m*; **cash price** N Bar(-zahlungs)preis *m*; **cash purchase** N Barkauf *m*; **cash receipts** PL (*in shop*) Bareinnahmen *pl*; **cash reduction** N **cash discount**; **cash register** N Registrierkasse *f*; **cash reserves** PL Bargeldreserven *pl*; **cash sale** N Barverkauf *m*; **cash transaction** N Bargeldtransfer *m*

casing ['keɪsɪŋ] N (*Tech*) Gehäuse *nt*; (*of cylinder, tyre*) Mantel *m*; (*of sausage*) Haut *f*, Darm *m*

casino [kəˈsiːnəʊ] N (Spiel)kasino *nt*, Spielbank *f*

cask [kɑːsk] N Fass *nt*

casket ['kɑːskɪt] N Schatulle *f*; (*for cremated ashes*) Urne *f*; (*US*, = *coffin*) Sarg *m*, Totenschrein *m* (*geh*)

Caspian Sea ['kæspɪənsiː] N Kaspisches Meer

Cassandra [kəˈsændrə] N (*Myth*) Kassandra *f*; **despite all the ~s** allen Kassandrarufen *or* Unkenrufen zum Trotz

cassava [kəˈsɑːvə] N Maniok *m*

casserole ['kæsərəʊl] **N** (*Cook*) Schmortopf *m*, Kasserolle *f*; **a ~ of lamb** eine Lammkasserolle **VT** schmoren

cassette [kæˈset] N Kassette *f*

cassette: cassette deck N Kassettendeck *nt*; **cassette player, cassette recorder** N Kassettenrekorder *m*; **cassette tape** N Kassette *f*

cassock ['kæsək] N Talar *m*, Soutane *f*

cast [kɑːst] *vb*: *pret, ptp* **cast** **N a** (*of dice, net, line*) Wurf *m*

b (= *mould*) (Guss)form *f*; (= *object moulded*) Abdruck *m*; (*in metal*) (Ab)guss *m* **c** (= *plaster cast*) Gipsverband *m* **d** (*Theat*) Besetzung *f*; **~ (in order of appearance)** Darsteller *pl* (in der Reihenfolge ihres Auftritts *or* Auftretens); **the ~ includes several famous actors** das Stück ist mit mehreren berühmten Schauspielern besetzt; **who's in the ~?** wer spielt mit?

e the ~ of sb's features jds Gesichtsschnitt *m*; ~ of mind *or* thought Gesinnung *f* **f** (*Med*, = *squint*) schielender Blick; **to have a ~ in one eye** auf einem Auge schielen **g** (*of worm*) aufgeworfene Erde; (*of bird*) Gewölle *nt*
h (= *tinge*) Schimmer *m*
VT a (*lit liter, fig*, = *throw*) werfen; *anchor, net, fishing lines* auswerfen; *horoscope* erstellen; **to ~ one's vote** seine Stimme abgeben; **a picture of the bishop ~ing his vote** ein Bild des Bischofs bei der Stimmabgabe; **to ~ lots** (aus)losen; **to ~ in one's lot with sb** sich auf jds (*acc*) Seite stellen; **to ~ one's eyes over sth** einen Blick auf etw (*acc*) werfen; **to ~ a critical/sceptical eye on sth** etw kritisch/skeptisch begutachten; **to ~ a greedy eye** *or* **greedy eyes on sth** gierige Blicke auf etw (*acc*) werfen; **to ~ the blame on sb** jdm die Schuld geben, die Schuld auf jdn abwälzen; **to ~ a shadow** (*lit, fig*) einen Schatten werfen (*on* auf +*acc*)
b (= *shed*) **to ~ its skin** sich häuten; **to ~ a shoe** ein Hufeisen *nt* verlieren; **to ~ its feathers** (*form*) sich mausern; **to ~ its leaves** (*form*) die Blätter abwerfen; **to ~ its young** (*form*) (Junge) werfen
c (*Tech, Art*) gießen → **mould**[1]
d (*Theat*) *play* besetzen; *parts also* verteilen; **he was well/badly ~** die Rolle passte gut/schlecht zu ihm; **he was ~ for the part of Hamlet** er sollte den Hamlet spielen; **I don't know why they ~ him as the villain** ich weiß nicht, warum sie ihm die Rolle des Schurken gegeben *or* zugeteilt haben; **to ~ oneself as** sich darstellen als
VI a (*Fishing*) die Angel auswerfen
b (*Theat*) die Rollen verteilen, die Besetzung vornehmen

▶ **cast about** (*Brit*) *or* **around for** VI +*prep obj* zu finden versuchen; *for new job etc also* sich umsehen nach; **he was casting about** *or* **around (in his mind) for something to say/for an excuse** er suchte nach Worten/nach einer Ausrede

▶ **cast aside** VT *sep cares, prejudices, inhibitions, habits* ablegen; *old clothes etc* ausrangieren; *person* fallen lassen

▶ **cast away** VT *sep* wegwerfen; **to be cast away** (*Naut*) gestrandet sein; **he was cast away on a desert island** er wurde auf eine einsame Insel verschlagen

▶ **cast back** VI (*fig*) **to cast back (in one's mind)** im Geiste zurückdenken (*to* an +*acc*) **VT** *sep* **to cast one's thoughts** *or* **mind back** seine Gedanken zurückschweifen lassen (*to* in +*acc*)

▶ **cast down** VT *sep eyes* niederschlagen; (*liter,* = *throw down*) *weapons* hinwerfen; **to be cast down** (*fig*) niedergeschlagen sein

▶ **cast off** VI *sep* **a** (= *get rid of*) abwerfen; *friends* fallen lassen **b** *stitches* abketten **c** (*Naut*) losmachen **VI a** (*Naut*) losmachen **b** (*Knitting*) abketten

▶ **cast on** (*Knitting*) **VT** *sep* anschlagen **VI** anschlagen

▶ **cast out** VT *sep* (*liter*) vertreiben; *demons* austreiben

▶ **cast up** VT *sep* **a** **to cast one's eyes up (to the heavens)** seine Augen (zum Himmel) emporrichten **b** (= *wash up*) *flotsam, sailors* anspülen; **they were cast up on a desert island** sie wurden auf einer einsamen Insel an Land gespült **c** (= *refer to*) *sb's misdemeanours etc* aufbringen; **to cast sth up at sb** jdm etw vorhalten

castanets [ˌkæstə'nets] PL Kastagnetten *pl*

castaway ['kɑːstəweɪ] N (*lit, fig*) Schiffbrüchige(r) *mf*

caste [kɑːst] **N** Kaste *f*; **to lose ~** an Rang verlieren, absteigen; **he lost ~ with his friends** er verlor in den Augen seiner Freunde *or* bei seinen Freunden an Ansehen **ADJ** *attr mark, system* Kasten-; **a high/low ~ family** eine Familie, die einer hohen/niedrigen Kaste angehört

castellan ['kæstələn] N Kastellan *m*

castellated ['kæstəleɪtɪd] ADJ mit (Türmen und) Zinnen

caster ['kɑːstə'] N = **castor**

caster sugar N (*Brit*) Sandzucker *m*

castigate ['kæstɪgeɪt] VT *person* (*verbally*) geißeln; (*old: physically*) züchtigen

castigation [ˌkæstɪ'ɡeɪʃən] N (*verbal*) Geißelung *f*; (*old: physical*) Züchtigung *f*

Castile [kæ'stiːl] N Kastilien *nt*

Castilian [kæ'stɪljən] **ADJ** kastilisch **N a** (*Ling*) Kastilisch *nt* **b** (= *person*) Kastilier(in) *m(f)*

casting ['kɑːstɪŋ] N **a** (*Fishing*) Auswerfen *nt*; (*Tech, Art*, = *act, object*) (Ab)guss *m*; (*in plaster*) Abdruck *m*, Abguss *m* **b** (*Theat*) Rollenverteilung *f*, Besetzung *f*

casting: casting couch N (*hum*) Besetzungscouch *f* (*hum inf*); **she got the part through the ~** sie bekam die Rolle, weil sie mit dem Regisseur geschlafen hat; **casting director** N Besetzungsleiter(in) *m(f)*; **casting vote** N ausschlaggebende Stimme; **he used his ~** seine Stimme gab den Ausschlag

cast iron N Gusseisen *nt* **ADJ cast-iron a** (*lit*) gusseisern **b** (*fig*) *will, constitution* eisern; *case, alibi* hieb- und stichfest

castle ['kɑːsl] **N a** Schloss *nt*; (= *medieval fortress*) Burg *f*; **to build ~s in the air** Luftschlösser bauen **b** (*Chess*) Turm *m* **VI** (*Chess*) rochieren

castling ['kɑːslɪŋ] N (*Chess*) Rochade *f*

cast: cast-off ADJ *clothes* abgelegt *attr*; **cast-offs** PL (*Brit inf*) abgelegte Kleider *pl*; **she's one of his ~** (*fig inf*) sie ist eine seiner ausrangierten Freundinnen (*inf*)

castor ['kɑːstə'] **N a** (*Brit, for sugar, salt etc*) Streuer *m* **b** (= *wheel*) Rolle *f*, Rad *nt*

castor oil N Rizinus(öl) *nt*

castrate [kæs'treɪt] VT kastrieren; (*fig*) *text* verstümmeln

castrati [kæs'trɑːtiː] *pl of* **castrato**

castration [kæs'treɪʃən] N Kastration *f*

castrato [kæs'trɑːtəʊ] N *pl* **castrati** Kastrat *m*

casual ['kæʒʊl] **ADJ a** (= *not planned*) zufällig; *acquaintance, glance* flüchtig; **we were in the area, so we paid them a ~ visit** wir waren gerade in der Gegend und haben sie bei der Gelegenheit besucht
b (= *offhand, careless*) lässig; *attitude* gleichgültig; *remark* beiläufig; (= *lacking emotion*) gleichgültig; **it was just a ~ remark** das war nicht so ernst gemeint, das habe ich/hat er *etc* nur so gesagt; **he was very ~ about it** es war ihm offensichtlich gleichgültig; (*in reaction*) das hat ihn kalt gelassen *or* nicht tangiert (*inf*); **you shouldn't be so ~ about it** du solltest das nicht so leicht *or* auf die leichte Schulter nehmen; **he tried to sound ~** er tat so, als ob ihm das nichts ausmachen würde; **he had a rather ~ manner for a policeman** für einen Polizisten war er ziemlich salopp *or* lässig; **the ~ observer** der oberflächliche Betrachter
c (= *informal*) zwanglos; *discussion, chat also* ungezwungen; *clothes* leger; **a ~ shirt** ein Freizeithemd *nt*; **wear** Freizeitkleidung *f*; **he was wearing ~ clothes** er war leger gekleidet
d (= *irregular*) *work, worker, labourer* Gelegenheits-; (= *occasional*) *drug user, sexual partner* gelegentlich; *affair, relationship* locker; **~ drinker** Gelegenheitstrinker(in) *m(f)*; **~ friendship** oberflächliche Freundschaft; **~ sex** Gelegenheitssex *m*, freie Liebe
N a casuals PL (= *shoes*) Slipper *pl* **b** (= *casual worker*) Gelegenheitsarbeiter(in) *m(f)*; **~s** Aushilfen *pl*
c (*also* **football casual**) Fußballrowdy *m*

casually ['kæʒʊlɪ] ADV (= *without planning*) zufällig; (= *without emotion*) ungerührt; (= *incidentally, in an offhand manner*) beiläufig; (= *without seriousness*) lässig; (= *informally*) zwanglos; *dressed* leger

casualness ['kæʒʊlnɪs] N (= *informality*) Zwanglosigkeit *f*; (= *carelessness*) Lässigkeit *f*; (= *lack of emotion*) Ungerührtheit *f*, Schnodderigkeit *f*

casualty ['kæʒʊltɪ] N **a** (*lit, fig*) Opfer *nt*; (*injured also*) Verletzte(r) *mf*; (*killed also*) Tote(r) *mf*; **were there many casualties?** gab es viele Opfer?; (*Mil*) gab es hohe Verluste? **b** (*also* **casualty unit**) Notaufnahme *f*; **to go to ~** in die Notaufnahme gehen; **to be in ~** in der Notaufnahme sein

casualty: casualty list N Verlustliste *f*; **casualty ward** N Unfallstation *f*

casuist ['kæzjʊɪst] N Kasuist *m*

casuistry ['kæzjʊɪstrɪ] N Kasuistik *f*

cat[1] [kæt] N **a** Katze *f*; (= *tiger etc*) (Raub)katze *f*; **the (big) ~s** die großen Katzen; **to let the ~ out of the bag** die Katze aus dem Sack lassen; **they fight like ~ and dog** die sind *or* die vertragen sich wie Hund und Katze; **to play a ~-and-mouse game with sb** mit jdm Katz und Maus spielen; **there isn't room to swing a ~** (*inf*) man kann sich nicht rühren(, so eng ist es); **a ~ may look at a king** (*prov*) es wird doch noch erlaubt sein zu gucken!; **to be on ~ on hot bricks, to be like a ~ on a hot tin roof** wie auf glühenden Kohlen sitzen; **to look like the ~ that got the cream** sich freuen wie ein Schneekönig (*inf*); **that's put the ~ among the pigeons!** da hast du *etc* aber was (Schönes) angerichtet!; **he thinks he's the ~'s whiskers** (*Brit inf*) *or* **the ~'s meow** (*US inf*) er hält sich für wer weiß was; **he doesn't have a ~ in hell's chance of winning** er hat nicht die geringste Chance zu gewinnen; **when** *or* **while the ~'s away the mice will play** (*Prov*) wenn die Katze aus dem Haus ist, tanzen die Mäuse (*Prov*); **has the ~ got your tongue?** (*inf*) du hast wohl die Sprache verloren?
b (*inf,* = *woman*) Katze *f*
c (= *whip*) (neunschwänzige) Katze *f*
d (*dated US sl*) Typ *m* (*inf*)
e (*inf:* = *caterpillar tractor*) Raupe *f*

cat[2] [kæt] N (*Aut inf*) *abbr* **catalytic converter** Kat *m*

catabolism [kə'tæbəlɪzm] N Abbaustoffwechsel *m*, Katabolismus *m* (*spec*)

cataclysm ['kætəklɪzəm] N Verheerung *f*; (*fig*) Umwälzung *f*

cataclysmic [ˌkætə'klɪzmɪk] ADJ verheerend; (*fig*) umwälzend

catacombs ['kætəkuːmz] PL Katakomben *pl*

catafalque ['kætəfælk] N Katafalk *m*

catalepsy ['kætəlepsɪ] N Katalepsie *f*, Starrsucht *f*

cataleptic [ˌkætə'leptɪk] ADJ kataleptisch

catalogue, (*US*) **catalog** ['kætəlɒg] **N** Katalog *m* **VT** katalogisieren

catalysis [kə'tæləsɪs] N Katalyse *f*

catalyst ['kætəlɪst] N (*lit, fig*) Katalysator *m*

catalytic [ˌkætə'lɪtɪk] ADJ (*lit, fig*) katalytisch

catalytic converter N (*Aut*) Katalysator *m*

catamaran [ˌkætəmə'ræn] N Katamaran *m*

cat-and-dog ADJ **to lead a ~ life** wie Hund und Katze leben

cat-and-mouse ADJ **to play ~** *or* **a ~ game with sb** mit jdm Katz und Maus spielen

catapult ['kætəpʌlt] **N a** (*Brit:* = *slingshot*) Schleuder *f*; (*Mil, Aviat*) Katapult *nt or m*; **~ launching** (*Aviat*) Katapultstart *m* **VT** schleudern, katapultieren; (*Aviat*) katapultieren **VI** geschleudert *or* katapultiert werden

cataract ['kætərækt] N **a** (= *rapids*) Katarakt *m* **b** (*Med*) grauer Star

catarrh [kə'tɑː'] N Katarr(h) *m*

catarrhal [kə'tɑːrəl] ADJ katarr(h)alisch

catastrophe [kə'tæstrəfɪ] N Katastrophe *f*; **to end in ~** verhängnisvoll *or* in einer Katastrophe enden; **to be heading for ~** auf eine Katastrophe zusteuern; **to be the final ~ for sb** jdm schließlich zum Verhängnis werden

catastrophic [ˌkætə'strɒfɪk] ADJ katastrophal; *event, decision, course also* verhängnisvoll

catastrophically [ˌkætə'strɒfɪkəl] ADV *fail* katastrophal; **to go ~ wrong** katastrophal schief gehen

catatonia [ˌkætə'təʊnɪə] N Katatonie *f*

catatonic [ˌkætə'tɒnɪk] (*Med*) **ADJ** katatonisch **N** Katatoniker(in) *m(f)*

cat: catbird N (*US*) amerikanische Spottdrossel; **cat burglar** N Fassadenkletterer *m*; **catcall** (*Theat*) **N** **~s** *pl* Pfiffe und Buhrufe *pl* **VI** pfeifen

catch [kætʃ] *vb*: pret, ptp **caught** **N** **a** (*of ball etc*) **to make a (good) ~** (gut) fangen; **good ~!** gut gefangen!; **it was a difficult ~** das war schwer zu fangen; **he missed an easy ~** er hat einen leichten Ball nicht gefangen **b** (*Fishing, Hunt*) Fang *m*; (*of trawler etc also*) Fischzug *m*; **he didn't get a ~** er hat nichts gefangen; **he's a good ~** (*fig inf*) er ist ein guter Fang; (*for marriage also*) er ist eine gute Partie **c** (= *children's game*) Fangen *nt* **d** (= *trick, snag*) Haken *m*; **where's the ~?** wo liegt *or* ist (da) der Haken?; **there's a ~ in it somewhere!** die Sache hat irgendwo einen Haken, da ist irgendwo ein Haken dabei; **~ question** Fangfrage *f* **e** (= *device for fastening*) Verschluss(vorrichtung *f*) *m*; (= *hook*) Haken *m*; (= *latch*) Riegel *m* **f** (= *break in voice*) Stocken *nt*; **with a ~ in one's voice** mit stockender Stimme **g** (*Mus*) Kanon *für Singstimmen mit heiter-komischem Text* **h** (= *fragment*) Bruchstück *nt*

VT **a** *object* fangen; *batsman* durch Abfangen des Balls ausscheiden lassen **b** *fish, mice* fangen; *thief, offender* fassen, schnappen (*inf*), erwischen (*inf*); *escaped animal* (ein)fangen; (*inf: = manage to see*) erwischen (*inf*); **to ~ sb's arm, to ~ sb by the arm** jdn am Arm fassen; **she held it up to ~ the light** sie hielt es gegen das Licht; **glass which ~es the light** Glas, in dem sich das Licht spiegelt; **to ~ sight/a glimpse of sb/sth** jdn/etw erblicken *or* zu sehen kriegen (*inf*); **to ~ sb's attention/eye** jdn auf sich (*acc*) aufmerksam machen; **to be caught between two people/alternatives** zwischen zwei Menschen/Möglichkeiten hin und her gerissen sein; **he was caught between envy and admiration** er war zwischen Neid und Bewunderung hin und her gerissen **c** (= *take by surprise*) erwischen, ertappen; **to ~ sb at sth** jdn bei etw erwischen; **to ~ sb by surprise** jdn überraschen; **to be caught unprepared** nicht darauf vorbereitet sein; **to ~ sb at a bad time** jdm ungelegen kommen; **I caught him flirting with my wife** ich habe ihn (dabei) erwischt, wie er mit meiner Frau flirtete; **I caught myself feeling sorry for him** ich habe mich dabei ertappt, dass er mir Leid tat; **you won't ~ me signing any contract** (*inf*) ich unterschreibe doch keinen Vertrag; **you won't ~ me in that restaurant** (*inf*) in das Restaurant gehe ich garantiert *or* bestimmt nicht; **(you won't) ~ me doing that again** (*inf*) das mache ich bestimmt nicht wieder!; **you won't ~ me falling for that trick again** (*inf*) auf den Trick falle ich nicht noch einmal herein; **aha, caught you** hab ich dich doch erwischt (*inf*); (*with question*) ha, reingefallen (*inf*); **caught in the act** auf frischer Tat ertappt; (*sexually*) in flagranti erwischt; **we were caught in a storm** wir wurden von einem Unwetter überrascht; **to ~ sb on the wrong foot** *or* **off balance** (*fig*) jdn überrumpeln **d** (= *take*) *bus, train etc* nehmen **e** (= *be in time for*) *train, bus* erreichen, kriegen (*inf*); **can I still ~ the post?** kommt der Brief noch mit?; **if you want to ~ the 4 o'clock post ...** wenn das mit der Vieruhrleerung mitsoll ...; **if I hurry I'll ~ the end of the film** wenn ich mich beeile kriege ich das Ende des Films noch mit (*inf*) **f** (= *become entangled*) hängen bleiben mit; **a nail caught her dress** ihr Kleid blieb an einem Nagel hängen; **I caught my finger in the car door** ich habe mir den Finger in der Wagentür eingeklemmt; **he caught his foot in the grating**

er ist mit dem Fuß im Gitter hängen geblieben **g** (*with stitches*) mit ein paar Stichen befestigen; **to ~ a dress (in) at the waist** ein Kleid an der Taille fassen **h** (= *understand, hear*) mitkriegen (*inf*) **i** **to ~ an illness** sich (*dat*) eine Krankheit zuziehen *or* holen (*inf*); **he's always ~ing cold(s)** er erkältet sich leicht; **you'll ~ your death (of cold)!** du holst dir den Tod! (*inf*) **j** (= *portray*) *mood, atmosphere etc* einfangen **k** **to ~ one's breath** (*after exercise etc*) Luft holen, verschnaufen; **to ~ sb a glancing blow** jdn seitlich erwischen; **the blow/ball caught him on the arm** der Schlag/Ball traf ihn am Arm; **she caught him one on the nose** (*inf*) sie haute ihm auf die Nase; **you'll ~ it!** (*Brit inf*) es setzt was! (*inf*), du kannst (aber) was erleben! (*inf*); **he caught it all right!** (*Brit inf*) (*physically*) der hat vielleicht eine Abreibung bekommen! (*inf*); (*verbally*) der hat aber was zu hören bekommen! (*inf*)

VI **a** (*with ball*) fangen **b** (*fire*) in Gang kommen, brennen; (*wood etc*) Feuer fangen, brennen; (*Cook*) anbrennen **c** (= *get stuck*) klemmen, sich verklemmen; (= *get entangled*) hängen bleiben, sich verfangen; **her dress caught in the door** sie blieb mit ihrem Kleid in der Tür hängen

▶**catch at** VI +prep obj (= *grab for*) greifen nach; *opportunity* ergreifen

▶**catch on** VI (*inf*) **a** (= *become popular*) ankommen; (*fashion also*) sich durchsetzen; (*book etc also*) einschlagen **b** (= *understand*) kapieren (*inf*)

▶**catch out** VT sep (*fig*) überführen; (*with trick question etc*) hereinlegen (*inf*); (*Sport*) abfangen; **I caught you out there!** du bist durchschaut; (*with trick question*) jetzt bist du aber reingefallen (*inf*); **to catch sb out in a lie** jdn beim Lügen ertappen

▶**catch up** **VI** aufholen; **to catch up on one's sleep** Schlaf nachholen; **to catch up on** *or* **with one's work** Arbeit nachholen; **to catch up with sb** (*running, in work etc*) jdn einholen; **hurry, they're catching up!** beeil dich, sie holen auf!; **you've got a lot of catching up to do** du musst noch eine Menge nachholen

VT sep **a** **to catch sb up** (*walking, working etc*) jdn einholen **b** (= *snatch up*) (vom Boden) hochheben; *hair* hochstecken; **she caught up her skirts** sie raffte *or* schürzte ihre Röcke **c** **to get caught up in sth** (= *entangled*) sich in etw (*dat*) verheddern *or* verfangen; *in traffic* in etw (*acc*) kommen; *in discussion* in etw (*acc*) verwickelt werden

catch: catch-22 N auswegslose Falle, Sackgasse *f*; **a ~ situation** (*inf*) eine Zwickmühle; **catchall** N **a** (*US: = drawer etc*) Schublade *f* für Krimskrams (*inf*) **b** (= *phrase, clause etc*) allgemeine Bezeichnung/Klausel/allgemeiner Rahmen *etc*; **catch-as-catch-can** N (*Sport*) Catch-as-catch-can *nt*; **catch crop** N Zwischenfrucht *f*

catcher ['kætʃə'] N Fänger *m*; **he's a good ~** er ist gut im Fangen, er fängt gut

catching ['kætʃɪŋ] ADJ (*Med, fig*) ansteckend

catchment area ['kætʃmənt'ɛərɪə] N Einzugsgebiet *nt*, Einzugsbereich *m*

catchment basin ['kætʃmənt'beɪsn] N Einzugsgebiet *nt*

catch: catchpenny ADJ (*dated*) publikumswirksam, zugkräftig; **catch phrase** N Schlagwort *nt*, Slogan *m*; **catch question** N (*inf*) Fangfrage *f*; **catch quota** N Fangquote *f*

catchup ['kætʃəp] N (*US*) = **ketchup**

catch: catchweight ADJ (*Sport*) ohne Gewichtsklasse; **catchword** N Schlagwort *nt*

catchy ['kætʃɪ] ADJ (+er) *tune, slogan* eingängig; *title* einprägsam

catechism ['kætɪkɪzəm] N (= *instruction*) Katechese *f*; (*fig*) Verhör *nt*; (= *book*) Katechismus *m*

catechize ['kætɪkaɪz] VT katechisieren

categorical [ˌkætɪ'gɒrɪkəl] ADJ *statement, denial* kategorisch; **he was quite ~ about it** er hat das mit Bestimmtheit gesagt; **~ imperative** kategorischer Imperativ

categorically [ˌkætɪ'gɒrɪkəlɪ] ADV *state, deny* kategorisch; *say* mit Bestimmtheit

categorization [ˌkætɪgərəraɪ'zeɪʃən] N Kategorisierung *f*

categorize ['kætɪgəraɪz] VT kategorisieren

category ['kætɪgərɪ] N Kategorie *f*, Klasse *f*; **Category A prisoner** (*Brit*) ≈ Schwerverbrecher(in) *m(f)*

cater ['keɪtə'] VI (= *provide food*) die Speisen und Getränke liefern

▶**cater for** VI +prep obj **a** (= *serve with food*) mit Speisen und Getränken versorgen; *coach party etc* (mit Speisen und Getränken) bedienen; **weddings and functions catered for** wir richten Hochzeiten und andere Veranstaltungen aus; **that café caters mainly for students** das Café ist hauptsächlich auf Studenten eingestellt **b** (= *provide for*) ausgerichtet *or* eingestellt sein auf (+*acc*); (*also* **cater to**) *needs, tastes* gerecht werden (+*dat*), etwas zu bieten haben (+*dat*); **to cater for all tastes** jedem Geschmack gerecht werden, für jeden (Geschmack) etwas zu bieten haben; **a region which caters more for old people** eine Gegend, die mehr für alte Menschen tut *or* die alten Menschen mehr zu bieten hat; **a resort which caters for children** ein kinderfreundlicher Urlaubsort **c** (= *expect, be prepared for*) **I hadn't catered for that** darauf bin ich/war ich nicht eingestellt

cater-corner(ed) [ˌkeɪtə'kɔːnə'(-əd)] ADJ, ADV (*US*) diagonal

caterer ['keɪtərə'] N (= *company*) Lieferfirma *f* für Speisen und Getränke; (*for parties etc*) Partyservice *m*; (= *owner, manager*) Gastronom(in) *m(f)*

catering ['keɪtərɪŋ] N Versorgung *f* mit Speisen und Getränken (*for +gen*); (= *trade*) Gastronomie *f*; **who's doing the ~?** wer liefert das Essen und die Getränke?; **~ trade** (Hotel- und) Gaststättengewerbe *nt*

caterpillar ['kætəpɪlə'] N **a** (*Zool*) Raupe *f* **b** **~®** (*Tech*) Raupe(nkette) *f*, Gleiskette *f*; (= *vehicle*) Raupenfahrzeug *nt*

caterpillar track® N Raupenkette *f*, Gleiskette *f*

caterpillar tractor® N Raupenfahrzeug *nt*, Gleiskettenfahrzeug *nt*

caterwaul ['kætəwɔːl] VI jaulen

caterwauling ['kætəwɔːlɪŋ] N Gejaule *nt*

cat: cat fight N (*esp US inf, between women*) Gezänk *nt*, Gezerfe *nt*; **catfish** N Wels *m*, Katzenfisch *m*; **cat flap** N Katzenklappe *f*; **catgut** N Katgut *nt*

catharsis [kə'θɑːsɪs] N **a** (*Med*) Darmreinigung *f*, Darmentleerung *f* **b** (*Liter, Philos*) Katharsis *f*, Läuterung *f*

cathartic [kə'θɑːtɪk] **ADJ** **a** (*Med*) abführend **b** (*Liter, Philos*) kathartisch **N** (*Med*) Abführmittel *nt*

cathedral [kə'θiːdrəl] N Dom *m*; (*esp in England, France, Spain*) Kathedrale *f*; **~ town/city** Domstadt *f*

Catherine ['kæθərɪn] N Katharina *f*

Catherine wheel N Feuerrad *nt*

catheter ['kæθɪtə'] N Katheter *m*

catheterize ['kæθɪtəraɪz] VT katheterisieren

cathode ['kæθəʊd] N Kat(h)ode *f*

cathode: cathode ray N Kat(h)odenstrahl *m*; **cathode-ray tube** N Kat(h)odenstrahlröhre *f*

Catholic ['kæθəlɪk] **ADJ** (*Eccl*) katholisch; **the ~ Church** die katholische Kirche **N** Katholik(in) *m(f)*

catholic ['kæθəlɪk] ADJ (= *varied*) vielseitig; **he's a man of very ~ tastes** er ist (ein) sehr vielseitig interessiert(er Mensch)

Catholicism [kə'θɒlɪsɪzəm] N Katholizismus *m*

cat: catkin N (*Bot*) Kätzchen *nt*; **catlick** N (*inf*) Katzenwäsche *f*; **catlike** ADJ katzenhaft, katzengleich; **cat litter** N Katzenstreu *f*; **catmint** N Katzenminze *f*; **catnap** N to have a ~ ein Nickerchen *nt* machen (*inf*), **VI** dösen; **catnip** N Katzenminze *f*; **cat-o'-nine-tails** N neunschwänzige Katze

CAT scan [ˈkætˌskæn] N Computertomografie *f*

cat's cradle N Abnehmespiel *nt*, Fadenspiel *nt*

cat's-eye [ˈkætsˌaɪ] N (*Miner*) Katzenauge *nt*

Catseye® [ˈkætsˌaɪ] N (*Brit Aut*) Katzenauge *nt*, Rückstrahler *m*

cat's-paw [ˈkætspɔː] N Handlanger *m*

cat's pyjamas PL (*US*) → **cat's whiskers**

catsuit [ˈkætsuːt] N einteiliger Hosenanzug

catsup [ˈkætsəp] N (*US*) → **ketchup**

cat's whiskers PL (*inf*) to be the ~ spitze sein (*inf*); he thinks he's the ~ er hält sich für etwas Besonderes

cattail [ˈkætˌteɪl] N (*US*) Rohrkolben *m*, Kanonenputzer *m* (*inf*)

cattery [ˈkætərɪ] N (*for boarding*) Katzenpension *f*; (*for breeding*) Katzenzucht *f*

cattiness [ˈkætɪnɪs] N (*fig*) Gehässigkeit *f*, Boshaftigkeit *f*

cattle [ˈkætl] PL Rind(vieh) *nt*; 500 head of ~ 500 Rinder, 500 Stück Vieh; "cattle crossing" „Vorsicht Viehtrieb!"; they were treated like ~ sie wurden wie Vieh behandelt

cattle: cattle breeding N Rinderzucht *f*; **cattle car** N (*US Rail*) Viehwaggon *m*; **cattle-grid** N Weiderost *m*, Viehtor *nt*; **cattleman** N Rinderzüchter *m*; **cattle market** N (*lit*) Viehmarkt *m*; (*fig inf*) = beauty contest etc) Fleischbeschau *f* (*inf*); (*for pick-ups*) Abschleppladen *m* (*inf*); **cattle prod** N Knüppel *m* zum Viehtreiben; **cattle range** N Weideland *nt*, Viehtrift *f*; **cattle rustler** N Viehdieb *m*; **cattle shed** N Viehstall *m*; **cattle show** N Rinder(zucht)schau *f*; **cattle truck** N (*Aut*) Viehanhänger *m*; (*Rail*) Viehwagen *m*

catty [ˈkætɪ] ADJ (+er) gehässig, boshaft

catty-corner(ed) [ˌkætɪˈkɔːnə(-əd)] ADJ, ADV (*US*) = **cater-corner(ed)**

catwalk [ˈkætwɔːk] N Steg *m*, Brücke *f*; (*for models*) Laufsteg *m*

Caucasian [kɔːˈkeɪzɪən] ADJ kaukasisch N Kaukasier(in) *m(f)*

Caucasus [ˈkɔːkəsəs] N Kaukasus *m*

caucus [ˈkɔːkəs] N (= *committee*) Gremium *nt*, Ausschuss *m*; (*US: = meeting*) Sitzung *f*

caudal [ˈkɔːdl] ADJ Schwanz-, kaudal (*spec*); the ~ vertebrae die Schwanzwirbel *pl*; the ~ fin die Schwanzflosse

caught [kɔːt] pret, ptp of **catch**

caul [kɔːl] N Glückshaube *f*

cauldron [ˈkɔːldrən] N großer Kessel *m*; (= *witch's cauldron*) (Hexen)kessel *m*

cauliflower [ˈkɒlɪflaʊə] N Blumenkohl *m*

cauliflower cheese N Blumenkohl *m* mit Käsesoße

cauliflower ear N Boxerohr *nt*

caulk [kɔːk] VT seams, joints abdichten; (*on ship*) kalfatern

caulking [ˈkɔːkɪŋ] N Material *nt* zum Abdichten; (*Naut*) Teer *m*

causal [ˈkɔːzəl] ADJ kausal, ursächlich; ~ relationship Kausalzusammenhang *m*

causality [kɔːˈzælɪtɪ] N Kausalität *f*

causally [ˈkɔːzəlɪ] ADV kausal, ursächlich; they are ~ connected dazwischen besteht ein Kausalzusammenhang

causation [kɔːˈzeɪʃən] N Kausalität *f*; (*of particular event*) Ursache *f*; the law of ~ das Kausalgesetz *or* -prinzip

causative [ˈkɔːzətɪv] ADJ factor verursachend; (*Gram*) kausativ N (*Gram*) Kausativ *nt*

cause [kɔːz] ✿ 17.2, 26.3 N a Ursache *f* (of für); ~ and effect Ursache und Wirkung; what

was the ~ of the fire? wodurch ist das Feuer entstanden?

b (= *reason*) Grund *m*, Anlass *m*; she has no ~ to be angry sie hat keinen Grund, sich zu ärgern; the ~ of his failure der Grund für sein Versagen; with/without (good) ~ mit (triftigem)/ohne (triftigen) Grund; not without ~ nicht ohne Grund; there's no ~ for alarm es besteht kein Grund *or* Anlass zur Aufregung; you have every ~ to be worried du hast allen Anlass zur Sorge; you have good ~ for complaint Sie haben allen Grund zur Klage, Sie beklagen sich zu Recht

c (= *purpose, ideal*) Sache *f*; to make common ~ with sb mit jdm gemeinsame Sache machen; to work for *or* in a good ~ sich für eine gute Sache einsetzen; he died for the ~ of peace er starb für den Frieden *or* für die Sache des Friedens; in the ~ of justice für die (Sache der) Gerechtigkeit, im Namen der Gerechtigkeit; it's all in a good ~ es ist für eine gute Sache

d (*Jur*: = *action*) Fall *m*, Sache *f*

VT verursachen; to ~ sb grief jdm Kummer machen; to ~ sb to do sth (*form*) jdn veranlassen, etw zu tun (*form*)

cause célèbre N Cause célèbre *f*

causeway [ˈkɔːzweɪ] N Damm *m*

caustic [ˈkɔːstɪk] ADJ (*Chem*) ätzend, kaustisch; (*fig*) ätzend; remark bissig; he was very ~ about the project er äußerte sich sehr bissig über das Projekt

caustically [ˈkɔːstɪklɪ] ADV say, remark bissig; his new book is ~ funny sein neues Buch ist auf bissige Art lustig

caustic soda N Ätznatron *nt*

cauterization [ˌkɔːtəraɪˈzeɪʃən] N (*Med*) Kaustik *f*, Kauterisation *f*

cauterize [ˈkɔːtəraɪz] VT (*Med*) kauterisieren

caution [ˈkɔːʃən] N a (= *circumspection*) Vorsicht *f*, Umsicht *f*, Bedacht *m*; "caution!" „Vorsicht!"; to act with ~ umsichtig *or* mit Bedacht vorgehen, Vorsicht walten lassen b (= *warning*) Warnung *f*; (*official*) Verwarnung *f* c (*inf*) to be a real ~ zum Piepen sein (*inf*) **VT** to ~ sb jdn warnen (*against* vor +*dat*); (*officially*) jdn verwarnen; to ~ sb against doing sth jdn davor warnen, etw zu tun

cautionary [ˈkɔːʃənərɪ] ADJ belehrend; sign Warn-; a ~ tale eine Geschichte mit Moral

caution money N (*Brit*) Kaution *f*

cautious [ˈkɔːʃəs] ADJ vorsichtig; to play a ~ game Vorsicht walten lassen; to give sth a ~ welcome etw mit Zurückhaltung *or* verhaltener Zustimmung aufnehmen; ~ optimism vorsichtiger *or* verhaltener Optimismus

cautiously [ˈkɔːʃəslɪ] ADV move, say, react vorsichtig; welcome verhalten; accept mit Vorbehalten; ~ optimistic verhalten optimistisch

cautiousness [ˈkɔːʃəsnɪs] N Vorsicht *f*

cavalcade [ˌkævəlˈkeɪd] N Kavalkade *f*

cavalier [ˌkævəˈlɪə] N (= *horseman, knight*) Kavalier *m*; **Cavalier** (*Hist*) Kavalier *m* ADJ a the **Cavalier resistance** (*Hist*) der Widerstand der Kavaliere b (= *offhand*) person, nature, attitude, approach unbekümmert; disregard, overruling also ungeniert, kaltlächelnd; ... he said in his ~ fashion ... sagte er leichthin; treat it seriously, don't be so ~ nehmen Sie das ernst, und gehen Sie nicht so leichthin darüber hinweg

cavalierly [ˌkævəˈlɪəlɪ] ADV unbekümmert, kalt lächelnd; say leichthin

cavalry [ˈkævəlrɪ] N Kavallerie *f*, Reiterei *f*

cavalry: cavalryman N Kavallerist *m*; **cavalry officer** N Kavallerieoffizier *m*; **cavalry twill** N Reitertrikot *m*, strapazierfähiger Hosenstoff

cave¹ [keɪv] N to keep ~ (dated Brit Sch sl) Schmiere stehen (*inf*)

cave² [keɪv] N Höhle *f* **VI** to go caving auf Höhlenexpedition(en) gehen; he did a lot of caving in his youth in seiner Jugend hat er viel Höhlenforschung betrieben

▶ **cave in** VI a (= *collapse*) (roof, wall) einstürzen; (*fig: scheme etc*) zusammenbrechen b (*inf*: = *surrender, yield*) nachgeben, kapitulieren

caveat [ˈkævɪæt] N Vorbehalt *m*; to enter a ~ (*Jur*) Einspruch einlegen

caveat emptor [ˈkævɪætˈemptɔː] N (*Jur*) Ausschluss *m* der Gewährleistung

cave: cave dweller N Höhlenbewohner *m*; **cave-in** N Einsturz *m*; (= *place*) Einsturzstelle *f*; **caveman** N Höhlenmensch *m*; (*fig*) Tier *nt* (*inf*), Urmensch *m*; ~ instincts Urinstinkte *pl*; **cave painting** N Höhlenmalerei *f*

caver [ˈkeɪvə] N Höhlenforscher(in) *m(f)*

cavern [ˈkævən] N Höhle *f*

cavernous [ˈkævənəs] ADJ a cellar, pit, darkness tief; hole gähnend; mouth riesig; eyes tief liegend; cheeks eingefallen, hohl; voice hohl (tönend); yawn herzhaft, breit b mountain etc höhlenreich, voller Höhlen

caviar(e) [ˈkævɪɑː] N Kaviar *m*

cavil [ˈkævɪl] VI kritteln; to ~ at sth an etw (*dat*) herumkritteln

cavity [ˈkævɪtɪ] N Hohlraum *m*, Höhlung *f*; (*in tooth*) Loch *nt*; nasal/chest ~ (*Anat*) Nasen-/Brusthöhle *f*

cavity block N Hohlraumziegel *m*

cavity wall N Hohlwand *f*; ~ insulation Schaumisolierung *f*

cavort [kəˈvɔːt] VI tollen, toben; to ~ about herumtollen *or* -toben

cavy [ˈkeɪvɪ] N Meerschweinchen *nt*

caw [kɔː] **VI** krächzen N (heiserer) Schrei

cawing [ˈkɔːɪŋ] N Krächzen *nt*, Gekrächz(e) *nt*

cay [keɪ] N (kleine) Insel, Koralleninsel *f*

cayenne pepper [keɪˈenˈpepə] N Cayennepfeffer *m*

CB abbr of **Citizens' Band** CB; **CB radio** CB-Funk *m*

CBC abbr of **Canadian Broadcasting Corporation**

CBE (*Brit*) abbr of **Commander of the Order of the British Empire**

CBI (*Brit*) abbr of **Confederation of British Industry** ≈ BDI

CBS abbr of **Columbia Broadcasting System** CBS

CC (*Brit*) a abbr of **County Council** b abbr of **Cricket Club**

cc¹ abbr of **cubic centimetre** cc, cm³

cc² abbr of **carbon copy** N Kopie *f* **VT** eine Kopie senden an (+*acc*); **cc:** ... Kopie (an): ...

CCTV N ABBR of **closed-circuit television**

CD a abbr of **compact disc** CD *f*; **CD player** CD-Spieler *m*; **CD case** CD-Hülle *f* b abbr of **corps diplomatique** c abbr of **civil defence** d (*US*) abbr of **Congressional District**

CDC (*US*) abbr of **Centers for Disease Control and Prevention**

CDC

Die **Centers for Disease Control and Prevention**, kurz **CDC**, bilden eine US-Bundesbehörde, die für viele Aspekte der öffentlichen Gesundheit zuständig ist. Zu ihren Aufgaben gehört das Festlegen und Verschärfen von Schadstoffgrenzwerten und Sicherheitsstandards für Umwelt oder Arbeitsplätze, das Sammeln und Analysieren von Daten, die für das Gesundheitswesen relevant sind, sowie die Vorsorge gegen übertragbare Krankheiten und deren Kontrolle. Der Hauptsitz der **CDC** ist in Atlanta, Georgia. Im Ausland wurde die US-Seuchenkontrollbehörde vor allem durch ihre Vorreiterrolle bei der Beobachtung der Ausbreitung des HIV-Virus und der Identifizierung von dessen Übertragungswegen bekannt.

Cdr abbr of **Commander**

CD-ROM [ˈsiːdiːˈrɒm] abbr of **compact disk - read only memory** CD-ROM *f*; ~ drive CD-ROM-Laufwerk *nt*

CDT **a** (US) abbr of **Central Daylight Time** **b** (Brit Sch) abbr of **Craft, Design and Technology** ≈ Arbeitslehre f

CDTV abbr of **compact disc television** CDTV nt

cease [siːs] **VI** enden, aufhören; (noise, shouting etc) verstummen; **we shall not ~ from our endeavours** (liter) wir werden in unserem Streben nicht nachlassen (geh); **without ceasing** ohne Pause, unaufhörlich; **to ~ from doing sth** (form) von etw ablassen (geh) **VT** beenden; fire, payments, production einstellen; **to ~ doing sth** aufhören, etw zu tun; **to ~ to exist** aufhören zu bestehen; **~ fire!** Feuer halt! **N without ~** (liter) unaufhörlich, ohne Unterlass (liter)

cease-fire [ˈsiːsˈfaɪə] N Feuerpause or -einstellung f; (longer) Waffenruhe f, Einstellung f der Kampfhandlungen; **to give the ~** den Befehl zur Feuereinstellung geben

ceaseless [ˈsiːslɪs] ADJ (= endless) endlos, unaufhörlich; (= relentless) vigilance unablässig

ceaselessly [ˈsiːslɪslɪ] ADV (= endlessly) unaufhörlich; (= relentlessly) unablässig

cecum [ˈsiːkəm] N = **caecum**

cedar [ˈsiːdə] N **a** (= tree) Zeder f; **~ of Lebanon** Libanonzeder f **b** (also **cedarwood**) Zedernholz nt

cede [siːd] VT territory abtreten (to an +acc); **to ~ a point in an argument** in einem Punkt or in einer Sache nachgeben

cedilla [sɪˈdɪlə] N Cedille f

Ceefax® [ˈsiːfæks] N Videotext der BBC

ceiling [ˈsiːlɪŋ] N **a** (Zimmer)decke f → **hit VT** I **b** (Aviat, = cloud ceiling) Wolkenhöhe f; (= aircraft's ceiling) Gipfelhöhe f **c** (fig, = upper limit) ober(st)e Grenze, Höchstgrenze f; **price ~** oberste Preisgrenze; **to put a ~ on sth** etw nach oben begrenzen

celadon [ˈselədɒn] **N** Seladon nt **ADJ** seladongrün

celandine [ˈseləndaɪn] N **a** (= greater celandine) Schöllkraut nt **b** (= lesser celandine) Scharbockskraut nt

celeb [sɪˈleb] N (inf) Promi m (inf)

celebrant [ˈselɪbrənt] N (Eccl) Zelebrant m

celebrate [ˈselɪbreɪt] ✪ 25.1, 25.2 **VT a** feiern; event, birthday also begehen **b** (= extol) sb's name, deeds feiern, preisen (geh) **c** mass, ritual zelebrieren; communion feiern **VI** feiern

celebrated [ˈselɪbreɪtɪd] ADJ gefeiert (for wegen), berühmt (for für)

celebration [ˌselɪˈbreɪʃən] N **a** (= party, festival) Feier f; (= commemoration, jubilee also) Gedenkfeier f; (= act of celebrating) Feiern nt; **during the centenary ~s** während der Hundertjahrfeier(n); **in ~ of** zur Feier (+gen) **b** (= praise) Verherrlichung f **c** (of mass, ritual) Zelebration f; (of communion) Feier f

celebratory [ˌselɪˈbreɪtərɪ] ADJ meal, drink zur Feier des Tages

celebrity [sɪˈlebrɪtɪ] N Berühmtheit f; (= person also) berühmte Persönlichkeit f

celeriac [səˈlærɪæk] N (Knollen)sellerie f

celerity [sɪˈlerɪtɪ] N (form) Geschwindigkeit f

celery [ˈselərɪ] N Stangensellerie m or f; **three stalks of ~** drei Stangen Sellerie; **~ hearts** Sellerieherzen pl

celesta [sɪˈlestə], **celeste** [sɪˈlest] N (Mus) Celesta f

celestial [sɪˈlestɪəl] ADJ himmlisch; (Astron) Himmels-

celibacy [ˈselɪbəsɪ] N Zölibat nt or m; (fig) Enthaltsamkeit f

celibate [ˈselɪbɪt] **ADJ** (Rel) keusch, zölibatär (spec); (fig) enthaltsam **N to be a ~** im Zölibat leben

cell [sel] N (all senses) Zelle f; **~ wall** Zellwand f

cellar [ˈselə] N Keller m; **he keeps an excellent ~** er hat einen ausgezeichneten Weinkeller

cellarage [ˈselərɪdʒ] N (= cellar space) Kellerfläche f; (= storage cost) Lagerkosten pl

cell culture N (Biol) Zellkultur f

cellist [ˈtʃelɪst] N Cellist(in) m(f)

cello, 'cello [ˈtʃeləʊ] N Cello nt

Cellophane® [ˈseləfeɪn] N Cellophan® nt

cellphone [ˈselfəʊn] N (esp US) Handy nt, Mobiltelefon nt

cellular [ˈseljʊlə] ADJ **a** zellenförmig, zellular, Zell- **b** (Tex) aus porösem Material

cellular phone N Funktelefon nt; (= mobile phone) Handy nt, Mobiltelefon nt

cellulite [ˈseljʊˌlaɪt] N Cellulitis f

celluloid [ˈseljʊlɔɪd] N Zelluloid nt; **~ heroes** Zelluloidhelden pl; **on ~** auf der Leinwand

cellulose [ˈseljʊləʊs] **N** Zellulose f, Zellstoff m **ADJ** Zellulose-

Celsius [ˈselsɪəs] ADJ Celsius-; **30 degrees ~** 30 Grad Celsius

Celt [kelt, selt] N Kelte m, Keltin f

Celtic [ˈkeltɪk, ˈseltɪk] **ADJ** keltisch **N** (Ling) Keltisch nt

cembalo [ˈtʃembələʊ] N (Mus) Cembalo nt

cement [səˈment] **N a** (Build) Zement m; (inf: = concrete) Beton m **b** (= glue) Leim m, Klebstoff m; (for holes etc, fig) Kitt m **c** (of tooth) (Zahn-)zement m **VT a** (Build) zementieren; (= glue) leimen, kitten; (fig) festigen, zementieren

cement mixer N Betonmischmaschine f

cemetery [ˈsemɪtrɪ] N Friedhof m

cenotaph [ˈsenətɑːf] N Mahnmal nt, Ehrenmal nt, Kenotaph m

censer [ˈsensə] N (Eccl) Rauchfass, Räuchergefäß nt

censor [ˈsensə] **N** Zensor m **VT** zensieren; (= remove) chapter herausnehmen

censorious [senˈsɔːrɪəs] ADJ remark, glance strafend; **he was very ~ of the new policy** er kritisierte die neue Politik scharf

censorship [ˈsensəʃɪp] N Zensur f; **press ~, ~ of the press** Pressezensur f

censure [ˈsenʃə] **VT** tadeln **N** Tadel m; **vote of ~** Tadelsantrag m

census [ˈsensəs] N Zensus m, Volkszählung f; (Bibl) Schätzung f; (= traffic census) Verkehrszählung f; **to take a ~ (of the population)** eine Volkszählung durchführen

cent [sent] N Cent m; **I haven't a ~** (US) ich habe keinen Cent; **to put in one's two ~s' worth** (esp US) seinen Senf dazugeben (inf)

centaur [ˈsentɔː] N Zentaur m

centenarian [ˌsentɪˈneərɪən] **ADJ** hundertjährig **N** Hundertjährige(r) mf, Zentenar m (geh)

centenary [senˈtiːnərɪ] N (= anniversary) hundertster Jahrestag; (= birthday) hundertster Geburtstag; (= 100 years) Jahrhundert nt; **she has just celebrated her ~** sie ist gerade hundert Jahre alt geworden; **~ celebrations** Hundertjahrfeier f

centennial [senˈtenɪəl] **ADJ** hundertjährig, hundertjährlich **N** (esp US) Hundertjahrfeier f, Zentenarfeier f (geh)

center N (US) = **centre**

centesimal [senˈtesɪməl] ADJ zentesimal, hundertteilig

centigrade [ˈsentɪgreɪd] ADJ Celsius-; **one degree ~** ein Grad Celsius

centigramme, (US) centigram [ˈsentɪgræm] N Zentigramm nt

centilitre, (US) centiliter [ˈsentɪˌliːtə] N Zentiliter m or nt

centimetre, (US) centimeter [ˈsentɪˌmiːtə] N Zentimeter m or nt

centipede [ˈsentɪpiːd] N Tausendfüßler m

central [ˈsentrəl] **ADJ a** zentral, Zentral-; (= main, chief) Haupt-; **the ~ area of the city** das Innenstadtgebiet; **~ London** das Zentrum von London; **our house is very ~** unser Haus liegt sehr zentral **b** (fig) importance, figure, issue zentral; (role) wesentlich, zentral; **to be ~ to sth** das Wesentliche an etw (dat) sein; **he plays a ~ role** or **part in ...** er spielt eine zentrale or wesentliche Rolle bei ... **N** (US: = ex-

change, operator) (Telefon)zentrale f, Fernamt nt

central: Central African Republic N Zentralafrikanische Republik; **Central America** N Mittelamerika nt; **Central American ADJ** mittelamerikanisch **N** Mittelamerikaner(in) m(f); **Central Asian** ADJ zentralasiatisch; **central casting** N (esp US Film) Castingagentur f; **straight out of ~** (fig) wie eine klassische Figur aus dem Film; **Central Committee** N (Pol) Zentralkomitee nt; **Central Europe** N Mitteleuropa nt; **Central European ADJ** mitteleuropäisch **N** Mitteleuropäer(in) m(f); **Central European Time** N mitteleuropäische Zeit; **central government** N Zentralregierung f; **central heating** N Zentralheizung f

centralism [ˈsentrəlɪzəm] N (esp Pol) Zentralismus m

centralist [ˈsentrəlɪst] ADJ (esp Pol) zentralistisch

centrality [senˈtrælɪtɪ] N (= central location) zentrale Lage; (fig: = importance) zentrale Bedeutung

centralization [ˌsentrəlaɪˈzeɪʃən] N Zentralisierung f

centralize [ˈsentrəlaɪz] VT zentralisieren

central locking [ˌsentrəlˈlɒkɪŋ] N Zentralverriegelung f

centrally [ˈsentrəlɪ] ADV zentral; **~ heated** zentralbeheizt; **~ planned economy** zentral gesteuerte or geplante Wirtschaft

central: central nervous system N Zentralnervensystem nt; **central processing unit** N (Comput) Zentraleinheit f; **central reservation** N Mittelstreifen m, Grünstreifen m; **Central Standard Time** N Central Standard Time f; **central station** N Hauptbahnhof m; **central unit** N (Comput) Zentraleinheit f

centre, (US) center [ˈsentə] **N a** (= chief place) Zentrum nt

b (= middle, Pol) Mitte f; (of circle) Mittelpunkt m; (= town centre) Stadtmitte f; (= city centre) Zentrum nt, City f; **~ of gravity** Schwerpunkt m; **~ of attention** or **attraction** Hauptanziehungspunkt m, Hauptattraktion f; (= person) Mittelpunkt m der Aufmerksamkeit; **she always wants to be the ~ of attraction** sie will immer im Mittelpunkt stehen; **the man at the ~ of the controversy** der Mann im Mittelpunkt der Kontroverse; **left of ~** (Pol) links der Mitte; **politician/party of the ~** Politiker(in) m(f)/Partei f der Mitte; **the ~ of the field** (Sport) das Mittelfeld; **let's go into the ~** komm, wir gehen in die Stadt!

c (= community centre, sports centre, shopping centre) Zentrum nt, Center nt

d (Rugby) mittlerer Dreiviertelspieler; (Basketball, Netball) Center m

VT a (also Comput) zentrieren; **to feel ~d** (person) ausgeglichen sein

b (= concentrate) konzentrieren; **to be ~d on sth** sich auf etw (acc) konzentrieren

c (Sport) ball zur Mitte (ab)spielen

▶ **centre up** VT sep zentrieren

▶ **centre (up)on** VI +prep obj (thoughts, problem, talk etc) kreisen um, sich drehen um

centre, (US) center: centre bit N (Tech) Zentrumbohrer m; **centreboard, (US) centerboard** N (Naut) (Kiel)schwert nt; **centre court, center court** (US) N (Tennis) Centre- or Center-Court m; **centrefold, (US) centerfold** N doppelseitiges Bild in der Mitte einer Zeitschrift; **centrefold girl, (US) centerfold girl** N weibliches Aktmodell, dessen Foto auf den Mittelseiten einer Zeitschrift abgedruckt ist; **centre forward** N (Sport) Mittelstürmer(in) m(f); **centre half** N (Sport) Stopper(in) m(f); **centre line** N Mittellinie f, Mitte f; **centre party** N Partei f der Mitte; **centrepiece, (US) centerpiece** N (on table) Tafelaufsatz m; (fig) (of meeting, talks, treaty, statement) Kernstück nt; (of novel, work) Herzstück nt; (of show) Hauptattraktion f; **the ~ of this week's events was ...** im Mittelpunkt des Geschehens dieser Woche stand ...; **centre three-quarter** N (*Rugby*) mittlerer Dreiviertelspieler, mittlere Dreivertelspielerin

centrifugal [ˌsentrɪˈfjʊɡəl] ADJ zentrifugal; ~ **force** Zentrifugal- *or* Fliehkraft *f*

centrifuge [ˈsentrɪfjuːʒ] N (*Tech*) Zentrifuge *f*, Schleuder *f*

centripetal [ˌsentrɪˈpiːtl] ADJ zentripetal; ~ **force** Zentripetalkraft *f*

centrist [ˈsentrɪst] N Anhänger(in) *m(f)* der politischen Mitte; (= *politician*) Politiker(in) *m(f)* der Mitte

centuries-old [ˈsentjʊrɪzˈəʊld] ADJ jahrhundertealt

centurion [senˈtjʊərɪən] N Zenturio *m*

century [ˈsentjʊrɪ] N **a** Jahrhundert *nt*; **in the twentieth** ~ im zwanzigsten Jahrhundert; (*written*) im 20. Jahrhundert **b** (*Cricket*) Hundert *f*

CEO (*US*) *abbr of* **chief executive officer**

cep [sep] N (*Bot*) Steinpilz *m*

cephalic [sɪˈfælɪk] ADJ (*form*) Kopf-, Schädel-

ceramic [sɪˈræmɪk] ADJ keramisch; ~ **hob** Glaskeramikkochfeld *nt* **N** Keramik *f*

ceramics [sɪˈræmɪks] N **a** *sing* (= *art*) Keramik *f* **b** *pl* (= *articles*) Keramik(en *pl*) *f*, Keramikwaren *pl*

cereal [ˈsɪərɪəl] N **a** (= *crop*) Getreide *nt*; ~ **crop** Getreideernte *f*; **the growing of ~s** der Getreideanbau; **maize, rye and other ~s** Mais, Roggen und andere Getreidearten **b** (= *food*) Cornflakes *pl*/Müsli *nt*/Müesli *nt* (*Sw*) *etc*

cerebellum [ˌserɪˈbeləm] N Kleinhirn *nt*, Zerebellum *nt* (*spec*)

cerebral [ˈserɪbrəl] ADJ (*Physiol*) zerebral; (= *intellectual*) geistig; *person* durchgeistigt, vergeistigt; ~ **palsy** zerebrale Lähmung

cerebration [ˌserɪˈbreɪʃən] N (*usu hum*) Reflexion *f*

cerebrum [ˈserəbrəm] N Großhirn *nt*, Zerebrum *nt* (*spec*)

ceremonial [ˌserɪˈməʊnɪəl] ADJ zeremoniell **N** Zeremoniell *nt*

ceremonially [ˌserɪˈməʊnɪəlɪ] ADV feierlich, zeremoniell

ceremonious [ˌserɪˈməʊnɪəs] ADJ förmlich, zeremoniös (*geh*)

ceremoniously [ˌserɪˈməʊnɪəslɪ] ADV mit großem Zeremoniell

ceremony [ˈserɪmənɪ] ✪ 24.3 N **a** (= *event etc*) Zeremonie *f*, Feier(lichkeiten *pl*) *f* **b** (= *formality*) Förmlichkeit(en *pl*) *f*; **to stand on** ~ förmlich sein

cerise [səˈriːz] ADJ kirschrot, cerise *pred* **N** Kirschrot *nt*

cert¹ [sɜːt] *abbr of* **certificate**

cert² [sɜːt] N (*Brit inf*) **a (dead)** ~ eine todsichere Sache (*inf*); **it's a dead ~ he'll be coming** er kommt todsicher (*inf*)

certain [ˈsɜːtən] ✪ 15.1, 16.1, 26.3 ADJ **a** (= *positive, convinced*) sicher; (= *inevitable, guaranteed*) bestimmt, gewiss; **are you ~ of** *or* **about that?** sind Sie sich (*dat*) dessen sicher?; **is he ~?** weiß er das genau?; **there's no ~ cure for this disease/for inflation** für *or* gegen diese Krankheit/gegen die Inflation gibt es kein sicheres Mittel; **for ~** ganz sicher, ganz genau; **I don't know for ~, but I think ...** ich weiß ihn nicht ganz sicher, aber ich glaube ...; **I can't say for ~** ich kann das nicht genau *or* mit Sicherheit sagen; **he is ~ to come** er wird ganz bestimmt *or* gewiss kommen; **we are ~ to succeed** wir werden ganz bestimmt Erfolg haben; **to make ~ of sth** (= *check*) sich einer Sache (*gen*) vergewissern, eine nachprüfen; (= *ensure*) für etw sorgen; **to make ~ of a seat** sich (*dat*) einen Platz sichern; **will you please make ~?** vergewissern Sie sich bitte noch einmal; **be ~ to tell him** vergessen Sie nicht, ihm das zu sagen; **there is ~ to be strong opposition to the proposal** es wird sicher starken Widerstand gegen den Vorschlag geben; **that was ~ to happen** das musste ja so kommen; **to my ~**

knowledge ich bin mir ganz sicher **b** *attr* (= *not named or specified*) gewiss; *reason, conditions* bestimmt; **a ~ gentleman** ein gewisser Herr; **to a ~ extent** *or* **degree** in gewisser Hinsicht, zu einem bestimmten Grade; **of a ~ age** in einem gewissen Alter **PRON** einige; ~ **of you/them** einige von euch/ihnen

certainly [ˈsɜːtənlɪ] ✪ 26.1, 26.3 ADV (= *admittedly*) sicher(lich); (= *positively, without doubt*) bestimmt, gewiss (*geh*); **it is ~ true that ...** es ist sicherlich richtig, dass ...; ~ **not!** ganz bestimmt nicht, auf keinen Fall!; **I ~ will not!** ich denke nicht daran!; ~! sicher!, gewiss! (*geh*)

certainty [ˈsɜːtəntɪ] N **a** (= *sure fact*) Gewissheit *f*; **to know for a ~ that ...** mit Sicherheit wissen, dass ...; **he was faced with the ~ of defeat** er sah seiner sicheren Niederlage entgegen; **his success is a ~** er wird mit Sicherheit Erfolg haben, sein Erfolg ist gewiss; **the ultimate ~ of death** die letztliche Gewissheit des Todes; **there are no certainties in modern Europe** in einem modernen Europa ist nichts gewiss; **will it happen? – yes, it's a ~** wird das passieren? – ja, mit Sicherheit; **it's a ~ that ...** es ist absolut sicher, dass ... **b** *no pl* (= *conviction*) Gewissheit *f*, Sicherheit *f*

CertEd (*Brit*) *abbr of* **Certificate in Education**

certifiable [ˌsɜːtɪˈfaɪəbl] ADJ *fact, claim* nachweisbar **b** (*Psych*) unzurechnungsfähig; (*inf*, = *mad*) nicht zurechnungsfähig

certificate [səˈtɪfɪkɪt] N Bescheinigung *f*, Nachweis *m*; (*of qualifications*) Zeugnis *nt*, Urkunde *f*; (*of health*) Zeugnis *nt*; (= *marriage certificate*) Trauschein *m*; (*of baptism*) Taufschein *m*; (= *share certificate*) Zertifikat *nt*; (*Film*) Freigabe *f*

certification [ˌsɜːtɪfɪˈkeɪʃən] N **a** (*of film*) Klassifizierung *f* **b** (*Jur*, = *document*) Beglaubigung *f*

certified [ˈsɜːtɪfaɪd] ADJ: **certified accountant** N (*Brit*) konzessionierte(r) Buchprüfer(in) *m(f)*, konzessionierte(r) Steuerberater(in) *m(f)*; **certified mail** N Einschreiben *nt*; **certified milk** N (*US*) Vorzugsmilch *f*; **certified public accountant** N (*US*) geprüfter Buchhalter, geprüfte Buchhalterin

certify [ˈsɜːtɪfaɪ] VT **a** (= *confirm*) bescheinigen, bestätigen; (*Jur*) beglaubigen; **this is to ~ that ...** hiermit wird bescheinigt *or* bestätigt, dass ...; **she was certified dead** sie wurde für tot erklärt; **certified as a true copy** beglaubigte Abschrift; **the painting has been certified (as) genuine** das Gemälde wurde als echt erklärt; **certified cheque** *or* (*US*) **check** gedeckter Scheck **b** (*Psych*) für unzurechnungsfähig erklären; (= *put in asylum*) in eine Anstalt einweisen; **he should be certified** (*inf*) der ist doch nicht ganz zurechnungsfähig (*inf*) **VI to ~ to sb/sth** sich für jdn/etw verbürgen

certitude [ˈsɜːtɪtjuːd] N Gewissheit *f*, Sicherheit *f*

cervical [ˈsɜːvɪkəl, səˈvaɪkəl] ADJ zervikal (*spec*)

cervical cancer N Gebärmutterhalskrebs *m*

cervical smear N Abstrich *m*

cervix [ˈsɜːvɪks] N (*of uterus*) Gebärmutterhals *m*

Cesarean, Cesarian [sɪˈzɛərɪən] N (*US*) = **Caesarean**

cesium N (*US*) = **caesium**

cessation [seˈseɪʃən] N Ende *nt*; (*of hostilities*) Einstellung *f*; ~ **of the heartbeat** Herzstillstand *m*

cession [ˈseʃən] N Abtretung *f*; ~ **of land/territory** Gebietsabtretung(en *pl*) *f*

cesspit [ˈsespɪt] N = **cesspool a**

cesspool [ˈsespuːl] N **a** Senk- *or* Jauchegrube *f*, Latrine *f* **b** (*fig*) Sumpf *m*; **a ~ of vice** ein Sündenpfuhl *m*

cestode [ˈsestəʊd], **cestoid** [ˈsestɔɪd] N (*Zool*) Bandwurm *m*

CET *abbr of* **Central European Time** MEZ

cetacean [sɪˈteɪʃən] N Wal *m*, Zetazee *f* (*spec*) **ADJ** Wal(fisch)-, Zetazeen- (*spec*)

Ceylon [sɪˈlɒn] N Ceylon *nt*

Ceylonese [ˌsiːlɒˈniːz] ADJ ceylonesisch **N** Ceylonese *m*, Ceylonesin *f*

CF (*US*) *abbr of* **cost and freight** cf

cf *abbr of* **confer** vgl

c/f *abbr of* **carry forward**

CFC *abbr of* **chlorofluorocarbon** FCKW *m*

CFE a (*Brit*) *abbr of* **college of further education** Weiterbildungseinrichtung *f* **b** *abbr of* **Conventional Forces in Europe** Konventionelle Streitkräfte *pl* in Europa, CFE

CFI (*US*) *abbr of* **cost, freight and insurance** cif

CFO *abbr of* **chief financial officer** Finanzdirektor(in) *m(f)*

CFS (*Med*) *abbr of* **chronic fatigue syndrome** CFS

CG (*US*) *abbr of* **coastguard**

cg *abbr of* **centigram(s)** *of* **centigramme(s)** cg

CGA (*Comput*) *abbr of* **colour graphics adaptor** CGA *m*

ch a *abbr of* **chapter** Kap **b** *abbr of* **central heating** ZH

cha-cha [ˈtʃɑːtʃɑː] N Cha-Cha-Cha *m* **VI** Cha-Cha-Cha tanzen

Chad [tʃæd] N der Tschad

chador [ˈtʃɑːdɔː] N Tschador *m*

chafe [tʃeɪf] N **a** (= *rub, abrade*) (auf)scheuern, wund scheuern; **his shirt ~d his neck** sein (Hemd)kragen scheuerte (ihn) **b** (*fig*) aufregen, nervös machen **VI a** (= *rub*) sich aufscheuern *or* wund scheuern; (= *cause soreness*) scheuern; **her skin ~s easily** ihre Haut wird leicht wund; **the rope was chafing against the railings** das Seil scheuerte an der Reling **b** (*fig*) sich ärgern (*at, against* über +*acc*); **he ~d at having to take orders from her** es ging ihm gegen den Strich, dass er von ihr Befehle entgegennehmen musste **N** wund gescheuerte Stelle

chafer [ˈtʃeɪfə] N Käfer *m*

chaff¹ [tʃɑːf] N **a** (= *husks of grain*) Spreu *f* → **wheat b** (= *straw*) Häcksel *m or nt*

chaff² N **a** (= *banter, also* **chaffing**) Scherze *pl*, Flachserei *f* (*inf*) **VT** aufziehen (*about* mit)

chaffinch [ˈtʃæfɪntʃ] N Buchfink *m*

chagrin [ˈʃæɡrɪn] N Ärger *m*, Verdruss *m* (*geh*) **VT** ärgern, verdrießen (*geh*); **he was much ~ed by the news** die Nachricht bekümmerte *or* verdross (*geh*) ihn sehr

chain [tʃeɪn] N **a** Kette *f*; ~s (*lit, fig*: = *fetters*) Ketten *pl*, Fesseln *pl*; (*Aut*) (Schnee)ketten *pl*; ~ **of office** Amtskette *f*; **to keep a dog on a** ~ einen Hund an der Kette halten; **to pull** *or* **yank sb's** ~ (*esp US fig*) jdn necken; **in** ~**s** in Ketten **b** (*of mountains*) (Berg)kette *f*, (Gebirgs)kette *f* (*of arms etc*) Kette *f*; ~ **of shops** Ladenkette *f*; **to make a** ~ eine Kette bilden; ~ **of events** Kette von Ereignissen; ~ **of command** (*Mil*) Befehlskette *f* **c** (= *measure of length*) Messkette *f* **VT** (*lit, fig*) anketten, festketten; *dog* an die Kette legen, anketten; **to** ~ **sb/sth to sth** jdn/etw an etw (*acc*) ketten

▶ **chain up** VT *sep prisoner* in Ketten legen; *dog* an die Kette legen, anketten

chain *in cpds* Ketten-; **chain bridge** N Ketten- *or* Hängebrücke *f*; **chain drive** N Kettenantrieb *m*, Kettengetriebe *f*; **chain gang** N Truppe *f* aneinander geketteter Sträflinge, Sträflingskolonne *f*; **chain letter** N Kettenbrief *m*; **chain lightning** N Linienblitz *m*; **chain-link fence** N Maschendrahtzaun *m*; **chain mail** N Kettenhemd *nt*; **chain reaction** N Kettenreaktion *f*; **chain saw** N Kettensäge *f*; **chain-smoke** VI eine (Zigarette) nach der anderen rauchen, kettenrauchen *infin only*; **chain smoker** N Kettenraucher(in) *m(f)*; **chain stitch** N (*Sew*) Kettenstich *m*; **chain store** N Kettenladen *m*

chair [tʃɛə] N **a** (= *seat*) Stuhl *m*; (= *armchair*) Sessel *m*; (= *sedan chair*) Sänfte *f*; **please take a** ~ bitte nehmen Sie Platz! **b** (*in committees etc*) Vorsitz *m*; **to be in/take the** ~ den Vorsitz führen; **to address the** ~ sich an den Vorsitzenden/die Vorsitzende wenden; **all questions**

through the ~, please bitte alle Fragen (direkt) an den Vorsitzenden richten! **c** (= *professorship*) Lehrstuhl *m* (of für) **d** (= *electric chair*) (elektrischer) Stuhl VT a *meeting* den Vorsitz führen bei **b** (*Brit*, = *carry in triumph*) auf den Schultern (davon)tragen

chair: chairborne ['tʃeəbɔːn] ADJ **to be ~** (*inf*) einen Schreibtischjob haben; **chairbound** ['tʃeəbaʊnd] ADJ an den Rollstuhl gefesselt; **chairlift** N Sessellift *m*; **chairman** N Vorsitzende(r) *mf*; **Mr/Madam Chairman** Herr Vorsitzender/Frau Vorsitzende; **chairmanship** N Vorsitz *m*; **under the ~ of** unter (dem) Vorsitz von; **chairperson** N Vorsitzende(r) *mf*; **chair umpire** N (*Tennis*) Stuhlschiedsrichter(in) *m(f)*; **chairwoman** N Vorsitzende *f*

chaise [ʃeɪz] N (*Hist*) Einspänner *m*

chaise longue [ʃeɪz'lɒŋ] N Chaiselongue *f*

chalet ['ʃæleɪ] N Chalet *nt*; (*in motel etc*) Apartment *nt*

chalice ['tʃælɪs] N (*poet, Eccl*) Kelch *m*

chalk [tʃɔːk] N Kreide *f*; (= *limestone also*) Kalkstein *m*; **white as ~** kreidebleich; **not by a long ~** (*Brit, inf*) bei weitem nicht, noch nicht einmal annähernd; **the biggest by a long ~** (*Brit inf*) bei weitem der Größte; **they're as different as ~ and cheese** (*Brit*) sie sind (so verschieden) wie Tag und Nacht VT *message etc* mit Kreide schreiben; *luggage etc* mit Kreide kennzeichnen; *billiard cue* mit Kreide einreiben

▶**chalk up** VT *sep* **a** (*lit*) (mit Kreide) aufschreiben, notieren **b** (*fig*, = *gain, win*) *success, victory* verbuchen; *medal* einheimsen **c** (*fig*, = *mark up as credit*) anschreiben (*inf*)

chalk: chalk dust N Kreidestaub *m*; **chalkface** N (*Brit Sch hum*) **at the ~** im Klassenzimmer

chalkiness ['tʃɔːkɪnɪs] N Kalkigkeit *f*; (= *chalky content*) Kalkhaltigkeit *f*

chalk pit N Kalk(stein)bruch *m*

chalky ['tʃɔːkɪ] ADJ (+*er*) (= *containing chalk*) kalkhaltig; (= *like chalk*) kalkartig; (= *covered with chalk*) voller Kalk

challenge ['tʃælɪndʒ] N a (*to duel, match etc*) Herausforderung *f* (*to* an +*acc*); (*fig*, = *demands*) Anforderung(en *pl*) *f*; **to issue a ~ to sb** jdn herausfordern; **this job is a ~** bei dieser Arbeit ist man gefordert; **I see this task as a ~** ich sehe diese Aufgabe als Herausforderung; **the ~ of modern life** die Anforderungen des heutigen Lebens; **those who rose to the ~** diejenigen, die sich der Herausforderung stellten; **the office job presented no ~ for him** die Bürotätigkeit stellte keine Ansprüche an ihn *or* forderte ihn nicht; **the ~ of the unknown** der Reiz des Unbekannten

b (= *bid: for leadership etc*) Griff *m* (*for* nach); **a direct ~ to his authority** eine direkte Infragestellung seiner Autorität

c (*Mil*, = *of sentry*) Anruf *m*, Werdaruf *m*

d (*Jur*, = *of witness*) Ablehnung *f*

VT a *person, champion (to duel, race etc)* herausfordern; *world record etc* überbieten wollen; **to ~ sb to do sth** wetten, dass jd etw nicht (tun) kann; **he ~d her to run a marathon** er wettete, dass sie keinen Marathonlauf machen würde; **to ~ sb to a duel** jdn zum Duell fordern; **to ~ sb to a game** jdn zu einer Partie herausfordern

b (*fig*, = *make demands on*) fordern

c (*fig*) *remarks, sb's authority* infrage *or* in Frage stellen, anfechten

d (*sentry*) anrufen

e (*Jur*) *witnesses* ablehnen; *evidence, verdict* anfechten

challengeable ['tʃælɪndʒəbl] ADJ anfechtbar

-challenged [-'tʃælɪndʒd] ADJ SUF (*usu hum*) **vertically-challenged** zu kurz geraten (*hum*); **intellectually-challenged** beschränkt, geistig minderbemittelt (*inf*); **follically-challenged** mit spärlichem Haarwuchs, oben ohne (*hum inf*)

challenger ['tʃælɪndʒə'] N (*to duel, match etc*) Herausforderer *m*, Herausforderin *f*; **a ~ of traditional beliefs** einer, der überkommene Glaubenssätze infrage *or* in Frage stellt

challenging ['tʃælɪndʒɪŋ] ADJ (= *provocative*) herausfordernd; (= *thought-provoking*) reizvoll; (= *demanding*) anspruchsvoll, fordernd; **a ~ idea** eine reizvolle Vorstellung; **I don't find this work very ~** diese Arbeit fordert mich nicht

challengingly ['tʃælɪndʒɪŋlɪ] ADV **a** (= *defiantly*) herausfordernd; **he looked ~ at the doctor** er sah den Arzt herausfordernd an **b** (= *demandingly*) extrem; **a ~ difficult game** ein schwieriges Spiel, das eine echte Herausforderung darstellt

chamber ['tʃeɪmbə'] N **a** (*old*, = *room*) Gemach *nt* (*old*), Raum *m*; (= *bedroom*) Schlafgemach *nt* (*old*); **~ of horrors** Horrorkabinett *nt* **b** (*Brit*) **~s** *pl* (*of solicitor*) Kanzlei *f*; (*of judge*) Dienst- *or* Amtszimmer *nt* **c** **Chamber of Commerce** Handelskammer *f*; **the Upper/Lower Chamber** (*Parl*) die Erste/Zweite Kammer **d** (*Anat*) (Herz)kammer *f* **e** (*of revolver*) Kammer *f*

chamberlain ['tʃeɪmbəlɪn] N Kammerherr *m*

chamber: chambermaid N Zimmermädchen *nt*, Kammerzofe *f* (*old*); **chamber music** N Kammermusik *f*; **chamber orchestra** N Kammerorchester *nt*; **chamber pot** N Nachttopf *m*

chambray ['tʃæmbreɪ] N (*US*) = **cambric**

chameleon [kə'miːlɪən] N (*Zool, fig*) Chamäleon *nt*

chamfer ['tʃæmfə'] N Fase *f*, Schrägkante *f* VT abfasen, abschrägen

chamois ['ʃæmwɑː] N **a** (= *leather*) Gamsleder *nt*; **a ~ (leather)** ein Ledertuch *nt*, ein Fensterleder *nt* **b** (*Zool*) Gämse *f*

champ¹ [tʃæmp] VT (*animals*) geräuschvoll mahlen *or* kauen; (*people*) mampfen (*inf*); **to ~ at the bit** (*lit*) an der Gebissstange kauen; (*fig*) vor Ungeduld fiebern

champ² N (*inf*) Meister(in) *m(f)*, Champion *m*; **listen, ~** hör zu, Meister

champagne [ʃæm'peɪn] N Sekt *m*, Schaumwein *m*; (= *French champagne*) Champagner *m*; **~ bucket** Sektkübel *m*, Sektkühler *m*; **~ glass** Sekt-/Champagnerglas *nt*; **~ lifestyle** Luxusleben *nt* ADJ (*also* **champagne-coloured**, (*US*) **champagne-colored**) champagner(farben)

champers ['ʃæmpəz] N (*dated Brit inf*) Schampus *m* (*inf*)

champion ['tʃæmpjən] N a (*Sport*) Meister(in) *m(f)*, Champion *m*; **~s** (= *team*) Meister *m*; **world ~** Weltmeister(in) *m(f)*; **boxing ~** Boxchampion *m*; **heavyweight ~ of the world** Weltmeister *m* im Schwergewicht **b** (*of a cause*) Verfechter *m* ADJ a (= *prizewinning*) siegreich; *dog, bull, show animal* preisgekrönt; **~ boxer** erfolgreicher Boxer; **~ horse** (*Racing*) Turfsieger *m*; (*Show-jumping*) siegreiches Turnierpferd *m* **b** (*N Engl, inf*) klasse *inv* (*inf*), prima *inv* (*inf*) VT *person, action, cause* eintreten für, sich engagieren für

championship ['tʃæmpjənʃɪp] N a (*Sport*) Meisterschaft *f* **b** **championships** PL (= *event*) Meisterschaftskämpfe *pl* **c** (= *support*) Eintreten *nt*, Engagement *nt* (*of* für)

chance [tʃɑːns] ⊙ 16.2, 16.3 N a (= *coincidence*) Zufall *m*; (= *luck, fortune*) Glück *nt*; **by ~** durch Zufall, zufällig; **a game of ~** ein Glücksspiel *nt*; **would you by any ~ be able to help?** könnten Sie mir wohl *or* vielleicht behilflich sein?; **to leave things to ~** die Dinge dem Zufall überlassen; **to trust to ~** auf sein Glück vertrauen

b (= *possibility*) Aussicht(en *pl*) *f*, Chance(n *pl*) *f*; (= *probability, likelihood*) Möglichkeit *f*; **(the) ~s are that …** aller Wahrscheinlichkeit nach …, wahrscheinlich …; **the ~s are against that happening** vieles spricht dagegen *or* die Wahrscheinlichkeit ist gering, dass das eintritt; **what are the ~s of him agreeing?** wie sind die Aussichten *or* wie stehen die Chancen, dass er zustimmt?; **what are the ~s of his coming?** wie groß ist die Wahrscheinlichkeit, dass er kommt?; **is there any ~ of us meeting again?** könnten wir uns vielleicht wiedersehen?; **is**

there any ~ he might be lost? besteht die Möglichkeit, dass er sich verirrt hat?; **on the ~ of finding her at home** in der Hoffnung, sie zu Hause anzutreffen; **he doesn't stand** *or* **hasn't got a ~** er hat keine(rlei) Chance(n); **he doesn't stand a ~ of winning** er hat keine Chance zu gewinnen; **he has a good ~ of winning** er hat gute Aussicht zu gewinnen, er hat gute Siegeschancen; **to be in with a ~** eine Chance haben; **no ~!** (*inf*) nee! (*inf*), ist nicht drin (*inf*); **will you lend me £50? – sorry, no ~** (*inf*) leihst du mir £ 50? – bedaure, nichts zu machen *or* ist nicht drin (*inf*)

c (= *opportunity*) Chance *f*; **the ~ of a lifetime** eine einmalige Chance; **you won't get another ~ of going there** *or* **to go there** die Gelegenheit, dahin zu fahren, bietet sich (dir) nicht noch einmal; **you won't get another ~** das ist eine einmalige Gelegenheit; **I had the ~ to go** *or* **of going** ich hatte (die) Gelegenheit, dahin zu gehen; **now's your ~!** das ist deine Chance!; **this is my big ~** das ist DIE Chance für mich; **to take one's ~** die Gelegenheit nutzen; **to have an eye to the main ~** (*pej*) nur auf seinen Vorteil bedacht sein; **he never had a ~ in life** er hat im Leben nie eine Chance gehabt; **give me a ~!** nun mach aber mal langsam (*inf*); **to give sb a ~ to explain** du hast mir ja nie die Chance gegeben, das zu erklären; **~ would be a fine thing!** (*inf*) schön wärs!

d (= *risk*) Risiko *nt*; **to take a ~** es darauf ankommen lassen; **aren't you taking a bit of a ~?** ist das nicht ein bisschen riskant?; **he's not taking any ~s** er geht kein Risiko ein ATTR zufällig; **~ meeting** zufällige Begegnung VI **it ~d that …** es traf *or* fügte (geh) sich, dass …

VT **a** **to ~ to do sth** zufällig etw tun **b** **I'll ~ it!** (*inf*) ich versuchs mal (*inf*); **to ~ one's arm** (*inf*) (et)was riskieren; **to ~ one's luck** (= *have a try*) sein Glück versuchen; (= *risk*) das Glück herausfordern; **I'll just have to ~ that happening** das muss ich eben riskieren

▶**chance (up)on** VI +prep obj *person* zufällig begegnen (+*dat*), zufällig treffen; *thing* zufällig stoßen auf (+*acc*)

chancel ['tʃɑːnsəl] N Chor *m*, Altarraum *m*

chancellery ['tʃɑːnsələrɪ] N (= *offices*) Kanzleramt *nt*; (= *position*) Kanzlerschaft *f*

chancellor ['tʃɑːnsələ'] N (*Jur, Pol, Univ*) Kanzler *m*; **Chancellor (of the Exchequer)** (*Brit*) Schatzkanzler(in) *m(f)*, Finanzminister(in) *m(f)*

chancellorship ['tʃɑːnsələʃɪp] N Kanzlerschaft *f*

chancer ['tʃɑːnsə'] N (*inf*) Windhund *m* (*inf*)

chancery ['tʃɑːnsərɪ] N **ward in ~** Mündel *nt* in Amtsvormundschaft

Chancery Division ['tʃɑːnsərɪdɪvɪʒən] N (*Brit Jur*) *für Grundstücks-, Erbschaftssachen etc zuständige Abteilung des High Court of Justice*

chancre ['ʃæŋkə'] N Schanker *m*

chancy ['tʃɑːnsɪ] ADJ (+*er*) (*inf*, = *risky*) riskant

chandelier [ʃændə'lɪə'] N Kronleuchter *m*

chandler ['tʃɑːndlə'] N (*for candles*) Kerzenmacher *m*; (= *shop*) Kerzenladen *m*; **ship's ~** Schiffsausrüster *m*

change [tʃeɪndʒ] ⊙ 19.3 N a (= *alteration*) Veränderung *f*; (= *modification also*) Änderung *f* (*to* +*gen*); **a ~ for the better** ein Fortschritt *m*, eine Verbesserung; **a ~ for the worse** ein Rückschritt *m*, eine Verschlechterung; **~ of address** Adressen- *or* Anschriftenänderung *f*; **a ~ in the weather** eine Wetterveränderung; **a ~ of air** eine Luftveränderung; **a ~ is as good as a rest** (*prov*) Abwechslung wirkt *or* tut Wunder; **no ~** unverändert; **I need a ~ of scene** ich brauche Tapetenwechsel; **to make ~s (to sth)** (an etw *dat*) (Ver)änderungen *pl* vornehmen; **to make a ~/a major ~ in sth** etw ändern/bedeutend verändern; **the ~ of life** die Wechseljahre; **he needs a ~ of clothes** er müsste sich mal wieder umziehen; **I didn't have a ~ of clothes with me**

ich hatte nichts zum Wechseln mit; **a ~ of job** ein Stellenwechsel *m*

b (= *variety*) Abwechslung *f*; **(just) for a ~** zur Abwechslung (mal); **that makes a ~** das ist mal was anderes; (*iro*) das ist ja was ganz Neues!; **it'll make a nice ~** das wäre eine nette Abwechslung → **ring**

c *no pl* (= *changing*) Veränderung *f*; **those who are against ~** diejenigen, die gegen jegliche Veränderung sind; **the constant ~ will only confuse people** der ständige Wechsel verwirrt die Leute nur

d (*of one thing for another*) Wechsel *m*; **~ of career** Berufswechsel *m*; **a ~ of government** ein Regierungswechsel *m*, ein Wechsel *m* in der Regierung; **a wheel ~** ein Radwechsel *m*

e *no pl* (= *money*) Wechselgeld *nt*; (= *small change*) Kleingeld *nt*; **can you give me ~ for a pound?** können Sie mir ein Pfund wechseln?; **I haven't got any ~** ich habe kein Kleingeld; **I haven't got ~ for £5** ich kann auf £ 5 nicht rausgeben or £ 5 nicht wechseln; **you won't get much ~ out of £5** von £ 5 wird wohl nicht viel übrig bleiben; **keep the ~** der Rest ist für Sie; **you won't get much ~ out of him** (*fig*) aus ihm wirst du nicht viel rauskriegen

f (*St Ex*) **Change** Börse *f*

VT a (*by substitution*) wechseln; *address, name* ändern; **to ~ trains/buses** *etc* umsteigen; **to ~ one's clothes** sich umziehen; **to ~ a wheel/the oil** Rad-/Ölwechsel vornehmen, ein Rad/das Öl wechseln; **to ~ a baby's nappy** (*Brit*) or **diaper** (*US*), **to ~ a baby** (bei einem Baby) die Windeln wechseln, ein Baby wickeln; **to ~ the sheets** or **the bed** die Bettwäsche wechseln, das Bett neu beziehen; **to ~ one's seat** den Platz wechseln, sich woanders hinsetzen; **to ~ hands** den Besitzer wechseln; **would you ~ the record?** (*lit, fig*) kannst du (mal) eine andere Platte auflegen?; **to ~ places with sb** mit jdm den Platz tauschen; **she ~d places with him/Mrs Brown** und sie tauschten die Plätze; **I wouldn't ~ places with him for the world** ich möchte or würde um nichts in der Welt mit ihm tauschen

b (= *alter*) (ver)ändern; *person, ideas* ändern; (= *transform*) verwandeln; **to ~ sb/sth into sth** jdn/etw in etw (*acc*) verwandeln; **you won't be able to ~ her** du kannst sie nicht ändern; **a chameleon can ~ its colour** das Chamäleon kann seine Farbe wechseln

c (= *exchange: in shop etc*) umtauschen; **she ~d the dress for one of a different colour** sie tauschte das Kleid gegen ein andersfarbiges um; **he ~d his Rolls Royce for a Jaguar** er vertauschte seinen Rolls Royce mit einem Mini → **guard**

d *money* (*into smaller money*) wechseln; (*into other currency*) (ein)wechseln, (um)tauschen

e (*Brit Aut*) **to ~ gear** schalten

VI a (= *alter*) sich ändern; (*town, person also*) sich verändern; **you've ~d!** du hast dich aber verändert!; **he will never ~** er wird sich nie ändern, der ändert sich nie!; **to ~ from sth into ...** sich aus etw in ... (*acc*) verwandeln

b (= *change clothes*) sich umziehen; **she ~d into an old skirt** sie zog sich einen alten Rock an; **I'll just ~ out of these old clothes** ich muss mir noch die alten Sachen ausziehen

c (= *change trains etc*) umsteigen; **you ~ at York** in York müssen Sie umsteigen; **all ~!** Endstation!, alle aussteigen!

d (*Brit Aut*: = *change gear*) schalten; (*traffic lights*) umspringen (*to* auf +*acc*)

e (*from one thing to another*) (*seasons*) wechseln; **to ~ to a different system** auf ein anderes System umstellen, zu einem anderen System übergehen; **I ~d to philosophy from chemistry** ich habe von Chemie zu Philosophie gewechselt; **do you want to ~ with me?** (*places*) möchten Sie mit mir tauschen?

▶ **change around** VT SEP = **change round** VT

▶ **change down** VI (*Brit Aut*) einen niedrigeren Gang einlegen, in einen niedrigeren Gang schalten, (he)runterschalten

▶ **change over** **VI a** (= *change to sth different*) sich umstellen (*to* auf +*acc*); **we have just changed over from gas to electricity** hier or bei uns ist gerade von Gas auf Strom umgestellt worden **b** (= *exchange places, activities etc*) wechseln; (*Sport also*) die Seiten wechseln; **do you mind if I change over?** (*TV*) hast du was dagegen, wenn ich umschalte? **VT** *sep* austauschen

▶ **change round** (*esp Brit*) **VI** = **change over** VI **b** **VT** *sep room* umräumen; *furniture* umstellen; *tyres* austauschen, auswechseln

▶ **change up** VI (*Brit Aut*) einen höheren Gang einlegen, in einen höheren Gang schalten, höher schalten (*inf*); **to change up into top** in den höchsten Gang schalten

changeability [ˌtʃeɪndʒəˈbɪlɪtɪ] N Unbeständigkeit *f*, Veränderlichkeit *f*

changeable [ˈtʃeɪndʒəbl] ADJ *person, character* unbeständig; *weather* veränderlich, wechselhaft; *mood, winds* wechselnd

changeless [ˈtʃeɪndʒlɪs] ADJ unveränderlich

changeling [ˈtʃeɪndʒlɪŋ] N (= *child*) Wechselbalg *m*

change machine N Geldwechsler *m*

changeover [ˈtʃeɪndʒəʊvə] N Umstellung *f* (*to* auf +*acc*); (*of governments*) Regierungswechsel *m*; (*in relay race*) (Stab)wechsel *m*; (*of teams changing ends*) Seitenwechsel *m*

changing [ˈtʃeɪndʒɪŋ] ADJ sich verändernd, wechselnd; **the fast-changing market** der sich schnell ändernde Markt **the ~ of the Guard** die Wachablösung

changing room N (*in store*) Ankleideraum *m*, Kabine *f*; (*Sport*) Umkleideraum *m*, Umkleidekabine *f*

channel [ˈtʃænl] **N a** (= *watercourse*) (Fluss)bett *nt*; (= *strait*) Kanal *m*; (= *deepest part of river etc*) Fahrrinne *f*; **the (English) Channel** der Ärmelkanal

b (*fig, usu pl*) (*of bureaucracy etc*) Dienstweg *m*; (*of information etc*) Kanal *m*; (*of thought, interest etc*) Bahn *f*; **if you go through the right ~s** wenn Sie sich an die richtigen Stellen wenden; **to go through the official ~s** den Dienstweg gehen; **you'll have to go through ~s** (*US*) Sie werden den Dienstweg einhalten müssen; **through the usual ~s** auf den üblichen Wege

c (= *groove*) Furche *f*, Rinne *f*

d (*TV, Rad*) Kanal *m*, Programm *nt*

VT a (= *dig out, furrow*) *way, course* sich (*dat*) bahnen

b (= *direct*) *water, river* (hindurch)leiten (*through* durch)

c (*fig*) *efforts, interest* lenken (*into* auf +*acc*); *energy also* kanalisieren; *crowd* dirigieren

▶ **channel off** VT *sep* (*lit*) ableiten; (*fig*) abzweigen

channel: Channel ferry N (*Brit*) Kanalfähre *f*; **channel-hop** VI (*Brit TV inf*) ständig umschalten or den Kanal wechseln, zappen (*inf*); **channel-hopping** N (*Brit TV inf*) ständiges Umschalten, Zappen *nt* (*inf*); **Channel Islander** N Bewohner(in) *m(f)* der Kanalinseln; **Channel Islands** PL Kanalinseln *pl*; **channel-surf** VI (*esp US TV inf*) = **channel-hop**; **channel-surfing** N (*esp US TV inf*) = **channel-hopping**; **Channel Tunnel** N Kanaltunnel *m*

chant [tʃɑːnt] **N** (*Eccl, Mus*) Gesang *m*, Cantus *m*; (= *monotonous song*) Sprechgesang *m*, Singsang *m*; (*of football fans etc*) Sprechchor *m*; **tribal ~s** Stammesgesänge *pl* **VT** im (Sprech)chor rufen; (*Eccl*) singen **VI** Sprechchöre anstimmen; (*Eccl*) singen

chanterelle [ˈtʃæntərel] N Pfifferling *m*

chanticleer [ˈtʃæntɪkliːə] N (*old*) Hahn *m*

chaos [ˈkeɪɒs] N Chaos *nt*, Durcheinander *nt*; **complete ~** ein totales Durcheinander

chaotic [keɪˈɒtɪk] ADJ chaotisch

chaotically [keɪˈɒtɪklɪ] ADV chaotisch; **the papers had been scattered ~ about the room** die Papiere lagen kreuz und quer im ganzen Raum verteilt; **such people can be ~ untidy** bei sol-

chen Leuten kann das reinste Chaos herrschen

chap¹ [tʃæp] **N** (*Med, of skin*) **he's got ~s on his hands** seine Hände sind aufgesprungen or rau **VI** (*skin*) aufspringen **VT** spröde machen; **~ped lips** aufgesprungene or raue Lippen *pl*

chap² N (*Brit inf*: = *man*) Kerl *m* (*inf*), Typ *m* (*inf*); **old ~** alter Junge (*inf*) or Knabe (*inf*); **poor little ~** armer Kleiner!, armes Kerlchen!; **now look here (you) ~s** hört mal zu, Jungs (*inf*)

chap³ *abbr of* **chapter** Kap.

chapel [ˈtʃæpəl] **N a** Kapelle *f*; (*Sch, Univ*, = *service*) Andacht *f*; **~ of rest** Kapelle in einem Bestattungsunternehmen, wo Tote aufgebahrt werden **b** (= *nonconformist church*) Sektenkirche *f* **c** (*Press, of union*) Betriebsgruppe innerhalb der Gewerkschaft der Drucker und Journalisten

chaperon(e) [ˈʃæpərəʊn] **N a** (*for propriety*) Anstandsdame *f*, Anstandswauwau *m* (*hum inf*) **b** (= *escort*) Begleiter(in) *m(f)* **c** (*esp US*: = *supervisor*) Aufsichts- or Begleitperson *f* **VT a** (*for propriety*) begleiten, Anstandsdame spielen bei **b** (= *escort*) begleiten **c** (*esp US*: = *supervise*) beaufsichtigen

chaplain [ˈtʃæplɪn] N Kaplan *m*

chaplaincy [ˈtʃæplənsɪ] N Amt *nt* or Stelle *f* eines Kaplans; (= *building*) Diensträume *pl* eines Kaplans

chaplet [ˈtʃæplɪt] N (*of flowers etc*) Kranz *m*

chappy [ˈtʃæpɪ] N (*inf*) Kerlchen *nt* (*inf*)

chaps [tʃæps] PL lederne Reithosen *pl*, Cowboyhosen *pl*

chapstick® [ˈtʃæpstɪk] N Lippenbalsam *m*, Labello® *m*

chapter [ˈtʃæptə] **N a** (*of book*) Kapitel *nt*; **to give ~ and verse (for sth)** (*fig*) etw genau belegen **b** (*fig*) Kapitel *nt*; **a ~ of accidents** eine Serie von Unfällen **c** (*Eccl*) Kapitel *nt* **d** (*esp US*, = *branch*) Ortsgruppe *f*

chapterhouse N (*Eccl*) Kapitel(saal *m*) *nt*

char¹ [tʃɑː] VT (= *burn black*) verkohlen

char² (*Brit, inf*) N (*also* **charwoman, charlady**) Putzfrau *f* VI putzen; **to ~ for sb** bei jdm putzen

char³ N (= *fish*) Saibling *m*

char⁴ N (*Brit, inf*, = *tea*) Tee *m*

charabanc, char-à-banc [ˈʃærəbæŋ] N (*old*) offener Omnibus für Ausflugsfahrten

character [ˈkærɪktə] **N a** (= *nature*) Charakter *m*; (*of people*) Wesen *nt no pl*, Wesensart *f*; **there's quite a difference in ~ between them** sie sind wesensmäßig sehr verschieden; **to be in ~ for sb** typisch für jdn sein; **it is out of ~ for him to behave like that** solches Benehmen ist untypisch für ihn; **it's out of ~ for him to do that** es ist eigentlich nicht seine Art, so etwas zu tun; **to be of good/bad ~** ein guter/schlechter Mensch sein

b *no pl* (= *strength of character*) Charakter *m*; **a man of ~** ein Mann von Charakter

c *no pl* (= *individuality, of towns etc*) Charakter *m*; (*of person*) Persönlichkeit *f*; **she/it has no ~** sie/es hat keine eigene Note; **her face is full of ~** sie hat ein Charaktergesicht

d (*in novel*) (Roman)figur *f*, (Roman)gestalt *f*; (*Theat*) Gestalt *f*

e (= *person in public life*) Persönlichkeit *f*, Gestalt *f*; (= *original person*) Original *nt*; (*inf*, = *person*) Typ *m* (*inf*), Type *f* (*inf*)

f (= *reference*) Zeugnis *nt*

g (*Typ, Comput*) Zeichen *nt*; (*Chinese etc also*) Schriftzeichen *nt*; **to type 100 ~s per minute** 100 Anschläge pro Minute machen; **Gothic ~s** gotische Schrift

character *in cpds* (*Theat*) Charakter-; **character actor** N Charakterdarsteller *m*; **character assassination** N Rufmord *m*

characteristic [ˌkærɪktəˈrɪstɪk] ADJ charakteristisch, typisch (*of* für) **N** (*typisches*) Merkmal, Charakteristikum *nt*; (*Math*) Charakteristik *f*, Kennziffer *f*; **one of the main ~s of his style is ...** besonders charakteristisch für seinen Stil ist

..., eines der Hauptmerkmale seines Stils ist ...; **he has all the ~s of the true aristocrat** er hat alle Züge des echten Aristokraten

characteristically [ˌkærɪktəˈrɪstɪkəlɪ] ADV typisch

characterization [ˌkærɪktəraɪˈzeɪʃən] N *(in a novel etc)* Personenbeschreibung *f*; *(of one character)* Charakterisierung *f*

characterize [ˈkærɪktəraɪz] VT **a** *(= be characteristic of)* kennzeichnen, charakterisieren **b** *(= describe)* beschreiben

characterless [ˈkærɪktəlɪs] ADJ *person* nichts sagend, farblos; *room* nichts sagend, nichts Besonderes *pred*; *wine* fade

character: character part N Charakterrolle *f*; **character reference** N Referenz *f*; **character set** N *(Comput)* Zeichensatz *m*; **character sketch** N Charakterstudie *f*; **character space** N *(Comput)* Zeichenplatz *m*; **character string** N *(Comput)* Zeichenkette *f*; **character witness** N *(Jur)* Leumundszeuge *m*, Leumundszeugin *f*

charade [ʃəˈrɑːd] N Scharade *f*; *(fig)* Farce *f*, Affentheater *nt (inf)*

char-broiled [ˈtʃɑːbrɔɪld] ADJ *(US)* = **char-grilled**

charcoal [ˈtʃɑːkəʊl] N Holzkohle *f*; *(= drawing)* Kohlezeichnung *f*; *(= pencil)* Kohle(stift *m*) *f*

charcoal: charcoal-burner N *(= person)* Köhler *m*, Kohlenbrenner *m (rare)*; *(= stove)* Holzkohlenofen *m*; **charcoal drawing** N Kohlezeichnung *f*; **charcoal grey**, *(US)* **charcoal gray** N Schwarzgrau *nt*; **charcoal-grey**, *(US)* **charcoal-gray** ADJ schwarzgrau

charge [tʃɑːdʒ] N **a** *(Jur, = accusation)* Anklage *f (of wegen)*; **convicted on all three ~s** in allen drei Anklagepunkten für schuldig befunden; **to bring a ~ against sb** gegen jdn Anklage erheben, jdn unter Anklage stellen; **to press ~s (against sb)** (gegen jdn) Anzeige erstatten; **what is the ~?** wessen werde ich/wird er etc beschuldigt?; **to be on a murder ~** unter Mordanklage stehen; **he was arrested on a ~ of murder** er wurde wegen *or* unter Mordverdacht festgenommen; **to give sb in ~** *(form)* jdn in polizeilichen Gewahrsam bringen *(form)*; **it was laid to his ~** *(form)* es wurde ihm angelastet *or* zur Last gelegt; **to be on a ~** *(soldier)* eine Disziplinarstrafe verbüßen; **to put a soldier on a ~** über einen Soldaten eine Disziplinarstrafe verhängen, einen Soldaten verknacken *(inf)*; **you're on a ~, Smith!** das gibt eine Disziplinarstrafe, Smith!

b *(= attack: of soldiers, bull etc)* Angriff *m*; *(= trumpet call)* Signal *nt*; **to sound the ~** zum Angriff blasen

c *(= fee)* Gebühr *f*; **what's the ~?** was kostet das?; **what's your ~?** was verlangen Sie?; **to make a ~ (of £5) for sth** (£ 5 für) etw berechnen *or* in Rechnung stellen; **he made no ~ for mending my watch** er hat mir für die Reparatur der Uhr nichts berechnet; **there's an extra ~ for delivery** die Lieferung wird zusätzlich berechnet; **his ~s are quite reasonable** seine Preise sind ganz vernünftig; **free of ~** kostenlos, gratis; **delivered free of ~** Lieferung frei Haus

d *(= explosive charge)* (Spreng)ladung *f*; *(in firearm, Elec, Phys)* Ladung *f*; **to put a battery on ~** eine Batterie aufladen; **to be on ~** aufgeladen werden; **it still gives me a ~** *(fig inf)* das macht mir noch immer Spaß

e *(= position of responsibility)* Verantwortung *f (of für)*; **to be in ~** verantwortlich sein, die Verantwortung haben; **who is in ~?** wer ist hier der Verantwortliche?; **look, I'm in ~ here** hören Sie mal zu, hier bestimme ich!; **to be in ~ of sth** für etw die Verantwortung haben; *of department* etw leiten; **to give sb ~ of sth** jdm die Verantwortung für etw übertragen; *of department* jdm die Leitung von etw übertragen; **while in ~ of a motor vehicle** *(form)* am Steuer eines Kraftfahrzeuges; **the man in ~** der Verantwortliche, die verantwortliche Person; **the children were placed in their aunt's ~** die Kinder wurden der Obhut der Tante anvertraut; **the**

children in *or* **under her ~** die ihr anvertrauten Kinder; **to take ~ of sth** etw übernehmen; **to take ~** das Kommando übernehmen; **he took ~ of the situation** er nahm die Sache in die Hand; **I've been given ~ of this class** diese Klasse wurde mir anvertraut

f *(= ward)* *(= child)* Schützling *m*; *(of authorities)* Mündel *nt*; *(= patient)* Patient(in) *m(f)*

g *(= financial burden)* **to be a ~ on sb** jdm zur Last fallen

VT a *(with +gen)* *(Jur)* anklagen; *(fig)* beschuldigen; **to ~ sb with doing sth** jdm vorwerfen, etw getan zu haben; **to find sb guilty/not guilty as ~d** jdn im Sinne der Anklage für schuldig/nicht schuldig befinden

b *(attack)* stürmen; *troops* angreifen; *(bull etc)* losgehen auf *(+acc)*; *(Sport)* goalkeeper, player angehen; **the forwards ~d the defence** die Stürmer griffen die Deckung an

c *(= ask in payment)* berechnen; **I won't ~ you for that** das kostet Sie nichts, ich berechne Ihnen nichts dafür

d *(= record as debt)* in Rechnung stellen; **~ it to the company** stellen Sie das der Firma in Rechnung, das geht auf die Firma *(inf)*; **please ~ all these purchases to my account** bitte setzen Sie diese Einkäufe auf meine Rechnung

e *firearm* laden; *(Phys, Elec)* battery (auf)laden

f *(form, = command)* **to ~ sb to do sth** jdn beauftragen *or* anweisen *(form)*, etw zu tun

g *(form, = give as responsibility)* **to ~ sb with sth** jdn mit etw beauftragen

VI a *(= attack)* stürmen; *(at people)* angreifen *(at sb jdn)*; *(bull)* losgehen *(at sb auf jdn)*; **~!** vorwärts!

b *(inf, = rush)* rennen; **he ~d into a brick wall** er rannte gegen eine Mauer; **he ~d into the room/upstairs** er stürmte ins Zimmer/die Treppe hoch

▶ **charge up** VT *sep* **a** *(= record as debt)* in Rechnung stellen *(to sb jdm)*; **I'll charge the expenses up** das geht auf Geschäftskosten **b** *(Elec)* aufladen

chargeable [ˈtʃɑːdʒəbl] ADJ **a** *(Jur)* crime, offence strafbar; **to be ~ with sth** für etw angeklagt werden können **b** **to be ~ to sb** auf jds Kosten *(acc)* gehen; **are these expenses ~?** geht das auf Geschäftskosten?

charge: charge account N Kunden(kredit)-konto *nt*; **charge-cap** VT *(Brit)* **the council was ~ped** der Stadtrat wurde ein Höchstsatz für die Kommunalsteuer auferlegt; **charge-capping** N *(Brit)* Festlegung eines Kommunalsteuer-Höchstsatzes durch die Zentralregierung; **charge card** N Kundenkreditkarte *f*

charged [tʃɑːdʒd] ADJ *(lit, fig)* geladen; *(Elec also)* aufgeladen; **~ with emotion** emotionsgeladen

chargé d'affaires [ˈʃɑːʒeɪdæˈfeə] N Chargé d'affaires *m*

charge: charge hand N Vorarbeiter(in) *m(f)*; **charge nurse** N *(Brit)* Stationsleiter(in) *m(f)* *(im Pflegedienst)*

charger [ˈtʃɑːdʒə] N **a** *(= battery charger)* Ladegerät *nt* **b** *(= horse)* Ross *nt* **c** *(old, = dish)* Platte *f*

charge sheet N Anklageprotokoll *nt*

char-grilled [ˈtʃɑːgrɪld] ADJ *(Brit)* vom Holzkohlengrill

charily [ˈtʃɛərɪlɪ] ADV vorsichtig

chariness [ˈtʃɛərɪnɪs] N Vorsicht *f*

chariot [ˈtʃærɪət] N Wagen *m*, Streitwagen *m* *(liter)*

charioteer [ˌtʃærɪəˈtɪə] N Wagenlenker *m*

charisma [kæˈrɪzmə] N Charisma *nt*

charismatic [ˌkærɪzˈmætɪk] ADJ charismatisch

charitable [ˈtʃærɪtəbl] ADJ menschenfreundlich, gütig; *(= dispensing charity)* trust, organization Wohltätigkeits-, karitativ; *(= financially generous, tolerant)* großzügig; *thought, remark etc* freundlich; **to have ~ status** als gemeinnützig anerkannt sein; *(= give) etw* eine gute Tat; **he wasn't very ~ about his boss** er äußerte sich nicht gerade schmeichelhaft über seinen Chef; **I'm feeling ~ today, here's £5** ich habe heute meinen

sozialen Tag, hier hast du £ 5; **to take a ~ view of sth** etw milde betrachten

charitably [ˈtʃærɪtəblɪ] ADV großzügig; *say etc* freundlich

charity [ˈtʃærɪtɪ] N **a** *(= Christian virtue)* tätige Nächstenliebe, Barmherzigkeit *f* **b** *(= tolerance, kindness)* Menschenfreundlichkeit *f*; **for ~'s sake, out of ~** aus reiner Menschenfreundlichkeit; **~ begins at home** *(Prov)* man muss zuerst an seine eigene Familie/sein eigenes Land *etc* denken **c** *(= alms)* **to live on ~** von Almosen leben **d** *(= charitable society)* Wohltätigkeitsverein *m*, karitative Organisation; *(= charitable purposes)* Wohlfahrt *f*; **to work for ~** für die Wohlfahrt arbeiten; **a collection for ~** eine Sammlung für wohltätige *or* karitative Zwecke

charity in *cpds* Wohltätigkeits-

charlady [ˈtʃɑːleɪdɪ] N *(Brit)* Putz- *or* Reinemachefrau *f*

charlatan [ˈʃɑːlətən] N Scharlatan *m*

Charlemagne [ˈʃɑːləmeɪn] N Karl der Große

Charles [tʃɑːlz] N Karl *m*

charleston [ˈtʃɑːlstən] N Charleston *m*

charley horse [ˈtʃɑːlɪhɔːs] N *(US, inf)* steifes Bein

Charlie [ˈtʃɑːlɪ] N *dim of* **Charles**

charlie [ˈtʃɑːlɪ] *(Brit)* N **a** *(inf: = fool)* Heini *m (inf)*, Blödmann *m (inf)*; **I felt a real ~** ich kam mir richtig blöd vor *(inf)*; **I must have looked a proper ~** ich muss ziemlich dumm aus der Wäsche geguckt haben *(inf)* **b** *(sl: = cocaine)* Koks *m (inf)*, Candy *m (sl)*

Charlotte [ˈʃɑːlət] N **a** Charlotte *f* **b** *(Cook)* **charlotte** Charlotte *f*; **charlotte russe** Charlotte Malakoff

charm [tʃɑːm] N **a** *(= attractiveness)* Charme *m no pl*; *(of person also)* Anziehungskraft *f*; *(of cottage, village, countryside)* Reiz *m*; **feminine ~s** (weibliche) Reize *pl*; **he succumbed to her ~s** er erlag ihrem Charme; **to turn on the ~** seinen (ganzen) Charme spielen lassen

b *(= spell)* Bann *m*; **it worked like a ~** das hat hervorragend geklappt

c *(= amulet)* Talisman *m*; *(= trinket)* Anhänger *m*

VT a *(= attract, please)* bezaubern; **to ~ one's way into sth** sich in etw *(acc)* einschmeicheln; **to ~ one's way out of sth** sich mit Charme vor etw *(dat)* drücken; **to ~ sth out of sb** jdm etw abschmeicheln; **he could ~ the birds out of** *or* **from the trees** *(prov)* er könnte mit seinem Charme alles erreichen

b *(= cast spell on)* bannen; *snakes* beschwören; **to lead a ~ed life** einen Schutzengel haben

▶ **charm away** VT *sep fears, worries etc* zerstreuen

charm bracelet N Armband *nt* mit Anhängern

charmed circle [tʃɑːmdˈsɜːkl] N *(liter)* illustrer Kreis

charmer [ˈtʃɑːmə] N **to be a real ~** wirklich charmant sein

charming [ˈtʃɑːmɪŋ] ADJ reizend, charmant; **~!** *(iro)* wie reizend! *(iro)*, na, das ist ja reizend! *(iro)*

charmingly [ˈtʃɑːmɪŋlɪ] ADV reizend; **she behaved/welcomed us quite ~** sie war/begrüßte uns äußerst charmant

charmless [ˈtʃɑːmlɪs] ADJ *place* wenig reizvoll; *person* unsympathisch

charm offensive N Charmeoffensive *f*

charnel house [ˈtʃɑːnlhaʊs] N *(old)* Leichenhalle *f*; *(for bones)* Beinhaus *nt*

chart [tʃɑːt] N **a** Tabelle *f*; *(= graph, diagram)* Schaubild *nt*, Diagramm *nt*; *(= map, weather chart)* Karte *f*; **on a ~** in einer Tabelle/einem Diagramm; **to keep a ~ of sth** etw in eine Tabelle eintragen/in einem Diagramm erfassen **b** **charts** PL *(= top twenty)* Hitliste *f*, Charts *pl* **VT** *(= make a map of)* kartografisch erfassen; *(= record progress of)* auswerten; *(= keep a chart of)* aufzeichnen, erfassen; *(= plan)* festlegen; **to**

~ **the progress of a team** den Erfolg eines Teams aufzeichnen **VI** (= reach pop charts: singer, song) in die Charts pl or die Hitliste kommen

charter ['tʃɑːtə'] **N a** Charta f; (= town charter, Univ also) Gründungsurkunde f; (of a society) Satzung f; (= permission to become established) Charter f or m, Freibrief m **b** (Naut, Aviat etc, = hire) **on** ~ gechartert; **the plane is available for** ~ das Flugzeug kann gechartert werden **VT** plane, bus etc chartern

charter in cpds Charter-

chartered accountant [,tʃɑːtəd'kauntənt] N (Brit) staatlich geprüfter Bilanzbuchhalter, staatlich geprüfte Bilanzbuchhalterin

charter: charter flight N Charterflug m; **charter party** N Chartergesellschaft f; **charter plane** N Charterflugzeug nt

chart topper N (= hit record) Spitzenreiter m

charwoman ['tʃɑːˌwʊmən] N (Brit) = **charlady**

chary ['tʃeərɪ] ADJ (+er) (= cautious) vorsichtig; (= sparing) zurückhaltend (of mit); **I'd be ~ of taking lifts from strangers if I were you** an deiner Stelle würde ich nicht so ohne weiteres mit Fremden mitfahren; **he is ~ of giving praise** er ist mit Lob zurückhaltend

Charybdis [kə'rɪbdɪs] N Charybdis f

Chas abbr of **Charles**

chase[1] [tʃeɪs] **N** Verfolgungsjagd f; (Hunt) Jagd f; (Horse Racing: = steeplechase) Hindernisrennen nt; **a (high-speed) car** ~ eine Verfolgungsjagd im Auto; **to give** ~ die Verfolgung aufnehmen; **to give** ~ **to sb** jds Verfolgung aufnehmen; **the thrill of the** ~ die Jagdlust; **the ~ for the championship** der Kampf um die Meisterschaft; **to cut to the** ~ (esp US inf) zum Kern der Sache kommen
VT jagen; (= follow) verfolgen; member of opposite sex hinterherlaufen (+dat), nachlaufen (+dat); **he's been chasing that girl for months** er ist schon seit Monaten hinter der Frau her; **to** ~ **one's own tail** (fig) seine Zeit und Energie verschwenden
VI to ~ **after sb** hinter jdm herrennen (inf); (in vehicle) hinter jdm herrasen (inf); **to** ~ **around** herumrasen (inf)

▶ **chase away** or **off VI** losrasen (inf); (on foot also) losrennen **VT** sep wegjagen; (fig) sorrow etc vertreiben

▶ **chase down** VT SEP **a** (= track down) aufspüren; thing auftreiben **b** (US, = catch) aufspüren, erwischen

▶ **chase up** VT sep person rankriegen (inf); information etc ranschaffen (inf); **we'll have to chase them up a bit (about ...)** wir werden ihnen ein bisschen Dampf machen müssen (wegen ...)

chase[2] VT (Tech) silver, metal ziselieren

chaser ['tʃeɪsə'] N **a** (= pursuer) Verfolger m **b** (= drink) **have a whisky** ~ trinken Sie einen Whisky dazu

chasm ['kæzəm] N (Geol) Spalte f, Kluft f (also fig); **a yawning** ~ ein gähnender Abgrund; **the future lay before him, a great black** ~ die Zukunft tat sich wie ein riesiger dunkler Abgrund vor ihm auf

chassis ['ʃæsɪ] N Chassis nt; (Aut also) Fahrgestell nt

chaste [tʃeɪst] ADJ (+er) (= pure, virtuous) keusch; (= simple, unadvanced) style, elegance schlicht

chastely ['tʃeɪstlɪ] ADV kiss keusch, unschuldig; dress schlicht

chasten ['tʃeɪsn] VT nachdenklich stimmen, zur Einsicht bringen; pride, stubborn nature zügeln; ~**ed by ...** durch ... zur Einsicht gelangt

chasteness ['tʃeɪstnɪs] N (of person, relationship) Keuschheit f; (= simplicity: of style) Schlichtheit f

chastening ['tʃeɪsnɪŋ] ADJ thought, experience ernüchternd

chastise [tʃæs'taɪz] VT (physically) züchtigen (geh); (verbally) schelten

chastisement ['tʃæstɪzmənt] N (physical) Züchtigung f (geh); (verbal) Schelte f

---

chastity ['tʃæstɪtɪ] N (= sexual purity) Keuschheit f; (= virginity also) Unberührtheit f, Reinheit f

chastity belt N Keuschheitsgürtel m

chasuble ['tʃæzjʊbl] N Messgewand nt, Kasel f

chat [tʃæt] **N** Unterhaltung f; (about unimportant things also) Plauderei f, Schwatz m (inf); **could we have a ~ about it?** können wir uns mal darüber unterhalten?; **she dropped in for a ~** sie kam für ein Schwätzchen rein (inf) **VI** plaudern; (two people also) sich unterhalten

▶ **chat up** VT sep (Brit inf) person einreden auf (+acc); prospective girl-/boyfriend sich heranmachen an (+acc), anquatschen (inf)

chatelaine ['ʃætəleɪn] N **a** (of castle, = housekeeper) Schlossverwalterin f; (= owner) Schlossherrin f **b** (old) Gürtel, an dem ein Schlüsselbund getragen wird

chat room N (Comput) Chatroom m

chat show N (Brit) Talkshow f

chattels ['tʃætlz] PL (Jur) bewegliches Vermögen, bewegliche Habe; **all his (goods and)** ~ seine gesamte Habe

chatter ['tʃætə'] **N** (of person) Geschwätz nt, Geplapper nt; (of birds, monkeys) Geschnatter nt; (of teeth) Klappern nt **VI** (person) schwatzen, schwätzen (esp S Ger), plappern; (birds, monkeys) schnattern; (teeth) klappern

chatterbox ['tʃætəbɒks] N Quasselstrippe f (inf)

chattering ['tʃætərɪŋ] **N** Geschwätz nt **ADJ the** ~ **classes** (Brit pej inf) das Bildungsbürgertum

chatty ['tʃætɪ] ADJ (+er) person geschwätzig, schwatzhaft; **written in a ~ style** im Plauderton geschrieben

chat-up line ['tʃætʌplaɪn] N Anmacherspruch m, Aufreiße f (inf)

chauffeur ['ʃəʊfə'] N Chauffeur m, Fahrer m; ~-**driven** mit Fahrer or Chauffeur; **to be** ~-**driven** einen Fahrer haben

chauffeuse [ʃəʊ'fɜːz] N Chauffeuse f, Fahrerin f

chauvinism ['ʃəʊvɪnɪzəm] N Chauvinismus m

chauvinist ['ʃəʊvɪnɪst] **N** (= jingoist) Chauvinist(in) m(f); (= male chauvinist) männlicher Chauvinist **ADJ** chauvinistisch; **(male)** ~ **pig** Chauvinistenschwein nt (inf)

chauvinistic [ʃəʊvɪ'nɪstɪk] ADJ chauvinistisch

cheap [tʃiːp] **ADJ** (+er) **a** also ADV(= inexpensive) billig; **I got it** ~ ich habe es billig gekriegt; **it's going** ~ es ist billig zu haben; **it doesn't come** ~ es ist nicht billig; ~ **and cheerful** preiswert; **it's** ~ **at the price** es ist spottbillig; **to hold sth** ~ etw gering achten; **human life is** ~ ein Menschenleben ist nicht viel wert
b (= poor quality) billig, minderwertig; **everything they sell is** ~ **and nasty** sie verkaufen nur Ramsch
c (fig, = mean, shallow, sexually cheap) joke, flattery, thrill, girl billig; person, behaviour, appearance ordinär; **to feel** ~ sich (dat) schäbig vorkommen; **how can you be so** ~! wie kannst du nur so gemein sein!; **to make oneself** ~ sich entwürdigen; (by loose living) sich wegwerfen **N on the** ~ auf die billige Tour (inf); **to buy sth on the** ~ (inf) etw für einen Pappenstiel (inf) or einen Apfel und ein Ei (inf) kaufen; **to make sth on the** ~ (inf) etw ganz billig produzieren

cheapen ['tʃiːpən] **VT** (lit) verbilligen, herabsetzen; (fig) herabsetzen, schlecht machen; **to** ~ **oneself** sich entwürdigen **VI** billiger werden, sich verbilligen

cheapie ['tʃiːpɪ] N, ADJ (inf) = **cheapo**

cheap-jack ['tʃiːpdʒæk] ADJ Ramsch- (pej)

cheaply ['tʃiːplɪ] ADV buy, sell, furnish, decorate billig; make, produce, eat, live günstig

cheapness ['tʃiːpnɪs] N **a** (= inexpensiveness) billiger Preis **b** (= poor quality) Billigkeit f, Minderwertigkeit f **c** (fig, of joke) Billigkeit f; (of person, behaviour) ordinäre Art

cheapo ['tʃiːpəʊ] (inf) **N** Billigartikel m, billiges Ding (inf) **ADJ** Billig-; ~ **video** Billigvideo nt

---

cheap shot N unfaire Bemerkung; **that was a** ~ das war unfair, das ging unter die Gürtellinie (inf)

cheapskate ['tʃiːpskeɪt] N (inf) Knicker m, Knauser m (inf)

cheat [tʃiːt] **VT** betrügen; authorities also täuschen; **to** ~ **death** dem Tod von der Schippe springen; **to** ~ **sb out of sth** jdn um etw betrügen; **to feel** ~**ed** sich betrogen fühlen **VI** betrügen; (in exam, game etc) mogeln (inf), schummeln (Sch inf); (in card games also) falsch spielen, mogeln (inf) **N a** (= person) Betrüger(in) m(f); (in exam, game etc) Mogler(in) m(f) (inf), Schummler(in) m(f) (Sch inf); (in card games also) Falschspieler(in) m(f), Mogler(in) m(f) (inf) **b** (= dishonest trick) Betrug m, Täuschung f

▶ **cheat on** VI +prep obj betrügen

cheater ['tʃiːtə'] N (US, = person) = **cheat N a**

cheating ['tʃiːtɪŋ] **N** Betrügen nt, Betrug m; (in exam, game etc) Mogeln m (inf), Schummeln nt (Sch inf); (in card games also) Falschspielen nt, Mogeln m (inf) **ADJ** betrügerisch

Chechen ['tʃetʃən] **N** pl **Chechens** or **Chechen** Tschetschene m, Tschetschenin f **ADJ** tschetschenisch; **the** ~ **Republic** die Tschetschenische Republik

Chechenia [tʃe'tʃiːnɪə], **Chechnya** ['tʃetʃnɪə] N Tschetschenien nt

check [tʃek] **N a** (= examination) Überprüfung f, Kontrolle f; **to give sth a** ~ etw überprüfen or nachsehen; **to make a** ~ **on sb/sth** jdn/etw überprüfen, bei jdm/etw eine Kontrolle durchführen; **a random** ~ eine Stichprobe; **to keep a** ~ **on sb/sth** jdn/etw überwachen or kontrollieren
b (= restraint) Hemmnis nt, Erschwernis f; (Mil, to army) Hindernis nt, Sperre f; **an efficient** ~ **on population growth** ein wirksames Mittel zur Eindämmung des Bevölkerungswachstums; **to hold** or **keep sb in** ~ jdn in Schach halten; **to keep one's temper in** ~ sich beherrschen; **(a system of)** ~**s and balances** ein Sicherungssystem nt; **to act as a** ~ **on sth** etw unter Kontrolle (dat) halten
c (= pattern) Karo(muster) nt; (= square) Karo nt
d (Chess) Schach nt; **to be in** ~ im Schach stehen; **to put sb in** ~ jdm Schach bieten
e (US, = cheque) Scheck m; (= bill) Rechnung f; ~ **please** bitte (be)zahlen
f (US: = room) (Rail) Gepäckaufbewahrung f; (Theat) Garderobe f; (= ticket, Rail) (Gepäck-) schein m; (Theat) (Garderoben)marke f
g (US, = tick) Haken m
VT a (= examine) überprüfen, checken (inf); (in book also) nachsehen; (US also) tickets also kontrollieren; **to** ~ **whether** or **if ...** nachprüfen, ob ...
b (= act as control on) kontrollieren; (= stop) enemy, advance aufhalten; anger unterdrücken, beherrschen; **I was going to say it, but I just managed to** ~ **myself in time** ich wollte es sagen, aber ich konnte mich gerade noch beherrschen
c (Chess) Schach bieten (+dat)
d (Aviat) luggage einchecken, abfertigen lassen; (US) coat etc abgeben; (US Rail) luggage (= register) aufgeben; (= deposit) abgeben, zur Aufbewahrung geben
e (US, = tick) abhaken
VI a (= make sure) nachfragen (with bei); (= have a look) nachsehen, nachgucken; **I was just** ~**ing** ich wollte nur nachprüfen
b (= stop, pause) stocken; (horse) scheuen

▶ **check back** VI (= look back in records) zurückgehen (in zu), nachsehen (in in +dat); (= re-contact) rückfragen (with bei)

▶ **check in VI** (at airport) sich bei der Abfertigung melden, einchecken; (at hotel) sich anmelden; **what time do you have to check in?** wann musst du am Flughafen sein? **VT** sep (at airport) luggage abfertigen lassen, einchecken; (at hotel) person anmelden; **he isn't checked in at this hotel** er wohnt nicht in diesem Hotel; **they checked me in at a first-class hotel** ich wurde in einem erstklassigen Hotel untergebracht

► **check off** VT *sep* (*esp US*) abhaken

► **check on** VI +*prep obj* = **check up on**

► **check out** VI sich abmelden; (= *leave hotel*) abreisen; (= *sign out*) sich austragen; (= *clock out*) stempeln, stechen VT *sep* **a** *figures, facts, persons* überprüfen; **check it out with the boss** klären Sie das mit dem Chef ab; **check out our new range** (*inf*) sehen Sie sich (*dat*) unser neues Sortiment an **b** (*hotel*) *guest* abfertigen

► **check over** VT *sep* überprüfen

► **check through** VT *sep* **a** *account, proofs* durchsehen, durchgehen **b** **they checked my bags through to Berlin** mein Gepäck wurde nach Berlin durchgecheckt

► **check up** VI überprüfen

► **check up on** VI +*prep obj* überprüfen; *person also* Nachforschungen anstellen über (+*acc*); (= *keep a check on*) *sb* kontrollieren

checkable ['tʃekəbl] ADJ kontrollierbar, nachprüfbar

checkback ['tʃekbæk] N Rückfrage *f*

checkbook ['tʃekbʊk] N (*US*) Scheckbuch *nt*

checked [tʃekt] ADJ **a** (*in pattern*) kariert; ~ **pattern** Karomuster *nt* **b** (*Phon*) *syllable* geschlossen; *vowel* in geschlossener Silbe (stehend)

checker ['tʃekə'] N **a** (*of documents etc*) Prüfer(in) *m(f)* **b** (*US, in supermarket*) Kassierer(in) *m(f)* **c** (*US, for coats etc*) Garderobenfrau *f*/-mann *m*

checkerboard ['tʃekəbɔːd] N (*US*) Damebrett *nt*; (= *chessboard*) Schachbrett *nt*

Checker cab® ['tʃekəˌkæb] N (*US, Aut*) *US-Taxi mit Schachbrettmusterstreifen an den Seiten*

checkered ADJ (*US*) = **chequered**

checkers ['tʃekəz] N (*US*) Damespiel *nt*; **to play** ~ Dame spielen

check-in (desk) ['tʃekɪn(ˌdesk)] N Abfertigung *f*, Abfertigungsschalter *m*; (*Aviat*) Abflugschalter *m*; (*US, in hotel*) Rezeption *f*, Anmeldung *f*

checking ['tʃekɪŋ] N Überprüfung *f*, Kontrolle *f*; **it needs more** ~ es muss gründlicher überprüft werden; ~ **account** (*US*) Girokonto *nt*; ~ **slip** Kontrollabschnitt *m*

check: **check list** N Prüf- or Checkliste *f*; **checkmate** N Schachmatt *nt*; ~**!** (*Chess*) matt!; (*fig*) aus!; **he found himself in** ~ (*lit, fig*) er war matt gesetzt VT matt setzen; **checkout** N (*in supermarket*) Kasse *f* **b** (= *leaving of hotel*) Auschecken *nt no pl*; **checkpoint** N Kontrollpunkt *m*; **Checkpoint Charlie** Checkpoint Charlie *m*, Ausländerübergang *m* Friedrichstraße; **checkroom** N (*US, Theat*) Garderobe *f*; (*Rail*) Gepäckaufbewahrung *f*; **checkup** N (*Med*) Untersuchung *f*, Check-up *m*; **to have a ~/go for a** ~ einen Check-up machen lassen

---

cheddar ['tʃedə'] N Cheddar(käse) *m*

---

cheek [tʃiːk] N **a** Backe *f*, Wange *f* (*liter*); **to be ~ by jowl (with sb)** Tuchfühlung mit jdm haben, auf Tuchfühlung (mit jdm) sein; **to dance ~ to** ~ Wange an Wange tanzen; ~ **pouch** Futtertasche *f*; **to turn the other** ~ die andere Wange hinhalten **b** (= *buttock*) Backe *f* **c** (*Brit*: = *impudence*) Frechheit *f*, Unverschämtheit *f*, Dreistigkeit *f*; **to have the ~ to do sth** die Frechheit or Stirn haben, etw zu tun, sich erfrechen, etw zu tun; **they gave him a lot of ~** sie waren sehr frech zu ihm; **enough of your ~!** jetzt reichts aber!; **of all the ~!, the ~ of it!** so eine Frechheit or Unverschämtheit! VT (*Brit*) **to ~ sb** frech sein zu jdm or gegen jdn

cheekbone ['tʃiːkbəʊn] N Wangenknochen *m*, Jochbein *nt* (*spec*)

-cheeked [-'tʃiːkd] ADJ *suf* -backig; **rosy--cheeked** rotbackig

cheekily ['tʃiːkɪlɪ] ADV frech, vorwitzig, dreist

cheekiness ['tʃiːkɪnɪs] N Frechheit *f*, Dreistigkeit *f*, Vorwitz *m* (*geh*); (*of person also*) freche Art

cheeky ['tʃiːkɪ] ADJ (+*er*) (*Brit*) frech, vorwitzig, dreist; *remark, person, smile also* schnippisch; *hat, dress* kess, flott; *driving* schneidig, schnittig, frech; **it's a bit ~ asking for another pay rise so soon** es ist etwas unverschämt, schon wieder eine Gehaltserhöhung zu verlangen; ~ **girl** freche Göre

cheep [tʃiːp] N Piep *m*, Piepser *m* VI piepsen

cheer [tʃɪə'] N **a** Hurra- or Beifallsruf *m*; (= *cheering*) Hurrageschrei *nt*, Jubel *m*; **to give three ~s for sb** jdn dreimal hochleben lassen, ein dreifaches Hurra auf jdn ausbringen; **three ~s for Mike!** ein dreifaches Hurra für Mike!; ~**!** (*inf*: = *your health*) prost!; (*Brit inf*: = *goodbye*) tschüs(s)! (*inf*); (*Brit inf*: = *thank you*) danke schön! **b** (= *comfort*) Aufmunterung *f*, Ermutigung *f*; **the news gave us some** ~ die Nachricht munterte uns auf; **words of** ~ aufmunternde Worte, Zuspruch *m* **c** (*old*) **be of good** ~ seid guten Mutes or wohlgemut (*old*) **d** (*old*, = *food etc*) **good** ~ Tafelfreude(n *pl*) *f* (*old*) VT **a** *person* zujubeln (+*dat*); *thing, event* bejubeln **b** (= *gladden*) aufmuntern, aufheitern, froh machen VI jubeln, hurra or Hurra rufen

► **cheer on** VT *sep* anspornen, anfeuern

► **cheer up** VT *sep* aufmuntern, aufheitern; *room, place* aufheitern; **he needed a bit of cheering up** er brauchte etwas Aufmunterung or Aufheiterung; **tell him that, that'll cheer him up** sag ihm das, dann freut er sich VI (*person*) vergnügter or fröhlicher werden, bessere Laune bekommen; (*things*) besser werden; **cheer up!** lass den Kopf nicht hängen!, nun lach doch mal!; **cheer up, it's not that bad** Kopf hoch or nur Mut, so schlimm ist es auch wieder nicht

cheerful ['tʃɪəfʊl] ADJ fröhlich, vergnügt; *person also* gut gelaunt, heiter (*geh*); *place, colour etc* heiter; *prospect, news* erfreulich; *tune* fröhlich; **to be ~ about sth** in Bezug auf etw optimistisch sein; **you're a ~ one, aren't you?** (*iro*) du

---

bist (mir) vielleicht ein schöner Miesmacher (*inf*); **that's ~!** (*iro*) das ist ja heiter!

cheerfully ['tʃɪəfʊlɪ] ADV fröhlich, vergnügt; *decorated* lustig, heiter; **I could ~ strangle him!** den könnte ich glatt umbringen

cheerfulness ['tʃɪəfʊlnɪs] N Fröhlichkeit *f*; (*of person also*) gute Laune, Vergnügtheit *f*, Frohsinn *m* (*geh*); (*of place, colour etc*) Heiterkeit *f*; (*of prospect, news*) Erfreulichkeit *f*; (*of tune*) fröhlicher Charakter

cheerily ['tʃɪərɪlɪ] ADV fröhlich, vergnügt; ~ **coloured** lustig angemalt

cheering ['tʃɪərɪŋ] N Jubel *m*, Jubeln *nt*, Hurrageschrei *nt*; (= *cheering on*) anfeuernde Zurufe *pl* ADJ **a** *news, prospect* beglückend **b** *crowds* jubelnd

cheerio ['tʃɪərɪ'əʊ] INTERJ (*esp Brit, inf*) **a** (= *goodbye*) Wiedersehen (*inf*), Servus (*S Ger, Aus*); (*to friends*) tschüs(s) (*inf*) **b** (= *your health*) prost

cheerleader ['tʃɪəliːdə'] N Anführer *m*

cheerless ['tʃɪəlɪs] ADJ freudlos, trüb; *person* trübselig, trübsinnig; *prospect* trübe, düster, traurig; *scenery* grau

cheers [tʃɪəz] INTERJ → **cheer** N a

cheery ['tʃɪərɪ] ADJ (+*er*) fröhlich, vergnügt; *tune, colour also* lustig

cheese [tʃiːz] N Käse *m*; **a big** ~ (*inf*) ein hohes Tier (*inf*); **hard ~!** (*dated inf*) Künstlerpech! (*inf*); **say ~!** (*Phot*) bitte recht freundlich, sag „cheese"

cheese in *cpds* Käse-; **cheeseboard** N Käsebrett *nt*; (= *course*) Käseplatte *f*; **cheeseburger** N Cheeseburger *m*; **cheesecake** N (*Cook*) Käsekuchen *m*; (*sl*: = *female photos*) (nacktes) Fleisch (*inf*); **cheesecloth** N Käseleinen *nt*, indische Baumwolle *f*

cheesed off [tʃiːzd'ɒf] ADJ (*Brit, inf*) angeödet (*inf*); **I'm ~ with this job/her** diese Arbeit/sie ödet mich an (*inf*) or stinkt mir (*inf*)

cheese: cheeseparing N Pfennigfuchserei *f* (*inf*), Knauserei *f* ADJ knauserig, knickerig (*inf*); **cheese straw** N (*Brit*) kleine Käsestange

cheesy ['tʃiːzɪ] ADJ (+*er*) käsig; **to taste** ~ nach Käse schmecken; **a ~ taste** ein Käsegeschmack; **a ~ smile** ein Pepsodentlächeln *nt* (*inf*) **b** (*inf*, = *shoddy*) mies (*inf*)

cheetah ['tʃiːtə] N Gepard *m*

chef [ʃef] N Küchenchef *m*; (*as profession*) Koch *m*; (= *head chef*) Chefkoch *m*

Chelsea bun [ˌtʃelsɪ'bʌn] N (*Brit*) Hefeteigbrötchen mit Rosinen

Chelsea Pensioner [ˌtʃelsɪ'penʃənə'] N (*Brit*) *Armeeangehöriger im Ruhestand, der im „Chelsea Royal Hospital" wohnt*

chemical ['kemɪkəl] ADJ chemisch; ~ **accident** Chemieunfall *m*; ~ **castration** chemische Kastration N Chemikalie *f*

chemical engineer N Chemieingenieur(in) *m(f)*

chemical engineering N Chemotechnik *f*

chemically ['kemɪkəlɪ] ADV chemisch

chemical toilet N Chemietoilette *f*

chemical warfare N chemische Krieg(s)führung

chemise [ʃə'miːz] N Unterkleid *nt*

chemist ['kemɪst] N **a** (= *expert in chemistry*) Chemiker(in) *m(f)* **b** (*Brit: in shop*) Drogist(in) *m(f)*; (*dispensing*) Apotheker(in) *m(f)*; ~**'s shop** Drogerie *f*; (*dispensing*) Apotheke *f*

chemistry ['kemɪstrɪ] N **a** Chemie *f*; (= *chemical make-up*) chemische Zusammensetzung; ~ **set** Chemiebaukasten *m* **b** (*fig*) Verträglichkeit *f*; **the good ~ between them** ihre gute Verträglichkeit; **the ~ between us was perfect** wir haben uns sofort vertragen, es hat sofort zwischen uns gefunkt (*inf*); **the ~'s all wrong (between us)** wir sind einfach zu verschieden; **the ~ of physical attraction/of love** das Kräftespiel der körperlichen Anziehung/in der Liebe

chemotherapy [ˌkiːməʊˈθerəpɪ] N Chemotherapie f

chenille [ʃəˈniːl] N Chenille f

cheque, (US) **check** [tʃek] ✪ 20.7 N Scheck m; **a ~ for £100** ein Scheck über £ 100; **to pay by ~** mit (einem) Scheck bezahlen

cheque account N Girokonto nt

chequebook, (US) **checkbook** [ˈtʃekbʊk] N Scheckheft nt, Scheckbuch nt; **~ journalism** Scheckbuchjournalismus m

cheque card N Scheckkarte f

chequered, (US) **checkered** [ˈtʃekəd] ADJ (lit) kariert; (= dappled) gefleckt, gesprenkelt; (fig) career, history, past bewegt

chequered flag, (US) **checkered flag** N (Motor Racing) Zielflagge f

cherish [ˈtʃerɪʃ] VT **a** person liebevoll sorgen für; **to love and to ~** zu lieben und zu ehren **b** feelings, hope hegen; idea, illusion sich hingeben (+dat); **I shall always ~** that memory/present die Erinnerung (daran)/das Geschenk wird mir immer lieb und teuer sein; **to ~ sb's memory** jds Andenken in Ehren halten

cherished [ˈtʃerɪʃt] ADJ dream, belief, ambition lang gehegt, größte(r, s); **this is one of my ~ memories** daran erinnere ich mich gern zurück; **her most ~ possessions** die Dinge, an denen sie am meisten hängt

Cherokee (Indian) [ˈtʃerəʊkiː(ˈɪndɪən)] N Tscherokese m, Tscherokesin f

cheroot [ʃəˈruːt] N Stumpen m

cherry [ˈtʃerɪ] **N** Kirsche f; (= colour) Kirschrot nt; **wild ~** Vogelkirsche f; **life isn't exactly a bowl of cherries for her right now** das Leben ist für sie im Moment kein Zuckerlecken ADJ (colour) kirschrot; (Cook) Kirsch-

cherry in cpds Kirsch-; **cherry blossom** N Kirschblüte f; **cherry bomb** N (US) Knallerbse f; **cherry brandy** N Cherry Brandy m; **cherry orchard** N Kirschgarten m; **cherry-pick** (fig inf) **VT** die Rosinen heraussuchen aus (inf) **VI** sich (dat) die Rosinen heraussuchen; **cherry picker** N (= vehicle) Bockkran m; **cherry-red** ADJ kirschrot; **cherry tomato** N Kirschtomate f, Cherrytomate f

cherub [ˈtʃerəb] N **a** pl **-im** [ˈtʃerəbɪm] (Eccl) Cherub m **b** pl **-s** (Art) Putte f, Putto m (form); (= baby) Engelchen nt

chervil [ˈtʃɜːvɪl] N Kerbel m

Cheshire cat [ˌtʃeʃəˈkæt] N **to grin like a ~** breit grinsen

chess [tʃes] N Schach(spiel) nt

chess: chessboard N Schachbrett nt; **chessman**, **chesspiece** N Schachfigur f; **chess piece** N Schachfigur f; **chess set** N Schachspiel nt

chest¹ [tʃest] N (for tea, tools etc) Kiste f; (= piece of furniture, for clothes, money etc) Truhe f; **~ of drawers** Kommode f

chest² N (Anat) Brust f, Brustkorb m (esp Med); **the boxer's broad ~** der breite Brustkasten des Boxers; **to measure sb's ~** jds Brustweite or Brustumfang messen; **to get sth off one's ~** (fig inf) sich (dat) etw von der Seele reden, etw loswerden; **to have a weak ~** schwach auf der Brust sein (inf); **a cold on the ~** (Brit) a ~ **cold** Bronchialkatarr(h) m; **~ pains** Schmerzen pl in der Brust

-chested [-ˈtʃestɪd] ADJ suf -brüstig; **flat-chested** flachbrüstig

chesterfield [ˈtʃestəfiːld] N Chesterfieldsofa nt

chest infection N Lungeninfekt m

chestnut [ˈtʃesnʌt] **N a** (= nut, tree) Kastanie f **b** (= colour) Kastanienbraun nt **c** (= horse) Fuchs m **d** (inf, = old joke) alte or olle Kamelle (inf) ADJ (colour) hair kastanienbraun, rötlich braun; **a ~ horse** ein Fuchs m

chest specialist N Facharzt m/-ärztin f für Lungenkrankheiten, Lungenfacharzt m/-ärztin f

chesty [ˈtʃestɪ] ADJ (+er) (Brit inf) person erkältet, grippig (inf); cough rau, schnarrend; **I'm a bit ~**

---

this morning ich habs heute etwas auf der Brust (inf)

cheval glass [ʃəˈvælglɑːs] N Standspiegel m (zum Kippen)

chevron [ˈʃevrən] N Winkel m

chew [tʃuː] **N** Kauen nt; **to have a good ~ on sth** auf or an etw (dat) gründlich herumkauen **VT** kauen; **this meat requires a lot of ~ing** an or bei diesem Fleisch muss man viel (herum-) kauen; **that dog's been ~ing the carpet again** der Hund hat schon wieder am Teppich genagt; **don't ~ your fingernails** kaue nicht an deinen Nägeln; **she always ~s her nails when she's nervous** immer, wenn sie nervös ist, kaut sie an den Nägeln; **to ~ the fat** (inf) tratschen (inf) → **cud**

▶ **chew away** **VI** lange herumkauen (at an or auf +dat); **the rats have been chewing away at the woodwork** die Ratten haben am Holz herumgenagt **VT** sep wegfressen

▶ **chew off** or **out** VT sep (US, inf) zur Schnecke machen (inf)

▶ **chew on** VI +prep obj **a** (lit) (herum)kauen auf (+dat) **b** (also **chew over**: inf) facts, problem sich (dat) durch den Kopf gehen lassen

▶ **chew up** VT sep **a** (lit) aufessen, fertig essen; (animal) auffressen; pencil etc zerkauen; ground, road surface zerstören; paper zerfressen, zermalmen **b** (inf, = tell off) fertig machen (inf), runterputzen (inf)

chewing gum [ˈtʃuːɪŋɡʌm] N Kaugummi m or nt

chewy [ˈtʃuːɪ] ADJ meat zäh; pasta kernig; sweets weich

chiaroscuro [kɪˌɑːrəsˈkʊərəʊ] N Chiaroscuro nt, Helldunkel nt

chic [ʃiːk] ADJ (+er) schick, elegant **N** Chic m, Schick m

chicane [ʃɪˈkeɪn] N (Sport) Schikane f

chicanery [ʃɪˈkeɪnərɪ] N (= trickery) Machenschaften pl; (legal) Winkelzüge pl

Chicano [tʃɪˈkɑːnəʊ] N (= Mexican American) pl **Chicanos** Chicano m

chichi [ˈtʃiːʃiː] ADJ (inf) todschick (inf), auf schön gemacht (inf); dress etc verspielt, niedlich

chick [tʃɪk] N **a** (of chicken) Küken nt; (= young bird) Junge(s) nt **b** (inf, = child) Kleine(s) nt **c** (inf, = girl) Mieze f (inf); **she's some ~** sie ist nicht ohne (inf)

chicken [ˈtʃɪkɪn] **N a** Huhn nt; (for roasting, frying) Hähnchen nt; **she's no ~** (inf) sie ist nicht mehr die Jüngste; **~ liver** Hühner- or Geflügelleber f; **to run around like a headless ~** wie ein kopfloses Huhn herumlaufen; **don't count your ~s (before they're hatched)** (Prov) man soll den Tag nicht vor dem Abend loben (Prov); **it's a ~-and egg situation** (inf) das ist eine Zwickmühle **b** (inf, = coward) feiges Huhn (inf), Feigling m ADJ (inf) feig; **he's ~** er ist ein Feigling or ein feiges Huhn (inf); **he's too ~ to do it** er ist zu feig

▶ **chicken out** VI (inf) kneifen (inf)

chicken in cpds Hühner-; **chicken farmer** N Hühnerzüchter m; **chicken feed** N **a** (lit) Hühnerfutter nt **b** (inf, = insignificant sum) paar Cent; **they expect us to work for ~** sie erwarten, dass wir für 'n Appel und 'n Ei arbeiten (inf); **chicken flu** N Hühnergrippe f; **chicken-hearted**, **chicken-livered** ADJ feige, hasenherzig (old, liter); **chickenpox** N Windpocken pl; **chicken run** N Hühnerhof m, Auslauf m; **chickenshit** (US, sl) **N** **a** (= coward) Angsthase m (inf), Memme f (pej inf) **b** no pl to be ~ (= be worthless) Scheiße sein (sl), einen Dreck wert sein (inf) ADJ **a** (= cowardly) feige **b** (= worthless) beschissen (inf); **chicken wire** N Hühnerdraht m

chick: chick flick N (inf) Frauenfilm m, Schnulze f (inf pej); **chick lit** N (inf) Frauenroman m, Frauenbuch nt; **chickpea** N Kichererbse f; **chickweed** N Sternmiere f

chicle [ˈtʃɪkl] N Chiclegummi m

---

chicory [ˈtʃɪkərɪ] N Chicorée f or m, Schikoree f or m; (in coffee) Zichorie f

chide [tʃaɪd] pret **chid** (old) or **chided** [tʃɪd, ˈtʃaɪdɪd] ptp **chided** or **chidden** (old) [ˈtʃɪdn] VT schelten, rügen

chief [tʃiːf] **N** pl **-s a** (of organization) Leiter(in) m(f), Chef(in) m(f) (inf); (of clan) Oberhaupt nt; (of tribe) Häuptling m; (of gang) Anführer(in) m(f); (inf, = boss) Boss m (inf), Chef m; **~ of police** Polizeipräsident(in) or -chef(in) m(f); **~ of staff** (Mil) Stabschef(in) m(f); **~ of state** Staatschef(in) m(f) **b** (Her) Schildhaupt nt **c** in ~ hauptsächlich ADJ **a** (= most important) Haupt-, wichtigste(r, s), bedeutendste(r, s); **the ~ thing** das Wichtigste, die Hauptsache; **~ reason** Hauptgrund m **b** (= most senior) Haupt-, Ober-, erste(r); **~ clerk** Bürochef m; **~ executive officer** Generaldirektor m; **Chief Secretary (to the Treasury)** (Brit, Pol) stellvertretender Finanzminister, stellvertretende Finanzministerin; **~ of staff** (General)stabschef(in) m(f)

chief constable N (Brit) Polizeipräsident(in) m(f) or -chef(in) m(f)

chief justice N (Brit) ≈ Oberrichter(in) m(f); (US) Oberster Bundesrichter, Oberste Bundesrichterin

chiefly [ˈtʃiːflɪ] ADV hauptsächlich, in erster Linie, vor allem

chieftain [ˈtʃiːftən] N (of tribe) Häuptling m; (of clan) Oberhaupt nt, Älteste(r) m; (of robber band) Hauptmann m; **the village ~** der Dorfälteste

---

CHIEF WHIP

Im britischen Parlamentssystem sind die **Chief Whips** (Fraktionsführer) die Abgeordneten, die für die Einhaltung der Parteidisziplin im Unterhaus sorgen. Sowohl die Regierungspartei wie auch die Opposition haben einen **Chief Whip**, der die Abgeordneten seiner Partei über die Parlamentsgeschäfte auf dem Laufenden hält, der den Parteichef über die Ansichten der Hinterbänkler informiert und der vor allem darauf achtet, dass alle Abgeordneten bei wichtigen Abstimmungen auch anwesend sind und ihre Stimme abgeben. Diese letzte Aufgabe ist gerade dann besonders wichtig, wenn die Regierung nur über eine knappe Mehrheit im Unterhaus verfügt.

---

chiffon [ˈʃɪfɒn] **N** Chiffon m ADJ Chiffon-

chignon [ˈʃiːnjɒn] N Nackenknoten m, Chignon m

chihuahua [tʃɪˈwaʊwɑː] N Chihuahua m

chilblain [ˈtʃɪlbleɪn] N Frostbeule f

child [tʃaɪld] N pl **children** (lit, fig) Kind nt; **when I was a ~** in or zu meiner Kindheit; **she was with ~** (old, liter) sie trug ein Kind unter ihrem Herzen (old, liter); **the ~ of ignorance** das Produkt der Unwissenheit

child in cpds Kinder-; **child abuse** N Kindesmisshandlung f; (sexually) Notzucht f mit Kindern; **child abuser** N jd, der Kinder misshandelt (sexually) Kinderschänder(in) m(f); **child allowance** N (Brit inf) Kindergeld nt; **child-bearing** **N** Mutterschaft f, Kinderkriegen nt (inf); **ten years of ~ exhausted her** zehn Jahre mit kleinen Kindern erschöpften sie ADJ **of ~ age** im gebärfähigen Alter; **good ~ hips** gebärfreudiges Becken; **child bed** N (old) Kind- or Wochenbett nt; **to be in ~** im Wochenbett liegen; **child benefit** N (Brit) Kindergeld nt; **childbirth** N Geburt f, Gebären nt; **to die in ~** bei der Geburt sterben; **child bride** N kindliche or sehr junge Braut; **childcare** N Kinderfürsorge f; (= social work department) Jugendfürsorge f, Jugendhilfe f; **child-friendly** ADJ kinderfreundlich; **child guidance** N Erziehungsberatung f; (= social work agency) Erziehungsberatungsstelle f; **childhood**

N Kindheit f; **to be in one's second ~** seine zweite Kindheit erleben

childish ['tʃaɪldɪʃ] ADJ (pej) kindisch

childishly ['tʃaɪldɪʃlɪ] ADV (pej) kindisch; **~ simple** kinderleicht

childishness ['tʃaɪldɪʃnɪs] N (pej) kindisches Gehabe

child: child labour, (US) **child labor** N Kinderarbeit f; **childless** ADJ kinderlos; **childlike** ADJ kindlich; **child lock** N Kindersicherung f; **childminder** N (Brit) Tagesmutter f; **childminding** N (Brit) Beaufsichtigung f von Kindern; **child molester** N Person, die Kinder (sexuell) belästigt; **child prodigy** N Wunderkind nt; **childproof** ADJ kindersicher; **Child Protection Register** N (Brit) von örtlichen Sozialbehörden geführte Liste von Kindern, die dem Kinderschutzprogramm unterstellt sind; **child reduction** N Kinderermäßigung f

children ['tʃɪldrən] pl of **child**

child: child-resistant ADJ bruchsicher; **child seat** N Kindersitz m; **child sex** N Kindersex m attr Kindersex-; **~ tourism** Kindersextourismus m; **~ abuser** Kinderschänder(in) m(f); **child's play** N ein Kinderspiel nt; **child's seat** N = **child seat**; **Child Support Agency** N (Brit) staatliche Organisation, die sich um Unterhaltszahlungen für Kinder kümmert; **child welfare** N Jugendfürsorge f; **Child Welfare Centre** Kinderabteilung f im Gesundheitsamt

Chile ['tʃɪlɪ] N Chile nt

Chilean ['tʃɪlɪən] ADJ chilenisch N Chilene m, Chilenin f

chill [tʃɪl] N a Frische f; **there's quite a ~ in the air** es ist ziemlich frisch; **the sun took the ~ off the water** die Sonne hat das Wasser ein bisschen erwärmt; **you should take the ~ off the wine** Sie sollten den Wein nicht so eiskalt servieren

b (Med) fieberhafte Erkältung; (= shiver) Schauder m, Frösteln nt; **to catch a ~** sich verkühlen

c (fig) **a distinct ~ in East/West relations** eine deutliche Abkühlung der Ost-West-Beziehungen; **his presence cast a ~ over the meeting** durch seine Anwesenheit wurde das Treffen sehr kühl or frostig

ADJ (lit) kühl, frisch; (fig liter) reception kühl, frostig

VT a (lit) wine, meat kühlen; **I was ~ed to the bone** or **marrow** die Kälte ging mir bis auf die Knochen

b (fig) blood gefrieren lassen; enthusiasm etc abkühlen

► **chill out** VI (inf) relaxen (sl)

chill cabinet N (Brit) Kühlvitrine f

chiller ['tʃɪlə'] N (inf) Gruselgeschichte f; (= film) Gruselfilm m

chilli, (US) **chili** ['tʃɪlɪ] N Peperoni pl; (= spice, meal) Chili m

chill(i)ness ['tʃɪl(ɪ)nɪs] N (lit) Kühle f, Frische f; (fig) Kühle f, Frostigkeit f

chilling ['tʃɪlɪŋ] ADJ look frostig, eisig; prospect, thought äußerst unerquicklich, beunruhigend; reminder, message, warning, words schrecklich, Schrecken erregend; sight, story, account grauenhaft, Schauder erregend

chillingly ['tʃɪlɪŋlɪ] ADV (+adj) beunruhigend, beängstigend; reminiscent, similar schrecklich; (+vb) Schauder erregend; **the voice was ~ familiar** die Stimme klang auf beunruhigende Art vertraut; **they have ~ demonstrated how ...** sie haben auf erschreckende Weise gezeigt, wie ...

chill-out ['tʃɪlaʊt] ADJ (inf) music zum Relaxen (inf); **~ room** Ruheraum m (in dem sich die Besucher eines Rave Clubs erholen können), Chill-out m (sl)

chilly ['tʃɪlɪ] ADJ (+er) weather kühl, frisch; manner, look, smile etc kühl, frostig; **to feel ~** frösteln, frieren; **I feel ~** mich fröstelt, mir ist kühl

chime [tʃaɪm] N Glockenspiel nt, Geläut nt; (of doorbell) Läuten nt no pl VT schlagen VI läuten

► **chime in** VI (inf) sich einschalten

► **chime in with** VI +prep obj (plans) in Einklang stehen mit

chimera [kaɪ'mɪərə] N Chimäre f; (fig) Schimäre f

chimerical [kaɪ'merɪkəl] ADJ schimärisch

chimney ['tʃɪmnɪ] N Schornstein m; (on factory also) Schlot m; (= open fireplace) Kamin m; (of lamp) Zylinder m; (of stove) Rauchfang m; (Mountaineering) Kamin m

chimney: chimney breast N Kaminvorsprung m; **chimneypiece** N Kaminsims m; **chimneypot** N Schornsteinkopf m; **chimney stack** N Schornstein m; **chimney sweep** N Schornsteinfeger m

chimp [tʃɪmp] (inf), **chimpanzee** [ˌtʃɪmpæn'ziː] N Schimpanse m

chin [tʃɪn] N Kinn nt; **to have a weak/strong ~** wenig Kinn/ein ausgeprägtes Kinn haben; **to keep one's ~ up** die Ohren steif halten (inf), **keep your ~ up!** Kopf hoch!, nur Mut!; **he took it on the ~** (fig inf) er hats mit Fassung getragen; (Sport) **to ~ the bar** einen Klimmzug machen

China ['tʃaɪnə] N China nt

china ['tʃaɪnə] N Porzellan nt ADJ Porzellan-; **~ cabinet** Porzellanvitrine f

china: china blue N Kobaltblau nt; **china clay** N Kaolin m; **Chinaman** N Chinese m; (US, pej) Schlitzauge nt; **China Sea** N East/South ~ Ost-/Südchinesisches Meer; **Chinatown** N Chinesenviertel nt; **chinaware** N Porzellanware(n pl) f

chinchilla [tʃɪn'tʃɪlə] N Chinchilla f; (= fur) Chinchilla(pelz) m

Chinese [tʃaɪ'niːz] N a (= person) Chinese m, Chinesin f b (= language, fig, = gibberish) Chinesisch nt c (inf, = restaurant) Chinarestaurant nt; (= meal) chinesisches Essen ADJ chinesisch; **~ restaurant** Chinarestaurant nt

Chinese: Chinese cabbage N Chinakohl m; **Chinese lantern** N Lampion m; **Chinese leaves** N Chinakohl m; **Chinese puzzle** N ein Gegenstand zum Zusammensetzen als Geduldsspiel; **Chinese red** N Zinnoberrot nt; **Chinese studies** PL Sinologie f; **Chinese wall** N (fig) unüberwindliches Hindernis; **Chinese whispers** N stille Post; **to have a game of ~** stille Post spielen; **Chinese white** N Chinesischweiß nt

chink¹ [tʃɪŋk] N Riss m, Ritze f; (in door) Spalt m; **a ~ of light** ein dünner Lichtstreifen or -strahl; **the ~ in sb's armour** (fig) jds schwacher Punkt VT (US) stopfen

chink² N (= sound) Klirren nt; (of coins) Klimpern nt VT klirren mit; coins klimpern mit VI klirren; (coins) klimpern

Chink [tʃɪŋk] N (pej) Schlitzauge nt, Chinese m, Chinesin f

chinkie ['tʃɪŋkɪ] (inf) N (= restaurant) Chinarestaurant nt; (= meal) chinesisches Essen ADJ (esp pej) restaurant, meal chinesisch

chin: chinless ADJ **to be ~** (lit) ein fliehendes Kinn haben; (fig) willensschwach sein; **~ wonder** (hum) leicht vertrottelter Vertreter der Oberschicht; **chin rest** N Kinnstütze f; **chin strap** N Kinnriemen m

chintz [tʃɪnts] N Chintz m ATTR curtains Chintz-

chintzy ['tʃɪntsɪ] ADJ (+er) schmuck; (pej) kitschig

chin-up ['tʃɪnʌp] N Klimmzug m

chinwag ['tʃɪnwæg] N (Brit, inf) Schwatz m (inf)

chip [tʃɪp] N a Splitter m; (of glass also) Scherbe f; (of wood) Span m; **chocolate ~s** ≈ Schokoladenstreusel pl; **he's a ~ off the old block** er ist ganz der Vater; **to have a ~ on one's shoulder** einen Komplex haben (about wegen); **sb with a ~ on his shoulder** jd, der sich ständig angegriffen fühlt

b (Brit: = potato stick) Pomme frite m or nt usu pl; (US, = potato slice) Chip m usu pl

c (in crockery, furniture etc) abgeschlagene or abgestoßene Ecke or Stelle; **this cup has a ~** diese Tasse ist angeschlagen

d (in poker etc) Chip m, Spielmarke f; **to cash in one's ~s** (euph) den Löffel abgeben (euph inf); **he's had his ~s** (inf) er hat ausgespielt (inf); **to be in the ~s** (US, inf) Kleingeld haben (inf), flüssig sein (inf); **when the ~s are down** wenn es drauf ankommt

e **to give the ball a ~** (Golf, Tennis) den Ball chippen

f (Comput, = microchip) Chip nt

VT a cup, stone anschlagen; varnish, paint abstoßen; wood beschädigen; (= chip off) wegschlagen, abstoßen

b (Sport) ball chippen

VI (cup etc) angeschlagen werden, Macken/eine Macke bekommen (inf); (paint) abspringen; (stone) splittern; **this pottery ~s easily** diese Keramik ist schnell angeschlagen

► **chip away** VT sep weghauen; **the woodpecker chipped away the bark** der Specht hackte die Rinde ab VI **the sculptor chipped away until ...** der Bildhauer meißelte am Stein herum, bis ...

► **chip away at** VI +PREP OBJ authority, system unterminieren; debts reduzieren, verringern; **to chip away at sb's image** jds Image ankratzen, jdn demontieren

► **chip in** VI (inf) a (= interrupt) sich einschalten b (= contribute) **he chipped in with £3** er steuerte £ 3 bei; **would you like to chip in?** würdest du gerne etwas beisteuern?

► **chip off** VT sep paint etc wegschlagen; piece of china abstoßen, abschlagen VI (paint etc) absplittern

chip basket N Frittiersieb nt

chipboard ['tʃɪpbɔːd] N Spanholz nt; piece of ~ Spanplatte f

chipmunk ['tʃɪpmʌŋk] N Backenhörnchen nt

chipolata [tʃɪpə'lɑːtə] N (Brit) Cocktailwürstchen nt

chip pan N Fritteuse f

chipped [tʃɪpt] ADJ a cup, bone, tooth, enamel, step angeschlagen, abgestoßen, beschädigt; paint, nail varnish abgesplittert; **to be badly ~** stark angeschlagen sein b (Brit, Cook) **~ potatoes** Pommes frites pl

Chippendale ['tʃɪpəndeɪl] ADJ Chippendale-; **~ chair** Chippendalestuhl m

chippie ['tʃɪpɪ] N = **chippy** b

chippings ['tʃɪpɪŋz] PL Splitter pl; (of wood) Späne pl; (= road chippings) Schotter m

chippy ['tʃɪpɪ] N (inf) a (= joiner) Schreiner m b (= chip shop) Frittenbude f (inf), Pommesbude f (inf)

chip shot N (Golf) Chip(shot) m; (Tennis) Chip m

chiromancer ['kaɪərəmænsə'] N Chiromant(in) m(f)

chiromancy ['kaɪərəmænsɪ] N Chiromantie f

chiropodist [kɪ'rɒpədɪst] N Fußpfleger(in) m(f)

chiropody [kɪ'rɒpədɪ] N Fußpflege f

chiropractic [ˌkaɪərə'præktɪk] N Chiropraktik f

chiropractor ['kaɪərəʊˌpræktə'] N Chiropraktiker(in) m(f)

chirp [tʃɜːp] VI (birds) zwitschern; (crickets) zirpen N (of birds) Piepser m; (= chirping) Piepsen nt no pl, Zwitschern nt no pl; (of crickets) Zirpen nt no pl; **I don't want to hear another ~ out of you** ich möchte keinen Muckser mehr von dir hören (inf)

chirpy ['tʃɜːpɪ] ADJ (+er) (inf) munter

chirrup ['tʃɪrəp] N = **chirp**

chisel ['tʃɪzl] N Meißel m; (for wood) Beitel m VT meißeln; (in wood) stemmen; **her finely ~led features** ihr fein geschnittenes Gesicht

chit¹ [tʃɪt] N junges Ding; **she's a mere ~ of a girl** sie ist ja noch ein halbes Kind

chit² N (also **chit of paper**) Zettel m

chitchat ['tʃɪttʃæt] N (inf) Geschwätz nt, Gerede nt

chivalric ['ʃɪvəlrɪk] ADJ ritterlich

chivalrous ADJ , **chivalrously** ADV ['ʃɪvəlrəs, -lɪ] ritterlich

chivalry ['ʃɪvəlrɪ] N Ritterlichkeit f; (medieval concept) Rittertum nt; ~ **is not dead** es gibt noch Kavaliere

chives [tʃaɪvz] N Schnittlauch m

chivvy ['tʃɪvɪ] VT (Brit, inf: also **chivvy along** or **up**) antreiben; **to ~ sb into doing sth** jdn dazu antreiben, etw zu tun

chlorate ['klɔːreɪt] N Chlorat nt

chloric ['klɔːrɪk] ADJ chlorig, chlorhaltig

chloric acid N Chlorsäure f

chloride ['klɔːraɪd] N Chlorid nt; ~ **of lime** Chlorkalk m

chlorinate ['klɒrɪneɪt] VT water chloren

chlorination [klɒrɪ'neɪʃən] N (of water) Chloren nt

chlorine ['klɔːriːn] N Chlor nt

chlorofluorocarbon [ˌklɒrəʊfluərə'kɑːbən] N Chlorfluorkohlenwasserstoff m

chloroform ['klɒrəfɔːm] **N** Chloroform nt **VT** mit Chloroform betäuben, eine Chloroformnarkose geben (+dat)

chlorophyll ['klɒrəfɪl] N Chlorophyll nt

choc ['tʃɒk] N (Brit inf) Praline f; **box of ~s** Schachtel f Pralinen

choc-ice ['tʃɒkaɪs] N Eismohrle nt (Eiscreme mit Schokoladenüberzug)

chock [tʃɒk] **N** Bremskeil m, Bremsklotz m; (Naut) (under boat) Bock m; (for cables) Lippe f, Lippklampe f; **~s away** Bremsklötze weg **VT** wheel blockieren; boat aufbocken

chock-a-block ['tʃɒkəblɒk] ADJ (esp Brit inf), **chock-full** ['tʃɒkfʊl] ADJ (inf) knüppelvoll (inf), gerammelt voll (inf)

chocoholic [ˌtʃɒkə'hɒlɪk] N (inf) Schokoladensüchtige(r) mf; **to be a ~** nach Schokolade süchtig sein

chocolate ['tʃɒklɪt] **N** **a** Schokolade f; (hot or drinking) ~ Schokolade f, Kakao m; **a ~** eine Praline **b** (= colour) Schokoladenbraun nt **ADJ** Schokoladen-; (= chocolate-coloured) schokoladenbraun; ~ **pudding** Schokoladenkuchen m; (= whip) Schokoladenpudding m; ~ **sauce** Schokoladensoße f

chocolate: chocolate bar N (= slab) Tafel f Schokolade; (= Mars® bar etc) Schokoladenriegel m; **chocolate biscuit** N Schokoladenkeks m; **chocolate box** N Pralinenschachtel f; **chocolate-box** ADJ look, picture Postkarten-; **chocolate cake** N Schokoladenkuchen m; **chocolate-coloured** ADJ schokoladenbraun; **chocolate-flavoured** ADJ mit Schokoladengeschmack; **chocolate fudge cake** N Schokoladencremetorte f

choice [tʃɔɪs] ✪ 1.1, 10.1, 18.3 **N** **a** (= act of, possibility of choosing) Wahl f; **it's your ~** du hast die Wahl; **to make a ~** eine Wahl treffen; **to take one's ~** sich (dat) etwas aussuchen; **I didn't do it from ~** ich habe es mir nicht ausgesucht; **he had no** or **little ~ but to obey** er hatte keine (andere) Wahl or es blieb ihm nichts anderes übrig, als zu gehorchen; **if I had the ~ I would ...** wenn ich die Wahl hätte, würde ich ...; **the prize is a holiday of your** (own) ~ zu gewinnen ist eine Urlaubsreise an einen Ort Ihrer Wahl

b (= person, thing chosen) Wahl f; **it was your ~** du wolltest es ja so

c (= variety to choose from) Auswahl f (of an +dat, von)

ADJ **a** (Comm) goods, fruit, wine Qualitäts-, erstklassig

b language (= elegant) gewählt; (euph, = vulgar) der/die/das sich gewaschen hat (inf)

choicest ['tʃɔɪsəst] ADJ allerfeinste(r, s), auserlesen

choir ['kwaɪə'] N **a** Chor m; **you are singing to the ~** (US: inf) du rennst offene Türen ein **b** (Archit) Chor(raum) m

choir in cpds Chor-; **choirboy** N Chor- or Sängerknabe m; **choir loft** N Chorempore f; **choir master** N Chorleiter m; **choir practice** N Chorprobe f; **choir school** N Konvikt nt für Sängerknaben; **choir stall** N Chorstuhl m; **choir stalls** PL Chorgestühl nt

choke [tʃəʊk] **VT** **a** person ersticken; (= throttle) (er)würgen, erdrosseln; **don't eat so fast, you'll ~ yourself** iss nicht so schnell, sonst erstickst du daran; **to ~ the life out of sb/sth** (lit, fig) jdm/einer Sache den Garaus machen; **in a voice ~d with tears/emotion** mit tränenersticker/tief bewegter Stimme **b** (fig) pipe, tube, street verstopfen; fire, plants ersticken **VI** ersticken (on an +dat); **he was choking with laughter/anger** er erstickte fast or halb vor Lachen/Wut **N** (Aut) Choke m, Starterzug m; **give it a bit of ~** zieh den Choke etwas heraus

▶ **choke back** VT sep feelings, tears, reply unterdrücken

▶ **choke down** VT sep hinunterschlucken

▶ **choke off** VT sep **a** supplies drosseln; **raising taxes could choke off the recovery** eine Steuererhöhung könnte den Erholungsprozess beeinträchtigen **b** (inf) person (= interrupt) das Wort abschneiden +dat; (= put off) abwimmeln (inf) **c** (inf, = make fed up) **I'm choked off** mir stinkts! (inf)

▶ **choke up** VT sep **a** (= block) pipe, drain etc verstopfen **b** (usu pass) voice ersticken; **you sound a bit choked up** du klingst etwas verschnupft **c** (inf) **to get/be choked up** (inf) ganz fuchsig (inf) werden/sein (about wegen)

choke chain N Stachelhalsband nt

choked [tʃəʊkt] ADJ (inf) pikiert

chokedamp ['tʃəʊkdæmp] N (Brit) Ferch m, böse or giftige Wetter pl

choker ['tʃəʊkə'] N (= collar) Vatermörder m; (= necklace) enger Halsreif; (of velvet etc) Kropfband nt

choking ['tʃəʊkɪŋ] ADJ **a** smoke, fumes beißend; ~ **dust** Staub m, der einem die Luft zum Atmen nimmt **b** sob, moan, gasp erstickt

choler ['kɒlə'] N (old, = bile) (gelbe) Galle; (= bad temper) Zorn m

cholera ['kɒlərə] N Cholera f

choleric ['kɒlərɪk] ADJ cholerisch, leicht aufbrausend

cholesterol [kə'lestərɒl] N Cholesterin nt

chomp [tʃɒmp] VT laut mahlen; (person) mampfen (inf)

choo-choo ['tʃuːtʃuː] N (baby-talk, = train) Puffpuff f (baby-talk)

choose [tʃuːz] pret **chose**, ptp **chosen** **VT** **a** (= select) (aus)wählen, sich (dat) aussuchen; **to ~ a team** eine Mannschaft auswählen or zusammenstellen; **they chose him as their leader** or **to be their leader** sie wählten ihn zu ihrem Anführer; **in a few well-chosen words** in wenigen wohlgesetzten Worten

b (= decide, elect) **to ~ to do sth** es vorziehen, etw zu tun; **may I come earlier? – if you ~ to** darf ich früher kommen? – wenn Sie wollen

VI **a** **to ~ (between** or **among/from)** wählen or eine Wahl treffen (zwischen +dat/aus or unter +dat); **there is nothing** or **little to ~ between them** sie sind gleich gut; **there aren't many to ~ from** die Auswahl ist nicht sehr groß

b (= decide, elect) **as/if you** wie/wenn Sie wollen

choos(e)y ['tʃuːzɪ] ADJ (+er) wählerisch

chop¹ [tʃɒp] **N** **a** (= blow) Schlag m

b (Cook) Kotelett nt

c (Sport) harter (Kurz)schlag; (Karate) Karateschlag m

d (= waves) Klatschen nt, Schlagen nt

e (inf) **to get the ~** (= be axed) dem Rotstift zum Opfer fallen; (= be fired) rausgeschmissen werden (inf); **to give sb the ~** jdn rausschmeißen (inf); **to be for the ~** (= going to be axed)

gestrichen werden; (= going to be fired) auf der Abschussliste stehen (inf)

VT **a** (= cut) hacken; meat, vegetables etc klein schneiden; **to ~ one's way through the undergrowth** sich (dat) einen Weg durchs Dickicht schlagen

b (Sport) ball (ab)stoppen; (Wrestling etc) opponent einen Schlag versetzen (+dat)

▶ **chop at** VT +prep obj hacken or schlagen nach; (with axe) einhacken auf (+acc)

▶ **chop back** VT sep zurück- or wegschneiden

▶ **chop down** VT sep tree fällen

▶ **chop off** VT sep abhacken, abschlagen, abhauen

▶ **chop up** VT sep zerhacken, zerkleinern; (fig) country aufteilen; company aufspalten

chop² VI **a** (Naut, wind) drehen, umspringen **b** (fig) **to ~ and change (one's mind)** ständig seine Meinung ändern; **if they keep ~ping and changing the team ...** wenn sie ständig die Spieler wechseln ...

chop chop ADV, INTERJ (inf) hopp, hopp (inf)

chophouse ['tʃɒphaʊs] N Steakhaus nt

chopper ['tʃɒpə'] N **a** (= axe) Hackbeil nt **b** (inf, = helicopter) Hubschrauber m **c** (= bicycle) BMX-Rad nt; (inf, = motorcycle) Maschine f (inf)

choppers ['tʃɒpəz] PL (inf, = teeth) Beißerchen pl (inf)

chopping ['tʃɒpɪŋ]: **chopping block** N Hackklotz m; (for wood, executions etc) Block m; **chopping board** N (Brit) Hackbrett m; **chopping knife** N (Brit) Hackmesser nt; (with rounded blade) Wiegemesser nt

choppy ['tʃɒpɪ] ADJ (+er) sea kabbelig; wind böig, wechselhaft

chops [tʃɒps] PL (of dog) Lefzen pl; (inf, of person) Visage f (inf)

chop: chopstick N Stäbchen nt; **chop suey** ['tʃɒp'suːɪ] N Chopsuey nt

choral ['kɔːrəl] ADJ Chor-; ~ **society** Gesangverein m, Chor m

chorale [kɒ'rɑːl] N Choral m

chord [kɔːd] N **a** (Mus) Akkord m; **to strike the right ~** (fig) den richtigen Ton treffen; **to strike a sympathetic ~** (fig) auf Verständnis stoßen **b** (Geometry) Sehne f **c** (Anat) Band nt

chordal ['kɔːdl] ADJ (Mus) Akkord-

chore [tʃɔː'] N lästige Pflicht; **~s** pl Hausarbeit f; **to do the ~s** den Haushalt machen, die Hausarbeit erledigen

choreograph ['kɒrɪəʊɡrɑːf] VT choreografieren

choreographer [ˌkɒrɪ'ɒɡrəfə'] N Choreograf(in) m(f)

choreographic [ˌkɒrɪəʊ'ɡræfɪk] ADJ choreografisch

choreography [ˌkɒrɪ'ɒɡrəfɪ] N Choreografie f

chorister ['kɒrɪstə'] N (Kirchen)chormitglied nt; (= boy) Chorknabe m

chortle ['tʃɔːtl] **VI** gluckern, glucksen; **he was chortling over the article** er lachte in sich hinein or vor sich hin, als er den Artikel las **N** Gluckser m

chorus ['kɔːrəs] **N** **a** (= refrain) Refrain m **b** Chor m; (of opera) Opernchor m; (= dancers) Tanzgruppe f; **she's one** – sie singt im Chor/ sie ist bei der Tanzgruppe; **in ~** im Chor; **he was greeted with a ~ of good morning, sir** als er hereinkam, riefen alle im Chor: Guten Morgen! **VT** im Chor singen/sprechen/rufen

chorus: chorus girl N Revuetänzerin f or -girl nt; **chorus line** N Revue f

chose [tʃəʊz] pret of **choose**

chosen ['tʃəʊzn] ptp of **choose** ADJ **the ~ people** das auserwählte Volk; **the ~ few** die wenigen Auserwählten

choux pastry ['ʃuː'peɪstrɪ] N Brandteig m

chow [tʃaʊ] N (inf, = food) was zu mampfen (inf)

chow(chow) ['tʃaʊ(tʃaʊ)] N (= dog) Chow-Chow m

chowder ['tʃaʊdə'] N sämige Fischsuppe

chow mein [tʃaʊ'meɪn] N *gebratene Nudeln mit Pilzen, Fleisch, Shrimps etc*

Christ [kraɪst] **N** Christus *m* **INTERJ** *(sl)* Herrgott *(inf)*

christen ['krɪsn] VT **a** *(= baptize)* taufen; **to ~ sb after sb** jdn nach jdm (be)nennen **b** *(inf, = use for first time)* einweihen

Christendom ['krɪsndəm] N *(old)* die Christenheit

christening ['krɪsnɪŋ] N Taufe *f*; **~ robe** Taufkleid *nt*

Christian ['krɪstɪən] **N** Christ *m* **ADJ** *(lit, fig)* christlich

Christianity [ˌkrɪstɪ'ænɪtɪ] N **a** *(= faith, religion)* Christentum *nt*, christlicher Glaube; *(= body of Christians)* Christenheit *f* **b** *(= being a Christian)* Christlichkeit *f*, Frömmigkeit *f*; **his ~ did not prevent him from doing it** sein christlicher Glaube hinderte ihn nicht daran(, das zu tun) **c** *(= Christian character)* christliche Haltung *or* Gesinnung

Christianize ['krɪstɪənaɪz] VT christianisieren

Christian: Christian name N Vor- *or* Rufname *m*; **to be on ~ terms** sich mit Vornamen anreden; **Christian Science** N Christian Science *f*; **Christian Scientist** N Anhänger(in) *m(f)* der Christian Science

Christlike ['kraɪstlaɪk] ADJ christusgleich

Christmas ['krɪsməs] ✪ 23.2 N Weihnachten *nt*; **are you going home for ~?** fährst du (über) Weihnachten nach Hause?; **what did you get for ~?** was hast du zu Weihnachten bekommen?; **merry** *or* **happy ~!** frohe *or* fröhliche Weihnachten!; **it's as if ~ had come early!** das ist wie Ostern und Weihnachten zusammen

Christmas: Christmas bonus N Weihnachtsgratifikation *f (geh)*, Weihnachtsgeld *nt*; **Christmas box** N *(Brit)* Trinkgeld *nt* zu Weihnachten, ≈ Neujahrsgeld *nt*; **Christmas cake** N *Früchtekuchen mit Zuckerguss zu Weihnachten*; **Christmas card** N Weihnachtskarte *f*; **Christmas carol** N Weihnachtslied *nt*; **Christmas Day** N der erste Weihnachtstag; **on ~** an Weihnachten, am ersten (Weihnachts)feiertag; **Christmas Eve** N Heiligabend *m*; **on ~** Heiligabend; **Christmas Island** N Weihnachtsinsel *f*; **Christmas present** N Weihnachtsgeschenk *nt*; **Christmas pudding** N Plumpudding *m*; **Christmas rose** N Christrose *f*; **Christmas stocking** N *Strumpf, in den Weihnachtsgeschenke gelegt werden*

Christmassy ['krɪsməsɪ] ADJ *(inf)* weihnachtlich

Christmas: Christmas time N Weihnachtszeit *f*; **at ~** zur *or* in der Weihnachtszeit; **Christmas tree** N Weihnachtsbaum *m*, Christbaum *m (esp S Ger)*

chromatic [krə'mætɪk] ADJ *(Art, Mus)* chromatisch

chrome [krəʊm] N Chrom *nt*

chrome steel N Chromstahl *m*

chromium ['krəʊmɪəm] N Chrom *nt*

chromium: chromium plate N Chromschicht *f*; **chromium-plated** ADJ verchromt; **chromium plating** N Verchromung *f*

chromosome ['krəʊməsəʊm] N Chromosom *nt*

chronic ['krɒnɪk] ADJ **a** *disease, invalid, liar, underfunding, overcrowding etc* chronisch; **Chronic Fatigue Syndrome** chronisches Erschöpfungssyndrom **b** *(inf, = terrible)* schlecht, miserabel *(inf)*

chronically ['krɒnɪklɪ] ADV *ill, depressed, underfunded, overcrowded* chronisch

chronicle ['krɒnɪkl] **N** Chronik *f*; **Chronicles** *pl (Bibl)* Bücher *pl* der Chronik **VT** aufzeichnen; *historic events also* eine Chronik (+gen) verfassen

chronicler ['krɒnɪklə'] N Chronist *m*

chronograph ['krɒnəgrɑːf] N Chronograph *m*; *(= stopwatch)* Zeitmesser *m*

chronological [ˌkrɒnə'lɒdʒɪkəl] ADJ chronologisch; **in ~ order** in chronologischer Reihenfolge

chronologically [ˌkrɒnə'lɒdʒɪkəlɪ] ADV chronologisch; **~ arranged** in chronologischer Reihenfolge

chronology [krə'nɒlədʒɪ] N zeitliche Abfolge, Chronologie *f (form)*; *(= list of dates)* Zeittafel *f*

chronometer [krə'nɒmɪtə'] N Chronometer *m*

chrysalis ['krɪsəlɪs] N *pl* **-es** *(Biol)* Puppe *f*; *(= covering)* Kokon *m*

chrysanthemum [krɪ'sænθəməm], **chrysanth** [krɪ'sænθ] *(inf)* N Chrysantheme *f*

chub [tʃʌb] N *pl* – Döbel *m*, Aitel *m*

Chubb lock® ['tʃʌblɒk] N *(Brit)* Sicherheitsschloss *nt*

chubby ['tʃʌbɪ] ADJ *(+er)* pummelig, rundlich; **~ cheeks** Pausbacken *pl*

chubby-cheeked ['tʃʌbɪ'tʃiːkd] ADJ pausbäckig

chuck¹ [tʃʌk] **VT** *(inf)* **a** *(= throw)* schmeißen *(inf)* **b** *(inf)* girlfriend etc Schluss machen mit; *job* hinschmeißen *(inf)*; **~ it!** *(= stop it)* Schluss jetzt! **c to ~ sb under the chin** jdm einen Kinnstüber versetzen **N** *(inf, = dismissal)* Rausschmiss *m (inf)*; **to give sb the ~** jdn rausschmeißen *(inf)*, jdn an die Luft setzen *(inf)*; **he got the ~** er ist rausgeflogen *(inf)*, den haben sie an die Luft gesetzt *(inf)*

▶ **chuck about** *(Brit)* *or* **around** VT *sep (inf)* rumschmeißen (mit) *(inf)*

▶ **chuck away** VT *sep (inf, = throw out)* wegschmeißen *(inf)*; *(= waste) money* aus dem Fenster schmeißen *(inf)*

▶ **chuck in** VT *sep (Brit inf) job* hinschmeißen *(inf)*, an den Nagel hängen *(inf)*; **to chuck it (all) in** den Laden hinschmeißen *(inf)*

▶ **chuck out** VT *sep (inf)* rausschmeißen *(inf)*; *useless articles also* wegschmeißen *(inf)*; **to be chucked out** rausfliegen *(of aus) (inf)*

▶ **chuck up** VT *sep (Brit inf) job* hinschmeißen *(inf)*

chuck² N *(Tech)* Spannfutter *nt*

chuck³ N *(dated US, inf, = food)* Essen *nt*

chucker-out ['tʃʌkər'aʊt] N *(inf)* Rausschmeißer *m (inf)*

chuckle ['tʃʌkl] **N** leises Lachen, Kichern *nt no pl*; **to have a good ~ about sth** sich *(dat)* eins lachen über etw *(acc) (inf)* **VI** leise in sich *(acc)* hineinlachen, sich *(dat)* eins lachen *(inf)*; **to ~ away** vor sich hin lachen *or* kichern

chuck wagon N *(dated US inf)* Proviantwagen *m* mit fahrbarer Küche

chuffed [tʃʌft] ADJ *(Brit inf)* vergnügt und zufrieden; *(= flattered)* gebauchpinselt *(inf) (about wegen)*; **I was dead ~** ich freute mich darüber wie ein Schneekönig *(inf)*; **to be ~ with oneself** auf sich *(acc)* selbst stolz sein; **to look ~ with oneself** sehr zufrieden aussehen

chug [tʃʌg] **N** Tuckern *nt* **VI** tuckern

▶ **chug along** VI entlangtuckern; *(fig inf)* gut vorankommen

chukka, chukker ['tʃʌkə'] N *(Polo)* Chukka *nt*, Chukker *nt*

chum [tʃʌm] N *(inf)* Kamerad *m*, Kumpel *m (inf)*, Spezi *m (S Ger)*

▶ **chum up** VI sich anfreunden

chummy ['tʃʌmɪ] ADJ *(+er) (inf)* kameradschaftlich; **to be ~ with sb** mit jdm sehr dicke sein *(inf)*; **to get ~ with sb** sich mit jdm anfreunden

chump [tʃʌmp] N **a** *(inf)* Trottel *m*, dummes Stück *m*, Hornochse *m (inf)* **b** **he's off his ~** *(Brit, inf)* der hat 'ne Meise *(inf)*

chump chop N Kotelett *nt*

chunder ['tʃʌndə'] VI *(inf)* kotzen *(sl)*

chunk [tʃʌŋk] N großes Stück; *(of meat)* Batzen *m*; *(of stone)* Brocken *m*

chunky ['tʃʌŋkɪ] ADJ *(+er) (inf) legs, arms* stämmig; *person also* untersetzt, gedrungen; *knitwear* dick, klobig; *book* kompakt; *glass* massiv; *jewellery* klotzig

Chunnel ['tʃʌnəl] N *(inf)* Kanaltunnel *m*

church [tʃɜːtʃ] N Kirche *f*; *(= service)* die Kirche; **to go to ~** in die Kirche gehen; **the Church Fathers** die Kirchenväter; **the Church of England** die anglikanische Kirche; **he has gone into** *or* **entered the Church** er ist Geistlicher geworden; **Church calendar** Kirchenkalender *m*, Kalendarium *nt*

church in *cpds* Kirchen-; **churchgoer** ['tʃɜːtʃgəʊə'] N Kirchgänger(in) *m(f)*; **churchgoing** ['tʃɜːtʃgəʊɪŋ] ADJ **a – family** eine Familie, die regelmäßig in die Kirche geht; **church hall** N Gemeindehalle *f*; **churchman** N *(= clergyman)* Geistliche(r), Seelsorger *m*; *(= churchgoer)* Kirchgänger *m*; **church mode** N *(Mus)* Kirchentonart *f*; **church mouse** N **as poor as a ~** arm wie eine Kirchenmaus; **church school** N Konfessionsschule *f*; **church service** N Gottesdienst *m*; **churchwarden** N Gemeindevorsteher *m*

churchy ['tʃɜːtʃɪ] ADJ *(+er) (inf) person* kirchlich

churchyard ['tʃɜːtʃjɑːd] N Friedhof *m*, Kirchhof *m (old, dial)*

churl ['tʃɜːl] N ungehobelter Kerl, Rüpel *m*

churlish ADJ , **churlishly** ADV ['tʃɜːlɪʃ, -lɪ] ungehobelt

churlishness ['tʃɜːlɪʃnɪs] N ungehobeltes Benehmen

churn [tʃɜːn] **N** *(for butter)* Butterfass *nt*; *(Brit, = milk churn)* Milchkanne *f* **VT a to ~ butter** buttern, Sahne buttern **b** *(= agitate) sea, mud etc* aufwühlen **VI** *(water, mud)* wirbeln, strudeln; *(wheels, rage etc)* wühlen; *(propeller)* wirbeln, sich wild drehen; **his stomach was ~ing** sein Magen revoltierte; **the ~ing sea** die stampfende See

▶ **churn away** VI sich wild drehen; *(engine)* stampfen

▶ **churn out** VT *sep* am laufenden Band produzieren

▶ **churn up** VT *sep* aufwühlen

chute [ʃuːt] N **a** Rutsche *f*; *(= garbage chute)* Müllschlucker *m* **b** *(= rapid in river)* Stromschnelle *f* **c** *(inf, = parachute)* Fallschirm *m* **d** *(in playground)* Rutschbahn *f*, Rutsche *f*

chutney ['tʃʌtnɪ] N Chutney *m*

chutzpah ['hʊtspə] N Chuzpe *f*

CI *abbr* of **Channel Islands**

CIA *abbr* of **Central Intelligence Agency** CIA *m*

ciabatta [tʃə'bætə] N Ciabatta *nt*

ciborium [sɪ'bɔːrɪəm] N Ziborium *nt*

cicada [sɪ'kɑːdə] N Zikade *f*

cicatrix ['sɪkətrɪks] N *pl* **cicatrices** [sɪkə'traɪsiːz] wildes Fleisch, Granulationsgewebe *nt (spec)*; *(= scar)* Narbe *f*

cicerone [ˌtʃɪtʃə'rəʊnɪ] N Cicerone *m*

CID *(Brit) abbr* of **Criminal Investigation Department** ≈ Kripo *f*

cider ['saɪdə'] N Apfelwein *m*, Cidre *m*; **hard ~** *(US)* Apfelwein *m (voll vergoren)*; **sweet ~** süßer Apfelwein *(teilweise vergoren)*, Rauscher *m (dial)*; **rough ~** Apfelwein *m (mit größerem Alkoholgehalt)*

cider: cider apple N Mostapfel *m*; **cider press** N Apfelpresse *f*

cif *abbr* of **cost, insurance and freight** cif

cig [sɪg] N *(inf) (= cigarette)* Zigarette *f*; *(= cigar)* Zigarre *f*

cigar [sɪ'gɑː'] N Zigarre *f*

cigar: cigar box N Zigarrenkiste *f*; **cigar cutter** N Zigarrenabschneider *m*

cigarette [ˌsɪgə'ret] N Zigarette *f*

cigarette: cigarette box N Zigarettenschachtel *f*; **cigarette case** N Zigarettenetui *nt*; **cigarette end** N Zigarettenstummel *m*; **cigarette holder** N Zigarettenspitze *f*; **cigarette lighter** N Feuerzeug *nt*; **cigarette machine** N Zigarettenautomat *m*; **cigarette paper** N Zigarettenpapier *nt*

cigarillo [sɪgə'rɪləʊ] N Zigarillo *m or nt*

cigar: cigar lighter N (in car) Zigarettenanzünder m; **cigar-shaped** ADJ zigarrenförmig

ciggy ['sɪgɪ] N (inf) Glimmstängel m (inf), Kippe f (inf)

C-in-C abbr of **Commander in Chief**

cinch [sɪntʃ] **N** **a** (US, = saddle girth) Sattelgurt m **b** (inf) **it's a ~** (= easy) das ist ein Kinderspiel or ein Klacks (inf); (esp US, = certain) es ist todsicher (inf) **VT** (US) **a** **to ~ a horse** den Sattelgurt anziehen **b** (inf) deal regeln (sl)

cinder ['sɪndə'] N **~s** pl Asche f; (lumpy) Schlacke f; (still burning) glühendes Kohlestück; **burnt to a ~** (Brit fig) verkohlt

Cinderella [,sɪndə'relə] N (lit, fig) Aschenputtel nt

cinder track N Aschenbahn f

cineaste ['sɪnɪæst] N Cineast(in) m(f), Kinoliebhaber(in) m(f)

cine ['sɪnɪ]: **cine camera** N (Brit) (Schmal)filmkamera f; **cine film** N (Brit) Schmalfilm m

cinema ['sɪnəmə] N (esp Brit) Kino nt; (= films collectively also) Film m; **at/to the ~** im/ins Kino

cinema (esp Brit): **cinema complex** N Kinocenter nt; **cinemagoer** N Kinogänger(in) m(f); **cinema-going** **N** **the popularity of ~** die Beliebtheit des Kinos **ADJ** **the ~ public** das Kinopublikum, die Kinogänger pl; **cinema-loving** ADJ kinofreudig

Cinemascope® ['sɪnəməskəʊp] N Cinemascope nt

cinematic [sɪnə'mætɪk] ADJ filmisch; **~ art** Filmkunst f

cinematograph [,sɪnə'mætəgrɑ:f] N (dated) Kinematograf m (dated)

cinephile ['sɪnɪfaɪl] N Kinoliebhaber(in) m(f)

Cineplex® ['sɪnɪpleks] N Mulitplex-Kino nt

cine projector N (Brit) Filmprojektor m

Cinerama® [,sɪnə'rɑ:mə] N Cinerama® nt

cinerary ['sɪnərərɪ] ADJ Aschen-

cinerary urn ['sɪnərərɪ-] N Urne f

cinnabar ['sɪnəbɑ:'] N Zinnober m

cinnamon ['sɪnəmən] **N** Zimt m **ADJ** attr **a** cake, biscuit Zimt- **b** (colour) zimtfarben

CIO (US) abbr of **Congress of Industrial Organizations** amerikanischer Gewerkschaftsdachverband

cipher ['saɪfə'] **N** **a** (= Arabic numeral) Ziffer f, Zahl f **b** (= zero) Null f **c** (= nonentity) Niemand m no pl **d** (= code) Chiffre f, Kode m, Code m; **in ~** chiffriert **e** (= monogram) Monogramm nt, Namenszeichen nt **VT** (= encode) verschlüsseln, chiffrieren

cipher clerk N (De)chiffreur(in) m(f)

cipher officer N (army) Fernmeldeoffizier(in) m(f); (secret service etc) (De)chiffreur(in) m(f)

circ abbr of **circa** ca.

circa ['sɜ:kə] PREP zirka, circa

circle ['sɜ:kl] **N** **a** Kreis m; **to stand in a ~** im Kreis stehen; **to go round in ever decreasing ~s** (lit) Spiralen drehen; (fig) sich unablässig im Kreis drehen; **to have come** or **turned full ~** (lit) sich ganz herumgedreht haben, eine Volldrehung gemacht haben; (fig) wieder da sein, wo man angefangen hat; **we're just going round in ~s** (fig) wir bewegen uns nur im Kreise; **to come full ~** (fig) zum Ausgangspunkt zurückkehren; **things have come full ~** der Kreis hat sich geschlossen; **when the seasons have come full ~** wenn sich der Kreis der Jahreszeiten schließt

b (of hills etc) Ring m, Kette f; (round the eyes) Ring m (round unter +dat); (in gymnastics) Welle f; **a Celtic stone ~** ein keltischer Steinkreis

c (Brit, Theat) Rang m → **dress circle, upper circle**

d (= group of persons) Kreis m, Zirkel m (geh); **a close ~ of friends** ein enger Freundeskreis; **in political ~s** in politischen Kreisen; **the family ~** der engste Familienkreis; **the whole family ~** die ganze Familie; **he's moving in different ~s now** er verkehrt jetzt in anderen Kreisen

VT **a** (= surround) umgeben

b (= move around) kreisen um; **the enemy ~d the town** der Feind kreiste die Stadt ein

c (= draw a circle round) einen Kreis or Kringel machen um; **he ~d several of the addresses** er machte einen Kreis um mehrere der Anschriften; **~d in red** rot umkringelt

VI (= fly in a circle) kreisen

▶ **circle around** VI (people) umhergehen or -wandern; (birds) Kreise ziehen; (vehicle) kreisen, Runden drehen; (ship, plane) kreisen; **the wolves circled around, waiting** die Wölfe kreisten lauernd um uns/sie/das Lager etc

circlet ['sɜ:klɪt] N Reif m

circlip ['sɜ:klɪp] N Sicherungsring m

circuit ['sɜ:kɪt] **N** **a** (= journey around etc) Rundgang m/-fahrt f/-reise f (of um); **to make a ~ of sth** um etw herumgehen/-fahren, einen Rundgang/eine Rundfahrt um etw machen; **three ~s of the racetrack** drei Runden auf der Rennbahn; **they made a wide ~ to avoid the enemy** sie machten einen großen Bogen um den Feind

b (of judges etc) Gerichtsbezirk m; **to go on ~** den (Gerichts)bezirk bereisen; **he is on the eastern ~** er bereist or hat den östlichen (Gerichts)bezirk

c (Theat) Theaterring m or -kette f; **to travel the ~** die Theater (der Reihe nach) bereisen

d (Elec) Stromkreis m; (= apparatus) Schaltung f

e (Sport, = track) Rennbahn f

f **the professional golf/tennis ~** die Golf-/Tennisturnierrunde (der Berufsspieler)

VT track, course eine Runde drehen um

circuit: circuit board N (Tech) Platine f, Leiterplatte f; **circuit breaker** N Stromkreisunterbrecher m; **circuit court** N Bezirksgericht, das an verschiedenen Orten eines Gerichtsbezirks Sitzungen abhält; **circuit diagram** N Schaltplan m; **circuit judge** N Richter m an einem Bezirksgericht

circuitous [sɜ:'kjʊɪtəs] ADJ umständlich; **~ path** Schlängelpfad m

circuitously [sɜ:'kjʊɪtəslɪ] ADV umständlich; **the road winds ~** die Straße schlängelt sich

circuitousness [sɜ:'kjʊɪtəsnɪs] N Umständlichkeit f; (of route) Gewundenheit f

circuitry ['sɜ:kətrɪ] N Schaltkreise pl

circuit training N Circuittraining nt, Zirkeltraining nt

circuity [sɜ:'kjʊətɪ] N = **circuitousness**

circular ['sɜ:kjʊlə'] **ADJ** object kreisförmig, rund; **~ motion** Kreisbewegung f; **~ tour** Rundfahrt f/-reise f; **a ~ tour of the island** eine Inselrundfahrt; **~ argument** Zirkelschluss m **N** (in firm) Rundschreiben nt, Rundbrief m; (single copy) Umlauf m; (= printed advertisement) Wurfsendung f → also **circular letter**

circularize ['sɜ:kjʊləraɪz] VT person durch Rundschreiben informieren; letter, memo zirkulieren lassen

circular: circular letter N Rundschreiben nt, Rundbrief m; **circular saw** N Kreissäge f; **circular stair, circular staircase** N Wendeltreppe f

circulate ['sɜ:kjʊleɪt] **VI** **a** (water, blood, money) fließen, zirkulieren; (traffic) fließen; (news, rumour) kursieren, in Umlauf sein **b** (person: at party) die Runde machen **VT** news, rumour verbreiten, in Umlauf bringen; memo etc zirkulieren lassen; water pumpen

circulating ['sɜ:kjʊleɪtɪŋ]: **circulating capital** N flüssiges Kapital, Umlaufkapital nt; **circulating library** N Fahrbücherei f; **circulating medium** N (Fin) Zahlungs- or Umlaufsmittel nt

circulation [,sɜ:kjʊ'leɪʃən] **N** **a** (= act of circulating) (Med) Kreislauf m, Zirkulation f; (of traffic) Ablauf m, Fluss m; (of money also) Umlauf m; (of news, rumour) Kursieren nt; **to have poor ~** Kreislaufstörungen haben; **to put notes into ~** Banknoten in Umlauf bringen; **this coin was** withdrawn from or taken out of ~ diese Münze wurde aus dem Verkehr gezogen; **new words which come into ~** Wörter, die neu in Umlauf kommen; **he's back in ~ now** (inf) er mischt wieder mit (inf); **to be out of ~** (inf) (person) von der Bildfläche or in der Versenkung verschwunden sein; (criminal, politician) aus dem Verkehr gezogen worden sein; **the ideas then in ~** die Ideen, die damals im Schwang(e) waren

b (of newspaper etc) Auflage(nziffer) f; **for private ~** zum privaten Gebrauch

circulatory [,sɜ:kjʊ'leɪtərɪ] ADJ Kreislauf-; **~ system** Blutkreislauf m

circum- ['sɜ:kəm-] PREF um-, um ... herum

circumcise ['sɜ:kəmsaɪz] VT beschneiden

circumcision [,sɜ:kəm'sɪʒən] N Beschneidung f; **the Circumcision** (Eccl) der Tag der Beschneidung des Herrn

circumference [sə'kʌmfərəns] N Umfang m; **the tree is 10 ft in ~** der Baum hat einen Umfang von 10 Fuß

circumflex ['sɜ:kəmfleks] N Zirkumflex m

circumlocution [,sɜ:kəmlə'kju:ʃən] N Weitschweifigkeit f; (= evasiveness) Umschreibung f, Drumherumreden nt (inf)

circumlocutory [,sɜ:kəmlə'kju:tərɪ] ADJ weitschweifig; expression umschreibend

circumnavigate [,sɜ:kəm'nævɪgeɪt] VT the globe umfahren; (in yacht also) umsegeln; cape, island also umschiffen

circumnavigation ['sɜ:kəm,nævɪ'geɪʃən] N Fahrt f (of um); (in yacht also) Umsegelung f; **~ of the globe** Fahrt f um die Welt; Weltumsegelung f

circumnavigator [,sɜ:kəm'nævɪgeɪtə'] N **~ of the globe** Weltumsegler(in) m(f)

circumscribe ['sɜ:kəmskraɪb] VT **a** (Math) einen Kreis umbeschreiben (+dat) **b** (= restrict) eingrenzen

circumscription [,sɜ:kəm'skrɪpʃən] N **a** (= restriction) Eingrenzung f **b** (on coin) Umschrift f

circumspect ['sɜ:kəmspekt] ADJ umsichtig

circumspection [,sɜ:kəm'spekʃən] N Umsicht f

circumspectly ['sɜ:kəmspektlɪ] ADV umsichtig

circumstance ['sɜ:kəmstəns] N **a** Umstand m; **in** or **under the ~** unter diesen Umständen; **in** or **under no ~s** unter gar keinen Umständen, auf keinen Fall; **in certain ~s** unter Umständen, eventuell; **what were the ~s surrounding the case?** wie waren die näheren Umstände des Falls?; **a victim of ~** ein Opfer nt der Umstände; **he was forced by ~ to do it** die Umstände zwangen ihn, es zu tun **b** **circumstances** PL (= financial condition) finanzielle Verhältnisse pl, Umstände pl (form); **in poor ~s** in ärmlichen Verhältnissen **c** → **pomp**

circumstantial [,sɜ:kəm'stænʃəl] ADJ **a** (= detailed) report, statement ausführlich, detailliert **b** (Jur) case auf Indizienbeweisen beruhend; **~ evidence** Indizienbeweis m; **the case against him is purely ~** der Fall beruht allein auf Indizienbeweisen **c** (= secondary) nebensächlich

circumstantiate [,sɜ:kəm'stænʃɪeɪt] VT (form) belegen

circumvent [,sɜ:kəm'vent] VT umgehen

circumvention [,sɜ:kəm'venʃən] N Umgehung f

circus ['sɜ:kəs] N Zirkus m; (in place names) Platz m

cirrhosis [sɪ'rəʊsɪs] N Zirrhose f

cirrus ['sɪrəs] N pl **cirri** ['sɪraɪ] Zirruswolke f

CIS abbr of **Commonwealth of Independent States** GUS f

cisalpine ['sɪz'ælpaɪn] ADJ zisalpin

cissy ['sɪsɪ] N = **sissy**

Cistercian [sɪs'tɜ:ʃən] **N** Zisterzienser m **ADJ** Zisterzienser-

cistern ['sɪstən] N Zisterne f; (of WC) Spülkasten m

citable ['saɪtəbl] ADJ anführbar, zitierbar

citadel ['sɪtədl] N Zitadelle f

citation [saɪ'teɪʃən] N **a** (= quote) Zitat nt; (= act of quoting) Zitieren nt **b** (Mil) Belobigung f, lobende Erwähnung **c** (Jur) Vorladung f (vor Gericht)

cite [saɪt] VT **a** (= quote) anführen, zitieren **b** (Mil) belobigen, lobend erwähnen (for wegen) **c** (Jur) vorladen; **he was ~d to appear** er wurde vorgeladen, er erhielt eine Vorladung; **he was ~d as the co-respondent** (= mentioned) er wurde als der Dritte in der Scheidungssache genannt

citify ['sɪtɪfaɪ] VT verstädtern

citizen ['sɪtɪzn] N **a** Bürger(in) m(f) **b** (of a state) (Staats)bürger(in) m(f); **French ~** französischer Staatsbürger, französische Staatsbürgerin, Franzose m, Französin f; **~ of the world** Weltbürger(in) m(f)

citizenry ['sɪtɪznrɪ] N (liter) Bürgerschaft f

Citizens' Advice Bureau N (Brit) ≈ Bürgerberatungsstelle f

CITIZENS' ADVICE BUREAU

1939 wurden in Großbritannien **Citizens' Advice Bureaus** errichtet, die die Bürger über die Kriegssonderregelungen informieren sollten. Nach dem Krieg wurde daraus ein allgemeiner kostenloser Beratungsdienst, der der Öffentlichkeit bei einer ganzen Palette von Problemen mit Rat und Tat zur Seite steht. Heutzutage beschäftigen sich diese Bürgerberatungsstellen überwiegend mit Schuldenproblemen, Wohnungssuche, Sozialhilfe, Sozialdiensten und Verbraucherschutz. Der öffentlich finanzierte Service verfügt über Hunderte von örtlichen Beratungsstellen, die von jeweils einem voll bezahlten leitenden Mitarbeiter sowie speziell geschulten ehrenamtlichen Kräften betrieben werden.

---

citizen: citizen's arrest N Festnahme durch eine Zivilperson; **Citizens' Band** N CB-Funk m; **Citizen's Charter** N (Brit) 1991 von der britischen Regierung zur Verbesserung öffentlicher Dienstleistungen eingesetzte Charta

citizenship ['sɪtɪznʃɪp] N Staatsbürgerschaft f

citrate ['sɪtreɪt] N Zitrat nt

citric acid ['sɪtrɪkæsɪd] N Zitronensäure f

citron ['sɪtrən] N (= fruit) Zitrone f; (= tree) Zitronenbaum m

citrus ['sɪtrəs] N Zitrusgewächs nt; **~ fruits** Zitrusfrüchte pl

city ['sɪtɪ] N Stadt f, Großstadt f; **towns and cities** Städte und Großstädte; **the ~ of Glasgow** die Stadt Glasgow **b** (in London) **the City** die City, das Banken- und Börsenviertel

city: city boy N Großstadtkind nt, Großstadtjunge m; **city-bred** ADJ in der (Groß)stadt aufgewachsen; **city centre**, (US) **city center** N Stadtmitte f, Stadtzentrum nt, Innenstadt f, City f; **city council** N Stadtrat m; **city councillor**, (US) **city councilor** [n] Stadtrat m/-rätin f, Stadtratsmitglied nt; **city desk** N (Brit) Finanz- und Wirtschaftsabteilung f (einer Redaktion); (US) Abteilung f für Lokalnachrichten; **city dweller** N Stadtbewohner(in) m(f); **city editor** N (Brit) Wirtschaftsredakteur(in) m(f); (US) Lokalredakteur(in) m(f); **city father** N Stadtverordnete(r) m; **the ~s** die Stadtväter pl; **city hall** N Rathaus nt; (US, = municipal government) Stadtverwaltung f; **city life** N (Groß)stadtleben nt; **city manager** N (US) Oberstadtdirektor(in) m(f)

CITY NICKNAMES

Amerikanische Städte haben oft Spitznamen, die auch häufig verwendet werden. New York ist allgemein unter „The Big Apple" bekannt (**apple** ist ein Slangausdruck für eine Großstadt), Chicago ist „The Windy City" (weil hier heftige Winde vom Michigansee her wehen), New Orleans „The Big Easy"

(wegen des dortigen Lebensrhythmus), und Detroit ist „Motown" (da es für seine Motorenindustrie bekannt ist).
Einige Städte werden auf ihre Initialen reduziert, wie „LA" für Los Angeles und „Big D" für Dallas. Bei anderen Städten werden Namensteile weggelassen, so bei „Vegas" für Las Vegas, oder zu Kurzversionen zusammengezogen, wie bei „Frisco" statt San Francisco und „Philly" statt Philadelphia.

city: city page N (Brit) Wirtschaftsseite f; **city person** N (Groß)stadtmensch m; **cityscape** N (Groß)stadtlandschaft f; **city slicker** N (pej inf) feiner Pinkel aus der (Groß)stadt (pej inf); (dishonest) schlitzohriger Großstädter (pej inf); **city state** N Stadtstaat m; **City Technology College** N (Brit) ≈ technische Fachschule; **city treasurer** N Stadtkämmerer m/-kämmerin f; **city type** N (Groß)stadtmensch m

civet ['sɪvɪt] N (= substance) Zibet m; (= cat) Zibetkatze f

civic ['sɪvɪk] ADJ rights, virtues bürgerlich, Bürger-; duties, responsibilities als Bürger; guard, authorities Stadt-, städtisch; event, reception der Stadt

civic centre N (Brit) Verwaltungszentrum nt einer Stadt

civics ['sɪvɪks] N sing Staatsbürgerkunde f

civies ['sɪvɪz] PL (inf) = **civvies**

civil ['sɪvl] ADJ **a** (= of society) bürgerlich; duties staatsbürgerlich, Bürger-; unrest, conflict in der Bevölkerung **b** (= polite) höflich; (in behaviour also) aufmerksam, zuvorkommend; **to be ~ to sb** höflich zu jdm sein; **cigar? – very ~ of you** Zigarre? – sehr zuvorkommend (von Ihnen) **c** (Jur) zivilrechtlich **d** (= civilian) aircraft, aviation zivil

civil: Civil Aviation Authority N Behörde f für Zivilluftfahrt; **civil defence**, (US) **civil defense** N Zivilschutz m; **~ worker** Beauftragte(r) mf des Zivilschutzes; **civil disobedience** N ziviler Ungehorsam; **~ campaign** Kampagne f für zivilen Ungehorsam; **civil engineer** N Bauingenieur(in) m(f); **civil engineering** N Hoch- und Tiefbau m

civilian [sɪ'vɪlɪən] N Zivilist(in) m(f) ADJ zivil, Zivil-; **in ~ clothes** in Zivil; **~ casualties** Verluste pl unter der Zivilbevölkerung

civility [sɪ'vɪlɪtɪ] N Höflichkeit f

civilization [sɪvɪlaɪ'zeɪʃən] N **a** (= civilized world) Zivilisation f; **all ~** die ganze zivilisierte Welt; **~!, the explorer exclaimed** Menschen!, rief der Forscher aus **b** (= state: of Greeks etc) Kultur f **c** (= act) Zivilisierung f

civilize ['sɪvɪlaɪz] VT zivilisieren; person also Kultur beibringen (+dat)

civilized ['sɪvɪlaɪzd] ADJ **a** zivilisiert; **all ~ nations** alle Kulturnationen **b** working hours, conditions, hour zivil; (= cultured) lifestyle, age etc kultiviert; **a more ~ place to live in** ein etwas zivilerer Ort zum Leben; **brandy after dinner, very ~** Weinbrand nach dem Essen, sehr gepflegt

civil: civil law N Zivilrecht nt, bürgerliches Recht; **civil liberty** N Bürgerrecht nt; **civil liberties group** Bürgerrechtsgruppe f; **civil list** N Zivilliste f

civilly ['sɪvlɪ] ADV (= politely) höflich, zuvorkommend

civil: civil marriage N standesamtliche Trauung, Ziviltrauung f; **civil rights** PL (staats)bürgerliche Rechte pl ATTR march, campaign, demonstration Bürgerrechts-; **civil servant** N ≈ Staatsbeamte(r) m, Staatsbeamtin f; **civil service** N ≈ Staatsdienst m (ohne Richter und Lehrer); (= civil servants collectively) Beamtenschaft f; **civil union** N gleichgeschlechtliche Ehe; **civil war** N Bürgerkrieg m

civvies ['sɪvɪz] PL (inf) Zivil nt; **he put his ~ on** er schmiss sich in Zivil (inf)

civvy street ['sɪvɪ'striːt] N (Brit, inf) Zivilleben nt; **on ~** im Zivilleben

CJ abbr of **chief justice**

CJD abbr of **Creutzfeldt-Jakob disease** CJK f

---

cl abbr of **centilitre(s)** cl

clack [klæk] N Klappern nt, Geklapper nt VI klappern

clad [klæd] (old) pret, ptp of **clothe** ADJ (liter) gekleidet; **~ with tiles** mit Ziegeln gedeckt ADJ suf fur-/silk-clad in Pelze/Seide gekleidet; **iron-/steel-clad** mit Eisen/Stahl verkleidet; **ivy-clad** efeubewachsen; **snow-clad** schneebedeckt

claim [kleɪm] ❂ 17.1 VT **a** (= demand as one's own or due) Anspruch m erheben auf (+acc); social security, benefits, sum of money (= apply for) beantragen; (= draw) beanspruchen; lost property abholen; **he ~ed diplomatic immunity** er berief sich auf seine diplomatische Immunität; **to ~ sth as one's own** etw für sich beanspruchen, Anspruch auf etw (acc) erheben; **both armies ~ed the victory** beide Armeen nahmen den Sieg für sich in Anspruch; **territories ~ed by the Arabs** von den Arabern beanspruchte Gebiete; **the fighting ~ed many lives** die Kämpfe forderten viele Menschenleben; **does anyone ~ this wallet?** gehört diese Brieftasche jemandem?
b (= profess, assert) behaupten; **he ~s to have seen you** er behauptet, Sie gesehen zu haben, er will Sie gesehen haben; **the club can ~ a membership of ...** der Verein kann ... Mitglieder vorweisen; **the advantages ~ed for this technique** die Vorzüge, die man dieser Methode zuschreibt
c one's attention, interest in Anspruch nehmen
VI **a** (Insur) Ansprüche geltend machen; (for damage done by people) Schadenersatz m verlangen
b (for expenses etc) **to ~ for sth** sich (dat) etw zurückgeben or -zahlen lassen; **you can ~ for your travelling expenses** Sie können sich (dat) Ihre Reisekosten zurückerstatten lassen
N **a** (= demand) Anspruch m; (= pay claim, Ind) Forderung f; **his ~ to the throne/title/property etc** sein Anspruch auf den Thron/Titel/das Grundstück etc; **my ~ to fame is that ...** mein Anspruch auf Ruhm begründet sich darauf, dass ...; **I have many ~s on my time** meine Zeit ist or ich bin sehr in Anspruch genommen; **you have no ~ on me** du hast keine Ansprüche an mich (zu stellen); **children have first ~ on their parents** die Kinder müssen an erster Stelle stehen, die Kinder müssen vorgehen; **to lay ~ to sth** Anspruch auf etw (acc) erheben; **to put in a ~ (for sth)** etw beantragen; (Insur) Ansprüche geltend machen; **they put in a ~ for extra pay** sie forderten einen Zuschlag; **we want the ~ back-dated** wir wollen das Geld rückwirkend; **he put in an expenses ~ for £100** er reichte Spesen in Höhe von £ 100 ein; **the ~s were all paid** (Insur) der Schaden wurde voll ersetzt
b (= assertion) Behauptung f; **to make a ~** eine Behauptung aufstellen; **have you heard his ~?** haben Sie gehört, was er behauptet?; **the exaggerated ~s made for the new washing powder** die übertriebenen Eigenschaften, die man diesem neuen Waschpulver zuschreibt; **the book makes no ~ to be original** das Buch erhebt keinen Anspruch auf Originalität; **I make no ~ to be a genius** ich erhebe nicht den Anspruch, ein Genie zu sein
c (Min) Claim m (Anteil an einem Goldfeld etc) → **stake**

▸ **claim back** VT sep zurückfordern; **to claim sth back (as expenses)** sich (dat) etw zurückzahlen or -geben or -erstatten lassen

claimant ['kleɪmənt] N (for social security etc) Antragsteller(in) m(f); (for inheritance etc) Anspruchsteller(in) m(f) (to auf +acc); (Jur) Kläger(in) m(f); **a ~ to a title/throne** ein Titel-/Thronanwärter m, eine Titel-/Thronanwärterin

claim form N Antragsformular nt

clairvoyance [kleə'vɔɪəns] N Hellsehen nt, Hellseherei f

clairvoyant [kleə'vɔɪənt] N Hellseher(in) m(f) ADJ hellseherisch; **I'm not ~** ich bin (doch) kein Hellseher!

clam [klæm] N Venusmuschel f; **he shut up like a ~** aus ihm war kein Wort mehr herauszubekommen

▶ **clam up** VI (inf) keinen Piep (mehr) sagen (inf); **he clammed up on me** ich habe kein Wort mehr aus ihm herausgekriegt (inf)

clambake ['klæmbeɪk] N (US) Muschelessen nt am Strand; (inf, = party) Fete f (inf)

clamber ['klæmbə'] VI klettern, kraxeln (esp S Ger); **to ~ up a hill** auf einen Berg klettern, einen Berg hinaufklettern; **the baby ~ed all over the sofa** das Baby krabbelte auf dem Sofa herum ◆ N Kletterei f, Kraxelei f (esp S Ger)

clamminess ['klæmɪnɪs] N Feuchtigkeit f, Klammheit f

clammy ['klæmɪ] ADJ (+er) feucht, klamm; **a ~ handshake** ein feuchter Händedruck

clamor N (US) = **clamour**

clamorous ['klæmərəs] ADJ (liter) a mob lärmend b demands lautstark; applause tosend

clamour, (US) **clamor** ['klæmə'] N a (= noise) Lärm m, Lärmen nt; **the ~ of the battlefield** der Kampf- or Schlachtenlärm b (= demand) lautstark erhobene Forderung (for nach); **a ~ against sth** ein Aufschrei m gegen etw; **constant ~ against the EC** ständiges Geschrei gegen die EG ◆ VI **to ~ for sth** nach etw schreien; **to ~ against sth** sich gegen etw empören; **the paper ~ed against the government** die Zeitung wetterte gegen die Regierung; **the men were ~ing to go home** die Männer forderten lautstark die Heimkehr

clamp¹ [klæmp] N Schraubzwinge f; (Med, Elec) Klemme f; (for illegally parked car) Parkkralle f ◆ VT (ein)spannen; illegally parked car eine Parkkralle befestigen an (+dat)

▶ **clamp down** VT sep (lit) festmachen ◆ VI (fig, on expenses etc) gewaltig bremsen (inf); (police, government) rigoros durchgreifen

▶ **clamp down on** VI +prep obj person an die Kandare nehmen; expenditure, activities einen Riegel vorschieben (+dat); news broadcasts unterdrücken; **the government clamped down on private radio stations** die Regierung holte zum Schlag gegen private Rundfunksender aus

clamp² N (Brit, of potatoes) Miete f

clampdown ['klæmpdaʊn] N Schlag m (on gegen); **he ordered a ~ on the porn merchants** er hat dafür gesorgt, dass es den Pornohändlern an den Kragen ging (inf); **the ~ has made tax evasion almost impossible** das harte Durchgreifen hat Steuerhinterziehung fast unmöglich gemacht

clan [klæn] N (lit, fig) Clan m

clandestine [klæn'destɪn] ADJ geheim; meeting, society Geheim-; rendezvous heimlich

clandestinely [klæn'destɪnlɪ] ADV im Geheimen

clang [klæŋ] N Klappern nt; (of hammer) Hallen nt, Dröhnen nt; (of swords) Klirren nt ◆ VI klappern; (hammer) hallen, dröhnen; (swords) klirren ◆ VT klappern mit; cymbal schlagen; bell läuten

clanger ['klæŋə'] N (Brit, inf) Fauxpas m, Schnitzer m (inf); **to drop a ~** ins Fettnäpfchen treten (inf)

clangor ['klæŋgə'] N (US) = **clangour**

clangorous ['klæŋgərəs] ADJ (liter) hallend

clangour ['klæŋgə'] N Hallen nt; (irritating) Getöse nt

clank [klæŋk] N Klirren nt ◆ VT klirren mit ◆ VI klirren

clannish ['klænɪʃ] ADJ group klüngelhaft, verfilzt (inf); person cliquenbewusst; **the office staff became unbearably ~** im Büro entwickelte sich eine unerträgliche Cliquenwirtschaft

clansman ['klænzmən] N pl **-men** [-mən] Clanmitglied nt; **all the McTaggart clansmen** alle Mitglieder des Clans McTaggart

clap¹ [klæp] N (inf) Tripper m; **to catch a dose of the ~** sich (dat) was or den Tripper (weg)holen (inf)

clap² N Klatschen nt no pl; (no pl: = applause) (Beifall)klatschen nt; **a ~ of thunder** ein Donnerschlag m; **give him a ~!** klatscht ihm Beifall!, alle(s) klatschen!; **the audience gave him a big ~** das Publikum klatschte (ihm) begeistert Beifall; **a ~ on the back** ein Schlag m auf die Schulter ◆ VT a (= applaud) Beifall klatschen (+dat) b **to ~ one's hands** in die Hände klatschen; **to ~ sb on the back** jdm auf die Schulter klopfen c (= put quickly) **he ~ped his hand over my mouth** er hielt mir den Mund zu; **to ~ sb into prison** jdn ins Gefängnis stecken; **to ~ eyes on sb/sth** (inf) jdn/etw zu sehen kriegen (inf) ◆ VI (Beifall) klatschen

▶ **clap on** VT sep handcuffs anlegen (prep obj +dat); **to clap on one's hat** sich (dat) den Hut aufstülpen; **to clap on sail** (Naut) Beisegel setzen; **to clap on the brakes** (Aut) auf die Bremse latschen (inf)

▶ **clap to** VT always separate door zuklappen ◆ VI (door) zuklappen

clapboard ['klæpbɔ:d] N Schindel f

clapped-out ['klæptaʊt] ADJ attr, **clapped out** ['klæpt'aʊt] (inf) klapprig; **a ~ old car** ein klappriges Auto, eine alte Klapperkiste (inf); **I feel really clapped out** (Brit inf) ich bin total geschafft (inf)

clapper ['klæpə'] N (of bell) (Glocken)klöppel m; **to go/drive/work like the ~s** (Brit, inf) ein Mordstempo draufhaben (inf)

clapperboard ['klæpəbɔ:d] N (Film) (Synchron)klappe f

clapping ['klæpɪŋ] N (Beifall)klatschen nt, Beifall m

claptrap ['klæptræp] N (inf) Geschwafel nt (inf)

claque [klæk] N (Theat) Claque f, Claqueure pl

claret ['klærət] N a (= wine) roter Bordeauxwein b (= colour) Weinrot nt ◆ ADJ weinrot

clarification [ˌklærɪfɪ'keɪʃən] N a (= explanation) Klarstellung f; **the whole issue needs a lot more ~** die Sache bedarf noch der Klärung; **I'd like a little ~ on this point** ich hätte diesen Punkt gerne näher erläutert; **in** or **as ~** zur Klarstellung b (of wine) Klärungsprozess m

clarificatory [klærɪfɪ'keɪtərɪ] ADJ erklärend

clarified ['klærɪfaɪd] ADJ butter, sugar raffiniert; stock, wine geklärt

clarify ['klærɪfaɪ] VT a (= explain) klären, klarstellen; text erklären; statement näher erläutern; **the matter has now clarified itself** die Sache hat sich jetzt geklärt b butter, sugar raffinieren; stock, wine (wine) sich klären

clarinet [ˌklærɪ'net] N Klarinette f

clarinettist [ˌklærɪ'netɪst] N Klarinettist(in) m(f)

clarion ['klærɪən] N (liter) Fanfare f; **a ~ call for reform** ein Ruf m nach Reformen; **a ~ call to action** ein Aufruf m zum Handeln

clarity ['klærɪtɪ] N Klarheit f

clash [klæʃ] VI a (armies, demonstrators) zusammenstoßen; **the chairman ~ed with the committee at the last meeting** der Vorsitzende hatte auf der letzten Sitzung eine Auseinandersetzung mit dem Komitee; **unions ~ with government over pay** in der Tariffrage gibt es einen Konflikt zwischen Gewerkschaften und Regierung b (colours) nicht harmonieren, sich beißen; (interests) kollidieren, aufeinander prallen; (programmes, films) sich überschneiden; **our personalities** or **we ~ too much** wir passen einfach nicht zusammen c (cymbals etc: also **clash together**) aneinanderschlagen; (swords) klirrend aneinanderschlagen ◆ VT cymbals, swords schlagen ◆ N a (of armies, demonstrators etc) Zusammenstoß m; (between people, parties) Konflikt m; **there's bound to be a ~ between the chairman and the vice-chairman** zwischen dem Vorsitzenden und seinem Stellvertreter muss es ja zu einem Zusammenstoß kommen b (of personalities) grundsätzliche Verschiedenheit, Unvereinbarkeit f; **we want to avoid a ~ of personalities in the office** wir wollen keine Leute im Büro, die absolut nicht miteinander harmonieren; **it's such a ~ of personalities** sie sind charakterlich grundverschieden; **I don't like that ~ of red and turquoise** mir gefällt diese Zusammenstellung von Rot und Türkis nicht; **a ~ of interests** eine Interessenkollision c (of swords) Aufeinanderprallen nt

clasp [klɑ:sp] N a (on brooch etc) (Schnapp-) verschluss m b (with one's arms) Umklammerung f; (with hand) Griff m c (Mil, of medals) Ansteckabzeichen nt, Metallspange f auf dem Ordensband ◆ VT a (= hold) (er)greifen; **to ~ sb's hand** jds Hand ergreifen; **to ~ one's hands (together)** die Hände falten; **with his hands ~ed in prayer** mit zum Gebet gefalteten Händen; **with his hands ~ed behind his back** mit auf dem Rücken verschränkten Händen; **to ~ sb in one's arms** jdn in die Arme nehmen or schließen; **they lay ~ed in each other's arms** sie lagen sich in den Armen; **to ~ sb to one's chest** jdn ans Herz drücken b (= fasten with a clasp) befestigen, zuschnappen lassen; **she ~ed the bracelet round her wrist** sie legte ihr Armband an

clasp knife N Taschenmesser nt

class [klɑ:s] ✪ 5.2 N a (= group, division) Klasse f; **what ~ are you travelling?** in welcher Klasse reisen Sie?; **he's not in the same ~ as his brother** sein Bruder ist eine Klasse besser; **they're just not in the same ~** man kann sie einfach nicht vergleichen; **in a ~ by himself/itself** or **of his/its own** weitaus der/das Beste b (= social rank) gesellschaftliche Stellung, Stand m (dated), Klasse f (Sociol); **the ruling ~** die herrschende Klasse, die Herrschenden pl; **considerations of ~** Standeserwägungen pl (dated), Klassengesichtspunkte pl; **it was ~ not ability that determined who ...** (die gesellschaftliche) Herkunft und nicht die Fähigkeiten bestimmten wer ...; **what ~ is he from?** aus welcher Schicht or Klasse kommt er?; **are you ashamed of your ~?** schämst du dich deines Standes (dated) or deiner Herkunft?; **~ and educational background** Klassenzugehörigkeit und Erziehung; **we were talking about ~** wir sprachen über die gesellschaftlichen Klassen c (Sch, Univ) Klasse f; **I don't like her ~es** ihr Unterricht gefällt mir nicht; **you should prepare each ~ in advance** du solltest dich auf jede (Unterrichts)stunde vorbereiten; **to take a Latin ~** Latein unterrichten or geben; (Univ) ein Lateinseminar etc abhalten; **the French ~** (= lesson) die Französischstunde; (= people) die Französischklasse; **an evening ~** ein Abendkurs m; **eating in ~** Essen während des Unterrichts; **the ~ of 1980** der Jahrgang 1980, die Schul-/ Universitätsabgänger etc des Jahres 1980 d (Bot, Zool) Klasse f e (Brit, Univ, of degree) Prädikat nt; **a first-class degree** ein Prädikatsexamen nt; **second-/third- -class degree** ≈ Prädikat Gut/Befriedigend f (inf, = quality, tone) Stil m; **to have ~** Stil haben, etwas hermachen (inf); (person) Format haben; **that gives the place a bit of ~** das macht (doch) (et)was her (inf); **I see we've got a bit of ~ in tonight, two guys in dinner jackets** heute Abend haben wir ja vornehme or exklusive Gäste, zwei Typen im Smoking ◆ ADJ (inf, = excellent) erstklassig, exklusiv; **to be a ~ act** große Klasse sein (inf) ◆ VT einordnen, klassifizieren; **he was ~ed with the servants** er wurde genauso eingestuft wie die Diener ◆ VI eingestuft werden, sich einordnen lassen

class: **class action** N (US Jur) Klage im Interesse einer Gruppe von Beteiligten, Gruppenklage f; **class-conscious** ADJ standesbewusst, klassenbewusst; **class-consciousness** N Standesbewusstsein nt, Klassenbewusstsein nt; **class distinction** N gesellschaftlicher Unterschied, Klassenunterschied m; **there is too**

much ~ die gesellschaftlichen Unterschiede/ Klassenunterschiede sind zu groß; **class feeling** N (= *antagonism*) Klassenantagonismus *m*; (= *solidarity*) Solidarität *f*, Klassenbewusstsein *nt*

classic ['klæsɪk] ADJ (*lit, fig*) klassisch; **it was ~!** (*inf*) das war geradezu klassisch!; **a ~ example of sth** ein klassisches Beispiel für etw; **~ car** klassischer Wagen N Klassiker *m*

classical ['klæsɪkəl] ADJ klassisch; (= *in the style of classical architecture*) klassizistisch; *education* humanistisch; *method, solution also* altbewährt; **~ music** klassische Musik; **the ~ world** die antike Welt; **a ~ scholar** ein Altphilologe *m*

classically ['klæsɪkəlɪ] ADV klassisch

classicism ['klæsɪsɪzəm] N Klassik *f*; (= *style of classic architecture*) Klassizismus *m*

classicist ['klæsɪsɪst] N Altphilologe *m*/-philologin *f*

classics ['klæsɪks] N *sing* (*Univ*) Altphilologie *f*

classifiable ['klæsɪfaɪəbl] ADJ klassifizierbar

classification [ˌklæsɪfɪ'keɪʃən] N Klassifizierung *f*, Einteilung *f*

classified ['klæsɪfaɪd] ADJ in Klassen or Gruppen eingeteilt; **~ ad**(**vertisement**) Kleinanzeige *f*; **~ information** (*Mil*) Verschlusssache *f*; (*Pol*) Geheimsache *f*; **~ results** (*Brit, Sport*) (Spiel)ergebnisse *pl*; **~ section** (*Press*) Kleinanzeigenteil *m* N **the ~s** die Kleinanzeigen *pl*

classify ['klæsɪfaɪ] VT a (= *categorize*) klassifizieren, (nach Klassen or Gruppen) ordnen b *information* für geheim erklären

classiness ['klæsɪnɪs] N (*inf*) Exklusivität *f*

classism ['klɑːsɪzəm] N Klassendiskriminierung *f*

class: classless ADJ *society* klassenlos; **class list** N (*Brit, Univ*) Benotungsliste *f*; **classmate** N Klassenkamerad(in) *m(f)*, Mitschüler(in) *m(f)*; **class reunion** N Klassentreffen *nt*; **classridden** ADJ *society* von Klassengegensätzen beherrscht; **classroom** N Klassenzimmer *nt*; **classroom assistant** N Assistenzlehrkraft *f*; **class size** (*Sch*) Klassenstärke *f*; **class society** N Klassengesellschaft *f*; **class struggle** N Klassenkampf *m*; **class system** N Klassensystem *nt*; **class thinking** N Klassendenken *nt*; **class war(fare)** N Klassenkrieg *m*

CLASS SYSTEM

Auch wenn sich das strenge Klassensystem des Viktorianischen Zeitalters im 20. Jahrhundert etwas gelockert hat, ist die britische Gesellschaft doch noch immer stark von einer Trennung der sozialen Klassen gekennzeichnet. In Großbritannien wird die Zugehörigkeit zu einer Klasse durch Geburt, Ausbildung, Beruf und Vermögen bestimmt, wobei auch Lebensstil und Akzent eine Rolle spielen. Auch wenn die Schaffung einer „klassenlosen Gesellschaft" das erklärte Ziel vieler Politiker ist, findet in der Öffentlichkeit relativ wenig Diskussion über das Klassensystem oder über Strategien zur Überwindung der Klassenschranken statt.

classy ['klɑːsɪ] ADJ (+*er*) (*inf*) nobel (*inf*), exklusiv; **~ hotel** eine Nobelherberge (*inf*); **a ~ woman** eine Klassefrau (*inf*)

clatter ['klætə] N Klappern *nt*, Geklapper *nt*; (*of hooves also*) Trappeln *nt*, Getrappel *nt*; **her workbox fell with a ~ to the ground** mit lautem Klappern fiel der Nähkasten zu Boden VI klappern; (*hooves also*) trappeln; **the box of tools went ~ing down the stairs** der Werkzeugkasten polterte die Treppe hinunter; **the cart ~ed over the cobbles** der Wagen polterte or rumpelte über das Pflaster VT klappern mit

clause [klɔːz] N a (*Gram*) Satz *m* b (*Jur etc*) Klausel *f*

claustrophobia [ˌklɔːstrə'fəubɪə] N Klaustrophobie *f*, Platzangst *f* (*inf*)

claustrophobic [ˌklɔːstrə'fəubɪk] ADJ klaustrophob(isch) (*Psych*); **it's so ~ in here** hier kriegt man Platzangst (*inf*); **I get this ~ feeling** ich kriege Platzangst (*inf*); **a room of ~ proportions** ein Zimmer, in dem man Platzangst kriegt (*inf*)

clave [kleɪv] *ptp of* **cleave** [2]

clavichord ['klævɪkɔːd] N Klavichord *nt*

clavicle ['klævɪkl] N Schlüsselbein *nt*

claw [klɔː] N Kralle *f*; (*of lions, birds of prey also, of excavator*) Klaue *f*; (*of lobster etc*) Schere *f*, Zange *f*; (*of hammer*) Nagelklaue *f*; **to show one's ~s** (*fig*) die Krallen zeigen; **to get one's ~s into sb** (*inf*) (dauernd) auf jdm herumhacken; **once a woman like that has got her ~s into a man …** wenn eine Frau die erst einmal einen Mann in den Klauen hat … VT kratzen; **badly ~ed** schlimm zerkratzt; **the mole ~s its way through the soil** der Maulwurf wühlt sich durch das Erdreich; **they ~ed their way out from under the rubble** sie wühlten sich aus dem Schutt hervor; **he ~ed his way to the top** (*fig*) er hat sich an die Spitze durchgeboxt; **two women, cats, ~ing each other** zwei Frauen, die wie Hyänen aufeinander losgingen VI **to ~ at sth** sich an etw (acc) krallen; **he ~ed desperately for the handle** er krallte verzweifelt nach der Klinke

▶ **claw back** VT *sep* (*taxman etc*) sich (dat) zurückholen

▶ **claw out** VT *sep* auskratzen

claw: clawback N (*for individual*) Rückerstattung *f*; **from this sale the government got a £3m ~** aus diesem Verkauf flossen 3 Millionen Pfund in die Staatskasse zurück; **claw hammer** N Tischlerhammer *m*; **claw mark** N Kratzer *m*

clay [kleɪ] N Lehm *m*; **to have feet of ~** or (*US*) **feet** einen Makel auf seiner weißen Weste haben → *also* **potter** [1]

clay court N (*Tennis*) Sandplatz *m*

clayey ['kleɪɪ] ADJ lehmig; *soil also* Lehm-

claymore ['kleɪmɔː] N zweischneidiges Langschwert

clay: clay pigeon N Tontaube *f*; **clay pigeon shooting** N Tontaubenschießen *nt*; **clay pipe** N Tonpfeife *f*

clean [kliːn] ADJ (+*er*) a (= *not dirty, also bomb*) sauber; **to wash/wipe/brush sth ~** etw abwaschen/-reiben/-bürsten; **to wipe a disk ~** (*Comput*) alle Daten von einer Diskette löschen; **she has very ~ habits, she's a very ~ person** sie ist sehr sauber b (= *new, not used*) *sheets, paper* sauber, neu; (*Typ*) *proof* sauber; **I want to see a nice ~ plate** ich will einen schön leer gegessenen Teller sehen; **the vultures picked the carcass/bone ~** die Geier nagten den Kadaver bis aufs Skelett ab/nagten den Knochen ganz ab; **to make a ~ start** ganz von vorne anfangen; (*in life*) ein neues Leben anfangen; **to have a ~ record** (*with police*) nicht vorbestraft sein, eine weiße Weste haben (*inf*); **he has a ~ record** gegen ihn liegt nichts vor; **to start again with a ~ sheet** einen neuen Anfang machen, ein neues Kapitel aufschlagen; **a ~ driving licence** ein Führerschein *m* ohne Strafpunkte; **to be ~ for six months** (*criminal*) er ist seit sechs Monaten sauber; (*from drink*) er ist seit sechs Monaten trocken; (*from drugs*) er ist seit sechs Monaten clean; **he's ~, no guns** (*inf*) alles in Ordnung, nicht bewaffnet c (= *not obscene*) *joke* stubenrein; *film* anständig; **keep television ~** das Fernsehen muss sauber or anständig bleiben; **good ~ fun** ein harmloser, netter Spaß d (= *well-shaped*) *lines* klar e (= *regular, even*) *cut* sauber, glatt; **a ~ break** (*also Med*) ein glatter Bruch; (*fig*) ein klares Ende; **a ~ break with the past** ein klarer Bruch mit der Vergangenheit f (*Sport*) *fight, match* sauber, fair; *boxer* fair g (= *acceptable to religion*) rein h **to make a ~ breast of sth** etw gestehen, sich (dat) etw von der Seele reden; **to have ~ hands** (*fig*) eine reine Weste haben → **sweep**
ADV glatt; **I ~ forgot** das habe ich glatt(weg) vergessen (*inf*); **he got ~ away** er verschwand spurlos; **he got ~ away from the rest of the field** er ließ das übrige Feld weit hinter sich; **the ball/he went ~ through the window** der Ball flog glatt/er flog achtkantig durch das Fenster; **to cut ~ through sth** etw ganz durchschneiden/durchschlagen *etc*; **to come ~** (*inf*) auspacken (*inf*); **to come ~ about sth** etw gestehen; **we're ~ out (of matches)** es sind keine (Streichhölzer) mehr da
VT sauber machen; (*with cloth also*) abwischen; *carpets also* reinigen; (= *remove stains etc*) säubern; *clothes also* säubern (*form*); (= *dry-clean*) reinigen; *nails, paintbrush, furniture also, dentures, old buildings* reinigen; *window, shoes* säubern, reinigen (*form*); *fish, wound* säubern; *chicken* ausnehmen; *vegetables* putzen; *apple, grapes etc* säubern (*form*); (= *wash*) (ab)waschen; (= *wipe*) abwischen; *cup, plate etc* säubern (*form*); *car* waschen, putzen; **the cat is ~ing itself** die Katze putzt sich; **to ~ one's hands** (= *wash*) sich (dat) die Hände waschen or (*wipe*) abwischen or (*scrape, with grease remover*) säubern; **to ~ one's teeth** sich (dat) die Zähne putzen or (*with toothpick*) säubern; **to ~ one's face** (= *wash*) sich (dat) das Gesicht waschen or (*wipe*) abwischen; **the dirt off your face** wisch dir den Schmutz vom Gesicht!; **~ your shoes before you come inside** putz dir die Schuhe ab, bevor du reinkommst!; **to ~ a room** ein Zimmer sauber machen, in einem Zimmer putzen; **clothes which are easy to ~** pflegeleichte Kleider *pl*
VI reinigen; **this paint ~s easily** diese Farbe lässt sich leicht reinigen; **brand X ~s better** die Marke X reinigt gründlicher
N **to give sth a ~** → vt

▶ **clean down** VT *sep car, lorry* waschen; *walls* abwaschen

▶ **clean off** VT *sep* (= *wash*) abwaschen; (= *rinse*) abspülen; (= *wipe*) abwischen; (= *scrape, rub*) abreiben; *dirt, barnacles, rust* entfernen, abmachen (*inf*) VI sich abwaschen *etc* lassen

▶ **clean out** VT *sep* a (*lit*) gründlich sauber machen; (*with water also*) ausspülen; *stables also* ausmisten; *carburettor* reinigen; *stomach* auspumpen or -räumen b (*inf*) (= *to make penniless*) *person* ausnehmen (wie eine Weihnachtsgans) (*inf*); (= *to rob, burgle*) *bank, house, flat* ausräumen (*inf*); **to clean out the bank** (*when gambling*) die Bank sprengen; **to be cleaned out** abgebrannt sein (*inf*) c (*inf, = buy all stock*) **to clean sb out** jdm alles wegkaufen

▶ **clean up** VT *sep* a (*lit*) sauber machen; *old building, old painting* reinigen; *mess* aufräumen; **to clean oneself up** sich sauber machen b (*fig*) **the new mayor cleaned up the city** der neue Bürgermeister hat für Sauberkeit in der Stadt gesorgt; **to clean up television** den Bildschirm (von Gewalt, Sex etc) säubern → **act** N d VI a (*lit*) aufräumen b (*inf*) abkassieren (*inf*), absahnen (*inf*); **he certainly cleaned up on that sale** bei dem Verkauf hat er kräftig abgesahnt (*inf*)

clean: clean-break divorce N *Scheidung, bei der die Frau auf Unterhaltszahlungen verzichtet und dafür Vermögenswerte wie z.B. das Haus überschrieben bekommt*; **clean-cut** ADJ klar umrissen; *sort of person* gepflegt; **the ~ lines of his new suit** der klare or einfache Schnitt seines neuen Anzuges; **~ features** klare Gesichtszüge *pl*

cleaner ['kliːnə] N a (= *person*) Reinemachefrau *f*, Gebäudereiniger *m* (*form*); **a firm of office ~s** eine Büroreinigungsfirma; **the ~s come once a week** das Reinigungspersonal kommt einmal pro Woche b (= *shop*) **~'s** Reinigung *f*; **to take sb to the ~'s** (*inf*, = *con, trick*) jdn übers Ohr hauen (*inf*), jdn reinlegen (*inf*); (= *defeat easily*) jdn in die Pfanne hauen (*inf*) c (= *thing*) Reiniger *m* → **vacuum cleaner** d (= *substance*) Reiniger *m*, Reinigungsmittel *nt*

cleaning ['kli:nɪŋ] N **the ladies who do the ~** die Frauen, die (hier) sauber machen; **~ fluid** Reinigungsflüssigkeit *f*

cleaning lady N Reinemachefrau *f*

clean-limbed ['kli:n'lɪmd] ADJ gut gebaut

cleanliness ['klenlɪnɪs] N Reinlichkeit *f*; **~ is next to godliness** (*Prov*) Sauberkeit ist alles!

clean-living ['kli:n'lɪvɪŋ] ADJ anständig, sauber

cleanly¹ ['kli:nlɪ] ADV sauber; **the bone broke ~** es war ein glatter Knochenbruch

cleanly² ['klenlɪ] ADJ (*+er*) sauber; *person* reinlich

cleanness ['kli:nnɪs] N **a** Sauberkeit *f* **b** (*of joke*) Anständigkeit *f*, Stubenreinheit *f*; (*of film*) Anständigkeit *f*; (*Typ, of proof*) Sauberkeit *f* **c** (*of outline*) Klarheit *f* **d** (*of break etc*) Sauberkeit *f*, Glätte *f*; **because of the ~ of the break** weil es ein glatter Bruch war

clean-out ['kli:naʊt] N **to give sth a ~** etw sauber machen

clean room N (*Ind*) Reinraum *m*

cleanse [klenz] VT reinigen; (*spiritually*) läutern (*of* von)

cleanser ['klenzə'] N (= *detergent*) Reiniger *m*, Reinigungsmittel *nt*; (*for skin*) Reinigungscreme *f*, Reinigungsmilch *f*

clean-shaven ['kli:n'ʃeɪvn] ADJ glatt rasiert

cleansing ['klenzɪŋ] ADJ *agent* Reinigungs-; **~ cream/milk** Reinigungscreme *f*/-milch *f*; **~ lotion** Reinigungslotion *f*

cleansing department N Stadtreinigung *f*

cleanup ['kli:nʌp] N **a** **give yourself a good ~ before you come down to dinner** wasch dich erst einmal, bevor du zum Essen kommst; **to give sth a ~** etw sauber machen; **~ operation/ costs** Säuberungsaktion *f*/-kosten *pl* **b** (*by police*) Säuberung *f* **c** (*sl*, = *profit*) Schnitt *m* (*inf*)

| **clear** [klɪə'] |
| ☼ 26.1, 26.3 |

1 ADJECTIVE	4 TRANSITIVE VERB
2 NOUN	5 INTRANSITIVE VERB
3 ADVERB	6 PHRASAL VERBS

1 – ADJECTIVE (*+er*)

a generally klar; *complexion* rein; *conscience* rein, gut *attr*; *photograph* scharf; **on a clear day** bei klarem Wetter

b = obvious klar; **to be clear to sb** jdm klar sein; **it's still not clear to me why** es ist mir immer noch nicht klar, warum, ich bin immer noch im Unklaren (darüber), warum; **a clear case of murder** ein klarer *or* eindeutiger Fall von Mord; **to have a clear advantage** eindeutig *or* klar im Vorteil sein; **you weren't very clear** du hast dich nicht sehr klar ausgedrückt; **is that clear?** alles klar?; **let's get this clear, I'm the boss** eins wollen wir mal klarstellen, ich bin hier der Chef; **as clear as mud** (*inf*) klar wie Kloßbrühe (*inf*)

♦ **to make + clear to make oneself** *or* **one's meaning clear** sich klar ausdrücken; **do I make myself clear?** habe ich mich klar (genug) ausgedrückt?; **to make it clear to sb that ...** es jdm (unmissverständlich) klarmachen, dass ...; **to make sb clear to sb** (= *explain*) jdm etw klarmachen; **I wish to make it clear that ...** (= *state unequivocally*) ich möchte einmal ganz klar sagen, dass ...

c = sure **to be clear on** *or* **about sth** (sich *dat*) über etw (*acc*) im Klaren sein; **if you're not clear about something, ask me** falls Ihnen etwas unklar ist *or* falls Sie sich über etwas nicht im Klaren sind, fragen Sie bitte mich

d = free **to be clear of sth** frei von etw sein; **I want to keep the weekend clear** ich möchte mir das Wochenende freihalten; **we're now clear of debts** jetzt sind wir schuldenfrei *or* frei von Schulden, jetzt haben wir keine Schulden mehr; **he's clear of all suspicion** er ist frei von jedem Verdacht; **she is clear of cancer** sie hat keinen Krebs mehr

e = unobstructed *road, way* frei; **is it clear now?** (*of road*) ist jetzt frei?; **there's not an inch of clear space on his desk** auf seinem Schreibtisch ist überhaupt kein Platz

f = not touching **jack the car up until the wheel is clear** heb den Wagen an, bis das Rad nicht mehr den Boden berührt

♦ **clear of**

= away from **the bottom of the door should be about 3 mm clear of the floor** zwischen Tür und Fußboden müssen etwa 3 mm Luft sein; **park at least 20 cm clear of the pavement** parken Sie wenigstens 20 cm vom Bürgersteig entfernt; **OK, keep going, you're clear of the wall** in Ordnung, fahr, bis zur Mauer ist noch ein ganzes Stück Platz; **hold his head well clear of the water** den Kopf gut über Wasser halten; **the mortars landed well clear of us** die Mörser schlugen ein ganzes Stück neben uns ein

= beyond **the plane climbed until it was clear of the clouds** das Flugzeug stieg auf, bis es aus den Wolken heraus war; **the car was clear of the town** das Auto hatte die Stadt hinter sich gelassen; **at last we were/got clear of the prison walls** endlich hatten wir die Gefängnismauern hinter uns

g = ahead (*Brit*) **Rangers are now three points clear** Rangers liegen jetzt mit drei Punkten Vorsprung an der Spitze; **Rangers are now three points clear of Celtic** Rangers liegt jetzt drei Punkte vor Celtic

h = complete voll, vollständig; **three clear days** drei volle Tage

i = net klar; **a clear profit** ein Reingewinn *m*; **a clear majority** eine klare Mehrheit; **to have a clear lead** klar führen

2 – NOUN

♦ **in clear** in Klartext

♦ **in the clear to be in the clear** (= *free from suspicion*) frei von jedem Verdacht sein; **we're not in the clear yet** (= *not out of debt, difficulties*) wir sind noch nicht aus allem heraus; **this puts Harry in the clear** damit ist Harry entlastet

3 – ADVERB

a = distinctly **loud and clear** laut und deutlich

b = completely **he got clear away** er verschwand spurlos; **he kicked the ball clear across the field** er schoss den Ball quer über das Spielfeld

c = away **he kicked the ball clear** er klärte; **the helicopter lifted him clear** der Hubschrauber brachte ihn außer Gefahr; **he leapt clear of the burning car** er rettete sich durch einen Sprung aus dem brennenden Auto; **I'll come when I get clear of all this work** ich komme, wenn ich diese ganze Arbeit erledigt *or* hinter mir habe

♦ **to steer/keep clear to steer** *or* **keep clear of sb** jdm aus dem Wege gehen; **to steer** *or* **keep clear of sth** etw meiden; **to steer** *or* **keep clear of a place** um einen Ort einen großen Bogen machen; **you'd better steer** *or* **keep clear of that pub** um die Kneipe würde ich lieber einen großen Bogen machen; **I prefer to keep clear of town during the rush hour** während der Hauptverkehrszeit meide ich die Stadt nach Möglichkeit; **exit, keep clear** Ausfahrt freihalten!; **dangerous chemicals, keep clear** Vorsicht, giftige Chemikalien!; **keep clear of the testing area** Versuchsgebiet nicht betreten!

♦ **to stand clear** zurücktreten, zurückbleiben; **stand clear of the doors!** bitte von den Türen zurücktreten!

4 – TRANSITIVE VERB

a = remove obstacles from *pipe* reinigen; *blockage* beseitigen; *land, road, railway line* räumen; (*Comput*) *screen* löschen; *one's conscience* erleichtern; **to clear the table** den Tisch abräumen; **to clear the decks (for action)** (*fig*) alles startklar machen; **to clear a space for sth** für etw Platz schaffen; **to clear the way for sb/sth** den Weg für jdn/etw frei machen; **to clear the streets of beggars** die Bettler von den Straßen vertreiben; **to clear a way through the crowd** sich (*dat*) einen Weg durch die Menge bahnen; **to clear a room** (*of people*) ein Zimmer räumen; (*of things*) ein Zimmer ausräumen; **her singing cleared the room in no time** ihr Gesang ließ die Leute fluchtartig den Raum verlassen; **to clear the court** den Gerichtssaal räumen lassen; **to clear the ground for further talks** den Boden für weitere Gespräche bereiten

b = clear away *snow, rubbish* räumen; **he cleared all the rubbish off his desk, he cleared his desk of all the rubbish** er räumte den ganzen Kram von seinem Schreibtisch

c letterbox leeren

d = free from guilt (*Jur*) (= *find innocent*) *person* freisprechen; *one's/sb's name* rein waschen; **that clears him** das beweist seine Unschuld; **he will easily clear himself** er wird seine Unschuld leicht beweisen können

e = get past or over **he cleared the bar easily** er übersprang die Latte mit Leichtigkeit; **the horse cleared the gate easily** das Pferd nahm das Gatter mit Leichtigkeit; **the door should clear the floor by 3 mm** zwischen Tür und Fußboden müssen 3 mm Luft sein; **raise the car till the wheel clears the ground** das Auto anheben, bis das Rad den Boden nicht mehr berührt; **the ship's keel only just cleared the reef** der Kiel des Schiffes kam an dem Riff nur um Haaresbreite vorbei

f = purify *blood* reinigen; **to clear one's head** (wieder) einen klaren Kopf bekommen

g Ftbl etc (*Brit*) **to clear the ball** klären

h = make profit of machen, rausholen (*inf*); **I didn't even clear my expenses** ich habe nicht einmal meine Ausgaben wieder hereinbekommen

i debt begleichen, zurückzahlen

j stock räumen; **"half price, to clear"** „Restposten zum halben Preis"

k = approve abfertigen; *ship* klarieren; *expenses, appointment* bestätigen; *goods* zollamtlich abfertigen; **to clear a cheque** *or* (*US*) **check** bestätigen, dass ein Scheck gedeckt ist; **you'll have to clear that with management** Sie müssen das mit der Firmenleitung regeln *or* abklären; **cleared by security** von den Sicherheitsbehörden für unbedenklich erklärt; **to clear a plane for take-off** einem Flugzeug die Starterlaubnis erteilen, ein Flugzeug zum Start freigeben

5 – INTRANSITIVE VERB

(*weather*) aufklaren, schön werden; (*mist, smoke*) sich auflösen; (*crystal ball*) sich klären

6 – PHRASAL VERBS

▶ **clear away** VT sep wegräumen VI **a** (*mist etc*) sich auflösen, sich legen **b** (= *clear away the dishes*) den Tisch abräumen

▶ **clear off** VT sep *debts* begleichen, zurückzahlen; *mortgage* abzahlen, abtragen; *arrears of work* aufarbeiten VI (*Brit inf*) abhauen (*inf*), verschwinden (*inf*)

▶ **clear out** VT sep *cupboard, room, unwanted objects* ausräumen; **he cleared everyone out of the room** er schickte alle aus dem Zimmer VI (*inf*) **a** (= *leave*) verschwinden (*inf*) **b** (= *leave home etc*) ausziehen, sich absetzen (*inf*)

▶ **clear up** VT sep **a** *point, matter* klären; *mystery, crime* aufklären, aufdecken; *doubts* beseitigen **b** (= *tidy*) aufräumen; *litter* wegräumen VI **a** (*weather*) (sich) aufklären; (*rain*) aufhören **b** (= *tidy up*) aufräumen

---

clearance ['klɪərəns] N **a** (= *act of clearing*) Entfernen *nt*, Beseitigung *f* → *also* **slum clearance** **b** (= *free space*) Spielraum *m*; (= *headroom*) lichte Höhe **c** (*Ftbl etc*) **it was a good ~ by the defender** der Verteidiger hat gut geklärt **d** (*of cheque*) Bestätigung *f* der Deckung **e** (*by customs*) Abfertigung *f*; (*by security*) Unbedenklichkeitserklärung *f*; (= *document*) Unbedenklichkeitsbescheinigung *f*; **get your security**

~ first Sie müssen erst noch von den Sicherheitsorganen für unbedenklich erklärt werden; **the despatch was sent to the Foreign Office for ~** der Bericht wurde zur Überprüfung ans Außenministerium geschickt; **~ to land** Landeerlaubnis f; **~ for takeoff** Startfreigabe f **f** (Naut) Klarierung f; **~ outwards** Ausklarierung f; **~ inwards** Einklarierung f

clearance: clearance certificate N (Naut) Verzollungspapiere pl; **clearance sale** N (Comm) Räumungsverkauf m

clear-cut ['klɪə'kʌt] ADJ **a** decision, distinction, answer, policy, victory klar; issue, problem klar umrissen **b** features scharf

clear-headed ['klɪə'hedɪd] ADJ person, decision besonnen

clearing ['klɪərɪŋ] N (in forest) Lichtung f

clearing: clearing bank N (Brit) Clearingbank f; **clearing house** N Clearingstelle f

clearly ['klɪəlɪ] ✪ 15.1 ADV **a** (= distinctly) klar; **~ visible** klar or gut zu sehen; **to stand out ~ from the rest** sich deutlich vom Übrigen hervorheben or abheben **b** (= obviously) eindeutig; **is that so? – ~** ist das der Fall? – natürlich or selbstverständlich; **~ we cannot allow …** wir können keinesfalls zulassen …; **this ~ can't be true** das muss eindeutig falsch sein, das kann auf keinen Fall stimmen

clearness ['klɪənɪs] N **a** (of water, soup, sky, head, eyes, weather etc) Klarheit f; (of complexion, conscience) Reinheit f; (of colour) Kräftigkeit f; (of photograph) Schärfe f **b** (of sound) Klarheit f **c** (to one's understanding: = distinctness, obviousness) Klarheit f

clear: clear round N (Showjumping) Null-Fehler-Ritt m; **to do a ~** den Parcours fehlerfrei durchreiten; **clear-sighted** ADJ (fig) klar- or scharfsichtig; **clear-sightedness** N (fig) Klar- or Scharfsicht f; **clear-up rate** N (Police) Aufklärungsrate f; **clearway** f (Brit) Straße f mit Halteverbot, Schnellstraße f

cleat [kliːt] N (on shoes) Stoßplatte f; (made of metal) Absatzeisen nt; (on gangplank etc) Querleiste f; (for rope) Klampe f

cleavage ['kliːvɪdʒ] N **a** (= split) Spalte f, Kluft f (geh), (fig) Spaltung f, Kluft f **b** (of woman's breasts) Dekolletee nt, Dekolleté nt

cleave¹ [kliːv] pret **clove** or **cleft** or **cleaved**, ptp **cleft** or **cloven** VT spalten; **to ~ in two** in zwei Teile spalten; **to ~ a way through sth** sich (dat) einen Weg durch etw bahnen VI **a** **to ~ through the waves** die Wellen durchschneiden **b** (Biol) sich spalten

cleave² VI pret **cleaved** or **clave**, ptp **cleaved** (= adhere) festhalten (to an +dat), beharren (to auf +dat); **through all the difficulties they ~d fast to each other** (liter) durch alle Schwierigkeiten hindurch hielten sie fest zusammen

cleaver ['kliːvə'] N Hackbeil nt

clef [klef] N (Noten)schlüssel m

cleft [kleft] pret, ptp of **cleave ¹** ADJ gespalten; **a ~ chin** ein Kinn nt mit Grübchen; **to be in a ~ stick** in der Klemme sitzen (inf) N Spalte f, Kluft f (geh), (in chin) Grübchen nt; (fig) Spaltung f, Kluft f

cleft: cleft lip N Hasenscharte f; **cleft palate** N Gaumenspalte f, Wolfsrachen m

clematis ['klemətɪs] N Waldrebe f, Klematis f

clemency ['klemənsɪ] N Milde f (towards sb jdm gegenüber); **the prisoner was shown ~** dem Gefangenen wurde eine milde Behandlung zuteil

clement ['klemənt] ADJ mild (towards sb jdm gegenüber)

clementine ['kleməntaɪn] N (= fruit) Klementine f

clench [klentʃ] VT **a** fist ballen; teeth zusammenbeißen; (= grasp firmly) packen; **to ~ sth between one's teeth** etw zwischen die Zähne klemmen; **to ~ sth in one's hands** etw mit den Händen umklammern; **~ed-fist salute** Arbeiterkampfgruß m **b** → **clinch VT a**

Cleopatra [ˌkliːə'pætrə] N Kleopatra f

clerestory ['klɪəstɔːrɪ] N (Archit) Lichtgaden m

clergy ['klɜːdʒɪ] PL Klerus m, Geistlichkeit f, die Geistlichen pl; **to join the ~** Geistlicher werden

clergyman ['klɜːdʒɪmən] N pl **-men** [-mən] Geistliche(r) m, Pastor m, Pfarrer m

clergywoman ['klɜːdʒɪˌwʊmən] N pl **-women** [-wɪmɪn] N Geistliche f, Pastorin f, Pfarrerin f

cleric ['klerɪk] N Geistliche(r) m

clerical ['klerɪkəl] ADJ **a** **~ work/job** Schreib- or Büroarbeit f; **~ worker** Schreib- or Bürokraft f; **~ staff** Schreibkräfte pl, Büropersonal nt; **~ error** Versehen nt; (in figures, wording etc) Schreibfehler m; **~ duties** Büroarbeiten pl; **~ inaccuracies** Versehen nt, Nachlässigkeit f; **the ~ branch of the civil service** ≈ die mittlere Beamtenlaufbahn **b** (Eccl) geistlich

clerical collar N Stehkragen m (des Geistlichen), Priesterkragen m

clericalism ['klerɪkəlɪzəm] N Klerikalismus m

clerihew ['klerɪhjuː] N Clerihew nt, witziger Vierzeiler

clerk [klɑːk, (US) klɜːrk] N **a** (Büro)angestellte(r) mf **b** (= secretary) Schriftführer(in) m(f); **Clerk of the Court** (Brit Jur) Protokollführer(in) m(f); **~ of works** (Brit) Bauleiter(in) m(f) **c** (US, = shop assistant) Verkäufer(in) m(f) **d** (US, in hotel) Hotelsekretär(in) m(f)

clever ['klevə'] ADJ **a** (= mentally bright) schlau; animal also klug; **to be ~ at French** gut in Französisch sein; **how ~ of you to remember my birthday!** wie aufmerksam von dir, dass du an meinen Geburtstag gedacht hast! **b** (= ingenious, skilful, witty) klug; person, move in chess also geschickt; idea also schlau; device, machine raffiniert, geschickt; **to be ~ at sth** in etw (dat) geschickt sein; **he is ~ at raising money** er ist geschickt, wenn es darum geht, Geld aufzubringen; **to be ~ with one's hands** geschickte Hände haben **c** (= cunning, smart) schlau, clever (inf)

clever-clever ['klevə'klevə'] ADJ (inf) ausgeklügelt; person oberschlau (inf)

clever clogs ['klevə'klɒgz] N (inf) Schlauberger m (inf)

clever Dick N (Brit inf) Schlaumeier m (inf), Schlaukopf m (inf)

cleverly ['klevəlɪ] ADV geschickt; (= wittily) schlau, klug; **he very ~ remembered it** schlau wie er war, hat er es nicht vergessen

cleverness ['klevənɪs] N **a** (= intelligence) Schlauheit f; (of animal also) Klugheit f **b** (= skill, ingenuity) Klugheit f; (of person, move in chess also) Geschicktheit f; (of idea) Schlauheit f; (of device, machine) Raffiniertheit f **c** (= cunning) Schläue pl, Cleverness f

clew [kluː] N **a** (of thread) Knäuel nt **b** (Naut, of sail) Schothorn nt; (of hammock) Schlaufe f **c** **= clue** VT **a** thread aufwickeln **b** (Naut) **to ~ (up)** aufgeien

cliché ['kliːʃeɪ] N Klischee nt; **~-ridden** voller Klischees

clichéd ['kliːʃeɪd] ADJ klischeehaft

click¹ [klɪk] N **a** Klicken nt; (of joints) Knacken nt; (of light switch) Knipsen nt; (of fingers) Knipsen nt, Schnipsen nt; (of latch, key in lock) Schnappen nt; (tongue, Phon) Schnalzen nt; **he turned with a sharp ~ of his heels** er drehte sich um und klappte zackig die Hacken zusammen VI **a** (= make clicking noise) klicken; (joints) knacken; (light switch) knipsen; (fingers) knipsen, schnipsen; (latch, key in lock) schnappen; (tongue, Phon) schnalzen; (high heels) klappern **b** (inf, = be understood) funken (inf); **suddenly it all ~ed (into place)** plötzlich hatte es gefunkt (inf) **c** (inf, = get on well) funken (inf); **they ~ed right from the moment they first met** zwischen ihnen hatte es vom ersten Augenblick an gefunkt (inf); **some people you ~ with straight away** mit manchen Leuten versteht man sich auf Anhieb

d (inf, = catch on) ankommen (inf) (with bei) VT **heels** zusammenklappen; fingers schnippen mit; tongue schnalzen mit; **to ~ a door shut** eine Tür zuklinken; **to ~ sth into place** etw einschnappen lassen

▶ **click on** VI **a** (inf, = understand) es schnallen (inf); **he just didn't click on** er hat es einfach nicht geschnallt (inf) **b** (Comput) **to click on the mouse** mit der Maus klicken; **to click on an icon** ein Icon anklicken

click² N usu pl (US inf) Kilometer m

clickable ['klɪkəbl] ADJ (Comput) icon, image anklickbar

clicker ['klɪkə'] N (US inf: = remote control) Fernbedienung f

client ['klaɪənt] N **a** Kunde m, Kundin f; (of solicitor) Klient(in) m(f); (of barrister) Mandant(in) m(f) **b** (US, receiving welfare) Bezieher(in) m(f)

clientele [ˌkliːɒn'tel] N Kundschaft f, Klientel f; **the regular ~** die Stammkundschaft

client state N (Pol) Satellitenstaat m

cliff [klɪf] N Klippe f; (along coast also) Kliff nt; (inland also) Felsen m; **the ~s of Cornwall** die Kliffküste Cornwalls; **the ~s of Dover** die Felsen von Dover

cliff: cliff dweller N vorgeschichtlicher Höhlenbewohner im Colorado-Cañon; **cliffhanger** N Superthriller m (inf); **cliffhanging** ADJ conclusion spannungsgeladen; **clifftop** N Felskuppe f; **a house on a ~** ein Haus oben auf einem Felsen ADJ **~ walk** Spaziergang m auf der Felskuppe; **~ scenery** Felsenlandschaft f

climacteric [klaɪ'mæktərɪk] N (Med) Klimakterium nt; (fig) (Lebens)wende f, Wendepunkt m (im Leben)

climactic [klaɪ'mæktɪk] ADJ **the conclusion was ~ in the extreme** der Schluss war ein absoluter Höhepunkt; **a ~ scene** ein Höhepunkt

climate ['klaɪmɪt] N (lit, fig) Klima nt; **the two countries have very different ~s** die beiden Länder haben (ein) sehr unterschiedliches Klima; **America has many different ~s** Amerika hat viele verschiedene Klimazonen; **to move to a warmer ~** in eine wärmere Gegend or in eine Gegend mit wärmerem Klima ziehen; **the ~ of public opinion** die Stimmung in der Öffentlichkeit, das öffentliche Klima

climatic [klaɪ'mætɪk] ADJ klimatisch, Klima-

climatologist [ˌklaɪmə'tɒlədʒɪst] N Klimaforscher(in) m(f)

climatology [ˌklaɪmə'tɒlədʒɪ] N Klimatologie f, Klimakunde f

climax ['klaɪmæks] N (all senses) Höhepunkt m; (sexual also) Orgasmus m; **this brought matters to a ~** damit erreichte die Angelegenheit ihren Höhepunkt

climb [klaɪm] VT **a** (also **climb up**) klettern auf (+acc); wall also, hill steigen auf (+acc); mountains also besteigen; ladder, steps hoch- or hinaufsteigen; pole, cliffs hochklettern; **my car can't ~ that hill** mein Auto schafft den Berg nicht or kommt den Berg nicht hoch; **to ~ a rope** an einem Seil hochklettern **b** (also **climb over**) wall etc steigen or klettern über (+acc) VI klettern; (as mountaineer) bergsteigen; (into train, car etc) steigen; (road) ansteigen; (aircraft) (auf)steigen; (sun) steigen; (prices) steigen, klettern (inf); **when the sun had ~ed to its highest point** als die Sonne am höchsten stand; **he ~ed to the top of his profession** er hat den Gipfel seiner beruflichen Laufbahn erklommen N **a** (= climbing) **we're going out for a ~** wir machen eine Kletter- or Bergtour; (as mountaineers) wir gehen bergsteigen; **that was some ~!** das war eine Kletterei!; **Ben Lomond is an easy ~** Ben Lomond ist leicht zu besteigen; **I've never done that ~** den habe ich noch nicht bestiegen **b** (of aircraft) Steigflug m; **the plane went into a steep ~** das Flugzeug zog steil nach oben

▶ **climb down** VI **a** (*person, from tree, wall*) herunterklettern; (*from horse, mountain*) absteigen; (*from ladder*) heruntersteigen; (*road*) abfallen **b** (= *admit error*) nachgeben; **it'll be a pleasure to make him climb down** es wird ein Vergnügen sein, ihn von seinem hohen Ross herunterzuholen VI +*prep obj tree, wall* herunterklettern von; *ladder* heruntersteigen; *mountain etc* absteigen

▶ **climb in** VI einsteigen; (*with difficulty also*) hineinklettern

▶ **climb up** VI = **climb** VI VI +*prep obj ladder etc* hinaufsteigen; *tree, wall* hochklettern

climbable ['klaɪməbl] ADJ besteigbar

climb-down ['klaɪmdaʊn] N (*fig*) Abstieg *m*; **it was quite a ~ for the boss to have to admit that he was wrong** der Chef musste ziemlich zurückstecken und zugeben, dass er Unrecht hatte

climber ['klaɪmə'] N **a** (= *mountaineer*) Bergsteiger(in) *m(f)*; (= *rock climber*) Kletterer(in) *m(f)* **b** (= *social climber*) sozialer Aufsteiger, soziale Aufsteigerin **c** (= *plant*) Kletterpflanze *f*

climbing ['klaɪmɪŋ] ADJ **a** Berg(steiger)-; (= *rock climbing*) Kletter-; *accident, partner* beim Bergsteigen; **we are going on a ~ holiday** wir gehen im Urlaub zum Bergsteigen/Klettern; **~ club** Bergsteiger-/Kletterklub *m*; **~ speed** (*Aviat*) Steiggeschwindigkeit *f* **b** *plant* Kletter- **N a** Bergsteigen *nt*; (= *rock climbing*) Klettern *nt*; **to go ~** bergsteigen/klettern gehen, zum Bergsteigen/Klettern gehen; **we did a lot of ~** wir sind viel geklettert **b** (*pej: also* **social climbing**) sozialer Aufstieg

climbing: climbing frame N Klettergerüst *nt*; **climbing irons** ['klaɪmɪŋˌaɪənz] PL Steigeisen *pl*; **climbing plant** N Kletter- *or* Schlingpflanze *f*; **climbing wall** N Kletterwand *f*

clime [klaɪm] N (*old, liter*) Himmelsstrich (*old, liter*), Landstrich (*geh*) *m*; **in these ~s** in diesen Breiten; **he moved to warmer ~s** er zog in wärmere Breiten

clinch [klɪntʃ] VT **a** (*Tech: also* **clench**) *nail* krumm schlagen **b** *argument* zum Abschluss bringen; **to ~ the deal** den Handel perfekt machen, den Handel besiegeln; **that ~es it** damit ist der Fall erledigt VI (*Boxing*) in den Clinch gehen, clinchen **N** (*Boxing, fig*) Clinch *m*; **in a ~** im Clinch (*inf*)

clincher ['klɪntʃə'] N (*inf*) ausschlaggebendes Argument; **that was the ~** das gab den Ausschlag

cling¹ [klɪŋ] *pret, ptp* **clung** VI **a** (= *hold on tightly*) sich festklammern (*to* an +*dat*), sich klammern (*to* an +*acc*); (*to opinion also*) festhalten (*to* an +*dat*); (= *remain close*) sich halten (*to* an +*acc*); (*clothes, fabric*) sich anschmiegen (*to* +*dat*); (*smell*) haften (*to* an +*dat*), sich setzen (*to* in +*acc*); **~ on tight!** halt dich gut fest!; **to ~ together** sich aneinander klammern; (*lovers*) sich umschlingen, sich umschlungen halten; **in spite of all the difficulties they've clung together** trotz aller Schwierigkeiten haben sie zusammengehalten; **she clung around her father's neck** sie hing ihrem Vater am Hals; **the boat clung to the shoreline** das Schiff hielt sich dicht an die Küste; **women who ~** Frauen, die sich an einen klammern

cling² **N** Klingen *nt*; (*of cash register*) Klingeln *nt* VI klingen; (*cash register*) klingeln

clingfilm ['klɪŋfɪlm] N Frischhaltefolie *f*

clinging ['klɪŋɪŋ] ADJ *garment* sich anschmiegend; *smell* lange haftend, hartnäckig; **she's the ~ sort** sie ist wie eine Klette (*inf*)

clinging vine N (*inf*) Klette *f* (*inf*)

cling(stone) peach ['klɪŋ(stəʊn)'piːtʃ] N Klingstone *m* (*nicht steinlösende Pfirsichsorte*)

clingy ['klɪŋɪ] ADJ (+*er*) *person* anhänglich; *thing* haftend

clinic ['klɪnɪk] N **a** Klinik *f* **b** (= *medical course*) klinischer Unterricht, Klinik *f*

clinical ['klɪnɪkəl] ADJ **a** (*Med*) klinisch; **~ tests** *or* **trials** klinische Tests *pl* **b** (*fig*: = *sterile*)

room, atmosphere steril, kalt; (= *detached, dispassionate*) klinisch, nüchtern; *sb's appearance* streng

clinical depression N klinische Depression

clinically ['klɪnɪkəlɪ] ADV *dead, test, prove, observe* klinisch; *insane, obese* krankhaft; **~ depressed** klinisch depressiv

clinical thermometer N Fieberthermometer *nt*

clink¹ [klɪŋk] VT klirren lassen; (= *jingle*) klimpern mit; **she ~ed a coin against the window** sie schlug mit einer Münze gegen die Scheibe, dass es klirrte; **to ~ glasses with sb** mit jdm anstoßen VI klirren; (= *jingle*) klimpern; **the spoon ~ed against the glass** der Löffel stieß klirrend an das Glas **N** *no pl* Klirren *nt*, Klimpern *nt*; **the ~ of glasses as they drank to his health** das Klingen der Gläser, als auf sein Wohl getrunken wurde

clink² N (*inf*: = *prison*) Knast *m* (*inf*); **in ~** im Knast

clinker ['klɪŋkə'] N **a** (*from fire*) Schlacke *f*; **a ~** ein Stück Schlacke **b** (= *brick*) Klinker *m*

clinker-built ['klɪŋkəbɪlt] ADJ (*Naut*) klinkergebaut

clip¹ [klɪp] **N a** (*for holding things*) Klammer *f* **b** (= *jewel*) Klips *m* **c** (*of gun*) Ladestreifen *m* VT **to ~ on** anklemmen; *papers also* anheften; **to ~ sth onto sth** etw an etw (*acc*) anklemmen/-heften; **to ~ two things together** zwei Dinge zusammenklemmen/-heften VI **to ~ on (to sth)** (an etw *acc*) angeklemmt werden; **to ~ together** zusammengeklemmt werden

clip² VT **a** (= *trim*) scheren; *dog also* trimmen; *hedge also, fingernails* schneiden; *wings* stutzen; **to ~ sb's wings** (*fig*) jdm einen Dämpfer aufsetzen; **they'll find that a young baby will ~ their wings a bit** sie werden merken, dass das Kleinkind sie recht unbeweglich macht **b** (*also* **clip out**) *article from paper* ausschneiden; (*also* **clip off**) *hair* abschneiden; **he ~ped a few seconds off the lap record** er hat ein paar Sekunden um Rundenrekord unterboten **c** (*Brit*) *ticket* lochen, knipsen, entwerten **d** **to ~ (the ends of) one's words** abgehackt sprechen **e** (= *hit*) treffen; (= *graze: car, bullet*) streifen; **he ~ped him round the ear** er gab ihm eine Ohrfeige; **the left jab just ~ped his chin** die linke Gerade streifte sein Kinn **N a** (= *hit*) **to give the sheep a ~** die Schafe scheren; **to give the hedge a ~** die Hecke scheren *or* (be-) schneiden; **to give one's fingernails a ~** sich (*dat*) die Fingernägel schneiden **b** (= *sound*) Klappern *nt* **c** (= *hit*) Schlag *m*; **he gave him a ~ round the ear** er gab ihm eins hinter die Ohren (*inf*) **d** (*inf*: = *high speed*) **at a fair ~** mit einem Mordszahn (*inf*); **he made off at a fair ~** er legte ganz schön los (*inf*) **e** (*from film*) Ausschnitt *m*, Clip *m*

clip: clip art N (*Comput*) Clip-Art *f*; **clipboard** **N a** (= *board*) Klemmbrett *nt*, Manuskripthalter *m* **b** (*Comput*) Zwischenablage *f*; **clip-clop** N **the ~ of hooves** das Getrappel der Hufe; **clip frame** N Wechselrahmen *m*; **clip joint** N (*sl*) Nepplokal *nt* (*inf*); **clip-on** ADJ *brooch* mit Klips; *tie* zum Anstecken; **~ earrings** Klips *pl*; **~ sunglasses** Sonnenklip *m*, Sonnenvorstecker *m*

clipped [klɪpt] ADJ *accent* abgehackt; **~ form** Kurzform *f*

clipper ['klɪpə'] N (*Naut*) Klipper *m*; (*Aviat*) Clipper *m*

clippers ['klɪpəz] PL (*also* **pair of clippers**) Schere *f*; (*for hedge also*) Heckenschere *f*; (*for hair*) Haarschneidemaschine *f*; (*for fingernails*) Zwicker *m*, Nagelzange *f*

clippie ['klɪpɪ] N (*Brit, inf*) Schaffnerin *f*

clipping ['klɪpɪŋ] N (= *newspaper clipping*) Ausschnitt *m*; **nail ~s** abgeschnittene Nägel *pl*

clique [kliːk] N Clique *f*, Klüngel *m* (*inf*)

cliquish ['kliːkɪʃ] ADJ cliquenhaft, klüngelhaft (*inf*)

cliquishness ['kliːkɪʃnɪs] N Cliquenwirtschaft *f*, Klüngel *m* (*inf*)

clitoris ['klɪtərɪs] N Klitoris *f*, Kitzler *m*

Cllr (*Brit*) *abbr of* **Councillor**

cloak [kləʊk] **N** (*lit*) Umhang *m*; (*fig*, = *disguise*) Deckmantel *m*; (= *veil: of secrecy etc*) Schleier *m*; **under the ~ of darkness** im Schutz der Dunkelheit VT (*fig*) verhüllen; **fog ~ed the town** die Stadt war in Nebel gehüllt

cloak: cloak-and-dagger ADJ mysteriös, geheimnisumwittert; **~ play** Kriminalstück *nt*; **a ~ operation** eine Nacht-und-Nebel-Aktion; **cloakroom** N **a** (*Brit: for coats*) Garderobe *f* **b** (*Brit, euph*) Waschraum *m* (*euph*)

clobber ['klɒbə'] (*inf*) **N** (*Brit: = belongings*) Zeug *nt* (*inf*); (= *clothes*) Klamotten *pl* (*inf*) VT **a** (= *hit, defeat*) **to get ~ed** eins übergebraten kriegen (*inf*); **to ~ sb one** jdm ein paar vor den Latz knallen (*inf*) **b** (= *charge a lot*) schröpfen; **the taxman really ~ed me** das Finanzamt hat mir ganz schön was abgeknöpft (*inf*)

clobbering ['klɒbərɪŋ] N (*inf*: = *beating, defeat*) Tracht *f* Prügel (*inf*), Dresche *f* (*inf*); **to get a ~** Dresche (*inf*) oder eine Tracht Prügel (*inf*) beziehen; (*fig: from the taxman*) ganz schön geschröpft werden *or* was abgeknöpft kriegen (*inf*)

cloche [klɒʃ] N **a** (= *hat*) Topfhut *m* **b** (*for plants*) Folien-/Glasschutz *m*

cloche tunnel N Folientunnel *m*

clock [klɒk] **N a** Uhr *f*; **round the ~** rund um die Uhr; **against the ~** (*Sport*) nach *or* auf Zeit; **to work against the ~** gegen die Uhr arbeiten; **to beat the ~** schneller als vorgesehen fertig sein; **to put the ~ back/forward** *or* **on** (*lit*) die Uhr zurückstellen/vorstellen; **to put** *or* **turn the ~ back** (*fig*) die Zeit zurückdrehen; **to watch the ~** (*inf*) dauernd auf die Uhr sehen **b** (*inf*, = *speedometer, milometer*) Tacho *m* (*inf*); (*of taxi*) Uhr *f*; **it's got 100,000 miles on the ~** es hat einen Tachostand von 100.000 Meilen VT **a** (*Sport*) **he clocked four minutes for the mile** er lief die Meile in vier Minuten; **he's ~ed the fastest time this year** er ist die schnellste Zeit dieses Jahres gelaufen/gefahren **b** (*inf*: = *hit*) **to ~ed him one** er hat ihm eine runtergehauen (*inf*) **c** (*Brit inf*: = *see*) sehen **d** (*Brit inf*) *mileage* **to ~ back** (*in betrügerischer Absicht*) den Meilenzähler zurückdrehen

▶ **clock in** VI (*Sport*) **he clocked in at 3 minutes 56 seconds** seine Zeit war 3 Minuten 56 Sekunden

▶ **clock in** *or* **on** VI (*den Arbeitsbeginn*) stempeln *or* stechen VT *sep* **to clock sb on** für jdn stempeln *or* stechen

▶ **clock off** *or* **out** VI (*das Arbeitsende*) stempeln *or* stechen VT *sep* **to clock sb out** für jdn stempeln *or* stechen

▶ **clock up** VT *sep* **a** (*athlete, competitor*) *time* laufen/fahren/schwimmen etc **b** *speed, distance* fahren **c** (*inf*) *success* verbuchen; **that's another successful deal to clock up to Jim** noch ein erfolgreiches Geschäft, das Jim für sich verbuchen kann; **to clock up overtime** Überstunden machen

clock *in cpds* Uhr(en)-; **clock card** N Stechkarte *f*; **clock face** N Zifferblatt *nt*; **clock golf** N Uhrengolf *nt*; **clock hour** N volle Stunde; **clockmaker** N Uhrmacher(in) *m(f)*; **clock radio** N Radiouhr *f*; **clock tower** N Uhrenturm *m*; **clock-watcher** N **she's a terrible ~** sie sieht *or* guckt dauernd auf die Uhr; **clock-watching** N Auf-die-Uhr-Schauen *nt*; **clockwise** ADJ, ADV im Uhrzeigersinn; **in a ~ direction** im Uhrzeigersinn; **clockwork** **N** (*of clock*) Uhrwerk *nt*; (*of toy*) Aufziehmechanismus *m*; **driven by ~** zum Aufziehen; **like ~** wie am Schnürchen ATTR *a train, car* aufziehbar, zum Aufziehen **b** **~ precision** äußerste Genauigkeit; **with ~ regularity** mit der Regelmäßigkeit eines Uhrwerks; **he arrives every day at 9.30**

with ~ **regularity** er kommt jeden Tag pünktlich auf die Minute um 9.30 Uhr

clod [klɒd] N **a** (*of earth*) Klumpen *m* **b** (*fig:* = *person, also* **clodpole**) Trottel *m*; **this silly great** ~ dieser Obertrottel (*inf*)

clodhopper ['klɒd,hɒpə'] N (*inf*) **a** (= *person*) Trampel *m* (*inf*), Tollpatsch *m* **b** (= *shoe*) Quadratlatschen *m* (*inf*)

clodhopping ['klɒd,hɒpɪŋ] ADJ (*inf*) *person* trampelig (*inf*), tölpelhaft, schwerfällig; ~ **shoes/boots** klobige Schuhe *pl*/Stiefel *pl*

clog [klɒg] N (= *shoe*) Holzschuh *m*; ~**s** *pl* (*modern*) Clogs *pl*; ~ **dance** Holzschuhtanz *m*; **to pop one's** ~**s** (*Brit inf*) den Löffel abgeben (*inf*) VT (*also* **clog up**) *pipe, drain etc* verstopfen; *mechanism, wheels* blockieren; ~**ged with traffic** verstopft VI (*also* **clog up**, *pipe etc*) verstopfen; (*mechanism etc*) blockiert werden

cloggy ['klɒgɪ] ADJ (*inf*) klumpig

cloister ['klɔɪstə'] N **a** (= *covered walk*) Kreuzgang *m* **b** (= *monastery*) Kloster *nt* VR **to** ~ **oneself (away)** sich von der Welt abkapseln

cloistered ['klɔɪstəd] ADJ **a** (*fig*) weltabgeschieden; *way of thinking* weltfremd *or* -fern (*liter*); **to lead a** ~ **life** (= *isolated*) in klösterlicher Abgeschiedenheit leben; (= *sheltered*) ein streng *or* klösterlich behütetes Leben führen **b** (*Archit*) **a** ~ **courtyard** ein Klosterhof *m* mit Kreuzgang

clone [kləʊn] N (*also Comput, fig:* = *person*) Klon *m* VT klonen

clonk [klɒŋk] (*inf*) VT hauen N (= *blow*) Schlag *m*; (= *sound*) Plumps *m*

close¹ [kləʊs] ADJ (+*er*) **a** (= *near*) nahe (*to* +*gen*), in der Nähe (*to* +*gen*, *von*); **is Glasgow** ~ **to Edinburgh?** liegt Glasgow in der Nähe von Edinburgh?; **the buildings which are** ~ **to the station** die Gebäude in der Nähe des Bahnhofs *or* in Bahnhofsnähe; **in** ~ **proximity** in unmittelbarer Nähe (*to* +*gen*); **in such** ~ **proximity (to one another)** so dicht zusammen; **you're very** ~ (*in guessing etc*) du bist ganz dran; ~ **combat** Nahkampf *m*; **at** ~ **quarters** aus unmittelbarer Nähe; **he chose the** ~**st cake** er nahm den Kuchen, der am nächsten lag; **we use this pub because it's** ~/**the** ~**st** wir gehen in dieses Lokal, weil es in der Nähe/am nächsten ist **b** (*in time*) nahe (bevorstehend); **nobody realized how** ~ **a nuclear war was** es war niemandem klar, wie nahe ein Atomkrieg bevorstand **c** (*fig*) *friend, co-operation, connection etc* eng; *relative* nahe; *resemblance* groß, stark; **they were very** ~ **(to each other)** sie waren *or* standen sich *or* einander (*geh*) sehr nahe **d** (= *not spread out*) *handwriting, print* eng; *texture, weave* dicht, fest; *grain* dicht, fein; *ranks* dicht, geschlossen; (*fig*) *argument* lückenlos, stichhaltig; *reasoning, game* geschlossen **e** (= *exact, painstaking*) *examination, study* eingehend, genau; *translation* originalgetreu; *watch* streng, scharf; *arrest* scharf; **now pay** ~ **attention to me** jetzt hör mir gut zu; **you have to pay very** ~ **attention to the traffic signs** du musst genau auf die Verkehrszeichen achten; **to keep a** ~ **lookout for sb/sth** scharf nach jdm/etw Ausschau halten **f** (= *stuffy*) schwül; (*indoors*) stickig **g** (= *almost equal*) *fight, result* knapp; **a** ~**(-fought) match** ein (ganz) knappes Spiel; **a** ~ **finish** ein Kopf-an-Kopf-Rennen *nt*; **a** ~ **election** ein Kopf-an-Kopf-Rennen *nt*, eine Wahl mit knappem Ausgang; **it was a** ~ **thing** *or* **call** das war knapp!; **the vote/election was too** ~ **to call** der Ausgang der Abstimmung/Wahl war völlig offen **h** ~ **on** nahezu; ~ **on sixty/midnight** an die sechzig/kurz vor Mitternacht ADV (+*er*) nahe; (*spatially also*) dicht; ~ **by** in der Nähe; ~ **by us** in unserer Nähe; **stay** ~ **to me** bleib dicht bei mir; ~ **to the water/ground** nahe *or* dicht am Wasser/Boden; ~ **by the bridge** nahe (bei) der Brücke; **he followed** ~ **behind me** er ging dicht hinter mir; **don't stand too** ~ **to the fire** stell dich nicht zu nahe *or*

dicht ans Feuer; **to be** ~ **to tears** den Tränen nahe sein; ~ **together** dicht *or* nahe zusammen; **my exams were so** ~ **together** meine Prüfungen lagen so kurz hintereinander; **the** ~**r the exams came the more nervous he got** je näher die Prüfung rückte, desto nervöser wurde er; **that brought the two brothers** ~**r together** das brachte die beiden Brüder einander näher; **please stand** ~**r together** bitte rücken Sie näher *or* dichter zusammen; **this pattern comes** ~/~**st to the sort of thing we wanted** dieses Muster kommt dem, was wir uns vorgestellt haben, nahe/am nächsten; **what does it look like (from)** ~ **up?** wie sieht es von nahem aus?; **if you get too** ~ **up ...** wenn du zu nahe herangehst ...

N (*in street names*) Hof *m*; (*of cathedral etc*) Domhof *m*; (*Scot:* = *outside passage*) offener Hausflur

close² [kləʊz] VT **a** (= *shut*) schließen; *eyes, door, shop, window, curtains also* zumachen; (*permanently*) *business, shop etc* schließen; *factory* stilllegen; (= *block*) *opening etc* verschließen; *road* sperren; **"closed"** „geschlossen"; **sorry, we're** ~**d** tut uns Leid, wir haben geschlossen *or* zu; **don't** ~ **your mind to new ideas** du solltest dich neuen Ideen nicht verschließen; **to** ~ **one's eyes/ears to sth** sich gegenüber blind/taub stellen; **to** ~ **ranks** (*Mil, fig*) die Reihen schließen; **to** ~ **the gap between ...** die Diskrepanz zwischen ... beseitigen **b** (= *bring to an end*) *church service, meeting* schließen, beenden; *affair, discussion also* abschließen; *bank account etc* auflösen; *sale* abschließen; **the matter is** ~**d** der Fall ist abgeschlossen **c** (*Elec*) *circuit* schließen

VI **a** (= *shut, come together*) sich schließen; (*door, window, box, lid, eyes, wound also*) zugehen; (= *can be shut*) schließen, zugehen; (*shop, factory*) schließen, zumachen; (*factory: permanently*) stillgelegt werden; **his eyes** ~**d** die Augen fielen ihm zu; (*in death*) seine Augen schlossen sich **b** (= *come to an end*) schließen; (*tourist season*) aufhören, enden, zu Ende gehen; (*Theat, play*) auslaufen **c** (= *approach*) sich nähern, näher kommen; (*boxers etc*) aufeinander losgehen; **the battleship** ~**d to within 100 metres** das Kriegsschiff kam bis auf 100 Meter heran **d** (*Comm,* = *accept offer*) abschließen, zu einem Abschluss kommen **e** (*St Ex*) schließen; **the shares** ~**d at £5** die Aktien erreichten eine Schlussnotierung von £ 5

N Ende *nt*, Schluss *m*; **to come to a** ~ enden, aufhören, zu Ende gehen; **to draw to a** ~ sich dem Ende nähern, dem Ende zugehen; **to draw** *or* **bring sth to a** ~ etw beenden; **at/towards** (*Brit*) *or* **toward** (*US*) **the** ~ **of (the) day** am/gegen Ende des Tages; **at the** ~ **(of business)** bei Geschäfts- *or* (*St Ex*) Börsenschluss

▶ **close around** VI +*prep obj* umschließen, sich schließen um; **the waters closed around the drowning man** die Wellen schlugen über dem Ertrinkenden zusammen

▶ **close down** VI **a** (*business, shop etc*) schließen, zumachen (*inf*); (*factory: permanently*) stillgelegt werden **b** (*Rad, TV*) das Programm beenden; **programmes close down at about 12** Sendeschluss (ist) gegen 24 Uhr; **we're now closing down for the night** (und) damit ist unser heutiges Programm beendet VT *sep shop etc* schließen; *factory* (*permanently*) stilllegen

▶ **close in** VI (*evening, winter*) anbrechen; (*night, darkness*) hereinbrechen; (*days*) kürzer werden; (*enemy etc*) bedrohlich nahe kommen; **the troops closed in around the enemy** die Truppen zogen sich um den Feind zusammen; **to close in on sb** (*gang, individual etc*) jdm auf den Leib rücken; **the walls were slowly closing in on him** die Wände kamen langsam auf ihn zu; **the police are closing in on him** die Polizei zieht das Netz um ihn zu; (*physically*) die Polizisten umzingeln ihn VT *sep* umgeben, umfrieden (*geh*)

▶ **close off** VT *sep* abriegeln, (ab)sperren; (= *separate off*) *area of office etc* abteilen, abtrennen

▶ **close on** VI +*prep obj* einholen

▶ **close round** VI +*prep obj* (*esp Brit*) = **close around**

▶ **close up** VI **a** (*line of people*) aufschließen, zusammenrücken; (*Mil*) aufschließen; (*wound*) (sich) schließen **b** (= *lock up*) ab- *or* zuschließen, ab- *or* zusperren VT *sep* **a** *house, shop* zumachen; *house also* verschließen; *shop also* ab- *or* zuschließen, ab- *or* zusperren **b** (= *block up*) zumachen

▶ **close with** VI +*prep obj* **a** *enemy* zum Nahkampf übergehen mit; *boxer etc* ringen *or* kämpfen mit **b** (= *strike bargain with*) handelseinig sein *or* werden mit; (= *accept*) *offer* eingehen auf

close-cropped [,kləʊs'krɒpt] ADJ *hair* kurz geschnitten

closed [kləʊzd]: **closed circuit** N geschlossener Stromkreis; **closed-circuit television** N interne Fernsehanlage; (*for supervision*) Fernsehüberwachungsanlage *f*; **closed-door** ADJ *meeting, session* hinter verschlossenen Türen

close-down ['kləʊzdaʊn] N **a** (*of shop, business etc*) (Geschäfts)schließung *f*; (*of factory*) Stilllegung *f* **b** (*Rad, TV*) Sendeschluss *m*

closed [kləʊzd]: **closed primary** N (*US Pol*) Vorwahl mit Fraktionszwang, bei der nur Mitglieder der eigenen Partei gewählt werden können; **closed scholarship** N an eine bestimmte Schule gebundenes Stipendium; **closed season** N Schonzeit *f*; **closed session** N (*Jur*) Sitzung *f* unter Ausschluss der Öffentlichkeit; **closed set** N (*Math*) abgeschlossene Menge; **closed shop** N Closedshop *m*; **we have a** ~ wir haben Gewerkschaftszwang

close [kləʊs]: **close-fisted** ADJ geizig, knauserig (*inf*); **close-fitting** ADJ eng anliegend, eng sitzend; **close-grained** ADJ fein gemasert; **close-harmony singers** PL Vokalgruppe *f* (*die im Barbershop-Stil singt*); **close-harmony singing** N Gesang *m* in geschlossener Harmonie; **close-knit** ADJ *comp* **closer-knit** *community* eng *or* fest zusammengewachsen

closely ['kləʊslɪ] ADV **a** eng, dicht; *work, connect* eng; *woven* fest; *related* nah(e), eng; *follow* (*in time*) dicht; **he was** ~ **followed by a policeman** ein Polizist ging dicht hinter ihm; **she held the baby** ~ sie drückte das Baby (fest) an sich; ~ **reasoned** schlüssig dargestellt *or* -gelegt; **the match was** ~ **contested** die Spielausgang war hart umkämpft **b** (= *attentively*) *watch, listen etc* genau; *study also* eingehend; *guard* scharf, streng; **a** ~**-guarded secret** ein streng gehütetes Geheimnis

close-mouthed [,kləʊs'maʊðd] ADJ verschwiegen

closeness ['kləʊsnɪs] N **a** (= *nearness, in time*) Nähe *f*; **she could feel his** ~ **to her** sie konnte seine Nähe fühlen **b** (*fig, of friendship*) Innigkeit *f*; **thanks to the** ~ **of their co-operation ...** dank ihrer engen Zusammenarbeit ...; **the** ~ **of their relationship/resemblance caused problems** ihre enge Beziehung/ihre große Ähnlichkeit verursachte Probleme **c** (*fig: of reasoning*) Schlüssigkeit *f*; (*Sport, of game*) Geschlossenheit *f*; **the** ~ **of the print/weave** die große Druck-/(Ge)webedichte **d** (*of examination, interrogation*) Genauigkeit *f*; (*of watch*) Strenge *f*; (*of translation*) Textnähe *f or* -treue *f* **e** **the** ~ **(of the air)** die Schwüle; (*indoors*) die stickige Luft **f** (*race etc*) knapper Ausgang; **the** ~ **of the finish** der knappe Ausgang des Rennens

close [kləʊs]: **close-run** ADJ *comp* **closer-run** *race* mit knappem Ausgang; **it was a** ~ **thing** es war eine knappe Sache; **close season** N **a** (*Ftbl*) Saisonpause *f* **b** (*Hunt, Fishing*) Schonzeit *f*; **close-set** ADJ *comp* **closer-set** *eyes* eng zusammenstehend; *print* eng; **close-shaven** ADJ glatt rasiert

closet ['klɒzɪt] vb: pret, ptp **closeted** ['klɒzɪtɪd] **N a** (US) Wandschrank m; **to come out of the ~** (fig) (man) sich als Homosexueller outen; (woman) sich als Lesbe outen **b** (dated: = water closet) Klosett nt **c** (old: = small room) Kabinett nt, Nebenzimmer nt **VT to be ~ed** hinter verschlossenen Türen sitzen (with sb mit jdm); **I ~ed myself in my study** ich habe mich in meinem Arbeitszimmer vergraben **ADJ** attr (= secret) heimlich

close-up ['kləʊsʌp] **N** Nahaufnahme f; **in ~** in Nahaufnahme; (of face) in Großaufnahme **ATTR** shot, view Nah–; lens für Nahaufnahmen

closing ['kləʊzɪŋ] **N a** (= shutting) Schließung f; (of factory: permanently) Stilllegung f **b** (St Ex) Börsenschluss m **ADJ a** remarks, words etc abschließend, Schluss–; **~ arguments** (Jur) Schlussplädoyers pl **b** (St Ex) **~ prices** Schlusskurse pl, Schlussnotierungen pl

closing: closing balance sheet N (Fin) Schlussbilanz f; **closing date N** (for competition etc) Einsendeschluss m; **closing-down sale** ['kləʊzɪŋ'daʊnseɪl] **N** (Comm) Räumungsverkauf m; **closing scene N** (Theat, TV) Schlussszene f; **closing time N** Geschäfts- or Ladenschluss m; (Brit, in pub) Polizei- or Sperrstunde f; **when is ~?** wann schließt die Bank/ das Geschäft/der Laden/das Lokal etc?

closure ['kləʊʒə'] **N a** (= act of closing) Schließung f; (of road) Sperrung f; (of wound, incision) Schließen nt; (of factory, mine etc also) Stilllegung f **b** (Parl) Schluss m der Debatte; **to move the ~** den Schluss der Debatte beantragen; **to apply the ~ to a debate** das Ende einer Debatte erklären

clot [klɒt] **N a** (of blood) (Blut)gerinnsel nt; (of milk) (Sahne)klumpen m **b** (Brit inf: = person) Trottel m **VT** blood zum Gerinnen bringen **VI** (blood) gerinnen; (milk) dick werden

cloth [klɒθ] **N a** Tuch nt, Stoff m; (as book cover) Leinen nt; **a nice piece of ~** ein schöner Stoff, ein gutes Tuch; **~ of gold** goldenes Tuch **b** (= dishcloth, tea cloth etc) Tuch nt; (for cleaning also) Lappen m; (= tablecloth) Tischdecke f, Tischtuch nt **c** no pl (Eccl) **a man of the ~** ein geistlicher Herr; **the ~** der geistliche Stand, die Geistlichkeit

cloth: clothbound ADJ book in Leinen (gebunden); **cloth cap** N Schlägermütze f

clothe [kləʊð] pret, ptp **clad** (old) or **clothed** VT **a** (usu pass: = dress) kleiden; **she appeared ~d in white** (liter) sie erschien (ganz) in Weiß **b** (= provide clothes for) anziehen **c** (fig liter) kleiden (liter); **~d in glory** mit Ruhm bedeckt; **the hills ~d in mist** die nebelverhangenen Hügel

cloth: cloth-eared ADJ (inf) doof (inf); **cloth-ears** N sing (inf) Doofmann m (inf)

clothes [kləʊðz] **PL a** (= garments) Kleider pl; (= clothing, outfit also) Kleidung f no pl; **his mother still washes his ~** seine Mutter macht ihm immer noch die Wäsche; **with one's ~ on** angezogen, (voll) bekleidet; **with one's ~ off** ausgezogen; **you can't swim properly with your ~ on** mit or in Kleidern kann man nicht richtig schwimmen; **to put on/take off one's ~** sich an-/ausziehen **b** (= bedclothes) Bettzeug nt

clothes: clothes basket N Wäschekorb m; **clothes brush** N Kleiderbürste f; **clothes drier, clothes dryer** N Wäschetrockner m; **clothes hanger** N Kleiderbügel m; **clothes horse** N Wäscheständer m; **she's a real ~** (inf) sie hat einen Kleiderfimmel (inf); **clothes line** N Wäscheleine f; **clothes moth** N Kleidermotte f; **clothes peg,** (US) **clothes pin** N Wäscheklammer f; **clothes pole, clothes prop** N Wäschestütze f; **clothes shop** N Bekleidungsgeschäft nt

clothier ['kləʊðɪə'] N (= seller of clothes, for men) Herrenausstatter m; (for women) Modegeschäft nt or -salon m

clothing ['kləʊðɪŋ] N Kleidung f

clotted ['klɒtɪd] ADJ **hair ~ with mud** mit Schlamm verklebtes Haar

clotted cream N Sahne f (aus erhitzter Milch)

clottish ['klɒtɪʃ] ADJ (inf) trottelig; **a ~ thing to do** eine Eselei

cloud [klaʊd] **N a** Wolke f; **low ~(s) delayed takeoff** tief hängende Wolken verzögerten den Start; **to have one's head in the ~s** in höheren Regionen schweben; (momentarily) geistesabwesend sein; **to be up in the ~s** (inf) überglücklich sein; **to be on ~ nine** (inf) im siebten Himmel sein or schweben (inf); **every ~ has a silver lining** (Prov) kein Unglück ist so groß, es hat sein Glück im Schoß (Prov) **b** (of smoke, dust etc) Wolke f; (of insects) Schwarm m, Haufen m; (of gas, smoke from fire) Schwaden m; **~ of dust/smoke** Staub-/Rauchwolke f; **a ~ of controversy/confusion surrounded the whole matter** die ganze Angelegenheit wurde von Kontroversen überschattet/ nebulöses Durcheinander herrschte in der ganzen Angelegenheit; **the ~ of suspicion hanging over him suddenly dispersed** der Verdacht, der über ihm schwebte, verflog plötzlich; **he's been under a ~ for weeks** (= under suspicion) seit Wochen haftet ein Verdacht an ihm; (= in disgrace) die Geschichte hängt ihm schon wochenlang nach; **the ~s are gathering** (lit, fig) es braut sich etwas zusammen **c** (in liquid, marble) Wolke f **VT** (lit) sky, view verhängen (geh); mirror trüben; **a ~ed sky** ein bewölkter Himmel **b** (fig: = cast gloom on) prospect, sb's enjoyment trüben; face, expression umwölken (geh); (= mar, spoil) friendship, sb's future überschatten; (= make less clear) mind, judgement, awareness trüben; nature of problem verschleiern; **to ~ the issue** (= complicate) es unnötig kompliziert machen; (= hide deliberately) die Angelegenheit verschleiern **VI** = **cloud over**

▶ **cloud over** VI (sky) sich bewölken, sich bedecken; (mirror etc) (sich) beschlagen, anlaufen; **his face clouded over** seine Stirn umwölkte sich (geh)

▶ **cloud up** VI (mirror etc) beschlagen; **it's clouding up** (weather) es bezieht sich **VT** sep **the steam clouded up the windows** die Fenster beschlugen (vom Dampf)

cloud: cloud bank N Wolkenwand f; **cloudburst** N Wolkenbruch m; **cloud-capped** ADJ (liter) **~ mountains/peaks** die wolkenverhangenen Berge/Gipfel; **cloud chamber** N Nebelkammer f; **cloud-cuckoo-land** N Wolkenkuckucksheim nt; **you're living in ~ if you think ...** du lebst auf dem Mond, wenn du glaubst ... (inf)

cloudiness ['klaʊdɪnɪs] **N a** (of sky) Bewölkung f **b** (of liquid, diamond, glass, plastic etc) Trübung f; (of eyes) Trübheit f **c** (of argument, position, point of view) Unklarheit f

cloudless ['klaʊdlɪs] ADJ sky wolkenlos

cloudy ['klaʊdɪ] ADJ (+er) **a** sky wolkig, bewölkt, bedeckt; weather grau; **we had only three ~ days** wir hatten nur drei Tage, an denen es bewölkt war; **it's getting ~** es bewölkt sich; **the weather will be ~** es ist mit Bewölkung zu rechnen **b** liquid, diamond, glass, eyes etc trüb **c** (= unclear) argument, position, point of view diffus, unklar

clout [klaʊt] **N a** (inf: = blow) Schlag m; **to give sb a ~** jdm eine runterhauen (inf); **to give sth a ~** auf etw (acc) schlagen or hauen (inf); **to give sb a ~ round the ears** jdm eine Ohrfeige geben (inf); **to give oneself a ~ on the knee, to give one's knee a ~** sich (dat) aufs Knie hauen (inf); (against door etc) sich (dat) das Knie (an)stoßen or anschlagen **b** (political, industrial) Schlagkraft f **VT** (inf) schlagen, hauen (inf); **to ~ sb one** jdm eine runterhauen (inf) or eins verpassen (inf)

clove[1] [kləʊv] **N a** Gewürznelke f; **oil of ~s** Nelkenöl nt **b** **~ of garlic** Knoblauchzehe f

clove[2] pret of **cleave**[1]

clove hitch N Webeleinstek m

cloven ['kləʊvn] PTP of **cleave**[1]

cloven hoof N Huf m der Paarhufer or -zeher; (of devil) Pferdefuß m; **pigs have cloven hooves** Schweine sind Paarzeher

clover ['kləʊvə'] N Klee m; **to be/live in ~** wie Gott in Frankreich leben

cloverleaf ['kləʊvəli:f] N (Bot, Mot) Kleeblatt nt

clown [klaʊn] **N a** (in circus etc) Clown m; (inf: = foolish person also) Kasper m, Hanswurst m; (pej) Idiot m, Trottel m; **to act the ~** den Clown or Hanswurst spielen, herumkaspern (inf) **VI** (also **clown about** or **around**) herumblödeln (inf) or -kaspern (inf)

clownish ['klaʊnɪʃ] ADJ albern, clownesk (geh)

cloy [klɔɪ] VI (lit, fig) zu süßlich sein/werden; (pleasures) an Reiz verlieren

cloying ['klɔɪɪŋ] ADJ (lit) übermäßig süß; **~ sentimentality** gefühlsduselige Sentimentalität

cloyingly ['klɔɪɪŋlɪ] ADV süßlich; **~ sentimental** gefühlsduselig sentimental

cloze test ['kləʊz,test] N Wortergänzungstest m, Lückentest m

club [klʌb] **N a** (= weapon) Knüppel m, Prügel m, Keule f; (= golf club) Golfschläger m; (= Indian club) Keule f **b** **clubs** PL (Cards) Kreuz nt; **the ace/nine of ~s** (das) Kreuzass/(die) Kreuzneun **c** (= society) Klub m, Verein m; (= tennis club, golf club, gentleman's club, night club) Klub m, Club m; (Ftbl) Verein m; **to be in the ~** (inf) in anderen Umständen sein (inf); **to get sb in the ~** (inf) jdm ein Kind machen (inf); **join the ~!** (inf) gratuliere! du auch!; **the London ~ scene** das Nachtleben von London **VT** einknüppeln auf (+acc), knüppeln **VI** **to go ~bing** Nachtklubs besuchen

▶ **club together** VI (Brit) zusammenlegen

clubbable ['klʌbəbl] ADJ geeignet, in einen Klub aufgenommen zu werden; (= sociable) gesellschaftsfähig

clubby ['klʌbɪ] ADJ (inf) gesellig

club: club class N (Aviat) Clubklasse f, Businessklasse f; **club foot** N Klumpfuß m; **clubfooted** ADJ klumpfüßig; **clubhouse** N Klubhaus nt; **clubland** N (of gentlemen's clubs) Klubviertel nt (vornehmer Stadtteil, in dem sich besonders viele Klubs befinden); (esp Brit: of nightclubs) Vergnügungsviertel nt; **clubman** N he isn't much of a ~ er interessiert sich nicht besonders für Klubs; **club member** N Vereins- or Klubmitglied nt; **club room** N Klubraum nt; **club sandwich** N Clubsandwich nt

cluck [klʌk] **VI** gackern; (hen: to chicks) glucken **N** Gackern nt; (of hen to chicks) Glucken nt

clue [klu:] N Anhaltspunkt m, Hinweis m; (in police search also: = object) Spur f; (in crosswords) Frage f; **to find a/the ~ to sth** den Schlüssel zu etw finden; **I'll give you a ~** ich gebe dir einen Tipp; **I haven't a ~!** (inf) (ich hab) keine Ahnung!

▶ **clue up** VT sep (inf) person informieren; **to get clued up on** or **about sth** sich mit etw vertraut machen; **to be clued up on** or **about sth** über etw (acc) im Bilde sein; (about subject) mit etw vertraut sein

clueless ['klu:lɪs] ADJ (inf) ahnungslos, unbedarft (inf); expression, look ratlos

cluelessly ['klu:lɪslɪ] ADV (inf) ratlos

clump [klʌmp] **N a** (of trees, flowers etc) Gruppe f; (of earth) Klumpen m; **a ~ of shrubs** ein Gebüsch nt **b** (inf: = blow) Schlag m, Hieb m **VT** (inf: = hit) schlagen, hauen (inf) **VI** trampeln; (inf) schlagen, hauen (inf); **to ~ about** herumtrampeln; (in snow, mud etc) herumstapfen

clumpy ['klʌmpɪ] ADJ shoes klobig

clumsily ['klʌmzɪlɪ] ADV **a** ungeschickt; (= in an ungainly way) schwerfällig; act ungeschickt **b** (= inelegantly) written, translated etc schwerfällig, unbeholfen **c** (= awkwardly, tactlessly) ungeschickt, unbeholfen; compliment also plump

clumsiness ['klʌmzɪnɪs] **N a** Ungeschicklichkeit f; (= ungainliness) Schwerfälligkeit f **b** (of tool, shape) Unförmigkeit f; (of prose, translation etc) Schwerfälligkeit f, Unbeholfenheit f **c** (= awkwardness: of apology, excuse etc) Plumpheit f

clumsy ['klʌmzɪ] ADJ (+er) **a** ungeschickt; (= all thumbs also) tollpatschig; (= ungainly) schwerfällig **b** (= unwieldy) plump; tool also wuchtig, klobig; shape also unförmig, klobig; (= inelegant) prose, translation etc schwerfällig, unbeholfen; (= careless) mistake dumm **c** (= awkward, tactless) plump, ungeschickt

cling [klɪŋ] pret, ptp of **cling** [1]

clunk [klʌŋk] **N** dumpfes Geräusch **VI** **the door ~ed shut** die Tür schloss sich mit einem dumpfen Geräusch

clunker ['klʌŋkə'] N (US, pej inf: = car) Kiste f (pej inf), Mühle f (pej inf)

clunky ['klʌŋkɪ] ADJ klobig

cluster ['klʌstə'] **N** (of trees, flowers, houses) Gruppe f, Haufen m; (of curls, bananas) Büschel nt; (of bees, people, grapes) Traube f; (of islands) Gruppe f; (of diamonds) Büschel nt; (Phon) Häufung f; **the flowers grow in a ~ at the top of the stem** die Blumen sitzen or wachsen doldenförmig am Stängel; (of roses etc) mehrere Blüten wachsen am gleichen Stiel **VI** (people) sich drängen or scharen; **they all ~ed round to see what he was doing** alle drängten or scharten sich um ihn, um zu sehen, was er tat

cluster bomb N Splitterbombe f

clutch[1] [klʌtʃ] **N** **a** (= grip) Griff m **b** (Aut) Kupplung f; **to let in/out the ~** ein-/auskuppeln; **~ pedal** Kupplungspedal nt **c** (fig) **to fall into sb's ~es** jdm in die Hände fallen, jdm ins Netz gehen; **to be in sb's ~es** in jds Gewalt (dat) sein; **to have sb in one's ~es** jdn im Netz or in den Klauen haben; **he escaped her ~es** er entkam ihren Klauen **VT** (= grab) umklammern, packen; (= hold tightly) umklammert halten; **to ~ sth in one's hand** etw umklammern

▶**clutch at** VI +prep obj (lit) schnappen nach (+dat), greifen; (= hold tightly) umklammert halten; (fig) sich klammern an (+acc) → **straw**

clutch[2] N (of chickens) Brut f; (of eggs) Gelege nt

clutch bag N Unterarmtasche f

clutter ['klʌtə'] **N** (= confusion) Durcheinander nt; (= disorderly articles) Kram m (inf); **the ~ of bottles and crockery in the kitchen** das Durcheinander von Flaschen und Geschirr in der Küche; **his desk was in a ~** auf seinem Schreibtisch war ein fürchterliches Durcheinander; **his essay was a ~ of unrelated details** sein Aufsatz war ein Sammelsurium or Wirrwarr von zusammenhangslosen Einzelheiten **VT** (also **clutter up**) zu voll machen (inf)/stellen; painting, photograph überladen; mind voll stopfen; **to be ~ed with sth** (mind, room, drawer etc) mit etw voll gestopft sein; (floor, desk etc) mit etw übersät sein; (painting etc) mit etw überladen sein; **the floor was terribly ~ed** auf dem Fußboden lag alles verstreut; **his desk was dreadfully ~ed** sein Schreibtisch war ganz voll

cm abbr of **centimetre** cm

Cmdr abbr of **Commander**

CNAA abbr of **Council for National Academic Awards**

CND abbr of **Campaign for Nuclear Disarmament**

CNN abbr of **Cable News Network** CNN no art

CO abbr of **Commanding Officer**

Co **a** abbr of **company** KG f **b** abbr of **county**

co- [kəʊ-] PREF Mit-, mit-

c/o **a** abbr of **care of** bei, c/o **b** abbr of **carried over** Übertr.

coach [kəʊtʃ] **N** **a** (horsedrawn) Kutsche f; (= state coach) (Staats)karosse f; **~ and four** Vierspänner m **b** (Rail) (Eisenbahn)wagen m, Waggon m **c** (Brit: = motor coach) (Reise)bus m; **by ~** mit dem Bus; **~ travel/journeys** Busreisen pl; **~ driver** Busfahrer m **d** (= tutor) Nachhilfelehrer(in) m(f); (Sport) Trainer m **VT** **a** (Sport) trainieren **b** **to ~ sb for an exam** jdn aufs Examen vorbereiten; **he had been ~ed in what to say** man hatte mit ihm eingeübt, was er sagen sollte

coach: coach box N (Kutsch)bock m; **coach-builder** N (Brit) Karosseriebauer m;

coach-building N (Brit) Karosseriebau m; **coach house** N (old) Remise f

coaching ['kəʊtʃɪŋ] N (Sport) Trainerstunden pl; (Tennis) Training nt; (= tutoring) Nachhilfe f

coach: coachload N (Brit) = **busload; coachman** N Kutscher m; **coach party** N (Brit) Busreisegruppe f; **coach station** N (Brit) Busbahnhof m; **coach trip** N (Brit) Busfahrt f; **coachwork** N (Brit) Karosserie f

coagulate [kəʊ'ægjʊleɪt] **VI** (blood) gerinnen, koagulieren (spec); (jelly) fest werden; (paint) zähflüssig werden, eindicken **VT** blood gerinnen lassen; milk dick werden lassen; jelly fest werden lassen

coagulation [kəʊˌægjʊ'leɪʃən] N (of blood) Gerinnen nt, Gerinnung f, Koagulation f (spec); (of milk) Dickwerden nt; (of jelly) Festwerden nt; (of paint) Eindicken nt

coal [kəʊl] N Kohle f; **we still burn ~** wir heizen noch mit Kohle; **as black as ~** kohlrabenschwarz; **to carry** or **take ~s to Newcastle** (Brit Prov) Eulen nach Athen tragen (Prov); **to haul** (Brit) or **drag sb over the ~s** jdm eine Standpauke halten, jdm die Leviten lesen; **to heap ~s of fire on sb's head** feurige Kohlen auf jds Haupt (dat) sammeln

coal in cpds Kohlen-; **coal bed** N Kohlenflöz m; **coal bin**, **coal bunker** N Kohlenkasten m; **coal-black** ADJ kohlrabenschwarz; **coal cellar** N Kohlenkeller m; **coal dust** N Kohlenstaub m, (Kohlen)grus m

coalesce [ˌkəʊə'les] VI (Phys, Chem) sich verbinden, eine Verbindung eingehen; (fig) sich vereinigen, zusammengehen; (views, opinions etc) sich verquicken (geh)

coalescence [ˌkəʊə'lesəns] N (Phys, Chem) Verbindung f; (fig) Vereinigung f; (of views, opinions etc) Verquickung f (geh)

coal: coalface N (Brit) Streb m; **men who work at the ~** Männer, die im Streb or vor Ort arbeiten; **workers at the ~** (fig) diejenigen, die die Arbeit machen; **coalfield** N Kohlenrevier nt; **coal fire** N Kamin m; **a ~ heats better** ein Kohlenfeuer wärmt besser; **coal-fired** ADJ Kohle(n)-; **~ power station** Kohlekraftwerk nt; **coal hod** N Kohleneimer m; **coal hole** N Kohlenbunker m

coalition [ˌkəʊə'lɪʃən] N Koalition f; **~ government** Koalitionsregierung f

coal: coal man N Kohlenmann m; **coal merchant** N Kohlenhändler m; **coal mine** N Grube f, Zeche f, Kohlenbergwerk nt; **coal miner** N Bergmann m, Kumpel m (inf); **coalmining** N Kohle(n)bergbau m; **the ~ industry** der Kohle(n)bergbau; **~ area** Kohlenrevier nt; **coal pit** N = **coal mine; coal scuttle** N Kohleneimer m, Kohlenkasten m; **coal seam** N Kohlenflöz nt; **coal shed** N Kohlenschuppen m; **coal strike** N Bergarbeiterstreik m; **coal tar** N Kohlenteer m; **coal tar soap** N Teerseife f; **coal tip** N (Brit) Kohlenhalde f; **coal tit** N (Orn) Tannenmeise f; **coal yard** N Kohlenhof m

coarse [kɔːs] ADJ (+er) **a** (= not delicate, in texture) grob; sand, sugar also grobkörnig; features also derb; **~ sandpaper** grobes Schmirgelpapier **b** (= uncouth) gewöhnlich; person, manners also grob, ungehobelt, ungeschliffen; laugh derb; joke derb, unanständig **c** (= common) food derb, einfach; **~ red wine** einfacher (Land)rotwein

coarse: coarse fish N Süßwasserfisch m (mit Ausnahme aller Lachs- und Forellenarten); **coarse fishing** N Angeln nt von Süßwasserfischen; **coarse-grained** ['kɔːs'greɪnd] ADJ grobfaserig; **~ fibre** grobe Faser f; **~ paper** ungeleimtes Papier, Zeitungspapier nt

coarsely ['kɔːslɪ] ADV **a** (= in large pieces) chop, grate, grind grob; **~ woven cloth** grob gewobener Stoff **b** (= uncouthly) laugh, joke, speak derb; behave ungehobelt

coarsen ['kɔːsn] **VT** person derber machen; skin gerben **VI** (person) derber werden; (skin) gröber werden

coarseness ['kɔːsnɪs] N **a** (of texture) Grobheit f **b** (fig: = vulgarity) Gewöhnlichkeit f; (of person, manners also) Grobheit f, Ungeschliffenheit f; (of joke also) Unanständigkeit f; (of sb's language) Derbheit f; **the ~ of his laugh** sein derbes Lachen

coast [kəʊst] **N** **a** Küste f, Gestade nt (poet); **at the ~** an der Küste; **on the ~** am Meer; **we're going to the ~** wir fahren an die Küste or ans Meer; **the ~ is clear** (fig) die Luft ist rein **VI** **a** (car, cyclist, in neutral) (im Leerlauf) fahren; (= cruise effortlessly) dahinrollen; (athlete) locker laufen; (US, on sled) hinunterrodeln **b** (fig) **to be ~ing along** mühelos or spielend vorankommen; **he was just ~ing up to the exam** er steuerte ohne große Mühe aufs Examen zu

coastal ['kəʊstəl] ADJ Küsten-; **~ traffic** Küstenschifffahrt f

coaster ['kəʊstə'] **N** **a** (Naut) Küstenmotorschiff nt **b** (= drip mat) Untersetzer m **c** (US, = sled) (Rodel)schlitten m; (= roller-coaster) Achterbahn f, Berg- und Talbahn f

coaster brake N (US) Rücktrittbremse f

coast: coastguard N Küstenwache f; **the ~s** die Küstenwacht; **~ boat/station** Küstenwachtboot nt/-posten m; **coastline** N Küste f

coat [kəʊt] **N** **a** (= outdoor garment) Mantel m; (= doctor's coat etc also) (Arzt)kittel m; (= jacket of suit etc also) Jacke f; (for men also) Jackett nt; **~ and skirt** Kostüm nt **b** (Her) **~ of arms** Wappen nt **c** **~ of mail** Panzerhemd nt; (of chain mail) Kettenhemd nt **d** (of animal) Fell nt; **winter ~** Winterfell nt **e** (of paint, tar etc, = application) Anstrich m; (= actual layer) Schicht f; **give it a second ~** (of paint) streich es noch einmal **VT** (with paint etc) streichen; (with chocolate, icing etc) überziehen; **to be ~ed with dust/mud** mit einer Staub-/Schmutzschicht überzogen sein, eine Staub-/Schmutzschicht haben; **my hands were ~ed with grease/flour** meine Hände waren voller Schmiere/Mehl; **his tongue was ~ed** seine Zunge war belegt; **~ed paper** gestrichenes Papier; **the chassis was ~ed with an anti-rust preparation** das Chassis war mit einem Rostschutzmittel beschichtet or (sprayed) gespritzt

coat hanger N Kleiderbügel m

coating ['kəʊtɪŋ] N Überzug m, Schicht f; (of paint) Anstrich m

coat: coatless ADJ ohne Mantel; **coat stand** N Garderobenständer m; **coat-tails** PL Rockschöße pl

co-author ['kəʊ'ɔːθə'] N Mitautor(in) m(f), Mitverfasser(in) m(f); **they were ~s of the book** sie haben das Buch gemeinsam geschrieben

coax [kəʊks] VT überreden; **to ~ sb into doing sth** jdn beschwatzen (inf) or dazu bringen, etw zu tun; **he ~ed the engine into life** er brachte den Motor mit List und Tücke in Gang; **you have to ~ the fire** du musst dem Feuer ein bisschen nachhelfen; **to ~ sth out of sb** jdm etw entlocken

coaxing ['kəʊksɪŋ] **N** gutes Zureden, Zuspruch m; **with a little ~ the engine/fire started** mit etwas List und Tücke kam der Motor/das Feuer in Gang **ADJ** einschmeichelnd

coaxingly ['kəʊksɪŋlɪ] ADV **to ask ~** mit einschmeichelnder Stimme fragen; **however ~ he spoke to him ...** sosehr sie auch versuchte, ihn zu überreden ...

cob [kɒb] N **a** (= horse) kleines, gedrungenes Pferd **b** (= swan) (männlicher) Schwan **c** (also cobnut) (große) Haselnuss **d** (= corn) (Mais)kolben m; (= bread) rundes Brot; **corn on the ~** Maiskolben m; **a ~ of coal** ein Stück Eier- or Nusskohle

cobalt ['kəʊbɒlt] N Kobalt nt

cobalt-blue ['kəʊbɒltblu:] ADJ kobaltblau

cobber ['kɒbə'] N (Austral, inf) Kumpel m (inf)

cobble ['kɒbl] N (*also* **cobblestone**) Kopfstein *m* VT a shoe flicken b a ~d street eine Straße mit Kopfsteinpflaster

▶ **cobble together** VT *sep* (*inf*) essay etc zusammenschustern

cobbler ['kɒblə'] N a Schuster *m*, Flickschuster *m* b (= drink) Cobbler *m*; (esp US: = fruit pie) Obst mit Teig überbacken

cobblers ['kɒbləz] PL (Brit, inf: = rubbish) Scheiße *f* (inf), Mist *m* (inf); **(what a load of old) ~!** was für ein Haufen Mist! (inf)

cobblestone ['kɒblstəʊn] N = **cobble** N

COBOL ['kəʊbɒl] abbr of **common business oriented language** COBOL

cobra ['kəʊbrə] N Kobra *f*

cobweb ['kɒbweb] N (= single thread, threads) Spinn(en)webe *f*; (= full cobweb) Spinnennetz *nt*; **a brisk walk will blow away the ~s** (fig) ein ordentlicher Spaziergang und man hat wieder einen klaren Kopf

cobwebbed ['kɒbwebd] ADJ voller Spinnweben

coca ['kəʊkə] N a (= shrub) Koka *f* b no pl (= dried leaves) Kokablätter pl, Koka *f*

cocaine [kə'keɪn] N Kokain *nt*

coccyx ['kɒksɪks] N Steißbein *nt*

cochineal [ˌkɒtʃɪ'niːl] N (= insect, colouring) Koschenille *f*

cochlear ['kɒklɪə'] ADJ kochlear

cock [kɒk] N a (= rooster) Hahn *m*; (= weathercock) Wetterhahn *m*; **(the) ~ of the walk** or **roost** der Größte (inf) b (= male bird) Männchen *nt* c (= tap) (Wasser)hahn *m* d (of rifle) Hahn *m* e (of hat) schiefer Sitz f (Brit, inf: = mate) Kumpel *m* (inf) g (sl: = penis) Schwanz *m* (sl) VT a **to ~ the gun** den Hahn spannen b **ears** spitzen; **the parrot ~ed its head to one side** der Papagei legte seinen Kopf schief or auf die Seite; **to ~ a snook at sb** (Brit) (lit) jdm eine lange Nase machen; (fig) zeigen, dass man auf jdn pfeift

▶ **cock up** VT *sep* (Brit, inf: = mess up) versauen (inf)

cockade [kɒ'keɪd] N Kokarde *f*

cock: cock-a-doodle-doo N Kikeriki *nt*; **cock-a-hoop** ADJ ganz aus dem Häuschen, außer sich vor Freude; **cock-a-leekie (soup)** N Lauchsuppe *f* mit Huhn

cockamamie [ˌkɒkə'meɪmɪ] ADJ (US, inf: = poor quality) mies (inf)

cock-and-bull story [ˌkɒkən'bʊlˌstɔːrɪ] N Lügengeschichte *f*; **to give sb a ~** jdm eine Lügengeschichte erzählen

cockatoo [ˌkɒkə'tuː] N Kakadu *m*

cockatrice ['kɒkətrɪs] N Basilisk *m*

cockchafer ['kɒktʃeɪfə'] N Maikäfer *m*

cockcrow ['kɒkkrəʊ] N (old: = dawn) Hahnenschrei *m*; **at ~** beim ersten Hahnenschrei

cocked [kɒkt] ADJ **~ hat** (with two points) Zweispitz *m*; (with three points) Dreispitz *m*; **to knock sb into a ~ hat** (= beat up) aus jdm Kleinholz machen; (= outdo) jdn total an die Wand spielen; **this painting knocks all the others into a ~ hat** (inf) dieses Gemälde stellt alle anderen in den Schatten

cocker ['kɒkə'] N (also **cocker spaniel**) Cocker(spaniel) *m*

cockerel ['kɒkərəl] N junger Hahn

cock: cockeyed ['kɒkaɪd] ADJ (inf) a (= crooked) schief b (= absurd) idea verrückt, widersinnig; **cockfight** N Hahnenkampf *m*; **cockhorse** N (old) Steckenpferd *nt*

cockily ['kɒkɪlɪ] ADV (inf) großspurig

cockiness ['kɒkɪnɪs] N (inf) Großspurigkeit *f*

cockle ['kɒkl] N a (= shellfish) also **cockleshell** Herzmuschel *f* b (= boat) kleines Boot, Nussschale *f* c **it warmed the ~s of my heart** es wurde mir warm ums Herz

cockney ['kɒknɪ] N a (= dialect) Cockney *nt* b (= person) Cockney *m* ADJ Cockney-

cockpit ['kɒkpɪt] N a (Aviat, of racing car) Cockpit *nt*; (Naut: on yacht) Plicht *f*, Cockpit *nt* b (for cockfighting) Hahnenkampfplatz *m*

cockroach ['kɒkrəʊtʃ] N Küchenschabe *f*, Kakerlak *m*

cockscomb ['kɒkskəʊm] N a (Orn, Bot) Hahnenkamm *m* b = **coxcomb**

cock: cock sparrow N (männlicher) Spatz; **cocksucker** ['kɒkˌsʌkə'] N (pej, vulgar) Schwanzlutscher(in) *m(f)* (pej); **cocksure** ADJ (ganz) sicher, fest überzeugt; **don't you be so ~** sei dir deiner Sache (gen) nicht zu sicher; **to be ~ of oneself** von sich (dat) selber or selbst sehr überzeugt sein

cocktail ['kɒkteɪl] N Cocktail *m*; **we're invited for ~s** wir sind zum Cocktail eingeladen

cocktail in cpds Cocktail-; **cocktail bar** N Cocktailbar *f*; **cocktail cabinet** N Hausbar *f*; **cocktail lounge** N Cocktailbar *f*; **cocktail stick** N Cocktailspieß *m*; **cocktail waiter** N (esp US) Getränkekellner *m*; **cocktail waitress** N (esp US) Getränkekellnerin *f*

cockup ['kɒkʌp] N (Brit, inf) **to be a ~** in die Hose gehen (inf); **to make a ~ of sth** bei or mit etw Scheiße bauen (inf)

cocky ['kɒkɪ] ADJ (+er) (inf) anmaßend, großspurig; **he was so ~ before the exams** er tat so großspurig vorm Examen

cocoa ['kəʊkəʊ] N Kakao *m*

cocoa bean N Kakaobohne *f*

cocomat ['kəʊkəmæt] N Kokosmatte *f*

coconut ['kəʊkənʌt] N Kokosnuss *f* ATTR Kokos-

coconut: coconut matting N Kokosläufer *m*; **coconut oil** N Kokosöl *nt*; **coconut palm** N Kokospalme *f*; **coconut shy** N Wurfbude *f*; **coconut tree** N Kokospalme *f*

cocoon [kə'kuːn] N Kokon *m*; (fig, of scarves, blankets etc) Hülle *f*; **the old warships were put in ~s** die alten Kriegsschiffe wurden mit Planen abgedeckt VT einhüllen; ship etc abdecken; **she looks well ~ed against the wind** sie ist gut gegen den Wind eingemummt

COD abbr of **cash** (Brit) or **collect** (US) **on delivery**

cod[1] [kɒd] N Kabeljau *m*; (in Baltic) Dorsch *m*

cod[2] ADJ (Brit: = not genuine) vorgetäuscht

coda ['kəʊdə] N Koda *f*

coddle ['kɒdl] VT a child, invalid umhegen, verhätscheln b (Cook) eggs im Backofen pochieren

code [kəʊd] N a (= cipher) Kode *m*, Code *m*, Chiffre *f*; **in ~** verschlüsselt, chiffriert; **to put into ~** verschlüsseln, chiffrieren; **to break a secret ~** einen Geheimkode knacken b (Jur) Gesetzbuch *nt*, Kodex *m* c (= rules, principles) Kodex *m*; **~ of honour/behaviour** Ehren-/Sittenkodex *m*; **~ of conduct** Verhaltenskodex *m*; **~ of practice** Verfahrensregeln pl d post or zip (US) ~ Postleitzahl *f* e (Comput) Kode *m*, Code *m* f (Ling, Sociol) Code *m*, Kode *m* VT verschlüsseln, chiffrieren; (Comput) kodieren

code breaker N Kodeknacker *m*

coded ['kəʊdɪd] ADJ a (= in code) message, warning, instructions kodiert, verschlüsselt; **in ~ form** in kodierter or verschlüsselter Form b (= indirect) criticism, attack, reference versteckt; **in ~ lan-**

guage in verschlüsselter or kodierter Sprache c (Telec) signal kodiert

codeine ['kəʊdiːn] N Kodein *nt*

code: code letter N Kodebuchstabe *m*; **code name** N Deckname *m*; **code number** N Kennziffer *f*

co-dependent [ˌkəʊdɪ'pendənt] (esp US, Psych) N Koabhängige(r) *mf* ADJ koabhängig

code word N Kodewort *nt*; (Comput also) Passwort *nt*, Kennwort *nt*

codex ['kəʊdeks] N pl **codices** Kodex *m*

codfish ['kɒdfɪʃ] N = **cod**[1]

codger ['kɒdʒə'] N (inf) komischer (alter) Kauz

codices ['kəʊdɪsiːz] pl of **codex**

codicil ['kəʊdɪsɪl] N Kodizill *nt*

codify ['kəʊdɪfaɪ] VT laws kodifizieren

coding ['kəʊdɪŋ] N a Chiffrieren *nt*; **a new ~ system** ein neues Chiffriersystem; **I don't understand the ~** ich verstehe den Kode nicht b (Comput: = codes) Kodierung(en pl) *f*

cod: cod-liver oil N Lebertran *m*; **codpiece** N Hosenbeutel *m*

co-driver ['kəʊdraɪvə'] N Beifahre(in) *m(f)*

codswallop ['kɒdzwɒləp] N (Brit, inf) Stuss *m* (dated inf)

co-ed, coed ['kəʊ'ed] N (inf, Brit: = school) gemischte Schule, Koedukationsschule *f*; (dated US: = girl student) Schülerin *f* or Studentin *f* einer gemischten Schule ADJ school gemischt, Koedukations- ADV **to go ~** Koedukation einführen

coedit [ˌkəʊ'edɪt] VT book mit herausgeben

coedition [ˌkəʊɪ'dɪʃən] N gemeinsame Ausgabe

coeditor ['kəʊ'edɪtə'] N Mitherausgeber(in) *m(f)*

coeducation ['kəʊˌedjʊ'keɪʃən] N Koedukation *f*

coeducational ['kəʊˌedjʊ'keɪʃənl] ADJ teaching koedukativ; school Koedukations-

coefficient [ˌkəʊɪ'fɪʃənt] N (Math, Phys) Koeffizient *m*

coerce [kəʊ'ɜːs] VT zwingen; **to ~ sb into doing sth** jdn dazu zwingen or nötigen (geh), etw zu tun

coercion [kəʊ'ɜːʃən] N Zwang *m*; (Jur) Nötigung *f*

coercive [kəʊ'ɜːsɪv] ADJ Zwangs-

coeval [kəʊ'iːvəl] (form) ADJ der gleichen Periode or Zeit (with wie); manuscripts, authors etc also zeitgenössisch attr N Zeitgenosse *m*

coexist [ˌkəʊɪg'zɪst] VI koexistieren (Pol, Sociol, geh), nebeneinander bestehen; **to ~ with** or **alongside sb/sth** neben or mit jdm/etw bestehen or existieren

coexistence [ˌkəʊɪg'zɪstəns] N Koexistenz *f*

coexistent [ˌkəʊɪg'zɪstənt] ADJ koexistent (geh), nebeneinander bestehend; **the two states are now peacefully ~** die beiden Staaten leben jetzt friedlich nebeneinander or in friedlicher Koexistenz

coextensive [ˌkəʊɪk'stensɪv] ADJ (in time) zur gleichen Zeit; (in area) flächengleich; (in length) längengleich; (fig) concepts bedeutungs- or inhaltsgleich; **to be ~ with sth** mit etw zusammenfallen; (spatially) sich mit etw decken

C of E abbr of **Church of England**

coffee ['kɒfɪ] N Kaffee *m*; **two ~s, please** zwei Kaffee, bitte

coffee in cpds Kaffee-; **coffee bar** N Café *nt*; **coffee bean** N Kaffeebohne *f*; **coffee break** N Kaffeepause *f*; **coffee cake** N Mokkakuchen *m*; **coffee cup** N Kaffeetasse *f*; **coffee filter** N Kaffeefilter *m*; **coffee grinder** N Kaffeemühle *f*; **coffee grounds** PL Kaffeesatz *m*; **coffee house** N (also Hist) Kaffeehaus *nt*; **coffee machine** N (= coffee maker) Kaffeemaschine *f*; (= vending machine) Kaffee-Verkaufsautomat *m*; **coffee maker** N Kaffeemaschine *f*; **coffee percolator** N Kaffeemaschine *f*; **coffeepot** N Kaffeekanne *f*; **coffee table** N Couchtisch *m*; **coffee-table** ADJ **~ book**

Bildband *m*; **coffee whitener** N Kaffeeweißer *m*

coffer ['kɒfə'] N **a** Truhe *f* **b** (*fig*) **the ~s** die Schatulle, das Geldsäckel; (*of state*) das Staatssäckel **c** (*Archit*) Kassette *f*

cofferdam ['kɒfədæm] N Caisson *m*

coffin ['kɒfɪn] N Sarg *m*

coffin dodger N (*hum inf*) Scheintote(r) *mf* (*sl*)

cog [kɒg] N (*Tech*) Zahn *m*; (= *cogwheel*) Zahnrad *nt*; **he's only a ~ in the machine** (*fig*) er ist nur ein Rädchen im Getriebe; **each employee is a vital ~ in the company** jeder einzelne Angestellte ist ein wichtiger Teil in der Firma

cogency ['kəʊdʒənsɪ] N Stichhaltigkeit *f*

cogent ['kəʊdʒənt] ADJ stichhaltig; *argument, reason also* zwingend; *reasoning also* überzeugend

cogently ['kəʊdʒəntlɪ] ADV stichhaltig

cogitate ['kɒdʒɪteɪt] **VI** (*about, (up)on* über +*acc*) nachdenken, grübeln **VT** nachdenken über +*acc*; (= *devise*) ersinnen

cogitation [ˌkɒdʒɪ'teɪʃən] N Nachdenken *nt*

cognac ['kɒnjæk] N Kognak *m*; (*French*) Cognac *m*

cognate ['kɒgneɪt] ADJ verwandt; **N** (*Ling*) urverwandt (*Ling*) verwandtes Wort, urverwandte Sprache; **"night" is a ~ of "Nacht"** „night" ist mit „Nacht" verwandt

cognition [kɒg'nɪʃən] N Erkenntnis *f*; (*visual*) Wahrnehmung *f*

cognitive ['kɒgnɪtɪv] ADJ *powers, faculties* kognitiv

cognizance ['kɒgnɪzəns] N (*form*) **a** (= *conscious knowledge, awareness*) Kenntnis *f*; (= *range of perception*) Erkenntnisbereich *m*; **to take ~ of sth** etw zur Kenntnis nehmen **b** (= *jurisdiction*) Zuständigkeit *f*, Befugnis *f*; (*Jur*) Gerichtsbarkeit *f*

cognizant ['kɒgnɪzənt] ADJ (*form*) **a** (= *aware, conscious*) **to be ~ of sth** sich (*dat*) einer Sache (*gen*) bewusst sein **b** (= *having jurisdiction*) zuständig

cognoscente [ˌkɒgnəʊ'ʃentɪ] N *pl* **cognoscenti** [ˌkɒgnəʊ'ʃentiː] Kenner *m*

cog: cog railway N (*US*) Zahnradbahn *f*; **cogwheel** N Zahnrad *nt*

cohabit [kəʊ'hæbɪt] VI (*esp Jur*) in nichtehelicher *or* nicht ehelicher Lebensgemeinschaft leben, zusammenleben

cohabitant [kəʊ'hæbɪtənt] N Lebensgefährte *m*/-gefährtin *f*

cohabitation [ˌkəʊhæbɪ'teɪʃən] N eheähnliche Gemeinschaft

cohabitee [ˌkəʊhæbɪ'tiː] N *Partner(in) in einer nichtehelichen Lebensgemeinschaft*

coheir ['kəʊ'εə'] N Miterbe *m* (*to* +*gen*); **they were ~s to the fortune** sie waren gemeinsame Erben des Vermögens

coheiress ['kəʊ'εərɪs] N Miterbin *f* (*to* +*gen*)

cohere [kəʊ'hɪə'] **VI a** (*lit*) zusammenhängen **b** (*fig, community*) ein Ganzes *or* eine Einheit bilden; (*essay, symphony etc*) in sich geschlossen sein; (*argument, reasoning, style*) kohärent *or* zusammenhängend sein

coherence [kəʊ'hɪərəns] N **a** (*lit*) Kohärenz *f* **b** (*of community*) Zusammenhalt *m*; (*of essay, symphony etc*) Geschlossenheit *f*; (*of argument, reasoning, style*) Kohärenz *f*; **his speech lacked ~** seiner Rede (*dat*) fehlte der Zusammenhang **c** (*fig: = comprehensibility*) **after five whiskies he lacked ~** nach fünf Whiskys gab er nur noch unzusammenhängendes Zeug von sich

coherent [kəʊ'hɪərənt] ADJ **a** (= *comprehensible*) zusammenhängend; **incapable of ~ speech** unfähig, zusammenhängend zu sprechen **b** (= *cohesive*) *logic, reasoning etc* kohärent, schlüssig; *case* schlüssig

coherently [kəʊ'hɪərəntlɪ] ADV **a** (= *comprehensibly*) zusammenhängend **b** (= *cohesively*) kohärent, schlüssig

cohesion [kəʊ'hiːʒən] N (*Sci*) Kohäsion *f*; (*fig also*) Zusammenhang *m*; (*of group*) Zusammenhalt *m*, Geschlossenheit *f*

cohesive [kəʊ'hiːsɪv] ADJ (*Sci*) Binde-, Kohäsiv-; (*fig*) geschlossen

cohesively [kəʊ'hiːsɪvlɪ] ADV (*Sci*) kohäsiv; (*fig*) *write, argue* im Zusammenhang

cohort ['kəʊhɔːt] N Kohorte *f*, Trupp *m*

COHSE ['kəʊzɪ] (*Brit dated*) *abbr of* **Confederation of Health Service Employees** *Gewerkschaft der Angestellten des Gesundheitsdienstes*

coif [kɔɪf] N (*Hist, Eccl*) Haube *f*; (= *skullcap*) Kappe *f*

coiffed [kɔɪft] ADJ frisiert

coiffure [kwɒ'fjʊə'] N Haartracht *f*, Coiffure *f* (*geh*)

coiffured [kwɒ'fjʊəd] ADJ = **coiffed**

coil [kɔɪl] **N a** (*of rope, wire etc*) Rolle *f*; (*in light bulb*) Glühdraht *m*; (*on loop*) Windung *f*; (*of smoke*) Kringel *m*; (*of hair*) Kranz *m*; **she wore her hair in ~s** (*round head*) sie hatte eine Gretchenfrisur; (*round ears*) sie trug ihr Haar in Schnecken; **the sinewy ~s of the snake** die kraftvoll gespannte Spirale des Schlangenkörpers **b** (*Elec*) Spule *f* **c** (= *contraceptive*) Spirale *f* **VT** aufwickeln, aufrollen; *wire* aufspulen, aufwickeln; **to ~ sth round sth** etw um etw wickeln; **the python ~ed itself around the rabbit/(up) in the basket** die Pythonschlange umschlang das Kaninchen/rollte sich im Korb zusammen **VI** sich ringeln; (*smoke also*) sich kringeln; (*river*) sich schlängeln *or* winden

coil spring N Sprungfeder *f*

coin [kɔɪn] **N a** Münze *f* **b** *no pl* Münzen *pl*; **in the ~ of the realm** in der Landeswährung; **I'll pay you back in the same ~** (*Brit fig*) das werde ich dir in gleicher Münze heimzahlen; **the other side of the ~** (*fig*) die Kehrseite der Medaille; **they are two sides of the same ~** das sind zwei Seiten derselben Sache **VT** *money, phrase* prägen; **to be ~ing money** *or* **it (in)** (*fig inf*) er prägt richtig Geld (*inf*); **..., to ~ a phrase** ..., um mich mal so auszudrücken

coinage ['kɔɪnɪdʒ] N **a** (= *act*) Prägen *nt*, Prägung *f*; (= *coins*) Münzen *pl*, Hartgeld *nt no pl*; (= *system*) Währung *f* **b** (*fig*) Prägung *f*, Neuschöpfung *f*

coin box N (= *telephone*) Münzfernsprecher *m*; (= *box*) Geldkasten *m*; (*on telephone, meter*) Münzzähler *m*

coincide [ˌkəʊɪn'saɪd] VI (*in time, place*) zusammenfallen; (*in area*) sich decken; (= *agree*) übereinstimmen; **the two concerts ~** die beiden Konzerte finden zur gleichen Zeit statt

coincidence [kəʊ'ɪnsɪdəns] N **a** Zufall *m*, Fügung *f* (*geh*); **what a ~!** welch ein Zufall!; **it is no ~ that ...** es ist kein Zufall, dass ..., es ist nicht von ungefähr, dass ... **b** (= *occurring or coming together, in time*) Zusammentreffen *nt*; (*in place*) Zusammenfall *m*; (= *agreement*) Übereinstimmung *f*

coincident [kəʊ'ɪnsɪdənt] ADJ (*in time*) zusammentreffend; (*in place*) zusammenfallend; (= *agreeing*) übereinstimmend

coincidental ADJ , **coincidentally** ADV [kəʊˌɪnsɪ'dentl, -təlɪ] zufällig

coin-operated ['kɔɪn'ɒpəreɪtɪd] ADJ Münz-; **~ machine** Münzautomat *m*

coin slot N Münzeinwurf *m*

coir [kɔɪə'] N Kokosfaser *f*, Coir *nt or f*

coital ['kɔɪtəl] ADJ (*form*) Koitus-; → *also* **postcoital**

coition [kəʊ'ɪʃən], **coitus** ['kɔɪtəs] N (*form*) Koitus *m*, Akt *m*

coitus interruptus ['kɔɪtəsˌɪntə'rʌptəs] N Coitus interruptus *m*

coke¹ [kəʊk] N Koks *m*

coke² N (*inf*, = *cocaine*) Koks *m* (*inf*)

Coke® [kəʊk] N (*inf*) (Coca-)Cola® *f*, Coke® *nt*

col¹ [kɒl] N Sattel *m*, Pass *m*

col² *abbr of* **column** Sp.

Col *abbr of* **Colonel**

COLA ['kəʊlə] (*US, Fin*) *abbr of* **cost-of-living adjustment** Dynamisierung *f* auf der Basis veränderter Lebenshaltungskosten

colander ['kʌləndə'] N Seiher *m*, Sieb *nt*

cold [kəʊld] **7.5** **ADJ** (+*er*) **a** kalt; **~ meats** Aufschnitt *m*; **I am ~** mir ist kalt, ich friere; **my hands are ~/are getting ~** ich habe/kriege kalte Hände; **the room is/the nights are getting ~** das Zimmer wird/die Nächte werden kalt; **don't get ~** pass auf, dass du nicht frierst!; **if you get ~** wenn es dir zu kalt wird, wenn du frierst; **your coffee is getting ~** dein Kaffee wird kalt **b** (*fig*) kalt; *answer, reception* betont kühl; *colour* kalt; *personality* kühl; (= *dispassionate, not sensual*) kühl; **to be ~ to sb** jdn kühl behandeln; **that leaves me ~** das lässt mich kalt **c** (*inf*, = *unconscious*) bewusstlos; (= *knocked out*) k. o.; **to be out ~** bewusstlos/k. o. sein; **to knock sb out ~** jdn k. o. schlagen **d** (*inf, in guessing*) kalt; **you're still ~** immer noch kalt **e** (*Hunt*) *scent* kalt **f** (*phrases*) **in ~ blood** kaltblütig; **~ comfort** ein schwacher Trost; **to get/have ~ feet** (*fig inf*) kalte Füße kriegen/haben (*inf*); **to get/have ~ feet about doing sth** Muffe kriegen/haben, etw zu tun (*inf*); **he's a ~ fish** er ist ein kalter Fisch (*inf*); **to give sb the ~ shoulder** (*inf*) jdm die kalte Schulter zeigen; **to be in a ~ sweat** vor Angst schwitzen; **that brought him out in a ~ sweat** dabei brach ihm der kalte Schweiß *or* der Angstschweiß aus; **to throw ~ water on sb's plans** (*inf*) jdm eine kalte Dusche geben; **to throw ~ water on sb's hopes** (*inf*) jds Hoffnungen (*dat*) einen Dämpfer aufsetzen **ADV to come to sth ~** unvorbereitet an eine Sache herangehen; **to learn/know sth ~** (*US*) etw gut lernen/können; **he stopped ~ when ...** (*US*) er hielt unvermittelt an, als ...; **she quit her job ~** sie hat glatt *or* eiskalt gekündigt (*inf*); **he was turned down ~** er wurde glatt abgelehnt **N a** Kälte *f*; **to feel the ~** kälteempfindlich sein; **don't go out in this ~!** geh nicht raus bei dieser Kälte!; **to be left out in the ~** (*fig*) ausgeschlossen werden, links liegen gelassen werden; **to feel left out in the ~** sich ausgeschlossen fühlen **b** (*Med*) Erkältung *f*; (= *runny nose*) Schnupfen *m*; **a heavy** *or* **bad ~** eine schwere Erkältung; **to have a ~** erkältet sein; (= *runny nose*) einen Schnupfen haben; **to get** *or* **catch a ~** sich erkälten, sich (*dat*) eine Erkältung holen; **to catch ~** sich erkälten; **~ in the head** (*Brit*) head ~ Kopfgrippe *f*; **~ on the chest** (*Brit*) chest ~ Bronchialkatarr(h) *m*

cold: cold-blooded ADJ (*Zool, fig*) kaltblütig; **~ animal** Kaltblüter *m*; **to be ~ about sth** etw kaltblütig tun; **cold-bloodedly** ['kəʊld'blʌddlɪ] ADV kaltblütig; **cold box** N (*Brit*) Kühlbox *f*; **cold call** N (*Comm*) (*on phone*) Vertreteranruf *m*; (= *visit*) Vertreterbesuch *m*; **cold calling** N (*Comm*) (*on phone*) Kundenwerbung *f* per Telefon; (= *visiting*) Vertreterbesuche *pl*; **cold chisel** N Kaltmeißel *m*; **cold cream** N Coldcream *f or nt*, halbfette Feuchtigkeitscreme; **cold cuts** PL (*US*) Aufschnitt *m*; **cold frame** N (*Hort*) Frühbeet *nt*; **cold fusion** N (*Phys*) kalte Fusion; **cold-hearted** ADJ kaltherzig

coldly ['kəʊldlɪ] ADV (*lit, fig*) kalt; *answer, receive* betont kühl; **they ~ planned the murder** der Mord wurde von ihnen kaltblütig geplant

coldness ['kəʊldnɪs] N (*lit, fig*) Kälte *f*; (*of answer, reception, welcome*) betonte Kühle; **the unexpected ~ of the weather** die unerwartete Kälte; **the ~ with which they planned the murder** die Kaltblütigkeit, mit der sie den Mord planten

cold: cold room N Kühlraum *m*; **cold selling** N Cold Selling *nt*; **cold shoulder** N (*inf*) **to give sb the ~** jdm die kalte Schulter zeigen;

cold-shoulder VT (*inf*) die kalte Schulter zeigen (+*dat*); **cold snap** N (*Met*) Kälteeinbruch *m*; **cold sore** N (*Med*) Bläschenausschlag *m*; **cold start** N (*Aut, Comput*) Kaltstart *m*; **cold storage** N Kühllagerung *f*; **to put sth into** ~ (*lit, food*) etw kühl lagern; (*fig*) idea, plan etw auf Eis legen; **cold store** N Kühlhaus *nt*; **cold turkey** (*inf*) ADJ **a** ~ **cure** ein kalter Entzug (*sl*) **b** **to come off drugs** ~ einen kalten Entzug machen (*sl*); **cold war** N kalter Krieg; **cold warrior** N kalter Krieger; **cold-weather payment** N (*Brit*) Brennstoffbeihilfe *f*

coleslaw ['kəʊlslɔː] N Krautsalat *m*

colic ['kɒlɪk] N Kolik *f*

coliseum [ˌkɒlɪ'siːəm] N Kolosseum *nt*

collaborate [kə'læbəreɪt] VI **a** (= work together) zusammenarbeiten; **they asked him to** ~ sie baten ihn mitzuarbeiten, sie baten um seine Mitarbeit; **to** ~ **with sb on** or **in sth** mit jdm bei etw zusammenarbeiten **b** (with enemy) kollaborieren; **he was suspected of collaborating** er wurde der Kollaboration verdächtigt

collaboration [kə,læbə'reɪʃən] N **a** (= working together) Zusammenarbeit *f*; (of one party) Mitarbeit *f*; **helpful** ~ Mithilfe *f* **b** (with enemy) Kollaboration *f* **c** (= piece of work) Gemeinschaftsproduktion *f*

collaborative [kə'læbərətɪv] ADJ gemeinschaftlich

collaboratively [kə'læbərətɪvlɪ] ADV gemeinschaftlich; **to work** ~ zusammenarbeiten

collaborator [kə'læbəreɪtə'] N **a** Mitarbeiter(in) *m(f)* **b** (with enemy) Kollaborateur(in) *m(f)*

collage [kɒ'lɑːʒ] N Collage *f*

collapse [kə'læps] VI **a** (person) zusammenbrechen; (mentally, = have heart attack also) einen Kollaps erleiden or haben; **his health** ~d er hatte einen Kollaps; **they all** ~**d with laughter** sie konnten sich alle vor Lachen nicht mehr halten; **she** ~**d onto her bed, exhausted** sie plumpste erschöpft aufs Bett
b (= fall down, cave in) zusammenbrechen; (building, wall, roof also) einstürzen; (lungs) zusammenfallen, kollabieren
c (fig: = fail) zusammenbrechen; (negotiations) scheitern; (civilization) untergehen; (prices) stürzen, purzeln (inf); (government) zu Fall kommen, stürzen; (plans) scheitern, zu Fall kommen; (hopes) sich zerschlagen; **his whole world** ~**d about him** eine ganze Welt stürzte über ihm zusammen; **their whole society** ~**d** ihre ganze Gesellschaftsordnung brach zusammen
d (= fold, table, umbrella, bicycle etc) sich zusammenklappen lassen; (telescope, walking stick) sich zusammenschieben lassen; (life raft) sich zusammenlegen or -falten lassen
VT table, umbrella, bicycle etc zusammenklappen; telescope, walking stick zusammenschieben; life raft zusammenlegen or -falten
N **a** (of person) Zusammenbruch *m*; (= nervous breakdown also, heart attack) Kollaps *m*
b (of object) Zusammenbruch *m*; (of building, wall, roof also) Einsturz *m*; (of lungs) Kollaps *m*
c (fig: = failure) Zusammenbruch *m*; (of negotiations also) Scheitern *nt*; (of civilization) Untergang *m*; (of government) Sturz *m*; (of hopes) Zerschlagung *f*

collapsible [kə'læpsəbl] ADJ table, bicycle etc zusammenklappbar, Klapp-; telescope, walking stick zusammenschiebbar; life raft zusammenlegbar, zusammenfaltbar, Falt-; ~ **umbrella** zusammenschiebbarer Schirm, Taschenschirm *m*, Knirps® *m*

collar ['kɒlə'] N **a** Kragen *m*; **he got hold of him by the** ~ er packte ihn am Kragen; ~ **stud** Kragenknopf *m* **b** (for dogs) Halsband *nt*; (for horses) Kum(me)t *nt* **c** (= chain and insignia) Hals- or Ordenskette *f* **d** (Mech, on pipe etc) Bund *m* VT (= capture) fassen; (= latch onto) abfangen, schnappen (inf)

collarbone ['kɒləbəʊn] N Schlüsselbein *nt*

collate [kɒ'leɪt] VT **a** data, information zusammentragen **b** (Typ) kollationieren, zusammentragen

collateral [kɒ'lætərəl] ADJ **a** (= connected but secondary) evidence, questions etc zusätzlich, Zusatz-; events Begleit- **b** (= parallel, side by side) states etc nebeneinander liegend; (fig) aims etc Hand in Hand gehend **c** descent, branch of family seitlich, kollateral (spec) **d** (Fin) security zusätzlich N (Fin) (zusätzliche) Sicherheit

collateral: collateral loan N (Fin) Lombardkredit *m*, Lombarddarlehen *nt*; **collateral security** N (Fin) Nebensicherheit *f*, Nebenbürgschaft *f*

collation [kɒ'leɪʃən] N **a** (= collating) Vergleich *m*, Kollationieren *nt*; (Typ) Kollationieren *nt*, Zusammentragen *nt* **b** (form: = meal) Imbiss *m*

colleague ['kɒliːg] N Kollege *m*, Kollegin *f*; **my** ~**s at work** meine Arbeitskollegen

collect[1] ['kɒlekt] N (Eccl) Kirchen- or Tagesgebet *nt*

collect[2] [kə'lekt] ✪ 27.2 VT **a** (= accumulate) ansammeln; (furniture) dust anziehen; empty glasses, exam papers, tickets etc einsammeln; litter aufsammeln; prize bekommen; belongings zusammenpacken or -sammeln; (= assemble) sammeln; one's thoughts sammeln, ordnen; information sammeln, zusammentragen; volunteers zusammenbringen; **she** ~**ed a lot of praise/five points for that** das hat ihr viel Lob/fünf Punkte eingebracht or eingetragen; **to** ~ **interest** Zinsen bringen
b (= pick up, fetch) things, persons abholen (from bei)
c stamps, coins sammeln
d taxes einziehen; money, jumble for charity sammeln; rent, fares kassieren; debts eintreiben
VI **a** (= gather) sich ansammeln; (dust) sich absetzen
b (= collect money) sammeln; (for charity) sammeln
c (Comm: = call for goods) abholen
ADJ (US) → collect cable, collect call
ADV (US) **to pay** ~ bei Empfang bezahlen; **to call** ~ ein R-Gespräch führen; **to pay** ~ **on delivery** bei Lieferung bezahlen; (through post) per Nachnahme bezahlen

▶ **collect together** VT sep zusammensammeln; information zusammentragen; team of people auf- or zusammenstellen; **the officer collected his men together** der Offizier rief seine Leute zusammen

▶ **collect up** VT sep einsammeln; litter aufsammeln; belongings zusammenpacken or -sammeln

collect cable N (US) vom Empfänger bezahltes Telegramm

collect call N (US) R-Gespräch *nt*

collected [kə'lektɪd] ADJ **a the** ~ **works of Oscar Wilde** Oscar Wildes gesammelte Werke **b** (= calm) ruhig, gelassen

collectedly [kə'lektɪdlɪ] ADV ruhig, gelassen

collection [kə'lekʃən] N **a** (= group of people, objects) Ansammlung *f*; (of stamps, coins etc) Sammlung *f*; **they're an odd** ~ **of people** das ist ein seltsamer Verein (inf)
b (= collecting, of facts, information) Zusammentragen *nt*; (of goods, person) Abholung *f*; (of mail) Abholung *f*; (from letter box) Leerung *f*; (of stamps, coins) Sammeln *nt*; (of money, jumble for charity) Sammlung *f*; (in church) Kollekte *f*; (of rent, fares) Kassieren *nt*; (of taxes) Einziehen *nt*; (of debts) Eintreiben *nt*; **the police organized the** ~ **of all firearms** die Polizei ließ alle Schusswaffen einsammeln; **to hold a** ~ **for sb/ sth** für jdn/etw eine Sammlung durchführen; **bill for** ~ Inkassowechsel *m*
c (Fashion) Kollektion *f*

collective [kə'lektɪv] ADJ **a** kollektiv, Kollektiv-; responsibility, agreement, action also gemeinsam; ~ **ticket** Sammelfahrschein *m* **b** (= accumulated) wisdom, discoveries, experience gesamt attr; **the** ~ **unconscious** das kollektive Unbe-

wusste N Kollektiv *nt*; (= farm also) Produktionsgenossenschaft *f*

collective bargaining N Tarifverhandlungen *pl*

collective farm N landwirtschaftliche Produktionsgenossenschaft

collectively [kə'lektɪvlɪ] ADV gemeinsam, zusammen; (in socialist context also) kollektiv

collective noun N (Gram) Kollektivum *nt*, Sammelbegriff *m*

collective security N (Pol) kollektive Sicherheit

collectivism [kə'lektɪvɪzəm] N Kollektivismus *m*

collectivist [kə'lektɪvɪst] N Kollektivist(in) *m(f)* ADJ kollektivistisch

collectivize [kə'lektɪvaɪz] VT kollektivieren

collector [kə'lektə'] N **a** (of taxes) Einnehmer(in) *m(f)*; (of rent, cash) Kassierer(in) *m(f)*; (= ticket collector) Bahnbediensteter, der die abgefahrenen Fahrkarten einsammelt **b** (of stamps, coins etc) Sammler(in) *m(f)*; ~**'s** (item, piece, price) Sammler-, Liebhaber-; ~**'s car** Liebhaberauto *nt*

colleen ['kɒliːn] N (Ir) junges Mädchen, Mädel *nt*

college ['kɒlɪdʒ] N **a** (= part of university) College *nt*, Institut *nt*; **to go to** ~ (= university) studieren; **to start** ~ sein Studium beginnen; **we met at** ~ wir haben uns im Studium kennen gelernt **b** (of music, agriculture, technology etc) Fachhochschule *f*; **College of Art** Kunstakademie *f* **c** (= body) **College of Cardinals** Kardinalskollegium *nt*; **College of Physicians/Surgeons** Ärztebund *m*, Ärztekammer *f*

COLLEGE

College ist ein allgemeiner Oberbegriff für höhere Bildungsinstitute. In Großbritannien kann er sich auf Einrichtungen beziehen, in denen man in einzelnen Fachbereichen, wie Kunst oder Musik, einen Hochschulabschluss erwerben kann, aber ebenso auf Schulen ohne weiteren Abschluss, z. B. für Sekretärinnen oder Friseure. Einige britische Universitäten, darunter Oxford und Cambridge, setzen sich aus **Colleges** zusammen. In diesen **collegiate universities** sorgen die **Colleges** für die Unterbringung und Ausbildung der Studenten, auch wenn die Universität dann die Abschlüsse verleiht. Zu den bekanntesten **Colleges** zählen wohl das King's College in Cambridge und das Magdalen College in Oxford. In den USA werden die Universitäten in Verwaltungseinheiten unterteilt, die als **Colleges** bezeichnet werden: zum Beispiel das „College of Arts and Sciences" oder das „College of Medicine". **Graduate schools**, die normalerweise Teil einer Universität sind, bieten auf dem **bachelor** aufbauende Studiengänge zur weiteren Spezialisierung an. **Junior** oder **community colleges** sind Institute, an denen man nach zweijähriger Studienzeit einen berufsbezogenen Abschluss machen kann; sie bieten auch Weiterbildungen für Berufstätige an → DEGREE, OXBRIDGE

---

collegiate [kə'liːdʒɪt] ADJ College-; ~ **life** das Collegeleben, das Leben auf dem College; **Oxford is a** ~ **university** Oxford ist eine auf dem College-System aufgebaute Universität

collide [kə'laɪd] VI **a** (lit) zusammenstoßen or -prallen; (Naut) kollidieren; **they** ~**d head-on** sie stießen frontal zusammen; **to** ~ **with sb** mit jdm zusammenstoßen; **to** ~ **with sth** gegen etw prallen **b** (fig, person) eine heftige Auseinandersetzung haben (with mit); (interest, demands) kollidieren

collie ['kɒlɪ] N Collie *m*

collier ['kɒlɪə'] N **a** Bergmann *m*, Kumpel *m* (inf) **b** (= coal ship) Kohlenschiff *nt*

colliery ['kɒlɪərɪ] N Grube *f*, Zeche *f*

collimate ['kɒlɪmeɪt] VT kollimieren

collision [kə'lɪʒən] N (lit) Zusammenstoß m, Zusammenprall m; (fig) Zusammenstoß m, Konflikt m, Kollision (Neut) Kollision f; **on a ~ cours** (lit, fig) auf Kollisionskurs; **to be in ~ with sth** etw zusammenstoßen; **to come into ~ with sth** (lit, fig) mit etw zusammenstoßen; (Naut) mit etw kollidieren

collision dama... ...nsur) Schadenersatzverzichtklaus... ...nen

collocate ['kɒlə...' ... (G... ...ebeneinander stellen; **to be ~d** nebeneinander stehen

collocation [kɒlə'keɪʃən] N (Gram) Kollokation f

colloquial [kə'ləʊkwɪəl] ADJ umgangssprachlich

colloquialism [kə'ləʊkwɪəlɪzəm] N umgangssprachlicher Ausdruck

colloquially [kə'ləʊkwɪəlɪ] ADV umgangssprachlich

colloquium [kə'ləʊkwɪəm] N Kolloquium nt

colloquy ['kɒləkwɪ] N (form) Gespräch nt; (Liter) Dialog m; **in ~** im Gespräch

collude [kə'luːd] VI gemeinsame Sache machen (**with** mit)

collusion [kə'luːʒən] N (geheime) Absprache; **they're acting in ~** sie haben sich abgesprochen; **there's been some ~ between those two pupils** diese beiden Schüler haben zusammengearbeitet

collusive [kə'luːsɪv] ADJ **~ behaviour** geheime Absprachen pl; **~ business practices** geheime Geschäftsabsprachen pl

collywobbles ['kɒlɪˌwɒblz] PL (inf) **the ~** (= upset stomach) Bauchgrimmen nt (inf); (= nerves) ein flaues Gefühl im Magen

Cologne [kə'ləʊn] N Köln nt ADJ Kölner, kölnisch

cologne [kə'ləʊn] N Kölnischwasser nt, Eau de Cologne nt

colon[1] ['kəʊlən] N (Anat) Dickdarm m

colon[2] N (Gram) Doppelpunkt m; (old, Typ) Kolon nt

colonel ['kɜːnl] N Oberst m; (as address) Herr Oberst

colonial [kə'ləʊnɪəl] ADJ Kolonial-, kolonial; **~ architecture** Kolonialstil m; **~ type** Typ m des Herrenmenschen (iro) N Bewohner(in) m(f) einer Kolonie/der Kolonien

colonialism [kə'ləʊnɪəlɪzəm] N Kolonialismus m

colonialist [kə'ləʊnɪəlɪst] ADJ kolonialistisch N Kolonialist(in) m(f)

colonist ['kɒlənɪst] N Kolonist(in) m(f), Siedler(in) m(f)

colonization [ˌkɒlənaɪ'zeɪʃən] N Kolonisation f

colonize ['kɒlənaɪz] VT kolonisieren

colonized ['kɒlənaɪzd] ADJ kolonisiert

colonnade [ˌkɒlə'neɪd] N Kolonnade f, Säulengang m

colony ['kɒlənɪ] N Kolonie f

colophon ['kɒləfən] N Kolophon m, Signet nt

color etc (US) = **colour** etc

Colorado beetle [ˌkɒlə'rɑːdəʊ'biːtl] N Kartoffelkäfer m

colorant ['kʌlərənt] N (US) = **colourant**

coloration [ˌkʌlə'reɪʃən] N Färbung f

coloratura [kɒlərə'tʊərə] N Koloratur f

color guard N (US) = **colour party**

coloscopy [kə'lɒskəpɪ] N (Med) Koloskopie f

colossal [kə'lɒsl] ADJ riesig, ungeheuer, gewaltig; fool, cheek, mistake ungeheuer; car, man, park, lake, city riesig; prices, damage, building also kolossal

colossally [kə'lɒsəlɪ] ADV (= immensely) (+adj) wahnsinnig, unheimlich; (+vb) enorm, extrem; **~ expensive** wahnsinnig teuer

colosseum [kɒlɪ'siːəm] N Kolosseum nt

colossi [kə'lɒsaɪ] pl of **colossus**

Colossians [kə'lɒʃəns] N (Epistle to the) **~** Kolosserbrief m

colossus [kə'lɒsəs] N pl **colossi** or **-es** (= statue) Koloss m; (= person also) Riese m; **this ~ of the world of music** dieser Gigant or Titan der Musik

colostomy [kə'lɒstəmɪ] N (Med) Kolostomie f; **~ bag** Kolostomiebeutel m

colour, (US) **color** ['kʌlə'] N a (lit, fig) Farbe f; **what ~ is it?** welche Farbe hat es?; **red/yellow in ~** rot/gelb; **the film was in ~** der Film war in Farbe; **~ illustration** farbige Illustration; **a good sense of ~** ein guter Farbensinn; **let's see the ~ of your money first** (inf) zeig erst mal dein Geld her (inf); **the ~ of a note** (Mus) die Klangfarbe eines Tons → **glowing**

b (= complexion) (Gesichts)farbe f; **to change ~** die Farbe wechseln; **to get one's ~ back** wieder Farbe bekommen; **to bring the ~ back to sb's cheeks** jdm wieder Farbe geben; **to have a high ~** (Brit) eine gesunde Gesichtsfarbe haben; (= look feverish) rot im Gesicht sein; **he had gone a funny ~** er nahm eine komische Farbe an

c (racial) Hautfarbe f; **I don't care what ~ he is** seine Hautfarbe interessiert mich nicht; **people of ~** (dated) Farbige pl

d **colours** PL (= paints) Farben pl; **a box of ~s** ein Mal- or Tuschkasten m

e (fig: = bias: of newspaper, report) Färbung f

f (of place, period etc) Atmosphäre f; **to add ~ to a story** einer Geschichte (dat) Farbe geben; **the pageantry and ~ of Elizabethan England** der Prunk und die Farbenpracht des Elisabethanischen England

g (= appearance of truth) **to lend ~ to a tale** eine Geschichte ausschmücken

h **colours** PL (= symbols of membership) Farben pl; (Sport) (Sport)abzeichen nt; (= flag) Fahne f; **the regimental ~s** die Regimentsfahne; **to serve with/join the ~s** (old) der Fahne dienen (dated)/den bunten Rock anziehen (dated); **to nail one's ~s to the mast** (fig) Farbe bekennen; **to nail one's ~s to sb's mast** (fig) sich zu jdm bekennen; **to sail under false ~s** (fig) unter falscher Flagge segeln; **to show one's true ~s** (fig) sein wahres Gesicht zeigen

VT a (lit) anmalen; (Art) kolorieren; (= dye) färben

b (fig) beeinflussen; (= bias deliberately) färben

VI a (leaves) sich (ver)färben

b (person: also **colour up**) rot werden, erröten

▶ **colour in** VT sep anmalen; (Art) kolorieren

colourant, (US) **colorant** ['kʌlərənt] N Farbstoff m

colour, (US) **color** in cpds Farb-; (racial) Rassen-; (Mil) Fahnen-; **colour bar** N Rassenschranke f; (in country also) Rassenschranken pl; **to operate a ~** Rassentrennung praktizieren; **colour--blind** ADJ farbenblind; **colour blindness** N Farbenblindheit f; **colour-code** VT farbig kennzeichnen or kodieren; **colour coordination** N farbliche Abstimmung; **colour copy** N Farbkopie f

coloured, (US) **colored** ['kʌləd] ADJ a bunt; fabric, walls also farbig b (fig, = biased) gefärbt; (= exaggerated) ausgeschmückt; **a highly ~ account** ein reichlich ausgeschmückter Bericht c person, race farbig; (= of mixed blood) gemischtrassig N Farbige(r) mf; (of mixed blood) Mischling m

-coloured, (US) **-colored** ADJ suf **yellow-/red--coloured** gelb/rot; **straw-/dark-coloured** strohfarben/dunkel

colourfast, (US) **colorfast** ['kʌləfɑːst] ADJ farbecht

colourful, (US) **colorful** ['kʌləfʊl] ADJ a (lit) bunt; spectacle farbenfroh or -prächtig b (fig) style of writing, account etc farbig, anschaulich; life, historical period (bunt) bewegt; personality (bunt) schillernd; **his ~ past** seine bunte or bewegte Vergangenheit c (euph: = vulgar) language derb

colourfully, (US) **colorfully** ['kʌləfəlɪ] ADV (= brightly) dressed, painted, decorated bunt b (= excitingly) describe, write anschaulich c (euph: = vulgarly) swear heftig

colourfulness, (US) **colorfulness** ['kʌləfʊlnɪs] N a (lit) Buntheit f; (of spectacle) Farbenpracht f b (fig, of style of writing, account) Farbigkeit f, Anschaulichkeit f; (of sb's life, historical period) Bewegtheit f; **the ~ of his character** sein schillernder Charakter

colouring, (US) **coloring** ['kʌlərɪŋ] N a (= complexion) Gesichtsfarbe f, Teint m b (= substance) Farbstoff m c (= painting) Malen nt (= coloration) Farben pl e (fig, of news, facts etc) Färbung f

colouring book, (US) **coloring book** N Malbuch nt

colouring set, (US) **coloring set** N Mal- or Tuschkasten m; (= box of crayons) Schachtel f Buntstifte

colourist, (US) **colorist** ['kʌlərɪst] N Farbkünstler(in) m(f)

colourless, (US) **colorless** ['kʌlələs] ADJ (lit, fig) farblos; existence also grau

colourlessly, (US) **colorlessly** ['kʌlələslɪ] ADV (lit) farblos; (fig) neutral

colourlessness, (US) **colorlessness** ['kʌlələsnɪs] N Farblosigkeit f

colour, (US) **color**: **colour party** N Fahnenträgerkommando nt; **colour photograph** N Farbfoto nt; **colour postcard** N bunte Ansichtskarte; **colour retention** N (of clothes, paint) Farbechtheit f; **colour scheme** N Farbzusammenstellung f; **colour sergeant** N (Mil) Fahnenträger m; **colour supplement** N Farbbeilage f, Magazin nt; **colour television** N Farbfernsehen nt; (= set) Farbfernseher m; **colour transparency** N Farbdia nt; **colour-wash**, (US) **colorwash** N Farbtünche f

colt [kəʊlt] N Hengstfohlen nt; (dated fig: = youth) junger Dachs (inf)

Co Ltd abbr of **company limited** GmbH f

coltsfoot ['kəʊltsfʊt] N pl **-s** (Bot) Huflattich m

columbine ['kɒləmbaɪn] N (Bot) Akelei f

Columbus [kə'lʌmbəs] N Kolumbus m

Columbus Day N (US) amerikanischer Feiertag am zweiten Montag im Oktober, an dem die Entdeckung Amerikas durch Kolumbus gefeiert wird

column ['kɒləm] N a (Archit, of smoke, water etc) Säule f; **~ of mercury** Quecksilbersäule f b (of figures, names) Kolonne f; (= division of page) Spalte f, Kolumne f; (spec); (= article in newspaper) Kolumne f c (of vehicles, soldiers etc) Kolonne f

columnist ['kɒləmnɪst] N Kolumnist(in) m(f)

coma ['kəʊmə] N Koma nt; **to be in a ~** im Koma liegen; **to go** or **fall into a ~** ins Koma fallen

comatose ['kəʊmətəʊs] ADJ komatös

comb [kəʊm] N a (also Tech, of fowl) Kamm m b (= act) **to give one's hair a ~** sich kämmen; **your hair could do with a ~** du könntest dich (auch) mal wieder kämmen c (= honeycomb) Wabe f VT a hair, wool kämmen; horse striegeln; **to ~ one's hair** sich (dat) die Haare kämmen, sich kämmen b (= search) durchkämmen; newspapers durchforsten

▶ **comb out** VT sep a hair auskämmen b mistakes ausmerzen; useless stuff aussortieren

▶ **comb through** VI +prep obj hair kämmen; files, book etc durchgehen; shops durchstöbern

combat ['kɒmbæt] N Kampf m; **ready for ~** kampfbereit, einsatzbereit VT (lit, fig) bekämpfen VI kämpfen

combatant ['kɒmbətənt] N (lit, fig) Kombattant m

combat: combat dress N Kampfanzug m; **combat fatigue** N Kriegsmüdigkeit f

combative ['kɒmbətɪv] ADJ (= pugnacious) kämpferisch; (= competitive) aggressiv

combat: combat jacket N Feldjacke f, Kampfjacke f; **combat knife** N Kampfmesser nt; **combat mission** N Kampfeinsatz m;

combat plane N Kampfflugzeug *nt;* **combats** ['kɒmbæts] PL (*inf*) Tarnhose *f,* Kampfhose *f;* **combat troops** PL Kampftruppen *pl;* **combat trousers** PL (*Brit*) Tarnhose *f,* Kampfhose *f;* **combat unit** N (*esp US*) Kampfverband *m,* Kampfeinheit *f;* **combat zone** N Kampfgebiet *nt* or -zone *f*

combination [ˌkɒmbɪ'neɪʃən] N **a** Kombination *f;* (= *combining, of organizations, people etc*) Vereinigung *f,* Zusammenschluss *m;* (*of events*) Verkettung *f;* **in** ~ zusammen, gemeinsam; **an unusual colour** ~ eine ungewöhnliche Farbzusammenstellung; **pink is a** ~ **of red and white** Rosa ist eine Mischung aus Rot und Weiß; those two boys together are a nasty ~ diese beiden Jungen zusammen sind ein übles Duo **b** **combinations** PL (= *undergarment*) Kombination *f,* Hemdhose *f* **c** (= *motorcycle combination*) Motorrad *nt* mit Beiwagen **d** (*for lock*) Kombination *f*

combination: combination lock N Kombinationsschloss *nt;* **combination sandwich** N (*US*) gemischt belegtes Sandwich

combine [kəm'baɪn] **VT** kombinieren, verbinden; **couldn't we** ~ **the two suggestions?** lassen sich die beiden Vorschläge nicht kombinieren *or* miteinander verbinden?; **your plan** ~**s the merits of the other two** Ihr Plan vereinigt die Vorzüge der beiden anderen **VI** sich zusammenschließen; (*Chem*) sich verbinden; **to** ~ **against sb** sich gegen jdn verschwören **N** ['kɒmbaɪn] **a** (*Econ*) Firmengruppe *f,* Konzern *m;* (*in socialist countries*) Kombinat *nt* **b** (*Agr: also* **combine harvester**) Mähdrescher *m*

combined [kəm'baɪnd] ADJ gemeinsam; *talents, efforts* vereint; *forces* vereinigt; ~ **with** in Kombination mit; (*esp clothes, furniture*) kombiniert mit; **a** ~ **clock and wireless** eine Radiouhr; **a** ~ **radio and tape recorder** Radio *nt* und Tonband *nt* in einem; (*Ski*) **downhill** ~ Kombinationsabfahrt *f;* ~ **event** (*Sport*) Mehrkampf *m;* (*Ski*) Kombination *f;* ~ **honours** (*Brit, Univ*) Doppelstudium *nt;* ~ **operations** (*Mil*) gemeinsame Operation; ~ **time** (*Sport*) Gesamtzeit *f*

combining form [kəm'baɪnɪŋfɔːm] N Affix *nt,* Wortbildungselement *nt*

combo ['kɒmbəʊ] N (*Mus*) Combo *f*

combustibility [kəmˌbʌstɪ'bɪlɪtɪ] N Brennbarkeit *f*

combustible [kəm'bʌstɪbl] ADJ brennbar **N** brennbarer Stoff

combustion [kəm'bʌstʃən] N Verbrennung *f*

combustion chamber N Brennkammer *f*

come [kʌm] *pret* **came,** *ptp* **come** **VI** **a** (= *approach*) kommen; ~**!** (*form:* = *come in*) herein!; ~ **and get it!** (das) Essen ist fertig!, Essen fassen! (*esp Mil*); **to** ~ **and go** kommen und gehen; (*vehicle*) hin- und herfahren; **the picture/sound** ~**s and goes** das Bild/der Ton geht immerzu weg; **I don't know whether I'm coming or going** ich weiß nicht (mehr), wo mir der Kopf steht (*inf*); ~ **and see me soon** besuchen Sie mich bald einmal; **he has** ~ **a long way** er hat einen weiten Weg hinter sich; (*fig*) er ist weit gekommen; **the project has** ~ **a long way** das Projekt ist schon ziemlich weit; **he came running into the room** er kam ins Zimmer gerannt; **he came hurrying into the room** er eilte ins Zimmer; **he came laughing into the room** er kam lachend ins Zimmer; **coming!** ich komme (gleich)!, komm ja schon!; ~ ~**!**, ~ **now!** (*fig*) komm(, komm)!, na, na!; **Christmas is coming** bald ist Weihnachten

b (= *arrive*) kommen; (= *reach, extend*) reichen (**to** an/in/bis *etc* +*acc*); **they came to a town/ castle** sie kamen in eine Stadt/zu einem Schloss; **it came to me that ...** mir fiel ein, dass ...

c (= *have its place*) kommen; **May** ~**s before June** Mai kommt vor Juni; **the adjective must** ~ **before the noun** das Adjektiv muss vor dem Substantiv stehen; **where does your name** ~ **in the list?** an welcher Stelle auf der Liste steht Ihr Name?; **that must** ~ **first** das muss an erster Stelle kommen; **all the other candidates**

came far behind die anderen Bewerber waren weit abgeschlagen

d (= *happen*) geschehen; ~ **what may** ganz gleich, was geschieht, komme, was (da) mag (*geh*); **you could see it coming** das konnte man ja kommen sehen, das war ja zu erwarten; **she had it coming to her** (*inf*) das musste ja so kommen; **you've got it coming to you** (*inf*) mach dich auf was gefasst!; **recovery came slowly** nur allmählich trat eine Besserung ein **e** **how** ~? (*inf*) wieso?, weshalb?; **how** ~ **you're so late?, how do you** ~ **to be so late?** wieso *etc* kommst du so spät? **f** (= *be, become*) werden; **his dreams came true** seine Träume wurden wahr; **the handle has** ~ **loose** der Griff hat sich gelockert; **it** ~**s less expensive to shop in town** es ist *or* kommt billiger, wenn man in der Stadt einkauft; **everything came all right in the end** zuletzt *or* am Ende wurde doch noch alles gut **g** (*Comm:* = *be available*) erhältlich sein; **milk now** ~**s in plastic bottles** es gibt jetzt Milch in Plastikflaschen **h** (+*infin:* = *be finally in a position to*) **I have** ~ **to believe him** inzwischen *or* mittlerweile glaube ich ihm; **I'm sure you will** ~ **to agree with me** ich bin sicher, dass du mir schließlich zustimmst; (**now**) ~ **to think of it** wenn ich es mir recht überlege **i** **the years/weeks to** ~ die kommenden *or* nächsten Jahre/Wochen; **in days to** ~ in Zukunft; **in time to** ~ in künftigen Zeiten; **the life (of the world) to** ~ das ewige Leben **j** (*inf uses*) ... ~ **next week** nächste Woche ...; **I've known him for three years** ~ **January** im Januar kenne ich ihn drei Jahre; **how long have you been away?** – **a week** ~ **Monday** wie lange bist du schon weg? – (am) Montag acht Tage (*inf*) *or* eine Woche; ~ **Monday I'll be ...** Montag in acht Tagen (*inf*) *or* in einer Woche bin ich ...; ~ **again?** wie bitte?; **she is as vain as they** ~ sie ist so eingebildet wie nur was (*inf*) **k** (*inf:* = *have orgasm*) kommen (*inf*) **VT** (*Brit inf:* = *act as if one were*) spielen; **don't** ~ **the innocent with me** spielen Sie hier bloß nicht den Unschuldigen!, kommen Sie mir bloß nicht auf die unschuldige Tour (*inf*)!; **he tried to** ~ **the innocent with me** er hat versucht, den Unschuldigen zu markieren (*inf*), er hat es auf die unschuldige Tour versucht (*inf*); **don't** ~ **that game** *or* **that (with me)!** kommen Sie mir bloß nicht mit DER Tour! (*inf*), DIE Masche bei mir nicht! (*inf*); **that's coming it a bit strong!** das ist reichlich übertrieben **N** (*sl:* = *semen*) Saft *m* (*sl*)

▶ **come about** VI **a** *impers* (= *happen*) passieren; **how does it come about that you are here?** wie kommt es, dass du hier bist?; **this is why it came about** das ist so gekommen; **this is how it came about ...** das kam so ... **b** (*Naut, wind*) drehen; (*ship*) beidrehen

▶ **come across** **VI** **a** (= *cross*) herüberkommen **b** (= *be understood*) verstanden werden; (*message, speech*) ankommen **c** (= *make an impression*) wirken; **he wants to come across as a tough guy** (*inf*) er will gerne den starken Mann (*inf*) **d** (*inf:* = *do what is wanted*) mitmachen (*inf*) **VI** +*prep obj* (= *find or meet by chance*) treffen auf (+*acc*); **if you come across my watch ...** wenn du zufällig meine Uhr siehst

▶ **come across with** VI +*prep obj* (*inf*) *information* rausrücken mit (*inf*); *money* rausrücken (*inf*)

▶ **come after** **VI** +*prep obj* **a** (= *follow in sequence, be of less importance than*) kommen nach; **the noun comes after the verb** das Substantiv steht nach *or* hinter dem Verb **b** (= *pursue*) hinterherkommen (+*dat*) **c** (= *follow later*) nachkommen **VI** (= *follow later*) nachkommen

▶ **come along** VI **a** (= *hurry up, make an effort etc: also* **come on**) kommen **b** (= *attend, accompany*) kommen; **come along with me** kommen Sie mal (bitte) mit **c** (= *develop: also* **come on**) **to be coming along** sich machen, vorangehen; (*person*) sich machen; **how is your broken arm?** – **it's coming**

along nicely was macht dein gebrochener Arm? – dem gehts ganz gut *or* prima; **the bulbs are coming along nicely** die Blumenzwiebeln wachsen gut; **the new apprentice is coming along nicely** der neue Lehrling macht sich gut; **my play isn't coming along at all well** mein Stück macht überhaupt keine Fortschritte **d** (= *arrive, turn up*) kommen, auftauchen; (*chance etc*) sich ergeben

▶ **come apart** VI (= *fall to pieces*) kaputtgehen, auseinander fallen; (= *be able to be taken apart*) zerlegbar sein; **it just came apart in my hands** es ist in meinen Händen in Stücke gegangen

▶ **come (a)round** VI **a** **the road was blocked and we had to come round by the farm** die Straße war blockiert, so dass *or* sodass wir einen Umweg über den Bauernhof machen mussten **b** (= *call round*) vorbeikommen *or* -schauen **c** (= *recur*) **your birthday will soon come round again** du hast ja bald wieder Geburtstag; **Christmas has come round again** nun ist wieder Weihnachten **d** (= *change one's opinions*) es sich (*dat*) anders überlegen; **eventually he came round to our way of thinking** schließlich machte er sich (*dat*) unsere Denkungsart zu Eigen **e** (= *regain consciousness*) wieder zu sich (*dat*) kommen **f** **to come round to doing sth** (= *get round*) dazu kommen, etw zu tun **g** (= *throw off bad mood*) wieder vernünftig werden (*inf*) **h** (*Naut, boat*) wenden

▶ **come at** VI +*prep obj* (= *attack*) *sb* losgehen auf (+*acc*); (= *approach*) *runway* anfliegen; *problem* angehen

▶ **come away** VI **a** (= *leave*) (weg)gehen; **come away with me for a few days** fahr doch ein paar Tage mit mir weg!; **come away from there!** komm da weg!; **come away in!** (*Scot*) kommen Sie doch rein! **b** (= *become detached*) abgehen

▶ **come back** VI **a** (= *return*) zurückkommen; (= *drive back*) zurückfahren; **to come back to what I was saying** um noch einmal auf das zurückzukommen, was ich vorhin gesagt habe; **we always come back to the same difficulty** wir stoßen immer wieder auf dieselbe Schwierigkeit; **can I come back to you on that one?** kann ich später darauf zurückkommen?; **the colour is coming back to her cheeks** langsam bekommt sie wieder Farbe; **will his memory ever come back?** wird er je das Gedächtnis wiedererlangen? **b** (= *return to one's memory*) **his name is coming back to me** langsam erinnere ich mich wieder an seinen Namen; **ah yes, it's all coming back** ach ja, jetzt fällt mir alles wieder ein; **your German will very quickly come back** du wirst ganz schnell wieder ins Deutsche reinkommen (*inf*) **c** (= *become popular again*) wieder in Mode kommen **d** (= *make a comeback*) **they thought Sinatra would never come back** man glaubte, Sinatra würde niemals ein Come-back machen; **they came back into the game with a superb goal** sie fanden mit einem wunderbaren Tor ins Spielgeschehen zurück **e** (= *reply*) reagieren; **she came back at him with a fierce accusation** sie entgegnete ihm mit einer heftigen Anschuldigung

▶ **come before** VI +*prep obj* (*Jur, person*) gebracht werden vor (+*acc*); **his case came before the court** sein Fall wurde vor Gericht gebracht

▶ **come between** VI +*prep obj* *people, lovers* treten zwischen (+*acc*); **I never let anything come between me and my evening pint** ich lasse mich durch nichts von meinem abendlichen Bier(chen) abhalten; **he tried to come between the two fighting men** er versuchte, die beiden Kampfhähne zu trennen

▶ **come by** **VI** +*prep obj* (= *obtain*) kriegen; *illness, bruise* sich (*dat*) holen; *idea* kommen auf (+*acc*) **VI** (= *visit*) vorbeikommen

▶ **come close to** VI +*prep obj* = **come near to**

►**come down** VI **a** (*from ladder, stairs*) herunterkommen; (*aircraft also*) landen; (*from mountain also*) absteigen; (*snow, rain*) fallen; **come down from there at once!** komm da sofort runter!; **we came down to 6,000 metres** wir gingen auf 6.000 m runter

b (= *be demolished: building etc*) abgerissen werden; (= *fall down*) (he)runterfallen

c (= *drop, prices*) sinken, runtergehen (*inf*); (*seller*) runtergehen (*to* auf +*acc*)

d (= *be a question of*) ankommen (*to* auf +*acc*); **it all comes down to something very simple** das ist letzten Endes ganz einfach; **when you come** *or* **it comes down to it** letzten Endes

e (= *lose social rank*) sinken, absteigen; **you've come down in the world a bit** du bist aber ganz schön tief gesunken

f (= *reach*) reichen (*to* bis auf +*acc*, zu); **her hair comes down to her shoulders** die Haare gehen *or* fallen ihr bis auf die Schultern; **the dress comes down to her ankles** das Kleid geht ihr bis zu den Knöcheln

g (= *be transmitted: tradition, story etc*) überliefert werden

h (*from university*) **when did you come down?** wann bist du von der Uni runter? (*inf*), wann haben Sie die Universität verlassen?; (*for vacation*) seit wann habt ihr Semesterferien?

i (*dated US, inf: = be about to happen*) **there's a bank robbery coming down next week** für nächste Woche ist ein Banküberfall geplant

►**come down on** VI +*prep obj* **a** (= *punish, rebuke*) rannehmen (*inf*), zusammenstauchen (*inf*) → **brick** **b** (= *decide in favour of*) setzen auf (+*acc*); **he came down on the side of expansion** er setzte auf Expansion; **you've got to come down on one side or the other** du musst dich so oder so entscheiden

►**come down with** VI +*prep obj illness* kriegen

►**come for** VI +*prep obj* kommen wegen

►**come forward** VI **a** (= *make oneself known*) sich melden **b** **to come forward with help/money** Hilfe/Geld anbieten; **to come forward with a good suggestion** mit einem guten Vorschlag kommen

►**come from** VI +*prep obj* kommen aus; (*suggestion*) kommen *or* stammen von; **where does he/it come from?** wo kommt er/das her?

►**come in** VI **a** (= *enter*) (he)reinkommen; (*person also*) eintreten; **come in!** herein!; **to come in out of the cold** aus der Kälte kommen

b (= *arrive*) ankommen, eintreffen; (*train also*) einfahren; (*ship also*) einlaufen

c (*tide*) kommen

d (*report, information etc*) hereinkommen; **a report has just come in of …** uns ist gerade eine Meldung über … zugegangen

e (= *become seasonable*) **when do strawberries come in?** wann ist die Zeit für Erdbeeren?, wann gibt es (frische) Erdbeeren?

f (*fashions, vogue*) aufkommen, in Mode kommen

g (*in a race*) **he came in fourth** er wurde Vierter, er belegte den vierten Platz; **where did he come in?** wie Wievielte ist er denn geworden?, welchen Platz hat er belegt?

h (*Pol: = be elected to power*) **when the socialists came in** als die Sozialisten ans Ruder *or* an die Regierung kamen

i (= *be received as income*) **he has £15,000 coming in every year** er kriegt (*inf*) *or* hat £ 15.000 im Jahr; **we have no money coming in at the moment** im Moment kommt kein Geld herein

j (= *have a part to play*) **where do I come in?** welche Rolle spiele ich dabei?; **… but where does your brother come in?** … aber was hat dein Bruder mit der ganzen Sache zu tun?; **that will come in handy** (*inf*) *or* **useful** das kann ich/man noch gut gebrauchen

k (*Telec*) **come in, Panda 5** Panda 5, melden!

►**come in for** VI +*prep obj attention, admiration* erregen; *criticism etc also* hinnehmen *or* einstecken müssen

►**come in on** VI +*prep obj venture, scheme etc* mitmachen bei, sich beteiligen an (+*dat*)

►**come into** VI +*prep obj* **a** (= *inherit*) *legacy etc* erben **b** (= *be involved*) **I don't see where I come into all this** ich verstehe nicht, was ich mit der ganzen Sache zu tun habe; **this is a donation, publicity doesn't come into it** es handelt sich hier um eine Spende, Publicity ist dabei nicht im Spiel **c** (*in fixed collocations*) **to come into one's own** zeigen, was in einem steckt; **to come into being** *or* **existence** entstehen; **to come into bud** zu knospen beginnen; **to come into sb's possession** in jds Besitz (*acc*) gelangen

►**come near to** VI +*prep obj* **to come near to doing sth** nahe daran *or* drauf und dran sein, etw zu tun; **he came near to (committing) suicide** er war *or* stand kurz vor dem Selbstmord

►**come of** VI +*prep obj* **a** (= *result from*) **nothing came of it** es ist nichts daraus geworden, es führte zu nichts; **that's what comes of disobeying!** das kommt davon, wenn man nicht hören will! **b** (= *be descended from*) kommen *or* stammen aus

►**come off** VI **a** (*person: off bicycle etc*) runterfallen

b (*button, handle, paint etc*) abgehen; (= *be removable also*) sich abnehmen lassen

c (*stains, marks*) weg- *or* rausgehen

d (= *take place*) stattfinden; **her wedding didn't come off after all** aus ihrer Hochzeit ist nun doch nichts geworden

e (*plans etc*) klappen (*inf*); (*attempts, experiments etc also*) glücken, gelingen

f (= *acquit oneself*) abschneiden; **he came off well in comparison to his brother** im Vergleich zu seinem Bruder ist er gut weggekommen; **he always came off badly in fights** bei Schlägereien zog er immer den Kürzeren; **several companies are likely to come off badly with the new tax laws** mehrere Firmen kommen in der neuen Steuergesetzgebung schlecht weg

g (*sl: = have orgasm*) kommen (*inf*); **eventually he came off** endlich kam es ihm (*sl*)

VI +*prep obj* **a** *bicycle, horse etc* fallen von

b (*button, paint, stain*) abgehen von

c *case, assignment etc* abgeben; **to come off the gold standard** (*Fin*) vom Goldstandard abgehen

d **to come off sth** (*drugs, medication*) aufhören mit etw

e (= *be removed from price of*) runtergehen von (*inf*)

f (*inf*) **come off it!** nun mach mal halblang! (*inf*)

►**come on** VI **a** (= *follow*) nachkommen

b = **come along** **a** **come on!** komm!; **come ON!** komm schon!

c (= *continue to advance*) zukommen (*towards* auf +*acc*)

d (*Brit: = progress, develop*) = **come along c**

e (= *start, night*) hereinbrechen; (*storm*) ausbrechen, einsetzen; **it came on to rain, the rain came on** es begann zu regnen, es fing an zu regnen; **I've a cold coming on** ich kriege eine Erkältung; **winter etc is coming on** es wird Winter etc

f (*Jur, case*) verhandelt werden

g (*Sport: player*) ins Spiel kommen; (*Theat, actor*) auftreten, auf die Bühne kommen; (*play*) gegeben werden

h (*inf*) **she's coming on seventeen** sie wird siebzehn

i (*inf: = make impression, behave*) **he tries to come on like a tough guy** er versucht, den starken Mann zu mimen (*inf*); **he came on with this bit about knowing the director** er gab damit an, den Direktor zu kennen; **to come on strong** groß auftreten (*inf*)

VI +*prep obj* = **come (up)on**

►**come on to** VI +*prep obj* (*esp US inf: = make advances to*) anmachen (*inf*)

►**come out** VI **a** (= *leave*) (he)rauskommen; **to come out of a room/meeting etc** aus einem Zimmer/einer Versammlung etc kommen; **can you come out tonight?** kannst du heute Abend weg?; **do you want to come out with me?** gehst du mit mir weg?; **he asked her to come out for a meal/drive** er lud sie zum Essen/einer Spazierfahrt ein; **to come out fighting** (*fig*) sich kämpferisch geben

b (= *be published, marketed, book, magazine*) erscheinen, herauskommen; (*new product*) auf den Markt kommen; (*film*) (in den Kinos) anlaufen; (= *become known, exam results*) herauskommen, bekannt werden; (*news*) bekannt werden

c (*Ind*) **to come out (on strike)** in den Streik treten, streiken

d (*Phot, film, photograph*) **the photo of the hills hasn't come out very well** das Foto von den Bergen ist nicht sehr gut geworden; **let's hope the photos come out** hoffentlich sind die Bilder was geworden (*inf*) *or* gut geworden; **you always come out well in photos** du bist sehr fotogen; **all the details have come out clearly** alle Einzelheiten kommen klar (he)raus

e (= *show itself*) sich zeigen; **his arrogance comes out in everything he says** bei allem, was er sagt, kommt seine Arroganz durch

f (*splinter, stains, dye etc*) (he)rausgehen

g (*Math: problems, divisions etc*) aufgehen

h (= *total, average*) betragen; **the total comes out at £500** das Ganze beläuft sich auf (+*acc*) *or* macht (*inf*) £ 500

i (*in exams etc*) **he came out third in French** er wurde Drittbester in Französisch

j (*stars, sun, flowers*) (he)rauskommen; **no sooner had the words come out than …** kaum waren die Worte heraus, als …

l (= *go into society: girl*) debütieren

m (= *be released: prisoner*) (he)rauskommen

n (*homosexual*) sich outen; (*man also*) sich als Homosexueller bekennen; (*woman also*) sich als Lesbe bekennen

o **his face came out in spots** er bekam lauter Pickel im Gesicht; **he came out in a rash** er bekam einen Ausschlag; **he came out in a sweat** ihm brach der Schweiß aus

p **to come out against/in favour of** *or* **for sth** sich gegen/für etw aussprechen, etw ablehnen/befürworten

q **to come out of sth badly/well** bei etw schlecht/nicht schlecht wegkommen; **she came out of the interview well** sie hat bei dem Vorstellungsgespräch einen guten Eindruck gemacht; **to come out on top** sich durchsetzen, Sieger bleiben

►**come out with** VI +*prep obj truth, facts* rausrücken mit (*inf*); *remarks, nonsense* loslassen (*inf*)

►**come over** VI **a** (*lit*) herüberkommen; **he came over to England** er kam nach England

b (= *change one's opinions, allegiance*) **he came over to our side** er trat auf unsere Seite über; **he came over to our way of thinking** er machte sich unsere Denkungsart zu Eigen

c (*inf: = become suddenly*) werden; **I came over (all) queer** *or* **funny** mir wurde ganz komisch (*inf*) *or* ganz merkwürdig

d (= *be understood*) = **come across VI b**

e (= *make an impression*) = **come across VI c**

VI +*prep obj* (*feelings*) überkommen; **I don't know what came over her to speak like that!** ich weiß nicht, was über sie gekommen ist, so zu reden!; **what's come over you?** was ist denn (auf einmal) mit dir los?, was ist in dich gefahren?

►**come through** VI **a** (*phone call, order*) durchkommen; **your expenses haven't come through yet** (= *been cleared*) wir haben Ihre Ausgaben noch nicht durchgekriegt; **your papers haven't come through yet** Ihre Papiere sind noch nicht fertig; **his divorce has come through** seine Scheidung ist durch (*inf*) **b** (= *survive*) durchkommen **c** (= *be successful*) **to come through for sb** für jdn da sein; **they came through on their promises** sie haben ihre Versprechen gehalten VI +*prep obj* (= *survive*) *illness, danger* überstehen

►**come to** VI **a** (= *regain consciousness: also* **come to oneself**) wieder zu sich kommen

b (*Naut*) beidrehen VI +*prep obj* **a** **that will**

never come to much daraus wird nie etwas werden; **that won't come to much** daraus wird nicht viel werden; **that didn't come to anything** daraus ist nichts geworden

b *impers* **when it comes to mathematics ...** wenn es um Mathematik geht, ...; **when it comes to choosing, he ...** wenn er die Wahl hat *or* vor die Wahl gestellt wird, ...; **if it comes to that we're sunk** wenn es dazu kommt, sind wir verloren; **come to that** *or* **if it comes to that, he's just as good** was das betrifft *or* an(be)langt, ist er genauso gut; **let's hope it never comes to a court case** *or* **to court** wollen wir hoffen, dass es nie zum Prozess kommt; **it comes to the same thing** das kommt *or* läuft auf dasselbe hinaus

c *(price, bill)* **how much does it come to?** wie viel macht das?; **it comes to £20** es kommt auf *or* beläuft sich auf £ 20; **it comes to much less/more than I thought** es kommt viel billiger/teurer, als ich dachte

d *(= touch on)* *point, subject etc* kommen auf *(+acc)*; *(= tackle)* *problem, job etc* herangehen an *(+acc)*

e *(in certain collocations)* **to come to a decision** zu einer Entscheidung kommen; **it's coming to something when ...** es will schon etwas heißen, wenn ...; **what are things** *or* **what is the world coming to!** wohin soll das noch führen! → **blow** [1], **light** *etc*

▶ **come together** VI zusammenkommen, sich treffen; **he and his wife have come together again** er ist wieder mit seiner Frau zusammen; **it's all coming together for him** *(inf)* es regelt sich jetzt alles für ihn *(inf)*

▶ **come under** VI *+prep obj* **a** *(= be subject to)* **to come under sb's influence/domination** unter jds Einfluss/Herrschaft geraten; **this shop has come under new management** dieser Laden hat einen neuen Besitzer/Pächter; **this comes under another department** das ist Sache einer anderen Abteilung **b** *category, heading* kommen unter *(+acc)*

▶ **come up** VI **a** *(lit)* hochkommen; *(upstairs)* hoch- *or* raufkommen; *(diver, submarine)* nach oben kommen; *(sun, moon)* aufgehen; **do you come up to town often?** kommen Sie oft in die Stadt?; **he came up (to Oxford) last year** *(Univ)* er studiert seit letztem Jahr (in Oxford); **you've come up in the world** du bist ja richtig vornehm geworden!; **he came up to me with a smile** er kam lächelnd auf mich zu **b** *(supplies, troops etc)* herangeschafft werden **c** *(Jur, case)* verhandelt werden, drankommen *(inf)*; *(accused)* vor Gericht kommen **d** *(plants)* herauskommen **e** *(matter for discussion)* aufkommen, angeschnitten werden; *(name)* erwähnt werden; **I can't do it as I'm afraid something has come up** ich bin leider verhindert, ich kann leider nicht **f** *(number in lottery etc)* gewinnen; **to come up for sale/auction** *etc* zum Verkauf/zur Auktion *etc* kommen; **my contract will soon come up for renewal** mein Vertrag muss bald verlängert werden **g** *(post, job)* frei werden **h** *(exams, election)* bevorstehen **i** *(= be vomited)* wieder hochkommen **j** *(= shine, show colour)* herauskommen

▶ **come up against** VI *+prep obj* stoßen auf *(+acc)*; *opposing team* treffen auf *(+acc)*; **his plan was doing well until he came up against the directors** sein Vorhaben machte gute Fortschritte, bis er an die Geschäftsleitung geriet; **the new teacher keeps coming up against the headmaster** der neue Lehrer gerät ständig mit dem Direktor aneinander

▶ **come (up)on** VI *+prep obj* **a** *(lit, = attack by surprise)* überfallen; *(fig, disaster)* hereinbrechen über *(+acc)* **b** *(= find)* stoßen auf *(+acc)*

▶ **come up to** VI *+prep obj* **a** *(= reach up to)* gehen *or* reichen bis zu *or* an *(+acc)*; **the water came up to his knees** das Wasser ging *or* reichte ihm bis an die Knie *or* bis zu den Knien **b** *(= equal)* hopes erfüllen; *expectations*

entsprechen *(+dat)* **c** *(inf: = approach)* **she's coming up to twenty** sie wird bald zwanzig; **we're coming up to 150 km/h** wir haben gleich 150 km/h drauf *(inf)*; **it's just coming up to 10 o'clock** es ist gleich 10 Uhr

▶ **come up with** VI *+prep obj* *answer* haben; *idea, solution also* kommen auf *(+acc)*; *plan* sich *(dat)* ausdenken, entwickeln; *suggestion* machen, bringen; **I can't come up with any answers either** ich habe auch keine Antwort; **let me know if you come up with anything** sagen Sie mir Bescheid, falls Ihnen etwas einfällt

come-at-able [kʌmˈætəbl] ADJ *(inf)* leicht erreichbar

Comeback [ˈkʌmbæk] N **a** *(Theat etc, fig)* Come-back *nt*, Comeback *nt*; **to make** *or* **stage a ~** ein Come-back versuchen/machen **b** *(inf, = redress)* Anspruch *m* auf Schadenersatz; *(= reaction)* Reaktion *f*; **we've got no ~ in this situation** wir können da nichts machen

Comecon [ˈkɒmɪkɒn] *abbr of* **Council for Mutual Economic Aid** Comecon *m or nt*

comedian [kəˈmiːdɪən] N Komiker(in) *m(f)*; *(fig also)* Witzbold *m*

comedic [kəˈmiːdɪk] ADJ komisch

comedienne [kəˌmiːdɪˈen] N Komikerin *f*; *(= actress)* Komödiendarstellerin *f*

comedown [ˈkʌmdaʊn] N *(inf)* Abstieg *m*

comedy [ˈkɒmɪdɪ] N **a** *(Theat)* Komödie *f*, Lustspiel *nt*; **~ programme** Unterhaltungsprogramm *nt*; **~ writer** Lustspielautor(in) *m(f)* *or* *(classical)* -dichter(in) *m(f)*; **"Comedy of Errors"** „Komödie der Irrungen"; **the entire deal was just a ~ of errors** *(fig)* bei dem Geschäft ging aber auch alles daneben; **low ~** Klamauk *m*; **high ~** echte *or* gekonnte Komödie; **to act in ~** Komödiendarsteller(in) *m(f)* sein **b** *(fig)* Komödie *f*, Theater *nt* *(inf)*

come-hither [kʌmˈhɪðə'] ADJ *(inf)* **she gave him a ~ look** sie warf ihm einladende *or* aufmunternde Blicke zu

comeliness [ˈkʌmlɪnɪs] N *(liter)* Wohlgestalt *f* *(liter)*

comely [ˈkʌmlɪ] ADJ *(+er)* *(liter)* wohlgestaltet *(geh)*

come-on [ˈkʌmɒn] N *(inf: = lure, enticement)* Köder *m* *(fig)*; **to give sb the ~** *(woman)* jdn anmachen *(inf)*

comer [ˈkʌmə'] N **this competition is open to all ~s** an diesem Wettbewerb kann sich jeder beteiligen; **"open to all ~s"** „Teilnahme für jedermann"

comestible [kəˈmestɪbl] N *usu pl* Nahrungsmittel *pl* ADJ essbar; **~ goods** Nahrungsmittel *pl*

comet [ˈkɒmɪt] N Komet *m*

come-to-bed [ˈkʌmtəbed] ADJ **she/he has ~ eyes** *(inf)* sie/er hat Schlafzimmeraugen *(inf)*

comeuppance [ˌkʌmˈʌpəns] N *(inf)* **to get one's ~** die Quittung kriegen *(inf)*

comfit [ˈkʌmfɪt] N *(old)* Konfekt *nt*, Zuckerwerk *(old)* *nt*

comfort [ˈkʌmfət] N **a** Komfort *m*, Bequemlichkeit *f*; **relax in the ~ of a leather armchair** entspannen Sie sich in unseren behaglichen Ledersesseln; **he likes his ~s** er liebt seinen Komfort *or* seine Bequemlichkeit; **to live in ~** komfortabel leben; **an apartment with all modern ~s** eine Wohnung mit allem Komfort

b *(= consolation)* Beruhigung *f*, Trost *m*; **to take ~ from the fact that ...** sich mit dem Gedanken *or* sich damit trösten, dass ...; **your presence is/you are a ~ to me** es beruhigt mich sehr, dass Sie da sind; **it is a ~ to know that ...** es ist tröstlich *or* beruhigend zu wissen, dass ...; **it is no ~** *or* **of little ~ to know that ...** es ist nicht sehr tröstlich zu wissen, dass ...; **some ~ you are!** *(iro)* das ist ja ein schöner Trost! *(iro)*, du bist gut! *(iro)*; **small ~** schwacher Trost; **a pipe is a great ~ to me** Pfeiferauchen hat etwas sehr Beruhigendes; **your poems brought a little ~ to my life** Ihre Gedichte haben ein wenig Trost in mein Leben gebracht; **too close for ~** bedrohlich nahe

VT *(= console)* trösten; **the child needed a lot of ~ing** es dauerte eine ganze Weile, bis das Kind sich trösten ließ; **he stayed with the injured man to ~ him** er blieb bei dem Verletzten, um ihm Beistand zu leisten; **the hot soup ~ed him a little** nach der heißen Suppe fühlte er sich etwas wohler

comfortable [ˈkʌmfətbl] ADJ **a** *armchair, bed, shoes, life, position* bequem; *room, hotel etc* komfortabel; *temperature* angenehm; **to make sb/oneself ~** es jdm/sich bequem machen; *(= make at home)* es jdm/sich gemütlich machen; **the sick man had a ~ night** der Kranke hatte *or* verbrachte eine ruhige Nacht; **the patient/his condition is ~** der Patient/er ist wohlauf, **are you ~?, asked the nurse** liegen/sitzen *etc* Sie bequem?, fragte die Schwester; **are you too hot? – no, I'm just ~** ist es Ihnen zu heiß? – nein, es ist angenehm so

b *(fig)* *income, pension* ausreichend; *life* geruhsam, angenehm; *majority, lead* sicher; *winner* überlegen; *figure* mollig; **he's very ~ to be with** bei ihm fühlt man sich sehr wohl; **she had quite a ~ feeling about it** sie hatte ein gutes Gefühl dabei; **to feel ~ with sb/sth** sich bei jdm/etw wohl fühlen; **I'm not very ~ about it** mir ist nicht ganz wohl bei der Sache; **I'm not too ~ about giving her the job** mir ist nicht ganz wohl bei dem Gedanken, ihr die Stelle zu geben; **in ~ circumstances** *(= well-off)* gut situiert

comfortably [ˈkʌmfətblɪ] ADV **a** *lie, sit, dress, fit etc* bequem; *furnished, upholstered* komfortabel **b** *(fig)* *win, lead* sicher; *live* geruhsam, angenehm; *afford* gut und gern; *claim, say* ruhig; **they are ~ off** es geht ihnen gut

comfort eating N Essen *nt* als Trost

comforter [ˈkʌmfətə'] N **a** *(= person)* Tröster(in) *m(f)*; **my wife was my ~ in times of stress** in schweren Zeiten war meine Frau mein Beistand **b** *(dated: = scarf)* Wollschal *m* **c** *(= dummy, teat)* Schnuller *m* **d** *(US: = quilt)* Deckbett *nt*

comfort food N Essen *nt*, das als Trost dient

comforting [ˈkʌmfətɪŋ] ADJ tröstlich, beruhigend; **a ~ cup of tea** eine Tasse Tee zur Beruhigung

comfortless [ˈkʌmfətlɪs] ADJ **a** *chair etc* unbequem; *room, hotel* ohne Komfort **b** *(fig)* *person* ungemütlich; *life* unbequem; *thought, prospect* unerfreulich, unangenehm

comfort station N *(US)* Bedürfnisanstalt *f*, öffentliche Toilette

comfort zone N Bereich, in dem man sich sicher fühlt **two goals in two minutes put Rangers in the ~** nach zwei Toren in zwei Minuten fühlten Rangers sich sicher

comfy [ˈkʌmfɪ] ADJ *(+er)* *(inf)* *chair* bequem; *hotel, flat, room* gemütlich; **are you ~?** sitzt/liegst du bequem?; **make yourself ~** machen Sie es sich *(dat)* bequem *or* gemütlich *(inf)*

comic [ˈkɒmɪk] ADJ komisch; **~ actor** Komödiendarsteller(in) *m(f)*, Komöde *m* *(geh)*; **~ verse** humoristische Gedichte *pl* N **a** *(= person)* Komiker(in) *m(f)* **b** *(= magazine)* Comicheft(chen) *nt* **c** *(US)* **~s** Comics *pl*

comical ADJ , **comically** ADV [ˈkɒmɪkəl, -ɪ] komisch, ulkig

comic: comic book N Comicbuch *nt*; **comic opera** N komische Oper; **comic relief** N befreiende Komik; **comic strip** N Comicstrip *m*

coming [ˈkʌmɪŋ] N Kommen *nt*; **you can sense the ~ of spring** man fühlt *or* spürt das Herannahen des Frühlings; **the first/second ~ (of the Lord)** die Ankunft/Wiederkunft des Herrn; **the ~ of a new manager** die Ankunft eines neuen Geschäftsführers; **~ and going/~s and goings** Kommen und Gehen *nt*; **~ of age** Erreichung *f* der Volljährigkeit ADJ *(lit, fig)* kommend; *year, week also* nächst; **a ~ politician** einer der kommenden Männer in der Politik; **the ~ election** die bevorstehende Wahl; **it's the ~ thing** *(inf)* das ist zur Zeit groß im Kommen *(inf)*

coming-out [ˈkʌmɪŋˈaʊt] N gesellschaftliches Debüt, (offizielle) Einführung in die Gesellschaft; (of homosexual, lesbian) Coming-out nt; ~ **party** Debütantinnenparty f

comma [ˈkɒmə] N Komma nt

command [kəˈmɑːnd] **VT a** (= order) befehlen, den Befehl geben (sb jdm); **he ~ed that the prisoners be released** er befahl, die Gefangenen freizulassen

b (= be in control of) army, ship befehligen, kommandieren

c (= be in a position to use) money, resources, vocabulary verfügen über (+acc), gebieten über (+acc) (geh); **to ~ sb's services** jds Dienste or Hilfe in Anspruch nehmen

d to ~ sb's admiration/respect jdm Bewunderung/Respekt abnötigen, jds Bewunderung/Respekt erheischen (geh); **antiques ~ a high price** Antiquitäten stehen hoch im Preis

e (= overlook) valley überragen; view bieten (of über +acc)

VI a (= order) befehlen

b (Mil, Naut: = to be in command) das Kommando führen

N a (= order) Befehl m; **at/by the ~ of** auf Befehl +gen; **at the word of ~** auf Kommando; **on ~** auf Befehl or Kommando

b (Mil: = power, authority) Kommando nt, Befehlsgewalt f; **to be in ~** das Kommando or den (Ober)befehl haben (of über +acc); **to take ~** das Kommando übernehmen (of +gen); **the new colonel arrived to take ~** of his regiment der neue Oberst kam, um sein Regiment zu übernehmen; **during/under his ~** unter seinem Kommando; **the battalion is under the ~ of ...** das Bataillon steht unter dem Kommando von ... or wird befehligt von ...; **to be second in ~** zweiter Befehlshaber sein

c (Mil: = troops) Kommando nt; (= district) Befehlsbereich m; (= command post) Posten m

d (Comput) Befehl m

e (fig: = possession, mastery) Beherrschung f; ~ **of the seas** Seeherrschaft f; **the gymnast's remarkable ~ over his body** die bemerkenswerte Körperbeherrschung des Turners; **his ~ of English is excellent** er beherrscht das Englische ausgezeichnet; **to have sb/sth at one's ~** über jdn/etw verfügen or gebieten (geh); **I am at your ~** ich stehe zu Ihrer Verfügung; **to be in ~ (of oneself)** sich unter Kontrolle haben

commandant [ˌkɒmənˈdænt] N (Mil) Kommandant(in) m(f)

command economy N Kommandowirtschaft f

commandeer [ˌkɒmənˈdɪə] VT (Mil) men einziehen; (from another battalion, fig) abbeordern, abkommandieren; stores, ship, car etc (lit, fig) beschlagnahmen, requirieren

commander [kəˈmɑːndə] N **a** Führer(in) m(f); (Mil, Aviat) Befehlshaber(in) m(f), Kommandant(in) m(f); (Naut) Fregattenkapitän(in) m(f); (Brit, Police) Distriktleiter der Londoner Polizei **b** (of order of chivalry) Komtur m

commander in chief N pl **commanders in chief** Oberbefehlshaber(in) m(f)

commanding [kəˈmɑːndɪŋ] ADJ **a** (= in charge) position Befehls- **b** (= dominant, powerful) position führend; personality gebieterisch; voice, tone Kommando- (pej); **to be in a ~ position** eine führende Stellung haben; **to have a ~ lead** überlegen führen **c** (of place) beherrschend; ~ **heights** Kommandohöhen pl

commandingly [kəˈmɑːndɪŋlɪ] ADV speak gebieterisch

commanding officer N (Mil) befehlshabender Offizier

command language N (Comput) Befehlssprache f

command line N (Comput) Befehlszeile f

commandment [kəˈmɑːndmənt] N (esp Bibl) Gebot nt; **to break a ~** gegen ein Gebot verstoßen

command module N (Space) Kommandokapsel f

commando [kəˈmɑːndəʊ] N pl **-s** (Mil) (= soldier) Angehörige(r) m eines Kommando(trupp)s; (= unit) Kommando(trupp m) nt

command: command paper N (Brit: Parl) (dem Parlament vorgelegter) Kabinettsbeschluss m; **command performance** N (Theat) königliche Galavorstellung; **command post** N (Mil) Kommandoposten m

commemorate [kəˈmeməreɪt] VT gedenken (+gen); **a festival to ~ the event** eine Feier zum Gedenken an das Ereignis

commemoration [kəˌmeməˈreɪʃən] N Gedenken nt; **in ~ of** zum Gedenken an (+acc)

commemorative [kəˈmemərətɪv] ADJ Gedenk-; ~ **plaque** Gedenktafel f

commence [kəˈmens] (form) **VI** beginnen **VT** beginnen (obj mit +dat); legal proceedings eröffnen; **to ~ doing** or **to do sth** mit etw anfangen

commencement [kəˈmensmənt] N **a** (form) Beginn m **b** (Univ, Cambridge, Dublin, US) Abschlussfeier f (zur Verleihung der Diplome etc)

commend [kəˈmend] **VT a** (= praise) loben; (= recommend) empfehlen; **it has much/little to ~ it** es ist sehr/nicht sehr empfehlenswert **b** (= entrust, Bibl) spirit, soul befehlen (to +dat); ~ **me to Mr Smith** (form) empfehlen Sie mich Herrn Smith (form) **VR** sich empfehlen (to +dat)

commendable [kəˈmendəbl] ADJ lobenswert, löblich

commendably [kəˈmendəblɪ] ADV lobenswerterweise

commendation [ˌkɒmenˈdeɪʃən] N (no pl: = praise) Lob nt; (= award) Auszeichnung f; (= official recognition) Belobigung f

commendatory [kəˈmendətrɪ] ADJ anerkennend

commensurate [kəˈmenʃərɪt] ADJ entsprechend (with +dat); **to be ~ with sth** einer Sache (dat) entsprechen; **they made salaries ~ with those in comparable professions** die Gehälter wurden denen in vergleichbaren Berufen angeglichen

commensurately [kəˈmenʃərətlɪ] ADV entsprechend, angemessen

comment [ˈkɒment] ✪ 6.3 **N** (= remark) Bemerkung f (on, about über +acc, zu); (official) Kommentar m (on zu); (no pl: = talk, gossip) Gerede nt; (= textual or margin note etc) Anmerkung f; **no ~** kein Kommentar!; **to make a ~** eine Bemerkung machen, einen Kommentar abgeben **VI** sich äußern (on über +acc, zu), einen Kommentar abgeben (on zu); **need I ~?** Kommentar überflüssig! **VT** bemerken, äußern

commentary [ˈkɒməntərɪ] N Kommentar m (on zu); **he used to do commentaries on football matches** früher war er Reporter bei Fußballspielen; **I don't want a running ~ from you** ich brauche deine ständigen Kommentare nicht

commentary box N (Sport) Kommentatorenbox f

commentate [ˈkɒmenteɪt] VI (Rad, TV) Reporter(in) m(f) sein (on bei)

commentator [ˈkɒmenteɪtə] N **a** (Rad, TV) Reporter(in) m(f) **b** (on texts etc) Interpret(in) m(f); (of Bible) Exeget(in) m(f)

commerce [ˈkɒmɜːs] N **a** Handel m; (between countries also) Handelsverkehr m; **in the world of ~** im Geschäftsleben; **he is in ~** er ist Geschäftsmann **b** (form: = dealings) Verkehr m

commercial [kəˈmɜːʃəl] **ADJ** Handels-; custom also, ethics, training kaufmännisch; language, premises, vehicle Geschäfts-; production, radio, project, success, attitude, farming, whaling, fishing kommerziell; (pej) film, music etc kommerziell; **the ~ world** die Geschäftswelt; **of no ~ value** ohne Verkaufswert; **to think in ~ terms** kaufmännisch denken; **it makes good ~ sense** das lässt sich kaufmännisch durchaus vertreten; **has Christmas become too ~?** ist Weihnachten zu kommerziell geworden? **N** (Rad, TV) Werbespot m; **during the ~s** während der (Fernseh)werbung

commercial: commercial art N Werbegrafik f; **commercial artist** N Werbegrafiker(in) m(f); **commercial bank** N Handelsbank f; **commercial break** N Werbepause f; **commercial centre**, (US) **commercial center** N Handelszentrum nt; **commercial college** N Fachschule f für kaufmännische Berufe; **commercial court** N Handelsgericht nt

commercialese [kəˌmɜːʃəˈliːz] N Wirtschaftssprache f

commercialism [kəˈmɜːʃəlɪzəm] N Kommerzialisierung f; (connected with art, literature also) Kommerz m

commercialization [kəˌmɜːʃəlaɪˈzeɪʃən] N Kommerzialisierung f

commercialize [kəˈmɜːʃəlaɪz] VT kommerzialisieren

commercially [kəˈmɜːʃəlɪ] ADV geschäftlich; manufacture, succeed kommerziell; **to be ~ minded** kaufmännisch veranlagt or kommerziell eingestellt (usu pej) sein

commercial: commercial paper N (Fin) kurzfristiges Handelspapier; **commercial television** N kommerzielles Fernsehen; **commercial traveller**, (US) **commmercial traveler** N Handelsvertreter(in) m(f); **commercial usage** N Usance f, Handelsbrauch m; **commercial vehicle** N Nutzfahrzeug nt

commie [ˈkɒmɪ] (pej inf) **N** Rote(r) mf (pej inf) **ADJ** rot (pej inf)

commingle [kɒˈmɪŋgl] VI (liter) sich vermischen; (colours) ineinander verschwimmen

commis chef [ˈkɒmɪʃef] N Küchengehilfe m, Küchengehilfin f

commiserate [kəˈmɪzəreɪt] VI mitfühlen (with mit); **we ~ with you on the loss of your husband** wir nehmen Anteil am Tode Ihres Gatten

commiseration [kəˌmɪzəˈreɪʃən] N Mitgefühl nt no pl, (An)teilnahme f no pl; **my ~s** herzliches Beileid (on zu)

commissar [ˈkɒmɪsɑː] N Kommissar m

commissariat [ˌkɒmɪˈsɛərɪət] N **a** (Mil) Intendantur f **b** (in former USSR etc) Kommissariat nt

commissary [ˈkɒmɪsərɪ] N **a** (Mil) Intendant m **b** (= delegate) Beauftragte(r) m **c** (US, Comm) Laden m in Lagern/auf Baustellen etc

commission [kəˈmɪʃən] **N a** (= committing) Begehen nt (form)

b (for building, painting etc) Auftrag m

c (Comm) Provision f; **on ~**, **on a ~ basis** auf Provision(sbasis); **to charge ~** (bank etc) eine Kommission berechnen

d (Mil) Patent nt

e (= special committee) Kommission f, Ausschuss m; ~ **of inquiry** Untersuchungskommission f or -ausschuss m

f (Naut, fig: = use) **to put into ~** in Dienst stellen; **to take out of ~** aus dem Verkehr ziehen; **in/out of ~** in/außer Betrieb

g (form: = task, errand) Erledigung f; **I was given a ~ to recruit new members** ich wurde (damit) beauftragt, neue Mitglieder zu werben

h the (EC) Commission die EG-Kommission **VT a** person beauftragen; book, painting in Auftrag geben; **to ~ sb to do sth** jdn damit beauftragen, etw zu tun

b (Mil) sb zum Offizier ernennen; officer ernennen

c ship in Dienst stellen; power station etc in Betrieb nehmen; ~**ing ceremony** Eröffnungszeremonie f

commission agent N Kommissionär(in) m(f)

commissionaire [kəˌmɪʃəˈnɛə] N Portier m

commissioned officer N Offizier m

commissioner [kəˈmɪʃənə] N **a** (= member of commission) Ausschussmitglied nt **b** (of police) Polizeipräsident(in) m(f) **c** (Jur) ~ **for oaths** Notar(in) m(f)

commissioning editor [kəˈmɪʃənɪŋˈedɪtə] N Redakteur(in) m(f)

commit [kəˈmɪt] **VT a** (= perpetrate) begehen; **the crimes they ~ted against humanity** ihre

Verbrechen gegen die Menschlichkeit
b **to ~ sb (to prison/to a home)** jdn ins Gefängnis/in ein Heim einweisen; **to have sb ~ted (to an asylum)** jdn in eine Anstalt einweisen lassen; **to ~ sb for trial** jdn einem Gericht überstellen; **to ~ sb/sth to sb's care** jdn/etw jds Obhut (*dat*) anvertrauen; **to ~ sth to writing** *or* **to paper** etw zu Papier bringen
c (= *involve, obligate*) festlegen (*to* auf +*acc*); **to ~ troops to a battle** Truppen in ein Gefecht schicken; **to ~ resources/manpower to a project** Mittel/Arbeitskräfte für ein Projekt einsetzen; **that doesn't ~ you to buying the book** das verpflichtet Sie nicht zum Kauf des Buches
d (*Parl*) *bill* an den (zuständigen) Ausschuss überweisen
VI **to ~ to sb/sth** sich jdm gegenüber/zu etw verpflichten
VR sich festlegen (*to* auf +*acc*); **to ~ oneself on an issue** sich in einer Frage festlegen; **you have to ~ yourself totally to the cause** man muss sich voll und ganz für die Sache einsetzen *or* engagieren; **I don't want to ~ myself** ich möchte mich nicht festlegen; **the government has ~ted itself to (undertake) far-reaching reforms** die Regierung hat sich zu weitreichenden *or* weit reichenden Reformen bekannt *or* verpflichtet; **... without ~ting myself to the whole contract** ... ohne damit an den ganzen Vertrag gebunden zu sein

commitment [kəˈmɪtmənt] N **a** (= *obligation*) Verpflichtung *f*; (= *dedication*) Engagement *nt*; **his family ~s** seine familiären Verpflichtungen *pl*; **his teaching ~s** seine Lehrverpflichtungen *pl*; **there's no ~ (to buy)** es besteht kein(erlei) Kaufzwang; **to make a ~ to do sth** (*form*) sich verpflichten, etw zu tun; **the trainer demands one hundred per cent ~ from his team** der Trainer verlangt von seiner Mannschaft hundertprozentigen Einsatz; **his ~ to his job is total** er geht völlig in seiner Arbeit auf; **political/military ~** politisches/militärisches Engagement; **he is frightened of ~** (*in relationship*) er hat Angst davor, sich festzulegen
b (*Parl, of bill*) Überweisung *f* an den (zuständigen) Ausschuss

committal [kəˈmɪtl] N **a** (*to prison, asylum etc*) Einweisung *f*; **his ~ for trial** seine Überstellung ans Gericht; **~ proceedings** gerichtliches Voruntersuchung **b** (*of crime etc*) Begehen *nt* (*form*) **c** **~ to memory** Auswendiglernen *nt*; (*of single fact*) Sicheinprägen *nt* **d** (*Parl*) = **commitment b**

committed [kəˈmɪtɪd] ADJ (= *dedicated*) engagiert; **he is so ~ to his work that ...** er geht so in seiner Arbeit auf, dass ...; **all his life he has been ~ to this cause** er hat sich sein Leben lang für diese Sache eingesetzt

committee [kəˈmɪtɪ] N Ausschuss *m* (*also Parl*), Komitee *nt*; **to be** *or* **sit on a ~** in einem Ausschuss *or* Komitee sein *or* sitzen; **Committee of 100** (*Brit*) Komitee der Hundert; **~ meeting** Ausschusssitzung *f*; **~ member** Ausschussmitglied *nt*

committeeman [kəˈmɪtɪmæn] N *pl* **-men** [-men] (*esp US*) **a** (= *member of committee*) Komiteemitglied *nt* **b** (*Pol*) lokaler Parteiführer

committee stage N (*Brit Parl*) **the bill didn't reach the ~** der Gesetzentwurf ist gar nicht erst an den (zuständigen) Ausschuss gelangt; **the ~ lasted weeks** der Gesetzentwurf wurde mehrere Wochen im Ausschuss verhandelt

committeewoman [kəˈmɪtɪwʊmən] N *pl* **-women** [-wɪmɪn] (*esp US*) **a** (= *member of committee*) Komiteemitglied *nt* **b** (*Pol*) lokale Parteiführerin

commode [kəˈməʊd] N **a** (= *chest of drawers*) Kommode *f* **b** (= *night-commode*) (Nacht)stuhl *m*

commodious [kəˈməʊdɪəs] ADJ geräumig

commodity [kəˈmɒdɪtɪ] N Ware *f*; (*agricultural*) Erzeugnis *nt*; **basic** *or* **staple commodities** (*natural*) Grundstoffe *pl*; (*St Ex*) Rohstoffe *pl*; (*manufactured*) Bedarfsgüter *pl*; (= *foodstuffs*) Grund-

nahrungsmittel *pl*; **electricity is a ~ which every country needs** Strom ist ein (Versorgungs)gut, das jedes Land braucht

commodity exchange N (*St Ex*) Warenbörse *f*

commodity futures PL (*St Ex*) Warentermingeschäft *nt*

commodity market N Rohstoffmarkt *m*

commodore [ˈkɒmədɔːʳ] N (*Naut*) Flottil+lenadmiral *m*; (= *senior captain*) Kommodore *m*; (*of yacht club*) Präsident *m*

common [ˈkɒmən] ❂ 5.5 **ADJ** (+*er*) **a** (= *shared by many*) gemeinsam; *property also* Gemein-, gemeinschaftlich; **~ land** Allmende *f*; **~ prostitute** Straßendirne *f*; **it is ~ knowledge that ...** es ist allgemein bekannt, dass ...; **it is to the ~ advantage that ...** es ist von allgemeinem Nutzen, dass ...; **very little/no ~ ground** kaum eine/keine gemeinsame Basis; **to find ~ ground (with sb)** eine gemeinsame Basis finden (mit jdm); **sth is ~ to everyone/sth** alle haben/etw hat etw gemein
b (= *frequently seen or heard etc*) häufig; *word also* weitverbreitet, weit verbreitet; *experience also* allgemein; *animal, bird* häufig *pred*, häufig anzutreffend *attr*; *belief, custom, animal, bird* (weit)verbreitet, weit verbreitet; (= *customary, usual*) normal; **it's quite a ~ sight** das sieht man ziemlich häufig; **it's ~ for visitors to feel ill here** Besucher fühlen sich hier häufig krank; **nowadays it's quite ~ for the man to do the housework** es ist heutzutage ganz normal, dass der Mann die Hausarbeit macht
c (= *ordinary*) gewöhnlich; **the ~ man** der Normalbürger; **the ~ people** die einfachen Leute; **a ~ soldier** ein einfacher *or* gemeiner (*dated*) Soldat; **the ~ run of mankind** die (breite) Masse; **the ~ touch** das Volkstümliche; **he has the ~ touch** er kann gut mit Menschen umgehen; **the Book of Common Prayer** (*Eccl*) die Agende; **it's only ~ decency to apologize** es ist nur recht und billig, dass man sich entschuldigt
d (= *vulgar, low-class*) gewöhnlich; **to be as ~ as muck** (*Brit inf*) schrecklich gewöhnlich *or* ordinär sein
N **a** (= *land*) Anger *m*, Gemeindewiese *f*
b **nothing out of the ~** nichts Besonderes
c **to have sth in ~ (with sb/sth)** etw (mit jdm/etw) gemein haben; **to have a lot/nothing in ~** viel/nichts miteinander gemein haben, viele/keine Gemeinsamkeiten haben; **we do at least have that in ~** wenigstens das haben wir gemein; **in ~ with many other people/towns/countries** (ebenso *or* genauso) wie viele andere (Leute)/Städte/Länder ...; **I, in ~ with ...** ich, ebenso wie ...

Common Agricultural Policy N gemeinsame Agrarpolitik

commonalty [ˈkɒmənəltɪ] N (*form*) **the ~** die Bürgerlichen *pl*

common: common carrier N (*Comm*: = *transport company*) öffentliches Transportunternehmen; (*Telec*) Telefongesellschaft *f*; **common cold** N Schnupfen *m*; **common core** (*Sch*) Pflichtfächer *pl*; **common currency** N **to be ~** allgemein bekannt sein; (*rumour*) überall umgehen; **to become ~** allgemein bekannt werden; **common denominator** N (*Math, fig*) gemeinsamer Nenner; **lowest ~** (*Math, fig*) kleinster gemeinsamer Nenner; **common divisor** N gemeinsamer Teiler; **common Entrance (Examination)** N Aufnahmeprüfung *f* (*für eine britische Public School*)

commoner [ˈkɒmənəʳ] N **a** Bürgerliche(r) *mf* **b** (*Brit, Univ*) Student, der kein Universitätsstipendium erhält

common: common factor N gemeinsamer Teiler; **common fraction** N gemeiner Bruch; **common gender** N (*Gram*) doppeltes Geschlecht; **common law** N Gewohnheitsrecht *nt*; **common-law** ADJ **she is his ~ wife** sie lebt mit ihm in eheähnlicher Gemeinschaft; **the law regarded her as his ~ wife** vor dem Gesetz galt ihre Verbindung als eheähnliche Gemeinschaft

commonly [ˈkɒmənlɪ] ADV **a** (= *often*) häufig; (= *widely*) gemeinhin, weithin; **a ~ held belief** eine weitverbreitete *or* weit verbreitete Ansicht; **it is ~ believed that ...** es wird allgemein angenommen, dass ...; **(more) ~ known as ...** besser bekannt als ... **b** (= *vulgarly*) gewöhnlich, ordinär

common: Common Market N Gemeinsamer Markt; **Common Marketeer** N Befürworter(in) *m(f)* des Gemeinsamen Marktes; **common multiple** N gemeinsame(s) Vielfache(s); **the lowest** *or* **least ~** das kleinste gemeinsame Vielfache

commonness [ˈkɒmənnɪs] N **a** (= *frequency*) Häufigkeit *f*; (*of word also*) weite Verbreitung, Geläufigkeit *f*; (*of experience also*) Allgemeinheit *f* **b** (= *vulgarity*) Gewöhnlichkeit *f*; (*of person also*) ordinäre Art

common: common noun N Gattungsbegriff *m*; **common-or-garden** ADJ (*Brit*) Feld-, Wald- und Wiesen- (*inf*); *topic, novel etc* ganz gewöhnlich; **commonplace** ADJ alltäglich; (= *banal*) banal **N** Gemeinplatz *m*; **a ~** (= *frequent sight or event*) etwas Alltägliches; **common room** N Aufenthalts- *or* Tagesraum *m*; (*for teachers*) Lehrerzimmer *nt*; (*Univ*) Dozentenzimmer *nt*

Commons [ˈkɒmənz] PL **the ~** (*Parl*) das Unterhaus → **house**

commons [ˈkɒmənz] PL **on short ~** auf Kurzration gesetzt

common: common sense N gesunder Menschenverstand; **common-sense** ADJ vernünftig; *attitude also* gesund; **it's the ~ thing to do** das ist das Vernünftigste; **common stock** N (*US St Ex*) Stammaktien *pl*; **common time** N Viervierteltakt *m*; **commonweal** N (*form*) Gemeinwohl *nt*

commonwealth [ˈkɒmənwelθ] N **a** Staat *m*, Gemeinwesen *nt*; (*US*) *Bezeichnung für die US-Bundesstaaten Kentucky, Massachusetts, Pennsylvania und Virginia* **the Commonwealth of Australia** der Australische Bund; **the (British) Commonwealth**, **the Commonwealth of Nations** das Commonwealth; **Commonwealth of Independent States** Gemeinschaft *f* Unabhängiger Staaten **b** (*Hist*) **the Commonwealth** *die englische Republik unter Cromwell*

COMMONWEALTH

Das **Commonwealth**, offiziell **Commonwealth of Nations**, ist ein freiwilliger Zusammenschluss souveräner Staaten, die vormals fast alle britische Kolonien waren. Im Moment gibt es 51 Mitglieder, darunter Großbritannien, Australien, Kanada, Indien, Jamaika, Neuseeland, Pakistan und Südafrika, die zusammen ein Viertel der Weltbevölkerung stellen. Alle Mitgliedsstaaten erkennen den britischen Monarchen als Oberhaupt des Commonwealth an. Bei der jährlichen **Commonwealth Conference** werden verschiedene politische und wirtschaftliche Fragen beraten. Die Mitgliedsstaaten werden in einem anderen Commonwealth-Staat nicht durch eine Botschaft, sondern durch ein Hochkommissariat, genannt **High Commission**, vertreten.

Commonwealth Games PL Commonwealth-Spiele *pl*

commotion [kəˈməʊʃən] N Aufregung *f usu no indef art*; (= *noise*) Lärm *m*, Spektakel *m*; **to cause a ~** Aufsehen erregen; **to make a ~** Theater machen (*inf*); (= *noise*) Krach machen

comms [kɒmz] N = **communication d**

communal [ˈkɒmjuːnl] ADJ **a** (*of a community*) Gemeinde-; **~ life** Gemeinschaftsleben *nt* **b** (= *owned, used in common*) gemeinsam; *bathroom, kitchen also* Gemeinschafts-

communally [ˈkɒmjuːnəlɪ] ADV gemeinsam; **to be ~ owned** Gemein- *or* Gemeinschaftseigentum sein

communard [ˈkɒmjʊˌnɑːd] N Kommunarde *m*, Kommunardin *f*

commune[1] [kə'mjuːn] VI **a** (= *communicate*) Zwiesprache halten; **to ~ with the spirits** mit den Geistern verkehren **b** (*esp US Eccl, Catholic*) kommunizieren, die Kommunion empfangen; (*Protestant*) das Abendmahl empfangen

commune[2] ['kɒmjuːn] N Kommune *f*; (= *administrative division also*) Gemeinde *f*

communicable [kə'mjuːnɪkəbl] ADJ **a** *disease* übertragbar **b** *ideas, knowledge* kommunizierbar, vermittelbar

communicant [kə'mjuːnɪkənt] N (*Eccl*) Kommunikant(in) *m(f)*

communicate [kə'mjuːnɪkeɪt] VT *news etc* übermitteln; *ideas, feelings* vermitteln; *illness* übertragen (*to* auf +*acc*) VI **a** (= *be in communication*) in Verbindung *or* Kontakt stehen; **the ship was unable to ~ with the shore** das Schiff konnte keine Verbindung zum Festland herstellen **b** (= *convey or exchange thoughts*) sich verständigen, kommunizieren; **the inability of modern man to ~** die Unfähigkeit des heutigen Menschen zur Kommunikation **c** (*rooms*) verbunden sein; **communicating door** Verbindungstür *f* **d** (*Eccl, Catholic*) kommunizieren; (*Protestant*) das Abendmahl empfangen

communication [kə,mjuːnɪ'keɪʃən] N **a** (= *communicating*) Verständigung *f*, Kommunikation *f*; (*of ideas, information*) Vermittlung *f*; (*of disease*) Übertragung *f*; (= *contact*) Verbindung *f*; **system/means of ~** Kommunikationssystem *nt*/-mittel *nt*; **to be in ~ with sb** mit jdm in Verbindung stehen (*about* wegen) **b** (= *exchanging of ideas*) Verständigung *f*, Kommunikation *f*; **~ breakdown** Zusammenbruch *m* der Kommunikation **c** (= *letter, message*) Mitteilung *f* **d** **~s** (= *roads, railways, telegraph lines etc*) Kommunikationswege *pl*, Kommunikationsnetz *nt*; **all ~s with the mainland have been cut off** sämtliche Verbindungen zum Festland sind unterbrochen; **they're trying to restore ~s** man versucht, die Verbindung wieder herzustellen **e** **~s** (*Telec*) Telekommunikation *f* **f** (*between rooms etc*) Verbindung *f*

communication: communication cord N (*Brit, Rail*) ≈ Notbremse *f*; **communication gap** N Kommunikationslücke *f*; **communication problem** N Kommunikationsproblem *nt*; **communication skills** PL Kommunikationsfähigkeit *f*

communications [kə,mjuːnɪ'keɪʃənz] N: **communications package** N Kommunikationssoftware *f*; **communications satellite** N Kommunikations- *or* Nachrichtensatellit *m*; **communications software** N Kommunikationssoftware *f*; **communications technology** N Nachrichtentechnik *f*

communication trench N Verbindungsgraben *m*

communicative [kə'mjuːnɪkətɪv] ADJ mitteilsam, gesprächig

communicator [kə'mjuːnɪkeɪtə'] N Kommunikator(in) *m(f)*

communion [kə'mjuːnɪən] N **a** (= *intercourse, exchange of feelings etc*) Zwiesprache *f*; (*with spirits*) Verkehr *m*; **a sense of ~ with nature** ein Gefühl *nt* der Verbundenheit mit der Natur **b** (= *religious group*) Gemeinde *f*; (= *denomination*) Religionsgemeinschaft *f*; **the ~ of saints/the faithful** die Gemeinschaft der Heiligen/Gläubigen **c** (*Eccl: also* **Communion**, *Protestant*) Abendmahl *nt*; (*Catholic*) Kommunion *f*; **to receive** *or* **take ~** die Kommunion/das Abendmahl empfangen

communion: communion rail N Kommunionsbank *f*; **communion service** N Abendmahlsgottesdienst *m*; **communion table** N Abendmahlstisch *m*

communiqué [kə'mjuːnɪkeɪ] N Kommuniqué *nt*, Kommunikee *nt*, (amtliche) Verlautbarung *f*

communism ['kɒmjʊnɪzəm] N Kommunismus *m*

communist ['kɒmjʊnɪst] N Kommunist(in) *m(f)* ADJ kommunistisch

Communist China N das Kommunistische China, Rotchina *nt*

communistic [,kɒmjʊ'nɪstɪk] ADJ prokommunistisch; (*esp US*: = *communist*) kommunistisch

Communist Manifesto N Kommunistisches Manifest

Communist Party N kommunistische Partei

community [kə'mjuːnɪtɪ] N **a** (= *social, cultural etc group*) Gemeinschaft *f*; (*ethnic also*) Bevölkerungsgruppe *f*; **the ~ at large** das ganze Volk; **the great ~ of nations** die große Völkergemeinschaft; **a sense of ~** (ein) Gemeinschaftsgefühl *nt*; **to work in the ~** im Sozialbereich tätig sein **b** (= *the public*) Allgemeinheit *f* **c** (*Eccl, of monks, nuns*) (Ordens)gemeinschaft *f* **d** (= *holding in common*) **the ~ of love** die Liebesgemeinschaft; **they have no ~ of interests** sie haben keine gemeinsamen Interessen

community: community association N (*Brit*) Bürgerverein *m*; **community care** N (*Brit, Social*) **a** (= *home care*) häusliche Pflege **b** (*also* **community care programme**) kommunales Fürsorgeprogramm; **community centre**, (*US*) **community center** N Gemeindezentrum *nt*; **community charge** N (*Brit, dated*) Kopfsteuer *zur Finanzierung der Stadt- und Gemeindeverwaltungen*; **community chest** N (*US*) Wohltätigkeits- *or* Hilfsfonds *m*; **community college** N (*US*) *College zur Berufsausbildung und Vorbereitung auf ein Hochschulstudium*; **community home** N Fürsorgeanstalt *f*; **community relations** PL das Verhältnis zwischen den Bevölkerungsgruppen; **community service** N (*Jur*) Sozialdienst *m*; **community singing** N gemeinsames Singen; **community spirit** N Gemeinschaftssinn *m*; **community worker** N Sozialberufler(in) *m(f)*

communize ['kɒmjʊnaɪz] VT kommunistisch machen

commutable [kə'mjuːtəbl] ADJ (*Jur*) umwandelbar

commutation [,kɒmjʊ'teɪʃən] N **a** (*Jur*) Umwandlung *f* **b** **~ ticket** (*US*) Zeitnetzkarte *f*

commutator ['kɒmjʊteɪtə'] N (*Elec*) Kommutator *m*

commute [kə'mjuːt] VT (*all senses*) umwandeln VI (= *travel as commuter*) pendeln

commuter [kə'mjuːtə'] N Pendler(in) *m(f)*; **the ~ belt** das Einzugsgebiet, der Einzugsbereich; **a ~ belt** ein städtischer Einzugsbereich; **~ traffic** Pendlerverkehr *m*; **~ train** Pendlerzug *m*

commuting [kə'mjuːtɪŋ] N Pendeln *nt*; (= *commuter traffic*) Pendelverkehr *m*; **I hate ~** ich hasse es zu pendeln; **within ~ distance** nahe genug, um zu pendeln

comp [kɒmp] N (*Typ inf*) Setzer(in) *m(f)*

compact[1] [kəm'pækt] ADJ (+*er*) kompakt; *style of writing, prose also* gedrängt; *soil, snow* fest; **the print is too ~** der Druck ist zu eng, es ist zu eng bedruckt VT *snow, soil* festtreten/-walzen/-fahren *etc* **b** (*fig liter*) **to be ~ed of ...** sich aus ... zusammensetzen

compact[2] ['kɒmpækt] N **a** (= *powder compact*) Puderdose *f* **b** (*US*, = *car*) Kompaktauto *nt or* -wagen *m* **c** (= *camera*) Kompaktkamera *f*

compact[3] ['kɒmpækt] N (*form:* = *agreement*) Vereinbarung *f*, Übereinkunft *f*

compact camera N Kompaktkamera *f*

compact disc N Compactdisc *f*, Compact Disc *f*; **~ player** CD-Spieler *m*

compactly [kəm'pæktlɪ] ADV kompakt; *expressed* gedrängt; *printed* eng

compactness [kəm'pæktnɪs] N Kompaktheit *f*; (*of style also*) Gedrängtheit *f*; (*of print*) Dichte *f*, Enge *f*

companion [kəm'pænjən] N **a** (= *person with one*) Begleiter(in) *m(f)*; **~s in arms** Kampfgefährten *pl*, Waffenbrüder *pl* (*geh*); **my ~s on the journey** meine Reisegefährten *pl*; **travelling/ holiday/drinking ~** Reisebegleiter(in) *m(f)*/Urlaubsgefährte *m*, -gefährtin *f*/Zechgenosse *m*, -genossin *f*

b (= *friend*) Freund(in) *m(f)*, Kamerad(in) *m(f)*; **his elder brother is not much of a ~ for him** sein älterer Bruder ist ihm kein richtiger Freund; **a faithful ~ for fifty years** ein treuer Gefährte über fünfzig Jahre **c** (= *one of pair of objects*) Pendant *nt* **d** (= *lady companion*) Betreuerin *f* **e** (= *handbook*) **"the Gardener's Companion"** „der Ratgeber für den Gartenfreund“ **f** (*of order of knighthood*) Ritter *m* **ATTR** passend; *volume* Begleit-; **they have just brought out a ~ set of Dickens** in derselben Reihe ist jetzt eine Dickens-Ausgabe erschienen

companionable [kəm'pænjənəbl] ADJ freundlich

companionably [kəm'pænjənəblɪ] ADV vertraut; *smile also* freundlich

companion: companion piece N Pendant *nt* (*to* zu); **companion set** N (= *fire irons*) Kaminbesteck *nt*; **companionship** N Gesellschaft *f*; **companionway** N (*Naut*) Niedergang *m*

company ['kʌmpənɪ] ✪ 25.1 N **a** Gesellschaft *f*; **to keep sb ~** jdm Gesellschaft leisten; **to keep ~ with sb** mit jdm verkehren; **I enjoy ~** ich bin gern in Gesellschaft, ich habe gern Gesellschaft; **I enjoy his ~** ich bin gern mit ihm zusammen; **female ~** Damengesellschaft *f*; **he arrived with female ~** er kam in Damenbegleitung; **he's good ~** seine Gesellschaft ist angenehm; **he came along just for (the) ~** er kam bloß mit, um Gesellschaft zu haben; **he doesn't know how to behave in ~** er weiß nicht, wie man sich in Gesellschaft benimmt; **I/he in ~ with ...** ich/er, genauso wie ...; **she is not fit for your sister** use sist nicht der richtige Umgang für deine Schwester; **a man is known by the ~ he keeps** (*prov*) sage mir, mit wem du umgehst, so sage ich dir, wer du bist (*prov*); **she has a cat, it's ~ for her** sie hält sich eine Katze, da hat sie (wenigstens) Gesellschaft; **you'll be in good ~ if ...** wenn du ..., bist du in guter Gesellschaft **b** (= *guests*) Besuch *m* **c** (*Comm*) Firma *f*, Gesellschaft *f*; **Smith & Company, Smith & Co.** Smith & Co.; **shipping ~** Schifffahrtsgesellschaft *f*, Reederei *f*; **publishing ~** Verlagshaus *nt*, Verlag *m*; **a printing/ clothes ~** ein Druckerei-/Textilbetrieb *m*; **that's paid for by the ~** das bezahlt die Firma **d** (*Theat*) (Schauspiel)truppe *f* **e** (*Naut*) **ship's ~** Besatzung *f* **f** (*Mil*) Kompanie *f* **ATTR** Firmen-; **he has a ~ BMW** er hat einen BMW als Firmenwagen

company: company car N Firmenwagen *m*; **company commander** N (*Mil*) Kompaniechef *m*; **company director** N Direktor(in) *m(f)*, Firmenchef(in) *m(f)*; **company law** N Gesellschaftsrecht *nt*; **company lawyer** N (*for company law*) Gesellschaftsrechtler(in) *m(f)*; (*within company*) Hausjurist(in) *m(f)*; **company loyalty** N Firmentreue *f*; **company man** N treues *or* loyales Firmenmitglied; **company policy** N Geschäftspolitik *f*; **company secretary** N (*Brit, Comm*) Prokurist(in) *m(f)*; **company sergeant major** N (*Mil*) Kompaniefeldwebel *m*; **company time** N Arbeitszeit *f*

comparable ['kɒmpərəbl] ADJ vergleichbar (*with, to* mit)

comparably ['kɒmpərəblɪ] ADV ähnlich

comparative [kəm'pærətɪv] ADJ **a** *religion, philology etc* vergleichend; **~ literature** vergleichende Literaturwissenschaft, Komparatistik *f* **b** **the ~ form** (*Gram*) der Komparativ, die erste Steigerungsstufe **c** (= *relative*) relativ; **to live in ~ luxury** relativ luxuriös leben N (*Gram*) Komparativ *m*

comparatively [kəm'pærətɪvlɪ] ✪ 5.1 ADV **a** vergleichend **b** (= *relatively*) verhältnismäßig, relativ

compare [kəm'pɛə'] ✪ 5.1, 5.3, 26.3 VT vergleichen (*with, to* mit); **~d with** *or* **to** im Vergleich zu, verglichen mit; **they cannot be ~d** man kann sie nicht vergleichen, sie lassen sich nicht vergleichen; **his car is not to be** or **can't be ~d with my new one** sein Wagen ist überhaupt kein Vergleich zu meinem neuen Auto; **to ~ notes** Eindrücke/Erfahrungen austauschen **VI** sich vergleichen lassen (*with* mit); **it ~s badly/well** es schneidet vergleichsweise schlecht/ gut ab; **it doesn't ~ very well at all** es schneidet im Vergleich überhaupt nicht gut ab; **how do the two cars ~ in terms of speed?** wie sieht ein Geschwindigkeitsvergleich der beiden Wagen aus?; **the old car can't ~ in terms of speed with the new one** in puncto Geschwindigkeit lässt sich der alte Wagen nicht mit dem neuen vergleichen **N** **beyond** or **without ~** unvergleichlich; **beautiful beyond ~** unvergleichlich schön

comparison [kəmˈpærɪsn] ✪ 5.2, 5.5, 26.3 N **a** Vergleich *m* (*to* mit); **in** or **by ~** vergleichsweise; **in** or **by ~ with** im Vergleich zu; **to make** or **draw a ~** einen Vergleich anstellen; **to bear** or **stand ~** einem Vergleich standhalten, einen Vergleich aushalten; **there's no ~** das ist gar kein Vergleich **b** (*Gram*) Steigerung *f*; **degree of ~** Steigerungsstufe *f*

comparison shopping N (*Comm*) preisbewusstes Einkaufen

compartment [kəmˈpɑːtmənt] N (*in fridge, desk etc*) Fach *nt*; (*Rail*) Abteil *nt*; (*Naut*) Schott *nt*, Schotte *f*; (*fig*) (Schub)fach *nt*

compartmentalize [ˌkɒmpɑːˈtmentəlaɪz] VT aufsplittern

compartmentalized [ˌkɒmpɑːˈtmentəlaɪzd] ADJ *subject* gegliedert; **their excessively ~ view of life** ihre übertrieben genau gegliederte Lebensanschauung

compass [ˈkʌmpəs] N **a** Kompass *m*; **by the ~** nach dem Kompass **b** **compasses** PL (*also* **pair of compasses**) Zirkel *m* **c** (*fig*: = *extent*) Rahmen *m*; (*of human mind, experience*) Bereich *m*; (*Mus, of voice*) Umfang *m* VT = **encompass ~ed about with enemies** (*form*) von Feinden umzingelt

compass: compass bearing N Kompasspeilung *f*; **compass card** N Kompassscheibe *f*, Windrose *f*; **compass course** N Navigationskurs *m*

compassion [kəmˈpæʃən] N Mitgefühl *nt*, Mitleid *nt* (*for* mit); (*esp Bibl*) Erbarmen *nt* (*on, for* mit)

compassionate [kəmˈpæʃənɪt] ADJ mitfühlend, voller Mitgefühl or Mitleid; **on ~ grounds** aus familiären Gründen

compassionate leave N Beurlaubung *f* wegen einer dringenden Familienangelegenheit

compassionately [kəmˈpæʃənɪtlɪ] ADV voll Mitgefühl

compass rose N Windrose *f*

compatibility [kəmˌpætəˈbɪlɪtɪ] N Vereinbarkeit *f*, Kompatibilität *f* (*geh*); (*Med*) Verträglichkeit *f*, Kompatibilität *f* (*spec*); (*Comput*) Kompatibilität *f*; **their ~/lack of ~ was obvious** es war offensichtlich, dass die beiden gut/schlecht zueinander passten

compatible [kəmˈpætɪbl] ADJ vereinbar, kompatibel (*geh*); (*Med*) verträglich, kompatibel (*spec*); *people* zueinander passend; *colours, furniture* passend; (*Comput*) kompatibel; **to be ~** (*people*) zueinander passen; (*colours, furniture*) zusammenpassen; (*plan*) vereinbar sein; **a salary ~ with the dangers of the job** ein Gehalt, das den Gefahren des Berufs entspricht; **such action would not be ~ with democracy** ein solches Vorgehen ist nicht mit dem Demokratieverständnis zu vereinen; **an IBM-compatible computer** ein IBM-kompatibler Computer

compatibly [kəmˈpætɪblɪ] ADV **to be ~ matched** gut zueinander passen

compatriot [kəmˈpætrɪət] N Landsmann *m*, Landsmännin *f*

compel [kəmˈpel] VT **a** (= *force*) zwingen; **I feel ~led to tell you …** ich sehe mich (dazu) gezwungen or veranlasst, Ihnen mitzuteilen, … **b** *admiration, respect* abnötigen (*from sb* jdm); *obedience* erzwingen (*from sb* von jdm)

compellable [kəmˈpeləbl] ADJ (*Jur*) *witness* aussagepflichtig

compelling [kəmˈpelɪŋ] ADJ zwingend; *performance, personality, eyes* bezwingend; **to make a ~ case for sth** schlagende Beweise für etw liefern; **the novel makes ~ reading** der Roman ist äußerst spannend zu lesen

compellingly [kəmˈpelɪŋlɪ] ADV *write, tell* spannend; *persuasive* umwerfend; **~ attractive** unwiderstehlich; **he presented his case ~** er legte seinen Fall mit zwingender Logik dar

compendious [kəmˈpendɪəs] ADJ *notes etc* umfangreich

compendium [kəmˈpendɪəm] N Handbuch *nt*, Kompendium *nt*; **~ of games** Spielemagazin *nt*

compensate [ˈkɒmpənseɪt] **VT** (= *recompense*) entschädigen; (*Mech*) ausgleichen **VI** (*Psych*) kompensieren

▶ **compensate for** VI +*prep obj* (*in money, material goods etc*) ersetzen; (= *make up for, offset*) wieder wettmachen or ausgleichen; (*Psych*) kompensieren; **he was awarded £900 to compensate for the damage** er erhielt £ 900 Schadenersatz or -ausgleich

compensating [ˈkɒmpənseɪtɪŋ] ADJ ausgleichend, Ausgleichs-; **~ errors** *pl* sich gegenseitig aufhebende Fehler

compensation [ˌkɒmpənˈseɪʃən] N (= *damages*) Entschädigung *f*; (*fig*) Ausgleich *m*; (*Psych*) Kompensation *f*; **he had the ~ of knowing that …** er hatte die Genugtuung zu wissen, dass …; **in ~** als Entschädigung/Ausgleich/Kompensation

compensatory [kəmˈpensətərɪ] ADJ kompensierend, ausgleichend; *education* kompensatorisch; (*Psych*) kompensatorisch

comper [ˈkɒmpə] N (*inf*) jd, der regelmäßig an Preisausschreiben teilnimmt

compère [ˈkɒmpeə] (*Brit*) **N** Conférencier *m* **VT** **to ~ a show** bei einer Show der Conférencier sein

compete [kəmˈpiːt] VI **a** (*firm, country*) konkurrieren; **to ~ with each other** sich (gegenseitig) Konkurrenz machen; **to ~ for sth** um etw kämpfen or (*esp Comm*) konkurrieren; **able to ~ industrially** industriell konkurrenzfähig; **his poetry can't ~ with Eliot's** seine Gedichte können sich nicht mit denen Eliots messen; **he can't ~ (any more)** er kann nicht mehr mithalten **b** (*Sport*) teilnehmen; **to ~ for the championship** um die Meisterschaft kämpfen; **to ~ with/against sb** gegen jdn kämpfen or antreten

competence [ˈkɒmpɪtəns], **competency** [ˈkɒmpɪtənsɪ] N **a** Fähigkeit *f*; (*of lawyer, scientist etc also, Ling*) Kompetenz *f*; **to do sth with surprising ~** etw mit erstaunlichem Geschick tun; **his ~ in handling money/dealing with awkward clients** sein Geschick im Umgang mit Geld/schwierigen Kunden; **what level of ~ has the class reached in Spanish?** auf welchem Stand ist die Klasse in Spanisch? **b** (= *income*) Einkommen *nt* **c** (*Jur*) Zuständigkeit *f*

competent [ˈkɒmpɪtənt] ADJ **a** fähig, befähigt (*in* zu); (*in a particular field*) kompetent; (= *adequate*) *knowledge, understanding* angemessen, adäquat; **his English is quite ~** sein Englisch ist recht gut; **to be/feel ~ to do sth** kompetent or fähig sein/sich kompetent or fähig fühlen, etw zu tun; **to do a ~ job** gute Arbeit leisten **b** (*Jur*) zuständig; *evidence, witness* zulässig **c** (*form*: = *relevant*) **to be ~/not ~** (*business, question*) von/ohne or nicht von Belang sein

competently [ˈkɒmpɪtəntlɪ] ADV geschickt, kompetent

competition [ˌkɒmpɪˈtɪʃən] N **a** *no pl* Konkurrenz *f* (*for* um); **to keep an eye on the ~** die Konkurrenz beobachten; **unfair ~** unlauterer Wettbewerb; **a spirit of ~** Wettbewerbs- or Kon-

kurrenzdenken *nt*; **to be in ~ with sb** mit jdm wetteifern or (*esp Comm*) konkurrieren; **to be driven by ~** unter Konkurrenzdruck stehen **b** (= *contest*) Wettbewerb *m*; (*in newspapers etc*) Preisausschreiben *nt*; **beauty/swimming ~** Schönheitskonkurrenz *f* or -wettbewerb *m*/Schwimmwettbewerb *m*

competitive [kəmˈpetɪtɪv] ADJ **a** *person, attitude* vom Konkurrenzdenken geprägt; *sport* (Wett)kampf-; **~ advantage/disadvantage** Wettbewerbsvorteil *m*/-nachteil *m*; **~ spirit** Wettbewerbs- or Konkurrenzgeist *m*; (*of team*) Kampfgeist *m*; **he's a very ~ sort of person** er genießt Wettbewerbssituationen; (*in job etc*) er ist ein sehr ehrgeiziger Mensch; **the exam system encourages children to be too ~** das Prüfungssystem regt die Kinder zu sehr zum Konkurrenzdenken an; **the recruitment procedure is not ~** die Stellenvergabe erfolgt nicht auf Grund eines Auswahlverfahrens; **to gain a ~ advantage** or **edge over sb** jdm gegenüber einen Wettbewerbsvorteil erzielen; **a ~ examination** eine Auswahlprüfung **b** (*Comm*) *business, prices, salaries* wettbewerbs- or konkurrenzfähig; **a highly ~ market** ein Markt mit starker Konkurrenz; **retailing is highly ~** der Einzelhandel ist stark wettbewerbsbetont or -orientiert; **~ bidding** Ausschreibungswettbewerb *m*; **~ tendering** freie Ausschreibung

competitively [kəmˈpetɪtɪvlɪ] ADV **a** **to be ~ priced** im Preis wettbewerbsfähig sein **b** *swim, ski, play etc* in Wettkämpfen

competitiveness [kəmˈpetɪtɪvnɪs] N (= *competitive spirit*) Wettbewerbs- or Konkurrenzgeist *m*; (*of product, company, prices*) Wettbewerbsfähigkeit *f*

competitor [kəmˈpetɪtə] N **a** (*Sport, in contest*) Teilnehmer(in) *m(f)*; (*for job*) Mitbewerber(in) *m(f)*; **to be a ~** teilnehmen **b** (*Comm*) Konkurrent(in) *m(f)*; **our ~s** unsere Konkurrenz or Konkurrenten

compilation [ˌkɒmpɪˈleɪʃən] N Zusammenstellung *f*; (*of material*) Sammlung *f*; (*of dictionary*) Abfassung *f*

compile [kəmˈpaɪl] VT zusammenstellen, erstellen (*form*); *material* sammeln, zusammentragen; *dictionary* verfassen; (*Comput*) kompilieren

compiler [kəmˈpaɪlə] N (*of dictionary*) Verfasser(in) *m(f)*; (*Comput*) Compiler *m*; **who's the ~ of this list?** wer hat diese Liste zusammengestellt?

comping [ˈkɒmpɪŋ] N (*inf*) regelmäßige Teilnahme an Preisausschreiben

complacence [kəmˈpleɪsəns], **complacency** [kəmˈpleɪsnsɪ] N Selbstzufriedenheit *f*, Selbstgefälligkeit *f*

complacent [kəmˈpleɪsənt] ADJ selbstzufrieden or -gefällig; **don't get ~ just because …** jetzt werde bloß nicht selbstgefällig or überheblich, nur weil …

complacently [kəmˈpleɪsntlɪ] ADV selbstzufrieden or -gefällig; **those who ~ accept their parents' beliefs** diejenigen, die die Ansichten ihrer Eltern unreflektiert übernehmen

complain [kəmˈpleɪn] VI sich beklagen, klagen (*about* über +*acc*); (= *to make a formal complaint*) sich beschweren, Beschwerde einlegen (*about* über +*acc, to* bei); **to ~ that …** sich darüber beklagen/beschweren, dass …; **(I) can't ~** (*inf*) ich kann nicht klagen (*inf*); **stop ~ing!** beklag dich nicht dauernd!; **to ~ of sth** über etw (*acc*) klagen; **to ~ of not having enough time** über Zeitmangel klagen; **she's always ~ing** sie muss sich immer beklagen, sie hat immer etwas zu klagen

complainant [kəmˈpleɪnənt] N Beschwerdeführer(in) *m(f)*; (*in court*) Kläger(in) *m(f)*

complaint [kəmˈpleɪnt] N **a** Klage *f*; (= *formal complaint*) Beschwerde *f* (*to* bei); **I have no cause for ~** ich kann mich nicht beklagen; **I wouldn't have any ~(s) if …** ich würde mich nicht beklagen, wenn …; **to lodge a ~ against sb with the police** jdn bei der Polizei anzeigen, gegen jdn Anzeige erstatten **b** (= *illness*) Beschwerden *pl*; **a very rare ~** eine sehr seltene Krankheit, ein sehr seltenes Leiden

complaisance [kəm'pleɪzəns] N (*liter*) Gefälligkeit *f*

complaisant ADJ , **complaisantly** ADV [kəm'pleɪzənt, -lɪ] gefällig, entgegenkommend; *smile* wohlwollend

complement ['kɒmplɪmənt] **N** **a** (= *addition*) Ergänzung *f* (*to* +*gen*); (*to perfect sth*) Vervollkommnung *f* (*to* +*gen*); (= *colour*) Komplementärfarbe *f* (*to zu*) **b** (= *full number*) volle Stärke; (= *crew of ship*) Besatzung *f*; **the battalion didn't have its full ~ of soldiers** das Bataillon hatte seine Sollstärke nicht; **we've got our full ~ in the office now** unser Büro ist jetzt komplett *or* voll besetzt **c** (*Gram*) Ergänzung *f* **d** (*Math*: = *angle*) Ergänzungswinkel *m* **VT** ['kɒmplɪment] **a** (= *add to*) ergänzen; (= *make perfect*) vervollkommnen, abrunden; (*colour*) herausbringen; **to ~ each other** sich ergänzen; (*colours*) aufeinander abgestimmt sein **b** (*Gram*) die Ergänzung bilden zu **c** (*Math*) zu 90° ergänzen

complementary [ˌkɒmplɪ'mentərɪ] ADJ *colour* Komplementär-; *angle* Ergänzungs-; **a ~ pair** ein zusammengehöriges Paar; **two ~ characters** zwei einander ergänzende Charaktere; **they are ~ to each other** sie ergänzen sich *or* einander; **they have ~ interests** ihre Interessen ergänzen sich

complementary: complementary colour, (*US*) **complementary color** N Komplementärfarbe *f*; **complementary medicine** N Komplementärmedizin *f*

complete [kəm'pliːt] ADJ **a** (= *entire, whole*) ganz *attr*; *set also, wardrobe, deck of cards* vollständig, komplett; (= *having the required numbers*) vollzählig; *edition* Gesamt-; **my happiness/disappointment was ~** mein Glück/meine Enttäuschung war vollkommen; **my life is now ~** mein Leben ist erfüllt; **our victory was ~** unser Sieg war vollkommen; **the ~ works of Shakespeare** die gesammelten Werke Shakespeares; **no classical collection is ~ without Beethoven's ninth symphony** eine Sammlung klassischer Musik wäre ohne Beethovens neunte Sinfonie nicht zu denken; **a very ~ account** ein sehr umfassender *or* detaillierter Bericht; **are we ~?** sind wir vollzählig? **b** *attr* (= *total, absolute*) völlig; *failure, beginner, disaster, flop also, victory* total; *surprise, shambles also* komplett; *satisfaction also, approval* voll; **we were ~ strangers** wir waren uns *or* einander völlig fremd; **we were in ~ agreement** wir stimmten völlig überein **c** (= *finished*) fertig; **his novel is not yet ~** sein Roman ist noch nicht abgeschlossen; **my life's work is now ~** mein Lebenswerk ist nun vollbracht **d** **~ with** komplett mit; **he came ~ with rucksack and boots** er erschien komplett ausgerüstet mit Rucksack und Stiefeln **e** *sportsman, gardener etc* perfekt **VT** **a** (= *make whole*) *collection, set* vervollständigen, komplettieren; *team* vollzählig machen; *education, meal* abrunden; **to ~ our numbers** damit wir vollzählig sind; **that ~s my collection** damit ist meine Sammlung vollständig **b** (*fig*) *happiness* vollkommen machen; **and to ~ their misery ...** und zu allem Unglück ... **c** (= *finish*) beenden, abschließen, zum Abschluss *or* zu Ende bringen; *building, work* fertigstellen; *prison sentence* verbüßen; **~ this phrase** ergänzen Sie diesen Ausspruch; **it's not ~d yet** es ist noch nicht fertig **d** *form, questionnaire* ausfüllen

completely [kəm'pliːtlɪ] ADV völlig, vollkommen; **he's ~ wrong** er irrt sich gewaltig, er hat völlig Unrecht; **he's not ~ normal** er ist nicht ganz normal

completeness [kəm'pliːtnɪs] N Vollständigkeit *f*; **the design has a sense of ~ about it** das De-

sign erscheint vollendet *or* vollkommen; **a work which demonstrates the ~ of his talent** ein Werk, das sein vollendetes Talent beweist

completion [kəm'pliːʃən] N **a** (= *finishing*) Fertigstellung *f*; (*of work also*) Beendigung *f*; (*of project, course, education*) Abschluss *m*; (*of prison sentence*) Verbüßung *f*; **to be near ~** kurz vor dem Abschluss stehen; **to bring sth to ~** etw zum Abschluss bringen; **we need more people for the ~ of the work** wir brauchen noch mehr Leute, um die Arbeit zum Abschluss zu bringen; **on ~ of the course** am Ende *or* nach Abschluss des Kurses; **on ~ of the contract/sale** bei Vertrags-/Kaufabschluss; **~ date** Fertigstellungstermin *m* **b** (= *making whole*) Vervollständigung *f*; (*of education, meal*) Abrundung *f*; (*of happiness etc*) Vervollkommnung *f* **c** (= *filling in: of form etc*) Ausfüllen *nt*

complex ['kɒmpleks] ADJ **a** komplex; *person, mind, issue, question, problem, poem also* vielschichtig; *theory, task, system also, machine, pattern* differenziert, kompliziert; *situation also, paragraph* verwickelt, kompliziert **b** (*Gram*) **a ~ sentence** ein Satzgefüge *nt* **N a** Komplex *m*; **industrial ~** Industriekomplex *m* **b** (*Psych*) Komplex *m*; **he has a ~ about his ears** er hat Komplexe *or* einen Komplex wegen seiner Ohren; **don't get a ~ about it** deswegen brauchst du keine Komplexe zu bekommen

complexion [kəm'plekʃən] N **a** Teint *m*; (= *skin colour*) Gesichtsfarbe *f* **b** (*fig*: = *aspect*) Anstrich *m*, Aspekt *m*; **to put a new/different etc ~ on sth** etw in einem neuen/anderen *etc* Licht erscheinen lassen; **of a different political/religious ~** mit anderen politischen/religiösen Anschauungen

complexity [kəm'pleksɪtɪ] N Komplexität *f*; (*of person, mind, issue, question, problem, poem also*) Vielschichtigkeit *f*; (*of theory, task, system also, machine, pattern*) Differenziertheit *f*, Kompliziertheit *f*

compliance [kəm'plaɪəns] N Einverständnis *nt*; (*with rules etc*) Einhalten *nt* (*with* +*gen*); (= *submissiveness*) Willfährigkeit *f* (*geh*), Fügsamkeit *f*; **in ~ with the law/our wishes etc** dem Gesetz/unseren Wünschen *etc* gemäß

compliant [kəm'plaɪənt] ADJ entgegenkommend, gefällig; (= *submissive*) nachgiebig, willfährig (*geh*)

complicate ['kɒmplɪkeɪt] VT komplizieren

complicated ['kɒmplɪkeɪtɪd] ADJ kompliziert

complication [ˌkɒmplɪ'keɪʃən] N Komplikation *f*; (= *complicated nature*) Kompliziertheit *f*

complicit [kəm'plɪsɪt] ADJ **a** (= *knowing*) *look, wink, silence* wissend **b** (= *involved*) **to be ~ in sth** an etw (*dat*) beteiligt *or* in etw (*acc*) verwickelt sein; **he was ~ in allowing it to happen** er war mitverantwortlich dafür, dass es passieren konnte

complicity [kəm'plɪsɪtɪ] N Mittäterschaft *f* (*in bei*)

compliment ['kɒmplɪmənt] **N a** Kompliment *nt* (*on zu, wegen*); **to pay sb a ~** jdm ein Kompliment machen; **that's quite a ~, coming from you** wenn Sie das sagen, heißt das schon etwas *or* ist das wahrhaftig ein Kompliment; **(give) my ~s to the chef** mein Lob *or* Kompliment dem Koch/der Köchin **b** **compliments** PL (*form*) Grüße *pl*; **give him my ~s** empfehlen Sie mich ihm (*dated form*); **to pay one's ~s to sb** (*on arrival*) jdn begrüßen; (*on departure*) sich jdm empfehlen (*dated form*); (= *visit*) jdm einen Höflichkeitsbesuch abstatten (*form*); **the ~s of the season** frohes Fest; **"with the ~s of Mr X/the management"** „mit den besten Empfehlungen von Herrn X/der Geschäftsleitung"; **"with the ~s of the publishers"** „zur gefälligen Kenntnisnahme, der Verlag" **VT** ['kɒmplɪment] ein Kompliment/Komplimente machen (+*dat*) (*on wegen, zu*)

complimentary [ˌkɒmplɪ'mentərɪ] ADJ **a** (= *praising*) schmeichelhaft; **~ close** Schlussformel

f; **to be ~ about sb/sth** sich schmeichelhaft über jdn/etw äußern, jdn/etw loben **b** (= *free*) *seat, ticket* Frei-; **~ copy** Freiexemplar *nt*; (*of magazine*) Werbenummer *f*

compliments slip ['kɒmplɪmənts,slɪp] N (*Comm*) Empfehlungszettel *m*

compline ['kɒmplɪn] N (*Eccl*) Komplet *f*

comply [kəm'plaɪ] ⚙ 11.3 VI (*person*) einwilligen; (*object, system etc*) die Bedingungen erfüllen, den Bedingungen entsprechen; **to ~ with sth** einer Sache (*dat*) entsprechen; (*system*) in Einklang mit etw stehen; **to ~ with the terms of a treaty** die Vertragsbedingungen erfüllen; **to ~ with a request/a wish/instructions** einer Bitte/einem Wunsch/den Anordnungen nachkommen (*form*) *or* entsprechen (*form*); **to ~ with sb's wishes** sich jds Wünschen (*dat*) fügen; **to ~ with a time limit** eine Frist einhalten; **to ~ with the rules** sich an die Regeln halten

component [kəm'pəʊnənt] **N** Teil *nt*, Bestandteil *m*; (*Chem, Phys*) Komponente *f* ADJ **a** **~ part** ein (Bestand)teil *m*; **the ~ parts** die Bestand- *or* Einzelteile *pl*; **the ~ parts of a machine/sentence** die einzelnen Maschinen-/Satzteile *pl*

comport [kəm'pɔːt] (*form*) **VR** sich verhalten **VI** **to ~ with** sich vereinbaren lassen mit

comportment [kəm'pɔːtmənt] N Verhalten *nt*; **to study ~** Anstandsunterricht nehmen

compose [kəm'pəʊz] VT **a** *music* komponieren; *letter* abfassen, aufsetzen; *poem* verfassen **b** (= *constitute, make up*) bilden; **to be ~d of** sich zusammensetzen aus; **water is ~d of ...** Wasser besteht aus ... **c** **to ~ oneself** sich sammeln; **to ~ one's features** sich wieder in die Gewalt bekommen; **to ~ one's thoughts** Ordnung in seine Gedanken bringen **d** (*Typ*) setzen

composed [kəm'pəʊzd] ADJ (= *calm*) beherrscht, gelassen

composedly [kəm'pəʊzədlɪ] ADV beherrscht, gelassen

composer [kəm'pəʊzə] N **a** (*Mus*) Komponist(in) *m(f)* **b** (*of letter, poem etc*) Verfasser(in) *m(f)*

composite ['kɒmpəzɪt] ADJ **a** zusammengesetzt; **~ motion** Sammelantrag *m*; **~ material** Verbund(werk)stoff *m*; **~ structure** gegliederter Aufbau **b** (*Bot*) Korbblütler-; *flower* zur Familie der Korbblütler gehörig **c** (*Math*) *number* teilbar **N** (*Bot*) Korbblütler *m*

composite photograph N Fotomontage *f*

composition [ˌkɒmpə'zɪʃən] N **a** (= *act of composing, of music*) Komponieren *nt*; (*of letter*) Abfassen *nt*, Aufsetzen *nt*; (*of poem*) Verfassen *nt*; **music of his own ~** selbst komponierte Musik; **verse of her own ~** selbst verfasste Verse *pl* **b** (= *arrangement, Mus, Art*) Komposition *f*; (*Mus*: = *theory of composition also*) Kompositionslehre *f* **c** (*Sch*: = *essay*) Aufsatz *m* **d** (= *constitution, make-up*) Zusammensetzung *f*; (*of sentence*) Aufbau *m*, Konstruktion *f*; **to change the ~ of sth** die Zusammensetzung einer Sache (*gen*) ändern; **to decide on the ~ of sth** etw zusammenstellen; **this medicine is a ~ of ...** dieses Medikament setzt sich aus ... zusammen; **there is a touch of madness in his ~** (*old, liter*) in ihm findet sich die Anlage zum Wahnsinn **e** (= *artificial substance*) Kunststoff *m* **f** (*Typ*) Setzen *nt*; **~ by hand** Handsatz *m*, manueller Satz **g** (*Jur*) Vergleich *m*

compositional [ˌkɒmpə'zɪʃənl] ADJ Kompositions-; **~ style** Kompositionsstil *m*

composition in *cpds* Kunst-; **composition rubber** N synthetischer Kautschuk; **composition sole** N Kunststoffsohle *f*

compositor [kəm'pɒzɪtə] N (*Typ*) (Schrift)setzer(in) *m(f)*

compos mentis ['kɒmpəs'mentɪs] ADJ **I'm never really ~ first thing in the morning** frühmorgens ist mein Verstand noch nicht so klar *or* bin ich noch nicht voll da (*inf*); **he's quite ~** er ist voll zurechnungsfähig; **he's not quite ~** er ist nicht voll zurechnungsfähig, er ist nicht ganz bei Trost (*inf*)

compost ['kɒmpɒst] N Kompost *m*; **~ heap** Komposthaufen *m*

composure [kəm'pəʊʒə'] N Beherrschung *f*, Fassung *f*; **to lose one's ~** die Beherrschung verlieren; **to regain one's ~** seine Selbstbeherrschung wiederfinden

compote ['kɒmpəʊt] N Kompott *nt*

compound¹ ['kɒmpaʊnd] N (*Chem*) Verbindung *f*; (*Gram*) Kompositum *nt*, zusammengesetztes Wort

ADJ **a** (*Chem*) **~ substance** Verbindung *f* **b** (*Gram*) *tense, word* zusammengesetzt

VT [kəm'paʊnd] **a** (*rare, = combine*) verbinden; (*Chem*) mischen; **to be ~ed of ...** (*liter*) sich zusammensetzen aus ...

b (*Jur*) *debt* begleichen, tilgen; *quarrel* beilegen; **to ~ a crime** ein Verbrechen wegen erhaltener Entschädigung nicht verfolgen

c (*= make worse*) verschlimmern; *problem* verstärken, vergrößern; **this only ~s our difficulties** das erschwert unsere Lage *or* Situation noch zusätzlich

VI [kəm'paʊnd] einen Vergleich schließen; (*with creditors*) sich vergleichen; **to ~ with sb for sth** sich mit jdm auf etw (*acc*) einigen

compound² ['kɒmpaʊnd] N (*= enclosed area*) Lager *nt*; (*in prison*) Gefängnishof *m*; (*= living quarters*) Siedlung *f*; (*in zoo*) Gehege *nt*

compound: compound eye N (*Zool*) Facetten- *or* Netzauge *nt*; **compound fraction** N (*Math*) Doppelbruch *m*; **compound fracture** N (*Med*) offener *or* komplizierter Bruch

compounding ['kɒmpaʊndɪŋ] N (*Ling*) Zusammensetzungen *pl*

compound: compound interest N (*Fin*) Zinseszins *m*; **compound number** N (*Math*) zusammengesetzte Zahl; **compound sentence** N (*Gram*) Satzgefüge *nt*; (*of two or more main clauses*) Satzreihe *f*, Parataxe *f*

comprehend [,kɒmprɪ'hend] VT **a** (*= understand*) begreifen, verstehen **b** (*= include*) enthalten, umfassen, einschließen

comprehensibility [,kɒmprɪ,hensɪ'bɪlɪtɪ] N Verständlichkeit *f*

comprehensible [,kɒmprɪ'hensəbl] ADJ verständlich; **the graffiti is not ~** das Graffito ist nicht verständlich *or* zu verstehen

comprehension [,kɒmprɪ'henʃən] N **a** (*= understanding*) Verständnis *nt*; (*= ability to understand*) Begriffsvermögen *nt*; **that is beyond my ~** das übersteigt mein Begriffsvermögen; (*behaviour*) das ist mir unbegreiflich **b** (*= inclusion*) Aufnahme *f* **c** (*= school exercise*) Fragen *pl* zum Textverständnis

comprehensive [,kɒmprɪ'hensɪv] ADJ umfassend; **to go ~** (*Brit Sch*) (eine) Gesamtschule werden; **(fully) insurance** Vollkasko(versicherung *f*) *nt*; **are you ~?** (*Insur*) sind Sie vollkaskoversichert?, haben Sie Vollkasko? (*inf*) N (*Brit*) Gesamtschule *f*

comprehensively [,kɒmprɪ'hensɪvlɪ] ADV umfassend

comprehensiveness [,kɒmprɪ'hensɪvnɪs] N Ausführlichkeit *f*; **the ~ of his report** sein umfassender Bericht

comprehensive school N (*Brit*) Gesamtschule *f*

währleisten. Auch wenn es immer noch einige **grammar schools** gibt, sind die meisten staatlichen Schulen in Großbritannien heutzutage **comprehensive schools.**

compress¹ [kəm'pres] **VT** komprimieren (*into* auf +*acc*); *air etc also, data* verdichten; *materials* zusammenpressen (*into* zu) **VI** sich verdichten, sich komprimieren lassen

compress² ['kɒmpres] N Kompresse *f*, feuchter Umschlag

compressed air [kəm'prest'eə'] N Druck- *or* Pressluft *f*

compression [kəm'preʃən] N Verdichtung *f*, Kompression *f*; (*of information etc*) Komprimieren *nt*; **the gas is in a state of very high ~** das Gas ist stark verdichtet *or* komprimiert

compression: compression bandage N Druck- *or* Kompressionsverband *m*; **compression ratio** N Verdichtungs- *or* Kompressionsverhältnis *nt*

compressor [kəm'presə'] N Kompressor *m*, Verdichter *m*; **~ program** (*Comput*) Verdichtungsprogramm *nt*

comprise [kəm'praɪz] VT bestehen aus, umfassen

compromise ['kɒmprəmaɪz] N Kompromiss *m*; **to come to** *or* **reach** *or* **make a ~** zu einem Kompromiss kommen *or* gelangen, einen Kompromiss schließen; **one has to make ~s** man muss auch mal Kompromisse schließen **ADJ** *attr* Kompromiss-; **~ decision** Kompromissentscheidung *f*; **~ solution** Kompromisslösung *f* **VI** Kompromisse schließen (*about* in +*dat*); **we agreed to ~** wir einigten uns auf einen Kompromiss **VT** **a** *sb* kompromittieren; **to ~ oneself** sich kompromittieren; **to ~ one's reputation** seinem guten Ruf schaden; **to ~ one's principles** seinen Prinzipien untreu werden **b** (*= imperil*) gefährden

compromising ['kɒmprəmaɪzɪŋ] ADJ kompromittierend

comptroller [kən'trəʊlə'] N (*form*) Rechnungsprüfer *m*, Bücherrevisor *m*; **Comptroller of the Queen's Household** *Beamter des Rechnungshofes, der die königlichen Finanzen überprüft*

compulsion [kəm'pʌlʃən] N Zwang *m*, Druck *m*; (*Psych*) innerer Zwang; **under ~** unter Druck *or* Zwang; **you are under no ~** Sie sind nicht gezwungen, niemand zwingt Sie

compulsive [kəm'pʌlsɪv] ADJ zwanghaft, Zwangs-; *neurosis* Zwangs-; *behaviour* zwanghaft; **the ~ buying of ...** der krankhafte Zwang, ... zu kaufen; **~ buying as a form of disease** Kaufzwang, eine Art Krankheit; **he has a ~ desire to ...** es steht unter dem Zwang, zu ...; **he is a ~ eater/shopper** er hat die Esssucht/Kaufsucht, er leidet an einem Esszwang/Kaufzwang; **he is a ~ liar** er hat einen krankhaften Trieb zu lügen; **she's a ~ talker** sie muss unbedingt reden; **it makes ~ reading/viewing** das muss man einfach lesen/sehen; **this ~ TV-watching ruins every conversation** diese ständige Fernsehsucht zerstört jede Unterhaltung!

compulsively [kəm'pʌlsɪvlɪ] ADV **a** *lie, gamble, eat, talk* zwanghaft; **to act ~** unter einem (inneren) Zwang handeln **b** (*= irresistibly*) **~ readable/watchable** faszinierend zu lesen/anzusehen

compulsorily [kəm'pʌlsərɪlɪ] ADV zwangsweise

compulsory [kəm'pʌlsərɪ] ✪ 10.3 ADJ obligatorisch; *liquidation, measures* Zwangs-; *subject, member* Pflicht-; **that is ~** das ist Pflicht *or* obligatorisch; **education is ~** es besteht (allgemeine) Schulpflicht; **~ registration** Meldepflicht *f*; **~ retirement** Zwangspensionierung *f*; **the compulsories** PL (*Ice-Skating etc*) die Pflicht

compulsory: compulsory purchase N Enteignung *f*; **compulsory purchase order** N Enteignungsbeschluss *m*; **to put a ~ on a place** die Enteignung eines Grundstückes verfügen; **compulsory service** N (*US*) Wehrpflicht *f*

compunction [kəm'pʌŋkʃən] N (*liter*) Schuldgefühle *pl*, Gewissensbisse *pl*; **without the slightest ~** ohne sich im Geringsten schuldig zu fühlen

computation [,kɒmpjʊ'teɪʃən] N Berechnung *f*, Kalkulation *f*

computational [,kɒmpjʊ'teɪʃənəl] ADJ Computer-

computational linguistics N *sing* Computerlinguistik *f*

compute [kəm'pjuːt] VT berechnen (*at* auf +*acc*), errechnen

computer [kəm'pjuːtə'] N Computer *m*, Rechner *m*; (*for data processing also*) Datenverarbeitungsanlage *f*; **to put/have sth on ~** etw im Computer speichern/(gespeichert) haben; **it's all done by ~** das geht alles per Computer; **~ skills** Computerkenntnisse *pl*

computer in *cpds* Computer-; **computer age** N Computerzeitalter *nt*; **computer-aided** ADJ rechnergestützt; **computer-aided design** N rechnergestützter Entwurf; **computer-assisted** N computergestützt

computerate [kəm'pjuːtərɪt] ADJ **to be ~** sich mit Computern auskennen

computer: computer-based ADJ auf Computerbasis; **computer code** N Maschinenkode *m*; **computer-controlled** ADJ rechnergesteuert; **computer crash** N Computerabsturz *m*; **computer crime** N Computerkriminalität *f*; **computer dating** N Partnervermittlung *f* per Computer; **~ agency** *or* **bureau** Partnervermittlungsbüro *nt* auf Computerbasis; **computer-designed** ADJ durch Computer *or* mit Computerunterstützung entworfen; **computer error** N Computerfehler *m*

computerese [kəm,pjuːtə'riːz] N (*inf*: *= jargon*) Computerjargon *m*

computer: computer freak N (*inf*) Computerfreak *m* (*inf*); **computer game** N Computerspiel *nt*; **computer games software** N Software *f* für Computerspiele; **computer-generated** ADJ *image, graphics* computergeneriert; **computer graphics** N *sing* Computergrafik *f*, grafische Datenverarbeitung

computerization [kəm'pjuːtəraɪ'zeɪʃən] N (*of information etc*) Computerisierung *f*; **the ~ of the factory** die Umstellung der Fabrik auf Computer

computerize [kəm'pjuːtəraɪz] VT *information* computerisieren; *company, accounting methods* auf Computer *or* EDV umstellen

computerized axial tomography [kəm'pjuːtəraɪzd 'æksɪəl tə'mɒɡrəfɪ] N Computertomografie *f*

computer: computer language N Computersprache *f*; **computer literacy** N Computerkenntnisse *pl*; **computer literate** ADJ **to be ~** sich mit Computern auskennen; **computer model** N Computermodell *nt*; **computer nerd** N (*pej inf*) Computerfreak *m* (*sl*); **computer network** N Computernetzwerk *nt*; (*larger also*) Rechnerverbund *m*; **computer-operated** ADJ computergesteuert; **computer operator** N Operator(in) *m(f)*, Bildschirmarbeiter(in) *m(f)*; **computer peripheral** N Peripheriegerät *nt*; **computer printout** N (*Computer*)ausdruck *m*; **computer program** N (*Computer*)programm *nt*; **computer programmer** N Programmierer(in) *m(f)*; **computer projection** N Hochrechnung *f*; **computer science** N Informatik *f*; **computer scientist** N Informatiker(in) *m(f)*; **computer search** N Suche *f* per Computer; (*in criminal contexts*) Rasterfahndung *f*; **computer sex** N Computersex *m*; **computer studies** PL Computerwissenschaft *f*; **computer-typeset** VT im Computersatz herstellen; **computer typesetting** N Computersatz *m*; **computer virus** N Computervirus *m*

computing [kəm'pjuːtɪŋ] N **a** (*= subject*) Computerwissenschaft *f*; **her husband's in ~** ihr Mann ist in der Computerbranche **b** (*= act*)

Berechnung *f* **ATTR** *problem, task* rechnerisch; **~ speed** Rechen- *or* Operationsgeschwindigkeit *f*

comrade [ˈkɒmrɪd] N Kamerad *m*; (*Pol*) Genosse *m*, Genossin *f*

comrade-in-arms [ˈkɒmrɪdɪnˈɑːmz] N Waffenbruder *m* (*old*), Kriegskamerad *m*

comradely [ˈkɒmrɪdlɪ] ADJ kameradschaftlich

comradeship [ˈkɒmrɪdʃɪp] N Kameradschaft (-lichkeit) *f*; **the spirit of ~** der Kameradschaftsgeist

comsat [ˈkɒmsæt] *abbr of* **communications satellite**

Con (*Pol*) *abbr of* **Conservative**

con¹ [kɒn] VT (*rare:* = *learn*) sich (*dat*) einprägen

con² ADV, N → **pro³**

con³ VT (*Naut*) steuern, lenken

con⁴ (*inf*) **N** Schwindel *m*, Beschiss *m* (*inf*); **it's a ~!** das ist alles Schwindel *or* Beschiss (*inf*) **VT** hereinlegen (*inf*), bescheißen (*inf*); **he ~ned her out of all her money** er hat sie um ihr ganzes Geld gebracht; **to ~ sb into doing sth** jdn durch einen faulen Trick dazu bringen, dass er etw tut (*inf*); **don't let him ~ you into believing it** lass dir das bloß nicht von ihm aufbinden (*inf*) *or* einreden; **he ~ned his way through the security check** er hat sich durch die Sicherheitskontrolle gemogelt (*inf*)

con⁵ (*inf*) *abbr of* **convict** Knastbruder *m* (*inf*)

con artist N (*inf*) Schwindler(in) *m(f)*

conc *abbr of* **concessions** Erm.

concatenation [kɒnˌkætɪˈneɪʃən] N Verkettung *f*

concave [ˈkɒnkeɪv] ADJ konkav; *mirror* Konkav-, Hohl-

concavity [kɒnˈkævɪtɪ] N Konkavität *f*

concavo-convex [kɒnˌkeɪvəʊkɒnˈveks] ADJ konkav-konvex

conceal [kənˈsiːl] VT (= *hide*) *object, emotions, thoughts* verbergen; (= *keep secret*) verheimlichen (*sth from sb* jdm etw); **why did they ~ this information from us?** warum hat man uns diese Informationen vorenthalten?; **to ~ the fact that ...** (die Tatsache) verheimlichen, dass ...; **the chameleon was completely ~ed against its background** das Chamäleon war nicht mehr von seiner Umgebung zu unterscheiden

concealed [kənˈsiːld] ADJ verborgen; *lighting, wiring, turning, entrance* verdeckt; *camera* versteckt, Geheim-

concealment [kənˈsiːlmənt] N (*of facts*) Verheimlichung *f*; (*of evidence*) Unterschlagung *f*; (*of criminal*) Gewährung *f* von Unterschlupf (*of an* +*acc*); **to come out of ~** aus dem Versteck auftauchen; **to stay in ~** sich versteckt halten

concede [kənˈsiːd] **VT** (= *yield, give up*) *privilege* aufgeben; *lands* abtreten (*to an* +*acc*); **to ~ a right to sb** jdm ein Recht überlassen; **to ~ victory to sb** vor jdm kapitulieren; **to ~ a match** (= *give up*) aufgeben, sich geschlagen geben; (= *lose*) ein Match abgeben; **to ~ a penalty** einen Elfmeter verursachen; **to ~ a point to sb** jdm in einem Punkt Recht geben; (*Sport*) einen Punkt an jdn abgeben

b (= *admit, grant*) zugeben, einräumen (*form*); *privilege* einräumen (*to sb* jdm); *right* zubilligen, zugestehen (*to sb* jdm); **it's generally ~d that ...** es ist allgemein anerkannt, dass ...; **to ~ defeat** sich geschlagen geben **VI** nachgeben, kapitulieren

conceit [kənˈsiːt] N **a** (= *pride*) Einbildung *f*; **he's full of ~** er ist schrecklich eingebildet **b** **he is wise in his own ~** (*liter*) er dünkt sich weise (*liter*) **c** (*liter*) Konzetto *nt*

conceited [kənˈsiːtɪd] ADJ eingebildet

conceitedly [kənˈsiːtɪdlɪ] ADV *say* eingebildet; **he ~ claimed ...** eingebildet wie er ist, hat er behauptet ...

conceitedness [kənˈsiːtɪdnɪs] N Eingebildetheit *f*, Einbildung *f*

conceivable [kənˈsiːvəbl] ADJ denkbar, vorstellbar; **it is hardly ~ that ...** es ist kaum denkbar, dass ..., man kann sich (*dat*) kaum vor-

stellen, dass ...; **it's not ~ that she would have gone without us** ich kann mir nicht vorstellen, dass sie ohne uns gegangen ist

conceivably [kənˈsiːvəblɪ] ADV **she may ~ be right** es ist durchaus denkbar, dass sie Recht hat; **will it happen? – ~** wird das geschehen? – das ist durchaus denkbar

conceive [kənˈsiːv] **VT** **a** *child* empfangen **b** (= *imagine*) sich (*dat*) denken *or* vorstellen; *idea, plan* haben; *novel* die Idee haben zu; **it was originally ~d as quite a different sort of book** ursprünglich war das Buch ganz anders geplant *or* konzipiert (*geh*); **the idea was ~d in a Paris café** die Idee (dazu) wurde in einem Pariser Café geboren; **the way he ~s his role** seine Vorstellung *or* Auffassung von seiner Rolle; **she ~s it to be her duty** sie erachtet (*geh*) *or* betrachtet es als ihre Pflicht; **I can't ~ why** ich verstehe *or* begreife nicht, warum **c** **to ~ a dislike for sb/sth** eine Abneigung gegen jdn/etw entwickeln; **to ~ a passion for sb/sth** eine Leidenschaft für jdn/etw entdecken **VI** (*woman*) empfangen

▸**conceive of** VI +*prep obj* sich (*dat*) vorstellen; **who first conceived of the idea?** wer hatte die Idee zuerst?, wem kam die Idee zuerst?; **he absolutely refuses to conceive of cheating** Betrug käme ihm überhaupt nicht in den Sinn

concentrate [ˈkɒnsəntreɪt] **VT** **a** konzentrieren (*on* auf +*acc*); **to ~ all one's energies on sth** sich (voll und) ganz auf etw (*acc*) konzentrieren; **to ~ one's mind on sth** seine Gedanken *or* sich auf etw (*acc*) konzentrieren; **a spell in prison will certainly ~ his mind** eine Gefängnisstrafe wird ihm sicher zu denken geben; **it's amazing how he's ~d so much material into one novel** es ist erstaunlich, wie viel Material er in einem Roman zusammengedrängt hat

b (*Mil*) *troops* konzentrieren

c (*Chem*) konzentrieren

VI **a** (= *give one's attention*) sich konzentrieren; **to ~ on doing sth** sich darauf konzentrieren, etw zu tun

b (*people*) sich sammeln; (*troops also*) sich konzentrieren

ADJ (*Chem*) konzentriert

N (*Chem*) Konzentrat *nt*

concentrated [ˈkɒnsəntreɪtɪd] ADJ **a** *liquid, substance* konzentriert; **in a ~ form** in konzentrierter Form; **~ orange juice** Orangensaftkonzentrat *nt* **b** (= *concerted*) *effort, attack* konzentriert

concentration [ˌkɒnsənˈtreɪʃən] N **a** Konzentration *f*; **powers of ~** Konzentrationsfähigkeit *f* **b** (= *gathering*) Ansammlung *f* **c** (*Chem*) Konzentration *f*

concentration camp N Konzentrationslager *nt*, KZ *nt*

concentric [kənˈsentrɪk] ADJ *circles* konzentrisch

concept [ˈkɒnsept] N Begriff *m*; (= *conception*) Vorstellung *f*; **the ~ of evil** der Begriff des Bösen; **our ~ of the world** unser Weltbild *nt*; **his ~ of marriage** seine Vorstellungen von der Ehe; **the ~ behind the play was good** das Stück war gut konzipiert (*geh*), das Stück war in der Anlage *or* vom Konzept her gut

concept album N (*Mus*) Konzeptalbum *nt*

conception [kənˈsepʃən] N **a** (= *forming ideas*) Vorstellung *f* **b** (= *idea*) Vorstellung *f*; (= *way sth is conceived*) Konzeption *f*; **what's your ~ of the ideal life?** was ist Ihrer Vorstellung nach ein ideales Leben?; **the Buddhist ~ of life/nature/morality** die buddhistische Auffassung vom Leben/Vorstellung von der Natur/Moralvorstellung; **the classical ~ of beauty** das klassische Schönheitsideal; **they have a totally different ~ of justice** sie haben eine völlig unterschiedliche Auffassung *or* Vorstellung von Gerechtigkeit; **in their ~ they are ...** sie sind von der Konzeption her ...; **he has no ~ of how difficult it is** er macht sich (*dat*) keinen Begriff davon *or* er hat keine Vorstellung, wie schwer das ist

c (*of child*) die Empfängnis, die Konzeption (*form*)

conceptual [kənˈseptjʊəl] ADJ *thinking* begrifflich; **is this a ~ possibility?** ist ein solcher Begriff überhaupt denkbar?

conceptual art N Conceptart *f*, Konzeptkunst *f*

conceptualism [kənˈseptjʊəlɪzəm] N Konzeptualismus *m*

conceptualization [kənˌseptjʊələˈzeɪʃən] N Begriffsbildung *f*; **the ~ of experience** die begriffliche Erfassung der Erfahrung

conceptualize [kənˈseptjʊəlaɪz] **VT** in Begriffe fassen **VI** begrifflich denken

conceptually [kənˈseptjʊəlɪ] ADV begrifflich; **X is ~ impossible** X ist begrifflich undenkbar; **it only exists ~** das existiert nur in der Vorstellung

concern [kənˈsɜːn] ❀ 26.2 **N** **a** (= *relation, connection*) **do you have any ~ with banking?** haben Sie etwas mit dem Bankwesen zu tun?; **to have no ~ with sth** mit etw nichts zu tun haben **b** (= *business, affair*) Angelegenheit(en *pl*) *f*; (= *matter of interest and importance to sb*) Anliegen *nt*; **the day-to-day ~s of government** die täglichen Regierungsgeschäfte; **it's no ~ of his** das geht ihn nichts an; **what ~ is it of yours?** was geht Sie das an?

c (*Comm*) Konzern *m* → **going ADJ c**

d (= *share*) Beteiligung *f*

e (= *anxiety*) Sorge *f*, Besorgnis *f*; **a look of ~** ein besorgter *or* sorgenvoller Blick; **the situation in the Middle East is causing ~** die Lage im Nahen Osten ist Besorgnis erregend; **there's some/no cause for ~** es besteht Grund/kein Grund zur Sorge; **to do sth out of ~ for sb** etw aus Sorge um jdn tun; **he showed great ~ for your safety** er war *or* zeigte sich (*geh*) sehr um Ihre Sicherheit besorgt; **don't you feel any ~ for the starving millions?** berührt Sie die Tatsache, dass Millionen am Verhungern sind, überhaupt nicht?

f (= *importance*) Bedeutung *f*; **a matter of great ~** eine Angelegenheit von immenser Bedeutung; **issues of national ~** Fragen *pl* von nationalem Interesse; **to be of little/great ~ to sb** jdm nicht/sehr wichtig sein

VT **a** (= *be about*) handeln von; **it ~s the following issue** es geht um die folgende Frage; **the last chapter is ~ed with ...** das letzte Kapitel behandelt ...

b (= *be the business of, involve*) angehen, betreffen; (= *affect*) betreffen; **that doesn't ~ you** das betrifft Sie nicht; (*as snub*) das geht Sie nichts an; **to whom it may ~** (*on certificate*) Bestätigung *f*; (*on reference*) Zeugnis *nt*; **the countries ~ed with oil production** die Länder, die mit der Ölproduktion zu tun haben; **where money/honour is ~ed** wenn es um Geld/die Ehre geht; **as far as the money is ~ed** was das Geld betrifft *or* angeht; **is it important? – not as far as I'm ~ed** ist es denn wichtig? – was mich betrifft nicht; **as far as he is ~ed it's just another job, but ...** für ihn ist es nur ein anderer Job, aber ...; **as far as I'm ~ed you can do what you like** von mir aus kannst du tun und lassen, was du willst; **where we are ~ed** wo es um uns geht; (= *in so far as we are affected*) wo wir betroffen sind; **the department ~ed** (= *relevant*) die zuständige Abteilung; (= *involved*) die betreffende Abteilung; **who are the people ~ed in this report?** wer sind die Leute, um die es in diesem Bericht geht?; **the persons ~ed** die Betroffenen, die betreffenden Personen; **my brother is the most closely ~ed** mein Bruder ist am meisten davon betroffen; **the men ~ed in the robbery** die in den Überfall verwickelten Männer **c** (= *interest*) **he is only ~ed with facts** ihn interessieren nur die Fakten; (= *is only dealing with*) ihm geht es nur um die Fakten; **to ~ oneself with *or* about sth** sich für etw interessieren; **I'm not ~ed now *or* I don't want to ~ myself now with the economic aspect of the problem** mir geht es jetzt nicht um den ökonomischen Aspekt des Problems

d (= *have at heart*) **we should be ~ed more with** *or* **about quality** Qualität sollte uns ein größeres Anliegen sein; **a mother is naturally ~ed about the wellbeing of her children** das Wohl ihrer Kinder ist einer Mutter natürlich ein Anliegen; **he's not at all ~ed with** *or* **about her wellbeing** ihr Wohl kümmert ihn überhaupt nicht; **there's no need for you to ~ yourself about that** darum brauchen Sie sich nicht zu kümmern

e (= *worry: usu pass*) **to be ~ed about sth** sich (*dat*) um etw Sorgen machen, um etw besorgt sein; **I was very ~ed to hear about your illness** ich habe mir Sorgen gemacht, als ich von Ihrer Krankheit hörte; **he was ~ed by the news** die Nachricht beunruhigte ihn; **don't ~ yourself** machen Sie sich keine Sorgen; **I was very ~ed about** *or* **for your safety** ich war sehr um Ihre Sicherheit besorgt; **I am ~ed to hear that ...** es beunruhigt mich, dass ...; **~ed parents** besorgte Eltern; **a ~ed look** ein besorgter Blick

concerning [kənˈsɜːnɪŋ] PREP bezüglich, hinsichtlich, betreffs (*form*) (*all +gen*); **~ your request ...** apropos Ihrer Anfrage ..., was Ihre Anfrage betrifft ...; **~ what?** worüber?

concert¹ [ˈkɒnsət] N **a** (*Mus*) Konzert *nt*; **were you at the ~?** waren Sie in dem Konzert?; **Madonna in ~** Madonna live **b** (*of voices etc*) **in ~** im Chor, gemeinsam **c** (*fig*) **in ~** gemeinsam; **to work in ~ with sb** mit jdm zusammenarbeiten

concert² [kənˈsɜːt] VT *efforts* vereinen

concerted [kənˈsɜːtɪd] ADJ *efforts, action, attack* gemeinsam, konzertiert (*esp Pol*); **with their ~ efforts ...** mit vereinten Kräften ...; **to take ~ action** gemeinsam vorgehen; **to make a ~ attack** gemeinsam *or* geballt angreifen

concert: concertgoer N Konzertbesucher(in) *m(f)* *or* -gänger(in) *m(f)*; **concert grand** N Konzertflügel *m*; **concert hall** N Konzerthalle *f* *or* -saal *m*

concertina [ˌkɒnsəˈtiːnə] **N** Konzertina *f* **VI** sich wie eine Ziehharmonika zusammenschieben

concertmaster [ˈkɒnsətmæstəʳ] N (*US*) Konzertmeister *m*

concerto [kənˈtʃɜːtəʊ] N Konzert *nt*, Concerto *nt*

concert: concert performer N Konzertkünstler(in) *m(f)*; **concert pianist** N Pianist(in) *m(f)*; **concert pitch** N Kammerton *m*; **concert tour** N Konzerttournee *f*

concession [kənˈseʃən] N Zugeständnis *nt*, Konzession *f* (*to an +acc*); (*Comm*) Konzession *f*; **to make ~s to sb** jdm Konzessionen *or* Zugeständnisse machen

concessionaire [kənˌseʃəˈneəʳ] N (*Comm*) Konzessionär *m*

concessionary [kənˈseʃənərɪ] ADJ (*Comm*) Konzessions-; (= *reduced*) *rates, fares* verbilligt

concessive [kənˈsesɪv] ADJ (*Gram*) konzessiv, Konzessiv-

conch [kɒntʃ] N große, spiralige Meeresschnecke (*used as trumpet*) Trompetenschnecke *f*, Tritonshorn *nt* (*also Myth*)

conchy [ˈkɒntʃɪ] N (*pej sl*) Kriegsdienstverweigerer *m*, Drückeberger *m* (*pej inf*)

concierge [ˈkɒnsɪɛːʒ] N Portier *m*, Portiersfrau *f*

conciliate [kənˈsɪlɪeɪt] VT **a** (= *placate*) besänftigen; (= *win the goodwill of*) *person* versöhnlich stimmen **b** (= *reconcile*) *opposing views* auf einen Nenner bringen, in Einklang bringen

conciliation [kənˌsɪlɪˈeɪʃən] N **a** (= *resolution: of dispute, differences, Pol, Ind*) Schlichtung *f*; **~ board** Schlichtungskommission *f* **b** (= *appeasement: of person*) Besänftigung *f*

conciliator [kənˈsɪlɪeɪtəʳ] N Vermittler(in) *m(f)*

conciliatory [kənˈsɪlɪətərɪ] ADJ (= *intended to reconcile*) versöhnlich; (= *placatory*) beschwichtigend, besänftigend

concise [kənˈsaɪs] ADJ präzis(e), exakt; **~ dictionary** Handwörterbuch *nt*

concisely [kənˈsaɪslɪ] ADV präzis(e), exakt

conciseness [kənˈsaɪsnɪs], **concision** [kənˈsɪʒən] N Präzision *f*, Exaktheit *f*

conclave [ˈkɒnkleɪv] N **a** Klausur *f*; **in ~** in Klausur; **to meet in ~** eine Klausurtagung abhalten **b** (*Eccl*) Konklave *nt*

conclude [kənˈkluːd] ✪ 26.1 **VT a** (= *end*) *meeting, letter, speech* beenden, schließen; *meal* abschließen, beenden; **this, gentlemen, ~s our business** meine Herren, sind wir mit unserer Besprechung am Ende; **and now, to ~ tonight's programmes** zum Abschluss unseres heutigen Abendprogramms

b (= *arrange*) *treaty, transaction, deal* abschließen

c (= *infer*) schließen, folgern (*from* aus); **what did you ~?** was haben Sie daraus geschlossen *or* gefolgert?

d (= *decide, come to conclusion*) zu dem Schluss kommen; **what have you ~d about his suggestion?** zu welchem Schluss sind Sie in Bezug auf seinen Vorschlag gekommen?

VI (*meetings, events*) enden; (*letter, speech etc also*) schließen; **to ~ I would like to say ...**, **I would like to ~ by saying ...** abschließend möchte ich sagen ...

concluding [kənˈkluːdɪŋ] ADJ *remarks, words* abschließend, Schluss-; **~ bars/lines** Schlusstakte/-zeilen *pl*; **the ~ stages of the tournament** die letzten Durchgänge des Turniers

conclusion [kənˈkluːʒən] ✪ 26.1, 26.3 N **a** (= *end*) Abschluss *m*; (*of essay, novel etc*) Schluss *m*; **in ~** zum (Ab)schluss, abschließend **b** (= *settling: of treaty etc*) Abschluss *m*, Zustandekommen *nt* **c** Schluss(folgerung *f*) *m*; **what do you draw** *or* **reach from all this?** welchen Schluss *or* welche Schlussfolgerung ziehen Sie daraus *or* aus alldem?; **let me know your ~s** lassen Sie mich wissen, zu welchem Schluss Sie gekommen sind; **a hasty ~** ein voreiliger Schluss; **one is forced to the ~ that ...** man kommt unweigerlich zu dem Schluss, dass ... **d** (*Logic*) Folgerung *f*

conclusive [kənˈkluːsɪv] ADJ (= *convincing*) schlüssig, überzeugend; (= *decisive, final*) endgültig; (*Jur*) *evidence* einschlägig; *proof* schlüssig, eindeutig

conclusively [kənˈkluːsɪvlɪ] ADV (= *convincingly*) schlüssig, überzeugend; (= *decisively*) endgültig; *prove* eindeutig, unwiderleglich; **this settles this issue ~** damit ist die Sache endgültig beigelegt

concoct [kənˈkɒkt] VT **a** (*Cook etc*) zusammenstellen, (zu)bereiten; (*hum*) kreieren, zurechtzaubern **b** (*fig*) sich (*dat*) zurechtlegen; *scheme, plan also* ausbrüten *or* -hecken; *excuse also* sich (*dat*) ausdenken; *new dress, hat* zaubern

concoction [kənˈkɒkʃən] N **a** (= *food*) Kreation *f*, Zusammenstellung *f*; (= *drink*) Gebräu *nt*; **one of her little ~s** eines ihrer Spezialrezepte **b** (= *story etc*) Erdichtung *f*; (*Fashion*) Zauberei *f*, Spielerei *f*; **the plot is an amazing ~ of bizarre events** der Plot ist eine erstaunliche Verkettung der merkwürdigsten Ereignisse

concomitant [kənˈkɒmɪtənt] **ADJ to be ~ with sth** von etw begleitet werden **N** Begleiterscheinung *f*

concord [ˈkɒnkɔːd] N (= *harmony*) Eintracht *f*; (*about decision etc*) Einvernehmen *nt*, Übereinstimmung *f*

concordance [kənˈkɔːdəns] N **a** (= *agreement*) Übereinstimmung *f*; **in ~ with your specifications** (*form*) Ihren Angaben *or* Anweisungen gemäß **b** (*Bibl, Liter*) Konkordanz *f*

concordant [kənˈkɔːdənt] ADJ (*form*) übereinstimmend; **to be ~ with** entsprechen (+*dat*)

concordat [kənˈkɔːdæt] N Konkordat *nt*

concourse [ˈkɒnkɔːs] N **a** (*liter, of people*) Menschenmenge *f*, Menschenauflauf *m*; (*of two rivers*) Zusammenfluss *m* **b** (= *place*) Eingangshalle *f*; (*US, in park*) freier Platz; **station ~** Bahnhofshalle *f*

concrete¹ [ˈkɒŋkriːt] ADJ *object, evidence, example, proposals, measures* konkret; **a chair is a ~**

object ein Stuhl ist gegenständlich *or* etwas Gegenständliches; **could you put your argument in a more ~ form?** könnten Sie etwas konkreter werden?

concrete² **N** (*Build*) Beton *m*; **nothing is set** *or* **embedded in ~ yet** (*fig*) es ist noch nichts definitiv festgelegt **ADJ** Beton- **VT** *wall, floor* betonieren

concretely [kənˈkriːtlɪ] ADV konkret; **to express sth ~/more ~** etw konkretisieren/konkreter ausdrücken

concrete: concrete mixer N Betonmischmaschine *f*; **concrete music** N konkrete Musik; **concrete noun** N Konkretum *nt*; **concrete poetry** N Bilderlyrik *f*

concretion [kənˈkriːʃən] N (= *coalescence*) Verschmelzung *f*; (*Geol also*) Konkretion *f*; (*Med*) Konkrement *nt*

concubine [ˈkɒŋkjʊbaɪn] N **a** (*old*) Konkubine *f*, Mätresse *f* **b** (*in polygamy*) Konkubine *f*, Nebenfrau *f*

concupiscence [kənˈkjuːpɪsəns] N Lüsternheit *f*

concupiscent [kənˈkjuːpɪsənt] ADJ lüstern

concur [kənˈkɜːʳ] VI **a** (= *agree*) übereinstimmen; (*with a suggestion etc*) beipflichten (*with +dat*); (*Math*) zusammenlaufen; **John and I ~red** John und ich waren einer Meinung; **I ~ with that** ich pflichte dem bei **b** (= *happen together*) zusammentreffen, auf einmal eintreten

concurrence [kənˈkʌrəns] N **a** (= *accordance*) Übereinstimmung *f*; (= *agreement, permission*) Einverständnis *nt*, Zustimmung *f* **b** (*of events*) Zusammentreffen *nt* **c** (*Math*) Schnittpunkt *m*; **at the ~ of the two lines** im Schnittpunkt der beiden Geraden

concurrent [kənˈkʌrənt] ADJ **a** (= *occurring at the same time*) gleichzeitig; **to be ~ with sth** mit etw zusammentreffen, zur gleichen Zeit wie etw stattfinden **b** (= *acting together*) vereint, gemeinsam **c** (= *in agreement*) übereinstimmend; *interpretation, statement also* gleich lautend; **to be ~ with sth** mit etw übereinstimmen **d** (*Math*) zusammenlaufend; (= *intersecting*) sich schneidend

concurrently [kənˈkʌrəntlɪ] ADV gleichzeitig; **the two sentences to run ~** (*Jur*) unter gleichzeitigem Vollzug beider Freiheitsstrafen

concuss [kənˈkʌs] VT (*usu pass*) **to be ~ed** eine Gehirnerschütterung haben

concussion [kənˈkʌʃən] N Gehirnerschütterung *f*

condemn [kənˈdem] ✪ 26.3 VT **a** (= *censure*) verurteilen

b (*Jur: = sentence*) verurteilen; **to ~ sb to death/10 years' imprisonment** jdn zum Tode/zu 10 Jahren Gefängnis verurteilen; **the ~ed man** der zum Tode Verurteilte; **the ~ed cell** die Todeszelle

c (*fig*) verdammen, verurteilen (*to* zu)

d (= *declare unfit*) *building, slums* für abbruchreif erklären; *ship* für nicht mehr seetüchtig erklären; **these houses are/should be ~ed** diese Häuser stehen auf der Abrissliste/sollten abgerissen werden; **the fruit was ~ed as unfit for consumption** das Obst wurde für den Verzehr ungeeignet erklärt

e (*US, Jur*) beschlagnahmen; *land* enteignen

condemnation [ˌkɒndem'neɪʃən] ✪ 14 N **a** Verurteilung *f*; (*fig also*) Verdammung *f*; **what a ~ was it for a min** ein Armutszeugnis **b** (*of slums, ship*) Kondemnation *f* (*spec*); **the new council was responsible for the immediate ~ of some of the old city slums** die neue Stadtverwaltung war dafür verantwortlich, dass einige der alten Slums sofort auf die Abrissliste kamen **c** (*US Jur*) Beschlagnahme *f*; (*of land*) Enteignung *f*

condemnatory [kɒndem'neɪtərɪ] ADJ aburteilend; *frown* missbilligend; *criticism* verdammend; *conclusion* vernichtend

condensation [ˌkɒndenˈseɪʃən] N **a** (*of vapour*) Kondensation *f*; (= *liquid formed*) Kondensat *nt*; (*on window panes etc*) Kondenswasser *nt*; **the**

windows/walls are covered with ~ die Fenster/Wände sind beschlagen **b** (= *short form*) Kurzfassung *f*; (= *act*) Kondensierung *f*, Zusammenfassung *f*

condense [kən'dens] **VT** **a** (= *reduce*) kondensieren **b** (*Phys*) *gas* kondensieren; (= *compress*) verdichten; *rays* bündeln **c** (= *shorten*) zusammenfassen; **in a very ~d form** in sehr gedrängter Form **VI** (*gas*) kondensieren, sich niederschlagen

condensed milk [kən'denst'mɪlk] N Kondensmilch *f*, Büchsen- *or* Dosenmilch *f*

condenser [kən'densə'] N (*Elec, Phys*) Kondensator *m*; (*Opt*) Kondensor *m*, Sammellinse *f*

condescend [ˌkɒndɪ'send] VI **a** (= *stoop*) sich herab- *or* herbeilassen; **to ~ to do sth** sich herab- *or* herbeilassen, etw zu tun, geruhen (*geh, iro*) *or* so gnädig sein, etw zu tun **b** **to ~ to sb** jdn herablassend behandeln; **he doesn't like being ~ed to** er lässt sich nicht gerne von oben herab behandeln

condescending [ˌkɒndɪ'sendɪŋ] ADJ (*pej*) herablassend, von oben herab *pred*; **to be ~ to** *or* **toward(s) sb** jdn von oben herab *or* herablassend behandeln

condescendingly [ˌkɒndɪ'sendɪŋlɪ] ADV (*pej*) herablassend, von oben herab

condescension [ˌkɒndɪ'senʃən] N (*pej*) Herablassung *f*; (= *attitude also*) herablassende Haltung

condiment ['kɒndɪmənt] N Würze *f*

condition [kən'dɪʃən] **N** **a** (= *determining factor*) Bedingung *f* (*also Jur, Comm*); (= *prerequisite*) Voraussetzung *f*; **~s of sale** Verkaufsbedingungen *pl*; **on ~ that ...** unter der Bedingung *or* Voraussetzung, dass ...; **on one/this ~** unter einer/der Bedingung *or* Voraussetzung; **on what ~?** zu welchen Bedingungen?, unter welchen Voraussetzungen?; **on no ~** auf keinen Fall; **to make ~s** Bedingungen stellen; **he made it a ~ that ...** er machte es zur Bedingung, dass ...
b **conditions** PL (= *circumstances*) Verhältnisse *pl*, Zustände *pl* (*pej*); **working ~s** Arbeitsbedingungen *pl*; **living ~s** Wohnverhältnisse *pl*; **weather ~s** die Wetterlage; **in** *or* **under (the) present ~s** bei den derzeitigen Verhältnissen
c *no pl* (= *state*) Zustand *m*; **he is in good/bad ~** er ist in guter/schlechter Verfassung; **it is in good/bad ~** es ist in gutem/schlechtem Zustand; **he is in a critical ~** sein Zustand ist kritisch; **not in your ~!** nicht in deinem Zustand!; **he is in no ~ to make the journey** er ist nicht reisefähig; **the car is in no ~ to make such a long journey** so wie das Auto ist, kann man damit keine Reise machen; **you're in no ~ to drive** du bist nicht mehr fahrtüchtig; **to be in/out of ~** eine gute/keine Kondition haben; **to keep in/get into ~** in Form bleiben/kommen; (*Sport also*) seine Kondition beibehalten/sich (*dat*) eine gute Kondition antrainieren; **in an interesting ~** (*dated hum inf*) in anderen Umständen; **to change one's ~** (= *old*) sich verehelichen (*dated*); **the human ~** die Situation des Menschen *or* der Menschen
d (*Med*) Beschwerden *pl*; **heart/thyroid ~** Herz-/Schilddrüsenleiden *nt*; **he has a heart ~** er ist herzkrank
e (*old*: = *rank*) Stand *m*, Schicht *f*; **in every ~ of life** aus allen Ständen
VT **a** (*esp pass*: = *determine*) bedingen, bestimmen; **to be ~ed by** bedingt sein durch, abhängen von
b (= *bring into good condition*) *hair, athlete, animal* in Form bringen; **~ing powder** Aufbaumittel *nt*
c (*Psych etc*, = *train*) konditionieren; (= *accustom*) gewöhnen; **they have become ~ed to believe it** sie sind so konditioniert, dass sie es glauben; **~ed reflex** *or* **response** bedingter Reflex

conditional [kən'dɪʃənl] **ADJ** **a** mit Vorbehalt, bedingt, vorbehaltlich; (*Comm, Jur*) *sale* mit Auflagen; **a ~ yes** ein Ja mit Vorbehalt; **to be ~ (up)on sth** von etw abhängen **b** (*Gram*) konditional, Konditional-, Bedingungs-; **the ~ mood/**

tense der Konditional **N** (*Gram*) Konditional *m*

conditional access N (*TV*) Empfang *m* nur für Abonnenten

conditional discharge N (*Jur*) Entlassung *f* auf Bewährung

conditionally [kən'dɪʃnəlɪ] ADV unter *or* mit Vorbehalt

conditioner [kən'dɪʃənə'] N (*for hair*) Pflegespülung *f*; (*for washing*) Weichspüler *m*

conditioning shampoo [kən'dɪʃənɪŋʃæm'puː] N Pflegeshampoo *nt*

condo ['kɒndəʊ] N (*US, inf*) = **condominium b**

condole [kən'dəʊl] VI **to ~ with sb** (**on** *or* **upon sth**) jdm (zu etw) sein Mitgefühl aussprechen; (*on death also*) jdm (zu etw) kondolieren

condolence [kən'dəʊləns] N Beileid *nt no pl*, Anteilnahme *f*, Kondolenz *f no pl* (*pej*); **message/letter of ~** Kondolenzbotschaft *f*/-brief *m*; **book of ~(s)** Kondolenzbuch *nt*; **please accept my ~s on the death of your mother** (meine) aufrichtige Anteilnahme zum Tode Ihrer Mutter

condom ['kɒndɒm] N Kondom *nt or m*, Präservativ *nt*

condominium ['kɒndə'mɪnɪəm] **N** **a** (*Pol*) Kondominium *nt*; (= *rule also*) Kondominat *nt* **b** (*US, = apartment house*) ≈ Haus *nt* mit Eigentumswohnungen, Eigentumsblock *m*; (= *single apartment*) ≈ Eigentumswohnung *f*

condone [kən'dəʊn] VT (= *overlook*) (stillschweigend) hinwegsehen über (+*acc*); (= *approve*) (stillschweigend) dulden

condor ['kɒndɔː'] N Kondor *m*

conduce [kən'djuːs] VI **to ~ to** (*form*) förderlich sein (+*dat*)

conducive [kən'djuːsɪv] ADJ förderlich, dienlich (*to* +*dat*)

conduct ['kɒndʌkt] **N** **a** (= *behaviour*) Verhalten *nt*, Benehmen *nt* (*towards* gegenüber); (*of children also*) Betragen *nt*; (*of prisoner*) Führung *f*; **the rules of ~** die Verhaltensregeln
b (= *management*) Führung *f*; (*of conference, commission of inquiry*) Leitung *f*; (*of investigation*) Durchführung *f*; **his ~ of the war** seine Kriegsführung; **their ~ of the campaign** die Art, wie sie die Kampagne durchführen/durchgeführt haben
VT [kən'dʌkt] **a** (= *guide*) führen; (*ceremoniously*) geleiten (*geh*); **~ed tour (of)** (*of country*) Gesellschaftsreise *f* (durch); (*of building*) Führung *f* (durch)
b (= *direct, manage*) *war, campaign, correspondence, conversation* führen; *meeting, business also* leiten; *investigation* durchführen; *private affairs* handhaben; **he ~ed his own defence** er übernahm seine eigene Verteidigung
c (*Mus*) dirigieren
d (*Phys, Physiol*) leiten; *lightning* ableiten, erden **VI** [kən'dʌkt] **a** (*Mus*) dirigieren
b (*Phys*) leiten
VR [kən'dʌkt] sich verhalten, sich benehmen; (*prisoner*) sich führen; **her husband ~ed himself abominably** ihr Mann führte sich unmöglich auf

conductible [kən'dʌktɪbl] ADJ (*Phys*) leitfähig

conduction [kən'dʌkʃən] N (*Phys, Physiol*) Leitung *f* (*along* durch *or* (*Physiol*) entlang)

conductive [ˌkɒnd'ʌktɪv] ADJ leitfähig, leitend

conductivity [ˌkɒndʌk'tɪvɪtɪ] N (*Phys, Physiol*) Leitfähigkeit *f*

conductor [kən'dʌktə'] N **a** (*Mus*) Dirigent(in) *m(f)*; (*of choir also*) Leiter(in) *m(f)* **b** (= *bus, tram conductor*) Schaffner *m*; (*US, Rail*: = *guard*) Zugführer *m* **c** (*Phys*) Leiter *m*; (= *lightning conductor*) Blitzableiter *m*

conductor rail N (*Fahr*)leitung(sschiene) *f*

conductress [kən'dʌktrɪs] N (*on bus etc*) Schaffnerin *f*

conduct sheet ['kɒndʌkt-] N (*Mil*) militärische Beurteilung

conduit ['kɒndɪt] N Leitungsrohr *nt*; (*Elec*) Rohrkabel *nt*

cone [kəʊn] N **a** Kegel *m*; (*Geol*: *of volcano*) (Berg)kegel *m*; (= *storm cone*) Windsack *m*; (= *traffic cone*) Pylon *m* (*form*), Leitkegel *m*; (*Space*: = *nose cone*) Nase *f*; **a ~ of light** ein Lichtkegel *m* **b** (*Bot*) Zapfen *m* **c** (= *ice-cream cone*) (Eis)tüte *f*

▸ **cone off** VT *sep* mit Pylonen absperren

cone-shaped ['kəʊn'ʃeɪpt] ADJ kegelförmig

cone sugar N Hutzucker *m*

coney N = **cony**

confab ['kɒnfæb] N (*inf*) kleine Besprechung; **we'd better have a quick ~** wir bekakeln das am besten mal schnell (*inf*)

confection [kən'fekʃən] N **a** (= *sweets*) Konfekt *nt*, Zucker- *or* Naschwerk *nt* (*old*) **b** (*Comm*: = *item of ladies' clothing*) modischer Artikel; **a charming little ~ from Dior** eine bezaubernde kleine Kreation von Dior

confectioner [kən'fekʃənə'] N (= *maker*) Konditor *m*, Zuckerbäcker *m* (*old*); (= *seller also*) Süßwarenverkäufer(in) *m(f)*; **~'s (shop)** Süßwarenladen *m*

confectioner's custard [kən'fekʃənəz-] N Puddingmasse *f*

confectioner's sugar N (*US*) Puderzucker *m*

confectionery [kən'fekʃənərɪ] N Konditorwaren *pl*, Süßwaren *pl*; (= *chocolates*) Konfekt *nt*

confederacy [kən'fedərəsɪ] N (*Pol*, = *confederation*) Bündnis *nt*; (*of nations*) Staatenbund *m*, Konföderation *f*; **the Confederacy** (*US, Hist*) die Konföderierten Staaten von Amerika

confederate [kən'fedərɪt] **ADJ** *system* konföderiert; *nations also* verbündet; **the Confederate States** (*US, Hist*) die Konföderierten Staaten von Amerika **N** (*Pol*: = *ally*) Verbündete(r) *m*, Bündnispartner *m*, Bundesgenosse *m*; (*pej*: = *accomplice*) Komplize *m* (*pej*); **the Confederates** (*US, Hist*) die Konföderierten *pl*

confederation [kən,fedə'reɪʃən] **N** **a** (*Pol*) = *alliance*) Bündnis *nt*, Bund *m*; (= *system of government*) Staatenbund *m*, Konföderation *f*; **the Swiss Confederation** die Schweizerische Eidgenossenschaft **b** (= *association*) Bund *m*; **Confederation of British Industry** Verband *m* der britischen Industrie

confer [kən'fɜː'] **VT** (*on, upon sb* jdm) *title, degree* verleihen; *power also* übertragen **VI** sich beraten, konferieren (*geh*)

conference ['kɒnfərəns] N **a** Konferenz *f*; (*more informal*) Besprechung *f*; **to be in a ~ (with)** eine Besprechung *or* Konferenz haben (mit); **to get round the ~ table** sich an den Konferenztisch setzen; **to get sb to the ~ table** jdn an den Konferenztisch bringen; **I'm sorry, he's in ~** tut mir Leid, er ist in *or* bei einer Konferenz/Besprechung **b** (= *convention*) Konferenz *f*, Tagung *f*

conference call N (*Telec*) Konferenzschaltung *f*

conference room N Konferenzzimmer *nt*

conferencing ['kɒnfərənsɪŋ] N (*Telec*) Konferenzschaltungen *pl*

conferment [kən'fɜːmənt], **conferral** [kən'fɜːrəl] N (*of title, degree*) Verleihung *f*

conferrable [kən'fɜːrəbl] ADJ übertragbar

confess [kən'fes] **VT** **a** (= *acknowledge*) gestehen, zugeben; *ignorance, mistake also* bekennen, beichten (*hum inf*) **b** (*Eccl*) *sins* bekennen; (*to priest*) beichten; (*priest*) *penitent* die Beichte abnehmen (+*dat*) **VI** (= *admit*) gestehen (*to* +*acc*); **to ~ to sth** etw gestehen, sich zu etw bekennen; **if you did it, you might as well ~** wenn du es warst, warum gestehst du es (dann) nicht? **b** (*Eccl*) **to ~ to sb/to sth** jdm/etw (*acc*) beichten

confessed [kən'fest] ADJ (= *admitted*) *plan* zugegeben, erklärt, eingestanden; (= *having confessed*) *criminal* geständig; (= *self-confessed*) *revolutionary* erklärt; *alcoholic, criminal* eigenen Eingeständnisses, nach eigenen Angaben

confessedly [kən'fesɪdlɪ] ADV zugegebenermaßen

confession [kənˈfeʃən] N **a** (= admission) Eingeständnis nt; (of guilt, crime etc) Geständnis nt; **on his own ~** laut eigener Aussage; **to make a full ~ of sth to sb** (Jur also) jdm ein volles Geständnis einer Sache (gen) ablegen; **I have a ~ to make** ich muss dir etwas beichten (inf) or gestehen; (Jur) ich möchte ein Geständnis ablegen; **"confessions of a ... "** „Bekenntnisse eines/einer ...“; **~ magazine** Zeitschrift f mit Geschichten, die das Leben schrieb **b** (Eccl: of sins) Beichte f, (Schuld- or Sünden-) bekenntnis nt; general = allgemeines Sündenbekenntnis; **~ of faith** Glaubensbekenntnis nt; **to make one's ~** seine Sünden bekennen; **to hear ~** (die) Beichte hören **c** (= faith) (Glaubens)bekenntnis nt, Konfession f; **what ~ are you?** welche Konfession or Glaubenszugehörigkeit haben Sie?

confessional [kənˈfeʃənl] N Beichtstuhl m; **the secrecy of the ~** das Beichtgeheimnis

confessor [kənˈfesəʳ] N **a** (Eccl) Beichtvater m **b** Edward the Confessor Edward der Bekenner

confetti [kənˈfetiː] N , no pl Konfetti nt

confidant [ˌkɒnfɪˈdænt] N Vertraute(r) m

confidante [ˌkɒnfɪˈdænt] N Vertraute f

confide [kənˈfaɪd] VT anvertrauen (to sb jdm)

▶**confide in** VI +prep obj **a** (= tell secrets to) sich anvertrauen (+dat); **to confide in sb about sth** jdm etw anvertrauen **b** (old: = trust) sein Vertrauen setzen in (+acc), bauen auf (+acc)

confidence [ˈkɒnfɪdəns] ✪ 19.4 N **a** (= trust) Vertrauen nt; (in sb's abilities also) Zutrauen nt (in zu); (= confident expectation) Zuversicht f; **to have (every/no) ~ in sb/sth** (volles/kein) Vertrauen zu jdm/etw haben or ein jdm/etw setzen; **they have no ~ in his ability/the future** sie haben kein Vertrauen or Zutrauen zu seinen Fähigkeiten/kein Vertrauen in die Zukunft; **I have every ~ that ...** ich bin ganz zuversichtlich, dass ...; **to put one's ~ in sb/sth** auf jdn/etw bauen, sich auf jdn/etw verlassen; **I wish I had your ~** ich wünschte, ich hätte deine Zuversicht(lichkeit); **we look with ~ ...** wir schauen zuversichtlich ...; **can you leave your car here with ~?** kann man hier sein Auto beruhigt abstellen?; **he talked with ~ on the subject** er äußerte sich sehr kompetent zu dem Thema; **I can't talk with any ~ about ...** ich kann nichts Bestimmtes über (+acc) ... sagen; **in the full ~ that ...** im festen Vertrauen darauf, dass ...; **issue of ~** (Parl) Vertrauensfrage f; **to give a vote of ~** (Parl) das Vertrauen aussprechen; **to ask for a vote of ~** (Parl) die Vertrauensfrage stellen; **motion/vote of no ~** Misstrauensantrag m/-votum nt **b** (= self-confidence) (Selbst)vertrauen nt, Selbstsicherheit f **c** (= confidential relationship) Vertrauen nt; **in (strict) ~** (streng) vertraulich; **to take sb into one's ~** jdn ins Vertrauen ziehen; **to be or enjoy sb's ~** jds Vertrauen besitzen or genießen **d** (= information confided) vertrauliche Mitteilung

confidence: confidence building N Vertrauensbildung f; **confidence-building** ADJ vertrauensbildend; **confidence trick** N = con trick; **confidence trickster** N = con man

confident [ˈkɒnfɪdənt] ADJ **a** (= sure) überzeugt, zuversichtlich (of +gen); look etc zuversichtlich; **to be ~ of success** or **succeeding** vom Erfolg überzeugt sein, zuversichtlich or überzeugt sein, dass man gewinnt; **to be/feel ~ about sth** in Bezug auf etw zuversichtlich sein; **it will happen – are you ~?** es wird geschehen – sind Sie davon überzeugt or dessen sicher?; **to be ~ in sb/sth** Vertrauen zu jdm/etw haben, jdm/einer Sache vertrauen; **~ in her love** ihrer Liebe gewiss (geh) **b** (= self-assured) (selbst)sicher; **to be in a ~ mood** sich seiner sicher fühlen

confidential [ˌkɒnfɪˈdenʃəl] ADJ **a** information, whisper vertraulich; **to treat sth as ~** etw vertraulich behandeln; **to keep sth ~** etw für sich behalten **b** (= enjoying sb's confidence) **~ secre-**
tary Privatsekretär(in) m(f); **~ agent** Sonderbeauftragte(r) mf mit geheimer Mission **c** (= inclined to confide) vertrauensselig

confidentiality [ˌkɒnfɪˌdenʃɪˈælɪtɪ] N Vertraulichkeit f

confidentially [ˌkɒnfɪˈdenʃəlɪ] ADV vertraulich, im Vertrauen

confidently [ˈkɒnfɪdəntlɪ] ADV **a** zuversichtlich; look forward also vertrauensvoll **b** (= self--confidently) selbstsicher; (= with conviction) mit Überzeugung

confiding [kənˈfaɪdɪŋ] ADJ vertraulich; **he's not a ~ sort of person** er vertraut sich keinem an

confidingly [kənˈfaɪdɪŋlɪ] ADV vertraulich

configuration [kənˌfɪgjʊˈreɪʃən] N Konfiguration f (form); (Geog) Form f, Gestalt f; (Sci) Struktur f, Aufbau m; (Astron) Anordnung f, Aspekt m (spec); (Comput) Konfiguration f

configure [kənˈfɪgəʳ] VT (Comput) konfigurieren

confine [kənˈfaɪn] VT **a** (= keep in) person, animal (ein)sperren; flood eindämmen; **to be ~d to the house** nicht aus dem Haus können; **to be ~d to barracks/one's room** Kasernen-/Stubenarrest m haben **b** (= limit) remarks beschränken (to auf +acc); **to ~ oneself to doing sth** sich darauf beschränken, etw zu tun; **the damage was ~d to ...** der Schaden beschränkte or erstreckte sich nur auf (+acc) ...; **he finds the job too confining** er fühlt sich in dem Job beschränkt or eingeengt; **lions are ~d to Africa** Löwen gibt es nur in Afrika **c** (dated pass: in childbirth) **to be ~d** niederkommen (old) **confines** [ˈkɒnfaɪnz] PL (of space, thing etc) Grenzen pl; (of marriage) Fesseln pl; (of system) enge Grenzen pl

confined [kənˈfaɪnd] ADJ space beschränkt, begrenzt; atmosphere beengend

confinement [kənˈfaɪnmənt] N **a** (= imprisonment) (= act) Einsperren nt; (in hospital) Einweisung f; (of animals) Gefangenhalten nt; (= state) Eingesperrtsein nt; (in jail) Haft f; (of animals) Gefangenschaft f; (Mil) Arrest m (also hum); **to barracks/one's room** Kasernen-/Stubenarrest m; **to put sb in ~** jdn einsperren; **to keep sb in close ~** jdn in strengem Gewahrsam halten **b** (= restriction) Beschränkung f (to auf +acc) **c** (dated: = childbirth) Entbindung f, Niederkunft f (old)

confirm [kənˈfɜːm] VT **a** (= verify) bestätigen; **this has ~ed me in my decision** das hat meinen Entschluss bekräftigt; **his new play ~s him as our leading playwright** sein neues Stück stellt wieder unter Beweis, dass er unser führender Schauspieldichter ist **b** (= strengthen) bestärken; one's resolve also bekräftigen **c** (Eccl) konfirmieren; Roman Catholic firmen

confirmation [ˌkɒnfəˈmeɪʃən] N **a** Bestätigung f; **a letter in ~ of** ein Brief m zur or als Bestätigung (+gen) **b** (Eccl) Konfirmation f; (of Roman Catholics) Firmung f; **~ classes** Konfirmanden-/Firmunterricht m

confirmatory [kənˈfɜːmətərɪ] ADJ bestätigend

confirmed [kənˈfɜːmd] ADJ **a** erklärt; nonsmoker, meat-eater, atheist überzeugt; bachelor eingefleischt **b** booking bestätigt

confirming bank [kənˈfɜːmɪŋˌbæŋk] N bestätigende Bank

confiscate [ˈkɒnfɪskeɪt] VT beschlagnahmen, konfiszieren; **to ~ sth from sb** jdm etw abnehmen

confiscation [ˌkɒnfɪsˈkeɪʃən] N Beschlagnahme f, Konfiszierung f

confiscatory [ˌkɒnfɪsˈkeɪtərɪ] ADJ **they have ~ powers** sie sind zur Beschlagnahme befugt

conflagration [ˌkɒnfləˈgreɪʃən] N (of forest, towns) Feuersbrunst f (geh); (of building) Großbrand m

conflate [kənˈfleɪt] VT zusammenfassen

conflation [kənˈfleɪʃən] N Zusammenfassung f

conflict [ˈkɒnflɪkt] N Konflikt m; (of moral issues, ideas also) Widerstreit m, Zwiespalt m; (between two accounts etc) Widerspruch m; (= fight-
ing) Zusammenstoß m; **to be in ~ with sb/sth** mit jdm/etw im Konflikt liegen, im Widerspruch zu jdm/etw stehen; **the ego is always in ~ with the id** das Ich ist immer im Widerstreit mit dem Es; **to come into ~ with sb/sth** mit jdm/etw in Konflikt geraten; **open/armed ~** offener Konflikt/bewaffneter Zusammenstoß; **border ~** Grenzkonflikt m; **~ of interests/ opinions** Interessen-/Meinungskonflikt m **VI** [kənˈflɪkt] im Widerspruch stehen (with zu), widersprechen (with +dat); **their opinions on the subject** stehen in diesem Punkt stehen ihre Ansichten im Widerspruch zueinander

conflicting [kənˈflɪktɪŋ] ADJ widersprüchlich

confluence [ˈkɒnfluəns] N (of rivers) Zusammenfluss m

conform [kənˈfɔːm] VI **a** (things: = comply with) entsprechen (to +dat); (people: socially) sich anpassen (to an +acc); (things, people: to rules etc) sich richten (to nach); (= agree) übereinstimmen, konform gehen (with mit) **b** (Brit, Eccl) sich (der englischen Staatskirche dat) unterwerfen

conformance [kənˈfɔːməns] N = conformity

conformism [kənˈfɔːmɪzəm] N Konformismus m

conformist [kənˈfɔːmɪst] ADJ konformistisch N Konformist m (also Brit Eccl)

conformity [kənˈfɔːmɪtɪ] N **a** (= uniformity) Konformismus m **b** (= compliance) Übereinstimmung f; (of manners) Konformismus m; (socially) Anpassung f (with an +acc); **in ~ with sth** einer Sache (dat) entsprechend or gemäß; **to be in ~ with sth** einer Sache (dat) entsprechen; **to bring sth into ~ with sth** etw mit etw in Einklang or Übereinstimmung bringen

confound [kənˈfaʊnd] VT **a** (= amaze) verblüffen **b** (= throw into confusion) verwirren, durcheinander bringen **c** (liter: = mistake for sth else) verwechseln **d** (inf) **~ it!** vermaledeit (dated) or verflixt (inf) noch mal!; **~ him!** der vermaledeite (dated) or verflixte (inf) Kerl!

confounded [kənˈfaʊndɪd] ADJ (inf) vermaledeit (dated inf), verflixt (inf); cheek also verflucht (inf); noise also Heiden- (inf); nuisance elend (inf)

confoundedly [kənˈfaʊndɪdlɪ] ADV (dated inf) verflucht (inf)

confront [kənˈfrʌnt] VT **a** (= face) danger, enemy, the boss gegenübertreten (+dat); (fig) problems, issue also begegnen (+dat); (= stand or be confronting) wall of ice etc gegenüberstehen (+dat); (problems, decisions) sich stellen (+dat) **b** (= bring face to face with) konfrontieren; **to ~ sb with sb/sth** jdn jdm gegenüberstellen, jdn mit jdm/etw konfrontieren; **to be ~ed with sth** mit etw konfrontiert sein, vor etw (dat) stehen; **(when) ~ed with** angesichts (+gen)

confrontation [ˌkɒnfrʌnˈteɪʃən] N Konfrontation f (also Pol); (defiant also) Auseinandersetzung f; (with witnesses, evidence etc) Gegenüberstellung f

Confucian [kənˈfjuːʃən] ADJ konfuzianisch N Konfuzianer(in) m(f)

Confucianism [kənˈfjuːʃənɪzm] N Konfuzianismus m

Confucius [kənˈfjuːʃəs] N Konfuzius m, Konfutse m

confuse [kənˈfjuːz] VT **a** (= bewilder, muddle) people konfus machen, verwirren, durcheinander bringen; (= make unclear) situation verworren machen; **am I confusing you?** bringe ich Sie durcheinander?, verwirrt Sie das?; **don't ~ the issue!** bring (jetzt) nicht alles durcheinander! **b** (= mix up) people verwechseln; matters, issues also durcheinander bringen; **to ~ two problems** zwei Probleme durcheinanderbringen or miteinander verwechseln

confused [kənˈfjuːzd] ADJ **a** (= muddled) wirr, konfus; person also verwirrt; (through old age, after anaesthetic etc) wirr im Kopf; idea, report, situ-

ation also verworren; *sound, jumble* wirr **b** (= *embarrassed*) verwirrt, verlegen, betreten

confusedly [kən'fju:zɪdlɪ] ADV verwirrt; (= *in disorder also*) wirr; (= *embarrassedly also*) verlegen, betreten

confusing [kən'fju:zɪŋ] ADJ verwirrend

confusingly [kən'fju:zɪŋlɪ] ADV verwirrend; **~, he then contradicted himself** verwirrenderweise widersprach er sich dann

confusion [kən'fju:ʒən] N **a** (= *disorder*) Durcheinander *nt*, Wirrwarr *m*, Unordnung *f*; (= *jumble*) Wirrwarr *m*; **to be in ~** in Unordnung sein, durcheinander sein; **scenes of ~** allgemeines *or* wildes Durcheinander; **to retreat in ~** (*Mil*) einen ungeordneten Rückzug antreten; **to throw everything into ~** alles durcheinander bringen; **in the ~ of the battle** im Durcheinander der Schlacht; **to run about in ~** wild durcheinander laufen
b (= *perplexity*) Verwirrung *f*, Unklarheit *f*; (= *mental confusion, after drugs, blow on head etc*) Verwirrtheit *f*; (*through old age etc*) Wirrheit *f*; **in the ~ of the moment** im Eifer des Gefechts
c (= *embarrassment*) Verlegenheit *f*; (*at being found out*) Betroffenheit *f*; **to be covered in ~** vor Verlegenheit erröten
d (= *mixing up*) Verwechslung *f*

confutation [kɒnfju:'teɪʃən] N Widerlegung *f*

confute [kən'fju:t] VT widerlegen

conga ['kɒŋgə] N Conga *f*

congeal [kən'dʒi:l] VI erstarren, starr werden; (*glue, mud*) hart *or* fest werden; (*blood*) gerinnen; (*fig: = with fear*) erstarren VT erstarren lassen (*also fig*); *glue, mud* hart werden lassen; *blood* gerinnen lassen

congenial [kən'dʒi:nɪəl] ADJ **a** (= *pleasant*) ansprechend; *person also* sympathisch; *place, job also, atmosphere* angenehm; **to be ~ to sb** (*place, atmosphere, environment, work*) jdm zusagen **b** (*liter: = of like nature*) kongenial (*liter*), geistesverwandt

congenital [kən'dʒenɪtl] ADJ angeboren, kongenital (*spec*); **~ defect** Geburtsfehler *m*; **~ liar** (*inf*) Erzlügner(in) *m(f)* (*inf*)

congenitally [kən'dʒenɪtəlɪ] ADV (*Med*) *deaf, blind, disabled* von Geburt an; *obese* anlagebedingt; (*fig*) *lazy, incapable, stupid, optimistic, dishonest* von Natur aus

conger ['kɒŋgəʳ] N (*also* **conger eel**) Seeaal *m*

congeries [kən'dʒi:ri:z] N *sing* (*liter*) Konglomerat *nt*, Ansammlung *f*, Anhäufung *f*

congested [kən'dʒestɪd] ADJ überfüllt; (*with traffic*) verstopft; (*with people also*) voll; *pavement* übervoll; (= *highly populated*) über(be)völkert; **his lungs are ~** in seiner Lunge hat sich Blut angestaut *or* ist es zu einem Blutstau gekommen

congestion [kən'dʒestʃən] N (= *traffic, pedestrians*) Stau *m*, Stockung *f*; (*in corridors etc*) Gedränge *nt*; (= *overpopulation*) Übervölkerung *f*; (*Med*) Blutstau *m*, Blutandrang *m*; **the ~ in the city centre is getting so bad ...** die Verstopfung in der Innenstadt nimmt derartige Ausmaße an ...

congestion charge N City-Maut *f*

congestive [kən'dʒestɪv] ADJ (*Med*) Stauungs-; **~ heart failure** Stauungsinsuffizienz *f*

conglomerate [kən'glɒmərɪt] N (*also Geol, Comm*) Konglomerat *nt* ADJ *nation* zusammengewürfelt; *language* Misch-; **~ rock** (*Geol*) Konglomeratgestein *nt* VI [kən'glɒməreɪt] sich zusammenballen, sich vereinigen, verschmelzen

conglomeration [kən,glɒmə'reɪʃən] N Ansammlung *f*, Haufen *m*; (*of ideas*) Gemisch *nt*

Congo ['kɒŋgəʊ] N Kongo *m*; **the Democratic Republic of the ~** die Demokratische Republik Kongo; **the People's Republic of the ~** die Volksrepublik Kongo

Congolese [,kɒŋgəʊ'li:z] ADJ kongolesisch N Kongolese *m*, Kongolesin *f*

congrats [kən'græts] INTERJ (*dated inf*) gratuliere!

congratulate [kən'grætjʊleɪt] VT gratulieren (*+dat*) (*also on birthday, engagement etc*), beglückwünschen (*on* zu); **you are to be ~d on not having given up** man kann Ihnen nur gratulieren, dass Sie nicht nachgegeben haben

congratulation [kən,grætjʊ'leɪʃən] ✪ 23.6, 24.1, 24.2, 24.3, N Gratulation *f*, Gratulieren *nt*; **letter/message of ~** Glückwunschbrief *m*/-botschaft *f*, Gratulationsbrief *m*/-botschaft *f*

congratulations [kən,grætjʊ'leɪʃənz] PL Glückwunsch *m*, Glückwünsche *pl*; **to offer/send one's ~** gratulieren, jdn beglückwünschen/jdm seine Glückwünsche senden INTERJ (ich) gratuliere!, herzlichen Glückwunsch!; (*iro*) gratuliere!; **~ on ...!** herzlichen Glückwunsch *or* herzliche Glückwünsche zu ...!

congratulatory [kən'grætjʊlətərɪ] ADJ *card, telegram* Glückwunsch-; *look, tone* anerkennend; **I wrote him a ~ letter on ...** ich gratulierte ihm brieflich zu ...; **she bought me a ~ drink** sie lud mich ein, um mit mir darauf zu trinken *or* anzustoßen

congregate ['kɒŋgrɪgeɪt] VI sich sammeln; (*on a particular occasion*) sich versammeln; **to be ~d in ...** sich sammeln/versammeln in (*+dat*) ...

congregation [,kɒŋgrɪ'geɪʃən] N **a** Versammlung *f*; (*not planned*) Ansammlung *f*; (= *people in cities etc*) Zusammenballung *f* **b** (*Eccl*) Gemeinde *f*; (*of cardinals*) Kongregation *f*

congregational [,kɒŋgrɪ'geɪʃənl] ADJ **a** **Congregational** kongregationalistisch **b** (*of a congregation*) Gemeinde-

Congregationalism [,kɒŋgrɪ'geɪʃənəlɪzəm] N Kongregationalismus *m*

Congregationalist [,kɒŋgrɪ'geɪʃənəlɪst] N Kongregationalist(in) *m(f)*

congress ['kɒŋgres] N **a** (= *meeting*) Kongress *m*, Tagung *f*; (*of political party*) Parteitag *m* **b** **Congress** (*US etc, Pol*) der Kongress

congressional [kɒŋ'greʃənl] ADJ *delegate, meeting* Kongress-

Congressional district N (*US Pol*) Kongresswahlbezirk *m*

Congressional Record N (*US Pol*) Veröffentlichung *f* der Kongressdebatten

Congressman ['kɒŋgresmən] N *pl* **-men** [-mən] Kongressabgeordnete(r) *m*

Congresswoman ['kɒŋgres,wʊmən] N *pl* **-women** [-wɪmɪn] Kongressabgeordnete *f*

congruence ['kɒŋgrʊəns] N Kongruenz *f*, Übereinstimmung *f*; (*Geometry*) Deckungsgleichheit *f*, Kongruenz *f*

congruent ['kɒŋgrʊənt] ADJ **a** = **congruous** **b** (*Math*) *number* kongruent; (*Geometry also*) deckungsgleich

congruity [kəŋ'gru:ɪtɪ] N Übereinstimmung *f*, Kongruenz *f* (*geh*)

congruous ['kɒŋgrʊəs] ADJ **a** (= *corresponding*) sich deckend, übereinstimmend; **to be ~ with sth** sich mit etw decken **b** (= *appropriate, proper*) vereinbar

conic ['kɒnɪk] ADJ **a** (*Math*) Kegel-, konisch **b** (*also* **conical**) kegelförmig, Kegel-, konisch

conic projection N (*Geog*) Kegelprojektion *or* -abbildung *f*

conic section N (*Math*) Kegelschnitt *m*

conifer ['kɒnɪfəʳ] N Nadelbaum *m*, Konifere *f* (*spec*); **~s** Nadelhölzer *pl*

coniferous [kə'nɪfərəs] ADJ *tree, forest* Nadel-

conjectural [kən'dʒektʃərəl] ADJ auf Vermutungen *or* Mutmaßungen beruhend; **a conclusion which must remain ~** ein Schluss, der Vermutung *or* Mutmaßung bleiben muss; **it is entirely ~** es ist reine Vermutung

conjecture [kən'dʒektʃəʳ] VT vermuten, mutmaßen (*geh*) VI Vermutungen *or* Mutmaßungen anstellen, mutmaßen (*geh*); **it was just as scientists had ~d** es verhielt sich geradeso, wie es die Wissenschaftler gemutmaßt *or* vermutet hatten N Vermutung *f*, Mutmaßung *f* (*geh*); **what will come next is a matter of** *or* **for ~** was folgt, das kann man nur vermuten *or* das bleibt unserer Vermutung überlassen

conjoin [kən'dʒɔɪn] VT (*form*) verbinden

conjoined [kən'dʒɔɪnd] ADJ (*form*) verbunden, verknüpft; (= *at the same time*) *events* zusammentreffend

conjoint ADJ, **conjointly** ADV [kən'dʒɔɪnt, -lɪ] gemeinsam

conjugal ['kɒndʒʊgəl] ADJ *rights, bliss, duties* ehelich; *state* Ehe-; **~ affection** Gattenliebe *f*

conjugate ['kɒndʒʊgeɪt] VT (*Gram*) konjugieren, beugen VI (*Gram*) sich konjugieren lassen; (*Biol*) konjugieren

conjugation [,kɒndʒʊ'geɪʃən] N (*Gram, Biol*) Konjugation *f*

conjunct [kən'dʒʌŋkt] ADJ (= *joined*) verbunden; (= *combined*) vereint, gemeinsam; (*Jur*) befangen

conjunction [kən'dʒʌŋkʃən] N **a** (*Gram*) Konjunktion *f*, Bindewort *nt* **b** (= *association*) Verbindung *f*; (= *co-occurrence: of events*) Zusammentreffen *nt*; **in ~** zusammen; **in ~ with the new evidence** in Verbindung mit dem neuen Beweismaterial; **the programme was broadcast in ~ with the NBC** die Sendung wurde von NBC übernommen; **the programme was produced in ~ with the NBC** das Programm wurde in Zusammenarbeit mit NBC aufgezeichnet **c** (*Astron*) Konjunktion *f*

conjunctive [kən'dʒʌŋktɪv] ADJ (*Gram, Anat*) Binde-

conjunctivitis [kən,dʒʌŋktɪ'vaɪtɪs] N (*Med*) Bindehautentzündung *f*, Konjunktivitis *f* (*spec*)

conjuncture [kən'dʒʌŋktʃəʳ] N Zusammentreffen *nt*

conjure[1] [kən'dʒʊəʳ] VT (*liter: = appeal to*) beschwören

conjure[2] ['kʌndʒəʳ] VI zaubern; **a name to ~ with** ein Name, der Wunder wirkt *or* der eine Ausstrahlung hat VT zaubern; *image, memory* heraufbeschwören; **to ~ something out of nothing** etwas aus dem Nichts herbeizaubern

▶ **conjure away** VT *sep* (*lit, fig*) wegzaubern

▶ **conjure up** VT *sep ghosts, spirits* beschwören; (*fig*) *memories etc* heraufbeschwören; (= *provide, produce*) hervorzaubern; *meal* zusammenzaubern

conjurer ['kʌndʒərəʳ] N Zauberer, Zauberkünstler(in) *m(f)*

conjuring ['kʌndʒərɪŋ] N Zaubern *nt*; (= *performance*) Zauberei *f*; **~ trick** Zaubertrick *m*, (Zauber)kunststück *nt*

conjuror ['kʌndʒərəʳ] N = **conjurer**

conk [kɒŋk] (*inf*) N (*esp Brit: = nose*) Zinken *m* (*inf*) VT (= *hit*) hauen (*inf*)

▶ **conk out** VI (*inf*) es aufstecken (*inf*), den Geist aufgeben; (*person, = faint*) umkippen (*inf*); (= *die*) ins Gras beißen (*inf*)

conker ['kɒŋkəʳ] N (*Brit, inf*) (Ross)kastanie *f*; **~s** (= *game*) *Spiel, bei dem zwei Spieler mit an Fäden befestigten Kastanien wechselseitig versuchen, die Kastanie des Gegenspielers zu treffen und zu zerstören*

con man N *pl* **con men** (*inf*) Schwindler *m*, Bauernfänger *m* (*inf*); (*pretending to have social status*) Hochstapler *m*; (*promising marriage*) Heiratsschwindler *m*

connect [kə'nekt] ✪ 17.2, 27.5 VT **a** (= *join*) verbinden (*to, with* mit); (*Elec etc: also* **connect up**) *appliances, subscribers* anschließen (*to* an *+acc*); **I'll ~ you** (*Telec*) ich verbinde (Sie); **to be ~ed** (*two things*) miteinander verbunden sein; (*several things*) untereinander verbunden sein; **to ~ to earth** erden; **~ed by telephone** telefonisch verbunden → **parallel**
b (*fig: = associate*) in Verbindung *or* Zusammenhang bringen; **I always ~ Paris with springtime** ich verbinde Paris immer mit Frühling; **these things are ~ed in my mind** diese Dinge gehören für mich zusammen; **I'd never ~ed them** ich hatte sie nie zueinander in Beziehung gesetzt

c (*esp pass*: = *link*) *ideas, theories etc* verbinden; **to be ~ed with** eine Beziehung haben zu, in einer Beziehung *or* in Verbindung stehen zu; (= *be related to*) verwandt sein mit; **he's ~ed with the BBC/university** er hat mit der BBC/der Universität zu tun; **to be ~ed by marriage** verschwägert sein; **to be ~ed** (*ideas etc*) in Beziehung zueinander stehen; (*firms*) geschäftlich miteinander verbunden sein; **loosely ~ed facts** lose verknüpfte Fakten

VI **a** (= *join, two rooms*) eine Verbindung haben (*to, with* zu); (*two parts, wires etc*) Kontakt haben; **to ~ with sb/sb's ideas** jdn/jds Gedanken verstehen; **~ing rooms** angrenzende Zimmer *pl* (*mit Verbindungstür*)

b (*Rail, Aviat etc*) Anschluss haben (*with an* +*acc*); **~ing flight** Anschlussflug *m*

c (*inf*: = *hit*) (*fist etc*) landen (*inf*) (*with auf* +*dat*); (*golf club etc*) treffen (*with* +*acc*); **he really ~ed** er hat voll getroffen

▶ **connect up** VT *sep* (*Elec etc*) anschließen (*to, with an* +*acc*)

connecting: connecting cord [kəˈnektɪŋ-ˌkɔːd] N (*Elec*) Verbindungsschnur *f*; **connecting rod** [kəˈnektɪŋˌrɒd] N Pleuel- *or* Kurbelstange *f*

connection [kəˈnekʃən] N **a** Verbindung *f* (*to, with* zu, mit); (= *telephone line also, wire*) Leitung *f*; (*to mains*) Anschluss *m* (*to an* +*acc*); (= *connecting part*) Verbindung(sstück *nt*) *f*; **parallel/series** Parallel-/Reihenschaltung *f*; **~ charge** (*Telec*) Anschlussgebühr *f*

b (*fig*: = *link*) Zusammenhang *m*, Beziehung *f* (*with* zu); **in this ~** in diesem Zusammenhang; **in ~ with** in Zusammenhang mit

c (= *relationship, business connection*) Beziehung *f*, Verbindung *f* (*with* zu); (= *family connection*) familiäre Beziehung; (*old, form*: = *relative*) (entfernter) Verwandter, (entfernte) Verwandte; **to have ~s** Beziehungen haben; **there is some family ~** sie/wir *etc* sind weitläufig miteinander verwandt

d (*Rail etc*) Anschluss *m*

connective [kəˈnektɪv] **N** (*Gram*) Bindewort *nt* **ADJ** verbindend

connective tissue N Bindegewebe *nt*

connector [kəˈnektə'] N (= *device*) Verbindungsstück *nt*, Anschluss *m*; (*Elec*) Lüsterklemme *f*

connexion [kəˈnekʃən] N = **connection**

conning tower [ˈkɒnɪŋtaʊə'] N Kommandoturm *m*

connivance [kəˈnaɪvəns] N (= *tacit consent*) stillschweigendes Einverständnis; (= *dishonest dealing*) Schiebung *f*; **his ~ at the wrongdoing** seine Mitwisserschaft bei dem Vergehen; **to do sth in ~ with sb** etw mit jds Wissen tun; **to be in ~ with sb** mit jdm gemeinsame Sache machen

connive [kəˈnaɪv] VI **a** (= *conspire*) sich verschwören, gemeinsame Sache machen; **he's a conniving little wretch** (*inf*) er ist ein hinterhältiger Tropf (*inf*) **b** (= *deliberately overlook*) **to ~ at sth** etw stillschweigend dulden; **to ~ at a crime** einem Verbrechen Vorschub leisten

connoisseur [ˌkɒnəˈsɜː'] N Kenner *m*, Connaisseur *m* (*geh*); **~ of wines/women** Wein-/Frauenkenner *m*

connotation [ˌkɒnəʊˈteɪʃən] N Assoziation *f*, Konnotation *f* (*spec*); **the ~s of this word** die mit diesem Wort verbundenen Assoziationen, die Konnotationen dieses Wortes (*spec*)

connotative [ˈkɒnəteɪtɪv] ADJ *meaning* Neben-, assoziativ, konnotativ (*spec*)

connote [kɒˈnəʊt] VT suggerieren

connubial [kəˈnjuːbɪəl] ADJ ehelich, Ehe-

conquer [ˈkɒŋkə'] VT **a** *lit country* erobern; *enemy, nation* besiegen **b** (*fig*) *difficulties, feelings, disease* bezwingen, besiegen; *sb's heart* erobern; *mountain* bezwingen

conquering [ˈkɒŋkərɪŋ] ADJ *hero* siegreich

conqueror [ˈkɒŋkərə'] N (*of country, heart*) Eroberer *m*, Eroberin *f*; (*of enemy, difficulties, feelings, disease*) Sieger(in) *m(f)* (*of über* +*acc*), Besieger(in) *m(f)*; (*of difficulties, feelings, mountains*)

Bezwinger(in) *m(f)*; **William the Conqueror** Wilhelm der Eroberer

conquest [ˈkɒŋkwest] N Eroberung *f*; (*of enemy etc, disease*) Sieg *m* (*of über* +*acc*), Bezwingung *f*; (*inf*: = *person*) Eroberung *f*

Cons *abbr of* **Conservative**

consanguinity [ˌkɒnsæŋˈgwɪnɪtɪ] N Blutsverwandtschaft *f*

conscience [ˈkɒnʃəns] N Gewissen *nt*; **to have a clear/easy/bad/guilty ~** ein reines/gutes/schlechtes/böses Gewissen haben (*about* wegen); **doesn't telling lies give you a guilty ~?** haben Sie keine Gewissensbisse *or* kein schlechtes Gewissen, wenn Sie lügen?; **with an easy ~** mit ruhigem Gewissen, ruhigen Gewissens (*geh*); **he has no ~ about lying** er macht sich (*dat*) kein Gewissen daraus, zu lügen; **it/he will be on your ~ all your life** Sie werden das/ihn Ihr Leben lang auf dem Gewissen haben; **she/it is on my ~** ich habe ihretwegen/deswegen Gewissensbisse; **it's still on my ~** (= *I still haven't done it*) es steht mir noch bevor; **my ~ won't let me do it** das kann ich mit meinem Gewissen nicht vereinbaren; **in (all)** ~ allen Ernstes; **I can't in all ~ ...** ich kann unmöglich ...; **let your ~ be your guide!** hör auf dein Gewissen; **it's between you and your ~** das musst du mit dir selbst *or* mit deinem Gewissen abmachen

conscience: conscience clause N (*Jur*) ≈ Gewissensklausel *f*; **conscience money** N **his donation looks like ~** mit der Spende will er wohl sein Gewissen beruhigen; **conscience-stricken** ADJ schuldbewusst

conscientious [ˌkɒnʃɪˈenʃəs] ADJ **a** (= *diligent*) gewissenhaft; (= *conscious of one's duty*) pflichtbewusst **b** (*Mil*) **he refused to go as a ~ objection** er weigerte sich aus Gewissensgründen hinzugehen → **conscientious objector**

conscientiously [ˌkɒnʃɪˈenʃəslɪ] ADV *practise, exercise* gewissenhaft; *obey* pflichtschuldigst

conscientiousness [ˌkɒnʃɪˈenʃəsnɪs] N Gewissenhaftigkeit *f*; (= *sense of duty*) Pflichtbewusstsein *nt*, Pflichtgefühl *nt*

conscientious objector N (*Mil*) Wehrdienst- *or* Kriegsdienstverweigerer *m* (*aus Gewissensgründen*)

conscious [ˈkɒnʃəs] ADJ **a** (*Med*) bei Bewusstsein **b** (= *aware*) bewusst (*also Psych*); **the ~ mind** das Bewusstsein; **to be/become ~ of sth** sich (*dat*) einer Sache (*gen*) bewusst sein/werden; **I was/became ~ that** es war/wurde mir bewusst, dass; **politically** ~ politisch bewusst; **environmentally** ~ umweltbewusst **c** (= *deliberate*) *effort etc* bewusst; *humour also* absichtlich

-conscious ADJ *suf* -bewusst; **weight-conscious** gewichtsbewusst

consciously [ˈkɒnʃəslɪ] ADV bewusst; (= *deliberately also*) absichtlich

consciousness [ˈkɒnʃəsnɪs] N **a** (*Med*) Bewusstsein *nt*; **to lose ~** das Bewusstsein verlieren, bewusstlos werden; **to regain ~** das Bewusstsein wiedererlangen, wieder zu sich kommen **b** (= *awareness*) Bewusstsein *nt*, Wissen *nt*; **her ~ of her abilities** das Wissen um ihre Fähigkeiten **c** (= *conscious mind*) Bewusstsein *nt*; **to be ~-raising** den Bewusstseinsgrad erhöhen, bewusstseinserweiternd sein

-consciousness N *suf* -bewusstheit *f*

conscript [kənˈskrɪpt] **VT** einziehen, einberufen; *army* ausheben **N** [ˈkɒnskrɪpt] (*Brit*) Wehrpflichtige(r) *m*

conscripted [kənˈskrɪptɪd] ADJ *soldier* eingezogen, einberufen; *troops* aus Wehrpflichtigen bestehend; *workers, labourers* zwangsverpflichtet

conscription [kənˈskrɪpʃən] N Wehrpflicht *f*; (= *act of conscripting*) Einberufung *f*; (*of army*) Aushebung *f*

consecrate [ˈkɒnsɪkreɪt] VT (*lit, fig*) weihen

consecration [ˌkɒnsɪˈkreɪʃən] N Weihe *f*; (*in Mass*) Wandlung *f*

consecutive [kənˈsekjʊtɪv] ADJ **a** aufeinander folgend; *numbers* fortlaufend; **on four ~ days**

vier Tage hintereinander; **this is the third ~ morning he's been late** er ist jetzt dreimal hintereinander morgens zu spät gekommen **b** (*Gram*) *clause* Konsekutiv-, Folge-

consecutively [kənˈsekjʊtɪvlɪ] ADV nacheinander, hintereinander; *numbered* fortlaufend

consensual [kənˈsensjʊəl] ADJ **a** (*Jur*) **to be ~** auf (bloßer) mündlicher Übereinkunft beruhen; **~ contract** obligatorischer Vertrag **b** (*Physiol*) Reflex-, unwillkürlich

consensus [kənˈsensəs] N Übereinstimmung *f*; (= *accord also*) Einigkeit *f*; **what's the ~?** was ist die allgemeine Meinung?; **the ~ is that ...** man ist allgemein der Meinung, dass ...; **there's a ~ (of opinion) in favour of ...** die allgemeine Mehrheit ist für ...; **cabinet decisions are based on ~** Entscheidungen des Kabinetts beruhen auf einem Mehrheitsbeschluss; **there was no ~ (among them)** sie waren sich nicht einig, es gab keinen Konsens unter ihnen (*form*); **~ politics** Politik *f* des Konsensus *or* Miteinander

consent [kənˈsent] **☉** 9.3, 11.2 **VI** zustimmen (*to* +*dat*), einwilligen (*to in* +*acc*); **to ~ to do sth** sich bereit erklären, etw zu tun; **to ~ to sb doing sth** einwilligen *or* damit einverstanden sein, dass jd etw tut; **homosexuality between ~ing adults** homosexuelle Beziehungen zwischen erwachsenen Männern **N** Zustimmung *f* (*to* zu), Einwilligung *f* (*to in* +*acc*); **it/he is by common** *or* **general ~ ...** man hält es/ihn allgemein für ...; **to be chosen by general ~** einstimmig gewählt werden; **by mutual** *or* **common ~** in gegenseitigem Einverständnis → **age** N **c**

consent form N (*Med*) Einverständniserklärung *f*

consequence [ˈkɒnsɪkwəns] **☉** 26.3 N **a** (= *result, effect*) Folge *f*; (*of actions also*) Konsequenz *f*; **in ~** folglich; **in ~ of** infolge (+*gen*); **in ~ of which** infolgedessen; **and the ~ is that we have ...** und folglich haben wir ...; **as a ~ of ...** als Folge (+*gen*); **with the ~ that he ...** was zur Folge hatte *or* mit dem Erfolg, dass er ...; **to face** *or* **take the ~s** die Folgen *or* Konsequenzen tragen

b (= *importance*) Wichtigkeit *f*, Bedeutung *f*; **a person of ~** eine bedeutende *or* wichtige Persönlichkeit; **did he have anything of ~ to say?** hatte er irgend etwas Wichtiges zu sagen?; **he's (a man) of no ~** er hat nichts zu sagen; **it's of no ~** das spielt keine Rolle; **that's of no ~ to me** das ist mir einerlei; **of what ~ is that to you?** was tangiert Sie das? (*inf*)

c consequences SING (= *game*) Schreibspiel, *bei dem auf gefaltetem Papier ein nicht bekannter Vorsatz ergänzt wird*

consequent [ˈkɒnsɪkwənt] ADJ *attr* daraus folgend, sich daraus ergebend; (*temporal*) darauf folgend; **to be ~ upon sth** (*form, liter*) sich aus etw ergeben

consequential [ˌkɒnsɪˈkwenʃəl] ADJ **a** = **consequent b** (= *self-important*) wichtigtuerisch; *smile, tone also* überheblich **c** (= *logically consistent*) folgerichtig

consequentially [ˌkɒnsɪˈkwenʃəlɪ] ADV (= *as a result*) daraufhin

consequently [ˈkɒnsɪkwəntlɪ] **☉** 26.3 ADV folglich

conservancy [kənˈsɜːvənsɪ] N **a** (*Brit*, = *board*) Schutzbehörde *f*; (*for ports, rivers etc*) Wasserschutzamt *nt*; (*for forests*) Forstamt *nt* **b** (= *official conservation*) Erhaltung *f*, Schutz *m*

conservation [ˌkɒnsəˈveɪʃən] N **a** (= *preservation*) Erhaltung *f*, Schutz *m*; **~ technology** Umweltschutztechnik *f* **b** (*Phys*) Erhaltung *f*

conservation area N Naturschutzgebiet *nt*; (*in town*) unter Denkmalschutz stehendes Gebiet

conservationist [ˌkɒnsəˈveɪʃənɪst] N Umweltschützer(in) *m(f)*; (*as regards old buildings etc*) Denkmalpfleger(in) *m(f)*

conservatism [kənˈsɜːvətɪzəm] N Konservatismus *m*

conservative [kənˈsɜːvətɪv] **ADJ a** *person, style* konservativ; (= *cautious, moderate*) vorsichtig; **at**

a ~ estimate bei vorsichtiger Schätzung **b** (*Pol*) konservativ; **the Conservative Party** (*Brit*) die Konservative Partei **N** (*Pol: also* **Conservative**) Konservative(r) *mf*; **I'm a ~ in such matters** in solchen Dingen bin ich konservativ

conservatively [kən'sɜːvətɪvlɪ] ADV konservativ; *estimate, invest* vorsichtig

conservatoire [kən'sɜːvətwɑː'] N Konservatorium *nt*

conservatory [kən'sɜːvətrɪ] N **a** Wintergarten *m* **b** (*esp US, Mus etc*) Konservatorium *nt*

conserve [kən'sɜːv] VT erhalten, bewahren, konservieren; *building* erhalten; *one's strength* schonen; *strength, energy* (auf)sparen

conserves [kən'sɜːvz] PL Eingemachte(s) *nt*

consider [kən'sɪdə'] ✿ 21.4, 26.1, 26.3 VT **a** (= *reflect upon*) *plan, idea, offer* sich (*dat*) nachdenken über (+*acc*); *possibilities* sich (*dat*) überlegen; **I'll ~ the matter** ich werde mir die Sache überlegen *or* durch den Kopf gehen lassen **b** (= *have in mind*) in Erwägung ziehen; **we're ~ing a few changes** wir ziehen ein paar Änderungen in Erwägung; **I'm ~ing going abroad** ich spiele mit dem Gedanken, ins Ausland zu gehen, ich erwäge einen Auslandsaufenthalt (*geh*); **he is being ~ed for the job** er wird für die Stelle in Erwägung *or* Betracht gezogen **c** (= *entertain*) in Betracht ziehen; **he refused even to ~ the possibility** er verwarf die Möglichkeit sofort, er weigerte sich, die Möglichkeit überhaupt in Betracht zu ziehen; **I won't even ~ the idea of ...** der Gedanke, zu ..., kommt für mich überhaupt nicht in Betracht; **I won't even ~ it!** ich denke nicht daran!; **would you ~ £500?** hielten Sie £ 500 für angemessen?; **I'm sure he would never ~ doing anything criminal** ich bin überzeugt, es käme ihm nie in den Sinn, etwas Kriminelles zu tun **d** (= *think of*) denken an (+*acc*); **~ George** denken Sie an George; **~ my position** überlegen Sie sich meine Lage; **~ this case, for example** nehmen Sie zum Beispiel diesen Fall; **~ how he must have felt** überlegen Sie sich, wie ihm zumute *or* zu Mute gewesen sein muss; **~ how much you owe him** denken Sie daran *or* bedenken Sie, wie viel Sie ihm schulden; **have you ~ed going by train?** haben Sie daran gedacht, mit dem Zug zu fahren? **e** (= *take into account*) denken an (+*acc*); *cost, difficulties, dangers also, facts* bedenken, berücksichtigen; *person, feelings also* Rücksicht nehmen auf (+*acc*); **when one ~s that ...** wenn man bedenkt, dass ...; **all things ~ed** alles in allem **f** (= *regard as, deem*) betrachten als; *person* halten für; **to ~ sb to be** *or* **as ...** jdn als ... betrachten, jdn für ... halten; **to ~ oneself lucky/honoured** sich glücklich schätzen/geehrt fühlen; **~ it (as) done!** schon so gut wie geschehen!; **(you can) ~ yourself sacked** betrachten Sie sich als entlassen; **I ~ it an honour** ich betrachte es als besondere Ehre **g** (= *look at*) (eingehend) betrachten

considerable [kən'sɪdərəbl] ADJ beträchtlich, erheblich; *amount of money, achievement also* ansehnlich; *loss also, interest, income* groß; (*used admiringly*) *number, size, achievement, effort etc* beachtlich; **to a ~ extent** *or* **degree** weitgehend; **to face ~ difficulties** mit beträchtlichen *or* erheblichen *or* gewaltigen Schwierigkeiten konfrontiert sein; **for a** *or* **some ~ time** für eine ganze Zeit

considerably [kən'sɪdərəblɪ] ADV (*in comparisons*) *changed, older, better, grown* beträchtlich, um einiges; (= *very*) *upset, impressed* höchst

considerate [kən'sɪdərɪt] ADJ rücksichtsvoll (*to(wards)*) gegenüber); (= *kind*) aufmerksam

considerately [kən'sɪdərɪtlɪ] ADV *behave, say* rücksichtsvoll

consideration [kən,sɪdə'reɪʃən] ✿ 26.1 N **a** *no pl* (= *careful thought*) Überlegung *f*; **I'll give it my ~** ich werde es mir überlegen **b** *no pl* (= *regard, account*) **to take sth into ~** etw bedenken, etw berücksichtigen; *factors also* etw in Erwägung ziehen; **taking everything into**

~ alles in allem; **to leave sth out of ~** etw außer Acht lassen; **your request/the matter is under ~** Ihr Gesuch/die Sache wird zurzeit geprüft (*form*), wir gehen der Sache zurzeit nach; **in ~ of** (= *in view of*) mit Rücksicht auf (+*acc*), in Anbetracht (+*gen*); (= *in return for*) als Dank für **c** *no pl* (= *thoughtfulness*) Rücksicht *f* (*for* auf +*acc*); **to show** *or* **have ~ for sb/sb's feelings** Rücksicht auf jdn/jds Gefühle nehmen; **his lack of ~ (for others)** seine Rücksichtslosigkeit (anderen gegenüber) **d** (= *sth taken into account*) Erwägung *f*, Gesichtspunkt *m*, Faktor *m*; **money is a minor ~/not a ~/his first ~** Geld spielt eine unbedeutendere Rolle/keine Rolle/bei ihm die größte Rolle; **it's a ~** das wäre zu überlegen **e** (= *reward, payment*) Entgelt *nt*, Gegenleistung *f*, kleine Anerkennung (*hum*); **for a ~** gegen Entgelt, für eine Gegenleistung *or* kleine Anerkennung (*hum*)

considered [kən'sɪdəd] ADJ *opinion* ernsthaft

considering [kən'sɪdərɪŋ] **PREP** für (+*acc*), wenn man ... (*acc*) bedenkt **CONJ** wenn man bedenkt; **~ (that) he's been ill ...** wenn man bedenkt, dass er krank war ..., dafür, dass er krank war ... **ADV** eigentlich; **it's not too bad ~** es ist eigentlich gar nicht so schlecht; **yes it is, ~** ach ja, eigentlich schon

consign [kən'saɪn] VT **a** (*Comm*, = *send*) versenden, verschicken; (= *address*) adressieren (*to* an +*acc*); **the goods are ~ed to ...** die Waren sind für ... bestimmt **b** (= *commit*) übergeben (*to* +*dat*); (= *entrust also*) anvertrauen; **it was ~ed to the rubbish heap** es landete auf dem Abfallhaufen; **to ~ a child to sb's care** ein Kind in jds Obhut (*acc*) geben

consignee [ˌkɒnsaɪ'niː] N (*Comm*) Empfänger *m*

consigner [kən'saɪnə'] N = consignor

consignment [kən'saɪnmənt] N (*Comm*) **a** (*of goods*) Versendung *f*, Verschickung *f*; **goods for ~ abroad** ins Ausland gehende Ware; **on ~** in Kommission; (*overseas*) in Konsignation **b** (= *goods*) Sendung *f*; (*bigger*) Ladung *f*

consignment note N (*Comm*) Frachtbrief *m*

consignor [kən'saɪnə'] N (*Comm*) Versender *m*

consist [kən'sɪst] VI **a** (= *be composed*) **to ~ of** bestehen aus **b** (= *have as its essence*) **to ~ in sth** in etw (*dat*) bestehen; **his happiness ~s in helping others** sein Glück besteht darin, anderen zu helfen

consistency [kən'sɪstənsɪ] N **a** *no pl* Konsequenz *f*; (*of statements*) Übereinstimmung *f*; Vereinbarkeit *f*; (*of argument*) Logik *f*, Folgerichtigkeit *f*; **his statements lack ~** seine Aussagen widersprechen sich *or* sind nicht miteinander vereinbar **b** *no pl* (= *uniformity, of quality*) Beständigkeit *f*; (*of performance, results*) Stetigkeit *f*; (*of method, style*) Einheitlichkeit *f* **c** (*of substance*) Konsistenz *f*; (*of liquids also*) Dicke *f*; (*of glue, dough, rubber etc also*) Festigkeit(sgrad *m*) *f*; **beat it to a thick ~** zu einer festen Masse schlagen

consistent [kən'sɪstənt] ADJ **a** konsequent; *statements* übereinstimmend, miteinander vereinbar; (= *logical*) *argument* logisch, folgerichtig; (= *constant*) *failure* ständig, stetig **b** (= *uniform*) *quality* beständig; *performance, results* gleich bleibend, stetig; *method, style* einheitlich **c** (*in agreement*) **to be ~ with sth** einer Sache (*dat*) entsprechen; **what you're saying now is not ~ with what you said before** was Sie jetzt sagen, widerspricht dem *or* lässt sich mit dem nicht vereinbaren, was Sie davor gesagt haben

consistently [kən'sɪstəntlɪ] ADV **a** *argue, behave* konsequent; (= *constantly*) *fail* ständig; *refuse, deny, oppose, reject* hartnäckig **b** (= *uniformly*) einheitlich, durchweg **c** (*in agreement*) entsprechend (*with* +*dat*)

consolation [ˌkɒnsə'leɪʃən] N Trost *m no pl*; (= *act*) Tröstung *f*; **it is some ~ to know that ...** es ist tröstlich *or* ein Trost zu wissen, dass ...; **that's a big ~!** (*iro*) das ist ein schwacher Trost!; **old age has its ~s** das Alter hat auch seine gu-

ten Seiten; **a few words of ~** ein paar tröstende Worte

consolation prize N Trostpreis *m*

consolatory [kən'sɒlətərɪ] ADJ tröstlich, tröstend

console¹ [kən'səʊl] VT trösten; **to ~ sb for sth** jdn über etw (*acc*) hinwegtrösten

console² [ˈkɒnsəʊl] N **a** (= *control panel*) (Kontroll)pult *nt*; (*of organ*) Spieltisch *m* **b** (= *cabinet*) Schrank *m*, Truhe *f*; **our TV is a ~ (model)** wir haben eine Fernsehtruhe **c** (= *ornamental bracket*) Konsole *f*

console table N Konsoltischchen *nt*

consolidate [kən'sɒlɪdeɪt] VT **a** (= *confirm*) festigen **b** (= *combine*) zusammenlegen, vereinigen; *companies* zusammenschließen; *funds, debts* konsolidieren; **~d balance sheet** konsolidierte Bilanz

consolidated fund N (*Brit Fin*) konsolidierter Staatsfonds, unablösbare Anleihe

consolidation [kən,sɒlɪ'deɪʃən] N **a** (= *strengthening*) Festigung *f* **b** (= *amalgamation*) Zusammenlegung *f*, Vereinigung *f*; (*of companies*) Zusammenschluss *m*; (*of funds, debts*) Konsolidierung *f*

consoling [kən'səʊlɪŋ] ADJ tröstlich, tröstend

consols [ˈkɒnsɒlz] PL (*Brit, Fin*) Konsols *pl*, konsolidierte Staatsanleihen *pl*

consommé [kɒn'sɒmeɪ] N Kraftbrühe *f*, Konsommee *f* (*old*)

consonance [ˈkɒnsənəns] N (*Mus*) Konsonanz *f*; (*Poet*) Konsonantengleichklang *m*; (*fig, of agreement, ideas*) Einklang *m*, Harmonie *f*; (= *consistency*) Übereinstimmung *f*

consonant [ˈkɒnsənənt] **N** (*Phon*) Konsonant *m*, Mitlaut *m*; **~ shift** Lautverschiebung *f* **ADJ** (*Mus*) konsonant (*with* zu); **to be ~ with sth** (*fig*) mit etw in Einklang zu bringen sein

consonantal [ˌkɒnsə'næntl] ADJ konsonantisch

consort [ˈkɒnsɔːt] **N** (*form:* = *spouse*) Gemahl(in) *m(f)* (*form*), Gatte *m* (*form*), Gattin *f* (*form*) → **prince consort** **VI** (*form*) **to ~ with sb** (= *associate*) verkehren (*with* mit) **b** (= *be consistent*) passen (*with* zu), sich vereinbaren lassen (*with* mit)

consortium [kən'sɔːtɪəm] N Konsortium *nt*

conspicuous [kən'spɪkjʊəs] ADJ *person, clothes, behaviour* auffällig, auffallend; (= *easily visible*) *road signs* deutlich sichtbar, auffällig; (= *obvious*) *lack of sympathy etc* deutlich, offensichtlich, auffallend; (= *outstanding*) *bravery* bemerkenswert, hervorragend; **to be/make oneself ~** auffallen; **to feel ~** den Eindruck haben aufzufallen; **why don't you put it in a more ~ position?** warum stellen Sie es nicht irgendwohin, wo es eher auffällt?; **to be/not to be ~ for sth** sich/sich nicht gerade durch etw auszeichnen; **he was ~ by his absence** er glänzte durch Abwesenheit; **he showed a ~ lack of tact** er fiel durch sein mangelndes Taktgefühl (unangenehm) auf

conspicuous consumption N Prestigekäufe *pl*

conspicuously [kən'spɪkjʊəslɪ] ADV **a** (= *prominently*) gut sichtbar **b** (= *noticeably*) *silent, uneasy* auffällig, auffallend; *successful* bemerkenswert; **to be ~ lacking in sth** etw offenkundig nicht haben; **to be ~ absent** (*person*) durch Abwesenheit glänzen; **the government has ~ failed to intervene** es wurde übel vermerkt, dass die Regierung nicht eingegriffen hat

conspicuousness [kən'spɪkjʊəsnɪs] N (*of person, clothes, behaviour*) Auffälligkeit *f*; (= *visibility: of road signs etc*) deutliche Sichtbarkeit, Auffälligkeit *f*; (= *obviousness: of lack of sympathy etc*) Deutlichkeit *f*

conspiracy [kən'spɪrəsɪ] N Verschwörung *f*, Komplott *nt*, Konspiration *f* (*form*); (*Jur*) (strafbare) Verabredung *f*; **~ to defraud** Verabredung *f* zum Betrug; **~ to murder** Mordkomplott *nt*; **a ~ of silence** ein verabredetes Schweigen; **he**

thinks it's all a ~ against him er meint, man hätte sich gegen ihn verschworen

conspiracy theory N Verschwörungstheorie f

conspirator [kən'spɪrətə'] N Verschwörer(in) m(f)

conspiratorial ADJ , **conspiratorially** **ADV** [kən,spɪrə'tɔ:rɪəl, -lɪ] **ADJ** verschwörerisch

conspire [kən'spaɪə'] VI **a** (people) sich verschwören, sich zusammentun, konspirieren (form) (against gegen); **to ~ (together) to do sth** sich verabreden or heimlich planen, etw zu tun **b** (events) zusammenkommen, sich verschwören (geh); (fate etc) sich verschwören (against gegen)

constable ['kʌnstəbl] N (Brit: = police constable) Polizist(in) m(f); (in address) Herr Wachtmeister, Frau Wachtmeisterin

constabulary [kən'stæbjʊlərɪ] N (Brit) Polizei f no pl

constancy ['kʌnstənsɪ] N **a** (of support, supporter) Beständigkeit f, Konstanz f (liter); (of feelings) Unveränderlichkeit f, Unwandelbarkeit f; (of friend, lover) Treue f; (also **constancy of purpose**) Ausdauer f **b** (of temperature etc) Beständigkeit f

constant ['kʌnstənt] **ADJ** **a** (= continuous) quarrels, interruptions, noise dauernd, ständig, konstant (geh); **we have ~ hot water** wir haben ständig heißes Wasser **b** (= unchanging) temperature gleichmäßig, gleich bleibend, konstant; **x remains ~ while y ...** x bleibt konstant, während y ...; **the price is not ~** der Preis bleibt nicht gleich or konstant **c** (= steadfast) affection, devotion unwandelbar, beständig; friend, supporter, lover treu **N** (Math, Phys, fig) Konstante f, konstante Größe

constant load N (Tech) Grundlast f

constantly ['kʌnstəntlɪ] ADV (an)dauernd, ständig

constellation [,kʌnstə'leɪʃən] N Sternbild nt, Konstellation f (also fig)

consternation [,kʌnstə'neɪʃən] N (= dismay) Bestürzung f; (= concern, worry) Sorge f; (= fear and confusion) Aufruhr m; **to my great ~** zu meiner großen Bestürzung; **in ~** bestürzt; **to cause ~** (state of £, sb's behaviour) Grund zur Sorge geben; (news) Bestürzung auslösen; **with a look of ~ on his face** mit bestürzter Miene; **the news filled me with ~** ich war bestürzt, als ich das hörte

constipate ['kʌnstɪpeɪt] VT Verstopfung f hervorrufen bei, verstopfen

constipated ['kʌnstɪpeɪtɪd] ADJ bowels verstopft; **he is ~** er hat Verstopfung, er ist verstopft (inf); **it'll make you ~** davon bekommst du Verstopfung, das stopft

constipation [,kʌnstɪ'peɪʃən] N , no pl Verstopfung f

constituency [kən'stɪtjʊənsɪ] N (Pol) Wahlkreis m

constituent [kən'stɪtjʊənt] **ADJ** **a** (Pol) assembly konstituierend **b** attr part, element einzeln; **~ part** or **element** (of machine, matter) Bestandteil m **N** **a** (Pol) Wähler(in) m(f) **b** (= part, element) Bestandteil m **c** (Ling) Satzteil m

constitute ['kʌnstɪtju:t] VT **a** (= make up) bilden, ausmachen; **society is so ~d that ...** die Gesellschaft ist so aufgebaut, dass ... **b** (= amount to) darstellen; **that ~s a lie** das ist eine glatte Lüge **c** (= set up, give legal authority to) committee, court einrichten, konstituieren (form) **d** (form: = appoint) ernennen or bestimmen zu; **he ~d himself my bodyguard** er spielte meinen Leibwächter

constitution [,kʌnstɪ'tju:ʃən] N **a** (Pol) Verfassung f; (of club etc) Satzung f **b** (of person) Konstitution f, Gesundheit f; **to have a strong/ weak ~** eine starke/schwache Konstitution haben **c** (= way sth is made) Aufbau m; (= what sth is made of) Zusammensetzung f **d** (= setting up: of committee etc) Einrichtung f

---

Großbritannien hat anders als die Bundesrepublik Deutschland oder die Vereinigten Staaten keine niedergeschriebene Verfassung. Stattdessen setzt sich die britische **constitution** aus Gesetzen zusammen, die entweder verabschiedet (**statute law**) oder durch Gerichtsbeschluss entschieden worden sind (**common law**); außerdem umfasst sie eine Vielzahl von Regeln und Bräuchen, die die Basis für die Regierungsarbeit bilden. Die Gesetze der Verfassung können, wie jedes andere Gesetz, durch Parlamentsbeschlüsse modifiziert oder abgeschafft werden.

---

constitutional [,kʌnstɪ'tju:ʃənl] **ADJ** **a** (Pol) reform, crisis, theory Verfassungs-; monarchy, monarch konstitutionell; government, action verfassungsmäßig; **~ law** Verfassungsrecht nt; **~ change** Verfassungsänderung f; **it's not ~** das ist verfassungswidrig **b** (Med) konstitutionell (spec), körperlich bedingt; (fig) dislike etc naturgegeben or -bedingt **N** (hum inf) Spaziergang m; **to go for a/one's ~** einen/seinen Spaziergang machen

constitutionally [,kʌnstɪ'tju:ʃənəlɪ] ADV (Pol) verfassungsmäßig; (= as the constitution says also) nach der Verfassung; (= in accordance with the constitution) verfassungsgemäß; (Med) körperlich; (fig) von Natur aus

constrain [kən'streɪn] VT zwingen; one's temper zügeln

constrained [kən'streɪnd] ADJ (= forced) gezwungen; **to feel ~ by sth** sich durch etw eingeengt sehen; **to be/feel ~ to do sth** gezwungen sein/sich gezwungen sehen, etw zu tun

constraint [kən'streɪnt] N **a** (= compulsion) Zwang m **b** (= restriction) Beschränkung f, Einschränkung f; **to place ~s on sth** einer Sache (dat) Zwänge auferlegen **c** (in manner etc) Gezwungenheit f; (= embarrassment) Befangenheit f

constrict [kən'strɪkt] VT **a** (= compress) einzwängen, einengen; muscle zusammenziehen; vein verengen **b** (= hamper, limit) movements behindern, einschränken (also fig); breathing behindern; (rules, traditions etc) einengen; outlook, view etc beschränken

constriction [kən'strɪkʃən] N **a** (of muscles) Zusammenziehen nt; **he had a feeling of ~ in his chest** er hatte ein Gefühl der Enge in der Brust **b** (= limiting, of movements) Behinderung f; (caused by rules, traditions etc) Einengung f; (of outlook, view etc) Beschränkung f

constrictive [kən'strɪktɪv] ADJ garment beengend; environment einengend; ideology eng; amendments einschränkend

constrictor [kən'strɪktə'] N **a** (= muscle) Schließmuskel m, Konstriktor m (spec) **b** (= snake) Boa (constrictor) f

construct [kən'strʌkt] **VT** bauen; bridge, machine also konstruieren; (Geometry) konstruieren; sentence bilden, konstruieren; novel, play etc aufbauen; theory entwickeln, konstruieren **N** ['kʌnstrʌkt] Gedankengebäude nt

construction [kən'strʌkʃən] N **a** (of building, road) Bau m; (of bridge, machine also, of geometrical figures) Konstruktion f; (of novel, play etc) Aufbau m; (of theory) Entwicklung f, Konstruktion f; **in course of** or **under ~** in or im Bau **b** (= way sth is constructed) Struktur f; (of building) Bauweise f; (of machine, bridge) Konstruktion f; (of novel, play etc) Aufbau m **c** (= sth constructed) Bau m, Bauwerk nt; (= bridge, machine) Konstruktion f; **primitive ~s** primitive Bauten **d** (= interpretation) Deutung f; **to put a wrong ~ on sth** etw falsch auffassen or auslegen; **I don't know what ~ to put on it** ich weiß nicht, wie ich das auffassen soll **e** (Gram) Konstruktion f; **sentence ~** Satzbau m

constructional [kən'strʌkʃənl] ADJ baulich; technique, tool Bau-; fault, toy Konstruktions-

---

construction: **construction industry** N Bauindustrie f; **construction site** N Baustelle f, Baugelände nt; **construction worker** N Bauarbeiter(in) m(f)

constructive [kən'strʌktɪv] ADJ konstruktiv

constructively [kən'strʌktɪvlɪ] ADV konstruktiv; critical auf konstruktive Art; **he suggested, not very ~, that ...** er machte den nicht gerade konstruktiven Vorschlag, zu ...

construe [kən'stru:] **VT** **a** (Gram) words analysieren; sentence also zerlegen; **in English it is ~d as an adjective** im Englischen wird das als Adjektiv betrachtet **b** (= interpret) auslegen, auffassen **VI** (Gram, sentence) sich zerlegen or aufgliedern or analysieren lassen

consubstantiation [,kʌnsəb,stænʃɪ'eɪʃən] N (Eccl) Konsubstantiation f

consuetude [,kʌnswɪ'tju:d] N (form) normative Kraft des Faktischen (form)

consul ['kʌnsəl] N Konsul m

consular ['kʌnsjʊlə'] ADJ konsularisch

consulate ['kʌnsjʊlɪt] N Konsulat nt

consul general N pl **-s -** Generalkonsul m

consulship ['kʌnsəlʃɪp] N Konsulat nt

consult [kən'sʌlt] **VT** **a** (= ask) sich besprechen mit, konsultieren; lawyer, doctor etc konsultieren, zurate or zu Rate ziehen; dictionary nachschlagen in (+dat), konsultieren (geh); map nachsehen auf (+dat); oracle befragen; horoscope nachlesen; clock sehen auf (+acc); **he might have ~ed me** das hätte er auch mit mir besprechen können, er hätte mich auch konsultieren können; **you don't have to ~ me about every little detail** Sie brauchen mich nicht wegen jeder Kleinigkeit zu fragen; **he did it without ~ing anyone** er hat das getan, ohne jemanden zu fragen **b** (form: = consider) bedenken **VI** (= confer) sich beraten, beratschlagen; **to ~ together (over sth)** (etw) gemeinsam beraten; **to ~ with sb** sich mit jdm beraten

consultancy [kən'sʌltənsɪ] N (= act) Beratung f; (= business) Beratungsbüro nt

consultant [kən'sʌltənt] **N** (Brit Med) Facharzt m/-ärztin f (am Krankenhaus); (other professions) Berater(in) m(f) **ADJ** attr beratend

consultation [,kʌnsəl'teɪʃən] N (= meeting) Beratung f, Besprechung f, Konsultation f (form); (of doctor, lawyer) Konsultation f (of +gen), Beratung f (of mit); **in ~ with** in gemeinsamer Beratung mit; **to have a ~ with one's doctor/lawyer** seinen Arzt/Rechtsanwalt konsultieren; **to hold a ~ (with sb)** sich (mit jdm) beraten, eine Besprechung (mit jdm) abhalten

consultative [kən'sʌltətɪv] ADJ document beratend, konsultativ (form); **in a ~ capacity** in beratender Funktion

consulting [kən'sʌltɪŋ] ADJ engineer, architect, psychiatrist beratend

consulting hours PL (Med) Sprechstunde f

consulting room N (Med) Sprechzimmer nt

consumable [kən'sju:məbl] N Konsumgut nt, Verbrauchsgut nt; **~s** (Comput) Verbrauchsmaterial nt

consume [kən'sju:m] VT **a** food, drink zu sich nehmen, konsumieren (form); food also verzehren (geh), aufessen, vertilgen (hum inf); (Econ) konsumieren **b** (= destroy, fire) vernichten; (= use up) fuel, money verbrauchen; energy aufbrauchen, verzehren (geh); time in Anspruch nehmen; **he was ~d with desire/jealousy** er wurde von Begierde/Eifersucht verzehrt (geh); **he was ~d with rage** die Wut fraß ihn nahezu auf

consumer [kən'sju:mə'] N Verbraucher(in) m(f), Konsument(in) m(f) (form)

consumer in cpds Verbraucher-; **consumer advice centre** N Verbraucherzentrale f; **consumer credit** N Verbraucherkredit m; **consumer demand** N (konsumptive (spec)) Nachfrage; **consumer durables** PL (langlebige) Gebrauchsgüter pl; **consumer goods** PL Konsumgüter pl; **consumer group** N Verbrauchergruppe f

consumerism [kən'sjuːmərɪzəm] N Konsumismus *m*, Konsumdenken *nt*; **the age of ~** das Konsumzeitalter

consumer: consumer protection N Verbraucherschutz *m*; **consumer research** *f*; **consumer resistance** N Kaufunlust *f*; **Consumers' Association** N (*Brit*) britischer Verbraucherverband; **consumer society** N Konsumgesellschaft *f*

consuming [kən'sjuːmɪŋ] ADJ *ambition, interest* glühend, brennend; *desire, passion also* verzehrend (*geh*)

consummate [kən'sʌmɪt] ADJ *skill, folly* vollendet, vollkommen; *politician* unübertrefflich; **with ~ ease** mit spielender Leichtigkeit VT ['kɒnsəmeɪt] *marriage* vollziehen

consummately [kən'sʌmɪtlɪ] ADV (*form*) a (= *skilfully*) vollendet; **the film is a ~ acted piece** der Film ist ein schauspielerisch hervorragend umgesetzt b (= *supremely*) unübertrefflich; **he's ~ manipulative** er ist ein Meister der Manipulation

consummation [ˌkɒnsə'meɪʃən] N a (*of marriage*) Vollzug *m* b (*fig, = peak*) Höhepunkt *m*; (= *fulfilment*) Erfüllung *f*

consumption [kən'sʌmpʃən] N a (*of fuel etc*) Konsum *m*; (*of food also*) Verzehr *m* (*geh*); (*of non-edible products*) Verbrauch *m*; **the letter is for private ~ only** (*inf*) der Brief ist nur für den privaten Gebrauch; **not fit for human ~** zum Verzehr ungeeignet; **world ~ of oil** Weltölverbrauch *m*; **his daily ~ of two bottles of wine** sein täglicher Konsum von zwei Flaschen Wein b (*Med old*) Auszehrung *f* (*old*), Schwindsucht *f*

consumptive [kən'sʌmptɪv] (*old*) N Schwindsüchtige(r) *mf* ADJ schwindsüchtig

contact ['kɒntækt] ✪ 21.1 N a Kontakt *m*; (*touching also*) Berührung *f*; (= *communication also*) Verbindung *f*; **to be in ~ with sb/sth** (= *be touching*) jdn/etw berühren; (*in communication*) mit jdm/etw in Verbindung *or* Kontakt stehen; **to keep in ~ with sb** mit jdm in Kontakt bleiben; **to come into ~ with sb/sth** (*lit, fig*) mit jdm/etw in Berührung kommen; *with disease carrier also* mit jdm in Kontakt kommen; **he has no ~ with his family** er hat keinen Kontakt zu seiner Familie; **frequent ~ with death** häufige Berührung mit dem Tod; **on ~ with air/water** wenn es mit Luft/Wasser in Berührung kommt; **I'll get in ~** ich werde mich melden (*inf*), **I'll get in(to) ~ with you** ich werde mich mit Ihnen in Verbindung setzen; **how can we get in(to) ~ with him?** wie können wir ihn erreichen?; **to make ~** (*two things*) sich berühren; (*wires, wheels etc*) in Berührung *or* Kontakt (miteinander) kommen; (*two people, = get in touch*) sich miteinander in Verbindung setzen; (*by radio etc*) eine Verbindung herstellen; (*psychologically*) Kontakt bekommen; **he could make ~ by radio** er konnte sich durch Funk in Verbindung setzen; **as soon as the glue makes ~ (with the surface)** sobald der Klebstoff mit der Fläche in Berührung *or* Kontakt kommt; **to make ~ with sb/sth** (= *touch*) jdn/etw berühren, mit jdm/etw in Berührung kommen; (*wire, wheels etc also*) mit jdm/etw in Kontakt kommen; (= *get in touch with*) sich mit jdm/etw in Verbindung setzen; (*psychologically*) Kontakt zu jdm/etw bekommen; **I finally made ~ with him at his office** ich habe ihn schließlich im Büro erreicht; **to lose ~ (with sb/sth)** den Kontakt *or* die Verbindung (zu jdm/etw) verlieren; **point of ~** (*Math, fig*) Berührungspunkt *m* b (*Elec*) (= *act*) Kontakt *m*; (= *equipment*) Kontakt- *or* Schaltstück *nt*; **to make/break ~** den Kontakt herstellen/unterbrechen c (= *person*) Kontaktperson *f* (*also Med*); (*in espionage*) Verbindungsmann *m*, V-Mann *m*; **~s** *pl* Kontakte *pl*, Verbindungen *pl*; **to make ~s** er hat einen nützlichen Kontakt hergestellt VT *person, agent, lawyer* sich in Verbindung setzen mit; (*for help*) *police* sich wenden an (+*acc*)

I've been trying to ~ you for hours ich versuche schon seit Stunden, Sie zu erreichen; **he doesn't want to be ~ed unless it's urgent** er möchte, dass man sich nur in dringenden Fällen mit ihm in Verbindung setzt

contact: contact allergy N Kontaktallergie *f*; **contact breaker** N Unterbrecher *m*; **contact flight** N Sichtflug *m*; **contact lens** N Kontaktlinse *f*; **contact man** N Kontakt- *or* Mittelsmann *m*; **contact poison** N Kontakt- *or* Berührungsgift *nt*; **contact print** N (*Phot*) Kontaktabzug *m*; **contact sport** N Kontaktsport *m*

contagion [kən'teɪdʒən] N (= *contact*) Ansteckung *f*; (= *disease*) Ansteckungskrankheit *f*; (= *epidemic*) Seuche *f* (*also fig*); (*fig: = spreading influence*) schädlicher Einfluss

contagious [kən'teɪdʒəs] ADJ (*Med, fig*) ansteckend; *disease also* direkt übertragbar; **he's not ~** (*Med*) seine Krankheit ist nicht ansteckend; (*hum*) er ist nicht giftig (*inf*)

contain [kən'teɪn] VT a (= *hold within itself*) enthalten; **the envelope ~ed money** im Umschlag befand sich Geld, der Umschlag enthielt Geld b (= *have capacity for: box, bottle, room*) fassen c (= *control*) *emotions, oneself* beherrschen; *tears* zurückhalten; *laughter* unterdrücken; *disease, inflation, sb's power* in Grenzen halten; *epidemic, flood* aufhalten, unter Kontrolle bringen; *enemy* in Schach halten; (*Sport*) in Schach halten; *attack* abwehren; **he could hardly ~ himself** er konnte kaum an sich (*acc*) halten d (*Math*) *angle* einschließen

container [kən'teɪnə'] N a Behälter *m*; (= *bottle, jar etc also*) Gefäß *nt* b (*Comm, for transport*) Container *m* ADJ *attr* Container-; **by ~ lorry** per Container

containerization [kən,teɪnəraɪ'zeɪʃən] N (*of goods*) Verpackung *f* in Container; (*of ports*) Umstellung *f* auf Container

containerize [kən'teɪnəraɪz] VT *freight* in Container verpacken; *port* auf Container umstellen

containment [kən'teɪnmənt] N (*Mil*) In-Schach-Halten *nt*; (*of attack*) Abwehr *f*; **their efforts at ~ (of the rebels)** ihre Bemühungen, die Rebellen in Schach zu halten

contaminate [kən'tæmɪneɪt] VT verunreinigen, verschmutzen; (= *poison*) vergiften; (*radioactivity*) verseuchen, kontaminieren (*spec*); (*fig*) *mind* verderben; **the oranges were ~d by poison** in den Orangen befanden sich Giftstoffe

contamination [kən,tæmɪ'neɪʃən] N , *no pl* Verunreinigung *f*, Verschmutzung *f*; (*by poison*) Vergiftung *f*; (*by radioactivity*) Verseuchung *f*, Kontaminierung *f* (*spec*); (= *substance*) Giftstoffe *pl*; (*fig*) schädlicher Einfluss (*of* auf +*acc*); (*fig: = contaminated state*) Verdorbenheit *f*

contango [kən'tæŋgəʊ] N (*Fin*) Report *m*

contd *abbr of* **continued** Forts., Fortsetzung *f*

contemplate ['kɒntempleɪt] VT a (= *look at*) betrachten b (= *think about, reflect upon*) nachdenken über (+*acc*); (= *consider*) *changes, a purchase, action, accepting an offer* in Erwägung ziehen, erwägen (*geh*); *a holiday* denken an (+*acc*); **he ~d the future with some misgivings** er sah der Zukunft mit einem unguten Gefühl entgegen; **he would never ~ violence** der Gedanke an Gewalttätigkeit würde ihm nie kommen; **it's too awful to ~** schon der Gedanke (daran) ist zu entsetzlich c (= *expect*) voraussehen d (= *intend*) **to ~ doing sth** daran denken, etw zu tun

contemplation [ˌkɒntem'pleɪʃən] N , *no pl* a (= *act of looking*) Betrachtung *f* b (= *act of thinking*) Nachdenken *nt* (*of* über +*acc*); (= *deep thought*) Besinnung *f*, Betrachtung *f*, Kontemplation *f* (*esp Rel*); **a life of ~** ein beschauliches *or* kontemplatives (*esp Rel*) Leben; **deep in ~** in Gedanken versunken c (= *expectation*) Erwartung *f*

contemplative [kən'templətɪv] ADJ a (= *thoughtful*) *look, person* nachdenklich; *mood also* besinnlich b *life, religious order* beschaulich, kontemplativ

contemplatively [kən'templətɪvlɪ] ADV nachdenklich; *sit also* in Gedanken

contemporaneous [kən,tempə'reɪnɪəs] ADJ gleichzeitig stattfindend *attr*; **a manuscript ~ with ...** ein Manuskript aus derselben Zeit *or* Epoche wie ...; **events ~ with the rebellion** Ereignisse zur Zeit des Aufstandes

contemporary [kən'tempərərɪ] ADJ a (= *of the same time*) *events* gleichzeitig; *records, literature, writer* zeitgenössisch; (= *of the same age*) *manuscript* gleich alt; **records ~ with the invasion** Aufzeichnungen aus der Zeit der Invasion b (= *of the present time*) *life* heutig; *art, design* zeitgenössisch, modern N Altersgenosse *m*/-genossin *f*; (*in history*) Zeitgenosse *m*/-genossin *f*; (*at university*) Kommilitone *m*, Kommilitonin *f*

contempt [kən'tempt] N a Verachtung *f*; (= *disregard also*) Geringachtung *f*, Geringschätzung *f* (*for* von); **to hold in ~** verachten; **to bring into ~** in Verruf bringen; **in ~ of public opinion** die öffentliche Meinung außer Acht lassend, ohne Ansehen der öffentlichen Meinung; **beneath ~** unter aller Kritik b (*Jur, also* **contempt of court**) Missachtung *f* (der Würde) des Gerichts, Ungebühr *f* vor Gericht; (*through non-appearance*) Ungebühr *f* durch vorsätzliches Ausbleiben; (*by press*) Beeinflussung *f* der Rechtspflege; **to be in ~ (of court)** das Gericht *or* die Würde des Gerichts missachten

contemptible [kən'temptəbl] ADJ verachtenswert, verächtlich

contemptuous [kən'temptjʊəs] ADJ *manner, gesture, look* geringschätzig, verächtlich; *person* herablassend; *laugh, sneer, remark, reference* verächtlich; **to be ~ of sb/sth** jdn/etw verachten; **she was quite ~ of my offer** sie reagierte ziemlich verächtlich auf mein Angebot

contemptuously [kən'temptjʊəslɪ] ADV *say, look, laugh, spit* verächtlich

contend [kən'tend] VI a (= *compete*) kämpfen; **to ~ (with sb) for sth** (mit jdm) um etw kämpfen; **then you'll have me to ~ with** dann bekommst du es mit mir zu tun; **but I've got two directors to ~ with** aber ich habe es mit zwei Direktoren zu tun b (= *cope*) **to ~ with sb/sth** mit jdm/etw fertig werden VT behaupten

contender [kən'tendə'] N Kandidat(in) *m(f)*, Anwärter(in) *m(f)* (*for* auf +*acc*); (*for job also*) Bewerber(in) *m(f)* (*for* um); (*Sport*) Wettkämpfer(in) *m(f)* (*for* um)

contending [kən'tendɪŋ] ADJ *emotions* widerstreitend; **the ~ parties** (*in dispute, lawsuit*) die streitenden Parteien *pl*

content¹ [kən'tent] ADJ *pred* zufrieden (*with* mit); **to be/feel ~** zufrieden sein; **she's quite ~ to stay at home** sie bleibt ganz gern zu Hause N Zufriedenheit *f* VT *person* zufrieden stellen; **to ~ oneself with** sich zufrieden geben *or* begnügen *or* abfinden mit; **to ~ oneself with doing sth** sich damit zufrieden geben *or* begnügen *or* abfinden, etw zu tun

content² ['kɒntent] N a **contents** PL (*of room, one's pocket, book etc*) Inhalt *m*; **(table of) ~s** Inhaltsverzeichnis *nt* b *no pl* (= *substance, component*) Gehalt *m*; (*of speech, book etc also*) Inhalt *m*; **gold/vitamin ~** Gold-/Vitamingehalt *m*

contented, **contentedly** [kən'tentɪd, -lɪ] ADJ, ADV zufrieden

contentedness [kən'tentɪdnɪs] N = **contentment**

contention [kən'tenʃən] N a (= *dispute*) Streit *m*; **~s** Streitigkeiten *pl*; **the matter in ~** die strittige Angelegenheit; **that is no longer in ~** das steht nicht mehr zur Debatte b (= *argument*) Behauptung *f*; **it is my ~ that ...** ich behaupte, dass ... c (*in contest*) **to be in ~ (for sth)** Chancen (auf etw (*acc*)) haben

contentious [kən'tenʃəs] ADJ *subject, issue* strittig, umstritten; *view* umstritten, kontrovers; *decision, proposal, legislation* umstritten; *person* streitlustig, streitsüchtig

contentiously [kən'tenʃəslɪ] ADV kontrovers

contentment [kən'tentmənt] N Zufriedenheit f

content provider N (*Comput*) Content Provider *m*

contest ['kɒntest] **N** (*for um*) Kampf *m*; (= *competition also*) Wettkampf *m*, Wettstreit *m* (*geh*); (= *beauty contest etc*) Wettbewerb *m*; **boxing** ~ Boxkampf *m*; **election** ~ Wahlkampf *m*; **it's no** ~ das ist ein ungleicher Kampf; **it was a real** ~ **of skill** es kam dabei wirklich aufs Können an **VT** [kən'test] **a** (= *fight over*) kämpfen um; (= *fight against, oppose*) kämpfen gegen; (*Parl*) *election* teilnehmen an (+*dat*); **to** ~ **a seat** (*Parl*) um einen Wahlkreis kämpfen; **the seat was not** ~**ed** es gab keinen Kampf um den Wahlkreis **b** (= *dispute*) *statement* bestreiten, angreifen; *measure* angreifen; (*Jur*) *will, right, legal action* anfechten; **a** ~**ed measure** eine umstrittene Maßnahme; **to** ~ **sb's right to do sth** jdm das Recht streitig machen *or* jds Recht anfechten, etw zu tun **VI** [kən'test] kämpfen (*for um*)

contestant [kən'testənt] N (Wettbewerbs)teilnehmer(in) *m(f)*; (*Parl, in quiz*) Kandidat(in) *m(f)*; (*Sport*) (Wettkampf)teilnehmer(in) *m(f)*; (*Mil*) Kämpfende(r) *m*; **the** ~**s in the election** die Wahlkandidaten

context ['kɒntekst] **✪** 26.2 N Zusammenhang *m*, Kontext *m* (*geh*); **(taken) out of** ~ aus dem Zusammenhang *or* Kontext (*geh*) gerissen; **in the broader European** ~ im weiteren europäischen Zusammenhang *or* Kontext (*geh*) *or* Rahmen; **in this** ~ in diesem Zusammenhang; **in an office** ~ im Rahmen eines Büros

context-sensitive [ˌkɒntekst'sensɪtɪv] ADJ (*Comput*) kontextsensitiv

contextual [kən'tekstjʊəl] ADJ kontextuell (*form*); *meaning* aus dem Zusammenhang *or* Kontext (*geh*) ersichtlich

contextualize [kən'tekstjʊəlaɪz] VT in einen Zusammenhang *or* Kontext (*geh*) setzen

contiguity [ˌkɒntɪ'gjʊɪtɪ] N (unmittelbare) Nachbarschaft

contiguous [kən'tɪgjʊəs] ADJ (*form*) aneinander grenzend, sich berührend; (*in time*) (unmittelbar) aufeinander folgend; **the estates are** ~ die Grundstücke grenzen aneinander

continence ['kɒntɪnəns] N **a** (*Med*) Kontinenz f (*spec*), Fähigkeit f Stuhl und/oder Urin zurückzuhalten **b** (= *abstinence*) Enthaltsamkeit f

continent[1] ['kɒntɪnənt] ADJ (= *self-controlled*) mäßig, beherrscht, maßvoll; (*sexually*) (sexuell) enthaltsam; **the old lady was not** ~ (*Med*) die alte Dame konnte ihre Darmtätigkeit/Blasentätigkeit nicht mehr kontrollieren

continent[2] N (*Geog*) Kontinent *m*, Erdteil *m*; (= *mainland*) Festland *nt*; **the Continent (of Europe)** (*Brit*) Kontinentaleuropa *nt*; **on the Continent** in Europa, auf dem Kontinent

continental [ˌkɒntɪ'nentl] **ADJ a** (*Geog*) kontinental **b** (*Brit*, = *European*) europäisch; *holidays* in Europa **N** (Festlands)europäer(in) *m(f)*

continental: continental breakfast N kleines Frühstück; **continental drift** N (*Geog*) Kontinentaldrift f; **continental quilt** N Steppdecke f; **continental shelf** N (*Geog*) Kontinentalschelf *m*, Kontinentalsockel *m*

contingency [kən'tɪndʒənsɪ] N **a** möglicher Fall, Eventualität f; **in this** ~, **should this** ~ **arise** in diesem Fall, für diesen Fall, sollte dieser Fall eintreten; **to provide for all contingencies** alle Möglichkeiten einplanen, alle Eventualitäten berücksichtigen; **a** ~ **plan** ein Ausweichplan *m*; ~ **planning** Planung f für Eventualfälle **b** (*Philos*) Kontingenz f

contingency fee N (*US, Jur*) Erfolgshonorar *nt*

contingency fund N Eventualfonds *m*

contingent [kən'tɪndʒənt] **ADJ** **a** ~ **upon** (*form*) abhängig von; **to be** ~ **upon** abhängen von **b** (*Philos*) kontingent **N** Kontingent *nt*; (= *section*) Gruppe f; (*Mil*) Trupp *m*

continual [kən'tɪnjʊəl] ADJ (= *frequent*) dauernd, ständig; (= *unceasing*) ununterbrochen, pausenlos

continually [kən'tɪnjʊəlɪ] ADV (= *repeatedly*) (an)dauernd, ständig; (= *ceaselessly*) ununterbrochen, pausenlos

continuance [kən'tɪnjʊəns] N **a** (= *duration*) Dauer f **b** = **continuation a**

continuation [kən,tɪnjʊ'eɪʃən] N **a** Fortsetzung f, Fortführung f; **the** ~ **of the human race** der Weiterbestand *or* Fortbestand der menschlichen Rasse; **the Government's** ~ **in office** das Verbleiben der Regierung im Amt **b** (= *retention: of arrangement etc*) Beibehaltung f **c** (= *resumption*) Fortsetzung f, Wiederaufnahme f **d** (= *sth continued*) Fortsetzung f, Weiterführung f

continue [kən'tɪnjuː] **VT** **a** (= *carry on*) fortfahren mit; *policy, tradition, struggle* fortsetzen, fortführen, weiterführen; *activity, piece of work, meal* fortsetzen, weitermachen mit; **to** ~ **doing** *or* **to do sth** etw weiter tun, fortfahren, etw zu tun; **to** ~ **to fight/sing/read/eat, to** ~ **fighting/singing/reading/eating** weiterkämpfen/-singen/-lesen/-essen; **her condition** ~**s to improve** ihr Befinden bessert sich ständig

b (= *resume*) fortsetzen; *conversation, work, journey also* wieder aufnehmen; **to be** ~**d** Fortsetzung folgt; ~**d on p 10** weiter *or* Fortsetzung auf Seite 10

c (= *prolong*) *line* verlängern, weiterführen

VI (= *go on, person*) weitermachen; (*crisis, speech*) fortdauern, (an)dauern; (*influence*) fortdauern, andauern; (*weather*) anhalten; (*road, forest etc*) weitergehen, sich fortsetzen; (*concert etc*) weitergehen; **to** ~ **on one's way** weiterfahren; (*on foot*) weitergehen; **he** ~**d after a short pause** er redete/schrieb/las *etc* nach einer kurzen Pause weiter; **to** ~ **with one's work** seine Arbeit fortsetzen, mit seiner Arbeit weitermachen; **please** ~ bitte machen Sie weiter; (*in talking*) fahren Sie fort; **to** ~ **to be obstinate/cheerful** weiterhin starrköpfig/fröhlich bleiben; **he** ~**s to be optimistic** er ist nach wie vor optimistisch; **to** ~ **at university/with a company/as sb's secretary** auf der Universität/bei einer Firma/jds Sekretärin bleiben; **to** ~ **in office** im Amt verbleiben; **his influence** ~**d after his death** sein Einfluss überdauerte seinen Tod

continuing [kən'tɪnjuːɪŋ] ADJ ständig, fortgesetzt; *process* stetig, kontinuierlich (*geh*)

continuity [ˌkɒntɪ'njuːɪtɪ] N **a** Kontinuität f; **the story lacks** ~ der Geschichte fehlt der rote Faden **b** (*Film*) Anschluss *m*; (*Rad*) (verbindende) Ansagen *pl*

continuity announcer N (*TV, Rad*) Ansager(in) *m(f)*

continuity girl N Scriptgirl *nt*

continuo [kən'tɪnjʊəʊ] N Continuo *nt*; **to play the** ~ Continuo spielen

continuous [kən'tɪnjʊəs] ADJ dauernd, ständig, kontinuierlich (*geh*); *line* durchgezogen, ununterbrochen; *rise, movement etc* stetig, stet *attr* (*geh*), gleichmäßig; (*Math*) *function* stetig; **to be in** ~ **use** ständig in Benutzung sein; **a** ~ **stream of people** ein ununterbrochener Andrang von Menschen; **a** ~ **stream of phone calls** eine ununterbrochene Flut von Anrufen; ~ **assessment** Beurteilung f der Leistungen während des ganzen Jahres; ~ **paper** (*Comput*) Endlospapier *nt*; (*pre-printed*) Endlosformular *nt*; ~ **performance** (*Film*) durchgehende Vorstellung; ~ **tense** (*Gram*) Verlaufsform f; **present/past** ~ (*Gram*) erweitertes Präsens/Präteritum; ~ **text** Fließtext *m*

continuously [kən'tɪnjʊəslɪ] ADV (= *repeatedly*) dauernd, ständig, kontinuierlich (*geh*); (= *ceaselessly*) ununterbrochen; *rise, move* stetig, gleichmäßig

continuum [kən'tɪnjʊəm] N Kontinuum *nt*

contort [kən'tɔːt] VT **a** *one's features, metal* verziehen (*into zu*); *limbs* verrenken, verdrehen; **a**

face ~**ed with pain** ein schmerzverzerrtes Gesicht; **a** ~**ed smile** ein verkrampftes Lächeln **b** (*fig*) *words* verdrehen; *report also* verzerren

contortion [kən'tɔːʃən] N (*esp of acrobat*) Verrenkung f; (*of features*) Verzerrung f; **mental** ~**s** geistige Verrenkungen *pl or* Klimmzüge *pl*; **he resorted to elaborate verbal** ~**s to avoid telling the truth** er hat sich gedreht und gewendet, um nicht die Wahrheit sagen zu müssen

contortionist [kən'tɔːʃənɪst] N Schlangenmensch *m*

contour ['kɒntʊə] **N** **a** (= *outline*) Kontur f, Umriss *m* **b** **contours** PL (= *shape*) Konturen *pl*; **the** ~**s of her body** ihre Konturen **c** (*Geog*) Höhenlinie f **VT** *road* der Gegend anpassen; *land* hügelig anlegen; *map* mit Höhenlinien versehen

contoured ['kɒntʊəd] ADJ konturenreich, geschwungen; ~ **seat** den Körperformen angepasster Sitz

contour (*Geog*): **contour line** N Höhenlinie f; **contour map** N Höhenlinienkarte f; **contour sheet** N (*US*) Spannbettlaken *nt*, Spannbetttuch *nt*

contra- ['kɒntrə-] PREF Gegen-, Kontra-; (*Mus, = pitched lower*) Kontra-

contraband ['kɒntrəbænd] **N**, *no pl* (= *goods*) Konterbande f, Schmuggelware f; (*form, = smuggling*) Schleichhandel *m*, Schmuggeln *nt*; ~ **of war** Kriegskonterbande f **ADJ** Schmuggel-; ~ **goods** Konterbande f, Schmuggelware f

contraception [ˌkɒntrə'sepʃən] N Empfängnisverhütung f

contraceptive [ˌkɒntrə'septɪv] **N** empfängnisverhütendes Mittel; (= *sheath*) Verhütungsmittel *nt*, Präventivmittel *nt* (*form*) **ADJ** empfängnisverhütend; *pill* Antibaby-; *advice* über Empfängnisverhütung

contract[1] ['kɒntrækt] **N** **a** (= *agreement*) Vertrag *m*, Kontrakt *m* (*old*); (= *document also*) Vertragsdokument *nt*; (*Comm, = order*) Auftrag *m*; (= *delivery contract*) Liefervertrag *m*; **to enter into** *or* **make a** ~ **(with sb)** (mit jdm) einen Vertrag eingehen *or* (ab)schließen; **to be under** ~ unter Vertrag stehen (*to bei, mit*); **to be bound by** ~ vertraglich gebunden sein (*to an* +*acc*); **to put work out to** ~ Arbeiten außer Haus machen lassen; **to take out a** ~ **on sb** (*to kill*) einen Killer auf jdn ansetzen; **terms of** ~ Vertragsbedingungen *or* -bestimmungen *pl*

b (*Bridge*) Kontrakt *m* → **contract bridge** **ADJ** *price, work* vertraglich festgelegt *or* vereinbart; ~ **work** Auftragsarbeit f

VT [kən'trækt] **a** (= *acquire*) *debts* machen, ansammeln; *illness* erkranken an (+*dat*); *vices, habit* sich (*dat*) zulegen, entwickeln, annehmen; *passion* entwickeln

b (= *enter into*) *marriage, alliance* schließen, eingehen

VI [kən'trækt] **a** (*Comm*) **to** ~ **to do sth** sich vertraglich verpflichten, etw zu tun

b (*form, = make an arrangement*) sich verbünden

▶ **contract in** VI sich anschließen (-*to* +*dat*); (*into insurance scheme*) beitreten (-*to* +*dat*)

▶ **contract out** **VI** (= *withdraw*) austreten, aussteigen (*inf*) (*of aus*); (= *not join*) sich nicht anschließen (*of* +*dat*); (*out of insurance scheme*) nicht beitreten (*of* +*dat*) **VT** *sep* (*Comm*) *work* außer Haus machen lassen (*to von*), vergeben (*to an* +*acc*)

contract[2] [kən'trækt] **VT** **a** *muscle, metal etc* zusammenziehen; *brow* in Falten legen, hochziehen; *pupil* verengen **b** (*Ling*) zusammenziehen, kontrahieren (*spec*) (*into zu*) **VI** (*muscle, metal etc*) sich zusammenziehen; (*pupil also*) sich verengen; (*fig, influence, business*) (zusammen-)schrumpfen

contract bridge N Kontrakt-Bridge *nt*

contracted [kən'træktɪd] ADJ zusammengezogen; (*Ling also*) verkürzt; *brow* gerunzelt; (*fig*) engstirnig

contraction [kən'trækʃən] N **a** (*of metal, muscles*) Zusammenziehen *nt*, Zusammenziehung *f*; (*of pupils*) Verengung *f*; (*fig*) Schrumpfung *f* **b** (*Ling*) Kontraktion *f* **c** (*in childbirth*) ~s Wehen *pl* **d** (*form: = acquisition, of debts*) Ansammlung *f*; (*of habit*) Entwicklung *f*, Annahme *f*; **his ~ of polio** seine Erkrankung an Kinderlähmung

contract: contract killing N Auftragsmord *m*; **contract law** N , *no pl* Vertragsrecht *nt*; **contract note** N (*St Ex*) Schlussschein *m*

contractor [kən'træktə'] N (= *individual*) Auftragnehmer *m*, beauftragter Elektriker/Monteur *etc*; (= *company also*) beauftragte Firma; (= *building contractor*) Bauunternehmer *m*; (= *company*) Bauunternehmen *nt*, Bauunternehmer *m*; **that is done by outside ~s** damit ist eine andere Firma beauftragt

contractual [kən'træktʃʊəl] ADJ vertraglich

contractually [kən'træktʃʊəlɪ] ADV vertraglich; **~ binding** vertraglich bindend

contradict [ˌkɒntrə'dɪkt] ✪ 26.3 VT (*person*) widersprechen (+*dat*); (*event, action, statement also*) im Widerspruch stehen zu; **to ~ oneself** sich (*dat*) widersprechen; **he ~ed every word I said** er widersprach mir bei jedem Wort; **he can't stand being ~ed** er duldet keinen Widerspruch

contradiction [ˌkɒntrə'dɪkʃən] N Widerspruch *m* (*of zu*); (= *act of contradicting*) Widersprechen *nt*; **full of ~s** voller Widersprüchlichkeiten; **to give a flat ~** einfach *or* rundheraus widersprechen (+*dat*)

contradictory [ˌkɒntrə'dɪktərɪ] ADJ *person* widersprüchlich; *statements also* (sich) widersprechend; **to be ~ to sth** einer Sache (*dat*) widersprechen, zu etw im Widerspruch stehen; **it is ~ to claim that ...** es ist ein Widerspruch, zu behaupten ...; **he was in a ~ mood** er war voller Widerspruchsgeist

contradistinction [ˌkɒntrədɪs'tɪŋkʃən] N (*form*) **in ~ to** im Gegensatz *or* Unterschied zu

contraflow ['kɒntrəfləʊ] N (*Mot*) Gegenverkehr *m* ADJ Gegenverkehrs-

contrail ['kɒntreɪl] N (*Aviat*) Kondensstreifen *m*

contraindication [ˌkɒntrəˌɪndɪ'keɪʃən] N (*Med*) Kontraindikation *f*, Gegenanzeige *f*

contralto [kən'træltəʊ] N (= *voice*) Alt *m*; (= *singer also*) Altist(in) *m(f)* ADJ *voice* Alt-; **the ~ part** die Altstimme, der Alt

contraption [kən'træpʃən] N (*inf*) Apparat *m* (*inf*); (= *vehicle also*) Vehikel *nt* (*inf*), Kiste *f* (*inf*)

contrapuntal [ˌkɒntrə'pʌntl] ADJ kontrapunktisch

contrarian [kən'treərɪən] (*form*) N Querdenker(in) *m(f)*, Nonkonformist(in) *m(f)* ADJ nonkonformistisch

contrarily [kən'treərɪlɪ] ADV (= *perversely*) widerborstig; (*of horse etc*) widerspenstig

contrariness [kən'treərɪnɪs] N Widerborstigkeit *f*; (*of person also*) Widerspruchsgeist *m*; (*of horse*) Widerspenstigkeit *f*

contrary¹ ['kɒntrərɪ] ✪ 22, 26.2, 26.3 ADJ **a** (= *opposite*) entgegengesetzt; *effect, answer also* gegenteilig; (= *conflicting*) *views, statements also* gegensätzlich; (= *adverse*) *winds, tides* widrig; **in a ~ direction** in entgegengesetzter Richtung; **sth is ~ to sth** etw steht im Gegensatz zu etw; **it is ~ to our agreement** es entspricht nicht unseren Abmachungen; **to run ~ to sth** einer Sache (*dat*) zuwiderlaufen; **~ to nature** wider die Natur; **~ to our hopes/intentions** wider all unsere Hoffnungen/Absichten, entgegen unseren Hoffnungen/Absichten; **~ to what I expected** entgegen meinen Erwartungen

N Gegenteil *nt*; **on the ~** im Gegenteil; **the ~ of what I expected** das Gegenteil von dem, was ich erwartet hatte; **unless you hear to the ~** sofern Sie nichts Gegenteiliges hören; **statement/evidence to the ~** gegenteilige Aussage/gegenteiliger Beweis; **quite the ~** ganz im Gegenteil

contrary² [kən'treərɪ] ADJ widerborstig, widerspenstig; *person also* voll Widerspruchsgeist; *horse* widerspenstig

contrast ['kɒntrɑːst] ✪ 5.1 N **a** (= *contrasting*) Gegenüberstellung *f*

b Gegensatz *m* (*with, to zu*); (*visual, = striking difference of opposites*) Kontrast *m* (*with, to zu*); **by** *or* **in ~** im Gegensatz dazu; **to be in ~ with** *or* **to sth** im Gegensatz/in Kontrast zu etw stehen; **the red is a good ~** das Rot stellt einen guten Kontrast dar; **she's quite a ~ to her sister** es besteht ein ziemlicher Gegensatz *or* Unterschied zwischen ihr und ihrer Schwester; **the ~ between the state of the £ now and last year** der Unterschied zwischen dem jetzigen Stand des Pfundes und seinem Wert im letzten Jahr; **and now, by way of ~** und nun etwas ganz anderes; **what a ~!** welch ein Gegensatz!

c (*Art, Phot, TV*) Kontrast *m*

VT [kən'trɑːst] einen Vergleich anstellen (*with* zwischen +*dat*), gegenüberstellen (*with* +*dat*)

VI [kən'trɑːst] im Gegensatz *or* in Kontrast stehen (*with* zu), kontrastieren (*with* mit); (*colours also*) sich abheben (*with* von), abstechen (*with* von); **to ~ unfavourably with sth** bei einem Vergleich mit *or* im Vergleich zu etw schlecht abschneiden; **his promises and his actions ~ sharply** seine Versprechungen und seine Handlungsweise stehen in scharfem Kontrast *or* Gegensatz zueinander; **blue and yellow ~ nicely** Blau und Gelb ergeben einen hübschen Kontrast

contrasting [kən'trɑːstɪŋ] ADJ *opinions, lifestyle etc* gegensätzlich, kontrastierend (*form*); *colours* kontrastierend, Kontrast-

contrastive [kən'trɑːstɪv] ADJ gegenüberstellend; (*Ling*) kontrastiv

contravene [ˌkɒntrə'viːn] VT *law, custom etc* (*action, behaviour*) verstoßen gegen, verletzen; (*person also*) zuwiderhandeln (+*dat*)

contravention [ˌkɒntrə'venʃən] N Verstoß *m* (*of gegen*), Verletzung *f* (*of* +*gen*); (*of law also*) Übertretung *f* (*of* +*gen*); **to be in ~ of ...** gegen ... verstoßen; **to act in ~ of sth** einer Sache (*dat*) zuwiderhandeln

contre-jour ['kɒntrəʒʊə'] ADJ (*Phot*) Gegenlicht-; **~ shot** Gegenlichtaufnahme *f*

contretemps ['kɒntrətɒŋ] N , *no pl* Zwischenfall *m*; (= *unexpected hitch also*) kleines Missgeschick

contribute [kən'trɪbjuːt] VT beitragen (*to* zu); *food, money, supplies* beisteuern (*to* zu); (*to charity*) spenden (*to* für); *time, talent* zur Verfügung stellen (*to* +*dat*); *press article also, information* liefern (*to* für), beisteuern (*to* +*dat*); **to ~ one's share** sein(en) Teil dazu beitragen

VI beitragen (*to* zu); (*to pension fund etc*) einen Beitrag leisten (*to* zu); (*to present*) beisteuern (*to* zu); (*to charity*) spenden (*to* für); (*to newspaper, conference, society etc*) einen Beitrag leisten (*to* zu); (*regularly: to a magazine etc*) mitwirken (*to* an +*dat*); **do you want me to ~?** möchten Sie, dass ich etwas dazu beisteuere *or* (*to charity*) etwas spende?

contribution [ˌkɒntrɪ'bjuːʃən] N Beitrag *m* (*to* zu); (= *donation also*) Spende *f* (*to* für); **to make a ~ to sth** einen Beitrag zu etw leisten; **the beer is my ~** das Bier stelle ich; **I appreciate the ~ of so much of your time/effort** ich weiß es zu schätzen, dass Sie Ihre Zeit so großzügig zur Verfügung gestellt/solche Anstrengungen unternommen haben

contributor [kən'trɪbjʊtə'] N (*to magazine etc*) Mitarbeiter(in) *m(f)* (*to* an +*dat*); (*of goods, money*) Spender(in) *m(f)*; **to be a ~ to a newspaper** für eine Zeitung schreiben; **to be a ~ to an appeal** auf einen Appell hin etwas spenden

contributory [kən'trɪbjʊtərɪ] ADJ **a** **it's certainly a ~ factor/cause** es ist sicherlich ein Faktor, der dazu beiträgt *or* der mit eine Rolle spielt; **to be a ~ cause of a disease** ein Faktor sein, der zu einer Krankheit beiträgt; **to be ~ to sth** zu etw beitragen **b** *pension scheme* beitragspflichtig

contributory negligence N (*Jur*) Mitverschulden *nt*

con trick N (*inf*) Schwindel *m*

contrite ADJ , **contritely** ADV [kən'traɪt, -lɪ] reuig, zerknirscht

contrition [kən'trɪʃən] N Reue *f*; **act of ~** (*Eccl*) Buße *f*

contrivance [kən'traɪvəns] N **a** (= *device*) Vorrichtung *f*; (*mechanical*) Gerät *nt*, Apparat *m* **b** (= *devising, scheming*) Planung *f*; (= *invention*) Erfindung *f*; (= *inventiveness*) Findigkeit *f*, Erfindungsgabe *f*; **a plan of his ~** ein seinem Kopf entstammender Plan; **a device of his ~** ein von ihm erfundenes Gerät **c** (= *plan, scheme*) List *f*

contrive [kən'traɪv] VT **a** (= *devise*) *plan, scheme* entwickeln, entwerfen, ersinnen; (= *make*) fabrizieren; **to ~ a means of doing sth** einen Weg finden, etw zu tun **b** (= *manage, arrange*) bewerkstelligen, zuwege *or* zu Wege bringen; *meeting also* arrangieren; **to ~ to do sth** es fertig bringen (*also iro*) *or* zuwege *or* zu Wege bringen, etw zu tun; **can you ~ to be here at three o'clock?** können Sie es so einrichten, dass Sie um drei Uhr hier sind?; **he always ~s to get his own way** er versteht (es) immer, seinen Kopf durchzusetzen

contrived [kən'traɪvd] ADJ gestellt; *style also* gekünstelt

control [kən'trəʊl] N **a** *no pl* (= *management, supervision*) Aufsicht *f* (*of* über +*acc*); (*of money, fortune*) Verwaltung *f* (*of* +*gen*); (*of situation, e-motion, language*) Beherrschung *f* (*of* +*gen*); (= *self-control*) (Selbst)beherrschung *f*; (= *physical control*) (Körper)beherrschung *f* (*of* +*gen*); (= *authority, power*) Gewalt *f*, Macht *f* (*over* über +*acc*); (*over territory*) Gewalt *f* (*over* über +*acc*); (= *regulation, of prices, disease, inflation*) Kontrolle *f* (*of* +*gen*); (*of traffic*) Regelung *f* (*of* +*gen*); (*of pollution*) Einschränkung *f* (*of* +*gen*); **his ~ of the ball** seine Ballführung; **to be in ~ of sth, to have ~ of sth** (= *be in charge of, business, office*) etw leiten, etw unter sich (*dat*) haben; *money* etw verwalten; **to have ~ of sb** jdn unter Kontrolle haben; *children* jdn beaufsichtigen; **I'm in ~ here** ich habe hier die Leitung; **to be in ~ of sth, to have sth under ~** (= *deal successfully with*) etw in der Hand haben; *class also* etw unter Kontrolle haben; *situation also* Herr einer Sache (*gen*) sein, etw beherrschen; *car, inflation, disease, pollution* etw unter Kontrolle haben; **to be in ~ of oneself** sich in der Hand *or* in der Gewalt haben; **to be in ~ of one's emotions** Herr über seine Gefühle sein, Herr seiner Gefühle sein; **to have some/no ~ over sb/sth** (= *have influence over*) Einfluss/keinen Einfluss auf jdn/etw haben; *over money* Kontrolle/keine Kontrolle über etw (*acc*) haben; **she has no ~ over how the money is spent/what her children do** sie hat keinen Einfluss darauf, wie das Geld ausgegeben wird/was ihre Kinder machen; **to lose ~ (of sth)** etw nicht mehr in der Hand haben, (*über etw acc*) die Gewalt *or* Herrschaft verlieren; *of business* die Kontrolle (*über etw acc*) verlieren; *of car* die Kontrolle *or* Herrschaft (*über etw acc*) verlieren; **to lose ~ of oneself** die Beherrschung verlieren; **to lose ~ of the situation** nicht mehr Herr der Lage sein; **to keep ~ (of oneself)** sich unter Kontrolle halten; **to be/get out of ~** (*child, class*) außer Rand und Band sein/geraten; (*situation*) außer Kontrolle sein/geraten; (*car*) nicht mehr zu halten sein; (*inflation, prices, disease, pollution*) sich jeglicher Kontrolle (*dat*) entziehen/nicht mehr zu halten *or* zu bremsen (*inf*) sein; (*fire*) nicht unter Kontrolle sein/außer Kontrolle geraten; **the car spun out of ~** der Wagen begann sich ganz unkontrollierbar zu drehen; **under state ~** unter staatlicher Kontrolle *or* Aufsicht; **to bring** *or* **get sth under ~** etw unter Kontrolle bringen; *situation* Herr einer Sache (*gen*) werden; *car* etw in seine Gewalt bringen; **to be under ~** unter Kontrolle sein; (*children, class*) sich benehmen; (*car*) (wieder) lenkbar sein; **everything** *or* **the situation is under ~** wir/sie *etc* haben die Sache im Griff (*inf*); **the situation was beyond their ~** die Sache war ihnen völlig aus der Hand geglitten, sie hatten die Sache nicht mehr in der Hand; **he was beyond his parents' ~** er war seinen Eltern über den Kopf gewachsen; **circumstances beyond our** ~ nicht in unserer Hand liegende Umstände

b (= *check*) Kontrolle *f* (*on* +*gen*, über +*acc*); **wage/price ~s** Lohn-/Preiskontrolle *f*

c (= *control room*) die Zentrale; (*Aviat*) der Kontrollturm

d (= *knob, switch*) Regler *m*; (*of vehicle, machine*) Schalter *m*; **to be at the ~s** (*of spaceship, airliner*) am Kontrollpult sitzen; (*of small plane, car*) die Steuerung haben; **to take over the ~s** die Steuerung übernehmen

e (*Sci*, = *person*) Kontrollperson *f*; (= *animal*) Kontrolltier *nt*; (= *group*) Kontrollgruppe *f*

f (*Spiritualism*) *Geist einer Persönlichkeit, dessen Äußerungen das Medium wiedergibt*

g (*Comput*) **~-F1** Control-F1

VT **a** (= *direct, manage*) kontrollieren; *business* führen, leiten, unter sich (*dat*) haben; *sea* beherrschen; *organization* in der Hand haben; *animal, child, class* fertig werden mit; *car* steuern, lenken; *traffic* regeln; *emotions, movements* beherrschen, unter Kontrolle halten; *hair* bändigen; **to ~ oneself/one's temper** sich beherrschen; ~ **yourself!** nimm dich zusammen!; **please try to ~ your children/dog** bitte sehen Sie zu, dass sich Ihre Kinder benehmen/sich Ihr Hund benimmt

b (= *regulate, check*) *prices, rents, growth etc* kontrollieren; *temperature, speed* regulieren; *disease* unter Kontrolle bringen; *population* eindämmen, im Rahmen halten

control: **control centre**, (*US*) **control center** N Kontrollzentrum *nt*; **control character** N (*Comput*) Steuerzeichen *nt*; **control column** N Steuersäule *f* (*form*), Steuerknüppel *m*; **control desk** N Steuer- or Schaltpult *nt*; (*TV, Rad*) Regiepult *nt*; **control experiment** N Kontrollversuch *m*; **control freak** N (*inf*) **most men are total ~s** die meisten Männer müssen immer alles unter Kontrolle haben; **control group** N (*Med, Psych*) Kontrollgruppe *f*; **control key** N (*Comput*) Steuerungstaste *f*; **control knob** N (*on TV etc*) Kontrollknopf *m*

controllable [kən'trəʊləbl] ADJ kontrollierbar, zu kontrollieren *pred*; *child, animal* lenkbar

controlled [kən'trəʊld] ADJ *emotion, movement, voice* beherrscht; *passion* gezügelt; *conditions, rent* kontrolliert; *prices* gebunden; *temperature* geregelt; ~ **drugs** or **substances** verschreibungspflichtige Medikamente *pl*

controller [kən'trəʊlə'] N **a** (= *director, Rad*) Intendant(in) *m(f)*; (*Aviat*) (Flug)lotse *m*, (Flug-)lotsin *f* **b** (= *financial head*) Leiter *m* des Finanzwesens

control: **control lever** N (*Mot, Tech*) Schalthebel *m*; (*Aviat*) Steuerknüppel *m*; **control light** N Kontrolllampe *f*

controlling [kən'trəʊlɪŋ] ADJ *attr factor* beherrschend; *body* Aufsichts-; ~ **interest** Mehrheitsanteil *m*

control: **control measures** PL Überwachungsmaßnahmen *pl*; **control panel** N Schalttafel *f*, Schaltblende *f*; (*on aircraft, TV*) Bedienungsfeld *nt*; (*on machine*) Steuer- or Bedienungs- or Betriebspult *nt*; (*on car*) Armaturenbrett *nt*; **control point** N Kontrollpunkt *m*, Kontrollstelle *f*; **control rod** N Regelstab *m*; **control room** N Kontrollraum *m*; (*Naut also*) Kommandoraum *m*; (*Mil*) (Operations)zentrale *f*; (*of police*) Zentrale *f*; **control stick** N = **control column**; **control tower** N (*Aviat*) Kontrollturm *m*; **control unit** N (*Comput*) Steuerwerk *nt*, Steuereinheit *f*

controversial [ˌkɒntrə'vɜːʃəl] ADJ *speech, person, figure etc* kontrovers; (= *debatable*) *matter, decision also* umstritten, strittig; **it is still ~ whether ...** es ist immer noch umstritten, ob ...; **he is deliberately ~** er gibt sich bewusst kontrovers

controversially [ˌkɒntrə'vɜːʃəlɪ] ADV kontroverserweise; **more ~, he claims that ...** er behauptet, was noch umstrittener ist, dass ...

controversy [ˈkɒntrəvɜːsɪ, kən'trɒvəsɪ] N Kontroversen *pl*, Streit *m*; **there was a lot of ~ about it** es gab deswegen große Kontroversen or Differenzen; **to lead to ~** Anlass zu Kontrover-

sen geben; **statements/facts that are beyond ~** völlig unumstrittene Behauptungen/Tatsachen

controvert [ˈkɒntrəvɜːt] VT (*form*) anfechten, bestreiten

contumacious [ˌkɒntjʊ'meɪʃəs] ADJ (*form*) verstockt; (= *insubordinate*) rebellisch

contumaciously [ˌkɒntjʊ'meɪʃəslɪ] ADV (*form*) verstockt; (= *insubordinately*) rebellisch

contumacy [ˈkɒntjʊməsɪ] N (*form*) Verstocktheit *f*; (= *insubordination*) Gehorsamsverweigerung *f*

contumely [ˈkɒntjʊmɪlɪ] N , *no pl* (*form*, = *abuse*) Schmähen *nt* (*geh*); (= *insult*) Schmähung *f* (*geh*)

contuse [kən'tjuːz] VT (*form*) quetschen, prellen

contusion [kən'tjuːʒən] N Quetschung *f*, Kontusion *f* (*spec*)

conundrum [kə'nʌndrəm] N (*lit, fig*) Rätsel *nt*

conurbation [ˌkɒnɜː'beɪʃən] N Ballungsgebiet *nt* or -raum *m* or -zentrum *nt*, Conurbation *f* (*spec*)

convalesce [ˌkɒnvə'les] VI genesen (*from, after* von); **while convalescing** während der Genesung(szeit)

convalescence [ˌkɒnvə'lesəns] N Genesung *f*; (= *period*) Genesungszeit *f*

convalescent [ˌkɒnvə'lesənt] **N** Rekonvaleszent(in) *m(f)* (*form*), Genesende(r) *mf* **ADJ** genesend; **to be ~** auf dem Wege der Besserung sein

convalescent home N Genesungsheim *nt*

convection [kən'vekʃən] N Konvektion *f*

convector [kən'vektə'] N (*also* **convector heater**) Heizlüfter *m*

convene [kən'viːn] **VT** *meeting* einberufen; *group of people* zusammenrufen, versammeln **VI** zusammenkommen, sich versammeln; (*parliament, court*) zusammentreten

convener [kən'viːnə'] N *Person, die Versammlungen einberuft* (*Brit, Ind*) Gewerkschaftsvertreter(in) *m(f)* (*der für die Vetrauensleute in einem Betrieb zuständig ist*)

convenience [kən'viːnɪəns] N **a** *no pl* (= *usefulness, advantageousness*) Annehmlichkeit *f*; (= *functionalness*) Zweckmäßigkeit *f*; **for the sake of ~** aus praktischen Gründen

b *no pl* **for your ~** zum gefälligen Gebrauch; **these chairs are for the ~ of customers** diese Stühle sind für unsere Kunden gedacht; **I'm not changing it for** or **to suit his ~** ich werde es seinetwegen or nur um es ihm recht zu machen nicht ändern; **he did not find that date to his ~** der Termin passte ihm nicht or kam ihm nicht gelegen; **at your own ~** zu einem Ihnen angenehmen Zeitpunkt, wann es Ihnen passt (*inf*); **at your earliest ~** (*Comm*) möglichst bald, baldmöglichst (*form*)

c (= *convenient thing, amenity*) Annehmlichkeit *f*; **a house with all modern ~s** ein Haus mit allem modernen Komfort

d (*Brit, form*, = *public convenience*) (öffentliche) Toilette, Bedürfnisanstalt *f* (*dated form*)

convenience foods PL Fertiggerichte *pl*

convenient [kən'viːnɪənt] ADJ (= *useful, functional*) zweckmäßig, praktisch; *area, house* (*for shops etc*) günstig gelegen; *time* günstig, passend; **at a more ~ time** zu einem passenderen or günstigeren Zeitpunkt; **if it is ~** wenn es Ihnen (so) passt; **if it is ~ to** or **for you** wenn es Ihnen (so) passt, wenn es Ihnen keine Umstände macht; **a time ~ for all of us** ein Ort, der/eine Zeit, die uns allen passt or für uns alle günstig ist; **is tomorrow ~ (to** or **for you)?** passt (es) Ihnen morgen?, geht es morgen?; **he sat down on a ~ chair** er setzte sich auf den Stuhl, der gerade da stand; **the trams are very ~** (= *nearby*) die Straßenbahnhaltestellen liegen sehr günstig; (= *useful*) die Straßenbahn ist sehr praktisch; **a ~ place to stop** eine geeignete or günstige Stelle zum Anhalten; **is there a ~ train?** gibt es einen geeigneten or passenden Zug?; **her resignation was most ~ (for him)** ihr

Rücktritt kam (ihm) äußerst gelegen; **how ~!** sehr günstig!

conveniently [kən'viːnɪəntlɪ] ADV günstigerweise; *situated* günstig, vorteilhaft; (= *usefully*) *designed* praktisch, zweckmäßig; **he very ~ arrived home early** er kam früh nach Hause, was äußerst günstig war; **it ~ started to rain** wie bestellt, fing es an zu regnen; **the house is ~ close to the shops** das Haus liegt in praktischer Nähe der Läden; **he ~ forgot to post the letter** (*iro*) er hat praktischerweise vergessen, den Brief aufzugeben

convent [ˈkɒnvənt] N (Frauen)kloster *nt*; **to enter a ~** ins Kloster gehen

convention [kən'venʃən] N **a** Brauch *m*, Sitte *f*; (= *social rule*) Konvention *f*; ~ **requires** or **demands that ...** die Sitte or der Brauch will es so, dass ...; **it's a ~ that ...** es ist so üblich or Sitte or Brauch, dass ...; **it's a social ~** es ist gesellschaftlicher Brauch; (= *point of etiquette*) es ist eine gesellschaftliche Konvention; **a disregard for ~** eine Missachtung der Konventionen **b** (= *agreement*) Abkommen *nt* **c** (= *conference*) Tagung *f*, Konferenz *f*; (*Pol*) Versammlung *f*

conventional [kən'venʃənl] ADJ *dress, attitudes, warfare, weapons* konventionell; *person, behaviour also* konventionsgebunden; *philosophy, beliefs, theory, manner, technique* herkömmlich; *theatre, music, style* traditionell; *symbol, mealtimes* normalerweise üblich; **it is ~ to do sth** es ist normalerweise üblich, etw zu tun; ~ **medicine** konventionelle Medizin; **in the ~ sense** im herkömmlichen Sinn

Conventional Forces in Europe PL konventionelle Streitkräfte *pl* in Europa

conventionality [kən,venʃə'nælɪtɪ] N (*of dress, attitudes*) Konventionalität *f*; (*of person, behaviour also*) Konventionsgebundenheit *f*; (*of philosophy, beliefs, theory, manner, technique*) Herkömmlichkeit *f*; (*of theatre, music, style*) traditionelle Art

conventionally [kən'venʃnəlɪ] ADV *dress, behave, live* konventionell; *written, built, designed* traditionell; ~ **one would be expected to ...** herkömmlicherweise würde erwartet, dass man ...

convention centre, (*US*) **convention center** N Tagungszentrum *nt*, Kongresszentrum *nt*

conventioneer [kən,venʃə'nɪə'] N (*esp US*) Konferenzteilnehmer(in) *m(f)*

convent school N Klosterschule *f*

converge [kən'vɜːdʒ] VI (*roads, lines*) zusammenlaufen (*at in* or *an* +*dat*); (*rivers also*) zusammenströmen (*at in* or *an* +*dat*); (*Math, Phys*) konvergieren (*at in* +*dat*); (*fig, views etc*) sich aneinander annähern, konvergieren (*geh*); **to ~ on sb/sth/New York** von überallher zu jdm/etw/nach New York strömen

convergence [kən'vɜːdʒəns] N (*of roads, lines*) Zusammenlaufen *nt*; (*of rivers also*) Zusammenströmen *nt*; (*Math, Phys*) Konvergenz *f*; (*fig, of views etc*) Annäherung *f*; **point of ~** Schnittpunkt *m*; (*of rays*) Brennpunkt *m*; (*of rivers*) Zusammenfluss *m*

convergent [kən'vɜːdʒənt], **converging** [kən'vɜːdʒɪŋ] ADJ *roads, lines* zusammenlaufend; *rivers also* zusammenströmend; (*Math, Phys*) konvergent (*form*), konvergierend; (*fig*) *views etc* sich (aneinander) annähernd

conversant [kən'vɜːsənt] ADJ *pred* ~ **with sth** mit etw vertraut

conversation [ˌkɒnvə'seɪʃən] N Gespräch *nt*, Unterhaltung *f*; (*Sch*) Konversation *f*; **to make ~** sich unterhalten; (= *small talk*) Konversation machen; **to get into/be in ~ with sb** mit jdm ins Gespräch kommen/im Gespräch sein; **deep in ~** ins Gespräch vertieft; **to have a ~/several ~s with sb (about sth)** sich mit jdm/mehrmals mit jdm (über etw *acc*) unterhalten; **he has no ~** mit ihm kann man sich nicht unterhalten; **his ~ is so amusing** er ist ein unterhaltsamer Gesprächspartner; **a subject of ~** ein Gesprächsthema *nt*; **words used only in ~** Wörter, die nur in der gesprochenen Sprache gebraucht werden; **we only mentioned it in ~** wir haben das nur gesprächsweise erwähnt; **the art of ~** die Kunst der gepflegten Konversation or Unterhaltung

conversational [ˌkɒnvəˈseɪʃənl] ADJ *tone, style* Unterhaltungs-, Plauder-, leger; **~ German** gesprochenes Deutsch; **his tone was quiet and ~** er sagte es in ruhigem Gesprächston; **that gave him a ~ opening** das ermöglichte es ihm, sich in die Unterhaltung einzuschalten or (*to get talking*) eine Unterhaltung anzufangen

conversationalist [ˌkɒnvəˈseɪʃnəlɪst] N guter Unterhalter or Gesprächspartner, gute Unterhalterin or Gesprächspartnerin; **not much of a ~** nicht gerade ein Konversationsgenie

conversationally [ˌkɒnvəˈseɪʃnəlɪ] ADV *write* im Plauderton

conversation: conversation mode N (*Comput*) Dialogbetrieb *m*; **conversation piece** N Gesprächsgegenstand *m*; **conversation stopper** N **that was a real ~** das brachte die Unterhaltung zum Erliegen

converse¹ [kənˈvɜːs] VI (*form*) sich unterhalten, konversieren (*old*)

converse² [ˈkɒnvɜːs] ADJ umgekehrt; (*Logic also*) konvers (*spec*); *opinions etc* gegenteilig ◼ N (*= opposite*) Gegenteil *nt*; (*Logic*, *= proposition*) Umkehrung *f*, Konverse *f* (*spec*); **the ~ is true** das Gegenteil trifft zu; **quite the ~** ganz im Gegenteil

conversely [kɒnˈvɜːslɪ] ADV umgekehrt

conversion [kənˈvɜːʃən] N **a** (*= transformation*) Konversion *f* (*into* in +*acc*); (*Fin, Sci also*) Umwandlung *f*; (*of measures*) Umrechnung *f* (*into* in +*acc*); (*of van, caravan etc*) Umrüstung *f*, Umbau *m*; (*= model*) Spezialausführung *f*; (*of building*) Umbau *m* (*into* zu); (*of appliances*) Umstellung *f* (*to auf* +*acc*); **the attic flat is a ~** die Wohnung ist ein ausgebauter Dachstock; **~ table** Umrechnungstabelle *f* **b** (*Rel, fig*) Bekehrung *f*, Konversion *f* (*to* zu)

convert [ˈkɒnvɜːt] ◼ N (*lit, fig*) Bekehrte(r) *mf*; (*to another denomination*) Konvertit *m*; **to become a ~ to sth** (*lit, fig*) sich zu etw bekehren

◼ VT [kənˈvɜːt] **a** (*= transform*) konvertieren (*into* in +*acc*); (*Fin, Sci also*) umwandeln (*into* in +*acc*); (*Rugby*) verwandeln; *measures* umrechnen (*into* in +*acc*); *van, caravan etc* umrüsten, umbauen (*into* zu); *attic* ausbauen (*into* zu); *building* umbauen (*into* zu); *appliance* umstellen (*to auf* +*acc*); **a sofa that can be ~ed into a bed** ein Sofa, das sich in ein Bett verwandeln lässt; **most of the town has now been ~ed to natural gas** der größte Teil der Stadt ist jetzt auf Erdgas umgestellt

b (*Rel, fig*) bekehren (*to* zu); (*to another denomination*) konvertieren

◼ VI [kənˈvɜːt] sich verwandeln lassen (*into* in +*acc*)

converted [kənˈvɜːtɪd] ADJ *barn, chapel* umgebaut; *loft* ausgebaut → **preach**

converter [kənˈvɜːtəʳ] N (*Elec*) Konverter *m*; (*for AC/DC*) Stromgleichrichter *m*

convertibility [kənˌvɜːtəˈbɪlɪtɪ] N (*of currency*) Konvertierbarkeit *f*, Konvertibilität *f*; (*of appliances*) Umstellbarkeit *f*

convertible [kənˈvɜːtəbl] ADJ verwandelbar; *currency* konvertibel, konvertierbar; *car* mit aufklappbarem Verdeck; *appliances* umstellbar; **a ~ sofa** ein Sofa, das sich in ein Bett verwandeln lässt ◼ N (*= car*) Kabriolett *nt*, Kabrio *nt*

convex [kɒnˈveks] ADJ *lens, mirror* konvex, Konvex-

convexity [kɒnˈveksɪtɪ] N Konvexität *f*

convey [kənˈveɪ] VT **a** (*= transport*) befördern; *goods* spedieren; *water* leiten **b** (*= make known or felt*) *opinion, idea* vermitteln; (*= make understood*) *meaning* klarmachen; (*= transmit*) *message, order, best wishes* übermitteln, überbringen; **what does this poem/music ~ to you?** was sagt Ihnen dieses Gedicht/diese Musik?; **words cannot ~ what I feel** was ich empfinde, lässt sich nicht mit Worten ausdrücken; **try to ~ to him**

that he should ... versuchen Sie doch, ihm klarzumachen, dass er ... sollte **c** (*Jur*) *property* übertragen (*to auf* +*acc*)

conveyance [kənˈveɪəns] N **a** (*= transport*) Beförderung *f*; (*of goods also*) Spedition *f*; **~ of goods** Gütertransport *m*; **mode of ~** Beförderungsmittel *nt* **b** (*old, form, = vehicle*) Gefährt *nt* **c** (*Jur*) (Eigentums)übertragung *f* (*to auf* +*acc*); (*= document*) Übertragungsurkunde *f*

conveyancing [kənˈveɪənsɪŋ] N (*Jur*) (Eigentums)übertragung *f*

conveyor [kənˈveɪəʳ] N (*of message etc*) Überbringer(in) *m(f)*; (*Tech*) Förderer *m*

conveyor belt N Fließband *nt*; (*for transport, supply*) Förderband *nt*

conveyor-belt [kənˈveɪəbelt] ADJ (*fig*) Fließband-; **a ~ hospital** ein Krankenhaus, in dem die Patienten wie am Fließband abgefertigt werden

convict [ˈkɒnvɪkt] ◼ N Sträfling *m*, Zuchthäusler(in) *m(f)* ◼ VT [kənˈvɪkt] **a** (*Jur*) *person* verurteilen (*of* wegen), für schuldig erklären (*of* +*gen*); **a ~ed criminal** ein verurteilter Verbrecher, eine verurteilte Verbrecherin; **to get sb ~ed** jds Verurteilung (*acc*) bewirken **b** (*actions etc: = betray*) überführen; **to stand ~ed by one's own actions** durch sein Handeln überführt werden ◼ VI [kənˈvɪkt] jdn verurteilen; **the jury refused to ~** die Geschworenen lehnten es ab, einen Schuldspruch zu fällen

conviction [kənˈvɪkʃən] N **a** (*Jur*) Verurteilung *f*; **five previous ~s** fünf Vorstrafen; **to get a ~** (*police, prosecution*) einen Schuldspruch erreichen **b** (*= belief, act of convincing*) Überzeugung *f*; **to be open to ~** sich gern eines Besseren belehren lassen; **to carry ~** überzeugend klingen; **his speech lacked ~** seine Rede klang wenig überzeugend; **he's a socialist by ~** er ist ein überzeugter Sozialist; **he did it in the ~ that ...** er tat es in der Überzeugung, dass ...; **a man of strong ~s** ein Mann, der feste Anschauungen vertritt; **his fundamental political/moral ~s** seine politische/moralische Gesinnung → **courage**

convince [kənˈvɪns] ◎ 6.2, 15.1, 26.2 VT überzeugen; **I'm trying to ~ him that ...** ich versuche, ihn davon zu überzeugen, dass ...

convinced [kənˈvɪnst] ADJ überzeugt

convincing ADJ , **convincingly** ADV [kənˈvɪnsɪŋ, -lɪ] ◎ 26.1, 26.3 überzeugend

convivial [kənˈvɪvɪəl] ADJ heiter und unbeschwert; *person also* fröhlich; (*= sociable*) gesellig

conviviality [kənˌvɪvɪˈælɪtɪ] N unbeschwerte Heiterkeit *f*; (*of person*) Fröhlichkeit *f*; (*= sociability*) Geselligkeit *f*

convocation [ˌkɒnvəˈkeɪʃən] N (*form, = calling together*) Einberufung *f*; (*= meeting, Eccl*) Versammlung *f*

convoke [kənˈvəʊk] VT *meeting* einberufen; (*Parl also*) zusammentreten lassen

convolute [ˈkɒnvəluːt] ADJ *shell* spiralig aufgewunden; *petal, leaf* eingerollt

convoluted [ˌkɒnvəˈluːtɪd] ADJ **a** (*= involved*) verwickelt; *plot also* verschlungen; *theory also* kompliziert; *style* gewunden **b** (*= coiled*) gewunden; *shell* spiralig aufgewunden

convolution [ˌkɒnvəˈluːʃən] N *usu pl* (*= coil*) Windung *f*; (*of plot*) Verschlungenheit *f no pl*; (*of style*) Gewundenheit *f*; (*of theory*) Kompliziertheit *f*

convolvulus [kənˈvɒlvjʊləs] N Winde *f*

convoy [ˈkɒnvɔɪ] ◼ N **a** (*= escort*) Konvoi *m*, Geleit *nt*; **under ~** mit Geleitschutz, unter Konvoi; **one of our ~ was torpedoed** eines unserer Geleitboote or Begleitboote wurde torpediert; **to be on ~ duty** als Geleitschutz abgeordnet sein **b** (*vehicles under escort, ships*) Konvoi *m*; (*= ships also*) Verband *m*; **in ~** im Konvoi/Verband ◼ VT Geleitschutz geben (+*dat*), begleiten; **the ships were ~ed across** die Schiffe wurden unter Konvoi hinübergebracht

convulse [kənˈvʌls] VT (*earthquake, war etc*) *land* erschüttern; (*fig also*) erschüttern; *muscles* krampfhaft zusammenziehen; **to be ~d with laughter/in pain** sich vor Lachen schütteln/vor Schmerzen winden; **a face ~d with rage** ein vor Wut verzerrtes Gesicht; **a joke which ~d the audience** ein Witz, bei dem sich das Publikum vor Lachen bog

convulsion [kənˈvʌlʃən] N **a** (*Med*) Schüttelkrampf *m no pl*, Konvulsion *f* (*spec*); (*of crying*) Weinkrampf *m no pl* **b** (*caused by social upheaval etc*) Erschütterung *f* **c** (*inf, of laughter*) **to go into/be in ~s** sich biegen or schütteln vor Lachen; **he had the audience in ~s** er rief beim Publikum wahre Lachstürme hervor

convulsive [kənˈvʌlsɪv] ADJ konvulsiv(isch) (*spec*), Krampf-; *movement also* krampfhaft; **~ laughter** Lachkrämpfe *pl*

convulsively [kənˈvʌlsɪvlɪ] ADV krampfartig; **she sobbed ~** sie wurde von Schluchzern geschüttelt

cony, coney [ˈkəʊnɪ] N **a** (*US*) Kaninchen *nt* **b** (*also* **cony skin**) Kaninchenfell *nt*

coo [kuː] ◼ VI (*pigeon, fig*) gurren ◼ VT gurren, girren ◼ N Gurren *nt*, Girren *nt* ◼ INTERJ (*Brit, inf*) ui

cooee [ˈkuːiː] ◼ INTERJ huhu ◼ VI huhu rufen

cook [kʊk] ◼ N Koch *m*, Köchin *f*; **she is a good ~/very plain ~** sie kocht gut/einfache Kost; **too many ~s (spoil the broth)** (*Prov*) viele Köche verderben den Brei (*Prov*); **to be chief ~ and bottle-washer** (*inf: = dogsbody*) (das) Mädchen für alles sein (*inf*)

◼ VT **a** *food, meal* machen, zubereiten; (*in water, milk etc*) kochen; (*= fry, roast*) braten; *pie, pancake also* backen; **how are you going to ~ the duck?** wie willst du die Ente zubereiten?; **a ~ed meal/supper** eine warme Mahlzeit/ein warmes Abendessen; **a ~ed breakfast** ein Frühstück *nt* mit warmen Gerichten; **to ~ sb's/one's goose** (*fig inf*) jdm/sich die Tour vermasseln (*inf*); **our goose is ~ed** (*fig inf*) wir sitzen in der Tinte (*inf*)

b (*inf, = falsify*) *accounts* frisieren (*inf*)

◼ VI (*person, food*) kochen; (*= fry, roast*) braten; (*pie*) backen; **it will ~ quickly** das ist schnell gekocht; **the pie takes half an hour to ~** die Pastete ist in einer halben Stunde fertig; **what's ~ing?** (*fig inf*) was ist los?

▶ **cook up** VT *sep* (*fig inf*) *story, excuse* sich (*dat*) einfallen lassen, zurechtbasteln (*inf*); **cooked-up story** Lügenmärchen *nt*

cookbook [ˈkʊkbʊk] N Kochbuch *nt*

cooker [ˈkʊkəʳ] N **a** (*esp Brit, = stove*) Herd *m* **b** (*= apple*) Kochapfel *m*

cooker hood N (*Brit*) Abzugshaube *f*

cookery [ˈkʊkərɪ] N Kochen *nt* (*also Sch*), Kochkunst *f*; **French ~** französische Küche; **~ classes** Kochkurs *m*, Kochkurse *pl*

cookery book N Kochbuch *nt*

cookhouse [ˈkʊkhaʊs] N (*Naut*) Kombüse *f*; (*Mil*) Feldküche *f*

cookie, cooky [ˈkʊkɪ] N **a** (*US, = biscuit*) Keks *m*, Plätzchen *nt*; **that's the way the ~ crumbles** (*inf: also Brit*) so ist das nun mal (im Leben), das ist der Lauf der Welt or der Dinge; **to get caught with one's hands in the ~ jar** (*fig inf*) ertappt werden (*inf*) **b** (*inf, = smart person*) Typ *m*; **he's a pretty tough ~** er ist ein ziemlich zäher Typ; **smart ~** cleveres Köpfchen

cookie cutter (*US*) ◼ N (*Cook*) Ausstechform *f* ◼ ADJ (*fig inf*) einfallslos

cooking [ˈkʊkɪŋ] N Kochen *nt*; (*= food*) Essen *nt*; **plain ~** einfaches Essen, Hausmannskost *f*; **French ~** die französische Küche, französisches Essen; **his ~ is atrocious** er kocht miserabel

cooking *in cpds* Koch-; **cooking apple** N Kochapfel *m*; **cooking chocolate** N Blockschokolade *f*; **cooking facilities** PL Kochgelegenheit *f*; **cooking foil** N Backfolie *f*; **cooking salt** N Kochsalz *nt*

cook: cook-off N (*US*) Kochwettbewerb *m*; **cookout** N (*US*) Kochen *nt* am Lagerfeuer;

(*on barbeque*) Grillparty *f*; **cookware** N Kochgeschirr *nt*, Töpfe und Pfannen *pl*

cooky N = cookie

cool [kuːl] ADJ (+er) **a** *water, weather, drink* kühl; *clothes* luftig, leicht; **serve ~** kalt *or* (gut) gekühlt servieren; **it's nice to slip into something ~** es ist angenehm, in etwas Luftiges *or* Leichtes schlüpfen zu können; **"keep in a ~ place"** „kühl aufbewahren" **b** (= *calm, unperturbed*) *person, manner* besonnen; *voice* kühl; **to keep ~**, **to keep a ~ head** einen kühlen Kopf behalten; **keep ~!** reg dich nicht auf!, (nur) ruhig Blut!; **as ~ as you please** mit kühler Gelassenheit, in aller Seelenruhe **c** (= *audacious*) kaltblütig, unverfroren (*pej*), kaltschnäuzig (*inf*); **as ~ as you please** mit größter Unverfrorenheit (*pej*), seelenruhig; **that was very ~ of him** da hat er sich ein starkes Stück geleistet; **a ~ customer** (*inf*) ein cooler Typ (*inf*) **d** (= *unenthusiastic, unfriendly*) *greeting, reception, look* kühl; **to be ~ to(wards)** sb jdm gegenüber kühl verhalten; **play it ~!** immer mit der Ruhe!; **she decided to play it ~** sie entschied sich, ganz cool kühl zu machen **e** *colour* kalt; **~ green** kaltes Grün **f** (*inf, with numbers etc*) glatt (*inf*); **he earns a ~ thirty thousand a year** er verdient glatte dreißigtausend im Jahr (*inf*) **g** (*inf, = great, smart*) *idea, disco, pub, dress etc* stark (*inf*), cool (*sl*); **to act ~** sich cool geben (*sl*); **to look ~** cool aussehen (*sl*) **N a** (*lit, fig*) Kühle *f*; **in the ~ of the evening** in der Abendkühle; **to keep sth in the ~** etw kühl aufbewahren **b** (*inf*) **keep your ~!** reg dich nicht auf!, immer mit der Ruhe!; **to lose one's ~** durchdrehen (*inf*); **he doesn't have the ~ to be a TV announcer** er hat nicht die Nerven für einen Fernsehansager **VT a** kühlen; (= *cool down*) abkühlen; *wine* kühlen, kalt stellen **b** (*inf*) **~ it!** (= *don't get excited*) reg dich ab! (*inf*), mach mal langsam (*inf*); (= *don't cause trouble*) mach keinen Ärger! (*inf*); **tell those guys to ~ it** sag den Typen, sie sollen keinen Ärger machen (*inf*); **I think we should ~ it** ich glaube wir sollten etwas langsamer treten (*inf*) **VI** (*lit, fig*) abkühlen; (*anger*) verrauchen, sich legen; (*enthusiasm, interest*) nachlassen; **he has ~ed toward(s) her** er ist ihr gegenüber kühler geworden

▶ **cool down VI a** (*lit*) abkühlen; (*weather also, person*) sich abkühlen **b** (*feelings etc*) sich abkühlen; (*anger also*) verrauchen; (*critical situation, person:* = *calm down*) sich beruhigen; **look, just cool down will you!** komm, reg dich (bloß wieder) ab! (*inf*); **to let things cool down** die Sache etwas ruhen lassen **VT** *sep a food, drink* abkühlen; (= *let cool down*) abkühlen lassen; **to cool oneself down** sich abkühlen **b** *situation* beruhigen; **put him in a cell, that'll cool him down** steck ihn in eine Zelle, dann wird er sich schon wieder beruhigen

▶ **cool off VI a** (*liquid, food*) abkühlen; (*person*) sich abkühlen **b** (*fig*) (sich) abkühlen; (*enthusiasm, interest*) nachlassen; (= *become less angry*) sich beruhigen; (= *become less friendly*) kühler werden (*about or towards sb* jdm gegenüber)

coolant ['kuːlənt] N Kühlmittel *nt*

cool: cool bag N Kühltasche *f*; **cool box** N Kühlbox *f*

cooler ['kuːlə'] N **a** (*for milk etc*) Kühlapparat *m*; (*for wine*) Kühler *m* **b** (*inf, = prison*) Bau *m* (*inf*)

cool-headed [kuːl'hedɪd] ADJ kühl (und besonnen)

coolie ['kuːlɪ] N (*pej*) Kuli *m*

cooling ['kuːlɪŋ] ADJ *drink, shower* kühlend; *effect* (ab)kühlend; *affection* abnehmend; *enthusiasm, interest* nachlassend; **~ fan** Lüfter *m*

cooling-off ['kuːlɪŋ'ɒf] N (*in relationship etc*) Abkühlung *f*; **there's been a distinct ~ (of interest) about this project** das Interesse an diesem Projekt hat merklich nachgelassen

cooling-off period N **a** (*gesetzlich festgelegter*) *Zeitraum für Schlichtungsverhandlungen (bei Arbeitskämpfen)* **b** (*in relationship etc*) Zeit *f* zur Abkühlung

cooling tower N Kühlturm *m*

cool jazz N Cooljazz *m*, Cool Jazz *m*

coolly ['kuːlɪ] ADV **a** (= *calmly*) ruhig, gefasst, besonnen **b** (= *unenthusiastically, in an unfriendly way*) kühl **c** (= *audaciously*) kaltblütig, unverfroren (*pej*), kaltschnäuzig (*inf*)

coolness ['kuːlnɪs] N **a** (*of water, weather, drink*) Kühle *f*; (*of clothes*) Luftigkeit *f*, Leichtigkeit *f* **b** (= *calmness, of person, manner*) Besonnenheit *f*; (*of voice*) Kühle *f* **c** (= *audacity, impudence*) Kaltblütigkeit *f*, Unverfrorenheit *f* (*pej*), Kaltschnäuzigkeit *f* (*inf*) **d** (= *unfriendliness: of greeting, reception, look*) Kühle *f*

coomb [kuːm] N Tal(mulde *f*) *nt*

coon [kuːn] N **a** (*Zool*) Waschbär *m* **b** (*pej sl*) Nigger *m* (*pej*)

coop [kuːp] N (*also* **hen coop**) Hühnerstall *m*; **to fly the ~** (*fig inf*) sich aus dem Staub machen (*inf*)

▶ **coop up** VT *sep person* einsperren; *several people* zusammenpferchen (*inf*)

co-op ['kəʊ'ɒp] N (= *society*) Genossenschaft *f*; (= *shop*) Coop *m*, Konsum *m*

cooper ['kuːpə'] N Böttcher *m*, Küfer *m* (*dial*)

cooperate [kəʊ'ɒpəreɪt] VI kooperieren, zusammenarbeiten; (= *go along with, not be awkward*) mitmachen; **to ~ toward(s) a common end** auf ein gemeinsames Ziel hinarbeiten; **even the weather ~d in making it a day to remember** auch das Wetter trug dazu bei, es zu einem denkwürdigen Tag zu machen; **if the weather ~s** wenn das Wetter mitmacht

cooperation [kəʊˌɒpə'reɪʃən] N Kooperation *f*, Zusammenarbeit *f*; (= *help*) Mitarbeit *f*, Kooperation *f*; **we produced this model in ~ with ...** wir haben dieses Modell in Gemeinschaftsarbeit *or* Kooperation *or* gemeinsam mit ... produziert; **to increase ~ between EC countries** um die Kooperation *or* Zusammenarbeit zwischen EG-Ländern zu fördern; **with the ~ of all members then ...** wenn alle Mitglieder mitmachen, dann ...

cooperative [kəʊ'ɒpərətɪv] ADJ **a** (= *prepared to comply*) kooperativ; (= *prepared to help*) hilfsbereit; **if any member does not have a ~ attitude** wenn ein Mitglied nicht bereit ist mitzumachen **b** *firm* auf Genossenschaftsbasis; **~ farm** Bauernhof *m* auf Genossenschaftsbasis **N** Genossenschaft *f*, Kooperative *f*; (*also* **cooperative farm**) Bauernhof *m* auf Genossenschaftsbasis

cooperative bank N (*US*) Genossenschaftsbank *f*

cooperatively [kəʊ'ɒpərətɪvlɪ] ADV (= *jointly*) gemeinsam; (= *obligingly*) hilfsbereit; **to work ~ with sb** mit jdm zusammenarbeiten

cooperative society N Genossenschaft *f*, Kooperative *f*

coopt [kəʊ'ɒpt] VT selbst (hinzu)wählen, kooptieren (*spec*); **he was ~ed onto the committee** er wurde vom Komitee selbst dazugewählt

coordinate [kəʊ'ɔːdnɪt] ADJ gleichwertig; (*in rank*) gleichrangig; (*Gram*) nebengeordnet (*with zu*); **~** (*Math etc*) Koordinate *f*; (= *equal*) etwas Gleichwertiges; **~s** (= *clothes*) Kleidung *f* zum Kombinieren **VT** [kəʊ'ɔːdɪneɪt] **a** *movements, muscles, pieces of work* koordinieren; (*two people, firms*) operations *etc also* aufeinander abstimmen; *thoughts also* ordnen; **to ~ one thing with another** eine Sache auf eine andere abstimmen **b** (*Gram*) nebenordnen, koordinieren; **coordinating conjunction** nebenordnende *or* koordinierende Konjunktion

coordinated [kəʊ'ɔːdɪneɪtɪd] ADJ **a** *person, action, effort, approach, operation* koordiniert; **to be badly ~** (*person*) eine Koordinationsschwäche haben **b** (= *matching*) *clothes, designs* aufeinander abgestimmt; **colour-coordinated** (*clothes*) farblich aufeinander abgestimmt

coordinate geometry [kəʊ'ɔːdnɪt-] N (*Math*) analytische Geometrie

coordination [kəʊˌɔːdɪ'neɪʃən] N Koordination *f*, Koordinierung *f*; **in ~ with** in Abstimmung mit; **to have little** *or* **no ~** eine Koordinationsstörung haben

coordinator [kəʊ'ɔːdɪneɪtə'] N Koordinator(in) *m(f)*; (*Gram*) koordinierende *or* nebenordnende Konjunktion

coot [kuːt] N Wasserhuhn *nt*; **bald as a ~** völlig kahl; **to be as bald as a ~** eine Platte haben (*inf*)

cootie ['kuːtɪ] N (*US, inf*) Laus *f*

co-owner ['kəʊ'əʊnə'] N Mitbesitzer(in) *m(f)*, Miteigentümer(in) *m(f)*

co-ownership ['kəʊ'əʊnəʃɪp] N Mitbesitz *m*

cop [kɒp] **N a** (*inf, = policeman*) Polizist(in) *m(f)*, Bulle *m* (*pej inf*); **to play ~s and robbers** Räuber und Gendarm spielen **b** (*Brit, inf, = arrest*) **it's a fair ~** jetzt hats mich erwischt (*inf*) **c** (*Brit, inf*) **it's not much ~** das ist nichts Besonderes **VT** (*inf, = catch*) *sb* schnappen (*inf*), erwischen (*inf*); *clout, thump* fangen (*inf*); **he ~ped one right on the nose** er fing eine genau auf der Nase (*inf*); **when they found out he didn't have a licence he really ~ped it** (*Brit*) als sie herausfanden, dass er keinen Führerschein hatte, war er dran (*inf*); **hey, ~ a load of this!** he, hör dir das mal an! (*inf*)

▶ **cop out** VI (*inf*) aussteigen (*inf*) (*of aus*)

copartner ['kəʊ'pɑːtnə'] N Teilhaber(in) *m(f)*, Partner *m*

copartnership ['kəʊ'pɑːtnəʃɪp] N Teilhaberschaft *f*, Partnerschaft *f*

copayment [kəʊ'peɪmənt] N (*US*) Zuzahlung *f* (*zu Medikamenten etc*)

cope¹ [kəʊp] N **a** (*Eccl*) Pluviale *nt* **b** (*Archit*) = coping

cope² [kəʊp] VI zurechtkommen; (*with work*) es schaffen; **to ~ with** (*problems, children, difficult person*) fertig werden mit, zurechtkommen mit; **how do you ~ all by yourself?** wie werden Sie so allein fertig?, wie kommen Sie so allein zurecht?; **I can't ~ with all this work** ich bin mit all der Arbeit überfordert; **she can't ~ with the stairs any more** sie schafft die Treppe nicht mehr

Copenhagen [ˌkəʊpn'heɪgən] N Kopenhagen *nt*

Copernican [kə'pɜːnɪkən] ADJ kopernikanisch

Copernicus [kə'pɜːnɪkəs] N Kopernikus *m*

copestone ['kəʊpstəʊn] N **a** (*Archit*) Abdeckplatte *f* **b** (*fig, of career etc*) Krönung *f*; (*of theory*) Schlussstein *m*

copier ['kɒpɪə'] N (= *copyist*) Kopist(in) *m(f)*; (= *imitator also*) Nachmacher(in) *m(f)*; (*of writer, painter also*) Imitator(in) *m(f)*; (= *machine*) Kopiergerät *nt*, Kopierer *m* (*inf*)

co-pilot ['kəʊpaɪlət] N Kopilot(in) *m(f)*

coping ['kəʊpɪŋ] N (*Archit*) Mauerkrone *f*

coping: coping saw N Laubsäge *f*; **coping stone** N = copestone

copious ['kəʊpɪəs] ADJ *supply* groß, reichlich; *information, details, illustrations* zahlreich; *writer* fruchtbar; **~ amounts of sth** reichliche Mengen von etw *or* an etw (*dat*); **to weep ~ tears** Ströme *or* eine Flut von Tränen vergießen

copiously ['kəʊpɪəslɪ] ADV reichlich; **she wept ~** sie vergoss Ströme von Tränen

copiousness ['kəʊpɪəsnɪs] N (*of supply*) Größe *f*, Reichlichkeit *f*; (*of information, details*) Fülle *f*, Reichtum *m*; (*of writer*) Fruchtbarkeit *f*

cop-out ['kɒpaʊt] N (*inf, = going back on sth*) Rückzieher *m*; (= *deliberate evasion*) Ausweichmanöver *nt*; **this solution/translation is just a ~** diese Lösung/Übersetzung weicht dem Problem nur aus

copper ['kɒpə'] N **a** (= *metal*) Kupfer *nt*; **~ ore** Eisenerz *nt*; **~ sulphate** Kupfersulfat *nt*, Kupfervitriol *nt* **b** (= *colour*) Kupferrot *nt* (*esp Brit, inf, = coin*) Cent *m*; **~s** Kleingeld *nt* **d** (*inf, = policeman*) Polizist(in) *m(f)*, Bulle *m* (*pej inf*)

e (*for boiling clothes etc*) Kupferkessel *f*, Waschkessel *m*

copper: copper beech N Rotbuche *f*; **copper-bottomed** ADJ mit Kupferboden; (*Fin, fig*) gesund; **copper-coloured** ADJ kupferfarben; **copper mine** N Kupfermine *f*; **coppernob** N (*inf*) Rotkopf *m* (*inf*); **copperplate** VT verkupfern N **a** (= *plate for engraving*) Kupferplatte *f*; (= *engraving*) Kupferstich *m* **b** (= *handwriting*) lateinische (Ausgangs)schrift ADJ ~ **engraving** Kupferstich *m*; (= *process also*) Kupferstechen *nt*; ~ **(hand)writing** lateinische (Ausgangs)schrift; **in your best ~ writing** in deiner besten Sonntagsschrift; **copper-plating** N Verkupferung *f*; **coppersmith** N Kupferschmied *m*

coppery ['kɒpərɪ] ADJ kupfern, kupferrot

coppice ['kɒpɪs] N = **copse**

copra ['kɒprə] N Kopra *f*

coprocessor ['kəʊ'prəʊsesə'] N (*Comput*) Koprozessor *m*; **maths ~** Arithmetikprozessor *m*

co-produce [ˌkəʊprə'djuːs] VT *film, album* koproduzieren

co-production [ˌkəʊprə'dʌkʃən] N Koproduktion *f*

coprophilia ['kɒprəfɪlɪə] N Koprophilie *f*

copse [kɒps] N Wäldchen *nt*

cop shop N (*Brit, inf*) Bullerei *f* (*sl*), Wache *f*

copter ['kɒptə'] N (*inf*) Hubschrauber *m*

Coptic ['kɒptɪk] ADJ koptisch

copula ['kɒpjʊlə] N Kopula *f*, Satzband *nt*

copulate ['kɒpjʊleɪt] VI kopulieren

copulation [ˌkɒpjʊ'leɪʃən] N Kopulation *f*

copulative ['kɒpjʊlətɪv] (*Gram*) N Kopula *f* ADJ kopulativ

copy ['kɒpɪ] N **a** Kopie *f* (*also Comput*); (*of document, separately written or typed also*) Abschrift *f*; (*typed carbon also*) Durchschlag *m*; (*handwritten carbon also*) Durchschrift *f*; (*Phot*) Abzug *m*; **to take** *or* **make a ~ of sth** eine Kopie/Zweitschrift *etc* von etw machen; **to write out a fair ~** etw ins Reine schreiben, eine Reinschrift herstellen

b (*of book etc*) Exemplar *nt*; **have you got a ~ of today's "Times"?** hast du die „Times" von heute?

c (*Press etc, = subject matter*) Stoff *m*; (= *material to be printed*) Artikel *m*; (*Typ*) (Manu)skript *nt*; **that's always good ~** das zieht immer; **this murder story will make good ~** aus diesem Mord kann man etwas machen

d (*in advertising*) Werbetext *m*; **who did the ~ for this campaign?** wer hat den Text/die Texte für diese Werbekampagne gemacht?; **he writes good ~** er schreibt gute Werbetexte

VI (= *imitate*) nachahmen; (*Sch etc*) abschreiben VT **a** (= *make a copy of*) kopieren (*also Comput*); *document* (*separately written/typed*) eine Abschrift anfertigen von; (*typed/handwritten carbon*) einen Durchschlag/eine Durchschrift machen von; (*Phot*) abziehen; (= *write out again*) abschreiben; **to ~ sth to a disk** etw auf eine Diskette kopieren

b (= *imitate*) nachmachen; *gestures, person also* nachahmen; **they always ~ Ford** sie machen Ford immer alles nach

c (*Sch etc*) *sb else's work* abschreiben; (*by painting*) abmalen; **to ~ Brecht** (*von*) Brecht abschreiben

d (= *send a copy to*) einen Durchschlag/eine Durchschrift senden an (+*acc*)

copy: copybook N Schönschreibheft *nt* → **blot** ADJ mustergültig, wie es/er/sie im Lehrbuch steht; **a ~ landing** eine Bilderbuchlandung; **copy boy** N (*Press*) Laufjunge *m*; **copycat** N (*inf*) Nachahmer(in) *m(f)*; (*with written work*) Abschreiber(in) *m(f)*; **she's a terrible ~** sie macht immer alles nach; sie schreibt immer ab; **~!** Nachmachen gilt nicht! (*inf*) ADJ *attr* **his was a ~ crime** er war ein Nachahmungstäter; **copy desk** N (*Press*) Redaktionstisch *m*; **copy-edit** VT (*Press*) redigieren; (*in publishing also*) lektorieren, bearbeiten; **copy**

editor N (*Press*) Redakteur(in) *m(f)*; (*publishing also*) Lektor(in) *m(f)*, Manuskriptbearbeiter(in) *m(f)*

copyist ['kɒpɪɪst] N Kopist(in) *m(f)*

copy (*Comput*): **copy-protected** ADJ *disk* kopiergeschützt; **copy protection** N Kopierschutz *m*

copyreader ['kɒpiːdə'] N = **copy editor**

copyright ['kɒpɪraɪt] N Copyright *nt*, Urheberrecht *nt*; **out of ~** urheberrechtlich nicht mehr geschützt ADJ urheberrechtlich geschützt VT *book* urheberrechtlich schützen; (*author*) urheberrechtlich schützen lassen

copy: copy typist N Schreibkraft *f*; **copywriter** N Werbetexter(in) *m(f)*

coquetry ['kɒkɪtrɪ] N Koketterie *f*

coquette [kə'ket] N kokettes Mädchen, kokette Frau

coquettish [kə'ketɪʃ] ADJ kokett, kess

coquettishly [kə'ketɪʃlɪ] ADV kokett

cor [kɔː'] INTERJ (*Brit, inf*) Mensch (*inf*), Mann (*sl*)

coracle ['kɒrəkl] N *kleines ovales Ruderboot aus mit Leder bezogenem Flechtwerk*

coral ['kɒrəl] N **a** Koralle *f*; **~ necklace** Korallenkette *f* **b** (= *colour*) Korallenrot *nt*

coral *in cpds* Korallen-; **coral-coloured** ADJ korallenfarbig; **coral island** N Koralleninsel *f*; **coral reef** N Korallenriff *nt*; **Coral Sea** N Korallenmeer *nt*; **coral snake** N Korallennatter *f*

cor anglais ['kɔːr'ɒŋgleɪ] N (*esp Brit*) Englischhorn *nt*

corbel ['kɔːbəl] N Kragstein *m*, Konsole *f*

cord [kɔːd] N **a** Schnur *f*; (*for clothes*) Kordel *f*; (*Elec*) Schnur *f* **b** **cords** PL (*also* **a pair of cords**) Kordhosen *pl* **c** (*Tex*) → **corduroy** **a** (*Anat*) → **spinal, umbilical, vocal** ATTR (*Brit*) Kord-; **~ jacket** Kordjacke *f*; **~ trousers** Kordhosen *pl*

cordage ['kɔːdɪdʒ] N , *no pl* Tauwerk *nt*

corded ['kɔːdɪd] ADJ (= *ribbed*) gerippt

cordial ['kɔːdɪəl] ADJ freundlich, höflich; *dislike* heftig N (= *drink*) Fruchtsaftkonzentrat *nt*; (*alcoholic*) Fruchtlikör *m*

cordiality [ˌkɔːdɪ'ælɪtɪ] N Freundlichkeit *f*, Höflichkeit *f*

cordially ['kɔːdɪəlɪ] ADV freundlich, höflich; **~ yours** mit freundlichen Grüßen; **they ~ dislike him** er ist ihnen zutiefst unsympathisch

cordite ['kɔːdaɪt] N Cordit *nt*

cordless ['kɔːdlɪs] ADJ *telephone* schnurlos

cordon ['kɔːdn] N **a** Kordon *m*, Postenkette *f*; **to put a ~ round sth** einen Kordon um etw ziehen, etw (hermetisch) abriegeln **b** (= *ribbon of an Order*) Kordon *m*, (*Ordens*)band *nt* **c** (*Hort*) Kordon *m*, Schnurbaum *m* VT = **cordon off**

▶ **cordon off** VT *sep area, building* absperren, abriegeln

cordon bleu [ˌkɔːdɒn'blɜː'] N (*Cook, = award*) Meisterkochdiplom *nt*; (= *chef, cook*) Meisterkoch *m*, Meisterköchin *f* ADJ *cook* vorzüglich; *recipe, dish, meal* delikat, exquisit; **she's taking a ~ cookery course** sie macht einen Kochkurs für die feine Küche (mit)

cordon sanitaire [ˌkɔːdnsani'tɛə'] N (*Med, Pol*) Cordon sanitaire *m*

corduroy ['kɔːdərɔɪ] N Kordsamt *m*; **~s** Kord(samt)hosen *pl*

corduroy *in cpds* Kord(samt)-; **corduroy road** N Knüppeldamm *m*

CORE [kɔː'] (*US*) abbr of **Congress of Racial Equality** *Verband zur Bekämpfung von Rassendiskriminierung*

core [kɔː'] N (*lit, fig*) Kern *m*; (*of apple, pear*) Kernhaus *nt*, Butzen *m* (*dial*); (*of rock*) Innere(s) *nt*; (*of nuclear reactor*) Kern *m*; **rotten/English to the ~** (*fig*) durch und durch schlecht/englisch; **shaken/shocked to the ~** zutiefst erschüttert/schockiert; **to get to the ~ of the matter** (*fig*) zum Kern der Sache kommen ADJ

attr issue Kern-; (*Sch*) *subject* Haupt-, Pflicht-; *curriculum* Haupt-; **~ business** (*Comm*) Kerngeschäft *nt* VT *fruit* entkernen; *apple, pear* das Kernhaus (+*gen*) entfernen *or* ausschneiden

corelate VTI = **correlate**

coreligionist ['kɔːrɪ'lɪdʒənɪst] N Glaubensgenosse *m*/-genossin *f*

corer ['kɔːrə'] N (*Cook*) Apfelstecher *m*

co-respondent [ˌkəʊrɪs'pɒndənt] N (*Jur*) Mitbeklagte(r) *or* Dritte(r) *mf* (*im Scheidungsprozess*), Scheidungsgrund *m* (*hum*)

core: core time N Kernzeit *f*; **core vocabulary** N Grundwortschatz *m*

Corfu [kɔː'fuː] N Korfu *nt*

corgi ['kɔːgɪ] N Corgi *m*

coriander [ˌkɒrɪ'ændə'] N Koriander *m*

Corinth ['kɒrɪnθ] N Korinth *nt*

Corinthian [kə'rɪnθɪən] ADJ korinthisch N **a** Korinther(in) *m(f)* **b** (*Eccl*) **~s** +*sing vb* Korinther *f*

Coriolanus [ˌkɒrɪə'leɪnəs] N Coriolan *m*

cork [kɔːk] N **a** *no pl* (= *substance*) Kork *m* **b** (= *stopper*) Korken *m*; **put a ~ in it!** (*inf*) halt die Klappe! (*inf*) **c** (*Fishing: also* **cork float**) Schwimmer *m* VT (*also* **cork up**) *bottle, wine* zu- *or* verkorken ADJ Kork-, korken (*rare*); **~ flooring** Kork(fuß)boden *m*

corkage ['kɔːkɪdʒ] N Korkengeld *nt*

corked [kɔːkt] ADJ **the wine is ~** der Wein schmeckt nach Kork

corker ['kɔːkə'] N (*dated inf*) **a ~** einsame Klasse (*inf*)

corking ['kɔːkɪŋ] ADJ (*dated Brit, inf*) Klasse- (*inf*); **a ~ game** ein Klassespiel *nt* (*inf*)

cork: cork oak N Korkeiche *f*; **corkscrew** N Korkenzieher *m*; **corkscrew curls** PL Korkenzieherlocken *pl*; **cork shoes** PL Schuhe *pl* mit Korksohlen; **cork tile** N Korkfliese *f*; **cork-tipped** ADJ *cigarette* mit Korkfilter; **cork tree** N Korkbaum *m*

corky ['kɔːkɪ] ADJ Kork-, korkartig; *taste* Kork-, korkig

corm [kɔːm] N Knolle *f*

cormorant ['kɔːmərənt] N Kormoran *m*

Corn (*Brit*) abbr of **Cornwall**

corn¹ [kɔːn] N **a** *no pl* (*Brit, = cereal*) Getreide *nt*, Korn *nt* **b** (= *seed of corn*) Korn *nt* **c** *no pl* (*esp US, = maize*) Mais *m* → **cob**

corn² N (*on foot*) Hühnerauge *nt*; **~ plaster** Hühneraugenpflaster *nt*; **to tread on sb's ~s** (*fig*) jdm auf die Hühneraugen treten

corn³ N (*inf, = sentiment etc*) Kitsch *m*, sentimentales Zeug *nt*; (= *trite humour*) olle Kamellen *pl* (*inf*)

corn: cornball N (*US, inf*) N Gefühlsdusel *m* (*inf*) ADJ gefühlsduselig (*inf*), kitschig, schmalzig; **Corn Belt** N (*Geog*) Getreidegürtel *m*; **corn bread** N (*US*) Maisbrot *nt*; **corn bunting** N (*Orn*) Grauammer *f*; **corn chandler** N Kornhändler *m*; **corncob** N Maiskolben *m*; **corn-coloured** ADJ strohfarben, strohgelb; **corncrake** N (*Orn*) Wachtelkönig *m*; **corncrib** N (*US*) Maisspeicher *m*; **corn dodger** N (*US*) Maisfladen *m*; **corn dog** N (*US, Cook*) *mit Maismehl paniertes Bratwürstchen*

cornea ['kɔːnɪə] N Hornhaut *f*, Cornea *f* (*spec*)

corneal ['kɔːnɪəl] ADJ Hornhaut-; **~ lenses** Linsen *pl*

corned beef ['kɔːnd'biːf] N Cornedbeef *nt*, Corned Beef *nt*

corner ['kɔːnə'] N **a** (*generally, Boxing*) Ecke *f*; (*of sheet also*) Zipfel *m*; (*of mouth, eye*) Winkel *m*; (= *sharp bend in road*) Kurve *f*; (*fig, = awkward situation*) Klemme *f* (*inf*); **at** *or* **on the ~** an der Ecke; **the teacher made him stand in the ~** der Lehrer stellte ihn in die Ecke; **it's just round the ~** (= *near*) es ist gleich um die Ecke; (*inf: = about to happen*) das steht kurz bevor; (*fig, recovery etc*) das wird bald eintreten; **to turn the ~** (*lit*) um die Ecke biegen; **we've turned the ~ now** (*fig*) wir sind jetzt über den Berg; **the pag-**

es are curling up at the ~s die Seiten haben Eselsohren; **out of the ~ of one's eye** aus dem Augenwinkel (heraus); **he always has a cigarette hanging out of the ~ of his mouth** er hat immer eine Zigarette im Mundwinkel (hängen); **to cut ~s** (lit) Kurven schneiden; (fig) das Verfahren abkürzen; **to drive** or **force sb into a ~** (fig) jdn in die Enge treiben; **to fight one's ~** (esp Brit, fig) für seine Sache kämpfen; **to have sb in one's ~** (fig) jdn auf seiner Seite haben; **all four ~s of the world** alle vier Winde; **he has travelled to all four ~s of the world** er hat die ganze Welt bereist; **in every ~ of Europe/the globe/the house** in allen (Ecken und) Winkeln Europas/der Erde/des Hauses; **an attractive ~ of Britain** eine reizvolle Gegend Großbritanniens
b (= out-of-the-way place) Winkel m; **have you got an odd ~ somewhere where I could store my books?** hast du irgendwo ein Eckchen or Plätzchen, wo ich meine Bücher lagern könnte?
c (Comm, = monopoly) Monopol nt; **to make/have a ~ in sth** das Monopol für or auf etw (acc) erwerben/haben
d (Ftbl) Ecke f, Eckball m, Corner m (Aus); **to take a ~** eine Ecke ausführen
VT a (lit, fig, = trap) in die Enge treiben
b (Comm) **the market** monopolisieren
VI (= take a corner: person) Kurven/die Kurve nehmen; **this car ~s well** dieses Auto hat eine gute Kurvenlage

corner in cpds Eck-; **corner cabinet** N Eckschrank m; **corner chair** N Eckstuhl m

cornered ['kɔːnəd] ADJ eckig; (fig) in die Ecke getrieben

-cornered [-'kɔːnəd] ADJ suf -eckig; **three-cornered** dreieckig

corner flag N (Sport) Eckfahne f

corner hit N (Hockey) Eckschlag m

cornering ['kɔːnərɪŋ] N (of car) Kurvenlage f; (of driver) Kurventechnik f

corner: **corner kick** N (Ftbl) Eckstoß m; **corner post** N (Ftbl) Eckfahne f; **corner seat** N (Rail) Eckplatz m; **corner shop** N Laden m an der Ecke; **cornerstone** N (lit, fig) Grundstein m, Eckstein m; **corner store** N (US) = **corner shop**; **corner table** N Tisch m in der Ecke, Ecktisch m; **cornerways**, **cornerwise** ADV über Eck, diagonal

cornet ['kɔːnɪt] N **a** (Mus) Kornett nt **b** (= ice-cream cornet) (Eis)tüte f

corn: **corn exchange** N Getreidebörse f; **corn-fed** ADJ mit Getreide gefüttert; **cornfield** N (Brit) Korn- or Weizenfeld nt; (US) Maisfeld nt; **cornflakes** PL Cornflakes pl; **cornflour** N (Brit) Stärkemehl nt; **cornflower** **N a** Kornblume f **b** (= colour) Kornblumenblau nt **ADJ** (also **cornflower blue**) kornblumenblau

cornice ['kɔːnɪs] N (Archit: of wall, column) (Ge-)sims nt; (fig, of snow) Wechte f

corniche ['kɔːnɪʃ, kɔːˈniːʃ] N Küstenstraße f

Cornish ['kɔːnɪʃ] ADJ kornisch, aus Cornwall **N** (Ling) Kornisch nt

Cornishman ['kɔːnɪʃmən] N pl **-men** [-mən] Bewohner m Cornwalls

Cornish pasty n (Brit) Gebäckstück aus Blätterteig mit Fleischfüllung

Cornishwoman ['kɔːnɪʃwʊmən] N pl **-women** [-wɪmɪn] Bewohnerin f Cornwalls

corn: **cornmeal** N (US) Maismehl nt; **corn oil** N (Mais)keimöl nt; **corn plaster** N Hühneraugenpflaster nt; **corn pone** N (US) = **corn bread**; **corn poppy** N Klatschmohn m, Mohnblume f; **corn shock** N (Getreide)garbe f; **cornstarch** N (US) Stärkemehl nt; **corn syrup** N (US) (Mais)sirup m

cornucopia [ˌkɔːnjʊˈkəʊpɪə] N (Myth, = horn-shaped container) Füllhorn nt; (fig, = abundance) Fülle f

Cornwall ['kɔːnwəl] N Cornwall nt

corn whisky N (US) Maiswhisky m

corny ['kɔːnɪ] ADJ (+er) (inf) joke blöd (inf); (= sentimental) kitschig; **what a ~ old joke!** der Witz hat (so) einen Bart (inf)

corolla [kəˈrɒlə] N (Bot) Blumenkrone f, Korolla f (spec)

corollary [kəˈrɒlərɪ] **N** (logische) Folge, Korollar nt (also Math); **this would prove, as a ~, that ...** damit würde dann gleichzeitig auch bewiesen, dass ... **ADJ** Begleit-

corona [kəˈrəʊnə] N (Astron, of sun, moon etc) Hof m; (= part of sun's atmosphere) Korona f; (of tooth) Krone f; (Bot) Nebenkrone f; (= cigar) Corona f

coronary ['kɒrənərɪ] **ADJ** (Med) Koronar- (spec); **~ failure** Herzversagen nt (inf), Koronarinsuffizienz f **N** Herzinfarkt m

coronary: **coronary artery** N (Med) Kranzarterie f; **coronary thrombosis** N (Med) Herzinfarkt m; **coronary vessel** N (Med) (Herz-)kranzgefäß nt, Koronargefäß nt (spec)

coronation [ˌkɒrəˈneɪʃən] **N a** Krönung f **b** in cpds Krönungs-; **~ robes** Krönungsgewänder pl

coroner ['kɒrənə] N Beamter, der Todesfälle untersucht, die nicht eindeutig eine natürliche Ursache haben ~'s **inquest** Untersuchung nicht eindeutig natürlicher Todesfälle ~'s **jury** Untersuchungskommission bei nicht eindeutig natürlichen Todesfällen

coronet ['kɒrənɪt] N Krone f; (= jewellery) Krönchen nt

corp. abbr of **corporation**

corporal[1] ['kɔːpərəl] N (abbr **corp**) (Mil) Stabsunteroffizier m

corporal[2] ADJ körperlich; pleasures, needs leiblich

corporal punishment N Prügel- or Körperstrafe f

corporate ['kɔːpərɪt] ADJ **a** (= of a group) gemeinsam, korporativ; **~ action/decision** geschlossenes or gemeinsames Vorgehen/gemeinsame Entscheidung; **to work for the ~ good** für das Gemeinwohl arbeiten; **to take out ~ membership of another society** als geschlossene Gruppe Mitglied eines anderen Vereins werden
b (of a corporation) korporativ; (of a company) Firmen-; (Jur) Korporations-; **I'm not a ~ man** ich bin ein Mensch, der sich in großen Firmen nicht wohl fühlt; **the ~ life of an organization** das Leben in einer großen Vereinigung; **I was meaning "we" in the ~ sense** ich meinte „wir" als Firma; **our ~ liabilities** unsere Verbindlichkeiten als Firma; **to move up the ~ ladder** in der Firma aufsteigen; **~ body** Körperschaft f; **~ finance** Unternehmensfinanzen pl; **~ financing** Unternehmensfinanzierung f; **~ planning** Unternehmensplanung f

corporate: **corporate hospitality** N Unterhaltung und Bewirtung von Firmenkunden; **corporate identity** N Firmenimage nt; **corporate law** N Gesellschaftsrecht nt; **corporate lawyer** N (working for corporation) Firmenanwalt m/-anwältin f; (= specialist in corporate law) Anwalt m/Anwältin f für Gesellschaftsrecht

corporately ['kɔːpərɪtlɪ] ADV **a** (= collectively) gemeinsam **b** (Comm) körperschaftlich; **to be ~ owned** einer Firma (dat) gehören; **he has plenty of capital, both ~ and privately** er hat jede Menge Kapital, sowohl geschäftlich als auch privat

corporate raider N Firmenaufkäufer(in) m(f)

corporate tax N Körperschaftsteuer f

corporation [ˌkɔːpəˈreɪʃən] **N a** (= municipal corporation) Gemeinde f, Stadt f; **the Mayor and Corporation** der Bürgermeister und die Stadt
b (Brit Comm: = incorporated company) Handelsgesellschaft f; (US, Comm, = limited liability company) Gesellschaft f mit beschränkter Haftung; **private ~** (Comm) Privatunternehmen nt; **public ~** (Comm) staatliches Unternehmen **c** (Brit, hum, = large belly) Schmerbauch m

corporation: **corporation bus** N Stadtbus m, städtischer Omnibus; **corporation property** N gemeindeeigener Besitz; **corporation tax** N Körperschaftsteuer f; **corporation tram** N städtische Straßenbahn; **corporation transport** N städtisches Verkehrsmittel

corporatism ['kɔːpərɪtɪzəm] N **the growth of ~** die steigende Zahl der Großunternehmen; **a sense of ~** ein Zusammengehörigkeitsgefühl nt innerhalb des/eines Unternehmens

corporeal [kɔːˈpɔːrɪəl] ADJ körperlich

corps [kɔːʳ] N pl – (Mil) Korps nt

corps de ballet N Corps de Ballet nt

corps diplomatique ['kɔːˌdɪpləʊmæˈtiːk] N diplomatisches Korps → **diplomatic corps**

corpse [kɔːps] **N** Leiche f, Leichnam m (geh) **VI** (Theat sl) einen Lachanfall bekommen

corpulence ['kɔːpjʊləns] N Korpulenz f

corpulent ['kɔːpjʊlənt] ADJ korpulent

corpus ['kɔːpəs] N **a** (= collection) Korpus m; (of opinions) Paket nt **b** (= main body) Großteil m; **the main ~ of his work** der Hauptteil seiner Arbeit **c** (Fin) Stammkapital nt

Corpus Christi ['kɔːpəsˈkrɪstɪ] N (Eccl) Fronleichnam m

corpuscle ['kɔːpʌsl] N Korpuskel nt (spec); **blood ~** Blutkörperchen nt

corpuscular [kɔːˈpʌskjuːlə] ADJ Korpuskular- (spec)

corpus delicti ['kɔːpəsdɪˈlɪktaɪ] N (Jur) Corpus Delicti nt; (= corpse) Leiche f

corral [kəˈrɑːl] **N** Korral m **VT** cattle in den Korral treiben

correct [kəˈrekt] **ADJ a** (= right) richtig; answer, pronunciation also korrekt; time also genau; **to be ~** (person) Recht haben; **to be ~ in one's estimates/assessment** richtig schätzen/einschätzen; **am I thinking that ...?** gehe ich recht in der Annahme, dass ...?; **~ money** or **change only** nur abgezähltes Geld, nur passenden Betrag
b (= proper, suitable, perfectly mannered) korrekt; **it's the ~ thing to do** das gehört sich so; **she was ~ to reject the offer** es war richtig, dass sie das Angebot abgelehnt hat
VT a korrigieren; person, pronunciation, error etc also berichtigen, verbessern; bad habit sich/jdm abgewöhnen; **to ~ proofs** Korrektur lesen; **~ me if I'm wrong** sie können mich gern berichtigen; **I stand ~ed** ich nehme alles zurück
b (old, by punishment, scolding) maßregeln; (by corporal punishment) züchtigen

correcting fluid [kəˈrektɪŋˌfluːɪd] N Korrekturflüssigkeit f

correction [kəˈrekʃən] N **a** Korrektion f, Korrektur f; (of person, pronunciation, error etc also) Berichtigung f, Verbesserung f; (of bad habit) Abgewöhnung f; **~ of proofs** Korrekturlesen nt; **I am open to ~** ich lasse mich gerne berichtigen; **to do one's ~s** (Sch) die Verbesserung machen; **~ key** Korrekturtaste f; **~ tape** (on typewriter) Korrekturband nt **b** (old, by punishment, scolding) Maßregelung f; (by corporal punishment) Züchtigung f; **house of ~** Besserungsanstalt f

correctional [kəˈrekʃənəl] ADJ (US) **~ officer** Justizvollzugsbeamte(r) m/-beamtin f; **the ~ system** das Justizvollzugssystem; **~ facility** Justizvollzugsanstalt f, Strafanstalt f

correctitude [kəˈrektɪtjuːd] N = **correctness b**

corrective [kəˈrektɪv] **ADJ** korrigierend; **to take ~ action** korrigierend eingreifen; **to have ~ surgery** sich einem korrigierenden Eingriff unterziehen **N** (Pharm, fig) Korrektiv nt

correctly [kəˈrektlɪ] ADV **a** (= accurately) richtig; answer, pronounce also korrekt; **he had ~ assumed that ...** er hatte richtigerweise angenommen, dass ...; **if I remember ~** wenn ich mich recht entsinne **b** (= in proper way) behave, speak, dress korrekt

correctness [kəˈrektnɪs] N **a** (= accuracy) Richtigkeit f **b** (of behaviour etc) Korrektheit f

correlate ['kɒrɪleɪt] **VT** *two things* zueinander in Beziehung setzen, korrelieren (*geh*); **to ~ sth with sth** etw mit etw in Beziehung setzen, etw mit etw korrelieren (*geh*) **VI** (*two things*) sich entsprechen; **to ~ with sth** mit etw in Beziehung stehen

correlation [ˌkɒrɪˈleɪʃən] N (= *correspondence*) Beziehung *f*; (= *close relationship*) enger or direkter Zusammenhang; (*Math, Statistics*) Korrelation *f*

correlative [kɒˈrelətɪv] **N** Korrelat *nt* **ADJ** (= *directly related*) entsprechend; (*Gram*) korrelativ

correspond [ˌkɒrɪsˈpɒnd] ✪ 5.4 VI **a** (= *be equivalent*) entsprechen (*to*, *with +dat*); (*two or more: to one another*) sich entsprechen; (= *be in accordance also*) sich decken (*with* mit); **your version doesn't ~** Ihre Version deckt sich nicht damit **b** (= *exchange letters*) korrespondieren (*with* mit)

correspondence [ˌkɒrɪsˈpɒndəns] N **a** (= *agreement, equivalence*) Übereinstimmung *f* (*between* zwischen, *with* mit) **b** (= *letter-writing*) Korrespondenz *f*; (= *letters also*) Briefe *pl*; (*in newspaper*) Leserzuschriften or -briefe *pl*; **to be in ~ with sb** mit jdm in Korrespondenz stehen (*form*), mit jdm korrespondieren; (*private*) mit jdm in Briefwechsel stehen, mit jdm korrespondieren (*geh*)

correspondence: correspondence card N Briefkarte *f*; **correspondence chess** N Fernschach *nt*; **correspondence column** N (*Press*) Leserbriefspalte *f*; **correspondence course** N Fernkurs *m*; **correspondence school** N Fernlehrinstitut *nt*

correspondent [ˌkɒrɪsˈpɒndənt] **N a** (= *letter-writer*) Briefschreiber(in) *m(f)*; **to be a good/bad ~** ein eifriger Briefschreiber sein/schreibfaul sein; **according to my ~** wie man mir geschrieben hat **b** (*Press*) Korrespondent(in) *m(f)* **c** (*Comm*) Entsprechung *f*, Gegenstück *nt* **ADJ** entsprechend

corresponding [ˌkɒrɪsˈpɒndɪŋ] ADJ entsprechend

correspondingly [ˌkɒrɪsˈpɒndɪŋlɪ] ADV (dem-) entsprechend

corridor ['kɒrɪdɔː'] N Korridor *m*; (*in building also, in train, bus*) Gang *m*; **in the ~s of power** an den Schalthebeln der Macht

corridor train N D-Zug *m*

corrie ['kɒrɪ] N (*Geol*) Kar *m*

corrigendum [kɒrɪˈdʒendəm] N *pl* **corrigenda** [kɒrɪˈdʒendə] Corrigendum *nt* (*geh*)

corroborate [kəˈrɒbəreɪt] VT bestätigen; *theory also* bekräftigen, erhärten, untermauern

corroboration [kəˌrɒbəˈreɪʃən] N Bestätigung *f*; (*of theory also*) Bekräftigung *f*, Erhärtung *f*, Untermauerung *f*; **in ~ of** zur Untermauerung or Unterstützung (*+gen*); **through lack of ~** (*Jur*) mangels unterstützenden Beweismaterials; (*from witnesses*) mangels bestätigender Zeugenaussagen

corroborative [kəˈrɒbərətɪv] ADJ bestätigend; *evidence* erhärtend, untermauernd *all attr*; **to be ~ of sth** etw bestätigen/untermauern

corroboree [kəˈrɒbərɪ] N (*Austral*) *Tanzritual der Aborigines* (*fig*) rauschendes Fest

corrode [kəˈrəʊd] **VT** *metal* zerfressen; (*fig*) zerstören **VI** (*metal*) korrodieren

corroded [kəˈrəʊdɪd] ADJ korrodiert

corrosion [kəˈrəʊʒən] N Korrosion *f*; (*fig*) Zerstörung *f*

corrosive [kəˈrəʊzɪv] **ADJ** korrosiv; (*fig*) zerstörend **N** Korrosion verursachendes Mittel

corrugated ['kɒrəgeɪtɪd] ADJ gewellt; **~ cardboard** dicke Wellpappe

corrugated iron N Wellblech *nt*

corrugated paper N Wellpappe *f*

corrugation [ˌkɒrəˈgeɪʃən] N Welle *f*

corrupt [kəˈrʌpt] **ADJ** verdorben, verworfen, schlecht; (= *open to bribery*) korrupt, bestechlich; *text, language* verderbt, korrumpiert; (*Comput*) *disk* nicht lesbar, kaputt; **morally ~** mora-

lisch verdorben or schlecht **VT** (*morally*) verderben; (*ethically*) korrumpieren; (*form: = bribe*) bestechen, korrumpieren; (*Comput*) *data* kaputt or unlesbar machen, zerstören; **to become ~ed** (*text, language*) korrumpiert werden; **to ~ sb's morals** jdn moralisch verderben

corruptible [kəˈrʌptəbl] ADJ korrumpierbar; (= *bribable also*) bestechlich

corruption [kəˈrʌpʃən] N **a** (= *act, of person*) Korruption *f*; (*by bribery also*) Bestechung *f*; (*Comput, of data*) Zerstörung *f* **b** (= *corrupt nature*) Verdorbenheit *f*, Verderbtheit *f*; (*by bribery*) Bestechlichkeit *f*; (*of morals*) Verfall *m*; (*of language, text*) Korrumpierung *f* **c** (*form, = decay of bodies etc*) Zersetzung *f*, Fäulnis *f*

corruptly [kəˈrʌptlɪ] ADV korrupt

corsage [kɔːˈsɑːʒ] N **a** (= *bodice*) Mieder *nt* **b** (= *flowers*) Ansteckblume *f*

corsair ['kɔːsɛə'] N (= *ship*) Piratenschiff *nt*, Korsar *m*; (= *pirate*) Pirat *m*, Korsar *m*

corselet [kɔːsəˈlet] N (= *corset*) Korselett *nt* **b** → **corslet**

corset ['kɔːsɪt] N , **corsets** *pl* Korsett *nt*; (*to give wasp waist*) Schnürmieder *nt*

corseted ['kɔːsɪtɪd] ADJ geschnürt

corsetry ['kɔːsɪtrɪ] N Miederwarenherstellung *f*; (= *corsets*) Miederwaren *pl*

Corsica ['kɔːsɪkə] N Korsika *nt*

Corsican ['kɔːsɪkən] **ADJ** korsisch; **~ holiday** Urlaub *m* auf Korsika; **she is** ~ sie ist Korsin **N a** Korse *m*, Korsin *f* **b** (*Ling*) Korsisch *nt*

corslet, corselet ['kɔːslɪt] N Brust- (und Rücken)panzer *m*

cortège [kɔːˈteɪʒ] N (= *retinue*) Gefolge *nt*; (= *procession*) Prozession *f*; (= *funeral cortège*) Leichenzug *m*

cortex ['kɔːteks] N *pl* **cortices** (*Anat, of brain*) Hirnrinde *f*; (*of kidney*) Nierenrinde *f*; (*Bot*) Kortex *m*

cortical ['kɔːtɪkl] ADJ (*Anat, Bot*) kortikal

cortices ['kɔːtɪsiːz] *pl of* **cortex**

cortisone ['kɔːtɪzəʊn] N Kortison *nt*, Cortison *nt*

corundum [kəˈrʌndəm] N (*Geol*) Korund *m*

coruscate ['kɒrəskeɪt] VI funkeln

coruscating ['kɒrəskeɪtɪŋ] ADJ brilliant, geistsprühend

corvette [kɔːˈvet] N (*Naut*) Korvette *f*

cos[1] [kɒz] *abbr of* **cosine** cos

cos[2] [kɒs] N (*also* **cos lettuce**) Romanasalat *m*, römischer Salat *m*

cos[3] [kəz] CONJ (*inf*) = **because**

cosec ['kəʊsek] *abbr of* **cosecant** cosec

cosecant ['kəʊsekænt] N Kosekans *m*

cosh [kɒʃ] **VT** auf den Schädel schlagen, eins über den Schädel ziehen (*+dat*) (*inf*) **N** (= *instrument*) Totschläger *m*; (= *blow*) Schlag *m* (auf den Kopf)

cosignatory ['kəʊˈsɪgnətərɪ] N Mitunterzeichner(in) *m(f)*

cosily, (*US*) **cozily** ['kəʊzɪlɪ] ADV **a** (= *snugly*) *furnished, decorated* behaglich **b** (= *comfortably*) *sit, settle* behaglich **c** (= *intimately*) *chat, gossip* gemütlich

cosine ['kəʊsaɪn] N Kosinus *m*

cosiness, (*US*) **coziness** ['kəʊzɪnɪs] N Gemütlichkeit *f*, Behaglichkeit *f*; (= *warmth*) mollige Wärme *f*; (*of chat*) Freundschaftlichkeit *f*, Traulichkeit *f* (*dated*)

COSLA ['kɒzlə] (*Scot*) *abbr of* **Convention of Scottish Local Authorities**

cosmetic [kɒzˈmetɪk] **ADJ** (*lit, fig*) kosmetisch **N** Kosmetikum *nt*, Schönheitspflegemittel *nt*

cosmetician [kɒzməˈtɪʃən] N Kosmetiker(in) *m(f)*

cosmetic surgery N kosmetische Chirurgie *f*; **she's had ~** sie hat eine Schönheitsoperation gehabt

cosmic ['kɒzmɪk] ADJ kosmisch; **~ dust** Weltraumnebel *m*

cosmogony [kɒzˈmɒgənɪ] N Kosmogonie *f*

cosmography [kɒzˈmɒgrəfɪ] N Kosmografie *f*

cosmologist [kɒzˈmɒlədʒɪst] N Kosmologe *m*, Kosmologin *f*

cosmology [kɒzˈmɒlədʒɪ] N Kosmologie *f*

cosmonaut ['kɒzmənɔːt] N Kosmonaut(in) *m(f)*

cosmopolitan [ˌkɒzməˈpɒlɪtən] **ADJ** kosmopolitisch, international **N** Kosmopolit *m*, Weltbürger *m*

cosmos ['kɒzmɒs] N **a** Kosmos *m* **b** (*Bot*) Kosmee *f*

cossack ['kɒsæk] **N** Kosak(in) *m(f)* **ADJ** Kosaken-

cossack hat N Kosakenmütze *f*

cosset ['kɒsɪt] VT verwöhnen

cossie, cozzie ['kɒzɪ] N (*Brit inf*) Badeanzug *m*

cost [kɒst] *vb: pret, ptp* **cost** **VT a** (*lit, fig*) kosten; **how much does it ~?** wie viel kostet es?; **how much will it ~ to have it repaired?** wie viel kostet die Reparatur?; **it ~ (him) a lot of money** das hat (ihn) viel Geld gekostet; **designer clothes ~ money** Designerkleidung kostet Geld; **driving without a seat belt ~ him dear** Fahren ohne Sicherheitsgurt kam ihn teuer zu stehen; **it ~ him a great effort/a lot of time** es kostete ihn viel Mühe/viel Zeit; **that mistake could ~ you your life** der Fehler könnte dich das Leben kosten; **~ what it may** koste es, was es wolle; **politeness doesn't ~ (you) anything** es kostet (dich) nichts, höflich zu sein; **it'll ~ you** (*inf*) das kostet dich was (*inf*) **b** *pret, ptp* **costed** (= *work out cost of*) *project etc* veranschlagen **c** *pret, ptp* **costed** (*Comm, = put a price on*) *articles for sale* auspreisen (*at* zu) **N a** (*lit*) Kosten *pl* (*of* für); **to bear the ~ of sth** die Kosten für etw tragen, für die Kosten von etw aufkommen; **the ~ of electricity/petrol these days** die Strom-/Benzinpreise heutzutage; **to buy sth at great ~** etw zu einem hohen Preis kaufen; **at little ~ to oneself** ohne große eigene Kosten; **to buy sth at ~** etw zum Selbstkostenpreis kaufen; **~ containment** Kostendämpfung *f*; **~ of manufacture** Produktions- or Herstellungskosten *pl*; **~ of sales** Verkaufskosten *pl* **b** (*fig*) Preis *m*; **at all ~s, at any ~** um jeden Preis; **whatever the ~** kostet es, was es wolle; **at the ~ of one's health/job/marriage** *etc* auf Kosten seiner Gesundheit/Stelle/Ehe *etc*; **at great/little personal ~** unter großen/geringen eigenen Kosten; **he found out to his ~ that ...** er machte die bittere Erfahrung, dass ... **c costs** PL (*Jur*) Kosten *pl*; **to be ordered to pay ~s** zur Übernahme der Kosten verurteilt werden

▶ **cost out** VT *sep* (kostenmäßig) kalkulieren

Costa Brava ['kɒstə'brɑːvə] N Costa Brava *f*

cost: cost accountant N Kostenbuchhalter(in) *m(f)*; **cost accounting** N Kalkulation *f*

Costa del Sol ['kɒstədel'sɒl] N Costa del Sol *f*

co-star ['kəʊstɑː'] **N** (*Film, Theat*) einer der Hauptdarsteller; **Burton and Taylor were ~s** Burton und Taylor spielten die Hauptrollen **VT** *the film* **~s R. Burton** der Film zeigt R. Burton in einer der Hauptrollen **VI** als Hauptdarsteller auftreten

Costa Rica ['kɒstə'riːkə] N Costa Rica *nt*

Costa Rican ['kɒstə'riːkən] **ADJ** costa-ricanisch **N** Costa-Ricaner(in) *m(f)*

cost: cost-benefit analysis N Kosten-Nutzen-Analyse *f*; **cost centre** N Kostenstelle *f*; **cost clerk** N Angestellte(r) *mf* in der Kostenbuchhaltung; **cost-conscious** ADJ kostenbewusst; **cost-covering** ADJ (*Fin*) kostendeckend; **cost-cutting** **N** Kostenverringerung *f* **ADJ** *attr* **~ exercise** Kosten dämpfende Maßnahmen *pl*; **cost-effective** ADJ rentabel, kosteneffizient (*spec*); **cost-effectively** ADV rentabel; **cost-effectiveness** N Rentabilität *f*, Kosteneffizienz *f* (*spec*)

coster(monger) ['kɒstə(ˌmʌŋgə')] N (Brit) Straßenhändler m

costing ['kɒstɪŋ] N Kalkulation f; ~ **department** Kostenbuchhaltung f, betriebliches Rechnungswesen

costive ['kɒstɪv] ADJ (form, = constipated) verstopft; (= constipating) stopfend

costliness ['kɒstlɪnɪs] N Kostspieligkeit f; (in business, industry) hoher Kostenaufwand; **the ~ of buying a new car** die mit dem Kauf eines neuen Wagens verbundenen hohen Kosten

costly ['kɒstlɪ] ADJ teuer, kostspielig; tastes, habits teuer; ~ **in terms of time/labour** zeitaufwendig or -aufwändig/arbeitsintensiv; **running a car is a ~ business** ein Auto zu unterhalten ist eine teure Angelegenheit

cost: cost of living N Lebenshaltungskosten pl; **cost-of-living adjustment** N (US, Fin) Dynamisierung f auf der Basis veränderter Lebenshaltungskosten (inf); **cost-of-living bonus** N Lebenshaltungskostenzuschlag m; **cost-of- -living index** N Lebenshaltungsindex m; **cost-plus** ADJ **calculated on a ~ basis** unter Einbeziehung einer Gewinnspanne berechnet; **cost price** N Selbstkostenpreis m; **cost-saving** ADJ Kosten sparend

costume ['kɒstjuːm] N Kostüm nt; (= bathing costume) Badeanzug m

costume: costume ball N Kostümfest nt; **costume drama** N **a** (= play) Schauspiel nt in historischen Kostümen; (= film) Kostümfilm m, Historienfilm m; (= series) Serie f in historischen Kostümen **b** (= genre, Theat) Schauspiele pl in historischen Kostümen; (Film) Kostümfilme pl; (TV) Serien pl in historischen Kostümen; **costume jewellery** N Modeschmuck m; **costume piece, costume play** N Schauspiel nt in historischen Kostümen; **costume ring** N Modeschmuckring m

costumier [kɒs'tjuːmɪə'], (US) **costumer** [kɒs'tjuːmə'] N **a** (= theatrical costumier) Kostümverleih m **b** (form, = dressmaker) Schneider(in) m(f)

cosy, (US) **cozy** ['kəʊzɪ] ADJ (+er) room, atmosphere, restaurant gemütlich, behaglich; (= warm) mollig warm; (fig) chat gemütlich, traulich (dated); relationship traut; **to feel ~** (person) sich wohl und behaglich fühlen; (room etc) einen behaglichen or gemütlichen Eindruck machen; **I'm very ~ here** ich fühle mich hier sehr wohl, ich finde es hier sehr gemütlich; **a ~ little tête-à-tête** (fig) ein trautes Tete-à-tête or Tête-à-tête; **warm and ~** mollig warm **N** (= tea cosy, egg cosy) Wärmer m **VI to ~ up to sb** (inf) mit jdm auf Schmusekurs gehen (inf)

cot [kɒt] N (esp Brit: = child's bed) Kinderbett nt; (US, = camp bed) Feldbett nt

cot death N (Brit) Krippentod m, plötzlicher Kindstod

cote [kəʊt] N (= dovecote) Taubenschlag m; (= sheepcote) Schafstall m

coterie ['kəʊtərɪ] N Clique f; (= literary coterie) Zirkel m

cotill(i)on [kə'tɪljən] N Kotillon m

cotta ['kɒtə] N (Eccl) Chorhemd nt

cottage ['kɒtɪdʒ] N **a** Cottage nt, Häuschen nt; (US, in institution) Wohneinheit f **b** (sl: for gays) Klappe f (sl)

cottage: cottage cheese N Hüttenkäse m; **cottage hospital** N (Brit) kleines Krankenhaus für leichtere Fälle; **cottage industry** N Manufaktur f, Heimindustrie f; **cottage loaf** N (Brit) eine Art rundes, hohes Weißbrot; **cottage pie** N Hackfleisch mit Kartoffelbrei überbacken

cottager ['kɒtɪdʒə'] N (Brit) Cottagebewohner(in) m(f)

cotter (pin) ['kɒtə(ˌpɪn)] N Splint m

cotton ['kɒtn] **N** Baumwolle f; (= plant) Baumwollstrauch m; (= fibre) Baumwollfaser f; (= fabric) Baumwollstoff m; (= sewing thread) (Baumwoll)garn nt ADJ Baumwoll-, baumwollen; clothes, fabric also aus Baumwolle

▶ **cotton on** VI (Brit inf) es kapieren (inf), es schnallen (inf); **to cotton on to sth** etw checken (inf); **has he cottoned on yet?** hat er es endlich kapiert (inf) or geschnallt? (inf)

▶ **cotton to** VI +prep obj (US inf) plan, suggestion gut finden

cotton in cpds Baumwoll-; **cotton batting** N (US) Gaze f; **Cotton Belt** N (Geog) Baumwollzone f; **cotton bud** N (Brit) Wattestäbchen nt; **cotton cake** N Futtermittel nt; **cotton candy** N (US) Zuckerwatte f; **cotton gin** N Entkörnungsmaschine f (für Baumwolle); **cotton grass** N Wollgras nt; **cotton mill** N Baumwollspinnerei f; **cotton pad** N Wattepad nt; **cotton picker** N Baumwollpflücker(in) m(f); (= machine) Baumwollpflückmaschine f; **cotton-picking** ADJ (US, inf) verflucht (inf); **cotton plant** N Baumwollstaude f or -strauch m; **cotton print** N (= fabric) bedruckter Baumwollstoff; **cottonseed** N Baumwollsamen m; **cottonseed cake** N = cotton cake; **cottonseed oil** N Baumwollsamenöl nt; **cottontail** N (US) Kaninchen nt, Karnickel nt; **cottonwood** N Pyramidenpappel f; **cotton wool** N (Brit) Watte f; **to wrap sb (up) in ~** (fig) jdn in Watte packen; **my brain feels like ~** ich kann überhaupt nicht klar denken

cotyledon [ˌkɒtɪ'liːdən] N Keimblatt nt

couch [kaʊtʃ] **N** Sofa nt; (= studio couch) Schlafcouch f; (= doctor's couch) Liege f; (= psychiatrist's couch) Couch f; (poet, = bed) Lager nt **VT** **a** (= put in words) request formulieren, abfassen **b** (= lower) spear, lance anlegen **VI** (liter, lion, cat etc) lauern, auf der Lauer liegen

couchant ['kuːʃənt] ADJ (Her) liegend

couchette [kuːʃet] N (Rail) Liegewagen(platz) m

couch grass N Quecke f

couch potato N (inf) Dauerglotzer(in) m(f) (inf), Couchpotato f

cougar ['kuːgə'] N Puma m, Kuguar m

cough [kɒf] **N** Husten m; **he has a bit of a ~** er hat etwas Husten **VI** **to give a warning ~** sich warnend räuspern; **a smoker's ~** Raucherhusten m **VI** husten **VT** blood husten

▶ **cough out** VT sep aushusten, ausspucken

▶ **cough up** **VT** sep (lit) aushusten **VT** insep (fig inf) money rausrücken (inf), ausspucken (inf), rüberkommen mit (sl) **VI** (fig inf) blechen (inf), ausspucken (inf)

cough: cough drop N Hustenpastille f; **cough mixture** N Hustensaft m or -mittel nt; **cough sweet** N (Brit) Hustenbonbon nt; **cough syrup** N Hustensaft m

could [kʊd] ❂ 1.1, 1.2, 2.2, 4, 9.1, 15.3, 26.3 pret of **can** [1]

couldn't ['kʊdnt] contr of **could not**

coulomb ['kuːlɒm] N Coulomb nt

council ['kaʊnsl] **N** (= body of representatives) Rat m; (= meeting) Sitzung f, Beratung f; **city/ town ~** Stadtrat m; **to be on the ~** im Rat sitzen, Ratsmitglied sein; **to hold ~** Beratungen abhalten, Rat halten (old); ~ **of war** Kriegsrat m; **Council of Europe** Europarat m; **Council of Ministers** (Pol) Ministerrat m **ADJ** attr ~ **meeting** Ratssitzung f

council (Brit): **council chamber** N Sitzungssaal m des Rats; **council estate** N Sozialwohnungssiedlung f; **council flat** N Sozialwohnung f; **council house** N Sozialwohnung f; **council housing** N sozialer Wohnungsbau

councillor, (US) **councilor** ['kaʊnsələ'] N Ratsmitglied nt; (= town councillor) Stadtrat m/-rätin f; **Smith** Herr Stadtrat/Frau Stadträtin Smith

council tax N (Brit) Kommunalsteuer f

council tenant N (Brit) Bewohner(in) m(f) einer Sozialwohnung

counsel ['kaʊnsəl] **N** **a** (form, = advice) Rat (-schlag) m; **to hold or take ~ with sb over** or **about sth** mit jdm etw beraten or beratschlagen; **to keep one's own ~** seine Meinung für sich behalten, mit seiner Meinung zurückhalten; ~**s of perfection** schlaue Ratschläge **b** pl - (Jur) Rechtsanwalt m; ~ **for the defence/prosecution** Verteidiger(in) m(f)/Vertreter(in) m(f) der Anklage, ≈ Staatsanwalt m/-anwältin f; ~ **on both sides** Verteidigung und Anklage **VT** **a** (form) person beraten; (= advise) action empfehlen, raten zu; **to ~ sb to do sth** jdm raten or empfehlen, etw zu tun **b** (in social work etc) beraten

counselling, (US) **counseling** ['kaʊnsəlɪŋ] N Beratung f; (Sociol) soziale Beratung; (by therapist) Therapie f; **to need ~** professionelle Hilfe brauchen; **to go for** or **have ~** zur Beratung/ Therapie gehen; **to give sb ~** jdm professionelle Hilfe zukommen lassen, jdn beraten/therapieren

counsellor, (US) **counselor** ['kaʊnsələ'] N **a** (= adviser) Berater(in) m(f) **b** (US, Ir, = lawyer) Rechtsanwalt m/-anwältin f

count[1] [kaʊnt] **N** **a** (with numbers) Zählung f; (Sport) Auszählen nt; (of votes) (Stimmen)zählung f, (Stimmen)auszählung f; **I'll have a ~** ich zähle es mal (ab); **she lost ~ when she was interrupted** sie kam mit dem Zählen durcheinander, als sie unterbrochen wurde; **I've lost all ~ of her boyfriends** ich habe die Übersicht über ihre Freunde vollkommen verloren; **to keep ~ (of sth)** (etw) mitzählen; (= keep track) die Übersicht (über etw acc)) behalten; **she couldn't keep ~ of them** sie verlor die Übersicht; **at the last ~ there were twenty members** bei der letzten Zählung waren es zwanzig Mitglieder; **all together now, on the ~ of three** und jetzt alle zusammen, bei drei gehts los; **I'll come and look for you after a ~ of ten** ich zähle bis zehn und dann komme und suche ich dich; **he was out for the ~, he took the ~** (Sport) er wurde ausgezählt; (fig) er war k. o.; **he took a ~ of eight** (Sport) er ging bis acht zu Boden **b** (Jur, = charge) Anklagepunkt m; **on that ~** (fig) in dem Punkt; **you're wrong on both ~s** Sie haben in beiden Punkten Unrecht; **on all ~s** in jeder Hinsicht **c** no pl (= notice) **don't take any ~ of what he says** hören Sie nicht auf das, was er sagt; **she never takes much/any ~ of him** sie nimmt wenig/keinerlei Notiz von ihm **VT** **a** (with numbers) (ab)zählen; (= count again) nachzählen; votes (aus)zählen; **to ~ ten** bis zehn zählen; **I only ~ed ten people** ich habe nur zehn Leute gezählt; **to ~ the cost** (lit) auf die Kosten achten, jeden Pfennig umdrehen; **she'll help anyone without ~ing the cost to herself** sie hilft jedem, ohne an sich selbst zu denken **b** (= consider) ansehen, betrachten; (= include) mitrechnen, mitzählen; **to ~ sb (as) a friend/among one's friends** jdn als Freund ansehen/zu seinen Freunden zählen; **you should ~ yourself lucky to be alive** Sie sollten froh und glücklich sein or Sie können noch von Glück sagen, dass Sie noch leben; **ten people (not) ~ing the children** zehn Leute, die Kinder (nicht) mitgerechnet or eingerechnet; **to ~ sth against sb** etw gegen jdn anrechnen **VI** **a** (with numbers) zählen; **to ~ to ten** bis zehn zählen; ~**ing from today** von heute an (gerechnet) **b** (= be considered) betrachtet or angesehen werden; (= be included) mitgerechnet or mitgezählt werden; (= be important) wichtig sein; **the children don't ~** die Kinder zählen nicht; **he doesn't ~ amongst her friends** er zählt nicht zu ihren Freunden; **that doesn't ~** das zählt nicht; **every minute/it all ~s** jede Minute ist/das ist alles wichtig; **appearance ~s a lot** es kommt sehr auf die äußere Erscheinung an; **to ~ against sb** gegen jdn sprechen

▶ **count down** **VI** den Countdown durchführen; **they started counting down last night** sie haben gestern abend mit dem Countdown angefangen; **to count down to blast-off** bis zum Abschuss (der Rakete) rückwärts zählen **VT** sep **to count a rocket down** den Countdown (für eine Rakete) durchführen

▶ **count for** VI +prep obj **to count for a lot** sehr viel bedeuten; **to count for nothing** nichts gelten

▶ **count in** VT sep mitzählen; person also mitrechnen, berücksichtigen, einplanen; **to count sb in on sth** davon ausgehen or damit rechnen, dass jd bei etw mitmacht; **you can count me in!** Sie können mit mir rechnen, da mache ich mit

▶ **count off** VT sep VI abzählen

▶ **count on** VI +prep obj (= depend on) rechnen mit, sich verlassen auf (+acc); **to count on doing sth** die Absicht haben, etw zu tun; **to count on being able to do sth** damit rechnen, etw tun zu können; **you can count on him to help you** du kannst auf seine Hilfe zählen

▶ **count out** VT sep **a** (Sport) auszählen **b** money, books etc abzählen **c** (Brit, Parl) **to count the House** eine Sitzung des Unterhauses wegen zu geringer Abgeordnetenzahl vertagen **d** (inf, = exclude) **(you can) count me out (of that)!** ohne mich!, da mache ich nicht mit!; **count him out of it** plane ihn besser nicht ein

▶ **count up** VT sep zusammenzählen or -rechnen

▶ **count upon** VI +prep obj = **count on**

count² N Graf m

countable ['kaʊntəbl] ADJ zählbar (also Gram)

countdown ['kaʊntdaʊn] N Count-down m, Countdown m; **to start the ~** mit dem Countdown beginnen

countenance ['kaʊntɪnəns] N **a** (old, form: = face) Angesicht nt (old, Eccl), Antlitz nt (old); (= expression) Gesichtsausdruck m; **to keep one's ~** (fig) die Fassung or Haltung bewahren; **to lose ~** (fig) das Gesicht verlieren; **to put sb out of ~** jdn aus der Fassung bringen **b** (= support) to give/lend ~ **to sth** einer Sache ermutigen/unterstützen VT behaviour gutheißen; plan, suggestion also, person unterstützen

counter ['kaʊntə] N **a** (in shop) Ladentisch m, Tresen m (N Ger); (in café) Theke f; (in bank, post office) Schalter m; **to sell/buy sth under/over the ~** etw unter dem/über den Ladentisch verkaufen/bekommen; **medicines which can be bought over the ~** Medikamente, die man rezeptfrei bekommt; **under-the-counter deals** (fig) dunkle Geschäfte pl, Schiebereien pl **b** (= small disc for games) Spielmarke f **c** (Tech) Zähler m **d** (Sport, Fencing) Parade f; (Boxing also) Konter m **e** (= reply) Entgegnung f, Erwiderung f, Replik f (geh) **f** (= opposing force) Gegengewicht nt (to zu) VT (= retaliate against) antworten auf (+acc), kontern (also Sport); **how dare you ~ my orders!** (= countermand) wie können Sie es wagen, meine Anweisungen or (Mil) Befehle aufzuheben; **to ~ the loss** den Verlust wettmachen or ausgleichen VI kontern (also Sport) ADV ~ **to** gegen (+acc); **to go** or **run ~ to sb's wishes** jds Wünschen (dat) zuwiderlaufen; **the results are ~ to expectations** die Ergebnisse widersprechen den Erwartungen

counter: counteract VT (= make ineffective) neutralisieren; (= act in opposition to) entgegenwirken (+dat); disease bekämpfen; **counteraction** N (making ineffective) Neutralisierung f; (= offsetting) Gegenwirkung f; (against disease) Bekämpfung f; **counteractive** ADJ entgegenwirkend, Gegen-; ~ **measures** Gegenmaßnahmen pl; **counterargument** N Gegenargument nt; **counterattack** N Gegenangriff m VT einen Gegenangriff starten gegen; (= argue against) kontern, beantworten VI einen Gegenangriff starten, zurückschlagen; **counterattraction** N Gegenattraktion f (to zu); (on TV etc) Konkurrenzprogramm nt; **counterbalance** N Gegengewicht nt VT ausgleichen; **counterblast** N (fig: = reaction) heftige Gegenreaktion (to auf +acc); **countercharge** N **a** (Jur) Gegenklage f **b** (Mil) Gegenattacke f;

countercheck N Gegenkontrolle f; **counterclaim** N (Jur) Gegenanspruch m; **counter clerk** N (in bank, booking office etc) Angestellte(r) mf im Schalterdienst; (in post office etc) Schalterbeamte(r) m/-beamtin f; **counterclockwise** ADJ, ADV (US) = **anti-clockwise**; **counterculture** N Gegenkultur f; **counterespionage** N Gegenspionage f, Spionageabwehr f; **counterexample** N Gegenbeispiel nt

counterfeit ['kaʊntəfiːt] ADJ gefälscht; (fig) falsch; ~ **money/coins** Falschgeld nt N Fälschung f VT fälschen; (fig) vortäuschen

counterfoil ['kaʊntəfɔɪl] N Kontrollabschnitt m

counter: counterinflationary ADJ (Econ) antiinflationär; **counterinsurgency** N Kampf m gegen Aufständische; ~ **measures** Maßnahmen pl gegen Aufständische; **counterinsurgent** N Antiguerillakämpfer(in) m(f); **counterintelligence** N = **counterespionage**; **counterirritant** N (Med) Gegenreizmittel nt

countermand ['kaʊntəmɑːnd] VT order aufheben, widerrufen; attack, plan rückgängig machen; **unless ~ed** bis auf gegenteilige Anweisung or (Mil) Order

counter: countermarch (Mil) N Rückmarsch m VI zurückmarschieren; **countermeasure** N Gegenmaßnahme f; **counteroffensive** N (Mil) Gegenoffensive f; **counteroffer** N Gegenangebot nt; **counterpane** N Tagesdecke f; **counterpart** N (= equivalent) Gegenüber nt; (= complement) Gegenstück nt, Pendant nt; **counterplot** N Gegenanschlag m VI einen Gegenanschlag planen; **counterpoint** N (Mus, fig) Kontrapunkt m VT (fig) einen Kontrapunkt bilden zu; **counterpoise** N **a** (= weight) Gegengewicht nt; (= force, fig) Gegenkraft f **b** no pl (= equilibrium, fig) Gleichgewicht nt; **to be in ~** im Gleichgewicht sein VT (lit, fig) ausgleichen; **counterproductive** ADJ unsinnig, widersinnig; criticism, measures, policies destruktiv, kontraproduktiv; **that wouldn't help us at all, in fact it would be** ~ das würde uns nicht weiterbringen, sondern sogar das Gegenteil bewirken or es wäre sogar kontraproduktiv; **Counter-Reformation** N (Hist) Gegenreformation f; **counter-revolution** N Gegen- or Konterrevolution f; **counter-revolutionary** ADJ konterrevolutionär; **countershaft** N (Tech) Vorgelegewelle f; **countersign** N (Mil) Parole f, Kennwort nt VT cheque etc gegenzeichnen; **countersignature** N Gegenunterschrift f; **countersink** N (= tool) Versenker m, Spitzsenker m VT hole senken; screw versenken; **counter staff** PL (in shop) Verkäufer pl; **counterstroke** N Gegenschlag m; **countersunk** ADJ screw Senk-; **countertenor** N (Mus) Kontratenor m; **counterterrorism** N Terrorismusbekämpfung f; **counterweight** N Gegengewicht nt

countess ['kaʊntɪs] N Gräfin f

counting house ['kaʊntɪŋhaʊs] N (old) Kontor nt

countless ['kaʊntlɪs] ADJ unzählig attr, zahllos attr; ~ **millions of ...** unzählige or zahllose Millionen von ...

count palatine N pl -s - Pfalzgraf m

countrified ['kʌntrɪfaɪd] ADJ ländlich, bäuerlich

country ['kʌntrɪ] N **a** (= state) Land nt; (= people also) Volk nt; **his own ~** seine Heimat; **to die for one's ~** für sein Land sterben; **to go to the ~** Neuwahlen ausschreiben **b** no pl (as opposed to town) Land nt; (= scenery, countryside also) Landschaft f; **in/to the ~** auf dem/aufs Land; **the surrounding ~** das umliegende Land, die Umgebung; **this is good hunting/fishing ~** das ist eine gute Jagd-/Fischgegend; **this is mining ~** dies ist ein Bergbaugebiet; **we're back in familiar ~ again** (fig) wir befinden uns wieder auf vertrautem Boden

country in cpds Land-; **country and western** N Country-und-Western-Musik f; **country--and-western** ADJ Country- und Western-;

country-born ADJ auf dem Land geboren; **country-bred** ADJ auf dem Land aufgewachsen; animals auf dem Land gezogen; **country bumpkin** N (pej) Bauerntölpel (inf), Bauer (pej inf) m; (= girl) Bauerntrampel nt (inf); **country club** N Klub auf dem Lande; **country code** N **a** (= telephone prefix) internationale Vorwahl **b** (Brit: = set of rules) Verhaltenskodex m für Besucher auf dem Lande; **country cousin** N Vetter m/Base f vom Lande; **country dance** N Volkstanz m; **country dancing** N Volkstanz m; **to go** ~ zum Volkstanz gehen; **country dweller** N Landbewohner(in) m(f); **country folk** PL Leute pl vom Lande; **country gentleman** N Landbesitzer m; **country gentry** PL Landadel m; **country house** N Landhaus nt; **country life** N das Landleben, das Leben auf dem Lande; **countryman** N **a** (= compatriot) Landsmann m; **his fellow countrymen** seine Landsleute **b** (= country dweller) Landmann m; **country mile** N (US inf) **to miss sth by a** ~ etw um Längen verpassen; **country music** N Countrymusik f; **country people** PL Leute pl vom Land(e); **country road** N Landstraße f; **country seat** N Landsitz m; **countryside** N (= scenery) Landschaft f, Gegend f; (= rural area) Land nt; **it's beautiful ~** das ist eine herrliche Landschaft or Gegend; **to live in the middle of the ~** mitten auf dem Land leben; **Countryside Commission** N (Brit) Kommission f zum Schutz ländlicher Gebiete; **country town** N Kleinstadt f; **country-wide** ADJ landesweit, im ganzen Land; **countrywoman** N **a** (= compatriot) Landsmännin f **b** (= country dweller) Landfrau f

county ['kaʊntɪ] N (Brit) Grafschaft f; (US) (Verwaltungs)bezirk m ADJ (Brit) family zum Landadel gehörend; accent, behaviour vornehm; occasion für den Landadel; **the ~ set** die feinen Pinkel (inf)

county: county borough N (Brit) Stadt mit grafschaftlichen Rechten; **county council** N (Brit) Grafschaftsrat m; **county court** N (Brit) Grafschaftsgericht nt; **county seat** N (US) Hauptstadt eines Verwaltungsbezirkes; **county town** N (Brit) Hauptstadt einer Grafschaft

coup [kuː] N **a** (= successful action) Coup m **b** (= coup d'état) Staatsstreich m, Coup d'Etat m

coup: coup de grâce [ˌkuːdəˈɡrɑːs] N (lit, fig) Gnadenstoß m; (with gun) Gnadenschuss m; **coup d'état** ['kuːdeɪtɑː] N = **coup b**

coupé ['kuːpeɪ] N (= car) Coupé nt, Kupee nt

couple ['kʌpl] N **a** (= pair) Paar nt; (= married couple) Ehepaar nt; **courting** ~**s** Liebespaare pl; **in** ~**s** paarweise → **happy a** **b** (inf) **a** ~ (= two) zwei; (= several) ein paar, einige; **a** ~ **of letters/friends** etc ein paar or einige Briefe/Freunde etc; **we had a** ~ **in the pub** wir haben in der Kneipe ein paar getrunken; **a** ~ **of times** ein paar Mal; **it took a** ~ **of minutes/hours** es hat einige or ein paar Minuten/ungefähr zwei Stunden gedauert VT **a** (= link) names, circuit verbinden; carriages etc koppeln; **smoking** ~**d with poor diet ...** Rauchen in Verbindung mit schlechter Ernährung ... **b** (= mate) animals paaren VI (= mate) sich paaren

▶ **couple on** VT sep anhängen

▶ **couple up** VT sep ankoppeln

coupler ['kʌplə] N (Comput) Koppler m

couples therapy N (US) Eheberatung f

couplet ['kʌplɪt] N Verspaar nt

coupling ['kʌplɪŋ] N **a** (= linking) Verbindung f; (of carriages etc) Kopplung f; **the continual ~ of his name with ...** dass sein Name ständig mit ... in Verbindung gebracht wird/wurde **b** (= mating) Paarung f **c** (= linking device) Kupplung f

coupon ['kuːpɒn] N **a** (= voucher) Gutschein m; (= ration coupon) (Zuteilungs)schein m **b** (Ftbl) Totoschein m, Wettschein m **c** (Fin) Kupon m

courage [ˈkʌrɪdʒ] N Mut *m*, Courage *f* (*inf*); **I haven't the ~ to refuse** ich habe einfach nicht den Mut, nein *or* Nein zu sagen; **take ~!** (*liter*) nur Mut!; **to take ~ from sth** sich durch etw ermutigt fühlen; **to lose one's ~** den Mut verlieren; **to have/lack the ~ of one's convictions** Zivilcourage/keine Zivilcourage haben; **to take one's ~ in both hands** sein Herz in beide Hände nehmen

courageous [kəˈreɪdʒəs] ADJ mutig; (= *with courage of convictions*) couragiert

courageously [kəˈreɪdʒəslɪ] ADV *fight, resist* mutig; *criticize, denounce* couragiert

courgette [kʊəˈʒet] N (*Brit*) Zucchini *f*

courier [ˈkʊrɪə] N **a** (= *messenger*) Kurier *m*; **by ~** per Kurier **b** (= *tourist guide*) Reiseleiter(in) *m(f)*

course[1] [kɔːs] ✪ 9.2, 11.3 N **a** (= *direction, path, of plane, ship*) Kurs *m*; (*of river*) Lauf *m*; (*fig, of illness, relationship*) Verlauf *m*; (*of history*) Lauf *m*; (*of action etc, = way of proceeding*) Vorgehensweise *f*; **to set (one's) ~ for a place** Kurs auf einen Ort nehmen; **to change** *or* **alter ~** den Kurs wechseln *or* ändern; **to be on/off ~** auf Kurs sein/vom Kurs abgekommen sein; **to be on ~ for sth** (*fig*) gute Aussichten auf etw (*acc*) haben; **to let sth take** *or* **run its ~** einer Sache (*dat*) ihren Lauf lassen, etw (*acc*) seinen Lauf nehmen lassen; **the affair has run its ~** die Angelegenheit ist zu einem Ende gekommen; **the ~ of true love ne'er did run smooth** (*prov*) Liebe geht oft seltsame Wege (*prov*); **which ~ of action did you take?** wie sind Sie vorgegangen?; **that was an unwise ~ of action** es war unklug, so vorzugehen; **the best ~ (of action) would be ...** das Beste wäre ...; **we have no other ~ (of action) but to ...** es bleibt uns nichts anderes übrig als zu ...; **to take a middle ~** einen gemäßigten Kurs einschlagen
b **in the ~ of his life/the next few weeks/the meeting** *etc* während seines Lebens/der nächsten paar Wochen/der Versammlung *etc*; **in the ~ of the/this conversation** im Laufe der Zeit/Unterhaltung; **it's in the ~ of being done** es wird gerade gemacht; **in the ~ of shaving** beim Rasieren; **in the ordinary ~ of things, you could expect ...** unter normalen Umständen könnte man erwarten ...; **to be in the ~ of nature** in der Natur der Sache liegen → **due**
c **of ~** (= *admittedly*) natürlich; (= *naturally, obviously also*) selbstverständlich; **of ~!** natürlich!, selbstverständlich!, klar! (*inf*); **of ~ I will!** aber natürlich *or* selbstverständlich werde ich, klar, ich komme (*inf*); **don't you like me? – of ~ I do** magst du mich nicht? – doch, natürlich; **he's rather young, of ~, but ...** er ist natürlich ziemlich jung, aber ...
d (*Sch, Univ*) Studium *nt*; (= *summer course etc*) Kurs(us) *m*; (*at work*) Lehrgang *m*; (*Med, of treatment*) Kur *f*; **to go on a French ~** einen Französischkurs(us) besuchen; **a ~ in first aid** ein Kurs über erste Hilfe, ein Erste-Hilfe-Kurs; **a ~ of lectures, a lecture ~** eine Vorlesungsreihe; **a ~ of pills/treatment** eine Pillenkur/eine Behandlung
e (*Sport*, = *race course*) Kurs *m*; (= *golf course*) Platz *m*; **to stay** *or* **last the ~** (*lit*) das Rennen durchhalten; (*fig*) bis zum Ende durchhalten
f (*Cook*) Gang *m*; **first ~** erster Gang; **a three-course meal** ein Essen *nt* mit drei Gängen
g (*Build*) Schicht *f*.
h (*Naut, = sail*) Untersegel *nt*

course[2] VT (*Hunt*) *hare, stag* hetzen, jagen VI **a** (*blood, tears*) strömen **b** (*Hunt, fig*) hetzen, jagen; **to go coursing** auf Hetzjagd gehen

courser [ˈkɔːsə] N **a** (= *dog*) Hatz- *or* Hetzhund *m* **b** (*poet, = horse*) (schnelles) Ross (*liter*)

coursing [ˈkɔːsɪŋ] N (*Sport*) Hetzjagd *f*, Hatz *f*, Hetze *f*

court [kɔːt] N **a** (*Jur, also* **court of justice** *or* **law**) Gericht *nt*; (= *body of judges also*) Gerichtshof *m*; (= *room*) Gerichtssaal *m*; **Court of Session** (*Scot*) *höchstes schottisches Zivilgericht* **to appear in ~** vor Gericht erscheinen; **the evi-**

dence was ruled out of ~ das Beweismaterial wurde nicht zugelassen; **his suggestion was ruled out of ~** (*fig*) sein Vorschlag wurde verworfen; **to take sb to ~** jdn verklagen *or* vor Gericht bringen; **to go to ~ over a matter** eine Sache vor Gericht bringen, mit einer Sache vor Gericht gehen; **the case comes up in ~ next week** der Fall wird nächste Woche verhandelt; **Sir James is still in ~** Sir James ist noch beim Gericht; **to give sb his/her day in ~** (*inf*) jdm die Möglichkeit geben, sich zur Sache zu äußern; **to be laughed out of ~** (*inf*) verlacht werden → **settle**
b (*royal*) Hof *m*; **to be presented at ~** bei Hofe vorgestellt werden; **the Court of St James** der englische Königshof; **to hold ~ in ...** (*film star etc*) Hof halten in ...
c (*Sport*) Platz *m*; (*for squash*) Halle *f*; (= *marked-off area*) Spielfeld *nt*; (= *service court etc*) Feld *nt*; **grass/hard ~** Rasen-/Hartplatz *m*; **on ~** auf dem Platz/in der Halle; **out of the ~** außerhalb des Spielfeldes
d (= *courtyard, Univ, = quadrangle*) Hof *m*; **inner ~** Innenhof *m*
e (*old form, = courtship*) Hof *m*; **to pay ~ to a woman** einer Frau (*dat*) den Hof machen
VT **a** (*dated*) *woman* umwerben, werben um, den Hof machen (+*dat*)
b (*fig*) *person's favour* werben um, buhlen um (*pej*); *danger, defeat* herausfordern
VI (*dated, man*) auf Freiersfüßen gehen (*dated, hum*); **they were ~ing at the time** zu der Zeit gingen sie zusammen; **she's ~ing** sie hat einen Freund; **are you ~ing?** hast du jemanden?

COURT

In England, Wales und Nordirland werden Schwerverbrechen und Verfahren, bei denen der Angeklagte auf „nicht schuldig" plädiert, im **Crown Court** vor einem Richter und zwölf Geschworenen verhandelt. Weniger schwere Straftaten werden in einem **magistrates' court** vor einem **magistrate** ohne Geschworene verhandelt. Die meisten Zivilfälle werden vor lokalen Gerichten verhandelt, wobei sich der **High Court** mit den schwerwiegenderen oder komplexeren Zivilrechtsangelegenheiten befasst. Berufungen können sowohl in Strafwie in Zivilfällen beim **Court of Appeal** eingelegt werden, und kommen in letzter Instanz vor das Oberhaus.
Die schottische Rechtsprechung ist anders angelegt. Hier befasst sich der **High Court of Justiciary** mit den Schwerverbrechen und **sheriff courts** mit den weniger schweren Straftaten. Der oberste Gerichtshof für Zivilrecht ist der **Court of Session**.
In den USA kümmern sich Bundesgerichte um Straftaten gegen das Bundesrecht; hier werden Fälle aus verschiedenen Staaten behandelt. Straftaten gegen die Gesetze eines Bundesstaates werden dagegen vor Gerichten im jeweiligen Staat verhandelt. Jeder Staat hat sein eigenes Rechtssystem und kann eigene Gesetze erlassen, mit der Einschränkung, dass diese nicht gegen die Verfassung der USA oder Bundesgesetze verstoßen dürfen. Es gibt keine unterschiedlichen Gerichte für Straf- und Zivilangelegenheiten. Die meisten Bundesstraffälle werden in **district courts** verhandelt, zwölf **Courts of Appeal** sind zuständig für die Berufungsfälle der untergeordneten Bundesgerichte. Oberste Gerichtshöfe für sowohl Bundes- wie Staatsrecht sind die **Supreme Courts**, einer in jedem Staat und einer für den Bund. Im Bundesstaatsrecht sind diesen **Appelate Courts** (Berufungsgerichte) untergeordnet, darunter county oder **city courts**, die sich mit Fällen der allgemeinen Rechtsprechung befassen.

---

court: court battle N (*Jur*) Rechtsstreit *m*, gerichtliche Auseinandersetzung; **court card** N (*Brit*) Bildkarte *f*; **court case** N (*Jur*) Gerichtsverfahren *nt*, Prozess *m*; **court circular** N Hofnachrichten *pl*; **court correspondent** N

(*Brit, Press*) Hofberichterstatter(in) *m(f)*; **court dress** N Hoftracht *f*

courteous ADJ , **courteously** ADV [ˈkɜːtɪəs, -lɪ] höflich

courtesan [ˌkɔːtɪˈzæn] N Kurtisane *f*

courtesy [ˈkɜːtɪsɪ] N Höflichkeit *f*; **(by) ~ of** freundlicherweise zur Verfügung gestellt von; **the air was fresh (by) ~ of a large hole in the roof** die Luft war ziemlich frisch, was einem großen Loch im Dach zu verdanken war; **would you do me the ~ of shutting up!** würden Sie mir den Gefallen tun und den Mund halten!

courtesy: courtesy bus N gebührenfreier Bus, Hotelbus *m*; **courtesy light** N (*Aut*) Innenleuchte *f*; **courtesy title** N Höflichkeitstitel *m*; **courtesy visit** N Höflichkeitsbesuch *m*

court: court fees PL Gerichtskosten *pl*; **court guide** N Hofkalender *m*; **court hearing** N (*Jur*) Gerichtsverhandlung *f*; **courthouse** N (*Jur*) Gerichtsgebäude *nt*

courtier [ˈkɔːtɪə] N Höfling *m*

courtliness [ˈkɔːtlɪnɪs] N (= *politeness*) Höflichkeit *f*; (= *refinement*) Vornehmheit *f*

courtly [ˈkɔːtlɪ] ADJ *manners* höflich; *grace, elegance* vornehm; **~ love** Minne *f*

court: court martial N *pl* **court martials** *or* **courts martial** (*Mil*) Militärgericht *nt*; (*in wartime also*) Kriegsgericht *nt*; **to be tried by ~** vor das/ein Militär-/Kriegsgericht gestellt werden *or* kommen; **court-martial** VT vor das/ein Militär-/Kriegsgericht stellen (*for wegen*); **court order** N (*Jur*) gerichtliche Verfügung; **I'll get a ~** ich werde eine gerichtliche Verfügung beantragen; **court reporter** N **a** (*Jur, = stenographer*) Gerichtsschreiber(in) *m(f)* **b** (*Brit, Press*) = **court correspondent**; **courtroom** N (*Jur*) Gerichtssaal *m*

courtship [ˈkɔːtʃɪp] N (*dated*) (Braut)werbung *f* (*dated*) (*of* um); **during their ~** während er um sie warb *or* freite (*dated*)

court: court shoe N Pumps *m*; **court tennis** N (*US*) Tennis *nt*; **courtyard** N Hof *m*

couscous [ˈkuːskuːs] N Couscous *m*

cousin [ˈkʌzn] N (*male*) Cousin *m*, Vetter *m* (*dated*); (*female*) Cousine *f*, Kusine *f*, Base *f* (*old*); **Kevin and Susan are ~s** Kevin und Susan sind Cousin und Cousine

cousinly [ˈkʌznlɪ] ADJ verwandtschaftlich

couture [kuːˈtjʊə] N Couture *f*

couturier [kuːˈtjʊərɪə] N Couturier *m*

cove[1] [kəʊv] N (*Geog*) (kleine) Bucht

cove[2] N (*dated Brit inf, = fellow*) Kerl *m* (*inf*); **odd ~** komischer Kauz

coven [ˈkʌvn] N Hexenzirkel *m*; (= *meeting*) Hexensabbat *m*

covenant [ˈkʌvɪnənt] N Schwur *m*; (*Bibl*) Bund *m*; (*Jur*) Verpflichtung *f* zu regelmäßigen Spenden; **to swear a solemn ~ that ...** feierlich schwören, dass ... VT **to ~ to do sth** durch ein Abkommen versprechen, etw zu tun; (*Jur*) sich vertraglich verpflichten, etw zu tun VI ein Abkommen/einen Bund schließen

Coventry [ˈkɒvəntrɪ] N **to send sb to ~** (*Brit, inf*) jdn schneiden (*inf*)

cover [ˈkʌvə] N **a** (= *lid*) Deckel *m*; (*of lens*) (Schutz)kappe *f*; (= *loose cover: on chair*) Bezug *m*; (= *cloth: for typewriter, umbrella etc*) Hülle *f*; (*on lorries, tennis court*) Plane *f*; (= *sheet: over merchandise, shop counter*) Decke *f*, Tuch *nt*; (= *blanket, quilt*) (Bett)decke *f*; **he put a ~ over her/it** er deckte sie/es zu; **she pulled the ~s up to her chin** sie zog die Decke bis ans Kinn (hoch)
b (*of book*) Einband *m*; (*of magazine*) Umschlag *m*; (= *dust cover*) (Schutz)umschlag *m*; **to read a book from ~ to ~** ein Buch von Anfang bis Ende *or* von der ersten bis zur letzten Seite lesen; **on the ~** auf dem Einband/Umschlag; (*of magazine*) auf der Titelseite, auf dem Titel(blatt)
c (*Comm, = envelope*) Umschlag *m*; **under separate ~** getrennt; **under plain ~** in neutralem Umschlag

d no pl (= shelter, protection) Schutz m (from vor +dat, gegen); (Mil) Deckung f (from vor +dat, gegen); **to take ~** (from rain) sich unterstellen, Schutz suchen (from vor +dat); (Mil) in Deckung gehen (from vor +dat); **under the ~ of the trees** im Schutz der Bäume; **these plants/ the car should be kept under ~** diese Pflanzen sollten/das Auto sollte abgedeckt sein or (under roof) durch ein Dach geschützt sein; **to get oneself under ~** sich unterstellen; (for longer period) Unterschlupf finden; **under ~ of darkness** im Schutz(e) der Dunkelheit; **to give sb ~** (Mil) jdm Deckung geben

e (Hunt) Deckung f; **to break ~** aus der Deckung hervorbrechen

f (Brit: = place at meal) Gedeck nt; **she laid ~s for six** sie deckte für sechs Personen, sie legte sechs Gedecke auf

g (Brit) (Comm, Fin) Deckung f; (= insurance cover) Versicherung f; **to operate without ~** ohne Deckung arbeiten; **to take out ~ for a car** ein Auto versichern; **to take out ~ against fire** eine Feuerversicherung abschließen; **to get ~ for sth** etw versichern (lassen); **do you have adequate ~?** sind Sie ausreichend versichert?

h (= assumed identity) Tarnung f; (= front organization also) Deckung f; **under ~ as** getarnt als; **to operate under ~** als Agent tätig sein; **to blow sb's ~** jdn enttarnen

i (Mus: also **cover version**) Coverversion f

VT **a** (= put cover on) bedecken; (= cover over) zudecken; (with loose cover) chair etc beziehen; **a ~ed wagon/way** ein Planwagen m/überdachter Weg; **to ~ one's head** den Kopf bedecken; **the car ~ed us in mud** das Auto bespritzte uns von oben bis unten mit Schlamm; **the mountain was ~ed with** or **in snow** der Berg war schneebedeckt or mit Schnee bedeckt; **you're all ~ed with dog hairs** du bist voller Hundehaare; **to ~ oneself in** or **with glory** Ruhm ernten; **to ~ oneself with ridicule** sich lächerlich machen; **~ed in** or **with shame** zutiefst beschämt

b (= hide) surprise verbergen; mistake, tracks also verdecken; **to ~ one's face in** or **with one's hands** sein Gesicht in den Händen verstecken or verbergen

c (= protect) decken; **to ~ one's back** or **rear** or (US inf) **ass** (fig) sich absichern; **he only said that to ~ himself** er hat das nur gesagt, um sich abzudecken or zu decken

d (= point a gun at etc) door etc sichern; sb decken; (= be on guard near) sichern; **to keep sb ~ed** in Schach halten; **I've got you ~ed!** (with gun etc) ich hab auf dich angelegt; (fig, Chess etc) ich hab dich

e (Fin) loan decken; expenses, costs also abdecken; (Insur) versichern; **will £30 ~ the drinks?** reichen £ 30 für die Getränke?; **he gave me £30 to ~ the drinks** er gab mir £ 30 für Getränke

f (= take in, include) behandeln; (law also) erfassen; (= allow for, anticipate) possibilities, eventualities vorsehen; **what does your travel insurance ~ you for?** was deckt deine Reiseversicherung ab?; **to ~ the waterfront** (esp US) einen weiten Bereich abdecken

g (Press, = report on) berichten über (+acc)

h (= travel) miles, distance zurücklegen

i (salesman etc) territory zuständig sein für

j (Mus) song neu interpretieren

k (animals: = copulate with) decken

l (= play a higher card than) überbieten

▶ **cover for** VI +prep obj **a** absent person vertreten, einspringen für **b** (= protect) decken

▶ **cover in** VT sep **a** (= fill in) grave etc auffüllen, zuschütten **b** (= roof in) überdachen

▶ **cover over** VT sep **a** (= put a cover over) zudecken; (for protection) tennis court abdecken; (= roof over) überdachen

▶ **cover up** **VI** **a** (= wrap up) sich einmummen **b** (= conceal a fact) alles vertuschen or verheimlichen; **don't try to cover up** versuchen Sie nicht, Ihren Fehler zu vertuschen; **to cover up for sb** jdn decken **VT** sep **a** child zudecken; object also, tennis court abdecken **b** (= hide) truth, facts vertuschen, verheimlichen

coverage ['kʌvərɪdʒ] N , no pl **a** (in media) Berichterstattung f (of über +acc); **to give full ~ to an event** ausführlich über ein Ereignis berichten; **the games got excellent TV ~** die Spiele wurden ausführlich im Fernsehen gebracht **b** (Insur) Versicherung f; **this policy gives you full ~ for …** diese Versicherung bietet Ihnen volle Deckung bei …

cover: cover address N Deckadresse f; **coverall** N usu pl (US) Overall m; **cover charge** N Kosten pl für ein Gedeck

covered market [ˌkʌvəd ˈmɑːkɪt] N überdachter Markt

cover girl N Titel(bild)mädchen nt, Covergirl nt

covering ['kʌvərɪŋ] N Decke f; (= floor covering) Belag m; **a ~ of dust/snow** eine Staub-/Schneedecke; **what kind of ~ did you put over the hole?** womit haben Sie das Loch ab- or zugedeckt?

covering: covering agreement N Mantelvertrag m; **covering letter** N (Brit) Begleitbrief m

coverlet ['kʌvəlɪt] N Tagesdecke f

cover letter N (US) = **covering letter**

cover: cover note N Deckungszusage f, vorläufiger Versicherungsschein; **cover organization** N Deckorganisation f; **cover price** N Einzel(exemplar)preis m; **cover shot** N (Phot) Totale f; (for magazine) Titelfoto nt; **cover story** N (of paper) Titelgeschichte f; (of spy) Geschichte f

covert ['kʌvət] **ADJ** threat, attack versteckt; glance also verstohlen; surveillance heimlich **N** Versteck nt → **draw**²

covertly ['kʌvətlɪ] ADV threaten, attack versteckt; glance also verstohlen; film, watch heimlich

cover-up ['kʌvərʌp] N Vertuschung f, Verschleierung f; **the Watergate ~** die Vertuschung von Watergate

cover version N (Mus) Coverversion f

covet ['kʌvɪt] **VT** begehren **VI** begehrlich or begierig sein

covetable ['kʌvɪtəbl] ADJ begehrenswert

covetous ['kʌvɪtəs] ADJ begehrlich; **to be ~ of sth** (liter) etw begehren

covetously ['kʌvɪtəslɪ] ADV begehrlich

covetousness ['kʌvɪtəsnɪs] N Begierde f (of auf +acc), Begehren nt (of nach)

covey ['kʌvɪ] N (of partridges) Kette f

coving ['kəʊvɪŋ] N Wölbung f

cow¹ [kaʊ] N **a** Kuh f; **a ~ elephant** eine Elefantenkuh; **till the ~s come home** (fig inf) bis in alle Ewigkeit (inf); **you'll be waiting till the ~s come home** (fig inf) da kannst du warten, bis du schwarz wirst (inf); **to have a ~** (US, inf) die Fassung verlieren, sich aufregen **b** (pej inf: = woman, stupid) Kuh f (inf); (nasty) gemeine Ziege (inf); **cheeky/lazy/nosey ~!** freches/faules/neugieriges Stück! (inf)

cow² VT person, animal einschüchtern, verschüchtern; **she had a ~ed look about her** sie machte einen eingeschüchterten or verschüchterten Eindruck; **to ~ sb into submission** jdn (durch Einschüchterung) gefügig machen

coward ['kaʊəd] N Feigling m

cowardice ['kaʊədɪs], **cowardliness** ['kaʊədlɪnɪs] N Feigheit f

cowardly ['kaʊədlɪ] ADJ feig(e)

cow: cowbell N Kuhglocke f; **cowboy** N **a** Cowboy m; **to play ~s and Indians** Indianer spielen; **the little boy was wearing a ~ outfit** der kleine Junge war als Cowboy verkleidet **b** (fig inf, incompetent) Pfuscher m; (= dishonest) Gauner m (inf); **a ~ outfit** ein windiges Unternehmen (inf); **cowboy hat** N Cowboyhut m; **cowcatcher** N (Rail) Schienenräumer m; **cow dung** N Kuhmist m

cower ['kaʊə] VI sich ducken; (squatting) kauern; **to ~ before sb** vor jdm ducken; **he stood ~ing in a corner** er stand geduckt in einer Ecke; **the ~ing peasants** die geduckten Bauern

▶ **cower away** VI (furchtsam) ausweichen (from +dat)

▶ **cower down** VI sich niederkauern

cow: cowgirl N Cowgirl nt; **cowhand** N Hilfscowboy m; (on farm) Stallknecht m; **cowherd** N Kuhhirte m; **cowhide** N **a** (untanned) Kuhhaut f; (no pl: = leather) Rindsleder nt **b** (US, = whip) Lederpeitsche f

cowl [kaʊl] N **a** (= monk's hood) Kapuze f **b** (= chimney cowl) (Schornstein)kappe f

cowlick ['kaʊlɪk] N Tolle f

cowling ['kaʊlɪŋ] N (Aviat) Motorhaube f

cowl neck N Schalrollkragen m

cowman ['kaʊmən] N pl **-men** [-mən] **a** (= farm labourer) Stallbursche m; (US, = cattle rancher) Viehzüchter m

co-worker ['kəʊ'wɜːkə] N Kollege m, Kollegin f

cow: cow parsley N Wiesenkerbel m; **cowpat** N Kuhfladen m; **cowpoke** N (US, inf) Kuhheini m (pej inf), Cowboy m; **cowpox** N Kuhpocken pl; **cowpuncher** N (US, inf) Cowboy m

cowrie, cowry ['kaʊrɪ] N Kaurischnecke f

cow: cowshed N Kuhstall m; **cowslip** N (Brit: = primrose) Schlüsselblume f; (US, = kingcup) Sumpfdotterblume f

cox [kɒks] **N** Steuermann m **VT** crew Steuermann sein für **VI** steuern

coxcomb ['kɒkskəʊm] N (old) Stutzer m (old)

coxless ['kɒkslɪs] ADJ ohne Steuermann

coxswain ['kɒksn] N **a** (in rowing) = **cox** N **b** (Naut: of lifeboat etc) Boot(s)führer m

coy [kɔɪ] ADJ (+er) **a** (= affectedly shy) verschämt; (= coquettish) neckisch, kokett; (= evasive) zurückhaltend; **to be ~ about sth** (= shy) in Bezug auf etw (acc) verschämt tun; (= evasive) sich ausweichend zu etw äußern

coyly ['kɔɪlɪ] ADV (= shyly) smile, look schüchtern, verschämt; (= evasively) say, answer, refuse ausweichend

coyness ['kɔɪnɪs] N (= shyness) Verschämtheit f; (= coquettishness) neckisches or kokettes Benehmen; (= evasiveness) ausweichende Haltung

coyote [kɔɪˈəʊtɪ] N Kojote m

coypu ['kɔɪpuː] N Sumpfbiber m

cozy ADJ (US) = **cosy**

cozzie ['kɒzɪ] N (Brit, inf) = **cossie**

CP abbr of **Communist Party** KP f

cp abbr of **compare** vgl.

CPA (US) abbr of **certified public accountant**

CPI (US) abbr of **Consumer Price Index**

cpi abbr of **characters per inch** cpi

Cpl abbr of **Corporal**

CP/M abbr of **control program/monitor** CP/M

CPO abbr **a** (Naut) of **chief petty officer** Oberfähnrich m zur See **b** (Police) of **crime prevention officer**

CPR abbr of **cardiopulmonary resuscitation** HLW f

cps abbr of **characters per second** cps, Zeichen pl pro Sekunde

CPU abbr of **central processing unit** CPU f, Zentraleinheit f

crab¹ [kræb] N **a** Krabbe f; (small also) Krebs m; (as food) Krabbe f; **to catch a ~** (Rowing) einen Krebs fangen **b** (= crab louse) Filzlaus f **c** (Gymnastics) Brücke f

crab² VI nörgeln

crab apple N (= fruit) Holzapfel m; (= tree) Holzapfelbaum m

crabbed ['kræbd] ADJ **a** = **crabby** **b** handwriting kritzelig, unleserlich

crabby ['kræbɪ] ADJ (+er) person griesgrämig, mürrisch

crab: crab grass N Fingerhirse f; **crab louse** N Filzlaus f; **crabmeat** N Krabbenfleisch nt; **crabwise** ADV seitwärts

crack [kræk] **N** **a** Riss m; (between floorboards etc) Ritze f; (= wider hole etc) Spalte f; (= fine line: in pottery, glass etc) Sprung m; **leave the window**

open a ~ lass das Fenster einen Spalt offen; **at the ~ of dawn** in aller Frühe; **to fall** or **slip through the ~s** (US fig) durch die Maschen schlüpfen **b** (= sharp noise, of wood etc breaking) Knacks m; (of gun, whip) Knall(en nt no pl) m; (of thunder) Schlag m; **at the ~ of doom** beim Jüngsten Gericht **c** (= sharp blow) Schlag m; **to give sb a ~ on the head** jdm eins auf den Kopf geben; **to give oneself a ~ on the head** sich (dat) den Kopf anschlagen **d** (inf, = gibe) Stichelei f; (= joke) Witz m; **to make a ~ about sb/sth** einen Witz über jdn/ etw reißen **e** (inf, = attempt) **to have a ~ at sth** etw mal probieren (inf) **f** (Drugs) Crack nt **g** (Ir, Brit inf) tolle Zeit; **tourists come to Ireland for the ~** die Touristen kommen wegen der tollen Atmosphäre nach Irland **h** (Brit vulg: = vagina) Fotze f (vulg) **ADJ** attr erstklassig; (Mil) Elite-; **~ shot** Meisterschütze m, Meisterschützin f **VT a** (= make a crack in) glass, china, pottery einen Sprung machen in (+acc); bone anbrechen, anknacksen (inf); skin, ground rissig machen; ground, ice einen Riss/Risse machen in (+acc); **to ~ a rib** sich (dat) eine Rippe anbrechen **b** (= break) nuts, safe knacken; (fig inf) code knacken; case, problem lösen; **to ~ (open) a bottle** einer Flasche (dat) den Hals brechen; **I've ~ed it** (= solved it) ich habs! **c** joke reißen **d** whip knallen mit; finger, joint knacken mit; **to ~ the whip** (fig) die Peitsche schwingen, ein strenges Regiment führen **e** (= hit sharply) schlagen; **he ~ed his head against the pavement** er krachte mit dem Kopf aufs Pflaster **f** (= distil) petroleum kracken; **~ing plant** Krackanlage f **VI a** (= get a crack, pottery, glass) einen Sprung/Sprünge bekommen, springen; (ice, road) einen Riss/Risse bekommen; (lips, skin) spröde or rissig werden; (bones) einen Knacks bekommen (inf); (= break) brechen; **at last his stern face ~ed and he laughed** schließlich verzog sich seine ernste Miene zu einem Lachen **b** (= make a cracking sound, twigs, joints) knacken, krachen; (whip, gun) knallen **c** (= hit sharply) schlagen, krachen **d** (= break: voice) (with emotion) versagen; **his voice is ~ing/beginning to ~** (boy) er ist im/ kommt in den Stimmbruch **e** (inf) **to get ~ing** loslegen (inf), sich daranmachen; **to get ~ing with** or **on sth** mit etw loslegen (inf), sich an etw (acc) machen; **get ~ing!** los jetzt!; (= speed up) mach(t) mal ein bisschen Dampf! (inf) **f** **to crack up VI b** he ~ed under the strain er ist unter der Belastung zusammengebrochen

▶ **crack down** VI **a** (whip) niederknallen, niederkrachen **b** (= clamp down) hart durchgreifen (on bei)

▶ **crack open** VT sep aufbrechen; **to crack open the champagne** die Sektkorken knallen lassen

▶ **crack up** VI **a** (= break into pieces) zerbrechen; (road surface, lips) aufspringen, rissig werden; (ice) brechen; (machine, plane) auseinander brechen, auseinander fallen; (make-up) rissig werden **b** (fig inf, person) durchdrehen (inf); (under strain) zusammenbrechen; (= have a mental breakdown) einen Nervenzusammenbruch haben; (organization) auseinander fallen, zusammenbrechen; (= lose ability, strength: athlete etc) abbauen; **I/he must be cracking up** (hum) so toll ist er/es dann auch wieder nicht; **she cracked up in the witness box** sie brach an der Zeugenbank zusammen **VT** sep (inf) **he's/it's not all he's/it's cracked up to be** so toll ist er/es dann auch wieder nicht; **he's cracked up to be some sort of genius** er wird als eine Art Genie gepriesen

crackajack N, ADJ (US) = **crackerjack**

crackbrained ['krækbreɪnd] ADJ (inf) verrückt, irre

crackdown N (inf) scharfes Durchgreifen; **to order a ~ on sth** anordnen, bei etw scharf durchzugreifen

cracked [krækt] ADJ **a** glass, plate, ice gesprungen; rib, bone angebrochen, angeknackst (inf); (= broken) gebrochen; surface, walls, make-up rissig; lips, skin aufgesprungen **b** (Brit inf, = mad) übergeschnappt (inf)

cracked wheat N Weizenschrot m or nt

cracker ['krækə'] N **a** (= biscuit) Kräcker m **b** (= firecracker) Knallkörper m; (= Christmas cracker) Knallbonbon nt **c crackers** PL (= nut crackers) Nussknacker m **d** (Brit inf) (= woman) tolle Frau (inf); (= man) toller Mann (inf); (= thing) tolles Ding (inf)

crackerjack, (US) **crackajack** ['krækədʒæk] **N** (= person) Kanone f (inf); (= thing) Knüller m (inf) **ADJ** bombig (inf)

crackers ['krækəz] ADJ pred (Brit, inf) übergeschnappt (inf); **to go ~** überschnappen (inf)

crack house N Bezugsstelle f für Crack, Crackhaus nt

cracking ['krækɪŋ] ADJ (inf) pace scharf; (dated, = good) novel klasse inv (inf), fantastisch, phantastisch

crackjaw ['krækdʒɔ:] (inf) **ADJ** attr word, name zungenbrecherisch **N** Zungenbrecher m

crackle ['krækl] **VI** (dry leaves) rascheln; (paper also) knistern; (fire) knistern, prasseln; (twigs, telephone line) knacken; (machine gun) knattern; (bacon) brutzeln; **the line was crackling so much** es knackte so stark in der Leitung **VT** paper rascheln or knistern mit **N a** (= crackling noise, of dry leaves) Rascheln nt; (of paper also) Knistern nt; (of fire also) Knistern nt, Prasseln nt; (of twigs, telephone line) Knacken nt; (of machine gun) Knattern nt; (of bacon) Brutzeln nt **b** (on china, porcelain) Craquelé m or nt, Krakelee m or nt

crackleware ['kræklweə'] N Krakeleeporzellan nt, Craqueléporzellan nt

crackling ['kræklɪŋ] N , no pl **a** = **crackle** N a **b** (Cook) Kruste f (des Schweinebratens)

cracknel ['kræknl] N (harter) Keks

crackpot ['krækpɒt] (inf) **N** Spinner(in) m(f) (inf), Irre(r) mf **ADJ** verrückt, irre

cracksman ['kræksmən] N pl **-men** [-mən] (sl) Safeknacker m

crackup ['krækʌp] N (inf) Zusammenbruch m

cradle ['kreɪdl] **N** (= cot, fig: = birthplace) Wiege f; (= support, of phone) Gabel f; (for invalids) Schutzgestell nt (zum Abhalten des Bettzeugs von Verletzungen); (for ship) (Ablauf)schlitten m; (Build, for window-cleaners) Hängegerüst nt; (in sea rescues) Hosenboje f; (for mechanic under car) Schlitten m; **from the ~ to the grave** von der Wiege bis zur Bahre; **right from the ~** von klein auf, von Kindesbeinen an **VT a** (= hold closely) an sich (acc) drücken; **he was cradling his injured arm** er hielt sich (dat) seinen verletzten Arm; **to ~ sb/sth in one's arms/lap** jdn/etw fest in den Armen/auf dem Schoß halten; **the baby lay ~d in her lap** das Baby lag (geborgen) in ihrem Schoß; **he ~d the telephone under his chin** er klemmte sich (dat) den Hörer unters Kinn; **the way he ~s the guitar** wie er die Gitarre zärtlich hält **b** receiver auflegen

cradle: cradle cap N Milchschorf m; **cradle snatcher** N (inf) **what a ~ he/she is!** (fig) der könnte ja ihr Vater/sie könnte ja seine Mutter sein!; **cradle-snatching** N (inf) **she is known for ~** sie angelt sich dauernd viel jüngere Männer (inf); **cradlesong** N Wiegenlied nt

craft [krɑ:ft] N **a** (= handicraft) Kunsthandwerk nt; (as trade) Kunstgewerbe nt; (= trade) Handwerk nt, Gewerbe nt; **it's a real ~** das ist eine echte Kunst → **art[1]** **b** (= guild) (Handwerker-) innung f, (Handwerks)zunft f (Hist) **c** no pl (= skill) Kunst f **d** no pl (= cunning) List f; **to ob-**

tain sth by ~ sich (dat) etw erlisten, etw durch List bekommen **e** pl **craft** (= boat) Boot nt

craft fair N Kunstgewerbemarkt m

craftily ['krɑ:ftɪlɪ] ADV schlau, clever

craftiness ['krɑ:ftɪnɪs] N Schlauheit f, Cleverness f

craftsman ['krɑ:ftsmən] N pl **-men** [-mən] Kunsthandwerker m; **he's a real ~** er ist ein echter Künstler

craftsmanship ['krɑ:ftsmənʃɪp] N Handwerkskunst f; (of person also) handwerkliches Können, Kunstfertigkeit f; **there's no ~ left these days** heutzutage gibt es einfach keine Handwerkskunst mehr

craftsperson ['krɑ:ftspɜ:sən] N pl **-people** [-pi:pl] Kunstgewerbler(in) m(f), Kunsthandwerker(in) m(f)

craftswoman ['krɑ:ftswʊmən] N pl **-women** [-wɪmɪn] Kunsthandwerkerin f

craft union N Handwerkergewerkschaft f

crafty ['krɑ:ftɪ] ADJ (+er) schlau, clever; **he's a ~ one** (inf) er ist ein ganz Schlauer (inf); **he's as ~ as a fox** er ist ein schlauer Fuchs; **he took a ~ glance at ...** er riskierte einen verstohlenen Blick auf (+acc) ...

crag [kræg] N Fels m

craggy ['krægɪ] ADJ (+er) (= rocky) felsig; (= jagged) zerklüftet; face kantig; **he was good-looking in a ~ sort of way** er sah eine herbe, kantige Art gut aus

cragsman ['krægzmən] N pl **-men** [-mən] Kletterer m, geübter Bergsteiger

crake [kreɪk] N Ralle f

cram [kræm] **VT a** (= fill) voll stopfen, voll packen; (= stuff in) hineinstopfen (in(to) +acc); people hineinzwängen (in(to) in +acc); **the room was ~med (with furniture)** der Raum war (mit Möbeln) voll gestopft; **we were all ~med into one room** wir waren alle in einem Zimmer zusammengepfercht; **he ~med his hat (down) over his eyes** er zog sich (dat) den Hut tief ins Gesicht **b** (for exam) Latin verbs etc pauken (inf), büffeln (inf); (= teach for exam) pupil pauken mit (inf) **VI** (= swot) pauken (inf), büffeln (inf)

▶ **cram in** VI (people) sich hinein-/hereindrängen or -quetschen or -zwängen (-to in +acc)

cram-full ['kræmfʊl] ADJ (inf) voll gestopft (of mit), gestopft voll (inf)

crammer ['kræmə'] N (= tutor) Einpauker m; (= student) Büffler(in) m(f) (inf); (= book) Paukbuch nt; (= school) Paukschule f

cramp[1] [kræmp] **N** (Med) Krampf m; **to have ~ in one's leg** einen Krampf im Bein haben; **to have the ~s** (US) Krämpfe haben **VT a** (also **cramp up**) persons zusammenpferchen, einpferchen; writing eng zusammenkritzeln **b** (fig, = hinder) behindern; **to ~ sb's style** jdm im Weg sein **c** (= give cramp to) Krämpfe pl verursachen in (+dat)

cramp[2] N (also **cramp iron**) Bauklammer f **VT** klammern

cramped [kræmpt] ADJ **a** space eng, beschränkt; flat, accommodation, room beengt; coach, train, plane überfüllt; **we are very ~ (for space)** wir sind räumlich sehr beschränkt **b** position, person, muscle, limb verkrampft **c** handwriting eng zusammengekritzelt

crampon ['kræmpɒn] N Steigeisen nt

cranberry ['krænbərɪ] N Preiselbeere f, Kronsbeere f; **~ sauce** Preiselbeersoße f

crane [kreɪn] **N a** Kran m; **~ driver** Kranführer(in) m(f) **b** (Orn) Kranich m **VT to ~ one's neck** den Hals recken, sich (dat) fast den Hals verrenken (inf) **VI** (also **crane forward**) den Hals or den Kopf recken

cranefly ['kreɪnflaɪ] N Schnake f

cranesbill ['kreɪnzbɪl] N (Bot) Storchschnabel m

crania ['kreɪnɪə] pl of **cranium**

cranial ['kreɪnɪəl] ADJ (Anat) Schädel-, kranial (spec)

cranium ['kreɪnɪəm] N pl **crania** (Anat) Schädel m, Cranium nt (spec)

crank[1] [kræŋk] N (= eccentric person) Spinner(in) m(f) (inf); (US, = cross person) Griesgram m

crank[2] **N** (Mech) Kurbel f **VT** (also **crank up**) ankurbeln

crankcase ['kræŋkkeɪs] N (Aut) Kurbelgehäuse nt

crankiness ['kræŋkɪnɪs] N **a** (= eccentricity) Verrücktheit f **b** (esp US, = bad temper) Griesgrämigkeit f

crankshaft ['kræŋkʃɑːft] N (Aut) Kurbelwelle f

cranky ['kræŋkɪ] ADJ (+er) **a** (= eccentric) verrückt **b** (esp US, = bad-tempered) griesgrämig

cranny ['krænɪ] N Ritze f, Spalte f → **nook**

crap [kræp] **N a** (sl) Scheiße f (vulg); **to go for/have a ~** scheißen gehen/scheißen (vulg) **b** (inf, = rubbish) Scheiße f (inf); **a load of ~** große Scheiße (inf) **VI** (sl) scheißen (vulg) **ADJ** attr (inf) joke, job etc Scheiß- (inf)

▶ **crap out** VI (inf) kneifen (of vor +dat)

crap game N (US) Würfelspiel nt (mit zwei Würfeln)

crappy ['kræpɪ] ADJ (+er) (inf) beschissen (inf), Scheiß- (inf)

craps [kræps] N (US) Würfelspiel nt; **to shoot ~** Würfel spielen

crapshooter ['kræpʃuːtə'] N Würfelspieler(in) m(f)

crash [kræʃ] **N a** (= noise) Krach(en nt no pl) m no pl; (of thunder, cymbals also, of drums) Schlag m; **there was a ~ upstairs** es hat oben gekracht; **the vase fell to the ground with a ~** die Vase fiel krachend zu Boden; **a ~ of thunder** ein Donnerschlag m; **the ~ of the waves against ...** das Krachen der Wellen gegen ... **b** (= accident) Unfall m, Unglück nt; (= collision also) Zusammenstoß m; (with several cars) Karambolage f; (= plane crash) (Flugzeug)unglück nt; **to be in a (car)** ~ in einen (Auto)unfall verwickelt sein; **to have a** ~ (mit dem Auto) verunglücken, einen (Auto)unfall haben; (= cause it) einen Unfall verursachen or bauen (inf); **the impact of the** ~ die Wucht des Aufpralls; (into another car) die Wucht des Zusammenstoßes **c** (Fin) Zusammenbruch m; (St Ex) Börsenkrach m **ADV** krach; **he went ~ into a tree** er krachte gegen einen Baum; **~, bang, wallop!** (inf) bums! (inf), krach! (inf) **VT** car, bicycle einen Unfall haben mit; plane abstürzen mit; **if you let him use your car he's bound to ~ it** wenn du ihm dein Auto gibst, fährt er es dir bestimmt kaputt (inf); **to ~ one's car into sth** mit dem Auto gegen etw krachen or knallen (inf); **the car was found ~ed** das Auto wurde demoliert aufgefunden **b** (with particle: = bang) **stop ~ing the plates around** hör auf, mit den Tellern zu scheppern (inf); **he ~ed the cymbals together** er schlug scheppernd die Becken zusammen; **he ~ed his head against the windscreen** er krachte mit dem Kopf gegen die Windschutzscheibe; **he ~ed the car through the barrier** er fuhr mit dem Auto voll durch die Absperrung (inf) **c** (inf: = gatecrash) **to ~ a party** uneingeladen zu einer Party gehen, in eine Party hineinplatzen **VI a** (= have an accident) verunglücken, einen Unfall haben; (plane) abstürzen; **to ~ into sth** gegen etw (acc) krachen or knallen (inf) **b** (with particle: = move with a crash) krachen; **to ~ to the ground/through sth** zu Boden/durch etw krachen; **they went ~ing through the undergrowth** sie brachen krachend durchs Unterholz; **his fist ~ed into Tom's face** seine Faust landete krachend in Toms Gesicht; **the whole roof came ~ing down (on him)** das ganze Dach krachte auf ihn herunter; **his whole world ~ed about him** or **his ears** seine ganze Welt brach zusammen **c** (Fin) Pleite machen (inf); (Comput) abstürzen; **when Wall Street ~ed** als Wall Street zusammenbrach, beim Börsenkrach der Wall Street

d (inf: also **crash out**) (= sleep) knacken (sl); (= fall asleep) einknacken (sl); (= become unconscious) zusammenklappen (inf)

crash: **crash barrier** N Leitplanke f; **crash course** N Schnell- or Intensivkurs m; **crash diet** N Radikalkur f; **crash dive** N Schnelltauchmanöver nt; **crash-dive** VI schnelltauchen; **crash helmet** N Sturzhelm m

crashing ['kræʃɪŋ] ADJ (dated inf) **he's/it's a ~ bore** er/es ist fürchterlich or zum Einschlafen langweilig (inf)

crashingly ['kræʃɪŋlɪ] ADV (dated inf) schrecklich

crash: **crash-land** VI eine Bruchlandung machen, bruchlanden **VT** eine Bruchlandung machen mit, bruchlanden mit; **crash-landing** N Bruchlandung f; **crash programme** N Intensivprogramm nt

crass [kræs] ADJ (+er) (= stupid, unsubtle) krass; ignorance also haarsträubend; (= coarse) behaviour unfein, derb; **must you be so ~ about it?** müssen Sie sich so krass ausdrücken?

crassly ['kræslɪ] ADV krass; behave unfein

crassness ['kræsnɪs] N (= insensitivity) Krassheit f; (= coarseness) Derbheit f

crate [kreɪt] **N** (also inf: = car, plane) Kiste f; (= beer crate, milk crate) Kasten m **VT** goods (in Kisten/eine Kiste) (ver)packen

crater ['kreɪtə'] N Krater m

cravat(te) [krə'væt] N Halstuch nt

crave [kreɪv] VT (liter: = beg) erbitten; mercy also erflehen; (= desire) attention, drink etc sich sehnen nach; **to ~ sb's pardon** (form) jdn um Verzeihung anflehen; **ladies and gentlemen, may I ~ your indulgence?** (form) meine Damen und Herren, darf ich um Ihre werte Aufmerksamkeit bitten?; **may I ~ your indulgence a moment longer?** (form) darf ich Ihre Geduld noch etwas länger in Anspruch nehmen?

▶ **crave for** VI +prep obj sich sehnen nach

craven ['kreɪvən] (liter) **ADJ** feig(e); **a ~ coward** ein elender Feigling, eine feige Memme (geh) **N** Memme f (geh)

cravenly ['kreɪvənlɪ] ADV (liter) feige, feigherzig (old)

craving ['kreɪvɪŋ] N Verlangen nt; **to have a ~ for sth** Verlangen nach etw haben; **pregnant women have strange ~s** schwangere Frauen haben eigenartige Gelüste

crawfish ['krɔːfɪʃ] N = **crayfish b**

crawl [krɔːl] **N a** (on hands and knees) Kriechen nt; (= slow speed) Schnecken- or Kriechtempo nt; (Brit inf: = pub-crawl) Kneipenbummel m; **it was a long ~** wir mussten lange kriechen; (in car) wir sind lange nur im Kriechtempo vorangekommen; **we could only go at a ~** wir kamen nur im Schnecken- or Kriechtempo voran; **to join the ~ to the coast** sich der (Auto)schlange zur Küste anschließen **b** (= swimming stroke) Kraul(stil) m, Kraulen nt; **to do the ~** kraulen; **she's very fast at the ~** sie ist sehr schnell im Kraulen **VI a** (person, traffic) kriechen; (baby, insects also) krabbeln; (time also) schleichen; **he tried to ~ away** er versuchte wegzukriechen **b** (= be infested) wimmeln (with von); **the meat was ~ing with flies** das Fleisch wimmelte nur so von Fliegen; **the street was ~ing with police** auf der Straße wimmelte es von Polizisten **c** spiders make/he makes my flesh or skin ~ wenn ich Spinnen/ihn sehe, kriege ich eine Gänsehaut **d** (inf: = suck up) kriechen (to vor +dat); **he went ~ing to teacher** er ist gleich zum Lehrer gerannt

crawler ['krɔːlə'] N **a** (Brit inf: = sycophant) Kriecher(in) m(f) **b** **crawlers** PL (= rompers) Spielanzug m

crawler lane N (Brit, Aut) Kriechspur f

crawling ['krɔːlɪŋ] ADJ insect, movement kriechend, krabbelnd; **a baby at the ~ stage** ein Baby im Krabbelalter → also **crawl**

crawl space N (US) niedriger Keller; (under roof) Zwischendecke f

crayfish ['kreɪfɪʃ] N **a** (freshwater) Flusskrebs m **b** (saltwater: also **crawfish**) Languste f

crayon ['kreən] **N a** (= pencil) Buntstift m; (= wax crayon) Wachs(mal)stift m; (= chalk crayon) Pastellstift m, Malkreide f; (= picture) Pastell nt, Kreide- or Pastellzeichnung f **VT** (mit Bunt-/Wachsmal-/Pastellstiften) zeichnen or malen

▶ **crayon in** VT sep drawing ausmalen

craze [kreɪz] **N** Fimmel m (inf); **it's all the ~** (inf) das ist große Mode; **there's a ~ for collecting old things just now** es ist zur Zeit große Mode, alte Sachen zu sammeln **VT a** (= make insane) **a ~d gunman** ein Amokschütze m; **to be half ~d with grief** vor Schmerz halb wahnsinnig sein; **he had a ~d look on his face** er hatte den Gesichtsausdruck eines Wahnsinnigen **b** pottery, glazing rissig machen **VI** (pottery) rissig werden

crazily ['kreɪzɪlɪ] ADV **a** skid, bounce, whirl wie verrückt; lean, tilt unwahrscheinlich **b** (= madly) verrückt

craziness ['kreɪzɪnɪs] N Verrücktheit f

crazy ['kreɪzɪ] ADJ (+er) **a** verrückt (with vor +dat); **to send** or **drive sb ~** jdn verrückt or wahnsinnig machen; **to go ~** verrückt or wahnsinnig werden; **to act ~** sich wie verrückt or wahnsinnig aufführen; **that's ~** das ist doch verrückt!; **like ~** (inf) wie verrückt (inf); **it/you would be ~ to do that** es wäre wirklich verrückt, das zu tun **b** (inf, = enthusiastic) verrückt (inf); **to be ~ about sb/sth** ganz verrückt or wild auf jdn/etw sein (inf); **football-crazy** fußballverrückt (inf); **to be ~ for sb** verrückt nach jdm sein (inf) **c** angle, tilt unwahrscheinlich

crazy: **crazy bone** N (US) Musikantenknochen m; **crazy golf** N (Brit) Minigolf nt; **crazy house** N (US inf) Irrenhaus nt; **crazy paving** N Mosaikpflaster nt; **crazy quilt** N (US) Flickendecke f

CRC abbr of **camera-ready copy**

CRE N (Brit) abbr of **Commission for Racial Equality** Kommission f für Rassengleichheit

creak [kriːk] **N** Knarren nt no pl; (of hinges, bed springs) Quietschen nt no pl; (of knees etc) Knacken nt no pl; **to give a loud ~** laut knarren/quietschen/knacken; **a series of ~s** knarrende/quietschende/knackende Geräusche **VI** knarren; (hinges, bed springs) quietschen; (knees etc) knacken

creaky ['kriːkɪ] ADJ (+er) **a** (lit) knarrend; hinges, bed springs quietschend; knees etc knackend **b** (fig) plot, thriller etc verstaubt

cream [kriːm] **N a** Sahne f, Rahm m (S Ger); (= cream pudding, artificial cream) Creme f, Krem f; **~ of tomato/chicken soup** Tomaten-/Hühnercremesuppe f; **~ of tartar** Weinstein m **b** (= lotion) Creme f **c** (= colour) Creme(farbe f) nt; **a skirt in a pale shade of ~** ein blass-cremefarbener Rock **d** (fig: = best) die Besten; (of society also) Creme f, Elite f; **our rivals take the ~ of the applicants** unsere Konkurrenz sahnt die besten Bewerber ab; **the ~ of the crop** (= people) die Elite; (= things) das Nonplusultra; **the ~ of society** die Creme der Gesellschaft; **to take the ~** den Rahm abschöpfen **ADJ a** (colour) creme inv, cremefarben or -farbig **b** (= made with cream) Sahne-, Creme-; **~ soups** Cremesuppen pl **VT a** (= put cream on) face etc eincremen **b** butter, eggs etc cremig rühren; potatoes pürieren; **~ed potatoes** Kartoffelpüree nt **c** (= skim) milk entrahmen **d** (= allow to form a cream) milk aufrahmen lassen **e** (US, inf: = defeat easily) in die Pfanne hauen (inf) **VI** (milk) aufrahmen

▶ **cream off** VT sep (lit) abschöpfen; (fig) profits also, the best absahnen

cream: cream bun N Eclair *nt*; **cream cake** N Sahnetorte *f*, Cremetorte *f*; (*small*) Sahnetörtchen *nt*, Cremetörtchen *nt*; **cream cheese** N (Doppelrahm)frischkäse *m*

creamer ['kriːmə] N **a** (*US: = jug*) Sahnekännchen *nt* **b** (*= skimming machine*) Milchzentrifuge *or* -schleuder *f* **c** (*= dried milk*) Milchpulver *nt*

creamery ['kriːmərɪ] N Molkerei *f*; (*= shop*) Milchgeschäft *nt*

cream: cream puff N Windbeutel *m*; **cream soda** N Sodawasser *nt* mit Vanillegeschmack; **cream tea** N Nachmittagstee *m*

creamy ['kriːmɪ] ADJ (+er) **a** (*= tasting of cream*) sahnig; (*= smooth*) cremig; **a ~ complexion** ein zarter Teint **b** (*= cream-coloured*) creme(farben *or* -farbig)

crease [kriːs] **N** **a** Falte *f*; (*= deliberate fold, in material also*) Kniff *m*; (*in paper also*) Falz *m*, Kniff *m*; (*ironed: in trousers etc*) (Bügel)falte *f*; **to be a mass of ~s** völlig zerknittert sein; **to put a ~ in a pair of trousers** eine Falte in eine Hose bügeln **b** (*Sport*) Linie *f* **VT** (*deliberately*) *clothes* Falten/eine Falte machen in (+*acc*); *material, paper* Kniffe/einen Kniff machen in (+*acc*); *paper* falzen; (*unintentionally*) zerknittern; **smartly ~d trousers** Hosen mit sauberen Bügelfalten **VI** knittern; **his face ~d with laughter** er fing an zu lachen

▸ **crease up** VI (*inf, with laughter*) sich kringeln (*inf*)

crease-proof ['kriːspruːf], **crease-resistant** ['kriːsrɪzɪstənt] ADJ knitterfrei

create [kriːˈeɪt] **VT** **a** (*= bring into existence*) schaffen; *new style, fashion also* kreieren; *the world, man* erschaffen; *draught, noise, fuss* verursachen; *difficulties* machen; *problems* (*person*) schaffen; (*action, event*) verursachen, hervorbringen; *impression* machen; (*Comput*) *file* anlegen; **to ~ a sensation** eine Sensation sein; **to ~ a fuss** Theater machen (*inf*) **b** (*= appoint*) *peer* ernennen; **peers can only be ~d by the reigning monarch** nur der regierende Monarch kann jemanden in den Adelsstand erheben; **to ~ sb baron** jdn zum Baron erheben *or* ernennen **VI** (*Brit, inf*) Theater machen (*inf*)

creation [kriːˈeɪʃən] N **a** *no pl* (*= bringing into existence*) Schaffung *f*; (*of new style, fashion also*) Kreation *f*; (*of the world, man*) Erschaffung *f*; (*of draught, noise, fuss*) Verursachung *f*; (*of problems, by person*) Schaffen *nt*; (*by action, event*) Verursachung *f* **b** *no pl* (*= appointment: of peer*) Erhebung *f*, Ernennung *f* **c** *no pl* **the Creation** die Schöpfung; **all ~, the whole of ~** die Schöpfung, alle Kreatur *f*, alle Geschöpfe *pl* **d** (*= created object, Art*) Werk *nt*; (*Fashion*) Kreation *f*

creationism [kriːˈeɪʃənɪzəm] N Kreationismus *m*

creationist [kriːˈeɪʃənɪst] **N** Kreationist(in) *m(f)* **ADJ** kreationistisch

creative [kriːˈeɪtɪv] ADJ *power, skill etc* schöpferisch; *approach, attitude, person* kreativ; **the ~ use of language** kreativer Sprachgebrauch

creative accounting N kreative Buchführung *f* (*um einen falschen Eindruck vom erzielten Gewinn zu erwecken*)

creatively [kriːˈeɪtɪvlɪ] ADV kreativ

creativeness [ˌkriːˈeɪtɪvnɪs], **creativity** [ˌkriːeɪˈtɪvɪtɪ] N schöpferische Begabung *or* Kraft; (*of person also, of approach, attitude*) Kreativität *f*

creative thinking N kreatives Denken

creative toys PL Spielzeug *nt* zum Gestalten und Werken

creative writing N dichterisches Schreiben

creator [kriːˈeɪtə] N Schöpfer(in) *m(f)*

creature [ˈkriːtʃə] N **a** Geschöpf *nt*, (Lebe)wesen *nt*, Kreatur *f*; **what a beautiful ~!** welch ein herrliches Geschöpf!; **all dumb ~s** die stumme Kreatur; **she's a funny ~** sie ist ein komisches Geschöpf; **there wasn't a ~ in sight** nirgends regte sich etwas, kein Lebewesen war zu sehen **b** (*= subordinate person*) Geschöpf *nt*

creature comforts PL leibliches Wohl

crèche [kreɪʃ] N **a** (*Brit: = day nursery*) (Kinder-) krippe *f or* -hort *m*; (*esp US: = children's home*) Kinderheim *nt* **b** (*= crib*) Krippe *f*

cred [kred] → **street cred**

credence ['kriːdəns] N **a** *no pl* (*= belief*) Glaube *m*; **to lend ~ to sth** etw glaubwürdig erscheinen lassen *or* machen; **worthy of ~** glaubwürdig; **to give** *or* **attach ~ to sth** einer Sache (*dat*) Glauben schenken; **letter of ~** Beglaubigungsschreiben *nt* **b** (*Eccl: also* **credence table**) Kredenz *f*

credentials [krɪˈdenʃəlz] PL (*= references*) Referenzen *pl*, Zeugnisse *pl*; (*= identity papers*) (Ausweis)papiere *pl*; **to present one's ~** seine Papiere vorlegen

credibility [ˌkredəˈbɪlɪtɪ] N Glaubwürdigkeit *f*; **his ~ rating is pretty low** er wird als nicht sehr glaubwürdig eingestuft

credibility gap N Glaubwürdigkeitslücke *f*; **his ~ widened** er verlor immer mehr an Glaubwürdigkeit

credible ['kredɪbl] ADJ glaubwürdig

credibly ['kredɪblɪ] ADV glaubhaft

credit ['kredɪt] **N** **a** *no pl* (*Fin*) Kredit *m*; (*in pub, hotel, shop etc*) Stundung *f*; **the bank will let me have £5,000 ~** die Bank räumt mir einen Kredit von £ 5.000 ein; **to buy on ~** auf Kredit kaufen; **his ~ is good** er ist kreditwürdig; (*in small shop*) er ist vertrauenswürdig; **to give sb (unlimited) ~** jdm (unbegrenzt) Kredit geben; **we can't give you ~** (*bank*) wir können Ihnen keinen Kredit geben; (*corner shop etc*) wir können Ihnen nichts stunden; **pubs do not usually give ~** in Lokalen bekommt man normalerweise nichts gestundet; **letter of ~** Kreditbrief *m*, Akkreditiv *nt*

b (*Fin: = money possessed by person, firm*) (Gut-) haben *nt*; (*Comm: = sum of money*) Kreditposten *m*; **to be in ~** Geld *nt* auf dem Konto haben; **to keep one's account in ~** sein Konto nicht überziehen; **the ~s and debits** Soll und Haben *nt*; **how much have we got to our ~?** wie viel haben wir auf dem Konto?; **~ arrangements** Kreditvereinbarungen *pl*

c (*= standing*) Ansehen *nt*; **a man of good ~** ein angesehener Mann

d *no pl* (*= honour*) Ehre *f*; (*= recognition*) Anerkennung *f*; (*Sch, Univ: = distinction*) Auszeichnung *f*; **he's a ~ to his family** er macht seiner Familie Ehre; **that's to his ~** das ehrt ihn; **well, all ~ to you for not succumbing** alle Achtung, dass Sie nicht nachgegeben haben; **at least he has this to his ~** das spricht immerhin für ihn; **her generosity does her ~** ihre Großzügigkeit macht ihr alle Ehre; **to reflect great ~ on sb** jdm große Ehre machen; **to come out of sth with ~** ehrenvoll aus etw hervorgehen; **to get all the ~** die ganze Anerkennung *or* Ehre einstecken; **I do all the work and he gets all the ~** ich mache die Arbeit, und ihm wird es als Verdienst angerechnet; **the ~ for that should go to him** das ist sein Verdienst; **to take the ~ for sth** das Verdienst für etw in Anspruch nehmen; **~ where ~ is due** (*prov*) Ehre, wem Ehre gebührt (*prov*)

e *no pl* (*= belief*) Glaube *m*; **to give ~ to sth** etw glauben, einer Sache (*dat*) Glauben schenken; **to lend ~ to sth** etw glaubwürdig erscheinen lassen *or* machen; **to gain ~** an Glaubwürdigkeit gewinnen; **I gave you ~ for more sense** ich habe Sie für vernünftiger gehalten; **worthy of ~** glaubwürdig

f (*esp US, Univ*) Schein *m*; **to take** *or* **do ~s** Scheine machen

g credits PL (*Film etc*) Vor-/Nachspann *m*; (*in book*) Herausgeber- und Mitarbeiterverzeichnis *nt*

VT **a** (*= believe*) glauben; **would you ~ it!** ist das denn zu glauben!, ist das denn die Möglichkeit! **b** (*= attribute*) zuschreiben (+*dat*); **I ~ed him with more sense** ich habe ihn für vernünftiger gehalten; **he was ~ed with having invented it** die Erfindung wurde ihm zugeschrieben; **he was ~ed with having found the solution** es wurde als sein Verdienst angerechnet *or* es wurde ihm zugute gehalten, diese Lösung gefunden zu ha-

ben; **it's ~ed with (having) magic powers** ihm werden Zauberkräfte zugeschrieben **c** (*Fin*) gutschreiben; **to ~ a sum to sb's account** jds Konto (*dat*) einen Betrag gutschreiben (lassen); **he had been ~ed with £100** ihm waren £ 100 gutgeschrieben worden

creditable ['kredɪtəbl] ADJ **a** (*= praiseworthy*) lobenswert, anerkennenswert **b** (*= credible*) glaublich

creditably ['kredɪtəblɪ] ADV löblich

credit: credit account N Kreditkonto *nt*; **credit agency** N (*giving credit*) Finanzierungsinstitut *nt*; (*for credit investigation*) Kreditschutzverein *m*; **credit balance** N Kontostand *m*, Saldo *m*; **credit bureau** N (*US*) = **credit agency**; **credit card** N Kreditkarte *f*; **credit check** N Überprüfung *f* der Kreditwürdigkeit; **to run a ~ on sb** jds Kreditwürdigkeit überprüfen; **credit control** N Kreditüberwachung *f*; **credit entry** N Gutschrift *f*; **credit facilities** PL Kreditmöglichkeiten *pl*; **credit hour** N (*US: Univ*) anrechenbare (Vorlesungs)stunde *f*; **credit interest** N Habenzinsen *pl*; **credit limit** N Kreditgrenze *f*; **credit line** N **a** (*Fin*) Kreditrahmen *m* **b** (*= sources*) Herkunfts- *or* Quellenangabe *f*; **credit note** N Gutschrift *f*

creditor ['kredɪtə] N Gläubiger *m*

credit: credit page N Herausgeber- und Mitarbeiterverzeichnis *nt*; **credit rating** N Kreditwürdigkeit *f*; **to have a good/bad ~** als kreditwürdig/als nicht kreditwürdig eingestuft werden; **credit-rating agency** N Kreditschutzverein *m*, ≈ Schufa *f*; **credit report** N Kreditauskunft *f*; **credit risk** N **to be a good/ poor ~** ein geringes/großes Kreditrisiko darstellen; **credit sales** PL Kreditkäufe *pl*; **credit side** N (*lit, fig*) Habenseite *f*; **on the ~ he's young** für ihn spricht, dass er jung ist; **credit squeeze** N Kreditbeschränkung *or* -knappheit *f*; **credit standing** N Kreditwürdigkeit *f*; **credit terms** PL Kreditbedingungen *pl*; **credit titles** PL (*Film*) = **credit** N **g**; **credit union** N Kreditgenossenschaft *f*; **creditworthiness** N Kreditwürdigkeit *f*; **creditworthy** ADJ kreditwürdig

credo ['kreɪdəʊ] N (*lit, fig*) Kredo *nt*, Credo *nt*, Glaubensbekenntnis *nt*

credulity [krɪˈdjuːlɪtɪ] N , *no pl* Leichtgläubigkeit *f*

credulous, credulously ADJ, ADV ['kredjʊləs, -lɪ] leichtgläubig

creed [kriːd] N (*Eccl: = prayer*) Glaubensbekenntnis *nt*; (*as part of service, fig also*) Kredo *nt*, Credo *nt*

creek [kriːk] N (*esp Brit: = inlet*) (kleine) Bucht; (*US, = brook*) Bach *m*; **to be up the ~ (without a paddle)** (*inf, = be in trouble*) in der Tinte sitzen (*inf*); (*= be completely wrong*) auf dem falschen Dampfer sein (*inf*)

creel [kriːl] N Korb *m*

creep [kriːp] *vb: pret, ptp* **crept** **VI** **a** (*= move quietly or slowly*) schleichen; (*with the body close to the ground, insects*) kriechen; (*plants, horizontally*) kriechen; (*vertically*) klettern, sich ranken; **ivy is a ~ing plant** Efeu ist eine Kletterpflanze; **~ing paralysis** schleichende Lähmung; **~ing inflation** schleichende Inflation; **the water level crept higher and higher** der Wasserspiegel kletterte immer höher **b** **the story made my flesh ~** bei der Geschichte überlief es mich kalt *or* bekam ich eine Gänsehaut

N **a** (*inf: = unpleasant person*) Widerling *m* (*inf*), widerlicher *or* fieser Typ (*inf*); **you little ~!** du fieser Typ (*inf*) **b** (*inf*) **he gives me the ~s** er ist mir nicht geheuer; **this old house gives me the ~s** in dem alten Haus ist es mir nicht geheuer

▸ **creep in** VI (sich) hinein-/hereinschleichen (*-to in* +*acc*); (*mistakes, doubts*) sich einschleichen (*-to in* +*acc*)

▸ **creep over** VI +*prep obj* (*feeling, doubt etc*) beschleichen, überkommen; (*pleasant feeling*) überkommen

▶ **creep up** VI **a** (*person*) sich heranschleichen (*on* an +*acc*); (*prices, inflation*) (in die Höhe) klettern **b** **to creep up on sb** (*time, exam*) langsam auf jdn zukommen; **old age is creeping up on him** er wird langsam alt

creeper ['kriːpə'] N **a** (= *plant, along ground*) Kriechpflanze *f*; (*upwards*) Kletterpflanze *f* **b** (= *bird*) Baumläufer *m* **c** **creepers** PL (*US*) Schuhe mit dicken Gummisohlen, Leisetreter *pl* (*inf*)

creepy ['kriːpɪ] ADJ (+*er*) (= *frightening*) unheimlich; *story, place also* gruselig

creepy-crawly ['kriːpɪ'krɔːlɪ] (*inf*) **ADJ** *insect* krabbelig (*inf*), kribbelnd, krabbelnd; *feeling* unheimlich **N** Krabbeltier *nt*

cremate [krɪ'meɪt] VT einäschern, kremieren (*rare*)

cremation [krɪ'meɪʃən] N Einäscherung *f*, Kremation *f*

crematorium [ˌkremə'tɔːrɪəm], (*esp US*) **crematory** ['kremə,tɔːrɪ] N Krematorium *nt*

crème de la crème ['kremdəlæ'krem] N Crème de la Crème *f*

crème de menthe ['kremdə'mɒnθ] N Pfefferminzlikör *m*

crenellated ['krenɪleɪtɪd] ADJ *battlements* mit Zinnen versehen, kreneliert (*spec*); *moulding, pattern* zinnenartig

crenellation [ˌkrenɪ'leɪʃən] N *usu pl* (*on castle*) Zinnen *pl*, Krenelierung *f* (*spec*); (*on moulding*) Zinnenmuster *nt*

Creole ['kriːəʊl] **N a** (*Ling*) Kreolisch *nt* **b** (= *person*) Kreole *m*, Kreolin *f* **ADJ** kreolisch; **he is ~** er ist Kreole

creolized ['kriːəlaɪzd] ADJ kreolisiert

creosote ['krɪəsəʊt] **N** Kreosot *nt* **VT** mit Kreosot streichen

crêpe [kreɪp] **N a** (*Tex*) Krepp *m*, Crêpe *f* **b** (*Cook*) Crêpe *m* **c** = **crêpe rubber** **d** = **crêpe paper** **ADJ** (= *made of crêpe*) Krepp-

crêpe: crêpe bandage N elastische Binde, elastischer Verband; **crêpe de Chine** [ˌkrepdə'ʃiːn] N Crêpe de Chine *m*, Chinakrepp *m*; **crêpe paper** N Krepppapier *nt*; **crêpe rubber** N Kreppgummi *m*; **crêpe-soled** ['kreɪp'səʊld] ADJ mit Kreppsohle(n), Krepp-; **crêpe suzette** [ˌkreɪpsuː'zet] N Crêpe Suzette *f*

crepitate ['krepɪteɪt] VI (*liter*) prasseln

crept [krept] *pret, ptp of* **creep**

crepuscular [krɪ'pʌskjʊlə'] ADJ (*liter*) dämmerig; **~ animals** (*Zool*) Dämmerungstiere *pl*

crescendo [krɪ'ʃendəʊ] **N** (*Mus*) Crescendo *nt*; (*fig*) Zunahme *f*; **~ of excitement** Anschwellen *nt* der Aufregung **VI** (*Mus, fig*) anschwellen

crescent ['kresnt] **N** Halbmond *m*; (*in street names*) Weg *m* (*halbmondförmig verlaufende Straße*) **ADJ** **the ~ moon** die Mondsichel

crescent-shaped ['kresnt'ʃeɪpt] ADJ halbmond- or sichelförmig

cress [kres] N (Garten)kresse *f*; (= *watercress*) Brunnenkresse *f*

crest [krest] **N a** (*of bird*) Haube *f*; (*of cock*) Kamm *m*; (*on hat etc*) Federbusch *m*; (= *plume on helmet*) Helmbusch *m* **b** (*Her*) Helmzierde *f*; (= *coat of arms*) Wappen *nt* **c** (*of wave, hill, Anat: of horse etc*) Kamm *m*; (*fig: of excitement, popularity*) Höhepunkt *m*, Gipfel *m*; (*Phys, of oscillation*) Scheitel(punkt) *m*; **he's riding on the ~ of a wave** (*fig*) er schwimmt im Augenblick oben **VT** (= *reach the crest of*) erklimmen

crested ['krestɪd] ADJ *notepaper, seal* verziert; (*Orn*) Hauben-; **~ coot** Kammblessralle *f*

crested tit N Haubenmeise *f*

crestfallen ['krest,fɔːlən] ADJ geknickt, niedergeschlagen

cretaceous [krɪ'teɪʃəs] ADJ Kreide-, kretazeisch (*spec*); **the ~ age** (*Geol*) die Kreide(zeit)

Cretan ['kriːtən] **ADJ** kretisch **N** Kreter(in) *m(f)*

Crete [kriːt] N Kreta *nt*

cretin ['kretɪn] N (*Med*) Kretin *m*; (*inf*) Schwachkopf *m* (*inf*)

cretinism ['kretɪnɪzəm] N (*Med*) Kretinismus *m*; (*inf*) Schwachsinn *m*, Idiotie *f*

cretinous ['kretɪnəs] ADJ (*Med*) kretinoid; (*inf*) schwachsinnig

cretonne [kre'tɒn] N Cretonne *f or m*

Creutzfeldt-Jakob disease [ˌkrɔɪtsfelt'jækɒb-dɪˌziːz] N , *no pl* Creutzfeldt-Jakob-Krankheit *f*

crevasse [krɪ'væs] N (Gletscher)spalte *f*

crevice ['krevɪs] N Spalte *f*

crew[1] [kruː] **N a** Mannschaft *f*; (*also Sport*) Crew *f*; (*including officers: of ship also, of plane, tank*) Besatzung *f*, Crew *f*; **50 passengers and 20 ~** 50 Passagiere und 20 Mann Besatzung; **the ground ~** (*Aviat*) das Bodenpersonal; **is Mary your ~?** macht Mary Vorschotmann? **b** (*Brit inf: = gang*) Bande *f*; **they were a motley ~** sie waren ein bunt zusammengewürfelter Haufen (*inf*) **VI** **to ~ for sb** bei jdm den Vorschotmann machen **VT** *yacht* die Mannschaft or Crew sein von; (*one person in race*) den Vorschotmann machen auf (+*dat*)

crew[2] (*old*) *pret of* **crow**

crew: crew cut N Bürstenschnitt *m*; **crew member** N Mitglied *nt* der Mannschaft, Besatzungsmitglied *nt*; **crew neck** N runder Halsausschnitt; (*also* **crew-neck pullover** or **sweater**) Pullover *m* mit rundem Halsausschnitt

crib [krɪb] **N a** (= *cradle*) Krippe *f*; (*US:* = *cot*) Kinderbett *nt* **b** (= *manger*) Krippe *f*, Raufe *f*; (*fig: = nativity scene*) Krippe *f* **c** (*US:* = *maize bin*) Trockengerüst *nt* für Maiskolben **d** (*esp Brit Sch:* = *cheating aid*) Spickzettel *m* (*inf*); (*inf:* = *plagiarism*) Anleihe *f* (*inf*) **VI** (*esp Brit Sch inf*) abschreiben (*inf*), spicken (*inf*); **to ~ from sb** von jdm abschreiben (*inf*) **VT** (*esp Brit Sch inf*) abschreiben (*inf*); **to ~ sth from sb** etw von jdm abschreiben (*inf*)

cribbage ['krɪbɪdʒ] N Cribbage *nt*

crib death N (*US*) Krippentod *m*, plötzlicher Kindstod

crick [krɪk] **N a** **~ in one's neck/back** ein steifes Genick/ein steifer Rücken **VT** **to ~ one's neck/back** sich (*dat*) ein steifes Genick/einen steifen Rücken zuziehen

cricket[1] ['krɪkɪt] N (= *insect*) Grille *f*

cricket[2] N (*Sport*) Kricket *nt*; **that's not ~** (*fig inf*) das ist nicht fair

---

CRICKET

Cricket wird oft als typisch englisches Spiel angesehen, obwohl es in ganz Großbritannien und dem Commonwealth sehr beliebt ist. Es wird überwiegend im Sommer auf großen Spielfeldern im Freien, den so genannten **cricket pitches**, gespielt. Dabei treten zwei Teams mit jeweils elf Spielern gegeneinander an. Das Regelwerk ist ziemlich komplex.

Jedes Team schlägt abwechselnd den Ball möglichst weit weg und versucht dann, mit **runs** Punkte zu erzielen. Die gegnerische Mannschaft, die **fielders**, versuchen dabei, den Ball zu fangen oder abzustoppen, damit der **batsman** der Schlagmann, keinen Punkt machen kann. Wenn der Ball das Tor berührt oder gefangen wird, ohne nach dem Abschlag den Boden berührt zu haben, ist der Schlagmann draußen und muss ersetzt werden. Sind alle zehn Schlagmänner im Aus, wechseln die Mannschaften die Rollen; jetzt muss das andere Team aufschlagen. Die Mannschaft, die die meisten **runs** punkten konnte, gewinnt. Wie bei Baseball in den USA, wird Kricket oft als Metapher für viele Aspekte des englischen Lebensstils herangezogen. Zahlreiche Ausdrücke haben Eingang in die Alltagssprache gefunden, z. B. „to be on a sticky wicket" (in der Klemme sein) und „to knock someone for six" (jemanden umhauen).

---

cricket *in cpds* Kricket-; **cricket bat** N (Kricket)schlagholz *nt*

cricketer ['krɪkɪtə'] N Kricketspieler(in) *m(f)*

cricketing ['krɪkɪtɪŋ] ADJ Kricket-; **England's ~ heroes** Englands Krickethelden

cricket: cricket match N Kricketspiel *nt*; **cricket pitch** N Kricketfeld *nt*

cri de c"oe)ur ['kriːdəˈkɜː'] N verzweifelter Stoßseufzer

crier ['kraɪə'] N (= *town crier*) Ausrufer *m*; (= *court crier*) Gerichtsdiener *m*

crikey ['kraɪkɪ] INTERJ (*dated Brit, inf*) Mann (*inf*)

crime [kraɪm] **N a** Straftat *f*; (= *murder, robbery with violence etc also, fig*) Verbrechen *nt*; **it's not a ~!** das ist nicht verboten; **it's a ~ to throw away all that good food** es ist eine Sünde or eine Schande, all das gute Essen wegzuwerfen **b** *no pl* Verbrechen *nt*; **~ and punishment** Verbrechen und Verbrechensverfolgung; **to lead a life of ~** kriminell leben; **~ is on the increase** die Zahl der Verbrechen nimmt zu; **~ doesn't pay** Verbrechen lohnen sich nicht

Crimea [kraɪ'mɪə] N (*Geog*) Krim *f*; (*inf*, = *Crimean War*) der Krimkrieg

Crimean [kraɪ'mɪən] **N** (= *person*) Krimbewohner(in) *m(f)* **ADJ** Krim-; **she's ~** sie kommt von der Krim

crime: crime fighter N Kriminalitätsbekämpfer(in) *m(f)*; **crime fighting** N Kriminalitätsbekämpfung *f*; **crime-fighting** ADJ Kriminalitätsbekämpfungs-, zur Kriminalitätsbekämpfung; **crime of passion** N Mord *m* aus Eifersucht; **crime prevention** N Verbrechensverhütung *f*, präventive Verbrechensbekämpfung (*form*), Kriminalitätsprävention *f*; **crime prevention officer** N Beamte(r) *m*/Beamtin *f* für Kriminalitätsprävention or Verbrechensverhütung; **crime rate** N Verbrechensrate *f*; **crime spree** N **to go on a ~** auf Verbrechenstour gehen; **crime story** N Kriminalgeschichte *f*, Krimi *m* (*inf*); **crime wave** N Verbrechenswelle *f*

criminal ['krɪmɪnl] **N** Straftäter(in) *m(f)* (*form*), Kriminelle(r) *mf*; (*guilty of capital crimes also, fig*) Verbrecher(in) *m(f)* **ADJ** **a** kriminell, verbrecherisch; *action also* strafbar; **~ law** Strafrecht *nt*; **to take ~ proceedings against sb** strafrechtlich gegen jdn vorgehen; **to have a ~ record** vorbestraft sein **b** (*fig*) kriminell; **it's ~ to stay in this weather** es ist eine Schande, bei diesem Wetter drinnen zu bleiben

criminal: criminal assault N Körperverletzung *f*; **criminal charge** N Anklage *f* wegen eines Verbrechens; **she faces ~s** sie wird eines Verbrechens angeklagt, sie muss sich vor Gericht wegen eines Verbrechens verantworten; **criminal code** N Strafgesetzbuch *nt*; **criminal court** N Strafkammer *f*, Gericht *nt* für Strafsachen; **criminal damage** N strafbare Sachbeschädigung *f*; **Criminal Investigation Department** N (*Brit*) Kriminalpolizei *f*

criminality [ˌkrɪmɪ'nælɪtɪ] N Kriminalität *f*

criminalization [ˌkrɪmɪnəlaɪ'zeɪʃən] N Kriminalisierung *f*

criminalize ['krɪmɪnəlaɪz] VT kriminalisieren

criminal lawyer N Anwalt *m*/Anwältin *f* für Strafsachen; (*specializing in defence*) Strafverteidiger(in) *m(f)*

criminally ['krɪmɪnəlɪ] ADV kriminell, verbrecherisch; **~ liable** (*Jur*) strafrechtlich verantwortlich, schuldfähig; **he thought she behaved quite ~** (*fig*) seiner Meinung nach hat sie sich kriminell verhalten

criminal: criminal negligence N grobe Fahrlässigkeit, Fahrlässigkeitsdelikt *nt*; **criminal offence**, (*US*) **criminal offense** N strafbare Handlung; **Criminal Records Office** N Kriminaldienststelle *f* zur Führung der Verbrecherkartei

criminologist [ˌkrɪmɪ'nɒlədʒɪst] N Kriminologe *m*, Kriminologin *f*

criminology [ˌkrɪmɪ'nɒlədʒɪ] N Kriminologie *f*

crimp [krɪmp] VT *hair* (mit der Brennschere) wellen

Crimplene® ['krɪmpliːn] N ≈ knitterfreier Trevira®

crimson ['krɪmzn] ADJ purpurn, purpurrot; *sky* blutrot, purpurrot; (*through blushing*) knallrot (*inf*), dunkelrot; **to turn** *or* **go ~** (*person, face*) knallrot (*inf*) *or* dunkelrot werden *or* anlaufen; (*sky*) sich blutrot färben N Purpur *nt*, Purpurrot *nt*

cringe [krɪndʒ] VI **a** (= *shrink back*) zurückschrecken (*at* vor +*dat*); (*fig*) schaudern; **to ~ before sb** vor jdm zurückweichen *or* -schrecken; **he ~d at the thought** er *or* ihn schauderte bei dem Gedanken; **he ~d when she mispronounced his name** er zuckte zusammen, als sie seinen Namen falsch aussprach **b** (= *humble oneself, fawn*) katzbuckeln, kriechen (*to* vor +*dat*); **to go cringing to sb** zu jdm gekrochen kommen; **a cringing person** ein Kriecher *m*; **cringing behaviour** kriecherisches Benehmen

cringe-making ['krɪndʒˌmeɪkɪŋ] ADJ extrem peinlich

crinkle ['krɪŋkl] N (Knitter)falte *f*; (*in skin*) Fältchen *nt* VT *paper, foil, dress etc* (zer)knittern; *cardboard, plastic etc* knicken; *edge of paper* wellen VI (= *wrinkle, paper, foil, dress etc*) knittern; (*face, skin*) (Lach)fältchen bekommen; (*edges of paper*) sich wellen, wellig werden; (= *curl: hair*) sich krausen; **his eyes ~d when he smiled** er bekam tausend Fältchen um die Augen, wenn er lächelte

crinkled ['krɪŋkld] ADJ *leaf, paper, clothes* zerknittert, zerknautscht; *face* faltig, runzelig; **the paper was all ~** das Papier war ganz zerknittert

crinkly ['krɪŋklɪ] ADJ (+er) (*inf, wrinkled*) *paper, foil etc* zerknittert; *edges* wellig; *hair* krauselig (*inf*)

crinoline ['krɪnəlɪn] N Krinoline *f*

cripes [kraɪps] INTERJ (*dated Brit, inf*) Mann (*inf*)

cripple ['krɪpl] N Krüppel *m* VT *person* zum Krüppel machen; *arm, legs etc* verkrüppeln; *ship, plane* aktionsunfähig machen; (*fig*) *industry, exports* lahm legen, lähmen; *person* lähmen; **the ship was ~d** das Schiff war nicht mehr aktionsfähig; **~d with rheumatism** von Rheuma praktisch gelähmt; **to be ~d for life** lebenslang ein Krüppel sein; **to be emotionally ~d** ein emotionaler Krüppel sein

crippling ['krɪplɪŋ] ADJ *pain* lähmend; *guilt, depression* lähmend; *taxes, repayments* erdrückend; *strikes* alles lähmend *attr*; **a ~ disease** ein Leiden, das einen bewegungsunfähig macht; **a ~ blow** (*lit, fig*) ein schwerer Schlag

cripplingly ['krɪplɪŋlɪ] ADV *expensive* unerschwinglich

crisis ['kraɪsɪs] N *pl* **crises** ['kraɪsiːz] Krise *f* (*also Med*); **to reach ~ point** den Höhepunkt erreichen; **that was a ~ in his life** (= *decisive moment*) das war ein entscheidender Punkt in seinem Leben; (= *emotional crisis*) das war eine Krise in seinem Leben; **at this time of ~** in dieser krisenreichen *or* schweren Zeit; **in times of ~** in Krisenzeiten

crisis: crisis centre N Einsatzzentrum *nt* (*für Krisenfälle*); **rape ~** Beratungsstelle *f* (*für Frauen, die Opfer einer Vergewaltigung geworden sind*); **crisis management** N Krisenmanagement *nt*

crisp [krɪsp] ADJ (+er) *apple, lettuce* knackig, fest; *bread, biscuits, bacon* knusprig; *snow* verharscht; *leaves* trocken; *appearance* adrett, frisch; *curls, clothes* steif; *manner, voice, style of writing, remark* knapp; *air, weather, colour* frisch; *sound* klar; (*Sport*) *shot* sauber; *ten-pound note* brandneu; **a ~ dry white wine** ein leichter, trockener Weißwein; **a ~ spring morning** ein frischer Frühlingsmorgen N (*Brit: = potato crisp*) Chip *m*; **to burn sth to a ~** etw verbrutzeln lassen; *toast* etw verkohlen lassen; **burned** *or* **blackened to a ~** völlig verbrutzelt; *toast* völlig verkohlt VT (*also* **crisp up**) *bread* aufbacken

crispbread ['krɪspbred] N Knäckebrot *nt*

crispen (up) ['krɪspn('ʌp)] VT *sep bread* aufbacken; *blouse etc* auffrischen

crisper ['krɪspə] N (*in fridge*) Gemüsefach *nt*

crisply ['krɪsplɪ] ADV knackig; *baked, fried* knusprig; *starched* steif; *dressed* adrett, frisch; *write, speak* knapp; **the snow crunched ~ under his feet** der Schnee knirschte unter seinen Füßen; **the notes rang out ~** die Töne kamen klar

crispness ['krɪspnɪs] N (*of apple, lettuce*) Knackigkeit *f*, Festheit *f*; (*of bread, biscuits, bacon*) Knusprigkeit *f*; (*of snow*) Verharschtheit *f*; (*of leaves*) Trockenheit *f*; (*of clothes*) Steifheit *f*; (*of manner, voice, style of writing*) Knappheit *f*; (*of air, weather*) Frische *f*; (*of sound*) Klarheit *f*; (*Sport, of shot*) Sauberkeit *f*

crispy ['krɪspɪ] ADJ (+er) (*inf*) knusprig

crisscross ['krɪskrɒs] N Kreuzundquer *nt* ADJ *pattern* Kreuz- ADV kreuz und quer VT mit einem Kreuzmuster versehen

crit [krɪt] N (*inf, of book etc*) Kritik *f*

criterion [kraɪ'tɪərɪən] N *pl* **criteria** [kraɪ'tɪərɪə] Kriterium *nt*; **then, by the same ~, he is guilty too** dann ist er ebenso schuldig

critic ['krɪtɪk] N Kritiker(in) *m(f)*; **literary ~** Literaturkritiker(in) *m(f)*; **he's a terrible ~** (= *very critical*) er ist schrecklich kritisch; **he's his own worst ~** er kritisiert sich selbst am meisten, er ist sein schlimmster Kritiker; **she is a strong/ constant ~ of the government** sie kritisiert die Regierung heftig/ständig *or* heftig/ständig an der Regierung

critical ['krɪtɪkəl] ADJ **a** (= *fault-finding, discriminating*) kritisch; **the book was a ~ success** das Buch kam bei den Kritikern an; **the book met with ~ acclaim** das Buch fand Anklang bei den Kritikern *or* wurde in den Kritiken gelobt; **~ reviews** Kritiken *pl*; **~ edition** kritische Ausgabe; **to cast a ~ eye over sth** sich (*dat*) etw kritisch ansehen; **to be ~ of sb/sth** jdn/etw kritisieren **b** (= *dangerous, Sci*) kritisch; (= *crucial also*) entscheidend; (*Med*) *person* in kritischem Zustand; **it is ~ (for us) to understand what is happening** es ist (für uns) von entscheidender Bedeutung zu wissen, was vorgeht; **of ~ importance** von entscheidender Bedeutung; **to be on the ~ list** (*Med*) in kritischem Zustand sein

critically ['krɪtɪkəlɪ] ADV **a** (= *finding fault*) kritisch **b** *ill* schwer **c** (= *crucially*) **to be ~ important** von entscheidender Bedeutung sein **d** (*Art, Liter etc*) **~ acclaimed** in den Kritiken gelobt

critical mass N (*Phys*) kritische Masse; (*fig*) Mindestanforderung *f*; **to reach ~** (*fig*) einen kritischen Punkt erreichen

critical path N kritischer Pfad; **~ analysis** kritische Pfadanalyse

criticism ['krɪtɪsɪzəm] ✪ 26.3 N Kritik *f*; **literary ~** Literaturkritik *f*; **to come in for a lot of ~** schwer kritisiert werden; **the decision is open to ~** das ist eine sehr anfechtbare Entscheidung

criticize ['krɪtɪsaɪz] ✪ 26.3 VI kritisieren VT kritisieren; **to ~ sb for sth** jdn für etw kritisieren; **I ~d her for always being late** ich kritisierte sie dafür, dass sie immer zu spät kommt

critique [krɪ'tiːk] N Kritik *f*

critter ['krɪtə] N (*US, dial*) = creature

croak [krəʊk] N (*of frog*) Quaken *nt no pl*; (*of raven, person*) Krächzen *nt no pl* VI (*frog*) quaken; (*raven, person*) krächzen VT **a** (*person*) krächzen **b** (*inf*: = *die*) **he ~ed it** er ist abgekratzt (*inf*)

croaky ['krəʊkɪ] ADJ (+er) (*inf*) *voice* krächzend; **you sound a bit ~** du klingst etwas heiser

Croat ['krəʊæt] N (= *person*) Kroate *m*, Kroatin *f*; (*Ling*) Kroatisch *nt*

Croatia [krəʊ'eɪʃə] N Kroatien *nt*

Croatian [krəʊ'eɪʃən] N = Croat ADJ kroatisch; **she is ~** sie ist Kroatin

crochet ['krəʊʃeɪ] N (*also* **crochet work**) Häkelei *f*; **~ hook** Häkelnadel *f*; **to do a lot of ~** viel häkeln VTI häkeln

crock¹ [krɒk] N (= *jar*) Topf *m*; (= *pottery chip*) Scherbe *f*; **what a ~ of shit!** (*US sl*) was für ein Haufen Scheiße (*sl*)

crock² N (*inf, = vehicle*) Kiste *f* (*inf*); (= *person*) Wrack *nt* (*inf*); (= *horse*) Klepper *m*; **an old ~s race** ein Oldtimerrennen *nt*

crocked [krɒkt] ADJ (*US inf*) breit (*sl*)

crockery ['krɒkərɪ] N (*Brit*) Geschirr *nt*

crocodile ['krɒkədaɪl] N **a** Krokodil *nt* **b** (*Brit, Sch*) **to walk in a ~** zwei und zwei hintereinander gehen; **the long ~ of little girls** der lange Zug kleiner Mädchen, die zwei und zwei hintereinander gehen

crocodile: crocodile clip N Krokodilklemme *f*; **crocodile tears** PL Krokodilstränen *pl*; **to shed ~** Krokodilstränen vergießen

crocus ['krəʊkəs] N Krokus *m*

Croesus ['kriːsəs] N Krösus *m*; **to be as rich as ~** ein (richtiger) Krösus sein

croft [krɒft] N (*esp Scot*) kleines Pachtgrundstück; (= *house*) Kate *f*

crofter ['krɒftə] N (*esp Scot*) Kleinpächter(in) *m(f)*

crofting ['krɒftɪŋ] (*esp Scot*) N Bewirtschaftung *von kleinen Pachtgrundstücken* ADJ *attr* community von Kleinpächtern

Crohn's disease ['krəʊnzdɪˌziːz] N (*Med*) Morbus Crohn *m*

croissant ['krwɑːsɒŋ] N Hörnchen *nt*

crone [krəʊn] N Tante *f* (*inf*)

crony ['krəʊnɪ] N Freund(in) *m(f)*, Spießgeselle (*hum*) *m*

cronyism ['krəʊnɪɪzəm] N, *no pl* (*pej*) Vetternwirtschaft *f* (*pej*)

crook¹ [krʊk] N **a** (= *dishonest person*) Gauner *m* (*inf*) **b** (= *staff, of shepherd*) Hirtenstab *m*, Krummstab *m*; (*of bishop also*) Bischofsstab *m* → **hook c** (= *bend, in road, river*) Biegung *f*; (*in arm*) Beuge *f* VT *finger* krümmen; *arm* beugen; **she only has to ~ her (little) finger and he comes running** sie braucht nur mit dem kleinen Finger zu winken und schon kommt er angerannt

crook² ADJ (*Austral, inf*) **a** (= *sick*) krank; **he's with the flu/a cold** er hat die Grippe/eine Erkältung; **he feels ~** er fühlt sich mies (*inf*) *or* lausig (*inf*); **he is ~** es geht ihm mies (*inf*) **b** (= *not functioning*) kaputt (*inf*); (= *not good*) mies (*inf*) **c** (= *angry*) wild (*inf*); **to go ~ at** *or* **on sb** wegen jdm wild werden

crooked [krʊkɪd] ADJ (*lit, = bent*) krumm; (= *tilted, sloping also*) *smile* schief; (*fig inf*: = *dishonest*) *method* krumm; *person* unehrlich; **your hat's ~** dein Hut sitzt schief

crookedly ['krʊkɪdlɪ] ADV *hang, smile, grin* schief

croon [kruːn] VT (= *sing softly*) leise *or* sanft singen; (*usu pej, sentimentally*) gefühlvoll *or* schmalzig (*pej inf*) singen VI (= *sing softly*) leise *or* sanft singen; (*usu pej, sentimentally*) Schnulzen (*pej inf*) *or* sentimentale Lieder singen

crooner ['kruːnə] N Sänger *m* (sentimentaler Lieder), Schnulzensänger *m* (*pej inf*)

crop [krɒp] N **a** (= *produce*) Ernte *f*; (= *species grown*) (Feld)frucht *f*; (*fig*: = *large number*) Schwung *m*; **the cereal ~s were destroyed** die Getreideernte wurde zerstört; **the barley ~ is looking good** die Gerste steht gut; **a good ~ of fruit/potatoes** eine gute Obst-/Kartoffelernte; **the beef ~** die Rindfleischproduktion; **to be in** *or* **under/out of ~** bebaut/nicht bebaut sein; **he grows a different ~ every year** er baut jedes Jahr etwas anderes an; **to bring the ~s in** die Ernte einbringen; **a ~ of students/problems** (*inf*) eine Reihe von Studenten/Problemen **b** (*of bird*) Kropf *m* **c** (*of whip*) Stock *m*; (= *hunting crop*) Reitpeitsche *f* **d** (= *hairstyle*) Kurzhaarschnitt *m*; **to give sb a close ~** jdm die Haare gehörig stutzen VT *hair* stutzen; *horse's or dog's tail also* kupieren; *photographs* zuschneiden; **her husband was ~ped from the photograph** ihr Mann war auf dem Foto weggeschnitten; **it's best to keep the grass ~ped short** man sollte das Gras kurz halten; **the goat ~ped the grass** die Ziege fraß das Gras ab; **~ped hair, hair ~ped short** kurz geschnittenes Haar

▶**crop out** VI auftauchen; (*minerals*) zutage or zu Tage treten

▶**crop up** VI aufkommen; **something's cropped up** es ist etwas dazwischengekommen; **he was ready for anything that might crop up** er war auf alle Eventualitäten gefasst

crop: crop circle N Kornkreis m; **crop-dusting** ['krɒpdʌstɪŋ] N Schädlingsbekämpfung f (*aus dem Flugzeug*); **crop failure** N Missernte f

cropper ['krɒpə] N **a** (= *person*) Anbauer m; **these plants are poor ~s** diese Pflanzen bringen nicht viel Ertrag **b** (*Brit inf*) **to come a ~** (*lit*: = *fall*) hinfliegen (*inf*); (*fig*: = *fail*) auf die Nase fallen

crop: crop rotation N Fruchtwechsel m; **crop-sprayer** N (= *person*) Schädlingsbekämpfer(in) m(f); (= *plane*) Schädlingsbekämpfungsflugzeug nt; (= *tractor*) Schädlingsbekämpfungsfahrzeug nt, Besprühungsfahrzeug nt; **crop-spraying** N Schädlingsbekämpfung f (*durch Besprühen*)

croquet ['krəʊkeɪ] N Krocket(spiel) nt; **~ lawn** Krocketrasen m

croquette [krəʊ'ket] N Krokette f

crosier, crozier ['krəʊʒɪə] N Bischofsstab m, Hirtenstab m, Krummstab m

cross[1] [krɒs] ⊘ 27.7 N **a** Kreuz nt; **to make one's ~** sein Kreuz(chen) machen or setzen; **to make the sign of the Cross** das Kreuzzeichen machen or schlagen; **the Cross and the Crescent** Kreuz und Halbmond; **to bear/take up one's ~** (*fig*) sein Kreuz tragen/auf sich (*acc*) nehmen; **we all have our ~ to bear** wir haben alle unser Kreuz zu tragen **b** (= *bias*) **on the ~** schräg; **to be cut on the ~** schräg geschnitten sein **c** (= *hybrid*) Kreuzung f; (*fig*) Mittelding nt; **a ~ between a laugh and a bark** eine Mischung aus Lachen und Bellen **d** (*Ftbl*) Flanke f; **to hit a ~ to sb** jdm zuflanken **e** (*Boxing*) Seitwärtshaken m **ATTR** (= *transverse*) street, line etc Quer- **VT a** (= *go across*) road, river, mountains überqueren; (*on foot*) picket line etc überschreiten; country, desert, room durchqueren; **to ~ the road** über die Straße gehen, die Straße überqueren; **to ~ sb's path** (*fig*) jdm über den Weg laufen; **it ~ed my mind that ...** es fiel mir ein, dass ..., mir kam der Gedanke, dass ...; **a smile ~ed her lips** ein Lächeln kam über ihre Lippen; **don't ~ your bridges until you come to them** (*prov*) lass die Probleme auf dich zukommen; **we'll ~ that bridge when we come to it** lassen wir das Problem mal auf uns zukommen, das sind ungelegte Eier (*inf*); **they have clearly ~ed the boundary into terrorism** sie haben eindeutig die Grenze zum Terrorismus überschritten **b** (= *put at right-angles, intersect*) kreuzen; **to ~ one's legs** die Beine übereinander schlagen; **to ~ one's arms** die Arme verschränken; **the lines are ~ed, we have a ~ed line** (*Telec*) die Leitungen überschneiden sich; **line AB ~es line CD at point E** AB schneidet CD in E; **to ~ sb's palm with silver** jdm ein Geldstück in die Hand drücken; **keep your fingers ~ed for me!** (*inf*) drück or halt mir die Daumen! (*inf*); **I'm keeping my fingers ~ed (for you)** (*inf*) ich drücke or halte (dir) die Daumen (*inf*) **c** (= *put a line across*) letter, t einen Querstrich machen durch; (*Brit*) cheque ≈ zur Verrechnung ausstellen; **a ~ed cheque** ein Verrechnungsscheck m; **to ~ sth through** etw durchstreichen → **dot d** (= *make the sign of the Cross*) **to ~ oneself** sich bekreuzigen; **~ my/your heart** (*inf*) Ehrenwort, Hand aufs Herz **e** (= *mark with a cross*) ankreuzen **f** (= *go against*) plans durchkreuzen; **to ~ sb**

jdn verärgern; **to be ~ed in love** in der Liebe enttäuscht werden **g** *animal, fruit* kreuzen **VI a** (*across road*) hinübergehen, die Straße überqueren; (*across Channel etc*) hinüberfahren; **"cross now"** „gehen"; **to ~ at the green light** bei Grün über die Straße gehen **b** (= *intersect*) sich kreuzen; (*lines also*) sich schneiden; **our paths have ~ed several times** (*fig*) unsere Wege haben sich öfters gekreuzt **c** (*letters etc*) sich kreuzen

▶**cross off** VT sep streichen (*prep obj* aus, von)

▶**cross out** VT sep ausstreichen

▶**cross over** **VI a** (= *cross the road*) hinübergehen, die Straße überqueren **b** (= *change sides*) übergehen, überwechseln (*to* zu) **VI** +*prep obj* road, street überqueren

cross[2] ADJ (+*er*) böse, sauer (*inf*); **to be ~ with sb** mit jdm or auf jdn böse sein

cross: cross-action N (*Jur*) Widerklage f; **crossbar** N (*of bicycle*) Stange f; (*Sport*) Querlatte f; **crossbeam** N (= *girder*) Querbalken m; (*Sport*) Schwebebalken m; **cross-bench** N usu pl (*Parl*) Bank, wo die weder zur Regierungs- noch zur Oppositionspartei gehörenden Abgeordneten sitzen; **cross-bencher** ['krɒsbentʃə] N (*Parl*) Abgeordneter, der weder der Regierungs- noch der Oppositionspartei angehört; **crossbill** N (*Orn*) Kreuzschnabel m; **crossbones** PL gekreuzte Knochen pl (*unter einem Totenkopf*) ▶ **skull**; **crossbow** N (Stand)armbrust f; **cross brace** N Kreuz- or Querverstrebung f; **crossbred** ADJ (*Zool, Biol*) gekreuzt; **crossbreed** (*Zool, Biol*) N Kreuzung f **VT** kreuzen; **cross-Channel** ADJ attr ferries, swimmer Kanal-; **a ~ swim** ein Durchschwimmen nt des Kanals; **crosscheck** N Gegenprobe f **VT** facts, figures überprüfen; equation die Gegenprobe machen bei; **cross-compiler** N (*Comput*) Crosscompiler m; **cross-country** ADJ Querfeldein-; **~ ski** Langlaufski m; **~ skier** Langläufer(in) m(f); **~ skiing** Langlauf m; **~ ski track** (Langlauf)loipe f ADV querfeldein N (= *race*) Querfeldeinrennen nt; **cross-court** (*Tennis*) ADV hit cross, diagonal über den Platz ADJ **to hit** or **play a ~ forehand** die Vorhand cross schlagen; **cross-cultural** ADJ multikulturell; **crosscurrent** N Gegenströmung f; **cross-dress** VI sich als Transvestit kleiden; **cross-dresser** N Transvestit m; **cross-dressing** N Transvestismus m; **cross-examination** N Kreuzverhör nt (*of* über +*acc*); **cross-examine** VT ins Kreuzverhör nehmen; **cross-eyed** ADJ schielend; **to be ~** schielen; **cross-fertilization** N , no pl (*Bot*) Kreuzbefruchtung f, Fremdbestäubung f; (*fig*) gegenseitige Befruchtung; **cross-fertilize** VT (*Bot*) kreuzbefruchten; **crossfield** ADJ **~ pass** (*Ftbl, Hockey*) Querpass m; **crossfire** N Kreuzfeuer nt; **to be caught in the ~** (*lit, fig*) ins Kreuzfeuer geraten; **cross-gartered** ADJ (*old*) mit kreuzweise geschnürten Waden; **cross-grained** ADJ wood quer gefasert; (= *grumpy*) mürrisch; (= *perverse*) querköpfig; **cross hairs** PL Fadenkreuz nt; **crosshatch** VT mit Kreuzlagen schattieren; **crosshatching** N Kreuzschattierung f

crossing ['krɒsɪŋ] N **a** (= *act*) Überquerung f; (= *sea crossing*) Überfahrt f **b** (= *crossing place*) Übergang m; (= *crossroads*) Kreuzung f

crossing point N (*of border*) Grenzübergang m

cross: cross-keys PL (*Her*) gekreuzte Schlüssel pl; **crosskick** N (*Ftbl*) Querpass m (nach innen); **cross-legged** ADJ, ADV mit gekreuzten Beinen; (*on ground*) im Schneidersitz; **cross liability** N (*Jur*) beiderseitige Haftpflicht

crossly ['krɒslɪ] ADV böse, verärgert

cross: cross-match VT (*Med*) kreuzen; **cross-matching** N (*Med*) Kreuzprobe f; **crossover** N (*Rail*) Gleiskreuzung f; (*Mus*) Crossover m; **a jazz-rap ~** ein Jazz-Rap-Crossover m; **cross-party** ADJ (*Pol*) talks zwischen den Parteien, parteiübergreifend; support, committee überparteilich; **crosspatch** N (*inf*) Brummbär m (*inf*); **crosspiece** N (= *bar*) Querstange f;

cross-ply ADJ Diagonal- N (*inf*) Diagonalreifen m; **cross-pollinate** VT fremdbestäuben; **cross-pollination** N Fremdbestäubung f; **cross-purposes** PL **to be** or **talk at ~** aneinander vorbeireden; **he was at ~ with her** sie haben aneinander vorbeigeredet; **cross-question** VT = **cross-examine**; **cross-rate** N (*St Ex*) Kreuznotierung f, Kreuzkurs m; **cross-refer** VT verweisen (*to* auf +*acc*); **cross-reference** N (Quer)verweis m (*to* auf +*acc*) **VT** = **cross-refer**; **crossroads** N sing or pl (*lit*) Kreuzung f; (*fig*) Scheideweg m; **cross section** N Querschnitt m; **to draw sth in ~** etw im Querschnitt zeichnen; **a ~ of the population** ein Querschnitt durch die Bevölkerung; **cross-stitch** N (*Sew*) Kreuzstich m **VT** im Kreuzstich arbeiten; **cross sum** N (*Math*) Quersumme f; **crosstalk** N , no pl **a** (*witty*) Wortgefecht nt, Wortgefechte pl **b** (*Telec*) Nebensprechen nt; **cross-town** ADJ (*US*) quer durch die Stadt; **crosswalk** N (*US*) Fußgängerüberweg m; **crossways** ADV = **crosswise**; **crosswind** N Seitenwind m; **crosswise** ADV quer; **crossword (puzzle)** N Kreuzworträtsel nt; **crosswort** N Kreuzlabkraut nt

crotch [krɒtʃ] N **a** (*in tree etc*) Gabelung f **b** (*of trousers*) Schritt m; (*Anat*) Unterleib m; **a kick in the ~** ein Tritt zwischen die Beine; **she wears her skirts about an inch below the ~** ihre Röcke reichen nur ein Paar Zentimeter über den Po (*inf*)

crotchet ['krɒtʃɪt] N **a** (*Brit, Mus*) Viertelnote f; **~ rest** Viertelpause f **b** (*inf*: = *cross person*) Miesepeter m

crotchety ['krɒtʃɪtɪ] ADJ (*inf*: = *cross*) schlecht gelaunt, miesepetrig (*inf*); child quengelig (*inf*)

crouch [kraʊtʃ] VI sich zusammenkauern, kauern; **to ~ down** sich niederkauern N Hocke f; (*of animal*) Kauerstellung f

croup[1] [kru:p] N , no pl (*Med*) Krupp m, Kehlkopfdiphtherie f

croup[2] N (*of horse*) Kruppe f

croupier ['kru:pɪeɪ] N Croupier m

crouton ['kru:tɒn] N Croûton m

crow[1] [krəʊ] N **a** (*Orn*) Krähe f; **as the ~ flies** (in der) Luftlinie; **to eat ~** (= *US, inf*) zu Kreuze kriechen **b** (*inf*) = **crowbar**

crow[2] N **a** (*of cock, baby*) Krähen nt no pl; (*of person*) J(a)uchzer m; **a ~ of delight** ein Freudenjauchzer m **VI a** (*of cock* or *old*) crew, ptp crowed (*cock*) krähen **b** pret, ptp crowed (*baby*) krähen; (*person*) j(a)uchzen; (*fig*, = *boast*) sich brüsten, angeben (*about* mit); (= *exult*) hämisch frohlocken (*over* über +*acc*)

crow: crowbar N Brecheisen nt; **crowberry** N Krähenbeere f

crowd [kraʊd] N **a** Menschenmenge f; (*Sport, Theat*) Zuschauermenge f; **to be swept along by the ~** von der or in der Menge mitgerissen werden; **to get lost in the ~(s)** in der Menge verloren gehen; **~s of people** Menschenmassen pl, große Menschenmengen pl; **that would pass in a ~** (*fig*) das geht (durch), wenn man nicht zu genau hinsieht; **to get a good ~ at a match** bei einem Spiel eine Menge Zuschauer haben; **there was quite a ~** es waren eine ganze Menge Leute da; **a whole ~ of us** ein ganzer Haufen von uns (*inf*) **b** (= *set of people, clique*) Clique f, Haufen m (*inf*); **the university ~** die Uni-Haufen (*inf*), die Uni-Clique; **the usual ~** die üblichen Leute; **I'm not one of that ~** ich gehöre nicht zu diesem Haufen (*inf*) or zu denen; **they're a nice ~** sie sind ein netter Haufen (*inf*) **c** no pl (= *the masses*) **the ~** die (breite) Masse; **to go with** or **follow the ~** mit der Herde laufen; **he hates to be just one of the ~** sie geht nicht gern in der Masse unter **VI** (sich) drängen; **to ~ (a)round** sich herumdrängen; **to ~ together** sich zusammendrängen; **to ~ in** (sich) hereindrängen; **to ~ (a)round sb/sth** (sich) um jdn/etw herumdrängen **VT a to ~ the streets** die Straßen bevölkern;

to ~ a room with furniture ein Zimmer mit Möbeln voll stopfen; **it will really ~ the office having three new people** mit drei neuen Leuten wird es im Büro sicherlich eng werden; **to ~ things together** Dinge eng zusammendrängen **b** (inf: = harass) **to ~ sb** jdn drängeln, jdm auf den Füßen stehen (inf); (creditors) jdn bedrängen

▶ **crowd out** VT sep (= not let in) wegdrängen; (= make leave) herausdrängen; (Press) article etc verdrängen; **the pub was crowded out** das Lokal war gerammelt voll (inf) or proppenvoll (inf)

crowd control N , no pl **~ was becoming difficult** die Kontrolle der Massen wurde schwierig; **expert in ~** Sicherheitsexperte m/-expertin f

crowded ['kraʊdɪd] ADJ **a** (= filled with people) train, shop etc überfüllt; **the streets/shops/trains are** ~ es ist voll auf den Straßen/in den Geschäften/in den Zügen; **~ with people** voller Menschen; **a room ~ with children** ein Zimmer voller Kinder; **to play to a ~ house** (Theat) vor vollem Haus spielen; **the holiday was ~ with incidents** die Ferien waren sehr ereignisreich; **a mind ~ with facts** eine Ansammlung von Faktenwissen (im Kopf) **b** (= overpopulated) city, district überbevölkert; conditions beengt; **it's a ~ profession** es ist ein überfüllter Berufszweig

crowd: crowd pleaser ['kraʊdpliːzə°] N (= person) Publikumsliebling m; (= event etc) Publikumserfolg m; **crowd puller** ['kraʊdpʊlə°] N Kassenmagnet m; **crowd scene** N (Theat) Massenszene f; **crowd trouble** N , no pl Massenausschreitungen pl

crowfoot ['krəʊfʊt] N (Bot) Hahnenfuß m

crown [kraʊn] N **a** (for royalty) Krone f; **~ of thorns** Dornenkrone f; **the Crown** die Krone; **to wear the ~** auf dem Thron sitzen; **to be heir to the ~** Thronfolger(in) m(f) sein; **to succeed to the ~** die Thronfolge antreten **b** (= coin) Krone f **c** (= top) (of head) Wirbel m; (= skull) Schädel m; (= head measurement) Kopf(umfang) m; (of hat) Kopf m; (of road) Wölbung f; (of arch) Scheitelpunkt m; (of roof) First m; (of tooth, tree) Krone f; (of hill) Kuppe f **d** (= size of paper) englisches Papierformat (ca. 45 × 38 cm²) **e** (fig: = climax, completion) Krönung f **VT a** king, queen krönen; **he was ~ed king** er ist zum König gekrönt worden **b** (= top) **the hill is ~ed with trees** die Bergkuppe ist mit Bäumen bewachsen; **the cake was ~ed with marzipan decorations** der Kuchen war zur Krönung des Ganzen (noch) mit Marzipanfiguren geschmückt; **to be ~ed with success** (fig) von Erfolg gekrönt sein **c** (fig: = form climax to) krönen; **to ~ it all it began to snow** (inf) zur Krönung des Ganzen begann es zu schneien; **that ~s everything!** (inf) das ist doch der Gipfel or die Höhe! (inf) **d** (in draughts etc) eine Dame bekommen mit **e** tooth eine Krone machen für; **the tooth had been ~ed before** der Zahn hatte schon vorher eine Krone gehabt **f** (inf: = hit) eine runterhauen (+dat) (inf)

crown: Crown Agent N (Brit Pol) Mitglied des Entwicklungshilfeausschusses; **crown cap** N = crown cork; **crown colony** N Kronkolonie f; **crown cork** N Kron(en)korken m; **crown court** N Bezirksgericht für Strafsachen

crowned head [ˌkraʊnd'hed] N gekröntes Haupt

crown green bowling N (Brit) ≈ Boule nt

crowning ['kraʊnɪŋ] N Krönung f ADJ success, achievement krönend; **her hair was her ~ glory** ihr Haar war ihre größte Zierde; **that symphony was his ~ glory** diese Sinfonie war die Krönung seines Werkes

crown: crown jewels PL Kronjuwelen pl; **crown lands** PL königliche Ländereien pl, Ländereien pl (also **Crown law** (Brit Jur) Strafrecht nt; **crown prince** N Kronprinz m; **crown princess** N Kronprinzessin f; **crown wheel** N Kronenrad m, Kammrad nt;

crown witness N Zeuge m/Zeugin f der Anklage

crow's: crow's feet PL Krähenfüße pl; **crow's nest** N (Naut) Mastkorb m; (on foremast) Krähennest nt, Ausguck m

crozier N = crosier

crucial ['kruːʃəl] ADJ **a** (= decisive) entscheidend (to für) **b** (= very important) äußerst wichtig **c** (Med) incision etc kreuzförmig

crucially ['kruːʃəlɪ] ADV ausschlaggebend; different bedeutend; **~ important** von entscheidender Bedeutung; **~, he is 10 years older than she is** von entscheidender Bedeutung ist, dass er 10 Jahre älter ist als sie

cruciate ['kruːʃɪeɪt] ADJ kreuzförmig; **~ ligament** Kreuzband nt

crucible ['kruːsɪbl] N (Schmelz)tiegel m

crucible steel N Tiegelgussstahl m

crucifix ['kruːsɪfɪks] N Kruzifix nt

crucifixion [ˌkruːsɪ'fɪkʃən] N Kreuzigung f

cruciform ['kruːsɪfɔːm] ADJ kreuzförmig

crucify ['kruːsɪfaɪ] VT **a** (lit) kreuzigen **b** (fig inf) play, author verreißen; person in der Luft zerreißen (inf) **c** (= mortify) the flesh abtöten

crud [krʌd] N (inf) **a** (= dirt) Dreck m (lit, fig) **b** (pej: = person) Scheißkerl m (pej)

cruddy ['krʌdɪ] ADJ (+er) (inf) blöd (inf), bescheuert (inf)

crude [kruːd] ADJ (+er) **a** (= unprocessed) Roh-, roh **b** (= vulgar) expression, story etc ordinär, derb **c** (= unsophisticated) method, model, implement primitiv; sketch grob; manners ungehobelt, grob; attempt unbeholfen **N** Rohöl nt

crudely ['kruːdlɪ] ADV **a** (= vulgarly) ordinär, derb **b** (= unsophisticatedly) primitiv; behave ungehobelt; (= approximately) estimate, draw grob; **to put it ~** um es ganz grob auszudrücken

crudeness ['kruːdnɪs], **crudity** ['kruːdɪtɪ] N **a** (= vulgarity) Derbheit f **b** (= lack of sophistication) (of method, model, implement) Primitivität f; (of sketch) Grobheit f; (of manners) Ungehobeltheit(s) nt (of +gen, in +dat); (of attempt) Unbeholfenheit f

crude oil N Rohöl nt

crudités ['kruːdɪteɪz] PL rohes Gemüse, serviert mit Dips

cruel [krʊəl] ADJ grausam (to zu); remark, wit, critic, winter also unbarmherzig; **to be ~ to animals** ein Tierquäler sein; **to be ~ to one's dog** seinen Hund quälen; **that is ~ to animals** das ist Tierquälerei; **don't be ~!** sei nicht so gemein!; **sometimes you have to be ~ to be kind** manchmal ist es letzten Endes besser, wenn man hart ist

cruelly ['krʊəlɪ] ADV (+vb) grausam; (+adj) auf grausame Art

cruelty ['krʊəltɪ] N Grausamkeit f (to gegenüber); (of remark, critic also) Unbarmherzigkeit f; **~ to children** Kindesmisshandlung f; **~ to animals** Tierquälerei f; **physical ~** Grausamkeit f; **mental ~** seelische Grausamkeit

cruelty-free ADJ cosmetics nicht an Tieren getestet

cruet ['kruːɪt] N **a** (= set) Gewürzständer m, Menage f; (for oil) Krügchen nt; **would you pass the ~?** könnten Sie mir bitte die Gewürze reichen? **b** (Eccl) Krügchen nt

cruise [kruːz] VI **a** (person) eine Kreuzfahrt machen; (ship) kreuzen, eine Kreuzfahrt machen **b** (= travel at cruising speed) (car) Dauergeschwindigkeit fahren; (aircraft) mit Reisegeschwindigkeit fliegen; (athlete) locker laufen; (= drive around) herumfahren; **the car ~s happily along at 90** 90 ist eine ideale Fahrgeschwindigkeit für das Auto; **we were cruising along the road** wir fuhren (gemächlich) die Straße entlang; **we are now cruising at a height/speed of** ... wir fliegen nun in einer Flughöhe/mit einer Reisegeschwindigkeit von ...; **the cyclist ~d down the hill** der Radfahrer rollte den Berg hinunter

c (fig) **to ~ to victory** einen leichten Sieg erringen **VT** (ship) befahren; (car) streets fahren auf (+dat); area abfahren **N** Kreuzfahrt f; **to go on** or **for a ~** eine Kreuzfahrt machen

cruise control N (Aut) Tempomat m, Tempostat m

cruise missile N Cruisemissile nt, Marschflugkörper m

cruiser ['kruːzə°] N (Naut) Kreuzer m; (= pleasure cruiser) Vergnügungsjacht f

cruiserweight ['kruːzəweɪt] N (Boxing) Halbschwergewicht nt

cruising ['kruːzɪŋ] N Kreuzfahrten pl; **to go ~** eine Kreuzfahrt/Kreuzfahrten machen

cruising: cruising altitude N Reiseflughöhe f; **cruising speed** N Reisegeschwindigkeit f; **cruising yacht** N Vergnügungsjacht f

cruller ['krʌlə°] N (US Cook) eine Art Berliner

crumb [krʌm] **N a** (of bread etc) Krümel m, Krume f, Brösel m; (= half eaten) Krume f; **can you spare a ~?** haben Sie eine Scheibe Brot für einen hungrigen Menschen?; **~s from the rich man's/master's table** Brosamen, die von des Reichen/des Herren Tisch fallen; **a few ~s of information** ein paar Informationsbrocken; **that's one ~ of comfort** das ist (wenigstens) ein winziger Trost **b** (inf: = fool) Depp m (inf); (= brute) Lump m (inf) **INTERJ** **~s!** (inf) Mensch! (inf), Mensch Meier! (inf) **VT** (Cook) fish etc panieren

crumble ['krʌmbl] **VT** zerkrümeln, zerbröckeln; **to ~ sth into/onto sth** etw in/auf etw (acc) krümeln or bröckeln **VI** (brick, earth) bröckeln; (bread, cake etc) krümeln; (also **crumble away**) (earth, building) zerbröckeln; (fig) (resistance, opposition) sich auflösen, schmelzen; (hopes) schwinden; (plans) ins Wanken geraten **N** (Brit Cook) Obst nt mit Streusel; (= topping) Streusel pl; **apple/rhubarb ~** mit Streuseln bestreutes, überbackenes Apfel-/Rhabarberdessert

crumbly ['krʌmblɪ] ADJ (+er) stone, earth bröcklig; cake, bread krümelig, bröselig

crummy ['krʌmɪ] ADJ (+er) (inf) mies (inf), Scheiß- (sl)

crumpet ['krʌmpɪt] N **a** (Cook) süßes, pfannkuchenartiges Gebäck **b** (dated esp Brit inf: = women) Miezen pl (inf); **he fancied a bit of ~** ihm war nach ein bisschen Sex; **she's a nice bit of ~** sie ist sehr sexy

crumple ['krʌmpl] VT (also **crumple up**) paper, dress, fabric (= crease) zer- or verknittern, zerknautschen; (= screw up) zusammenknüllen; metal eindrücken; **the force of the impact ~d the bonnet/car** die Wucht des Aufpralls drückte die Kühlerhaube ein/quetschte das Auto zusammen **VI** (fig: = collapse) zusammenbrechen; (= get creased: paper) krumpeln, knittern; (car, metal) zusammengedrückt werden; **her face ~d** ihr Gesicht verzog sich (zum Weinen)

crumple zone N Knautschzone f

crunch [krʌntʃ] **VT a** biscuit etc mampfen (inf) **b** **he ~ed the beetle/ice/gravel underfoot** der Käfer zerknackte/das Eis zersplitterte/der Kies knirschte unter seinen Füßen; **to ~ the gears** (Aut) die Gänge reinwürgen (inf) **c** (Comput) numbers verarbeiten **VI a** (gravel, snow etc) knirschen; (gears) krachen; **he ~ed across the gravel** er ging mit knirschenden Schritten über den Kies **b** **he was ~ing on a carrot** er mampfte eine Möhre (inf); **he ~ed into the apple** er biss knackend in den Apfel **N a** (= sound) Krachen nt; (of footsteps, gravel etc) Knirschen nt; **the two cars collided with a ~** die zwei Autos krachten zusammen (inf); **~!** Krach! **b** (inf: = car crash) Zusammenstoß m **c** (inf: = moment of reckoning) **the ~** der große Krach; **when it comes to the ~** wenn der entscheidende Moment kommt; **this is the ~** jetzt ist der spannende Moment; **it's/we've come to**

the ~ jetzt kommt es drauf an, jetzt geht es hart auf hart

▶ **crunch up** VT *sep* (= *eat*) *carrot etc* zerbeißen; (= *crush noisily*) *garbage etc* (krachend) zermahlen

crunchy ['krʌntʃɪ] ADJ (+er) *apple* knackig; *biscuit* knusprig; *snow* verharscht

crupper ['krʌpə'] N **a** (*of harness*) Schweifriemen *m* **b** (= *hindquarters*) Kruppe *f*

crusade [kru:'seɪd] N (*Hist, fig*) Kreuzzug *m*; (= *evangelical crusade*) Missions- *or* Glaubensfeldzug *m* VI (*Hist, fig*) einen Kreuzzug/Kreuzzüge führen; (*as evangelist*) missionieren

crusader [kru:'seɪdə'] N (*Hist*) Kreuzfahrer *m*, Kreuzritter *m*; (*fig*) Apostel *m*; (= *evangelical crusader*) Glaubensjünger(in) *m(f)*

crush [krʌʃ] N **a** (= *crowd*) Gedrängel *nt*; **it'll be a bit of a ~** es wird ein bisschen eng werden

b (*inf*) (= *infatuation*) Schwärmerei *f*; (= *object of infatuation*) Schwarm *m*; **to have a ~ on sb** für jdn schwärmen, in jdn verschossen sein (*inf*); **schoolgirl ~** Schulmädchenschwärmerei *f*

c (= *drink*) Saftgetränk *nt*

VT **a** (= *squeeze, press tightly*) quetschen; (= *damage*) *soft fruit etc* zerdrücken, zerquetschen; *finger, toes etc* quetschen; (*rock, car etc*) *sb* zerquetschen; (= *kill*) zu Tode quetschen; (= *grind, break up*) *spices, garlic* (zer)stoßen; *ice* stoßen; *ore, stone* zerkleinern, zerstampfen; *scrap metal, garbage* zusammenpressen; (= *crease*) *clothes, paper* zerknittern, zerdrücken; (= *screw up*) *paper* zerknüllen; **~ed pineapple** *klein geschnetzelte Ananas* **I was ~ed between two enormous men in the plane** ich war im Flugzeug zwischen zwei fetten Männern eingequetscht *or* eingeklemmt; **she ~ed the child to her breast** sie drückte das Kind fest an die Brust; **to ~ sb into sth** jdn in etw (*acc*) quetschen; **to ~ sth into sth** etw in etw (*acc*) stopfen

b (*fig*) *enemy, hopes, self-confidence, sb* vernichten; *revolution, opposition* niederschlagen; (= *oppress*) *people, peasants* unterdrücken; **she ~ed him with one glance** sie sah ihn vernichtend an, sie warf ihm einen vernichtenden Blick zu; **to ~ sb's spirit** jdn brechen

VI **a** (*crowd*) (sich) drängen; **they ~ed into the car** sie quetschten *or* drängten sich in das Auto

b (*clothes, fabric*) knittern, knautschen (*inf*)

▶ **crush in** VT *sep* hineinstopfen (*prep obj, -to in* +*acc*) VI hineindrängen

▶ **crush out** VT *sep juice etc* auspressen, ausquetschen (*inf*)

▶ **crush up** VT *sep* **a** (= *pulverize*) zerstoßen **b** (= *pack tightly together*) zusammendrücken *or* -quetschen; **we were (sitting) all crushed up** wir saßen alle zusammengequetscht

crush barrier N Absperrung *f*, Barrikade *f*

crushing ['krʌʃɪŋ] ADJ *defeat* zerschmetternd; *blow, look, reply* vernichtend; *experience* niederschmetternd

crushingly ['krʌʃɪŋlɪ] ADV schrecklich

crush-resistant ['krʌʃrɪzɪstənt] ADJ knitterfrei

crust [krʌst] N (*all senses*) Kruste *f*; **the earth's ~** die Erdkruste; **to earn a ~** (*inf*) seinen Lebensunterhalt verdienen VI verkrusten; **~ed port** Portwein *m* mit Kruste

crustacean [krʌs'teɪʃən] N Schalentier *nt*, Krustazee *f* (*spec*) ADJ *characteristics, class* der Schalentiere *or* Krustazeen (*spec*); *appearance* krebsähnlich

crusted ['krʌstɪd] ADJ mit einer Kruste überzogen, krustig; *blood* verkrustet

crustily ['krʌstɪlɪ] ADV (*fig*) barsch

crusty ['krʌstɪ] ADJ (+er) knusprig; (*fig*: = *irritable*) barsch

crutch [krʌtʃ] N **a** (*for walking*) Krücke *f*; **to use sb/sth as a ~** (*fig*) sich an jdn/etw klammern **b** (*Naut*) Baumstütze *f*, Baumschere *f* **c** = **crotch** b

crux [krʌks] N (*of matter, problem*) Kern *m*; **this is the ~ (of the matter)** das ist der springende Punkt

cry [kraɪ] N **a** (= *inarticulate shout*) Schrei *m*; (= *call*) Ruf *m*; **to give** *or* **utter a ~** (auf)schreien, einen Schrei ausstoßen; **a ~ of fear/pain** ein Angst-/Schmerzensschrei *m*; **a ~ for help** ein Hilferuf *m*; **he gave a ~ for help** er rief um Hilfe → **far**

b (*of animal*) Schrei *m*; (*Hunt: of hounds*) Geheul *nt*, Gebell *nt*; **the pack is in full ~** die Meute hetzt laut bellend *or* heulend hinter der Beute her; **to be in full ~** voll in Aktion sein (*inf*); **to be in full ~ after sb** (*fig*) sich mit großem Geheul auf jdn stürzen

c (= *slogan*) Parole *f*; (= *battle cry*) Schlachtruf *m*

d (= *outcry*) **a ~ for sth** ein Ruf *m* nach etw; **a ~ against sth** ein Protest *m* gegen etw

e (= *weep*) **a ~ will do you good** weine ruhig, das wird dir gut tun; **to have a good ~** sich einmal richtig ausweinen *or* ausheulen (*inf*); **to have a little ~** ein bisschen weinen

VI **a** (= *weep*) weinen (*inf*); (*baby*) schreien; **she was ~ing for her teddy bear** sie weinte nach ihrem Teddy; **... or I'll give you something to ~ about** ... und dann weißt du, warum du heulst (*inf*)

b (= *call*) rufen; (*louder*) schreien; (*Hunt: hounds*) heulen; (*animal, bird*) schreien; **to ~ for help** um Hilfe rufen/schreien; **she cried for a nurse/for somebody to come** sie rief/schrie nach einer Krankenschwester/nach jemandem

VT **a** (= *shout out*) rufen; (*louder*) schreien; **to ~ mercy** (*old, liter*) um Gnade flehen; **he cried to me to go away** er rief mir zu, dass ich verschwinden sollte → **crying, wolf**

b (= *announce*) ausrufen

c (= *weep*) *bitter tears etc* weinen; **to ~ one's eyes/heart out** sich (*dat*) die Augen ausweinen/herzzerreißend weinen; **to ~ oneself to sleep** sich in den Schlaf weinen; **to ~ on sb's shoulder** sich an jds Schulter *or* bei jdm ausweinen

▶ **cry down** VT *sep* (= *decry*) herabsetzen

▶ **cry off** VI (*Brit*) einen Rückzieher machen, aussteigen (*inf*); **to ~ off from sth** aus etw aussteigen (*inf*), etw (wieder) abblasen (*inf*)

▶ **cry out** VI **a** (= *call out*) aufschreien; **to cry out to sb** jdm etwas zuschreien; **he cried out to me to fetch help** er schrie mir zu, ich sollte Hilfe holen; **well, for crying out loud!** (*inf*) na, das darf doch wohl nicht wahr sein! (*inf*) **b** (*fig*) **to be crying out for sth** nach etw schreien; (= *be suitable for also*) sich (geradezu) zu etw anbieten; **that building is just crying out to be turned into a pub** dieses Gebäude schreit (geradezu) danach, dass man es in ein Lokal verwandelt

▶ **cry up** VT *sep* **it's/he's not all it's/he's cried up to be** so großartig ist es/er dann auch wieder nicht

crybaby ['kraɪbeɪbɪ] N (*inf*) Heulsuse *f* (*inf*)

crying ['kraɪɪŋ] ADJ (*fig*: = *outrageous*) *injustice* schreiend; *need* dringend; **it is a ~ shame** es ist jammerschade *or* ein Jammer N (= *weeping*) Weinen *nt*; (*of baby*) Schreien *nt*

cryogen ['kraɪədʒən] N Kühlmittel *nt*

crypt [krɪpt] N Krypta *f*; (= *burial crypt*) Gruft *f*

cryptic ['krɪptɪk] ADJ *remark etc* hintergründig, rätselhaft, schleierhaft; *clue, riddle etc* verschlüsselt; **you're being very ~** du drückst dich sehr rätselhaft *or* schleierhaft aus

cryptically ['krɪptɪkəlɪ] ADV hintergründig, rätselhaft, schleierhaft; **~ worded** (*letter, remark*) hintergründig *etc* formuliert; *clue* verschlüsselt formuliert

crypto- ['krɪptəʊ] PREF Krypto-, krypto-

cryptogram ['krɪptəʊgræm] N Kryptogramm *nt*

cryptographer [krɪp'tɒgrəfə'] N Kryptograf(in) *m(f)*

cryptographic [ˌkrɪptəʊ'græfɪk] ADJ kryptografisch, in Geheimschrift verschlüsselt

cryptography [krɪp'tɒgrəfɪ] N Kryptografie *f*

crystal ['krɪstl] N (*Chem, Rad*) Kristall *m*; (*on watch*) (Uhr)glas *nt*; (= *crystal glass*) Kristall *nt*; (= *quartz*) (Quarz)kristall *m* ADJ **a** (= *crystalline*) Kristall-, kristallin; (= *like a crystal*) kristallartig; (= *crystal-glass*) Kristall-, kristallen; (= *quartz*) Quarzkristall- **b** (*fig*) *waters* kristallklar, glasklar

crystal: crystal ball N Glaskugel *f*; **I don't have a ~** (*inf*) ich bin (doch) kein Hellseher; **you didn't see that ~, did you?** (*inf*) das hast du wohl nicht vorausgesehen?; **crystal-ball gazer** N Hellseher(in) *m(f)*; **crystal-ball gazing** N Hellseherei *f*; **crystal-clear** ADJ (*lit, fig*) glasklar, völlig klar, vollständig klar; **crystal detector** N (*Rad*) Kristalldetektor *m*; **crystal gazer** N Hellseher(in) *m(f)*; **crystal gazing** N Hellseherei *f* ADJ **all these crystal-gazing so-called experts** alle diese so genannten Experten, die aus dem Kaffeesatz wahrsagen; **crystal lattice** N Kristallgitter *nt*

crystalline ['krɪstəlaɪn] ADJ kristallin; **~ lens** (*Augen*)linse *f*

crystallization [ˌkrɪstəlaɪz'eɪʃən] N **a** (*lit*) Kristallisierung *f*; (*out of another substance*) Auskristallisierung *f* **b** (*fig*) (Heraus)kristallisierung *f*; (= *crystallized form*) kristallisierte Form; **after the ~ of these ideas into a theory** nachdem sich aus diesen Gedanken eine Theorie herauskristallisiert hatte

crystallize ['krɪstəlaɪz] VT (*lit*) zum Kristallisieren bringen; (= *separating out*) auskristallisieren; *fruit* kandieren; (*fig*) (feste) Form geben (+*dat*) VI (*lit*) kristallisieren; (= *separate out*) (sich) auskristallisieren; (*fig*) feste Form annehmen; **this theory ~d out of many years' research** diese Theorie hat sich nach jahrelanger Forschung herauskristallisiert

crystallized ['krɪstəlaɪzd] ADJ kristallisiert; *fruit* kandiert

crystallography [ˌkrɪstə'lɒgrəfɪ] N Kristallografie *f*

crystal set N (*Rad*) Detektorempfänger *m*

CSA (*Brit*) abbr of **Child Support Agency**

CSE (*Brit*) abbr of **Certificate of Secondary Education**

C section [ˌsiː'sekʃən] N (*inf*) Kaiserschnitt *m*

CS gas N ≈ Tränengas *nt*

CST abbr of **Central Standard Time**

ct a abbr of **cent b** abbr of **carat**

cub [kʌb] N **a** (*of animal*) Junge(s) *nt* **b** Cub (= *Cub Scout*) Wölfling *m* **c** (= *cub reporter*) junger Reporter, junge Reporterin **d** (*inf*, = *boy*) grüner Junge VI werfen

Cuba ['kjuːbə] N Kuba *nt*

Cuban ['kjuːbən] ADJ kubanisch N Kubaner(in) *m(f)*

Cuban heel N Blockabsatz *m*

cubbyhole ['kʌbɪhəʊl] N **a** (= *compartment*) Fach *nt* **b** (= *room*) Kabäuschen *nt*, Kabuff *nt*

cube [kjuːb] N **a** (= *shape, object*) Würfel *m* **b** (*Math: = power of three*) dritte Potenz; **the ~ of 3 is 27** die dritte Potenz von 3 ist 27, 3 hoch 3 ist 27 VT **a** (*Math*) in die dritte Potenz erheben, hoch 3 nehmen; **four ~d** vier hoch drei **b** (*Cook*) würfelig *or* in Würfel schneiden

cube root N Kubikwurzel *f*

cube sugar N Würfelzucker *m*

cubic ['kjuːbɪk] ADJ **a** (*of volume*) Kubik-, Raum-; **~ content** Raum- *or* Kubikinhalt *m*; **~ metre/foot** Kubikmeter *m or nt*/Kubikfuß *m* **b** (*Math*) kubisch; **~ equation** Gleichung *f* dritten Grades

cubic capacity N Fassungsvermögen *nt*; (*of engine*) Hubraum *m*

cubicle ['kjuːbɪkəl] N Kabine *f*; (*in dormitory etc also*) Alkoven *m*; (*in toilets*) (Einzel)toilette *f*

cubic measure N Raum- *or* Kubikmaß *nt*

cubiform ['kjuːbɪfɔːm] ADJ (*form*) kubisch, würfelförmig

cubism ['kjuːbɪzəm] N Kubismus *m*

cubist ['kjuːbɪst] N Kubist(in) *m(f)* ADJ kubistisch

cubit ['kjuːbɪt] N Elle *f*

cub: Cub mistress N Wölflingsmutter *f*; **cub reporter** N junger Reporter, junge Reporterin; **Cub Scout** N Wölfling *m*

cuckold [ˈkʌkəld] **N** Hahnrei *m* (*old*), betrogener Ehemann **VT** zum Hahnrei machen (*old*), betrügen, Hörner aufsetzen (+*dat*)

cuckoo [ˈkʊkuː] **N** Kuckuck *m* **ADJ** *pred* (*inf*) meschugge (*inf*); **to go ~** überschnappen (*inf*)

cuckoo: cuckoo clock N Kuckucksuhr *f*; **cuckoopint** [ˈkʊkuːpaɪnt] N (*Bot*) Gefleckter Aronsstab; **cuckoo spit** N (= *secretion*) Kuckucksspeichel *m*; (= *insect*) Schaumzikade *f*

cucumber [ˈkjuːkʌmbəʳ] N (Salat)gurke *f*; **as cool as a ~** seelenruhig

cud [kʌd] N wiedergekäutes Futter; **to chew the ~** (*lit*) wiederkäuen; (*fig*) vor sich hin grübeln, sinnieren

cuddle [ˈkʌdl] **N** Liebkosung *f*; **to give sb a ~** jdn in den Arm nehmen; **to need a ~** Zärtlichkeit brauchen, geknuddelt (*inf*) or liebkost werden wollen; **to have a ~** schmusen **VT** in den Arm nehmen; (*amorously also*) schmusen mit **VI** schmusen

▸ **cuddle down** VI sich kuscheln

▸ **cuddle up** VI sich kuscheln (*to, against* an +*acc*); **to cuddle up beside sb** sich neben jdm zusammenkuscheln; **to cuddle up in bed** sich im Bett zusammenkuscheln, sich ins Bett kuscheln; **I'm cold – well, cuddle up then** mir ist kalt – na, dann kuschel dich ran (*inf*); **we all had to cuddle up in the tent to keep warm** wir mussten uns alle im Zelt aneinander kuscheln, um es warm zu haben

cuddlesome [ˈkʌdlsəm] ADJ = **cuddly**

cuddly [ˈkʌdlɪ] ADJ (+*er*) (= *wanting a cuddle*) verschmust (*inf*), anschmiegsam; (= *good to cuddle*) *toy, doll* zum Liebhaben, knuddelig (*inf*); *person* knuddelig (*inf*); **to be in a ~ mood** in einer verschmusten Laune or in Schmuselaune sein

cuddly toy N Schmusetier *nt* (*inf*)

cudgel [ˈkʌdʒəl] **N** (*Brit*) Knüppel *m*; **to take up the ~s for** or **on behalf of sb/sth** (*fig*) für jdn/ etw eintreten or eine Lanze brechen, für jdn/ etw auf die Barrikaden gehen **VT** prügeln; **to ~ one's brains** (*fig*) sich (*dat*) das (Ge)hirn zermartern

cue [kjuː] **N** **a** (*Theat, fig*) Stichwort *nt*; (*action*) (Einsatz)zeichen *nt*; (*Film, TV*) Zeichen *nt* zum Aufnahmebeginn; (*Mus*) Einsatz *m*; (*written:* = *preceding bars*) Hilfsnoten *pl*; **to give sb his ~** (*Theat*) jdm das or sein Stichwort geben; (*action*) jdm das (Einsatz)zeichen geben; (*Mus*) jdm den Einsatz geben; **that sounds like a ~ for a song** das hört sich ganz nach einem Lied an; **whenever he hears the word "strike" that's his ~ to launch into an attack on the unions** das Wort „Streik" ist für ihn jedesmal (das) Stichwort für einen Angriff auf die Gewerkschaften; **to take one's ~ from sb** sich nach jdm richten; **right on ~** (*Theat*) genau aufs Stichwort; (*fig*) wie gerufen **b** (*Billiards*) Queue *nt* **VT** (*Theat*) das Stichwort geben (+*dat*); (*with gesture etc*) das Einsatzzeichen geben (+*dat*); (*Film, TV*) Zeichen geben (+*dat*); (*Mus*) *player* den Einsatz geben (+*dat*); *trumpet flourish etc* den Einsatz geben für; **~!** (*Film, TV*) ab!

▸ **cue in** VT *sep* den Einsatz geben (+*dat*); (*Film, TV*) *scene* abfahren lassen; *tape etc* (zur rechten Zeit) einspielen

cue: cue ball N Spielball *m*; **cue card** N (*TV*) Neger *m*; **cue rest** N Stütze *f* für das Queue

cuff¹ [kʌf] **N** **a** Manschette *f*; **off the ~** aus dem Handgelenk, aus dem Stegreif **b** (*US: of trousers*) (Hosen)aufschlag *m* **c** *usu pl* (*inf:* = *handcuff*) Handschelle *f* **d** (*dated US, inf:* = *credit*) **on the ~** auf Stottern (*inf*)

cuff² **VT** (= *strike*) einen Klaps geben (+*dat*), eins um die Ohren geben (*inf*) **N** (= *blow*) Klaps *m*

cuff link N Manschettenknopf *m*

cu.ft. *abbr* of **cubic foot/feet**

cu.in. *abbr* of **cubic inch(es)**

cuirass [kwɪˈræs] N Kürass *m*, Brustharnisch *m*

cuirassier [ˌkwɪrəˈsɪəʳ] N Kürassier *m*

cuisine [kwɪˈziːn] N Küche *f*

cul-de-sac [ˈkʌldəsæk] N Sackgasse *f*

culinary [ˈkʌlɪnərɪ] ADJ kulinarisch; *skill, talents etc* im Kochen

cull [kʌl] **N** **a** (= *selection*) Auswahl *f* **b** (= *killing of surplus*) Erlegen überschüssiger Tierbestände, Reduktionsabschuss *m*; **~ of seals** Robbenschlag *m* **c** (= *rejected item*) Ausschuss *m* **VT** **a** (= *collect*) entnehmen (*from* +*dat*); *legends* (zusammen)sammeln (*from* aus) **b** (= *kill as surplus*) (als überschüssig) erlegen; **to ~ seals** Robbenschlag *m* betreiben **c** (= *pick*) *flowers* pflücken

cullender N = **colander**

cullet [ˈkʌlɪt] N Bruchglas *nt*

culminate [ˈkʌlmɪneɪt] **VI** (*Astron*) kulminieren, den or seinen Höchst-/Tiefststand erreichen; (*fig*) (= *reach a climax: career, music etc*) gipfeln, kulminieren (*geh*) (*in* in +*dat*); (= *end*) herauslaufen (*in* auf +*acc*), enden (*in* mit) **VT** (*US*) den Höhepunkt or Gipfel (+*gen*) darstellen

culmination [ˌkʌlmɪˈneɪʃən] N (*Astron*) Kulminationspunkt *m*, Höchst-/Tiefststand *m*; (*fig*) (= *high point: of career etc*) Höhepunkt *m*; (= *end*) Ende *nt*, Ausgang *m*

culottes [kjuːˈlɒts] PL Hosenrock *m*; **a pair of ~** ein Hosenrock

culpability [ˌkʌlpəˈbɪlɪtɪ] N (*form*) Schuld *f*

culpable [ˈkʌlpəbl] ADJ (*form*) schuldig

culpable homicide N (*Jur*) fahrlässige Tötung

culpable negligence N (*Jur*) grobe Fahrlässigkeit

culprit [ˈkʌlprɪt] N Schuldige(r) *mf*; (*Jur*) Täter(in) *m(f)*; (*inf*) (= *person causing trouble*) Übeltäter(in) *m(f)*; (= *thing causing trouble*) Übeltäter *m*

cult [kʌlt] **N** (*Rel, fig*) Kult *m*; **to make a ~ of sth** (einen) Kult mit etw treiben **ATTR** Kult-

cultivable [ˈkʌltɪvəbl] ADJ kultivierbar

cultivate [ˈkʌltɪveɪt] VT **a** (*lit*) kultivieren; *soil* bebauen, kultivieren; *crop, fruit etc* anbauen; *beard* wachsen lassen **b** (*fig*) *friendship, links etc* pflegen, kultivieren; *art, skill, taste* entwickeln; *sb* sich (*dat*) warm halten (*inf*), die Beziehung zu ... pflegen; **a connection like that is definitely worth cultivating** es lohnt sich bestimmt, so eine Verbindung aufrechtzuerhalten; **to ~ one's mind** sich bilden

cultivated [ˈkʌltɪveɪtɪd] ADJ (*Agr, fig*) kultiviert

cultivation [ˌkʌltɪˈveɪʃən] **N** **a** (*lit*) Kultivieren *nt*, Kultivierung *f*; (*of crop, fruit etc*) Anbau *m*; **to be under ~** bebaut werden **b** (*fig*) (*of friendship, links etc*) Pflege *f* (*of* von); (*of art, skill*) Entwicklung *f*; (*of person*) Bemühung *f* (*of* um); **his constant ~ of influential friendships** seine ständigen Bemühungen um einflussreiche Freunde **c** (= *cultivated state*) Kultiviertheit *f*

cultivator [ˈkʌltɪveɪtəʳ] **N** **a** (= *machine*) Kultivator *m*, Grubber *m* **b** (= *person*) **a ~ of the soil/ of new friendships** jemand, der den Boden bebaut/neue Freundschaften pflegt

cult movie N Kultfilm *m*

cultural [ˈkʌltʃərəl] ADJ Kultur-; *resemblances, events* kulturell; **~ differences** kulturelle Unterschiede *pl*, Kulturunterschiede *pl*; **what sort of ~ activities are there?** was wird kulturell geboten?; **we enjoyed a very ~ evening** wir hatten einen kulturell sehr anspruchsvollen Abend; **could you not do something a little more ~ with your spare time?** könntest du deine Freizeit nicht etwas kultivierter gestalten or verbringen?

culturally [ˈkʌltʃərəlɪ] ADV kulturell

culture [ˈkʌltʃəʳ] **N** **a** Kultur *f*; **physical ~** (*dated*) Körperkultur *f* (*dated*); **a man of/of no ~** ein kultivierter/unkultivierter Mann, ein Mann mit/ohne Kultur; **to study German ~** die deutsche Kultur studieren; **a ~ of dependency, a dependency ~** eine Kultur der Abhängigkeit;

the company ~ die Unternehmenskultur **b** (*Agr, Biol, Med*) Kultur *f*; (*of animals*) Zucht *f* **VT** (*Biol, Med*) eine Kultur anlegen von

culture area N Kulturraum *m*

cultured [ˈkʌltʃəd] ADJ kultiviert; (*Agr, Biol, Med*) gezüchtet

culture dish N (*Biol, Med*) Kulturschale *f*

cultured pearl N Zuchtperle *f*

culture: culture fluid N (*Biol, Med*) Nährlösung *f*; **culture gap** N Kulturlücke *f*; **culture medium** N (*Biol, Med*) Kulturmedium *nt*, (künstlicher) Nährboden; **culture shock** N Kulturschock *m*; **culture vulture** N (*hum*) Kulturfanatiker(in) *m(f)*

culvert [ˈkʌlvət] N unterirdischer Kanal, (Abwasser)kanal *m*; (*for cables*) Kabeltunnel *m*

cum [kʌm] PREP in einem, gleichzeitig; **a sort of sofa-cum-bed** eine Art von Sofa und Bett in einem

cumbersome [ˈkʌmbəsəm] ADJ *clothing, coat* (be)hinderlich; *spacesuit, movements, gesture, style, piece of music* schwerfällig; *vehicle* unhandlich (*inf*), schwer zu manövrieren; *suitcases, parcels* sperrig, unhandlich; *procedure, regulations* beschwerlich, mühselig; **it's so ~ having to wear all this heavy clothing** es ist so lästig, dass man alle diese schweren Kleidungsstücke tragen muss

cumbersomely [ˈkʌmbəsəmlɪ] ADV *move, write* schwerfällig; *phrased also* umständlich; *dressed* hinderlich

cumbrous [ˈkʌmbrəs] ADJ = **cumbersome**

cumin [ˈkʌmɪn] N Kreuzkümmel *m*

cummerbund [ˈkʌməbʌnd] N Kummerbund *m*

cumulation [ˌkjuːmjʊˈleɪʃən] N Anhäufung *f*, Häufung *f*

cumulative [ˈkjuːmjʊlətɪv] ADJ gesamt, kumulativ (*geh*); **the ~ debts of ten years** die Schulden, die sich im Lauf von zehn Jahren angehäuft haben/hatten

cumulative evidence N (*Jur*) Häufung *f* von Beweisen/Zeugenaussagen

cumulative interest N (*Fin*) Zins und Zinseszins

cumulatively [ˈkjuːmjʊlətɪvlɪ] ADV kumulativ

cumulative voting N Wählen *nt* durch Kumulieren or Stimmenhäufung or nach dem Kumulierungssystem

cumulonimbus [ˈkjuːmjələʊˈnɪmbəs] N Kumulonimbus *m*

cumulus [ˈkjuːmjələs] N Kumulus *m*

cuneiform [ˈkjuːnɪfɔːm] ADJ keilförmig; *characters, inscription* in Keilschrift; **~ writing** Keilschrift *f* **N** Keilschrift *f*

cunnilingus [ˌkʌnɪˈlɪŋgəs] N Cunnilingus *m*

cunning [ˈkʌnɪŋ] **N** (= *cleverness*) Schlauheit *f*, Listigkeit *f*, Gerissenheit *f*; (*liter:* = *skill*) (Kunst-)fertigkeit *f*, Geschick *nt* **ADJ** **a** *plan* schlau; *person* schlau, gerissen; *smile, expression* verschmitzt, verschlagen (*pej*); (= *ingenious*) *gadget* schlau or clever (*inf*) ausgedacht **b** (*US, inf*) drollig

cunningly [ˈkʌnɪŋlɪ] ADV schlau; (*with reference to people also*) gerissen; *smile, look* verschmitzt, verschlagen (*pej*); (= *ingeniously*) geschickt; **a ~ designed little gadget** ein geschickt or clever ausgedachtes Ding

cunt [kʌnt] N (*vulg*) (= *vagina*) Fotze *f* (*vulg*), Möse *f* (*vulg*); (= *intercourse*) Fick *m* (*vulg*); (*term of abuse*) Arsch *m* (*vulg*); **she's a nice bit of ~** sie ist eine geile Fotze (*vulg*)

cup [kʌp] **N** **a** Tasse *f*; (= *goblet*) Pokal *m*, Kelch *m*; (= *mug*) Becher *m*; (*Eccl*) Kelch *m*; **in his ~s** (*dated inf*) angezecht **b** (= *cupful*) Tasse *f*; (*Cook, standard measure*) 8 fl oz = 0,22 l; **a ~ of tea/water** eine Tasse Tee/ Wasser; **that's just/that's not my ~ of tea** (*fig inf*) das ist genau/ist nicht mein Fall; **she's not everyone's ~ of tea** ihre Art gefällt nicht jedem **c** (= *prize, football cup etc*) Pokal *m*; **they're out of the Cup** sie sind aus dem Pokal(wettbewerb) ausgeschieden

d (= *drink*) Mix *m*, Becher *m*
e (*Bot: of flower*) Kelch *m*; (*of bra*) Körbchen *nt*; (*Golf*) Metallbüchse *f* (*im Loch*); (*Med: = cupping glass*) Schröpfkopf *m*
f (*fig liter: = portion*) Kelch *m*; **to drain the ~ of sorrow** (**to the dregs**) den Kelch des Leidens (bis zur Neige) leeren (*liter*); **my ~ is overflowing** *or* (*liter*) **runneth over** (*Bibl*) ich bin über alle Maßen glücklich, mein Glück ist vollkommen **VT a** *hands* hohl machen; **~ped hand** hohle Hand; **he ~ped his hands and blew into them** er blies sich (*dat*) in die Hände; **to ~ sth in one's hands** etw in den hohlen Händen halten; **he ~ped his chin in his hand** er stützte das Kinn in die Hand; **to ~ one's** *or* **a hand to one's ear** die Hand ans Ohr halten; **to ~ one's hands around sth** etw mit der hohlen Hand umfassen
b (*Med*) schröpfen
c (*Golf*) einlochen mit
cup: **cup-and-ball** N Fangbecherspiel *nt*; **cupbearer** N Mundschenk *m*
cupboard ['kʌbəd] N Schrank *m*
cupboard love N fauler Schmus (*inf*), Zweckfreundlichkeit *f*
cup: **cupcake** N *kleiner, runder Kuchen*; **Cup Final** N Pokalendspiel *nt*; (*international also*) Cupfinale *nt*; **Cup Finalist** N Teilnehmer(in) *m(f)* am Pokalendspiel; **cupful** N *pl* **cupsful, cupfuls** Tasse *f* (voll)
cupid ['kjuːpɪd] N Amorette *f*; **Cupid** Amor *m*; **Cupid's dart** (*liter*) Amors Pfeil *m* (*liter*), Liebespfeil *m*
cupidity [kjuː'pɪdɪtɪ] N (*liter*) Begierde *f* (*pej*), Gier *f* (*pej*)
Cupid's bow ['kjuːpɪdzbəʊ] ADJ bogenförmig geschwungen; **~ mouth** Kussmund *m*, Herzmund *m*
cup match N Pokalspiel *nt*
cupola ['kjuːpələ] N (*Archit*) Kuppel *f*; (*roof also*) Kuppeldach *nt*; (= *furnace*) Kupolofen *m*
cuppa ['kʌpə] N (*Brit, inf*) Tasse Tee *f*, Tässchen Tee *nt* (*inf*)
cupping ['kʌpɪŋ] N (*Med*) Schröpfen *nt*
cupping glass N (*Med*) Schröpfkopf *m*
cupreous ['kjuːprɪəs] ADJ kupfern
cuprite ['kjuːpraɪt] N Kupferoxid *nt*, Rotkupfererz *nt*
cupronickel ['kjuːprəʊ'nɪkl] N Kupfernickel *nt*, Kupfer-Nickel-Legierung *f*
cuprous ['kjuːprəs] ADJ kupfern
cup: **cup size** N (*of bra*) Körbchengröße *f*; **cup tie** N Pokalspiel *nt*
cupule ['kjuːpjuːl] N (*Bot*) Becher *m*, Cupula *f* (*spec*)
Cup Winner N Pokalsieger(in) *m(f)*; **~s' Cup** (*Ftbl*) Europapokal *m* der Pokalsieger
cur [kɜː'] N (*pej: = dog*) Köter *m* (*pej*); (*old, = man*) Kanaille *f* (*dated pej*), Hundsfott *m* (*dated pej*)
curability [,kjʊərə'bɪlɪtɪ] N Heilbarkeit *f*
curable ['kjʊərəbl] ADJ heilbar
Curaçao [,kjʊərə'səʊ] N Curaçao *m*
curacy ['kjʊərəsɪ] N (*Catholic*) Anstellung *f* als Kurat; (*Protestant*) Anstellung *f* als Vikar(in)
curate ['kjʊərɪt] N (*Catholic*) Kurat *m*; (*Protestant*) Vikar(in) *m(f)*; **it's like the ~'s egg** es ist streckenweise gar nicht so schlecht
curative ['kjʊərətɪv] ADJ Heil-, heilend; **~ powers** Heilkräfte *pl* **N** Heilmittel *nt*
curator [kjʊə'reɪtə'] N **a** (*of museum etc*) Kustos *m* **b** (*Jur: = guardian*) Kurator *m*, Vormund *m*
curatorial [,kjʊərə'tɔːrɪəl] ADJ **the museum's ~ team** die Kustoden *pl* des Museums
curb [kɜːb] **N a** (*of harness*) (= *bit*) Kandare *f*; (= *chain*) Kinnkette *f*, Kandarenkette *f* **b** (*fig*) Behinderung *f*; **to put a ~ on sb** jdn im Zaum *or* in Schranken halten; **to put a ~ on sth** etw einschränken; **this acted as a ~ on his musical development** das (be)hinderte seine musikalische Entwicklung **c** (*esp US: =* curb-

stone) = **kerb** **VT a** *horse* zügeln **b** (*fig*) zügeln; *immigration, investment etc* in Schranken halten, bremsen (*inf*)
curb: **curb bit** N Kandare *f*; **curb market** N (*US St Ex*) Freiverkehr *m*; **curb rein** N Kandarenzügel *m*; **curb roof** N (*Archit*) Mansardendach *nt*; **curb service** N (*US*) Bedienung *f* am Fahrzeug; **curbstone** N (*esp US*) = **kerbstone**
curcuma ['kɜːkjʊmə] N (*Bot*) Kurkuma *f*, Gelbwurz *f*
curd [kɜːd] N (*often pl*) Quark *m* **VT** gerinnen lassen **VI** gerinnen
curd cheese N Weißkäse *m*
curdle ['kɜːdl] **VT** (*lit, fig*) gerinnen lassen; **to ~ sb's blood** jdm das Blut in den Adern gerinnen lassen **VI** gerinnen; **his blood ~d** das Blut gerann ihm in den Adern
curdy ['kɜːdɪ] ADJ (= *coagulated*) geronnen, dick; (= *lumpy*) klumpig
cure [kjʊə'] **VT a** (*Med*) *illness, person* heilen, kurieren (*inf*); **to be/get ~d** (**of sth**) (von etw) geheilt *or* kuriert (*inf*) sein/werden; **he used to be an alcoholic but he's been ~d** er war früher Alkoholiker, aber jetzt ist er geheilt *or* kuriert (*inf*)
b (*fig*) *inflation, ill etc* abhelfen (+*dat*); **to ~ sb of sth** jdm etw austreiben, jdn von etw kurieren; **I'll ~ him!** dem werde ich das schon austreiben!
c *food* haltbar machen; (= *salt*) pökeln; (= *smoke*) räuchern; (= *dry*) trocknen; *skins, tobacco* trocknen
VI a (= *be healed*) heilen
b (*food, bacon, fish*) **it is left to ~** (= *to salt*) es wird zum Pökeln eingelegt; (= *to smoke*) es wird zum Räuchern aufgehängt; (= *to dry*) es wird zum Trocknen aufgehängt *or* ausgebreitet
N a (*Med*) (= *remedy*) (Heil)mittel *nt* (for gegen); (= *treatment*) Heilverfahren *nt* (for sb für jdn, for sth gegen etw); (= *recovery*) Heilung *f*; (= *health cure*) Kur *f*; (*fig: = remedy*) Mittel *nt* (for gegen); **to take the ~** zur *or* in Kur gehen, eine Kur machen; **beyond ~** (*patient*) unheilbar krank; *illness* unheilbar; (*fig*) *state of affairs, laziness etc* hoffnungslos; **there's no ~ for that** (*lit*) das ist unheilbar; (*fig*) dagegen kann man nichts machen
b (*Eccl: = spiritual care*) **the ~ of souls** die Seelsorge
cure-all ['kjʊərɔːl] N (*lit, fig*) Allheilmittel *nt*
cureless ['kjʊəlɪs] ADJ unheilbar
curettage [,kjʊərə'tiːdʒ] N (*Med*) Ausschabung *f*, Kürettage *f*
curet(te) [kjʊə'ret] N (*Med*) Kürette *f*
curfew ['kɜːfjuː] N Ausgangssperre *f*, Ausgehverbot *nt*; (*old: = evening bell*) Abendglocke *f*; **to be under ~** unter Ausgangssperre *or* Ausgehverbot stehen; **to impose a ~** eine Ausgangssperre *or* ein Ausgehverbot verhängen; **to lift the ~** die Ausgangssperre *or* das Ausgehverbot aufheben; **is the ~ still on?** ist noch Ausgangssperre?
Curia ['kjʊərɪə] N Kurie *f*
curie ['kjʊərɪ] N (*Phys*) Curie *nt*
curio ['kjʊərɪəʊ] N Kuriosität *f*
curiosity [,kjʊərɪ'ɒsɪtɪ] N **a** *no pl* (= *inquisitiveness*) Neugier *f*; (*for knowledge*) Wissbegier(de) *f*; **out of** *or* **from ~** aus Neugier; **~ killed the cat** (*Prov*) sei nicht so neugierig **b** (= *object, person*) Kuriosität *f*
curiosity shop N Kuriositätenladen *m*
curious ['kjʊərɪəs] ADJ **a** (= *inquisitive*) neugierig; **I'm ~ to know what he'll do** ich bin mal gespannt, was er macht; **I'm ~ to know how he did it** ich bin neugierig zu erfahren, wie er das gemacht hat; **I'd be ~ to know how you got on** ich wüsste (ganz) gern, wie du zurechtgekommen bist; **the neighbours were ~ to know ...** die Nachbarn wollten (nur) zu gerne wissen ...; **I'm ~ about him** ich möchte gern mehr über ihn erfahren *or* herausfinden; **why do you ask? – I'm just ~** warum fragst du? – nur so
b (= *odd*) sonderbar, seltsam, eigenartig; **how ~!** wie seltsam!; **it's ~ the way he already knew**

that sonderbar *etc*, dass er das schon gewusst hat
curiously ['kjʊərɪslɪ] ADV **a** (= *inquisitively*) neugierig **b** (= *oddly*) *behave, speak etc* seltsam, eigenartig, merkwürdig, sonderbar; *disappeared* auf sonderbare *or* merkwürdige Weise; *unconcerned* seltsam, merkwürdig; **they are ~ similar** sie ähneln sich merkwürdig *or* auf seltsame Weise; **it was ~ quiet** es war merkwürdig ruhig; **any sense of humour is ~ absent** seltsamerweise *or* eigenartigerweise fehlt jeglicher Sinn für Humor; **~ enough** merkwürdigerweise; **~ (enough), he didn't object** merkwürdigerweise hatte er nichts dagegen
curiousness ['kjʊərɪəsnɪs] N **a** = **curiosity a b** (= *oddness*) Merkwürdigkeit *f*, Sonderbarkeit *f*
curl [kɜːl] **N** (*of hair*) Locke *f*; **in ~s** in Locken, gelockt; (*tight*) gekräuselt, kraus; **a ~ of smoke** ein Rauchkringel *m*; **with a ~ of his lip** mit gekräuselten Lippen; **its tail was just a little ~** es hatte nur ein kleines Kringelschwänzchen **VT** *hair* locken; (*with curlers*) in Locken legen; (*in tight curls*) kräuseln; *lip* (*person*) kräuseln; (*animal*) hochziehen; *edges* umbiegen; **he ~ed the ball into the back of the net** er zirkelte den Ball mit einem Bogenschuss ins Netz **VI a** (*hair*) sich locken; (*tightly*) sich kräuseln; (*naturally*) lockig sein; (*paper*) sich wellen; (*wood*) sich verziehen; (*road*) sich schlängeln, sich winden; **his lip ~ed** er kräuselte die Lippen; **it's enough to make your hair ~** (*fig inf*) da stehen einem ja die Haare zu Berge (*inf*) **b** (*Sport*) Curling spielen
▶ **curl up** **VI a** (*animal, person*) sich zusammenrollen *or* -kugeln; (*hedgehog*) sich einigeln; (*paper*) sich wellen; (*metal*) sich rollen; (*leaf*) sich hochbiegen; **his moustache curls up at the ends** sein Schnurrbart ist nach oben gezwirbelt; **to curl up in bed/in an armchair** sich ins Bett/in einen Sessel kuscheln; **to curl up with a good book** es sich (*dat*) mit einem guten Buch gemütlich machen
b **the smoke curled up** der Rauch ringelte sich hoch
c (*inf*) **the way he behaves just makes me want to curl up** es macht mich krank, wie er sich benimmt (*inf*); **I just wanted to curl up and die** (*out of embarrassment etc*) ich wäre am liebsten im Boden versunken
VT *sep ends of moustache, piece of paper etc* wellen; *metal* rollen; *edges* hochbiegen; **to curl oneself/itself up** sich zusammenkugeln/zusammenringeln
curl cloud N (*Met*) Cirruswolke *f*
curler ['kɜːlə'] N **a** (= *hair curler*) Lockenwickel *m*, Lockenwickler *m*; **to put one's ~s in** sich (*dat*) die Haare eindrehen *or* auf (Locken-)wickler drehen; **have you never seen her in ~s?** hast du sie noch nie mit Lockenwickeln gesehen?; **my hair was in ~s, I had my ~s in** ich hatte Lockenwickel *or* Lockenwickler im Haar **b** (*Sport*) Curlingspieler(in) *m(f)*
curlew ['kɜːljuː] N Brachvogel *m*
curlicue ['kɜːlɪkjuː] N Schnörkel *m*
curling ['kɜːlɪŋ] N (*Sport*) Curling *nt*, Eisschießen *nt*; **~ stone** Curlingstein *m*, Eisstock *m*
curling tongs ['kɜːlɪŋtɒŋz], (*US*) **curling iron** ['kɜːlɪŋaɪən] PL Lockenschere *f*, Brennschere *f*; (*electric*) Lockenstab *m*
curlpaper ['kɜːlpeɪpə'] N (Papier)lockenwickel *m*
curly ['kɜːlɪ] ADJ (+*er*) *hair* lockig; (*tighter*) kraus; *tail* geringelt; *lettuce* kraus; *leaf* gewellt; *pattern, writing* verschnörkelt; **she was much curlier** ihr Haar war viel lockiger **N** (*inf, = person*) Krauskopf *m*
curly: **curly bracket** N geschweifte Klammer *f*; **curly-haired** ADJ lockig, lockenköpfig; (*tighter*) krausköpfig; **curly-head** N (*inf*) Lockenkopf *m*; (*tighter*) Krauskopf *m*; **curly-headed** ADJ = **curly-haired**
currant ['kʌrənt] N **a** (= *dried fruit*) Korinthe *f* **b** (*Bot*) Johannisbeere *f*; **~ bush** Johannisbeerstrauch *m*

currant bun N Rosinenbrötchen *nt*

currency ['kʌrənsɪ] N **a** (*Fin*) Währung *f*; **foreign** ~ Devisen *pl* **b** Verbreitung *f*; (*of word, expression*) Gebräuchlichkeit *f*; **to gain** ~ sich verbreiten, um sich greifen; **to give** ~ **to a rumour/theory** ein Gerücht/eine Theorie verbreiten *or* in Umlauf setzen

currency: currency appreciation N Geldaufwertung *f*; **currency depreciation** N Geldabwertung *f*; **currency market** N Devisenmarkt *m*; **currency snake** N Währungsschlange *f*; **currency speculator** N Währungsspekulant(in) *m(f)*; **currency trader** N Devisenhändler(in) *m(f)*; **currency trading** N Devisenhandel *m*

current ['kʌrənt] ADJ (= *present*) augenblicklich, gegenwärtig; *policy, price* aktuell; *research, month, week* laufend; *edition* letzte(r, s); (= *prevalent*) *opinion* verbreitet; *spelling, word* gebräuchlich; **to be no longer** ~ nicht mehr aktuell sein; (*coins*) nicht mehr in Umlauf sein; **a** ~ **rumour** ein Gerücht, das zur Zeit in Umlauf ist; ~ **affairs** Tagespolitik *f*, aktuelle Fragen *pl*, Aktuelle(s) *nt*; **in** ~ **use** allgemein gebräuchlich **N** **a** (*of water*) Strömung *f*, Strom *m*; (*of air*) Luftströmung *f*, Luftstrom *m*; **with/against the** ~ mit dem/gegen den Strom; **air/ocean** ~ Luft-/Meeresströmung *f or* -strom *m* **b** (*Elec*) Strom *m* **c** (*fig: of events, opinions etc*) Tendenz *f*, Trend *m*; **to go against the** ~ **of popular opinion** gegen den Strom *or* die Strömung der öffentlichen Meinung anschwimmen; **to go with the** ~ **of popular opinion** mit dem Strom *or* der Strömung der öffentlichen Meinung schwimmen; **if you try to go against the** ~ **of events** wenn Sie versuchen, gegen den Strom der Ereignisse anzuschwimmen; **the** ~ **of public feeling is now in favour of/against ...** die öffentliche Meinung tendiert zur Befürwortung/Ablehnung von ...; **a politician who ignores the** ~ **of popular opinion** ein Politiker, der die Tendenz(en) der öffentlichen Meinung *or* den Trend (in) der öffentlichen Meinung unbeachtet lässt

current: current account N Girokonto *nt*; **current assets** PL Umlaufvermögen *nt*; **current-carrying** ['kʌrəntˌkæriŋ] ADJ (*Elec*) Strom führend; **current collector** N (*Rail etc*) Stromabnehmer *m*; **current expenses** PL laufende Ausgaben *pl*; **current liabilities** PL kurzfristige Verbindlichkeiten *pl*

currently ['kʌrəntlɪ] ADV momentan, zur Zeit, gegenwärtig; **it is** ~ **thought that ...** die aktuelle Meinung ist, dass ...

current meter N (*Elec*) Stromzähler *m*

current price N (*Fin*) Tages- *or* Marktpreis *m*; (*St Ex*) Tageskurs *m*

curricle ['kʌrɪkl] N offener Zweispänner

curricula [kə'rɪkjʊlə] *pl of* **curriculum**

curricular [kə'rɪkjʊlə] ADJ *activities* lehrplanmäßig

curriculum [kə'rɪkjʊləm] N *pl* **curricula** Lehrplan *m*; **to be on the** ~ auf dem Lehrplan stehen

curriculum vitae [kə'rɪkjʊləm'viːtaɪ] N (*Brit*) Lebenslauf *m*

currish ['kɜːrɪʃ] ADJ (*dated*) *behaviour* hundsföttisch (*dated*)

curry¹ ['kʌrɪ] (*Cook*) **N** (= *spice*) Curry *m or nt*; (= *dish*) Curry *nt*; ~ **sauce** Currysauce *f* **VT** mit Curry zubereiten

curry² VT *horse* striegeln; *leather* zurichten; **to** ~ **favour (with sb)** sich (bei jdm) einschmeicheln *or* lieb Kind machen

currycomb ['kʌrɪkəʊm] **N** Striegel *m* **VT** striegeln

curry powder N Currypulver *nt*

curse [kɜːs] **N** **a** (= *malediction*) Fluch *m*; **to be under a** ~ unter einem Fluch stehen; **to put sb under a** ~ jdn mit einem Fluch belegen, einen Fluch über jdn aussprechen; **a** ~ *or* **a thousand** ~**s on this pen/him!** (*old, hum*) den Füller/den soll doch der Kuckuck holen! (*inf*), dieser ver-
maledeite Füller/Mensch! (*old*); ~**s!** (*inf*) verflucht! (*inf*) **b** (= *swearword*) Fluch *m* **c** (*fig: = affliction*) Fluch *m*; (*inf: = nuisance*) Plage *f* (*inf*); **it's the** ~ **of my life** das ist der Fluch meines Lebens; **the** ~ **of drunkenness** der Fluch des Alkohols; **the** ~ (*inf: = menstruation*) die Tage *pl* (*inf*); **she has the** ~ (*inf*) sie hat ihre Tage (*inf*) **VT** **a** (= *put a curse on*) verfluchen; ~ **you/it!** (*inf*) verflucht! (*inf*), verdammt! (*inf*), Mist! (*inf*); **I could** ~ **you for forgetting it** ich könnte dich verwünschen, dass du das vergessen hast; **where is he now,** ~ **the man** *or* ~ **him!** (*inf*) wo steckt er jetzt, der verfluchte Kerl! (*inf*); ~ **these trains!** (*inf*) diese verfluchten Züge! (*inf*) **b** (= *swear at or about*) fluchen über (+*acc*) **c** (*fig: = afflict*) **to be** ~**d with sb/sth** mit jdm/etw geschlagen *or* gestraft sein **VI** fluchen; **he started cursing and swearing** er fing an, wüst zu schimpfen und zu fluchen

cursed ['kɜːsɪd] ADJ (*inf*) verflucht (*inf*)

cursive ['kɜːsɪv] ADJ kursiv, Kursiv-; ~ **writing** Kursivschrift *f* **N** Kursivschrift *f*

cursively ['kɜːsɪvlɪ] ADV kursiv

cursor ['kɜːsə] N (*Comput*) Cursor *m*; ~ **control** Cursorsteuerung *f*; ~ **movements** Cursorbewegungen *pl*

cursorily ['kɜːsərɪlɪ] ADV *glance* flüchtig; *inspect, investigate also* oberflächlich

cursoriness ['kɜːsərɪnɪs] N (*of glance*) Flüchtigkeit *f*; (*of inspection, investigation also*) Oberflächlichkeit *f*

cursory ['kɜːsərɪ] ADJ *glance* flüchtig; *inspection, investigation also* oberflächlich

curst [kɜːst] ADJ (*old*) = **cursed**

curt [kɜːt] ADJ (+*er*) *person* kurz angebunden, barsch; *verbal reply also* knapp; *letter, nod, refusal* kurz, knapp; **to be** ~ **with sb** zu jdm kurz angebunden sein

curtail [kɜː'teɪl] VT kürzen

curtailment [kɜː'teɪlmənt] N Kürzung *f*

curtain ['kɜːtn] **N** **a** Vorhang *m*; (= *net curtain*) Gardine *f*; **to draw** *or* **pull the** ~**s** (= *open*) den Vorhang/die Vorhänge aufziehen; (= *close*) den Vorhang/die Vorhänge zuziehen **b** (*Theat*) Vorhang *m*; **to drop the** ~ den Vorhang fallen lassen; **the** ~ **rises/falls** *or* **drops** der Vorhang hebt sich/fällt; **the** ~ **rises on a scene of domestic harmony** der Vorhang hebt sich und gibt den Blick auf eine Szene häuslichen Glücks frei; **to take the** ~ (*inf*) vor den Vorhang treten; **to bring the** ~ **down on sth** (*fig*) den Vorhang endgültig über etw (*acc*) fallen lassen **c** (*fig: of mystery*) Schleier *m*; **a** ~ **of smoke/flames/rain** eine Rauch-/Flammen-/Regenwand; **if you get caught it'll be** ~**s for you** (*inf*) wenn sie dich erwischen, ist für dich der Ofen aus (*inf*) *or* bist du weg vom Fenster (*inf*) **VT** mit Vorhängen/einem Vorhang ausstatten; **a** ~**ed bed** ein Himmelbett *nt*

▶ **curtain off** VT *sep* durch einen Vorhang/Vorhänge abtrennen

curtain: curtain call N (*Theat*) Vorhang *m*; **to take a** ~ vor den Vorhang treten; **curtain hook** N Gardinengleithaken *m*; **curtain pole** N Vorhangstange *f*; **curtain rail** N Vorhangschiene *f*; **curtain-raiser** N (*Theat*) kurzes Vorspiel; **curtain ring** N Gardinenring *m*; **curtain rod** N Gardinenstange *f*; **curtain runner** N Vorhangschiene *f*; (*for curtain rings*) Gardinenstange *f*

curtly ['kɜːtlɪ] ADV *reply, nod* kurz, knapp; *refuse* kurzerhand

curtness ['kɜːtnɪs] N (*of person*) Barschheit *f*; (*of remark, reply, letter, refusal*) Kürze *f*, Knappheit *f*

curtsey, (*US*) **curtsy** ['kɜːtsɪ] **N** Knicks *m*; (*to royalty*) Hofknicks *m*; **to drop a curts(e)y** einen Knicks/Hofknicks machen **VI** knicksen (*to* vor +*dat*)

curvaceous [kɜː'veɪʃəs] ADJ üppig; *figure also* kurvenreich
---
curvaceously [kɜː'veɪʃəslɪ] ADV üppig, prall

curvature ['kɜːvətʃə] N Krümmung *f*; (*misshapen*) Verkrümmung *f*; ~ **of the spine** (*normal*) Rückgratkrümmung *f*; (*abnormal*) Rückgratverkrümmung *f*; **the** ~ **of space** die Raumkrümmung

curve [kɜːv] **N** Kurve *f*; (*of body, vase etc*) Rundung *f*, Wölbung *f*; (*of river*) Biegung *f*; (*of archway*) Bogen *m*; **there's a** ~ **in the road** die Straße macht einen Bogen; **the price** ~ die Preiskurve; **her** ~**s** (*inf*) ihre Kurven *or* Rundungen *pl* (*inf*) **VT** biegen; (= *build with a curve*) *arch, roof, side of ship* wölben; **gravity** ~**s the path of light** die Gravitation krümmt den Lichtweg; **he** ~**d the ball around the wall** er zirkelte den Ball um die Mauer herum **VI** **a** (*line, road*) einen Bogen machen; (*river*) eine Biegung machen; **her lips** ~**d into a smile** ihre Lippen verzogen sich zu einem Lächeln; **the road** ~**s around the city** die Straße macht einen Bogen um die Stadt; **to make a ball** ~ **(through the air)** einen Ball anschneiden, einem Ball einen Drall geben **b** (= *be curved*) (*space, horizon*) gekrümmt sein; (*side of ship, surface, arch*) sich wölben; (*hips, breasts*) sich runden; (*metal strip etc*) sich biegen

curveball ['kɜːvbɔːl] N (*US Baseball*) *Ball, der bogenförmig vom Werfer zum Schlagmann geworfen wird*

curved [kɜːvd] ADJ *line* gebogen; *table legs etc* also geschwungen; *horizon* gekrümmt; *surface, arch, sides of ship* gewölbt; *hips* rund; **space is** ~ der Raum ist gekrümmt

curvet [kɜː'vet] **N** Kruppade *f* **VI** eine Kruppade springen

curvilinear ['kɜːvɪ'lɪnɪə] ADJ (= *full of curves*) *tracery etc* mit vielen Rundungen *or* Kurven; (= *curved*) *motion, course* gewunden; (*Geometry*) *figure* krummlinig begrenzt

curvy ['kɜːvɪ] ADJ (+*er*) (*inf*) *road, figure* kurvenreich

cushion ['kʊʃən] **N** Kissen *nt*; (= *pad, fig: = buffer*) Polster *nt*; (*Billiards*) Bande *f*; **a stroke off the** ~ ein Stoß *m* gegen die Bande; **a** ~ **of air/moss** ein Luftkissen *nt*/Moospolster *nt* **VT** ~ **cover** Kissenüberzug *m*, Kissenbezug *m* **VT** **a** (= *absorb, soften*) *fall, blow* auffangen, dämpfen; (*fig*) *disappointment* dämpfen **b** (*fig: = protect*) **to** ~ **sb against sth** jdn gegen etw abschirmen, jdn vor etw (*dat*) behüten; **he** ~**ed the vase against his chest** er barg die Vase an seiner Brust **c** (*Billiards*) *ball* gegen die Bande spielen

cushioned ['kʊʃənd] ADJ **a** (= *padded*) Polster-, gepolstert **b** (*fig: = comfortable*) bequem

cushioning ['kʊʃənɪŋ] ADJ **to have a** ~ **effect** (stoß)dämpfend wirken; (*fig*) mildernd wirken

cushy ['kʊʃɪ] ADJ (+*er*) (*inf*) bequem; **to have a** ~ **time of it, to be onto a** ~ **number** eine ruhige Kugel schieben (*inf*); **a** ~ **job** ein gemütlicher *or* ruhiger Job; **that job is a** ~ **number** in dem Job reißt man sich (*dat*) kein Bein aus (*inf*)

cusp [kʌsp] N (*of tooth*) Höcker *m*; (*of moon*) Spitze *f* (der Mondsichel); (*Astrol*) Eintritt in ein neues Zeichen; **on the** ~ **of** (*fig*) an der Schwelle zu

cuspid ['kʌspɪd] N Eckzahn *m*

cuspidor ['kʌspɪdɔː] N (*US*) Spucknapf *m*

cuss [kʌs] (*inf*) **N a** (= *person*) Kauz *m* (*inf*) **b** **he's not worth a (tinker's)** ~ der ist keinen roten Heller wert (*inf*); **he doesn't care a (tinker's)** ~ **(about it)** das ist ihm völlig Wurst (*inf*) *or* schnuppe (*inf*) **c** (= *oath*) Fluch *m* **VI** fluchen; **to** ~ **and swear** schimpfen und fluchen

cussed ['kʌsɪd] ADJ (*inf*) stur

cussedness ['kʌsɪdnɪs] N (*inf*) Sturheit *f*; **out of sheer** ~ aus lauter *or* reiner Sturheit

cussword ['kʌswɜːd] N (*US, inf*) Kraftausdruck *m*, Schimpfwort *nt*

custard ['kʌstəd] N (= *pouring custard*) ≈ Vanillesoße *f*; (= *set custard*) ≈ Vanillepudding *m*

custard: custard apple N (*Bot*) Zimt- *or* Rahmapfel *m*; **custard cream (biscuit)** N

Doppelkeks m (mit Vanillecremefüllung); **custard pie** N (in slapstick) Sahnetorte f; **custard powder** N (for pouring custard) ≈ Vanillesoßenpulver nt; (for set custard) ≈ Vanillepuddingpulver nt; **custard tart** N ≈ Puddingtörtchen nt

custodial [kʌsˈtəʊdɪəl] ADJ (form) **a** duties etc als Aufseher **b** ~ **sentence** Gefängnisstrafe f

custodian [kʌsˈtəʊdɪən] N (of building, park, museum) Aufseher(in) m(f), Wächter(in) m(f); (of treasure, tradition, cultural heritage, world peace etc) Hüter(in) m(f)

custody [ˈkʌstədɪ] N **a** (= keeping, guardianship) Obhut f; (of person) Obhut f, Aufsicht f (of über +acc); (of object) Obhut f, Aufbewahrung f (of +gen, with bei); (Jur, of children) Sorgerecht nt (of für, über +acc); (= guardianship) Vormundschaft f (of für, über +acc); **to put** or **place sth in sb's** ~ etw jdm zur Aufbewahrung anvertrauen, etw in jds Obhut (acc) or Gewahrsam (acc) geben; **the mother was awarded** ~ **of the children after the divorce** der Mutter wurde bei der Scheidung das Sorgerecht für or über die Kinder zugesprochen; **he is in the** ~ **of his aunt** seine Tante hat die Vormundschaft für or über ihn; **the country's future is placed in the** ~ **of its teachers** die Zukunft des Landes liegt in den Händen der Lehrer; **whilst these goods are in the** ~ **of the police** während sich die Gegenstände in Polizeiaufbewahrung befinden **b** (= police detention) (polizeilicher) Gewahrsam, Haft f; **to take sb into** ~ jdn verhaften; **he will be kept in** ~ **until** ... er wird inhaftiert bleiben, bis ...

custom [ˈkʌstəm] **N** **a** (= established behaviour, convention) Sitte f, Brauch m; ~ **demands** ... es ist Sitte or Brauch ...; **as** ~ **has it** wie es Sitte or (der) Brauch ist; **our** ~s unsere Bräuche pl, unsere Sitten und Gebräuche pl **b** (= habit) (An)gewohnheit f; **it was his** ~ **to rest each afternoon** er pflegte am Nachmittag zu ruhen (geh); **as was his** ~ wie er es gewohnt war, wie er es zu tun pflegte (geh) **c** no pl (Comm: = patronage) Kundschaft f; **to get sb's** ~ jdn als Kunden gewinnen; **to take one's** ~ **elsewhere** (als Kunde) anderswo hingehen, woanders Kunde werden; **we get a lot of** ~ **from tourists** wir haben viele Touristen als Kunden, viele unserer Kunden sind Touristen **d** **customs** PL (= duty, organization) Zoll m; (the) **Customs** der Zoll; **the Customs and Excise Department** die britische Zollbehörde; **to go through** ~s durch den Zoll gehen; **to get sth through the** ~s etw durch den Zoll bekommen **e** (Jur) Gewohnheitsrecht nt; **that is** ~ **and practice** das ist allgemein üblich
ADJ (US) suit, shoes maßgefertigt; carpenter auf Bestellung arbeitend; ~ **tailor** Maßschneider(in) m(f)

customarily [ˈkʌstəmərəlɪ] ADV normaler- or üblicherweise

customary [ˈkʌstəmərɪ] ADJ (= conventional) üblich; (= habitual) gewohnt; **it's** ~ **to apologize** man entschuldigt sich normalerweise or gewöhnlich; **it's** ~ **to wear a tie** man trägt normalerweise or gewöhnlich eine Krawatte; ~ **laws** Gewohnheitsrecht nt

custom-built [ˈkʌstəmbɪlt] ADJ speziell angefertigt

custom car N speziell angefertigtes Auto, Spezialauto nt

customer [ˈkʌstəmə] N **a** (Comm: = patron) Kunde m, Kundin f; **our** ~s unsere Kundschaft; **the** ~ **is always right** der Kunde ist König **b** (inf, = person) Kunde m (inf)

customer base N Kundenstamm m

customer service(s) N Kundendienst m; ~ **department** Kundendienstabteilung f

custom house N (esp Hist) Zollamt nt

customize [ˈkʌstəmaɪz] VT car etc individuell aufmachen

custom-made [ˈkʌstəmmeɪd] ADJ clothes, shoes maßgefertigt, nach Maß; furniture, car speziell angefertigt

customs: customs clearance N Zollabfertigung f; **to get** ~ **for sth** etw zollamtlich abfertigen lassen; **customs declaration** N Zollerklärung f; **customs duty** N Zoll(abgabe f) m; **customs house** N Zollamt nt; **customs inspection** N Zollkontrolle f; **customs officer** N Zollbeamte(r) m, Zollbeamtin f; **customs union** N Zollunion f

cut [kʌt]	
vb: pret, ptp **cut**	
1 NOUN	4 INTRANSITIVE VERB
2 ADJECTIVE	5 PHRASAL VERBS
3 TRANSITIVE VERB	

1 – NOUN

a = result of cutting Schnitt m; (= wound) Schnittwunde f, Schnitt m; **he was treated for minor cuts and bruises** er wurde wegen kleinerer Schnittwunden und Prellungen behandelt; **to make a cut in sth** in etw (acc) einen Einschnitt machen

b = act of cutting Schnitt m; (with sword, whip) Hieb m, Schlag m; **a cut from his sword** ein Schlag mit seinem Schwert; **his hair could do with a cut** seine Haare könnten mal wieder geschnitten werden; **he's/it's a cut above the rest of them** er/es ist den anderen um einiges überlegen; **the cut and thrust of politics/publishing** das Spannungsfeld der Politik/der Trubel des Verlagswesens; **the cut and thrust of the debate** die Hitze der Debatte

c = reduction (in prices) Senkung f, Herabsetzung f; (in quality) Verminderung f; (in quantity, length etc) Verringerung f; (in expenses, salaries, expenditure, budget etc) Kürzung f; (in working hours, holidays) (Ver)kürzung f; (in programme, text, film) Kürzung f; (in production, output) Einschränkung f; **a cut in prices/taxes** eine Senkung der Preise/Steuern (gen), eine Preis-/Steuersenkung; **a 1% cut in interest rates** eine 1%ige Senkung des Zinssatzes; **he had to take a cut in (his) salary** er musste eine Gehaltskürzung hinnehmen; **the censor had made so many cuts** die Zensur hatte so viel gestrichen

d of clothes, hair Schnitt m; (of jewel) Schliff m

e of meat Stück nt

f = share (inf) Anteil m, Teil m; **to get one's cut** seinen Teil or Anteil bekommen; **to take one's cut** sich (dat) seinen Teil or Anteil nehmen; **a cut of the profits/proceeds** ein Teil m der Gewinne/Einnahmen

g = gibe Spitze f, spitze Bemerkung; **that remark was a cut at me** diese Bemerkung war auf mich gemünzt; **the unkindest cut of all** (prov) der schlimmste Schlag

h Mus Track m; **a cut from her forthcoming album** ein Track m von ihrem nächsten Album

i = route, waterway (= short route) Abkürzung f; (= connecting alleyway etc) Verbindungsweg m; (= canal) Kanal m

j = woodcut Holzschnitt m

k Elec Unterbrechung f (in +gen); (planned) Sperre f; **power/electricity cut** Stromausfall m; (planned) Stromsperre f

l Cards Abheben nt; **it's your cut** du hebst ab

m Sport **to give a cut to the ball** den Ball anschneiden

2 – ADJECTIVE

geschnitten; bread (auf)geschnitten; grass gemäht; prices ermäßigt, herabgesetzt; **to have a cut finger/hand/lip** eine Schnittwunde am Finger/an der Hand/an der Lippe haben; **finely cut features** fein geschnittene Züge pl; **a well-cut dress** ein gut geschnittenes Kleid; **cut flowers** Schnittblumen pl; **hand-cut crystal** handgeschliffenes Kristall; **the cut version of a film** die gekürzte or (= censored also) zensierte Fassung eines Films → **half-cut**

3 – TRANSITIVE VERB

a = make cut in (with knife, scissors) schneiden; fabric zuschneiden; cake anschneiden; rope durchschneiden; (Naut) kappen; grass mähen;

to cut one's finger/lip/leg sich (dat) am Finger/an der Lippe/am Bein schneiden; (with knife, razor etc also) sich (dat) in den Finger/in die Lippe/ins Bein schneiden; **to cut one's nails** sich (dat) die Nägel schneiden; **to cut oneself (shaving)** sich (beim Rasieren) schneiden; **to cut sth in half/three** etw halbieren/dritteln, etw in zwei/drei Teile schneiden; **the road cuts the village in two** die Straße schneidet das Dorf in zwei Teile; **to cut a hole in sth** ein Loch in etw (acc) schneiden; **to cut to pieces** zerstückeln; sb's reputation zerstören; (gunfire) enemy lines auseinander reißen; **to cut open** aufschneiden; **he cut his head open** er hat sich (dat) den Kopf aufgeschlagen; **to have** or **get one's hair cut** sich (dat) die Haare schneiden lassen; **to cut sb free/loose** jdn losschneiden

b = cut off abschneiden; (with sword, axe) abschlagen, abhacken

c = make by cutting steps schlagen, hauen; channel, trench graben, ausheben; figure (in wood) schnitzen (in aus); (in stone) hauen (in aus); glass, crystal, diamond schleifen; suit, dress, skirt zuschneiden; key anfertigen; **to cut one's coat according to one's cloth** (prov) sich nach der Decke strecken; **to cut a fine/sorry figure** eine gute/schlechte Figur machen or abgeben

d = break off electricity abstellen; gas (ab)sperren, abstellen; power supply unterbrechen; ties, links abbrechen; **to cut all one's ties** (fig) alle Verbindungen abbrechen (with zu)

e = skip lecture, class schwänzen (inf); **to cut school** die Schule schwänzen (inf)

f = intersect (line) schneiden; (path, road) kreuzen

g = reduce prices senken, herabsetzen; quality vermindern; quantity reduzieren; working hours, holidays (ver)kürzen; expenses, salary, text, programme, film kürzen; production, output verringern, einschränken

h = remove part of programme, text, film streichen; **to cut and paste text** (Comput) Text ausschneiden und einfügen; **they cut him from the team** sie warfen ihn aus dem Team

i = censor film Teile streichen aus

j = cause pain or suffering to schmerzen; **the wind cut his face** der Wind schnitt ihm ins Gesicht → **quick N a**

k Cards **to cut the cards/the pack** abheben

l Sport ball (an)schneiden

m = edit film schneiden, cutten

n Mus record pressen; (singer) machen

o = stop engine abstellen; (inf) noise aufhören mit; **cut the crap!** (sl) hör mit dem Scheiß auf! (inf)

p = divide **if we cut the profits three ways** wenn wir den Gewinn dritteln or unter drei verteilen or aufteilen

q = manage (inf) **he can't cut it** er bringts nicht (inf)

r set structures

♦ **to cut sb/sth short to cut sb short** jdm das Wort abschneiden; **to cut sth short** etw vorzeitig abbrechen; **to cut a long story short** kurz und gut, der langen Rede kurzer Sinn

♦ **to cut sb dead** (Brit) jdn wie Luft behandeln

♦ **to cut a tooth** zahnen, einen Zahn bekommen; **to cut one's teeth on sth** (fig) sich (dat) die (ersten) Sporen mit or an etw (dat) verdienen

♦ **to cut it fine** (Brit) don't cut it too fine with your essay lass es mit deinem Aufsatz nicht auf die letzte Minute ankommen; **£10 would be cutting it rather fine** £ 10 wären etwas knapp (bemessen); **2.20 would be cutting it a bit fine** 2.20 Uhr wäre ein bisschen knapp; **aren't you cutting it a bit fine?** ist das nicht ein bisschen knapp?

♦ **to cut one's losses** eine Sache abschließen, ehe der Schaden (noch) größer wird

4 – INTRANSITIVE VERB

a instrument (knife, scissors) schneiden; (lawn mower) mähen, schneiden; **to cut loose** (Naut) losmachen; *(fig)* sich losmachen; *(US, inf)* loslegen *(inf)*

♦ **to cut both ways** *(fig)* ein zweischneidiges Schwert sein

♦ **to cut and run** abhauen *(inf)*, die Beine in die Hand nehmen *(inf)*

b [material] **paper cuts easily** Papier lässt sich leicht schneiden

c = intersect *(lines, roads)* sich schneiden

d Film *(= change scenes)* überblenden *(to* zu); *(= stop filming)* aufhören, abbrechen; **cut!** Schnitt!, aus! → **chase**

e Cards abheben; **to cut for dealer** den Geber auslosen *(durch Ziehen einer Karte)*

f Sport den Ball/die Bälle *(an)*schneiden; **to cut at a ball** einen Ball anschneiden

5 – PHRASAL VERBS

▶ **cut across** VI +prep obj **a** *(lit)* hinübergehen/-fahren *etc (prep obj* über +*acc)*; **you can cut across here** Sie können hier hinüber; **if you cut across the fields** wenn Sie über die Felder gehen; **to cut across country** querfeldein gehen/fahren *etc* **b** *(fig)* theory *etc* widersprechen *(prep obj +dat)*; **this problem cuts across all ages** dieses Problem betrifft alle Altersgruppen

▶ **cut along** VI *(dated inf)* sich auf die Socken machen *(inf)*

▶ **cut away** VT sep wegschneiden; **the dress was cut away at the back** das Kleid war hinten or im Rücken *(tief)* ausgeschnitten

▶ **cut back** VI **a** *(= go back)* zurückgehen; *(in car)* zurückfahren; *(Film)* zurückblenden **b** *(= reduce expenditure etc)* sich einschränken; **to cut back on expenses** *etc* die Ausgaben *etc* einschränken; **to cut back on production** die Produktion zurückschrauben; **to cut back on smoking/sweets** weniger rauchen/Süßigkeiten essen VT sep **a** plants zurückschneiden **b** production zurückschrauben; *outgoings* einschränken; *programme* kürzen

▶ **cut down** VT sep **a** tree fällen; corn schneiden; *person (with sword)* (mit dem Schwert) niederstrecken

b *(= make smaller)* number, expenses einschränken; text zusammenstreichen *(to* auf +*acc)*; **to cut sb down to size** jdn auf seinen Platz verweisen

c usu pass *(= kill)* dahinraffen *(geh)*; **a young man cut down in his prime** ein junger Mann, der im Frühling seiner Jahre dahingerafft wurde *(liter)*

VI *(= reduce intake, expenditure etc)* sich einschränken; **to cut down on sth** etw einschränken; **to cut down on smoking** das Rauchen einschränken; **to cut down on sweets** weniger Süßigkeiten essen

▶ **cut in** VI **a** *(= interrupt)* sich einschalten *(on* in +*acc)*; **to cut in on sb** jdn unterbrechen; **to cut in on sth** sich in etw *(acc)* einschalten

b *(= cut towards the centre) (blade)* einschneiden; **to cut in on sb's market** sich in jds Revier *(acc)* drängen *(inf)*; **he cut in to the centre of the pitch** er zog ins Mittelfeld herüber

c *(Aut) (= swerve in front)* sich direkt vor ein anderes/das andere Auto hineindrängen; **to cut in in front of sb** jdn schneiden; **he cut in so sharply that the car behind had to swerve** er zog so schnell herüber, dass das nachfolgende Auto ausweichen musste

VT sep **to cut sb in on sth** jdn an etw *(dat)* beteiligen

▶ **cut into** VI +prep obj **a** *(= make a cut in)* cake, meat anschneiden **b** *(= swerve into)* line of traffic sich drängeln in *(+acc)*; woods, alleyway schnell einbiegen in *(+acc)* **c** *(= interrupt)* conversation fallen in *(+acc)* **d** *(fig) (= make inroads into)* savings ein Loch reißen in *(+acc)*; holidays verkürzen

▶ **cut off** VT sep **a** *(with knife etc)* abschneiden; *(with sword etc)* abschlagen; **to cut off sb's head** jdm den Kopf abschlagen

b town, supply abschneiden; allowance sperren; **to cut off the enemy's retreat/supplies** dem Feind den Rückzug/die Zufuhr abschneiden;

his deafness cut him off from others seine Taubheit schnitt ihn von der Umwelt ab; **we're very cut off out here** wir leben hier draußen sehr abgeschieden

c *(= disinherit)* enterben; **to cut sb off without a penny** jdn enterben

d *(= disconnect)* gas, telephone *etc* abstellen; **we've been cut off** *(Telec)* wir sind unterbrochen worden

e *(= break off)* discussion, relations abbrechen; **to cut sb off in the middle of a sentence** jdn mitten im Satz unterbrechen

▶ **cut out** VI *(engine, radio transmission)* aussetzen

VT sep **a** *(= remove by cutting)* ausschneiden; *malignant growth* herausschneiden

b *(= form by cutting)* coat, dress zuschneiden; **they had cut out a path through the jungle** sie hatten *(sich dat)* einen Weg durch den Dschungel geschlagen or gebahnt

c *(= delete)* (heraus)streichen; *(= not bother with)* verzichten auf *(+acc)*, sich *(dat)* schenken; smoking, swearing *etc* aufhören mit, sein lassen *(inf)*; rival ausstechen; **double glazing cuts out the noise** Doppelfenster verhindern, dass der Lärm hereindringt; **cut it out!** *(inf)* hör auf damit!, lass das (sein)! *(inf)*; **cut out the nonsense** lass den Unsinn; **and you can cut out the self-pity for a start!** und mit Selbstmitleid brauchst du gar nicht erst zu kommen or anzufangen!

d *(fig)* **to be cut out for sth** zu etw geeignet or gemacht sein; **to be cut out to be sth** dazu geeignet sein, etw zu sein or zu werden; **he's not cut out to be a doctor** er ist nicht zum Arzt geeignet, er hat nicht das Zeug zum Arzt

e **to have one's work cut out** alle Hände voll zu tun haben

▶ **cut through** VT sep he couldn't cut his way through es gelang ihm nicht durchzukommen; **we cut through the housing estate** wir gingen/ fuhren durch die Siedlung; **the boat cut through the waves** das Boot bahnte sich seinen Weg durch die Wellen

▶ **cut up** VI **to cut up rough** *(Brit inf)* Krach schlagen *(inf)* VT sep **a** meat aufschneiden; wood spalten; *(fig)* enemy, army vernichten **b** *(Aut)* **to cut sb up** jdn schneiden

---

cut-and-dried [ˌkʌtənˈdraɪd] ADJ *(fig)* festgelegt; **~ opinions** festgelegte Meinungen *pl*; **as far as he's concerned the whole issue is now ~** für ihn ist die ganze Angelegenheit erledigt; **it's not quite ~** so eindeutig ist das nicht

cut-and-paste [ˌkʌtənˈpeɪst] ADJ *(US)* **a ~ job** eine zusammengestückelte Arbeit *(usu pej)*

cutaneous [kjuːˈteɪnɪəs] ADJ kutan *(spec)*

cutaway [ˈkʌtəweɪ] N Cut(away) *m* ADJ **~ coat** Cut(away) *m*; **~ drawing** Schnittdiagramm *nt*

cutback [ˈkʌtbæk] N **a** Kürzung *f* **b** *(Film)* Rückblende *f*

cute [kjuːt] ADJ *(+er)* **a** *(inf: = sweet)* süß, niedlich **b** *(esp US inf: = clever)* idea, gadget dufte *(inf)*, prima *(inf)*; *(= shrewd)* person, move schlau, gerissen, clever *(inf)*; **that was pretty ~ of him** das hat er ganz schön schlau hingekriegt *(inf)*

cutely [ˈkjuːtlɪ] ADV **a** *(= sweetly)* süß, niedlich **b** *(= cleverly)* designed, made prima *(inf)*, toll *(inf)*; *(= shrewdly)* schlau, gerissen

cutesy [ˈkjuːtsɪ] ADJ *(pej inf)* person zuckersüß; painting, clothes kitschig

cutey [ˈkjuːtɪ] N → **cutie**

cut glass N geschliffenes Glas

cut-glass [ˈkʌtɡlɑːs] ADJ **a** *(lit)* aus geschliffenem Glas **b** accent vornehm

cuticle [ˈkjuːtɪkl] N *(of nail)* Nagelhaut *f*; *(Anat)* Epidermis *f*; *(Bot)* Kutikula *f*; **~ remover** Nagelhautentferner *m*

cutie [ˈkjuːtɪ] N *(esp US inf)* *(= attractive person)* flotter Käfer *(inf)*, dufte Biene *(inf)*; *(= child)* süßer Fratz *(inf)*; *(= shrewd person)* gewitzter Typ, Schlitzohr *m (pej)*

cutie-pie [ˈkjuːtɪpaɪ] N *(esp US, inf)* süßer Fratz *(inf)*

cutlass [ˈkʌtləs] N Entermesser *nt*

cutler [ˈkʌtlə] N Messerschmied *m*

cutlery [ˈkʌtlərɪ] N , *no pl (esp Brit)* Besteck *nt*

cutlet [ˈkʌtlɪt] N *(= boneless chop)* Schnitzel *nt*; *(= fish fillet)* (Fisch)schnitzel *nt*; *(of chopped meat)* (paniertes) Hacksteak

cut: cut loaf N aufgeschnittenes Brot; **cutoff** N **a** *(Tech, device)* Ausschaltmechanismus *m* **b** *(also* **cutoff point**) Trennlinie *f*; **cutout** N **a** *(= model)* Ausschneidemodell *nt*; *(= figure, doll)* Ausschneidepuppe *f*; **his characters are just cardboard ~s** seine Figuren sind einfach nur oberflächlich; **~ book** Ausschneidebogen *m* **b** *(of engine)* Aussetzen *nt*; **it has an automatic ~** es setzt automatisch aus **c** *(Elec)* Sperre *f* ADJ **a** model *etc* zum Ausschneiden **b** *(Elec)* Abschalt-; **~ device** Abschaltautomatik *f*; **cut-price** ADJ zu Schleuderpreisen; **~ offer** Billigangebot *nt*; **cut-rate** ADJ zu verbilligtem Tarif; **cut sheet feed** N *(Comput)* Einzelblatteinzug *m*

cutter [ˈkʌtə] N **a** *(= tool)* Messer *nt*; **a pair of (wire) ~s** eine Drahtschere; *(Elec)* ein Seitenschneider *m* **b** *(of clothes)* Zuschneider(in) *m(f)*; *(of jewel)* Schleifer(in) *m(f)*; *(of glass)* Glasschneider(in) *m(f)*; *(Film)* Cutter(in) *m(f)* **c** *(= boat)* Kutter *m*; *(US: = coastguard's boat)* Boot *nt* der Küstenwache **d** *(US: = sleigh)* leichter Pferdeschlitten

cut-throat [ˈkʌtθrəʊt] N *(= murderous type)* Verbrechertyp *m* ADJ **a** competition, business unbarmherzig, mörderisch **b** **~ razor** (offenes) Rasiermesser

cutting [ˈkʌtɪŋ] N **a** Schneiden *nt*; *(of grass)* Mähen *nt*; *(of cake)* Anschneiden *nt*; *(of rope)* Durchschneiden *nt*, Kappen *nt*; *(of garment)* Zuschneiden *nt*, Zuschnitt *m*; *(= cutting off)* Abschneiden *nt*; *(with sword)* Abschlagen *nt* **b** *(= shaping)* *(of steps)* Schlagen *nt*; *(of channel, trench)* Graben *nt*; *(of figure) (in wood)* Schnitzen *nt (in aus)*; *(in stone)* Hauen *nt (in aus)*; *(of glass, crystal, jewel)* Schliff *m*; *(of key)* Anfertigung *f*; *(of record)* Pressen *nt*, Herstellung *f* **c** *(= snubbing: of person)* Schneiden *nt*; *(of lecture, class)* Schwänzen *nt (inf)* **d** *(= reduction, of prices)* Senkung *f*, Herabsetzung *f*; *(of quality)* Verminderung *f*; *(of quantity)* Reduzierung *f*; *(of working hours)* Verkürzung *f*; *(of expenses, salary)* Kürzung *f* **e** *(= editing, Film)* Schnitt *m*; *(of production)* Drosselung *f*; *(of part of text)* Streichung *f* **f** *(Brit: = road cutting, railway cutting)* Durchstich *m* **g** *(Brit: = clipping) (from newspaper)* Ausschnitt *m*; *(of cloth)* Schnipsel *m*, Stückchen (Stoff) *nt* **h** *(Hort)* Ableger *m*; **to take a ~** einen Ableger nehmen ADJ **a** blade, edge scharf; **to be at the ~ edge of sth** in etw *(dat)* führend sein **b** *(fig)* wind, cold schneidend; remark, tongue scharf, spitz; **to be ~ to sb** jdm gegenüber spitze Bemerkungen machen

cutting: cutting board N *(US)* = **chopping board**; **cutting edge** N **a** *(= blade)* Schneide *f*, Schnittkante *f* **b** no pl *(= most advanced stage)* letzter Stand *(of gen)*; **cutting room** N *(Film)* Schneideraum *m*; **to end up on the ~ floor** *(fig)* im Papierkorb enden

cuttlebone [ˈkʌtlbəʊn] N Schulp *m*

cuttlefish [ˈkʌtlfɪʃ] N Tintenfisch *m*, Sepie *f*, Kuttelfisch *m*

cut up ADJ *(inf: = upset)* **he was very ~ about it** das hat ihn schwer getroffen or ziemlich mitgenommen

CV abbr of **curriculum vitae**

cwm [kuːm] N Kar *nt*

CWO abbr of **cash with order**

cwt abbr of **hundredweight**

cyanide [ˈsaɪənaɪd] N Zyanid *nt*, Blausäuresalz *nt*; **~ poisoning** Blausäurevergiftung *f*

cyber- ['saɪbə-]: **cybercafé** N Internetcafé *nt*, Cybercafé *nt*; **cybernetic** ADJ kybernetisch; **cybernetics** N *sing* Kybernetik *f*; **cyberpet** N Tamagotchi *m*, elektronisches Haustier; **cyberpunk** N (*Liter*) Cyberpunk *m*; **cybersex** N Cybersex *m*; **cyberspace** N Cyberspace *m*

cyborg ['saɪbɔːg] N Cyborg *m*, Robotermensch *m*

cyclamen ['sɪkləmən] N Alpenveilchen *nt*, Zyklamen *nt* (*spec*)

cycle ['saɪkl] **N** **a** Zyklus *m*, Kreislauf *m*; (*of events*) Gang *m*; (*of poems, songs*) Zyklus *m*; (*Elec*) Periode *f*; **life ~** Lebenszyklus *or* -kreislauf *m*; **the moon's ~** der Mondwechsel **b** (= *bicycle*) (Fahr)rad *nt*; (*inf*: = *motorbike*) Maschine *f* (*sl*) **VI** mit dem (Fahr)rad fahren

cycle: cycle clip N Fahrradklammer *f*; **cycle lane** N (Fahr)radweg *m*; **cycle path** N (Fahr)radweg *m*

cycler ['saɪklə'] N (*US*) = **cyclist**

cycle: cycle race N Radrennen *nt*; **cycle rack** N Fahrradständer *m*; **cycle shed** N Fahrradstand *m*; **cycle track** N (= *path*) (Fahr)radweg *m*; (*for racing*) Radrennbahn *f*; **cycleway** N (Fahr)radweg *m*

cyclic(al) ['saɪklɪk(əl)] ADJ zyklisch; (*Elec*) periodisch

cycling ['saɪklɪŋ] N Radfahren *nt*; **I enjoy ~** ich fahre gern Rad

cycling: cycling cape N Radmantel *m*, Radcape *nt*; **cycling holiday** N Urlaub *m* mit dem Fahrrad; **cycling shorts** PL Radlerhose *f*; **cycling tour** N Radtour *f*

cyclist ['saɪklɪst] N (Fahr)radfahrer(in) *m(f)*; (= *motor cyclist*) Motorradfahrer(in) *m(f)*

cyclometer [saɪ'klɒmɪtə'] N Kilometerzähler *m*

cyclone ['saɪkləʊn] N Zyklon *m*; **~ cellar** (*US*) *tiefer Keller zum Schutz vor Zyklonen*

cyclonic [saɪ'klɒnɪk] ADJ zyklonartig

cyclopaedia [ˌsaɪkləʊ'piːdɪə] N Enzyklopädie *f*

Cyclops ['saɪklɒps] N Zyklop *m*

cyclorama [ˌsaɪklə'rɑːmə] N Rundhorizont *m*

cygnet ['sɪgnɪt] N Schwanjunge(s) *nt*

cylinder ['sɪlɪndə'] N (*Math, Aut*) Zylinder *m*; (*of revolver, typewriter*) Walze *f*; **a four-cylinder car** ein Vierzylinder *m*, ein vierzylindriges Auto; **to be firing on all ~s** (*lit*) auf allen Zylindern laufen; (*fig*) in Fahrt sein; **he's only firing on two ~s** (*fig*) er bringt nicht seine volle Leistung

cylinder: cylinder block N (*Aut*) Zylinderblock *m*; **cylinder capacity** N (*Aut*) Hubraum *m*; **cylinder head** N (*Aut*) Zylinderkopf *m*; **cylinder head gasket** N (*Aut*) Zylinderkopfdichtung *f*

cylindrical ADJ , **cylindrically** ADV [sɪ'lɪndrɪkəl, -ɪ] zylindrisch

cymbal ['sɪmbəl] N Beckenteller *m*; **~s** Becken *nt*; **to play the ~s** das Becken schlagen

cynic ['sɪnɪk] N **a** Zyniker(in) *m(f)*; **don't be such a ~** sei nicht so zynisch **b** Cynic (*Philos*) Kyniker *m*, Zyniker *m*

cynical ['sɪnɪkəl] ADJ **a** zynisch; **he was very ~ about it** er äußerte sich sehr zynisch dazu **b** Cynical (*Philos*) kynisch, zynisch

cynically ['sɪnɪklɪ] ADV zynisch

cynicism ['sɪnɪsɪzəm] N **a** *no pl* Zynismus *m* **b** (= *cynical remark*) zynische Bemerkung **c** Cynicism (*Philos*) Kynismus *m*, Zynismus *m*

cynosure ['saɪnəʃʊə'] N **to be the ~ of all eyes** (*liter*) alle Blicke auf sich ziehen *or* vereinigen

cypher N, VT = **cipher**

cypress ['saɪprɪs] N Zypresse *f*

Cyprian ['sɪprɪən] N (*old*) = **Cypriot**

Cypriot ['sɪprɪət] **a** zypriotisch, zyprisch **N** Zypriot(in) *m(f)*, Zyprer(in) *m(f)*

Cyprus ['saɪprəs] N Zypern *nt*

Cyrillic ['sɪrɪlɪk] ADJ kyrillisch

cyst [sɪst] N Zyste *f*

cystic fibrosis [ˌsɪstɪkfaɪ'brəʊsɪs] N Mukoviszidose *f*

cystitis [sɪs'taɪtɪs] N Blasenentzündung *f*, Zystitis *f* (*spec*)

cytology [saɪ'tɒlədʒɪ] N Zytologie *f*, Zellenlehre *f*

cytoplasm ['saɪtəʊplæzm] N Zytoplasma *nt*, Zellplasma *nt*

CZ (*US*) *abbr of* **Canal Zone** Kanalzone *f*, *Gebiet um den Panamakanal*

czar [zɑː'] N Zar *m*

czarevitch ['zɑːrəvɪtʃ] N Zarewitsch *m*

czarina [zɑː'riːnə] N Zarin *f*

czarism ['zɑːrɪzəm] N Zarismus *m*

czarist ['zɑːrɪst] **ADJ** zaristisch **N** Zarist(in) *m(f)*

Czech [tʃek] **ADJ** tschechisch **N** **a** Tscheche *m*, Tschechin *f* **b** (*Ling*) Tschechisch *nt*

Czechoslovak [tʃekəʊ'sləʊvæk] **ADJ** tschechoslowakisch **N** Tschechoslowake *m*, Tschechoslowakin *f*

Czechoslovakia [tʃekəʊslə'vækɪə] N die Tschechoslowakei

Czechoslovakian [tʃekəʊslə'vækɪən] ADJ, N = **Czechoslovak**

Czech Republic N Tschechische Republik, Tschechien *nt*

D

D, d [di:] N D *nt*, d *nt*; (*Sch, as a mark*) ausreichend; **D sharp** Dis *nt*, dis *nt*; **D flat** Des *nt*, des *nt* → *also* **major, minor, natural**

D (*US Pol*) abbr of **Democratic** dem.

d **a** (*Brit, old*) abbr of **pence** **b** abbr of **died** gest.

'd = **had, would**

DA (*US*) abbr of **District Attorney**

D/A abbr of **deposit account**

dab¹ [dæb] **N** **a** (= *small amount*) Klecks *m*; (*applied with puff, of cream etc*) Tupfer *m*; (*of liquid, perfume, glue etc*) Tropfen *m*; (*of butter*) Klacks *m*; **a ~ of powder/ointment** *etc* etwas *or* ein bisschen Puder/Salbe *etc*; **to give sth a ~ of paint** etw überstreichen **b** **dabs** PL (*Brit inf*: = *fingerprints*) Fingerabdrücke *pl* **VT** (*with powder etc*) betupfen; (*with towel etc*) tupfen; **to ~ one's eyes** sich (*dat*) die Augen tupfen; **she ~bed ointment/powder on her face/the wound** sie betupfte sich (*dat*) das Gesicht/die Wunde mit Salbe/Puder

▶ **dab at** VI +*prep obj* betupfen

▶ **dab off** VT *sep* abtupfen

▶ **dab on** VT *sep* auftragen (*prep obj* auf +*acc*)

dab² N (= *fish*) Kliesche *f*, Scharbe *f*

dab³ ADJ (*inf*) **to be a ~ hand at sth** gut in etw (*dat*) sein; **to be a ~ hand at doing sth** sich darauf verstehen, etw zu tun

dabble ['dæbl] **VT** **to ~ one's hands/feet in the water** mit den Händen/Füßen im Wasser plan(t)schen **VI** **a** (*with hands, feet*) plan(t)schen **b** (*fig*) **to ~ in/at sth** sich (nebenbei) mit etw beschäftigen; **are you a serious photographer? – no, I only ~ (in it)** beschäftigen Sie sich ernsthaft mit der Fotografie? – nein, nur so nebenbei; **he ~s in stocks and shares/antiques** er versucht sich an der Börse/in Antiquitäten

dabbler ['dæblə'] N Amateur(in) *m(f)*

dabchick ['dæbtʃɪk] N Steißfuß *m*

da capo [dɑː'kɑːpəʊ] ADV (*Mus*) da capo, noch einmal

dace [deɪs] N *pl* - Weißfisch *m*

dacha ['dætʃə] N Datscha *f*, Datsche *f*

dachshund ['dækshʊnd] N Dackel *m*, Dachshund *m* (*rare*)

Dacron® ['dækrɒn] N (*US*) Dacron® *nt*

dactyl ['dæktɪl] N (*Zool*) Zehe *f*, Finger *m*; (*Liter*) Daktylus *m*

dactylic [dæk'tɪlɪk] ADJ daktylisch

dad [dæd] N (*inf*) Vater *m*; (*affectionately also*) Vati *m* (*inf*), Papa *m* (*inf*)

Dada [dɑːdɑː] N (*Art*) Dada *m*

Dadaism ['dɑːdɑːɪzm] N (*Art*) Dadaismus *m*

daddy ['dædɪ] N (*inf*) Papa *m* (*inf*), Vati *m* (*inf*); **the ~ of them all** (*inf*) der Größte

daddy-longlegs [ˌdædɪ'lɒŋlegz] N *pl* - (*Brit*) Schnake *f*; (*US*) Weberknecht *m*

dado ['deɪdəʊ] N (*of pedestal*) Basis *f*; (*of wall*) Paneel *nt*

daemon ['diːmən] N (*liter*) = **demon**

daff [dæf] N (*Brit, inf*) = **daffodil**

daffodil ['dæfədɪl] N Osterglocke *f*, Narzisse *f*

daffy ['dæfɪ] ADJ (+*er*) (*inf*) = **daft**

daft [dɑːft] ADJ (+*er*) doof, blöd, bekloppt (*all inf*); **~ in the head** (*inf*) blöd (*inf*), bekloppt (*inf*); **what a ~ thing to do** so was Doofes *or* Blödes *or* Beklopptes (*all inf*); **he's ~ about her/about football** (*inf*) er ist verrückt nach ihr/nach Fußball (*inf*); **to go ~** verblöden; **he's ~ enough to believe anything** er ist so blöd, er glaubt alles

daftie ['dɑːftɪ], **daft ha'porth** ['dɑːfteɪpəθ] N (*Brit, inf*) Dussel *m* (*inf*)

daftness ['dɑːftnɪs] N (*inf*) Blödheit *f*, Doofheit *f* (*both inf*)

dag [dæg] N (*inf*: = *shred*) Zottel *m*, Zipfel *m*, Fetzen *m* (*all inf, pej*)

dagger ['dægə'] N **a** Dolch *m*; **to be at ~s drawn with sb** (*fig*) mit jdm auf (dem) Kriegsfuß stehen; **to look ~s at sb** (*Brit*) jdn mit Blicken durchbohren **b** (*Typ*) Kreuz *nt*

dago ['deɪgəʊ] N (*pej*) Südländer(in) *m(f)*, Kanake *m* (*pej sl*), *verächtliche Bezeichnung für Spanier, Portugiesen oder Südamerikaner*

daguerreotype [də'gerəʊtaɪp] N Daguerreotypie *f* **VT** nach dem Daguerreotypieverfahren fotografieren

dahlia ['deɪlɪə] N Dahlie *f*

Dáil Éireann [daɪl'ɛərən] N *Unterhaus der Republik Irland*

daily ['deɪlɪ] ADJ täglich; **~ newspaper** Tageszeitung *f*; **~ wage** Tagelohn *m*; **~ grind** täglicher Trott; **~ life** der Alltag; **he is employed on a ~ basis** er ist tageweise angestellt; (*labourer*) er ist als Tagelöhner beschäftigt, er steht im Tagelohn ADV täglich; **three times ~** dreimal täglich **N** **a** (= *newspaper*) Tageszeitung *f* **b** (*also* **daily help, daily woman**) Putzfrau *f*

daily bread N (*fig*: = *livelihood*) tägliches Brot; **to earn one's ~** sich (*dat*) sein Brot verdienen

daily dozen N (*inf*) Morgengymnastik *f*

daintily ['deɪntɪlɪ] ADV zierlich; *hold, walk, move* anmutig

daintiness ['deɪntɪnɪs] N Zierlichkeit *f*; (*of movement, manners etc*) Anmutigkeit *f*, Geziertheit *f* (*pej*)

dainty ['deɪntɪ] ADJ (+*er*) **a** zierlich; *lace, handkerchief* niedlich; *movement, music* anmutig; **she has ~ little ways** bei *or* an ihr ist alles fein und zierlich **b** *food* appetitlich; **~ morsel** Appetithappen *m* **c** (= *refined*) geziert, etepetete (*inf*) **N** Leckerei *f*

daiquiri ['daɪkərɪ] N *Cocktail aus Rum, Limonensaft und Zucker*

dairy ['dɛərɪ] N Molkerei *f*; (*on farm*) Milchkammer *f*; (= *shop*) Milchgeschäft *nt*

dairy: dairy butter N Markenbutter *f*; **dairy cattle** PL Milchvieh *nt*; **dairy cow** N Milchkuh *f*; **dairy farm** N auf Milchviehhaltung spezialisierter Bauernhof; **dairy farming** N Milchviehhaltung *f*; **dairy herd** N Herde *f* Milchkühe; **dairy husbandry** N Milchwirtschaft *f*; **dairy ice cream** N Milchspeiseeis *nt*

dairying ['dɛərɪŋ] N Milchwirtschaft *f*

dairy: dairymaid N Melkerin *f*; (= *worker*) Molkereiangestellte *f*; **dairyman** N Melker *m*; (= *worker*) Molkereiangestellte(r) *m*; (= *milkman*) Milchmann *m*; **dairy produce** N , **dairy products** PL Milch- *or* Molkereiprodukte *pl*

dais ['deɪs] N Podium *nt*

daisy ['deɪzɪ] N Gänseblümchen *nt*; **to be pushing up the daisies** (*inf*) sich (*dat*) die Radieschen von unten besehen (*hum*)

daisy chain N Kette *f* aus Gänseblümchen

daisywheel ['deɪzɪwiːl] N (*Typ, Comput*) Typenrad *m*; **~ typewriter** Typenradschreibmaschine *f*

daisywheel printer N Typenraddrucker *m*

dale [deɪl] N (*N Engl, liter*) Tal *nt*

dalesman ['deɪlzmən] N *pl* **-men** [-mən], **daleswoman** ['deɪlzwʊmən] N *pl* **-women** [-wɪmɪn] *Bewohner(in) des Gebiets der Dales in Yorkshire*

dalliance ['dælɪəns] N (*liter*) Tändelei *f* (*liter*)

dally ['dælɪ] VI **a** (= *waste time*) (herum)trödeln, bummeln; (= *flirt*) **to ~ with sb** mit jdm schäkern; **to ~ with an idea** mit einem Gedanken liebäugeln

Dalmatia [dæl'meɪʃə] N Dalmatien *nt*

Dalmatian [dæl'meɪʃən] ADJ dalmatinisch, dalmatisch **N** **a** (= *person*) Dalmatiner(in) *m(f)* **b** (= *dog*) Dalmatiner *m*

daltonism ['dɔːltənɪzəm] N Farbenblindheit *f*, Daltonismus *m* (*dated spec*), Rotgrünblindheit *f*

dam¹ [dæm] **N** (*lit, fig*) Damm *m*; (= *reservoir*) Stausee *m* **VT** (*also* **dam up**) **a** *river, lake* (auf)stauen; *valley* eindämmen **b** (*fig*) *flow of words* eindämmen; *feelings* aufstauen

dam² N (= *mother*) Muttertier *nt*

damage ['dæmɪdʒ] **N** **a** Schaden *m* (*to an* +*dat*); **to do a lot of ~** großen Schaden anrichten; **to do sb/sth a lot of ~** jdm/einer Sache (*dat*) großen Schaden zufügen; **the ~ to his pride/ego/reputation** die Verletzung seines Stolzes/Erschütterung seines Selbstbewusstseins/Schädigung seines Rufs; **it did no ~ to his reputation** das hat seinem Ruf nicht geschadet; **the ~ is done** (*fig*) es ist passiert **b** **damages** PL (*Jur*) Schaden(s)ersatz *m* **c** (*inf*: = *cost*) **what's the ~?** was kostet der Spaß? (*inf*)

VT schaden (+*dat*); *health, reputation, relations also* schädigen; *machine, car, furniture, fruit, tree* beschädigen; **to ~ one's eyesight** sich (*dat*) die Augen verderben; **smoking can ~ your health** Rauchen ist gesundheitsschädlich, Rauchen schadet Ihrer Gesundheit; **to ~ one's chances** sich (*dat*) die Chancen verderben

damaged ['dæmɪdʒd] ADJ beschädigt, schadhaft (*geh*); (= *broken*) defekt

damage control, **damage limitation** N Schadensbegrenzung *f*

damaging ['dæmɪdʒɪŋ] ADJ schädlich; *remarks* abträglich; **to be ~ to sb/sth** sich auf jdn/etw schädigend *or* schädlich auswirken, schädlich für jdn/etw sein; **that was a ~ blow to his pride** das hat seinem Stolz einen empfindlichen Schlag versetzt

damascene ['dæməsiːn] VT damaszieren; **~d blades** Damaszener Klingen *pl*

Damascus [də'mɑːskəs] N Damaskus *nt*; **~ steel** Damaszener Stahl *m*

damask ['dæməsk] **N** **a** Damast *m* **b** ~ **(steel)** Damaszener Stahl *m* **ADJ** **a** Damast-, aus Damast; ~ **tablecloth** Damasttischdecke *f* **b** (*liter: colour*) rosig

damask rose N Damaszenerrose *f*

Dam Buster N *jd, der während des 2. Weltkriegs mit speziell angefertigten Bomben Staudämme zerstörte*

dame [deɪm] **N** **a** **Dame** (*Brit*) *Titel der weiblichen Träger des „Order of the British Empire"* **b** (*old lady*) Dame *f*; **Dame Fortune** (*esp Brit*) Frau Fortuna *f* **c** (*Theat, in pantomime*) (komische) Alte **d** (*US, inf*) Weib *nt* (*inf*)

damfool ['dæm'fuːl] ADJ *attr* (*inf*) idiotisch (*inf*)

dammit ['dæmɪt] INTERJ (*inf*) verdammt (*inf*), Teufel noch mal (*inf*); **it weighs 2 kilos as near as ~** es wiegt so gut wie 2 Kilo

damn [dæm] **INTERJ** (*inf*) verdammt (*inf*)
N (*inf*) **he doesn't care** *or* **give a ~** er schert sich den Teufel *or* einen Dreck (darum) (*inf*); **I don't give a ~** das ist mir piepegal (*inf*) *or* scheißegal (*inf*); **it's not worth a ~** das ist keinen Pfifferling wert
ADJ *attr* (*inf*) verdammt; **it's one ~ thing after another** verdammt noch mal, da kommt aber auch eins nach dem andern; **it's a ~ nuisance** das ist ein verdammter Mist (*inf*), das ist wirklich zu blöd (*inf*); **a ~ sight better/worse** verdammt viel besser/schlechter (*inf*); **I can't see a ~ thing** verdammt (noch mal), ich kann überhaupt nichts sehen (*inf*); **I couldn't see a ~ thing** das war vielleicht ein Mist, ich konnte überhaupt nichts sehen (*inf*)
ADV (*inf*) verdammt; **I should ~ well hope/think so** das will ich aber auch stark hoffen/ich doch stark annehmen (*inf*); **pretty ~ good/quick** verdammt gut/schnell (*inf*); **you're ~ right** du hast völlig recht; **~ all** nicht die Bohne (*inf*); **I've done ~ all today** ich hab heute null Komma nichts gemacht (*inf*)
VT **a** (*Rel*) verdammen
b (= *bring condemnation, ruin on*) das Genick brechen (+*dat*); (*evidence*) überführen
c (= *judge and condemn*) verurteilen; **book etc** verreißen; **to ~ sb/sth with faint praise** jdn/etw auf eine Weise loben, die ihn/es bloßstellt
d (*inf*) ~ **him/you!** (*annoyed*) verdammt! (*inf*); (*indifferent*) der kann/du kannst mich mal! (*inf*); ~ **him for forgetting** so ein (verdammter) Mist, er hats vergessen (*inf*); ~ **Richard, he's pinched my book** der verdammte Richard hat mein Buch geklaut (*inf*); ~ **it!** verdammt (noch mal)! (*inf*); ~ **it all!** zum Donnerwetter! (*inf*); (*in surprise*) Donnerwetter! (*inf*), Teufel auch! (*inf*); **well, I'll be ~ed!** Donnerwetter! (*inf*); **I'll be ~ed if I'll go there** ich denk nicht (im Schlaf) dran, da hinzugehen (*inf*); **I'll be ~ed if I know** weiß der Teufel (*inf*)

damnable ADJ , **damnably** ADV ['dæmnəbl, -ɪ] grässlich

damnation [dæm'neɪʃən] **N** (*Eccl*) (= *act*) Verdammung *f*; (= *state of damnation*) Verdammnis *f* **INTERJ** (*inf*) verdammt (*inf*)

damned [dæmd] **ADJ** **a** *soul* verdammt **b** (*inf*) = **damn** ADJ **ADV** = **damn** ADV **N** (*Eccl, liter*) **the ~** *pl* die Verdammten *pl*

damnedest ['dæmdɪst] N **to do** *or* **try one's ~** (*inf*) verdammt noch mal sein Möglichstes tun (*inf*)

damning ['dæmɪŋ] ADJ vernichtend; *evidence* belastend; **he was pretty ~ about it** er hat sich ziemlich vernichtend darüber geäußert

Damocles ['dæməkliːz] N **sword of ~** Damoklesschwert *nt*

damp [dæmp] **ADJ** (+*er*) feucht; **a ~ squib** (*fig*) ein Reinfall *m* **N** **a** (= *dampness*) Feuchtigkeit *f* **b** (*Min*) (= *chokedamp*) Schlagwetter *nt*; (= *firedamp*) Grubengas *nt* **VT** **a** befeuchten, anfeuchten **b** (*fig*) *enthusiasm etc* dämpfen **c** *sounds, vibrations* dämpfen; (*also* **damp down**) *fire* ersticken

damp course N Dämmschicht *f*

dampen ['dæmpən] VT = **damp** VT a, b

damper ['dæmpə] **N** **a** (*of chimney*) (Luft)klappe *f*; (*of piano*) Dämpfer *m* **b** **to put a ~ on sth** einer Sache (*dat*) einen Dämpfer aufsetzen **c** (*Austral: = bread*) Fladenbrot *nt*

dampish ['dæmpɪʃ] ADJ etwas feucht

damply ['dæmplɪ] ADV feucht

dampness ['dæmpnɪs] N Feuchtigkeit *f*

damp-proof ['dæmppruːf] ADJ feuchtigkeitsbeständig; ~ **course** Dämmschicht *f*

damsel ['dæmzəl] **N** (*obs, liter*) Maid *f* (*obs, liter*)

damselfly ['dæmzəlflaɪ] N Seejungfer *f*, Schlankjungfer *f*

damson ['dæmzən] N (= *fruit*) Damaszenerpflaume *f*; (= *tree*) Damaszenerpflaumenbaum *m*

Dan [dæn] N (*Sport*) Dan *m*

dance [dɑːns] **N** **a** (= *movement*) Tanz *m*; ~ **class** Tanzstunde *f*; **the Dance of Death** der Totentanz; **may I have the next ~?** darf ich um den nächsten Tanz bitten?; **she's led him a merry ~** sie hat ihn ja ganz schön an der Nase herumgeführt; (= *caused a lot of trouble*) ihretwegen hat er sich (*dat*) die Hacken abgelaufen **b** (= *ball*) Tanz *m*, Tanzabend *m*; **public** = öffentliche Tanzveranstaltung; **end-of-term** = Semesterball *m*; **to give** *or* **hold a ~** einen Tanz(-abend) veranstalten; (*privately*) eine Tanzparty geben; **to go to a ~** tanzen gehen, zum Tanzen gehen
VT tanzen; **to ~ attendance on sb** jdn von hinten und vorn bedienen (*inf*)
VI **a** (= *perform dance*) tanzen; **would you like to ~?** möchten Sie tanzen?
b (= *move here and there*) **to ~ about** (herum-)tänzeln; **to ~ up and down** auf- und abhüpfen; **to ~ for joy** einen Freudentanz aufführen
c (*fig*) tanzen; (*boat on waves*) schaukeln

dance in *cpds* Tanz-; **dance band** N Tanzkapelle *f*; **dance floor** N Tanzboden *m*; (*in restaurant*) Tanzfläche *f*; **dance hall** N Tanzsaal *m*; **dance music** N Tanzmusik *f*

dancer ['dɑːnsə] N Tänzer(in) *m(f)*

dancing ['dɑːnsɪŋ] **N** Tanzen *nt* **ATTR** Tanz-; ~ **dervish** tanzender Derwisch; ~ **shoe** Tanzschuh *m*; **put on your ~ shoes!** (*fig*) mach dich hübsch *or* zurecht!

dancing: dancing girl N Tänzerin *f*; **dancing master** M Tanzlehrer *m*; **dancing partner** N Tanzpartner(in) *m(f)*; **dancing step** N Tanzschritt *m*

D and C *abbr of* **dilation and curettage** Dilation und Kürettage *f* (*spec*), Ausschabung *f*

dandelion ['dændɪlaɪən] N Löwenzahn *m*

dandelion clock ['dændɪlaɪən,klɒk] N Pusteblume *f*

dander ['dændə] N (*inf*) **to get sb's ~ up** jdn auf die Palme bringen (*inf*); **to get one's ~ up** seine *or* die Borsten aufstellen (*inf*)

dandified ['dændɪfaɪd] ADJ stutzerhaft

dandle ['dændl] VT schaukeln (*on* auf +*dat*)

dandruff ['dændrəf] N Schuppen *pl*

dandruffy ['dændrəfɪ] ADJ *hair* schuppig

dandy ['dændɪ] **N** Dandy *m*, Stutzer *m* (*dated*), Geck *m* (*dated*) **ADJ** (*dated esp US inf*) prima (*inf*)

Dane [deɪn] N Däne *m*, Dänin *f*

dang [dæŋ] (*dated inf*) ADJ, ADB, VT = **damn** ADJ, ADV, VT d

danger ['deɪndʒə] **N** **a** Gefahr *f*; **he loves ~** er liebt die Gefahr; **the ~s of smoking** die mit dem Rauchen verbundenen Gefahren; **to put sb/sth in ~** jdn/etw in Gefahr bringen, jdn/etw gefährden; **to run into ~** in Gefahr geraten; **to be in ~ of doing sth** Gefahr laufen, etw zu tun; **the species is in ~ of extinction** die Art ist vom Aussterben bedroht; **out of ~** außer Gefahr; **there is a ~ of fire** es besteht Feuergefahr; **there is a ~ of his getting lost** es besteht die Gefahr, dass er sich verirrt; **he ran the ~ of being recognized** er lief Gefahr, erkannt zu werden; **there is no ~ of that** die Gefahr besteht nicht; **to be a ~ to sb/sth** für jdn/etw eine Gefahr bedeuten; **he's a ~ to himself** er bringt sich selbst in Gefahr
b **"danger"** „Achtung, Lebensgefahr!"; (*Mot*) „Gefahrenstelle"; **"danger, high-tension cables"** „Achtung, Hochspannung!"; **"danger, ice"** „Glatteisgefahr"; **"danger, keep out"** „Zutritt verboten, Lebensgefahr!"; **the signal was at ~** (*Rail*) das Signal stand auf Rot

danger: danger area N Gefahrzone *f* *or* -bereich *m*; **danger list** N **on/off the ~** in/außer Lebensgefahr; **danger money** N Gefahrenzulage *f*; **to get ~** eine Gefahrenzulage kriegen

dangerous ['deɪndʒrəs] ADJ gefährlich; *driving* rücksichtslos; **these prisoners are not ~ to the public** diese Gefangenen stellen keine Gefahr für die Öffentlichkeit dar; **the Bronx can be a ~ place** die Bronx kann gefährlich sein; ~ **drugs** gefährliche Medikamente; (= *illegal*) Drogen *pl*; **the lion was injured but still ~** der Löwe war verletzt, aber er stellte immer noch eine Gefahr dar; **to be ~ to health** gesundheitsgefährdend sein; **to be a ~ driver** rücksichtslos fahren; **this is a ~ game we're playing** wir spielen hier gefährlich; **a little knowledge** *or* **learning is a ~ thing** (*prov*) Halbwissen ist gefährlich

dangerously ['deɪndʒrəslɪ] ADV gefährlich; *low, high* bedenklich; *drive* rücksichtslos; **the deadline is getting ~ close** der Termin rückt bedenklich nahe; **she was ~ ill** sie war todkrank, sie schwebte in Lebensgefahr; **let's live ~ for once** lass uns einmal etwas riskieren

danger: danger point N Gefahrengrenze *f*; **to reach ~** die Gefahrengrenze erreichen; **danger signal** N (*lit, fig*) Warnsignal *nt*; (*Rail*) Deckungssignal *nt* vor Gefahr (*spec*); **danger zone** N Gefahrenzone *f*

dangle ['dæŋgl] **VT** baumeln lassen; **to ~ sth in front of** *or* **before sb** (*fig*) jdm etw verlockend in Aussicht stellen **VI** baumeln

dangling ['dæŋglɪŋ] ADJ baumelnd; ~ **participle** (*Gram*) Partizip mit falschem Bezug

Danish ['deɪnɪʃ] **ADJ** dänisch **N** (= *language*) Dänisch *nt*; **the ~** *pl* (= *people*) die Dänen

Danish blue (cheese) N Blauschimmelkäse *m*

Danish pastry N Plundergebäck *nt*

dank [dæŋk] ADJ (unangenehm) feucht

Dante ['dæntɪ] N Dante *m*

Dantean ['dæntɪən] ADJ dantisch

Dantesque [dæn'tesk] ADJ dantesk

Danube ['dænjuːb] N Donau *f*

dapper ['dæpə] ADJ gepflegt, gediegen

dapple ['dæpl] VT sprenkeln

dappled ['dæpld] ADJ **a** (= *patchy*) light gefleckt; ~ **with sunlight** mit Sonnenlicht gesprenkelt; ~ **shade** Halbschatten *m* **b** (= *mottled*) *horse* scheckig

dapple grey (horse), (*US*) **dapple gray (horse)** N Apfelschimmel *m*

DAR *abbr of* **Daughters of the American Revolution** Töchter *pl* der amerikanischen Revolution

Darby and Joan ['dɑːbɪən'dʒəʊn] PL *glückliches, älteres Ehepaar* ~ **club** Altenklub *m*

Dardanelles [,dɑːdə'nelz] PL Dardanellen *pl*

dare [deə] **⚙** 14 **VI** (= *be bold enough*) es wagen; (= *have the confidence*) sich trauen; **you/he wouldn't ~!** du wirst dich/er wird sich schwer hüten; **you ~!** untersteh dich!; **how ~ you!** was fällt dir ein!
VT **a** **to ~ (to) do sth** (es) wagen, etw zu tun, sich trauen, etw zu tun; **I didn't ~ (to) go upstairs** ich habe mich nicht getraut, die Treppe hinaufzugehen, ich habe mich nicht die Treppe hinauf getraut; **he wouldn't ~ say anything bad about his boss** er wird sich hüten *or* sich untersehen, etwas Schlechtes über seinen Chef zu sagen; **he ~ not** *or* **~n't do it** das wagt er nicht!; **she ~s to dress differently (from the others)** sie hat den Mut, sich anders (als die anderen) anzuziehen; **how ~ you say such**

things? wie kannst du es wagen *or* was unterstehst du dich, so etwas zu sagen?; **don't you ~ say that to me** untersteh dich, das zu mir zu sagen; **~ you do it?** trauen Sie sich?

b **I ~ say it gets quite cold here** ich könnte mir denken, dass es hier ziemlich kalt wird; **I ~ say he'll be there** es kann (gut) sein, dass er dort sein wird; **he's bound to be there – I ~ say** er ist sicher dort – das kann gut sein; **he was very sorry – I ~ say** es tat ihm sehr Leid – das glaube ich gerne

c (= *challenge*) **go on, I ~ you!** (trau dich doch, du) Feigling!; **are you daring me?** wetten, dass? (*inf*); **(I) ~ you to jump off** spring doch, du Feigling!

d (*rare,* = *face the risk of*) riskieren; *danger* trotzen (+*dat*)

N Mutprobe *f*; **to do sth for a ~** etw als Mutprobe tun

daredevil ['dɛə,devl] **N** Waghals *m* **ADJ** waghalsig

daresay [,dɛə'seɪ] (*esp Brit*) = **dare say → dare VT b**

daring ['dɛərɪŋ] **ADJ** **a** (= *courageous*) *person, move* mutig, kühn (*geh*); *attempt* kühn (*geh*); *escape* waghalsig; **at least she was ~ enough to attempt it** sie hat sich wenigstens getraut, es zu versuchen **b** (= *audacious*) *person* wagemutig; *writer, clothes, film, book* gewagt; **a ~ low-cut dress** ein Kleid mit gewagtem Ausschnitt **N** Wagemut *m*, Kühnheit *f* (*geh*); (*of statement*) Gewagtheit *f*

daringly ['dɛərɪŋlɪ] **ADV** mutig, kühn (*geh*); **a ~ low-cut dress** ein Kleid mit einem gewagten Ausschnitt

dark [dɑːk] ☯ 16.1 **ADJ** (+*er*) **a** *room, house, street, cloud, colour, hair, eyes, skin* dunkel; **it will not be ~ for half an hour yet** es wird erst in einer halben Stunde dunkel; **it's getting ~** es wird dunkel; **~ blue/grey** dunkelblau/-grau; **a ~ blue** ein dunkles Blau

b (= *sad, gloomy*) *days, period, mood* düster, finster; **to think ~ thoughts** düsteren Gedanken nachhängen

c (= *sinister*) *corner, secret* dunkel; *forces* dunkel, finster; *look, threat* finster; **from ~est Peru** aus dem finstersten Peru; **the ~ side of sth** die Schattenseite einer Sache (*gen*); **she flashed a ~ glance at me** sie warf mir einen finsteren Blick zu; **to drop ~ hints** dunkle Andeutungen machen; **~ deed** Übeltat *f*

d (*old,* = *secret*) geheim; **to keep sth ~** etw geheim halten

e (*Phon*) velar, dunkel

N **a** **the ~** (= *darkness*) die Dunkelheit; **he was sitting in the ~** er saß im Dunkeln; **they aren't afraid of the ~** sie haben keine Angst im Dunkeln *or* vor der Dunkelheit; **after/before ~** nach/vor Einbruch der Dunkelheit; **until ~** bis zum Einbruch der Dunkelheit; **we'll be back after ~** wir kommen wieder, wenn es dunkel ist

b (*fig*) **to be in the ~ (about sth)** keine Ahnung (von etw) haben; **to keep** *or* **leave sb in the ~ (about sth)** jdn (über etw *acc*) im Dunkeln lassen; **we must keep him in the ~** er darf nichts davon wissen; **to work in the ~** im Dunkeln tappen

dark: dark age N (= *era*) dunkles Zeitalter; **the Dark Ages** das frühe Mittelalter; **to be living in the ~s** (*pej*) im finstersten Mittelalter leben; **dark chocolate** N Zartbitterschokolade *f*; **dark-complexioned** [,dɑːkəm'plekʃənd] **ADJ** mit dunklem Teint; **Dark Continent** N **the ~** der Schwarze Erdteil

darken ['dɑːkən] **VT** **a** (*lit*) dunkel machen; *sky* verdunkeln; (*before storm*) verfinstern; **to ~ one's hair/eyelashes** sich (*dat*) die Haare/Wimpern dunkel färben; **the sun ~ed her skin** die Sonne hat ihre Haut gebräunt **b** (*fig*) trüben; *future* trüben, verdüstern; **never ~ my door again!** lassen Sie sich hier nicht mehr blicken! **VI** **a** (*lit*) dunkel werden; (*sky*) sich verdunkeln; (*before storm*) sich verfinstern **b** (*fig, at-*

mosphere, mood) sich trüben, sich verdüstern; (*face, eyes*) sich verfinstern

dark: dark-eyed ADJ dunkeläugig; **dark glasses** PL Sonnenbrille *f*; (*of blind person*) dunkle Brille; **dark horse** N (*fig*) stilles Wasser; (= *unexpected winner*) unbekannte Größe

darkie, **darky** ['dɑːkɪ] N (*pej inf*) Schwarze(r) *mf*

darkish ['dɑːkɪʃ] ADJ *colour, complexion* ziemlich dunkel; **the car was a ~ colour/~ green** der Wagen hatte eine dunkle/dunkelgrüne Farbe

darkly ['dɑːklɪ] ADV (+*vb*) düster, finster; (+*adj*) auf finstere Weise; **to mutter/hint ~** dunkle Bemerkungen/Andeutungen machen; **a ~ comic novel** ein finster-komischer Roman

dark matter N (*Astron*) dunkle Materie, Dunkelmaterie *f*

darkness ['dɑːknɪs] N **a** (*lit*) Dunkelheit *f*; (*of night*) Finsternis *f*, Dunkelheit *f*; **in total ~** in totaler *or* völliger Dunkelheit, in tiefem Dunkel (*geh*); **the house was in ~** das Haus lag im Dunkeln **b** (*fig,* = *sinisterness*) Finsterkeit *f* **c** (*fig,* = *gloominess, sadness*) Düsterkeit *f*

dark: darkroom N (*Phot*) Dunkelkammer *f*; **dark-skinned** ADJ dunkelhäutig

darky N (*pej inf*) = **darkie**

darling ['dɑːlɪŋ] **N a** Schatz *m*; (*esp child*) Schätzchen *nt*; **he is mother's ~/the ~ of the crowds** er ist Mamas Liebling/der Publikumsliebling; **she's a little ~** sie ist ein süßer kleiner Schatz; **that cat is a little ~** diese Katze ist ein liebes kleines Tierchen; **be a ~ and ...** sei so lieb *or* nett und ..., sei ein Schatz und ... **b** (*form of address*) Liebling *m*, Schatz *m*, Schätzchen *nt* **ADJ** *cat, dress etc* süß, goldig; *wife etc* lieb; *house* reizend

darn¹ [dɑːn] (*Sew*) **N** gestopfte Stelle **VT** stopfen

darn² (*also* **darned**) (*inf*) **ADJ** *cheek, nerve* verdammt (*inf*); **a ~ sight better/worse** ein ganzes Ende besser/schlechter (*inf*) **ADV** verdammt (*inf*), verflixt (*inf*); **he'd better make ~ sure** er sollte verdammt noch mal dafür sorgen (*inf*); **pretty ~ quick** verdammt schnell (*inf*); **you're ~ right** du hast völlig Recht; **you know ~ well what I mean** du weißt verdammt genau, was ich meine (*inf*); **we'll do just as we ~ well please** wir machen genau das, was wir wollen; **~ near impossible** so gut wie unmöglich **VT** **~ it!** verflixt noch mal! (*inf*); **~ him!** zum Kuckuck mit ihm! **N** **I don't give a ~** das ist mir völlig schnurz (*inf*)

darned [dɑːnd] ADJ, ADV (*inf*) = **darn² ADJ, ADV**

darner ['dɑːnə] N **a** (= *needle*) Stopfnadel *f* **b** (= *darning egg*) Stopfei *nt*; (= *darning mushroom*) Stopfpilz *m*

darning ['dɑːnɪŋ] N Stopfen *nt*; (= *things to be darned*) Flick- *or* Stopfsachen *pl*, Flickarbeit *f*; **I've a lot of ~ to do** ich habe viel zu stopfen

darning mushroom N Stopfpilz *m*

darning needle N Stopfnadel *f*

dart [dɑːt] **N a** (*movement*) Satz *m*; **the fish made a ~ for the shelter of the weeds** der Fisch schnellte ins schützende Seegras; **with a ~ of its tongue the chameleon caught its prey** die Zunge schnellte heraus, und das Chamäleon hatte seine Beute gefangen; **he felt a ~ of pain when he thought of her** ein plötzlicher Schmerz durchzuckte ihn, als er an sie dachte **b** (= *weapon*) Pfeil *m*; (*fig: of sarcasm etc*) Spitze *f*; (*Sport*) (Wurf)pfeil *m* **c** (*liter, of serpent*) (Gift)zahn *m*; (*of bee*) Stachel *m* **d** (*Sew*) Abnäher *m* **VI** flitzen; (*fish*) schnellen; **to ~ out** (*person*) hinausflitzen; (*fish, tongue*) herausschnellen; **to ~ in** (*person*) hereinstürzen; (*into water: otter etc*) hineinstürzen; **he ~ed behind a bush** er ~de hinter einen Busch; **he ~ed off** *or* **away** er flitzte davon; **her eyes ~ed round the room** ihre Blicke schossen blitzschnell im Zim-

mer hin und her; **her thoughts were ~ing about** ihre Gedanken schwirrten umher **VT** *look* werfen; **to ~ a glance at sb** jdm einen Blick zuwerfen; **to ~ a glance at sth** einen Blick auf etw (*acc*) werfen; **the snake ~ed its tongue out** die Schlange ließ ihre Zunge hervorschnellen

dart board N Dartscheibe *f*

darting ['dɑːtɪŋ] ADJ blitzschnell

darts [dɑːts] **N** *sing* Darts *nt*, Pfeilwurfspiel *nt*; **a game of ~** ein Dartspiel *nt*

Darwinian [dɑː'wɪnɪən] **N** Darwinist(in) *m(f)* **ADJ** darwinistisch

Darwinism ['dɑːwɪnɪzəm] N Darwinismus *m*

dash [dæʃ] **N a** (= *sudden rush*) Jagd *f*; **he made a ~ for the door/across the road** er stürzte auf die Tür zu/über die Straße; **she made a ~ for it** sie rannte, so schnell sie konnte; **to make a ~ for freedom** versuchen, in die Freiheit zu entkommen; **his ~ for freedom was unsuccessful** sein Versuch, in die Freiheit zu entkommen, war vergeblich; **it was a mad ~ to the hospital** wir/sie *etc* eilten Hals über Kopf zum Krankenhaus

b (= *hurry*) Hetze *f*

c (= *style, vigour*) Schwung *m*, Elan *m*; **to cut a ~** eine schneidige Figur machen

d (= *small amount*) **a ~ of** etwas, ein bisschen; (*of vinegar, spirits*) etwas, ein Schuss *m*; (*of seasoning etc*) etwas, eine Prise; (*of lemon*) ein Spritzer *m*; **a ~ of colour** (*Brit*) *or* **color** (*US*) ein Farbtupfer *m*; **a ~ of mystery** etwas Geheimnisvolles

e (*Typ*) Gedankenstrich *m*

f (*in morse*) Strich *m*

g (*Aut*) Armaturenbrett *nt*

VT **a** (= *throw violently*) schleudern; **to ~ sth to pieces** etw in tausend Stücke zerschlagen; **he ~ed his head on the floor when he fell** er schlug beim Hinfallen mit dem Kopf auf dem Boden auf; **the ship was ~ed against the rocks** das Schiff wurde gegen die Klippen geschleudert

b (= *discourage*) *sb's hopes* zunichte machen; **that ~ed his spirits** das hat ihn völlig geknickt

c (*inf*) = **darn² VT**

VI **a** (= *rush*) sausen (*inf*); **to ~ into/across a room** in ein Zimmer/quer durch ein Zimmer stürzen *or* stürmen; **to ~ away/back/up** fort-/zurück-/hinaufstürzen

b (= *knock, be hurled*) schlagen; (*waves*) peitschen

INTERJ **~ (it)!** (*inf*) verflixt! (*inf*), (verflixter) Mist! (*inf*)

▶ **dash off** **VI** losstürzen; **sorry to have to dash off like this** es tut mir Leid, dass ich so forthetzen muss **VT** *sep letter, essay* hinwerfen; *drawing also* mit ein paar Strichen hinwerfen

dashboard ['dæʃbɔːd] N Armaturenbrett *nt*

dashed [dæʃt] ADJ, ADV = **darn² ADV, VT**

dashing ['dæʃɪŋ] (*dated*) ADJ **a** (= *showy, stylish*) *person* schneidig, flott; *moustache, clothes* schneidig; **to cut a ~ figure** flott *or* schneidig aussehen **b** (= *spirited*) *person* temperamentvoll; (= *dynamic*) dynamisch; *action* unerschrocken; **a ~ young officer** ein zackiger junger Offizier

dashpot ['dæʃpɒt] N (*Tech*) Pralltopf *m*

dastardly ['dæstədlɪ] ADJ niederträchtig, gemein

DAT N *abbr of* **digital audio tape** DAT *nt*; **~ cassette** DAT-Kassette *f*

data ['deɪtə] *pl of* **datum** *usu with sing vb* Daten *pl*; **the actual ~ is quite surprising** die eigentlichen Daten sind recht erstaunlich; **a piece of ~** eine Angabe; (*Math*) ein (Zahlen)wert *m*; **we have a significant amount of ~ on ...** wir haben einen beträchtlichen Datenbestand über ... (+*acc*)

data: data bank N Datenbank *f*; **database** N Datenbank *f*; **we have a large ~ of ...** wir haben große Datenbestände an ... (*dat*); **~ manager** Datenbankmanager(in) *m(f)*; **data block** N Datenblock *m*; **data buffer** N Datenpuffer *m*; **data capture** N Datenerfassung *f*; **data carrier** N Datenträger *m*; **data collection** N Datenerfassung *f*; **data file** N Datei *f*; **data-handling system** N Datenerfassungssystem *nt*; **data input** N Dateneingabe *f*; **data network** N Datennetz *nt*; **data pen** N (*Comput*) Lichtgriffel *m*; **data processing** N Datenverarbeitung *f*; **data protection** N Datenschutz *m*; **data protection act** N Datenschutzgesetz *m*; **data retrieval** N Datenabruf *m*; **data switch** N Datenschalter *m*; **data switching** N Datenvermittlung *f*; **data transfer** N Datentransfer *m*; **data transmission** N Datenübertragung *f*

date¹ [deɪt] N (= *fruit*) Dattel *f*; (= *tree*) Dattelpalme *f*

date² N **a** (= *time of event*) Datum *nt*; (= *historical date*) Geschichts- *or* Jahreszahl *f*; (*for appointment*) Termin *m*; ~ **of birth** Geburtsdatum *nt*; **what's the ~ today?** der Wievielte ist heute?, welches Datum haben wir heute?; **what ~ is Easter this year?** auf welches Datum fällt Ostern dieses Jahr?; **what is the ~ of that letter?** von wann ist der Brief datiert?; **to fix** *or* **set a ~ (for sth)** einen Termin (für etw) festsetzen; **to ~** bis heute, bis dato (*form, dated*); **the band's UK tour ~s are: …** die Band tritt an den folgenden Daten in Großbritannien auf: … **b** (*on coins, medals etc*) Jahreszahl *f* **c** (= *appointment*) Verabredung *f*; (*with girlfriend etc*) Rendezvous *nt*; **who's his ~?** mit wem trifft er sich?; **his ~ didn't show up** diejenige, mit der er ausgehen wollte, hat ihn versetzt (*inf*); **to make a ~ with sb** sich mit jdm verabreden; **she's out on a ~** sie hat eine Verabredung *or* ein Rendezvous; **I've got a lunch ~ today** (*with friend*) ich habe mich heute zum Mittagessen verabredet; (*on business*) ich muss heute Mittag an einem Arbeitsessen teilnehmen

VT a (= *put date on*) mit dem Datum versehen; *letter etc also* datieren; **a letter ~d the seventh of August** ein vom siebten August datierter Brief; **a coin ~d 1390** eine Münze von 1390 **b** (= *establish age of*) *work of art etc* datieren; **that hat really ~s you** an dem Hut sieht man, wie alt Sie sind **c** (= *take out*) *girlfriend etc* ausgehen mit; (*regularly*) gehen mit (*inf*)

VI a to ~ back to zurückdatieren auf (+*acc*); **to ~ from** zurückgehen auf (+*acc*); (*antique etc*) stammen aus **b** (= *become old-fashioned*) veralten **c** (= *have boyfriend etc*) einen Freund/eine Freundin haben; (*couple*) miteinander gehen; **he didn't ~ much when he was at school** in seiner Schulzeit ging er nur selten mit Mädchen aus

dated [ˈdeɪtɪd] ADJ altmodisch; *clothes, manners also* überholt

date: dateless ADJ **a** *manuscript* undatiert, ohne Jahreszahl **b** (= *never old-fashioned*) zeitlos; **date line** N (*Geog*) Datumsgrenze *f*; (*Typ*) Datumszeile *f*; **date palm** N Dattelpalme *f*; **date rape** N *Vergewaltigung nach einem Rendezvous*; **date-rape drug** N Date-Rape-Droge *f*, Vergewaltigungsdroge *f*; **date sugar** N Palmzucker *m*; **date stamp** N Datumsstempel *m* **VT** mit Datumsstempel versehen

dating bar N (*US*) *Lokal, in dem sich Singles treffen*

dative [ˈdeɪtɪv] N Dativ *m*; **in the ~** im Dativ **ADJ** Dativ-, dativisch; **~ object** Dativobjekt *nt*; **the ~ case** der Dativ

datum [ˈdeɪtəm] N *pl* **data** (*rare*) Faktum *nt*, Datum *nt*

daub [dɔːb] **VT** *walls, canvas, face* beschmieren; *paint, slogans, make-up* schmieren; (= *coat with grease etc*) *axle* einschmieren; (= *coat with mud, clay*) *walls* bewerfen; (= *spread on*) *grease, mud, clay* streichen **N a** (*Build*) Bewurf *m* **b** (*pej, = bad picture*) Kleckserei *f*

dauber [ˈdɔːbə] N (*pej*) Kleckser(in) *m(f)*

daughter [ˈdɔːtə] N (*lit, fig*) Tochter *f*

daughterboard [ˈdɔːtəˌbɔːd] N (*Comput*) Zusatzplatine *f*

daughter-in-law [ˈdɔːtərɪnlɔː] N *pl* **daughters-in-law** Schwiegertochter *f*

daunt [dɔːnt] VT entmutigen; **to be ~ed by sth** sich von etw entmutigen lassen; **nothing ~ed** unverzagt

daunting [ˈdɔːntɪŋ] ADJ entmutigend

dauntless [ˈdɔːntlɪs] ADJ unerschrocken, beherzt; *courage* unbezähmbar

davenport [ˈdævnpɔːt] N **a** (*esp US, = sofa*) Sofa *nt*, Couch *f* **b** (*Brit, = desk*) Sekretär *m*

David [ˈdeɪvɪd] N David *m*

davit [ˈdævɪt] N (*Naut*) Davit *m or nt*

Davy [ˈdeɪvɪ] N *dim of* **David**

Davy Jones' locker [ˈdeɪvɪˌdʒəʊnzɪzˈlɒkə] N der Meeresgrund

Davy lamp N (Gruben)sicherheitslampe *f*

dawdle [ˈdɔːdl] VI (= *be too slow*) trödeln; (= *stroll*) bummeln; **to ~ on the way** unterwegs trödeln; **to ~ over one's work** bei der Arbeit bummeln *or* trödeln

▶ **dawdle along** VI dahinbummeln; (+*prep obj*) entlangbummeln

▶ **dawdle away** VT *sep time* vertrödeln

dawdler [ˈdɔːdlə] N Trödler(in) *m(f)*; (*as regards work also*) Bummelant(in) *m(f)* (*inf*)

dawdling [ˈdɔːdlɪŋ] ADJ **we were stuck behind a ~ lorry** wir saßen hinter einem Lastwagen fest, der im Bummeltempo fuhr

dawn [dɔːn] N **a** (*lit, fig*) (Morgen)dämmerung *f*, Morgenröte *f* (*liter*); (*no art: time of day*) Tagesanbruch *m*, Morgengrauen *nt*; **at ~** bei Tagesanbruch, im Morgengrauen; **it's almost ~** es ist fast Morgen, es dämmert schon bald; **from ~ to dusk** von morgens bis abends

VI a day was already ~ing es dämmerte schon; **the day ~ed rainy** der Tag fing mit Regen an; **the day will ~ when …** (*fig*) der Tag wird kommen, wo … **b** (*fig, new age etc*) dämmern, anbrechen; (*hope*) erwachen **c** (*inf*) **to ~ (up)on sb** jdm dämmern, jdm zum Bewusstsein kommen; **it ~ed on him that …** es wurde ihm langsam klar, dass …, es dämmerte ihm, dass …

dawn: dawn chorus N Morgenkonzert *nt* der Vögel; **dawn patrol** N (*Aviat*) Morgenpatrouille *f*; **dawn raid** N **a** (*by police*) Razzia *f* (*in den frühen Morgenstunden*); (*Mil*) Überraschungsangriff *m* **b** (*Fin*) plötzlicher Aufkauf von Aktien

day [deɪ] N **a** Tag *m*; **he's coming in three ~s' time** *or* **in three ~s** er kommt in drei Tagen; **it will arrive any ~ now** es muss jeden Tag kommen; **what ~ is it today?** welcher Tag ist heute?, was haben wir heute?; **what ~ of the month is it?** der Wievielte ist heute?; **twice a ~** zweimal täglich *or* am Tag; **the ~ before yesterday** vorgestern; **the ~ after/before, the following/previous ~** am Tag danach/zuvor, am (darauf) folgenden/vorhergehenden Tag; **the ~ after tomorrow** übermorgen; **this ~ week** (*Brit inf*) heute in acht Tagen (*inf*); **from that ~ on (-wards)** von dem Tag an; **from this ~ forth** (*old*) von diesem Tage an; **two years ago to the ~** auf den Tag genau vor zwei Jahren; **one ~** eines Tages; **one ~ we went swimming, and the next …** einen Tag gingen wir schwimmen, und den nächsten …; **one of these ~s** irgendwann (einmal), eines Tages; **~ in, ~ out** tagein, tagaus; **they went to London for the ~** sie machten einen Tagesausflug nach London; **for ~s on end** tagelang; **~ after ~** Tag für Tag, tagtäglich; **~ by ~** jeden Tag, täglich; **the other ~** neulich; **at the end of the ~** (*fig*) letzten Endes; **to live from ~ to ~** von einem Tag auf den andern leben; **all of ~s** ausgerechnet heute; **some ~ soon** demnächst; **I remember it to this ~** daran erinnere ich mich noch heute; **he's fifty if he's a ~** (*esp Brit*) er ist mindestens *or* wenigstens fünfzig; **all ~** den ganzen Tag; **to travel during the ~** *or* **by ~** tagsüber *or* während des Tages reisen; **at that time of ~** zu der Tageszeit; **to work ~ and night** Tag und Nacht arbeiten;

good ~! guten Tag!; (= *goodbye*) auf Wiedersehen!; **(the) ~ is done** (*liter*) der Tag ist vorüber; **to be paid by the ~** tageweise bezahlt werden; **let's call it a ~** machen wir Schluss; **some time during the ~** irgendwann im Laufe des Tages; **to have a nice ~** einen schönen Tag verbringen; **to have a lazy ~** einen Tag faulenzen; **have a nice ~!** viel Spaß!; (*esp US, said by storekeeper etc*) schönen Tag noch!; **did you have a nice ~?** wars schön?; **did you have a good ~ at the office?** wie wars im Büro?; **to have a good/bad ~** einen guten/schlechten Tag haben; **what a ~!** (*terrible*) so ein fürchterlicher Tag!; (*lovely*) so ein herrlicher Tag!; **on a wet/dry ~** an einem regnerischen/trockenen Tag; **to work an eight-hour ~** einen Achtstundentag haben, acht Stunden am Tag arbeiten; **it's all in the** *or* **a ~'s work!** das ist (doch) selbstverständlich; **that'll be the ~** das möcht ich sehen *or* erleben → **make 1 g**

b (*period of time: often pl*) **these ~s** heute, heutzutage; **what are you doing these ~s?** was machst *or* treibst du denn so?; **in this ~ and age** heutzutage; **the taking point of the ~** das Tagesgespräch; **in ~s to come** künftig, in künftigen Zeiten *or* Tagen (*geh*); **from his young ~s** von Kindesbeinen *or* frühester Jugend an; **in his younger ~s** als er noch jünger war; **in Queen Victoria's ~, in the ~s of Queen Victoria** zu Königin Viktorias Zeiten; **the happiest ~s of my life** die glücklichste Zeit meines Lebens; **those were the ~s** das waren noch Zeiten; **in the old ~s** früher; **in the good old ~s** in der guten alten Zeit; **it's early ~s yet** es ist noch zu früh; **during the early ~s of the war** in den ersten Kriegstagen; **he/this material has seen better ~s** er/dieser Stoff hat (auch) schon bessere Zeiten *or* Tage gesehen; **to end one's ~s in misery** im Elend sterben **c** (*with poss adj: = lifetime, best time*) **famous in her ~** in ihrer Zeit berühmt; **it has had its ~** das hat seine Glanzzeit überschritten; **his ~ will come** sein Tag wird kommen; **everything has its ~** für alles kommt einmal die richtige Zeit **d** *no pl* (= *contest, battle*) **to win** *or* **carry the ~** den Sieg bringen; **to lose/save the ~** den Kampf verlieren/retten

day: day bed N Ruhebett *nt*; **day boarder** N (*Brit, Sch*) Externe(r) *mf*; **daybook** N (*Comm*) Journal *nt*, Tagebuch *nt*; **day boy** N (*Sch*) Externe(r) *m*; **daybreak** N Tagesanbruch *m*; **at ~** bei Tagesanbruch; **daycare** N **to be in ~** (*child*) in einer Tagesstätte untergebracht sein; (*old person*) in einer Altentagesstätte untergebracht sein; **day(care) centre**, (*US*) **day(care) center** N (*for children*) Tagesstätte *f*; (*for old people*) Altentagesstätte *f*; **day coach** N (*US*) (Eisenbahn)personenwagen *m*; **daydream** N Tagtraum *m*, Träumerei *f* **VI** (mit offenen Augen) träumen; **day excursion** N Tagesausflug *m*; **dayfly** N Eintagsfliege *f*; **day girl** N (*Sch*) Externe *f*; **day hospital** N Tagesklinik *f*; **day job** N Hauptberuf *m*; **don't give up the ~** (*hum*) häng deinen Beruf nicht gleich an den Nagel (*inf*); **day labourer**, (*US*) **day laborer** N Tagelöhner(in) *m(f)*

daylight [ˈdeɪlaɪt] N **a** (= *daybreak*) Tagesanbruch *m* **b** Tageslicht *nt*; **it is still ~** es ist noch hell; **it was broad ~** es war heller *or* helllichter Tag; **in broad ~** am hellen *or* helllichten Tage; **I'd like to get there in ~** ich möchte gern bei Tag ankommen; **to beat the living ~s out of sb** (*inf*) jdn windelweich schlagen (*inf*); **to scare the living ~s out of sb** (*inf*) jdm einen fürchterlichen Schreck einjagen (*inf*)

daylight: daylight robbery N (*Brit inf*) Halsabschneiderei *f* (*inf*), offener Diebstahl; **daylight saving time** N (*esp US*) Sommerzeit *f*

day: daylong ADJ den ganzen Tag dauernd; **day nurse** N Tagesschwester *f*; **day nursery** N Kindertagesstätte *f*; (*in private house*) Kinderzimmer *nt*; **day-old** ADJ *baby* einen Tag alt; *strike, ceasefire* seit einem Tag andauernd; *food, newspaper* vom Vortag; **day pupil** N (*Sch*) Externe(r) *mf*; **dayrate** N Tagessatz *m*; **day release** N (*Brit*) *tageweise Freistellung von An-*

gestellten zur Weiterbildung; **day release course** N (*Brit*) Tageskurs *m* für Berufstätige; **day return (ticket)** N (*Brit, Rail*) Tagesrückfahrkarte *f*

days [deɪz] ADV (*esp US*) tagsüber

day: day school N Tagesschule *f*; **day shift** N Tagschicht *f*; **to be on** *or* **work ~** Tagschicht arbeiten; **day ticket** N (*Brit, Rail*) Tagesrückfahrkarte *f*

daytime ['deɪtaɪm] **N** Tag *m*; **in the ~** bei Tage, tagsüber, während des Tages **ATTR** am Tage; *raid* am hellen *or* hellichten Tage; **what's your ~ phone number?** unter welcher Nummer sind Sie tagsüber erreichbar?; **~ course** Tageskurs *m*; **~ job** Tagesjob *m*; **~ television** Fernsehen *nt* während des Tages, Vor- und Nachmittagsprogramm *nt*

daytimes ['deɪtaɪmz] ADV (*US*) am Tag, bei Tag

day: day-to-day ADJ täglich; *occurrence* alltäglich; **on a ~ basis** tageweise; **day trader** N (*St Ex*) Tagesspekulant(in) *m(f)*, Daytrader(in) *m(f)*; **day trading** N (*St Ex*) Tagesspekulation *f*, Daytrading *nt*; **day trip** N Tagesausflug *m*; **day-tripper** N Tagesausflügler(in) *m(f)*

daze [deɪz] N Benommenheit *f*; **in a ~** ganz benommen **VT** benommen machen

dazed [deɪzd] ADJ benommen

dazzle ['dæzl] VT (*lit, fig*) blenden

dazzler ['dæzlə'] N (*fig*) Blender(in) *m(f)*, Angeber(in) *m(f)*

dazzling ['dæzlɪŋ] ADJ (*lit*) blendend

dazzlingly ['dæzlɪŋlɪ] ADV (*lit, fig*) blendend; **~ beautiful** strahlend schön

dB *abbr of* **decibel** dB

DC a *abbr of* **direct current b** *abbr of* **District of Columbia**

DCC® N *abbr of* **digital compact cassette** DCC *f*

DCI N (*Brit, Police*) *abbr of* **Detective Chief Inspector**

DD *abbr of* **Doctor of Divinity** Dr. theol.

D/D *abbr of* **direct debit**

D-day ['diːdeɪ] N (*Hist, fig*) der Tag X

DDT *abbr of* **dichloro-diphenyl-trichloroethane** DDT *nt*

deacon ['diːkən] N Diakon *m*; (= *elder*) Kirchenälteste(r) *m*

deaconess ['diːkənes] N Diakonin *f*; (= *elder*) Kirchenälteste *f*

deaconry ['diːkənrɪ] N Diakonat *nt*

deactivate [diːˈæktɪveɪt] VT entschärfen

dead [ded] **ADJ a** tot; *plant* abgestorben, tot; **he has been ~ for two years** er ist seit zwei Jahren tot; **to drop (down)** *or* **fall down ~** tot umfallen; **to shoot sb ~** jdn erschießen *or* totschießen (*inf*); **over my ~ body** (*inf*) nur über meine Leiche (*inf*); **you're ~ meat (if you come back here)** (*inf*) du bist ein toter Mann(, wenn du noch mal hierhin zurückkommst) (*inf*) **b** (= *not sensitive*) *limbs* abgestorben, taub; **my hand's gone ~** ich habe kein Gefühl in meiner Hand; **to be ~ from the neck up** (*inf*) nur Stroh im Kopf haben (*inf*); **to be ~ to the world** tief und fest schlafen **c** (= *without activity etc*) *town, season* tot; *business* flau **d** (*Elec*) *cable* stromlos; (*Telec*) tot; **to go ~** ausfallen **e** (= *burned out*) *fire* aus *pred*; *match* abgebrannt **f** (*inf*: = *finished with*) (*Typ*) *copy* abgesetzt; **are these glasses/bottles ~?** können diese Gläser/Flaschen weg? **g** (*Sport*) *ball* tot **h** (= *obsolete*) *language etc* tot; *custom* ausgestorben; **to be ~ and buried, to be ~ in the water** tot und begraben sein **i** (= *absolute, exact*) total, völlig; **~ silence** Totenstille *f*; **~ calm** (*Naut*) absolute *or* totale Windstille; **~ centre** die genaue *or* exakte Mitte; **she was in a ~ faint** sie war völlig bewusstlos; **to come to a ~ stop** völlig zum Stillstand kommen; **he's the ~ spit of his father** (*sl*)

er ist seinem Vater wie aus dem Gesicht geschnitten → **cert, set**
j *colour* tot, stumpf, matt; *sound* dumpf
k (*Typ*) **~ key** unbelegte Taste *f*
l (*inf,* = *exhausted*) tot (*inf*), völlig kaputt (*inf*); **she looked half ~** sie sah völlig kaputt *or* fertig aus (*inf*); **I'm ~ on my feet** ich bin zum Umfallen kaputt (*inf*)
ADV a (= *exactly*) genau; **~ straight** schnurgerade; **to be ~ on time** auf die Minute pünktlich kommen; (*clock*) auf die Minute genau gehen; **their arrows were ~ on target** ihre Pfeile trafen genau ins Ziel **b** (*Brit inf:* = *very*) total (*inf*), völlig; **~ drunk** total betrunken, stockvoll (*inf*); **~ tired** totmüde; **you're ~ right** Sie haben völlig Recht; **he was ~ lucky** er hat Schwein gehabt (*inf*), er hat irrsinnig Glück gehabt; **~ slow** ganz langsam; "**dead slow**" „Schritt fahren"; **to be ~ certain about sth** (*inf*) bei etw todsicher sein; **he's ~ against it** er ist total dagegen **c to stop ~** abrupt stehen bleiben *or* (*talking*) innehalten
N a the ~ *pl* die Toten *pl* **b in the ~** *or* **at ~ of night** mitten in der Nacht; **in the ~ of winter** mitten im Winter

dead: dead account N (*Fin*) umsatzloses *or* unbewegtes Konto; **dead-and-alive** ADJ (*inf*) *party, place* tot, langweilig; **dead-ball line** N (*Rugby*) Feldauslinie *f*; **dead beat** (*Brit inf*) völlig kaputt (*inf*), total fertig (*inf*); **deadbeat N** (= *down-and-out*) Gammler(in) *m(f)*; (= *failure*) Versager(in) *m(f)* **~ dad** *Vater, der seiner Unterhaltspflicht nicht nachkommt*; **dead centre**, (*US*) **dead center** N genaue Mitte; **to hit sth ~** etw genau in die Mitte treffen; **dead duck to be a ~** passé sein; **politically he's/it's a ~** politisch ist er/es gestorben (*inf*)

deaden ['dedn] VT *shock* auffangen; *pain* mildern; *force, blow* abschwächen; *nerve, passions* abtöten; *sound, noise* dämpfen; *mind, feeling* abstumpfen

dead: dead end N Sackgasse *f*; **to come to a ~** (*lit, road*) in einer Sackgasse enden; (*driver*) an eine Sackgasse kommen; (*fig*) in eine Sackgasse geraten; **dead-end** ADJ *attr* **~ street** (*esp US*) Sackgasse *f*; **to be in ~ street** (*fig*) keine Chancen haben; **~ kids** Gassenkinder *pl*; **a ~ job** ein Job *m* ohne Aufstiegsmöglichkeiten; **dead hand** N **the ~ of bureaucracy/the state** die schwere Last der Bürokratie/des Staates; **dead heat** N totes Rennen; **dead leg** N (*inf*) taubes Bein; **dead letter** N (*lit*) unzustellbarer Brief; (*Jur*) toter Buchstabe; **deadline** N (letzter) Termin; **to fix** *or* **set a ~** eine Frist setzen; **to work to a ~** auf einen Termin hinarbeiten; **he was working to a six o'clock ~** um sechs Uhr musste er die Arbeit fertig haben; **can you meet the ~?** können Sie den Termin *or* die Frist einhalten?; **copy ~** (*Press*) Redaktionsschluss *m*

deadliness ['dedlɪnɪs] N (*of poison, weapon*) tödliche Wirkung; (*of wit, sarcasm*) vernichtende Wirkung; (*of... = boringness*) tödliche Langeweile; (= *awfulness*) Entsetzlichkeit *f*

deadlock ['dedlɒk] N **to reach (a) ~** in eine Sackgasse geraten; **to end in ~** sich festfahren; **to break the ~** aus der Sackgasse herauskommen

deadlocked ['dedlɒkt] ADJ *negotiations, talks* festgefahren

deadly ['dedlɪ] **ADJ** (+*er*) **a** (= *lethal*) *poison, weapon, disease, attack, force* tödlich; **to be ~ to sb** tödliche Folgen für jdn haben; **a ~ combination of ...** eine tödliche Mischung von ...; **assault with a ~ weapon** (*Jur*) Körperverletzung *f* mit einer gefährlichen Waffe; **to play a ~ game** ein tödliches Spiel spielen **b** (= *devastating*) *logic, look* vernichtend; (= *unerring*) *accuracy* tödlich; *bowler, striker* treffsicher **c** (*inf,* = *boring*) todlangweilig (*inf*) **d** (= *complete*) *silence, enemies, rivals* tödlich; **to be in ~ earnest** es todernst meinen; **their ~ en-**

emy ihr Todfeind *m*; **that made the competition even deadlier** dadurch wurde die Konkurrenz noch mörderischer; **the (seven) ~ sins** (*Bibl*) die (sieben) Todsünden *pl*
ADV (= *extremely*) **~ dull** todlangweilig (*inf*); **he was ~ serious** er meinte es todernst; **~ cold** eisig kalt; **~ pale** totenbleich; **~ poisonous** tödlich

deadly nightshade N Tollkirsche *f*

dead: dead man's handle N SIFA-Schalttaste *f*, Totmannkurbel *f*; **dead march** N Totenmarsch *m*; **dead men's shoes** N **to wait for ~** warten, bis eine Stelle frei wird

deadness ['dednɪs] N (*of limbs*) Taubheit *f*; (*of colour*) Langweiligkeit *f*; **nothing compares with the ~ of Blackpool in winter** nichts ist so öde wie Blackpool im Winter

dead: dead nettle N (*Bot*) Taubnessel *f*; **deadpan ADJ** *face* unbewegt; *style, humour* trocken; **with a ~ expression** mit unbeweglicher Miene **N** (= *face, expression*) unbewegliche Miene; **dead reckoning** N (*Naut*) Koppelung *f*; **Dead Sea** N Totes Meer; **~ scrolls** *pl* Schriftrollen *pl* vom Toten Meer; **dead weight** N (*Tech*) Eigengewicht *nt*, Totgewicht *nt*; **the box/she was a ~** die Kiste/sie war furchtbar schwer; **Dead White (European) Male** N (*esp US*) *abwertender Ausdruck für (das Kulturleben dominierende) Weiße (europäischer Abstammung)*; **deadwood** N (*lit*) morsches Holz; (*Naut*) Totholz *nt*; (*fig*) Ballast *m*; **to get rid of the ~** (*people*) die Nieten loswerden (*inf*)

deaf [def] **ADJ** (+*er*) (*lit, fig*) taub; **as ~ as a (door)post** stocktaub; **he was ~ to her pleas** er blieb gegen alle ihre Bitten taub, er verschloss sich ihren Bitten; **to turn a ~ ear to sb/sth** sich jdm/einer Sache (*dat*) gegenüber taub stellen; **our pleas fell on ~ ears** unsere Bitten fanden kein Gehör **N the ~** *pl* die Tauben *pl*

deaf: deaf aid N Hörgerät *nt*; **deaf-and-dumb** ADJ taubstumm; **~ language** Taubstummensprache *f*

deafen ['defn] VT (*lit*) taub machen; (*fig*) betäuben

deafening ['defnɪŋ] ADJ *noise* ohrenbetäubend; *row* lautstark; **a ~ silence** ein eisiges Schweigen

deaf-mute ['def'mjuːt] N Taubstumme(r) *mf*

deafness ['defnɪs] N (*lit, fig*) Taubheit *f* (*to* gegenüber)

deal¹ [diːl] ◊ 26.1 **N** (= *amount*) Menge *f*; **a good** *or* **great ~ of** eine Menge, (ziemlich) viel; **not a great ~ of** nicht (besonders) viel; **there's still a (good** *or* **great) ~ of work left to do** es ist noch ein schönes Stück *or* eine Menge Arbeit zu tun; **there's a good** *or* **great ~ of truth in what he says** es ist schon ziemlich viel Wahres an dem, was er sagt; **it says a good ~ for him (that ...)** es spricht sehr für ihn(, dass ...); **and that's saying a great ~** und damit ist schon viel gesagt; **to mean a great ~ to sb** jdm viel bedeuten
ADV a good *or* **great ~** viel; **not a great ~** nicht viel; **to learn/travel/talk a great ~** viel lernen/reisen/reden; **did you swim much? – not a great ~** seid ihr viel geschwommen? – nicht besonders viel; **a good ~ more important** viel wichtiger

deal² *vb: pret, ptp* **dealt N a** (*also* **business deal**) Geschäft *nt*, Handel *m*; (= *arrangement*) Handel *m*, Abkommen *nt*, Deal *m* (*inf*); **to do** *or* **make a ~ with sb** mit jdm ein Geschäft *or* einen Deal (*inf*) machen, mit jdm ein Geschäft abschließen; **it's a ~** abgemacht!; **it's a done ~** (*US*) es ist beschlossene Sache; **I'll make** *or* **do a ~ with you** ich schlage Ihnen ein Geschäft vor; **I never make ~s** ich lasse mich nie auf Geschäfte ein; **are you forgetting our ~?** hast du unsere Abmachung vergessen?; **he got a bad ~ on that car** mit dem Auto hat er ein schlechtes Geschäft gemacht → **big**
b (*inf*) **to give sb a fair ~** jdn anständig behandeln; **the workers have always had a bad ~** die Arbeiter sind immer schlecht behandelt worden; **a better ~ for the lower paid** bessere Be-

dingungen für die schlechter bezahlten Arbeiter; **the management offered us a new ~** die Firmenleitung hat uns ein neues Angebot gemacht

c (*Cards*) **it's your ~** Sie geben **VT a** (*also* **deal out**) *cards* geben, austeilen **b** *drugs* dealen (*inf*)

c → **blow**[1]

VI a (*Cards*) geben, austeilen **b** (*in drugs*) dealen (*inf*)

▶ **deal in VI** +*prep obj* (*Comm*) *goods, stolen property, pornography* handeln mit; **this is an organization dealing in terror** diese Organisation hat sich dem Terror verschrieben; **we deal only in facts** wir beschränken uns auf die Tatsachen **VT** *sep* (*Cards*) *player* Karten geben (+*dat*)

▶ **deal out VT** *sep* verteilen (*to* an +*acc*); *cards* (aus)geben (*to* +*dat*); **to deal out punishment** Strafen verhängen; **to deal out criticism** Kritik üben

▶ **deal with** ✪ 26.3 **VI** +*prep obj* **a** (= *do business with*) verhandeln mit

b (= *manage, handle*) sich kümmern um; *job* sich befassen mit; *emotions* umgehen mit; (*successfully*) fertig werden mit; (*Comm*) *orders* erledigen; (= *be responsible for*) zuständig sein für; **let's deal with the adjectives first** behandeln wir zuerst die Adjektive; **to know how to deal with sb** wissen, wie man mit jdm fertig wird *or* mit jdm umgeht; **you bad boy, I'll deal with you later** (*inf*) dich knöpf *or* nehm ich mir später vor, du Lausebengel! (*inf*); **the problem has been successfully dealt with** man ist gut mit dem Problem fertiggeworden; **if we don't deal with the problem soon** wenn wir uns nicht bald mit dem Problem befassen; **to deal with a case** (*judge*) einen Fall verhandeln; (*lawyer*) sich mit einem Fall befassen

c (= *be concerned with, book, film etc*) handeln von; (*author*) sich beschäftigen *or* befassen mit

deal³ N (= *wood*) Kiefern- *or* Tannenholz *nt* **ADJ** *attr* aus Kiefern- *or* Tannenholz

dealer ['di:lə'] **N a** (*Comm*) Händler(in) *m(f)*; (= *wholesaler*) Großhändler(in) *m(f)*; **a ~ in furs** ein Pelzhändler **b** (*in drugs*) Dealer(in) *m(f)* (*inf*) **c** (*Cards*) Kartengeber *m*

dealing ['di:lɪŋ] **N a** (= *trading*) Handel *m*; (*on stock exchange*) Handel *m*, Transaktionen *pl*; (*in drugs*) Dealen *nt*; **he is involved in drug ~** er ist in den Drogenhandel verwickelt **b** (*of cards*) Geben, Aus- *or* Verteilen *nt* **c dealings** PL (*Comm*) Geschäfte *pl*; (*generally*) Umgang *m*; **to have ~s with sb** mit jdm zu tun haben; (*Comm also*) Geschäftsbeziehungen zu jdm haben; **he had secret ~s with the Mafia** er stand heimlich mit der Mafia in Verbindung

dealing room N (*Fin*) Geschäftsraum *m* für Devisengeschäfte

dealt [delt] *pret, ptp of* **deal²**

dean [di:n] **N** (*Eccl, Univ*) Dekan(in) *m(f)*

deanery ['di:nərɪ] **N a** Dekanat *nt* **b** (*Eccl, = house*) Dekanei *f*

deanship ['di:nʃɪp] **N** (*Eccl, Univ*) Dekanat *nt*

dear [dɪə'] **ADJ** (+*er*) **a** (= *loved*) lieb, teuer (*liter*); **I hold him/it ~** er/es ist mir lieb und teuer; **she is a ~ friend of mine** sie ist eine sehr gute Freundin von mir; **it is ~ to my heart** es liegt mir sehr am Herzen; **that is my ~est wish** das ist mein sehnlichster *or* innigster Wunsch; **my ~ fellow** mein lieber Freund; **you are very ~ to me** du bist mir lieb und teuer; **these memories are very ~ to him** diese Erinnerungen sind ihm teuer

b (= *lovable, sweet*) *child* lieb, süß, reizend; *thing* süß, entzückend, reizend; **what a ~ little dress/baby/kitten** was für ein süßes *or* entzückendes Kleidchen/Kind/Kätzchen

c (*in letter-writing etc*) **~ Daddy/John** lieber Vati/John!; **~ Sir** sehr geehrter Herr X!; **~ Madam** sehr geehrte Frau X!; **~ Sir or Madam** sehr geehrte Damen und Herren!; **~ Mr Kemp** sehr geehrter Herr Kemp!; (*less formal*) lieber Herr Kemp!; **Dear John letter** (*esp US, inf*) Abschiedsbrief *m*

d (= *expensive*) *goods, shop* teuer; *prices* hoch; **to get ~er** (*goods*) teurer werden

INTERJ **~ ~!, ~ me!** (ach) du liebe Zeit!, (du) meine Güte!; **oh ~!** oje!, ach du meine Güte *or* du liebe Zeit!

N **hello/thank you ~** hallo/vielen Dank; **Robert ~** (mein lieber) Robert; **yes, ~** (*husband to wife etc*) ja, Schätzchen *or* Liebling; **Edward, my ~** mein lieber Edward; **my ~est** mein Teuerster (*geh*), mein Teuerster (*geh*), (meine) Liebste, (mein) Liebster; **are you being served, ~?** (*inf*) werden Sie schon bedient?; **give it to me, there's a ~** (*Brit inf*) gib es mir, sei (doch) so lieb *or* gut; **be a ~** (*inf*) sei so lieb *or* gut; **poor ~** die Arme, der Arme; **your mother is a ~** (*inf*) deine Mutter ist ein Engel (*inf*) *or* richtig lieb; **her little boy is such a ~** ihr kleiner Junge ist so ein süßer Knopf (*inf*); **this old ~ came up to me** (*Brit*) dieses Muttchen kam zu mir her (*inf*)

ADV (*lit, fig*) *buy, pay, sell* teuer; **this will cost them ~** das wird sie teuer zu stehen kommen

dearie, deary ['dɪərɪ] **N** (*inf*) *usu not translated* (*woman to child*) Kleine(r, s); **thanks for your help, ~** (*to child*) vielen Dank für deine Hilfe, mein Kind

dearly ['dɪəlɪ] **ADV a** (= *greatly*) *love* von ganzem Herzen; *hope* sehr; **~ beloved** (*form, Eccl*) geliebt; (*addressing congregation*) liebe Gemeinde, liebe Brüder und Schwestern; **I would ~ love to marry** ich würde liebend gern heiraten; **I ~ wish I had more money** ich wünschte, ich hätte mehr Geld; **I should ~ love** *or* **like to live here** ich würde für mein Leben gern hier wohnen **b** (*fig*) **he paid ~ (for it)** er hat es teuer bezahlt; **~ bought** teuer erkauft; **to cost sb ~** jdn teuer zu stehen kommen

dearness ['dɪənɪs] **N a** (= *expensiveness*) hoher Preis **b** (= *being loved*) **her ~ to him** dass sie ihm lieb und teuer war

dearth [dɜ:θ] **N** Mangel *m* (*of* an +*dat*); **~ of ideas** Gedankenarmut *f*; **there is no ~ of young men** an jungen Männern ist *or* herrscht kein Mangel

deary N = **dearie**

death [deθ] ✪ 24.4 **N** Tod *m*; (*of plans, hopes etc*) Ende *nt*; **~ by drowning/hanging** Tod durch Ertrinken/Erhängen; **~ to all traitors!** Tod allen Verrätern!; **~ as in life** im Tod wie im Leben; **to be afraid of ~** sich vor dem Tod fürchten; **to be burned to ~** verbrennen; (*at stake*) verbrannt werden; **to starve to ~** verhungern; **to bleed to ~** verbluten; **to freeze to ~** erfrieren; **how many ~s were there?** wie viele Tote *or* Todesfälle gab es?; **to die a hero's ~** den Heldentod sterben; **she died a horrible ~** sie starb einen schrecklichen Tod; **a fight to the ~** ein Kampf auf Leben und Tod; **to put sb to ~** jdn hinrichten; **to do sb to ~** (*old*) jdn umbringen; **this type of novel has been done to ~** diese Art von Roman ist schon zu Tode geritten worden; **to drink oneself to ~** sich zu Tode trinken; **to work oneself to ~** sich totarbeiten; **he works his men to ~** er schindet seine Leute zu Tode; **to be at ~'s door** an der Schwelle des Todes stehen; **it will be the ~ of you** (*inf*) das wird den Tod sein; **he will be the ~ of me** (*inf, = he's so funny*) ich lach mich noch einmal tot über ihn (*inf*); (= *he's annoying*) er bringt mich noch ins Grab; **to catch one's ~ (of cold)** (*inf*) sich (*dat*) den Tod holen; **I am sick to ~ of all this** (*inf*) das alles hängt mir gründlich zum Halse raus, ich bin das alles gründlich satt *or* leid; **he looked like ~ warmed up** (*Brit inf*) *or* **over** (*US inf*) er sah wie der Tod auf Urlaub aus (*inf*)

death: death agony N Todeskampf *m*; **deathbed N** Sterbebett *nt*; **to be on one's ~** auf dem Sterbebett liegen; **deathbed scene N** Szene *f* am Sterbebett; **death bell N** Totenglocke *f*; **death benefit N** (*Insur*) Versicherungsprämie *f* im Todesfall; **deathblow N** (*lit, fig*) Todesstoß *m*; **death camp N** Vernichtungslager *nt*; **death cell N** (*Brit*) Todeszelle *f*; **death certificate N** Sterbeurkunde *f*, Totenschein *m*; **death chair N** elektrischer Stuhl;

death cup N (*Bot*) Grüner Knollenblätterpilz; **death-dealing ADJ** *blow, missile* tödlich; **death-defying ADJ** todesverachtend, todesmutig; **death duties PL** (*Brit*) Erbschaftssteuern *pl*; **death grant N** (*Brit Hist*) Sterbegeld *nt*; **death instinct N** (*Psych*) Todestrieb *m*; **death knell N** (*fig*) Todesstoß *m* → **knell**; **deathless ADJ** unsterblich; **deathlike ADJ** totenähnlich

deathly ['deθlɪ] **ADJ** **~ hush** *or* **silence** Totenstille *f*; **~ pallor** Totenblässe *f* **ADV** **~ pale** totenblass; **~ cold** eiskalt; **~ quiet** totenstill

death: death mask N Totenmaske *f*; **death metal N** (*Mus*) Death Metal *m*; **death penalty N** Todesstrafe *f*; **death rate N** Sterbeziffer *f*; **death rattle N** Todesröcheln *nt*; **death ray N** Todesstrahl *m*; **death roll N** Verlust- *or* Gefallenenliste *f*; **death row N** Todestrakt *m*; **death sentence N** Todesurteil *nt*; **death's head N** (*on flag etc*) Totenkopf *m*; **death's head moth N** Totenkopf *m*, Totenkopfschwärmer *m*; **death squad N** Todeskommando *nt*; **death taxes PL** (*US*) = **death duties**; **death threat N** Morddrohung *f*; **death throes** (*lit, fig*) Todeskampf *m*; **in his ~** im Todeskampf; **death toll N** Zahl *f* der (Todes-)opfer *or* Toten; **deathtrap N** Todesfalle *f*; **death warrant N** Hinrichtungsbefehl *m*; (*fig*) Todesurteil *nt*; **to sign one's own ~** (*fig*) sein eigenes Todesurteil unterschreiben *or* unterzeichnen; **deathwatch N** Totenwache *f*; **deathwatch beetle N** Totenuhr *f*, Klopfkäfer *m*; **death wish N** Todeswunsch *m*

deb [deb] **N** (*inf*) Debütantin *f*

débâcle [de'bɑ:kl] **N** Debakel *nt* (*over* bei)

debag [ˌdi:'bæg] **VT** (*Brit, inf*) die Hosen runterziehen (+*dat*)

debar [dɪ'bɑ:'] **VT** (*from club, competition*) ausschließen (*from* von); **to ~ sb from doing sth** jdn davon ausschließen, etw zu tun

debark [dɪ'bɑ:k] **VI** sich ausschiffen, an Land gehen **VT** ausschiffen; *troops* landen

debarkation [ˌdi:bɑ:'keɪʃən] **N** Ausschiffung *f*, Landung *f*; (*of troops*) Landen *nt*

debarment [dɪ'bɑ:mənt] **N** Ausschluss *m*; **his ~ from the club** sein Ausschluss aus dem Klub

debase [dɪ'beɪs] **VT a** *person* erniedrigen, entwürdigen **b** *virtues, qualities* mindern, herabsetzen **c** *metal* verschlechtern; *coinage* den Wert mindern (+*gen*)

debased [dɪ'beɪst] **ADJ** verderbt; *quality, value* minderwertig; *word, expression* abgegriffen

debasement [dɪ'beɪsmənt] **N a** (*of person*) Erniedrigung *f*, Entwürdigung *f* **b** (*of virtues, qualities*) Minderung *f*, Herabsetzung *f* **c** (*of metal*) Verschlechterung *f*; (*of coinage*) Wertminderung *f*

debatable [dɪ'beɪtəbl] **ADJ** fraglich; *frontier* umstritten; **it's a ~ point whether ...** es ist fraglich, ob ...

debate [dɪ'beɪt] **VT** *question* debattieren, diskutieren **VI** debattieren, diskutieren (*with* mit, *about* über *acc*); **he was debating with himself whether or not to go** er überlegte hin und her, ob er gehen sollte **N** (*debate*) *f*; **after much ~** nach langer Debatte; **the ~ was on** *or* **about ...** die Debatte ging über ... (*acc*); **the death penalty was under ~** zur Debatte stand die Todesstrafe; **to be open to ~** zur Debatte stehen

debater [dɪ'beɪtə'] **N** Debattierer(in) *m(f)*

debating [dɪ'beɪtɪŋ] **N** Debattieren *nt*, Diskutieren *nt* **ADJ** *attr* Debattier-; **~ society** Debattierklub *m*

debauch [dɪ'bɔ:tʃ] **VT** verderben **N** Orgie *f*

debauched [dɪ'bɔ:tʃt] **ADJ** *person, look* verderbt; *life* zügellos, ausschweifend

debauchee [ˌdebɔ:'tʃi:] **N** Wüstling *m*, Lüstling *m*

debauchery [dɪ'bɔ:tʃərɪ] **N** Ausschweifung *f*, Debauche *f* (*old*); **a life of ~** ein zügelloses *or* ausschweifendes Leben

debenture [dɪ'bentʃə'] **N** (*Fin*) Schuldschein *m*; (*Customs*) Rückzollschein *m*

debenture: debenture bond N Schuldverschreibung f, Obligation f; **debenture holder** N Obligationär(in) m(f); **debenture stock** N Schuldverschreibungen pl, Obligationen pl

debilitate [dɪ'bɪlɪteɪt] VT schwächen

debilitating [dɪ'bɪlɪteɪtɪŋ] ADJ schwächend; lack of funds, war, depression etc lähmend; shyness, self-doubt hinderlich, hemmend; **to have a ~ effect on sb/sth** jdn/etw schwächen

debility [dɪ'bɪlɪtɪ] N Schwäche f

debit ['debɪt] N Schuldposten m, Debet nt; ~ **account** Debetkonto nt; ~ **balance** Debetsaldo m; ~ **and credit** Soll nt und Haben nt; **to enter sth to the ~ side of an account** etw auf der Sollseite verbuchen; **on the ~ side** (fig) auf der Minusseite VT **~ sb's/sb's account (with a sum)**, **to ~ (a sum) to sb/sb's account** jdn/jds Konto (mit einer Summe) belasten or debitieren (form)

debit: debit card N Kundenkarte f; **debit entry** N Abbuchung f

deboard [dɪ'bɔːd] (US) VI (from train, bus, plane) aussteigen; (from boat) ausschiffen VT train, bus, plane aussteigen aus; boat ausschiffen aus

debonair [ˌdebə'neə'] ADJ flott

debone [diː'bəʊn] VT meat vom Knochen lösen; fish entgräten

debouch [dɪ'baʊtʃ] VI (troops) hervorbrechen, debouchieren (old); (river) münden, sich ergießen

Debrett [də'bret] N ≈ Gotha m

debrief [ˌdiː'briːf] VT befragen; **to be ~ed** Bericht erstatten

debriefing [ˌdiː'briːfɪŋ] N (also **debriefing session**) Einsatzbesprechung f (nach dem Flug etc)

debris ['debriː] N Trümmer pl, Schutt m; (Geol) Geröll nt

debt [det] N (= money owed, obligation) Schuld f; ~ **of honour** (Brit) or **honor** (US) Ehrenschuld f, Verschuldung f der öffentlichen Hand; **to be in ~** verschuldet sein (to gegenüber); **to be £5 in ~** £ 5 Schulden haben (to bei); **he is in my ~** (for money) er hat Schulden bei mir; (for help etc) er steht in meiner Schuld; **to run** or **get into ~** Schulden machen, sich verschulden; **to get out of ~** aus den Schulden herauskommen; **to be out of ~** schuldenfrei sein; **to repay a ~** (lit, fig) eine Schuld begleichen; **I shall always be in your ~** ich werde ewig in Ihrer Schuld stehen ATTR Schulden-; ~ **relief/forgiveness** Schuldenerlass m; ~ **burden** Schulden pl

debt: debt collection agency N Inkassobüro nt; **debt collector** N Inkassobeauftragte(r) mf, Schuldeneintreiber(in) m(f) (inf)

debtor ['detə'] N Schuldner(in) m(f)

debt: debt relief N Schuldenerleichterung m; **debt rescheduling** ['detrɪ'ʃedʒʊəlɪŋ] N Umschuldung f

debug [ˌdiː'bʌg] VT **a** mattress entwanzen **b** (= remove technical faults from) die Fehler beseitigen bei **c** (= remove bugging equipment from) entwanzen (Comput) entwanzen; **~ging program** Fehlerkorrekturprogramm nt, Debugger m

debugger [ˌdiː'bʌgə'] N (Comput) Debugger m

debunk [ˌdiː'bʌŋk] VT claim entlarven; myth aufdecken; politician vom Sockel stoßen

debus [diː'bʌs] VTI aus dem/einen Bus aussteigen

début ['deɪbjuː] N (lit, fig) Debüt nt; **to make one's ~** (in society) in die Gesellschaft eingeführt werden; (Theat) sein Debüt geben; (fig) sein Debüt geben; **~ album** Debütalbum nt VI (Theat) debütieren, sein Debüt geben; (fig) sein Debüt geben

débutante ['debjʊtɑːnt] N Debütantin f

Dec abbr of **December** Dez.

dec abbr of **deceased** gest.

decade ['dekeɪd] N **a** (= ten years) Jahrzehnt nt, Dekade f **b** (Eccl, of rosary) Gesätz nt

decadence ['dekədəns] N Dekadenz f

decadent ['dekədənt] ADJ dekadent N (Liter) Vertreter(in) m(f) der Dekadenz, Décadent m (geh)

decaff ['diːkæf] N abbr of **decaffeinated** (inf) Koffeinfreie(r) m (inf)

decaffeinated [diː'kæfɪneɪtɪd] ADJ koffeinfrei, entkoffeiniert

decagramme, (US) **decagram** ['dekəgræm] N Dekagramm nt

decal [dɪ'kæl] N (US) Abziehbild nt; (process) Abziehen nt

decalcify [ˌdiː'kælsɪfaɪ] VT entkalken

decalitre, (US) **decaliter** ['dekə,liːtə'] N Dekaliter m or nt

decalogue ['dekəlɒg] N Dekalog m

decametre, (US) **decameter** ['dekə,miːtə'] N Dekameter nt

decamp [dɪ'kæmp] VI **a** (Mil) das Lager abbrechen **b** (inf) verschwinden, sich aus dem Staube machen (inf)

decant [dɪ'kænt] VT umfüllen, dekantieren (form)

decanter [dɪ'kæntə'] N Karaffe f

decapitate [dɪ'kæpɪteɪt] VT enthaupten (geh), köpfen, dekapitieren (form); **she was ~d in the accident** bei dem Unfall wurde ihr der Kopf abgetrennt

decapitation [dɪ,kæpɪ'teɪʃən] N Enthauptung f (geh)

decarbonization ['diː,kɑːbənaɪ'zeɪʃən] N (Aut) Entkohlung f, Dekarbonisierung f

decarbonize [ˌdiː'kɑːbənaɪz] VT pistons etc dekarbonisieren, entkohlen

decasyllable ['dekəsɪləbl] N Zehnsilber m

decathlete [dɪ'kæθliːt] N Zehnkämpfer m

decathlon [dɪ'kæθlən] N Zehnkampf m

decay [dɪ'keɪ] VI **a** (lit) verfallen; (Phys) zerfallen; (= rot, dead body, flesh, vegetable matter) verwesen; (food) schlecht werden, verderben; (tooth) faulen, verfallen; (bones, wood) verfallen, morsch werden **b** (fig) verfallen; (health also) sich verschlechtern; (beauty also) verblühen, vergehen; (civilization, race) untergehen; (friendship) auseinander gehen, zerfallen; (one's faculties) verkümmern; (business, family) herunterkommen VT food schlecht werden lassen, verderben; tooth faulen lassen, schlecht werden lassen; wood morsch werden lassen N **a** (lit: = action) Verfall m; (Phys) Zerfall m; (= rotting, of dead body, flesh, vegetable matter) Verwesung f; (of food) Schlechtwerden nt; (of bones, wood) Morschwerden nt; **tooth** ~ Zahnfäule f, Karies f; **to fall into** ~ in Verfall geraten, verfallen **b** (= decayed part or area) Fäule f, Fäulnis f **c** (fig) Verfall m; (of friendship, civilization) Zerfall m; (of race, family, business) Untergang m; (of faculties) Verkümmern nt

decayed [dɪ'keɪd] ADJ wood etc morsch; tooth faul; food schlecht; body, vegetable matter verwest

decd abbr of **deceased** gest.

decease [dɪ'siːs] (Jur, form) N Ableben nt (form) VI sterben, verscheiden (geh)

deceased [dɪ'siːst] (Jur, form) ADJ ge- or verstorben; **John Brown,** ~ der verstorbene John Brown N **the** ~ der/die Tote or Verstorbene; (pl) die Toten or Verstorbenen pl

deceit [dɪ'siːt] N Betrug m no pl, Täuschung f; **these unending ~s** diese endlosen Täuschungsmanöver; **a character full of** ~ ein durch und durch falscher Charakter

deceitful [dɪ'siːtfʊl] ADJ falsch, betrügerisch

deceitfully [dɪ'siːtfəlɪ] ADV betrügerischerweise; behave betrügerisch; **she had** ~ **lured him to her house** sie hatte ihn auf hinterlistige Weise in ihr Haus gelockt

deceitfulness [dɪ'siːtfʊlnɪs] N Falschheit f; (= deceitful acts) Betrügereien pl

deceivable [dɪ'siːvəbl] ADJ leicht zu täuschen(d)

deceive [dɪ'siːv] VT täuschen, trügen (geh); one's wife, husband betrügen; **to ~ sb into doing sth** jdn durch Täuschung dazu bringen, etw zu tun; **are my eyes deceiving me - is it really you?** täuschen mich meine Augen, oder bist du es wirklich?; **to ~ oneself** sich (dat) selbst etwas vormachen VI trügen (geh), täuschen

deceiver [dɪ'siːvə'] N Betrüger(in) m(f)

decelerate [diː'seləreɪt] VI (car, train) langsamer werden; (driver) die Geschwindigkeit herabsetzen; (production) sich verlangsamen VT verlangsamen

deceleration ['diː,selə'reɪʃən] N (of car, train) Langsamerwerden nt; (by driver) Herabsetzung f der Geschwindigkeit; (of production) Verlangsamung f

December [dɪ'sembə'] N Dezember m → also **September**

decency ['diːsənsɪ] N (= good manners etc) Anstand m; (of dress etc) Anständigkeit f; (of behaviour) Schicklichkeit f; ~ **demands that ...** der Anstand fordert, dass ...; **it's only common ~ to ...** es gehört sich einfach, zu ...; **have you no sense of ~?** haben Sie denn kein Anstandsgefühl!; **for ~'s sake** anstandshalber; **he could have had the ~ to tell me** er hätte es mir anständigerweise auch sagen können; **I hope you'll have the ~ to tell me** ich hoffe, du wirst die Anständigkeit besitzen, es mir zu sagen

decent ['diːsənt] ADJ (all senses) anständig; **are you ~?** (inf) bist du schon salonfähig? (inf); **to do the ~ thing** das einzig Anständige tun; **it was ~ of you to come** es war sehr anständig von Ihnen zu kommen; **to give sb a ~ burial** jdn ordentlich begraben

decently ['diːsəntlɪ] ADV treat, pay, live anständig; dress also schicklich (geh); bury richtig, mit Anstand; **you can't ~ ask him to do it now** Sie können ihn jetzt kaum bitten, es zu tun

decentralization ['diː,sentrəlaɪ'zeɪʃən] N Dezentralisierung f

decentralize [diː'sentrəlaɪz] VTI dezentralisieren

decentralized [diː'sentrəlaɪzd] ADJ dezentral

deception [dɪ'sepʃən] N **a** (= act of deceiving) Täuschung f, Betrug m (of an +dat); (of wife etc) Betrug m **b** (= state of being deceived) Täuschung f **c** (= that which deceives) Täuschung f

deceptive [dɪ'septɪv] ADJ irreführend; similarity täuschend; simplicity trügerisch; **to be ~** täuschen, trügen (geh); **appearances are** or **can be ~** der Schein trügt

deceptively [dɪ'septɪvlɪ] ADV simple, easy täuschend; strong, powerful überraschend; gentle, mild trügerisch, täuschend; **to look ~ like sb/sth** jdm/einer Sache täuschend ähnlich sehen

deceptiveness [dɪ'septɪvnɪs] N Täuschende(s) nt; **the ~ of the effects of perspective** die trügerischen Effekte der Perspektive; **beware of the ~ of statistics** Vorsicht, Statistiken sind irreführend

decibel ['desɪbel] N Dezibel nt

decide [dɪ'saɪd] ✪ 8.2 VT **a** (= come to a decision) (sich) entscheiden; (= take it into one's head) beschließen, sich entschließen; **what did you ~?** (yes or no) wie habt ihr euch entschieden?; (what measures) was habt ihr beschlossen?; **did you ~ anything?** habt ihr irgendwelche Entscheidungen getroffen?; **you must ~ what to do** du musst (dich) entscheiden, was du tun willst; **you can't suddenly ~ you're going to leave home** du kannst nicht plötzlich beschließen, dass du einfach von zu Hause weggehst; **I have ~d we are making a big mistake** ich bin zu der Ansicht gekommen, dass wir einen großen Fehler machen; **I'll ~ what we do!** ich bestimme, was wir tun!; **she always wants to ~ everything** sie will immer alles bestimmen; **the car seems to have ~d it's not going to start** das Auto scheint beschlossen zu haben, nicht anzuspringen; **the weather hasn't ~d what it's going to do yet** das Wetter hat (sich) noch nicht entschlossen, was es will **b** (= *settle*) *question, war etc* entscheiden; **to ~ sb's fate** jds Schicksal bestimmen, (über) jds Schicksal entscheiden **c to ~ sb to do sth** jdn veranlassen, etw zu tun; **that eventually ~d me** das hat schließlich für mich den Ausschlag gegeben **VI** (sich) entscheiden; **I don't know, YOU ~** ich weiß nicht, entscheiden or bestimmen SIE!; **I don't know, I can't ~** ich kann mich nicht entscheiden; **to ~ for/ against sth** sich für/gegen etw entscheiden; **to ~ for** or **in favour** (*Brit*) or **favor** (*US*) **of/against sb** (*Jur*) zu jds Gunsten/Ungunsten or für/gegen jdn entscheiden

▸ **decide on** VI +*prep obj* sich entscheiden für

decided [dɪˈsaɪdɪd] ADJ **a** (= *clear, definite*) *improvement* entschieden; *difference, advantage* deutlich **b** (= *determined*) *manner* entschlossen, bestimmt; **he is a man of ~ views** er hat sehr fest gefügte Ansichten

decidedly [dɪˈsaɪdɪdlɪ] ADV entschieden; **she is ~ lazy** sie ist (ganz) entschieden faul; **he's ~ uncomfortable about it** es ist ihm gar nicht wohl dabei; **a ~ dangerous** ausgesprochen gefährlich; **a ~ different view** eine ganz andere Ansicht; **she was ~ unhappy about it** sie war wirklich nicht glücklich damit

decider [dɪˈsaɪdə] N (*Brit*) **a the ~ was that ...** was den Ausschlag gab, war dass ..., ausschlaggebend war, dass ... **b** (= *game*) Entscheidungsspiel *nt*; (= *goal*) Entscheidungstreffer *m*

deciding [dɪˈsaɪdɪŋ] ADJ entscheidend; *factor also* ausschlaggebend; **the ~ game** das Entscheidungsspiel

deciduous [dɪˈsɪdjʊəs] ADJ *leaves* die jedes Jahr abfallen; *antler* das abgeworfen wird; ~ **tree/forest** Laubbaum *m*/-wald *m*

decimal [ˈdesɪməl] ADJ Dezimal-; **to three ~ places** auf drei Dezimalstellen; **to go ~** sich auf das Dezimalsystem umstellen N Dezimalzahl *f*; ~**s** Dezimalzahlen *pl*

decimal currency N Dezimalwährung *f*

decimalization [ˌdesɪməlaɪˈzeɪʃən] N Umstellung *f* auf das Dezimalsystem, Dezimalisierung *f* (*form*)

decimalize [ˈdesɪməlaɪz] VT *system, currency* auf das Dezimalsystem umstellen, dezimalisieren (*form*)

decimal: decimal point N Komma *nt*; **decimal system** N Dezimalsystem *nt*

decimate [ˈdesɪmeɪt] VT dezimieren

decipher [dɪˈsaɪfə] VT (*lit, fig*) entziffern

decipherable [dɪˈsaɪfərəbl] ADJ (*lit, fig*) entzifferbar

decision [dɪˈsɪʒən] N **a** Entscheidung *f* (*on* über +*acc*), Entschluss *m*; (*esp of committee etc*) Beschluss *m*; (*of judge*) Entscheidung *f*; **to make a ~** eine Entscheidung treffen or fällen, einen Entschluss/Beschluss fassen; **she always wants to make all the ~s** sie will immer über alles bestimmen; **I can't make your ~s for you** ich kann nicht für dich entscheiden; **it's your ~** das musst du entscheiden; **I can't give you a ~ now** ich kann das jetzt nicht entscheiden; **to come to a ~** zu einer Entscheidung kommen; **I've come to the ~ that it's a waste of time** ich bin zu dem Schluss gekommen, dass es Zeitverschwendung ist; **~s, ~s!** immer diese Entscheidungen! **b** *no pl* (*of character*) Entschlusskraft *f*, Entschlossenheit *f*; **a man of ~** ein Mann von Entschlusskraft; **to act with ~** entschlossen handeln

decision: decision-maker N Entscheidungsträger(in) *m(f)*; **decision-making** N Entscheidungsfindung *f*; **to show an aptitude for ~** Entschlusskraft zeigen; **he's hopeless at ~** er kann einfach keine Entscheidungen treffen ADJ *attr* ~ **skills** or **abilities** Entschlusskraft *f*; **the ~ process** der Prozess der Entscheidungsfindung

decisive [dɪˈsaɪsɪv] ADJ **a** (= *crucial*) entscheidend; *factor* ausschlaggebend, entscheidend; *rejection* entschieden **b** (= *resolute*) *manner, answer* bestimmt, entschlossen; *person* entschlussfreudig

decisively [dɪˈsaɪsɪvlɪ] ADV **a** (= *crucially, conclusively*) *change, influence* entscheidend; *defeat* deutlich; *reject* entschieden **b** (= *resolutely*) *say* bestimmt, entschlossen; *act* entschlossen

decisiveness [dɪˈsaɪsɪvnɪs] N **a** (= *crucial importance*) entscheidende Bedeutung; **a victory of such ~** ein so entscheidender Sieg **b** (= *resoluteness*) Bestimmtheit *f*, Entschlossenheit *f*

deck [dek] N **a** (*Naut*) Deck *nt*; **on ~** auf Deck; **to go up on ~** an Deck gehen; **to go (down) below ~(s)** unter Deck gehen **b** (*of bus, plane*) Deck *nt*; **top** or **upper ~** Oberdeck *nt* **c** (*inf*, = *floor*) Boden *m* **d** (*Cards*) **a ~ of cards** ein Kartenspiel **e** (*of record player*) Laufwerk *nt*; (= *part of hi-fi unit*) Plattenspieler *m* **f** (*esp US*: = *veranda*) Veranda *f* VT (*also* **deck out**) schmücken; **to ~ oneself out in one's Sunday best** sich in seinen Sonntagsstaat werfen (*inf*), sich herausputzen; **all ~ed out in his Sunday best** ganz fesch in seinem Sonntagsstaat

deck: deck cabin N Deckkabine *f*; **deck cargo** N Deckladung *f*; **deck chair** N Liegestuhl *m*

-decker [ˈdekə] N *suf* -decker *m*; (*Naut*) **a three-decker** ein Dreidecker *m* → **single-decker, double-decker**

deck: deck hand N Deckshelfer(in) *m(f)*; **deckhouse** N Deckshaus *nt*

decking [ˈdekɪŋ] N (*esp US*: = *wooden flooring*) Deck *nt*

deckle edge [ˈdekledʒ] N Büttenrand *m*

deckle-edged [ˈdekledʒd] ADJ mit Büttenrand; *paper* Bütten-

deck tennis N Decktennis *nt*

declaim [dɪˈkleɪm] VI deklamieren; **to ~ against sth** gegen etw wettern VT deklamieren, vortragen

declamation [ˌdekləˈmeɪʃən] N Deklamation *f*; (*against sth*) Tirade *f*

declamatory [dɪˈklæmətərɪ] ADJ deklamatorisch, pathetisch

declarable [dɪˈkleərəbl] ADJ *goods* verzollbar

declaration [ˌdekləˈreɪʃən] N Erklärung *f*; (*Cards*) Ansage *f*; (*Customs*) Deklaration *f* (*form*); ~ **of intent** Absichtserklärung *f*; ~ **of love** Liebeserklärung *f*; ~ **of bankruptcy** Konkursanmeldung *f*; **to make/sign a ~** eine Erklärung abgeben/unterzeichnen; ~ **of war** Kriegserklärung *f*; ~ **of the results** (*Pol*) Bekanntgabe *f* des Ergebnisses/der Ergebnisse

declare [dɪˈkleə] ✪ 26.2 VT **a** *intentions* erklären, kundtun (*geh*); *results* bekannt geben, veröffentlichen; *goods* angeben, deklarieren (*form*); **have you anything to ~?** haben Sie etwas zu verzollen?; **to ~ one's income** sein Einkommen angeben; **to ~ one's love (for sb)** (jdm) eine Liebeserklärung machen; **to ~ one's support (for sb/sth)** seine Unterstützung (für jdn/etw) zum Ausdruck bringen; **to ~ war (on sb)** (jdm) den Krieg erklären; **to ~ a state of emergency** den Notstand erklären or ausrufen; **to ~ independence** sich für unabhängig erklären; **to ~ sb bankrupt** jdn für bankrott erklären; **I ~ this motorway officially open** ich erkläre diese Autobahn für offiziell eröffnet; **he ~d the meeting closed** er erklärte die Sitzung für geschlossen; **to ~ sb the winner** jdn zum Sieger erklären; **he ~d himself fit to play** er erklärte sich für spielfähig **b** (= *assert*) erklären, beteuern, versichern VI **a** ~ **for/against sb/sth** sich für/gegen jdn/etw erklären; **well I (do) ~!** (*dated*) ist es denn die Möglichkeit! **b** (*Sport*) die Runde für beendet erklären

declared [dɪˈkleəd] ADJ erklärt

declaredly [dɪˈkleərɪdlɪ] ADV erklärtermaßen

déclassé, déclassée [deɪˈklæseɪ] ADJ heruntergekommen; (*in status*) sozial abgesunken

declassification [ˌdɪˌklæsɪfɪˈkeɪʃən] N (*of information*) Freigabe *f*

declassify [diːˈklæsɪfaɪ] VT *information* freigeben

declension [dɪˈklenʃən] N (*Gram*) Deklination *f*

declinable [dɪˈklaɪnəbl] ADJ (*Gram*) deklinierbar

decline [dɪˈklaɪn] ✪ 12.3 N **a** (*in standards, birthrate, business, sales, prices*) Rückgang *m*; (*of empire, a party's supremacy*) Untergang *m*, Niedergang *m*; ~ **in performance** (*Sport*) Leistungsabfall *m*; **to be on the** or **in ~, to go** or **fall into ~** (*business*) zurückgehen; (*empire*) verfallen **b** (*Med*) Verfall *m*; **she went into a ~** es ging bergab mit ihr VT **a** *invitation, honour* ablehnen; **he ~d to come** er hat es abgelehnt, zu kommen **b** (*Gram*) deklinieren VI **a** (*empire*) verfallen; (*fame*) verblassen; (*health*) sich verschlechtern; (*prices, business*) zurückgehen; (*importance, significance, value*) geringer werden; (*custom*) aussterben; (*popularity, enthusiasm, interest*) abnehmen; (*population, influence*) abnehmen, zurückgehen; **cases of real poverty are declining** Fälle von echter Armut gibt es immer weniger **b** (= *refuse, say no*) ablehnen **c** (= *slope: ground*) abfallen **d** (*sun*) untergehen; (*liter, life, day*) zur Neige gehen (*liter*); **in his declining years** gegen Ende seiner Tage (*liter*) **e** (*Gram*) dekliniert werden

declivity [dɪˈklɪvɪtɪ] N Abschüssigkeit *f*

declutch [diːˈklʌtʃ] VI auskuppeln

decoction [dɪˈkɒkʃən] N Abkochung *f*, Absud *m*; (*Pharm*) Dekokt *nt* (*spec*)

decode [ˌdiːˈkəʊd] VT dekodieren, dechiffrieren, entschlüsseln; (*Comput, TV*) dekodieren

decoder [ˌdiːˈkəʊdə] N (*Comput, TV*) Dekoder *m*, Decoder *m*, Dekodierer *m*

decoke [ˌdiːˈkəʊk] VT entrußen

decollate [ˈdiːkɒleɪt] VT (*Comput*) trennen

decollator [ˈdiːkɒleɪtə] N (*Comput*) Formulartrenner *m*, Trennmaschine *f*

décolletage [deɪˈkɒltɑːʒ], **décolleté¹** [deɪˈkɒlteɪ] N Dekolleté *nt*, Dekolletee *nt*, (*tiefer*) Ausschnitt

décolleté² ADJ dekolletiert, (*tief*) ausgeschnitten

decolonize [diːˈkɒlənaɪz] VT entkolonisieren

decommission [ˌdiːkəˈmɪʃən] VT *power plant* stilllegen; *arms* ausmustern; *warship* außer Dienst nehmen

decommissioning [ˌdiːkəˈmɪʃənɪŋ] N (*of arms*) Ausmusterung *f*

decompose [ˌdiːkəmˈpəʊz] VT (*Chem, Phys*) zerlegen; (= *rot*) zersetzen VI zerlegt werden; (= *rot*) sich zersetzen

decomposed [ˌdiːkəmˈpəʊzd] ADJ (= *rotten*) verfault, faul; *corpse* verwest; *food* verfault

decomposition [ˌdiːkɒmpəˈzɪʃən] N (*Phys: of light*) Zerlegung *f*; (*Chem also*) Abbau *m*; (= *rotting*) Zersetzung *f*, Verfaulen *nt*

decompress [ˌdiːkəmˈpres] VT **a** *diver* einer Dekompression (*dat*) unterziehen **b** *picture, signal, data* dekomprimieren VI sich einer Dekompression (*dat*) unterziehen

decompression [ˌdiːkəmˈpreʃən] N Dekompression *f*, Druckverminderung *f*

decompression: decompression chamber N Dekompressionskammer *f*; **decompression sickness** N Dekompressions- or Taucherkrankheit *f*

decongestant [ˌdiːkənˈdʒestənt] ADJ abschwellend N abschwellendes Mittel; (*drops etc*) Nasentropfen *pl*/-spray *nt*

deconsecrate [ˌdiːˈkɒnsɪkreɪt] VT dekonsekrieren

deconstruct [ˌdiːkənˈstrʌkt] VT (*esp Liter*) dekonstruieren

decontaminate [ˌdiːkənˈtæmɪneɪt] VT entgiften, dekontaminieren; *(from radioactivity)* entseuchen

decontamination [ˈdiːkənˌtæmɪˈneɪʃən] N Entgiftung f, Dekontamination f; *(from radioactivity)* Entseuchung f, Dekontamination f

decontextualize [ˌdiːkənˈtekstjʊəlaɪz] VT *(form)* aus dem Zusammenhang nehmen

decontrol [ˌdiːkənˈtrəʊl] VT *(Comm)* trade, prices freigeben

décor [ˈdeɪkɔːʳ] N *(in room)* Ausstattung f; *(Theat)* Dekor m or nt; **he did his front room with Victorian ~** er richtete sein vorderes Zimmer im viktorianischen Stil ein

decorate [ˈdekəreɪt] VT **a** cake, hat verzieren; street, building, Christmas tree schmücken; room tapezieren; *(= paint)* (an)streichen; *(for special occasion)* dekorieren **b** soldier dekorieren, auszeichnen

decorating [ˈdekəreɪtɪŋ] N Tapezieren nt; *(= painting)* Streichen nt

decoration [ˌdekəˈreɪʃən] N **a** *(of cake, hat)* Verzierung f; *(of street, building, Christmas tree)* Schmücken nt; *(of room)* Tapezieren nt; *(= painting)* (An)streichen nt; *(for special occasion)* Dekoration f **b** *(= ornament, on cake, hat etc)* Verzierung f; *(on Christmas tree, building, in street)* Schmuck m no pl; **Christmas ~s** Weihnachtsdekorationen pl or -schmuck m; **interior ~** Innenausstattung f; **his secretary is just for ~** seine Sekretärin ist nur zur Dekoration da **c** *(Mil)* Dekoration f, Auszeichnung f

decorative [ˈdekərətɪv] ADJ dekorativ

decorator [ˈdekəreɪtəʳ] N *(Brit)* Maler(in) m(f)

decorous [ˈdekərəs] ADJ action, behaviour geziemend, schicklich; dress schicklich

decorously [ˈdekərəslɪ] ADV behave geziemend, schicklich; dress schicklich

decorum [dɪˈkɔːrəm] N Anstand m, Dekorum nt *(old, form)*; **to have a sense of ~** Gefühl für Anstand haben; **to behave with ~** sich mit gebührendem Anstand benehmen

decouple [ˌdiːˈkʌpl] VT entkoppeln

decoy [ˈdiːkɔɪ] N *(lit, fig)* Köder m; *(person)* Lockvogel m; **to act as a ~** als Köder fungieren, Lockvogel spielen; **police ~** Lockvogel m der Polizei; **~ manoeuvre** *(Brit)* or **maneuver** *(US)* Falle f VT person locken; **to ~ sb into doing sth** jdn durch Lockmittel dazu bringen, etw zu tun

decrease [diːˈkriːs] VI abnehmen; *(figures, output, life expectancy, birth rate, production)* zurückgehen, abnehmen; *(strength, enthusiasm, intensity)* nachlassen; *(in knitting)* abnehmen; **in decreasing order of importance** in der Reihenfolge ihrer Bedeutung; **it ~s in value** es verliert an Wert VT verringern, reduzieren N [ˈdiːkriːs] Abnahme f; *(in figures, output, life expectancy, birth rate, production)* Rückgang m; *(in strength, enthusiasm, intensity)* Nachlassen nt; **~ in speed** Verminderung or Abnahme f der Geschwindigkeit; **to be on the ~** abnehmen

decreasingly [diːˈkriːsɪŋlɪ] ADV immer weniger; **~ popular** immer unbeliebter

decree [dɪˈkriː] N Anordnung f, Verordnung f, Verfügung f; *(Pol: of king etc)* Erlass m; *(Eccl)* Dekret nt; *(Jur)* Verfügung f; *(of tribunal, court)* Entscheid m, Urteil nt; **by royal ~** auf königlichen Erlass; **by government ~** auf Erlass der Regierung; **to issue a ~** einen Erlass herausgeben VT verordnen, verfügen; **he ~d an annual holiday on 1st April** er erklärte den 1. April zum (ständigen) Feiertag

decree absolute N *(Jur)* endgültiges Scheidungsurteil

decree nisi [dɪˌkriːˈnaɪsaɪ] N *(Jur)* vorläufiges Scheidungsurteil

decrepit [dɪˈkrepɪt] ADJ staircase, car etc altersschwach; building baufällig, heruntergekommen; industry heruntergekommen; person altersschwach, klapprig *(inf)*

decrepitude [dɪˈkrepɪtjuːd] N *(of staircase, car etc)* Altersschwäche f; *(of building)* Baufälligkeit

f; *(of person)* Altersschwäche f, Klapprigkeit f *(inf)*; *(of industry)* heruntergekommener Zustand

decriminalization [ˌdiːkrɪmɪnəlaɪˈzeɪʃən] N Entkriminalisierung f

decriminalize [diːˈkrɪmɪnəlaɪz] VT entkriminalisieren

decry [dɪˈkraɪ] VT schlecht machen

decrypt [diːˈkrɪpt] VT *(Comput, Telec)* entschlüsseln

dedicate [ˈdedɪkeɪt] VT **a** church weihen **b** book, music, song widmen *(to sb* jdm); **to ~ oneself** or **one's life to sb/sth** sich or sein Leben jdm/einer Sache widmen, sich einer Sache hingeben; **~d to the memory of ...** zum Gedenken an ...

dedicated [ˈdedɪkeɪtɪd] ADJ **a** attitude hingebungsvoll; service, fans treu; *(in one's work)* engagiert; **a ~ nurse/teacher** etc eine Krankenschwester/eine Lehrerin etc, die mit Leib und Seele bei der Sache ist; **to become a top-class dancer you have to be really ~** um ein erstklassiger Tänzer zu werden, muss man wirklich mit Leib und Seele dabei sein; **he is completely ~, he thinks of nothing but his work** er hat sich völlig seiner Arbeit verschrieben, er denkt an nichts anderes; **it's very ~ of you to stay on this late, Robinson** das ist sehr aufopfernd von Ihnen, so lange zu bleiben, Robinson; **she's ~ to her students** sie engagiert sich sehr für ihre Studenten; **to be a ~ follower of fashion** immer mit der neuesten Mode gehen; **he is a ~ follower of football** er ist ein ausgesprochener Fußballanhänger

b **~ word processor** dediziertes Textverarbeitungssystem

dedicatee [ˌdedɪkəˈtiː] N Person, der etwas gewidmet wird

dedication [ˌdedɪˈkeɪʃən] N **a** *(= quality)* Hingabe f *(to an +acc)* **b** *(= act: of church)* Einweihung f, Weihe f; **they admired his ~ of his life to helping the poor** sie bewunderten, dass er sein Leben in den Dienst der Armen stellte **c** *(in book)* Widmung f

dedicator [ˈdedɪkeɪtəʳ] N Widmende(r) mf, Zueigner(in) m(f) *(geh)*

deduce [dɪˈdjuːs] VT folgern, schließen *(from* aus); *(Logic)* deduzieren *(from* von)

deducible [dɪˈdjuːsɪbl] ADJ zu schließen, ableitbar *(from* aus); logisch deduzierbar *(from* von)

deduct [dɪˈdʌkt] VT abziehen *(from* von); *(from wages also)* einbehalten; **to ~ sth from the price** etw vom Preis ablassen; **to ~ sth for expenses** etw für Spesen zurückbehalten; **to ~ income tax at source** Einkommensteuer einbehalten; **after ~ing 5%** nach Abzug von 5%

deductible [dɪˈdʌktəbl] ADJ abziehbar, *(= tax deductible)* absetzbar

deduction [dɪˈdʌkʃən] N **a** *(= act of deducting)* Abziehen nt, Abzug m; *(= sth deducted, from price)* Nachlass m *(from* für, auf +acc); *(from wage)* Abzug m **b** *(= act of deducing)* Folgern nt, Folgerung f; *(= sth deduced)* (Schluss)folgerung f; *(Logic)* Deduktion f; **by a process of ~** durch Folgern

deductive [dɪˈdʌktɪv] ADJ deduktiv

deed [diːd] N **a** Tat f, Handlung f; *(= feat)* Tat f, Leistung f; **good ~** gute Tat; **evil ~** Übeltat f; **in word and ~** in Wort und Tat **b** **in ~** tatsächlich, in der Tat; **he is master in ~ if not in name** er ist der eigentliche or tatsächliche Herr, wenn auch nicht offiziell or nach außen hin **c** *(Jur)* Übertragungsurkunde f; **the ~s of a house** die Übertragungsurkunde eines Hauses; **~ of covenant** Vertragsurkunde f VT *(US)* überschreiben *(to* auf +acc)

deed poll N (einseitige) Absichtserklärung

deejay [ˈdiːdʒeɪ] N *(inf)* Diskjockey m

deem [diːm] VT **to ~ sb/sth (to be) sth** jdn/etw für etw erachten *(geh)* or halten; **it was ~ed necessary** es wurde für nötig gehalten, man hielt es für nötig; **he was ~ed worthy of the award** *(geh)* er wurde des Preises für würdig er-

achtet *(geh)* or gehalten; **he was ~ed too ill to leave hospital** man hielt ihn für zu krank, um das Krankenhaus zu verlassen

deep [diːp] ADJ *(+er)* **a** water, hole, wound tief; **the pond/snow was 4 feet ~** der Teich war/der Schnee lag 4 Fuß tief; **a two-foot ~ trench** ein zwei Fuß tiefer Graben; **two feet ~ in snow** mit zwei Fuß Schnee bedeckt; **two feet ~ in water** zwei Fuß tief unter Wasser; **the ~ end** *(of swimming pool)* das Tiefe; **to go off (at) the ~ end** *(fig inf)* auf die Palme gehen *(inf)*; **to go or jump in at the ~ end** *(fig)* sich kopfüber in die Sache stürzen; **to be thrown in at the ~ end** *(fig)* gleich zu Anfang richtig ranmüssen *(inf)*

b shelf, cupboard tief; *(= wide)* border, edge breit; **a plot of ground 15 metres ~** ein 15 Meter tiefes Stück Land; **the spectators stood ten ~** die Zuschauer standen zu zehnt hintereinander

c voice, sound, note, colour tief

d breathing, sigh tief

e *(fig)* mystery, sleep, secret, mourning tief; *(= profound)* thinker, book, remark, writer tiefsinnig; *(= heartfelt)* concern, relief, interest groß; sorrow *(empfunden)*; *(= devious)* person verschlagen, hintergründig; dealings undurchsichtig; **~est sympathy** aufrichtiges Beileid; **~ down, she knew he was right** im Innersten wusste sie, dass er Recht hatte; **~ in conversation** ins Gespräch vertieft; **~ in thought/a book** in Gedanken/in ein Buch vertieft or versunken; **~ in debt** hoch verschuldet; **~ in recession** mitten in einer Rezession; **we had a ~ and meaningful relationship** wir hatten eine tiefer gehende und sinnvolle Beziehung; **to be in ~ trouble** in großen Schwierigkeiten sein

ADV *(+er)* tief; **~ into the night** bis tief in die Nacht hinein; **~ in enemy territory** tief auf feindlichem Gebiet; **to breathe ~** tief atmen; **he's in it pretty ~** *(inf)* er steckt or hängt ganz schön tief da drin *(inf)*; **passions are running ~** die Gefühle schlagen hohe Wellen

N **a** *(liter)* **the ~** das Meer, die See **b** **in the ~ of winter** mitten im tiefsten Winter

deepen [ˈdiːpən] VT *(lit, fig)* vertiefen; concern, sorrow vergrößern, vertiefen; love, friendship vertiefen, verstärken; colour dunkler machen; mystery vergrößern; crisis, recession verschärfen; sound tiefer machen VI *(lit, fig)* sich vergrößern, tiefer werden; *(sorrow, concern, interest)* zunehmen, größer werden; *(colour, sound, voice)* tiefer werden; *(mystery)* größer werden; *(rift, divisions)* sich vertiefen; *(crisis, recession)* sich verschärfen

deepening [ˈdiːpənɪŋ] ADJ sorrow, concern etc zunehmend, wachsend; friendship, love also sich vertiefend; crisis, recession sich verschärfend; colour, mystery sich vertiefend, tiefer werdend N *(of hole, mystery)* Vergrößerung f; *(of sorrow, interest, concern)* Zunahme f; *(of friendship, love)* Vertiefung f; *(of crisis, recession)* Verschärfung f

deep: **deep-dyed** [ˈdiːpˈdaɪd] ADJ *(inf)* eingefleischt, unverbesserlich, Erz-; **deep-fat fryer** N Fritteuse f; **deep-freeze** VT einfrieren; **deepfreeze** [ˈdiːpˈfriːz] N Tiefkühltruhe f; *(upright)* Gefrierschrank m; **deep-freezing** N Einfrieren nt, Tiefgefrieren nt; **deep-frozen** ADJ tiefgefroren; **~ foods** Tiefkühlkost f; **deep-fry** VT frittieren, im schwimmenden Fett backen; **deep grammar** N Tiefengrammatik f; **deep kiss** N Zungenkuss m; **deep-laid** ADJ comp deeper-laid plot (sorgfältig) ausgetüftelt *(inf)* or ausgearbeitet

deeply [ˈdiːplɪ] ADV **a** *(lit)* tief; **~ embedded** or **ingrained dirt** tief sitzender Schmutz

b *(fig)* concerned, worried zutiefst, äußerst; unhappy, suspicious, unpopular äußerst; regret, move, shock, involved, grateful zutiefst; interested höchst; love sehr, innig; think gründlich; **~ religious** tiefreligiös; **~ committed** stark engagiert; **they are ~ embarrassed by it** es ist ihnen äußerst peinlich; **to be ~ in love** sehr verliebt sein; **to fall ~ in love** sich sehr verlieben; **~ in debt** hoch verschuldet; **a ~ ingrained prejudice** ein fest verwurzeltes Vorurteil; **to go ~ into a matter** sich gründlich mit einer Sache befassen

deepness ['di:pnɪs] N (lit, fig) Tiefe f; (of border, edge) Breite f; (= profundity, of thinker, remark etc) Tiefsinnigkeit f; (of concern, relief, interest) Größe f

deep: deep-pan pizza [ˌdi:pæn'pi:tsə] N Pfannenpizza f; **deep-ray therapy** N Tiefenbestrahlung f; **deep-rooted** ADJ comp **deeper-rooted** (fig) tief verwurzelt; **deep-sea** ADJ Tiefsee-; ~ **drilling** Tiefseebohrung f; **deep-sea diver** N Tiefseetaucher(in) m(f); **deep-sea fishery**, **deep-sea fishing** N Hochseefischerei f; **deep-seated** ADJ comp **deeper-seated** tief sitzend; **deep-set** ADJ comp **deeper-set** tief liegend; **Deep South** N Tiefer Süden; **deep space** N der äußere Weltraum; **deep structure** N (Ling) Tiefenstruktur f; **deep-throated** ['di:pˌθrəʊtɪd] ADJ kehlig

deer [dɪə'] N pl - (= roe deer) Reh nt; (= stag) Hirsch m; (collectively) Rotwild nt; **there are a lot of** ~ **in the forest** im Wald gibt es viel Rotwild

deer: deerhound N Deerhound m; **deer park** N Wildpark m; **deerskin** N Hirsch-/Rehleder nt; **deerstalker** N a (= person) jd, der auf die Pirsch geht b (= hat) ≈ Sherlock-Holmes-Mütze f; **deerstalking** N Pirschen nt, Pirsch f; **to go** ~ auf die Pirsch gehen

de-escalate [ˌdi:'eskəleɪt] VT deeskalieren

de-escalation [ˌdi:eskə'leɪʃən] N Deeskalation f

deface [dɪ'feɪs] VT verunstalten

de facto [deɪ'fæktəʊ] ADJ, ADV de facto

defamation [ˌdefə'meɪʃən] N Diffamierung f, Verleumdung f; ~ **of character** Rufmord m

defamatory [dɪ'fæmətərɪ] ADJ diffamierend, verleumderisch

defame [dɪ'feɪm] VT diffamieren, verleumden

default [dɪ'fɔ:lt] N a (= failure to appear, Jur) Nichterscheinen nt vor Gericht; (Sport) Nichtantreten nt; (= failure to perform duty) Versäumnis f; (= failure to pay) Nichtzahlung f; **judgement by** ~ (Jur) Versäumnisurteil nt; **to win by** ~ kampflos gewinnen b (= lack, absence) Mangel m; **in** ~ **of, due to** ~ **of** in Ermangelung +gen c ['di:fɔ:lt] (Comput) Default m, Voreinstellung f VI (= not appear, Jur) nicht erscheinen; (Sport) nicht antreten; (= not perform duty, not pay) säumig sein; **to** ~ **in one's payments** seinen Zahlungsverpflichtungen nicht nachkommen; **it always** ~**s to the C drive** (Comput) es wird immer das Laufwerk C angesprochen ATTR ['di:fɔ:lt] (Comput) parameter voreingestellt; ~ **drive** Standardlaufwerk nt

defaulter [dɪ'fɔ:ltə'] N (Jur) nicht erscheinende Partei; (Sport) nicht antretender Spieler, nicht antretende Spielerin; (on payment) Säumige(r) mf, säumiger Zahler; (Mil, Naut) Straffällige(r) mf

defeat [dɪ'fi:t] N (= defeating) Besiegung f, Sieg m (= über +acc); (of motion, bill) Ablehnung f; (of hopes, plans) Vereitelung f; (= being defeated) Niederlage f; **their** ~ **of the enemy** ihr Sieg über den Feind; **their** ~ **by the enemy** ihre Besiegung or Niederlage durch den Feind; **to admit** ~ sich geschlagen geben; **to suffer a** ~ eine Niederlage erleiden VT army, team besiegen, schlagen; government eine Niederlage beibringen (+dat), besiegen; motion, bill ablehnen; hopes, plans vereiteln; **to** ~ **one's own ends** or **object** sich (dat or acc) ins eigene Fleisch schneiden; **that would be** ~**ing the purpose of the exercise** dann verliert die Übung ihren Sinn; **it** ~**s me why ...** (inf) es will mir einfach nicht in den Kopf, warum ... (inf)

defeatism [dɪ'fi:tɪzəm] N Defätismus m

defeatist [dɪ'fi:tɪst] N Defätist m ADJ defätistisch

defecate ['defəkeɪt] VI den Darm entleeren, defäkieren (form)

defecation [ˌdefə'keɪʃən] N Entleerung f des Darms, Defäkation f (form)

defect¹ ['di:fekt] N Fehler m, Schaden m; (in mechanism also) Defekt m; (physical = körperlicher Schaden or Defekt; **hearing** ~ Gehörfehler m, Gehörschaden m; **sight** ~ Sehfehler m, Sehschwäche f; **character** ~ Charakterfehler m

defect² [dɪ'fekt] VI (Pol) sich absetzen; (fig) abtrünnig werden, abfallen; **to** ~ **to the enemy** zum Feind überlaufen

defection [dɪ'fekʃən] N (Pol) Überlaufen nt; (fig) Abtrünnigkeit f, Abfall m

defective [dɪ'fektɪv] ADJ a material, goods etc fehlerhaft; machine, gene defekt; (fig) fehlerhaft; hearing, sight mangelhaft, gestört; **he has a** ~ **heart valve** er hat einen Herzklappenfehler b (Gram) unvollständig, defektiv c (mentally) ~ geistesgestört N a (Gram) Defektivum nt b (= retarded person) Geistesgestörte(r) mf

defence, (US) **defense** [dɪ'fens] N a no pl Verteidigung f no pl; **in his** ~ zu seiner Verteidigung; **to come to sb's** ~ jdn verteidigen; **to put up** or **make a spirited** ~ **of sb/sth** jdn/etw mutig verteidigen; **his only** ~ **was ...** seine einzige Rechtfertigung war ... b (= form of protection) Abwehr- or Schutzmaßnahme f; (Mil, = fortification etc) Befestigung f, Verteidigungsanlage f; **as a** ~ **against** als Schutz gegen; **his** ~**s were down** er war wehrlos; **she caught me when my** ~**s were down** sie erwischte mich in einem schwachen Augenblick (inf) c (Jur, Sport) Verteidigung f; **to play in** ~ in der Verteidigung spielen

defence, (US) **defense: defence counsel** N Verteidiger(in) m(f); **defence expenditure** N Verteidigungsausgaben pl; **defenceless**, (US) **defenseless** ADJ schutzlos; **defenceman** [dɪ'fensmən] N pl -**men** (Ice hockey) Verteidiger m; **defence mechanism** N (Physiol, Psych) Abwehrmechanismus m; **defence minister** N Verteidigungsminister(in) m(f); **defence system** N (Biol) Abwehrsystem nt; **defence witness** N Zeuge m/Zeugin f der Verteidigung, Entlastungszeuge(in) m(f)

defend [dɪ'fend] VT verteidigen (also Jur) (against gegen); **to** ~ **oneself** sich verteidigen

defendant [dɪ'fendənt] N Angeklagte(r) mf; (in civil cases) Beklagte(r) mf ADJ angeklagt, beklagt

defender [dɪ'fendə'] N Verteidiger(in) m(f); **Defender of the Faith** Fidei Defensor m

defending [dɪ'fendɪŋ] ADJ ~ **counsel** Verteidiger(in) m(f); **the** ~ **champions** die Titelverteidiger pl

defenestration [di:ˌfenɪ'streɪʃən] N (form, hum) Fenstersturz m; **the Defenestration of Prague** der Prager Fenstersturz

defense etc (US) = **defence** etc

defensible [dɪ'fensɪbl] ADJ a (lit) wehrhaft; **because of its position the town wasn't** ~ die Stadt war wegen ihrer Lage nicht zu verteidigen b (= justifiable) behaviour, argument vertretbar, zu verteidigen pred

defensive [dɪ'fensɪv] ADJ defensiv (also fig); **a good** ~ **player** ein guter Verteidiger N (Mil) Verteidigungs- or Abwehraktion f; **to be on the** ~ (Mil, fig) in der Defensive sein; **to put sb on the** ~ (fig) jdn in die Defensive drängen; **to go onto the** ~ (fig) sich in die Defensive begeben

defensively [dɪ'fensɪvlɪ] ADV (also Sport) defensiv

defer¹ [dɪ'fɜ:'] VT (= delay) verschieben; event also verlegen; **to** ~ **doing sth** es verschieben, etw zu tun

defer² VI (= submit) **to** ~ **to sb** sich jdm beugen or fügen; **to** ~ **to sb's wishes** sich jds Wünschen (dat) fügen

deference ['defərəns] N Achtung f, Respekt m; **out of** or **in** ~ **to** aus Achtung (dat) or Respekt (dat) vor; **with all due** ~ **to you** bei aller schuldigen Achtung or allem schuldigen Respekt Ihnen gegenüber

deferential [ˌdefə'renʃəl] ADJ ehrerbietig, respektvoll; **to be** ~ **to sb** jdm mit Respekt or Achtung begegnen

deferentially [ˌdefə'renʃəlɪ] ADV ehrerbietig, respektvoll

deferment [dɪ'fɜ:mənt] N Verschiebung f, (of event also) Verlegung f

deferred [dɪ'fɜ:d]: **deferred annuity** N nach bestimmter Zeit fällige Rente; **deferred pay** N (Mil) einbehaltener Sold; (Naut) einbehaltene Heuer; **deferred payment** N Ratenzahlung f; **deferred shares** PL Nachzugsaktien pl; **deferred taxation** N Steuerrückstellung f; **deferred terms** PL (US) Abzahlungssystem nt; **on** ~ auf Abzahlung or Raten

defiance [dɪ'faɪəns] N Trotz m (of sb jdm gegenüber); (of order, law, death, danger) Missachtung f (of +gen); **an act of** ~ eine Trotzhandlung; **in** ~ **of sb/sth** jdm/etw zum Trotz; **his** ~ **of my orders caused an accident** weil er meine Anordnungen missachtete, gab es einen Unfall; **that is in** ~ **of gravity/logic** das widerspricht den Gesetzen der Schwerkraft/Logik

defiant [dɪ'faɪənt] ADJ child, answer trotzig; (= rebellious) aufsässig; (= challenging) attitude herausfordernd

defiantly [dɪ'faɪəntlɪ] ADV declare, announce, stare trotzig, herausfordernd; reject trotzig; resist standhaft

defibrillator [di:'fɪbrɪleɪtə'] N (Med) Defibrillator m

deficiency [dɪ'fɪʃənsɪ] N (= shortage) Mangel m; (Fin) Defizit nt, Fehlbetrag m; (= defect: in character, system) Schwäche f; **vitamin/iron** ~ Vitamin-/Eisenmangel m

deficiency: deficiency disease N (Med) Mangelkrankheit f; **deficiency guarantee** N (Fin) Ausfallbürgschaft f; **deficiency payment** N (Fin) Ausgleichszahlung f

deficient [dɪ'fɪʃənt] ADJ unzulänglich; **sb/sth is** ~ **in sth** jdm/einer Sache fehlt es an etw (dat); **a diet** ~ **in iron** eine Ernährung, die nicht genug Eisen enthält → **mentally**

deficit ['defɪsɪt] N Defizit nt

deficit financing N (Fin) Defizitfinanzierung f, Finanzierung f durch Staatsverschuldung

deficit spending N (Fin) Deficit-Spending nt

defile¹ ['di:faɪl] N Hohlweg m VI hintereinander marschieren

defile² [dɪ'faɪl] VT (= pollute, sully) verschmutzen, verunreinigen; (= desecrate) schänden, entweihen

defilement [dɪ'faɪlmənt] N Verschmutzung f, Verunreinigung f; (= desecration) Schändung f, Entweihung f

definable [dɪ'faɪnəbl] ADJ definierbar; conditions, boundaries, duties etc bestimmbar

define [dɪ'faɪn] VT a (= describe) definieren; conditions, boundaries, powers, duties bestimmen, festlegen b (= show in outline) betonen; clearly ~d scharf; **the path is not very well** ~d der Weg ist nicht sehr deutlich; **to be clearly** ~d **against the sky** sich klar or scharf gegen den Himmel abzeichnen

definite ['defɪnɪt] ADJ a (= fixed, concrete, explicit) definitiv; answer, decision klar, eindeutig; agreement, date, plan, intention, wish fest, definitiv; command, request bestimmt; **is that** ~? ist das sicher?; (= agreed by contract etc also) steht das fest?; **there has been an improvement, that's** ~ es ist eindeutig eine Verbesserung eingetreten; **for** ~ (say, know) mit Bestimmtheit b (= distinct, pronounced) mark, stain, lisp deutlich; advantage, improvement klar, eindeutig; problem, possibility echt c (= positive, decided) tone, manner bestimmt; **she was very** ~ **about it** sie war sich (dat) sehr sicher d (Gram) definitiv

definite article N (Gram) bestimmter Artikel

definitely ['defɪnɪtlɪ] ✪ 8.2 ADV a (= finally) decide, say endgültig; **it's not** ~ **arranged/agreed yet** es steht noch nicht fest b (= clearly) eindeutig; (= *certainly*) bestimmt; (= *whatever happens*) auf jeden Fall; **~ not** auf keinen Fall; **she has ~ put on weight** sie hat eindeutig zugenommen; **he ~ wanted to come** er wollte bestimmt kommen; **that is ~ wrong** das ist bestimmt nicht richtig; **that's ~ an improvement/an advantage** das ist ganz sicherlich eine Verbesserung/ein Vorteil **c** (= *emphatically*) say nachdrücklich, bestimmt

definiteness ['defɪnɪtnɪs] N Bestimmtheit *f*; (*of answer, decision*) Klarheit *f*, Eindeutigkeit *f*

definition [defɪ'nɪʃən] N **a** (*of word, concept*) Definition *f*; **by ~** per definitionem, definitionsgemäß **b** (*of powers, duties, boundary*) Festlegung *f*, Bestimmung *f* **c** (*Phot, TV*) Bildschärfe *f*; (*Rad*) Tonschärfe *f*; (*Opt, of lens*) Schärfe *f*

definitive [dɪ'fɪnɪtɪv] ADJ (= *decisive*) victory, answer entschieden; (= *authoritative*) book maßgeblich (on für); (= *defining*) term beschreibend; **~ laws** Rahmengesetze *pl* N (= *stamp*) Briefmarke *f* einer Dauerserie

definitively [dɪ'fɪnɪtɪvlɪ] ADV definitiv

deflate [di:'fleɪt] VT tyre, balloon die Luft ablassen aus; **to ~ the currency** (*Fin*) eine Deflation herbeiführen; **to ~ sb's confidence/ego** jds Selbstvertrauen/Ego (*dat*) einen Dämpfer aufsetzen; **he felt a bit ~d when ...** es war ein ziemlicher Dämpfer für ihn, dass ... VI (*Fin*) eine Deflation herbeiführen

deflation [di:'fleɪʃən] N (*of tyre, ball*) Luftablassen *nt* (*of aus*); (*Fin*) Deflation *f*

deflationary [di:'fleɪʃənərɪ] ADJ (*Fin*) Deflations-, deflationistisch; **~ policy** Deflationspolitik *f*

deflect [dɪ'flekt] VT ablenken; ball ablenken, abfälschen; steam, air current ableiten, ablenken; (*Phys*) light beugen VI (*compass needle*) ausschlagen; (*projectile*) abweichen

deflection [dɪ'flekʃən] N Ablenkung *f*; (*of ball*) Ablenkung *f*, Abfälschung *f*; (*of air current*) Ableitung *f*; (*Phys, of light*) Beugung *f*

deflective [dɪ'flektɪv] ADJ ablenkend; (*Phys*) beugend

deflector [dɪ'flektə'] N Deflektor *m*, Ablenkvorrichtung *f*

defloration [di:flɔː'reɪʃən] N (*liter, of girl*) Entjungferung *f*, Defloration *f*

deflower [di:'flaʊə'] VT (*liter*) girl entjungfern, deflorieren

defog [di:'fɒg] NT windscreen freimachen

defogger [di:'fɒgə'] N (*Aut*) Gebläse *nt*

defoliant [di:'fəʊlɪənt] N Entlaubungsmittel *nt*

defoliate [di:'fəʊlɪeɪt] VT entlauben, entblättern

defoliation [di:fəʊlɪ'eɪʃən] N Entlaubung *f*

deforest [di:'fɒrɪst] VT entwalden

deforestation [di:fɒrɪ'steɪʃən] N Entwaldung *f*

deform [dɪ'fɔːm] VT deformieren, verunstalten; (*Tech*) verformen; mind, tastes verderben

deformation [di:fɔː'meɪʃən] N Deformierung *f*, Deformation *f*, Verunstaltung *f*; (*Tech*) Verformung *f*

deformed [dɪ'fɔːmd] ADJ deformiert, verunstaltet; (*Tech*) verformt; person deformiert, missgestaltet; mind krankhaft

deformity [dɪ'fɔːmɪtɪ] N Deformität *f*, Verunstaltung *f*; (*of person*) Deformität *f*, Missgestalt *f*; (*of mind*) Krankhaftigkeit *f*

defraud [dɪ'frɔːd] VT betrügen, hintergehen; **to ~ sb of sth** jdn um etw betrügen or bringen

defrauder [dɪ'frɔːdə'] N Betrüger(in) *m(f)*

defray [dɪ'freɪ] VT tragen, übernehmen

defrayal [dɪ'freɪəl], **defrayment** [dɪ'freɪmənt] N Übernahme *f*

defrock [di:'frɒk] VT aus dem Priesteramt verstoßen

defrost [di:'frɒst] VT fridge abtauen; food auftauen VI (*fridge*) abtauen; (*food*) auftauen

defroster [di:'frɒstə'] N Defroster *m*, Entfroster *m*

deft [deft] ADJ (*+er*) flink, geschickt

---

deftly ['deftlɪ] ADV geschickt

deftness ['deftnɪs] N Flinkheit *f*, Geschicktheit *f*

defunct [dɪ'fʌŋkt] ADJ person verstorben; (*fig*) institution etc eingegangen; idea untergegangen; law außer Kraft

defuse [di:'fju:z] VT (*lit, fig*) entschärfen

defy [dɪ'faɪ] VT **a** (= *refuse to submit to, disobey*) person sich widersetzen (+*dat*); (*esp child*) trotzen (+*dat*); orders, law, death, danger verachten, trotzen (+*dat*)
b (*fig, = make impossible*) widerstehen (+*dat*); **to ~ definition** nicht definiert werden können; **to ~ description** jeder Beschreibung spotten; **that defies belief!** das ist ja unglaublich!; **to ~ gravity/logic** den Gesetzen der Schwerkraft/Logik widersprechen; **to ~ the odds to do sth** etw entgegen allen Erwartungen tun; **she defies her age** or **the years and wears the latest fashions** sie trägt ihrem Alter zum Trotz die neueste Mode
c (= *challenge*) **I ~ you to do it/to buy one more cheaply** machen Sie es doch/kaufen Sie doch einen Billigeren, wenn Sie können

degeneracy [dɪ'dʒenərəsɪ] N Degeneration *f*

degenerate [dɪ'dʒenərɪt] ADJ degeneriert; people, morals also entartet N [dɪ'dʒenərɪt] degenerierter Mensch VI [dɪ'dʒenəreɪt] degenerieren; (people, morals also) entarten; **the demonstration ~d into violence** die Demonstration artete in Gewalttätigkeiten aus

degenerateness [dɪ'dʒenərɪtnɪs] N Degeneration *f*

degeneration [dɪdʒenə'reɪʃən] N Degeneration *f*; (of people, morals also) Entartung *f*

degenerative [dɪ'dʒenərətɪv] ADJ (*Med*) degenerativ (spec)

degradable [dɪ'greɪdəbl] ADJ waste abbaubar

degradation [degrə'deɪʃən] N Erniedrigung *f*; (*Geol*) Erosion *f*; (*Chem*) Abbau *m*; **the appalling ~ of the jails** die schrecklich entwürdigenden Zustände in den Gefängnissen

degrade [dɪ'greɪd] VT erniedrigen; (*esp Mil, =* lower in rank*) degradieren; (*Geol*) erodieren; (*Chem*) abbauen; **to ~ oneself** sich erniedrigen; **I wouldn't ~ myself by doing that** ich würde mich nicht dazu erniedrigen, das zu tun VI (*Chem, = break down*) sich abbauen

degrading [dɪ'greɪdɪŋ] ADJ erniedrigend

degree [dɪ'griː] N **a** (= *unit of measurement*) Grad *m* no *pl*; **an angle of 90 ~s** ein Winkel *m* von 90 Grad; **it was 35 ~s in the shade** es waren 35 Grad im Schatten
b (= *extent: of risk, uncertainty etc*) Maß *nt*; **some** or **a ~ of** ein gewisses Maß an (+*dat*); **to some ~, to a (certain) ~** einigermaßen, zu einem gewissen Grad, in gewissem Maße; **to a high ~** in hohem Maße; **to such a ~ that ...** so sehr or in solchem Maße, dass ...; **to what ~ was he involved?** wie weit or in welchem Maße war er verwickelt?
c (= *step in scale*) Grad *m*; **by ~s** nach und nach; **first ~ murder** (*Jur*) Mord *m*; **second ~ murder** (*Jur*) Totschlag *m*
d (*Univ*) akademischer Grad; **first ~** erster akademischer Grad; **to get one's ~** einen akademischen Grad erhalten; **to do a ~** studieren; **when did you do your ~?** wann haben Sie das Examen gemacht?; **I'm taking** or **doing a language ~** ~ in **languages** ich studiere Sprachwissenschaften; **I've got a ~ in Business Studies** ich habe einen Hochschulabschluss in Wirtschaftslehre
e (= *position in society*) Rang *m*, Stand *m*

DEGREE

Mit **degree** bezeichnet man in den englischsprachigen Ländern den Grad der universitären Ausbildung. Der erste erreichbare Grad ist dabei ein **bachelor degree** nach einem vierjährigen Studium, der mit dem Magisterabschluss in Deutschland vergleichbar ist. Die am häufigsten verliehenen Grade sind

---

der **Bachelor of Arts** (BA oder auch manchmal in den USA AB) für Geisteswissenschaften, und **Bachelor of Science** (BSc in Großbritannien, BS in den USA) für Naturwissenschaften.

Den meisten Hochschulabsolventen in Großbritannien wird ein **honours degree** verliehen. Wenn man die dafür notwendige Note nicht erreicht hat oder sich für einen verkürzten Studiengang eingeschrieben hat, bekommt man einen **ordinary** oder **pass degree**. Die **honours degrees** werden in den folgenden Abstufungen verliehen: **first class** für die Note 1, **upper second** (2-1), **lower second** (2-2) und **third** für die Note 3. In den USA werden die Hochschulabschlüsse zwar nicht benotet, doch bekommen die besten Studenten Ehrentitel (**cum laude, magna cum laude** oder **summa cum laude**). Wenn man lieber einen praxisorientierten und berufsspezifischen Studiengang absolvieren möchte, kann man nach einer zweijährigen Ausbildung an einem **junior** oder **community college** einen **associate degree** erwerben.

Nach einem **bachelor degree** kann man in einem stärker wissenschafts- und forschungsorientierten Studiengang einen höheren akademischen Titel erwerben, einen sogenannten **master's degree**. Der höchste Titel, der verliehen werden kann, ist ein **doctorate**. Meist wird er in Geisteswissenschaften erworben, und die Doktoranden dürfen ihren Namen dann mit einem **PhD** oder **DPhil** schmücken.

---

degree: degree ceremony N (*Brit, Univ*) Graduierungsfeier *f*; **degree course** N Universitätskurs, der mit dem ersten akademischen Grad abschließt; **degree day** N Tag *m* der Gradverleihung

dehumanize [di:'hju:mənaɪz] VT entmenschlichen

dehydrate [di:haɪ'dreɪt] VT Wasser entziehen (+*dat*), dehydrieren (spec)

dehydrated [di:haɪ'dreɪtɪd] ADJ dehydriert (spec); foods also getrocknet; eggs also pulverisiert; person, skin dehydriert (spec), ausgetrocknet; **~ milk** Trockenmilch *f*; **~ vegetables** Dörrgemüse *nt*

dehydration [di:haɪ'dreɪʃən] N Austrocknung *f*, Dehydration *f* (spec); (of vegetables, milk etc) Trocknung *f*, Dehydration *f* (spec)

de-ice [di:'aɪs] VT enteisen

de-icer [di:'aɪsə'] N Enteiser *m*; (= spray for cars) Defroster *m*

deictic ['daɪktɪk] ADJ (*Ling*) deiktisch

deification [di:ɪfɪ'keɪʃən] N Vergötterung *f*

deify ['di:ɪfaɪ] VT vergöttern

deign [deɪn] VT **to ~ to do sth** geruhen or sich herablassen, etw zu tun; **he didn't ~ to** er ließ sich nicht dazu herab

deinstall [di:ɪn'stɔːl] VT software deinstallieren

deism ['di:ɪzəm] N Deismus *m*

deist ['di:ɪst] N Deist(in) *m(f)*

deity ['di:ɪtɪ] N Gottheit *f*; **the Deity** Gott *m*

deixis ['daɪksɪs] N (*Ling*) Deixis *f*

déjà vu ['deɪʒɑː'vuː] N Déjà-vu-Erlebnis *nt*; **a feeling** or **sense of ~** das Gefühl, das schon einmal gesehen zu haben

deject [dɪ'dʒekt] VT deprimieren

dejected ADJ , **dejectedly** ADV [dɪ'dʒektɪd, -lɪ] niedergeschlagen, deprimiert

dejection [dɪ'dʒekʃən] N Niedergeschlagenheit *f*, Depression *f*

de jure [di:'dʒʊərɪ] ADJ, ADV de jure

dekko ['dekəʊ] N (*Brit, inf*) kurzer Blick (at auf +*acc*); **let's have a ~ (at it)** (= show me) lass (das) mal sehen; (= let's go and see it) gucken wir uns das mal an

delay [dɪ'leɪ] VT **a** (= *postpone*) verschieben, aufschieben; orgasm hinauszögern; **to ~ doing sth** es verschieben or aufschieben, etw zu tun; **he ~ed paying until ...** er wartete so lange mit dem Zahlen, bis ...; **he ~ed writing the letter** er schob den Brief auf; **rain ~ed play** der Beginn des Spiels verzögerte sich wegen Regens **b** (= *hold up*) *person, train, traffic* aufhalten **VI** (= *wait*) warten; **if you ~ too long in booking** wenn Sie zu lange mit der Buchung warten; **to ~ in doing sth** es verschieben *or* aufschieben, etw zu tun; **he ~ed in paying the bill** er schob die Zahlung der Rechnung hinaus; **don't ~!** verlieren Sie keine Zeit!, tun Sie es unverzüglich!; **don't ~ in sending it in** senden Sie es unverzüglich ein **N** (= *hold-up*) Aufenthalt *m*; (*to traffic*) Stockung *f*; (*to train, plane*) Verspätung *f*; (= *time lapse*) Verzögerung *f*; **roadworks are causing ~s of up to 1 hour** Straßenbauarbeiten verursachen Staus bis zu 1 Stunde; **"delays possible (until ...)"** „Staugefahr! (bis ...)"; **there are ~s to all flights** alle Flüge haben Verspätung; **a split second's ~** eine Verzögerung von einem Bruchteil einer Sekunde; **without ~** unverzüglich; **without further ~** ohne weitere Verzögerung

delayed [dɪˈleɪd] ADJ (= *postponed*) verschoben, aufgeschoben, hinausgezögert; (= *late*) verspätet; (*TV, Rad*) broadcast zeitversetzt

delayed-action [dɪˈleɪdˌækʃ(ə)n] ADJ attr *bomb, mine* mit Zeitzünder; **~ shutter release** (*Phot*) Selbstauslöser *m*

delayer [dɪˈleɪə(r)] N **a** (= *person*) jd, der Zeit zu gewinnen sucht **b** (= *reason for delay*) Verzögerungsgrund *m*

delaying [dɪˈleɪɪŋ] ADJ action verzögernd, hinhaltend, Verzögerungs-; **~ tactics** Verzögerungs- *or* Hinhaltetaktik *f*

dele [ˈdiːlɪ] **VT** streichen, tilgen (*geh*) **N** Deleatur *nt*, Deleaturzeichen *nt*

delectable [dɪˈlektəbl] ADJ köstlich; (*fig*) reizend

delectation [ˌdiːlekˈteɪʃ(ə)n] N **for sb's ~** als besonderen Genuss für jdn

delegate [ˈdelɪgeɪt] **VT** person delegieren; *authority, power* übertragen (*to sb* jdm); *responsibility, job* delegieren (*to sb* an jdn); **to ~ sb to do sth** jdn dazu abordnen *or* damit beauftragen, etw zu tun **VI** delegieren; **you must ~ more** Sie sollten mehr delegieren **N** [ˈdelɪgət] Delegierte(r) *mf*

delegation [ˌdelɪˈgeɪʃ(ə)n] N **a** (*of responsibility etc*) Delegation *f*; **he's no good at ~** er kann einfach nicht delegieren **b** (= *group of delegates*) Delegation *f*, Abordnung *f*

delete [dɪˈliːt] **VT** streichen (*from* von); (*Comput*) löschen; **"delete where applicable"** „Nichtzutreffendes *or* nicht Zutreffendes (bitte) streichen"

delete key N (*Comput*) Löschtaste *f*

deleterious [ˌdelɪˈtɪərɪəs] ADJ (*form*) schädlich (*to* für)

deletion [dɪˈliːʃ(ə)n] N Streichung *f*; (*Comput*) Löschung *f*; **to make a ~** etwas streichen; **he made several ~s in the text** er strich mehrere Stellen im Text; **who made those ~s?** wer hat das gestrichen?

delft [delft] N Delfter Fayencen *pl*

deli [ˈdelɪ] N (*inf*) = **delicatessen**

deliberate [dɪˈlɪbərɪt] **ADJ** **a** (= *intentional*) absichtlich; *action, attempt, insult, lie* bewusst; **spot the ~ mistake** suchen Sie den versteckten Fehler **b** (= *cautious, thoughtful*) besonnen; *action, decision, judgement* (wohl) überlegt; (= *slow*) *movement, step, voice* bedächtig **VI** [dɪˈlɪbəreɪt] (= *ponder*) nachdenken (*on, upon* über +*acc*); (= *discuss*) sich beraten (*on, upon* über +*acc*, wegen) **VT** [dɪˈlɪbəreɪt] (= *ponder*) bedenken, überlegen; (= *discuss*) beraten

deliberately [dɪˈlɪbərɪtlɪ] ✪ 18.4 ADV **a** (= *intentionally*) bewusst, absichtlich; *plan* vorsätzlich; **it looks as if the blaze was started ~** es sieht so aus, als sei der Brand vorsätzlich gelegt worden **b** (= *cautiously, thoughtfully*) act überlegt; (= *steadily*) *move* bedächtig

deliberateness [dɪˈlɪbərɪtnɪs] N **a** (= *intentional nature*) Absichtlichkeit *f* **b** (= *thoughtfulness, cautiousness*) Besonnenheit *f*; (*of action*) Überlegtheit *f*; (= *slowness*) Bedächtigkeit *f*

deliberation [dɪˌlɪbəˈreɪʃ(ə)n] N **a** (= *consideration*) Überlegung *f* (*on* zu); **after due/careful ~** nach reiflicher/sorgfältiger Überlegung **b** **deliberations** PL (= *discussions*) Beratungen *pl* (*of, on* in +*dat*, über +*acc*) **c** (= *purposefulness, slowness*) Bedächtigkeit *f*

deliberative [dɪˈlɪbərətɪv] ADJ speech abwägend; **~ body** Beratungsorgan *nt*; **~ assembly** beratende Versammlung; **~ process** Beratungsprozess *m*

delicacy [ˈdelɪkəsɪ] N **a** = **delicateness** **b** (= *food*) Delikatesse *f*, Leckerbissen *m*

delicate [ˈdelɪkɪt] ADJ **a** (= *fine, dainty*) fein; *colour* zart; *food* delikat; *flavour* fein; (= *fragile*) *person, bones, china* zerbrechlich; *fabric, flower, stomach* empfindlich; *health, person* zart; **in a ~ condition** (*dated euph*) in anderen Umständen; **she's feeling a bit ~ after the party** nach der Party fühlt sie sich etwas angeschlagen **b** (= *sensitive*) *person* feinfühlig; *manner* feinfühlig, delikat; *instrument* empfindlich; *task* fein; *playing* gefühlvoll; **he has a ~ touch** (*pianist, artist*) er hat sehr viel Gefühl **c** (= *requiring skilful handling*) *operation, subject, situation* heikel, delikat **delicates** PL (= *fabrics*) Feinwäsche *f*

delicately [ˈdelɪkɪtlɪ] ADV **a** (= *daintily*) zart; **she took it ~ from him** sie nahm es ihm mit einer grazilen Bewegung ab; **a ~ pretty girl** ein zartes, hübsches Mädchen **b** (= *subtly*) *spiced, scented* fein; *coloured* zart; **~ flavoured** (*Brit*) *or* **flavored** (*US*) mit einem delikaten Geschmack; **a soup ~ flavoured** (*Brit*) *or* **flavored with nutmeg** (*US*) eine fein mit Muskat gewürzte Suppe **c** (= *tactfully*) taktvoll **d** (= *with precision*) fein; **she picked her way ~ over the rocks** vorsichtig suchte sie sich einen Weg über die Felsen

delicateness [ˈdelɪkɪtnɪs] N **a** (= *daintiness*) Zartheit *f*; (= *fragility*) Zerbrechlichkeit *f*; (*of fabric, flower, liver*) Empfindlichkeit *f*; (*of health, person*) Zartheit *f* **b** (= *sensitivity, of person*) Feinfühligkeit *f*; (*of instrument*) Empfindlichkeit *f*; (*of task*) Feinheit *f*; **the ~ of his playing** sein gefühlvolles Spiel **c** (*of operation, subject, situation*) heikle Natur *f* **d** (= *subtlety: of flavour*) Feinheit *f*

delicatessen [ˌdelɪkəˈtesn] N Feinkostgeschäft *nt*

delicious [dɪˈlɪʃəs] ADJ **a** food etc köstlich, lecker (*inf*) **b** (= *delightful*) herrlich; **in ~ anticipation** voll herrlicher Vorfreude

deliciously [dɪˈlɪʃəslɪ] ADV **a** (= *tastily*) tender, creamy köstlich **b** (= *delightfully*) warm, fresh, fragrant herrlich

delight [dɪˈlaɪt] **N** Freude *f*; **to my ~** zu meiner Freude; **he takes great ~ in doing that** es bereitet ihm große Freude, das zu tun; **to give sb great ~** jdn sehr freuen; **it's a ~ to watch, it's a ~ to watch him** es ist eine Freude, ihm zuzusehen **VT** person, ear, eye etc erfreuen → **delighted VI** sich erfreuen (*in* an +*dat*); **she ~s in doing that** es bereitet ihr große Freude, das zu tun

delighted [dɪˈlaɪtɪd] ✪ 3.2, 11.3, 13, 19.5, 24.1, 24.3, 25.1 ADJ (*with* über +*acc*) erfreut, entzückt; **to be ~** sich sehr freuen (*at* über +*acc*, *that* dass); **absolutely ~** hocherfreut, ganz entzückt; **~ to meet you!** sehr angenehm!; **we will be ~ to accept (your invitation)** wir nehmen Ihre Einladung gern an; **I'd be ~ to help you** ich würde Ihnen sehr gern helfen

delightful [dɪˈlaɪtfʊl] ADJ reizend; *weather, party, meal* wunderbar

delightfully [dɪˈlaɪtfəlɪ] ADV wunderbar

delimit [diːˈlɪmɪt] VT abgrenzen

delimitation [ˌdiːlɪmɪˈteɪʃ(ə)n] N Abgrenzung *f*

delimiter [diːˈlɪmɪtə(r)] N (*Comput*) Trennzeichen *nt*, Delimiter *m*

delineate [dɪˈlɪnɪeɪt] VT (= *draw*) skizzieren; *boundary, border* einzeichnen; (= *describe*) beschreiben, darstellen

delineation [dɪˌlɪnɪˈeɪʃ(ə)n] N Skizzierung *f*; (*of boundary, border*) Einzeichnung *f*; (= *description*) Beschreibung *f*, Darstellung *f*

delinquency [dɪˈlɪŋkwənsɪ] N Kriminalität *f*, Delinquenz *f* (*spec*) → **juvenile delinquency**

delinquent [dɪˈlɪŋkwənt] **ADJ** **a** straffällig **b** *bill* überfällig; *account* rückständig **N** Delinquent(in) *m(f)* → **juvenile delinquent**

delirious [dɪˈlɪrɪəs] ADJ (*Med*) im Delirium; (*fig*) im Taumel; **to be ~ with joy** im Freudentaumel sein

deliriously [dɪˈlɪrɪəslɪ] ADV **a** (= *ecstatically*) scream, cheer ekstatisch; **~ happy** euphorisch; **I fell ~ in love with her** ich verliebte mich unsterblich in sie **b** (*Med*) rave im Delirium

delirium [dɪˈlɪrɪəm] N (*Med*) Delirium *nt*; (*fig*) Taumel *m*

delirium tremens [dɪˈlɪrɪəmˈtremenz] N Delirium tremens *nt*, Säuferwahn(sinn) *m*

delist [ˌdiːˈlɪst] VT streichen (*von einer Liste*); (*St Ex*) aus der Notierung streichen

deliver [dɪˈlɪvə(r)] **VT** **a** *goods* liefern; *note, message* zustellen, überbringen; (*on regular basis*) *papers etc* zustellen; (*on foot*) austragen; (*by car*) ausfahren; **to ~ sth to sb** jdm etw liefern/überbringen/zustellen; **he ~ed the goods to the door** er lieferte die Waren ins Haus; **~ed free of charge** frei Haus (geliefert); **to ~ sb/sth into sb's care** jdn/etw in jds Obhut (*acc*) geben; **to ~ the goods** (*fig inf*) es bringen (*sl*), es schaffen **b** (*liter, = rescue*) befreien; **~ us from evil** (*Bibl*) erlöse uns von dem Übel *or* Bösen **c** (= *pronounce*) *speech, sermon, lecture* halten; *ultimatum* stellen; *verdict* sprechen, verkünden; *warning* aussprechen **d** (*Med*) baby zur Welt bringen; (*old*) woman entbinden; **to be ~ed of a son** (*old*) eines Jungen genesen (*old*) **e** (= *hand over: also* **deliver up**) aushändigen, übergeben; **to ~ a town into the hands of the enemy** eine Stadt dem Feind ausliefern → **stand** **f** (= *aim, throw*) blow versetzen, landen (*inf*); ball werfen; **Ali ~ed a punch to Bugner's jaw** Ali landete einen Schlag an Bugners Kinn (*inf*); **to ~ a broadside** eine Breitseite abfeuern **VI** **a** (*lit*) liefern **b** (*fig inf, = be good enough*) es bringen (*sl*); **they didn't ~** sie brachtens nicht (*sl*)

deliverable [dɪˈlɪvərəbl] ADJ goods lieferbar

deliverance [dɪˈlɪvərəns] N (*liter*) Befreiung *f* (*from* von), Erlösung *f* (*from* von)

deliverer [dɪˈlɪvərə(r)] N **a** (*Comm*) Lieferant *m* **b** (*liter, = rescuer*) Erlöser *m*, Retter *m*

delivery [dɪˈlɪvərɪ] ✪ 20.5 N **a** (*of goods*) (Aus)lieferung *f*; (*of parcels, letters*) Zustellung *f*; **please allow 28 days for ~** die Lieferzeit kann bis zu 28 Tagen betragen; **to take ~ of a package** ein Paket in Empfang nehmen **b** (*Med*) Entbindung *f* **c** (*of speaker*) Vortrag *m*, Vortragsweise *f* **d** (*liter, = rescue*) Rettung *f*, Befreiung *f* **e** (*of punch, blow*) Landung *f* (*inf*); (*Cricket*) Wurf *m*

delivery: delivery boy N Bote *m*; (*for newspapers*) Träger *m*; **delivery charge** N Lieferkosten *pl*; (*for mail*) Zustellgebühr *f*; **delivery contract** N Liefervertrag *m*; **delivery man** N Lieferant *m*; **delivery note** N Lieferschein *m*; **delivery output** N Förderleistung *f*; **delivery room** N Kreißsaal *m*, Entbindungssaal *m*; **delivery service** N Zustelldienst *m*; **delivery time** N Lieferzeit *f*; **delivery van** N Lieferwagen *m*

dell [del] N kleines bewaldetes Tal

delouse [ˌdiːˈlaʊs] VT entlausen

Delphic [ˈdelfɪk] ADJ (*lit, fig*) delphisch; **the ~ oracle** das Delphische Orakel, das Orakel von Delphi

delphinium [delˈfɪnɪəm] N Rittersporn *m*

delta [ˈdeltə] N Delta *nt*

delta: delta ray N (*Phys*) Deltastrahl *m*; **delta rhythm**, **delta wave** N (*Physiol*) Deltawelle *f*; **delta wing** N (*Aviat*) Deltaflügel *m*

delude [dɪˈluːd] VT täuschen, irreführen (*with* mit); **to ~ sb into thinking sth** jdn dazu verleiten, etw zu glauben; **to ~ oneself** sich (*dat*) Illusionen machen, sich (*dat*) etwas vormachen; **stop deluding yourself that ...** hör auf, dir vorzumachen, dass ...; **don't ~ yourself that ...** mach dir doch nicht vor, dass ...

deluded [dɪˈluːdɪd] ADJ voller Illusionen; **poor ~ girl** arme Irre

deluge [ˈdeljuːdʒ] N (*lit*) Überschwemmung *f*; (*of rain*) Guss *m*; (*fig, of complaints, letters etc*) Flut *f*; **the Deluge** (*Bibl*) die Sintflut VT (*lit, fig*) überschwemmen, überfluten

delusion [dɪˈluːʒən] N Illusion *f*, Irrglaube *m* *no pl*; (*Psych*) Wahnvorstellung *f*; **to be** *or* **labour** (*Brit*) *or* **labor** (*US*) **under a ~** in einem Wahn leben; **to have ~s of grandeur** den Größenwahn haben

delusive [dɪˈluːsɪv], **delusory** [dɪˈluːsərɪ] ADJ irreführend, täuschend, trügerisch

de luxe [dɪˈlʌks] de-Luxe-, De-Luxe-; **~ hotel/ model** Luxushotel/-modell *nt*; **~ version** De-Luxe-Ausführung *f*

delve [delv] VI (*into subject*) sich eingehend befassen (*into* mit); (*into book*) sich vertiefen (*into* in +*acc*); **to ~ in(to) one's pocket/a drawer** tief in die Tasche/eine Schublade greifen; **to ~ into the past** die Vergangenheit erforschen

Dem (*US, Pol*) abbr of **Democratic**

demagnetize [ˌdiːˈmæɡnɪtaɪz] VT entmagnetisieren

demagogic [ˌdeməˈɡɒɡɪk] ADJ demagogisch

demagogue, (*US*) **demagog** [ˈdeməɡɒɡ] N Demagoge *m*, Demagogin *f*

demagoguery [ˌdeməˈɡɒɡərɪ], **demagogy** [ˈdeməɡɒɡɪ] N Demagogie *f*

demand [dɪˈmɑːnd] ✪ 10.1 VT verlangen, fordern (*of, from* von); (*situation, task etc*) erfordern, verlangen; *time* beanspruchen; **they ~ed his resignation** sie forderten seinen Rücktritt; **he ~ed money** er wollte Geld haben; **he ~ed to know what had happened** er verlangte zu wissen, was passiert war; **he ~ed to see my passport** er wollte meinen Pass sehen

N **a** (= *firm request*) Forderung *f*, Verlangen *nt* (*for* nach); (= *claim for better pay, of kidnapper etc*) Forderung *f* (*for* nach); **by popular ~** auf allgemeinen Wunsch; **to be available on ~** auf Wunsch erhältlich sein; **abortion on ~** Abtreibung *f* auf Wunsch; **to make ~s on sb** Forderungen *or* Ansprüche an jdn stellen; **he makes too many ~s on my time** er nimmt mich zu sehr in Beschlag (*inf*); **he makes too many ~s on my pocket** er liegt mir zu sehr auf der Tasche (*inf*)

b *no pl* (*Comm*) Nachfrage *f*; **to create (a) ~ for a product** Nachfrage für ein Produkt schaffen; **there's no ~ for it** es ist nicht gefragt, es besteht keine Nachfrage danach; **to be in (great) ~** (*article, person*) sehr gefragt sein

demand: demand bill N (*Fin*) Sichtwechsel *m*; **demand deposit** N (*Fin*) Sichteinlage *f*, kurzfristige Einlage

demander [dɪˈmɑːndə] N **a** (= *requester*) Fordernde(r) *mf* **b** (= *buyer*) Käufer(in) *m(f)*

demanding [dɪˈmɑːndɪŋ] ADJ *child, job* anstrengend; *task also, teacher, boss* anspruchsvoll; **physically/mentally ~** körperlich/geistig anstrengend

demand: demand management N Steuerung *f* der Nachfrage; **demand note** N Zahlungsaufforderung *f*

de-manning [ˌdiːˈmænɪŋ] N (*Brit, of industry*) Personal- *or* Stellenabbau *m*

demarcate [ˈdiːmɑːkeɪt] VT abgrenzen, demarkieren

demarcation [ˌdiːmɑːˈkeɪʃən] N Abgrenzung *f*, Demarkation *f*; **~ line** Demarkationslinie *f*; **~ dispute** Streit *m* um den Zuständigkeitsbereich

démarche [ˈdeɪmɑːʃ] N Demarche *f*

dematerialize [ˌdiːməˈtɪərɪəlaɪz] VT entmaterialisieren VI sich entmaterialisieren

demean [dɪˈmiːn] VR **a** (= *lower*) sich erniedrigen; **I will not ~ myself by doing that** ich werde mich nicht dazu hergeben, das zu tun **b** (= *behave*) sich benehmen *or* verhalten VT erniedrigen

demeaning [dɪˈmiːnɪŋ] ADJ erniedrigend

demeanour, (*US*) **demeanor** [dɪˈmiːnə] N (= *behaviour*) Benehmen *nt*, Auftreten *nt*; (= *bearing*) Haltung *f*

demented [dɪˈmentɪd] ADJ verrückt, wahnsinnig; **~ with worry** verrückt vor Angst

dementia [dɪˈmenʃɪə] N Schwachsinn *m*, Demenz *f* (*spec*); **~ praecox** Jugendirresein *nt*, Dementia praecox *f* (*spec*)

demerara (sugar) [ˌdeməˈreərə(ˈʃuːɡə)] N brauner Rohrzucker

demerge [ˌdiːˈmɜːdʒ] VT *company* entflechten

demerit [diːˈmerɪt] N Schwäche *f*, Fehler *m*; (*dated US*, = *black mark*) Minuspunkt *m*

demesne [dɪˈmeɪn] N Grundbesitz *m*; **to hold sth in ~** etw in Besitz haben

demi [ˈdemɪ] PREF Halb-, halb-; **~god** Halbgott *m*, Halbgöttin *f*

demijohn [ˈdemɪdʒɒn] N Demijohn *m*; (*in wickerwork*) bauchige Korbflasche

demimonde [ˌdemɪˈmɒnd] N Halbwelt *f*

demilitarization [ˈdiːˌmɪlɪtəraɪˈzeɪʃən] N Entmilitarisierung *f*

demilitarize [ˌdiːˈmɪlɪtəraɪz] VT entmilitarisieren; **~d zone** entmilitarisierte Zone

demise [dɪˈmaɪz] N (= *death*) Tod *m*; (*of person also*) Ableben *nt* (*geh*); (*fig, of institution, newspaper etc*) Ende *nt*

demisemiquaver [ˌdemɪsemɪˈkweɪvə] N Zweiunddreißigstelnote *f*

demission [dɪˈmɪʃən] N (*of office, function*) Niederlegung *f*; (*of minister*) Demission *f* (*geh*), Rücktritt *m*

demist [diːˈmɪst] VT *windscreen* freimachen

demister [ˌdiːˈmɪstə] N Gebläse *nt*

demitasse [ˈdemɪtæs] N (*US*, = *cup*) Mokkatasse *f*; (= *coffee*) Kaffee *m*

demi-vegetarian [ˌdemɪvedʒɪˈteərɪən] N Halbvegetarier(in) *m(f)*

demiworld N Halbwelt *f*

demo [ˈdeməʊ] N abbr of **demonstration** Demo(nstration) *f* ADJ attr **~ disk** Demodiskette *f*; **~ tape** Demoband *nt*

demob [ˌdiːˈmɒb] (*Brit*) N abbr of **demobilization** Entlassung *f* aus dem Kriegsdienst VT abbr of **demobilize** aus dem Kriegsdienst entlassen, demobilisieren

demobilization [ˈdiːˌməʊbɪlaɪˈzeɪʃən] N (*of army*) Demobilmachung *f*, Demobilisierung *f*; (*of soldier*) Entlassung *f* aus dem Kriegsdienst, Demobilisierung *f*

demobilize [diːˈməʊbɪlaɪz] VT aus dem Kriegsdienst entlassen, demobilisieren

democracy [dɪˈmɒkrəsɪ] N Demokratie *f*

democrat [ˈdeməkræt] N Demokrat(in) *m(f)*

democratic [ˌdeməˈkrætɪk] ADJ **a** demokratisch; **the Social Democratic Party** die Sozialdemokratische Partei; **the Christian Democratic Party** die Christlich-Demokratische Partei **b** **Democratic** (*US, Pol, candidate, nomination, convention*) der Demokratischen Partei; **the Democratic Party** die Demokratische Partei

democratically [ˌdeməˈkrætɪkəlɪ] ADV demokratisch; **~ accountable** dem Volk verantwortlich; **Democratically controlled** (*US, Pol*) von den Demokraten kontrolliert

democratize [dɪˈmɒkrətaɪz] VT demokratisieren

demographer [dɪˈmɒɡrəfə] N Demograf(in) *m(f)*

demographic [ˌdeməˈɡræfɪk] ADJ demografisch

demography [dɪˈmɒɡrəfɪ] N Demografie *f*

demolish [dɪˈmɒlɪʃ] VT *building* ab- *or* einreißen, abbrechen; *fortifications* niederreißen; (*fig*) *opponent, theory* zunichte machen, vernichten; *myth* zerstören; (*hum*) *cake etc* vertilgen

demolition [ˌdeməˈlɪʃən] N Abbruch *m*

demolition: demolition area N = **demolition zone**; **demolition squad** N Abbruchkolonne *f*; **demolition work** N Abbrucharbeiten *pl*; **demolition zone** N Abbruchgebiet *nt*

demon [ˈdiːmən] N (= *evil spirit*) Dämon *m*; (*fig, = person*) Dämon(in) *m(f)*; (*inf, = child*) Teufel *m*; **to work like a ~** wie besessen arbeiten; **he's a ~ player** er ist ein teuflisch guter Spieler (*inf*); **the Demon Drink** König Alkohol *m*

demoniac [dɪˈməʊnɪæk] ADJ dämonisch N Besessene(r) *mf*

demoniacal [ˌdiːməʊˈnaɪəkəl] ADJ dämonisch

demonic [dɪˈmɒnɪk] ADJ dämonisch

demonize [ˈdiːmənaɪz] VT dämonisieren

demonstrable [ˈdemənstrəbl] ADJ beweisbar, offensichtlich

demonstrably [ˈdemənstrəblɪ] ADV nachweislich

demonstrate [ˈdemənstreɪt] VT **a** *truth, emotions, needs, goodwill, skill, bravery* zeigen, beweisen; (*by experiment, example*) demonstrieren, zeigen **b** *appliance etc* vorführen; *operation* vorführen, demonstrieren VI (*Pol etc*) demonstrieren

demonstration [ˌdemənˈstreɪʃən] N **a** (*of truth, emotions, needs, goodwill, skill, bravery*) Beweis *m*; (*by experiment, example*) Demonstration *f*; (*of appliance etc*) Vorführung *f*; (*of operation*) Vorführung *f*, Demonstration *f*; **to give a ~ of sth** (*by experiment, example*) etw demonstrieren; *of operation also, of gadget* etw vorführen; **he gave us a ~** er zeigte es uns **b** (*Pol etc*) Demonstration *f*; **to hold/break up a ~** eine Demonstration veranstalten *or* durchführen/auflösen ATTR **~ project** Demonstrationsprojekt *nt*

demonstration car N Vorführwagen *m*

demonstration model N Vorführmodell *m*

demonstrative [dɪˈmɒnstrətɪv] ADJ (*also Gram*) demonstrativ

demonstrator [ˈdemənstreɪtə] N **a** (*Comm*) Vorführer(in) *m(f)* (von technischen Geräten), Propagandist(in) *m(f)*; (*Sch, Univ*) Demonstrator *m* **b** (*Pol*) Demonstrant(in) *m(f)*

demoralization [dɪˌmɒrəlaɪˈzeɪʃən] N Entmutigung *f*; (*of troops etc*) Demoralisierung *f*

demoralize [dɪˈmɒrəlaɪz] VT entmutigen; *troops etc* demoralisieren

demoralizing [dɪˈmɒrəlaɪzɪŋ] ADJ entmutigend; (*for troops etc*) demoralisierend

demote [dɪˈməʊt] VT (*Mil*) degradieren (*to* zu); (*in business etc*) zurückstufen; **to be ~d** (*Sport*) absteigen; **~d to captain** zum Hauptmann degradiert

demotic [dɪˈmɒtɪk] ADJ **a** *Greek* demotisch **b** (= *of the people*) volkstümlich

demotion [dɪˈməʊʃən] N (*Mil*) Degradierung *f*; (*in business etc*) Zurückstufung *f*; (*Sport*) Abstieg *m*

demotivate [ˌdiːˈməʊtɪveɪt] VT demotivieren

demount [ˌdiːˈmaʊnt] VT (= *take to pieces*) auseinander nehmen, zerlegen; *machinery* abmontieren

demur [dɪˈmɜː] VI Einwände erheben, Bedenken haben (*to, at* gegen); (*Jur*) Einspruch erheben *or* einlegen N (*form*) Einwand *m*, Bedenken *pl*; (*Jur*) Einspruch *m*; **without ~** widerspruchslos

demure [dɪˈmjʊə] ADJ (+*er*) sittsam

demurely [dɪˈmjʊəlɪ] ADV sittsam

demureness [dɪˈmjʊənɪs] N Sittsamkeit *f*

demurrage [dɪˈmʌrɪdʒ] N (*Comm*, = *charge*) (Über)liegegeld *nt*; (= *time*) Überliegezeit *f*

demutualize [ˌdiːˈmjuːtjʊəlaɪz] VI (*Fin*) sich in eine Kapitalgesellschaft umwandeln

demystification [ˌdiːmɪstɪfɪˈkeɪʃən] N Entmystifizierung f

demystify [diːˈmɪstɪfaɪ] VT entmystifizieren

demythologize [ˈdiːmɪˈθɒlədʒaɪz] VT entmythologisieren

den [den] N **a** (of lion, tiger etc) Höhle f, Versteck nt; (of fox) Bau m **b** ~ **of iniquity** or **vice** Lasterhöhle f; ~ **of thieves** Spelunke f, Räuberhöhle f (hum) → **gambling den, opium den** **c** (= study) Arbeitszimmer nt; (= private room) gemütliches Zimmer, Bude f (inf)

denationalization [ˈdiːˌnæfnəlaɪˈzeɪʃən] N Entstaatlichung f

denationalize [diːˈnæfnəlaɪz] VT entstaatlichen

denature [diːˈneɪtʃəʳ] VT denaturieren; (= make unfit for eating, drinking also) ungenießbar machen

denazification [ˈdiːˌnætsɪfɪˈkeɪʃən] N Entnazifizierung f

denazify [diːˈnætsɪfaɪ] VT entnazifizieren

dendrite [ˈdendraɪt] N Dendrit m

deniability [dɪˌnaɪəˈbɪlɪtɪ] N (esp US Pol) Möglichkeit f zu leugnen or alles abzustreiten; **a way of preserving** ~ eine Möglichkeit, ein Hintertürchen offenzulassen

deniable [dɪˈnaɪəbl] ADJ bestreitbar

denial [dɪˈnaɪəl] N **a** (of accusation, guilt) Leugnen nt; ~ **of (the existence of) God** Gottesleugnung f; **the government issued an official** ~ die Regierung gab ein offizielles Dementi heraus; **to be in** ~ **about sth** etw abstreiten; **to be in** ~ (Psych) sich der Realität verschließen **b** (= refusal, of request etc) Ablehnung f, abschlägige Antwort; (official) abschlägiger Bescheid; (of rights) Verweigerung f **c** (= disowning) Verleugnung f; **Peter's** ~ **of Christ** die Verleugnung des Petrus **d** (= self-denial) Selbstverleugnung f

denier [ˈdenɪəʳ] N (of stockings) Denier nt

denigrate [ˈdenɪɡreɪt] VT verunglimpfen

denigration [ˌdenɪˈɡreɪʃən] N Verunglimpfung f

denim [ˈdenɪm] N **a** Jeansstoff m, Köper m **b** **denims** PL Bluejeans pl, Blue Jeans pl, Jeans pl **ADJ** attr Jeans-; ~ **jacket** Jeansjacke f; ~ **suit** Jeansanzug m

denitrification [ˌdiːnaɪtrɪfɪˈkeɪʃən] N Entstickung f

denizen [ˈdenɪzn] N Bewohner(in) m(f); (= person) Einwohner(in) m(f); ~**s of the forest** Waldbewohner pl; ~**s of the deep** Bewohner pl der Tiefe

Denmark [ˈdenmɑːk] N Dänemark nt

denominate [dɪˈnɒmɪneɪt] VT benennen, bezeichnen

denomination [dɪˌnɒmɪˈneɪʃən] N **a** (Eccl) Konfession f **b** (= name, naming) Benennung f, Bezeichnung f **c** (of money) Nennbetrag m; (of weight, measures) Einheit f **d** (= class, kind) Klasse f, Gruppe f

denominational [dɪˌnɒmɪˈneɪʃənl] ADJ (Eccl) konfessionell, Konfessions-; ~ **school** Konfessionsschule f

denominator [dɪˈnɒmɪneɪtəʳ] N (Math) Nenner m

denotation [ˌdiːnəʊˈteɪʃən] N **a** (Philos, of term, concept) Denotation f, Begriffsumfang m; (of word) Bedeutung f **b** (= name: of object) Bezeichnung f; (= symbol) Symbol nt

denotative [dɪˈnəʊtətɪv] ADJ (Ling) denotativ

denote [dɪˈnəʊt] VT bedeuten; symbol, word bezeichnen; (Philos) den Begriffsumfang angeben von

dénouement [dɪˈnuːmɒŋ] N (Theat, Liter) (Auf)lösung f; (fig) Ausgang m

denounce [dɪˈnaʊns] VT **a** (= accuse publicly) anprangern, brandmarken; (= inform against) anzeigen, denunzieren (sb to sb jdn bei jdm) **b** (= condemn as evil) alcohol, habit etc verurteilen, denunzieren (geh) **c** treaty (auf)kündigen

denouncement [dɪˈnaʊnsmənt] N = **denunciation**

---

dense [dens] ADJ (+er) **a** (= thick) fog, smoke, forest dicht (also Phys); crowd dicht gedrängt **b** prose, language, style, book, film (= concentrated) gedrängt; (= over-complex) überladen **c** (inf) person (= of low intellect) beschränkt (inf); (= slow) begriffsstutzig (inf), schwer von Begriff (inf)

densely [ˈdenslɪ] ADV populated, wooded dicht; ~ **packed** (crowd) dicht gedrängt

denseness [ˈdensnɪs] N **a** (= thickness) Dichte f **b** (= concentrated nature) Gedrängtheit f; (= excessive complexity) Überladenheit f

densify [ˈdensɪfaɪ] **VT** verdichten **VI** sich verdichten

density [ˈdensɪtɪ] N Dichte f; **population** ~ Bevölkerungsdichte f

dent [dent] **N** (in metal) Beule f, Delle f (inf); (in wood) Kerbe f, Delle f (inf); **that made a** ~ **in his savings** (inf) das hat ein Loch in seine Ersparnisse gerissen; **that made a bit of a** ~ **in his pride/confidence** (inf) das hat seinen Stolz/sein Selbstbewusstsein ganz schön angeknackst (inf)
VT hat, car, wing einbeulen, verbeulen; wood, table eine Delle machen in (+acc); (inf) pride, confidence anknacksen (inf); image, reputation schaden (+dat); hopes, profits dahinschwinden lassen; ~**ed cans are usually cheaper** eingebeulte Dosen sind meist billiger
VI (metal etc) sich einbeulen; (wood, table) eindellen

dental [ˈdentl] **ADJ** **a** Zahn-; treatment zahnärztlich; training zahnmedizinisch (form) **b** (Ling) Dental-, dental; ~ **sound** Dentallaut m **N** (Ling) Dental m, Zahnlaut m

dental: dental assistant N Zahnarzthelfer(in) m(f); **dental floss** N Zahnseide f; **dental hygiene** N Zahnpflege f; **dental hygienist** [ˈdentlhaɪˈdʒiːnɪst] N zahnmedizinischer Fachhelfer, zahnmedizinische Fachhelferin; **dental nurse** N Zahnarzthelfer(in) m(f); **dental surgeon** N Zahnarzt m/-ärztin f; **dental technician** N Zahntechniker(in) m(f)

dentifrice [ˈdentɪfrɪs] N Zahnpasta f

dentist [ˈdentɪst] N Zahnarzt m, Zahnärztin f; **at the** ~**('s)** beim Zahnarzt

dentistry [ˈdentɪstrɪ] N Zahnmedizin f, Zahnheilkunde f

dentition [denˈtɪʃən] N (= process of teething) Zahnen nt, Dentition f (spec); (= arrangement of teeth) Gebissform f

dentures [ˈdentʃəz] PL Zahnprothese f; (full) Gebiss nt

denude [dɪˈnjuːd] VT (of trees etc) entblößen (of +gen); (fig also) berauben (of +gen)

denunciation [dɪˌnʌnsɪˈeɪʃən] N (= accusation) Anprangerung f, Brandmarkung f; (= informing) Denunziation f; (= condemnation) Verurteilung f; (of treaty) (Auf)kündigung f; **the book is a sustained** ~ **of ...** das Buch ist eine einzige Anklage gegen ...

Denver boot [ˌdenvəˈbuːt] N (inf, = car clamp) Parkkralle f

deny [dɪˈnaɪ] ✪ 15.1, 26.3 VT **a** charge, accusation etc bestreiten, leugnen, (ab)leugnen; existence of God leugnen; (officially) dementieren; **do you** ~ **having said that?** bestreiten or leugnen Sie, das gesagt zu haben?; **there's no** ~**ing it** das lässt sich nicht bestreiten or leugnen; **I** ~ **that there is a real need for it** ich bestreite, dass ein echtes Bedürfnis danach besteht; **to** ~ **liability** keine Haftung übernehmen
b (= refuse) **to** ~ **sb's request** jdm seine Bitte abschlagen; **to** ~ **sb his rights** jdm seine Rechte vorenthalten; **to** ~ **sb aid/a privilege** jdm Hilfe/ein Privileg versagen; **to** ~ **sb access (to sth)** jdm den Zugang (zu etw) verwehren; **to** ~ **sb credit** jdm den Kredit verweigern; **I can't** ~ **her anything** ich kann ihr nichts abschlagen; **I had to** ~ **myself the pleasure of seeing him** ich musste mir das Vergnügen, ihn zu sehen, versagen; **why should I** ~ **myself these little comforts?** warum sollte ich mir das bisschen Komfort nicht gönnen?

---

c (= disown) leader, religion, principles verleugnen **d** **to** ~ **oneself** sich selbst verleugnen

deodorant [diːˈəʊdərənt] **ADJ** desodor(is)ierend **N** Deodorant nt

deodorize [diːˈəʊdəraɪz] VT desodor(is)ieren

deontology [ˌdiːɒnˈtɒlədʒɪ] N Pflichtethik f, Deontologie f

deoxidize [diːˈɒksɪdaɪz] VT desoxidieren

deoxygenate [diːˈɒksɪdʒəneɪt] VT Sauerstoff entziehen (+dat); ~**d blood** sauerstoffarmes Blut

deoxyribonucleic acid [dɪˈɒksɪˌraɪbəʊnjuːˈkleɪkˌæsɪd] N Desoxyribonukleinsäure f

dep. abbr of **departs, departure** (in timetables etc) Abf.

depart [dɪˈpɑːt] **VI** **a** (= go away) weggehen; (on journey) abreisen; (by bus, car etc) wegfahren; (train, bus etc) abfahren; **he** ~**s for Rome tomorrow morning** er reist morgen früh nach Rom ab; **the bus** ~**s from the bus station** der Bus fährt vom or am Busbahnhof ab; **the train at platform 6** ~**ing for ...** der Zug auf Bahnsteig 6 nach ...; **guests are asked to sign the register before they** ~ Gäste werden gebeten, vor der Abreise einen Meldezettel auszufüllen; **to be ready to** ~ (person) start- or abfahrbereit sein; **the visitors were about to** ~ die Gäste waren im Begriff aufzubrechen; **to** ~ **on one's way** (liter, old) sich aufmachen, aufbrechen **b** (= deviate: from opinion etc) abweichen (from von)
VT **a** (train, bus etc) abfahren aus **b** (liter) **to** ~ **this earth** or **life** aus dieser Welt or diesem Leben scheiden (liter)

departed [dɪˈpɑːtɪd] **ADJ** **a** (liter, = dead) verstorben, verschieden (geh) **b** (= bygone) friends verloren **N** **the (dear)** ~ der/die (liebe) Verstorbene; (pl) die (lieben) Verstorbenen pl

department [dɪˈpɑːtmənt] N **a** (generally) Abteilung f; (Geog: in France) Departement nt; (in civil service) Ressort nt; **Department of Employment** (Brit) **Department of Labor** (US) Arbeitsministerium nt; **Department of State** (US) Außenministerium nt; **that's not my** ~ (fig) dafür bin ich nicht zuständig **b** (Sch, Univ) Fachbereich m

departmental [ˌdiːpɑːˈmentl] ADJ Abteilungs-; (Sch, Univ) Fachbereichs-; (in civil service) committee des Ressorts; ~ **manager** Abteilungsleiter(in) m(f); ~ **head** (Sch, Univ) Fachbereichsleiter(in) m(f); **the minister's new** ~ **responsibilities** das neue Ressort des Ministers; **the money for** ~ **budgets** das Geld für die Haushalte der einzelnen Abteilungen

departmentalism [ˌdiːpɑːˈmentəlɪzəm] N Gliederung f in Abteilungen

departmentalize [ˌdiːpɑːˈmentəlaɪz] VT in Abteilungen einteilen or (auf)gliedern

departmentally [ˌdiːpɑːˈmentəlɪ] ADV abteilungsweise

department store N Kaufhaus nt, Warenhaus nt

departure [dɪˈpɑːtʃəʳ] N **a** (of person) Weggang m; (on journey) Abreise f (from aus); (of vehicle) Abfahrt f; (of plane) Abflug m; **to be on the point of** ~ im Aufbruch (begriffen) sein; **there are three** ~**s daily for Stockholm** (by plane) es gibt täglich drei Flüge nach Stockholm; "**departures**" „Abfahrt"; (at airport) „Abflug"; **at the hour of our** ~ **from this life** (liter) in der Stunde unseres Dahinscheidens (liter)
b (fig, from custom, principle, truth) Abweichung nt (from von), Abgehen nt (from von)
c (fig, = change in policy etc) neue Richtung f; **this marks a significant** ~ **from his previous way of life** hiermit ändert sich sein bisheriger Lebensstil grundlegend

departure: departure board N (Rail) Abfahrtstafel f; (Aviat) Abfluganzeige f; **departure gate** N Flugsteig m; **departure language** N (Ling) Ausgangssprache f; **departure lounge** N Abflughalle f; (for single flight) Warteraum m; **departure signal** N Abfahrtssignal *nt*; **departure time** N (*Aviat*) Abflugzeit *f*; (*Rail, bus*) Abfahrtzeit *f*

depend [dɪ'pend] ⏱ 6.3 VI **a** (= *be determined by*) abhängen (*on sb/sth* von jdm/etw); **the price ~s on the quantity you buy** der Preis hängt von der Menge ab, die Sie kaufen); **it ~s on what you mean by reasonable** es kommt darauf an, was Sie unter vernünftig verstehen; **how long are you staying? – it ~s** wie lange bleiben Sie? – das kommt darauf an; **it all ~s on …** das kommt ganz auf … an; **~ing on his mood** je nach seiner Laune; **~ing on how late we arrive** je nachdem, wie spät wir ankommen **b** (= *rely*) sich verlassen (*on, upon* auf +*acc*); **you may ~ (up)on his coming** Sie können sich darauf verlassen, dass er kommt; **you can ~ (up)on it!** darauf können Sie sich verlassen!; **you can ~ (up)on it that he'll forget** du kannst dich darauf verlassen, dass er es vergisst **c** (*person*: = *be dependent on*) **to ~ on** abhängig sein von, angewiesen sein auf (+*acc*); **they have to ~ on the grandparents for childcare** sie sind darauf angewiesen, dass die Großeltern sich um die Kinder kümmern

dependability [dɪˌpendə'bɪlɪtɪ] N Zuverlässigkeit *f*, Verlässlichkeit *f*

dependable [dɪ'pendəbl] ADJ zuverlässig, verlässlich

dependably [dɪ'pendəblɪ] ADV zuverlässig, verlässlich

dependant, dependent [dɪ'pendənt] N Abhängige(r) *mf*; **do you have ~s?** haben Sie (abhängige) Angehörige?

dependence [dɪ'pendəns] N Abhängigkeit *f* (*on, upon* von); **drug/alcohol ~** Drogen-/Alkoholabhängigkeit *f*

dependency [dɪ'pendənsɪ] N **a** (= *country*) Schutzgebiet *nt*, Kolonie *f* **b** = **dependence a**

dependent [dɪ'pendənt] ADJ **a** (= *reliant, also Gram, Math*) abhängig; **financially ~** finanziell abhängig; **~ on insulin** insulinabhängig; **to be ~ on** or **upon sb/sth** von jdm/etw abhängig sein; **heavily ~ on the tourist trade** stark vom Tourismus abhängig; **to be ~ on charity/sb's goodwill** auf Almosen/jds Wohlwollen angewiesen sein; **to be ~ on** or **upon sb/sth for sth** für etw auf jdn/etw angewiesen sein; **to be ~ on** or **upon sb/sth to do sth** auf jdn/etw angewiesen sein, um etw zu tun; **to have ~ children** Kinder haben, für deren Unterhalt man aufkommen muss **b** **to be ~ on** or **upon sb/sth** (= *determined by*) von jdm/etw abhängen; **your success is ~ (up)on the effort you put in** der Erfolg hängt davon ab, wie viel Mühe du dir gibst **N** = **dependant**

depeople [ˌdiː'piːpl] VT entvölkern

depersonalize [diː'pɜːsənəlaɪz] VT entpersönlichen, depersonalisieren (*Psych*)

depict [dɪ'pɪkt] VT darstellen; (*in words also*) beschreiben

depiction [dɪ'pɪkʃən] N Darstellung *f*; (*in words also*) Beschreibung *f*

depilatory [dɪ'pɪlətərɪ] ADJ enthaarend, Enthaarungs-; **~ cream** Enthaarungscreme *f* **N** Enthaarungsmittel *nt*

deplane [diː'pleɪn] VT (*aus dem Flugzeug*) ausladen **VI** (*aus dem Flugzeug*) aussteigen, von Bord gehen

deplenish [dɪ'plenɪʃ] VT *supplies etc* verringern

deplete [dɪ'pliːt] VT **a** (= *exhaust*) erschöpfen; (= *reduce*) vermindern, verringern; *funds* verringern; **certain substances ~ the ozone layer** bestimmte Stoffe bauen die Ozonschicht ab; **our supplies are somewhat ~d** unsere Vorräte sind ziemlich erschöpft; **the larder is rather ~d** die Speisekammer ist ziemlich leer; **the audience had become somewhat ~d** die Zuschauerreihen hatten sich ziemlich gelichtet **b** (*Med*) **to ~ the body of sth** dem Körper etw entziehen

depletion [dɪ'pliːʃən] N **a** (= *exhausting*) Erschöpfung *f*; (= *reduction*) Verminderung *f*, Verringerung *f*; (*of funds*) Verringerung *f*; (*of stock,*

membership) Abnahme *f* **b** (*Med*) Mangel *m* (*of* an +*acc*)

deplorable [dɪ'plɔːrəbl] ADJ (= *dreadful*) schrecklich; (= *disgraceful*) schändlich; **this joke is in ~ taste** dieser Witz ist schrecklich geschmacklos; **it is ~ that …** es ist eine Schande or unerhört, dass …

deplorably [dɪ'plɔːrəblɪ] ADV schrecklich; **the press are acting ~** es ist eine Schande, wie die Presse sich verhält; **it is in ~ bad taste** es zeugt von bedauernswert schlechtem Geschmack

deplore [dɪ'plɔː'] VT (= *regret*) bedauern, beklagen; (= *disapprove of*) missbilligen; **his attitude is to be ~d** seine Haltung ist bedauerlich

deploy [dɪ'plɔɪ] **VT a** (*Mil, = use, employ*) einsetzen; (= *position*) aufstellen; **the number of troops/missiles ~ed in Germany** die Zahl der in Deutschland stationierten Streitkräfte/Raketen **b** (*fig*) *resources, staff, arguments* einsetzen **VI** (*Mil*) sich aufstellen, aufmarschieren

deployment [dɪ'plɔɪmənt] N **a** (*Mil, = using*) Einsatz *m*; (= *positioning*) Aufstellung *f*, Stationierung *f* **b** (*fig, of resources, staff, arguments*) Einsatz *m*

deplume [ˌdiː'pluːm] VT *bird* rupfen

depoliticize [ˈdiː'pɒlɪtɪsaɪz] VT entpolitisieren

deponent [dɪ'pəʊnənt] **N** (*Ling*) Deponens *nt*; (*Jur*) vereidigter Zeuge **ADJ** **~ verb** Deponens *nt*

depopulate [ˌdiː'pɒpjʊleɪt] VT entvölkern

depopulation ['diːˌpɒpjʊ'leɪʃən] N Entvölkerung *f*

deport [dɪ'pɔːt] **VT** *prisoner* deportieren; *foreign national* abschieben **VR** (= *behave*) sich benehmen or verhalten

deportation [ˌdiːpɔː'teɪʃən] N (*of prisoner*) Deportation *f*; (*of foreign national*) Abschiebung *f*

deportation order N Abschiebungsanordnung *f*

deportee [dɪpɔː'tiː] N Deportierte(r) *mf*; (= *alien awaiting deportation*) Abzuschiebende(r) *mf*

deportment [dɪ'pɔːtmənt] N **a** Haltung *f*; (= *behaviour*) Verhalten *nt*, Benehmen *nt*; **lessons in ~** Haltungsschulung *f*, Anstandsunterricht *m*

depose [dɪ'pəʊz] **VT** absetzen; *sovereign also* entthronen **VI** (*Jur*) unter Eid aussagen

deposit [dɪ'pɒzɪt] **VT a** (= *put down*) hinlegen; (*upright*) hinstellen; **the turtle ~s her eggs in the sand** die Schildkröte legt ihre Eier im Sand ab **b** *money, valuables* deponieren (*in or with* bei); **I ~ed £500 in my account** ich zahlte £ 500 auf mein Konto ein **c** (*Geol*) ablagern **N a** (*Fin, in bank*) Einlage *f*, Guthaben *nt*; **to have £500 on ~** ein Guthaben or eine Einlage von £ 500 haben **b** (*Comm, = part payment*) Anzahlung *f*; (= *returnable security*) Sicherheit *f*, Kaution *f*; (*for bottle*) Pfand *nt*; **to put down a ~ of £1000 on a car** eine Anzahlung von £ 1000 für ein Auto leisten, £ 1000 für ein Auto anzahlen; **to leave a ~** eine Sicherheit or Kaution hinterlegen; **to lose one's ~** (*Pol*) seine Kaution verlieren **c** (*Chem: in wine, Geol*) Ablagerung *f*; (= *accumulation of ore, coal, oil*) (*Lager*)stätte *f*; **to form a ~** sich ablagern; **calcium ~s** Kalziumvorräte *pl*; **fat ~s** Fettablagerungen *pl*

deposit account N Sparkonto *nt*

depositary [dɪ'pɒzɪtərɪ] N Treuhänder(in) *m(f)*

deposit copy N (= *book*) Belegexemplar *nt* (*für öffentliche Bibliotheken*)

deposition [ˌdiːpə'zɪʃən] N **a** (*of sovereign*) Entthronung *f*, Absetzung *f*; (*of official*) Absetzung *f* **b** (*Jur*) Aussage *f* unter Eid **c** (*Art, Rel*) **~ from the cross** Kreuzabnahme *f*

depositor [dɪ'pɒzɪtə'] N Deponent(in) *m(f)*, Einzahler(in) *m(f)*

depository [dɪ'pɒzɪtərɪ] N Verwahrungsort *m*; (= *warehouse*) Lagerhaus *nt*

deposit slip N Einzahlungsbeleg *m*

depot ['depəʊ] N **a** (= *bus garage etc*) Depot *nt*; (= *store*) Lager(haus) *nt*, Depot *nt* **b** (*US, Rail*) Bahnhof *m*

depot ship N Versorgungsschiff *nt*

depravation [ˌdeprə'veɪʃən] N **a** (= *depraving*) Verderbung *f* **b** (= *depravity*) Verderbtheit *f*, Verworfenheit *f*

deprave [dɪ'preɪv] VT verderben

depraved [dɪ'preɪvd] ADJ verderbt, verkommen, verworfen

depravity [dɪ'prævɪtɪ] N Verderbtheit *f*, Verworfenheit *f*

deprecate ['deprɪkeɪt] VT (*form*) missbilligen

deprecating ADJ , **deprecatingly** ADV ['deprɪkeɪtɪŋ, -lɪ] missbilligend

deprecation [deprɪ'keɪʃən] N (*form*) Missbilligung *f*

deprecatory ['deprɪkətə rɪ] N = **deprecating**

depreciable [dɪ'priːʃəbl] ADJ (*Fin*) abschreibbar

depreciate [dɪ'priːʃɪeɪt] **VT a** *value* mindern; *exchange rate* abwerten; **to ~ a currency** die Kaufkraft einer Währung mindern; **to ~ a property** den Wert einer Immobilie mindern **b** (= *belittle*) herabsetzen, herabwürdigen **VI** an Wert verlieren; (*currency*) an Kaufkraft verlieren; (*exchange rate*) fallen, sinken; **the pound has ~d by 8%** das Pfund ist um 8% gefallen

depreciation [dɪˌpriːʃɪ'eɪʃən] N **a** (*of property, value*) Wertminderung *f*; (*in accounting*) Abschreibung *f*; (*of currency*) Kaufkraftverlust *m* **b** (= *belittlement*) Herabsetzung *f*, Herabwürdigung *f*

depreciatory [dɪ'priːʃɪətərɪ] ADJ abschätzig, herabsetzend

depredate ['deprɪdeɪt] VT (= *plunder*) plündern; (= *vandalize*) verwüsten

depredation [ˌdeprɪ'deɪʃən] N *usu pl* Verwüstung *f*

depress [dɪ'pres] **VT a** *person* deprimieren; *immune system* schwächen; (= *discourage*) entmutigen **b** (= *press down*) *lever* niederdrücken, herunterdrücken; *push button* drücken, betätigen **c** (*Comm*) *market* schwächen; *prices* fallen lassen; *sales* zurückgehen lassen

depressant [dɪ'presnt] **N** Beruhigungsmittel *nt*, Sedativ(um) *nt* (*spec*) **ADJ** beruhigend, dämpfend, sedativ (*spec*)

depressed [dɪ'prest] **ADJ a** (= *despondent*) deprimiert (*about* über +*acc*); (*Med*) depressiv; **to look ~** niedergeschlagen or bedrückt aussehen; **to feel ~** sich deprimiert or niedergeschlagen fühlen **b** (*Econ*, = *run-down*) *market* flau, schleppend; *economy, industry* geschwächt; *region* Not leidend; *share prices* fallend; *sales* rückläufig; **~ area** Notstandsgebiet *nt*; **the ~ state of the property market** die schlechte Marktlage bei Immobilien **c** (*form*, = *sunken*) tief liegend

depressing [dɪ'presɪŋ] ADJ deprimierend, bedrückend; **these figures make ~ reading** es ist deprimierend, diese Zahlen zu lesen

depressingly [dɪ'presɪŋlɪ] ADV deprimierend; **it all sounded ~ familiar** es hörte sich alles nur zu vertraut an; **~, the costs are too high** deprimierenderweise sind die Kosten zu hoch

depression [dɪ'preʃən] N **a** Depression *f*; (*Med*) Depressionen *pl* **b** (*of lever*) Herunteror Niederdrücken *nt*; (*of key, push button*) Drücken *nt*, Betätigen *nt* **c** (*in ground*) Vertiefung *f*, Senke *f*, Mulde *f* (*Met*) Tief(druckgebiet) *nt*; **a deep ~** ein ausgedehntes Tief(druckgebiet) *nt* **e** (*Econ*) Flaute *f*; (*St Ex*) Baisse *f*; **the Depression** die Weltwirtschaftskrise

depressive [dɪ'presɪv] **ADJ** depressiv **N** an Depressionen Leidende(r) *mf*; **to be a ~** depressiv sein

depressurize [diː'preʃəraɪz] VT den Druck herabsetzen in (+*dat*); **should the cabin become ~d** bei Druckverlust in der Kabine …

deprivation [ˌdeprɪ'veɪʃən] N **a** (= *depriving*) Entzug *m*; (= *loss*) Verlust *m*; (*Psych*) Deprivation f; (of rights) Beraubung f **b** (= state) Entbehrung f; (= lack of necessities) Mangel m; **the ~s of the war** die Entbehrungen des Krieges

deprive [dɪ'praɪv] VT **to ~ sb of sth** (of sth one has) jdn einer Sache (gen) berauben; (of sth to which one has a right) jdm etw vorenthalten; **we were ~d of our rights/freedom** wir wurden unserer Rechte/Freiheit beraubt; **they were ~d of a decent education** ihnen wurde eine anständige Erziehung vorenthalten; **I wouldn't want to ~ you of the pleasure of seeing her** ich möchte dir das Vergnügen, sie zu sehen, nicht vorenthalten; **the team was ~d of the injured Owen** die Mannschaft musste ohne den verletzten Owen auskommen; **she was ~d of sleep/oxygen** sie litt an Schlafmangel/Sauerstoffmangel; **they are ~d of any sense of national identity** ihnen fehlt jedes Gefühl für nationale Identität; **to ~ oneself of sth** sich (dat) etw nicht gönnen

deprived [dɪ'praɪvd] ADJ person, background benachteiligt; childhood arm; area (wirtschaftlich) benachteiligt; **the ~ areas of the city** die Armenviertel der Stadt

deprogramme, (US) **deprogram** [di:'prəʊɡræm] VT cult member entprogrammieren

dept abbr of department Abt.

depth [depθ] N **a** Tiefe f; **the ~s of the ocean** die Tiefen des Ozeans; **at a ~ of 3 feet** in einer Tiefe von 3 Fuß, in 3 Fuß Tiefe; **don't go out of your ~** geh nicht zu tief rein!; **to be out of one's ~** (lit) den Boden unter den Füßen verlieren; (fig also) ins Schwimmen geraten
b (of knowledge, feeling, colour) Tiefe f; **the ~ of his feelings for her** die Tiefe seiner Gefühle für sie; **he had no idea of the ~ of feeling against him** er hatte keine Ahnung, wie abgrundtief die Abneigung gegen ihn war; **they now understood the ~ of feeling on this issue** sie wussten jetzt, wie sehr dieses Thema die Gemüter bewegte; **he has ~ of character** er hat Charakterstärke; **the wine has ~ of character** der Wein hat viel Charakter; **in ~** eingehend, intensiv; interview ausführlich → **in-depth**
c (fig) **~(s)** Tiefen pl; **in the ~s of despair** in tiefster Verzweiflung; **in the ~s of winter/the forest** im tiefsten Winter/Wald; **in the ~s of the countryside** auf dem flachen Land; **in the ~s of recession** mitten in der Rezession; **from the ~s of the earth** aus den Tiefen der Erde (geh); **to sink to new ~s** so tief wie nie zuvor sinken

depth charge N Wasserbombe f

depthless ['depθlɪs] ADJ unermesslich tief, unendlich; (fig) oberflächlich

depth: depth of field N (Phot) Tiefenschärfe f; **depth psychology** N Tiefenpsychologie f

deputation [ˌdepjʊ'teɪʃən] N (= act) Abordnung f; (= people also) Delegation f

depute [dɪ'pju:t] VT person abordnen, delegieren; **to be ~d to do sth** dazu abgeordnet or delegiert werden, etw zu tun

deputize ['depjʊtaɪz] VI vertreten (for sb jdn), als Vertreter(in) fungieren (for sb für jdn) VT ernennen, abordnen

deputy ['depjʊtɪ] N **a** Stellvertreter(in) m(f) **b** (in deputation) Delegierte(r) mf **c** (also **deputy sheriff**) Hilfssheriff m **d** (in France) Deputierte(r) mf; (US, in foreign parliaments) Abgeordnete(r) mf ADJ attr stellvertretend

derail [dɪ'reɪl] VT zum Entgleisen bringen, entgleisen lassen; (fig) plan, negotiations scheitern lassen; **to be ~ed** entgleisen VI entgleisen

derailleur gears [dɪ'reɪljə'ɡɪəz], **derailleurs** [dɪ'reɪljəz] (inf) PL Kettenschaltung f

derailment [dɪ'reɪlmənt] N Entgleisung f

derange [dɪ'reɪndʒ] VT **a** (= make insane) verrückt or wahnsinnig machen; mind, senses verwirren **b** plan durcheinander bringen, umwerfen

deranged [dɪ'reɪndʒd] ADJ mind gestört, verwirrt, verstört; person, gunman geistesgestört

derangement [dɪ'reɪndʒmənt] N **a** Geistesgestörtheit f **b** (of order) Unordnung f, Durcheinander nt

Derby ['dɑ:bɪ, (US) 'dɜ:bɪ] N **a** (US: also **Derby hat**) Melone f **b** (= local Derby) (Lokal)derby nt **c** (Racing) Derby nt

deregulate [di:'reɡjʊleɪt] VT deregulieren; buses etc dem freien Wettbewerb überlassen

deregulation [di:reɡjʊ'leɪʃən] N Deregulierung f; (of buses etc) Wettbewerbsfreiheit f (of für)

derelict ['derɪlɪkt] ADJ (= abandoned) verlassen, aufgegeben; (= ruined) verfallen, heruntergekommen N **a** (Naut) (treibendes) Wrack **b** (= person) Obdachlose(r) mf

dereliction [ˌderɪ'lɪkʃən] N **a** (= state: of property) Verfall m, Heruntergekommenheit f **b** **~ of duty** Pflichtversäumnis nt

derestricted [ˌdi:rɪ'strɪktɪd] ADJ road, area ohne Geschwindigkeitsbegrenzung or -beschränkung

deride [dɪ'raɪd] VT sich lustig machen über (+acc), verspotten

derider [dɪ'raɪdə'] N Verspotter(in) m(f), Spötter(in) m(f)

deriding [dɪ'raɪdɪŋ] ADJ spöttisch, höhnisch

de rigueur [dərɪ'ɡɜ:'] ADJ pred unerlässlich

derision [dɪ'rɪʒən] N Hohn m, Spott m; **object of ~** Zielscheibe f des Spotts; **to be greeted with ~** spöttisch or mit Spott aufgenommen werden

derisive [dɪ'raɪsɪv] ADJ spöttisch, höhnisch; (= malicious) hämisch, verächtlich

derisively [dɪ'raɪsɪvlɪ] ADV spöttisch, höhnisch; (= maliciously) verächtlich

derisory [dɪ'raɪsərɪ] ADJ **a** amount, offer lächerlich **b** = derisive

derivable [dɪ'raɪvəbl] ADJ (Ling, Philos, Chem) ableitbar

derivation [ˌderɪ'veɪʃən] N Ableitung f; (Chem) Derivation f; **this text has its ~ from Kafka's novels** dieser Text basiert auf Kafkas Romanen; **whatever the true ~ of this story may be** woher diese Geschichte auch immer ursprünglich stammt

derivative [dɪ'rɪvətɪv] ADJ abgeleitet; (Ling, Chem) abgeleitet, derivativ; (fig) style, composition, literary work etc nachgeahmt, imitiert; **~ markets** (Fin) Markt m für Derivate; **~ products** (Fin) Derivate pl N **a** Ableitung f; (Ling also, Chem) Derivat nt **b** (Fin) Derivat nt

derive [dɪ'raɪv] VT idea, name, origins her- or ableiten (from von); profit, benefit ziehen (from aus); satisfaction, comfort, pleasure, energy gewinnen (from aus); income beziehen (from aus); **this word is ~d from the Greek** dieses Wort stammt aus dem Griechischen VI **to ~ from** sich her- or ableiten von; (power, fortune) beruhen auf (+dat), herkommen or -rühren von; (ideas) kommen or stammen von; **this ~s from the fact that ...** das beruht auf der Tatsache, dass ...

dermatitis [ˌdɜ:mə'taɪtɪs] N Hautentzündung f, Dermatitis f

dermatologist [ˌdɜ:mə'tɒlədʒɪst] N Hautarzt m, Hautärztin f, Dermatologe m, Dermatologin f

dermatology [ˌdɜ:mə'tɒlədʒɪ] N Dermatologie f; **~ clinic** Hautklinik f

dermatosis [ˌdɜ:mə'təʊsɪs] N Hautkrankheit f, Dermatose f (spec)

derogate ['derəɡeɪt] VI **to ~ from sth** (form) einer Sache (dat) Abbruch tun

derogation [ˌderə'ɡeɪʃən] N (form, of power, dignity etc) Beeinträchtigung f, Schmälerung f, Abbruch m (of, from gen)

derogatory [dɪ'rɒɡətərɪ] ADJ abfällig, abschätzig

derrick ['derɪk] N Derrickkran m, Montagekran m; (above oil well) Bohrturm m

derring-do ['derɪŋ'du:] N (old) Verwegenheit f, Tollkühnheit f; **deeds of ~** verwegene or tollkühne Taten

derringer ['derɪndʒə'] N Derringer m or f

derv [dɜ:v] N (Brit) Diesel(kraftstoff) m, Dieselöl nt

dervish ['dɜ:vɪʃ] N Derwisch m

DES abbr of **Department of Education and Science** Bildungs- und Wissenschaftsministerium nt

desalinate [di:'sælɪneɪt] VT entsalzen

desalination [di:sælɪ'neɪʃən] N, **desalinization** [di:sælɪnaɪ'zeɪʃən] N Entsalzung f

desalination plant N Meerwasserentsalzungsanlage f

desalinize [di:'sælɪnaɪz] VT entsalzen

desalt [di:'sɔ:lt] VT (esp US) entsalzen

desalting plant [di:'sɔ:ltɪŋplɑ:nt] N (esp US) Meerwasserentsalzungsanlage f

descale [di:'skeɪl] VT entkalken

descant ['deskænt] N (Mus) Diskant m; **~ recorder** Sopranflöte f VI [des'kænt] sich auslassen or verbreiten (upon über +acc), ausgiebig kommentieren

descend [dɪ'send] VI **a** (= go down, person) hinuntergehen, hinabschreiten (geh); (lift, vehicle) hinunterfahren; (road) hinunterführen, hinuntergehen; (hill) abfallen; (from horse) absteigen; (Astron) untergehen; **in ~ing order of importance** nach Wichtigkeit geordnet
b (= have as ancestor) abstammen (from von)
c (= pass by inheritance, property) übergehen (from von, to auf +acc); (customs) überliefert werden (from von, to auf +acc); (rights) vererbt werden (from von, to auf +acc)
d (= attack suddenly) herfallen (on, upon über +acc), überfallen (on, upon sb jdn); (disease, illness) heimsuchen (on, upon sb jdn); (= come over, sadness etc) befallen (on, upon sb jdn); (silence) sich senken (on, upon über +acc)
e (inf, = visit) **to ~ (up)on sb** jdn überfallen (inf); **thousands of fans are expected to ~ on the city** man erwartet, dass tausende or Tausende von Fans die Stadt überlaufen
f (= lower oneself) **to ~ to sth** sich zu etw herablassen; **I'd never ~ to sarcasm** ich würde mich nicht dazu herablassen, sarkastisch zu werden; **he even ~ed to bribery** er scheute selbst vor Bestechung nicht zurück; **to ~ into anarchy/chaos/civil war** in Anarchie/Chaos/einen Bürgerkrieg versinken
VT **a** stairs hinuntergehen or -steigen, hinabschreiten (geh)
b **to be ~ed from** abstammen von

descendant [dɪ'sendənt] N **a** Nachkomme m **b** (Astron, Astrol) **in the ~** im Deszendenten

descender [dɪ'sendə'] N (Typ) Unterlänge f

descent [dɪ'sent] N **a** (= going down, of person) Hinuntergehen nt, Absteigen nt; (from mountain, of plane, into underworld) Abstieg m; (of gymnast) Abgang m; (= slope: of road) Abfall m; **during the ~ of the mountain** während des Abstiegs vom Berg; **the road made a sharp ~** die Straße fiel steil ab; **~ by parachute** Fallschirmabsprung m; **the ~ from the cross** (Art, Rel) die Kreuzabnahme
b (= ancestry) Abstammung f, Herkunft f; **of noble ~** von adliger Abstammung or Herkunft; **he claims direct ~ from ...** er behauptet, direkt von ... abzustammen
c (of property) Vererbung f, Übertragung f (to auf +acc); (of customs) Überlieferung f (to auf +acc)
d (Mil, fig, = attack) Überfall m (on auf +acc)
e (inf, = visit) Überfall m (inf)
f (fig, into crime etc) Absinken nt (into in +acc); (into chaos, civil war, madness) Versinken nt (into in +acc)

descramble [di:'skræmbl] VT (Telec) entschlüsseln

describe [dɪ'skraɪb] VT **a** (= give description of) beschreiben, schildern; **~ him for us** beschreiben Sie ihn uns (dat); **which cannot be ~d** was unbeschreiblich ist; **to ~ oneself/sb as ...** sich/jdn als ... bezeichnen; **he ~s himself as an intellectual** er bezeichnet sich als Intellektueller; **the police ~ him as dangerous/a terrorist** die Polizei bezeichnet ihn als gefährlich/(einen)

Terroristen; **he is ~d as being tall with short fair hair** er wird als groß mit kurzen blonden Haaren beschrieben **b** (*Math*) beschreiben

description [dɪ'skrɪpʃən] N **a** Beschreibung *f*; (*of event, situation*) Schilderung *f*, Beschreibung *f*; **she gave a detailed ~ of what had happened** sie beschrieb ausführlich, was vorgefallen war; **this is beyond ~** das ist ja unbeschreiblich; **to answer (to)** *or* **fit the ~ of ...** der Beschreibung als ... entsprechen; **they answer** *or* **fit the ~ of the suspects** auf sie trifft die Beschreibung der Verdächtigen zu; **do you know anyone of this ~?** kennen Sie jemanden, der dieser Beschreibung entspricht *or* auf den diese Beschreibung zutrifft?

b (= *sort*) Art *f*; **vehicles of every ~** *or* **of all ~s** Fahrzeuge aller Art **c** (*Math*) Beschreibung *f*

descriptive [dɪ'skrɪptɪv] ADJ **a** beschreibend; *account, adjective, passage* anschaulich; **~ writing** Beschreibung *f*; **his ~ powers** sein Talent zur Beschreibung; **to be ~ of sth** etw beschreiben **b** *linguistics, science etc* deskriptiv

descriptively [dɪs'krɪptɪvli] ADV anschaulich; (*Sci, Ling*) deskriptiv; **the name is not ~ accurate** der Name ist keine genaue Beschreibung; **it is known, ~, as ...** es ist anschaulicherweise unter dem Namen ... bekannt

descriptivism [dɪ'skrɪptɪvɪzəm] N (*Ling, Philos*) Deskriptivismus *m*

descriptivist [dɪ'skrɪptɪvɪst] (*Ling, Philos*) **N** Deskriptivist(in) *m(f)* **ADJ** deskriptivistisch

descry [dɪ'skraɪ] VT (*form, liter*) gewahren (*geh*), erblicken

desecrate ['desɪkreɪt] VT entweihen, schänden

desecration [desɪ'kreɪʃən] N Entweihung *f*, Schändung *f*

desecrator ['desɪkreɪtə'] N Schänder(in) *m(f)*; (*of graves*) Grabschänder(in) *m(f)*

desegregate [di:'segrɪgeɪt] VT *schools, sport* desegregieren; **~d schools** gemischtrassige Schulen *pl*

desegregation ['di:segrɪ'geɪʃən] N Aufhebung *f* der Rassentrennung (*of in +dat*), Desegregation *f*

deselect [di:sɪ'lekt] VT *MP etc* nicht wieder (als Kandidat) aufstellen

desensitize [di:'sensɪtaɪz] VT (*Phot*) lichtunempfindlich machen; (*Med*) desensibilisieren; **to become ~d to sth** (*fig*) einer Sache (*dat*) gegenüber abstumpfen

desert[1] ['dezət] **N** (*lit, fig*) Wüste *f* **ADJ** *attr* Wüsten-; **~ landscape** Wüstenlandschaft *f*; **~ warfare** Wüstenkrieg *m*

desert[2] [dɪ'zɜ:t] **VT** (= *leave*) verlassen; (= *abandon*) *person, cause, party* im Stich lassen; **by the time the police arrived the place was ~ed** als die Polizei eintraf, war niemand mehr da; **in winter the place is ~ed** im Winter ist der Ort verlassen; **to ~ the army** von der Armee desertieren **VI** (*Mil, fig*) desertieren, Fahnenflucht begehen; **to ~ from the army** von der Armee desertieren; **to ~ to the rebels** zu den Rebellen überlaufen

desert boots ['dezət-] PL Boots *pl*

deserted [dɪ'zɜ:tɪd] ADJ (= *abandoned*) verlassen; *place* unbewohnt, (wie) ausgestorben; *street* menschenleer; (= *lonely*) *person* verlassen, einsam

deserter [dɪ'zɜ:tə'] N (*Mil, fig*) Deserteur(in) *m(f)*

desertion [dɪ'zɜ:ʃən] N **a** (= *act*) Verlassen *nt*; (*Jur: of wife, family*) böswilliges Verlassen; (*Mil*) Desertion *f*, Fahnenflucht *f*; (*fig*) Fahnenflucht *f*; **~ to the enemy** Überlaufen *nt* zum Feind **b** (= *state*) Verlassenheit *f*

desert island ['dezət-] N einsame *or* verlassene Insel

desert rat ['dezət-] N (*Brit, fig inf*) Wüstensoldat *m*

deserts [dɪ'zɜ:ts] PL Verdienste *pl*; (= *reward: also* iro) verdiente Belohnung; (= *punishment*) verdiente Strafe; **according to one's ~** nach seinen Verdiensten; **to get one's just ~** bekommen, was man verdient hat, seine gerechte Belohnung bekommen

deserve [dɪ'zɜ:v] **VT** verdienen; **he ~s to win** er verdient den Sieg; **he ~s to be punished** er verdient es, bestraft zu werden; **she ~s better** sie hat etwas Besseres verdient; **to get what one ~s** bekommen, was man verdient hat **VI** **he ~s well of his country** (*form*) sein Land ist ihm zu Dank verpflichtet

deserved [dɪ'zɜ:vd] ADJ (wohl)verdient

deservedly [dɪ'zɜ:vɪdlɪ] ADV verdientermaßen; **and ~ so** und das zu Recht

deserving [dɪ'zɜ:vɪŋ] ADJ *person, action, cause* verdienstvoll; *winner* verdient; **the ~ poor** die Bedürftigen; **to be ~ of sth** etw verdient haben

deshabille [dezə'bi:l] N = **dishabille**

desiccate ['desɪkeɪt] VT trocknen

desiccated ['desɪkeɪtɪd] ADJ getrocknet; (*fig*) vertrocknet

desiccation [desɪ'keɪʃən] N Trocknung *f*, Trocknen *nt*

desideratum [dɪzɪdə'rɑ:təm] N *pl* **desiderata** [dɪzɪdə'rɑ:tə] Desiderat(um) *nt* (*liter*), Erfordernis *nt*

design [dɪ'zaɪn] **N** **a** (= *planning, shaping etc, of building, book, picture etc*) Entwurf *m*; (*of dress*) Design *nt*, Entwurf *m*; (*of car, machine, plane etc*) Konstruktion *f*; **it's still at the ~ stage** es befindet sich noch in der Konstruktion *or* im Konstruktionsstadium; **it was a good/faulty ~** es war gut/schlecht konstruiert; **a new ~** (*Aut*) ein neues Modell

b *no pl* (*as subject:* = *art of designing*) Design *nt* **c** (= *pattern: on pottery, material*) Muster *nt* **d** (= *intention*) Plan *m*, Absicht *f*; *evil* **~s** böse Absichten; **by ~** (*rather than accident*) absichtlich (und nicht zufällig); **to have ~s on sb/sth** mit jdm/etw etwas im Sinn haben, es auf jdn/etw abgesehen haben; **he has ~s on her** er hat etwas mit ihr vor

VT **a** (= *plan, draw*) entwerfen; *machine* konstruieren; **a well ~ed machine** eine gut durchkonstruierte Maschine; **car seats ~ed for maximum safety** Autositze, die für maximale Sicherheit konstruiert sind

b (= *intend*) **to be ~ed for sb/sth** für jdn/etw bestimmt *or* konzipiert sein; **the dictionary is ~ed for beginners** das Wörterbuch ist für Anfänger bestimmt *or* konzipiert; **a peace plan ~ed to end the civil war** ein Friedensplan, der den Bürgerkrieg beenden soll; **this magazine is ~ed to appeal to young people** diese Zeitschrift soll junge Leute ansprechen; **the legislation is ~ed as a consumer protection measure** die Gesetzgebung soll dem Verbraucherschutz dienen

VI planen, Pläne *or* Entwürfe machen **ADJ** *attr* Design-; **~ technology** Designtechnik *f*

designate ['dezɪgneɪt] **VT** **a** (= *name*) kennzeichnen, benennen; (= *appoint*) bestimmen, ernennen, designieren (*form*); **to ~ sb as sth** jdn zu etw ernennen **b** (= *indicate, specify, mark*) festlegen, bestimmen; **to be ~d for sth** für etw bestimmt sein; **smoking is permitted in ~d areas** Rauchen ist in den dafür bestimmten Bereichen erlaubt; **to be the ~d driver** als Fahrer bestimmt sein **ADJ** ['dezɪgnɪt] **the Prime Minister ~** der designierte Premierminister

designation [dezɪg'neɪʃən] N **a** (= *naming*) Kennzeichnung *f*, Benennung *f*; (= *appointment*) Bestimmung *f*, Ernennung *f* **b** (= *indicating*) Bestimmung *f*, Festlegung *f*

designedly [dɪ'zaɪnɪdlɪ] ADV absichtlich, vorsätzlich

design engineer N Designingenieur(in) *m(f)*

designer [dɪ'zaɪnə'] **N** Designer(in), Gestalter(in) *m(f)*; (= *fashion designer*) Modeschöpfer(in) *m(f)*; (*of machines etc*) Konstrukteur(in) *m(f)*; (*Theat*) Bühnenbildner(in) *m(f)* **ADJ** *attr* Designer-; **~ clothes** Designerkleider *pl*, Designerklamotten *pl* (*pej*)

designer: designer baby N Designerbaby *nt*; **designer drug** N Modedroge *f*, Designerdro-

ge *f*; **designer stubble** N (*hum*) Dreitagebart *m* (*inf*)

design fault N Designfehler *m*

designing [dɪ'zaɪnɪŋ] ADJ intrigant, hinterhältig

desirability [dɪzaɪərə'bɪlɪtɪ] N Wünschbarkeit *f*; **they discussed the ~ of launching the product in July** sie erörterten, ob es wünschenswert sei, das Produkt im Juli auf den Markt zu bringen; **in his eyes this only increased her ~** das machte sie in seinen Augen umso begehrenswerter; **in order to increase the ~ of these houses** um die Attraktivität dieser Häuser zu erhöhen

desirable [dɪ'zaɪərəbl] ADJ **a** wünschenswert; *action, progress* erwünscht; *goal* erstrebenswert **b** *position, offer, house* reizvoll, attraktiv **c** *woman* begehrenswert

desirably [dɪ'zaɪərəblɪ] ADV *located* reizvoll; *equipped, furnished* attraktiv; *male, sexy, feminine* begehrenswert

desire [dɪ'zaɪə'] ☼ 8.3 **N** Wunsch *m* (*for* nach); (= *longing*) Sehnsucht *f* (*for* nach); (*sexual*) Verlangen *nt* (*for* nach), Begehren *nt* (*for* nach); **her sexual ~s** ihre sexuellen Wünsche; **a ~ for peace/revenge** der Wunsch *m* nach Frieden/Rache; **the ~ to please** der Wunsch zu gefallen; **heart's ~** Herzenswunsch *m*; **I have no ~ to see him** ich habe kein Verlangen, ihn zu sehen; **I have no ~ to cause you any trouble** ich möchte Ihnen keine Unannehmlichkeiten bereiten

VT wünschen; *object* sich (*dat*) wünschen; *woman* begehren; *peace* haben wollen, verlangen nach; **if ~d** auf Wunsch; **to have the ~d effect** die gewünschte Wirkung haben; **cut the wood to the ~d length** das Holz auf die gewünschte Länge zuschneiden; **it leaves much** *or* **a lot to be ~d** das lässt viel *or* einiges zu wünschen übrig; **it leaves something to be ~d** es lässt zu wünschen übrig; **to ~ sb to do sth** (*form, = request*) jdn bitten *or* ersuchen, etw zu tun

desirous [dɪ'zaɪərəs] ADJ (*form*) **to be ~ of sth** etw wünschen; **to be ~ of doing sth** den Wunsch haben, etw zu tun

desist [dɪ'zɪst] VI (*form*) Abstand nehmen, absehen (*from doing sth* davon, etw zu tun, *from sth* von etw)

desk [desk] N Schreibtisch *m*; (*for pupils, master*) Pult *nt*; (*in shop, restaurant*) Kasse *f*; (*in hotel*) Empfang *m*; (*Press*) Ressort *nt*

desk: desk-bound ADJ an den Schreibtisch gebunden; **desk clerk** N (*US*) Empfangschef *m*, Empfangsdame *f*; **desk diary** N Tischkalender *m*; **desk editor** N Lektor(in) *m(f)*, Manuskriptbearbeiter(in) *m(f)*; (*Press*) Ressortchef(in) *m(f)*; **deskill** [di:'skɪl] VT *job* vereinfachen (*sodass die Arbeit keine oder kaum Fachkenntnisse mehr erfordert*); **desk job** N Bürojob *m*; **desk pad** N Schreibunterlage *f*

desktop ['desktɒp] N Arbeitsfläche *f*

desktop: desktop computer N Desktopcomputer *m*, Desktop-Computer *m*, Tischrechner *m*; **desktop publishing** N Desktop-Publishing *nt*

desk work N Schreibarbeit *f*

desolate ['desəlɪt] **ADJ** **a** *place* (= *bleak*) trostlos; (= *devastated*) verwüstet; *landscape* trostlos, öde; *beauty* einsam **b** (= *lonely, sad*) *person* trostlos; *feeling, cry* verzweifelt; **she looked ~** sie wirkte trostlos; **he was ~ without her** ohne sie fühlte er sich einsam und verlassen **VT** ['desəleɪt](*liter*) *place* verwüsten

desolately ['desəlɪtlɪ] ADV trostlos

desolation [desə'leɪʃən] N **a** (*of country by war*) Verwüstung *f* **b** (*of landscape*) Trostlosigkeit *f* **c** (= *grief*) Trostlosigkeit *f*; (= *friendlessness*) Verlassenheit *f*

despair [dɪ'speə'] **N** Verzweiflung *f* (*about, at* über +*acc*); **to be filled with ~** Verzweiflung überkam *or* ergriff ihn; **to be in ~** verzweifelt sein; **she looked at him in ~** sie sah ihn verzweifelt *or* voller Verzweiflung an; **in ~, she gave up** in ihrer Verzweiflung gab sie auf; **his ~**

of ever being able to return home seine Verzweiflung darüber, vielleicht nie mehr nach Hause zurückkehren zu können; **to be the ~ of sb** jdn zur Verzweiflung bringen [VI] verzweifeln, alle Hoffnung aufgeben; **to ~ of doing sth** alle Hoffnung aufgeben, etw zu tun; **to ~ of sth** alle Hoffnung auf etw (*acc*) aufgeben; **I ~ of you** du bringst *or* treibst mich zur Verzweiflung; **I ~ at their incompetence** mit ihrer Unfähigkeit bringen *or* treiben sie mich (noch) zur Verzweiflung; **to make sb ~** jdn zur Verzweiflung bringen *or* treiben

despairing ADJ , **despairingly** ADV [dɪsˈpɛərɪŋ, -lɪ] verzweifelt

despatch [dɪˈspætʃ] VT, N (*esp Brit*) = **dispatch**

desperado [ˌdespəˈrɑːdəʊ] N *pl* **-(e)s** Desperado *m*

desperate [ˈdespərɪt] ADJ **a** verzweifelt; *criminal* zum Äußersten entschlossen; *measure, situation* verzweifelt, extrem; *solution* extrem; **don't do anything ~!** mach keine Dummheiten!; **to get** *or* **grow ~** verzweifeln, in Verzweiflung geraten; **I haven't had a cigarette for hours, I'm getting ~** (*inf*) ich habe schon seit Stunden keine mehr geraucht, jetzt brauche ich aber dringend eine; **things are ~** die Lage ist extrem; **the company's ~ financial position** die extrem gespannte Finanzlage der Firma; **the ~ plight of the refugees** die schreckliche Not der Flüchtlinge; **to be ~ to do sth** etw unbedingt tun wollen; **to be ~ for sb to do sth** unbedingt wollen, dass jd etw tut; **to be ~ for sth** etw unbedingt *or* dringend brauchen

b (= *urgent*) *need, shortage* dringend; **her ~ need to be liked** ihr verzweifeltes Bedürfnis, gemocht zu werden; **to be in ~ need of sth** etw dringend brauchen; **a building in ~ need of repair** ein Gebäude, das dringend repariert werden muss

c (*inf hum*) **are you going out with Jane? you must be ~!** du gehst mit Jane aus? dir muss es ja wirklich schlecht gehen!; **I'm not that ~!** so schlimm ist es auch wieder nicht!

desperately [ˈdespərɪtlɪ] ADV **a** (= *frantically*) *fight, look for, hope, try* verzweifelt

b (= *urgently*) *need* dringend; *want* unbedingt; **to be ~ in need of sb/sth** jdn/etw dringend brauchen; **he ~ wanted to become a film maker** er wollte unbedingt Filmemacher werden

c (= *extremely*) *difficult* extrem; *important, sad* äußerst; **I'm ~ ill** schwer krank; **his son was ~ ill with cancer** sein Sohn war schwer krebskrank; **to be ~ worried (about sth)** sich (*dat*) (über etw *acc*) schreckliche Sorgen machen; **I'm not ~ worried** ich mache mir keine allzu großen Sorgen; **I'm not ~ keen to do sth** etw unbedingt tun wollen; **I'm not ~ keen on ...** ich bin nicht besonders scharf auf (*acc*) ...; **~ unhappy** todunglücklich; **to try ~ hard to do sth** verzweifelt versuchen, etw zu tun; **to be ~ in love (with sb)** unsterblich (in jdn) verliebt sein

desperation [ˌdespəˈreɪʃən] N Verzweiflung *f*; **an act of ~** eine Verzweiflungstat; **in (sheer) ~** aus (reiner) Verzweiflung; **to drive sb to ~** jdn zur Verzweiflung bringen *or* treiben

despicable [dɪˈspɪkəbl] ADJ verabscheuungswürdig; *person* verachtenswert, widerwärtig, ekelhaft

despicably [dɪˈspɪkəblɪ] ADV (+*vb*) abscheulich; (+*adj*) verachtenswert

despise [dɪˈspaɪz] VT verachten; *food also* verschmähen; **to ~ oneself (for sth)** sich selbst (wegen etw) verachten; **she ~d herself for deceiving him** sie verachtete sich dafür, dass sie ihn betrogen hatte

despising ADJ , **despisingly** ADV [dɪˈspaɪzɪŋ, -lɪ] verächtlich, voller Verachtung, verachtungsvoll

despite [dɪˈspaɪt] PREP trotz (+*gen*); **in ~ of** (*old, liter*) trotz, ungeachtet (+*gen*); **~ his warnings** seinen Warnungen zum Trotz; **~ what she says** trotz allem, was sie sagt; **I smiled ~ myself** ich konnte mir ein Lächeln nicht verkneifen

despoil [dɪˈspɔɪl] VT *person* berauben (*of gen*); *countryside* ausplündern

despondence [dɪˈspɒndəns], **despondency** [dɪˈspɒndənsɪ] N Niedergeschlagenheit *f*, Mutlosigkeit *f*

despondent [dɪˈspɒndənt] ADJ niedergeschlagen, mutlos; **to be** *or* **feel ~ about sth** über etw (*acc*) bedrückt sein; **to grow ~** den Mut verlieren

despondently [dɪˈspɒndəntlɪ] ADV niedergeschlagen, mutlos

despot [ˈdespɒt] N (*lit, fig*) Despot(in) *m(f)*

despotic ADJ , **despotically** ADV [desˈpɒtɪk, -əlɪ] (*lit, fig*) despotisch, herrisch

despotism [ˈdespətɪzəm] N Despotie *f*; (*as ideology*) Despotismus *m*

des res [ˈdezˈrez] N (*hum inf*) attraktiver Wohnsitz

dessert [dɪˈzɜːt] N Nachtisch *m*, Dessert *nt*; **for ~** als *or* zum Nachtisch

dessert: dessert apple N Dessertapfel *m*; **dessert plate** N Dessertteller *m*; **dessertspoon** N Dessertlöffel *m*; **dessert wine** N Dessertwein *m*

destabilization [ˌdiːsteɪbɪlaɪˈzeɪʃən] N Destabilisierung *f*

destabilize [diːˈsteɪbɪlaɪz] VT destabilisieren

destination [ˌdestɪˈneɪʃən] N (*of person*) Reiseziel *nt*; (*of goods*) Bestimmungsort *m*; (*fig, of person*) Bestimmung *f*; (*of money*) Zweck *m*; **port of ~** Bestimmungshafen *m*; **to know one's ~ in life** seine Bestimmung kennen

destine [ˈdestɪn] VT **a** (= *set apart, predestine*) *person* bestimmen, ausersehen; *object* bestimmen; **to be ~d to do sth** dazu bestimmt *or* ausersehen sein, etw zu tun; **to be ~d for sth** zu etw bestimmt sein **b** *usu pass* (= *be fated*) **we were ~d to meet** das Schicksal hat es so gewollt, dass wir uns begegnen; **I was ~d never to see them again** ich sollte sie nie (mehr) wiedersehen

destined [ˈdestɪnd] ADJ **~ for** (*ship, person*) unterwegs nach; *goods* für; **where is the cargo ~ for?** wo geht diese Fracht hin?

destiny [ˈdestɪnɪ] N **a** *no art* (= *determining power*) Schicksal *nt*, Vorsehung *f*; **Destiny** das Schicksal, die Vorsehung **b** (= *individual fate, fated event*) Schicksal *nt*, Geschick *nt*, Los *nt*; **the destinies of Germany during this period** die Geschicke Deutschlands während dieser Zeit; **to control one's own ~** sein Schicksal selbst in die Hand nehmen; **it was his ~** es war sein Schicksal *or* Los; **will it be our ~ to meet again?** wird uns das Schicksal (je) wieder zusammenführen?

destitute [ˈdestɪtjuːt] ADJ **a** (= *poverty-stricken*) mittellos; **to be utterly ~** bettelarm sein **b** (= *lacking*) bar (*of +gen*) **N** **the ~** *pl* die Mittellosen, die, die im Elend leben

destitution [ˌdestɪˈtjuːʃən] N (bittere) Not, Elend *nt*; (*esp financial*) Mittellosigkeit *f*

destroy [dɪˈstrɔɪ] VT **a** (*lit*: = *wreck, ruin*) zerstören; *box, toy, watch etc* kaputtmachen; *documents, trace* vernichten; **to ~ oneself** sich zugrunde *or* zu Grunde richten; **to be ~ed by fire** durch Brand vernichtet werden **b** (= *kill*) vernichten; *animal* einschläfern **c** (*fig*: = *put an end to*) zerstören; *influence, hopes, chances* zunichte machen, vernichten; *reputation, mood, beauty* ruinieren; *morals* zersetzen; **to ~ sb** jdn zugrunde *or* zu Grunde richten

destroyer [dɪˈstrɔɪə*] N (*Naut*) Zerstörer *m*

destruct [dɪˈstrʌkt] VI (*esp Space*) sich selbst zerstören

destruct button N Knopf *m* zur Selbstzerstörung

destructible [dɪˈstrʌktəbl] ADJ vernichtbar

destruction [dɪˈstrʌkʃən] N **a** (= *destroying, of town, building, hope*) Zerstörung *f*; (*of enemy, people, insects, documents*) Vernichtung *f*; (*of reputation*) Ruinierung *f*, Zerstörung *f*; (*of character,*

soul) Zerstörung *f*, Zersetzung *f* **b** (= *damage: caused by war, fire*) Verwüstung *f*, Zerstörung *f*

destructive [dɪˈstrʌktɪv] ADJ **a** (*lit*) *power, nature, war, wind* zerstörerisch; *effect* zerstörend; *person, behaviour, tendencies* destruktiv; **~ weapon** Vernichtungswaffe *f*; **the ~ force** *or* **power of ...** die Zerstörungskraft von ...; **~ urge** (*Psych*) Destruktionstrieb *m*; **to be ~ of** *or* **to sth** (*also fig*) etw zerstören; **these air strikes are highly ~ of human life** diese Luftangriffe fordern viele Menschenleben; **environmentally ~ projects** umweltzerstörende Projekte

b (*fig*) *power, emotion, influence, behaviour, criticism* destruktiv; **the ~ power of gossip** die Destruktivität von Tratsch; **a mutually ~ relationship** eine Beziehung, in der sich beide gegenseitig zerstören; **the economically ~ effect of inflation** die schädliche Auswirkung der Inflation auf die Wirtschaft

destructively [dɪˈstrʌktɪvlɪ] ADV destruktiv; **to be ~ critical** destruktive Kritik üben

destructiveness [dɪˈstrʌktɪvnɪs] N **a** (*of fire, war*) zerstörende Wirkung; (*of weapon*) Zerstörungskraft *f*; (*of person, child etc*) Destruktivität *f* (*esp Psych*), Zerstörungswut *f* **b** (*of criticism*) Destruktivität *f*, zersetzende Wirkung

destructor [dɪˈstrʌktə*] N (*Tech: also* **refuse destructor**) Müllverbrennungsanlage *f*

desuetude [dɪˈsjʊɪtjuːd] N (*form*) **to fall into ~** außer Gebrauch kommen

desulphurization, (*US*) **desulfurization** [ˌdiːsʌlfərəˈzeɪʃən] N Entschwefelung *f*; **~ plant** Entschwefelungsanlage *f*

desultorily [ˈdesəltərɪlɪ] ADV halbherzig; *chat, talk, dance* zwanglos; *announce, answer, point out* beiläufig; **they walked ~ toward(s) the house** sie schlenderten auf das Haus zu

desultoriness [ˈdesəltərɪnɪs] N (*of manner, approach, attempt*) Halbherzigkeit *f*; (*of conversation*) Zwanglosigkeit *f*; (*of reading*) Flüchtigkeit *f*

desultory [ˈdesəltərɪ] ADJ *reading* flüchtig; *manner, approach, attempt* halbherzig; *firing* vereinzelt, sporadisch; *applause* schwach; **to have a ~ conversation** eine zwanglose Unterhaltung führen; **in (a) ~ fashion** halbherzig

detach [dɪˈtætʃ] VT **a** (= *separate, unfasten*) *rope, cart* loslösen (*from von*); *section of form, document* abtrennen (*from von*); *part of machine, wooden leg, collar, hood* abnehmen (*from von*); *lining* herausnehmen (*from aus*); *coach from train* abhängen (*from von*); **to ~ oneself from a group** sich von einer Gruppe lösen *or* trennen; **a section became ~ed from ...** ein Teil löste sich von ... **b** (*Mil, Naut*) abkommandieren

detachable [dɪˈtætʃəbl] ADJ *part of machine, collar, legs* abnehmbar; *section of document* abtrennbar (*from von*); *lining* ausknöpfbar; (*with zip*) ausreißbar; *lens* auswechselbar

detached [dɪˈtætʃt] ADJ **a** (= *unbiased*) *opinion* distanziert, unvoreingenommen; (= *unemotional*) *manner, person, expression* kühl, distanziert **b** (*Brit*) **~ house** allein stehendes Haus, Einzelhaus *nt*

detachment [dɪˈtætʃmənt] N **a** (= *act of separating, of part of machine*) Abnehmen *nt*; (*of section of form, document*) Abtrennen *nt*; (*of rope, cart*) Loslösen *nt* **b** (= *lack of emotion*) Distanz *f*; (= *objectivity*) Abstand *m* **c** (*Mil*) Sonderkommando *nt*, Abordnung *f*

detail [ˈdiːteɪl] ✪ 19.1, 20.1, 21.3, 26.3 **N** **a** Detail *nt*; (*particular*) Einzelheit *f*; (= *part of painting, photo etc*) Ausschnitt *m*; (= *insignificant circumstance*) unwichtige Einzelheit; **in ~** im Detail, in Einzelheiten; **in great ~** in allen Einzelheiten, ausführlich; **in every ~** mit *or* in allen Einzelheiten; **every ~ was taken care of** jede Kleinigkeit wurde beachtet; **there's one little ~ you've forgotten** eine Kleinigkeit haben Sie (noch) vergessen; **please send me further ~s** bitte schicken Sie mir nähere *or* weitere Einzelheiten; **I didn't want to hear the ~s** ich wollte die Einzelheiten (gar) nicht hören; **to go into ~s** auf Einzelheiten eingehen, ins Detail gehen; **his attention to ~** seine Aufmerksamkeit für das Detail **ⓑ** (*Mil*) Sondertrupp *m* **VT ⓐ** *facts, story* ausführlich *or* genau berichten; **the specifications are fully ~ed on page 3** die genaue Ausführung wird auf Seite 3 aufgeführt **ⓑ** (*Mil*) *troops* abkommandieren (*for* zu, *to do* um zu tun)

detail drawing N Detailzeichnung *f*

detailed ['di:teɪld] ADJ *information, description, discussion, instructions* ausführlich; *report, account, plan, proposal* ausführlich, detailliert; *analysis, study, examination* eingehend; *investigation* eingehend, gründlich; *knowledge, work, results, map, picture* detailliert; (= *precise*) genau; **~ accounts** (*Fin*) genau geführte Geschäftsbücher; **they gave a more ~ account of what they had seen** sie beschrieben ausführlicher, was sie gesehen hatten; **he demanded ~ accounts of her spending** er verlangte eine genaue Aufstellung ihrer Ausgaben; **to have a ~ look at sth** etw genau untersuchen

detain [dɪ'teɪn] VT (= *keep back*) aufhalten; (*police*) in Haft nehmen; **to be ~ed** (= *be arrested*) verhaftet werden; (= *be in detention*) sich in Haft or in polizeilichem Gewahrsam befinden; **to ~ sb for questioning** jdn zur Vernehmung festhalten

detainee [diːteɪ'niː] N Häftling *m*

detect [dɪ'tekt] VT entdecken, herausfinden; (= *see, make out*) ausfindig machen; *crime* aufdecken; *disease* feststellen; *a tone of sadness, movement, noise* wahrnehmen; *mine, gas* aufspüren; **do I ~ a note of irony?** höre ich da nicht eine gewisse Ironie (heraus)?

detectable [dɪ'tektəbl] ADJ (= *able to be found*) *trace* feststellbar; (= *discernible*) wahrnehmbar; *effect, sign* erkennbar; **no ~ difference** kein erkennbarer Unterschied

detection [dɪ'tekʃən] N **ⓐ** (*of criminal*) Entlarvung *f*; (*of crime*) Entdeckung *f*, Aufdeckung *f*; (*of fault*) Entdeckung *f*; Feststellung *f*; (*of disease*) Feststellung *f*; (= *detective work*) Ermittlungsarbeit *f*; **to avoid** *or* **escape ~** nicht entdeckt werden; (*criminal*) nicht gefasst werden, nicht dingfest gemacht werden; (*mistake*) dem Aufmerksamkeit (*dat*) entgehen; **he tried to escape ~ by ...** er versuchte, unentdeckt zu bleiben, indem ...; **a brilliant piece of ~** ein glänzendes Stück Detektivarbeit **ⓑ** (*of gases, mines*) Aufspürung *f*

detective [dɪ'tektɪv] N Detektiv(in) *m(f)*; (= *police detective*) Kriminalbeamte(r) *m*/-beamtin *f*

detective: detective agency N Detektivbüro *nt*, Detektei *f*; **detective chief inspector** N (*Brit*) Kriminaloberinspektor(in) *m(f)*; **detective chief superintendent** N (*Brit*) Kriminalhauptkommissar(in) *m(f)*; **detective constable** N (*Brit*) Kriminalbeamte(r) *m*/-beamtin *f*; **detective inspector** N Kriminalinspektor(in) *m(f)*; **detective sergeant** N Kriminalmeister(in) *m(f)*; **detective story** N Kriminalgeschichte *f*, Kriminalroman *m*, Krimi *m* (*inf*); **detective superintendent** N (*Brit*) Kriminalkommissar(in) *m(f)*; **detective work** N kriminalistische Arbeit

detector [dɪ'tektə'] N (*Rad, Tech*) Detektor *m*

detector van N (*Rad, Tech*) Funkmesswagen *m*

détente [deɪ'tɑːnt] N Entspannung *f*, Détente *f*

detention [dɪ'tenʃən] N **ⓐ** (= *captivity*) Haft *f*, Gewahrsam *m*; (= *act*) Festnahme *f*; (*Mil*) Arrest *m*; (*Sch*) Nachsitzen *nt*; **to give a pupil two hours' ~** einen Schüler zwei Stunden nachsitzen lassen; **he's in ~** (*Sch*) er sitzt nach **ⓑ** (= *being held up, delayed*) Verzögerung *f*, Aufenthalt *m*

detention centre, (*US*) **detention center** N Jugendstrafanstalt *f*

deter [dɪ'tɜː'] VT (= *prevent*) abhalten, hindern; (= *discourage*) abschrecken; **to ~ sb from sth** jdn von etw abhalten or an etw (*dat*) hindern; **to ~ sb from doing sth** jdn davon abhalten or daran hindern, etw zu tun; **he won't be ~red**

(**by the cost**) er lässt sich (von den Kosten) nicht abschrecken; **don't let him ~ you** lassen Sie sich nicht von ihm abhalten *or* abbringen

detergent [dɪ'tɜːdʒənt] N Reinigungs- *or* Säuberungsmittel *nt*; (= *soap powder etc*) Waschmittel *nt* ADJ reinigend

deteriorate [dɪ'tɪərɪəreɪt] VI sich verschlechtern; (*materials*) verderben; (*species*) entarten; (*morals, brickwork*) verfallen

deterioration [dɪ,tɪərɪə'reɪʃən] N Verschlechterung *f*; (*of materials*) Verderben *nt*; (*of species*) Entartung *f*; (*of morals, brickwork*) Verfall *m*

determent [dɪ'tɜːmənt] N Abschreckung *f* (*from* von); (= *means*) Abschreckungsmittel *nt*

determinable [dɪ'tɜːmɪnəbl] ADJ **ⓐ** *quantity* bestimmbar **ⓑ** (*Jur*) befristet

determinant [dɪ'tɜːmɪnənt] ADJ determinierend *attr*, entscheidend N ausschlaggebender Faktor; (*Math, Biol etc*) Determinante *f*

determinate [dɪ'tɜːmɪnɪt] ADJ *number, period etc* bestimmt, begrenzt; *concept* festgelegt; *direction* bestimmt

determination [dɪ,tɜːmɪ'neɪʃən] N **ⓐ** (= *firmness of purpose*) Entschlossenheit *f*; **he has great ~** er ist ein Mensch von großer Entschlusskraft; **he showed fierce ~** er zeigte wilde Entschlossenheit; **there is an air of ~ about him** er hat etwas Entschlossenes an sich **ⓑ** (= *determining*) Determinierung *f*; (*of character, future*) Bestimmung *f*, Determinierung *f*; (*of cause, nature, position*) Ermittlung *f*, Bestimmung *f*; (*of frontiers*) Festlegung *f*, Festsetzung *f*

determinative [dɪ'tɜːmɪnətɪv] (*Gram*) N Determinativ(um) *nt* ADJ determinativ

determine [dɪ'tɜːmɪn] VT **ⓐ** (= *be a decisive factor in*) *sb's character, future etc* bestimmen, determinieren **ⓑ** (= *settle, fix*) *conditions, price* festlegen, festsetzen **ⓒ** (= *ascertain*) *cause, nature, position* ermitteln, bestimmen **ⓓ** (= *resolve*) beschließen **ⓔ** (*Jur*) *contract* beenden

▶ **determine on** VI +*prep obj course of action, alternative* sich entschließen zu; **to determine on doing sth** beschließen *or* sich entschließen, etw zu tun

determined [dɪ'tɜːmɪnd] ⚙ 8.2 ADJ entschlossen; *look* fest entschlossen; **he is a ~ opponent/ supporter of capital punishment** er ist ein entschiedener Gegner/Befürworter der Todesstrafe; **to make a ~ effort** *or* **attempt to do sth** sein Möglichstes tun, um etw zu tun; **he is ~ that ...** er hat (fest) beschlossen, dass ...; **to be ~ to do sth** fest entschlossen sein, etw zu tun, etw unbedingt tun wollen; **they are ~ to see that the people responsible are brought to justice** sie wollen unbedingt dafür sorgen, dass die Verantwortlichen vor Gericht gebracht werden; **he's ~ to make me lose my temper** er legt es darauf an, dass ich wütend werde; **you seem ~ to exhaust yourself** du scheinst dich mit aller Gewalt kaputtmachen zu wollen

determinedly [dɪ'tɜːmɪndlɪ] ADV (+*vb*) entschlossen; *say* bestimmt, resolut; (+*adj*) entschieden; (= *stubbornly*) beharrlich; **Brian remained ~ optimistic** Brian ließ sich seinen Optimismus nicht nehmen

determiner [dɪ'tɜːmɪnə'] N (*Gram*) Bestimmungswort *nt*

determining [dɪ'tɜːmɪnɪŋ] ADJ entscheidend, bestimmend

determinism [dɪ'tɜːmɪnɪzəm] N Determinismus *m*

determinist [dɪ'tɜːmɪnɪst] ADJ deterministisch N Determinist(in) *m(f)*

deterministic [dɪ,tɜːmɪ'nɪstɪk] ADJ deterministisch

deterrence [dɪ'terəns] N Abschreckung *f*

deterrent [dɪ'terənt] N (*also Mil*) Abschreckungsmittel *nt*; **to act as a ~** als Abschreckung(smittel) dienen (*to* für); **to be a ~** abschrecken ADJ abschreckend, Abschreckungs-; **~ effect** Abschreckungseffekt *m*

detest [dɪ'test] VT verabscheuen, hassen; **I ~ having to get up early** ich hasse es, früh aufstehen zu müssen

detestable [dɪ'testəbl] ADJ widerwärtig, abscheulich; *character also* verabscheuungswürdig

detestably [dɪ'testəblɪ] ADV widerwärtig, abscheulich

detestation [,diːtes'teɪʃən] N Abscheu *m* (*of* vor +*dat*)

dethrone [diː'θrəʊn] VT entthronen

dethronement [diː'θrəʊnmənt] N Entthronung *f*

detonate ['detəneɪt] VI (*fuse*) zünden; (*bomb*) detonieren VT zur Explosion bringen; **detonating device** Detonator *m*

detonation [,detə'neɪʃən] N Zündung *f*

detonator ['detəneɪtə'] N Zünd- *or* Sprengkapsel *f*; (*Rail*) Nebelsignal *nt*

detour ['diːtʊə'] N **ⓐ** (*in road, also fig*) Umweg *m*; (*in river*) Schleife *f*, Bogen *m*; (*from a subject*) Abschweifung *f*; **to make a ~** einen Umweg machen **ⓑ** (*for traffic*) Umleitung *f* VT *traffic* umleiten VI (= *make a detour*) einen Umweg machen

detox ['diːtɒks] (*inf*) N (= *treatment*) Entzug *m* (*inf*); ~ **centre** (*Brit*) *or* **center** (*US*) Entzugsklinik *f*; ~ **programme** (*Brit*) *or* **program** (*US*) Entzugsprogramm *nt* (*inf*) VI Entzug machen (*inf*)

detoxification [,diːtɒksɪfɪ'keɪʃən] N Entgiftung *f*

detoxify [diː'tɒksɪfaɪ] VT entgiften

detract [dɪ'trækt] VI **to ~ from sth** etw beeinträchtigen, einer Sache (*dat*) Abbruch tun; *from pleasure, merit also* etw schmälern

detraction [dɪ'trækʃən] N Beeinträchtigung *f* (*from gen*), Schmälerung *f* (*from gen*)

detractor [dɪ'træktə'] N Kritiker(in) *m(f)*

detrain [diː'treɪn] VT ausladen VI (*troops*) aussteigen

detribalize [diː'traɪbəlaɪz] VT die Stammesstruktur auflösen in (+*dat*); **as Africa becomes increasingly ~d** mit dem zunehmenden Verfall der Stammesstruktur in Afrika

detriment ['detrɪmənt] N Schaden *m*, Nachteil *m*; **to the ~ of sth** zum Schaden einer Sache (*gen*), zum Schaden von etw; **to sb's ~** zu jds Nachteil; **I don't know anything to his ~** ich weiß nichts Nachteiliges über ihn; **without ~ to** ohne Schaden für

detrimental [,detrɪ'mentl] ADJ (*to health, reputation*) schädlich (*to dat*); *effect* nachteilig, schädlich (*to für*); *influence* schädlich; (*to case, cause, one's interest*) abträglich (*to dat*); **to be ~ to sb/ sth** jdm/einer Sache (*dat*) schaden; **this could have a ~ effect** das könnte sich nachteilig auswirken

detritus [dɪ'traɪtəs] N (*Geol*) Geröll *nt*; (*fig*) Müll *m*

de trop [də'trəʊ] ADJ fehl am Platz, überflüssig

detumescent [,diːtjʊ'mesnt] ADJ (*form*) abschwellend

deuce¹ [djuːs] N **ⓐ** (*Cards*) Zwei *f* **ⓑ** (*Tennis*) Einstand *m*; **after ten ~s** nachdem es zehnmal Einstand gegeben hatte; **to be at ~** den Einstand erreicht haben

deuce² N (*dated inf*) Teufel *m* → **devil** N c

deuced ['djuːsɪd] (*dated inf*) ADJ verteufelt (*dated inf*), verdammt (*inf*); **that ~ dog** dieser verdammte Hund (*inf*) ADV **it was ~ difficult** es war verteufelt schwierig (*dated inf*)

deucedly ['djuːsɪdlɪ] ADV (*dated inf*) verteufelt (*dated inf*)

deus ex machina ['deɪəseks'mækɪnə] N Deus ex Machina *m*

deuterium [djuː'tɪərɪəm] N Deuterium *nt*

Deuteronomy [,djuːtə'rɒnəmɪ] N das fünfte Buch Mose(s), Deuteronomium *nt* (*spec*)

Deutschmark ['dɔɪtʃmɑːk], **Deutsche Mark** [,dɔɪtʃə'mɑːk] N (*Hist*) D-Mark *f*, Deutsche Mark *f*

devaluate [diːˈvæljʊeɪt] VT = **devalue**

devaluation [ˌdɪvæljʊˈeɪʃən] N Abwertung f

devalue [diːˈvæljuː] VT abwerten

devastate [ˈdevəsteɪt] VT **a** (lit) town, land verwüsten; (fig) opposition vernichten; economy zugrunde or zu Grunde richten **b** (inf, = overwhelm) umhauen (inf); **I was ~d** das hat mich umgehauen (inf); **they were ~d by the news** die Nachricht hat sie tief erschüttert

devastating [ˈdevəsteɪtɪŋ] ADJ **a** (= destructive) consequence, war, attack, storm, disease verheerend; **to be ~ to** or **for sth**, **to have a ~ effect on sth** verheerende Folgen für etw haben **b** (fig) effect schrecklich; news niederschmetternd; criticism, report, attack, performance unschlagbar; defeat vernichtend; woman, wit umwerfend (inf); **a ~ blow/loss** ein vernichtender Schlag/ Verlust; **to be ~ to** or **for sb** jdn niederschmettern; **to be in ~ form** in unschlagbarer Form sein

devastatingly [ˈdevəsteɪtɪŋlɪ] ADV (lit) vernichtend; (fig) attractive, effective, witty, funny umwerfend (inf); accurate, frank verheerend; **the author demolished these arguments ~** der Autor machte diese Argumente total zunichte

devastation [ˌdevəˈsteɪʃən] N Verwüstung f

develop [dɪˈveləp] VT **a** mind, body entwickeln **b** argument, thesis, outlines (weiter)entwickeln, weiter ausführen; original idea (weiter)entwickeln; plot of novel (= unfold) entfalten; (= fill out) weiterentwickeln, ausbauen; (Mus) theme durchführen **c** natural resources, region, ground, new estate erschließen; old part of a town sanieren; new series, new model entwickeln; business (from scratch) aufziehen; (= expand) erweitern, ausbauen; **they plan to ~ this area into a ...** es ist geplant, dieses Gebiet als ... zu erschließen **d** liking, taste, talent entwickeln; cold sich (dat) zuziehen **e** (Phot, Math) entwickeln

VI **a** (person, region, country) sich entwickeln; **to ~ into sth** sich zu etw entwickeln, etw werden **b** (illness, tendency, feeling) sich entwickeln; (talent, plot etc) sich entfalten **c** (Phot) entwickelt werden **d** (event, situation) sich entwickeln; **it later ~ed that he had never seen her** später stellte sich heraus or zeigte es sich, dass er sie nie gesehen hatte

developer [dɪˈveləpə'] N **a** = **property developer b** (Phot) Entwickler m **c** late ~ Spätentwickler(in) m(f)

developing [dɪˈveləpɪŋ] ADJ crisis, storm aufkommend; industry neu entstehend; interest wachsend; foetus, embryo sich entwickelnd; society, economy sich entwickelnd; **the ~ world** die Entwicklungsländer pl N **a** = **development a**, **d b** (Phot) Entwickeln nt

developing: **developing bath** N Entwicklerbad nt; **developing country** N Entwicklungsland nt; **developing tank** N Entwicklerschale f

development [dɪˈveləpmənt] N **a** (of person, mind, body) Entwicklung f **b** (= way subject, plot etc is developed) Ausführung f; (of interests) Entfaltung f; (of argument etc) (Weiter)entwicklung f; (Mus) Durchführung f **c** (= change in situation) Entwicklung f; **new ~s in ...** neue Entwicklungen in ...; **to await (further) ~s** neue Entwicklungen abwarten **d** (of area, site, new town) Erschließung f; (of old part of town) Sanierung f; (of industry, from scratch) Entwicklung f; (= expansion) Ausbau m; **industrial ~** Gewerbegebiet nt; **residential ~** Wohnsiedlung f; **office ~** Bürokomplex m; **business ~** Geschäftszentrum nt; **we live in a new ~** wir leben in einer neuen Siedlung; **unauthorized ~** illegale Baumaßnahmen pl **e** (Phot, Math) Entwicklung f

developmental [dɪveləpˈmentl] ADJ Entwicklungs-; **~ stage** Entwicklungsphase f

development: **development area** N Entwicklungsgebiet nt; (in town) Erschließungsgebiet nt; (in old town) Sanierungsgebiet nt; **development company** N (Wohnungs)baugesellschaft f; **development costs** PL Erschließungskosten pl; **development cycle** N (Comm, Biol) Entwicklungszyklus m; **development grant** N Entwicklungsförderung f

deviancy [ˈdiːvɪənsɪ] N abweichendes Verhalten, Devianz f

deviant [ˈdiːvɪənt] ADJ behaviour abweichend, deviant (spec) N jd, der von der Norm abweicht, Deviant m (spec)

deviate [ˈdiːvɪeɪt] VI **a** (person: from truth, former statement, routine) abweichen (from von) **b** (ship, plane, projectile) vom Kurs abweichen or abkommen; (deliberately) vom Kurs abgehen

deviation [ˌdiːvɪˈeɪʃən] N Abweichen nt, Abweichung f; **~ from the norm** Abweichung f von der Norm

deviationism [ˌdiːvɪˈeɪʃənɪzəm] N Abweichlertum nt

deviationist [ˌdiːvɪˈeɪʃənɪst] ADJ abweichend N Abweichler(in) m(f)

device [dɪˈvaɪs] N **a** (= gadget etc) Gerät nt; (= extra fitment) Vorrichtung f; (explosive) ~ Sprengkörper m; **nuclear ~** atomarer Sprengkörper; **a rhetorical ~** ein rhetorischer Kunstgriff **b** **to leave sb to his own ~s** jdn sich (dat) selbst überlassen **c** (= emblem) Emblem nt; (= motto) Motto nt, Devise f

devil [ˈdevl] N **a** (= evil spirit) Teufel m **b** (= person, child) Teufel m (inf); (= object, screw etc) Plage f; (= daring person) Teufelskerl m; **you poor ~!** (du) armer Teufel!; **you little ~!** du kleiner Satansbraten!; **shall I have another? – go on, be a ~** soll ich noch einen trinken etc? – los, nur zu, riskier! (inf); **be a ~ and say yes** riskier mal was und sag ja or Ja **c** (inf, as intensifier) **I had a ~ of a job getting here** es war verdammt schwierig, hierher zu kommen (inf); **he had a ~ of a time selling his car** er hatte schreckliche Schwierigkeiten, sein Auto zu verkaufen; **I live a ~ of a long way away** ich wohne verdammt weit weg; **the ~ of it is ...** das Ärgerliche daran ist ... (inf); **how/ what/why/who the ~ ...?** wie/was/warum/wer zum Teufel or in drei Teufels Namen ...?; **to work like the ~** wie ein Pferd schuften (inf); **to run/drive like the ~** wie ein geölter Blitz sausen/fahren (inf); **there will be the ~ to pay** das dicke Ende kommt nach **d** (in expressions) **(to be) between the Devil and the deep blue sea** (sich) in einer Zwickmühle (befinden); **go to the ~!** (inf) scher dich zum Teufel! (inf); **the ~ take him/it** (old inf) der Teufel soll ihn/es holen, hols der Teufel (inf); **the ~ finds work for idle hands** (Prov) Müßiggang ist aller Laster Anfang (Prov); **to sell one's soul to the ~** dem Teufel seine Seele verkaufen; **he has the ~ in him today** ihn reitet heute der Teufel; **speak** or **talk** (Brit) **of the ~!** wenn man vom Teufel spricht!; **give the ~ his due** das muss der Neid ihm lassen; **to have the ~'s own luck** or **the luck of the ~** (inf) ein Schweineglück (inf) or unverschämtes Glück haben; **better the ~ you know (than the ~ you don't)** (prov) von zwei Übeln wählt man besser das, was man schon kennt; **(the) ~ take the hindmost** den Letzten beißen die Hunde (Prov) VI (Jur, Typ, Liter etc) Handlangerdienste tun VT (Cook) kidneys scharf gewürzt grillen

devil fish N (= ray) Rochen m; (= octopus) Tintenfisch m

devilish [ˈdevlɪʃ] ADJ teuflisch; chuckle, grin schalkhaft, verschmitzt ADV (dated inf, = extremely) verteufelt (dated inf); **~ funny** urkomisch

devilishly [ˈdevlɪʃlɪ] ADV **a** = **devilish** ADV **b** chuckle, grin schalkhaft, verschmitzt

devilishness [ˈdevlɪʃnɪs] N Teuflische(s) nt (of an +dat); (of chuckle, grin) Schalkhaftigkeit f, Verschmitztheit f

devil-may-care [ˌdevlmeɪˈkeə'] ADJ leichtsinnig, vollständig unbekümmert; **he's got a ~ attitude to life** seine Lebenseinstellung ist „Nach mir die Sintflut"

devilment [ˈdevlmənt] N (grober) Unfug; **just for ~** aus lauter Übermut; **her eyes twinkled with ~** ihre Augen blitzten voller Übermut

devilry [ˈdevlrɪ] N **a** (= mischief) (grober) Unfug **b** (= black magic) Teufelskunst f **c** (= extreme wickedness, cruelty) Teufelei f

devil: **devil's advocate** N des Teufels Advokat m, Advocatus Diaboli m; **to play ~** den Advocatus Diaboli spielen; **devil's food cake** N (esp US) schwere Schokoladentorte; **devils-on-horseback** [ˌdevlzɒnˈhɔːsbæk] PL (Cook) mit Speckscheiben umwickelte Backpflaumen auf Toast

devious [ˈdiːvɪəs] ADJ **a** (= deceitful, sly) person verschlagen, hinterhältig; means, method hinterhältig, krumm (inf); business, plan, game, attempt trickreich; **by ~ means** auf die krumme Tour (inf); **to have a ~ mind** (= be cunning) ganz schön schlau sein; **his/her ~ mind** seine/ihre verschlungenen Gehirnwindungen **b** (= tortuous) route, way gewunden; **by a ~ route** auf einem Umweg

deviously [ˈdiːvɪəslɪ] ADV (+vb) mit List und Tücke

deviousness [ˈdiːvɪəsnɪs] N **a** (= deceitfulness) Verschlagenheit f, Hinterhältigkeit f; **the ~ of his mind** seine verschlungenen Gedankengänge pl **b** (= tortuousness) Gewundenheit f

devise [dɪˈvaɪz] VT **a** scheme, style sich (dat) ausdenken; way, means finden; plan schmieden; strategy, policy ausarbeiten **b** (Jur) hinterlassen, vermachen N (Jur) Vermächtnis nt, Hinterlassenschaft f

devitalization [diːvaɪtəlaɪˈzeɪʃən] N Schwächung f

devitalize [diːˈvaɪtəlaɪz] VT schwächen

devoid [dɪˈvɔɪd] ADJ **~ of** bar +gen, ohne

devoir [dəˈvwɑː] N (form, liter) **a** (= duty) Pflicht f; **to do one's ~** seine Pflicht tun **b** (= respect) Höflichkeit f

devolution [ˌdiːvəˈluːʃən] N **a** (of power) Übertragung f (from ... to von ... auf +acc); (Pol) Dezentralisierung f **b** (Jur, of property, = active devolving) Übertragung f; (= being devolved) Übergang m **c** (Biol) Rückentwicklung f, Degeneration f

---

DEVOLUTION

Innerhalb des politischen Systems Großbritanniens bezieht sich der Begriff **devolution** auf den Dezentralisierungsprozess, das Delegieren von Machtbefugnissen aus dem traditionellen Regierungssitz in London in die Hauptstädte von Schottland (Edinburgh) und Wales (Cardiff). Allerdings ist heftig umstritten, wie weit dieser Prozess gehen soll. Einige hätten am liebsten eigene gesetzgebende Versammlungen für Schottland und Wales innerhalb des Verbandes von Großbritannien, während die Nationalisten anstelle der **devolution** absolute Unabhängigkeit und Eigenstaatlichkeit fordern.

---

devolve [dɪˈvɒlv] (on, upon auf +acc) VI (duty, property etc) übergehen; **the cost of the operation ~s upon the patient** die Kosten für die Operation muss der Patient tragen; **it ~d on me to take the final decision** die endgültige Entscheidung fiel mir zu; **the union ~d into a looser confederation of states** die Union löste sich in einen lockeren Staatenbund auf VT duty, power etc übertragen; **a ~d government** eine dezentralisierte Regierung

devote [dɪˈvəʊt] VT time, life, oneself, book, chapter, attention widmen (to dat); thought verwenden (to auf +acc); one's energies konzentrieren (to auf +acc); building verwenden (to für); resources bestimmen (to für)

devoted [dɪ'vəʊtɪd] ADJ *wife, husband, mother, father* liebend; *servant, follower, fan* treu; *admirer* eifrig; **~ care** hingebungsvolle Pflege; **30 years of ~ service** dreißig Jahre treuer Dienste (*gen*); **to be ~ to sb** jdn innig lieben; (*servant, fan*) jdm treu ergeben sein; **they are ~ to one another** sie lieben sich innig; **to be ~ to a cause** sich völlig für eine Sache engagieren; **to be ~ to one's family** in seiner Familie völlig aufgehen

devotedly [dɪ'vəʊtɪdlɪ] ADV hingebungsvoll; *serve, follow* treu; *support* eifrig

devotee [ˌdevəʊ'tiː] N Anhänger(in) *m(f)*; (*of a writer*) Verehrer(in) *m(f)*; (*of music, poetry*) Liebhaber(in) *m(f)*

devotion [dɪ'vəʊʃən] N **a** (*to friend, wife etc*) Ergebenheit *f* (*to* gegenüber); (*to work*) Hingabe *f* (*to an* +*acc*); **~ to duty** Pflichteifer *m* **b** (*of part of building, time etc*) (*to* für) Verwendung *f*; (*of resources*) Bestimmung *f* **c devotions** PL (*Rel*) Andacht *f*; **to be at one's ~s** in Andacht versunken sein

devotional [dɪ'vəʊʃənl] ADJ *book, literature* religiös; **~ objects** Devotionalien *pl*

devour [dɪ'vaʊə] VT (*lit, fig*) verschlingen; **I could ~ you** ich habe dich zum Fressen gern, du bist wirklich zum Fressen; **to be ~ed by jealousy/an all-consuming passion** von Eifersucht/einer unersättlichen Leidenschaft verzehrt werden

devouring [dɪ'vaʊərɪŋ] ADJ *hunger, passion* verzehrend

devout [dɪ'vaʊt] ADJ *person, Christian, Muslim* fromm; *Christianity, Catholicism, Marxist, environmentalist, follower* überzeugt; *supporter* treu; *opponent* eingeschworen; **it was my father's ~ wish/hope that ...** es war der inständige Wunsch/die sehnliche Hoffnung meines Vaters, dass ..., mein Vater wünschte sich inständig/hoffte sehnlich, dass ... N **the ~** die Frommen

devoutly [dɪ'vaʊtlɪ] ADV **a** (*Rel*, +*adj*) tief; (+*vb*) fromm; **~ religious** tiefreligiös; **a ~ Christian prince** ein frommer christlicher Prinz; **he ~ followed the Catholic faith** er blieb dem katholischen Glauben treu **b** (= *sincerely*) believe ernsthaft; *wish* sehnlich; *hope* inständig

dew [djuː] N Tau *m*

dewater [diː'wɔːtə] VT entwässern

dew: dewberry ['djuːbərɪ] N Brombeere *f*; **dewclaw** N Afterkralle *f*, Afterklaue *f*; **dewdrop** N Tautropfen *m*; **dewfall** N (*poet, liter*) Taufall *m*; (= *film of dew*) Tauschleier *m* (*poet*); **dewlap** N (*on cow*) Wamme *f*; (*hum, on person*) Doppelkinn *nt*; **dew point** N (*Phys*) Taupunkt *m*; **dew pond** N *flacher Teich, der sich aus Regenwasser bildet*

dewy ['djuːɪ] ADJ (+*er*) *grass, morning* taufeucht; *skin* taufrisch; **her eyes were ~** ihre Augen hatten einen feuchten Schimmer

dewy-eyed ['djuːɪaɪd] ADJ (= *innocent, naive*) naiv; (= *trusting*) vertrauensselig; **to go or get all ~** feuchte Augen bekommen

dexterity [deks'terɪtɪ] N Geschick *nt*

dexterous, **dextrous** ['dekstrəs] ADJ geschickt

dexterously ['dekstrəslɪ] ADV geschickt

dextrose ['dekstrəʊz] N Dextrose *f*, Traubenzucker *m*

DFC *abbr of* **Distinguished Flying Cross** *Militärorden für hervorragende Piloten*

DFE (*Brit*) *abbr of* **Department for Education** Ministerium *nt* für Bildung und Erziehung

dg *abbr of* **decigram(s)** *or* **decigramme(s)** dg

dhow [daʊ] N D(h)au *f*

DHSS (*Brit, old*) *abbr of* **Department of Health and Social Security** Ministerium *nt* für Gesundheit und Soziales

diabetes [ˌdaɪə'biːtiːz] N Zuckerkrankheit *f*, Diabetes *m*, Zucker *no art* (*inf*)

diabetic [ˌdaɪə'betɪk] ADJ **a** zuckerkrank, diabetisch (*spec*); **~ patient** Diabetespatient(in) *m(f)*; **~ coma** Diabetikerkoma *nt* **b** *beer, choco-*

late, drugs, clinic für Diabetiker **N** Zuckerkranke(r) *mf*, Diabetiker(in) *m(f)*

diabolic [ˌdaɪə'bɒlɪk], **diabolical** [ˌdaɪə'bɒlɪkəl] ADJ **a** (*form,* = *satanic*) *forces* diabolisch (*geh*), teuflisch; **with ~al cunning** mit ungeheurer Gerissenheit; **~ possession** Besessenheit *f* durch den Teufel **b** (*inf,* = *appalling*) entsetzlich; **~al weather** Sauwetter *nt* (*inf*)

diabolically [ˌdaɪə'bɒlɪkəlɪ] ADV **a** (*inf.* = *incredibly*) *clever, difficult* teuflisch (*inf*); *cunning* ungeheuer; **~ bad** entsetzlich (schlecht) **b** (= *wickedly*) *grin, smile* boshaft

diachronic [ˌdaɪə'krɒnɪk] ADJ diachron

diacritic [ˌdaɪə'krɪtɪk] ADJ diakritisch **N** diakritisches Zeichen

diacritical [ˌdaɪə'krɪtɪkəl] ADJ diakritisch

diadem ['daɪədem] N Diadem *nt*

diaeresis, (*US*) **dieresis** [daɪ'erɪsɪs] N Diärese *f*; (= *sign*) Trema *nt*

diagnose ['daɪəgnəʊz] VT (*Med, fig*) diagnostizieren

diagnosis [ˌdaɪəg'nəʊsɪs] N *pl* **diagnoses** [ˌdaɪəg'nəʊsiːz] Diagnose *f*; **to make a ~** eine Diagnose stellen

diagnostic [ˌdaɪəg'nɒstɪk] ADJ diagnostisch; **~ test bay** Diagnosestand *m*

diagnostician [ˌdaɪəgnɒs'tɪʃən] N Diagnostiker(in) *m(f)*

diagnostics [ˌdaɪəg'nɒstɪks] N *sing or pl* Diagnose *f*; **~ program** (*Comput*) Diagnoseprogramm *nt*

diagonal [daɪ'ægənl] ADJ diagonal **N** Diagonale *f*

diagonally [daɪ'ægənlɪ] ADV diagonal; (*loosely:* = *crossways*) schräg; **he crossed the street ~** er ging schräg über die Straße; **~ across sth** (*walk*) schräg über etw (*acc*); *be placed* schräg über etw (*dat*); **~ across from** *or* **opposite sb/sth** jdm/einer Sache (*dat*) schräg gegenüber

diagram ['daɪəgræm] N (*Math*) Diagramm *nt*; (*of machine etc*) Diagramm *nt*, Schaubild *nt*; (= *chart: of figures etc*) grafische Darstellung; **as shown in the ~** wie das Diagramm/die grafische Darstellung zeigt

diagrammatic [ˌdaɪəgrə'mætɪk] ADJ diagrammatisch; **in ~ form** in einem Schaubild *or* Diagramm dargestellt; (*chart*) grafisch dargestellt

dial ['daɪəl] ⊘ 27.1, 27.2, 27.7 N **a** (*of clock*) Zifferblatt *nt*; (*of speedometer, pressure gauge*) Skala *f*; (*Telec*) Wähl- *or* Nummernscheibe *f*; (*on radio etc*) (Frequenzbereich-)Einstellskala *f* **b** (*inf,* = *face*) Visage *f* (*inf*) **VT** (*Telec*) wählen; **to ~ direct** durchwählen; **you can ~ London direct** man kann nach London durchwählen; **to ~ 999** den Notruf wählen; **to ~ a wrong number** eine falsche Nummer wählen, sich verwählen **VI** (*Telec*) wählen

dialect ['daɪəlekt] **N** Dialekt *m*; (*local, rural also*) Mundart *f*; **the country people spoke in ~** die Landbevölkerung sprach Dialekt; **the play is in ~** das Stück ist in Dialekt *or* Mundart geschrieben **ATTR** Dialekt-; **~ word** Dialektausdruck *m*

dialectal [ˌdaɪə'lektl] ADJ dialektal; (*local, rural also*) mundartlich

dialectical [ˌdaɪə'lektɪkəl] ADJ dialektisch; **~ materialism** dialektischer Materialismus

dialectician [ˌdaɪəlek'tɪʃən] N Dialektiker(in) *m(f)*

dialectic(s) [ˌdaɪə'lektɪk(s)] N *with sing vb* Dialektik *f*

dialling ['daɪəlɪŋ]: **dialling code** N (*Brit Telec*) Vorwahl(nummer) *f*, Ortsnetzkennzahl *f* (*form*); **dialling tone** N (*Brit, Telec*) Amtszeichen *nt*

dialogue, (*US*) **dialog** ['daɪəlɒg] N (*all senses*) Dialog *m*; **~ box** (*Comput*) Dialogfeld *nt*; **~ coach** Dialogregisseur(in) *m(f)*

dial tone N (*US, Telec*) Amtszeichen *nt*

dial-up ['daɪəlʌp] ADJ *attr* (*Comput*) Wähl-; **~ link** Wählverbindung *f*; **~ modem** (Wähl)modem *nt*

dialysis [daɪ'æləsɪs] N Dialyse *f*

diamanté [ˌdaɪə'mæntɪ] N Strass *m*; (*rare,* = *fabric*) *mit Pailletten besetzter Stoff*

diameter [daɪ'æmɪtə] N Durchmesser *m*; **to be one foot in ~** einen Durchmesser von einem Fuß haben; **what's its ~?** welchen Durchmesser hat es?, wie groß ist es im Durchmesser?

diametrical [ˌdaɪə'metrɪkəl] ADJ (*Math, fig*) diametral

diametrically [ˌdaɪə'metrɪkəlɪ] ADV **~ opposed (to sth)** (einer Sache *dat*) völlig *or* diametral (*geh*) entgegengesetzt; **their views are ~ opposed** sie haben völlig entgegengesetzte Ansichten

diamond ['daɪəmənd] N **a** Diamant *m* → **rough diamond** **b** **diamonds** PL (*Cards*) Karo *nt*; **the ace/seven of ~s** das Karoass/die Karosieben **c** (*Baseball*) Innenfeld *nt* **d** (*Math,* = *rhombus*) Raute *f*

diamond *in cpds* Diamant-; **~ bracelet** Diamantarmband *nt*; **diamond cutter** N Diamantschneider(in) *m(f)*; (*Ind*) Diamantschleifer(in) *m(f)*; **diamond cutting** N Diamantschleifen *nt*; **diamond drill** N Diamantbohrer *m*; **diamond jubilee** N 60-jähriges Jubiläum *nt*; **diamond merchant** N Diamantenhändler(in) *m(f)*; **diamond-shaped** ADJ rautenförmig; **diamond wedding** N diamantene Hochzeit

Diana [daɪ'ænə] N Diana *f*

dianthus [daɪ'ænθəs] N *pl* **dianthuses** (*Bot*) Nelke *f*

diapason [ˌdaɪə'peɪzən] N (*also Mus*) Diapason *m or nt*; **open ~** Prinzipal *nt*; **stopped ~** gedacktes Prinzipal

diaper ['daɪəpə] N (*US*) Windel *f*

diaphanous [daɪ'æfənəs] ADJ durchscheinend

diaphragm ['daɪəfræm] N (*Anat, Phys, Chem*) Diaphragma *nt*; (*abdominal*) Zwerchfell *nt*, Diaphragma *nt*; (*Phot*) Blende *f*; (*in telephone*) Membran *f*; (= *contraceptive*) Pessar *nt*

diarist ['daɪərɪst] N (*of personal events*) Tagebuchschreiber(in) *m(f)*; (*of contemporary events*) Chronist(in) *m(f)*

diarrhoea, (*US*) **diarrhea** [ˌdaɪə'riːə] N Durchfall *m*, Diarrhö(e) *f*; **~ verbal** = geistiger Dünnschiss (*sl*); **the speaker had verbal ~** der Redner hatte geistigen Dünnschiss (*sl*)

diary ['daɪərɪ] N (*of personal experience*) Tagebuch *nt*; (*for noting dates*) (Termin)kalender *m*; **to keep a ~** Tagebuch führen; **desk/pocket ~** Schreibtisch-/Taschenkalender *m*; **I've got it in my ~** es steht in meinem (Termin)kalender

diaspora [daɪ'æspərə] N Diaspora *f*

diastole [daɪ'æstəlɪ] N Diastole *f*

diastolic [daɪə'stɒlɪk] ADJ (*Physiol*) *blood pressure* diastolisch

diatonic [ˌdaɪə'tɒnɪk] ADJ diatonisch

diatribe ['daɪətraɪb] N Schmährede *f*

dibble ['dɪbl] **N** Pflanzholz *nt*, Setzholz *nt* **VT** *plant* setzen, pflanzen; *hole* machen, graben

dibs [dɪbz] PL (*sl*) **a** (= *claim*) Recht *nt*, Anspruch *m*; **I have ~ on that piece of cake** das Stück Kuchen steht mir zu **b** (= *money*) Knete *f* (*inf*)

dice [daɪs] **N** *pl* - Würfel *m*; **to play ~** Würfel spielen, würfeln; **to roll the ~** würfeln; **~ cup** *or* **box** Würfelbecher *m*; **no ~** (*esp US inf*) (das) ist nicht drin (*inf*) **VI** würfeln; **to ~ with death/danger** mit dem Tode/der Gefahr spielen **VT** (*Cook*) würfelig *or* in Würfel schneiden

dicey ['daɪsɪ] ADJ (*inf*) riskant

dichotomy [dɪ'kɒtəmɪ] N Trennung *f*, Dichotomie *f*

dick [dɪk] N **a** (*inf,* = *detective*) Schnüffler(in) *m(f)* (*inf*); **private ~** Privatdetektiv(in) *m(f)* → **clever dick** **b** (*sl,* = *penis*) Schwanz *m* (*sl*)

dickens ['dɪkɪnz] N (*euph inf,* = *devil*) Teufel *m* → **devil** N **c**

Dickensian [dɪ'kenzɪən] ADJ *character, novel* dickenssch *attr*; (= *old-fashioned*) *building, style* antiquiert; **it's all very ~** das ist alles wie aus einem Roman von Dickens

dicker ['dɪkə] VI (US) feilschen

dickey, **dicky** ['dɪkɪ] N **a** (inf, on shirt) Hemdbrust f; (= bow tie) Fliege f **b** (also **dickey seat**) Notsitz m (in einem Zweisitzer)

dickhead ['dɪkhed] N (sl pej) Idiot m (pej)

dicky ['dɪkɪ] ADJ (inf) heart angeknackst (inf); **I feel a bit ~** (dated) ich bin ziemlich ab (inf) or erschossen (inf) **N** = **dickey**

dickybird ['dɪkɪbɜːd] N (Brit, baby-talk) Piepmatz m (baby-talk); **I haven't heard a ~ from him** (inf) ich habe keinen Ton von ihm gehört

dicta ['dɪktə] pl of **dictum**

Dictaphone® ['dɪktəfəʊn] N Diktaphon nt, Diktafon nt

dictate [dɪk'teɪt] **VT** diktieren; **reason/common sense ~s that ...** die Vernunft/der gesunde Menschenverstand sagt uns, dass ... **VI** diktieren **N** ['dɪkteɪt] usu pl Diktat nt; (of reason) Gebote pl

▶**dictate to** VI +prep obj person diktieren (+dat), Vorschriften machen (+dat); **I won't be dictated to** ich lasse mir nicht diktieren, ich lasse mir keine Vorschriften machen

dictation [dɪk'teɪʃən] N (also Sch) Diktat nt; **to take (down) ~** ein Diktat aufnehmen; **to read at ~ speed** in Diktiertempo lesen

dictator [dɪk'teɪtə] N **a** (Pol, fig) Diktator(in) m(f) **b** (of letter, passage) Diktierende(r) mf

dictatorial ADJ , **dictatorially** ADV [ˌdɪktə'tɔːrɪəl, -ɪ] diktatorisch

dictatorship [dɪk'teɪtəʃɪp] N (Pol, fig) Diktatur f

diction ['dɪkʃən] N **a** (Liter) Diktion f; **poetic ~** poetische Sprache **b** (= way of speaking) Diktion f

dictionary ['dɪkʃənrɪ] N Wörterbuch nt

dictum ['dɪktəm] N pl **dicta** Diktum nt

did [dɪd] PRET of **do²**

didactic [dɪ'dæktɪk] ADJ didaktisch

didactically [dɪ'dæktɪkəlɪ] ADV didaktisch

diddle ['dɪdl] VT (Brit inf) übers Ohr hauen (inf), beschummeln; **you have been ~d** man hat Sie übers Ohr gehauen; **to ~ sb out of sth** jdm etw abgaunern (inf)

diddler ['dɪdlə] N (inf) Spitzbube m, Gauner m

diddly-squat ['dɪdlɪ'skwɒt] N (US inf) nix (inf); **I don't think any of these films mean ~** ich glaube nicht, dass diese Filme irgendwas bedeuten

diddums ['dɪdəmz] INTERJ (inf) du Armer/Arme

didn't ['dɪdənt] = **did not** → **do²**

didst [dɪdst] (obs) = **didst thou** → **do²**

die¹ [daɪ] **VI** **a** (lit) sterben; (soldier) fallen, sterben; (motor, engine) absterben; (planet) vergehen; **to ~ of** or **from hunger/pneumonia/grief** vor Hunger/an Lungenentzündung/vor or aus Kummer sterben; **to ~ for one's country** für sein Land sterben; **he ~d from his injuries** er erlag seinen Verletzungen; **to ~ by one's own hand** von eigener Hand sterben, Hand an sich (acc) legen; **he ~d of a broken heart** er starb an einem gebrochenen Herzen; **he ~d happy/a hero** er starb glücklich/als Held; **to be dying** im Sterben liegen; **never say ~!** nun nicht aufgeben!; **to ~ laughing** (inf) sich totlachen (inf); **I'd rather** or **sooner ~!** (inf) lieber würde ich sterben!; **a dress to ~ for** (inf) ein unwiderstehliches or umwerfendes (inf) Kleid

b (fig inf: = long) **to be dying to do sth** darauf brennen, etw zu tun, brennend gern etw tun wollen; **I'm dying to know what happened** ich bin schrecklich gespannt zu hören, was passiert ist; **he's dying to meet you** er möchte Sie brennend gern kennen lernen; **she's dying to get home** sie brennt darauf, heimzukommen; **I'm dying for a cigarette** ich brauche jetzt unbedingt eine Zigarette; **I'm dying of thirst** ich verdurste fast; **I'm dying for him to visit** ich kann seinen Besuch kaum noch abwarten

c (fig, love) vergehen, ersterben (geh), erlöschen (geh); (memory) (ver)schwinden; (custom) aussterben; (empire) untergehen; **the secret ~d with him** er nahm das Geheimnis mit ins Grab;

old habits ~ **hard** alte Gewohnheiten legt man nur schwer ab

VT **to ~ a hero's/a violent death** den Heldentod/eines gewaltsamen Todes sterben; **to ~ the death** (plan etc) sterben (inf)

▶**die away** VI (sound, voice) schwächer or leiser werden; (wind) nachlassen, sich legen; (anger) sich legen, vergehen

▶**die back** VI absterben

▶**die down** VI nachlassen; (fire) herunterbrennen; (flames) kleiner werden; (storm, wind) sich legen, nachlassen; (noise) leiser werden, schwächer werden; (emotion also) sich legen; (quarrel, protest) nachlassen, schwächer werden

▶**die off** VI (hin)wegsterben; (animals, people also) (der Reihe nach) sterben

▶**die out** VI aussterben

die² N **a** pl **dice** (form) Würfel m; **the ~ is cast** (prov) die Würfel sind gefallen → also **dice b** **c** **-s** (Tech) Gesenk nt, Gussform f; (in minting) Prägestempel m

die casting N (= article) Spritzguss m, Spritzgussstück nt; (= process) Spritzgussverfahren nt

die-hard ['daɪhɑːd] **N** zäher Kämpfer, zähe Kämpferin; (= resistant to change) Ewiggestrige(r) mf ADJ zäh; (pej) reaktionär

dielectric [ˌdaɪɪ'lektrɪk] ADJ dielektrisch

dieresis N (US) = **diaeresis**

diesel ['diːzəl] N (= train) Dieseltriebwagen m; (= car) Diesel m; (= fuel) Dieselöl nt, Diesel no art

diesel: **diesel-electric** ADJ dieselelektrisch; **diesel engine** N Dieselmotor m; **diesel oil** N Dieselöl nt; **diesel train** N Dieseltriebwagen m

die: **die sinker** N Werkzeugmacher(in) m(f); **die stamp** N Prägestempel m

diet¹ ['daɪət] **N** Nahrung f; (= special diet) Diät f; (= slimming diet) Schlankheitskur f; **there's nothing wrong with my ~** meine Ernährung ist völlig in Ordnung; **to put sb on a ~/a special ~** jdm eine Schlankheitskur/eine Diät verordnen; **to be/go on a ~** eine Schlankheitskur machen; **high protein ~** proteinreiche Diät; **he lives on a ~ of hamburgers and chips** er ernährt sich von Hamburgern und Pommes frites; **to be fed (on) a ~ of sth** (fig) etw dauernd eingetrichtert bekommen; **she lives on a ~ of TV soap operas** sie macht nichts anderes als sich Fernsehserien anzusehen **VI** eine Schlankheitskur machen

diet² N (= assembly) Abgeordnetenversammlung f; **the German/Japanese ~** der deutsche/japanische Reichstag; **the Diet of Worms** der Reichstag zu Worms

dietary ['daɪətərɪ] ADJ Ernährungs-; **~ habits** Ernährungsgewohnheiten pl; **~ deficiency** ernährungsbedingte Mangelerscheinung

dietary fibre, (US) **dietary fiber** N Ballaststoff m

dietetic [ˌdaɪə'tetɪk] ADJ Diät-, diätetisch; **~ foods** Diätnahrungsmittel pl

dietetics [ˌdaɪə'tetɪks] N sing Diätlehre f, Diätetik f

dietician [ˌdaɪə'tɪʃən] N Diätist(in) m(f), Ernährungswissenschaftler(in) m(f)

diet sheet N Diät-/Schlankheits(fahr)plan m

differ ['dɪfə] VI **a** (= be different) sich unterscheiden (from von); **tastes ~** die Geschmäcker sind verschieden; **I ~ from you in that** ich unterscheide mich von Ihnen darin, dass ... **b** (= disagree) **to ~ with sb on** or **over sth** über etw (acc) anderer Meinung sein als jd; **we ~ed sharply over that** darin waren wir völlig verschiedener Meinung → **agree, beg**

difference ['dɪfrəns] ✪ 5.4 N **a** Unterschied m; (in age) (Alters)unterschied m (in, between zwischen +dat); **that makes a big ~** das ist für mich ein großer Unterschied; **to make a ~ to** or **in sth** einen Unterschied bei etw machen; **that makes a big** or **a lot of ~**, **that makes all the ~** das ändert die Sache völlig, das gibt

der Sache (dat) ein ganz anderes Gesicht; **cooperation makes all the ~** Zusammenarbeit macht viel aus; **a bottle of wine would make all the ~** es fehlt nur noch eine Flasche Wein dazu; **it makes all the ~ in the world** da liegt der entscheidende Unterschied; **what ~ does it make if ...?** was macht es schon, wenn ...?; **what ~ is that to you?** was macht dir das aus?; **it makes no ~, it doesn't make any ~** es ist egal; **it makes no ~ to me** das ist mir egal or einerlei; **for all the ~ it makes** obwohl es ja eigentlich egal ist; **I can't tell the ~** ich kann keinen Unterschied erkennen; **a job with a ~** (inf) ein Job, der mal was anderes ist

b (between numbers, amounts) Differenz f; **to pay the ~** die Differenz or den Rest(betrag) bezahlen; **to split the ~** sich (dat) die Differenz or den Rest(betrag) teilen

c (= quarrel) Differenz f, Auseinandersetzung f; **a ~ of opinion** eine Meinungsverschiedenheit; **to settle** or **resolve one's ~s** die Differenzen or Meinungsverschiedenheiten beilegen

different ['dɪfrənt] ADJ **a** andere(r, s), anders pred (from, to als); **two people, things** verschieden, unterschiedlich; **completely ~** völlig verschieden; (= changed) völlig verändert; **that's ~!** das ist was anderes!; **in what way are they ~?** wie unterscheiden sie sich?; **to feel (like) a ~ person** ein ganz anderer Mensch sein; **to do something ~** etwas anderes tun; **that's quite a ~ matter** das ist etwas völlig anderes; **she's quite ~ from what you think** sie ist ganz anders, als Sie denken; **he wants to be ~** er will unbedingt anders sein or etwas Besonderes sein

b (= various) verschieden

ADV think anders; **he doesn't know any ~** er kennt es nicht anders; (with behaviour) er weiß es nicht besser

differential [ˌdɪfə'renʃəl] ADJ (= different) rates of pay, treatment, diagnosis, effects unterschiedlich; (= distinguishing) feature unterscheidend; **~ pricing** (Comm) Preisdiskriminierung f **N** **a** (= difference) Unterschied m (between zwischen); (Math) Differenzial nt, Differential nt; **wage/ salary ~** Lohn-/Gehaltsunterschiede or -differenzen pl **b** (Aut) Differenzial(getriebe) nt, Differential(getriebe) nt

differential: **differential calculus** N (Math) Differenzialrechnung f, Differentialrechnung f; **differential coefficient** N (Math) Ableitung f; **differential equations** PL (Math) Differenzialgleichungen pl, Differentialgleichungen pl; **differential gear** N (Aut) Differenzial(getriebe) nt, Differential(getriebe) nt

differentially [ˌdɪfə'renʃəlɪ] ADV (Tech) differenzial, differential

differentiate [ˌdɪfə'renʃɪeɪt] ✪ 5.1 **VT** unterscheiden; (Math) differenzieren; **to ~ x and y/x from y** x und y voneinander/x von y unterscheiden **VI** unterscheiden, einen Unterschied machen, differenzieren; (two things: = become different) sich unterschiedlich or anders entwickeln; **to ~ between people** einen Unterschied zwischen Menschen machen

differentiation [ˌdɪfərenʃɪ'eɪʃən] N Unterscheidung f, Differenzierung f

differently ['dɪfrəntlɪ] ADV anders (from als); (from one another) unterschiedlich; **I was never treated ~ from the men** ich wurde nie anders als die Männer behandelt; **we all react ~ to stress** wir reagieren alle anders or unterschiedlich auf Stress; **~ priced seating areas** unterschiedlich teure Sitzbereiche; **~ priced books** Bücher mit unterschiedlichen Preisen

differently-abled [ˌdɪfrəntlɪ'eɪbld] ADJ (euph) behindert

difficult ['dɪfɪkəlt] ✪ 5.1, 26.3 ADJ **a** (= hard) question, task, time schwer, schwierig; situation, writer, book schwierig; **there's nothing ~ about it** das ist doch gar nicht schwer; **the ~ thing is that ...** die Schwierigkeit liegt darin, dass ...; **it was a ~ decision to make** es war eine schwere or schwierige Entscheidung; **it is not ~ to imagine** es ist nicht schwer, sich (dat) das vorzustellen; **it was ~ for him to leave her** es fiel ihm schwer, sie zu verlassen; **it's ~ for youngsters** or **youngsters find it ~ to get a job** junge Leute haben Schwierigkeiten, eine Stelle zu finden; **it's ~ to see what they could have done** es lässt sich schwer vorstellen, was sie hätten tun können; **it's ~ to deny that** es lässt sich kaum leugnen; **he's ~ to get on with** es ist schwer, mit ihm auszukommen; **it's ~ being a man today** es ist schwer, heute ein Mann zu sein; **to make it ~ for sb (to do sth)** es jdm nicht leicht machen(, etw zu tun); **to have a ~ time (doing sth)** Schwierigkeiten haben(, etw zu tun); **she's having a ~ time now she's on her own** jetzt, wo sie allein ist, hat sie es schwer; **to put sb in a ~ position** jdn in eine schwierige Lage bringen **b** (= *awkward*) *person, child* schwierig; **to be ~ (about sth)** (wegen etw) Schwierigkeiten machen; **he's just trying to be ~** er will nur Schwierigkeiten machen

difficulty ['dɪfɪkəltɪ] N Schwierigkeit f; **with/ without ~** mit/ohne Schwierigkeiten; **he had ~ (in) setting up in business** es fiel ihm schwer or nicht leicht, sich selbstständig zu machen; **she had great ~ (in) breathing** sie konnte kaum atmen; **there was some ~ (in) finding him** es war schwierig or nicht leicht, ihn zu finden; **the ~ is (in) choosing** or **to choose** die Wahl ist nicht leicht; **they hadn't appreciated the ~ of finding somewhere to live** sie hatten nicht bedacht, wie schwierig es sein würde, eine Wohnung zu finden; **in ~** or **difficulties** in Schwierigkeiten; **to get into difficulties** in Schwierigkeiten geraten; **to get out of difficulties** Schwierigkeiten überwinden

diffidence ['dɪfɪdəns] N Bescheidenheit f, Zurückhaltung f; (*of smile*) Zaghaftigkeit f

diffident ['dɪfɪdənt] ADJ zurückhaltend, bescheiden; *smile* zaghaft; **he was ~ about offering his help** er hat zaghaft seine Hilfe angeboten

diffidently ['dɪfɪdəntlɪ] ADV zaghaft

diffract [dɪ'frækt] VT beugen

diffraction [dɪ'frækʃən] N Diffraktion f, Beugung f

diffuse [dɪ'fjuːz] **VT** *light, heat, gas, rays* ausstrahlen, verbreiten; *fluid* ausgießen, ausschütten; (*Chem*) diffundieren, verwischen; *perfume* verbreiten, verströmen; (*fig*) *knowledge, custom, news* verbreiten; *tension* verringern, abbauen **VI** ausstrahlen, sich ver- or ausbreiten; (*fluid*) sich ausbreiten; (*Chem*) diffundieren, sich vermischen; (*perfume, odour*) ausströmen; (*fig, custom, news*) sich verbreiten; (*tension*) sich verringern **ADJ** [dɪ'fjuːs] **a** *gas, rays, light* diffus; *feeling* undeutlich, vage **b** (= *verbose*) *style, writer* langatmig, weitschweifig

diffused [dɪ'fjuːzd] ADJ verbreitet; *lighting* indirekt

diffuseness [dɪ'fjuːsnɪs] N (*of style*) Weitschweifigkeit f

diffuser [dɪ'fjuːzə'] N (*for light*) (Licht)diffusor m

diffusion [dɪ'fjuːʒən] N (*of light, heat, rays, fluid etc*) Ausbreitung f; (*Chem*) Diffusion f; (*of perfume, odour*) Ausströmung f; (*of knowledge, custom, news*) Verbreitung f

dig [dɪg] *vb*: *pret, ptp* **dug VT a** *ground* graben; *garden* umgraben; *grave* ausheben; *trench, hole, tunnel etc* graben, ausheben; **to ~ potatoes** Kartoffeln roden; **they dug their way out of prison** sie gruben sich (*dat*) einen (Flucht)tunnel aus dem Gefängnis **b** (= *poke, thrust*) bohren (*sth into sth* etw in etw *acc*); **to ~ sb in the ribs** jdm or jdn in die Rippen stoßen **c** (*inf*, = *enjoy*) stehen auf (+*dat*) (*inf*); (= *understand*) kapieren (*inf*) **VI a** (*person*) graben; (*dog, pig*) wühlen, graben; (*Tech*) schürfen; (*Archeol*) (aus)graben, Ausgrabungen machen; **to ~ for minerals** Erz schürfen; **to ~ in one's pockets for sth** in seinen Taschen nach etw suchen or wühlen; **to ~ deep** (*Sport, fig*) auf seine letzten Reserven zurückgreifen; (*fig, in one's memory*) lange überlegen; (= *investigate*) gründlich nachforschen

b (*inf*, = *taunt*) **to ~ at sb** jdn anschießen or anmotzen (*inf*) **N a** (*Brit: with hand, elbow*) Puff m, Stoß m; **to give sb a ~ in the ribs** jdm einen Rippenstoß geben **b** (*Brit:* = *sarcastic remark*) Seitenhieb m, Spitze f; **to have a ~ at sb/sth** eine spitze Bemerkung über jdn/etw machen **c** (*Archeol*) (Aus)grabung f; (= *site*) Ausgrabungsstätte f

▶ **dig around** VI (*inf*) herumsuchen

▶ **dig in** **VI a** (*also* **dig oneself in**: *Mil, fig*) sich eingraben; **the pickets are digging in for a long strike** die Streikposten stellen sich auf einen langen Streik ein **b** (*inf*, = *eat*) reinhauen (*inf*) **VT** *sep* **a** *compost* unter- or eingraben **b** (*Mil*) *troops, tanks* eingraben **c** **to dig one's heels in** (*lit*) die Hacken in den Boden stemmen; (*fig*) sich auf die Hinterbeine stellen (*inf*)

▶ **dig into** VI +*prep obj* **a** (*inf*) *cake, pie* herfallen über (+*acc*) (*inf*) **b** *sb's past* wühlen in (+*dat*) **c** **to dig (deep) into one's pockets** or **purse** (*fig*) tief in die Tasche greifen

▶ **dig out** VT *sep* (*lit, fig*) ausgraben (*of* aus)

▶ **dig over** VT *sep soil, garden* umgraben

▶ **dig up** VT *sep* **a** *earth* aufwühlen; *lawn, garden* umgraben **b** *plants, treasure, body, idea* ausgraben; *weeds* (aus)jäten; (*fig*) *fact, information* ausgraben, auftun; *solution* finden; **where did you dig her up?** (*inf*) wo hast du die denn aufgegabelt? (*inf*)

digest [daɪ'dʒest] **VT** (*lit, fig*) verdauen **VI** verdauen **N** ['daɪdʒest] **a** (*of book, facts*) Digest m or nt, Auswahl f **b** (*Jur*) Gesetzessammlung f

digestible [dɪ'dʒestɪbl] ADJ verdaulich

digestion [dɪ'dʒestʃən] N Verdauung f

digestive [dɪ'dʒestɪv] **ADJ** Verdauungs- **N a** (*US*: = *aperitif*) Aperitif m **b** (*Brit*) = **digestive biscuit**

digestive biscuit N (*Brit*) Keks aus Roggenmehl

digestive system Verdauungsapparat m or -system nt

digger ['dɪgə'] N **a** (*person*, = *miner*) Bergmann m, Goldgräber m; (= *navvy*) Straßenarbeiter m; (*Tech*, = *excavator*) Bagger m **b** (*inf*) australischer/neuseeländischer Soldat; (*Austral, inf*, = *pal*) Kumpel m

diggings ['dɪgɪŋz] PL **a** (*Min*) Bergwerk nt; (= *minerals*) Funde pl; (*Archeol*) Grabungsort m **b** (*dated US*) = **digs**

digicam ['dɪdʒɪkæm] N (*Comput*) Digitalkamera f

digit ['dɪdʒɪt] N **a** (= *finger*) Finger m; (= *toe*) Zehe f; (*Math*) Ziffer f; **a four-digit number** eine vierstellige Zahl

digital ['dɪdʒɪtəl] **ADJ a** *clock, computer* Digital-; **~ display** Digitalanzeige f; **~ technology** Digitaltechnik f **b** (*Anat*) Finger- **N** (*of piano, organ*) Taste f

digital: digital audio tape N DAT-Band nt; **digital cable** N (*TV*) Digitalkabel nt; **digital camera** N digitale Kamera, Digitalkamera f; **digital compact cassette** N digitale Compactkassette f, DCC f

digitalin [ˌdɪdʒɪ'teɪlɪn] N Digitalis nt

digitalis [ˌdɪdʒɪ'teɪlɪs] N Digitalis f

digitalization [ˌdɪdʒɪtəlaɪ'zeɪʃən] N Digitalisierung f

digitally ['dɪdʒɪtəlɪ] ADV digital; **~ remastered** digital aufbereitet; **~ recorded** im Digitalverfahren aufgenommen

digital: digital radio N digitales Radio; **digital recording** N Digitalaufnahme f; **digital television, digital TV** N digitales Fernsehen

digitize ['dɪdʒɪtaɪz] VT (*Comput*) digitalisieren

digitizer ['dɪdʒɪtaɪzə'] N (*Comput*) Digitalisierer m

dignified ['dɪgnɪfaɪd] ADJ *person* (ehr)würdig; *behaviour, manner, face* würdevoll; **he maintained a ~ silence** er schwieg würdevoll; **she made a ~ exit** sie machte einen würdevollen Abgang

dignify ['dɪgnɪfaɪ] VT ehren, auszeichnen; **to ~ sb/sth with the name of ...** jdn/etw mit dem anspruchsvollen Namen ... belegen

dignitary ['dɪgnɪtərɪ] N Würdenträger(in) m(f); **the local dignitaries** die Honoratioren am Ort

dignity ['dɪgnɪtɪ] N (*of person, occasion, work*) Würde f; **to die with ~** in Würde sterben; **to stand on one's ~** förmlich sein; **to lose one's ~** sich blamieren; **that would be beneath my ~** das wäre unter meiner Würde **b** (= *high rank, post*) Rang m, (hohe) Stellung f; (= *title*) Würde f

digraph ['daɪgræf] N Digraph m

digress [daɪ'gres] VI abschweifen

digression [daɪ'greʃən] N Abschweifung f, Exkurs m; **this by way of a ~** aber das nur nebenbei

digressive [daɪ'gresɪv] ADJ abschweifend, abweichend

digs [dɪgz] PL (*Brit*) Bude f (*inf*); **to be** or **live in ~** ein möbliertes Zimmer or eine Bude (*inf*) haben

dihedral [daɪ'hiːdrəl] **ADJ** zweiflächig **N** V-Winkel m; (*Aviat*) V-Stellung f

dike [daɪk] N, VT = **dyke**

dilapidated [dɪ'læpɪdeɪtɪd] ADJ *building* verfallen, heruntergekommen, baufällig; *book, clothes* schäbig

dilapidation [dɪˌlæpɪ'deɪʃən] N **a** (*of building*) Baufälligkeit f, Verfall m; (*of book, clothes*) Schäbigkeit f; **in a state of ~** in schlechtem Zustand **b** (*Geol*) Verwitterung f

dilatation [ˌdaɪlə'teɪʃən], **dilation** [daɪ'leɪʃən] N Ausdehnung f, Erweiterung f; (*of pupils*) Erweiterung f; **~ and curettage** Dilation und Kürettage f (*spec*), Ausschabung f

dilate [daɪ'leɪt] **VT** weiten, dehnen; **~d pupils** erweiterte Pupillen pl **VI** sich weiten, sich dehnen; (*pupils*) sich erweitern; **to ~ (up)on** (*talk at length*) sich verbreiten über (+*acc*)

dilatoriness ['dɪlətərɪnɪs] N Langsamkeit f, Zögern nt (*in doing sth* etw zu tun)

dilatory ['dɪlətərɪ] ADJ **a** *person* langsam; *reply* verspätet; **to be ~ in sth** (*dat*) Zeit lassen; **he was rather ~ in answering** er ließ sich mit der Antwort Zeit **b** (= *delaying*) **~ policy** Hinhaltepolitik f; **~ tactics** Hinhalte- or Verzögerungstaktik f

dildo ['dɪldəʊ] N Godemiché m

dilemma [daɪ'lemə] N Dilemma nt; **to be in a ~** sich in einem Dilemma befinden, in der Klemme sitzen (*inf*); **to place sb in a ~** jdn in eine Klemme (*inf*) or ein Dilemma bringen; **he is faced with a serious ~** er steht vor einem ernsten Dilemma

dilettante [ˌdɪlɪ'tæntɪ] **N** pl **dilettanti** [ˌdɪlɪ'tæntɪ] Amateur(in) m(f), Dilettant(in) m(f); (*Art*) Kunstliebhaber(in) m(f) **ADJ** amateurhaft, stümperhaft

dilettantism [ˌdɪlɪ'tæntɪzəm] N Dilettantismus m, Kunstliebhaberei f

diligence ['dɪlɪdʒəns] N (*in work etc*) Fleiß m; (= *keenness*) Eifer m

diligent ['dɪlɪdʒənt] ADJ *person* (*in work etc*) fleißig; (= *keen*) eifrig; *search, work* sorgfältig, genau; **to be ~ in doing sth** etw eifrig tun

diligently ['dɪlɪdʒəntlɪ] ADV fleißig; (= *keenly*) eifrig; (= *carefully*) sorgfältig

dill [dɪl] N Dill m

dill pickle N saure Gurke (*mit Dill eingelegt*)

dilly-dally ['dɪlɪdælɪ] VI (*over work etc*) trödeln; (*when walking also*) bummeln; **without ~ing** ohne zu trödeln/bummeln; **no ~ing!** ein bisschen dalli!

dilute [daɪ'luːt] **VT** *orange juice, milk etc* verdünnen; *colour* dämpfen, abschwächen; (*fig*) mildern, (ab)schwächen; *power, influence* schwächen; **~ to taste** nach Geschmack verdünnen **ADJ** verdünnt

dilution [daɪ'luːʃən] N (*of orange juice, milk etc*) Verdünnung f; (*of colour*) Dämpfung f, Abschwächung f; (*fig*) Milderung f; (*of power, influence*) Schwächung f

diluvial [daɪˈluːvɪəl], **diluvian** [daɪˈluːvɪən] ADJ (Sint)flut-, sintflutartig

dim [dɪm] ADJ (+er) **a** (= not bright) light, lamp schwach, trüb; metal matt, glanzlos; (= badly lit) room dämmerig, dunkel; **the room grew ~** im Zimmer wurde es dunkel

b (= vague) figure, shape undeutlich; outline schwach, undeutlich; memory, recollection dunkel; **I have a ~ memory or recollection of it** ich erinnere mich nur (noch) dunkel daran; **to have a ~ awareness of sth** sich (dat) einer Sache (gen) nur undeutlich bewusst sein

c (= gloomy) prospects, outlook schlecht; **it's a ~ lookout for him** es sieht sehr schlecht für ihn aus; **to take a ~ view of sth** mit etw gar nicht einverstanden sein

d (inf, = stupid) beschränkt (inf), schwer von Begriff (inf)

e (liter) eyes trüb (liter)

VT **a** (= turn down) light dämpfen; lamp verdunkeln; **to ~ the lights** (Theat) das Licht langsam ausgehen lassen; **to ~ one's headlights** (esp US) abblenden

b (= make dull) colour dämpfen, decken; sound dämpfen; metal mattieren; sight, mind, senses, memory trüben; beauty verblassen lassen; glory beeinträchtigen

VI **a** (light) schwach or trübe werden; (lamp) verlöschen, dunkler werden

b (= become dull, colour) gedämpft or matter werden; (sound) leiser werden; (metal) mattiert werden; (memory) nachlassen; (beauty) verblassen; (glory) verblassen, vergehen; (sight) nachlassen, getrübt werden

▶ **dim out** VT sep (US) city verdunkeln

dime [daɪm] N (US) Zehncentstück nt; **it's not worth a ~** (inf) das ist keinen (roten) Heller or keine fünf Pfennig wert; **they're a ~ a dozen** (inf) das ist Dutzendware; **~ novel** Groschen- or Schundroman m

dimension [daɪˈmenʃən] N Dimension f; (= measurement) Abmessung en pl, Maß nt; **a problem of vast ~s** ein Problem größten Ausmaßes; **this adds a new ~ to his work** das gibt seiner Arbeit eine neue Dimension

-dimensional [-daɪˈmenʃənl] ADJ suf -dimensional; **one-/two-/three-dimensional** ein-/zwei-/dreidimensional

dime store N (US) Billigladen m, Billigkaufhaus nt

diminish [dɪˈmɪnɪʃ] VT **a** (= reduce) verringern; price, authority herabsetzen; value, strength (ver)mindern; number verkleinern; enthusiasm dämpfen; reputation schmälern; power einschränken

b (Mus) (um einen Halbton) vermindern; **~ed** vermindert

VI (= be reduced) sich verringern; (speed, authority, strength) abnehmen, sich vermindern; (price) fallen, sinken; (value) sich vermindern, sich verringern; (number) sich verkleinern; (enthusiasm) nachlassen; (reputation) schlechter werden; **law of ~ing returns** (Econ) Gesetz nt von der fallenden Profitrate; **to ~ in size** kleiner werden; **to ~ in value** im Wert sinken, an Wert verlieren

diminishable [dɪˈmɪnɪʃəbl] ADJ reduzierbar

diminished responsibility [dɪˌmɪnɪʃtrɪspɒnsəˈbɪlɪtɪ] N (Jur) verminderte Zurechnungsfähigkeit

diminuendo [dɪˌmɪnjʊˈendəʊ] ADV diminuendo N Diminuendo nt

diminution [ˌdɪmɪˈnjuːʃən] N (in general) Verringerung f; (of reputation) Schmälerung f; (in enthusiasm) Nachlassen nt

diminutive [dɪˈmɪnjʊtɪv] ADJ winzig, klein; (Gram) diminutiv **N** (Gram) Verkleinerungsform f, Diminutiv(um) nt; (of name) Kurzform f

dimity [ˈdɪmɪtɪ] N Dimitz m

dimly [ˈdɪmlɪ] ADV **a** shine schwach; **~ lit** schwach beleuchtet **b** (= vaguely) undeutlich; see verschwommen; **the peninsula was ~ visible** man konnte die Halbinsel gerade noch ausmachen; **I was ~ aware that ...** es war mir undeut-

lich bewusst, dass ...; **she ~ remembered it** sie erinnerte sich (noch) dunkel daran; **in the ~-remembered past** in dunkler Vorzeit

dimmer [ˈdɪmə] N (Elec) Dimmer m; (US, Aut) Abblendschalter or -hebel m; **~s** pl (US Aut) Abblendlicht nt; (= sidelights) Begrenzungsleuchten pl

dimmer switch N Dimmer m

dimness [ˈdɪmnɪs] N **a** (of light) Schwäche f, Trübheit f; (of metal) Mattheit f; **the ~ of the room** das Halbdunkel or Dämmerlicht im Zimmer **b** (= vagueness, of figure, shape) Undeutlichkeit f; (of outline, eyesight, memory) Schwäche f; (of eyes) Trübheit f **c** **the ~ of his prospects** die schlechten Aussichten pl **d** (inf, = stupidity) Beschränktheit f (inf)

dim-out [ˈdɪmaʊt] N (US) Verdunkelung f

dimple [ˈdɪmpl] **N** (on cheek, chin) Grübchen nt; (= depression) Delle f, Vertiefung f; (on water) Kräuselung f VI (cheeks) Grübchen bekommen; (person) Grübchen zeigen; (surface) sich einbeulen; (water) sich kräuseln VT **a smile ~d her cheeks** sie lächelte und zeigte dabei ihre Grübchen

dimpled [ˈdɪmpld] ADJ cheek, chin mit Grübchen; **she gave him a ~ smile** als sie ihn anlächelte, sah man ihre Grübchen

dimply [ˈdɪmplɪ] ADJ face voll(er) Grübchen

dim: dimwit [ˈdɪmwɪt] N (inf) Schwachkopf m (inf); **dim-witted** ADJ (inf) blöd (inf), dämlich (inf)

din [dɪn] **N** Lärm m, Getöse nt; **an infernal ~** ein Höllenlärm or -spektakel m VT **to ~ sth into sb** jdm etw einbläuen VI **the noise was still ~ning in his ears** der Lärm dröhnte ihm immer noch in den Ohren

dinar [ˈdiːnɑː] N Dinar m

din-dins [ˈdɪndɪnz] N (baby-talk) Happi(-Happi) nt (baby-talk); **your ~ is ready** jetzt gibts Happi(-Happi); **what's for ~?** was gibts zu füttern? (inf)

dine [daɪn] VI speisen, dinieren (old, geh) (on etw); **they ~d on caviare every night** sie aßen jeden Abend Kaviar; **to ~ in** zu Hause essen; **to ~ out** außer Haus or auswärts speisen; **he ~d out on that story for months** diese Geschichte hat ihm monatelang Einladungen zum Essen verschafft VT bewirten, beköstigen → also **wine** VT

diner [ˈdaɪnə] N **a** (= person) Speisende(r) mf; (in restaurant) Gast m **b** (= café etc) Esslokal nt **c** (Rail) Speisewagen m

diner-out [ˌdaɪnəˈraʊt] N pl diners-out jd, der auswärts isst

dinette [daɪˈnet] N Essecke f

ding-a-ling [ˈdɪŋəˈlɪŋ] N **a** Klingeling nt; (= fire engine) Tatütata nt **b** (US, inf, = fool) Depp m (inf)

dingbats [ˈdɪŋbæts] PL (Austral sl: = delirium tremens) Säuferwahn m (hum), Wahnvorstellungen pl; **to give sb the ~** jdn nervös machen

ding-dong [ˈdɪŋˈdɒŋ] **N** Bimbam nt ADJ (fig) battle hin und her wogend

ding(e)y, dinghy [ˈdɪŋgɪ] N Ding(h)i nt; (collapsible) Schlauchboot nt

dinginess [ˈdɪndʒɪnɪs] N Unansehnlichkeit f

dingle [ˈdɪŋgl] N baumbestandene Mulde

dingo [ˈdɪŋgəʊ] N Dingo m, australischer Wildhund

dingy[1] [ˈdɪndʒɪ] ADJ (+er) building, room, street, area düster, trüb; (= dirty) schmuddelig; colour schmutzig; **wallpaper with ~ yellow stripes** Tapeten mit schmutzig gelben Streifen

dingy[2] [ˈdɪŋgɪ] N = **ding(e)y**

dining [ˈdaɪnɪŋ]: **dining car** N Speisewagen m; **dining chair** N Esszimmerstuhl m; **dining hall** N Speisesaal m; **dining room** N Esszimmer nt; (in hotel) Speiseraum m; **dining table** N Esstisch m

dink [dɪŋk] N **a** (inf) abbr of double income, no kids **~s** pl Doppelverdiener pl ohne Kinder **b** (dated US, pej, = Vietnamese) Vietnamese m, Vietnamesin f

dinkum [ˈdɪŋkəm] N (Austral, inf) ADJ echt; **a (fair) ~ Aussie** ein waschechter Australier, eine waschechte Australierin ADV echt

dinky[1] [ˈdɪŋkɪ] ADJ **a** (Brit, inf: = cute) schnuckelig (inf) **b** (US inf: = small) winzig **c** (also **Dinky** ®) Modell-; **~ car** Modellauto nt

dinky[2] N (inf) abbr of double income, no kids yet **dinkies** pl noch kinderlose Doppelverdiener pl

dinky-di [ˈdɪŋkɪˈdaɪ] ADJ (Austral) typisch, echt

dinner [ˈdɪnə] ✪ 25.1, 25.2 N (= evening meal) (Haupt)mahlzeit f, Abendessen nt; (formal) (Abend)essen nt; (= lunch) Mittagessen nt; (for cat, dog) Fressen nt; **to be at ~** beim Essen sein, (gerade) essen; **to be eating or having one's ~** zu Abend/Mittag essen; (dog, cat) (gerade) fressen; **we're having people to ~** wir haben Gäste zum Essen; **~'s ready** das Essen ist fertig; **to finish one's ~** zu Ende essen; **what time do you finish ~?** wann bist du mit dem Essen fertig?; **to go out to ~** (in restaurant) auswärts or außer Haus essen (gehen); (at friends') zum Essen eingeladen sein; **to give a ~ in sb's honour** ein Essen zu jds Ehren geben; **a formal ~** ein offizielles Essen

dinner: dinner bell N (Essens)glocke f; **the ~ has gone** es hat (zum Essen) geläutet; **dinner-dance** N Abendessen mit Tanz; **dinner dress** N kleines Abendkleid; **dinner duty** N **to do ~** Tischaufsicht haben; **dinner jacket** N Smokingjacke f; **dinner knife** N Tafelmesser nt; **dinner money** N (Brit Sch) Essensgeld nt; **dinner party** N Abendgesellschaft f (mit Essen); **to have or give a small ~** ein kleines Essen geben; **dinner plate** N Tafelteller m; **dinner service, dinner set** N Tafelservice nt; **dinner suit** N Smoking m; **dinner table** N Tafel f; **we were already sitting at the ~** wir hatten schon zum Essen Platz genommen; **dinner theater** N (US) Restaurant mit Theatervorführung; **dinnertime** N Essenszeit f; **dinner trolley, dinner wagon** N Servierwagen m

dinosaur [ˈdaɪnəsɔː] N Dinosaurier m

dinosaurian [ˌdaɪnəˈsɔːrɪən] ADJ Dinosaurier-; **~ fossils** Dinosaurierfossilien pl

dint [dɪnt] **N a by ~ of** durch, kraft (+gen); **we succeeded by ~ of working 24 hours a day** wir schafften es, indem wir 24 Stunden pro Tag arbeiteten **b** = **dent** VT = **dent**

diocesan [daɪˈɒsɪsən] ADJ Diözesan-; **~ bishop** Diözesanbischof m

diocese [ˈdaɪəsɪs] N Diözese f, Bistum nt

diode [ˈdaɪəʊd] N Diode f

Dionysian [ˌdaɪəˈnɪzɪən] ADJ dionysisch

Dionysus [ˌdaɪəˈnaɪsɪs] N Dionysos m

dioptre, (US) diopter [daɪˈɒptə] N Dioptrie f

diorama [ˌdaɪəˈrɑːmə] N Diorama nt

dioxide [daɪˈɒksaɪd] N Dioxid nt

dioxin [daɪˈɒksɪn] N Dioxin nt

Dip abbr of **diploma**

dip [dɪp] VT **a** (in(to) +acc) (into liquid) tauchen; pen, hand, brush (ein)tauchen; bread (ein)tunken, stippen (inf); candles ziehen; sheep in Desinfektionslösung baden, dippen; **to ~ sth in flour/egg** etw in Mehl/Ei wälzen

b (into bag, basket) hand stecken

c (Brit Aut) headlights abblenden; **~ped headlights** Abblendlicht nt; **her lights are ~ped** sie fährt mit Abblendlicht

d **to ~ one's flag** (Naut) die Flagge dippen VI (ground) sich senken; (temperature, pointer on scale, prices) fallen, sinken; (boat) tauchen; **the sun ~ped behind the mountains** die Sonne verschwand hinter den Bergen

N a (= swim) **to go for a or to have a ~** kurz or schnell mal schwimmen gehen, kurz reinspringen; **after a or her ~ she lay and sunbathed** nach einem kurzen Bad sonnte sie sich

b (= liquid, for cleaning animals) Desinfektionslösung f; (Tech) Lösung f

c (in ground, = hollow) Bodensenke f; (= slope) Abfall m; **the road took a ~** die Straße fiel ab

d (*in prices etc*) Fallen *nt*, Sinken *nt*; **to take a ~** fallen, sinken

e (*Phys: also* **angle of dip**) Inklination *f*, Neigungswinkel *m*

f (*Naut, of flag*) Dippen *nt*

g (*Cook*) Dip *m*; **a garlic ~** ein Knoblauchdip → **lucky dip**

h (= *candle*) gezogene Kerze

i (*Sport*) Beugestütz *m*

j (*inf*, = *pickpocket*) Taschendieb *m*, Langfinger *m* (*inf*)

▶ **dip into** VI +*prep obj* **a** (*lit*) **she dipped into her bag for her keys** sie griff in ihre Tasche, um ihre Schlüssel zu holen **b** (*fig*) **to dip into one's pocket** tief in die Tasche greifen; **to dip into one's savings** seine Ersparnisse angreifen, an seine Ersparnisse gehen **c** *book* einen kurzen Blick werfen in (+*acc*)

Dip. Ed. ['dɪp'ed] (*Brit Univ*) *abbr of* **Diploma in Education** Diplom *nt* in Pädagogik *or* Erziehungswissenschaften

diphtheria [dɪfˈθɪərɪə] N Diphtherie *f*

diphthong ['dɪfθɒŋ] N Diphthong *m*

diphthongize ['dɪfθɒŋaɪz] VTI diphthongieren

diploid ['dɪplɔɪd] ADJ (*Biol*) *cell, nucleus* diploid

diploma [dɪˈpləʊmə] N Diplom *nt*; **teacher's ~** Lehrerdiplom *nt*; **to hold a ~ in** ein Diplom haben in (+*dat*)

diplomacy [dɪˈpləʊməsɪ] N (*Pol, fig*) Diplomatie *f*; **to use ~** diplomatisch vorgehen

diplomat ['dɪpləmæt] N (*Pol, fig*) Diplomat(in) *m(f)*

diplomatic [ˌdɪpləˈmætɪk] ADJ (*lit, fig*) diplomatisch

diplomatically [ˌdɪpləˈmætɪkəlɪ] ADV (*lit, fig*, = *tactfully*) diplomatisch; (= *by diplomatic means*) auf diplomatischem Wege; (= *at a diplomatic level*) auf diplomatischer Ebene

diplomatic: diplomatic bag N (*Brit*) Diplomatenpost *f*; **diplomatic corps** N diplomatisches Korps; **diplomatic immunity** N Immunität *f*; **diplomatic pouch** N (*US*) = **diplomatic bag**; **diplomatic service** N diplomatischer Dienst

diplomatist [dɪˈpləʊmətɪst] N = **diplomat**

dip needle N Inklinationsnadel *f*

dipolar [daɪˈpəʊlə] ADJ zweipolig

dipole ['daɪpəʊl] N Dipol *m*

dipper ['dɪpə] N **a** (= *ladle*) Schöpflöffel *m*, Kelle *f* **b** (*Tech*, = *person*) Eintaucher(in) *m(f)* **c** (*Orn*) Taucher *m*, Tauchente *f* **d** (*Tech*, = *bulldozer*) Bagger *m*; (= *scoop*) Schaufel *f* **e** (*at fair: also* **Big Dipper**) Achterbahn *f* **f** (*Brit, Aut, for headlamps*) Abblendschalter *m* **g** (*US, Astron*) **the Big** *or* **Great/Little Dipper** der Große/Kleine Wagen *or* Bär

dipping shot N (*Ftbl*) Aufsetzer *m*

dippy ['dɪpɪ] ADJ (*inf*) plemplem (*inf*), meschugge (*inf*)

dip rod N (*US*) = **dipstick**

dipso ['dɪpsəʊ] N *abbr of* **dipsomaniac**

dipsomania [ˌdɪpsəʊˈmeɪnɪə] N Trunksucht *f*

dipsomaniac [ˌdɪpsəʊˈmeɪnɪæk] N Trunksüchtige(r) *mf*

dipstick ['dɪpstɪk] N Ölmessstab *m*

DIP switch ['dɪpswɪtʃ] N (*Comput*) DIP-Schalter *m*

dip switch N (*Aut*) Abblendschalter *m*

diptera ['dɪptərə] PL Dipteren *pl* (*spec*), Zweiflügler *pl*

dipterous ['dɪptərəs] ADJ zweiflüg(e)lig

diptych ['dɪptɪk] N Diptychon *nt*

dire [daɪə] ADJ **a** (= *serious*) *consequences* verheerend; *warning, prediction, threat* unheilvoll; *effects* katastrophal; *situation* miserabel; (= *desperate*) verzweifelt; **the ~ state of the property market** die miserable Lage auf dem Immobilienmarkt; **in ~ poverty** in äußerster Armut; **to do sth out of ~ necessity** etw aus dringender Notwendigkeit tun; **to be in ~ need of sth** etw dringend brauchen; **to be in ~ straits** in einer ernsten

---

Notlage sein; **the economy is in ~ straits** die Wirtschaftslage ist katastrophal **b** (*inf*, = *awful*) mies (*inf*); **the standard is pretty ~** das Niveau ist unter aller Kritik (*inf*)

direct [daɪˈrekt] ✪ 27.1, 27.3 ADJ **a** direkt; *link, result, heir, contact* direkt, unmittelbar; *responsibility, cause, danger* unmittelbar; *train* durchgehend; *opposite* genau; **as a ~ result of** als eine unmittelbare Folge von; **~ line of descent** Abstammung *f* in direkter Linie; **to be a ~ descendant of sb** von jdm in direkter Linie abstammen, ein direkter Nachkomme von jdm sein; **to pay by ~ debit** (*Brit*) *or* **deposit** (*US*) per Einzugsauftrag bezahlen; **to impose ~ rule (on the Irish/from London)** (Irland/von London aus) direkt regieren; **~-grant school** (*Brit*) Privatschule mit staatlicher Unterstützung; **avoid ~ sunlight** direkte Sonneneinstrahlung meiden; **to take a ~ hit** einen Volltreffer einstecken; **they are willing to hold ~ talks with the government** sie sind bereit, mit der Regierung direkt zu verhandeln

b (= *blunt*) *person, remark* direkt, offen; *refusal, denial* glatt

c (*Gram*) **~ speech** (*Brit*) *or* **discourse** (*US*) direkte Rede

VT **a** (= *address, aim*) *remark, letter* richten (*to* an +*acc*); *efforts, look* richten (*towards* +*acc*); *anger* auslassen (*towards* an +*acc*); *money* zufließen lassen (*to* +*dat*); **the violence was ~ed against the police** die Gewalttätigkeiten richteten sich gegen die Polizei; **to ~ sb's attention to sb/sth** jds Aufmerksamkeit auf jdn/etw lenken; **can you ~ me to the town hall?** können Sie mir den Weg zum Rathaus sagen?

b (= *supervise, control*) *person's work, business* leiten, lenken; *traffic* regeln

c (= *order*) anweisen (*sb to do sth* jdn, etw zu tun); (*Jur*) *jury* Rechtsbelehrung erteilen (+*dat*); **to ~ that sth (should) be done** anordnen, dass etw getan wird; **the judge ~ed the jury to ...** der Richter belehrte die Schöffen darüber, dass ...; **to be taken as ~ed by your doctor** (*Med*) nach ärztlicher Verordnung einzunehmen

d *film, play* Regie führen bei; *group of actors* dirigieren; *radio/TV programme* leiten

ADV direkt

direct: direct access N (*Comput*) Direktzugriff *m*; **direct action** N direkte Aktion; **to take ~** direkt handeln; **direct current** N (*Elec*) Gleichstrom *m*; **direct-debit mandate** N (*Fin*) Abbuchungsauftrag *m*; **direct dialling** N Durchwahl *f*; **direct flight** N Direktflug *m*; **direct hit** N (*Mil, fig*) Volltreffer *m*

direction [dɪˈrekʃən] N **a** (*lit, fig*, = *way*) Richtung *f*; **in every ~/all ~s** in jede Richtung/alle Richtungen; **in the wrong/right ~** (*lit, fig*) in die falsche/richtige Richtung; **in the ~ of Hamburg/the hotel** in Richtung Hamburg/des Hotels; **what ~ did he go in?** in welche Richtung ist er gegangen/gefahren?; **a sense of ~** (*lit*) Orientierungssinn *m*; (*fig*) ein Ziel *nt* im Leben; **new ~s in modern philosophy** neue Wege in der modernen Philosophie

b (= *management: of company etc*) Leitung *f*, Führung *f*

c (*of film, actors*) Regie *f*; (*of play also*) Spielleitung *f*; (*of radio/TV programme*) Leitung *f*; **under the ~ of** unter der Regie von

d directions PL (= *instructions*) Anweisungen *pl*; (*to a place*) Angaben *pl*; (*for use*) (Gebrauchs)anweisung *or* -anleitung *f*; (*in recipe etc*) Hinweise *pl*

directional [dɪˈrekʃənl] ADJ Richtungs-; **~ stability** Richtungsstabilität *f*

directional: directional antenna N Richtantenne *f*; **directional microphone** N Richtmikrofon *nt*; **directional radio** N Richtfunk *m*, Peilfunk *m*

direction: direction finder N Peilantenne *f*; **direction indicator** N (*Aut*) Winker *m*; (*flashing*) Blinker *m*

directionless [dɪˈrekʃənlɪs] ADJ *activity* ziellos; *person* unschlüssig, unentschlossen

directive [dɪˈrektɪv] N Direktive *f*, Weisung *f*

---

directly [dɪˈrektlɪ] ADV **a** direkt; *above, below, opposite, related* direkt, unmittelbar; **to be ~ linked** *or* **connected (to sth)** in einem direkten *or* unmittelbaren Zusammenhang (mit etw) stehen; **A is not ~ related to B** zwischen A und B besteht kein direkter Zusammenhang; **he is ~ descended from X** er stammt in direkter Linie von X ab; **~ responsible** unmittelbar verantwortlich **b** (= *bluntly*) *say* direkt, offen; *refuse, deny* glatt **c** (= *at once*) sofort; (= *shortly*) gleich CONJ (= *as soon as*) sobald; **he'll come ~ he's ready** er kommt, sobald er fertig ist

direct-mail advertising [daɪˈrektˈmeɪlˈædvətaɪzɪŋ] N Postwurfsendungen *pl*

direct marketing N Direktmarketing *nt*

directness [daɪˈrektnɪs] N Direktheit *f*

direct object N (*Gram*) direktes Objekt, Akkusativobjekt *nt*

director [dɪˈrektə] N **a** (*of company, institution*) Direktor(in) *m(f)*, Leiter(in) *m(f)*; (*Univ*) Rektor(in) *m(f)*; **~ of studies** Studienberater(in) *m(f)*; **~ of music** Musikdirektor(in) *m(f)*; **~ of Public Prosecutions** Oberstaatsanwalt *m*/-anwältin *f* **b** (*Rad, TV*) Direktor(in) *m(f)*; (*Film, Theat*) Regisseur(in) *m(f)* **c** (*Mil*) Richtgerät *nt*

directorate [daɪˈrektərɪt] N (= *period of office*) Dienstzeit *f* als Direktor; (= *board of directors*) Aufsichtsrat *m*

director general N Generaldirektor(in) *m(f)*

director's chair N (*Film*) Regiestuhl *m*

director's cut N (*Film*) vom Regisseur geschnittene Fassung

directorship [daɪˈrektəʃɪp] N Direktorstelle *f* or -posten *m*; **under his ~** unter seiner Leitung

directory [dɪˈrektərɪ] ✪ 27.1 N **a** Adressbuch *nt*; (= *telephone directory*) Telefonbuch *nt*; (= *trade directory*) Branchenverzeichnis *nt*; **~ inquiries** (*Brit*) *or* **assistance** (*US*) (*Telec*) (Fernsprech-) auskunft *f* **b** (*Comput*) Inhaltsverzeichnis *nt*, Directory *nt*; **to change directories** das Directory wechseln **c** (*Hist*) **the Directory** das Direktorium

direct: direct product N (*Math*) Skalarprodukt *nt*; **direct taxation** N direkte Besteuerung

dirge [dɜːdʒ] N Grab- *or* Trauer- *or* Klagegesang *m*

dirigible ['dɪrɪdʒɪbl] N (lenkbares) Luftschiff ADJ lenkbar

dirk [dɜːk] N (*Scot*) Dolch *m*

dirt [dɜːt] N **a** Schmutz *m*; (= *soil*) Erde *f*; (= *excrement*) Dreck *m*; **to be covered in ~** völlig verschmutzt sein; **to eat ~** (*fig*) sich widerspruchslos demütigen *or* beleidigen lassen; **to treat sb like ~** jdn wie (den letzten) Dreck behandeln (*inf*); **he looked at me as though I was a piece of ~** er sah mich an, als wäre ich ein Stück Dreck (*inf*) **b** (*fig*, = *obscenity*) Schmutz *m*; **to dig up** *or* **dig (the) ~ on sb** (*inf*) jdn in den Schmutz ziehen; **he wanted to get all the ~ he could on his opponent** er wollte seinen Gegner so richtig schlecht wie möglich machen

dirt: dirt-cheap ADJ, ADV (*inf*) spottbillig (*inf*); **it was going ~** es war spottbillig zu haben; **dirt farmer** N (*US*) Kleinbauer *m*, Kleinbäuerin *f*

dirtily ['dɜːtɪlɪ] ADV **a** schmutzig **b** (*fig*, = *meanly*) gemein, schäbig; (= *obscenely*) schmutzig

dirtiness ['dɜːtɪnɪs] N Schmutzigkeit *f*; (*of story also*) Unanständigkeit *f*

dirt: dirt road N unbefestigte Straße; **dirt track** N Feldweg *m*; (*Sport*) Aschenbahn *f*; **dirt-track racing** N Aschenbahnrennen *nt*

dirty ['dɜːtɪ] ADJ (+*er*) **a** (*lit*) schmutzig; **to get sth ~** etw schmutzig machen; **~ mark** Schmutzfleck *m*

b (*with colours*) schmutzig; **~ grey** schmutzig grau; **~ white** schmutzig weiß; **~ green** olivgrün **c** (*pej*, = *underhand*) *job, business, dealings* schmutzig; *player, competitor* unfair; (*emph inf*, = *despicable*) gemein; **~ play** Foulspiel *nt*; **to do the ~ deed** (*Brit usu hum*) die Übeltat vollbringen

d (= *obscene, smutty*) *book, film, word* unanständig; *joke* schmutzig; *person* obszön; **a ~ mind** eine schmutzige Fantasie; **~ old man** (*pej, hum*) alter Lustmolch (*inf*); **people for whom "liberalism" is a ~ word** Leute, für die „Liberalismus" ein Schimpfwort ist

e to give sb a ~ look (*inf*) jdm einen bösen *or* giftigen (*inf*) Blick zuwerfen

VT (= *soil*) beschmutzen; (*Brit*: = *foul up*) *machine parts, spark plugs* verschmutzen

N to do the ~ on sb (*Brit inf*) jdn reinlegen (*inf*)

dirty: dirty trick N gemeiner Trick; **~s campaign** Diffamierungskampagne f; **dirty weekend** N (*hum inf*) Liebeswochenende *nt*; **dirty work** N to do sb's ~ (*lit*) die Schmutzarbeit für jdn machen; (*fig*) sich (*dat*) für jdn die Finger schmutzig machen

dis, diss [dɪs] VT (*sl*) **to ~ sb** jdn blöd anreden (*inf*)

disability [ˌdɪsəˈbɪlɪtɪ] N **a** (= *handicap, injury etc*) Behinderung f **b** (*Jur*) Rechtsunfähigkeit f

disability living allowance N (*Brit*) Beihilfe f für Erwerbsunfähige

disability pension N Erwerbsunfähigkeitsrente f

disable [dɪsˈeɪbl] VT **a** *person* zum/zur Behinderten machen **b** *tank, gun* unbrauchbar machen; *ship* kampfunfähig machen **c** (*Jur*, = *make incapable*) rechtsunfähig machen; (= *disqualify*) für unfähig erklären (*from doing sth* etw zu tun)

disabled [dɪsˈeɪbld] ADJ **a** behindert; **severely/partially ~** schwer/leicht behindert; **physically ~** körperbehindert; **mentally ~** geistig behindert; **~ ex-serviceman** Kriegsversehrte(r) *m*; **~ toilet** Behindertentoilette f **b** *tank, gun* unbrauchbar; *ship* nicht seetüchtig **c** (*Jur*) nicht rechtsfähig **PL the ~** die Behinderten *pl*; **the war ~** die Kriegsversehrten *pl*

disablement [dɪsˈeɪblmənt] N **a** Behinderung f **b** (*of tank, gun, ship*) Unbrauchbarmachen *nt*

disabuse [ˌdɪsəˈbjuːz] VT **to ~ sb of sth** jdn von etw befreien

disaccord [ˌdɪsəˈkɔːd] **N** (= *disagreement*) Uneinigkeit f; (= *contradiction*) Widerspruch *m* **VI** (= *disagree*) nicht übereinstimmen

disaccustom [ˌdɪsəˈkʌstəm] VT **to ~ sb to sth** jdm etw abgewöhnen

disadvantage [ˌdɪsədˈvɑːntɪdʒ] N Nachteil *m*; (= *detriment also*) Schaden *m*; **to be at a ~** benachteiligt *or* im Nachteil sein; **he felt at a ~** er fühlte sich benachteiligt; **to put sb at a ~** jdn benachteiligen; **to show oneself at a ~** sich von einer ungünstigen *or* unvorteilhaften Seite zeigen; **it would be to your ~** es wäre zu Ihrem Nachteil

disadvantaged [ˌdɪsədˈvɑːntɪdʒd] ADJ benachteiligt

disadvantageous ADJ , **disadvantageously** ADV [ˌdɪsædvɑːnˈteɪdʒəs, -lɪ] nachteilig

disaffected [ˌdɪsəˈfektɪd] ADJ entfremdet; **to become ~** sich entfremden

disaffection [ˌdɪsəˈfekʃən] N Entfremdung f (*with* von)

disagio [dɪsˈædʒɪəʊ] N (*Fin*) Disagio *nt*, Abschlag *m*

disagree [ˌdɪsəˈgriː] ✪ 12.1 VI **a** (*with person, views*) nicht übereinstimmen; (*with plan, suggestion etc*) nicht einverstanden sein; (*two people*) sich (*dat*) nicht einig sein **b** (= *quarrel*) eine Meinungsverschiedenheit haben **c** (= *be different: figures, reports*) nicht übereinstimmen **d** (*climate, food*) **to ~ with sb** jdm nicht bekommen; **garlic ~s with me** ich vertrage keinen Knoblauch, Knoblauch bekommt mir nicht

disagreeable [ˌdɪsəˈgriːəbl] ADJ unangenehm; *person* unsympathisch

disagreeableness [ˌdɪsəˈgriːəblnɪs] N Unangenehme(s) *nt*, unangenehme Art; (*of person*) unsympathische Art

disagreeably [ˌdɪsəˈgriːəblɪ] ADV unangenehm

disagreement [ˌdɪsəˈgriːmənt] N **a** (*with opinion, between opinions*) Uneinigkeit f; **to be in ~ with sb** mit jdm nicht einer Meinung sein; **we are in ~** wir sind verschiedener Meinung; **there is still ~** es herrscht noch Uneinigkeit **b** (= *quarrel*) Meinungsverschiedenheit f **c** (*between figures, reports*) Diskrepanz f

disallow [ˌdɪsəˈlaʊ] VT *evidence, expenses* nicht anerkennen; *claim* zurückweisen, nicht anerkennen; *plan etc* ablehnen; (*Sport*) *goal* nicht anerkennen, nicht geben

disambiguate [ˌdɪsæmˈbɪgjʊeɪt] VT *text etc* eindeutig machen, disambiguieren (*spec*)

disappear [ˌdɪsəˈpɪə] **VI** verschwinden; (*worries, fears, difficulties*) verschwinden, sich in nichts auflösen; (*memory*) schwinden; (*objections*) sich zerstreuen; **he ~ed from sight** er verschwand; **to make sth ~** etw verschwinden lassen; **to do a ~ing trick** (*inf*) sich verdünnisieren (*inf*), sich verdrücken (*inf*); **to ~ into thin air** sich in Luft auflösen **VT** (*esp Pol inf*) verschwinden lassen **PL the ~ed** die Verschwundenen *pl*

disappearance [ˌdɪsəˈpɪərəns] N Verschwinden *nt*

disappoint [ˌdɪsəˈpɔɪnt] VT enttäuschen

disappointed [ˌdɪsəˈpɔɪntɪd] ✪ 14 ADJ enttäuscht; **she was ~ to find/learn that ...** sie war enttäuscht, als sie feststellte/erfuhr, dass ...; **to be ~ that ...** enttäuscht (darüber) sein, dass ...; **to be ~ in** *or* **with** *or* **by sb/sth** von jdm/etw enttäuscht sein; **he was ~ in love** er erlebte eine Enttäuschung in der Liebe; **he was ~ at having to pull out of the race** er war enttäuscht (darüber), dass er aus dem Rennen ausscheiden musste

disappointing [ˌdɪsəˈpɔɪntɪŋ] ADJ enttäuschend; **how ~!** so eine Enttäuschung!

disappointingly [ˌdɪsəˈpɔɪntɪŋlɪ] ADV enttäuschend; (*introducing sentence*) leider; **she performed ~** sie enttäuschte; **rather ~, he didn't have the opportunity** es war ziemlich enttäuschend, dass er keine Gelegenheit dazu hatte, leider hatte er keine Gelegenheit dazu

disappointment [ˌdɪsəˈpɔɪntmənt] N Enttäuschung f; (*of ambition*) Nichterfüllung f

disapprobation [ˌdɪsæprəˈbeɪʃən] N Missbilligung f

disapproval [ˌdɪsəˈpruːvl] N Missbilligung f; **murmur of ~** missbilligendes Gemurmel

disapprove [ˌdɪsəˈpruːv] **VI** missbilligen **VI** dagegen sein; **if you don't ~, I'd like to ...** wenn Sie nichts dagegen haben, würde ich gerne ...; **to ~ of sb** jdn ablehnen; **to ~ of sth** etw missbilligen; **he ~s of children smoking** er missbilligt es, wenn Kinder rauchen

disapproving [ˌdɪsəˈpruːvɪŋ] ADJ *look, glance, person* missbilligend; **to make ~ noises** sein Missfallen zum Ausdruck bringen; **to be ~ of sb/sth** jdn/etw missbilligen

disapprovingly [ˌdɪsəˈpruːvɪŋlɪ] ADV missbilligend

disarm [dɪsˈɑːm] **VT** (*lit, fig*) entwaffnen **VI** (*Mil*) abrüsten

disarmament [dɪsˈɑːməmənt] N Abrüstung f

disarmer [dɪsˈɑːmə] N Abrüstungsbefürworter(in) *m(f)*

disarming [dɪsˈɑːmɪŋ] ADJ entwaffnend

disarmingly [dɪsˈɑːmɪŋlɪ] ADV entwaffnend; **~ simple** verblüffend einfach

disarrange [ˈdɪsəˈreɪndʒ] VT durcheinander bringen

disarranged [ˈdɪsəˈreɪndʒd] ADJ unordentlich

disarrangement [ˌdɪsəˈreɪndʒmənt] N Unordnung f

disarray [ˌdɪsəˈreɪ] **N** Unordnung f; **to be in ~** (*troops*) in Auflösung (begriffen) sein; (*thoughts, organization, political party*) durcheinander *or* in Unordnung sein; (*person*) aufgelöst sein; (*clothes*) in unordentlichem Zustand sein **VT** in Unordnung bringen

disassemble [ˈdɪsəˈsembl] VT auseinander nehmen; *prefabricated building* abbauen

disassociate [ˈdɪsəˈsəʊʃɪeɪt] VT = **dissociate**

disaster [dɪˈzɑːstə] N Katastrophe f; (*Aviat, Min, Rail*) Unglück *nt*, Katastrophe f; (= *fiasco*) Fiasko *nt*, Desaster *nt*; **doomed to ~** zum Untergang verdammt *or* verurteilt → *also* **recipe**

disaster: disaster area N Katastrophengebiet *nt*; (*fig*: = *person*) Katastrophe f; **disaster fund** N Katastrophenfonds *m*; **disaster movie** N Katastrophenfilm *m*

disastrous [dɪˈzɑːstrəs] ADJ *earthquake, flood, accident* katastrophal, verheerend; *marriage, day, consequence* katastrophal; **dinner was ~** das Abendessen war eine Katastrophe; **to be ~ for sb/sth** katastrophale Folgen für jdn/etw haben

disastrously [dɪˈzɑːstrəslɪ] ADV katastrophal; **it all went ~ wrong** es was eine Katastrophe; **we performed ~** unsere Leistung war katastrophal (schlecht); **they fared ~ in the elections** sie schnitten bei den Wahlen katastrophal schlecht ab

disavow [ˈdɪsəˈvaʊ] VT verleugnen; *one's words* ableugnen

disavowal [ˌdɪsəˈvaʊəl] N Verleugnung f; (*of one's words*) Ableugnung f

disband [dɪsˈbænd] **VT** auflösen **VI** (*army, club*) sich auflösen; (*soldiers, club members*) auseinander gehen

disbar [dɪsˈbɑː] VT (*Jur*) die Lizenz entziehen (+*dat*)

disbelief [ˈdɪsbəˈliːf] N Ungläubigkeit f; (*Rel*) Unglaube *m*; **in ~** ungläubig

disbelieve [ˈdɪsbəˈliːv] VT nicht glauben

disbeliever [ˈdɪsbəˈliːvə] N Ungläubige(r) *mf*

disbelieving ADJ , **disbelievingly** ADV [ˈdɪsbəˈliːvɪŋ, -lɪ] ungläubig

disburden [dɪsˈbɜːdn] VT (*lit, fig*) entlasten

disburse [dɪsˈbɜːs] VT aus(be)zahlen

disbursement [dɪsˈbɜːsmənt] N Auszahlung f

disc, (*esp US*) **disk** [dɪsk] N **a** (= *flat, circular object*) (runde) Scheibe; (*Anat*) Bandscheibe f; (*Mil*, = *identity disc*) (Erkennungs)marke f → **slip b** (= *record, Comput*) Platte f; (= *CD*) CD f → *also* **disk**

discard [dɪsˈkɑːd] **VT a** *unwanted article, person* ausrangieren; *idea, plan* verwerfen; (= *take off*) *coat* ausziehen; *antlers, leaves* abwerfen **b** (*Cards*) abwerfen **VI** (*Cards*) abwerfen **N a** (*Cards*) Abwerfen *nt* **b** (*Ind, Comm*) Ausschuss *m*, Ausschussware f

disc: disc brake N Scheibenbremse f; **disc camera** N Disc-Kamera f

discern [dɪˈsɜːn] VT (*with senses*) wahrnehmen; (*mentally*) erkennen; **he was too young to ~ right from wrong** er war zu jung, um Recht von Unrecht unterscheiden zu können

discernible [dɪˈsɜːnəbl] ADJ (*with senses*) wahrnehmbar; (*mentally*) erkennbar

discernibly [dɪˈsɜːnəblɪ] ADV erkennbar

discerning [dɪˈsɜːnɪŋ] ADJ *clientele, reader* anspruchsvoll, kritisch; *eye, ear* fein

discernment [dɪˈsɜːnmənt] N **a** (= *ability to discern, observation*) feines Gespür; (*discriminating taste*) kritisches Urteilsvermögen **b** (= *act of discerning, with senses*) Wahrnehmung f; (*mentally*) Erkennen *nt*

discharge [dɪsˈtʃɑːdʒ] **VT a** *employee, prisoner, patient* entlassen; *accused* freisprechen; **he ~d himself (from hospital)** er hat das Krankenhaus auf eigene Verantwortung verlassen

b (= *emit, Elec*) entladen; *liquid, gas (pipe etc)* ausstoßen; *workers* ausströmen lassen; (*Med*) ausscheiden, absondern; **the factory was discharging toxic gas into the atmosphere** aus der Fabrik strömten giftige Gase in die Atmosphäre; **the tanker was discharging oil into the Channel** das Öl lief aus dem Tanker in den (Ärmel)kanal; **how much oil has been ~d?** wie viel Öl ist ausgelaufen?; (*deliberately*) wie viel Öl hat man abgelassen?

c (= *unload*) *ship, cargo* löschen; **the bus ~d its passengers** die Passagiere stiegen aus dem Bus aus

d (*gun*) abfeuern
e *debt* begleichen; *duty* nachkommen (+*dat*); *function, obligations* erfüllen; **~d bankrupt** entlasteter Konkursschuldner
VI (*wound, sore*) eitern
N ['dɪstʃɑːdʒ] **a** (= *dismissal, of employee, prisoner, patient*) Entlassung *f*; (*of accused*) Freispruch *m*; (*of soldier*) Abschied *m*
b (*Elec*) Entladung *f*; (*of gas*) Ausströmen *nt*; (*of liquid: Med*) (*vaginal*) Ausfluss *m*; (*of pus*) Absonderung *f*
c (*of cargo*) Löschen *nt*
d (*of debt*) Begleichung *f*; (*of duty, function*) Erfüllung *f*; (*of bankrupt*) Entlastung *f*

disc harrow N Scheibenegge *f*

disciple [dɪ'saɪpl] N (*lit*) Jünger *m*; (*fig*) Schüler(in) *m(f)*, Jünger(in) *m(f)* (*usu iro*)

disciplinarian [ˌdɪsɪplɪ'nɛərɪən] N Zuchtmeister(in) *m(f)*; **to be a strict ~** eiserne Disziplin halten

disciplinary [ˌdɪsɪ'plɪnərɪ] ADJ Disziplinar-; *matters* disziplinarisch; **~ proceedings** or **procedures** Disziplinarverfahren *nt*; **~ measures/ powers** Disziplinarmaßnahmen *pl*/-gewalt *f*; **he has no ~ problems in his class** in seiner Klasse hat er keine Schwierigkeiten mit der Disziplin; **the worst ~ record in the League** das längste Disziplinarstrafregister in der Liga; **a school with a firm ~ code** eine Schule mit einer strengen Disziplin; **to take ~ action** Disziplinarmaßnahmen ergreifen; **they face ~ action/ charges** gegen sie werden Disziplinarmaßnahmen ergriffen/wird ein Disziplinarverfahren eröffnet

discipline ['dɪsɪplɪn] **N** (*all senses*) Disziplin *f*; (= *punishment*) disziplinarische Maßnahmen *pl*; **to maintain ~** die Disziplin aufrechterhalten **VT** **a** (= *train, make obedient*) disziplinieren; *reactions, emotions* in Zucht or unter Kontrolle halten; **to ~ oneself to do sth** sich dazu anhalten or zwingen, etw zu tun **b** (= *punish*) bestrafen; (*physically*) züchtigen

disciplined ['dɪsɪplɪnd] ADJ diszipliniert; **we gave a ~ performance** wir spielten diszipliniert

disc jockey N Diskjockey *m*

disclaim [dɪs'kleɪm] VT **a** (= *deny*) abstreiten, (weit) von sich (*dat*) weisen; **to ~ all** or **any responsibility** jede Verantwortung von sich weisen **b** (*Jur*) *a right* verzichten auf (+*acc*)

disclaimer [dɪs'kleɪmə'] N **a** Dementi *nt*; **to issue a ~** eine Gegenerklärung abgeben **b** **to put in a ~ of sth** (*Jur*) eine Verzichterklärung auf etw (*acc*) abgeben

disclose [dɪs'kləʊz] VT *secret* enthüllen; *intentions, news, details, identity* bekannt geben

disclosure [dɪs'kləʊʒə'] N **a** (*of secret*) Enthüllung *f*; (*of intentions, news, details, identity*) Bekanntgabe *f* **b** (= *fact etc revealed*) Mitteilung *f*

disco ['dɪskəʊ] N Disko *f*, Disco *f*; **~ dancing** Diskotanzen *nt*

discography [dɪs'kɒgrəfɪ] N Diskografie *f*

discolor VTI (*US*) = **discolour**

discoloration [dɪsˌkʌlə'reɪʃən] N Verfärben *nt*; (= *mark*) Verfärbung *f*

discolour, (*US*) **discolor** [dɪs'kʌlə'] **VT** verfärben **VI** sich verfärben

discoloured, (*US*) **discolored** [dɪs'kʌləd] ADJ verfärbt; **his left temple was bruised and ~** an seiner linken Schläfe hatte er einen Bluterguss

discomfit [dɪs'kʌmfɪt] VT Unbehagen verursachen (+*dat*)

discomfiture [dɪs'kʌmfɪtʃə'] N Unbehagen *nt*

discomfort [dɪs'kʌmfət] N (*lit*) Beschwerden *pl*; (*fig*, = *uneasiness, embarrassment*) Unbehagen *nt*; **to feel some ~** sich nicht wohl fühlen; **the injury gives me a little ~ now and again** die Verletzung verursacht mir ab und zu leichte Beschwerden; **much to my ~ he offered to pay** es war mir sehr unangenehm, dass er zahlen wollte; **the ~s of camping** die Unannehmlichkeiten des Zeltens

discompose ['dɪskəm'pəʊz] VT (*form*) **a** (= *disarrange*) in Unordnung bringen; (*fig*) *person*

durcheinander bringen **b** (= *agitate*) (völlig) aus der Fassung bringen, verwirren

disconcert [ˌdɪskən'sɜːt] VT beunruhigen

disconcerting [ˌdɪskən'sɜːtɪŋ] ADJ beunruhigend

disconcertingly [ˌdɪskən'sɜːtɪŋlɪ] ADV beunruhigend; (*introducing sentence*) irritierenderweise

disconnect ['dɪskə'nekt] VT *pipe etc* trennen; *TV, iron* ausschalten; (= *cut off supply of*) *gas, electricity* abstellen; **to ~ a call** (*Telec*) ein Gespräch unterbrechen; **I've been ~ed** (*for nonpayment*) man hat mir das Telefon/den Strom/das Gas *etc* abgestellt; (*in mid-conversation*) das Gespräch ist unterbrochen worden

disconnected [ˌdɪskə'nektɪd] ADJ unzusammenhängend; *phrases, sentences* unzusammenhängend, zusammenhanglos; **~ events** nicht miteinander zusammenhängende Ereignisse

disconsolate [dɪs'kɒnsəlɪt] ADJ untröstlich; (= *gloomy*) niedergeschlagen; **to grow ~** verzweifeln, verzagen

disconsolately [dɪs'kɒnsəlɪtlɪ] ADV untröstlich; (= *gloomily*) niedergeschlagen

discontent ['dɪskən'tent] N Unzufriedenheit *f*

discontented ['dɪskən'tentɪd] ADJ unzufrieden (*with, about* mit)

discontentedly [ˌdɪskən'tentɪdlɪ] ADV unzufrieden

discontentment ['dɪskən'tentmənt] N Unzufriedenheit *f*

discontinuation [ˌdɪskənˌtɪnjʊ'eɪʃən] N Aufgabe *f*; (*of class, conversation, treatment*) Abbruch *m*; (*Comm, of line*) (Produktions)einstellung *f*; (*of production, Jur, of case, proceedings*) Einstellung *f*

discontinue ['dɪskən'tɪnjuː] VT aufgeben; *class, conversation, treatment* abbrechen; *project* einstellen, aufgeben; *use* beenden; (*Comm*) *line* auslaufen lassen, die Produktion einstellen von; *production* einstellen; (*Jur*) *case, proceedings* einstellen; **a ~d line** (*Comm*) eine ausgelaufene Serie

discontinuity [ˌdɪskɒntɪ'njuːɪtɪ] N mangelnde Kontinuität, Diskontinuität *f* (*geh*); **a certain amount of ~** ein gewisser Mangel an Kontinuität; **to reduce any ~ to a minimum** die Kontinuität möglichst wenig unterbrechen

discontinuous ADJ , **discontinuously** ADV [ˌdɪskən'tɪnjʊəs, -lɪ] nicht kontinuierlich

discord ['dɪskɔːd] N **a** Uneinigkeit *f* **b** (*Mus*) Disharmonie *f*

discordance [dɪs'kɔːdəns] N **a** Uneinigkeit *f* **b** (*of colours, sounds, music*) Disharmonie *f*

discordant [dɪs'kɔːdənt] ADJ *opinions, colours* nicht miteinander harmonierend; *sound* misstönend; *meeting, atmosphere* unharmonisch; (*Mus*) disharmonisch; **to strike a ~ note** (*fig*) einen falschen Ton anschlagen

discotheque ['dɪskəʊtek] N Diskothek *f*

discount ['dɪskaʊnt] **⊙ 20.3** **N** **a** (*on article*) Rabatt *m*; (*for cash*) Skonto *nt* or *m*; **to give a ~ on sth** Rabatt or Prozente (*inf*) auf etw (*acc*) geben; **to give a 5% ~** jdm 5% Rabatt/ Skonto geben; **at a ~** auf Rabatt/Skonto; **~ for cash** Skonto or Rabatt bei Barzahlung **b** **to be at a ~** (*Fin*) unter pari sein; (*fig*) nicht or wenig gefragt sein **VT** **a** (*Comm*) *sum of money* nachlassen; *bill, note* diskontieren; **~ed bill** Diskontwechsel *m* **b** [dɪs'kaʊnt] *person's opinion* unberücksichtigt lassen; **to ~ sth as an exaggeration/as untrue** etw als Übertreibung/als unwahr abtun

discountable [dɪs'kaʊntəbl] ADJ (*Fin*) diskontfähig, diskontierbar

discount: discount broker N Wechselmakler(in) *m(f)*; **discount house** N **a** (*Fin*) Diskontbank *f* **b** (= *store*) Discountgeschäft *nt* or -laden *m*; **discount market** N (*Fin*) Diskontmarkt *m*; **discount rate** N (*Fin*) Diskontsatz *m*; **discount store** N Discounter *m*, Discountgeschäft *nt* or -laden *m*

discourage [dɪs'kʌrɪdʒ] VT **a** (= *dishearten*) entmutigen; **to become ~d (by)** entmutigt werden

(*von*); (= *generally disheartened*) mutlos werden (*durch*) **b** (= *dissuade*) **to ~ sb from doing sth** jdm abraten, etw zu tun; (*successfully*) jdn davon abbringen, etw zu tun **c** (= *deter, hinder*) abhalten; *friendship, advances, plan, speculation, investment* zu verhindern suchen; *praise, evil* abwehren; *pride* nicht ermutigen; *smoking* unterbinden; **the weather ~d people from going away** das Wetter hielt die Leute davon ab wegzufahren

discouragement [dɪs'kʌrɪdʒmənt] N **a** (= *depression*) Mutlosigkeit *f* **b** (= *dissuasion*) Abraten *nt*; (*with success*) Abbringen *nt* **c** (= *deterrence, hindrance*) Abhaltung *f*; (*of friendship*) Verhinderung *f*; (*of praise*) Abwehr *f* **d** (= *discouraging thing*) **to be a ~** entmutigend sein

discouraging [dɪs'kʌrɪdʒɪŋ] ADJ entmutigend; **he was rather ~ about her chances** er äußerte sich ziemlich entmutigend über ihre Chancen

discouragingly [dɪs'kʌrɪdʒɪŋlɪ] ADV entmutigend

discourse ['dɪskɔːs] **N** Diskurs *m* (*geh*) **VI** einen Diskurs geben (*geh*); (= *converse*) einen Diskurs führen (*geh*)

discourse analysis N (*Ling*) Diskursanalyse *f*

discourteous [dɪs'kɜːtɪəs] ADJ unhöflich

discourteously [dɪs'kɜːtɪəslɪ] ADV unhöflich; **we were ~ ignored** wir wurden unhöflicherweise ignoriert

discourteousness [dɪs'kɜːtɪəsnɪs], **discourtesy** [dɪs'kɜːtɪsɪ] N Unhöflichkeit *f*

discover [dɪs'kʌvə'] VT entdecken; *culprit* finden; *secret, truth* herausfinden; *cause* feststellen; (*after search*) *house, book* ausfindig machen, entdecken; (= *notice*) *mistake, loss* feststellen, bemerken; **did you ever ~ who ...?** haben Sie jemals herausgefunden, wer ...?

discoverer [dɪs'kʌvərə'] N Entdecker(in) *m(f)*

discovery [dɪs'kʌvərɪ] N Entdeckung *f*

discredit [dɪs'kredɪt] **VT** **a** (= *cast slur/doubt on*) diskreditieren **b** (= *disbelieve*) keinen Glauben schenken (+*dat*) **N** **a** *no pl* (= *dishonour, disbelief*) Misskredit *m*; **to bring ~ (up)on sb/sth** jdn/ etw in Misskredit bringen **b** **to be a ~ to sb** eine Schande für jdn sein

discreditable [dɪs'kredɪtəbl] ADJ diskreditierend; **to be ~ to sb** jdn diskreditieren, jdn in Misskredit bringen

discreditably [dɪs'kredɪtəblɪ] ADV diskreditierend

discredited [dɪs'kredɪtɪd] ADJ diskreditiert

discreet [dɪ'skriːt] ADJ diskret; *inquiry* diskret, taktvoll; *account* taktvoll; *elegance* unaufdringlich; *jewellery, tie, dress, decoration* dezent; **at a ~ distance** in einer diskreten Entfernung; **to maintain a ~ presence** eine unauffällige Präsenz aufrechterhalten; **to keep** or **maintain a ~ silence** diskret schweigen; **to be ~ about sth** etw diskret behandeln

discreetly [dɪ'skriːtlɪ] ADV diskret; *dressed, decorated* dezent; **~, she said nothing** taktvollerweise sagte sie nichts

discreetness [dɪ'skriːtnɪs] N Diskretheit *f*; (*of account*) taktvolle Art; (*of jewellery, tie, dress, decoration*) dezente Art

discrepancy [dɪs'krepənsɪ] N Diskrepanz *f* (*between* zwischen +*dat*)

discrete [dɪ'skriːt] ADJ diskret

discretion [dɪ'skreʃən] N **a** Diskretion *f*; **~ is the better part of valour** (*Brit Prov*) Vorsicht ist die Mutter der Porzellankiste (*inf*) **b** (= *freedom of decision*) Ermessen *nt*; **to leave sth to sb's ~** etw in jds Ermessen (*acc*) stellen; **use your own ~** Sie müssen nach eigenem Ermessen handeln; **to be at sb's ~** in jds Ermessen (*dat*) stehen; **to do sth at one's ~** etw nach eigenem Ermessen tun

discretionary [dɪ'skreʃənərɪ] ADJ Ermessens-; **~ powers** Ermessensspielraum *m*

discriminate [dɪ'skrɪmɪneɪt] **VI** **a** (= *be discriminating*) kritisch sein; (= *distinguish*) unterscheiden (*between* zwischen +*dat*) **b** (= *make unfair* *distinction*) Unterschiede machen (*between* zwischen +*dat*); **to ~ in favour** (*Brit*) or **favor** (*US*) **of/against sb** jdn bevorzugen/benachteiligen **VT** unterscheiden, einen Unterschied machen zwischen (+*dat*); **to ~ good from bad** Gut und Böse unterscheiden können

▶ **discriminate against** VI +*prep obj* diskriminieren; **they were discriminated against** sie wurden diskriminiert

discriminating [dɪˈskrɪmɪneɪtɪŋ] ADJ **a** (= *discerning*) *person* anspruchsvoll, kritisch; *judgement, eye* kritisch; *palate* fein; **a ~ ear** ein feines Gehör **b** (*Fin*) *tax, tariff* diskriminierend

discrimination [dɪˌskrɪmɪˈneɪʃən] N **a** (= *differential treatment*) Diskriminierung *f*; **racial ~** Rassendiskriminierung *f*; **sex(ual)/religious ~** Diskriminierung *f* auf Grund des Geschlechts/der Religion **b** (= *differentiation*) Unterscheidung *f* (*between* zwischen +*dat*) **c** (= *discernment*) kritisches Urteilsvermögen

discriminatory [dɪˈskrɪmɪnətərɪ] ADJ diskriminierend

discursive [dɪˈskɜːsɪv], **discursory** [dɪˈskɜːsərɪ] ADJ **a** *style* weitschweifig **b** (*Philos*) diskursiv

discus [ˈdɪskəs] N Diskus *m*; **in the ~** (*Sport*) im Diskuswerfen; **~ thrower** Diskuswerfer(in) *m(f)*

discuss [dɪˈskʌs] VT besprechen; *politics, theory* diskutieren; *in essay, speech etc* erörtern, diskutieren; **I don't want to ~ it any further** ich möchte darüber nicht weiter reden, ich möchte das nicht weiter diskutieren; **I am not willing to ~ it** ich bin nicht gewillt, darüber zu diskutieren

discussant [dɪˈskʌsənt] N (*US*) Diskussionsteilnehmer(in) *m(f)*

discussion [dɪˈskʌʃən] N Diskussion *f* (*of, about* über +*acc*); (= *meeting*) Besprechung *f*; **after much** or **a lot of ~** nach langen Diskussionen; **to be under ~** zur Diskussion stehen; **that is still under ~** das ist noch in der Diskussion; **open to ~** zur Diskussion gestellt; **a subject for ~** ein Diskussionsthema *nt*; **to come up for ~** zur Diskussion gestellt werden; **~ document** or **paper** Diskussionspapier *nt*; **~ group** Diskussionsgruppe *f*

disdain [dɪsˈdeɪn] **VT** *sb* verachten; *sth also* verschmähen; **he ~ed to notice them** er hielt es für unter seiner Würde, ihnen Beachtung zu schenken **N** Verachtung *f*; **with ~** verächtlich

disdainful [dɪsˈdeɪnfʊl] ADJ, **disdainfully** [dɪsˈdeɪnfəlɪ] ADV herablassend; *look* verächtlich

disease [dɪˈziːz] N (*lit, fig*) Krankheit *f*

diseased [dɪˈziːzd] ADJ (*lit, fig*) krank; *tissue, plant* befallen

disembark [ˌdɪsɪmˈbɑːk] **VT** ausschiffen **VI** von Bord gehen

disembarkation [ˌdɪsembɑːˈkeɪʃən] N Landung *f*

disembodied [ˈdɪsɪmˈbɒdɪd] ADJ körperlos; *voice* geisterhaft; *head, hand* (vom Körper) abgetrennt

disembowel [ˌdɪsɪmˈbaʊəl] VT die Eingeweide herausnehmen (+*dat*); (= *murder*) den Bauch aufschlitzen (+*dat*)

disempower [ˌdɪsɪmˈpaʊə] VT entkräften

disenchant [ˈdɪsɪnˈtʃɑːnt] VT ernüchtern; **he became ~ed with her/it** sie/es ernüchterte ihn

disenfranchise [ˈdɪsɪnˈfræntʃaɪz] VT **a** *person* die bürgerlichen Ehrenrechte aberkennen (+*dat*); *town* das Recht nehmen, einen Abgeordneten ins Parlament zu senden (+*dat*) **b** (*Comm*) die Konzession entziehen (+*dat*)

disenfranchisement [ˈdɪsɪnˈfræntʃaɪzmənt] N (*of person*) Aberkennung *f* der bürgerlichen Ehrenrechte; (*of town*) Entzug *m*, des Rechts, einen Abgeordneten ins Parlament zu senden

disengage [ˌdɪsɪnˈgeɪdʒ] **VT a** (= *extricate*) losmachen, lösen (*from* aus) **b** (*Tech*) ausrücken (*form*); **to ~ the clutch** (*Aut*) auskuppeln **c** (*Mil, from country*) abziehen; (*from battle*) abziehen, abrücken lassen **VI a** (*Tech*) ausrücken (*form*) **b** (*Mil*) auseinander rücken (*opponents*)

sich trennen **c** (*Fencing*) sich (aus seiner Bindung) lösen

disengagement [ˌdɪsɪnˈgeɪdʒmənt] N **a** (= *extrication*) Lösung *f* **b** (*Tech*) Ausrücken *nt* (*form*); **~ of the clutch** das Auskuppeln **c** (*Mil*) Abzug *m*

disentail [ˈdɪsɪnˈteɪl] VT (*Jur*) das Fideikommiss (+*gen*), auflösen

disentangle [ˈdɪsɪnˈtæŋgl] VT (*lit, fig*) entwirren; *problem, mystery also* enträtseln; **to ~ oneself (from sth)** (*lit*) sich (aus etw) lösen; (*fig*) sich (von etw) lösen

disestablish [ˌdɪsɪsˈtæblɪʃ] VT *the Church* vom Staat trennen

disestablishment [ˌdɪsɪsˈtæblɪʃmənt] N Trennung *f* (vom Staat)

disfavour, (*US*) **disfavor** [dɪsˈfeɪvə] N **a** (= *displeasure*) Ungnade *f*; (= *dislike*) Missfallen *nt*; **to fall into/be in ~ (with)** in Ungnade fallen/sein (bei); **to look with ~ (up)on sb/sth** jdn/etw mit Missfallen betrachten **b** (= *disadvantage*) **in/to his ~** zu seinen Ungunsten

disfigure [dɪsˈfɪgə] VT verunstalten; *person also* entstellen; *city, landscape* verschandeln

disfigurement [dɪsˈfɪgəmənt] N Verunstaltung *f*; (*of person also*) Entstellung *f*; (*of city, landscape*) Verschandelung *f*

disfranchise [dɪsˈfræntʃaɪz] VT = **disenfranchise**

disfranchisement [dɪsˈfræntʃaɪzmənt] N = **disenfranchisement**

disgorge [dɪsˈgɔːdʒ] **VT** *food* ausspucken, ausspeien; (*stomach*) ausstoßen; (*fig, = spew forth*) ausspeien; (*river*) *waters* ergießen; (= *give up*) her(aus)geben or herausrücken; **the train ~d its passengers** die Passagiere strömten aus dem Zug; **the ship is disgorging its cargo of weapons** aus dem Schiff werden Waffen ausgeladen **VI** (*river*) aus einer Schlucht austreten

disgrace [dɪsˈgreɪs] **N a** *no pl* (= *dishonour, shame*) Schande *f*; **in ~** mit Schimpf und Schande; (*as a punishment*) zur Strafe; **to bring ~ (up)on sb** jdm Schande machen or bringen; **to be in/fall into ~** in Ungnade (gefallen) sein/fallen (*with* bei)
b (= *cause of shame, thing*) Schande *f* (*to* für), Blamage *f* (*to* für); (*person*) Schandfleck *m* (*to* +*gen*); **you're a complete ~!** mit dir kann man sich wirklich nur blamieren!; **the cost of rented accommodation is a ~** es ist eine Schande, wie teuer Mietwohnungen sind
VT Schande machen (+*dat*); *country, family* Schande bringen über (+*acc*); **don't ~ us!** mach uns keine Schande!, blamier uns nicht!; **to ~ oneself** sich blamieren; (*child, dog*) sich schlecht benehmen; **he ~d himself by losing his temper** zu seiner Schande verlor er die Beherrschung; **to be ~d** blamiert sein; (*politician, officer etc*) in Unehre gefallen sein

disgraceful [dɪsˈgreɪsfʊl] ADJ erbärmlich (*schlecht*); *behaviour, scenes, negligence* skandalös; **it's quite ~ how/that ...** es ist wirklich eine Schande, wie/dass ...

disgracefully [dɪsˈgreɪsfəlɪ] ADV schändlich; **~ low wages** erbärmlich niedrige Löhne

disgruntle [dɪsˈgrʌntl] VT verstimmen

disgruntled [dɪsˈgrʌntld] ADJ verstimmt

disgruntlement [dɪsˈgrʌntlmənt] N Verstimmung *f*

disguise [dɪsˈgaɪz] **VT** unkenntlich machen; *voice* verstellen; *vehicle, aircraft, building* tarnen; *fear, dislike* verbergen; *taste* kaschieren; *facts, mistakes, interest* verschleiern; **to ~ oneself/sb as** sich/jdn verkleiden als; **superstition ~d as faith** Aberglaube, der unter dem Deckmantel des Glaubens daherkommt **N** (*lit*) Verkleidung *f*; (*of vehicle, aircraft, building*) Tarnung *f*; (*fig*) Deckmantel *m*; **in ~** verkleidet, getarnt; **in the ~ of** verkleidet als/getarnt als/unter dem Deckmantel von

disgust [dɪsˈgʌst] **N** Ekel *m*; (*at sb's behaviour*) Entrüstung *f*, Empörung *f*; **in ~** voller Ekel/ Empörung; **much to his ~ they left** sehr zu sei-

ner Empörung gingen sie **VT** (*person, sight*) anekeln, anwidern; (*actions*) empören

disgusted [dɪsˈgʌstɪd] ADJ angeekelt; (*at sb's behaviour*) empört; **to be ~ with sb** empört über jdn sein; **to be ~ with sth** angewidert von etw sein; **I was ~ with myself** ich war mir selbst zuwider

disgustedly [dɪsˈgʌstɪdlɪ] ADV angewidert; (= *angrily*) empört

disgusting [dɪsˈgʌstɪŋ] ADJ **a** (= *revolting*) *behaviour* widerlich; (= *physically nauseating*) ekelhaft; *taste, smell, person* widerlich, ekelhaft; **it looks ~** es sieht widerlich or ekelhaft aus **b** (= *offensive*) *book, film, photo* anstößig, widerlich; (= *obscene*) obszön; **don't be ~** sei nicht so ordinär **c** (= *disgraceful*) unerhört; **it's ~ that...** es ist unerhört or eine Schande, dass ...

disgustingly [dɪsˈgʌstɪŋlɪ] ADV widerlich, ekelhaft; **~ rich** stinkreich

dish [dɪʃ] **N a** Schale *f*; (*for serving*) Schüssel *f*, Schale *f* **b** **dishes** PL (= *crockery*) Geschirr *nt*; **to do the ~es** Geschirr spülen, abwaschen **c** (= *food*) Gericht *nt*; **fish/pasta ~es** Fisch-/Nudelgericht *pl* **d** (*Elec*) Parabolreflektor *m*; (*also* **dish aerial** (*Brit*) or **antenna** (*US*)) Parabolantenne *f*, Schüssel *f* (*inf*) **e** (*inf, girl*) klasse Frau (*inf*), scharfe Braut (*sl*); (*man*) toller Typ (*inf*), scharfer Typ (*sl*) **VT a** (= *serve*) anrichten **b** **to ~ the dirt on sb** (*inf*) jdn in den Dreck ziehen (*inf*)

▶ **dish out** VT *sep* (*inf*) austeilen; **he can really dish it out** er kann ganz schön austeilen (*inf*)

▶ **dish up** **VT** *sep* **a** (*lit*) auf dem Teller anrichten; (*in bowls*) auftragen **b** (*fig inf*) *story, news* auftischen (*inf*) **VI** anrichten

dishabille [ˌdɪsəˈbiːl] N (*form*) **in various degrees of ~** mehr oder weniger hüllenlos

disharmony [ˈdɪsˈhɑːmənɪ] N (*lit, fig*) Disharmonie *f*

dish: dishcloth [ˈdɪʃklɒθ] N (*for drying*) Geschirrtuch *nt*; (*for washing*) Spüllappen *m* or -tuch *nt*; **dish drainer** [ˈdɪʃˌdreɪnə] N Abtropfständer *m*

dishearten [dɪsˈhɑːtn] VT entmutigen; **don't be ~ed!** nun verlieren Sie nicht gleich den Mut!, nur Mut!

disheartening ADJ, **dishearteningly** ADV [dɪsˈhɑːtnɪŋ, -lɪ] entmutigend

dished [dɪʃt] ADJ (*Tech*) konkav (gewölbt); *wheels* gestürzt

dishevelled, (*US*) **disheveled** [dɪˈʃevəld] ADJ unordentlich; *hair* zerzaust; *person, appearance* ungepflegt; **to be in a ~ state** ziemlich mitgenommen aussehen

dish mop N Spülbürste *f*

dishonest [dɪsˈɒnɪst] ADJ unehrlich; (= *cheating*) *businessman* unredlich, unehrlich; (= *lying*) verlogen; *plan, scheme* unlauter

dishonestly [dɪsˈɒnɪstlɪ] ADV (= *not truthfully*) unehrlich; *pretend, claim* unehrlicherweise; (= *deceitfully*) betrügerisch; (= *with intent to deceive*) in betrügerischer Absicht; **to obtain money ~** sich auf betrügerische Weise Geld verschaffen

dishonesty [dɪsˈɒnɪstɪ] N Unehrlichkeit *f*; (= *cheating: of businessman*) Unredlichkeit *f*, Unehrlichkeit *f*; (= *lying*) Verlogenheit *f*; (*of plan, scheme*) Unlauterkeit *f*

dishonour, (*US*) **dishonor** [dɪsˈɒnə] **N** Schande *f*, Unehre *f*; **to bring ~ (up)on sb** Schande über jdn bringen **VT a** (= *disgrace*) schänden, entehren; *family* Schande machen (+*dat*) **b** (*Comm, Fin*) *cheque* nicht honorieren; *bill* nicht bezahlen **c** *agreement* nicht einhalten; *promise* nicht einlösen or einhalten

dishonourable, (*US*) **dishonorable** [dɪsˈɒnərəbl] ADJ unehrenhaft; **it was ~ of him to do that** es war unehrenhaft, dass er das getan hat

dishonourable discharge, (*US*) **dishonorable discharge** N (*Mil*) unehrenhafte Entlassung; **to be given a ~** (*Mil*) unehrenhaft entlassen werden

dishonourableness, *(US)* **dishonorableness** [dɪsˈɒnərəblnɪs] N Unehrenhaftigkeit *f*

dishonourably, *(US)* **dishonorably** [dɪsˈɒnərəblɪ] ADV unehrenhaft

dish: dishpan N *(US)* Abwaschschüssel *f*; **dishpan hands** PL raue und rissige Hände *pl*; **dishrack** N Geschirrständer *m*; *(in dishwasher)* (Einsatz)korb *m*; **dishtowel** N *(US, Scot)* Geschirrtuch *nt*; **dishwasher** N *(= person)* Tellerwäscher(in) *m(f)*, Spüler(in) *m(f)*; *(= machine)* (Geschirr)spülmaschine *f*; **dishwasher-proof** ADJ spülmaschinenfest; **dishwater** N Abwasch- *or* Spülwasser *nt*; **this coffee tastes like ~** der Kaffee schmeckt wie Abwasch- *or* Spülwasser

dishy [ˈdɪʃɪ] ADJ *(+er)* *(inf)* woman, man scharf *(sl)*, toll *(inf)*

disillusion [ˌdɪsɪˈluːʒən] VT desillusionieren; **I hate to ~ you, but ...** es tut mir Leid, Ihnen Ihre Illusionen rauben *or* Sie desillusionieren zu müssen, aber ... N Desillusion *f*

disillusionment [ˌdɪsɪˈluːʒənmənt] N Desillusionierung *f*

disincentive [ˌdɪsɪnˈsentɪv] N Entmutigung *f*; **to be a ~ to sth** keinen Anreiz für etw bieten; **to be a ~ to do sth** keinen Anreiz dafür bieten, etw zu tun; **it acts as a ~** es hält die Leute ab

disinclination [dɪsɪnklɪˈneɪʃən] N Abneigung *f*, Unlust *f*

disinclined [ˈdɪsɪnˈklaɪnd] ADJ abgeneigt

disinfect [ˌdɪsɪnˈfekt] VT desinfizieren

disinfectant [ˌdɪsɪnˈfektənt] N Desinfektionsmittel *nt* ADJ desinfizierend, Desinfektions-

disinfection [ˌdɪsɪnˈfekʃən] N Desinfektion *f*

disinformation [dɪsɪnfɔːˈmeɪʃən] N Desinformation *f*

disingenuous [ˌdɪsɪnˈdʒenjʊəs] ADJ unaufrichtig

disingenuously [ˌdɪsɪnˈdʒenjʊəslɪ] ADV unaufrichtig, unehrlich; say, remark unaufrichtigerweise; **the finance ministry claims ~ that it did not know this was going on** das Finanzministerium behauptet wider besseren Wissens, dass es über die Vorgänge nicht informiert gewesen sei

disingenuousness [ˌdɪsɪnˈdʒenjʊəsnɪs] N Unaufrichtigkeit *f*

disinherit [ˈdɪsɪnˈherɪt] VT enterben

disinheritance [ˈdɪsɪnˈherɪtəns] N Enterbung *f*

disintegrate [dɪsˈɪntɪgreɪt] VI zerfallen; *(rock, cement)* auseinander bröckeln; *(road surface)* rissig werden; *(car)* sich in seine Bestandteile auflösen; *(group, institution)* sich auflösen; *(marriage, society, theory)* zusammenbrechen; *(family)* auseinander gehen; **to ~ into civil war/chaos** in den Bürgerkrieg/ins Chaos versinken VT zerfallen lassen; rock, cement auseinander bröckeln lassen; road surface brüchig werden lassen; group, institution auflösen; theory zusammenbrechen lassen

disintegration [dɪsɪntɪˈgreɪʃən] N Zerfall *m*; *(of rock, cement)* Auseinanderbröckeln *nt*; *(of road surface)* Rissigkeit *f*; *(of group, institution, family)* Auflösung *f*; *(of marriage, society, theory)* Zusammenbruch *m*

disinter [ˌdɪsɪnˈtɜː] VT ausgraben

disinterest [dɪsˈɪntrəst] N Desinteresse *nt* *(in an +dat)*

disinterested [dɪsˈɪntrɪstɪd] ADJ **a** *(= impartial)* unvoreingenommen, unparteiisch **b** *(= uninterested)* desinteressiert

disinterestedly [dɪsˈɪntrɪstɪdlɪ] ADV **a** *(= impartially)* unvoreingenommen, unparteiisch; **we reason ~ from the facts we observe** wir urteilen unvoreingenommen auf Grundlage der von uns beobachteten Fakten **b** *(= uninterestedly)* look, say gelangweilt; **I watched ~ as the train pulled into the station** ich beobachtete gelangweilt, wie der Zug in den Bahnhof einfuhr

disinterestedness [dɪsˈɪntrɪstɪdnɪs] N **a** *(= impartiality)* Unvoreingenommenheit *f* **b** *(= lack of concern)* Desinteresse *nt*

disinterment [ˌdɪsɪnˈtɜːmənt] N Ausgrabung *f*

disjointed [dɪsˈdʒɔɪntɪd] ADJ **a** *(= incoherent)* sentences, words, thoughts unzusammenhängend, zusammenhanglos; film, programme unzusammenhängend **b** *(= disunited)* society zerrissen; team uneinig; play unzusammenhängend

disjointedly [dɪsˈdʒɔɪntɪdlɪ] ADV unzusammenhängend, zusammenhanglos

disjointedness [dɪsˈdʒɔɪntɪdnɪs] N **a** *(= incoherence)* Zusammenhanglosigkeit *f* **b** *(= disunity, of society)* Zerrissenheit *f*; *(of team)* Uneinigkeit *f*

disjunctive [dɪsˈdʒʌŋktɪv] *(Gram)* ADJ disjunktiv N Disjunktion *f*

disk N *(Comput)* Platte *f*; *(= floppy disk)* Diskette *f*; **on ~** auf Platte/Diskette

disk *(Comput)*: **disk controller** N Plattencontroller *m*; **disk drive** N Diskettenlaufwerk *nt*; *(= hard disk drive)* Festplattenlaufwerk *nt*

diskette [dɪsˈket] N *(Comput)* Diskette *f*

disk: diskless [ˈdɪsklɪs] ADJ *(Comput)* plattenlos; **disk operating system** N *(Comput)* Betriebssystem *nt*; **disk space** N *(Comput)* Speicherkapazität *f*

dislike [dɪsˈlaɪk] VT nicht mögen, nicht gern haben; **to ~ doing sth** etw ungern *or* nicht gern tun; **to ~ sb doing sth** es nicht gern haben *or* sehen, wenn jd etw tut; **I ~ him/it intensely** ich mag ihn/es überhaupt nicht; **I don't ~ it** ich habe nichts dagegen N Abneigung *f* *(of gegen)*; **likes and ~s** Vorlieben und Abneigungen; **to take a ~ to sb/sth** eine Abneigung gegen jdn/etw entwickeln; **he had taken an instant ~ to John** er konnte John auf Anhieb nicht leiden

dislocate [ˈdɪsləʊkeɪt] VT *(Med)* verrenken, ausrenken; *(fig)* plans durcheinander bringen; **to ~ one's shoulder** sich *(dat)* den Arm auskugeln

dislocation [ˌdɪsləʊˈkeɪʃən] N *(Med)* Verrenkung *f*; *(of shoulder)* Auskugeln *nt*; *(fig, of plans)* Durcheinanderbringen *nt*

dislodge [dɪsˈlɒdʒ] VT obstruction, stone lösen; *(= prise, poke out)* herausstochern; *(= knock out)* herausschlagen *or* -klopfen; person verdrängen; *(Mil)* enemy verdrängen; **a few stones have been ~d** einige Steine haben sich gelöst

disloyal [dɪsˈlɔɪəl] ADJ illoyal; **to be ~ to sb** jdm gegenüber nicht loyal sein

disloyalty [dɪsˈlɔɪəltɪ] N Illoyalität *f* *(to gegenüber)*

dismal [ˈdɪzməl] ADJ **a** *(= depressing)* place, building, day, prospect, weather trostlos; thought trüb; **it makes ~ reading** es ist bedrückend zu lesen; **the ~ science** *(= economics)* politische Ökonomie **b** *(= poor)* performance kläglich, miserabel; prospects miserabel; **the ~ state of the economy** die miserable Wirtschaftslage; **to be a ~ failure** kläglich scheitern

dismally [ˈdɪzməlɪ] ADV **a** *(= depressingly)* say, think, look trübselig; grey, monotonous trostlos; morale was ~ **low** die Moral war deprimierend schlecht **b** *(= badly)* fail kläglich; **the world champion performed ~** der Weltmeister zeigte eine klägliche Leistung

dismantle [dɪsˈmæntl] VT *(= take to pieces)* auseinander nehmen; scaffolding abbauen; *(permanently)* ship abwracken; arms factory, machinery demontieren; *(fig)* apartheid etc demontieren

dismast [dɪsˈmɑːst] VT entmasten

dismay [dɪsˈmeɪ] N Bestürzung *f*; **in ~** bestürzt; **to my ~ I discovered that ...** zu meiner Bestürzung stellte ich fest, dass ... VT bestürzen

dismember [dɪsˈmembə] VT *(lit)* animal, body zerstückeln; *(Med)* zergliedern; *(fig)* empire zersplittern

dismemberment [dɪsˈmembəmənt] N *(lit)* Zergliederung *f*; *(fig)* Zersplitterung *f*

dismiss [dɪsˈmɪs] VT **a** *(from job)* entlassen **b** *(= allow to go)* entlassen; assembly auflösen, auf-
heben; **~!** wegtreten!; **"class ~ed"** „ihr dürft gehen" **c** *(= brush aside)* point, objection, speculation, claims abtun; **to ~ sth from one's mind** etw verwerfen; **to ~ sb from one's mind** sich *(dat)* jdn aus dem Kopf schlagen; **to ~ sth out of hand** etw pauschal abtun **d** *(Jur)* accused entlassen; appeal abweisen; **to ~ a case** die Klage abweisen; **to ~ charges against sb** die Klage gegen jdn abweisen **e** *(Sport)* batsman, team ausschlagen; **he was ~ed for 52 runs** er wurde nach 52 Läufen ausgeschlagen

dismissal [dɪsˈmɪsəl] N **a** *(= firing: from job)* Entlassung *f* **b** *(= permission to leave)* Entlassung *f*; *(of assembly)* Auflösung *f* **c** *(= brushing aside: of point, objection, speculation, claim)* Abtun *nt* **d** *(Jur, of accused)* Entlassung *f*; *(of appeal)* Abweisung *f*, Einstellung *f*; *(of case, charges)* Abweisung *f* **e** *(Sport, of batsman, team)* Ausschlagen *nt*

dismissive [dɪsˈmɪsɪv] ADJ remark wegwerfend; gesture abweisend; **to be ~ of sb** jdn heruntermachen; **to be ~ of sth** etw abtun

dismissively [dɪsˈmɪsɪvlɪ] ADV abweisend; say abweisend, wegwerfend

dismount [dɪsˈmaʊnt] VI absteigen VT **a** rider abwerfen **b** *(Tech)* machine, gun abmontieren

disobedience [ˌdɪsəˈbiːdɪəns] N Ungehorsam *m* *(to gegenüber)*

disobedient [ˌdɪsəˈbiːdɪənt] ADJ ungehorsam

disobey [ˌdɪsəˈbeɪ] VT parents, teacher nicht gehorchen *(+dat)*; officer den Gehorsam verweigern *(+dat)*; rule, law übertreten

disoblige [ˌdɪsəˈblaɪdʒ] VT keinen Gefallen tun *(+dat)*

disobliging ADJ , **disobligingly** ADV [ˌdɪsəˈblaɪdʒɪŋ, -lɪ] ungefällig

disorder [dɪsˈɔːdə] N **a** Durcheinander *nt*; *(in room etc)* Unordnung *f*, Durcheinander *nt*; **in ~** durcheinander, in Unordnung; **to retreat in ~** *(Mil)* einen ungeordneten Rückzug antreten **b** *(Pol, = rioting)* Unruhen *pl* **c** *(Med)* Funktionsstörung *f*, **eating ~** Störung *f* des Essverhaltens; **kidney ~** Nierenleiden *nt*; **mental ~** Geistesstörung *f*; **sleep ~** Schlafstörung *f*; **stomach ~** Magenbeschwerden *pl* VT **a** *(= mess up)* durcheinander bringen; room in Unordnung bringen **b** *(Med)* angreifen

disordered [dɪsˈɔːdəd] ADJ **a** *(= untidy)* room unordentlich; hair, plans, papers wirr; *(fig, = disorderly)* life, world, existence ungeordnet **b** *(= disturbed)* mind, behaviour, imagination gestört; **mentally ~** geistesgestört

disorderliness [dɪsˈɔːdəlɪnɪs] N **a** *(= untidiness, of room, desk)* Unordentlichkeit *f*; *(of queue, process, row)* Ungeordnetheit *f* **b** *(= unruliness, of person)* Wildheit *f*; *(of crowd, event)* Undiszipliniertheit *f*; *(of conduct)* Ungehörigkeit *f*

disorderly [dɪsˈɔːdəlɪ] ADJ **a** *(= untidy)* room, desk unordentlich; queue, row ungeordnet **b** *(= unruly)* person wild; crowd, event undiszipliniert; conduct, behaviour ungehörig; **~ yobbos** *(inf)* randalierende Halbstarke; **to become ~** *(person, crowd)* außer Rand und Band geraten; **the rally became ~** bei der Kundgebung kam es zu Ausschreitungen → also **drunk** ADJ **c** *(= badly organised)* process ungeordnet

disorderly: disorderly behaviour, *(US)* **disorderly behavior** N *(Jur)* ungebührliches *or* ungehöriges Benehmen; **disorderly conduct** N = **disorderly behaviour**; **disorderly house** N *(Jur, = brothel)* öffentliches Haus; *(= gambling den)* Spielhölle *f*; **to keep a ~** ein öffentliches Haus unterhalten

disorganization [dɪsɔːgənaɪˈzeɪʃən] N Desorganisation *f*; *(= state of confusion)* Durcheinander *nt*

disorganize [dɪsˈɔːgənaɪz] VT durcheinander bringen

disorganized [dɪsˈɔːgənaɪzd] ADJ systemlos; life, person chaotisch; filing system etc durcheinander pred, ungeordnet; **he/the office is completely ~** bei ihm/im Büro geht alles drunter und drüber

disorient [dɪsˈɔːrɪənt], **disorientate** [dɪsˈɔːrɪənteɪt] VT (*lit, fig*) verwirren, desorientieren

disorientation [dɪsˌɔːrɪənˈteɪʃən] N Verwirrung f, Desorientierung f

disown [dɪsˈəʊn] VT verleugnen; *signature* nicht (als seine eigene) anerkennen; *suggestion* nicht wahrhaben wollen; **I'll ~ you if you go out in that hat** wenn du mit dem Hut ausgehst, tue ich so, als ob ich nicht zu dir gehöre

disparage [dɪsˈpærɪdʒ] VT herabsetzen; *work, achievements also* schmälern

disparagement [dɪsˈpærɪdʒmənt] N Herabsetzung f; (*of work, achievements also*) Schmälerung f

disparaging ADJ , **disparagingly** ADV [dɪsˈpærɪdʒɪŋ, -lɪ] abschätzig, geringschätzig

disparate [ˈdɪspərɪt] ADJ ungleich, disparat (*geh*)

disparity [dɪsˈpærɪtɪ] N Ungleichheit f, Disparität f (*geh*)

dispassion [dɪsˈpæʃən] N Objektivität f

dispassionate [dɪsˈpæʃənɪt] ADJ (= *impartial*) unvoreingenommen, objektiv; (= *unemotional*) unbewegt, leidenschaftslos

dispassionately [dɪsˈpæʃənɪtlɪ] ADV (= *impartially*) unvoreingenommen, objektiv; (= *unemotionally*) unbewegt, leidenschaftslos

dispatch [dɪsˈpætʃ] VT a (= *send*) *letter, goods etc* senden, schicken; *person, troops etc* (ent)senden, schicken b (= *deal with*) *job etc* (prompt) erledigen c (= *kill*) töten d (*inf*) *food* fertig werden mit (*inf*) N [dɪsˈpætʃ, ˈdɪspætʃ] a (*of letter, goods etc*) Senden nt, Schicken nt; (*of person, troops etc*) Entsendung f; **date of ~** Absendedatum nt b (= *message, report*) Depesche f; (*Press*) Bericht m; **to be mentioned in ~es** (*Mil*) in den Kriegsberichten erwähnt werden c (= *dealing with: of job etc*) prompte Erledigung d (= *promptness*) Promptheit f; **with ~** prompt

dispatch: dispatch box N (*Brit, Parl*) Depeschenkassette f; **dispatch documents** PL (*Comm*) Versandpapiere pl; **dispatch goods** PL Eilgut nt; **dispatch note** N (*in advance*) Versandanzeige f; (*with goods*) Begleitschein m; **dispatch rider** N (= *motorcyclist*) Melder(in) m(f), Meldefahrer(in) m(f)

dispel [dɪsˈpel] VT *clouds, fog* auflösen, vertreiben; *doubts, fears, gloom* zerstreuen; *sorrows* vertreiben; *myth* zerstören; *impression, notion* ein Ende machen (+*dat*)

dispensability [dɪsˌpensəˈbɪlɪtɪ] N Entbehrlichkeit f

dispensable [dɪsˈpensəbl] ADJ entbehrlich

dispensary [dɪsˈpensərɪ] N (*in hospital*) (Krankenhaus)apotheke f; (*in chemist's*) Apothekenabteilung f; (= *clinic*) Dispensarium nt

dispensation [ˌdɪspenˈseɪʃən] N a (= *handing out*) Verteilung f; (*of charity*) Austeilung f; **~ of justice** Rechtsprechung f b (= *exemption*) Dispensation f; (*Eccl*) Dispens f; **special ~** Sonderregelung f c (= *system, regime*) System nt; (*Rel*) Glaubenssystem nt; **~ of Providence** Fügung f der Vorsehung *or* des Schicksals

dispense [dɪsˈpens] VT a verteilen, austeilen (*to an* +*acc*); *advice* erteilen; (*machine*) *product, money* ausgeben; **to ~ justice** Recht sprechen b (*Pharm*) *medicine* abgeben; *prescription* zubereiten c (*form, = exempt*) dispensieren, befreien; **to ~ sb from doing sth** jdn davon befreien *or* dispensieren, etw zu tun (*Pharm*) Medizin abgeben, dispensieren (*form*)

▶ **dispense with** VI +*prep obj* verzichten auf (+*acc*); **I could/couldn't dispense with that** ich könnte darauf gut/nicht verzichten, ich könnte ohne das auskommen/nicht auskommen; **that can be dispensed with** das ist entbehrlich

dispenser [dɪsˈpensəʳ] N a (*Pharm*) Apotheker(in) m(f) b (= *container*) Spender m; (= *slot machine*) Automat m

dispensing chemist's [dɪˌspensɪŋˈkemɪsts] N Apotheke f

dispersal [dɪsˈpɜːsəl] N (= *scattering*) Verstreuen nt; (*Bot: of seed*) Verteilung f; (= *dispelling*) (*of crowd, mist*) Zerstreuung f, Auflösung f; (*of oil slick*) Auflösung f; (*Opt: of light*) Streuung f; (*Chem: of particles*) Dispersion f; (*fig*) (*of knowledge etc*) Verbreitung f; (*of efforts*) Verzettelung f, Zersplitterung f

dispersant [dɪsˈpɜːsənt] N Lösungsmittel nt

disperse [dɪsˈpɜːs] VT (= *scatter widely*) verstreuen; (*Bot*) *seed* verteilen; (= *dispel*) *crowd, mist* zerstreuen, auflösen; *oil slick* auflösen; (*Opt*) *light* streuen; (*Chem*) *particles* dispergieren; (*fig*) *knowledge etc* verbreiten VI sich zerstreuen *or* auflösen; (*oil slick*) sich auflösen

dispersion [dɪsˈpɜːʃən] N = dispersal

dispirit [dɪsˈpɪrɪt] VT entmutigen

dispirited ADJ , **dispiritedly** ADV [dɪsˈpɪrɪtɪd, -lɪ] entmutigt

dispiriting ADJ , **dispiritingly** ADV [dɪsˈpɪrɪtɪŋ, -lɪ] entmutigend

displace [dɪsˈpleɪs] VT a (= *move*) verschieben; *people* vertreiben b (= *replace*) ablösen, ersetzen c (*Naut, Phys*) *water, air etc* verdrängen d (*in office*) verdrängen, ausbooten (*inf*)

displaced: displaced emotion N verlagertes Gefühl; **displaced person** N Vertriebene(r) mf

displacement [dɪsˈpleɪsmənt] N a (= *act of moving*) Verschiebung f; (*of people*) Vertreibung f; (*Naut, Phys: of air, water*) Verdrängung f; (= *volume displaced, Phys*) verdrängte Menge; (*Naut*) Verdrängung f b (= *replacement*) Ablösung f, Ersatz m c (= *distance sth is moved*) Verschiebung f; (*Geol, of rocks*) Dislokation f

displacement: displacement activity N (*Psych*) Ersatzbefriedigung f; **displacement ton** N (*Naut*) Verdrängungstonne f

display [dɪsˈpleɪ] VT a (= *show*) *object* zeigen; *interest, courage* zeigen, beweisen; *ignorance* an den Tag legen, beweisen; (*ostentatiously*) *new clothes etc* vorführen; *feelings* zur Schau stellen; *power* demonstrieren; *exam results, notice* aushängen b (*Comm*) *goods* ausstellen c (*Typ, Press*) hervorheben VI Imponiergehabe zeigen; (*birds*) balzen N a (*of object*) Zeigen nt; (*of interest, courage*) Zeigen nt, Beweis m; (*of ignorance*) Beweis m; (*ostentatious, of new clothes etc*) Vorführung f; (*of feelings*) Zurschaustellung f; (*of power*) Demonstration f; **to make a great ~ of sth** etw groß zur Schau stellen; **to make a great ~ of doing sth** etw betont auffällig tun; **to be/go on ~** ausgestellt sein/werden; **the painting goes on public ~ today** das Gemälde wird heute öffentlich ausgestellt; **these are only for ~** die sind nur zur Ansicht; **I hope we don't have another ~ (of temper)** ich hoffe, wir kriegen nicht noch einmal denselben Tanz *or* dieselbe Schau (*inf*); **she was not given to public ~s of emotion** sie zeigte ihre Gefühle nicht gerne in der Öffentlichkeit b (= *exhibition of paintings etc*) Ausstellung f; (= *dancing display etc*) Vorführung f; (= *military, air display*) Schau f; **firework ~** (öffentliches) Feuerwerk c (*Comm*) Auslage f, Display nt d (*Zool*) Imponiergehabe nt; (*of bird*) Balz f e (= *visual display*) Anzeige f

display: display advertisement N Displayanzeige f; **display advertising** N Displaywerbung f; **display cabinet** N Schaukasten m; **display case** N Vitrine f; **display pack** N Displaypackung f; **display unit** N (*Comput*) (Daten)sichtgerät nt, Bildschirmgerät nt; **display window** N Schaufenster nt

displease [dɪsˈpliːz] VT missfallen (+*dat*), nicht gefallen (+*dat*); (= *annoy*) verstimmen, verärgern; **to be ~d with sth** verärgert über etw (*acc*) sein; **he was rather ~d to hear that ...** er hörte nur sehr ungern, dass ...; **I was not ~d with my efforts** ich war mit meinen Bemühungen nicht unzufrieden

displeasing [dɪsˈpliːzɪŋ] ADJ unangenehm; **to be ~ to sb** jdm missfallen *or* nicht gefallen; (= *annoy*) jdn verstimmen *or* verärgern; **the idea**

was not ~ to her der Gedanke war ihr gar nicht so unangenehm

displeasure [dɪsˈpleʒəʳ] N Missfallen nt (*at* über +*acc*)

disport [dɪsˈpɔːt] VR (*old*) sich ergötzen (*old*)

disposability [dɪˌspəʊzəˈbɪlɪtɪ] N (freie) Verfügbarkeit f

disposable [dɪsˈpəʊzəbl] ADJ a (= *throwaway*) Wegwerf-; **~ razor** Wegwerfrasierer m; **~ nappy** (*Brit*) Wegwerfwindel f; **~ syringe/needle** Einwegspritze f/-nadel f; **all acupuncture needles are now ~** alle Akupunkturnadeln werden heute nach Gebrauch weggeworfen; **~ contact lenses** Kontaktlinsen pl zum Wegwerfen b (*fig, = unimportant*) *person, music, art* unbedeutend c (= *available*) verfügbar **disposables** PL (= *containers*) Einwegbehälter pl; (= *nappies*) Wegwerfwindeln pl

disposable assets PL (*Fin*) disponibles (*spec*) *or* frei verfügbares Vermögen

disposable income N verfügbares Einkommen

disposal [dɪsˈpəʊzəl] N a Loswerden nt; (*by selling also*) Veräußerung f; (*of unwanted person or goods, of litter, body*) Beseitigung f; (*of question, matter*) Erledigung f, Regelung f b (= *control: over resources, funds, personnel*) Verfügungsgewalt f; **the means at sb's ~** die jdm zur Verfügung stehenden Mittel; **to put sth at sb's ~** jdm etw zur Verfügung stellen; **to be at sb's ~** jdm zur Verfügung stehen; **we had the entire staff/building at our ~** die ganze Belegschaft/das ganze Gebäude stand uns zur Verfügung c (*form: = arrangement, of ornaments, furniture*) Anordnung f, Arrangement nt; (*Mil, of troops*) Aufstellung f

dispose [dɪsˈpəʊz] VT a (*form, = arrange*) *shrubs, ornaments* anordnen; *people, troops* aufstellen; *papers* ordnen b (= *make willing*) **to ~ sb to do sth** jdn geneigt machen, etw zu tun VI → **propose VI b**

▶ **dispose of** VI +*prep obj* a (= *get rid of*) *furniture* loswerden; (*by selling*) veräußern, loswerden; *unwanted person, goods* beseitigen, loswerden; *litter, body* beseitigen; *opponent, difficulties* aus dem Weg schaffen; *question, matter* erledigen, regeln b (= *have at disposal*) *fortune, time* verfügen über (+*acc*) c (= *kill*) eliminieren

disposed [dɪsˈpəʊzd] ADJ (*form*) a **to be ~ to do sth** (= *prepared*) bereit sein, etw zu tun; (= *inclined*) etw tun wollen; **to be well** *or* **favourably** (*Brit*) *or* **favorably** (*US*) **~ to(wards) sb** jdm wohlgesinnt sein; **to be well** *or* **favourably** (*Brit*) *or* **favorably** (*US*) **~ to(wards) sth** einer Sache (*dat*) wohlwollend gegenüberstehen → *also* **ill-disposed** b (*form, = arranged*) angeordnet; **the choir was ~ in the most original way** der Chor war sehr originell aufgestellt

disposition [ˌdɪspəˈzɪʃən] N a (*form: = arrangement*) (*of buildings, ornaments*) Anordnung f; (*of forces*) Aufstellung f; (*Jur: of money, property*) Verfügung f b (= *temperament*) Veranlagung f; **her cheerful/friendly ~** ihre fröhliche/freundliche Art

dispossess [ˌdɪspəˈzes] VT enteignen

dispossession [ˌdɪspəˈzeʃən] N Enteignung f

disproportion [ˌdɪsprəˈpɔːʃən] N Missverhältnis nt

disproportionate [ˌdɪsprəˈpɔːʃnɪt] ADJ **to be ~ (to sth)** in keinem Verhältnis (zu etw) stehen; **a ~ amount of money** ein unverhältnismäßig hoher Geldbetrag; **a ~ amount of time** eine unverhältnismäßig lange Zeit

disproportionately [ˌdɪsprəˈpɔːʃnɪtlɪ] ADV (+*adj*) unverhältnismäßig; *affect* unverhältnismäßig stark; *suffer* unverhältnismäßig viel; **~ large numbers of ...** unverhältnismäßig viele ...; **immigrants were ~ represented** Einwanderer stellten einen unverhältnismäßig großen Anteil dar; **the new tax will fall ~ on the poor** die neue Steuer wird die Armen unverhältnismäßig stark belasten

disprovable [dɪsˈpruːvəbl] ADJ widerlegbar

disprove [dɪsˈpruːv] ○ 26.3 VT widerlegen

disputable [dɪˈspjuːtəbl] ADJ sehr zweifelhaft, disputabel

disputant [dɪˈspjuːtənt] N Disputant(in) m(f)

disputation [ˌdɪspjuːˈteɪʃən] N Disput m, Kontroverse f

disputatious [ˌdɪspjuːˈteɪʃəs] ADJ streitbar, streitlustig

dispute [dɪˈspjuːt] **VT a** (= argue against) statement bestreiten, anfechten; claim to sth, will anfechten; **I would ~ that** das möchte ich bestreiten **b** (= debate) question, subject sich streiten über (+acc); **the issue was hotly ~d** das Thema wurde hitzig diskutiert **c** (= contest) championship, possession kämpfen um; territory beanspruchen **VI** (= argue) streiten **N** [dɪˈspjuːt, ˈdɪspjuːt] **a** no pl (= arguing, controversy) Disput m, Kontroverse f; **to be beyond ~** außer Frage stehen; **there is some ~ about which horse won** es ist umstritten, welches Pferd gewonnen hat; **the two countries are in ~ over boundaries** zwischen den beiden Ländern gibt es Grenzstreitigkeiten; **a territory in** or **under ~** ein umstrittenes Gebiet; **to be open to ~** anfechtbar or umstritten sein; **the case is in** or **under ~** (Jur) der Fall wird verhandelt **b** (= quarrel, argument) Streit m **c** (Ind) Auseinandersetzung f; **the union is in ~ with the management** zwischen Gewerkschaft und Betriebsleitung bestehen Unstimmigkeiten; **wages ~** Tarifauseinandersetzungen pl

disqualification [dɪsˌkwɒlɪfɪˈkeɪʃən] N **a** Ausschluss m; (Sport) Disqualifikation f; **~ (from driving)** Führerscheinentzug m **b** (= disqualifying factor) Grund m zur Disqualifikation

disqualify [dɪsˈkwɒlɪfaɪ] VT **a** (= make ineligible) untauglich or ungeeignet machen (from für); (Sport etc) disqualifizieren, ausschließen; **to ~ sb from driving** jdm den Führerschein entziehen; **that disqualifies you from criticizing him** das nimmt Ihnen jedes Recht, ihn zu kritisieren

disquiet [dɪsˈkwaɪət] VT beunruhigen **N** (also **disquietude**) Unruhe f

disquisition [ˌdɪskwɪˈzɪʃən] N (lange, ausführliche) Abhandlung or (speech) Rede (on über +acc)

disregard [ˌdɪsrɪˈɡɑːd] **VT** ignorieren; remark, feelings also nicht beachten; danger, advice, authority also missachten **N** Nichtbeachtung f (for gen), Missachtung f (for gen); (for danger) Missachtung f; (for money) Geringschätzung f (for gen); **to show complete ~ for sth** etw völlig außer Acht lassen

disrelish [dɪsˈrelɪʃ] (form) **N** Abneigung f, Widerwillen m (for gegen) **VT** einen Widerwillen haben gegen

disrepair [ˌdɪsrɪˈpɛə] N Baufälligkeit f; **in a state of ~** baufällig; **to fall into ~** verfallen

disreputable [dɪsˈrepjʊtəbl] ADJ person, hotel, bar verrufen; clothes schäbig; conduct unehrenhaft; area anrüchig, verrufen; **~ woman** leichtes Mädchen

disreputably [dɪsˈrepjʊtəblɪ] ADV behave (= dishonourably) übel, gemein; (= not respectably) anstößig

disrepute [ˌdɪsrɪˈpjuːt] N schlechter Ruf; **to bring sth into ~** etw in Verruf bringen; **to fall into ~** in Verruf kommen or geraten

disrespect [ˌdɪsrɪˈspekt] N Respektlosigkeit f (for gegenüber); **to show ~ for sth** keinen Respekt vor etw (dat) haben; **I don't mean any ~, but ...** ich will nicht respektlos sein, aber ...; **no ~ to ...** bei allem Respekt vor (+dat) ...

disrespectful [ˌdɪsrɪˈspektfʊl] ADJ respektlos (to gegenüber)

disrespectfully [ˌdɪsrɪˈspektfəlɪ] ADV respektlos; **I don't mean that ~** das ist nicht respektlos gemeint

disrobe [dɪsˈrəʊb] **VI** (judge) seine Gewänder ablegen; (form, hum, = undress) sich entkleiden, sich entblättern (hum inf) **VT** (form, hum, = undress) entkleiden

disrupt [dɪsˈrʌpt] VT stören; lesson, meeting, conversation, train service also unterbrechen; **their lives were ~ed (by it)** das brachte ihr Leben durcheinander, das stellte ihr Leben auf den Kopf

disruption [dɪsˈrʌpʃən] N Störung f; (of lesson, meeting, conversation, train service also) Unterbrechung f

disruptive [dɪsˈrʌptɪv] ADJ behaviour, influence störend; effect zerstörerisch; **~ pupils** Schüler, die den Schulbetrieb stören; **to be a ~ influence** einen störenden Einfluss ausüben; **to be ~ to sb/sth** sich störend auf jdn/etw auswirken; **~ action** (Ind) Störaktionen pl

dissatisfaction [ˈdɪsˌsætɪsˈfækʃən] N Unzufriedenheit f

dissatisfied [dɪsˈsætɪsfaɪd] ADJ unzufrieden (with mit)

dissect [dɪˈsekt] VT plant präparieren; animal sezieren, präparieren; (fig) report, theory sezieren, zergliedern

dissection [dɪˈsekʃən] N **a** (= act) (of plant) Präparation f; (of animal) Sektion f; (fig, of report, theory) Zergliederung f **b** (= plant or animal dissected) Präparat nt

dissemble [dɪˈsembl] **VT** (= cover up) verbergen; (= feign) vortäuschen, heucheln **VI** (liter) sich verstellen; (= feign illness) simulieren

dissembler [dɪˈsemblə] N Heuchler(in) m(f)

disseminate [dɪˈsemɪneɪt] VT verbreiten

dissemination [dɪˌsemɪˈneɪʃən] N Verbreitung f

dissension [dɪˈsenʃən] N Meinungsverschiedenheit f, Differenz f; **to cause ~** zu Meinungsverschiedenheiten or Differenzen führen; (person) Meinungsverschiedenheiten or Differenzen verursachen

dissent [dɪˈsent] **VI a** (= oppose) anderer Meinung sein, differieren (geh); **I strongly ~ from what he says** ich muss dem, was er sagt, entschieden widersprechen **b** (Eccl) sich weigern, die Staatskirche anzuerkennen **N a** (= opposition) Dissens m; (fig) Nichtübereinstimmung f; **to voice/express one's ~ (with sth)** erklären, dass man (mit etw) nicht übereinstimmt; **there was remarkably little ~** es gab bemerkenswert wenig Widerspruch **b** (Eccl) Weigerung f die (englische) Staatskirche anzuerkennen

dissenter [dɪˈsentə] N Abweichler(in) m(f); (Eccl also) Dissenter m

dissentient [dɪˈsenʃɪənt] ADJ (form) = **dissenting**

dissenting [dɪˈsentɪŋ] ADJ attr opinion abweichend; **there was not a single ~ voice** es wurde keine Gegenstimme laut

dissert [dɪˈsɜːt], **dissertate** [ˈdɪsəteɪt] VI (form) (in writing) eine Abhandlung schreiben (on über +acc); (in speech) einen Vortrag halten (on über +acc)

dissertation [ˌdɪsəˈteɪʃən] N wissenschaftliche Arbeit; (for PhD) Dissertation f; (fig) Vortrag m

disservice [dɪsˈsɜːvɪs] N **to do oneself/sb a ~** sich/jdm einen schlechten Dienst erweisen

dissidence [ˈdɪsɪdəns] N Opposition f; (Pol) Dissidententum nt

dissident [ˈdɪsɪdənt] **N** Dissident(in) m(f), Regimekritiker(in) m(f) **ADJ** dissident, regimekritisch

dissimilar [dɪˈsɪmɪlə] ADJ unterschiedlich, verschieden (to von); two things verschieden; **not ~ (to sb/sth)** (jdm/einer Sache) nicht ungleich or (in appearance) nicht unähnlich

dissimilarity [ˌdɪsɪmɪˈlærɪtɪ] N Unterschiedlichkeit f, Verschiedenheit f; (in appearance also) Unähnlichkeit f

dissimulate [dɪˈsɪmjʊleɪt] **VT** verbergen **VI** sich verstellen

dissimulation [dɪˌsɪmjʊˈleɪʃən] N Verstellung f, Heuchelei f

dissipate [ˈdɪsɪpeɪt] **VT a** (= dispel) fog auflösen; heat ableiten; doubts, fears zerstreuen; tension lösen **b** energy, efforts verschwenden, vergeuden; fortune verschwenden **VI** (clouds, fog) sich auflösen; (crowd, doubts, fear also) sich zerstreuen; (tension) sich lösen

dissipated [ˈdɪsɪpeɪtɪd] ADJ person, behaviour, society zügellos; life, activity ausschweifend; face verlebt

dissipation [ˌdɪsɪˈpeɪʃən] N **a** (= debauchery) Ausschweifung f; **a life of ~** ein ausschweifendes Leben **b** (= dispersal: of doubts, fears) Zerstreuung f **c** (= wasting, of energy, efforts) Verschwendung f, Vergeudung f; (of fortune) Verschwendung f

dissociate [dɪˈsəʊʃɪeɪt] ○ 26.2 VT trennen, dissoziieren (geh, Chem) (from von); **to ~ oneself from sb/sth** sich von jdm/etw distanzieren; **two aspects which have become largely ~d** zwei Aspekte, die sich weitgehend voneinander gelöst haben

dissociation [dɪˌsəʊsɪˈeɪʃən] N Trennung f, Dissoziation f (geh, Chem, Psych)

dissoluble [dɪˈsɒljʊbl] ADJ (Chem) löslich, dissolubel (spec)

dissolute [ˈdɪsəluːt] ADJ person zügellos; way of life ausschweifend, zügellos; appearance verlebt

dissoluteness [ˈdɪsəluːtnɪs] N (of person, way of life) Zügellosigkeit f; (of appearance) Verlebtheit f

dissolution [ˌdɪsəˈluːʃən] N **a** (Chem, Jur, Pol) Auflösung f **b** (of relationship) Auflösung f; (of faith) Abbröckeln nt

dissolve [dɪˈzɒlv] **VT a** (lit, Jur, Pol, fig) auflösen; marriage scheiden, auflösen **b** (Film) überblenden (into in or auf +acc) **VI a** (lit, Jur, Pol) sich (auf)lösen; (fig) sich in nichts auflösen; **it ~s in water** es ist wasserlöslich, es löst sich in Wasser; **to ~ into tears** in Tränen zerfließen; **to ~ into laughter** in Lachen ausbrechen **b** (Film) überblenden (into in or auf +acc) **N** (Film) Überblendung f

dissolvent [dɪˈzɒlvənt] **ADJ** lösend **N** Lösungsmittel nt

dissonance [ˈdɪsənəns] N (Mus, fig) Dissonanz f

dissonant [ˈdɪsənənt] ADJ (Mus) dissonant; (fig) opinions, temperaments unvereinbar; colours disharmonisch

dissuade [dɪˈsweɪd] VT **to ~ sb from sth** jdn von etw abbringen, jdm etw ausreden; **to ~ sb from doing sth** jdn davon abbringen or jdm ausreden, etw zu tun; **he wouldn't be ~d** ließ sich nicht davon abbringen, er ließ sich nicht ausreden

dissuasion [dɪˈsweɪʒən] N Abraten nt

dissuasive [dɪˈsweɪsɪv] ADJ abratend; **he was very ~** er riet sehr davon ab

dissuasiveness [dɪˈsweɪsɪvnɪs] N (of person) Abraten nt; **the ~ of his tone** sein abratender Ton; **the ~ of his arguments** seine abratenden Argumente

distaff [ˈdɪstɑːf] N **a** (in spinning) Spinnrocken m, Kunkel f **b** on the **~ side** mütterlicherseits

distance [ˈdɪstəns] **N a** (in space) Entfernung f; (= gap, interval) Abstand m, Distanz f (geh); (= distance covered) Strecke f, Weg m; **we now measure ~ in feet** wir geben Entfernungen jetzt in Fuß an; **at a ~ of two feet** in zwei Fuß Entfernung; **stopping ~** Bremsweg m; **the ~ between the eyes/railway lines** der Abstand zwischen den Augen/Eisenbahnschienen; **at an equal ~ from the middle** gleich weit von der Mitte entfernt; **the ~ between London and Glasgow is ...** die Entfernung zwischen London und Glasgow beträgt ...; **what's the ~ between London and Glasgow?** wie weit ist es von London nach Glasgow?; **I don't know the exact ~** ich weiß nicht genau, wie weit es ist; **we covered the ~ between London and Glasgow in five hours** wir haben für die Strecke London-Glasgow fünf Stunden gebraucht; **he went with me (for) part of the ~** er ging einen Teil der Strecke or des Weges mit mir; **in the**

(far) ~ (ganz) in der Ferne, (ganz) weit weg; **to gaze into the** ~ in die Ferne starren; **he admired her at** *or* **from a** ~ (*fig*) er bewunderte sie aus der Ferne; **it's within walking** ~ es ist zu Fuß erreichbar; **it's no** ~ es ist überhaupt nicht weit, es ist nur ein Katzensprung (*inf*); **a short** ~ **away** ganz in der Nähe; **it's quite a** ~ **(away)** es ist ziemlich weit (entfernt *or* weg); **we drove 600 miles – that's quite a** ~ wir sind 600 Meilen gefahren – das ist eine ganz schöne Strecke; **the race is over a** ~ **of 3 miles** das Rennen geht über eine Distanz von 3 Meilen; **to go the** ~ durchhalten, es durchstehen; **the fight went the** ~ der Kampf ging über alle Runden; **to keep one's** ~ **(from sb/sth)** Abstand (von jdm/etw) halten **b** (*in time*) **from** *or* **at a** ~ **of 400 years** aus einem Abstand von 400 Jahren; **at this** ~ **in time** nach einem so langen Zeitraum **c** (*fig, in social rank*) Unterschied *m*; **to keep sb at a** ~ jdn auf Distanz halten; **to keep one's** ~ **(from sb)** (*= be aloof*) auf Distanz (zu jdm) bleiben, Abstand *or* Distanz (zu jdm) wahren (*geh*) **VT a** (*Sport etc*) **= outdistance** **b** **to** ~ **oneself/sb from sb/sth** sich/jdn von jdm/etw distanzieren; **television may** ~ **the public from reality** das Fernsehen kann die Öffentlichkeit der Wirklichkeit entfremden

distanced ['dɪstənst] ADJ (*lit, fig*) distanziert

distance: distance event N Langstreckenlauf *m*; **distance runner** N Langstreckenläufer(in) *m(f)*

distant ['dɪstənt] ADJ **a** (*in space*) *horizon, land, region, mountains* fern; *galaxies* weit entfernt; *sound* entfernt; *relative, resemblance* entfernt; **with views of** ~ **mountains** mit Aussicht auf die Berge in der Ferne; **we had a** ~ **view of the church** wir sahen die Kirche in der Ferne; **he is somewhat** ~ **from the day-to-day operations** er hat dem täglichen Betrieb ziemlich wenig zu tun; **I felt so** ~ **from her** ich fühlte mich so weit weg von ihr; **to come** *or* **finish a** ~ **second/third (to sb/sth)** (*in race, competition*) weit abgeschlagen auf dem zweiten/dritten Platz (hinter jdm/etw) landen; **profits came a** ~ **second to preserving jobs** Gewinne lagen an zweiter Stelle, weit hinter der Arbeitsplatzerhaltung **b** (*in time, age*) *past, future* fern; *memory* entfernt, schwach; *days* weit zurückliegend; **it's a** ~ **prospect** (*fig*) es liegt noch in weiter Ferne; **in the not too** *or* **very** ~ **future** in nicht allzu ferner Zukunft **c** (*= reserved*) *person, voice* distanziert; **they are emotionally** ~ **from their families** sie haben ein emotional distanziertes Verhältnis zu ihren Familien **d** (*= distracted*) *person, look, mind* abwesend; **there was a** ~ **look in her eyes** sie hatte einen abwesenden Blick **ADV** (*in time, space*) entfernt; **a mile** ~ **from our house** eine Meile von unserem Haus entfernt; **dawn was still an hour** ~ es war noch eine Stunde bis zum Morgengrauen

distantly ['dɪstəntlɪ] ADV **a** ~ **related (to sb)** entfernt *or* weitläufig (mit jdm) verwandt **b** (*= far away*) entfernt, weit weg; *see in* **the Ferne**; (*fig*) *remember* entfernt; **a buzzer sounded** ~ weit weg war ein Summer zu hören; **to be** ~ **aware of sth** sich (*dat*) einer Sache (*gen*) vage bewusst sein **c** (*= unemotionally*) distanziert **d** (*= distractedly*) abwesend

distaste [dɪs'teɪst] N Widerwille *m* (*for* gegen)

distasteful [dɪs'teɪstfʊl] ADJ *task* unangenehm; *photo, magazine* geschmacklos; **to be** ~ **to sb** jdm zuwider *or* unangenehm sein; **he found the idea** ~ der Gedanke war ihm zuwider

distastefully [dɪs'teɪstfʊlɪ] ADV angewidert

distemper¹ [dɪs'tempə'] N (*= paint*) Temperafarbe *f* **VT** mit Temperafarbe streichen

distemper² N **a** (*Vet*) Staupe *f* **b** (*old, = ill temper*) Verstimmung *f*

distend [dɪs'tend] **VT** *balloon* (auf)blasen; *sails, stomach* (auf)blähen **VI** sich blähen

distension [dɪs'tenʃən] N Blähen *nt*; (*of stomach*) (Auf)blähung *f*

---

distil, (*US*) **distill** [dɪs'tɪl] **VT a** (*Chem*) destillieren; *whisky etc* brennen, destillieren; (*fig*) herausarbeiten, (heraus)destillieren **b** (*= drip slowly*) tropfenweise ausscheiden *or* absondern **VI a** (*Chem*) sich herausdestillieren; (*whisky*) gebrannt werden; (*fig*) sich herauskristallisieren **b** (*= drip slowly*) langsam heraustropfen, herauströpfeln

distillate ['dɪstɪlɪt] N (*Chem, Ind*) Destillat *nt*

distillation [,dɪstɪ'leɪʃən] N **a** (*Chem etc, = act*) Destillation *f*; (*of whisky etc also*) Brennen *nt*; (*= product*) Destillat *nt* **b** (*fig, = act*) Verarbeitung *f*; (*= product*) Destillat *nt*

distilled [dɪs'tɪld] ADJ destilliert; *spirits also* gebrannt; *essence* (heraus)destilliert; (*fig*) *wisdom* herausdestilliert

distiller [dɪs'tɪlə'] N Destillateur *m*, (Branntwein)brenner *m*

distillery [dɪs'tɪlərɪ] N Destillerie *f*, (Branntwein)brennerei *f*

distinct [dɪs'tɪŋkt] ADJ **a** (*= different*) *parts, groups, types, areas, phases* verschieden, unterschiedlich; ~ **from** anders als; **to be** ~ **from sth** sich von etw unterscheiden; **disciplines** ~ **from one another** voneinander getrennte Disziplinen; **to keep A** ~ **from B** A und B auseinander halten *or* voneinander trennen; **as** ~ **from** im Unterschied zu; **what he thinks, as** ~ **from what he says** was er denkt, im Unterschied dazu, was er sagt **b** (*= definite*) *sign, change, memory, lack, improvement* deutlich; *flavour* bestimmt; *image, sound* klar, deutlich; **to have** ~ **memories of sb/sth** sich deutlich an jdn/etw erinnern; **to get the** ~ **idea** *or* **impression that ...** den deutlichen Eindruck bekommen, dass ...; **to have the** ~ **feeling that ...** das bestimmte Gefühl haben, dass ...; **to have a** ~ **advantage (over sb)** (jdm gegenüber) klar *or* deutlich im Vorteil sein; **there is a** ~ **possibility that ...** es besteht eindeutig die Möglichkeit, dass ...; **a** ~ **personality** eine ausgeprägte Persönlichkeit

distinction [dɪs'tɪŋkʃən] N **a** (*= difference*) Unterschied *m*; (*= act of distinguishing*) Unterscheidung *f*; **to make** *or* **draw a** ~ **(between two things)** (zwischen zwei Dingen) unterscheiden *or* einen Unterschied machen **b** *no pl* (*= preeminence*) (hoher) Rang *m*, Distinktion *f* (*dated geh*); (*= refinement*) Vornehmheit *f*; **she has an air of** ~ **about her** sie hat etwas Vornehmes *or* Distinguiertes (*geh*) (an sich); **a pianist of** ~ ein Pianist von Rang; **he has the** ~ **of being the oldest living person** er zeichnet sich dadurch aus, dass er der älteste Mensch ist **c** (*Sch, Univ, = grade*) Auszeichnung *f*; **he got a** ~ **in French** er hat das Französischexamen mit Auszeichnung bestanden; **he was awarded several academic** ~**s** ihm sind mehrere akademische Auszeichnungen verliehen worden

distinctive [dɪs'tɪŋktɪv] ADJ *style, flavour, smell, gesture, walk etc* unverwechselbar, unverkennbar; *feature, pattern* unverkennbar; *sound* typisch, unverkennbar; *voice, dress* (*= characteristic*) charakteristisch; (*= unmistakable*) unverwechselbar; (*= striking*) *colour, plumage* auffällig; ~ **features** (*of person*) besondere Kennzeichen; **she had a very** ~ **voice** sie hatte eine ganz unverwechselbare *or* besondere Stimme; **with his** ~ **irony** mit der ihm eigenen *or* für ihn charakteristischen Ironie; **there's something** ~ **about them** an ihnen ist etwas Besonderes; ~ **to sb/sth** charakteristisch für jdn/etw

distinctively [dɪs'tɪŋktɪvlɪ] ADV unverwechselbar; ~ **dressed** auffällig gekleidet; **music which is** ~ **American** Musik mit ausgeprägt amerikanischen Zügen; **there is nothing** ~ **Christian about this philosophy** an dieser Philosophie ist nichts ausgesprochen Christliches

distinctiveness [dɪs'tɪŋktɪvnɪs] N (*= unmistakableness*) Unverwechselbarkeit *f*; (*= characteristic nature*) charakteristische Art; (*= striking nature*) Auffälligkeit *f*

distinctly [dɪs'tɪŋktlɪ] ADV **a** (*= clearly*) *remember, hear, see, speak* deutlich **b** (*= decidedly*) dif-

---

ferent, better entschieden, eindeutig; *American, English, modern* ausgeprägt; *odd, uncomfortable, uneasy, nervous* ausgesprochen; *limited, cool, unhappy* eindeutig; *possible* durchaus; **he is** ~ **lacking in imagination** ihm mangelt es eindeutig an Fantasie

distinctness [dɪs'tɪŋktnɪs] N **a** (*= difference*) Verschiedenheit *f*, Unterschiedlichkeit *f*; (*= separateness*) Getrenntheit *f* **b** (*= clarity*) Deutlichkeit *f*

distinguish [dɪs'tɪŋgwɪʃ] **VT a** (*= make different*) unterscheiden; **only the length of their hair** ~**es the twins** die Zwillinge unterscheiden sich nur durch ihre Haarlänge **b** (*= tell apart*) unterscheiden, auseinander halten; **he can't** ~ **green from** *or* **and red** er kann Rot nicht von Grün unterscheiden, er kann Rot und Grün nicht auseinander halten **c** (*= make out*) *landmark, shape* erkennen, ausmachen; (*amongst others*) *voice* heraushören **VI to** ~ **between** unterscheiden zwischen (+*dat*), einen Unterschied machen zwischen (+*dat*) **VR** sich auszeichnen, sich hervortun

distinguishable [dɪs'tɪŋgwɪʃəbl] ADJ **a** (*= easily told apart*) unterscheidbar; **to be (barely)** ~ **from sth** (kaum) von etw zu unterscheiden sein; **to be** ~ **by sth** an etw (*dat*) erkennbar sein; **it is easily** *or* **readily** ~ es ist leicht zu unterscheiden; (*= recognizable*) es ist leicht *or* gut zu erkennen; **the two types are easily/no longer** ~ die beiden Arten sind leicht/nicht mehr auseinander zu halten *or* voneinander zu unterscheiden **b** (*= discernible*) *shape, voice, words, figure* erkennbar, zu erkennen

distinguished [dɪs'tɪŋgwɪʃt] ADJ **a** (*= eminent*) *guest, professor* angesehen; *scholar, writer* namhaft, angesehen; *career* glänzend; *history* ruhmreich; ~ **service** verdienstvolle Laufbahn, (*Mil*) Dienst *m* mit Auszeichnung; **the** ~ **company of ...** die hervorragende Gesellschaft (+*gen*) ...; **to be** ~ **for sth** sich durch etw auszeichnen **b** (*= refined*) *person, appearance* distinguiert (*geh*); **to look** ~ distinguiert (*geh*) *or* vornehm aussehen

distinguishing [dɪs'tɪŋgwɪʃɪŋ] ADJ kennzeichnend, charakteristisch; **he has no** ~ **features** er hat keine besonderen Kennzeichen; **the** ~ **feature of his work is ...** was seine Arbeit auszeichnet *or* kennzeichnet, ist ...

distort [dɪs'tɔːt] **VT** verzerren (*also Phys*); *truth, words* verdrehen; *reality, history* verzerrt darstellen; *facts* verzerrt darstellen, verdrehen; *judgement* trüben, beeinträchtigen **VI** verzerrt werden

distorted [dɪs'tɔːtɪd] ADJ **a** (*= unclear, inaccurate*) *sound, view, picture, report* verzerrt; **she has an entirely** ~ **impression of events** sie sieht die Ereignisse völlig verzerrt; **she has a** ~ **image of what is normal** sie hat ein verzerrtes Bild davon, was normal ist **b** (*= deformed, twisted*) *joints, bones, plants* verformt; *mouth, face* entstellt

distortion [dɪs'tɔːʃən] N Verzerrung *f* (*also Phys*); (*of truth, words*) Verdrehung *f*; (*of reality, history*) verzerrte Darstellung; (*of facts*) verzerrte Darstellung, Verdrehung *f*; (*of judgement*) Trübung *f*, Beeinträchtigung *f*

distract [dɪs'trækt] **VT a** (*= divert attention of*) ablenken; **to** ~ **sb's attention** jdn ablenken **b** (*old, = amuse*) zerstreuen, die Zeit vertreiben (+*dat*)

distracted [dɪs'træktɪd] ADJ (*= preoccupied*) abwesend, zerstreut; (*= worried, anxious*) besorgt, beunruhigt; (*= grief-stricken, distraught*) außer sich (*with* vor +*dat*); **she screamed like one** ~ sie schrie wie eine Irre

distractedly [dɪs'træktɪdlɪ] ADV abwesend, zerstreut; (*= in distress*) verzweifelt

distraction [dɪs'trækʃən] N **a** *no pl* (*= lack of attention*) Unaufmerksamkeit *f* **b** (*= interruption: from work etc*) Ablenkung *f* **c** (*= entertainment*) Zerstreuung *f* **d** (*= anxiety*) Ruhelosigkeit *f*, Unruhe *f*; (*= distraught state*) Verstörung *f*; **to love sb to** ~ jdn wahnsinnig lieben; **to drive sb to** ~ jdn zum Wahnsinn *or* zur Verzweiflung treiben

distrain [dɪ'streɪn] VI (Jur) **to ~ upon sb's goods** jds Eigentum beschlagnahmen

distraint [dɪ'streɪnt] N (Jur) Beschlagnahmung f, Beschlagnahme f; **~ order** Beschlagnahmungsverfügung f

distraught [dɪ'strɔːt] ADJ verzweifelt, außer sich (dat) pred; look, voice verzweifelt

distress [dɪ'stres] **N a** Verzweiflung f; (physical) Leiden nt; (mental, cause of distress) Kummer m, Sorge f; **to be in great ~** sehr leiden; **to cause sb ~** jdm Sorge/starke Schmerzen bereiten **b** (= great poverty) Not f, Elend nt **c** (= danger) Not f; **to be in ~** (ship) in Seenot sein; (plane) in Not sein; **~ call** Notsignal nt **VT** (= worry) Kummer machen (+dat), Sorge bereiten (+dat); **don't ~ yourself** machen Sie sich (dat) keine Sorgen!; **the thought ~ed him enormously** der Gedanke bekümmerte ihn sehr

distressed [dɪ'strest] ADJ **a** (= upset) bekümmert; (= grief-stricken) erschüttert (about von) **b** (= poverty-stricken) **~ area** Notstandsgebiet nt

distressing [dɪ'stresɪŋ] ADJ (= upsetting) Besorgnis erregend; (stronger) erschreckend; (= regrettable) betrüblich

distressingly [dɪ'stresɪŋlɪ] ADV (= unfortunately) leider, bedauerlicherweise; common, familiar, high, low erschreckend; groan Mitleid erregend; **~, it took him six hours to die** so dauerte sechs quälende Stunden, bis er gestorben war

distress: distress rocket N Notrakete f; **distress signal** N Notsignal nt

distributable [dɪ'strɪbjuːtəbl] ADJ verteilbar, austeilbar

distributary [dɪ'strɪbjʊtərɪ] **N** (Geog) Nebenarm m, Flussarm m eines Deltas **ADJ** Verteiler-; **~ network** Verteilernetz nt

distribute [dɪ'strɪbjuːt] VT verteilen (to an +acc); information verbreiten; (Comm) goods vertreiben (to, among an +acc); drugs handeln mit (to bei); films verleihen (to an +acc); dividends ausschütten (to an +acc); **the cells are widely ~d throughout the body** die Zellen sind im ganzen Körper verbreitet; **your weight should be evenly ~d** Ihr Gewicht sollte gleichmäßig verteilt sein

distributing agent N (Groß)handelsvertreter(in) m(f)

distribution [ˌdɪstrɪ'bjuːʃən] **N a** (= act) Verteilung f; (of information) Verbreitung f; (Comm: of goods) Vertrieb m; (= dealing: of drugs) Handel m; (of mit) (of films) Verleih m; (of dividends) Ausschüttung f; **~ network** Vertriebsnetz nt; **~ rights** Vertriebsrechte pl **b** (= spread) Verbreitung f; **geographical ~** geografische Verteilung f

distribution box N (Elec) Verteilerkasten m, Abzweigdose f

distributive [dɪ'strɪbjʊtɪv] (Gram) **ADJ** distributiv **N** Distributivum nt

distributor [dɪ'strɪbjʊtə'] **N a** Verteiler(in) m(f); (Comm, = wholesaler) Großhändler m; (= retailer) Händler(in) m(f); (of films) Verleih(er) m; **~ discount** Händlerrabatt m **b** (Aut) Verteiler m

distributorship [dɪs'trɪbjʊtəʃɪp] N (Comm, = company) Vertriebsgesellschaft f; (= right to supply) Vertrieb m

district ['dɪstrɪkt] N (of country) Gebiet nt; (of town) Stadtteil m, Viertel nt; (= geographical area) Gegend f; (= administrative area) (Verwaltungs)bezirk m; **shopping/business ~** Geschäftsviertel nt

---

DISTRICT OF COLUMBIA

Der **District of Columbia** ist der Sitz der Regierung der Vereinigten Staaten von Amerika. Er gehört zu keinem Staat, sondern ist ein vollständig autonomer Bezirk im Osten des Landes. Er umfasst ungefähr 180 km², genau die Fläche, über die sich die Landeshauptstadt Washington erstreckt. Die Abkürzung DC wird daher hinter den Namen den Hauptstadt gestellt: Washington, DC.

---

district: district attorney N (US) Bezirksstaatsanwalt m/-anwältin f; **District Commissioner** N hoher Regierungsbeamter in einer Kolonie; **district council** N (Brit) Bezirksregierung f; **district court** N (US, Jur) Bezirksgericht nt; **district judge** N (US) Richter(in) m(f) an einem (Bundes)bezirksgericht; **district manager** N (Comm) Bezirksdirektor(in) m(f); **district nurse** N (Brit) Gemeindeschwester f; **district surveyor** N Bauinspektor(in) m(f), Beamte(r) m/Beamtin f des regionalen Bauaufsichtsamtes

distrust [dɪs'trʌst] **VT** misstrauen (+dat) **N** Misstrauen nt (of gegenüber)

distrustful [dɪs'trʌstfʊl] ADJ misstrauisch (of gegenüber)

disturb [dɪ'stɜːb] **VT a** (= interrupt) person, sleep, silence, balance stören; **the pain ~ed my sleep** vor Schmerzen habe ich schlecht geschlafen; **sorry to ~ you** entschuldigen Sie bitte die Störung **b** (= alarm) person beunruhigen **c** waters bewegen; sediment aufwirbeln; papers durcheinander bringen; (fig) peace of mind stören; **to ~ the peace** die Ruhe stören **VI** stören; **"please do not ~"** „bitte nicht stören"

disturbance [dɪ'stɜːbəns] **N a** (political, social) Unruhe f; (in house, street) (Ruhe)störung f; **to cause** or **create a ~** Unruhe or eine Ruhestörung verursachen; **~ of the peace** Störung f des Friedens **b** (= interruption: in work, routine) Störung f **c** no pl (= disarranging, of papers) Durcheinanderbringen nt; (of liquid) Bewegung f; (fig, of peace of mind) Störung f; **emotional ~** seelische Störung f **d** no pl (= alarm, uneasiness) Unruhe f; **I don't want to cause any ~ but …** ich will Sie ja nicht beunruhigen, aber …

disturbed [dɪ'stɜːbd] ADJ **a** (= interrupted, turbulent) night, times unruhig; **pregnant women tend to have more ~ sleep than other people** Schwangere schlafen oft unruhiger als andere Menschen; **separate beds can eliminate ~ sleep** getrennte Betten können Schlafstörungen verhindern **b** (Psych, = unbalanced, unhappy) person, behaviour, childhood, background gestört; **emotionally/mentally ~** seelisch/geistig gestört **c** (= worried) person beunruhigt, besorgt (about, at, by über +acc); **he was ~ that …** es beunruhigte or besorgte ihn, dass …; **I was ~ to hear of his accident** ich war beunruhigt, als ich von seinem Unfall erfuhr

disturber [dɪ'stɜːbə'] N Störer(in) m(f), Störenfried m; (= troublemaker) Unruhestifter(in) m(f)

disturbing [dɪ'stɜːbɪŋ] ADJ (= alarming) beunruhigend; (= distracting) störend; **some viewers may find these scenes ~** einige Zuschauer könnten an diesen Szenen Anstoß nehmen

disturbingly [dɪ'stɜːbɪŋlɪ] ADV beunruhigend; (introducing sentence) beunruhigenderweise

disulphide, (US) **disulfide** [daɪ'sʌlfaɪd] N Disulfid nt

disunite ['dɪsjuː'naɪt] VT spalten, entzweien

disunity [ˌdɪs'juːnɪtɪ] N Uneinigkeit f

disuse ['dɪs'juːs] N **to fall into ~** nicht mehr benutzt werden; (custom) außer Gebrauch kommen; **rusty from ~** wegen mangelnder Benutzung verrostet

disused ['dɪs'juːzd] ADJ building leer stehend; mine, quarry, railway line stillgelegt; vehicle, machine nicht mehr benutzt

disyllabic [ˌdaɪsɪ'læbɪk] ADJ word zweisilbig

ditch [dɪtʃ] **N a** Graben m **b** (Aviat inf) Bach m (sl) **VT** (inf, = get rid of) person abhängen (inf); employee, boyfriend abservieren (inf); plan, project baden gehen lassen (inf); car stehen lassen; old manuscript, unwanted object wegschmeißen (inf); **to ~ a plane** eine Maschine im Bach landen (sl) **VI** (Aviat inf) in den Bach gehen

ditchwater ['dɪtʃˌwɔːtə'] N abgestandenes, fauliges Wasser; **(as) dull as ~** (inf) stinklangweilig (inf)

dither ['dɪðə'] **N to be all of a ~, to be in a ~** ganz aufgeregt or am Rotieren (inf) sein **VI** zaudern, schwanken; **to ~ over sth** mit etw zaudern; **to ~ over how/whether …** schwanken, wie/ob …; **stop ~ing (about) and get on with it!** jetzt lass doch dieses ewige Hin und Her und fang endlich mal an!

dithery ['dɪðərɪ] ADJ (inf) unentschlossen

dithyrambs ['dɪθɪræmz] PL Dithyramben pl

ditsy ['dɪtsɪ] ADJ (esp US, inf) = **ditzy**

ditto ['dɪtəʊ] N **I'd like coffee – ~ (for me)** (inf) ich möchte Kaffee – dito or ich auch; **the restaurants are expensive here, and ~ the cinemas** die Restaurants hier sind teuer und die Kinos auch; **~ marks, ~ sign** Wiederholungszeichen nt

ditty ['dɪtɪ] N Liedchen nt, Weise f

ditzy ['dɪtsɪ] ADJ (esp US inf) albern; blonde doof (inf)

diuretic [ˌdaɪjʊə'retɪk] **ADJ** harntreibend, diuretisch (spec) **N** harntreibendes Mittel, Diuretikum nt (spec)

diurnal [daɪ'ɜːnl] **ADJ** (liter, = of the daytime) Tages-; **the earth's ~ rotation** die tägliche Umdrehung der Erde **N** (Eccl) Diurnal(e) nt

div abbr of **dividend**

diva ['diːvə] N Diva f, Primadonna f

divan [dɪ'væn] N Diwan m; **~ bed** Liege f

dive [daɪv] vb: pret **dived** or (US) **dove**, ptp **dived** **N a** (by swimmer) Sprung m; (by plane) Sturzflug m; (Ftbl) Hechtsprung m; **~rs are only allowed to make two ~s a day** Taucher dürfen nur zweimal am Tag unter Wasser; **that was the deepest ~ yet** das war die bisher größte Tauchtiefe; **to make a ~ for sth** (fig inf) sich auf etw (acc) stürzen; **to take a ~** (inf) (pound, dollar etc) absacken (inf); (confidence, hopes) sich in nichts auflösen; (Ftbl) eine Schwalbe machen (sl) **b** (pej inf, = club etc) Spelunke f (inf) **VI a** (person, from diving board) springen; (from side of lake, pool etc) (mit dem Kopf voraus) springen, hechten; (under water) tauchen; (submarine) untertauchen; (plane) einen Sturzflug machen; (birds, from air) einen Sturzflug machen; (in water) tauchen; (prices) stürzen; **to ~ for pearls** nach Perlen tauchen; **the goalkeeper ~d for the ball** der Torwart hechtete nach dem Ball; **~!** (Naut) auf Tauchstation! **b** (inf) **he ~d into the crowd** er tauchte in der Menge unter; **he ~d under the table** er verschwand blitzschnell unter dem Tisch; **to ~ for cover** eilig in Deckung gehen; **he ~d into a taxi** er stieg eilig in ein Taxi; **he ~d into his bag** er fischte eilig in seiner Tasche

▶ **dive in** VI **a** (swimmer) (mit dem Kopf voraus) hineinspringen **b** (inf, = start to eat) **dive in!** hau(t) rein! (inf)

dive: dive-bomb VT im Sturzflug bombardieren; **dive bomber** N Sturzkampfbomber m, Stuka m; **dive bombing** N Sturzkampfbombardierung f

diver ['daɪvə'] **N a** Taucher(in) m(f); (off high board) Turmspringer(in) m(f); (off springboard) Kunstspringer(in) m(f) **b** (bird) Taucher m

diverge [daɪ'vɜːdʒ] VI abweichen (from von), divergieren (geh, Math); (two things) voneinander abweichen

divergence [daɪ'vɜːdʒəns] N Divergenz f (geh, Math), Auseinandergehen nt; (from a standard etc) Abweichung f

divergent [daɪ'vɜːdʒənt] ADJ views unterschiedlich, auseinander gehend; interests unterschiedlich, voneinander abweichend; **to take** or **follow ~ paths** unterschiedliche Wege gehen; **to be ~ from** sth von etw abweichen; **~ response** (Psych) divergente Reaktion

divergent thinking N (Psych) divergentes Denken

divers ['daɪvɜːz] ADJ attr mehrere, diverse

diverse [daɪ'vɜːs] **ADJ a** (with singular noun) group gemischt, bunt zusammengewürfelt; society, population gemischt; range, selection breit, vielfältig **b** (with plural noun) people, areas, elements, backgrounds verschieden, unterschiedlich; *interests* vielfältig; **celebrities as ~ as ...** so verschiedene *or* unterschiedliche Berühmtheiten wie ...

diversification [daɪ,vɜːsɪfɪ'keɪʃən] N (= *change, variety*) Abwechslung f; (*of business etc*) Diversifikation f

diversified [daɪ'vɜːsɪfaɪd] ADJ (= *varied*) verschieden, verschiedenartig; *risk* verteilt; *company* diversifiziert

diversify [daɪ'vɜːsɪfaɪ] VT abwechslungsreich(er) gestalten; *interests* breit(er) fächern; *business etc* diversifizieren ◼ VI (*Comm*) diversifizieren; **to ~ into new products** sich auf neue Produkte umstellen

diversion [daɪ'vɜːʃən] N **a** (*of traffic, stream*) Umleitung f; (= *relaxation*) Unterhaltung f; **for ~** zur Unterhaltung *or* Zerstreuung; **it's a ~ from work** es ist eine angenehme Abwechslung von der Arbeit **c** (*Mil, fig, = sth that distracts attention*) Ablenkung f; **to create a ~** ablenken; **as a ~** um abzulenken

diversionary [daɪ'vɜːʃnəri] ADJ Ablenkungs-; **~ attack** *or* **raid** Ablenkungsangriff m; **~ manoeuvre** Ablenkungsmanöver nt

diversity [daɪ'vɜːsɪti] N Vielfalt f; **~ of opinion** Meinungsvielfalt f; **the ~ of her interests** die Vielfältigkeit ihrer Interessen

divert [daɪ'vɜːt] VT **a** *traffic, stream* umleiten; *attention* ablenken; *conversation* in eine andere Richtung lenken; *blow* abwenden; *money* abzweigen; *resources, investment* umlenken **b** (= *amuse*) unterhalten

diverting [daɪ'vɜːtɪŋ] ADJ unterhaltsam, kurzweilig

divest [daɪ'vest] VT **a** (*of clothes, leaves*) berauben; **to ~ oneself of sth** sich einer Sache (*gen*) entledigen; **to ~ sb of sth** jdn einer Sache (*gen*) berauben; **to be ~ed of sth** einer Sache (*gen*) entledigt/beraubt werden; **he ~ed her of her coat** (*hum, form*) er nahm ihr den Mantel ab **b** (= *strip of office/(his) rank*) jdn des *or* seines Amtes/seiner Würden entkleiden (*geh*)

divestiture [daɪ'vestɪtʃə], **divestment** [daɪ'vestmənt] N (*form*) **a** (= *deprivation*) (*of clothes*) Entkleidung f, Entblößung f; (*of rights*) Beraubung f **b** (*Fin: of investment*) Veräußerung f

dividable [dɪ'vaɪdəbl] ADJ teilbar

divide [dɪ'vaɪd] VT **a** (= *separate*) trennen **b** (= *split into parts: also* **divide up**,) *money, work, property, kingdom, room* teilen (*into* in +*acc*); (*in order to distribute*) aufteilen; **the river ~s the city into two** der Fluss teilt die Stadt; **the pastry in half** den Teig in zwei Hälften teilen; **she ~d the cake into five pieces** sie teilte den Kuchen in fünf Stücke (auf); **the book can be ~d into three main parts** das Buch kann in drei Hauptteile gegliedert werden **c** (= *share out*) *money, time, food* verteilen; **she ~d the food evenly among the children** sie verteilte das Essen gleichmäßig an die Kinder **d** (*Math*) dividieren, teilen; **to ~ 6 into 36, to ~ 36 by 6** 36 durch 6 teilen *or* dividieren; **what is 12 ~d by 3?** was ist 12 (geteilt *or* dividiert) durch 3? **e** (= *cause disagreement among*) *friends* entzweien **f** (*Brit, Parl*) **to ~ the House** durch Hammelsprung abstimmen lassen ◼ VI **a** (*river, road, room, cells*) sich teilen; (*book etc*) sich gliedern (*into* in +*acc*); **to ~ into groups** sich in Gruppen aufteilen; (= *be classified*) sich gliedern lassen; **the policy of ~ and rule/conquer** die Politik des „divide et impera"/Teilen und Besiegens **b** (*Math, number*) sich teilen *or* dividieren lassen (*by* durch); **we're learning to ~** wir lernen Teilen *or* Dividieren; **he's no good at dividing** er kann nicht teilen *or* dividieren **c** (*Brit, Parl*) **the House ~d** das Parlament stimmte durch Hammelsprung ab; **~, ~!** abstimmen!

◼ N (*Geog*) Wasserscheide f; **the Great Divide** (*Geog*) die (nord)amerikanische Wasserscheide; (*fig*) die Kluft; (= *death*) der Tod; **to cross the Great Divide** (*fig*) den Schritt über die Schwelle tun; (= *die*) die Schwelle des Todes überschreiten; **the racial/social/cultural ~** die Kluft zwischen den Rassen/Gesellschaftsschichten/Kulturen

▶ **divide off** ◼ VI sich (ab)trennen; (= *be separable*) sich (ab)trennen lassen ◼ VT sep (ab)trennen

▶ **divide out** VT sep aufteilen (*among* unter +*acc or dat*)

▶ **divide up** ◼ VI = **divide VI a** ◼ VT sep = **divide VT b, c**

divided [dɪ'vaɪdɪd] ADJ **a** (= *partitioned*) *city, country* geteilt; **~ skirt** Hosenrock m **b** (= *disunited*) *nation, country, society* geteilt, gespalten; *government, opposition* zerstritten; *opinion* geteilt; **to have ~ loyalties** nicht zu vereinbarende Pflichten haben; **children of divorced parents have ~ loyalties** Scheidungskinder fühlen sich zwischen den Eltern hin- und hergerissen; **my mind is ~** ich kann mich nicht entscheiden; **to be ~ on** *or* **over sth** (*people*) sich in etw (*dat*) *or* über etw (*acc*) nicht einig sein; **opinion was ~ (on whether ...)** die Meinungen waren geteilt (darüber, ob ...)

divided highway N (*US*) ≈ Schnellstraße f

dividend ['dɪvɪdend] N **a** (*Fin*) Dividende f; **to pay ~s** (*fig*) sich bezahlt machen **b** (*Math*) Dividend m

dividend coupon, dividend warrant N (*Fin*) Dividendenschein m, Gewinnanteilschein m

dividers [dɪ'vaɪdəz] PL Stechzirkel m

dividing [dɪ'vaɪdɪŋ] ADJ (ab)trennend

dividing line N (*lit, fig*) Trenn(ungs)linie f

dividing wall N Trennwand f

divination [,dɪvɪ'neɪʃən] N Prophezeiung f, Weissagung f

divine [dɪ'vaɪn] ADJ (*Rel, fig inf*) göttlich; **~ worship** Anbetung f Gottes ◼ N Theologe m; (= *priest*) Geistliche(r) m ◼ VT **a** (= *foretell*) *the future* weissagen, prophezeien **b** (*liter, = make out*) *sb's intentions* erahnen, erspüren (*liter*) **c** (= *find*) *water, metal* aufspüren

divinely [dɪ'vaɪnli] ADV **a** (*Rel, by God*) appointed, inspired von Gott; **~ ordained** von Gott gewollt; **~ noble/wise** göttlich edel/weise **b** (*fig inf*) *funny, decadent etc* göttlich (*inf*)

diviner [dɪ'vaɪnə] N **a** (*of future*) Wahrsager(in) m(f) **b** = **water diviner**

diving ['daɪvɪŋ] N (*under water*) Tauchen nt; (*into water*) Springen nt; (*Sport*) Wasserspringen nt

diving: diving bell N Taucherglocke f; **diving board** N (Sprung)brett nt; **diving header** N (*Ftbl*) Flug- *or* Hechtkopfball m; **diving suit** N Taucheranzug m

diving rod [daɪvɪŋ'rɒd] N Wünschelrute f

divinity [dɪ'vɪnɪti] N **a** (= *divine quality*) Göttlichkeit f **b** (= *theology*) Theologie f; (*Sch*) Religion f; **doctor of ~** (*Brit*) Doktor der Theologie **c** (= *divine being*) göttliches Wesen, Gottheit f

divisible [dɪ'vɪzəbl] ADJ teilbar (*by* durch)

division [dɪ'vɪʒən] N **a** (= *act of dividing, state of being divided*) Teilung f; (*Math*) Teilen nt, Division f; **we're learning ~** wir lernen Teilen *or* Dividieren; **he can't do ~** er kann nicht teilen *or* dividieren; **the ~ of labour** (*Brit*) *or* **labor** (*US*) die Arbeitsteilung **b** (*Mil*) Division f **c** (= *result of dividing, in administration*) Abteilung f; (*in box, case*) Fach nt; (= *part*) Teil m; (= *category*) Kategorie f; **the bank's European ~** die für Europa zuständige Abteilung der Bank; **the sales ~** die Verkaufsabteilung **d** (= *that which divides: in room*) Trennwand f; (*fig: between social classes etc*) Schranke f; (= *dividing line: lit, fig*) Trennungslinie f **e** (*fig, = discord*) Uneinigkeit f **f** (*Brit, Parl*) **to call for a ~** eine Abstimmung durch Hammelsprung verlangen **g** (*Sport*) Liga f

Divisional Court [dɪ,vɪʒənl'kɔːt] N (*Brit, Jur*) Berufungsgericht mit zwei oder mehr Richtern

division bell [dɪ'vɪʒən,bel] N (*Parl*) Klingel, mit der die Abgeordneten zur Abstimmung gerufen werden

division sign N (*Math*) Teilungszeichen nt

divisive [dɪ'vaɪsɪv] ADJ *issue, figure* kontrovers, umstritten; *influence, effect* polarisierend; **to be ~** Uneinigkeit schaffen; **a ~ general election** eine Wahl, die das Land in zwei Lager spaltet

divisor [dɪ'vaɪzə] N (*Math*) Divisor m

divorce [dɪ'vɔːs] N (*Jur*) Scheidung f (*from* von); (*fig*) Trennung f; **he wants a ~** er will sich scheiden lassen; **to get a ~ (from sb)** sich (von jdm) scheiden lassen ◼ VT **a** *husband, wife* sich scheiden lassen von; **to get ~d** sich scheiden lassen **b** (*fig*) trennen ◼ VI sich scheiden lassen; **they ~d last year** sie haben sich letztes Jahr scheiden lassen

divorcé [dɪ'vɔːseɪ] N geschiedener Mann, Geschiedene(r) m

divorce court N Scheidungsgericht nt

divorced [dɪ'vɔːst] ADJ (*Jur*) geschieden (*from* von); **to be ~ from sth** (*fig*) keine(rlei) Beziehung zu etw haben; **she's completely ~ from reality** sie ist völlig wirklichkeitsfremd

divorcee [dɪ,vɔː'siː] N Geschiedene(r) mf, geschiedener Mann, geschiedene Frau; **she is a ~** sie ist geschieden

divorce proceedings PL Scheidungsprozess m

divorce settlement N (*mutually agreed*) Scheidungsvergleich m; (*imposed by court*) Scheidungsurteil nt

divot ['dɪvɪt] N *vom Golfschläger etc ausgehacktes Rasenstück*

divulge [daɪ'vʌldʒ] VT preisgeben (*sth to sb* jdm etw)

divvy ['dɪvɪ] (*Brit, inf*) dim of **dividend** Dividende f

▶ **divvy up** (*inf*) ◼ VT sep (= *divide up*) aufteilen ◼ VI aufteilen

Diwali [dɪ'wɑːlɪ] N Diwali nt

Dixie ['dɪksɪ] N (*also* **Dixieland**) Dixie(land) m ADJ der Südstaaten

---

DIXIE

Dixie ist der Spitzname für die Südstaaten der USA. Insbesondere wird er für die elf Staaten verwandt, die sich vormals während des amerikanischen Bürgerkrieges zu den Konföderierten Staaten von Amerika zusammengeschlossen hatten: Alabama, Arkansas, Georgia, Florida, Louisiana, Mississippi, North Carolina, South Carolina, Tennessee, Texas und Virginia. **Dixie** wird auch adjektivisch eingesetzt, wenn man Besonderheiten der Südstaaten und ihrer Einwohner beschreiben möchte: „Scarlett O'Hara was the epitome of Dixie femininity" (etwa: „ ... war der Inbegriff einer Südstaatenschönheit"). Der Name **Dixie** stammt ursprünglich wohl aus Louisiana, weil dort auf der Rückseite der Zehn-Dollar-Noten die Zahl auf französisch mit „dix" angegeben war. Andere Mutmaßungen verweisen auf die imaginäre Mason-Dixon Linie, die einst den Norden vom Süden trennte → MASON-DIXON LINE

---

dixie ['dɪksɪ] N (*Brit Mil sl*) Gulaschkanone f (*inf*); (*for eating*) Essgeschirr nt

Dixie cup® N (*US*) Pappbecher m

DIY [diːaɪ'waɪ] (*Brit*) abbr of **do-it-yourself** ◼ N Do-it-yourself nt, Heimwerken nt; **she was doing some ~ over the weekend** sie machte am Wochenende einige Heimwerkerarbeiten ◼ ADJ *product* für Heimwerker; **~ chain** Baumarktkette f; **~ fan** *or* **enthusiast** Heimwerker(in) m(f), Do-it-yourself-Fan m; **~ kit** (*for household jobs*) Heimwerkerausrüstung f; (*for businesses etc*) Starterpaket nt; (*for car etc*) Bausatz m; **~ work** Heimwerkerarbeiten pl; **this is an easy ~ job** das kann man leicht selber machen; **you can tell it's a ~ job** man kann sehen, dass hier ein Heimwerker am Werk war; **~ home improvements** eigenhändige Modernisierung; **they opted for a ~ divorce** sie entschieden sich, ihre Scheidung selbst zu vereinbaren; **~ justice** Selbstjustiz *f*

DIY shop, **DIY store** N Baumarkt *m*, Heimwerkermarkt *m*

dizzily ['dɪzɪlɪ] ADV **a** (= *giddily*) benommen; **my head spun ~** mir war entsetzlich schwindelig; **share prices rose ~** die Aktienkurse stiegen auf Schwindel erregende Höhen **b** (*fig inf*: = *foolishly*) dümmlich

dizziness ['dɪzɪnɪs] N Schwindel *m*; **bout** or **fit of ~** Schwindelanfall *m*

dizzy ['dɪzɪ] ADJ (+*er*) **a** (= *giddy*) schwindelig; **I'm (feeling) ~** mir ist schwindelig (*from* von); **she started to feel ~** ihr wurde schwindelig; **~ spell** Schwindelanfall *m*; **it makes me ~ to think of it** mir wird ganz schwindelig bei dem Gedanken; **she was ~ with success** der Erfolg hatte sie benommen gemacht; **when you're ~ with desire** wenn dir vor Begehren ganz schwindelig ist

b (*fig*) *height, speed* Schwindel erregend; **to rise to ~ heights** zu Schwindel erregenden Höhen aufsteigen

c (= *foolish*) *person* hirnlos; *action* verrückt; **delightfully ~** herrlich verrückt; **a ~ blonde** ein dummes Blondchen (*inf*)

VT *person* verwirren

DJ a *abbr of* **dinner jacket b** *abbr of* **disc jockey**

dl *abbr of* **decilitre(s)** dl

D Lit *abbr of* **Doctor of Letters** Dr. phil.

DM a (*Hist*) *abbr of* **Deutschmark** DM **b** *abbr of* **Doctor of medicine** Dr. med.

dm *abbr of* **decimetre(s)** dm

D-Mark ['diːmɑːk] N (*Hist*) *abbr of* **Deutschmark** D-Mark *f*

D Mus *abbr of* **Doctor of Music**

DMZ *abbr of* **demilitarized zone** entmilitarisierte Zone

DNA *abbr of* **de(s)oxyribonucleic acid** DNS *f*

DNA: DNA fingerprinting, **DNA profiling** N = **genetic fingerprinting**; **DNA testing** N DNS-Tests *pl*

DNF (*Athletics*) *abbr of* **did not finish**

D-notice ['diːnəʊtɪs] N (*Brit, Pol*) offizielles Verbot an die Presse, bestimmte für die innere Sicherheit wichtige Informationen zu veröffentlichen

DNS (*Athletics*) *abbr of* **did not start**

do¹ [dəʊ] N (*Mus*) Do *nt*

do² [duː]	
vb: pret **did**, *ptp* **done**	
1 AUXILIARY VERB	4 NOUN
2 TRANSITIVE VERB	5 PLURAL NOUN
3 INTRANSITIVE VERB	6 PHRASAL VERBS

1 – AUXILIARY VERB

There is no equivalent in German to the use of **do** in questions, negative statements and negative commands.

a interrogative, negative **do you understand?** verstehen Sie?; **I don't** or **do not understand** ich verstehe nicht; **what did he say?** was hat er gesagt?; **didn't you** or **did you not know?** haben Sie das nicht gewusst?; **don't be silly!** sei nicht albern!

b in question tags **oder**; **you know him, don't you?** Sie kennen ihn doch?, Sie kennen ihn (doch, oder)?; **you don't know him, do you?** Sie kennen ihn also nicht, oder?; **so you know them, do you?** (*in surprise*) Sie kennen sie also wirklich or tatsächlich!; **he does understand, doesn't he?** das versteht er doch, oder?; **he didn't go, did he?** er ist (doch) nicht gegangen, oder?

c substitute for another verb **you speak better German than I do** Sie sprechen besser Deutsch als ich; **he likes cheese and so do I** er isst gern

Käse und ich auch; **he doesn't like cheese and neither do I** er mag keinen Käse und ich auch nicht; **I don't like cheese but he does** ich mag keinen Käse, aber er schon; **they said he would go and he did** sie sagten, er würde gehen und das tat er (dann) auch

d in tag responses **do you see them often? – yes, I do/no, I don't** sehen Sie sie oft? – ja/ nein; **do you serve food? – yes, we do** gibts bei Ihnen Essen? – ja; **you didn't go, did you? – yes, I did** Sie sind nicht gegangen, oder? – doch; **they speak French – oh, do they?** sie sprechen Französisch – ja?, ach, wirklich or tatsächlich?; **they speak German – do they really?** sie sprechen Deutsch – wirklich?; **may I come in? – do!** darf ich hereinkommen? – ja, bitte; **shall I open the window? – no, don't!** soll ich das Fenster öffnen? – nein, bitte nicht!; **who broke the window? – I did** wer hat das Fenster eingeschlagen? – ich

e for emphasis **DO come!** (*esp Brit*) kommen Sie doch (bitte)!; **DO shut up!** (*esp Brit*) (nun) sei doch (endlich) ruhig!; **do tell him that ...** (*esp Brit*) sagen Sie ihm doch (bitte), dass ...; **well do I remember him!** und ob ich mich an ihn erinnere!; **it's very expensive, but I DO like it** es ist zwar sehr teuer, aber es gefällt mir nun mal; **so you DO know them!** Sie kennen sie also doch!

2 – TRANSITIVE VERB

a tun, machen; **I've done a stupid thing** ich habe da was Dummes gemacht or getan; **to do sth again** etw noch (ein)mal tun or machen; **sorry, it's impossible, it can't be done** tut mir Leid, (ist) ausgeschlossen, es lässt sich nicht machen; **can you do it by yourself?** schaffst du das allein?, kannst du das allein machen?; **we did the journey in eight hours** wir haben die Fahrt in acht Stunden geschafft

♦ **do** +noun phrase **to do the housework/one's homework** die Hausarbeit/seine Hausaufgaben machen; **who did the choreography/the cover design?** wer hat die Choreografie/den Umschlagentwurf gemacht?; **we'll have to get someone to do the roof** wir müssen jemanden bestellen, der das Dach macht (*inf*)

Note that a more specific verb may be required in German.

could you do this letter please tippen Sie bitte diesen Brief; **you do the painting and I'll do the papering** du streichst an und ich tapeziere; **he does the film crits for the magazine** er schreibt die Filmkritiken für die Zeitschrift; **to do the flowers** die Blumen arrangieren; **to do one's make-up** sich schminken; **to do one's hair** sich frisieren, sich (*dat*) die Haare (zurecht)machen (*inf*); **to do one's nails** sich (*dat*) die Nägel machen or (*varnish*) lackieren; **to do one's teeth** (*Brit*) sich (*dat*) die Zähne putzen; **to do the dishes** spülen, den Abwasch machen; **to do the washing** Wäsche waschen; **to do the ironing** bügeln

♦ **do + anything/something** **he knows it's a mistake but he can't do anything about it** er weiß, dass es ein Fehler ist, aber er kann nichts dagegen machen or daran ändern; **are you doing anything this evening?** haben Sie heute Abend schon etwas vor?; **we'll have to do something about this/him** wir müssen da/ wir müssen mit ihm etwas tun or unternehmen; **do something for me, will you ... shut up** tu mir bloß den (einen) Gefallen und halt den Mund; **does that do anything for you?** (*inf*) macht dich das an? (*inf*); **Brecht doesn't do anything for me** Brecht lässt mich kalt (*inf*) or sagt mir nichts

♦ **do + everything** **I've done everything I can** ich habe alles getan, was ich kann

♦ **do + nothing** **I've got nothing to do** ich habe nichts zu tun; **I shall do nothing of the sort** ich werde nichts dergleichen tun; **he does nothing but complain** er nörgelt immer nur, er tut nichts als nörgeln (*inf*)

♦ **do** with wh- phrase **what's to be done?** was ist da zu tun?; **but what can you do?** aber was

kann man da machen?; **what do you want me to do (about it)?** und was soll ich da tun or machen?; **well, do what you can** mach or tu (eben), was du kannst; **what have you done to him?** was haben Sie mit ihm gemacht?; **now what have you done!** was hast du jetzt bloß wieder angestellt or gemacht?; **what are you doing on Saturday?** was machen or tun Sie am Sonnabend?; **what do I have to do to get through to him?** was muss ich tun, um zu ihm durchzukommen?; **what shall we do for money?** wie machen wir es mit Geld?; **how do you do it?** wie macht man das?; (*in amazement*) wie machen Sie das bloß?

♦ **that's done it** (*inf*) so, da haben wir's!, da haben wir die Bescherung! (*inf*)

♦ **that does it!** jetzt reichts mir!

b as job, profession **what does your father do?** was macht Ihr Vater (beruflich)?

c = provide service, product **what can I do for you?** was kann ich für Sie tun?; (*by shop assistant*) was darfs sein?; **sorry, we don't do lunches** wir haben leider keinen Mittagstisch; **we do a wide range of herbal teas** wir führen eine große Auswahl an Kräutertees; **we only do one style of gloves** (= *sell*) wir haben or führen nur eine Sorte Handschuhe; (= *produce*) wir stellen nur eine Sorte Handschuhe her; **who did the food for your reception?** wer hat bei Ihrem Empfang für das Essen gesorgt?

d = complete, finish (*in pret, ptp only*) **the work's done now** die Arbeit ist gemacht or getan or fertig; **what's done cannot be undone** was geschehen ist, kann man nicht ungeschehen machen; **I haven't done** (*Brit*) or **I'm not done telling you what I think of you** mit dir bin ich noch lange nicht fertig; **done!** (= *agreed*) abgemacht!; **are you done?** (*inf*) bist du endlich or schon (*iro*) fertig?

♦ **over and done with** **it's all over and done with** (= *is finished*) das ist alles erledigt; (= *has happened*) das ist alles vorbei or überstanden

e = study, cover durchnehmen, haben; **we've done Milton** wir haben Milton gelesen or durchgenommen; **I've never done any German** ich habe nie Deutsch gelernt or gehabt

f Cook machen (*inf*); **to do the cooking** kochen; **how do you like your steak done?** wie möchten Sie Ihr Steak?; **well done** durch(gebraten); **is the meat done?** ist das Fleisch fertig (gebraten) or durch?

g = solve lösen; *sum, crossword, puzzle etc* lösen, machen

h = take customer drannehmen; **the barber said he'd do me next** der Friseur sagte, er würde mich als Nächsten drannehmen

i Theat, Film *part* spielen; **to do Hamlet** den Hamlet spielen; **to do a play** (= *put on*) ein Stück aufführen; **to do a film** (= *produce*) einen Film machen or drehen

j = take off, mimic nachmachen; **he does a brilliant Charlie Chaplin** er kann Charlie Chaplin hervorragend nachmachen; **she does the worried mother very convincingly** sie spielt die besorgte Mutter sehr überzeugend

k = visit, see sights of *city, country, museum* besuchen, abhaken (*inf*)

l Aut etc fahren, machen (*inf*); **this car does or can do** or **will do 100** das Auto fährt or macht (*inf*) 100

m = treat (*Brit inf*) **they do you very well at that hotel** in dem Hotel ist man gut untergebracht or aufgehoben; **they do you very well at that restaurant** in dem Restaurant isst man sehr gut

♦ **to do oneself well** es sich (*dat*) gut gehen lassen

n = be suitable for (*inf*) passen (*sb* jdm); (= *be sufficient for*) reichen (*sb* jdm); **that will do me nicely** das reicht dicke (*inf*) or allemal

o = cheat (*inf*) übers Ohr hauen (*inf*), reinlegen (*inf*); **you've been done!** du bist reingelegt or übers Ohr gehauen worden (*inf*); **I was done for £80** für £ 80 hat man mich ganz schön übers Ohr gehauen (*inf*)

p = burgle (*inf*) einbrechen in (+*acc*); **the office was done last night** im Büro ist gestern Nacht ein Bruch gemacht worden (*sl*)

q = hurt (Brit inf) **I'll do you!** dir besorg ichs noch! (inf)

r = tire out (inf) **I'm absolutely done (in)!** ich bin völlig geschafft or erledigt or fertig (all inf)

s = take (inf drugs) nehmen

t in prison (inf 6 years etc) sitzen, abreißen (inf)

u = translate (old, liter) **done into (the) English by ...** ins Englische übertragen von ...

3 – INTRANSITIVE VERB

a = act **do as I do** mach es wie ich; **he did well to take advice** er tat gut daran, sich beraten zu lassen; **he did right** er hat richtig gehandelt, es war richtig von ihm; **he did right/well to go** es war richtig/gut, dass er gegangen ist

b = get on, fare **how are you doing?** wie gehts (Ihnen)?; **I'm not doing so badly** es geht mir gar nicht so schlecht; **the patient is doing very well** dem Patienten geht es recht ordentlich; **he's doing well at school** er ist gut in der Schule; **his business is doing well** sein Geschäft geht gut; **the roses are doing well this year** die Rosen stehen dieses Jahr gut; **when my uncle died I did quite well** als mein Onkel starb, bin ich ganz gut dabei weggekommen

♦ **how do you do?** (on introduction) guten Tag/Abend!, angenehm! (form)

♦ **what's doing?** (inf) was ist los?

c = be suitable gehen; **that will never do!** das geht nicht!; **this room will do** das Zimmer geht (inf) or ist in Ordnung; **will it do if I come back at 8?** geht es, wenn ich um 8 Uhr zurück bin?; **it doesn't do to keep a lady waiting** es gehört sich nicht or es geht nicht, dass man eine Dame warten lässt; **will she/it do?** geht sie/das?

♦ **to do as/for this coat will do for or as a cover** dieser Mantel geht als Decke

d = be sufficient reichen; **can you lend me some money? – will £10 do?** können Sie mir etwas Geld leihen? – reichen £ 10?; **yes, that'll do** ja, das reicht

♦ **to make do** you'll have to make do with £10 £ 10 müssen Ihnen reichen, Sie werden mit £ 10 auskommen müssen

♦ **that'll do!** jetzt reichts aber!

4 – NOUN (Brit inf)

a = event Veranstaltung f, Sache f (inf); (= party) Fete f (inf); **she had a big do for her eighteenth birthday** an ihrem achtzehnten Geburtstag stieg bei ihr eine Riesenfete (inf)

b = swindle (Brit) Schwindel m; **the whole thing was a do from start to finish** die ganze Sache war von vorne bis hinten ein Schwindel

5 – dos PLURAL NOUN

the dos and don'ts was man tun und nicht tun sollte; **fair dos** (inf) gleiches Recht für alle

6 – PHRASAL VERBS

▶ **do away with** VI +prep obj **a** custom, law, nuclear weapons abschaffen; document vernichten; building abreißen; **to do away with the need for sth** etw überflüssig or unnötig machen; **it does away with the need to wear protective clothing** das macht Schutzkleidung überflüssig or unnötig **b** (inf: = kill) umbringen

▶ **do by** VI +prep obj **to do well/badly by sb** jdn gut/schlecht behandeln; **do as you would be done by** (Prov) was du nicht willst, dass man dir tu, das füg auch keinem andern zu (Prov) → **hard** ADV **b**

▶ **do down** VT sep (Brit) herunter machen, schlecht machen

▶ **do for** VI +prep obj (inf) **a** (= finish off) person fertig machen; project zunichte machen; **to be done for** (person) erledigt or fertig (inf) sein; (project) gestorben sein (inf) **b** (charlady) putzen für or bei

▶ **do in** VT sep (inf) **a** (= kill) um die Ecke bringen (inf) **b** (usu pass: = exhaust) **to be or feel done in** fertig or geschafft sein (inf)

▶ **do out** VT sep **a** room auskehren or -fegen **b** **to do sb out of a job** jdn um eine Stelle

bringen; **to do sb out of £100** jdn um £ 100 bringen or erleichtern (inf)

▶ **do over** VT sep **a** (= redecorate) (neu) herrichten **b** (inf, = beat up) zusammenschlagen; (= rob, burgle) ausrauben **c** (US, = do again) noch einmal machen

▶ **do up** VI (dress etc) zugemacht werden VT sep **a** (= fasten) zumachen; tie binden **b** (= parcel together) goods zusammenpacken; **books done up in brown paper** in Packpapier eingewickelte Bücher **c** house, room (neu) herrichten; **her hair was done up in ringlets** ihr Haar war in Ringellocken gelegt

▶ **do with** VI +prep obj **a** (= need) brauchen; **do you know what I could do with?** weißt du, was ich jetzt brauchen könnte?; **I could do with a cup of tea** ich könnte eine Tasse Tee gebrauchen or vertragen (inf); **it could do with a clean** es müsste mal sauber gemacht werden **b** (inf: = tolerate) ausstehen, vertragen; **I can't be doing with this noise** ich kann den Lärm nicht vertragen or ausstehen

c **he has to do with the steel industry** er hat mit der Stahlindustrie zu tun; **what has that got to do with it?** was hat das damit zu tun?; **I won't have anything to do with it!** ich möchte nichts damit zu tun haben!; **that has or is nothing to do with you!** das geht Sie gar nichts an!; **it has something to do with money** es hat etwas mit Geld zu tun; **it has something to do with her being adopted** es hat etwas damit zu tun, dass sie adoptiert wurde; **it/this debate has to do with ...** dabei/in dieser Debatte geht es um ...; **money has a lot to do with it** Geld spielt eine große Rolle dabei

d **what have you done with my gloves/your hair?** was hast du mit meinen Handschuhen/deinem Haar gemacht?

e **he doesn't know what to do with himself** er weiß nicht, was er mit sich anfangen soll; **the children can always find something to do with themselves** die Kinder finden immer etwas, womit sie sich beschäftigen können

f **to be done with sb/sth** (= finished) mit jdm/etw fertig sein

▶ **do without** VI +prep obj auskommen ohne; **I can do without your advice** Sie können sich Ihren Rat sparen; **I could have done without that!** das hätte mir (wirklich) erspart bleiben können; **you'll have to do without** Sie müssen ohne auskommen

do³ written abbr of **ditto**

DOA abbr of **dead on arrival**

doable ['duːəbl] ADJ (inf) machbar

d.o.b. abbr of **date of birth**

Doberman (pinscher) ['dəʊbəmən('pɪnʃə')] N Dobermann(pinscher) m

doc [dɒk] (inf) abbr of **doctor** (as address) Herr/Frau Doktor

docile ['dəʊsaɪl] ADJ sanftmütig; animal fromm; acceptance widerstandslos

docilely ['dəʊsaɪlɪ] ADV sanftmütig

docility [dəʊˈsɪlɪtɪ] N Sanftmut f

dock¹ [dɒk] **N** a Dock nt; (for berthing) Pier m, Kai m; ~**s** pl Hafen m; **my car is in** ~ (inf) mein Wagen ist in der Werkstatt VT docken (spec); (Space also) ankoppeln (with an +acc) VI a (Naut) anlegen **b** (Space, two spacecraft) docken (spec), ankoppeln; **the space shuttle** ~**ed with Russia's space station** die Raumfähre koppelte or dockte (spec) an die russische Raumstation an

dock² N (Jur) Anklagebank f; **to stand in the** ~ auf der Anklagebank sitzen; **"prisoner in the** ~**"** „Angeklagte(r)"

dock³ VT a dog's tail kupieren; horse's tail stutzen **b** wages kürzen; points abziehen; **to** ~ **£50 off sb's wages** jds Lohn um £ 50 kürzen; **he was** ~**ed 6 points for cheating** ihm wurden 6 Punkte wegen Mogeln abgezogen **N** kupierter Schwanz; (of horse) gestutzter Schweif

dock⁴ N (Bot) Ampfer m

docker ['dɒkə'] N (Brit) Hafenarbeiter m, Docker m

docket ['dɒkɪt] **N** a (on document, parcel etc) Warenbegleitschein m, Laufzettel m **b** (Jur, = judgements register) Urteilsregister nt; (= list of cases) Liste der Gerichtstermine **c** (= customs certificate) Zollinhaltserklärung f VT a contents, judgement, information etc zusammenfassen, eine Kurzfassung geben or herstellen von **b** contents angeben; (= put docket on) crate mit einem Warenbegleitschein or Laufzettel versehen

dock gates PL Hafeneingang m; (in water) Docktor nt

docking ['dɒkɪŋ] N (Space) Docking nt (spec), Ankoppelung f

docking: docking manoeuvre N (Space) (An)koppelungsmanöver nt; **docking station** PL a (Space) (Welt)raumstation f **b** (for digital camera) Dockingstation f; **docking techniques** PL (Space) (An)koppelungstechnik f; **docking time** N Liegezeit f

dock: dock labourer N Hafenarbeiter m; **dockland** N Hafenviertel nt; **dock strike** N Hafenarbeiterstreik m; **dock worker** N Hafenarbeiter m; **dockyard** N Werft f

Doc Martens® [dɒkˈmɑːtənz] PL Springerstiefel pl

doctor ['dɒktə'] **N** a (Med) Arzt m, Ärztin f, Doktor(in) m(f) (inf); **Doctor Smith** Doktor Smith; **yes,** ~ ja, Herr/Frau Doktor; **the** ~**'s** (= surgery) der Arzt; **to go to the** ~ zum Arzt gehen; **to send for the** ~ den Arzt holen; **he is a** ~ er ist Arzt; **a woman** ~ eine Ärztin; **he's under a** ~ **in London** (inf) er ist bei einem Arzt in London in Behandlung; **to be under** ~**'s orders** in ärztlicher Behandlung sein; **it's just what the** ~ **ordered** (fig inf) das ist genau das Richtige **b** (Univ etc) Doktor m; **to get one's** ~**'s degree** promovieren, seinen Doktor machen; ~ **of Law/of Science** etc Doktor der Rechte/der Naturwissenschaften etc; **Dear Doctor Smith** Sehr geehrter Herr Dr./Sehr geehrte Frau Dr. Smith VT a cold behandeln; **to** ~ **oneself/sb** an sich (dat)/jdm herumdoktern **b** (inf, = castrate) kastrieren **c** (= tamper with) accounts frisieren; text verfälschen; **the food's/wine's been** ~**ed** dem Essen/Wein ist etwas beigemischt worden

doctoral thesis ['dɒktərəl'θiːsɪs] N Doktorarbeit f

doctorate ['dɒktərɪt] N Doktorwürde f; ~ **in science/philosophy** Doktor(titel) m in Naturwissenschaften/Philosophie; **to gain one's** ~ die Doktorwürde verliehen bekommen; **to take one's** ~ seinen Doktor machen; **he's still doing his** ~ er sitzt immer noch an seiner Doktorarbeit

doctrinaire [ˌdɒktrɪˈnɛə'] ADJ doktrinär

doctrinal [dɒkˈtraɪnl] ADJ doktrinell; **on** ~ **matters** in Sachen der Doktrin

doctrine ['dɒktrɪn] N Doktrin f, Lehre f

docudrama ['dɒkjʊˌdrɑːmə] N Dokumentarspiel nt

document ['dɒkjʊmənt] **N** Dokument nt, Urkunde f VT a history, fact, life dokumentieren; case beurkunden, (urkundlich) belegen; **the theory is well** ~**ed** die Theorie ist gut belegt **b** ship mit Papieren versehen

documentary [ˌdɒkjʊˈmentərɪ] **ADJ** a dokumentarisch, urkundlich **b** (Film, TV) a ~ **film** ein Dokumentarfilm m; **in** ~ **form** in Form einer Dokumentation **N** (Film, TV) Dokumentarfilm m

documentary credit N (Fin) Dokumentenakkreditiv nt

documentary evidence N (Jur) urkundliche Beweise pl

documentation [ˌdɒkjʊmenˈteɪʃən] N Dokumentation f

docu-soap ['dɒkjʊsəʊp] N (TV) Dokusoap f

DOD (US) abbr of **Department of Defense** Verteidigungsministerium nt

dodder ['dɒdə'] VI tapern

dodderer ['dɒdərə'] N (esp Brit inf) Tattergreis m (inf)

doddering ['dɒdərɪŋ], **doddery** ['dɒdərɪ] ADJ (esp Brit) person taperig

doddle ['dɒdl] N (Brit inf) **it was a ~** es war ein Kinderspiel

dodge [dɒdʒ] **N a** (lit) Sprung m zur Seite, rasches Ausweichen; (Ftbl, Boxing) Ausweichen nt **b** (= trick) Trick m, Kniff m; (= ingenious plan) Glanzidee f (inf); **to know all the ~s** mit allen Wassern gewaschen sein

VT blow, ball, question, difficulty ausweichen (+dat); tax umgehen; (= shirk) work, military service sich drücken vor (+dat); **to ~ the issue** der (eigentlichen) Frage ausweichen or aus dem Weg gehen

VI ausweichen; **to ~ out of sight** blitzschnell verschwinden, sich blitzschnell verdrücken (inf); **to ~ out of the way** (of car, blow) zur Seite springen; **to ~ behind a tree** hinter einen Baum springen; **to ~ through the traffic** sich durch den Verkehr schlängeln

dodgem ['dɒdʒəm] N (Auto)scooter m; **did you go on the ~s?** bist du (Auto)scooter gefahren?

dodger ['dɒdʒə'] **N a** (= trickster) Schlawiner m (inf) → **artful b** (Naut) Wetterschutz m

dodgery ['dɒdʒərɪ] N (= trick) Kniff m, Trick m; (= fib) Schwindel m

dodgy ['dɒdʒɪ] ADJ (Brit, inf) **a** (= dubious, uncertain) person zweifelhaft, zwielichtig; deal, business, practices zwielichtig; area, loan zweifelhaft; plan unsicher; situation vertrackt (inf), verzwickt (inf); weather unbeständig; **there's something ~ about him** er ist nicht ganz koscher (inf); **there's something ~ about this business** die Sache ist nicht ganz astrein (inf); **it's a ~ business** (= uncertain) es ist eine unsichere Sache; **he's on ~ ground** er befindet sich auf unsicherem Boden

b (= weak) back, heart schwach; (= damaged) tyre, car/boat etc part defekt; **he has a ~ stomach from eating oysters** er hat Austern gegessen und sich damit den Magen verdorben

c (= near-the-knuckle) remark anstößig

dodo ['dəʊdəʊ] **N a** Dodo m, Dronte f; **as dead as a ~** mausetot **b** (US, inf, = silly person) Trottel m (inf)

DOE a (Brit) abbr of **Department of the Environment** Umweltministerium nt **b** (US) abbr of **Department of Energy** Energieministerium nt

doe [dəʊ] N (roe deer) Reh nt, Ricke f; (red deer) Hirschkuh f; (rabbit) (Kaninchen)weibchen nt; (hare) Häsin f

doer ['du:ə'] **N a** (= author of deed) Täter(in) m(f); **he's a great ~ of crosswords** (inf) er macht sehr gerne Kreuzworträtsel **b** (= active person) Mann m/Frau f der Tat, Macher(in) m(f) (inf); **he's more of a ~ than a thinker** er ist eher ein Mann der Tat als der Theorie

does [dʌz] 3rd pers sing of **do**²

doeskin ['dəʊskɪn] N Rehfell nt; (treated) Rehleder nt

doesn't ['dʌznt] contr of **does not**

doff [dɒf] VT hat ziehen, lüften; (old) garment ablegen

dog [dɒg] **N a** Hund m; **the ~s** (Brit, Sport) das Hunderennen

b (fig) **it's a ~'s life** es ist ein Hundeleben; **to go to the ~s** (person, business, district, institution) vor die Hunde gehen (inf); **give a ~ a bad name (and hang him)** wer einmal ins Gerede or in Verruf kommt(, dem hängt das sein Leben lang an); **~ in the manger** (Brit) Spielverderber(in) m(f); **~-in-the-manger attitude** (Brit) missgünstige Einstellung; **every ~ has his day** jeder hat einmal Glück im Leben; **it's (a case of) ~ eat ~** es ist ein Kampf aller gegen alle; **~-eat-dog society** Ellenbogengesellschaft f; **you can't teach an old ~ new tricks** der Mensch ist ein Gewohnheitstier; **let sleeping ~s lie** schlafende Hunde soll man nicht we-

cken; **to put on the ~** (dated US, inf) auf fein machen (inf); **~'s dinner** or **breakfast** (inf) Schlamassel m (inf); **he made a complete ~'s breakfast of it** (inf) er hat dabei totalen Mist gebaut (inf); **to work like a ~** (inf) wie ein Pferd arbeiten (inf)

c (= male fox, wolf) Rüde m

d (inf, = man) **lucky ~** Glückspilz m; **dirty ~** gemeiner Hund; **sly ~** gerissener Hund (inf); **there's life in the old ~ yet** noch kann man ihn nicht zum alten Eisen werfen; **Tom Jones, you old ~!** Tom Jones, du alter Schwerenöter! → **top dog**

e (Tech, = clamp) Klammer f

f (US, inf, = failure) Pleite f (inf)

g (inf, = unattractive woman) Schreckschraube f (inf)

VT **a** (= follow closely) **to ~ sb** or **sb's footsteps** jdm hart auf den Fersen sein/bleiben

b (= harass) verfolgen; **~ged by controversy/injury** von Kontroversen/Verletzungen verfolgt

dog: dog basket N Hundekorb m; **dog biscuit** N Hundekuchen m; **dog breeder** N Hundezüchter(in) m(f); **dog breeding** N Hundezucht f; **dogcart** N Dogcart m; **dog-cheap** ADJ, ADV (inf) spottbillig (inf); **dog collar** N (lit) Hundehalsband nt; (vicar's) Kollar nt; **dog days** PL Hundstage pl; **dog-eared** ['dɒgɪəd] ADJ mit Eselsohren; **dog-end** N (inf) Kippe f (inf); **dog fancier** N Hundefreund(in) m(f); (= breeder, seller) Hundezüchter(in) m(f); **dogfight** N (Aviat) Luftkampf m; **dogfish** N Hundshai m; **dog food** N Hundefutter nt; **dog fox** N Fuchsrüde m

dogged ['dɒgɪd] ADJ person zäh, beharrlich; determination, resistance, pursuit, battle, refusal hartnäckig; persistence zäh; **they have been ~ in their search** sie haben beharrlich gesucht

doggedly ['dɒgɪdlɪ] ADV beharrlich; fight also hartnäckig; **~ determined** hartnäckig

doggedness ['dɒgɪdnɪs] N Beharrlichkeit f, Zähigkeit f; (of resistance, pursuit, refusal) Hartnäckigkeit f

doggerel ['dɒgərəl] N (also **doggerel verse**) Knittelvers m

doggie, doggy ['dɒgɪ] **N** (inf) kleiner Hund, Hündchen nt **ADJ** Hunde-; (= dog loving) hundenärrisch; **I'm not really a ~ person** ich bin kein großer Freund von Hunden; **~ smell** Hundegeruch m

doggie bag N (Beutel für) Essensreste, die nach Hause mitgenommen werden

doggo ['dɒgəʊ] ADV (inf) **to lie ~** sich nicht mucksen (inf); (= go underground) von der Bildfläche verschwinden (inf)

doggone [ˌdɒgˈgɒn] INTERJ (US, inf) **~ (it)!** verdammt noch mal! (inf)

doggoned [ˌdɒgˈgɒn(d)] ADJ (US, inf) verdammt (inf)

doggy N (inf) = **doggie**

doggy fashion ADV (inf) **have sex** wie die Hunde

doggy paddle N **to do (the) ~** paddeln, Hundepaddeln machen

dog: dog handler N Hundeführer(in) m(f); **doghouse** N Hundehütte f; **he's in the ~** (inf) er ist in Ungnade; (with wife) bei ihm hängt der Haussegen schief; **dog iron** N Kaminbock m; **dog Latin** N Küchenlatein nt; **doglead** N Hundeleine f; **dogleg** N Knick m; (in road also) scharfe Kurve; (in pipe also) starke Krümmung; **dog licence**, (US) **dog license** N Hundemarke f; **a ~ costs ...** die Hundesteuer beträgt ...; **doglike** ADJ hundeähnlich; **~ devotion** hündische Ergebenheit

dogma ['dɒgmə] N Dogma nt

dogmatic [dɒgˈmætɪk] ADJ dogmatisch; **~ theology** Dogmatik f; **to be very ~ about sth** in etw (dat) sehr dogmatisch sein

dogmatically [dɒgˈmætɪkəlɪ] ADV dogmatisch

dogmatism ['dɒgmətɪzəm] N Dogmatismus m

dogmatize ['dɒgmətaɪz] VTI (Rel, fig) dogmatisieren

do-gooder ['du:'gʊdə'] N (pej) Weltverbesserer m, Weltverbesserin f

dog: dog paddle N = **doggy paddle**; **dog rose** N Hundsrose f

dogsbody ['dɒgzbɒdɪ] N (Brit) **she's/he's the general ~** sie/er ist (das) Mädchen für alles

dog: dog show N Hundeausstellung f; **dogsled** N Hundeschlitten m; **Dog Star** N Hundsstern m, Sirius m; **dog's-tooth check** [ˌdɒgztu:θˈtʃek], **dog-tooth check** N Hahnentrittmuster nt; **dog tag** N (US, Mil inf) Erkennungsmarke f, Hundemarke f (inf); **dog-tired** ADJ hundemüde; **dogtooth** N (Archit) Hundszahn m; **dog track** N Hunderennbahn f; **dogtrot** N gemächlicher or leichter Trott; **dogwatch** N (Naut) Hundewache f; **dogwood** N Hartriegel m, Hornstrauch m

doily ['dɔɪlɪ] N (Spitzen- or Zier)deckchen nt

doing ['du:ɪŋ] N **a** Tun nt; **this is your ~** das ist dein Werk; **it was none of my ~** ich hatte nichts damit zu tun; **that takes some ~** da gehört (schon) etwas dazu; **there is a difference between ~ and saying** zwischen Taten und Worten besteht ein Unterschied **b doings** PL (inf) Handlungen pl, Taten pl **c doings** PL (inf Brit: = thing) Dingsbums nt (inf)

do-it-yourself ['du:ɪtjə'self] ADJ, N = **DIY**

dol abbr of **dollar**

Dolby® ['dɒlbɪ] N Dolby® nt

doldrums ['dɒldrəmz] PL **a** (Geog, area) Kalmengürtel m or -zone f; (weather) Windstille f, Kalme f **b to be in the ~** (people) Trübsal blasen (inf), (business etc) in einer Flaute stecken

dole [dəʊl] N (Brit inf) Arbeitslosenunterstützung f, Alu f (inf), Stütze f (inf); **to go/be on the ~** stempeln (gehen)

► **dole out** VT sep austeilen, verteilen

doleful ['dəʊlfʊl] ADJ person, face, look, expression tieftraurig, trübselig; eyes, voice, sigh tieftraurig; song klagend

dolefully ['dəʊlfəlɪ] ADV tieftraurig, trübselig

dole money N (Brit inf) Arbeitslosenunterstützung f, Stütze f (inf)

dolichocephalic ['dɒlɪkəʊse'fælɪk] ADJ dolichozephal

doll [dɒl] **N a** Puppe f; **~'s pram** (Brit) or **baby carriage** (US) Puppenwagen m **b** (dated esp US inf, = girl) Mädchen nt; (= pretty girl) Puppe f (inf); **thanks Betty, you're a ~** danke Betty, du bist klasse (inf)

► **doll up** VT sep (inf) herausputzen; **to doll oneself up, to get dolled up** sich aufdonnern (inf); **she was dolled up for the party** sie war für die Party aufgedonnert (inf)

dollar ['dɒlə'] N Dollar m

dollar: dollar area N Dollarraum m, Dollarblock m; **dollar bill** N Dollarnote f; **dollar diplomacy** N Finanzdiplomatie f; **dollar gap** N Dollarlücke f; **dollar rate** N Dollarkurs m; **dollar sign** N Dollarzeichen nt

dollish ['dɒlɪʃ] ADJ puppenhaft

dollop ['dɒləp] N (inf) Schlag m (inf)

doll's house, (US) **doll house** N Puppenhaus nt

dolly ['dɒlɪ] **N a** (inf, = doll) Püppchen nt **b** (= wheeled frame) (Transport)wagen m; (Film, TV) Dolly m, Kamerawagen m; (Rail) Schmalspurrangierlokomotive f **c** (for washing clothes) Wäschestampfer m **d** (Tech, for rivet) Gegenhalter m **e** (inf: = girl) Puppe f **f** (Sport inf) lahmer Ball (inf) **ADJ** (Sport inf) shot lahm; catch leicht

► **dolly in** N (Film, TV) VT sep vorfahren VI vorfahren

► **dolly out** (Film, TV) VT sep zurückfahren VI zurückfahren

dolly bird N (dated Brit inf) Puppe f ADJ attr puppig

dolman ['dɒlmən] N Dolman m; **~ sleeve** angeschnittener Ärmel

dolomite ['dɒləmaɪt] N Dolomit m; **the Dolomites** die Dolomiten pl

dolphin ['dɒlfɪn] N Delphin *m*, Delfin *m*

dolphinarium [ˌdɒlfɪ'nɛərɪəm] N Delphinarium *nt*, Delfinarium *nt*

dolt [dəʊlt] N Tölpel *m*

doltish ['dəʊltɪʃ] ADJ tölpelhaft, dumm

domain [dəʊ'meɪn] N **a** (*lit*, *= estate*) Gut *nt*; (*belonging to state, Crown*) Domäne *f*; **the Crown ~s** die Ländereien der Krone **b** (*fig*) Domäne *f* → **public c** (*Math*) Funktionsbereich *m* **d** (*Comput*) Domäne *f*, Domain *nt*

domain name N (*Comput*) Domainname *m*

dome [dəʊm] N **a** (*Archit, on building*) Kuppel *f* **b** (*of heaven, skull*) Gewölbe *nt*; (*of hill*) Kuppe *f*; (*of branches*) Kuppel *f* **c** (*lid, cover etc*) Haube *f*

domed [dəʊmd] ADJ *forehead, ceiling* gewölbt; *roof* kuppelförmig; **~ stadium** Stadion *nt* mit Kuppeldach

domestic [də'mestɪk] ADJ **a** (*= household*) häuslich; **the ~ arrangements** die häusliche Situation; **~ chores** *or* **duties** Hausarbeit *f*; **his wife has always taken care of his ~ needs** seine Frau hat zu Hause immer alles für ihn gemacht; **everything of a ~ nature** alles, was den Haushalt angeht; **she was never very ~, she was never a very ~ sort of person** sie war nie ein sehr häuslicher Mensch; **~ activities** *or* **things take up a lot of time** der Haushalt nimmt viel Zeit in Anspruch; **in the interests of ~ harmony** im Interesse des Familienfriedens; **~ bliss** häusliches Glück; **~ quarrel** Ehekrach *m*; **~ appliances** Haushaltsgeräte *pl*; **for ~ use** für den Hausgebrauch; **~ rubbish** (*Brit*) *or* **garbage** (*US*) Hausmüll *m* **b** (*esp Pol, Comm, = within a country*) consumption, production, spending, sales, demand *etc* inländisch; *the Inland; currency inländisch; problems* im Inland; *news* aus dem Inland; *issues, affairs* innenpolitisch; **he was more interested in foreign affairs than in ~ affairs** er interessierte sich mehr für Außenpolitik als für Innenpolitik **N** **a** (*= servant*) Hausangestellte(r) *mf* **b** (*inf: = quarrel*) Ehekrach *m*

domestically [də'mestɪkəlɪ] ADV **a** (*esp Pol, Comm*) inländisch; *grown, produced* im Inland; **to be ~ owned** inländischen/einen inländischen Besitzer haben; **~ and internationally** im In- und Ausland **b** (*= in the home*) im Haushalt; **~ inclined** häuslich veranlagt

domestic animal N Haustier *nt*

domesticate [də'mestɪkeɪt] VT *wild animal* domestizieren; (*hum*) *person* domestizieren; (*= house-train*) *dog, cat* stubenrein machen

domesticated [də'mestɪkeɪtɪd] ADJ *animal, species* domestiziert; *person* häuslich

domestication [dəmestɪ'keɪʃən] N (*of wild animal, hum: of person*) Domestikation *f*, Domestizierung *f*; **the ~ of cats doesn't take long** es dauert nicht lange, bis man Katzen stubenrein gemacht hat

domestic: domestic cat N Hauskatze *f*; **domestic dog** N Haushund *m*; **domestic economy** N (*Pol*) Binnenwirtschaft *f*; **domestic flight** N Inlandflug *m*; **domestic fuel** N Brennstoff *m* für private Haushalte

domesticity [ˌdəʊmes'tɪsɪtɪ] N häusliches Leben

domestic: domestic market N (*Pol, Comm*) Binnenmarkt *m*; **domestic policy, domestic politics** N Innenpolitik *f*; **domestic rates** PL (*Brit Econ, Hist*) Kommunalabgaben *pl*; **domestic science** N (*esp old Brit Sch*) Hauswirtschaftslehre *f*; **~ college/teacher** (*esp old Brit, Sch*) Hauswirtschaftsschule *f*/-lehrer(in) *m(f)*; **domestic servant** N Hausangestellte(r) *mf*; **domestic service** N Arbeit *f* als Hausangestellte(r); **to be in ~** als Hausangestellte(r) arbeiten; **domestic staff** N Hauspersonal *nt*; **domestic supply** N Hausanschluss *m*; **they had no ~ of water** sie hatten keinen Wasseranschluss im Haus; **domestic violence** N Gewalt *f* in der Familie; **one in ten women is a victim of ~** eine von zehn Frauen ist Opfer

häuslicher Gewalt *or* wird zu Hause misshandelt

domicile ['dɒmɪsaɪl] (*form*) **N** (*Admin*) Wohnsitz *m*; (*Fin*) Zahlungs- *or* Erfüllungsort *m* **VT** (*Admin*) unterbringen (*with* bei, *in* +*dat*); (*Fin*) domizilieren (*at* bei); **he is currently ~d in Berlin** er ist zur Zeit in Berlin wohnhaft (*form*)

domiciliary [ˌdɒmɪ'sɪlɪərɪ] ADJ *care* häuslich, im Haus; **~ visit** (*of doctor*) Hausbesuch *m*; **~ expenses** Haushaltskosten *pl*

dominance ['dɒmɪnəns] N Vorherrschaft *f* (*over* über +*acc*), Dominanz *f* (*over* über +*acc*) (*also Biol*)

dominant ['dɒmɪnənt] ADJ **a** *person, role, class, feature* dominierend; *partner, figure, position, issue, personality* dominierend, beherrschend; *nation, culture, ideology, species, trend, theme* dominierend, vorherrschend; *gene* dominant; **the ~ factor** der wichtigste *or* dominierende Faktor; **to be ~** *or* **the ~ force in sth** etw dominieren; **they are ~ in the world market** sie beherrschen den Weltmarkt; **~ male** (*animal*) männliches Leittier; (*fig hum, man*) Platzhirsch *m* **b** (*Mus*) dominant; **~ seventh** Dominantseptakkord *m* **N a** (*Biol*) dominantes Gen **b** (*Mus*) Dominante *f*

dominate ['dɒmɪneɪt] VI dominieren VT beherrschen; (*colour, feature*) beherrschen, dominieren; (*species, gene*) dominieren

domination [ˌdɒmɪ'neɪʃən] N (Vor)herrschaft *f*; **under the ~ of the Romans** unter römischer Herrschaft; **his ~ of his younger brothers** sein dominierendes Verhalten seinen jüngeren Brüdern gegenüber; **her ~ of the conversation/game** die Tatsache, dass sie die Unterhaltung/das Spiel beherrschte

dominatrix [ˌdɒmɪ'neɪtrɪks] N *pl* **dominatrices** *or* **dominatrixes** Domina *f*

domineer [ˌdɒmɪ'nɪə'] VI tyrannisieren (*over sb* jdn)

domineering [ˌdɒmɪ'nɪərɪŋ] ADJ herrisch; *mother-in-law, husband etc also* herrschsüchtig

Dominican[1] [də'mɪnɪkən] (*Geog*) ADJ dominikanisch **N** Dominikaner(in) *m(f)*

Dominican[2] (*Eccl*) **N** Dominikaner *m* ADJ Dominikaner-, dominikanisch; **~ monastery** Dominikanerkloster *nt*

Dominican Republic N Dominikanische Republik

dominion [də'mɪnɪən] N **a** *no pl* Herrschaft *f* (*over* über +*acc*); **to have ~ over sb** Macht über jdn haben **b** (*= territory*) Herrschaftsgebiet *nt*; **overseas ~s** überseeische Gebiete *pl*; **the Dominion of Canada** das Dominion Kanada

Dominion Day N *gesetzlicher Feiertag in Kanada zur Erinnerung an die Übertragung der vollen politischen Autonomie*

domino ['dɒmɪnəʊ] N *pl* **-es a** Domino(stein) *m*; **a game of ~es** ein Dominospiel *nt*; **to play ~es** Domino spielen **b** (*= costume, mask*) Domino *m*

domino effect N Dominowirkung *f* or -effekt *m*

domino theory N Dominoeffekt *m*

don[1] [dɒn] N (*Brit, Univ*) *Universitätsdozent(in) besonders in Oxford und Cambridge*

don[2] VT *garment* anziehen, anlegen (*dated*); *hat* aufsetzen

donate [də'neɪt] VT *money, blood, kidney* spenden; *gifts to a charity also* stiften; *time* zur Verfügung stellen VI spenden; **to ~ to charity** für wohltätige Zwecke spenden

donation [də'neɪʃən] N (*= act of giving: of money, gifts, blood*) Spenden *nt*; (*= gift*) Spende *f*; **to make a ~ of 50p/£10,000** 50 Pence/£ 10.000 spenden

done [dʌn] *ptp of* **do**[2] ADJ **a** (*= finished*) *work* erledigt; (*= cooked*) *vegetables* gar; *meat* durch; *cake* durchgebacken; **to get sth ~** (*= finished*) etw fertig kriegen; **is it ~ yet?** ist es schon erledigt?; **~!** (*= agreed*) abgemacht!; **a ~ deal** (*US*) eine abgekartete Sache **b** (*Brit inf, = tired out*) **I'm ~ (in)** ich bin geschafft (*inf*) or fertig **c** **it's not**

the ~ thing, that's not ~ das tut man nicht (*inf, = used up*) **the butter is (all) ~** die Butter ist alle

donee [dəʊ'niː] N (*Jur*) Schenkungsempfänger(in) *m(f)*, Beschenkte(r) *mf*

doner kebab ['dɒnəkə'bæb] N Döner(kebab) *m*

dong [dɒŋ] N **a** (*= sound of bell*) Bimbam *nt* **b** (*= currency*) Dong *m* **c** (*sl: = penis*) Apparat *m* (*inf*)

dongle ['dɒŋgl] N (*Comput*) Dongle *m*, Kopierschutzstecker *m*

Don Juan [ˌdɒn'dʒuːən] N (*lit, fig*) Don Juan *m*

donkey ['dɒŋkɪ] N Esel *m*

donkey: donkey derby N Eselrennen *nt*; **donkey engine** N (*Rail*) (kleines) Hilfsaggregat; **donkey jacket** N *dicke (gefütterte) Jacke*; **donkey ride** N Ritt *m* auf dem/einem Esel, Eselsritt *m*

donkey's years ['dɒŋkɪz'jɜːz] PL (*inf*) ewig und drei Tage (*inf*), eine Ewigkeit (*inf*); **she's been here for ~** (*inf*) sie ist schon ewig und drei Tage (*inf*) or eine Ewigkeit hier

donkey-work ['dɒŋkɪwɜːk] N Routinearbeit *f*, Dreckarbeit *f* (*inf*)

donnish ['dɒnɪʃ] (*Brit: usu pej*) ADJ professoral; **a ~ type** ein typischer Gelehrter

donor ['dəʊnə'] N (*Med, to charity*) Spender(in) *m(f)*

donor card N Organspenderausweis *m*

donor organ N Spenderorgan *nt*

do-nothing ['duː'nʌθɪŋ] **N** Faulenzer(in) *m(f)*, Nichtstuer(in) *m(f)* ADJ faul

don't [dəʊnt] *contr of* **do not**

don't-know [ˌdəʊnt'nəʊ] N (*in opinion poll*) **30% were ~** 30% hatten keine Meinung

donut ['dəʊnʌt] N (*esp US*) = **doughnut**

doodah ['duːdɑː], (*US*) **doodad** ['duːdæd] N (*inf*) Dingsbums *nt* (*inf*), Dingsda *nt* (*inf*)

doodle ['duːdl] VI Männchen malen VT kritzeln N Gekritzel *nt*

doodlebug ['duːdlbʌg] N **a** (*Brit, = bomb*) V1-Rakete *f* **b** (*US, = larva*) Ameisenlarve *f*

doohickey ['duːhɪkɪ] N (*US, inf, = thingummy*) Dings(bums) *nt*

doolally [duː'lælɪ] ADJ (*inf*) plemplem *pred* (*inf*)

doom [duːm] **N a** (*= fate*) Schicksal *nt*; (*= ruin*) Verhängnis *nt*; **to go to one's ~** seinem Verhängnis entgegengehen; **to send sb to his ~** jdn ins Verhängnis stürzen; **he met his ~** das Schicksal ereilte ihn; **~ and gloom** tiefster Pessimismus; **it's all ~ and gloom with him at the moment** er sieht zur Zeit alles nur schwarz; **it's not all gloom and ~** so schlimm ist es ja alles gar nicht VT verurteilen, verdammen; **to be ~ed** verloren sein; **the project was ~ed from the start** das Vorhaben war von Anfang an zum Scheitern verurteilt; **the ~ed ship** das dem Untergang geweihte Schiff; **~ed to die** dem Tode geweiht; **~ed to failure** zum Scheitern verurteilt; **this country was ~ed to become a second-rate nation** dieses Land war dazu verdammt, zur Zweitrangigkeit abzusinken

doomsday ['duːmzdeɪ] N der Jüngste Tag; **... otherwise we'll be here till ~** (*inf*) ... sonst sind wir in zwanzig Jahren noch hier

door [dɔː'] N **a** Tür *f*; (*= entrance: to cinema etc*) Eingang *m*; **there's someone at the ~** da ist jemand an der Tür; **was that the ~?** hat es geklingelt/geklopft?; **to answer the ~** die Tür aufmachen; **to see sb to the ~** jdn zur Tür bringen; **to stand in the ~** in der Tür stehen; **to be on the ~** (*bouncer etc*) Türsteher sein; (*collecting ticket money etc*) Türdienst haben; **to pay at the ~** (*Theat etc*) an der (Abend)kasse zahlen; **"doors open 2.20"** „Einlass 14.20 Uhr“; **to go from ~ to ~** (*= salesman etc*) von Tür zu Tür gehen, Klinken putzen (*inf*); **he lives three ~s away** er wohnt drei Häuser weiter; **it takes 7 hours from ~ to ~** man braucht 7 Stunden von Tür zu Tür

b (*phrases*) **by** *or* **through the back ~** durch ein Hintertürchen; **to have a foot** *or* **toe in the ~** mit einem Fuß *or* Bein drin sein; **to lay sth at sb's ~** jdm etw vorwerfen *or* anlasten; **to be at death's ~** an der Schwelle des Todes stehen (*geh*); **to leave the ~ open to** *or* **for further negotiations** die Tür zu weiteren *or* für weitere Verhandlungen offen lassen; **to open the ~ to sth** einer Sache (*dat*) Tür und Tor öffnen; **to show sb the ~** jdm die Tür weisen; **to shut** *or* **slam the ~ in sb's face** jdm die Tür vor der Nase zumachen; **to shut** *or* **close the ~ on sth** etw ausschließen; **we don't want to shut any ~s** wir möchten uns (*dat*) keine Möglichkeiten verbauen; **when one ~ shuts, another ~ opens** (*prov*) irgendwie geht es immer weiter; **out of ~s** im Freien; **behind closed ~s** hinter verschlossenen Türen

door *in cpds* Tür-; **doorbell** N Türglocke *or* -klingel *f*; **there's the ~** es hat geklingelt; **door chain** N Sicherheitskette *f*

do-or-die ['duːɔː'daɪ] ADJ verbissen

door: doorframe N Türrahmen *m*; **doorhandle** N Türklinke *f*; (= *knob*) Türknauf *m*; **doorkeeper** N (*of hotel, block of flats*) Portier *m*; **doorknob** N Türknauf *m*; **doorknocker** N Türklopfer *m*; **doorman** N Portier *m*; **doormat** N Fußmatte *f*, Abtreter *m*; (*fig*) Fußabtreter *m*; **door money** N Eintrittsgeld *nt*; **doornail** N **as dead as a ~** mausetot; **door opener** N Türöffner *m*; **doorplate** N Türschild *nt*; **doorpost** N Türpfosten *m*; **deaf as a ~** stocktaub; **doorscraper** N Kratzeisen *nt*, Fußabstreifer *m* (*aus Metall*); **doorstep** N Eingangsstufe *f*; (*hum*: = *hunk of bread*) dicke Scheibe Brot; **the bus stop is just on my ~** (*fig*) die Bushaltestelle ist direkt vor meiner Tür **VT** (*Brit, Press*) zu Hause aufsuchen und interviewen; (*Pol*) zu Hause besuchen, um Wahlwerbung zu machen; **doorstepping** ['dɔːstepɪŋ] N , *no pl* (*Brit, Press*) *agressive Interviewtechnik, bei der Journalisten unangemeldet und ungebeten jdn zu Hause aufsuchen* (*Pol*) *Methode der Wahlwerbung, bei der Politiker von Haus zu Haus gehen, um die Bewohner für ihre Partei zu gewinnen*; **doorstop(per)** N Türanschlag *m*; **door-to-door** ADJ *attr*, **door to door** ADJ *pred* **a ~ salesman** Vertreter *m* **b** *delivery* von Haus zu Haus; **how's that for ~ service?** na, ist das nicht ein Service?; **police are carrying out ~ inquiries** die Polizei befragt alle Anwohner; **doorway** N (*of room*) Tür *f*; (*of building, shop*) Eingang *m*; (*fig, to success etc*) Weg *m*

dope [dəʊp] **N a** *no pl* (*inf*, = *drugs*) Rauschgift *nt*, Stoff *m* (*inf*), Drogen *pl*; (*Sport*) Aufputschmittel *nt*; **he failed a ~ test** er fiel bei der Dopingkontrolle auf **b** *no pl* (*inf*, = *information*) Information(en) *f(pl)*; **to have ~ on sb** Informationen über jdn haben **c** (*inf*, = *stupid person*) Esel *m* (*inf*), Trottel *m* (*inf*) **d** (= *varnish*) Lack *m* **e** (*for explosives*) Benzinzusatz(mittel *nt*) *m* **VT** *person*; *food, drink* präparieren, ein Betäubungsmittel untermischen (+*dat*)

▶**dope up** VT **to be doped up on** *or* **with Valium®** (*inf*) mit Valium® voll gestopft sein (*inf*)

dope: dopehead N (*inf*) Junkie *m* (*inf*); **dope peddler, dope pusher** N Drogenhändler(in) *m(f)*, Dealer(in) *m(f)* (*inf*); **dope test** N (*inf Sport*) Dopingkontrolle *f*

dopey, dopy ['dəʊpɪ] ADJ (+*er*) (*inf*, = *stupid*) bekloppt (*inf*), blöd (*inf*); (= *sleepy, half-drugged*) benommen, benebelt (*inf*)

doping ['dəʊpɪŋ] N (*Sport*) Doping *nt*

Doppler effect ['dɒplər‚fekt] N Dopplereffekt *m*

Doric ['dɒrɪk] ADJ (*Archit*) dorisch

dork [dɔːk] N (*inf pej*) Idiot *m*, Trottel *m* (*both inf pej*)

dorm [dɔːm] (*inf*) *abbr of* **dormitory**

dormancy ['dɔːmənsɪ] N (*form*: = *inactivity*) (*of volcano*) Untätigkeit *f*; (*of plant*) Ruhe *f*; (*of virus*) Inaktivität *f*

dormant ['dɔːmənt] ADJ *volcano* untätig; *animal, plant, bud* ruhend; (*Banking*) *account* ruhend; *energy* verborgen, latent; *passion* schlummernd; **~ state** Ruhezustand *m*; **to remain ~** ruhen; (*disease, virus*) schlummern; **the ~ season** die Ruhezeit; **to lie ~** (*project, idea, work of art*) brachliegen; **to let a matter lie ~** eine Sache ruhen *or* liegen lassen

dormer (window) ['dɔːmə('wɪndəʊ)] N Mansardenfenster *nt*

dormice ['dɔːmaɪs] *pl of* **dormouse**

dormitory ['dɔːmɪtrɪ] N Schlafsaal *m*; (*US*, = *building*) Wohnheim *nt*; **~ suburb** *or* **town** Schlafstadt *f*

Dormobile® ['dɔːməbiːl] N Wohnmobil *nt*, Campingbus *m*

dormouse ['dɔːmaʊs] N *pl* **dormice** Haselmaus *f*

Dors (*Brit*) *abbr of* **Dorset**

dorsal ['dɔːsl] ADJ Rücken-, dorsal (*spec*) N (*Phon*) Dorsal(laut) *m*

dorsal fin N Rückenflosse *f*

dory ['dɔːrɪ] N (*US*) *Ruderboot mit spitzem Bug und schmalem Heck*

DOS [dɒs] (*Comput*) *abbr of* **disk operating system** DOS *nt*

dosage ['dəʊsɪdʒ] N Dosis *f*; (= *giving of medicine*) Dosierung *f*; **~ meter** Dosimeter *nt*

dose [dəʊs] N **a** (*Med*) Dosis *f*; (*fig, of punishment etc*) Ration *f*; **give him a ~ of medicine** gib ihm Medizin; **he needs a ~ of his own medicine** (*fig*) man sollte es ihm mit gleicher Münze heimzahlen; **in small/large ~s** (*fig*) in kleinen/großen Mengen; **she's all right in small ~s** sie ist nur (für) kurze Zeit zu ertragen **b** (*inf*, = *venereal disease*) Tripper *m*; **to catch a ~** sich (*dat*) etwas holen (*inf*), sich (*dat*) den Tripper holen **c** (*inf*, = *bout of illness*) Anfall *m*; **she's just had a ~ of the flu** sie hat gerade Grippe gehabt **VT** *person* Arznei geben (+*dat*); **I've tried dosing myself with cough mixture** ich habe versucht, mich mit Hustensaft zu kurieren

dosh [dɒʃ] N (*inf*, = *money*) Moos *nt* (*sl*), Knete *f* (*sl*)

doss [dɒs] (*Brit, inf*) N Schlafplatz *m*, Bleibe *f* (*inf*) **VI** (*also* **doss down**) pennen (*inf*), sich hinhauen (*inf*); **to ~ down for the night** sich für die Nacht einquartieren (*inf*)

dosser ['dɒsə'] N (*Brit, inf*) Penner(in) *m(f)* (*inf*), Stadtstreicher(in) *m(f)*

dosshouse ['dɒshaʊs] N (*Brit, inf*) Penne *f* (*inf*), Obdachlosenheim *nt*

dossier ['dɒsɪeɪ] N Dossier *m or nt*; **they are keeping a ~ on him** sie haben ein Dossier über ihn angelegt

dost [dʌst] (*obs*) *2nd pers sing of* **do²**

DOT (*US*) *abbr of* **Department of Transportation** Verkehrsministerium *nt*

dot [dɒt] N **a** Punkt *m*; (*on material*) Tupfen *m*, Punkt *m*; **morse code is made up of ~s and dashes** das Morsealphabet besteht aus kurzen und langen Signalen; **~, dash, ~** (*morse*) kurz, lang, kurz; **~, ~, ~** (*in punctuation*) drei Punkte **b** (*phrases*) **to arrive on the ~** auf die Minute pünktlich (an)kommen; **on the ~ of 9pm** um Punkt 21 Uhr; **at 3 o'clock on the ~** haargenau *or* auf die Minute genau um 3 Uhr; **she has lived here since the year ~** (*Brit, inf*) sie lebt schon ewig *or* schon seit ewigen Zeiten hier **VT a** **to ~ an i** einen i-Punkt setzen; **to ~ one's i's and cross one's t's** (*fig*) peinlich genau *or* penibel sein; **a ~ted bow tie** eine gepunktete Fliege; **the ~ted line** punktierte Linie; **to tear along the ~ted line** an der *or* entlang der punktierten Linie abtrennen; **to sign on the ~ted line** (*fig*) seine formelle Zustimmung geben, formell zustimmen **b** (= *sprinkle*) verstreuen; **a field ~ted with flowers** ein mit Blumen übersätes Feld; **hotels ~ted around the island** über die Insel verstreute Hotels; **pictures ~ted around the room** im Zimmer verteilte Bilder **c** **to ~ sb one** (*inf*) jdm eine langen (*inf*)

dotage ['dəʊtɪdʒ] N Senilität *f*, Altersschwäche *f*; **to be in one's ~** in seiner zweiten Kindheit sein, senil sein; **he's spending his ~ in the south of France** er verbringt seinen Lebensabend in Südfrankreich

dotcom, dot.com [dɒt'kɒm] N (*Comput*) Internetfirma *f*

dot command N (*Comput*) Punktbefehl *m*

dote on ['dəʊtɒn] VI +*prep obj* abgöttisch lieben

dotgone, dot.gone [dɒtgɒn] N (*Comput*) gescheiterte Internetfirma

doth [dʌθ] (*obs*) *3rd pers sing of* **do²**

doting ['dəʊtɪŋ] ADJ **her ~ parents** ihre sie abgöttisch liebenden Eltern; **a ~ old fool** ein vernarrter alter Trottel

dot matrix (printer) N Matrixdrucker *m*, Nadeldrucker *m*

dottle ['dɒtl] N Tabakrest *m*

dotty ['dɒtɪ] ADJ (+*er*) (*Brit, inf*) kauzig, schrullig; **to be ~ about sb/sth** (= *like*) nach jdm/etw verrückt sein

double ['dʌbl] ADV **a** (= *twice as much*) *charge, cost, pay* doppelt so viel; *count* doppelt; **~ the size (of)** doppelt so groß (wie); **~ the amount** doppelt so viel; **we paid her ~ what she was getting before** wir zahlten ihr das Doppelte von dem, was sie vorher bekam; **they charge ~ what they used to** sie berechnen doppelt so viel wie früher; **he took ~ the time it took me** er brauchte doppelt so lange wie ich; **he's ~ your age** er ist doppelt so alt wie du; **six is twelve** zweimal sechs ist zwölf; **to see ~** doppelt sehen **b** **to bend ~** sich krümmen; **she was bent ~ with laughter/pain** sie krümmte sich vor Lachen/Schmerzen; **to fold sth ~** etw einmal falten
ADJ a (= *twice as much*) doppelt; **to pay a ~ amount** das Doppelte bezahlen; **a ~ gin/whisky** *etc* ein doppelter Gin/Whisky *etc* **b** (= *having two similar parts, in pairs*) Doppel-; **~ bottom** doppelter Boden; **the egg had a ~ yolk** das Ei hatte zwei Dotter; **it is spelled with a ~ 'p'** es wird mit Doppel-p *or* mit zwei p geschrieben; **my phone number is 9, ~ 3, 2, 4** meine Telefonnummer ist neun drei drei zwei vier *or* neun dreiunddreißig vierundzwanzig **c** (*Bot*) *flower* gefüllt **N a** (= *twice a quantity, number, size etc*) das Doppelte, das Zweifache; **~ or quits** doppelt oder nichts; **he earns the ~ of what I do** er verdient doppelt so viel wie ich **b** (= *person*) Ebenbild *nt*, Doppelgänger(in) *m(f)*; (*Film, Theat*, = *stand-in*) Double *nt*; (= *actor taking two parts*) Schauspieler, der eine Doppelrolle spielt; **I saw your ~** ich habe einen Doppelgänger/eine Doppelgängerin von dir gesehen; **I've got the ~ of that clock** ich habe genau die gleiche Uhr **c** **at the ~** (*also Mil*) im Laufschritt; (*fig*) im Eiltempo; **on the ~** (*fig*) auf der Stelle **d** (*Cards*, = *increase*) Verdoppelung *f*; (*Bridge*) Kontra *nt*; (= *hand*) *Blatt, das die Verdoppelung/das Kontra rechtfertigt* (*in racing*) Doppelwette *f*; (*in dice*) Pasch *m*; (*in dominoes*) Doppelstein *m*, Pasch *m* **VT a** (= *increase twofold*) verdoppeln **b** (= *fold in two*) *piece of paper* (einmal) falten **c** (*Film, Theat*) **he ~s the roles of courtier and hangman** er hat die Doppelrolle des Höflings und Henkers; **the producer decided to ~ the parts of pimp and judge** der Produzent beschloss, die Rollen des Zuhälters und des Richters mit demselben Schauspieler zu besetzen **d** (*Naut*, = *sail round*) umsegeln **e** (*Cards*) verdoppeln; (*Bridge*) kontrieren **VI a** (= *increase twofold*) sich verdoppeln **b** (*Mus*) zwei Instrumente spielen; **he ~s on flute and clarinet** er spielt Flöte und Klarinette **c** (*Film, Theat*) **to ~ for sb** jds Double sein, jdn doubeln; **who is doubling for him?** wer doubelt ihn?, wer ist sein Double?; **he ~s as the butler**

and the duke er hat die Doppelrolle des Butlers und Herzogs; **this bedroom ~s as a study** dieses Schlafzimmer dient auch als Arbeitszimmer

d (*Cards*) verdoppeln; (*Bridge*) kontrieren

▶ **double back** **VI** (*person*) kehrtmachen, zurückgehen/-fahren; (*animal*) kehrtmachen, zurücklaufen; (*road, river*) sich zurückwinden *or* -schlängeln **VT** *sep blanket* umschlagen; *page* umknicken

▶ **double over** **VI** = double up VI a **VT** *sep* = double back VT

▶ **double up** **VI** **a** (= *bend over*) sich krümmen; (*with laughter*) sich biegen, sich kringeln (*inf*); **he doubled up when the bullet hit him** er klappte (*inf*) *or* brach zusammen, als die Kugel ihn traf

b (= *share room*) das Zimmer/Büro *etc* gemeinsam benutzen; (= *share bed*) in einem Bett schlafen; **you'll have to double up with Mary** du musst dir ein Zimmer mit Mary teilen

c (*esp Brit, Betting*) den Einsatz bis zum ersten Gewinn verdoppeln

d (= *have two roles*) **to double up as ...** auch als ... dienen

VT *sep* **a** *paper* falten, knicken; *blanket* zusammenlegen

b **the bullet/blow doubled him up** von der Kugel/dem Schlag getroffen, brach er zusammen

double: double act N (*esp Theat,* = *performers*) Zweigespann *nt;* (= *performance*) Zweiershow *f;* **double-acting** ADJ doppelt wirksam; **double agent** N Doppelagent(in) *m(f);* **double album** N (*Mus*) Doppelalbum *nt;* **double bar** N (*Mus*) Doppelstrich *m;* **double-barrelled,** (*US*) **double-barreled** [ˌdʌblˈbærəld] ADJ Doppel-; **double-barrelled name,** (*US*) **double-barreled name** N Doppelname *m;* **double-barrelled shotgun,** (*US*) **double-barreled shotgun** N doppelläufiges Gewehr, Zwilling *m;* **double bass** N Kontrabass *m;* **double bassoon** N Kontrafagott *nt;* **double bed** N Doppelbett *nt;* **double bend** N S-Kurve *f;* **double bill** N Vorstellung *f* mit zwei Filmen/Stücken; **double bind** N Zwickmühle *f;* **double-blind** ADJ (*Sci*) Doppelblind-; **~ experiment** Doppelblindversuch *m;* **double bluff** N (= *deception*) doppelter Bluff; **double boiler** N (*US*) Turmtopf *m;* **double-book** VT *room, seat* zweimal reservieren; *flight* zweimal buchen; **I'm very sorry, I've ~ed your seat** es tut mir sehr Leid, ich habe einen Platz für Sie reserviert, der schon vergeben war; **double-breasted** ADJ zweireihig; **~ jacket/suit** Zweireiher *m;* **double check** N doppelte Überprüfung; **in spite of all his ~s** obwohl er alles doppelt *or* noch einmal überprüft hatte; **double-check** VT I noch einmal (über)prüfen; **double chin** N Doppelkinn *nt;* **double-click** (*Comput*) **VT** doppelklicken **VI** doppelklicken (*on auf +acc*); **double-clutch** VI (*US*) = double-declutch; **double consonant** N Doppelkonsonant *m;* **double cream** N Schlagsahne *f;* **double-cross** (*inf*) **VT** ein Doppelspiel *or* falsches Spiel treiben mit; **the ~ing swines!** diese falschen Hunde! (*inf*) **N** Doppelspiel *nt;* **double-crosser** N (*inf*) falscher Freund *or* Hund (*inf*); **double-date** VT **he's double-dating me** er trifft sich außer mit mir noch mit einer anderen; **double-dealer** N Betrüger(in) *m(f);* **double-dealing** **N** Betrügerei(en) *f(pl)* **ADJ** betrügerisch; **double-decker** N (*all senses*) Doppeldecker *m;* **double-declutch** VI (*Aut*) mit Zwischengas schalten; **double density** ADJ (*Comput*) *disk* mit doppelter Dichte; **double doors** PL Flügeltür *f;* **double Dutch** N (*esp Brit*) Kauderwelsch *nt;* **to talk ~** Unsinn *or* Kauderwelsch reden; **it was ~ to me** das waren für mich böhmische Dörfer; **double eagle** N (*US*) alte amerikanische Goldmünze mit einem Wert von 20 Dollar; **double-edged** ADJ (*lit, fig*) *remark, compliment* zweischneidig; **tourism is ~ or is a ~ sword** der Tourismus ist ein zweischneidiges Schwert; **double entendre** ['duːblɑ̃ːnˈtɑ̃ːndr] N (*esp*

Brit) Zweideutigkeit *f;* **double-entry bookkeeping** N doppelte Buchführung; **double exposure** N doppelt belichtetes Foto; **double fault** N (*Tennis*) Doppelfehler *m;* **double feature** N Programm *nt* mit zwei Hauptfilmen; **double figures** PL zweistellige Zahlen *pl;* **double first** N (*Brit, Univ*) **he got a ~** er bestand beide Fächer mit „sehr gut"; **double flat** N (*Mus*) Doppel-b *nt;* **double glaze** VT mit Doppelverglasung versehen; **double glazing** N Doppelfenster *pl;* **double Gloucester** N *englische Käsesorte;* **double-header** N (*US, Sport*) Doppelspieltag *m;* **double helix** N (*Chem*) Doppelhelix *f;* **double honours (course)** N (*Brit, Univ*) ≈ Doppelstudium *nt;* **double indemnity** N (*US Insur*) Verdoppelung der Lebensversicherungssumme bei Unfalltod; **double jeopardy** N (*US Jur*) doppelte Strafverfolgung wegen derselben Tat; **double-jointed** ADJ äußerst elastisch, sehr gelenkig; **double knitting (wool)** N Sportwolle *f;* **double knot** N Doppelknoten *m;* **double life** N Doppelleben *nt;* **double lock** N Doppelschloss *nt;* **double-lock** VT zweimal abschließen; **double meaning** N **it has a ~** es ist doppeldeutig; **double negative** N doppelte Verneinung; **double-page spread** N Doppelseite *f;* **double-park** VI in der zweiten Reihe parken; **double parking** N Parken *nt* in der zweiten Reihe; **double pneumonia** N doppelseitige Lungenentzündung; **double-quick** (*inf*) **ADV** im Nu, in null Komma nichts (*inf*) **ADJ** **in ~ time** im Nu, in null Komma nichts (*inf*); **double reed** N (*Mus*) doppeltes Rohrblatt; **double room** N Doppelzimmer *nt*

doubles ['dʌblz] N *sing or pl* (*Sport*) Doppel *nt;* **to play ~** im Doppel spielen

double: double saucepan N Turmtopf *m;* **double sharp** N (*Mus*) Doppelkreuz *nt;* **double-sided** ADJ (*Comput*) *disk* zweiseitig; *poster* doppelseitig; **~ (adhesive) tape** Doppelklebeband *nt;* **double-space** VT (*Typ*) mit doppeltem Zeilenabstand drucken; **double spacing** N doppelter Zeilenabstand; **doublespeak** N (*pej*) doppelzüngiges Gerede; **double standard** N Doppelmoral *f;* **society applies ~s** die Gesellschaft misst mit zweierlei Maß; **double star** N Doppelstern *m;* **double stop** **N** (*Mus*) Doppelgriff *m* **VI** mit Doppelgriff spielen; **double stopping** N (*Mus*) Doppelgriffe *pl;* **double strike** N (*Comput, printing*) Doppeldruck *m*

doublet ['dʌblɪt] N **a** Wams *nt* **b** (*Ling*) Dublette *f*

double: double take N **he did a ~** er musste zweimal hingucken; **double talk** N (*ambiguous*) zwei- *or* doppeldeutiges Gerede; (*deceitful*) doppelzüngiges Gerede; **double taxation** N Doppelbesteuerung *f;* **doublethink** N widersprüchliches Denken; **double ticket** N Eintrittskarte *f* für zwei Personen; **double time** N (*Mil*) Laufschritt *m;* **double-tongue** VI (*Mus*) mit Doppelzunge blasen; **double-tonguing** N Doppelzunge *f;* **double vision** N (*Med*) Doppeltsehen *nt;* **he suffered from ~** er sah doppelt; **double wedding** N Doppelhochzeit *f;* **double whammy** N Doppelschlag *m;* **double windows** PL Doppelfenster *pl;* **double yellow lines** PL *gelbe Doppellinie am Fahrbahnrand zur Kennzeichnung des absoluten Halteverbots* **it is illegal in Britain to park on ~** in Großbritannien ist es verboten, auf gelben Doppellinien zu parken

doubloon [dʌˈbluːn] N Dublone *f*

doubly ['dʌblɪ] ADV doppelt; **to work ~ hard** doppelt so hart arbeiten; **to make ~ sure (that ...)** ganz sichergehn(, dass ...); **~ so** umso mehr; **this road is dangerous, ~ so when it's icy** diese Straße ist gefährlich, umso mehr bei Glatteis

doubt [daʊt] ✪ 15.1, 16.1, 26.3 **N** Zweifel *m;* **to have one's ~s as to** *or* **about sth** (so) seine Bedenken hinsichtlich einer Sache (*gen*) haben; **I have my ~s about her** ich habe bei ihr (so) meine Bedenken; **I have no ~s about tak-**

ing the job ich habe keine Bedenken, die Stelle anzunehmen; **there's no ~ about it** daran gibt es keinen Zweifel; **I have no ~ about it** ich bezweifle das nicht; **I have ~s whether he will come** ich bezweifle, dass er kommt; **to cast ~ on sth** etw in Zweifel ziehen; **there is room for ~** es ist durchaus nicht sicher; **to be open to ~** fragwürdig sein; **his reputation is in ~** sein Ruf wird infrage *or* in Frage gestellt; **to be in (some) ~ about sth** Zweifel an etw (*dat*) haben; **to be in little ~ as to sth** keine Bedenken hinsichtlich einer Sache (*gen*) haben; **I am in no ~ as to what** *or* **about what he means** ich bin mir völlig im Klaren darüber, was er meint; **the outcome is still in ~** das Ergebnis ist noch ungewiss; **when in ~** im Zweifelsfall; **no ~ he will come tomorrow** höchstwahrscheinlich kommt er morgen; **without (a) ~** ohne Zweifel; **I knew beyond ~ that ...** ich wusste ohne jeden Zweifel, dass ...; **it must be proved beyond reasonable ~** es muss ganz unzweifelhaft bewiesen werden

VT bezweifeln; *sb's honesty, truth of statement* anzweifeln, Zweifel haben an (+*dat*); **to ~ sb's word** jds Wort anzweifeln; **I'm sorry I ~ed you** (*what you said*) es tut mir Leid, dass ich dir nicht geglaubt habe; (*your loyalty etc*) es tut mir Leid, dass ich an dir gezweifelt habe; **I ~ it (very much)** das möchte ich (doch stark) bezweifeln, das bezweifle ich (sehr); **I don't ~ it** das bezweifle ich (auch gar) nicht; **I ~ whether he will come** ich bezweifle, dass er kommen wird

VI Zweifel haben *or* hegen

doubter ['daʊtə'] N Skeptiker(in) *m(f),* Zweifler(in) *m(f)*

doubtful ['daʊtfʊl] ✪ 16.1, 16.2 ADJ **a** (*usu pred:* = *unconvinced*) *person* unsicher; **I'm still ~** ich habe noch Bedenken; **to be ~ about sth** an etw (*dat*) zweifeln; **to be ~ about doing sth** Bedenken haben, ob man etw tun soll; **I was ~ whether I could ever manage it** ich bezweifelte, ob ich es je schaffen könnte; **to be ~ of sb/sth** jdm/einer Sache (*dat*) nicht trauen

b (= *unlikely*) *reconciliation, improvement, victory* unwahrscheinlich; **it is ~ that...** es ist unsicher *or* zweifelhaft, ob ...

c (= *questionable, dubious*) *reputation* zweifelhaft, fragwürdig; *future, outcome* ungewiss; *joke, taste, quality, value* zweifelhaft; **information of ~ reliability/origin** zweifelhafte Informationen; **it is ~ whether this could be managed** es ist fraglich, ob das zu schaffen wäre

d (*Sport,* = *unlikely to play*) **he is ~ for tonight's match** es ist fraglich, ob er heute Abend spielen kann; **she is a ~ starter for Saturday's race** es ist fraglich, ob sie in dem Rennen am Samstag starten wird

doubtfully ['daʊtfəlɪ] ADV **a** (= *uncertainly*) unsicher **b** (= *questionably, dubiously*) *attributed* fraglicherweise

doubtfulness ['daʊtfʊlnɪs] N **a** (= *uncertainty, of person*) Unsicherheit *f* **b** (= *unlikeliness, of improvement, victory*) Unwahrscheinlichkeit *f* **c** (= *dubiousness*) Zweifelhaftigkeit *f,* Fragwürdigkeit *f;* (*of future, outcome*) Ungewissheit *f;* (*of joke, taste*) Zweifelhaftigkeit *f*

doubting Thomas [ˌdaʊtɪŋˈtɒməs] N ungläubiger Thomas

doubtless ['daʊtlɪs] ✪ 26.3 ADV sicherlich; **this is ~ true** das stimmt sicherlich

douche [duːʃ] N Spülung *f,* Irrigation *f* (*spec*); (= *instrument*) Irrigator *m* **VI** eine Spülung machen **VT** spülen

dough [dəʊ] N **a** Teig *m* **b** (*inf,* = *money*) Kohle *f* (*inf*)

dough: doughball N Kloß *m;* **doughboy** N (*dated US Mil sl*) Landser *m* (*inf*); **dough hook** N (*Cook*) Knethaken *m;* **doughnut** N (*Brit*) Berliner (Pfannkuchen) *m,* Krapfen *m* (*S Ger, Aus*); **doughnutting** ['dəʊnʌtɪŋ] N (*Brit Parl inf*) Situation, in der sich wenige anwesende Abgeordnete im Unterhaus um den Redner gruppieren, um im Fernsehen den Eindruck eines vollen Hauses zu vermitteln

doughty ['daʊtɪ] ADJ (*liter*) kühn, tapfer

doughy ['dəʊɪ] ADJ **a** *consistency* zäh, teigig; (*pej*) *bread* klitschig, nicht durchgebacken **b** (*pej*) *complexion* käsig

Douglas fir [ˌdʌgləsˈfɜː'], **Douglas pine** [-'paɪn] N Douglastanne *f*

dour ['dʊə'] ADJ (= *silent, unfriendly*) verdrießlich; *struggle* hart, hartnäckig

dourly ['dʊəlɪ] ADV verdrießlich; (= *stubbornly*) hartnäckig

douse [daʊs] VT **a** (= *pour water over*) Wasser schütten über (+*acc*); (= *put into water*) ins Wasser tauchen; *plants* reichlich wässern; **to ~ sb/ sth in** *or* **with petrol** jdn/etw mit Benzin übergießen **b** *light* ausmachen, löschen

dove[1] [dʌv] N (*lit, fig*) Taube *f*

dove[2] [dəʊv] (*US*) pret of **dive**

dove [dʌv-]: **dove-coloured**, (*US*) **dove-colored** ADJ taubenblau; **dovecot(e)** N ['dʌvkɒt] Taubenschlag *m*; **dove-grey** ADJ taubengrau

Dover sole [ˌdəʊvə'səʊl] N Seezunge *f*

dovetail ['dʌvteɪl] N Schwalbenschwanz *m*; **~ joint** Schwalbenschwanzverbindung *f* **VT** (schwalbenschwanzförmig) überblatten; (*fig*) *plans* koordinieren **VI** (*plans*) übereinstimmen

dowager ['daʊədʒə'] N (*adlige*) Witwe; **~ duchess** Herzoginwitwe *f*

dowdiness ['daʊdɪnɪs] N absoluter Mangel an Schick

dowdy ['daʊdɪ] ADJ (+*er*) ohne jeden Schick

dowel ['daʊəl] N Dübel *m*

dower house ['daʊəhaʊs] N *Haus für eine Witwe*

Dow-Jones average [ˌdaʊ'dʒəʊnz'ævərɪdʒ] N Dow-Jones-Index *m*

---

down[1] [daʊn]

1 ADVERB	4 ADJECTIVE
2 PREPOSITION	5 TRANSITIVE VERB
3 NOUN	

1 – ADVERB

When **down** is an element in a phrasal verb, eg **get down, sit down, stand down, write down,** look up the verb.

a indicating movement (*towards speaker*) herunter; (*away from speaker*) hinunter; (*downstairs*) nach unten; **to jump down** herunter-/hinunterspringen; **on his way down from the summit** auf seinem Weg vom Gipfel herab/hinab; **on the way down to London** auf dem Weg nach London runter (*inf*); **all the way down to the bottom** bis ganz nach unten; **down!** (*to dog*) Platz!

♦ **down with ...!** nieder mit ...!

b indicating static position unten; **down there** da unten; **I'll stay down here** ich bleibe hier unten; **down in the valley** unten im Tal; **it needs a bit of paint down at the bottom** es muss unten herum neu gestrichen werden; **don't kick a man when he's down** (*fig*) man soll jemanden nicht fertig machen, wenn er schon angeschlagen ist *or* wenns ihm dreckig geht (*inf*); **head down** mit dem Kopf nach unten; **the sun was down** die Sonne war untergegangen; **the blinds were down** die Jalousien waren unten *or* heruntergelassen; **John isn't down yet** (= *still in bed*) John ist noch nicht unten; **I'll be down in a minute** ich komme sofort runter; **to be down for the count** (*Boxing*) ausgezählt werden; **I've been down with flu** ich habe mit Grippe (im Bett) gelegen → **dump N d**

c = to or in another place (*usu not translated*) **he came down from London yesterday** er kam gestern aus London; **he's down in London/at his brother's** er ist in London/bei seinem Bruder; **he lives down South** er wohnt im Süden; **we're going down South** wir fahren in den Süden; **we're going down to the seaside/to Dover** wir fahren an die See/nach Dover

d = below previous level **his temperature is down** sein Fieber ist zurückgegangen; **his shoes were**

worn down seine Schuhe waren abgetragen; **the price of meat is down on last week** der Fleischpreis ist gegenüber der letzten Woche gefallen; **interest rates are down to/by 3%** der Zinssatz ist auf/um 3% gefallen; **I'm £20 down on what I expected** ich habe £ 20 weniger als ich dachte; **he's down to his last £10** er hat nur noch £ 10; **they're still three goals down** sie liegen immer noch mit drei Toren zurück → **luck**

e in writing **I've got it down in my diary** ich habe es in meinem Kalender notiert; **let's get it down on paper** schreiben wir es auf, halten wir es schriftlich fest; **when you see it down on paper** wenn man es schwarz auf weiß sieht; **to be down for the next race** für das nächste Rennen gemeldet sein; **it's down for next month** es steht für nächsten Monat auf dem Programm

f indicating range or succession (*usu not translated*) **from the biggest down** vom Größten angefangen; **down through the ages** von jeher

♦ **down to** (= *until*) bis zu; **from 1700 down to the present** seit 1700 bis zur Gegenwart; **right down to the present day** bis zum heutigen Tag; **from the chairman (all the way) down to the doorman** vom Vorsitzenden bis (herunter) zum Pförtner

g indicating responsibility

♦ **to be down to sb/sth** (= *caused by*) an jdm/ etw liegen; **any mistakes are down to us** irgendwelche Fehler liegen an uns; **it's down to you to decide** (= *your responsibility*) die Entscheidung liegt bei Ihnen

h as deposit **to pay £20 down** £ 20 anzahlen; **I've put down a deposit on a new bike** ich habe eine Anzahlung für ein neues Fahrrad gemacht; **how much do they want down?** was verlangen sie als Anzahlung?

2 – PREPOSITION

a indicating movement downwards **to go/come down the hill/the stairs** *etc* den Berg/die Treppe *etc* hinuntergehen/herunterkommen; **he ran his finger down the list** er ging (mit dem Finger) die Liste durch; **her hair fell loose down her back** sie trug ihr Haar offen über die Schultern

b at a lower part of **he's already halfway down the hill** er ist schon auf halbem Wege nach unten; **the other skiers were further down the slope** die anderen Skifahrer waren weiter unten; **she lives just down the street** sie wohnt ein Stückchen weiter die Straße entlang

c = along **he was walking/coming down the street** er ging/kam die Straße entlang; **if you look down this road, you can see ...** wenn Sie diese Straße hinunterblicken, können Sie ... sehen

d = throughout **down the centuries** durch die Jahrhunderte (hindurch)

e = to, in, at (*Brit inf*) **he's gone down the pub** er ist in die Kneipe gegangen; **she's down the shops** sie ist einkaufen gegangen; **he works down the garage** er arbeitet in der Autowerkstatt

3 – NOUN (= *dislike*)

♦ **to have a down on sb** (*inf*) jdn auf dem Kieker haben (*inf*) → **up**

4 – ADJECTIVE (*inf*)

a = depressed **he was (feeling) a bit down** er fühlte sich ein wenig down (*inf*) *or* niedergeschlagen

b = not working **to be down** außer Betrieb sein; (*Comput*) abgestürzt sein

5 – TRANSITIVE VERB

opponent niederschlagen, zu Fall bringen; *enemy planes* abschießen, (he)runterholen (*inf*); *beer etc* runterkippen *or* -schütten (*inf*); **to down tools** die Arbeit niederlegen

---

down[2] N (= *feathers*) Daunen *pl*, Flaumfedern *pl*; (= *fine hair*) Flaum *m*

down[3] N *usu pl* (*Geog*) Hügelland *nt no pl*; **on the ~(s)** im Hügelland

down: **down-and-out** N (= *tramp*) Penner(in) *m(f)* (*inf*) ADJ heruntergekommen; *appearance also* abgerissen; **down arrow** N (*Comput*) Abwärtspfeil *m*; **downbeat** N *Taktstockführung, die den ersten betonten Taktteil anzeigt*, erster Taktteil ADJ (*fig*) *ending* undramatisch; *mood* gedrückt; **down-bow** N (*Mus*) Abstrich *m*; **downcast** ADJ **a** (= *depressed*) *person, expression* niedergedrückt, entmutigt **b** *eyes* niedergeschlagen; *look* gesenkt N (*Min*) Wetterschacht *m*; **downdraught**, (*US*) **downdraft** N (*Met*) Fallwind *m*; (*Tech*) Fallstrom *m*

downer ['daʊnə'] N **a** (*Drugs inf*) Downer *m* (*sl*), Beruhigungsmittel *nt* **b** (*inf:* = *depressing experience*) **for divorced people, Christmas can be a ~** für Geschiedene kann Weihnachten einen Tiefpunkt bedeuten; **she's on a real ~ just now** sie ist zur Zeit richtig depressiv

down: **downfall** N **a** Sturz *m*, Fall *m*; (*of empire*) Fall *m*, Untergang *m*; (= *cause of ruin: drink etc*) Ruin **b** (*of rain*) heftiger Niederschlag, Platzregen *m*; **downgrade** N (*Rail*) Gefälle *nt*; **to be on the ~** (*fig*) auf dem absteigenden Ast sein; (*health, quality*) sich verschlechtern **VT** *hotel, job, work* herunterstufen; *person* degradieren; **down-hearted** ADJ niedergeschlagen, entmutigt; **downhill** ADV (*lit, fig*) bergab; **to go ~** (*road*) bergab führen *or* gehen; (*vehicle*) herunterfahren; (*person on foot*) heruntergehen; **he/his health/the economy is going ~** mit ihm/seiner Gesundheit/der Wirtschaft geht es bergab; **things just went steadily ~** es ging immer mehr bergab ADJ **a** *road, path* bergab führend; **~ slope** Abhang *m*; **the path is ~ for two miles** der Weg führt zwei Meilen bergab; **the ~ path to drug addiction** der abschüssige Weg in die Drogensucht; **they had not noticed her gradual ~ path** sie hatten nicht bemerkt, wie es mit ihr langsam bergab ging; **it's all ~ (after thirty)** (= *gets worse*) es geht (ab dreißig) nur noch bergab; **it was ~ all the way** *or* **all ~ after that** (= *got easier*) danach wurde alles viel einfacher **b** (*Ski*) **~ competition** *or* **race** Abfahrtslauf *m*; **~ course** Abfahrtsstrecke *f*; **~ skiing** Abfahrtslauf *m* N (*Ski*) Abfahrtslauf *m*

Downing Street ['daʊnɪŋˌstriːt] N die Downing Street; (= *the government*) die britische Regierung

---

DOWNING STREET

Downing Street ist die Straße in London, in der sich der offizielle Wohnsitz des britischen Premierministers (Nr. 10) und der des Finanzministers (Nr. 11) befinden. **Downing Street**, oder auch **Number Ten** oder **Ten Downing Street** wird in den Medien häufig als Synonym für den Premierminister, die Regierung oder das Kabinett verwendet: „Downing Street has strenuously denied these allegations", „A statement from Number Ten is expected later this afternoon".

---

down: **downlighter** ['daʊnˌlaɪtə'] N Deckenstrahler *m*; **down line** N (*Rail*) *Eisenbahnlinie von der Stadt aufs Land oder aus der Hauptstadt heraus*; **download** (*Comput*) **VT** (herunter)laden **VI** **it won't ~** Runterladen ist nicht möglich ATTR *font, character* ladbar; **downloadable** ADJ (*Comput*) ladbar; **down-market** ADJ *product* für den Massenmarkt; *service* weniger anspruchsvoll; **this restaurant is more ~** dieses Restaurant ist weniger exklusiv ADV **to go ~** sich auf den Massenmarkt ausrichten; **down payment** N (*Fin*) Anzahlung *f*; **down-pipe** N Abflussrohr *nt*, Fallrohr *nt*; **downplay** VT herunterspielen (*inf*), bagatellisieren; **downpour** N Platzregen *m*, Wolkenbruch *m*; **downright** ADV *dangerous, silly, hostile, dull etc* ausgesprochen; *rude, disgusting* geradezu ADJ **a ~ lie** eine glatte Lüge; **his ~ rudeness** seine ausgesprochene Unverschämtheit; **downriver** ADV flussabwärts (*from* von); **~ from Bonn** unterhalb von Bonn; **downshift** VI *in eine* schlechter bezahlte Stelle überwechseln, runterschalten (inf); **downside** N Kehrseite f; **downsize** ['daʊnsaɪz] VT business, workforce verkleinern; **~d economy** durch Rationalisierung und Stellenabbau gekennzeichnete wirtschaftliche Lage VI (company) sich verkleinern; **downsizing** (Comput) N Downsizing nt; (Comm also) Stellenabbau m; **downspout** N Abflussrohr nt, Fallrohr nt

Down's syndrome ['daʊnz'sɪndrəʊm] (Med) N Downsyndrom nt ATTR **a ~ baby** ein an Downsyndrom leidendes Kind

down: downstage ADV (= towards the front of the stage) zum vorderen Teil der Bühne; (= at the front of the stage) im vorderen Teil der Bühne; **downstairs** ADV go, come nach unten, die Treppe hinunter; fall die Treppe hinunter; be, sleep, eat etc unten ADJ ['daʊnsteəz] **the ~ phone/rooms** das Telefon/die Zimmer unten; **~ flat** (Brit) or **apartment** Parterrewohnung f; **our ~ neighbours** (Brit) or **neighbors** (US) die Nachbarn unter uns; **the woman/the people ~** die Frau/die Leute von unten; **downstate** (US) ADJ im Süden (des Bundesstaates); **in ~ Illinois** im Süden von Illinois ADV move, go in den Süden (des Bundesstaates); live, be situated im Süden (des Bundesstaates) N der Süden (des Bundesstaates); **downstream** ADV flussabwärts, stromabwärts (from von); **downstroke** N (in writing) Abstrich m; (Mech, of piston) Ansaugtakt m; **downswept** ADJ wings abwärts gerichtet; **downswing** N Abwärtsschwingen nt; **down-the-line** ADJ (inf: = uncompromising) vorbehaltlos; **downtime** N Ausfallzeit f; **down-to-earth** ADJ attitude, approach nüchtern; **he's very ~** (= practical) er steht mit beiden Füßen auf der Erde; **downtown** (esp US) ADV go in die (Innen)stadt, in Stadtzentrum; live, be situated in der (Innen)stadt, im Stadtzentrum ADJ **~ Chicago** die Innenstadt or das Stadtzentrum von Chicago; **the ~ area** das Stadtzentrum; **down train** N Zug, der von der Stadt aufs Land fährt oder von der Hauptstadt abgeht; **downtrend** N (Econ) Abwärtstrend m; **to be in** or **on a ~** sich im Abwärtstrend befinden; **downtrodden** ADJ people unterdrückt, geknechtet; **downturn** N (in prices, business) Rückgang m, Abflauen nt; **to take a ~** zurückgehen, abflauen; **his fortunes took a ~** sein Glücksstern sank; **down under** (inf) N (= Australia) Australien nt; (= New Zealand) Neuseeland nt ADV be, live in Australien/Neuseeland; go nach Australien/Neuseeland

downward ['daʊnwəd] ADV (also **downwards**) look, point, extend, move nach unten; **to work ~(s)** sich nach unten vorarbeiten; **to slope gently ~(s)** sanft abfallen; **face ~(s)** (person) mit dem Gesicht nach unten; (book) mit der aufgeschlagenen Seite nach unten; **movement ~(s)** (in price, value) Rückgang m; **to move ~(s)** (figure, rate) sinken, fallen; **everyone from the Queen ~(s)** jeder, bei der Königin angefangen; **our estimates have been revised ~(s)** unsere Kalkulation wurde nach unten korrigiert; **to spiral ~(s)** (prices) stürzen; **the economy is spiralling** (Brit) or **spiraling** (US) **~(s)** mit der Wirtschaft geht es rapide bergab ADJ stroke nach unten; **she made a bold ~ stroke with the paintbrush** sie machte einen kühnen Pinselstrich nach unten; **~ movement** Abwärtsbewegung f; **apply foundation in a ~ direction** tragen Sie die Grundierung von oben nach unten auf; **~ slope** Abhang m; **~ gradient** (Brit) or **grade** (US) Gefälle nt; **~ trend** Abwärtstrend m; **~ spiral** stetiger Rückgang; **he's on the ~ path** (fig) mit ihm gehts bergab; **the dollar resumed its ~ path** or **slide against the yen** der Dollar fiel weiter gegen den Yen; **a ~ slide in prices** ein Preisrutsch m; **to take a ~ turn** sich zum Schlechteren wenden; **to put ~ pressure on wages/prices** die Löhne/Preise (nach unten) drücken

downwind ['daʊnwɪnd] ADV move, drift mit dem Wind; sail vor dem Wind; stand, be in Windrichtung (of, from +gen)

downy ['daʊnɪ] ADJ (+er) **a** (= filled with feathers) daunengefüllt; (= covered with feathers) flaumig **b** (fig) skin, hair, leaf, peach flaumig; **fine ~ hair** ein feiner Flaum

dowry ['daʊrɪ] N Mitgift f

dowse¹ ['daʊs] VT = **douse**

dowse² ['daʊz] VI (= divine) mit einer Wünschelrute suchen

dowser ['daʊzə'] N Wünschelrutengänger(in) m(f)

dowsing rod ['daʊzɪŋrɒd] N Wünschelrute f

doxology [dɒkˈsɒlədʒɪ] N Lobpreisung f, Verherrlichung f Gottes

doyen ['dɔɪən] N Nestor m; (of diplomatic corps) Doyen m

doyenne ['dɔɪən] N Nestorin f; (of diplomatic corps) Doyenne f

doz abbr of **dozen**

doze [dəʊz] N Nickerchen nt; **to have a ~** dösen, ein Nickerchen machen VI (vor sich hin) dösen

▶ **doze off** VI einschlafen, einnicken

dozen ['dʌzn] N Dutzend nt; **80p a ~** 80 Pence das Dutzend; **two ~ eggs** zwei Dutzend Eier; **half a ~** sechs, ein halbes Dutzend; **~s** jede Menge; (fig inf) eine ganze Menge; **~s of times** (inf) x-mal (inf), tausendmal; **there are ~s like that** (inf) das gibts wie Sand am Meer; **there were ~s like this one** (inf) es gab dutzende or Dutzende solcher Vorfälle; **~s of people came** (inf) dutzende or Dutzende von Leuten kamen

dozily ['daʊzɪlɪ] ADV verschlafen, schläfrig

doziness ['daʊzɪnɪs] N Verschlafenheit f, Schläfrigkeit f

dozy ['daʊzɪ] ADJ (+er) **a** (= sleepy) schläfrig, verschlafen **b** (Brit inf, = stupid) dösig (inf)

DP abbr of **data processing** DV f

D Phil abbr of **Doctor of Philosophy** Dr. phil.

dpi (Comput) abbr of **dots per inch** dpi

DPP abbr of **Director of Public Prosecutions**

DPT [ˌdiːpiːˈtiː] N (Med) Dreifachimpfung f gegen Diphtherie, Keuchhusten und Wundstarrkrampf

dpt abbr of **department** Abt

DQ (Athletics) abbr of **Disqualified**

Dr abbr of **doctor** Dr.

drab [dræb] ADJ (+er) trist; life, activities eintönig; **~ brown** graubraun N **a** no pl (Tex) grober, graubrauner Wollstoff **b** → **dribs and drabs**

drably ['dræblɪ] ADV dressed trist; painted in tristen Farben; **~ uniform** deprimierend eintönig

drabness ['dræbnɪs] N Tristheit f; (of life, activities) Eintönigkeit f

drachma ['drækmə], (pl) 'drækmiː] N pl **-e** or **-s** Drachme f

draconian [drəˈkəʊnɪən] ADJ drakonisch

draft [drɑːft] N **a** (= rough outline) Entwurf m **b** (Fin, Comm) Wechsel m, Tratte f **c** (Mil, = group of men) Sonderkommando nt **d** (US Mil, = group of conscripts) Rekruten pl; (= conscription) Einberufung (zum Wehrdienst) **e** (US) = **draught** **f** (Comput) Draft(druck) m, Schnellschrift f VT **a** letter, speech, bill, contract entwerfen **b** (US, Mil) conscript einziehen, einberufen (into zu); **to ~ sb to do sth** (Mil) jdn dazu abkommandieren, etw zu tun; (fig) jdn dazu abtragen, etw zu tun; **he was ~ed into the England squad** er wurde für die englische Nationalmannschaft aufgestellt attr (Comput) Draft-; **~ mode** Draft-Modus m, Draftmodus m

draft: draft board N (US Mil) Einberufungsbehörde f; (= panel) Einberufungsausschuss m; **draft call** N (US Mil) Einberufungsbescheid m; **draft card** N (US, Mil) Wehrpass m; **draft dodger** N (US, Mil) Wehrpflichtiger, der sich vor dem Wehrdienst drückt, Drückeberger m (pej inf)

draftee ['drɑːftiː] N (US, Mil) Wehrpflichtige(r) m(f)

draftiness etc (US) = **draughtiness** etc

draft: draft letter N Entwurf m eines/des Briefes; **draft version** N Entwurf m

drag [dræg] N **a** (= object pulled along, for dredging etc) Suchanker m; (Naut: = cluster of hooks) Dregganker m, Draggen m; (Naut: = dragnet) Schleppnetz nt; (= heavy sledge) Lastschlitten m; (Agr, = harrow) schwere Egge **b** (= resistance, Aviat) Luft- or Strömungswiderstand m; (Naut) Wasserwiderstand m **c** (= brake) Hemmklotz m, Hemmschuh m **d** (= slow laborious progress) **it was a long ~ up to the top of the hill** es war ein langer, mühseliger Aufstieg zum Gipfel, der Aufstieg auf den Gipfel war ein furchtbarer Schlauch (inf) **e** (inf, = burden) **to be a ~ on sth** eine Belastung für etw sein **f** (inf) **what a ~!** (boring) Mann, ist das/der/die/das langweilig! (inf); (nuisance) so'n Mist (inf); **what a ~ having to go back!** so'n Mist, dass wir zurückmüssen (inf); **the film was a real ~** der Film war stinklangweilig (inf); **she thought his girlfriend was a real ~** sie fand, dass seine Freundin echt langweilig war (inf) **g** (inf, = pull on cigarette) Zug m (on, at an +dat); **give me a ~** lass mich mal ziehen, gib mir mal 'n Zug (inf); **he took a long ~ on his cigarette** er zog lange an seiner Zigarette **h** (inf, = women's clothing worn by men) (von Männern getragene) Frauenkleidung f; **in ~ in** Frauenkleidung, im Fummel (sl), als Tunte (inf) **i** (dated US inf, = influence) Einfluss m; **to use one's ~** seinen Einfluss ausüben **j** (US inf, = street) **the main ~** die Hauptstraße VT **a** person, object schleppen, schleifen, ziehen; **he ~ged her out of/into the car** er zerrte sie aus dem/in das Auto; **she ~ged me to the library every Friday** sie schleppte mich jeden Freitag in die Bücherei; **the dog was ~ging its broken leg (behind it)** der Hund schleifte sein gebrochenes Bein hinter sich her; **to ~ one's feet** or **heels** (lit) (mit den Füßen) schlurfen; (fig) die Sache schleppen lassen; **she accused the government of ~ging its feet on reforms** sie beschuldigte die Regierung, die Reformen zu verzögern; **to ~ anchor** (Naut) vor Anker treiben **b** river absuchen VI **a** (= trail along) schleifen; (feet) schlurfen; (Naut, anchor) treiben **b** (= lag behind: person) hinterherhinken **c** (fig, time, work) sich hinziehen; (play, book) sich in die Länge ziehen; (conversation) sich (mühsam) hinschleppen

▶ **drag along** VT sep person mitschleppen; **to drag oneself along** sich mühsam dahinschleppen

▶ **drag apart** VT sep auseinander zerren, trennen

▶ **drag away** VT sep (lit, fig) wegschleppen or -ziehen; **you'll have to drag him away from the television** den muss man mit Gewalt vom Fernsehen wegziehen; **if you can drag yourself away from the television for a second ...** wenn du dich vielleicht mal für eine Sekunde vom Fernsehen losreißen könntest ...

▶ **drag behind** VT +prep obj **to drag sb/sth behind one** jdn/etw hinter sich (dat) herschleppen or herschleifen VI (fig) zurückbleiben, hinterherhinken

▶ **drag down** VT sep (lit) herunterziehen; (fig) mit sich ziehen; **he is trying to drag me down with him** er versucht, mich mit sich zu ziehen; **to drag sb down to one's own level** (fig) jdn auf sein eigenes Niveau herabziehen; **he was dragged down by the scandal** der Skandal führte fast zu seinem Ruin; **his illness is dragging him down** seine Krankheit macht ihn fertig (inf); **you shouldn't let these things drag you down so** du solltest dich dadurch nicht so entmutigen lassen

▶ **drag in** VT sep **a** (lit) hineinziehen; **look what the cat's dragged in** (fig inf) sieh mal, wer da kommt **b** (fig) subject aufs Tapet bringen; remark anbringen

▸ **drag off** VT sep (lit) wegzerren or -ziehen; (fig) wegschleppen; **to drag sb off to a concert** jdn in ein Konzert schleppen

▸ **drag on** VI sich in die Länge ziehen; (meeting, lecture also) sich hinziehen; (conversation) sich hinschleppen; **it dragged on for 3 hours** es zog sich über 3 Stunden hin

▸ **drag out** VT sep **a** meeting, discussion etc in die Länge ziehen **b** (= extract) **eventually I had to drag it out of him** schließlich musste ich es ihm aus der Nase ziehen (inf)

▸ **drag up** VT sep **a** scandal, story ausgraben; person aufgabeln (inf), auftun (inf) **b** (inf) child mehr schlecht als recht aufziehen

drag: drag and drop N (Comput) Drag-and--Drop nt; **drag artist** N (inf) Travestiekünstler(in) m(f); **drag coefficient** N Luftwiderstandsbeiwert m

dragée ['dræʒeɪ] N (Med: = sweet) Dragee nt

drag factor N Widerstandsbeiwert m

draggy ['drægɪ] ADJ (inf) anödend (inf)

drag lift N (Ski) Schlepplift m

dragline N Schleppleine f, Schleppseil nt

dragnet ['drægnet] N (for fish) Schleppnetz nt; (= police hunt) großangelegte Polizeiaktion

dragoman ['drægəʊmən] N Dragoman m

dragon ['drægən] N (lit, fig inf) Drache m

dragonfly ['drægən,flaɪ] N Libelle f

dragoon [drə'guːn] **N** (Mil) Dragoner m **VT to ~ sb into doing sth** jdn zwingen or mit Gewalt dazu bringen, etw zu tun

drag: drag queen N (inf) Tunte f (inf); **drag race** N Beschleunigungsrennen nt; **dragrope** N Schlepptau nt; **drag show** N Transvestitenshow f

dragster ['drægstə'] N Dragster m (sl)

drain [dreɪn] **N a** (= pipe) Rohr nt; (under sink etc) Abfluss(rohr nt) m; (under the ground) Kanalisationsrohr nt; (= drain cover) Rost m; **open ~** (Abfluss)rinne f; **to pour money down the ~** (fig inf) das Geld zum Fenster hinauswerfen; **this country/company is going down the ~** (inf) dieses Land/diese Firma geht vor die Hunde (inf); **I had to watch all our efforts go down the ~** ich musste zusehen, wie alle unsere Bemühungen zunichte (gemacht) wurden; **to laugh like a ~** (Brit, inf) sich kaputtlachen **b** (on resources, finances etc) Belastung f (on +gen); **looking after her father has been a great ~ on her energy** die Pflege ihres Vaters hat sehr an ihren Kräften gezehrt → **brain drain** **VT a** (lit) drainieren; land, marshes entwässern; vegetables abgießen; (= let drain) abtropfen lassen; mine auspumpen; reservoir trockenlegen; boiler, radiator das Wasser ablassen aus; engine oil ablassen **b** (fig) **such emotions ~ our energy** solche Gefühle zehren an unseren Kräften; **to feel ~ed** sich ausgelaugt fühlen; **to ~ a country of resources** ein Land auslaugen or auspowern; **to ~ sb dry** jdn ausnehmen (inf) **c** (= empty) glass austrinken, leeren **VI a** (vegetables, dishes) abtropfen; (land into river) entwässert werden **b** (fig) **the blood/colour** (Brit) or **color** (US) **~ed from his face** das Blut/die Farbe wich aus seinem Gesicht; **his face ~ed of all colour** (Brit) or **color** (US) er wurde wachsbleich

▸ **drain away** VI (liquid) ablaufen; (strength) dahinschwinden; (tension) sich lösen **VT** sep liquid ableiten

▸ **drain off** VT sep abgießen; (= let drain) abtropfen lassen

drainage ['dreɪnɪdʒ] **N a** (= draining) Dränage f, Drainage f; (of land) Entwässerung f **b** (= system) Entwässerungssystem nt; (in house, town) Kanalisation f **c** (= sewage) Abwasser nt **d** (Geol) Drain(ier)ung f (spec), Entwässerung f

drainage: drainage area, **drainage basin** N (Geol) Einzugsgebiet f; **drainage channel** N

(Build) Entwässerungsgraben m, Abzugsgraben m; **drainage tube** N (Med) Drain m, Drän m

drainer ['dreɪnə'] N (for dishes) Abtropfständer m, Abtropfbrett nt

drain: drain hose N (of washing machine) Abflussschlauch m; **draining board**, (US) **drain board** N Ablauf m; **drainpipe** N Abflussrohr nt; **drainpipes**, **drainpipe trousers** PL Röhrenhosen pl

drake [dreɪk] N Erpel m, Enterich m → **duck**[1]

dram [dræm] N **a** (= measure, Pharm) ≈ Drachme f (old) **b** (Brit: = small drink) Schluck m (Whisky)

drama ['drɑːmə] N (= art, play, incident) Drama nt; (no pl: = quality of being dramatic) Dramatik f; **18th-century German ~** das deutsche Drama des 18. Jahrhunderts; **family ~** (= TV series) Familienserie f; **to make a ~ out of a crisis** eine Krise dramatisieren

drama: drama critic N Theaterkritiker(in) m(f); **drama-doc** N (TV) Dokumentarspiel nt; **drama queen** N (pej inf) Schauspielerin f (pej inf); **drama school** N Schauspielschule f; **drama student** N Schauspielschüler(in) m(f)

dramatic [drə'mætɪk] **ADJ a** dramatisch; change einschneidend, dramatisch; **there was a ~ improvement (in it)** es verbesserte sich dramatisch **b** (Theat) dramatisch; **~ works** dramatische Werke pl, Dramen pl; **~ criticism** Theaterkritik f; **his ~ ability** seine schauspielerischen Fähigkeiten; **~ art** Theater nt; **the ~ arts** das Theater; **~ film** Filmdrama nt **b dramatics** PL **a** (= theatricals) Theater nt **b** (= histrionics) **his/her etc ~s** sein/ihr etc theatralisches Getue

dramatically [drə'mætɪkəlɪ] ADV **a** (= radically) increase, improve, fall, reduce dramatisch, enorm; change dramatisch, einschneidend; different radikal; effective extrem; worse, better dramatisch; **this plan is ~ different from the last one** dieser Plan unterscheidet sich radikal or dramatisch vom letzten; **a country of ~ changing landscapes** ein Land, in dem sich die Landschaft immer wieder dramatisch verändert **b** (= theatrically) theatralisch; **he paused ~** er machte eine theatralische Pause **c** (Theat) dramatisch; **~, it was very effective** dramatisch gesehen war es sehr wirkungsvoll

dramatis personae ['dræmətɪspɜː'səʊnaɪ] PL Personen pl der Handlung, dramatis personae pl (old)

dramatist ['dræmətɪst] N Dramatiker(in) m(f)

dramatization [dræmətaɪ'zeɪʃən] N Bühnen-/Fernsehbearbeitung f, Dramatisierung f

dramatize ['dræmətaɪz] **VT a** novel für die Bühne/das Fernsehen bearbeiten, dramatisieren **b** (= make vivid) event dramatisieren **VI a** (novel etc) sich für die Bühne/das Fernsehen bearbeiten lassen **b** (= exaggerate) übertreiben

drank [dræŋk] pret of **drink**

drape [dreɪp] **VT a** drapieren; window mit Vorhängen versehen; person hüllen; altar drapieren, behängen; **to ~ sth over sth** etw über etw (acc) drapieren; **she ~d herself over the sofa** (inf) sie drapierte sich malerisch auf das Sofa; **she opened the door ~d only in a towel** sie machte die Tür auf, nur in ein Badetuch gehüllt **N a drapes** PL (US) Gardinen pl **b** (= way sth hangs) Fall m

draper ['dreɪpə'] N (Brit) Textilkaufmann m/-frau f; **~'s (shop)** Textilgeschäft nt

drapery ['dreɪpərɪ] N **a** (Brit, = cloth etc) Stoff m; (= business: also **drapery shop**) Stoffladen m **b** (= hangings) Draperie f (old); (on wall) Behang m; (around bed etc) Vorhänge pl; (clothing, fig liter) Gewand nt

drastic ['dræstɪk] ADJ drastisch; solution radikal, drastisch; consequences schwerwiegend, schwer wiegend; surgery radikal; change, reform einschneidend, radikal; improvement einschneidend; **to make ~ changes in sth** etw radikal ändern; **to take ~ action** or **measures** drastische Maßnahmen ergreifen

drastically ['dræstɪkəlɪ] ADV drastisch; change, different radikal; **to go ~ wrong** total schief gehen; **they're ~ short of supplies** ihre Vorräte sind bedrohlich knapp

drat [dræt] INTERJ (inf) **~ (it)!** verflixt! (inf); **~ that child!** dieses verflixte Kind! (inf)

dratted ['drætɪd] ADJ (inf) verflixt (inf)

draught, (US) **draft** [drɑːft] **N a** (Luft)zug m; (= through draught) Durchzug m; (for fire) Zug m; **there's a terrible ~ in here** hier zieht es fürchterlich; **I'm sitting in a ~** ich sitze im Zug; **are you in a ~?** zieht's Ihnen?; **there's a ~ blowing round the back of my neck** mir zieht's im Genick; **open the flues to increase the ~** mach die Klappen auf, damit der Ofen mehr Zug bekommt; **he's beginning to feel the ~** (fig inf) ihm wird allmählich das Geld knapp **b** (= swallow, drink) Zug m; **a ~ of mead** ein Schluck m Met **c** (= draught beer) Fassbier nt; **on ~** vom Fass **d** (Naut) Tiefgang m **e** (Med) sleeping **~** Schlaftrunk m **f** (of fish) Fischzug m **g draughts** PL (Brit, = game) Damespiel nt; (+pl vb: = pieces) Damesteine pl **h** (= rough sketch) = **draft** N **a**

draught, (US) **draft: draught animal** N Zugtier nt; **draught beer** N Fassbier nt, Bier nt vom Fass

draughtboard N (Brit) Damebrett nt

draught excluder N (Brit) Dichtungsmaterial nt

draughtiness, (US) **draftiness** ['drɑːftɪnɪs] N Zugigkeit f

draught net N (for fishing) Zugnetz nt

draughtproof, (US) **draftproof** ['drɑːftpruːf] ADJ windows, doors dicht; room gegen Zugluft geschützt

draughtproofing, (US) **draftproofing** ['drɑːftpruːfɪŋ] N Zugluftisolierung f; (= material) Isoliermaterial nt gegen Zugluft

draughtsman, (US) **draftsman** ['drɑːftsmən] N pl **-men** [-mən] **a** (of plans) Zeichner m; (of documents, treaty etc) Verfasser m **b** (Brit, in game) Damestein m

draughtsmanship, (US) **draftsmanship** ['drɑːftsmənʃɪp] N **his brilliant ~** sein hervorragendes zeichnerisches Können; **the power of his ~ shows that ...** an der Qualität seiner Zeichnung kann man sehen, dass ...

draughtswoman, (US) **draftswoman** ['drɑːftswʊmən] N pl **-women** [-wɪmɪn] (of plans) Zeichnerin f; (of documents, treaty etc) Verfasserin f

draughty, (US) **drafty** ['drɑːftɪ] ADJ (+er) zugig; **it's ~ in here** hier zieht es

draw[1] [drɔː] pret **drew**, ptp **drawn** **VT** (lit, fig) zeichnen; line ziehen; **we must ~ the line somewhere** (fig) irgendwo muss Schluss sein; **I ~ the line at cheating** (personally) Mogeln kommt für mich nicht in Frage; (in others) beim Mogeln hörts bei mir auf; **some people just don't know where to ~ the line** (fig) manche Leute wissen einfach nicht, wie weit sie gehen können; **to ~ a line between** (fig) einen Unterschied machen zwischen **VI** zeichnen

draw[2] [drɔː]	
vb: pret **drew**, ptp **drawn**	
1 TRANSITIVE VERB	3 NOUN
2 INTRANSITIVE VERB	4 PHRASAL VERBS

1 – TRANSITIVE VERB

a = move by pulling ziehen; bolt zurückschieben; bow spannen; curtains (= open) aufziehen; (= shut) zuziehen; **he drew his chair nearer the fire** er rückte seinen Stuhl näher an den Kamin heran; **he drew her close to him** er zog sie an sich; **he drew his finger along the edge of the table** er fuhr mit dem Finger die Tischkante entlang; **he drew the smoke into his lungs** er machte einen (tiefen) Lungenzug

b = move by pulling behind coach, cart ziehen

c = bring bringen; **her shouts drew me to the scene** ihr Rufen brachte mich an den Ort des Geschehens; **to draw sth to a close** etw zu Ende bringen, etw beenden

d = extract *teeth, sword, gun* ziehen; *knife* ziehen, zücken; *cork* herausziehen; **with drawn sword** mit gezogenem *or* gezücktem Schwert; **it was like drawing teeth** (*fig*) es war Schwerstarbeit

e = take holen; *wine (from barrel)* zapfen; **to draw water from a well** Wasser aus einem Brunnen holen; **to draw a (deep) breath** (tief) Luft holen; **to draw a long breath** einmal tief Luft holen; **to draw inspiration from sb/sth/ somewhere** sich von jdm/von etw/von irgendwas inspirieren lassen; **to draw strength from sth** Kraft aus etw schöpfen; **to draw comfort from sth** sich mit etw trösten; **he's bitten her – has he drawn blood?** er hat sie gebissen – blutet sie?

♦ **to draw money/a salary/a pension to draw money from the bank** Geld (vom Konto) abheben; **to draw the dole/a big salary** Arbeitslosenunterstützung/ein großes Gehalt beziehen; **to draw one's pension** seine Rente bekommen

f = elicit **her singing drew tears from the audience** ihr Singen rührte die Zuhörer zu Tränen; **her singing drew tremendous applause from the audience** ihr Singen rief brausenden Beifall hervor; **the play has drawn a lot of criticism** das Theaterstück hat viel Kritik auf sich (*acc*) gezogen; **to draw a smile/a laugh from sb** jdm ein Lächeln/ein Lachen entlocken; **my letter drew an angry reply from him** auf meinen Brief reagierte er mit einer ungehaltenen Antwort

♦ **to be drawn** (*person*) **he refuses to be drawn** (= *will not speak*) aus ihm ist nichts herauszubringen; (= *will not be provoked*) er lässt sich auf nichts ein; **I won't be drawn on that issue** zu dem Thema möchte ich mich nicht äußern

g = attract *interest* erregen; *customer, crowd* anlocken; **to draw fire** (*lit, fig*) unter Feuer genommen werden; **to feel drawn toward(s) sb** sich zu jdm hingezogen fühlen; **to draw sb into sth** jdn in etw (*acc*) hineinziehen *or* verwickeln; **to draw sb away from sb/sth** jdn von jdm/etw weglocken → **attention a**

h = formulate *conclusion, comparison* ziehen; *distinction* treffen; **you can draw whatever conclusion you like** du kannst daraus schließen, was du willst

i Naut **the boat draws 4 metres** das Boot hat 4 Meter Tiefgang

j = tie (*Sport*) **to draw a match** sich unentschieden trennen, unentschieden spielen

k = choose at random ziehen; **the first correct entry drawn from the hat** die erste richtige Einsendung, die gezogen wird; **we've been drawn (to play) away/at home** wir sind für ein Auswärtsspiel/Heimspiel gezogen worden; **France has been drawn against Scotland** Frankreich ist für ein Spiel gegen Schottland gezogen worden; **to draw a raffle** eine Auslosung vornehmen

l Cards **to draw a card from the pack** eine Karte vom Haufen abheben *or* nehmen; **to draw trumps** Trümpfe herauszwingen

m Cook *fowl* ausnehmen → **hang VT e**

n Hunt *fox* aufstöbern; **to draw a covert** ein Tier aus seinem Versteck aufstöbern *or* aufjagen

2 – INTRANSITIVE VERB

a = move (*person, time, event*) kommen; **he drew to one side** er ging/fuhr zur Seite; **to draw round the table** sich um den Tisch versammeln; **to draw to an end** *or* **to a close** zu Ende gehen; **to draw ahead of the other runners** er zog den anderen Läufern davon; **the two horses drew level** die beiden Pferde zogen gleich

♦ **to draw near** herankommen (*to* an +*acc*); **he drew nearer** *or* **closer (to it)** er kam (immer) näher (heran); **Christmas is drawing nearer** Weihnachten rückt näher

b = allow airflow (*chimney, pipe*) ziehen

c = tie (*Sport*) unentschieden spielen; **they drew 2-2** sie trennten sich *or* sie spielten 2:2 unentschieden; **the teams drew for second place** im Kampf um den 2. Platz trennten sich die Mannschaften unentschieden; **Scotland drew with Ireland** Schottland und Irland trennten sich *or* spielten unentschieden

d Cards **to draw for partners** die Partner durch Kartenziehen bestimmen

e = infuse (*tea*) ziehen

3 – NOUN

a = random selection (= *lottery*) Ziehung *f*, Ausspielung *f*; (*for sports competitions*) Auslosung *f*, Ziehung *f* → **luck**

b = tie (*Sport*) Unentschieden *nt*; **the match ended in a draw** das Spiel endete unentschieden *or* mit einem Unentschieden; **the team had five wins and two draws** die Mannschaft hat fünfmal gewonnen und zweimal unentschieden gespielt

c = attraction (*play, film etc*) (Kassen)schlager *m*, Knüller *m* (*inf*); (*person*) Attraktion *f*; **the pay was the big draw of the job** die Bezahlung war das Attraktive an der Stelle

d in shooting

♦ **the draw to be quick on the draw** (*lit*) schnell mit der Pistole sein, schnell (den Revolver) ziehen; (*fig*) schlagfertig sein; **to beat sb to the draw** schneller sein als jd; (*lit: cowboy etc*) schneller ziehen als jd

4 – PHRASAL VERBS

► **draw alongside** VI heranfahren/-kommen (+*prep obj* an +*acc*)

► **draw apart** VI (= *move away*) sich lösen; (*couple*) sich auseinander leben; (*from political party etc*) abrücken

► **draw aside** VT *sep person* beiseite nehmen; *curtains* zur Seite ziehen

► **draw away** VI **a** (= *move off, car etc*) losfahren; (*procession*) sich entfernen **b** (= *move ahead: runner etc*) davonziehen (*from sb* jdm) **c** (= *move away: person*) sich entfernen; **she drew away from him when he put his arm around her** sie rückte von ihm ab, als er den Arm um sie legte VT *sep person* weglocken; *object* wegnehmen

► **draw back** VI zurückweichen VT *sep* zurückziehen; *curtains also* aufziehen

► **draw down** VT *sep blinds* herunterlassen; **to draw sth down on oneself** (*fig*) etw auf sich (*acc*) ziehen

► **draw in** VI **a** (*train*) einfahren; (*car*) anhalten **b** (= *get shorter: days*) kürzer werden; **the nights are starting to draw in** die Abende werden wieder länger VT *sep* **a** *breath, air* einziehen **b** (= *attract, gain*) *crowds* anziehen **c** **to draw in one's claws** (*lit, fig*) die Krallen einziehen → **horn d** (= *pull on*) *reins* anziehen

► **draw into** VT (= *involve*) hineinziehen; **I don't want to be drawn into your problems** ich möchte nicht in Ihre Probleme verwickelt *or* hineingezogen werden; **the country is refusing to be drawn into the war** das Land lässt sich nicht in den Krieg hineinziehen; **I tried to draw him into the conversation** ich versuchte, ihn am Gespräch zu beteiligen

► **draw off** VI (*car*) losfahren VT *sep* **a** *gloves, garment* ausziehen **b** *excess liquid* abgießen

► **draw on** VI as **the night drew on** mit fortschreitender Nacht; **the time is drawing on** es wird spät VI +*prep obj* (= *use as source: also* **draw upon**) sich stützen auf (+*acc*); **you'll have to draw on your powers of imagination** Sie müssen Ihre Fantasie *or* Phantasie zu Hilfe nehmen; **the author draws on his experiences in the desert** der Autor schöpft aus seinen Erfahrungen in der Wüste VT *sep* (= *put on*) *stockings, gloves* anziehen

► **draw out** VI **a** (*train*) ausfahren; (*car*) herausfahren (*of* aus) **b** (= *become longer: days*) länger werden VT *sep* **a** (= *take out*) herausziehen; *money* ab-

heben **b** (= *make longer*) ziehen **c** (= *prolong*; **a long-drawn-out meeting** eine sehr in die Länge gezogene Besprechung **d** (= *cause to speak*) **to draw sb out of his shell** jdn aus der Reserve locken

► **draw over** VI **the policeman told the driver to draw over (to the side of the road)** der Polizist sagte dem Autofahrer, er solle an den Straßenrand fahren

► **draw together** VT *sep threads* miteinander verknüpfen; *bits of argument also* in einen Zusammenhang bringen

► **draw up** VI (= *stop: car*) (an)halten VT *sep* **a** (= *formulate*) entwerfen; *contract, agreement* entwerfen, aufsetzen; *will* aufsetzen; *list* aufstellen **b** *chair* heranziehen; *boat* aufschleppen (*spec*), an Land ziehen; **to draw oneself up (to one's full height)** sich (zu seiner vollen Größe) aufrichten **c** (= *set in line*) *troops* aufstellen **d** (= *make stop*) **this thought drew him up short** dieser Gedanke ließ ihn mit einem Ruck innehalten

► **draw upon** VI +*prep obj* = **draw on** VI +*prep obj*

---

drawback ['drɔːbæk] N Nachteil *m*

drawbridge ['drɔːbrɪdʒ] N Zugbrücke *f*

drawee [drɔː'iː] N (*Fin*) Bezogene(r) *mf*, Trassat *m* (*spec*)

drawer N **a** [drɔː'] (*in desk etc*) Schublade *f* → **chest** [1] **b** ['drɔːə'] (*person: of pictures*) Zeichner(in) *m(f)* **c** ['drɔːə'] (*of cheque etc*) Aussteller(in) *m(f)*, Trassant *m* (*spec*) **d** **drawers** [drɔːz] PL (*dated, hum, for men*) Unterhose(n) *f(pl)*; (*for women also*) Schlüpfer *m*

drawing ['drɔːɪŋ] N Zeichnung *f*; **I'm no good at ~** ich bin nicht gut im Zeichnen, ich kann nicht gut zeichnen

drawing: drawing board N Reißbrett *nt*; **the project is still on the ~** (*fig*) das Projekt ist noch in der Planung; **it's back to the ~** (*fig*) das muss noch einmal ganz neu überdacht werden; **drawing paper** N Zeichenpapier *nt*; **drawing pen** N Zeichenfeder *f*; **drawing pin** N (*Brit*) Reißzwecke *f*; **drawing room** N Wohnzimmer *nt*; (*in mansion*) Salon *m*; **drawing table** N Zeichentisch *m*

drawl [drɔːl] VI schleppend sprechen VT schleppend aussprechen N schleppende Sprache; **a Texan ~** schleppendes Texanisch; **a southern ~** ein schleppender südlicher Dialekt

drawn [drɔːn] ptp of **draw**[1] or **draw**[2] ADJ **a** *curtains* zugezogen; *blinds* heruntergezogen **b** (= *haggard, from tiredness*) abgespannt; (*from worry*) abgehärmt **c** *game, match* unentschieden

drawn butter N (*Cook*) Buttersoße *f*

drawstring ['drɔːstrɪŋ] N Kordel *f* zum Zuziehen

dray [dreɪ] N Rollwagen *f*

dray: drayhorse N Zugpferd *nt*; (*in brewery*) Brauereipferd *nt*; **drayman** N Rollkutscher *m*

dread [dred] VT sich fürchten vor (+*dat*), große Angst haben vor (+*dat*); **I'm ~ing Christmas this year** dieses Jahr graut es mir schon vor Weihnachten; **a ~ed disease** eine gefürchtete Krankheit; **and now the ~ed moment, here are the exam results** der mit Schrecken erwartete Augenblick ist da, hier sind die Examensergebnisse; **I ~ to think what may happen** ich wage nicht daran zu denken, was passieren könnte; **I ~** *or* **I'm ~ing seeing her again** ich denke mit Schrecken an ein Wiedersehen mit ihr; **he ~s going to the dentist** er hat schreckliche Angst davor, zum Zahnarzt zu gehen N **a sense of ~** ein Angstgefühl *nt*; **the thought filled me with ~** bei dem Gedanken wurde mir angst und bange; **to live in ~ of the secret police** in ständiger Angst vor der Geheimpolizei leben; **to live in ~ of being found out** in ständiger Angst davor leben, entdeckt zu werden ADJ (*liter*) gefürchtet

dreadful ['dredfʊl] ✪ 7.3 ADJ schrecklich, furchtbar; *person* schrecklich; *weather* scheußlich, furchtbar; **a ~ business** eine schreckliche Angelegenheit; **what a ~ thing to happen** wie entsetzlich *or* furchtbar, dass das passieren musste; **to feel ~** (= *ill*) sich elend fühlen; **I feel ~ (about it)** (= *mortified*) es ist mir schrecklich peinlich; **I feel ~ about letting you down** es ist mir schrecklich unangenehm, Sie im Stich zu lassen

dreadfully ['dredfəlɪ] ADV schrecklich; *behave also* furchtbar; **to treat sb ~** jdn scheußlich behandeln; **something was ~ wrong** etwas stimmte ganz und gar nicht

dreadlocks ['dredlɒks] PL Dreadlocks *pl*

dreadnought ['drednɔːt] N (*Naut*) Dreadnought *m*

dream [driːm] ✪ 12.3 *vb*: pret, ptp **dreamt** (*Brit*) *or* **dreamed** **N** **a** Traum *m*; **to have a bad ~** schlecht träumen; **the whole business was like a bad ~** die ganze Angelegenheit war wie ein böser Traum; **sweet ~s!** träum was Schönes!, träume süß!; **to have a ~ about sb/sth** von jdm/etw träumen; **to see sb/sth in a ~** jdn/etw im Traum sehen; **life is a ~** das Leben ist nur ein Traum; **it worked like a ~** (*inf*) das ging wie im Traum

b (*when awake*) **lost in ~s** traumverloren; **she goes round in a ~** sie lebt wie im Traum; **to be in a ~** (mit offenen Augen) träumen

c (= *fantasy, vision*) Traum *m*; **the house/woman of his ~s** das Haus/die Frau seiner Träume, sein Traumhaus/seine Traumfrau; **she was happy beyond her wildest ~s** sie war so glücklich, wie sie es in ihren kühnsten Träumen nicht für möglich gehalten hätte; **never in my wildest ~s did I think I'd win** ich hätte in meinen kühnsten Träumen nicht gedacht, dass ich gewinnen würde; **in your ~s!** (*inf*) das hättest du wohl gern!; **to have ~s of becoming rich** davon träumen, reich zu werden; **to make a ~ come true for sb, to make sb's ~ come true** jdm einen Traum erfüllen; **all his ~s came true** all seine Träume gingen in Erfüllung; **it was a ~ come true** es war ein Traum, der wahrgeworden war; **I have a ~ of a better world** ich träume von einer besseren Welt; **it's just idle ~s** das sind nichts als Wunschträume

d (*inf*) Schatz *m*; **darling, you're a ~!** Liebling, du bist ein Schatz; **a ~ of a hat** ein traumhaft schöner Hut; **a ~ of a girl** ein Schatz *m* von einem Mädchen; **a ~ of a father** ein toller Vater

VI (*lit, fig*) träumen (*about, of* von); **I'm sorry, I was ~ing** es tut mir Leid, ich habe geträumt; **~ on!** (*inf*) träum du nur weiter!

VT (*lit, fig*) träumen; *dream haben*; **he ~s of being free one day** er träumt davon, eines Tages frei zu sein; **I would never have ~ed of doing such a thing** ich hätte nicht im Traum daran gedacht, so etwas zu tun; **I wouldn't ~ of it** das würde mir nicht im Traum einfallen; **I wouldn't ~ of telling her** es fiele mir nicht im Traum ein, es ihr zu erzählen; **who would have ~ed it would be so complicated** wer hätte es sich träumen lassen, dass es so kompliziert sein würde; **I never ~ed (that) he would come** ich hätte mir nie *or* nicht träumen lassen, dass er kommen würde

ADJ *attr* Traum-; **~boat** (*dated sl*) Traummann *m*; **~ job** Traumjob *m*; **~land** Traumland *nt*; **~ world** Traumwelt *f*

▶ **dream away** VT *sep time* verträumen; **one's life** mit Träumen verbringen

▶ **dream up** VT *sep* (*inf*) *idea* sich (*dat*) einfallen lassen *or* ausdenken; **where did you dream that up?** wie bist du denn bloß darauf gekommen?

dreamer ['driːmə'] N Träumer(in) *m(f)*

dreamily ['driːmɪlɪ] ADV verträumt

dreaminess ['driːmɪnɪs] N Verträumtheit *f*

dreamless ['driːmlɪs] ADJ *sleep* traumlos

dreamlike ['driːmlaɪk] ADJ traumähnlich; *music* traumhaft; **~ quality** Verträumtheit *f*

dreamt [dremt] (*Brit*) pret, ptp of **dream**

dream: dream ticket N (*inf*: *Pol etc, individual*) ideale Besetzung; (*pair*) Traumpaar *nt*; (*group*) ideales Team; **dream world** N Traumwelt *f*

dreamy ['driːmɪ] ADJ (+er) **a** *smile, look, music, voice, person* verträumt; *idea* versponnen; **a ~ look came into the mother's eyes** der Blick der Mutter wurde verträumt **b** (*inf, = lovely*) traumhaft

drear [drɪə'] ADJ (*poet*) = **dreary**

drearily ['drɪərɪlɪ] ADV (+vb) eintönig; *say* monoton; *stare* trüb; (+adj) trostlos; **it rained ~ all day** es war trostlos, wie es den ganzen Tag regnete; **it was ~ familiar** es war nur allzu vertraut

dreariness ['drɪərɪnɪs] N Trostlosigkeit *f*; (*of job, life*) Eintönigkeit *f*

dreary ['drɪərɪ] ADJ (+er) *place* trostlos; *hour, day, month* trostlos, öde; *job, life* eintönig, monoton; *clothes* langweilig; *play, book* langweilig, öde

dredge[1] [dredʒ] **N** **a** Bagger *m*; (*net*) Schleppnetz *nt*; (*vessel*) = **dredger** [1] **VT** *river, canal* ausbaggern, schlämmen

▶ **dredge up** VT *sep* (*lit*) ausbaggern; (*fig*) *unpleasant facts, painful memories* ans Licht holen, hervorkramen

dredge[2] VT (*Cook*) bestäuben, bestreuen

dredger[1] ['dredʒə'] N (= *ship*) Schwimmbagger *m*; (= *machine*) Bagger *m*

dredger[2] N (*Cook*) Streuer *m*; (*also* **sugar dredger**) Zuckerstreuer *m*

dredging[1] ['dredʒɪŋ] N Ausbaggern *nt*

dredging[2] N (*Cook*) Bestreuen *nt*

dregs [dregz] PL **a** (*Boden*)satz *m*; **to drink the ~ of sth** etw bis auf den letzten Tropfen austrinken **b** (*fig*) Abschaum *m*; **the ~ of society** der Abschaum der Gesellschaft

drench [drentʃ] VT **a** (= *soak*) durchnässen; **I'm absolutely ~ed** ich bin durch und durch nass; **to be ~ed in sweat** schweißgebadet sein; **to be ~ed in blood** vor Blut triefen; **to get ~ed to the skin** bis auf die Haut nass werden **b** (*Vet*) Arznei einflößen (+dat)

drenching ['drentʃɪŋ] **N** **to get a ~** bis auf die Haut nass werden **ADJ** **he's been working out in the ~ rain all day** er hat den ganzen Tag draußen im strömenden Regen gearbeitet

Dresden ['drezdən] N (*also* **Dresden china**) ≈ Meißner Porzellan *nt*

dress [dres] **N** **a** (*for woman*) Kleid *nt* **b** *no pl* (= *clothing*) Kleidung *f*; **articles of ~** Kleidungsstücke *pl*; **to be in eastern ~** orientalisch gekleidet sein **c** *no pl* (= *way of dressing*) Kleidung *f*, Kleider *pl*; **to be outrageous/careless in one's ~** sich ausgefallen/nachlässig kleiden

VT **a** (= *clothe*) *child* anziehen; *family* kleiden; *recruits etc* einkleiden; **to get ~ed** sich anziehen; **are you ~ed?** bist du schon angezogen?; **he's old enough to ~ himself** er ist alt genug, um sich allein anzuziehen; **to ~ sb in sth** jdm etw anziehen; **she ~es herself with great fastidiousness** sie kleidet sich sehr sorgfältig; **~ed in black** in Schwarz, schwarz gekleidet; **~ed in a sailor's uniform** im Matrosenanzug; **he was ~ed in a suit** er trug einen Anzug; **to be ~ed for the country/for the town/for tennis** fürs Land/für die Stadt/zum Tennisspielen angezogen sein; **~ed to kill** (*inf*) todschick aufgemacht (*inf*)

b (*Theat*) *play* Kostüme entwerfen für **c** (= *arrange, decorate*) (*Naut*) *ship* beflaggen; (*Comm*) *shop window* dekorieren; **to ~ sb's hair** jdm das Haar frisieren **d** (*Cook*) *salad* anmachen; *food for table* anrichten; *chicken* brat- *or* kochfertig machen; **~ed crab** farcierter Krebs **e** *skins* gerben; *material* appretieren; *timber* hobeln; *stone* schleifen **f** *wound* verbinden **g** *troops* ausrichten **h** (*Agr*) *fields* vorbereiten

VI **a** sich anziehen *or* kleiden; **to ~ in black** sich schwarz kleiden; **she ~es very well** sie kleidet sich sehr gut; **to ~ for dinner** sich zum Essen umziehen **b** (*soldiers*) sich ausrichten; **right, ~!** rechts, richt't euch!

▶ **dress down** **VT** *sep* **a** *horse* striegeln **b** **to dress sb down** jdn herunterputzen (*inf*) **VI** sich betont lässig kleiden

▶ **dress up** **VI** **a** (*in smart clothes*) sich fein machen, sich schön anziehen **b** (*in fancy dress*) sich verkleiden; **he came dressed up as Santa Claus** er kam als Weihnachtsmann (verkleidet); **to dress up as a pirate** sich als Pirat verkleiden; **it's just his old plan dressed up in a new way** das ist bloß sein alter Plan in einem neuen Gewand **VT** *sep* **a** (= *disguise*) verkleiden **b** (= *smarten*) *person* herausputzen; **dress yourself up a bit!** mach dich ein bisschen schön!

dressage ['dresɑːʒ] N Dressur *f*

dress: dress circle N erster Rang; **dress coat** N Frack *m*; **dress code** N Kleiderordnung *f*; **dress designer** N Modezeichner(in) *m(f)*

dresser[1] ['dresə'] N **a** (*Theat*) Garderobier *m*, Garderobiere *f* **b** (*Med*) *his* ~ sein Assistent bei der Operation **c** (*tool, for wood*) Hobel *m*; (*for stone*) Schleifstein *m* **d** (*Comm: also* **window-dresser**) Dekorateur(in) *m(f)* **e** **she's a stylish ~** sie kleidet sich stilvoll

dresser[2] N **a** Anrichte *f* **b** (*US, = dressing table*) Frisierkommode *f*

dress form N Schneiderpuppe *f*

dressing ['dresɪŋ] N **a** (= *act*) Anziehen *nt*, Ankleiden *nt* **b** (*Med: = bandage, ointment*) Verband *m* **c** (*Cook*) Soße *f*, Dressing *nt* **d** (*Agr*) Dünger *m*; **a ~ of phosphate** Phosphatdünger *m* **e** (*of material*) Appretieren *nt*; (*of stone*) Schleifen *nt*; (*of leather*) Gerben *nt*; (*of wood*) Hobeln *nt*; (*for material*) Appreturmittel *nt*; (*for leather*) Gerbmittel *nt*

dressing: dressing-down N (*inf*) Standpauke *f* (*inf*); **to give sb a ~** jdn herunterputzen (*inf*), jdm eine Standpauke halten (*inf*); **to get a ~** eins auf den Deckel *or* das Dach kriegen (*inf*); **dressing gown** N Morgenrock *m*, Morgenmantel *m*; (*in towelling*) Bademantel *m*; **dressing room** N (*in house*) Ankleidezimmer *nt*; (*Theat*) (Künstler)garderobe *f*; (*Sport*) Umkleidekabine *f*; **dressing station** N Verbandsplatz *m*; **dressing table** N Frisiertoilette *or* -kommode *f*; **dressing-table set** N Toilettengarnitur *f*

dress: dressmaker N (Damen)schneider(in) *m(f)*; **dressmaking** N Schneidern *nt*; **dress parade** N (*Mil*) Parade *f* in Galauniform; **dress pattern** N (*Sew*) Schnittmuster *nt*; **dress rehearsal** N (*lit, fig*) Generalprobe *f*; **dress sense** N **he has no ~ at all** er hat keinen Sinn dafür, wie man sich gut anzieht; **her ~ is appalling** sie zieht sich fürchterlich an; **dress shield** N Arm- *or* Schweißblatt *nt*; **dress shirt** N Frackhemd *nt*; **dress suit** N Abendanzug *m*; **dress uniform** N Galauniform *f*; **dress watch** N elegante Uhr

dressy ['dresɪ] ADJ (+er) (*inf*) *clothes* elegant; *person* elegant angezogen; *event* vornehm; **do you think I look/a long skirt would be too ~?** meinst du, dass ich zu fein angezogen bin/ein langer Rock übertrieben wäre?

drew [druː] pret of **draw** [1] *or* **draw** [2]

dribble ['drɪbl] **VI** **a** (*liquids*) tropfen **b** (*baby, person*) sabbern; (*animal*) geifern **c** (*Sport*) dribbeln **d** (*people*) **to ~ back/in etc** kleckerweise zurückkommen/hereinkommen etc (*inf*) **VT** **a** (*Sport*) **to ~ the ball** mit dem Ball dribbeln **b** (*baby etc*) kleckern; **to ~ saliva** sabbern; **he ~d milk down his chin** er kleckerte sich (*dat*) Milch übers Kinn **N** **a** (*of water*) ein paar Tropfen; **a slow ~ of water was still coming out of the pipe** es tröpfelte immer noch etwas aus der Leitung **b** (*of saliva*) Tropfen *m* **c** (*Sport*) Dribbling *nt*

dribbler ['drɪblə'] N **a** (*Sport*) Dribbelkünstler(in), Dribbler(in) *m(f)* **b** **he's a terrible ~** (*baby*) er kleckert ständig (*inf*)

driblet ['drɪblɪt] N (= *drop*) Tropfen *m*; **in ~s** kleckerweise (*inf*); **~s of intelligence began to**

come through Informationen fingen an durchzusickern

dribs and drabs ['drɪbzən'dræbz] **PL in ~** kleckerweise (inf)

dried [draɪd] pret, ptp of **dry** ADJ vegetables, herbs, apricots etc getrocknet; blood eingetrocknet; **~ yeast** Trockenhefe f; **~ egg** Trockenei nt, Eipulver nt; **~ milk** Trockenmilch f, Milchpulver nt

dried: dried flowers PL Trockenblumen pl; **dried fruit** N Dörrobst nt, Backobst nt

dried-up [draɪd'ʌp] ADJ **a** (pej inf: = wizened) verhutzelt; **a ~ old spinster** eine vertrocknete alte Jungfer **b** (= stale) food eingetrocknet **c** river bed, oasis ausgetrocknet; well versiegt → also **dry up**

drier N = **dryer**

drift [drɪft] **VI a** (Naut, Aviat, snow) treiben; (sand) wehen; (Rad) verschwimmen; **to ~ off course** abtreiben; **rally drivers have a technique of ~ing round corners** Rallyefahrer haben eine Technik, sich durch Kurven tragen zu lassen

b (fig, person) sich treiben lassen; **to let things ~** die Dinge treiben lassen; **to let things ~ into marriage/crime** er schlitterte in die Ehe/in eine kriminelle Laufbahn hinein (inf); **he ~ed from job to job** er ließ sich planlos von Job zu Job treiben; **he was ~ing aimlessly along** (in life etc) er lebte planlos in den Tag hinein, er ließ sich plan- und ziellos treiben; **the nation was ~ing toward(s) a crisis** das Land trieb auf eine Krise zu; **young people are ~ing away from the villages** junge Leute wandern aus den Dörfern ab; **to ~ apart** (people) sich auseinander leben; **we're ~ing apart** wir leben uns immer mehr auseinander; **the audience started ~ing away** das Publikum begann wegzugehen

VT treiben; (wind) snow also vor sich her treiben

N a (of air, water current) Strömung f; **the ~ of the current** (speed) die (Stärke der) Strömung; (direction) die Strömung(srichtung)

b (= mass caused by drifting, of sand, fallen snow) Verwehung f; (of leaves) Haufen m

c (of ship, aircraft) (Ab)drift f, Abweichung f; **to allow for ~** Abdriften or Abweichung (mit) einkalkulieren

d (Geol: = deposits) Geschiebe nt; **glacial ~** Moräne f

e (= tendency) **the ~ towards the cities** der Drang in die Städte; **the ~ of policy away from this reform** das grundsätzliche Abrücken von dieser Reform; **the ~ of support away from him** die nachlassende Unterstützung für ihn

f (= general meaning: of questions) Richtung f, Tendenz f; **I caught the ~ of what he said** ich verstand, worauf er hinauswollte; **if you get my ~** wenn Sie mich richtig verstehen

g (Ling) Tendenz f

▶ **drift off** VI **to drift off (to sleep)** einschlafen; (= doze) eindämmern

drift anchor N (Naut) Treibanker m

drifter ['drɪftə'] N **a** (= person) Gammler(in) m(f); **he's a bit of a ~** ihn hälts nirgends lange **b** (boat) Drifter m

drift ice N Treibeis nt

drifting ['drɪftɪŋ] N (= drifting snow) Schneeverwehungen pl

drifting mine N Treibmine f

drift: drift net N Treibnetz nt; **drift sand** N Treibsand m; **driftwood** N Treibholz nt

drill[1] [drɪl] **N a** (for metal, wood, oil, dentist's) Bohrer m **b** (Mil) Drill m; (= marching etc) Exerzieren nt; **we get ~ every morning** jeden Morgen müssen wir exerzieren

VT (for metal, wood, oil, dentist's) **to ~** bohren; teeth anbohren **b** bohren; **to ~ for oil** nach Öl bohren; **have they started ~ing yet?** haben sie schon mit den Bohrungen angefangen?

▶ **drill down** VI (in die Tiefe) bohren; **we kept drilling down until we hit oil** wir bohrten bis wir auf Öl stießen; **we drilled down 500 feet** wir bohrten in eine Tiefe von 500 Fuß

drill[2] **N a** no pl (esp Mil, also fig) Drill m; (= marching etc) Exerzieren nt; **we get ~ every morning** jeden Morgen müssen wir exerzieren

b (in grammar etc) Drillübung f; **pattern ~** Patterndrill m

c (inf, = procedure) **they went through the ~** sie übten den Ablauf; **they all knew the ~** sie wussten alle, was sie tun mussten; **he doesn't know the ~** er weiß nicht, wie der Laden läuft (inf) or wie die Sache angefasst werden muss

VT a soldiers drillen; (in marching etc) exerzieren

b **to ~ pupils in grammar** mit den Schülern Grammatik pauken

c **manners were ~ed into me as a child** man hat mir als Kind gute Manieren eingedrillt (inf); **I ~ed into him that ...** ich habe es ihm eingebläut, dass ... (inf)

VI (Mil) gedrillt werden; (marching etc) exerzieren

drill[3] (Agr) **N a** (= furrow) Furche f **b** (= machine) Drillmaschine f **VT** drillen

drill[4] N (Tex) Drillich m

drill bit N Bit nt, Bohrspitze f

drill ground N Exerzierplatz m

drilling ['drɪlɪŋ] N (for oil) Bohrung f; (by dentist) Bohren nt; **when does ~ start?** wann fangen die Bohrungen an?; **~ operations begin next week** die Bohrungen fangen nächste Woche an

drilling platform N Bohrplattform f

drilling rig N Bohrturm m; (at sea) Bohrinsel f

drill sergeant N Ausbilder m

drily ['draɪlɪ] ADV **a** (= with dry humour) say, laugh trocken; (= unemotionally) say nüchtern; **~ witty** trocken-geistreich; **~ ironic** trocken-ironisch **b** cough, kiss trocken

drink [drɪŋk] vb: pret **drank**, ptp **drunk** **N a** (= liquid to drink) Getränk nt; **food and ~** Essen und Getränke; **may I have a ~?** kann ich etwas zu trinken haben?; **would you like a ~ of water?** möchten Sie etwas Wasser?; **to give sb a ~** jdm etwas zu trinken geben; **~s can** Getränkedose f

b (= glass of alcoholic drink) Glas nt, Drink m; **have a ~!** trink doch was or einen!; **can I get you a ~?** kann ich Ihnen etwas zu trinken holen?; **let's have a ~** trinken wir was; **I need a ~!** ich brauche was zu trinken!; **he likes a ~** er trinkt gern (einen); **he's had a good ~** (inf) er hat ein paar über den Durst getrunken; **the ~s are on me** die Getränke zahle or spendiere ich; **the ~s are on the house** die Getränke gehen auf Kosten des Hauses; **to ask friends in for ~s** Freunde auf ein Glas or einen Drink einladen

c no pl (= alcoholic liquor) Alkohol m; **the ~ problem** der Alkoholismus; **he has a ~ problem** er trinkt; **~ caused his downfall** der Alkohol hat ihn ruiniert; **to be the worse for ~** betrunken sein; **to take to ~** zu trinken anfangen; **his worries drove him to ~** vor lauter Sorgen fing er an zu trinken; **she drove him to ~** sie war der Grund, warum er zu trinken anfing; **it's enough to drive you to ~!** da könnte man wirklich zum Trinker werden

d (esp Naut, Aviat inf: = sea) Bach m (sl); **three planes went down into the ~** drei Flugzeuge gingen in den Bach (sl)

VT trinken; **would you like something to ~?** möchten Sie etwas zu trinken (haben)?; **is the water fit to ~?** ist das Trinkwasser?, kann man das Wasser trinken?; **he ~s all his wages** er vertrinkt seinen ganzen Lohn; **to ~ oneself silly** sich dumm und dämlich trinken (inf) or saufen (inf); **to ~ oneself into a stupor** sich sinnlos besaufen (inf); **this car ~s petrol** dieses Auto säuft das Benzin nur so (inf); **they drank the pub dry** (Brit) sie tranken die Kneipe leer → **table N a**

VI trinken; **he doesn't ~** er trinkt nicht, er trinkt keinen Alkohol; **his father drank** sein Vater hat getrunken or war Trinker; **to go out ~ing** einen trinken gehen; **one shouldn't ~ and drive** nach dem Trinken soll man nicht fahren; **~ing and driving** Alkohol am Steuer; **to ~** auf jdn trinken; (to one's neighbour at table etc) jdm zuprosten or zutrinken; **to ~ to sth** auf etw (acc) trinken; **I'll ~ to that** darauf trinke ich

▶ **drink away** VT sep fortune vertrinken; sorrows im Alkohol ersäufen

▶ **drink down** VT sep hinuntertrinken, hinunterschlucken

▶ **drink in** VT sep **a** (plants etc) water aufsaugen; (person) air einsaugen, einatmen; sunshine in sich (acc) aufsaugen **b** (fig) a sight, his words etc (begierig) in sich aufnehmen

▶ **drink off** VT sep austrinken, leeren; **he drank off the wine in one long gulp** er trank den Wein in einem Zug aus

▶ **drink up** **VI** austrinken; **drink up!** trink aus! **VT** sep austrinken

drinkable ['drɪŋkəbl] ADJ **a** (= not poisonous) trinkbar; **~ water** Trinkwasser nt **b** (= palatable) genießbar, trinkbar; **a very ~ little wine** ein sehr süffiges Weinchen

drink: drink-driver N (Brit) angetrunkener Autofahrer, angetrunkene Autofahrerin; **drink-driving** (Brit) **N** Trunkenheit f am Steuer ATTR charge, conviction wegen Trunkenheit am Steuer; campaign gegen Trunkenheit am Steuer; **the number of ~ offences** die Zahl der Fälle von Trunkenheit am Steuer

drinker ['drɪŋkə'] N Trinker(in) m(f); **he's a heavy ~** er ist ein starker Trinker

drinking ['drɪŋkɪŋ] **N** Trinken nt; **there had been some heavy ~ at the party** auf der Party war viel getrunken worden; **his ~ caused his marriage to break up** an seiner Trunksucht ging seine Ehe in die Brüche; **underage ~** der Alkoholkonsum von Minderjährigen

ADJ Trink-, Sauf- (inf); **~ habits** Trinkgewohnheiten pl; **~ session** or bingee (inf) Trinkgelage nt; **~ bout** or **spree** Sauftour f (inf); **when his wife died he went on a ~ bout for three months** als seine Frau starb, hat er drei Monate lang nur getrunken; **they are ~ friends** sie gehen oft zusammen einen trinken (inf); **I'm not really a ~ man** ich trinke eigentlich nicht viel Alkohol

drinking: drinking age N Mindestalter für den Alkoholkonsum in der Öffentlichkeit; **drinking chocolate** N Trinkschokolade f; **drinking club** N Klub, in dem Alkohol ausgeschenkt wird; **drinking companion** N Zechkumpan(in) m(f); **drinking den** N Kaschemme f (pej); **drinking fountain** N Trinkwasserbrunnen m; **drinking glass** N Trinkglas nt; **drinking horn** N Trinkhorn nt; **drinking laws** PL Gesetze über den Alkoholkonsum; **drinking problem** N Alkoholproblem nt; **drinking song** N Trinklied nt; **drinking station** N (at marathon) Verpflegungsstation f; **drinking straw** N Trinkhalm m, Strohhalm m; **drinking trough** N Wassertrog m; **drinking-up time** N (Brit) die letzten zehn Minuten vor der Polizeistunde; **drinking water** N Trinkwasser nt

drinks machine N Getränkeautomat m

drink-up time N (Brit) Zeit, innerhalb derer Gäste ihre Getränke nach Schließung des Lokals austrinken können

drip [drɪp] **VI** (water, tap) tropfen; **to be ~ping with sweat** schweißüberströmt or schweißgebadet sein; **to be ~ping with blood** vor Blut triefen; **sweat was ~ping off his forehead** der Schweiß triefte ihm von der Stirn; **the walls were ~ping with water** die Wände waren triefnass; **his voice was ~ping with sarcasm** seine Stimme triefte nur so vor or von Sarkasmus; **she was ~ping with jewellery** (Brit) or **jewelry** (US) sie strotzte nur so von Schmuck

VT liquid träufeln, tropfen; **he was ~ping water/blood all over the carpet** Wasser/sein Blut tropfte überall auf den Teppich; **his clothes were ~ping water all over the carpet** von seinen Kleidern tropfte Wasser überall auf den Teppich; **careful, you're ~ping paint on my coat** pass auf, die Farbe tropft mir auf den Mantel!

N a (= sound: of water, rain, tap) Tropfen nt **b** (= drop) Tropfen m **c** (Med) Infusionsapparat m, Tropf m (inf); **to be on a ~** eine Infusion bekommen, am Tropf hängen (inf) **d** (inf: person) Waschlappen m (inf)

drip: drip coffee N (US) Filterkaffee m; **drip-dry** ADJ shirt bügelfrei VT tropfnass aufhängen VI bügelfrei sein; "drip-dry" (on label) „bügelfrei"; **let it ~** hängen Sie es tropfnass auf; **drip-feed** (Med) N künstliche Ernährung VT künstlich ernähren

dripping ['drɪpɪŋ] ADJ **a** (= soaking) **~ (wet)** tropfnass **b** tap tropfend; gutter undicht N **a** (Brit Cook) Bratenfett nt **b** (= action of water etc) Tropfen nt

dripping pan N (Cook) Fettpfanne f

drippy ['drɪpɪ] ADJ (+er) (inf) **a** person doof (inf); singer, film, novel schmalzig **b** (US, = rainy) day regnerisch

drivability [ˌdraɪvə'bɪlɪtɪ] N (Aut, = performance) Fahreigenschaften pl; (= ease of handling) Fahrkomfort m

drive [draɪv] vb: pret **drove**, ptp **driven** N **a** (Aut: = journey) (Auto)fahrt f; **to go for a ~** ein bisschen (raus)fahren; **to go for a ~ to the coast** ans Meer fahren; **he took her for a ~ in his new car** er machte mit ihr eine Spazierfahrt in seinem neuen Auto; **it's about one hour's ~ from London** es ist etwa eine Stunde Fahrt von London (entfernt) **b** (into house: also **driveway**) Einfahrt f, Zufahrt f; (longer) Auffahrt f, Zufahrt f **c** (Golf, Tennis) Treibschlag m **d** (Psych etc) Trieb m; **sex ~** Geschlechts- or Sexualtrieb m **e** (= energy) Schwung m, Elan m, Tatendrang m; **you're losing your ~** Ihr Elan or Schwung lässt nach; **he has no ~** er hat keinen Elan or Schwung **f** (Comm, Pol etc) Aktion f; **this is part of a ~ to attract new members** das ist Teil einer Mitgliederwerbeaktion; **recruitment ~** Anwerbungskampagne f; **fundraising ~** Sammelaktion f; **the ~ toward(s) democracy** die starke Entwicklung zur Demokratie hin → **export** VI **g** (Mil: = offensive) kraftvolle Offensive **h** (Mech, = power transmission) Antrieb m; **front-wheel/rear-wheel ~** Vorderrad-/Hinterradantrieb m **i** (Aut) Steuerung f; **left-hand ~** Linkssteuerung f **j** (Cards) → **whist** **k** (Comput) Laufwerk nt VT **a** (= cause to move) people, animals, dust, clouds etc treiben; **to ~ sb out of the country** jdn aus dem Land (ver)treiben; **to ~ a nail/stake into sth** einen Nagel/Pfahl in etw (acc) treiben; **the gale drove the ship off course** der Sturm trieb das Schiff vom Kurs ab **b** cart, car, train fahren; **he ~s a taxi (for a living)** er ist Taxifahrer, er fährt Taxi (inf) **c** (= convey in vehicle) person fahren; **I'll ~ you home** ich fahre Sie nach Hause; **could you ~ us there?** können Sie uns dahin fahren? **d** (= provide power for, operate) motor (belt, shaft) antreiben; (electricity, fuel) betreiben; (Comput) steuern; **a car ~n by electricity** ein Auto nt mit Elektroantrieb **e** (Tennis, Golf) ball driven (spec); **to ~ the ball** einen Treibball spielen **f** (= cause to be in a state or to become) treiben; **to ~ sb round the bend** (Brit inf) or **mad** jdn verrückt machen; **to ~ sb to murder** jdn zum Mord treiben; **I was ~n to it** ich wurde dazu getrieben; **who/what drove you to do that?** wer/was trieb or brachte Sie dazu(, das zu tun)? **g** (= force to work hard) person hart herannehmen, schinden (pej); **you're driving him too hard** Sie nehmen ihn zu hart ran, Sie schinden ihn zu sehr (pej); **he ~s himself very hard** er fordert sich selbst sehr stark **h** tunnel treiben; well ausheben; nail schlagen VI **a** (= travel in vehicle) fahren; **can you** or **do you ~?** fahren Sie Auto?; **he's learning to ~** er lernt Auto fahren; **to ~ at 50 km an hour** mit (einer Geschwindigkeit von) 50 km in der Stunde fahren; **to ~ on the right** rechts fahren; **did you come by train? – no, we drove** sind Sie mit der Bahn gekommen? – nein, wir sind mit dem Auto gefahren; **it's cheaper to ~** mit dem Auto ist es billiger **b** (= move violently) schlagen, peitschen; **the rain was driving into our faces** der Regen peitschte uns (dat) ins Gesicht

▶**drive along** VI (vehicle, person) dahinfahren VT sep (wind, current) person, boat (voran)treiben

▶**drive at** VI +prep obj (fig, = intend, mean) hinauswollen auf (+acc); **what are you driving at?** worauf wollen Sie hinaus?

▶**drive away** VI (car, person) wegfahren VT sep (lit, fig) person, cares vertreiben

▶**drive back** VI (car, person) zurückfahren VT sep **a** (= cause to retreat) person zurückdrängen; enemy zurücktreiben, zurückdrängen **b** (= convey back in vehicle) person zurückfahren

▶**drive home** VT sep nail einschlagen, einhämmern; argument einhämmern; **she drove home her point that ...** sie legte eindringlich und überzeugend dar, dass ...; **how can I drive it home to him that it's urgent?** wie kann ich (es) ihm nur klarmachen, dass es dringend ist?

▶**drive in** VI (car, person) (hinein)fahren; **he drove into the garage** er fuhr in die Garage VT sep nail (hin)einschlagen, (hin)einhämmern; screw (r)eindrehen

▶**drive off** VI **a** (person, car) weg- or abfahren **b** (Golf) abschlagen VT sep **a** person, enemy vertreiben **b** **she was driven off in a big Mercedes** sie fuhr in einem großen Mercedes weg; **he was driven off in an ambulance** er wurde in einem Krankenwagen weggebracht or abtransportiert

▶**drive on** VI (person, car) weiterfahren VT sep (= incite, encourage) person antreiben; (to do sth bad) anstiften

▶**drive out** VI heraus-/hinausfahren; **he drove out onto the street** er fuhr auf die Straße (hinaus) VT sep person hinaustreiben or jagen; evil thoughts austreiben

▶**drive over** VI hinüberfahren VT always separate (in car) person überfahren; **he drove his family over to see us** er hat seine Familie (mit dem Auto) zu uns gebracht VI +prep obj dog überfahren

▶**drive up** VI (car, person) vorfahren; **a car drove up outside the house** ein Auto fuhr vor dem Haus vor

drive: drive belt N Treibriemen m; **drive-by** ADJ shooting, crime, murder aus dem fahrenden Auto heraus (begangen); **drive-in** N cinema (esp Brit) Autokino nt; **~ bank** Bank f mit Autoschalter; **~ restaurant** Drive-in-Restaurant nt; **to watch a ~ movie** sich (dat) einen Film im Autokino ansehen N (= restaurant) Drive-in-Restaurant nt

drivel ['drɪvl] N (pej) Blödsinn m, Kokolores m (inf); **what a lot of ~!** das ist ja kompletter Blödsinn!; **mindless ~** leeres Gefasel (pej) VI Unsinn reden; **what's he ~ling** (Brit) or **~ing** (US) **(on) about?** was faselt er da?, worüber labert er da? (inf)

driven ['drɪvn] ptp of **drive**

-driven ['drɪvn] ADJ suf -betrieben; **battery-driven** batteriebetrieben; **computer-driven** computergesteuert; **steam-driven train** Zug m mit Dampflokomotive

driver ['draɪvə] N **a** (of car, taxi, lorry, bus) Fahrer(in) m(f); (Brit: of locomotive) Führer(in) m(f); (of coach) Kutscher(in) m(f); **~'s seat** (lit) Fahrersitz m; **to be in the ~'s seat** (fig) das Steuer führen, die Zügel in der Hand haben **b** (of animals) Treiber(in) m(f) **c** (= golf club) Driver m **d** (Comput) Treiber m

driver's license N (US) Führerschein m

drive: drive shaft N Antriebswelle f; (Aut) Kardanwelle f; **drive-through**, (esp US) **drive-thru** N Drive-thru m ADJ restaurant mit Drive-thru; drugstore mit Autoschalter; **driveway** N Auffahrt f; (longer) Zufahrtsstraße f or -weg m; **drive wheel** N Antriebsrad nt, Treibrad nt

driving ['draɪvɪŋ] N Fahren nt; **his ~ is awful** er fährt schrecklich schlecht; **I do a lot of ~ in my job** in meinem Beruf muss ich sehr viel fahren; **~ is her hobby** Autofahren ist ihr Hobby; **I**

don't like ~ ich fahre nicht gern (Auto); **~ position** Fahrposition f ADJ **a** (= motivating) ambition brennend; **to be the ~ force behind sth** die treibende Kraft bei etw sein **b** **~ rain** peitschender Regen; **~ snow** Schneetreiben nt

driving: driving ban N Führerscheinentzug m; **he was given a two-year ~** ihm wurde der Führerschein für zwei Jahre entzogen; **driving conditions** PL Straßenverhältnisse pl; **driving distance** N **to be within easy ~** mit dem Auto leicht erreichbar sein; **driving experience** N Fahrpraxis f; **driving instructor** N Fahrlehrer(in) m(f); **driving iron** N (Golf) Driving-Iron m; **driving lesson** N Fahrstunde f; **driving licence** N (Brit) Führerschein m

---

DRIVING LICENCE, DRIVER'S LICENSE

In Großbritannien erhält ein Führerscheinanwärter erst einmal eine vorübergehende Fahrerlaubnis, die **provisional licence**. In einem Führerschein, der **driving licence**, ist kein Foto des Inhabers, und dieser ist auch nicht verpflichtet, das Papier beim Fahren mit sich zu führen. Allerdings muss es auf Verlangen innerhalb von sieben Tagen auf der Polizeiwache vorgelegt werden. Eine volle Fahrerlaubnis behält seine Gültigkeit bis zum siebzigsten Geburtstag des Inhabers und muss danach alle drei Jahre erneuert werden.

In den USA ist es von Staat zu Staat verschieden, ab wann man einen Führerschein, die **driver's license**, erwerben darf - von 15 bis 21 reicht die Spanne. Allerdings können Führerscheinanwärter schon davor **learners' permits** oder **junior licenses** erhalten, mit denen Jugendlichen das Autofahren unter bestimmten Umständen erlaubt ist, zum Beispiel für den Schulweg. Der Führerschein muss immer mitgeführt werden, da er häufig dazu dient, Identität oder Alter des Inhabers auszuweisen. Normalerweise gilt die **driver's license** vier bis sechs Jahre und muss danach erneuert werden.

---

driving: driving mirror N Rückspiegel m; **driving offence**, (US) **driving offense** N Verkehrsdelikt nt; **driving range** N (Golf) Drivingrange m; **driving school** N Fahrschule f; **driving seat** N Fahrersitz m; **to be in the ~** (fig) das Steuer führen, die Zügel in der Hand haben; **to put sb in the ~** (fig) jdm die Führung übergeben; **we need to put our party back in the ~** wir müssen unsere Partei wieder an die Macht bringen; **driving style** N Fahrweise f; **driving test** N Fahrprüfung f; **to take/fail/pass one's ~** die Fahrprüfung machen/nicht bestehen/bestehen; **driving wheel** N (Brit) Antriebsrad nt

drizzle ['drɪzl] N Nieselregen m, Sprühregen m VI nieseln VT (pour over) träufeln; **~ oil over the salad** Öl auf den Salat träufeln

drizzly ['drɪzlɪ] ADJ **~ weather** Nieselwetter nt; **it's ~** es nieselt

droll ADJ , **drolly** ADV [drəʊl, -lɪ] komisch, amüsant

dromedary ['drɒmɪdərɪ] N Dromedar nt

drone [drəʊn] N **a** (= bee, fig) Drohne f **b** (= sound, of bees) Summen nt; (of engine, aircraft) Brummen nt **c** (= monotonous way of speaking) monotone Stimme **d** (Mus, = bass voice part) Bass m; (of bagpipes) Brummer m; (sound) Bordun(ton) m **e** (Aviat, = robot plane) ferngesteuertes Flugzeug VI **a** (bee) summen; (engine, aircraft) brummen **b** (= speak monotonously: also **drone away** or **on**) eintönig sprechen; (in reciting) leiern; **he ~d on and on for hours** er redete stundenlang in seinem monotonen Tonfall; **we had to listen to him droning on about politics** wir mussten seinem monotonen Geschwafel über Politik zuhören (inf)

▶ **drone out** VT *sep speech* monoton vortragen; (*reciting*) leiern

drongo ['drɒŋɡəʊ] N **a** (*esp Austral, pej inf, = person*) Schwachkopf *m* (*pej inf*) **b** (= *bird*) Drongo *m*

drool [druːl] VI sabbern; (*animal*) geifern

▶ **drool over** VI +*prep obj* richtig verliebt sein in (+*acc*); **everyone is drooling over the huge reward offered** alle sind scharf auf die hohe Belohnung; **he sat there drooling over a copy of Playboy** er geilte sich an einem Playboyheft auf (*sl*)

droop [druːp] VI **a** (*lit, person*) vornübergebeugt stehen, krumm stehen, sich schlecht halten; (*shoulders*) hängen; (*head*) herunterfallen; (*eyelids*) herunterhängen; (*with sleepiness*) zufallen; (*flowers*) die Köpfe hängen lassen; (*feathers, one's arms, breasts*) schlaff herunterhängen; (*rope, roof etc*) durchhängen **b** (*fig, one's interest, energy*) erlahmen; (*audience etc*) erschlaffen, schlaff werden; **his spirits were beginning to ~** sein Mut begann zu schwinden *or* sinken; **the heat made him ~** die Hitze machte ihn schlaff *or* matt **VT** head hängen lassen **N** (*lit, of body*) Gebeugtsein *nt*; (*of eyelids*) Schwere *f*; **I recognized her by the familiar ~ of her shoulders** ich habe sie an ihren hängenden Schultern erkannt

drooping ['druːpɪŋ] ADJ **a** head, shoulders, breasts, feathers, leaves, tail hängend; hand, branches herunterhängend; moustache nach unten hängend; flowers welk; eyelids herunterhängend; (*with sleep*) schwer; roof durchhängend **b** **a drink to revive his ~ spirits** ein Schluck, um seine (geschwundenen) Lebensgeister wieder zu wecken

droopy ['druːpɪ] ADJ **a** schlaff; tail herabhängend; moustache nach unten hängend; eyelids herunterhängend; (*with sleep*) schwer **b** (*inf, = tired, weak*) schlaff, schlapp (*inf*)

---

drop [drɒp]

| 1 NOUN | 3 INTRANSITIVE VERB |
| 2 TRANSITIVE VERB | 4 PHRASAL VERBS |

1 – NOUN

a of liquid Tropfen *m*; **drop by drop** tropfenweise; **a drop of blood** ein Blutstropfen *m*, ein Tropfen *m* Blut; **just a drop for me** für mich nur einen Tropfen; **a drop of wine?** ein Schlückchen *nt* Wein?; **it's a drop in the ocean** *or* **bucket** (*fig*) das ist ein Tropfen auf den heißen Stein; **eye drops** Augentropfen *pl*

b = fall (*in temperature, prices*) Rückgang *m* (*in gen*); (*sudden*) Sturz *m* (*in gen*); (*in blood pressure*) Absinken *nt*; **a drop in prices** ein Preisrückgang *m*/-sturz *m*; **20% is quite a drop** 20%, das ist stark gefallen; **he took a big drop in salary when he changed jobs** als er die Stelle wechselte, nahm er eine beträchtliche Gehaltsverschlechterung in Kauf; **a sudden/noticeable drop in temperature** ein plötzlicher/merklicher Temperaturabfall

c = vertical distance (= *difference in level*) Höhenunterschied *m*; (= *fall*) Sturz *m*, Fall *m*; **a drop of ten feet** ein Höhenunterschied von zehn Fuß; **there's a drop of ten feet down to the ledge** bis zu dem Felsvorsprung geht es zehn Fuß hinunter; **it's a nasty drop** es geht tief hinunter; **it was a sheer drop from the top of the cliff into the sea** die Klippen fielen schroff zum Meer ab

d = delivery (*of supplies, arms*) Abwurf *m*; (*of drugs etc*) Lieferung *f*; (= *parachute jump*) (Ab-)sprung *m*; **the Red Cross made a drop of medical supplies into the flood zone** das Rote Kreuz warf Medikamente über dem Überschwemmungsgebiet ab

e of gallows Falltür *f*

f Theat (*also*) **drop curtain** Vorhang *m*

g = hiding place (*for secret mail*) toter Briefkasten

h = advantage **to have the drop on sb** jdn ausstechen können; **to get the drop on sb** sich (*dat*) einen Vorteil gegenüber jdm verschaffen

i = sweet Drops *m*

2 – TRANSITIVE VERB

a = cause to fall in drops liquid tropfen

b = allow to fall fallen lassen; bomb, supplies, pamphlets, burden abwerfen; parachutist absetzen; voice senken; curtsy machen; (*Knitting*) stitch fallen lassen; (= *lower*) hemline herunterlassen; (*Theat*) curtain herunterlassen; **I dropped my watch** meine Uhr ist runtergefallen; **don't drop it!** lass es nicht fallen!; **he dropped his heavy cases on the floor** er setzte *or* stellte seine schweren Koffer auf dem Boden ab; **drop that gun!** lass die Pistole fallen!; **to drop a letter in the postbox** (*Brit*) *or* **mailbox** (*US*) einen Brief einwerfen *or* in den Briefkasten werfen; **the boys dropped their trousers** (*Brit*) *or* **pants** die Jungen ließen ihre Hosen herunter

c = kill bird abschießen; (*sl*) person abknallen (*inf*)

d = set down (*from car*) person absetzen; thing abliefern; (*from boat*) cargo löschen

e = utter casually remark, name fallen lassen; clue geben; hint machen; **he let drop that he was going to get married** (*by mistake*) es rutschte ihm raus, dass er heiraten wollte (*inf*); (*deliberately*) er erwähnte so nebenbei, dass er heiraten wollte

f = send postcard, note, line schreiben; **to drop sb a note** *or* **a line** jdm ein paar Zeilen schreiben

g = omit word, reference auslassen; (*deliberately*) weglassen (*from in* +*dat*); programme absetzen; **this word drops the "e" in the plural** bei diesem Wort fällt das „e" im Plural weg; **the paper refused to drop the story** die Zeitung weigerte sich, die Geschichte fallen zu lassen; **he drops his aitches** er verschluckt immer das „h"

h = abandon work, habit, lifestyle aufgeben; idea, plan fallen lassen, aufgeben; discussion, conversation abbrechen; candidate, minister, friend fallen lassen; girlfriend Schluss machen mit; (*Jur*) case niederschlagen; **you'll find it hard to drop the habit** es wird Ihnen schwer fallen, sich (*dat*) das abzugewöhnen; **you'd better drop the idea** schlagen Sie sich (*dat*) das aus dem Kopf; **to drop sb from a team** jdn aus einer Mannschaft nehmen; **let's drop the subject** lassen wir das Thema; **let's drop it!** lassen wir das!; **drop it!** (*inf*) hör auf (damit)!; **drop everything (and come here immediately)!** (*inf*) lass alles stehen und liegen (und komm sofort her)!

i = lose money verlieren, loswerden (*inf*); **she dropped the first three games** (*Tennis*) sie gab die ersten drei Spiele ab

j = give birth to (*animal*) werfen

3 – INTRANSITIVE VERB

a = drip (*liquid*) (herunter)tropfen

b = fall (*object*) (herunter)fallen; (*Theat: curtain*) fallen; (*rate, temperature etc*) sinken; (*wind*) sich legen; (*voice*) sich senken; **don't let it drop** lass es nicht fallen; **to drop astern** (*Naut*) zurückfallen; **Britain has dropped from fifth to tenth in the league** Großbritannien ist vom fünften auf den zehnten Ligaplatz (zurück)gefallen → penny, pin

c to the ground (*person*) fallen; (= *collapse*) umfallen, umkippen (*inf*); **to drop to the ground** sich zu Boden fallen lassen; **to drop to one's knees** auf die Knie fallen *or* sinken; **she dropped into an armchair** sie sank in einen Sessel, sie ließ sich in einen Sessel fallen; **I'm ready to drop** (*inf*) ich bin zum Umfallen müde (*inf*); **she danced till she dropped** (*inf*) sie tanzte bis zum Umfallen (*inf*) *or* Gehtnichtmehr (*inf*); **to drop dead** tot umfallen; **drop dead!** (*inf, expressing contempt*) geh zum Teufel! (*inf*); **small businesses were dropping like flies in the recession** (*inf*) während der Rezession gingen kleine Geschäfte massenweise ein (*inf*)

d = end (*conversation etc*) aufhören; **to let sth drop** etw auf sich beruhen lassen; **you can't just let** the matter drop Sie können die Sache nicht einfach auf sich beruhen lassen; **shall we let it drop?** sollen wir es darauf beruhen lassen?

4 – PHRASAL VERBS

▶ **drop across** or **around** VI (*inf*) vorbeikommen/-gehen; **we dropped around to see him** wir sind bei ihm vorbeigegangen; **drop around and see us some time** kommen Sie doch mal (bei uns) vorbei

▶ **drop away** VI **a** (= *become fewer: numbers*) people have been dropping away at recent meetings in letzter Zeit sind immer weniger Leute zu den Versammlungen gekommen **b** (*cliffs*) jäh *or* steil *or* schroff abfallen

▶ **drop back** VI zurückfallen

▶ **drop behind** VI zurückfallen VI +*prep obj* **to drop behind sb** hinter jdn zurückfallen

▶ **drop by** VI (*inf*) vorbeikommen, hereinschauen

▶ **drop down** VI (= *fall*) herunterfallen; **he dropped down behind the hedge** er duckte sich hinter die Hecke; **he dropped down onto his knees** er sank in *or* fiel auf die Knie; **to drop down dead** tot umfallen; **the cliffs drop down to the sea** die Klippen fallen jäh *or* steil zum Meer (hin) ab; **he has dropped down to eighth overall** er ist insgesamt auf den achten Platz zurückgefallen VI *sep* fallen lassen

▶ **drop in** VI (*inf, = visit casually*) vorbeikommen, hereinschauen; **I've just dropped in for a minute** ich wollte nur mal kurz hereinschauen; **drop in on the Smiths** schauen Sie doch mal bei den Smiths herein; **to drop in at the pub** der Kneipe (*dat*) einen Besuch abstatten

▶ **drop off** VI **a** (= *fall down*) abfallen; (= *come off: handle etc*) abgehen **b** (= *fall asleep*) einschlafen; (*for brief while*) einnicken **c** (*sales*) zurückgehen; (*speed, interest, popularity*) nachlassen, zurückgehen VI *sep* (= *set down from car etc*) person absetzen; parcel abliefern

▶ **drop out** VI **a** (*of box etc*) herausfallen (*of aus*) **b** (*from competition etc*) ausscheiden (*of aus*); **to drop out of a race** (*before it*) an einem Rennen nicht teilnehmen; (*during it*) aus dem Rennen ausscheiden; **he dropped out of the philosophy course** er gab den Kurs in Philosophie auf; **to drop out of society** aus der Gesellschaft aussteigen (*inf*); **to drop out of school** (*Brit*) die Schule vorzeitig verlassen; (*US: out of university*) die Universität vorzeitig verlassen; **he decided to drop out** er beschloss auszusteigen (*inf*) **c** the "t" drops out das „t" fällt weg

▶ **drop over** VI (*inf*) = drop across

---

drop: drop ball N (*Ftbl*) Schiedsrichterball *m*; **drop bottom** N Bodenklappe *f*; **drop ceiling** N Hängedecke *f*; **drop cloth** N (*US*: = dust cover) Staubdecke *f*; **drop curtain** N (*Theat*) (Fall)vorhang *m*; **drop-dead gorgeous** ADJ (*inf*) umwerfend (*inf*); **drop forge** VT (*Metal*) gesenkschmieden; **drop goal** N (*Rugby*) Tor *nt* durch Dropkick; **drop hammer** N Fallhammer *m*; **drop handlebars** PL Rennlenker *m*; **drop-in centre** N (*Brit*) Tagesstätte *f*; **drop kick** N (*Rugby*) Dropkick *m*; **drop-leaf table** N Tisch *m* mit herunterklappbaren Seitenteilen

droplet ['drɒplɪt] N Tröpfchen *nt*

droplet infection N (*Med*) Tröpfcheninfektion *f*

dropout ['drɒpaʊt] N (*from society*) Aussteiger(in) *m(f)* (*inf*); (*pej*) Asoziale(r) *mf*; (= *university dropout*) Studienabbrecher(in) *m(f)*; **the ~ rate at universities** die Zahl der Studienabbrecher

dropper ['drɒpə] N (*Med*) Pipette *f*; (*on bottle*) Tropfer *m*

droppings ['drɒpɪŋz] PL Kot *m*; (*of horse*) Äpfel *pl* (*inf*); (*of sheep*) Bohnen *pl*, Köttel *pl* (*inf*)

drop: drop scene N (*Theat*) (Zwischen)vorhang *m*; **drop seat** N Klappsitz *m*; **drop shot** N (*Tennis*) Stoppball *m*

dropsical ['drɒpsɪkəl] ADJ wassersüchtig

dropsy ['drɒpsɪ] N Wassersucht f

drop zone N (for supplies) Abwurfgebiet nt; (for parachutists) Absprunggebiet nt

drosophila [drəʊˈsɒfɪlə] N Drosophila f, Taufliege f

dross [drɒs] N , no pl (Metal) Schlacke f; (fig) Schund m; **money is but ~** Geld ist eitel und nichtig

drought [draʊt] N Dürre f; **three ~s in as many years** drei Dürrekatastrophen in ebenso vielen Jahren

drove[1] [drəʊv] N (of animals) Herde f; (of people) Schar f; **they came in ~s** sie kamen in hellen Scharen

drove[2] pret of **drive**

drover ['drəʊvə'] N Viehtreiber(in) m(f)

drown [draʊn] VI ertrinken VT a person, animal ertränken; **to be ~ed** ertrinken; **he looks like a ~ed rat** (inf) er sieht wie eine gebadete Maus aus (inf); **to ~ one's sorrows (in drink)** seine Sorgen (im Alkohol) ertränken; **to ~ one's whisky** seinen Whisky verwässern b (= submerge, flood) land überschwemmen, überfluten c (= render inaudible: also **drown out**) noise, voice übertönen; speaker niederschreien

drowning ['draʊnɪŋ] ADJ person ertrinkend; **a ~ man will clutch at a straw** (Prov) dem Verzweifelten ist jedes Mittel recht N Ertrinken nt; **there were three ~s here last year** im letzten Jahr sind hier drei Leute ertrunken

drowse [draʊz] VI (vor sich (acc) hin) dösen or dämmern N Halbschlaf m, Dämmerschlaf m

▶ **drowse off** VI eindämmern, eindösen (inf)

drowsily ['draʊzɪlɪ] ADV schläfrig; (after sleep) verschlafen

drowsiness ['draʊzɪnɪs] N Schläfrigkeit f; (after sleep) Verschlafenheit f; **to cause ~** schläfrig machen

drowsy ['draʊzɪ] ADJ (+er) a (= sleepy) person schläfrig; (after sleep) verschlafen; voice verschlafen; **to grow** or **become ~** schläfrig werden; **to feel ~** sich schläfrig fühlen; **she was still ~ with sleep** sie war noch verschlafen b (= soporific) afternoon träge; countryside schläfrig; **I spent a ~ evening in front of the telly** ich habe den Abend vor dem Fernseher verdöst

drub [drʌb] VT (= thrash) person (ver)prügeln, schlagen; (= defeat) schlagen

drubbing ['drʌbɪŋ] N a (= thrashing) Prügel pl; **to give sb a ~** jdm eine Tracht Prügel verpassen b (= defeat) Niederlage f; **to take a good ~** ganz schön Prügel kriegen (inf); **they suffered a 5-0 ~** sie wurden vernichtend mit 5:0 geschlagen

drudge [drʌdʒ] N (= person) Arbeitstier nt (inf); (= job) stumpfsinnige Plackerei or Schufterei (inf); **some see a lexicographer as a harmless ~** manche sehen Lexikografen als Menschen, die nur brav vor sich hin schuften (inf) VI sich placken, schuften (inf)

drudgery ['drʌdʒərɪ] N stumpfsinnige Plackerei or Schufterei (inf); **it's sheer ~** es ist eine einzige Plackerei

drug [drʌg] N a (Med, Pharm) Medikament nt, Arzneimittel nt; (inducing unconsciousness) Betäubungsmittel nt; (Sport) Dopingmittel nt; **he's on ~s** (Med) er muss Medikamente nehmen; **to put sb on ~s** jdm Medikamente verordnen b (= addictive substance) Droge f, Rauschgift nt; **to be on ~s** drogen- or rauschgiftsüchtig sein; **to take ~s** Drogen or Rauschgift nehmen → **hard drug, soft** i c (Comm, = unsaleable goods) **a ~ on the market** (old) eine unverkäufliche Ware; (in shop) ein Ladenhüter m VT a (Med) patient Medikamente geben (+dat); (= render unconscious) person, animal betäuben; **to ~ oneself up to the eyeballs on tranquillizers** (Brit inf) sich mit Beruhigungsmitteln voll pumpen (inf) b **to ~ sth** (food, drink) ein Betäubungsmittel in etw (acc) mischen

drug: drug abuse N Drogenmissbrauch m; **drug abuser** N **to be a ~** Drogenmissbrauch m betreiben; **drug addict** N Drogen- or Rauschgiftsüchtige(r), Drogen- or Rauschgiftabhängige(r) mf; **drug addiction** N Rauschgiftsucht f, Drogenabhängigkeit or -sucht f; **drug baron** N Drogenbaron m; **drug culture** N Drogenkultur f; **drug dealer** N Drogenhändler(in) m(f), Dealer(in) m(f) (inf); **drug dependency** N Drogenabhängigkeit f

drugged [drʌgd] ADJ food, drink mit einem Betäubungsmittel versetzt; **to be ~** (person) unter Beruhigungsmitteln stehen; **he seemed ~** er schien wie betäubt; **her whisky was ~** in ihrem Whisky waren K.O.-Tropfen; **he awoke from a long ~ sleep** er erwachte aus einer langen, tiefen Betäubung; **~ with sleep** schlaftrunken; **~ with fatigue** vor Müdigkeit ganz benommen

druggie ['drʌgɪ] N (inf) Drogenkonsument(in) m(f), Drogi m (inf)

druggist ['drʌgɪst] N (US) Drogist(in) m(f)

drug: drug industry N (Pharm) Arzneimittelindustrie f; **drug pusher** N Dealer(in) m(f) (inf); **drug runner** N Drogenschmuggler(in) m(f); **drug squad** N Rauschgiftdezernat nt, Drogenfahndung f; **~ officer** Drogenfahnder(in) m(f)

drugs: drugs raid N Drogenrazzia f; **drugs ring** N Drogen(händler)ring m; **drugs test** N Dopingtest m; **drugs testing** N Dopingkontrolle f

drug: drugstore N (US) Drugstore m; **drug taker** N **to be a ~** Drogen or Rauschgift nehmen; **drug taking** N Einnehmen nt von Drogen or Rauschgift; **drug test** N (Sport) Dopingkontrolle f; **drug traffic, drug trafficking** N Drogenhandel m; **drug trafficker** N Drogenschieber(in) m(f); **drug treatment** N (Med) medikamentöse Behandlung; **drug user** N Drogenbenutzer(in) m(f)

druid ['druːɪd] N Druide m

drum [drʌm] N a (Mus) Trommel f; **Joe Jones on ~s** am Schlagzeug: Joe Jones; **the ~s** die Trommeln pl; (pop, jazz) das Schlagzeug; **to beat** or **bang the ~ for sb/sth** (fig) die Trommel für jdn/etw rühren b (for oil, petrol) Tonne f; (cylinder for wire) Trommel f, Rolle f; (Tech: = machine part) Trommel f, Walze f; (Phot) Entwicklertrommel f; (Archit: = wall) Tambour m, Trommel f; (= shaft) Säulentrommel f c (Anat: also **ear drum**) Trommelfell nt VI (Mus, fig, rain etc) trommeln VT **to ~ one's fingers on the table** mit den Fingern auf den Tisch trommeln

▶ **drum into** VT always separate **to drum sth into sb** jdm etw eintrichtern (inf) or einpauken (inf); tidiness etc eindrillen (inf)

▶ **drum out** VT sep (out of army, club) ausstoßen

▶ **drum up** VT sep enthusiasm, interest wecken; support, customers gewinnen; **to drum up business** Aufträge an Land ziehen (inf)

drum: drumbeat N Trommelschlag m; **drum brake** N Trommelbremse f; **drumfire** N (Mil) Trommelfeuer nt; **drumhead** N Trommelfell nt; **drumhead court martial** N Standgericht nt; **drum kit** N Schlagzeug nt; **drum major** N Tambourmajor m; **drum majorette** N (US) Tambourmajorin f

drummer ['drʌmə'] N a (in orchestra) Trommelschläger(in) m(f); (in band, pop group) Schlagzeuger(in) m(f); (Mil, in parade etc) Trommler(in) m(f) b (US, inf) Vertreter(in) m(f)

drummer boy N Trommler m

drumstick ['drʌmstɪk] N a (Mus) Trommelschlägel or -stock m b (on chicken etc) Keule f

drunk [drʌŋk] ptp of **drink** ADJ (+er) a (= inebriated) betrunken; **he was slightly ~** er war leicht betrunken or etwas angetrunken; **to get ~ betrunken werden** (on von); (on purpose) sich betrinken (on mit); **to be ~ on wine** von Wein betrunken sein; **to be as ~ as a lord** or **skunk** (inf) blau wie ein Veilchen sein (inf); **to be ~ and disorderly** (Jur) durch Trunkenheit öffentliches Ärgernis erregen b (fig) **to be ~ with** or **on success** vom Erfolg berauscht sein; **to be ~ with** or **on power/freedom/joy** im Macht-/Freiheits-/Freudenrausch sein N Betrunkene(r) mf; (habitual) Trinker(in) m(f), Säufer(in) m(f) (inf)

drunkard ['drʌŋkəd] N Trinker(in) m(f), Säufer(in) m(f) (inf)

drunk driver N (esp US) angetrunkener Autofahrer, angetrunkene Autofahrerin

drunk driving, drunken driving N (esp US) Trunkenheit f am Steuer

drunken ['drʌŋkən] ADJ person betrunken; (habitually) versoffen (inf); state, voice verloffen; night, evening, party feuchtfröhlich; **a ~ man** ein Betrunkener; **~ violence** Gewalttätigkeiten pl unter Alkoholeinfluss; **a ~ brawl** eine Schlägerei zwischen Betrunkenen; **a ~ argument** ein Streit m im Suff (inf); **in a ~ rage** or **fury** in einem Wutanfall im Vollrausch; **in a ~ stupor** im Vollrausch, sinnlos betrunken

drunkenly ['drʌŋkənlɪ] ADV betrunken; behave wie ein Betrunkener/eine Betrunkene

drunkenness ['drʌŋkənnɪs] N (= state) Betrunkenheit f; (= habit, problem) Trunksucht f

drunkometer [drʌŋˈkɒmɪtə'] N (US) = Breathalyzer®

dry [draɪ] VT pret, ptp **dried** trocknen; fruit also dörren; skin abtrocknen; **to ~ oneself** sich abtrocknen; **he dried his hands/feet** er trocknete sich (dat) die Hände/Füße ab, er trocknete seine Hände/Füße ab; **to ~ the dishes** das Geschirr abtrocknen; **to ~ one's eyes** sich (dat) die Tränen abwischen VI a (= become dry) trocknen; **the washing was hanging up to ~ in the sun** die Wäsche trocknete in der Sonne b (= dry dishes) abtrocknen ADJ a thing, weather, period, country trocken; soil, river, lake ausgetrocknet; well versiegt; **to run ~** (river) austrocknen; (well) versiegen; **~ period** or **spell** Trockenperiode f; **the ~ season** die Trockenzeit f; **to rub oneself ~** sich abrubbeln; **to rub sth ~** etw abtrocknen or trockenreiben; **to wipe sth ~** etw abtrocknen or trockenwischen; **as ~ as a bone** knochentrocken; **~ shampoo** Trockenshampoo nt → **high ADJ a** b mouth, throat, lips, eyes, cough trocken; **to feel/be ~** (inf, = thirsty) Durst haben, eine trockene Kehle haben; **there wasn't a ~ eye in the house** es blieb kein Auge trocken c (Cook) ingredients trocken; **~ mustard** Senfpulver nt; **~ bread** trocken Brot d cow trockenstehend; **her breasts are ~** sie hat keine Milch e (inf, = anti-alcohol) state, country alkoholfrei f (= ironic, wry) humour, wit trocken g voice ausdruckslos; sound trocken; **her voice was harsh and ~** ihre Stimme klang hart und trocken h (= uninspired, dull) book, speech, lecture trocken; **as ~ as dust** todlangweilig, knochentrocken (inf) i wine, sherry, cider trocken N **in the ~** im Trockenen; **come into the ~** komm ins Trockene; **to give sth a ~** etw trocknen

▶ **dry off** VI (clothes etc) trocknen, trocken werden VT sep abtrocknen

▶ **dry out** VI a (clothes, ground, skin etc) austrocknen b (inf, alcoholic) eine Entziehungskur machen VT sep clothes trocknen; ground, skin austrocknen

▶ **dry up** VI a (stream, well) austrocknen, versiegen; (moisture) trocknen; (inspiration, source of income) versiegen; (author) keine Ideen mehr haben; **then business started drying up** dann wurden die Aufträge immer spärlicher b (= dry dishes) abtrocknen c (actor) stecken bleiben (inf); (speaker) den Faden verlieren d (inf, = be quiet) **dry up!** halt den Mund! (inf) VT sep mess aufwischen; dishes abtrocknen; (sun) well, river bed austrocknen

dryad ['draɪæd] N Dryade f

dry: **dry-as-dust** ADJ fürchterlich trocken, staubtrocken; **dry battery** N (*Elec*) Trockenbatterie *f*; **dry cell** N (*Elec*) Trockenelement *nt*; **dry cell battery** N Trockenbatterie *f*; **dry-clean** `VT` chemisch reinigen; **to have a dress ~ed** ein Kleid chemisch reinigen lassen; "**dry-clean only**" (*on label*) chemisch reinigen! `VI` **will it ~?** lässt es sich chemisch reinigen?; **dry-cleaner's** N chemische Reinigung; **dry-cleaning** N chemische Reinigung; **dry dock** N (*Naut*) Trockendock *nt*

dryer ['draɪə'] N (*for clothes*) Wäschetrockner *m*; (= *spin dryer*) Wäscheschleuder *f*; (*for hands*) Händetrockner *m*; (*for hair*) Föhn *m*, Haartrockner *m*; (*over head*) Trockenhaube *f*; (*in paint*) Trockenstoff *m*

dry: **dry farming** N Trockenfarmsystem *nt*; **dry-fly fishing** N Trockenfliegenfischen *nt*; **dry ginger** N (*mixer*) Ingwerlimonade *f*; **dry goods** PL (*Comm*) Kurzwaren *pl*; **dry ice** N Trockeneis *nt*

drying ['draɪɪŋ]: **drying cupboard** N (Wäsche)trockenschrank *m*; **drying room** N Trockenboden *m*, Trockenkeller *m*; **drying-up** N Abtrocknen *nt*; **to do the ~** abtrocknen

dry land N fester Boden; **I'll be glad to be on ~ again** ich bin froh, wenn ich wieder festen Boden unter den Füßen habe

dryly ['draɪlɪ] ADV = drily

dry measure N Trockenmaß *nt*

dryness ['draɪnɪs] N (*all senses*) Trockenheit *f*

dry: **dry nurse** N Säuglingsschwester *f*; **dry-roasted** ADJ *peanuts* trocken geröstet; **dry rot** N (*Haus- or Holz*)schwamm *m*; **dry run** N Probe *f*; (*Mil*) Trockentraining *nt*; **dry-shod** ADJ, ADV mit trockenen Füßen; **to cross sth ~** etw trockenen Fußes überqueren; **dry ski slope** N Trockenskipiste *f*; **dry-stone wall** N Bruchsteinmauer *f*; **dry valley** N Trockental *nt*; **dry weight** N Trockengewicht *nt*

DS (*Brit, Police*) abbr of **Detective Sergeant**

DSC abbr of **Distinguished Service Cross** *Auszeichnung für besondere Verdienste*

DSc abbr of **Doctor of Science** Dr. rer. nat.

DSM abbr of **Distinguished Service Medal** *Auszeichnung für besondere Verdienste*

DSO (*Brit*) abbr of **Distinguished Service Order** *Auszeichnung für besondere Verdienste*

DSS

Das **DSS (Department of Social Security)** ist das Ministerium, das für die Durchführung der Sozialfürsorgepolitik der britischen Regierung verantwortlich ist. Es teilt sich in eine Reihe ausführender Behörden auf, darunter die **Benefits Agency**, die staatliche Sozialhilfe ausschüttet, die **Contributions Agency**, die die Sozialversicherungsbeiträge einsammelt, und die **Child Support Agency**, deren Aufgabe das Eintreiben von Unterhaltszahlungen vom jeweilig unterhaltspflichtigen Elternteil nach einer Trennung oder Scheidung ist → NATIONAL INSURANCE.

DST (*esp US*) abbr of **daylight saving time**

DTI (*Brit*) abbr of **Department of Trade and Industry** ≈ Wirtschaftsministerium *nt*

DTP abbr of **desktop publishing** DTP *nt*

DTs ['di:'ti:z] abbr of **delirium tremens to have the ~** vom Saufen den Tatterich haben (*inf*)

dual ['djʊəl] ADJ (= *double*) doppelt, Doppel-; (= *two kinds of*) zweierlei; **his ~ role as ...** in seiner Doppelrolle als ...; **it has a ~ function** es hat doppelte or zweierlei Funktion

dual: **dual carriageway** N (*Brit*) Straße mit Mittelstreifen und Fahrbahnen in beiden Richtungen, ≈ Schnellstraße *f*; **dual citizenship** N doppelte Staatsangehörigkeit *f*; **dual controls** PL (*Aut*) Doppelsteuerung *f*; **dual economy** N duale Volkswirtschaft

dualism ['djʊəlɪzəm] N Dualismus *m*

dualist ['djʊəlɪst] N Dualist(in) *m(f)*

dualistic [,djʊə'lɪstɪk] ADJ dualistisch

duality [djʊ'ælɪtɪ] N Dualität *f*

dual: **dual nationality** N doppelte Staatsangehörigkeit; **dual personality** N (*Psych*) gespaltene Persönlichkeit; **dual pricing** N deglomerative Preisdifferenzierung; **dual-purpose** ADJ zweifach verwendbar

dub[1] [dʌb] VT `a` **to ~ sb a knight** jdn zum Ritter schlagen `b` (= *nickname*) taufen `c` *film* synchronisieren; **the film was ~bed into French** der Film war französisch synchronisiert

► **dub in** VT *sep* (*Film*) *sound* synchron (zum Bild) aufnehmen

dub[2] [dʌb] N (*US, inf*) Tollpatsch *m*

Dubai [du:'baɪ] N Dubai *nt*

dubber ['dʌbə'] N (*Film*) Synchronsprecher(in) *m(f)*

dubbin ['dʌbɪn] N Lederfett *nt*

dubbing ['dʌbɪŋ] N (*Film*) Synchronisation *f*

dubiety [dju:'baɪətɪ] N (*form*) Zweifel *pl*

dubious ['dju:bɪəs] ADJ `a` (= *questionable*) *reputation, person* zweifelhaft; *business deal* fragwürdig, zweifelhaft; *idea, claim, statement, basis* fragwürdig; *attribution* fraglich; **it seems ~ that...** erscheint fragwürdig, dass ...; (= *suspicious*) es erscheint verdächtig, dass ...; **of ~ origin** zweifelhaften Ursprungs; **of ~ benefit/quality** von zweifelhaftem Nutzen/zweifelhafter Qualität; **it sounds ~** ich habe da meine Zweifel; **to have the ~ honour** (*Brit*) or **honor** (*US*) or **distinction/pleasure of doing sth** (*usu iro*) die zweifelhafte Ehre/das zweifelhafte Vergnügen haben, etw zu tun

`b` (= *uncertain, unconvinced*) unsicher; **I was ~ at first, but he convinced me** ich hatte zuerst Bedenken, aber er überzeugte mich; **I was ~ that** or **whether ...** ich bezweifelte, dass ...; **he's ~ whether he should come** er weiß nicht or ist im Zweifel, ob er kommen soll; **to be ~ about sth** etw anzweifeln; **I'm very ~ about it** ich habe da doch starke Zweifel; **he sounded ~** er klang zweifelnd or skeptisch; **she looked ~** sie blickte skeptisch drein; **he gave me a ~ look** er sah mich zweifelnd an

dubiously ['dju:bɪəslɪ] ADV `a` (= *questionably*, +*vb*) fraglicherweise; (+*adj*) fragwürdig; **costly and ~ effective treatment** teure Behandlungen von zweifelhafter Wirksamkeit `b` (= *uncertainly*) *look* zweifelnd, skeptisch; *say, suggest* zweifelnd, unsicher

dubiousness ['dju:bɪəsnɪs] N `a` (= *questionable nature, of reputation, origin*) Zweifelhaftigkeit *f*; (*of deal, claim, statement etc*) Fragwürdigkeit *f* `b` (= *uncertainty: of person*) Unsicherheit *f*; **there was a certain ~ in his voice** es lag ein gewisser Zweifel in seiner Stimme

ducal ['dju:kəl] ADJ herzoglich; **~ palace** Herzogspalast *m*

ducat ['dʌkɪt] N (*Hist*) Dukaten *m*

duchess ['dʌtʃɪs] N Herzogin *f*

duchy ['dʌtʃɪ] N Herzogtum *nt*

duck[1] [dʌk] `N` `a` (*bird*) Ente *f*; **wild ~** Wildente *f*; **roast ~** gebratene Ente, Entenbraten *m*; **to play ~s and drakes** (*Brit*) Steine (über das Wasser) springen lassen; **to play ~s and drakes with sth** (*Brit*: = *squander*) mit etw furchtbar aasen (*inf*); **to take to sth like a ~ to water** bei etw gleich in seinem Element sein; **it's (like) water off a ~'s back to him** das prallt alles an ihm ab `b` (*Brit, inf*) = duckie `c` **a funny-looking old ~** (*dated esp Brit inf*) eine komische alte Tante (*inf*) `d` (*Mil inf*) Amphibienfahrzeug *nt* `e` (*Cricket*) **he made** or **scored a ~** er hat keinen Punkt erzielt; **to be out for a ~** ohne Punktgewinn aus sein

`VI` `a` (*also* **duck down**) sich ducken; **he ~ed down out of sight** er duckte sich, so dass er nicht mehr zu sehen war; **he ~ed under the water** er tauchte (im Wasser) unter; **they ~ed for cover** sie duckten sich, um in Deckung zu gehen

`b` **he ~ed out of the room** er verschwand aus

dem Zimmer; **she ~ed out of the rain** sie suchte Schutz vor dem Regen; **to ~ and dive** or **weave** (*also fig*) Ausweichmanöver machen

`VT` `a` (= *push under water*) untertauchen `b` **to ~ one's head** den Kopf einziehen `c` (= *avoid*) *difficult question, blow, challenge* ausweichen (+*dat*); *responsibility* sich drücken vor (+*dat*) (*inf*)

► **duck out of** VI +*prep obj* (= *back out of*) sich drücken vor (+*dat*) (*inf*)

duck[2] N `a` (*Tex*) Segeltuch *nt* `b` **ducks** PL Segeltuchhosen *pl*

duck: **duckbill, duck-billed platypus** N Schnabeltier *nt*; **duckboard** N Lattenrost *m*; **duck-egg blue** N zartes Blau

duckie ['dʌkɪ] N (*dated Brit inf*) *often not translated*, Süße(r) *mf*; **are you all right, ~?** na, alles in Ordnung?

ducking ['dʌkɪŋ] N (*in water*) Untertauchen *nt*, Tauchen *nt*; **to give sb a ~** jdn untertauchen or tunken

ducking: **ducking and diving** N (*inf*) Ausweichmanöver *pl*; (*verbal also*) Ausflüchte *pl*; **~ is all part of political life** Ausweichmanöver gehören zur Politik; **ducking stool** N Sitz auf einem Balken, mit dem Übeltäter zur Strafe ins Wasser getaucht wurden

duckling ['dʌklɪŋ] N Entenküken, Entlein *nt*; **roast ~** gebratene junge Ente → ugly duckling

duck pond N Ententeich *m*

ducks [dʌks] N (*Brit, inf*) = duckie

duck: **duck shooting** N Entenjagd *f*; **duck soup** N (*US inf fig*) Kinderspiel *nt* (*inf*); **to be ~ in Kinderspiel sein** (*for für*); **duckweed** N Entenflott *nt*, Entengrütze *f*, Wasserlinse *f*

ducky N (*Brit, inf*) = duckie

duct [dʌkt] N `a` (*Anat*) Röhre *f*; **tear ~** Tränenkanal *m* `b` (*for liquid, gas*) (Rohr)leitung *f*, Rohr *nt*; (*Elec*) Rohr *nt*, Röhre *f*

ductile ['dʌktaɪl] ADJ `a` *metal* hämmerbar; (= *stretchable*) dehnbar, streckbar `b` (*fig liter*) *person* leicht lenkbar

ductless gland ['dʌktlɪs'glænd] N endokrine or innersekretorische Drüse

dud [dʌd] (*inf*) `ADJ` `a` (= *useless*) nutzlos; (= *worthless*) *person* unfähig; *company* völlig unrentabel; *script* mies (*inf*); **~ mine/shell/bomb/bullet** Blindgänger *m*; **~ equipment/batteries** Geräte/Batterien, die nichts taugen; **a ~ scheme** ein totaler Reinfall

`b` (= *counterfeit*) *note, coin, antique* gefälscht; *cheque, loan* ungedeckt; **a ~ note** (*Brit*) or **bill** (*US*) eine Blüte (*inf*); **~ £10 notes** (*Brit*) falsche or gefälschte 10-Pfund-Scheine

`N` (= *bomb, shell, grenade*) Blindgänger *m*; (= *coin*) Fälschung *f*; (= *note*) Blüte *f* (*inf*); (= *person*) Niete *f* (*inf*), Versager(in) *m(f)*; **this watch/battery is a ~** diese Uhr/Batterie taugt nichts

dude [dju:d] N (*US*) `a` (*inf*, = *man*) Kerl *m* (*inf*) `b` (*dated*: = *dandy*) Dandy *m* `c` (*dated*: = *city type*) Städter *m*, feiner Stadtpinkel (*pej inf*)

dude ranch N (*US*) Touristenranch *f*, Ferienranch *f*

DUDE RANCH

Eine **dude ranch** ist eine Ranch im Westen der USA, auf der man als Tourist den Wilden Westen hautnah erleben kann. Die Ranch kann noch wirklich bewirtschaftet werden, es kann sich aber auch um ein reines Freizeitunternehmen handeln. Wer echte Cowboyluft schnuppern möchte, kann zu Pferde durch die Prärie reiten, bei der Rancharbeit helfen und am Lagerfeuer deftige Mahlzeiten einnehmen. **Dude** bezeichnet im amerikanischen Slang einen geschniegelten Städter oder Ostküstenbewohner. In der Filmkomödie „City Slickers" von 1991 mit Billy Crystal geht es genau um solch eine Gruppe Städter von der Ostküste, die auf einer **dude ranch** richtige Abenteuer erleben wollen.

dudgeon ['dʌdʒən] N **in high ~** sehr empört, sehr aufgebracht

duds [dʌdz] PL (inf, = clothes) Klamotten pl (inf)

due [djuː] ✪ 17.2 ADJ **a** (= expected, scheduled) fällig; **to be ~** (plane, train, bus) ankommen sollen; (elections, results) anstehen; **the train was ~ ten minutes ago/is ~ to arrive at 10.32** der Zug sollte vor 10 Minuten ankommen/soll um 10.32 Uhr ankommen; **when is the baby ~?** wann soll das Baby kommen?; **the results are ~ at the end of the month** die Ergebnisse stehen Ende des Monats an or sind Ende des Monats fällig; **he is ~ back in London tomorrow** er soll morgen nach London zurückkommen; **to be ~ in** (train, bus) ankommen sollen; (ferry) einlaufen sollen; **to be ~ out** (magazine, CD) herauskommen sollen; **he is ~ to speak about now** er müsste jetzt gerade seine Rede halten; **the building is ~ to be demolished** das Gebäude soll demnächst abgerissen werden; **he is ~ for a rise** (Brit) or **raise** (US) ihm steht eine Gehaltserhöhung zu; **she is ~ for promotion** sie ist mit einer Beförderung an der Reihe; **the prisoner is ~ for release** or **~ to be released** der Gefangene soll jetzt entlassen werden; **the car is ~ for a service** das Auto muss zur Inspektion; **you look ~ for a haircut** du müsstest mal zum Friseur gehen; **the carpet looks ~ for a clean** der Teppich müsste gereinigt werden; **~ date** (Fin) Fälligkeitstermin m; (for baby) erwarteter Geburtstermin

b (= proper) attention, consideration gebührend; care nötig; **after ~ consideration** nach reiflicher Überlegung; **to drive with ~ care and attention** mit der gebotenen Vorsicht fahren; **driving without ~ care and attention** (Jur) fahrlässiges Verhalten im Straßenverkehr; **in ~ course** or **time** (= eventually) zu gegebener Zeit; **every home will have a computer in ~ course** auf die Dauer wird jeder Haushalt einen Computer besitzen; **~ credit** die gebührende Anerkennung; **~ credit for his achievements** die Anerkennung, die ihm für seine Leistungen gebührt; **the council, to give them ~ credit, have tried their best to plan ahead** die Stadt, das muss man ihr lassen, hat ihr Bestes getan, um vorauszuplanen; **with (all) ~ respect** bei allem Respekt (to für) → credit N d

c (= owed) **to be ~** (money) ausstehen; **to be ~ to sb** (money, leave, respect) jdm zustehen; **to fall ~** (Fin: loan, debt) fällig werden; **I'm ~ some leave, I've got some leave ~ to me** mir steht etwas Urlaub zu; **the respect ~ to his age** der seinem Alter gebührende Respekt; **the respect ~ from a son to his father** der Respekt, den ein Sohn seinem Vater schuldet; **my thanks are ~ to Mr Dobbs** mein Dank gilt Herrn Dobbs; **to be ~ a couple of days off** ein paar freie Tage verdient haben

d **~ to** (= owing to) auf Grund +gen, aufgrund +gen, wegen +gen; (= caused by) durch; **what's it ~ to?** worauf ist es zurückzuführen?; **closed ~ to repairs** wegen Reparaturarbeiten geschlossen; **his death was ~ to natural causes** er ist eines natürlichen Todes gestorben; **his failure was entirely ~ to himself/his carelessness** an seinem Versagen war nur er selbst/seine Nachlässigkeit schuld

N ADV (= precisely) **~ north/south/east/west** direkt nach Norden/Süden/Osten/Westen; **~ east of the village** in Richtung Osten des Dorfes

dues PL (= subscription, fees) (Mitglieds-)beitrag m; **to pay one's ~s** (fig) seinen Verpflichtungen nachkommen

b **to give him his ~, he did at least try** eins muss man ihm lassen, er hat es wenigstens versucht; **to give him his ~, he had no idea about it** man muss gerechterweise zugeben, dass er davon keine Ahnung hatte → devil N d

duel ['djuːəl] N (lit, fig) Duell nt; **~ of wits** geistiger Wettstreit VI sich duellieren; (German students) eine Mensur schlagen; **~ling** (Brit) or **~ing** (US) **pistols** Duellierpistolen pl

duellist, (US) **duelist** ['djuːəlɪst] N Duellant m

due process N (Jur) **a** **~ (of law)** (US) ordentliches Gerichtsverfahren **b** **~ of law** ordnungsgemäßes Verfahren

duet [djuːˈet] N Duo nt; (for voices) Duett nt; **violin ~** Geigenduo nt

duff¹ [dʌf] N (Cook) Mehlpudding m → plum duff

duff² ADJ (Brit, inf) machine, watch (= useless) nutzlos; (= broken) kaputt (inf); idea blöd (inf); film, book, record, job mies (inf); loan faul (inf); company unrentabel; opponent unfähig; **I'll bet you it's a ~ one** ich wette, dass es nichts taugt **N** (esp US, inf, = buttocks) Hintern m (inf), Arsch m (vulg); **to get off one's ~** seinen Arsch in Bewegung setzen (sl)

▶ **duff up** VT sep (Brit, inf) zusammenschlagen (inf)

duffel ['dʌfl]: **duffel bag** N Matchbeutel or -sack m; **duffel coat** N Dufflecoat m

duffer ['dʌfə] N (Brit, inf) **a** (esp Sch) Blödmann m (inf); **to be a ~ at football/French** eine Niete im Fußball/in Französisch sein (inf) **b** (= silly old man) (alter) Trottel (inf)

dug¹ [dʌg] N (of animal) Zitze f

dug² pret, ptp of **dig**

dugout ['dʌgaʊt] N (Mil) Schützengraben m, Unterstand m; (also **dugout canoe**) Einbaum m

duke [djuːk] N Herzog m

dukedom ['djuːkdəm] N (= territory) Herzogtum nt; (= title) Herzogswürde f

dukes [djuːks] PL (dated sl, = fists) Fäuste pl; **put up your ~** zeig mal deine Fäuste (inf)

dulcet ['dʌlsɪt] ADJ (liter, hum, iro) wohlklingend, melodisch; **so nice to hear her/his ~ tones again** (hum, iro) wie nett, ihre liebliche/seine sonore Stimme wieder zu hören (hum, iro)

dulcimer ['dʌlsɪmə] N Cymbal nt, Hackbrett nt

dull [dʌl] ADJ (+er) **a** (= not bright or shiny) light trüb; glow schwach; colour matt, trüb; eyes matt, glanzlos; hair, skin, metal, paintwork stumpf, matt; weather, day trüb, grau; sky bedeckt; **the sea was a ~ grey** das Meer war mattgrau; **it will be ~ at first** (weather forecast) es wird anfangs bewölkt

b (= boring) langweilig; **deadly ~, as ~ as ditchwater** or **dishwater** todlangweilig; **there's never a ~ moment** man langweilt sich keinen Augenblick

c (= vague, muffled) sound, thud, ache, sensation dumpf; **he fell to the ground with a ~ thud** er schlug dumpf auf den Boden auf

d (= listless) person, mood träge; gaze, expression lustlos; (St Ex, Comm) market flau; trading schleppend; **I felt ~ and sleepy** ich fühlte mich träge und müde

e (= slow-witted) langsam; **the ~est boy in the class** der schwächste Schüler in der Klasse; **his senses/intellectual powers are growing ~** seine Sinne/geistigen Kräfte lassen langsam nach

f (form, = blunt) knife, blade stumpf

VT **a** (= lessen) pain betäuben; grief lindern; senses, mind, sensitivity abstumpfen; vision, hearing trüben, schwächen; impression schwächen; pleasure dämpfen; **emotionally ~ed** (emotional) abgestumpft

b (= make less bright) light, colour dämpfen; metal, paintwork stumpf werden lassen

c (= muffle) sound dämpfen

d (form, = blunt) knife, blade stumpf machen

VI (light) schwächer werden; (colour) verblassen; (eyes) sich trüben

dullard ['dʌləd] N Dummkopf m

dullness ['dʌlnɪs] N **a** (of light) Trübheit f; (of colours, eyes) Mattheit f; (of hair, paintwork, metal) Stumpfheit f; (of weather, day) Trübheit f; (of sky) Bedecktheit f **b** (= boring nature) Langweiligkeit f **c** (of sound, thud) Dumpfheit f **d** (= listlessness, of person) Trägheit f; (of expression) Lustlosigkeit f; (St Ex, Comm, of market) Flauheit f **e** (= slow-wittedness) Langsamkeit f **f** (form, = bluntness) Stumpfheit f

dully ['dʌlɪ] ADV **a** (= dimly) gleam, glint matt, schwach **b** (= without enthusiasm) say, look lustlos **c** (= vaguely) throb, ache, feel dumpf **d** (= boringly) langweilig

duly ['djuːlɪ] ADV **a** (= properly) elect, note, sign ordnungsgemäß, vorschriftsmäßig; **to be ~ grateful/sympathetic/impressed** gebührend dankbar/mitfühlend/beeindruckt sein; **I was ~ surprised** ich war entsprechend überrascht **b** (= as expected) wie erwartet; (= in due course) dann auch; **he ~ obliged** wie erwartet tat er es auch, er tat es dann auch; **she ~ went to China in April** wie erwartet fuhr sie im April nach China, so fuhr sie dann im April nach China

dumb [dʌm] ADJ (+er) **a** (= mute) stumm; (= silent, speechless) sprachlos; (liter, = silent) rage, recognition wortlos, stumm; **~ animals** (unsere stummen Freunde,) die Tiere; **she was struck ~** (fig) es verschlug ihr die Sprache; **she was struck ~ with fear/shock** die Angst/der Schock verschlug ihr die Sprache; **he was in a ~ rage** er war stumm vor Wut; **don't give me that ~ insolence!** sieh mich nicht so unverschämt an!

b (esp US, inf, = stupid) dumm, doof (inf); **that was a ~ thing to do/say** wie kann man nur so etwas Dummes machen/sagen!; **he did one ~ thing after another** er machte eine Dummheit nach der anderen; **to act** or **play ~** sich dumm stellen

▶ **dumb down** VT sep simplifizieren

dumb: **dumbbell** N (Sport) Hantel f; **dumb blonde** N (pej inf) dümmliche Blondine f (pej); **dumb cluck** N (inf, = fool) Doofi m (inf)

dumbfound ['dʌmfaʊnd] VT verblüffen; **I'm ~ed!** ich bin sprachlos!

dumbly ['dʌmlɪ] ADV stumm

dumbness ['dʌmnɪs] N **a** Stummheit f **b** (esp US, inf, = stupidity) Doofheit f (inf), Dummheit f

dumbo ['dʌmbəʊ] N (inf, = stupid person) Doofkopp m (inf)

dumb: **dumb show** N (Theat) pantomimische Einlage in einem Stück **in ~** in Mimik; **dumb terminal** N (Comput) Idiotterminal nt, dummes Terminal; **dumb waiter** N Speiseaufzug m; (= trolley) Serviertisch m, stummer Diener

dum-dum ['dʌmdʌm] N (inf) Doofie m (inf)

dumdum (bullet) ['dʌmdʌm('bʊlɪt)] N Dumdum(geschoss) nt

dummy ['dʌmɪ] **N** **a** (= sham object) Attrappe f; (Comm) Schaupackung f, Attrappe f; (for clothes) Schaufenster- or Kleider)puppe f; (of book) Blindband m → **ventriloquist's dummy**, **tailor's dummy** **b** (Brit, = baby's teat) Schnuller m **c** (Cards, = person) Dummy m; (= cards) Tisch m **d** (inf, = fool) Dummkopf m, Idiot m (inf), Doofie m (inf) **e** (Ftbl etc) Finte f; **to sell sb a ~** jdn antäuschen ADJ attr (= not real) unecht; **it's just a ~ grenade** das ist nur die Attrappe einer Granate; **a ~ company** eine Scheinfirma; **a ~ bomb/weapon** eine Bomben-/Waffenattrappe; **~ pills** Placebos pl

dummy run N Probe f; (of air attack) Übung f

dump [dʌmp] **N** **a** (Brit, = pile of rubbish) Schutthaufen m, Abfallhaufen m; (= place) Müllplatz m, Müllkippe f **b** (Mil) Depot nt **c** (pej inf, = town) Kaff nt (inf); (= house, building) Dreckloch nt (pej inf); (= school etc) Sauladen m (pej inf) **d** (inf) **to be (down) in the ~s** deprimiert or down (inf) sein **e** (Comput) Dump m, Abzug m **f** (sl) **to go for a ~** (Brit) or **take a ~** auf Scheißhaus gehen (sl)

VT **a** (= get rid of) rubbish abladen; **they ~ed the waste/bodies overboard** sie warfen den Abfall/die Leichen über Bord

b (= put down, let fall) load, rubbish abladen; bags etc (= leave) lassen; (= leave) lassen; **where can I ~ these books?** wo kann ich diese Bücher lassen?; **to ~ sb/sth on sb** jdn/etw bei jdm abladen

c (inf, = abandon, get rid of) person, girlfriend abschieben; *car* abstellen, loswerden; *sth unwanted* abladen

d (*Comm*) *goods* zu Dumpingpreisen verkaufen

e (*Comput*) ausgeben, abziehen, dumpen

▶ **dump down** VT *sep* fallen lassen

▶ **dump off** VT *sep* (*inf*) **will you dump me off on the way home?** kannst du mich auf der Rückfahrt absetzen?

▶ **dump on** VI +*prep obj* (*inf*) **to dump on sb** (= *mistreat*) jdn von oben herab behandeln; (= *offload problems*) seine ganzen Probleme bei jdm abladen (*inf*)

dumper ['dʌmpə'] N (= *dump truck*) Kipper *m*

dumping ['dʌmpɪŋ] N **a** (*of load, rubbish*) Abladen *nt*; **"no ~"** (*Brit*) „Schuttabladen verboten!" **b** (*Comm*) Dumping *nt*

dumping: dumping ground N Müllkippe *f*, Schuttabladeplatz *m*; (*fig*) Abladeplatz *m*; **dumping price** N (*Comm*) Dumpingpreis *m*

dumpling ['dʌmplɪŋ] N **a** (*Cook*) Kloß *m*, Knödel *m* **b** (*inf*, = *person*) Dickerchen *nt* (*inf*)

Dumpster® ['dʌmpstə'] N (*US*) (Müll)container *m*

dump truck N Kipper *m*

dumpy ['dʌmpɪ] ADJ pummelig; *glasses* klein und massiv

dun¹ [dʌn] ADJ graubraun **N** Graubraun *nt*

dun² VT mahnen; **to ~ sb for payment** bei jdm eine Zahlung anmahnen

dunce [dʌns] N (*Sch*) langsamer Lerner *or* Schüler; (= *stupid person*) Dummkopf *m*; **to be a ~ at maths** eine Niete *or* schlecht in Mathe sein (*inf*); **the ~ of the class** das Schlusslicht der Klasse; **~'s cap** *spitzer Papierhut, der früher zur Strafe dem schlechtesten Schüler aufgesetzt wurde*

dunderhead ['dʌndəhed] N Dummkopf *m*, Dummerjan *m* (*inf*)

dune [djuːn] N Düne *f*

dung [dʌŋ] **N** Dung *m*; (*of birds*) Dreck *m*; (*Agr*, = *manure*) Mist *m*, Dünger *m* **VT** *field* düngen, misten

dungarees [ˌdʌŋɡə'riːz] (*esp Brit*) PL (*workman's, child's*) Latzhose *f*; **a pair of ~** eine Latzhose

dung: dung beetle N Mistkäfer *m*; **dung cart** N Mistkarren *m*

dungeon ['dʌndʒən] N Verlies *nt*, Kerker *m*

dung: dung fork N Mistgabel *f*; **dung heap**, **dunghill** ['dʌŋhɪl] N Mist- *or* Dunghaufen *m*

dunk [dʌŋk] VT (ein)tunken

dunning letter ['dʌnɪŋˌletə'] N Mahnbrief *m*

dunno ['dʌnəʊ] = (**I**) **don't know**

duo ['djuːəʊ] N Duo *nt*

duodenal [ˌdjuːəʊ'diːnl] ADJ **~ ulcer** Zwölffingerdarmgeschwür *nt*

duodenum [ˌdjuːəʊ'diːnəm] N Zwölffingerdarm *m*, Duodenum *nt* (*spec*)

dupe [djuːp] VT betrügen, überlisten, übertölpeln; **he was ~d into believing it** er fiel darauf rein **N** Betrogene(r) *mf*

duple ['djuːpl] ADJ (*Mus*) **~ time** Zweiertakt *m*

duplex ['djuːpleks] ADJ (*Elec*, *Tech*) doppelt; (*Comput*) Duplex-; **~ operation** Duplexbetrieb *m* **N** (*esp US*) = **duplex apartment**, **duplex house**

duplex apartment N (*esp US*) zweistöckige Wohnung

duplex house N (*US*) Zweifamilienhaus *nt*

duplicate ['djuːplɪkeɪt] VT **a** (= *make a copy of*) *document* ein Duplikat *nt* *or* eine Zweitschrift anfertigen von

b (= *make copies of: on machine*) kopieren, vervielfältigen

c (= *repeat*) *action etc* wiederholen, noch einmal machen; (*wastefully*) doppelt *or* zweimal machen; *success* wiederholen; **that is merely duplicating work already done** da wird doch nur schon Erledigtes noch einmal gemacht

N ['djuːplɪkɪt] (*of document*) Duplikat *nt*, Kopie

f; (*of work of art*) Kopie *f*; (*of key etc*) Zweitschlüssel *m*; **in ~** in doppelter Ausfertigung **ADJ** ['djuːplɪkɪt] doppelt, zweifach; **a ~ copy of the text** ein Duplikat *nt* *or* eine Kopie des Textes; **a ~ receipt** eine Empfangsbescheinigung in doppelter Ausfertigung; **a ~ key** ein Zweitschlüssel *m*

duplicating machine ['djuːplɪkeɪtɪŋməʃiːn] N Vervielfältigungsapparat *m*

duplication [ˌdjuːplɪ'keɪʃən] N (*of documents, act*) Vervielfältigung *f*; (= *duplicate*) Kopie *f*; (= *double*) Doppel *nt*; (*of efforts, work*) Wiederholung *f*; **save expenses by avoiding ~ of effort** tun Sie nichts zweimal, sparen Sie Kosten

duplicator ['djuːplɪkeɪtə'] N = **duplicating machine**

duplicitous [djuː'plɪsɪtəs] ADJ falsch, betrügerisch

duplicity [djuː'plɪsɪtɪ] N Doppelspiel *nt*

durability [ˌdjʊərə'bɪlɪtɪ] N **a** (*of product, material, finish*) Strapazierfähigkeit *f*, Haltbarkeit *f* **b** (*of peace, relationship*) Dauerhaftigkeit *f*

durable ['djʊərəbl] ADJ **a** (= *tough*) *product, material, finish* strapazierfähig, haltbar; **CDs are more ~ than tapes** CDs halten länger als Kassetten **b** (= *lasting*) *peace, solution, relationship* dauerhaft

durable goods PL langlebige Güter *pl*

duration [djʊə'reɪʃən] N (*of play, war etc*) Länge *f*, Dauer *f*; **for the ~ of** für die Dauer (+*gen*); **of long/short ~** von langer/ kurzer Dauer; **after a struggle of six years' ~** nach sechsjährigem Kampf; **he joined up for the ~** er hat sich bis zum Ende verpflichtet; **it looks as though we are here for the ~** (*inf*) es sieht so aus, als ob wir bis zum Ende hier sind

duress [djʊə'res] N Zwang *m*; **he signed the form under ~** er hat die Unterschrift unter Zwang geleistet

Durex® ['djʊəreks] N Gummi *m* (*inf*)

during ['djʊərɪŋ] PREP während (+*gen*)

durst [dɜːst] (*obs*) *pret* of **dare**

durum ['djʊərəm] N , **durum wheat** N Hartweizen *m*

dusk [dʌsk] N (= *twilight*) (Abend)dämmerung *f*; (= *gloom*) Finsternis *f*; **at/shortly after ~** bei/ kurz nach Einbruch der Dunkelheit

duskiness ['dʌskɪnɪs] N Dunkelheit *f*

dusky ['dʌskɪ] ADJ (+*er*) (*liter*) *room, evening, skin, colour* dunkel; *person* dunkelhäutig; *light* schwach; **the light in the room was ~** es war dämmerig im Zimmer; **~ pink** altrosa

dust [dʌst] **N** , *no pl* **a** Staub *m*; **covered in ~** staubbedeckt; **to make** *or* **raise a lot of ~** (*lit, fig*) eine Menge Staub aufwirbeln; **to gather ~** (*lit, fig*) verstauben; **a speck of ~** ein Körnchen *nt* Staub; **clouds of interstellar ~** staubförmige interstellare Materie; **when the ~ had settled** (*fig*) als sich die Wogen wieder etwas geglättet hatten; **we'll let the ~ settle first** (*fig*) wir warten, bis sich die Wogen geglättet haben → **bite**

VT a

b **to give sth a ~** etw abstauben

VT *furniture* abstauben; *room* Staub wischen in (+*dat*); **it's (all) done and ~ed** (*Brit fig inf*) das ist (alles) unter Dach und Fach

b (*Cook*) bestäuben

c (*Police*) **to ~ sth for prints** etw zur Abnahme von Fingerabdrücken einstauben

VI (*housewife etc*) Staub wischen; **she spent the morning ~ing** sie verbrachte den Morgen mit Staubwischen

▶ **dust down** VT *sep person, sb's clothes* (*with brush*) abbürsten; (*with hand*) abklopfen; (*fig*) herunterputzen; **to dust oneself down** sich abbürsten; (*dat*) den Staub abklopfen; (*fig*) sich rein waschen

▶ **dust off** VT *sep dirt* abwischen, wegwischen; *table, surface, person* abstauben; **to dust oneself off** sich (*dat*) den Staub abklopfen; (*fig*) sich rein waschen

▶ **dust out** VT *sep cup* auswischen

dust: dust bag N Staubbeutel *m*; **dust-bath** N Staubbad *nt*; **dustbin** N (*Brit*) Mülltonne *f*; **dustbin man** N (*Brit*) = **dustman**; **dust bowl** N Trockengebiet *nt*; **dustcart** N (*Brit*) Müllwagen *m*; **dust cloud** N Staubwolke *f*; **dust-cloth** N Staubtuch *nt*, Staublappen *m*; **dust coat** N Kittel *m*; **dust cover** N (*on book*) (Schutz)umschlag *m*; (*on furniture*) Schonbezug *m*; **dust devil** N kleiner Wirbelsturm

duster ['dʌstə'] N **a** Staubtuch *nt*; (*Sch*) (Tafel-)schwamm *m* **b** (*Naut*) Schiffsflagge → **red duster** **c** (*US: also* **duster coat**) Kittel *m*

dust-free ['dʌstfriː] ADJ staubfrei

dustiness ['dʌstɪnɪs] N Staubigkeit *f*

dusting ['dʌstɪŋ] N **a** Staubwischen *nt*; **to do the ~** Staub wischen; **when I've finished the ~** wenn ich mit Staubwischen fertig bin **b** (*Cook etc*, = *sprinkling*) (Be)stäuben *nt*; **a ~ of snow** eine dünne Schneedecke

dusting-powder ['dʌstɪŋˌpaʊdə'] N Talkpuder *m*

dust: dust jacket N (Schutz)umschlag *m*; **dustman** N (*Brit*) Müllmann *m*; **the dustmen come on Fridays** freitags ist Müllabfuhr; **dust-pan** N Kehr- *or* Müllschaufel *f*; **dust-proof** ADJ staubdicht; **dustsheet** N (*Brit*) Tuch *nt* (*zum Abdecken von Möbeln*); **dust storm** N Staubsturm *m*; **dust trap** N Staubfänger *m*; **dust-up** N (*dated inf*) Streit *m*, (handgreifliche) Auseinandersetzung

dusty ['dʌstɪ] ADJ (+*er*) **a** (= *full of dust, covered in dust*) staubig; *furniture, book, photograph* verstaubt **b** *colour* schmutzig; **~ reds and browns** schmutzige Rot- und Brauntöne; **~ blue** graublau; **~ pink** altrosa **c** (*inf*) *answer* schroff **d** **not too** *or* **so ~** (*inf*) gar nicht so übel (*inf*)

Dutch [dʌtʃ] ADJ niederländisch (*esp form*), holländisch; **~ cheese** Holländer Käse; **a ~ man** ein Niederländer *m* (*esp form*), ein Holländer *m*; **a ~ woman** eine Niederländerin (*esp form*), eine Holländerin *f*; **he is ~** er ist Niederländer (*esp form*) *or* Holländer; **she is ~** sie ist Niederländerin (*esp form*) *or* Holländerin; **~ master** (*Art*) Meister *m* der Holländischen Schule; **the ~ School** (*Art*) die Holländische Schule

N a (= *people*) **the ~** die Niederländer (*esp form*) *or* Holländer *pl*

b (= *language*) Niederländisch *nt*, Holländisch *nt*; **to be in ~ (with sb)** (*US, inf*) (bei jdm) schlecht angeschrieben sein → *also* **double Dutch, English**

ADV to go ~ (with sb) (*inf*, = *share the cost*) (mit jdm) getrennte Kasse machen; **she insisted upon going ~** sie bestand darauf, dass wir getrennte Kasse machen *or* dass jeder für sich bezahlt

Dutch: Dutch auction N *Versteigerung mit stufenweise erniedrigtem Ausbietungspreis*; **Dutch barn** N (*Brit*) offene Scheune; **Dutch cap** N (= *diaphragm*) Pessar *nt*; **Dutch courage** N (*inf*) **to get** *or* **give oneself ~** sich (*dat*) Mut antrinken (*from mit*); **I can't do it without some ~** ich kann es nicht, ohne mir vorher ein bisschen Mut anzutrinken; **all they need is a bit of ~** sie müssen sich nur ein bisschen Mut antrinken; **Dutch door** N (*US*) quer geteilte Tür; **Dutch East Indies** PL Niederländisch-Ostindien *nt*; **Dutch elm disease** N Ulmensterben *nt*; **Dutchman** N Niederländer *m* (*esp form*), Holländer *m*; **if he's a professional footballer, then I'm a ~** wenn er ein Profifußballer ist, dann fresse ich einen Besen (*inf*); **Dutch metal** N unechtes Blattgold, Rauschgold *nt*; **Dutch oven** N Schmortopf *m*; **Dutch Reformed Church** N Niederländische Reformierte Kirche; **Dutch treat** N (*inf*) Kinobesuch/Essen *etc* mit getrennter Kasse **we settled on a ~** wir einigten uns darauf, getrennte Kasse zu machen; **Dutch uncle** N **to talk to sb like a ~, to be sb's ~** jdm eine Standpauke halten (*inf*); **Dutchwoman** N Niederländerin *f* (*esp form*), Holländerin *f*

dutiable ['djuːtɪəbl] ADJ zollpflichtig

dutiful ['djuːtɪfʊl] ADJ *child* gehorsam; *husband, employee* pflichtbewusst; **a ~ visit** ein Pflichtbesuch *m*; **your ~ son** (*old, form, in letters*) dein treuer Sohn (*old, form*); **with a ~ nod** mit einem gehorsamen Nicken

dutifully ['djuːtɪfəlɪ] ADV pflichtbewusst; (= *obediently*) treu und brav; **we all laughed ~** wir alle lachten brav

duty ['djuːtɪ] ⊘ 10.1, 19.2, 19.5 N **a** Pflicht *f*; **to do one's ~** seine Pflicht tun; **to do one's ~ by sb** seine Pflicht gegenüber jdm tun *or* erfüllen; **it is my ~ to say** *or* **I am (in) ~ bound to say that ...** es ist meine Pflicht zu sagen, dass ...; **one's ~ to one's parents** seine Pflicht (und Schuldigkeit) seinen Eltern gegenüber; **it is my painful ~ to admit ...** ich habe die schwere *or* traurige Pflicht, Ihnen zu gestehen ...; **you don't know? but it's your ~ to know!** du weißt das nicht? aber es ist deine verdammte Pflicht und Schuldigkeit, es zu wissen! (*inf*); **to make it one's ~ to do sth** es sich (*dat*) zur Pflicht machen, etw zu tun **b** (= *responsibility*) Aufgabe *f*, Pflicht *f*; **to take up one's duties** seine Pflichten aufnehmen; **to report for ~** sich zum Dienst melden; **to be on ~** (*doctor etc*) im Dienst sein; (*Sch etc*) Aufsicht haben; **who's on ~ tomorrow?** wer hat morgen Dienst/Aufsicht?; **he went on ~ at 9** sein Dienst fing um 9 an; **to be off ~** nicht im Dienst sein; **he comes off ~ at 9** sein Dienst endet um 9; **I'm off ~ on Tuesday** Dienstag habe ich dienstfrei; **he was called for overseas ~** er wurde nach Übersee eingezogen; **to return to ~** den Dienst wieder aufnehmen; **night ~** Nachtdienst *m*; **he's been neglecting his duties as a husband** er hat seine ehelichen Pflichten vernachlässigt; **the box does ~ for a table** die Kiste dient als Tisch **c** (*Fin*, = *tax*) Zoll *m*; **to pay ~ on sth** Zoll auf etw (*acc*) zahlen → **estate duty**

duty call N a ~ ein Höflichkeitsbesuch *m*

duty-free [djuːtɪ'friː] ADJ zollfrei ADV zollfrei N ~**s** *pl* (*inf*) zollfreie Waren *pl*

duty-free: duty-free allowance N Warenmenge, die man zollfrei einführen kann; **duty-free shop** N Duty-free-Shop *m*, Dutyfreeshop *m*; **duty-free shopping** N Einkauf *m* von zollfreien Waren

duty: duty NCO N UvD *m*; **duty officer** N Offizier *m* vom Dienst; **duty roster** N Dienstplan *m*

duvet ['djuːveɪ] N (= *quilt*) Steppdecke *f*

DV *abbr of* **deo volente** so Gott will

DVD N ABBR *of* **digital versatile** *or* **video disc** DVD *f*

DVD: DVD player N DVD-Player *m*; **DVD-Rom** N DVD-Rom *f*

DVLA (*Brit*) *abbr of* **Driver and Vehicle Licensing Agency** Kfz-Steuer- und Führerscheinbehörde *f*

dwarf [dwɔːf] N *pl* **dwarves** [dwɔːvz] Zwerg *m*; (= *tree*) Zwergbaum *m*; (= *star*) Zwerg(stern) *m* ADJ *person* zwergenhaft; ~ **shrubs** Zwergsträucher *pl* VT **a** (*skyscraper, person*) klein erscheinen lassen, überragen; (*through achievements, ability etc*) in den Schatten stellen; **to be ~ed by sb/sth** neben jdm/etw klein erscheinen **b** (*Hort*) *tree* klein züchten

dwarf galaxy N Zwerggalaxie *f*

dwarf star N Zwerg(stern) *m*

dweeb [dwiːb] N (*esp US inf*) mickeriger Typ (*inf*)

dwell [dwel] *pret, ptp* **dwelt** VI **a** (*liter*, = *live*) weilen (*geh*), leben, wohnen **b** (*fig*) **the memory dwelt in his mind** die Erinnerung haftete in seinem Gedächtnis

▶**dwell (up)on** VI +*prep obj* **a** (= *spend time on*) verweilen bei, sich länger aufhalten bei; (*in thought*) verweilen bei, länger nachdenken über (+*acc*); **to dwell (up)on the past** sich ständig mit der Vergangenheit befassen; **let's not dwell (up)on it** wir wollen uns nicht (länger) damit aufhalten **b** (*Mus*) *note* halten

dweller ['dwelə'] N Bewohner(in) *m(f)*

dwelling ['dwelɪŋ] N (*form: also* **dwelling place**) Wohnsitz *m* (*form*), Wohnung *f*; ~ **house** Wohnhaus *nt*

dwelt [dwelt] *pret, ptp of* **dwell**

DWEM [dwem] N (*esp US*) *abbr of* **Dead White (European) Male**

dwindle ['dwɪndl] VI (*strength, relevance*) schwinden, abnehmen; (*interest*) nachlassen; (*numbers, audiences*) zurückgehen, abnehmen; (*supplies, stocks*) schrumpfen, zur Neige gehen

▶**dwindle away** VI (*strength, person*) dahinschwinden; (*supplies*) zusammenschrumpfen

dwindling ['dwɪndlɪŋ] ADJ schwindend; *interest* nachlassend; *population, numbers, audiences* zurückgehend; *stocks, supplies* schwindend; **the prime minister's ~ popularity** die sinkende Beliebtheit des Premierministers N Schwinden *nt*; (*of stocks, population*) Rückgang *m*; (*of interest*) Nachlassen *nt*

dye [daɪ] N Farbstoff *m*; **hair ~** Haarfärbmittel *nt*; **food ~** Lebensmittelfarbe *f*; **the ~ will come out in the wash** die Farbe geht bei der Wäsche heraus VT färben; ~**d blonde hair** blond gefärbtes Haar VI (*cloth etc*) sich färben lassen

dyed-in-the-wool ['daɪdɪnðə,wʊl] ADJ Erz-, durch und durch *pred*; *attitude* eingefleischt; **he's a ~ conservative/romantic** er ist ein Erzkonservativer/-romantiker, er ist durch und durch konservativ/romantisch

dyer ['daɪə'] N Färber(in) *m(f)*; ~**'s and cleaner's** Färberei und Reinigung *f*

dye: dyestuffs PL Farbstoffe *pl*; **dyeworks** N *sing or pl* Färberei *f*

dying ['daɪɪŋ] *prp of* **die** ADJ **a** (*lit*) *person* sterbend; *animal* verendend, sterbend; *plant* eingehend; (= *last*) *breath, wish, words* letzte(r, s); **until** *or* **till** *or* **to one's ~ day** bis an sein Lebensende **b** (*fig*, = *declining*) *tradition, industry, art* aussterbend; (= *final*) *days, minutes* letzte(r, s); *fire, embers* verglühend; **to be a ~ breed** langsam aussterben; **regular customers are a ~ breed** regelmäßige Kunden gibt es fast nicht mehr; **the ~ minutes of the game** die letzten Spielminuten N **the ~** *pl* die Sterbenden

dyke, (*US*) **dike** [daɪk] N **a** (= *channel*) (Entwässerungs)graben *m*, Kanal *m* **b** (= *barrier*) Deich *m*, Damm *m*; (= *causeway*) Fahrdamm *m* **c** (*sl*, = *lesbian*) Lesbe *f* (*inf*) VT *land* eindeichen; *river* eindämmen

dykey ['daɪkɪ] ADJ (*inf*) lesbisch

dynamic [daɪ'næmɪk] ADJ (*also Phys*) dynamisch N Dynamik *f*

dynamically [daɪ'næmɪkəlɪ] ADV (*also Phys*) dynamisch

dynamics [daɪ'næmɪks] N *sing or pl* Dynamik *f*

dynamism ['daɪnəmɪzəm] N Dynamismus *m*; (*of person*) Dynamik *f*

dynamite ['daɪnəmaɪt] N (*lit*) Dynamit *nt*; (*fig*) Zünd- *or* Sprengstoff *m*; **she is ~** sie ist eine Wucht (*inf*); **that story is pure ~** diese Geschichte ist der reinste Zündstoff VT *rocks, bridge* sprengen

dynamo ['daɪnəməʊ] N Dynamo *m*; (*Aut*) Lichtmaschine *f*; **she's a human ~** sie steckt voller Dynamik

dynastic [daɪ'næstɪk] ADJ dynastisch

dynasty ['dɪnəstɪ] N Dynastie *f*

dysentery ['dɪsɪntrɪ] N Dysenterie *f*, Ruhr *f*

dysfunction [dɪs'fʌŋkʃən] N Funktionsstörung *f*, Fehlfunktion *f*; **liver ~** Funktionsstörung *f* der Leber

dysfunctional [dɪs'fʌŋkʃənəl] ADJ *family, background* dysfunktional; *childhood* zerrüttet

dyslexia [dɪs'leksɪə] N Legasthenie *f*

dyslexic [dɪs'leksɪk] ADJ legasthenisch; **she is ~** sie ist Legasthenikerin N Legastheniker(in) *m(f)*

dysmenorrhoea [,dɪsmenə'rɪə] N Dysmenorrhö(e) *f*

dyspepsia [dɪs'pepsɪə] N Dyspepsie *f*, Verdauungsstörung *f*; **nervous ~** nervöse Magenschwerden *pl*

dyspeptic [dɪs'peptɪk] ADJ dyspeptisch N jd, der an Dyspepsie leidet

dysphasia [dɪs'feɪzɪə] N Dysphasie *f*

dystopia [dɪs'təʊpɪə] N Dystopie *f*

dystrophy ['dɪstrəfɪ] N Dystrophie *f*, Ernährungsstörung *f*

E

E, e [iː] N E *nt*, e *nt*; (*Mus*) E *nt*, e *nt*; **E flat** Es *nt*, es *nt*; **E sharp** Eis *nt*, eis *nt* → **minor**

E *abbr of* **east** O

e- [iː] PREF (= *electronic*) E-, e-

each [iːtʃ] ADJ jede(r, s); **~ one of us** jeder von uns; **~ and every one of us** jeder Einzelne von uns; **~ and every boy** jeder einzelne Junge (ohne Ausnahme)

PRON **a** jede(r, s); **~ of them gave their** *or his* **opinion** sie sagten alle ihre Meinung, jeder (von ihnen) sagte seine Meinung; **a little of ~ please** ein bisschen von jedem, bitte; **we ~ had our own ideas about it** jeder von uns hatte seine eigene Vorstellung davon

b **~ other** sich, einander (*geh*); **they haven't seen ~ other for a long time** sie haben sich *or* einander lange nicht gesehen; **they wrote (to) ~ other** sie haben sich (*dat*) *or* einander geschrieben; **we visit ~ other** wir besuchen uns (gegenseitig), wir besuchen einander; **they were sorry for ~ other** sie bedauerten sich gegenseitig, sie bedauerten einander; **the respect they have for ~ other** die Achtung, die sie voreinander haben; **the love they have for ~ other** die Liebe, die sie füreinander empfinden; **you must help ~ other** ihr müsst einander helfen *or* euch gegenseitig helfen; **on top of ~ other** aufeinander; **next to ~ other** nebeneinander; **they went to ~ other's houses** sie besuchten einander zu Hause

ADV je; **we gave them one apple ~** wir haben ihnen je einen Apfel gegeben; **two classes of 20 pupils ~** zwei Klassen mit je 20 Schülern; **the books are £10 ~** die Bücher kosten je £ 10; **carnations at one euro ~** Nelken zu einem Euro das Stück

each way (*Brit, Horseracing etc*) ADJ **~ bet** Wetteinsatz *m* auf alle drei Gewinnplätze ADV **to bet on** *or* **back a horse ~** auf alle drei Gewinnplätze setzen; **I had £10 ~ on Black Velvet** ich hatte £ 10 auf Black Velvet auf allen drei Gewinnplätzen gesetzt

eager [ˈiːgə] ADJ *person, discussion, pursuit* eifrig; *face, eyes* erwartungsvoll; *response* begeistert; **the ~ looks on their faces** der erwartungsvolle Ausdruck in ihren Gesichtern; **in ~ anticipation** voll gespannter Erwartung; **to be ~ to do sth** darauf erpicht sein, etw zu tun, etw unbedingt tun wollen; **he was ~ to help** er war äußerst willig zu helfen; **children who are ~ to learn** Kinder, die lerneifrig *or* lernbegierig *or* lernwillig sind; **she is ~ to please** sie ist darum bemüht, alles richtig zu machen; **he was ~ to please her** er war eifrig bedacht, sie zufrieden zu stellen; **to be ~ for sth** auf etw (*acc*) erpicht *or* aus sein; **~ for knowledge** wissbegierig; **he was ~ for work** er wollte unbedingt Arbeit haben; **to be ~ for sb to do sth** unbedingt wollen, dass jd etw tut; **to be ~ for sth to happen** es kaum erwarten können, dass etw geschieht

eager beaver N (*inf*) Arbeitstier *nt* (*inf*)

eagerly [ˈiːgəlɪ] ADV eifrig; *await, anticipate* gespannt; *accept, agree* bereitwillig; **~ awaited** mit Spannung erwartet; **we look forward ~ to the day when ...** wir warten ungeduldig auf den Tag, an dem ...

eagerness [ˈiːgənɪs] N Eifer *m*; **with ~** eifrig; **~ for power/vengeance** Macht-/Rachgier *f*; **~ for**

combat Kampflust *f*; **~ for friendship** Suchen *nt* nach Freundschaft; **such was his ~ to please ...** er war so darauf bedacht zu gefallen, ...; **such was his ~ to help ...** seine Bereitwilligkeit zu helfen war so groß, ...

eagle [ˈiːgl] N **a** Adler *m*; **to keep an ~ eye on sb/sth** ein wachsames Auge auf jdn/etw werfen; **under the ~ eye of ...** unter dem wachsamen Blick (+*gen*) ...; **nothing escapes her ~ eye** nichts entgeht ihrem wachsamen Blick **b** (*Golf*) Eagle *nt* VT (*Golf*) **to ~ a hole** ein Eagle *nt* spielen

eagle-eyed [ˈiːglaɪd] ADJ **the ~ detective** der Detektiv mit seinen Adleraugen

Eagle Scout N (*US*, = *person*) ein Pfadfinder *des höchsten Ranges in den USA* (= *rank*) *höchster Rang für Pfadfinder in den USA*

eaglet [ˈiːglɪt] N Adlerjunge(s) *nt*

E & OE *abbr of* **errors and omissions excepted**

ear¹ [ɪə] N **a** (*Anat, fig*) Ohr *nt*; **to keep one's ~s open** die Ohren offen halten; **to keep an ~ to the ground** die Ohren aufsperren *or* offen halten; **to be all ~s** ganz Ohr sein; **she was listening with only half an ~** sie hörte nur mit halbem Ohr zu; **your ~s must have been burning** Ihnen müssen die Ohren geklungen haben; **to lend an ~** zuhören; **to lend an ~ to sb** jdm sein Ohr leihen; **to find a sympathetic ~** ein offenes Ohr finden; **to lend a sympathetic ~** verständnisvoll zuhören; **if that came to** *or* **reached his ~s** wenn ihm das zu Ohren kommt; **he has the ~ of the prime minister** der Premierminister hört auf ihn; **it goes in one ~ and out the other** das geht zum einen Ohr hinein und zum anderen wieder hinaus; **to be up to one's ~s in debt/work** bis über beide *or* die Ohren in Schulden/Arbeit stecken; **he's got money/houses** *etc* **coming out of his ~s** (*inf*) er hat Geld/Häuser *etc* ohne Ende (*inf*); **it all came crashing down around his ~s** (*inf*) um ihn herum brach alles zusammen; **he'll be out on his ~** (*inf*) dann fliegt er raus (*inf*); **to bend sb's ~** (*inf*) jdn voll quatschen (*inf*), jdn voll sülzen (*sl*)

b (= *sense of hearing*) Gehör *nt*, Ohr *nt*; **to have a good ~ for music** ein feines Gehör für Musik haben; **to play it by ~** (*lit*) nach (dem) Gehör spielen; **to play it by ~** (*fig*) improvisieren

ear² N (*of grain, plant*) Ähre *f*; (*of maize*) Kolben *m*

ear: earache N Ohrenschmerzen *pl*; **eardrops** PL (*Med*) Ohrentropfen *pl*; **eardrum** N Trommelfell *nt*

-eared [-ɪəd] ADJ *suf* **long-/short-eared** lang-/kurzohrig

ear: earflap N Ohrenschützer *m*; **earful** N (*inf*) **to get an ~** mit einer Flut von Beschimpfungen überschüttet werden; **to give sb an ~** jdn herunterputzen (*inf*), jdn zusammenstauchen (*inf*); **earhole** N (*Brit, inf*) Ohr *nt*, Löffel *m* (*inf*); **to give sb a clip** *or* **clout round the ~** jdm ein paar *or* eins hinter die Löffel geben (*inf*)

earl [ɜːl] N Graf *m*

earldom [ˈɜːldəm] N (= *land*) Grafschaft *f*; (= *title*) Grafentitel *m*; (= *rank*) Grafenstand *m*

earlier [ˈɜːlɪə] ADJ *comp of* **early** früher; **in ~ times** früher, in vergangenen Zeiten; **at an ~**

date früher, eher; **in his/her ~ years he/she had ...** in jüngeren Jahren hatte er/sie ...; **her ~ dislike gave way to hatred** aus ihrer anfänglichen Abneigung wurde Hass

ADV **~ (on)** früher; (= *just now*) vorhin; **~ (on) in the novel** an einer früheren Stelle in dem Roman; **this is what we talked about ~ (on)** darüber haben wir vorhin schon gesprochen; **her parents had died four years ~** ihre Eltern waren vier Jahre früher *or* vorher *or* zuvor gestorben; **~ (on) today** heute (vor einigen Stunden); **~ (on) this month/year** früher in diesem Monat/in diesem Jahr; **I cannot do it ~ than Thursday** ich kann es nicht vor Donnerstag *or* eher als Donnerstag machen

ear lobe N Ohrläppchen *nt*

early [ˈɜːlɪ] ADV **a** **~ (on)** früh; **~ in 1915/in February** Anfang 1915/Februar; **~ (on) in the year/(the) winter** Anfang des Jahres/des Winters; **~ (on) in the war** in der Anfangsphase des Krieges; **~ (on) in his/her/their** *etc* **life** in jungen Jahren; **~ (on) in the race** zu Anfang des Rennens; **~ (on) in the evening/morning** am frühen Abend/Morgen; **he got up very ~ in the morning** er stand sehr früh (am Morgen) auf; **as ~ as** (= *already*) schon; **she learned to read as ~ as four** sie lernte schon mit vier Jahren lesen; **~ this month/year** Anfang des Jahres; **~ next month/year** Anfang nächsten Monats/Jahres; **~ today/this morning** heute früh; **the earliest he can come is tomorrow** er kann frühestens morgen kommen

b (= *before the expected time*) früher (als erwartet); (= *before the appointed time*) zu früh; (= *earlier than usual*) früh; **she left ten minutes ~** sie ist zehn Minuten früher gegangen; **to be five minutes/an hour ~** fünf Minuten/eine Stunde zu früh kommen; **he was ~ for the meeting** er kam zu früh zu der Besprechung; **he left school ~** (*went home*) er ging früher von der Schule nach Hause; (*finished education*) er ging vorzeitig von der Schule ab; **to get up/go to bed ~** früh aufstehen/ins Bett gehen; **good morning, you're ~ today** guten Morgen, Sie sind heute ja früh dran; **~ to bed, ~ to rise (makes a man healthy, wealthy and wise)** (*Prov*) früh ins Bett und früh heraus, frommt dem Leib, dem Geist, dem Haus (*Prov*) → **bright b**

ADJ (+*er*) **a** früh; **it was ~ evening when we finished** wir waren am frühen Abend fertig; **we went for an ~ morning drive** *or* **a drive in the ~ morning** wir machten eine Spritztour am frühen Morgen; **we had an ~ lunch** wir aßen früh zu Mittag; **in ~ summer/autumn** zu Sommer-/Herbstanfang, im Frühsommer/Frühherbst; **in ~ spring/winter** zu Frühlings-/Winteranfang; **the ~ years/months/days** die ersten Jahre/Monate/Tage; **in ~ January/August** *etc* Anfang Januar/August *etc*; **in the ~ 60s/1980s** *etc* Anfang der sechziger/achtziger *etc* Jahre *or* Sechziger-/Achtzigerjahre *etc*; **to have an ~ night** früh ins Bett gehen; **to keep ~ hours** früh ins Bett gehen und früh aufstehen; **the ~ hours** die frühen Morgenstunden; **until** *or* **into the ~ hours** bis in die frühen Morgenstunden; **her ~ life** in jungen Jahren; **his ~ work** seine frühen Werke, sein Frühwerk *nt*; **at an ~ age** in jungen Jahren; **from an ~ age** von klein auf; **since ~ childhood** seit seiner/ihrer *etc* frühen Kindheit; **in his ~**

teens im frühen Teenageralter; **to be in one's ~ thirties/forties** etc Anfang dreißig/vierzig etc sein; **it's too ~ to say/to say whether ...** es ist noch zu früh, um etwas zu sagen/um zu sagen, ob ...; **it is too ~ to know what his motives are** man weiß noch nicht, welche Motive er hat; **it's too ~ for a final decision** es ist zu früh, um eine endgültige Entscheidung zu fällen; **only her voice has changed from those ~ days** nur ihre Stimme ist anders als damals zu Anfang; **it's ~ days (yet)** (esp Brit) wir/sie etc sind noch im Anfangsstadium; **~ identification** (Med) Früherkennung f

b (= before expected time) flowers früh blühend; cabbage, peas etc, crop früh; death vorzeitig; marriage früh; menopause verfrüht; **~ vegetables** Frühgemüse nt; **an ~ spring** ein zeitiger Frühling

c (from historical perspective) settlers, man frühgeschichtlich; **the ~ church** die Urkirche f; **~ Christians** Urchristen pl; **an ~ form of hypnotherapy** eine Frühform der Hypnotherapie; **~ baroque** Frühbarock m

d (= soon) at an ~ date bald; **at the earliest possible moment** so bald wie irgend möglich; **to promise ~ delivery** baldige Lieferung versprechen → **convenience b**

early: early bath N **to send sb for an ~** (Brit, Ftbl, Rugby) jdn vom Feld schicken; **to take an ~** (Brit fig: = withdraw) sich frühzeitig zurückziehen; **early bird** N (in morning) Frühaufsteher(in) m(f); (arriving etc) Frühankömmling m; **it's the ~ that catches the worm** (Prov) Morgenstund hat Gold im Mund (Prov); **early closing** N it's ~ today die Geschäfte haben or sind heute nachmittag geschlossen; **early retirement** N vorgezogener or vorzeitiger Ruhestand; **to take ~** vorzeitig in den Ruhestand gehen; **to have taken ~** Frührentner(in) m(f) sein; **early riser** N Frühaufsteher(in) m(f); **early warning (sign** or **signal)** N Vorwarnung f; **early warning system** N Frühwarnsystem nt

ear: earmark N (on animal) Ohrmarke f VT (fig) vorsehen, bestimmen; **ear-minded** [ˈɪəˌmaɪndɪd] ADJ (Psych) auditiv, vorwiegend mit Gehörsinn begabt; **earmuffs** PL Ohrenschützer pl

earn [ɜːn] VT money, praise, rest verdienen; (Fin) interest bringen; **to ~ one's keep/a living** Kost und Logis/seinen Lebensunterhalt verdienen; **to ~ a** or **one's crust** (Brit) seine Brötchen verdienen; (inf); **this ~ed him a lot of money/respect** das trug ihm viel Geld/große Achtung ein, damit verdiente er sich (dat) viel Geld/große Achtung; **he's ~ed it** das hat er sich (dat) verdient; **~ing capacity** Verdienstmöglichkeiten pl; **~ing value** Ertragswert m

earned income [ˈɜːndˈɪnkʌm] N Arbeitseinkommen nt

earner [ˈɜːnə] N **a** (= person) Verdiener(in) m(f); **big ~s** Großverdiener pl **b** (Brit, inf) Einnahmequelle f; **that video shop is a nice little ~** der Videoladen wirft ganz schön was ab (inf)

earnest [ˈɜːnɪst] ADJ person ernst, ernsthaft; voice ernst; hope, desire aufrichtig, innig; conversation, discussion ernsthaft; **it shall be my ~ prayer that ...** ich werde aufrichtig dafür beten, dass ...; **they were in ~ conversation** sie unterhielten sich ernsthaft

N in ~ a (= for real) richtig; **then she started crying in ~** dann fing sie erst an richtig zu weinen; **to be in ~ about sth** (= serious) etw ernst meinen; **is he in ~ about it?** ist es ihm ernst damit?; **this time I'm in ~** diesmal meine ich es ernst, diesmal ist es mein Ernst

b ~ **(money)** (Jur, = deposit) Handgeld nt

c (= guarantee) Pfand nt (of +gen); **an ~ of one's good intentions** ein (Unter)pfand seiner guten Absichten

earnestly [ˈɜːnɪstlɪ] ADV say, ask ernst, ernsthaft; talk, discuss, work, try ernsthaft; explain im Ernst, ernsthaft; hope aufrichtig, innig; look ernst

earnestness [ˈɜːnɪstnɪs] N Ernsthaftigkeit f; (of voice) Ernst m; (of desire, prayer) Innigkeit f

earnings [ˈɜːnɪŋz] PL (of person) Verdienst m; (of a business) Ertrag m

ear: ear, nose and throat ADJ attr Hals-Nasen-Ohren-; **~ specialist** Hals-Nasen-Ohren-Facharzt m/-ärztin f; **earphones** PL Kopfhörer pl; **earpiece** N Hörer m; **ear piercing** N Durchstechen nt der Ohrläppchen; **ear-piercing** ADJ scream ohrenbetäubend; **earplug** N Ohrwatte f, Ohropax® nt; **earring** N Ohrring m; **earshot** N out of/within ~ außer/in Hörweite; **ear-splitting** ADJ sound, scream ohrenbetäubend

earth [ɜːθ] **N a** (= world) Erde f; **the ~, Earth** die Erde; **on ~** auf der Erde, auf Erden (liter); **to the ends of the ~** bis ans Ende der Welt; **where/who** etc **on ~ ...?** (inf) wo/wer etc ... bloß?; **what on ~ ...?** (inf) was in aller Welt ...?; **nothing on ~ will stop me now** keine Macht der Welt hält mich jetzt noch auf; **there's no reason on ~ why ...** es gibt keinen erdenklichen Grund, warum ...; **heaven on ~** der Himmel auf Erden; **did the ~ move for you, darling?** (hum inf) war es wahnsinnig schön für dich, Liebling? (hum inf); **it cost the ~** (Brit inf) das hat eine schöne Stange Geld gekostet (inf); **it won't cost the ~** (Brit inf) es wird schon nicht die Welt kosten (inf); **to pay the ~** (Brit inf) ein Vermögen bezahlen

b (= ground) Erde f; **to fall to ~** zur Erde fallen; **to come back** or **down to ~ (again)** (fig) wieder auf den Boden der Tatsachen (zurück-)kommen; **to bring sb down to ~ (with a bump)** (fig) jdn (unsanft) wieder auf den Boden der Tatsachen zurückholen

c (= soil) Erde f

d (Brit, Elec) Erde f

e (of fox, badger etc) Bau m; **to go to ~** (Brit) (fox) im Bau verschwinden; (criminal etc) untertauchen; **to run sb/sth to ~** (Brit fig) jdn/etw ausfindig machen or aufstöbern

VT (Brit, Elec) erden

▶ **earth up** VT sep plant ausgraben

earth: earthbound ADJ erdgebunden; **earth closet** N Trockenabort m

earthen [ˈɜːθən] ADJ irden

earthenware [ˈɜːθənwɛə] **N** (= material) Ton m; (= dishes etc) Tongeschirr nt ADJ aus Ton, Ton-; **~ crockery** Tongeschirr nt

earthiness [ˈɜːθɪnɪs] N Derbheit f; (of person) Urtümlichkeit f

earthling [ˈɜːθlɪŋ] N (pej) Erdenwurm m

earthly [ˈɜːθlɪ] ADJ **a** (= of this world) irdisch **b** (inf, = possible) **there is no ~ reason to think ...** es besteht nicht der geringste Grund für die Annahme ...; **there's no ~ reason why ...** es gibt nicht den geringsten Grund, warum ...; **this thing is of no ~ use** das Ding hat nicht den geringsten Nutzen **N** (inf) **she doesn't stand an ~** sie hat nicht die geringste Chance

earth: earthman N (Sci-Fi) Erdenmensch m, Terraner(in) m(f); **earth mother** N (Myth) Erdmutter f; (fig) Urmutter f; **earth-moving equipment** N Maschinen pl für Erdbewegungen; **earthperson** N (Sci-Fi) Erdbewohner(in) m(f); **earthquake** N Erdbeben nt; **earth sciences** PL Geowissenschaften pl; **earth-shattering** ADJ (fig) welterschütternd; **earth tremor** N Erdstoß m; **earthward** ADJ in Richtung Erde; **in an ~ direction** in Richtung Erde (also **earthwards**) in Richtung Erde ADV; **earthwork** N (Build) Erdarbeiten pl; (Mil) Schanzwerk nt, Schanze f; **earthworm** N Regenwurm m

earthy [ˈɜːθɪ] ADJ **a** colour erdfarben; flavour, smell erdig; **~ browns** erdfarbene Brauntöne pl **b** (fig) person urtümlich; humour, language, book, play derb; approach robust

ear: ear trumpet N Hörrohr nt; **earwax** N Ohrenschmalz nt; **earwig** N Ohrwurm m; **earwitness** N Ohrenzeuge m/-zeugin f (to gen)

ease [iːz] **N a** (= freedom from discomfort) Behagen nt; **I never feel at ~ in this dress** ich fühle mich in diesem Kleid nie ganz wohl; **I've never felt at ~ with computers** Computer waren mir nie so richtig geheuer; **I am never at ~ in his company** in seiner Gesellschaft fühle ich mich immer befangen or fühle ich mich nie frei und ungezwungen; **to be** or **feel at ~ with oneself** sich (in seiner Haut) wohl fühlen; **to put** or **set sb at (his/her) ~** jdm die Befangenheit nehmen; **to put** or **set sb's mind at ~** jdn beruhigen; **my mind is at ~ now** jetzt bin ich beruhigt; **to take one's ~** sich (dat) bequem machen; **(stand) at ~!** (Mil) rührt euch! → **ill-at-ease**

b (= absence of difficulty) Leichtigkeit f; **with (the greatest of) ~** mit (größter) Leichtigkeit; **for ~ of use/access/reference** um die Benutzung/den Zugang/das Nachschlagen zu erleichtern

c (= absence of work) Muße f; **he lives a life of ~** er führt ein Leben der Muße

VT a (= relieve) pain lindern; mind erleichtern; **to ~ the burden on sb** jdm eine Last abnehmen

b (= make less, loosen) rope, strap lockern, nachlassen; dress etc weiter machen; pressure, tension verringern; situation entspannen; fears zerstreuen; problem abhelfen (+dat)

c **to ~ a key into a lock** einen Schlüssel behutsam in ein Schloss stecken or einführen; **to ~ off the clutch** (Aut) die Kupplung behutsam kommen lassen; **he ~d the car into gear** er legte behutsam einen Gang ein; **he ~d the lid off** er löste den Deckel behutsam ab; **he ~d his broken leg up onto the stretcher** er hob sein gebrochenes Bein behutsam auf die Trage; **he ~d his way toward(s) the door** (= slowly) er bewegte sich langsam zur Tür; (= unobtrusively) er bewegte sich unauffällig zur Tür; **he ~d his way through the hole** er schob sich vorsichtig durch das Loch

VI nachlassen; (situation) sich entspannen; (prices) nachgeben; **he ~d down into second gear** er schaltete behutsam in den zweiten Gang zurück

▶ **ease off** or **up VI a** (= slow down, relax) langsamer werden; (driver) verlangsamen; (situation) sich entspannen; **ease up a bit!** (etwas) langsamer!, sachte, sachte!; **the doctor told him to ease up a bit at work** der Arzt riet ihm, bei der Arbeit etwas kürzer zu treten; **things usually ease up a little just after Christmas** nach Weihnachten wird es normalerweise etwas ruhiger or geruhsamer; **there'll be no easing up until we've finished!** es wird keine Ruhepause geben, bis wir fertig sind **b** (pain, rain) nachlassen

easel [ˈiːzl] N Staffelei f

easily [ˈiːzɪlɪ] ADV **a** (= without difficulty) leicht; **~ accessible** (place) leicht zu erreichen; **they now have ~ available travel** sie können jetzt ohne Schwierigkeiten reisen; **he learnt to swim ~** er lernte mühelos schwimmen

b (= possibly) can, may leicht; could, might gut; **dishwashers can ~ ruin hand-painted china** Spülmaschinen können bemaltes Porzellan leicht ruinieren; **she might/could ~ decide to cancel** es könnte gut sein, dass sie sich entscheidet abzusagen; **it could just as ~ happen here** es könnte genauso gut hier passieren

c (= unquestionably, with figures) gut und gerne; (+ superl) eindeutig, mit Abstand; **it's ~ 25 miles** es sind gut und gerne 25 Meilen; **they are ~ the best** sie sind eindeutig or mit Abstand die Besten

d (= in a relaxed manner) talk, breathe ganz entspannt

easiness [ˈiːzɪnɪs] N Leichtigkeit f

east [iːst] **N the ~, the East** (also Pol) der Osten; **in the ~** im Osten; **to the ~** nach or gen (liter) Osten; **to the ~ of** östlich von, im Osten von; **the wind is coming from the ~** der Wind kommt von Ost(en) or aus (dem) Osten; **the ~ of France** der Osten Frankreichs, das östliche Frankreich; **the south and ~ of the square** die Südseite und die Ostseite des Platzes;

East-West relations Ost-West-Beziehungen *pl*; **of/between East and West** von/zwischen Osten und Westen → *also* **Far East, Middle East, Near East**

ADV (= *eastward*) nach Osten, ostwärts; **the kitchen faces ~** die Küche liegt nach Osten; **~ of Paris/the river** östlich von Paris/des Flusses **ADJ** Ost-; **~ coast** Ostküste *f*; **~ wind** *m*; **~ window** Ostfenster *nt*; **Salford East** Salford Ost

east: East Africa N Ostafrika *nt*; **East Anglia** N *die englischen Grafschaften Norfolk und Suffolk sowie Teile von Essex und Cambridgeshire*; **East Asia** N Ostasien *nt*; **East Berlin** N Ostberlin *nt*; **East Berliner** N Ostberliner(in) *m(f)*; **eastbound** **ADJ** (in) Richtung Osten; **the ~ carriageway of the M4** (*Brit*) die M4 in Richtung Osten; **to be ~** nach Osten unterwegs sein, ostwärts fahren **ADV** nach Osten, (in) Richtung Osten; **East End** N **the ~** der (Londoner) Osten; **East Ender** N Bewohner(in) *m(f)* des Londoner Ostens

Easter ['iːstə'] **N** Ostern *nt*; **at ~** an *or* zu Ostern **ADJ** *attr* Oster-

Easter: Easter bunny N Osterhase *m*; **Easter Day** N Ostersonntag *m*; **Easter egg** N Osterei *nt*; **Easter Island** N Osterinsel *f*

easterly ['iːstəlɪ] **ADJ** östlich, Ost-; **an ~ wind** ein Ostwind *m*, ein Wind *m* aus östlicher Richtung; **in an ~ direction** in östlicher Richtung **N** (= *wind*) Ostwind *m*, Ost *m* (*poet*) **ADV** nach Osten

Easter Monday N Ostermontag *m*

eastern ['iːstən] **ADJ** Ost-, östlich; *attitude* orientalisch; **the Eastern bloc** der Ostblock; **Eastern Europe** Osteuropa *nt*

easterner ['iːstənə'] N (*esp US*) Oststaatler(in) *m(f)*; **he's an ~** er kommt aus dem Osten

easternmost ['iːstənməʊst] **ADJ** östlichste(r, s)

Easter Sunday N Ostersonntag *m*

east: East Europe N (*esp US*) Osteuropa *nt*; **East European** **ADJ** osteuropäisch **N** Osteuropäer(in) *m(f)*; **East German** **ADJ** ostdeutsch; **the ~ government** (*Hist*) die Regierung der DDR **N** Ostdeutsche(r) *mf*; **East Germany** N Ostdeutschland *nt* (= *GDR*) die DDR; **East Indian** **ADJ** ostindisch; (= *East Caribbean*) ostkaribisch; **East Indies** PL Ostindien *nt* (*old*), die Malaiische Archipel; **east-north-east** **ADV** Ostnordosten; **~ of Munich/the lake** ostnordöstlich von München/des Sees; **East Side** N **the (Lower) ~** die East Side (*der Osten von Manhattan*); **east-southeast** **ADV** Ostsüdosten *m* **ADV** nach Ostsüdosten; **~ of Munich/the lake** ostsüdöstlich von München/des Sees; **East Timor** N Osttimor *m*; **eastward** ADV (*also* **eastwards**) ostwärts, nach Osten, (in) Richtung Osten **ADJ** *direction* östlich; *route* nach Osten, (in) Richtung Osten; **eastwardly** ADV, ADJ = **eastward**

easy ['iːzɪ] **ADJ** (+*er*) **a** (= *simple*) leicht; *task, job* leicht, einfach; *option, solution, answer* einfach; **finding somewhere to eat is an ~ task** es ist leicht *or* einfach, ein Restaurant zu finden; **it's no ~ task** es ist nicht einfach; **it's ~ to forget that ...** man vergisst leicht, dass ...; **it's ~ for her** sie hat es leicht; **it's ~ for her to do it** sie kann es leicht tun; **that's ~ for you to say** du hast gut reden; **to make ~ reading** leicht zu lesen sein; **he was an ~ winner** er hat mühelos gewonnen; **to be far from ~** *or* **none too ~** alles andere als leicht sein, nicht gerade leicht sein; **that's the ~ part** das ist das Einfache; **it's an ~ (enough) mistake to make** den Fehler kann man leicht machen, das kann einem leicht passieren; **to be within ~ reach of sth** etw leicht erreichen können; **in** *or* **by ~ stages** (= *step by step*) Schritt für Schritt; (= *gradually*) nach und nach; **as ~ as pie** *or* **as ABC** *or* **as falling off a log** kinderleicht; **easier said than done** leichter gesagt als getan; **~ credit** leicht erhältliche Kredite; **on ~ terms** (*Comm*) zu günstigen Bedingungen; **to go for the ~ option**, **to take the ~ way out** es sich (*dat*) leicht machen; **she is ~ to work with/get on with** mit

ihr kann man gut arbeiten/auskommen; **she opted for the ~ life** sie machte sich (*dat*) das Leben leicht; **~ living** ein sorgenfreies Leben; **to have it ~**, **to have an ~ time (of it)** es leicht haben; **to have an ~ ride** es leicht haben; **he will not be given an ~ ride** man wird es ihm nicht leicht machen; **~ prey** eine leichte Beute; **to be ~ meat** (*inf*) eine leichte Beute sein **b** (= *not harsh*) **to be ~ on the eye/ear** angenehm anzusehen/anzuhören sein; **he/she is ~ on the eye** (*inf*) er/sie sieht gut aus; **to be ~ on the stomach** leicht verdaulich sein **c** (= *relaxed*) *temperament, conversation, laugh, smile, voice* ungezwungen; *relationship* unbefangen; *tone* lässig; **at an ~ pace** in gemütlichem Tempo; **he had a quick and ~ laugh** er lachte schnell und ungezwungen; **to be on ~ terms with sb** mit jdm auf vertrautem Fuß stehen; **I'm ~** (*Brit, inf*) mir ist alles recht, ist mir egal (*inf*); **stand ~!** (*Brit Mil*) rührt euch!; **I don't feel ~ about it** (= *uncomfortable*) es ist mir nicht recht, mir ist dabei nicht wohl **d** (*pej inf*: = *promiscuous*) **she's ~** sie ist immer zu haben; **she wasn't like the ~ girls he had known** sie war anders als die leichten Mädchen, die er gekannt hatte; **to be an ~ make** (*US*) *or* **lay** (*sl*) jeden ranlassen (*inf*); **woman of ~ virtue** (*dated euph*, = *prostitute*) Freudenmädchen *nt* **ADV** (*inf*) **to go ~ on sb** nicht so streng mit jdm sein; **to go ~ on sth** mit etw sparsam umgehen; **to go ~ on the brakes/one's liver** die Bremsen/seine Leber schonen; **to take it ~**, **to take things ~** (= *rest*) sich schonen; **take it ~!** (= *calm down*) immer mit der Ruhe!; (*esp US, when saying goodbye*) machs gut!; **~ does it** immer sachte

easy: easy-care ADJ pflegeleicht; **easy chair** N Sessel *m*; **easy come, easy go** INTERJ wie gewonnen, so zerronnen (*Prov*); **easy-come easy-go** ADJ unbekümmert; **easy-going** ADJ (= *not anxious*) gelassen; (= *lax*) lax, lässig; **easy listening** N leichte Musik, Unterhaltungsmusik *f*; **easy-listening** ADJ *album, CD* mit leichter Musik, mit Unterhaltungsmusik; **~ music** leichte Musik, Unterhaltungsmusik *f*; **easy money** N leicht verdientes Geld; **you can make ~** Sie können leicht Geld machen; **easy-on-the-pocket** ADJ erschwinglich; **easy-peasy** [ˌiːzɪ'piːzɪ] ADJ (*Brit inf, baby-talk*) kinderleicht; **easy street** N (*inf*) **to be on ~** im Wohlstand leben; **easy touch** N **to be an ~** (*inf*) nicht nein *or* Nein sagen können

eat [iːt] *vb: pret* **ate**, *ptp* **eaten** **VT** (*person*) essen, fressen (*pej inf*); (*animal*) fressen; **to ~ one's breakfast** frühstücken; **to ~ one's lunch/dinner** zu Mittag/Abend essen; **he ate his way through ...** er aß sich durch ...; **he's ~ing us out of house and home** (*inf*) der isst *or* frisst uns noch arm *or* die Haare vom Kopf (*inf*); **to ~ one's words** (alles,) was man gesagt hat, zurücknehmen; **he was forced to ~ his words** er musste alles zurücknehmen; **he won't ~ you** (*inf*) er wird dich schon nicht fressen (*inf*); **what's ~ing you?** (*inf*) was hast du denn? → **alive a** **VI** essen, fressen (*pej inf*); (*animal*) fressen; **I haven't ~en for ages** ich habe schon ewig nichts mehr gegessen **N** (*inf*) **eats** PL Fressalien *pl* (*inf*); **time for ~s!** Fütterung der Raubtiere! (*inf*)

▶ **eat away** VT *sep* (*sea*) auswaschen; (*acid*) zerfressen

▶ **eat away at** VI +*prep obj* **a** (*waves, sea*) auswaschen; (*acid, rust, pest*) anfressen; (*rot, damp*) angreifen **b** (*fig*) *revenue* auffressen; *finances* angreifen; *society* zerstören

▶ **eat into** VI +*prep obj* *metal* anfressen; *capital* angreifen; *market share, profits* verringern; *life, time* verkürzen

▶ **eat out** **VI** zum Essen ausgehen **VT** *sep* **to eat one's heart out** Trübsal blasen, sich vor Gram verzehren (*geh*); **Michael Parkinson, eat your heart out** Michael Parkinson, da kannst du vor Neid erblassen

▶ **eat out of** VI +*prep obj* **she had them eating out of her hand** (*fig*) sie fraßen ihr aus der Hand

▶ **eat up** **VT** *sep* **a** (*lit*) aufessen; (*animal*) auffressen **b** (*fig*, = *use up, consume*) verbrauchen, fressen (*inf*); **this car eats up the miles** der Wagen gibt ganz schön was her (*inf*) **c** **he was eaten up with envy** der Neid nagte *or* zehrte an ihm **VI** aufessen

eatable ['iːtəbl] ADJ essbar, genießbar

eat-by date ['iːtbaɪdeɪt] N Haltbarkeitsdatum *nt*

eaten ['iːtn] *ptp of* **eat**

eater ['iːtə'] N **a** Esser(in) *m(f)* **b** (= *apple*) Essapfel *m*

eatery ['iːtərɪ] N (*hum inf*, = *restaurant etc*) Esslokal *nt*, Fresslokal *nt* (*hum inf*)

eating ['iːtɪŋ] N Essen *nt*; **to make good ~** gut zum Essen sein

eating: eating apple N Essapfel *m*; **eating disorder** N Essstörung *f*; **eating house** N Gasthaus *nt*; **eating place** N Esslokal *nt*

eau de Cologne ['əʊdəkə'ləʊn] N Kölnischwasser *nt*, Eau de Cologne *nt*

eaves ['iːvz] PL Dachvorsprung *m*

eavesdrop ['iːvzdrɒp] VI (heimlich) lauschen; **to ~ on a conversation** ein Gespräch belauschen

eavesdropper ['iːvzdrɒpə'] N Lauscher(in) *m(f)*

eavesdropping ['iːvzdrɒpɪŋ] N heimliches Lauschen *or* Horchen; **electronic ~** (*esp Pol*) Lauschangriff *m* (*on* auf +*acc*), Lauschoperation *f* (*on* gegen)

ebb [eb] **N** Ebbe *f*; **the tide is on the ~** es ist Ebbe; **~ and flow** Ebbe und Flut *f*; (*fig*) Auf und Ab *nt*; **at a low ~** (*fig*) auf einem Tiefstand; **their popularity is at its lowest ~** ihre Beliebtheit hat einen absoluten Tiefpunkt erreicht **VI** **a** (*tide*) zurückgehen; **to ~ and flow** (*lit, fig*) kommen und gehen **b** (*fig: also* **ebb away**, *enthusiasm etc*) abebben, verebben; (*life*) zu Ende gehen

ebb tide N Ebbe *f*

Ebola [ɪ'bəʊlə], **Ebola virus** N (*Med*) Ebola-Virus *nt or m*, Ebolavirus *nt or m*

ebonite ['ebənaɪt] N Ebonit *m*

ebony ['ebənɪ] N Ebenholz *nt* **ADJ** *colour* schwarz wie Ebenholz; *material* aus Ebenholz; *hair, face* ebenholzfarben

e-book ['iːbʊk] N Onlinebuch *nt*

ebullience [ɪ'bʌlɪəns] N Überschwänglichkeit *f*

ebullient [ɪ'bʌlɪənt] ADJ *person* überschwänglich; *spirits, mood* übersprudelnd; *optimism* unbändig

e-business [ˌiː'bɪznɪs] N **a** (= *company*) Internetfirma *f* **b** (= *commerce*) E-Business *nt*, elektronischer Geschäftsverkehr

EC *abbr of* **European Community** EG *f*

ECB *abbr of* **European Central Bank** EZB *f*

eccentric [ik'sentrik] **ADJ** (*also Tech*) exzentrisch; *taste* ausgefallen **N** **a** (= *oddball*) Exzentriker(in) *m(f)* **b** (*Tech*) Exzenter *m*

eccentrically [ik'sentrikəlɪ] ADV (*also Tech*) exzentrisch; *dress, decorate* ausgefallen; **she ~ rejected it** merkwürdigerweise war sie dagegen

eccentricity [ˌeksən'trɪsɪtɪ] N (*all senses*) Exzentrizität *f*

Eccles cake ['ekəlzˌkeɪk] N (*Brit*) *mit Dörrobst gefülltes Gebäck*

Ecclesiastes [ɪˌkliːzɪ'æstiːz] N (*der Prediger*) Salomo *m*

ecclesiastic [ɪˌkliːzɪ'æstɪk] N Kleriker *m*

ecclesiastical [ɪˌkliːzɪ'æstɪkəl] ADJ kirchlich

ECG *abbr of* **electrocardiogram** EKG *nt*

echelon ['eʃəlɒn] N (*Mil*, = *formation*) Staffelung *f*, Echelon *m* (*old*); **the higher ~s** die höheren Ränge *pl*

echo ['ekəʊ] **N** Echo *nt*, Widerhall *m*; (*fig*) Anklang *m* (*of an* +*acc*); (*Comput*) Rückmeldung *f*;

he was cheered to the ~ er bekam brausenden or rauschenden Beifall **VT** sound zurückwerfen; (fig) wiedergeben **VI** (sounds) widerhallen; (room, footsteps) hallen; **to ~ with sth** von etw widerhallen; **her words ~ed in his ears** ihre Worte hallten ihm in den Ohren

echo chamber N Hallraum m; (for electric guitar) Nachhallerzeuger m

echolocation [ˌekəʊləʊ'keɪʃən] N Echoortung f

echo sounder N Echolot nt

ECJ N ABBR of **European Court of Justice** Europäischer Gerichtshof

éclair [eɪ'klɛəʳ] N Eclair nt, Liebesknochen m

eclampsia [ɪ'klæmpsɪə] N (Med) Eklampsie f

eclectic [ɪ'klektɪk] ADJ eklektisch

eclecticism [ɪ'klektɪsɪzəm] N Eklektizismus m

eclipse [ɪ'klɪps] **N** (Astron) Eklipse f (spec), Finsternis f; (fig) (of fame, theory) Verblassen nt; (of person) Niedergang m; **~ of the sun/moon** Sonnen-/Mondfinsternis f; **to be in ~** (sun, moon) verfinstert sein; (fig) in der Versenkung verschwunden sein **VT** (Astron) verfinstern; (fig) in den Schatten stellen

eco- ['iːkəʊ-] PREF Öko-, öko-

ecocide ['iːkəʊsaɪd] N Umweltzerstörung f

ecoconscious [ˌiːkəʊ'kɒnʃəs] ADJ ökobewusst, umweltbewusst

ecofriendly [ˌiːkəʊ'frendlɪ] ADJ (Brit) umweltfreundlich

ecohome ['iːkəʊhəʊm] N Ökohaus nt

E.coli [iː'kəʊlaɪ] N (Med) E-coli f

ecological [ˌiːkəʊ'lɒdʒɪkəl] ADJ problem, balance, impact ökologisch; **~ disaster** Umweltkatastrophe f; **~ damage** Umweltschäden pl; **~ system** Ökosystem nt; **~ group** Umweltorganisation f; **~ party** Umweltpartei f

ecologically [ˌiːkəʊ'lɒdʒɪkəlɪ] ADV ökologisch; **~ harmful** umweltschädlich; **~ minded/aware** umweltbewusst

ecologist [ɪ'kɒlədʒɪst] N Ökologe m, Ökologin f

ecology [ɪ'kɒlədʒɪ] N Ökologie f

e-commerce ['iːkɒmɜːs] N Onlinehandel m, E-Commerce m

economic [ˌiːkə'nɒmɪk] ADJ **a** (= financial) Wirtschafts-; **~ crisis** Wirtschaftskrise f; **~ growth** Wirtschaftswachstum nt; **~ news** Nachrichten pl aus der Wirtschaft; **~ policy** Wirtschaftspolitik f; **~ recovery** Wirtschaftsaufschwung m, wirtschaftlicher Aufschwung; **~ system** Wirtschaftssystem nt **b** (= cost-effective) price, rent wirtschaftlich; system wirtschaftlich, rentabel; **it is not ~ to do this** es ist nicht rentabel, das zu tun; **to be ~ for sb** sich für jdn rentieren

economic aid N Wirtschaftshilfe f

economical [ˌiːkə'nɒmɪkəl] ADJ sparsam, wirtschaftlich; **to be ~ with sth** mit etw haushalten or Haus halten, mit etw sparsam umgehen; **they were ~ with the truth** sie haben es mit der Wahrheit nicht so genau genommen; **an ~ style** (Liter) ein prägnanter Stil

economically [ˌiːkə'nɒmɪkəlɪ] ADV **a** (= financially) depressed, powerful, important wirtschaftlich; **after the war, the country suffered ~** nach dem Krieg litt die Wirtschaft des Landes; **we can't compete ~** unsere Wirtschaft ist nicht konkurrenzfähig; **~ viable** rentabel; **the most powerful state** die größte Wirtschaftsmacht **b** (= thriftily) sparsam; **to use sth ~** mit etw wirtschaftlich or sparsam umgehen **c** (= in few words) prägnant; **to get the point across ~** das Argument knapp fassen

economic indicator N Wirtschaftsindikator m

economic migrant, **economic refugee** N Wirtschaftsflüchtling m

economics [ˌiːkə'nɒmɪks] N **a** sing or pl Volkswirtschaft f, Wirtschaftswissenschaften pl; (= social economics) Volkswirtschaft f; (in management studies) Betriebswirtschaft f **b** pl (= economic aspect) Wirtschaftlichkeit f, Ökonomie f; **the ~ of the situation** die wirtschaftliche Seite der Situation

economist [ɪ'kɒnəmɪst] N Wirtschaftswissenschaftler(in) m(f); (= social economist) Volkswirt(in) m(f), Volkswirtschaftler(in) m(f); (in management studies) Betriebswirt(in) m(f), Betriebswirtschaftler(in) m(f)

economize [ɪ'kɒnəmaɪz] VI sparen

▶ **economize on** VI +prep obj sparen

economy [ɪ'kɒnəmɪ] N **a** (system) Wirtschaft f no pl; (from a monetary aspect) Konjunktur f; **what is the state of the ~?** wie ist die Wirtschaftslage/Konjunktur?

b (= saving: in time, money) Sparmaßnahme f, Einsparung f; **fuel ~** geringer Kraftstoffverbrauch; **a false ~** falsche Sparsamkeit; **economies of scale** Einsparungen pl durch erhöhte Produktion; **to make economies** zu Sparmaßnahmen greifen, Einsparungen machen

c (= thrift) Sparsamkeit f; **to practise** (Brit) or **practice** (US) ~ Sparsamkeit walten lassen; **~ of language/expression** knappe Sprache/Ausdrucksweise; **with ~ of effort** mit sparsamem Krafteaufwand

economy: economy class N Touristenklasse f; **economy drive** N Sparmaßnahmen pl; **we'll have to have an ~** wir werden Sparmaßnahmen ergreifen müssen; **economy size** N Sparpackung f

eco: ecosphere N Ökosphäre f; **ecosystem** N Ökosystem nt; **ecotourism** N Ökotourismus m; **eco-warrior** N (inf) Ökokämpfer(in) m(f)

ecru [e'kruː] ADJ naturfarben, ekrü

ecstasy ['ekstəsɪ] N **a** Ekstase f, Verzückung f; **to be in ~** ekstatisch or verzückt sein; **to go into ecstasies over sth** über etw (acc) in Ekstase or Verzückung geraten; **~! she sighed** welche Wonne! seufzte sie **b** (= drug) Ecstasy nt

ecstatic [eks'tætɪk] ADJ ekstatisch, verzückt

ecstatically [eks'tætɪkəlɪ] ADV ekstatisch; listen also verzückt; **~ happy** überglücklich

ECT abbr of **electroconvulsive therapy** Elektroschock m, Elektrokrampftherapie f

ectomorph ['ektəʊmɔːf] N ektomorpher Konstitutionstyp

ectopic [ek'tɒpɪk] ADJ **~ pregnancy** ektopische or ektope Schwangerschaft

ectoplasm ['ektəʊplæzəm] N Ektoplasma nt

ECU, ecu ['eɪkjuː] N abbr of **European Currency Unit** ECU m, Ecu m

Ecuador ['ekwədɔːʳ] N Ecuador nt, Ekuador nt

Ecuador(i)an [ˌekwə'dɔːr(ɪ)ən] **ADJ** ecuadorianisch, ekuadorianisch **N** Ecuadorianer(in) m(f), Ekuadorianer(in) m(f)

ecumenical [ˌiːkjʊ'menɪkəl] ADJ (form) ökumenisch; **~ council** Ökumenischer Rat

ecumenically [ˌiːkjʊ'menɪkəlɪ] ADV (form) ökumenisch; (introducing a sentence) vom ökumenischen Standpunkt aus

ecumenicism [ˌiːkjʊ'menɪsɪzm] N (form) Ökumenismus m

eczema ['eksɪmə] N Ekzem nt, (Haut)ausschlag m

ed a abbr of **editor** Hrsg., Herausgeber(in) m(f) **b** abbr of **edition** Ausg., Ausgabe f **c** abbr of **edited** hg., herausgegeben

Edam ['iːdæm] N Edamer (Käse) m

eddy ['edɪ] **N** Wirbel m; (of water also) Strudel m; **the wind swept up eddies of dust** der Wind wirbelte Staubwolken auf **VI** wirbeln; (water also) strudeln

edelweiss ['eɪdlvaɪs] N Edelweiß nt

edema [ɪ'diːmə] N (esp US) Ödem nt

Eden ['iːdn] N (also fig) **Garden of ~** Garten m Eden

edge [edʒ] **N a** (of knife, razor) Schneide f; **to take the ~ off sth** (fig, sensation) etw der Wirkung (gen) berauben; pain etw lindern; **that took the ~ off my appetite** das nahm mir erst einmal den Hunger; **the noise sets my teeth on ~** das Geräusch geht mir durch und durch; **his arrogance sets my teeth on ~** seine Arroganz bringt mich auf die Palme (inf); **to be on**

~ nervös sein; **my nerves are on ~** ich bin schrecklich nervös; **there was an ~ to his voice** seine Stimme klang ärgerlich; **to have the ~ on sb/sth** jdm/etw überlegen sein; **but the professional had the ~** aber der Profi war eben besser; **it gives her/it that extra ~** darin besteht eben der kleine Unterschied; **to lose one's ~** seine Überlegenheit verlieren

b (= outer limit) Rand m; (of brick, cube) Kante f; (of lake, river) Ufer nt, Rand m; (of sea) Ufer nt; (of estates etc) Grenze f; **a book with gilt ~s** ein Buch mit Goldschnitt; **the trees at the ~ of the road** die Bäume am Straßenrand; **the film had us on the ~ of our seats** der Film war unheimlich spannend; **to be on the ~ of disaster** am Rande des Untergangs stehen; **to live life on the ~** gefährlich leben; **rough ~s** (fig) kleine Mängel pl

VT a (= put a border on) besetzen, einfassen; **to ~ a coat with fur** einen Mantel mit Pelz verbrämen; **~d in black** mit einem schwarzen Rand

b (= sharpen) tool, blade schärfen, schleifen, scharf machen

c to ~ one's way toward(s) sth (slowly) sich allmählich auf etw (acc) zubewegen; (carefully) sich vorsichtig auf etw (acc) zubewegen; **she ~d her way through the crowd** sie schlängelte sich durch die Menge; **the prisoner ~d his way along the wall** der Gefangene schob sich langsam an der Wand entlang

VI sich schieben; **to ~ toward(s) the door** sich zur Tür stehlen; **to ~ away** sich davonstehlen; **to ~ away from sb/sth** sich allmählich immer weiter von jdm/etw entfernen; **to ~ up to sb** sich an jdn heranmachen; **he ~d past me** er drückte or schob sich an mir vorbei

▶ **edge out VT** sep (of job, position etc) beiseite drängen; **Germany edged England out of the final** Deutschland verdrängte England aus dem Endspiel **VI** **she edged out onto the balcony** sie tastete sich auf den Balkon vor; **the driver edged out onto the main road** der Fahrer fuhr vorsichtig auf die Hauptstraße

▶ **edge up VT** sep prices etc hoch drücken **VI** (prices etc) hoch gehen

edgeways ['edʒweɪz] ADV mit der Schmalseite voran; **I couldn't get a word in ~** ich bin überhaupt nicht zu Wort gekommen

edginess ['edʒɪnɪs] N Nervosität f

edging ['edʒɪŋ] N Borte f, Einfassung f

edging shears PL Rasenschere f

edgy ['edʒɪ] ADJ (+er) person nervös

edibility [ˌedɪ'bɪlɪtɪ] N Essbarkeit f, Genießbarkeit f

edible ['edɪbl] ADJ essbar, genießbar; **very ~!** durchaus genießbar!

edict ['iːdɪkt] N Erlass m; (Hist) Edikt nt

edification [ˌedɪfɪ'keɪʃən] N Erbauung f; **for the ~ of …** zur Erbauung des/der …

edifice ['edɪfɪs] N (lit, fig) Gebäude nt; (fig also) Gefüge nt

edify ['edɪfaɪ] VT erbauen

edifying ['edɪfaɪɪŋ] ADJ erbaulich; **this is not a very ~ spectacle** das ist kein besonders erbaulicher Anblick

Edinburgh ['edɪnbərə] N Edinburg(h) nt

EDINBURGH FESTIVAL

Das **Edinburgh Festival** findet jedes Jahr im August statt. Es dauert drei Wochen und ist mittlerweile eines der größten Kunst- und Theaterfestivals der Welt. Neben dem offiziellen Festivalprogramm, in dem Künstler internationalen Ranges präsentiert werden, gibt es auch noch das Edinburgh Festival **Fringe**, wo man eine riesige Palette der verschiedensten Kunstformen vom Traditionellen über das Abenteuerliche bis hin zum Bizarren erleben kann. Zur selben Zeit wie das Internationale Festival und die **Fringe** findet im Edinburgh Castle der **Military Tattoo**, ein Treffen internationaler Dudelsackgruppen, statt.

edit ['edɪt] **VT** *series, author, newspaper, magazine* herausgeben, edieren; *newspaper story, book, text* redigieren, bearbeiten; *film, tape* schneiden, cutten; (*Comput*) editieren; **~ed by: ...** (*Film*) Schnitt: ... **VI** redigieren, redaktionell arbeiten

▶ **edit out** VT *sep* herausnehmen; (*from film, tape*) herausschneiden; *character (from story)* herausstreichen

editable ['edɪtəbl] ADJ (*Comput*) *file* editierbar

editing ['edɪtɪŋ] N (*of series, author, newspaper, magazine*) Herausgabe *f*, Edieren *nt*; (*of newspaper story, book, text*) Redaktion *f*, Bearbeitung *f*; (*of film, tape*) Schnitt *m*; (*Comput*) Editieren *nt*

edition [ɪ'dɪʃən] N Ausgabe *f*, Edition *f*; (= *impression*) Auflage *f*

editor ['edɪtə'] N (*of text, newspaper, magazine, series, author*) Herausgeber(in) *m(f)*; (*publisher's*) (Verlags)lektor(in) *m(f)*; (*Film*) Cutter(in) *m(f)*; (*Comput*) Editor *m*; **political ~** politischer Redakteur *m*, politische Redakteurin *f*; **sports ~** Sportredakteur(in) *m(f)*; **~ in chief** Herausgeber(in) *m(f)*; (*of newspaper*) Chefredakteur(in) *m(f)*; **the ~s in our educational department** die Redaktion unserer Schulbuchabteilung; **the ~ of this passage obviously misunderstood** der, der diese Stelle redigierte, hat offensichtlich nicht richtig verstanden

editorial [edɪ'tɔ:rɪəl] ADJ **a** (= *editing*) *work, task, budget, board* redaktionell; **~ department** or **office** Redaktion *f*; **~ staff** Redaktionsangestellte *pl*; (= *department*) Redaktion *f*; **~ meeting** Redaktionsbesprechung *f* **b** (= *involving opinions*) *control, problems, questions* redaktionell; **~ page** Kommentarseite *f*; **the ~ pages** der Kommentarteil; **the paper's ~ policy** die redaktionelle Linie der Zeitung **N a** (= *article*) Leitartikel *m* **b** (= *department*) Redaktion *f*

editorial assistant N Redaktionsassistent(in) *m(f)*

editorial comment N (*Press*) Kommentare *pl* der Redaktion; (= *leaders*) Leitartikel *pl*

editorially [edɪ'tɔ:rɪəlɪ] ADV redaktionell; (= *as an editor*) als Redakteur(in); **we are not able to comment** wir können keine redaktionellen Kommentare abgeben; **~ the paper will focus on Europe** in ihren Kommentaren wird die Zeitung sich auf Europa konzentrieren

editorship ['edɪtəʃɪp] N (*of newspaper, magazine*) Chefredaktion *f*; **under the ~ of ...** unter ... als Herausgeber(in)

EDP *abbr of* **electronic data processing** EDV *f*

EDT (*US*) *abbr of* **Eastern Daylight Time** östliche Sommerzeit in den USA und Kanada

educable ['edjʊkəbl] ADJ erziehbar; (*academically*) ausbildbar

educate ['edjʊkeɪt] VT **a** (*Sch, Univ*) erziehen; **the parents' role in educating their children** die Rolle der Eltern bei der Erziehung ihrer Kinder; **he's hardly ~d at all** er ist ziemlich ungebildet; **he was ~d at Eton** er ist in Eton zur Schule gegangen **b** *public* informieren; **we need to ~ our children about drugs** wir müssen dafür sorgen, dass unsere Kinder über Drogen Bescheid wissen **c** *the mind* schulen; *one's tastes* (aus)bilden

educated ['edjʊkeɪtɪd] ADJ gebildet; **to make an ~ guess** eine fundierte *or* wohl begründete Vermutung anstellen; **an ~ mind** ein gebildeter Geist

education [edjʊ'keɪʃən] N Erziehung *f*; (= *studies, training*) Ausbildung *f*; (= *knowledge, culture*) Bildung *f*; **Ministry of Education** Ministerium *nt* für Erziehung und Unterricht, Kultusministerium *nt*; **lecturer in ~** Dozent(in) *m(f)* für Pädagogik; **College of Education** pädagogische Hochschule; (*for graduates*) Studienseminar *nt*; (*local*) **~ authority** Schulbehörde *f*; **to study ~** Pädagogik *or* Erziehungswissenschaften studieren; **if the government neglects ~** wenn die Regierung das Erziehungs- und Ausbildungswesen vernachlässigt; **the ~ budget** der Etat für das Erziehungs- und Ausbildungswesen; **~ is free** die Schulausbildung ist kostenlos; **his ~ was interrupted** seine Ausbildung wurde unter-

brochen; **to get an ~** eine Ausbildung bekommen; **the ~ he received at school** seine Schulbildung; **she had a university ~** sie hatte eine Universitätsausbildung; **a literary/scientific ~** eine literarische/naturwissenschaftliche Bildung; **she had little ~** sie war ziemlich ungebildet

educational [edjʊ'keɪʃənl] ADJ **a** (= *academic*) *needs* erzieherisch; (*at school level*) *needs, achievement* schulisch; **~ system** (= *institutions*) Bildungswesen *nt*; (= *structure*) Bildungssystem *nt*; **~ opportunities** Ausbildungschancen *pl*; **~ institution** or **establishment** Bildungsanstalt *f*; **~ standards** (*in schools*) Unterrichtsniveau *nt*; (*of country*) Bildungsniveau *nt*; **~ qualification** (Ausbildungs)abschluss *m* **b** (= *teaching*) *issue* pädagogisch; **~ theory** Pädagogik *f*, Unterrichtstheorie *f*; **~ method** or **methodology** Erziehungsmethode *f*; **~ supplies** Unterrichtsmaterial *nt* **c** (= *educative, instructive*) *experience, video* lehrreich; *day also* informativ; **~ trip** (= *school trip*) Klassenfahrt *f*; (*for adults*) Bildungsreise *f*; **~ leave** Bildungsurlaub *m*; **~ film** Lehrfilm *m*; **~ book** Lehrbuch *nt*; (*for schools*) Schulbuch *nt*; **~ experience** lehrreiche Erfahrung; **~ toy** pädagogisch wertvolles Spielzeug; **~ game** Lernspiel *nt*; **~ material** Lehrmittel *pl*

educational adviser N (*Brit, Sch, Admin*) Unterrichtsberater(in) *m(f)*

educationalist [edjʊ'keɪʃnəlɪst] N Pädagoge *m*, Pädagogin *f*, Erziehungswissenschaftler(in) *m(f)*

educationally [edjʊ'keɪʃnəlɪ] ADV pädagogisch; (= *relating to school*) schulisch; **~ subnormal** lernbehindert; **to stimulate the youngsters ~** die Jugendlichen durch Lernen stimulieren

educational: educational park N (*US*) Gesamtschulanlage *f*; **educational psychologist** N Schulpsychologe *m*/-psychologin *f*; **educational psychology** N Schulpsychologie *f*; **educational publisher** N Schulbuchverlag *m*; **educational television** N Schulfernsehen *nt*; (*for adults*) Bildungssendungen *pl*

educationist [edjʊ'keɪʃnɪst] N = **educationalist**

educative ['edjʊkətɪv] ADJ erzieherisch

educator ['edjʊkeɪtə'] N Pädagoge *m*, Pädagogin *f*, Erzieher(in) *m(f)*; **an ~ of the young** ein Erzieher *m*/eine Erzieherin der Jugend

educe [ɪ'dju:s] VT (*form*) ableiten (*from sth* von etw), entlocken (*from sb* jdm)

edutainment [edjʊ'teɪnmənt] N Edutainment *nt*

Edward ['edwəd] N Eduard *m*

Edwardian [ed'wɔ:dɪən] ADJ *house, furniture, clothes* Edwardianisch, aus der Zeit Eduards VII.; **the ~ era** die Edwardianische Zeit, die Zeit Eduards VII.; **~ England** England in der Zeit Eduards VII. **N** (= *person*) Zeitgenosse *m*/Zeitgenossin *f* Eduards VII.

EEC N (*dated*) *abbr of* **European Economic Community** EG *f*, EWG *f* (*dated*)

EEG *abbr of* **electroencephalogram** EEG *nt*

eek [i:k] INTERJ i, igitt

eel [i:l] N Aal *m* → **slippery**

e'en [i:n] ADV (*poet*) *contr of* **even**[1]

EENT (*US, Med*) *abbr of* **eye, ear, nose and throat ~ specialist** Augen- und HNO-Arzt *m*/-Ärztin *f*

e'er [ɛə'] ADV (*poet*) *contr of* **ever**

eerie, eery ['ɪərɪ] ADJ (*+er*) unheimlich

eerily ['ɪərɪlɪ] ADV (*+vb*) unheimlich; (*+adj*) auf unheimliche Weise; **the whole town was ~ quiet** in der ganzen Stadt herrschte eine unheimliche Stille; **sometimes they were ~ similar** manchmal bestand eine unheimliche Ähnlichkeit zwischen ihnen

EET *abbr of* **Eastern European Time** OEZ *f*

efface [ɪ'feɪs] VT auslöschen; **to ~ oneself** sich zurückhalten

effect [ɪ'fekt] **N a** (= *result*) Wirkung *f*, Effekt *m*; (= *repercussion*) Auswirkung *f*; **the ~ of an**

acid on metal die Wirkung einer Säure auf Metall; **alcohol has the ~ of dulling your senses** Alkohol bewirkt eine Abstumpfung der Sinne; **the ~ of this rule will be to prevent ...** diese Regelung wird die Verhinderung von ... bewirken *or* zur Folge haben; **the ~ of this is that ...** das hat zur Folge, dass ...; **the ~s of radioactivity on the human body** die Auswirkungen radioaktiver Strahlen auf den menschlichen Körper; **to feel the ~s of the recession** die Auswirkungen der Rezession spüren; **to feel the ~s of the drugs** die Wirkung der Drogen spüren; **to no ~** erfolglos, ergebnislos; **to such good ~ that ...** so wirkungsvoll, dass ...; **to have an ~ on sb/sth** eine Wirkung auf jdn/etw haben; **to have a good ~ (on sb/sth)** eine gute Wirkung (auf jdn/etw) haben; **to have no ~** keine Wirkung haben; **to take ~** (*drug*) wirken; **with immediate ~** mit sofortiger Wirkung; **with ~ from 3 March** mit Wirkung vom 3. März **b** (= *impression*) Wirkung *f*, Effekt *m*; **to create an ~** eine Wirkung *or* einen Effekt erzielen; **~s of light** (*Art*) Lichteffekte *pl*; **the sword was only for ~** der Degen war nur zum Effekt da; **he paused for ~** er machte eine effektvolle Pause **c** (= *meaning*) **his letter is to the ~ that ...** sein Brief hat zum Inhalt, dass ...; **we received a letter to the ~ that ...** wir erhielten ein Schreiben des Inhalts, dass ...; **he used words to that ~** sinngemäß drückte er sich so aus; **... or words to that ~** ... oder etwas in diesem Sinne *or* etwas Ähnliches **d** **effects** PL (= *property*) Effekten *pl* **e** (= *reality*) **in ~** in Wirklichkeit, im Effekt **f** (*of laws*) **to be in ~** gültig *or* in Kraft sein; **to come into** or **take ~** in Kraft treten; **to put sth into ~** etw in Kraft setzen; **to remain in ~** in Kraft bleiben **VT a** bewirken, herbeiführen; **to ~ change** Veränderungen herbeiführen; **to ~ an entry** (*form*) sich (*dat*) Zutritt verschaffen; **to ~ an escape** fliehen **b** (*form*) *sale, purchase* tätigen; *payment* leisten; *insurance* abschließen; *settlement* erzielen

effective [ɪ'fektɪv] ADJ **a** (= *successful*) *way, method, action, measures* effektiv, wirksam; *means, treatment, vaccine, deterrent* wirksam; *strategy, policy, government, politician* effektiv; **to be ~ in pain relief** Schmerzlinderung bewirken; **to be ~ in doing sth** bewirken, dass etw geschieht; **to be ~ against sth** (*drug*) gegen etw wirken **b** (= *striking*) *decoration, pattern, combination* wirkungsvoll; **to look ~** wirkungsvoll aussehen, gut wirken **c** (= *actual*) *control, increase* effektiv, tatsächlich; (*Econ, Fin*) *demand, interest rate* effektiv, tatsächlich; *leader* eigentlich; *income* wirklich, tatsächlich; **they have ~ control of the area** sie haben das Gebiet praktisch unter Kontrolle **d** (= *operative*) wirksam, in Kraft; **a new law, ~ from** or **becoming ~ on 1 August** ein neues Gesetz, das am 1. August in Kraft tritt; **~ date** In-Kraft-Treten *nt* **e** (*Mil*) *troops* einsatzbereit

effectively [ɪ'fektɪvlɪ] ADV **a** (= *successfully*) wirksam; *function, work, teach* effektiv **b** (= *strikingly*) wirkungsvoll **c** (= *in effect*) effektiv, praktisch

effectiveness [ɪ'fektɪvnɪs] N **a** (= *successfulness*) Wirksamkeit *f*; (*of strategy, government, politician*) Effektivität *f* **b** (= *striking effect*) Wirkung *f*

effectual [ɪ'fektjʊəl] ADJ (*form*) wirksam

effectually [ɪ'fektjʊəlɪ] ADV (*form*) wirksam; **we solved the problem more ~** wir haben das Problem besser gelöst

effectuate [ɪ'fektjʊeɪt] VT bewirken

effeminacy [ɪ'femɪnəsɪ] N feminines Wesen, Effemination *f* (*geh*)

effeminate [ɪ'femɪnɪt] ADJ feminin, effeminiert (*geh*)

effervesce [efə'ves] VI sprudeln; (*fig, person*) überschäumen

effervescence [ˌefəˈvesns] N (lit) Sprudeln nt; (fig) Überschäumen nt, überschäumendes Temperament

effervescent [ˌefəˈvesnt] ADJ sprudelnd; (fig) überschäumend

effete [ɪˈfiːt] ADJ schwach; person saft- und kraftlos

efficacious [ˌefɪˈkeɪʃəs] ADJ (form) wirksam; **to be ~ for/against sth** bei etw wirksam sein; **to prove ~ in the treatment of sth** sich in der Behandlung von etw als wirksam erweisen

efficacy [ˈefɪkəsɪ] N Wirksamkeit f

efficiency [ɪˈfɪʃənsɪ] N (of person) Fähigkeit f, Tüchtigkeit f; (of machine, factory, organization, system) Leistungsfähigkeit f; (of method) Wirksamkeit f; (of engine) (= power) Leistungsfähigkeit f; (= economy) Sparsamkeit f; (of service) Effizienz f (geh); (of use) Rationalität f; **jobs were lost as part of an ~ drive** Stellen wurden wegrationalisiert; **software that improves the ~ of translators** Software, die die Leistungsfähigkeit von Übersetzern erhöht

efficient [ɪˈfɪʃənt] ADJ person fähig, tüchtig; system, machine, company, organization leistungsfähig; car, engine (= powerful) leistungsfähig; (= economical) sparsam, verbrauchsarm; service gut, effizient (geh); method wirksam; way, use rationell; **work is organized in the most logical and ~ way** die Arbeit wird so logisch und rationell wie möglich organisiert; **to be ~ in or at (doing) sth** etw gut können; **she's ~ at dealing with difficult customers** sie kann gut mit schwierigen Kunden umgehen; **the body is remarkably ~ at dealing with such things** der Körper wird mit diesen Dingen bemerkenswert gut fertig; **they are less ~ at turning sunlight into e-lectricity** bei der Umwandlung von Sonnenlicht in elektrischen Strom sind sie weniger effektiv

efficiently [ɪˈfɪʃəntlɪ] ADV effektiv; **to work more ~** rationeller arbeiten; **quickly and ~** schnell und effizient (geh)

effigy [ˈefɪdʒɪ] N Bildnis nt; **to burn sb in ~** jds Puppe verbrennen

effing [ˈefɪŋ] (euph sl) ADJ Scheiß- (inf) N **~ and blinding** Fluchen nt, Geschimpfe nt VI (only in -ing form) **he was ~ and blinding** er erging sich in wüsten Schimpfereien

efflorescent [ˌefləˈresnt] ADJ (Chem) ausblühend, effloreszierend (spec); (Bot) aufblühend

effluence [ˈefluəns] N Abwasser nt

effluent [ˈefluənt] ADJ ausfließend; gas ausströmend N (from a lake) Ausfluss m; (= sewage) Abwasser nt

effluvium [eˈfluːvɪəm] N Ausdünstung f

▶**eff off** [ˈefˈɒf] VI (euph sl) sich verpissen (sl)

effort [ˈefət] N **a** (= attempt) Versuch m; (= strain, hard work) Anstrengung f, Mühe f; (Mech) Leistung f; **to make an ~ to do sth** den Versuch unternehmen, etw zu tun, sich bemühen, etw zu tun; **to make the ~ to do sth** sich (dat) die Mühe machen, etw zu tun; **to make every ~ or a great ~ to do sth** sich sehr bemühen or anstrengen, etw zu tun; **to make every possible ~ to do sth** jede nur mögliche Anstrengung or große Anstrengung unternehmen or machen, etw zu tun; **to make little ~ to do sth** sich (dat) wenig Mühe geben, etw zu tun; **he made no ~ to be polite** er machte sich (dat) nicht die Mühe, höflich zu sein; **it's an ~ (to get up in the morning)** es kostet einige Mühe or Anstrengung(, morgens aufzustehen); **getting up was an ~** das Aufstehen kostete einige Mühe or Anstrengung; **he had to double his ~s** er musste seine Anstrengungen verdoppeln; **if it's not too much of an ~ for you** (iro) wenn es dir nicht zu viel Mühe macht; **with an ~** mühsam; **with a great ~ of will** mit einer gewaltigen Willensanstrengung; **come on, make an ~** komm, streng dich an; **it's well worth the ~** die Mühe lohnt sich wirklich

b (= campaign) Aktion f; **the famine relief ~** die Hilfsaktion gegen die Hungersnot

c (inf) Unternehmen nt; **it was a pretty poor ~** das war eine ziemlich schwache Leistung; **it's not bad for a first ~** das ist nicht schlecht für den Anfang; **what did you think of his latest ~?** was halten Sie von seinem jüngsten Unternehmen?; **his first ~ at making a film** sein erster Versuch, einen Film zu drehen; **best film went to a strange Swedish ~** die Auszeichnung für den besten Film ging an ein merkwürdiges schwedisches Machwerk

effortless [ˈefətlɪs] ADJ movement, victory, ease, style mühelos; charm, elegance natürlich, ungezwungen; **~ superiority** natürliche Überlegenheit

effortlessly [ˈefətlɪslɪ] ADV mühelos; chat ungezwungen

effortlessness [ˈefətlɪsnɪs] N Mühelosigkeit f

effrontery [ɪˈfrʌntərɪ] N Unverschämtheit f; **how can you have the ~ to deny the charge?** dass Sie die Frechheit besitzen, den Vorwurf abzustreiten!

effusion [ɪˈfjuːʒən] N (lit, fig) Erguss m

effusive [ɪˈfjuːsɪv] ADJ überschwänglich; (= gushing) exaltiert; **to be ~ in one's praise of or for sb** jdn überschwänglich loben

effusively [ɪˈfjuːsɪvlɪ] ADV überschwänglich

effusiveness [ɪˈfjuːsɪvnɪs] N Überschwänglichkeit f

E-fit [ˈiːfɪt] N Computer-Phantombild nt

EFL [ˈiːef ˈel] abbr of **English as a Foreign Language** Englisch als Fremdsprache; **~ teacher** Lehrer(in) m(f) für Englisch als Fremdsprache

EFT abbr of **electronic funds transfer** elektronische Geldüberweisung

EFTA [ˈeftə] abbr of **European Free Trade Association** EFTA f

EFTPOS [ˈeftpɒs] abbr of **electronic funds transfer at point of sale**

eg abbr of **exempli gratia** (= for example) z. B.

EGA (Comput) abbr of **enhanced graphics adapter** EGA m

egad [ɪˈgæd] INTERJ (old, hum) fürwahr (old, hum)

egalitarian [ɪˌgælɪˈtɛərɪən] ADJ egalitär; **an ~ relationship between teacher and students** eine gleichberechtigte Beziehung zwischen Lehrer und Schülern N Verfechter(in) m(f) des Egalitarismus

egalitarianism [ɪˌgælɪˈtɛərɪənɪzəm] N Egalitarismus m

egg [eg] N Ei nt; **to put all one's ~s in one basket** (prov) alles auf eine Karte setzen; **as sure as ~s is ~s** (inf) so sicher wie das Amen in der Kirche (inf); **to have ~ on or all over one's face** (fig inf) dumm dastehen (inf); **he's a good/bad ~** (dated inf) er ist ein famoser Kerl (dated)/ein übler Kunde (inf)

▶**egg on** VT sep anstacheln; **don't egg him on!** jetzt stachel ihn doch nicht auch noch an!

egg: **egg and dart** N Eierstab m (spec); **egg--and-spoon race** N Eierlauf m; **eggbeater** N Schneebesen m; **egg cosy,** (US) **egg cozy** N Eierwärmer m; **egg cup** N Eierbecher m; **egg custard** N Eiercreme f; **egg flip** N Ei-Flip m; **egghead** N (pej inf) Intellektuelle(r) mf, Eierkopf m (pej inf); **eggplant** N (esp US) Aubergine f; **egg rack** M (in fridge) Eierleiste f; **egg roll** N Eibrötchen nt; **egg sandwich** N Sandwich nt mit Ei; **eggs Benedict** N, no pl (Cook) pochierte Eier und Schinken auf Toast mit Sauce hollandaise; **eggshell** N Eierschale f; **he acts as if he's walking on ~s** er führt einen wahren Eiertanz auf ADJ Eierschalen-; **egg-shell-blue** ADJ eierschalenblau; **egg slicer** N Eierschneider m; **egg spoon** N Eierlöffel m; **egg timer** N Eieruhr f; **egg tooth** N (Zool) Eierzahn m; **egg whisk** N Schneebesen m; **egg white** N Eiweiß nt; **egg yolk** N Eidotter m, Eigelb nt

egis [ˈiːdʒɪs] N (US) = aegis

eglantine [ˈegləntaɪn] N Weinrose f

ego [ˈiːgəʊ] N (Psych) Ego nt, Ich nt; (= self-esteem) Selbstbewusstsein nt; (= conceit) Einbil-

dung f; **this will boost his ~** das wird sein Selbstbewusstsein stärken, das wird ihm Auftrieb geben; **he has a monstrously big ~** er hat ein total übersteigertes Selbstbewusstsein; **his ~ won't allow him to admit he is wrong** sein Stolz lässt ihn nie zugeben, dass er Unrecht hat

egocentric(al) [ˌegəʊˈsentrɪk(əl)] ADJ egozentrisch, ichbezogen

egoism [ˈegəʊɪzəm] N Egoismus m, Selbstsucht f

egoist [ˈegəʊɪst] N Egoist(in) m(f), selbstsüchtiger Mensch

egoistical [ˌegəʊˈɪstɪkəl] ADJ egoistisch, selbstsüchtig, eigennützig

egomania [ˌiːgəʊˈmeɪnɪə] N Egomanie f, übersteigerte Ichbezogenheit

egomaniac [ˌiːgəʊˈmeɪnɪæk] N Egomane m, Egomanin f

egotism [ˈegəʊtɪzəm] N Ichbezogenheit f, Egotismus m

egotist [ˈegəʊtɪst] N Egotist(in) m(f), ichbezogener Mensch

egotistic(al) [ˌegəʊˈtɪstɪk(əl)] ADJ von sich eingenommen, ichbezogen, egotistisch

ego trip N (inf) Egotrip m (inf); **to be on an ~** auf einem Egotrip sein

egregious [ɪˈgriːdʒəs] ADJ ausgemacht, ungeheuerlich

egret [ˈiːgrɪt] N (Orn) Reiher m; (= ornament) Reiherfeder f

Egypt [ˈiːdʒɪpt] N Ägypten nt

Egyptian [ɪˈdʒɪpʃən] ADJ ägyptisch N **a** Ägypter(in) m(f) **b** (Ling) Ägyptisch nt

Egyptology [ˌiːdʒɪpˈtɒlədʒɪ] N Ägyptologie f

eh [eɪ] INTERJ **a** (inviting repetition) **I've found a gold mine – eh?** ich habe eine Goldmine entdeckt – was? or hä? (inf) **b** (inviting agreement) **it's good, eh?** gut, nicht?

eider [ˈaɪdə] N Eiderente f

eiderdown [ˈaɪdədaʊn] N (= quilt) Federbett nt, Daunendecke f; (= feathers) Daunen pl, Flaumfedern pl

eidetic [aɪˈdetɪk] ADJ eidetisch

eight [eɪt] ADJ acht; **to be behind the ~ ball** (US, inf) in der Patsche sitzen (inf) → **six** N **a** Acht f → **six** **b** (Rowing) Achter m **c** **to have had one over the ~** (inf) einen über den Durst or einen zu viel getrunken haben (inf)

eighteen [ˈeɪˈtiːn] ADJ achtzehn N Achtzehn f

eighteenth [ˈeɪˈtiːnθ] ADJ achtzehnte(r, s) N (= fraction) Achtzehntel nt; (of series) Achtzehnte(r, s) → **sixteenth**

eighth [eɪtθ] ADJ achte(r, s) N (= fraction) Achtel nt; (of series) Achte(r, s) → **sixth**

eighth note N (US, Mus) Achtelnote f, Achtel nt

eightieth [ˈeɪtɪɪθ] ADJ achtzigste(r, s) N (= fraction) Achtzigstel nt; (of series) Achtzigste(r, s) → **sixtieth**

eightsome (reel) [ˈeɪtsəm(ˈriːl)] N schottischer Volkstanz für 8 Tänzer

eighty [ˈeɪtɪ] ADJ achtzig N Achtzig f → **sixty**

Eire [ˈɛərə] N Irland nt, Eire nt

either [ˈaɪðə, ˈiːðə] ♦ 26.2 PRON **a** (= one or other) eine(r, s) (von beiden); **there are two boxes on the table, take ~ (of them)** auf dem Tisch liegen zwei Schachteln, nimm eine davon; **if on ~ side of the road there is a line of trees** wenn eine Straßenseite mit Bäumen bestanden ist

b (= each, both) jede(r, s), beide pl; **~ day would suit me** beide Tage passen mir; **which bus will you take? – ~ (will do)** welchen Bus wollen Sie nehmen? – das ist egal; **she offered me tea and coffee, but I don't drink ~ (of them)** sie bot mir Tee und Kaffee an, aber ich trinke keines von beiden or ich trinke beides nicht; **on ~ side of the street** auf beiden Seiten der Straße; **it wasn't in ~ (box)** es war in keiner der beiden (Kisten)

ADV **CONJ** **a** (*after neg statement*) auch nicht; **he sings badly and he can't act ~** er ist ein schlechter Sänger, und spielen kann er auch nicht; **I have never heard of him – no, I haven't ~** ich habe noch nie von ihm gehört – ich auch nicht

b **~ ... or** entweder ... oder; (*after a negative*) weder ... noch; **he must be ~ lazy or stupid** er muss entweder faul oder dumm sein; **~ be quiet or go out!** entweder bist du ruhig oder du gehst raus!; **I have never been to ~ Paris or Rome** ich bin weder in Paris noch in Rom gewesen

c (= *moreover*) **she inherited some money and not an insignificant amount** ~ sie hat Geld geerbt, und (zwar) gar nicht so wenig

ejaculate [ɪˈdʒækjʊleɪt] **VT** **a** (= *utter*) ausstoßen, ausrufen **b** (*Physiol*) ejakulieren, ausspritzen **VI** **a** (= *cry out*) aufschreien **b** (*Physiol*) ejakulieren **N** [ɪˈdʒækjʊlɪt] Ejakulat *m*

ejaculation [ɪˌdʒækjʊˈleɪʃən] **N** **a** (= *cry*) Ausruf *m* **b** (*Physiol*) Ejakulation *f*, Samenerguss *m*

ejaculatory [ɪˈdʒækjʊlətərɪ] **ADJ** *style, language* stoßhaft; (*Physiol*) Ejakulations-; **~ control** Ejakulationskontrolle *f*

eject [ɪˈdʒekt] **VT** **a** (= *throw out*) *heckler, tenant* hinauswerfen **b** *cartridge* auswerfen; (*Tech*) ausstoßen, auswerfen; *pilot* herausschleudern **VI** (*pilot*) den Schleudersitz betätigen

ejecta [ɪˈdʒektə] **PL** (*Geol, Astrol*) Auswurf *m*; (*of vulcano*) ausgeschleuderte Materie

ejection [ɪˈdʒekʃən] **N** Hinauswurf *m*; (*of cartridge*) Auswerfen *nt*; (*Tech*) Ausstoß *m*; **~ is the pilot's last resort** Betätigung des Schleudersitzes ist die letzte Rettung für den Piloten

ejectment [ɪˈdʒektmənt] **N** Hinauswurf *m*; (*Jur*) Herausgabeklage *f*

ejector [ɪˈdʒektəʳ] **N** (*on gun*) Auswerfer *m*, Ejektor *m*

ejector seat, (*US*) **ejection seat** **N** (*Aviat*) Schleudersitz *m*

eke out [ˈiːkaʊt] **VT** *sep food, supplies* strecken, verlängern; *money, income* aufbessern; **to ~ a living** sich (recht und schlecht) durchschlagen

EKG **N** (*US*) = **ECG**

el [el] **N** (*US*) *abbr of* **elevated railroad** Hochbahn *f*

elaborate [ɪˈlæbərɪt] **ADJ** **a** (= *complex, overcomplex*) *machine, equipment, procedure, ritual, system, network* kompliziert; (= *sophisticated*) ausgeklügelt; *scheme* groß angelegt; *precautions, efforts, plans* umfangreich; (= *sophisticated*) *preparations* ausführlich; *cooking, ceremony, design* aufwändig, aufwendig; **an ~ meal** ein großes Menü; **an ~ hoax/plot** ein ausgeklügelter Schwindel/Plan **b** (= *lavish, ornate*) *costume, design, furniture, style* kunstvoll

VT [ɪˈlæbəreɪt] **a** (= *expand in words*) *statement, remark* weiter ausführen; **to ~ sth further** auf etw *acc* näher eingehen

b (= *develop*) *system, plan, theory* ausarbeiten; (= *refine*) verfeinern, ausfeilen **VI** **would you care to** *or* **could you ~ on that?** könnten Sie darauf näher eingehen?; **there's no need to ~** Sie brauchen nichts weiter zu sagen; **it isn't a statement I want to ~ on** zu dieser Feststellung möchte ich mich nicht weiter äußern

elaborately [ɪˈlæbərɪtlɪ] **ADV** **a** (= *carefully*) sorgfältig; (= *in detail*) ausführlich; (= *complexly*) kompliziert; **an ~ staged press conference** eine mit großem Aufwand veranstaltete Pressekonferenz; **~ casual** betont lässig **b** (= *ornately, lavishly*) kunstvoll; **~ costumed** aufwändig *or* aufwendig kostümiert

elaborateness [ɪˈlæbərɪtnɪs] **N** **a** (= *complexity*) Kompliziertheit *f*; (*of cooking, ceremony, design*) Aufwändigkeit *f*, Aufwendigkeit *f*; (*of scheme*) groß angelegte Art; (*of precautions, plan*) Umfang *m*; (= *sophisticated nature: of plans, preparations*) Ausführlichkeit *f* **b** (= *ornateness, lavishness*) kunstvolle Art

elaboration [ɪˌlæbəˈreɪʃən] **N** (*of system, plan, theory,* = *working out*) Ausarbeitung *f*; (= *refine-*

ment) Verfeinerung *f*, Ausfeilung *f*; (= *description: of details etc*) nähere Ausführung; (= *that which elaborates: details etc*) Ausschmückung *f*; **an author who goes in for a great deal of tedious ~** ein Schriftsteller, der eine Menge langatmiger Beschreibungen bringt

élan [eɪˈlæn] **N** Elan *m*

elapse [ɪˈlæps] **VI** vergehen, verstreichen

elastic [ɪˈlæstɪk] **ADJ** (*lit, fig*) elastisch; **~ waist** Taille *f* mit Gummizug **N** Gummi(band *nt*) *m*; (*US, = rubber band*) Gummi *m*; **a piece of ~** ein Gummiband *nt*

elasticated [ɪˈlæstɪkeɪtɪd] **ADJ** elastisch; **~ waist** Gummibund *m*; (*of garment*) Taille *f* mit Gummizug

elastic band **N** (*esp Brit*) Gummiband *nt*

elasticity [ˌiːlæsˈtɪsɪtɪ] **N** Elastizität *f*

elastic stockings **PL** Gummistrümpfe *pl*

Elastoplast® [ɪˈlæstəʊplɑːst] **N** (*Brit*) Hansaplast® *nt*

elate [ɪˈleɪt] **VT** begeistern, in Hochstimmung versetzen

elated [ɪˈleɪtɪd] **ADJ** begeistert

elation [ɪˈleɪʃən] **N** Begeisterung (*at* über +*acc*), Hochstimmung *f*; (*of crowd*) Jubel *m*, Begeisterung *f*; **a mood of such ~** eine solche Hochstimmung

elbow [ˈelbəʊ] **N** **a** Ellbogen *m*; **since he's been rubbing ~s with senators** (*esp US*) seit er sich in Senatorenkreisen bewegt **b** (*of pipe, river, road*) Knie *nt* **VT** **to ~ one's way forward** sich durchdrängen; **he ~ed his way through the crowd** er boxte sich durch die Menge; **to ~ sb aside** jdn beiseite stoßen; **he ~ed me in the stomach** er stieß mir *or* mich mit dem Ellbogen in den Magen; **to ~ one's way to the top** (*fig*) sich nach oben durchboxen (*inf*), die Ellbogen gebrauchen, um an die Spitze zu kommen

▶ **elbow out** **VT** *sep* (*fig*) hinausdrängeln

elbow grease **N** (*inf*) Muskelkraft *f*

elbowing [ˈelbəʊɪŋ] **N** (*Ice hockey*) Ellbogencheck *m*

elbow: elbow rest **N** Armstütze *f*; **elbowroom** **N** (*inf: lit, fig*) Ellbogenfreiheit *f* (*inf*)

elder[1] [ˈeldəʳ] **ADJ** *attr comp of* **old** **a** (= *older*) *brother etc* ältere(r, s) **b** (= *senior*) **Pliny the ~** Plinius der Ältere, der ältere Plinius **N** **a** **respect your ~s and betters** du musst Respekt vor Älteren haben **b** (*of tribe, Church*) Älteste(r) *m* **c** (*Presbyterian*) Gemeindeälteste(r) *mf*, Presbyter(in) *m(f)*

elder[2] **N** (*Bot*) Holunder *m*

elderberry [ˈeldəberɪ] **N** Holunderbeere *f*; **~ wine** Holunderwein *m*

elderflower [ˈeldəflaʊəʳ] **N** Holunder *m*, Holunderblüte *f*

elderly [ˈeldəlɪ] **ADJ** ältlich, ältere(r, s) *attr*

elder statesman **N** (alt)erfahrener Staatsmann

eldest [ˈeldɪst] **ADJ** *attr superl of* **old** älteste(r, s) **N** **the ~** der/die/das Älteste; (*pl*) die Ältesten *pl*; **the ~ of four children** das älteste von vier Kindern; **my ~** (*inf, = son*) mein Ältester; (= *daughter*) meine Älteste

El Dorado, **eldorado** [ˌeldəˈrɑːdəʊ] **N** *pl* **-dos** (El)dorado *nt*, Paradies *nt* (*fig*)

elec **a** *abbr of* **electricity** **b** *abbr of* **electric** elektr.

elect [ɪˈlekt] **VT** **a** (*by vote*) wählen; **he was ~ed chairman/MP** er wurde zum Vorsitzenden/Abgeordneten gewählt; **to ~ sb to the Senate** jdn in den Senat wählen **b** (= *choose*) (er)wählen, sich entscheiden für; **to ~ to do sth** sich dafür entscheiden, etw zu tun; **to ~ French nationality** sich für die französische Staatsangehörigkeit entscheiden **ADJ** **the president ~** der designierte *or* künftige Präsident **PL** (*esp Rel*) **the ~** die Auserwählten *pl*

elected [ɪˈlektɪd] **ADJ** gewählt

election [ɪˈlekʃən] **N** Wahl *f*; **his ~ to the chairmanship** seine Wahl zum Vorsitzenden

election *in cpds* Wahl-; **~ victory/defeat** Wahlsieg *m*/-niederlage *f*; **election campaign** **N** Wahlkampf *m*

electioneer [ɪˌlekʃəˈnɪəʳ] **VI** als Wahlhelfer arbeiten, Wahlhilfe leisten; **he's just ~ing for X** er macht nur Wahlpropaganda für X

electioneering [ɪˌlekʃəˈnɪərɪŋ] **N** (= *campaign*) Wahlkampf *m*; (= *propaganda*) Wahlpropaganda *f* **ADJ** Wahl-; **~ campaign** Wahlkampf *m*; **~ speech** Wahlkampfrede *f*

elective [ɪˈlektɪv] **ADJ** **a** *democracy* mit Wahlen; **~ assembly** Wahlversammlung *f*; **~ dictatorship** gewählte Diktatur; **~ office/post** Amt, *das/ Posten, der durch Wahl besetzt wird* **he has never won/held ~ office** er ist noch nie zu einem Amt gewählt worden **b** (*Med*) *surgery* nicht unbedingt notwendig; *abortion* nicht medizinisch indiziert **c** (*US: Sch, Univ* = *optional*) *course* wahlfrei; **~ subject** Wahlfach *nt* **N** (*US: Sch, Univ*) Wahlfach *nt*

elector [ɪˈlektəʳ] **N** **a** Wähler(in) *m(f)* **b** (*Hist*) **Elector** Kurfürst *m* **c** (*US*) Wahlmann *m*

electoral [ɪˈlektərəl] **ADJ** Wahl-; **~ boundaries** Grenzen *pl* der Wahlbezirke; **~ defeat/victory** Wahlniederlage *f*/-sieg *m*; **~ fraud** Wahlbetrug *m*; **~ process** Wahlverfahren *nt*; **~ support** Unterstützung *f* durch die Wähler; **~ system** Wahlsystem *nt*; **the ~ map** (*lit*) die Aufteilung der Wahlbezirke; (*fig*) die Stimmenverteilung in den Wahlbezirken

electoral college **N** Wahlausschuss *m*; **the ~, the Electoral College** (*US, in presidential election*) das Wahlmännergremium

---

ELECTORAL COLLEGE

Amerikaner wählen ihren Präsidenten und Vizepräsidenten nicht direkt; stattdessen werden **electors** gewählt, Wahlmänner, die sich verpflichtet haben, für bestimmte Kandidaten zu stimmen. Zusammen bilden die Wahlmänner das von der Verfassung vorgeschriebene **electoral college**. In diesem Gremium hat jeder Staat so viele Stimmen, wie die Gesamtzahl seiner Senatoren und Abgeordneten. Jede Partei wählt eine Gruppe von Wahlmännern, und am Tag der Präsidentschaftswahl stimmt die amerikanische Öffentlichkeit für die Gruppe, die den Kandidaten unterstützt, den sie als Sieger sehen möchte. Da die siegreiche Gruppe dann alle Stimmen eines Staates für den Kandidaten ihrer Partei abgibt, wäre es theoretisch möglich, dass ein Kandidat die Mehrheit der Stimmen aus der Bevölkerung erhält und trotzdem die Präsidentschaftswahl verliert, da zu wenige Wahlmänner für ihn stimmen.

---

electoral district **N** Wahlbezirk *m*

electoral law **N** Wahlrecht *nt*

electorally [ɪˈlektərəlɪ] **ADV** (= *in the election*) bei der Wahl; (= *with the electorate*) bei den Wählern

electoral register, **electoral roll** **N** Wählerverzeichnis *nt*

electoral vote **N** (*US, Pol*) Stimme *f* für die Präsidentschaftswahl

electorate [ɪˈlektərɪt] **N** Wähler *pl*, Wählerschaft *f*

Electra complex [ɪˈlektrəˌkɒmpleks] **N** (*Psych*) Elektrakomplex *m*

electric [ɪˈlektrɪk] **ADJ** **a** (*lit, = powered by electricity, generated*) elektrisch; (= *carrying electricity*) Strom-; **~ car/vehicle** Elektroauto *nt*; **~ razor** Elektrorasierer *m*; **~ mixer/kettle** elektrischer Mixer/Wasserkocher **b** (*fig, = exciting*) *atmosphere, mood* wie elektrisiert; **the effect was ~** das hatte eine tolle Wirkung **N** **a** (*inf, = electricity*) Elektrizität *f*, Elektrik *f* (*inf*) **b** **electrics** **PL** Strom *m*; (*Aut*) Elektrik *f*

electrical [ɪˈlektrɪkəl] **ADJ** *components, fault, power, failure, activity, signal* elektrisch; **~ equipment/ goods** Elektrogeräte *pl*; **~ appliance** Elektrogerät *nt*; **~ system** Elektrik *f*; **~ fittings** Elektroinstallationen *pl*

electrical: electrical energy N Elektroenergie *f*, elektrische Energie; **electrical engineer** N Elektrotechniker(in) *m(f)*; (*with degree*) Elektroingenieur(in) *m(f)*; **electrical engineering** N Elektrotechnik *f*; **the ~ industry** die elektrotechnische Industrie; **electrical fitter** N Elektromonteur(in) *m(f)*

electrically [ɪˈlektrɪkəlɪ] ADV elektrisch; **an ~ powered car** ein Wagen *m* mit Elektroantrieb; **~ operated/controlled** elektrisch betätigt/gesteuert

electrical storm N Gewitter *nt*

electric: electric-arc welding N Lichtbogenschweißung *f*; **electric bill** N (*inf*) Stromrechnung *f*; **electric blanket** N Heizdecke *f*; **electric blue** N Stahlblau *nt*; **electric-blue** ADJ stahlblau; **electric cable** N Stromkabel *nt*; **electric chair** N elektrischer Stuhl; **electric charge** N elektrische Ladung; **electric circuit** N Stromkreislauf *m*; **electric cooker** N Elektroherd *m*; **electric current** N elektrischer Strom; **electric eel** N Zitteraal *m*; **electric eye** N Photozelle *f*; **electric fence** N Elektrozaun *m*; **electric field** N elektrisches Feld; **electric fire** N elektrisches Heizgerät; **electric furnace** N (= *blast furnace*) elektrischer Hochofen; (= *kiln*) elektrischer Brennofen; **electric guitar** N elektrische Gitarre, E-Gitarre *f*; **electric heater** N elektrisches Heizgerät

electrician [ɪlekˈtrɪʃən] N Elektriker(in) *m(f)*

electricity [ɪlekˈtrɪsɪtɪ] N Elektrizität *f*; (= *electric power for use*) (elektrischer) Strom; **to have ~ connected** Stromanschluss *or* elektrischen Strom bekommen; **to turn on/off the ~** den Strom an-/abschalten

electricity: electricity (generating) board (*Brit*) N Elektrizitätswerk *nt*; **electricity meter** N Stromzähler *m*; **electricity strike** N Streik *m* in den Elektrizitätswerken

electric: electric light N elektrisches Licht; **electric lighting** N elektrische Beleuchtung; **electric motor** N Elektromotor *m*; **electric organ** N elektrische Orgel; **electric plug** N (Strom)stecker *m*; **electric ray** N (*Zool*) Zitterrochen *m*; **electric shock** N elektrischer Schlag, Stromschlag *m*; (*Med*) Elektroschock *m* 🔲 ADJ *attr* **~ treatment** Elektroschocktherapie *f*; **to give sb a ~ treatment** jdn mit Elektroschock behandeln; **electric socket** N (Strom)steckdose *f*; **electric storm** N Gewitter *nt*; **electric toothbrush** N elektrische Zahnbürste; **electric train** N Elektrozug *m*; (= *model train set*) elektrische Eisenbahn; **electric window** N (*Aut*) elektrischer Fensterheber; **electric wiring** N Stromleitungen *pl*, elektrische Leitungen *pl*

electrification [ɪˌlektrɪfɪˈkeɪʃən] N Elektrifizierung *f*

electrify [ɪˈlektrɪfaɪ] VT **a** (*Rail*) elektrifizieren **b** (= *charge with electricity*) unter Strom setzen **c** (*fig*) elektrisieren

electrifying [ɪˈlektrɪfaɪɪŋ] ADJ (*fig*) elektrisierend

electro- [ɪˈlektrəʊ-] PREF Elektro-

electro: electrocardiogram [ɪˌlektrəʊˈkɑːdɪəʊgræm] N Elektrokardiogramm *nt*; **electrocardiograph** [ɪˌlektrəʊˈkɑːdɪəʊgrɑːf] N Elektrokardiograf *m*; **electrochemical** [ɪˌlektrəʊˈkemɪkəl] ADJ elektrochemisch; **electroconvulsive therapy** [ɪˌlektrəʊkənˈvʌlsɪvˈθerəpɪ] N Elektroschocktherapie *f*

electrocute [ɪˈlektrɪkjuːt] VT durch einen (Strom)schlag töten; (= *execute*) durch den *or* auf dem elektrischen Stuhl

electrocution [ɪˌlektrəˈkjuːʃən] N Tötung *f* durch Stromschlag; (= *execution*) Hinrichtung *f* durch den elektrischen Stuhl

electrode [ɪˈlektrəʊd] N Elektrode *f*

electro: electrodynamics N Elektrodynamik *f*; **electroencephalogram** N Elektroenze-

phalogramm *nt*; **electroencephalograph** N Elektroenzephalograf *m*

electrolysis [ɪlekˈtrɒlɪsɪs] N Elektrolyse *f*

electrolyte [ɪˈlektrəʊlaɪt] N Elektrolyt *m*

electro: electromagnet N Elektromagnet *m*; **electromagnetic** ADJ elektromagnetisch; **electromagnetism** N Elektromagnetismus *m*

electron [ɪˈlektrɒn] N Elektron *nt*

electron: electron beam N Elektronenstrahl *m*; **electron camera** N Elektronenkamera *f*; **electron gun** N Elektronenkanone *f*

electronic [ɪlekˈtrɒnɪk] ADJ elektronisch; *information* elektronisch gespeichert; **the ~ age** das elektronische Zeitalter

electronically [ɪlekˈtrɒnɪkəlɪ] ADV elektronisch; **to be available ~** in elektronischer Form vorhanden sein

electronic: electronic banking N elektronischer Geldverkehr; **electronic brain** N Elektronen(ge)hirn *nt*; **electronic data processing** N (*Comput*) elektronische Datenverarbeitung; **electronic engineering** N Elektronik *f*; **~ company** Elektronikfirma *f*; **electronic flash** N (*Phot*) Elektronenblitz *m*; **electronic funds transfer** N elektronische (Geld)überweisung; **~ system** elektronisches Überweisungssystem; **electronic game** N Elektronikspiel *nt*; **electronic keyboard** N (*Mus*) elektronisches Keyboard; (*on computer*) elektronische Tastatur; **electronic mail** N elektronische Post; **electronic mailbox** N elektronischer Briefkasten; **electronic music** N elektronische Musik; **electronic news gathering** N elektronischer Nachrichtendienst; **electronic point of sale** N elektronisches Kassenterminal; **~ system** System *nt* mit elektronischen Kassenterminals; **electronic publishing** N elektronisches Publizieren

electronics [ɪlekˈtrɒnɪks] N **a** *sing* (*subject*) Elektronik *f* **b** *pl* (*of machine etc*) Elektronik *f*

electronic: electronic surveillance N elektronische Überwachung; **electronic tag** N elektronische Marke, elektronisches Kennzeichen; (*for prisoner*) elektronische Fußfessel; **electronic tagging** N elektronische Markierung *or* Kennzeichnung; (*for prisoners*) elektronische Fußfesseln *pl*; **electronic transfer of funds** N elektronische (Geld)überweisung

electron microscope N Elektronenmikroskop *nt*

electroplate [ɪˈlektrəʊpleɪt] VT galvanisieren N no *pl* Galvanisierung *f*; **is it silver? – no,** ~ ist das Silber? – nein, nur versilbert

electroplated [ɪˈlektrəʊpleɪtɪd] ADJ (galvanisch) versilbert/verchromt *etc*

electroscope [ɪˈlektrəʊskəʊp] N Elektroskop *nt*

electroshock therapy [ɪˌlektrəʊʃɒkˈθerəpɪ] N Elektroschocktherapie *or* -behandlung *f*

electrostatic [ɪˌlektrəʊˈstætɪk] ADJ elektrostatisch

electrotherapy [ɪˌlektrəʊˈθerəpɪ] N (*Med*) Elektrotherapie *f*

elegance [ˈelɪgəns] N Eleganz *f*

elegant [ˈelɪgənt] ADJ elegant; *style also* gewandt; *book* elegant geschrieben; **an ~ solution** eine elegante Lösung

elegantly [ˈelɪgəntlɪ] ADV elegant; *shaped also* harmonisch; *written also* gewandt; **~ simple** bestechend einfach

elegiac [elɪˈdʒaɪək] ADJ elegisch N usu *pl* (*Liter*) elegischer Vers, Vers *m* im elegischen Versmaß

elegize [ˈelɪdʒaɪz] VI (in Elegien) klagen (*upon* über +*acc*)

elegy [ˈelɪdʒɪ] N Elegie *f*

element [ˈelɪmənt] N (*all senses*) Element *nt*; **the ~s of mathematics** die Grundbegriffe *pl* *or* Anfangsgründe *pl* (*geh*) der Mathematik; **one of the key ~s of the peace plan** einer der grundlegenden Bestandteile des Friedensplans; **an ~ of danger** ein Gefahrenelement *nt*; **the ~ of chance** das Zufallselement; **an ~ of truth** eine

Spur *or* ein Element *nt* von Wahrheit; **the personal ~** das persönliche Element; **a hooligan/ criminal ~** ein paar Rowdys/Kriminelle; **the (four) ~s** die (vier) Elemente; **to be in one's ~** in seinem Element sein; **to be out of one's ~** (*with group of people*) sich fehl am Platze fühlen; (*with subject*) sich nicht auskennen

elemental [ˌelɪˈmentl] ADJ **a** (*liter*) *truth, life, feeling, drive* elementar; *art* urwüchsig; **~ force** Elementargewalt *f*, Naturgewalt *f*; **~ powers** Elementarkräfte *pl*; **the ~ energies** (*of the four elements*) die Energien *pl* der vier Elemente **b** (*Chem*) elementar

elementary [ˌelɪˈmentərɪ] ADJ **a** (= *simple*) *rules* einfach, elementar; (= *basic*) *idea, fact, precautions* grundlegend; **a few ~ rules** einige Grundregeln; **sometimes the cause is quite ~** manchmal ist die Ursache ganz einfach *or* simpel; **~ mistake** Grundfehler *m*, grober Fehler; **~, my dear Watson** elementar, lieber Watson **b** (*pej*, = *rudimentary*) primitiv; **his acting is about as ~ as you can get** primitiver als er kann man gar nicht spielen **c** (*Sch*) *level* elementar; **~ skills/knowledge** Grundkenntnisse *pl*; **~ reading and writing** Grundkenntnisse *pl* im Lesen und Schreiben; **~ computer skills** grundlegende Computerkenntnisse *pl*; **~ maths** Elementarmathematik *f*; **a rather ~ knowledge of science** einige Grundkenntnisse in Naturwissenschaften

elementary: elementary education N Grundschulbildung *f*; **elementary particle** N (*Phys*) Elementarteilchen *nt*; **elementary particle physics** N (*Phys*) Elementarteilchenphysik *f*; **elementary school** N (*US*, = *primary school*) Grundschule *f*; **elementary schooling** N (*US*) Grundschulbildung *f*; **elementary student** N (*US*) Grundschüler(in) *m(f)*; **elementary teacher** N (*US*) Grundschullehrer(in) *m(f)*

elephant [ˈelɪfənt] N Elefant *m* → **pink** [1] ADJ a, **white elephant**

elephantiasis [ˌelɪfənˈtaɪəsɪs] N Elefantiasis *f*, Elephantiasis *f*

elephantine [ˌelɪˈfæntaɪn] ADJ (= *heavy, clumsy*) schwerfällig, wie ein Elefant; (= *large*) riesig, elefantös (*hum*); **~ memory** Elefantengedächtnis *nt* (*inf*)

elephant seal N (*Zool*) See-Elefant *m*

elevate [ˈelɪveɪt] VT **a** (= *raise*) heben; (= *increase*) *blood pressure etc* erhöhen; **by elevating the house a full 3 feet above ...** indem man das Haus ganze 3 Fuß über (+*acc*) ... setzt **b** (*fig*) *mind* erbauen; *soul* erheben; **elevating reading** erbauliche Lektüre; **an elevating prospect** eine erfreuliche Aussicht; **to ~ the condition of the people** die Lebensbedingungen des Volkes verbessern **c** **to ~ sb to the peerage** jdn in den Adelsstand erheben; **since he's been ~d to top management** (*hum*) seit er ins Spitzenmanagement berufen worden ist

elevated [ˈelɪveɪtɪd] ADJ **a** (= *raised*) *situation, platform, level, pressure, rate* erhöht; **~ train, ~ railway** (*Brit*) *or* **railroad** (*US*) Hochbahn *f*; **an ~ monorail track** eine Einschienenhochbahn; **the ~ section of the M4** die als Hochstraße gebaute Strecke der M4 **b** (= *exalted, lofty*) *status, tone, style, language* gehoben; *thoughts* erhaben

elevation [ˌelɪˈveɪʃən] N **a** (*to*) Hebung *f*; (*to higher rank*) Erhebung *f* (*to in* +*acc*); (*Eccl*) Elevation *f* **b** (*of thought*) Erhabenheit *f*; (*of position, style*) Gehobenheit *f* **c** (*above sea level*) Höhe *f* über dem Meeresspiegel *or* über N.N.; (*hill etc*) (Boden)erhebung *f*, Anhöhe *f* **d** **angle of ~** Höhen- *or* Elevationswinkel *m* **e** (*of gun*) Elevation *f*, Erhöhung *f* **f** (*Archit*, = *drawing*) Aufriss *m*; **front ~** Frontansicht *f*, Fassadenaufriss *m*

elevator [ˈelɪveɪtə] N **a** (*US*) Fahrstuhl *m*, Lift *m*, Aufzug *m* **b** (= *storehouse*) Silo *m* **c** (*Aviat*) Höhenruder *nt* **d** (*with buckets etc*) Aufzug *m*; (= *hoist*) Winde *f*

elevator shoe N Schuh *m* mit Plateausohle

eleven [ɪˈlevn] **N a** (= number) Elf f; **the ~ plus** (old Brit, Sch) Aufnahmeprüfung in einer weiterführende Schule **b** (Sport) Elf f; **the German ~** die deutsche (National)elf; **the second ~** die zweite Mannschaft **ADJ** elf → also **six**

elevenses [ɪˈlevnzɪz] **N** sing or pl (Brit) zweites Frühstück

eleventh [ɪˈlevnθ] **ADJ** elfte(r, s); **at the ~ hour** (fig) in letzter Minute, fünf Minuten vor zwölf **N** (= fraction) Elftel nt, Elfte(r, s); (of series) Elfte(r, s) → also **sixth**

elf [elf] **N** pl **elves** Elf m, Elfe f; (mischievous) Kobold m

elfin [ˈelfɪn] **ADJ a** (= attractive) elfenhaft **b** (Myth) elfisch

elfish [ˈelfɪʃ] **ADJ** elfenhaft; (= mischievous) koboldhaft

elicit [ɪˈlɪsɪt] **VT** entlocken (from sb jdm); support gewinnen (from sb jds); **to ~ public sympathy** die Sympathie der Öffentlichkeit gewinnen

elide [ɪˈlaɪd] **VT** elidieren, auslassen **VI** elidiert werden, wegfallen

eligibility [ˌelɪdʒəˈbɪlɪtɪ] **N a** Berechtigung f; **because of his undoubted ~ for the post** da er für die Stelle zweifelsohne in Frage kommt/kam **b** Wählbarkeit f

eligible [ˈelɪdʒəbl] **ADJ a** infrage or in Frage kommend; (for competition etc) teilnahmeberechtigt; (for student flights, grants etc) berechtigt; (for membership) aufnahmeberechtigt; **to be ~ for parole** für Bewährung infrage or in Frage kommen; **to be ~ for a job/an office** für einen Posten/ein Amt infrage or in Frage kommen; **to be ~ for a pension** pensionsberechtigt sein; **an ~ bachelor** ein begehrter Junggeselle **b** (= able to be elected) wählbar

eliminate [ɪˈlɪmɪneɪt] **VT a** (= remove) ausschließen; competitor ausschalten; inflation, poverty, waste ein Ende machen (+dat); danger, problem beseitigen; (Physiol) ausscheiden, eliminieren; (Math) eliminieren; **our team/candidate was ~d in the second round** unsere Mannschaft/unser Kandidat schied in der zweiten Runde aus **b** (= kill) enemy ausschalten, eliminieren

elimination [ɪˌlɪmɪˈneɪʃən] **N a** (= removal) Ausschluss m, Ausscheidung f; (of competitor) Ausschaltung f; (of inflation, poverty, waste) Beendung f; (of danger, problem) Beseitigung f; (Physiol) Ausscheidung f, Elimination f (spec); (Math) Elimination f; **by (a) process of ~** durch negative Auslese; **our ~ by the German team** die Ausschaltung unserer Mannschaft durch die deutsche **b** (= killing: of enemy) Ausschaltung f, Eliminierung f

elision [ɪˈlɪʒən] **N** Elision f

elite [eɪˈliːt] **N** (often pej) Elite f **ADJ** Elite-; **~ group** Elitegruppe f, Elite f; **~ unit** Eliteeinheit f; **~ force** Elitetruppe f; **~ troops** Elitetruppen pl; **an ~ group of scholars** eine Elite der Gelehrten

elitism [eɪˈliːtɪzəm] **N** Elitedenken nt

elitist [eɪˈliːtɪst] **ADJ** elitär **N** elitär Denkende(r) mf; **he's an ~** er denkt elitär

elixir [ɪˈlɪksəʳ] **N** Elixier nt, Auszug m; **~ of life** Lebenselixier nt

Elizabeth [ɪˈlɪzəbəθ] **N** Elisabeth f

Elizabethan [ɪˌlɪzəˈbiːθən] **ADJ** elisabethanisch **N** Elisabethaner(in) m(f)

elk [elk] **N** Elch m

ellipse [ɪˈlɪps] **N** Ellipse f

ellipsis [ɪˈlɪpsɪs] **N** pl **ellipses** [ɪˈlɪpsiːz] (Gram) Ellipse f

elliptic(al) [ɪˈlɪptɪk(əl)] **ADJ a** (Math etc) orbit, path elliptisch **b** (fig) account, reference andeutungsweise; style unklar; essay, book, play kryptisch (geh); **she gives an elliptical account of the tragedy** sie berichtet nur andeutungsweise von der Tragödie

elliptically [ɪˈlɪptɪkəlɪ] **ADV a** (Math) elliptisch; **planets move round ~** die Planeten haben eine

elliptische Umlaufbahn **b** (fig) speak andeutungsweise; write kryptisch (geh)

elm [elm] **N** Ulme f

El Niño [elˈniːnjəʊ] **N** El Niño m

elocution [ˌeləˈkjuːʃən] **N** Sprechtechnik f; **teacher of ~** Sprecherzieher(in) m(f); **~ lessons** Sprechunterricht m

elocutionist [ˌeləˈkjuːʃənɪst] **N** Sprecherzieher(in) m(f)

elongate [ˈiːlɒŋgeɪt] **VT** verlängern; (= stretch out) lang ziehen, strecken **VI** länger werden

elongated [ˈiːlɒŋgeɪtɪd] **ADJ** (= extra length added) verlängert; (= stretched) neck ausgestreckt; shape länglich; body lang gestreckt; orbit elliptisch

elongation [ˌiːlɒŋˈgeɪʃən] **N** Verlängerung f; (= stretching) Ausstrecken nt

elope [ɪˈləʊp] **VI** durchbrennen or ausreißen, um zu heiraten (inf)

elopement [ɪˈləʊpmənt] **N** Durchbrennen nt (inf) or Ausreißen nt (inf), um zu heiraten

eloquence [ˈeləkwəns] **N** (of person) Redegewandtheit f; (of speech, words) Gewandtheit f; (of statement, tribute, plea) Wortgewandtheit f; (fig, of testimony, gesture, silence) Beredtheit f; **phrased with such ~** so gewandt ausgedrückt

eloquent [ˈeləkwənt] **ADJ a** (= persuasive) speech, words gewandt; statement, tribute, plea wortgewandt; person redegewandt; **his lawyer made an ~ plea for leniency** sein Anwalt bat mit gewandten Worten um Milde; **to be ~ about or on sth** mit schönen Worten über etw (acc) reden; **to be ~ in describing/recommending sth** etw mit gewandten or schönen Worten beschreiben/empfehlen; **to wax ~ (about or on sth)** (von etw) schwärmen **b** (fig) hands, voice ausdrucksvoll; gesture beredt; silence beredt, viel sagend; **to be ~ or give ~ testimony to sth** ein beredtes Zeugnis für etw sein, etw beredt bezeugen; **to be ~ proof of sth** ein überzeugender Beweis für etw sein

eloquently [ˈeləkwəntlɪ] **ADV a** (= persuasively) speak, express, write mit beredten Worten; demonstrate deutlich; **very ~ put or phrased** sehr gewandt ausgedrückt **b** (fig) gesture, smile beredt

else [els] **ADV a** (after pron) andere(r, s); **anybody ~ would have done it** jeder andere hätte es gemacht; **is there anybody ~ there?** (in addition) ist sonst (noch) jemand da?; **since John doesn't want it, does anybody ~ want it?** da John es nicht will, will jemand anders es haben?; **somebody ~** sonst jemand, jemand anders; **is there somebody ~?, she asked** ist da jemand anders?, fragte sie; **I'd prefer something ~** ich möchte lieber etwas anderes; **I'd prefer anything ~** alles andere wäre mir lieber; **have you anything ~ to say?** haben Sie sonst noch etwas zu sagen?; **do you find this species anywhere ~?** findet man die Gattung sonst wo or auch anderswo?; **but they haven't got anywhere ~ to go** aber sie können sonst nirgends anders hingehen; **this is somebody ~'s umbrella** dieser Schirm gehört jemand anders; **something ~** etwas anderes, sonst etwas; **that car is something ~** (inf) das Auto ist einfach Spitze (inf); **if all ~ fails** wenn alle Stricke reißen; **above all ~** vor allen Dingen; **will there be anything ~, sir?** (in shop) darf es sonst noch etwas sein?; (butler) haben Sie sonst noch Wünsche?; **everyone/everything ~** alle anderen/alles andere; **everywhere ~** überall sonst

b **somewhere** or **someplace** (esp US) **~** woanders, anderswo; (with motion) woandershin, anderswohin; **from somewhere ~** anderswoher, woandersher, von woanders

c (after pron, neg) **nobody ~, no one ~** sonst niemand, niemand anders; **nobody ~ understood** sonst hat es niemand verstanden, niemand anders hat es verstanden; **nothing ~** sonst nichts, nichts anderes; **nothing ~ would be good enough** alles andere wäre nicht gut genug; **what do you want? – nothing ~, thank you** was möchten Sie? – danke, nichts weiter; **that this is a result of the cold and nothing ~**

dass dies allein auf die Kälte zurückzuführen ist; **if nothing ~, you'll enjoy it** auf jeden Fall wird es dir Spaß machen; **there's nothing ~ for it but to ...** da gibt es keinen anderen Ausweg, als zu ...; **nowhere ~** sonst nirgends or nirgendwo, nirgendwo anders; (with motion) sonst nirgendwohin, nirgendwo anders hin; **there's not much ~ we can do** wir können kaum etwas anderes tun; **I can think of little ~** ich kann fast an nichts anderes mehr denken

d (after interrog) **where ~?** wo sonst?, wo anders?; **who ~?** wer sonst?; **who ~ but John could have done a thing like that?** wer anders als John hätte so etwas tun können?; **what ~?** was sonst?; **how ~ can I do it?** wie kann ich es denn sonst or anders machen?; **what ~ could I have done?** was hätte ich sonst tun können?

e (adv of quantity) **they sell books and toys and much ~** (Brit) sie führen Bücher, Spielzeug und vieles andere; **there is little ~ to be done** da bleibt nicht viel zu tun übrig

f (= otherwise, if not) sonst, andernfalls; **do it now (or) ~ you'll be punished** tu es jetzt, sonst setzt es Strafe or oder es setzt Strafe; **do it or ~ ...!** mach das, sonst or oder ...!; **he's either a genius or ~ he's completely mad** er ist entweder ein Genie oder aber völlig verrückt

elsewhere [ˌelsˈweəʳ] **ADV** woanders, anderswo (inf); **to go ~** woandershin gehen; **her thoughts were ~** sie war mit ihren Gedanken woanders

ELT abbr of **English Language Teaching** → also **TEFL**

elucidate [ɪˈluːsɪdeɪt] **VT** text erklären; issue Licht werfen auf (+acc), erhellen; situation erhellen; point näher ausführen; mystery aufklären, aufhellen

elucidation [ɪˌluːsɪˈdeɪʃən] **N** (of text) Erklärung f; (of issue, situation) Erhellung f; (of point) nähere Ausführung; (of mystery) Aufklärung f, Aufhellung f

elucidatory [ɪˈluːsɪdətərɪ] **ADJ** erklärend

elude [ɪˈluːd] **VT** observation, justice sich entziehen (+dat); sb's gaze ausweichen (+dat); police, enemy entkommen (+dat), entwischen (+dat); **to ~ capture** entkommen; **the principle ~d his grasp** er konnte das Prinzip nicht erfassen; **sleep ~d her** sie konnte keinen Schlaf finden; **the name ~s me** der Name ist mir entfallen; **the title still ~s him** der Titel fehlt ihm immer noch

elusive [ɪˈluːsɪv] **ADJ a** truth schwer fassbar; goal, target, success schwer erreichbar; (= unattainable) unerreichbar; **happiness seems to be an ~ state for some people** Glück scheint für manche Menschen ein unerreichbarer Zustand zu sein; **there was an ~ quality about Robert** Robert hatte etwas schwer Fassbares an sich (dat); **financial success proved ~** der finanzielle Erfolg wollte sich nicht einstellen; **his answer to my question was ~** er antwortete mir ausweichend **b** person schwer zu erreichen; animal scheu; prey schwer zu fangen; **he remained ~** er blieb unauffindbar

elusively [ɪˈluːsɪvlɪ] **ADV** (+adj) auf undefinierbare Art; (+vb) undefinierbar; answer ausweichend

elusiveness [ɪˈluːsɪvnɪs] **N** (of thoughts) Flüchtigkeit f; (of happiness) Unerreichbarkeit f; **the ~ of this concept** die Schwierigkeit, diesen Begriff zu definieren; **the ~ of his answer** seine ausweichende Antwort

elves [elvz] pl of **elf**

Elysian [ɪˈlɪzɪən] **ADJ a** (Myth) elysisch; **the ~ fields** pl Elysium nt **b** (fig) paradiesisch, himmlisch

'em [əm] **PRON** (inf) = **them**

emaciated [ɪˈmeɪsɪeɪtɪd] **ADJ** abgezehrt, ausgezehrt, stark abgemagert; **to become ~** stark abmagern

emaciation [ɪˌmeɪsɪˈeɪʃən] **N** Auszehrung f, starke Abmagerung

E-mail, e-mail [ˈiːmeɪl] **N** E-Mail f **VT** **to ~ sb** jdm eine E-Mail schicken; **to ~ sth** etw per E-Mail schicken, etw mailen (inf)

emanate ['emaneɪt] VI ausgehen (*from* von); (*odour*) ausströmen, ausgehen (*from* von); (*documents, instructions*) stammen (*from* aus); **according to instructions emanating from regional headquarters** (*form*) nach Anweisungen der Bezirksstelle

emanation [ˌema'neɪʃən] N Ausgehen *nt*; (*of odour*) Ausströmen *nt*, Ausgehen *nt*; (*Rel*) Emanation *f*

emancipate [ɪ'mænsɪpeɪt] VT *women* emanzipieren; *slaves* freilassen; *country, people* befreien; (*fig*) emanzipieren, befreien, frei machen; **to ~ oneself** sich emanzipieren

emancipated [ɪ'mænsɪpeɪtɪd] ADJ *woman, outlook* emanzipiert; *slave* freigelassen

emancipation [ɪˌmænsɪ'peɪʃən] N **a** (*lit, fig*) Emanzipation *f*; (*of slave*) Freilassung *f*; (*of country, people*) Befreiung *f*

emasculate [ɪ'mæskjʊleɪt] VT **a** (= *weaken*) entkräften **b** (*lit*) man entmannen

emasculated [ɪ'mæskjʊleɪtɪd] ADJ *style etc* (saftund) kraftlos

emasculation [ɪˌmæskjʊ'leɪʃən] N **a** (= *weakening*) Entkräftung *f*, Schwächung *f* **b** (*lit*) Entmannung *f*, Kastration *f*

embalm [ɪm'bɑːm] VT *corpse* einbalsamieren

embalming fluid [ɪm'bɑːmɪŋ'fluːɪd] N Balsamierflüssigkeit *f*

embank [ɪm'bæŋk] VT *river* eindämmen, eindeichen

embankment [ɪm'bæŋkmənt] N (Ufer)böschung *f*; (*along path, road*) Böschung *f*; (*for railway*) Bahndamm *m*; (*holding back water*) (Ufer-)damm *m*, Deich *m*; (= *roadway beside a river*) Ufer(straße *f*) *nt*

embargo [ɪm'bɑːgəʊ] **N** *pl* **-es a** Embargo *nt* (*against* gegen); **oil/arms/trade ~** Öl-/Waffen-/Handelsembargo *nt*; **to impose** *or* **place** *or* **put an ~ on sth** etw mit einem Embargo belegen, ein Embargo über etw (*acc*) verhängen; **to lift an ~ on sth** ein Embargo über etw (*acc*) aufheben; **the country is under an economic ~** über das Land wurde ein Wirtschaftsembargo verhängt **b** (*fig*) Sperre *f*; **to put an ~ on further spending** alle weiteren Ausgaben sperren **VT** *trade, goods* mit einem Embargo belegen

embark [ɪm'bɑːk] **VI a** einschiffen; *goods also* verladen **VI a** (*Naut*) sich einschiffen; (*troops*) eingeschifft werden **b** (*fig*) **to ~ up(on) sth** etw anfangen, etw beginnen

embarkation [ˌembɑː'keɪʃən] N **a** Einschiffung *f* **b** (*of cargo*) Verladung *f*, Übernahme *f*

embarkation officer N Verladeoffizier *m*

embarkation papers N Bordpapiere *pl*

embarrass [ɪm'bærəs] VT **a** in Verlegenheit bringen, verlegen machen; (*generosity etc*) beschämen; **she was ~ed by the question** die Frage war ihr peinlich **b** (*obs, = hamper*) **he was ~ed by his cumbersome greatcoat** er wurde durch seinen unförmigen Übermantel behindert

embarrassed [ɪm'bærəst] ADJ verlegen; **he looked a bit ~** er sah etwas verlegen aus; **I am/feel so ~ (about it)** es ist mir so peinlich; **she was ~ to be seen with him** or about being seen with him es war ihr peinlich, mit ihm gesehen zu werden; **it's nothing to be ~ about, there's no need to feel ~ (about it)** das braucht einem nicht peinlich zu sein; **I was ~ for him** es war mir seinetwegen peinlich; **to be financially ~** in einer finanziellen Verlegenheit sein

embarrassing [ɪm'bærəsɪŋ] ADJ peinlich; *generosity etc* beschämend

embarrassingly [ɪm'bærəsɪŋlɪ] ADV auf peinliche Weise; (*introducing sentence*) peinlicherweise; **the play flopped ~** das Stück war ein peinlicher Reinfall; **it was ~ bad** es war so schlecht, dass es schon peinlich war; **~ candid remarks** Bemerkungen von peinlicher Offenheit; **~ for him, his wife came in at the wrong moment** es war peinlich für ihn, dass seine Frau im falschen Moment hereinkam

embarrassment [ɪm'bærəsmənt] N Verlegenheit *f*; (*through generosity also*) Beschämung *f*; **to cause ~ to sb** jdn in Verlegenheit bringen, jdn verlegen machen; **to be a constant source of ~ to sb** jdn ständig in Verlegenheit bringen; **to my great ~ she ...** sie ..., was mir sehr peinlich war; **she's an ~ to her family** sie blamiert die ganze Familie (*inf*); **financial ~** finanzielle Verlegenheit; **an ~ of riches** ein verwirrender Reichtum

embassy ['embəsɪ] N Botschaft *f*

embattled [ɪm'bætld] ADJ **a** (= *besieged*) belagert; (= *fought over*) umkämpft; (= *fighting*) kämpfend **b** (*fig*) *person, government* bedrängt

embed [ɪm'bed] VT **a** einlassen; **the car was firmly ~ded in the mud** das Auto steckte im Schlamm fest; **the bullet ~ded itself in the wall** die Kugel bohrte sich in die Wand; **to be (deeply) ~ded in sth** (*fig*) (tief) in etw (*dat*) verwurzelt sein **b** (*Comput*) **~ded commands** eingebettete Befehle **c** (*Ling*) **~ded clauses** eingeschobene Gliedsätze

embellish [ɪm'belɪʃ] VT (= *adorn*) schmücken, verschönern; (*fig*) *tale, account* ausschmücken; *truth* beschönigen

embellishment [ɪm'belɪʃmənt] N Schmuck *m*; (= *act*) Verschönerung *f*; (*of story*) Ausschmückung *f*; (*of truth*) Beschönigung *f*; (*of handwriting*) Verzierung *f*, Schnörkel *m*; (*Mus*) Verzierung *f*

embers ['embəz] PL Glut *f*, → **fan** [1]

embezzle [ɪm'bezl] VT unterschlagen, veruntreuen (*from* +*dat*)

embezzlement [ɪm'bezlmənt] N Unterschlagung *f*

embezzler [ɪm'bezlə] N jd, *der Unterschlagungen/eine Unterschlagung begangen hat* **he admitted to being an ~** er gab zu, Geld unterschlagen *or* veruntreut zu haben

embitter [ɪm'bɪtə] VT *person* verbittern; *relations* trüben, vergiften

emblazon [ɪm'bleɪzən] VT **a** (*Her*) schmücken, (ver)zieren **b** (= *display boldly*) *name* stolz hervorheben; **the name "Jones" was ~ed on the cover** der Name „Jones" prangte auf dem Umschlag **c** (= *extol*) überschwänglich preisen

emblem ['embləm] N Emblem *nt*; (*of political party, trade also*) Wahrzeichen *nt*

emblematic [ˌemblə'mætɪk] ADJ emblematisch (*of* für)

embodiment [ɪm'bɒdɪmənt] N **a** Verkörperung *f*; **to be the ~ of evil** das Böse in Person sein **b** (= *inclusion*) Aufnahme *f*, Eingliederung *f*

embody [ɪm'bɒdɪ] VT **a** (= *give form to*) *one's thoughts* ausdrücken, Ausdruck geben (+*dat*), in Worte kleiden **b** *spirit, principles, one's ideal* verkörpern **c** (= *include*) enthalten

embolden [ɪm'bəʊldən] VT ermutigen, Mut machen (+*dat*); **to ~ sb to do sth** jdn dazu ermutigen *or* jdm Mut machen, etw zu tun; **to be ~ed to do sth** dazu ermutigt werden, etw zu tun

embolism ['embəlɪzəm] N (*Med*) Embolie *f*

embonpoint [ˌɒmbɒm'pwɑːŋ] N (*hum euph*) Embonpoint *m or nt* (*dated*), Leibesfülle *f*

emboss [ɪm'bɒs] VT *metal, leather* prägen; *silk, velvet* gaufrieren; **the cover is ~ed with his name** sein Name ist auf den Einband aufgeprägt

embossed [ɪm'bɒst] ADJ *lettering, paper, leather* geprägt; *design* erhaben; **an ~ silver tray** ein Silbertablett *nt* mit Relief; **~ with a design** mit aufgeprägtem Muster; **~ in silver** mit Silberprägung; **~ wallpaper** Prägetapete *f*

embouchure ['ɒmbʊʃʊə'] N (*Mus*) Mundstück *nt*; (*of player*) Mundstellung *f*

embrace [ɪm'breɪs] ✪ 26.3 **VT a** (= *hug*) umarmen, in die Arme schließen; **they ~d each other** sie umarmten sich *or* einander **b** (= *seize eagerly*) *religion* annehmen; *opportunity* wahrnehmen, ergreifen; *cause* sich annehmen (+*gen*); *offer* annehmen, ergreifen; **he ~d the idea of an integrated Europe** er machte sich (*dat*) den Gedanken eines integrierten Europas zu eigen **c** (= *include*) umfassen, erfassen; **an all-embracing role** eine allumfassende Rolle **VI** sich umarmen **N** (= *hug*) Umarmung *f*; **a couple locked in a tender ~** ein Paar in zärtlicher Umarmung; **he held her in his ~** er hielt sie umschlungen; **his ~ of the Catholic faith** sein Bekenntnis zum katholischen Glauben; **death's ~** (*liter*) die Arme des Todes

embracery [ɪm'breɪsərɪ] N (*Jur*) Bestechungsversuch *m*

embrasure [ɪm'breɪʒə'] N (*in parapet*) Schießscharte *f*; (*of door, window*) Laibung *f*

embrocation [ˌembrəʊ'keɪʃən] N Einreibemittel *nt*

embroider [ɪm'brɔɪdə'] **VT** *cloth* besticken; *pattern* sticken; (*fig*) *facts, truth* ausschmücken; **to ~ a design on sth** ein Muster auf etw (*acc*) (auf)sticken **VI** sticken

embroidered [ɪm'brɔɪdəd] ADJ **a** (*lit*) *material, cushion, tablecloth etc* bestickt (*with* mit); *design* (auf)gestickt (*on* auf +*acc*); **~ in gold** goldbestickt; **a design ~ in silk and wool** ein mit Wolle und Seide gesticktes Muster **b** (*fig, = embellished*) *story, version* ausgeschmückt

embroidery [ɪm'brɔɪdərɪ] N **a** Stickerei *f* **b** (*fig*) Ausschmückungen *pl*

embroidery: embroidery frame N Stickrahmen *m*; **embroidery thread** N Stickgarn *nt*

embroil [ɪm'brɔɪl] VT **to ~ sb in sth** jdn in etw (*acc*) hineinziehen; **to become ~ed in a dispute** in einen Streit verwickelt *or* hineingezogen werden

embroilment [ɪm'brɔɪlmənt] N Verwicklung *f* (*in* in +*acc*)

embryo ['embrɪəʊ] N Embryo *m*; (*esp fig*) Keim *m*; **in ~** (*lit, fig*) im Keim; (*animal*) als Embryo

embryologist [ˌembrɪ'ɒlədʒɪst] N Embryologe *m*, Embryologin *f*

embryology [ˌembrɪ'ɒlədʒɪ] N Embryologie *f*

embryonic [ˌembrɪ'ɒnɪk] ADJ embryonisch; (*esp fig*) keimhaft

emcee ['em'siː] **N** Conférencier *m*; (*on TV also*) Showmaster(in) *m(f)*; (*at private functions*) Zeremonienmeister(in) *m(f)* **VT** *show* als Conférencier *etc* leiten

emend [ɪ'mend] VT *text* verbessern, korrigieren

emendation [ˌiːmen'deɪʃən] N Verbesserung *f*, Korrektur *f*

emerald ['emərəld] **N a** (= *stone*) Smaragd *m* **b** (= *colour*) Smaragdgrün *nt* **ADJ** smaragden, Smaragd-; (*colour also*) smaragdgrün; **~ ring** Smaragdring *m*

Emerald Isle N **the ~** die Grüne Insel

emerge [ɪ'mɜːdʒ] ✪ 17.2 **VI a** (= *come out*) auftauchen; **he ~d from behind the shed** er tauchte hinter dem Schuppen auf; **one arm ~d from beneath the blanket** ein Arm tauchte unter der Decke hervor; **he ~d from the house/a meeting** er kam aus dem Haus/aus einer Besprechung; **we ~d into the bright daylight** wir kamen heraus in das helle Tageslicht; **the country is emerging from civil war** das Land hat den Bürgerkrieg überwunden; **the economy is starting to ~ from the recession** die Wirtschaft beginnt sich von der Rezession zu erholen; **to ~ unscathed** ungeschoren davonkommen; **to ~ victorious** siegreich hervorgehen; **he ~d (as) the winner** er ging als Sieger hervor **b** (= *come into being*) *life, new nation etc* entstehen; **life ~d from the sea** das Leben entstammt dem *or* kommt aus dem Meer **c** (*truth, nature of problem etc*) sich herausstellen, herauskommen (*from* bei); (*facts*) sich herausstellen, an den Tag kommen; **it ~s that ...** es stellt sich heraus, dass ...; **but what will ~ from all this?** aber was wird sich aus all dem ergeben?

emergence [ɪ'mɜːdʒəns] N Auftauchen *nt*; (*of new nation etc*) Entstehung *f*; (*of theory, school of thought*) Aufkommen *nt*

emergency [ɪˈmɜːdʒənsɪ] **N** (= *crisis*) Notfall *m*; (*particular situation*) Notlage *f*; **in an ~, in case of ~** im Notfall; **to be prepared for any ~** für den Notfall vorbereitet sein; **state of ~** Notstand *m*; **to declare a state of ~** den Notstand erklären *or* ausrufen; **to declare a state of ~ in an area** eine Gegend zum Notstandsgebiet erklären; **the doctor's been called out on an ~** der Arzt ist zu einem Notfall gerufen worden **ADJ a** (= *in/for an emergency*) Not-; *meeting, talks, debate* außerordentlich; *repair* notdürftig; **~ regulations** Notverordnung *f*; **~ appeal** Notaufruf *m*; **~ committee** Notkomitee *nt*; **~ rations** Notverpflegung *f*; **an ~ repair has been done on the car** das Auto ist notdürftig repariert worden; **we had an ~ meeting in the garden** wir hielten schnell eine Lagebesprechung im Garten ab; **to undergo ~ surgery** sich einer Notoperation unterziehen; **to be given ~ treatment** (*in hospital*) auf der Unfallstation behandelt werden; **~ plan/procedure** Plan *m*/Maßnahmen *pl* für den Notfall; **for ~ use only** nur für den Notfall **b** (= *for a disaster*) Katastrophen-; **~ aid** *or* **relief** Katastrophenhilfe *f*; **~ fund** Katastrophenfonds *m*; **~ airlift** Luftbrücke *f* **c** (= *for state of emergency*) Notstands-; **~ measures** *or* **action** Notstandsmaßnahmen *pl*; **~ powers** Notstandsvollmachten *pl*; **~ law** Notstandsgesetz *nt*

emergency in *cpds* Not-; **emergency brake** N Notbremse *f*; **emergency call** N Notruf *m*; **emergency centre**, (*US*) **emergency center** N Rettungszentrum *nt* des Noteinsatzes; **emergency clause** N Dringlichkeits- *or* Notklausel *f*; **emergency cord** N (*Rail*) Notbremse *f*; **emergency doctor** N Notarzt *m*/-ärztin *f*; **emergency exit** N Notausgang *m*; **emergency landing** N Notlandung *f*; **emergency number** N (*Telec*) Notruf *m*; (*after plane crash etc*) Sondertelefon *nt*; (*for technical help*) Hotline *f*; **emergency room** N (*US*) Unfallstation *f*; **emergency service** N Notdienst *m*, Hilfsdienst *m*; **emergency services** PL Notdienst *m*, Notdienste *pl*; **emergency stop** N (*Aut*) Vollbremsung *f*; **emergency telephone** N Notruftelefon *nt*; **emergency telephone number** N (*Telec*) Notrufnummer *f*; (*after plane crash etc*) Nummer *f* des Sondertelefons; (*of individual*) Nummer *f* für dringende Notfälle; (*for technical help*) Hotlinenummer *f*; **emergency ward** N Unfallstation *f*

emergent [ɪˈmɜːdʒənt] ADJ (*form*) *democracy, nation, country* jung, aufstrebend; *movement, group* aufstrebend; *sexuality, womanhood* erwachend

emeritus [ɪˈmerɪtəs] ADJ emeritiert; **~ professor, professor ~** Professor emeritus *m*

emery [ˈemərɪ] N Schmirgel *m*

emery: **emery board** N Papiernagelfeile *f*; **emery cloth** N Schmirgelleinwand *f*; **emery paper** N Schmirgelpapier *nt*

emetic [ɪˈmetɪk] **N** Brechmittel *nt*, Emetikum *nt* (*spec*); **ADJ** Brechreiz erregend, emetisch (*spec*)

emigrant [ˈemɪɡrənt] **N** Auswanderer *m*, Auswanderin *f*; (*esp for political reasons*) Emigrant(in) *m(f)* **ADJ** *attr* Auswanderer-, Emigranten-; **~ country** Auswandererland *nt*

emigrate [ˈemɪɡreɪt] VI auswandern; (*esp for political reasons*) emigrieren

emigration [emɪˈɡreɪʃən] N Auswanderung *f*; (*esp for political reasons*) Emigration *f*

émigré [ˈemɪɡreɪ] N Emigrant(in) *m(f)*

eminence [ˈemɪnəns] **N a** (= *distinction*) hohes Ansehen; **doctors of ~** (hoch) angesehene Ärzte *pl*; **to achieve ~** hohes Ansehen erlangen **b** (*of ground*) Erhebung *f*, Anhöhe *f* **c** (*Eccl*) **His/Your Eminence** Seine/Eure Eminenz

éminence grise [ˈemɪnɒ̃sˈɡriːz] N graue Eminenz

eminent [ˈemɪnənt] ADJ **a** (= *distinguished, prominent*) *person* angesehen, bedeutend; **to be ~ in a particular field** auf einem bestimmten Gebiet führend sein **b** (*form*, = *notable*) ausge-

sprochen; **you showed ~ good sense in coming to us** es war ausgesprochen vernünftig von Ihnen, zu uns zu kommen; **in an ~ degree** in ausgesprochen hohem Maße

eminently [ˈemɪnəntlɪ] ADV (= *extremely*) *sensible, readable* ausgesprochen; *practical* äußerst; *desirable* überaus; **~ suitable** *or* **suited** vorzüglich geeignet; **~ respectable** hoch angesehen; **an ~ forgettable speech** eine Rede, die man getrost vergessen kann; **it seems to me ~ reasonable** ich finde es durchaus berechtigt; **to be ~ qualified for sth/to do sth** sich vorzüglich für etw eignen/dazu eignen, etw zu tun; **to be ~ capable of sth** eindeutig zu etw fähig sein

emir [eˈmɪə] N Emir *m*

emirate [ˈemɪrɪt] N Emirat *nt*

emissary [ˈemɪsərɪ] N Emissär *m*, Abgesandte(r) *mf*

emission [ɪˈmɪʃən] N Ausstrahlung *f*, Abstrahlung *f*; (*of fumes, X-rays*) Emission *f* (*spec*); (*of sound*) Abgabe *f*; (*of gas, smell*) Verströmen *nt*, Ausströmen *nt*; (*of liquid*) Ausströmen *nt*; (*gradual*) Absonderung *f*, Abscheidung *f*; (*of vapour, smoke: continuous*) Abgabe *f*; (*of lava*) Ausstoßen *nt*; (*of sparks*) Versprühen *nt*

emit [ɪˈmɪt] VT **a** *light* ausstrahlen, abstrahlen; *radiation* aussenden, emittieren (*spec*); *sound* abgeben; *gas, smell* verströmen, ausströmen; *vapour, smoke* (*continuously*) abgeben; *lava, cry* ausstoßen; *liquid* (*gradually*) absondern, abscheiden; *sparks* versprühen **b** *banknotes* ausgeben

Emmy [ˈemɪ] N (= *award*) Emmy *f*

emollient [ɪˈmɒlɪənt] (*Med*) **N** Linderungsmittel *nt* **ADJ** lindernd

emolument [ɪˈmɒljʊmənt] N *usu pl* (*form*) Vergütung *f*; (= *fee*) Honorar *nt*; (= *salary*) Bezüge *pl*

emote [ɪˈməʊt] VI seine Gefühle ausdrücken; (*actor*) Gefühle mimen

emoticon [ɪˈməʊtɪkən] N (*Comput*) Gefühlssymbol *nt*

emotion [ɪˈməʊʃən] **N a** Gefühl *nt*, Emotion *f*, Gefühlsregung *f*; **to dissociate ~ from reason** Verstand und Gefühl trennen **b** *no pl* (= *state of being moved*) (Gemüts)bewegung *f*, Bewegtheit *f*; **to show no ~** unbewegt bleiben; **in a voice full of ~** mit bewegter Stimme; **there was absolutely no ~ in his voice** seine Stimme war völlig emotionslos

emotional [ɪˈməʊʃənl] ADJ **a** (= *related to emotions, psychological*) *needs, security, involvement, detachment, reaction, energy* emotional; *problem, stress, trauma, abuse* seelisch; *support, development* psychologisch; **to go through ~ turmoil/an ~ upheaval** einen Aufruhr der Gefühle erleben; **~ state** Gemütszustand *m*; **his ~ wellbeing** sein seelisches Wohl; **~ life** Seelenleben *nt*; **~ intensity** Gefühlsintensität *f*; **on an ~ level** auf emotionaler Ebene; **to be on an ~ high** in Hochstimmung sein; **to be at an ~ low** ein seelisches Tief durchmachen; **~ wreck** seelisches Wrack **b** (= *emotive*) *issue, impact, experience, situation* emotional **c** (= *influenced by feelings*) *person, behaviour* (*characteristically*) emotional, gefühlsbetont; (*in particular situation*) emotional, gefühlvoll; *decision* gefühlsmäßig; *scene, response, reaction* emotional; *farewell, welcome* gefühlvoll; *appeal, speech* emotional, gefühlsbetont; **he made an ~ appeal to his wife** er appellierte gefühlsbetont an seine Frau; **the ~ appeal of a product** die gefühlsmäßige Anziehungskraft einer Ware; **to be ~ about sth** sich über etw (*acc*) erregen *or* aufregen; **to become** *or* **get ~** sich erregen *or* aufregen; **~ outburst** Gefühlsausbruch *m*

emotional: emotional baggage N seelischer Ballast; **emotional blackmail** N psychologische Erpressung; **emotional cripple** N emotionaler Krüppel

emotionalism [ɪˈməʊʃnəlɪzəm] N Gefühlsbetontheit *f*, Rührseligkeit *f*

emotionally [ɪˈməʊʃnəlɪ] ADV **a** (= *psychologically*) seelisch; (= *from an emotional point of view*) *involved* gefühlsmäßig; **I don't want to get ~ in-**

volved (with her) ich will mich (bei ihr) nicht ernsthaft engagieren; **~ disturbed** seelisch gestört; **an ~ deprived child** ein Kind ohne Nestwärme; **~ I was a wreck** ich war ein seelisches Wrack; **physically and ~** körperlich und seelisch **b** (= *emotively, in an emotional manner*) emotional; (= **~ charged** (*atmosphere, debate*) spannungsgeladen

emotionless [ɪˈməʊʃənlɪs] ADJ *face, voice etc* ausdruckslos; *person* gefühllos, emotionslos

emotive [ɪˈməʊtɪv] ADJ *issue* emotional; *language, word* emotional gefärbt

empanel VT = **impanel**

empathize [ˈempəθaɪz] VI sich hineinversetzen *or* einfühlen (*with* in +*acc*)

empathy [ˈempəθɪ] N Einfühlungsvermögen *nt*, Empathie *f*

emperor [ˈempərə] N Kaiser *m*; (*in Rome also*) Imperator *m*

emperor penguin N Kaiserpinguin *m*

emphasis [ˈemfəsɪs] N **a** (= *vocal stress*) Betonung *f*; **the ~ is on the first syllable** die Betonung *or* der Ton liegt auf der ersten Silbe; **to lay** *or* **put ~ on a word** ein Wort betonen; **to say sth with ~** etw mit Nachdruck *or* nachdrücklich betonen **b** (= *importance*) Betonung *f*, (Schwer)gewicht *nt*; **to lay ~** *or* **place** *or* **put the ~ on sth** etw betonen; **to lay ~** *or* **place** *or* **put the ~ on doing sth** Wert darauf legen, etw zu tun; **this year the ~ is on femininity** dieses Jahr liegt der Akzent *or* die Betonung auf Weiblichkeit; **there is too much ~ on research** die Forschung steht zu sehr im Vordergrund; **a change of ~** eine Akzentverschiebung

emphasize [ˈemfəsaɪz] ✪ 26.3 VT *word, syllable, hips* betonen; *point, importance, difference, need* also hervorheben; **it cannot be too strongly ~d that ...** man kann gar nicht genug betonen, dass ...

emphatic [ɪmˈfætɪk] ADJ **a** (= *forceful*) entschieden; *response* nachdrücklich, entschieden; *denial* energisch; *tone, stress, gesture* nachdrücklich; **his response was immediate and ~** er antwortete sofort und mit Nachdruck; **the accused responded with an ~ denial** in seiner Antwort leugnete der Angeklagte es energisch *or* entschieden; **the answer is an ~ no** die Antwort lautet ganz entschieden nein; **their answer was an ~ yes** sie bejahten es mit Nachdruck; **to be ~ (that ...)** (*person*) darauf bestehen(, dass ...); **to be ~ about sth** auf etw (*dat*) bestehen; **he was ~ in his defence of it** er verteidigte es mit Nachdruck; **they were ~ in denying their involvement** sie leugneten entschieden *or* energisch, dass sie daran beteiligt waren **b** (= *decisive*) *victory, win, winner* klar, überzeugend; *defeat* schwer; *result, approval* eindeutig

emphatically [ɪmˈfætɪkəlɪ] ADV **a** (= *forcefully*) *say* nachdrücklich, mit Nachdruck; *nod* nachdrücklich, entschieden; *reply, reject* entschieden; *deny* energisch, entschieden; **most ~** mit allem Nachdruck **b** (= *definitely*) eindeutig; **most ~** ganz eindeutig; **~ not** auf (gar) keinen Fall

empire [ˈempaɪə] **N a** Reich *nt*; (*worldwide*) Weltreich *nt*, Imperium *nt*; **the Holy Roman Empire** das Heilige Römische Reich (deutscher Nation); **the British Empire** das Britische Weltreich, das Empire **b** (*fig, esp Comm*) Imperium *nt*; **his business/publishing ~** sein Geschäfts-/Verlagsimperium *nt* **ADJ** *attr* **Empire** Empire-; **Empire style/furniture** Empirestil *m*/-möbel *pl*

empire: empire-builder N (*fig*) jd, der sich ein kleines Imperium aufbaut; **empire-building** N (*fig*) Schaffung *f* eines eigenen kleinen Imperiums

empiric [emˈpɪrɪk] **ADJ** = **empirical** **N** Empiriker(in) *m(f)*

empirical [emˈpɪrɪkəl] ADJ empirisch

empirically [emˈpɪrɪkəlɪ] ADV empirisch; (*introducing sentence*) empirisch gesehen

empiricism [emˈpɪrɪsɪzəm] N Empirismus *m*; (*method*) Empirie *f*

empiricist [emˈpɪrɪsɪst] N Empiriker(in) *m(f)*

emplacement [ɪmˈpleɪsmənt] N (*Mil*) Stellung *f*

employ [ɪmˈplɔɪ] **VT a** *person* beschäftigen; (= *take on*) anstellen; *private detective* beauftragen; **he has been ~ed with us for 15 years** er ist schon seit 15 Jahren bei uns
b (= *use*) *means, method, tactics, skill, force, cunning* anwenden, einsetzen; *word, concept* verwenden; *time* verbringen; **you can surely find a better way of ~ing your time** Sie können doch bestimmt Besseres mit Ihrer Zeit anfangen; **they ~ed the services of a chemist to help them** sie zogen einen Chemiker heran, um ihnen zu helfen
c to be ~ed in doing sth damit beschäftigt sein, etw zu tun
N to be in the ~ of sb (*form*) bei jdm beschäftigt sein, in jds Diensten stehen (*geh*)

employable [ɪmˈplɔɪəbl] ADJ *person* anstellbar, zu beschäftigen *pred*

employee [ˌɪmplɔɪˈiː] N Angestellte(r) *mf*; **~s and employers** Arbeitnehmer und Arbeitgeber; **the ~s** (*of one firm*) die Belegschaft, die Beschäftigten *pl*; **~ rights** Arbeitnehmerrechte *pl*

employer [ɪmˈplɔɪə] N Arbeitgeber(in) *m(f)*, Brötchengeber *m* (*hum inf*); (*Comm, Ind*) Unternehmer(in) *m(f)*; Arbeitgeber(in) *m(f)*; (*of domestics, servants, civil servants*) Dienstherr(in) *m(f)*; **~s' federation** Arbeitgeberverband *m*; **~'s contribution** Arbeitgeberanteil *m*; **~'s liability insurance plan** Arbeitgeberhaftpflichtversicherung *f*

employment [ɪmˈplɔɪmənt] N **a** (An)stellung *f*, Arbeit *f*; **to take up ~ with sb** eine Stelle bei jdm annehmen; **to be without ~** stellungslos or ohne Arbeit sein; **to seek ~** Arbeit or eine Stelle suchen; **to seek ~ with sb** sich bei jdm bewerben; **to leave one's ~** seine Stelle aufgeben; **out of ~** stellungslos, arbeitslos; **how long is it since you were last in ~?** wann hatten Sie Ihre letzte Stellung?; **conditions/contract/place of ~** Arbeitsbedingungen *pl*/-vertrag *m*/-platz *m*; **~ market** Arbeits- or Stellenmarkt *m*; **to find ~ for sb** Arbeit or eine Anstellung für jdn finden; **what kind of ~ are you looking for?** welche Art von Tätigkeit suchen Sie?
b (= *act of employing*) Beschäftigung *f*; (= *taking on*) Anstellung *f*, Einstellen *nt*
c (= *use, of means, method, skill, force, cunning*) Anwendung *f*, Einsatz *m*; (*of word, concept*) Verwendung *f*

employment: employment agency N Stellenvermittlung *f*; **employment exchange** N (*dated*), **employment office** N Arbeitsamt *nt*; **employment programme**, (*US*) **employment program** N Beschäftigungsprogramm *nt*

emporium [emˈpɔːrɪəm] N Warenhaus *nt*

empower [ɪmˈpaʊə] VT **a to ~ sb to do sth** jdn ermächtigen, etw zu tun; (*Jur*) jdm (die) Vollmacht erteilen, etw zu tun; **to be ~ed to do sth** ermächtigt or befugt sein, etw zu tun; (*Jur*) die Vollmacht haben, etw zu tun **b** (= *make powerful*) *women, minorities etc* stärken

empress [ˈempris] N Kaiserin *f*

emptiness [ˈemptinis] N Leere *f*, Leerheit *f*; (*of life etc*) Leere *f*

empty [ˈempti] ADJ (+*er*) **a** leer; (= *unoccupied*) *house* leer stehend *attr*; *seat, chair, space, place* frei; **apart from them the room was ~** außer ihnen war niemand im Zimmer; **there were no ~ seats on the bus** im Bus waren keine Plätze frei; **she was staring into ~ space** sie starrte ins Leere; **the house was just an ~ shell** das Haus bestand nur aus nackten Mauern; **on an ~ stomach** mit leerem Magen; *take drug, drink alcohol* auf leeren Magen; **to be running on ~** (*person, organization etc*) am Ende sein; **my car is running on ~** ich habe kein Benzin mehr; **~ vessels make the most sound** (*Prov*) die am wenigsten zu sagen haben, reden am meisten → *also* **empty-headed, empty-handed**
b (= *devoid*) **the parks are ~ of children** in den Parks sind keine Kinder; **she was left ~ of feel-**

---

ing sie hatte keine Gefühle mehr; **a sentence ~ of sense** ein sinnloser Satz; **~ of all expression** völlig ausdruckslos
c (*fig, = meaningless, dreary*) *words, phrase, marriage, gesture, promise, threat, feeling* leer; *dream, hope* verloren; *life, days, weeks* leer, unausgefüllt; (= *expressionless*) *face, expression, eyes* leer, ausdruckslos; **~ rhetoric** leeres Gerede; **an ~ exercise** eine leere Formalität; **to feel ~** ein leeres Gefühl or ein Gefühl *nt* der Leere haben; **that ~ feeling** dieses leere Gefühl, dieses Gefühl der Leere
N *usu pl* **empties** Leergut *nt*
VT a leeren; *container* (ent)leeren; *box, room* ausräumen; *house* räumen; *glass, bottle* leeren; (*by drinking*) austrinken; *pond, tank* ablassen, leeren; *lorry* abladen; **her singing emptied the hall in ten minutes flat** mit ihrem Singen schaffte sie es, dass der Saal innerhalb von zehn Minuten leer war; **the burglars emptied the shop** die Einbrecher haben den Laden ausgeräumt
b (= *pour*) *liquid, contents* ausgießen, leeren; **he emptied it into another container** er goss es in ein anderes Gefäß um
VI (*water*) auslaufen, abfließen; (*rivers*) münden, sich ergießen (*liter*) (*into* in +*acc*); (*theatre, streets*) sich leeren; **the sink is not ~ing properly** der Ausguss läuft nicht richtig ab

▶ **empty out** VT *sep* ausleeren

empty: empty-handed ADJ **to return ~** mit leeren Händen zurückkehren, unverrichteter Dinge zurückkehren; **empty-headed** ADJ strohdumm; **she's an ~ girl** sie hat Stroh im Kopf; **empty nester** N *usu pl* Elternteil, dessen Kinder (*erwachsen und*) aus dem Haus sind; **empty nest syndrome** N *Syndrom bei Eltern, wenn ihre Kinder (erwachsen und) aus dem Haus sind*

Empyrean [empɪˈriːən] N **the ~** (*liter*) das Empyreum *nt* (*liter*)

EMS *abbr of* **European Monetary System** EWS *nt*

EMU *abbr of* **European Monetary Union** EWU *nt*

emu [ˈiːmjuː] N Emu *m*

emulate [ˈemjʊleɪt] VT **a** (= *imitate*) nacheifern (+*dat*), nachstreben (+*dat*); **I tried to ~ his success** ich versuchte, es ihm gleichzutun **b** (*Comput*) emulieren

emulation [ˌemjʊˈleɪʃən] N **a** Nacheiferung *f*; **in ~ of sb** in dem Bestreben, es jdm gleichzutun **b** (*Comput*) Emulation *f*

emulsifier [ɪˈmʌlsɪfaɪə] N Emulgator *m*

emulsify [ɪˈmʌlsɪfaɪ] **VT** emulgieren, zu einer Emulsion verbinden **VI** emulgieren

emulsion [ɪˈmʌlʃən] N **a** Emulsion *f* **b** (*also* **emulsion paint**) Emulsionsfarbe *f*

enable [ɪˈneɪbl] VT **a** (= *make able*) **to ~ sb to do sth** es jdm ermöglichen or möglich machen, etw zu tun, jdn in den Stand setzen, etw zu tun (*geh*); **what ~s the seal to stay under water so long?** wodurch ist der Seehund fähig, so lange unter Wasser zu bleiben? **b** (*Jur, = authorize*) *measures, reforms* anordnen; **to ~ sb to do sth** jdn (dazu) ermächtigen, etw zu tun

enabling [ɪˈneɪblɪŋ] ADJ **a** ~ **legislation** Ermächtigungsgesetze *pl*; ~ **act/law** Ermächtigungsgesetz *nt* **b** (= *empowering*) **to play an ~ role in sth** etw möglich machen; ~ **technology** Hilfstechnologie *f*

enact [ɪˈnækt] VT **a** (*Pol*) *law* erlassen; **it is hereby ~ed that ...** es wird hiermit verfügt, dass ... **b** (= *perform*) *play* aufführen; *role* darstellen, spielen; **the scene which was ~ed yesterday** (*fig*) die Szene, die sich gestern abgespielt hat

enactment [ɪˈnæktmənt] N (*of law*) Erlass *m*; (*of regulation*) Verordnung *f*, Verfügung *f*; (*of play*) Aufführung *f*

enamel [ɪˈnæməl] **N** Email *nt*, Emaille *f* (*inf*); (= *paint*) Email(le)lack *m*; (*of tiles etc*) Glasur *f*; (*of teeth*) Zahnschmelz *m*; (= *nail enamel*) Nagellack *m* **VT** emaillieren **ADJ** *pot, pan* Email(le)-; ~ **paint** Email(le)lack *m*

---

enamelled, (*US*) **enameled** [ɪˈnæməld] ADJ emailliert; ~ **jewellery** (*Brit*) **enameled jewelry** (*US*) Email(le)schmuck *m*

enamelware [ɪˈnæməlˌweə] N Email(le)waren *pl*

enamour, (*US*) **enamor** [ɪˈnæmə] VT **to be ~ed of sb** (= *in love with*) in jdn verliebt sein; **to be ~ed of sth** (= *taken by*) von etw angetan or entzückt sein; **she was not exactly ~ed of the idea** sie war von der Idee nicht gerade begeistert

en bloc [ãˈblɒk] ADV en bloc; **to resign ~** geschlossen zurücktreten

enc = **enc(l)**

encamp [ɪnˈkæmp] **VI** das Lager aufschlagen **VT where the troops were ~ed** wo die Truppen ihr Lager bezogen hatten

encampment [ɪnˈkæmpmənt] N Lager *nt*

encapsulate [ɪnˈkæpsjʊleɪt] VT (*Pharm*) in Kapseln abfüllen; (*fig, = express in condensed form*) zusammenfassen

encase [ɪnˈkeɪs] VT verkleiden (*in* mit); *wires* umgeben (*in* mit); (*Cook*) *cake* überziehen (*in* mit); (*in pastry etc*) einhüllen (*in* in +*acc*); **her arms were ~d in plaster** ihre Arme waren eingegipst or in einem Gipsverband

encash [ɪnˈkæʃ] VT *cheque etc* einlösen

encashment [ɪnˈkæʃmənt] N (*of cheque etc*) Einlösung *f*

encephalitis [ˌensefəˈlaɪtɪs] N Gehirnentzündung *f*

enchain [ɪnˈtʃeɪn] VT (*lit*) in Ketten legen; **to be ~ed** (*fig*) gefangen sein

enchant [ɪnˈtʃɑːnt] VT **a** (= *delight*) bezaubern, entzücken; **to be ~ed by sth** von etw or über etw (*acc*) entzückt sein **b** (= *put under spell*) verzaubern; **the ~ed wood** der Zauberwald

enchanting ADJ, **enchantingly** ADV [ɪnˈtʃɑːntɪŋ, -lɪ] bezaubernd, entzückend

enchantment [ɪnˈtʃɑːntmənt] N **a** (= *delight*) Entzücken *nt* **b** (= *charm*) Zauber *m*

enchantress [ɪnˈtʃɑːntrɪs] N Zauberin *f*; (= *enchanting woman*) bezaubernde Frau

encipher [ɪnˈsaɪfə] VT chiffrieren

encircle [ɪnˈsɜːkl] VT (= *surround*) umgeben, umfassen; (*belt*) umschließen, umfassen; (*troops*) einkreisen, umfassen; *building* umstellen; **his arm ~d her waist** er hielt ihre Taille umfasst; **the house was ~d by trees** das Haus ist von Bäumen umstanden

encirclement [ɪnˈsɜːklmənt] N (*Mil*) Einkreisung *f*, Umfassung *f*; (*in a valley*) Einkesselung *f*; (*of building*) Umstellung *f*

encircling [ɪnˈsɜːklɪŋ] **N** (*Mil*) Umfassung *f*, Einkreisen *nt*; (*in valley*) Einkesseln *nt*; (*of building*) Umstellung *f* **ADJ** *walls etc* umgebend; *hills, forest* umliegend (*liter*); *gloom* allumfassend; ~ **war** Einkesselungskrieg *m*; ~ **movement** (*Mil*) Einkreisungs- or Umfassungsmanöver *nt*

enc(l) *abbr of* **enclosure(s)** Anl.

enclave [ˈenkleɪv] N Enklave *f*

enclitic [ɪnˈklɪtɪk] N Enklitikon *nt*

enclose [ɪnˈkləʊz] **☉** 20.2, 20.3, 20.7, 21.1 VT **a** (= *shut in*) einschließen; (= *surround*) umgeben; (*with fence etc*) *ground* einzäunen, einfrieden (*geh*) **b** (*in a parcel, envelope*) beilegen (*in, with dat*), beifügen (*in, with dat*); **to ~ sth in a letter** einem Brief etw beilegen; **I am enclosing the original with the translation** anbei die Übersetzung sowie den Originaltext; **I ~d your letter with mine** ich habe Ihren Brief mit meinem mitgeschickt

enclosed [ɪnˈkləʊzd] ADJ **a** (= *confined*) *space, area* geschlossen; *garden* abgeschlossen, eingefriedet (*geh*); *waters* von Land umschlossen **b** (*in letter, parcel*) *form, cheque, photo, details* beiliegend; ~ **with** or **in the letter** dem Brief beigelegt; **a phot was ~ in the letter** dem Brief lag ein Foto bei; **please find ~ a cheque for the sum of £25** (*Brit*) or **a check for the sum of 25 dollars** (*US*) in der Anlage or beiliegend finden Sie einen Scheck über £ 25/25 dollars **c** (=

separate, sheltered) existence behütet; *(community* geschlossen

enclosed order N *(Rel)* geschlossener Orden

enclosure [ɪnˈkləʊʒəʳ] N **a** *(= ground enclosed)* eingezäuntes Grundstück or Feld, Einfriedung f; *(for animals)* Gehege nt; **the ~** *(on racecourse)* der Zuschauerbereich **b** *(act)* Einzäunung f, Einfried(ig)ung f *(geh)* **c** *(= fence etc)* Umzäunung f; **~ wall** Umfassungsmauer f **d** *(= document etc enclosed)* Anlage f

encode [ɪnˈkəʊd] VT *(also Comput)* kodieren

encoder [ɪnˈkəʊdəʳ] N *(also Comput)* Kodierer m, Kodiergerät nt

encomium [ɪnˈkəʊmɪəm] N *(form)* Lobrede f, Laudatio f *(geh)*

encompass [ɪnˈkʌmpəs] VT **a** *(liter, = surround)* umfassen *(by* mit) **b** *(= include)* umfassen **c** *(liter, = bring about)* downfall herbeiführen

encore [ˈɒŋkɔːʳ] INTERJ da capo, Zugabe N Zugabe f, Dakapo nt, Dacapo nt; **to call for/give an ~** eine Zugabe verlangen/geben VT *piece* als Zugabe verlangen; *artiste* um eine Zugabe bitten VI eine Zugabe geben

encounter [ɪnˈkaʊntəʳ] VT *enemy, opposition* treffen or stoßen auf (+acc); *difficulties, resistance* stoßen auf (+acc); *danger* geraten in (+acc); *(liter) person* begegnen (+dat), treffen; **to ~ enemy fire** unter feindlichen Beschuss geraten N Begegnung f, Treffen nt; *(in battle)* Zusammenstoß m; **chance ~** zufällige Begegnung; **sexual ~** sexuelle Erfahrung; **close ~** *(Space, = near miss)* Beinahezusammenstoß m; *(with aliens)* unheimliche Begegnung

encounter group N *(Psych)* Selbsterfahrungsgruppe f

encourage [ɪnˈkʌrɪdʒ] VT *person* ermutigen, ermuntern; *(= motivate)* anregen; *(= give confidence)* Mut machen (+dat), ermutigen; *arts, industry, projects, investments* fördern; *(Sport) team, competitor* anfeuern, anspornen; *bad habits* unterstützen; **~ participation** zum Mitmachen anregen; **we don't want to ~ suspicion** wir wollen keinen Verdacht erregen; **to be ~d by sth** durch etw neuen Mut schöpfen; **he's lazy enough as it is, please don't ~ him** er ist schon faul genug, bitte ermuntern or unterstützen Sie ihn nicht noch; **that will ~ bad habits** das wird zu schlechten Gewohnheiten führen; **to ~ sb to do sth** jdn ermutigen or ermuntern, etw zu tun; **you'll only ~ him to think ...** er wird dann nur noch eher glauben, dass ...; **this ~s me to think that maybe ...** das lässt mich vermuten, dass vielleicht ...

encouragement [ɪnˈkʌrɪdʒmənt] N Ermutigung f, Ermunterung f; *(= motivation)* Anregung f; *(= support)* Unterstützung f, Förderung f; **to give sb (a lot of) ~** jdn (sehr) ermuntern; **he doesn't need any ~** ihn braucht man nicht zu ermuntern; **an ~ to buy** ein Kaufanreiz m

encouraging [ɪnˈkʌrɪdʒɪŋ] ADJ ermutigend; **I found him very ~** er hat mir sehr viel Mut gemacht

encouragingly [ɪnˈkʌrɪdʒɪŋlɪ] ADV *smile, nod, say, speak* ermutigend; *(+adj)* erfreulich; *(introducing sentence)* erfreulicherweise; **more/less ~, they ...** es ist ermutigender/weniger ermutigend, dass sie ...

encroach [ɪnˈkrəʊtʃ] VI **to ~ (up)on** *(land)* vordringen in (+acc); *sphere, rights* eingreifen in (+acc); *privileges* übergreifen auf (+acc); *time* in Anspruch nehmen

encroachment [ɪnˈkrəʊtʃmənt] N *(on land)* Vordringen nt; *(on rights)* Eingriff m; *(on privileges)* Übergriff m; *(on time)* Beanspruchung f

encrust [ɪnˈkrʌst] VT *(fig, with pearls)* besetzen; **~ed with earth/cement** erd-/zementverkrustet; **a jewel-encrusted brooch** eine juwelenbesetzte Brosche; **~ed with ice** vereist

encrustation [ɪnkrʌsˈteɪʃən] N Kruste f, Verkrustung f; *(fig, with diamonds, pearls, lace)* Besatz m; *(with ice etc)* Überzug m

encrypt [ɪnˈkrɪpt] VT *(Comput, Telec, TV)* verschlüsseln

encryption [ɪnˈkrɪpʃən] N *(Comput, Telec, TV)* Verschlüsselung f

encumber [ɪnˈkʌmbəʳ] VT *beladen;* *(with debts)* belasten; **~ed property** *(Fin)* belasteter Grundbesitz

encumbrance [ɪnˈkʌmbrəns] N *(also Jur)* Belastung f; *(person)* Last f; **to be an ~ to sb** *(luggage)* jdn behindern; *(person)* eine Last für jdn sein; *(dependent, responsibility)* eine Belastung für jdn sein

encyclical [ɪnˈsɪklɪkəl] N Enzyklika f

encyclop(a)edia [ɪnˌsaɪklə(ʊ)ˈpiːdɪə] N Lexikon nt, Enzyklopädie f

encyclop(a)edic [ɪnˌsaɪklə(ʊ)ˈpiːdɪk] ADJ enzyklopädisch

end [end] N **a** Ende nt; *(of finger)* Spitze f; **at the ~ of the procession** am Schluss or Ende der Prozession; **our house is the fourth from the ~** unser Haus ist das viertletzte; **to the ~s of the earth** bis ans Ende der Welt; **from ~ to ~** von einem Ende zum anderen; **who'll meet you at the ~?** wer holt dich ab, wenn du ankommst?; **Lisa's on the other ~ (of the phone)** Lisa ist am Telefon; **to keep one's ~ up** *(inf, = stay cheerful)* sich nicht unterkriegen lassen *(inf);* *(= do one's share)* das seine or Seine tun; **to stand on ~** *(barrel, box etc)* hochkant stehen; *(hair)* zu Berge stehen; **for hours on ~** stundenlang ununterbrochen; **the ships collided ~ on** *(Brit)* die Schiffe fuhren aufeinander auf; **~ to ~** mit den Enden aneinander; **to change ~s** *(Sport)* die Seiten wechseln; **to make (both) ~s meet** *(fig)* zurechtkommen *(inf),* sich über Wasser halten; **to see no further than the ~ of one's nose** nicht weiter sehen als seine Nase (reicht); **how are things at your ~?** wie sieht es bei Ihnen aus?; **we've got some problems at this ~** wir haben hier or bei uns einige Probleme; **to have one's ~ away** *(Brit sl)* kräftig durchziehen *(sl)* → **rope, tether b** *(= remnant, of rope)* Ende nt, Rest m; *(of candle, cigarette)* Stummel m; **just a few odd ~s left** nur noch ein paar Reste

c *(= conclusion)* Ende nt; **at the ~** schließlich; **the ~ of the month** das Monatsende; **at/toward(s) the ~ of December** Ende/gegen Ende Dezember; **at the ~ of (the) winter/the war** am Ende des Winters/des Krieges; **at the ~ of the opera/the book** am Schluss der Oper/des Buches; **at the ~ of three weeks** nach drei Wochen; **they'll be paid at the ~ of the job** sie werden bezahlt, wenn sie mit der Arbeit fertig sind; **at the ~ of the day** *(fig)* letzten Endes, schließlich und endlich; **until or to the ~ of time** bis ans Ende aller Tage; **is there no ~ to this?** hört das denn nie auf?; **as far as I'm concerned, that's the ~ of the matter!** für mich ist die Sache erledigt; **we shall never hear the ~ of it** das werden wir noch lange zu hören kriegen; **to be at an ~** zu Ende sein; **to be at the ~ of one's patience/strength** mit seiner Geduld/seinen Kräften am Ende sein; **to watch a film to the ~** einen Film bis zu Ende ansehen; **to read a book to the ~** ein Buch bis zu Ende lesen; **that's the ~ of him** er ist erledigt or fertig *(inf);* **that's the ~ of that** das ist damit erledigt; **to bring to an ~** zu Ende bringen, beenden; *relations* ein Ende setzen (+dat), beenden; **to come to an ~** zu Ende gehen; **to get to the ~ of the road/book** ans Ende der Straße/zum Schluss des Buches kommen; **this is the ~ of the road for the government** das bedeutet das Ende für die Regierung; **at the ~ of the road** or **line many businesses will go bankrupt** letzten Endes werden viele Firmen Pleite machen *(inf);* **in the ~** schließlich, zum Schluss; **to put an ~ to sth** einer Sache *(dat)* ein Ende setzen; **to come to a bad ~** ein böses Ende nehmen; **to meet one's ~** den Tod finden; **he met a violent ~** er starb einen gewaltsamen Tod; **were you with him at the ~?** warst du zum Schluss or am Ende bei ihm?

d *(inf phrases)* **we met no ~ of famous people** *(esp Brit)* wir trafen viele berühmte Leute; **to think no ~ of sb** *(esp Brit)* große Stücke auf jdn

halten; **it pleased her no ~** *(esp Brit)* das hat ihr maßlos or irrsinnig *(inf)* gefallen; **you're the ~** *(Brit)* *(= annoying)* du bist der letzte Mensch *(inf);* *(= funny)* du bist zum Schreien *(inf)*

e *(= purpose)* Ziel nt, Zweck m; **with this ~ in view** mit diesem Ziel vor Augen; **to what ~?** *(form)* zu welchem Zweck?; **an ~ in itself** Selbstzweck no art; **the ~ justifies the means** *(prov)* der Zweck heiligt die Mittel *(prov)*

ADJ attr letzte(r, s); **the ~ house** das Endhaus, das letzte Haus

VT beenden; *speech, one's days also* beschließen; **the novel to ~ all novels** der größte Roman aller Zeiten; **the deal to ~ all deals** das beste Geschäft aller Zeiten; **to ~ it all** *(= commit suicide)* Schluss machen

VI enden; **we'll have to ~ soon** wir müssen bald Schluss machen; **we ~ed with a song** zum Schluss sangen wir ein Lied; **to be ~ing** zu Ende gehen; **to ~ by doing sth** schließlich etw tun; **where's it all going to ~?** wo soll das nur hinführen?; **to ~ in an "s"** auf „s" enden; **each leg ~s in a claw** jedes Bein läuft in eine Klaue aus; **an argument which ~ed in a fight** ein Streit, der mit einer Schlägerei endete

▶ **end off** VT sep abschließen, beschließen

▶ **end up** VI enden, landen *(inf);* **to end up doing sth** schließlich etw tun; **to end up (as) a lawyer** schließlich Rechtsanwalt werden; **to end up (as) an alcoholic** als Alkoholiker enden; **to end up a criminal** schließlich zum Verbrecher werden; **we ended up at Joe's** wir waren or landeten *(inf)* schließlich bei Joe; **you'll end up in trouble** Sie werden noch Ärger bekommen

endanger [ɪnˈdeɪndʒəʳ] VT gefährden

endangered [ɪnˈdeɪndʒəd] ADJ *species, animal, plant* vom Aussterben bedroht

end consumer N End- or Letztverbraucher(in) m(f)

endear [ɪnˈdɪəʳ] VT beliebt machen *(to* bei); **to ~ oneself to sb** sich bei jdm beliebt machen

endearing [ɪnˈdɪərɪŋ] ADJ *person, quality* liebenswert; *habit, trait, manner* nett, liebenswert; *smile* gewinnend

endearingly [ɪnˈdɪərɪŋlɪ] ADV liebenswert; *smile* gewinnend

endearment [ɪnˈdɪəmənt] N **term of ~** Kosename m, Kosewort nt; **words of ~** liebe Worte pl

endeavour, *(US)* **endeavor** [ɪnˈdevəʳ] N *(= attempt)* Anstrengung f, Bemühung f; *(liter, = striving)* (Be)streben nt no pl *(geh);* **all human ~** das gesamte Streben des Menschen; **to make an ~ to do sth** sich nach Kräften bemühen, etw zu tun; **in an ~ to please** um ihr eine Freude zu machen VT sich anstrengen, sich bemühen, bestrebt sein *(geh)*

endemic [enˈdemɪk] ADJ ·(lit, fig) endemisch; **~ to** endemisch in *(dat);* **petty embezzling seems to be ~ here** kleine Unterschlagungen scheinen hier eine Krankheit zu sein

endgame [ˈendgeɪm] N Endspiel nt

ending [ˈendɪŋ] N *(of story, book, events)* Ausgang m; *(of day)* Abschluss m; *(= last part)* Ende nt, Schluss m; *(of word)* Endung f; **a story with a happy ~** eine Geschichte mit einem Happy End or Happyend; **the dispute had a happy ~** der Streit ging gut aus

endive [ˈendaɪv] N *(Winter)*endivie f, Endiviensalat m

endless [ˈendlɪs] ADJ **a** *(= interminable, unlimited)* period, stream, series, talk, patience endlos; *variety* unendlich; *supply* unbegrenzt; **an ~ round of meetings** Besprechungen, die kein Ende nehmen wollen; **the list is ~** die Liste nimmt kein Ende **b** *(= countless)* meetings, arguments, questions, problems unzählig; **the possibilities are ~** es gibt unendlich viele Möglichkeiten **c** *(= continuous)* road, stretch endlos (lang); *queue* endlos lang; *expanse* unendlich; *desert, forest* endlos, unendlich

endlessly [ˈendlɪslɪ] ADV **a** *(= without stopping)* talk, discuss, argue endlos; *listen, play, sit* ewig **b** *(= again and again)* repeat, recycle endlos, immer wieder `c` (= *without limit*) *stretch* endlos; *fascinating, curious, long* unendlich

endocrine ['endəʊkraɪn] ADJ endokrin; ~ **gland** endokrine Drüse

endocrinologist [ˌendəʊkraɪ'nɒlədʒɪst] N Endokrinologe m, Endokrinologin f

endocrinology [ˌendəʊkraɪ'nɒlədʒɪ] N Endokrinologie f

endomorph ['endəʊmɔːf] N Pykniker(in) m(f)

endomorphic ['endəʊmɔːfɪk] ADJ pyknisch

endorphin [ˌen'dɔːfɪn] N Endorphin nt

endorse [ɪn'dɔːs] **⊘** 11.1 VT `a` *document, cheque* auf der Rückseite unterzeichnen, indossieren `b` (*Brit, Jur*) *driving licence* eine Strafe vermerken auf (+*dat*); **I had my licence ~d** ich bekam einen Strafvermerk auf meinem Führerschein `c` (= *approve*) billigen, unterschreiben (*inf*); *product, company* empfehlen; **I ~ that** dem stimme ich zu, dem pflichte ich bei

endorsee [ɪnˌdɔː'siː] N (*Fin*) Indossatar m

endorsement [ɪn'dɔːsmənt] N `a` (*on cheque, bill of exchange*) Indossament nt; (*on policy*) Zusatz m, Nachtrag m `b` (*Brit, Jur, on driving licence*) Strafvermerk m auf dem Führerschein `c` (*of opinion*) Billigung f; (*for product, company*) Empfehlung f; **the committee's ~ of the idea** die Billigung der Idee durch das Komitee

endorser [ɪn'dɔːsə'] N (*Fin*) Indossar m

endoscope ['endəʊskəʊp] N Endoskop nt

endoscopy [ˌen'dɒskəpɪ] N Endoskopie f

endow [ɪn'daʊ] VT `a` *institution, church* eine Stiftung machen an (+*acc*); (*Univ, Sch*) *prize, chair* stiften; **an ~ed school** *eine mit Stiftungsgeldern gebaute und finanzierte Schule* `b` (*fig*) *usu pass* **to ~ sb with sth** jdm etw geben or schenken; **to be ~ed with a natural talent for singing** ein sängerisches Naturtalent sein; **the poor lad is not very well ~ed** (*inf: with intelligence*) mit dem armen Bengel ist nicht viel los; **she's well ~ed** (*hum*) sie ist von der Natur reichlich ausgestattet (worden)

endowment [ɪn'daʊmənt] N `a` Stiftung f; **~s** Stiftungsgelder pl `b` (= *natural talent etc*) Begabung f; **his/her physical ~s** (*hum*) womit ihn/sie die Natur ausgestattet hat

endowment: endowment assurance N Versicherung f auf den Erlebensfall, Erlebensversicherung f; **endowment mortgage** N Hypothek f mit Lebensversicherung; **endowment policy** N Lebensversicherungspolice f

end: endpapers PL Vorsatzblätter pl; **end product** N Endprodukt nt; (*fig*) Produkt nt; **end result** N Endergebnis nt; **end table** N (*for couch*) kleiner Tisch; **end terrace** N (*Brit*) Reiheneckhaus nt

endue [ɪn'djuː] VT versehen, begaben (*liter*); **to be ~d with sth** über etw (*acc*) verfügen, mit etw begabt sein

endurable [ɪn'djʊərəbl] ADJ erträglich

endurance [ɪn'djʊərəns] N Durchhaltevermögen nt; **to have great powers of ~** großes Durchhaltevermögen haben; **what a feat of ~** welche Ausdauer!; **he was tried beyond ~** er wurde über die Maßen gereizt; **his suffering was beyond ~** sein Leiden war unerträglich

endurance: endurance race N (*Sport*) Rennen, bei dem es vor allem auf die Ausdauer ankommt; **endurance test** N Belastungsprobe f; (*fig*) Durchhaltetest m

endure [ɪn'djʊə'] VT `a` (= *undergo*) *pain, insults, losses, tribulations, hardship* erleiden `b` (= *put up with*) ertragen; *agony* aushalten, ertragen; **it was more than I could ~** ich konnte es nicht mehr ertragen; **she can't ~ being laughed at** sie kann es nicht vertragen or haben (*inf*), wenn man über sie lacht VI bestehen; (*work, memories also*) Bestand haben

enduring [ɪn'djʊərɪŋ] ADJ dauerhaft; *love, belief* beständig, dauerhaft; *popularity* bleibend

end user N (*esp Comput*) Endbenutzer m

endways ['endweɪz], **endwise** ['endwaɪz] ADV mit dem Ende nach vorne or zuerst; (= *end to*

---

end) mit den Enden aneinander; **put it ~ on** legen Sie es mit dem Ende or der Spitze an

ENE *abbr of* **east-north-east** ONO

enema ['enɪmə] N Klistier nt, Einlauf m; (= *syringe*) Klistierspritze f

enemy ['enəmɪ] **N** (*lit, fig*) Feind(in) m(f); **to make enemies** sich (*dat*) Feinde machen or schaffen; **to make an ~ of sb** sich (*dat*) jdn zum Feind(e) machen; **he is his own worst ~** er schadet sich (*dat*) selbst am meisten ADJ *attr* feindlich; *position, advance, morale* des Feindes; **destroyed by ~ action** vom Feind or durch Feindeinwirkung (*form*) zerstört

enemy-occupied [ˌenəmɪ'ɒkjupaɪd] N vom Feind besetzt

energetic [ˌenə'dʒetɪk] ADJ `a` *person* (= *enthusiastic, lively*) energiegeladen; (= *active*) aktiv; **to be more/very ~** mehr/viel Energie haben; **if I'm feeling ~** wenn ich die Energie habe `b` *activity* (= *full of action*) energiegeladen; (= *strenuous*) anstrengend; *performance* schwungvoll; *campaign* aktiv; *action, effort* energisch, entschlossen; **~ sport** Bewegungssport m; **do something ~** machen Sie etwas Aktives

energetically [ˌenə'dʒetɪkəlɪ] ADV `a` *deny, protest, campaign, work* energisch `b` *run, dance, jump* voller Energie; **she nodded her head ~** sie nickte nachdrücklich

energize ['enədʒaɪz] VT *rocket motor, particle* Antrieb geben (+*dat*); (*Elec*) unter Strom setzen; (*fig*) *person* neue Energie geben (+*dat*); *economy* ankurbeln; **to be ~d by sth** (*fig*) von etw in Schwung gebracht werden

energy ['enədʒɪ] N Energie f; **he put his speech over with a lot of ~** er hielt seine Rede mit viel Schwung; **chocolate gives you ~** Schokolade gibt neue Energie; **to concentrate one's energies on doing sth** seine ganze Kraft dafür aufbieten, etw zu tun; **to devote all one's energies to sth** seine ganze Energie or Kraft für etw einsetzen; **I haven't the ~** mir fehlt die Energie dazu; **to conserve one's energies** mit seinen Kräften haushalten or Haus halten or sparsam umgehen; **to save one's ~ for sth** seine Kräfte für etw aufsparen

energy: energy balance N (*of body*) Energiehaushalt m; **energy conservation** N Energieeinsparung f; **energy crisis** N Energiekrise f; **energy efficiency** N Energieeffizienz f; **energy-efficient** ADJ energieeffizient; **energy-giving** ADJ *food* Energie spendend; **energy-intensive** ADJ energieintensiv; **energy-saving** ADJ Energie sparend; **~ measures** Energiesparmaßnahmen pl; **energy supplies** PL Energievorräte pl

enervate ['enəveɪt] VT (*physically*) entkräften, schwächen; (*mentally*) entnerven, enervieren (*geh*)

enervating ['enəveɪtɪŋ] ADJ strapazierend

enfant terrible [ɒnfɒnte'riːblə] N *pl* **-s -s** Enfant terrible nt

enfeeble [ɪn'fiːbl] VT schwächen; **~d by** geschwächt durch

enfeeblement [ɪn'fiːblmənt] N Schwächung f

enfold [ɪn'fəʊld] VT einhüllen (*in* in +*acc*); **to ~ sb in one's arms** jdn in die Arme schließen

enforce [ɪn'fɔːs] VT `a` durchführen, Geltung verschaffen (+*dat*); *one's claims, rights* geltend machen; *discipline* sorgen für, schaffen; *decision, policy, ban, ruling* durchsetzen; *measures* durchführen; *sanctions* verhängen; **the police ~ the law** die Polizei sorgt für die Einhaltung der Gesetze; **to ~ silence/obedience** sich (*dat*) Ruhe/Gehorsam verschaffen; **to ~ sth (up)on sb** jdm etw aufzwingen `b` (*rare, = give force to*) *demand* Nachdruck verschaffen (+*dat*); *argument* stützen, untermauern

enforceable [ɪn'fɔːsəbl] ADJ durchsetzbar

enforcement [ɪn'fɔːsmənt] N (*of law, policy, ruling*) Durchführung f; (*of obedience*) Erzwingung f

enfranchise [ɪn'fræntʃaɪz] VT `a` (= *give vote to*) das Wahlrecht geben or erteilen (+*dat*); **to be**

~d wahlberechtigt sein `b` (= *set free*) *slaves* freilassen

enfranchisement [ɪn'fræntʃɪzmənt] N `a` (*Pol*) Erteilung f des Wahlrechts; **after the ~ of women** nachdem die Frauen das Wahlrecht erhalten hatten `b` (*of slave*) Freilassung f

engage [ɪn'geɪdʒ] VT `a` *servant, workers* anstellen, einstellen; *singer, performer* engagieren; *lawyer* sich (*dat*) nehmen; **to ~ the services of sb** jdn anstellen/engagieren; *of lawyer* sich (*dat*) jdn nehmen `b` *room* mieten, sich (*dat*) nehmen `c` *attention, interest* in Anspruch nehmen; **to ~ sb in conversation** jdn in ein Gespräch verwickeln `d` **to ~ oneself to do sth** (*form*) sich verpflichten, etw zu tun `e` *the enemy* angreifen, den Kampf eröffnen gegen `f` (*Tech*) *gear wheels* ineinander greifen lassen; **to ~ a gear** (*Aut*) einen Gang einlegen; **to ~ the clutch** (ein)kuppeln; **to ~ four-wheel drive** den Allradantrieb zuschalten
VI `a` (*form, = promise*) sich verpflichten (*to do* zu tun) `b` (*gear wheels*) ineinander greifen; (*clutch*) fassen `c` **to ~ in sth** sich in etw (*dat*) beteiligen; **to ~ in conversation** sich unterhalten; **to ~ in politics** sich politisch betätigen; **to ~ with sb/sth** mit jdm/etw in Beziehung treten; **to ~ in competition with sb** in Wettbewerb mit jdm treten `d` (*Mil*) angreifen; **to ~ with the enemy** den Feind angreifen

engaged [ɪn'geɪdʒd] **⊘** 24.2, 27.3 ADJ `a` (= *betrothed*) **~ (to be married)** verlobt (*to* mit); **the couple** die Verlobten pl; **to get** or **become ~ (to sb)** sich (mit jdm) verloben `b` *toilet, seat, taxi* besetzt; (*Brit Telec*) *line, number, telephone* besetzt `c` (*form, = busy*) *person* beschäftigt; **to be otherwise ~** (*at future time*) etwas anderes vorhaben; (*at present*) anderweitig beschäftigt sein; **to be ~ in sth** mit etw beschäftigt sein; *in criminal activities* in etw (*acc*) verwickelt sein; **the parties in the dispute** die am Streit beteiligten Parteien; **to be ~ in doing sth** dabei sein, etw zu tun; **we are actively ~ in trying to find a solution** wir bemühen uns aktiv um eine Lösung; **to be ~ on sth** mit etw befasst or beschäftigt sein

engaged tone N (*Telec*) Besetztzeichen nt

engagement [ɪn'geɪdʒmənt] **⊘** 24.2, 25.2 N `a` (= *appointment*) Verabredung f; (*of actor etc*) Engagement nt; **public/social ~s** öffentliche/gesellschaftliche Verpflichtungen pl; **a dinner ~** eine Verabredung zum Essen `b` (= *betrothal*) Verlobung f `c` (*form, = undertaking*) Verpflichtung f `d` (*Mil*) Gefecht nt, Kampf m `e` (*of parts of machine*) Ineinandergreifen nt

engagement: engagement diary N Terminkalender m; **engagement ring** N Verlobungsring m

engaging [ɪn'geɪdʒɪŋ] ADJ *person* angenehm; *smile* gewinnend; *character, personality* einnehmend; *manner* einnehmend, angenehm; **he is such an ~ character** er hat so ein einnehmendes Wesen

en garde [ɒn'gɑːd] INTERJ en garde

engender [ɪn'dʒendə'] VT (*fig*) erzeugen

engenderment [ɪn'dʒendəmənt] N Erzeugung f

engine ['endʒɪn] N `a` Maschine f; (*of car, plane etc*) Motor m; (*of ship*) Maschine f `b` (*Rail*) Lokomotive f, Lok f `c` (*Comput: = search engine*) Suchmaschine f

engine: engine block N Motorblock m; **engine compartment** N Motorraum m

-engined [-'endʒɪnd] ADJ *suf* -motorig; **single-/twin-engined** ein-/zweimotorig; **front-/rear-/diesel-engined** mit Front-/Heck-/Dieselmotor

engine driver N (*Brit*) Lok(omotiv)führer(in) m(f)

engineer [ˌendʒɪ'nɪə'] **N** `a` (*Tech*) Techniker(in) m(f); (*with university degree etc*) Ingenieur(in) m(f); **the Engineers** (*Mil*) die Pioniere pl `b`

(*Naut, on merchant ships*) Maschinist(in) *m(f)*; (*in Navy*) (Schiffs)ingenieur(in) *m(f)* **c** (*US, Rail*) Lokführer(in) *m(f)* **d** (*fig, of scheme*) Arrangeur(in) *m(f)* **VT a** (*Tech*) konstruieren **b** (*fig*) *election, campaign, coup* organisieren; *downfall, plot* arrangieren, einfädeln; *success, victory* in die Wege leiten; (*Sport*) *goal* einfädeln; **to ~ a scheme** einen Plan aushecken

engineering [ˌendʒɪˈnɪərɪŋ] N **a** (*Tech*) Technik *f*; (= *mechanical engineering*) Maschinenbau *m*; (= *engineering profession*) Ingenieurwesen *nt*; **the ~ of the building** die Konstruktion des Gebäudes; **he's in ~** er ist Ingenieur; **a brilliant piece of ~** eine Meisterkonstruktion; **a triumph of ~** ein Triumph *m* der Technik **b** (*fig, of election, campaign, coup*) Organisation *f*; (*of downfall, plot*) Arrangement *nt*; (= *manoeuvring*) Arrangements *pl*

engineering: engineering department N technische Abteilung; (*mechanical*) Abteilung *f* für Maschinenbau; **engineering faculty** N (*Univ*) Fakultät *f* für Maschinenbau; **engineering industries** PL Maschinenindustrie *f*; **engineering worker** N Techniker(in) *m(f)*; **engineering works** N *sing or pl* Maschinenfabrik *f*

engineer officer N technischer Offizier, technische Offizierin

engine: engine mountings PL Motoraufhängung *f*; **engine oil** N Motoröl *nt*; **engine room** N (*Naut*) Maschinenraum *m*; **engine shed** N (*Brit*) Lokomotivschuppen *m*

England [ˈɪŋɡlənd] **N** England *nt* **ADJ** *attr* **the ~ team** die englische Mannschaft

English [ˈɪŋɡlɪʃ] **ADJ** englisch; **he is ~** er ist Engländer; **he's an ~ teacher** (*teaching English*) er ist Englischlehrer; (*English by nationality*) er ist ein englischer Lehrer; **~ translator** englischer Übersetzer, englische Übersetzerin; (*foreign*) Übersetzer(in) *m(f)* für Englisch; **(full) ~ breakfast** englisches Frühstück **N a the ~** *pl* die Engländer *pl* **b** (*Ling*) Englisch *nt*; (= *the English language in general, English grammar*) Englisch *nt*, das Englische; (*as university subject*) Anglistik *f*; **can you speak ~?** können Sie Englisch?; **he doesn't speak ~** er spricht kein Englisch; **"English spoken"** „hier wird Englisch gesprochen"; **they were speaking ~** sie unterhielten sich auf Englisch; **he speaks very good ~** er spricht ein sehr gutes Englisch; **in ~** auf *or* in (*inf*) Englisch; **in good/modern-day ~** in gutem/modernem Englisch; **to translate sth into/from ~** etw ins Englische/aus dem Englischen übersetzen; **is that ~?** (= *correct*) ist das richtig?; **that's not ~** das ist verkehrt, das ist falsches Englisch; **~/teaching ~ as a foreign language** (*abbr* **EFL/TEFL**) Englisch als Fremdsprache; **the King's/Queen's ~** die englische Hochsprache → **old English, plain ADJ b**

English: English Channel N Ärmelkanal *m*; **English flute** N (*Mus*) Blockflöte *f*; **English Heritage** N (*Brit*) Organisation für die Pflege von Denkmälern und historischen Bauwerken in England; **English horn** N (*Mus*: = *cor anglais*) Englischhorn *nt*; **Englishman** N Engländer *m*; **an ~'s home is his castle** (*Prov*) für den Engländer ist sein Haus seine Burg; **English muffin** N (*US, Cook*) flaches Milchbrötchen, das meist getoastet gegessen wird; **English speaker** N Englischsprachige(r) *mf*; **English-speaking** ADJ englischsprachig; **Englishwoman** N Engländerin *f*

Eng Lit [ˈɪŋˈlɪt] *abbr of* **English Literature** engl. Lit.

engorged [ɪnˈɡɔːdʒd] ADJ angeschwollen; **sth is ~ with blood** in etw (*dat*) staut sich das Blut; **the blood vessels that allow the penis to become ~** die Blutgefäße, die den Penis anschwellen lassen

engraft [ɪnˈɡrɑːft] VT **a** (*Bot*) aufpfropfen (*into, on, upon* auf +*acc*); **b** (*fig geh*) *principles* verankern (*into* in +*dat*)

engrave [ɪnˈɡreɪv] VT *glass, metal, stone, wood* gravieren; *design, letter, names* eingravieren; (*fig*) einprägen

engraved [ɪnˈɡreɪvd] ADJ *glass, metal, plaque* graviert; *design, letter, name* eingraviert; **~ plates** (*Typ*) (Kupfer)stiche *pl*; **beautifully ~ with flowers** mit einem hübschen eingravierten Blumenmuster; **her name is ~ on my heart** ich werde ihren Namen immer im Herzen bewahren; **it is ~ on my memory** es hat sich mir unauslöschlich eingeprägt

engraver [ɪnˈɡreɪvə(r)] N Graveur(in) *m(f)*; (*on stone*) Steinhauer(in) *m(f)*; (*on wood*) Holzschneider(in) *m(f)*

engraving [ɪnˈɡreɪvɪŋ] N **a** (= *process*) Gravieren *nt*; (*on rock, stone*) Einmeißeln *nt*; (*on wood*) Einschnitzen *nt*, Einkerben *nt*; **~ needle** Graviernadel *f* **b** (= *copy*) (Kupfer-/Stahl)stich *m*; (*from wood*) Holzschnitt *m*; (= *design*) Gravierung *f*; (*on wood, stone*) eingemeißelte Verzierung/Schrift *etc*

engross [ɪnˈɡrəʊs] VT *person, attention* gefangen nehmen; **to become ~ed in one's book/one's work** sich in sein Buch/seine Arbeit vertiefen; **to be ~ed in one's (own) thoughts/in conversation** in Gedanken/ins Gespräch vertieft sein

engrossing [ɪnˈɡrəʊsɪŋ] ADJ fesselnd

engulf [ɪnˈɡʌlf] VT verschlingen; (*fig: feeling, pain*) übermannen; **to be ~ed by flames** in Flammen stehen

enhance [ɪnˈhɑːns] VT verbessern; *price, value, attraction, chances* erhöhen

enigma [ɪˈnɪɡmə] N Rätsel *nt*

enigmatic [ˌenɪɡˈmætɪk] ADJ rätselhaft

enigmatically [ˌenɪɡˈmætɪkəlɪ] ADV rätselhaft; **he replied somewhat ~** er gab eine etwas rätselhafte Antwort; **he describes himself, ~, as an old man** er beschreibt sich rätselhafterweise als einen alten Mann

enjambement [ɪnˈdʒæmmənt] N (*Poet*) Enjambement *nt*

enjoin [ɪnˈdʒɔɪn] VT (*form*) **to ~ sb to silence/caution, to ~ silence/caution on sb** jdn eindringlich zur Ruhe/zur Vorsicht mahnen; **to ~ on sb the need for sth** jdm die Notwendigkeit einer Sache eindringlich vor Augen stellen; **to ~ sb to do sth/from doing sth** jdn eindringlich mahnen, etw zu tun/etw nicht zu tun

enjoy [ɪnˈdʒɔɪ] ♦ 7.2 **VT a** (= *take pleasure in*) genießen; **he ~s swimming/reading** er schwimmt/liest gern, Lesen/Schwimmen macht ihm Spaß; **he ~s being rude to people** es macht ihm Spaß *or* ihm macht es Spaß, zu Leuten unhöflich zu sein; **he ~ed writing the book** es hat ihm Freude gemacht, das Buch zu schreiben; **I've ~ed talking to you** es war mir eine Freude, mit Ihnen zu unterhalten, es war nett, sich mit Ihnen zu unterhalten; **I ~ed the book/concert** das Buch/Konzert hat mir gefallen; **he ~ed the meal** das Essen hat

ihm gut geschmeckt; **I ~ your company/the company of women** ich bin gerne mit Ihnen/mit Frauen zusammen; **I didn't ~ it at all** es hat mir überhaupt keinen Spaß gemacht; **the author didn't mean his book to be ~ed** dem Verfasser ging es nicht darum, dass man an seinem Buch Spaß *or* Vergnügen haben sollte; **to ~ life** das Leben genießen; **I ~ed a very pleasant weekend in the country** ich habe ein sehr angenehmes Wochenende auf dem Land verbracht; **did you ~ your meal?** hat Ihnen das Essen gefallen?; **I really ~ed my meal** ich habe das Essen richtig genossen **b** *rights, freedom, advantages, respect, confidence* genießen; *income, success* haben; *good health, reputation, support* sich erfreuen (+*gen*) (*geh*) **VR to ~ oneself** sich amüsieren; **~ yourself!** viel Spaß!, amüsieren Sie sich gut!

enjoyable [ɪnˈdʒɔɪəbl] ADJ nett; *film, book* unterhaltsam, nett; *evening, meal* angenehm

enjoyably [ɪnˈdʒɔɪəblɪ] ADV (= *pleasantly*) auf angenehme Art; (= *entertainingly*) unterhaltsam; (= *with enjoyment*) mit Vergnügen

enjoyment [ɪnˈdʒɔɪmənt] N **a** Vergnügen *nt*, Spaß *m* (*of an* +*dat*); **he got a lot of ~ from the book** das Buch machte ihm großen Spaß; **she gets a lot of ~ from reading** Lesen macht ihr großen Spaß *or* bringt ihr viel Freude **b** (*of rights, income, fortune*) Genuss *m*

enlarge [ɪnˈlɑːdʒ] **VT** vergrößern; *hole, field of knowledge* erweitern; *organ, pore* vergrößern, erweitern; *membership, majority also* erhöhen **VI a** sich vergrößern **b to ~ (up)on sth** auf etw (*acc*) näher eingehen

enlarged [ɪnˈlɑːdʒd] ADJ vergrößert; *organ, pore also, community* erweitert; **an ~ force** verstärkte Truppen *pl*; **an ~ print** (*Phot*) eine Vergrößerung; **~ edition** erweiterte Ausgabe

enlargement [ɪnˈlɑːdʒmənt] N **a** (*Phot*) Vergrößerung *f* **b** (= *process*) Vergrößerung *f*; (*of hole, field of knowledge*) Erweiterung *f*; (*Med: of organ*) Erweiterung *f*, Vergrößerung *f*; (*of membership, majority*) Erhöhung *f*

enlarger [ɪnˈlɑːdʒə(r)] N (*Phot*) Vergrößerungsapparat *m*

enlighten [ɪnˈlaɪtn] VT aufklären (*on, as to, about* über +*acc*); (*spiritually*) erleuchten; **let me ~ you** darf ich es Ihnen erklären?

enlightened [ɪnˈlaɪtnd] ADJ *person, society* aufgeklärt; (= *progressive*) *person, approach, policy* progressiv, fortschrittlich; **in this ~ age, in these ~ times** (*usu iro*) in diesem aufgeklärten Zeitalter

enlightening [ɪnˈlaɪtnɪŋ] ADJ aufschlussreich

enlightenment [ɪnˈlaɪtnmənt] N Aufklärung *f*; (*spiritual*) Erleuchtung *f*; **the Enlightenment** die Aufklärung; **the age of Enlightenment** das Zeitalter der Aufklärung

enlist [ɪnˈlɪst] **VI** (*Mil etc*) sich melden (*in* zu) **VT** *soldiers, recruits* einziehen; *supporters, collaborators* anwerben, gewinnen; *assistance, sympathy, support* gewinnen; **could I ~ your aid?** darf ich Sie um Hilfe bitten?; **I had to ~ his help** ich musste seine Hilfe in Anspruch nehmen

enlisted man [ɪnˈlɪstɪdˈmæn] *pl* **enlisted men** N (*US*) gemeiner Soldat

enlistment [ɪnˈlɪstmənt] N (*of soldiers, recruits, = enlisting*) Meldung *f*; (= *being enlisted*) Einziehung *f*; (*of supporters, collaborators*) Anwerbung *f*, Gewinnung *f*; (*of assistance, support*) Gewinnung *f*

enliven [ɪnˈlaɪvn] VT beleben

en masse [ˌɑ̃ˈmæs] ADV **a** (= *everybody together*) alle zusammen; **to resign ~** geschlossen zurücktreten **b** (= *in large numbers, things*) in großen Mengen; (*people*) in großen Gruppen; **the flowers looked lovely ~** die vielen Blumen sahen schön zusammen aus

enmesh [ɪnˈmeʃ] VT (*lit*) in einem Netz fangen; (*fig*) verstricken; **to get ~ed in sth** (*fig*) in etw (*acc*) verstrickt werden

enmity [ˈenmɪtɪ] N Feindschaft *f*

ennoble [ɪˈnəʊbl] VT (*lit*) adeln, in den Adelsstand erheben; (*fig*) *mind, person* erheben (*geh*)

ennui [ˈɒnwiː] N , *no pl* (*liter*) Ennui *m* (*liter*)

enormity [ɪˈnɔːmɪtɪ] N **a** *no pl* (*of action, offence*) ungeheures Ausmaß **b** (*of crime*) Ungeheuerlichkeit *f*

enormous [ɪˈnɔːməs] ADJ *object* enorm, riesig; *animal* riesig; *person* (= *fat*) ungeheuer dick; (= *tall*) riesig groß; *amount, success, profits, losses, range, choice* riesig; *number, quantity, variety, effort, relief* ungeheuer; *difference* riesig, gewaltig; **an ~ great thing** (*inf*) ein Riesending *nt* (*inf*); **she was wearing an ~ great ruby** sie trug einen riesig großen Rubin; **he has ~ talent/an ~ talent for ...** er hat enorm viel Talent/ein enorm großes Talent für ...; **~ amounts** *or* **sums of money** Unsummen *pl*; **an ~ amount of work** eine Unmenge Arbeit; **an ~ amount of pain** ungeheure Schmerzen *pl*; **it means an ~ amount to me** es bedeutet mir ungeheuer viel; **an ~ number of, ~ numbers of** ungeheuer viele; **he was a lovely lad with ~ potential** er war ein netter Junge, aus dem enorm viel hätte werden können

enormously [ɪˈnɔːməslɪ] ADV (+*vb*) enorm; (+*adj*) ungeheuer

enough [ɪˈnʌf] **ADJ a** (*before noun*) (= *sufficient*) genug; **~ sugar/apples** genug *or* genügend Zucker/Äpfel; **~ trouble/problems** (= *more would be unwelcome*) genug Ärger/Probleme
b (*after noun: form*) **proof ~** Beweis genug
PRON genug (*of* von); **I had not seen ~ of his work** ich hatte noch nicht genug von seiner Arbeit gesehen; **I hope it's ~** ich hoffe, es reicht *or* genügt; **two years was ~** zwei Jahre reichten, zwei Jahre waren lange genug; **have you ~ to pay the bill?** haben Sie genug, um die Rechnung zu bezahlen?; **we have ~ to live on** wir haben genug zum Leben, es reicht uns zum Leben; **this noise is ~ to drive me mad** dieser Lärm macht mich noch ganz verrückt; **one song was ~ to show he couldn't sing** ein Lied genügte, um zu zeigen, dass er nicht singen konnte; **it is ~ for us to know that ...** es genügt uns zu wissen, dass ...; **I've got ~ to worry about** ich habe genug Sorgen; **we've made ~ of a mess here** wir haben hier genug angerichtet; **~ is ~** was zu viel ist, ist zu viel; **~ said** mehr braucht man nicht zu sagen; **to have had ~** (= *be fed up*) genug haben (*of* von); **I've had ~** ich habe genug; (*in exasperation*) jetzt reichts mir aber (*inf*); **one can never have ~ of this music** von dieser Musik kann man nie genug kriegen; **that's ~!** jetzt reicht es aber!, jetzt ist es aber genug!
ADV a (= *sufficiently*) genug; **to be punished ~** genug bestraft sein; **he is good ~ to win** er ist gut genug, um zu gewinnen; **he knows well ~ what I said** er weiß ganz genau, was ich gesagt habe
b (= *reasonably, fairly*) **it is common ~ for children to overeat** es kommt durchaus häufig vor, dass Kinder zu viel essen; **to be happy ~** einigermaßen zufrieden sein; **to be happy ~ to do sth** etw so weit ganz gern tun; **she sounded sincere ~** sie schien so weit ganz ehrlich; **easy ~** nicht allzu schwer; **it is easy ~ to make them yourself** man kann sie ohne weiteres selbst machen; **he drove off happily ~** er ist ganz fröhlich weggefahren; **I like it well ~** es gefällt mir so weit ganz gut; **easily ~** ohne größere Schwierigkeiten → *also* **fair¹ ADJ a**
c oddly *or* **funnily ~** komischerweise; **interestingly ~** interessanterweise → *also* **sure ADV b**

en passant [ˌɑ̃ˈpæsɑ̃] ADV **a** (*liter*) *mention, refer to* beiläufig, nebenbei; **it can be dealt with ~** es kann nebenbei erledigt werden **b** (*introducing remark*) nebenbei bemerkt

enquire *etc* [ɪnˈkwaɪə'] = **inquire** *etc*

enquirer [ɪnˈkwaɪərə'] N = **inquirer**

enquiring [ɪnˈkwaɪərɪŋ] ADJ = **inquiring**

enquiringly [ɪnˈkwaɪərɪŋlɪ] ADV = **inquiringly**

enquiry [ɪnˈkwaɪərɪ] ✪ 20.2 N = **inquiry**

enrage [ɪnˈreɪdʒ] VT wütend machen; **it ~s me to think that ...** es macht mich wütend, wenn ich daran denke, dass ...

enraged [ɪnˈreɪdʒd] ADJ wütend, aufgebracht (*at, by* über +*acc*); **he was ~ to see that ...** er war wütend, als er sah, dass ...

enrapture [ɪnˈræptʃə'] VT entzücken, bezaubern

enraptured [ɪnˈræptʃəd] ADJ hingerissen, entzückt (*at, by* von)

enrich [ɪnˈrɪtʃ] VT bereichern; *soil, food* anreichern; **to ~ oneself** sich bereichern; **to ~ one's life** sein Leben bereichern

enriched [ɪnˈrɪtʃt] ADJ (*also Phys*) angereichert; *person* bereichert; **~ with vitamins** mit Vitaminen angereichert

enrichment [ɪnˈrɪtʃmənt] N Bereicherung *f*; (*of soil*) Anreicherung *f*

enrol, (*US*) **enroll** [ɪnˈrəʊl] **VT** einschreiben; *members* aufnehmen; *schoolchild* (*school, headmaster*) anmelden; (*parents*) anmelden; (*Univ*) immatrikulieren **VI** sich einschreiben; (*in the army*) sich melden (*in* zu); (*for course, at school*) sich anmelden; (*Univ*) sich immatrikulieren *or* einschreiben

enrolment, (*US*) **enrollment** [ɪnˈrəʊlmənt] N **a** (= *enrolling*) Einschreibung *f*; (*of members*) Aufnahme *f*; (*of schoolchild, by school, headmaster*) Aufnahme *f*; (*by parents*) Anmeldung *f*; (*Univ*) Immatrikulation *f* **b** (= *being enrolled*) Einschreibung *f*; (*in the army*) Meldung *f*; (*for course, at school*) Anmeldung *f*; (*Univ*) Immatrikulation *f*, Einschreibung *f* **c** (= *have an ~ of X* (*evening class*) eine (Gesamt)teilnehmerzahl von X haben; (*university*) X immatrikulierte Studenten haben; (*school*) eine (Gesamt)schülerzahl von X haben

en route [ɒnˈruːt] ADV unterwegs; **~ to/for/from** auf dem Weg zu/nach/von

ensconce [ɪnˈskɒns] VR sich niederlassen, sich häuslich niederlassen (*in* in +*dat*); **he was ~d in the front room** er hatte sich in dem vorderen Zimmer (häuslich) niedergelassen

ensemble [ɑ̃ːnˈsɑ̃ːmbl] N **a** (*Mus, Theat*) Ensemble *nt*; **~ acting** *or* **playing** schauspielerisches Zusammenspiel **b** (*Fashion*) Ensemble *nt* **c** (= *collection: of people, things*) Ansammlung *f*

enshrine [ɪnˈʃraɪn] VT (*fig*) bewahren

enshroud [ɪnˈʃraʊd] VT (*liter.* = *shroud*) (*lit*) einhüllen; (*fig*) umgeben; **the case remains ~d in mystery** der Fall bleibt weiterhin von einem Geheimnis umgeben

ensign [ˈensaɪn] N **a** (= *flag*) Nationalflagge *f* **b** (*Mil Hist*) Fähnrich *m* **c** (*US, Naut*) Fähnrich *m* zur See

enslave [ɪnˈsleɪv] VT zum Sklaven machen; **he is ~d by the system** das System hat ihn zum Sklaven gemacht; **she is ~d by her routine** sie ist zur Sklavin ihrer Routine geworden

enslavement [ɪnˈsleɪvmənt] N (*lit*) Versklavung *f*; (*fig*) sklavische Abhängigkeit (*to* von)

ensnare [ɪnˈsnɛə'] VT (*lit*) fangen; (*fig, woman*) umgarnen; (*charms*) berücken, bestricken; **his leg became ~d in the ropes** sein Bein verfing sich in den Seilen

ensue [ɪnˈsjuː] VI folgen (*from, on* aus); **it ~s that ...** daraus folgt, dass...; **I don't know what ~d** ich weiß nicht, was daraufhin geschah

ensuing [ɪnˈsjuːɪŋ] ADJ darauf folgend *attr*; *months, weeks also* folgend *attr*

en suite [ɒnˈswiːt] ADJ **room with ~ bathroom, ~ room** Zimmer *nt* mit eigenem Bad

ensure [ɪnˈʃʊə'] VT sicherstellen; (= *secure*) sichern; **will you ~ that I get a seat?** sorgen Sie dafür, dass ich einen Platz bekomme?

ENT abbr *of* **ear, nose and throat ~ department** HNO-Abteilung *f*; **~ specialist** HNO-Arzt *m*/ -Ärztin *f*

entablature [ɪnˈtæblətʃʊə'] N Gebälk *nt*

entail [ɪnˈteɪl] VT **a** *expense, inconvenience, changes* mit sich bringen; *risk, difficulty, loss* verbunden sein mit, mit sich bringen; (= *involve*)

work erforderlich machen; **what is ~ed in buying a house?** was ist zum Hauskauf alles erforderlich?; **this will ~ (my) buying a new car** das bringt mit sich *or* macht es erforderlich, dass ich mir ein neues Auto kaufen muss **b** (*Logic*) **if x = y, not x ~s not y** wenn x = y ist, so folgt daraus, dass nicht x nicht = y ist **c** (*Jur*) **to ~ an estate** ein Gut als Fideikommiss vererben; **~ed estate** unveräußerliches Erbgut, Fideikommiss *nt*

entangle [ɪnˈtæŋgl] VT **a** (= *catch up*) verfangen; **to become ~d in sth** sich in etw (*dat*) verfangen; **their feet were ~d in the ropes** sie hatten sich mit den Füßen in den Seilen verfangen **b** (= *get into a tangle*) *hair* verwirren; *wool, thread, ropes* verwickeln, verwirren; **to become ~d** sich verwirren, sich verwickeln *or* verheddern (*inf*) **c** (*fig, in affair etc*) verwickeln, verstricken (*in* in +*acc*); **he became ~d in his own words** er verhaspelte sich (*inf*)

entanglement [ɪnˈtæŋglmənt] N **a** (*lit, no pl*: = *enmeshing*) Verfangen *nt*; (= *tangle, of ropes etc*) Durcheinander *nt*; (*esp Mil, of barbed wire*) Verhau *m* **b** (*fig, in affair etc*) Verwicklung *f*; **legal ~** Rechtskonflikt *m*; **he wanted to avoid any ~ with domestic politics** er wollte sich aus der Innenpolitik heraushalten; **she didn't want any romantic ~** sie wollte nicht in eine Romanze verwickelt werden

enter [ˈentə'] **VT a** (*towards speaker*) hereinkommen in (+*acc*); (*away from speaker*) hineingehen in (+*acc*); (= *walk into*) *building etc* betreten, eintreten in (+*acc*); (= *drive into*) *car park, motorway* einfahren in (+*acc*); (= *turn into*) *road etc* einbiegen in (+*acc*); (= *flow into: river, sewage etc*) münden in (+*acc*); (= *penetrate: bullet etc*) eindringen in (+*acc*); (= *climb into*) *train* einsteigen in (+*acc*); (= *cross border of*) *country* einreisen in (+*acc*); **to ~ harbour** (in den Hafen) einlaufen; **the dispute is ~ing its fifth year** die Auseinandersetzung zieht sich jetzt schon ins fünfte Jahr hin; **the thought never ~ed my head** *or* **mind** so etwas wäre mir nie eingefallen; **that idea HAD ~ed my mind** (*iro*) auf diesen Gedanken bin ich tatsächlich gekommen
b (= *join, become a member of*) eintreten in (+*acc*); **to ~ the Army/Navy** zum Heer/zur Marine gehen; **to ~ the Church** Geistlicher werden; **to ~ a school** in eine Schule eintreten; **to ~ university** ein Studium beginnen; **to ~ a profession** einen Beruf ergreifen
c (= *record*) eintragen (*in* in +*acc*); (*Comput*) *data* eingeben; **to ~ sb's/one's name** jdn/sich eintragen; **~ these purchases under my name** (*Comm*) tragen Sie diese Käufe auf meinen Namen ein
d (= *enrol, for school, exam etc*) *pupil* anmelden; (*for race, contest etc*) *horse* melden; *competitor* anmelden; **I ~ed him in the competition** ich meldete ihn zu dem Wettbewerb an
e (= *go in for*) *race, contest* sich beteiligen an (+*dat*); **only amateurs could ~ the race** es konnten nur Amateure an dem Rennen teilnehmen
f (= *submit*) *appeal, plea* einlegen; **to ~ an action against sb** (*Jur*) gegen jdn einen Prozess anstrengen *or* einleiten
VI a (*towards speaker*) hereinkommen; (*away from speaker*) hineingehen; (= *walk in*) eintreten; (*into bus etc*) einsteigen; (= *drive in*) einfahren; (= *penetrate: bullet etc*) eindringen; (= *into country*) einreisen
b (*Theat*) auftreten
c (*for race, exam etc*) sich melden (*for* zu)
N (*Comput*) **hit ~** Enter drücken

▶ **enter into** VI +*prep obj* **a** *relations, negotiations, discussions* aufnehmen; *contract, alliance* schließen, eingehen; **to enter into conversation with sb** ein Gespräch mit jdm anknüpfen; **to enter into correspondence with sb** mit jdm in Briefwechsel treten → **spirit b** (= *figure in*) eine Rolle spielen bei

▶ **enter up** VT *sep* eintragen

▶ **enter (up)on** VI +*prep obj career, duties* antreten; *new era* eintreten in (+*acc*); *subject* eingehen auf (+*acc*); *transaction* abschließen

enteric [enˈterɪk] ADJ Darm-; ~ **infection** Darmentzündung *f*

enteric fever N (Unterleibs)typhus *m*

enteritis [ˌentəˈraɪtɪs] N Dünndarmentzündung *f*

enter key N (*Comput*) Enter-Taste *f*

enterprise [ˈentəpraɪz] N **a** *no pl* (= *initiative, ingenuity*) Initiative *f*; (= *adventurousness*) Unternehmungsgeist *m* **b** (= *project, undertaking, Comm, = firm*) Unternehmen *nt*; **free/public/private ~** (*system*) freies/öffentliches/privates Unternehmertum

enterprise zone N wirtschaftliches Fördergebiet

enterprising [ˈentəpraɪzɪŋ] ADJ *person* (= *adventurous*) unternehmungslustig; (= *resourceful*) einfallsreich; *company* geschäftstüchtig; *idea, scheme* einfallsreich, originell; **that was ~ of her** da war sie aber unternehmungslustig/einfallsreich

enterprisingly [ˈentəpraɪzɪŋlɪ] ADV (= *adventurously*) unternehmungslustig; (= *resourcefully*) einfallsreich; **he very ~ started his own business** unternehmungslustig, wie er war, machte er sein eigenes Geschäft auf

entertain [ˌentəˈteɪn] VT **a** (= *offer hospitality to*) einladen; (*to meal*) bewirten; **to ~ sb to dinner** jdn zum Essen einladen **b** (= *amuse*) unterhalten; (*humorously, with jokes*) belustigen **c** *thought, intention* sich tragen mit; *suspicion, doubt* hegen; *hope* nähren; *suggestion, proposal, offer, possibility* in Erwägung ziehen VI **a** (= *have visitors*) Gäste haben **b** (*comedian, conjurer etc*) unterhalten

entertainer [ˌentəˈteɪnə'] N Unterhalter(in) *m(f)*, Entertainer(in) *m(f)*

entertaining [ˌentəˈteɪnɪŋ] ADJ (= *fun*) unterhaltsam; (= *amusing*) amüsant N die Bewirtung von Gästen; **she does a lot of ~** sie hat oft Gäste; **business ~** die Bewirtung von Geschäftspartnern

entertainingly [ˌentəˈteɪnɪŋlɪ] ADV (= *in a fun way*) unterhaltsam; (= *amusingly*) amüsant

entertainment [ˌentəˈteɪnmənt] N **a** (= *amusement*) Unterhaltung *f*; (*professional*) Entertainment *nt*; **for my own ~** nur so zum Vergnügen, zu meinem Privatvergnügen; **the cinema is a great form of ~** das Kino bietet tolle Unterhaltung; **the film is good ~** der Film ist sehr unterhaltsam; **the world of ~** die Unterhaltungsbranche **b** (= *performance*) Darbietung *f*

entertainment: entertainment allowance N ≈ Aufwandspauschale *f*; **entertainment tax** N Vergnügungssteuer *f*; **entertainment value** N **to have good ~** großen Unterhaltungswert haben; (*person*) sehr unterhaltend sein

enthral, enthrall (*US*) [ɪnˈθrɔːl] VT begeistern, berücken; (*exciting story etc also*) packen, fesseln; **he was (held) ~led by her beauty** er war von ihrer Schönheit gefesselt *or* bezaubert *or* berückt (*geh*)

enthralling [ɪnˈθrɔːlɪŋ] ADJ spannend; *story also* packend

enthrone [ɪnˈθrəʊn] VT inthronisieren; *bishop* feierlich einsetzen; **to sit ~d** thronen

enthronement [ɪnˈθrəʊnmənt] N Inthronisation *f*, Inthronisierung *f*; (*of bishop*) Einsetzung *f*

enthuse [ɪnˈθjuːz] VI schwärmen (*over von*)

enthusiasm [ɪnˈθjuːzɪæzəm] N **a** Begeisterung *f*, Enthusiasmus *m* (*for für*); **she showed little ~ for the scheme** sie zeigte sich von dem Plan nicht sehr begeistert; **she has great ~ for life** sie hat sehr viel Lebensfreude; **I can't work up any ~ for going out** ich kann mich gar nicht dafür begeistern, auszugehen; **I can't work up any ~ for the idea** ich habe mich für die Idee nicht begeistern; **the idea filled her with ~** die Idee begeisterte sie

b (= *interest*) Interesse *nt*; (= *passion*) Leiden-

schaft *f*; **photography is one of her many ~s** Fotografieren ist eines ihrer vielen Interessen/Leidenschaften; **he has many ~s** er kann sich für viele Dinge begeistern

enthusiast [ɪnˈθjuːzɪæst] N Enthusiast(in) *m(f)*; **he's a sports/football/rock-and-roll ~** er ist begeisterter Sportler/Fußballfreund *m*/Rock 'n' Roll-Anhänger *m*

enthusiastic [ɪnˌθjuːzɪˈæstɪk] ✪ 7.3, 14 ADJ begeistert, enthusiastisch; **he was very ~ about the plan** er war von dem Plan äußerst begeistert; **to be ~ about doing sth** etw mit Begeisterung tun; (*in future*) sich darauf freuen, etw zu tun; **he was ~ in his praise of it** er lobte es begeistert; **they had been a little too ~ when buying the ingredients** sie waren beim Einkaufen der Zutaten ein bisschen über das Ziel hinausgeschossen; **to be less than ~ (about sth)** nicht gerade (von etw) begeistert sein; **to be less than ~ about doing sth** nicht gerade wild darauf sein, etw zu tun; **to wax ~ (about sth)** (über etw *acc*) in Begeisterung geraten

enthusiastically [ɪnˌθjuːzɪˈæstɪkəlɪ] ADV begeistert, mit Begeisterung

entice [ɪnˈtaɪs] VT locken; (= *lead astray*) verführen, verleiten; **to ~ sb to do sth** *or* **into doing sth** jdn dazu verführen *or* verleiten, etw zu tun; **to ~ sb away** jdn weglocken

enticement [ɪnˈtaɪsmənt] N (= *act*) Lockung *f*; (= *leading astray*) Verführung *f*; (= *lure*) Lockmittel *nt*; (*fig*) Verlockung *f*

enticing [ɪnˈtaɪsɪŋ] ADJ verlockend; *look* verführerisch

enticingly [ɪnˈtaɪsɪŋlɪ] ADV verlockend, verführerisch; **the wine is ~ aromatic** der Wein hat ein verlockendes Aroma; **they have an ~ simple way of life** sie haben einen beneidenswert einfachen Lebensstil

entire [ɪnˈtaɪə'] ADJ **a** (= *whole, complete*) ganz; *cost, career gesamt* **b** (= *intact*) vollständig **c** (= *uncastrated*) nicht kastriert

entirely [ɪnˈtaɪəlɪ] ADV **a** (= *exclusively*) *depend, devote* ganz, ausschließlich; **the accident was ~ the fault of the other driver** der andere Fahrer hatte die ganze Schuld an dem Unfall; **to be made ~ of ...** ganz *or* ausschließlich aus ... bestehen; **he lived ~ on bread and milk** er lebte ausschließlich *or* nur von Brot und Milch; **that is ~ a matter for the police/the school authorities** dafür ist allein die Polizei/die Schulbehörde zuständig

b (*emph, = totally*) völlig; **I agree ~** ich stimme voll und ganz zu; **I don't agree ~** ich bin nicht ganz der (gleichen) Meinung; **~ free (of charge)** ganz umsonst; **it has been ~ free of serious problems** damit hat es keinerlei ernste Probleme gegeben; **~ possible** durchaus möglich; **to be ~ convinced by sb/sth** von jdm/etw völlig *or* ganz überzeugt sein; **to be another matter ~ or a different matter ~** etwas ganz *or* völlig anderes sein

entirety [ɪnˈtaɪərətɪ] N Gesamtheit *f*; **in its ~** in seiner Gesamtheit

entitle [ɪnˈtaɪtl] VT **a** *book* betiteln; **it is ~d ...** es hat den Titel ... **b** (= *give the right*) **to ~ sb to sth** jdn zu etw berechtigen; *to compensation, legal aid, holiday* jdm den Anspruch auf etw (*acc*) geben; **to ~ sb to do sth** jdn dazu berechtigen, etw zu tun; **to be ~d to sth** das Recht auf etw (*acc*) haben; *to compensation, legal aid, holiday* Anspruch auf etw (*acc*) haben; **to be ~d to do sth** das Recht haben, etw zu tun; **I'm ~d to my own opinion** ich kann mir meine eigene Meinung bilden; **to be ~d to vote** wählen können, das Wahlrecht haben

entitlement [ɪnˈtaɪtlmənt] N Berechtigung *f* (*to zu*); (*to compensation, legal aid, holiday etc*) Anspruch *m* (*to auf* +*acc*); **what is your holiday ~?** (*Brit*) wie viel Urlaub steht Ihnen zu?

entity [ˈentɪtɪ] N Wesen *nt*; **legal ~** juristische Person; **living ~** Lebewesen *nt*; **as a separate ~** als ein eigenständiges Gebilde

entomb [ɪnˈtuːm] VT beisetzen, bestatten; **the mausoleum which ~s his body** das Mausoleum, in dem er beigesetzt ist

entomologist [ˌentəˈmɒlədʒɪst] N Entomologe *m*, Entomologin *f*

entomology [ˌentəˈmɒlədʒɪ] N Entomologie *f*, Insektenkunde *f*

entourage [ˌɒntʊˈrɑːʒ] N Gefolge *nt*, Entourage *f* (*geh*)

entr'acte [ˈɒntrækt] N Zwischenspiel *nt*

entrails [ˈentreɪlz] PL (*lit*) Eingeweide *pl*, (*fig, of watch etc*) Innereien *pl* (*hum*)

entrain [ɪnˈtreɪn] VT *troops* (in Eisenbahnwaggons) verladen VI (in den Zug) einsteigen

entrance¹ [ɪnˈtrɑːns] VT in Entzücken *or* Verzückung versetzen; **to be ~d** verzückt sein; **to be ~d by/with sth** von etw entzückt sein

entrance² [ˈentrəns] N **a** (= *way in*) Eingang *m*; (*for vehicles*) Einfahrt *f*; (= *hall*) Eingangshalle *f*, Entree *nt* (*geh*)

b (= *entering*) Eintritt *m*; (*Theat*) Auftritt *m*; **on his ~** bei seinem Eintritt/Auftritt; **to make an ~** in Erscheinung treten; **he likes to make an ~** er setzt sich gern in Szene; **to make one's ~** (*Theat*) auftreten; (*fig*) erscheinen; **his ~ into politics** sein Einstieg *m* in die Politik

c (= *admission*) Eintritt *m* (*to in* +*acc*); (*to club etc*) Zutritt *m* (*to zu*); (*to school*) Aufnahme *f* (*to in* +*acc*); **to gain ~ to a university** die Zulassung zu einer Universität erhalten; **children get free ~ (to the zoo)** Kinder haben freien Eintritt (im Zoo)

entrance: entrance card N Eintrittskarte *f*; **entrance examination** N Aufnahmeprüfung *f*; **entrance fee** N (*for museum etc*) Eintrittsgeld *nt*; (*for competition*) Teilnahmegebühr *f*; (*for club membership*) Aufnahmegebühr *f*; **entrance hall** N Eingangshalle *f*; **entrance qualifications** PL Zulassungsanforderungen *pl*; **entrance ticket** N Eintrittskarte *f*; **entrance visa** N Einreisevisum *nt*

entrancing [ɪnˈtrɑːnsɪŋ, -lɪ] ADJ bezaubernd

entrancingly [ɪnˈtrɑːnsɪŋlɪ] ADV bezaubernd; **it's ~ simple** es ist bestechend einfach

entrant [ˈentrənt] N (*to profession*) Berufsanfänger(in) *m(f)* (*to in* +*dat*); (*in contest*) Teilnehmer(in) *m(f)*; (*in exam*) Prüfling *m*

entrap [ɪnˈtræp] VT **a** (= *catch*) (in einer Falle) fangen **b** (= *induce*) **to ~ sb into doing sth** jdn dazu verführen *or* verleiten, etw zu tun

entrapment [ɪnˈtræpmənt] N **a** (= *state of being entrapped*) Gefangensein *nt* in einer Falle **b** (= *entrapping*) Fangen *nt* in einer Falle, Fallenstellen *nt* **c** (= *inducement*) (geschickte) Verführung (*etw Böses/Kriminelles zu tun*)

entreat [ɪnˈtriːt] VT inständig *or* dringend bitten, anflehen (*for um*); **listen to him, I ~ you** ich bitte Sie inständig *or* ich flehe Sie an, ihn anzuhören

entreatingly [ɪnˈtriːtɪŋlɪ] ADV flehentlich

entreaty [ɪnˈtriːtɪ] N dringende *or* flehentliche Bitte; **they resisted my entreaties** sie blieben gegen alle meine Bitten taub; **a look of ~** ein flehender Blick; **a gesture of ~** eine flehende Gebärde

entrecôte (steak) [ˈɒntrəkəʊt(ˌsteɪk)] N Entrecote *nt*

entrée [ˈɒntreɪ] N **a** (*Brit:* = *starter*) Vorspeise *f*; (*esp US:* = *main course*) Hauptgericht *nt* **b** (*to club etc*) Zutritt *m*

entrench [ɪnˈtrentʃ] VT (*Mil*) eingraben, verschanzen

entrenched [ɪnˈtrentʃd] ADJ **a** (= *established*) *position* unbeugsam; *ideas* festgefügt; *belief, attitude* fest verwurzelt; *interests* etabliert; *power, bureaucracy* etabliert, festgesetzt; *behaviour, person* inflexibel; **deeply ~ beliefs/prejudices** tief verwurzelte Überzeugungen/Vorurteile *pl*; **to be/become ~ in sth** (*word, custom*) sich in etw (*dat*) eingebürgert haben/einbürgern; (*idea, prejudice*) sich in etw (*dat*) festgesetzt haben/festsetzen; (*belief*) in etw (*dat*) verwurzelt sein/sich in etw (*dat*) verwurzeln; **you're too ~ in**

the past Sie sind zu sehr in der Vergangenheit verhaftet
b (*Mil*) eingegraben, verschanzt; **to take up ~ positions** sich verschanzen

entrenchment [ɪn'trentʃmənt] N (*Mil*) Verschanzung *f*

entrepôt ['ɒntrəpəʊ] N (= *warehouse*) Lagerhalle *f*; (= *port*) Umschlaghafen *m*

entrepreneur [,ɒntrəprə'nɜː'] N Unternehmer(in) *m(f)*

entrepreneurial [,ɒntrəprə'nɜːrɪəl] ADJ unternehmerisch

entrepreneurship [,ɒntrəprə'nɜːʃɪp] N Unternehmertum *nt*

entropy ['entrəpɪ] N Entropie *f*

entrust [ɪn'trʌst] VT anvertrauen (*to sb* jdm); **to ~ a child to sb's care** ein Kind jds Obhut anvertrauen; **to ~ sb with a task** jdn mit einer Aufgabe betrauen; **to ~ sb with money/a secret** jdm Geld/ein Geheimnis anvertrauen

entry ['entrɪ] N **a** (*into* in +*acc*) (= *coming or going in*) Eintritt *m*; (*by car etc*) Einfahrt *f*; (*into country*) Einreise *f*; (*into club, school etc*) Aufnahme *f*; (*Theat*) Auftritt *m*; **point of ~** (*of bullet etc*) Einschussstelle *f*; (*of inlet pipe etc*) Anschlussstelle *f*; **port of ~** Einreisehafen *m*; (= *airport*) Landeflughafen *m*; **to make an/one's ~** auftreten; **"no ~"** (*on door etc*) „Zutritt verboten"; (*on one-way street*) „keine Einfahrt"
b (= *way in*) Eingang *m*; (*for vehicles*) Einfahrt *f*
c (*in diary, account book, dictionary etc*) Eintrag *m*; **the dictionary has 30,000 entries** das Wörterbuch enthält 30.000 Stichwörter; **to make an ~ against sb** (*Fin*) einen Betrag von jds Konto abbuchen
d (*for race etc: of competitor*) Meldung *f*; (*for competition: of piece of work*) Einsendung *f*; **there is a large ~ for the 200m** für die 200 m sind viele Meldungen eingegangen; **the closing date for entries is Friday** der Einsendeschluss ist Freitag

entry: entry form N Anmeldeformular *nt*; **entry-level** ADJ *model, position* für Einsteiger; **~ prices** Einführungspreise *pl*; **~ workers** neu eingestellte Arbeiter *pl*; **entry course** Anfängerkurs *m*; **entry permit** N Passierschein *m*; (*into country*) Einreiseerlaubnis *f*; **entry phone** N Türsprechanlage *f*; **entry qualifications** PL Zulassungsanforderungen *pl*; **entry visa** N Einreisevisum *nt*; **entryway** N (*US*) Eingang *m*; (*for vehicles*) Einfahrt *f*

entwine [ɪn'twaɪn] **VT** (= *twist together*) stems, ribbons ineinander schlingen; **they ~d their hands** sie schlangen ihre Hände ineinander; **to be ~d with sth** (*fig*) mit etw verflochten sein; **to be ~d in sth** (*acc*) verwickelt sein **VI** sich ineinanderschlingen *or* -winden

E number N E-Nummer *f*

enumerate [ɪ'njuːməreɪt] VT aufzählen

enumeration [ɪ,njuːmə'reɪʃən] N Aufzählung *f*

enunciate [ɪ'nʌnsɪeɪt] VTI artikulieren

enunciation [ɪ,nʌnsɪ'eɪʃən] N Artikulation *f*

enuresis [,enjə'riːsɪs] N (*Med spec*) Enurese *f*

envelop [ɪn'veləp] VT einhüllen; **flames ~ed the house** das Haus war von Flammen eingehüllt; **he was ~ed in a black cloak** er war in einen schwarzen Umhang gehüllt

envelope ['envələʊp] N **a** (Brief)umschlag *m*; (*large: for packets etc*) Umschlag *m* **b** (*of balloon, Biol*) Hülle *f*; (*of airship*) Außenhaut *f*; (*of insect*) Hautpanzer *m*

enveloping [ɪn'veləpɪŋ] ADJ alles umhüllend; **the all-enveloping fog** die dichte Nebelhülle

envelopment [ɪn'veləpmənt] N Einhüllung *f*

envenom [ɪn'venəm] VT (*lit, fig*) vergiften

enviable ADJ , **enviably** ADV ['envɪəbl, -ɪ] beneidenswert

envious ['envɪəs] ADJ *person, glance* neidisch; **to be ~ of sb** auf jdn neidisch sein, jdn beneiden; **to be ~ of sth** auf etw (*acc*) neidisch sein; **I felt ~ of her success** ich beneidete sie um ihren Erfolg; **he is ~ that you are more successful** er ist

neidisch, weil du erfolgreicher bist; **to cast ~ eyes** *or* **an ~ eye at sth** etw neiderfüllt betrachten

enviously ['envɪəslɪ] ADV neidisch, neiderfüllt

environment [ɪn'vaɪərənmənt] N Umwelt *f*; (*of town etc, physical surroundings*) Umgebung *f*; (= *social, cultural surroundings*) Milieu *nt*, Umwelt *f*; **working-class ~** Arbeitermilieu *nt*; **cultural/hostile ~** kulturelle/feindliche Umwelt; **Department of the Environment** (*Brit*) Umweltministerium *nt*; **Secretary** (*US*) *or* **Minister** (*Brit*) **of the Environment** Umweltminister(in) *m(f)*

Environment Agency N (*Brit*) Umweltbehörde *f*

environmental [ɪn,vaɪərən'mentl] ADJ **a** (= *ecological*) Umwelt-; **~ awareness** Umweltbewusstsein *nt*; **~ concerns** Sorgen *pl* um die Umwelt; **~ damage/pollution** Umweltschäden *pl*/-verschmutzung *f*; **~ disaster** Umweltkatastrophe *f*; **~ effects/impact** Auswirkungen *pl*/Auswirkung *f* auf die Umwelt, Folgen *pl* für die Umwelt; **~ issues** *or* **matters** Umweltfragen *pl* **b** (= *protecting the environment*) Umweltschutz-; **~ group** Umweltschutzorganisation *f*; **~ movement** Umweltschutzbewegung *f* **c** (= *relating to surroundings*) umgebungsbedingt; **~ change** eine Veränderung in der Umgebung

environmental health N (*Brit*) öffentliches Gesundheitswesen; **Environmental Health Department** ≈ Gesundheitsamt *nt*; **Environmental Health Officer** ≈ Beamte(r) *m*/Beamtin *f* des öffentlichen Gesundheitsdienstes; **Environmental Health Service** ≈ öffentlicher Gesundheitsdienst

environmentalism [ɪn,vaɪərən'mentəlɪzəm] N Umweltbewusstsein *nt*

environmentalist [ɪn,vaɪərən'mentəlɪst] **N** Umweltschützer(in) *m(f)* **ADJ** Umwelt-; **~ movement/issues** Umweltbewegung *f*/-themen *pl*

environmentally [ɪn,vaɪərən'mentəlɪ] ADV **a** (= *ecologically*) im Hinblick auf die Umwelt, umwelt-; **~ correct/sound** umweltgerecht; **~ sensitive** umweltempfindlich; **~ conscious** *or* **aware** umweltbewusst; **~ harmful** umweltschädlich; **~ friendly/unfriendly** umweltfreundlich/-feindlich; **we must protect the planet ~** wir müssen die Umwelt unseres Planeten schützen **b** (= *through living conditions*) durch die Umgebung; **~ acquired/induced** umgebungsbedingt

Environmental Protection Agency N (*US, Admin*) staatliche Umweltbehörde *der USA*

environment-friendly [ɪn,vaɪərənmənt'frendlɪ] ADJ umweltfreundlich

environs [ɪn'vaɪərənz] PL Umgebung *f*; **Rome and its ~** Rom und Umgebung

envisage [ɪn'vɪzɪdʒ] **◐** 8.1 VT sich (*dat*) vorstellen; **do you ~ any price rises in the near future?** halten Sie Preisanstiege in nächster Zukunft für wahrscheinlich?

envoi ['envɔɪ] N (*of poem*) Zueignungs- *or* Schlussstrophe *f*

envoy ['envɔɪ] N Bote *m*, Botin *f*; (= *diplomat*) Gesandte(r) *mf*

envoy extraordinary N Sonderbeauftragte(r) *mf*

envy ['envɪ] **N** Neid *m*; **his car was the ~ of his friends** seine Freunde beneideten ihn um sein Auto; **a laboratory which would be the ~ of every scientist** ein Labor, das der Neid eines jeden Wissenschaftlers wäre **VT** *person* beneiden; **to ~ sb sth** jdn um *or* wegen etw beneiden; **that's a job I don't ~** das ist eine Arbeit, um die ich niemanden beneiden

enzyme ['enzaɪm] N Enzym *nt*, Ferment *nt*

---

ligt oder diskriminiert werden. Eine andere Behörde, die „Commission for Racial Equality" soll dafür sorgen, dass niemand wegen seiner Religions- oder Rassenzugehörigkeit oder seiner Hautfarbe diskriminiert wird.
Die **Equal Employment Opportunity Commission** oder kurz **EEOC** ist die Gleichstellungsbehörde der US-Regierung, die gleiche Rechte und Chancen am Arbeitsplatz für alle garantieren soll, unabhängig von Rasse, Religion, Geschlecht, Hautfarbe oder Alter. Arbeitgeber, die gegen den Gleichstellungsgrundsatz verstoßen, können bei Bundesgerichten verklagt werden.

Eolithic [,iːəʊ'lɪθɪk] ADJ eolithisch

eon ['iːɒn] N (*US*) = **aeon**

EP *abbr of* **extended play** EP *f*

EPA (*US*) *abbr of* **Environmental Protection Agency**

epaulette ['epɔːlet] N Epaulette *f*, Schulterstück *nt*

épée [eɪ'peɪ] N (*Fecht*)degen *m*

ephebe ['ɪfiːb] N Ephebe *m*

ephemera [ɪ'femərə] PL Eintagsfliegen *pl* (*fig*), kurzlebige Erscheinungen

ephemeral [ɪ'femərəl] ADJ ephemer (*geh, Zool*), kurzlebig; *happiness also* flüchtig

epic ['epɪk] **ADJ** *poetry* episch; *novel* monumental; *performance, match, struggle* gewaltig; *journey* lang und abenteuerlich; **~ film** Monumentalfilm *m*; **of ~ proportions** von monumentalen Ausmaßen **N** (= *poem*) Epos *nt*, Heldengedicht *nt*; (= *film, novel*) Epos *nt*, monumentaler Film/Roman; (= *match*) gewaltiges Spiel; **an ~ of the screen** (*Film*) ein Filmepos *nt*

epicentre, (*US*) **epicenter** ['epɪsentə'] N Epizentrum *nt*

epicure ['epɪkjʊə'] N Feinschmecker(in) *m(f)*

epicurean [,epɪkjʊə'riːən] **ADJ** epikureisch (*geh*) **N** Epikureer *m* (*geh*), Genussmensch *m*

epicycle ['epɪsaɪkl] N Epizykel *m*

epicyclic [,epɪ'saɪklɪk] ADJ epizyklisch

epidemic [,epɪ'demɪk] **N** Epidemie *f* (*also fig*), Seuche *f* **ADJ** epidemisch

epidemiological [,epɪdiːmɪə'lɒdʒɪkəl] ADJ epidemiologisch

epidemiologist [,epɪdiːmɪ'ɒlədʒɪst] N Epidemiologe *m*, Epidemiologin *f*

epidemiology [,epɪdiːmɪ'ɒlədʒɪ] N Epidemiologie *f*

epidermis [,epɪ'dɜːmɪs] N Epidermis *f*, Oberhaut *f*

epidural [,epɪ'djʊərəl] **ADJ** epidural **N** Epiduralanästhesie *f*

epiglottis [,epɪ'glɒtɪs] N Kehldeckel *m*, Epiglottis *f* (*spec*)

epigram ['epɪɡræm] N (= *saying*) Epigramm *nt*, Sinngedicht *nt*

epigrammatic(al) [,epɪɡrə'mætɪk(əl)] ADJ epigrammatisch

epigraph ['epɪɡrɑːf] N Epigraf *nt*, Inschrift *f*; (*at beginning of book, chapter*) Motto *nt*, Sinnspruch *m*

epilepsy ['epɪlepsɪ] N Epilepsie *f*

epileptic [,epɪ'leptɪk] **ADJ** epileptisch; **~ fit** epileptischer Anfall; **he is ~** er ist Epileptiker **N** Epileptiker(in) *m(f)*

epilogue, (*US*) **epilog** ['epɪlɒg] N Epilog *m*, Nachwort *nt*; (*Rad, TV*) Wort *nt* zum Tagesausklang

Epiphany [ɪ'pɪfənɪ] N das Dreikönigsfest

episcopacy [ɪ'pɪskəpəsɪ] N (*Eccl*) Episkopat *nt*; **the ~** das Episkopat, die Gesamtheit der Bischöfe

episcopal [ɪ'pɪskəpəl] ADJ bischöflich, episkopal (*spec*); **~ conference** Bischofskonferenz *f*

Episcopal Church N Episkopalkirche *f*

episcopalian [ɪ,pɪskə'peɪlɪən] **ADJ** zur Episkopalkirche gehörig **N Episcopalian** Mitglied *nt* der Episkopalkirche, Episkopale(r) *mf* (*form*); **the Episcopalians** die Episkopalkirche

episiotomy [ə,pi:zɪ'ɒtəmɪ] N Dammschnitt *m*, Episiotomie *f*

episode ['epɪsəʊd] N Episode *f*; (*of story, TV, Rad*) Fortsetzung *f*; (= *incident*) Begebenheit *f*, Vorfall *m*

episodic [,epɪ'sɒdɪk] ADJ episodenhaft, episodisch; *novel* in Episoden

epistemic [,epɪ'sti:mɪk] ADJ (*Philos*) epistemisch (*spec*)

epistemological [ɪ,pɪstɪmə'lɒdʒɪkəl] ADJ erkenntnistheoretisch, epistemologisch (*spec*)

epistemology [ɪ,pɪstɪ'mɒlədʒɪ] N Erkenntnistheorie *f*, Epistemologie *f* (*spec*)

epistle [ɪ'pɪsl] N (*old, iro*) Epistel *f*; (*Bibl*) Brief *m* (*to an +acc*)

epistolary [ɪ'pɪstələrɪ] ADJ Brief-; ~ *novel* Briefroman *m*

epitaph ['epɪtɑ:f] N Epitaph *nt*; (*on grave also*) Grabinschrift *f*

epithalamium [,epɪθə'leɪmɪəm] N *pl* **-a** *or* **-ums** Hochzeitsgedicht *nt*, Epithalamium *nt* (*spec*)

epithet ['epɪθet] N Beiname *m*, Epitheton *nt* (*geh*); (= *insulting name*) Schimpfname *m*

epitome [ɪ'pɪtəmɪ] N **a** (*of virtue, wisdom etc*) Inbegriff *m* (*of +gen*, an +*dat*) **b** (*rare, of book*) Epitome *f* (*spec*)

epitomize [ɪ'pɪtəmaɪz] VT verkörpern

epoch ['i:pɒk] N Zeitalter *nt* (*also Geol*), Epoche *f*

epoch-making ['i:pɒk'meɪkɪŋ] ADJ Epoche machend, epochal

eponym ['epənɪm] N (*Ling*) Eponym *nt*

eponymous [ɪ'pɒnɪməs] ADJ namengebend; ~ *hero* (*of novel*) Titelheld *m*

EPOS ['i:pɒs] abbr of **electronic point of sale** elektronisches Kassenterminal

epoxy resin [ɪ'pɒksɪ'rezɪn] N Epoxydharz *nt*

EPROM ['i:prɒm] (*Comput*) abbr of **erasable programmable read only memory** EPROM *m or nt*

Epsom salts ['epsəm'sɔːlts] PL (Epsomer) Bittersalz *nt*

equable ['ekwəbl] ADJ *climate* gleichmäßig; *person, temperament* ausgeglichen; (= *placid*) gleichmütig

equably ['ekwəblɪ] ADV ausgeglichen; (= *placidly*) gleichmütig

equal ['i:kwəl] **ADJ** **a** (= *identical*) *parts, number, value, importance etc* gleich; **an ~ amount of land** gleich viel Land; **~ numbers of men and women** gleich viele Männer und Frauen; **A and B are of ~ value** A hat den gleichen Wert wie B; **to be of ~ importance** gleich wichtig sein; **to be ~ in size (to)** gleich groß sein (wie); **two halves are ~ to one whole** zwei Halbe sind gleich ein Ganzes; **a is ~ to b** a ist gleich b; **an amount ~ to the purchase price** eine dem Kaufpreis entsprechende Summe; **with ~ enthusiasm** mit gleich großer Begeisterung; **other things being ~** wenn nichts dazwischenkommt; **education is a good thing, other things being ~** Bildung an sich ist etwas Gutes

b (= *without discrimination*) *opportunities, rights, pay, access* gleich; **~ opportunities (for men and women)** Chancengleichheit *f* (für Männer und Frauen); **~ rights for women** die Gleichberechtigung der Frau; **on ~ terms** *or* an **~ footing** (*meet, compete*) als Gleichgestellte; (= *under the same conditions*) unter den gleichen Bedingungen; **to be on ~ terms (with sb)** (mit jdm) gleichgestellt sein; **to put sb on an ~ footing (with sb)** jdn (mit jdm) gleichstellen; **the relationship should be put on a more ~ footing** das Verhältnis sollte einen unter Gleichgestellten werden; **all men are ~, but some are more ~ than others** (*hum*) alle Menschen sind gleich, nur einige sind gleicher (*hum*)

c (= *capable*) **to be ~ to the situation/task** der Situation/Aufgabe gewachsen sein; **to feel ~ to sth** sich zu etw imstande *or* im Stande *or* in der Lage fühlen

N (*in rank*) Gleichgestellte(r) *mf*; **she is his ~** sie ist ihm ebenbürtig; **our ~s** unseresgleichen; **to treat sb as an ~** jdn als ebenbürtig behandeln; **to have no ~** nicht seinesgleichen haben; (= *be unsurpassed*) unübertroffen sein

VI **three times three ~s nine** drei mal drei (ist) gleich neun; **let x ~ 3** wenn x gleich 3 ist, x sei (gleich) 3

VT (= *match, rival*) gleichkommen (+*dat*); **he ~led** (*Brit*) *or* **~ed** (*US*) **his brother in generosity** er kam seinem Bruder an Großzügigkeit gleich; **not to be ~led** (*Brit*) *or* **~ed** (*US*) unvergleichlich; (= *unsurpassed*) unübertroffen; **this show is not to be ~led** (*Brit*) *or* **~ed** (*US*) **by any other** diese Show hat nicht ihresgleichen; **there is nothing to ~ it** nichts kommt dem gleich

equality [ɪ'kwɒlɪtɪ] N Gleichheit *f*

equalize ['i:kwəlaɪz] **VT** *chances, opportunities* ausgleichen; *incomes, prices, interest rates* angleichen **VI** (*Sport*) ausgleichen; **the equalizing goal** (*Brit*) das Ausgleichstor

equalizer ['i:kwəlaɪzə'] N **a** (*Brit Sport*) Ausgleich *m*; (*Ftbl etc*) Ausgleichstor *nt* or -treffer *m*; **to score** *or* **get the ~** den Ausgleich erzielen **b** (*US, hum inf*: = *gun*) Kanone *f* (*sl*)

equally ['i:kwəlɪ] ✪ 26.1, 26.2, ADV **a** (= *evenly*) *divide, share* gleichmäßig; **~ spaced** in gleichmäßigen Abständen; (*in time*) in regelmäßigen Abständen

b (= *to the same extent, in the same way*) (+*adj*) ebenso, genauso; **they are ~ (as) successful** sie sind genauso erfolgreich; **men and women must become ~ responsible** Männer und Frauen müssen die gleiche Verantwortung übernehmen; **all foreigners should be treated ~** alle Ausländer sollten gleich behandelt werden; **they look ~ good in contemporary settings** sie sehen in einer modernen Umgebung genauso gut aus; **to apply/occur ~** gleichermaßen gelten/vorkommen

c (*introducing sentence*: = *by the same token*) ebenso; **~ one must concede that ...** ebenso muss man zugeben, dass ..., man muss aber auch zugeben, dass ...; **she cannot marry him, but ~ she cannot live alone** sie kann ihn nicht heiraten, sie kann aber auch nicht allein leben

equals sign ['i:kwəlz'saɪn] N Gleichheitszeichen *nt*

equanimity [,ekwə'nɪmɪtɪ] N Gleichmut *m*, Gelassenheit *f*; **with ~** gleichmütig, gelassen; **to recover one's ~** seine Gelassenheit wiedergewinnen, das seelische Gleichgewicht wieder finden

equate [ɪ'kweɪt] VT **a** (= *identify*) gleichsetzen, identifizieren (*with* mit); (= *compare, treat as the same*) auf die gleiche Stufe stellen, als gleichwertig hinstellen *or* betrachten; **do not ~ physical beauty with moral goodness** du musst *or* darfst Schönheit nicht mit gutem Charakter gleichsetzen; **to ~ liberalism and conservatism** Liberalismus mit Konservatismus gleichsetzen **b** (*Math*) gleichsetzen (*to* mit)

equation [ɪ'kweɪʒən] N (*Math, fig*) Gleichung *f*; **the ~ of religion and morality** die Gleichsetzung von Religion mit Moralität; **to balance the ~ between work and leisure** Arbeit und Freizeit ins rechte Gleichgewicht bringen; **that doesn't even enter the ~** das steht doch überhaupt nicht zur Debatte

equator [ɪ'kweɪtə'] N Äquator *m*; **at the ~** am Äquator

equatorial [,ekwə'tɔːrɪəl] ADJ äquatorial, Äquatorial-

Equatorial Guinea N Äquatorialguinea *nt*

equerry [ɪ'kwerɪ] N (= *personal attendant*) persönlicher Diener (*eines Mitgliedes der königlichen Familie*); (*in charge of horses*) königlicher Stallmeister

equestrian [ɪ'kwestrɪən] ADJ Reit-, Reiter-; ~ *act* Reit- *or* Pferdenummer *f*; **~ events** Reitveranstaltung *f*; (*tournament*) Reitturnier *nt*; **~ statue** Reiterstandbild *nt*

equestrianism [ɪ'kwestrɪənɪzəm] N Pferdesport *m*, Reiten *nt*

equidistant ['i:kwɪ'dɪstənt] ADJ gleich weit entfernt (*from* von)

equilateral ['i:kwɪ'lætərəl] ADJ gleichseitig

equilibrium ['i:kwɪ'lɪbrɪəm] N Gleichgewicht *nt*; **the political ~ of East Asia** das politische Gleichgewicht in Ostasien; **to keep/lose one's ~** das Gleichgewicht halten/verlieren; **in ~** im Gleichgewicht

equine ['ekwaɪn] ADJ Pferde-; ~ *sports* Pferdesport *m*

equinoctial [,i:kwɪ'nɒkʃəl] ADJ *gales, tides* äquinoktial

equinox ['i:kwɪnɒks] N Tagundnachtgleiche *f*, Äquinoktium *nt*; **the spring/autumn ~** die Frühjahrs-/Herbst-Tagundnachtgleiche

equip [ɪ'kwɪp] VT *ship, soldier, astronaut, army, worker* ausrüsten; *household, kitchen* ausstatten; **the building is also ~ped as a sports hall** das Gebäude ist auch als Sporthalle ausgestattet; **to ~ sb for life** (*fig*) jdm das (nötige) Rüstzeug fürs Leben mitgeben; **to ~ oneself with sth** sich mit etw ausrüsten; **to ~ oneself with a good education** sich (*dat*) eine gute Ausbildung verschaffen; **he is well ~ped for the job** (*fig*) er hat die nötigen Kenntnisse *or* das nötige Rüstzeug für die Stelle; **you are better ~ped than I to tackle chemistry translations** du bringst für Chemieübersetzungen das bessere Rüstzeug mit

equipage ['ekwɪpɪdʒ] N Equipage *f*

equipment [ɪ'kwɪpmənt] N , *no pl* **a** (= *objects*) (*of person*) Ausrüstung *f*; **laboratory ~** Laborausstattung *f*; **office ~** Büroeinrichtung *f*; **electrical ~** Elektrogeräte *pl*; **kitchen ~** Küchengeräte *pl* **b** (= *action of equipping*: *of ship, soldier, astronaut, army, worker*) Ausrüstung *f* **c** (*mental, intellectual*) (geistiges) Rüstzeug

equipoise ['ekwɪpɔɪz] N (*form*: = *equilibrium*) Gleichgewicht *nt*

equitable ['ekwɪtəbl] ADJ fair, gerecht, recht und billig

equitableness ['ekwɪtəblnɪs] N Fairness *f*, Billigkeit *f*

equitably ['ekwɪtəblɪ] ADV gerecht

equity ['ekwɪtɪ] N **a** Fairness *f*, Billigkeit *f* **b** **equities** PL (*Fin*) Stammaktien *pl*, Dividendenpapiere *pl*; **equities market** Aktienmarkt *m* **c** (*Jur*) Billigkeitsrecht *nt*, billiges Recht; **~ of redemption** Aktienrecht *nt* des Hypothekenschuldners **d** (*Brit, Theat*) **Equity** britische Schauspielergewerkschaft

equity: equity capital N (*Fin*) Eigenkapital *nt*, Nettoanteil *m*; **Equity card** N (*Brit Theat*) Mitgliedskarte der Schauspielergewerkschaft; **equity stake** N (*Fin*) Kapitalbeteiligung *f*

equivalence [ɪ'kwɪvələns] N Äquivalenz *f*, Entsprechung *f*

equivalent [ɪ'kwɪvələnt] **ADJ** **a** (= *equal*) gleich, gleichwertig, äquivalent; **that's ~ to saying ...** das ist gleichbedeutend damit, zu sagen ...; **to be ~ in meaning** die gleiche Bedeutung haben **b** (= *corresponding*) entsprechend, äquivalent; **the ~ institution in America** die entsprechende Einrichtung in Amerika, das amerikanische Äquivalent dazu; **an ~ salary in 1985 would have been ...** ein entsprechendes Gehalt wäre im Jahre 1985 ... gewesen; **it is ~ to £30** das entspricht £ 30; **... or the ~ value in francs ...** oder der Gegenwert in Francs

c (*Chem*) gleichwertig; (*Geometry*) äquivalent **d** **that's ~ to lying** das ist so viel wie gelogen; **as an au pair she is ~ to nanny and maid** als Aupair ist sie Kindermädchen und Dienstmädchen in einer Person

N Äquivalent *nt*; (= *counterpart*) Gegenstück *nt*, Pendant *nt*; (= *person*) Pendant *nt*; **that is the ~ of ...** das entspricht ... (*dat*); **what is the ~ in euros?** was ist der Gegenwert in Euro?; **the American ~ of the British public school** das amerikanische Gegenstück *or* Pendant zur britischen Public School; **the German ~ of the**

English custom die deutsche Entsprechung zu dem englischen Brauch; **... or the ~ in cash** ...oder der Gegenwert in bar

equivocal [ɪˈkwɪvəkəl] ADJ *(form)* **a** (= *ambiguous, vague) reply, response* zweideutig; *statement, comment* unklar, vage; *position* unklar, unbestimmt; *results, research* unklar; *evidence* nicht schlüssig; **she was ~** sie legte sich nicht fest; **he was more ~** er drückte sich unklarer aus **b** (= *ambivalent) attitude* zwiespältig, ambivalent; *person* ambivalent; (= *undecided*) unentschieden; **to be ~ about sth** keine klare Meinung zu etw haben; **public opinion is ~ about it** die öffentliche Meinung ist darüber geteilt

equivocally [ɪˈkwɪvəkəlɪ] ADV **a** (= *ambiguously*) zweideutig **b** (= *unclearly*) unklar

equivocate [ɪˈkwɪvəkeɪt] VI ausweichen, ausweichend antworten

equivocation [ɪˌkwɪvəˈkeɪʃən] N Ausflucht *f*, doppelsinnige *or* ausweichende Formulierung; **without ~** ohne Ausflüchte

ER **a** *abbr of* **Elizabeth Regina** **b** *(US) abbr of* **e-mergency room**

ERA *(US) abbr of* **Equal Rights Amendment** *Verfassungsartikel zur Gleichberechtigung*

era [ˈɪərə] N Ära *f*, Epoche *f*; *(Geol)* Erdzeitalter *nt*; **the Christian ~** (die) christliche Zeitrechnung; **the end of an ~** das Ende einer Ära

eradicate [ɪˈrædɪkeɪt] VT ausrotten

eradication [ɪˌrædɪˈkeɪʃən] N Ausrottung *f*

erasable [ɪˈreɪzəbl] ADJ löschbar; **~ programmable read only memory** *(Comput)* löschbarer programmierbarer Festwertspeicher

erase [ɪˈreɪz] VT ausradieren; *(from tape, Comput)* löschen; *(from the mind)* streichen *(from aus)*; *(sl, = kill)* erledigen *(sl)*

erase head N *(on tape recorder)* Löschkopf *m*

eraser [ɪˈreɪzə] N Radiergummi *nt or m*

erasure [ɪˈreɪʒə] N (= *act*) Auslöschen *nt*, Ausradieren *nt*; *(from tape)* Löschen *nt*; (= *sth erased*) ausradierte Stelle, Radierstelle *f*; *(on tape)* gelöschte Stelle

ere [ɛə] *(old, poet)* **PREP** ehe, bevor; **~ now** bisher; **~ long** binnen kurzem **CONJ** ehe, bevor

erect [ɪˈrekt] VT *wall, building* bauen; *statue, memorial, altar* errichten *(to sb* jdm); *machinery, traffic signs, collapsible furniture* aufstellen; *scaffolding* aufstellen, aufbauen; *tent* aufschlagen; *mast, flagpole* aufrichten; *(fig) barrier* errichten, aufbauen; *system* aufstellen ADJ **a** (= *upright) person, posture, plant* aufrecht; *head* hoch erhoben; *stem* gerade; *tail* erhoben; *ears* aufgestellt; **to stand ~** gerade stehen; **to walk ~** aufrecht gehen **b** *(Physiol) penis* erigiert, steif; *clitoris, nipples* erigiert, aufgerichtet

erectile [ɪˈrektaɪl] ADJ Schwell-, erektil; **~ tissue** Schwellkörper *m*

erection [ɪˈrekʃən] N **a** (= *act of erecting, of wall, building*) (Er)bauen *nt*; *(of statue, memorial, altar)* Errichten *nt*; *(of machinery, traffic signs, collapsible furniture)* Aufstellen *nt*; *(of tent)* Aufschlagen *nt*; *(of mast, flagpole)* Aufrichten *nt*; *(fig, of barrier)* Errichten *nt*, Aufbauen *nt*; *(of system)* Aufstellen *nt* **b** (= *building*) Gebäude *nt*, Bau *m* **c** *(Physiol)* Erektion *f*

erectly [ɪˈrektlɪ] ADV aufrecht

erg [ɜːɡ] N Erg *nt*

ergo [ˈɜːɡəʊ] ADV *(form, hum)* ergo, also

ergonomic ADJ , **ergonomically** ADV [ˌɜːɡəʊˈnɒmɪk, -əlɪ] ergonomisch

ergonomics [ˌɜːɡəʊˈnɒmɪks] N *sing* Ergonomie *f*, Arbeitswissenschaft *f*

ergot [ˈɜːɡət] N Mutterkorn *nt*, Hungerkorn *nt*

ergotism [ˈɜːɡətɪzəm] N *(Med)* Mutterkornvergiftung *f*, Ergotismus *m*

erica [ˈerɪkə] N *(Bot)* Erika *f*, Heidekraut *nt*

Erin [ˈɪərɪn] N *(poet)* Irland *nt*

ERM N *abbr of* **exchange rate mechanism**

ermine [ˈɜːmɪn] N (= *animal*) Hermelin *nt*; (= *fur*) Hermelin *m*

Ernie [ˈɜːnɪ] *abbr of* **Electronic Random Number Indicator Equipment**

erode [ɪˈrəʊd] VT *(glacier, water, sea)* auswaschen, erodieren *(spec)*; *(acid)* ätzen; *(rust)* wegfressen, anfressen; *(fig) confidence, power, values, beliefs* untergraben; *authority* unterminieren; *differentials* aushöhlen; *value* abtragen, untergraben VI *(value)* abgetragen werden

erogenous [ɪˈrɒdʒənəs] ADJ erogen; **~ zones** erogene Zonen *pl*

erosion [ɪˈrəʊʒən] N *(by water, glaciers, rivers)* Erosion *f*, Abtragung *f*; *(by acid)* Ätzung *f*; *(fig, of love etc)* Schwinden *nt*; *(of power, values, beliefs)* Untergrabung *f*; *(of authority)* Unterminierung *f*; *(of differentials)* Aushöhlen *nt*; *(of value)* Abtragung *f*, Untergrabung *f*; **an ~ of confidence in the pound** ein Vertrauensverlust *m or* -schwund *m* des Pfundes

erosive [ɪˈrəʊzɪv] ADJ *effect of sea etc* abtragend; *effect of acid* ätzend

erotic [ɪˈrɒtɪk] ADJ erotisch; *love also* sinnlich; *pose also* aufreizend; **an ~ dancer** ein Erotiktänzer *m*, eine Erotiktänzerin *f*; **he's a very ~ person** er ist sehr erotisch

erotica [ɪˈrɒtɪkə] PL Erotika *pl*

erotically [ɪˈrɒtɪkəlɪ] ADV erotisch; **~ charged** erotisch geladen

eroticism [ɪˈrɒtɪsɪzəm] N Erotik *f*

eroticize [ɪˈrɒtɪsaɪz] VT erotisieren

err [ɜː] VI **a** (= *be mistaken*) sich irren; **to ~ in one's judgement** in seinem Urteil fehlgehen, sich in seinem Urteil irren; **to ~ is human(, to forgive divine)** *(Prov)* Irren ist menschlich(, Vergeben göttlich) *(Prov)*; **it is better to ~ on the side of caution** man sollte im Zweifelsfall lieber zu vorsichtig sein **b** (= *sin*) sündigen, Verfehlungen begehen **c** *(Rel, = stray)* abgehen, in die Irre gehen

errand [ˈerənd] N (= *shopping etc*) Besorgung *f*; *(to give a message etc)* Botengang *m*; (= *task*) Auftrag *m*; **to send sb on an ~** jdn auf Besorgungen/einen Botengang schicken; **to go on** *or* **run ~s (for sb)** (für jdn) Besorgungen/Botengänge machen; **to be out on an ~** Besorgungen/einen Botengang machen, etwas erledigen; **~ of mercy** Rettungsaktion *f*

errand boy N Laufbursche *m*, Laufjunge *m*

errant [ˈerənt] ADJ (= *erring) ways* sündig, verfehlt; *husband* dat untreu; *members* abtrünnig; *(hum) Marxist, Freudian* fehlgeleitet, auf Irrwegen

errata [eˈrɑːtə] *pl of* **erratum**

erratic [ɪˈrætɪk] ADJ unberechenbar; *progress, pattern, rhythm, pulse, breathing* ungleichmäßig; *performance* variabel; *movement* unkontrolliert; **to be (very) ~** *(sales, figures)* (stark) schwanken; **his ~ driving** sein unberechenbarer Fahrstil; **his work is rather ~** er ist in seiner Arbeit recht wechselhaft; **public transport here is very ~** die öffentlichen Verkehrsmittel verkehren hier nur sehr unregelmäßig; **we work ~ hours** wir haben unregelmäßige Arbeitszeiten

erratically [ɪˈrætɪkəlɪ] ADV *behave, drive* unberechenbar; **to work ~** *(person)* ungleichmäßig arbeiten; *(machine)* unregelmäßig arbeiten; **the ~ brilliant hockey team** die hervorragende, jedoch sehr wechselhaft spielende Hockey-Mannschaft

erratum [eˈrɑːtəm] N *pl* **errata** Erratum *nt*

erring [ˈɜːrɪŋ] ADJ = **errant b**

erroneous [ɪˈrəʊnɪəs] ADJ falsch; *assumption, belief, impression* irrig

erroneously [ɪˈrəʊnɪəslɪ] ADV fälschlicherweise

error [ˈerə] ✪ 18.3, 20.6, 20.7 N **a** (= *mistake*) Fehler *m*; **~ in calculation** Rechenfehler *m*; **~ of compass** (magnetische) Abweichung *m*; **~s and omissions excepted** *(Comm)* Irrtum vorbehalten; **a pilot ~** ein Fehler *m* des Piloten; **the ~ rate** die Fehlerquote, die Fehlerrate; **~ in fact** *(Jur)* Tatsachenirrtum *m*; **~ in form** *(Jur)* Formfehler *m*; **~ in law** *(Jur)* Rechtsirrtum *m* → **margin b** (= *wrongness*) Irrtum *m*; **to be in ~** im Irrtum sein, sich im Irrtum befinden; **in ~** (=

---

wrongly, accidentally) irrtümlicherweise; **to see the ~ of one's ways** seine Fehler einsehen

error message N *(Comput)* Fehlermeldung *f*

ersatz [ˈeəzæts] ADJ Ersatz-; **~ religion** Ersatzreligion *f*; **~ coffee** Kaffee-Ersatz *m* N Ersatz *m*

Erse [ɜːs] N , *no pl* Gälisch *nt*

erstwhile [ˈɜːstwaɪl] ADJ *(old, liter)* vormalig, einstig, ehemalig ADV *(old, liter)* vormals, ehedem, einst

eructate [ɪˈrʌkteɪt] VI *(hum, form)* aufstoßen

eructation [ˌɪrʌkˈteɪʃən] N *(hum, form)* Aufstoßen *nt*; **an ~** ein Rülpser *m (inf)*

erudite [ˈerʊdaɪt] ADJ gelehrt; *person also* gebildet, belesen

eruditely [ˈerʊdaɪtlɪ] ADV gelehrt

erudition [ˌerʊˈdɪʃən] N Gelehrsamkeit *f*; **a work of great ~** ein sehr gelehrtes Werk

erupt [ɪˈrʌpt] VI *(volcano, war, quarrel)* ausbrechen; *(spots)* zum Vorschein kommen; *(fig, person)* explodieren; **to ~ in(to) violence** in Gewalttätigkeit ausarten; **the district ~ed in riots** in dem Bezirk brachen Unruhen aus; **the crowd ~ed into applause/laughter** die Menge brach in Applaus/Gelächter aus; **he ~ed in anger** er bekam einen Wutanfall; **her face had ~ed in spots** sie hatte im ganzen Gesicht Pickel bekommen

eruption [ɪˈrʌpʃən] N *(of volcano, anger, war, violence)* Ausbruch *m*; *(Med, of spots, rash)* Eruption *f (spec)*, Ausbruch *m*, Auftreten *nt*; (= *rash etc)* Hautausschlag *m*, Eruption *f (spec)*

erysipelas [ˌerɪˈsɪpɪləs] N *(Wund)rose *f*

ESA *(Space) abbr of* **European Space Agency**

escalate [ˈeskəleɪt] VT *war* ausweiten, eskalieren; *costs* sprunghaft erhöhen VI sich ausweiten, um sich greifen, eskalieren; *(costs)* eskalieren, in die Höhe schnellen

escalation [ˌeskəˈleɪʃən] N Eskalation *f*

escalator [ˈeskəleɪtə] N Rolltreppe *f*

escalator clause N Gleitklausel *f*

escalope [ˈeskələp] N Schnitzel *nt*

escapable [ɪˈskeɪpəbl] ADJ vermeidbar

escapade [ˌeskəˈpeɪd] N Eskapade *f*

escape [ɪˈskeɪp] VI **a** (= *get away*) flüchten, fliehen *(from aus)*, entfliehen *(geh) (from +dat)*; *(from pursuers, captivity)* entkommen *(from +dat)*; *(from prison, camp, cage, stall etc)* ausbrechen *(from aus)*; *(bird)* entfliegen *(from +dat)*; *(water)* auslaufen *(from aus)*; *(gas)* ausströmen *(from aus)*; **to stop the prisoners escaping** um Gefängnisausbrüche zu verhindern; **he was shot dead while trying to ~** er wurde bei einem Fluchtversuch erschossen; **an ~d prisoner/tiger** ein entflohener Häftling/entsprungener Tiger; **he ~d from the fire** er ist dem Feuer entkommen; **I've got you now, she said, and I won't let you ~** jetzt habe ich dich, sagte sie, und du entkommst mir so schnell nicht; **I just feel I have to ~ from this place** ich habe einfach das Gefühl, dass ich hier wegmuss; **she has to be able to ~ from her family sometimes** sie muss ab und zu die Möglichkeit haben, ihrer Familie zu entfliehen; **a room which I can ~ to** ein Zimmer, in das ich mich zurückziehen kann; **to ~ from oneself** vor sich *(dat)* selber fliehen; **it's no good trying to ~ from the world** es hat keinen Zweck, vor der Welt fliehen zu wollen; **he's trying to ~ from life on the streets** er versucht, von dem Leben auf der Straße wegzukommen; **to ~ from reality** der Wirklichkeit entfliehen *(geh)*; **to ~ from poverty** der Armut entkommen

b (= *get off, be spared*) davonkommen; **these cuts will affect everyone, nobody will ~** diese Kürzungen betreffen alle, keiner wird ungeschoren davonkommen; **the others were killed, but he ~d** die anderen wurden getötet, aber er kam mit dem Leben davon

VT **a** *pursuers* entkommen *(+dat)*

b (= *avoid) consequences, punishment, disaster, detection* entgehen *(+dat)*; **no department will ~ these cuts** keine Abteilung wird von diesen Kürzungen verschont bleiben; **he narrowly ~d**

injury er ist gerade noch unverletzt davongekommen; **he narrowly ~d death** er ist dem Tod mit knapper Not entronnen; **he narrowly ~d being run over** er wäre um ein Haar *or* um Haaresbreite überfahren worden; **to ~ the worst** vom Schlimmsten verschont bleiben; **but you can't ~ the fact that ...** aber du kannst nicht leugnen *or* abstreiten, dass ...

c (= *be unnoticed, forgotten by*) **his name ~s me** sein Name ist mir entfallen; **nothing ~s him** ihm entgeht nichts; **to ~ notice** unbemerkt bleiben; **it had not ~d her (attention)** es war ihr *or* ihrer Aufmerksamkeit nicht entgangen

d the thoughtless words which ~d me die unbedachten Worte, die mir herausgerutscht *or* entfahren sind

N a (*from prison etc*) Ausbruch *m*, Flucht *f*; (= *attempted escape*) Ausbruchsversuch *m*, Fluchtversuch *m*; (*from a country*) Flucht *f* (*from* aus); (*fig, from reality, one's family etc*) Flucht *f* (*from* vor); **to make one's ~** ausbrechen, entfliehen; **the ~ was successful** der Ausbruchs- *or* Fluchtversuch glückte *or* war erfolgreich; **the increasing number of ~s** die zunehmende Zahl von Ausbruchsfällen; **with this security system ~ is impossible** dieses Sicherheitssystem macht Ausbrechen unmöglich; **what are their chances of ~?** wie sind ihre Fluchtmöglichkeiten?, wie sind ihre Chancen zu entkommen?; **there's been an ~ from London Zoo** aus dem Londoner Zoo ist ein Tier ausgebrochen; **to have a miraculous ~** (*from accident, illness*) auf wunderbare Weise davonkommen; **fishing/music is his ~** Angeln/Musik ist seine Zuflucht; **otherwise I don't get any ~ from the demands of my family** sonst habe ich überhaupt keine Abwechslung von den Ansprüchen meiner Familie; **there's no ~** (*fig*) es gibt keinen Ausweg *or* kein Entrinnen (*geh*) → **lucky**

b (*of water*) Ausfließen *nt*; (*of gas*) Ausströmen *nt*; (*of steam, gas, in a machine*) Entweichen *nt*; **due to an ~ of gas** aufgrund *or* auf Grund ausströmenden Gases

c (*Comput*) **hit ~** Escape drücken

escape: escape artist N Entfesselungskünstler(in) *m(f)*; **escape attempt**, **escape bid** N Fluchtversuch *m*; **escape chute** N (*on plane*) Notrutsche *f*; **escape clause** N (*Jur*) Rücktrittsklausel *f*

escapee [ɪskeɪˈpiː] N entflohener Häftling

escape: escape hatch N (*Naut*) Notluke *f*; **escape key** N (*Comput*) Escape-Taste *f*; **escape mechanism** N Abwehrmechanismus *m*

escapement [ɪˈskeɪpmənt] N (*of clock*) Hemmung *f*

escape: escape pipe N Überlaufrohr *nt*; (*for gas, steam*) Abzugsrohr *nt*; **escape plan** N Fluchtplan *m*; **escape-proof** ADJ ausbruchsicher; **escape road** N Ausweichstraße *f*; **escape route** N Fluchtweg *m*; **escape valve** N Sicherheitsventil *nt*; **escape velocity** N (*Space*) Fluchtgeschwindigkeit *f*

escapism [ɪˈskeɪpɪzəm] N Wirklichkeitsflucht *f*, Eskapismus *m* (*spec*)

escapist [ɪˈskeɪpɪst] N jd, der vor der Wirklichkeit flieht, Eskapist(in) *m(f)* ADJ eskapistisch; **~ fantasy** unrealistische Fantasien *or* Phantasien *pl*

escapologist [ˌeskəˈpɒlədʒɪst] N Entfesselungskünstler(in) *m(f)*

escarpment [ɪˈskɑːpmənt] N Steilhang *m*; (*Geol*) Schichtstufe *f*; (*as fortification*) Böschung *f*

eschatological [ˌeskətəˈlɒdʒɪkəl] ADJ eschatologisch

eschatology [ˌeskəˈtɒlədʒɪ] N Eschatologie *f*

eschew [ɪsˈtʃuː] VT (*old, liter*) scheuen, (ver)meiden; *wine etc* sich enthalten (+*gen*); *temptation* aus dem Wege gehen (+*dat*)

escort [ˈeskɔːt] N a Geleitschutz *m*; (*escorting vehicles, ships etc*) Eskorte *f*, Geleitschiff *nt*/-schiffe *pl*; (= *police escort*) Begleitmannschaft *f*, Eskorte *f*; (= *guard of honour*) Eskorte *f*; **under ~** unter Bewachung; **motorcycle ~** Motorrades-

korte *f* b (= *male companion*) Begleiter *m*; (= *hired female*) Hostess *f* VT [ɪˈskɔːt] begleiten; (*Mil, Naut*) *general* eskortieren, Geleit(schutz) geben (+*dat*)

escort: escort agency N Hostessenagentur *f*; **escort duty** N Geleitdienst *m*; **to be on ~** Geleitschutz geben; **escort fighter** N (*Aviat*) Begleitjäger *m*; **escort party** N Eskorte *f*; **escort vessel** N (*Naut*) Geleitschiff *nt*

escrow [ˈeskrəʊ] N **~ account** Anderkonto *nt*; **to put money in ~** Geld auf ein Anderkonto legen

escutcheon [ɪˈskʌtʃən] N Wappen *nt*; **it is a blot on his ~** das ist ein Fleck auf seiner weißen Weste

ESE *abbr of* **east-south-east** OSO

Eskimo [ˈeskɪməʊ] (*pej*) ADJ Eskimo-, eskimoisch **N a** Eskimo *m*, Eskimofrau *f* b (*Ling*) Eskimosprache *f*

Eskimo dog N Eskimohund *m*

ESL *abbr of* **English as a Second Language**

ESN *abbr of* **educationally subnormal**

esophagus N (*esp US*) = **oesophagus**

esoteric [ˌesəˈterɪk] ADJ esoterisch

ESP *abbr of* **extrasensory perception** ASW *f*

esp. *abbr of* **especially** bes.

espadrille [ˌespəˈdrɪl] N Espadrille *f*

espalier [ɪˈspæljə] N (= *trellis*) Spalier *nt*; (= *tree*) Spalierbaum *m*; (*method*) Anbau *m* von Spalierobst

especial [ɪˈspeʃəl] ADJ besondere(r, s)

especially [ɪˈspeʃəlɪ] **★** 26.3 ADV **a** (= *particularly*) besonders; **I ~ liked the beginning** der Anfang hat mir besonders gut gefallen; **to try ~ hard** sich besonders viel Mühe geben; **not ~** nicht besonders; **(more) ~ as ...** besonders *or* vor allem, weil ...; **~ in summer** vor allem im Sommer; **you ~ ought to know** gerade du solltest das wissen; **why Jim ~?** warum ausgerechnet *or* gerade Jim? b (= *specifically*) speziell, eigens; **I came ~ to see you** ich bin eigens gekommen, um dich zu sehen; **to do sth ~ for sb/sth** etw speziell *or* extra für jdn/etw tun

Esperanto [ˌespəˈræntəʊ] N Esperanto *nt*

espionage [ˌespɪəˈnɑːʒ] N Spionage *f*

esplanade [ˌespləˈneɪd] N (Strand)promenade *f*

espousal [ɪˈspaʊzəl] N **a** (*old, = marriage*) Vermählung *f*; (= *betrothal*) Verlobung *f* b (*of cause etc*) Parteinahme *f* (*of* für)

espouse [ɪˈspaʊz] VT **a** (*old, form*) *woman* sich vermählen mit, zur Frau nehmen; (= *get betrothed to*) sich anverloben (+*dat*) (*old*); **to become ~d to sb** jdm angetraut/anverlobt werden b (*fig*) *cause, views* Partei ergreifen für, eintreten für; *views* befürworten

espresso [eˈspresəʊ] N **~ (coffee)** Espresso *m*; **~ bar** Espresso(bar *f*) *nt*

esprit de corps [eˈspriːdəˈkɔː] N Korpsgeist *m*

espy [ɪˈspaɪ] VT (*old, liter*) erspähen, erblicken

esquire [ɪˈskwaɪə] N (*abbr* **Esq**) (*Brit: on envelope*) **als Titel nach dem Namen, unter anderer Titel angegeben wird** **James Jones, Esq** Herrn James Jones

essay¹ [eˈseɪ] (*form*) VT (= *try*) (aus)probieren N Versuch *m*

essay² [ˈeseɪ] N Essay *m or nt*; (*esp Sch*) Aufsatz *m*

essayist [ˈeseɪɪst] N Essayist(in) *m(f)*

essayistic [ˌeseɪˈɪstɪk] ADJ essayistisch

essence [ˈesəns] N **a** (*Philos*) Wesen *nt*, Essenz *f*; (= *substratum*) Substanz *f* b (= *most important quality*) Wesen *nt*, Wesentliche(s) *nt*, Kern *m*; **in ~ the theories are very similar** die Theorien sind im Wesentlichen *or* in ihrem Kern *or* essenziell (*geh*) *or* essentiell (*geh*) sehr ähnlich; **how would you describe the situation, in ~?** wie würden Sie die Situation im Wesentlichen beschreiben?; **speed/time is of the ~** Geschwindigkeit/Zeit ist von entscheidender Bedeutung; **the ~ of his thought** der Kern *or* die Essenz seines Denkens; **the note contained the ~ of what he had said** die

Notiz enthielt den Kern dessen, was er gesagt hatte; **he embodies the very ~ of Japanese spirit** er verkörpert den Inbegriff des japanischen Geistes; **the novel captures the ~ of life in the city** der Roman fängt das Leben in der Stadt perfekt ein; **the ~ of Liberalism** die Essenz des Liberalismus

c (= *extract: Chem, Cook*) Essenz *f*

essential [ɪˈsenʃəl] **★** 10.1 ADJ **a** (= *necessary, vital*) (unbedingt *or* absolut) erforderlich *or* notwendig; *services, supplies* lebenswichtig; **it is ~ to act quickly** schnelles Handeln ist unbedingt *or* absolut erforderlich; **it is ~ that he come(s)** es ist absolut *or* unbedingt erforderlich, dass er kommt, er muss unbedingt kommen; **it is ~ that you understand this** du musst das unbedingt verstehen; **do it now – is it really ~?** mach es jetzt – ist das wirklich unbedingt nötig?; **this is of ~ importance** dies ist von entscheidender Bedeutung; **certain vitamins are ~ for good health** bestimmte Vitamine sind für die Gesundheit unerlässlich; **she's become ~ to me** sie ist mir unentbehrlich geworden; **the ~ thing is to ...** wichtig ist vor allem, zu ...

b (= *of the essence, basic*) wesentlich, essenziell (*geh*), essentiell (*geh*); (*Philos*) essenziell, essentiell, wesenhaft; *question, role* entscheidend; **~ features** wesentliche Eigenschaften *pl*; **the ~ feature of his personality** der Grundzug *or* der grundlegende Zug seiner Persönlichkeit; **I don't doubt his ~ goodness** ich zweifle nicht an, dass er im Grunde ein guter Mensch ist; **to establish the ~ nature of the problem** feststellen, worum es im Kern bei diesem Problem eigentlich geht; **to establish the ~ nature of the disease** feststellen, worum es sich bei dieser Krankheit eigentlich handelt

N a (= *necessary thing*) **a compass is an ~ for mountain climbing** ein Kompass ist unbedingt notwendig zum Bergsteigen; **the first ~ is to privatize the industry** als erstes muss die Industrie unbedingt privatisiert werden; **just bring the ~s** bring nur das Allernotwendigste mit; **with only the bare ~s** nur mit dem Allernotwendigsten ausgestattet

b **essentials** PL (= *most important points*) wichtige Punkte *pl*, Essentials *pl*; **the ~s of German grammar** die Grundlagen *pl or* die Grundzüge *pl* der deutschen Grammatik

essentially [ɪˈsenʃəlɪ] ADV (= *fundamentally*) im Wesentlichen; (= *basically, at heart*) im Grunde genommen; **~, they are saying that ...** im Wesentlichen sagen sie, dass ...; **she was an ~ good woman** im Grunde genommen war sie eine gute Frau

essential oils [ɪˈsenʃəlˈɔɪlz] PL (*Chem*) ätherische Öle *pl*

EST (*US*) *abbr of* **Eastern Standard Time** Ostküstenzeit *f*

est a *abbr of* **established** gegr. **b** *abbr of* **estimated** gesch.

establish [ɪˈstæblɪʃ] **★** 15.1 VT **a** (= *found, set up*) gründen; *government* bilden; *laws* geben, schaffen; *custom, new procedure* einführen; *relations* herstellen, aufnehmen; *links* anknüpfen; *post* einrichten, schaffen; *power, authority* sich (*dat*) verschaffen; *peace* stiften; *order* (wieder) herstellen; *list* (*in publishing*) aufstellen, zusammenstellen; *reputation* sich (*dat*) verschaffen; *precedent* setzen; *committee* einsetzen; **once he had ~ed his power as Emperor** als er seine Macht als Kaiser begründet hatte; **his father ~ed him in business** sein Vater ermöglichte ihm den Start ins Geschäftsleben; **to ~ one's reputation as a scholar/writer** sich (*dat*) einen Namen als Wissenschaftler(in)/Schriftsteller(in) machen

b (= *prove*) *fact, innocence* beweisen, nachweisen; *claim* unter Beweis stellen; **we have ~ed that ...** wir haben bewiesen *or* gezeigt, dass ...

c (= *determine*) *identity, facts* ermitteln, feststellen

d (= *gain acceptance for*) *product, theory, ideas* Anklang *or* Anerkennung finden für; *one's rights* Anerkennung finden für; **if we can ~ our prod-**

uct on the market wenn wir unser Produkt auf dem Markt etablieren können

VR (*in business, profession*) sich etablieren, sich niederlassen; **he has now firmly ~ed himself in the company** er ist jetzt in der Firma fest etabliert; **he seems to have ~ed himself as an expert** er scheint sich (*dat*) einen Ruf als Experte verschafft zu haben

established [ɪˈstæblɪʃt] ADJ *order, authority, religion* bestehend, etabliert; *rules* bestehend; *business, company* etabliert, eingeführt; *clientele* fest; *reputation* gesichert; *tradition* althergebracht; *name, brand* etabliert; **it's an ~ practice or custom** es ist allgemein üblich; **this is our ~ procedure** so gehen wir normalerweise vor; **firmly ~** (*reputation, peace*) völlig gesichert; *company, name* fest etabliert; **a well ~ business** ein fest etabliertes *or* gut eingeführtes Geschäft; **well** *or* **firmly ~ as sth** (= *recognized*) allgemein als etw anerkannt; **Indian food is now firmly ~ as a favourite** (*Brit*) *or* **favorite** (*US*) die indische Küche hat sich einen festen Platz als Lieblingsessen erobert; **it's an ~ fact that ...** es steht fest, dass ...; **this is ~ truth** das ist die unbestrittene Wahrheit; **~ 1850** (*Comm etc*) gegründet 1850

Established Church N Staatskirche *f*

establishing shot [ɪˈstæblɪʃɪŋʃɒt] N (*Film*) Eröffnungsszene *f*

establishment [ɪˈstæblɪʃmənt] N **a** (= *setting up, of relations, links*) Aufnahme *f*, Herstellung *f*; (*of committee*) Bildung *f*, Einsetzung *f*; (*of post*) Schaffung *f*, Einrichtung *f*; (*of peace*) Herstellung *f*; (*of order*) Herstellung *f*, Schaffung *f*; (*of publisher's list*) Bildung *f*; (*of power, authority*) Festigung *f*, (Wieder)herstellung *f*; (*of reputation*) Begründung *f*
b (= *proving*) Beweis *m*; **the lawyer devoted a lot of time to the ~ of a few basic facts** der Rechtsanwalt verwandte viel Zeit darauf, ein paar Tatsachen unter Beweis zu stellen
c (= *determining*) Ermittlung *f*; **~ of the truth** Wahrheitsfindung *f*
d (= *institution etc*) Institution *f*; (= *hospital, school etc*) Anstalt *f*, Institution *f*; **the school is a very modest ~** die Schule ist sehr bescheiden; **commercial ~** kommerzielles Unternehmen
e (= *household*) Haus *nt*, Haushalt *m*; **to keep up a large ~** ein großes Haus führen
f (*Mil, Naut etc: personnel*) Truppenstärke *f*; **war/ peace ~** Kriegs-/Friedensstärke *f*
g **the Establishment** das Establishment; **~ person** (Erz)konservative(r) *mf*; **~ figure** Mitglied *nt or* Angehörige(r) *mf* des Establishments

estate [ɪˈsteɪt] N **a** (= *land*) Gut *nt*; **country ~** Landgut *nt*; **family ~** Familienbesitz *m* **b** (*Jur: = possessions*) Besitz *m*, Besitztümer *pl*, Eigentum *nt*; (*of deceased*) Nachlass *m*, Erbmasse *f*; **to leave one's ~ to sb** jdm seinen ganzen Besitz vermachen *or* hinterlassen; **personal ~** persönliches Eigentum → **real** ADJ **c** (*esp Brit*, = *housing estate*) Siedlung *f*; (= *trading estate*) Industriegelände *nt* **d** (= *order, rank*) Stand *m*; **the three ~s** die drei Stände; **person of high ~** (*old*) Standesperson *f* (*old*); **the holy ~ of matrimony** (*Brit Rel*) der heilige Stand der Ehe **e** (*Brit*) = **estate car**

estate: estate agent N (*Brit*) Grundstücks- *or* Immobilienmakler(in) *m(f)*; **estate-bottled** ADJ *wine* vom Erzeuger abgefüllt; **"estate bottled"** Erzeugerabfüllung *f*; **estate car** N (*Brit*) Kombi(wagen) *m*; **estate duty** N Erbschaftssteuer *f*

esteem [ɪˈstiːm] **VT a** (= *consider*) ansehen, betrachten **b** (= *think highly of*) *person* hoch schätzen; *qualities* schätzen; **my ~ed colleague** (*form*) mein verehrter Herr Kollege (*form*), meine verehrte Frau Kollegin (*form*) **N** Wertschätzung *f*; **to hold sb/sth in (high) ~** jdn/etw (hoch) schätzen, viel von jdm/etw halten; **to be held in low/great ~** wenig/ sehr geschätzt werden; **he went down in my ~** er ist in meiner Achtung gesunken

ester [ˈestə] N (*Chem*) Ester *m*

esthete *etc* (*esp US*) N = **aesthete** *etc*

Est(h)onia [eˈstəʊnɪə] N Estland *nt*
Est(h)onian [eˈstəʊnɪən] ADJ estnisch **N a** Este *m*, Estin *f* **b** (*Ling*) Estnisch *nt*

estimable [ˈestɪməbl] ADJ **a** (= *deserving respect*) schätzenswert **b** (= *that can be estimated*) (ab)schätzbar

estimate [ˈestɪmɪt] **N a** (= *approximate calculation*) Schätzung *f*; (= *valuation: by antique dealer etc*) Taxierung *f*; **what's your ~ of our chances of success?** wie schätzen Sie unsere Erfolgschancen ein?; **£100/it is just an ~** £ 100/das ist nur geschätzt; **at a rough ~** grob geschätzt, über den Daumen gepeilt (*inf*); **at a conservative ~** vorsichtig geschätzt; **at the lowest ~** mindestens, wenigstens
b (*Comm, of cost*) (Kosten)voranschlag *m*; **to get an ~** einen (Kosten)voranschlag einholen
c estimates PL (= *government costs*) Haushalt *m*, Budget *nt*
VT [ˈestɪmeɪt] *cost, price* (ein)schätzen; *distance, speed* schätzen; **his wealth is ~d at ...** sein Vermögen wird auf ... geschätzt; **his wealth is hard to ~** sein Vermögen lässt sich schwer schätzen; **I ~ she must be 40** ich schätze sie auf 40, ich schätze, dass sie 40 ist; **I ~ we'll need 30 people/£300** ich schätze, wir brauchen 30 Leute/ £ 300
VI [ˈestɪmeɪt] schätzen; **I'm just estimating** das schätze ich nur

estimation [ˌestɪˈmeɪʃən] N **a** Einschätzung *f*; **in my ~** meiner Einschätzung nach **b** (= *esteem*) Achtung *f*; **to hold sb in high ~** jdn hoch achten, viel von jdm halten; **he went up/down in my ~** er ist in meiner Achtung gestiegen/gesunken

estimator [ˈestɪmeɪtə] N (*Insur etc*) Schätzer(in) *m(f)*

estivate *etc* (*US*) VB = **aestivate** *etc*

Estonia *etc* = **Est(h)onia** *etc*

estoppel [ɪˈstɒpl] N (*Jur*) rechtshemmender Einwand

estragon [ˈestrəɡɒn] N (*Bot*) Estragon *m*

estrange [ɪˈstreɪndʒ] VT *person* entfremden (*from +dat*); **to be/become ~d from sb/sth** sich von jdm/ etw entfremdet haben/entfremden; **they are ~d** (*married couple*) sie haben sich auseinander gelebt; **his ~d wife** seine von ihm getrennt lebende Frau

estrangement [ɪˈstreɪndʒmənt] N Entfremdung *f* (*from* von)

estrogen [ˈiːstrəʊdʒən] N (*US*) = **oestrogen**

estuary [ˈestjʊərɪ] N Mündung *f*

estuary English N (*Brit*) (*von Jugendlichen*) *in Südengland gesprochene Variante des Cockney*

ET (*US*) *abbr of* **Eastern Time** Ostküstenzeit *f*

ETA *abbr of* **estimated time of arrival** voraussichtliche Ankunft

et al [etˈæl] ADV et al

etcetera [ɪtˈsetərə] ADV (*abbr* **etc**) und so weiter, et cetera

etch [etʃ] **VI** ätzen; (*in copper*) in Kupfer stechen; (*in other metals*) radieren **VT** ätzen; (*in copper*) in Kupfer stechen; (*in other metals*) radieren; **the windows were ~ed with the vehicle registration number** das Autokennzeichen war in die Scheiben eingeätzt; **the event was ~ed on her mind** das Ereignis hatte sich ihr ins Gedächtnis eingegraben

etching [ˈetʃɪŋ] N **a** (= *picture*) Ätzung *f*; (*in copper*) Kupferstich *m*; (*in other metals*) Radierung *f*; **come up and see my ~s** (*hum*) wollen Sie noch mit heraufkommen und sich (*dat*) meine Briefmarkensammlung ansehen? (*hum*) **b** (= *process*) Ätzen *nt*; (*in copper*) Kupferstechen *nt*; (*in other metals*) Radieren *nt*

ETD *abbr of* **estimated time of departure** voraussichtliche Abfahrt; (*Aviat*) voraussichtlicher Abflug

eternal [ɪˈtɜːnl] ADJ **a** (= *everlasting, immutable*) ewig; **the Eternal City** die Ewige Stadt; **the ~ triangle** das Dreiecksverhältnis **b** (= *incessant*) endlos, ewig (*inf*); **can't you stop this ~ quar-**

relling? könnt ihr nicht mit der ewigen Streiterei aufhören? (*inf*) **c** (= *God*) der Ewige; (= *God*) der Ewige

eternally [ɪˈtɜːnəlɪ] ADV ewig; *optimistic, cheerful* immer; **damned ~** auf ewig verdammt; **to be ~ grateful (to sb/for sth)** (jdm/für etw) ewig dankbar sein

eternity [ɪˈtɜːnɪtɪ] N (*lit, fig: inf*) Ewigkeit *f*; (*Rel, = the future life*) das ewige Leben; **from here to ~** bis in alle Ewigkeit; **for all ~** in alle Ewigkeit; **it seemed an ~** es kam mir wie eine Ewigkeit vor

eternity ring N Memoryring *m*

ethane [ˈiːθeɪn] N Äthan *nt*

ethanol [ˈeθənɒl] N Äthanol *nt*

ether [ˈiːθə] N (*Chem, poet*) Äther *m*

ethereal [ɪˈθɪərɪəl] ADJ **a** (= *light, delicate, spiritual*) ätherisch **b** (= *of the upper air*) *regions* himmlisch

ethic [ˈeθɪk] N Ethik *f*, Ethos *nt*

ethical [ˈeθɪkəl] ADJ **a** (= *morally right*) ethisch *attr*; (*of ethics*) Moral-; **~ philosophy** Moralphilosophie *f*; **~ values** moralische Werte *pl*; **it is not ~ to ...** es ist unethisch *or* unmoralisch, zu ...; **~ behaviour** (*Brit*) *or* **behavior** (*US*) ethisch einwandfreies Verhalten **b** (= *available only on prescription*) *medicine etc* verschreibungspflichtig

ethically [ˈeθɪkəlɪ] ADV ethisch; (= *with correct ethics*) *act, behave etc* ethisch einwandfrei

ethics [ˈeθɪks] N **a** *sing* (= *study, system*) Ethik *f* **b** *pl* (= *morality*) Moral *f*; **the ~ of abortion** die moralischen *or* ethischen Aspekte *pl* der Abtreibung

Ethiopia [ˌiːθɪˈəʊpɪə] N Äthiopien *nt*

Ethiopian [ˌiːθɪˈəʊpɪən] ADJ äthiopisch **N** Äthiopier(in) *m(f)*

ethnic [ˈeθnɪk] ADJ **a** (= *racial*) ethnisch; **~ clashes** ethnische Konflikte *pl*; **~ violence** Rassenkrawalle *pl*; **~ Germans** Volksdeutsche *pl* **b** (= *traditional*) *atmosphere* urtümlich; *fabric, clothes* folkloristisch; **~ music** Folklore *f*; **in Zambia she bought several pairs of ~ earrings** in Sambia kaufte sie mehrere Paare der dort typischen Ohrringe; **books on ~ food** Bücher über das Essen in verschiedenen Kulturen **N**

ethnics PL Mitglieder *pl* einer ethnischen Gruppe

ethnically [ˈeθnɪklɪ] ADV ethnisch

ethnic cleansing N (*euph*) ethnische Säuberung

ethnographer [eθˈnɒɡrəfə] N Völkerkundler(in) *m(f)*

ethnography [eθˈnɒɡrəfɪ] N (beschreibende) Völkerkunde, Ethnografie *f*

ethnologist [eθˈnɒlədʒɪst] N Ethnologe *m*, Ethnologin *f*

ethnology [eθˈnɒlədʒɪ] N (vergleichende) Völkerkunde, Ethnologie *f*

ethologist [ɪˈθɒlədʒɪst] N Verhaltensforscher(in) *m(f)*

ethology [ɪˈθɒlədʒɪ] N Verhaltensforschung *f*, Ethologie *f*

ethos [ˈiːθɒs] N Gesinnung *f*, Ethos *nt*

ethyl [ˈiːθaɪl] N Äthyl *nt*

ethylene [ˈeθɪliːn] N Äthylen *nt*

etiolate [ˈiːtɪəʊleɪt] VT (*Bot*) etiolieren (*spec*); (= *enfeeble*) auszehren

etiology *etc* (*esp US*) N = **aetiology** *etc*

etiquette [ˈetɪket] N Etikette *f*; **rules of ~** Verhaltensregeln *pl*; **a breach of ~** ein Verstoß *m* gegen die Etikette; **court ~** Hofetikette *f*; **that's not in accordance with medical ~** das entspricht nicht dem Berufsethos eines Arztes

Eton [ˈiːtən]: **Eton collar** N breiter, steifer, weißer Umlegekragen; **Eton crop** N Bubikopf *m*, Herrenschnitt *m*

Etonian [iːˈtəʊnɪən] (*Brit*) **N** Schüler *m* am Eton College **ADJ** des Eton College

Etruscan [ɪˈtrʌskən] ADJ etruskisch **N a** Etrusker(in) *m(f)* **b** (*Ling*) Etruskisch *nt*

et seq. *abbr of* **et sequentia** f., und folgende

ETV (*US*) *abbr of* **Educational Television** ≈ Schulfernsehen *nt*

etymological ADJ , **etymologically** ADV [ˌetɪməˈlɒdʒɪkəl, -lɪ] etymologisch

etymology [ˌetɪˈmɒlədʒɪ] N Etymologie *f*

EU *abbr of* **European Union** EU *f*

eucalyptus [ˌjuːkəˈlɪptəs] N Eukalyptus *m*; ~ (oil) Eukalyptusöl *nt*

Eucharist [ˈjuːkərɪst] N (*Eccl: = service*) Abendmahlsgottesdienst *m*; the ~ das (heilige) Abendmahl, die Eucharistie

Eucharistic [ˌjuːkəˈrɪstɪk] ADJ eucharistisch; the ~ liturgy die Abendmahlsliturgie; the ~ sacrament das Sakrament des heiligen Abendmahls

Euclid [ˈjuːklɪd] N Euklid *m*

Euclidean [juːˈklɪdɪən] ADJ euklidisch

eugenics [juːˈdʒenɪks] N *sing* Eugenik *f*

eulogistic [ˌjuːləˈdʒɪstɪk] ADJ (*form*) lobrednerisch

eulogize [ˈjuːlədʒaɪz] VT eine Lobesrede halten auf (+*acc*)

eulogy [ˈjuːlədʒɪ] N Lobesrede *f*, Eloge *f* (*liter*)

eunuch [ˈjuːnək] N Eunuch *m*

euphemism [ˈjuːfəmɪzəm] N Euphemismus *m*, Hüllwort *nt*; **a ~ for sth** ein Euphemismus *m* or verhüllender Ausdruck für etw

euphemistic [juːfəˈmɪstɪk] ADJ euphemistisch, verhüllend

euphemistically [juːfəˈmɪstɪkəlɪ] ADV euphemistisch, verhüllend; **to be ~ described/known as ...** beschönigend als ... bezeichnet werden/bekannt sein

euphonic [juːˈfɒnɪk], **euphonious** [juːˈfəʊnɪəs] ADJ euphonisch, wohlklingend

euphonium [juːˈfəʊnɪəm] N Euphonium *nt*

euphony [ˈjuːfənɪ] N (*Mus, Ling*) Euphonie *f*, Wohlklang *m*

euphoria [juːˈfɔːrɪə] N Euphorie *f*

euphoric [juːˈfɒrɪk] ADJ euphorisch

Euphrates [juːˈfreɪtiːz] N Euphrat *m*

Eurailpass [ˈjʊəreɪlpɑːs] N *Dauerfahrkarte, die Nicht-Europäer zur Benutzung aller (west)europäischen Eisenbahnen berechtigt*

Eurasia [jʊəˈreɪʃə] N Eurasien *nt*

Eurasian [jʊəˈreɪʃn] ADJ eurasisch N Eurasier(in) *m(f)*

Euratom [jʊəˈrætəm] *abbr of* **European Atomic Energy Community** Euratom *f*

eureka [jʊəˈriːkə] INTERJ heureka

eurhythmics [juːˈrɪðmɪks] N *sing* Eurhythmie *f*

euro [ˈjʊərəʊ] N (*= currency*) Euro *m*

Euro-, euro- [ˈjʊərəʊ] PREF Euro-, euro-; **Eurocentric** eurozentrisch

Eurobond [ˈjʊərəʊbɒnd] N Eurobond *m*

Eurocheque, (*US*) **Eurocheck** [ˈjʊərəʊtʃek] N Euroscheck *m*

Eurocrat [ˈjʊərəʊkræt] N Eurokrat(in) *m(f)*

Eurodollar [ˈjʊərəʊdɒlə] N Eurodollar *m*

Euroland [ˈjʊərəʊlænd] N (*inf*) Eurozone *f*, Euroland *nt* (*inf*)

Euro MP N (*inf*) Europaabgeordnete(r) *mf*

Europe [ˈjʊərəp] N Europa *nt*

European [jʊərəˈpiːən] ADJ europäisch; ~ standard (*Ind*) europäische Norm N Europäer(in) *m(f)*

European: European Central Bank N Europäische Zentralbank; **European Commission** N Europäische Kommission; **European Community** N Europäische Gemeinschaft; **European Court of Justice** N Europäischer Gerichtshof; **European Currency Unit** N Europäische Währungseinheit; **European Economic Community** N Europäische Wirtschaftsgemeinschaft; **European Free Trade Association** N Europäische Freihandelszone; **European Monetary Union** N Europäische Währungsunion; **European Parliament** N Europäisches Parlament, Europaparlament *nt*; **European Union** N Europäische Union

Euro-sceptic [ˈjʊərəʊˌskeptɪk] N Euroskeptiker(in) *m(f)*

Eurotunnel [ˈjʊərəʊˌtʌnl] N Eurotunnel *m*, Kanaltunnel *m*

Eurovision [ˈjʊərəʊvɪʒn] N Eurovision *f*; ~ Song Contest Eurovisions-Schlagerwettbewerb *m*

Eustachian tube [juːˈsteɪʃənˈtjuːb] N eustachische Röhre

EU standard [ˌiːjuːˈstændəd] N EU-Norm *f*

euthanasia [juːθəˈneɪzɪə] N Euthanasie *f*

evacuate [ɪˈvækjʊeɪt] VT **a** (*= leave*) fort, house räumen **b** (*= clear*) *danger area* räumen; *civilians, women, children* evakuieren (*from* aus, *to* nach) **c** *bowels* entleeren VI **all the villagers had to ~** alle Bewohner mussten das Dorf räumen

evacuation [ɪˌvækjʊˈeɪʃən] N (*of fort, house, danger area*) Räumung *f*; (*of civilians, women, children*) Evakuierung *f*

evacuee [ɪˌvækjʊˈiː] N Evakuierte(r) *mf*

evade [ɪˈveɪd] VT **a** *blow* ausweichen (+*dat*); *pursuit, pursuers* sich entziehen (+*dat*), entkommen (+*dat*) **b** *obligation, justice, capture* sich entziehen (+*dat*); *military service* umgehen, sich entziehen (+*dat*); *question, issue* ausweichen (+*dat*); *difficulty, person, sb's glance* ausweichen (+*dat*), (ver)meiden; *sb's vigilance* entgehen (+*dat*); **to ~ taxes** Steuern hinterziehen; **he successfully ~d the authorities for several years** mehrere Jahre kamen die Behörden ihm nicht auf die Spur; **if you try to ~ paying import duty** wenn Sie versuchen, den Einfuhrzoll zu umgehen; **a concept which somehow ~s precise definition** ein Begriff, der sich einer genauen Definition entzieht

evaluate [ɪˈvæljʊeɪt] VT *house, painting, worth etc* schätzen (*at* auf +*acc*); *damages* festsetzen (*at* auf +*acc*); *chances, situation, effectiveness, usefulness* einschätzen, beurteilen; *evidence, results* auswerten; *pros and cons* (gegeneinander) abwägen; *contribution, achievement, work, performance* beurteilen; (*Med*) *patient* untersuchen (und die Diagnose stellen)

evaluation [ɪˌvæljʊˈeɪʃən] N (*of house, painting, worth etc*) Schätzung *f*; (*of damages*) Festsetzung *f*; (*of situation, chances, effectiveness, usefulness*) Einschätzung *f*, Beurteilung *f*; (*of evidence, results*) Auswertung *f*; (*of pros and cons*) Abwägung *f*; (*of contribution, achievement, work, performance*) Beurteilung *f*; (*Med: of patient*) Untersuchung (und Diagnosestellung) *f*; **in my** ~ nach meiner Einschätzung; **on ~ of the evidence it became clear that ...** die Auswertung or Sichtung des Beweismaterials machte klar, dass ...

evaluative [ɪˈvæljʊətɪv] ADJ (*form*) wertend

evanescence [ˌiːvəˈnesəns] N (*Liter*) Vergänglichkeit *f*

evanescent [ˌiːvəˈnesənt] ADJ (*Liter*) vergänglich

evangelic(al) [ˌiːvænˈdʒelɪk(əl)] ADJ evangelikal

evangelist [ɪˈvændʒəlɪst] N (*Bibl*) Evangelist(in) *m(f)*; (*= preacher*) Prediger(in) *m(f)*; (*= itinerant*) Wanderprediger(in) *m(f)*

evangelize [ɪˈvændʒəlaɪz] VT evangelisieren, bekehren VI das Evangelium predigen

evaporate [ɪˈvæpəreɪt] VI **a** (*liquid*) verdampfen, verdunsten **b** (*fig: = disappear*) sich in nichts or in Luft auflösen; (*hopes*) sich zerschlagen, schwinden VT *liquid* verdampfen or verdunsten (lassen); **evaporating dish** Abdampfschale *f*

evaporated milk [ɪˈvæpəreɪtɪdˈmɪlk] N Kondens- or Büchsenmilch *f*

evaporation [ɪˌvæpəˈreɪʃən] N Verdampfung *f*, Verdampfen *nt*; (*fig*) Schwinden *nt*

evasion [ɪˈveɪʒən] N **a** (*of question etc*) Ausweichen *nt* (*of* vor +*dat*) **b** (*= evasive answer etc*) Ausflucht *f*

evasive [ɪˈveɪsɪv] ADJ ausweichend; **he was (very) ~** er wich (dauernd) aus; **they were ~ about it** sie redeten drum herum; **she was ~ about her intentions** sie war ausweichend, was ihre Ab-

sichten betraf; **to take ~ action** ein Ausweichmanöver machen

evasively [ɪˈveɪsɪvlɪ] ADV ausweichend

evasiveness [ɪˈveɪsɪvnɪs] N ausweichendes Verhalten; (*of answers*) ausweichende Antworten *pl*, Herumgerede *nt* (*pej*)

Eve [iːv] N Eva *f*

eve[1] [iːv] N Vorabend *m*; **on the ~ of** am Tage vor (+*dat*), am Vorabend von or +*gen*

eve[2] N (*obs, poet*) Abend *m*

even[1] [ˈiːvən] ✪ 26.1, 26.3 ADJ **a** *surface, ground* eben; **to make sth ~** (*ground, earth*) etw ebnen; **the concrete has to be ~ with the ground** der Beton muss eben mit dem Boden abschließen **b** (*= regular*) *layer etc, voice* gleichmäßig; *progress* stetig; *breathing, pulse* regelmäßig, gleichmäßig; *temper* ausgeglichen **c** *quantities, distances, values* gleich; **they are an ~ match** sie sind einander ebenbürtig; **I will get ~ with you for that** das werde ich dir heimzahlen; **that makes us ~** (*in game*) damit steht es unentschieden; (*fig*) damit sind wir quitt; **the odds** or **chances are about ~** die Chancen stehen etwa fifty-fifty (*inf*); **he has an ~ chance of winning** seine Gewinnchancen stehen fifty-fifty (*inf*); **to break ~** die Kosten decken; **to give sb an ~ break** (*esp US*) jdm eine Chance geben; **never give a sucker an ~ break** (*dated US inf*) gib einem Trottel keine Chance (*inf*) **d** *number* gerade; **~ money** *Wette, bei der die doppelte Einsatzsumme als Gewinn ausgezahlt wird* **I'll give you ~ money he's late** (*inf*) ich gehe jede Wette mit dir ein, dass er zu spät kommt **e** (*= exact*) genau; **let's make it an ~ hundred** nehmen wir eine runde Zahl und sagen 100 ADV **a** sogar, selbst; **that's good going, ~ for you** sogar or selbst für dich ist das allerhand; **they ~ denied its existence** sie leugneten sogar seine Existenz; **it'll be difficult, impossible ~** das wird schwierig sein, wenn nicht (so)gar unmöglich **b** (*with comp adj*) sogar noch; **that's ~ better/more beautiful** das ist sogar (noch) besser/schöner **c** (*with neg*) **not ~** nicht einmal; **without ~ a smile** ohne auch nur zu lächeln; **he didn't ~ answer the letter** er hat den Brief (noch) nicht einmal beantwortet **d** **~ if** sogar or selbst wenn; **~ though** obwohl; **~ if you were a millionaire** sogar or selbst wenn du ein Millionär wärst; **~ though I live alone I'm not lonely** obwohl ich allein lebe, bin ich nicht einsam; **but ~ then** aber sogar or selbst dann; **~ as I spoke someone knocked at the door** noch während ich redete, klopfte es an der Tür; **~ as ... so** (*old*) genau wie ... so; **~ so** (aber) trotzdem VT *surface* glatt or eben machen, glätten

▶ **even out** VI **a** (*prices*) sich einpendeln **b** (*ground*) eben werden, sich ebnen VT *sep* **a** *prices* ausgleichen **b** *ground, cement* ebnen, glätten **c** *tax burden, wealth* gleichmäßig verteilen; **that should even things out a bit** dadurch müsste ein gewisser Ausgleich erzielt werden; **that will even things out between us** damit sind wir wohl wieder quitt

▶ **even up** VT *sep sum* aufrunden (*to* auf +*acc*); **that will even things up** das wird die Sache etwas ausgleichen VI (*= pay off debt*) Schulden begleichen (*with* bei); **can we even up later?** können wir später abrechnen?

even[2] N (*obs, poet*) Abend *m*

even-handed ADJ , **even-handedly** ADV [ˌiːvnˈhændɪd, -lɪ] gerecht, fair

evening [ˈiːvnɪŋ] N Abend *m*; **in the ~** abends, am Abend; **this/tomorrow/yesterday ~** heute/morgen/gestern Abend; **that ~** an jenem Abend; **that ~ was ...** jener Abend war ...; **on the ~ of the twenty-ninth** am 29. abends; **one ~ as I ...** eines Abends, als ich ...; **every Monday ~** jeden Montagabend; **all ~** den ganzen Abend (lang or über); **the ~ of his life** (*liter*) sein Lebensabend

evening: evening class N Abendkurs *m*; **to go to** *or* **take -es** *or* **an ~ in French** einen Abendkurs in Französisch besuchen; **evening dress** N (men's) Abendanzug *m*, Gesellschaftsanzug *m*; (women's) Abendkleid *nt*; **evening gown** N Abendkleid *nt*; **evening meal** N (Brit) Abendessen *nt*; **evening paper** N Abendzeitung *f*; **evening star** N Abendstern *m*

evenly ['i:vənlı] ADV **a** (= unvaryingly, equally) gleichmäßig; *divide* in gleiche Teile; **the contestants were ~ matched** die Gegner waren einander ebenbürtig; **your weight should be ~ balanced (between your two feet)** Sie sollten Ihr Gewicht gleichmäßig (auf beide Füße) verteilen; **to be ~ divided between A and B** (property) zu gleichen Teilen zwischen A und B aufgeteilt sein; **my time is ~ divided between work and leisure activities** meine Zeit ist zu gleichen Teilen in Arbeit und Freizeit aufgeteilt; **public opinion seems to be ~ divided** die öffentliche Meinung scheint in zwei gleich große Lager gespalten zu sein
b (= calmly) *say, look* at gelassen

evenness ['i:vənnıs] N **a** (of ground) Ebenheit *f*
b (= regularity) Gleichmäßigkeit *f*; (of progress) Stetigkeit *f*; (of breathing, pulse) Regelmäßigkeit *f*, Gleichmäßigkeit *f*; (of temper) Ausgeglichenheit *f*

evens ['i:vənz] ADJ **it's ~ that ...** (inf) die Chancen stehen fifty-fifty, dass ... (inf)

evensong ['i:vənsɒŋ] N Abendgottesdienst *m*

event [ɪ'vent] N **a** (= happening) Ereignis *nt*; **~s are taking place in Belfast which ...** in Belfast geschehen *or* ereignen sich Dinge, die ...; **in the normal course of ~s** normalerweise; **~s have proved us right** die Ereignisse haben uns Recht gegeben; **it's quite an ~** das ist wirklich ein Ereignis; **it's easy to be wise after the ~** hinterher ist man immer klüger → **happy event**
b (= organized function) Veranstaltung *f*; (Sport) Wettkampf *m*; **what is your best ~?** in welcher Disziplin sind Sie am besten?
c (= case) Fall *m*; **in the ~ of her death** im Falle ihres Todes; **in the ~ of war/fire** im Falle eines Krieges/Brandes, im Kriegs-/Brandfall; **in the ~ of my not returning, ...** sollte ich nicht wiederkommen, ...; **in the unlikely ~ that ...** falls, was sehr unwahrscheinlich ist, ...; **he said he wouldn't come, but in the ~ he did** er sagte, er würde nicht kommen, aber er kam dann schließlich doch; **but in any ~ I can't give you my permission** aber ich kann dir jedenfalls nicht meine Erlaubnis geben; **but in any ~ you have my permission** aber Sie haben auf alle Fälle meine Erlaubnis; **in either ~** in jedem Fall; **at all ~s** auf jeden Fall

even-tempered ['i:vən'tempəd] ADJ ausgeglichen

eventer [ɪ'ventə'] N (Sport) Militaryreiter(in) *m(f)*

eventful [ɪ'ventfʊl] ADJ ereignisreich; *life, period also* bewegt

eventide ['i:vəntaɪd] N (obs, poet) Abendzeit *f*

eventide home N Altenheim *nt*

eventing [ɪ'ventɪŋ] N (Sport) Military *f*

eventual [ɪ'ventfʊəl] ADJ **the decline and ~ collapse of the Roman Empire** der Niedergang und schließlich vollkommene Zerfall des Römischen Reiches; **he predicted the ~ fall of the government** er hat vorausgesagt, dass die Regierung am Ende *or* schließlich zu Fall kommen würde; **the ~ success of the project is not in doubt** es besteht kein Zweifel, dass das Vorhaben letzten Endes Erfolg haben wird; **he lost to the ~ winner** er verlor gegen den späteren Gewinner

eventuality [ɪ,ventʃʊ'ælɪtɪ] N (möglicher) Fall, Eventualität *f*; **in the ~ of fire** im Brandfall; **be ready for any ~** sei auf alle Eventualitäten gefasst

eventually [ɪ'ventʃʊəlɪ] ADV schließlich; (= one day) eines Tages; (= in the long term) auf lange Sicht; **they will take decisions on savings and ~**

on redundancies sie werden Entscheidungen über Einsparungen und schließlich auch Entlassungen treffen; **~ your child will leave home** eines Tages wird Ihr Kind von zu Hause weggehen; **this will ~ cause problems** das bringt auf lange Sicht Probleme

ever ['evə'] ADV **a** je(mals); **not ~** nie; **nothing ~ happens** es passiert nie etwas; **it hardly ~ snows here** hier schneit es kaum (jemals); **if I ~ catch you doing that again** wenn ich dich noch einmal dabei erwische; **if you ~ see her** wenn Sie sie je sehen sollten; **seldom, if ~** selten, wenn überhaupt; **he's a rascal if ~ there was one** er ist ein richtiggehender kleiner Halunke; **as if I ~ would** als ob ich das jemals täte; **don't you ~ say that again!** sag das ja nie mehr!; **neither of us had ~ ridden a horse** keiner von uns war schon jemals geritten; **have you ~ been to Glasgow?** bist du schon einmal in Glasgow gewesen?; **have you ~ known him tell a lie?** haben Sie ihn (schon) jemals lügen hören?; **did you ~ see** *or* **have you ~ seen anything so strange?** hast du schon jemals so etwas Merkwürdiges gesehen?; **more beautiful than ~ (before)** schöner denn je (zuvor); **the best soup I have ~ tasted** die beste Suppe, die ich je(mals) gekostet habe; **the first ... ~ der** *etc* allererste ...; **the first man ~ to walk on the moon** der erste Mensch, der je(mals) den Mond betrat; **I'll never, ~ forgive myself** das werde ich mir nie im Leben verzeihen
b (= at all times) **since I was a boy** seit ich ein Junge war; **~ since I have lived here ...** seitdem ich hier lebe ...; **~ since (then)** seit der Zeit, seitdem; **for ~** für immer, für alle Zeit (-en); **it seemed to go on for ~ (and ~)** es schien ewig zu dauern; **for ~ and a day** für alle Zeiten, ewig und drei Tage (inf); **~ increasing power** ständig wachsende Macht; **an ~ present feeling** ein ständiges Gefühl; **he was ~ the troublemaker** er war ein ewiger Unruhestifter; **all she ~ does is complain** sie tut nichts anderes als sich ständig zu beschweren
c (intensive) **be he ~ so charming** wenn er auch noch so liebenswürdig ist, sei er auch noch so liebenswürdig; **come as quickly as ~ you can** komm so schnell du nur kannst; **she's the best grandmother ~** sie ist die beste Großmutter, die es gibt; **did you ~!** (inf) also so was!
d **what ~ shall we do?** was sollen wir bloß machen?; **when ~ will they come?** wann kommen sie denn bloß *or* endlich?; **why ~ not?** warum denn bloß nicht? → **whatever, wherever** *etc*
e (inf) **so/such** unheimlich; **~ so slightly drunk** ein ganz klein wenig betrunken; **he's ~ such a nice man** er ist ein ungemein netter Mensch; **I am ~ so sorry** es tut mir schrecklich Leid; **thank you ~ so much** ganz herzlichen Dank
f (old, = always) allzeit (old, liter)
g (in letters) **yours ~** *or* **~ yours, Wendy** viele Grüße, Ihre Wendy

Everest ['evərest] N **(Mount) ~** der (Mount) Everest

Everglades ['evəgleɪdz] N **the ~** die Everglades

evergreen ['evəgriːn] ADJ *trees, shrubs, leaves* immergrün; (fig) *topic* immer aktuell N Nadelbaum *m*, immergrüner Busch

evergreen facility N (Fin) Revolvingkredit *m*

everlasting [,evə'lɑːstɪŋ] ADJ **a** *God, life, torment* ewig; *gratitude* immer während; *glory* unvergänglich; **to his ~ shame** zu seiner ewigen Schande **b** (inf, = constant) ewig (inf) N **from ~ to ~ thou art God** Du bist Gott von Ewigkeit zu Ewigkeit

everlasting flower N Strohblume *f*, Immortelle *f*

everlastingly [,evə'lɑːstɪŋlɪ] ADV (liter) ewig

evermore [,evə'mɔː'] ADV **a** (liter, = always) auf immer und ewig; **for ~** in alle Ewigkeit **b** (= increasingly) zunehmend; *rise, fall* immer mehr; **it becomes ~ the responsibility of the individual** dafür wird der Einzelne zunehmend selbst verantwortlich

every ['evrɪ] ADJ **a** jede(r, s); **you must examine ~ one** Sie müssen jeden (Einzelnen) untersuchen; **~ man for himself** jeder für sich; **in ~ way** (= in all respects) in jeder Hinsicht; (= by every means) mit allen Mitteln; **he is ~ bit as clever as his brother** er ist ganz genauso schlau wie sein Bruder; **~ bit as much** ganz genauso viel; **~ single time** jedes einzelne Mal; **~ single time I ...** immer wenn ich ...
b (= all possible) **I have ~ confidence in him** ich habe unbedingtes *or* uneingeschränktes Vertrauen zu ihm; **I have/there is ~ hope that ...** ich habe allen Grund/es besteht aller Grund zu der Hoffnung, dass ...; **we wish you ~ success/happiness** wir wünschen Ihnen alles (nur erdenklich) Gute/viel Glück und Zufriedenheit; **there was ~ prospect of success** es bestand alle Aussicht auf Erfolg; **to make ~ effort to do sth** sich alle Mühe geben *or* sich sehr bemühen, etw zu tun
c (indicating recurrence) **~ fifth day, ~ five days** jeden fünften Tag, alle fünf Tage; **~ other day** jeden zweiten Tag, alle zwei Tage; **write on ~ other line** bitte jede Zeile Zwischenraum lassen; **write on ~ other page** bitte jede zweite Seite beschreiben; **once ~ week** einmal jede *or* pro Woche; **one in ~ twenty people** jeder zwanzigste Mensch; **~ so often, ~ once in a while, ~ now and then** *or* **again** hin und wieder, ab und zu, gelegentlich
d (after poss adj) **they catered to his ~ whim** sie erfüllten ihm jeden Wunsch; **his ~ word** jedes seiner Worte, jedes Wort, das er sagte

everybody ['evrɪbɒdɪ] PRON jeder(mann), alle *pl*; **~ has finished** alle sind fertig; **it's not ~ who can afford a video recorder** nicht jeder kann sich (dat) einen Videorekorder leisten; **~ knows ~ else here** hier kennt jeder jeden; **~ knows that** das weiß (doch) jeder

everyday ['evrɪdeɪ] ADJ alltäglich; *reality* täglich; **~ clothes** Alltagskleidung *f*; **to be an ~ occurrence** (all)täglich vorkommen; **for ~ use** für den täglichen Gebrauch; **words in ~ use** Wörter *pl* der Alltagssprache; **~ language** Alltagssprache *f*; **~ people** ganz normale Menschen; **~ life** *or* **living** der Alltag; **~ world** Alltagswelt *f*

everyman ['evrɪmæn] N Durchschnittsmensch *m*; **language that ~ and everywoman can understand** eine Sprache, die der Durchschnittsmensch verstehen kann

everyone ['evrɪwʌn] ✪ 26.2 PRON = **everybody**

everything ['evrɪθɪŋ] N alles; **~ possible/old** alles Mögliche/Alte; **~ you have** alles, was du hast; **is ~ all right?** ist alles in Ordnung?; **time is ~** Zeit ist kostbar; **money isn't ~** Geld ist nicht alles; **money is ~ to him** Geld bedeutet ihm alles → **mean³ a**

everywhere ['evrɪweə'] ADV überall; (with direction) überallhin; **from ~** überallher, von überall; **~ you look there's a mistake** wo man auch hinsieht, findet man Fehler

evict [ɪ'vɪkt] VT *tenants, squatters* zur Räumung zwingen (from +gen); **they were ~ed** sie wurden zum Verlassen ihrer Wohnung gezwungen

eviction [ɪ'vɪkʃən] N Ausweisung *f*

eviction order N Räumungsbefehl *m*

evidence ['evɪdəns] N **a** Beweis *m*, Beweise *pl*; **show me your ~** welche Beweise haben Sie?; **what ~ is there to support this theory?** welche Anhaltspunkte gibt es, die diese Theorie untermauern?; **according to ~ of our senses** nach dem, was wir mit unseren Sinnen erkennen können; **there is no ~ of ...** es deutet nichts auf ... hin; **there is no ~ that ...** es deutet nichts darauf hin, dass ...; **these marks are ~ of life on Mars** diese Spuren sind Beweis *or* ein Zeichen *nt* dafür, dass es auf dem Mars Leben gibt; **a scratch was the only ~ of the fight** ein Kratzer war der einzige Beweis für den Kampf; **the car bore ~ of having been in an accident** das Auto trug deutliche Spuren eines Unfalls
b (Jur) Beweismaterial *nt*; (object, dagger etc) Beweisstück *nt*; (= testimony) Aussage *f*; **the lawyers are still collecting ~** die Anwälte holen immer noch Beweise ein; **we haven't got any ~**

wir haben keinerlei Beweise; **there wasn't e-nough** ~ die Beweise *or* Indizien reichten nicht aus; **for lack of** ~ aus Mangel an Beweisen, mangels Beweisen (*form*); **on the ~ available …** aufgrund *or* auf Grund des vorhandenen Beweismaterials …; **not admissible as** ~ als Beweismittel nicht zulässig; **all the ~ was against him** alles sprach *or* die Tatsachen sprachen gegen ihn; **to give** ~ **(for/against sb)** (für/gegen jdn) aussagen; **to give** ~ **for the defence** (*Brit*) *or* **defense** (*US*)**/prosecution** für die Verteidigung/die Anklage aussagen; **piece of** ~ (= *statement*) Zeugenaussage *f*; (= *object*) Beweisstück *or* -mittel *nt* → **queen's evidence**, **state's evidence**

[c] **to be in** ~ sichtbar sein; **poverty was still (very) much in** ~ es gab immer noch sichtlich viel Armut; **his father was nowhere in** ~ sein Vater war nirgends zu sehen; **she likes to be very much in** ~ sie hat es gern, gesehen und beachtet zu werden; **a statesman very much in ~ at the moment** ein Staatsmann, der zur Zeit stark beachtet wird

[VT] zeugen von

evident ADJ , **evidently** ADV ['ɛvɪdənt, -lɪ] offensichtlich

evil ['iːvl] [N] [a] Böse(s) *nt*; **good and ~ in Victorian England** das Gute und das Böse im viktorianischen England; **the conflict between good and** ~ der Kampf zwischen Gut und Böse; **there was never any trace of ~ in her** an ihr war nie etwas Böses; **the ~ in the universe** das Übel in der Welt; **to wish sb no** ~ jdm nichts Böses wünschen; **to speak** ~ **of sb** schlecht von jdm reden

[b] (= *bad thing or activity*) Übel *nt*; **a necessary** ~ ein notwendiges Übel; **the lesser/greater of two ~s** das kleinere/größere Übel; **social ~s** soziale Missstände *pl*; **a sermon on the ~s of drink** eine Predigt über das Laster des Trinkens

[ADJ] [a] (= *bad, wicked*) *person, tongue* böse; *example, influence, reputation* schlecht; ~ **deed** Übeltat *f*; **the country's most ~ terrorists** die schlimmsten Terroristen des Landes; **with ~ intent** mit *or* aus böser Absicht; **the ~ weed** (*hum*, = *tobacco*) das Kraut (*inf*); (= *smoking*) das Rauchen; **to put off the ~ day/moment** den schrecklichen Tag/Augenblick hinauszögern

[b] (= *devilish*) *spirit, spell, power* böse; *place* verhext

[c] (= *unpleasant*) *smell, taste* übel

evil: evildoer N Übeltäter(in) *m(f)*, Bösewicht *m* (*dated*); **evil eye** N **the** ~ der böse Blick; **to give sb the** ~ jdn mit dem bösen Blick ansehen

evilly ['iːvlɪ] ADV bösartig; ~ **motivated** durch das Böse motiviert

evil: evil-minded ADJ bösartig; **evil-smelling** ADJ übel riechend

evince [ɪˈvɪns] VT an den Tag legen; *surprise, desire also* bekunden

eviscerate [ɪˈvɪsəreɪt] VT ausnehmen; *person* entleiben

evocation [ˌevəˈkeɪʃən] N Heraufbeschwören *nt*, Wachrufen *nt*

evocative [ɪˈvɒkətɪv] ADJ atmosphärisch; *name* wohlklingend; **scent can be very** ~ ein Duft kann viele Erinnerungen heraufbeschwören; **to be** ~ **of sth** etw heraufbeschwören

evocatively [ɪˈvɒkətɪvlɪ] ADV atmosphärisch; **the islands ~ known as the South Seas** die Inseln, die unter dem atmosphärischen Namen Südsee bekannt sind

evoke [ɪˈvəʊk] VT heraufbeschwören; *memory also* wachrufen; *admiration, response* hervorrufen

evolution [ˌiːvəˈluːʃən] N [a] (= *development, Biol*) Evolution *f*, Entwicklung *f*; **the ~ of events in Vietnam** die Entwicklung in Vietnam; **theory of** ~ Evolutionstheorie *f* [b] *often pl* (*of troops*) Bewegung *f*; (*of dancers, skaters*) Figur *f*, Bewegung *f*

evolutionary [ˌiːvəˈluːʃnərɪ] ADJ evolutionär; ~ **theory** Evolutionstheorie *f*

evolutionism [ˌiːvəˈluːʃənɪzəm] N Evolutionismus *m*

evolutionist [ˌiːvəˈluːʃnɪst] [N] Evolutionist(in) *m(f)* [ADJ] evolutionistisch

evolve [ɪˈvɒlv] [VT] *system, theory, plan* entwickeln [VI] sich entwickeln, sich herausbilden

ewe [juː] N Mutterschaf *nt*

ewer ['juːə'] N Wasserkrug *m*

ex¹ [eks] N (*inf*) Verflossene(r) *mf* (*inf*)

ex² *abbr of* **example** Bsp., Beispiel *nt*

ex- [eks-] PREF [a] ehemalig, Ex-; ~**president** früherer Präsident, frühere Präsidentin, Expräsident(in) *m(f)*; ~**wife** frühere Frau, Exfrau *f*; ~**Yugoslavia** das frühere Jugoslawien [b] ~**factory** ab Werk → **ex officio**, **ex works**

exacerbate [ek'sæsəbeɪt] VT *person* verärgern; *pain, disease, problem* verschlimmern; *hate* vergrößern; *resentment, discontent* vertiefen; *situation, crisis, tensions* verschärfen

exacerbation [ek,sæsə'beɪʃən] N (*of pain, disease, problem*) Verschlimmerung *f*; (*of situation, crisis, tensions*) Verschärfung *f*

exact [ɪgˈzækt] [ADJ] [a] (= *precise*) genau; *translation* wörtlich; **to be ~ about sth** etw genau darlegen; **do you have the ~ amount?** ist es passend?; **please have the ~ fare ready** bitte Fahrgeld abgezählt bereithalten; **they won't know the ~ nature of the problem until tomorrow** sie werden erst morgen erfahren, worum es sich bei dem Problem genau handelt; **until this ~ moment** bis genau zu diesem Augenblick; **the ~ thing I want** genau das, was ich will; **the ~ same thing** genau das gleiche; **the ~ opposite** das genaue Gegenteil; **he's 47 to be ~** er ist 47, um genau zu sein; **they evolved from reptiles, dinosaurs to be ~** sie stammen von Reptilien ab, genau(er) gesagt, von Dinosauriern; **or to be more ~** oder, genauer gesagt [b] (= *meticulous*) *person* genau, exakt; **to be very ~ in one's work** sehr genau arbeiten; ~ **science** (*lit, fig*) exakte Wissenschaft

[VT] (*form*) *money, obedience, revenge* fordern; *payment* eintreiben; *promise* abverlangen (*from sb* jdm); *guarantee, assurance* verlangen (*from* von); **to ~ a high price** (*fig*) einen hohen Preis fordern

exacting [ɪgˈzæktɪŋ] ADJ *person, work, task* anspruchsvoll; *standards, demands* hoch; *detail* peinlich genau; **to be very** ~ sehr viel verlangen; **he's very ~ about cleanliness** er ist peinlich genau, was Sauberkeit angeht, er nimmt es mit der Sauberkeit sehr genau

exactingness [ɪgˈzæktɪŋnɪs] N **because of his ~ as a teacher** da er ein so anspruchsvoller Lehrer ist

exaction [ɪgˈzækʃən] N [a] (= *act, of money*) Eintreiben *nt*; (*of promises*) Abverlangen *nt*; (*of obedience*) Fordern *nt* [b] (= *money exacted*) Forderung *f*; (= *excessive demand*) überzogene Forderung

exactitude [ɪgˈzæktɪtjuːd] N Genauigkeit *f*, Exaktheit *f*

exactly [ɪgˈzæktlɪ] ✪ 17.2 ADV genau; **I wanted to know ~ where my mother was buried** ich wollte genau wissen, wo meine Mutter begraben war; **that's ~ what I was thinking** genau das habe ich auch gedacht; **at ~ five o'clock** um Punkt fünf Uhr; **at ~ 9.43 a.m./the right time** genau um 9.43 Uhr/zur richtigen Zeit; **I want to get things ~ right** ich will genau richtig machen; **who ~ will be in charge?** wer wird eigentlich die Verantwortung haben?; **that's not ~ what I mean** das ist nicht genau das, was ich meine; **the ~ same** genau der/die/das Gleiche; **you mean we are stuck? – ~** wir sitzen also fest? – stimmt genau; **is she sick? – not** ~ ist sie krank? – eigentlich nicht; **not** ~ (*iro*, = *hardly*) nicht gerade; **his father was not ~ poor/pleased** sein Vater war nicht gerade arm/erfreut; **it's not a ~ comedy** es ist nicht gerade eine Komödie

exactness [ɪgˈzæktnɪs] N Genauigkeit *f*

exaggerate [ɪgˈzædʒəreɪt] [VT] [a] (= *overstate*) übertreiben; **he ~d what really happened** er hat das, was wirklich geschehen war, übertrieben dargestellt; **he tends to ~ his own importance** er neigt dazu, sich wichtig zu tun [b] (= *intensify*) *effect* verstärken; *similarity* hervorheben [VI] übertreiben

exaggerated [ɪgˈzædʒəreɪtɪd] ADJ übertrieben; **to have an ~ view of sth** etw überschätzen; **to have an ~ sense of one's own importance** eine übertrieben hohe Meinung von sich haben

exaggeratedly [ɪgˈzædʒəreɪtɪdlɪ] ADV übertrieben

exaggeration [ɪg,zædʒə'reɪʃən] ✪ 26.1 N Übertreibung *f*; **a bit of an** ~ eine leichte Übertreibung, leicht übertrieben

exalt [ɪgˈzɔːlt] VT [a] (*in rank or power*) erheben [b] (= *praise*) preisen

exaltation [ˌegzɔːl'teɪʃən] N (= *feeling*) Begeisterung *f*, Exaltation *f* (*liter*)

exalted [ɪgˈzɔːltɪd] ADJ [a] *position, style* hoch; **at** *or* **on a less ~ level** auf nicht ganz so gehobener Ebene; **the ~ ranks of …** die erhabenen Ränge der …; **to be in ~ company** sich in gehobener Gesellschaft befinden; **she moves only in the most ~ circles** sie bewegt sich nur in den besten Kreisen [b] *mood, person* exaltiert, überschwänglich

exam [ɪgˈzæm] N Prüfung *f*

examination [ɪg,zæmɪ'neɪʃən] N [a] (*Sch etc*) Prüfung *f*; (*Univ*) Examen *nt*, Prüfung *f*; **geography** ~ Geografieprüfung *f*; ~ **nerves** *pl* Prüfungsangst *f*

[b] (= *study, inspection*) Prüfung *f*, Untersuchung *f*; (*of machine, premises, passports*) Kontrolle *f*; (*of question*) Untersuchung *f*; (*of accounts*) Prüfung *f*; **on closer** ~ bei genauer(er) Prüfung *or* Untersuchung; **it was found on ~ that …** die Untersuchung ergab, dass …; **the matter is still under** ~ die Angelegenheit wird noch geprüft *or* untersucht

[c] (*Med*) Untersuchung *f*; **she underwent a thorough** ~ sie wurde gründlich untersucht [d] (*Jur, of suspect, accused, witness*) Verhör *nt*; (*of case, documents*) Untersuchung *f*; **legal** ~ Verhör *nt*

examine [ɪgˈzæmɪn] ✪ 26.1 VT [a] (*for auf +acc*) untersuchen; *documents, accounts* prüfen; *machine, passports, luggage* kontrollieren; **you need (to have) your head ~d** (*inf*) du solltest dich mal auf deinen Geisteszustand untersuchen lassen [b] *pupil, candidate* prüfen (*in in +dat, on über +acc*) [c] (*Med*) untersuchen [d] (*Jur*) *suspect, accused, witness* verhören

examinee [ɪg,zæmɪ'niː] N (*Sch*) Prüfling *m*; (*Univ*) (Examens)kandidat(in) *m(f)*

examiner [ɪgˈzæmɪnə'] N (*Sch, Univ*) Prüfer(in) *m(f)*; **board of ~s** Prüfungsausschuss *m*

example [ɪgˈzɑːmpl] ✪ 26.1, 26.2 N Beispiel *nt*; **for** ~ zum Beispiel; **to set a good/bad** ~ ein gutes/schlechtes Beispiel geben, mit gutem/schlechtem Beispiel vorangehen; **his conduct should be an ~ to us** sein Verhalten sollte uns ein Beispiel sein; **a leader who is an ~ to his men** ein Führer, der seinen Männern als Beispiel dient *or* mit leuchtendem Beispiel vorangeht; **to follow sb's** ~ jds Beispiel folgen; **to take sth as an** ~ sich (*dat*) ein etw als Beispiel nehmen; **to make an ~ of sb** an jdm ein Exempel statuieren; **to punish sb as an ~ to others** jdn exemplarisch bestrafen

exasperate [ɪgˈzɑːspəreɪt] VT zur Verzweiflung bringen, auf die Palme bringen (*inf*); **to become** *or* **get ~d** verzweifeln (*with an +dat*), sich aufregen (*with über +acc*); ~**d by his lack of attention** verärgert über seine mangelnde Aufmerksamkeit

exasperating [ɪgˈzɑːspəreɪtɪŋ] ADJ ärgerlich; *delay, difficulty, job* leidig *attr*; *person* nervig (*inf*); **it's so ~ not to be able to buy a newspaper** es ist wirklich zum Verzweifeln, dass man keine Zeitung bekommen kann; **she can be so ~!** sie kann einen wirklich zur Verzweiflung *or* auf die Palme (*inf*) bringen!

exasperatingly [ɪgˈzɑːspəreɪtɪŋlɪ] ADV **this train/student is ~ slow** es ist zum Verzweifeln, wie langsam dieser Zug fährt/dieser Student ist

exasperation [ɪgˌzɑːspəˈreɪʃən] N Verzweiflung f (*with* über +*acc*); **he cried out in ~** er schrie verzweifelt auf

excavate [ˈekskəveɪt] **VT** *ground* ausschachten; (*machine*) ausbaggern; (*Archeol*) *remains* ausgraben; *site* Ausgrabungen machen auf (+*dat*); *trench, graves* ausheben **VI** (*Archeol*) Ausgrabungen machen

excavation [ekskəˈveɪʃən] N **a** (*Archeol*) (Aus)grabung f; **~s** (= *site*) Ausgrabungsstätte f **b** (*of tunnel etc*) Graben nt

excavator [ˈekskəveɪtəʳ] N (= *machine*) Bagger m; (*Archeol*: = *person*) Ausgräber(in) m(f)

exceed [ɪkˈsiːd] VT **a** (*in value, amount, length of time*) übersteigen, überschreiten (*by* um); **the guests ~ed 40 in number** die Zahl der Gäste überstieg 40; **to ~ 5 kilos in weight** das Gewicht von 5 kg übersteigen or überschreiten; **a fine not ~ing £500** eine Geldstrafe bis zu £ 500 **b** (= *go beyond*) hinausgehen über (+*acc*); *expectations, desires* übertreffen, übersteigen; *limits, powers, speed limit* überschreiten

exceedingly [ɪkˈsiːdɪŋlɪ], **exceeding** (*old*) [ɪkˈsiːdɪŋ] ADV (+*adj, adv*) äußerst, ausgesprochen; **we had an ~ good lunch** wir aßen ausgesprochen gut zu Mittag; **my aunt felt the cold ~** meine Tante litt außerordentlich unter der Kälte

excel [ɪkˈsel] **VI** sich auszeichnen, sich hervortun **VT** übertreffen (*in* in +*dat*, *an* +*dat*); **to ~ oneself** (*often iro*) sich selbst übertreffen

excellence [ˈeksələns] N **a** (= *high quality*) hervorragende Qualität, Vorzüglichkeit f; **artistic/academic ~** höchste künstlerische/wissenschaftliche Qualität; **the ~ of the essay** der ausgezeichnete or hervorragende Aufsatz; **we strive for ~** wir streben hervorragende Qualität an **b** (= *excellent feature*) Vorzug m, hervorragende Eigenschaft

Excellency [ˈeksələnsɪ] N Exzellenz f; **Your/His ~** Eure/Seine Exzellenz

excellent [ˈeksələnt] ⚙ 19.2 ADJ ausgezeichnet, hervorragend; **I passed my exams – ~!** ich habe meine Prüfungen bestanden – ausgezeichnet!

excellently [ˈeksələntlɪ] ADV ausgezeichnet, hervorragend

excelsior [ekˈselsɪɔːʳ] N (*US*, = *shavings*) Holzwolle f

except [ɪkˈsept] **PREP** **a** außer (+*dat*); **what can they do – wait?** was können sie (anders) tun als warten?; **who could have done it ~ him?** wer hätte es außer ihm denn getan? **b** **~ for** abgesehen von, bis auf (+*acc*); **~ that ...** außer or nur dass ...; **~ for the fact that** abgesehen davon, dass ...; **~ if** es sei denn(, dass), außer wenn; **~ when** außer wenn **CONJ** **a** (= *only*) doch; **I'd refuse – I need the money** ich würde ablehnen, doch ich brauche das Geld **b** (*old, form,* = *unless*) es sei denn(, dass); **~ he be a traitor** es sei denn, er wäre ein Verräter **VT** ausnehmen; **to ~ sb from sth** jdn bei etw ausnehmen; **none ~ed** ohne Ausnahme

excepting [ɪkˈseptɪŋ] PREP außer; **not ~ X** ohne X auszunehmen or auszuschließen, X nicht ausgenommen; **always ~ ...** natürlich mit Ausnahme (+*gen*) ...

exception [ɪkˈsepʃən] N **a** Ausnahme f; **to make an ~** eine Ausnahme machen; **to make an ~ of/for sb** eine Ausnahme bei jdm/für jdn machen; **without ~** ohne Ausnahme; **with the ~ of** mit Ausnahme von; **this case is an ~ to the rule** dieser Fall ist eine Ausnahme, das ist ein Ausnahmefall; **the ~ proves the rule, this is the ~ that proves the rule** (*prov*) Ausnahmen bestätigen die Regel (*prov*); **these strokes of luck are the ~** diese Glücktreffer sind die Ausnahme; **with this ~** mit der einen Ausnahme; **sb/sth is no ~** jd/etw ist or bildet keine Aus-

nahme **b to take ~ to sth** Anstoß m an etw (*dat*) nehmen

exceptionable [ɪkˈsepʃənəbl] ADJ (*form*) **a** (= *arguable*) anfechtbar, bestreitbar **b** (= *objectionable*) anstößig

exceptional [ɪkˈsepʃənl] ADJ **a** (= *outstanding*) *person, talent, achievement* außergewöhnlich, außerordentlich; (= *outstandingly good*) *teacher, quality, performance etc* hervorragend; (= *outstandingly high*) *value, amount* außergewöhnlich hoch; **of ~ quality/talent/value/courage** außergewöhnlich gut/talentiert/wertvoll/mutig; **an ~ amount of money** außergewöhnlich viel Geld; **it takes ~ courage** dazu gehört außergewöhnlich viel Mut; **his work is ~ in its poetic quality** seine Werke sind von einer außergewöhnlichen Poesie **b** (= *unusual*) *circumstances, situation, powers* außergewöhnlich; *person, weather* ungewöhnlich; **~ case** Ausnahmefall m; **in ~ cases, in** or **under ~ circumstances** in Ausnahmefällen; **~ child** (*US, Sch*) hoch begabtes Kind

exceptionally [ɪkˈsepʃənlɪ] ADV **a** (= *extraordinarily*) außergewöhnlich, außerordentlich **b** (= *unusually, as an exception*) ausnahmsweise

excerpt [ˈeksɜːpt] **N** Auszug m, Exzerpt nt **VT** (*Liter, Mus*) exzerpieren

excess [ɪkˈses] **N** **a** Übermaß nt (*of an* +*dat*); **an ~ of caution** allzu viel Vorsicht; **an ~ of details** allzu viele Einzelheiten; **to eat/drink to ~** übermäßig essen/trinken; **to carry sth to ~** etw übertreiben; **don't do anything to ~** man soll nichts übertreiben; **he does everything to ~** er übertreibt bei allem **b** **excesses** PL Exzesse pl; (*drinking, sex etc*) Ausschweifungen pl; (*brutalities*) Ausschreitungen pl **c** (= *amount left over*) Überschuss m; **~ of demand over supply** Nachfrageüberschuss m **d** **to be in ~ of** hinausgehen über (+*acc*), überschreiten; **a figure in ~ of ...** eine Zahl über (+*dat*) ... **e** (*esp Brit Insur*) Selbstbeteiligung f **ADJ** *water, salt, energy* überschüssig; *alcohol* zu viel; **~ fat** Fettpolster nt, überschüssiges Fett

excess: **excess baggage** N Übergewicht nt; **excess capacity** N Überkapazität f; **excess charge** N zusätzliche Gebühr; (*for letter etc*) Nachgebühr f; **excess demand** N Nachfrageüberschuss m; **excess fare** N Nachlösegebühr f; **I had to pay an ~** ich musste nachlösen; **excess freight** N Überfracht f

excessive [ɪkˈsesɪv] ADJ übermäßig; *price, profits, speed* überhöht; *demands* übertrieben; **an ~ amount of, ~ amounts of** übermäßig viel; **to spend an ~ amount of time on sth** übermäßig viel Zeit auf etw (*acc*) verwenden; **~ levels of lead** ein zu hoher Bleigehalt; **~ drinking** übermäßiger Alkoholgenuss; **~ use of the clutch** zu häufiger Gebrauch der Kupplung; **avoid ~ exposure to the sun** setzen Sie sich nicht so lange der Sonne aus; **that's (a bit) ~!** das geht (etwas) zu weit!, das ist (etwas) übertrieben!

excessively [ɪkˈsesɪvlɪ] ADV (+*vb*) übermäßig; *drink, eat* zu viel; (+*adj*) *bright, boring, ugly* äußerst, ausgesprochen; **to worry ~** sich übermäßig große Sorgen machen; **~ so** allzu sehr; **he's confident, perhaps ~ so** er ist selbstbewusst, vielleicht sogar zu selbstbewusst

excess: **excess postage** N Nachgebühr f, Strafporto nt (*inf*); **excess production** N Überproduktion f; **excess profit** N Übergewinn m; **~s tax** (*Econ*) Übergewinnsteuer f; **excess supply** N Angebotsüberschuss m; **excess weight** N Übergewicht nt; **to lose ~** überflüssige Pfunde abnehmen

exchange [ɪksˈtʃeɪndʒ] **VT** *books, glances, seats* tauschen; *foreign currency* wechseln, umtauschen (*for in* +*acc*); *information, views, secrets, experiences, hostages, phone numbers* austauschen; **to ~ words** einen Wortwechsel haben; **to ~ letters** einen Briefwechsel führen; **to ~ blows** sich schlagen; **to ~ fire (with)** einen Schusswechsel haben (mit); **to ~ greetings** sich grüßen; **to ~ insults** sich gegenseitig beleidigen; **to ~ gifts**

sich (gegenseitig) beschenken; **to ~ one thing for another** eine Sache gegen eine andere austauschen or (*in shop*) umtauschen **N** **a** (*of goods, stamps*) Tausch m; (*of prisoners, views, secrets, diplomatic notes*) Austausch m; (*of one bought item for another*) Umtausch m; **an ~ of fire** ein Schusswechsel m; **in ~** dafür; **in ~ for money** gegen Geld or Bezahlung; **in ~ for a table** für einen Tisch; **in ~ for lending me your car** dafür, dass Sie mir Ihr Auto geliehen haben; **that's not a fair ~ for my bike** das ist kein fairer Tausch für mein Rad; **to lose by the ~** einen schlechten Tausch machen; **fair ~ is no robbery** (*Prov*) Tausch ist kein Raub (*Prov*) **b** (*Fin,* = *act*) Wechseln nt; (= *place*) Wechselstube f **c** (*St Ex*) Börse f **d** (*telephone*) **~** Fernvermittlungsstelle f (*form*), Fernamt nt; (*in office etc*) (Telefon)zentrale f **e** (= *altercation*) Wortwechsel m

exchangeable [ɪksˈtʃeɪndʒəbl] ADJ austauschbar (*for* gegen); *goods bought* umtauschbar (*for* gegen); **goods bought in the sale are not ~** Ausverkaufsware ist vom Umtausch ausgeschlossen

exchange: **exchange broker** N (*St Ex*) Devisenmakler(in) m(f); **exchange control** N (*Fin*) Devisenkontrolle f; **exchange market** N (*Fin*) Devisenmarkt m; **exchange rate** N Wechselkurs m; **Exchange Rate Mechanism** N (*Fin*) Wechselkursmechanismus m; **exchange student** N Austauschstudent(in) m(f); **exchange teacher** N Austauschlehrer(in) m(f); **exchange value** N Tauschwert m; **exchange visit** N (*Sch etc*) Austauschbesuch m; **to be on an ~** einen Austauschbesuch machen

exchequer [ɪksˈtʃekəʳ] N Finanzministerium nt; (*esp in GB*) Schatzamt nt; (*inf, personal*) Finanzen pl (*inf*) → **chancellor**

excisable [ekˈsaɪzəbl] ADJ steuerpflichtig

excise¹ [ˈeksaɪz] N **a** Verbrauchssteuer f (*on* auf +*acc*, für); **~ on beer/tobacco** Bier-/Tabaksteuer f **b** (*Brit:* = *department*) *Verwaltungsabteilung für indirekte Steuern*

excise² [ekˈsaɪz] VT (*Med*) herausschneiden, entfernen (*also fig*)

excise [ˈeksaɪz]: **excise duties** PL Verbrauchssteuern pl; **excise licence** N (*Brit*) Schankkonzession f; **exciseman** N Steuereinnehmer m; **excisewoman** N Steuereinnehmerin f

excision [ekˈsɪʒən] N (*Med, fig*) Entfernung f

excitability [ɪkˌsaɪtəˈbɪlɪtɪ] N Erregbarkeit f; (*Med*) Reizbarkeit f

excitable [ɪkˈsaɪtəbl] ADJ **a** *person, animal* leicht erregbar; **in an ~ state** erregt; **to become** or **get ~** erregt werden **b** (*Med*) reizbar

excite [ɪkˈsaɪt] VT **a** *person, animal* aufregen, aufgeregt machen; (= *rouse enthusiasm in*) begeistern; **the news had clearly ~d him** er war wegen der Nachricht sichtlich aufgeregt; **the whole village was ~d by the news** das ganze Dorf war über die Nachricht in Aufregung; **the prospect doesn't exactly ~ me** ich finde die Aussicht nicht gerade begeisternd **b** (*Physiol*) *nerve* reizen; (*sexually*) erregen **c** *sentiments, passion, admiration* erregen; *interest, curiosity* wecken, erregen; *imagination, appetite* anregen; **the issue has ~d a great deal of fierce debate** das Thema hat viele heiße Debatten ausgelöst

excited [ɪkˈsaɪtɪd] ADJ **a** aufgeregt; (= *agitated*) erregt; (= *enthusiastic*) begeistert; **(sexually)** ~ (sexuell) erregt; **he was ~ to hear of this development** er wurde aufgeregt, als er von dieser Entwicklung erfuhr; **to be ~ about sth** von etw begeistert sein; (= *looking forward*) sich auf etw (*acc*) freuen; **to become** or **get ~ (about sth)** sich (über etw *acc*) aufregen; (= *enthuse*) sich (über etw *acc*) begeistern; **to get ~** (*sexually*) erregt werden; **aren't you ~ about what's going to happen?** sind Sie nicht gespannt, was passieren wird?; **it was nothing to get ~ about**

es war nichts Besonderes; **he is ~ at the prospect of working for himself** er freut sich darauf, selbstständig zu arbeiten **b** (*Phys*) *atom* angeregt

excitedly [ɪkˈsaɪtɪdlɪ] ADV aufgeregt

excitement [ɪkˈsaɪtmənt] N **a** Aufregung *f*; **there was great ~ when ...** es herrschte große Aufregung, als ...; **a mood of ~** eine Spannung; **a shriek of ~** ein aufgeregter Schrei; **in the ~ of the match** in der Aufregung des Spiels, im Eifer des Gefechts; **she only did it for (a bit of) ~** sie hat es nur getan, um ein bisschen Aufregung zu haben; **what's all the ~ about?** wozu die ganze Aufregung?; **to be in a state of high ~** in heller Aufregung sein; **his novel has caused great ~** sein Roman hat große Begeisterung ausgelöst; **he enjoys paragliding and other such ~s** Paragliding und ähnlich aufregende Dinge machen ihm Spaß **b** (*Physiol*) Reizung *f*; (*sexual*) Erregung *f*

exciting [ɪkˈsaɪtɪŋ] ADJ aufregend; *player, artist* sensationell; *prospect* reizvoll; (*= full of suspense*) spannend; (*sexually*) erregend; **it's very ~ to find new talent** es ist sehr aufregend *or* spannend, neue Talente zu entdecken; **there is something ~ about this** das hat etwas Aufregendes an sich; **~ for** *or* **to sb** aufregend für jdn; **visually ~** visuell reizvoll

excitingly [ɪkˈsaɪtɪŋlɪ] ADV (*+adj*) aufregend; (*+vb*) auf aufregende Weise; **the film ~ portrays the last days of the war** der Film ist eine spannende Darstellung der letzten Kriegstage

excl **a** *abbr of* **excluding** **b** *abbr of* **exclusive** exkl.

exclaim [ɪkˈskleɪm] **VI** **he ~ed in surprise when he saw it** er schrie überrascht auf, als er es sah; **she ~ed at the sight of such extravagance** beim Anblick solcher Extravaganz entfuhr ihr ein Aufschrei; **at last! she ~ed** endlich! rief sie (aus)

exclamation [ˌekskləˈmeɪʃən] N Ausruf *m* (*also Gram*); **an ~ of horror** ein Schreckensschrei *m*

exclamation mark, (*US*) **exclamation point** N Ausrufezeichen *nt*

exclamatory [ɪkˈsklæmətərɪ] ADJ exklamatorisch; **~ remarks** Ausrufe *pl*

exclude [ɪkˈskluːd] VT ausschließen; **to ~ sb from the team/an occupation** jdn aus der Mannschaft/von einer Beschäftigung ausschließen; **to ~ a child from school** ein Kind vom Schulunterricht ausschließen; **to ~ sb from doing sth** jdn davon ausschließen, etw zu tun; **if we don't ~ the possibility that ...** wenn wir die Möglichkeit nicht ausschließen, dass ...; **the price ~s VAT** (*Brit*) der Preis versteht sich ausschließlich Mehrwertsteuer; **£200 excluding VAT** (*Brit*) £ 200 ohne Mehrwertsteuer; **the meal costs £15 excluding wine** das Essen kostet £ 15 ohne Wein; **everything excluding the house** alles außer *or* ausgenommen das Haus

exclusion [ɪkˈskluːʒən] N Ausschluss *m* (*from* von); (*from school*) Ausschluss *m* von Unterricht; **she thought about her job to the ~ of everything else** sie dachte ausschließlich an ihre Arbeit

exclusionary [ɪksˈkluːʒənərɪ] ADJ (*form*) ausschließend

exclusion: exclusion clause N (*Insur*) Haftungsausschlussklausel *f*; **exclusion order** N (*Jur, against suspected terrorist, football hooligan*) Einreiseverbot *nt*; (*against spouse*) Hausverbot *nt*

exclusive [ɪkˈskluːsɪv] **ADJ** **a** (*= select*) exklusiv **b** (*= unshared, unique*) *use, control* alleinig, ausschließlich; *story* exklusiv; **~ interview** Exklusivinterview *nt*; **~ offer** Exklusivangebot *nt*; **an offer ~ to our readers/to Smith's** ein Exklusivangebot für unsere Leser/bei Smith; **~ property** Alleineigentum *nt*; **~ rights to sth** Alleinrechte *pl* an etw (*dat*); (*Press*) Exklusivrechte *pl* an etw (*dat*); **~ rights to coverage of the Olympic Games** Exklusivrechte für die Berichterstattung bei den Olympischen Spielen; **to have ~ use of a room** einen Raum für sich allein haben; **this**

is the **~ preserve of the privileged** das ist die ungeteilte Domäne der Privilegierten **c** (*= not inclusive*) exklusive *inv*; **our terms are ~** unsere Bedingungen verstehen sich exklusive; **~ of taxes/postage and packing** (*Comm*) exklusive Steuern/Porto und Verpackung; **mutually ~** einander ausschließend; **they are mutually ~** sie schließen einander aus **N** (*Press, = story*) Exklusivbericht *m*; (*= interview*) Exklusivinterview *nt*; **the story was a Times ~** die Geschichte wurde exklusiv von der Times gebracht

exclusively [ɪkˈskluːsɪvlɪ] ADV ausschließlich; (*Press*) exklusiv; **details were ~ revealed by Hello** Einzelheiten wurden in Hello enthüllt; **an (almost) ~ white population** eine (fast) ausschließlich weiße Bevölkerung; **to be available ~ (from/to)** ausschließlich *or* exklusiv (bei/für) erhältlich sein

exclusiveness [ɪkˈskluːsɪvnɪs] N Exklusivität *f*

exclusivity [ˌɪkskluːˈsɪvɪtɪ] N Exklusivität *f*

excommunicate [ˌekskəˈmjuːnɪkeɪt] VT exkommunizieren

excommunication [ˈekskəˌmjuːnɪˈkeɪʃən] N Exkommunikation *f*

ex-convict [ˈeksˈkɒnvɪkt] N ehemaliger Häftling

excoriate [ɪkˈskɔːrɪeɪt] VT (*form*: *= criticize severely*) *person, organization* attackieren; *idea* verurteilen

excrement [ˈekskrɪmənt] N Kot *m*, Exkremente *pl*

excrescence [ɪksˈkresns] N Gewächs *nt*, Auswuchs *m* (*also fig*)

excreta [ɪkˈskriːtə] PL Exkremente *pl*

excrete [ɪkˈskriːt] VT ausscheiden, absondern

excretion [ɪkˈskriːʃən] N (*= act*) Ausscheidung *f*, Exkretion *f*; (*= substance*) Exkret *nt*

excruciating [ɪkˈskruːʃɪeɪtɪŋ] ADJ **a** (*lit, = unbearable*) *pain, noise, silence* unerträglich; *cramp, headache also, sight, experience* fürchterlich, entsetzlich; *death* qualvoll; **I was in ~ pain** ich hatte unerträgliche Schmerzen **b** (*fig*) *experience, boredom* unerträglich; *joke* entsetzlich; *detail* schrecklich; **an ~ pun** ein entsetzlicher Kalauer

excruciatingly [ɪkˈskruːʃɪeɪtɪŋlɪ] ADV **a** (*lit, = unbearably*) *painful* unerträglich; **walking was ~ painful** das Gehen bereitete unerträgliche Schmerzen **b** (*fig, = extremely*) fürchterlich, entsetzlich; **~ funny** urkomisch, zum Schreien (*inf*)

exculpate [ˈekskʌlpeɪt] VT (*form*) *person* freisprechen, exkulpieren (*liter*) (*from* von); **to ~ oneself** sich rechtfertigen

excursion [ɪkˈskɜːʃən] N Ausflug *m*; (*fig, into a subject also*) Exkurs *m*; **to go on an ~** einen Ausflug machen

excursionist [ɪkˈskɜːʃənɪst] N Ausflügler(in) *m(f)*

excursion: excursion ticket N verbilligte Fahrkarte (zu einem Ausflugsort); **excursion train** N Sonderzug *m*

excusable [ɪkˈskjuːzəbl] ADJ verzeihlich, entschuldbar

excuse [ɪkˈskjuːz] **VT** **a** (*= seek to justify*) *action, person* entschuldigen; **such rudeness cannot be ~d** so eine Unhöflichkeit ist nicht zu entschuldigen; **to ~ oneself** sich entschuldigen (*for sth* für *or* wegen etw); **he ~d himself for being late** er entschuldigte sich, dass er zu spät kam; **he ~d himself by saying that his English wasn't very good** er entschuldigte sich mit seiner Entschuldigung sagte er, er spreche nicht gut Englisch **b** (*= pardon*) **to ~ sb** jdm verzeihen; **to ~ sb for having done sth** jdm verzeihen, dass er etw getan hat; **well, I think I can be ~d for believing him** nun, man kann es mir wohl nicht übel nehmen, dass ich ihm geglaubt habe; **~ me for interrupting** entschuldigen *or* verzeihen Sie bitte die Störung; **if you will ~ the expression** wenn Sie mir den Ausdruck gestatten; **~ me!** (*= sorry, to get attention, go past, after sneezing etc*) Entschuldigung!, entschuldigen Sie!; (*indig-*

nant) erlauben Sie mal!; **well, ~ me for asking!** entschuldige, dass ich gefragt habe! **c** (*= set free from obligation*) **to ~ sb from (doing) sth** jdn von einer Sache befreien, jdm etw erlassen; **he is ~d attendance** er muss nicht unbedingt anwesend sein; (*pupil*) er ist vom Schulbesuch befreit; **you are ~d** (*to children*) ihr könnt gehen; **can I be ~d?** darf ich mal verschwinden (*inf*)?; **he ~d himself and left the room** er entschuldigte sich und ging aus dem Zimmer; **and now if you will ~ me I have work to do** und nun entschuldigen Sie mich bitte, ich habe zu arbeiten **N** [ɪkˈskjuːs] **a** (*= justification*) Entschuldigung *f*; **there's no ~ for it** dafür gibt es keine Entschuldigung; **they had no ~ for attacking him** sie hatten keinen Grund, ihn anzugreifen; **to give sth as an ~** etw zu seiner Entschuldigung anführen *or* vorbringen; **he gave two reasons as an ~ for his action** er gab zwei Gründe zur Entschuldigung für seine Tat an **b** (*= pretext*) Ausrede *f*, Entschuldigung *f*; **to make ~s for sb/sth** jdn/etw entschuldigen; **they made ~s for not having done anything about it** sie brachten Ausreden an, warum sie nichts dagegen unternommen hatten; **I have a good ~ for not going** ich habe eine gute Ausrede *or* Entschuldigung, warum ich nicht hingehen kann; **it was raining – well, that's your ~** es hat geregnet – das ist wohl deine Ausrede *or* Entschuldigung; **~s, ~s!** das sind alles Ausreden!; **you're full of ~s** du hast immer eine Ausrede; **he's only making ~s** er sucht nur nach einer Ausrede; **a good ~ for a party** ein guter Grund, eine Party zu feiern **c** **excuses** PL (*= apology*) Entschuldigung *f*; **to offer one's ~s** sich entschuldigen **d** **an ~ for a steak** ein jämmerliches *or* armseliges Steak

excuse-me [ɪkˈskjuːzmiː] N (*= dance*) Tanz *m* mit Abklatschen

ex-directory [ˌeksdaɪˈrektərɪ] ADJ (*Brit*) **to be ~** nicht im Telefonbuch stehen

ex dividend ADV (*St Ex*) ohne Anrecht auf Dividende

ex-dividend [ˈeksˈdɪvɪdend] ADJ (*St Ex*) **~ share** Aktie *f* ohne Anrecht auf Dividende

execrable ADJ , **execrably** ADV [ˈeksɪkrəbl, -ɪ] scheußlich, abscheulich

execrate [ˈeksɪkreɪt] VT **a** (*= hate*) verabscheuen **b** (*= curse*) verfluchen, verwünschen

execration [ˌeksɪˈkreɪʃən] N **a** (*= hatred*) Abscheu *m* **b** (*= curse*) Fluch *m*, Verwünschung *f*

executable [ˈeksɪkjuːtəbl] ADJ ausführbar; **~ file** (*Comput*) ausführbare Datei, Programmdatei *f*

executant [ɪgˈzekjʊtənt] N Ausführende(r) *mf*

execute [ˈeksɪkjuːt] VT **a** *plan, order, task etc* durchführen, ausführen; *movement, dance* ausführen; *duties* erfüllen, wahrnehmen; *purpose* erfüllen; (*Comput*) *command* abarbeiten, ausführen **b** (*Mus, = perform*) vortragen; *cadenza etc* ausführen; (*Art*) ausführen **c** *criminal* hinrichten **d** (*Jur*) *will* vollstrecken, ausführen; *contract* ausfertigen; (*= sign*) *document* unterzeichnen

execution [ˌeksɪˈkjuːʃən] N **a** (*= carrying out, of plan, order, task etc*) Durchführung *f*, Ausführung *f*; (*of movement, dance*) Ausführung *f*; (*of duties*) Erfüllung *f*, Wahrnehmung *f*; **to put sth into ~** etw ausführen; **in the ~ of his duties** bei der Ausübung seines Amtes **b** (*Mus*) Vortrag *m*; (*= musician's skill*) Ausführung *f*; (*Art*) Ausführung *f* **c** (*= punishment*) Hinrichtung *f*, Exekution *f* **d** (*Jur, of will, judgement*) Vollstreckung *f*; (*of contract*) Ausfertigung *f*; (*= signing*) Unterschreiben *nt*

executioner [ˌeksɪˈkjuːʃnə] N Henker *m*, Scharfrichter *m*

executive [ɪgˈzekjʊtɪv] **N** **a** (*Admin, Comm: = person*) leitender Angestellter, leitende Angestellte, Manager(in) *m(f)*; **junior ~** leitender Angestellter, leitende Angestellte; **senior ~** Geschäftsführer(in) *m(f)*; **he's a Shell ~** er ist ein leitender Angestellter bei Shell; **business ~s** leitende Geschäftsleute *pl*

b (Comm, Pol, = managing group) Vorstand m; **the party's/union's National Executive (Committee)** der Partei-/Gewerkschaftsvorstand; **to be on the ~** Vorstandsmitglied or im Vorstand sein **c the ~** (Pol, part of government) die Exekutive **ADJ a** (= managerial) position, post leitend; **~ power** Exekutivgewalt f; **the ~ branch (of government)** die Exekutive (der Regierung); **~ decision** Managemententscheidung f; **~ function** Führungsfunktion f; **~ role** Führungsrolle f; **~ ability** Führungsqualität f; **he has ~ ability** er hat das Zeug zum Manager; **~ pay** or **salaries** Gehälter pl der leitenden Angestellten **b** (= luxury, for executives) für gehobene Ansprüche

executive: executive board N (Admin, Comm) Vorstand m; **executive briefcase** N Diplomatenkoffer m; **executive burnout** N Managerkrankheit f; **executive car** N Wagen m der gehobenen Mittelklasse; **executive chair** N Chefsessel m; **executive chairman** N Vorstandsvorsitzender m; **executive committee** N Vorstand m; **executive council** N Vorstand m; **the Executive Council** (Pol) der Exekutivrat; **executive director** N Vorstandsmitglied nt; **executive jet** N Privatjet m (für Manager); **executive lounge** N (at airport) VIP-Salon m; **executive mansion** N, **Executive Mansion** (US, = White House) der Amtssitz des Präsidenten; (= State Governor's house) der Amtssitz des Gouverneurs; **executive member** N Vorstandsmitglied nt; **executive officer** N Erster Offizier; **executive order** N (US) Rechtsverordnung f; **executive president** N Präsident(in) m(f) mit Exekutivgewalt; **executive producer** N (Film, Theat) geschäftsführender Produzent, geschäftsführende Produzentin; **executive relief** N (euph) Sex für leitende Angestellte; **executive secretary** N Direktionssekretär(in) m(f); **executive session** N (US, Parl) Senatssitzung f (unter Ausschluss der Öffentlichkeit); **executive suite** N (in office) Vorstandsetage f; **executive toy** N Managerspielzeug nt

---

EXECUTIVE PRIVILEGE

Das **executive privilege** ist das Recht des US-Präsidenten, bestimmte Informationen über die Aktivitäten seines Büros vor dem Kongress oder der Justiz geheim zu halten. Es wird normalerweise im Interesse der nationalen Sicherheit angewandt oder um private Regierungsgespräche vertraulich zu behandeln. Dieses Privileg kann nicht aus persönlichen Gründen angeführt werden. Einige Präsidenten haben versucht, für ihre Amtszeit das absolute **executive privilege** zu erhalten, was ihnen jedoch von den Gerichten verwehrt wurde. Im Watergate-Skandal berief sich Präsident Nixon auf dieses Privileg, um Bandmitschnitte von Telefongesprächen nicht einem Untersuchungsausschuss des US-Senats übergeben zu müssen, doch der oberste Gerichtshof hob in diesem Fall das Recht auf.

---

executor [ɪɡˈzekjʊtə'] N (of will) Testamentsvollstrecker m

executrix [ɪɡˈzekjʊtrɪks] N Testamentsvollstreckerin f

exegesis [ˌeksɪˈdʒiːsɪs] N Exegese f, Auslegung f

exegetical [ˌeksɪˈdʒetɪkəl] ADJ exegetisch

exemplary [ɪɡˈzemplərɪ] ADJ **a** (= excellent) vorbildlich, beispielhaft (in sth in etw dat) **b** (= as a deterrent) punishment, sentence exemplarisch

exemplary damages PL (Jur) über den verursachten Schaden hinausgehende Entschädigung, Bußgeld nt

exemplification [ɪɡˌzemplɪfɪˈkeɪʃən] N Erläuterung f, Veranschaulichung f, Exemplifizierung f (geh)

exemplify [ɪɡˈzemplɪfaɪ] VT erläutern, veranschaulichen

exempt [ɪɡˈzempt] ADJ befreit (from von); **diplomats are ~** Diplomaten sind ausgenommen; **could I be made ~ (from that)?** könnte ich davon befreit werden? **VT** person, business befreien; **to ~ sb from doing sth** jdn davon befreien, etw zu tun; **to ~ sth from a ban** etw von einem Verbot ausnehmen

exemption [ɪɡˈzempʃən] N Befreiung f; **~ from taxes** Steuerfreiheit f

exercise [ˈeksəsaɪz] **N a** no pl (of right) Wahrnehmung f; (of physical, mental power) Ausübung f; (of patience, mental faculties) Übung f; (of imagination) Anwendung f; **in the ~ of his duties** bei der Ausübung seiner Pflichten **b** (bodily or mental, drill, Mus etc) Übung f; **stomach ~s** Übungen pl für die Bauchmuskeln; **to do one's ~s in the morning** Morgengymnastik machen **c** no pl (physical) Bewegung f; **physical ~** (körperliche) Bewegung; **a dog needs a lot of ~** ein Hund braucht viel Bewegung; **people who don't take** or **get enough ~** Leute, die sich nicht genug bewegen or die nicht genug Bewegung bekommen; **I need to get some ~** ich brauche ein wenig Bewegung; **what form of ~ do you do?** wie halten Sie sich fit? **d** (= activity) **it was a pointless ~** es war völlig sinnlos; **it was a useful ~ in public relations** für die Publicrelations war es nützlich; **that's just an ~ in window-dressing** (fig) das ist alles nur Schau **e** (Mil) usu pl Übung f; **to go on ~s** eine Übung machen **f exercises** PL (US, = ceremonies) Feierlichkeiten pl **VT a** body, mind üben, trainieren; (Mil) troops exerzieren; horse bewegen; dog spazieren führen; **I'm not saying this just to ~ my voice** ich sage das nicht zum Spaß **b** (= use) one's authority, control, power ausüben; a right geltend machen, ausüben; patience, tact, discretion üben; influence ausüben (on auf +acc); talents Gebrauch machen von; **to ~ care in doing sth** Vorsicht walten lassen, wenn man etw tut **VI if you ~ regularly ...** wenn Sie sich viel bewegen ...; **you don't ~ enough** du hast zu wenig Bewegung; **he was exercising on the parallel bars** er turnte (gerade) am Barren

exercise: exercise bike N Heimtrainer m; **exercise book** N Heft nt

exerciser [ˈeksəsaɪzə'] N (= machine) Trainingsgerät nt; (= bigger) Fitness-Center nt; (= person) Trainer(in) m(f) (inf)

exercise yard N Hof m

exercycle [ˈeksəsaɪkl] N Heimtrainer m

exert [ɪɡˈzɜːt] VT pressure, influence, power, control ausüben (on auf +acc); authority aufbieten, einsetzen (on bei); force gebrauchen, anwenden; **to ~ a force on sth** eine Kraft auf etw (acc) ausüben **VR** sich anstrengen

exertion [ɪɡˈzɜːʃən] **N a** (= effort) Anstrengung f; **by one's own ~s** durch eigene Anstrengungen **b** (of force, strength) Anwendung f, Einsatz m; (of authority) Aufgebot nt, Einsatz m; (of influence, power, control) Ausübung f; **the ~ of force/pressure on sth** die Ausübung von Kraft/Druck auf etw (acc); **rugby requires strenuous physical ~** Rugby fordert unermüdlichen körperlichen Einsatz; **after the day's ~s** nach des Tages Mühen

exeunt [ˈeksɪʌnt] VI (Theat) ab; **~ Brutus and Cassius** Brutus und Cassius ab

exfoliate [eksˈfəʊlɪeɪt] VT skin durch Peeling entfernen, abschleifen VI Peeling nt machen

exfoliation [eksˌfəʊlɪˈeɪʃən] N Peeling nt

ex gratia [eksˈɡreɪʃə] ADJ payment ohne Anerkennung der Rechtspflicht

exhalation [ˌekshəˈleɪʃən] N (of breath) Ausatmen nt; (of gas) Verströmen nt

exhale [eksˈheɪl] VT **a** (= breathe out) ausatmen **b** (= give off) smoke abgeben; gas, vapour ablassen, abgeben VI ausatmen

exhaust [ɪɡˈzɔːst] VT **a** (= use up completely) erschöpfen; **we have ~ed the subject** wir haben das Thema erschöpfend behandelt **b** (= tire) erschöpfen; **the children are/this job is ~ing me** die Kinder sind/diese Arbeit ist eine Strapaze für mich **N a** (esp Brit Aut etc) Auspuff m **b** no pl (= gases) Auspuffgase pl

exhausted [ɪɡˈzɔːstɪd] ADJ **a** (= very tired) erschöpft (from von); **from laughing and singing** vom Lachen und Singen erschöpft; **she was ~ from digging the garden** sie war erschöpft, weil sie den Garten umgegraben hatte **b** (= finished, used up) supplies, resources, funds, oilfield, mine erschöpft; ammunition, savings aufgebraucht; **his patience was ~** er war mit seiner Geduld am Ende

exhaust fumes PL Auspuffgase pl, Abgase pl

exhausting [ɪɡˈzɔːstɪŋ] ADJ anstrengend; activity, work, journey also strapaziös; **grief is ~** Trauern ist erschöpfend

exhaustion [ɪɡˈzɔːstʃən] N Erschöpfung f

exhaustive [ɪɡˈzɔːstɪv] ADJ umfassend, erschöpfend; list vollständig; search gründlich

exhaustively [ɪɡˈzɔːstɪvlɪ] ADV research, cover, prove, speak, describe erschöpfend, ausführlich; complete, thorough äußerst

exhaust: exhaust pipe N (esp Brit) Auspuffrohr nt; **exhaust system** N (esp Brit) Auspuff m

exhibit [ɪɡˈzɪbɪt] VT **a** paintings etc, goods ausstellen; membership card vorzeigen, vorweisen **b** skill, ingenuity zeigen, beweisen, an den Tag legen; reaction zeigen VI ausstellen **N a** (in an exhibition) Ausstellungsstück nt **b** (Jur) Beweisstück nt

exhibition [ˌeksɪˈbɪʃən] **N a** (of paintings, furniture etc) Ausstellung f; (of articles for sale) Auslage f **b** (= act of showing: of a technique, film etc) Vorführung f **c what an ~ of bad manners!** was für schlechte Manieren!; **did you see her at the party last night? - what an ~!** hast du sie auf der Party gestern Abend gesehen? - die hat sich vielleicht aufgeführt!; **to make an ~ of oneself** ein Theater machen (inf); **am I making an ~ of myself?** benehm ich mich daneben? **d** (Brit, Univ = grant) Stipendium nt

exhibition centre, (US) **exhibition center** N Ausstellungszentrum nt; (for trade fair) Messegelände nt

exhibitioner [ˌeksɪˈbɪʃənə'] N (Brit, Univ) Stipendiat(in) m(f)

exhibitionism [ˌeksɪˈbɪʃənɪzəm] N Exhibitionismus m

exhibitionist [ˌeksɪˈbɪʃənɪst] N Exhibitionist(in) m(f) ADJ exhibitionistisch

exhibition match N (Sport) Schaukampf m

exhibitor [ɪɡˈzɪbɪtə'] N Aussteller(in) m(f)

exhilarate [ɪɡˈzɪləreɪt] VT in Hochstimmung versetzen; (news also) (freudig) erregen; (sea air etc) beleben, erfrischen

exhilarated [ɪɡˈzɪləreɪtɪd] ADJ laugh erregt, aufgeregt; **to feel ~** in Hochstimmung sein

exhilarating [ɪɡˈzɪləreɪtɪŋ] ADJ experience erregend, aufregend; activity aufregend; feeling, sensation berauschend; air, breeze belebend; **it is ~ to run along an empty beach** es ist berauschend, einen leeren Strand entlangzulaufen

exhilaration [ɪɡˌzɪləˈreɪʃən] N Hochgefühl nt; **the ~ of flying** das Hochgefühl beim Fliegen

exhort [ɪɡˈzɔːt] VT ermahnen

exhortation [ˌeɡzɔːˈteɪʃən] N Ermahnung f

exhumation [ˌekshjuːˈmeɪʃən] N Exhumierung f

exhume [eksˈhjuːm] VT exhumieren

exigence [ˈeksɪdʒəns], **exigency** [ɪɡˈzɪdʒənsɪ] **N a** usu pl (= requirement) (An)forderung f; (of situation) Erfordernis nt **b** (= emergency) Notlage f **c** (= urgency) Dringlichkeit f

exigent [ˈeksɪdʒənt] ADJ (= urgent) zwingend, dringend; (= exacting) master streng, gestreng (old)

exiguity [ˌeɡzɪˈɡjuːɪtɪ] N (form) Winzigkeit f; (= meagreness) Knappheit f

exiguous [ɪgˈzɪgjʊəs] ADJ *(form) savings, income, revenue* knapp, dürftig

exile ['eksaɪl] **N a** (= *person*) Verbannte(r) *mf* **b** (= *banishment*) Exil *nt*, Verbannung *f*; **to go into ~** ins Exil gehen; **in ~** im Exil **VT** verbannen *(from aus)*, ins Exil schicken; **the ~d former president** der im Exil lebende frühere Präsident

exist [ɪgˈzɪst] **VI a** (= *to be*) existieren, bestehen; **does God ~?** existiert Gott?; **~s alles, was ist** *or* **existiert**; **it only ~s in her imagination** das gibt es *or* das existiert nur in ihrer Fantasie; **I want to live, not just ~** ich möchte leben, nicht einfach nur existieren; **it doesn't ~** das gibt es nicht; **to cease to ~** zu bestehen aufhören; **to continue to ~** fortbestehen, weiter bestehen; **doubts still ~** noch bestehen Zweifel; **the understanding which ~s between the two countries** das Einvernehmen zwischen den beiden Ländern; **there ~ many people who ...** es gibt viele Leute, die ...; **there ~s a tradition that ...** es gibt den Brauch, dass ...; **there ~s the possibility** *or* **the possibility ~s that ...** es besteht die Möglichkeit, dass ... **b** (= *live*) leben *(on von)*; **we cannot ~ without water** wir können ohne Wasser nicht leben *or* existieren; **can life ~ on Mars?** kann auf dem Mars Leben existieren?; **she ~s on very little** sie kommt mit sehr wenig aus; **is it possible to ~ on such a small salary?** kann man denn von so einem kleinen Gehalt leben? **c** (= *be found*) vorkommen; **the natural resources which ~ in the Antarctic** die Bodenschätze, die in der Antarktis vorkommen

existence [ɪgˈzɪstəns] **N a** Existenz *f*; *(of custom, tradition, institution)* Bestehen *nt*, Existenz *f*; **to be in ~** existieren, bestehen; **to come into ~** entstehen; *(person)* auf die Welt kommen; **to go out of ~** zu bestehen *or* existieren aufhören; **do you believe in the ~ of God?** glauben Sie daran, dass Gott existiert?, glauben Sie an die Existenz Gottes?; **the continued ~ of slavery** das Weiterbestehen *or* der Fortbestand der Sklaverei; **the only one in ~** der Einzige, den es gibt **b** (= *life*) Leben *nt*, Dasein *nt*, Existenz *f*; **a miserable ~** ein elendes Leben, ein trostloses Dasein; **means of ~** Lebensunterhalt *m*

existent [ɪgˈzɪstənt] ADJ existent, *conditions, laws* bestehend; **to be ~** existieren; **dinosaurs are no longer ~** Dinosaurier gibt es nicht mehr

existential [ˌegzɪsˈtenʃəl] ADJ existentiell, existenziell

existentialism [ˌegzɪsˈtenʃəlɪzəm] N Existentialismus *m*, Existenzialismus *m*

existentialist [ˌegzɪsˈtenʃəlɪst] **N** Existentialist(in) *m(f)*, Existenzialist(in) *m(f)* **ADJ** existentialistisch, existenzialistisch

existing [ɪgˈzɪstɪŋ] ADJ bestehend; *circumstances* gegenwärtig

exit ['eksɪt] **N a** *(from stage, life)* Abgang *m*; *(from room)* Hinausgehen *nt (from aus)*; *(from competition)* Ausscheiden *nt*; *(from sb's life)* Scheiden *nt (geh)*; **to make an/one's ~** *(from stage)* abgehen; *(from room)* hinausgehen; **he made a very dramatic ~** sein Abgang war sehr dramatisch **b** (= *way out*) Ausgang *m*; *(for vehicles)* Ausfahrt *f* **VI** hinausgehen; *(from stage)* abgehen; *(from competition)* ausscheiden; *(Comput)* das Programm/die Datei *etc* verlassen, aussteigen *(inf)*; **~ the king** *(Theat)* der König (tritt) ab **VT a** *(US)* *train* verlassen, aussteigen aus; *place* hinausgehen aus **b** *(Comput)* *program, file* verlassen, aussteigen aus *(inf)*

exit: exit permit N Ausreisegenehmigung *f*; **exit poll** N *bei Wahlen unmittelbar nach Verlassen der Wahllokale durchgeführte Umfrage*

exitus ['eksɪtəs] N *(Med)* Exitus *m* *(spec)*, Tod *m*

exit visa N Ausreisevisum *nt*

exodus ['eksədəs] N **a** *(from a country)* Abwanderung *f*; *(Bibl: of Hebrews, also fig)* Exodus *m*; **general ~** allgemeiner Aufbruch **b** **~ of capital** Kapitalabwanderung *f* **c** *(Bibl)* **Exodus** 2. Buch Mosis *or* Mose, Exodus *m*

ex officio [ˌeksəˈfɪʃɪəʊ] *(form)* **ADJ** **an ~ member** ein Mitglied von Amts wegen **ADV** von Amts wegen

exonerate [ɪgˈzɒnəreɪt] VT entlasten *(from von)*

exoneration [ɪgˌzɒnəˈreɪʃən] N Entlastung *f (from von)*

exorbitance [ɪgˈzɔːbɪtəns] N *(of price)* Unverschämtheit *f*; *(of demands also)* Maßlosigkeit *f*, Übertriebenheit *f*

exorbitant [ɪgˈzɔːbɪtənt] ADJ überhöht; *price also* unverschämt; *demand* maßlos, übertrieben; **that's ~!** das ist Wucher!

exorbitantly [ɪgˈzɔːbɪtntlɪ] ADV **~ priced** *or* **expensive** maßlos teuer; **they are paid ~** sie werden unverschämt gut bezahlt; **they charge ~** sie verlangen unverschämte Preise

exorcism ['eksɔːsɪzəm] N Geisterbeschwörung *f*, Exorzismus *m*, Austreibung *f* böser Geister

exorcist ['eksɔːsɪst] N Exorzist(in) *m(f)*

exorcize ['eksɔːsaɪz] VT exorzieren; *evil spirit also* austreiben

exoskeleton [ˌeksəʊˈskelɪtən] N Außenskelett *nt*

exoteric [ˌeksəʊˈterɪk] ADJ exoterisch

exotic [ɪgˈzɒtɪk] ADJ exotisch; **~ dancer** exotischer Tänzer, exotische Tänzerin; **~ holidays** *(esp Brit)* *or* **vacation** *(US)* Urlaub *m* in exotischen Ländern **N** *(Bot)* exotische Pflanze, Exot(e) *m*

exotica [ɪgˈzɒtɪkə] PL Exotika *pl*; **a museum of ~** *(fig)* ein Raritätenkabinett *nt*

exotically [ɪgˈzɒtɪkəlɪ] ADV exotisch; **~ named** mit exotischem Namen

exoticism [ɪgˈzɒtɪsɪzəm] N Exotik *f*, Exotische *nt*

expand [ɪkˈspænd] **VT** *metal, gas, liquid, empire, chest* ausdehnen, expandieren; *business, trade, production* erweitern, expandieren; *knowledge, mind, algebraic formula, membership* erweitern; *influence, experience* vergrößern; *summary, notes* weiter ausführen; *ideas* entwickeln **VI** *(solids, gases, liquids, universe)* sich ausdehnen, expandieren; *(business, trade, economy, empire)* expandieren, wachsen; *(volume of trade, exports, production)* zunehmen, expandieren; *(knowledge, experience, influence)* zunehmen, wachsen; *(fields of knowledge, study, mind)* breiter werden; *(horizons)* sich erweitern; **we want to ~** wir wollen expandieren *or* (uns) vergrößern; **the market is ~ing** der Markt wächst; **we've ~ed into the European market** wir sind in den europäischen Markt vorgedrungen; **~ing watchstrap** Gliederarmband *nt*

▶ **expand (up)on** VT *subject* weiter ausführen; **could you expand on that?** könnten Sie das weiter ausführen?

expandable [ɪkˈspændəbl] ADJ erweiterbar

expanded polystyrene [ɪkˈspændɪd-] N Styropor® *nt*

expander [ɪkˈspændəʳ] N Expander *m*

expanse [ɪkˈspæns] N Fläche *f*; *(of ocean etc)* Weite *f no pl*; **a vast ~ of grass** eine riesige Grasfläche; **an ~ of woodland** ein Waldgebiet *nt*

expansion [ɪkˈspænʃən] N *(of liquid, gas, metal, universe, property)* Ausdehnung *f*, Expansion *f*; *(of business, trade, production)* Erweiterung *f*, Expansion *f*; *(territorial, economic, colonial)* Expansion *f*; *(of subject, idea)* Entwicklung *f*; *(Math, of knowledge, membership)* Erweiterung *f*; *(of experience, influence)* Vergrößerung *f*; *(of summary, notes)* Ausweitung *f*

expansion *(Comput)*: **expansion board** N Erweiterungsplatine *f*; **expansion card** N Erweiterungskarte *f*

expansionism [ɪkˈspænʃənɪzəm] N Expansionspolitik *f*

expansionist [ɪkˈspænʃənɪst] **ADJ** expansionistisch, Expansions-; **~ policy** Expansionspolitik *f* **N** Expansionspolitiker(in) *m(f)*

expansion: expansion joint N *(Tech)* Dehn(ungs)fuge *f*; **expansion slot** N *(Comput)* Erweiterungssteckplatz *m*

expansive [ɪkˈspænsɪv] ADJ **a** (= *communicative*) *person, mood* mitteilsam; *welcome* herzlich; **to be in an ~ mood** in gesprächiger Stimmung sein **b** *(form, = broad, extensive)* *area, lawn* ausgedehnt; *view* weit; *gesture* ausladend; *role* umfassend **c** (= *expanding, growing*) *economy* expandierend; *business* expansiv; **~ phase** Expansionsphase *f*; **to have ~ ambitions (for sth)** Expansionspläne (für etw) haben **d** *(Phys)* expansiv

expansively [ɪkˈspænsɪvlɪ] ADV **a** (= *warmly*) *say* herzlich; *smile* breit; **b** (= *enthusiastically*) begeistert **b** (= *in detail*) ausführlich

ex parte [eksˈpɑːtɪ] ADJ, ADV *(Jur)* einseitig, (seitens) einer Partei

expat ['ekspæt] N, ADJ = **expatriate** N, ADJ

expatiate [ɪkˈspeɪʃɪeɪt] VI sich verbreiten *(on über +acc)*

expatiation [ɪkˌspeɪʃɪˈeɪʃən] N weitläufige Erörterung

expatriate [eksˈpætrɪət] **N** im Ausland Lebende(r) *mf*; **British ~s** im Ausland lebende Briten; **the ~s in Abu Dhabi** die Ausländer in Abu Dhabi; **I'm an ~ too** ich bin hier auch im Exil *(hum)* **ADJ** *person, family* im Ausland lebend; **~ workers** ausländische Arbeitskräfte; **~ community** Ausländergemeinde *f* **VT** [eksˈpætrɪeɪt] *person* ausbürgern, expatriieren *(geh)*

expect [ɪkˈspekt] 🟳 6.2, 8.1, 10.2, 16.2, 26.3 **VT a** (= *anticipate*) erwarten; *esp sth bad* rechnen mit; **that was to be ~ed** das war zu erwarten, damit war zu rechnen; **I know what to ~** ich weiß, was mich erwartet; **we were ~ing war in 1939** 1939 haben wir mit Krieg gerechnet; **to ~ the worst** mit dem Schlimmsten rechnen; **I ~ed as much** das habe ich erwartet, damit habe ich gerechnet; **he failed as (we had) ~ed** er fiel, wie erwartet, durch; **he got first prize as was to be ~ed** wie erwartet, bekam er den ersten Preis; **to ~ to do sth** erwarten *or* damit rechnen, etw zu tun; **I didn't ~ to gain his sympathy** ich habe kein Mitleid von ihm erwartet; **he ~s to be elected** er rechnet damit, gewählt zu werden; **it is ~ed that ...** es wird erwartet, dass ..., man rechnet damit, dass ...; **it is hardly to be ~ed that ...** es ist kaum zu erwarten *or* damit zu rechnen, dass ...; **the talks are ~ed to last two days** die Gespräche sollen zwei Tage dauern; **she is ~ed to resign tomorrow** es wird erwartet, dass sie morgen zurücktritt; **I was ~ing him to come** ich habe eigentlich erwartet, dass er kommt; **you can't ~ me to agree to that!** Sie erwarten doch wohl nicht, dass ich dem zustimme!; **I'll ~ to see you tomorrow then** dann sehen wir uns also morgen; **at that price, what did you ~?** was hast du denn zu dem *or* für den Preis erwartet? **b** (= *suppose*) denken, glauben; **will they be on time? – yes, I ~ so/no, I ~ not** kommen sie pünktlich? – ja, ich glaube schon *or* ich denke doch/nein, ich glaube nicht; **this work is very tiring – yes, I ~ it is** diese Arbeit ist sehr anstrengend – (ja,) das glaube ich; **I ~ it will rain** höchstwahrscheinlich wird es regnen, es wird wohl regnen; **I ~ you'd like a drink** Sie möchten sicher etwas trinken, ich nehme an, Sie möchten etwas trinken; **I ~ you're tired** Sie werden sicher müde sein; **I ~ he turned it down** er hat wohl abgelehnt, ich nehme an, er hat abgelehnt; **well, I ~ he's right** er wird schon Recht haben; **well, I ~ it's all for the best** das ist wohl nur gut so; **I ~ it was your father who phoned** ich nehme an, es war dein Vater, der angerufen hat **c** (= *demand*) **to ~ sth of** *or* **from sb** etw von jdm erwarten; **to ~ sb to do sth** erwarten, dass jd etw tut; **I ~ you to be obedient** ich erwarte von dir Gehorsam; **what do you ~ me to do about it?** was soll ich da tun?; **don't ~ me to**

feel sorry erwarte von mir kein Mitleid; **are we ~ed to tip the waiter?** müssen wir dem Kellner Trinkgeld geben?

d (= *await*) *person, thing, action, baby* erwarten; **I will be ~ing you tomorrow** ich erwarte dich morgen; **I am ~ing them for supper** ich erwarte sie zum Abendessen; **we'll ~ you when we see you** (*inf*) wenn wir ihr kommt, dann kommt ihr (*inf*); **you'll have to ~ me when you see me** (*inf*) wenn ich da bin, bin ich da! (*inf*)

VI **she's ~ing** sie ist in anderen Umständen, sie bekommt *or* erwartet ein Kind

expectancy [ɪk'spektənsɪ] N Erwartung *f*

expectant [ɪk'spektənt] ADJ **a** (= *eagerly waiting*) erwartungsvoll **b** (= *future*) *mother, father, parents* werdend

expectantly [ɪk'spektəntlɪ] ADV erwartungsvoll; *wait* gespannt

expectation [ˌekspek'teɪʃən] N **a** (= *act of expecting*) Erwartung *f*; **in ~ of** in Erwartung (+*gen*); **in the confident ~ of an easy victory** fest im einem leichten Sieg rechnend **b** (= *that expected*) Erwartung *f*; **against** *or* **contrary to all ~(s)** wider Erwarten; **to exceed all ~(s)** alle Erwartungen übertreffen; **to come up to sb's ~s** jds Erwartungen (*dat*) entsprechen **c** (= *prospect*) Aussicht *f* **d** **~ of life** Lebenserwartung *f*

expected [ɪk'spektɪd] ADJ erwartet; *relief, profit also* erhofft; **the contract will provide an ~ 900 new jobs** es wird erwartet, dass der Auftrag 900 Arbeitsplätze schaffen wird

expectorant [ɪk'spektərənt] N Expektorans *nt* (*spec*)

expectorate [ɪk'spektəreɪt] VTI (*form*) ausspeien

expedience [ɪk'spiːdɪəns], **expediency** [ɪk'spiːdɪənsɪ] N **a** (= *self-interest*) Zweckdenken *nt*, Berechnung *f* **b** (*of measure etc*, = *politic nature*) Zweckdienlichkeit *f*; (= *advisability*) Ratsamkeit *f*

expedient [ɪk'spiːdɪənt] ADJ **a** (= *politic*) zweckdienlich; (= *advisable*) angebracht, ratsam **N** Notbehelf *m*, Hilfsmittel *nt*

expediently [ɪk'spiːdɪəntlɪ] ADV zweckmäßigerweise

expedite ['ekspɪdaɪt] VT **a** (= *hasten*) beschleunigen, vorantreiben; **see what you can do to ~ matters** sehen Sie zu, ob Sie die Sache beschleunigen können **b** (*rare*) *letters* expedieren (*spec*)

expedition [ˌekspɪ'dɪʃən] N **a** Expedition *f*; (*Mil*) Feldzug *m*; **shopping ~** Einkaufstour *f*; **to go on an ~** auf (eine) Expedition *or* Forschungsreise gehen; **to go on a shopping ~** eine Einkaufstour machen **b** *no pl* (*old, form*, = *speed*) Eile *f*; **with ~** eilends (*old, form*)

expeditionary [ˌekspɪ'dɪʃənrɪ] ADJ Expeditions-; **~ force** (*Mil*) Expeditionskorps *nt*

expeditious [ˌekspɪ'dɪʃəs] ADJ schnell, prompt

expeditiously [ˌekspɪ'dɪʃəslɪ] ADV schnell, prompt; **as ~ as possible** so schnell wie möglich, schnellstens

expel [ɪk'spel] VT **a** *person* vertreiben; (*officially, from country*) ausweisen (*from* aus); (*from school*) verweisen (*from* von, +*gen*); (*from society*) ausstoßen, ausschließen; *evil* austreiben **b** *gas, liquid* ausstoßen; **to ~ one's breath** ausatmen

expend [ɪk'spend] VT **a** (= *spend, employ*) *money* ausgeben, verwenden; *time, energy, care* aufwenden (*on* für, *on doing sth* um etw zu tun), verwenden (*on* auf +*acc*, *on doing sth* darauf, etw zu tun) **b** (= *use up*) *resources* verbrauchen

expendability [ɪkˌspendə'bɪlɪtɪ] N (*form, of device, object*) Entbehrlichkeit *f*; (*of person also*) Überflüssigkeit *f*

expendable [ɪk'spendəbl] (*form*) ADJ *device, object* entbehrlich; *person also* überflüssig; **an ~ luxury** ein überflüssiger Luxus **N** *usu pl* **~s** entbehrliche Dinge *pl*

expenditure [ɪk'spendɪtʃəʳ] N **a** (= *money spent*) Ausgaben *pl* **b** (= *spending, of money*) Ausgabe *f*; (*of time, energy*) Aufwand *m* (*on* an

+*dat*); **the ~ of money on ...** Geld auszugeben für ...; **~ of time/energy** Zeit-/Energieaufwand *m*

expense [ɪk'spens] N **a** Kosten *pl*; **at my ~** auf meine Kosten; **at public ~** auf Staatskosten; **at great ~** mit hohen Kosten; **it's a big ~** es ist eine große Ausgabe; **to go to the ~ of buying a car** (viel) Geld für ein Auto anlegen; **they went to the ~ of installing a lift** sie gaben viel Geld dafür aus, einen Lift einzubauen; **to go to great ~ to repair the house** es sich (*dat*) etwas kosten lassen, das Haus instand *or* in Stand zu setzen

b (*Comm, usu pl*) Spesen *pl*; **to incur ~s** Unkosten haben; **your ~s will be covered** Ihre Unkosten werden Ihnen vergütet; **put it on ~s** schreiben Sie es auf die Spesenrechnung; **it's all on ~s** das geht alles auf Spesen

c (*fig*) **at sb's ~**, **at the ~ of sb** auf jds Kosten (*acc*); **at the ~ of sth** auf Kosten einer Sache (*gen*); **to get rich at the ~ of others/the poor** sich auf Kosten anderer/der Armen bereichern; **at the ~ of quality** auf Kosten der Qualität

expense: expense account N Spesenkonto *nt*; **this will go on his ~** das geht auf Spesen; **expense-account** ADJ *attr* **~ lunch** Mittagessen *nt* auf Spesen; **~ lifestyle** Leben *nt* auf Spesen; **~ people who stay in this hotel** (*inf*) in diesem Hotel wohnen nur Spesenreiter (*inf*); **expenses form** N Formular *nt* zur Spesenabrechnung; **expenses-paid** ADJ auf Geschäftskosten; **an all-expenses-paid holiday** ein Gratisurlaub *m*

expensive [ɪk'spensɪv] ADJ teuer; **the least ~ seats** die billigsten Plätze; **they were too ~ for most people to buy** sie konnten sich die meisten Leute konnten sie sich nicht leisten; **childcare is an ~ business** Kinderbetreuung ist eine teure *or* kostspielige Angelegenheit; **to have ~ tastes** einen teuren Geschmack haben

expensively [ɪk'spensɪvlɪ] ADV teuer; **both boys had been privately, and ~, educated** beide Jungen hatten teure Privatschulen besucht; **she lived ~ but quietly** sie lebte ein aufwändiges *or* aufwendiges, aber ruhiges Leben; **~ priced** teuer

expensiveness [ɪk'spensɪvnɪs] N (*of goods, travel, services etc*) hoher Preis, Kostspieligkeit *f*; (*of living somewhere*) Kostspieligkeit *f*; **the ~ of her tastes** ihr teurer Geschmack; **the increasing ~ of basic commodities** die ständige Verteuerung von Grundbedarfsmitteln

experience [ɪk'spɪərɪəns] ⊙ 19.2 **N** **a** (= *knowledge, wisdom acquired*) Erfahrung *f*; **~ of life** Lebenserfahrung *f*; **~ shows** *or* **proves that ...** die Erfahrung lehrt, dass ...; **to know sth from ~** etw aus Erfahrung wissen; **to learn/ speak from ~** aus eigener Erfahrung lernen/ sprechen; **from my own personal ~** aus eigener Erfahrung; **he has no ~ of grief** er hat nie Kummer erfahren *or* erlebt; **he has no ~ of living in the country** er kennt das Landleben nicht; **I gained a lot of useful ~** ich habe viele nützliche Erfahrungen gemacht; **to have an ~** eine Erfahrung machen

b (= *practice, skill*) Erfahrung *f*; **he has had no practical ~** ihm fehlt die Praxis, er hat keine praktischen Kenntnisse *or* keine praktische Erfahrung; **to have ~ of a technique** Erfahrung in einer Methode haben; **have you had any ~ of driving a bus?** haben Sie Erfahrung im Busfahren?; **~ in a job/in business** Berufs-/Geschäftserfahrung *f*; **to have a lot of teaching ~** große Erfahrung als Lehrer(in) haben; **he lacks ~** ihm fehlt die Praxis *or* praktische Erfahrung; **he is working in a factory to gain ~** er arbeitet in einer Fabrik, um praktische Erfahrungen zu sammeln

c (= *event experienced*) Erlebnis *nt*; **I had a nasty ~** mir ist etwas Unangenehmes passiert; **the trial was a very nasty ~** der Prozess war eine sehr unangenehme Sache; **it was a painful ~** es war schmerzlich (*geh*); **to suffer some terrible ~s** viel durchmachen; **what an ~!** das war vielleicht etwas!; **it was a new ~ for me** es war völlig neu für mich

VT **a** (= *suffer, undergo*) *pain, grief, hunger* erfahren, erleben; *difficult times, recession* durchmachen; *problems, symptoms* haben; **to ~ difficulties** auf Schwierigkeiten stoßen, Schwierigkeiten haben

b (= *feel*) fühlen, spüren, empfinden

experienced [ɪk'spɪərɪənst] ADJ *person* erfahren; *staff, teacher, driver etc also* mit Erfahrung; **we need someone more ~** wir brauchen jemanden mit mehr Erfahrung *or* jemanden, der mehr Erfahrung hat; **an ~ eye** ein geschulter Blick; **to be ~ in sth** etw (*dat*) Erfahrung haben *or* erfahren sein; **they are ~ in helping elderly people** sie haben Erfahrung darin, älteren Leuten zu helfen

experiential [ɪkˌspɪərɪ'enʃəl] ADJ auf Erfahrung beruhend

experiment [ɪk'sperɪmənt] **N** (*Chem, Phys, fig*) Versuch *m*, Experiment *nt*; **to do an ~** einen Versuch *or* ein Experiment machen; **as an ~** versuchsweise, als Versuch **VI** (*Chem, Phys, fig*) experimentieren (*on, with* mit)

experimental [ɪkˌsperɪ'mentl] ADJ (*also Sci, Med, Tech etc*) experimentell; **~ theatre** (*Brit*) *or* **theater** (*US*)/**cinema** Experimentiertheater *nt*/-kino *nt*; **~ physics/psychology** Experimentalphysik *f*/-psychologie *f*; **~ laboratory/period** Versuchslabor *nt*/-zeit *f*; **to be at an** *or* **in the ~ stage** sich im Versuchs- *or* Experimentierstadium befinden; **on an ~ basis** versuchsweise; **he argued for an ~ lifting of the ban** er argumentierte dafür, das Verbot versuchsweise aufzuheben

experimentally [ɪkˌsperɪ'mentəlɪ] ADV **a** (= *as an experiment*) versuchsweise **b** (*Chem, Phys etc*, = *by experiment*) experimentell; *use* in Versuchen

experimentation [ɪkˌsperɪmen'teɪʃən] N Experimentieren *nt*

expert ['ekspɜːt] **N** Experte *m*, Expertin *f*; (= *professional*) Fachmann *m*, Fachfrau *f*; (*Jur*) Sachverständige(r) *mf*; **he is an ~ on the subject/at that sort of negotiation** er ist Fachmann *or* Experte auf dem Gebiet/für solche Verhandlungen; **~ in geology** Fachmann *m*/Fachfrau *f* für Geologie, Geologieexperte *m*/-expertin *f*; **an ~ at chess** ein Schachexperte *m*, eine Schachexpertin; **she is an ~ on wines/oriental philosophy** sie ist eine Weinexpertin/ eine Expertin auf dem Gebiet der orientalischen Philosophie; **with the eye of an ~** mit fachmännischem Blick; **to get the advice of ~s** Experten/Sachverständige zurate *or* zu Rate ziehen; **~'s report** Sachverständigenbericht *m*, Gutachten *nt*; **OK, you do it, you're the ~** gut, machen Sies, Sie sind der Fachmann; **he's an ~ at saying the wrong thing** (*iro*) er versteht es meisterhaft, genau das Falsche zu sagen

ADJ **a** (= *skilled*) *driver, carpenter, accountant etc* meisterhaft; **she's an ~ typist** sie ist perfekt im Maschinenschreiben; **he is ~ at** *or* **in skiing** er ist ein perfekter Skifahrer; **he is ~ at forgeries** *or* **an ~ forger** er kann meisterhaft fälschen; **he is ~ at this operation** er führt diese Operation meisterhaft aus; **to be ~ at** *or* **in doing sth** es hervorragend verstehen, etw zu tun; **people sufficiently ~ in interpreting the data** Leute, die sich in der Interpretation der Daten genügend auskennen

b (= *specialist, of an expert*) *approach, work, job, advice, help, attention, treatment* fachmännisch; *opinion* eines Fachmanns; (*Jur*) eines Sachverständigen; **his ~ hands** seine erfahrenen Hände; **an ~ eye** der Blick des Fachmanns; **to run** *or* **cast an ~ eye over sth** etw fachmännisch begutachten; **we need your ~ touch** wir brauchen Ihr fachmännisches Können; **an ~ opinion** ein Gutachten *nt*; **what's your ~ opinion?** (*also iro*) was meinen Sie als Fachmann *or* Experte dazu?

expertise [ˌekspɜː'tiːz] N Sachverstand *m*, Sachkenntnis *f* (*in* in +*dat*, *auf dem Gebiet* +*gen*); (= *manual skills*) Geschick *nt* (*in* bei)

expertly ['ekspɜːtlɪ] ADV (= skilfully) meisterhaft; drive, manoeuvre geschickt, gekonnt; repair fachmännisch; (= using expert knowledge) judge, examine sachverständig; **the job was ~ done** die Arbeit wurde fachmännisch ausgeführt

expert system N (Comput) Expertensystem nt

expert witness N Sachverständige(r) mf

expiate ['ekspɪeɪt] VT sühnen

expiation [ˌekspɪ'eɪʃən] N **in ~ of** als Sühne für

expiatory ['ekspɪətərɪ] ADJ Sühne-; **~ offering** Sühneopfer nt

expiration [ˌekspaɪə'reɪʃən] N **a** = **expiry b** (of breath) Ausatmen nt, Ausatmung f

expire [ɪk'spaɪə] VI **a** (lease, passport) ablaufen, ungültig werden; (time limit) ablaufen, zu Ende gehen **b** (liter, = die) seinen Geist aufgeben (liter) **c** (= breathe out) ausatmen

expiry [ɪk'spaɪərɪ] N Ablauf m; **on the ~ of** nach Ablauf (+gen); **date of ~, ~ date** Ablauftermin m; (of voucher, special offer) Verfallsdatum nt

explain [ɪk'spleɪn] ✪ 26.3 VT erklären (to sb jdm); motives, situation, thoughts erläutern, erklären; mystery aufklären; **it's all right, I can ~ everything** schon gut, ich kann das alles erklären; **that is easy to ~, that is easily ~ed** das lässt sich leicht erklären; **he wanted to see me but wouldn't ~ why** er wollte mich sehen, sagte aber nicht, warum or aus welchem Grunde; **so that ~s why he didn't react** ach, das erklärt, warum er nicht reagiert hat **VR** (= justify) sich rechtfertigen; **he'd better ~ himself** ich hoffe, er kann das erklären; **I think you'd better start ~ing yourself** was hast du zu deiner Entschuldigung zu sagen?; **~ yourself!** was soll das?, kannst du das erklären? **VI** es erklären; **please ~** bitte erklären Sie das; **I think you've got some ~ing to do** ich glaube, Sie müssen da einiges erklären

▸ **explain away** VT sep eine Erklärung finden für

explainable [ɪk'spleɪnəbl] ADJ erklärlich; **this is easily ~** das lässt sich leicht erklären; **that is ~ by ...** das lässt sich durch ... erklären

explanation [ˌeksplə'neɪʃən] ✪ 26.1 N **a** Erklärung f; (of motives, situation, thoughts) Erläuterung f, Erklärung f; (of mystery) Aufklärung f; **it needs some/a little ~** es bedarf einer Erklärung/einer kurzen Erklärung, man muss das etwas/ein wenig erklären; **he gave a long ~ of what he meant** er erklärte lange, was er meinte; **what is the ~ of this?** wie ist das zu erklären? **b** (= justification) Erklärung f, Rechtfertigung f; **has he anything to say in ~ of his conduct?** kann er irgendetwas zur Erklärung seines Verhaltens vorbringen?

explanatory [ɪk'splænətərɪ] ADJ erklärend; **a few ~ notes** ein paar Anmerkungen zur Erklärung

expletive [ɪk'spliːtɪv] N (= exclamation) Ausruf m; (= oath) Kraftausdruck m, Fluch m; (Gram, = filler word) Füllwort nt **ADJ ~ word** (Gram) Füllwort nt

explicable [ɪk'splɪkəbl] ADJ erklärbar

explicate ['eksplɪkeɪt] VT (form) erläutern, ausführen

explication [ˌeksplɪ'keɪʃən] N (form) Erläuterung f, Ausführung f

explicit [ɪk'splɪsɪt] ADJ person, statement, description (klar und) deutlich; orders eindeutig; instructions, commitment, agreement, support, reference ausdrücklich; (esp sexually) details, description, picture, photograph eindeutig; **sexually ~** sexuell explizit; **in ~ detail** in allen Einzelheiten; **there is no ~ mention of it** es wird nicht ausdrücklich erwähnt; **speaking to MPs, he was more ~** als er zu den Abgeordneten sprach, ging er näher darauf ein; **he was ~ about his intentions** er machte seine Absichten ganz deutlich; **he was very ~ in his explanations** seine Erklärungen waren sehr deutlich; **she was quite ~ in discussing details of the operation** sie diskutierte die Einzelheiten der Operation in aller Deutlichkeit; **in ~ terms** klar und deutlich

explicitly [ɪk'splɪsɪtlɪ] ADV **a** state, say deutlich, ausdrücklich **b** forbid, reject, mention, acknowledge ausdrücklich; (+adj) eindeutig; **~ political activities** eindeutig politische Aktivitäten; **~ anti-Semitic** unverhohlen antisemitisch; **~ sexual photographs** sexuell explizite Fotos

explode [ɪk'spləʊd] VI **a** (lit) explodieren **b** (fig) explodieren; **to ~ with anger** vor Wut platzen (inf), in die Luft gehen (inf); **to ~ with laughter** in schallendes Gelächter ausbrechen, losplatzen (inf); **to ~ into life** (engine, game) plötzlich in Gang kommen; (crisis) plötzlich aufflammen **VT a** bomb, plane sprengen; dynamite, gas zur Explosion bringen **b** (fig) theory zu Fall bringen; **to ~ a myth** einen Mythos entlarven

exploded [ɪk'spləʊdɪd] ADJ **~ diagram** Explosionszeichnung f; **~ view** Einzelteildarstellung f, Explosionsdarstellung f

exploit ['eksplɔɪt] N (heroic) Heldentat f; **~s** (= adventures) Abenteuer pl **VT** [ɪk'splɔɪt] **a** (= use unfairly) workers ausbeuten; friend, sb's credulity, good nature, weakness ausnutzen **b** (= make use of) talent, the situation, opportunity ausnutzen, ausnützen (dial); coal seam ausbeuten; land, natural resources, technology nutzen

exploiter [ɪk'splɔɪtə] N (lit, fig) Ausbeuter(in) m(f)

exploitation [ˌeksplɔɪ'teɪʃən] N **a** (= unfair treatment, of workers) Ausbeutung f; (of friend, sb's credulity, good nature, weakness) Ausnutzung f **b** (= utilization, of land, natural resources, technology) Nutzung f; (of coal seam) Ausbeutung f; (of talent, situation, opportunity) Ausnutzung f

exploration [ˌeksplɔː'reɪʃən] N (of country, area) Erforschung f, Exploration f (geh); (of small area, town) Erkundung f; (of topic, possibilities) Untersuchung f, Sondierung f, Exploration f; **a voyage of ~** (lit, fig) eine Entdeckungsreise; **on his ~s** auf seinen Erkundungen

exploratory [ɪk'splɔrətərɪ] ADJ approach, stage exploratorisch; **~ talks** or **discussions/meeting** Sondierungsgespräche pl/-gespräch nt; **he emphasized that the talks were only ~** er betonte, dass es sich nur um Sondierungsgespräche handelte; **~ trip/expedition** Erkundungsfahrt f/-expedition f; **~ digging/drilling** Probegrabungen pl/-bohrungen pl; **~ work** Vorarbeiten pl; **~ surgery, an ~ operation** (Med) eine Explorationsoperation

explore [ɪk'splɔː] VT **a** country, forest, unknown territory erforschen, erkunden, explorieren (geh); (Med) untersuchen **b** (fig) question, implications, prospects untersuchen, sondieren; possibilities, options prüfen, sondieren; **to ~ common ground** Gemeinsamkeiten herausarbeiten **VI** to go exploring auf Entdeckungsreise gehen; **he went off into the village to ~** er ging auf Entdeckungsreise ins Dorf

explorer [ɪk'splɔːrə] N Forscher(in) m(f), Forschungsreisende(r) mf

explosion [ɪk'spləʊʒən] N **a** Explosion f; (= noise) Knall m, Explosion f **b** (fig, of anger) Wutausbruch m **c** (fig, in prices, figures etc) Explosion f

explosive [ɪk'spləʊzɪv] N Sprengstoff m **ADJ a** (lit) gas, mixture explosiv; **~ device** Sprengsatz m; **~ charge** Sprengladung f; **~ power** or **force** Sprengkraft f **b** (fig, = volatile) situation, issue, problem, mixture explosiv, brisant; argument, reaction heftig; person, temper aufbrausend **c** (fig) = sudden) noise, applause explosionsartig; start explosiv; **~** = rapid) growth explosionsartig **d** (Phon) Verschluss-, explosiv

explosively [ɪk'spləʊsɪvlɪ] ADV **a** (lit) react, erupt explosiv **b** (fig) grow explosionsartig; say, ask wütend; laugh schallend; **his dance is ~ energetic** er tanzt mit einer explosionsartigen Energie

expo ['ekspəʊ] N abbr of exposition Ausstellung f

exponent [ɪk'spəʊnənt] N **a** (of theory) Vertreter(in) m(f), Exponent(in) m(f) **b** (Math) Exponent m, Hochzahl f

exponential [ˌekspəʊ'nenʃəl] ADJ growth exponentiell; (Math) Exponential-; **~ function** Exponentialfunktion f; **~ series** Exponentialreihe f

exponentially [ˌekspəʊ'nenʃəlɪ] ADV grow, increase exponentiell

export [ɪk'spɔːt] VT exportieren (also Comput), ausführen; **countries which ~ oil** Öl exportierende Länder pl **VI** exportieren, ausführen; **~ or die** wer nicht exportiert, geht unter **VI** exportieren, ausführen **N** ['ekspɔːt] Export m, Ausfuhr f; **ban on ~s** Exportverbot nt, Ausfuhrverbot nt **ADJ** ['ekspɔːt] attr Export-, Ausfuhr-; **~ ban** Exportverbot nt, Ausfuhrverbot nt

exportable [ɪk'spɔːtəbl] ADJ exportfähig

exportation [ˌekspɔː'teɪʃən] N Export m, Ausfuhr f

export ['ekspɔːt]: **export director** N Exportdirektor(in) m(f); **export drive** N Exportkampagne f; **export duty** N Export- or Ausfuhrzoll m

exporter [ɪk'spɔːtə] N Exporteur m (of von); (= country) Exportland nt (of für)

export ['ekspɔːt]: **export licence**, (US) **export license** N Ausfuhrgenehmigung f, Ausfuhrlizenz f, Exportgenehmigung f; **export manager** N Exportleiter(in) m(f); **export permit** N Ausfuhrerlaubnis f, Exporterlaubnis f; **export regulations** PL Ausfuhrbestimmungen pl; **export trade** N Exporthandel m

expose [ɪk'spəʊz] VT **a** (= uncover) rocks, remains freilegen; electric wire freilegen; (fig) nerve bloß- or freilegen **b** (to danger, rain, sunlight, radiation) aussetzen (to dat); **not to be ~d to heat** vor Hitze (zu) schützen; **to ~ oneself to criticism** sich der Kritik aussetzen **c** (= display) one's ignorance offenbaren; one's wounds (vor)zeigen; **to ~ oneself** (indecently) sich entblößen; **darling, you're exposing yourself** du zeigst etwas (zu) viel, Liebling **d** (= reveal) abuse, treachery aufdecken; scandal, plot enthüllen, aufdecken; person, imposter, murderer, thief entlarven; **to ~ sb/sth to the press** jdn/etw der Presse ausliefern **e** (Phot) belichten

exposé [ek'spəʊzeɪ] N Exposé nt, Exposee nt; (of scandal etc) Aufdeckung f

exposed [ɪk'spəʊzd] ADJ **a** (= unprotected) position, location, hillside, garden ungeschützt; (Mil) troops, flank ungedeckt; (Mil, fig) position exponiert; **the house is very ~** or **in a very ~ position** das Haus steht sehr frei or ungeschützt; **~ to the wind** dem Wind ausgesetzt; **to feel ~** sich verletzlich fühlen; **to be ~ to sth** (person) einer Sache (dat) ausgesetzt sein; **the troops were ~ to attack** die Truppen waren nicht gegen einen Angriff gedeckt **b** (= bare) skin, part of body unbedeckt; nerve freigelegt; wiring, engine parts, brickwork frei liegend; **to be ~ to view** sichtbar sein; **a dress which leaves the back ~** ein Kleid, bei dem der Rücken frei bleibt; **to feel ~** (fig, = insecure) sich allen Blicken ausgesetzt fühlen

exposition [ˌekspə'zɪʃən] N **a** (of facts, theory) Darlegung f, Exposition f (geh); (explanatory) Erklärung f, Erläuterung f; (of literature, text) Kommentar m (of zu), Erläuterung f; (Mus) Exposition f **b** (= exhibition) Ausstellung f

expository [ɪk'spɒzɪtərɪ] ADJ darlegend

expostulate [ɪk'spɒstjʊleɪt] VI protestieren; **to ~ with sb** mit jdm disputieren

expostulation [ɪkˌspɒstjʊ'leɪʃən] N Protest m

exposure [ɪk'spəʊʒə] N **a** (to sunlight, air, danger) Aussetzung f (to +dat); **doctors are warning against excessive ~ of the skin to sunlight** die Ärzte warnen davor, die Haut zu sehr dem Sonnenlicht auszusetzen; **to be suffering from ~** (Med) an Unterkühlung leiden; **to die of ~** (Med) erfrieren **b** (= displaying) Entblößung f **c** (= unmasking, of person, thief, murderer) Entlarvung f; (of abuses, plots, vices, scandals, crime) Aufdeckung f; **to threaten sb with ~** drohen, jdn zu entlarven

d (= position of building) Lage f; **southern ~** Südlage f

e (Phot) Belichtung(szeit) f

f (Media) Publicity f; **his new film has been given a lot of ~** sein neuer Film hat viel Publicity bekommen

exposure meter N (Phot) Belichtungsmesser m

expound [ɪk'spaʊnd] VT theory, one's views darlegen, erläutern

express [ɪk'spres] ✪ 6.3, 24.4, 26.3 **VT a** = ausdrücken, zum Ausdruck bringen; (in words) wish, one's sympathy, appreciation also aussprechen (to sb jdm); **to ~ oneself** sich ausdrücken; **this ~es exactly the meaning of the phrase** das gibt genau die Bedeutung dieses Ausdrucks wieder; **I haven't the words to ~ my thoughts** mir fehlen die Worte, um meine Gedanken auszudrücken; **if I may ~ my opinion** wenn ich meine Meinung äußern darf; **the thought/feeling which is ~ed here** der Gedanke, der/das Gefühl, das hier zum Ausdruck kommt; **it is hard to ~ how delighted I am/how much I hate him** es ist schwer, in Worte zu fassen, wie sehr ich mich freue/wie sehr ich ihn hasse

b (= be expressive of) ausdrücken; **a face which ~es candour/pride** ein Gesicht, das Aufrichtigkeit/Stolz ausdrückt

c juice, breast milk auspressen, ausdrücken

d letter etc per Express or als Eilsendung schicken

ADJ a (= explicit) order, instruction, direction, permission ausdrücklich; (= specific) purpose, intention bestimmt; **on ~ orders from the Prime Minister** auf ausdrückliche Anordnung des Premierministers; **with the ~ intention of doing sth** mit der bestimmten Absicht, etw zu tun

b (= fast) **letter** Eilbrief m; **by ~ mail** per Eilzustellung; **~ service** Express- or Schnelldienst m; **an ~ laundry service** ein Wäscheschnelldienst m

ADV to send a letter/package ~ einen Brief/ein Paket als Eilsendung or per Express schicken

N a (= train) Schnellzug m; **the Orient Express** der Orientexpress; **to send goods by ~** Waren als Eilgut schicken

b (= bus, coach) Schnellbus m

express: express company N (US) Spedition f (für Expressgut); **express delivery** N Eilzustellung f; **express goods** PL Eilfracht f, Eilgut nt

expression [ɪk'spreʃən] N **a** (= expressing: of opinions, friendship, affection, joy) Äußerung f, Ausdruck m; **as an ~ of our gratitude** zum Ausdruck unserer Dankbarkeit; **to give ~ to sth** etw zum Ausdruck bringen; **from Cairo came ~s of regret at the attack** Kairo brachte Bedauern über den Angriff zum Ausdruck; **popular discontent which found ~ in acts of violence** allgemeine Unzufriedenheit, die sich in Gewalttaten äußerte

b (= feeling: in music, art etc) Ausdruck m; **you need to put more ~ into it** Sie müssen das ausdrucksvoller spielen; **to play sth with ~** etw ausdrucksvoll spielen

c (= phrase etc) Ausdruck m

d (of face) (Gesichts)ausdruck m; **you could tell by his ~ that ...** man konnte an seinem Gesichtsausdruck erkennen, dass ...; **a face devoid of ~** ein ausdrucksloses Gesicht

e (Math) Ausdruck m

expressionism [ɪk'spreʃənɪzəm] N Expressionismus m

expressionist [ɪk'spreʃənɪst] **N** Expressionist(in) m(f) **ADJ** expressionistisch

expressionistic [ɪk,spreʃə'nɪstɪk] ADJ expressionistisch

expressionless [ɪk'spreʃənlɪs] ADJ person unbewegt; face, eyes, look, voice ausdruckslos

expressive [ɪk'spresɪv] ADJ eyes, face, voice ausdrucksvoll; glance, look vielsagend; gestures, painting, music ausdrucksvoll, expressiv (geh);

language ausdrucksstark; **~ dance** Ausdruckstanz m; **your eyes are your most ~ feature** deine Augen sind das Ausdrucksvollste an dir; **to be ~ of sth** (form) etw ausdrücken; **the French term seemed more ~ of what she felt** das französische Wort schien ihre Gefühle besser auszudrücken or genauer wiederzugeben; **~ powers/abilities** Ausdrucksfähigkeit f or -vermögen nt

expressively [ɪk'spresɪvlɪ] ADV ausdrucksvoll, expressiv (geh)

expressiveness [ɪk'spresɪvnɪs] N Ausdruckskraft f; (of face also) Ausdrucksfähigkeit f

expressly [ɪk'spreslɪ] ADV **a** (= explicitly) forbid, state, exclude, allow ausdrücklich; **not ~ illegal** nicht ausdrücklich verboten **b** (= specifically) design, write, make speziell; **he did it ~ to annoy me** (= intentionally) er hat es absichtlich or bewusst getan, um mich zu ärgern

express: express train N Schnellzug m; **expressway** N Schnellstraße f

expropriate [eks'prəʊprɪeɪt] VT enteignen

expropriation [eks,prəʊprɪ'eɪʃən] N Enteignung f, Expropriation f (dated)

expulsion [ɪk'spʌlʃən] N (from a country) Ausweisung f (from aus); (driving out) Vertreibung f (from aus); (from school) Verweisung f (von der Schule); (of evil) Austreibung f (from aus)

expulsion order N Ausweisungsbefehl m

expunge [ɪk'spʌndʒ] VT (form) ausstreichen (from aus); (from records also) auslöschen (from aus)

expurgate ['ekspɜːgeɪt] VT zensieren, die anstößigen Stellen entfernen aus; **~d edition** gereinigte Fassung

exquisite [ɪk'skwɪzɪt] ADJ **a** (= very fine) object, ornament, jewellery, elegance exquisit, erlesen; food, wine, humour exquisit, köstlich; craftsmanship, painting, sculpture vorzüglich, erlesen; face, features, building, town, view bezaubernd; manners, taste ausgesucht, erlesen; tact, politeness feinste(r, s); **in ~ detail** im allerfeinsten Detail **b** (= intense) pleasure, pain, irony köstlich; relief überwältigend; **with ~ care** mit größter Sorgfalt

exquisitely [ɪk'skwɪzɪtlɪ] ADV **a** (= beautifully, delightfully) dress ausgesucht, erlesen; carved, crafted, made aufs kunstvollste or Kunstvollste; decorate mit erlesenem Geschmack; **~ detailed** aufs feinste or Feinste detailliert; **she danced ~** sie tanzte ganz hervorragend; **it was ~ timed** der Zeitpunkt war hervorragend gewählt; **~ beautiful** bezaubernd schön; **~ elegant** von exquisiter Eleganz **b** (= intensely, extremely) sensitive, delicate überaus, außerordentlich; painful, funny köstlich; polite ausgesucht

ex-serviceman [eks'sɜːvɪsmən] N pl **-men** [-mən] Exsoldat m, Veteran m

ex-servicewoman [eks'sɜːvɪswʊmən] N pl **-women** [-wɪmɪn] Exsoldatin f, Veteranin f

ext abbr of **extension** App.

extant [ek'stænt] ADJ (noch) vorhanden or existent

extemporaneous [ɪk,stempə'reɪnɪəs], **extemporary** [ɪk'stempərɪ] ADJ unvorbereitet, aus dem Stegreif

extempore [ɪks'tempərɪ] **ADV** speak aus dem Stegreif, unvorbereitet **ADJ** prayer improvisiert; **to give an ~ speech** eine Rede aus dem Stegreif halten, extemporieren (geh)

extemporize [ɪk'stempəraɪz] VTI aus dem Stegreif sprechen, extemporieren (geh); (Mus) improvisieren

extend [ɪk'stend] ✪ 22 **VT a** (= stretch out) arms ausstrecken; **to ~ one's hand** die Hand ausstrecken; **to ~ one's hand to sb** jdm die Hand ausstrecken; **to ~ a wire between two posts** einen Draht zwischen zwei Pfosten spannen **b** (= prolong) street, line, visit, passport, holidays, deadline, lease verlängern; **her tender care doubtless ~ed his life** ihre liebevolle Pflege hat sein Leben zweifellos verlängert **c** (= enlarge) research, powers, franchise ausdehnen, erweitern; knowledge erweitern, vergrö-

ßern; influence ausbauen; scheme ausweiten; house anbauen an (+acc); property vergrößern, erweitern; limits erweitern; frontiers of a country ausdehnen; **to ~ one's lead** seine Führung ausbauen; **in an ~ed sense of the term** im weiteren Sinne des Wortes

d (= offer) (to sb jdm) help gewähren; hospitality, friendship erweisen; invitation, thanks, condolences, congratulations aussprechen; **to ~ a welcome to sb** jdn willkommen heißen

e (usu pass: = make demands on) person, pupil, athlete fordern

VI a (wall, estate, garden) sich erstrecken; ausdehnen (to, as far as bis); (ladder, table) sich ausziehen lassen; (meetings etc: over period of time) sich ausdehnen or hinziehen; **a career that ~ed from 1974 to 1990** eine Laufbahn, die sich von 1974 bis 1990 erstreckte

b (= reach to) enthusiasm which ~s even to the children Begeisterung, die sich sogar auf die Kinder überträgt; **does that ~ to (include) me?** betrifft das auch mich?

extendable [ɪk'stendɪbl], **extensible** [ɪk'stensɪbl] ADJ object ausziehbar

extended [ɪk'stendɪd] ADJ **extended credit** N (Fin) verlängerter Kredit; **extended family** N Großfamilie f; **extended memory** N (Comput) erweiterter Arbeitsspeicher; **extended-play record** N Schallplatte f mit verlängerter Spielzeit

extension [ɪk'stenʃən] ✪ 27.4, 27.5, 27.7 N **a** (of property) Vergrößerung f; (of business, knowledge) Erweiterung f, Vergrößerung f; (of powers, franchise, research, frontiers) Ausdehnung f; (of road, line, period of time) Verlängerung f; (of house) Anbau m **b** (= addition to length of sth, of road, line, table, holidays, leave etc) Verlängerung f; (of house) Anbau m **c** (Telec) (Neben)anschluss m; **~ 3714** Apparat 3714 **d** (Logic, of word, concept) Extension f

extension: extension cable N Verlängerungskabel nt; **extension course** N (Univ) weiterführender Kurs; **extension ladder** N Ausziehleiter f; **extension lead** N Verlängerungsschnur f

extensive [ɪk'stensɪv] ADJ area, land, forest, settlement, tour ausgedehnt; plans, reforms, influence, powers, rights weitreichend, weit reichend; research, range, menu, collection, alterations, repairs, surgery umfangreich; burns, rash großflächig; damage beträchtlich; knowledge umfassend, umfangreich; experience reich, groß; network weit verzweigt; view weit; **the facilities available are very ~** es steht eine Vielzahl von Einrichtungen zur Verfügung; **the story got or was given ~ coverage in the papers** über diese Geschichte wurde in der Presse ausführlich berichtet; **we had fairly ~ discussions** wir haben es ziemlich ausführlich diskutiert; **to make ~ use of sth** etw häufig or viel benutzen

extensively [ɪk'stensɪvlɪ] ADV travel, write, work viel; use, grow häufig; research, report, write, discuss, quote ausführlich; modify, alter beträchtlich; restore zum großen Teil; **the clubhouse was ~ damaged** an dem Klubhaus entstand ein größerer or beträchtlicher Schaden; **the chassis was ~ modified** am Chassis wurden umfangreiche Änderungen vorgenommen; **this edition has been ~ revised** diese Ausgabe ist grundlegend überarbeitet worden; **I have quoted ~ from the article** ich habe umfangreiche Zitate aus dem Artikel verwendet; **the ~ reported or covered trial** der Prozess, über den ausführlich berichtet wurde

extensor [ɪk'stensə] N Streckmuskel m

extent [ɪk'stent] N **a** (= length) Länge f; (= size) Ausdehnung f

b (= range, scope, of knowledge, alterations, power, activities, commitments) Umfang m; (of damage, losses) Ausmaß nt, Umfang m; **debts to the ~ of £5,000** Schulden in Höhe von £ 5.000

c (= degree) Grad m, Maß nt; **to some ~** bis zu einem gewissen Grade; **to what ~** inwieweit; **to a certain ~** in gewissem Maße; **to a large/**

lesser ~ in hohem/geringerem Maße; **she was involved only to the ~ of investing a small a-mount** ihre Beteiligung beschränkte sich auf die Investition einer kleinen Summe; **to such an ~ that ...** dermaßen *or* derart, dass ...; **he was ruined to the ~ that he had to sell everything** er war dermaßen ruiniert, dass er alles verkaufen musste; **such was the ~ of the damage** so groß war der Schaden

extenuate [ɪkˈstenjʊeɪt] VT *guilt* verringern, mindern; *offence, conduct* beschönigen; **extenuating circumstances** mildernde Umstände

extenuation [ɪkˌstenjʊˈeɪʃən] N (= *act*) Verringerung *f*, Minderung *f*, Beschönigung *f*; (= *extenuating factor*) mildernde Umstände *pl*

exterior [ɪkˈstɪərɪəʳ] **N a** (*of house, box etc*) Außenseite *f*, Äußere(s) *nt*; (*of person*) Äußere(s) *nt*; **on the ~** außen **b** (*Film*) Außenaufnahme *f* **ADJ** Außen-; *surface also* äußere(r, s); **~ wall** Außenwand *f*; **~ lighting** Außenbeleuchtung *f*; **~ shots** Außenaufnahmen *pl*; **~ view** Außenansicht *f*; **~ decoration/paintwork** Außenanstrich *m*; **~ paint** Farbe *f* für Außenanstrich

exterior angle N (*Math*) Außenwinkel *m*

exterminate [ɪkˈstɜːmɪneɪt] VT ausrotten, vernichten; *disease, beliefs, ideas* ausrotten

extermination [ɪkˌstɜːmɪˈneɪʃən] N Ausrottung *f*, Vernichtung *f*; (*of disease, beliefs, ideas*) Ausrottung *f*

exterminator [ɪkˈstɜːmɪneɪtəʳ] N (= *person: of rats etc, pests*) Kammerjäger(in) *m(f)*; (= *poison etc*) Vernichtungsmittel *nt*

external [ek ˈstɜːnl] **ADJ a** (= *outer*) *layer, covering, similarity etc* äußere(r, s); *dimensions, angle, diameter* Außen-; *injury* äußerlich; *gills* außen liegend; **the ~ walls of the house** die Außenwände des Hauses; **~ appearance** Aussehen *nt*; **~ surface** Außenfläche *f*; **~ skeleton** Außenskelett *nt*; **for ~ use** (*Pharm*) zur äußerlichen Anwendung **b** (*fig, = from outside*) *influence, factor, event, reality* äußere(r, s), extern (*geh*); **~ pressures** Druck *m* von außen; **~ cause** äußerer Anlass; **the ~ world** die Außenwelt; **to be ~ to sth** außerhalb einer Sache liegen; (= *not part of sth*) nicht zu etw gehören; **reasons both internal and ~ to the company** Ursachen, die sowohl innerhalb als auch außerhalb des Unternehmens zu finden sind **c** (= *foreign*) *affairs, relations, policy* auswärtig; **the European commissioner for ~ affairs** der EG-Kommissar für auswärtige Angelegenheiten; **MI6, the ~ security service** MI6, der militärische Abschirmdienst **d** (= *independent*) *examiner, auditor, assessor, evaluator* extern **N externals** PL (*form*) Äußerlichkeiten *pl*

external: external borders PL (*of country*) Landesgrenzen *pl*; (*of area*) Außengrenzen *pl*; **external debt** N Auslandsverschuldung *f*; **external degree** N (*Brit, Univ*) Abschluss *m* nach einem Fernstudium

externalize [ek ˈstɜːnəlaɪz] VT externalisieren

externally [ek ˈstɜːnəlɪ] ADV **a** *apply, use* äußerlich; **zinc helps healing both internally and ~** Zink fördert den innerlichen sowie äußerlichen Heilprozess **b** (= *on the outside*) außen; (*of person, appearance*) äußerlich; (= *to the outside*) nach außen; (= *from the outside*) von außen; (*Comm, = outside the firm*) außer Haus; **~ mounted cameras** außen angebrachte Kameras; **~ imposed conditions** von außen auferlegte Bedingungen; **the two models are ~ identical** die beiden Modelle sind äußerlich identisch; **he remained ~ calm** er blieb nach außen hin *or* äußerlich ruhig **c** (*Pol, = in foreign policy*) außenpolitisch

external trade N Außenhandel *m*

extinct [ɪkˈstɪŋkt] ADJ **a** (= *gone forever*) *animal, species, tribe, custom, art form, type of person etc* ausgestorben; (*fig*) *way of life, empire* untergegangen; *language* tot; **that fish has been ~ for thousands of years** dieser Fisch ist schon seit tausenden *or* Tausenden von Jahren ausgestorben;

to be made ~ ausgerottet werden; **to become ~** (*also fig*) aussterben; **is the English gentleman ~?** gibt es den englischen Gentleman überhaupt noch? **b** *volcano* erloschen

extinction [ɪkˈstɪŋkʃən] N (*of race, family, animal, species, tribe*) Aussterben *nt*; (= *annihilation*) Ausrottung *f*; **threatened with** *or* **faced with** *or* **in danger of ~** vom Aussterben bedroht; **this animal was hunted to ~** diese Tierart wurde durch Jagen ausgerottet

extinguish [ɪkˈstɪŋgwɪʃ] VT *fire, candle* (aus)löschen; *cigarette* ausmachen; *light* löschen; *hopes, passion* zerstören; *debt* tilgen

extinguisher [ɪkˈstɪŋgwɪʃəʳ] N Feuerlöscher *m*, Löschgerät *nt*

extirpate [ˈekstɜːpeɪt] VT *lit, fig* (mit der Wurzel) ausrotten, (gänzlich) beseitigen

extirpation [ˌekstɜːˈpeɪʃən] N *lit, fig* Ausrottung *f*

extol [ɪkˈstəʊl] VT preisen, rühmen

extort [ɪkˈstɔːt] VT *money* erpressen (*from* von); *confession* erzwingen (*from* von); *secret* abpressen (*from* +*dat*)

extortion [ɪkˈstɔːʃən] N (*of money*) Erpressung *f*; (*of signature*) Erzwingung *f*; **this is sheer ~!** (*inf*) das ist ja Wucher!

extortionate [ɪkˈstɔːʃənɪt] ADJ *charge, rate, sum, amount* horrend; *tax, rent, bill* maßlos hoch; **~ prices** Wucherpreise *pl*, horrende *or* unverschämte *or* astronomische (*inf*) Preise *pl*; **~ rates of interest** Wucherzinsen *pl*; **I was charged an ~ amount for a ticket** ich musste einen Wucherpreis für eine Karte bezahlen

extortioner [ɪkˈstɔːʃənəʳ] N Erpresser(in) *m(f)*; (*charging high prices*) Wucherer(in) *m(f)*

extra [ˈekstrə] **ADJ a** (= *additional*) zusätzlich; **take an ~ pair of shoes (just in case)** nimm ein zusätzliches Paar Schuhe (als Reserve) mit; **we need an ~ chair** wir brauchen noch einen Stuhl; **I have set an ~ place at table** ich habe noch ein Gedeck aufgelegt; **if you're cold put an ~ pullover on** wenn du frierst, zieh dir noch einen Pullover an; **to work ~ hours** Überstunden machen; **to make an ~ effort** sich besonders anstrengen; **~ police/troops were called in** es wurde Verstärkung gerufen; **to go to ~ expense** sich zusätzlich in Unkosten stürzen; **take ~ care!** sei besonders vorsichtig!; **for ~ safety** für den speziellen *or* besonderen Schutz; **for ~ whiteness** für ein (noch) strahlenderes Weiß; **an ~ £3 a week** £ 3 mehr pro Woche; **send 75p ~ for postage and packing** schicken Sie zusätzlich 75 Pence für Porto und Verpackung; **we make an ~ charge** wir berechnen einen Zuschlag; **there is an ~ charge/no ~ charge for breakfast** das Frühstück wird zusätzlich/nicht zusätzlich berechnet; **ask if there will be any ~ costs** fragen Sie, ob noch zusätzliche Kosten hinzukommen; **available at ~ cost/at no ~ cost** gegen einen Aufpreis/ohne Aufpreis erhältlich; **~ bus** Sonderbus *m* **ADV a** (= *more money*) *pay, cost, charge* mehr; **you have to pay ~ for breakfast, breakfast costs ~** das Frühstück wird zusätzlich berechnet; **post and packing ~** zuzüglich Porto und Verpackung; **to charge ~** einen Zuschlag berechnen **b** (= *especially*) besonders; **he wanted to do ~ well in the exam** er wollte bei der Prüfung besonders gut abschneiden **N a** (= *special request*) Sonderwunsch *m* **b extras** PL (= *extra expenses*) zusätzliche Kosten *pl*, Nebenkosten *pl*; (*in restaurant*) zusätzliche Beilagen *pl*; (*for machine*) Zubehör *nt*; (*for car*) Extras *pl* → **optional c** (*Film, Theat*) Statist(in) *m(f)*, Komparse *m*, Komparsin *f* **d** (= *remainder*) **what shall we do with the ~?** was sollen wir mit dem Rest machen?

extra- PREF **a** (= *outside*) außer-; **~parliamentary** außerparlamentarisch **b** (= *especially*) besonders, extra; **~dry** (*wine*) herb; *champagne* extra dry; **~large** (*eggs, tomatoes*) besonders *or* extra groß; *T-shirt, underpants* übergroß; **an ~large size** eine Übergröße; **~smart** besonders schick, todschick (*inf*)

extract [ɪkˈstrækt] **VT a** (= *take out*) herausnehmen; *cork etc* (heraus)ziehen (*from* aus); *juice, minerals, oil, DNA, energy* gewinnen (*from* aus); *tooth* ziehen, extrahieren (*spec*); *bullet, foreign body* entfernen (*from* aus); **she ~ed herself from his arms** sie befreite sich aus seinen Armen **b** (*fig*) *information, secrets* entlocken (*from* +*dat*); *confession, money* herausholen (*from* aus); *permission, promise, concession* abringen (*from* +*dat*), erlangen (*from* von); *the meaning/moral of a book* herausarbeiten (*from* aus); **he is able to ~ himself from difficult situations** er kann sich aus schwierigen Lagen befreien **c** (*Math*) *square root* ziehen **d** *quotation, passage* herausziehen, exzerpieren (*geh*) **N** [ˈekstrækt] **a** (*from book etc*) Auszug *m*, Exzerpt *nt* **b** (*Med, Cook*) Extrakt *m*

extraction [ɪkˈstrækʃən] N **a** (= *process of extracting*) Herausnehmen *nt*; (*of cork etc*) (Heraus)ziehen *nt*; (*of juice, minerals, oil, DNA, energy*) Gewinnung *f*; (*of bullet, foreign body*) Entfernung *f*; (*of information, secrets*) Entlocken *nt*; (*of confession, money*) Herausholen *nt*; (*of permission, promise, concession*) Abringen *nt*, Erlangen *nt* **b** (*Dentistry: = act of extracting*) (Zahn)ziehen *nt*, Extraktion *f* (*spec*); **he had to have an ~** ihm musste ein Zahn gezogen werden **c** (= *descent*) Herkunft *f*, Abstammung *f*; **of Spanish ~** spanischer Herkunft *or* Abstammung

extractor [ɪkˈstræktəʳ] N (*for juice*) Presse *f*, Entsafter *m*; (*for dust*) Sauganlage *f*; (*of gun*) Auszieher *m*

extractor fan N Sauglüfter *m*

extractor hood N Dunstabzugshaube *f*

extracurricular [ˌekstrəkəˈrɪkjʊləʳ] ADJ außerhalb des Stundenplans; **~ activity** (*esp hum: in spare time*) Freizeitaktivität *f* (*hum*)

extraditable [ˈekstrədaɪtəbl] ADJ *offence* auslieferungsfähig; *person* auszuliefern *pred*, auszuliefernd *attr*

extradite [ˈekstrədaɪt] VT ausliefern

extradition [ˌekstrəˈdɪʃən] N Auslieferung *f*

extradition: extradition order N (= *request*) Auslieferungsantrag *m*; **extradition treaty** N Auslieferungsvertrag *m*; **extradition warrant** N Auslieferungsantrag *m*

extramarital [ˈekstrəˈmærɪtl] ADJ außerehelich

extramural [ˈekstrəˈmjʊərəl] ADJ (*Brit, Univ*) **~ department** selbstständige Abteilung für Teilzeitkurse, die allen zugänglich sind **I took an ~ course at the university** ich besuchte einen Teilzeitkurs an der Universität; **~ studies** Teilzeitstudium außerhalb des normalen Universitätsprogramms **~ activity** Zeitvertreib *m* neben dem Studium; (*esp hum: in spare time*) Freizeitaktivität *f* (*hum*)

extraneous [ɪkˈstreɪnɪəs] ADJ (*form*) **a** (= *from outside*) *noise* von außen; *influence* äußere(r, s), extern (*geh*); **~ matter** (*Tech, Med*) Fremdstoffe *pl*; (*solid*) Fremdkörper *pl* **b** (= *not relevant*) *matter, material, issue, detail, thought* irrelevant, unwesentlich; **~ matters/issues** Unwesentliches *nt*; **to avoid all ~ issues** alles vermeiden, was nicht zur Sache gehört; **to feel ~** (*person*) sich (*dat*) überflüssig vorkommen; **~ to sth** für etw irrelevant

extraordinaire [eksˌtrɔːdɪˈnɛəʳ] ADJ unvergleichlich; **George Kuchar, film maker ~** George Kuchar, der unvergleichliche Filmemacher

extraordinarily [ɪkˈstrɔːdnrɪlɪ] ADV außerordentlich; (= *unusually*) *high, low, good, difficult, well* ungemein; (*introducing sentence*) erstaunlicherweise

extraordinary [ɪkˈstrɔːdnrɪ] ADJ **a** (= *exceptional*) *person, career, quality* außergewöhnlich; *success, courage, skill* außerordentlich; (= *unusual, strange*) *behaviour, appearance, dress, action, speech* merkwürdig, eigenartig; *tale, adventure* seltsam; (= *amazing*) *insults, violence* erstaunlich; **there's nothing ~ about that** daran ist nichts Ungewöhnliches; **it's ~ to think that ...** es ist (schon) eigenartig, wenn man denkt, dass ...; **what an ~ thing to say!** wie kann man nur so etwas sagen!; **it's ~ how much he resembles his brother** es ist erstaunlich, wie sehr er seinem Bruder ähnelt **b** (*Brit, form, = special*) *measure, party, congress* außerordentlich; **~ meeting** Sondersitzung *f*

extraordinary general meeting N außerordentliche Hauptversammlung

extrapolate [ek'stræpəleɪt] VTI extrapolieren (*from* aus)

extrapolation [ekˌstræpəˈleɪʃən] N Extrapolation *f*

extrasensory ['ekstrə'sensərɪ] ADJ außersinnlich; **~ perception** außersinnliche Wahrnehmung

extra-special ['ekstrə'speʃəl] ADJ ganz besondere(r, s); **to take ~ care over sth** sich (*dat*) besonders viel Mühe mit etw geben; **to make something ~ to eat** etwas ganz Besonderes zu essen machen

extraterrestrial ['ekstrətɪ'restrɪəl] **ADJ** außerirdisch, extraterrestrisch **N** außerirdisches Lebewesen

extraterritorial ['ekstrəˌterɪ'tɔːrɪəl] ADJ exterritorial

extra time N (*Sport*) Verlängerung *f*; **we had to play ~** der Schiedsrichter ließ nachspielen

extrauterine pregnancy ['ekstrəˈjuːtəraɪn'pregnənsɪ] N (*Med*) Bauchhöhlenschwangerschaft *f*

extravagance [ɪk'strævəgəns] N **a** Luxus *m* no pl; (= wastefulness) Verschwendung *f*; **her ~** ihre Verschwendungssucht; **if you can't forgive her little ~s** wenn Sie es ihr nicht verzeihen können, dass sie sich ab und zu einen kleinen Luxus leistet; **the ~ of her tastes** ihr kostspieliger or teurer Geschmack; **the ~ of her daily life** ihr luxuriöses Alltagsleben; **a life of such ~** ein derart luxuriöser Lebensstil; **the ~ of a big wedding** der Aufwand einer großen Hochzeitsfeier **b** (of ideas, theories) Extravaganz *f*, Ausgefallenheit *f*; (of claim, demand) Übertriebenheit *f* **c** (= extravagant action or notion) Extravaganz *f*

extravagant [ɪk'strævəgənt] ADJ **a** (= wasteful) *person* verschwenderisch; *taste, habit* teuer; **to be ~ with electricity** verschwenderisch mit Strom umgehen, Strom verschwenden; **your ~ spending habits** deine Angewohnheit, das Geld mit vollen Händen auszugeben; **cooking a whole chicken may seem ~** es scheint vielleicht übertrieben, ein ganzes Huhn zu kochen; **it isn't really ~ to rent a car** es ist eigentlich kein Luxus, einen Mietwagen zu nehmen; **she judged it unnecessarily ~** sie hielt es für einen überflüssigen Luxus **b** (= lavish) *gift, luxury* teuer, extravagant; *price* überhöht; *lifestyle* aufwändig, aufwendig, luxuriös; *party, entertainment* aufwändig, aufwendig; *designs, style, dress* ausgefallen, extravagant **c** (= flamboyant) *person* extravagant; *behaviour, gesture, praise, contempt, claim, promise* übertrieben; (= absurd) *idea, theory* abwegig; **to be ~ in one's praise of sb/sth** jdn/etw übertrieben loben; **an obituary ~ in its praise** ein Nachruf voller übertriebener Bewunderung

extravagantly [ɪk'strævəgəntlɪ] ADV **a** (= lavishly) *entertain* aufwändig, aufwendig; *live* luxuriös; **~ expensive** maßlos teuer **b** (= extremely) *übertrieben; gifted* überaus; *praise, thank* überschwänglich; **his ~ eccentric behaviour** sein extravagantes or übertriebenes Verhalten **c** (= flamboyantly) *dress, behave* extravagant

extravaganza [ɪkˌstrævə'gænzə] N fantastische Dichtung or (Mus) Komposition *f*; (= show) Ausstattungsstück *nt*

extravehicular [ˌekstrəvɪ'hɪkjʊlə] ADJ (Space) außerhalb des Raumfahrzeugs

extravert ['ekstrəvɜːt] N, ADJ = **extrovert**

extreme [ɪk'striːm] **ADJ** **a** *caution, courage, pleasure, kindness, simplicity* äußerste(r, s); *discomfort, sensitivity, concern, joy, danger* größte(r, s); *example, conditions, behaviour, temperatures* extrem; (Pol) *right, left, views* extrem; *measures, method* drastisch; *difficulty, pressure* ungeheuer; *rudeness* maßlos; *poverty* bitterste(r, s); **to proceed with ~ caution** mit äußerster Vorsicht vorgehen; **to suffer ~ discomfort** größte Beschwerden haben; **in ~ old age** in äußerst hohem Alter; **of ~ importance/urgency** äußerst wichtig/dringend; **~ case** Extremfall *m*; **~ left-wing anarchists** linksextremistische Anarchisten; **fascists of the ~ right** extrem rechts stehende Faschisten; **the weather was pretty ~** es herrschten recht extreme Wetterbedingungen; **the ~ unction** (Rel) die Letzte Ölung **b** (= furthest) *end, tip, edge, north, south* äußerste(r, s); **the room at the ~ end of the corridor** das Zimmer ganz am Ende des Korridors; **at the ~ left of the picture** ganz links im Bild **N** Extrem *nt*; **the ~s of happiness and despair** höchstes Glück und tiefste Verzweiflung; **between these two ~s** zwischen diesen beiden Extremen; **~s of temperature** extreme Temperaturen *pl*; **in the ~** im höchsten Grade; **it is bewildering in the ~** es ist höchst or im höchsten Grade verwirrend; **to go from one ~ to the other** von einem Extrem ins andere fallen; **to go to ~s** es übertreiben; **I wouldn't go to that ~** so weit würde ich nicht gehen; **to take or carry sth to ~s** etw bis zum Extrem treiben; **to drive sb to ~s** jdn zum Äußersten treiben

extremely [ɪk'striːmlɪ] ADV äußerst; *important, high, low* extrem; **was it difficult? – ~!** war es schwierig? – sehr!

extreme sport N Extremsport *m*

extremism [ɪk'striːmɪzəm] N Extremismus *m*

extremist [ɪk'striːmɪst] **N** Extremist(in) *m(f)* **ADJ** *organization, element, view* extremistisch; *violence von* Extremisten; **~ leader** Extremistenführer(in) *m(f)*; **~ group** Extremistengruppe *f*; **right-wing ~ organisations** rechtsextremistische Organisationen

extremity [ɪk'stremɪtɪ] N **a** (= furthest point) äußerstes Ende; **at the northerly ~ of the continent** am nördlichsten Zipfel des Kontinents **b** **extremities** PL (= hands and feet) Extremitäten *pl* **c** (= extreme degree) **in the ~ of his despair** in tiefster or äußerster Verzweiflung **d** (= state of need, distress) Not *f*; **he was reduced to the ~ of having to sell his business** er musste zum äußersten Mittel schreiten und sein Geschäft verkaufen **e** (= extreme actions) **to resort to extremities** zu äußersten or extremen Mitteln greifen; **to drive sb to extremities** jdn zum Äußersten treiben

extricable [ɪk'strɪkəbl] ADJ herausziehbar (from aus), zu befreien(d) (from aus, von)

extricate ['ekstrɪkeɪt] VT befreien; (fig) retten; **to ~ oneself from sth** (lit, fig) sich aus etw befreien

extrication [ˌekstrɪ'keɪʃən] N (lit) Befreiung *f* (from aus); (fig) Rettung *f*

extrinsic [ek'strɪnsɪk] ADJ äußerlich; *factor, reason* äußere(r, s); *considerations* nicht hereinspielend

extroversion [ˌekstrəʊ'vɜːʃən] N Extravertiertheit *f*

extrovert ['ekstrəʊvɜːt] **ADJ** extravertiert **N** extravertierter Mensch, Extravertierte(r) *mf*

extroverted ['ekstrəʊvɜːtɪd] ADJ (esp US) extravertiert

extrude [ek'struːd] **VT** *sb, sth* ausstoßen; *metal* herauspressen; *plastic* extrudieren **VI** herausstehen (from aus)

extrusion [ɪk'struːʒən] N (Tech, of metal) Fließpressen *nt*; (of plastic) Extrudieren *nt*

exuberance [ɪg'zuːbərəns] N **a** (of person) Überschwänglichkeit *f*; (of joy, youth, feelings) Überschwang *m*; (of joy) überschwängliche Freude (at über +acc); **in his ~** (= rejoicing) in seiner überschwänglichen Freude, im Überschwang der Gefühle; **in their youthful ~** (= high spirits) in ihrem jugendlichen Überschwang **b** (= vitality: of prose, style) Vitalität *f* **c** (= abundance) Fülle *f*, Reichtum *m*

exuberant [ɪg'zuːbərənt] ADJ **a** (= irrepressible, energetic) *person, personality* überschwänglich; *esp child* übermütig; *mood* überschäumend; *voice* jubelnd; *style* übersprudelnd; *painting* lebhaft; *film, music, show* mitreißend; **he was/felt ~ (about his success)** er freute sich unbändig (über seinen Erfolg); **they were ~ after their victory** nach ihrem Sieg waren sie in Jubelstimmung; **rugs in ~ colours** (Brit) or **colors** (US) farbenfrohe Teppiche **b** *growth, foliage, flowers* üppig

exuberantly [ɪg'zuːbərəntlɪ] ADV überschwänglich; (esp of child) übermütig; *grow, decorate* üppig; **~ happy** überglücklich

exude [ɪg'zjuːd] **VI** (liquid) austreten (from aus); (blood, pus etc) abgesondert werden (from von) **VT** **a** *liquid* ausscheiden; *dampness, sap* ausscheiden, ausschwitzen; *smell* ausströmen **b** (fig, = radiate) *confidence, charisma* ausstrahlen; *optimism* verströmen; *enthusiasm* verbreiten; (pej) *charm* triefen vor

exult [ɪg'zʌlt] VI frohlocken; **~ing in his freedom** seine Freiheit genießend

exultant [ɪg'zʌltənt] ADJ *person, tone* jubelnd; *expression, smile, cry* triumphierend; **he was ~** er jubelte, er war in Jubelstimmung; **~ mood** Jubelstimmung *f*; **the mood was less than ~** es herrschte nicht gerade Jubelstimmung

exultantly [ɪg'zʌltəntlɪ] ADV jubelnd; *laugh* triumphierend

exultation [ˌegzʌl'teɪʃən] N Jubel *m*; **sing in ~** (Rel) jauchzet und frohlocket; **their ~ at the prospect** ihr Jubel über die Aussicht

ex works ADV (Brit) ab Werk

ex-works [eks'wɜːks] ADJ (Brit) **~ prices** Preise *pl* ab Werk

eye [aɪ] **N** **a** (of human, animal, electronic) Auge *nt*; **with tears in her ~s** mit Tränen in den Augen; **a gleam in sb's ~** ein Glitzern in jds Augen (dat); **with one's ~s closed/open** (lit, fig) mit geschlossenen/offenen Augen; **an ~ for an ~** Auge um Auge; **~s right!** (Mil) (die) Augen rechts!; **~s front!** (Mil) Augen geradeaus!; **as far as the ~ can see** so weit das Auge reicht; **to be all ~s** große Augen machen; **that's one in the ~ for him** (inf) da hat er eins aufs Dach gekriegt (inf); **to cast or run one's ~ over sth** etw überfliegen; **to cast one's ~s round a room** seine Blicke durch ein Zimmer wandern or schweifen lassen; **his ~ fell on a small door** sein Blick fiel auf eine kleine Tür; **to rest one's ~ on sth** seine Augen or den Blick auf etw (dat) ruhen lassen; **to look sb (straight) in the ~** jdm in die Augen sehen; **to set or clap** (inf) **~s on sb/sth** jdn/etw zu Gesicht bekommen; **a strange sight met our ~s** ein seltsamer Anblick bot sich uns; **(why don't you) use your ~s!** hast du keine Augen im Kopf?; **with one's own ~s** mit eigenen Augen; **in front of or before my very ~s** (direkt) vor meinen Augen; **it was there all the time right in front of my ~s** es lag schon die ganze Zeit da, direkt vor meiner Nase; **under the watchful ~ of the guard/their mother** unter der Aufsicht des Wächters/ihrer Mutter; **your ~s are bigger than your stomach** diese Augen sind größer als dein Magen; **you need ~s in the back of your head** da muss man hinten und vorne Augen haben; **I don't have ~s in the back of my head** ich hab doch hinten keine Augen; **to keep an ~ on sb/sth** (= look after) auf jdn/etw aufpassen; **the police are keeping an ~ on him** (= have him under surveillance) die Polizei beobachtet ihn; **to keep one's ~s on the ball/main objective** sich auf den Ball/die Hauptsache konzentrieren; **to take one's ~s off sb/sth** die Augen or den Blick von jdm/etw abwenden; **don't take your ~ off the ball** konzentrier dich auf den Ball; **don't take your ~s off the magician's left hand** lassen Sie die linke Hand des Zauberkünstlers nicht aus den Augen; **to have one's ~s fixed on sth** etw nicht aus den Augen lassen; **to keep one's ~s open or peeled** (inf) **or skinned** (inf) die Augen offen halten; **to keep an ~ open or out for sth** nach etw Ausschau halten; **to keep a watchful ~ on the situation** die Sache im Auge behalten; **to keep an ~ on expenditure** auf die Ausgaben achten or aufpassen; **to open sb's ~s to sb/sth** jdm die

Augen über jdn/etw öffnen; **to close** *or* **shut one's ~s to sth** die Augen vor etw (*dat*) verschließen; **to see ~ to ~ with sb** mit jdm einer Meinung sein; **to make ~s at sb** jdm schöne Augen machen; **to catch sb's ~** jds Aufmerksamkeit erregen; **the dress caught my ~** das Kleid fiel *or* stach mir ins Auge; **she would buy anything that caught her ~** sie kaufte alles, was ihr ins Auge fiel; **he was a monster in their ~s** in ihren Augen war er ein Scheusal; **in the ~s of the law** in den Augen des Gesetzes; **through sb's ~s** durch *or* mit jds Augen; **to look at a question through the ~s of an economist** eine Frage mit den Augen *or* aus der Sicht eines Volkswirts betrachten; **with a critical/an uneasy ~** mit kritischem/besorgtem Blick; **with an ~ to the future** im Hinblick auf die Zukunft; **with an ~ to buying sth** in der Absicht, etw zu kaufen; **to have an ~ to** *or* **for the main chance** jede Gelegenheit ausnutzen; **I've got my ~ on you** ich beobachte dich genau; **to have one's ~ on sth** (= *want*) auf etw (*acc*) ein Auge geworfen haben; **the ~s of the world** *or* **all ~s are on the police/the conference** die Polizei/die Konferenz steht im Blickpunkt der Öffentlichkeit; **I only have ~s for you** ich habe nur Augen für dich; **to have a keen ~ for sth** ein scharfes Auge für etw haben, einen scharfen Blick für etw haben; **she has an ~ for a bargain** sie hat einen Blick *or* ein Auge für günstige Käufe; **he has no ~ for beauty** ihm fehlt der Blick für Schönheit; **he has a good ~ for form** er hat ein Auge für Form; **you need an ~ for detail** man muss einen Blick fürs Detail haben; **to get one's ~ in** (*shooting*) sich einschießen; (*playing tennis etc*) sich einspielen; **to be up to one's ~s in work** (*Brit inf*) in Arbeit ersticken (*inf*); **to be up to one's ~s in debt** (*Brit inf*) bis über beide Ohren verschuldet sein (*inf*); **he's in it up to the ~s** (*inf*) er steckt bis zum Hals drin (*inf*); **my ~!** (*inf*) Unsinn!

b (*of needle*) Öhr *nt*; (*of potato, on peacock's tail*) Auge *nt*; (*of hurricane*) Auge *nt*; **in the ~ of the wind** (*Naut*) in *or* gegen den Wind; **the minister in the ~ of the storm** (*fig*) der Minister im Mittelpunkt der Kontroverse → **hook and eye**
VT anstarren; **to ~ sb up and down** jdn von oben bis unten mustern

▸ **eye up** VT *sep girls, boys* mustern, begutachten

eye: **eye appeal** N attraktive Gestaltung, optische Wirkung; **eyeball** **N** Augapfel *m*; **to be ~ to ~** sich Auge in Auge gegenüberstehen; **drugged up to the ~s** (*esp Brit inf*) total zugedröhnt (*inf*) **VT** (*inf*) aggressiv anstarren; **eyebath** N Augenbad *nt*; (= *container*) Augenbadewanne *f*; **eyebrow** N Augenbraue *f*; **to raise one's ~s** die Augenbrauen hochziehen; (*fig*) die Stirn runzeln (*at sth* über etw *acc*); **he never raised an ~** er hat sich nicht einmal gewundert; **that will raise a few ~s, there will be a few raised ~s (at that)** da werden sich einige wundern; **eyebrow pencil** N Augenbrauenstift *m*; **eye-catcher** N (*thing*) Blickfang *m*; **she's quite an ~** sie zieht alle Blicke auf sich; **eye-catching** ADJ auffallend; *publicity, poster* auffällig, ins Auge springend; **that's very ~** das fällt *or* springt wirklich ins Auge; **eye contact** N Blickkontakt *m*; **to make/avoid ~ with sb** Blickkontakt mit jdm aufnehmen/vermeiden; **eyecup** N (*US*) Augenbadewanne *f*

-eyed [-aɪd] ADJ *suf* -äugig; **green-eyed** grünäugig; **sad-eyed** mit traurigen Augen

eyedrops [ˈaɪdrɒps] PL Augentropfen *pl*

eyeful [ˈaɪfʊl] N **he got an ~ of soda water** er bekam Selterswasser ins Auge; **she's quite an ~** (*inf*) sie hat allerhand zu bieten (*inf*); **I opened the bathroom door and got quite an ~** ich öffnete die Badezimmertür und sah allerhand (*inf*)

eye: **eyeglass** N (*old*) Augenglas *nt* (*old*); **eyeglasses** PL (*US*, = *spectacles*) Brille *f*; **eyehole** N Guckloch *nt*; (*Tech*) kleine, runde Öffnung; **eyelash** N Augenwimper *f*; **eyelet** [ˈaɪlɪt] N Öse *f*; **eyelevel** ADJ *attr grill* in Augenhöhe; **eyelid** N Augenlid *nt*; **eyeliner** [ˈaɪlaɪnə] N Eyeliner *m*; **eye-minded** ADJ visuell, *vorwiegend mit Gesichtssinn begabt*; **eye-opener** N **a** **that was a real ~ to me** das hat mir die Augen geöffnet **b** (*US, inf*: = *drink*) (alkoholischer) Muntermacher; **eye patch** N Augenklappe *f*; **eyepiece** N Okular *nt*; **eyeshade** N Augenblende *f*, Schild *m*; **eye shadow** N Lidschatten *m*; **eyeshot** N Sicht- *or* Sehweite *f*; **within/out of ~** in/außer Sichtweite; **we are out of his ~** er kann uns nicht mehr sehen; **eyesight** N Sehkraft *f*, Sehvermögen *nt*; **to have good/poor ~** gute/schlechte Augen haben; **to lose one's ~** das Augenlicht verlieren (*geh*), erblinden; **his ~ is failing** seine Augen lassen nach, sein Sehvermögen lässt nach; **eye socket** N (*Anat*) Augenhöhle *f*; **eyesore** N Schandfleck *m*; **this settee is a real ~** dieses Sofa sieht fürchterlich aus; **eyestrain** N Überanstrengung *f or* Ermüdung *f* der Augen; **eye test** N Augentest *m or* -untersuchung *f*

Eyetie [ˈaɪtaɪ] N (*Brit pej sl*) Spag(h)ettifresser(in) *m(f)* (*pej inf*), Itaker *m* (*pej inf*)

eye: **eyetooth** N Eckzahn *m*, Augenzahn *m*; **I'd give my eyeteeth for that** darum würde ich alles geben; **eyewash** N (*Med*) Augenwasser *or* -bad *nt*; (*fig inf*) Gewäsch *nt* (*inf*); (= *deception*) Augenwischerei *f*; **eyewater** N (*Physiol*) Augenflüssigkeit *f*; **eyewitness** N Augenzeuge *m*/-zeugin *f*

eyrie [ˈɪərɪ] N Horst *m*

Ezekiel [ɪˈziːkɪəl] N (*Bibl*) Hesekiel *m*, Ezechiel *m*

e-zine [ˈiːziːn] N (*Comput*) Onlinemagazin *nt*, Internetmagazin *nt*

F

F, f [ef] N F *nt*, f *nt*; **F sharp** Fis *nt*, fis *nt*; **F flat** Fes *nt*, fes *nt* → **natural**

F *abbr of* **Fahrenheit** F

f **a** *abbr of* **foot** of **feet** **b** *abbr of* **feminine** f

FA *abbr of* **Football Association**

fa [fɑ:] N (*Mus*) Fa *nt*

fab [fæb] ADJ (*dated inf*) *abbr of* **fabulous** toll (*inf*), dufte (*dated inf*)

fable ['feɪbl] N Fabel *f*; (= *legend, body of legend*) Sage *f*; (*fig*, = *lie*) Märchen *nt*; **is it fact or ~?** ist es wahr oder erfunden?

fabled ['feɪbld] ADJ sagenhaft; **Cleopatra, ~ for her beauty** Kleopatra, berühmt für ihre Schönheit

fabric ['fæbrɪk] N **a** (*Tex*) Stoff *m* **b** (= *basic structure*: *of building*) Bausubstanz *f* **c** (*fig*: *of society etc*) Gefüge *nt*, Struktur *f*

fabricate ['fæbrɪkeɪt] VT **a** (= *invent*) *story* erfinden, ersinnen (*geh*); *quotation* erfinden; *evidence, confession* fälschen **b** (= *manufacture*) herstellen, fabrizieren

fabrication [ˌfæbrɪ'keɪʃən] N **a** (= *act of inventing*) Erfindung *f*; (*of evidence, confession*) Fälschung *f*; (= *story invented*) Erfindung *f*, Lügenmärchen *nt*; **it's (a) pure ~** das ist ein reines Märchen *or* (= *despite*) reine Erfindung **b** (= *manufacture*) Herstellung *f*, Fabrikation *f*

Fabrikoid® ['fæbrɪkɔɪd] N (*US*) Kunstleder *nt*, Skai® *nt*

fabulist ['fæbjʊlɪst] N (*Liter*, = *writer of fables*) Fabeldichter(in) *m(f)*; (= *writer of fantastical literature*) Fabulant(in) *m(f)*; (*fig*, = *liar*) Fabulierer(in) *m(f)*, Fabulant(in) *m(f)*

fabulous ['fæbjʊləs] ADJ sagenhaft (*inf*); (*inf*, = *wonderful also*) toll (*inf*), fabelhaft

fabulously ['fæbjʊləslɪ] ADV *wealthy, expensive* sagenhaft (*inf*); (*inf*, = *wonderfully*) fabelhaft, fantastisch (*inf*); **~ beautiful** hinreißend schön; **you can eat ~ well there** man kann dort fantastisch (*inf*) *or* fabelhaft essen

façade [fə'sɑ:d] N (*lit, fig*) Fassade *f*

face [feɪs] **N** **a** Gesicht *nt*; **to go red in the ~** rot anlaufen; **I don't want to see your ~ here again** ich möchte Sie hier nie wieder sehen; **we were standing ~ to ~** wir standen einander Auge in Auge *or* von Angesicht zu Angesicht (*geh*) gegenüber; **next time I see him ~ to ~** das nächste Mal, wenn ich ihm begegne; **to bring sb ~ to ~ with sb/sth** jdn mit jdm/etw konfrontieren; **to bring two people ~ to ~** zwei Leute einander gegenüberstellen *or* miteinander konfrontieren; **to come ~ to ~ with sb** jdn treffen; **to come ~ to ~ with sth** einer Sache (*dat*) ins Auge sehen; **he told him so to his ~** er sagte ihm das (offen) ins Gesicht; **he shut the door in my ~** er schlug mir die Tür vor der Nase zu; **he laughed in my ~** er lachte mir ins Gesicht; **the plan blew up in his ~** der Plan ging ins Auge; **to look sb in the ~** jdn ansehen; **to be able to look sb in the ~** jdm in die Augen sehen können; **to throw sth back in sb's ~** jdm etw wieder vorhalten; **in the ~ of great difficulties/much opposition** *etc* angesichts *or* (= *despite*) trotz größter Schwierigkeiten/starker Opposition *etc*; **courage in the ~ of the enemy** Tapferkeit vor dem Feind; **to be off** *or* **out of one's ~** (*Brit inf*: = *drunk, on drugs*) total zu sein (*inf*) → **flat¹**

b (= *expression*) Gesicht(sausdruck *m*) *nt*; **to make** *or* **pull a ~** das Gesicht verziehen; **to make** *or* **pull ~s/a funny ~** Gesichter *or* Grimassen/eine Grimasse machen *or* schneiden (*at sb* jdm); **to put a good ~ on it** gute Miene zum bösen Spiel machen; **to put a brave ~ on it** sich (*dat*) nichts anmerken lassen; (= *do sth one dislikes*) (wohl oder übel) in den sauren Apfel beißen; **he has set his ~ against that** er stemmt sich dagegen

c (= *prestige*) **loss of ~** Gesichtsverlust *m*; **to save (one's) ~** das Gesicht wahren; **to lose ~** das Gesicht verlieren

d (*of clock*) Zifferblatt *nt*; (= *rock face*) (Steil)wand *f*; (= *coalface*) Streb *m*; (= *typeface*) Schriftart *f*; (*of playing card*) Bildseite *f*; (*of coin*) Vorderseite *f*; (*of house*) Fassade *f*; **to put sth ~ up (-wards)/down(wards)** etw mit der Vorderseite nach oben/unten legen; **to be ~ up(wards)/down(wards)** (*person*) mit dem Gesicht nach oben/unten liegen; (*thing*) mit der Vorderseite nach oben/unten liegen; (*book*) mit der aufgeschlagenen Seite nach oben/unten liegen; **to work at the (coal) ~** vor Ort arbeiten; **to change the ~ of the world** die Welt völlig verändern; **the changing ~ of politics** das sich wandelnde Gesicht der Politik; **the unacceptable ~ of capitalism** die unannehmbare Seite des Kapitalismus; **he/it vanished off the ~ of the earth** (*inf*) er/es war wie vom Erdboden verschwunden; **I'm the luckiest person on the ~ of the earth** (*inf*) ich bin der glücklichste Mensch auf der Welt; **on the ~ of it** so, wie es aussieht

e (*inf*, = *effrontery*) **to have the ~ to do sth** die Stirn haben, etw zu tun

VT **a** (= *be opposite, have one's face towards*) gegenüber sein (+*dat*), gegenüberstehen/-liegen *etc* (+*dat*); (*window, door*) *north, south* gehen nach; *street, garden etc* liegen zu; (*building, room*) *north, south* liegen nach; *park, street* liegen zu; **to ~ the wall/light** zur Wand gekehrt/dem Licht zugekehrt sein; (*person*) mit dem Gesicht zur Wand/zum Licht stehen/sitzen *etc*; **sit down and ~ the front!** setz dich und sieh nach vorn!; **~ this way!** bitte sehen Sie hierher!; **he was facing me at dinner** er saß mir beim Essen gegenüber; **the picture/wall facing you** das Bild/die Wand Ihnen gegenüber; **facing one another** einander gegenüber; **to sit facing the front of the bus** in Fahrtrichtung sitzen

b (*fig*) *possibility, prospect* rechnen müssen mit; **to ~ death** dem Tod ins Auge sehen; **to ~ trial** vor Gericht gestellt werden; **to ~ financial ruin** vor dem finanziellen Ruin stehen; **to be ~d with sth** sich einer Sache (*dat*) gegenübersehen; **the problem facing us** das Problem, dem wir gegenüberstehen *or* mit dem wir konfrontiert sind; **you'll ~ a lot of criticism if you do that** Sie setzen sich großer Kritik aus, wenn Sie das tun; **to be ~d with a bill for £100** eine Rechnung über £ 100 präsentiert bekommen; **he is facing a charge of murder** er steht unter Mordanklage, er ist wegen Mordes angeklagt; **he ~s life in prison if convicted** wenn er für schuldig befunden wird, muss er mit lebenslänglich rechnen

c (= *meet confidently*) *situation, danger, criticism* sich stellen (+*dat*); *person, enemy* gegenübertreten (+*dat*); **he ~d defeat bravely** er hat sich

tapfer mit der Niederlage abgefunden; **to ~ (the) facts** den Tatsachen ins Auge blicken *or* sehen; **let's ~ it** machen wir uns doch nichts vor; **you'd better ~ it, you're not going to get the job** du musst dich wohl damit abfinden, dass du die Stelle nicht bekommst

d (*inf*, = *put up with, bear*) verkraften (*inf*); *another drink, cake etc* runterkriegen (*inf*); **I can't ~ another of these arguments** ich halte noch so einen Streit einfach nicht aus; **I can't ~ seeing anyone** ich kann einfach niemanden sehen; **I can't ~ it** (*inf*) ich bringe es einfach nicht über mich

e *building, wall* verblenden, verkleiden; (*Sew*) *garment* (mit Besatz) verstürzen

f (*Cards*) aufdecken

g *stone* glätten, (*plan*) schleifen

VI (*house, room*) liegen (*towards park* dem Park zu, *onto road* zur Straße, *away from road* nicht zur Straße); (*window*) gehen (*onto, towards* auf +*acc*, *so, away from* nicht auf +*acc*); **he was sitting facing away from me** er saß mit dem Rücken zu mir; **they were all facing toward(s) the window** sie saßen alle mit dem Gesicht zum Fenster (hin); **the house ~s south/toward(s) the sea** das Haus liegt nach Süden/zum Meer hin; **in which direction was he facing?** in welche Richtung stand er?; **you've parked facing in the wrong direction** Sie haben in der falschen Richtung geparkt; **the side of the house that ~s onto the road** die der Straße zugekehrte Seite des Hauses; **why was the house built facing away from the park?** warum wurde das Haus nicht mit Blick auf den Park gebaut?; **right ~!** (*Mil*) rechts um!

▶ **face about** VI (*US, Mil*) kehrtmachen

▶ **face out** VT *sep* durchstehen

▶ **face up to** VI +*prep obj fact, truth* ins Gesicht sehen (+*dat*); *danger* ins Auge sehen *or* blicken (+*dat*); *possibility* sich abfinden mit; *reality, problems* sich auseinander setzen mit; *responsibility* auf sich (*acc*) nehmen; **he won't face up to the fact that ...** er will es nicht wahrhaben, dass ...

face: **face card** N Bildkarte *f*; **face cloth** N Waschlappen *m*; **face cream** N Gesichtscreme *f*; **face flannel** N (*Brit*) Waschlappen *m*; **face guard** N Schutzmaske *f*; **faceless** ADJ *drawing* gesichtslos; (*fig*) anonym; **face-lift** N (*lit*) Gesichts(haut)straffung *f*, Facelift(ing) *nt*; (*fig, for car, building etc*) Verschönerung *f*; **to have a ~** (*lit*) das Gesicht liften *or* straffen lassen; (*fig*) ein neues Aussehen bekommen; **to give the house a ~** das Haus renovieren, das Haus einer Verschönerungsaktion unterziehen; **face mask** N **a** (*of diver etc*) (Gesichts)maske *f* **b** (*Cosmetics*) Gesichtsmaske *f or* -packung *f*; **face-off** N **a** (= *confrontation*) Konfrontation *f* **b** (*Ice hockey*) Bully *nt*; **face pack** N Gesichtspackung *f*; **face paints** PL Gesichtsfarbe *f*; **face powder** N Gesichtspuder *m*

facer ['feɪsə'] N (*Brit, inf*, = *difficulty*) harte Nuss (*inf*)

face: **face-saver** N Ausrede *f* um das Gesicht zu wahren; **face-saving** ADJ **a** ~ **measure/solution/tactic** eine Maßnahme/Lösung/Taktik, die dazu dient, das Gesicht zu wahren

facet ['fæsɪt] N (*lit*) Facette *f*; (*fig*) Seite *f*, Aspekt *m*

faceted ['fæsɪtɪd] ADJ facettiert, fassettiert

faceting ['fæsɪtɪŋ] N (Miner) Facettenschliff m, Fassettenschliff m

facetious [fə'siːʃəs] ADJ remark, speech, tone witzelnd, spöttisch, mokant; **to be ~ (about sth)** (über etw (acc)) Witze machen, sich (über etw (acc)) mokieren; **~ humour** Blödeleien pl; **if satire is merely ~** wenn Satire zur Blödelei wird; **I was just being ~** das war doch nur ein Witz or so eine Blödelei (inf)

facetiously [fə'siːʃəslɪ] ADV witzelnd; (= mockingly) spöttisch

face: face tissue N Kosmetiktuch nt; **face--to-face** ADJ persönlich; confrontation, contact direkt; **face value** (Fin) Nennwert m, Nominalwert m; **to take sth at (its) ~** (fig) etw für bare Münze nehmen; **to take sb at ~** jdm unbesehen glauben; **face worker** N (Min) Hauer m

facial ['feɪʃəl] ADJ Gesichts-; **~ hair** Gesichtsbehaarung f; **~ expression** Gesichtsausdruck m; **~ features** Gesichtszüge pl; **~ injuries** Gesichtsverletzungen pl, Verletzungen pl im Gesicht N kosmetische Gesichtsbehandlung f; **to have a ~** zur Gesichtsbehandlung gehen

facially ['feɪʃəlɪ] ADV alike vom Gesicht her; **to be ~ disfigured** entstellte Gesichtszüge haben; **~ disfigured people** Menschen mit entstellten Gesichtszügen; **~, she has changed little** ihr Gesicht hat sich kaum verändert

facile ['fæsaɪl] ADJ (pej) person, mind, work of art oberflächlich; optimism blind; task simpel; question vordergründig; comparison, answer billig; solution billig, simpel; remark nichts sagend; style flüssig; **it is ~ to suggest that...** es lässt sich natürlich leicht sagen, dass ...

facilitate [fə'sɪlɪteɪt] VT erleichtern; (= make possible) ermöglichen; **it would ~ matters** es würde die Sache erleichtern

facilitator [fə'sɪlɪteɪtə] N Vermittler(in) m(f); **the role of teachers as ~s** die Vermittlerrolle von Lehrern

facility [fə'sɪlɪtɪ] N **a** Einrichtung f; **to give sb every ~** jdm jede Möglichkeit bieten; **you will have every ~ for study** es wird Ihnen alles zur Verfügung stehen, was Sie zum Studium brauchen; **we have no ~ or facilities for disposing of toxic waste** wir haben keine Möglichkeit zur Beseitigung von Giftmüll; **a computer with the ~ to reproduce text** ein Computer, der Text wiedergeben kann; **a large hotel with all facilities** ein großes Hotel mit allem Komfort; **facilities for the disabled** Einrichtungen pl für Behinderte; **cooking facilities** Kochgelegenheit f; **toilet facilities** Toiletten pl
b no pl (= ease) Leichtigkeit f; (= dexterity) Gewandtheit f; **he has a great ~ for languages/maths** Sprachen fallen/Mathematik fällt ihm sehr leicht

facing ['feɪsɪŋ] N **a** (on wall) Verblendung f, Verkleidung f; (Sew) Besatz m **b** ADJ **on the ~ page** auf der gegenüberliegenden Seite

facsimile [fæk'sɪmɪlɪ] N Faksimile nt; (Telec) Faksimileübertragung f

fact [fækt] ✪ 15.1, 26 N **a** Tatsache f, Faktum nt (geh); (historical, geographical etc) Faktum nt; **hard ~s** nackte Tatsachen pl; **the true ~s** der wahre Sachverhalt; **~s and figures** Fakten und Zahlen; **he accepts the ~ that I don't eat meat** er akzeptiert es, dass ich kein Fleisch esse; **in view of the ~ that ...** angesichts der Tatsache, dass ...; **despite the ~ that ...** der Tatsache zum Trotz, dass ...; **to know for a ~ that** (es) ganz genau or sicher wissen, dass; **the ~ (of the matter) is that ...** die Sache ist die, dass ...; **the ~ remains that ...** es lässt sich nicht bestreiten, dass ...; **to stick to the ~s** bei den Tatsachen bleiben, sich an die Tatsachen or Fakten halten; **to look (the) ~s in the face** der Wirklichkeit or den Tatsachen (dat) ins Auge sehen; **the ~s of the case** (Jur) der Tatbestand, der Sachverhalt; **... and that's a ~** ... darüber besteht kein Zweifel!, ... Tatsache! (inf); **is that a ~?** tatsächlich?, Tatsache? (inf) → **face VT c**

b no pl (= reality) Wirklichkeit f, Realität f; **~ and fiction** Dichtung und Wahrheit; **based/founded on ~** auf Tatsachen beruhend
c in (point of) ~, in actual ~ eigentlich; (= in reality) tatsächlich, in Wirklichkeit; (= after all) (dann) doch; (to make previous statement more precise) nämlich; **in ~, as a matter of ~** eigentlich; (to intensify previous statement) sogar; **I don't suppose you know him? – in (actual) ~** or **as a matter of ~ I do** Sie kennen ihn nicht zufällig? – doch, eigentlich schon; **do you know him? – in (actual) ~** or **as a matter of ~ I do** kennen Sie ihn? – jawohl; **it sounds simple, but in (actual) ~** or **in point of ~ it's very difficult** es hört sich so einfach an, aber in Wirklichkeit ist es sehr schwer; **I'd meant to do some work but in ~ I was too tired** ich wollte eigentlich etwas arbeiten, war aber dann zu müde; **I thought I could give you a lift, but in (actual) ~ I won't be going** ich dachte, ich könnte dich mitnehmen, aber ich gehe doch nicht; **I'm going soon, in (actual) ~ tomorrow** ich reise bald ab, nämlich morgen; **it won't be easy, in ~** or **as a matter of ~ it'll be very difficult** es wird nicht einfach sein, es wird sogar sehr schwierig sein; **does it hurt? – as a matter of ~ it's very painful** tuts weh? – ja, und sogar ganz schön; **I bet you haven't done that! – as a matter of ~ I have!** du hast das bestimmt nicht gemacht! – und ob, aber ja doch!; **as a matter of ~ we were just talking about you** wir haben (nämlich) eben von Ihnen geredet; **do you know Sir Charles? – as a matter of ~ he's my uncle/yes, in ~ he's my uncle** kennen Sie Sir Charles? – ja, und er ist sogar/ja, er ist nämlich mein Onkel
d (Jur) **to be an accessory before/after the ~** sich der Beihilfe/Begünstigung schuldig machen

fact-based ['fæktbeɪst] ADJ auf Tatsachen beruhend

fact-finding ['fæktfaɪndɪŋ] ADJ **~ mission** Erkundungsmission f; **~ tour** Informations- or Erkundungsreise f; **~ team** Erkundungsgruppe f

faction ['fækʃən] N **a** (= group) (Partei)gruppe f; (Pol) Fraktion f; (= splinter group) Splittergruppe f **b** no pl (= strife) interne Unstimmigkeiten pl

factionalism ['fækʃənlɪzəm] N interne Streitigkeiten pl or Querelen pl

factious ['fækʃəs] ADJ (liter) streitsüchtig, händelsüchtig; quarrelling kleinlich, engherzig

factitious [fæk'tɪʃəs] ADJ künstlich, unecht; demand for goods hochgespielt

fact of life N **a** (= reality) harte Tatsache; **that's just a ~** so ist es nun mal im Leben **b** **facts of life** PL (sexual) Aufklärung f; **to tell** or **teach sb the facts of life** jdn aufklären; **to know the facts of life** aufgeklärt sein

factor ['fæktə] ✪ 26.1 N **a** Faktor m; **the scandal was a contributing ~ in his defeat** der Skandal trug zu seiner Niederlage bei; **to be a ~ in determining/deciding sth** etw mitbestimmen/mitentscheiden **b** (of sun cream) Faktor m; **I use ~ 10** ich verwende Schutzfaktor 10 **c** (= agent) Makler(in) m(f) **d** (Comm, for debts) Kommissionär(in) m(f) **e** (Math) Faktor m; **by a ~ of two/three** etc mit einem Faktor von zwei/drei etc **f** (Biol) Erbfaktor m **VI** (Comm) Schulden aufkaufen

▶ **factor in** VT SEP (esp US) berücksichtigen; **to factor sth into sth** etw in etw (acc) mit einbeziehen

factorize ['fæktəraɪz] VT in Faktoren zerlegen, faktorisieren

factory ['fæktərɪ] N Fabrik f; (plant also) Werk nt

factory: Factory Act N Arbeitsschutzgesetz nt; **factory farm** N industrieller Viehzuchtbetrieb, Großmästerei f; **factory farming** N industriell betriebene Viehzucht; **factory hand** N Fabrikarbeiter(in) m(f); **factory inspector** N Gewerbeaufsichtsbeamte(r) m, Gewerbeaufsichtsbeamtin f; **factory price** N Fabrikpreis

m; **factory ship** N Fabrikschiff nt; **factory worker** N Fabrikarbeiter(in) m(f)

factotum [fæk'təʊtəm] N Faktotum nt

factsheet ['fæktʃiːt] N Informationsblatt nt

factual ['fæktjʊəl] ADJ evidence auf Tatsachen beruhend; account, speech sachlich; **~ information** Sachinformationen pl; (= facts) Fakten pl; **~ error** Sachfehler m; **~ knowledge** Faktenwissen nt; **~ report** Tatsachenbericht m; **to have a ~ basis** auf Tatsachen beruhen; **the book is largely ~** das Buch beruht zum größten Teil auf Tatsachen

factually ['fæktjʊəlɪ] ADV write, speak sachlich; **~ accurate** sachlich richtig

faculty ['fækəltɪ] N **a** (= power of mind) Vermögen nt, Fähigkeit f, Kraft f; (= ability, aptitude) Begabung f, Talent nt; **mental faculties** geistige Fähigkeiten pl, Geisteskräfte pl; **~ of reason** Vernunft f; **~ of hearing/sight** Hör-/Sehvermögen nt; **to be in (full) possession of (all) one's faculties** im Vollbesitz seiner Kräfte sein; **to have a ~ for doing sth** ein Talent dafür haben, etw zu tun **b** (Univ) Fakultät f; **the medical ~, the ~ of medicine** die medizinische Fakultät; **the Faculty** (= staff) der Lehrkörper **c** (Eccl) Vollmacht f

fad [fæd] N Fimmel m, Tick m (inf); (= fashion) Masche f (inf); **it's just a ~** das ist nur ein momentaner Fimmel (inf) or Tick (inf); **that's the latest fashion ~** das ist die neuste Modemasche (inf); **her latest food ~** ihr neuester Fimmel in puncto Ernährung (inf); **her ~ for caviar** ihr Kaviarfimmel (inf); **his ~ for wearing an earring** sein Tick or Fimmel, einen Ohrring zu tragen (inf)

faddish ['fædɪʃ], **faddy** ['fædɪ] (inf) ADJ wählerisch

fade [feɪd] **VI a** (= lose colour) verblassen; (material, colour) verbleichen, verblassen; (on exposure to light) verschießen; (flower) verblühen; (= lose shine) seinen Glanz verlieren; **guaranteed not to ~** garantiert farbecht
b (fig, memory) verblassen; (sight, strength, inspiration, feeling) nachlassen, schwinden (geh); (hopes) zerrinnen; (smile) vergehen, verschwinden; (beauty) verblühen; (sound) verklingen, verhallen; (radio signal) schwächer werden; **hopes are fading of finding any more survivors** die Hoffnung, noch weitere Überlebende zu finden, wird immer geringer; **he ~d into obscurity** er geriet langsam in Vergessenheit; **to ~ into the background** (person) sich im Hintergrund halten; (fears) in den Hintergrund rücken
c (Rad, TV, Film) scene ausgeblendet werden; (cameraman) ausblenden; **to ~ to another scene** (allmählich) zu einer anderen Szene überblenden
d (Tech, brakes) nachlassen
VT a (= cause to lose colour) ausbleichen
b (Rad, TV, Film) ausblenden; **to ~ one scene (in)to another** von einer Szene (allmählich) in eine andere überblenden
N (Rad, TV, Film) Blende f

▶ **fade away** VI (sight) schwinden; (memory) verblassen, schwinden; (hopes) zerrinnen; (interest, strength, inspiration) nachlassen; (sound) verklingen, verhallen; (person) immer weniger or schwächer werden; (from memory of the public) aus dem Gedächtnis schwinden

▶ **fade in** (Rad, TV, Film) VI allmählich eingeblendet werden VT sep allmählich einblenden

▶ **fade out** VI **a** (Rad, TV, Film) abblenden **b** **to fade out of sb's life** aus jds Leben verschwinden VT sep (Rad, TV, Film) abblenden

▶ **fade up** VT sep (Rad, TV, Film) aufblenden; sound lauter werden lassen, anschwellen lassen

faded ['feɪdɪd] ADJ photograph, grandeur verblasst; colour, material verblichen; (after exposure to light) verschossen; flowers, beauty verblüht; **a pair of ~ jeans** verblichene Jeans pl

fade: fade-in N (Rad, TV, Film) Auf- or Einblendung f; **fadeless** ['feɪdlɪs] ADJ licht- or farbecht; (*fig:* = *eternal*) unvergänglich; **fade-out** N (*Rad, TV, Film*) Abblende *f*

faecal, (*US*) **fecal** ['fiːkəl] ADJ fäkal

faeces, (*US*) **feces** ['fiːsiːz] PL Kot *m*

faerie ['fɛərɪ] (*old*) N Fee *f* ADJ Elfen-; ~ **king/ queen** Elfenkönig *m*/-königin *f*

Faeroes ['fɛərəʊz] PL = **Faroes**

faery ['fɛərɪ] N, ADJ (*old*) = **faerie**

faff about ['fæfəˌbaʊt], **faff around** ['fæfəˌraʊnd] VI (*Brit, inf*) herumbosseln (*inf*)

fag [fæg] (*inf*) N **a** *no pl* (*Brit* = *drudgery*) Schinderei *f*, Plackerei *f* **b** (*Brit,* = *cigarette*) Kippe *f* (*inf*), Glimmstängel *m* (*dated inf*) **c** (*Brit, Sch*) *junger Internatsschüler, der einem älteren bestimmte Dienste zu leisten hat* **d** (*esp US sl:* = *homosexual*) Schwule(r) *m* (*inf*) VT (*Brit inf: also* **fag out**) erschöpfen, schlauchen (*inf*); **to be ~ged (out)** kaputt *or* geschafft sein (*inf*) VI (*Brit*) **a** (*also* **fag away**) sich abrackern (*inf*), sich abplagen **b** (*Sch*) *einem älteren Schüler Dienste leisten*

fag end (*Brit*) **a** (*inf,* = *cigarette end*) Kippe *f* (*inf*), Stummel *m* **b** (*inf,* = *last part*) letztes Ende; **the ~s of old policies** die kümmerlichen Reste der alten Politik

fag hag N (*US sl*) Schwulenfreundin *f* (*inf*)

fagot ['fægət] N (*esp US sl:* = *homosexual*) Schwule(r) *m* (*inf*)

Fahrenheit ['færənhaɪt] N Fahrenheit *nt*

FAI N ABBR *of* **Football Association of Ireland**

fail [feɪl] VI **a** (= *be unsuccessful*) keinen Erfolg haben; (*in mission, life etc*) versagen, scheitern; (*campaign, efforts, negotiations, plan, experiment, marriage*) fehlschlagen, scheitern; (*undertaking, attempt*) fehlschlagen, misslingen, missglücken; (*applicant, application*) nicht angenommen werden; (*election candidate, Theat: play*) durchfallen; (*business*) eingehen; (*charm, attempts at persuasion etc*) vergeblich *or* umsonst sein; **he ~ed in his attempt to take control of the company** sein Versuch, die Leitung der Firma zu übernehmen, schlug fehl *or* blieb erfolglos *or* missglückte; **he ~ed in his application for the post** seine Bewerbung wurde nicht angenommen; **to ~ in one's duty** seine Pflicht nicht tun; **to ~ by 5 votes** (*motion*) mit 5 Stimmen Mehrheit abgelehnt werden; (*person*) um 5 Stimmen geschlagen werden; **if all else ~s** wenn alle Stricke reißen; **to ~ miserably** *or* **dismally** kläglich scheitern

b (= *not pass exam*) durchfallen; **he ~ed in Latin** er fiel in Latein durch

c (= *fall short*) **where he/the essay ~s is in not being detailed enough** sein Fehler/der Fehler des Aufsatzes ist, dass er nicht ausführlich genug ist; **this report ~s in that it comes up with no clear proposals** dieser Bericht lässt es an klaren Vorschlägen fehlen; **where you ~ is that you lack relevant experience** Ihnen fehlt es an der notwendigen Erfahrung

d (= *grow feeble, health*) sich verschlechtern; (*hearing, eyesight*) nachlassen; (*invalid*) schwächer werden; **he is ~ing fast** sein Zustand verschlechtert sich zusehends

e (= *stop working, be cut off etc, generator, battery, radio, electricity, pump, engine*) ausfallen; (*brakes*) versagen; (*supply, wind*) ausbleiben; (*heart etc*) versagen, aussetzen; **the crops ~ed** es gab eine Missernte; (*completely*) die Ernte fiel aus

VT **a** *candidate* durchfallen lassen; *subject* durchfallen in (+*dat*); **to ~ an exam** eine Prüfung nicht bestehen, durch eine Prüfung fallen; **to ~ Latin** in Latein durchfallen

b (= *let down, person, memory*) im Stich lassen; (= *not live up to sb's expectations*) enttäuschen; **his heart ~ed him** sein Herz setzte aus; **words ~ me** mir fehlen die Worte

c **to ~ to do sth** etw nicht tun; (= *neglect*) (es) versäumen, etw zu tun; **she ~ed to lose weight** es gelang ihr nicht abzunehmen; **he ~ed to win support for his proposal** er konnte keine Unterstützung für seinen Vorschlag finden; **she never ~s to amaze me** sie versetzt mich immer wieder in Erstaunen; **I ~ to see why** es ist mir

völlig unklar, warum; (*indignantly*) ich sehe gar nicht ein, warum; **I ~ed to understand how/what ...** ich konnte nicht verstehen, wie/was ...

N a without ~ ganz bestimmt, auf jeden Fall; (= *inevitably*) garantiert, grundsätzlich

b (= *failed candidate, exam*) **there were ten ~s** zehn sind durchgefallen *or* durchgerasselt (*inf*); **she got a ~ in history** in Geschichte ist sie hängen geblieben (*inf*) *or* durchgefallen

failed [feɪld] ADJ *attempt, coup, marriage, bid* gescheitert; *bank, company* bankrott; *exam candidate* durchgefallen; *writer, actor* verhindert

failing [ˈfeɪlɪŋ] N Schwäche *f*, Fehler *m* PREP ~ **an answer** mangels (einer) Antwort (*geh*); **ask John if he knows, ~ him try Harry** fragen Sie John (danach), und wenn er es nicht weiß, versuchen Sie es bei Harry; **~ this/that** (oder) sonst, und wenn das nicht möglich ist; **~ which** ansonsten, widrigenfalls (*form*)

fail-safe [ˈfeɪlseɪf] ADJ (ab)gesichert; *method* hundertprozentig sicher; *mechanism, system* störungssicher

failure [ˈfeɪljə] N **a** (= *lack of success*) Misserfolg *m*; (*of campaign, efforts, negotiations, plan, experiment, marriage*) Fehlschlag *m*, Scheitern *nt*; (*of undertaking, attempt*) Fehlschlag *m*; (*of application*) Ablehnung *f*; (*in exam, Theat: of play*) Misserfolg *m*; (*of business*) Eingehen *nt*; **~ to do sth** vergeblicher Versuch, etw zu tun; **~ rate** (*in exams*) Misserfolgsquote *f*; (*of machine*) Fehlerquote *f*

b (= *unsuccessful person*) Versager(in) *m(f)*, Niete *f* (*inf*) (*at in +dat*); (= *unsuccessful thing*) Misserfolg *m*, Reinfall *m* (*inf*), Pleite *f* (*inf*); **I'm a bit of a ~ at making my own clothes** ich bin eine ziemliche Niete, wenn es darum geht, meine eigenen Kleider zu nähen (*inf*)

c (= *omission, neglect*) **because of his ~ to reply/act** weil er nicht geantwortet/gehandelt hat, weil er es versäumt *or* unterlassen hat zu antworten/zu handeln; **his ~ to notice anything** weil er nichts bemerkt hat; **~ to pay will result in prosecution** bei Nichteinbringungsfall erfolgt Anzeige (*form*); **~ to perform one's duty** Nichterfüllung *f* seiner Pflicht; **~ to appear** Nichterscheinen *nt* (*form*)

d (= *health*) Verschlechterung *f*; (*of hearing, eyesight*) Nachlassen *nt*; (*of invalid*) Nachlassen *nt* der Kräfte

e (= *breakdown, of generator, engine, electricity, pump, engine*) Ausfall *m*; (*of brakes*) Versagen *nt*; (*of supply, wind*) Ausbleiben *nt*; **heart/kidney/liver ~** Herz-/Nieren-/Leberversagen *nt*; **~ of crops** Missernte *f*; (*complete*) Ernteausfall *m*

fain [feɪn] ADV (*obs*) **I would ~** ich möchte ...

faint [feɪnt] ADJ (+*er*) **a** (= *weak, not pronounced*) schwach; *tracks, line, outline* undeutlich; *mark, stain, photocopy* blass; *colour* verblasst; *sound, call, steps, suspicion, hope, smile* leise; *resemblance* entfernt; *chance* gering; **the colours have gone ~** die Farben sind verblichen; **your voice is very ~** (*on telephone*) man hört dich kaum; **I never felt the ~est desire to cry** ich verspürte absolut nicht das Bedürfnis zu weinen; **I have a ~ memory** *or* **recollection of that day** ich kann mich schwach an den Tag erinnern; **she made a ~ attempt at a laugh** sie versuchte zaghaft zu lachen; **I haven't the ~est idea** (*emph*) ich habe nicht die leiseste *or* geringste Ahnung; **the ~ hearts** die Zaghaften *pl*, die Hasenfüße *pl* (*inf*); **~ heart never won fair lady** (*Prov*) → *also* **damn** VT **c**

b *pred* (*Med*) **she was** *or* **felt ~** sie war einer Ohnmacht nahe; **he was concerned that I might become ~** er machte sich Sorgen, dass ich ohnmächtig werden könnte; **he began to feel ~** ihm wurde schwach; **he was ~ with hunger** ihr war ganz schwach vor Hunger

VI (*Med,* = *pass out*) ohnmächtig werden, in Ohnmacht fallen (*with, from* vor +*dat*); **to ~ at the sight of blood** beim Anblick von Blut ohnmächtig werden

N (*Med*) Ohnmacht *f*; **she fell to the ground in a (dead) ~** sie fiel ohnmächtig zu Boden

faint-hearted [feɪntˈhɑːtɪd] ADJ zaghaft; **it's not for the ~** es ist nichts für ängstliche Gemüter *or* für Angsthasen (*inf*)

faint-heartedness [feɪntˈhɑːtɪdnɪs] N Zaghaftigkeit *f*

fainting fit [ˈfeɪntɪŋfɪt] N Ohnmachtsanfall *m*

faintly [ˈfeɪntlɪ] ADV **a** (= *weakly*) *glow, shine, burn* schwach; *smell, smile* leicht; (= *quietly*) *sound, speak, say, sigh* leise; **the words are just ~ visible** die Worte sind gerade noch sichtbar; **I could hear the siren ~** ich konnte die Sirene gerade noch hören **b** (= *slightly*) *absurd, condescending, disappointed, suspicious* leicht; **she felt ~ ridiculous** sie kam sich etwas lächerlich vor; **~ familiar** entfernt vertraut; **I do remember him ~** ich kann mich schwach an ihn erinnern

faintness [ˈfeɪntnɪs] N **a** Schwäche *f*; (*of tracks, line*) Undeutlichkeit *f*; **such was the ~ of the photocopy that ...** die Fotokopie war so blass, dass ...; **such was the ~ of his voice that ...** seine Stimme war so schwach, dass ...; **due to the ~ of the sound** weil der Ton so leise war; **the ~ of his resemblance to his father** seine entfernte Ähnlichkeit mit seinem Vater; **despite the ~ of her hope** obwohl sie nur eine leise Hoffnung hatte; **~ of heart** (*liter*) Verzagtheit *f* **b** (= *dizziness*) flaues Gefühl, Schwächegefühl *nt*

fair¹ [fɛə] ADJ (+*er*) **a** (= *just*) *person, fight, game, player, competition, price* fair (*to* or *on sb* jdm gegenüber, *gegen* jdn); *trial, conclusion* gerecht; **he tried to be ~ to everybody** er versuchte, allen gegenüber gerecht zu sein *or* (*give everybody their due*) allen gerecht zu werden; **that is a (very) ~ point** *or* **comment** das lässt sich (natürlich) nicht abstreiten; **it wouldn't be ~ to disturb the children's education** es wäre unfair, die Ausbildung der Kinder zu unterbrechen; **it is ~ to say that ...** man kann wohl sagen, dass ...; **to be ~, ...** man muss (fairerweise) dazusagen, dass ...; **it's only ~ for her to earn more than us** es ist doch nur gerecht *or* fair, dass sie mehr verdient als wir; **it's only ~ to ask him/to give him a hand** man sollte ihn fairerweise fragen/ihm fairerweise helfen; **it's only ~ to expect ...** man kann doch wohl zu Recht erwarten, ...; **~ enough!** na schön, na gut; **that's ~ enough** das ist nur recht und billig; **as is (only) ~** was nur recht und billig ist; **~'s ~** wir wollen doch fair bleiben; **by ~ means or foul** mit allen Mitteln, egal wie (*inf*)

b (= *quite considerable*) *sum* ziemlich groß; **~ amount of money** ziemlich viel Geld; **to have a ~ degree of competence** ziemlich kompetent sein; **to be a ~ size** ziemlich groß sein; **we were doing a ~ speed** wir fuhren ziemlich schnell; **it's a ~ distance** *or* **way** es ist ziemlich weit; **a ~ number of students** ziemlich viele Studenten; **a ~ chance of success** ziemlich gute Erfolgsaussichten

c (= *reasonable, shrewd*) *guess, assessment, idea* ziemlich gut; **he's a ~ judge of character** er hat eine ziemlich gute Menschenkenntnis; **to have a ~ knowledge of a subject** sich auf einem Gebiet ziemlich gut auskennen; **I had a pretty ~ idea of the answer to the question** ich wusste ziemlich genau, was die Antwort auf diese Frage war; **I've a ~ idea that he's going to resign** ich bin mir ziemlich sicher, dass er zurücktreten wird; **it's a ~ guess that he'll never agree** man kann ziemlich sicher annehmen, dass er nie zustimmen wird; **that's a ~ sample of ...** das ist ziemlich typisch für ...

d (= *average*) mittelmäßig; **how are you? – ~ to middling** (*Brit*) wie geht's dir? – mittelprächtig (*inf*) *or* so einigermaßen

e (= *fair-haired*) *person, hair* blond; (= *fair-skinned*) *person* hellhäutig; *skin* hell

f (*old, poet,* = *lovely*) *person* hold (*dated*); *place* schön; **the ~ sex** (*dated, hum*) das schöne Geschlecht

g (= *fine and dry*) *weather* heiter, schön; **the weather is set ~** das Wetter bleibt weiterhin schön

ADV **a** **to play ~** fair sein; (*Sport*) fair spielen;

to play ~ with or **by sb** sich jdm gegenüber fair verhalten → also **fair play**
b **~ and square** (win, lose) ganz klar; **they beat us ~ and square** sie haben uns deutlich geschlagen
c (dial, = pretty well) ganz schön (inf), vielleicht (inf); **it ~ took my breath away** das hat mir glatt den Atem verschlagen

fair² N (Jahr)markt m; (= funfair) Volksfest nt; (Comm) Messe f

fair: fair copy N Reinschrift f; **to write out a ~ of sth** etw ins Reine schreiben; **fair game** N (lit) jagdbares Wild; (fig) Freiwild nt; **the grouse is ~ between the months of ...** bejagt (spec) or gejagt werden; **fairground** N (for funfair) Festplatz m; **~ showman** Schausteller(in) m(f); **fair-haired** ADJ comp fairer-haired blond; **fair-haired boy** N (dated US) Lieblingskind nt, Liebling m

fairing ['fɛərɪŋ] N (Aviat, Aut) Stromlinienverkleidung f

fairly ['fɛəlɪ] ADV **a** (= moderately) ziemlich; **~ recently** erst kürzlich **b** (= justly) treat gerecht, fair; (= justifiably) claim zu Recht; describe, blame gerechterweise; (= equally) share gerecht **c** (= positively, really) geradezu; **we ~ flew along** wir sausten nur so dahin

fair-minded ['fɛəmaɪndɪd] ADJ gerecht

fairness ['fɛənɪs] N **a** (= justice) Gerechtigkeit f, Fairness f; **in all ~** gerechterweise, fairerweise; **in (all) ~ to him we should wait** wir sollten so fair sein und noch warten **b** (= lightness, of hair) Blondheit f; **the ~ of her skin** ihre Hellhäutigkeit

fair: fair play N (Sport, fig) faires Verhalten, Fairplay nt, Fair Play nt; **that's not ~** (fig) das ist nicht fair or gerecht; **fair-sized** ADJ recht groß; **fair-spoken** ADJ (geh) freundlich, höflich; **fair trade** N fairer Handel (mit Entwicklungsländern); (US) Preisbindung f; **fairway** N **a** (Naut) Fahrwasser nt or -rinne f **b** (Golf) Fairway nt; **fair-weather** ADJ a **~ friend** ein Freund, der nur in guten Zeiten ein Freund ist

fairy ['fɛərɪ] N **a** Fee f; good ~ gute Fee; **he's away with the fairies** (inf) der hat einen Schaden (inf) **b** (pej inf, = homosexual) Homo m (dated inf), Schwule(r) m (inf)

fairy: fairy cycle N Kinderfahrrad nt; **fairy footsteps** PL (iro inf) Stapfen nt; **fairy godmother** N (lit, fig) gute Fee; **fairyland** Märchenland nt; **fairy lights** PL bunte Lichter pl; **fairy-like** ADJ feenhaft; **fairy queen** N Elfenkönigin f; **fairy ring** N Hexentanzplatz m; (of mushrooms) Hexenring m; **fairy story**, **fairy tale** N (lit, fig) Märchen nt; **fairy-tale** ADJ (fig) romance, ending märchenhaft

fait accompli [ˌfeɪtə'kɒmpliː] N vollendete Tatsache, Fait accompli nt (geh); **to present sb with a ~** jdn vor vollendete Tatsachen stellen

faith [feɪθ] N **a** (= trust) Vertrauen nt (in zu); (in human nature, medicine, science etc, religious faith) Glaube m (in an +acc); **~ in God** Gottvertrauen nt; **to have ~ in sb** jdm (ver)trauen; **to have ~ in sth** Vertrauen in etw (acc) haben; **act of ~** Vertrauensbeweis m; **it was more an act of ~ than a rational decision** das war mehr auf gut Glück gemacht als eine rationale Entscheidung

b (= religion) Glaube m no pl, Bekenntnis nt **c** (= promise) **to keep/break ~ with sb** jdm treu bleiben/untreu werden, jdm die Treue halten/ brechen (geh) **d** (= sincerity, loyalty) Treue f; **to act in good/ bad ~** in gutem Glauben/böser Absicht handeln

faith cure N Heilung f durch Gesundbeten

faithful ['feɪθful] ADJ **a** (= loyal) person, animal, car, service treu; **to be/remain ~ to sb/sth** jdm/ einer Sache treu sein/bleiben; **to be ~ to one's promise** sein Versprechen treu halten; **to be ~ to sb's wishes** jds Wünsche treu erfüllen; **she is ~ to her own culture and religion** sie bleibt ihrer eigenen Kultur und Religion treu; **they are ~ to each other** sie sind einander treu
b (= accurate) adaptation, reproduction, copy originalgetreu; translation genau; **the translation is ~ to the original/the spirit of the original** die Übersetzung hält sich genau an das Original/ an den Geist des Originals
N **a** (= stalwart) treuer Anhänger, treue Anhängerin; **the party ~(s)** die treuen Anhänger der Partei
b **the ~** pl (Rel) die Gläubigen pl

faithfully ['feɪθfəlɪ] ADV **a** (= loyally) treu; (= conscientiously) gewissenhaft; (= steadfastly) standhaft; **to promise ~** ganz fest versprechen; **Yours ~** (Brit: on letter) hochachtungsvoll **b** (= accurately) restore originalgetreu; report, reflect, translate, reproduce genau

faithfulness ['feɪθfəlnɪs] N **a** (= loyalty) Treue f (to zu) **b** (= accuracy, of translation) Genauigkeit f; (of reproduction) Originaltreue f

faith: faith healer N Gesundbeter(in) m(f); **faith healing** N Gesundbeten nt; **faithless** ADJ treulos; **faithlessness** N Treulosigkeit f

fake [feɪk] ADJ unecht; certificate, banknote, painting gefälscht; **~ fur** Pelzimitation f; **a ~ suntan** Bräune f aus der Flasche **N** (= object) Fälschung f; (jewellery) Imitation f; (= person, trickster) Schwindler(in) m(f); (feigning illness) Simulant(in) m(f); **the passport/painting was a ~** der Pass/das Gemälde war gefälscht **VT** vortäuschen; picture, document, results, evidence etc fälschen; bill, burglary, crash fingieren; jewellery imitieren, nachmachen; elections manipulieren; **to ~ an illness** (eine Krankheit) simulieren or vortäuschen

▶**fake up** VT sep story erfinden; picture, passport fälschen

fakir ['fɑːkɪə'] N Fakir m

falcon ['fɔːlkən] N Falke m

falconer ['fɔːlkənə'] N Falkner(in) m(f)

falconry ['fɔːlkənrɪ] N Falknerei f; (= sport) Falkenjagd or -beize f

Falkland Islands ['fɔːklənd,aɪləndz], **Falklands** ['fɔːkləndz] PL Falklandinseln pl

fall [fɔːl] vb: pret **fell**, ptp **fallen** **N** **a** (lit, fig: = tumble) Fall m no pl, Sturz m; (= decline: of empire etc) Untergang m; **the Fall (of Man)** (Eccl) der Sündenfall; **to break sb's ~** jds Fall auffangen; **to have a ~** (hin)fallen, stürzen; **he had several ~s** er ist mehrmals hingefallen or gestürzt; **she had a bad ~** sie ist schwer gestürzt; **to head** or **ride for a ~** in sein Verderben rennen
b (= defeat, of town, fortress etc) Einnahme f, Eroberung f; (of Troy) Fall m; (of country) Zusammenbruch m; (of government) Sturz m
c **~ of rain/snow** Regen-/Schneefall m; **~ of rock** Steinschlag m; **there was another heavy ~ (of snow) last night** es hat heute Nacht wieder viel geschneit
d (of night) Einbruch m
e (= lowering) Sinken nt; (in temperature) Abfall m, Sinken nt; (sudden) Sturz m; (of barometer) Fallen nt; (sudden) Sturz m; (in wind) Nachlassen nt; (in revs, population, membership) Abnahme f; (in graph) Abfall m; (in morals) Verfall m; (of prices, currency, gradual) Sinken nt; (sudden) Sturz m; **~ in demand** (Comm) Nachfragerückgang m
f (= slope: of roof, ground) Gefälle nt; (steeper) Abfall m

g (= waterfall: also **falls**) Wasserfall m; **the Niagara Falls** der Niagarafall
h (Wrestling) Schultersieg m
i (= hang, of curtains etc) Fall m
j (US, = autumn) Herbst m; **in the ~** im Herbst
VI **a** (lit, fig: = tumble) fallen; (Sport, from a height, badly) stürzen; (object, to the ground) herunterfallen; **to ~ to one's death** tödlich abstürzen; **to ~ into a trap** in die Falle gehen
b (= hang down: hair, clothes etc) fallen; **her hair kept ~ing into her eyes** ihr fielen dauernd die Haare in die Augen
c (snow, rain) fallen
d (= drop, temperature, price) fallen, sinken; (population, membership etc) abnehmen; (voice) sich senken; (wind) sich legen, nachlassen; (land) abfallen; (graph, curve, rate) abnehmen; (steeply) abfallen; **her eyes fell** sie schlug die Augen nieder (geh); **his face fell** er machte ein langes Gesicht; **to ~ in sb's estimation** or **eyes** in jds Achtung (dat) sinken
e (= be defeated, country) eingenommen werden; (city, fortress) fallen, erobert or eingenommen werden; (government, ruler) gestürzt werden; **to ~ to the enemy** vom Feind eingenommen werden; (fortress, town also) vom Feind erobert werden
f (= be killed) fallen; **to ~ in battle** fallen
g (night) hereinbrechen; (silence) eintreten
h (Bibl) den Sündenfall tun; (old, girl) die Unschuld or Ehre verlieren (dated); **when Adam fell** nach Adams Sündenfall
i (= occur, birthday, Easter etc) fallen (on auf +acc); (accent) liegen (on auf +dat); (= be classified) gehören (under in +acc), fallen (under unter +acc); **it ~s under another category** das gehört in or fällt in eine andere Kategorie; **that ~s within/outside the scope of ...** das fällt in/ nicht in den Bereich +gen ..., das liegt innerhalb/außerhalb des Bereichs +gen ...
j (= be naturally divisible) zerfallen, sich gliedern (into in +acc); **to ~ into three sections** sich in drei Teile gliedern; **to ~ into categories** sich in Kategorien gliedern lassen
k (fig) **her eyes fell on a strange object** ihr Blick fiel auf einen merkwürdigen Gegenstand; **where do you think the responsibility/blame for that will ~?** wem wird Ihrer Meinung nach die Verantwortung dafür/die Schuld daran gegeben?
l (= become) werden; **to ~ asleep** einschlafen; **to ~ ill** krank werden, erkranken (geh); **to ~ in love with sb** sich in jdn verlieben; **to ~ out of love with sb** aufhören, jdn zu lieben; **she's forever ~ing in and out of love** sie verliebt sich dauernd neu
m (= pass into a certain state) **to ~ into decline** (building) verkommen; (economy) schlechter werden; **to ~ into ruin** (zur Ruine) verfallen; **to ~ into decay** verfallen; **to ~ into a deep sleep** in tiefen Schlaf fallen or sinken; **to ~ into temptation** in Versuchung geraten; **to ~ into conversation (with sb)** (mit jdm) ins Gespräch kommen; **to ~ into a state of unconsciousness** das Bewusstsein verlieren, in Ohnmacht fallen; **to ~ into a coma** in ein Koma fallen; **to ~ into disarray** in Unordnung geraten; **to ~ into bad habits** in schlechte Gewohnheiten verfallen; **to ~ apart** or **to pieces** (chairs, cars, book etc) aus dem Leim gehen (inf); (clothes, curtains) sich in Wohlgefallen auflösen (inf); (house) verfallen; (system, company, sb's life) aus den Fugen geraten or gehen; **I fell apart when he left me** meine Welt brach zusammen, als er mich verließ
n **to ~ to doing sth** (= start) anfangen, etw zu tun
o (in set constructions see also n, adj etc) **to ~ into the hands of sb** jdm in die Hände fallen; **to ~ among thieves** unter die Räuber fallen or geraten

▶**fall about** (also **fall about laughing**) VI (Brit inf) sich kranklachen (inf)

▶**fall away** VI **a** (ground) abfallen **b** (= come away, crumble: plaster, bricks, river bank) abbröckeln (from von) **c** = **fall off** **d** (anxiety, fears) weichen (geh) (from von) **e** (from party, church) abfallen

▶ **fall back** VI zurückweichen (*also Mil*)

▶ **fall back (up)on** VI +*prep obj* zurückgreifen auf (+*acc*)

▶ **fall behind** VI **a** (*in race, at school etc*) zurückbleiben (*prep obj* hinter +*dat*), zurückfallen (*prep obj* hinter +*acc*) **b** (*with rent, work etc*) in Rückstand *or* Verzug geraten

▶ **fall down** VI **a** (*person*) hinfallen; (*statue, vase*) herunterfallen; (= *collapse*: *house, scaffolding etc*) einstürzen **b** (*down stairs, cliff face*) hinunterfallen (*prep obj* +*acc*); **he fell right down to the bottom** er ist bis ganz nach unten gefallen **c** (*fig, = be inadequate: person, theory, plan*) versagen; **where he/the plan falls down is ...** woran es ihm/dem Plan fehlt, ist ..., woran es bei ihm/dem Plan hapert, ist ... (*inf*); **that was where we fell down** daran sind wir gescheitert

▶ **fall for** VI +*prep obj* **a** **I really fell for him/it** er/es hatte es mir angetan **b** (= *be taken in by*) *sales talk, propaganda* hereinfallen auf (+*acc*)

▶ **fall in** VI **a** (*into water etc*) hineinfallen **b** (= *collapse*) einstürzen **c** (*Mil, troops*) (in Reih und Glied) antreten; (*one soldier*) ins Glied treten; **fall in!** antreten!; **to fall in beside** *or* **alongside sb** sich jdm anschließen **d** (= *make friends*) **it didn't take long for us to fall in again** es dauerte nicht lange, bis wir uns wieder versöhnten

▶ **fall in with** VI +*prep obj* **a** (= *meet, join up with*) sich anschließen (+*dat*); *bad company* geraten in (+*acc*) **b** (= *agree to*) mitmachen bei; *request* unterstützen **c** (= *make friends with*) **I didn't fall back in with her for a year** ich habe mich ein Jahr lang nicht mit ihr versöhnt

▶ **fall off** VI **a** (*lit, person, object etc*) herunterfallen (*prep obj* von) **b** (= *decrease*) zurückgehen, abnehmen; (*supporters*) abfallen; (*speed*) sich verringern, abnehmen; (*support, enthusiasm*) nachlassen

▶ **fall on** VI +*prep obj* **a** (= *trip on*) *stone* fallen über (+*acc*) **b** (= *be the responsibility of, be borne by, duty, decision, task*) zufallen (+*dat*); (*blame*) treffen (+*acc*); **the responsibility falls on your shoulders** Sie tragen *or* haben die Verantwortung **c** (= *attack*) herfallen über (+*acc*) **d** (= *find*) stoßen auf (+*acc*)

▶ **fall out** VI **a** (*of bed, boat, window*) herausfallen; **to fall out of sth** aus etw fallen **b** (= *quarrel*) sich (zer)streiten; **the two countries fell out over the question of borders** zwischen den beiden Ländern kam es wegen Grenzstreitigkeiten zum Bruch **c** (*Mil*) wegtreten **d** (= *happen*) sich ergeben; **just wait and see how things fall out** wart erst mal ab, wie alles wird

▶ **fall over** VI (*person*) hinfallen; (= *collapse*) umfallen; (*statue, vase*) umfallen, umkippen VI +*prep obj* **a** (= *trip over*) *sth's legs* fallen über (+*acc*); **they were falling over each other to get the book** sie drängelten sich, um das Buch zu bekommen **b** **to fall over oneself to do sth** (*fast*) umbringen (*inf*) *or* sich (*dat*) die größte Mühe geben, etw zu tun; **to fall over backwards to do sth** sich (*förmlich*) überschlagen, etw zu tun (*inf*)

▶ **fall through** VI (*plan*) ins Wasser fallen, fehlschlagen

▶ **fall to** VI **a** (*inf, = start eating*) sich dranmachen (*inf*), reinhauen (*inf*); (= *start fighting, working*) loslegen (*inf*) **b** (= *be the responsibility of*) zufallen (+*dat*), obliegen (+*dat*) (*geh*)

▶ **fall upon** VI +*prep obj* = **fall on b-d**

fallacious [fə'leɪʃəs] ADJ irrig; *argument* trugschlüssig

fallacy ['fæləsɪ] N Irrtum *m*; (*in logic*) Fehlschluss *m*, Trugschluss *m*; **a popular ~** ein weit verbreiteter Irrtum

fall-back position ['fɔːlbækpəˌzɪʃən] N Rückfallposition *f*

fallen ['fɔːlən] *ptp* of **fall** ADJ *women, soldier, angel* gefallen; *leaf* abgefallen; *tree* umgestürzt; **~ idol** gefallener Götze *m*; **~ arches** *pl* (*Med*) Senkfüße *pl* PL **the Fallen** (*Mil*) die Gefallenen *pl*

fall guy N (*esp US inf*: = *victim*) armes Opfer, Angeschmierte(r) *mf* (*inf*); (= *scapegoat*) Sündenbock *m*

fallibility [ˌfælɪ'bɪlɪtɪ] N Fehlbarkeit *f*

fallible ['fæləbl] ADJ fehlbar, nicht unfehlbar

falling ['fɔːlɪŋ] ADJ (= *dwindling*) *prices, profits, rate, temperature, standards* sinkend, fallend; *population, membership* abnehmend

falling: falling-off N = **fall-off**; **falling-out** N (= *quarrel*) Streit *m*; **falling sickness** N (*old*) Fallsucht *f* (*old*); **falling star** N Sternschnuppe *f*

fall: fall line N (*Sci*) Fall-Linie *f*; **fall-off** N Rückgang *m*, Abnahme *f*; (*in numbers, attendances*) Abfall *m*; (*in speed*) Verringerung *f*; (*in enthusiasm, support*) Nachlassen *nt*

Fallopian tube [fə'ləʊpɪən'tjuːb] N Eileiter *m*

fallout ['fɔːlaʊt] N radioaktiver Niederschlag, Fallout *m*, Fall-out *m* (*spec*); (*fig*) Auswirkungen *pl* (*from* +*gen*); **~ shelter** Atomschutzbunker *m*

fallow[1] ['fæləʊ] ADJ **a** (*Agr*, = *unused*) brachliegend; **most of the fields are (lying) ~** die meisten Felder liegen brach; **to leave land ~, to let land lie ~** Land brachliegen lassen **b** (*fig*, = *inactive*) *period* unproduktiv

fallow[2] ADJ falb, gelbbraun

fallow deer N Damwild *nt*

false [fɔːls] ADJ (+*er*) **a** (= *wrong*) falsch; **to put a ~ interpretation on sth** etw falsch auslegen *or* deuten; **to prove ~** sich als falsch erweisen; **~ sense of security** ein falsches Gefühl der Sicherheit; **~ accounting** (*Jur*) Bücherfälschung *f*; **that's a ~ economy** das ist am falschen Ort gespart; **~ imprisonment/arrest** willkürliche Inhaftierung/Festnahme; **~ judgement** Fehlurteil *nt*; **~ statement** Falschaussage *f*; **under** *or* **by ~ pretences** (*Brit*) *or* **pretenses** (*US*) unter Vorspiegelung falscher Tatsachen; **~ god/prophet** falscher Gott/Prophet; **to bear ~ witness** (*old*) falsches Zeugnis ablegen (*Bibl, old*), eine falsche Aussage machen **b** (= *artificial, fake*) *nose, beard* falsch; *blood, eyelashes* künstlich; *papers* gefälscht; **~ bottom** (*of suitcase*) doppelter Boden *f*; **~ ceiling** Zwischendecke *f* **c** (*pej*, = *insincere*) *laughter, enthusiasm* gekünstelt; **~ modesty** falsche Bescheidenheit; **to ring ~** nicht echt klingen **d** (= *disloyal*) *friend, lover, wife, husband, servant* treulos; **to be ~ to sb** jdm untreu sein; (= *deceive*) jdn hintergehen ADV **to play sb ~** mit jdm ein falsches Spiel treiben

false: false alarm N falscher *or* blinder Alarm; **false beginner** N Lernende(r) mit Vorkenntnissen, der/die noch einmal von vorne anfängt; **false ceiling** N (*Archit*) Zwischen- *or* Unterdecke *f*; **false dawn** N **a** (*Astron*) Zodiakal- *or* Tierkreislicht *nt* **b** (*fig*) **the boom was a ~** der Aufschwung erweckte falsche Hoffnungen; **false friend** N (*Ling*) falscher Freund; **false front** N **a** (*Archit, also fig*) falsche Fassade **b** (*fig*) bloße Fassade, Mache *f* (*inf, pej*); **false-hearted** ADJ falsch, treulos

falsehood ['fɔːlshʊd] N **a** (= *lie*) Unwahrheit *f* **b** *no pl* (*of statement etc*) Unwahrheit *f*

false key N Dietrich *m*, Nachschlüssel *m*

falsely ['fɔːlslɪ] ADV **a** (= *wrongly*) *interpret, understand* falsch; *accused, convicted, imprisoned* zu Unrecht **b** (= *untruthfully, mistakenly*) *claim, report, think* fälschlicherweise **c** (+*adj*: = *artificially*) künstlich

false: False Memory Syndrome N (*Psych*) False-Memory-Syndrom *nt*; **false move** N falsche Bewegung; (*fig, = mistake*) Fehler *m*; **one ~ and you're dead** eine falsche Bewegung und du bist tot; **one ~, and ...** (*fig*) ein kleiner Fehler und ...; **false negative** N (*Med*) **~ (result)** falsch negative Diagnose

falseness ['fɔːlsnɪs] N **a** (*of statement etc*) Unrichtigkeit *f*, Falschheit *f*; (*of promise*) Unaufrichtigkeit *f*, Falschheit *f* **b** (= *artificiality*: of

pearls, eyelashes etc) Unechtheit *f* **c** (= *unfaithfulness*: of lover etc) Untreue *f*, Treulosigkeit *f*

false: false positive N (*Med*) **~ (result)** falsch positive Diagnose; **false pregnancy** N (*Med*) Scheinschwangerschaft *f*; **false rib** N falsche Rippe; **false start** N Fehlstart *m*; **false teeth** PL (künstliches) Gebiss, falsche Zähne *pl*

falsetto [fɔːl'setəʊ] N (= *voice*) Fistelstimme *f*; (*Mus*) Falsett *nt*; (= *person*) Falsettist *m* ADJ **voice** Fistelstimme *f*; (*Mus*) Falsettstimme *f* ADV **sing** im Falsett; **speak** mit einer Fistelstimme

falsies ['fɔːlsɪz] PL (*inf*) Gummibusen *m* (*inf*)

falsifiable ['fɔːlsɪfaɪəbl] ADJ (= *disprovable*) widerlegbar, falsifizierbar (*spec*)

falsification [ˌfɔːlsɪfɪ'keɪʃən] N **a** (Ver)fälschung *f* **b** (= *disproving*) Widerlegung *f*, Falsifikation *f* (*spec*)

falsify ['fɔːlsɪfaɪ] VT **a** *records, evidence, history* fälschen; *report* entstellen; *results, tests* verfälschen **b** (= *disprove*) widerlegen, falsifizieren (*spec*)

falsity ['fɔːlsɪtɪ] N (= *incorrectness*) Unrichtigkeit *f*; (= *artificiality*: of smile) Falschheit *f*; (= *unfaithfulness*) Treulosigkeit *f*

falter ['fɔːltə'] VI (*speaker*) stocken; (*steps, horse*) zögern

faltering ['fɔːltərɪŋ] ADJ *voice* stockend, stammelnd; (= *hesitating, wavering*) zögernd; (= *unsteady*) *steps* tastend; *economy* geschwächt; *campaign* halbherzig; *recovery* zögernd

falteringly ['fɔːltərɪŋlɪ] ADV *say* stockend, stammelnd; (= *hesitantly*) zögernd; (= *unsteadily*) *move, walk* taumelnd

fame [feɪm] N Ruhm *m*; **~ and fortune** Ruhm und Reichtum; **of ill ~** von üblem Ruf, berüchtigt; **to come to ~** Ruhm erlangen, zu Ruhm kommen; **to win ~ for sth** sich (*dat*) durch etw einen Namen machen; **is that the Joseph Heller of "Catch-22" ~?** ist das der berühmte Joseph Heller, der „Catch-22" geschrieben hat?; **Borg of Wimbledon 1979 ~** Borg, der sich 1979 in Wimbledon einen Namen gemacht hat

famed [feɪmd] ADJ berühmt

familial [fə'mɪlɪəl] ADJ familiär

familiar [fə'mɪlɪə'] ADJ **a** (= *usual, well-known*) *surroundings, sight, scene* gewohnt, vertraut; *figure, voice* vertraut; *street, person, feeling* bekannt; *phrase, title, song* geläufig, bekannt; *complaint, event, protest* häufig; (= *customary*) *form, course, pattern* üblich; **his face is ~** das Gesicht ist mir bekannt; **surrounded by ~ faces** von vertrauten Gesichtern umgeben; **the problems are all too ~** die Probleme sind nur allzu vertraut; **to be/seem ~ to sb** jdm bekannt sein/vorkommen; **it looks very ~** es kommt mir sehr bekannt vor; **to sound ~** sich bekannt anhören (*to sb* jdm); **that sounds ~** das habe ich doch schon mal gehört; **to be on ~ ground** Bescheid wissen; **to follow a ~ pattern** (*visit*) wie gewohnt verlaufen; (*negotiations*) den gewohnten Verlauf nehmen; (*interview*) wie üblich ablaufen **b** (= *conversant*) **I am ~ with the word/the town** das Wort/die Stadt ist mir bekannt *or* (*more closely*) vertraut; **I'm not ~ with computer language** ich bin mit der Computersprache nicht vertraut; **are you ~ with these modern techniques?** wissen Sie über diese modernen Techniken Bescheid?; **is he ~ with our customs?** ist er mit unseren Bräuchen vertraut?; **to make sb ~ with sth** jdn mit etw vertraut machen **c** (= *friendly*) *tone* familiär; *greeting* freundschaftlich; *gesture* familiär, vertraulich; (= *overfriendly*) familiär, plumpvertraulich; **the ~ form of address** die Anrede für Familie und Freunde, die vertraute Anrede; **to be on ~ terms with sb** mit jdm auf vertrautem Fuß stehen; **we're all on pretty ~ terms** wir haben ein ziemlich ungezwungenes Verhältnis zueinander; **~ language** Umgangssprache *f*; **~ expressions** umgangssprachliche Ausdrücke *pl*; **they're not the kind of people one wishes to become too ~ with** mit solchen Leuten möchte man sich nicht unbedingt näher einlassen

N **a** (liter, = friend) Vertraute(r) mf (liter) **b** (of witch etc) Hausgeist m

familiarity [fə‚mɪlɪˈærɪtɪ] **N** **a** no pl Vertrautheit f **b** (between people) vertrautes Verhältnis; (between colleagues etc) ungezwungenes or familiäres Verhältnis; (of tone etc) Familiarität f; (of greeting) Freundschaftlichkeit f; (of gesture) Vertraulichkeit f, Familiarität f; (pej: = overfriendliness) plumpe Vertraulichkeit, Familiarität f; **the ~ with which she greeted the head waiter** der vertraute Ton, in dem sie den Oberkellner begrüßte; **~ breeds contempt** (Prov) allzu große Vertrautheit erzeugt Verachtung **c** usu pl (= overfriendly action) plumpe Vertraulichkeit

familiarization [fə‚mɪlɪəraɪˈzeɪʃən] **N** (**process of**) ~ Gewöhnungsprozess m; **he is responsible for the ~ of all new employees with the procedures** er ist dafür verantwortlich, dass alle neuen Angestellten mit der Verfahrensweise vertraut gemacht werden

familiarize [fəˈmɪlɪəraɪz] **VT** **to ~ sb/oneself with sth** jdn/sich mit etw vertraut machen; **once you've ~d yourself with the job** wenn Sie sich eingearbeitet haben

familiarly [fəˈmɪljəlɪ] **ADV** **a** (= informally) familiär; (= in a friendly way) vertraulich; **he slapped me rather too ~ on the back** er klopfte mir plumpvertraulich auf den Rücken; **~ known as** or **called X** von Freunden und Verwandten X genannt **b** (+adj) gewohnt; **the ~ drab streets** die gewohnt tristen Straßen

family [ˈfæmɪlɪ] **N** **a** Familie f; (including cousins, aunts etc) Verwandtschaft f; (= lineage) Familie f, Haus nt, Geschlecht nt (geh); **to start a ~** eine Familie gründen; **they plan to add to their ~** sie planen Familienzuwachs; **has he any ~?** hat er Familie?; **it runs in the ~** das liegt in der Familie; **of good ~** aus guter Familie, aus gutem Hause; **he's one of the ~** er gehört zur Familie; **with just the immediate ~** im engsten Familienkreis; **a ~ of four** eine vierköpfige Familie **b** (of plants, animals, languages etc) Familie f; **the ~ of man** die Menschheit

ATTR Familien-; **~ business** Familienunternehmen nt; **a ~ friend** ein Freund/eine Freundin des Hauses or der Familie; **the ~ house** das Haus der Familie; **a ~ house** ein Einfamilienhaus nt; **the ~ silver** das Tafelsilber; **she's in the ~ way** (inf) sie ist in anderen Umständen; **~ conference** Familienrat m; **~ resemblance** Familienähnlichkeit f; **~ values** Familienwerte pl, familiäre Werte pl

family: family allowance N (dated) ≈ Kindergeld nt; **family butcher** N D. Crosby, Family Butcher D. Crosby, Fleischermeister; **our/the ~** unsere/die Stammfleischerei; **family circle** N **a** (= family members) Familienkreis m **b** (US, Theat) zweiter Rang; **family credit** N (Brit) Sozialleistung für Geringverdiener, um das Familieneinkommen auf einen Mindestbetrag anzuheben; **Family Division** N (Brit, Jur) für Familienrecht zuständige Abteilung des obersten Gerichts, ≈ Familiengericht nt; **family doctor** N Hausarzt m/-ärztin f; **family Health Services Authority** N (Brit) regionale Gesundheitsbehörde, ≈ Gesundheitsamt nt; **family hotel** N Familienpension f; **Family Income Supplement** N (dated) Beihilfe f (zum Lebensunterhalt) (für Familien); **family man** N (home-loving) häuslich veranlagter Mann; (with a family) Familienvater m; **family name** N Familienname m, Nachname m; **family planning** N Familienplanung f; **family planning clinic** N Familienberatungsstelle f; **family reunion** N Familientreffen nt; **family room** N (esp US: in house) Wohnzimmer nt **b** (Brit) (in pub) für Kinder zugelassener Raum in einem Lokal (in hotel) Familienzimmer nt; **family-size** ADJ in Haushaltsgröße; car, packet Familien-; house Einfamilien-; **family tree** N Stammbaum m

famine [ˈfæmɪn] **N** (lit) Hungersnot f; (fig) Knappheit f; **to die of ~** verhungern

famine relief N Hungerhilfe f

famish [ˈfæmɪʃ] **VI** (inf) verhungern

famished [ˈfæmɪʃt] **ADJ** (inf) verhungert, ausgehungert; **I'm absolutely ~** ich sterbe vor Hunger (inf)

famous [ˈfeɪməs] **ADJ** **a** berühmt (for durch, für); **so when's this ~ party going to be?** (iro) und wann soll diese tolle Party stattfinden? (inf); **~ last words!** (inf) man soll es nicht beschreien **b** (dated: = excellent) famos (dated)

famously [ˈfeɪməslɪ] **ADV** **a** (= notoriously) bekanntermaßen; **as X ~ declared** in den berühmten Worten von X; **the man who ~ said "no"** der Mann mit dem berühmten „nein"; **she was married eight times, most ~ to Paul Hassett** sie war achtmal verheiratet, wobei Paul Hassett der bekannteste ihrer Ehemänner war **b** (dated inf: = excellently) glänzend; **to get on** or **along ~ (with sb)** sich (mit jdm) glänzend verstehen; **they get on ~** sie kommen glänzend miteinander aus; **to do ~** sehr erfolgreich sein; **to go ~** bestens laufen

famulus [ˈfæmjʊləs] **N** Famulus m

fan¹ [fæn] **N** **a** (hand-held) Fächer m; (mechanical: = extractor fan, Aut: to cool engine) Ventilator m; (on scooter) Lüfterrad nt; (Aut: = booster) Gebläse nt; **then the shit will really hit the ~** (sl) dann ist die Kacke echt am Dampfen (sl) **b** (of peacock, fig) Fächer m; **to spread sth out in a ~** etw fächerförmig ausbreiten

VT **a** (wind) umwehen; (person) fächeln (+dat); **to ~ sb/oneself** jdm/sich (Luft) zufächeln; **to ~ the embers** die Glut anfachen; **to ~ the flames** (lit) das Feuer anfachen; (fig) Öl ins Feuer gießen; **to ~ the flames of resentment/violence** den Groll/die Gewalt schüren **b** cards fächerförmig ausbreiten; **the peacock ~ned its tail** der Pfau schlug ein Rad

▶ **fan out** **VI** (searchers etc) ausschwärmen **VT** sep feathers fächerförmig aufstellen; cards fächerförmig ausbreiten

fan² N (= supporter) Fan m, Anhänger(in) m(f); **I'm quite a ~ of yours** ich bin ein richtiger Verehrer von Ihnen

fan-assisted [ˈfænəˌsɪstɪd] **ADJ** **~ oven** Umluftherd m

fanatic [fəˈnætɪk] **N** Fanatiker(in) m(f) **ADJ** = **fanatical**

fanatical [fəˈnætɪkəl] **ADJ** fanatisch; **he is ~ about it/them** es geht/sie gehen ihm über alles; **I'm ~ about fitness** ich bin ein Fitnessfanatiker; **there was a ~ gleam in her eye** ihre Augen glänzten fanatisch

fanatically [fəˈnætɪkəlɪ] **ADV** (+adj) loyal, hostile auf fanatische Weise; (+vb) train, cheer fanatisch; **to be ~ against sth** or **opposed to sth** ein fanatischer Gegner von etw sein

fanaticism [fəˈnætɪsɪzəm] **N** Fanatismus m

fan belt N Keilriemen m

fanciable [ˈfænsɪəbl] **ADJ** (Brit, = attractive) attraktiv, anziehend

fancied [ˈfænsɪd] **ADJ** (= imaginary) eingebildet

fancier [ˈfænsɪə] **N** Liebhaber(in) m(f)

fanciful [ˈfænsɪfəl] **ADJ** story, idea fantastisch, phantastisch, abstrus; (= fancy) costume reich verziert; pattern, animal etc fantasievoll, phantasievoll; (= unrealistic) plan etc unrealistisch; visions überspannt; **I think you're being somewhat ~** ich glaube, das ist etwas weit hergeholt; **and I don't think it's ~ to claim that ...** und ich glaube nicht, dass es verstiegen ist zu behaupten, dass ...

fancifulness [ˈfænsɪfʊlnɪs] **N** (of story etc) Seltsamkeit f; (of person) blühende Fantasie or Phantasie f; (of costume) reiche Verzierung; (of pattern) Fantasiereichtum m, Phantasiereichtum m

fan club N Fanklub m

fancy [ˈfænsɪ] **VT** **a** (= like, be attracted by) **I ~ that car/the idea** (= like) das Auto/die Idee gefällt mir or hat es mir angetan; **he fancies a house on Crete** (= would like to have) er hätte gern ein Haus auf Kreta; **I don't ~ a house in Glasgow** ich möchte kein Haus in Glasgow haben; **I didn't ~ that job/that party** die Stelle/die Party hat mich nicht gereizt; **do you ~ a walk/steak/beer?** hast du Lust zu einem Spaziergang/auf ein Steak/auf ein Bier?; **she fancies (the idea of) doing that** (= would like to) sie würde or möchte das gern tun; (= feels like it) sie hätte Lust, das zu tun; **count me out, I don't ~ the idea** ohne mich, das ist nichts für mich; **I don't ~ the idea, but I'll have to do it** ich habe gar keine Lust dazu, aber ich muss es ja wohl tun; **I don't ~ THAT (idea)!** nur das nicht; **he fancies her as a wife** er hätte sie gern zur Frau; **he really fancies her** sie hat es ihm angetan; (sexually) er ist scharf auf sie (inf); **I don't ~ him** (sexually) ich finde ihn nicht attraktiv; **he fancies his chances** er meint, er hätte Chancen; **I don't ~ my chances of getting that job** ich rechne mir keine großen Chancen aus, die Stelle zu bekommen; **a bit of what you ~ does you good** man muss sich auch mal was Gutes gönnen

b (= imagine) meinen, sich (dat) einbilden; (= think) glauben; **he fancied he heard footsteps** er meinte, Schritte zu hören; **I rather ~ he has gone out** ich glaube, er ist weggegangen; **how long? – not long, I ~** wie lange? – nicht lange, denke or glaube ich

c (in exclamations) **~ doing that!** so was(, das) zu tun!; **~ him doing that!** nicht zu fassen, dass er das getan hat or tut!; **~ that!** (inf) (just) ~! (inf) (nein) so was!, denk mal an! (inf); **just ~, he ...** (inf) stell dir vor, er ...; **~ seeing you here!** so was, Sie hier zu sehen!; **~ him winning!** wer hätte gedacht, dass er gewinnt!

VR von sich eingenommen sein, sich für Wunder was halten (inf); **he fancies himself as an actor/expert** er hält sich für einen (guten) Schauspieler/einen Experten; **do you ~ yourself as a teacher?** kannst du dir dich als Lehrer vorstellen?; **they ~ themselves to be Europeans** sie halten sich für Europäer

N **a** (= liking) **to have a ~ for sth** Lust zu etw haben; (for food or drink) Lust auf etw (acc) haben; **she had a ~ for sports cars** sie hatte eine Vorliebe für Sportwagen; **a passing ~** nur so eine Laune; **he's taken a ~ to her/this car/the idea** sie/das Auto/die Idee hat es ihm angetan; **they took a ~ to each other** sie fanden sich sympathisch; **to take** or **catch sb's ~** jdn ansprechen, jdm gefallen; **they took a ~ to go swimming** sie bekamen Lust, schwimmen zu gehen; **to tickle sb's ~** jdn reizen; **just as the ~ takes me/you** etc ganz nach Lust und Laune; **he only works when the ~ takes him** er arbeitet nur, wenn ihm gerade danach ist

b no pl (= imagination) Fantasie f, Phantasie f; **to separate fact from ~** die Wirklichkeit von der Fantasie trennen; **that was just his ~** das hat er sich (dat) nur eingebildet

c (= notion, whim) **I have a ~ that ...** ich habe so ein Gefühl, dass ...; **he had a sudden ~ to go to Spain** ihn überkam eine plötzliche Laune, nach Spanien zu fahren

ADJ (+er) **a** (inf, = elaborate) clothes, shoes ausgefallen; pattern, hairdo, manoeuvre kunstvoll; food, gadget raffiniert; word, language hochtrabend; **nothing ~** nichts Ausgefallenes; **you won't get anything ~ there** dort bekommst du nur etwas ganz Einfaches; **he uses such ~ language** er drückt sich so gewählt aus; **how do you like our new computer? – very ~!** wie gefällt dir unser neuer Computer? – sehr beeindruckend!; **~ trick** toller Trick (inf); **~ footwork** (Ftbl) geschickte Beinarbeit; (in dancing) komplizierte Schritte pl; (fig) raffinierte Manöver pl **b** (often pej inf, = smart) house, car, clothes, shop schick (inf); school, restaurant nobel, schick (inf); **a ~ car** ein toller Schlitten (inf) **c** (inf: = high) price überhöht, gepfeffert (inf)

fancy: fancy dress N (Masken)kostüm nt; **is it ~?** geht man da verkleidet hin?; **they came in ~** sie kamen verkleidet or kostümiert; **fancy-dress** ATTR **~ ball** Maskenball m; **~ party** Kostümfest nt; **fancy-free** ADJ → **footloose**; **fancy goods** PL Geschenkartikel pl; **fancy man** N (= pimp) Zuhälter m; (= lover) Liebhaber *m*; **fancy woman** N Freundin *f*, Weibchen *nt* (*inf*); **fancywork** N feine Handarbeit

fandango [fæn'dæŋɡəʊ] N Fandango *m*

fanfare ['fænfeə'] N Fanfare *f*; **trumpet ~** Trompetenstoß *m*; **with a ~ of publicity** mit einer Aufsehen erregenden Werbekampagne

fanfold paper ['fænfəʊld'peɪpə'] N (*Comput*) Endlospapier *nt*

fang [fæŋ] N (*of snake*) Giftzahn *m*; (*of wolf, dog*) Fang *m*; (*of vampire*) Vampirzahn *m*; (*hum, of person*) Hauer *m* (*hum*)

fan: fan heater N Heizlüfter *m*; **fanlight** N Oberlicht *nt*; **fan mail** N Verehrerpost *f*

fanny ['fænɪ] N **a** (*esp US, inf*) Po *m* (*inf*) **b** (*Brit, sl*) Möse *f* (*vulg*)

fanny bag N (*US*) Gürteltasche *f*, Wimmerl *nt* (*dial*)

fan: fan oven N Umluftherd *m*; **fan-shaped** ADJ fächerförmig; **fantabulous** [fæn'tæbjʊləs] ADJ (*inf*) super(klasse)toll (*inf*); **fantail** N (= *pigeon*) Pfautaube *f*

fantasia [fæn'teɪzɪə] N Fantasie *f*

fantasize ['fæntəsaɪz] VI fantasieren, phantasieren; (= *dream*) Fantasie- or Phantasievorstellungen haben (*about* von)

fantastic [fæn'tæstɪk] **INTERJ** (*inf*) fantastisch!, toll! (*inf*); **you're pregnant? ~!** du bist schwanger? (das ist ja) toll! (*inf*) ▸ ADJ **a** (*inf*, = *wonderful*) fantastisch, toll (*inf*); **it was a ~ success** es war ein Riesenerfolg; **to look ~** fantastisch or fabelhaft aussehen; **to sound ~** sich fantastisch anhören **b** (*inf*, = *terrific, huge*) *range, profit* fantastisch; **a ~ amount of, ~ amounts of** unwahrscheinlich or wahnsinnig viel (*inf*); **at a ~ speed** unwahrscheinlich or wahnsinnig schnell (*inf*) **c** (= *fantastical, exotic*) *creature* fantastisch, phantastisch; **~ world** Fabelwelt *f* ▸ **trip** VT **c** **d** (= *unbelievable, improbable*) *story* unwahrscheinlich; *truth* unglaublich; **~ though that may seem** so unglaublich das auch scheinen mag; **it all seems a bit too ~ to me** es kommt mir alles etwas zu unglaublich vor

fantastical [fæn'tæstɪkl] ADJ (*liter*) *story, place, world* fantastisch, phantastisch; *account, architecture* seltsam, skurril (*geh*)

fantastically [fæn'tæstɪkəlɪ] ADV **a** (*inf*, = *extraordinarily*) *high, large, expensive, well etc* unwahrscheinlich (*inf*), wahnsinnig (*inf*) **b** (= *strikingly*) auffallend; (= *imaginatively*) fantasievoll, phantasievoll; (= *elaborately*) kunstvoll; **~ coloured** fantastisch or phantastisch bunt

fantasy ['fæntəsɪ] N **a** (= *imagination*) Fantasie *f*, Phantasie *f* **b** (= *illusion*) Fantasie *f*, Hirngespinst *nt* (*pej*); **that's pure ~** or **a ~** das ist reine Fantasie or bloß ein Hirngespinst **c** (*Mus, Liter*) Fantasie *f*

fan: fan tracery N fächerförmiges Maßwerk; **fan vaulting** N Fächergewölbe *nt*

fanzine ['fænzi:n] N Fanmagazin *nt*

FAO *abbr of* **for the attention of** z. Hd.

FAQ N (*Comput*) *abbr of* **frequently asked questions** häufig gestellte Fragen *pl*

far [fɑː'] ✪ 26.2 *comp* **further, farther**, *superl* **furthest, farthest** ADV **a** (*in distance*) weit; **we don't live ~** or **we live not ~ from here** wir wohnen nicht weit von hier; **I'll go with you as ~ as the gate** ich begleite dich bis zum Tor; **~ and wide** weit und breit; **from ~ and near** or **wide** von nah und fern; **~ above** hoch or weit über (+*dat*); **~ away** weit entfernt or weg; **I won't be ~ off** or **away** ich bin ganz in der Nähe; **~ away in the distance** weit in der Ferne; **I was** or **my thoughts were ~ away** ich war mit meinen Gedanken weit weg; **~ into the jungle** weit in den Dschungel hinein; **~ out** weit draußen; **have you come ~?** kommen Sie von weit her? **b** (*in time*) **as ~ back as I can remember** so weit ich (zurück)denken or mich erinnern kann; **as ~ back as 1945** schon (im Jahr) 1945; **~ into the night** bis spät in die Nacht; **~ into the future** bis weit in die Zukunft **c** (*in degree, extent*) weit; **how ~ have you got**

with your plans? wie weit sind Sie mit Ihren Plänen (gekommen)?; **~ longer/better** weit länger/besser; **it's ~ beyond what I can afford** das übersteigt meine Mittel bei weitem **d** (*in set phrases*) **as** or **so ~ as I'm concerned** was mich betrifft; **it's all right as ~ as it goes** das ist so weit ganz gut; **in so ~ as** insofern als; **~ and away the best, by ~ the best, the best by ~** bei weitem or mit Abstand der/die/das Beste; **better by ~** weit besser; **~ from satisfactory** alles andere als befriedigend; **~ from liking him I find him quite unpleasant** ich mag ihn nicht, ich finde ihn (im Gegenteil) sogar ausgesprochen unsympathisch; **~ from it!** ganz und gar nicht, (ganz) im Gegenteil; **~ be it from me to ...** es sei mir ferne, zu ...; **so ~** (= *up to now*) bisher, bis jetzt; (= *up to this point*) so weit; **so ~ this week I've seen him once/three times** diese Woche habe ich ihn erst einmal/ schon dreimal gesehen; **so ~ this week I haven't seen him at all** diese Woche habe ich ihn noch nicht gesehen; **so ~ so good** so weit, so gut; **so ~ and no further** bis hierher und nicht weiter; **to go ~** (*money, supplies, measures etc*) weit reichen; (= *last a long time also*) lange reichen; (*person*: = *succeed*) es weit bringen; **these measures won't go very ~ toward(s) stemming rising costs** diese Maßnahmen werden nicht viel dazu beitragen, die steigenden Kosten einzudämmen; **I would go so ~ as to say ...** ich würde so weit gehen zu sagen ...; **that's going too ~** das geht zu weit; **to carry a joke too ~** einen Spaß zu weit treiben; **that's carrying a joke too ~** da hört der Spaß auf; **not ~ out** (*in guess*) nicht schlecht; **~ out** (= *avant-garde, art*) hypermodern; *ideas* ausgefallen; (*inf*, = *fantastic*) echt geil (*sl*); **not ~ off** (*in space*) nicht weit; (*in guess, aim*) fast (getroffen); (= *almost*) nicht viel weniger; **the weekend isn't ~ off now** es ist nicht mehr lang bis zum Wochenende; **~ gone** (*inf*) schon ziemlich hinüber (*inf*) ▸ ADJ **a** (= *more distant of two*) weiter entfernt, hintere(r, s); **the ~ end of the room** das andere Ende des Zimmers; **the ~ window/door** das Fenster/die Tür am anderen Ende des Zimmers; **the ~ wall** die Wand am anderen Ende; **on the ~ side of** auf der anderen Seite von; **when he reached the ~ bank** als er am anderen Ufer ankam; **which of these cars is yours? – the ~ one** welches ist dein Auto? – das, das weiter weg ist; **which bed will you have? – the ~ one** welches Bett möchtest du? – das da drüben **b** (= *far-off*) *country, land* weit entfernt; **in the ~ distance** in weiter Ferne; **it's a ~ cry from ...** (*fig*) das ist etwas ganz anderes als ...

Faraday cage ['færədeɪˌkeɪdʒ] N (*Phys*) faradayscher Käfig

faraway, far-away ['fɑːrəweɪ] ADJ **a** (= *distant*) *place* entlegen; *town, region, country* fern; *sound, voice, person* weit entfernt; **a tiny, ~ voice** ein kleines Stimmchen in der Ferne; **a ~ relative** ein in der Ferne lebender Verwandter **b** (= *dreamy*) *look, voice* verträumt, versonnen

farce [fɑːs] N (*Theat, fig*) Farce *f*; **the election campaign degenerated into ~** der Wahlkampf wurde zur Farce

farcemeat ['fɑːsmiːt] N = **forcemeat**

farcical ['fɑːsɪkl] ADJ (*Theat*) possenhaft; (*fig*, = *absurd*) absurd, grotesk

fare [feə'] N **a** (= *charge*) Fahrpreis *m*; (*on plane*) Flugpreis *m*; (*on boat*) Preis *m* für die Überfahrt; (= *money*) Fahrgeld *nt*; **what is the ~?** was kostet die Fahrt/der Flug/die Überfahrt?; **~s, please!** noch jemand ohne (*inf*), noch jemand zugestiegen?; **have you got the right ~?** haben Sie das Fahrgeld passend?; **he gave me (the cost of/money for) the ~** er gab mir das Fahrgeld **b** (= *passenger*) Fahrgast *m* **c** (*old, form*, = *food*) Kost *f*; **traditional Christmas ~** ein traditionelles Weihnachtsessen; **vegetarian dishes are now standard ~ in most restaurants** vegetarische Gerichte gehören jetzt in den meisten Restaurants zum Angebot

▸ VI **he ~d well** es ging or erging (*geh*) ihm gut; **the dollar ~d well on the stock exchange today** der Dollar schnitt heute an der Börse gut ab; **~ thee well** (*old*) leb(e) wohl (*old*)

Far East N **the ~** der Ferne Osten

Far Eastern ADJ fernöstlich; **~ politics** Fernostpolitik *f*; **~ travel** Fernostreisen *pl*

fare: fare-dodger N Schwarzfahrer(in) *m(f)*; **fare stage** N Fahrzone *f*, Teilstrecke *f*, Zahlgrenze *f*

farewell [feə'wel] **N** Abschied *m*; **to say** or **make one's ~s** sich verabschieden; (*before a longer absence*) Abschied nehmen; **to bid sb ~** jdm Auf Wiedersehen or Lebewohl (*old*) sagen; **to say ~ to sth** (*old*) von etw Abschied nehmen ▸ **INTERJ** (*old*) lebt wohl (*old*); (*to friend, sweetheart*) leb(e) wohl (*old*)

farewell *in cpds* Abschieds-; **~ speech** Abschiedsrede *f*

fare zone N Tarifzone *f*

far: far-fetched ADJ weit hergeholt, an den Haaren herbeigezogen; **far-flung** ADJ **a** (= *distant*) abgelegen **b** (= *widely spread*) weit auseinander gezogen; **far gone** ADJ *night* weit fortgeschritten; *person* erschöpft, schwach; *clothes* abgetragen; *shoes* abgetreten → *also* **far**

farinaceous [ˌfærɪ'neɪʃəs] ADJ mehlhaltig

farm [fɑːm] **N** Bauernhof *m*; (*bigger*) Gutshof *m*; (*in US, Australia*, = *health farm*) Farm *f*; (= *fish farm*) Fischzucht *f*, Teichwirtschaft *f* (*form*); (= *mink farm etc*) (Pelztier)zuchtfarm *f*; **pig/chicken ~** Schweine-/Hühnerfarm *f*; **trout ~** Forellenzucht *f* ▸ **ATTR** landwirtschaftlich; **~ labourer** (*Brit*) or **laborer** (*US*) Landarbeiter(in) *m(f)*; **~ animals** Tiere *pl* auf dem Bauernhof ▸ **VT** *land* bebauen; *livestock* halten; *trout, mink etc* züchten ▸ **VI** Landwirtschaft betreiben; **man has been ~ing for thousands of years** der Mensch (be)treibt schon seit Jahrtausenden Ackerbau und Viehzucht

▸ **farm out** VT *sep work* vergeben (*on, to* an +*acc*); *children* in Pflege geben (*to* +*dat* bei)

farmer ['fɑːmə'] N Bauer *m*, Bäuerin *f*, Landwirt(in) *m(f)*; (*in US, Australia*) Farmer(in) *m(f)*; (= *mink farmer*) Züchter(in) *m(f)*; (= *fish farmer*) Teichwirt(in) *m(f)* (*form*); (= *gentleman farmer*) Gutsherr *m*; (= *tenant farmer*) Pächter(in) *m(f)*; **~'s wife** Bäuerin *f*; **~'s co-operative** landwirtschaftliche Genossenschaft

farm: farmhand N Landarbeiter(in) *m(f)*; **farmhouse** N Bauernhaus *nt*; **farmhouse loaf** N (*Brit*) großes, *in einer Kastenform gebackenes Weißbrot*

farming ['fɑːmɪŋ] N Landwirtschaft *f*; (*of crops also*) Ackerbau *m*; (*of animals also*) Viehzucht *f*

farm: farmland N Ackerland *nt*; **farm prices** PL Agrarpreise *pl*; **farmstead** N Bauernhof *m*, Gehöft *nt*; **farmyard** N Hof *m*

Far North N **the ~** der hohe Norden

faro ['feərəʊ] N Phar(a)o *nt*

Faroe Islands ['feərəʊˌaɪləndz], **Faroes** ['feərəʊz] PL Färöer *pl*

Faroese [ˌfeərəʊ'iːz] **N** **a** (= *person*) Färöer(in) *m(f)* **b** (*Ling*) Färöisch(e) *nt* ▸ ADJ färöisch; **the ~ people** die Färöer *pl*

far-off ['fɑːrɒf] **ADJ** **a** *days, time* (*in the past*) lange vergangen, weit zurückliegend; (*in the future*) weit entfernt **b** *place, country* fern, weit entfernt ▸ ADV in der Ferne

farrago [fə'rɑːɡəʊ] N Gemisch *nt*, Allerlei *nt*

far-reaching [ˌfɑː'riːtʃɪŋ] ADJ weitreichend, weit reichend

farrier ['færɪə'] N Hufschmied *m*

farrow ['færəʊ] **VT** *piglets* werfen ▸ **VI** ferkeln ▸ **N** Wurf *m*

far-seeing [ˌfɑː'siːɪŋ] ADJ weitblickend, weit blickend

Farsi ['fɑːsiː] N Farsi *nt*

far: far-sighted ADJ **a** (*lit*) weitsichtig **b** (*fig*) *person, policy* weitblickend, weit blickend; (= *taking precautionary measures*) umsichtig; *measures* auf weite Sicht geplant; **far-sightedness**

N **a** (*lit*) Weitsichtigkeit *f* **b** (*fig: of person, policy*) Weitblick *m*

fart [fɑːt] (*inf*) **N** **a** Furz *m* (*inf*) **b** (= *person*) **he's a boring old ~** er ist ein langweiliger alter Knacker (*inf*) **VI** furzen (*inf*)

▶ **fart about** *or* **around** VI (*inf*) **a** (= *rush around*) hin und her sausen (*inf*) **b** (= *loaf around*) herumbummeln (*inf*) **c** (= *mess around*) herumalbern (*inf*); **stop farting about** *or* **around and do some work** jetzt halte dich nicht länger auf und arbeite mal was (*inf*); **to fart about** *or* **around with sth** an etw (*dat*) herumfummeln (*inf*)

farther ['fɑːðə] *comp of* **far** ADV = **further** ADV **ADJ** weiter entfernt, hintere(r, s); **at the ~ end** am anderen Ende

farthermost ['fɑːðəməʊst] ADJ = **furthermost**

farthest ['fɑːðɪst] ADJ, ADV *superl of* **far the ~ point of the island** der am weitesten entfernte Punkt der Insel → **furthest ADV, ADJ**

farthing ['fɑːðɪŋ] N Farthing *m* (*ein Viertelpenny*)

farthingale ['fɑːðɪŋgeɪl] N Reifrock *m*, Krinoline *f*

fas *abbr of* **free alongside ship** frei Kai

fascia ['feɪʃə] N (*Brit, Aust*) Armaturentafel *f*

fascicle ['fæsɪkl], **fascicule** ['fæsɪkjuːl] N **a** (*Bot*) Büschel *nt*; (*Anat*) Bündel *nt* **b** (*of book*) Lieferung *f*, Faszikel (*old*) *m*

fascinate ['fæsɪneɪt] VT faszinieren; (= *enchant: skill, beauty, singer etc also*) begeistern, bezaubern; (= *hold spellbound: book, film, magician also*) fesseln; **old houses ~/this subject ~s me** ich finde alte Häuser/dieses Gebiet hochinteressant *or* faszinierend; **the audience watched/listened ~d** das Publikum sah/hörte gebannt zu; **it ~s me how well he does these things** ich finde es erstaunlich, wie gut er das macht

fascinating ['fæsɪneɪtɪŋ] ADJ faszinierend, hochinteressant; *beauty* bezaubernd

fascinatingly ['fæsɪneɪtɪŋlɪ] ADV faszinierend; *talk, describe* hochinteressant; *beautiful* bezaubernd; (*introducing sentence*) faszinierenderweise; **~ interesting** hochinteressant

fascination [ˌfæsɪ'neɪʃən] N Faszination *f*; (= *fascinating quality also*) Reiz *m*; **to listen/watch in ~** gebannt zuhören/zusehen; **to have** *or* **hold a ~ for sb** auf jdn einen besonderen Reiz ausüben; **his ~ with the cinema** der Reiz, den das Kino auf ihn ausübt, die Faszination, die das Kino auf ihn ausübt; **I don't understand the ~ of this book** ich verstehe nicht, was an diesem Buch so faszinierend ist; **she developed a ~ for Impressionist painting** impressionistische Malerei begann sie zu faszinieren

fascism ['fæʃɪzəm] N Faschismus *m*

fascist ['fæʃɪst] **N** Faschist(in) *m(f)* **ADJ** faschistisch

fascistic [fə'ʃɪstɪk] ADJ faschistisch

fash [fæʃ] VT (*Scot*, = *trouble*) ärgern; (= *worry*) aufregen

fashion ['fæʃən] **N** **a** *no pl* (= *manner*) Art (und Weise) *f*; **(in the) Indian ~** auf Indianerart, nach Art der Indianer; **in the usual ~** wie üblich; **in a similar ~** auf ähnliche Weise; **to behave in a strange ~** sich merkwürdig verhalten; **did it work/have you translated it? – after a ~** hat es geklappt/hast du es übersetzt? – so einigermaßen; **to do sth after** *or* **in a ~** etw recht und schlecht machen; **I can cook after a ~** ich kann so einigermaßen kochen; **a novel after** *or* **in the ~ of D.H. Lawrence** ein Roman im Stil von D. H. Lawrence; **in this ~** auf diese Weise, so **b** (*in clothing: = latest style*) Mode *f*; **(back) in ~** (wieder) modern; **it's the/all the ~** es ist Mode/große Mode; **to come into/go out of ~** in Mode/aus der Mode kommen; **a man of ~** ein modischer Herr; **the Paris ~s** die Pariser Mode; **she always wears the latest ~s** sie ist immer nach der neuesten Mode gekleidet; **~s in women's clothes** die Damenmode; **to set a ~** eine Mode aufbringen; **the ~ world** die Welt der Mode

(= *custom, of society*) Sitte *f*, Brauch *m*; (*of individual*) Gewohnheit *f*; **it was the ~ in those days** das war damals Sitte *or* Brauch

VT formen, gestalten; **to ~ sth after sth** etw einer Sache (*dat*) nachbilden

fashionable ['fæʃnəbl] ADJ *clothes, look, person* modisch; *restaurant, shop, area* schick; *idea, artist* zurzeit beliebt; **~ colour** (*Brit*) *or* **color** (*US*) Modefarbe *f*; **~ writer** Modeschriftsteller(in) *m(f)*; **to become ~** in Mode kommen, modern werden; **it became very ~** es wurde große Mode *or* sehr modern; **it's ~ to do that** es ist modern *or* in Mode, das zu tun; **the ~ set** *or* **people** die Schickeria

fashionably ['fæʃnəblɪ] ADV modisch

fashion: fashion-conscious ADJ modebewusst; **fashion designer** N Modezeichner(in) *m(f)*; **fashion magazine** N Modeheft *nt or* -zeitschrift *f*; **fashion model** N Mannequin *nt*; (= *man*) Dressman *m*; **fashion parade** N Mode(n)schau *f*; **fashion plate** N Modezeichnung *f*; **she looked like a ~** sie sah aus wie aus der Modezeitung; **fashion show** N Mode(n)schau *f*; **fashion victim** N (*pej inf*) Opfer *nt* der Mode, Fashion Victim *nt*; **fashionwear** ['fæʃnwɛə] N Modeartikel *pl*

fast¹ [fɑːst] **ADJ** (+*er*) **a** (= *quick*) schnell; **she's a ~ runner/reader** sie kann schnell laufen/lesen; **he's a ~ worker** (*lit*) er arbeitet schnell; (*fig*) er geht mächtig ran (*inf*); **to pull a ~ one** (**on sb**) (*inf*) jdn übers Ohr hauen (*inf*); **the ~ life** das hektische Leben; **~ train** (*Brit*) D-Zug *m* **b** **to be ~** (*clock, watch*) vorgehen; **to be five minutes ~** fünf Minuten vorgehen **c** *tennis court, squash ball etc* schnell **d** (*Phot*) *film* hochempfindlich; *lens* lichtstark **e** (*fig, = immoral*) *behaviour, person* locker, flott, ausschweifend (*pej*); **~ woman** leichtlebige Frau **ADV** **a** schnell **b** (*fig*) **to live ~** flott *or* locker leben **c** (*old*) **to follow ~ on sth** dicht auf etw (*acc*) folgen

fast² **ADJ** **a** (= *firm, secure*) fest; **to make a boat ~** ein Boot festmachen **b** *colour, dye* farbecht **c** (= *staunch*) *friend* gut **ADV** **a** (= *firmly, securely*) fest; **to stick ~** festsitzen; (*with glue*) festkleben; **to stand ~** standhaft *or* fest stehen; **to stand ~ by sb** (treu) zu jdm stehen; **to stand ~ by sth** an etw (*dat*) festhalten; **to hold ~ to sth** an etw (*dat*) festhalten; **to play ~ and loose with sb** mit jdm ein falsches *or* doppeltes Spiel treiben **b** (= *soundly*) **to be ~ asleep** tief *or* fest schlafen

fast³ **VI** (= *not eat*) fasten **N** Fasten *nt*; (= *period of fasting*) Fastenzeit *f*; **~ day** Fasttag *m*; **to break one's ~** das Fasten brechen

fast: fastback N (Wagen *m* mit) Fließheck *nt*; **fast-breeder reactor** N schneller Brüter

fasten ['fɑːsn] **VT** **a** (= *attach*) festmachen, befestigen (*to, onto* an +*dat*); (= *do up*) *parcel etc* zuschnüren; *buttons, buckle, dress etc* zumachen; (= *tighten*) *screw etc* anziehen; (= *lock*) *door* (ab)schließen; **to ~ one's seat belt** sich anschnallen; **to ~ two things together** zwei Dinge zusammenmachen (*inf*) *or* aneinander befestigen **b** (*fig*) *thoughts, attention* zuwenden (*on sb* jdm); **to ~ the blame on sb** die Schuld auf jdn schieben, jdm die Schuld in die Schuhe schieben (*inf*); **to ~ one's hopes on sb/sth** seine Hoffnungen auf jdn/etw setzen; **to ~ one's eyes on sb/sth** die Augen *or* den Blick auf jdn/etw heften **VI** sich schließen lassen; **the dress ~s at the back** das Kleid wird hinten zugemacht; **the door won't ~** die Tür lässt sich nicht schließen; **these two pieces ~ together** diese zwei Teile werden miteinander verbunden

▶ **fasten down** VT *sep* festmachen

▶ **fasten in** VT *sep* festschnallen (+*prep obj* in +*dat*)

▶ **fasten on** **VT** *sep* befestigen, festmachen (+*prep obj, -to* an +*dat*); *flower, badge* anheften (+*prep obj, -to* an +*dat*) **VI** +*prep obj* (= *concentrate on*) *person, subject* herumhacken auf (+*dat*)

(*inf*); **his eyes fastened on mine** er heftete seine Augen auf meine

▶ **fasten onto** VI +*prep obj* (*fig*) **to fasten onto sth** sich in etw (*acc*) verbeißen

▶ **fasten up** VT *sep dress etc* zumachen; **could you fasten me up?** (*inf*) kannst du mir zumachen? (*inf*)

fastener ['fɑːsnə], **fastening** ['fɑːsnɪŋ] N Verschluss *m*

fast food N Fastfood *nt*, Fast Food *nt*; **he lives mainly on ~** er ernährt sich hauptsächlich von Fastfood *or* Fast Food *or* von Schnellgerichten

fast-food ['fɑːstfuːd]: **fast-food chain** N Fastfoodkette *f*, Fast-Food-Kette *f*, Schnellimbisskette *f*; **fast-food outlet** N Fastfoodlokal *nt*, Fast-Food-Lokal *nt*, Schnellimbiss *m*; **fast-food restaurant** N Fastfoodrestaurant *nt*, Fast-Food-Restaurant *nt*, Schnellimbiss *m*

fast: fast forward N (*on tape deck*) Vorspultaste *f*; **fast-forward** VTI vorspulen

fastidious [fæs'tɪdɪəs] ADJ genau (*about* in Bezug auf +*acc*); (*pej*) pingelig (*inf*) (*about* in Bezug auf +*acc*)

fastidiously [fæs'tɪdɪəslɪ] ADV **a** (= *meticulously*) *check, copy, examine* mit äußerster Sorgfalt; **~ tidy** (*place*) sorgfältigst aufgeräumt; *person* penibel ordentlich; **~ clean** peinlich sauber **b** (*pej, = fussily*) pingelig (*inf*); **he wrinkled his nose ~** er rümpfte angewidert die Nase

fastidiousness [fæs'tɪdɪəsnɪs] N Sorgfalt *f*; (*pej: = fussiness*) Pingeligkeit *f* (*inf*)

fasting ['fɑːstɪŋ] N Fasten *nt*

fast lane N Überholspur *f*; **life in the ~** (*fig*) das hektische Leben; **those in the ~ of life** diese dynamischen Erfolgstypen (*inf*)

fastness ['fɑːstnɪs] N **a** (= *stronghold*) Feste *f*; **mountain ~** Bergfeste *f* **b** (*of colours*) Farbechtheit *f* **c** (= *immorality*) Liederlichkeit *f*

fast track N schnellster Weg; **~ carrier** Senkrechtkarriere *f*

fat [fæt] **ADJ** (+*er*) **a** (= *overweight*) *person, animal, stomach, arms, thighs* dick, fett (*pej*); **to get** *or* **become ~** dick werden; **to grow ~ (on sth)** (*fig, person, company, town*) (durch etw) reich werden; **it's** *or* **the show's not over until the ~ lady sings** (*hum inf*) das ist noch nicht das Ende **b** (= *thick*) *book, pile* dick; (*fig inf*) *profit, fee, salary* üppig, fett (*inf*); *wallet, cheque(book)* dick; (= *prosperous*) *year, period* fett **c** (= *fatty*) *meat* fett **d** (*inf: = stupid*) **can't you get it into your ~ head (that) ...** hast du Idiot es denn noch immer nicht gecheckt, dass ... (*inf*); **they can't get it into their silly ~ heads that ...** diesen Idioten will es nicht in den Kopf, dass ... (*inf*) → *also* **fathead** **e** (*iro inf*) **that's a ~ lot of good** *or* **use** das bringt doch überhaupt nichts; **a ~ lot of good thieving did you** das Stehlen hat dir überhaupt nichts gebracht (*inf*); **~ lot of help she was** sie war 'ne schöne Hilfe! (*iro inf*); **~ chance!** schön wärs!; **~ chance of that!** das kannst du dir abschminken! (*inf*) **N** (*Anat, Cook, Chem*) Fett *nt*; **reduce the ~ in your diet** reduzieren Sie den Fettgehalt Ihrer Ernährung; **to put on ~** Speck ansetzen (*inf*); **to run to ~** in die Breite gehen (*inf*); **to live off the ~ of the land** (*fig*) wie Gott in Frankreich *or* wie die Made im Speck leben; **the ~'s in the fire** (*fig*) jetzt ist der Teufel los (*inf*)

fatal ['feɪtl] ADJ **a** (= *causing death*) tödlich (*to, for* für); **he had a ~ accident** er ist tödlich verunglückt; **the illness is invariably ~** die Krankheit verläuft immer tödlich; **possibly ~ delays** Verzögerungen *pl*, die möglicherweise tödliche Folgen haben werden; **to prove ~** sich als tödlich erweisen; **~ accident inquiry** (*Scot*) Untersuchung *f* zur Unfallursache (*bei Unfällen mit Todesfolge*)

b (*fig, = disastrous*) *mistake, weakness, flaw, consequences* fatal, verhängnisvoll; (= *fateful*) *day, decision* verhängnisvoll; **to be** *or* **prove ~ to** *or* **for sb/sth** das Ende für jdn/etw bedeuten *or* sein; **it proved ~ to their diplomatic relations** es hatte verhängnisvolle Folgen für ihre diplomatischen Beziehungen; **in the end such methods will prove ~** solche Methoden werden sich letztendlich als verhängnisvoll herausstellen; **it's ~ to ask him, he always forgets** frag ihn bloß nicht, er vergisst es immer; **it would be ~ to do that** es wäre verhängnisvoll, das zu tun; **it was a ~ blow to our hopes** es hat unsere Hoffnungen zunichte gemacht; **her ~ attraction for him** die unheilvolle Anziehungskraft, die sie auf ihn ausübte

fatalism ['feɪtəlɪzəm] N Fatalismus m

fatalist ['feɪtəlɪst] N Fatalist(in) m(f)

fatalistic ADJ, **fatalistically** ADV [,feɪtə'lɪstɪk, -əlɪ] fatalistisch

fatality [fə'tælɪtɪ] N **a** Todesfall m; (in accident, war etc) (Todes)opfer nt; **there were no fatalities** es gab keine Todesopfer **b** (liter, = inevitability) Unabwendbarkeit f

fatally ['feɪtəlɪ] ADV **a** (= mortally) wounded, injured tödlich; **~ ill** todkrank; **they were ~ stabbed** sie wurden erstochen; **she overdosed ~** sie kam eine tödliche Überdosis **b** (= irrevocably) undermine, damage, weaken unwiderruflich; (= disastrously) verheerend; **the ~ incriminating tape** das Band mit dem fatalen Belastungsmaterial; **I was ~ attracted to him/it** er/es übte eine unheilvolle Anziehungskraft auf mich aus; **to be ~ flawed** fatale Mängel aufweisen

Fata Morgana ['fɑːtəmɔː'gɑːnə] N Fata Morgana f

fat-ass ['fætæs] (US, pej sl) N Fettsack m (pej inf), fettes Schwein (pej inf) ADJ fett (pej)

fat cat N (fig inf) überbezahlter Topmanager, überbezahlte Topmanagerin, fette Katze (inf)

fate [feɪt] N Schicksal nt; **the Fates** (Myth) die Parzen pl; **the examiners meet to decide our ~ next week** die Prüfer kommen nächste Woche zusammen, um über unser Schicksal zu entscheiden; **to leave sth to ~** etw dem Schicksal überlassen; **to leave sb to his ~** jdn seinem Schicksal überlassen; **to go to meet one's ~** seinem Schicksal entgegentreten; **to meet one's ~** vom Schicksal heimgesucht or ereilt (geh) werden; **to face a similar ~** einem ähnlichen Schicksal entgegensehen; **to meet with** or **suffer the same ~** das gleiche Schicksal haben or erleiden; **as sure as ~ it will go wrong** das geht garantiert schief; **as sure as ~ it went wrong** das ist natürlich prompt schief gegangen

fated ['feɪtɪd] ADJ unglückselig; project, plan zum Scheitern verurteilt; **to be ~** unter einem ungünstigen Stern stehen; **to be ~ to fail** or **to be unsuccessful** zum Scheitern verurteilt sein; **their plans were ~ to be forgotten** ihre Pläne waren dazu verurteilt, vergessen zu werden; **they were ~ never to meet again** es war ihnen bestimmt, sich nie wiederzusehen

fateful ['feɪtfʊl] ADJ day, night, moment, meeting, journey schicksalhaft; decision, consequence verhängnisvoll; words schicksalsschwer; **to be ~ for sb** jds Schicksal besiegeln

fathead ['fæthed] N (Brit inf) Dummkopf m, Blödmann m (inf)

fatheaded [,fæt'hedɪd] ADJ (Brit inf) dumm, blöd (inf)

father ['fɑːðə'] N **a** (lit, fig) Vater m (to sb jdm); **from ~ to son** vom Vater auf den Sohn; **like ~ like son** der Apfel fällt nicht weit vom Stamm; **(Old) Father Time** die Zeit (als Allegorie)
b ~s pl (= ancestors) Väter pl
c (= founder) Vater m; (= leader) Führer m, Vater m (liter); **the Fathers of the Church** die Kirchenväter pl
d (= God) **(our) Father** Vater m (unser)
e (= priest) Pater m; **the Holy Father** der Heilige Vater
VT a child, cub etc zeugen; (= admit paternity) die Vaterschaft anerkennen für; (fig) idea, plan Urheber (+gen) sein
b (= saddle with responsibility) **to ~ sth on sb** jdm die Verantwortung für etw aufhalsen (inf) or aufbürden

father: **Father Christmas** N (Brit) der Weihnachtsmann; **father confessor** N (Rel) Beichtvater m; **father figure** N Vaterfigur f; **fatherhood** N Vaterschaft f; **father-in-law** N pl **fathers-in-law** Schwiegervater m; **fatherland** N Vaterland nt; **fatherless** ADJ vaterlos

fatherly ['fɑːðəlɪ] ADJ väterlich, wie ein Vater

Father's Day N Vatertag m

fathom ['fæðəm] N Faden m VT **a** (lit) ausloten **b** (= understand) ermessen (geh); (inf: also **fathom out**) verstehen; **I just can't ~ him (out)** er ist mir ein Rätsel; **I couldn't ~ it (out)** ich kam der Sache nicht auf den Grund, ich kam nicht dahinter (inf); **we're trying to ~ (out) what ...** wir versuchen zu ergründen, was ...

fathomable ['fæðəməbl] ADJ (fig) fassbar; **less ~** weniger verständlich

fathomless ['fæðəmlɪs] ADJ (lit) abgrundtief; (fig, = boundless) unermesslich; (= incomprehensible) unergründlich

fatigue [fə'tiːg] N **a** Abspannung f, Erschöpfung f, Ermüdung f; **battle ~** Kampfmüdigkeit f; **compassion ~** Verdrossenheit f mit immer neuen Spendenaufrufen; **donor ~** Spendenmüdigkeit f **b** (Tech, = metal fatigue) Ermüdung f **c** (Mil, = fatigue duty) Arbeitsdienst m; **to be on ~** Arbeitsdienst haben **d fatigues** PL (Mil) Arbeitsanzug m; **in ~s** im Arbeitsanzug VT **a** (= tire) ermüden; (= exhaust) erschöpfen **b** (Tech) metal ermüden VI ermüden

fatigue: **fatigue dress** N Arbeitsanzug m; **in ~** im Arbeitsanzug; **fatigue duty** N Arbeitseinsatz m, Arbeitsdienst m; **fatigue party** N Arbeitskommando nt

fatiguing [fə'tiːgɪŋ] ADJ (= tiring) ermüdend; (= exhausting) erschöpfend

fatless ['fætlɪs] ADJ fettfrei, ohne Fett

fatling ['fætlɪŋ] N junges Masttier

fatness ['fætnɪs] N **a** (= overweight) Dicke f, Fettheit f (pej) **b** (= thickness, of book, pile, wad) Dicke f, Umfang m; (fig inf, of wallet, chequebook) Dicke f; (of profit, fee, salary) Üppigkeit f, Fettheit f (inf) **c** (fig, of land) Fruchtbarkeit f

fatso ['fætsəʊ] N (inf) Dicke(r) mf (inf), Fettsack m (pej inf)

fat-soluble ADJ (Chem) fettlöslich

fat stock N Mastvieh nt

fatted ['fætɪd] ADJ **to kill the ~ calf** einen Willkommensschmaus veranstalten

fatten ['fætn] VT (also **fatten up**) animals mästen; people herausfüttern (inf); (fig) profits erhöhen; budget aufstocken; **are you trying to ~ me up?** (inf) du willst mich wohl mästen? (inf) VI (also **fatten up** or **out**, animal) fett werden; (person) dick werden; (through overeating) sich mästen (inf)

fattener ['fætnə'] N Dickmacher m

fattening ['fætnɪŋ] ADJ food dick machend; **chocolate is ~** Schokolade macht dick

fatty ['fætɪ] ADJ (+er) fett; (= greasy) fettig; **~ deposits** Fettablagerungen pl; **~ tissue** Fettgewebe nt; **~ tumour** Fettgeschwulst f; **they have a fattier diet than us** sie ernähren sich fettreicher als wir N (inf) Dickerchen nt (inf)

fatty acid N Fettsäure f

fatty degeneration N (Med) Verfettung f

fatuity [fə'tjuːɪtɪ] N Albernheit f; (= remark, action also) törichte Bemerkung/Tat (geh)

fatuous ['fætjʊəs] ADJ töricht (geh), albern

faucet ['fɔːsɪt] N (US) Hahn m

faugh [fɔː] INTERJ (old) pfui

fault [fɔːlt] ⊙ 18.3 N **a** (= mistake, defect) Fehler m; (Tech) Defekt m; **generous to a ~** übermäßig großzügig; **to find ~ with sb/sth** etwas an jdm/etw auszusetzen haben; **he was at ~** er war im Unrecht; **my memory was at ~** mein Gedächtnis hat mich getrogen; **you were at ~ in not telling me** es war nicht recht von Ihnen, dass Sie mir das nicht gesagt haben **b** no pl **it won't be my/his ~ if ...** es ist nicht meine/seine Schuld, wenn ..., ich bin/er ist

nicht schuld, wenn ...; **whose ~ is it?** wer ist schuld (daran)?; **it's all your own ~** das ist Ihre eigene Schuld, Sie sind selbst schuld; **through no ~ of her own, she ...** es war nicht ihre eigene Schuld, dass sie ...
c (Geol) Verwerfung f
d (Tennis, Horseriding) Fehler m
VT **a** Fehler finden an (+dat), etwas auszusetzen haben an (+dat); **I can't ~ it/him** ich habe nichts daran/an ihm auszusetzen
b (Geol) eine Verwerfung verursachen in (+dat)
VI (Geol) sich verwerfen

fault: **fault-finder** N Krittler(in) m(f); **fault-finding** ADJ krittelig N Krittelei f

faultily ['fɔːltɪlɪ] ADV falsch

faultless ['fɔːltlɪs] ADJ **a** (= without mistakes) fehlerlos; English fehlerfrei, fehlerlos **b** (= immaculate) appearance tadellos, einwandfrei

faultlessly ['fɔːltlɪslɪ] ADV **a** (= without mistakes) speak, copy, translate fehlerfrei, fehlerlos **b** (= perfectly) dressed, executed tadellos; work, run, perform einwandfrei; fluent, loyal vollkommen

fault: **fault line** N (Geol) Verwerfungslinie f; **fault-tolerant** ADJ (Tech, Comput) fehlertolerant

faulty ['fɔːltɪ] ADJ (+er) (Tech, Biol) defekt; (Comm) fehlerhaft; reasoning, logic falsch, fehlerhaft

faun [fɔːn] N (Myth) Faun m

fauna ['fɔːnə] N Fauna f

faux pas [fəʊ'pɑː] N Fauxpas m

fava bean ['fɑːvəbiːn] N (US) dicke Bohne, Saubohne f

favorite son N (US, Pol) regionaler Spitzenkandidat

favour, (US) **favor** ['feɪvə'] ⊙ 11.2 N **a** no pl (= goodwill) Gunst f, Wohlwollen nt; **to win/lose sb's ~** jds Gunst (acc) erlangen (geh)/verscherzen; **to find ~ with sb** bei jdm Anklang finden; **to look with ~ on sth** einer Sache (dat) wohlwollend gegenüberstehen; **to be in ~ with sb** bei jdm gut angeschrieben sein; (fashion, pop star, writer etc) bei jdm beliebt sein, bei jdm ankommen; **to be/fall out of ~** in Ungnade (gefallen) sein/fallen; (fashion, pop star, writer etc) nicht mehr ankommen or beliebt sein (with bei)
b **to be in ~ of sth** für etw sein; **to be in ~ of doing sth** dafür sein, etw zu tun; **a point in his ~** ein Punkt zu seinen Gunsten, ein Punkt, der für ihn spricht; **the judge ruled in his ~** der Richter entschied zu seinen Gunsten; **he's got everything in his ~** es spricht alles für ihn; **all those in ~ raise their hands** alle, die dafür sind, Hand hoch; **he rejected socialism in ~ of the market economy** er lehnte den Sozialismus ab und bevorzugte statt dessen die Marktwirtschaft **balance** N f
c (= partiality) Vergünstigung f; **to show ~ to sb** jdn bevorzugen
d (= act of kindness) Gefallen m, Gefälligkeit f; **to ask a ~ of sb** jdn um einen Gefallen bitten; **to do sb a ~** jdm einen Gefallen tun; **do me a ~!** (inf) sei so gut!; **would you do me the ~ of returning my library books?** wären Sie bitte so freundlich und würden meine Bücher in die Bücherei zurückbringen?; **do me the ~ of shutting up!** (inf) tu mir einen Gefallen und halt den Mund!; **as a ~** aus Gefälligkeit; **as a ~ to him** ihm zuliebe; **to sell sexual ~s** (old, hum) Liebesgünste verkaufen (old, hum)
e (old, = ribbon etc) Schleife f
f (on wedding cake) Verzierung f, (Kuchen)dekoration f; (to take home) Tüllbeutel mit Zuckermandeln
VT **a** idea (= be in favour of) für gut halten; (= prefer) bevorzugen; **I ~ the second proposal** ich bin für den zweiten Vorschlag
b (= show preference) bevorzugen; (king etc) begünstigen
c (= oblige, honour) beehren (form); **to ~ sb with a smile** jdm gütigerweise ein Lächeln gewähren (geh)

d (= *be favourable for*) begünstigen
e (*US*, = *resemble*) ähneln (+*dat*)

favourable, (*US*) **favorable** ['feɪvərəbl] ○ 13
ADJ **a** (= *positive*) *response, reaction* positiv; *opinion, review, impression* positiv, günstig; **I haven't heard one ~ opinion on it** ich habe noch keine einzige positive Meinung dazu gehört; **her request met with a ~ response** ihre Bitte stieß auf Zustimmung; **most people were ~ to the idea** die meisten Leute standen der Idee positiv gegenüber; **she got a ~ mention in the report** sie wurde in dem Bericht lobend erwähnt
b (= *beneficial*) *terms, position, deal* günstig, vorteilhaft; *comparison* vorteilhaft; *mood* positiv; *climate, weather, conditions* günstig (*to* für); **to be given ~ treatment** bevorzugt behandelt werden; **to show sth in a ~ light** etw in einem günstigen Licht zeigen; **an atmosphere ~ to expansion** ein günstiges Klima für Expansion; **on ~ terms** zu günstigen Bedingungen; **conditions are ~ for development** für die Entwicklung herrschen günstige Bedingungen

favourableness, (*US*) **favorableness** ['feɪvərəblnɪs] N Günstigkeit *f*; **the ~ of his attitude** seine positive Einstellung

favourably, (*US*) **favorably** ['feɪvərəblɪ] ADV **a** (= *approvingly*) *respond* positiv; *receive, regard, think, judge* wohlwollend; **he was ~ impressed by it** er war davon sehr angetan; **her application had impressed him very ~** ihre Bewerbung hatte ihn sehr beeindruckt; **to look ~ (up)on sb/sth** jdn/etw wohlwollend behandeln; **to be ~ disposed** *or* **inclined to(wards) sb/sth** jdm/einer Sache gewogen sein (*geh*) **b** (= *advantageously*) günstig; **to compare ~ (with sth)** im Vergleich (mit etw) gut abschneiden

favoured, (*US*) **favored** ['feɪvəd] ADJ **a** **~ few** einige (wenige) Auserwählte; **a ~ friend** ein besonderer Freund

favourite, (*US*) **favorite** ['feɪvərɪt] ○ 7 **N** **a** (= *person*) Liebling *m*; (*Hist, pej*) Günstling *m*; **he is a universal ~** er ist allgemein beliebt; **which of her children is her ~?** welches Kind mag sie am liebsten *or* ist ihr Liebling? **b** (= *thing*) **this one is my ~** das habe ich am liebsten; **this book/dress is my ~** das ist mein Lieblingsbuch/-kleid; **we sang all the old ~s** wir holten all die alten Lieder gesungen **c** (*Sport*) Favorit(in) *m(f)*; **Chelsea are the ~s** Chelsea ist (der) Favorit **b** attr Lieblings-; **my ~ book/dress** mein Lieblingsbuch *nt*/-kleid *nt*

favouritism, (*US*) **favoritism** ['feɪvərɪtɪzəm] N Vetternwirtschaft *f* (*inf*), Günstlingswirtschaft *f*; (*in school*) Schätzchenwirtschaft *f* (*inf*), Lieblingswirtschaft *f*

fawn[1] [fɔːn] **N** **a** Hirschkalb *nt*; (*of roe deer*) Rehkitz *nt* **b** (= *colour*) Beige *nt* **ADJ** (*colour*) beige

fawn[2] VI (*dog*) (mit dem Schwanz) wedeln; (*fig, person*) katzbuckeln (*on, upon or over +dat*), herumscharwenzeln (*on, upon or over* um)

fawning ['fɔːnɪŋ] ADJ *person, manner* kriecherisch, liebedienernd; *dog* schwanzwedelnd

fax [fæks] **N** **a** (*also* **fax machine**) Fax *nt*, Telefax *nt*, Fernkopierer *m*; **to send sth by ~** etw per Fax *or* Telefax senden, etw faxen **b** (= *message, document*) Fax *nt*, Telefax *nt* **VT** faxen; **can you ~ us?** können Sie uns (*dat*) faxen?

▶**fax back** VT *sep document* zurückfaxen; **can you fax me back?** können Sie mir per Fax antworten?

fax: fax board N Faxkarte *f*; **fax bureau** N Faxbüro *nt*; **fax card** N = **fax board**; **fax machine** N = fax N a; **fax message** N Fax *nt*, Telefax *nt*; **fax number** N (Tele)faxnummer *f*; **faxshot** **N** Direktwerbung *f* per Fax; **to send out a ~** Werbemitteilungen per Fax senden **VT** Werbemitteilungen per Fax senden an (+*acc*)

fay [feɪ] N (*liter*, = *fairy*) Fee *f*

faze [feɪz] VT (*inf*) **a** (= *take aback*) verdattern (*inf*); **the question didn't ~ me at all** die Frage brachte mich keineswegs aus der Fassung **b** (= *daunt*) entmutigen; **do not be ~d by the en-**

trance exam lass dich von der Aufnahmeprüfung nicht abschrecken

FBI (*US*) *abbr of* **Federal Bureau of Investigation** FBI *nt*

FC *abbr of* **football club** FC *m*

FDA

Die **Food and Drug Administration**, kurz **FDA**, ist die älteste Verbraucherschutzbehörde in den USA. In ihren Aufgabenbereich fällt die Kontrolle von Nahrungsmitteln, Lebensmittelzusätzen, Medikamenten und Kosmetikartikeln sowie die Entscheidung darüber, ob deren Verzehr bzw. Gebrauch ungefährlich für den Verbraucher ist. Im Ausland ist die **FDA** besonders für ihre Vorreiterrolle bei der Prüfung von Ungefährlichkeit und Wirksamkeit neuer Arzneimittel bekannt, aber auch für die kontinuierliche Überwachung der Anwendung nach der Markteinführung.

FDD (*Comput*) *abbr of* **floppy disk drive**

FDR (*Aviat*) *abbr of* **flight-data recorder** Flug(daten)schreiber *m*

fealty ['fiːəltɪ] N (*Hist*) Lehnstreue *f*

fear [fɪə] **N** **a** Angst *f*, Furcht *f* (*for* +*dat*); **~s for the future** Zukunftsängste *pl*; **~ of death/failure** Todes-/Versagensangst *f*; **~ of flying** Flugangst *f*, Angst *f* vorm Fliegen; **~ of heights** Höhenangst *f*; **he has ~s for his sister's safety** er fürchtet für *or* um die Sicherheit seiner Schwester; **there are ~s that ...** es wird befürchtet, dass ...; **have no ~** (*old, hum*) fürchte dich nicht (*old, hum*); **with ~ and trembling** mit schlotternden Knien; **to be in ~ of sb/sth** Angst vor jdm/etw haben; **to go** *or* **live in ~ of sb/sth** in (ständiger) Angst vor jdm/etw leben; **he lived in ~ of being discovered** er lebte in ständiger Angst davor, entdeckt zu werden; **to be in ~ of one's life** um sein Leben bangen; **for ~ that ...** aus Angst, dass ...; **she talked quietly for ~ of waking the baby** sie sprach leise, um das Baby nicht aufzuwecken; **without ~ or favour** (*Brit*) *or* **favor** (*US*) ganz gerecht
b *no pl* (= *risk, likelihood*) **no ~!** (*inf*) nie im Leben! (*inf*); **there's no ~ of that happening again** keine Angst, das passiert so leicht nicht wieder; **there's not much ~ of his coming** wir brauchen kaum Angst zu haben, dass er kommt **c** (= *awe: of God*) Scheu *f*, Ehrfurcht *f*; **to put the ~ of God into sb** (*inf*) jdm gewaltig Angst einjagen (*inf*)
VT **a** (= *be afraid of*) (be)fürchten; **I ~ the worst** ich befürchte das Schlimmste; **he's a man to be ~ed** er ist ein Mann, den man fürchten muss; **many women ~ to go out at night** viele Frauen haben Angst davor, abends auszugehen
b (= *feel awe for*) *God* Ehrfurcht haben vor (+*dat*)
VI **to ~ for** fürchten für *or* um; **never ~!** keine Angst!

fearful ['fɪəfʊl] ADJ **a** (= *apprehensive*) ängstlich, bang; **he was ~ lest he fall/be discovered** (*old*) ihm bangte davor zu versagen/entdeckt zu werden; **to be ~ for one's/sb's life** um sein/jds Leben fürchten; **to be ~ of sb/sth** Angst vor jdm/etw (*dat*) haben; **I was ~ of waking her** ich befürchtete, dass ich sie aufwecken würde **b** (= *frightening*) furchtbar, schrecklich (*inf*) **c** (*dated inf*: = *terrible*) furchtbar, schrecklich (*inf*)

fearfully ['fɪəfʊlɪ] ADV **a** (= *apprehensively*) ängstlich **b** (*dated inf*: = *terribly*) *expensive, hot, loud etc* furchtbar (*inf*), schrecklich (*inf*)

fearfulness ['fɪəfʊlnɪs] N (= *apprehension*) Ängstlichkeit *f*

fearless ['fɪəlɪs] ADJ furchtlos; **~ of sth** ohne Angst *or* Furcht vor etw (*dat*); **to be ~ of heights/the consequences** keine Höhenangst/ keine Angst vor den Folgen haben, Höhen/die Folgen nicht fürchten

fearlessly ['fɪəlɪslɪ] ADV furchtlos

fearlessness ['fɪəlɪsnɪs] N Furchtlosigkeit *f*

fearsome ['fɪəsəm] ADJ Furcht erregend; **he was in a ~ rage** er hatte einen fürchterlichen Wutanfall

fearsomely ['fɪəsəmlɪ] ADV *efficient, powerful* erschreckend; **~ equipped with an array of weapons** mit einem Furcht einflößenden Waffenarsenal ausgerüstet

feasibility [ˌfiːzəˈbɪlɪtɪ] N **a** (*of plan etc*) Durchführbarkeit *f*, Machbarkeit *f*; **the ~ of doing sth** die Möglichkeit, etw zu tun; **I doubt the ~ of doing that** ich glaube nicht, dass das möglich *or* machbar ist **b** (= *plausibility: of story etc*) Wahrscheinlichkeit *f*

feasibility study N Machbarkeitsstudie *f*

feasible ['fiːzəbl] ADJ **a** (= *practicable*) möglich, machbar; *plan, proposition, alternative* durchführbar; *route* gangbar, möglich; **economically ~** wirtschaftlich machbar **b** (= *plausible*) *excuse, story, theory* plausibel, wahrscheinlich

feasibly ['fiːzəblɪ] ADV **a** (= *practicably*) **if it can ~ be done** wenn es machbar ist *or* praktisch möglich ist **b** (= *plausibly*) plausibel; **that could ~ be true** das könnte durchaus stimmen; **he could ~ still be alive** es ist durchaus möglich, dass er noch lebt

feast [fiːst] **N** **a** (= *banquet*) Festmahl *nt*, Festessen *nt*; (*Hist*) Festgelage *nt*; **a wedding ~** ein Hochzeitsmahl *nt* (*geh*); **a ~ for the eyes** eine Augenweide; **a ~ of entertainment** erstklassige Unterhaltung; **it's ~ or famine** (*fig*) alles oder nichts
b (*Eccl, Rel*) Fest *nt*; **~ day** Festtag *m*, Feiertag *m*; **movable/immovable ~** beweglicher/unbeweglicher Feiertag
VI (*lit*) Festgelage *pl*/ein Festgelage halten; **to ~ on sth** sich an etw (*dat*) gütlich tun; (*person also*) in etw (*dat*) schwelgen; (*fig*) sich an etw (*dat*) weiden
VT a *guest* festlich bewirten; **to ~ oneself** sich gütlich tun (*on* an +*dat*); (*person also*) schwelgen (*on* in +*dat*)
b **to ~ one's eyes on sb/sth** seine Augen an jdm/etw weiden

feat [fiːt] N Leistung *f*; (*heroic, courageous etc*) Heldentat *f*; (*skilful*) Kunststück *nt*, Meisterleistung *f*; **a ~ of courage/daring** eine mutige/wagemutige Tat

feather ['feðə] **N** Feder *f*; **~s** (= *plumage*) Gefieder *nt*; **~ headdress** Kopfschmuck *m* aus Federn; **as light as a ~** federleicht; **that's a ~ in his cap** das ist ein Ruhmesblatt *nt* für ihn; **you could have knocked me down with a ~** (*inf*) ich war wie vom Donner gerührt; **that'll make the ~s fly** das wird die Gemüter bewegen; **they are birds of a ~** sie sind von dem gleichen Schlag; **birds of a ~ stick** *or* **flock together** (*Prov*) Gleich und Gleich gesellt sich gern (*Prov*) → **white feather**
VT *arrow etc* mit Federn versehen; **to ~ one's nest** (*fig*) sein Schäfchen ins Trockene bringen
b (*Aviat*) *propeller* auf Segelstellung bringen **c** (*Rowing*) *oar* flach drehen **VI** (*Rowing*) das Ruderblatt flach drehen

feather: feather bed N mit Federn gefüllte Matratze; **featherbed** VT (*fig*) *person* verhätscheln; (*Ind, with grants*) verhätscheln; (*by overmanning*) unnötige Arbeitskräfte zugestehen (+*dat*); **featherbedding** N (*fig*) Hätscheln *nt*; (*with subsidies*) unnötige Subventionierung; **featherbrain** N Spatzenhirn *nt*; **featherbrained** ADJ dümmlich; **feather cut** N (= *hairstyle*) Stufenschnitt *m*; **feather duster** N Staubwedel *m*

feathered ['feðəd] ADJ gefiedert

featherweight ['feðəweɪt] N (*Boxing*) Federgewicht *nt*; (*fig*) Leichtgewicht *nt*; **~ champion** Meister *m* im Federgewicht

feathery ['feðərɪ] ADJ (+*er*) *fed(e)rig; feel, flakes* zart; **~ cloud** Federwolke *f*

feature ['fiːtʃə] **N** **a** (*facial*) (Gesichts)zug *m*; **to have strong/delicate ~s** markante/feine Gesichtszüge haben
b (= *characteristic*) Merkmal *nt*, Kennzeichen

nt, Charakteristikum nt; (of sb's character) Grundzug m; **a ~ of his style is ...** sein Stil ist durch ... gekennzeichnet; **a ~ of this book is ...** das Buch zeichnet sich durch ... aus; **special ~** Besonderheit f; **new ~** Neuheit f; **the main ~ of the recession** das Kennzeichnende an der Rezession

c (= focal point: of room, building etc) besonderes or herausragendes Merkmal; **~ fireplace** offener Kamin; **to make a ~ of sth** etw besonders betonen, etw zur Geltung bringen; **the main ~ of the new shopping mall** die Hauptattraktion des neuen Einkaufszentrums; **the old volcano, the dominant ~ of the island, ...** der die Insel dominierende alte Vulkan ...

d (Press) (Sonder)beitrag m, Feature nt; (Rad, TV) (Dokumentar)bericht m, Feature nt

e (= film) Spielfilm m

VT a (Press) story, picture bringen

b this film **~s an English actress** in diesem Film spielt eine englische Schauspielerin mit; **the album ~s their latest hit single** auf dem Album ist auch ihre neueste Hitsingle; **the room ~s a large fireplace** eine Besonderheit des Zimmers ist der große Kamin

VI a (= occur) vorkommen; **the story ~d on all today's front pages** die Geschichte war heute auf allen Titelseiten

b (Film) (mit)spielen

feature: **feature article** N Sonderbeitrag m, Feature nt; **feature film** N Spielfilm m; **feature-length** ADJ film mit Spielfilmlänge; **featureless** ADJ ohne besondere Merkmale; **feature story** N Sonderbericht m, Feature nt; **feature writer** N Feuilletonist(in) m(f)

Feb abbr of **February** Febr.

febrile ['fi:braɪl] ADJ fiebrig, fieberhaft

February ['februərɪ] N Februar m → **September**

fecal ['fi:kəl] ADJ (US) = **faecal**

feces ['fi:si:z] PL (US) = **faeces**

feckless ['feklɪs] ADJ nutzlos

fecund ['fi:kənd] ADJ (lit, fig) fruchtbar

fecundate ['fi:kəndeɪt] VT befruchten

fecundity [frˈkʌndɪtɪ] N (lit, fig) Fruchtbarkeit f

fed¹ [fed] pret, ptp of **feed**

fed² N (US, inf) FBI-Agent(in) m(f)

Fedayeen [fedɑˈjiːn] PL Freischärler pl

federal ['fedərəl] ADJ Bundes-; system etc föderalistisch; (US, Hist) föderalistisch; **~ state** Bundesstaat m; **~ bureau** Bundesamt nt; **the Federal Republic of Germany** die Bundesrepublik Deutschland; **Federal Insurance Contributions Act** (US) Gesetz über die Einbehaltung von Sozialversicherungsbeiträgen N (US) **a** (Hist) Föderalist m **b** (inf: in FBI) FBI-Agent(in) m(f)

> **FEDERAL**
>
> In den USA besagt der Begriff **federal** vor den Namen von Regierungsbehörden und Verantwortungsbereichen, dass diese Bundesbehörden und -kompetenzen sind und somit der US-Regierung in Washington unterstehen, nicht etwa den Regierungen der einzelnen Staaten. So verfolgt zum Beispiel das **Federal Bureau of Investigation**, besser bekannt als **FBI**, Verstöße gegen Bundesrecht, **federal law**.

federalism ['fedərəlɪzəm] N Föderalismus m

federalist ['fedərəlɪst] ADJ föderalistisch N Föderalist m

Federal Reserve Board N (US) Zentralbankrat m

Federal Trade Commission N (US) Bundesbehörde zur Bekämpfung des unlauteren Wettbewerbs und zur Durchführung der Kartellgesetze

federate ['fedəreɪt] VT zu einem Bund vereinigen or zusammenschließen, föderieren (rare) VI sich zu einem Bund zusammenschließen ADJ ['fedərɪt] verbündet, föderiert

federated ['fedəreɪtəd] ADJ state föderiert

federation [ˌfedəˈreɪʃən] N **a** (= act) Zusammenschluss m, Föderation f (rare) **b** (= league) Föderation f, Bund m

fedora [fɪˈdɔːrə] N Filzhut m

fed up ◊ 7.3 ADJ (inf) **I'm ~** ich habe die Nase voll (inf); **I'm ~ with him/it** er/es hängt mir zum Hals heraus (inf), ich habe ihn/es satt; **you look pretty ~** du siehst so aus, als hättest du die Nase voll (inf); **I'm ~ waiting for him** ich habe es satt or ich bin es leid, auf ihn zu warten

fee [fi:] N **a** Gebühr f; (of doctor, lawyer, artist, tutor) Honorar nt; (of stage performer) Gage f; (of director, administrator etc) Bezüge pl; (= membership fee) Beitrag m; **(school) ~s** Schulgeld nt; **on payment of a small ~** gegen geringe Gebühr **b** land held in **~ simple** (Jur) unbeschränkt vererbbares Land

feeble ['fi:bl] ADJ (+er) **a** (= weak) person schwach, schwächlich; light, voice schwach **b** (pej, = pathetic) person, effort, applause, support, smile schwach; attempt, performance kläglich; explanation, argument, idea wenig überzeugend; excuse faul (inf); joke lahm (inf); response halbherzig; **don't be so ~!** sei nicht so ein Waschlappen (inf)

feeble-minded [ˌfi:blˈmaɪndɪd] ADJ dümmlich

feebleness ['fi:blnɪs] N **a** (= weakness, of person) Schwäche f, Schwächlichkeit f; (of light, voice) Schwäche f **b** (pej, = pathetic nature) Kläglichkeit f; (of person, effort, applause, support) Schwäche f; (of excuse) Faulheit f (inf); (of joke) Lahmheit f (inf); (of response) Halbherzigkeit f; **the ~ of his argument** sein wenig überzeugendes Argument

feebly ['fi:blɪ] ADV shine, move, attempt, resist, applaud schwach; smile kläglich; say, explain wenig überzeugend; **he performed ~** er zeigte eine klägliche Leistung

feed [fi:d] vb: pret, ptp **fed** N **a** (= meal, of animals) Fütterung f; (of baby, inf: of person) Mahlzeit f; (= food, of animals) Futter nt; (inf, of person) Essen nt; **when is the baby's next ~?** wann wird das Baby wieder gefüttert?; **to have a good ~** (inf) tüchtig futtern (inf); **he's off his ~** (hum) er hat keinen Appetit

b (Theat) Stichwort nt

c (Tech, to machine) Versorgung f (to +gen); (to furnace) Beschickung f (to +gen); (to computer) Eingabe f (into in +acc)

VT a (= provide food for) person, army verpflegen; family ernähren; **I have three hungry mouths to ~** ich habe drei hungrige Münder zu stopfen (inf); **to ~ oneself** sich selbst verpflegen; **he ~s himself well** er isst gut

b (give food to) baby, invalid, animal füttern; plant düngen; **to (be able to) ~ oneself** (child) allein or ohne Hilfe essen (können); **to ~ sth to sb/an animal** jdm etw zu essen/einem Tier etw zu fressen geben; **they were fed to the lions** sie wurden den Löwen zum Fraß vorgeworfen

c (= supply) machine versorgen; furnace beschicken; computer füttern; meter Geld einwerfen in (+acc), füttern (hum); fire unterhalten, etwas legen auf (+acc); (fig) hope, imagination, rumour nähren, Nahrung geben (+dat); **two rivers ~ this reservoir** dieses Reservoir wird von zwei Flüssen gespeist; **he steals to ~ his heroin habit** er stiehlt, um sich mit Heroin zu versorgen; **blood vessels that ~ blood to the brain** Blutgefäße, die das Gehirn mit Blut versorgen; **to ~ sth into a machine** etw in eine Maschine geben; **to ~ information (in)to a computer** Informationen in einen Computer eingeben; **to ~ information to sb, to ~ sb (with) information** jdn mit Informationen versorgen; **to ~ sb lies** jdn systematisch belügen

d (Tech, = insert) führen; **to ~ sth along/ through a tube** etw an einem Röhrchen entlang/durch ein Röhrchen führen

e (Theat, fig) **to ~ sb (with) the right lines** jdm die richtigen Stichworte geben

VI (animal) fressen; (baby) gefüttert werden; (hum, person) futtern (inf)

▶ **feed back** VT sep facts, information zurückleiten (to an +acc); money zurückfließen lassen; (Elec) rückkoppeln; **by the time the information had been fed back to him** als die Informationen schließlich zu ihm zurückkamen; **to feed sth back into the computer** dem Computer etw wieder eingeben

▶ **feed in** VT sep tape, wire etc einführen (prep obj in +acc); facts, information eingeben (prep obj in +acc)

▶ **feed on** VI +prep obj sich (er)nähren von; (fig) sich nähren von VT sep +prep obj **to feed sb on sth** (animal, baby) jdn mit etw füttern; person jdn mit etw ernähren

▶ **feed up** VT sep animal mästen; **to feed sb up** jdn aufpäppeln → also **fed up**

feed: **feedback** N (Psych, Comput) Feed-back nt, Feedback nt, Rückmeldung f; (Elec) Rückkoppelung f; (fig) Reaktion f, Feed-back nt, Feedback nt; **~ of information** Rückinformation f; **everyone should try to get as much ~ as possible from the others** jeder sollte von den anderen möglichst viel Feed-back or Feedback bekommen; **to provide more ~ on sth** ausführlicher über etw (acc) berichten; **feedbag** N (US) Futtersack m; **to put on the ~** (inf) eine Mahlzeit einlegen

feeder ['fi:də] N **a** (= bottle) Flasche f; (for birds) Futterhalter m; (= net) Futternetz nt; **automatic ~** Futterautomat m

b (= eater) Esser(in) m(f); **the cow is a good ~** die Kuh frisst gut; **peonies are quite heavy ~s** (= need water/plant food) Pfingstrosen brauchen viel Wasser/Dünger

c (= device supplying machine) Zubringer m

d (= contributory source) (= river) Zu(bringer)-fluss m; (= road) Zubringer(straße f) m; (= air, bus, rail service) Zubringerlinie f; (Elec) Speiseleitung f, Feeder m

ATTR Zubringer-; **~ road** Zubringerstraße f; **~ pipe** Zuleitungsrohr nt; **~ line** (Rail, Aviat) Zubringerlinie f, Zubringerstrecke f; **~ service** Zubringerdienst m

feeding ['fi:dɪŋ]: **feeding bottle** N Flasche f; **feeding cup** N Schnabeltasse f; **feeding frenzy** N **a** (lit) Futterstreit m **b** (fig) **the press was in a ~** die Presse riss sich um die Story; **feeding ground** N Futterplatz m; **feeding time** N (for animal) Fütterungszeit f; (for baby) Zeit f für die Mahlzeit; **the baby's ~ was still an hour away** die nächste Mahlzeit des Säuglings war erst in einer Stunde fällig

feel [fi:l] ◊ 3.1, 6.2, 7.1, 8.4 vb: pret, ptp **felt** VT **a** (= touch) fühlen; (examining) befühlen; **to ~ one's way** sich vortasten; **I'm still ~ing my way (in my new job)** ich versuche noch, mich (in meiner neuen Stelle) zurechtzufinden; **to ~ one's way into sth** (fig) sich in etw (acc) einfühlen

b (= be aware of by touching, feeling) prick, sun etc fühlen, spüren; **I can't ~ anything in my left leg** ich habe kein Gefühl im linken Bein; **I felt it move** ich spürte, wie es sich bewegte

c (= be conscious of in oneself) regret, joy, fear etc fühlen, empfinden; effects spüren; **I felt myself blush** ich merkte or spürte, dass ich rot wurde; **he felt a sense of regret** er empfand Bedauern; **can't you ~ the sadness in this music?** können Sie nicht empfinden, wie traurig diese Musik ist?; **she felt his eyes on her** sie merkte or spürte, wie er sie ansah

d (= be affected by) heat, cold, insult, loss leiden unter (+dat); **I don't ~ the cold as much as he does** die Kälte macht mir nicht so viel aus wie ihm; **a right hook which he really felt** ein rechter Haken, der saß; **she's fallen, I bet she felt that!** sie ist hingefallen, das hat bestimmt wehgetan!; **I felt that!** (pain) das hat wehgetan!

e (= think) glauben; **what do you ~ about him/ it?** was halten Sie von ihm/davon?; **it was felt that ...** man war der Meinung, dass ...; **he felt it necessary** er hielt es für notwendig; **don't ~ you have to ...** glauben Sie nicht, Sie müssten ...; **I can't help ~ing that ...** ich kann mir nicht helfen, ich glaube, dass ...

VI a (*indicating physical or mental state: person*) sich fühlen; **to ~ well/ill/apprehensive** sich wohl/elend/unsicher fühlen; **I ~ sick** mir ist schlecht; **how do you ~ today?** wie fühlen Sie sich heute?; **to ~ convinced/certain** überzeugt/sicher sein; **to ~ hungry/thirsty/sleepy** hungrig/durstig/müde sein; **I ~ hot/cold** mir ist heiß/kalt; **I felt very touched by his remarks** ich war sehr gerührt von seinen Bemerkungen; **I ~ much better** ich fühle mich viel besser, es geht mir viel besser; **you'll ~ (all) the better for a bath** ein Bad wird Ihnen gut tun; **he doesn't ~ quite himself today** er ist heute nicht ganz auf der Höhe; **I felt sad/strange** mir war traurig/komisch zumute or zu Mute; **I felt as though I'd never been away** mir war, als ob ich nie weg gewesen wäre; **I felt as if I was going to be sick** ich dachte, mir würde schlecht werden; **how do you ~ about him?** (*emotionally*) was empfinden Sie für ihn?; **you can imagine what I felt like** or **how I felt** Sie können sich (*dat*) vorstellen, wie mir zumute or zu Mute war

b (= *feel to the touch: material, ground, bricks etc*) sich anfühlen; **to ~ hard/soft/rough etc** sich hart/weich/rau etc anfühlen; **the room/air ~s warm** das Zimmer/die Luft kommt einem warm vor; **my skin ~s tight** mir spannt die Haut; **the shirt ~s as though it's made of silk** das Hemd fühlt sich so an, als sei es aus Seide

c (= *think, have opinions*) meinen; **how do you ~ about the idea/going for a walk?** was halten Sie von ihm/der Idee/von einem Spaziergang?; **how do you ~ about these developments?** was meinen Sie zu dieser Entwicklung?; **that's just how I ~** das meine ich auch, ich bin genau derselben Meinung

d to ~ like (= *have desire for*) Lust haben auf (+*acc*); *food also* Appetit haben auf (+*acc*); **I ~ like something to eat** ich möchte jetzt gern etwas essen; **I ~ like going for a walk** ich habe Lust spazieren zu gehen; **I felt like screaming/crying/giving up** ich hätte am liebsten geschrien/geheult/aufgegeben, ich hätte schreien/heulen/aufgeben können; **if you ~ like it** wenn Sie Lust haben, wenn Sie wollen or gern möchten

e *impers* **what does it ~ like** or **how does it ~ to be all alone?** wie fühlt man sich or wie ist das so ganz allein?; **what does it ~ like** or **how does it ~ to be the boss?** wie fühlt man sich als Chef?, was ist das für ein Gefühl, Chef zu sein?; **it ~s like flying** es ist wie Fliegen

N *no pl* **a let me have a ~ (of it)!** lass (mich) mal fühlen!

b (= *quality when touched*) **it has a velvety/papery ~** es fühlt sich samten/wie Papier an; **he loved the ~ of her skin** er liebte es, wie sich ihre Haut anfühlte; **he recognizes things by their ~** er erkennt Dinge daran, wie sie sich anfühlen; **I don't like the ~ of wool against my skin** ich mag Wolle nicht auf der Haut; **I like the ~ of the sun on my face** ich spüre gerne die Sonne im Gesicht

c (= *quality*) **the room has a cosy ~** das Zimmer hat eine gemütliche Atmosphäre; **there's a nostalgic ~ to his music** seine Musik klingt nostalgisch

d (*fig*) **to get/have a ~ for sth** ein Gefühl *nt* für etw bekommen/haben; **to get the ~ for sth** ein Gefühl *nt* für etw bekommen; **you must get the ~ of the poem** Sie müssen sich in das Gedicht einfühlen

▶ **feel about** (*Brit*) or **around** VI umhertasten; (*in drawer, bag etc*) herumsuchen, herumtasten

▶ **feel for** VI +*prep obj* **a** (= *sympathize with*) (mit)fühlen mit, Mitgefühl haben mit; **I feel for you** Sie tun mir Leid **b** (= *search* or *grope for*) tasten nach; (*in pocket, bag etc*) kramen nach

▶ **feel up** VT *sep* (*esp US inf: sexually*) befummeln (*inf*)

▶ **feel up to** VI +*prep obj* sich gewachsen fühlen (+*dat*)

feeler ['fiːlə] **N a** (*Zool*) Fühler *m*; (*of sea animal*) Tentakel *m* or *nt* **b** (*fig*) Fühler *m*; **to put out ~s** seine Fühler ausstrecken **c feelers** PL (*also* **feeler gauge**) Fühl(er)lehre *f*

feelgood ['fiːlgʊd] ADJ *film, song* Feelgood-; **the ~ factor** (*Pol*) der Feelgood-Faktor

feeling ['fiːlɪŋ] **N a** (= *sense of touch*) Gefühl *nt*, Empfindung *f*; **I've lost all ~ in my right arm** ich habe kein Gefühl mehr im rechten Arm

b (= *physical, mental sensation, emotion*) Gefühl *nt*; **a ~ of pain/warmth** ein Gefühl *nt* des Schmerzes/der Wärme; **I had a ~ of isolation** ich kam mir ganz isoliert vor; **he doesn't have much ~ for his sister** er hat nicht viel für seine Schwester übrig; **his voice trembled with ~** seine Stimme bebte vor Gefühl; **I know the ~** ich weiß, wie das ist

c (= *presentiment*) (Vor)gefühl *nt*; **I've a funny ~ she won't come** ich hab so das Gefühl, dass sie nicht kommt

d (= *opinion: also* **feelings**) Meinung *f*, Ansicht *f* (*on* zu); **there was a general ~ that ...** man war allgemein der Ansicht, dass ...; **ill** or **bad ~** Verstimmung *f*; **good ~** Wohlwollen *nt*; **there's been a lot of bad ~ about this decision** wegen dieser Entscheidung hat es viel böses Blut gegeben

e (= *talent*) Gefühl *nt*

f ~s Gefühle *pl*; **to have ~s for sb** Gefühle für jdn haben; **you've hurt his ~s** Sie haben ihn verletzt; **no hard ~s!** ich nehme es dir nicht übel; **no hard ~s?** nimm es mir nicht übel

feet [fiːt] *pl of* **foot**

FEFC (*Brit*) *abbr of* **Further Education Funding Council** *Organisation, die über die Finanzierung der Erwachsenenbildung entscheidet*

feign [feɪn] VT vortäuschen; *friendship, interest, sympathy, feelings also* heucheln; **to ~ illness/madness** simulieren, sich krank/verrückt stellen; **to ~ sleep/death** sich schlafend/tot stellen

feigned [feɪnd] ADJ vorgeblich *attr*; *illness also* simuliert; *interest, sympathy etc also* vorgetäuscht, geheuchelt

feint [feɪnt] **N** (*Sport*) Finte *f*; **to make a ~** eine Finte anwenden (*at* gegenüber); **he made a ~ to the left and shot to the right** er hat links angetäuscht und nach rechts geschossen **VI** (*Sport*) fintieren, eine Finte anwenden (*also fig*); **he ~ed with the left and hit with the right** er hat links angetäuscht und rechts zugeschlagen

feint(-ruled) ['feɪnt(ruːld)] ADJ fein liniert

feisty ['faɪstɪ] ADJ (+*er*) (= *spirited*) robust; (*inf, = lively*) lebhaft, lebendig

felicitate [fɪ'lɪsɪteɪt] VT (*form*) beglückwünschen (*sb on sth* jdn zu etw), gratulieren (*sb on sth* jdm zu etw)

felicitation [fɪˌlɪsɪ'teɪʃən] **N** *usu pl* (*form*) Glückwunsch *m*; **my ~s** herzliche Glückwünsche, ich gratuliere

felicitous ADJ , **felicitously** ADV [fɪ'lɪsɪtəs, -lɪ] (*form*) glücklich

felicity [fɪ'lɪsɪtɪ] **N** (*form*) **a** (= *happiness*) Glück *nt*, Glückseligkeit *f* (*geh*) **b** (= *aptness*) **he expresses himself with ~** er drückt sich sehr glücklich aus; **the ~ of the expression** die glückliche Wahl des Ausdrucks

feline ['fiːlaɪn] ADJ (*lit*) Katzen-; *species* der Katzen; (*fig*) *grace, suppleness* katzenartig, katzenhaft; **~ eyes** Katzenaugen *pl* **N** Katze *f*

fell[1] [fel] *pret of* **fall**

fell[2] **N** (= *skin*) Fell *nt*, Balg *m*

fell[3] ADJ (*liter*) fürchterlich → **swoop**

fell[4] VT *tree* fällen, schlagen; *person* niederstrecken, zu Boden strecken; *animal* zur Strecke bringen

fell[5] **N** (*N Engl*, = *mountain*) Berg *m*; (= *moor*) Moorland *nt*

fellah ['felə] **N a** Fellache *m*, Fellachin *f* **b** = **fellow[1] a**

fellatio [fɪ'leɪʃɪəʊ] **N** Fellatio *f*

fellow[1] ['feləʊ] **N a** Mann *m*, Kerl *m* (*usu pej*), Typ *m* (*inf*); (*inf*, = *boyfriend*) Freund *m*, Typ *m* (*inf*); **a nice/friendly ~** ein netter/freundlicher Kerl; **a clever ~** ein gescheiter Bursche, ein cleverer Typ (*inf*); **poor ~!** der Arme!; **listen to me, ~** (*US, inf*) hör mal her, Mann (*inf*); **an old**

~ ein alter Mann or Knabe (*inf*); **look here, old ~** hör mal her, alter Junge (*inf*); **young ~** junger Bursche; **this journalist ~** dieser komische Journalist; **my dear ~** mein lieber Freund or Mann (*inf*); **who is this ~?** wer ist denn der Typ (*inf*) or Kerl da?; **this ~ here** dieser Herr, dieser Typ (*inf*); (*rude*) dieser Kerl hier; **I'm not the sort of ~ who ...** ich bin nicht der Typ, der ... (*sl*); **a ~ needs a bit of rest sometimes** (*inf*) man braucht doch auch mal 'ne Pause (*inf*)

b (= *comrade*) Kamerad *m*, Kumpel *m* (*inf*); (= *colleague*) Kollege *m*, Kollegin *f*; **~s in distress** Leidensgenossen *pl*; **to get together with one's ~s** mit seinesgleichen zusammenkommen

c (*Univ*) Fellow *m* → **research fellow**

d (*of a society*) Mitglied *nt*

e (*of things*: = *one of a pair*) Gegenstück *nt*

fellow[2] PREF **our ~ bankers/doctors** unsere Kollegen *pl* (im Bankwesen/in der Ärzteschaft), unsere Berufskollegen *pl*; **our ~ guests** die anderen Gäste; **~ inmates** Mitinsassen *pl*; **~ member** (*in club*) Klubkamerad(in) *m(f)*; (*in party*) Parteigenosse *m*/-genossin *f*; **~ passenger** Mitreisende(r) *mf*; **~ student** Kommilitone *m*, Kommilitonin *f*; **~ sufferer** Leidensgenosse *m*/-genossin *f*; **~ worker** Kollege *m*, Kollegin *f*, Mitarbeiter(in) *m(f)*; **~ writers** Schriftstellerkollegen *pl*; **our ~ communists** unsere kommunistischen Gesinnungsgenossen; **he is a ~ lexicographer** er ist auch Lexikograf; **"fellow Americans..."** „meine lieben amerikanischen Mitbürger..."

fellow: fellow being N Mitmensch *m*; **fellow citizen** N Mitbürger(in) *m(f)*; **fellow countryman** N (= *man*) Landsmann *m*; (= *woman*) Landsmännin *f*, Landsfrau *f*; **fellow countrymen** PL Landsleute *pl*; **fellow creature** N Mitmensch *m*; **fellow feeling** N Mitgefühl *nt*; (= *togetherness*) Zusammengehörigkeitsgefühl *nt*; **fellow men** PL Mitmenschen *pl*

fellowship ['feləʊʃɪp] **N a** *no pl* Kameradschaft *f*; (= *company*) Gesellschaft *f*; (*Eccl*) Gemeinschaft *f*; **... who lived without the ~ of other men** ..., der keinen Umgang mit anderen Menschen hatte; **there's no sense of ~ here** hier herrscht kein kameradschaftlicher Geist **b** (*Univ*, = *scholarship*) Forschungsstipendium *nt*; (= *job*) Position eines Fellow

fellow traveller, (*US*) **fellow traveler** N **a** (*lit*) Mitreisende(r) *mf* **b** (*Pol*) Sympathisant(in) *m(f)*

fell runner ['felrʌnə] N Geländeläufer(in) *m(f)* (*über bergiges Gebiet*)

felon ['felən] N (Schwer)verbrecher(in) *m(f)*

felonious [fɪ'ləʊnɪəs] ADJ verbrecherisch

felony ['felənɪ] N (schweres) Verbrechen

felspar ['felspɑː] N Feldspat *m*

felt[1] [felt] *pret, ptp of* **feel**

felt[2] **N** Filz *m* → **roofing** ADJ *attr* Filz-; **~ hat** Filzhut *m* **VI** (*wool etc*) (ver)filzen

felt-tip (pen) ['felttɪp('pen)] N Filzstift *m*, Filzschreiber *m*

felucca [fe'lʌkə] N Feluke *f*

female ['fiːmeɪl] ADJ **a** weiblich; *labour, rights* Frauen-; **a ~ doctor/student/dog** eine Ärztin/Studentin/Hündin; **~ bear** Bärenweibchen *nt*; **a ~ companion** eine Gesellschafterin; **a ~ football team** eine Damenfußballmannschaft; **a typical ~ attitude** typisch Frau **b** (*Tech*) *connector, plug* weiblich, Innen-; **~ screw** (Schrauben)mutter *f*, Mutterschraube *f*; **~ thread** Mutter- or Innengewinde *nt* **N a** (= *animal*) Weibchen *nt* **b** (*inf*: = *woman*) Frau *f*; (*pej*) Weib *nt* (*pej*), Weibsbild *nt* (*pej inf*); **a typical ~** eine typische Frau; **to eye up all the ~s** die Frauen or Miezen (*inf*) beäugen

female: female condom N Femidom® *nt*, Kondom *nt* für die Frau; **female impersonator** N Damen-Imitator *m*

Femidom® ['femɪdɒm] N Femidom® *nt*, Kondom *nt* für die Frau

feminine ['femɪnɪn] ADJ **a** *person, clothes, look, perfume, voice* feminin; *beauty, role, qualities, na-*

ture weiblich; (*Anat, Biol*) weiblich; **a ~ occupation** ein Frauenberuf *m*; **~ wiles** weibliche Listen *pl*; **his ~ side** seine weibliche *or* feminine Seite **b** (*Gram*) *noun, pronoun, ending* weiblich, feminin (*spec*) **N** (*Gram*) Femininum *nt*

feminine hygiene N Monatshygiene *f*; **~ products** Monatshygieneartikel *pl*

femininity [ˌfemɪˈnɪnɪtɪ] N Weiblichkeit *f*

feminism [ˈfemɪnɪzəm] N Feminismus *m*, Frauenrechtlertum *nt*

feminist [ˈfemɪnɪst] **N** Feminist(in) *m(f)* **ADJ** feministisch; **I've always been fairly ~** ich war schon immer ziemlich feministisch eingestellt; **the ~ movement** die Frauenbewegung

feminize [ˈfemɪnaɪz] VT weiblich machen, eine weibliche Note verleihen

femme fatale [ˌfæmfəˈtɑːl] N *pl* **femmes fatales** Femme fatale *f*

femur [ˈfiːmə'] N Oberschenkelknochen *m*

fen [fen] N Moor- *or* Sumpfland *nt*; **the Fens** *die Niederungen in East Anglia*

fence [fens] **N** **a** Zaun *m*; (*Sport*) Hindernis *nt*; **to sit on the ~** (*fig, = be neutral*) neutral bleiben, nicht Partei ergreifen; (= *be irresolute*) unschlüssig sein, zaudern; **on the wrong/other side of the ~** (*fig*) auf der verkehrten/anderen Seite; **to mend ~s** (*fig*) die Dinge bereinigen **b** (*inf, = receiver of stolen goods*) Hehler(in) *m(f)* **c** (*Tech*) Anschlag *m* **VT** **a** (*also* **fence in**) land einzäunen, umzäunen **b** (*Sport*) fechten gegen **c** (*inf*) hehlen; **until we find somebody to ~ stolen cars …** bis wir einen Hehler für gestohlene Autos finden … **VI** **a** (*Sport*) fechten **b** (*fig*) ausweichen; **to ~ with sb** sich (*dat*) mit jdm ein Wortgefecht liefern; (*evading questions*) jdm ausweichen **c** (*inf, = receive stolen goods*) hehlen, mit Diebesgut handeln

▸ **fence in** VT *sep* **a** (*lit*) einzäunen, umzäunen, mit einem Zaun umgeben **b** (*fig*) **to fence sb in** jdn in seiner Freiheit einschränken *or* beschränken, jds Freiheit beschneiden *or* einengen; **don't fence me in** lass mir meine Freiheit; **to feel fenced in by restrictions** sich von Beschränkungen eingeengt fühlen

▸ **fence off** VT *sep piece of land* abzäunen; **to fence oneself off (from sb)** (*fig*) sich (von jdm) absondern

fence-mending [ˈfensˌmendɪŋ] N (*esp Pol fig*) Bereinigung *f* der Lage

fencer [ˈfensə'] N Fechter(in) *m(f)*

fencing [ˈfensɪŋ] N **a** (*Sport*) Fechten *nt*; **~ instructor** Fechtlehrer(in) *or* -meister(in) *m(f)*; **~ school** Fechtschule *f* **b** (= *fences, material*) Zaun *m*, Einzäunung *f*

fend [fend] VI **to ~ for oneself** (= *provide*) für sich (selbst) sorgen, sich allein durchbringen; (= *defend*) sich (selbst) verteidigen; **could she ~ for herself in the city?** konnte sie sich in der Stadt allein durchschlagen?

▸ **fend off** VT *sep* abwehren; *attacker also* vertreiben; *criticism* zurückweisen; *competition* ausschalten

fender [ˈfendə'] N **a** (*in front of fire*) Kamingitter *nt* **b** (*US*) (*on car*) Kotflügel *m*; (*on bicycle etc*) Schutzblech *nt* **c** (*Naut*) Fender *m* **d** (*US, on train, streetcar*) Puffer *m*

fender-bender [ˈfendəˌbendə'] N (*US, inf*) kleiner Blechschaden

fenestration [ˌfenɪsˈtreɪʃən] N **a** (*Archit*) Fensteranordnung *f* **b** (*Med*) Fensterungsoperation *f*

fen fire N Irrlicht *nt*

feng shui [ˌfeŋˈʃuːɪ] N Feng Shui *nt*

fennel [ˈfenl] N (*Bot*) Fenchel *m*

feoff [fiːf] N (*old, form, = land*) Lehen *nt*

feral [ˈferəl] ADJ *attr animal, child* verwildert; (*fig*) *features, quickness* wild; **~ cat** Wildkatze *f*

ferment [ˈfɜːment] **N** **a** (= *fermentation*) Gärung *f*; (= *substance*) Ferment *nt*, Gärstoff *m* **b** (*fig*)

Unruhe *f*, Erregung *f*; **the city was in ~** es brodelte *or* gärte in der Stadt **VI** [fəˈment](*lit, fig*) gären; (*plan also*) (aus)reifen **VT** [fəˈment](*lit*) fermentieren, zur Gärung bringen; (*fig*) anwachsen lassen

fermentation [ˌfɜːmenˈteɪʃən] N **a** Gärung *f*; (*fig, of plan etc*) Ausreifen *nt* **b** (*fig, = excitement*) Aufregung *f*, Unruhe *f*

fermentation lock N Gärventil *nt*

fern [fɜːn] N Farn(kraut *nt*) *m*

ferocious [fəˈrəʊʃəs] ADJ **a** (= *fierce*) *animal, person, appearance* wild; *dog* äußerst bissig; (= *trained to attack*) scharf; *look, glare* grimmig; *battle, war* erbittert; *debate, argument* heftig; *attack* brutal; *competition, criticism* scharf, heftig; **a ~ beast** eine reißende Bestie; **to have a ~ temper** zu heftigen Wutanfällen neigen; **he came under ~ attack from the Opposition** er wurde von der Opposition aufs schärfste *or* Schärfste angegriffen **b** (= *vicious-looking*) *knife, dagger, teeth* Furcht erregend **c** (= *extreme*) *heat* glühend; *storm* heftig; *climate* unerträglich; *thirst* brennend; *energy* grimmig

ferociously [fəˈrəʊʃəslɪ] ADV **a** (= *violently*) *hit, fight, resist, argue* heftig; *criticize, attack* aufs schärfste *or* Schärfste; *glare* grimmig; *bark, roar* wütend; **~ determined** wild entschlossen; **the market is ~ competitive** auf dem Markt herrscht ein gnadenloser Wettbewerb **b** (*emph, = extremely*) *tough, difficult* äußerst

ferocity [fəˈrɒsɪtɪ] N (*of animal*) Wildheit *f*; (*of dog*) Bissigkeit *f*; (*of appearance, look, glare*) Grimmigkeit *f*; (*of battle, war, debate, argument, competition, criticism*) Heftigkeit *f*; (*of attack*) Brutalität *f*

ferret [ˈferɪt] **N** Frettchen *nt* **VI** **a** (*Sport: also* **go ferreting**) mit dem Frettchen jagen **b** (*also* ferret about *or* around) herumstöbern *or* -schnüffeln (*pej*); **she was ~ing (about *or* around) among my books** sie schnüffelte in meinen Büchern (herum); **he was ~ing (around) for information** er schnüffelte nach Informationen (herum)

▸ **ferret out** VT *sep* (*Brit inf*) aufstöbern, aufspüren

ferric [ˈferɪk] ADJ Eisen-; **~ oxide** Eisenoxid *nt*

Ferris wheel [ˈferɪsˌwiːl] N Riesenrad *nt*

ferrite [ˈferaɪt] N Ferrit *m*; **~ rod** Ferritstab *m*

ferrite-rod aerial [ˈferaɪtˌrɒdˈɛərɪəl] N Ferritantenne *f*

ferroconcrete [ˌferəʊˈkɒŋkriːt] N Eisen- *or* Stahlbeton *m*

ferrous [ˈferəs] ADJ Eisen-; **~ chloride** Eisenchlorid *nt*

ferrule [ˈferuːl] N (*of umbrella, cane*) Zwinge *f*, Ring *m*

ferry [ˈferɪ] **N** Fähre *f* **VT** **a** (*also* **ferry across** *or* **over**) (*by boat*) übersetzen; (*by plane, car etc*) transportieren, bringen; **to ~ sb across** *or* **over a river** jdn über einen Fluss setzen; **to ~ sb/sth back and forth** jdn/etw hin- und herbringen; **he ferried voters to and from the polls** er fuhr Wähler zum Wahllokal und wieder nach Hause **b** (= *deliver*) *plane* überführen

ferry: ferryboat N Fährboot *nt*; **ferryman** N Fährmann *m*

fertile [ˈfɜːtaɪl] ADJ **a** (*Agr, Biol*) *land, region, woman, man, animal* fruchtbar; *soil* ergiebig; *egg, ovum* befruchtungsfähig; **the ~ period** *or* **time** die fruchtbaren Tage *pl* **b** (*fig, = productive*) *mind, brain* produktiv; *imagination, period* fruchtbar; **the idea fell on ~ ground** der Gedanke fiel auf fruchtbaren Boden; **this is ~ ground for racists/ethnic hatred** das ist fruchtbarer Boden für Rassisten/Rassenhass

fertility [fəˈtɪlɪtɪ] N (*lit, fig*) Fruchtbarkeit *f*; (*of soil, seed also*) Ergiebigkeit *f*; (*fig, of mind, brain*) Produktivität *f*

fertility: fertility cult N Fruchtbarkeitskult *m*; **fertility drug** N Fruchtbarkeitspille *f*; **fertility symbol** N Fruchtbarkeitssymbol *nt*

fertilization [ˌfɜːtɪlaɪˈzeɪʃən] N Befruchtung *f*; (*of soil*) Düngung *f*

---

fertilize [ˈfɜːtɪlaɪz] VT *animal, egg, flower* befruchten; *land, soil* düngen

fertilizer [ˈfɜːtɪlaɪzə'] N Dünger *m*, Düngemittel *nt*; **artificial ~** Kunstdünger *m*

ferule [ˈferuːl] N **a** Stock *m* **b** = **ferrule**

fervency [ˈfɜːvənsɪ] N = **fervour**

fervent [ˈfɜːvənt] ADJ *supporter, belief, advocate, nationalist, socialist* leidenschaftlich; *admirer* glühend; *hope, prayer, wish, desire* inbrünstig (*geh*); **she is a ~ believer in free trade** sie glaubt leidenschaftlich an den freien Handel

fervently [ˈfɜːvəntlɪ] ADV leidenschaftlich; *hope, wish, pray* inbrünstig (*geh*); **~ religious** tiefreligiös

fervid [ˈfɜːvɪd] ADJ (*form*) = **fervent**

fervidly [ˈfɜːvɪdlɪ] ADV (*form*) = **fervently**

fervour, (*US*) **fervor** [ˈfɜːvə'] N Leidenschaftlichkeit *f*; (*of public speaker*) Leidenschaft *f*; (*of hope, prayer, wish*) Inbrunst *f* (*geh*)

fest [fest] N (*inf*) Festival *nt*; **film/jazz ~** Film-/Jazzfestival *nt*; **gore ~** (= *film*) blutrünstiger Film

fester [ˈfestə'] VI eitern, schwären (*old*); (*fig, insult, resentment etc*) nagen, fressen; **~ing sore** (*fig*) Eiterbeule *f*

festival [ˈfestɪvəl] N **a** (*Eccl etc*) Fest *nt*; **Church ~s** kirchliche Feste *pl*, kirchliche Feiertage *pl*; **Festival of Lights** Lichterfest *nt* **b** (*cultural*) Festspiele *pl*, Festival *nt*; **the Edinburgh Festival** das Edinburgher Festival; **the Salzburg Festival** die Salzburger Festspiele *pl*

festive [ˈfestɪv] ADJ festlich; **the ~ season** die Festzeit; **he was in (a) ~ mood** er war in festlicher Stimmung *or* in Festtagslaune

festivity [feˈstɪvɪtɪ] N **a** (= *gaiety*) Feststimmung *f*, Feiertagsstimmung *f*; **there was an air of ~ in the office** im Büro herrschte Feststimmung *f* **b** (= *celebration*) Feier *f*; **festivities** *pl* (= *festive proceedings*) Feierlichkeiten *pl*, Festivitäten *pl* (*hum*)

festoon [feˈstuːn] **N** Girlande *f*; (*in curtain etc, Archit*) Feston *m* **VT** **to ~ sb with sth** jdn mit etw behängen; **to ~ sth with sth** etw mit etw schmücken *or* verzieren; **to be ~ed with sth** mit etw behängt sein; **lace curtains ~ed the windows** Spitzengardinen schmückten die Fenster

feta (cheese) [ˈfetə(ˈtʃiːz)] N Feta(käse) *m*

fetal [ˈfiːtl] ADJ (*esp US*) = **foetal**

fetch [fetʃ] **VT** **a** (= *bring*) holen; (= *collect*) *person, thing* abholen; **would you ~ a handkerchief for me** *or* **me a handkerchief?** kannst du mir ein Taschentuch holen (gehen)?; **I'll ~ her from the station** ich hole sie vom Bahnhof ab; **she ~ed in the washing** sie holte die Wäsche herein; **he's upstairs, I'll ~ him down** er ist oben, ich hole ihn herunter **b** (= *bring in*) *£10 etc* (ein)bringen **c** (*inf*) **to ~ sb a blow** jdm eine langen (*inf*); (*accidentally: with rucksack etc*) jdn erwischen (*inf*) **VI** **a** **to ~ and carry for sb** bei jdm Mädchen für alles sein **b** (*Naut*) Kurs halten; (= *change course*) Kurs nehmen

▸ **fetch up** **VI** (*inf*) landen (*inf*) **VT** *sep* (*Brit, = vomit*) wieder von sich geben, erbrechen

fetching [ˈfetʃɪŋ] ADJ attraktiv, reizend; *smile* gewinnend, einnehmend

fetchingly [ˈfetʃɪŋlɪ] ADV attraktiv, reizend; *smile* gewinnend; *pretty* bezaubernd

fête [feɪt] **N** Fest *nt*; **village ~** Dorffest *nt* **VT** (= *make much of*) *sb, sb's success* feiern; **to ~ sb** (= *entertain*) zu jds Ehren ein Fest geben; **a much ~d actress** eine gefeierte Schauspielerin

fetid [ˈfetɪd] ADJ übel riechend

fetidness [ˈfetɪdnɪs] N Gestank *m*

fetish [ˈfetɪʃ] N Fetisch *m*; **to have a ~ for leather/cleanliness** einen Leder-/Sauberkeitstick haben (*inf*), ein Leder-/Sauberkeitsfetischist *m* sein; **to make a ~ of sth** einen Kult mit etw treiben, etw zum Fetisch machen *or* erheben

fetishism [ˈfetɪʃɪzəm] N Fetischismus *m*

fetishist [ˈfetɪʃɪst] N Fetischist(in) *m(f)*

fetishistic [ˌfetɪˈʃɪstɪk] ADJ fetischistisch

fetlock ['fetlɒk] N Fessel f; (joint) Fesselgelenk nt

fetter ['fetə'] **VT** prisoner fesseln; goat anpflocken; (fig) in Fesseln legen **N** ~s pl (Fuß)fesseln pl; (fig) Fesseln pl; **to put a prisoner in ~s** einen Gefangenen in Fesseln legen

fettle ['fetl] N **to be in fine or good ~** in bester Form sein; (as regards health also) in bester Verfassung or topfit (inf) sein

fettucine [,fetə'tʃiːnɪ] N , no pl Fettucine pl

fetus ['fiːtəs] N (US) = **foetus**

feu [fjuː] N (Scot) Lehen nt

feud [fjuːd] (lit, fig) **N** Fehde f; **to have a ~ with sb** mit jdm in Fehde liegen **VI** sich befehden, in Fehde liegen

feudal ['fjuːdl] ADJ Feudal-, feudal; ~ **system** Feudalsystem nt; ~ **landowner** Feudal- or Lehnsherr m

feudalism ['fjuːdəlɪzəm] N Feudalismus m, Lehnswesen nt

feu duty N (Scot) Lehnsabgabe f

fever ['fiːvə'] N **a** Fieber nt no pl; **tropical ~s** tropische Fieberkrankheiten pl; **to have a ~** eine Fieberkrankheit haben; (= high temperature) Fieber haben **b** (fig) Aufregung f, Erregung f, Fieber nt; **election ~** Wahlfieber nt, Wahlrausch m; **in a ~ of excitement** in fieberhafter Erregung

feverish ['fiːvərɪʃ] ADJ **a** (= frenzied, frantic) excitement, activity, haste, pace, effort fieberhaft; speculation wild; atmosphere, expectation fiebrig; **to be ~ with excitement** vor Aufregung fiebern; **to work at a ~ pace** in fieberhafter Eile arbeiten **b** (Med) person fiebrig; condition, illness fieberhaft; **to be ~** Fieber haben; ~ **dream** Fiebertraum m; ~ **sweat** Fieberschweiß m

feverishly ['fiːvərɪʃlɪ] ADV **a** (= frantically) work, try fieberhaft; (= agitatedly) await erregt; ~ **impatient** fiebernd vor Ungeduld; **the market is ~ busy** auf dem Markt herrscht eine fieberhafte Tätigkeit **b** sleep, toss fiebrig; talk im Fieber

feverishness ['fiːvərɪʃnɪs] N **a** (= frantic nature) Fieberhaftigkeit f **b** (Med) Fiebrigkeit f

fever pitch N **at ~** auf dem Siedepunkt; **to reach ~** am Siedepunkt angelangt sein, den Siedepunkt erreichen; **to be working at ~** auf Hochtouren arbeiten

few [fjuː] **ADJ** (+er) **a** (= not many) wenige; ~ **people come to see him** nur wenige Leute besuchen ihn; **with ~ exceptions** mit wenigen Ausnahmen; **we are very ~** wir sind nur sehr wenige or nur ein kleines Häufchen; ~ **and far between** dünn gesät; **as ~ as ten cigarettes a day can be harmful** schon or bereits zehn Zigaretten am Tag können schädlich sein; **as ~ as six objections** bloß sechs Einwände, nicht mehr als sechs Einwände; **how ~ they are!** wie wenige das sind!; **so ~ books** so wenige Bücher; **too ~ cakes** zu wenige Kuchen; **there were 3 too ~** es waren 3 zu wenig da; **10 would not be too ~** 10 wären nicht zu wenig; **he is one of the ~ people who ...** er ist einer der wenigen, die ...; **the exceptions are ~** es gibt nur wenige Ausnahmen; **such occasions are ~** solche Gelegenheiten sind selten or rar

b a ~ ein paar; **a very ~** nur ganz wenige; **a ~ more days** noch ein paar Tage; **a ~ times** ein paar Male; **there were quite a ~ waiting** ziemlich viele warteten; **he has quite a ~ girlfriends** er hat eine ganze Menge or ziemlich viele Freundinnen; **he's had a ~ (too many)** er hat einen über den Durst getrunken; **quite a ~ books** ziemlich viele Bücher, eine ganze Menge Bücher; **I saw a good ~** or **quite a ~ people** ich habe ziemlich viele Leute or eine ganze Menge Leute gesehen; **not a ~ people** nicht wenige Leute; **we'll go in a ~ minutes** wir gehen in ein paar Minuten; **in the next/past ~ days** in den nächsten/letzten paar Tagen; **every ~ days** alle paar Tage

PRON **a** (= not many) wenige; ~ **of them came** wenige von ihnen kamen; **some ~** gar nicht so wenige; **the Few** Kampfflieger, die an der Luftschlacht um England im zweiten Weltkrieg

teilnahmen **the lucky ~** die wenigen Glücklichen; **opera used to be an experience for the ~** Opern waren früher ein privilegierten Minderheit vorbehalten; **as ~ as you** genauso wenig wie du; **how ~ there are!** wie wenige das sind!; **however ~ there may be** wie wenig auch immer da ist; **I've got so/too ~ as it is** ich habe sowieso schon so/zu wenig(e); **so ~ have been sold** so wenige sind bis jetzt verkauft worden; **there are too ~ of you** ihr seid zu wenige

b a ~ ein paar; **I'll just take a ~** ich nehme nur ein paar; **a ~ more** ein paar mehr; **quite a ~ eine ganze Menge; **quite a ~ did not believe him** eine ganze Menge Leute or ziemlich viele Leute glaubten ihm nicht; **some ~** einige; **there are always the ~ who ...** es gibt immer einige wenige Leute or ein paar Leute, die ...; **the ~ who knew him** die wenigen, die ihn kannten

fewer ['fjuːə'] ADJ, PRON comp of **few** weniger; **no ~ than** nicht weniger als

fewest ['fjuːɪst] superl of **few** **ADJ** die wenigsten **PRON** die wenigsten, am wenigsten

fey [feɪ] ADJ (Scot) todgeweiht; (= clairvoyant) hellseherisch

fez [fez] N Fes m

ff abbr of **following** ff

FHSA (Brit) abbr of **Family Health Services Authority** ≈ Gesundheitsamt nt

fiancé [fɪ'ɑ̃ːŋseɪ] N Verlobte(r) m

fiancée [fɪ'ɑ̃ːŋseɪ] N Verlobte f

fiasco [fɪ'æskəʊ] N pl **-s**, (US also) **-es** Fiasko nt

fiat ['faɪæt] N **a** (= decree) Befehl m, Erlass m, Anordnung f; **nothing can be done by ~** nichts geschieht so einfach auf Befehl **b** (= authorization) Billigung f, Plazet nt

fiat money N Papiergeld nt ohne Deckung

fib [fɪb] (inf) **N** Flunkerei f (inf), Schwindelei f (inf); **that's a ~!** das ist geflunkert! (inf); **don't tell ~s** flunker or schwindel nicht! (inf) **VI** flunkern (inf), schwindeln (inf)

fibber ['fɪbə'] N (inf) Flunkerer m (inf), Schwindler(in) m(f) (inf)

fibbing ['fɪbɪŋ] N (inf) Flunkerei f (inf)

fibre, (US) **fiber** ['faɪbə'] N **a** Faser f **b** (= roughage) Ballaststoffe pl **c** (fig) **moral ~** Charakterstärke f; **he has no moral ~** er hat keinen inneren Halt, er hat kein Rückgrat; **with every ~ of one's being** mit jeder Faser seines Herzens

fibre, (US) **fiber: fibreboard**, (US) **fiberboard** N Faserplatte f; **fibreglass**, (US) **fiberglass** **N** Fiberglas nt, Glasfaser f **ADJ** aus Fiberglas or Glasfaser; **~-reinforced** glasfaserverstärkt; **fibreoptic cable**, (US) **fiberoptic cable** N faseroptisches Kabel, Glasfaserkabel nt; **fibre optics** N sing Faseroptik f; **fibre-tip pen** N (Brit) Faserschreiber m

fibroid ['faɪbrɔɪd] **ADJ** fibrös **N** Fibromyom nt

fibrositis [,faɪbrə'saɪtɪs] N Bindegewebsentzündung f

fibrous ['faɪbrəs] ADJ faserig

fibula ['fɪbjʊlə] N Wadenbein nt

FICA (US) abbr of **Federal Insurance Contributions Act** (Jur) Gesetz über die Einbehaltung von Sozialversicherungsbeiträgen **a third of Jack's salary went to ~** ein Drittel von Jacks Gehalt ging an die Sozialversicherung

fickle ['fɪkl] ADJ unbeständig, launenhaft; person also wankelmütig; weather also wechselhaft

fickleness ['fɪklnɪs] N Wechselhaftigkeit f, Unbeständigkeit f; (of person also) Wankelmütigkeit f

fiction ['fɪkʃən] N **a** no pl (Liter) Erzähl- or Prosaliteratur f; **you'll find that under ~** das finden Sie unter Belletristik; **work of ~** Erzählung f; (longer) Roman m; **light ~** (leichte) Unterhaltungsliteratur f; **romantic ~** Liebesromane pl **b** (= invention) (freie) Erfindung, Fiktion f; **that's pure ~** das ist frei erfunden; **total recycling is a ~** das totale Recycling gibt es nicht

fictional ['fɪkʃənl] ADJ **a** (= invented) erfunden; (Liter) character, hero, heroine, setting, account er-

funden, fiktiv; film, drama fiktional; **entirely ~** rein fiktiv, frei erfunden; **the party's unity was ~** die Einheit der Partei war eine Fiktion **b** (= relating to fiction) work erzählerisch; **his ~ writing** seine erzählenden Schriften; **a clever ~ device** ein geschickter erzählerischer Trick; **a ~ representation of historical events** eine dichterische Darstellung historischer Ereignisse

fictitious [fɪk'tɪʃəs] ADJ **a** (= false, nonexistent) name, address falsch; loan, case fingiert; **the job in the advertisement turned out to be ~** es stellte sich heraus, dass die ausgeschriebene Stelle gar nicht gab **b** (Liter, = imaginary) character, setting, story, event erfunden; **all characters in this film are (entirely) ~** alle Gestalten in diesem Film sind (frei) erfunden

fiddle ['fɪdl] **N** **a** (Mus inf) Fiedel f (inf), Geige f; **to play second ~** die zweite Geige spielen; **to play second ~ to sb** (fig) in jds Schatten (dat) stehen; **he refuses to play second ~** (fig) er will immer die erste Geige spielen; **as fit as a ~** kerngesund

b (Brit inf, = cheat, swindle) Manipulation f, Schiebung f; (with money) faule Geschäfte pl (inf); **it's a ~** das ist Schiebung!; **there are so many ~s going on** es wird so viel getrickst (inf) or manipuliert; **the accountants were well aware there had been some sort of ~** die Buchprüfer wussten ganz genau, dass da irgendetwas manipuliert or frisiert (inf) worden war; **tax ~** Steuermanipulation f; **to be on the ~** faule Geschäfte or krumme Dinger machen (inf)

c **it's a bit of a ~** (Brit: = quite tricky) es ist eine ziemliche Fummelei (inf)

VI **a** (Mus inf) fiedeln (inf), geigen **b** (= fidget, play around) herumspielen; **don't ~ with the engine if you don't know what you're doing** spiel nicht am Motor herum, wenn du dich damit nicht auskennst; **he sat there nervously fiddling with his tie/cigarette lighter** er saß da und spielte nervös an seinem Schlips herum/spielte mit seinem Feuerzeug herum; **put that thing down and stop fiddling!** leg das Ding weg und hör endlich mit der Fummelei auf! (inf)

c (= split hairs, be overprecise etc) Haare spalten, pingelig sein (inf)

VT (Brit inf) ~ accounts, results frisieren (inf); election manipulieren; **he ~d it so that ...** er hat es so hingebogen or getrickst (inf), dass ... **b** tune fiedeln (inf), geigen

INTERJ ach du liebe Zeit, ach du liebes Lottchen (hum inf)

▶ **fiddle about** (Brit) or **around** VI to fiddle about or around with sth an etw (dat) herumspielen or herumfummeln (inf); (= fidget with) mit etw herumspielen; **he dived under the bonnet and fiddled about** or **around for a while** er verschwand unter der Kühlerhaube und fummelte eine Weile herum (inf); **I'm not spending all day just fiddling around with this one little job!** ich werde doch nicht den ganzen Tag damit zubringen, an dieser einen Kleinigkeit rumzufummeln! (inf)

fiddle-faddle ['fɪdlfædl] INTERJ (dated, = nonsense) Quatsch (inf)

fiddler ['fɪdlə'] N **a** (Mus inf) Geiger(in) m(f) **b** (inf, = cheat) Schwindler(in) m(f), Betrüger(in) m(f)

fiddler crab N Winkerkrabbe f

fiddlesticks ['fɪdlstɪks] INTERJ (= nonsense) Unsinn, Quatsch (inf); (= bother) ach du liebe Zeit, du liebes Lottchen (hum inf)

fiddliness ['fɪdlɪnɪs] N (Brit inf, = intricacy) Kniffligkeit f (inf); (= awkwardness in use) Umständlichkeit f

fiddling ['fɪdlɪŋ] ADJ (= trivial) läppisch

fiddly ['fɪdlɪ] ADJ (+er) (Brit) (= intricate) job, task knifflig (inf); (= awkward to use) object, controls etc umständlich; **it is ~ to use** es ist (in der Benutzung) zu umständlich; **little ~ bits** umständliche Kleinteile pl

fidelity [fɪˈdelɪtɪ] N **a** Treue f (to zu) **b** (of translation etc) Genauigkeit f; (Rad etc) Klangtreue f

fidget [ˈfɪdʒɪt] **VI** (also **fidget about** or **a-round**: = be restless) zappeln; **to ~ with sth** mit etw herumspielen or herumfummeln (inf); **don't ~** zappel nicht so rum; **he sat there ~ing in his chair** er rutschte auf seinem Stuhl hin und her **N a** (= person) Zappelphilipp m (inf) **b** (inf) **to get the ~s** zappelig werden; **have you got the ~s?** was bist du für ein Zappelphilipp! (inf)

fidgety [ˈfɪdʒɪtɪ] ADJ zappelig; audience etc, legs, feet, hands unruhig

fiduciary [fɪˈdjuːʃɪərɪ] **ADJ** treuhänderisch; currency ungedeckt; **~ company** Treuhandgesellschaft f **N** Treuhänder(in) m(f)

fie [faɪ] INTERJ (old) pfui; **~ on you!** pfui!, schämen Sie sich!

fief [fiːf] N (Hist) Lehen nt

field [fiːld] **N a** (Agr) Feld nt, Acker m; (= area of grass) Wiese f; (for cows, horses etc) Weide f; **corn/wheat ~** Getreide-/Weizenfeld nt; **potato ~** Kartoffelacker m; **we had a picnic in a ~** wir machten auf einer Wiese Picknick; **he's working in the ~s** er arbeitet auf dem Feld or Acker; **the farm has 20 ~s** der Hof hat 20 Felder; **beasts of the ~** Feldtiere pl; **to cut across the ~s** quer über die Felder gehen
b (= coalfield, icefield, oilfield etc) Feld nt
c (for football etc: = ground) Platz m; **sports** or **games ~** Sportplatz m; **to take the ~** auf den Platz kommen, einlaufen
d (Mil) Feld nt; **~ of battle** Schlachtfeld nt; **noted for his bravery in the ~** für seine Tapferkeit im Feld bekannt; **to take the ~** zur Schlacht antreten
e (of study, work etc) Gebiet nt, Feld nt; **to be first in the ~ with sth** (Comm) als Erster etw auf den Markt bringen; **to lead the ~ (in sth)** (in etw dat) das Feld anführen; **in all the ~s of human endeavour** (liter) im gesamten menschlichen Trachten (liter); **studies in the ~ of medicine** Studien auf dem Gebiet der Medizin; **this is, of course, a very broad ~** das ist natürlich ein weites Feld; **what ~ are you in?** auf welchem Gebiet or in welchem Feld arbeiten Sie?; **his ~ is Renaissance painting** sein Spezialgebiet ist die Malerei der Renaissance
f (= area of practical observation or operation) Praxis f; **when a salesman goes out into the ~** wenn ein Verkäufer in den Außeneinsatz geht; **work in the ~** Feldforschung f; (of sales rep) Außendienst m; **to test sth in the ~** etw in der Praxis or vor Ort ausprobieren
g (Phys, Opt) Feld nt; **~ of vision** Blick- or Gesichtsfeld nt; **gravitational ~** Gravitationsfeld nt, Schwerefeld nt; **~ of force** Kraftfeld nt; **magnetic ~** Magnetfeld nt, magnetisches Feld
h (Sport: = competitors) Feld nt; (Cricket, Baseball) Fängerpartei f; **the rest of the ~** (in race) der Rest des Feldes, die übrigen Läufer; **there's quite a strong ~ for the race** das Teilnehmerfeld für das Rennen ist ziemlich stark; **to hold off a strong ~** sich gegen ein starkes Feld behaupten
i (Comput) Datenfeld nt; (on punch card) Feld nt
j (on flag, Her) Feld nt, Grund m
k **to play the ~** (inf) eine Beziehung nach der anderen haben
VT a (Cricket, Baseball etc) ball auffangen und zurückwerfen; (fig) question etc abblocken, abwehren; **he had to ~ calls from irate customers** er musste wütende Kunden am Telefon abwimmeln (inf)
b team, side aufs Feld or auf den Platz schicken
c (Pol) candidate aufstellen
VI (Cricket, Baseball etc) als Fänger spielen; **when we go out to ~** wenn wir die Fänger(partei) stellen

field: field ambulance N (Mil) Sanka m, Sanitätskraftwagen m; **field artillery** N Feldartillerie f; **field day** N **a** Manöver nt **b** (US: for school sports) (Schul)sportfest nt **c** (fig) I **had a ~** ich hatte meinen großen Tag; **to have a ~** einen inneren Reichsparteitag haben (inf); **with the score at 6-0 the Scots are having a ~ against the English** beim Stand von 6:0 machen die Schotten jetzt die Engländer nach allen Regeln der Kunst fertig (inf)

fielder [ˈfiːldə] N (Cricket, Baseball etc) Fänger(in) m(f)

field: field event N (Athletics) Disziplin, die nicht auf der Aschenbahn ausgetragen wird; **field games** PL Feldspiele pl; **field glasses** PL Feldstecher m; **field goal** N (US, Basketball) Korbwurf m aus dem Spielgeschehen; (Ftbl) Fieldgoal nt, Feldtor nt; **field gun** N (Mil) Feldgeschütz nt; **field hockey** N (US) Hockey nt; **field hospital** N (Mil) (Feld)lazarett nt; **field kitchen** N (Mil) Feldküche f; **field marshal** N (Mil) Feldmarschall m; **fieldmouse** N Feldmaus f; **field officer** N (Mil) Stabsoffizier m; **fieldpiece** N (Mil) Feldgeschütz nt; **field service** N (Comm) Außendienst m

fieldsman [ˈfiːldzmən] N pl **-men** [-mən] (Cricket) Fänger m

field: field sports PL **a** Sport m im Freien (Jagen und Fischen) **b** = field games; **field staff** N (Comm) Außendienstmitarbeiter(in) m(f); **field study** N Feldforschung f; **a** = eine Feldstudie; **field test** N Feldversuch m; **field-test** VT in einem Feldversuch/in Feldversuchen testen; **field trip** N Exkursion f; **field work** N **a** (of geologist, surveyor etc) Arbeit f im Gelände; (of sociologist etc) Feldarbeit f, Feldforschung f **b** (Mil) Feldbefestigung f, Schanze f; **field worker** N Praktiker(in) m(f)

fiend [fiːnd] N **a** (= evil spirit) Teufel m, Dämon m; (= person) Teufel m; **the Fiend** der böse Feind; **"sex ~ strikes again"** „Sexbestie schlägt wieder zu" **b** (inf, = addict) Fanatiker(in) m(f); **tennis ~** Tennisnarr m; **she's a fresh-air ~** sie ist Frischluftfanatikerin

fiendish [ˈfiːndɪʃ] ADJ **a** (= cruel) person, act, look teuflisch; delight, glee, laughter hämisch; **he took a ~ delight in doing it** es machte ihm eine höllische Freude, es zu tun **b** (inf, = cunning) plan, device, gadget höllisch raffiniert or clever (inf) **c** (inf, = very difficult) problem verzwickt (inf), höllisch schwer (inf)

fiendishly [ˈfiːndɪʃlɪ] ADV **a** (inf, = very) difficult, clever, complicated höllisch (inf), verteufelt (inf); funny wahnsinnig (inf); **it's ~ simple** es ist verblüffend einfach **b** (= evilly) mean, ambitious, laugh, grin teuflisch

fierce [fɪəs] ADJ (+er) animal wild, aggressiv; dog böse; person, look, appearance grimmig; fighting, battle, opposition, resistance, opponent, critic, rivals erbittert, heftig; debate, argument, storm heftig; attack, competition, criticism scharf; determination wild; loyalty unerschütterlich; pride, ambition, independence leidenschaftlich; heat, sun glühend; **the troops came under ~ attack** die Truppen wurden scharf angegriffen; **he has a ~ temper** er braust leicht or leicht auf

fiercely [ˈfɪəslɪ] ADV contest, oppose, fight, deny heftig; criticize scharf; defend, argue leidenschaftlich; say böse, grimmig; independent, competitive, proud, loyal äußerst; **to be ~ critical of sth** etw scharf kritisieren; **~ determined** wild entschlossen; **to oppose sth ~, to be ~ opposed to sth** einer Sache (dat) heftigen Widerstand entgegensetzen, heftigen Widerstand gegen etw leisten; **TV and radio stations compete ~ with one another** Fernseh- und Radiosender stehen in scharfem Wettbewerb miteinander; **the fire was burning ~** es brannte lichterloh

fierceness [ˈfɪəsnɪs] N **a** (of animal) Wildheit f; (of dog) Bösartigkeit f; (of person, look, appearance) Grimmigkeit f; (of temper) aufbrausende Art; (of fighting, battle, debate, opposition, rivalry, storm) Heftigkeit f; (of attack, competition, criticism) Schärfe f; (of sun) Gluthitze f; **the ~ of the heat** die Gluthitze, die glühende Hitze

fieriness [ˈfaɪərɪnɪs] N **a** (of temperament, character) Hitzigkeit f; (of person) Hitzköpfigkeit f,

Hitzigkeit f; (of speech, performance) Feurigkeit f **b** (= spiciness: of food) Feurigkeit f

fiery [ˈfaɪərɪ] ADJ (+er) **a** (= burning) inferno, furnace, heat glühend **b** colour, orange leuchtend; sunset rot glühend; hair feuerrot; **~ red** feuerrot **c** (Cook: = spicy) food, drink feurig **d** (= passionate) temperament, character hitzig; person hitzköpfig; speech, performance feurig; **a ~ redhead** ein hitziger Rotschopf; **to have a ~ temper** ein Hitzkopf m sein

fiesta [fɪˈestə] N Fiesta f

FIFA [ˈfiːfə] abbr of **Federation of International Football Associations** FIFA f

fife [faɪf] N (Mus) Querpfeife f

fifteen [fɪfˈtiːn] **ADJ** fünfzehn **N a** Fünfzehn f **b a** rugby = eine Rugbymannschaft; **the Welsh ~** die Rugbynationalmannschaft von Wales

fifteenth [fɪfˈtiːnθ] **ADJ** fünfzehnte(r, s) **N** Fünfzehnte(r, s); (= part, fraction) Fünfzehntel nt → also **sixteenth**

fifth [fɪfθ] **ADJ** fünfte(r, s); **~ rate** fünftrangig **N** Fünfte(r, s); (= part, fraction) Fünftel nt; (Mus) Quinte f; **to take the ~** (US, inf) die Aussage verweigern → also **sixth**

fifth: fifth column N fünfte Kolonne; **fifth columnist** N Angehörige(r) mf der fünften Kolonne, Kollaborateur(in) m(f)

fiftieth [ˈfɪftɪɪθ] **ADJ** fünfzigste(r, s) **N** Fünfzigste(r, s); (= part, fraction) Fünfzigstel nt → also **sixth**

fifty [ˈfɪftɪ] **ADJ** fünfzig **N** Fünfzig f → also **sixty**

fifty-fifty [ˈfɪftɪˈfɪftɪ] **ADV** halbe-halbe (inf), fifty-fifty (inf); **to go ~ (with sb)** (mit jdm) halbe-halbe or fifty-fifty machen (inf) **ADJ** **it was a ~ deal** bei dem Handel sollte fifty-fifty geteilt werden (inf); **they had ~ shares in the business** sie waren zu fünfzig Prozent an der Firma beteiligt; **he has a ~ chance of survival/victory** or hat eine fünfzigprozentige Überlebens-/Gewinnchance

fig [fɪg] N Feige f; **I don't care** or **give a ~** ich kümmere mich einen Dreck darum (inf); **I don't give a ~ what he thinks!** (Brit inf) seine Meinung kümmert mich einen (feuchten) Dreck (inf)

fig. abbr of **figure(s)** Abb.

fight [faɪt] vb: pret, ptp **fought** **N a** (lit, fig) Kampf m; (= fist fight, scrap) Rauferei f, Prügelei f, Schlägerei f; (Mil) Gefecht nt; (= argument, row) Streit m; **to have a ~ with sb** sich mit jdm schlagen; (= argue) sich mit jdm streiten; **to give sb a ~** (lit, fig) jdm einen Kampf liefern; **to put up a ~** (lit, fig) sich zur Wehr setzen; **to put up a good ~** (lit, fig) sich tapfer zur Wehr setzen, sich tapfer schlagen; **do you want a ~?** willst du was?, du willst dich wohl mit mir anlegen?; **if he wants a ~, then ...** (lit, fig) wenn er Streit sucht, dann ...; **a politician who enjoys a good ~** ein streitlustiger Politiker; **he won't give in without a ~** er ergibt sich nicht kampflos; **in the ~ against disease** im Kampf gegen die Krankheit; **the ~ for survival** der Kampf ums Überleben; **he lost his ~ for life** er verlor den Kampf um sein Leben; **the big ~** (*Boxing*) der große Kampf

b (= *fighting spirit*) Kampfgeist *m*; **there was no ~ left in him** sein Kampfgeist war erloschen; **to show ~** Kampfgeist zeigen

VI kämpfen; (= *have punch-up etc*) raufen, sich prügeln, sich schlagen; (= *argue: with wife etc*) sich streiten *or* zanken; **the dogs were ~ing over a bone** die Hunde rauften um einen Knochen; **to ~ against disease** Krankheiten bekämpfen; **to ~ for sb/sth** um jdn/etw kämpfen; **to ~ for what one believes in** für seine Überzeugungen eintreten *or* streiten; **to ~ for one's life** um sein Leben kämpfen; **to ~ for breath** nach Atem ringen; **to go down ~ing** sich nicht kampflos ergeben; **to ~ shy of sth** einer Sache (*dat*) aus dem Weg gehen; **I've always fought shy of claiming that ...** ich habe immer bewusst vermieden, zu behaupten ...

VT **a** *person* kämpfen mit *or* gegen; (= *have punch-up with*) sich schlagen mit, sich prügeln mit; (*in battle*) kämpfen mit, sich (*dat*) ein Gefecht *nt* liefern mit; **I'm prepared to ~ him/the government** (= *argue with, take on*) ich bin bereit, das mit ihm/der Regierung durchzukämpfen; **I'll ~ him on that one** dazu nehme ich es mit ihm auf; **you can't ~ the whole company** du kannst es nicht mit der ganzen Firma aufnehmen

b *fire, disease, cuts, policy, crime, inflation* bekämpfen; *decision* ankämpfen gegen; *corruption* angehen gegen; **there's no point in ~ing it, you can't win** es hat keinen Zweck, dagegen anzukämpfen, es ist aussichtslos; **she fought the urge to giggle** sie versuchte, sich das Kichern zu verkneifen

c **to ~ a duel** ein Duell *nt* austragen, sich duellieren; **to ~ pitched battles** sich (*dat*) offene Gefechte liefern; **to ~ political battles** politische Kämpfe austragen; **to ~ an action** (*Jur*) einen Prozess durchkämpfen *or* durchfechten; **to ~ one's way through the crowd** sich durch die Menge kämpfen → *also* **battle N**

d (*Mil, Naut*, = *control in battle*) *army, ships* kommandieren

▶ **fight back VI** (*in fight*) zurückschlagen; (*Mil*) sich verteidigen, Widerstand leisten; (*in argument*) sich wehren, sich zur Wehr setzen; (*after illness*) zu Kräften kommen; (*in sport*) zurückkämpfen **VT** *sep tears, doubts etc* unterdrücken; **he fought his way back into the match/to the top** er hat sich ins Spiel/wieder an die Spitze zurückgekämpft

▶ **fight down VT** *sep anxiety, anger* unterdrücken

▶ **fight off VT** *sep* (*Mil, fig*) *attack, disease, attacker* abwehren; *sleep* ankämpfen gegen; **I'm still trying to fight off this cold** ich kämpfe immer noch mit dieser Erkältung; **she has to keep fighting men off** sie muss dauernd Männer abwimmeln

▶ **fight on VI** weiterkämpfen

▶ **fight out VT** *sep* **to fight it out** es untereinander ausfechten

fightback ['faɪtbæk] N Come-back *nt*, Comeback *nt*

fighter ['faɪtə'] N **a** Kämpfer(in) *m(f)*, Streiter(in) *m(f)*; (*Boxing*) Fighter *m*; **he's a ~** (*fig*) er ist eine Kämpfernatur **b** (*Aviat*, = *plane*) Jagdflugzeug *nt*, Jäger *m*

fighter: fighter-bomber N Jagdbomber *m*; **fighter interceptor** N Abfangjäger *m*; **fighter pilot** N Jagdflieger *m*

fighting ['faɪtɪŋ] **N** (*Mil*) Kampf *m*, Gefecht *nt*; (= *punch-ups, scrapping etc*) Prügeleien *pl*, Raufereien *pl*; (= *arguments between husband and wife etc*) Streit *m*, Zank *m*; **~ broke out** Kämpfe brachen aus → **street fighting ADJ** *attr person* kämpferisch, streitlustig; **~ troops**, **~ forces** Kampftruppen *pl*; **~ line** Front *f*; **~ man** Krieger *m*, Kämpfer *m*; **~ strength** (*Mil*) Kampf- *or* Einsatzstärke *f*

fighting: fighting chance N faire Chancen *pl*; **he's in with *or* he has a ~** (*of winning*) wenn er sich anstrengt; **at least that gives you a ~** damit hast du wenigstens eine Chance; **fighting cock** N (*lit, fig*) Kampfhahn *m*; **fighting fit** ADJ (*Brit inf*) topfit (*inf*); **fighting spirit** N Kampfgeist *m*; **to have tremendous ~** ungeheuren Kampfgeist haben; **fighting weight** N (*Boxing*) Kampfgewicht *nt*

fig leaf N (*lit, fig*) Feigenblatt *nt*

figment ['fɪgmənt] N **a ~ of the imagination** pure Einbildung, ein Hirngespinst *nt*; **it's all a ~ of his imagination** das ist alles eine Ausgeburt seiner Fantasie *or* Phantasie

fig tree N Feigenbaum *m*

figurative ['fɪgjʊrətɪv] ADJ **a** (= *metaphorical*) *language* bildlich; *use, sense* übertragen; **in a ~ sense** im übertragenen Sinn **b** (*Art*) *art, painting, sculpture, artist* gegenständlich

figuratively ['fɪgjʊrətɪvlɪ] ADV in a übertragenen Sinn; **~ speaking** bildlich gesprochen; **I'm speaking ~ there** das ist natürlich nicht wörtlich gemeint

figure ['fɪgə'] **N** **a** (= *number*) Zahl; (= *digit*) Ziffer *f*; (= *sum*) Summe *f*; **to put a ~ on sth** etw konkret in Zahlen angeben; **could you put some sort of ~ on the salary?** können Sie mir die ungefähre Höhe des Gehaltes mitteilen?; **he didn't want to put a ~ on it** er wollte keine Zahlen nennen; **name your ~** nennen Sie Ihren Preis; **he's good at ~s** er ist ein guter Rechner; **a mistake in the ~s** ein Unstimmigkeit in den Zahlen; **have you seen last year's ~s?** haben Sie die Zahlen vom Vorjahr gesehen?; **Miss Jones, could you bring in the ~s for the Fotheringham contract?** Fräulein Jones, könnten Sie das Zahlenmaterial zum Fotheringham-Vertrag bringen?; **to reach double ~s** in die zweistelligen Zahlen gehen; **a three-figure sum** eine dreistellige Summe; **to sell for a high ~** für eine hohe Summe verkauft werden; **he earns well into six ~s** er hat gut und gern ein sechsstelliges Einkommen; **government ~s show that ...** die Zahlen der Regierung zeigen, dass ...; **the ~s work** (*inf*) es rechnet sich (*inf*)

b (*in geometry, dancing, skating*) Figur *f*; **~ (of) eight** Acht *f*

c (= *human form*) Gestalt *f*

d (= *shapeliness*) Figur *f*; **she has a good ~** sie hat eine gute Figur; **I'm dieting to keep my ~** ich lebe Diät, um meine Figur zu behalten; **to lose one's ~** seine Figur verlieren; **to get one's ~ back** seine alte Figur wiederbekommen; **what a ~!** (*was für*) eine tolle Figur!; **she's a fine ~ of a woman** sie ist eine stattliche Frau; **he's a fine ~ of a man** er ist ein Bild von einem Mann → **cut**

e (= *personality*) Persönlichkeit *f*; (= *character in novel etc*) Gestalt *f*; **the great ~s of history** die Großen der Geschichte; **a key public ~** eine Schlüsselfigur des öffentlichen Lebens; **~ of fun** Witzfigur *f*, lächerliche Erscheinung

f (= *statuette, model etc*) Figur *f*

g (*Liter*) **~ of speech** Redensart *f*, Redewendung *f*; **it's just a ~ of speech** das ist doch nur eine (leere) Redensart, das sagt man doch nur so

h (*Mus*) Figur *f*, Phrase *f*; (= *notation*) Ziffer *f*

i (= *illustration*) Abbildung *f*

VT **a** (= *decorate*) *silk etc* bemalen, mustern; **~d velvet** bedruckter Samt

b (*Mus*) *bass* beziffern; *melody* verzieren

c (= *imagine*) sich (*dat*) vorstellen, sich (*dat*) denken

d (*esp US inf*, = *think, reckon*) glauben, schätzen (*inf*)

e (*US, inf*, = *figure out*) schlau werden aus, begreifen

VI **a** (= *appear*) erscheinen, auftauchen; **where does pity ~ in your scheme of things?** wo rangiert Mitleid in deiner Weltordnung?; **he ~d in a play** er trat in einem Stück auf; **he ~d prominently in my plans** er spielte eine bedeutende Rolle in meinen Plänen

b (*inf*, = *make sense*) hinkommen (*inf*), hinhauen (*inf*); **that ~s** das hätte ich mir denken können; **it doesn't ~** das passt *or* stimmt nicht zusammen

▶ **figure on VI** +*prep obj* (*esp US*) rechnen mit

▶ **figure out VT** *sep* **a** (= *understand, make sense of*) begreifen, schlau werden aus; **I can't figure him out at all** ich werde überhaupt nicht schlau aus ihm; **I can't figure it out** ich werde daraus nicht schlau **b** (= *work out*) ausrechnen; *answer, how to do sth* herausbekommen; *solution* finden; **figure it out for yourself** das kannst du dir (leicht) selbst ausrechnen

figure: figure-conscious ADJ figurbewusst; **figurehead** N (*Naut, fig*) Galionsfigur *f*; **figure-hugging** ADJ figurbetont; **figure-skate** VI Eiskunst laufen; **figure skater** N Eiskunstläufer(in) *m(f)*; **figure skating** N Eiskunstlaufen *nt*

figurine ['fɪgəriːn] N Figurine *f*

Fiji ['fiːdʒiː] N Fidschiinseln *pl*

Fijian [fɪ'dʒiːən] **ADJ** fidschianisch **N** **a** Fidschiinsulaner(in) *m(f)* **b** (*Ling*) Fidschianisch *nt*

filament ['fɪləmənt] N (*Elec*) (Glüh- *or* Heiz)faden *m*; (*Bot*) Staubfaden *m*

filbert ['fɪlbət] N (*Bot*) (= *tree*) Haselnussstrauch *m*; (= *nut*) Haselnuss *f*

filch [fɪltʃ] VT (*inf*) filzen, mopsen, mausen (*all inf*)

file¹ [faɪl] **N** (= *tool*) Feile *f* **VT** feilen; **to ~ one's (finger)nails** sich (*dat*) die Fingernägel feilen

▶ **file down VT** *sep* abfeilen

file² **N** **a** (= *holder*) (Akten)hefter *m*, Aktenordner *m*; (*for card index*) Karteikasten *m*; **would you fetch it from the ~s** könnten Sie es bitte aus der Ablage holen; **it's in the ~s somewhere** das muss irgendwo bei den Akten sein

b (= *documents, information*) Akte *f* (*on sb über jdn, on sth zu etw*); **on ~** aktenkundig, bei den Akten; **have we got that on ~?** haben wir das bei den Akten?; **to open *or* start a ~ on sb/sth** eine Akte über jdn/zu etw anlegen; **to have/keep a ~ on sb/sth** eine Akte über jdn/zu etw haben/führen; **to keep sb/sth on ~** jds Unterlagen/die Unterlagen über etw (*acc*) zurückhalten; **to close the ~ on sb/sth** jds Akte/die Akte zu einer Sache schließen; **the Kowalski ~** die Akte Kowalski

c (*Comput*) Datei *f*, File *nt*; **data on ~** gespeicherte Daten; **to have sth on ~** etw im Computer gespeichert haben

d (*TV*) Archivbilder *pl*

VT **a** (= *put in file*) *letters* ablegen, abheften; **it's ~d under "B"** das ist unter „B" abgelegt

b (*Press*) *report* einsenden

c (*Jur*) *complaint* einreichen, erheben; (*law*)*suit* anstrengen; **to ~ a petition with a court** einen Antrag bei Gericht einreichen

VI **to ~ for divorce** die Scheidung einreichen; **to ~ for bankruptcy** Konkurs anmelden; **to ~ for custody (of the children)** das Sorgerecht (für die Kinder) beantragen

▶ **file away VT** *sep papers* zu den Akten legen; **to file sth away in one's memory** etw im Gedächtnis behalten

file³ **N** (= *row*) Reihe *f*; **in Indian *or* single ~** im Gänsemarsch; (*Mil*) in Reihe → **rank¹**

VI **to ~ in** hereinmarschieren *or* -kommen; **they ~d out of the classroom** sie gingen hintereinander *or* nacheinander aus dem Klassenzimmer; **the procession ~d under the archway** die Prozession zog unter dem Torbogen hindurch; **they ~d through the turnstile** sie kamen nacheinander durch das Drehkreuz; **the troops ~d past the general** die Truppen marschierten *or* defilierten am General vorbei; **the children ~d past the headmaster** die Kinder gingen in einer Reihe am Direktor vorbei; **a long line of refugees ~d over the bridge** eine lange Reihe von Flüchtlingen zog über die Brücke

file: file cabinet N (*US*) Aktenschrank *m*; **file-card** N Karteikarte *f*; **file clerk** N (*US*) Angestellte(r) *mf* in der Registratur; **file manage-ment** N (*Comput*) Dateiverwaltung *f*; **file manager** N (*Comput*) Dateimanager *m*; **file-name** N (*Comput*) Dateiname *m*; **file number** N Aktenzeichen *nt*; **file server** N (*Comput*) Fileserver *m*, Dateiserver *m*; **file size** N (*Comput*) Dateigröße *f or* -umfang *m*

filet [fɪˈleɪ] N (*US*) = **fillet**

file transfer protocol N (*Comput*) Dateitransferprotokoll *nt*

filial [ˈfɪlɪəl] ADJ *duties* des Kindes, als Kind; *piety, affection* kindlich; **with due ~ respect** mit dem Respekt, den eine Tochter/ein Sohn schuldig ist

filibuster [ˈfɪlɪbʌstə] (*esp US*) **N a** (= *speech*) Obstruktion *f*, Dauerrede *f* **b** (= *person*) = **filibusterer** **VI** filibustern, Obstruktion betreiben

filibusterer [ˈfɪlɪbʌstərə] N (*esp US*) Filibuster *m*, Dauerredner(in) *m(f)*, Obstruktionist(in) *m(f)*

filibustering [ˈfɪlɪbʌstərɪŋ] N (*esp US*) Verschleppungstaktik *f*, Obstruktionismus *m*

filigree [ˈfɪlɪgriː] **N** Filigran *nt* ADJ Filigran-; ~ **jewellery** Filigranschmuck *m*

filing [ˈfaɪlɪŋ] N **a** (*of documents*) Ablegen *nt*, Abheften *nt*; **who does your ~?** wer ist bei Ihnen für die Ablage zuständig?; **have you done the ~?** haben Sie die Akten schon abgelegt? **b** (*Jur*) Einreichung *f*

filing: filing cabinet N Aktenschrank *m or* -regal *nt*; **filing clerk** N (*esp Brit*) Angestellte(r) *mf* in der Registratur

filings [ˈfaɪlɪŋz] PL Späne *pl*

filing tray N Ablagekorb *m*

Filipino [fɪlɪˈpiːnəʊ] **N** Filipino *m*, Filipina *f* ADJ philippinisch

fill [fɪl] **VT a** *bottle, bucket, hole* füllen; *pipe* stopfen; *teeth* plombieren; (*wind*) *sails* blähen; (*fig*) (aus)füllen; **I had three teeth ~ed** ich bekam drei Zähne plombiert *or* gefüllt; **I need something to ~ my day** ich brauche etwas, um meinen Tag auszufüllen

b (= *permeate*) erfüllen; **~ed with anger/admiration** voller Zorn/Bewunderung, von Zorn/Bewunderung erfüllt (*geh*); **~ed with emotion** gefühlsgeladen; **the thought ~ed him with horror/hope** der Gedanke erfüllte ihn mit Entsetzen/Hoffnung

c *post, position* (*employer*) besetzen; (*employee*, = *take up*) einnehmen; (= *be in*) innehaben; *need* entsprechen (+*dat*); *role* übernehmen; **we are looking for a young man to ~ the post of assistant editor** wir suchen einen jungen Mann, der den Posten eines Redaktionsassistenten einnehmen soll; **I think she will ~ the job very nicely** ich denke, sie wird die Stelle sehr gut ausfüllen; **the position is already ~ed** die Stelle ist schon besetzt *or* vergeben

d *theatre, seats* füllen; **the lecture room was ~ed to capacity** der Hörsaal war bis auf den letzten Platz besetzt

VI sich füllen; **his eyes ~ed with tears** Tränen traten ihm in die Augen

N to drink one's ~ seinen Durst löschen; **to eat one's ~** sich satt essen; **to have had one's ~** gut satt sein; **I've had my ~ of him/it** (*inf*) ich habe von ihm/davon die Nase voll (*inf*), ich habe ihn/das satt; **she's had her ~ of disappointments** sie hat mehr als genug Enttäuschungen erlebt

▶ **fill in VI to fill in for sb** für jdn einspringen **VT** *sep* **a** *hole* auffüllen; *door, fireplace* zumauern; **to fill in the gaps in one's knowledge** seine Wissenslücken stopfen; **he's just filling in time until he gets another job** er überbrückt nur die Zeit, bis er eine andere Stelle bekommt **b** *form* ausfüllen; *name, address, missing word* eintragen; **could you fill in the details for me?** könnten Sie mir die Einzelheiten nennen? **c to fill sb in (on sth)** jdn (über etw *acc*) aufklären *or* ins Bild setzen

▶ **fill out VT a** (*sails etc*) sich blähen **b** (= *become fatter, person*) fülliger werden; (*cheeks, face*)

runder *or* voller werden **VT** *sep form* ausfüllen; *essay, article etc* strecken

▶ **fill up VI a** (*Aut*) (auf)tanken **b** (*hall, barrel etc*) sich füllen **VT** *sep* **a** *tank, cup* voll füllen; (*driver*) voll tanken; *hole* füllen, stopfen; **to fill sth right up** etw bis zum Rand (an)füllen; **he filled the glass up to the brim** er füllte das Glas randvoll; **fill her up!** (*Aut inf*) voll tanken bitte!; **that pie has really filled me up** ich fühle mich wirklich voll nach dieser Pastete; **you need something to fill you up** du brauchst was Sättigendes **b** *form* ausfüllen

filler [ˈfɪlə] **N a** (= *funnel*) Trichter *m* **b** (*Build*, = *paste for cracks*) Spachtelmasse *f* **c** (*Press, TV*) Füllsel *nt*, (Lücken)füller *m* **d** (*Chem, for plastics*) Füllstoff *m* **e** (*Ling*) ~ **(word)** Füllwort *nt*

filler cap N (*Brit*) Tankdeckel *m*

fillet [ˈfɪlɪt] **N a** (*Cook, of beef, fish*) Filet *nt*; ~ **of beef/lamb** Rinder-/Lammfilet *nt* **b** (*for the hair*) (Haar)band *nt* **VT** (*Cook*) filetieren; **~ed sole** Seezungenfilet *nt*

fillet steak N Filetsteak *nt*

filling [ˈfɪlɪŋ] **N a** (*in tooth*) Füllung *f*, Plombe *f*; **my ~'s come out** ich hab eine Füllung *or* Plombe verloren; **I had to have three ~s** ich musste mir drei Zähne plombieren *or* füllen lassen **b** (*Cook, in pie, tart*) Füllung *f* ADJ *food* sättigend

filling station N Tankstelle *f*

fillip [ˈfɪlɪp] N (*fig*) Ansporn *m*, Aufmunterung *f*; **to give sb a ~** jdn aufmuntern *or* ansporen; **to give sth a ~** einer Sache (*dat*) (neuen) Schwung geben; **this gave a ~ to our business** dadurch hat unser Geschäft einen Aufschwung genommen

fill-up [ˈfɪlʌp] N (*inf*) **do you want a ~?** soll ich nachschenken?

filly [ˈfɪlɪ] N Stutfohlen *nt*; (*dated inf*) Mädel *nt* (*dated*)

film [fɪlm] **N a** (= *motion picture*) Film *m*; **to make** *or* **shoot a ~** einen Film drehen *or* machen; **to make a ~** (*actor*) einen Film machen; **to go to (see) a ~** ins Kino gehen; **he's in ~s** er ist beim Film; **to go into ~s** zum Film gehen **b** (*Phot*) Film *m*; **get your holiday on ~** bannen Sie Ihre Ferien auf den Film; **I wish I'd got that on ~** ich wünschte, ich hätte das aufnehmen können; **to take a ~ of sth** einen Film über etw (*acc*) drehen *or* machen **c** (= *layer*) Film *m*; (*of dust*) Schicht *f*; (*of ice on water*) Schicht *f*; (*of mist, on the eye*) Schleier *m*; (= *thin membrane*) Häutchen *nt*; (*on teeth*) Belag *m*; (= *fine web*) feines Gewebe **VT** *play* verfilmen; *scene* filmen; *people* einen Film machen von; **he didn't know he was being ~ed** er wusste nicht, dass er gefilmt wurde **VI** filmen, drehen; **we start ~ing** *or* **~ing starts tomorrow** die Dreharbeiten fangen morgen an

▶ **film over** *or* **up VI** (*mirror, glass*) anlaufen

film: film archives PL Filmarchiv(e *pl*) *nt*; **film camera** N Filmkamera *f*; **film clip** N Filmausschnitt *m*; **film fan** N Filmliebhaber(in) *m(f)*, Filmfan *m*; **film festival** N Filmfestival *nt*, Filmfestspiele *pl*; **filmgoer** N Kinogänger(in) *m(f)*, Kinobesucher(in) *m(f)*; **film library** N Cinemathek *f*; **film maker** N Filmemacher(in) *m(f)*; **film rights** PL Filmrechte *pl*; **film script** N Drehbuch *nt*; **film sequence** N Filmsequenz *f*; **film set** N Filmset *nt*, Filmdekoration *f*; **filmset** VT (*Brit, Typ*) lichtsetzen, fotosetzen; **filmsetting** N (*Brit, Typ*) Lichtsatz *m*, Fotosatz *m*; **film star** N Filmstar *m*; **film strip** N Filmstreifen *m*; **film studio** N Filmstudio *nt*; **film test** N Probeaufnahmen *pl*; **to give sb a ~** Probeaufnahmen von jdm machen; **film version** N Verfilmung *f*

filmy [ˈfɪlmɪ] ADJ (+*er*) *clothing, fabric, curtains* hauchdünn

Filofax® [ˈfaɪləʊfæks] N Filofax® *m*

filter [ˈfɪltə] **N a** Filter *m*; (*Phot, Rad, Mech*) Filter *nt or m* **b** (*Brit, for traffic*) grüner Pfeil (*für Abbieger*) **VT** *liquids, air* filtern; *sunlight* durchschimmern lassen; *information* vorsortieren **VI a** (*light*) durchscheinen, durchschimmern; (*liq-*

uid, sound) durchsickern **b** (*Brit, Aut*) sich einordnen; **to ~ to the left** sich links einordnen

▶ **filter back VI** (*refugees etc*) allmählich zurückkommen

▶ **filter in VI** (*people*) langsam *or* allmählich eindringen; (*news*) durchsickern

▶ **filter out VI** (*people*) einer nach dem anderen herausgehen; (*news*) durchsickern **VT** *sep* (*lit*) herausfiltern; (*fig*) heraussieben

▶ **filter through VI** (*liquid, sound, news*) durchsickern; (*light*) durchschimmern, durchscheinen

filter: filter bag N Kaffeefilter *m*; **filter bed** N Klärbecken *nt*; **filter coffee** N Filterkaffee *m*; **filter lane** N (*Brit*) Spur *f* zum Einordnen, Abbiegespur *f*; **filter paper** N Filterpapier *nt*; **filter tip** N Filter *m*; **filter-tipped** ADJ ~ **cigarette** Filterzigarette *f*

filth [fɪlθ] N (*lit*) Schmutz *m*, Dreck *m*; (*fig*) Schweinerei *f* (*inf*), Sauerei *f* (*inf*); (= *people*) Dreckspack *nt* (*inf*), (Lumpen)gesindel *nt*; **the ~** (*pej sl*, = *police*) die Bullen *pl* (*sl*); **all the ~ they wrote about him in the papers** all der Unflat, der über ihn in der Zeitung geschrieben wurde; **less of your ~!** nicht so viele Schweinereien, bitte!; **she screamed ~ down the phone** sie rief Schweinereien ins Telefon (*inf*)

filthy [ˈfɪlθɪ] ADJ (+*er*) **a** (= *dirty*) dreckig, verschmutzt; **the kitchen is ~** die Küche starrt vor Dreck; **the room was ~ dirty** (*inf*) das Zimmer war völlig verdreckt (*inf*); **you're ~!** du bist ja ganz dreckig!; **to be ~ with mud** (*clothes, person*) mit Schlamm verschmutzt sein; **to live in ~ conditions** im Dreck leben

b (= *disgusting*) *substance, habit* ekelhaft, widerlich; *whisky is ~ stuff* Whisky ist ein ekelhaftes *or* widerliches Zeug; **you ~ liar!** du gemeiner Lügner!; **you ~ little slut!** (*sl*) du dreckige kleine Schlampe!; **~ rich** (*pej inf*) stinkreich (*inf*) → **lucre**

c (= *obscene*) *joke* dreckig, schmutzig; *language, expression* zotig; *book, magazine* obszön; **you've got a ~ mind!** du hast eine schmutzige Fantasie *or* Phantasie!

d (= *angry*) *look* bitterböse; **she gave me a ~ look** sie warf mir einen bitterbösen Blick zu; **he has a ~ temper** er kann sehr unangenehm werden; **to be in a ~ mood** eine miese Laune haben (*inf*)

e (*inf*: = *bad*) *night* scheußlich; **~ weather** Sauwetter *nt* (*inf*)

fin [fɪn] N **a** (*of fish*) Flosse *f* **b** (*Aviat*) Seitenleitwerk *nt*, Seitenflosse *f*; (*of bomb, rocket, ship*) Stabilisierungsfläche *f* **c** (*Aut, of radiator*) Kühlrippe *f* **d** (*for swimming*) Schwimmflosse *f*

finagle [fɪˈneɪgl] VT (*inf*) deichseln (*inf*); **to ~ sth out of sb** jdm etw abluchsen; **to ~ one's way out of sth** sich aus einer Sache herausmogeln

final [ˈfaɪnl] ADJ **a** (= *last*) letzte(r, s); ~ **round/match** letzte Runde/letztes Spiel; (*in a tournament*) Endrunde *f*/-spiel *nt*; ~ **bend/stretch** (*in stadium*) Zielkurve *f*/-gerade *f*; ~ **stage(s)** Endstadium *nt*; ~ **vowel/consonant** Schlussvokal *m*/-konsonant *m*; ~ **act/scene/chapter** Schlussakt *m*/-szene *f*/-kapitel *nt*; ~ **chord** Schlussakkord *m*; ~ **curtain** (*Theat*) Schlussvorhang *m*

b (= *definitive*) *result, outcome, decision, approval, version* endgültig; ~ **verdict** Endurteil *nt*; ~ **state** Endzustand *m*; ~ **score** Schlussstand *m*, Endergebnis *nt*; **the ~ results of their work** das Endergebnis ihrer Arbeit; **that's my ~ offer** das ist mein letztes Angebot; **the judges' decision is ~** die Preisrichter haben das letzte Wort; **that's not ~ yet** das steht noch nicht endgültig fest; **... and that's ~!** ... und damit basta! (*inf*) → **analysis a** → *also* **say 1 b**

c (= *ultimate*) *humiliation* größte(r, s); **this is the ~ insult** das ist der Gipfel; **the ~ irony is that he died two days before the book was completed** die Ironie des Schicksals wollte es schließlich, dass er zwei Tage vor Fertigstellung des Buchs starb; **he paid the ~ penalty for his crime** er bezahlte sein Verbrechen mit dem Leben

N **a** (*esp Sport*) Finale *nt*; (*of quiz, field event*) Endrunde *f*; (= *game*) Endspiel *nt*; (= *race*) Endlauf *m*; **to get to the ~** ins Finale kommen; **World Cup Final** (*Ftbl*) Endspiel *nt* der Fußballweltmeisterschaft; **the Olympic high jump ~** das olympische Finale im Hochsprung; **the ~s** das Finale, die Endrunde **b** **finals** PL (*Brit Univ*: = *examinations*) Abschlussprüfung *f* **c** (*Press*) **the late (night) ~** die letzte (Nacht)ausgabe

final: final clause N (*Gram*) Finalsatz *m*; **final curtain** N (*Theat*) **ten minutes before the ~** zehn Minuten vor Vorstellungsschluss; **the ~ falls on a horrific scene** bei Vorstellungsschluss bietet sich ein Bild des Schreckens; **final demand** N letzte Mahnung *f*; **final dividend** N (*Fin*) (Jahres)schlussdividende *f*

finale [fɪˈnɑːlɪ] N (*Mus, in opera*) Finale *nt*; (*Theat*) Schlussszene *f*; (*fig*) Finale *nt* (*geh*), (Ab)schluss *m*

final: final edition N (*Press*) letzte Ausgabe; **final examination** N Abschlussprüfung *f*; **Final Four** PL **the ~** (*US, Basketball*) die letzten Vier (*in der Basketballmeisterschaft*); **they have always played in the ~** sie waren immer unter den letzten Vier

finalist [ˈfaɪnəlɪst] N (*Sport*) Endrundenteilnehmer(in) *m(f)*, Finalist(in) *m(f)*; (*Univ*) Examenskandidat(in) *m(f)*

finality [faɪˈnælɪtɪ] N (*of decision etc*) Endgültigkeit *f*; (*of tone of voice*) Entschiedenheit *f*, Bestimmtheit *f*

finalization [ˌfaɪnəlaɪˈzeɪʃən] N Beendigung *f*; (*of plans, arrangements, details*) endgültige Festlegung; (*of deal, negotiations, sale*) endgültiger Abschluss; (*of draft*) endgültige Formgebung

finalize [ˈfaɪnəlaɪz] VT fertig machen, beenden; (= *determine*) plans, arrangements, details endgültig festlegen; deal, sale, negotiations zum Abschluss bringen; draft die endgültige Form geben (+*dat*); **to ~ a decision** eine endgültige Entscheidung treffen

finally [ˈfaɪnəlɪ] ✿ 26.1, 26.2 ADV **a** (= *eventually*) schließlich; (= *at last, expressing relief*) endlich **b** (= *lastly*) zum Schluss; (= *in conclusion, introducing a final point*) abschließend, zum Abschluss; **and ~ I must say ...** und abschließend möchte ich sagen ... **c** (= *definitively*) decide, settle endgültig

final: Final Solution N (*NS*) Endlösung *f*; **final whistle** N (*Ftbl*) Schlusspfiff *m*; **to blow the ~** das Spiel abpfeifen

finance [faɪˈnæns] **N** **a** Finanzen *pl*, Finanzor Geldwesen *nt*; **high ~** Hochfinanz *f*; **to study ~** (*academically*) Finanzwissenschaft studieren; (*as training*) eine Finanzfachschule besuchen **b** (= *money*) Geld *nt*, (Geld)mittel *pl*; **it's a question of ~** das ist eine Geldfrage *or* Frage der Finanzen; **~s** Finanzen *pl*, Finanz- *or* Einkommenslage *f*; **his ~s aren't sound** seine Finanzlage ist nicht gesund, seine Finanzen stehen nicht gut **VT** finanzieren

finance: finance company N Finanz(ierungs)gesellschaft *f*; **finance director** N Leiter(in) *m(f)* der Finanzabteilung; **finance plan** N Finanzierungsplan *m*

financial [faɪˈnænʃəl] ADJ **a** problems, difficulties, help, support finanziell; **it makes good or sound ~ sense** es ist finanziell sinnvoll; **~ resources** Geldmittel *pl* **b** (*St Ex, Econ*) Finanz-; **crisis/policy** Finanzkrise *f*/-politik *f*; **on the ~ markets** auf den Finanzmärkten; **~ news** Wirtschaftsnachrichten *pl*; **~ sector** Finanzsektor *m*; **~ adjustment** Finanzausgleich *m*; **~ status** Finanz- *or* Vermögenslage *f*

financial: financial accounting N (*Comm*) Finanzbuchhaltung *f*; **financial adviser** N Finanzberater(in) *m(f)*; **financial director** N (*Comm*) Leiter(in) *m(f)* der Finanzabteilung; **financial institution** N Geldinstitut *nt*, Finanzinstitut *nt*

financially [faɪˈnænʃəlɪ] ADV finanziell; (*introducing sentence*) finanziell gesehen; **the ~ troubled company** die in finanzielle Schwierigkeiten ge-

ratene Firma; **~ sound** finanziell solide; **the company is ~ sound** die Finanzlage der Firma ist gesund; **~ viable** rentabel; **to be ~ embarrassed** in Geldverlegenheit sein; **she's been struggling ~ for years** sie kommt seit Jahren finanziell kaum über die Runden; **~, things are a bit tight for me this month** diesen Monat bin ich etwas knapp bei Kasse (*inf*)

financial: financial management N (*Comm*) Finanzmanagement *nt*; **financial services** PL Finanzdienstleistungen *pl*; **financial statement** N (*Comm*) Abschluss *m*; (*annual*) Jahresabschluss *m*; **financial system** N Finanzwesen *nt*; **financial year** N (*Brit*) Geschäftsjahr *nt*, Finanzjahr *nt*

financier [faɪˈnænsɪə] N Finanzier *m*

finch [fɪntʃ] N Fink *m*

find [faɪnd] vb: pret, ptp found **VT** **a** finden; **it's nowhere to be found** es lässt sich nirgendwo finden *or* auftreiben (*inf*); **to ~ sb out or away** (= *not at home*) jdn nicht (zu Hause) antreffen; **hoping this letter ~s you in good health** in der Hoffnung, dass Sie gesund sind; **to ~ pleasure in sth** Freude an etw (*dat*) haben; **to ~ comfort in sth** Trost in etw (*dat*) finden; **we left everything as we found it** wir haben alles so gelassen, wie wir es vorgefunden haben; **he was found dead in bed** er wurde tot im Bett aufgefunden; **I can never ~ anything to say to him** ich weiß nie, was ich zu ihm sagen soll; **where am I going to ~ the money/time?** wo soll ich nur das Geld/die Zeit her?; **you must take us as you ~ us** Sie müssen uns so nehmen, wie wir sind; **if you can ~ it in you to ...** wenn Sie es irgend fertigbringen, zu ... **b** (= *supply*) besorgen (*sb sth* jdm etw); **go and ~ me a needle** hol mir doch mal eine Nadel; **did you ~ him what he wanted?** haben Sie bekommen, was er wollte?; **we'll have to ~ him a desk/secretary** wir müssen einen Schreibtisch/eine Sekretärin für ihn finden **c** (= *discover, ascertain*) feststellen; cause herausfinden; **we found the car wouldn't start** es stellte sich heraus, dass das Auto nicht ansprang; **I ~ I'm unable to ...** ich stelle fest, dass ich ... nicht kann; **you will ~ that I am right** Sie werden sehen, dass ich Recht habe; **it has been found that this is so** es hat sich herausgestellt, dass es so ist! **d** (= *consider to be*) finden; **I ~ Spain too hot** ich finde Spanien zu heiß; **I don't ~ it easy to tell you this** es fällt mir nicht leicht, Ihnen das zu sagen; **he always found languages easy/hard** ihm fielen Sprachen immer leicht/schwer; **I found all the questions easy** ich fand, dass die Fragen alle leicht waren; **did you ~ her a good worker?** fanden Sie, dass sie gut arbeitet?; **I ~ it impossible to understand him** ich kann ihn einfach nicht verstehen **e** **I found myself smiling** ich musste unwillkürlich lächeln; **I found myself wondering** ich machte mir so meine Gedanken; **I found myself thinking that ...** ich ertappte mich bei dem Gedanken, dass ...; **I ~ myself in an impossible situation/in financial difficulties** ich befinde mich in einer unmöglichen Situation/in finanziellen Schwierigkeiten; **one day he suddenly found himself out of a job** eines Tages war er plötzlich arbeitslos; **he awoke to ~ himself in prison/hospital** er erwachte und fand sich im Gefängnis/Krankenhaus wieder; **quite by accident I found myself in the park** ganz zufällig fand ich mich im Park wieder; **I found myself quite able to deal with it** ich stellte fest, dass ich durchaus fähig war, damit zurechtzukommen; **I found myself forced to turn back** ich sah mich gezwungen umzukehren **f** **this flower is found all over England** diese Blume findet man in ganz England, diese Blume ist in ganz England vorzufinden; **you don't ~ bears here any more** man findet hier keine Bären mehr, hier gibt es keine Bären mehr; **do you know where there is a florist's to be found?** wissen Sie, wo hier ein Blumenladen ist? **g** **£200 per week all found** £ 200 pro Woche,

(und freie) Kost und Logis **h** (*Jur*) **to ~ sb guilty/not guilty** jdn für schuldig/nicht schuldig befinden, jdn schuldig sprechen/freisprechen; **how do you ~ the accused?** wie lautet Ihr Urteil?; **the court has found that ...** das Gericht hat befunden, dass ... **i** (*Comput*) suchen; **~ and replace** suchen und ersetzen **VI** (*Jur*) **to ~ for/against the accused** den Angeklagten freisprechen/verurteilen, für/gegen den Angeklagten entscheiden **N** Fund *m*

▶ **find out** **VT** sep **a** answer, sb's secret herausfinden **b** (= *discover the misdeeds etc of*) person erwischen; (= *come to know about*) auf die Schliche kommen (+*dat*) (*inf*); **his wife has found him out** seine Frau ist dahinter gekommen; **don't get found out** lass dich nicht erwischen; **you've been found out** du bist entdeckt *or* ertappt (*inf*); **your sins will find you out** (*liter*) die Sonne bringt es an den Tag (*prov*) **VI** **a** es herausfinden; (= *discover misdeeds, dishonesty etc also*) dahinter kommen; **where is it? – find out for yourself!** wo ist es? – sieh doch selbst nach! **b** **to find out about sb/sth** (= *discover existence of*) jdn/etw entdecken; **to help children find out about other countries** Kindern dabei helfen, etwas über andere Länder herauszufinden

finder [ˈfaɪndə] N **a** (*of lost object*) Finder(in) *m(f)*; **~s keepers** (*inf*) wers findet, dem gehörts **b** (*of telescope*) Sucher *m*

finding [ˈfaɪndɪŋ] N **a** **~s** pl Ergebnis(se) *nt(pl)*; (*medical*) Befund *m*; **the ~s of the commission were as follows** die Kommission kam zu folgendem Ergebnis **b** (*Jur, = verdict*) Urteil(sspruch *m*) *nt*

fine[1] [faɪn] ADV **in ~** (*liter*) kurz und gut, kurzum

fine[2] **N** (*Jur*) Geldstrafe *f*; (*for less serious offences*) Geldbuße *or* -strafe *f*; (*driving*) Bußgeld *nt*; (*for minor traffic offences*) (gebührenpflichtige) Verwarnung **VT** (*Jur*) zu einer Geldstrafe verurteilen, mit einer Geldstrafe/-buße belegen; (*for driving offences also*) Bußgeld verhängen gegen; (*for minor traffic offences*) eine (gebührenpflichtige) Verwarnung erteilen (+*dat*); **he was ~d £100** er musste £ 100 Strafe bezahlen; **he was ~d for speeding** er hat einen Strafzettel für zu schnelles Fahren bekommen; **she was ~d for possession (of drugs)** sie wurde wegen Drogenbesitz zu einer Geldstrafe verurteilt

fine[3] ADJ (+*er*) **a** (= *excellent*) piece of work, example, painting, book, museum ausgezeichnet; building, town, view herrlich; person fein, trefflich (*geh*); performance, performer, player großartig, ausgezeichnet; **you're doing a ~ job** Sie machen Ihre Sache ganz ausgezeichnet; **they're in ~ health** sie erfreuen sich bester Gesundheit; **this is even ~r than her previous recording** das ist noch besser als ihre letzte Aufnahme; **she's a ~ woman** sie ist eine bewundernswerte *or* (*in stature*) stattliche Frau; **he is the ~st actor of our day** er ist der größte Schauspieler unserer Zeit; **the ~st English painting of its time** das beste *or* großartigste englische Gemälde seiner Zeit; **the ~st beaches in Spain** die herrlichsten *or* schönsten Strände Spaniens; **their ~st hour** ihre größte Stunde → **fettle, figure** N d, **form** N i **b** (= *acceptable: of things*) in Ordnung; **my coffee was ~** mein Kaffee war in Ordnung; **any more? – no, that's ~** *or* **it'll be ~** noch etwas? – nein, danke *or* es ist gut so; **everything's (just) ~** alles in (bester) Ordnung; **everything's going to be just ~** es wird schon alles gut gehen; **how was I? – you were ~** wie war ich? – gut; **these apples are ~ for cooking** diese Äpfel eignen sich (gut) zum Kochen; **it's ~ (for you) to interrupt me** Sie dürfen mich gerne unterbrechen; **it's ~ for men to cry** Männer dürfen auch weinen, es ist durchaus in Ordnung, wenn Männer weinen; **the doctor said it was ~ for me to play** der Arzt sagte, ich dürfte ohne weiteres spielen; **you look/the wallpaper looks ~ (to me)** (ich finde,)du siehst/die Tapete sieht gut aus; **your idea sounds ~** Ihre Idee hört sich gut an; **shall we have another beer? – sounds ~ to me** sollen wir noch ein Bier trinken? – ja, gute Idee; **he/she is ~** (= *managing OK*) er/sie kommt gut zurecht; (= *in good health*) es geht ihm/ihr gut; (= *things are going well*) mit ihm/ihr ist alles in Ordnung; **how are you?** – danke, gut; **a glass of water and I'll be ~** nach einem Glas Wasser wird es mir wieder gut gehen; **he's ~, he's done it before** es schafft es schon, er hat es schon ein-mal gemacht; **any questions? no? ~** noch Fra-gen? nein? gut; **that's ~ with** or **by me** ich habe nichts dagegen; **it'll take me a couple of days – that's ~ with me** ich werde ein paar Tage dafür brauchen – das ist in Ordnung; **anything she wanted was usually ~ with him** was sie auch im-mer wollte, er hatte meist nichts dagegen

c (= *high-quality*) *food* fein; *wine* erlesen, edel; *furniture, jewellery, clothes* ausgesucht; *china, por-celain, fabric* erlesen, ausgesucht; **the ~st ingre-dients** die erlesensten Zutaten

d (= *refined*) *lady, gentleman, manners* fein; (= *smart, large*) *house* vornehm; **she likes to play at being the ~ lady** sie spielt sich gern als feine Dame auf

e *weather, day* schön; **when it is/was ~** bei schönem Wetter; **all areas will be ~ tomorrow** morgen wird es überall schön; **one ~ day** eines schönen Tages

f (*iro*) *excuse, state, friend etc* schön (*iro*); **a ~ re-ward for all my work!** eine schöne Belohnung für meine ganze Mühe!; **a ~ friend you are!** du bist mir ja ein schöner Freund!; **a ~ time to re-member that!** ein feiner Augenblick, dich da-ran zu erinnern!; **that's all very ~, but ...** das ist ja alles schön und gut, aber ...; **that's ~ for you to say** du hast gut reden; **you're a ~ one to talk!** du kannst gerade reden!; **~ words** schöne Worte *pl*

g (= *thin*) *needle, thread* dünn, fein; *fabric, mate-rial* dünn; *hair, grain* fein; *handwriting* fein, zier-lich; *sieve, net, mesh, weave* fein(maschig); **a net with a ~ mesh** ein feinmaschiges Netz; **~ nib** spitze Feder; **a paper with very ~ grain** ein sehr feinkörniges Papier

h (= *in small particles*) *powder, dust, sand, mist* fein; **a ~ rain** Nieselregen *m*; **a ~ dusting of snow/flour** eine dünne Schneedecke/Mehl-schicht

i (= *delicate*) *china, fabric* fein; *features* fein, zart; *bones* zierlich

j (= *subtle, small*) *adjustment, detail, distinction, difference* fein; *print* klein; **in ~ print** klein ge-druckt; **to read the ~ print** das Kleingedruckte lesen; **the ~r points of English grammar** die Feinheiten der englischen Grammatik; **not to put too ~ a point on it** um ganz offen zu sein; **there's a ~ line between genius and madness** es besteht ein feiner Unterschied zwischen Genie und Wahnsinn

k *gold, silver* fein; **gold 98% ~** Gold mit 98% Feingehalt

ADV **a** (= *well*) *work* tadellos; **you're doing ~** Sie machen Ihre Sache gut; (*healthwise*) Sie ma-chen gute Fortschritte; **we get on ~** wir kom-men ausgezeichnet miteinander aus

b (= *thinly*) *cut, slice* fein, dünn → **cut 3 p**

▶**fine down** VT *sep wood etc* glätten; *text, novel etc* straffen (*to* zu); *theory* reduzieren (*to* auf +*acc*)

fine: fine art N *usu pl* schöne Künste *pl* **b** (= *skill*) Kunststück *nt*, echte Kunst; **he's got it down to a ~** er hat den Bogen heraus (*inf*); **fine cut** N (= *tobacco*) Feinschnitt *m*; **fine--drawn** ADJ **a** *thread* fein gesponnen or (*syn-thetic*) gezogen; *wire* fein gezogen **b** *features* fein (geschnitten); **fine-food shop** N Fein-kostgeschäft *nt*; **fine-grain, fine-grained** ADJ *wood, rock* fein gemasert; (*Phot*) *film, paper* fein-körnig

finely ['faɪnlɪ] ADV **a** (= *exquisitely*) *crafted, de-tailed, carved* fein

b (= *thinly, in small pieces*) *chop, grate, grind* fein,

---

slice dünn; **~ ground coffee** fein gemahlener Kaffee; **~ diced** fein gewürfelt, in feine Würfel geschnitten; **~ sliced** fein geschnitten, in dün-ne Scheiben geschnitten

c (= *subtly, delicately*) fein; **the case is ~ bal-anced** der Fall kann sich so oder so entschei-den; **a ~ judged speech** eine wohl ausgewoge-ne Rede; **~ drawn distinctions** feine Unter-schiede; **~ tuned** (*engine, machine*) genau einge-stellt; (*fig*) *military/party/administrative machine* gut geölt; (= *ultrasensitive*) hoch empfindlich

fine-mesh [faɪn'meʃ] ADJ *net* eng- or feinma-schig

fineness ['faɪnnɪs] N **a** (= *beauty, pleasantness*) Schönheit *f* **b** (= *high quality*) Güte *f*; (*of mind, novel*) Großartigkeit *f*; (= *elegance, delicacy*) Fein-heit *f*; (*of material*) Zartheit *f* **c** (*of sieve, net, mesh*) Feinmaschigkeit *f*; (*of dust, sand*) Feinheit *f* **d** (= *thinness*) Feinheit *f*, Dünnheit *f*; (*of nib*) Spitze *f*; **the ~ of the print** die kleine Schrift **e** (*of metal*) Feingehalt *m* **f** (*of adjustment, dis-tinction*) Feinheit *f*

finery ['faɪnərɪ] N **a** (*of dress*) Staat *m*; (*liter, of nature etc*) Pracht *f*; **she had never seen so much ~** sie hatte noch nie eine solche Pracht gesehen; **wedding guests in all their ~** Hoch-zeitsgäste in vollem Staat **b** (*Metal, = furnace*) Frischofen *m*

finesse [fɪ'nes] N **a** (= *skill, diplomacy*) Ge-wandtheit *f*, Geschick *nt* **b** (= *cunning*) Schlauheit *f*, Finesse *f* **c** (*Cards*) Schneiden *nt* **VI** (*Cards*) schneiden **VT** **a** (= *do with finesse*) *problem* geschickt lösen; (= *avoid*) ausweichen (+*dat*) **b** (*Cards*) schneiden

fine-tooth comb ['faɪntuːθkəʊm] N **to go o-ver sth with a ~** etw genau unter die Lupe neh-men; *area* etw durchkämmen; *room* etw gründ-lich durchsuchen

fine: fine-tune VT *engine* fein abstimmen; (*fig*) *projection etc* fein abstimmen; **fine-tuning** N (*lit*) Feinabstimmung *f*; (*fig also*) Detailarbeit *f*

finger ['fɪŋgə] N **a** Finger *m*; **she can twist him round her little ~** sie kann ihn um den (klei-nen) Finger wickeln; **to have a ~ in every pie** überall die Finger drin or im Spiel haben (*inf*), überall mitmischen (*inf*); **I forbid you to lay a ~ on him** ich verbiete Ihnen, ihm auch nur ein Härchen zu krümmen; **I didn't lay a ~ on her** ich habe sie nicht angerührt; **he wouldn't lift a ~ to help me** er würde keinen Finger rühren, um mir zu helfen; **he didn't lift a ~ (around the house)** er hat (im Haus) keinen Finger krumm gemacht (*inf*); **to point one's ~ at sb** mit dem Finger auf jdn zeigen; **to point the ~ or an accusing ~ at sb** (*fig*) mit Fingern auf jdn zei-gen; **to point the ~ of suspicion/blame at sb** jdn verdächtigen/beschuldigen; **I can't put my ~ on it, but ...** ich kann es nicht genau ausma-chen, aber ...; **you've put your ~ on it there** da haben Sie den kritischen Punkt berührt; **to put the ~ on sb** (*inf*) jdn verpfeifen (*inf*); **to get** or **pull one's ~ out** (*Brit inf*) Nägel mit Köpfen machen (*inf*); **pull your ~ out!** (*Brit inf*) es wird Zeit, dass du Nägel mit Köpfen machst! (*inf*); **to give sb the ~** (*esp US, inf*) jdm den Stinkefin-ger zeigen (*inf*) → **cross**

b (*of whisky etc*) Fingerbreit *m*

VT **a** (= *touch*) anfassen; (= *toy, meddle with*) befingern, herumfingern an (+*dat*)

b (*inf: = inform on*) verpfeifen

c (*Mus, = mark for fingering*) mit einem Finger-satz versehen; **to ~ the keys/strings** in die Tas-ten/Saiten greifen

finger: finger alphabet N Fingeralphabet *nt*; **fingerboard** N Griffbrett *nt*; **finger bowl** N Fingerschale *f*; **finger buffet** N Buffet *nt* mit Appetithappen; **finger-dry** VT **to ~ one's hair** sich (*dat*) die Haare mit den Fingern trocknen; **finger exercise** N Fingerübung *f*; **finger food** N Appetithappen *pl*; **finger hole** N (*in flute etc*) Griffloch *nt*

fingering ['fɪŋgərɪŋ] N **a** (*Mus, in the notation*) Fingersatz *m*; (*of keys, strings*) (Finger)technik *f*; **the ~ is very difficult** die Griffe sind sehr schwierig **b** (*of goods in shop etc*) Anfassen *nt*,

---

Berühren *nt*; (= *toying, meddling*) Befingern *nt* (*of, with* +*gen*), Herumfingern *nt* (*of, with* an +*dat*) **c** (*Tex*) Strumpfwolle *f*

finger: fingermark N Fingerabdruck *m*; **fin-gernail** N Fingernagel *m*; **finger paint** N Fin-gerfarbe *f*; **finger-paint** VT mit Fingerfarben malen; **fingerprint** **N** Fingerabdruck *m*; **to take sb's ~s** jdm Fingerabdrücke abnehmen **VT** **to ~ sb/sth** jdm/von etw Fingerabdrücke nehmen; **fingerprint expert** N Sachverstän-dige(r) *mf* für Fingerabdrücke; **fingerstall** N Fingerling *m*; **fingertip** N Fingerspitze *f*; **to have sth at one's ~s** (*fig, = know very well*) etw aus dem Effeff kennen (*inf*); (= *have at one's im-mediate disposal*) etw im kleinen Finger (*inf*) or parat haben; **everything you need is at your ~s** alles, was Sie brauchen, steht Ihnen zur Verfü-gung; **to one's ~s** (*fig*) durch und durch; **fin-gertip control** N (*of steering wheel etc*) mühe-lose Steuerung; **to have ~** sich mühelos bedie-nen lassen; **fingertip search** N Durchkäm-mungsaktion *f*

finickiness ['fɪnɪkɪnɪs] N (*of person*) Pingeligkeit *f* (*inf*); (*about language also*) Haarspalterei *f*; (*of task*) Kniff(e)ligkeit *f* (*inf*); **because of his ~ a-bout what he eats** weil er so wählerisch beim Essen ist

finicky ['fɪnɪkɪ] ADJ *person* schwer zufrieden zu stellen, pingelig (*inf*); (*about food, clothes etc*) wählerisch, pingelig (*inf*); *work, job* kniff(e)lig (*inf*); *detail* winzig; **he's a ~ eater** er ist beim Es-sen sehr wählerisch

finish ['fɪnɪʃ] **N** **a** (= *end*) Schluss *m*, Ende *nt*; (*of race*) Finish *nt*; (= *finishing line*) Ziel *nt*; **they never gave up, right to the ~** sie haben bis zum Schluss nicht aufgegeben; **from start to ~** von Anfang bis Ende; **he's got a good ~** (*Sport*) er hat einen starken Endspurt; **to be in at the ~** (*fig*) beim Ende dabei sein; **to fight to the ~** (*fig*) bis zum letzten Augenblick kämpfen

b (= *perfection, of manners*) Schliff *m*; (*of things*) Verarbeitung *f*, Ausfertigung *f*; **they lack the ~ of handmade ones** sie sind nicht so sorgfältig or sauber verarbeitet wie handgemachte; **it has a poor ~** die Verarbeitung or Ausfertigung ist schlecht

c (*of industrial products*) Finish *nt*; (= *final coat of paint*) Deckanstrich *m*; (*of material*) Appretur *f*; (*of paper*) Oberflächenfinish *nt*; (*of pottery*) Oberfläche *f*; (= *ornamental work*) Verzierung *f*; **paper with a gloss/matt ~** Hochglanz-/Matt-glanzpapier *nt*; **paint with a gloss/matt ~** Farbe *f* mit Hochglanzeffekt/mattem Glanz; **highly polished to give it a good ~** auf Hochglanz poliert

VT **a** beenden; *education, course* abschließen; *piece of work, business* erledigen, abschließen; **he's ~ed the painting/job** er ist mit dem Bild/ der Arbeit fertig; **to have ~ed doing sth** damit fertig sein, etw zu tun; **when I ~ eating ...** wenn ich mit dem Essen fertig bin, ...; **I've ~ed iron-ing** ich bin mit dem Bügeln fertig; **to ~ writing/ reading sth** etw zu Ende schreiben/lesen, etw fertig schreiben/lesen; **let me ~ eating** lass mich zu Ende essen, lass mich fertig essen; **to have ~ed sth** etw fertig haben; *task, course* etw fertig sein, etw beendet haben; **when do you ~ work?** wann machen Sie Feierabend or Schluss?; **I'm in a hurry to get this job ~ed** ich möchte diese Sache so schnell wie möglich zu Ende bringen; **she never lets him ~ (what he's saying)** sie lässt ihn nie ausreden; **Daddy, will you ~ (telling) that story?** Papa, erzählst du die Geschichte zu Ende or fertig?; **can I have that book when you've ~ed it?** kann ich das Buch haben, wenn du es ausgelesen hast?; **give me time to ~ my drink** lass mich austrin-ken; **~ what you're doing and we'll go** mach fertig, was du angefangen hast, und dann ge-hen wir; **the dollar ~ed the day up against the pound** bei Börsenschluss war der Dollar ge-genüber dem Pfund gestiegen

b (= *ruin*) ruinieren; (= *kill, inf: = exhaust*) ka-puttmachen (*inf*), den Rest geben (+*dat*) (*inf*); **another strike could ~ the firm** noch ein Streik könnte das Ende für die Firma bedeuten; **that**

last mile nearly ~ed me (inf) diese letzte Meile hat mir nahe den Rest gegeben (inf)
c (= put finishing touches to) den letzten Schliff geben (+dat); piece of handiwork verarbeiten; (= give a surface treatment to) surface, industrial product fertig bearbeiten, ein Finish geben (+dat); (= paint) anstreichen; car etc lackieren; **to ~ sth with a coat of varnish** etw zum Schluss (mit Firnis) lackieren; **the paintwork isn't very well ~ed** die Malerarbeiten wurden nicht sehr gut ausgeführt; **the metal is ~ed with a high-speed disc** das Metall wird mit einer schnell rotierenden Scheibe poliert; **the paper is ~ed on the glazing rollers** das Papier wird mit dem Kalander nachbearbeitet
VI **a** zu Ende or aus sein; fertig sein; (= come to an end, finish work) aufhören; (piece of music, story etc) enden; **when does the film ~?** wann ist der Film aus?; **my course ~es this week** mein Kurs geht diese Woche zu Ende; **we'll ~ by singing a song** wir wollen mit einem Lied schließen, zum Schluss singen wir ein Lied; **I've ~ed** ich bin fertig
b (Sport) das Ziel erreichen; **to ~ first/second** als erster/zweiter durchs Ziel gehen

▶ **finish off** **VI** **a** (= come to an end) aufhören, Schluss machen
b **to finish off with a glass of brandy** zum (Ab)schluss ein Glas Weinbrand trinken; **we finished off by singing ...** wir schlossen mit dem Lied ..., wir sangen zum (Ab)schluss ...
VT sep **a** piece of work fertig machen; job erledigen; **to finish off a painting** ein Bild zu Ende malen; **to finish off a letter** einen Brief zu Ende schreiben
b food, meal aufessen; drink austrinken
c (= kill) wounded animal, person den Gnadenstoß geben (+dat); (by shooting) den Gnadenschuss geben (+dat)
d (= do for) person den Rest geben, erledigen (inf); **the last mile just about finished me off** (inf) die letzte Meile hat mich ziemlich geschafft (inf) or fertig gemacht (inf)

▶ **finish up** **VI** **a** = **finish off** VI a, b **b** (= end up in a place) landen (inf); **he finished up a nervous wreck** er war zum Schluss ein Nervenbündel; **he finished up in third place** er landete auf dem dritten Platz (inf); **you'll finish up wishing you'd never started** du wünschst dir bestimmt noch, du hättest gar nicht erst angefangen; **I'll just finish up having to do it all again** zum Schluss muss ich doch alles nochmal machen **VT** sep = **finish off** VT b

▶ **finish with** VI +prep obj **a** (= no longer need) nicht mehr brauchen; **I've finished with the paper/book** ich habe mit der Zeitung/dem Buch fertig **b** (= want no more to do with) **I've finished with him** ich will nichts mehr mit ihm zu tun haben, ich bin fertig mit ihm (inf); (with boyfriend) ich habe mit ihm Schluss gemacht **c** **you wait till I've finished with you!** (inf) warte nur, dich knöpfe ich mir noch vor (inf)

finished ['fɪnɪʃt] ADJ **a** person fertig; **I'm nearly ~** ich bin fast fertig or so weit; **to be ~ doing sth** (US) damit fertig sein, etw zu tun; **when I was ~ eating** (US) als ich mit dem Essen fertig war; **to be ~ with sb/sth** jdm/etw fertig sein; (= have no) von jdm/etw nichts mehr wissen wollen; **I won't be ~ with him/it for some time yet** ich werde noch eine Weile mit ihm/damit zu tun haben; **I'm ~ with politics** mit der Politik ist es für mich vorbei
b (= used up) things aufgebraucht, alle (N Ger inf); (= over) activity, performance, trial zu Ende; **the wine is ~** es ist kein Wein mehr da; **when work was ~, we often dined out together** nach der Arbeit gingen wir oft zusammen essen; **those days are ~** die Zeiten sind vorbei
c (inf: = having no future) **to be ~** (jobholder, politician, sportsperson etc) erledigt sein (inf) (as als); **we're ~, it's ~ between us** es ist aus zwischen uns; **my career is ~** mit meiner Karriere ist es vorbei, meine Karriere ist am Ende; **the printed word is ~** das gedruckte Wort hat keine Zukunft mehr
d (= treated) product fertig bearbeitet; (with

paint) gestrichen; (with lacquer, varnish) lackiert; (with polish) poliert; clothing verarbeitet; **beautifully ~ wood** wunderschön verarbeitetes Holz; **the room is ~ in red** das Zimmer ist rot gestrichen
e (= fully made) product, work of art, film, building, dish, size fertig; **~ goods/products** Fertigprodukte pl; **the ~ result** das Endergebnis; **the ~ article** (= object) das fertige Produkt; (= piece of writing, work of art) die endgültige Version; (= accomplished performer) der perfekte Künstler, die perfekte Künstlerin; **they are not yet the ~ article** es fehlt ihnen noch einiges zur Perfektion

finisher ['fɪnɪʃə'] N **a** (Ftbl, Rugby, Hockey etc) **a good ~** ein guter Torschütze **b** (Athletics, Cycling etc) **to be a fast/strong ~** einen schnellen/starken Endspurt haben; **he is renowned as a fast ~** er ist für seinen schnellen Endspurt bekannt

finishing ['fɪnɪʃɪŋ] N **his ~ is excellent** (Ftbl, Rugby, Hockey etc) er ist ein ausgezeichneter Torschütze; (Cycling, Athletics) er ist ein ausgezeichneter Sprinter

finishing: finishing industry N (Tech) verarbeitende Industrie, Veredelungsindustrie f; **finishing line** N Ziellinie f; **finishing process** N (Tech) Veredelungsverfahren nt; **finishing school** N (Mädchen)pensionat nt

finite ['faɪnaɪt] ADJ **a** (= limited) set, amount, time, resources begrenzt; universe endlich; **a ~ number** eine begrenzte Zahl; (Math) eine endliche Zahl; **coal and oil are ~ resources** Kohle und Öl sind nicht erneuerbare Ressourcen; **there is a ~ limit to the weight a human can lift** ein Mensch kann höchstens ein bestimmtes Gewicht heben **b** (Rel, Philos) being, world endlich **c** (Gram) verb, clause finit

fink [fɪŋk] (dated US, sl) **N** **a** (= strikebreaker) Streikbrecher(in) m(f) **b** (= contemptible person) Saftsack m (inf) **VI** **to ~ on sb** jdn verpfeifen (inf)

Finland ['fɪnlənd] N Finnland nt

Finn [fɪn] N Finne m, Finnin f

Finnish ['fɪnɪʃ] ADJ finnisch; **he is ~** er ist Finne; **she is ~** sie ist Finnin **N** (Ling) Finnisch nt

Finno-Ugric ['fɪnəʊ'juːgrɪk], **Finno-Ugrian** ['fɪnəʊ'juːgrɪən] ADJ (Ling) finnisch-ugrisch, finnougrisch

fiord [fjɔːd] N Fjord m

fir [fɜː'] N Tanne f; (= wood) Tanne(nholz nt) f

fir cone N Tannenzapfen m

fire [faɪə'] **N** **a** Feuer nt; **the house was on ~** das Haus brannte; **to set ~ to sth, to set sth on ~** etw anzünden; (so as to destroy) etw in Brand stecken; **he'll never set the world** or **the Thames** (Brit) or **the heather** (Scot) **on ~** von ihm sind keine Sensationen zu erwarten; **to catch ~** Feuer fangen (also fig); (building, forest etc also) in Brand geraten; **"keep away from ~"** „von Feuer fern halten"; **when man discovered ~** als der Mensch das Feuer entdeckte; **you're playing with ~** (fig) du spielst mit dem Feuer; **to fight ~ with ~** (fig) mit den gleichen Waffen kämpfen; **to go through ~ and water** (fig) durchs Feuer gehen → **house**
b (= house fire, forest fire etc) Brand m; **there was a ~ next door** nebenan hat es gebrannt; **~! Feuer!, feurio** (old); **Glasgow has more ~s than any other city** in Glasgow brennt es häufiger als in anderen Städten; **to insure oneself against ~** eine Feuerversicherung abschließen
c (in grate) (Kamin)feuer nt; (= electric fire, gas fire) Ofen m; **they have an open ~** sie haben einen offenen Kamin
d (Mil) Feuer nt; **~!** Feuer!; **to open ~ on sb** das Feuer auf jdn eröffnen; **to be caught between two ~s** (lit, fig) zwischen zwei Feuer geraten; **to come under ~** (lit, fig) unter Beschuss geraten; **he came under ~ from the critics** er wurde von den Kritikern unter Beschuss genommen; **to draw ~ from sb** (lit) von jdm unter Feuer genommen werden; (fig) jds Kritik auf sich (acc) ziehen; **to be in the line of ~** (lit, fig)

in der Schusslinie stehen
e (= passion) Feuer nt; **he spoke with ~** er sprach mit Leidenschaft; **to have ~ in one's belly** von leidenschaftlicher Begeisterung erfüllt sein; **to be on ~** (fig) brennen (with vor +dat)
VT **a** (= burn to destroy) in Brand stecken
b pottery brennen
c furnace befeuern → **oilfired, gasfired**
d (fig) imagination beflügeln; passions entzünden, entfachen (geh); enthusiasm befeuern; **to ~ sb with enthusiasm** jdn begeistern, jdn in Begeisterung versetzen
e gun, arrow abschießen; shot abfeuern, abgeben; rocket zünden, abfeuern; **to ~ a gun at sb** auf jdn schießen; **to ~ a salute** Salut schießen; **she ~d an elastic (band) at me** sie schoss ein Gummiband auf mich ab; **to ~ questions at sb** Fragen auf jdn abfeuern
f (inf, = dismiss) feuern (inf)
VI **a** (= shoot) feuern, schießen (at auf +acc); **~!** (gebt) Feuer!
b (engine) zünden; **the engine is only firing on three cylinders** der Motor läuft nur auf drei Zylindern

▶ **fire away** VI (inf, = begin) losschießen (inf)

▶ **fire off** VT sep gun, round, shell, questions abfeuern; letter loslassen

▶ **fire up** VT sep machine, computer starten; **to be all fired up (about sth)** (esp US) (von etw) ganz begeistert sein

fire: fire alarm N Feueralarm m; (= apparatus) Feuermelder m; **fire appliance** N Feuerwehrfahrzeug nt; **firearm** N Feuer- or Schusswaffe f; **fireball** N **a** (of nuclear explosion) Feuerball m; (= lightning) Kugelblitz m **b** (= meteor) Feuerkugel f **c** (fig inf, = person) Energiebündel nt (inf); **firebomb** N Brandbombe f; **firebrand** N **a** Feuerbrand m (old) **b** (= mischief-maker) Unruhestifter(in) m(f), Aufwiegler(in) m(f); **firebreak** N (= strip of land) Feuerschneise f; (= wall) Brandmauer f; (= sandbags etc) (Schutz)wall m (gegen die Ausbreitung eines Feuers); **firebrick** N Schamottestein m; **fire brigade** N (Brit) Feuerwehr f; **firebug** N (inf) Feuerteufel m (inf), Brandstifter(in) m(f); **fire chief** N (esp Brit) Feuerwehrhauptmann m; **fire clay** N Schamotte f; **firecracker** N Knallkörper m; **firedamp** N (Min) Grubengas nt, schlagende Wetter pl; **fire department** N (US) Feuerwehr f; **firedog** N Kaminbock m; **fire door** N Feuertür f; **fire drill** N Probealarm m; (for firemen) Feuerübung f; **fire-eater** N Feuerfresser or -schlucker m; **fire engine** N Feuerwehrauto nt; **fire escape** N (= staircase) Feuertreppe f; (= ladder) Feuerleiter f; **fire exit** N Notausgang m; (= external stairs) Feuertreppe f; **fire-extinguisher** N Feuerlöscher m; **firefight** N (Mil) Schusswechsel m; **firefighter** N (= fireman) Feuerwehrmann or -frau f; (= voluntary helper) freiwilliger Helfer/freiwillige Helferin (bei der Feuerbekämpfung); **firefighting** ADJ attr techniques, team zur Feuerbekämpfung; **~ equipment** Feuerlöschgeräte pl; **~ operation** Feuerlöschaktion f; **firefly** N Leuchtkäfer m; **fireguard** N (Schutz)gitter nt (vor dem Kamin); **fire hazard** N **to be a ~** feuergefährlich sein; **these old houses are a ~** bei diesen alten Häusern besteht Brandgefahr; **fire hose** N Feuerwehrschlauch m; **firehouse** N (US) Feuerwache f, Feuerwehrzentrale f; **fire hydrant** N Hydrant m; **fire insurance** N Feuer- or Brandversicherung f; **fire irons** PL Kaminbesteck nt; **firelight** N Schein m des Feuers or der Flammen; **firelighter** N Feueranzünder m; **fireman** N **a** Feuerwehrmann m/-frau f; **to give sb a ~'s lift** jdn im Feuerwehrgriff tragen, jdn hochheben bzw tragen, indem man ihn über die Schulter wirft **b** (Rail) Heizer m; **fire marshal** N (US) Feuerwehrhauptmann m; **fireplace** N Kamin m; **fireplug** N (dated US) Hydrant m; **firepower** N (of guns, aircraft, army) Feuerkraft f; **fire prevention** N Brandschutz m; **fireproof** ADJ feuerfest VT materials feuerfest machen; **fire raiser** N (esp Brit) Brandstifter(in) m(f);

fire raising N (esp Brit) Brandstiftung f; **fire regulations** PL Brandschutzbestimmungen pl; **fire retardant** ADJ feuerhemmend N Feuerhemmer m; **fire risk** N Brandrisiko nt; **fire sale** N Ausverkauf m von Waren mit Brandschäden; **fire screen** N Ofenschirm m; **Fire Service** N Feuerwehr f; **fireside** N to sit by the ~ am Kamin sitzen; ~ **chair** Lehnsessel m; **fire station** N Feuerwache f, Feuerwehrzentrale f; **firestorm** N Feuersturm m; **firetrap** N Feuerfalle f; **fire truck** N (US) = **fire engine**; **firewall** N **a** (Comput) Firewall f **b** (= wall) Brandmauer f; **firewarden** N Feuerwehrmann m; **firewater** N (hum inf) Feuerwasser nt (inf); **firewoman** N Feuerwehrfrau f; **firewood** N Brennholz nt; **fireworks** PL Feuerwerkskörper pl; (= display) Feuerwerk nt; **there's going to be ~ at the meeting** (fig inf) bei dem Treffen werden die Funken fliegen

firing ['faɪrɪŋ] N **a** (of pottery) Brennen nt **b** (Mil) Feuer nt; (of gun, shot, rocket) Abfeuern nt; **the ~ of a salute** Salutschüsse pl **c** (inf, = dismissal) Rausschmiss m (inf) **d** (Aut, of engine) Zündung f

firing: firing line N (Mil) Feuer- or Schusslinie f; (fig) Schusslinie f; **to be in the ~** (lit, fig) in der Schusslinie stehen; **firing pin** N Schlagbolzen m; **firing squad** N Exekutionskommando nt

firm¹ [fɜːm] N Firma f; **~ of lawyers** Rechtsanwaltsbüro nt; **the Firm** (inf) die Mafia

firm² ADJ (+er) **a** (= solid) mattress, pillow, fruit, foundation etc fest; stomach, thighs straff; **the cake should be ~ to the touch** der Kuchen sollte sich fest anfühlen; **~ ground** or **going** (Horse Racing) harter Boden

b (= strong) hold, grip fest, sicher; handshake fest; (= steady) support, chair, ladder stabil; **to get** or **take a ~ hold on sth** etw festhalten; **to keep a ~ grip** or **hold on sth/oneself** (fig) etw fest/sich gut im Griff haben; **to have ~ control of sth** etw fest unter Kontrolle haben; **Liverpool took ~ control of the game** Liverpool beherrschte das Spiel; **to have a ~ grasp/understanding of sth** etw gut beherrschen/verstehen; **to gain a ~ foothold** (fig) festen Fuß fassen; **to have a ~ foothold** (fig) eine sichere Ausgangsposition haben; **you need a ~ base** or **foundation in any career** für jede Karriere braucht man eine stabile Basis or eine feste Grundlage; **they have no ~ foundations on which to build** sie haben keine feste Grundlage, auf der sie bauen können; **to put sth on a ~ footing** or **foundation** (economy, company etc) etw auf eine sichere Basis stellen

c (= definite) agreement, promise, commitment, belief, support fest; decision endgültig; evidence, information, conclusion sicher; news bestätigt; step entschlossen; **to set a ~ date for sth** einen festen Termin für etw vereinbaren; **it is my ~ belief** or **conviction that ...** ich bin der festen Überzeugung, dass ...; **to be a ~ believer in sth/that ...** fest an etw (acc) glauben/daran glauben, dass ...; **he's a ~ supporter** or **advocate of capital punishment** er ist ein entschiedener Befürworter der Todesstrafe; **~ Conservative supporters** überzeugte Anhänger der konservativen Partei

d (= strict) leader, father stark; leadership, policy, voice fest; manner, action entschlossen; measure durchgreifend; **this demands ~ leadership** das erfordert eine feste Führung; **to be ~ about sth** auf etw (dat) bestehen; **to be ~ with sb** jdm gegenüber bestimmt auftreten; **she's ~ with the children** sie ist streng mit den Kindern; **to take a ~ hand with sb** streng mit jdm umgehen; **children need a ~ hand** Kinder brauchen eine feste Hand; **to take a ~ stand** or **line** klar Stellung beziehen; **to take a ~ stand** or **line against sth** energisch gegen etw vorgehen

e ~ **friends** enge Freunde; **they are ~ friends** sie sind eng befreundet; **to become ~ friends with sb** sich eng mit jdm anfreunden; **to be a ~ favourite** (Brit) or **favorite** (US) (with sb) (bei jdm) sehr beliebt sein; **this restaurant is one of my ~ favourites** (Brit) or **favorites** (US) dies ist eines meiner Lieblingsrestaurants; **to be the ~**

favourite (Brit) or **favorite** (US) hoher Favorit sein; **the ~ favourite** (Brit) or **favorite** (US) **for a job** der aussichtsreichste Kandidat für einen Posten

f (Fin) price, currency stabil; **the pound was fairly ~ against the dollar** das Pfund blieb dem Dollar gegenüber relativ stabil

ADV **to hold sth ~** etw festhalten; **to hold ~** (Fin: prices, shares, currency) stabil bleiben; **to stand** or **hold ~** (= not give up) fest or standhaft bleiben; (troops) die Stellung halten; **you should stand ~ against such threats** Sie sollten sich durch solche Drohungen nicht beirren lassen

VT soil festdrücken

▶ **firm up** VT sep muscles kräftigen; thighs straffen; deal etc unter Dach und Fach bringen

firmament ['fɜːməmənt] N Firmament nt

firmly ['fɜːmlɪ] ADV **a** (= securely) place, hold, anchored, shut, established, set, stuck fest; fix sicher; **bake until ~ set** so lange backen, bis es fest (geworden) ist; **she had her sights ~ set on a career in politics** sie hatte sich eine Karriere in der Politik fest vorgenommen; **it was held ~ in place with a pin** es wurde von einer Nadel festgehalten; **these novels were ~ based on reality** diese Romane beruhten vollständig auf tatsächlichen Ereignissen; **~ established/in place** (fig) fest etabliert; **to be ~ in control of sth** etw fest in der Hand haben; **to be ~ committed to sth/to doing sth** sich voll für etw einsetzen/dafür einsetzen, etw zu tun; **~ held opinions** feste Ansichten

b (= definitely) say, tell bestimmt; reject entschieden; deny energisch; **I shall tell her quite ~ that ...** ich werde ihr klipp und klar sagen, dass ...

firmness ['fɜːmnɪs] N **a** (= solidity: of mattress, pillow, fruit, foundation etc) Festigkeit f; (of stomach, thighs) Straffheit f **b** (= strength: of hold, grip, handshake) Festigkeit f; (= steadiness: of support, chair, ladder) Stabilität f **c** (fig, of agreement, promise, commitment, belief, support) Festigkeit f; (of person, action, manner) Entschlossenheit f; (= strictness) Strenge f; **~ of character** Charakterstärke f; **it was thanks to his ~ of leadership** es war seiner festen Führung zu verdanken

firmware ['fɜːmwɛə'] N (Comput) Firmware f

first [fɜːst] ✪ 19.2, 26.1, 26.2 ADJ erste(r, s); **his ~ novel** sein Erstlingsroman m; **he was ~ in the queue** (Brit) or **in line** (US) er war der Erste in der Schlange; **he was ~ in Latin** er war der Beste in Latein; **who's ~?** wer ist der Erste? **I'm ~, I've been waiting longer than you** ich bin zuerst an der Reihe, ich warte schon länger als Sie; **the ~ time I saw her ...** als ich sie zum ersten Mal sah, ...; **is it your ~ time?** machst du das zum ersten Mal?; **there always has to be a ~ time** einmal ist immer das erste Mal; **we managed the very ~ time** wir haben es auf Anhieb geschafft; **in ~ place** (Sport etc) an erster Stelle; **to be** or **lie in ~ place** an erster Stelle liegen; **in the ~ place** zunächst or erstens einmal; **why didn't you say so in the ~ place?** warum hast du denn das nicht gleich gesagt?; **~ time around** beim ersten Mal

ADV **a** zuerst; (= before all the others) arrive, leave als erste(r, s); **~, take three eggs** zuerst or als Erstes nehme man drei Eier; **that's not what you said ~** zuerst hast du etwas anderes gesagt; **~ come ~ served** (prov) wer zuerst kommt, mahlt zuerst (Prov); **on a ~ come ~ served basis** nach dem Prinzip „wer zuerst kommt, mahlt zuerst"; **women and children ~** Frauen und Kinder zuerst; **ladies ~** Ladies first!, den Damen der Vortritt; **you (go) ~** nach Ihnen; **he says ~ one thing then another** er sagt mal so, mal so; **before he says anything I want to get in ~ with a few comments** bevor er irgendetwas sagt, möchte ich einige Bemerkungen anbringen; **what comes ~ in your order of priorities?** was steht bei Ihnen an erster Stelle?, was ist Ihnen am wichtigsten?; **but, darling, you know**

you always come ~ aber, mein Schatz, du weißt doch, dass du bei mir immer an erster Stelle stehst; **he always puts his job ~** seine Arbeit kommt bei ihm immer vor allen anderen Dingen

b (= before all else) als Erstes, zunächst; (in listing) erstens; **~ of all** (= before all else, mainly) vor allem; **~ (of all) I'm going for a swim** als Erstes or zu(aller)erst gehe ich schwimmen; **why can't I? – well, ~ of all** or **~ off** (inf), **it's not yours and secondly ...** warum denn nicht? – nun, zunächst or erstens einmal gehört es nicht dir und zweitens ...; **~ and foremost** zunächst; **~ and foremost, he is a writer** zuallererst ist er Schriftsteller; **~ and last he is an Englishman** er ist durch und durch Engländer

c (= for the first time) zum ersten Mal, das erste Mal; **when did you ~ meet him?** wann haben Sie ihn das erste Mal or zum ersten Mal getroffen?; **when this model was ~ introduced** zu Anfang or zuerst, als das Modell herauskam; **when it ~ became known that ...** als erstmals bekannt wurde, dass ...; **this work was ~ performed/published in 1997** dieses Werk wurde 1997 uraufgeführt/erstveröffentlicht

d (= before: in time) (zu)erst; **I must finish this ~** ich muss das erst fertig machen; **think ~ before you sign anything** überlegen Sie sich, bevor Sie etwas unterschreiben

e (in preference) eher, lieber; **I'd die ~!** eher or lieber würde ich sterben

f (Naut, Rail) **to travel ~** erster Klasse reisen

N **a** the ~ der/die/das Erste; (= former) der/die/das Erstere; **he was among the (very) ~ to arrive** er war unter den Ersten or Allerersten, die ankamen; **they were the ~ to congratulate me** sie gratulierten mir als Erste; **he was the ~ home/to finish** er war als Erster zu Hause/fertig; (in race) er ging als Erster durchs Ziel; **she wore a blouse and a skirt, but the ~ was too tight and the second too baggy** sie trug eine Bluse und einen Rock, aber erstere war zu eng und letzterer zu weit

b **this is the ~ I've heard of it** das ist mir ja ganz neu; **the ~ he knew about it was when he saw it in the paper** er hat erst davon erfahren, als er es in der Zeitung las

c **at ~** zuerst, zunächst; **from the ~** von Anfang an; **from ~ to last** von Anfang bis Ende

d (Brit, Univ) Eins f, Note f „Eins"; **he got a ~** er bestand (sein Examen) mit „Eins" or „sehr gut"; **he was supposed to get a ~** er war ein Einserkandidat

e **it's a ~** (= first time ever done) es ist das allererste Mal(, das so was gemacht wird); **it's a ~ for me/the firm** (= new experience) ich habe/die Firma hat noch nie so etwas gemacht; **this is a ~ for the city** das passiert zum ersten Mal in der Stadt

f (Aut) **~ (gear)** der erste (Gang); **in ~** im ersten (Gang)

g (US, Baseball) erstes Base or Mal → also **sixth**

first: **first aid** N erste Hilfe; **to give ~** erste Hilfe leisten; **first-aid box** N (Brit) Verband(s)kasten m; **first-aid kit** N Verband(s)kasten m; **first-aid post**, **first-aid station** N Sanitätswache f; **first-born** ADJ erstgeboren N Erstgeborene(r) mf; **first class** N (Rail, Post etc) erste Klasse ADJ PRED (= excellent) **he's ~ at cooking/tennis** er ist ein erstklassiger Koch/Tennisspieler; **that's absolutely ~!** das ist einfach Spitze! (inf); **first-class** ADJ ATTR **a** (= excellent) erstklassig; **he's a ~ cook** er ist ein erstklassiger Koch **b** (Rail, Aviat, Tourism) flight, train, ticket, cabin erster Klasse; **a ~ hotel** ein Erste-Klasse-Hotel nt, ein Hotel nt erster Klasse; **~ travel** Reisen pl erster Klasse; **a ~ ticket** eine Fahrkarte erster Klasse; **a ~ compartment** ein Erste-Klasse-Abteil nt; **~ passengers** Reisende pl in der ersten Klasse **c** (Post) **~ mail** bevorzugt beförderte Post **~ postage/stamp** Porto/Briefmarke f für die bevorzugt beförderte Post **~ letter** bevorzugt beförderter Brief **d** (Brit Univ) **~ (honours) degree** Examen nt mit „Eins" or „sehr gut"; **he graduated with ~ honours** er machte sein Examen mit „Eins" or

„sehr gut" **e** (*Sport*) *career, innings etc* in der obersten Spielklasse; ~ **cricket** die oberste Kricket-Spielklasse **to play** ~ **cricket** in der obersten Kricket-Spielklasse spielen **ADV a** (*Aviat, Naut, Rail*) *travel, fly* erster Klasse **b** (*Post*) **to send sth** ~ etw mit der bevorzugt beförderten Post schicken; **first costs** PL (*Comm*) Selbstkosten *pl*, Gestehungskosten *pl*; **first cousin** N Vetter *m or* Cousin *m*/Cousine *f or* Kusine *f* ersten Grades; **first-day cover** N Ersttagsbrief *m*; **first-degree burn** N Verbrennung *f* ersten Grades; **first edition** N Erstausgabe *f*; **first-foot** VT (*Scot*) einen Neujahrsbesuch abstatten (+*dat*); **first form** N (*Brit, Sch*) erste Klasse; **first-former** N (*Brit, Sch*) Erstklässler(in) *m(f)*; **first-generation** ADJ *citizen, computer* der ersten Generation; **first-hand** ADJ *information, experience, knowledge* aus erster Hand; **to have** ~ **knowledge of sth** etw aus eigener Erfahrung kennen; **they have** ~ **experience of charitable organizations** sie haben persönlich Erfahrungen mit Wohlfahrtsverbänden gemacht **ADV** *hear, learn, experience, witness* persönlich, aus erster Hand; *see* mit eigenen Augen; **they experienced police brutality** ~ *or* **at first hand** sie haben die Brutalität der Polizei am eigenen Leibe erfahren; **First Lady** N First Lady *f*; **first language** N Muttersprache *f*; **first lieutenant** N Oberleutnant *m*; **first light** N Tagesanbruch *m*, Morgengrauen *nt*; **at** ~ bei Tagesanbruch, im Morgengrauen

firstly ['fɜːstlɪ] ✪ 26.1, 26.2 ADV (= *in the first place*) zuerst; **they felt that their duty was** ~ **to the police** sie fühlten sich in erster Linie der Polizei verpflichtet; **why can't I?** – **well,** ~ **it's not yours and secondly** ... warum denn nicht? – nun, zunächst *or* erstens einmal gehört es nicht dir und zweitens ...

first: first mate N (*Naut*) Erster Offizier, Erste Offizierin; (*on small boats*) Bestmann *m*; **First Minister** N (*Brit, Pol*) Erster Minister, Erste Ministerin; **first name** N Vorname *m*; **they're on** ~ **terms** sie reden sich mit Vornamen an; **first night** N (*Theat*) Premiere *f*; ~ **nerves** Premierenfieber *nt*; **first-nighter** N Premierenbesucher(in) *m(f)*; **he is a** ~ er ist nicht vorbestraft; **first officer** N Erster Offizier, Erste Offizierin; **first-past-the-post system** N (*Pol*) Mehrheitswahlrecht *nt*; **first performance** N (*Theat*) Uraufführung *f*; (*Mus also*) Erstaufführung *f*; **first person** N ~ **the plural** die erste Person Plural; **the story is in the** ~ die Geschichte ist in der ersten Person geschrieben *or* wird von einem Icherzähler/einer Icherzählerin erzählt; **first-person** ADJ ~ **narrator** Icherzähler(in) *m(f)*; ~ **narrative** Icherzählung *f*; **first principles** PL Grundprinzipien *pl*; **to go back** *or* **return to** ~ zu den Grundlagen zurückkehren; **first-rate** ADJ erstklassig; **the orchestra was** ~ das Orchester hat ausgezeichnet gespielt; **they did a** ~ **job** sie haben erstklassige *or* ausgezeichnete Arbeit geleistet; **first refusal** N Vorkaufsrecht *nt*; **to give sb (the)** ~ jdm das Vorkaufsrecht einräumen; **to have (the)** ~ **on** das Vorkaufsrecht haben für; **first responder** N *usu pl* Ersthelfer *m*, Rettungskräfte *wie Feuerwehr, Polizei etc, die als erste am Unglücksort eintreffen*; **first school** N (= *Brit*) Grundschule *f*; **first-strike weapon** N Erstschlagwaffe *f*; **first thing** N **she just says the** ~ **that comes into her head** sie sagt einfach das, was ihr zuerst einfällt; **you don't have to buy the** ~ **you see** du brauchst nicht das zu kaufen, was du zuerst siehst; **the** ~ **(to do) is to ...** als Erstes muss man ...; **the** ~ **I knew about it was when James told me** ich erfuhr es erst, als James es mir erzählte; **the** ~ **I knew he'd taken the lot** ehe ich michs versah, hatte er alles genommen; **the** ~ **to remember is that she hates formality** man muss vor allem daran denken, dass sie Förmlichkeit nicht mag; ~**s first** eins nach dem anderen, immer (hübsch) der Reihe nach; (= *most important first*) das Wichtigste zuerst; **you have to put** ~**s first**

du musst wissen, was am wichtigsten ist; **he doesn't know the** ~ **about it/cars** davon/von Autos hat er nicht die geringste Ahnung **ADV** gleich; **I'll go** ~ **in the morning/when I get back** ich gehe gleich morgen früh/gleich, wenn ich wieder da bin; **I'm not at my best** ~ **(in the morning)** früh am Morgen bin ich nicht gerade in Hochform; **do it** ~ **before you forget** mach es gleich, ehe du es vergisst; **first-time buyer** N jd, *der zum ersten Mal ein Haus/eine Wohnung kauft*, Erstkäufer(in) *m(f)*; **first-timer** N (*inf*) **a** (= *novice*) Neuling *m* **b** (*Comm*) Erstkäufer(in) *m(f)*; **first violin** N erste Geige; **he plays** ~ er spielt erste Geige; **First World War** N **the** ~ der Erste Weltkrieg

firth [fɜːθ] N (*Scot*) Förde *f*, Meeresarm *m*

fir tree N Tannenbaum *m*

fiscal ['fɪskəl] ADJ finanziell; *measures* finanzpolitisch; ~ **crisis/policy** Finanzkrise/-politik *f*; ~ **reform** Steuerreform *f* N (*Scot, Jur*) Staatsanwalt *m*/-anwältin *f*

fiscal year N (*Fin*) Geschäftsjahr *nt*

fish [fɪʃ] N *pl* - *or* (*esp for different types*) **-es** Fisch *m*; ~ **and chips** Fisch und Pommes frites; **to drink like a** ~ (*inf*) wie ein Loch saufen (*inf*); **to have other** ~ **to fry** (*fig inf*) Wichtigeres zu tun haben; **like a** ~ **out of water** wie ein Fisch auf dem Trockenen; **neither** ~ **nor fowl** (*fig*) weder Fisch noch Fleisch; **he's a queer** ~ (*Brit inf*) er ist ein komischer Kauz; **there are plenty more** ~ **in the sea** (*fig inf*) es gibt noch mehr (davon) auf der Welt; **he's a big** ~ **in a small** *or* **little pond** er ist ein großes Tier am Ort (*inf*); **a little** ~ **in a big pond** nur einer von vielen; **The Fishes** (*Astron*) die Fische *pl* **VI** fischen; (*with rod also*) angeln; **to go** ~**ing** fischen/angeln gehen; **to go salmon** ~**ing** auf Lachsfang gehen **VT** fischen; (*with rod also*) angeln; **to** ~ **a river** in einem Fluss fischen/angeln; **to** ~ **a river dry** einen Fluss abfischen

▶ **fish for** VI +*prep obj* **a** (*lit*) fischen; (*with rod also*) angeln **b** (*fig*) *compliments* fischen nach; **they were fishing for information** sie waren auf Informationen aus

▶ **fish out** VT *sep* herausfischen *or* -angeln (*of or from sth* aus etw); **he fished it out from behind the cupboard** er angelte es hinter dem Schrank hervor

▶ **fish up** VT *sep* auffischen, herausziehen; (*fig, from memory etc*) hervorkramen *or* -holen

fish: fishbone N (Fisch)gräte *f*; **fishbowl** N Fischglas *nt*; **fish cake** N Fischfrikadelle *f*

fisher ['fɪʃə'] N **a** (*old, = fisherman*) Fischer *m*; ~**s of men** (*Bibl*) Menschenfischer *pl* (*Bibl*) **b** (= *animal*) Fischfänger *m*

fisherman ['fɪʃəmən] N *pl* **-men** [-mən] Fischer *m*; (*amateur*) Angler *m*; (= *boat*) Fischereiboot *nt*

fishery ['fɪʃərɪ] N (= *area*) Fischereizone *f or* -gewässer *nt*; (= *industry*) Fischerei *f*

fish: fisheye lens N (*Phot*) Fischauge *nt*; **fish farm** N Fischzucht(anlage) *f*; **fish farmer** N Fischzüchter(in) *m(f)*; **fish farming** N Fischzucht *f*; **fishfinger** N Fischstäbchen *nt*; **fish flour** N Fischmehl *nt*; **fish glue** N Fischleim *m*; **fish-hook** N Angelhaken *m*

fishing ['fɪʃɪŋ] N Fischen *nt*; (*with rod*) Angeln *nt*; (*as industry*) Fischerei *f*; ~ **(is) prohibited** Angeln verboten!

fishing: fishing boat N Fischerboot *nt*; **fishing fleet** N Fischereiflotte *f*; **fishing industry** N Fischindustrie *f*; **fishing line** N Angelschnur *f*; **fishing net** N Fischnetz *nt*; **fishing pole** N (*US*) Angelrute *f*; **fishing port** N Fischereihafen *m*; **fishing rod** N Angelrute *f*; **fishing tackle** N (*for sport*) Angelgeräte *pl*; (*for industry*) Fischereigeräte *pl*; **fishing village** N Fischerdorf *nt*

fish: fish knife N Fischmesser *nt*; **fish ladder** N Fischleiter *f*; **fish market** N Fischmarkt *m*; **fishmonger** ['fɪʃmʌŋgə'] N (*Brit*) Fischhändler(in) *m(f)*; **fishmonger's** N (*Brit*) Fischgeschäft *nt*; **fishnet stockings** PL Netzstrümpfe *pl*;

fish paste N Fischpaste *f*; **fishplate** N (*Rail*) Lasche *f*; **fish pond** N Fischteich *m*; **fish slice** N (*for serving*) Fischvorlegemesser *nt*; **fish stick** N (*US*) = **fishfinger**; **fish story** N (*US, inf*) Seemannsgarn *nt*; **fish tank** N (*in house*) Aquarium *nt*; (*on fish farm*) Fischteich *m*; **fishwife** N Fischfrau *f*; (*fig pej*) Marktweib *nt*

fishy ['fɪʃɪ] ADJ (+*er*) **a** ~ **smell** Fischgeruch *m*; **it smells rather** ~ es riecht ziemlich nach Fisch **b** (*inf*) verdächtig; *excuse, story* faul (*inf*); **there's something** ~ **about his story** an seiner Geschichte ist was faul (*inf*); **something** ~ **is going on here** hier ist was faul (*inf*)

fissile ['fɪsaɪl] ADJ spaltbar

fission ['fɪʃən] N (*Phys*) Spaltung *f*; (*Biol*) (Zell)teilung *f*

fissionable ['fɪʃnəbl] ADJ spaltbar

fission bomb N (konventionelle) Atombombe

fissure ['fɪʃə'] N Riss *m*; (*deep*) Kluft *f*; (*narrow*) Spalt *m*, Spalte *f*

fissured ['fɪʃəd] ADJ rissig; (= *with deep fissures*) zerklüftet

fist [fɪst] N Faust *f*; **to put one's** ~**s up** die Fäuste hochnehmen, in (Box)kampfstellung gehen

fistful ['fɪstfʊl] N Hand *f* voll; **a** ~ **of pound coins** eine Hand voll Pfundmünzen

fisticuffs ['fɪstɪkʌfs] PL (*dated inf*, = *fighting*) Handgreiflichkeiten *pl*; (= *boxing*) Boxen *nt*; **I'm not much good at** ~ ich tauge nicht viel mit den Fäusten; **resorting to** ~ **is no solution** handgreiflich (zu) werden ist keine Lösung

fit¹ [fɪt] ADJ (+*er*) **a** (= *suitable, suited for sth*) geeignet; *time, occasion* günstig; ~ **to eat** essbar; ~ **to drink** trinkbar; **is this meat still** ~ **to eat?** kann man dieses Fleisch noch essen?; ~ **for (human) consumption** zum Verzehr (durch Menschen) geeignet; ~ **for habitation** *or* **to live in** bewohnbar; **to be** ~ **to be seen** sich sehen lassen können; **she's not** ~ **to be a mother** sie ist als Mutter völlig ungeeignet; **this coat is** ~ **for the dustbin** (*Brit*) *or* **trash can** (*US*) dieser Mantel gehört in den Mülleimer

b (= *deserving*) **a man like that is not** ~ **to have such a good wife** ein Mann wie er verdient so eine gute Frau nicht *or* ist eine so gute Frau nicht wert; **you're not** ~ **to be spoken to** du bist es nicht wert *or* verdienst es nicht, dass man sich mit dir unterhält

c (= *right and proper*) richtig, angebracht; **I'll do as I think** *or* **see** ~ ich handle, wie ich es für richtig halte; **to see** ~ **to do sth** es für richtig *or* angebracht halten, etw zu tun; **he did not see** ~ **to cooperate** er hat es nicht für nötig gehalten zu kooperieren; **as is only** ~ wie es sich gehört; **it is only** ~ es ist nur recht und billig

d (*in health*) gesund; *sportsman etc* fit, in Form; **she is not yet** ~ **to travel** sie ist noch nicht reisefähig; **only the** ~**test survive** nur die Geeignetsten überleben; (*people*) nur die Gesunden überleben; (*in business etc*) nur die Starken können sich halten

e **to laugh** ~ **to burst** vor Lachen beinahe platzen; **to be** ~ **to drop** (*Brit*) zum Umfallen müde sein

N (*of clothes*) Passform *f*; **it is a very good/bad** ~ es sitzt *or* passt wie angegossen/nicht gut; **it's a bit of a tight** ~ (*clothes*) es ist etwas eng; (*timing, parking*) es geht gerade (noch)

VT a (*cover, sheet, net etc*) passen auf (+*acc*); (*key etc*) passen in (+*acc*); (*clothes etc*) passen (+*dat*); **this coat** ~**s you better** dieser Mantel passt Ihnen besser *or* sitzt bei Ihnen besser; **"one size** ~**s all"** „Einheitsgröße"; **that part won't** ~ **this machine** das Teil passt nicht für diese Maschine; **the washing machine won't** ~ **this space** die Waschmaschine passt nicht in diese Lücke; **to make a ring** ~ **sb** jdm einen Ring anpassen

b (= *be suitable for*) *sb's plans, a theory etc* passen in (+*acc*); *needs* erfüllen; *mood* passen zu

c **she was** ~**ted for her wedding dress** ihr Hochzeitskleid wurde ihr angepasst

d (= *put on, attach*) anbringen (*to an* +*dat*); *tyre, lock* montieren, anbringen; *double glazing* einsetzen, anbringen; (= *put in*) einbauen (*in* in +*acc*); (= *furnish, provide with*) ausstatten; **to ~ a key in the lock** einen Schlüssel ins Schloss stecken; **to ~ a bulb in its socket** eine Glühbirne in die Fassung drehen *or* schrauben; **to ~ a bolt to a door** eine Tür mit einem Riegel versehen; **to ~ a car with an alarm** eine Alarmanlage in ein Auto einbauen, ein Auto mit einer Alarmanlage ausstatten; **to have a new kitchen ~ted** eine neue Küche einbauen lassen

c (= *match*) *description, facts, circumstances* entsprechen (+*dat*); **to make the punishment ~ the crime** eine dem Vergehen angemessene Strafe verhängen

VI **a** (= *be right size, shape: dress etc, key*) passen; **my CV ~s on one page** mein Lebenslauf passt auf eine Seite *or* hat auf einer Seite Platz

b (= *correspond*) zusammenstimmen *or* -passen; **the facts don't ~** die Fakten sind widersprüchlich; **it all ~s** es passt alles zusammen; **there's still one piece of evidence that doesn't ~** da ist immer noch ein Indiz, das nicht dazupasst

▶ **fit in** **VI** **a** (= *find space for*) unterbringen; **you can fit five people into this car** in diesem Auto haben fünf Personen Platz

b (= *find time for*) *person* einen Termin geben (+*dat*); *meeting* unterbringen; (= *squeeze in*) einschieben; **Sir Charles could fit you in at 3 o'clock** um 3 Uhr hätte Sir Charles Zeit für Sie; **can you fit this meeting in(to) your schedule?** können Sie diese Konferenz noch in Ihrem Terminkalender unterbringen?

c (= *make harmonize*) **to fit sth in with sth** etw mit etw in Einklang bringen

d (= *fit, put in*) einsetzen, einbauen

VI **a** (= *go into place*) hineinpassen; **will we all fit in?** passen wir alle hinein?; **I can't get all the toys to fit in** ich kann die ganzen Spielsachen nicht hineinbekommen; **the clothes won't fit in(to) the case** die Sachen passen nicht in den Koffer

b (*plans, ideas, word*) passen; (*facts etc*) übereinstimmen; (= *match*) dazupassen; **there is one fact that doesn't fit in** da ist ein Punkt, der nicht ins Ganze passt; **how does this fit in?** wie passt das ins Ganze?; **I see, it all fits in now** jetzt passt alles zusammen; **suddenly everything fitted into place** plötzlich wurde alles klar; **to fit in with** (*plans, ideas*) in etw (*acc*) passen; (*facts*) mit etw übereinstimmen; (= *match*) zu etw passen; **does that fit in with your plans?** lässt sich das mit Ihren Plänen vereinbaren?; **he wants everybody to fit in with him/his plans** er will, dass sich jedermann nach ihm/seinen Plänen richtet

c (*people: = harmonize*) **he doesn't fit in here/with the others/with such a firm** er passt nicht hierhin/zu den anderen/in eine solche Firma; **she's the sort who fits in easily in any group** sie ist der Typ, der sich in jede Gruppe leicht einfügt; **the new director didn't fit in** der neue Direktor hat nicht in die Firma gepasst *or* nicht reingepasst (*inf*); **try to fit in (with the others)** versuche dich den anderen anzupassen; **she has problems fitting in** sie kann sich nicht gut anpassen

▶ **fit on** **VI** **a** (= *be right size, shape*) passen; **will it fit on?** passt es (darauf)? **b** (= *be fixed*) befestigt *or* angebracht sein; **where does this part fit on?** wo gehört dieses Teil drauf?, wo wird dieses Teil befestigt? **VI** *sep* **a** *dress* anprobieren; (*tailor*) anpassen (*prep obj* +*dat*) **b** (= *put in place, fix on*) anbringen

▶ **fit out** **VT** *sep* *expedition* ausrüsten; *ship* ausstatten; *person (for an expedition)* ausrüsten; (*with clothes etc*) ausstatten; **they've fitted one room out as an office** sie haben eines der Zimmer als Büro eingerichtet

▶ **fit up** **VT** *sep* **a** (= *fix up*) anbringen; (= *assemble*) zusammensetzen *or* -bauen **b** (= *supply with*) ausrüsten, ausstatten; (*with implements, weapons etc*) ausrüsten, ausstatten; **to fit sb/sth up with sth** jdn/etw mit etw versehen *or* ausstatten

fit² N (*Med, fig*) Anfall *m*; **~ of coughing/anger** Husten-/Wutanfall *m*; **in a ~ of anger** in einem

Anfall von Wut; **~ of remorse** Anwandlung *f or* Anfall *m* von Reue; **in** *or* **by ~s and starts** stoßweise; **he wrote this novel in ~s and starts** er hat diesen Roman in mehreren Anläufen geschrieben; **to be in ~s (of laughter)** sich vor Lachen biegen *or* kugeln (*inf*); **he'd have a ~** (*fig inf*) er würde (ja) einen Anfall kriegen (*inf*)

fitful ['fɪtfʊl] ADJ unbeständig; *working, progress* stoßweise; *sleep* unruhig; *sun* launenhaft (*geh*); *enthusiasm* sporadisch

fitfully ['fɪtfəlɪ] ADV *sleep* unruhig; *progress* stoßweise; *work* sporadisch; **the sun shone ~** die Sonne kam vereinzelt durch; **she slept only ~** sie wachte immer wieder auf

fitment ['fɪtmənt] N (*Brit*: = *furniture*) Einrichtungsgegenstand *m*; (*of machine, car*) Zubehörteil *nt*

fitness ['fɪtnɪs] N **a** (= *health*) Gesundheit *f*; (= *condition*) Fitness *f*, Kondition *f*; **~ training** Fitness- *or* Konditionstraining *nt*; **~ fanatic** *or* **freak** (*inf*) Fitnessfanatiker(in) *m(f)*; **~ test** (*Sport*) Fitness- *or* Konditionstest *m* **b** (= *suitability*) Eignung *f*; (*of remark etc*) Angemessenheit *f*; **~ for work** Erwerbsfähigkeit *f*; **~ for service** (*esp Mil*) Diensttauglichkeit *f*/-tauglichkeit *f*

fitted ['fɪtɪd] ADJ **a** **to be ~ with sth** (*room, vehicle*) mit etw ausgestattet sein; **a car ~ with a catalytic converter/an alarm** ein Auto mit (eingebautem) Katalysator/(eingebauter) Alarmanlage; **to be ~ as standard** zur serienmäßigen Ausstattung gehören

b (= *built-in*) Einbau-; *bedroom, bathroom* mit Einbauelementen; **~ wardrobe/cupboard** Einbauschrank *m*; **~ units** Einbauelemente *pl*; **~ kitchen** Einbauküche *f*

c (= *tailored*) *jacket, shirt* tailliert; **~ carpet** (*Brit*) Teppichboden *m*; **~ sheet** Spannbetttuch *nt*

d (*form*: = *suited*) **to be ~ to do sth** sich dazu eignen, etw zu tun; **he is well/ill ~ to be king** er eignet sich gut/schlecht zum König; **to be ~ for** *or* **to a task** sich für eine Aufgabe eignen; **these school-leavers are ill ~ for work** diese Schulabgänger sind nicht auf das Arbeitsleben vorbereitet

fitter ['fɪtə*] N **a** (*for clothes*) Schneider(in) *m(f)* **b** (*Tech, of engines*) Monteur(in) *m(f)*; (*for machines*) (Maschinen)schlosser(in) *m(f)*; (*not specially qualified*) Montagearbeiter(in) *m(f)*; (*of pipes etc*) Installateur(in) *m(f)*

fitting ['fɪtɪŋ] ADJ (= *suitable*) passend; *punishment, reward* angemessen; *expression also* angebracht; (= *seemly, becoming*) schicklich (*dated*); **it is not ~ for a young lady ...** es schickt sich nicht *or* ist nicht schicklich (*dated*) für eine junge Dame ... **N** **a** Anprobe *f*; **to go in for a ~** zur Anprobe gehen **b** (= *part*) Zubehörteil *nt*; (= *accessory*) Ausstattung *f*; (= *furniture also*) Einrichtung *f*; (= *pipes*) Installation *f*; **bathroom/office ~s** Badezimmer-/Büroeinrichtung *f*; **electrical ~s** Elektroinstallationen *pl*

fittingly ['fɪtɪŋlɪ] ADV (+*adj*) angemessen; *name, translate* passend; (*introducing sentence*) passenderweise; **a song ~ titled "Goodbye"** ein Lied mit dem passenden Titel „Goodbye"

fitting room N Anproberaum *m*; (= *cubicle*) Anprobekabine *f*

five [faɪv] ADJ fünf **N** Fünf *f* → *also* **six**

five: five-and-dime, five-and-ten N (*US*) billiges Kaufhaus; **five-a-side** ADJ *football* mit fünf Spielern pro Mannschaft; **~ team** Fünfermannschaft *f*, Fünf *f*; **fivefold** ADJ *increase, rise* fünffach **ADV** *increase, rise* um das Fünffache; **five-o'clock shadow** N *nachmittäglicher Anflug von Bartstoppeln*

fiver ['faɪvə*] N (*inf*) Fünfpfund-/Fünfdollarschein *m*

five: five-spot N (*US, inf*) Fünfdollarschein *m*; **five-star hotel** N Fünf-Sterne-Hotel *nt*; **five-year plan** N Fünfjahresplan *m*

fix [fɪks] **VT** **a** (= *make firm*) befestigen, festmachen (*sth to sth* etw an/auf etw *dat*); (= *put on, install*) *new aerial, new dynamo* anbringen; (*fig*) *ideas, images* verankern, festsetzen; **to ~ a stake in the ground** einen Pfahl im Boden veran-

kern; **to ~ the blame on sb** die Schuld auf jdn schieben, jdm die Schuld geben; **this image was firmly ~ed in his memory** diese Vorstellung war fest in seinem Gedächtnis verankert; **to ~ sth in one's mind** sich (*dat*) etw fest einprägen; **to ~ bayonets** die Bajonette aufpflanzen

b *eyes, attention* richten (*on, upon* auf +*acc*); *gun, camera, radar* richten (*on* auf +*acc*); **all eyes were/everybody's attention was ~ed on her** alle sahen sie wie gebannt an; **to ~ sb with an angry stare** (*liter*) jdn mit wütenden Blicken durchbohren; **to ~ sb with a look of concern** (*liter*) einen besorgten Blick auf jdn richten

c *date, price, limit* festsetzen, festlegen; (= *agree on*) ausmachen, beschließen; **nothing has been ~ed yet** es liegt noch nichts fest, es ist noch nichts fest (ausgemacht *or* beschlossen worden)

d (= *arrange*) arrangieren; *tickets, taxi etc* besorgen, organisieren (*inf*); **have you got anything ~ed for tonight?** haben Sie (für) heute Abend schon etwas vor?; **I ~ed it so that he could go to the concert** ich habe es arrangiert, dass er zu dem Konzert gehen kann

e (= *straighten out, sort out*) in Ordnung bringen, regeln; **don't worry, I'll ~ things with him** mach dir keine Gedanken, ich regle das mit ihm *or* ich bringe das in Ordnung

f (*inf, = get even with, sort out*) **I'll ~ him** dem werd ichs besorgen (*inf*); **the Mafia will ~ him** den wird sich (*dat*) die Mafia vornehmen (*inf*) *or* vorknöpfen (*inf*)

g (= *repair*) in Ordnung bringen, (ganz) machen (*inf*); (= *put in good order, adjust*) machen (*inf*)

h *drink, meal* machen; **to ~ one's hair/face** sich frisieren/schminken

i (*inf, = arrange dishonestly*) *race, fight, jury* manipulieren; *prices* absprechen; **the whole thing was ~ed** das war eine abgekartete Sache (*inf*)

j (*Chem, Phot*) fixieren

k (*Naut, Aviat*) *position* bestimmen; *submarine etc* orten

VI (*US inf*: = *intend*) vorhaben; **I'm ~ing to get married soon** ich habe vor, bald zu heiraten

N **a** (*inf, = tricky situation*) Patsche *f* (*inf*), Klemme *f* (*inf*); **to be in a ~** in der Patsche *or* Klemme sitzen (*inf*); **to get oneself into a ~** sich (*dat*) eine schöne Suppe einbrocken (*inf*)

b (*Naut*) Position *f*, Standort *m*; **to take a ~ on sth** etw orten; **to get a ~ on sb/sth** (*fig, = get clear about*) sich (*dat*) Klarheit über jdn/etw verschaffen

c (*inf: of drugs*) Druck *m* (*sl*); **to give oneself a ~** sich (*dat*) einen Schuss setzen (*inf*), sich (*dat*) einen Druck verpassen (*sl*); **I need my daily ~ of chocolate** (*inf*) ich brauche meine tägliche Schokoladenration

d (*inf*) **the fight/competition was a ~** der Kampf/Wettbewerb war eine abgekartete Sache (*inf*)

▶ **fix down** VT *sep* befestigen

▶ **fix on** **VI** *sep* festmachen (*prep obj* auf +*dat*); *badge etc also* anheften, anstecken; (= *fit on*) anbringen; (*by sewing*) annähen **VI** +*prep obj* (= *decide on*) sich entscheiden für

▶ **fix together** VT *sep* zusammenmachen (*inf*)

▶ **fix up** VT *sep* **a** *shelves* anbringen; *tent* aufstellen **b** (= *arrange*) arrangieren; *holidays etc* festmachen; (= *book*) *organized tour, hotel etc* buchen; **have you got anything fixed up for this evening?** haben Sie (für) heute Abend schon etwas vor? **c** **to fix sb up with sth** jdm etw besorgen *or* verschaffen; **we fixed them up for the night** wir haben sie für die Nacht untergebracht; **I stayed with him until I got myself fixed up (with a room)** ich habe bei ihm gewohnt, bis ich ein Zimmer hatte **d** (= *straighten out, sort out*) in Ordnung bringen, regeln **e** *room, house* einrichten

fixated [fɪk'seɪtɪd] ADJ fixiert (*on* auf +*acc*)

fixation [fɪk'seɪʃən] N **a** (*Psych*) Fixierung *f*; **she has a ~ about** *or* **on cleanliness** sie hat einen Sauberkeitsfimmel (*inf*) **b** (*Chem*) Fixierung *f*

fixative ['fɪksətɪv] N Fixativ *nt*

fixed [fɪkst] ADJ **a** (= *invariable*) *amount, time* fest(gesetzt); *position* unveränderlich; **at ~ intervals** in festen Abständen; **there's no ~ agenda** es gibt keine feste Tagesordnung; **with ~ bayonets** mit aufgepflanzten Bajonetten; **of no ~ abode** *or* **address** (*Jur*) ohne festen Wohnsitz; **~ exchange rate** (*Econ*) fester Wechselkurs; **~ menu** Tagesmenü *nt*; **~ price** Festpreis *m*
b *idea* fest; *smile, grin* starr; **to have a ~ idea** *or* **belief that ...** fest davon überzeugt *or* nicht davon abzubringen sein, dass ...; **a ~ stare** ein starrer Blick
c (= *rigged*) *election, game, match, race* manipuliert; **it's a ~ trial, the trial is ~** der Prozess ist eine abgekartete Sache; **the interview was ~** das Interview war gestellt; **the whole thing was ~** das war eine abgekartete Sache (*inf*)
d (*inf*) **how are we ~ for time?** wie siehts mit der Zeit aus?; **how are you ~ for food/money** *etc*? wie siehts bei dir mit Essen/Geld *etc* aus?; **how are you ~ for tonight?** was hast du (für) heute Abend vor?

fixed: fixed assets PL (*Comm*) feste Anlagen *pl*; **fixed capital** N Anlagevermögen *nt*; **fixed costs** PL (*Comm*) Fixkosten *pl*; **fixed- -interest** ADJ Festzins-; *stocks, investments* festverzinslich; **~ loan** Festzinsanleihe *f*

fixedly [ˈfɪksɪdlɪ] ADV *stare, look* starr, unverwandt

fixed: fixed-rate ADJ Festzins-; **~ mortgage** Festzinshypothek *f*; **fixed star** N Fixstern *m*; **fixed-term contract** N Zeitvertrag *m*, befristeter Vertrag; **fixed-wing** ADJ **~ aircraft** Starrflügelflugzeug *nt*

fixer [ˈfɪksə'] N (*Phot*) Fixiermittel *nt*

fixing bath [ˈfɪksɪŋˌbɑ:θ] N Fixierbad *nt*

fixings [ˈfɪksɪŋz] PL (*US, Cook*) Beilagen *pl*

fixity [ˈfɪksɪtɪ] N (*liter*) **his ~ of purpose** seine Zielstrebigkeit

fixture [ˈfɪkstʃə'] N **a** (*of a building etc*) **~s** Ausstattung *f*, unbewegliches Inventar (*form*); **~s and fittings** Anschlüsse und unbewegliches Inventar (*form*); **lighting ~s** elektrische Anschlüsse; **to be a ~** (*fig hum, person*) zum Inventar gehören **b** (*Brit, Sport*) Spiel *nt*

fixture list N (*Brit Sport*) Spielplan *m*

fizz [fɪz] **VI** (*champagne etc*) perlen, sprudeln, moussieren **N a** (*of champagne etc*) Perlen *nt*, Moussieren *nt* (= *drink*) Sprudel *m*; (*flavoured*) Limonade *f*, Brause *f* **c** (*dated Brit, inf*, = *champagne*) Schampus *m* (*dated inf*)

▶ **fizz up** VI (auf)sprudeln

fizzle [ˈfɪzl] **VI** zischen, spucken (*inf*)

▶ **fizzle out** VI (*firework, enthusiasm*) verpuffen; (*rocket*) vorzeitig verglühen; (*plan*) im Sande verlaufen

fizzy [ˈfɪzɪ] ADJ (+er) sprudelnd; **to be ~** sprudeln; **it's too ~** da ist zu viel Kohlensäure drin; **the soda water makes it ~** durch das Sodawasser sprudelt es; **a ~ drink** eine Brause

fjord [fjɔ:d] N Fjord *m*

flab [flæb] N (*inf*) Speck *m*; **to fight the ~** (*hum*) etwas für die schlanke Linie tun, sich trimmen

flabbergast [ˈflæbəgɑ:st] **VT** (*inf*) verblüffen, umhauen (*inf*); **I was ~ed to see him/at the price** ich war platt *or* von den Socken, als ich ihn sah/als ich den Preis erfuhr (*inf*)

flabbergasting [ˈflæbəgɑ:stɪŋ] ADJ pred (*inf*) unglaublich

flabbily [ˈflæbɪlɪ] ADV schlaff; *written* schwammig

flabbiness [ˈflæbɪnɪs] N (*of thighs, stomach, muscles, skin*) Schlaffheit *f* (*inf*); (*fig*: = *ineffectual nature*) Schlaffheit *f*

flabby [ˈflæbɪ] ADJ (+er) *thighs, stomach, muscles, skin* schlaff; *person also* schwabbelig (*inf*); (*fig*: = *ineffectual*) schlaff; **he's getting ~ (round the middle)** er setzt (um die Taille) Speck an

flaccid [ˈflæksɪd] ADJ (*liter*) schlaff; *prose* saftund kraftlos

flag¹ [flæg] **N a** Fahne *f*; (*small, on map, chart etc*) Fähnchen *nt*; (*national*) Fahne *f*, Flagge *f*; (*Naut*) Flagge *f*; (*for semaphore*) Signalflagge *or* -fahne *f*; **to fly the ~ (for)** (*fig*) die Fahne hochhalten (für); **to keep the ~ flying** (*lit, fig*) die Stellung halten; **to show the ~** seine Präsenz *or* (*fig also*) seine Anwesenheit dokumentieren; **~ of convenience** (*Naut*) Billigflagge *f* **b** (*for charity*) Fähnchen *nt* **c** (*of taxi*) **the ~ was down** das Taxi war besetzt; **he put the ~ down** er stellte auf „besetzt" **d** (= *paper marker*) Kennzeichen *nt* **VT** beflaggen

▶ **flag down** VT sep *taxi etc, person* anhalten

▶ **flag up** VT sep (*inf*, = *mark, indicate*) markieren

flag² VI erlahmen; (*interest, enthusiasm, strength etc also*) nachlassen; (*plant*) den Kopf/die Blätter hängen lassen; **he's ~ging** er lässt nach; (= *he is tiring*) er wird müde; **their spirits ~ged** ihr Mut sank; **the film starts ~ging toward(s) the middle** der Film lässt zur Mitte hin nach

flag³ N (*Bot*) Schwertlilie *f*; (= *sweet flag*) Kalmus *m*

flag⁴ N (*also* **flagstone**) Steinplatte *f*; (*for floor also*) Fliese *f* **VT** mit Steinplatten/Fliesen belegen; *floor also* fliesen

flag day N **a** (*Brit*) Tag, an dem eine Straßensammlung für einen wohltätigen Zweck durchgeführt wird **b** **Flag Day** (*US*) 14. Juni, Gedenktag der Einführung der amerikanischen Nationalflagge

flagellant [ˈflædʒələnt] N **a** (*Rel*) Flagellant *m* **b** (*form, for sexual gratification*) Flagellant *m*

flagellate [ˈflædʒəleɪt] VT geißeln

flagellation [ˌflædʒəˈleɪʃən] N Geißelung *f*

flagged [flægd] ADJ **a** *ship* beflaggt **b** *floor* gefliest

flag officer N (*Naut*) Flaggoffizier *m*

flagon [ˈflægən] N (= *bottle*) Flasche *f*; (= *jug*) Krug *m*

flagpole [ˈflægpəʊl] N Fahnenstange *f*; **to run an idea/a proposal up the ~** (*inf*) eine Idee/einen Vorschlag testen

flagrance [ˈfleɪgrəns], **flagrancy** [ˈfleɪgrənsɪ] N eklatante *or* krasse Offensichtlichkeit; (*of affair, defiance, disregard*) Unverhohlenheit *f*; **such was the ~ of this injustice ...** das war eine derart eklatante *or* krasse *or* himmelschreiende Ungerechtigkeit ...; **the unabashed ~ of his abuse of privilege** die unverhohlene Art, mit der er seine Privilegien missbraucht

flagrant [ˈfleɪgrənt] ADJ eklatant, krass; *injustice, crime also* himmelschreiend; *breach, violation* eklatant, flagrant (*geh*); *disregard, defiance, affair* unverhohlen, offenkundig

flagrantly [ˈfleɪgrəntlɪ] ADV *violate, abuse, disregard* ganz eindeutig *or* offensichtlich; *flirt* unverhohlen; **he is ~ indiscreet** er begeht offene Indiskretionen; **this is ~ unjust** das ist eine himmelschreiende Ungerechtigkeit

flag: flagship N (*lit, fig*) Flaggschiff *nt* **ADJ** *attr* Vorzeige-; **~ store** Vorzeigeladen *m*; **flagstaff** N Fahnen- *or* Flaggenmast *m*; **flag stop** N (*US*) Bedarfshaltestelle *f*; **flagstone** N (Stein)platte *f*; (*on floor also*) Fliese *f*; **flagwaver** N Hurrapatriot(in) *m(f)*, Chauvinist *m*; **flag-waving** **N** Hurrapatriotismus *m*, Chauvinismus *m*; **N** *speech* chauvinistisch

flail [fleɪl] **N** (Dresch)flegel *m* **VT** dreschen; **he ~ed his arms about** *or* **around wildly** er schlug wild (mit den Armen) um sich **VI to ~ (about)** herumfuchteln; **the dying deer with its legs ~ing in all directions** das verendende Reh, das mit seinen Läufen nach allen Richtungen ausschlug

flail tank N Minenräumpanzer *m*

flair [flɛə'] N (*for selecting the best etc*) Gespür *nt*, (feine) Nase (*inf*), Riecher *m* (*inf*); (= *talent*) Talent *nt*; (= *stylishness*) Flair *nt*; **his great ~ for business** sein großes Geschäftstalent

flak [flæk] N **a** Flakfeuer *nt* **b** (*fig*) **he's been getting a lot of ~ (for it)** er ist (dafür) mächtig unter Beschuss geraten (*inf*); **I'm not taking the ~ for this** ich lass mich deswegen nicht zur Sau machen (*inf*)

flake [fleɪk] **N** (*of snow, soap*) Flocke *f*; (*of paint, rust*) Splitter *m*; (*of plaster*) abgebröckeltes Stückchen; (*of metal, wood*) Span *m*; (*of skin*) Schuppe *f*; (*of fish*) Stückchen *nt* Fischfleisch; (*of almond*) Blättchen *nt*; (*of chocolate*) Raspel *m*; **~s of paint/plaster were falling off the ceiling** die Farbe blätterte/der Gips bröckelte von der Decke ab **VI** (*stone, plaster etc*) abbröckeln; (*paint*) abblättern **VT** (*Cook*) *chocolate, almonds* raspeln; *fish* in Stücke zerteilen

▶ **flake off** VI (*plaster*) abbröckeln; (*paint, rust etc*) abblättern, absplittern; (*skin*) sich schälen, sich abschuppen

▶ **flake out** VI (*inf*, = *become exhausted*) abschlaffen (*inf*); (= *pass out*) umkippen; (= *fall asleep*) einschlafen, einpennen (*inf*)

flak jacket N kugelsichere Weste

flaky [ˈfleɪkɪ] ADJ (+er) **a** *potatoes* flockig; *paint, plaster etc* brüchig; *crust* blättrig; *skin* schuppig **b** (*esp US*: = *mad, eccentric*) verrückt

flaky pastry N Blätterteig *m*

flamboyance [flæmˈbɔɪəns] N Extravaganz *f*; (*of lifestyle also*) Üppigkeit *f*; (*of colour*) Pracht *f*; (*of gesture*) Großartigkeit *f*

flamboyant [flæmˈbɔɪənt] ADJ extravagant; *lifestyle also* üppig, aufwendig, aufwändig; *plumage* farbenprächtig; *colours* prächtig; *gesture* großartig; **~ style** (*Archit*) Flamboyantstil *m*; (*of person*) extravagante Art; **in the ~ court of Louis XIV** am prunkvollen Hof Ludwigs XIV

flamboyantly [flæmˈbɔɪəntlɪ] ADV extravagant

flame [fleɪm] **N a** Flamme *f*; **the house was in ~s** das Haus stand in Flammen **b** (*of passion*) Flamme *f* (*geh*), Feuer *nt no pl* **c** (*inf*, = *sweetheart*) Flamme *f* (*inf*); **she's an old ~ of his** sie ist eine alte *or* ehemalige Flamme von ihm (*inf*) **VI** (*fire*) lodern, flammen (*geh*); (*fig: face, cheeks*) glühen; (*liter: colour*) leuchten; (*gem*) funkeln, gleißen (*liter*) **VT** (*Comput*) **to ~ sb** jdm eine Flame schicken

▶ **flame up** VI **a** (*fire*) auflodern **b** (*fig, person*) in Wut *or* Rage geraten; (*anger etc*) aufflammen, auflodern

flame-coloured [ˈfleɪmkʌləd] ADJ feuerfarben

flamenco [fləˈmɛŋkəʊ] **N** Flamenco *m* **ADJ** Flamenco-; **~ dancer** Flamencotänzer(in) *m(f)*

flame: flameproof [ˈfleɪmpru:f] ADJ feuerfest, feuersicher; *textiles* flammensicher; **flame-red** ADJ feuerrot; **flame retardant** ADJ, N = **fire retardant**; **flame test** N Flammprobe *f*; **flame-thrower** N Flammenwerfer *m*

flaming [ˈfleɪmɪŋ] ADJ **a** brennend, lodernd; (*fig*) *colour* leuchtend; *rage* hell; *passion* glühend; **he has ~ red hair** er hat feuerrotes Haar; **she was absolutely ~** (*Brit, inf*, = *angry*) sie kochte (vor Wut) (*inf*); **to have a ~ row (with sb)** sich (mit jdm) streiten, dass die Fetzen fliegen (*inf*) **b** (*Brit, inf, = bloody*) verdammt (*inf*), Scheiß- (*inf*); **it's a ~ nuisance** Mensch, das ist vielleicht ein Mist (*inf*); **it's a ~ waste of time** das ist eine verdammte Zeitverschwendung (*inf*); **it was there all the ~ time** Mensch *or* Scheiße, das war die ganze Zeit da (*inf*); **who does he ~ well think he is** verdammt noch mal, für wen hält der sich eigentlich? (*inf*)

flamingo [fləˈmɪŋgəʊ] N pl **-(e)s** Flamingo *m*

flammable [ˈflæməbl] ADJ leicht entzündbar, feuergefährlich

flan [flæn] N Kuchen *m*; **fruit ~** Obstkuchen *m*

flan case N Tortenboden *m*

Flanders [ˈflɑ:ndəz] N Flandern *nt*

Flanders poppy N (*Bot*) Klatschmohn *m*

flange [flændʒ] N (*on wheel etc*) Spurkranz *m*; (*Tech*, = *ring, collar*) Flansch *m*

flanged [flændʒd] ADJ gebördelt; *tube etc also* geflanscht

flank [flæŋk] **N** (*of animal, Mil*) Flanke *f*; (*of mountain, building*) Seite *f*, Flanke *f* (*old*) **VT b** (= *be at side of*) flankieren **b** (*Mil*) *the enemy* seitlich umgehen; **~ing movement** Flankenbewegung *f*

flannel ['flænl] **N a** Flanell *m* **b** (*Brit*, = *face flannel*) Waschlappen *m* **c** (*Brit, inf*, = *waffle*) Geschwafel *nt* (*inf*), Gelaber *nt* (*inf*) **d flannels** PL (= *trousers*) Flanellhose *f* ADJ Flanell-; **~ trousers** Flanellhose *f* **VI** (*Brit, inf*, = *waffle*) schwafeln (*inf*), labern (*inf*)

flannelette [ˌflænə'let] N (*Brit*) Baumwollflanell *m*; **~ sheet** Biberbetttuch *nt*

flap [flæp] **N a** (*of pocket*) Klappe *f*; (*of table*) ausziehbarer Teil; (*of tent*) Eingang *m*; (*Aviat*) (Lande)klappe *f*; **a ~ of skin** ein Hautfetzen *m*; (*Med*) ein Hautlappen *m* **b** (= *sound, of sails, sheeting etc*) Flattern *nt*, Knattern *nt*; (*of wings*) Schlagen *nt* **c** (= *motion*) **to give sth a ~** leicht auf etw (*acc*) klatschen **d** (*Brit inf*) helle Aufregung, Panik *f*; **to get in(-to) a ~** in helle Aufregung geraten, ins Flattern geraten (*inf*) **e** (*Phon*) geschlagener Laut **VI a** (*wings*) schlagen; (*door, shutters*) schlagen, klappern; (*sails, tarpaulin etc*) flattern; **his coat ~ped about his legs** der Mantel schlackerte ihm um die Beine (*inf*); **his ears were ~ping** (*inf*) er spitzte die Ohren **b** (*Brit inf*) in heller Aufregung sein; **to start to ~** in helle Aufregung geraten; **don't ~** reg dich nicht auf; **there's no need to ~** (das ist) kein Grund zur Aufregung; **she's been ~ping around all morning** sie rennt schon den ganzen Morgen wie ein aufgescheuchtes Huhn durch die Gegend (*inf*) **VT** **to ~ its wings** mit den Flügeln schlagen; **to ~ one's arms** mit den Armen rudern; **he ~ped the newspaper at the fly** er schlug *or* klatschte mit der Zeitung nach der Fliege
▶ **flap away** VI (*bird*) davonfliegen

flapjack ['flæpdʒæk] N (*US*) Pfannkuchen *m*; (*Brit*) Haferkeks *m*

flapper ['flæpə'] N *modisches Mädchen in den 20er Jahren*

flare [flɛə'] **N a** Auflodern *nt*; (*fig, of anger*) Aufbrausen *nt* **b** (= *signal*) Leuchtsignal *nt*; (*from pistol etc*) Leuchtrakete *f*, Leuchtkugel *f*; (= *fire, landing flare*) Leuchtfeuer *nt* **c** (*Fashion*) ausgestellter Schnitt; **a skirt with a slight ~** ein leicht ausgestellter Rock; **(a pair of) ~s** (*Brit inf*) eine Hose mit Schlag, eine Schlaghose **d** (= *solar flare*) Sonneneruption *f*, Fackel *f* **e** (*Phot*) Reflexlicht *nt* **VI a** (*match, torch*) aufleuchten; (*sunspot*) aufblitzen **b** (*trousers, skirts*) ausgestellt sein **c** (*nostrils*) sich blähen **d** (*fig, trouble, violence*) ausbrechen, aufflammen; **tempers ~d** die Gemüter erhitzten sich **VT** *nostrils* aufblähen
▶ **flare up** VI (*lit, fig: situation, affair*) aufflackern, auflodern; (*fig, person*) aufbrausen, auffahren; (*injury*) wieder Schwierigkeiten machen; (*fighting, epidemic*) ausbrechen; (*anger*) zum Ausbruch kommen; **his acne flared up** seine Akne trat wieder auf; **she flared up at me** sie fuhr mich an

flared [flɛəd] ADJ *trousers, skirt* ausgestellt; **~ nostrils** geblähte Nüstern

flare: flare path N (*Aviat*) Leuchtpfad *m*; **flare pistol** N Leuchtpistole *f*; **flare-up** N (*of situation*) Aufflackern *nt*, Auflodern *nt*; (*of person*) Aufbrausen *nt*; (*of fighting, epidemic*) Ausbruch *m*; (= *sudden dispute*) (plötzlicher) Krach

flash [flæʃ] **N a** (*of light*) Aufblinken *nt no pl*; (*very bright*) Aufblitzen *nt no pl*; (*of metal, jewels etc*) Blitzen *nt*, Blinken *nt no pl*; (*Mot*) Lichthupe *f no pl*; **there was a sudden ~ of light** plötzlich blitzte es hell auf; **to give sb a ~** (*Mot*) jdn (mit der Lichthupe) anblinken; **~ of lightning** Blitz *m*; **he gave two quick ~es with his torch** er blinkte zweimal kurz mit der Taschenlampe; **the ~es come at regular intervals** es blinkt in regelmäßigen Abständen; **three short ~es is the Morse sign for S** dreimal kurz blinken ist *or* drei kurze Blinkzeichen sind das Morsezeichen für S **b** (*fig*) (= *newsflash*) Kurzmeldung *f*; **~ of anger** Wutausbruch *m*; **~ of colour** (*Brit*) *or* **color** (*US*) Farbtupfer *m*; **in a ~** blitzartig, wie der Blitz; **as quick as a ~** blitzschnell; **a ~ in the pan** (*inf*) ein Strohfeuer *nt* **c** (*Mil, on uniform*) Abzeichen *nt* **d** (*Phot*) Blitz(licht *nt*) *m*; **to use a ~** Blitzlicht benutzen **e** (*US, inf*, = *torch*) Taschenlampe *f* **VI a** (*light*) aufblinken; (*very brightly*) aufblitzen; (*repeatedly: indicators etc*) blinken; (*metal, jewels, teeth*) blitzen; (*Mot*) die Lichthupe benutzen; **to ~ on and off** immer wieder aufblinken; **her eyes ~ed (with anger)** ihre Augen blitzten (wütend); **a message ~ed (up) onto the screen** eine Nachricht blinkte auf dem Bildschirm auf **b** (= *move quickly: vehicle, person*) sausen, schießen, flitzen (*all vi*); **a smile ~ed across his face** ein Lächeln huschte über sein Gesicht; **to ~ past** *or* **by** vorbeisausen *etc*; (*holidays etc*) vorbeifliegen; **the time ~ed past** die Zeit verflog im Nu; **the thought ~ed through my mind that ...** mir kam plötzlich der Gedanke, dass ..., es schoss mir durch den Kopf, dass ... **VT a** *light* aufblitzen *or* aufleuchten lassen; *SOS, message* blinken; **to ~ a torch on sb** jdn mit der Taschenlampe anleuchten; **to ~ a torch in sb's face** jdm mit der Taschenlampe ins Gesicht leuchten; **to ~ one's headlights** die Lichthupe betätigen; **to ~ one's headlights at sb, to ~ sb** jdn mit der Lichthupe anblinken; **she ~ed him a look of contempt/gratitude** sie blitzte ihn verächtlich/dankbar an; **he ~ed his famous smile** er ließ sein berühmtes Lächeln aufblitzen **b** (*inf*: = *show, wave*: also **flash around**) schwenken (*inf*), protzen mit; *diamond ring* blitzen lassen; *identity card* kurz vorzeigen; **don't ~ all that money around** wedel nicht so mit dem vielen Geld herum (*inf*); **those images were ~ed across television screens all around the world** diese Bilder wurden auf Fernsehschirmen in der ganzen Welt gezeigt ADJ (*inf*, = *showy*) protzig (*pej*); (= *smart*) schick
▶ **flash back** VI (*Film*) zurückblenden (*to* auf +*acc*); **his mind flashed back to the events of the last year** er erinnerte sich plötzlich an die Ereignisse des letzten Jahres

flash: flashback N (*Film*) Rückblende *f*; **flashbulb** N (*Phot*) Blitzbirne *f*; **flash burn** N Verbrennung *f* (*durch kurzzeitige Strahlungshitze*); **flash card** N (*Sch*) Leselernkarte *f*; **flashcube** N (*Phot*) Blitzwürfel *m*

flasher ['flæʃə'] N **a** (*Mot*) Lichthupe *f* **b** (*inf*, = *person exposing himself/herself*) Exhibitionist(in) *m(f)*

flash: flash flood N flutartige Überschwemmung; **flashforward** N (*Film*) Zeitsprung *m* (nach vorn); **flash gun** N Elektronenblitzgerät *nt*; **Flash Harry** N (*Brit inf*) Lackaffe *m* (*pej inf*)

flashily ['flæʃɪlɪ] ADV auffallend, auffällig

flashing ['flæʃɪŋ] N (*Build*) Verwahrung *f*, Kehlblech *nt*

flash: flashlight N **a** (*Phot*) Blitzlicht *nt* **b** (*esp US*, = *torch*) Taschenlampe *f* **c** (= *signal lamp*) Leuchtfeuer *nt*; **flash photography** N Blitz(licht)fotografie *f*; **flash point** N (*Chem*) Flammpunkt *m*; (*fig*) Siedepunkt *m*

flashy ['flæʃɪ] ADJ (+*er*) auffallend, auffällig

flask [flɑːsk] N Flakon *m*; (*Chem*) Glaskolben *m*; (*for spirits, carried in pocket*) Flachmann *m* (*inf*), Reiseflasche *f*; (= *vacuum flask*) Thermosflasche *f*

flat¹ [flæt] ADJ (+*er*) **a** flach; *tyre, nose, feet* platt; *surface* eben; **he stood ~ against the wall** er stand platt gegen die Wand gedrückt; **as ~ as a pancake** (*inf, tyre*) total platt; (*countryside*) total flach; (*girl*) flach wie ein (Plätt)brett, platt wie eine Flunder; **~ roof** Flachdach *nt*; **to fall ~ on one's face** auf die Nase fallen; **to lie ~** flach *or* platt liegen **b** (*fig*) fade; *painting, photo* flach, kontrastarm; *colour* matt, stumpf, glanzlos; *joke, remark* abgedroschen, öde, müde; *trade, market* lau, lahm, lustlos; *battery* leer; (= *stale*) *beer, wine* schal, abgestanden; **in a ~ voice** mit ausdrucksloser Stimme; **she felt a bit ~** sie fühlte sich ein bisschen daneben (*inf*), sie hatte zu nichts Lust; **to fall ~** (*joke*) nicht ankommen; (*play etc*) durchfallen **c** *refusal, denial* glatt, deutlich; **and that's ~** und damit basta **d** (*Mus*: = *out of tune*) *instrument* zu tief (gestimmt); *voice* zu tief **e** (*Comm*) Pauschal-; **~ rate** Pauschale *f*; (*internet*) Flatrate *f*; **to charge a ~ rate of interest** einen pauschalen Zinssatz berechnen; **to get a ~ rate of pay** pauschal bezahlt werden; **~ fare** Einheitstarif *m* ADV **a** *turn down, refuse* rundweg, kategorisch; **he told me ~ (out) that ...** er sagte mir klipp und klar, dass ... **b** (*Mus*) **to sing/play ~** zu tief singen/spielen **c** **in ten seconds ~** in sage und schreibe (nur) zehn Sekunden **d** **~ broke** (*inf*) total pleite (*inf*) **e** **~ out** (*inf*, = *exhausted*) total erledigt (*inf*); (= *asleep, drunk*) hinüber (*inf*); **to go ~ out** voll aufdrehen (*inf*); (*in car also*) Spitze fahren (*inf*); **to work** *or* **go ~ out** auf Hochtouren arbeiten; **to be lying ~ out** platt am Boden liegen **N a** (*of hand*) Fläche *f*; (*of blade*) flache Seite **b** (*Geog*) Ebene *f*; **on the ~** (= *on the plain*) in der Ebene; (= *on a flat surface*) auf ebener Fläche **c** (*Mus*) Erniedrigungszeichen *nt*, b *nt* **d** (*Aut*) Platte(r) *m* (*inf*), (Reifen)panne *f* **e** (*Theat*) Kulisse *f* **f** (*Sport*) **the ~** das Flachrennen; (= *season*) die Flachrennsaison

flat² N (*esp Brit*) Wohnung *f*

flat: flat-bed lorry N Tieflader *m*; **flatboat** Prahm *m*, Flachboot *nt*; **flat-bottomed** ['flæt,bɒtəmd] ADJ *boat, bowl* flach; **flat-chested** ADJ flachbrüstig; **flat dweller** N (*Brit*) Wohnungsbewohner(in) *m(f)*; **flat feet** PL Plattfüße *pl*; **flatfish** N Plattfisch *m*; **flatfoot** N (*inf*, = *policeman*) Polyp *m* (*inf*); **flat-footed** ADJ plattfüßig; **flat-hunting** N (*Brit*) Wohnungssuche *f*; **to go/be ~** auf Wohnungssuche gehen/sein; **flatiron** (*old*) Plätteisen *nt*; **flatlet** N (*Brit*) kleine Wohnung

flatly ['flætlɪ] ADV **a** (= *completely*) *refuse, deny, reject* kategorisch, rundweg; *contradict* aufs Schärfste; **to be ~ against** *or* **opposed to sth** etw rundweg ablehnen; (*in principle*) kategorisch gegen etw sein; **to be ~ opposed to doing sth** kategorisch dagegen sein, etw zu tun **b** (= *unemotionally*) *say, state* ausdruckslos, nüchtern

flatmate ['flætmeɪt] N (*Brit*) Mitbewohner(in) *m(f)*

flatness ['flætnɪs] N **a** Flachheit *f*; (*of nose*) Plattheit *f*; (*of surface*) Ebenheit *f* **b** (*fig*) Fadheit *f*; (*of painting, photo*) Flachheit *f*, Kontrastarmut *f*; (*of colour*) Stumpfheit *f*; (*of joke, remark*) Abgedroschenheit *f*; (*of trade, market*) Lustlosigkeit *f*; (*of beer, wine*) Schalheit *f* **c** (*of refusal, denial*) Deutlichkeit *f*, Direktheit *f*

flat: flat pack N (*Brit*: = *furniture*) flaches Paket; **it arrives as a ~** es kommt flach verpackt an; **flat-pack** ADJ **~ furniture** Möbel *pl* zur Selbstmontage; **flat paint** N Grundierfarbe *f*; **flat race** N Flachrennen *nt*; **flat racing** N Flachrennen *nt*; **flat screen** N (*Comput*) Flachbildschirm *m*; **flat season** N Flachrennsaison *f*

flatten ['flætn] **VT a** *path, road, field* ebnen, planieren; *metal* flach *or* platt hämmern *or* schlagen; (*storm etc*) *crops* zu Boden drücken, niederdrücken; *trees* umwerfen; *town* dem Erdboden gleichmachen **b** (*fig*, = *defeat*) vernichtend schlagen; (= *knock down*) niederschlagen; (= *demoralize, snub*) zu reduzieren; **that'll ~ him** das wird bei ihm die Luft rauslassen (*inf*) **VR** **to ~ oneself against sth** sich platt gegen *or* an etw drücken

▶**flatten out** **VI** (*countryside*) flach(er) *or* e-ben(er) werden; (*road*) eben(er) werden; (*Aviat*) ausschweben; (*fig, inflation, demand*) abflachen; (*prices*) nicht mehr so stark steigen **VT** *sep path* ebnen; *metal* glatt hämmern; *map, paper, fabric* glätten

flatter ['flætəˀ] **VT** schmeicheln (+*dat*); **it ~s your figure** das ist sehr vorteilhaft; **I was very ~ed by his remark** ich fühlte mich von seiner Bemerkung sehr geschmeichelt; **you can ~ yourself on being ...** Sie können sich (*dat*) etwas darauf einbilden, dass Sie ...; **he ~s himself he's a good musician** er bildet sich (*dat*) ein, ein guter Musiker zu sein; **don't ~ yourself!** bilde dir ja nichts ein!

flatterer ['flætərəˀ] **N** Schmeichler(in) *m(f)*

flattering ['flætərɪŋ] **ADJ** **a** (= *complimentary*) *remark* schmeichelhaft; *person* schmeichlerisch; **she was very ~ about you** sie hat sich sehr schmeichelhaft über Sie geäußert; **this was hardly ~ to her** das war nicht gerade schmeichelhaft für sie **b** (= *becoming, attractive*) *clothes, colour* vorteilhaft; *photograph* schmeichelhaft; **lighter hair shades are more ~ to your complexion** hellere Haarfarben sind vorteilhafter für Ihren Teint

flatteringly ['flætərɪŋlɪ] **ADV** **a** *say, write* schmeichlerisch **b** (= *becomingly, attractively*) *posed, dressed* vorteilhaft

flattery ['flætərɪ] **N** (= *compliments*) Schmeicheleien *pl*; **~ will get you nowhere** mit Schmeicheln kommst du nicht weiter

flattop **N** (*US, inf, = aircraft carrier*) Flugzeugträger *m*

flatulence ['flætjʊləns] **N** Blähung(en) *f(pl)*, Flatulenz *f* (*spec*); **to cause ~** Blähungen verursachen, blähen

flatulent ['flætjʊlənt] **ADJ** aufgebläht; *food* blähend

flat: flatware **N** (*US, = cutlery*) Besteck *nt*; (= *plates etc*) Geschirr *nt*; **flatwork** **N** (*US*) Mangelwäsche *f*; **flatworm** **N** Plattwurm *m*

flaunt [flɔːnt] **VT** *wealth, knowledge* zur Schau stellen, protzen mit; **she ~ed her body in front of him** sie stellte ihren Körper vor ihm zur Schau; **he ~ed his freedom before her** er prahlte vor ihr mit seiner Freiheit; **to ~ oneself** sich groß in Szene setzen

flautist ['flɔːtɪst] **N** Flötist(in) *m(f)*

flavour, (*US*) **flavor** ['fleɪvəˀ] **N** **a** (= *taste*) Geschmack *m*; (= *flavouring*) Aroma *nt*; (*fig*) Beigeschmack *m*; **strawberry-flavour ice cream** Eis *nt* mit Erdbeergeschmack; **with a lemon ~** mit Zitronengeschmack; **20 different ~s** 20 verschiedene Geschmackssorten; **the film gives the ~ of Paris in the twenties** der Film vermittelt die Atmosphäre des Paris der zwanziger Jahre *or* Zwanzigerjahre; **he/it is ~ of the month** (*inf*) er/es ist zurzeit Monat in (*inf*) **VT** Geschmack verleihen (+*dat*) *or* geben (+*dat*); **pineapple-flavoured** mit Ananasgeschmack

flavouring, (*US*) **flavoring** ['fleɪvərɪŋ] **N** (*Cook*) Aroma(stoff *m*) *nt*; **vanilla/rum ~** Vanille-/Rumaroma *f*

flavourless, (*US*) **flavorless** ['fleɪvəlɪs] **ADJ** fad(e), geschmacklos

flaw [flɔː] **N** (*lit*) Fehler *m*; (*fig also*) Mangel *m*; (*in sb's character also*) Mangel *m*, Defekt *m*; (*Jur, in contract etc*) (Form)fehler *m* **VT** *her argument was ~ed by lack of evidence* ihr Argument wurde durch Mangel an Beweisen entkräftet; *her beauty was not ~ed by the slightest imperfection* ihre Schönheit wurde durch keinen Mangel getrübt

flawed [flɔːd] **ADJ** fehlerhaft; **his logic was ~** seine Logik enthielt Fehler

flawless ['flɔːlɪs] **ADJ** *performance* fehlerlos; *behaviour* untadelig, tadellos; *complexion* makellos; *diamond* lupenrein; **~ English** fehlerloses *or* einwandfreies *or* tadelloses Englisch; **the weather was ~** das Wetter war ideal

flax [flæks] **N** (*Bot*) Flachs *m*

flaxen ['flæksən] **ADJ** *hair* flachsfarben; (*Tex*) flächse(r)n

flaxen-haired ['flæksən'hɛəd] **ADJ** flachsblond

flay [fleɪ] **VT** **a** (= *skin*) *animal* abziehen, häuten; *person* die Haut abziehen +*dat*; (= *beat*) verdreschen; (= *whip*) auspeitschen; **to ~ sb alive** jdn gründlich verdreschen **b** (*fig, = criticize*) kein gutes Haar lassen an (+*dat*), heruntermachen (*inf*)

flea [fliː] **N** Floh *m*; **to send sb off with a ~ in his/her ear** (*inf*) jdn wie einen begossenen Pudel abziehen lassen (*inf*)

flea: fleabag **N** **a** (*US, inf, = hotel*) Flohbude *f* (*inf*), Absteige *f* **b** (*inf, = person*) Schrulle *f* (*inf*); **fleabite** **N** Flohbiss *m*; **it's just a ~** (*fig*) das ist eine Kleinigkeit; **flea-bitten** **ADJ** voller Flohbisse; (*inf*) vergammelt (*inf*); **flea circus** **N** Flohzirkus *m*; **flea collar** **N** Flohhalsband *nt*; **flea market** **N** Flohmarkt *m*; **fleapit** **N** (*Brit, inf*) Flohkino *nt* (*inf*)

fleck [flek] **N** (*of red etc*) Tupfen *m*; (*of mud, paint*) (= *blotch*) Fleck(en) *m*; (= *speckle*) Spritzer *m*; (*of fluff, dust*) Teilchen *nt*, Flöckchen *nt* **VT** sprenkeln; (*with mud etc*) bespritzen; **~ed wool** melierte Wolle; **blue ~ed with white** blau mit weißen Tupfen *or* Punkten, blau und weiß gesprenkelt; **the sky was ~ed with little clouds** der Himmel war mit Schäfchenwolken übersät

flection ['flekʃən] **N** (*Gram*) Flexion *f*, Beugung *f*

flectional ['flekʃənəl] **ADJ** **~ ending** Flexionsendung *f*

fled [fled] *pret, ptp of* **flee**

fledged [fledʒd] **ADJ** *bird* flügge → **fully fledged**

fledgling ['fledʒlɪŋ] **N** (*Orn, = young bird*) Jungvogel *m* **ADJ** *democracy, organization, business* jung; *person* frisch gebacken (*inf*); **~ artist** Nachwuchskünstler(in) *m(f)*; **~ teacher/writer** Junglehrer(in) *m(f)*/-autor(in) *m(f)*; **their feminist movement is ~ at best** ihre Feministenbewegung steckt noch in den Kinderschuhen; **they began their ~ career on a shoestring** sie haben ganz klein mit sehr wenig Geld angefangen

flee [fliː] *pret, ptp* **fled** **VI** fliehen, flüchten (*from* vor +*dat*); **to ~ from temptation** der Versuchung entfliehen **VT** *town, country* fliehen *or* flüchten aus; *temptation, danger* entfliehen (+*dat*)

fleece [fliːs] **N** Vlies *nt*, Schaffell *nt*; (= *fabric, natural*) Schaffell *nt*; (*artificial*) Webpelz *m*, Plüsch *m* **VT** *sheep* scheren **b** (*fig inf*) **to ~ sb (out of his/her money)** jdn schröpfen

fleecy ['fliːsɪ] **ADJ** **a** *sheep, blanket, lining, garment* flauschig **b** (*fig*) *snow* flockig; **~ clouds** Schäfchenwolken *pl*

fleet¹ [fliːt] **N** **a** (*Naut*) Geschwader *nt*; (= *entire naval force*) Flotte *f*; **Fleet Air Arm** Marineluftwaffe *f*; **merchant ~** Handelsflotte *f* **b** (*of cars, coaches, buses etc*) (Fuhr)park *m*; **~ of trucks/taxis** er hat einen Lastwagenpark/ein Taxiunternehmen; **~ business** Firmenwagengeschäft *nt*

fleet² **ADJ** (+*er*) schnell, flink; **~ of foot, ~-footed** schnell- *or* leichtfüßig

fleet admiral **N** (*US*) Großadmiral *m*

fleetness ['fliːtnɪs] **N** **a** (= *quickness*) Schnelligkeit *f* **b** (*fig poet: = transience*) Flüchtigkeit *f* (*geh*), Vergänglichkeit *f*

fleeting ['fliːtɪŋ] **ADJ** *moment, thought* flüchtig; **a ~ visit** eine Stippvisite (*inf*); **to catch** *or* **get a ~ glimpse of sb/sth** einen flüchtigen Blick auf jdn/etw werfen können; **to make a ~ appearance** sich kurz sehen lassen; (*on TV*) kurz auftreten

fleetingly ['fliːtɪŋlɪ] **ADV** *wonder, smile, think, see* flüchtig; *visible* ganz kurz; **they were ~ here** sie waren ganz kurz hier

Fleet Street **N** (*Brit*) Fleet Street *f*; **he had a job on ~** er hatte einen Job als Journalist

Fleming ['flemɪŋ] **N** Flame *m*, Flämin *f*

Flemish ['flemɪʃ] **ADJ** flämisch **N** **a** **the ~** *pl* die Flamen *pl* **b** (*Ling*) Flämisch *nt*

flesh [fleʃ] **N** **a** Fleisch *nt*; (*of fruit*) (Frucht-)fleisch *nt*; (*of vegetable*) Mark *nt*; **to put on ~** (*animals*) zunehmen; (*person also*) Fleisch auf die Rippen bekommen (*inf*); **all that bare ~ on the beach** diese Fleischbeschau am Strand **b** (*fig*) one's own **~ and blood** sein eigen(es) Fleisch und Blut; **it was more than ~ and blood could bear** das war einfach nicht zu ertragen; **I'm only ~ and blood** ich bin auch nur aus Fleisch und Blut; **in the ~** in Person, in natura; **he's gone the way of all ~** er ist den Weg allen Fleisches gegangen; **to press the ~** (*inf*) Hände drücken; **to put ~ on an idea/a proposal** eine Idee/einen Vorschlag ausgestalten **c** (*Rel*) Fleisch *nt*; **sins of the ~** Sünden *pl* des Fleisches

▶**flesh out** **VT** *sep idea, proposal, thesis etc* ausgestalten; *details* eingehen auf (+*acc*)

flesh: flesh colour, (*US*) **flesh color** **N** Fleischfarbe *f*; **flesh-coloured**, (*US*) **flesh-colored** **ADJ** fleischfarben; **flesh-eating** **ADJ** Fleisch fressend

flesher ['fleʃəˀ] **N** **a** (= *knife*) Ausfleischmesser *nt* **b** (*esp Scot: = butcher*) Fleischer(in) *m(f)*, Metzger(in) *m(f)*

fleshings ['fleʃɪŋz] **PL** (= *tights*) Trikotstrumpfhose(n *pl*) *f*

fleshly ['fleʃlɪ] **ADJ** (+*er*) **a** (= *corporeal*) fleischlich, leiblich **b** (*fig: = sensual*) *pleasures, sin* fleischlich (*fig*), sinnlich **c** (= *worldly*) irdisch, menschlich

flesh wound **N** Fleischwunde *f*

fleshy ['fleʃɪ] **ADJ** (+*er*) **a** (= *fat*) *face, cheeks, nose* fleischig; *person* füllig **b** (= *consisting of flesh*) *fleischern*, aus Fleisch bestehend; (= *similar to flesh*) fleischartig; **~ tones** fleischfarbene Töne *pl*; (*in painting*) Fleischtöne *pl* **c** (*Bot*) *fruit, leaves* fleischig

fletch [fletʃ] **VT** *arrow* befiedern

fletcher ['fletʃəˀ] **N** Pfeilmacher(in) *m(f)*

fleur de lys [ˌflɜːdəˈliː] **N** *pl* **-s - -** [ˌflɜːdəˈliːz] bourbonische Lilie

flew [fluː] *pret of* **fly²** *or* **fly³**

flex [fleks] **N** (*Brit*) Schnur *f*; (*heavy duty*) Kabel *nt* **VT** *body, knees, arm etc* beugen; **to ~ one's muscles** (*lit, fig*) seine Muskeln spielen lassen

flexibility [ˌfleksɪˈbɪlɪtɪ] **N** **a** (*lit*) Biegsamkeit *f*, Elastizität *f* **b** (*fig*) Flexibilität *f*; (*of engine*) Elastizität *f*

flexible ['fleksəbl] **ADJ** **a** (*lit*) *material, object, limbs, joints, body* biegsam, elastisch; **~ coupling** (*Tech*) elastisches Gelenk **b** (*fig*) *person, approach, attitude, timetable, system* flexibel; *engine* elastisch; **~ working hours** gleitende Arbeitszeit, Gleitzeit *f*; **to work ~ hours** gleitende Arbeitszeit haben, Gleitzeit arbeiten; **to be ~ in one's approach** eine flexible Einstellung haben; **to be ~ about sth** in Bezug auf etw (*acc*) flexibel sein

flexibly ['fleksəblɪ] **ADV** **a** (*lit*) *connected, mounted* elastisch **b** (*fig*) *use, respond, interpret, work* flexibel

flexion ['flekʃən] **N** = **flection**

flexional ['flekʃənəl] **ADJ** = **flectional**

flex(i)time ['fleks(ɪ)taɪm] **N** Gleitzeit *f*

flexor (muscle) ['fleksə(mʌsl)] **N** Beuger *m*

flibbertigibbet [ˌflɪbətɪˈdʒɪbɪt] **N** (*junges*) Gänschen *nt*

flick [flɪk] **N** (*with finger*) Schnipsen *nt no pl*; (*of tail*) kurzer Schlag *m*; (*with whip*) Schnalzen *nt no pl*; **with a ~ of his fingers/the whip** mit einem Finger-/Peitschenschnalzen; **a ~ of the wrist** eine schnelle Drehung des Handgelenks **VT** *whip* schnalzen *or* knallen mit; *fingers* schnalzen mit; (*with whip*) *horse etc* leicht schlagen; (*with fingers*) *switch* anknipsen; *dust, ash* wegschnippen; (*with cloth*) wegwedeln; **she ~ed her hair out of her eyes** sie strich sich (*dat*) die Haare aus den Augen; **I'll just ~ a duster round the sitting room** (*inf*) ich wedel *or* geh eben mal mit dem Staubtuch durchs Wohnzimmer (*inf*); **she ~ed the light on** sie knipste das Licht an; **he ~ed the piece of paper onto the floor**

er schnipste das Papier auf den Fußboden **VI** the snake's tongue ~ed in and out die Schlange züngelte

▶ **flick off** VT *sep* wegschnippen; *(with duster)* wegwedeln

▶ **flick through** VI *+prep obj book* (schnell) durchblättern; *pages* (schnell) umblättern; *TV channels* (schnell) wechseln

flicker ['flɪkə'] **VI** *(flame, candle, light)* flackern; *(TV)* flimmern; *(needle on dial)* zittern; *(eyelid)* flattern, zucken; **the snake's tongue ~ed in and out** die Schlange züngelte; **a smile ~ed across his face** ein Lächeln huschte über sein Gesicht; **his eyes ~ed toward(s) the door** er blickte kurz zur Tür **N** *(of flame, candle, light)* Flackern *nt*; *(of TV)* Flimmern *nt*; *(of needle on dial)* Zittern *nt*; *(of eyelid)* Flattern *nt*; **a ~ of hope** ein Hoffnungsschimmer *m*; **without so much as the ~ of a smile** ohne (auch nur) den Anflug eines Lächelns

flicker-free ['flɪkə'fri:] ADJ *screen etc* flimmerfrei

flick knife N *(Brit)* Klappmesser *nt*, Schnappmesser *nt*

flicks [flɪks] PL *(inf)* Kintopp *m (inf)*; **to/at the ~** in den/im Kintopp *(inf)*

flier ['flaɪə'] N **a** *(Aviat, = pilot)* Flieger(in) *m(f)*; **to be a good/bad ~** *(person)* Fliegen gut/nicht vertragen; *(bird)* ein guter/schlechter Flieger sein **b** *(dated US) (= train)* Schnellzug *m*; *(= fast coach)* Expressbus *m* **c** **to take a ~** *(Brit, = leap)* einen Riesensprung *or* -satz machen; *(= fall)* der Länge nach hinfallen **d** *(Brit = flying start)* fliegender Start; **he got a ~** er hat einen fliegenden Start gemacht **e** *(= leaflet)* Flugblatt *nt*

flies [flaɪz] PL *(Brit: on trousers)* (Hosen)schlitz *m*

flight¹ [flaɪt] N **a** Flug *m*; **in ~** *(bird)* im Flug; *(Aviat)* in der Luft; **to ~** *(bird)* davonfliegen, auffliegen; **the principles of ~** die Prinzipien des Fliegens; **I'm getting the next ~ to Glasgow** ich nehme den nächsten Flug *or* das nächste Flugzeug nach Glasgow **b** *(group, of birds)* Schwarm *m*, Schar *f*; *(of aeroplanes)* Geschwader *nt*, Formation *f*; **to be in the top ~** *(fig)* zur Spitze gehören; **the top ~ of world tennis** die weltbesten Tennisspieler **c** *(of imagination)* Höhenflug *m*; **~ of fancy** geistiger Höhenflug **d** *(of stairs)* Treppe *f*; **he lives six ~s up** er wohnt sechs Treppen hoch; **a ~ of hurdles** eine Gruppe von Hürden; **he fell at the second ~** er fiel bei der zweiten Hürde **e** *(on dart, arrow)* Steuerfeder *f*

flight² N Flucht *f*; **to put the enemy to ~** den Feind in die Flucht schlagen; **to take (to) ~** die Flucht ergreifen; **the ~ of capital abroad** die Kapitalflucht ins Ausland; **to be in full ~** Hals über Kopf auf der Flucht sein; *(fig)* auf Hochtouren sein

flight: flight attendant N Flugbegleiter(in) *m(f)*, **flight bag** N Schultertasche *f*; **flight case** N Bordcase *nt*; **flight control** N *(Aviat)* Flugsicherung *f*; *(in aircraft)* Flugsteuerung *f*; **flight crew** N Flugbesatzung *f*; **flight deck** N **a** *(Naut)* Flugdeck *nt* **b** *(Aviat)* Cockpit *nt*; **flight engineer** N Bordingenieur(in) *m(f)*; **flight feather** N Schwungfeder *f*; **flightless** ADJ nicht flugfähig; **flight lieutenant** N *(Brit, Aviat)* Oberleutnant *m* der Luftwaffe; **flight log** N Bordbuch *nt*; **flight mechanic** N Bordmechaniker(in) *m(f)*; **flight number** N Flugnummer *f*; **flight path** N Flugbahn *f*; *(= route)* Flugroute *f*; **flight plan** N Flugablaufplan *m*; **flight recorder** N Flugschreiber *m*; **flight safety** N Flugsicherheit *f*; **flight sergeant** N Haupt- *or* Oberfeldwebel *m* (der Luftwaffe); **flight simulator** N Simulator *m*; **flight test** N Flugtest *m*; **flight-test** VT im Flug testen, flugtesten

flighty ['flaɪtɪ] ADJ *(+er) (= fickle)* unbeständig, flatterhaft; *(= empty-headed)* gedankenlos

flimflam ['flɪmflæm] N *(inf, = rubbish)* Blödsinn *m*; *(= lies)* Schwindel *m*

flimsily ['flɪmzɪlɪ] ADV *built, constructed* leicht, nicht solide; **a ~ bound book** ein schlecht gebundenes Buch

flimsiness ['flɪmzɪnɪs] N **a** *(= weak construction)* leichte *or* wenig solide Bauweise; *(of book)* schlechte *or* billige Aufmachung; **in spite of the ~ of the wings** trotz der leichten Bauweise der Tragflächen **b** *(= thinness: of material, garment)* Dünne *f* **c** *(fig, of excuse)* Fadenscheinigkeit *f*; *(of reason)* mangelnde Stichhaltigkeit; *(of evidence)* Dürftigkeit *f*

flimsy ['flɪmzɪ] ADJ *(+er)* **a** *(= fragile)* structure leicht gebaut, wenig solide; *material, cup, paper* dünn; *box* instabil; **~ of construction** nicht sehr stabil gebaut **b** *(= thin)* material, garment dünn, leicht; **a ~ dress** ein Fähnchen *nt* **c** *(fig)* evidence dürftig; *excuse* fadenscheinig; *reason* wenig stichhaltig; **on ~ grounds** ohne stichhaltige Gründe **N** *(= paper)* Durchschlagpapier *nt*; *(= document)* Durchschlag *m*

flinch [flɪntʃ] VI **a** *(= wince)* zurückzucken; **without ~ing** ohne mit der Wimper zu zucken **b** *(fig)* **to ~ from sth** vor etw *(dat)* zurückschrecken; **he ~ed from telling her the truth** er scheute sich, ihr die Wahrheit zu sagen

fling [flɪŋ] *vb: pret, ptp* **flung** **N** **a** *(= act of flinging)* Wurf *m*; Schleudern *nt* no *pl* **b** *(fig inf)* Anlauf *m*; **to give sth a ~** sich an etw *(dat)* versuchen, etw (aus)probieren; **youth must have its ~** die Jugend muss sich austoben; **to have a ~** *(= enjoy oneself)* sich austoben; **to have a last** *or* **final ~** sich noch einmal richtig austoben **c** *(inf: = relationship)* **to have a ~ (with sb)** eine Affäre (mit jdm) haben **d = Highland fling** **VT** *(lit, fig)* schleudern; **to ~ the window open** das Fenster aufstoßen; **the door was flung open** die Tür flog auf; **to ~ one's arms round sb's neck** jdm die Arme um den Hals werfen; **she flung herself into his arms** sie warf sich in seine Arme; **to ~ a coat round one's shoulders** sich *(dat)* einen Mantel über die Schulter(n) werfen; **to ~ oneself into a task** sich in eine Aufgabe stürzen; **to ~ oneself out of the window/off a bridge** sich aus dem Fenster/von einer Brücke stürzen; **to ~ oneself into a chair/ to the ground** sich in einen Sessel/auf den Boden werfen; **you shouldn't just ~ yourself at him** *(fig inf)* du solltest dich ihm nicht so an den Hals werfen

▶ **fling away** VT *sep* wegwerfen, wegschmeißen *(inf)*; *(fig)* money vergeuden, verschwenden

▶ **fling back** VT *sep* one's head zurückwerfen; *door* aufwerfen

▶ **fling down** VT *sep* *(lit)* runterschmeißen *(inf)*; **to fling down the gauntlet** den Fehdehandschuh hinwerfen *or* hinschleudern

▶ **fling off** VT *sep* *(lit)* coat abwerfen; *opponent* abschütteln; *(fig)* remark hinwerfen; *restraints* von sich werfen

▶ **fling out** VT *sep* unwanted object wegwerfen, wegschmeißen *(inf)*; *person* hinauswerfen, rausschmeißen *(inf)*

▶ **fling up** VT *sep* **a** *(= throw up)* hochwerfen; **to fling one's arms up in horror** entsetzt die Hände über dem Kopf zusammenschlagen **b** *(fig inf)* **to fling sth up at sb** jdm etw unter die Nase reiben

flint [flɪnt] N **a** *(for cigarette lighter)* Feuerstein *m* **b** *(= stone)* Feuerstein *m*, Flint(stein) *m*

flint: flint axe N (Feuer)steinbeil *nt*; **flint glass** N Flintglas *nt*; **flintlock** N Steinschlossgewehr *nt*

flinty ['flɪntɪ] ADJ *(+er)* **a** *(= hardhearted)* person hartherzig; *heart* steinern; *eyes, gaze* hart **b** *soil, ground* feuersteinhaltig

flip [flɪp] **N** **a** Schnipser *m*; **by the ~ of a coin** durch Hochwerfen einer Münze **b** *(= somersault)* Salto *m*; **backward ~** Salto rückwärts **c** *(Aviat inf)* Rundflug *m* **d** *(= drink)* Flip *m* **ADJ** *(inf, = flippant)* schnodderig *(inf)* **VT** schnippen, schnipsen; *switch* knipsen; *(inf) record* rumdrehen *(inf)*; **to ~ the pages (of a book)** die Seiten

(in einem Buch) umblättern; **to ~ a coin** eine Münze werfen; **to ~ one's lid** *(inf)* durchdrehen *(inf)*, aus dem Häuschen geraten *(inf)* **VI** *(inf)* durchdrehen *(inf)* **INTERJ** *(Brit, inf)* verflixt *(inf)*

▶ **flip off** VT *sep* wegschnipsen; *top, catch* aufklappen

▶ **flip over** **VT** *sep* umdrehen; *pages of book* wenden **VI** sich (um)drehen; *(plane)* sich in der Luft (um)drehen

▶ **flip through** VI *+prep obj book* durchblättern; *pages* umblättern

flip chart N Flipchart *f*

flip-flop ['flɪpflɒp] N **a** *(Sport)* Flickflack *m* **b** *(Elec)* Flipflop *m* **c** *(Brit: = sandal)* Gummilatsche *f (inf)*

flip pack N Klappschachtel *f*

flippancy ['flɪpənsɪ] N Leichtfertigkeit *f*; *(= disrespectfulness)* Schnodd(e)rigkeit *f*

flippant ['flɪpənt] ADJ *person, tone, attitude* leichtfertig; *remark also* hingeworfen; *(= disrespectful)* schnodd(e)rig *(inf)*; **to sound ~** sich leichtfertig anhören

flippantly ['flɪpəntlɪ] ADV *answer, say* leichtfertig; *(= disrespectfully)* schnodd(e)rig *(inf)*

flipper ['flɪpə'] N Flosse *f*; *(of diver)* (Schwimm)flosse *f*

flipping ['flɪpɪŋ] ADJ, ADV *(Brit inf emph)* verdammt *(inf)*

flip: flip side N *(of record)* B-Seite *f*; **flip switch** N Kippschalter *m*; **flip top** N Klappdeckel *m*; **flip-top bin** N Abfalleimer *m* mit Klappdeckel

flirt [flɜ:t] **VI** **a** flirten; **to ~ with an idea** mit einem Gedanken liebäugeln *or* spielen; **to ~ with danger/disaster** die Gefahr/das Unglück herausfordern **N** **he/she is just a ~** er/sie will nur flirten; **I'm a bit of a ~** ich flirte (für mein Leben) gern

flirtation [flɜ:'teɪʃən] N Flirt *m*; *(= flirting)* Flirten *nt*; **his ~ with death/danger** sein Spiel mit dem Tod/der Gefahr

flirtatious [flɜ:'teɪʃəs] ADJ *woman, behaviour* kokett; **she is very ~** sie flirtet gern

flirty ['flɜ:tɪ] ADJ **a** *woman, behaviour* kokett **b** *clothes* sexy

flit [flɪt] **VI** **a** *(bats, butterflies etc)* flattern, huschen; *(ghost, person, image)* huschen; **to ~ in and ~ted out** *(person)* rein- und rausflitzen; **an idea ~ted through my mind** ein Gedanke schoss mir *or* huschte mir durch den Kopf **b** *(Brit, = move house secretly)* bei Nacht und Nebel ausziehen, sich bei Nacht und Nebel davonmachen **c** *(Scot, N Engl, = move house)* umziehen **N** *(Brit)* **to do a (moonlight) ~** bei Nacht und Nebel umziehen

flitch [flɪtʃ] N Speckseite *f*; *(of halibut)* Heilbuttschnitte *f*

float [fləʊt] **N** **a** *(on fishing line, in cistern, carburettor, on aeroplane)* Schwimmer *m*; *(= anchored raft)* (verankertes) Floß, Schwimmplattform *f*; *(as swimming aid)* Schwimmkork *m*; *(of fish)* Schwimmblase *f*; *(on trawl net)* Korken *m* **b** *(= vehicle, in procession)* Festwagen *m*; *(for deliveries)* kleiner Elektrolieferwagen **c** *(= ready cash: in till)* Wechselgeld *nt* no *indef art* *(zu Geschäftsbeginn)*; *(= loan to start business)* Startkapital *nt*; *(= advance on expenses)* Vorschuss *m* **VI** **a** *(on water)* schwimmen; *(= move gently)* treiben; *(in air)* schweben; **the body ~ed (up) to the surface** die Leiche kam an die Wasseroberfläche; **it ~ed downriver** es trieb flussabwärts; **she ~ed down the aisle in a dream** sie schwebte wie im Traum zum Traualtar **b** *(Comm, currency)* floaten **VT** **a** *boat* zu Wasser bringen; **they ~ed the logs downstream** sie flößten die Baumstämme flussabwärts **b** *(Comm, Fin)* company gründen; *loan* lancieren; *shares* auf den Markt bringen; *bond issue* ausgeben; *currency* freigeben, floaten lassen; *(fig) ideas, suggestion* in den Raum stellen, zur Debatte stellen

▶**float around** VI (*rumour, news*) im Umlauf sein; (*person*) herumschweben (*inf*); (*things*) herumfliegen (*inf*)

▶**float away** or **off** VI (*on water*) abtreiben, wegtreiben; (*in air*) davonschweben; (*fig, person*) hinwegschweben

▶**float round** VI = **float around**

floatable [ˈfləʊtəbl] ADJ schwimmfähig; *river* flößbar

floatel [fləʊˈtel] N (*inf*) schwimmendes Hotel

floating [ˈfləʊtɪŋ] **ADJ** **a** *raft, logs* treibend; ~ **hotel/restaurant** schwimmendes Hotel/Restaurant **b** (*fig*) *population* wandernd **c** (*Fin*) *currency* freigegeben; ~ **exchange rate** floatender or frei schwankender Wechselkurs **d** (*Math, Comput*) Gleit-; ~ **accent** (*Comput*) fliegender Akzent; ~ **point** (*Comput*) Gleitpunkt *m*, Gleitkomma *nt* **e** (*Med*) *kidney* Wander-; *rib* frei **N** (*of currency*) Freigabe *f*, Floating *nt*

floating: floating bridge N Schiffsbrücke *f*; **floating capital** N Umlauf- or Betriebskapital *nt*; **floating debt** N schwebende Schuld; **floating dock** N Schwimmdock *nt*; **floating ice** N Treibeis *nt*; **floating light** N (= *ship*) Leuchtschiff *nt*; (= *buoy*) Leuchtboje *f*; **floating voter** N (*fig*) Wechselwähler *m*

flock[1] [flɒk] **N** **a** (*of sheep, geese, also Eccl*) Herde *f*; (*of birds*) Schwarm *m*, Schar *f* **b** (*of people*) Schar *f*, Haufen *m* (*inf*) **VI** in Scharen kommen; **to ~ in** hineinströmen or -drängen; **to ~ out** hinausströmen or -drängen; **to ~ around sb** sich um jdn scharen or drängen

flock[2] N (*Tex*) Flocke *f*

flock wallpaper N Velourstapete *f*

floe [fləʊ] N Treibeis *nt*, Eisscholle *f*

flog [flɒg] VT **a** (= *beat*) prügeln, schlagen; *thief, mutineer* auspeitschen; **you're ~ging a dead horse** (*esp Brit inf*) Sie verschwenden Ihre Zeit **b** (*Brit, inf*, = *sell*) verkloppen, verscherbeln, losschlagen (*all inf*)

▶**flog off** VT *sep* (*Brit, inf*) verscheuern (*inf*), verkloppen (*inf*)

flogging [ˈflɒgɪŋ] N Tracht *f* Prügel; (*Jur*) Prügelstrafe *f*; (*of thief, mutineer*) Auspeitschen *nt*; **to bring back** ~ die Prügelstrafe wieder einführen; **a public** ~ eine öffentliche Auspeitschung

flood [flʌd] **N** **a** (*of water*) Flut *f*; ~**s** Überschwemmung *f*, Hochwasser *nt*; (*in several places*) Überschwemmungen *pl*, Hochwasser *nt*; **the Flood** die Sintflut; **the river is in** ~ der Fluss führt Hochwasser; **she had a** ~ **in the kitchen** ihre Küche stand unter Wasser **b** (*fig*) Flut *f*, Schwall *m*; **she was in** ~**s of tears** sie war in Tränen gebadet; **the scene was bathed in a** ~ **of light** die Szene war lichtüberflutet **c** (*also* **flood tide**) Flut *f* **VT** **a** *fields, roads, town* überschwemmen, unter Wasser setzen; **the village/cellar was ~ed** das Dorf/der Keller war überschwemmt or stand unter Wasser; **to ~ the engine** den Motor absaufen lassen (*inf*) **b** (*storm, rain*) *river, stream* über die Ufer treten lassen **c** (*fig*) überschwemmen, überfluten; ~**ed with calls/complaints** mit Anrufen/Beschwerden überhäuft; ~**ed with light** lichtdurchflutet, von Licht durchflutet; **she was ~ed with relief** Erleichterung wallte in ihr auf **d** (*Comm*) **to ~ the market** den Markt überschwemmen **VI** **a** (*river*) über die Ufer treten; (*bath etc*) überfließen, überlaufen; (*cellar*) unter Wasser stehen; (*garden, land*) überschwemmt werden **b** (*people*) strömen; sich ergießen (*geh*); **the crowd ~ed into the streets** die Menge strömte auf die Straßen

▶**flood back** VI (*memories, feelings*) wieder aufwallen

▶**flood in** VI (*people, sunshine*) hineinströmen; (*water also*) hineinfließen; **the letters just flooded in** wir/sie *etc* hatten eine Flut von Briefen

▶**flood out** VT *sep house* überfluten, unter Wasser setzen; **the villagers were flooded out** die Dorfbewohner wurden durch das Hochwasser obdachlos

flood: flood control N Hochwasserschutz *m*; **flood disaster** N Flutkatastrophe *f*; **floodgate** N Schleusentor *nt*; **to open the** ~**s** (*fig*) Tür und Tor öffnen (*to* +*dat*)

flooding [ˈflʌdɪŋ] N Überschwemmung *f*

flood: floodlight vb: pret, ptp **floodlit** **VT** *buildings* anstrahlen; *football pitch* mit Flutlicht beleuchten; (*fig*, = *light brightly*) beleuchten **N** (= *device*) Scheinwerfer *m*; (= *light*) Flutlicht *nt*; **under ~s** unter or bei Flutlicht; **floodlighting** N Flutlicht(anlage *f*) *nt* **b** (*of building etc*) Beleuchtung *f*; **floodlit** pret, ptp of **floodlight** ADJ ~ **football match** Fußballspiel *nt* bei or unter Flutlicht; **flood plain** N Schwemmebene *f*; **flood tide** N Flut *f*

floor [flɔːʳ] **N** **a** Boden *m*; (*of room*) (Fuß)boden *m*; (= *dance floor*) Tanzboden *m*, Tanzfläche *f*; **ocean** ~ Meeresgrund *m*; **valley** ~ Talboden *m*; **stone-/tiled** ~ Stein-/Fliesenboden *m*; **to take to the** ~ (= *dance*) aufs Parkett or auf den Tanzboden gehen; **to take the** ~ (= *speak*) das Wort ergreifen; **to be given the** ~ (= *speak*) das Wort erhalten; **to hold** or **have the** ~ (*speaker*) das Wort haben **b** (= *storey: in apartment block etc*) Stock *m*, Stockwerk *nt*; **first** ~ (*Brit*) erster Stock; (*US*) Erdgeschoss *nt*, Erdgeschoß *nt* (*Aus*); **on the second** ~ (*Brit*) im zweiten Stock; (*US*) im ersten Stock **c** (*of prices etc*) Minimum *nt*; **property prices have fallen** or **dropped through the** ~ die Immobilienpreise sind in den Keller gefallen (*inf*) **d** (= *main part of chamber*) Plenar- or Sitzungssaal *m* (*also Parl*); (*of stock exchange*) Parkett *nt*; (= *people present*) Zuhörerschaft *f*; (*Parl*) Abgeordnete *pl*, Haus *nt*; **a question from the** ~ eine Frage aus der Zuhörerschaft; (*Brit Parl*) eine Frage aus dem Haus; ~ **of the House** (*Brit Parl*) Plenarsaal *m* des Unterhauses; **to cross the** ~ (*Brit Parl*) die Partei wechseln **VT** **a** *room etc* mit einem (Fuß)boden versehen **b** (= *knock down*) *opponent* zu Boden schlagen **c** (= *bewilder*) verblüffen; (= *defeat: question, problem etc*) schlagen (*inf*); **he looked completely ~ed** er sah völlig perplex aus

floor: floor area N Bodenfläche *f*; **floorboard** N Diele *f*, Bohle *f*; **floor cloth** N Scheuer- or Putzlappen *m*; **floor covering** N Bodenbelag *m*; **floor debate** N (*Parl*) Plenardebatte *f*; **floor exercise** N Bodenübung *f*

flooring [ˈflɔːrɪŋ] **N** **a** (= *floor*) (Fuß)boden *m* **b** (= *material*) Fußbodenbelag *m*

floor: floor lamp N Stehlampe *f*; **floor leader** N (*US: Parl*) Fraktionsführer(in) *m(f)*; **floor manager** N (*in store*) Abteilungsleiter(in) *m(f)* (*im Kaufhaus*); (*TV*) Aufnahmeleiter(in) *m(f)*; **floor model** N (verbilligtes) Ausstellungsstück; **floor plan** N Grundriss *m* (*eines Stockwerkes*); **floor polish** N Bohnerwachs *nt*; **floor polisher** N (= *tool*) Bohnerbesen *m*; **floor show** N Show *f*, Vorstellung *f* (*im Nachtklub oder Kabarett*); **floor space** N Stellraum *m*; **if you've got a sleeping bag we have plenty of** ~ wenn du einen Schlafsack hast, wir haben viel Platz auf dem Fußboden; **floor tile** N (Fuß)bodenfliese *f*/-platte *f*; **floor trading** N (*St Ex*) Parketthandel *m*; **floorwalker** N (*US Comm*) Ladenaufsicht *f*; **floor wax** N Bohnerwachs *nt*

floozie, **floozy** [ˈfluːzɪ] N (*inf*) Flittchen *nt* (*inf*), Schickse *f* (*inf*)

flop [flɒp] **VI** **a** (*person: = collapse*) sich fallen lassen; (*heavily*) sich hinplumpsen lassen (*inf*); **she ~ped into an armchair/onto the bed** sie ließ sich in einen Sessel/aufs Bett plumpsen (*inf*); **let's ~ now** (*inf*) komm, wir hauen uns in die Falle (*inf*) **b** (*thing: = fall*) fallen; (*heavily*) plumpsen **c** (*inf: = fail*) *scheme, plan* fehlschlagen, ein Reinfall *nt* sein (*inf*); (*play, book*) durchfallen;

the show ~**ped completely** die Show war ein totaler Reinfall; **he ~ped as Hamlet** als Hamlet war er ein Reinfall **N a** (*inf*, = *failure*) Reinfall *m*, Flop *m* (*inf*); **a disastrous** ~ ein totaler Reinfall **b** (= *movement*) Plumps *m* → **belly flop**

▶**flop around** VI herumzappeln; (*person: in slippers etc*) herumschlappen

flophouse [ˈflɒphaʊs] N (*dated US inf*) billige Absteige, Penne *f*

floppy [ˈflɒpɪ] **ADJ** (+*er*) schlaff, schlapp; *movement* schlaksig; *clothes* weit; *hair* wallend; *bow* weich; ~ **hat** Schlapphut *m*; ~ **ears** Schlappohren *pl* **N** (= *disk*) Floppydisk *f*, Floppy Disk *f*, Diskette *f*

floppy disk N (*Comput*) Floppydisk *f*, Floppy Disk *f*, Diskette *f*; ~ **drive** Diskettenlaufwerk *nt*

flora [ˈflɔːrə] N Flora *f*

floral [ˈflɔːrəl] **ADJ** **a** *fabric, print, wallpaper* geblümt; *fragrance, scent* blumig; ~ **design** or **pattern** Blumenmuster *nt* **b** (= *made of flowers*) Blumen-; ~ **arrangement/display** Blumenarrangement *nt*/-gesteck *nt*; ~ **tribute** Blumengruß *m*

Florence [ˈflɒrəns] N Florenz *nt*

Florentine [ˈflɒrəntaɪn] ADJ florentinisch

florescence [flɒˈresns] N Blüte *f*

floret [ˈflɒrət] N (*of flower*) (Einzel)blütchen *nt*; (*of cauliflower*) Röschen *nt*

florid [ˈflɒrɪd] ADJ (*usu pej*, = *ornate*) *language* blumig, schwülstig (*pej*); *wallpaper, tie* überladen; *music, architecture* reich verziert **b** (= *ruddy*) *person* rotgesichtig; *face, complexion* gerötet

florin [ˈflɒrɪn] N Florin *m*; (*Dutch*) Gulden *m*; (*dated Brit*) Zweishillingstück *nt*

florist [ˈflɒrɪst] N Blumenhändler(in) *m(f)*, Florist(in) *m(f)*; ~**'s (shop)** Blumengeschäft *nt*

floss [flɒs] **N** Flockseide *f*, Schappe *f*; (= *thread*) Florettgarn *nt*, ungezwirntes Seidengarn; (= *dental floss*) Zahnseide *f* **VT** *teeth* mit Zahnseide reinigen **VI** sich (*dat*) die Zähne mit Zahnseide reinigen

floss silk N Schappeseide *f*, Florettseide *f*

flotation [fləʊˈteɪʃən] N (*of ship*) Flottmachen *nt*; (*of log*) Flößen *nt*; (*Comm: of firm*) Gründung *f*; (*Metal*) Flotation *f*, Schwimmaufbereitung *f*

flotation collar N (*Space*) Schwimmkragen *m*

flotilla [fləˈtɪlə] N Flotille *f*

flotsam [ˈflɒtsəm] N Treibgut *nt*; **he was another of the city's** ~ er gehörte auch zu den Gestrandeten der Stadt, ~ **and jetsam** (*floating*) Treibgut *nt*; (*washed ashore*) Strandgut *nt*; **the** ~ **and jetsam of our society** die Gestrandeten *pl* or das Strandgut unserer Gesellschaft

flounce[1] [flaʊns] **VI** stolzieren; **to ~ in/out/around** herein-/heraus-/herumstolzieren **N** **she turned on her heel with a** ~ sie drehte sich pikiert auf dem Absatz um

flounce[2] **N** (= *frill*) Volant *m*, Rüsche *f* **VT** mit einem Volant/Volants or Rüschen besetzen

flounced [flaʊnst] ADJ *skirt, dress* mit Volants or Rüschen besetzt

flounder[1] [ˈflaʊndəʳ] N (= *fish*) Flunder *f*

flounder[2] **VI** **a** (*lit*) sich abstrampeln, sich abzappeln; **a stranded whale ~ing on the beach** ein gestrandeter Wal, der sich am Strand abquält; **we ~ed about in the mud** wir quälten uns mühselig im Schlamm **b** (*fig*) sich abzappeln (*inf*), sich abstrampeln (*inf*); **the company/economy was ~ing** der Firma/Wirtschaft ging es schlecht; **his career ~ed** mit seiner Karriere ging es abwärts; **to start to** ~ ins Schwimmen kommen; **to ~ through sth** sich durch etw wursteln or mogeln (*inf*); **he ~ed on** er wurstelte weiter

flour [ˈflaʊəʳ] **N** Mehl *nt* **VT** (*Cook*) *dough, rolling pin, one's hands* mit Mehl bestäuben

flour: flour bin N Mehlbüchse *f*; **flour dredger** N Mehlstreuer *m*

flourish [ˈflʌrɪʃ] **VI** (*plants etc, person*) (prächtig) gedeihen; (*business*) blühen, florieren; (*type of literature, painting etc*) seine Blütezeit haben;

(*writer, artist etc*) großen Erfolg haben, erfolgreich sein; **crime ~ed in poor areas** in den armen Gegenden gedieh das Verbrechen ► **VT** (= *wave about*) stick, book etc herumwedeln or -fuchteln mit, schwenken ► **N a** (= *curve, decoration etc*) Schnörkel *m* **b** (= *movement*) schwungvolle Bewegung, eleganter Schwung; **with a ~ of his stick** seinen Stock schwenkend; **she did/said it with a ~** sie tat es mit einer schwungvollen Bewegung/ sagte es mit viel Schwung **c** (*Mus*, = *fanfare*) Fanfare *f*; (= *decorative passage*) Verzierung *f*; **with a ~ of trumpets** mit einem Fanfarenstoß

flourishing ['flʌrɪʃɪŋ] ADJ florierend *attr*; *business also* gut gehend *attr*; *career* erfolgreich; *garden, plant* prächtig gedeihend *attr*; **how are you? – ~** wie gehts? – ausgezeichnet

flour: flour mill N (Korn)mühle *f*; **flour shaker** N Mehlstreuer *m*

floury ['flaʊərɪ] ADJ *face, hands, potatoes* mehlig

flout [flaʊt] VT sich hinwegsetzen über (+*acc*), missachten; *convention, society* pfeifen auf (+*acc*)

flow [fləʊ] ► **VI a** (*lit, fig*) fließen; (*tears*) strömen, fließen; (*prose*) flüssig sein; **where the river ~s into the sea** wo der Fluss ins Meer mündet; **tears were ~ing down her cheeks** Tränen liefen or flossen or strömten ihr übers Gesicht; **the wine ~ed freely all evening** der Wein floss den ganzen Abend in Strömen; **to make the conversation ~** ein lebhaftes Gespräch in Gang bringen; **to keep the traffic ~ing** den Verkehr nicht ins Stocken kommen lassen; **his words ~ed readily** er redete sehr flüssig; **to ~ in/out** (*water, people, money etc*) hinein-/herausströmen; **a surge of hatred ~ed through me** Hass wallte in mir auf **b** (*dress, hair etc*) fließen, wallen **c** (*tide*) steigen, hereinkommen ► **N a** Fluss *m*; (*of people*) Strom *m*; **the ~ of blood/traffic/information** der Blut-/Verkehrs-/ Informationsfluss; **against the ~ of the river** gegen den Strom; **to go with the ~** (*fig*) mit dem Strom schwimmen **b** **the tide is on the ~** die Flut kommt **c** (*of words etc*) Redefluss *m*; **the powerful ~ of his prose** seine wortgewaltige Prosa; **the ~ of conversation** der Gesprächsfluss; **he was in full ~** er war richtig in Fahrt

flow chart N Flussdiagramm *nt*

flower ['flaʊə'] ► **N a** Blume *f*; (= *blossom*) Blüte *f*; **"say it with ~s"** „lasst Blumen sprechen"; **no ~s by request** wir bitten von Blumenspenden abzusehen; **to be in ~** blühen, in Blüte stehen; **to come into ~** zu blühen anfangen **b** *no pl* (*fig*) Blüte *f*; **to be in the (full) ~ of youth** in der Blüte seiner Jugend stehen; **the ~ of British manhood** die Zierde der britischen Männer **c** (*Chem*) **~s of sulphur** Schwefelblume or -blüte *f* ► **VI** (*lit, fig*) blühen

flower: flower arrangement N Blumengesteck *nt*; **flower arranging** N Blumenstecken *nt*, Fertigen *nt* von Blumenarrangements; **flowerbed** N Blumenbeet *nt*; **flower child** N Blumenkind *nt*

flowered ['flaʊəd] ADJ *shirt, wallpaper* geblümt

flower: flower garden N Blumengarten *m*; **flower girl** N **a** (= *seller*) Blumenmädchen *nt* **b** (*at wedding etc*) Streukind *nt*; **flower head** N Blütenkopf *m*

flowering ['flaʊərɪŋ] ► **ADJ** Blüten-; **~ plant** Blütenpflanze *f*; **~ season** Blütezeit *f*; **~ shrub** Zierstrauch *m* ► **N** (*fig, of idea etc*) Blüte *f*

flower: flower people PL Blumenkinder *pl*; **flowerpot** N Blumentopf *m*; **flower power** N Flowerpower *f*, Flower-Power *f*; **flowerseller** N Blumenverkäufer(in) *m(f)*; **flower shop** N Blumenladen *m*, Blumengeschäft *nt*; **flower show** N Blumenschau *f*; **flower stalk** N Blütenstiel *m*

flowery ['flaʊərɪ] ADJ **a** *fabric, clothes, wallpaper* geblümt; *fragrance, perfume, scent* blumig; **a ~ field/meadow** ein Feld *nt*/eine Wiese voller

Blumen **b** (*fig*, = *elaborate*) *speech, language* blumig

flowing ['fləʊɪŋ] ADJ **a** *water* fließend **b** (= *long and loose*) *hair, beard, robe, gown* wallend; *skirt* fließend **c** (= *moving freely*) *movement, style, football* flüssig; (= *graceful*) *lines* fließend; **the ~ lines of the car** die schnittigen Linien des Autos

flown [fləʊn] *ptp of* fly² *of* fly³

fl. oz. *abbr of* **fluid ounce(s)**

flu, 'flu [fluː] N Grippe *f*; **to get** or **catch/have (the) ~** (die) or (eine) Grippe bekommen/haben

flub [flʌb] (*US inf*) ► **VT** verpfuschen, verpatzen (*both inf*) ► **VI** pfuschen, stümpern (*both inf*) ► **N** Schnitzer *m* (*inf*), grober Fehler

fluctuate ['flʌktjʊeɪt] VI schwanken; (*in number also*) fluktuieren

fluctuation [ˌflʌktjʊ'eɪʃən] N Schwankung *f*, Schwanken *nt no pl*; (*in number also*) Fluktuation *f*; (*fig, of opinions*) Schwanken *nt no pl*

flue [fluː] N Rauchfang *m*, Rauchabzug *m*; (*Mus: of organ, = pipe*) Labialpfeife *f*; (= *opening*) Kernspalt *m*; **~ brush** Stoßbesen *m*

fluency ['fluːənsɪ] N **a** (*in a foreign language*) fließendes Sprechen; **this job requires ~ in German** für diese Stelle ist fließendes Deutsch Voraussetzung; **~ in two foreign languages is a requirement** die Beherrschung von zwei Fremdsprachen ist Voraussetzung; **his ~ in English is inadequate** er spricht Englisch nicht fließend genug **b** (*in one's native language, of speaker, writer*) Gewandtheit *f*; (*of style*) Flüssigkeit *f* **c** (*of movement*) Flüssigkeit *f*

fluent ['fluːənt] ADJ **a** (*in a foreign language*) **to be ~** die Sprache fließend sprechen; **to be ~ in German** fließend Deutsch sprechen; **she is ~ in six languages** sie beherrscht sechs Sprachen fließend; **his English is not totally ~** er spricht nicht ganz fließend Englisch; **he is a ~ Japanese speaker, he speaks ~ Japanese** er spricht fließend Japanisch **b** (*in one's native language*) *writer, talker, debater* gewandt; *style* flüssig; *reader* fließend; **rage was making him ~** die Wut beflügelte seine Worte; **she speaks in ~ sentences** sie spricht in fließenden or flüssigen Sätzen **c** (= *moving freely*) *movement, action* flüssig; **Black Velvet is not the most ~ of jumpers** Black Velvet springt nicht besonders flüssig; **the match contained little ~ football** die Begegnung enthielt nur wenig flüssiges Spiel

fluently ['fluːəntlɪ] ADV **a** *speak, write* (*in a foreign language*) fließend; (*in one's native language*) flüssig; **to communicate ~ in Hebrew** sich fließend auf Hebräisch verständigen **b** (= *moving freely*) *jump, play* flüssig

fluey ['fluːɪ] ADJ (*Brit, inf*) **to feel ~** das Gefühl haben, dass man eine Grippe hat

fluff [flʌf] ► **N**, *no pl* (*on birds, young animals*) Flaum *m*; (*from material*) Fusseln *pl*; (= *dust*) Staubflocken *pl*; **a bit of ~** eine Fussel/eine Staubflocke; (*hum inf*) eine Mieze (*inf*) ► **VT a** (*also* **fluff out**) *feathers* aufplustern; *pillow* aufschütteln **b** *opportunity, lines in play, entrance* vermasseln (*inf*)

► **fluff up** VT *sep pillow etc* aufschütteln

fluffy ['flʌfɪ] ADJ (+*er*) **a** (= *soft*) *wool, slippers, sweater, towel* flauschig; *hair* locker; *kitten, rabbit* flaumweich; **a large ~ dog** ein großer, wolliger Hund; **~ white clouds** weiße Schäfchenwolken; **~ animal** or **toy** (= *soft toy*) Kuscheltier *nt* **b** (= *light*) *omelette, rice, mashed potatoes* locker; *egg, cake mixture* schaumig; **whip the eggs until ~** die Eier schaumig schlagen

fluid ['fluːɪd] ► **N** Flüssigkeit *f*; **loss of ~s** Flüssigkeitsverlust *m*; **she can only take ~s** sie kann nur flüssige Nahrung zu sich (*dat*) nehmen ► **ADJ a** (*lit*) flüssig **b** (*fig*) *movement* flüssig; *shape, painting* fließend **c** (*fig*, = *variable*) *situation* ungewiss; **his plans are still ~** seine Pläne stehen noch nicht fest

fluid assets [ˌfluːɪd'æsets] PL (*US, Fin*) Umlaufvermögen *nt*

fluidity [fluː'ɪdɪtɪ] N **a** (*lit, fig, of movement*) Flüssigkeit *f*; **the ~ of the painting** die fließenden Linien des Gemäldes **b** (*fig*: = *variability*: *of situation, plans*) Ungewissheit *f*

fluid ounce N Flüssigkeitsmaß (*Brit*: =28,4 *ml*, *US*: =29,6 *ml*)

fluish ['fluːɪʃ] ADJ = **fluey**

fluke¹ [fluːk] N (*inf*) Dusel *m* (*inf*), Schwein *nt* (*inf*); **by a ~** durch Dusel (*inf*); **it was a (pure) ~** das war (einfach) Dusel (*inf*)

fluke² N (*Naut*) Flunke *m*; (*of a whale's tail*) Fluke *f*; (*Fishing*: = *flounder*) Flunder *f*; (*Zool*: = *flatworm*) Plattwurm *m*

fluky ['fluːkɪ] ADJ (*inf*) *wind* wechselnd; **that was a ~ goal** das war ein Zufallstreffer

flume [fluːm] N **a** (= *ravine*) Klamm *f* **b** (= *channel*) Kanal *m* **c** (*in swimming pool*) schlauchförmige Wasserrutsche

flummox ['flʌməks] VT (*inf*) *person* durcheinander bringen, aus dem Konzept bringen (*inf*); **to be ~ed** durcheinander sein; **to be ~ed by sth** durch etw verwirrt sein, durch etw aus dem Konzept gebracht werden (*inf*)

flung [flʌŋ] *pret, ptp of* fling

flunk [flʌŋk] (*inf*) ► **VI** durchfallen (*inf*), durchrasseln (*inf*), durch die Prüfung fliegen (*inf*) ► **VT** *test* verhauen (*inf*); *candidate* durchfallen or durchrasseln lassen (*inf*); **to ~ German/an exam** in Deutsch/bei einer Prüfung durchfallen (*inf*)

flunk(e)y ['flʌŋkɪ] N Lakai *m*; (= *flatterer*) Radfahrer(in) *m(f)* (*inf*)

fluorescence [flʊə'resəns] N Fluoreszenz *f*

fluorescent [flʊə'resənt] ADJ (= *luminous*) *colour* leuchtend; *dye, paint, clothes* fluoreszierend; **~ display/screen** Leuchtanzeige *f*/-schirm *m*

fluorescent: fluorescent bulb N Leuchtstoffbirne *f*; **fluorescent light** N Leuchtstofflampe *f*, Neonlampe *f*; **fluorescent lighting** N Neonbeleuchtung *f*, Neonröhre *f*; **fluorescent tube** N Leuchtstoffröhre *f*

fluoridate ['flʊərɪdeɪt] VT mit Fluor versetzen, fluorieren

fluoridation [ˌflʊərɪ'deɪʃən] N Fluorzusatz *m* (*of* zu)

fluoride ['flʊəraɪd] N Fluorid *nt*; **~ toothpaste** Fluorzahnpasta *f*

fluorine ['flʊəriːn] N Fluor *nt*

fluorocarbon [ˌflʊərəʊ'kɑːbən] N Fluorkohlenwasserstoff *m*

fluorspar ['flʊəspɑː] N → **fluoride**

flurried ['flʌrɪd] ADJ **to become ~** sich aufregen, nervös werden

flurry ['flʌrɪ] ► **N a** (*of snow*) Gestöber *nt*; (*of rain*) Guss *m*; (*of wind*) Stoß *m*; **a ~ of blows** ein Hagel *m* von Schlägen **b** (*fig*) Aufregung *f*, Nervosität *f*; **in a ~** ganz aufgescheucht, in großer Aufregung; **a ~ of activity** eine Hektik; **a ~ of excitement** hektische Aufregung ► **VT** nervös machen, aufregen → **flurried**

flush¹ [flʌʃ] ► **N a** (= *lavatory flush*) (Wasser)spülung *f*; (= *water*) Schwall *m* **b** (= *blush*) Röte *f*; **the ~ of colour** (*Brit*) or **color** (*US*) **in her cheeks** die Farbe in ihren Wangen **c** (*of beauty, youth*) Blüte *f*; (*of joy*) Anfall *m*; (*of excitement, enthusiasm, panic*) Welle *f*; **in the (first) ~ of victory** im (ersten) Siegestaumel; **in the first ~ of youth** in der ersten Jugendblüte ► **VI a** (*person, face*) rot werden, rot anlaufen (*with* vor +*dat*); **to ~ crimson** dunkelrot anlaufen or werden **b** (*lavatory*) spülen ► **VT** spülen; (*also* **flush out**) *drain* durch- or ausspülen; **to ~ the lavatory** or **toilet** spülen, die Wasserspülung betätigen; **to ~ sth down the toilet** etw die Toilette hinunterspülen

► **flush away** VT *sep waste matter etc* wegspülen

► **flush out** VT *sep* **a** (*with water*) *sink, bottle* ausspülen, auswaschen; *dirt* wegspülen, wegschwemmen **b** *thieves, spies* aufstöbern, aufspüren; **they flushed them out of their hiding places** sie jagten sie aus ihren Verstecken

flush² ADJ pred **a** bündig; **cupboards ~ with the wall** Schränke, die mit der Wand abschließen; **to be ~ against the wall** direkt an der Wand stehen; **~ left/right** (text) links-/rechtsbündig **b** (inf) **to be ~** gut bei Kasse sein (inf)

flush³ VT game, birds aufstöbern, aufscheuchen

flush⁴ N (Cards) Flöte f, Sequenz f; (Poker) Flush m

flushed ['flʌʃt] ADJ (= red) face, cheeks rot, gerötet; **to be ~** (person) rot im Gesicht sein; **she arrived ~** sie kam mit einem roten Kopf an; **if your child is ~ and feverish** wenn Ihr Kind rot aussieht und Fieber hat; **~ with excitement/embarrassment/anger** rot vor Aufregung/Verlegenheit/Wut; **to be ~ with success/happiness** über seinen Erfolg/vor Glück strahlen; **white flowers ~ with pink** weiße, stellenweise rosa getönte Blüten

flushing ['flʌʃɪŋ] N (for lavatory) (Wasser)spülung f

fluster ['flʌstə] VT nervös machen; (= confuse) durcheinander bringen; **don't ~ me!** machen Sie mich nicht nervös!; **she got ~ed** sie wurde nervös, das brachte sie durcheinander; **to be ~ed** nervös or aufgeregt sein, durcheinander sein **N** **in a ~** nervös, aufgeregt; (= confused) durcheinander

flute [fluːt] **N** **a** (Mus) Querflöte f; (= organ stop) Flötenregister nt **b** **~ (glass)** Flöte f VT column, pillar kannelieren VI (person, voice) flöten

fluted ['fluːtɪd] ADJ column, pillar kanneliert; border, edge bogenförmig; **~ glass** (Sekt)flöte f

fluting ['fluːtɪŋ] N (Archit) Kannelierung f, Kanneluren pl; (of border, edge) Bogenform f

flutist ['fluːtɪst] N (US) = flautist

flutter ['flʌtə] VI **a** (flag, bird, butterfly) flattern (also Med); **her heart ~ed as he entered the room** sie bekam Herzklopfen, als er das Zimmer betrat; **to ~ away or off** davonflattern **b** (person) tänzeln; (nervously) flatterig sein; **to ~ around** herumtänzeln, nervös herumfuhrwerken (inf); **she ~ed into/out of the room** sie tänzelte ins Zimmer/aus dem Zimmer VT fan, piece of paper wedeln mit; (birds) wings flattern mit; one's eyelashes klimpern mit (hum inf); **to ~ one's eyelashes at sb** mit den Wimpern klimpern (hum), jdn mit einem tollen Augenaufschlag bezirzen **N** **a** Flattern nt (also Med); **this caused a ~ among the audience** dies verursachte leichte Unruhe im Publikum **b** (= nervousness) (all) in or of a ~ in heller Aufregung; **~ of anxiety/excitement** besorgte/aufgeregte Unruhe **c** (Brit inf) **to have a ~** (= gamble) sein Glück (beim Wetten) versuchen; **he likes his little ~ on a Friday night** er versucht Freitag abends gern sein Glück beim Wetten **d** (Aviat) Flattern nt

flutter kick N Wechselschlag m (beim Kraulen)

fluty ['fluːtɪ] ADJ (+er) voice flötend

fluvial ['fluːvɪəl] ADJ in Flüssen, fluvial (spec); **~ water** Flusswasser nt

flux [flʌks] N **a** (= state of change) Fluss m; **things are in a state of ~** die Dinge sind im Fluss; **to be in constant ~** ständig im Fluss sein **b** (Med: no pl) Ausfluss m; (Phys) Fluss m **c** (Metal) Flussmittel nt

fly¹ [flaɪ] N Fliege f; **they were dying like flies** sie starben wie die Fliegen; **small retailers are dropping like flies** kleine Einzelhändler gehen massenweise ein (inf); **he wouldn't hurt or harm a ~** er könnte keiner Fliege etwas zuleide or zu Leide tun; **that's the only ~ in the ointment** (inf) das ist das einzige Haar in der Suppe; **he's the ~ in the ointment** er ist Sand im Getriebe; **there are no flies on him** (Brit inf) ihn legt man nicht so leicht rein (inf); **to be a ~ on the wall** Mäuschen sein or spielen

fly² vb: pret flew, ptp flown VI **a** (person, bird, insect, aircraft etc) fliegen **b** (= move quickly, time) (ver)fliegen; (people)

sausen (inf), fliegen; (sparks) stieben, fliegen; **time flies!** wie die Zeit vergeht!; **the company is ~ing high** die Firma will hoch hinaus; **I'm already late, I must ~** ich bin schon spät dran, ich muss jetzt wirklich sausen (inf); **the door flew open** die Tür flog auf; **to ~ to sb's side** an jds Seite eilen; **to ~ into a rage** einen Wutanfall bekommen; **to ~ at sb** (inf) auf jdn losgehen; **to let ~ at sb** auf jdn losgehen; **he really let ~** er legte kräftig los; (verbally also) er zog kräftig vom Leder; **to knock or send sb/sth ~ing** jdn/etw umschmeißen (inf) or umwerfen; **he sent the ball ~ing over the wall** er schleuderte or schmiss (inf) den Ball über die Mauer; **to go ~ing** (person) hinfallen; (object) runterfallen; **stories are ~ing around the office** im Büro gehen Geschichten um **c to ~ in the face of authority/tradition** sich über jede Autorität/alle Traditionen hinwegsetzen; **to ~ in the face of reason** (person, organization) sich über jede Vernunft hinwegsetzen; (idea, theory etc) jeder Vernunft entbehren **d** (flag, hair) wehen VT **a** aircraft fliegen; kite steigen lassen **b** passengers, route, plane fliegen; Atlantic überfliegen **c** flag führen, wehen lassen → flag¹ **N** **to go for a ~** fliegen

▶**fly away** VI (bird) weg- or fortfliegen; (plane, person also) abfliegen; (fig, thoughts) wandern; (to zu)

▶**fly in** VI (troops, president, rescue plane etc) einfliegen; **we flew into Heathrow at night** wir sind abends in Heathrow angekommen; **she flew in from New York this morning** sie ist heute Morgen mit dem Flugzeug aus New York angekommen VT sep supplies, troops einfliegen

▶**fly off** VI **a** (plane, person) abfliegen, wegfliegen; (bird) wegfliegen, fortfliegen; **to fly off to the south** nach Süden fliegen; **a search plane flew off to look for them** ein Suchflugzeug flog los, um nach ihnen Ausschau zu halten; **as the plane flew off into the sunset** während das Flugzeug der untergehenden Sonne entgegenflog **b** (= come off, hat, lid etc) wegfliegen; (button) abspringen

▶**fly out** VI (troops, president, troop plane) ausfliegen; **as we flew out of Heathrow** als wir von Heathrow abflogen; **I'll fly out and come back by ship** ich werde hin fliegen und mit dem Schiff zurückkommen VT sep troops (to an area) hinfliegen; (out of an area) ausfliegen; **troops were flown out to the area** Truppen wurden in das Gebiet geflogen; **the company will fly you out** (into area) die Firma wird Sie hinfliegen; (out of area) die Firma wird Sie ausfliegen

▶**fly past** VI **a** (car, person) vorbeisausen or -flitzen (ceremonially) vorbeifliegen **c** (time) verfliegen VI +prep obj **to fly past sth** an etw (dat) vorbeifliegen

fly³ pret flew, ptp flown VI (= flee) fliehen, flüchten; **to ~ for one's life** um sein Leben laufen/fahren etc VT **to ~ the country** aus dem Land flüchten

fly⁴ N **a** (on trousers) (Hosen)schlitz m **b** = fly sheet **c** flies PL (Theat) Obermaschinerie f **d** = flywheel

fly⁵ (Brit inf) ADJ clever, gerissen **N** **to do sth on the ~** etw spontan tun

fly: **flyaway** ADJ hair fliegend, schwer zu bändigen; **fly-by-night** **N** **a** (= irresponsible man) Windhund m (inf); (= woman) leichtsinniges Ding (inf) **b** (= decamping debtor) flüchtiger Schuldner, flüchtige Schuldnerin ADJ **a** person unzuverlässig, unbeständig **b** (Fin, Comm) firm, operation zweifelhaft, windig (inf); **flycatcher** N **a** Fliegenschnäpper m **b** (= trap for flies) Fliegenfänger m; **fly-fishing** N Fliegenfischen nt; **fly half** N (Rugby) Halbspieler m

flying ['flaɪɪŋ] ADJ animal fliegend; glass, debris herumfliegend **N** Fliegen nt; **he likes ~** er fliegt gerne; **he's afraid of ~** er hat Angst vorm Fliegen or Flugangst

flying: **flying ambulance** N (= helicopter) Rettungshubschrauber m; (= plane) Rettungsflugzeug nt; **flying boat** N Flugboot nt; **flying bomb** N V-Rakete f; **flying buttress** N (Archit) Strebebogen m; **flying colours**, (US) **flying colors** PL **to pass with ~** glänzend abschneiden; **flying doctor** N fliegender Arzt (esp in Australien); **Flying Dutchman** N The ~ der Fliegende Holländer; **flying exhibition** N Wanderausstellung f; **flying fish** N Fliegender Fisch m; **flying fox** N Flughund m; **flying insect** N Fluginsekt nt; **flying jacket** N Fliegerjacke f; **flying leap** N (großer) Satz; **to take a ~** einen großen Satz machen; **flying machine** N (old, hum) Flugmaschine f; **flying officer** N (Brit) Oberleutnant m; **flying picket** N mobiler Streikposten; **flying saucer** N fliegende Untertasse; **flying squad** N Bereitschaftsdienst m; **flying start** N (Sport) fliegender Start; **to get off to a ~** (Sport) hervorragend wegkommen (inf); (fig) einen glänzenden Start haben; **flying suit** N Pilotenanzug m; **flying time** N Flugzeit f; **flying trapeze** N Trapez nt, Schwebereck nt; **flying visit** N Blitzbesuch m, Stippvisite f

fly: **flyleaf** N Vorsatzblatt nt; **flyover** N Überführung f; (US: = fly-past) Luftparade f; **flypaper** N Fliegenfänger m; **fly-past** N (Brit) Luftparade f; **flyposting** N illegales Plakatekleben; **fly sheet** N (= entrance) Überdach nt; (= outer tent) Überzelt nt; **fly spray** N Fliegenspray m; **fly swat(ter)** N Fliegenklatsche f; **fly-tipping** N illegales Müllabladen; **flytrap** N (Bot) Fliegenfalle f; **flyway** N (Orn) Zuglinie f; **flyweight** N (Boxing) Fliegengewicht nt; **flywheel** N Schwungrad nt

FM abbr **a** of frequency modulation FM **b** of field marshal **c** of foreign minister

f-number ['ef,nʌmbə] N (Phot) Blende f, Blendenzahl f

FO abbr of Foreign Office

foal [fəʊl] **N** Fohlen nt, Füllen nt; **in ~** trächtig VI fohlen

foam [fəʊm] **N** Schaum m; (of sea also) Gischt f VI schäumen; **to ~ at the mouth** (lit) Schaum vorm Mund or (animal) Maul haben; (fig, person) schäumen

▶**foam up** VI (liquid in container) schäumen

foam: **foam rubber** N Schaumgummi m; **foam sprayer** N Schaumlöscher m

foamy ['fəʊmɪ] ADJ (+er) **a** (= frothy) waves, beer schäumend **b** (liter, = resembling foam) schaumig

fob¹ [fɒb] VT (esp Brit) **to ~ sb off (with promises)** jdn (mit leeren Versprechungen) abspeisen; **to ~ sth off on sb, to ~ sb off with sth** jdm etw andrehen **N** (old: also **fob pocket**) Uhrtasche f

fob² [,efəʊ'biː] abbr of free on board

fob watch N Taschenuhr f

focal ['fəʊkəl] ADJ (fig) im Brennpunkt (stehend), fokal (geh)

focal: **focal length** N Brennweite f; **focal plane** N Brennebene f; **focal point** N (lit, fig) Brennpunkt m; **his family is the ~ of his life** seine Familie ist der Mittelpunkt seines Lebens, sein ganzes Leben dreht sich um seine Familie

fo'c'sle ['fəʊksl] N = forecastle

focus ['fəʊkəs] **N** pl foci ['fəʊkɪ] (Phys, Math, fig) Brennpunkt m; (of storm) Zentrum nt; (of earthquake, Med) Herd m; **in ~** (camera) (scharf) eingestellt; photo scharf; **to bring sth into ~** (lit) etw klar or scharf einstellen; (fig) topic etw in den Brennpunkt rücken; **out of ~** (lit, camera) unscharf eingestellt; photo unscharf; (fig) ideas vage; **to come into ~** ins Blickfeld rücken; **to keep sth in ~** (lit) etw scharf eingestellt im Suchfeld behalten; (fig) etw im Blickfeld behalten; **he/the new proposal was the ~ of attention** er/der neue Vorschlag stand im Mittelpunkt VT instrument einstellen (on auf +acc); light, heat rays bündeln; (fig) one's efforts, resources, energy konzentrieren (on auf +acc); **to ~ one's**

eyes on sb/sth den Blick auf jdn/etw richten; **to ~ one's attention/mind** sich konzentrieren; **I should like to ~ your attention (up)on a new problem** ich möchte Ihre Aufmerksamkeit auf ein neues Problem lenken **VI** (*light, heat rays*) sich bündeln; **to ~ on sth** sich auf etw (*acc*) konzentrieren; **his eyes ~ed on the book** sein Blick richtete sich auf das Buch; **I can't ~ properly** ich kann nicht mehr klar sehen

focus group N Fokusgruppe *f*

focus(s)ed ['fəʊkəst] ADJ (*fig*) fokussiert

fodder ['fɒdə'] N (*lit, fig*) Futter *nt*

foe [fəʊ] N (*liter*) Feind(in) *m(f)*, Widersacher(in) *m(f)* (*geh*)

FoE *abbr of* **Friends of the Earth**

foetal, (*esp US*) **fetal** ['fiːtl] ADJ fötal

foetid ['fiːtɪd] ADJ = **fetid**

foetus, (*esp US*) **fetus** ['fiːtəs] N Fötus *m*, Fetus *m*

fog [fɒg] **N** **a** Nebel *m*; **I am still in a ~** (*dated inf*) ich blicke immer noch nicht durch (*inf*) **b** (*Phot*) (Grau)schleier *m* **VT** **a** (*also* **fog up** *or* **over**) *mirror, glasses* beschlagen **b** (*Phot*) verschleiern **c** (*fig*) **to ~ the issue** die Sache vernebeln VI **a** (*also* **fog up** *or* **over**: *mirror, glasses*) beschlagen **b** (*Phot, negative*) einen Grauschleier bekommen

fog: fog bank N Nebelbank *f*; **fogbound** ADJ *ship, plane* durch Nebel festgehalten; *airport* wegen Nebel(s) geschlossen; **the main road to Edinburgh is ~** auf der Hauptstraße nach Edinburgh herrscht dichter Nebel

fogey ['fəʊgɪ] N (*inf*) **old ~** alter Kauz (*inf*); (= *woman*) Schrulle *f* (*inf*); **young ~** *junger Mensch, der sich bewusst konventionell benimmt und kleidet*, Junggreis *m* (*inf*)

foggy ['fɒgɪ] ADJ (*+er*) **a** (= *misty*) *day, weather, conditions* neb(e)lig **b** (*fig, = confused*) *brain* verwirrt; **in my ~ state** in meiner Verwirrung; **I haven't the foggiest (idea)** (*inf*) ich habe keinen blassen Schimmer (*inf*)

Foggy Bottom N (*US, hum inf*) *Scherzname für das amerikanische Außenministerium*

fog: foghorn N Nebelhorn *nt*; **a voice like a ~** (*inf*) eine dröhnende Stimme; **fog lamp, fog light** N Nebellampe *f*; (*Aut*) Nebelscheinwerfer *m*; **rear ~** (*Aut*) Nebelschlussleuchte *f*; **fog signal** N (*Naut, Rail*) Nebelsignal *nt*

FOIA (*US*) *abbr of* **Freedom of Information Act**

foible ['fɔɪbl] N Eigenheit *f*

foil¹ [fɔɪl] N **a** (= *metal sheet*) Folie *f*; (*of a mirror*) Spiegelfolie *f* ▸ **cooking foil, kitchen foil** **b** (*fig*) Hintergrund *m*, Folie *f*; **to act as a ~ to sth** einer Sache (*dat*) als Hintergrund *or* Folie dienen

foil² N (*Fencing*) Florett *nt*

foil³ VT *plans* durchkreuzen; *attempts* vereiteln; *person* einen Strich durch die Rechnung machen (*+dat*); **~ed again!** (*hum*) wieder nichts!; **he was ~ed in his attempts** ihm wurde ein Strich durch die Rechnung gemacht

foist [fɔɪst] VT **a** **to ~ sth (off) on sb** (*goods*) jdm etw andrehen; *task, responsibility* etw auf jdn abschieben; *opinions* jdm etw aufdrängen **b** **to ~ oneself (off) on sb** sich jdm aufdrängen

fold¹ [fəʊld] **N** Falte *f*; (*Geol, of the earth*) (Boden)falte *f*; **~s of skin** Hautfalten *pl*; **~s of fat** Fettwülste *pl* **VT** **a** (= *bend into folds*) *paper* (zusammen)falten; *blanket* zusammenlegen *or* -falten; **to ~ a newspaper in two/four** eine Zeitung falten/ zweimal falten; **to ~ sth flat** etw flach zusammenfalten **b** **to ~ one's arms** die Arme verschränken; **she ~ed her hands in her lap** sie faltete die Hände im Schoß zusammen **c** (= *wrap up*) einwickeln, einschlagen (*in* in *+acc*); **he ~ed the book in some paper** er schlug das Buch in Papier ein **d** **to ~ sb in one's arms** jdn in die Arme schließen

VI **a** (*chair, table*) sich zusammenklappen lassen; (*accidentally*) zusammenklappen **b** (= *close down: business*) eingehen; (*Theat, play*) abgesetzt werden

▸ **fold away** **VI** (*table, bed*) zusammenklappbar sein, sich zusammenlegen lassen **VT** *sep table, bed* zusammenklappen; *clothes* zusammenlegen; *newspaper* zusammenfalten

▸ **fold back** **VT** *sep shutters, door* zurückfalten; *sheet, bedclothes* auf- *or* zurückschlagen **VI** (*shutters, door*) zurückfalten, sich zurückfalten lassen

▸ **fold down** VT *sep chair* zusammenklappen; *corner* kniffen

▸ **fold in** VT *sep* (*Cook*) *flour, sugar* unterziehen, unterheben; **to fold sth into sth** etw unter etw (*acc*) heben *or* ziehen

▸ **fold over** VT *sep paper* umknicken; *blanket* umschlagen

▸ **fold up** VT *sep paper* zusammenfalten; *blanket also* zusammenlegen

fold² N (= *pen*) Pferch *m*; (*Eccl*) Herde *f*, Gemeinde *f*; **to return to the ~** (*fig*) in den Schoß der Gemeinde zurückkehren

foldaway ['fəʊldəweɪ] ADJ *attr* zusammenklappbar

folded ['fəʊldɪd] ADJ **a** *paper* (zusammen)gefaltet; *clothes, blanket, towel* (zusammen)gefaltet, zusammengelegt; *petal, leaf* geschlossen; **~ into a rectangle** zu einem Rechteck gefaltet **b** (= *crossed*) *hands* gefaltet; *arms* verschränkt; **to stand with one's arms ~** mit verschränkten Armen dastehen

folder ['fəʊldə'] N **a** (*for papers*) Aktendeckel *m*, Aktenmappe *f* **b** (*Comput*) Unterverzeichnis *nt* **c** (= *brochure*) Informationsblatt *nt*

folding ['fəʊldɪŋ] ADJ *attr* Klapp-; **~ bed** Klappbett *nt*; **~ chair** Klappstuhl *m*; (= *grille on lift*) Scherengittertür *f*; **~ table** Klapptisch *m*

folding: folding doors PL Falttür *f*; **folding money** N (*inf*) Papiergeld *nt*; **folding screen** N spanische Wand

foldout ['fəʊldaʊt] ADJ *attr section of book etc* ausklappbar

foliage ['fəʊlɪɪdʒ] N Blätter *pl*; (*of tree also*) Laub(werk) *nt*

foliation [ˌfəʊlɪ'eɪʃən] N **a** (*Bot*) Blattanordnung *f*; (= *development*) Blattbildung *f* **b** (*of book*) Foliierung *f*, Blattzählung *f* **c** (*Geol*) Schichtung *f* **d** (*Archit*) Laubwerk *nt*

folic acid [ˌfəʊlɪk'æsɪd] N Folsäure *f*

folio ['fəʊlɪəʊ] N **a** (= *sheet*) Folio *nt* **b** (= *volume*) Foliant *m*

folk [fəʊk] PL **a** (*also* **folks**: *inf, = people*) Leute *pl*; (= *people in general*) die Leute, man; **a lot of ~(s) believe ...** viele Leute/ glauben ...; **there were a lot of ~ at the concert** es waren eine Menge Leute bei dem Konzert; **come on, ~s** (*inf*) na los, Leute!; **the young/old ~** die Jungen/Alten; **old ~ can't ...** alte Menschen können nicht ... **b** (*inf: = relatives: also* **folks**) **my ~s** meine Leute (*inf*); **the old ~(s) stayed at home** die alten Herrschaften blieben zu Haus

folk: folk dance N Volkstanz *m*; **folklore** N Folklore *f*, Volkskunde *f*; **folk medicine** N Volksmedizin *f*; **folk memory** N (im Volk) lebendig gehaltene Überlieferungen *pl*; **folk music** N Volksmusik *f*; **folk singer** N Sänger(in) *m(f)* von Volksliedern; (*modern songs*) Folksänger(in) *m(f)*; **folk song** N Volkslied *nt*; (*modern*) Folksong *m*

folksy ['fəʊksɪ] ADJ **a** (= *rustic*) *music, culture, charm* volkstümlich; *clothes* bäuerlich; *furniture* rustikal **b** (*pej, = fake rustic*) auf rustikal gemacht (*pej*) **c** (*US, = affable, informal*) *person, manner* freundlich, herzlich; *speech, comment* volkstümlich

folk tale N Volksmärchen *nt*

follicle ['fɒlɪkl] N Follikel *nt*

follow ['fɒləʊ] ✪ 11.3 **VT** **a** *person, car, road, sign* folgen (*+dat*), nachgehen/-fahren *etc* (*+dat*); (= *pursue also*) verfolgen; (= *succeed*) fol-

gen (*+dat*), kommen nach; **he ~ed me about** er folgte mir überallhin; **he ~ed me out** er folgte mir nach draußen; **~ me** folgen Sie mir; (*by car also*) fahren Sie mir nach; **we're being ~ed** wir werden verfolgt; **to have sb ~ed** jdn verfolgen lassen; **his eyes ~ed her, he ~ed her with his eyes** er folgte ihr mit den Augen; **he arrived first, ~ed by the ambassador** er kam als Erster, gefolgt vom Botschafter; **he ~ed his father into the business** er folgte seinem Vater im Geschäft; **the earthquake was ~ed by looting** auf das Erdbeben folgte Plünderung; **the dinner will be ~ed by a concert** im Anschluss an das Essen findet ein Konzert statt; **the toast was ~ed by a vote of thanks** auf den Trinkspruch folgten Worte des Dankes; **to ~ the hounds** (mit den Hunden) auf die Jagd gehen; **~ that (if you can)!** (*said after a good performance etc*) das soll mir/ihm *etc* erst mal einer nachmachen!; **how do you ~ that?** das ist kaum zu überbieten; **I love lasagne ~ed by ice cream** besonders gern mag ich Lasagne und danach Eis; **potatoes are the most popular food, ~ed by white bread** Kartoffeln sind das beliebteste Essen, und an zweiter Stelle steht Weißbrot **b** (= *keep to*) *road, path* folgen (*+dat*), entlanggehen/-fahren *etc*; **the boat ~ed the coast** das Boot fuhr die Küste entlang; **the road ~s the valley** die Straße folgt dem Tal **c** (= *understand*) folgen (*+dat*); **do you ~ me?** können Sie mir folgen? **d** *profession* ausüben, nachgehen (*+dat*); *course of study, career* verfolgen; **to ~ the sea** (*liter*) zur See fahren **e** (= *conform to*) *fashion* mitmachen; *advice, instructions* befolgen, folgen (*+dat*); *party line* folgen (*+dat*); **to ~ (the dictates of) one's heart/ conscience** auf die Stimme seines Herzens/Gewissens hören **f** (= *read, watch regularly*) *serial* verfolgen; *strip cartoon* regelmäßig lesen; (= *take an interest in*) *progress, development, news* verfolgen; *athletics, swimming etc* sich interessieren für; (= *listen to attentively*) *speech* (genau) verfolgen; **to ~ the horses** sich für Pferderennen interessieren; **which team do you ~?** für welchen Verein sind Sie?; **the film ~s the fortunes of two women** der Film verfolgt das Schicksal zweier Frauen **VI** **a** (= *come after*) folgen (*on sth* auf etw *acc*); **as ~s** wie folgt; **his argument was as ~s** er argumentierte folgendermaßen; **to ~ in sb's footsteps** (*fig*) in jds Fußstapfen (*acc*) treten; **what is there to ~?** (*at meals*) was gibt es noch *or* (*planning the meal*) hinterher *or* anschließend?; **what ~s** das Folgende **b** (*results, deduction*) folgen (*from* aus); **it ~s from this that ...** hieraus folgt, dass ...; **it doesn't ~ that ...** daraus folgt nicht, dass ...; **that doesn't ~** nicht unbedingt! **c** (= *understand*) folgen; **I don't ~** das verstehe ich nicht, da komme ich nicht mit

▸ **follow on** VI **a** (= *come after*) später folgen *or* kommen; (*person*) nachkommen, später kommen **b** (*results*) folgen, sich ergeben (*from* aus) **c** (= *continue*) **the story follows on from his death** die Geschichte geht nach seinem Tod weiter; **she will follow on from where he left off** sie wird da weitermachen, wo er aufgehört hat **d** (*Cricket*) zwei Innenrunden hintereinander spielen

▸ **follow out** VT *sep idea, plan* zu Ende verfolgen, durchziehen

▸ **follow through** **VT** *sep argument* durchdenken, (zu Ende) verfolgen; *idea, plan, undertaking* (zu Ende) verfolgen, durchziehen **VI** **a** (*Sport*) durchschwingen **b** **to follow through with sth** (*with plan*) etw zu Ende verfolgen; (*with threat*) etw wahr machen

▸ **follow up** **VT** *sep* **a** (= *pursue, take further action on*) *request* nachgehen (*+dat*); *offer, suggestion* nachgehen (*+dat*), aufgreifen **b** (= *investigate further*) *suspect* näher beschäftigen *or* befassen mit; *suspect* Erkundigungen einziehen über (*+acc*); *candidate* in die engere Wahl nehmen; *matter* weiterverfolgen, sich näher befassen mit; *rumour* nachgehen (*+dat*); *patient* nachuntersuchen; (= *not lose track of*) *matter* im Auge behalten

c (= *reinforce*) *success, victory* fortsetzen, ausbauen; **to follow up words with deeds** auf Worte Taten folgen lassen; **he followed up the remark by punching him** er versetzte ihm zur Bekräftigung einen Schlag

d (= *get further benefit from*) *advantage* ausnutzen

VI a to follow up with sth etw folgen lassen

b (*Sport*) nachziehen

follower ['fɒləʊə] N (= *disciple*) Anhänger(in) m(f), Schüler(in) m(f); (= *servant*) Gefolgsmann m; **to be a ~ of fashion** sehr modebewusst sein; **he's a ~ of Blair** er ist Blair-Anhänger *or* ein Anhänger von Blair

following ['fɒləʊɪŋ] ✪ 20.2, 20.3, 26.2 **ADJ a** folgend; **the ~ day** der nächste *or* (darauf) folgende Tag; **he made the ~ remarks** er bemerkte Folgendes **b a ~ wind** Rückenwind m **N a** (= *followers*) Anhängerschaft f, Gefolgschaft f **b** he said the ~ er sagte Folgendes; **see the ~ for an explanation** (*in documents etc*) Erläuterungen hierzu finden Sie im Folgenden, Erklärungen im Folgenden; **the ~ is of note** Folgendes ist wichtig **PREP** nach

follow-my-leader ['fɒləʊmɪ'liːdə], (*US*) **follow-the-leader** ['fɒləʊðə'liːdə] N *Spiel, bei dem alle nachmachen müssen, was einer vormacht*

follow-through [ˌfɒləʊ'θruː] N (*Sport*) Durchziehen *nt*

follow-up ['fɒləʊʌp] N **a** Weiterverfolgen *nt*, Weiterführen f (*to +gen*) **b** (= *letter*) Nachfassschreiben *nt*; (*Press*) Fortsetzung f **c** (*Med*) Nachuntersuchung f

follow-up action N Folgemaßnahmen *pl*; **follow-up advertising** N Nachfasswerbung f; **follow-up album** N Nachfolgealbum *nt*; **follow-up care** N (*Med*) Nachbehandlung f; **follow-up interview** N zweites Vorstellungsgespräch *nt*; **follow-up meeting** N Folgetreffen *nt*; **follow-up operation** N (*Police*) Nachfassoperation f; (*Med*) zweite Operation; **follow-up phone call** N Anruf m zur Nachfrage *or* um nachzufragen; **follow-up question** N Folgefrage f; **follow-up study** N Nachfolgestudie f; **follow-up treatment** N (*Med*) Nachbehandlung f; **follow-up visit** N (*Med*) Nachuntersuchung f

folly ['fɒlɪ] N (= *foolishness, foolish thing*) Torheit f, Verrücktheit f; (= *building*) exzentrischer, meist völlig nutzloser Prachtbau; **it is sheer ~** (**to do that**) es ist der reinste Wahnsinn(, das zu tun)

foment [fəʊ'ment] VT *trouble, discord* schüren; (*Med*) mit feuchten Umschlägen behandeln

fomentation [ˌfəʊmen'teɪʃən] N (*of trouble, discord*) Schüren *nt*; (*Med*) feuchte Umschläge *pl*

fond [fɒnd] ADJ (+*er*) **a to be ~ of sb** jdn gern haben *or* mögen; **to be ~ of sth** etw mögen; **she is very ~ of animals** sie hat Tiere sehr gern, sie ist sehr tierlieb(end); **I'm not enormously ~ of Shaw's plays** ich bin kein großer Freund von Shaws Stücken; **the two were very ~ of each other** die beiden hatten *or* mochten einander sehr gern; **I am ~er of Michael than James, but I am ~est of Adrian** ich habe Michael lieber als James, aber Adrian habe ich am liebsten; **to become** *or* **grow ~ of sb/sth** jdn/etw lieb gewinnen; **he became very ~ of the garden** der Garten ist ihm sehr lieb geworden *or* sehr ans Herz gewachsen; **to be ~ of doing sth** etw gern tun; **she was ~ of shopping** sie ging gern einkaufen; **he is very ~ of telling us about the war** er erzählt uns mit Vorliebe vom Krieg

b (= *loving*) *husband, parent, relative, look, smile* liebevoll; *friend* lieb; **she gave him a ~ smile** sie lächelte ihn liebevoll an; **to bid sb a ~ farewell** sich liebevoll von jdm verabschieden; **they're saying their ~ farewells** sie nehmen zärtlich voneinander Abschied; **to have ~ memories of sth** schöne Erinnerungen an etw (*acc*) haben, sich gern an etw (*acc*) erinnern; **~est regards**

mit lieben Grüßen → **absence a**

c (= *fervent*) *hope, dream, wish* sehnlich; **his ~est wish** sein sehnlichster Wunsch, sein Herzenswunsch

d (= *foolish, vain*) *belief* naiv; *hope* töricht (*geh*); **in the ~ hope/belief that ...** in der vergeblichen Hoffnung, dass ...; **he has ~ hopes of winning** er bildet sich (*dat*) tatsächlich ein, gewinnen zu können

fondant ['fɒndənt] N Fondant *m*

fondle ['fɒndl] VT (zärtlich) spielen mit; (= *stroke*) streicheln; *person* schmusen mit

fondly ['fɒndlɪ] ADV **a** (= *affectionately*) liebevoll; **to remember sb ~** jdn in bester Erinnerung behalten; **to remember sth ~** sich gern an etw (*acc*) erinnern **b** (= *naively*) *imagine, believe* naiverweise; *hope* törichterweise (*geh*)

fondness ['fɒndnɪs] N (*for people*) Zuneigung f, Liebe f (*for* zu); (*for food, place, writer etc*) Vorliebe f (*for* für); (*for music, art*) Liebe f (*for* zu); **his ~ for** *or* **of swimming** seine Vorliebe fürs Schwimmen; **to remember sth/past times with ~** sehr gern an etw (*acc*)/an vergangene Zeiten zurückdenken

fondue ['fɒnduː] N Fondue *nt*; **~ set** Fondueset *nt*

font [fɒnt] N **a** (*Eccl*) Taufstein *m* **b** (*Typ*) Schrift f

fontanel(le) [ˌfɒntə'nel] N (*Physiol*) Fontanelle f

food [fuːd] N **a** Essen *nt*; (*for animals*) Futter *nt*; (= *nourishment*) Nahrung f; (= *foodstuff*) Nahrungsmittel *nt*; (= *groceries*) Lebensmittel *pl*; **the ~ is awful here** das Essen hier ist scheußlich; **dog and cat ~** Hunde- und Katzenfutter; **~ and drink** Essen und Trinken; **milk is a ~ rather than a drink** Milch ist eher ein Nahrungsmittel als ein Getränk; **canned ~s** Konserven *pl*; **I haven't any ~ in the house** ich habe nichts zu essen im Haus; **to be off one's ~** keinen Appetit haben; **they also do ~ at the pub** in der Kneipe gibt es auch Essen; **the very thought of ~ made her ill** wenn sie nur ans Essen dachte, wurde ihr schon schlecht

b (*fig*) Nahrung f; **~ for thought** Stoff *m* zum Nachdenken

food: food additives PL chemische Zusätze *pl*; **food aid** N Lebensmittelhilfe f; **food chain** N Nahrungskette f; **to get into the ~** in die Nahrungskette gelangen; **food court** N (*US*) Imbiss-Bereich *m* (*in einem Einkaufszentrum etc*)

foodie ['fuːdɪ] N (*inf*, = *food fanatic*) Kochkünstler(in) m(f), Kochfreak *m* (*inf*)

food: food parcel N Lebensmittelpaket *nt*; **food poisoning** N Lebensmittelvergiftung f; **food processor** N Küchenmaschine f; **food rationing** N Lebensmittelrationierung f; **food stamp** N (*US*) Lebensmittelmarke f; **foodstuff** N Nahrungsmittel *nt*; **food value** N Nährwert *m*

fool¹ [fuːl] **N a** Dummkopf *m*, Narr *m*, Närrin f; **don't be a ~!** sei nicht (so) dumm!; **some ~ of a civil servant** irgend so ein blöder *or* doofer Beamter (*inf*); **I was a ~ not to realize** wie konnte ich nur so dumm sein und das nicht merken; **have I been a ~!** war ich vielleicht dumm *or* blöd!, ich Idiot!; **he was a ~ not to accept** es war dumm von ihm, nicht anzunehmen; **he was ~ enough to ...** so dumm *or* blöd (*inf*) sein, zu ...; **to play** *or* **act the ~** Unsinn machen, herumalbern; **he made himself look a ~ in front of everyone** er machte sich vor allen lächerlich; **to make a ~ of sb** (*with ridicule*) jdn lächerlich machen; (*with a trick*) jdn zum Besten *or* zum Narren haben; **he made a ~ of himself at the party** er hat sich bei der Party blamiert; **to go on a ~'s errand** einen nutzlosen Gang tun; **to live in a ~'s paradise** in einem Traumland leben; **there's no ~ like an old ~** (*Prov*) Alter schützt vor Torheit nicht (*Prov*); **~s rush in (where angels fear to tread)** (*Prov*) blinder Eifer schadet nur (*Prov*) → **more, nobody**

b (= *jester*) Narr *m*

ADJ (*esp US, inf*) doof (*inf*), schwachsinnig (*inf*)

VI herumalbern, Blödsinn machen; **to ~ with sb/sth** mit jdm/etw spielen; **stop ~ing (around)!** lass den Blödsinn!; **I was only ~ing** das war doch nur Spaß

VT zum Narren haben *or* halten; (= *trick*) hereinlegen (*inf*); (*disguise, phoney accent etc*) täuschen; **you won't ~ me so easily** so leicht können Sie mich nicht hereinlegen (*inf*); **I was completely ~ed** darauf bin ich vollkommen hereingefallen; **you had me ~ed** ich habe das tatsächlich geglaubt; **who are you trying to ~?** wem willst du das weismachen?; **they ~ed him into believing that ...** sie haben ihm weisgemacht, dass ...; **they ~ed him into believing it** er hat es ihnen tatsächlich abgenommen

▶ **fool about** (*Brit*) *or* **fool around** VI **a** (= *waste time*) herumtrödeln; **he spends his time fooling about** *or* **around with his friends** er verschwendet seine ganze Zeit mit seinen Freunden **b** (= *play the fool*) herumalbern **c** **to fool about** *or* **around with sth** mit etw Blödsinn machen **d** (*sexually*) **he's fooling around with my wife** er treibt seine Spielchen mit meiner Frau; **she was fooling around** sie hat sich mit anderen eingelassen

fool² N (*Brit, Cook*) Sahnespeise aus Obstpüree

foolery ['fuːlərɪ] N Albernheit f

foolhardiness ['fuːlˌhɑːdɪnɪs] N Tollkühnheit f

foolhardy ['fuːlˌhɑːdɪ] ADJ tollkühn

foolish ['fuːlɪʃ] ADJ *person, decision, statement, action, mistake* dumm, töricht (*geh*); *question* dumm, blöd (*inf*); **he said his action had been ~** er sagte, dass er sich dumm verhalten *or* eine Dummheit gemacht hatte; **don't do anything ~** mach keinen Unsinn; **she had done something ~** sie hatte eine Dummheit gemacht; **what a ~ thing to do** wie kann man nur so dumm sein *or* so etwas Dummes tun; **to feel ~** sich (*dat*) dumm *or* albern vorkommen; **to look ~** dumm aussehen, sich lächerlich machen; **he's afraid of looking ~** er will sich nicht lächerlich machen *or* sich nicht blamieren; **to make sb look ~** jdn blamieren; **it made him look ~** dadurch hat er sich blamiert

foolishly ['fuːlɪʃlɪ] ADV (= *unwisely*) *behave, act* unklug, töricht (*geh*); *grin* dumm; *say* dummerweise; (*introducing sentence*) unklugerweise, törichterweise (*geh*); **you're being ~ romantic about it** deine romantische Einstellung dazu ist dumm

foolishness ['fuːlɪʃnɪs] N Dummheit f; **enough of this ~** lassen wir diese Dummheiten

foolproof ['fuːlpruːf] ADJ (= *infallible*) *method, system, test* unfehlbar; (= *idiot-proof*) *camera, recipe* narrensicher, idiotensicher (*inf*)

foolscap ['fuːlskæp] N (*also* **foolscap paper**) ≈ Kanzleipapier *nt*, *britisches Papierformat* (13¼ × 16½ *Zoll*)

fool's gold ['fuːls'gəʊld] N Katzengold *nt*

foot [fʊt] **N** *pl* **feet a** Fuß *m*; **to be on one's feet** (*lit, fig*) auf den Beinen sein; **to help sb back (on)to their feet** jdm wieder auf die Beine helfen; **to get back on one's feet** (*lit, fig*) wieder auf die Beine kommen; **the country is starting to get back on its feet again** das Land kommt langsam wieder auf die Beine; **on ~** zu Fuß; **to set ~ on dry land** den Fuß auf festen Boden setzen, an Land gehen; **I'll never set ~ here again!** hier kriegen mich keine zehn Pferde mehr her! (*inf*); **the first time he set ~ in the office** als er das erste Mal das Büro betrat; **to get** *or* **rise to one's feet** aufstehen; **to jump to one's feet** aufspringen; **to put one's feet up** (*lit*) die Füße hochlegen; (*fig*) es sich (*dat*) bequem machen; **he never puts a ~ wrong** (*gymnast, dancer*) bei ihm stimmt jeder Schritt; (*fig*) er macht nie einen Fehler; **to catch sb on the wrong ~** (*Sport*) jdn auf dem falschen Fuß erwischen; (*fig*) jdn überrumpeln; **to be dying** *or* **dead on one's feet** (*inf*) todmüde sein

b (*fig uses*) **to put one's ~ down** (= *act with decision or authority*) ein Machtwort sprechen; (= *forbid, refuse*) es strikt verbieten; (*Aut*) Gas geben; **to put one's ~ in it** ins Fettnäpfchen treten; **to put one's best ~ forward** (= *hurry*) die Beine unter den Arm nehmen; (= *do one's best*) sich anstrengen; **to find one's feet** sich eingewöhnen, sich zurechtfinden; **to fall on one's feet** auf die Beine fallen; **to have one's** or **both feet (firmly) on the ground** mit beiden Beinen (fest) auf der Erde stehen; **to keep one's feet on the ground** (*fig*) beide Beine auf der Erde halten; **to have one ~ in the grave** mit einem Bein im Grabe stehen; **to get/be under sb's feet** jdm im Wege stehen or sein; (*children also*) jdm vor den Füßen herumlaufen; **to get off on the right/wrong ~** einen guten/schlechten Start haben; **to have/get one's** or **a ~ in the door** einen Fuß in der Tür haben/in die Tür bekommen; **to get one's feet under the table** (*Brit inf*) sich etablieren; **to stand on one's own two feet** auf eigenen Füßen or Beinen stehen; **to sit at sb's feet** (*fig*) jds Jünger sein; **a nice area, my ~!** (*inf*) und das soll eine schöne Gegend sein!

c (*of stocking, list, page, stairs, hill, sewing machine etc*) Fuß *m*; (*of bed*) Fußende *nt*

d (*Measure*) Fuß *m*; **3 ~** or **feet wide/long** 3 Fuß breit/lang; **he's 6 ~ 3 ≈** er ist 1,90 m

e (*Poet*) (*Vers*)fuß *m*

f no pl (*Mil*) Infanterie *f*; **the 15th ~** das 15. Infanterieregiment; **ten thousand ~** (*Brit*) zehntausend Fußsoldaten *pl*

VT a to ~ it (*inf*, = *walk*) marschieren (*inf*)
b bill bezahlen, begleichen

footage ['futɪdʒ] N **a** (= *length*) Gesamtlänge *f* (*in Fuß*) **b** (*of film*) Filmmeter *pl*

foot-and-mouth (disease) ['futən'mauθ(dɪ-,zi:z)] N (*Brit*) Maul- und Klauenseuche *f*

football ['futbɔːl] N **a** Fußball *m*; (= *American football*) (American) Football *m* **b** (= *ball*) Fußball *m*, Leder *nt* (*inf*)

football: football boot N Fußballschuh *m*, Fußballstiefel *m*; **football casual** N Fußballprolo *m* (*inf*); **football coupon** N (*Brit*) Tippzettel *m*, Totoschein *m*

footballer ['futbɔːlə'] N **a** (*Brit*) Fußball(spieler)in *m(f)* **b** (*in American football*) Footballspieler *m*

football: football hooligan N Fußballrowdy or -hooligan *m*; **football hooliganism** N Fußballkrawalle *pl*

footballing ['futbɔːlɪŋ] ADJ Fußball-; **~ career** Fußballkarriere *f*; **~ countries** Fußball spielende Länder *pl*; **his ~ achievements** seine fußballerischen Leistungen

football pools PL Fußballtoto *nt* or *m* → **pool²** **c**

foot: foot bath N Fußbad *nt*; **footboard** N (*Rail, on coach*) Trittbrett *nt*; **foot brake** N Fußbremse *f*; **footbridge** N Fußgängerbrücke *f*

-footed [-futɪd] ADJ suf -füßig; **four-footed** vierfüßig

footer ['futə'] N (*Comput*) Fußzeile *f*

foot: footfall N Schritt *m*; **foot fault** N (*Tennis*) Fußfehler *m*; **footgear** N Fußbekleidung *f*; **foothills** PL (Gebirgs)ausläufer *pl*; **foothold** N Stand *m*, Halt *m*; (*fig*) sichere (Ausgangs)position; **he got** or **gained a ~ on the rock** er fand mit den Füßen Halt am Felsen; **to establish** or **gain a ~** (*fig*) Fuß fassen; **to lose one's ~** (*lit, fig*) den Halt verlieren

footie ['futɪ] N (*Brit, inf*) Fußball *m*

footing ['futɪŋ] N **a** (*lit*) Stand *m*, Halt *m*; **to lose one's ~** den Halt verlieren; **to miss one's ~** danebentreten

b (*fig*) (= *foundation, basis*) Basis *f*; (= *relationship*) Beziehung *f*, Verhältnis *nt*; **the business was on a secure ~** das Geschäft stand auf einer sicheren Basis; **we are trying to put training on a more scientific ~** wir versuchen, die Ausbildung wissenschaftlicher zu fundieren; **to be on a friendly ~ with sb** mit jdm auf freundschaftlichem Fuße stehen; **we want to put Britain on the same ~ as the rest of Europe** wir wollen Großbritannien mit dem restlichen Eu-

ropa gleichstellen; **on an equal ~ (with each other)** auf gleicher Basis; **to be on a war ~** sich im Kriegszustand befinden

c (*Archit*) Sockel *m*

footle ['fuːtl] VI **to ~ about** (*inf*) herumpusseln

footless ['fuːtlɪs] ADJ **a** (= *with no feet*) ohne Füße **b** (*fig, = unsubstantial*) nicht stichhaltig, nicht fundiert **c** (*inf: = inept*) ungeschickt

footlights ['futlaɪts] PL (*Theat*) Rampenlicht *nt*; **the lure of the ~** (*fig*) die Anziehungskraft der Bühne or der Bretter

footling ['fuːtlɪŋ] ADJ albern, dumm, läppisch

foot: footloose ADJ ungebunden, unbeschwert; **~ and fancy-free** frei und ungebunden; **footman** N Lakai *m*; **footmark** N Fußabdruck *m*; **footnote** N Fußnote *f*; (*fig*) Anmerkung *f*; **footpace** N Schritttempo *nt*; **at a ~** im Schritt; **footpath** N **a** (= *path*) Fußweg *m* **b** (*Brit, = pavement*) Bürgersteig *m*; **footplate** N Führerstand *m*; **footplate men**, **footplate workers** PL Lokomotivführer *pl*; **foot-pound** N *britische Maßeinheit für Drehmoment und Energie*; **footprint** N Fußabdruck *m*; (*fig, of machine*) Stellfläche *f*, Grundfläche *f*; **footprints** PL Fußspuren *pl*; **foot pump** N Fußpumpe *f*, Blasebalg *m*; **foot rot** N (*Vet*) Fußfäule *f*; **foot save** N (*Sport*) Fußabwehr *f*

Footsie ['futsɪ] N (*Fin inf*) Footsie(-Index) *m* (*inf*), Financial-Times-100-Index *m*

footsie ['futsɪ] N (*inf*) **to play ~ with sb** mit jdm füßeln

foot: footslog VI (*inf*) latschen (*inf*), marschieren; **footslogger** N (*Mil sl*) Fußsoldat *m*, Infanterist *m*; **~s** (*Mil sl*) Fußvolk *nt*; (*inf, = walkers*) Spaziergänger *pl*, Tippler *pl* (*inf*); **foot soldier** N Fußsoldat *m*, Infanterist *m*; **footsore** ADJ **to be ~** wunde Füße haben; **footstalk** N (*Bot*) Stängel *m*, Stiel *m*; **footstep** N Schritt *m*; **~ follow; footstool** N Schemel *m*, Fußbank *f*; **footwear** N Schuhe *pl*, Schuhwerk *nt*; **footwork** N , no pl (*Sport*) Beinarbeit *f*; (*fig*) Manöver *pl*

footy ['futɪ] N (*Brit, inf*) Fußball *m*

fop [fɒp] N (*dated*) Geck *m*, Stutzer *m* (*dated*)

foppish ['fɒpɪʃ] ADJ (*dated*) man geckenhaft (*pej*); **clothes** stutzerhaft

for¹ [fɔː'] **PREP a** (*intention*) für; (*purpose*) zu, für; (*destination*) nach; **a letter ~ me** ein Brief für mich; **clothes ~ children** Kleidung *f* für Kinder, Kinderkleidung *f*; **destined ~ greatness** zu Höherem bestimmt; **what ~?** wofür?, wozu?; **what is this knife ~?** wozu dient dieses Messer?; **he does it ~ pleasure** er macht es zum or aus Vergnügen; **what did you do that ~?** warum or wozu haben Sie das getan?; **a room ~ working in/ sewing** ein Zimmer zum Arbeiten/Nähen; **a bag ~ carrying books (in)** eine Tasche, um Bücher zu tragen; **fit ~ nothing** zu nichts nutze or zu gebrauchen; **to get ready ~ a journey** sich für eine Reise fertig machen; **ready ~ anything** zu allem bereit; **this will do ~ a hammer** das kann man als Hammer nehmen; **to go to Spain ~ one's holidays** nach Spanien in Urlaub fahren; **the train ~ Stuttgart** der Zug nach Stuttgart; **to leave ~ the USA** in die USA or nach Amerika abreisen; **he swam ~ the shore** er schwamm auf die Küste zu, er schwamm in Richtung Küste; **to make ~ home** sich auf den Heimweg machen

b (*indicating suitability*) **it's not ~ you to ask questions** Sie haben kein Recht, Fragen zu stellen; **it's not ~ me to say** es steht mir nicht zu, mich dazu zu äußern; **she's the woman** or **the one ~ me** sie ist die (richtige) Frau für mich; **married life is not ~ me** das Eheleben ist nichts für mich

c (= *representing, instead of*) **I'll speak to her ~ you if you like** wenn Sie wollen, rede ich an Ihrer Stelle or für Sie mit ihr; **I need someone to make up my mind ~ me** ich brauche jemanden, der die Entscheidung für mich trifft; **to act ~ sb** für jdn handeln; **D ~ Daniel** D wie Daniel; **agent ~ Renault** Vertreter(in) *m(f)* für Re-

nault; **she works ~ a bank** (*in the bank*) sie arbeitet bei or in einer Bank; (*outside the bank*) sie arbeitet für eine Bank

d (= *in defence, in favour of*) für; **are you ~ or against it?** sind Sie dafür oder dagegen?; **I'm all ~ it** ich bin ganz or sehr dafür; **I'm all ~ helping him** ich bin sehr dafür, ihm zu helfen; **the case ~ nuclear power** die Argumente für die Atomkraft

e (= *with regard to*) **anxious ~ sb** um jdn besorgt; **I'm very happy ~ you** ich freue mich sehr für euch; **~ my part** was mich betrifft; **as ~ him/ that** was ihn/das betrifft; **warm/cold ~ the time of year** warm/kalt für die Jahreszeit; **he is tall ~ his age** er ist groß für sein Alter; **what do you want ~ your birthday?** was wünschst du dir zum Geburtstag?; **it's all right** or **all very well ~ you (to talk)** Sie haben gut reden; **~ further information see page 77** weitere Informationen finden Sie auf Seite 77

f (= *because of*) aus; **~ this reason** aus diesem Grund; **he did it ~ fear of being left** er tat es aus Angst, zurückgelassen zu werden; **he is ~ famous ~ his jokes/his big nose** er ist für seine Witze bekannt/wegen seiner großen Nase berühmt; **to jump ~ joy** einen Freudensprung machen; **to go to prison ~ theft** wegen Diebstahls ins Gefängnis wandern; **to choose sb ~ his ability** jdn wegen seiner Fähigkeiten wählen; **if it were not ~ him** wenn er nicht wäre; **do it ~ me tu** es für mich

g (= *in spite of*) trotz (+*gen* or (*inf*) +*dat*); **~ all his wealth** trotz all seines Reichtums; **~ all that, you should have warned me** Sie hätten mich trotz allem warnen sollen

h (= *in exchange*) für; **to pay four euros ~ a ticket** vier Euro für eine Fahrkarte zahlen; **he'll do it ~ ten pounds** er macht es für zehn Pfund; **pound ~ pound** Pfund für Pfund

i (= *in contrast*) **~ every job that is created, two are lost** für jede Stelle, die neu geschaffen wird, gehen zwei verloren

j (*in time*) seit; (*with future tense*) für; **I have not seen her ~ two years** ich habe sie seit zwei Jahren nicht gesehen; **he's been here ~ ten days** er ist seit zehn Tagen hier; **I had/have known her ~ years** ich kannte/kenne sie schon seit Jahren; **then I did not see her ~ two years** dann habe ich sie zwei Jahre lang nicht gesehen; **he walked ~ two hours** er ist zwei Stunden lang marschiert; **I am going away ~ a few days** ich werde (für or auf) ein paar Tage wegfahren; **I shall be away ~ a month** ich werde einen Monat (lang) weg sein; **he won't be back ~ a week** er wird erst in einer Woche zurück sein; **I'll be back home ~ Christmas** Weihnachten bin ich wieder zu Hause; **can you get it done ~ Monday/this time next week?** können Sie es bis or für Montag/bis in einer Woche fertig haben?; **I've got a job ~ you ~ next week** ich habe für nächste Woche Arbeit für dich; **~ a while/time** (für) eine Weile/einige Zeit; **the meeting was scheduled ~ 9 o'clock** die Besprechung sollte um 9 Uhr stattfinden

k (*distance*) **the road is lined with trees ~ two miles** die Straße ist auf or über zwei Meilen mit Bäumen gesäumt; **we walked ~ two miles** wir sind zwei Meilen weit gelaufen; **there are roadworks on the M8 ~ two miles** auf der M8 gibt es eine zwei Meilen lange Baustelle; **~ miles** meilenweit; **~ mile upon mile** Meile um Meile

l (*with verbs*) **to pray ~ peace** für den or um Frieden beten; **to hope ~ news** auf Nachricht hoffen; **to look ~ sth** (nach) etw suchen → **vbs**

m (*after n: indicating liking, aptitude etc*) für; **a weakness ~ sweet things** eine Schwäche für Süßigkeiten; **his knack ~ saying the wrong thing** sein Talent, das Falsche zu sagen

n (*with infin clauses*) **~ this to be possible** damit dies möglich wird; **it's easy ~ him to do it** für ihn ist es leicht, das zu tun, er kann das leicht tun; **I brought it ~ you to see** ich habe es mitgebracht, damit Sie es sich (*dat*) ansehen können; **the best thing would be ~ you to leave** das Beste wäre, wenn Sie weggingen; **there's still time ~ him to come** er kann immer noch kommen; **their one hope is ~ him to return** ihre einzige Hoffnung ist, dass er zurückkommt

o (*phrases*) **to do sth ~ oneself** etw alleine tun; **~ example** zum Beispiel; **you're (in) ~ it!** (*inf*) jetzt bist du dran! (*inf*); **oh ~ a cup a tea!** jetzt eine Tasse Tee - das wäre schön!

CONJ denn; **~ it was too late** denn es war zu spät

ADJ pred (= *in favour*) dafür; **17 were ~, 13 against** 17 waren dafür, 13 dagegen

for² *abbr of* **free on rail** frei Bahn

forage ['fɒrɪdʒ] **N a** (= *fodder*) Futter *nt* **b** (= *search for fodder*) Futtersuche *f*; (*Mil*) Überfall *m* **VI** nach Futter suchen; (*Mil*) einen Überfall/Überfälle machen; (*fig*, = *rummage*) herumstöbern (*for* nach)

forage cap N Schiffchen *nt*

foray ['fɒreɪ] **N** (Raub)überfall *m*; (*Mil*) Ausfall *m*; (*fig*) Ausflug *m* (*into* in +*acc*); **to make a ~ into the European market** sich auf den europäischen Markt vorwagen **VI** Raubüberfälle/einen Raubüberfall machen; (*fig*) Ausflüge/einen Ausflug machen

forbad(e) [fə'bæd] *pret of* **forbid**

forbear¹ [fɔː'bɛəʳ] *pret* **forbore**, *ptp* **forborne** (*form*) **VI** I forbear from expressing my opinion ich verzichtete darauf or nahm Abstand davon, meine Meinung zu äußern; **we begged him to ~** wir baten ihn, darauf zu verzichten **VT** he forbore to make any comment er enthielt sich jeden Kommentars

forbear² ['fɔːbɛəʳ] **N** (*form*) Vorfahr(in) *m(f)*, Ahn(e) *m*, Ahne *f*

forbearance [fɔː'bɛərəns] **N** Nachsicht *f*

forbearing [fɔː'bɛərɪŋ] **ADJ** nachsichtig; (= *patient*) geduldig

forbid [fə'bɪd] **☉** 9.3, 9.5, 10.4 *pret* **forbad(e)**, *ptp* **forbidden** VT **a** (= *not allow*) verbieten; **to ~ sb to do sth** jdm verbieten, etw zu tun **b** (= *prevent*) verhindern, nicht erlauben; **my health ~s my attending** or **me from attending the meeting** meine Gesundheit erlaubt es nicht, dass ich an dem Treffen teilnehme; **God** or **Heaven ~!** Gott behüte or bewahre!; **Heaven ~ that she should come!** der Himmel bewahre uns davor, dass sie kommt!

forbidden [fə'bɪdn] **ADJ a** (= *prohibited*) love, food, goods verboten; **~ by law** gesetzlich verboten; **they are ~ to enter** sie dürfen nicht hereinkommen, es ist ihnen verboten, hereinzukommen; **smoking is (strictly) ~** Rauchen ist (streng) verboten; **preaching was ~ to women** Frauen durften nicht predigen, es war Frauen verboten zu predigen; **~ zone** Sperrzone *f*; **~ area** Sperrgebiet *nt*; **some cities and sites are ~ to foreigners** Ausländer dürfen manche Städte und Anlagen nicht betreten **b** (= *taboo*) **~ subject/word** Tabuthema *nt*/wort *nt*; **~ territory** or **ground** (*fig*) Tabu(thema) *nt*; **that's ~ territory** (*fig*) das ist tabu; **~ feelings** verbotene Gefühle *pl*

Forbidden City N **the ~** die Verbotene Stadt

forbidden fruit N verbotene Früchte *pl*; **~s are always the sweetest** verbotene Früchte schmecken am süßesten

forbidding [fə'bɪdɪŋ] **ADJ** person, expression Furcht einflößend; place, terrain unwirtlich; building, rocks, cliffs bedrohlich; task (= *uninviting*) wenig einladend; (= *overwhelming*) überwältigend; prospect düster; **the room was cold and ~** das Zimmer war kalt und unfreundlich

forbiddingly [fə'bɪdɪŋlɪ] **ADV** (= *off-puttingly*) (+*adj*) abstoßend; long, steep, expensive, difficult entmutigend; (+*vb*) say unfreundlich; look streng, unfreundlich; loom bedrohlich; **some find him ~ aloof** einige finden ihn unnahbar in seiner Strenge; **a ~ black cloud** eine bedrohlich schwarze Wolke

forbore [fɔː'bɔːʳ] *pret of* **forbear¹**

forborne [fɔː'bɔːn] *ptp of* **forbear¹**

force [fɔːs] **☉** 10.3, 26.1 **N a** no pl (= *physical strength, power*) Kraft *f*; (*of blow, impact, collision*) Wucht *f*; (= *physical coercion*) Gewalt *f*; (*Phys*) Kraft *f*; **to resort to ~** Gewalt anwenden; **to settle sth by ~** etw gewaltsam or durch Gewalt beilegen; **by sheer ~** durch reine Gewalt; **by** or **through sheer ~ of numbers** aufgrund or auf Grund zahlenmäßiger Überlegenheit; **there is a ~ 5 wind blowing** es herrscht Windstärke 5; **the ~ of the wind was so great he could hardly stand** der Wind war so stark, dass er kaum stehen konnte; **they were there in ~** sie waren in großer Zahl da; **they came in ~** sie kamen in großer Zahl or Stärke **b** no pl (*fig*) (*of argument*) Überzeugungskraft *f*; (*of music, phrase*) Eindringlichkeit *f*; (*of character*) Stärke *f*; (*of words*) Macht *f*; **that was ~ of habit** das war die Macht der Gewohnheit; **by** or **from ~ of habit** aus Gewohnheit; **by ~ of will** durch Willensanstrengung or Willenskraft; **the ~ of circumstances** der Druck der Verhältnisse; **I see the ~ of what he is saying** ich sehe ein, was er sagt, ist zwingend **c** (= *powerful thing, person*) Macht *f*; **Forces of Nature** Naturgewalten *pl*; **there are various ~s at work here** hier sind verschiedene Kräfte am Werk; **he is a powerful ~ in the reform movement** er ist ein einflussreicher Mann in der Reformbewegung → **life force d** (= *body of men*) **the ~s** (*Mil*) die Streitkräfte *pl*; **the (police) ~** die Polizei; **to join ~s** sich zusammentun → **sales force, work force e** **to come into/be in ~** in Kraft treten/sein **VT a** (= *compel*) zwingen; **to ~ sb/oneself to do sth** jdn/sich zwingen, etw zu tun; **he was ~d to resign** er wurde gezwungen zurückzutreten; (= *felt obliged to*) er sah sich gezwungen zurückzutreten; **he was ~d to conclude that ...** er sah sich zu der Folgerung gezwungen or gedrängt, dass ... **b** (= *extort, obtain by force*) erzwingen; **he ~d a confession out of** or **from me** er erzwang ein Geständnis von mir; **to ~ an error** (*Sport*) einen Fehler erzwingen, den Gegner ausspielen **c** (= *impose*) **to ~ sth (up)on sb** (*present, one's company*) jdm etw aufdrängen; conditions, obedience jdm etw auferlegen; conditions, decision, war jdm etw aufzwingen; **he ~d himself on her** (*sexually*) er tat ihr Gewalt an **d** (= *break open*) aufbrechen; **to ~ (an) entry** sich (*dat*) gewaltsam Zugang or Zutritt verschaffen **e** (= *push, squeeze*) **to ~ books into a box** Bücher in eine Kiste zwängen; **the liquid is ~d up the tube by a pump** die Flüssigkeit wird von einer Pumpe durch das Rohr nach oben gepresst; **if it won't open/go in, don't ~ it** wenn es nicht aufgeht/passt, wende keine Gewalt an; **to ~ one's way into sth** sich (*dat*) gewaltsam Zugang zu etw or in etw (*acc*) verschaffen; **to ~ one's way through** sich (*dat*) gewaltsam einen Weg bahnen; **to ~ a car off the road** ein Auto von der Fahrbahn drängen; **to ~ a bill through parliament** eine Gesetzesvorlage durch das Parlament peitschen **f** plants treiben **g** (= *produce with effort*) **to ~ a smile** gezwungen lächeln; **to ~ the pace** das Tempo forcieren; **don't ~ it** erzwingen Sie es nicht

▶ **force back** VT sep zurückdrängen; tears unterdrücken

▶ **force down** VT sep food sich (*dat*) hinunterquälen; aeroplane zur Landung zwingen; price drücken; laugh unterdrücken; lid of suitcase etc mit Gewalt zumachen

▶ **force off** VT sep lid mit Gewalt abmachen

▶ **force up** VT sep prices hoch treiben

forced [fɔːst] **ADJ a** (= *imposed*) Zwangs-; repatriation gewaltsam; marriage, resignation, withdrawal erzwungen; **~ sale** Zwangsverkauf *m*; (= *auction*) Zwangsversteigerung *f* **b** (= *contrived*) smile, laughter, conversation, wording gezwungen; behaviour gekünstelt; **to sound ~** sich gezwungen or unnatürlich anhören **c** plant getrieben

forced: forced entry N (= *break-in*) Einbruch *m*; **forced labour**, (*US*) **forced labor** N Zwangsarbeit *f*; **forced landing** N (*Aviat*) Notlandung *f*; **forced loan** N Zwangsanleihe *f*; **forced march** N (*Mil*) Gewaltmarsch *m*; **forced saving** N Zwangssparen *nt*

force-feed ['fɔːsfiːd] vb: pret, ptp **force-fed** **VT** zwangsernähren **N** (*Tech*) Druckschmierung *f*

forceful ['fɔːsfʊl] **ADJ a** (= *hard*) blow, kick kräftig, wuchtig **b** (= *vigorous*) person, manner, action energisch; character, personality stark; rejection, criticism, denial entschieden; speech, statement, language, style eindringlich; reminder eindringlich, nachdrücklich; argument (= *strong*) eindringlich; (= *convincing*) überzeugend; **he was ~ in his refusal** er weigerte sich entschieden; **she was ~ in her condemnation of the regime** sie verurteilte das Regime aufs schärfste or Schärfste

forcefully ['fɔːsfəlɪ] **ADV a** (= *forcibly*) remove, move mit Gewalt, gewaltsam; (= *violently*) push, knock heftig **b** (= *vigorously*) act, intervene energisch, entschlossen; argue eindringlich; deny, reject, criticize entschieden; say, demand, remind nachdrücklich, eindringlich; **it struck him ~ that ...** es fiel ihm sehr auf, dass ...

forcefulness ['fɔːsfʊlnɪs] **N a** (*of kick, punch*) Wucht *f* **b** (= *vigour, of person, manner, action, intervention*) energische or entschlossene Art *f*; (*of character, personality*) Stärke *f*; (*of rejection, criticism, denial*) Entschiedenheit *f*; (*of speech, statement, language, style*) Eindringlichkeit *f*; (*of argument*, = *strength*) Eindringlichkeit *f*; (= *conviction*) Überzeugungskraft *f*

force majeure [ˌfɔːsmæˈʒɜː] **N** höhere Gewalt; **to bow to ~** sich höherer Gewalt (*dat*) beugen

forcemeat ['fɔːsmiːt] **N** (*Cook*) Fleischfüllung *f*, Farce *f*

forceps ['fɔːseps] **PL** (also **pair of forceps**) Zange *f*; **~ delivery** Zangengeburt *f*

forcible ['fɔːsəbl] **ADJ a** (= *forced*) repatriation, removal gewaltsam; **~ feeding** Zwangsernährung *f* **b** (= *emphatic*) speech, declaration, language eindringlich; argument überzeugend; **a ~ reminder of sth** eine eindringliche or nachdrückliche Erinnerung an etw (*acc*)

forcible entry N Einbruch *m*

forcibly ['fɔːsəblɪ] **ADV a** (= *by force*) remove, restrain, separate gewaltsam, mit Gewalt; **to feed sb ~** jdn zwangsernähren **b** (= *powerfully*) eindringlich; argue, express eindringlich, nachdrücklich; **what struck me most ~ about this incident was ...** was mir an diesem Zwischenfall am meisten auffiel, war ...; **this was brought home to me ~ when ...** das wurde mir in vollem Ausmaß bewusst, als ...

forcing house ['fɔːsɪŋhaʊs] **N a** (*Agr etc*) Gewächshaus *nt* **b** (*fig*, = *school*) Lernfabrik *f*

ford [fɔːd] **N** Furt *f* **VT** durchqueren; (*on foot also*) durchwaten

fore [fɔːʳ] **N to the ~** im Vordergrund; **to come to the ~** ins Blickfeld geraten **ADJ** attr (Zool, Naut, Aviat: = *front*) vordere(r, s); **the ~ part of the ship** das Vorschiff; **~ watch** (*Naut*) Vorderwache *f* **ADV** (*Naut*) vorn; **~ and aft** längsschiffs **INTERJ** (*Golf*) Achtung!

fore-and-aft [ˌfɔːrəndˈɑːft] **ADJ** (*Naut*) **~ schooner** Gaffelschoner *m*; **~ sail** Schratsegel *nt*

forearm¹ ['fɔːrɑːm] **N** Unterarm *m*

forearm² [fɔːrˈɑːm] **VT** vorbereiten; **~ed with this information** mit diesen Informationen gerüstet or gewappnet → **forewarn**

forebear¹ ['fɔːbɛəʳ] **N** (*form*) Vorfahr(in) *m(f)*, Ahn(e) *m*, Ahne *f*

forebear² [fɔː'bɛəʳ] **VTI** = **forebear¹**

forebode [fɔː'bəʊd] **VT** (= *be portent of*) ein Zeichen or Omen sein für, ahnen lassen, deuten auf (+*acc*)

foreboding [fɔː'bəʊdɪŋ] **N** (= *presentiment*) (Vor)ahnung *f*, Vorgefühl *nt*; (= *feeling of disquiet*) ungutes Gefühl **ADJ** look Unheil verkündend

forebrain ['fɔːbreɪn] **N** Vorderhirn *nt*

forecast ['fɔːkɑːst] **VT** vorhersehen, voraussagen; (Met) voraussagen, vorhersagen **N** Voraussage f, Vorhersage f, Prognose f; (Met) Voraus- or Vorhersage f; **the ~ is good** der Wetterbericht or die Wettervorhersage ist günstig

forecaster ['fɔːkɑːstə'] **N** (Met) Meteorologe m, Meteorologin f; **economic ~** Wirtschaftsprognostiker(in) m(f)

forecastle ['fəʊksl] **N** (Naut) Vorschiff nt, Vorderdeck nt; (in Merchant Navy) Logis nt

foreclose [fɔː'kləʊz] **VT** loan, mortgage kündigen **VI to ~ on a loan/mortgage** ein Darlehen/ eine Hypothek kündigen; **to ~ on sb** jds Kredit/Hypothek kündigen

foreclosure [fɔː'kləʊʒə'] **N** Zwangsvollstreckung f (on bei)

forecourt ['fɔːkɔːt] **N** Vorhof m

foredeck ['fɔːdek] **N** Vor(der)deck nt

foredoomed [fɔː'duːmd] **ADJ** (form) **~ to fail** or **to failure** von vorneherein zum Scheitern verurteilt, tot geboren (fig inf)

forefather ['fɔːfɑːðə'] **N** Ahn m, Vorfahr m

forefinger ['fɔːfɪŋgə'] **N** Zeigefinger m

forefoot ['fɔːfʊt] **N** Vorderfuß m

forefront ['fɔːfrʌnt] **N in** or **at the ~ of** an der Spitze (+gen)

foregather [fɔː'gæðə'] **VI** zusammentreffen, sich versammeln

forego [fɔː'gəʊ] pret **forewent**, ptp **foregone VT** verzichten auf (+acc)

foregoing [fɔː'gəʊɪŋ] **ADJ** vorhergehend, vorangehend; **it can be seen from the ~ that ...** aus dem bisher Gesagten kann entnommen werden, dass ...

foregone [fɔː'gɒn] ptp of **forego ADJ** ['fɔːgɒn] **it was a ~ conclusion** es stand von vornherein fest

foreground ['fɔːgraʊnd] **N** (Art, Phot) Vordergrund m; **in the ~** im Vordergrund

forehand [fɔː'hænd] (Sport) **N** Vorhand f **ATTR** Vorhand-; **~ volley** Vorhandvolley m

forehead ['fɔːhed, 'fɒrɪd] **N** Stirn f

foreign ['fɒrən] **ADJ** **a** person, product ausländisch; food, customs, appearance fremdländisch; **to be ~** (person) Ausländer(in) sein; **a quarter of the population is ~** ein Viertel der Bevölkerung sind Ausländer or kommt aus dem Ausland; **~ countries** das Ausland; **he came from a ~ country** er kam aus dem Ausland; **~ travel** Auslandsreisen pl; **she was on her first ~ trip** sie machte zum ersten Mal eine Auslandsreise; **~ debt** Auslandsschuldung f; **~ investment** Auslandsinvestition f; **~ news** Auslandsnachrichten pl, Nachrichten pl aus dem Ausland
b (= alien) Fremd-; **~ matter** Fremdstoffe pl; **~ body** or **object** Fremdkörper m; **to be ~ to sb** jdm fremd sein; **behaviour that was ~ to his nature** ein Verhalten, das seiner Natur fremd war

foreign: foreign affairs PL (Pol) Außenpolitik f; **spokesman on ~** außenpolitischer Sprecher; **foreign agent N** (in espionage) ausländischer Agent; (Comm etc) Auslandsvertreter(in) m(f); **foreign aid N** Entwicklungshilfe f; **Foreign and Commonwealth Office N** (Brit) Außenministerium nt; **foreign-born ADJ** im Ausland geboren; **foreign correspondent N** Auslandskorrespondent(in) m(f); **foreign currency N** Devisen pl

foreigner ['fɒrənə'] **N** Ausländer(in) m(f)

foreign: foreign exchange N **a** (= currency) Devisen pl **b** (= system, trading) Devisenmarkt m, Devisenhandel m; (= location) Devisenbörse f; **on the ~s** an den Devisenbörsen **c** (= stock exchange) Auslandsbörse f; **foreign experience N** Auslandserfahrung f; **foreign language N** Fremdsprache f; **it was like a ~ to me** (fig) das waren böhmische Dörfer für mich (inf) **ATTR** film fremdsprachig; **~ assistant** Fremdsprachenassistent(in) m(f); **~ skills** Fremdsprachenkenntnisse pl; **foreign legion N** Fremdenlegion f; **Foreign Minister N** Außenminister(in) m(f); **foreign national N**

ausländische(r) Staatsangehörige(r) mf; **Foreign Office N** (Brit) Auswärtiges Amt; **foreign policy N** (Pol) Außenpolitik f; **foreign relations PL** (Pol) Auslandsbeziehungen pl; **Foreign Secretary N** (Brit) Außenminister(in) m(f); **foreign trade N** Außenhandel m

foreknowledge [fɔː'nɒlɪdʒ] **N** vorherige Kenntnis

foreland ['fɔːlənd] **N** Vorland nt; (= promontory) Landspitze f

foreleg ['fɔːleg] **N** Vorderbein nt

forelimb ['fɔːlɪm] **N** Vorderglied nt

forelock ['fɔːlɒk] **N** Stirnlocke f, Stirnhaar nt; **to touch** or **tug one's ~ (to sb)** (Brit) (jdm) seine Reverenz erweisen

foreman ['fɔːmən] **N** pl **-men** [-mən] (in factory) Vorarbeiter m; (on building site) Polier m; (Jur, of jury) Obmann m

foremast ['fɔːmɑːst] **N** (Naut) Fockmast m

foremost ['fɔːməʊst] **ADJ** **a** (= leading) authority, writer, scholar etc führend; **to be ~ in sth/in a field** in etw (dat)/auf einem Gebiet führend sein; **to be ~ in doing sth** führend darin sein, etw zu tun; **~ among them was John** John führte mit ihnen; **the thought which is ~ in his mind** der Gedanke, der ihn hauptsächlich beschäftigt **b** (Naut) vorderste(r, s) **ADV** **a** (= above all) vor allem → **first ADV b** **b** (= forwards) **to jump in feet/head ~** mit den Füßen/dem Kopf zuerst hineinspringen; **hold the spear point ~** halten Sie den Speer mit der Spitze nach vorn

forename ['fɔːneɪm] **N** Vorname m

forenoon ['fɔːnuːn] **N** (form) Vormittag m

forensic [fə'rensɪk] **ADJ** **a** evidence, test, laboratory forensisch; (Med) gerichtsmedizinisch **b** (form) skill forensisch

forensic: forensic expert N (Police) Spurensicherungsexperte m/-expertin f; **forensic medicine N** Gerichtsmedizin f, forensische Medizin

forensics [fə'rensɪks] **N** sing (= science) Kriminaltechnik f; (= medicine) Gerichtsmedizin f; (= police department) Spurensicherung f

forensic: forensic science N Kriminaltechnik f; **~ laboratory** kriminaltechnisches Labor; **forensic scientist N** Kriminaltechniker(in) m(f)

foreordain [ˌfɔːrɔː'deɪn] **VT = preordain**

forepaw N Vorderpfote f

foreplay ['fɔːpleɪ] **N** Vorspiel nt

forequarters ['fɔːkwɔːtəz] **PL** Vorderstücke pl

forerib N (Cook) Hochrippe f

forerunner ['fɔːrʌnə'] **N** (= precursor) Vorläufer m; **a ~ of things to come** ein Vorbote m der Zukunft

foresaid ['fɔːsed] **ADJ = aforesaid**

foresail ['fɔːseɪl] **N** (Naut) Focksegel nt

foresee [fɔː'siː] pret **foresaw** [fɔː'sɔː] ptp **foreseen** [fɔː'siːn] **VT** vorhersehen, voraussehen

foreseeable [fɔː'siːəbl] **ADJ** voraussehbar, absehbar; **in the ~ future** in absehbarer Zeit

foreshadow [fɔː'ʃædəʊ] **VT** ahnen lassen, andeuten

foresheet ['fɔːʃiːt] **N** (Naut) Fockschot f

foreshore ['fɔːʃɔː'] **N** Küstenvorland nt; (= beach) Strand m

foreshorten [fɔː'ʃɔːtn] **VT** (Art) perspektivisch zeichnen; (Phot) perspektivisch fotografieren

foreshortening [fɔː'ʃɔːtnɪŋ] **N** (Art) zeichnerische Verkürzung f; (Phot) fotografische Verkürzung

foresight ['fɔːsaɪt] **N** Weitblick m

foreskin ['fɔːskɪn] **N** Vorhaut f

forest ['fɒrɪst] **N** Wald m; (for lumber etc) Forst m; (fig) (of aerials etc) Wald m; (of ideas etc) Wust m, Menge f

forestage ['fɔːsteɪdʒ] **N** Vorbühne f

forestall [fɔː'stɔːl] **VT** sb, rival zuvorkommen (+dat); accident, eventuality vorbeugen (+dat);

crisis, danger, disaster abwenden; wish, desire im Keim ersticken; objection vorwegnehmen

forestation [fɒrɪ'steɪʃən] **N = afforestation**

forestay ['fɔːsteɪ] **N** (Naut) Fockstag nt

Forest Enterprise N (Brit) Landverwaltungsabteilung der Forstbehörde

forester ['fɒrɪstə'] **N** Förster(in) m(f)

forest ranger N (US) Förster(in) m(f)

forestry ['fɒrɪstrɪ] **N** Forstwirtschaft f

Forestry Commission (Brit), **Forestry Service** (US) **N** Forstverwaltung f

foretaste ['fɔːteɪst] **N** Vorgeschmack m; **to give sb a ~ of sth** jdm einen Vorgeschmack von etw geben

foretell [fɔː'tel] pret, ptp **foretold** [fɔː'təʊld] **VT** vorhersagen

forethought ['fɔːθɔːt] **N** Vorbedacht m

forever [fər'evə'] **ADV** **a** (= eternally) live, last, be grateful ewig; remember, go on immer; **she is ~ watchful** sie ist ewig wachsam; **Scotland ~!** ein Hoch auf Schottland! **b** (= irrevocably) go, disappear, change unwiderruflich; **the old social order was gone** – das alte Gesellschaftssystem war für immer verschwunden **c** (inf, = ages) **it takes ~** es dauert ewig (inf); **these old slate roofs go on** or **last ~** diese alten Schieferdächer halten ewig **d** (inf, = constantly) **to be ~ doing sth** (an)dauernd or ständig etw tun

forevermore [fər,evə'mɔː'] **ADV** (esp US) = **for evermore** → **evermore**

forewarn [fɔː'wɔːn] **VT** vorher warnen; **that should have ~ed him** das hätte ihm eine Vorwarnung sein sollen; **~ed is forearmed** (Prov) Gefahr erkannt, Gefahr gebannt (Prov)

forewent [fɔː'went] pret of **forego**

forewing ['fɔːwɪŋ] **N** Vorderflügel m

forewoman ['fɔːwʊmən] **N** pl **-women** [-wɪmɪn] Vorarbeiterin f; (Jur, of jury) Obmännin f

foreword ['fɔːwɜːd] **N** Vorwort nt

forfeit ['fɔːfɪt] **VT** **a** (esp Jur) one's rights etc verwirken **b** (fig) one's life, health, honour, sb's respect einbüßen; chance verpassen; right, place verlieren **N** (esp Jur) Strafe f, Buße f; (fig) Einbuße f; (in game) Pfand nt; **~s** sing (game) Pfänderspiel nt; **to pay a ~** (in game) ein Pfand (ab)geben; **his health was the ~ he paid** er zahlte mit seiner Gesundheit dafür **ADJ to be ~** (Jur) verfallen sein; (fig) verwirkt sein

forfeiture ['fɔːfɪtʃə'] **N** (Jur, fig) Verlust m, Einbuße f; (of claim) Verwirkung f

forgather [fɔː'gæðə'] **VI = foregather**

forgave [fə'geɪv] pret of **forgive**

forge [fɔːdʒ] **N** (= workshop) Schmiede f; (= furnace) Esse f **VT** **a** metal schmieden; (fig) friendship, alliance schließen; relationship aufbauen; plan schmieden; **to ~ economic/close links with sb/sth** Wirtschaftsbeziehungen/eine enge Bindung zu jdm/etw aufbauen **b** (= counterfeit) signature, banknote fälschen **N to ~ ahead (with sth)** (mit etw) vorwärts kommen or Fortschritte machen; **to ~ ahead** (in career) seinen Weg machen; (Sport) vorstoßen; **he ~d ahead of the rest of the field** er setzte sich weit vom Rest des Feldes

forger ['fɔːdʒə'] **N** Fälscher(in) m(f)

forgery ['fɔːdʒərɪ] **N** **a** (= act) Fälschen nt; **art/ cheque** (Brit) or **check** (US) **~** Kunst-/Scheckfälschung f; **to be prosecuted for ~** wegen Fälschung angeklagt sein **b** (= thing) Fälschung f; **the signature was a ~** die Unterschrift war gefälscht

forget [fə'get] ✪ 26.3 pret **forgot**, ptp **forgotten VT** skill, ability, language verlernen; **never to be forgotten** unvergesslich, unvergessen; **and don't you ~ it!** und dass du das ja nicht vergisst!; **he never lets you ~ it** either er sorgt dafür, dass du auch immer daran denkst; **to ~ to do sth** vergessen, etw zu tun; **I was ~ting you knew him** ich habe vergessen, dass Sie ihn kennen; **I ~ his name** sein Name ist mir entfallen; **I ~ what I wanted to say** es ist mir entfallen, was ich sagen wollte; **to ~ one's dif-**

ferences seine Meinungsverschiedenheiten ruhen lassen; **not ~ting ...** nicht zu vergessen ...; **~ it!** schon gut!; **you might as well ~ it** (*inf*) das kannst du vergessen (*inf*)

VI es vergessen; **don't ~!** vergiss (es) nicht!; **I never ~** ich vergesse nie etwas; **where has he gone? – I ~** wo ist er hingegangen? – ich habe es vergessen *or* es ist mir entfallen; **she drinks to ~** sie trinkt, um zu vergessen

VR (= *behave improperly*) sich vergessen, aus der Rolle fallen; (= *act unselfishly*) sich selbst vergessen

▶**forget about** VI +*prep obj* vergessen; **I've forgotten all about what he did** ich habe völlig vergessen, was er getan hat

forgetful [fə'ɡetfʊl] ADJ (= *absent-minded*) vergesslich; (*of one's duties etc*) achtlos, nachlässig (*of* gegenüber)

forgetfulness [fə'ɡetfʊlnɪs] N (= *absent-mindedness*) Vergesslichkeit *f*; (*of one's duties etc*) Achtlosigkeit *f*, Nachlässigkeit *f* (*of* gegenüber); **in a moment of ~** in einem Augenblick geistiger Abwesenheit

forget-me-not [fə'ɡetmɪnɒt] N (*Bot*) Vergissmeinnicht *nt*

forgettable [fə'ɡetəbl] ADJ **an eminently ~ second novel** ein zweiter Roman, den man getrost vergessen kann; **it was an instantly ~ game** es war ein Spiel, das man sofort vergessen konnte

forgivable [fə'ɡɪvəbl] ADJ verzeihlich, verzeihbar

forgivably [fə'ɡɪvəblɪ] ADV verzeihlich; **John was ~ tense** man konnte John seine Nervosität verzeihen; **~, she walked out without answering** sie verließ den Raum ohne zu antworten, was verzeihlich war

forgive [fə'ɡɪv] ✪ 18.1, 18.2 *pret* **forgave**, *ptp* **forgiven** [fə'ɡɪvn] **VT** *mistake, clumsiness* verzeihen, vergeben; *person* verzeihen (+*dat*), vergeben (+*dat*); *debt* erlassen; (*esp Eccl*) *sin* vergeben, erlassen; **to ~ sb sth** jdm etw verzeihen *or* vergeben; (*Eccl*) jdm etw vergeben *or* erlassen; **to ~ sb for sth** jdm etw verzeihen *or* vergeben; **to ~ sb for doing sth** jdm verzeihen *or* vergeben, dass er etw getan hat; **you could be ~n for thinking that ...** es ist durchaus verständlich, wenn Sie denken, dass ...; **~ me, but ...** Entschuldigung, aber ...; **I'll never ~ myself if anything happens to him** ich werde es mir nie verzeihen, wenn ihm etwas zustößt; **to ~ and forget** vergeben und vergessen

VI (*person*) verzeihen, vergeben

forgiveness [fə'ɡɪvnɪs] N , *no pl* (*quality*: = *willingness to forgive*) Versöhnlichkeit *f*; **to ask/beg (sb's) ~** (jdn) um Verzeihung *or* Vergebung (*esp Eccl*) bitten; **her complete ~ of them surprised him** es überraschte ihn, dass sie ihnen voll und ganz verzieh; **the ~ of sins** (*Eccl*) die Vergebung der Sünden; **~ of debt** Schuldenerlass *m*; **full of ~** versöhnlich

forgiving [fə'ɡɪvɪŋ] ADJ versöhnlich, nicht nachtragend

forgo [fɔ:'ɡəʊ] *pret* **forwent**, *ptp* **forgone** VT = **forego**

forgot [fə'ɡɒt] *pret of* **forget**

forgotten [fə'ɡɒtn] *ptp of* **forget**

fork [fɔ:k] **N a** (= *implement*) Gabel *f* **b** (*in tree*) Astgabel *f*; (*in road, railway*) Gabelung *f*; **take the left ~** nehmen Sie die linke Abzweigung **VT a** *ground* mit einer Gabel umgraben; (= *turn over*) *hay* wenden; **to ~ hay onto a cart** Heu mit einer Gabel auf einen Wagen werfen **b** *garden* gabeln (*inf*) **VI** (*roads, branches*) sich gabeln; **to ~ (to the) right** (*road*) nach rechts abzweigen; (*driver*) nach rechts abbiegen

▶**fork out** (*inf*) **VT** *sep* blechen (*inf*) **VI** blechen (*inf*)

▶**fork over** VT *sep ground* lockern; *hay* wenden

▶**fork up** VT *sep soil* mit einer Gabel umgraben; *hay* hochheben; *food* gabeln (*inf*)

forked [fɔ:kt] ADJ *tail, stick, branch* gegabelt; *tongue* gespalten; **to speak with (a) ~ tongue** (*fig*) mit gespaltener Zunge sprechen (*geh*)

forked lightning N Linienblitz *m*

fork: **fork-lift (truck)** ['fɔ:klɪft('trʌk)] (*inf*) N Gabelstapler *m*; **fork luncheon** N (*Brit*) Gabelfrühstück *nt*

forlorn [fə'lɔ:n] ADJ **a** (= *desolate*) verlassen; (= *miserable*) trostlos; **~ appearance** (*of house etc*) desolates *or* trostloses Aussehen; **a ~ figure** eine einsam und verlassen wirkende Gestalt; **her voice sounded ~** ihre Stimme klang einsam und verlassen; **the palaces stood empty and ~** die Paläste standen leer und verlassen da **b** (= *despairing*) *attempt, effort* verzweifelt; **it is a ~ hope** es ist ziemlich aussichtslos, es ist eine ziemlich aussichtslose Sache; **in the ~ hope of success/of finding a better life** in der verzweifelten Hoffnung auf Erfolg/ein besseres Leben

forlornly [fə'lɔ:nlɪ] ADV **a** *stand, wait* einsam und verlassen; *stare* verloren **b** *hope, try* (= *desperately*) verzweifelt; (= *vainly*) vergeblich

form [fɔ:m] **N a** *Form f*; **~ of government** Regierungsform *f*; **~ of life** Lebensform *f*; **the various ~s of energy** die verschiedenen Energieformen; **~ of address** Anrede *f*; **to choose another ~ of words** es anders formulieren; **~s of worship** Formen *pl* der Gottesverehrung; **a ~ of apology** eine Art der Entschuldigung; **a ~ of punishment** eine Form *or* Art der Bestrafung **b** (= *condition, style, guise*) Form *f*, Gestalt *f*; **in the ~ of** in Form von *or* +*gen*; (*with reference to people*) in Gestalt von *or* +*gen*; **medicine in tablet ~** Arznei in Tablettenform; **water in the ~ of ice** Wasser in Form von Eis; **the same thing in a new ~** das Gleiche in neuer Form *or* Gestalt; **the first prize will take the ~ of a trip to Rome** der erste Preis ist eine Reise nach Rom; **their discontent took various ~s** ihre Unzufriedenheit äußerte sich in verschiedenen Formen; **her letters are to be published in book ~** ihre Briefe sollen in Buchform *or* als Buch erscheinen **c** (= *shape*) Form *f*; (*of person*) Gestalt *f*; **to take ~** (*lit, fig*) Form *or* Gestalt annehmen **d** (*Art, Mus, Liter,* = *structure*) Form *f*; **~ and content** Form und Inhalt **e** (*Philos*) Form *f*; **the world of ~s** die Ideenwelt **f** (*Gram*) Form *f*; **the plural ~** die Pluralform, der Plural **g** *no pl* (= *etiquette*) (Umgangs)form *f*; **he did it for ~'s sake** er tat es der Form halber; **it's bad ~ so etwas tut man einfach nicht; **what's the ~?** (*inf*) was ist üblich? **h** (= *document*) Formular *nt*, Vordruck *m*; **printed ~** vorgedrucktes Formular **i** (= *physical condition*) Form *f*, Verfassung *f*; **to be in fine** *or* **good ~** gut in Form sein, in guter Form *or* Verfassung sein; **to be on/off ~** in/ nicht in *or* außer Form sein; **to be on top ~** in Höchstform sein; **he was in great ~ that evening** er war an dem Abend in Hochform; **to study (the) ~** (*Horse-racing*) die Form prüfen; **past ~** Papierform *f*; **on past ~** auf dem Papier **j** (*esp Brit,* = *bench*) Bank *f* **k** (*Brit, Sch*) Klasse *f* **l** *no pl* (*Brit inf,* = *criminal record*) **to have ~** vorbestraft sein **m** (*Tech,* = *mould*) Form *f* **n** (*US, Typ*) = **forme** **o** (*of hare*) Nest *nt*, Sasse *f* (*spec*) **VT a** (= *shape*) formen, gestalten (*into* zu); (*Gram*) *plural, negative* bilden; **he ~s his sentences well** er bildet wohlgeformte Sätze **b** (*train, mould*) *child, sb's character* formen **c** (= *develop*) *liking, desire, idea, habit* entwickeln; *friendship* schließen, anknüpfen; *opinion* sich (*dat*) bilden; *impression* gewinnen; *plan* ausdenken, entwerfen **d** (= *set up, organize*) *government, committee* bilden; *company, society, political party* gründen, ins Leben rufen **e** (= *constitute, make up*) *part, basis* bilden; **the committee is ~ed of ...** der Ausschuss wird von ... gebildet

f (= *take the shape or order of*) *circle, pattern* bilden; **to ~ a queue** (*Brit*) *or* **line** (*US*) eine Schlange bilden **VI a** (= *take shape*) Gestalt annehmen; **an idea ~ed in my mind** eine Idee nahm Gestalt an **b** (*esp Mil: also* **form up**) sich aufstellen *or* formieren, antreten; **to ~ into a queue** (*Brit*) *or* **line** (*US*)/**into two lines** eine Schlange/zwei Reihen bilden; **to ~ into a square** sich im Karree aufstellen; **to ~ into battle order** sich zur Schlachtordnung formieren

formal ['fɔ:məl] ADJ **a** *person, letter, relationship, behaviour, language* formell, förmlich; (= *official*) *talks, complaint, agreement, request* formell, offiziell; (= *ceremonial*) *occasion, reception* feierlich; **he made them a ~ bow** er verbeugte sich formell *or* feierlich vor ihnen; **to make a ~ apology** sich in aller Form entschuldigen; **the dinner was very ~** das Abendessen war sehr formell; **~ affair** *or* **occasion** formeller *or* feierlicher Anlass; **on ~ occasions** bei formellen *or* feierlichen Anlässen; **~ clothes** *or* **dress** (*for smart occasions*) Gesellschaftskleidung *f*; (*for work*) formelle Kleidung; **in ~ dress** formell gekleidet **b** (= *ordered*) *style, approach* formal; (= *severe*) streng; (*in design*) *garden, borders, square* regelmäßig angelegt; *room* formal eingerichtet; **~ gardens** formal angelegte Gartenanlagen *pl* **c** (= *proper*) *education, training* ordentlich; *qualifications* offiziell **d** (= *relating to form*) *logic, perfection, complexity, defect* formal

formaldehyde [fɔ:'mældɪhaɪd] N Formaldehyd *m*

formalin(e) ['fɔ:məlɪn] N Formalin *nt*

formalism ['fɔ:məlɪzəm] N Formalismus *m*

formalistic [,fɔ:mə'lɪstɪk] ADJ formalistisch

formality [fɔ:'mælɪtɪ] N **a** *no pl* (*of person, dress, greeting, language, ceremony etc*) Förmlichkeit *f* **b** (= *matter of form*) **it's a mere ~** es ist (eine) reine Formsache *or* Formalität; **let's dispense with the formalities** lassen wir die Formalitäten beiseite

formalize ['fɔ:məlaɪz] VT *rules, grammar* formalisieren; *agreement, arrangement* formell bekräftigen; *relationship* formell machen

formally ['fɔ:məlɪ] ADV **a** *speak, behave, dress* formell, förmlich; (= *officially*) *announce, agree, open, approve* formell, offiziell; *apologize* in aller Form; **~ courteous** förmlich und höflich; **~ dressed** formell gekleidet; **the pact still exists - at least ~** der Pakt besteht immer noch - zumindest der Form nach; **~ charged** (*Jur*) offiziell angeklagt; **~ binding** offiziell verbindlich **b** (*in design*) regelmäßig; **~ laid-out gardens** formal angelegte Gartenanlagen; **the chairs were ~ arranged in rows** die Stühle waren streng in Reihen angeordnet **c** (= *academically*) *teach, train* offiziell; (*in an educational establishment*) in einer Bildungsanstalt; **to teach sth ~** etw wissenschaftlich unterrichten; **he is ~ trained** er hat eine ordentliche Ausbildung

format ['fɔ:mæt] **N** (*as regards size*) Format *nt*; (*as regards content*) Aufmachung *f*; (*Rad, TV, of programme*) Struktur *f*; (*of computer data, recording*) Format *nt*; **page ~** Seitenformat *nt* **VT** (*Comput*) *disk, page, paragraph* formatieren

formation [fɔ:'meɪʃən] N **a** (= *act of forming*) Formung *f*, Gestaltung *f*; (*Gram: of plural etc*) Bildung *f*; (*of character*) Formung *f*; (*of government, committee*) Bildung *f*; (*of company, society*) Gründung *f*; (*of desire, idea, impression, habit etc*) Entwicklung *f*; (*of friendship*) Schließen *nt*, Anknüpfung *f*; (*of opinion*) Bildung *f*; (*of plan*) Entwurf *m* **b** (*of aircraft, dancers, troops*) Formation *f*; **battle ~** Gefechtsaufstellung *f*; **in close ~** (*Aviat*) im geschlossenen Verband; **to dance in ~** in Formation tanzen **c** (*Geol*) Formation *f*

formation: formation dancing N Formationstanzen *nt*; **formation flying** N Formationsflug *m*

formative ['fɔːmətɪv] **ADJ** **a** *influence, experience* prägend; **her ~ years** die charakterbildenden Jahre in ihrem Leben; **the most ~ experience of his life** die Erfahrung, die sein Leben entscheidend geprägt hat; **a ~ period** eine Zeit der Entwicklung **b** (*Gram*) **~ element** Wortbildungselement *nt* **N** (*Gram*) Wortbildungselement *nt*, Formativ *nt*

forme [fɔːm] **N** (*Brit, Typ*) (Satz)form *f*

former ['fɔːmə'] ✪ 26.2 **ADJ** **a** (= *previous*) *president, chairman, employee etc* früher; *home, prison, school, hospital etc* ehemalig; *country, place, strength, authority etc* früher; *times, years, days* vergangen; **~ President Richard Nixon** der frühere *or* ehemalige Präsident Richard Nixon; **his ~ wife** seine Exfrau; **her ~ husband** ihr Exmann *m*; **the radicals of ~ days** die Radikalen der Vergangenheit; **in ~ years** *or* **times** *or* **days** in früheren Zeiten

b (*as opposed to latter*) **the ~ option/alternative** *etc* die erstere Möglichkeit/Alternative *etc* **N** der/die/das erstere; (*more than one*) die ersteren *pl*; **of these two theories I prefer the ~** von diesen beiden Theorien ziehe ich (die) erstere vor

-former [-ˌfɔːmə'] **N** *suf* (*Brit, Sch*) -klässler(in) *m(f)*; **fifth-former** Fünftklässler(in) *m(f)*

formerly ['fɔːməlɪ] **ADV** früher; **she was more talkative than ~** sie war gesprächiger als sonst *or* vorher; **the ~ communist countries** die ehemals kommunistischen Länder; **the ~ busy office** das früher so geschäftige Büro; **we had ~ agreed that ...** wir hatten uns seinerzeit darauf geeinigt, dass ...

form: form feed N (*Comput*) Papiervorschub *m*; **form-fitting ADJ** eng anliegend

Formica® [fɔː'maɪkə] **N** Resopal® *nt*

formic acid ['fɔːmɪk'æsɪd] **N** Ameisensäure *f*

formidable ['fɔːmɪdəbl] **ADJ** (= *commanding respect*) *person* Achtung gebietend; *intellect, intelligence* überragend; (= *powerful, impressive*) *challenge, achievement, task, obstacle, strength, energy, height* gewaltig; *person, reputation* beeindruckend; *opponent* mächtig; *sight* überwältigend; *talents* außerordentlich; *team, combination* außerordentlich stark; **she is small but ~** sie ist klein aber oho (*inf*); **to be in ~ form** in absoluter Hochform sein

formidably ['fɔːmɪdəblɪ] **ADV** **a** (= *dauntingly*) enorm, außerordentlich; **~ equipped** außerordentlich gut ausgerüstet **b** (= *prodigiously, excellently*) hervorragend; **~ gifted** *or* **talented** außerordentlich begabt *or* talentiert; **~ efficient** überaus *or* außerordentlich effizient

form: formless ADJ **a** (= *amorphous*) formlos **b** (*pej, = unstructured*) *book, play, film, music* strukturlos, unstrukturiert; **formlessness N** **a** (= *amorphousness*) Formlosigkeit *f* **b** (*pej, = lack of structure*) Strukturlosigkeit *f*; **form letter N** (*Comput*) Formbrief *m*

formula ['fɔːmjʊlə] **N** *pl* **-s** *or* **-e** ['fɔːmjʊliː] **a** Formel *f* (*also Sci*); (*for lotion, medicine, soap powder*) Rezeptur *f*; **winning ~** Erfolgsrezept *nt*; **peace ~** Friedensformel *f*; **there's no sure ~ for success** es gibt kein Patentrezept für Erfolg; **they changed the ~ of the programme** sie änderten die Aufmachung des Programms; **all his books follow the same ~** alle seine Bücher sind nach demselben Rezept geschrieben **b** *no pl* (*also* **formula milk**) Säuglingsmilch *f*

Formula One N (*Motor Racing*) Formel 1

formulate ['fɔːmjʊleɪt] **VT** formulieren

formulation [ˌfɔːmjʊ'leɪʃən] **N** Formulierung *f*

formwork N (Ver)schalung *f*

fornicate ['fɔːnɪkeɪt] **VI** Unzucht treiben

fornication [ˌfɔːnɪ'keɪʃən] **N** Unzucht *f*

fornicator ['fɔːnɪkeɪtə'] **N** Hurer *m* (*inf*), Hurenbock *m* (*inf*); (*woman*) Hure *f* (*inf*)

forsake [fə'seɪk] *pret* **forsook** [fə'sʊk] *ptp* **forsaken** [fə'seɪkn]' **VT** verlassen; *bad habits* aufgeben, entsagen (+*dat*) (*geh*); **his charm never ~s him** sein Charme lässt ihn nie im Stich

forswear [fɔː'sweə'] *pret* **forswore** [fɔː'swɔː'] *ptp* **forsworn** [fɔː'swɔːn] **VT** **a** (= *renounce*) abschwören (+*dat*); **he has forsworn smoking** er hat hoch und heilig versprochen, nicht mehr zu rauchen **b** (= *deny*) unter Eid verneinen *or* leugnen

forsythia [fɔː'saɪθɪə] **N** Forsythie *f*

fort [fɔːt] **N** (*Mil*) Fort *nt*; **to hold the ~** (*fig*) die Stellung halten

forte¹ [fɔː'teɪ] **N** (= *strong point*) Stärke *f*, starke Seite

forte² (*Mus*) **ADV** laut, forte **ADJ** (= *played loudly*) laut *or* forte gespielt; (= *sung loudly*) laut *or* forte gesungen

forth [fɔːθ] **ADV** (*form, dated*) **a** (= *out*) heraus-; (= *forward*) hervor-; **to venture ~** sich hinauswagen; **to come ~** herauskommen; **to pour ~** (= *utter*) von sich (*dat*) geben; **to burst ~** (*person*) herausstürzen; (*sun*) hervorbrechen → **back ADV** → *also* **hold forth, put forth, set forth** *etc* **b** (= *onwards*) **from this time** *or* **day ~** von jetzt an; **from that day ~** von jenem Tag an; **and so ~** und so weiter

forthcoming [fɔːθ'kʌmɪŋ] **ADJ** (*form*) **a** *attr* (= *imminent*) *event, visit* bevorstehend; *album, book* in Kürze erscheinend; *film, play* in Kürze anlaufend; **a leaflet detailing the month's ~ events** eine Broschüre mit einer Programmvorschau für den Monat; **~ books/titles** geplante Neuerscheinungen *pl*; **our ~ titles for next year** Titel, die nächstes Jahr erscheinen; **"forthcoming attractions"** (*outside theatre/cinema*) „demnächst in diesem Theater/Kino"

b (= *available*) **to be ~** (*money, funds*) zur Verfügung gestellt werden; (*evidence*) geliefert werden; (*aid, support*) geleistet werden; (*details*) bekannt werden; **not to be ~** (*evidence, aid, support*) ausbleiben

c (= *communicative*) *person* mitteilsam; **to be ~ on** *or* **about sth** offen über etw (*acc*) reden; **not to be ~ on** *or* **about sth** sich über etw (*acc*) zurückhalten

forthright ['fɔːθraɪt] **ADJ** *person, manner* (= *direct*) direkt; (= *frank*) offen; (= *blunt*) *statement* unverblümt; *language* deutlich; **in ~ terms** unverblümt; **to be ~ in one's response** eine direkte Antwort geben; **to be ~ in saying sth** etw direkt sagen; **to be ~ about sth** sich unverblümt zu etw äußern

forthwith [ˌfɔːθ'wɪθ] **ADV** (*form*) umgehend, unverzüglich

fortieth ['fɔːtɪɪθ] **ADJ** vierzigste(r, s) **N** **a** (= *fraction*) Vierzigstel *nt*; (*in series*) Vierzigste(r, s) → *also* **sixth**

fortification [ˌfɔːtɪfɪ'keɪʃən] **N** **a** (= *act of fortifying*) (*of town*) Befestigung *f*; (*of wine*) Vergärung *f*; (*of food*) Anreicherung *f*; (*of person*) Bestärkung *f* **b** **fortifications PL** (*Mil*) Befestigungen *pl*, Festungsanlagen *pl*

fortified wine [ˌfɔːtɪfaɪd'waɪn] **N** weinhaltiges Getränk, Südwein *m*

fortifier ['fɔːtɪfaɪə'] **N** Stärkungsmittel *nt*

fortify ['fɔːtɪfaɪ] **VT** (*Mil*) *town* befestigen; *wine* mit zuckerreichem Most vergären; *food* anreichern; *person* bestärken; (*food, drink*) stärken; **fortified place** befestigte Stellung; **have a drink to ~ you** nehmen Sie einen Schluck zur Stärkung

fortissimo [fɔː'tɪsɪməʊ] (*Mus*) **ADV** fortissimo **ADJ** (= *played very loudly*) fortissimo gespielt; (= *sung very loudly*) fortissimo gesungen

fortitude ['fɔːtɪtjuːd] **N** (innere) Kraft *or* Stärke

Fort Knox [ˌfɔːt'nɒks] **N** Fort Knox *nt*; **they've turned their house into ~** sie haben aus ihrem Haus eine Festung gemacht

fortnight ['fɔːtnaɪt] **N** (*esp Brit*) vierzehn Tage, zwei Wochen; **a ~'s holiday** zwei Wochen *or* vierzehn Tage Urlaub

fortnightly ['fɔːtnaɪtlɪ] (*esp Brit*) **ADJ** vierzehntäglich, zweiwöchentlich; *newspaper, magazine also* alle zwei Wochen erscheinend; **~ visits** Besuche *pl* alle zwei Wochen; **a ~ cycle** ein Zyklus *m* von zwei Wochen; **at ~ intervals** in Ab-

ständen von zwei Wochen **ADV** alle vierzehn Tage, alle zwei Wochen

FORTRAN ['fɔːtræn] *abbr of* **formula translator** FORTRAN *nt*

fortress ['fɔːtrɪs] **N** Festung *f*

fortuitous **ADJ**, **fortuitously** **ADV** [fɔː'tjuːɪtəs, -lɪ] zufällig

fortuitousness [fɔː'tjuːɪtəsnɪs], **fortuity** [fɔː'tjuːɪtɪ] **N** Zufall *m*

fortunate ['fɔːtʃnɪt] **ADJ** *person, coincidence, choice* glücklich; *circumstances also* günstig; **we are ~ that/because ...** wir können von Glück reden *or* uns glücklich schätzen, dass/weil ...; **it is ~ that ...** es ist ein Glück, dass ...; **it was ~ for him/Mr Fox that...** es war sein Glück/ein Glück für Mr Fox, dass ...; **they were ~ to escape/survive** sie können von Glück sagen *or* sich glücklich schätzen, entkommen zu sein/überlebt zu haben; **I was ~ enough to go to a good school** ich hatte das Glück, eine gute Schule zu besuchen; **I have been unusually ~ in my parents and teachers** ich habe mit meinen Eltern und Lehrern ungewöhnlich großes Glück gehabt; **how ~!** welch *or* so ein Glück!

fortunately ['fɔːtʃnɪtlɪ] **ADV** glücklicherweise, zum Glück; **~ for me, my friend noticed it** zu meinem Glück hat mein Freund es bemerkt

fortune ['fɔːtʃuːn] **N** **a** (= *fate*) Schicksal *nt*, Geschick *nt*; (= *chance*) Zufall *m*; **she followed his ~s with interest** sie verfolgte sein Geschick mit Interesse; **the ~s of war** das Auf und Ab des Krieges; **he had the good ~ to have rich parents** er hatte das Glück, reiche Eltern zu haben; **by good ~** glücklicherweise, zum Glück; **by sheer good ~** rein zufällig; **~ has favoured** (*Brit*) *or* **favored** (*US*) **him** das Glück war ihm hold; **~ favours the brave** *or* **bold** (*Brit Prov*) das Glück ist nur dem Tüchtigen hold; **ill ~** Pech *nt*; **to tell sb's ~** jdm wahrsagen

b (= *money*) Reichtum *m*, Vermögen *nt*; **to come into/make a ~** ein Vermögen erben/machen; **to seek/make one's ~** sein Glück versuchen/machen; **to marry a ~** reich heiraten; **it costs a ~** es kostet ein Vermögen; **she spends a (small) ~ on clothes** sie gibt ein (kleines) Vermögen für Kleidung aus

fortune: fortune-hunter N Mitgiftjäger(in) *m(f)*; **fortune-teller N** Wahrsager(in) *m(f)*

forty ['fɔːtɪ] **ADJ** vierzig; **to have ~ winks** (*inf*) ein Nickerchen machen **N** Vierzig *f* → *also* **sixty**

forty-niner [ˌfɔːtɪ'naɪnə'] **N** *Goldgräber, der im Zuge des Goldrausches von 1849 nach Kalifornien ging*

forum ['fɔːrəm] **N** Forum *nt*

forward ['fɔːwəd] **ADV** **a** (*also* **forwards**, = *onwards, ahead*) vorwärts; (= *to the front, to particular point, out of line*) nach vorn; **please step ~** bitte vortreten; **to take two steps ~** zwei Schritte vortreten; **to rush ~** sich vorstürzen; **to go straight ~** geradeaus gehen; **~!** vorwärts!; **he drove backward(s) and ~(s) between the station and the house** er fuhr zwischen Haus und Bahnhof hin und her

b (*in time*) **from this time ~** (= *from then*) seitdem; (= *from now*) von jetzt an; **if we think ~ to the next stage** wenn wir an die vor uns liegende nächste Stufe denken

c (= *into prominence*) **to come ~** sich melden; **to bring ~ new evidence** neue Beweise *pl* vorlegen

ADJ **a** (*in place*) vordere(r, s); (*in direction*) Vorwärts-; **~ march** Vormarsch *m*; **~ gears** (*Aut*) Vorwärtsgänge *pl*; **this seat is too far ~** dieser Sitz ist zu weit vorn

b (*in time*) *planning* Voraus-; (*Comm*) *buying, price* Termin-; (= *well-advanced*) *season* (weit) fortgeschritten; *plants* früh *pred*; *children* frühreif; **I'd like to be further ~ with my work** ich wollte, ich wäre mit meiner Arbeit schon weiter; **good ~ thinking, Jones** gute Voraussicht, Jones

c (= *presumptuous, pert*) dreist

N (*Sport*) Stürmer(in) *m(f)*

VT **a** (= *advance*) *plans etc* vorantreiben; *career* voranbringen **b** (= *dispatch*) *goods* befördern, senden; (= *send on*) *letter, parcel* nachsenden; *information* weiterleiten; **please ~** bitte nachsenden; **we'll ~ your suggestions to the committee** wir werden Ihre Vorschläge an den Ausschuss weiterleiten

forwarder ['fɔːwədə'] N (= *person*) Spediteur(in) *m(f)*; (= *company*) Spedition *f*, Spediteur *m*

forwarding ['fɔːwədɪŋ]: **forwarding address** N Nachsendeadresse *f*; **forwarding agent** N (= *person*) Spediteur(in) *m(f)*; (= *company*) Spedition *f*, Spediteur *m*; **forwarding instructions** PL (*for goods*) Lieferanweisungen *pl*; (*for sending on mail*) Nachsendeanweisungen *pl*

forward: forward line N (*Sport*) Sturm *m*, Stürmerreihe *f*; **forward-looking** ADJ *person, attitude* fortschrittlich, progressiv; *plan, vision* vorausblickend

forwardness ['fɔːwədnɪs] N (= *presumption*) Dreistigkeit *f*

forward pass N (*Sport*) Vorwärtspass *m*

forward post N (*Mil*) Vorposten *m*

forwards ['fɔːwədz] ADV = **forward** ADV a

forward slash N (*Typ*) Schrägstrich *m*

forwent [fɔː'went] *pret* of **forgo**

Fosbury flop ['fɒzbrɪ'flɒp] N Fosburyflop *m*

fossil ['fɒsl] **N** (*lit*) Fossil *nt*; **he's an old ~!** (*inf*) er ist so verknöchert **ADJ** versteinert

fossil fuel N fossiler Brennstoff *m*

fossilization [ˌfɒsɪlaɪ'zeɪʃən] N Versteinerung *f*, Fossilierung *f* (*spec*); (*fig: of person*) Verknöcherung *f*

fossilized ['fɒsɪlaɪzd] ADJ versteinert; (*fig*) *person* verknöchert; *customs* verkrustet, starr

foster ['fɒstə'] ADJ *attr* (*Admin*) Pflege-; **she was placed in ~ care** sie wurde in Pflege gegeben, sie kam in eine Pflegestelle; **their children are in ~ care** ihre Kinder sind in Pflege **VI** Kinder/ein Kind in Pflege nehmen **VT** **a** *child* in Pflege nehmen; **when children are ~ed** wenn Kinder in Pflege or bei Pflegeeltern sind; **~ed children** Pflegekinder *pl*, Kinder *pl* in Pflege **b** (= *promote*) *music, drama, development* fördern; *image, friendship* pflegen; **a popular idea, ~ed by the media** eine populäre Idee, die von den Medien gefördert wird

▶ **foster out** VT *sep* in Pflege geben (*with* bei)

foster: foster brother N **a** Pflegebruder *m* **b** (*fed by same mother*) Milchbruder *m*; **foster child** N Pflegekind *nt*; **foster family** N Pflegefamilie *f*; **foster father** N Pflegevater *m*; **foster home** N Pflegestelle *f*; **she was placed in a ~** sie wurde in Pflege gegeben, sie kam in eine Pflegestelle; **foster mother** N **a** Pflegemutter *f* **b** (= *wet nurse*) Amme *f* **c** (= *apparatus*) Brutkasten *m*; **foster parents** PL Pflegeeltern *pl*; **he was placed with ~** er kam zu Pflegeeltern; **foster sister** N Pflegeschwester *f*

fought [fɔːt] *pret, ptp* of **fight**

foul [faʊl] ADJ **a** (= *disgusting*) *place, food, taste, breath* ekelhaft, widerlich; *water* faulig; *air* stickig; *smell* übel, ekelhaft **b** (= *dreadful*) *behaviour, crime* abscheulich; *temper* übel; *day* scheußlich (*inf*); **he was really ~ to her** er war wirklich gemein or fies (*inf*) zu ihr; **what a ~ thing (for you) to say about my sister** wie kannst du nur so etwas Gemeines über meine Schwester sagen; **she has a ~ temper** sie ist ein ganz übellauniger Mensch; **to be in a ~ mood** or **temper** eine ganz miese Laune haben (*inf*); **~ weather** scheußliches Wetter; (*Naut*) Sturm *m*; **~ luck** großes Pech; **~ deed** (*liter, hum*) Schandtat *f* **c** (= *offensive*) anstößig; **~ language** Schimpfwörter *pl*; **to have a ~ mouth** ein dreckiges Maul haben (*inf*) **d** (= *dishonest, unfair*) unredlich; (*Sport*, = *against the rules*) *shot* regelwidrig; *tackle* unerlaubt; (= *not valid*) ungültig; **~ ball** (*Baseball*) ungültiger Schlag; **to cry ~** sich über unfaire Behandlung beschweren → **fair** ADJ a **e** **to fall** or **run ~ of the law/authorities** mit

dem Gesetz/den Behörden in Konflikt geraten; **to fall** or **run ~ of sb** es sich (*dat*) mit jdm verderben; **to fall ~ of a ship** (*Naut*) mit einem Schiff kollidieren or zusammenstoßen **VT** **a** (= *dirty, pollute*) *air* verpesten; *beach* verschmutzen; (*dog*) *pavement* verunreinigen **b** (= *become entangled in*) *mechanism, device, propeller* sich verfangen in (+*dat*); *net, fishing line* verheddern; (= *clog*) *pipe* verstopfen; *chimney, gun barrel* blockieren **c** (*Sport*) foulen **d** (*Naut*, = *collide with*) *ship* rammen **e** (= *tarnish*) *person* entehren; *sb's reputation* beflecken **VI** **a** (= *become entangled*: *rope, line*) sich verheddern (*on, in* +*dat*) **b** (*Sport*) foulen, regelwidrig spielen **N** (*Sport*) Foul *nt*, Regelverstoß *m*; **technical/personal ~** (*Basketball*) technisches/persönliches Foul

▶ **foul up** VT *sep* (*inf*) versauen (*inf*)

fouler ['faʊlə'] N (*Sport*) Foulspieler(in) *m(f)*

foully ['faʊlɪ] ADV (= *horribly*) übel, schlimm

foul-mouthed ['faʊlmaʊðd] ADJ unflätig, vulgär

foulness ['faʊlnɪs] N **a** (= *disgusting nature, of place, food, taste, smell, breath*) Widerlichkeit *f*; (*of water*) Fauligkeit *f*; (*of air*) Stickigkeit *f* **b** (= *dreadfulness*) (*of behaviour, crime*) Abscheulichkeit *f*; (*of day, weather*) Scheußlichkeit *f* (*inf*); **the ~ of his behaviour** (*Brit*) or **behavior** (*US*) **to her, his ~ to her** sein gemeines Verhalten or seine Gemeinheit ihr gegenüber; **the ~ of her mood** ihre ganz üble Laune; **the ~ of her temper** ihre schreckliche Übellaunigkeit **c** (*of language*) Unflätigkeit *f*

foul play N **a** (*Sport*) unfaires or regelwidriges Spiel; (= *fouls*) Fouls *pl* **b** (*fig*) Unredlichkeiten *pl*; **the police do not suspect ~** die Polizei hat keinen Verdacht auf einen unnatürlichen or gewaltsamen Tod; **there was no evidence of ~** es gab keine Beweise, die auf Mord or einen gewaltsamen Tod schließen ließen

foul shot N (*Basketball*) Freiwurf *m*

foul-smelling [ˌfaʊl'smelɪŋ] ADJ übel riechend *attr*

foul-tempered [ˌfaʊl'tempəd] ADJ sehr übellaunig

found¹ [faʊnd] *pret, ptp* of **find**

found² VT **a** (= *set up*) gründen; *town, school, hospital* gründen, errichten **b** **to ~ sth (up)on sth** (*opinion, belief*) etw auf etw (*dat*) gründen or stützen; **our society is ~ed on this** darauf beruht or basiert unsere Gesellschaft, das ist die Grundlage unserer Gesellschaft; **the novel is ~ed on fact** der Roman beruht or basiert auf Tatsachen

found³ VT (*Metal*) *metal, glass* schmelzen und in eine Form gießen; *object* gießen

foundation [faʊn'deɪʃən] N **a** (= *act of founding, of business, colony*) Gründung *f*; (*of town, school*) Gründung *f*, Errichtung *f* **b** (= *institution*) Stiftung *f*; **~ research** = Forschungsstiftung *f* **c** **~s** *pl* (*Build, of house etc*) Fundament *nt*; (*of road*) Unterbau *m* **d** (*fig, = basis*) Grundlage *f*; **to be without ~** (*rumours, allegations*) jeder Grundlage entbehren; (*fears*) unbegründet sein; **to rock** or **shake sth to its ~s** etw bis in seine Grundfesten erschüttern **e** (= *make-up*) Grundierungscreme *f*

foundation: foundation cream N Grundierungscreme *f*; **Foundation Day** N (*Austral*) gesetzlicher Feiertag in Australien zur Erinnerung an die Landung der Briten am 26. Januar 1788; **foundation garment** N Mieder *nt*; **foundation stone** N Grundstein *m*

founder¹ ['faʊndə'] N (*of school, colony, organization etc*) Gründer(in) *m(f)*; (*of charity, museum*) Stifter(in) *m(f)*

founder² VI **a** (*ship: = sink*) sinken, untergehen **b** (*horse etc: = stumble*) straucheln, stolpern **c** (*fig: = fail, plan, project*) scheitern, fehlschlagen; (*hopes*) auf den Nullpunkt sinken

founder³ N (*Metal*) Gießer(in) *m(f)*

founder member N Gründungsmitglied *nt*

Founding Fathers ['faʊndɪŋ'fɑːðəz] PL (*US*) Väter *pl*

foundling ['faʊndlɪŋ] N Findling *m*, Findelkind *nt*; **~ hospital** Findelhaus *nt*, Findelheim *nt*

foundry ['faʊndrɪ] N Gießerei *f*

fount [faʊnt] N **a** (*liter: = fountain*) Born *m* (*poet*), Quelle *f*; (*fig, = source*) Quelle *f* **b** (*Typ*) Schrift *f*

fountain ['faʊntɪn] N Brunnen *m*; (*with upward jets also*) Springbrunnen *m*; (= *jet, spurt: of water, lava etc*) Fontäne *f*; (= *drinking fountain*) (Trinkwasser)brunnen *m*; (*fig, = source*) Quelle *f*; **~ of youth** Jungbrunnen *m*

fountain: fountainhead N (*of river*) Quelle *f*; (*fig*) Quelle *f*, Ursprung *m*; **fountain pen** N Füllfederhalter *m*, Füller *m*

four [fɔː'] **ADJ** vier; **open to the ~ winds** Wind und Wetter ausgesetzt; **scattered to the ~ winds** in alle vier Winde zerstreut; **the Four Hundred** (*US*) die oberen zehntausend **N** Vier *f*; **on all ~s** auf allen vieren; **will you make up a ~ for bridge?** haben Sie Lust, beim Bridge den vierten Mann zu machen? → *also* **six**

four: four-ball N (*Golf*) Vierer *m*; **four-colour**, (*US*) **four-color** ADJ (*Typ*) Vierfarb-; **~ advertisement** Vierfarbanzeige *f*; **~ printing** Vierfarbdruck *m*; **four-cycle** ADJ (*US*) = **four-stroke**; **four-dimensional** ADJ *attr* vierdimensional; **four-door** ADJ *attr* viertürig; **four-eyes** N *sing* (*hum inf*) Bebrille(r) *mf* (*hum inf*); (= *woman also*) Brillenschlange *f* (*hum inf*); **four-figure** ADJ *attr* vierstellig; **fourfold** ADV vierfach **ADJ** vierfach; **~ increase** um das Vierfache; **four-footed** ADJ vierfüßig; **four-four time** N (*Mus*) Viervierteltakt *m*; **four-handed** ADJ (*Mus*) vierhändig, für vier Hände, zu vier Händen; **four-in-hand** N Vierspänner *m*; **four-leaf clover**, **four-leaved clover** N vierblättriges Kleeblatt; **four-legged** ADJ vierbeinig; **four-letter word** N Vulgärausdruck *m*; **four-minute mile** N Vierminutenmeile *f*; **four-part** ADJ *attr series, programme* vierteilig; *plan* aus vier Teilen bestehend; (*Mus*) für vier Stimmen; *harmony, choir* vierstimmig; **four-poster (bed)** N Himmelbett *nt*; **fourscore** ADJ (*obs*) achtzig; **four-seater** ADV viersitzig **N** Viersitzer *m*; **foursome** N Quartett *nt*; (*Sport*) Viererspiel *nt*; **to go out in a ~** zu viert ausgehen; **foursquare** ADV **a** (*lit, = square*) viereckig **b** (*fig, = firm*) unerschütterlich **ADJ** **a** (*lit, = squarely*) fest **b** (*fig, = firmly*) stand fest, entschlossen; **four-star** ADJ Vier-Sterne-; **~ hotel/restaurant** Vier-Sterne-Hotel/-Restaurant *nt*; **four-star general** N (*US*) Vier-Sterne-General *m*; **four-star petrol** N (*Brit*) Super(benzin) *nt*; **four-stroke** ADJ **~ engine** Viertaktmotor *m*

fourteen ['fɔː'tiːn] **ADJ** vierzehn **N** Vierzehn *f* → *also* **sixteen**

fourteenth ['fɔː'tiːnθ] **ADJ** vierzehnte(r, s) **N** (= *fraction*) Vierzehntel *nt*; (*of series*) Vierzehnte(r, s) → *also* **sixteenth**

fourth [fɔːθ] **ADJ** vierte(r, s); **the ~ dimension** die vierte Dimension; **the ~ estate** die Presse **N** (= *fraction*) Viertel *nt*; (*in series*) Vierte(r, s); **to drive in ~** (*Aut*) im vierten Gang fahren; **we need a ~ for our game of bridge** wir brauchen noch einen vierten zum Bridge → *also* **sixth**

FOURTH OF JULY

Der **Fourth of July** (oder auch **Independence Day**) ist der wichtigste Feiertag in den Vereinigten Staaten, an dem der Unterzeichnung der Unabhängigkeitserklärung am 4. Juli 1776 gedacht wird, was als eigentliche Geburtsstunde der USA gilt. Daher sind die Feierlichkeiten recht patriotisch. Viele Bürger hissen die amerikanische Flagge vor ihrem Haus, und im ganzen Land wird mit öffentlichen Veranstaltungen gefeiert: Paraden, Picknicks und nicht zu vergessen das große Feuerwerk am Abend.

fourthly ['fɔːθlɪ] ADV viertens

four: four-way ADJ zu viert; **~ valve** Vierwegeventil *nt*; **four-way stop** N (*US Aut*) *Kreuzung, an der alle Verkehrsteilnehmer Vorfahrt gewähren müssen*; **four-wheel drive** N Vierradantrieb *m*

fowl [faʊl] N **a** (= *poultry*) Geflügel *nt*; (= *one bird*) Huhn *nt*/Gans *f*/Truthahn *m etc*; **to keep ~** Hühner *etc* halten; **roast ~** (*Cook*) Brathuhn *nt* **b the ~s of the air** (*liter*) die Vögel des Himmels **VI** (*also* **to go fowling**) auf Vogeljagd gehen

fowling piece ['faʊlɪŋpiːs] N Schrotflinte *f*

fowl pest N Hühnerpest *f*

fox [fɒks] N **a** (*lit, fig*) Fuchs *m*; **he's a sly ~** (*fig*) er ist ein schlauer Fuchs **b** (= *fox fur*) Fuchs(pelz) *m* **c** (*dated US, inf, = sexy woman*) scharfes Weib (*inf*) **VT** (= *deceive*) täuschen, reinlegen (*inf*); (= *bewilder*) verblüffen; **that's ~ed you, hasn't it?** da bist du baff, was? (*inf*)

fox: fox cub N Fuchsjunge(s) *nt*, Fuchswelpe *m*; **foxglove** N (*Bot*) Fingerhut *m*; **foxhole** N **a** Fuchsbau *m* **b** (*Mil*) Schützengraben *m*, Schützenloch *nt*; **foxhound** N Fuchshund *m*; **fox hunt** N Fuchsjagd *f* **VI** auf (die) Fuchsjagd gehen; **fox-hunting** N Fuchsjagd *f*; **to go ~** auf die *or* zur Fuchsjagd gehen; **fox terrier** N Foxterrier *m*; **foxtrot** N Foxtrott *m*

foxy ['fɒksɪ] ADJ (*+er*) (= *wily*) listig, pfiffig, verschlagen; **~ lady** (*dated US, inf*) scharfes Weib (*inf*)

foyer ['fɔɪeɪ] N (*in theatre*) Foyer *nt*; (*in hotel also*) Empfangshalle *f*; (*esp US, in apartment house*) Diele *f*

Fr *abbr* **a** of **Father** **b** of **Friar**

fracas ['frækɑː] N Aufruhr *m*, Tumult *m*

fraction ['frækʃən] N **a** (*Math*) Bruch *m* **b** (*fig*) Bruchteil *m*; **a ~ better/shorter** (um) eine Spur besser/kürzer; **move it just a ~ (of an inch)** verrücke es (um) eine Spur; **for a ~ of a second** einen Augenblick lang; **it missed me by a ~ of an inch** es verfehlte mich um Haaresbreite **c** (*Eccl*) Brechen *nt* des Brotes

fractional ['frækʃənl] ADJ **a** (*Math*) Bruch-; (*fig*) geringfügig; **~ part** Bruchteil *m* **b** (*Chem*) **~ distillation** fraktionierte Destillation

fractionally ['frækʃənəlɪ] ADV *less, slower* geringfügig; *ahead* um eine Nasenlänge; *behind* knapp; *rise, drop* um einen Bruchteil; **the dollar has dropped ~** *or* **is ~ down** der Dollarkurs ist geringfügig gefallen

fractious ['frækʃəs] ADJ verdrießlich; *child* aufsässig

fractiousness ['frækʃəsnɪs] N Verdrießlichkeit *f*; (*of child*) Aufsässigkeit *f*

fracture ['fræktʃə] N Bruch *m*; (*Med also*) Fraktur *f* (*spec*) **VT** brechen; **he ~d his shoulder** er hat sich (*dat*) die Schulter gebrochen; **~d skull** Schädelbruch *m* **VI** (*cheekbone etc*) brechen

fragile ['frædʒaɪl] ADJ *glass, china, object* zerbrechlich; *structure* fragil; *fabric* fein; *beauty, skin, child* zart; *elderly person* gebrechlich; *situation* heikel, unsicher; *confidence* schwach; *ceasefire, peace* brüchig; *health* zart, anfällig; *mental state, ego, economy* labil; *government, democracy* geschwächt; **"fragile (handle) with care"** „Vorsicht, zerbrechlich!"; **the ~ economic/political situation** die labile Wirtschaftslage/politische Situation; **to feel ~** (*inf*) sich angeschlagen fühlen; **to look ~** (*inf*) angeschlagen aussehen

fragility [frə'dʒɪlɪtɪ] N (*of glass, china, object*) Zerbrechlichkeit *f*; (*of beauty, skin, child*) Zartheit *f*; (*of fabric*) Feinheit *f*; (*of elderly person*) Gebrechlichkeit *f*; (*of health*) Zartheit *f*, Anfälligkeit *f*; (*of situation*) Unsicherheit *f*; (*of peace, ceasefire*) Brüchigkeit *f*; (*of mental state, economy*) Labilität *f*; (*of government, democracy*) geschwächter Zustand

fragment ['frægmənt] N **a** Bruchstück *nt*; (*of china, glass*) Scherbe *f*; (*of shell, food*) Stückchen *nt*; (*of paper, letter*) Schnipsel *m*; (*of programme, opera etc*) Bruchteil *m*; **he smashed it to ~s** er schlug es in Stücke; **the window smashed into ~s** das Fenster zersprang in Scherben; **~s of conversation** Gesprächsfetzen *pl* **b** (*esp Liter, Mus, = unfinished work*) Fragment *nt* **VI** [fræg'ment] (*rock, glass*) (zer)brechen, in Stücke brechen; (*fig*) (*hopes*) sich zerschlagen; (*society*) zerfallen **VT** [fræg'ment] *rock, glass* in Stücke brechen; (*with hammer etc*) in Stücke schlagen; (*fig*) *society* zerschlagen; *audience* aufsplittern; *market, industry, work* fragmentieren

fragmentary ['frægməntərɪ] ADJ (*lit, fig*) fragmentarisch, bruchstückhaft

fragmentation [ˌfrægmen'teɪʃən] N (*of rock, glass*) Zerbrechen *nt*; (*of society*) Fragmentierung *f*; (*of society*) Zerfall *m*; (*of hopes*) Zerschlagung *f*

fragmentation bomb N Splitterbombe *f*

fragmented [fræg'mentɪd] ADJ bruchstückhaft, (= *broken up*) unzusammenhängend, ohne Zusammenhang

fragrance ['freɪgrəns] N Duft *m*, Wohlgeruch *m*

fragrant ['freɪgrənt] ADJ duftend, wohlriechend; (*fig liter*) *memories* köstlich; **~ smell** Duft *m*; **the air was ~ with the scent of roses** der Duft von Rosen hing in der Luft

frail [freɪl] ADJ (*+er*) **a** (= *weak*) *person* gebrechlich; *health* zart, anfällig; **to be in ~ health** kränklich sein, gesundheitlich angeschlagen sein; **to look ~** schwach aussehen **b** (= *fragile*) *structure* fragil; *boat, aircraft* leicht gebaut; (*fig*) *hope* schwach; *ego* labil; **happiness is a ~ commodity** Glück ist eine unsichere Angelegenheit

frailty ['freɪltɪ] N **a** (= *weakness, of person*) Gebrechlichkeit *f*; (*of health*) Zartheit *f*, Anfälligkeit *f* **b** (= *fragility, of structure*) Fragilität *f*; (*of boat, aircraft*) leichte Bauart; (*fig, of hope*) Schwäche *f*; (*of ego*) Labilität *f*; **~, thy name is woman** Schwachheit, dein Name ist Weib

frame [freɪm] N **a** (= *basic structure, border of picture*) Rahmen *m*; (*of building*) (Grund)gerippe *nt*; (*of ship*) Gerippe *nt*; (*Typ*) Setzregal *nt*; (*Hort*) Mistbeet *nt*, Frühbeet *nt*; (*of spectacles: also* **frames**) Gestell *nt*; (*Billiards, = single game*) Spiel *nt*; (= *triangle*) Rahmen *m* **b** (*of human, animal*) Gestalt *f*; **her ~ was shaken by sobs** ihr Körper wurde von Schluchzen geschüttelt **c ~ of mind** (= *mental state*) Verfassung *f*; (= *mood*) Stimmung *f*, Laune *f*; **in a cheerful ~ of mind** in fröhlicher Stimmung *or* Laune; **in a relaxed ~ of mind** entspannt; **I am not in the right ~ of mind for singing** *or* **to sing** ich bin nicht in der (richtigen) Laune *or* Stimmung zum Singen **d** (*fig, = framework, system*) grundlegende Struktur *f*; **~ of reference** (*fig*) Bezugssystem *nt*; **within the ~ of ...** im Rahmen (*+gen*) ...; **this proposal is beyond the ~ of the peace agreement** dieser Vorschlag geht über den Rahmen des Friedensvertrags hinaus **e** (*Film, Phot*) (Einzel)bild *nt*; (*in comic strip*) Bild(chen) *nt* **f** (*TV*) Standbild *nt*, Rasterbild *nt* **g** (*Telec, Comput*) Datenübertragungsblock *m* **VT a** *picture* rahmen; (*fig*) *face etc* ein- *or* umrahmen; **he stood ~d in the door** er stand im Türrahmen; **a lake ~d by trees** ein ringsum von Bäumen umgebener See **b** (= *draw up, construct*) *constitution, law, plan* entwerfen; *idea* entwickeln; (= *express*) *answer, question* formulieren; *sentence* bilden; *words* bilden, formen; **she ~d the issue rather differently** sie stellte die Sache ganz anders dar **c** (*inf, = incriminate falsely*) **he said he had been ~d** er sagte, man habe ihm die Sache angehängt (*inf*) **VI** (= *develop*) sich entwickeln

frame house N Holzhaus *nt*, Haus *nt* mit Holzrahmen

frameless ['freɪmlɪs] ADJ *spectacles* randlos

framer ['freɪmə] N (Bilder)rahmer(in) *m(f)*

frame: frame rucksack N Rucksack *m* mit Traggestell; **frame saw** N Bügelsäge *f*; **frame story, frame tale** N (*Liter*) Rahmenerzählung

f; **frame tent** N Steilwandzelt *nt*; **frame-up** N (*inf*) Komplott *nt*; **framework** N (*lit*) Grundgerüst *nt*; (*fig, of essay, novel etc*) Gerüst *nt*, Gerippe *nt*; (*of society, government etc*) grundlegende Struktur *f*; **within the ~ of ...** im Rahmen (*+gen*) ...; **outside the ~ of ...** außerhalb des Rahmens (*+gen*) ...

framing ['freɪmɪŋ] N **a** (*action*) (Ein)rahmen *nt* **b** (= *frame*) Rahmen, Einfassung **c** (*TV*) Bildeinstellung *f*

franc [fræŋk] N Franc *m*

France [frɑːns] N Frankreich *nt*

franchise ['fræntʃaɪz] N **a** (*Pol*) Wahlrecht *nt* **b** (*Comm*) Lizenz *f*, Franchise *f* **VT** (*Comm*) *business, name* auf Lizenz vergeben

franchisee [ˌfræntʃaɪ'ziː] N (*Comm*) Lizenz- *or* Franchisenehmer(in) *m(f)*

franchiser, franchisor ['fræntʃaɪzə] N (*Comm*) Lizenz- *or* Franchisegeber(in) *m(f)*

Francis ['frɑːnsɪs] N Franz *m*; **St ~ of Assisi** der heilige Franziskus von Assisi

Franciscan [fræn'sɪskən] N Franziskaner(in) *m(f)* ADJ Franziskaner-; **~ monk/monastery** Franziskanermönch *m*/-kloster *nt*

Franco- [fræŋkəʊ-] *in cpds* Französisch-, Franko-; **Franco-British** ADJ französisch-britisch; **Franco-Canadian** ADJ frankokanadisch, französisch-kanadisch; **Franco-German** ADJ deutsch-französisch

Franconia [fræŋ'kəʊnɪə] N Franken *nt*

Franconian [fræŋ'kəʊnɪən] N **a** (= *person*) Franke *m*, Fränkin *f* **b** (= *dialect*) Fränkisch *nt* ADJ fränkisch

franco: francophile N Franzosenfreund(in) *m(f)*; **he is a ~** er ist frankophil; **francophilia** N Frankophilie *f*; **francophobe** N Franzosenfeind(in) *m(f)*; **francophobia** N Frankophobie *f*; **Francophone** ADJ frankophon, Französisch sprechend N Frankophone(r) *mf*, Französisch sprechende(r) *mf*; **Franco-Prussian** ADJ **the ~ War** der Deutsch-Französische Krieg

frangipane ['frændʒɪpeɪn], **frangipani** [ˌfrændʒɪ'pænɪ] N **a** (= *shrub*) Roter Jasmin(baum); (= *perfume*) Jasminparfüm *nt*

Franglais ['frɑ̃ːŋleɪ] N Franglais *nt*, Französisch *nt* mit vielen englischen Ausdrücken

frank[1] [fræŋk] ADJ (*+er*) *person* offen; *opinion also* ehrlich; *comment, discussion also* freimütig; **to be ~ with sb** ehrlich *or* offen mit *or* zu jdm sein; **he wasn't very ~ about it** er äußerte sich nicht sehr offen dazu; **to be (perfectly) ~ (with you)** um (ganz) ehrlich zu sein

frank[2] VT *letter* frankieren; (= *postmark*) *letter* stempeln

frank[2] N (*US inf*) → **frankfurter**

Frank [fræŋk] N (*Hist*) Franke *m*, Fränkin *f*

frankfurter ['fræŋkfɜːtə] N (= *sausage*) (Frankfurter) Würstchen *nt*

frankincense ['fræŋkɪnsens] N Weihrauch *m*

franking machine ['fræŋkɪŋməʃiːn] N Frankiermaschine *f*

Frankish ['fræŋkɪʃ] ADJ fränkisch N (*Ling*) Fränkisch *nt*

franklin ['fræŋklɪn] N (*Hist*) Freisasse *m*

frankly ['fræŋklɪ] ADV **a** (= *openly*) *say, talk, admit* offen **b** (= *to be frank*) offen *or* ehrlich gesagt; **quite ~, I don't care** um ganz ehrlich zu sein, es ist mir egal **c** (= *unapologetically*) **~ eccentric/male** unverhohlen exzentrisch/männlich

frankness ['fræŋknɪs] N Offenheit *f*; (*of opinion also*) Ehrlichkeit *f*; (*of discussion also*) Freimütigkeit *f*

frantic ['fræntɪk] ADJ **a** (= *distraught, desperate*) *person, phone call, search* verzweifelt; *shout, yell* erregt; *need, desire* heftig, übersteigert; **I was ~** ich war außer mir; **to become** *or* **get ~** außer sich (*dat*) geraten; (= *worried*) an den Rande der Verzweiflung geraten; **to be ~ with worry** vor Sorge außer sich (*dat*) sein; **to drive sb ~** jdn zur Verzweiflung treiben **b** (= *hectic*) *week, day* hektisch; **~ activity** (*generally*) hektisches

Treiben, Hektik *f*; (*particular instance*) fieberhafte Tätigkeit; **~ haste** fieberhafte Eile

frantically ['fræntɪkəlɪ] ADV **a** (= *desperately*) *try, search* verzweifelt **b** (= *hectically*) *work, run around* hektisch; *wave, scribble, scramble, run* wie wild; **she is ~ busy** sie hat wahnsinnig viel zu tun (*inf*)

frappé ['fræpeɪ] N Frappé *nt*

frat [fræt] N (*US Univ inf*) abbr of **fraternity**

fraternal [frə'tɜːnl] ADJ brüderlich; **~ twins** zweieiige Zwillinge *pl*

fraternity [frə'tɜːnɪtɪ] N **a** *no pl* Brüderlichkeit *f* **b** (= *community*) Vereinigung *f*, Zunft *f*; (*Eccl*) Bruderschaft *f*; (*US, Univ*) Verbindung *f*; **the legal/medical/teaching ~** die Juristen *pl*/Mediziner *pl*/Lehrer *pl*; **the hunting/sailing ~** die Jagd-/Segelfans *pl*; **the criminal ~** die Kriminellen *pl*, die Unterwelt → *also* **sorority**

fraternity pin N (*US, Univ*) Mitgliedsabzeichen *nt* (*einer Verbindung*)

fraternization [ˌfrætənaɪ'zeɪʃən] N (freundschaftlicher) Umgang, Verbrüderung *f* (*pej*); (*Mil also*) Fraternisierung *f*

fraternize ['frætənaɪz] VI (freundschaftlichen) Umgang haben, sich verbrüdern (*pej*) (*with* mit); (*Mil also*) fraternisieren (*with* mit)

fratricide ['frætrɪsaɪd] N Brudermord *m*; (= *person*) Brudermörder(in) *m(f)*

fraud [frɔːd] N **a** (*no pl*: = *trickery*) Betrug *m*; (= *trick*) Schwindel *m*, Betrug *m*; **~s** Betrügereien *pl* **b** (= *fraudulent person*) Betrüger(in) *m(f)*, Schwindler(in) *m(f)*; (*feigning illness*) Simulant(in) *m(f)*; (= *fraudulent thing*) (reiner) Schwindel, fauler Zauber (*inf*); **the whole thing was a ~** das ganze war (ein einziger) Schwindel or reiner Schwindel

Fraud Squad N (*Brit Police*) Betrugsdezernat *nt*

fraudulence ['frɔːdjʊləns], **fraudulency** ['frɔːdjʊlənsɪ] N Betrügerei *f*; (*of action*) betrügerische Art

fraudulent ['frɔːdjʊlənt] ADJ betrügerisch

fraudulently ['frɔːdjʊləntlɪ] ADV *act* betrügerisch; *obtain* auf betrügerische Weise

fraught [frɔːt] ADJ **a ~ with difficulty** voller Schwierigkeiten; **~ with danger** gefahrvoll, voller Gefahren; **~ with tension** spannungsgeladen, voller Spannung; **~ with meaning** bedeutungsschwer **b** (= *anxious*) *meeting, relationship, situation, atmosphere* gespannt; *person* angespannt; *time* nervenaufreibend

fray¹ [freɪ] N Schlägerei *f*; (*Mil*) Kampf *m*; **ready for the ~** (*lit, fig*) kampfbereit, zum Kampf bereit; **to be eager for the ~** (*lit, fig*) kampflustig sein; **to enter the ~** (*lit*) sich in den Kampf stürzen; (*fig*) sich in den Kampf or Streit einschalten

fray² VT *cloth* ausfransen; *cuff, rope* durchscheuern; **this can ~ the nerves** das kann einem ganz schön auf die Nerven gehen VI (*cloth*) (aus)fransen; (*cuff, trouser turn-up, rope*) sich durchscheuern; **tempers began to ~** die Gemüter begannen sich zu erhitzen or zu erregen; **to be ~ing at** or **around the edges** (*inf, alliance, marriage etc*) zu bröckeln beginnen

frayed [freɪd] ADJ *jeans etc* ausgefranst; (*fig*) gereizt, angespannt; **my nerves are quite ~** ich bin mit den Nerven runter or am Ende (*inf*); **tempers were ~** die Gemüter waren erhitzt; **I'm a bit ~ at** or **around the edges** (*inf*) ich bin ziemlich mit den Nerven runter (*inf*)

frazzle ['fræzl] N (*inf*) **burnt to a ~** (*Brit, toast, meat*) völlig verkohlt; (= *sunburnt*) von der Sonne total verbrannt; **worn to a ~** (= *exhausted*) total kaputt (*inf*); **to wear oneself to a ~** sich total kaputtmachen (*inf*) VT (*inf*) **a** (*US*: = *fray*) ausfransen **b** (*fig*, = *tire*) völlig erschöpfen or ermüden; **his nerves were ~d** er war mit den Nerven völlig am Ende (*inf*)

FRCP (*Brit*) abbr of **Fellow of the Royal College of Physicians** Mitglied *nt* des königlichen Ärzteverbands

FRCS (*Brit*) abbr of **Fellow of the Royal College of Surgeons** Mitglied *nt* des königlichen Chirurgenverbands

freak [friːk] N **a** (= *abnormal plant*) Missbildung *f*; (= *person, animal*) Missgeburt *f*, Missbildung *f*; **~ of nature** Laune *f* der Natur **b** (= *abnormal event*) außergewöhnlicher Zufall; (= *snowstorm etc*) Anomalie *f* **c** (*dated sl*: = *hippy*) ausgeflippter Typ (*sl*) **d** (*inf*) *jazz/movie* ~ Jazz-/Kinofreak *m* (*inf*); **health/fitness ~** Gesundheits-/Fitnessfreak *m* (*inf*) **e** (*inf*, = *weird person*) Irre(r) *mf*; **he looked at me as though I were some sort of ~** er sah mich an, als ob ich vom Mond wäre ADJ *weather, conditions* anormal, abnorm; *wave* ungewöhnlich hoch; *storm* ungewöhnlich stark; *accident, error* verrückt; *victory, goal* überraschend; (*Statistics*) *values* extrem VI (*inf*) ausflippen (*inf*)

▶ **freak out** VI ausflippen (*inf*); (*of society*) aussteigen VT sep **it freaked me out** dabei bin ich ausgeflippt (*inf*)

freakish ['friːkɪʃ] ADJ **a** → **freak** ADJ **b** (= *changeable*) *weather* verrückt (*inf*), launisch, unberechenbar; *person* ausgeflippt (*inf*); *hairstyle, idea* verrückt (*inf*), irre (*inf*)

freakishly ['friːkɪʃlɪ] ADV *warm* abnorm; *early also* überraschend; *bounce, deviate* verrückt (*inf*), unberechenbar, launisch

freak: freak-out N (*sl*) (*dated*: = *party*) Haschparty *f* (*inf*); (= *drug trip*) (Wahnsinns)trip *m* (*inf*); **freak show** N Monstrositätenshow *f*

freaky ['friːkɪ] ADJ (+*er*) (*inf*) durchgeknallt (*sl*)

freckle ['frekl] N Sommersprosse *f*

freckled ['frekld], **freckly** ['freklɪ] ADJ sommersprossig

Frederick ['fredrɪk] N Friedrich *m*

free [friː] ADJ (+*er*) **a** (= *at liberty, unrestricted*) *person, animal, state, activity, translation, choice* frei; **as ~ as a bird** or **(the) air** frei wie ein Vogel; **to set a prisoner ~** einen Gefangenen freilassen or auf freien Fuß setzen; **to go ~** (= *not be imprisoned*) frei ausgehen; (= *be set free*) freigelassen werden; **he is ~ to go** es steht ihm frei zu gehen; **you're ~ to choose** die Wahl steht Ihnen frei; **you're ~ to come too** Sie können ruhig auch kommen; **you're ~ to go now** Sie können jetzt gehen(, wenn Sie wollen); **you're ~ to decide** Sie können das selbst entscheiden; **I'm not ~ to do it** es steht mir nicht frei, es zu tun; **(do) feel ~ to help yourself/ask questions** nehmen Sie sich/fragen Sie ruhig; **feel ~!** (*inf*) bitte, gern(e)!; **to give sb a ~ hand** jdm freie Hand lassen; **he left one end of the rope ~** er ließ ein Ende des Seils lose; **his arms were left ~** (= *not tied*) seine Arme waren frei (gelassen); **~ elections** freie Wahlen *pl* → **rein** **b** (+*prep*) **~ from worry** sorgenfrei; **~ from blame/responsibility** frei von Schuld/Verantwortung; **~ of sth** frei von etw; **~ of** or **from pain** schmerzfrei; **~ of violence** gewaltlos; **~ of fear** ohne Angst; **a world ~ of nuclear weapons** eine Welt ohne Atomwaffen; **at last I was ~ of her** endlich war ich sie los **c** (= *costing nothing*) kostenlos, Gratis-; (*Comm*) gratis; **~ shares** Gratisaktien *pl*; **it's ~** das kostet nichts; **admission ~** Eintritt frei; **to get sth ~** etw umsonst bekommen; **we got in ~** or **for ~** (*inf*) wir kamen umsonst rein; **~, gratis and for nothing** gratis und umsonst; **I can tell you that for ~** (*inf*) das kann ich dir gratis sagen; **~ delivery** (porto)freier Versand; **~ alongside ship** (*Comm*) frei Kai; **~ on board** (*Comm*) frei Schiff **d** (= *not occupied*) *room, seat, hour, person* frei; **a few seats are kept ~** einige Plätze werden freigehalten; **I wasn't ~ earlier** ich hatte nicht eher Zeit; **this leaves our hands ~ for other issues** dadurch haben wir für andere Dinge Zeit; **if you've got a ~ hand could you carry this?** wenn du eine Hand frei hast, kannst du das tragen? **e** (= *lavish, profuse*) großzügig, freigebig; (= *licentious, improper*) *language, behaviour* frei, lose; (= *overfamiliar*) plumpvertraulich; **to be ~ with one's money** großzügig mit seinem Geld umgehen; **to be ~ with one's advice** Ratschläge erteilen; **to make ~ with other people's property** sich großzügig anderer Leute Sachen (*gen*) bedienen VT *prisoner* (= *release*) freilassen; (= *help escape*) befreien; *caged animal* freilassen; *nation* befreien; (= *untie*) *person* losbinden; *tangle* (auf)lösen; *pipe* freimachen; *rusty screw, caught fabric* lösen; (= *make available*) *person* freimachen; **to ~ sb from pain** jdn von seinen Schmerzen befreien; **to ~ oneself from sth** sich von etw freimachen

▶ **free up** VT (= *make available*) *person, time* freimachen; *money, resources* verfügbar machen

-free ADJ *suf* -frei; **alcohol-/rent-/tax-free** alkohol-/miet-/steuerfrei

free: free agent N **to be a ~** frei und ungebunden sein, ein freier Mensch sein; **free-and-easy** ADJ *attr*, **free and easy** ADJ *pred person, lifestyle, atmosphere, relationship* ungezwungen; (*morally*) locker; **free association** N freie Assoziation; **freebase** (*Drugs sl*) N Crack *nt* VT (= *smoke*) cocaine rauchen

freebie, freebee ['friːbiː] N (*inf*, = *promotional gift*) Werbegeschenk *nt*; **I got it as a ~** ich habe es gratis bekommen; **this is a ~** das ist gratis or umsonst

free: freeboard N Freibord *nt*; **freebooter** N Freibeuter *m*; **freeborn** ADJ frei geboren; **Free Church** N Freikirche *f*; **free climbing** N Freiklettern *nt*; **free collective bargaining** N Tarifautonomie *f*; **free currency** N (*Fin*) frei konvertierbare Währung

freedman ['friːdmæn] N *pl* **-men** [-men] befreiter or freigelassener Sklave

freedom ['friːdəm] N **a** Freiheit *f*; **~ of action/speech/worship** Handlungs-/Rede-/Religionsfreiheit *f*; **~ of association** Vereinsfreiheit *f*; **~ of the press** Pressefreiheit *f*; **~ of the seas** Freiheit *f* der Meere; **to give sb (the) ~ to do sth** jdm (die) Freiheit lassen, etw zu tun; **~ from sth** Freiheit *f* von etw **b** (= *frankness*) Offenheit *f*; (= *overfamiliarity*) plumpe (*inf*) or zu große Vertraulichkeit **c** (= *permission to use freely*) **the ~ of the city** die (Ehren)bürgerrechte *pl*; **to give sb the ~ of one's house** jdm sein Haus zur freien Verfügung stellen

freedom fighter N Freiheitskämpfer(in) *m(f)*

freedwoman ['friːdwʊmən] N *pl* **-women** [-wɪmɪn] befreite or freigelassene Sklavin

free: free enterprise N freies Unternehmertum; **free fall** N freier Fall; **in ~** (*Space, fig, economy etc*) in freiem Fall; **to go into ~** (*economy etc*) sich auf eine rasante Talfahrt begeben; **free-fall** VI frei fallen; **free-fall parachuting** N Fallschirmspringen *nt* mit freiem Fall; **free fight** N allgemeine Schlägerei

free-floating ADJ nicht gebunden, unabhängig; *currency, exchange rate* frei konvertierbar

Freefone® ['friːfəʊn] N (*Brit*) **call ~ 0800** rufen Sie gebührenfrei unter 0800 an

free: free-for-all N Gerangel *nt* (*inf*); (= *fight*) allgemeine Schlägerei; **to stop the situation becoming a ~** es unterbinden, dass jeder mitmischen kann; **free gift** N (Gratis)geschenk *nt*; **freehand** ADJ ~ *drawing* Freihandzeichnung *f*; ~ **sketch** Freihandskizze *f* ADV *paint, draw, cut* aus freier Hand; **free-handed** ADJ (= *generous*) großzügig, freigebig; **freehold** N Besitzrecht *nt*; **he bought the ~ of the house** er hat das Haus gekauft ADJ ~ **property** freier Grundbesitz; ~ **apartment** Eigentumswohnung *f*; ~ **house** Eigenheim *nt*; **the house is ~** das Haus ist nicht gepachtet und gehört dem Eigentümer uneingeschränkt ADV **to own sth ~** etw besitzen; **for sale ~** als Eigentumswohnung/Eigenheim zu verkaufen; **free house** N (*Brit*) *Wirtshaus, das nicht an eine bestimmte Brauerei gebunden ist*; **free kick** N (*Sport*) Freistoß *m*; **free labour,** (*US*) **free labor** (*nonunionized*) nicht organisierte Arbeitnehmer *pl*; **freelance** ADJ *journalist, photographer, writer* frei(schaffend), freiberuflich tätig; *work* freiberuflich; **I do a bit of ~ journalism** ich arbeite gelegentlich als freier Journalist; **most translators are ~** die meisten Übersetzer sind freiberuflich tätig ADV *work* freiberuflich; **she decided to go ~** sie entschloss sich, freiberuflich zu arbeiten N Freiberufler(in) *m(f)*; (*with particular firm*) freier Mitarbeiter, freie Mitarbeiterin VI freiberuflich arbeiten, freiberuflich tätig sein; **free list** N (*Theat*) Liste *f* der Empfänger von Freikarten; **freeload** VI (*inf*) schmarotzen (*on* bei); **freeloader** N (*inf*) Schmarotzer(in) *m(f)*; **free love** N freie Liebe

freely ['friːlɪ] ADV **a** *spend, give, lend, share* (= *liberally*) großzügig; (= *willingly*) bereitwillig; *refer* des Öfteren; *perspire* stark; **he was spending very ~** er gab das Geld mit vollen Händen aus; **to use sth ~** reichlich von etw Gebrauch machen; **I ~ admit that ...** ich gebe gern zu, dass ... **b** (= *unrestrictedly*) *move, operate* frei, ungehindert; *talk, speak, express oneself* frei, offen; *elected, contested* in freien Wahlen; *flow, travel* ungehindert; **to be ~ available** ohne Schwierigkeiten zu haben sein; **the wine was flowing ~** der Wein floss in Strömen

free: freeman N **a** (= *not a slave*) Freie(r) *m* **b** (*Brit*) ~ **of a city** Ehrenbürger(in) *m(f)* einer Stadt; **free market** N freier Markt; (*St Ex*) Freiverkehr *m*; **free market economy** N freie Marktwirtschaft; **free-marketeer** N Befürworter(in) *m(f)* des freien Marktes; **Freemason** N Freimaurer *m*; **freemasonry** N Freimaurerei *f*; **free port** N Freihafen *m*; **Freepost®** N "Freepost" = "Gebühr zahlt Empfänger"; **free-range** ADJ (*Brit*) *hen* frei laufend; *chicken, pig etc* aus Freilandhaltung; *produce* aus artgerechter Haltung; ~ **eggs** Eier *pl* von frei laufenden Hühnern; **free sample** N Gratisprobe *f*; **free sheet** N kostenlose Zeitung

freesia ['friːzɪə] N (*Bot*) Freesie *f*

free: free speech N Redefreiheit *f*; **free-spoken** ADJ freimütig; **freestanding** ADJ frei stehend; **it can be ~ or built-in** es kann frei stehen oder eingebaut werden; **freestyle** N (= *freestyle section*) Kür *f*; (*Swimming*) Freistil *m*; **the 200 metres** (*Brit*) **or meters** (*US*) ~ die 200 Meter Freistil ATTR ~ *swimming/wrestling* Freistilschwimmen/-ringen *nt*; **freethinker** N Freidenker(in) *m(f)*, Freigeist *m*; **freethinking** ADJ *person* freidenkerisch, freigeistig; **free time** N freie Zeit; (= *leisure*) Freizeit *f*; **if you have some ~** wenn Sie etwas Zeit haben; **free trade** N Freihandel *m*; **free-trade area** Freihandelszone *f*; **free-trader** N Freihändler(in) *m(f)*; **free throw** N (*Basketball*) Freiwurf *m*; **free TV** N frei empfangbares Fernsehen; **free verse** N freie Verse *pl*; **free vote** N (*esp Brit: Parl*) Abstimmung *f* ohne Fraktionszwang; **freeware** ['friːwɛəʳ] N (*Comput*) Freeware *f*; **freeway** N (*US*) Autobahn *f*; **freewheel** VI im Freilauf fahren N Freilauf *m*; **freewheeling, free-wheeling** ADJ *lifestyle, style, approach, atmosphere* ungezwungen, zwanglos; *person, community* frei, locker; *discussion* offen; **free will** N (*Philos*) freier Wille; **he did it of his own**

~ er hat es aus freien Stücken getan; **Free World** N **the** ~ die freie Welt

freezable ['friːzəbl] ADJ gefrierbar, einfrierbar

freeze [friːz] vb: pret **froze**, ptp **frozen** VI **a** (*Met*) frieren; (*water, liquids*) gefrieren; (*lakes, rivers*) zufrieren; (*pipes*) einfrieren; **it'll ~ hard tonight** es wird heute Nacht starken Frost geben; **to ~ to death** (*lit*) erfrieren; (*fig*) sich zu Tode frieren → **freezing, frozen** **b** (*fig*) (*blood*) erstarren, gerinnen; (*heart*) aussetzen; (*smile*) erstarren, gefrieren; **the sound made me ~** das Geräusch ließ mir das Blut in den Adern erstarren *or* gefrieren *or* gerinnen **c** (= *keep still*) in der Bewegung verharren *or* erstarren; **he froze in his tracks** er blieb wie angewurzelt stehen; **~!** keine Bewegung! **d** (*Cook*) **meat ~s well** Fleisch lässt sich gut einfrieren VT **a** *water* gefrieren; (*Med, Cook*) einfrieren **b** (*Econ*) *assets* festlegen; *credit, wages, programme, prices, bank account* einfrieren; (= *stop*) *film* anhalten **c** (*Med*) *wound* vereisen **d** (*fig*) **to ~ sb with a look** jdm einen eisigen Blick zuwerfen N **a** (*Met*) Frost *m*; **the big ~** der harte Frost **b** (*Econ*) Stopp *m*; **a wage(s) ~, a ~ on wages** ein Lohnstopp *m*; **a ~ on nuclear weapons testing** ein Atomwaffenteststopp *m*

▸ **freeze off** VT *sep* die kalte Schulter zeigen (+*dat*)

▸ **freeze onto** VI +*prep obj* (*US, inf*) **to freeze onto sb** sich wie eine Klette an jdn hängen *or* heften

▸ **freeze out** VT *sep* (*inf*) *person* herausekeln (*inf*)

▸ **freeze over** VI (*lake, river*) überfrieren; (*windscreen, windows*) vereisen

▸ **freeze up** VI zufrieren; (*pipes*) einfrieren; (*windscreen, windows*) vereisen VT *sep* **we were frozen up last winter** letztes Jahr waren alle unsere Leitungen eingefroren

freeze: freeze-dry VT gefriertrocknen; **freeze-frame** N (*Phot*) Standbild *nt*

freezer ['friːzəʳ] N Tiefkühltruhe *f*; (*upright*) Gefrierschrank *m*; (*Brit: = ice compartment of fridge*) Eisfach *nt*, (Tief)kühlfach *nt*, Gefrierfach *nt*

freeze-up ['friːzʌp] N **a** (*Met*) Dauerfrost *m* **b** (*esp US, of lakes, rivers etc*) **during the ~ a lot of birds perish** während Seen und Flüsse zugefroren sind, kommen viele Vögel ums Leben

freezing ['friːzɪŋ] ADJ **a** (*lit: = below zero*) *temperature* unter Null; ~ **conditions** Temperaturen *pl* unter null; ~ **weather** Frostwetter *nt*; ~ **rain** Eisregen *m*; **in ~ fog** bei Frost und Nebel **b** (= *extremely cold*) eiskalt, eisig kalt; *wind* eisig; **in the ~ cold** bei klirrender Kälte; **it's ~ (cold)** es ist eiskalt *or* eisig kalt; **I'm ~** mir ist eiskalt; **my hands/feet are ~** meine Hände/Füße sind eiskalt, ich habe eiskalte Hände/Füße N **a** (*Cook*) Einfrieren *nt* **b** (= *freezing point*) der Gefrierpunkt; **above/below ~** über/unter null, über/unter dem Gefrierpunkt; **to rise above ~** über null *or* über den Gefrierpunkt steigen; **to fall below ~** unter null *or* unter den Gefrierpunkt fallen

freezing point N Gefrierpunkt *m*; **below ~** unter null, unter dem Gefrierpunkt

freight [freɪt] N **a** (= *cargo*) Fracht *f*, Frachtgut *nt* **b** (= *transport of freight*) Frachtverkehr *m* **c** (*also* **freight charges**) Fracht *f*, Frachtkosten *pl*; ~ **paid** (*Comm*) frachtfrei, Fracht bezahlt; ~ **and delivery paid** (*US, Comm*) frachtfrei zum Bestimmungsort ADV **to send sth ~/air** etw als Frachtgut/per Luftfracht senden VT *goods* verfrachten

freightage ['freɪtɪdʒ] N (= *charge*) Fracht(gebühr) *f*

freight car N (*US, Rail*) Güterwagen *m*

freighter ['freɪtəʳ] N (*Naut*) Frachter *m*, Frachtschiff *nt*; (*Aviat*) Frachtflugzeug *nt*

freight: freight handler N Frachtverlader(in) *m(f)*; **freight plane** N Frachtflugzeug *nt*;

freight terminal N Fracht- *or* Güterterminal *nt*; **freight train** N Güterzug *m*

French [frentʃ] ADJ französisch; ~ **teacher** (*teaches French*) Französischlehrer(in) *m(f)*; (*comes from France*) französischer Lehrer, französische Lehrerin *f*; ~ **dictionary** ein Französischwörterbuch *nt*; **he is** ~ er ist Franzose; **she is** ~ sie ist Französin; **the ~ people** die Franzosen *pl*, das französische Volk N **a** (*Ling*) Französisch *nt*; **in** ~ auf französisch; **to speak ~** Französisch sprechen; **excuse my ~** (*hum inf*) entschuldigen Sie die Ausdrucksweise **b the** ~ *pl* die Franzosen *pl*

French: French Academy N **the** ~ die Académie Française; **French bean** N grüne Bohne; **French bread** N Baguette *nt*, Stangenbrot *nt*; **French-Canadian** ADJ **a** *person* frankokanadisch; **she is** ~ sie ist Frankokanadierin **b** *relations* frankokanadisch, französisch-kanadisch; (*Ling*) frankokanadisch, kanadisch-französisch **N** Frankokanadier(in) *m(f)* **a** (*Ling*) kanadisches Französisch *nt*; **French chalk** N Schneiderkreide *f*; **French cricket** N *dem Kricket ähnliches Kinderspiel*; **French doors** PL = **French windows**; **French dressing** N (*Cook*) **a** (*Brit, = oil and vinegar*) Vinaigrette *f* **b** (*US, = sweet, tomato-flavoured dressing*) French Dressing *nt*; **French Equatorial Africa** N Französisch-Äquatorialafrika *nt*; **French fried potatoes, French fries** PL Pommes frites *pl*; **French Guiana** N Französisch-Guayana *nt*; **French Guianan** [-gaɪˈænən] **N** Französisch-Guayaner(in) *m(f)* ADJ französisch-guayanisch; **French horn** N (*Mus*) (Wald)horn *nt*

frenchify ['frentʃɪfaɪ] VT französisieren; *clothes, restaurant* auf französisch machen (*inf*)

French: French kiss N Zungenkuss *m*; **French knickers** PL French Knickers *pl*; **French leave** N **to take** ~ sich französisch *or* auf Französisch empfehlen; **French letter** N (*Brit, inf*) Pariser *m* (*inf*); **French loaf** N Baguette *f*; **Frenchman** N Franzose *m*; **French marigold** N (*Bot*) Studentenblume *f*, Tagetes *f*; **French pastry** N Blätterteigteilchen *nt* mit Obst und Sahne; **French pleat** N französischer Zopf; **French polish** N Möbelpolitur *f* mit Schellack; **French-polish** VT lackieren; **French Revolution** N **the** ~ die Französische Revolution; **French Riviera** N **the** ~ die französische Riviera; **French roll** N *Damenfrisur, bei der das Haar seitlich zurückgekämmt und in einer länglichen Rolle aufgesteckt wird*; **French seam** N (*Sew*) französische Naht; **French stick** N Baguette *f*, Stangenbrot *nt*; **French toast** N **a** nur auf einer Seite gerösteter Toast **b** (*with egg*) in Ei getunktes gebratenes Brot; **French West Africa** N Französisch-Westafrika *nt*; **French windows** PL Verandatür *f*; **Frenchwoman** N Französin *f*

frenetic [frəˈnetɪk] ADJ *activity, pace, period* hektisch; *dancing* wild; *effort* verzweifelt

frenetically [frəˈnetɪklɪ] ADV (+*vb*) wie wild; *work* fieberhaft; *dance* frenetisch; **she is ~ busy** sie hat wahnsinnig viel zu tun (*inf*)

frenzied ['frenzɪd] ADJ *activity, efforts* hektisch, fieberhaft; *attack, passion, shouts* wild; *atmosphere* überreizt; *applause, crowd, fans, haste* rasend; **the gardens became the scene of ~ activity** in den Gärten herrschte hektische Betriebsamkeit

frenziedly ['frenzɪdlɪ] ADV *dance, shout* wie wild; *work* fieberhaft

frenzy ['frenzɪ] N Raserei *f*; **in a ~** in heller *or* wilder Aufregung; **he worked himself up into a ~** er steigerte sich in eine Raserei (hinein); **he worked the audience up into a ~** er brachte die Menge zur Raserei *or* zum Rasen; ~ **of activity** hektische Betriebsamkeit; ~ **of excitement** helle *or* wilde Aufregung

frequency ['friːkwənsɪ] N Häufigkeit *f*; (*Phys*) Frequenz *f*; **high/low** ~ Hoch-/Niederfrequenz *f*

frequency: frequency band N Frequenzband *nt*; **frequency distribution** N Häufigkeitsverteilung f; **frequency modulation** N Frequenzmodulation f

frequent ['fri:kwənt] ADJ häufig; *reports* zahlreich; *complaint, criticism* häufig geäußert; **she made ~ visits to Glasgow** sie reiste oft *or* häufig nach Glasgow; **take ~ breaks** machen Sie öfter *or* häufig eine Pause; **he is famous for his ~ changes of mind** er ist bekannt dafür, dass er häufig seine Meinung ändert; **her absences were ~** sie war oft *or* häufig abwesend; **do you suffer from ~ headaches?** haben Sie häufig *or* oft Kopfschmerzen?; **there are ~ trains** es verkehren viele Züge; **violent clashes were a ~ occurrence** es kam häufig *or* oft zu gewalttätigen Zusammenstößen

▪ VT [frɪ'kwent] *(form)* place (oft *or* häufig) besuchen; **he liked to ~ the bars** er hielt sich gern in den Bars auf; **a house which was ~ed by all sorts of famous people** ein Haus, in dem alle möglichen Berühmtheiten verkehrten

frequenter [frɪ'kwentə'] N *(of a house)* häufig gesehener Gast; *(of a pub)* Stammgast m; *(of a theatre, club)* häufiger Besucher, häufige Besucherin; **he's not a ~ of restaurants** er geht nicht oft ins Restaurant

frequent flyer N Vielflieger(in) m(f)

frequent-flyer [ˌfri:kwənt'flaɪə'] ADJ **~ programme** *(Brit) or* **scheme** Vielfliegerprogramm nt

frequently ['fri:kwəntlɪ] ADV oft, häufig; **I have ~ said/heard that** das habe ich schon öfter gesagt/gehört; **all too ~, ...** es kommt allzu oft *or* häufig vor, dass ...; **~ asked questions** *(Comput)* häufig gestellte Fragen pl

fresco ['freskəʊ] N *(= technique)* Freskomalerei f; *(= painting)* Fresko(gemälde) nt

fresh [freʃ] ADJ **a** *(= not stale)* food, clothes, taste, smell, breath frisch

b *(= new, recent)* instructions, news, wallpaper neu; *coat of paint, make-up, memories, scar* frisch; *(= additional, renewed)* allegations, reports, inquiries weitere(r, s); fighting, attack erneut; **~ supplies** Nachschub m; **a ~ outbreak of violence** erneute Ausschreitungen pl; **a ~ pot of tea** eine Kanne frisch aufgegossener Tee; **does your house need a ~ coat of paint?** muss Ihr Haus frisch gestrichen werden?; **we need some ~ faces** wir brauchen neue Gesichter; **to make a ~ start** einen neuen Anfang machen, neu anfangen; **to leave for ~ woods** *or* **fields (and pastures new)** einen Schlussstrich ziehen und anderswo neu anfangen; **to give ~ heart to sb** jdm neuen Mut geben; **the events were still ~ in his mind** *or* **memory** die Ereignisse waren ihm noch frisch im Gedächtnis *or* in Erinnerung

c *(= not dried, processed, frozen)* pasta, fruit, herbs, juice frisch; **~ milk** *(not UHT)* Frischmilch f; **~ meat** *(not frozen)* Frischfleisch nt; **~ orange juice** frisch gepresster Orangensaft

d *(= refreshed, not tired)* person, horse, face, complexion frisch; **as ~ as a daisy** taufrisch; **to feel ~** sich frisch fühlen

e *(= refreshing, original)* approach, style, writing erfrischend neu; **he has a ~ approach/~ ideas** er hat einen erfrischend neuen Ansatz/erfrischend neue Ideen

f *(= cool and invigorating)* morning, wind, breeze frisch; **it's a bit ~ today** heute ist es ziemlich frisch; **the air/water is cool and ~** die Luft/das Wasser ist kühl und erfrischend

g *(inf, = cheeky)* frech; *(= disrespectful)* pampig *(inf)*; **to be ~ with sb** frech zu jdm sein; **to get ~** frech werden; **don't get ~ with me!** komm mir bloß nicht frech!

▪ ADV **a** *(= straight)* young men ~ from *or* out of university junge Männer, die frisch *or* direkt von der Universität kommen; **I was ~ out of Oxford** ich hatte gerade mein Studium in Oxford beendet; **tourists ~ off the plane** Touristen, die gerade erst aus dem Flugzeug gestiegen sind; **milk ~ from the cows** Milch frisch von den Kühen; **cakes ~ from the oven** frisch aus dem Backofen, ofenfrische Kuchen; **to come ~ to sth** neu zu etw kommen

b *(inf)* **we're ~ out of cheese** uns ist gerade

der Käse ausgegangen; **they are ~ out of ideas** ihnen sind die Ideen ausgegangen, sie haben keine Ideen mehr

▸ **fresh up** VTIR *(US)* = freshen up

fresh: fresh air N frische Luft; **in the ~** an der frischen Luft; *(= outdoors)* im Freien; **to go out into the ~** an die frische Luft gehen; **to go for a breath of ~** frische Luft schnappen gehen; **I'm dying for a breath of ~** ich muss unbedingt frische Luft schnappen; **to be (like) a breath of ~** *(fig)* wirklich erfrischend sein; **it was a breath of ~ to read the article** es tat richtig gut, den Artikel zu lesen; **he has been a breath of ~ for us** er hat uns neuen Schwung gegeben; **fresh-baked** ADJ frisch gebacken

freshen ['freʃn] VI *(wind)* auffrischen; *(weather, air)* frisch werden ▪ VT **can I ~ your drink?** darf ich Ihnen noch nachschenken?; **chewing gum to ~ the breath** Kaugummi, um den Atem zu erfrischen

▸ **freshen up** VIR *(person)* sich frisch machen ▪ VT sep **a** child, invalid etc frisch machen; **that will freshen you up** das wird Sie erfrischen **b** room etc frischer aussehen lassen; team, image aufmöbeln *(inf)*

fresher ['freʃə'] N *(Brit Univ inf)* Erstsemester nt *(inf)*

fresh-faced [ˌfreʃ'feɪst] ADJ jung aussehend; **a ~ young man** ein junger Mann mit frischem Gesicht

freshly ['freʃlɪ] ADV frisch; **a ~ baked cake** ein frisch gebackener Kuchen; **the ~ dug grave** das frische Grab

freshman ['freʃmən] N pl **-men** [-mən] *(US, Univ)* Erstsemester nt *(inf)*; *(Sch)* Frischling m *(inf)*

freshness ['freʃnɪs] N **a** *(of food, fruit, wind, paint, breath, memories etc)* Frische f; *(of outlook)* Neuheit f **b** *(inf, = cheekiness)* Frechheit f; *(= lack of respect)* Pampigkeit f *(inf)*

freshness date N *(US)* (Mindest)haltbarkeitsdatum nt

fresh: freshwater ADJ attr **~ fish/eel** Süßwasserfisch m/-aal m; **~ harbour** *(Brit) or* **harbor** *(US)* Binnenhafen m; **fresh water** N *(not salty)* Süßwasser nt; *(not stale)* frisches Wasser

fret[1] [fret] VI **a** *(= become anxious)* sich *(dat)* Sorgen machen *(about um)*; *(baby)* unruhig sein; **don't ~** beruhige dich; **she ~s over** *or* **about the slightest thing** sie macht sich wegen jeder Kleinigkeit gleich Sorgen; **the child is ~ting for his mother** das Kind jammert nach seiner Mutter **b** *(horse)* **to ~ (at the bit)** sich (am Biss) reiben *or* scheuern ▪ VR sich *(dat)* Sorgen machen, sich aufregen ▪ N **to be in a ~** sich *(dat)* Sorgen machen, in Sorge sein

fret[2] VT wood etc laubsägen

fret[3] N *(on guitar etc)* Bund m

fretful ['fretfʊl] ADJ child quengelig; adult, behaviour wehleidig; *(= irritable, on edge)* genervt *(inf)*; tone klagend; *(= restless)* sleep unruhig

fretfully ['fretfəlɪ] ADV say wehleidig; cry kläglich

fretfulness ['fretfʊlnɪs] N *(of child)* Quengeligkeit f; *(of adult)* Wehleidigkeit f; *(= irritability)* Nervosität f *(inf)*

fret: fret saw N Laubsäge f; **fretwork** N *(in wood)* Laubsägearbeit f; *(Archit)* Mäander m

Freudian ['frɔɪdɪən] ADJ *(Psych, fig)* Freudsch attr, freudianisch; **very ~!** was Freud wohl dazu sagen würde! ▪ N Freudianer(in) m(f)

Freudian slip N freudsche Fehlleistung; *(spoken)* freudscher Versprecher

FRG abbr of **Federal Republic of Germany** BRD f

Fri abbr of **Friday** Fr.

friable ['fraɪəbl] ADJ bröckelig, krümelig

friableness ['fraɪəblnɪs] N Bröckeligkeit f, Krümeligkeit f

friar ['fraɪə'] N Mönch m; **Friar John** Bruder John; **Black Friars** Dominikaner pl; **Grey Friars** Franziskaner pl; **White Friars** Karmeliter pl

friary ['fraɪərɪ] N Mönchskloster nt

fricassee ['frɪkəsi:] N Frikassee nt ▪ VT frikassieren

fricative ['frɪkətɪv] ADJ Reibe-; **~ consonant** Reibelaut m ▪ N Reibelaut m

friction ['frɪkʃən] N **a** Reibung f; *(Phys)* Friktion f, Reibung f **b** *(fig)* Reibung f, Reibereien pl; **there is constant ~ between them** sie reiben sich ständig aneinander

friction: friction clutch N Friktionskupplung f, Reibungskupplung f; **friction feed** N *(Comput)* Friktionsvorschub m; **friction tape** N *(US)* Isolierband nt

Friday ['fraɪdɪ] N Freitag m → also **Tuesday**

fridge [frɪdʒ] N Kühlschrank m, Eisschrank m

fridge-freezer ['frɪdʒ'fri:zə'] N Kühl-Gefrierkombination f

fried [fraɪd] pret, ptp of **fry**[2] ADJ food, bread, rice gebraten; **~ egg** Spiegelei nt; **~ potatoes** Bratkartoffeln pl; **~ fish** Bratfisch m

friend [frend] N **a** Freund(in) m(f); *(less intimate)* Bekannte(r) m(f); **to become** *or* **make ~s with sb** sich mit jdm anfreunden, mit jdm Freundschaft schließen; **to make a ~ of sb** sich *(dat)* jdn zum Freund machen; **he makes ~s easily** er findet leicht Freunde; **she's a ~ of mine** sie ist eine Freundin/eine Bekannte von mir; **he's no ~ of mine** er ist nicht mein Freund; **to be ~s with sb** mit jdm befreundet sein, jds Freund(in) sein; **I'm not ~s with her any more** sie ist nicht mehr meine Freundin; **be a ~** sei so lieb; **we're just (good) ~s** da ist nichts, wir sind nur gut befreundet; **my honourable** *(Brit Parl)*/**learned** *(Jur)* **~** mein verehrter (Herr) Kollege, meine verehrte (Frau) Kollegin; **a ~ at court** *(fig)* ein einflussreicher Freund; **a ~ in need is a ~ indeed** *(Prov)* Freunde in der Not gehen tausend auf ein Lot *(Prov)*

b *(= helper, supporter)* Freund(in) m(f); **he's a ~ of the arts** er ist Förderer der schönen Künste; **the Friends of the National Theatre** die Freunde pl des Nationaltheaters

c *(Rel)* Friend Quäker(in) m(f); **Society of Friends** Quäker pl

friendless ['frendlɪs] ADJ ohne Freunde

friendliness ['frendlɪnɪs] N Freundlichkeit f; *(of welcome also)* Wärme f; *(of relations, attitude, advice)* Freundschaftlichkeit f

friendly ['frendlɪ] ADJ (+er) **a** *(= amiable)* person, smile, gesture, welcome, service, place freundlich; argument, advice, attitude freundschaftlich; cat, dog zutraulich; **she gave him a ~ smile** sie lächelte ihn freundlich an; **he gave me a ~ pat on the shoulder** er klopfte mir freundlich auf die Schulter; **to get a ~ welcome** freundlich begrüßt werden; **that wasn't a very ~ thing to do** das war nicht gerade sehr freundlich; **to be ~ to sb** freundlich *or* nett zu jdm sein; **to be ~ (with sb)** *(= to be friends)* (mit jdm) befreundet sein; **we're very/quite ~** wir sind eng befreundet/ganz gute Freunde; **~ relations** freundschaftliche Beziehungen pl; **to be on ~ terms with sb** mit jdm auf freundschaftlichem Fuße stehen; **to become** *or* **get ~ with sb** sich mit jdm anfreunden; **to get ~** *(inf: = intimate)* zärtlich werden → **user-friendly, environmentally**

b *(Pol)* country, nation freundlich; government, corporation freundlich gesinnt *(to +dat)*; **countries which are ~ to Libya** Länder, die Libyen freundlich gesinnt sind; **unions ~ to management** unternehmerfreundliche Gewerkschaften pl; **~ ports** Häfen pl in befreundeten Ländern ▪ N *(Sport: = match)* Freundschaftsspiel nt

friendly: friendly fire N *(Mil)* Beschuss m durch die eigene Seite; **Friendly Islands** PL Freundschaftsinseln pl; **friendly match** N *(Sport)* Freundschaftsspiel nt; **friendly society** N *(Brit)* Versicherungsverein m auf Gegenseitigkeit

friendship ['frendʃɪp] N Freundschaft f

fries [fraɪz] PL *(esp US, inf)* Fritten pl *(inf)*, Pommes pl *(inf)*

Friesian ['fri:ʒən] ADJ **a** friesisch **b** cattle Deutsche(r, s) Schwarzbunte(r, s) ▪ N **a** Friese *m*, Friesin *f* **b** (*Ling*) Friesisch *nt* **c** (= *cow*) Deutsche Schwarzbunte *f*

Friesian Islands PL Friesische Inseln *pl*

Friesland ['fri:slənd] N Friesland *nt*

frieze¹ [fri:z] N (*Archit*, = *picture*) Fries *m*; (= *thin band*) Zierstreifen *m*

frieze² N (*Tex*) Fries *m*

frigate ['frɪgɪt] N (*Naut*) Fregatte *f*

frigging ['frɪgɪn] (*sl*) **ADJ** verdammt (*inf*), Scheiß- (*inf*); **that ~ bus** der verdammte Bus (*inf*), der Scheißbus (*inf*) **ADV** verdammt (*inf*)

fright [fraɪt] N **a** Schreck(en) *m*; **to get or have a ~** sich erschrecken, einen Schreck bekommen; **to give sb a ~** jdm einen Schreck(en) einjagen, jdn erschrecken; **to take ~** es mit der Angst zu tun bekommen **b** (*inf*, = *person*) Vogelscheuche *f* (*inf*); **she looks a ~ in that hat** mit dem Hut sieht sie verboten *or* zum Fürchten aus (*inf*)

frighten ['fraɪtn] **VT** (= *give a sudden fright*) erschrecken, Angst einjagen (+*dat*); (= *make scared*) Angst machen (+*dat*), Angst einjagen (+*dat*); (*idea, thought*) ängstigen, Angst *or* Furcht einflößen (+*dat*); **I'm not easily ~ed** ich fürchte mich nicht so schnell, ich habe nicht so schnell Angst; (*with threats etc*) so schnell *or* leicht kann man mir keine Angst machen; **to be ~ed by sth** vor etw (*dat*) erschrecken; **to ~ sb into agreeing to sth** jdm solche Angst machen, dass er/sie einer Sache (*dat*) zustimmt; **to ~ the life out of sb** jdn zu Tode erschrecken **VI** she doesn't ~ easily so leicht fürchtet sie sich nicht; (*with threats etc*) so schnell *or* leicht kann man ihr keine Angst machen

▸ **frighten away** *or* **off** VT sep abschrecken; (*deliberately*) verscheuchen

frightened ['fraɪtnd] ADJ *person, animal* ängstlich, verängstigt; *voice, eyes, look* ängstlich, angsterfüllt; **to be ~ (of sb/sth)** Angst haben (vor jdm/etw); **are you ~ of the dark?** hast du Angst vor der Dunkelheit?; **don't be ~** hab keine Angst; **they were ~ (that) there would be another earthquake** sie hatten Angst (davor), dass es noch ein Erdbeben geben könnte; **to be ~ to do sth** Angst (davor) haben, etw zu tun; **I was too ~ to look** ich hatte zu viel Angst *or* war zu verängstigt, um hinzusehen; **to be ~ about *or* of doing sth** Angst davor haben, etw zu tun; **to be ~ to death *or* out of one's wits** zu Tode erschrocken sein; **to be ~ to death that...** Todesängste ausstehen, dass ...; **to be ~ to death of sb/sth** eine Todesangst vor jdm/ etw haben; **like a ~ rabbit** wie ein verängstigtes Kaninchen

frighteners ['fraɪtnəz] PL (*Brit, inf*) **to put the ~ on sb** jdm einen Schreck einjagen

frightening ['fraɪtnɪn] ADJ **a** (= *alarming*) *experience, incident* Furcht erregend; *situation, sight, prospect, feeling, thought, story* erschreckend; **it was a ~ situation** die Situation war zum Fürchten; **the most ~ sight** der entsetzlichste Anblick; **to look ~** zum Fürchten aussehen **b** (= *scary*) beängstigend; **life was more ~ when I was small** als ich noch klein war, hat das Leben mir mehr Angst gemacht; **it was a ~ place** der Ort war zum Fürchten; **it is ~ to think what could happen** es ist beängstigend, wenn man denkt, was alles passieren könnte

frighteningly ['fraɪtnɪnlɪ] ADV erschreckend; **more ~, one risked one's life** und was noch erschreckender war, es bestand Lebensgefahr

frightful ['fraɪtfʊl] ADJ (*inf*) schrecklich, furchtbar; **to look ~** zum Fürchten aussehen

frightfully ['fraɪtfəlɪ] ADV (*inf*) schrecklich, furchtbar; **she did ~ well at school** (*dated*) sie war in der Schule unheimlich gut (*inf*)

frightfulness ['fraɪtfʊlnɪs] N (*inf*) Schrecklichkeit *f*, Furchtbarkeit *f*

frigid ['frɪdʒɪd] ADJ **a** (*sexually*) frigide **b** (*form*: = *cold*) *place, air, night, weather* eiskalt; *temperature, silence, stare* eisig; *atmosphere, manner, smile* frostig

frigidity [frɪ'dʒɪdɪtɪ] N **a** (*sexual*) Frigidität *f* **b** (*form*: = *iciness*) eisige Kälte; (*fig, of atmosphere, manner, smile*) Frostigkeit *f*

frill [frɪl] N **a** (*on dress, shirt etc*) Rüsche *f*; (*on animal, bird*) Kragen *m*; (*round meat, on plant pot etc*) Manschette *f* **b** **~s** *pl* (*fig, = ornaments*) Kinkerlitzchen *pl* (*inf*), Verzierungen *pl*; **with all the ~s** mit allem Drum und Dran (*inf*); **a simple meal without ~s** ein schlichtes Essen

frilly ['frɪlɪ] ADJ (+*er*) **a** (*Tex*) *apron, cushion, clothing* mit Rüschen; **to be ~** Rüschen haben; **~ dress/blouse/underwear** Rüschenkleid *nt*/-bluse *f*/-unterwäsche *f* **b** (*fig*) *speech, style* blumig; *music, decoration* verschnörkelt

fringe [frɪndʒ] **N a** (*on shawl*) Fransenkante *f*, Fransen *pl* **b** (*Brit*, = *hair*) Pony *m* **c** (*fig, = periphery*) Rand *m*; **on the ~ of the forest** am Waldrand; **to live on the ~(s) of society** am Rande der Gesellschaft leben; **the ~s of a city** die Randbezirke *pl* einer Stadt → **lunatic fringe** **VT** mit Fransen versehen

fringe: fringe area N (*lit, fig*) Randgebiet *nt*; **fringe benefits** PL zusätzliche Leistungen *pl*

fringed [frɪndʒd] ADJ *skirt, shawl, jacket* mit Fransen; *lampshade* mit Fransenkante; **~ with *or* by sth** (*street, beach, lawn,* = *lined*) von etw gesäumt (*geh*); (= *surrounded*) von etw umsäumt (*geh*); **~ with silk** mit Seidenfransen

fringe: fringe event N Randveranstaltung *f*; **fringe group** N Randgruppe *f*; **fringe theatre**, (*US*) **fringe theater** N avantgardistisches Theater

frippery ['frɪpərɪ] N (*pej*, = *cheap ornament*) Flitter *m*, Kinkerlitzchen *pl* (*inf*); (= *trivialities*) belanglose Kleinigkeiten *pl*

Frisbee® ['frɪzbɪ] N Frisbee® *nt*

Frisian ['frɪsɪən] ADJ, N = **Friesian** ADJ a N a, b

frisk [frɪsk] **VI** (= *leap about*) umhertollen **VT** *suspect etc* durchsuchen, filzen (*inf*)

friskiness ['frɪskɪnɪs] N Verspieltheit *f*

frisky ['frɪskɪ] ADJ (+*er*) verspielt

frisson ['fri:sɒn] N (= *thrill*) Schauer *m*

fritillary [frɪ'tɪlərɪ] N (= *butterfly*) Perlmutterfalter *m*

fritter¹ ['frɪtə] VT (*Brit: also* **fritter away**) *money, time* vertun (*inf*), vergeuden, verplempern (*inf*)

fritter² N (*Cook*) Beignet *m*, Schmalzgebackenes *nt no pl* mit Füllung; **apple ~** Apfelbeignet *m*

frivolity [frɪ'vɒlɪtɪ] N Frivolität *f*; (*of appearance, writer*) unseriöse Art

frivolous ['frɪvələs] ADJ *person, attitude, remark* frivol, leichtfertig; *clothes, appearance, writer, scientist* unseriös; *object, activity* albern; **I spend a lot of money on ~ things** ich gebe viel Geld für unwichtige Dinge aus; **the ~ stories of the tabloids** die belanglosen Berichte in den Boulevardzeitungen

frivolously ['frɪvələslɪ] ADV frivol; *remark also* leichtfertig

frizz [frɪz] **VT** *hair* kräuseln **VI** sich kräuseln, kraus werden **N** Kraushaar *nt*

frizzle ['frɪzl] **VI** (= *sizzle*) brutzeln **VT** **a** *bacon etc* knusprig braten **b** *hair* kräuseln; **a man with ~d white hair** ein Mann mit weißem Kraushaar

frizz(l)y ['frɪz(l)ɪ] ADJ (+*er*) *hair* kraus

fro [frəʊ] ADV → **to, to-ing and fro-ing**

frock [frɒk] N Kleid *nt*; (*of monk*) Kutte *f*

frock coat N Gehrock *m*

frog¹ [frɒg] N **a** Frosch *m*; **to have a ~ in one's throat** einen Frosch im Hals haben; **he's a big ~ in a small pond** (*US*) er ist ein großes Tier am Ort (*inf*) **b** **Frog** (*Brit, pej inf*, = *French person*) Franzmann *m* (*dated inf*), Franzose *m*, Französin *f*

frog² N (= *fastening*) Paspelverschluss *m*

frogging ['frɒgɪn] N (= *fastenings*) Paspelverschlüsse *pl*

Froggy ['frɒgɪ] N (*Brit, pej inf*) Franzose *m*, Französin *f*, Franzmann *m* (*dated inf*)

frog: frog kick N Beinschlag *m* beim Brustschwimmen; **frogman** N Froschmann *m*; **frogmarch** VT (*Brit*) (ab)schleppen (*inf*), (weg)schleifen; (= *carry*) zu viert wegtragen; **they ~ed him in here** sie schleppten ihn herein (*inf*); **frogs' legs** PL (*Cook*) Froschschenkel *pl*; **frogspawn** N Froschlaich *m*

frolic ['frɒlɪk] vb: pret, ptp **frolicked** **VI** (*also* **frolic about** *or* **around**) herumtollen, herumtoben **N** (= *romp*) Herumtoben *nt*, Herumtollen *nt*; (= *gaiety*) Ausgelassenheit *f*; (= *prank*) Jux *m*, Scherz *m*, Spaß *m*

frolicsome ['frɒlɪksəm] ADJ übermütig, ausgelassen

from [frɒm] PREP **a** (*indicating starting place*) von (+*dat*); (*indicating place of origin*) aus (+*dat*); **he/ the train has come ~ London** er/der Zug ist von London gekommen; **he/it comes *or* is ~ Germany** er/es kommt *or* ist aus Deutschland; **where have you come ~ today?** von wo sind Sie heute gekommen?; **where does he come ~?, where is he ~?** woher kommt *or* stammt er?; **the train ~ Manchester** der Zug aus Manchester; **the train ~ Manchester to London** der Zug von Manchester nach London; **he's on the phone ~ London** er ruft aus London an; **~ house to house** von Haus zu Haus; **a representative ~ the company** ein Vertreter/eine Vertreterin der Firma

b (*indicating time, in past*) seit (+*dat*); (*in future*) ab (+*dat*), von (+*dat*) ... an; **~ last week until** *or* **to yesterday** von letzter Woche bis gestern; **~ ... on** ab ...; **~ now on** von jetzt an, ab jetzt; **~ then on** von da an; (*in past also*) seither; **~ his childhood** von Kindheit an, von klein auf; **he comes ~ time to time** er kommt von Zeit zu Zeit; **as ~ the 6th May** vom 6. Mai an, ab (dem) 6. Mai; **5 years ~ now** in 5 Jahren

c (*indicating distance*) von (+*dat*) (... weg); (*from town etc*) von (+*dat*) ... (entfernt); **the house is 10 km ~ the coast** das Haus ist 10 km von der Küste entfernt; **to work away ~ home** außer Haus arbeiten

d (*indicating sender, giver*) von (+*dat*); **tell him ~ me** richten Sie ihm von mir aus; **an invitation ~ the Smiths** eine Einladung von den Smiths; **"from ..."** (*on envelope, parcel*) „Absender ...", „Abs. ..."

e (*indicating removal*) von (+*dat*); (= *out of: from pocket, cupboard etc*) aus (+*dat*); **to take/grab etc sth ~ sb** jdm etw wegnehmen/wegreißen *etc*; **to steal sth ~ sb** jdm etw stehlen; **he took it ~ the top/middle/bottom of the pile** er nahm es oben vom Stapel/aus der Mitte des Stapels/ unten vom Stapel weg

f (*indicating source*) von (+*dat*); (= *out of*) aus (+*dat*); **where did you get that ~?** wo hast du das her?, woher hast du das?; **I got it ~ the supermarket/the library/Kathy** ich habe es aus dem Supermarkt/aus der Bücherei/von Kathy; **to drink ~ a stream/glass** aus einem Bach/Glas trinken; **quotation ~ "Hamlet"/the Bible/ Shakespeare** Zitat *nt* aus „Hamlet"/aus der Bibel/nach Shakespeare; **memories ~ his childhood** Erinnerungen aus seiner Kindheit; **translated ~ the English** aus dem Englischen übersetzt; **made ~ ...** aus ... hergestellt

g (= *modelled on*) nach (+*dat*); **painted ~ life** nach dem Leben gemalt

h (*indicating lowest amount*) ab (+*dat*); **~ £2/the age of 16 (upwards)** ab £ 2/16 Jahren (aufwärts); **dresses (ranging) ~ £60 to £80** Kleider *pl* zwischen £ 60 und £ 80

i (*indicating escape*) **he fled ~ the enemy** er floh vor dem Feind; **he got away ~ his pursuers** er entkam seinen Verfolgern; **he ran away ~ home** er rannte von zu Hause weg; **he escaped ~ prison** er entkam aus dem Gefängnis

j (*indicating change*) **things went ~ bad to worse** es wurde immer schlimmer; **he went ~ office boy to director** er stieg vom Laufjungen zum Direktor auf; **a price increase ~ one euro to two euros** eine Preiserhöhung von einem auf zwei Euro

k (*indicating difference*) **he is quite different ~ the others** er ist ganz anders als die andern; **to**

tell **black ~ white** Schwarz und Weiß auseinander halten; **I like all sports, ~ swimming to wrestling** ich mag alle Sportarten, von Schwimmen bis Ringen

I (= *because of, due to*) **to act ~ compassion** aus Mitleid handeln; **to die ~ cancer** an Krebs sterben; **weak ~ hunger** schwach vor Hunger; **weak ~ loss of blood** vom Blutverlust geschwächt

m (= *on the basis of*) **~ experience** aus Erfahrung; **to judge ~ recent reports ...** nach neueren Berichten zu urteilen ...; **your point of view** von Ihrem Standpunkt aus (gesehen); **to conclude ~ the information** aus den Informationen einen Schluss ziehen, von den Informationen schließen; **~ what I heard** nach dem, was ich gehört habe; **~ what I can see ...** nach dem, was ich sehen kann ...; **the look of things ...** (so) wie die Sache aussieht ...

n (*Math*) **3 ~ 8 leaves 5** 8 weniger 3 ist 5; **take 12 ~ 18** nimm 12 von 18 weg; **£10 will be deducted ~ your account** £ 10 werden von Ihrem Konto abgebucht

o (*in set phrases, see also other element*) **to prevent/stop sb ~ doing sth** jdn daran hindern/davon zurückhalten, etw zu tun; **he prevented me ~ coming** er hielt mich davon ab, zu kommen; **to suffer ~ sth** an etw (*dat*) leiden; **to shelter ~ the rain** sich vor dem Regen unterstellen; **to protect sb ~ sth** jdn vor etw (*dat*) schützen

p +adv von; **~ inside/underneath** von innen/unten

q +prep **~ above** or **over/across sth** über etw (*acc*) hinweg; **~ beneath** or **underneath sth** unter etw (*dat*) hervor; **~ out of sth** aus etw heraus; **~ before his mother's death** aus der Zeit vor dem Tod seiner Mutter; **~ among the trees** zwischen den Bäumen hervor; **~ inside/outside the house** von drinnen/draußen; **~ beyond the grave** aus dem Jenseits

frond [frɒnd] N (*of fern*) Farnwedel *m*; (*of palm*) Palmwedel *m*

front [frʌnt] **N a** (= *forward side, exterior*) Vorderseite *f*; (= *forward part, including interior*) Vorderteil *nt*; (*of house etc* = *façade*) Vorderfront *f*, Stirnseite *f*; (*of shirt, dress*) Vorderteil *nt*; (= *dickey*) Hemdbrust *f*; (*Theat*, = *auditorium*) Zuschauerraum *m*; **in ~** vorne; (*in line, race etc also*) an der Spitze; **in ~ of sb/sth** vor jdm/etw; **at the ~ of** (*inside*) vorne in (+*dat*); (*outside*) vor (+*dat*); (= *at the head of*) an der Spitze (+*gen*); **to be in ~** vorne sein; (*Sport*) vorn(e) or an der Spitze liegen; **look in ~ of you** blicken Sie nach vorne; **in ~ of you you can see ...** vor Ihnen können Sie ... sehen; **in** or **at the ~ of the train/class** vorne im Zug/Klassenzimmer; **he reached the ~ of the queue** (*Brit*) or **line** (*US*) er erreichte die Spitze der Schlange; **she spilled tea down the ~ of her dress** sie verschüttete Tee vorn über ihr Kleid

b (*Mil, Pol, Met*) Front *f*; **he fell at the ~** er ist an der Front gefallen; **they were attacked on all ~s** (*Mil*) sie wurden an allen Fronten angegriffen; (*fig*) sie wurden von allen Seiten angegriffen; **cold ~** (*Met*) Kaltluft(front) *f*; **we must present a common/united ~** wir müssen eine gemeinsame/geschlossene Front bieten; **on the wages ~** was die Löhne betrifft; **on the home** or **domestic ~** (*Pol*) im Inland

c (*Brit, of sea*) Strandpromenade *f*; (*of lake*) Uferpromenade *f*

d (= *outward appearance*) Fassade *f*; **to put on a bold ~** eine tapfere Miene zur Schau stellen; **to put on a calm ~** nach außen hin ruhig erscheinen; **it's just a ~** das ist nur Fassade

e (= *cover for illicit activity*) Tarnung *f*, Fassade *f*

f (*US*, = *figurehead of organization*) Galionsfigur *f*, Aushängeschild *nt*

g no pl (= *effrontery*) Stirn *f*; **to have the ~ to do sth** die Frechheit besitzen or die Stirn haben, etw zu tun

h (*poet*, = *brow, face*) Antlitz *nt* (*poet*)

ADV **~** vorne; **to move up ~** nach vorne rücken; **50% up ~** 50% Vorschuss; **to attack ~ and rear** von vorn und hinten angreifen; **eyes ~!** (*Mil*) Augen geradeaus! → *also* **upfront**

VI **the houses/windows ~ onto the street** die Häuser liegen/die Fenster gehen auf die Straße hinaus

VT a **cottages ~ed by well-kept lawns** Häuschen mit gepflegtem Rasen davor

b *organization, band* leiten

ADJ vorderste(r, s), Vorder-; *page* erste(r, s); **~ tooth/wheel/room** Vorderzahn *m*/-rad *nt*/-zimmer *nt*; **~ row** erste or vorderste Reihe; **the ~ end of the train** die Spitze des Zuges

frontage ['frʌntɪdʒ] N (*of building*) Front *f*, Vorderseite *f*; (= *ground in front of house*) Grundstück or Gelände *nt* vor dem Haus; **the shop has a ~ on two streets** der Laden hat Schaufenster auf or zu zwei Straßen hinaus; **because of its ~ onto the sea** weil es zur See hinaus liegt

frontage road N (*US*) → **service road**

frontal ['frʌntl] **ADJ** attr **a** (= *direct, head-on*) **assault** or **attack** Frontalangriff *m*; **~ challenge** direkte Herausforderung; **~ impact** or **collision** (*Aut*) Frontalzusammenstoß *m* **b** **~ nudity** (*TV, Film*) frontale Nacktszenen *pl*; (*Phot*) frontale Nacktaufnahmen *pl*; **(full) ~ nude shots** frontale Nacktaufnahmen *pl* **c** (*Met*) **~ system** Frontsystem *nt* **N a** (*Rel*) Altardecke *f* **b** = **full frontal**

frontal (*Anat, Med*): **frontal cortex** N Hirnrinde *f*; **frontal lobe** N Stirnlappen *m*; **frontal lobotomy** N Leukotomie *f*

front: **front bench** N (*Parl*) vorderste or erste Reihe (*wo die führenden Politiker sitzen*); **front burner** N **to be sb's ~** (*inf*) für jdn an erster Stelle kommen; **front crawl** N (*Swimming*) Kraulen *nt*, Kraulstil *m*; **front door** N Haustür *f*; **front drive** N (*Aut*) Frontantrieb *m*; **front end** N (*Comput*) Frontende *nt*; **front garden** N Vorgarten *m*

frontier ['frʌntɪə[r]] N Grenze *f*, Landesgrenze *f*; (= *boundary area*) Grenzgebiet *nt*; (*fig, of knowledge*) Grenze *f*; **to push back the ~s of science** auf wissenschaftliches Neuland vorstoßen

frontier in cpds Grenz-; **frontier dispute** N Grenzstreitigkeiten *pl*

frontiersman ['frʌntɪəzmən] N pl -men [-mən] Grenzbewohner *m*

frontier station N Grenzposten *m*

frontierswoman ['frʌntɪəzwʊmən] N pl -women ['wɪmɪn] Grenzbewohnerin *f*

frontispiece ['frʌntɪspiːs] N zweite Titelseite, Frontispiz *nt* (*obs*)

front: **front line** N Front(linie) *f*; **frontline** ADJ (*Mil*) Front-; (*fig*) *employees etc* in vorderster Front; **~ states** Anliegerstaaten *pl* (*an einem Kriegsschauplatz*); **~ troops** Fronttruppen *pl*; **front loader** N Frontlader *m*; **front man** N Mann *m* an der Spitze; (*pej*) Strohmann *m*; **front matter** N Titelei *f*; **front money** N (*US, paid upfront*) Vorschuss *m*; **front office** N (*US Comm*) Verwaltung *f*; **front organization** N Tarn- or Deckorganisation *f*; **front page** N erste Seite, Titelseite *f*; **to hit the ~** Schlagzeilen machen; **front-page** ADJ attr *news, story, report, headline, coverage* auf der ersten Seite; **~ picture** or **photograph** (*of magazine*) Titelbild *nt*; **to be** or **make ~ news** Schlagzeilen machen; **it's not exactly ~ news** das wird nicht gerade Schlagzeilen machen; **front rank** N **to be in the ~** (*fig*) zur Spitze zählen; **frontrunner** N **a** Läufer(in) *m(f)* an der Spitze; **he's by nature a ~** er läuft am liebsten an der Spitze **b** (*fig*) Spitzenreiter(in) *m(f)*; **front seat** N Platz *m* in der ersten Reihe; (*Aut*) Vordersitz *m*; (*fig*) Logenplatz *m*; **front view** N (*Tech*) Aufriss *m*; **front vowel** N (*Phon*) Vorderzungenvokal *m*; **front-wheel drive** N Vorderradantrieb *m*; **front woman** N Frau *f* an der Spitze; (*pej*) Strohfrau *f*

frosh [frɒʃ] N (*US inf*) (*Univ*) Erstsemester *nt* (*inf*); (*Sch*) Frischling *m* (*inf*)

frost [frɒst] **N a** *m*; (*on leaves etc*) Raureif *m*; **late ~s** späte Frostperioden *pl*; **ten degrees of ~** zehn Grad Kälte **b** (*fig*, = *cold manner*) Kühle *f*, Kälte *f*, Frostigkeit *f* **c** (*dated sl*, = *failure*) Pleite *f* (*inf*), Reinfall *m* **VT a** *glass* mattieren **b** (*esp US*) *cake* mit Zuckerguss überziehen, glasieren **c** (= *quick-freeze*) einfrieren, tiefkühlen

frost: **frostbite** N Frostbeulen *pl*; (*more serious*) Erfrierungen *pl*; **to suffer (from) ~** Frostbeulen/Erfrierungen haben; **frostbitten** ADJ *fingers, toes, person* erfroren; *crops, plants* durch Frost geschädigt; **people with ~ fingers** Leute mit Frostbeulen/Erfrierungen an den Fingern; **he was badly ~** er hatte sehr starke Erfrierungen; **frostbound** ADJ *ground* hart gefroren

frosted ['frɒstɪd] ADJ **a** (= *frost-covered*) *grass, trees, roofs* von Raureif bedeckt; *windows, windscreen* vereist **b** (*fig*) *eye shadow, nail varnish, lipstick* metallisch **c** (*esp US*, = *iced*) mit Zuckerguss überzogen, glasiert; (= *sugared*) *fruit* mit Zucker bestreut

frosted glass N Mattglas *nt*, Milchglas *nt*; **~ door** Matt- or Milchglastür *f*

frostily ['frɒstɪlɪ] ADV *say* frostig; *smile* kühl

frostiness ['frɒstɪnɪs] N (*of weather, fig, of welcome etc*) Frostigkeit *f*

frosting ['frɒstɪŋ] N (*esp US*, = *icing*) Zuckerguss *m*

frost line N Frostgrenze *f*

frost work N (*on window*) Eisblumen *pl*

frosty ['frɒstɪ] ADJ (+er) **a** (= *cold*) frostig; **~ night** Frostnacht *f*; **a clear and ~ night** eine frostklare Nacht; **~ weather** Frostwetter *nt* **b** (= *frost-covered*) *ground, grass* von Raureif bedeckt; (= *frozen*) *ground* gefroren **c** (*fig*) *person, reception, response, atmosphere* frostig, kühl; *look* eisig; *relations* unterkühlt

froth [frɒθ] **N a** (*on liquids, Med*) Schaum *m* **b** (= *light conversation, frivolities*) Firlefanz *m*; **the present ~ and commotion over the elections** der ganze Zirkus, der im Moment um die Wahlen gemacht wird **VI** schäumen; **the beer ~ed over the edge of the glass** der Schaum floss über den Rand des Bierglases; **a cup of ~ing coffee** eine Tasse Kaffee mit Schaum; **the dog was ~ing at the mouth** der Hund hatte Schaum vor dem Maul; **he was ~ing at the mouth (with rage)** er schäumte vor Wut

frothy ['frɒθɪ] ADJ (+er) **a** (= *bubbly*) *beer, milk shake, coffee, sea etc* schäumend; *mixture, cream* schaumig; **beer with a full ~ head** Bier mit einer großen Schaumkrone **b** (= *frilly*) duftig und voller Rüschen **c** (= *superficial*) *comedy, entertainment* leicht, seicht (*pej*)

frown [fraʊn] **N** Stirnrunzeln *nt* no pl; **to give a ~** die Stirn(e) runzeln; **... he said with a deep ~ ...** sagte er mit einem ausgeprägten Stirnrunzeln; **angry ~** finsterer Blick; **worried/puzzled ~** sorgenvoller/verdutzter Gesichtsausdruck, sorgenvolles/verdutztes Gesicht; **a worried ~ crossed his face** ein sorgenvoller Ausdruck huschte über sein Gesicht **VI** (*lit, fig*) die Stirn(e) runzeln (*at* über +*acc*)

▸ **frown (up)on** VI +prep obj (*fig*) *suggestion, idea* missbilligen, mit Stirnrunzeln betrachten; **this practice is frowned (up)on** diese Gewohnheit ist verpönt

frowning ['fraʊnɪŋ] ADJ *face, look, glance, expression* finster; **a ~ man** ein finster blickender Mann

frowsy, frowzy ['fraʊzɪ] ADJ (+er) (= *unkempt*) schlampig, schlud(e)rig

froze [frəʊz] pret of **freeze**

frozen ['frəʊzn] ptp of **freeze** ADJ **a** *ground, land, earth* gefroren; *pipe* eingefroren; *lock* zugefroren; **~ hard** hart gefroren; **~ (over)** (*lake, river*) zugefroren; **~ solid** ganz zugefroren **b** (*for preservation, Cook*) *vegetables, meat, meal* tiefgekühlt; (*Med*) *embryo, sperm* eingefroren; **~ yoghurt** gefrorener Jog(h)urt; **to keep sth ~** etw eingefroren lassen **c** (*inf*, = *very cold*) *person, part of body* eiskalt; **I'm ~** mir ist eiskalt; **to be ~ stiff** (*person, part of body*) steif gefroren sein; **~ to death** or **to the bone** völlig durchgefroren → **marrow** **d** (= *rigid*) *person, animal* starr; **~ in horror/with**

fear starr *or* steif vor Schreck/vor Angst; **I stood** *or* **was ~ to the spot** ich stand wie angewurzelt da; **a village ~ in time** ein Dorf, in dem die Zeit stehen geblieben ist; **he felt as if he was ~ in time** es war ihm, als sei die Zeit stehen geblieben
　e (*Econ*) prices, wages eingefroren; (*Fin*) account eingefroren

frozen: frozen assets PL (*Fin*) festliegendes Kapital, eingefrorene Guthaben *pl*; **frozen food** N Tiefkühlkost *f*; **~ compartment** Tiefkühlfach *nt*, Gefrierfach *nt*; **frozen shoulder** N (*Med*) steife Schulter; **frozen wastes** PL ewiges Eis

FRS abbr of **Fellow of the Royal Society**

fructification [ˌfrʌktɪfɪˈkeɪʃən] N (*lit, fig:* = making fruitful) Befruchtung *f*; (= forming fruit) Fruchtbildung *f*

fructify [ˈfrʌktɪfaɪ] VT (*lit, fig*) seed, writing befruchten VI Früchte tragen

frugal [ˈfruːgəl] ADJ **a** person, life genügsam; **to be ~ with one's money** sparsam mit seinem Geld umgehen **b** meal karg; food, diet frugal (*geh*), bescheiden

frugality [fruːˈgælɪtɪ] N **a** (of person) Genügsamkeit *f*; (= thrift) Sparsamkeit *f*; **a life of great ~** ein sehr genügsames Leben **b** (of meal) Kargheit *f*; (of food, diet) Bescheidenheit *f*, Frugalität *f* (*geh*)

frugally [ˈfruːgəlɪ] ADV live genügsam; use sparsam; eat sehr wenig

fruit [fruːt] N **a** (as collective) Obst *nt*; (*Bot, fig*) Frucht *f*; **is it a ~ or a vegetable?** ist es Obst oder Gemüse?; **what is your favourite** (*Brit*) *or* **favorite** (*US*) **~?** welches Obst magst du am liebsten?; **would you like some** *or* **a piece of ~?** möchten Sie etwas Obst?; **the ~s of the earth** die Früchte *pl* des Feldes; **to bear ~** (*lit, fig*) Früchte tragen; **the ~(s) of my labour/success** die Früchte *pl* meiner Arbeit/meines Erfolgs; **this project is the first ~ of our cooperation** dieses Projekt ist die erste Frucht unserer Zusammenarbeit (*geh*)
　b (dated Brit inf) old ~ alter Knabe (*inf*)
　c (US pej sl, = homosexual) Süße(r) *m* (*inf*), warmer Bruder (*inf*)
　VI Früchte tragen

fruit: fruit bat N Flughund *m*; **fruit bowl** N Obstschale *f*; **fruitcake** N englischer Kuchen; (esp Brit inf: = eccentric) Spinner(in) *m(f)* (*inf*); **as nutty as a ~** (esp Brit inf) total verrückt; **fruit cocktail** N Obstsalat *m*; **fruit cup** N **a** (= drink) Cocktail *m* mit Früchten **b** (US) Frucht- or Früchtebecher *m*; **fruit dish** N Obstteller *m*; **fruit drop** N Drops *m*, Früchtebonbon *m* or *nt*

fruiterer [ˈfruːtərəʳ] N (esp Brit) Obsthändler(in) *m(f)*

fruit: fruit farmer N Obstbauer *m*/-bäuerin *f*; **fruit farming** N Obstanbau *m*; **fruit fly** N Fruchtfliege *f*, Taufliege *f*

fruitful [ˈfruːtfʊl] ADJ **a** (= profitable) relationship, collaboration, talks, meeting fruchtbar; life, career produktiv; (= successful) attempt, inquiries erfolgreich; **it would be more ~ to wait until January** man hätte mehr davon, den Januar abzuwarten; **a ~ source of material** eine ergiebige Materialquelle **b** (*Agr, Bot*) land, plant, growth fruchtbar, ertragreich

fruitfully [ˈfruːtfəlɪ] ADV (= usefully) nutzbringend; (= advantageously) vorteilhaft

fruitfulness [ˈfruːtfʊlnɪs] N (lit, fig) Fruchtbarkeit *f*

fruition [fruːˈɪʃən] N (of aims, plans, ideas) Erfüllung *f*, Verwirklichung *f*; **to come to ~** sich verwirklichen; **to bring sth to ~** etw verwirklichen

fruit jar N Einmachglas *nt*, Einweckglas *nt*

fruit knife N Obstmesser *nt*

fruitless [ˈfruːtlɪs] ADJ **a** (= vain) search, talks, effort, morning, hour fruchtlos, erfolglos; attempt vergeblich; **to spend long and ~ hours searching** stundenlang vergeblich suchen; **it's a ~ exercise** es ist verlorene Mühe; **it is ~ to try** es ist

zwecklos *or* sinnlos, es zu versuchen; **to prove ~** sich als erfolglos *or* vergeblich erweisen **b** (*Bot*, = infertile) unfruchtbar

fruit: fruit machine N (*Brit*) Spielautomat *m*; **fruit salad** N Obstsalat *m*; (fig inf) Lametta *nt*; **fruit sugar** N Fruchtzucker *m*; **fruit tree** N Obstbaum *m*

fruity [ˈfruːtɪ] ADJ (+er) **a** taste, wine, oil, smell fruchtig **b** (= deep) voice volltönend **c** (inf, = lewd) remark, joke anzüglich **d** (inf, = crazy) bekloppt (*inf*); **she's ~** sie spinnt (*inf*) **e** (dated US, pej sl, = homosexual) schwul (*inf*)

frump [frʌmp] N (pej) Vogelscheuche *f* (*inf*); **old ~** alte Schachtel (*inf*)

frumpish [ˈfrʌmpɪʃ], **frumpy** [ˈfrʌmpɪ] ADJ (pej) ohne jeden Schick

frustrate [frʌˈstreɪt] VT person frustrieren; hopes zunichte machen; plans, plot durchkreuzen, zerstören; **he was ~d in his efforts** seine Anstrengungen waren umsonst *or* vergebens; **rescuers were ~d in their search by bad weather** die Retter wurden durch schlechtes Wetter bei der Suche behindert

frustrated [frʌˈstreɪtɪd] ADJ frustriert; **I get ~ when people criticize my work** es frustriert mich, wenn meine Arbeit kritisiert wird; **he's a ~ poet/intellectual** er wäre gern ein Dichter/Intellektueller

frustrating [frʌˈstreɪtɪŋ] ADJ frustrierend; **it's so ~** das ist alles so frustrierend, so ein Frust (*inf*)

frustratingly [frʌˈstreɪtɪŋlɪ] ADV slow, complex frustrierend

frustration [frʌˈstreɪʃən] N Frustration *f* no pl; (of hopes, plans, plot) Zerschlagung *f*; **the ~s of city life** die Frustration *or* der Frust (*inf*) des Stadtlebens; **he has had many ~s during the course of this project** er hat im Verlauf dieses Projektes viele Rückschläge erlebt

fry¹ [fraɪ] PL (= fish) kleine Fische *pl*

fry² VT **a** meat etc (in der Pfanne) braten; **to ~ an egg** ein Spiegelei machen, ein Ei in die Pfanne schlagen **b** (US, inf: = electrocute) auf dem elektrischen Stuhl hinrichten VI **a** (meat etc) braten; **we're absolutely ~ing in this heat** (inf) wir schmoren (in dieser Hitze) (*inf*) **b** (US, inf) auf dem elektrischen Stuhl hingerichtet werden N (US) Barbecue *nt*

▶ **fry up** VT sep (auf)braten, in die Pfanne hauen (*inf*)

frying pan [ˈfraɪŋˌpæn] N Bratpfanne *f*; **to jump out of the ~ into the fire** (Prov) vom Regen in die Traufe kommen (Prov)

fry-up [ˈfraɪʌp] N Pfannengericht *nt*; **to have a ~** sich (*dat*) etwas zusammenbrutzeln (*inf*)

f-stop [ˈefstɒp] N (*Phot*) Blende *f*

FT abbr of **Financial Times**

ft **a** abbr of **foot** ft **b** abbr of **feet** ft

FTC (US) abbr of **Federal Trade Commission**

FTP, ftp (*Comput*) abbr of **file transfer protocol** FTP *nt*

fuchsia [ˈfjuːʃə] N Fuchsie *f*

fuck [fʌk] (vulg) VT **a** (lit) ficken (*vulg*)
　b **you can get ~ed!**, **~ you!** leck mich am Arsch (*vulg*); **~ him!** der kann mich doch am Arsch lecken (*vulg*); **~ what he thinks!** ich scheiß was auf seine Meinung (*sl*); **~ this car!** dieses Scheißauto! (*inf*); **~ me, he didn't say that, did he?** leck mich am Arsch, das hat der wirklich gesagt? (*sl*)
　VI ficken (*vulg*)
　N **a** (lit) Fick *m* (*vulg*); **to have a ~** ficken (*vulg*); **she's a good ~** sie fickt gut (*vulg*)
　b **I don't give a ~** ich kümmere mich einen Scheiß darum (*inf*); **who/what/where the ~ is that?** wer/was/wo ist denn das, verdammt noch mal? (*inf*); **it hurts like ~** es tut verdammt weh (*inf*); **like ~ he will!** das werden wir erst noch sehen, verdammt noch mal! (*inf*); **shut the ~ up!** halt die Schnauze, verdammt noch mal! (*inf*)
　INTERJ (verdammte) Scheiße (*inf*), Herrgottsack (*S Ger vulg*)

▶ **fuck about** (Brit vulg) VI rumgammeln (*inf*); **to fuck about with sb** jdn verarschen (*inf*); **someone's been fucking about with the engine** verdammt, da hat irgend so ein Arsch am Motor rumgefummelt (*sl*) VT sep verarschen (*inf*)

▶ **fuck around** VI (vulg) **a** herumficken (*vulg*) **b** = **fuck about**

▶ **fuck off** VI (vulg) sich verpissen (*sl*); **fuck off!** verpiss dich! (*sl*), hau ab, du Arsch! (*sl*)

▶ **fuck up** (vulg) VT sep versauen (*inf*); piece of work, life verpfuschen (*inf*); **you've really fucked me up** (= let down, spoiled plans etc) du hast mir die Sache echt versaut (*inf*); **she is really fucked up** (psychologically) sie ist total verkorkst (*inf*); **heroin will really fuck you up** Heroin macht dich echt kaputt (*inf*) VI Scheiß machen (*inf*)

fuck-all [ˈfʌkɔːl] (vulg) N einen Scheiß (*sl*); **he knows ~ about it** er hat null Ahnung (*inf*); **it's got ~ to do with him** einen Scheiß hat das mit ihm zu tun (*sl*); **there was ~ to drink** es gab nichts zum Saufen (*inf*); **I've done ~ all day** ich hab den ganzen Tag nichts geschafft gekriegt (*inf*) ADJ attr **that's ~ use** das ist ja vielleicht ein Scheiß (*inf*) *or* total beknackt (*sl*) *or* fürn Arsch (*sl*); **he's got ~ idea how to do it** er hat null Ahnung, wie er das machen soll (*inf*)

fucker [ˈfʌkəʳ] N (vulg) Arsch *m* (*vulg*), Arschloch *nt* (*vulg*), Saftsack *m* (*inf*)

fucking [ˈfʌkɪŋ] (vulg) ADJ Scheiß- (*inf*); **this ~ machine** diese Scheißmaschine (*inf*); **~ hell!** verdammte Scheiße! (*inf*) ADV **a** (intensifying) **it's ~ cold** es ist arschkalt (*inf*); **a ~ awful film** ein total beschissener Film (*inf*) **b** (expressing annoyance) **I don't ~ believe this** verdammte Scheiße, das darf doch nicht wahr sein! (*inf*)

fuck-up [ˈfʌkʌp] N (vulg) **what a ~!** was für eine (totale) Scheiße! (*inf*); **there's been a ~** da hat einer Scheiße gebaut (*inf*)

fuddled [ˈfʌdld] ADJ (= muddled) verwirrt, verdattert (*inf*); (= tipsy) bedüdelt (*inf*), beschwipst, angesäuselt

fuddy-duddy [ˈfʌdɪˌdʌdɪ] (inf) ADJ verknöchert, verkalkt N komischer Kauz (*inf*); **an old ~** alter Kauz

fudge [fʌdʒ] N **a** (Cook) Fondant *m* **b** (Press, = space for stop press) Spalte *f* für letzte Meldungen; (= stop press news) letzte Meldungen *pl* **c** **her answer was a ~** ihre Antwort war ein Ausweichmanöver VT **a** (= fake up) story, excuse sich (*dat*) aus den Fingern saugen, (frei) erfinden **b** (= dodge) question, issue, problem ausweichen (+*dat*), um die Wege gehen (+*dat*) **c** **to ~ the books** die Bücher frisieren (*inf*)

fuel [fjʊəl] N Brennstoff *m*, Brennmaterial *nt*; (for vehicle) Kraftstoff *m*; (= petrol) Benzin *nt*; (Aviat, Space) Treibstoff *m*; (fig) Nahrung *f*; **to add ~ to the flames** *or* **fire** (fig) Öl in die Flammen *or* ins Feuer gießen; **what kind of ~ do you use in your central heating?** womit betreiben Sie Ihre Zentralheizung? → **solid fuel**
　VT **a** (= fill) stove, furnace etc mit Brennstoff versorgen; ships etc auftanken, betanken; (= use for fuel) betreiben; (= drive, propel) antreiben; (fig) conflict schüren; debate anfachen; inflation anheizen; speculation Nahrung geben (+*dat*); **power stations ~led** (Brit) *or* **~ed** (US) **by oil** mit Öl befeuerte Kraftwerke; **~led** (Brit) *or* **~ed** (US) **by memories** von Erinnerungen angefacht; **~led** (Brit) *or* **~ed** (US) **by drink** vom Alkohol angetrieben
　VI (ship, engine, aircraft) auftanken, Brennstoff/Treibstoff etc aufnehmen; **~ling stop** Landung *f* zum Auftanken

fuel: fuel cell N Brennstoffzelle *f*; **fuel cock** N Treibstoffhahn *m*; **fuel consumption** N Kraftstoff- or Benzinverbrauch *m*; **fuel gauge** N Benzinuhr *f*, Tankuhr *f*

fueling station [ˈfjʊəlɪŋˌsteɪʃən] N (US) Tankstelle *f*

fuel: fuel-injected ADJ Einspritz-; **~ engine** Einspritzmotor *m*; **fuel injection** N (Benzin)einspritzung *f*; **engine with ~** Einspritzmotor *m*; **fuel oil** N Gasöl *nt*; **fuel pipe** N Benzinleitung *f*; **fuel pump** N Benzinpumpe *f*; **fuel rod** N Brennstab *m*; **fuel shortage** N Brennstoffknappheit *f*; **fuel tank** N Öltank *m*

fug [fʌg] N (*esp Brit, inf*) Mief *m* (*inf*)

fuggy ['fʌgɪ] ADJ (*+er*) (*esp Brit, inf*) muffig, miefig (*inf*)

fugitive ['fjuːdʒɪtɪv] **N** (= *runaway*) Flüchtling *m* (*from* vor +*dat*); **he is a ~ from justice** er ist auf der Flucht vor der Justiz **ADJ** **a** (= *escaping*) flüchtig; **~ vehicle** Fluchtfahrzeug *nt* **b** (*liter, = fleeting*) thought, happiness, hour, visit flüchtig

fugue [fjuːg] N (*Mus*) Fuge *f*

fulcrum ['fʌlkrəm] N Dreh- *or* Stützpunkt *m*; (*fig, of argument, plan, organization*) Angelpunkt *m*

fulfil, (*US*) **fulfill** [fʊl'fɪl] VT erfüllen; *task, order* ausführen; *ambition* verwirklichen; **the prophecy was ~led** die Prophezeiung erfüllte sich; **being a mother didn't ~ her** sein fand im Muttersein keine Erfüllung; **to be** *or* **feel ~led** Erfüllung finden; **to ~ oneself** sich selbst verwirklichen

fulfilling [fʊl'fɪlɪŋ] ADJ **a ~ job** ein Beruf, in dem man Erfüllung findet

fulfilment, (*US*) **fulfillment** [fʊl'fɪlmənt] N Erfüllung *f*; **to bring sth to ~** etw zur Erfüllung bringen; **to come to ~** in Erfüllung gehen; (*life's work*) seine Erfüllung finden; **to lead to the ~ of sth** etw in Erfüllung gehen lassen

full [fʊl] **ADJ** (*+er*) **a** (= *filled*) room, theatre, train voll; **to be ~ of ...** voller (+*gen*) *or* voll von ... sein, voll sein mit ...; **he's ~ of good ideas** er steckt voll(er) guter Ideen; **a look ~ of hate** ein hasserfüllter Blick, ein Blick voller Hass; **his heart was ~** (*liter*) das Herz lief ihm über; **don't talk with your mouth ~** sprich nicht mit vollem Mund; **with his arms ~** mit voll geladenen Armen; **I have a ~ day ahead of me** ich habe einen ausgefüllten Tag vor mir; **I am ~ (up)** (*inf*) ich bin (papp)satt, ich bin voll (bis obenhin) (*inf*); **we are ~ up for July** wir sind für Juli völlig ausgebucht

b (= *maximum, complete*) voll; *description, report* vollständig; *understanding, sympathy* vollste(r, s); **at ~ speed** in voller Fahrt; **roses in ~ bloom** Rosen in voller Blüte; **to make ~ use of sth** etw voll ausnutzen; **that's a ~ day's work** damit habe ich *etc* den ganzen Tag zu tun; **I need a ~ night's sleep** ich muss mich (ein)mal gründlich ausschlafen; **to be in ~ flight** kopflos fliehen; **battalion at ~ strength** Bataillon in Sollstärke; **I waited two ~ hours** ich habe geschlagene zwei *or* zwei ganze Stunden gewartet; **the ~ details** die genauen *or* alle Einzelheiten; **a ~ colonel** ein Oberst *m*; **to run ~ tilt into sth** mit voller Wucht in etw (*acc*) *or* auf etw (*acc*) rennen; **to go at ~ tilt** rasen, Volldampf (*inf*) *or* volle Pulle (*inf*) fahren; **shots of the Rocky Mountains in ~ colour** (*Brit*) *or* **color** (*US*) schöne Farbaufnahmen von den Rocky Mountains

c (= *preoccupied*) **to be ~ of oneself** von sich (selbst) eingenommen sein, nur sich selbst im Kopf haben; **she was ~ of it** sie hat gar nicht mehr aufgehört, davon zu reden; **the papers were ~ of it for weeks** die Zeitungen waren wochenlang voll davon; **he's always so ~ of what he's going to do** er ist dauernd so von seinen Plänen dran (*inf*)

d (= *rounded*) lips, face voll; *figure, skirt etc* füllig; (*Naut*) sails voll, gebläht

ADV a (= *at least*) **it is a ~ five miles from here** es sind volle *or* gute fünf Meilen von hier

b (= *very, perfectly*) **I know ~ well that ...** ich weiß sehr wohl, dass ...

c (= *directly*) **to hit sb ~ in the face** jdn voll ins Gesicht schlagen; **to look sb ~ in the face** jdm voll in die Augen sehen; **she kissed him ~ on the mouth** sie küsste ihn voll auf den Mund

d ~ out (*work*) auf Hochtouren; *drive* mit Vollgas

N a in ~ ganz, vollständig; **to write one's name in ~** seinen Namen ausschreiben; **to pay in ~** den vollen Betrag bezahlen

b to the ~ vollständig, total

full: full age N (*Jur*) Mündigkeit *f*, Volljährigkeit *f*; **of ~** = mündig, volljährig; **fullback** N (*Sport*) Verteidiger(in) *m(f)*; **full beam** N (*Brit, Aut*) Fernlicht *nt*; **to drive (with one's headlights) on ~** mit Fernlicht fahren; **full-blooded** [fʊl'blʌdɪd] ADJ (= *vigorous*) kräftig; **he's a ~ German/Scot** er ist Vollblutdeutscher/-schotte; **full-blown** ADJ **a** (= *thoroughgoing*) recession, crisis, love affair, war richtiggehend; *scandal* ausgewachsen; *investigation* gründlich; *independence* voll; *heart attack* richtig; (= *fully qualified*) doctor voll qualifiziert; **the ~ disease** die Krankheit im Vollbild; **~ Aids** Vollbild-Aids *nt*; **b** (*Bot*) *flower* voll aufgeblüht; **full-bodied** ['fʊl'bɒdɪd] ADJ *wine* schwer, vollmundig; *woman* füllig; **full-court press** N (*US fig inf*) **to give sb the ~** jdn stark unter Druck setzen; **full-cream milk** N Vollmilch *f*; **full denture** N (*Med*) Vollprothese *f*; **full-dress** ['fʊldres] ADJ **a** *clothes* Gala-; **~ uniform** Galauniform *f* **b** (*fig, = important, ceremonious*) **~ debate** wichtige Debatte; **full employment** N Vollbeschäftigung *f*

fuller's earth [ˌfʊləz'ɜːθ] N Fullererde *f*, Bleicherde *f*

full: full-face **ADJ** *portrait* mit zugewandtem Gesicht; **~ photograph** En-Face-Foto *nt* (*spec*); **~ helmet** Integralhelm *m* **ADV** en face (*spec*); **she turned ~ to me** sie wandte sich mir voll zu; **she looked ~ at him** sie sah ihm direkt ins Gesicht; **full-faced** ADJ rundgesichtig; **full-flavoured**, (*US*) **full-flavored** ADJ vollmundig; **full-fledged** ADJ (*US*) = **fully fledged**; **full frontal** N Nacktdarstellung *f*; **full-frontal** ADJ Nackt-; (*fig*) *assault* direkt; **the ~ nudity in this play** die völlig nackten Schauspieler in diesem Stück; **~ photograph** Nacktfoto *nt*; **full-grown** ADJ ausgewachsen; **full house** N (*Theat*) ausverkaufte Vorstellung; (*Cards*) Fullhouse *nt*; **each night they played to a ~** sie spielten jeden Abend vor vollem Haus; **full-length** **ADJ** **a** *play, film, video* abendfüllend; *novel, album* vollständig **b** *coat, dress, skirt* (boden)lang; *boots* hoch; *curtains* bodenlang; **~ mirror** großer Spiegel *m*, (in dem man sich ganz sehen kann); **~ portrait** Ganzporträt *nt* **ADV** *lie* (lang) ausgestreckt; **to dive ~** einen Hechtsprung machen; **to stretch oneself ~** sich lang ausstrecken; **to fall ~** der Länge nach hinfallen; **full-lipped** ADJ volllippig; **full member** N Vollmitglied *nt*; **full moon** N Vollmond *m*; **full-mouthed** ['fʊl'maʊðd] ADJ *cattle* mit vollem Gebiss; (*fig*) *person* lautstark; **full name** N Vor- und Zuname *m*

fullness ['fʊlnɪs] N (*of detail, description*) Vollständigkeit *f*; (*of voice*) Klangfülle *f*; (*of colour*) Sattheit *f*; (*of sound*) Fülle *f*; (*of flavour*) Vollmundigkeit *f*; (*of skirt*) Fülle *f*, Weite *f*; **out of the ~ of his heart** (*liter*) aus der Fülle seines Herzens (*liter*); **this cut gives some ~ to the hairstyle** dieser Schnitt gibt der Frisur Fülle; **in the ~ of time** (= *eventually*) zu gegebener Zeit; (= *at predestined time*) da *or* als die Zeit gekommen war, da *or* als die Zeit erfüllt war

full: full-on **ADJ** (*inf*) total (*inf*); **full-page** ADJ *advertisement etc* ganzseitig; **full pay** N **to be suspended on ~** unter Fortzahlung der vollen Bezüge suspendiert sein; **full point** N (*Gram*) = **full stop**; **full professor** N (*Univ*) Ordinarius *m*; **full-scale** ADJ **a** (= *thoroughgoing*) war, riot, offensive, invasion richtiggehend; *investigation, inquiry, review* gründlich; *search* groß angelegt; *production* serienmäßig; *debate, negotiations, report* umfassend; **they are in ~ retreat** (*lit, fig*) sie haben auf der ganzen Linie den Rückzug angetreten **b** (= *life-size*) *drawing, model* in Originalgröße; **full-size(d)** ADJ *bicycle, violin etc* richtig (groß); **full-sized** ADJ *model, drawing* lebensgroß; **full stop** N (*esp Brit Gram*) Punkt *m*; **to come to a ~** zum völligen Stillstand kommen; **I'm not going, ~!** (*inf*) ich gehe nicht und damit basta (*inf*); **full term** N (*of pregnancy*) volle Schwangerschaftszeit; **full-term** **ADJ** *baby* nach der vollen Schwangerschaftszeit geboren; *pregnancy* von voller Länge; *delivery, birth* nach der vollen Schwangerschaftszeit **ADV** **to be carried ~** (*baby*) nach

der vollen Schwangerschaftszeit geboren werden; **to go ~** (*woman*) eine Schwangerschaft von voller Länge haben; **full time** **N** (*Sport*) reguläre Spielzeit; **at ~** nach Ablauf der regulären Spielzeit; **the whistle blew for ~** das Spiel wurde abgepfiffen **ADV** *work* ganztags; *study* voll; **full-time** ADJ **a** *secretary, worker* ganztags angestellt; **~ job** Ganztagsstelle *f*; **it's a ~ job** (*fig inf*) es hält einen ganz schön auf Trab (*inf*); **~ work** Ganztagsarbeit *f*; **~ student** Vollstudent(in) *m(f)*; **~ mother** Hausfrau *f* und Mutter *f* **b** (*Sport*) **the ~ score** der Schlussstand

fully ['fʊlɪ] ADV **a** (= *completely*) fit, aware, conscious völlig; *developed, operational, qualified* voll; *understand, recover* voll und ganz; *comply, participate* uneingeschränkt; *discuss, describe, answer, brief* ausführlich; **~ automatic** vollautomatisch; **~ pressurized** mit vollem Druckausgleich; **she was ~ aware of my thoughts** sie war sich meiner Gedanken voll (und ganz) bewusst; **~ booked** (ganz *or* völlig) ausgebucht; **~ clothed** (ganz) angezogen; **~ integrated** (*system, service*) voll integriert; (*racially*) ohne jegliche Rassentrennung; **a ~-equipped kitchen** eine komplett ausgestattete Küche; **~ illustrated** vollständig illustriert

b (= *at least*) **~ 200 years** volle *or* gute 200 Jahre; **~ one-quarter of the workers** ein volles *or* gutes Viertel der Arbeiter

fully: fully fashioned ['fʊlɪ'fæʃnd] ADJ *stocking, jumper* mit Passform; **fully fledged** ADJ **a** (*fig*) *member, citizen* richtig; *artist, atheist* richtiggehend; *party* eigenständig; *nazis* ausgewachsen (*inf*); *doctor, teacher etc* vollqualifiziert **b** (*Orn*) *bird* flügge; **fully paid-up** ADJ *member* (*lit*) ohne Beitragsrückstände; (*fig*) eingeschrieben; **fully qualified** ADJ vollqualifiziert *attr*

fulmar ['fʊlmə] N Eissturmvogel *m*

fulminate ['fʊlmɪneɪt] VI (*fig*) wettern, donnern

fulmination [ˌfʊlmɪ'neɪʃən] N Attacke *f*

fulsome ['fʊlsəm] ADJ *praise, tribute, compliment, manner, tone* (= *effusive*) überschwänglich; (= *exaggerated*) apology, support uneingeschränkt; **his most ~ praise** sein höchstes Lob; **he paid ~ tribute to her courage** er würdigte ihren Mut uneingeschränkt; **she was ~ in her praise of the children** sie lobte die Kinder überschwänglich

fulsomely ['fʊlsəmlɪ] ADV *praise, thank* (= *effusively*) überschwänglich; (= *exaggeratedly*) übertrieben; *write, say* in überschwänglichem Ton

fumble ['fʌmbl] **VI** (*also* **fumble about** *or* **around**) umhertasten *or* -tappen; **to ~ in the dark** im Dunkeln herumtasten *or* -tappen; **to ~ in one's pockets** in seinen Taschen wühlen; **to ~ (about) for sth** nach etw suchen *or* tasten; (*in case, pocket, drawer*) nach etw wühlen; **to ~ with sth** an etw (*dat*) herumfummeln; **to ~ for words** nach Worten suchen *or* ringen **VT** vermasseln (*inf*), verpfuschen (*inf*); **to ~ the ball** den Ball nicht sicher fangen

fumbler ['fʌmblə] N Stümper(in) *m(f)*

fumbling ADJ , **fumblingly** ADV ['fʌmblɪŋ, -lɪ] ungeschickt

fume [fjuːm] VI **a** (*liquids*) dampfen, rauchen; (*gases*) aufsteigen **b** (*fig inf, person*) wütend sein, kochen (*inf*)

fumes [fjuːmz] PL Dämpfe *pl*; (*of car*) Abgase *pl*; **petrol** (*Brit*) *or* **gas** (*US*) **~** Benzindämpfe *pl*

fumigate ['fjuːmɪgeɪt] VT ausräuchern

fun [fʌn] **N** (= *amusement*) Spaß *m*; **to have great ~ doing sth** viel Spaß daran haben, etw zu tun, viel Spaß an etw (*dat*) haben; **in ~** (= *as a joke*) im *or* als Scherz; **this is ~!** das macht Spaß *or* Freude!; **I'm not doing it for the ~ of it** ich mache das nicht zu meinem Vergnügen; **we just did it for ~** wir haben das nur aus *or* zum Spaß gemacht; **to spoil the ~** den Spaß verderben; **that takes all the ~ out of it** das nimmt einem den Spaß *or* die Freude daran; **it's ~ doing this/being with him** es macht Spaß, das zu tun/mit ihm zusammen zu sein; **it's not much ~ for the others though** es ist allerdings für die anderen nicht gerade ein Vergnügen;

life's not much ~ sometimes das Leben ist manchmal nicht gerade das reinste Vergnügen; **it's no ~ living on your own/being broke** es macht nicht gerade Spaß, allein zu leben/pleite (*inf*) zu sein; **you're no ~ to be with any more** es macht keinen Spaß mehr, mit dir zusammen zu sein; **he is great ~** man kriegt mit ihm viel Spaß *or* viel zu lachen (*inf*); **the children thought he was great** die Kinder fanden ihn sehr lustig; **the party was good ~** die Party hat viel Spaß gemacht; **what ~!** was für ein Spaß!; **that sounds like ~** das klingt gut; **I wasn't serious, I was just having a bit of ~** das hab ich nicht ernst gemeint, ich hab doch nur Spaß gemacht; **the children had ~ and games at the picnic** die Kinder haben beim Picknick viel Spaß gehabt; **that should be ~ and games** (*iro*) das kann ja (noch) heiter werden (*inf*); **to make ~ of** *or* **poke ~ at sb/sth** sich über jdn/ etw lustig machen; **we had ~ getting the car started** (*inf*) wir hatten ein bisschen Theater, ehe das Auto ansprang (*inf*); **like ~** (*US, inf*) (ja,) Pustekuchen! (*inf*)

ADJ *attr* (*inf*) **squash is a ~ game** Squash macht Spaß; **he's a real ~ person** er ist wirklich ein lustiger Kerl; **that sounds like a ~ idea** das hört sich prima an (*inf*)

function [ˈfʌŋkʃən] **N** **a** (*of heart, tool, word etc*) Funktion *f* **b** (*of person*) Aufgaben *pl*, Pflichten *pl*; **in his ~ as judge** in seiner Eigenschaft als Richter; **his ~ in life** seine Lebensaufgabe **c** (= *meeting*) Veranstaltung *f*; (= *reception*) Empfang *m*; (= *official ceremony*) Feier *f* **d** (*Math*) Funktion *f* **VI** funktionieren; (*heart, kidney, brain also*) arbeiten; **he can't ~ without his morning coffee** ohne seinen Kaffee am Morgen ist er nicht funktionsfähig; **to ~ as** fungieren als; (*person also*) die Rolle des/der ... spielen *or* ausfüllen; (*thing also*) dienen als

functional [ˈfʌŋkʃənəl] **ADJ** **a** (= *able to operate*) funktionsfähig **b** (= *utilitarian*) zweckmäßig, funktionell **c** (*Med*) Funktions-; **~ disorder** Funktionsstörung *f*

functionalism [ˈfʌŋkʃənəlɪzəm] **N** Funktionalismus *m*

functionally [ˈfʌŋkʃənəlɪ] **ADV** *designed* funktionell; **~ efficient** wirksam funktionierend; **~, they are identical/incompatible** sie sind in ihrer Funktion identisch/in ihren Funktionen unvereinbar; **he is ~ illiterate** er kann nicht gut genug lesen und schreiben, um im täglichen Leben zurechtzukommen

functionary [ˈfʌŋkʃə nərɪ] **N** Funktionär(in) *m(f)*

function: function key N (*Comput*) Funktionstaste *f*; **function room N** Veranstaltungsraum *m*

fund [fʌnd] **N** **a** (*Fin*) Fonds *m*; **to start a ~** einen Fonds einrichten *or* gründen
b **funds** PL Mittel *pl*, Gelder *pl*; **public ~s** öffentliche Mittel, Staatsgelder *pl*; **no ~s** (*Banking*) keine Deckung; **to be in ~** zahlungsfähig *or* bei Kasse (*inf*) sein; **to be pressed for ~s, to be short of ~s** knapp bei Kasse sein (*inf*); **at the moment I haven't the ~s** mir fehlen zur Zeit die Mittel *or* Gelder *pl*; **how are we off for ~s at the moment?** wie steht die Kasse zur Zeit?
c (= *supply: of wisdom, humour etc*) Schatz *m* (*of* von +*gen*), Vorrat *m* (*of an* +*dat*)
d **funds** PL (*Brit*, = *government securities*) Staatspapiere *pl*
VT a *debt* ausgleichen, bezahlen; (= *put up money for*) *scheme, project* finanzieren
b (= *invest*) *money* anlegen, investieren

fundage [ˈfʌndɪdʒ] **N** (*US sl*: = *money*) Knete *f* (*inf*)

fundament [ˈfʌndəmənt] **N** **a** (*lit, fig*: = *foundation*) Fundament *nt* **b** (*euph, hum*: = *buttocks*) vier Buchstaben (*inf*)

fundamental [ˌfʌndəˈmentl] ✪ 26.1 **ADJ** **a** (= *essential*) *issue, question, concept* grundlegend; *reason* eigentlich; *point* zentral; *feature, part* wesentlich; **~ principle/right/beliefs** Grundprinzip *nt*/-recht *nt*/-überzeugungen *pl*; **~ mathematical concepts** Grundbegriffe *pl* der Mathema-

tik; **of ~ importance** von grundlegender Bedeutung; **carbon is ~ to life** Kohlenstoff ist für alles Leben grundlegend; **~ to impressionism was the use of bright colours** die Verwendung von leuchtenden Farben war grundlegend für den Impressionismus
b (= *basic*) *problem, difference, contradiction* grundsätzlich; (= *basic and deep*) *change, revolution, shift* grundlegend, umwälzend; (= *elementary*) *mistake, error, flaw* grundlegend, fundamental; **I don't doubt his ~ goodness** ich zweifle nicht daran, dass er im Grunde ein guter Mensch ist; **his ~ ignorance of this subject** seine fundamentale Unkenntnis auf diesem Gebiet; **~ structure/form** Grundstruktur *f*/-form *f*; **~ research** Grundlagenforschung *f*
c (*Mus*) Grund-; **~ note/frequency** Grundton *m*/-frequenz *f*
PL **~s** (*of subject*) Grundbegriffe *pl*; (*of a problem*) Grundlagen *pl*; **the ~s of physics** die Grundbegriffe *pl* der Physik; **to get down to (the) ~s** bis zu den Grundlagen vordringen

fundamentalism [ˌfʌndəˈmentəlɪzəm] **N** Fundamentalismus *m*

fundamentalist [ˌfʌndəˈmentəlɪst] **ADJ** fundamentalistisch **N** Fundamentalist(in) *m(f)*

fundamentally [ˌfʌndəˈmentəlɪ] **ADV** **a** (= *essentially*) im Grunde (genommen); *different, wrong, flawed* grundlegend; **~ different views** grundlegend *or* vom Grund auf unterschiedliche Ansichten; **the treaty is ~ flawed** der Vertrag enthält grundlegende Fehler; **~, he is a bully** er ist im Grunde genommen ein Tyrann; **is man ~ good?** ist der Mensch im Grunde gut?; **~ important** von grundlegender Bedeutung **b** (= *radically*) *change, affect* grundlegend; *disagree* grundsätzlich; **I am ~ opposed to it** ich bin grundsätzlich dagegen; **we differ quite ~ on this** wir haben dazu grundverschiedene Ansichten

fundamental particle N (*Phys*) Elementarteilchen *nt*

fund: fundholding ADJ (*Brit*) **~ doctor** *or* **GP** *Arzt, der die Finanzen seiner Praxis selbst verwaltet*; **fundraiser N** Spendenbeschaffer(in) *m(f)*, Spendensammler(in) *m(f)*; **fundraising N** Geldbeschaffung *f*; **~ campaign** Aktion *f* zur Geldbeschaffung; (*for donations*) Spendenaktion *f*

funeral [ˈfjuːnə rəl] **N** Begräbnis *nt*, Beerdigung *f*, Beisetzung *f* (*form*); **were you at his ~?** waren Sie auf seiner Beerdigung?; **well, that's your ~** (*inf*) na ja, das ist dein persönliches Pech (*inf*), das ist dein Problem (*inf*)

funeral: funeral director N Beerdigungsunternehmer(in) *m(f)*; **funeral home N** (*US*) Leichenhalle *f*; **funeral march N** Trauermarsch *m*; **funeral parlour N** (*Brit*) Leichenhalle *f*; **funeral procession N** Leichenzug *m*; **funeral pyre N** Scheiterhaufen *m*; **funeral service N** Trauergottesdienst *m*

funereal [fjuːˈnɪərɪəl] **ADJ** traurig, trübselig; **~ silence** Grabesstille *f*

funfair [ˈfʌnfeəˈ] **N** Kirmes *f*

fungal [ˈfʌŋgəl] **ADJ** Pilz-; **~ infection** Pilzinfektion *f*

fungi [ˈfʌŋgaɪ] *pl of* **fungus**

fungicide [ˈfʌndʒɪsaɪd] **N** Fungizid *nt*, pilztötendes Mittel

fungoid [ˈfʌŋgɔɪd], **fungous** [ˈfʌŋgəs] **ADJ** schwammartig

fungus [ˈfʌŋgəs] **N** *pl* **fungi** (*Bot, Med*) Pilz *m*

fun house N (*esp US*) Rummelplatzattraktion *mit Räumen mit beweglichen Böden, Zerrspiegeln etc*

funicular (railway) [fjuːˈnɪkjʊlə(ˈreɪlweɪ)] **N** Seilbahn *f*

funk [fʌŋk] **N** **a** (*esp Brit, inf*, = *fear*) Schiss *m* (*inf*), Bammel *m* (*inf*); **to be in a (blue) ~** (vor Angst) die Hosen voll haben (*inf*), mächtig *or* ganz schön Schiss *or* Bammel haben (*inf*); **to put sb in a (blue) ~** jdm mächtig Bammel einjagen (*inf*) **b** (*Mus*) Funk *m* **VT** kneifen vor

(+*dat*) (*inf*); **he ~ed it** er hat (davor) gekniffen (*inf*)

funky [ˈfʌŋkɪ] **ADJ** (+*er*) **a** (*inf*) *music, person, clothes* geil (*sl*), funky (*sl*); **~ beat** (*inf*) Funkrhythmus *m* **b** (*dated US, sl*, = *terrified*) **to be ~** (fürchterlich) Schiss haben (*sl*) **c** (*esp Brit, inf*, = *cowardly*) feige, ängstlich **d** (*US inf*: = *smelly*) mufflig (*inf*); *air* miefig (*inf*)

fun-loving [ˈfʌnlʌvɪŋ] **ADJ** lebenslustig; **a ~ girl** (*euph*) ein lebenshungriges Mädchen

funnel [ˈfʌnl] **N** **a** (*for pouring*) Trichter *m* **b** (*Naut, Rail*) Schornstein *m*; **two-funnelled** (*Brit*) *or* **two-funneled** (*US*) **steamer** Dampfer *m* mit zwei Schornsteinen **c** (*US*, = *ventilation shaft etc*) Luftschacht *m* **VT** *liquid, grain* leiten; (*fig*) *attention, energies, information, funds* schleusen

funnies [ˈfʌnɪz] **PL** (*esp US inf*: *in newspaper*) Comics *pl*, Comic-Teil *m*

funnily [ˈfʌnɪlɪ] **ADV** **a** (= *strangely*) komisch, merkwürdig; **~ enough** komischerweise, merkwürdigerweise **b** (= *amusingly*) amüsant

funny [ˈfʌnɪ] **ADJ** (+*er*) **a** (= *comical*) komisch, lustig; *person* witzig; **don't try to be ~** (*inf*) mach keine Witze!; **don't get ~ with me** (*inf*) komm mir bloß nicht komisch; **to see the ~ side of sth** das Lustige an etw (*dat*) sehen; **what's so ~?** was ist denn so komisch *or* lustig?; **it's not ~!** das ist überhaupt nicht komisch *or* zum Lachen!
b (= *bizarre, odd*) komisch; **she gave him a ~ look** sie sah ihn komisch an; **to have ~ ideas about sth** merkwürdige Vorstellungen von etw haben; **there's something ~ about that place** der Ort ist irgendwie merkwürdig *or* seltsam; **I have a ~ feeling I'm going to regret this** ich habe das komische Gefühl, dass mir das noch Leid tun wird; **(it's) ~ (that) you should say that** komisch, dass Sie das sagen; **it's ~ but I feel as if I've known you a long time** komisch, ich habe das Gefühl, dass ich dich schon lange kenne; **(that's) ~! I thought he'd left** komisch! ich dachte, er ist schon weg; **the ~ thing is that he was right** das Komische ist, dass er Recht hatte; **to go all ~** (*inf*, = *go wrong*) verrückt spielen (*inf*); **I just feel a bit ~** (*inf*) mir ist ein bisschen komisch *or* mulmig (*inf*); **I feel ~ about seeing her again** (*inf*) mir ist komisch dabei zumute *or* zu Mute, sie wiederzusehen; **it's a ~ old world** ganz schön komisch *or* merkwürdig!; **~-peculiar** *or* **~-ha-ha?** (*inf*) komisch im Sinne von seltsam *or* lustig?
c (*inf*, = *mad*) *person* merkwürdig; **she's a bit ~ (in the head)** sie spinnt ein bisschen (*inf*)
d (*inf*, = *suspicious*) **~ business** *or* **tricks** faule Sachen *pl or* Tricks *pl* (*inf*); **there's something ~ going on here** hier ist doch was faul (*inf*); **don't try anything ~** keine faulen Tricks! (*inf*)
PL **the funnies** (*US Press inf*) die Cartoons *pl*, die Comicstrips *pl*

funny: funny bone N Musikantenknochen *m*; **funny cigarette N** (*inf*) Joint *m* (*inf*); **funny farm N** (*inf*) Klapsmühle *f* (*inf*); **funny girl N** (*inf*, = *comedienne*) Komikerin *f*; **funny handshake N** (*inf*) besonderer, von Freimaurern verwendeter Händedruck; **funny man N** (*inf*, = *comedian*) Komiker *m*; **funny money N** ein Wahnsinnsgeld *nt* (*inf*); **funny paper N** (*US*) Witzseiten *pl*

fun run N Volkslauf *m* (*oft für wohltätige Zwecke durchgeführt*)

fur [fɜː'] **N** **a** (*on animal*) Fell *nt*, Pelz *m*; (*for clothing*) Pelz *m*; **the cat has beautiful ~** die Katze hat ein wunderschönes Fell; **that will really make the ~ fly** (*inf*) da werden die Fetzen fliegen (*inf*); **a ~-lined coat** ein pelzgefütterter Mantel **b** **furs** PL Pelze *pl* **c** (*in kettle etc*) Kesselstein *m*; (*Med, on tongue*) Belag *m* **ATTR** Pelz-; **~ coat/collar** Pelzmantel *m*/-kragen *m*; **the ~ trade** der Pelzhandel

▶ **fur up VI** (*washing machine, veins, arteries*) verkalken; (*kettle, boiler*) verkalken, Kesselstein ansetzen; (*tongue*) pelzig werden **VT** *veins, arteries* verkalken lassen; **to be furred up** (*tongue*) belegt *or* pelzig sein; (*veins, arteries, washing machine, kettle, boiler*) verkalkt sein

furbelow ['fɜːbɪləʊ] N **a** (old) Falbel f, Faltenbesatz m **b** usu pl **~s** (pej) Firlefanz m

furbish ['fɜːbɪʃ] VT **a** (= polish) blank reiben, (auf)polieren **b** (= smarten up) aufpolieren

furious ['fjʊərɪəs] ADJ **a** (= very angry) person, letter, protest, reaction, row wütend; (= violent) argument, debate, attack, battle heftig; **he was ~ that they had ignored him** er war wütend darüber, dass sie ihn ignoriert hatten; **she was ~ to find that ...** sie war wütend, als sie feststellte, dass ...; **to be ~ about** or **at** or **over sth** wütend über etw (acc) sein; **to be ~ at** or **with sb (for doing sth)** wütend auf jdn sein(, weil er/sie etw getan hat); **she was ~ at being disturbed** sie war wütend darüber, dass sie gestört wurde; **he was ~ with himself for getting drunk** er war wütend auf sich, weil er sich betrunken hatte; **they came under ~ attack** sie wurden scharf angegriffen **b** (= tremendous) pace, speed rasend; **at a ~ pace** in rasendem Tempo; **the car was going at a ~ speed** das Auto fuhr rasend schnell; **the ~ pace of change** die rasend schnellen Veränderungen; **~ activity** wilde Hektik; **fast and ~** rasant; **the jokes came fast and ~** die Witze kamen Schlag auf Schlag; **the punches came fast and ~** es hagelte Schläge

furiously ['fjʊərɪəslɪ] ADV **a** (= angrily) react, argue, say wütend; **~ angry** fuchsteufelswild (inf) **b** (= frantically) work, scribble, beat, search wie wild; **her heart was beating ~** ihr schlug das Herz bis zum Hals; **to work fast and ~** hektisch arbeiten

furl [fɜːl] VT sail, flag einrollen; umbrella zusammenrollen

furlong ['fɜːlɒŋ] N Achtelmeile f

furlough ['fɜːləʊ] N (Mil, Admin) Urlaub m; **to go on ~** in Urlaub gehen

furn abbr of **furnished** möbl.

furnace ['fɜːnɪs] N Hochofen m; (Metal) Schmelzofen m; **this room is like a ~** dieses Zimmer ist ja das reinste Treibhaus

furnish ['fɜːnɪʃ] VT **a** house einrichten; **~ed room** möbliertes Zimmer; **~ed flat** (esp Brit) or **apartment** möblierte Wohnung; **to live in ~ed accommodation** zur Miete wohnen (in einer möblierten Wohnung); **~ing fabrics** Dekorationsstoffe pl **b** information, reason, excuse liefern, geben; **to ~ sb with sth** jdn mit etw versorgen, jdm etw liefern; with reason, excuse jdm etw liefern

furnishings ['fɜːnɪʃɪŋz] PL Mobiliar nt; (with carpets etc) Einrichtung f; **with ~ and fittings** voll eingerichtet

furniture ['fɜːnɪtʃə'] N Möbel pl; **a piece of ~** ein Möbelstück nt; **I must buy some ~** ich muss Möbel kaufen; **one settee and three chairs were all the ~ we had** unsere Einrichtung bestand nur aus einem Sofa und drei Stühlen; **if I stay here much longer, I'll become a part of the ~** wenn ich noch viel länger hier bleibe, gehöre ich bald zum Inventar

furniture: **furniture depository**, **furniture depot** (US) N Möbellager nt; **furniture remover** N Möbelspediteur m; **furniture van** N (Brit) Möbelwagen m

furore [fjʊə'rɔːrɪ], (US) **furor** ['fjʊrɔː'] N Protest(e) m(pl); **to cause a ~** einen Skandal verursachen

furred [fɜːd] ADJ tongue belegt, pelzig

furrier ['fʌrɪə'] N Kürschner(in) m(f)

furrow ['fʌrəʊ] N (Agr) Furche f; (Hort: for flowers etc) Rinne f; (on brow) Runzel f; (on sea) Furche f VT field pflügen; brow runzeln; (worries etc) furchen; (boats) sea Furchen ziehen in (+dat); **the old man's ~ed brow** die zerfurchte Stirn des alten Mannes

furry ['fɜːrɪ] ADJ (+er) **a** body, belly haarig; tail buschig; **~ animal** Tier nt mit Pelz; **~ friend** (hum) vierbeiniger Freund (hum); **the kitten is so soft and ~** das Kätzchen ist so weich und kuschelig; **the soft ~ skin of the seal** das weiche Fell des Seehundes **b** (= like fur) hat, slippers,

material, lining flauschig; **~ dice** Plüschwürfel pl; **~ toy** Plüschtier nt **c** (= coated) tongue belegt; (= scaly) kettle, pipe verkalkt

further ['fɜːðə'] ✪ 19.1, 26.1 ADV comp of **far a** (in place, time, fig) weiter; **~ on** weiter, weiter entfernt; **~ back** (in place, time) weiter zurück; (= in the past) früher; **nothing could be ~ from the truth** nichts könnte weiter von der Wahrheit entfernt sein; **nothing is ~ from my thoughts** nichts liegt mir ferner; **~ and ~ away** immer weiter weg; **to get ~ and ~ away** sich immer weiter entfernen; **we're no ~ advanced now** viel weiter sind wir jetzt (auch) nicht; **he has decided not to take the matter any ~** er hat beschlossen, die Angelegenheit auf sich beruhen zu lassen; **if we take this line of reasoning ~** wenn wir diese Argumente weiterverfolgen; **to look ~ ahead** (fig) weiter in die Zukunft schauen; **in order to make the soup go ~** um die Suppe zu strecken **b** (= more) **he didn't question me ~** er hat mich nicht weiter or mehr gefragt; **and ~ ...** und darüber hinaus ...; **~, I would like to say that ...** darüber hinaus möchte ich sagen, dass ...; **~ to your letter of ...** (Comm) Bezug nehmend auf or in Bezug auf Ihren Brief vom ... (form)

ADJ **a** = farther **b** (= additional) weiter; **to remand a case for ~ inquiry** (Jur) einen Fall zurückstellen, bis weitere Nachforschungen angestellt sind; **will there be anything ~?** kann ich sonst noch etwas für Sie tun?; **~ details** nähere or weitere Einzelheiten pl

VT one's interests, a cause fördern; process vorantreiben; **to ~ one's education** weiterbilden; **to ~ one's career** beruflich vorankommen

furtherance ['fɜːðə rə ns] N Förderung f; **in ~ of sth** zur Förderung einer Sache (gen)

further education N Weiterbildung f, Fortbildung f

furthermore ['fɜːðəmɔː'] ✪ 26.2, 26.3 ADV überdies, außerdem

furthermost ['fɜːðəməʊst] ADJ äußerste(r, s)

furthest ['fɜːðɪst] ADV am weitesten; **these fields are ~ (away) from his farm** diese Felder liegen am weitesten von seinem Hof entfernt; **this is the ~ north you can go** dies ist der nördlichste Punkt, den man erreichen kann; **those who came ~** die, die am weitesten gereist sind; **it was the ~ the Irish team had ever got** so weit war die irische Mannschaft noch nie gekommen; **here prices have fallen ~** hier sind die Preise am meisten or stärksten gefallen; **he went the ~ into this question** er drang am tiefsten in diese Frage ein

ADJ am weitesten entfernt; **the ~ of the three villages** das entfernteste von den drei Dörfern; **in the ~ depths of the forest** in den tiefsten Tiefen des Waldes; **5 km at the ~** höchstens 5 km; **the ~ way round** der weiteste Weg herum; **the ~ distance** die größte Entfernung; **taken to the ~ extent** (fig) zum Äußersten getrieben; **the ~ limits of endurance** die äußersten Grenzen des Durchhaltevermögens

furtive ['fɜːtɪv] ADJ action heimlich; behaviour, person heimlichtuerisch; (= suspicious) verdächtig; look verstohlen; **his ~ eyes** sein ausweichender Blick

furtively ['fɜːtɪvlɪ] ADV look, glance verstohlen; behave verdächtig

furtiveness ['fɜːtɪvnɪs] N (of action) Heimlichkeit f; (of behaviour, person) Heimlichtuerei f; (of look) Verstohlenheit f

fury ['fjʊərɪ] N **a** (of person) Wut f; (of storm also) Ungestüm nt; (of struggle, wind, passion) Heftigkeit f; **in a ~** wütend; **she flew into a ~** sie kam in Rage; **like ~** (inf) wie verrückt (inf) **b** (Myth) **the Furies** die Furien pl

furze [fɜːz] N Stechginster m

fuse, (US) **fuze** [fjuːz] VT **a** metals verschmelzen **b** (Brit, Elec) **to ~ the lights** die Sicherung durchbrennen lassen; **I've ~d the lights** die Sicherung ist durchgebrannt

c (fig) vereinigen, verbinden; (Comm) fusionieren

VI **a** (metals) sich verbinden; (atoms) verschmelzen; (bones) zusammenwachsen **b** (Brit, Elec) durchbrennen; **the lights ~d** die Sicherung war durchgebrannt **c** (fig: also **fuse together**) sich vereinigen

N **a** (Elec) Sicherung f; **to blow the ~s** die Sicherung durchbrennen lassen; **he'll blow a ~** (fig inf) bei dem brennen die Sicherungen durch (inf) **b** (Brit, Elec, = act of fusing) **there's been a ~ somewhere** irgendwo hat es einen Kurzschluss gegeben, da ist irgendwo ein Kurzschluss or Kurzer (inf) **c** (in bombs etc, Min) Zündschnur f; **to light the ~** die Zündschnur anzünden; **this incident lit the ~ which led to the war** dieser Zwischenfall war der Auslöser des Krieges; **she has got** or **is on a short ~** (fig inf) sie explodiert schnell or leicht

fuse box N Sicherungskasten m

fused [fjuːzd] ADJ plug etc gesichert

fuselage ['fjuːzəlɑːʒ] N (Flugzeug)rumpf m

fuse wire N Schmelzdraht m

fusilier [,fjuːzɪ'lɪə'] N (Brit) Füsilier m

fusillade [,fjuːzɪ'leɪd] N Salve f

fusion ['fjuːʒən] N (of metal, fig) Verschmelzung f, Fusion f; (Phys: also **nuclear fusion**) (Kern)fusion f, Kernverschmelzung f

fusion reactor N Fusionsreaktor m

fuss [fʌs] N Theater nt (inf); (= bother also) Umstände pl (inf), Aufheben(s) nt; (= lavish attention) Wirbel m (inf), Getue nt (inf)(of um); **I don't know what all the ~ is about** ich weiß wirklich nicht, was das ganze Getue or der ganze Wirbel soll (inf); **without (any) ~** ohne großes Theater (inf); **to cause a ~** Theater machen (inf); **to make a ~**, **to kick up a ~** Krach schlagen (inf); **to make a ~ about** or **over sth** viel Aufhebens or Wirbel (inf) um etw machen; **to make a ~ of sb** jdn viel Wirbel or Getue machen (inf); **to be in a ~** Zustände haben (inf); **a lot of ~ about nothing** viel Wirbel (inf) or Lärm um nichts

VI sich (unnötig) aufregen; (= get into a fuss) Umstände pl machen; **there's no need to ~ if your son doesn't wear a vest** Sie brauchen nicht gleich Zustände zu kriegen, nur weil Ihr Sohn kein Unterhemd anhat (inf); **don't ~, mother!** ist ja gut, Mutter!; **a mother who ~es unnecessarily** eine übertrieben besorgte Mutter; **with a crowd of attendants ~ing busily around her** mit einer Menge Bediensteter, die eifrig um sie herumhuschten

VT person nervös machen; (= pester) keine Ruhe lassen (+dat); **don't ~ me** lass mich in Ruhe, lass mir meine Ruhe

▶**fuss about** (Brit) or **around** VI herumfuhrwerken (inf)

▶**fuss over** VI +prep obj details Theater machen um; person bemuttern; guests, food sich (dat) große Umstände machen mit

fussbudget ['fʌsbʌdʒɪt] N (US, inf) = fusspot

fussed [fʌst] ADJ (Brit inf) **I'm not ~ (about it)** es ist mir egal; **he wasn't ~ about getting back to Belfast** es war ihm egal, ob er nach Belfast zurückging

fussily ['fʌsɪlɪ] ADV (pej) **a** (= painstakingly) adjust, check übertrieben sorgfältig; accurate peinlich; legalistic übertrieben **b** (= ornately) überladen; **~ designed wrought-iron gates** schmiedeeiserne Tore mit verschnörkeltem Muster; **~ dressed** verspielt gekleidet

fussiness ['fʌsɪnɪs] N **a** (= fastidiousness) peinliche Genauigkeit f; (= pettiness) Kleinlichkeit f; (= preciseness) Genauigkeit f; (= choosiness) wählerische Art; **because of his incredible ~ about what he eats** weil er so unglaublich wählerisch ist, was das Essen angeht **b** (pej: = overelaboration, of details, movements, acting) Übertriebenheit f; (of design, style) überladene Art; (of furnishings, dress) Verspieltheit f

fusspot ['fʌspɒt] N (*Brit inf*) Umstandskrä-
mer(in) *m(f)* (*inf*); (= *nag*) Nörgler(in) *m(f)*

fussy ['fʌsɪ] ADJ (*+er*) **a** (= *choosy*) wählerisch;
(= *petty*) kleinlich; (= *precise*) genau; **to be ~ a-
bout cleanliness/punctuality/one's appearance**
großen Wert auf Sauberkeit/Pünktlichkeit/sein
Äußeres legen; **he was ~ about his toilet paper**
er war sehr eigen, was sein Toilettenpapier an-
ging; **she is not ~ about her food** sie ist beim
Essen nicht wählerisch; **the child is a ~ eater**
das Kind ist beim Essen wählerisch; **I'm not ~**
(*inf*) das ist mir egal **b** (*pej*, = *overelaborate*) *design, style* überladen; *furnishings, dress* verspielt;
food kompliziert; *details, movements, gestures, acting* übertrieben

fustian ['fʌstɪən] **N** (*Tex*) Barchent *m* **ADJ** **a**
(*Tex*) aus Barchent **b** (*fig*, = *pompous*) schwülstig

fusty ['fʌstɪ] ADJ (*+er*) **a** (*pej*, = *old-fashioned*) *person, image, establishment* verstaubt **b** (= *musty*)
muffig

futile ['fjuːtaɪl] ADJ sinnlos; *plan, idea* nutzlos; *effort, attempt* (*usu attr*: = *in vain*) vergeblich; (*usu
pred*: = *pointless*) nutzlos

futility [fjuːˈtɪlɪtɪ] N Sinnlosigkeit *f*; (*of plan, idea*)
Nutzlosigkeit *f*; (*of effort, attempt*) Vergeblichkeit *f*

futon ['fuːtɒn] N Futon *m*

future ['fjuːtʃə] **N** **a** Zukunft *f*; **we will have to
see what the ~ holds** wir müssen abwarten *or*
sehen, was die Zukunft bringt; **they look to
the ~ with a certain anxiety** sie blicken mit einer gewissen Angst in die Zukunft; **in ~** in Zukunft; **it won't happen in the foreseeable/near
~** es wird in absehbarer/nächster Zeit nicht
passieren; **the strikes will continue into the
foreseeable ~** die Streiks werden auf absehba-
re Zeit anhalten; **in the distant/not too distant
~** in ferner/nicht allzu ferner Zukunft; **that is**
still very much in the ~ das liegt noch in weiter
Ferne; **what plans do you have for the ~?** was
für Zukunftspläne haben Sie?; **there is a
sound ~ in publishing** das Verlagswesen hat eine sichere Zukunft; **to have a/any ~** eine Zukunft haben; **no one had any faith in its ~** niemand glaubte daran, dass es eine Zukunft hatte; **there is a real ~ for me with this firm** ich habe in dieser Firma glänzende Aussichten; **her ~
lies** *or* **is in politics** ihre Zukunft liegt in der
Politik; **there's no ~ in this type of research**
diese Art von Forschung hat keine Zukunft
b (*Gram*) **the ~** das Futur, die Zukunft
c (*St Ex*) **futures** PL Termingeschäfte *pl*; **coffee ~s** Terminkontrakte *pl* in Kaffee; **commodi-
ty/financial ~s** Waren-/Finanzterminkontrakte
pl; **~s market** Terminmarkt *m*, Terminbörse *f*
ADJ *attr* **a** *generations, husband, wife, king, queen,
role* (zu)künftig; **at a** *or* **some ~ date** zu einem
späteren Zeitpunkt; **his ~ prospects/plans** seine Aussichten/Pläne für die Zukunft, seine
Zukunftsaussichten/-pläne; **in ~ years** in den
kommenden Jahren; **for ~ reference, ...** zu Ihrer Information, ...; **you can keep it for ~ reference** Sie können es behalten, um später darauf
Bezug zu nehmen; **~ life** Leben *nt* nach dem
Tod
b (*Gram*) **the ~ tense** das Futur, die Zukunft;
the ~ perfect die vollendete Zukunft

futurism ['fjuːtʃərɪzəm] N Futurismus *m*

futurist ['fjuːtʃərɪst] N Futurist(in) *m(f)*

futuristic [ˌfjuːtʃəˈrɪstɪk] ADJ futuristisch

futurity [fjuːˈtjʊərɪtɪ] N (*form*, = *future time*) Zukunft *f*

futurology [ˌfjuːtʃəˈrɒlədʒɪ] N Futurologie *f*

fuze N (*US*) = **fuse**

fuzz [fʌz] N **a** (*on peach, youth's chin etc*) Flaum
m; (*inf*, = *bushy beard etc*) Gemüse *nt* (*inf*); (=
frizzy hair) Wuschelkopf *m* **b** (*inf*, = *blur, blurred
sound*) Unschärfen *pl* **c** (*dated esp Brit inf*: = *police*) **the ~** die Bullen *pl* (*sl*)

fuzzily ['fʌzɪlɪ] ADV verschwommen; **~ worded**
unklar formuliert

fuzzy ['fʌzɪ] ADJ (*+er*) **a** (= *furry*) *material, sweater*
flauschig; (= *frizzy*) *hair* kraus; **~ dice** (*US*)
Plüschwürfel *pl* **b** (= *unclear*) *sound, voice, writing* undeutlich; *picture, idea, memory, distinction*
verschwommen, unscharf; *details* unklar; **to go
~** (*picture*) verschwimmen; **my brain was ~** ich
konnte nicht klar denken; **I'm a little ~ on
what happened** ich weiß nicht so genau, was
passiert ist; **his head was still ~ from the drink**
er war von dem Drink noch benebelt

fuzzy: fuzzy-headed ['fʌzɪˌhedɪd] ADJ (*inf*, =
not clear-thinking) nicht (ganz) klar im Kopf;
(*from headache, drugs, drink*) benebelt; **fuzzy
logic** N (*Comput*) Fuzzy Logic *f*; **fuzzy-wuzzy**
['fʌzɪˌwʌzɪ] N (*dated pej sl*) Krauskopf *m* (*inf*)

fwd *abbr of* **forward**

FWD, f.w.d. **a** *abbr of* **four-wheel drive** **b** *abbr
of* **front-wheel drive**

FWH, f.w.h. *abbr of* **flexible working hours**

f-word ['efˌwɜːd] N (*inf*) euphemistischer Bezug
auf das Wort „*fuck*" **I try not to use the ~ in
front of the children** ich versuche, vor den
Kindern möglichst keine schlimmen Flüche zu
gebrauchen; **the ~ was mentioned 35 times in
this short story** in dieser Kurzgeschichte steht
35mal „fuck"

FX [efˈeks] PL (*Film inf*) Spezialeffekte *pl*

FY (*Fin*) *abbr of* **fiscal year** (= *tax year*) Steuerjahr
nt; (= *financial year*) Geschäftsjahr *nt*

FYI *abbr of* **for your information** zu Ihrer Information

G

G, g [dʒiː] N **a** G nt, g nt **b** g's PL (= *gravitational force*) g nt **c** G (*US, inf,* = *one thousand dollars*) tausend Dollar *pl* **d** (*Mus*) G nt, g nt; **G sharp** Gis nt, gis nt; **G flat** Ges nt, ges nt → **major, minor**

G (*US*) abbr of **general audience** (*Film*) jugendfrei

g abbr of **gram(s)** of **gramme(s)** g

gab [gæb] (*inf*) N Gequassel nt (*inf*), Geschwätz nt; **to have a ~** (zusammen) quatschen (*inf*); **to have a ~ about sth** etw bequatschen (*inf*); **to have the gift of the ~** (= *talk a lot*) wie ein Wasserfall reden (*inf*); (= *be persuasive*) reden können, nicht auf den Mund gefallen sein VI quatschen (*inf*), quasseln (*inf*)

gabardine, gaberdine [ˌgæbəˈdiːn] N Gabardine m

gabble [ˈgæbl] (*Brit*) VI (*person*) brabbeln (*inf*); (*geese*) schnattern VT *poem, prayer* herunterrasseln (*inf*); *excuse, explanation* brabbeln (*inf*); **he ~d out his story** er rasselte seine Geschichte herunter N Gebrabbel nt (*inf*); (*of geese*) Geschnatter nt; **the speaker ended in a ~** der Redner rasselte das Ende herunter (*inf*)

▶ **gabble away** VI (*geese, people*) drauflosschnattern (*inf*)

▶ **gabble on** VI reden und reden, quasseln und quasseln (*inf*)

gabbler [ˈgæblə] N (*pej*) Brabbler m (*pej*), Schwätzer m (*pej*)

gabby [ˈgæbɪ] ADJ (*inf*) geschwätzig, schwatzhaft

gaberdine N = gabardine

gable [ˈgeɪbl] N Giebel m

gabled [ˈgeɪbld] ADJ Giebel-; **house/roof** Giebelhaus/-dach nt

gable: gable end N Giebelwand or -seite f; **gable window** N Giebelfenster nt

gad [gæd] INTERJ (by) ~! (*old*) bei Gott! (*old*)

▶ **gad about** (*Brit*) or **around** VI herumziehen (*prep obj* in +dat); **he's always gadding about** er ist ständig auf Achse (*inf*); **to gad about the country** im Land herumziehen or -reisen

gadabout [ˈgædəbaʊt] N rastloser Geist; (*who likes travelling*) Reiseonkel m/-tante f; **she's a real ~, out somewhere every evening** sie ist sehr unternehmungslustig, jeden Abend ist sie irgendwo anders

gadfly [ˈgædflaɪ] N (Vieh)bremse f

gadget [ˈgædʒɪt] N Gerät nt, Vorrichtung f, Apparat m; **with a lot of ~s** mit allen Schikanen (*inf*)

gadgeteer [ˌgædʒɪˈtɪə] N Liebhaber(in) m(f) von technischen Spielereien

gadgetry [ˈgædʒɪtrɪ] N Vorrichtungen pl, Geräte pl; (= *superfluous equipment*) technische Spielereien pl, Kinkerlitzchen pl (*inf*)

gadgety [ˈgædʒɪtɪ] ADJ *device* raffiniert, zweckvoll (konstruiert); *person* auf technische Spielereien versessen

gadzooks [gædˈzuːks] INTERJ (*old*) Kruzitürken (*old*)

Gael [geɪl] N Gäle m, Gälin f

Gaelic [ˈgeɪlɪk] ADJ gälisch N (*Ling*) Gälisch nt

Gaelic coffee N Irishcoffee m

gaff¹ [gæf] N **a** (*Fishing*) Landungshaken m, Gaff nt **b** (*Naut*) Gaffel f VT (*Fishing*) mit dem (Landungs)haken or Gaff an Land ziehen

gaff² N **to blow the ~** (*inf*) nicht dichthalten (*inf*); **he blew the ~ by saying that** als er das sagte, war alles raus (*inf*); **to blow the ~ on sth** etw ausquatschen (*inf*)

gaffe [gæf] N Fauxpas m; (*verbal*) taktlose Bemerkung; **to make a ~** einen Fauxpas begehen; (*by saying sth*) ins Fettnäpfchen treten (*inf*)

gaffer [ˈgæfə] N (*Brit*) **a** (= *foreman*) Vorarbeiter m, Vormann m; (= *boss*) Chef m, Boss m (*inf*), Alte(r) m(f) (*inf*) **b** (= *old man*) Alte(r) m, Opa m (*inf*)

gag [gæg] N **a** Knebel m; (*Med*) Mundsperre f; **to put a ~ on the press** die Presse mundtot machen **b** (= *joke*) Gag m VT **a** knebeln; (*Med*) die Mundsperre einlegen (+dat); (*fig*) *person* zum Schweigen bringen; *press etc* mundtot machen, knebeln VI **a** (= *joke*) Witze machen; (*comedian*) Gags machen; **..., he ~ged ...,** witzelte er **b** (= *retch*) würgen (*on an* +dat) **c to be ~ging for sth** (*inf*) scharf auf etw (*acc*) sein; **to be ~ging for it** (*sl*) geil wie Bock sein (*sl*)

gaga [ˈgɑːgɑː] ADJ (*Brit inf*) plemplem (*inf*), meschugge (*inf*); *old person* verkalkt (*inf*); **to go ~** (= *go senile*) verkalken (*inf*)

gage N, VT (*US*) = gauge

gagging order N (*lit, fig*) Maulkorberlass m

gaggle [ˈgægl] N (*of geese*) Herde f; (*hum, of people*) Schar f, Horde f VI schnattern

gag law, (*US*) **gag rule** N (*inf*) Maulkorbgesetz nt (*inf*), Maulkorberlass m (*inf*)

gaiety [ˈgeɪətɪ] N (= *cheerfulness*) Fröhlichkeit f, Heiterkeit f; (*usu pl:* = *merrymaking*) Vergnügung f

gaily [ˈgeɪlɪ] ADV **a** (= *happily*) fröhlich; (= *brightly*) *painted, dressed* farbenfroh; **~ coloured** (*Brit*) or **colored** (*US*) farbenfroh, farbenprächtig **b** (= *thoughtlessly*) unbekümmert, fröhlich (*inf*); *spend* ohne Rücksicht auf Verluste

gain [geɪn] N **a** no pl (= *advantage*) Vorteil m; (= *profit*) Gewinn m, Profit m; **the love of ~** Profitgier f (*pej*); **to do sth for ~** etw aus Berechnung (*dat*) or zum eigenen Vorteil tun; (*for money*) etw des Geldes wegen tun; **his loss is our ~** sein Verlust ist unser Gewinn, wir profitieren von seinem Verlust

b gains PL (= *winnings*) Gewinn m; (= *profits*) Gewinne pl

c (= *increase*) (in +gen) Zunahme f; (in speed) Erhöhung f; (in wealth) Steigerung f, Zunahme f; (in health) Besserung f; (in knowledge) Erweiterung f, Vergrößerung f; **~ in numbers** zahlenmäßiger Zuwachs; **~ in weight, weight ~** Gewichtszunahme f; **~ in sales** Absatzsteigerung f; **~ in height** Höhengewinn m

VT **a** (= *obtain, win*) gewinnen; *knowledge, wealth* erwerben; *advantage, respect, entry, access* sich (*dat*) verschaffen; *control, the lead* übernehmen; *marks, points* erzielen; *sum of money* verdienen; *liberty* erlangen; (= *achieve*) *nothing, a little etc* erreichen; **we ~ed something for ourselves** damit haben wir etwas für uns erreicht; **what does he hope to ~ by it?** was verspricht or erhofft er sich (*dat*) davon?; **to ~ independence** unabhängig werden; **to ~ sb's goodwill** jdn

wohlwollend stimmen; **to ~ sb's confidence** jds Vertrauen erlangen; **to ~ experience** Erfahrungen sammeln; **he ~ed a better view by climbing onto a wall** dadurch, dass er auf eine Mauer kletterte, hatte er einen besseren Ausblick; **they didn't ~ entry to the building** sie kamen nicht in das Gebäude hinein; **we ~ed an advantage over him** wir waren ihm gegenüber im Vorteil; **to ~ ground** (an) Boden gewinnen; (*disease*) um sich greifen, sich verbreiten; (*rumours*) sich verbreiten; **to ~ ground on sb** (= *get further ahead*) den Vorsprung zu jdm vergrößern; (= *catch up*) jdm gegenüber aufholen; **to ~ time** Zeit gewinnen; **how did he ~ such a reputation?** wie ist er zu diesem Ruf gekommen?; **he ~ed a reputation as ...** er hat sich (*dat*) einen Namen als ... gemacht

b (= *reach*) *other side, shore, summit* erreichen

c (= *increase*) **to ~ height** (an) Höhe gewinnen, höher steigen; **to ~ speed** schneller werden, beschleunigen; **to ~ strength** stärker werden; **she has ~ed weight/3 kilos** sie hat zugenommen/3 Kilo zugenommen; **as he ~ed confidence** als er sicherer wurde, als seine Selbstsicherheit wuchs or zunahm; **to ~ popularity** an Beliebtheit (*dat*) gewinnen; **my watch ~s five minutes each day** meine Uhr geht fünf Minuten pro Tag vor

VI **a** (*watch*) vorgehen

b (= *get further ahead*) den Vorsprung vergrößern; (= *close gap*) aufholen

c (= *profit: person*) profitieren (*by* von); **you can only ~ by it** das kann nur Ihr Vorteil sein, Sie können dabei nur profitieren; **society/the university would ~ from that** das wäre für die Gesellschaft/die Universität von Vorteil; **we stood to ~ from the decision** die Entscheidung war für uns von Vorteil

d **to ~ in confidence** mehr Selbstvertrauen bekommen; **to ~ in popularity** an Beliebtheit (*dat*) gewinnen; **to ~ in speed** schneller werden; **to ~ in height** (an) Höhe gewinnen; **to ~ in weight** zunehmen; **to ~ in prestige** an Ansehen gewinnen, sich (*dat*) größeres Ansehen verschaffen; **to ~ in strength** stärker werden

▶ **gain on** VI +prep obj (= *get further ahead*) den Vorsprung zu ... vergrößern; (= *close gap*) einholen; (= *catch up with*) *work, rust etc* fertig werden mit; **the disease was gaining on him** seine Krankheit schritt fort

gainer [ˈgeɪnə] N **I was the ~** ich habe dabei profitiert; **there were more losers than ~s** es gab mehr Verlierer als Gewinner; **the biggest ~ was the government** die Regierung hat am meisten (davon) profitiert

gainful [ˈgeɪnfʊl] ADJ *occupation etc* einträglich; **to be in ~ employment** erwerbstätig sein

gainfully [ˈgeɪnfʊlɪ] ADV *spend time* nutzbringend; **~ employed** erwerbstätig; **there was nothing that could ~ be said** man konnte nichts sagen, was noch etwas genutzt hätte

gainsay [ˌgeɪnˈseɪ] VT pret, ptp **gainsaid** [ˌgeɪnˈsed] widersprechen (+dat); *fact* (ab)leugnen, bestreiten; *evidence, argument* widerlegen; **if the facts cannot be gainsaid** es lässt sich/die Tatsachen lassen sich nicht leugnen; **there is no ~ing his honesty** seine Ehrlichkeit lässt sich nicht leugnen

'gainst [geɪnst] PREP = against

gait [geɪt] N Gang *m*; *(of horse)* Gangart *f*; **to have a rolling/shuffling ~** einen schaukelnden/ schlurfenden Gang haben; **with an unsteady ~** mit unsicheren Schritten

gaiter ['geɪtə'] N Gamasche *f*

gal¹ [gæl] N *(dated inf)* Mädel *nt (dated)*

gal² *abbr of* **gallon(s)**

gala ['gɑːlə] N *(= festive occasion)* großes Fest; *(Theat, Film, = ball)* Galaveranstaltung *f*; **swimming/sports ~** großes Schwimm-/Sportfest; **opening/closing ~** Eröffnungs-/Abschlussveranstaltung *f*

galactic [gə'læktɪk] ADJ galaktisch

gala day N Festtag *m*; *(for person)* großer Tag

gala dress N Gala *f*; *(= uniform also)* Galauniform *f or* -anzug *m*

Galahad ['gæləhæd] N Galahad *m*; *(fig)* Kavalier *m*, Ritter *m*

gala night N Galaabend *m*

galantine ['gæləntiːn] N *kalt servierte, glasierte Fleisch- oder Geflügelroulade*

gala occasion N festliche Veranstaltung

gala performance N Galavorstellung *f*, Festvorstellung *f*

galaxy ['gæləksɪ] N **a** *(Astron)* Milchstraße *f*, Sternsystem *nt*, Galaxis *f (spec)*; **the Galaxy** die Milchstraße, die Galaxis *(spec)* **b** *(fig)* Schar *f*, Heer *nt*

gale [geɪl] N **a** Sturm *m*; **it was blowing a ~** es stürmte, ein Sturm tobte *or* wütete; **~ force 8** Sturmstärke 8 **b** *(fig)* **~s of laughter** Lachsalven *pl*, stürmisches Gelächter

gale: gale-force winds PL orkanartige Winde; **gale warning** N Sturmwarnung *f*

Galicia [gə'lɪsɪə] N **a** *(in Eastern Europe)* Galizien *nt* **b** *(in Spain)* Galicien *nt*

Galician [gə'lɪsɪən] ADJ **a** *(in Eastern Europe)* galizisch **b** *(in Spain)* galicisch **▶** N **a** *(in Eastern Europe)* Galizier(in) *m(f)* **b** *(in Spain)* Galicier(in) *m(f)*

Galilean [ˌgælɪ'liːən] ADJ galiläisch **▶** N Galiläer(in) *m(f)*

Galilee ['gælɪliː] N Galiläa *nt*; **the Sea of ~** der See Genezareth, das Galiläische Meer

gall [gɔːl] N **a** *(Physiol)* Galle(nsaft *m*) *f* **b** *(= sore)* Wundstelle *f*; *(Bot)* Galle *f*; *(nut-shaped)* Gallapfel *m* **c** *(fig liter)* Bitternis *f (geh)* **d** *(inf)* Frechheit *f*; **to have the ~ to do sth** die Frechheit haben *or* besitzen, etw zu tun **▶** VT **a** *(= chafe)* wund reiben *or* scheuern; *(fig)* maßlos ärgern; **it ~s me that ...** es ärgert mich maßlos, dass ...

gallant ['gælənt] ADJ **a** *(= courageous)* person, effort, attempt, fight tapfer; **~ conduct** Tapferkeit *f* **b** *(= chivalrous)* person, gesture ritterlich **c** *(liter, = showy)* prächtig **▶** N ['gælənt, gə'lænt] *(Hist, = suitor)* Galan *m (old)*

gallantly ['gæləntlɪ] ADV **a** *(= courageously)* tapfer **b** *(= chivalrously)* ritterlich

gallantry ['gæləntrɪ] N **a** *(= bravery)* Tapferkeit *f*; *(= chivalry)* Edelmut *m* **b** *(= attentiveness to women)* Ritterlichkeit *f*, Galanterie *f* **c** *(= compliment)* Galanterie *f*, Artigkeit *f (dated)*

gall bladder N Gallenblase *f*

galleon ['gælɪən] N Galeone *f*

gallery ['gælərɪ] N **a** *(= balcony, corridor)* Galerie *f*; *(in church)* Empore *f*; *(Theat)* oberster Rang, Balkon *m*, Galerie *f*; **to play to the ~** *(fig)* sich in Szene setzen **b** *(Art)* (Kunst)galerie *f* **c** *(underground)* Stollen *m*

galley ['gælɪ] N **a** *(Naut, = ship)* Galeere *f*; **b** *(= kitchen)* Kombüse *f* **b** *(Typ, = tray)* (Setz)schiff *nt*; *(also* **galley proof**) Fahne *f*, Fahnenabzug *m*

galley slave N Galeerensklave *m*

Gallic ['gælɪk] ADJ gallisch; **the ~ Wars** der Gallische Krieg

Gallicism ['gælɪsɪzəm] N Gallizismus *m*

Gallicize ['gælɪsaɪz] VT französisieren

gallimaufry [ˌgælɪ'mɔːfrɪ] N *, no pl* Durcheinander *nt*, Mischmasch *m (inf)*

---

galling ['gɔːlɪŋ] ADJ äußerst ärgerlich; *experience* äußerst unangenehm; *person* unausstehlich; **this was especially ~ for him** das hat ihn besonders geärgert

gallivant [ˌgælɪ'vænt] VI sich amüsieren; **to ~ about** *or* **around** sich herumtreiben, herumzigeunern; **to ~ off** losziehen *(inf)*; **I was out ~ing last night** ich war gestern Abend bummeln *or* auf Achse *(inf)*

gallon ['gælən] N Gallone *f*

gallop ['gæləp] **N** Galopp *m*; **at a ~** im Galopp; **at full ~** im gestreckten Galopp; **to go for a ~** ausreiten; **after a quick ~ through Roman history, he ...** nachdem er das römische Geschichte im Galopp abgehandelt hatte, ... **VI** galoppieren, im Galopp reiten; **to ~ away** davongaloppieren; **we ~ed through our work/the agenda** wir haben die Arbeit im Galopp erledigt *(inf)*/ die Tagesordnung im Galopp abgehandelt *(inf)*; **to ~ through a book** ein Buch in rasendem Tempo lesen *(inf)* **VT** horse galoppieren lassen

galloping ['gæləpɪŋ] ADJ *(lit)* galoppierend; **at a ~ pace** *(lit)* im Galopp; *(fig)* in rasendem Tempo; **~ inflation** galoppierende Inflation

gallows ['gæləʊz] N Galgen *m*; **to send/bring sb to the ~** jdn an den Galgen bringen

gallows: gallows bird N *(inf)* Galgenvogel *m (inf)*; **gallows humour**, *(US)* **gallows humor** N Galgenhumor *m*

gallstone ['gɔːlstəʊn] N Gallenstein *m*

Gallup poll ['gæləp,pəʊl] N Meinungsumfrage *f*

galore [gə'lɔː'] ADV in Hülle und Fülle

galoshes [gə'lɒʃɪz] PL Gummischuhe *pl*, Galoschen *pl*

galumph [gə'lʌmf] VI *(inf)* trapsen *(inf)*

galvanic [gæl'vænɪk] ADJ **a** *(Elec)* galvanisch **b** *(fig)* movement zuckend; *(= stimulating)* mitreißend, elektrisierend

galvanism ['gælvənɪzəm] N Galvanismus *m*

galvanization [ˌgælvənəˈzeɪʃən] N Galvanisierung *f*, Galvanisation *f*

galvanize ['gælvənaɪz] VT **a** *(Elec)* galvanisieren **b** *(fig)* elektrisieren; **to ~ sb into action** jdn plötzlich aktiv werden lassen; **to ~ sb into doing** *or* **to do sth** jdm einen Stoß geben, etw sofort zu tun; **he was ~d into life by the news** die Nachricht hat ihm enormen Auftrieb gegeben

galvanized ['gælvənaɪzd] ADJ iron, steel galvanisiert

galvanometer [ˌgælvəˈnɒmɪtə'] N Galvanometer *nt*

Gambia ['gæmbɪə] N **(the) ~** Gambia *nt*

Gambian ['gæmbɪən] ADJ gambisch **N** Gambier(in) *m(f)*

gambit ['gæmbɪt] N **a** *(Chess)* Gambit *nt* **b** *(fig)* (Schach)zug *m*; **his favourite** *(Brit)* or **favorite** *(US)* **~ was to ...** was er am liebsten machte, war ...; **his opening ~ is ...** er fängt eine Unterhaltung mit ... an

gamble ['gæmbl] **N a** *(lit)* **I like the occasional ~** ich versuche gern mal mein Glück (im Spiel/bei Pferdewetten/bei Hundewetten *etc*); **to have a ~ on the horses/dogs** auf Pferde/ Hunde wetten; **to have a ~ on the stock exchange** an der Börse spekulieren **b** *(fig)* Risiko *nt*; **a political ~** ein politisches Wagnis; **it's a ~** es ist riskant *or* eine riskante Sache; **I'll take a ~ on it/him** ich riskiere es/es mit ihm; **he took a ~ in buying the house** beim Kauf des Hauses ist er ein Risiko eingegangen **VI a** *(lit)* (um Geld) spielen *(with mit)*, sich an Glücksspielen beteiligen; *(on horses etc)* wetten; **to ~ on the horses** bei Pferderennen wetten; **to ~ on the stock exchange** an der Börse spekulieren; **he made a lot of money gambling** er hat beim Glücksspiel *or (with cards)* beim Kartenspiel viel Geld gewonnen

b *(fig)* **to ~ on sth** sich auf etw *(acc)* verlassen; **she was gambling on his being late** sie hat sich darauf verlassen, dass er sich verspäten würde; **I was gambling on winning their support** ich verließ mich *or* spekulierte *(inf)* darauf,

---

dass sie mich unterstützen würden; **to ~ with sth** mit etw spielen, etw aufs Spiel setzen **VT a** money, fortune einsetzen; **to ~ sth on sth** etw auf etw *(acc)* setzen **b** *(fig)* aufs Spiel setzen

▶ gamble away VT sep verspielen

gambler ['gæmblə'] N *(lit, fig)* Spieler(in) *m(f)*; **he's a born ~** er ist eine Spielernatur; **Gamblers Anonymous** Anonyme Spieler *pl*

gambling ['gæmblɪŋ] N Spielen *nt* (um Geld); *(on horses etc)* Wetten *nt*; **to disapprove of ~** gegen das Glücksspiel/Wetten sein

gambling debts PL Spielschulden *pl*

gambling den, **gambling joint** N Spielhölle *f*

gambol ['gæmbəl] **N** Tollen *nt*, Tollerei *f*; *(of lambs)* Herumspringen *nt*; **to have a ~** herumtollen; herumspringen **VI** herumtollen; herumspringen

game¹ [geɪm] **N a** Spiel *nt*; *(= sport)* Sport(art *f*) *m*; *(= single game, of team sports, tennis)* Spiel *nt*; *(of table tennis)* Satz *m*; *(of billiards, board games etc, informal tennis match)* Partie *f*; **the wonderful ~ of football** Fußball, das wunderbare Spiel; **to have** *or* **play a ~ of football/tennis/chess** *etc* Fußball/Tennis/Schach *etc* spielen; **do you fancy a quick ~ of tennis/chess?** hättest du Lust, ein bisschen Tennis/Schach zu spielen?, hättest du Lust auf eine Partie Tennis/Schach?; **we had a quick ~ of cards after supper** nach dem Essen spielten wir ein bisschen Karten; **shall we play a ~ now?** wollen wir jetzt ein Spiel machen?; **to have a ~ with sb**, **to give sb a ~** mit jdm spielen; **winning the second set put him back in the ~ again** nachdem er den zweiten Satz gewonnen hatte, hatte er wieder Chancen; **he had a good ~** er spielte gut; **to be off one's ~** nicht in Form sein; **~ of chance** Glücksspiel *nt*; **~ of skill** Geschicklichkeitsspiel *nt*; **~ set and match to X** Satz und Spiel (geht an) X; **~ to X** Spiel X; **one ~ all** eins beide

b *(fig)* Spiel *nt*; *(= scheme, plan)* Absicht *f*, Vorhaben *nt*; **to play the ~** sich an die Spielregeln halten; **to play ~s with sb** mit jdm spielen; **he's just playing (silly) ~s** für ihn ist es nur ein Spiel; **the ~ is up** das Spiel ist aus; **to play sb's ~** jdm in die Hände spielen; **two can play at that ~**, **that's a ~ (that) two can play** wie du mir, so ich dir *(inf)*; **to beat sb at his own ~** jdn mit den eigenen Waffen schlagen; **to give the ~ away** alles verderben; **to see through sb's ~** jds Spiel durchschauen, jdm auf die Schliche kommen; **to spoil sb's little ~** jdm das Spiel verderben, jdm die Suppe versalzen *(inf)*; **I wonder what his ~ is?** ich frage mich, was er vorhat *or* im Schilde führt; **so that's your ~, is it?** darauf willst du also hinaus; **to be/keep ahead of the ~** *(fig)* um eine Nasenlänge voraus sein/bleiben; **to be out of the ~** *(inf, = be finished etc)* weg vom Fenster sein *(inf)*; **it's all part of the ~** das gehört alles dazu

c games PL *(= sports event)* Spiele *pl*

d games SING *(Sch)* Sport *m*; **to be good at ~s** gut in Sport sein

e *(inf, = business, profession)* Branche *f*; **how long have you been in this ~?** wie lange machen Sie das schon?; **the publishing ~** das Verlagswesen; **he's in the second-hand car ~** er macht in Gebrauchtwagen *(inf)*; **to be/go on the ~** *(esp Brit)* auf den Strich gehen *(inf)*

f *(inf, = difficult time)* Theater *nt (inf)*

g *(Hunt, Cook)* Wild *nt*

VI (um Geld) spielen

VT *(also* **game away**) verspielen

game² ADJ *(= brave)* mutig; **to be ~** *(= willing)* mitmachen, dabei sein; **to be ~ for sth** für etw bereit sein; **to be ~ to do sth** bereit sein, etw zu tun; **to be ~ for anything** für alles zu haben sein, zu allen Schandtaten bereit sein *(hum inf)*; **to be ~ for a laugh** jeden Spaß mitmachen

game³ ADJ *(= crippled)* lahm

game: game bag N Jagdtasche *f*; **game bird** N Federwild *nt no pl*; **the pheasant is a ~** der Fasan gehört zum Federwild

Gameboy® ['geɪmbɔɪ] N Gameboy® *m*

game: gamecock N Kampfhahn *m*; **game fish** N Sportfisch *m*; **gamekeeper** N Wildhüter(in) *m(f)*; **game laws** PL Jagdgesetz *nt*; **game licence**, (*US*) **game license** N Jagdschein *m*

gamely ['geɪmlɪ] ADV (= *bravely*) mutig

game: game park N Wildpark *m*; **game pie** N Wildpastete *f*; **game plan** N (*Sport*) Spielplan *m*; (*fig*) Strategie *f*; **game point** N Spielpunkt *m*; **game preserve** N Wildhegegebiet *nt*; **game reserve** N Wildschutzgebiet *or* -reservat *nt*; **game show** N (*TV*) Spielshow *f*

gamesmanship ['geɪmzmənʃɪp] N Ablenkungsmanöver *pl*; **political/diplomatic ~** politische/diplomatische Schläue

games [geɪmz]: **games master** N Sportlehrer *m*; **games mistress** N Sportlehrerin *f*; **games port** N (*Comput*) Spieleport *nt or m*; **games software** N Software *f* für Computerspiele

gamester ['geɪmstə'] N Spieler(in) *m(f)*

game theory N (*in business studies*) Spieltheorie *f*

game warden N Jagdaufseher *m*

gamin ['gæmɛ̃] N Straßenjunge *m*

gamine [gæ'mi:n] ADJ jungenhaft, knabenhaft

gaming ['geɪmɪŋ] N = **gambling ~ machine** Spielautomat *m*

gamma: gamma radiation N Gammastrahlung *f*; **gamma ray** ['gæmərei] N Gammastrahl *m*

gammon ['gæmən] N (= *bacon*) leicht geräucherter Vorderschinken; (= *ham*) (gekochter) Schinken; **~ steak** *dicke Scheibe Vorderschinken zum Braten oder Grillen*

gammy ['gæmɪ] ADJ (*Brit, inf*) lahm

gamp [gæmp] N (*dated hum*) Regenschirm *m*, Mussspritze *f* (*dated hum*)

gamut ['gæmət] N (*Mus*) Noten- *or* Tonskala *f*; (*fig*) Skala *f*; **to run the (whole) ~** of emotions die ganze Skala der Gefühle durchlaufen; **his facial expressions ran the ~ from pain to terror** sein Gesichtsausdruck durchlief die ganze Skala von Schmerz bis hin zu panischer Angst

gamy ['geɪmɪ] ADJ nach Wild schmeckend; (= *high*) angegangen; **~ taste** Wildgeschmack *m*; (= *high*) Hautgout *m* (*geh*), angegangener Geschmack

gander ['gændə'] N **a** Gänserich *m*, Ganter *m* (*dial*) **b** (*inf*) **to have** *or* **take a ~ at sth** auf etw (*acc*) einen Blick werfen; **let's have a ~!** gucken wir mal! (*inf*); (= *let me/us look*) lass mal sehen!

G and T, **G&T** [ˌdʒiːənˈtiː] N *abbr of* **gin and tonic** Gin Tonic *m*

gang [gæŋ] N Haufen *m*, Schar *f*; (*of workers, prisoners*) Kolonne *f*, Trupp *m*; (*of criminals, youths, terrorists*) Bande *f*, Gang *f*; (*of friends etc*: = *clique*) Clique *f*, Haufen *m* (*inf*); **there was a whole ~ of them** es war ein ganzer Haufen; **do you want to be in our ~?** möchtest du zu unserer Bande/Clique gehören?; **the Gang of Four** die Viererbande

▶ **gang up** VI sich zusammentun; **to gang up against** *or* **on sb** sich gegen jdn verbünden *or* verschwören; (*to fight*) geschlossen auf jdn *or* gegen jdn losgehen

gangbang ['gæŋbæŋ] (*inf*) N **a** (= *rape*) Gruppenvergewaltigung *f* **b** (*voluntary*) **she had six men round for a ~** sie wurde von sechs Männern durchgebumst (*inf*) VT **she was ~ed** (= *raped*) sie wurde Opfer einer Gruppenvergewaltigung; (*voluntarily*) sie wurde von mehreren Männern hintereinander gebumst (*inf*)

gangbanger ['gæŋbæŋə'] N (*US, inf*) Mitglied *nt* einer Straßenbande

gang boss N (*inf*) Vorarbeiter *m*, Vormann *m*

ganger ['gæŋə'] N Vorarbeiter *m*, Vormann *m*

Ganges ['gændʒiːz] N Ganges *m*

gangland ['gæŋlænd] N die Unterwelt ADJ Unterwelt-; **a ~ boss** ein Unterweltboss *m*

ganglia ['gæŋglɪə] *pl of* **ganglion**

gangling ['gæŋglɪŋ] ADJ schlaksig, hoch aufgeschossen

ganglion ['gæŋglɪən] N *pl* **ganglia a** (*Anat*) Ganglion *nt*; (*Med*) Überbein *nt*, Ganglion *nt* **b** (*fig, of activity*) Zentrum *nt*

gangplank ['gæŋplæŋk] N Laufplanke *f*, Landungssteg *m*

gang rape N Gruppenvergewaltigung *f*

gangrene ['gæŋgri:n] N Brand *m*, Gangrän *f or nt* (*spec*)

gangrenous ['gæŋgrɪnəs] ADJ brandig, gangränös (*spec*)

gangsta rap ['gæŋstəˌræp] N (*Mus*) Gangsta Rap *m*

gangster ['gæŋstə'] N Gangster(in) *m(f)*, Verbrecher(in) *m(f)*

gangsterism ['gæŋstərɪzəm] N Gangstertum *nt*, Verbrechertum *nt*

gangway ['gæŋweɪ] N **a** (*Naut, = gangplank*) Landungsbrücke *f*, Gangway *f*; (= *ladder*) Fallreep *nt* **b** (= *passage*) Gang *m* INTERJ Platz da

ganja ['gændʒə] N Ganja *nt*

gannet ['gænɪt] N (*Zool*) Tölpel *m*; **she's a real ~** (*inf*) sie ist ein richtiger Vielfraß

gantry ['gæntrɪ] N (*for crane*) Portal *nt*; (*on motorway*) Schilderbrücke *f*; (*Rail*) Signalbrücke *f*; (*for rocket*) Abschussrampe *f*

gaol [dʒeɪl] N, VT = **jail**

gaoler ['dʒeɪlə'] N = **jailer**

gap [gæp] N (*lit, fig*) Lücke *f*; (= *chink*) Spalt *m*; (*in surface*) Spalte *f*, Riss *m*; (*Geog*) Spalte *f*; (*Tech*: = *spark gap*) Abstand *m*; (*fig, in conversation, narrative*) Pause *f*; (= *gulf*) Kluft *f*; **to close the ~** (*in race*) (den Abstand) aufholen; **tax increases to close the ~ between spending and revenue** Steuererhöhungen, um die Lücke zwischen Ausgaben und Einnahmen zu schließen; **a ~ in one's knowledge** eine Bildungslücke; **a four-year ~**, **a ~ of four years** ein Abstand *m* von vier Jahren; **she returned to work after a ~ of five years** nach einer Pause von fünf Jahren ging sie wieder arbeiten

gape [geɪp] VI **a** (= *open mouth wide, person*) den Mund aufreißen *or* -sperren; (*bird*) den Schnabel aufsperren; (*chasm etc*) gähnen, klaffen; (*seam, wound*) klaffen **b** (= *stare: person*) starren, gaffen; **to ~ at sb/sth** jdn/etw (mit offenem Mund) anstarren; **the people stood and ~d** die Leute sperrten Mund und Nase auf (*inf*)

gaping ['geɪpɪŋ] ADJ **a** *mouth, beak* weit aufgesperrt; *hole* riesig; *wound* klaffend; *chasm, abyss* klaffend, *mouth* weit aufgerissen **b** (= *staring*) *person* gaffend; *eyes* weit aufgerissen

gap: gapless ADJ lückenlos; **gap-toothed** ADJ mit weiter Zahnstellung; (= *with teeth missing*) mit Zahnlücken

garage ['gæra:ʒ, (*US*) gə'ra:ʒ] N (*for parking*) Garage *f*; (*Brit*) (*for petrol*) Tankstelle *f*; (*for repairs etc*) (Reparatur)werkstatt *f*; **~ mechanic** (*Brit*) Kraftfahrzeug- *or* Kfz-Mechaniker(in) *m(f)* VT (*in einer Garage*) ab- *or* unterstellen; (= *drive into garage*) in die Garage fahren; **the car is kept ~d** das Auto wird in einer Garage aufbewahrt

garage: garage band N (*Mus*) Amateur-Rockband *f*; **garage sale** N *meist in einer Garage durchgeführter Verkauf von Haushaltsgegenständen und Trödel* → *also* **car-boot sale**

garaging ['gæra:ʒɪŋ, (*US*) gə'ra:ʒɪŋ] N Garagenplätze *pl*

garb [gɑ:b] N Gewand *nt* VT kleiden; **~ed all in black** ganz in Schwarz gekleidet

garbage ['gɑ:bɪdʒ] N (*lit: esp US*) Abfall *m*, Müll *m*; (*fig, = useless things*) Schund *m*, Mist *m* (*inf*); (= *nonsense*) Blödsinn *m*, Quatsch *m* (*inf*); (*Comput*) Garbage *m*; **~ in, ~ out** (*Comput*) garbage in, garbage out, Müll rein, Müll raus

garbage: garbage can N (*US*) Müll- *or* Abfalleimer *m*; (*outside*) Mülltonne *f*; **garbage col-**

lector N (*US*) Müllarbeiter *m*; **the ~s** die Müllabfuhr; **garbage disposal unit** N (*esp US*) Müllschlucker *m*; **garbage man** N (*US*) = **garbage collector**

garble ['gɑ:bl] VT (*deliberately*) *message* unverständlich machen; **to ~ one's words** sich beim Sprechen überschlagen

garbled ['gɑ:bld] ADJ *version, story* entstellt; *message, instructions* konfus; *words, speech, account* wirr; **in a ~ form** völlig entstellt; **the facts got a little ~** die Tatsachen sind etwas durcheinander geraten

garda ['gɑ:rdə] N *pl* **gardaí** ['gɑ:rdi:] (*Ir, = police*) Polizei *f*; (= *policeman/-woman*) Polizist(in) *m(f)*

garden ['gɑ:dn] N **a** Garten *m*; **the Garden of Eden** der Garten Eden; **everything in the ~ is lovely** *or* **rosy** (*fig*) es ist alles in Butter (*inf*) **b** (*often pl*: = *park*) Park *m*, Gartenanlagen *pl* VI im Garten arbeiten, Gartenarbeit machen, gärtnern

garden *in cpds* Garten-; **garden apartment** N (*US*) = **garden flat**; **garden burger** N Gemüseburger *m*; **garden centre**, (*US*) **garden center** N Gartencenter *nt*, Gärtnereimarkt *m*

gardener ['gɑ:dnə'] N Gärtner(in) *m(f)*

garden: garden flat N (*Brit*) Souterrainwohnung *f*; **garden frame** M Frühbeet *nt*; **garden gnome** N Gartenzwerg *m*

gardenia [gɑ:'di:nɪə] N Gardenie *f*

gardening ['gɑ:dnɪŋ] N Gartenarbeit *f*; **she loves ~** sie arbeitet gerne im Garten, sie gärtnert gerne; **~ tools** Gartengeräte *pl*

garden: garden party N Gartenparty *f or* -fest *nt*; **garden path** N **to lead sb up** (*esp Brit*) *or* **down** (*esp US*) **the ~** (*fig*) jdn an der Nase herumführen (*inf*); **garden produce** N (= *vegetables*) Gartengemüse *nt*; (= *fruit*) Gartenobst *nt*; **garden shears** PL Heckenschere *f*; **garden-variety** ADJ (*US, = ordinary*) gewöhnlich; (= *standard*) durchschnittlich

gargantuan [gɑ:'gæntjʊən] ADJ gewaltig, enorm

gargle ['gɑ:gl] VI gurgeln; (*with* mit) N (= *liquid*) Gurgelwasser *nt*

gargoyle ['gɑ:gɔɪl] N Wasserspeier *m*

garish ['gɛərɪʃ] ADJ (*pej*) *colours, neon sign* grell, schreiend; *clothes* knallbunt

garishly ['gɛərɪʃlɪ] ADV (*pej*) *dressed* in grellen Farben; *illuminated* grell; **~ coloured** (*Brit*) *or* **colored** (*US*) schreiend bunt, knallbunt

garishness ['gɛərɪʃnɪs] N (*pej*) grelle *or* schreiende Farben *pl*; (*of colours, illuminations*) Grellheit *f*

garland ['gɑ:lənd] N Kranz *m*; (= *festoon*) Girlande *f*; **a ~ of flowers** eine Blumengirlande VT bekränzen

garlic ['gɑ:lɪk] N Knoblauch *m*

garlic: garlic bread N Knoblauchbrot *nt*; **garlic clove** N Knoblauchzehe *f*; **garlic crusher** N Knoblauchpresse *f*

garlicky ['gɑ:lɪkɪ] ADJ *food* knoblauchhaltig; **~ taste** Knoblauchgeschmack *m*; **she's got ~ breath** ihr Atem riecht nach Knoblauch

garlic: garlic mushrooms PL *fritierte Pilze mit Knoblauch*; **garlic press** N Knoblauchpresse *f*; **garlic salt** N Knoblauchsalz *nt*

garment ['gɑ:mənt] N Kleidungsstück *nt*; (= *robe*) Gewand *nt* (*liter*); **all her ~s** ihre ganzen Kleider; **~ industry** (*US*) Bekleidungsindustrie *f*

garner ['gɑ:nə'] VT (*lit, fig*) (= *gather*) sammeln; *savings* ansammeln; *support* gewinnen; (= *store*) speichern

garnet ['gɑ:nɪt] N Granat *m*

garnish ['gɑ:nɪʃ] VT garnieren, verzieren; (*fig*) *story also, style* ausschmücken N Garnierung *f*

garnishing ['gɑ:nɪʃɪŋ] N (*Cook*) Garnierung *f*; (= *act also*) Garnieren *nt*; (*fig, of style, story etc*) Ausschmückung *f*

garret ['gærət] N (= *attic room*) Mansarde *f*, Dachkammer *f*; (= *attic*) Dachboden *m*

garrison ['gærɪsən] N Garnison *f* VT *troops* in Garnison legen; **to be ~ed** in Garnison liegen

garrison duty N Garnisonsdienst m
garrison town N Garnisonsstadt f
garrotte [gə'rɒt] VT (= execute) garrottieren, mit der Garrotte hinrichten; (= strangle) erdrosseln ▸ N Garrotte f
garrulity [gə'ruːlɪtɪ] N Geschwätzigkeit f, Schwatzhaftigkeit f
garrulous ['gærʊləs] ADJ geschwätzig, schwatzhaft
garrulously ['gærʊləslɪ] ADV to talk/chat etc ~ schwatzen, plappern
garryowen [ˌgærɪ'əʊɪn] N (Rugby) hohe Selbstvorlage
garter ['gɑːtə] N Strumpfband nt; (US, = strap for stocking) Strumpfhalter m; the (Order of the) Garter der Hosenbandorden
garter: garter belt N (US) Strumpf- or Hüftgürtel m; **garter snake** N Ringelnatter f; **garter stitch** N rechts-rechts gestricktes Muster; **5 rows** = 5 Reihen rechts-rechts gestrickt
gas [gæs] ▸ N ▸ a Gas nt; **to cook with ~** mit Gas kochen ▸ b (US, = petrol) Benzin nt; **to step on the ~** Gas geben ▸ c (= anaesthetic) Lachgas nt; **to have** (Brit) or **get** (US) ~ Lachgas bekommen ▸ d (Mil) (Gift)gas nt ▸ e (US Med: = wind) Blähungen pl ▸ f (inf: = talk) leeres Gefasel (inf); (boastful) großspuriges Gerede, Angeberei f; **to have a good ~** einen Schwatz halten ▸ g (inf) **it's/he's a ~** (= fantastic) es/er ist Klasse (inf); (= hilarious) es/er ist zum Schreien (inf) ▸ VT vergasen; **they were ~sed during their sleep** (accidentally) sie starben im Schlaf an Gasvergiftung; **to ~ oneself** den Gashahn aufdrehen, sich mit Gas vergiften ▸ VI (inf, = talk) schwafeln (inf), faseln (inf)
gas in cpds Gas-; **gasbag** N (inf) Quasselstrippe f (inf); **gas bracket** N Gasanschluss(stelle f) m, Gaszuleitungsrohr nt; (for light) Wandarm m; **gas chamber** N Gaskammer f; **gas cooker** N Gasherd m; **gas engine** N Gasmaschine f or -motor m
gaseous ['gæsɪəs] ADJ gasförmig
gas: gas field N Erdgasfeld nt; **gas fire** N Gasofen m; **gasfired** ADJ Gas-, gasbefeuert (form); **~ power station** Gaskraftwerk nt; **gas fitter** N Gasinstallateur(in) m(f); **gas fittings** PL Gasgeräte pl; **gas fixture** N fest installiertes Gasgerät; **gas guzzler** N (esp US inf) Säufer m, Benzinschlucker m (inf)
gash [gæʃ] ▸ N (= wound) klaffende Wunde; (in earth, tree) (klaffende) Spalte; (= slash) tiefe Kerbe; (in upholstery) tiefer Schlitz ▸ VT aufschlitzen; furniture, wood tief einkerben; **he fell and ~ed his head/knee** er ist gestürzt und hat sich (dat) dabei den Kopf/das Knie aufgeschlagen
gas: gas heater N Gasofen m; **gasholder** N Gasometer m, (Groß)gasbehälter m; **gas jet** N Gasdüse f
gasket ['gæskɪt] N (Tech) Dichtung f
gas: gas lamp N Gaslampe f; (in streets) Gaslaterne f; **gaslight** N ▸ a = gas lamp ▸ b no pl Gaslicht nt or -beleuchtung f; **gas lighter** N ▸ a Gasanzünder m ▸ b (for cigarettes etc) Gasfeuerzeug nt; **gas lighting** N Gasbeleuchtung f; **gas-lit** ADJ mit Gasbeleuchtung; **gas main** N Gasleitung f; **gasman** N Gasmann m (inf); **gas mantle** N (Gas)glühstrumpf m; **gas mask** N Gasmaske f; **gas meter** N Gaszähler m or -uhr f
gasoline ['gæsəʊliːn] N (US) Benzin nt
gasometer [gæ'sɒmɪtə] N Gasometer m, (Groß)gasbehälter m
gas oven N Gasherd m; (= gas chamber) Gaskammer f; **to put one's head in the ~** (= kill oneself, also hum) den Gashahn aufdrehen
gasp [gɑːsp] ▸ N (for breath) tiefer Atemzug; **the ~s of the runner** das Keuchen des Läufers; **to give a ~ (of surprise/fear** etc) (vor Überraschung/Angst etc) die Luft anhalten or nach Luft schnappen (inf); **a ~ went up at his audac-**

ity seine Verwegenheit verschlug den Leuten den Atem; **to be at one's last ~** in den letzten Zügen liegen; (= exhausted etc) auf dem letzten Loch pfeifen (inf); **this was the last ~ of the reform movement** das war das letzte Aufbäumen der Reformbewegung ▸ VI (continually) keuchen; (once) tief einatmen; (with surprise etc) nach Luft schnappen (inf); **to make sb ~** (lit, fig) jdm den Atem nehmen; **to ~ for breath** or **air** nach Atem ringen, nach Luft schnappen (inf); **he ~ed with astonishment** er war so erstaunt, dass es ihm den Atem verschlug; **heavens, no!, she ~ed** um Himmels willen, nein!, stieß sie hervor; **I'm ~ing for a cup of tea/a cigarette** (inf) ich lechze nach einer Tasse Tee/einer Zigarette (inf), ich brauche dringend eine Tasse Tee/eine Zigarette
▸**gasp out** VT sep hervorstoßen
gas pedal N (esp US) Gaspedal nt
gasper ['gɑːspə] N (Brit, inf) Glimmstängel m (dated inf)
gas: gas-permeable ADJ lenses gasdurchlässig; **gas pipe** N Gasrohr nt or -leitung f; **gas plasma** N Gasplasma nt; **gas pump** N (US) Zapfsäule f; **gas ring** N Gasbrenner m; (portable) Gaskocher m; **gas station** N (US) Tankstelle f; **gas stove** N Gasherd m; (portable) Gaskocher m
gassy ['gæsɪ] ADJ (+er) ▸ a (Sci) gasförmig; **it smells** ~ es riecht nach Gas ▸ b drink kohlensäurehaltig ▸ c (inf) person geschwätzig
gas: gas tank N (US) Benzintank m; **gas tap** N Gashahn m; **gastight** ADJ gasdicht
gastric ['gæstrɪk] ADJ Magen-, gastrisch (spec); **~ acid** Magensäure f
gastric: gastric flu, gastric influenza N Darmgrippe f; **gastric juices** PL Magensäfte pl; **gastric ulcer** N Magengeschwür nt
gastritis [gæs'traɪtɪs] N Magenschleimhautentzündung f, Gastritis f
gastro- ['gæstrəʊ-] PREF Magen-, Gastro- (spec)
gastroenteritis [ˌgæstrəʊˌentə'raɪtɪs] N Magen-Darm-Entzündung f, Gastroenteritis f (spec)
gastroenterologist ['gæstrəʊˌentəˌrɒlədʒɪst] N Gastroenterologe m, Gastroenterologin f
gastroenterology ['gæstrəʊˌentəˌrɒlədʒɪ] N Gastroenterologie f
gastronome ['gæstrənəʊm] N Feinschmecker(in) m(f)
gastronomic [ˌgæstrə'nɒmɪk] ADJ gastronomisch, kulinarisch
gastronomy [gæs'trɒnəmɪ] N Gastronomie f
gastropod ['gæstrəpɒd] N Bauchfüß(l)er m, Gastropode m (spec)
gastroscopy [gæs'trɒskəpɪ] N (Med) Gastroskopie f (spec), Magenspiegelung f
gaswoman ['gæswʊmən] N pl **-women** [-wɪmɪn] Frau f vom Gaswerk
gasworks ['gæswɜːks] N sing or pl Gaswerk nt
gat [gæt] N (US, sl) Kanone f (sl), Knarre f (sl)
gate [geɪt] ▸ N ▸ a Tor nt; (small, = garden gate) Pforte f; (= five-barred gate) Gatter nt; (in station) Sperre f; (in airport) Flugsteig m; (of level crossing) Schranke f; (Sport, = starting gate) Startmaschine f; (= sports ground entrance) Einlass m, Eingang m; **to open/shut the ~(s)** das Tor etc öffnen/schließen; **the ~s of heaven** das Himmelstor, die Himmelstür or -pforte ▸ b (Sport, = attendance) Zuschauerzahl f; (= entrance money) Einnahmen pl ▸ VT pupil, student Ausgangssperre erteilen (+dat)
-gate [-geɪt] SUF -Skandal m, -Affäre f; **Irangate** der Iran(gate)-Skandal, die Iran(gate)-Affäre
gateau ['gætəʊ] N pl **gateaux** ['gætəʊz] (esp Brit) Torte f
gate: gate-crash (inf) ▸ VT **to ~ a party/meeting** in eine Party/Versammlung reinplatzen (inf); (crowd: = to disrupt it) eine Party/Versammlung stürmen ▸ VI einfach so hingehen (inf); **gatecrasher** N ungeladener Gast; (at meeting) Eindringling m; **gatehouse** N Pförtnerhaus or -häuschen nt; **gatekeeper** N Pförtner(in)

m(f); (Rail) Schrankenwärter(in) m(f); **gate-leg(ged) table** N Klapptisch m; **gate money** N (Sport) Einnahmen pl; **gatepost** N Torpfosten m; **between you, me and the ~** (inf) unter uns gesagt; **gateway** N (lit, fig) Tor nt (to zu); (= archway, gate frame) Torbogen m; **gateway drug** N Einstiegsdroge f
gather ['gæðə] ▸ VT ▸ a (= collect, bring together) sammeln; crowd, people versammeln; flowers, cultivated fruit pflücken; potatoes, corn etc ernten; harvest einbringen; taxes einziehen; support gewinnen; (= collect up) broken glass, pins etc zusammenlesen, aufsammeln; one's belongings, books, clothes (zusammen)packen; **to ~ one's strength** Kräfte sammeln; **to ~ one's thoughts** seine Gedanken ordnen, sich sammeln; **velvet curtains ~ dust/dirt** Samtvorhänge sind Staub-/Schmutzfänger; **it just sat there ~ing dust** es stand nur da und verstaubte; **the serial ~ed a huge audience** die Serie gewann ein riesiges Publikum ▸ b (= increase) **to ~ speed** schneller werden, an Geschwindigkeit gewinnen; **to ~ strength** stärker werden ▸ c (= infer) schließen (from aus); **I ~ed that** das dachte ich mir; **I ~ from the papers that he has ...** wie ich aus den Zeitungen ersehe, hat er ...; **from what** or **as far as I can ~** (so) wie ich es sehe; **I ~ his report is very detailed** ich nehme an, dass sein Bericht sehr detailliert ist; **I ~ she won't be coming** ich nehme an, dass sie nicht kommt; **as you will have/might have ~ed ...** wie Sie bestimmt/vielleicht bemerkt haben ...; **as can be ~ed from my report** wie aus meinem Bericht hervorgeht or zu ersehen ist ▸ d (= draw) **to ~ sb into one's arms** jdn in die Arme nehmen or schließen; **he ~ed her to him** er zog sie an sich; **she ~ed her mink around her** sie hüllte sich in ihren Nerz ▸ e (Sew) kräuseln, raffen; (at seam) fassen ▸ f (Typ) zusammentragen, kollationieren (spec) ▸ VI ▸ a (= collect, people) sich versammeln; (objects, dust etc) sich (an)sammeln; (clouds) sich zusammenziehen; (storm) sich zusammenbrauen; **tears ~ed in her eyes** ihre Augen füllten sich mit Tränen ▸ b (= increase: darkness, force etc) zunehmen (in an +dat) ▸ c (abscess etc) sich mit Eiter füllen; (pus) sich sammeln ▸ N (Sew) Fältchen nt; **there were ~s at the waist (of the skirt)** der Rock war in der Taille gekräuselt or gerafft or gefasst
▸**gather (a)round** ▸ VI zusammenkommen; **come on, children, gather round!** kommt alle her, Kinder! ▸ VI +prep obj **they gathered (a)round the fire** sie versammelten or scharten sich um das Feuer
▸**gather in** VT sep ▸ a (= collect) einsammeln; crops einbringen; taxes einziehen; animals zusammentreiben ▸ b (Sew) cloth fassen
▸**gather together** ▸ VI zusammenkommen, sich versammeln ▸ VT sep einsammeln; one's belongings, books zusammenpacken; people versammeln; team zusammenstellen; animals zusammentreiben; **to gather oneself together** zu sich kommen; (for jump etc) sich bereitmachen (for zu)
▸**gather up** VT sep aufsammeln; one's belongings zusammenpacken; hair hochstecken; skirts (hoch)raffen; (fig) pieces auflesen; **he gathered himself up to his full height** er reckte sich zu voller Größe auf; **to gather up one's courage** seinen ganzen Mut zusammennehmen
gatherer ['gæðərə] N Sammler(in) m(f) → **hunter-gatherer**
gathering ['gæðərɪŋ] ▸ N ▸ a (= group) Gruppe f; (= assembly) Versammlung f; **family ~** Familientreffen nt; **a social ~** ein geselliges Beisammensein ▸ b (of people) Versammeln nt; (of objects) Sammeln nt; (of fruit) Pflücken nt; (of crops) Ernte f; (of speed) Zunahme f ▸ c (Sew) Fältchen nt ▸ ADJ ▸ a (= increasing) dusk, darkness, gloom zunehmend; storm, clouds aufziehend ▸ b (= assembling) crowd zusammenlaufend

gator, **'gator** [ˈgeɪtə] N (US inf) = **alligator**

GATT [gæt] (Hist) abbr of **General Agreement on Tariffs and Trade** GATT nt

gauche [gəʊʃ] ADJ (socially) unbeholfen, tölpelhaft; remark ungeschickt; (= clumsy) linkisch, ungeschickt

gauchely [ˈgəʊʃlɪ] ADV ungeschickt

gaucheness [ˈgəʊʃnɪs] N (socially) Unbeholfenheit f, Tölpelhaftigkeit f; (of remark) Ungeschicktheit f

gaucherie [ˈgəʊʃəri] N **a** = **gaucheness b** (= act) Tölpelei f; (= remark) ungeschickte Bemerkung

gaucho [ˈgaʊtʃəʊ] N Gaucho m

gaudily [ˈgɔːdɪlɪ] ADV painted, decorated, dressed knallig (inf), knallbunt; ~ **coloured** (Brit) or **colored** (US) knallbunt; **a** ~ **patterned carpet** ein Teppich m mit einem knallbunten Muster

gaudiness [ˈgɔːdɪnɪs] N (of colours) Knalligkeit f (inf); (of clothes, paint etc) Auffälligkeit f

gaudy [ˈgɔːdɪ] ADJ (+er) clothes, paint etc knallig (inf), auffällig bunt; colours knallig (inf)

gauge [geɪdʒ] **N a** (= instrument) Messgerät or -instrument nt; (to measure diameter, width etc) (Mess)lehre f; (for rings) Ringmaß nt; (to measure water level) Pegel m; **pressure/wind** ~ Druck-/Windmesser m
b (= thickness, width, of wire, sheet metal etc) Stärke f; (of bullet) Durchmesser m, Kaliber nt; (Rail) Spurweite f; **standard/narrow** ~ Normal-/Schmalspur f
c (fig) Maßstab m (of für)
VT a (Tech, = measure) messen
b (fig, = appraise) person's capacities, character, progress beurteilen; reaction, course of events abschätzen; situation abwägen; mood einschätzen; (= guess) schätzen; **I tried to** ~ **whether she was pleased or not** ich versuchte zu beurteilen, ob sie sich freute oder nicht

Gaul [gɔːl] N (= country) Gallien nt; (= person) Gallier(in) m(f)

Gaullism [ˈgəʊlɪzəm] N Gaullismus m

Gaullist [ˈgəʊlɪst] ADJ gaullistisch N Gaullist(in) m(f)

gaunt [gɔːnt] ADJ **a** (= haggard) hager; (= emaciated) abgezehrt **b** (liter, = stark) building trist; tree dürr und kahl; landscape öde

gauntlet[1] [ˈgɔːntlɪt] N **a** (of armour) Panzerhandschuh m; **to throw down/pick up** or **take up the** ~ (fig) den Fehdehandschuh hinwerfen/aufnehmen **b** (= glove) (Stulpen)handschuh m; (= part of glove) Stulpe f

gauntlet[2] N **to run the** ~ (fig) Spießruten laufen; **to (have to) run the** ~ **of sth** einer Sache (dat) ausgesetzt sein

gauntness [ˈgɔːntnɪs] N **a** (= haggardness) Hagerkeit f; (= emaciation) Abgezehrtheit f **b** (liter: = starkness, of building) Tristheit f; (of landscape) Öde f

gauze [gɔːz] N Gaze f; (Med also) (Verbands)mull m

gauzy [ˈgɔːzɪ] ADJ (+er) hauchfein or -zart

gave [geɪv] pret of **give**

gavel [ˈgævl] N Hammer m

gavotte [gəˈvɒt] N Gavotte f

gawk [gɔːk] (inf) N Schlaks m (inf) VI = **gawp**

gawkily [ˈgɔːkɪlɪ] ADV move, walk schlaksig, staksig (inf)

gawkiness [ˈgɔːkɪnɪs] N (of person, movement) Schlaksigkeit f, Staksigkeit f (inf); (of appearance) Unbeholfenheit f

gawky [ˈgɔːkɪ] ADJ (+er) person, movement schlaksig, staksig (inf); linkisch; animal unbeholfen, staksig (inf); appearance unbeholfen

gawp [gɔːp] VI (Brit inf) glotzen (inf), gaffen; **to** ~ **at sb/sth** jdn/etw anglotzen (inf) or angaffen; **what are you ~ing at?** was glotzt du da? (inf)

gay [geɪ] ADJ (+er) **a** (= homosexual) person schwul (inf); (= for homosexuals) rights für Schwule (inf); sex unter Schwulen; ~ **men and women** Schwule und Lesben pl (inf); ~ **movement**

Schwulenbewegung f; ~ **bar** Schwulenkneipe f; ~ **marriage** gleichgeschlechtliche Ehe, Homoehe f (inf); ~ **group** Schwulengruppe f; **the** ~ **community** die Schwulen pl
b (dated, = happy) fröhlich, unbekümmert; (= merry) party, time, atmosphere lustig; music lebhaft; (= colourful) paint, costumes bunt; **with** ~ **abandon** völlig unbekümmert, ohne Rücksicht auf Verluste (hum)
N Schwule(r) mf; ~ **lib** die Schwulenbewegung

Gaza Strip [ˈgɑːzəˈstrɪp] N Gazastreifen m

gaze [geɪz] **N** Blick m; **in the public** ~ im Blickpunkt der Öffentlichkeit **VI** starren; **to** ~ **at sb/sth** jdn/etw anstarren; **they** ~**d into each other's eyes** sie blickten sich tief in die Augen; **to** ~ **at oneself in the mirror** sich im Spiegel betrachten

▸ **gaze about** (Brit) or **around** VI um sich blicken; **he gazed about** or **around (him) at the strange scene** er sah sich (dat) erstaunt die seltsame Szene an

gazebo [gəˈziːbəʊ] N Gartenlaube f

gazelle [gəˈzel] N Gazelle f

gazette [gəˈzet] **N** (= magazine) Zeitung f, Gazette f (dated); (= government publication) Staatsanzeiger m, Amtsblatt nt **VT** im Staatsanzeiger bekannt geben

gazetteer [ˌgæzɪˈtɪə] N alphabetisches Ortsverzeichnis (mit Ortsbeschreibung)

gazump [gəˈzʌmp] VT (Brit) entgegen mündlicher Zusage ein Haus an einen Höherbietenden verkaufen

GB abbr of **Great Britain** GB nt, Großbritannien nt

gbh abbr of **grievous bodily harm**

GC (Brit) abbr of **George Cross** Tapferkeitsmedaille

GCE (Brit) abbr of **General Certificate of Education**

GCH abbr of **gas(fired) central heating** Gaszentralheizung f

GCHQ (Brit) abbr of **Government Communications Headquarters** Zentralstelle des britischen Nachrichtendienstes

GCSE (Brit) abbr of **General Certificate of Secondary Education**

> ### GCSE
>
> Das **General Certificate of Secondary Education** oder auch **GCSE** ist ein der mittleren Reife vergleichbarer Schulabschluss, den die meisten britischen Oberschüler mit sechzehn Jahren in einer Reihe von Fächern ablegen. Danach steigen sie entweder ins Berufsleben ein oder setzen ihre Schulausbildung bis zum A-Level-Abschluss fort. Die Abschlussnote beim **GCSE** setzt sich normalerweise aus einer Prüfungsnote und der kontinuierlichen Beurteilung der Jahresleistung zusammen, wobei Zensuren von A (die beste Note) bis G vergeben werden. Das schottische Äquivalent ist der **Standard Grade** → A LEVEL

Gdns abbr of **Gardens**

GDP abbr of **Gross Domestic Product** BIP nt

GDR (Hist) abbr of **German Democratic Republic** DDR f

gear [gɪə] **N a** (Aut etc) Gang m; ~**s** pl (= mechanism) Getriebe nt; (on bicycle) Gangschaltung f; **a bicycle with three** ~**s** ein Fahrrad nt mit Dreigangschaltung; **to put the car into** ~ einen Gang einlegen; **the car is/you're in** ~ der Gang ist drin (inf) or eingelegt; **the car is/you're not in** ~ das Auto ist im Leerlauf, es ist kein Gang drin (inf); **to leave the car in** ~ den Gang eingelegt lassen; **to leave the car out of** ~ das Auto im Leerlauf lassen; **to change** (esp Brit) or **shift** (US) ~ schalten; **to change** (esp Brit) or **shift** (US) **into third** ~ in den dritten Gang schalten, den dritten Gang einlegen; **to move up/down through the** ~**s** (durch die einzelnen Gänge) herauf-/herunterschalten; **the car jumps out of**

~ or **won't stay in** ~ der Gang springt heraus; **to move up a** ~ (fig) einen Gang zulegen (inf); **I am usually in bottom** ~ **in the mornings** (fig) morgens dauert bei mir alles länger; **she lives life in top** ~ sie lebt auf Hochtouren; **military production moved into high** ~ die Kriegsproduktion wurde auf Hochtouren gebracht; **to get one's brain in(to)** ~ (inf) seine Gehirnwindungen in Gang setzen → **arse a, ass**[2]
b (inf, = equipment) Ausrüstung f, Zeug nt (inf), Sachen pl (inf); (= tools) Gerät nt, Zeug nt (inf); (= belongings) Sachen pl (inf), Zeug(s) nt (inf); (= clothing) Sachen pl (inf)
c (Tech) Vorrichtung f → **landing gear, steering gear**
d (inf: = drugs) Stoff m (inf)
VT (fig) abstellen, ausrichten (to auf +acc); **to be** ~**ed to(wards) sb/sth** auf jdn/etw abgestellt sein; (person, needs, ambition) auf jdn/etw ausgerichtet sein; (= have facilities for) auf jdn/etw eingerichtet sein; **training is** ~**ed to make staff more efficient** die Ausbildung ist darauf ausgerichtet, das Personal effizienter zu machen
VI (Tech) eingreifen, im Eingriff sein

▸ **gear down VI** (driver) herunterschalten, in einen niedrigeren Gang schalten **VT** sep engine niedertouriger auslegen or machen; (fig) drosseln

▸ **gear up VI** heraufschalten, in einen höheren Gang schalten **VT** sep engine höhertourig auslegen or machen; **to gear oneself up for sth** (fig) sich auf etw (acc) einstellen

gear: ~ **gearbox** N Getriebe nt; **gear change** N Schalten nt

gearing [ˈgɪərɪŋ] N **a** (Aut) Auslegung f (der Gänge) **b** (Fin, of company) Verhältnis nt zwischen Eigen- und Fremdkapital

gear: ~ **gear lever** N Schaltknüppel m; (columnmounted) Schalthebel m; **gear ratio** N Übersetzung(sverhältnis nt) f; **gearshift** (US), **gear stick** N = **gear lever**; **gearwheel** N Zahnrad nt

gecko [ˈgekəʊ] N pl -**os** or -**oes** (Zool) Gecko m

GED (US Sch) abbr of **general equivalency diploma** auf dem zweiten Bildungsweg erworbener Oberschulabschluss

geddit [ˈgedɪt] INTERJ ~? (inf) kapiert? (inf)

gee [dʒiː] INTERJ **a** (esp US, inf) Mensch (inf), Mann (inf); ~ **whiz!** Mensch Meier! (inf) **b** (to horse) ~ **up!** hü!

gee-gee [ˈdʒiːdʒiː] N (baby-talk) Hottehü nt (inf)

geek [giːk] N (esp US inf) Waschlappen m (inf)

geeky [ˈgiːkɪ] ADJ (+er) (esp US, inf) dämlich (inf)

geese [giːs] pl of **goose**

geezer [ˈgiːzə] N (inf) Typ m (inf), Kerl m (inf); **old** ~ Opa m (inf)

Geiger counter [ˈgaɪgəˌkaʊntə] N Geigerzähler m

geisha (girl) [ˈgeɪʃə(ˌgɜːl)] N Geisha f

gel [dʒel] **N** Gel nt **VI** gelieren; (jelly etc also) fest werden; (fig) (plan, idea) Gestalt annehmen; (people) sich verstehen

gelatin(e) [ˈdʒelətiːn] N Gelatine f

gelatinous [dʒɪˈlætɪnəs] ADJ gelatine- or gallertartig

geld [geld] VT kastrieren, verschneiden

gelding [ˈgeldɪŋ] N kastriertes Tier, Kastrat m (spec); (= horse) Wallach m

gelignite [ˈdʒelɪgnaɪt] N Plastiksprengstoff m

gem [dʒem] N Edelstein m; (cut also) Juwel nt (geh); (fig, = person) Juwel nt; (of collection etc) Prachtstück or -exemplar nt; **thanks Pat, you're a** ~ danke, Pat, du bist ein Schatz; **that story is a real** ~ die Geschichte ist Spitzenklasse (inf) or einmalig gut; **every one a** ~ (inf) einer besser als der andere; **a** ~ **of a book/painting** (= splendid) ein meisterhaftes Buch/Gemälde; **she's a** ~ **of a girl/writer** sie ist ein reizendes Mädchen/eine hervorragende Schriftstellerin

Gemini [ˈdʒemɪnaɪ] N Zwillinge pl; **he's (a)** ~ er ist Zwilling

gemsbok ['gemzbɒk] N pl **-boks** or collectively **-bok** (Zool) Gemsantilope f

gemstone ['dʒɛmstəʊn] N Edelstein m

Gen abbr of **General** Gen.

gen [dʒen] N (Brit, inf) Informationen pl; **to give sb the ~ on** or **about sth** jdn über etw (acc) informieren; **to have some ~ on sth** Informationen über etw (acc) haben, etwas über etw (acc) wissen; **what's the ~ on this?** worum geht es hier?

▶ **gen up** (Brit, inf) **VI** **to gen up on sth** sich über etw (acc) informieren **VT** sep **to get genned up on sth** sich über etw (acc) informieren; **to be genned up on** or **about sth** sich in etw (dat) (sehr gut) auskennen

gender ['dʒendə'] N Geschlecht nt; **what ~ is this word?** welches Geschlecht hat dieses Wort?; **the feminine/masculine/neuter ~** das Femininum/Maskulinum/Neutrum

gender: gender-bender N (inf) **a** (Comput) = **gender changer** **b** (= person) **to be a ~** (man) feminin wirken; (woman) maskulin wirken; **gender changer** N (Comput) Stecker-Stecker--Adapter m; Buchse-Buchse-Adapter m; **gender issues** PL geschlechtsspezifische Fragen pl; **gender politics** PL Geschlechterpolitik f; **gender reassignment** N (form) Geschlechtsumwandlung f

gene [dʒi:n] N Gen nt, Erbfaktor m

genealogical [ˌdʒi:nɪə'lɒdʒɪkəl] ADJ genealogisch

genealogical tree N Stammbaum m

genealogist [ˌdʒi:nɪ'ælədʒɪst] N Genealoge m, Genealogin f, Stammbaumforscher(in) m(f)

genealogy [ˌdʒi:nɪ'ælədʒɪ] N Genealogie f, Stammbaumforschung f; (= ancestry) Stammbaum m

gene: gene bank N Genbank f; **gene pool** N Erbmasse f

genera ['dʒenərə] pl of **genus**

general ['dʒenərəl] **ADJ** allgemein; **to be ~** (= not detailed or specific: wording, proposals) allgemein gehalten sein; (= vague) unbestimmt or vage sein; (promises, clause) unverbindlich sein; (= widespread: custom, weather etc) weit verbreitet sein; **his ~ appearance** sein Aussehen im Allgemeinen; **this is not the ~ view** diese Ansicht wird nicht allgemein geteilt; **there was a ~ agreement among the two groups** die beiden Gruppen waren sich grundsätzlich einig; **it met with ~ approval** es wurde allgemein gebilligt; **the ~ attitude toward(s) the war is optimistic** es herrscht allgemein eine optimistische Einstellung zum Krieg; **to be in ~ use** allgemein verbreitet sein; **fortune tellers are so ~ in their statements** Wahrsager halten ihre Aussagen so allgemein; **the ~ plan** or **idea is that ...** wir hatten uns/sie hatten sich (dat) etc das so gedacht, dass ...; **the ~ idea of that is to ...** damit soll bezweckt werden, dass ..., es geht dabei darum, dass ...; **that was the ~ idea** so war das gedacht; **the ~ idea is to wait and see** wir/sie etc wollen einfach mal abwarten; **I've got the ~ idea (of it)** ich habe eine Vorstellung or ich weiß so ungefähr, worum es geht; **to give sb a ~ idea of a subject** jdm eine ungefähre Vorstellung von einem Thema geben; **in ~ terms, in a ~ sense** generell; **she recounted in very ~ terms the events of recent months** sie berichtete in groben Zügen von den Ereignissen der letzten Monate; **I spoke in a ~ way** ich habe ganz allgemein gesprochen; **in the ~ direction of the village** ungefähr in Richtung des Dorfes; **my ~ advice would be to leave them alone** grundsätzlich würde ich Ihnen raten, sie in Ruhe zu lassen; **as a ~ rule** im Allgemeinen; **a ~ ache** ein unbestimmter Schmerz; **~ labourer** ungelernter Arbeiter, ungelernte Arbeiterin; **~ drudge** Mädchen nt für alles; **~ reader** Durchschnittsleser(in) m(f)

N **a** **in ~** im Allgemeinen; **to go from the ~ to the particular** vom Allgemeinen ins Besondere gehen

b (Mil) General(in) m(f)

general: general anaesthetic, (US) **general anesthetic** N Vollnarkose f; **General Assembly** N (of United Nations) Voll- or Generalversammlung f; (Eccl) Generalsynode f; **General Certificate of Education** N (Brit) (= O level) ≈ mittlere Reife; (= A level) ≈ Reifezeugnis nt, ≈ Abitur nt; **General Certificate of Secondary Education** N (Brit) Abschluss m der Sekundarstufe, ≈ mittlere Reife; **general confession** N **the ~** (Rel) das allgemeine Sündenbekenntnis; **general dealer** N (US) = general store; **general degree** N nicht spezialisierter Studienabschluss; **general delivery** ADV (US, Canada, Post, = poste restante) postlagernd; **general election** N Parlamentswahlen pl; **general factotum** N Mädchen nt für alles; **general headquarters** N sing or pl (Mil) Generalkommando nt; **general holiday** N Feiertag m (für alle); **general hospital** N Allgemeinkrankenhaus nt

generalissimo [ˌdʒenərə'lɪsɪməʊ] N Generalissimus m

generalist ['dʒenərəlɪst] N Generalist(in) m(f)

generality [ˌdʒenə'rælɪtɪ] N **a** **to talk in generalities** ganz allgemein sprechen **b** (= general quality) Allgemeinheit f; (= general applicability) Allgemeingültigkeit f; **a rule of great ~** eine fast überall anwendbare Regel

generalization [ˌdʒenərəlaɪ'zeɪʃən] N Verallgemeinerung f

generalize ['dʒenərəlaɪz] **VI** verallgemeinern; **to ~ from sth** allgemeine Schlüsse aus etw ziehen; **to ~ about sth** etw verallgemeinern **VT** verallgemeinern

general: general knowledge **N** Allgemeinwissen nt or -bildung f **ATTR** zur Allgemeinbildung; **general linguistics** N sing allgemeine Sprachwissenschaft

generally ['dʒenərəlɪ] ADV **a** (= on the whole, for the most part) im Großen und Ganzen; **this is ~ true** das trifft im Großen und Ganzen zu **b** (= usually, as a rule) im Allgemeinen, meist; **they are ~ cheapest** sie sind meist or in der Regel am billigsten **c** (= widely) accepted, recognized allgemein; available überall, allgemein **d** (= in general) im Allgemeinen; **information on things ~ allgemeine Informationen; a few words on grants ~** ein paar Worte zu Stipendien allgemein or im Allgemeinen; **~ speaking** im Allgemeinen

general: general manager N Hauptgeschäftsführer(in) m(f); **general medicine** N Allgemeinmedizin f; **general meeting** N Generalversammlung f, Vollversammlung f; (of shareholders etc) Hauptversammlung f; **General Officer Commanding** N (Mil) Oberbefehlshaber(in) m(f); **general pardon** N Generalamnestie f; **general partnership** N (Jur) offene Handelsgesellschaft; **General Post Office** N (Brit, = building) Hauptpost(amt nt) f; (dated, = organization) Post f; **general practice** N (Brit, Med) (= work) Allgemeinmedizin f; **to be in ~ practice** (= place) allgemeinärztliche Praxis, Allgemeinpraxis f; **general practitioner** N Arzt m/Ärztin f für Allgemeinmedizin, praktischer Arzt, praktische Ärztin; **general public** N Öffentlichkeit f, Allgemeinheit f; **general-purpose** ADJ Universal-; **~ cleaner** Universalreiniger m; **general science** N (Sch) Naturwissenschaft f; **~ teacher** Naturwissenschaftslehrer(in) m(f); **General Secretary** N Generalsekretär(in) m(f)

generalship ['dʒenərəlʃɪp] N (Mil) **a** (= office) Generalsrang m; (= period of office) Dienstzeit f als General; **under his ~** als er General war **b** (= skill) Feldherrnkunst f

general: general staff N (Mil) Generalstab m; **general store** N Gemischtwarenhandlung f; **general strike** N Generalstreik m; **General Studies** PL (Brit, Sch) Kurs zur Vermittlung von Allgemeinwissen an spezialisierte Schüler

generate ['dʒenəreɪt] VT (lit, fig) erzeugen; heat, fumes also entwickeln; jobs schaffen; income einbringen; interest wecken; excitement hervorrufen; (Ling) generieren

generating station ['dʒenəreɪtɪŋˌsteɪʃən] Kraftwerk nt, Elektrizitätswerk nt

generation [ˌdʒenə'reɪʃən] N **a** (lit, fig) Generation f; **within a ~** in einer Generation **b** (= act of generating) Erzeugung f; (of jobs) Schaffung f

generational [ˌdʒenə'reɪʃənl] ADJ (within particular generation) der/einer Generation; **~ conflict/divide** Generationskonflikt m; **~ differences** Generationsunterschied m

generation gap N **the ~** Generationsunterschied m; (as an issue) Generationskonflikt m

generative ['dʒenərətɪv] ADJ (Biol) Zeugungs-, generativ (spec); (Elec) Erzeugungs-; **~ organs** (Biol) Zeugungsorgane pl

generative grammar N generative Grammatik, Erzeugungsgrammatik f

generator ['dʒenəreɪtə'] N Generator m

generic [dʒɪ'nerɪk] ADJ artmäßig; **~ name** or **term** Oberbegriff m; (Biol) Gattungsbegriff or -name m; **~ group** Gattung f

generically [dʒɪ'nerɪkəlɪ] ADV (Biol) gattungsmäßig; **they could be ~ described as ...** sie könnten unter dem Oberbegriff ... zusammengefasst werden

generic drug N Generikum nt

generosity [ˌdʒenə'rɒsɪtɪ] N **a** Großzügigkeit f; (of terms) Günstigkeit f **b** (= nobleness) Großmut m

generous ['dʒenərəs] ADJ **a** (= liberal) person, mood großzügig; **they were in a less ~ mood** sie waren weniger großzügig; **to be ~ in one's praise** mit Lob nicht geizen, voll des Lobes sein (geh); **to be ~ with one's time** großzügig mit seiner Zeit umgehen; **he was ~ in sharing his knowledge** er ließ andere an seinem Wissen großzügig teilhaben

b (= lavish) gift, hospitality, subsidy, prize, sum, offer großzügig; terms günstig; (= plentiful) portion, supply reichlich; **a ~ amount** or **helping of ...** eine reichliche Portion ...; **to be a ~ size** großzügig bemessen sein; **a ~ size 14** eine groß ausgefallene Größe 14; **with the ~ support of ...** mit großzügiger Unterstützung von ...; **the car has a ~ boot** (Brit) or **trunk** (US) der Wagen hat einen großzügigen Kofferraum

c (= kind) person, gesture, spirit großmütig; remarks wohlwollend; **she was ~ in defeat** sie war eine großmütige Verliererin; **they were ~ enough to overlook the mistake** sie waren so großzügig, den Fehler zu übersehen

generously ['dʒenərəslɪ] ADV **a** (= liberally) give, donate, provide großzügigerweise; reward großzügig; **to provide ~ for sb** großzügig für jdn sorgen; **please give ~ (to ...)** wir bitten um großzügige Spenden (für ...) **b** (= kindly) offer, agree großmütigerweise **c** (= amply) sized, proportioned, equipped großzügig; **~ cut shirts** weit or großzügig geschnittene Hemden; **to season ~** (Cook) reichlich würzen; **a ~ illustrated book** ein reich illustriertes Buch

generousness ['dʒenərəsnɪs] N **a** = generosity **b** (of portion, supply) Reichlichkeit f

genesis ['dʒenɪsɪs] N pl **geneses** ['dʒenɪsi:z] Entstehung f, Genese f (spec); **(the Book of) Genesis** (die) Genesis, das erste Buch Mose

genetic [dʒɪ'netɪk] ADJ genetisch; **does crime have a ~ cause?** ist Kriminalität erblich bedingt?; **~ information** Erbinformation f

genetically [dʒɪ'netɪkəlɪ] ADV genetisch; **~ engineered** genmanipuliert; **~ modified** gentechnisch verändert

genetic: genetic counselling, (US) **genetic counseling** N genetische Beratung; **genetic engineer** N Gentechniker(in) m(f); **genetic engineering** N Gentechnologie f; **genetic fingerprint** N genetischer Fingerabdruck; **genetic fingerprinting** N genetische Fingerabdrücke pl

geneticist [dʒɪ'netɪsɪst] N Vererbungsforscher(in) m(f), Genetiker(in) m(f)

genetics [dʒɪˈnetɪks] N *sing* Vererbungslehre *f*, Genetik *f*

Geneva [dʒɪˈniːvə] N Genf *nt*; **Lake ~** der Genfer See

Geneva Convention N Genfer Konvention *f*

genial [ˈdʒiːnɪəl] ADJ *person* (= *affable, cordial*) herzlich; (= *jovial*) leutselig; (= *sociable*) gesellig; *smile* freundlich; *company, atmosphere* angenehm; *warmth* wohltuend; **a ~ host** ein warmherziger Gastgeber; **a kind ~ face** ein freundlich lächelndes Gesicht; **in a ~ mood** gut aufgelegt

geniality [ˌdʒiːnɪˈælɪtɪ] N (*of person*) Herzlichkeit *f*; (= *good humour also*) gute Laune; (= *joviality*) Leutseligkeit *f*; (= *sociableness*) Gesellichkeit *f*; (*of smile*) Freundlichkeit *f*

genially [ˈdʒiːnɪəlɪ] ADV *smile, wave* freundlich; *laugh* herzlich; (= *jovially*) leutselig

genie [ˈdʒiːnɪ] N dienstbarer Geist; **the ~ is out of the bottle** (*fig*) der Geist ist aus der Flasche; **to let the ~ out of the bottle** (*fig*) den Geist aus der Flasche lassen; **to put the ~ back in the bottle** (*fig*) den Geist wieder in die Flasche bannen

genii [ˈdʒiːnɪaɪ] *pl of* **genius**

genital [ˈdʒenɪtl] ADJ Geschlechts-, Genital-, genital; **~ organs** Geschlechts- or Genitalorgane *pl*

genital herpes N Herpes genitalis *m*

genitalia [ˌdʒenɪˈteɪlɪə] PL (*form*) Genitalien *pl*

genitals [ˈdʒenɪtlz] PL Geschlechtsteile *pl*, Genitalien *pl*

genital warts PL Feigwarzen *pl*

genitive [ˈdʒenɪtɪv] N (*Gram*) Genitiv *m*; **in the ~** im Genitiv; Genitiv-; **~ object** Genitivobjekt *nt*; **~ case** Genitiv *m*

genitor [ˈdʒenɪtə] N (*Biol*) Erzeuger *m*

genius [ˈdʒiːnɪəs] N *pl* **-es** or **genii** a Genie *nt*; (= *mental or creative capacity*) Genius *m*, Schöpferkraft *f*; **her real ~ as a designer** ihre Genialität als Designerin; **a man of ~** ein genialer Mensch, ein Genie *nt*; **to have a ~ for sth/doing sth** (= *talent*) eine besondere Gabe für etw haben/dafür haben, etw zu tun; **her ~ for languages** ihre hohe Sprachbegabung; **she has a ~ for controversy** sie hat ein Talent dafür, Streit anzufangen; **a flash of ~** eine geniale Eingebung b (= *spirit: of period, country etc*) (Zeit)geist *m* c (= *bad influence*) **evil ~** böser Geist

Genoa [ˈdʒenəʊə] N Genua *nt*

Genoa cake N *mandelverzierter Früchtekuchen*

genocidal [ˌdʒenəʊˈsaɪdl] ADJ *war, campaign* völkermordähnlich; **~ crime** Völkermord- or Genozidverbrechen *nt*

genocide [ˈdʒenəʊsaɪd] N Völkermord *m*, Genozid *nt* (*geh*)

Genoese [ˌdʒenəʊˈiːz] ADJ genuesisch N Genuese *m*, Genuesin *f*

genome [ˈdʒiːnəʊm] N Genom *nt*

genotype [ˈdʒenəʊtaɪp] N Genotyp(us) *m*, Erbgut *nt*

genre [ˈʒɑːŋrə] N Genre *nt* (*geh*), Gattung *f*; (*Art: also* **genre painting**) Genremalerei *f*

gent [dʒent] N (*inf*) *abbr of* **gentleman** Herr *m*; **~s' shoes/outfitter** (*Comm*) Herrenschuhe *pl*/-ausstatter *m*; **"Gents"** (*Brit*, = *lavatory*) „Herren"; **where is the ~s?** wo ist die Herrentoilette?

genteel [dʒenˈtiːl] ADJ a (= *refined*) *person, institution, atmosphere, place* vornehm; *family, manners* vornehm, fein; **to live in ~ poverty** arm, aber vornehm leben → **shabby** b (= *overpolite*) geziert; (= *euphemistic*) *term, language* beschönigend N **the genteel** PL (*form*) die Vornehmen *pl*

genteelly [dʒenˈtiːlɪ] ADV vornehm; (= *overpolitely*) geziert

gentian [ˈdʒenʃɪən] N Enzian *m*

Gentile [ˈdʒentaɪl] N Nichtjude *m*, Nichtjüdin *f* ADJ nichtjüdisch, nicht jüdisch

gentility [dʒenˈtɪlɪtɪ] N Vornehmheit *f*

gentle [ˈdʒentl] ADJ (+er) a *person, disposition* sanft(mütig); *animal* zahm; *voice, eyes, manner, smile* sanft; *treatment* schonend; **to be ~ with sb** (*physically*) sanft or behutsam mit jdm umgehen; (*mentally*) sanft or einfühlsam mit jdm umgehen; **to be ~ with sth** vorsichtig or behutsam mit etw umgehen; **as ~ as a lamb** sanft wie ein Lamm; **she needs ~ treatment** sie muss behutsam behandelt werden; **the ~ or ~r sex** (*dated*) das zarte Geschlecht

b (= *light, soft*) *touch, caress* sanft, zart; *hand* sanft, behutsam; *movement, pressure, breeze, wind, rain* sanft, leicht; (= *low*) *heat* mäßig; (= *not severe*) *hill, slope, curve, landscape* sanft; *colour* sanft, zart; *sound* leise; *pace, stroll, exercise* gemächlich; **cook over a ~ heat** bei geringer Hitze kochen; **we made ~ progress** wir machten langsame, aber stetige Fortschritte

c (= *mild*) *detergent, lotion, cream* mild; **this detergent is ~ on the skin** dieses Putzmittel schont die Haut

d (= *subtle, discreet*) *mild*; *rebuke* sanft, mild; *persuasion* freundlich, sanft; **a ~ hint** eine zarte Andeutung; **a ~ reminder** ein zarter Wink, ein sanfter Hinweis; **to poke ~ fun at sb, to have a ~ dig at sb** jdn freundlich necken

e (= *wellborn*) **of ~ birth** (*dated form*) von edler or hoher Geburt

gentlefolk [ˈdʒentlfəʊk] PL (*dated*) vornehme or feine Leute *pl*

gentleman [ˈdʒentlmən] N *pl* **-men** [-mən] a (*well-mannered, well-born*) Gentleman *m*, Herr *m*; (*trustworthy*) Ehrenmann *m*, Gentleman *m*; **he's a real ~** er ist ein richtiger Gentleman; **be a ~ and take her home** sei ein richtiger Gentleman und bringe sie nach Hause b (= *man*) Herr *m*; **gentlemen!** meine Herren!; (*in business letter*) sehr geehrte Herren!; **gentlemen of the jury/press!** meine Herren Geschworenen/von der Presse! c (*dated: with private income*) Privatier *m*; (*Hist, rank*) Mann *m* von Stand; (*at court*) Höfling *m*; **~-farmer** Gutsbesitzer *m*

gentlemanly [ˈdʒentlmənlɪ] ADJ *man, manner, behaviour* ritterlich, gentlemanlike *pred*; **of ~ appearance** vornehm aussehend; **in an orderly and ~ way** ordentlich und wie Gentlemen/ein Gentleman; **in a ~ manner** in der Art von Gentlemen/eines Gentlemans; **that is hardly ~ conduct** dieses Verhalten gehört sich nicht für einen Gentleman

gentlemen's agreement [ˈdʒentlmənzə-ˈgriːmənt] N Gentlemen's Agreement *nt*; (*esp in business*) Vereinbarung *f* auf Treu und Glauben

gentlemen's club N [ˈdʒentlmənzˈklʌb] (*esp Brit*) *Klub, zu dem nur Männer bestimmter Gesellschaftsschichten zugelassen sind*

gentleness [ˈdʒentlnɪs] N a Sanftheit *f*; (*of animal*) Zahmheit *f*; (*of treatment*) Behutsamkeit *f*; (*of touch, colour*) Zartheit *f*, Sanftheit *f*; (*of pace, exercise*) Gemächlichkeit *f* b (= *mildness: of detergent, lotion, cream*) Milde *f* c (= *subtlety*) Milde *f*

gentlewoman [ˈdʒentlwʊmən] N *pl* **-women** [-wɪmɪn] (*dated*) Dame *f* (von Stand); (*at court*) Hofdame *f*; (*Hist*, = *attendant*) Zofe *f*

gently [ˈdʒentlɪ] ADV *say, smile, slope, fall* sanft; *move, shake, touch, caress, handle, press* sanft, behutsam; *knock* leise; *stroll* gemächlich; *climb* leicht; *simmer, cook* langsam; *treat* schonend; **you must tell him ~** du musst es ihm schonend beibringen; **it/she needs to be handled ~** damit/mit ihr muss man behutsam umgehen; **~ does it!** sachte, sachte!; **the doctor told me to take things ~** der Arzt sagte mir, dass ich es langsam angehen lassen soll (*inf*); **to simmer ~** auf kleiner Flamme langsam kochen (lassen)

gentrification [ˌdʒentrɪfɪˈkeɪʃən] N Aufwertung *f* (*durch Renovierungsarbeiten, Zuzug von sozial besser Gestellten etc*)

gentrify [ˈdʒentrɪfaɪ] VT *area* aufwerten (*durch Renovierungsarbeiten, Zuzug von sozial besser Gestellten etc*)

gentry [ˈdʒentrɪ] PL a Gentry *f*, niederer Adel b (*dated pej*: = *people*) Leute *pl*

genuflect [ˈdʒenjʊflekt] VI (*Rel*) eine Kniebeuge machen

genuflection, genuflexion [ˌdʒenjʊˈflekʃən] N (*Rel*) Kniebeuge *f*

genuine [ˈdʒenjʊɪn] ADJ a (= *authentic, not fake*) *picture, antique, coin, leather, refugee, democracy* echt; **the picture is ~** or **the ~ article** das Bild ist echt or ein Original; **this is the ~ article!** (*inf*: *beer, food etc*) das ist das Wahre!; **she's the ~ article, a cook who loves cooking** (*inf*) sie ist eine richtige Köchin, die das Kochen wirklich liebt

b (= *sincere*) *person, commitment, disbelief, astonishment, feeling* aufrichtig; *concern, interest, buyer* ernsthaft; *offer, friendship, relationship* ernst gemeint, ernsthaft; *Christian, Communist etc* überzeugt; *love, enthusiasm, difficulty* echt; *mistake* wirklich; **she looked at me in ~ astonishment** sie sah mich aufrichtig erstaunt an

c (= *natural, not affected*) *person* natürlich, ungekünstelt

genuinely [ˈdʒenjʊɪnlɪ] ADV wirklich; **he is ~ interested in making it work** er ist wirklich or ernsthaft daran interessiert, dass es klappt; **they are ~ concerned** sie machen sich ernsthafte Sorgen; **I'm ~ sorry that Peter has gone** es tut mir wirklich Leid, dass Peter gegangen ist

genuineness [ˈdʒenjʊɪnnɪs] N a (= *authenticity*) Echtheit *f* b (= *honesty, sincerity*) Aufrichtigkeit *f*; (*of concern, interest, offer, relationship*) Ernsthaftigkeit *f*; (*of love, enthusiasm*) Echtheit *f* c (= *naturalness*) Natürlichkeit *f*, Ungekünsteltheit *f*

genus [ˈdʒiːnəs] N *pl* **genera** (*Biol*) Gattung *f*

geocentric [ˌdʒiːəʊˈsentrɪk] ADJ geozentrisch

geochemistry [ˌdʒiːəʊˈkemɪstrɪ] N Geochemie *f*

geodesic [ˌdʒiːəʊˈdesɪk] ADJ geodätisch

geodesic dome N Traglufthalle *f*

geodesy [dʒiːˈɒdɪsɪ] N Geodäsie *f*

geographer [dʒɪˈɒgrəfə] N Geograf(in) *m(f)*

geographic(al) [dʒɪəˈgræfɪk(əl)] ADJ geografisch

geographically [dʒɪəˈgræfɪkəlɪ] ADV *isolated* geografisch; (*introducing sentence*) geografisch gesehen

geography [dʒɪˈɒgrəfɪ] N Geografie *f*; (*Sch also*) Erdkunde *f*; **policemen who knew the local ~** Polizisten, die sich vor Ort auskannten

geological [dʒɪəˈlɒdʒɪkəl] ADJ, **geologically** ADV [dʒɪəʊ-ˈlɒdʒɪkəl, -ɪ] geologisch

geologist [dʒɪˈɒlədʒɪst] N Geologe *m*, Geologin *f*

geology [dʒɪˈɒlədʒɪ] N Geologie *f*

geomancy [ˈdʒiːəʊmænsɪ] N Geomantie *f*

geometric(al) [dʒɪəʊˈmetrɪk(əl)] ADJ geometrisch

geometrically [dʒɪəʊˈmetrɪkəlɪ] ADV geometrisch

geometrician [ˌdʒɪəməˈtrɪʃən] N Fachmann *m*/-frau *f* für Geometrie, Geometer *m* (*old*)

geometry [dʒɪˈɒmɪtrɪ] N (*Math*) Geometrie *f*; **~ set** (Zirkelkasten *m* mit) Zeichengarnitur *f*

geophysics [dʒɪːəʊˈfɪzɪks] N *sing* Geophysik *f*

geopolitics [ˌdʒiːəʊˈpɒlɪtɪks] N *sing* Geopolitik *f*

Geordie [ˈdʒɔːdɪ] N (*inf*) Bewohner(in)/Dialekt *von Newcastle upon Tyne und Umgebung*

George [dʒɔːdʒ] N Georg *m*; **by ~!** (*dated Brit*) potz Blitz! (*dated inf*); (*indicating determination*) bei Gott! (*dated*)

georgette [dʒɔːˈdʒet] N Georgette *f or m*

Georgia [ˈdʒɔːdʒə] N (*US*) Georgia *nt*; (*in Europe*) Georgien *nt*, Grusinien *nt*

Georgian [ˈdʒɔːdʒɪən] ADJ a (*Brit*) *architecture, house, style, period* georgianisch; **the ~-style library** die Bibliothek im georgianischen Stil b (*Geog, in Europe*) georgisch; (*in USA*) *capital, people, state boundary etc* von Georgia; *person* aus Georgia N a (= *person*) (*in USA*) Einwohner(in) *m(f)* von Georgia; (*in Europe*) Georgier(in) *m(f)* **b** (*Ling*) Georgisch *nt*, Grusinisch *nt*

geostationary [ˌdʒiːəʊˈsteɪʃənərɪ] ADJ geostationär

geothermal [ˌdʒiːəʊˈθɜːməl] ADJ geothermal

geranium [dʒɪˈreɪnɪəm] N Geranie *f*

gerbil [ˈdʒɜːbɪl] N Wüstenspringmaus *f*

geriatric [ˌdʒerɪˈætrɪk] **ADJ** **a** (*Med*) patient geriatrisch; ~ **nurse** Altenpfleger(in) *m(f)* **b** (*pej inf*) altersschwach **N** **a** (*Med*) alter Mensch **b** (*pej inf*, = *senile person*) Tattergreis(in) *m(f)* (*pej inf*)

geriatric: geriatric care N Altenpflege *f*; **geriatric hospital** N geriatrische Klinik

geriatrician [ˌdʒerɪəˈtrɪʃən] N Facharzt *m*/-ärztin *f* für Geriatrie, Geriater(in) *m(f)*

geriatric medicine N Geratrie *f*, Altersheilkunde *f*

geriatrics [ˌdʒerɪˈætrɪks] N *sing* Geriatrie *f*, Altersheilkunde *f*

geriatric ward N Pflegestation *f* (*für alte Menschen*), Geriatriestation *f*

germ [dʒɜːm] N (*lit, fig*) Keim *m*; (*of particular illness also*) Krankheitserreger *m*; (*esp of cold*) Bazillus *m*; **don't spread your ~s around** behalte deine Bazillen für dich

German [ˈdʒɜːmən] **ADJ** deutsch; **he is ~** er ist Deutscher; **she is ~** sie ist Deutsche **N** **a** (= *person*) Deutsche(r) *mf*; **the ~s** die Deutschen **b** (*Ling*) Deutsch *nt*; ~ **lessons** Deutschunterricht *m*; **in ~** auf Deutsch; **to speak ~** Deutsch sprechen

German Democratic Republic N (*Hist*) Deutsche Demokratische Republik

germane [dʒɜːˈmeɪn] ADJ (*form*) von Belang (*geh*) (*to* für)

Germanic [dʒɜːˈmænɪk] ADJ **a** (= *German in character*) *voice, accent* deutsch klingend; (= *typically German*) *trait, style* (typisch) deutsch **b** (*Hist, Ling*) *language, people, tribe, society* germanisch

germanium [dʒɜːˈmeɪnɪəm] N (*Chem*) Germanium *nt*

Germanize [ˈdʒɜːmənaɪz] VT germanisieren; *word* eindeutschen

German: German measles N *sing* Röteln *pl*; **German shepherd (dog)**, (*US*) **German sheep dog** N Deutscher Schäferhund; **German-speaking** ADJ deutschsprachig; ~ **Switzerland** die deutschsprachige Schweiz, die Deutschschweiz; **German text**, **German type** N (*Typ*) Fraktur *f*, Frakturschrift *f*

Germany [ˈdʒɜːmənɪ] N Deutschland *nt*

germ: germ carrier N Bazillenträger *m*; **germ cell** N (*Biol*) Keimzelle *f*; **germ-free** ADJ keimfrei

germicidal [ˌdʒɜːmɪˈsaɪdl] ADJ keimtötend

germicide [ˈdʒɜːmɪsaɪd] N keimtötendes Mittel

germinal [ˈdʒɜːmɪnəl] ADJ (*fig*) aufkeimend (*geh*)

germinal disc N (*Biol*) Keimscheibe *f*

germinate [ˈdʒɜːmɪneɪt] VI keimen; (*fig*) aufkeimen (*geh*); **he let the idea ~ in his mind** er ließ die Idee in sich (*dat*) keimen VT (*lit, fig*) keimen lassen

germination [ˌdʒɜːmɪˈneɪʃən] N (*lit*) Keimung *f*; (*fig*) Aufkeimen *nt* (*geh*)

germ: germ-killer N keimtötendes Mittel; **germ layer** N (*Biol*) Keimblatt *nt*; **germproof** ADJ keimsicher, keimfrei; **germ warfare** N bakteriologische Kriegsführung, Bakterienkrieg *m*

gerontocracy [ˌdʒerɒnˈtɒkrəsɪ] N Gerontokratie *f*

gerontologist [ˌdʒerɒnˈtɒlədʒɪst] N Gerontologe *m*, Gerontologin *f*

gerontology [ˌdʒerɒnˈtɒlədʒɪ] N Gerontologie *f*

gerrymander [ˈdʒerɪmændə] (*Pol*) VT **to ~ constituency boundaries** Wahlkreisschiebungen vornehmen **N** Wahlkreisschiebung *f*

gerrymandering [ˈdʒerɪmændərɪŋ] N (*Pol*) Wahlkreisschiebungen *pl*

gerund [ˈdʒerənd] N Gerundium *nt*

gerundive [dʒɪˈrʌndɪv] N Gerundivum *nt*

Gestalt psychology [ɡəˈʃtæltsaɪˈkɒlədʒɪ] N Gestaltpsychologie *f*

Gestapo [ɡeˈstɑːpəʊ] N Gestapo *f*

gestate [dʒeˈsteɪt] VI (*lit form, animal*) trächtig sein, tragen (*form*); (*human*) schwanger sein; (*fig*) reifen VT tragen; (*fig*) in sich (*dat*) reifen lassen; *plan, idea* sich tragen mit (*geh*)

gestation [dʒeˈsteɪʃən] N (*lit, of animals*) Trächtigkeit *f*; (*of humans*) Schwangerschaft *f*; (*fig*) Reifwerden *nt*; **his book was 10 years in ~** der Reifungsprozess seines Buches dauerte 10 Jahre

gesticulate [dʒeˈstɪkjʊleɪt] VI gestikulieren; **to ~ at sb/sth** auf jdn/etw deuten

gesticulation [dʒeˌstɪkjʊˈleɪʃən] N (= *act*) Gestikulieren *nt*; (= *instance*) Gebärde *f* (*geh*), Geste *f*; **all his ~s** all sein Gestikulieren

gesture [ˈdʒestʃə] N (*lit, fig*) Geste *f*; **to make a ~** eine Geste machen; **a ~ of defiance/approval** eine herausfordernde/zustimmende Geste; **as a ~ of support/goodwill** als Zeichen der Unterstützung/des guten Willens; **his use of ~** seine Gestik VI gestikulieren; **to ~ at sb/sth** auf jdn/etw deuten; **he ~d with his head toward(s) the safe** er deutete mit dem Kopf auf den Safe VT **to ~ sb to do sth** jdm bedeuten *or* zu verstehen geben, etw zu tun

---

get [get]
pret **got**, *ptp* **got** *or* (*US*) **gotten**

1 TRANSITIVE VERB	3 REFLEXIVE VERB
2 INTRANSITIVE VERB	4 PHRASAL VERBS

1 – TRANSITIVE VERB

> When **get** is part of a set combination, eg. **get the sack**, **get hold of**, **get it right**, look up the other word.

a = receive bekommen, kriegen (*inf*); *sun, light, full force of blow* abbekommen, abkriegen (*inf*); *wound* sich (*dat*) zuziehen; *wealth, glory* kommen zu; *time, personal characteristics* haben (*from* von); **where did you get it (from)?** woher hast du das?; **this country gets very little rain** in diesem Land regnet es sehr wenig; **he wanted to get all the glory** er wollte all den Ruhm (haben); **he got the idea for his book while he was abroad/from an old document** die Idee zu dem Buch kam ihm, als er im Ausland war/hatte er von einem alten Dokument; **where did you get that idea?** wie kommst du denn auf die Idee?; **I got quite a surprise** ich war ziemlich überrascht; **I got quite a shock** ich habe einen ziemlichen Schock gekriegt (*inf*) *or* bekommen; **I get the feeling that ...** ich habe das Gefühl, dass ...

b = obtain by one's own efforts *object* sich (*dat*) besorgen; *visa, money* sich (*dat*) beschaffen *or* besorgen; (= *find*) *staff, finance, partner, job* finden; (= *buy*) kaufen; (= *buy and keep*) *large item, car, cat* sich (*dat*) anschaffen; **not to be able to get sth** etw nicht bekommen *or* kriegen (*inf*) können; **to get sb/oneself sth**, **to get sth for sb/oneself** jdm/sich etw besorgen; *job* jdm/sich etw verschaffen; **to need to get sth** etw brauchen; **I've still three to get** ich brauche noch drei; **to get a glimpse of sb/sth** jdn/etw kurz zu sehen bekommen; **you'll have to get a job/more staff** Sie müssen zusehen, dass Sie eine Stelle/mehr Personal bekommen *or* finden; **he's been trying to get a house/job** er hat versucht, ein Haus/eine Stelle zu bekommen; **why don't you get a place of your own?** (= *buy*) warum schaffen Sie sich (*dat*) nicht eine eigene Wohnung an?; (= *rent*) warum nehmen Sie sich (*dat*) nicht eine eigene Wohnung?; **he got himself a wife/a good job** er hat sich (*dat*) eine Frau zugelegt (*inf*)/einen guten Job verschafft; **what are you getting her for Christmas?** was schenkst du ihr zu Weihnachten?; **I got her a doll for Christmas** ich habe für sie eine Puppe zu Weihnachten besorgt; **we could get a taxi** wir könnten (uns *dat*) ein Taxi nehmen; **could you get me a taxi?** könnten Sie mir ein Taxi rufen *or* besorgen?; **we don't get a paper** wir haben keine Zeitung abonniert

c = fetch *person, doctor, object* holen; **to get sb from the station** jdn vom Bahnhof abholen; **can I get you a drink?** möchten Sie etwas zu trinken?; **I got him/myself a drink** ich habe ihm/mir etwas zu trinken geholt; **why don't you get a dictionary and look it up?** warum sehen Sie nicht in einem Wörterbuch nach?

d = catch bekommen, kriegen (*inf*); (*in children's game*) fangen; (= *take*) *train, bus* fahren mit; **to get sb by the arm/leg** jdn am Arm/Bein packen; **he's got it bad** (*inf*) den hats übel erwischt (*inf*); **get him!** (*to dog*) fass!; (*I've) got him!** (*inf*) ich hab ihn! (*inf*); **(I've) got it!** (*inf*) ich habs! (*inf*); **got you!** (*inf*) hab dich (erwischt)! (*inf*); **ha, ha, can't get me!** ha, ha, mich kriegst du nicht! (*inf*); **my big brother will get you!** (*inf*) mein großer Bruder, der zeigts dir *or* der macht dich fertig! (*inf*); **he's out to get you** (*inf*) er hats auf dich abgesehen (*inf*); **we'll get them yet!** (*inf*) die werden wir schon noch kriegen! (*inf*); **I'll get you for that!** (*inf*) das wirst du mir büßen!; **you've got me there!** (*inf*) da bin ich überfragt

e = hit treffen, erwischen (*inf*)

f *Rad, TV* bekommen, kriegen (*inf*)

g Telec (= *contact*) erreichen; *number* bekommen; (= *put through to, get for sb*) geben; **I'll get the number (for you)** (*switchboard*) ich verbinde Sie mit der Nummer; **get me 339/Mr Johnston please** (*to secretary*) geben Sie mir bitte 339/ Herrn Johnston; (*to switchboard*) verbinden Sie mich bitte mit 339/Herrn Johnston; **you've got the wrong number** Sie sind falsch verbunden

h = prepare *meal* machen; **I'll get you/myself some breakfast** ich mache dir/mir etwas zum Frühstück

i = eat essen; **to get breakfast** frühstücken; **to get lunch** zu Mittag essen; **to get a snack** eine Kleinigkeit essen

j = send, take bringen; **to get sb to hospital** jdn ins Krankenhaus bringen; **get the children to bed** bring die Kinder ins Bett; **they managed to get him home** sie schafften ihn nach Hause; **we'll get you there somehow** irgendwie kriegen wir dich schon dahin (*inf*); **where does that get us?** (*inf*) was bringt uns (*dat*) das? (*inf*); **this discussion isn't getting us anywhere** diese Diskussion führt zu nichts; **get the cat out of the room** tu die Katze aus dem Zimmer (*inf*); **to get sth to sb** jdm etw zukommen lassen; (= *take it oneself*) jdm etw bringen; **tell him to get it there as quickly as possible** er soll zusehen, dass das so schnell wie möglich dorthin gebracht wird

k = manage to move bekommen, kriegen (*inf*); **he couldn't get her up the stairs** er bekam *or* kriegte (*inf*) sie nicht die Treppe rauf; **he couldn't get himself out of bed** er kam nicht aus dem Bett

l = understand kapieren (*inf*), mitbekommen; (= *hear*) mitbekommen, mitkriegen (*inf*); (= *make a note of*) notieren; **I don't get it** (*inf*) da komme ich nicht mit (*inf*); **I don't get you** *or* **your meaning** ich verstehe nicht, was du meinst; **get it?** (*inf*) kapiert? (*inf*)

m = profit, benefit **what do you get from it?** was hast du davon?, was bringt es dir? (*inf*); **I don't get much from his lectures** seine Vorlesungen geben mir nicht viel; **he's only in it for what he can get** er will nur dabei profitieren

n in exclamations (*iro inf*) **get (a load of) that!** was sagst du dazu! (*inf*), hat man Töne! (*inf*); **get you!** (*regarding looks*) sag bloß! (*inf*), Junge, Junge! (*inf*); (*regarding ideas*) was du nicht sagst! (*inf*); **get her!** (*regarding looks*) was sagst du zu der da? (*inf*); (*iro*) sieh dir bloß die mal an! (*inf*); (*regarding ideas*) wie ist sie ganz schön clever! (*inf*); (*iro*) hör dir bloß das mal an! (*inf*)

o person (*inf*) (= *annoy*) ärgern, aufregen; (= *upset*) an die Nieren gehen (+*dat*) (*inf*); (= *thrill*) packen (*inf*); (= *amuse*) amüsieren

p to form passive (*inf*) werden; **when did it last get painted?** wann ist es zuletzt gestrichen worden?; **I got paid** ich wurde bezahlt

q set structures

♦ **to get sb to do sth** (= *have sth done by sb*) etw von jdm machen lassen; (= *persuade sb*) jdn dazu bringen, etw zu tun; **I'll get him to phone you back** ich sage ihm, er soll zurückrufen; (= *make him*) ich werde zusehen, dass er zurückruft; **you'll never get him to understand** du wirst es nie schaffen, dass er das versteht

♦ **to get sb + participle you'll get me/yourself thrown out** du bringst es so weit, dass ich hinausgeworfen werde/du hinausgeworfen wirst; **that'll get him disqualified** damit wird er disqualifiziert; **has she got the baby dressed yet?** hat sie das Baby schon angezogen?

♦ **to get sth done/made** *etc* **to get sth done** etw gemacht kriegen (*inf*); **to get the washing done** die Wäsche waschen; **to get some work done** Arbeit erledigen; **I'm not going to get much done** ich werde nicht viel geschafft kriegen (*inf*) *or* bekommen; **we ought to get it done soon** das müsste bald gemacht werden; **to get things done** was fertig kriegen (*inf*); **to get sth made for sb/oneself** jdm/sich etw machen lassen; **to get one's hair cut** sich (*dat*) die Haare schneiden lassen; **I got the bathroom cleaned this morning** ich habe heute Morgen das Bad geputzt; **I'll get the grass cut/the house painted soon** (*by sb else*) ich lasse bald den Rasen mähen/das Haus streichen; **did you get your expenses paid/your question answered?** haben Sie Ihre Spesen erstattet/eine Antwort auf Ihre Frage bekommen?

♦ **to get sth/sb + adjective** (= *cause to be*) **to get sb/sth/oneself ready** jdn/etw/sich fertig machen; **to get sth clean/open/shut** (*person*) etw sauber kriegen/aufkriegen/zukriegen (*inf*); **that'll get it clean** damit wird es sauber; **that'll get it open/shut** damit geht es auf/zu; **to get sb drunk** jdn betrunken machen *or* (*inf*) kriegen; **to get one's arm broken** sich (*dat*) den Arm brechen; **to get one's hands dirty** (*lit, fig*) sich (*dat*) die Hände schmutzig machen; **to get one's things packed** seine Sachen packen

♦ **to get sth to do sth I can't get the car to start** ich kriege das Auto nicht an (*inf*); **he can't get the sum to work out/the lid to stay open** er kriegt es nicht hin, dass die Rechnung aufgeht/dass der Deckel aufbleibt (*inf*); **can you get these two pieces to fit together?** können Sie die beiden Teile zusammen?; **can you get the wound to stop bleeding?** können Sie etwas machen, dass die Wunde nicht mehr blutet?; **once I've got this machine to work** wenn ich die Maschine erst einmal zum Laufen gebracht habe

♦ **to get sth/sb doing sth to get sth going** (*car, machine*) etw in Gang bringen; *party* etw in Fahrt bringen; **to get sb talking** jdn zum Sprechen bringen

♦ **to have got sth** (*Brit*: = *have*) etw haben

2 – INTRANSITIVE VERB

a = arrive kommen; **to get home** nach Hause kommen; **to get here** hier ankommen; **can you get to work by bus?** kannst du mit dem Bus zur Arbeit fahren?; **I've got as far as page 16** ich bin auf Seite 16

♦ **to get there** (*fig inf*, = *succeed*) es schaffen (*inf*); (= *understand*) dahinter kommen (*inf*); **now we're getting there** (*to the truth*) jetzt kommts raus! (*inf*); **how's the work going? – we're getting there!** wie geht die Arbeit voran? – langsam wirds was! (*inf*)

♦ **to get somewhere/nowhere** (*in job, career etc*) es zu etwas/nichts bringen; (*with work, in discussion etc*) weiterkommen/nicht weiterkommen; **to get somewhere/nowhere (with sb)** (bei jdm) etwas/nichts erreichen; **we're not getting anywhere by arguing like this** wir erreichen doch gar nichts, wenn wir uns streiten; **now we're getting somewhere** (*in project etc*) jetzt wird die Sache (*inf*); (*in interrogation, discussion etc*) jetzt kommen wir der Sache schon näher

♦ **to get nowhere fast** (*inf*) absolut nichts erreichen

♦ **to get far** (*lit*) weit kommen; (*fig*) es weit bringen; **you won't get far on £10** mit £ 10 kommst du nicht weit

b = become werden; **to get old/tired** *etc* alt/müde *etc* werden; **I'm getting cold/warm** mir wird es kalt/warm; **the weather is getting cold/warm** es wird kalt/warm; **to get dressed/shaved/washed** *etc* sich anziehen/rasieren/waschen *etc*; **to get married** heiraten; **to get free** sich befreien; **I'm getting bored** ich langweile mich langsam; **things can only get better** es kann nur besser werden; **to get lucky** (*inf*) Schwein haben (*inf*); **how lucky can you get?** so ein Glück!; **how stupid can you get?** wie kann man nur so dumm sein?

♦ **to get started** anfangen; **let's get started** fangen wir an!

♦ **to get + infinitive to get to know sb/sth** jdn/etw kennen lernen; **how did you get to know about that?** wie hast du davon erfahren?; **to get to like sb** jdn sympathisch finden; **to get to like sth** an etw (*dat*) Gefallen finden; **after a time you get to realize ...** nach einiger Zeit merkt man ...; **to get to do sth** (= *get chance to*) die Möglichkeit haben, etw zu tun; **to get to be ...** (mit der Zeit) ... werden; **to get to see sb/sth** jdn/etw zu sehen bekommen; **to get to work** sich an die Arbeit machen

♦ **to get + -ing to get working/scrubbing** *etc* anfangen zu arbeiten/schrubben *etc*; **you lot, get cleaning/working!** ihr da, ans Putzen/an die Arbeit!; **I got talking to him** ich kam mit ihm ins Gespräch; **to get going** (*person*, = *leave*) aufbrechen; (= *start working*) sich daranmachen; (= *start talking*) loslegen (*inf*); (*party etc*) in Schwung kommen; (*machine, fire etc*) in Gang kommen; **get going!** fang an!; (= *leave*) geh schon!

♦ **to have got to do sth** (= *be obliged to*) etw tun müssen; **I've got to** ich muss

3 – REFLEXIVE VERB

♦ **to get oneself ...**

= convey oneself gehen; (= *come*) kommen; **I had to get myself to the hospital** ich musste ins Krankenhaus (gehen); **how did you get yourself home?** wie bist du nach Hause gekommen?; **get yourself over here** komm hier rüber (*inf*)

with adjective sich ... machen; **to get oneself dirty/wet** sich schmutzig/nass machen; **to get oneself pregnant/fit** schwanger/fit werden

+ past participle **to get oneself washed/dressed** sich waschen/anziehen; **he managed to get himself promoted** er hat es geschafft, dass er befördert wurde; **he got himself hit in the leg** er wurde am Bein getroffen; **in order to get oneself elected** um gewählt zu werden; **you'll get yourself killed if you go on driving like that** du bringst dich noch um, wenn du weiter so fährst

4 – PHRASAL VERBS

▶ **get about** **VI** (*Brit*) (*prep obj* in +*dat*) **a** (*person*) sich bewegen können; (*to different places*) herumkommen **b** (*news*) sich herumsprechen; (*rumour*) sich verbreiten

▶ **get across** **VI a** (= *cross*) hinüberkommen; (+*prep obj*) *road, river* kommen über (+*acc*); **to get across to the other side** auf die andere Seite kommen *or* gelangen **b** (= *communicate: play, joke, comedian etc*) ankommen (*to* bei); (*teacher etc*) sich mitteilen (*to* +*dat*); (*idea, meaning*) klar werden, verständlich werden (*to* +*dat*)

VT *always separate* **a** (= *transport*) herüberbringen; (= *manage to get across*) herüberbekommen; (+*prep obj*) (herüber)bringen/-bekommen über (+*acc*) **b** (= *communicate*) *play, joke* ankommen mit (*to* bei); *one's ideas, concepts* verständlich machen, mitteilen (*to sb* jdm); **he got his message across (to them)** er machte es ihnen klar *or* verständlich

▶ **get ahead** **VI** (= *make progress*) vorankommen (*in* in +*dat*); (*in race*) sich einen Vorsprung verschaffen; (*from behind*) nach vorn kommen; **to get ahead of sb** jdn überflügeln; (*in race*) einen Vorsprung zu jdm gewinnen; (= *overtake*) jdn überholen; **if he gets too far ahead in his reading** wenn er im Lesen den anderen zu weit voraus ist; **to get ahead of schedule** schneller als geplant vorankommen

▶ **get along** **VI a** (= *go*) gehen; **I must be getting along** ich muss jetzt gehen, ich muss mich auf den Weg machen; **get along now!** nun geh/geht schon!; **get along with you!** (*inf*) jetzt hör aber auf! (*inf*)

b (= *manage*) zurechtkommen; **to get along without sb/sth** ohne jdn/etw auskommen *or* zurechtkommen

c (= *progress*) vorankommen; (*work, patient etc*) sich machen

d (= *be on good terms*) auskommen (*with* mit); **they get along quite well** sie kommen ganz gut miteinander aus

▶ **get around** **VI** = get about **VTI** +*prep obj* = get round VI b, d VT c, d

▶ **get around to** **VI** +*prep obj* = get round to

▶ **get at** **VI** +*prep obj* **a** (= *gain access to, reach*) herankommen an (+*acc*); *town, house* erreichen, (hin)kommen zu; (= *take, eat etc*) *food, money* gehen an (+*acc*); **put it where the dog won't get at it** stellen Sie es irgendwohin, wo der Hund nicht drankommt (*inf*); **don't let him get at the whisky** lass ihn nicht an den Whisky (ran); (*inf*) na, wenn ich den erwische! (*inf*); **the moths had got at the carpets** die Motten hatten sich an den Teppichen zu schaffen gemacht

b (= *discover, ascertain*) *truth* herausbekommen or -finden; *facts* kommen an (+*acc*)

c (*inf*, = *mean*) hinauswollen auf (+*acc*); **what are you getting at?** worauf willst du hinaus?

d (= *get at sb*) (*inf*, = *criticize*) an jdm etwas auszusetzen haben (*inf*); (= *nag*) an jdm herumnörgeln (*inf*); **he had the feeling that he was being got at** (*inf*) er hatte den Eindruck, dass man das galt *or* dass man ihm was an Zeug flicken wollte (*inf*); **are you trying to get at me?** hast du was an mir auszusetzen? (*inf*)

e (*inf*: = *corrupt*) beeinflussen; (*by threats*) unter Druck setzen (*inf*); (*by bribes*) schmieren (*inf*)

f (*inf*, = *start work on*) sich machen an (+*acc*)

▶ **get away** **VI** (= *leave*) wegkommen; (*prisoner, thief*) entkommen, entwischen (*from sb* jdm); (*sportsman: from start*) loskommen (*inf*); (*fig*, = *break away*) wegkommen (*inf*); (*from* von) **I must get away from here** ich muss hier weg (*inf*); **I'm looking forward to getting away** ich freue mich darauf, mal von hier wegzukommen; **I'd like to get away early today** ich würde heute gern früher gehen; **I just can't get away from him/my work** ich kann ihm/der Arbeit einfach nicht entrinnen; **you can't get away** *or* **there's no getting away from the fact that ...** man kommt nicht um die Tatsache herum, dass ...; **to get away from it all** sich von allem frei machen *or* losmachen; **get away (with you)!** (*inf*) ach, hör auf! (*inf*)

VT *always separate* (= *remove*) wegbekommen; (= *move physically*) *person* weg- *or* fortbringen; *objects* wegschaffen; **get her away from here/him** sehen Sie zu, dass sie hier/von ihm wegkommt; **get them away from danger** bringen Sie sie außer Gefahr; **get him away from the propeller** sehen Sie zu, dass er von dem Propeller weggeht; **get him/that dog away from me** schaff ihn mir/schaff mir den Hund vom Leib; **to get sth away from sb** (= *take away*) jdm etw weg- *or* abnehmen

▶ **get away with** **VI** +*prep obj* **a** (= *abscond with*) entkommen mit

b (*inf*, = *escape punishment for*) **you'll/he'll** *etc* **never get away with that** das wird nicht gut gehen; **he got away with it** er ist ungestraft *or* ungeschoren (*inf*) davongekommen, es ist gut gegangen; **the things he gets away with!** was er sich (*dat*) alles erlauben kann!; **to let sb get away with sth** jdm etw durchgehen lassen; **to**

let sb get away with doing sth es jdm durchgehen lassen, dass er etw tut

c (= *be let off with*) davonkommen mit

▶**get back** **VI** **a** (= *come back*) zurückkommen; (= *go back*) zurückgehen; **to get back (home)** nach Hause kommen; **to get back to bed/sleep** wieder ins Bett gehen/einschlafen; **to get back to work** (*after interruption etc*) wieder arbeiten können; (*after break*) wieder arbeiten gehen; **I ought to be getting back (home/to the office)** ich sollte (nach Hause/ins Büro) zurück(gehen); **I must be getting back (home)** ich muss nach Hause; **we soon got back to the subject of money** wir kamen bald auf das Thema Geld zurück

b (= *move backwards*) zurückgehen; **get back!** zurück(treten)!

VT sep **a** (= *recover*) money, possessions, person zurückbekommen; strength zurückgewinnen; **now that I've got you/it back** jetzt, wo ich dich/es wiederhabe

b (= *bring back*) zurückbringen; (= *put back in place*) zurücktun; **he took it out and can't get it back in** er hat es herausgenommen und kriegt es nicht wieder hinein

c (= *pay back*) **I'll get you back for that** das werde ich dir heimzahlen

▶**get back at** **VI** +*prep obj* (*inf*) sich rächen an (+*dat*); **to get back at sb for sth** jdm etw heimzahlen (*inf*)

▶**get back to** **VI** +*prep obj* (*esp Comm*, = *contact again*) sich wieder in Verbindung setzen mit; **I'll get back to you on that** ich werde darauf zurückkommen

▶**get behind** **VI** **a** (+*prep obj*) tree, person sich stellen hinter (+*acc*); desk sich setzen an (+*acc*); **to get behind the wheel** sich ans or hinter das Steuer setzen

b (*fig*) zurückbleiben; (*person*) ins Hintertreffen geraten; (+*prep obj*) zurückbleiben hinter (+*dat*); (*with schedule*) in Rückstand kommen; **to get behind with one's work/payments** mit seiner Arbeit/den Zahlungen in Rückstand kommen

c (= *support*) **the supporters got behind their team in the second half** in der zweiten Halbzeit fingen die Fans an, ihre Mannschaft anzufeuern

▶**get by** **VI** **a** (= *move past*) vorbeikommen (*prep obj* an +*dat*); **to let sb/a vehicle get by** jdn/ein Fahrzeug vorbeilassen

b (*fig*, = *pass unnoticed*) durchrutschen (*inf*); **how did that film get by the censors?** wie ist der Film nur durch die Zensur gekommen?

c (*inf*: = *pass muster, work, worker*) gerade noch annehmbar or passabel (*inf*) sein; (*knowledge*) gerade ausreichen; **she could just about get by in German** mit ihren Deutschkenntnissen könnte sie gerade so durchkommen (*inf*)

d (*inf*, = *manage*) durchkommen (*inf*); **she gets by on very little money** sie kommt mit sehr wenig Geld aus

▶**get down** **VI** **a** (= *descend*) heruntersteigen (*prep obj*, *from* von); (= *manage to get down, in commands*) herunterkommen (*prep obj*, *from* +*acc*); (*from horse, bicycle*) absteigen (*from* von); (*from bus*) aussteigen (*from* aus); **to get down the stairs** die Treppe hinuntergehen; **get down!** runter! (*inf*)

b (= *leave table*) aufstehen

c (= *bend down*) sich bücken; (*to hide*) sich ducken; **to get down on one's knees** auf die Knie fallen; **to get down on all fours** sich auf alle Viere begeben; **get down, somebody's shooting!** runter, da schießt jemand!

VT sep **a** (= *take down*) herunternehmen; trousers etc herunterziehen; (= *lift down*) herunterholen; (= *carry down*) herunterbringen; (= *manage to get down*) herunterbringen or -kriegen (*inf*)

b (= *reduce*) (*to* auf +*acc*) beschränken; (*as regards length*) verkürzen; temperature herunterbekommen; seller, price herunterhandeln

c (= *swallow*) food hinunterbringen; **get this down (you)!** (*inf*, = *eat/drink*) iss/trink das!

d (= *make a note of*) aufschreiben, notieren

e (*inf*, = *depress*) fertig machen (*inf*); **don't let it get you down** lass dich davon nicht unterkriegen (*inf*)

▶**get down to** **VI** +*prep obj* (= *start*) sich machen an (+*acc*), in Angriff nehmen; negotiations, consideration beginnen; (= *find time to do*) kommen zu; **to get down to business** zur Sache kommen

▶**get in** **VI** **a** (= *enter*) hereinkommen (*prep obj*, -*to* in +*acc*); (*into car, train etc*) einsteigen (*prep obj*, -*to* in +*acc*); (*into bath*) hineinsteigen; (*into bed*) sich hineinlegen; **to get in(to) the bath** in die Badewanne steigen; **to get into bed** sich ins Bett legen; **the smoke got in(to) my eyes** ich habe Rauch in die Augen gekriegt (*inf*) or bekommen; **he can't get in** er kann (*inf*) or kommt nicht hinein; **he got in between them** (*in bed*) er legte sich zwischen sie

b (= *arrive, train, bus*) ankommen (-*to* in +*dat*); (*plane*) landen

c (= *be admitted*) hineinkommen (-*to* in +*acc*); (*into school, profession*) ankommen, angenommen werden (-*to* in +*dat*)

d (*Pol*, = *be elected*) gewählt werden (-*to* in +*acc*), es schaffen (*inf*)

e (= *get home*) nach Hause kommen

f (*inf*: = *manage*) **to get in with a request** ein Gesuch anbringen; **he got in first/before me** er ist mir zuvorgekommen **VT** **a** sep (= *bring in*) hereinbringen (*prep obj*, -*to* in +*acc*); crops, harvest einbringen; taxes eintreiben; (= *fetch*) hereinholen (-*to* in +*acc*); (= *help enter*) hineinhelfen (+*dat*) (*prep obj*, -*to* in +*acc*)

b sep (= *receive*) forms etc bekommen; (= *submit*) forms einreichen; homework abgeben

c sep (= *plant*) (*prep obj*, -*to* in +*acc*) bulbs etc einpflanzen; seeds säen

d always separate (= *get admitted to, into club etc*) (*prep obj*, -*to* in +*acc*) (*as member*) zur Aufnahme verhelfen (+*dat*); (*as guest*) mitnehmen; **how did his parents get him in?** wie haben es seine Eltern geschafft, dass er angenommen wurde?

e always separate (= *get elected*) candidate zu einem Sitz verhelfen (+*dat*) (-*to* in +*dat*); party zu einem Wahlsieg verhelfen (+*dat*)

f sep (= *fit, insert into, find room for*) hineinbringen or -kriegen (*inf*) or -bekommen (-*to* in +*acc*); (*fig*) blow, punch, request, words anbringen; **it was hard to get a word in** es war schwer, auch nur ein Wort dazwischen zu kriegen (*inf*) or bekommen

g sep (= *get a supply*) groceries, coal holen, ins Haus bringen; **to get in supplies** sich (*dat*) Vorräte zulegen

h sep (= *send for*) doctor, plumber holen, kommen lassen; specialist, consultant etc zuziehen

i always separate **to get one's eye/hand in** in Übung kommen

▶**get in on** **VI** +*prep obj* (*inf*) mitmachen bei (*inf*), sich beteiligen an (+*dat*); **to get in on the act** mitmachen, mitmischen (*inf*) **VT** sep +*prep obj* beteiligen an (+*dat*); (= *let take part in*) mitmachen lassen bei

▶**get into** **VI** +*prep obj* → also **get in VI a-d** **a** rage, panic, debt, situation, company etc geraten in (+*acc*); fight verwickelt werden in (+*acc*); trouble, difficulties kommen or geraten in (+*acc*); (*inf*: = *upset*) fahren in (+*acc*) (*inf*); **what's got into him?** (*inf*) was ist bloß in ihn gefahren? (*inf*)

b bad habits sich (*dat*) angewöhnen; **to get into the habit** or **way of doing sth** sich (*dat*) angewöhnen, etw zu tun; **it's easy once you've got into the swing** or **way of it** es ist leicht, wenn Sie erst mal ein bisschen Übung darin haben

c (= *get involved in*) book sich einlesen bei; work sich einarbeiten in (+*acc*); **I just can't get into it** (*job*) ich kann mich einfach nicht einarbeiten

d (= *put on*) anziehen, schlüpfen in (+*acc*); (= *fit into*) hineinkommen or -passen in (+*acc*) **VT** +*prep obj* always separate **a I got the kids into bed** ich habe die Kinder ins Bett gebracht; **those results should get him into any university** mit den Zeugnissen müsste er auf

jeder Universität angenommen werden or ankommen; **his parents wanted to get him into a good school** seine Eltern wollten ihn auf eine gute Schule schicken; **that got the Liberals into Parliament** dadurch kamen die Liberalen ins Parlament; **he always tries to get it into the conversation that ...** er versucht immer, (es) in die Unterhaltung einfließen zu lassen, dass ...

b rage, debt, situation etc bringen in (+*acc*); **to get sb/oneself into trouble** jdn/sich in Schwierigkeiten (*acc*) bringen (*also euph*)

c **to get sb into bad habits** jdm schlechte Gewohnheiten beibringen; **who/what got you into the habit of getting up early?** wer hat Ihnen das angewöhnt/wieso haben Sie es sich angewöhnt, früh aufzustehen?

d **to get sb into a dress** jdm ein Kleid anziehen; (= *manage to put on*) jdn in ein Kleid hineinbekommen or -kriegen (*inf*)

▶**get in with** **VI** +*prep obj* (= *associate with*) Anschluss finden an (+*acc*); bad company geraten in (+*acc*); (= *ingratiate oneself with*) sich gut stellen mit

▶**get off** **VI** **a** (= *descend, from bus, train etc*) aussteigen (*prep obj* aus); (*from bicycle, horse*) absteigen (*prep obj* von); **to tell sb where to get off** (*inf*) jdm gründlich die Meinung sagen (*inf*); **he knows where he can get off!** (*inf*) der kann mich mal! (*inf*)

b (= *remove oneself*) (*prep obj* von) (*from premises*) weggehen, verschwinden; (*from lawn, ladder, sb's toes, furniture*) heruntergehen; (= *stand up: from chair*) aufstehen; **get off!** (= *let me go*) lass (mich) los!; **let's get off this subject** lassen wir das Thema! (*inf*); **he needs to get off his backside and find a job** (*inf*) er muss mal seinen Hintern heben (*inf*) und sich (*dat*) eine Stelle suchen

c (= *leave*) weg- or loskommen; **I must be getting off** ich muss los; **it's time you got off to school** es ist Zeit, dass ihr in die Schule geht; **to get off to an early start** früh wegkommen; **to get off to a good/bad start** (*Sport*) einen guten/schlechten Start haben; (*fig, person*) einen guten/schlechten Anfang machen; (*campaign etc*) sich gut/schlecht anlassen; **to get off on the right/wrong foot** einen guten/schlechten Start haben

d +*prep obj* (= *be excused*) homework, task etc nicht machen müssen; **to get off work/school** nicht zur Arbeit/Schule gehen müssen; **he got off tidying up his room** er kam darum herum, sein Zimmer aufräumen zu müssen (*inf*)

e (*fig*, = *escape, be let off*) davonkommen (*inf*); **to get off lightly/with a fine** billig/mit einer Geldstrafe davonkommen (*inf*)

f (= *fall asleep*) **to get off (to sleep)** einschlafen

g (*from work etc*) gehen können (*prep obj* in +*dat*); **I'll see if I can get off (work)** early ich werde mal sehen, ob ich früher (von der Arbeit) wegkann (*inf*); **what time do you get off work?** wann hören Sie mit der Arbeit auf? **VT** **a** sep (= *remove*) wegbekommen or -bringen or -kriegen (*inf*) (*prep obj* von); clothes, shoes ausziehen; (= *manage to get off*) herunterbekommen or -kriegen (*inf*) (*prep obj* von); cover, lid heruntertun (*prep obj* von); (= *manage to get off*) abbekommen (*prep obj* von); stains herausmachen (*prep obj* aus); (= *manage to get off*) herausbekommen or -kriegen (*inf*) or -bringen (*prep obj* aus); (= *take away from*) abnehmen (*prep obj* +*dat*); **I want to get all these books off my desk** ich möchte diese ganzen Bücher vom Tisch kriegen (*inf*); **get your dirty hands off my clean shirt** nimm deine schmutzigen Hände von meinem sauberen Hemd; **get your shoes off!** zieh die Schuhe aus!; **get him off me!** schaff ihn mir vom Leib! (*inf*); **get him off my property!** schaffen Sie ihn von meinem Grundstück!; **we need to get the homeless off the streets** wir müssen dafür sorgen, dass die Obdachlosen von der Straße kommen; **can't you get him off that subject?** können Sie ihn nicht von dem Thema abbringen?

b *always separate (from bus etc)* aussteigen lassen *(prep obj* aus); (= *manage to get off)* herausbekommen *or* -bringen *(prep obj* aus); *(from boat, roof, ladder etc)* herunterholen *(prep obj* von); (= *manage to get off)* herunterbringen *or* -bekommen, kriegen *(inf) (prep obj* von)

c *+prep obj always separate (inf, = obtain)* bekommen, kriegen *(inf) (prep obj* von); **I got that idea/pencil off John** ich habe die Idee/den Bleistift von John

d *sep (= send away)* mail, children losschicken; **to get sb/sth off to a good start** jdm/einer Sache zu einem guten Start verhelfen; **to get sb/sth off to a bad start** jdn/etw schon schlecht anfangen lassen; **to get sb off to school** jdn für die Schule fertig machen

e *always separate (= let off)* **that got him off school for the afternoon** dadurch musste er am Nachmittag nicht in die Schule; **that got her off doing the dishes** dadurch ist sie um den Abwasch herumgekommen

f *sep (= save from punishment)* accused *(lawyer)* freibekommen *or* -kriegen *(inf); (evidence etc)* entlasten; **only his good manners got him off** er ist nur wegen seines guten Benehmens davongekommen

g *always separate* **to get sb off (to sleep)** jdn zum Schlafen bringen

h *sep (from work etc)* day, afternoon freibekommen

▶ **get off on** [VI] *+prep obj (inf)* einen Kick bekommen von *(inf)*

▶ **get off with** [VI] *+prep obj (inf)* **a** (= *start a relationship with)* aufreißen *(inf)*; (= *have sex with)* bumsen mit *(inf)* **b** = **get away with c**

▶ **get on** [VI] **a** (= *climb on)* hinaufsteigen; *(+prep obj)* (hinauf)steigen auf *(+acc); (on bus, train etc)* einsteigen *(prep obj, -to* in *+acc); (on bicycle, horse etc)* aufsteigen *(prep obj, -to* auf *+acc)*; **get on the back and I'll give you a lift** steigen Sie hinten auf, dann nehme ich Sie mit

b (= *continue: with work etc)* weitermachen; (= *manage to get on)* weiterkommen

c (= *get late, old)* **time is getting on** es wird langsam spät; **he is getting on (in years)** er wird langsam alt

d → **get along a**

e (= *progress)* vorankommen; *(work, patient, pupil)* Fortschritte machen; (= *succeed)* Erfolg haben; **to get on in the world** es zu etwas bringen

f (= *fare, cope: in exam etc)* zurechtkommen; **how did you get on in the exam?** wie gings (dir) in der Prüfung?; **how are you getting on?** wie gehts?; **to get on without sb/sth** ohne jdn/etw zurechtkommen

g (= *have a good relationship)* sich verstehen, auskommen *(with* mit); **they don't get on (with each other)** sie kommen nicht miteinander aus, sie verstehen sich nicht

[VT] **a** *sep (prep obj* auf *+acc)* clothes, shoes anziehen; *hat, kettle* aufsetzen; *lid, cover* drauftun; *load (onto cart etc)* hinauftun; (= *manage to get on)* draufbekommen *or* -kriegen *(inf)*

b *always separate (on train, bus etc)* hineinsetzen; *(+prep obj, -to)* setzen in *(+acc);* (= *manage to get on)* hineinbekommen *or* -kriegen *(inf) (prep obj, -to* auf *+acc); (on bicycle, horse)* hinaufsetzen; *(prep obj, -to)* setzen auf *(+acc)*

▶ **get on for** [VI] *+prep obj (time, person in age)* zugehen auf *(+acc);* **he's getting on for 40** er geht auf die 40 zu; **there were getting on for 60 people there** es waren fast 60 Leute da

▶ **get on to** [VI] *+prep obj (inf)* **a** (= *get on track of)* person auf die Spur *or* Schliche kommen *(+dat) (inf); (dubious activity, double-dealing* aufdecken, herausfinden; **they got on to her trail** sie kamen ihr auf die Spur **b** (= *move on to)* next new subject übergehen zu **c** (= *contact)* sich in Verbindung setzen mit; **I'll get on to him about it** ich werde ihn daraufhin ansprechen

▶ **get onto** [VTI] *+prep obj* = **get on** VI a VT a, b

▶ **get on with** [VI] (= *continue)* weitermachen mit; (= *manage to get on with)* weiterkommen mit; **get on with it!** nun mach schon!;

(inf); **get on with what you're doing** mach weiter; **get on with your work, will you?** nun mach schon deine Arbeit!; **to let sb get on with sth** jdn etw machen lassen; **to leave sb to get on with it** jdn einfach machen lassen; **this will do to be getting on with** das tuts wohl für den Anfang *(inf)*

▶ **get out** [VI] **a** (= *leave)* herauskommen *(of* aus); (= *walk out)* hinausgehen *(of* aus); (= *drive out)* hinausfahren *(of* aus); (= *climb out)* herausklettern *or* -steigen *(of* aus); *(of bus, train, car)* aussteigen *(of* aus); (= *leave)* weggehen *(of* aus); *(fig) (of* aus); *(of business, scheme, contract)* aussteigen *(inf) (of* aus); *(of job)* wegkommen *(of* von); **he has to get out of the country/city** er muss das Land/die Stadt verlassen; **I just need to get out of the house for a while** ich muss nur mal eine Zeit lang aus dem Haus; **let's get out (of here)!** bloß weg hier! *(inf);* **get out!** raus! *(inf);* **get out of my house/room!** verlassen Sie mein Haus/Zimmer!, raus aus meinem Haus/Zimmer! *(inf);* **get out of my life!** ich will nichts mehr mit dir zu tun haben!; **the dog couldn't get out (of the hole)** der Hund kam (aus dem Loch) nicht mehr heraus; **I might need to get out in a hurry** es kann sein, dass ich schnell raus- *(inf)* *or* hinausmuss; **to get out of bed** aufstehen; **to get out while the going's good** gehen *or (of contract, affair etc)* aussteigen *(inf),* solange man das noch kann

b (= *go walking, shopping etc)* weggehen; **you ought to get out (of the house) more** Sie müssten mehr rauskommen *(inf);* **I'd like to get out into the countryside** ich würde gern irgendwo ins Grüne kommen; **to get out and about** herumkommen

c *(lit, fig, = escape, leak out) (of* aus) herauskommen; *(animal, prisoner)* entkommen; *(poisonous liquid, gas)* entweichen; *(news)* an die Öffentlichkeit dringen; **wait till the news gets out** warte, bis das herauskommt

[VT] *sep* **a** (= *remove) (of* aus) *cork, tooth, splinter, stain etc* herausmachen; *people* hinausbringen; (= *send out)* hinausschicken; (= *manage to get out)* hinausbekommen *or* -kriegen *(inf);* **I couldn't get him/it out of my head** *or* **mind** ich konnte ihn/es nicht vergessen; **get him out of my house/sight** schaff mir ihn aus dem Haus/aus den Augen!; **cold water will get the stain out** mit kaltem Wasser bekommen Sie *etc* den Fleck heraus

b (= *bring, take out)* herausholen *or* -nehmen *(of* aus); *car, boat, horse* herausholen *(of* aus)

c (= *withdraw)* money abheben *(of* von)

d (= *produce)* words, apology herausbekommen *or* -kriegen *(inf) or* -bringen

e (= *publish, present)* book, list etc herausbringen

f (= *borrow from library)* ausleihen *(of* aus)

g *(Sport)* batsman ausschlagen

h (= *derive)* **you only get out what you put in** Sie bekommen nur das zurück, was Sie hineinstecken

▶ **get out of** [VI] *+prep obj →* also **get out** VI a, c **a** (= *avoid, escape)* obligation, punishment herumkommen um; *difficulty* herauskommen aus; **you can't get out of it now** jetzt kannst du nicht mehr raus; **there's no getting out of paying tax** man kommt nicht darum herum, Steuern zu zahlen; **I have signed the contract and now I can't get out of it** ich habe den Vertrag unterschrieben, jetzt gibt es kein Zurück

b (= *become unaccustomed to)* **I've got out of the way of playing tennis** ich habe das Tennisspielen verlernt; **I'll get out of practice** ich verlerne es; **to get out of the habit of doing sth** sich *(dat)* abgewöhnen, etw zu tun; **it's hard to get out of the habit of waking up early** es ist schwer sich abzugewöhnen, früh aufzuwachen

[VT] *+prep obj always separate →* also **get out** VT a-c **a** (= *extract)* words, confession, truth herausbekommen *or* -bringen *or* -kriegen *(inf)* aus; **we could get nothing out of him** wir konnten nichts aus ihm herausbekommen

b (= *gain from)* profit machen bei; *money* herausholen aus; *benefit, knowledge, wisdom, much,*

little, nothing haben von; *pleasure* haben an *(+dat); happiness etc* finden in *(+dat);* **there's nothing to be got out of his lectures** von seinen Vorlesungen hat man nichts; **to get the best/most out of sb/sth** das Beste aus jdm herausholen/etw machen; **what can we get out of them/it?** wie können wir von ihnen/davon profitieren?

c **to get sb out of a habit** jdm eine Unsitte abgewöhnen; **to get sb out of (the habit of) doing sth** es jdm abgewöhnen, etw zu tun

▶ **get over** [VI] **a** (= *cross)* hinüberkommen *(prep obj* über *+acc);* (= *climb over)* hinübersteigen *or* -klettern; *(+prep obj)* steigen *or* klettern über *(+acc);* (= *manage to get over)* hinüberkommen; *(+prep obj)* kommen über *(+acc);* **they got over to the other side** sie kamen *or* gelangten auf die andere Seite

b *+prep obj (lit, fig, = recover from)* disappointment, loss, sb's cheek, fact, experience (hin)wegkommen über *(+acc); shock, surprise, illness* sich erholen von; **I can't get over the fact that ...** ich komme gar nicht darüber hinweg, dass ...; **I can't get over it** *(inf)* da komm ich nicht drüber weg *(inf)*

c *+prep obj* (= *overcome)* problem, nervousness, fear, handicap, obstacle überwinden

d (= *communicate, play, actor)* ankommen *(to* bei); *(speaker)* sich verständlich machen *(to +dat)*

[VT] **a** *always separate* (= *transport across)* person, animal, vehicle hinüberbringen *(prep obj* über *+acc);* (= *manage to get over)* hinüberbekommen *(prep obj* über *+acc);* (= *send)* hinüberschicken; (= *fetch)* holen; (= *help sb to cross, climb)* hinüberhelfen *(sb* jdm) *(prep obj* über *+acc)*

b *sep* (= *make comprehensible)* information, ideas etc verständlich machen *(to dat);* (= *impress upon)* klarmachen *(to dat);* **she gets her songs over well** sie kommt mit ihren Liedern gut an; **she got the news over (to them)** es gelang ihr, (ihnen) die Nachricht zu übermitteln

c = **get over with**

▶ **get over with** [VT] *always separate* hinter sich *(acc)* bringen; **let's get it over with** bringen wirs hinter uns; **to get sth over and done with** etw ein für alle Mal erledigen *or* hinter sich bringen

▶ **get past** [VI] = **get by a, b** [VT] *sep* vorbeibringen *(prep obj* an *+dat)*

▶ **get round** *(esp Brit)* [VI] **a** (= *drive, walk etc round)* herumkommen *(prep obj* um); **it's difficult to get round the shops in a wheelchair** es ist schwierig, im Rollstuhl durch die Geschäfte zu kommen

b *+prep obj* (= *evade, circumvent)* herumkommen um; *difficulty, law, regulations* umgehen

c *+prep obj* (= *persuade)* herumkriegen *(inf)*

d *+prep obj* **to get round the conference table** sich an einen Tisch setzen

[VT] *always separate* **a** (= *restore to consciousness)* to Bewusstsein *or* zu sich bringen

b (= *make agree)* herumbringen *or* -kriegen *(inf);* **I'm sure I can get her round to my way of thinking** ich bin sicher, dass ich sie überzeugen kann

c *+prep obj* **to get one's tongue round a word** ein Wort aussprechen können; **I still can't get my head round it** *(inf)* ich kann es immer noch nicht begreifen

d *+prep obj* **to get people (together) round the conference table** Leute an einem Tisch zusammenbringen

▶ **get round to** [VI] *+prep obj (esp Brit inf)* **to get round to sth** zu etw kommen; **to get round to doing sth** dazu kommen, etw zu tun

▶ **get through** [VI] **a** *(through gap, snow etc)* durchkommen *(prep obj* durch); **we only just got through with the car** wir kamen mit dem Auto gerade noch durch; **the news got through (to us)** die Nachricht kam (zu uns) durch

b (= *be accepted, pass)* durchkommen *(prep obj* bei); **to get through to the final** in die Endrunde kommen

c (*Telec*) durchkommen (*inf*) (*to sb* zu jdm, *to London/Germany* nach London/Deutschland)

d (= *communicate, be understood, person*) durchdringen (*to* zu); (*idea etc*) klar werden (*to* +*dat*); **he has finally got through to her** endlich hat er es geschafft, dass sie es begreift

e +*prep obj* (= *finish*) work fertig machen, erledigen; (= *manage to get through*) schaffen (*inf*); book fertig- or auslesen; bottle leer machen; **to get through doing sth** etw fertig machen; **when I've got through this** wenn ich damit fertig bin

f +*prep obj* (= *survive*) days, time herumbekommen or -kriegen (*inf*)

g +*prep obj* (= *consume, use up*) verbrauchen; clothes, shoes abnutzen; food aufessen, verputzen (*inf*); fortune durchbringen (*inf*)

VT *always separate* (= *get out of bed*) aus dem Bett holen; (= *help to stand up*) aufhelfen (+*dat*); (= *manage to get up*) hochbringen; **he couldn't get it up** (*inf*) er hat ihn nicht hochgekriegt (*inf*); **I'll get myself up in the morning** ich stehe morgen früh allein auf

b *always separate* (= *carry up*) hinaufbringen (*prep obj* +*acc*); (= *manage to get up*) hinaufbekommen or -kriegen (*inf*) (*prep obj* +*acc*); (= *help climb up*) hinaufhelfen (+*dat*) (*prep obj* auf +*acc*); (= *fetch*) heraufholen

c *sep* (= *gather*) steam aufbauen; **to get up speed** sich beschleunigen; **to get one's strength up, to get up one's strength** sich erholen, wieder neue Kräfte sammeln; **to get up an appetite** (*inf*) Hunger kriegen (*inf*) or bekommen

d *sep* (= *organize*) organisieren

e *always separate* (= *dress up, make attractive*) person, oneself zurechtmachen; article for sale aufmachen, herrichten; **to get oneself up as sb/sth** sich als jd/etw verkleiden; **to get sth up as sth** or **to look like sth** etw als etw aufmachen

▶ **get up against VI** +*prep obj* (*inf*, = *come in conflict with*) sich anlegen mit (*inf*)

▶ **get up to VI** +*prep obj* **a** (*lit, fig*, = *reach*) erreichen; standard herankommen an (+*acc*), kommen auf (+*acc*); page kommen bis; **as soon as he got up to me** sobald er neben mir stand

b (= *be involved in*) anstellen (*inf*); **to get up to mischief/all sorts** etwas/alles Mögliche anstellen; **what have you been getting up to?** was hast du getrieben? (*inf*)

VT +*prep obj always separate* (= *bring up to*) top of mountain hinaufbringen auf (+*acc*); standard bringen auf (+*acc*)

▶ **get through with VT** +*prep obj* (*inf*, = *finish*) hinter sich bringen; job, formalities, subject erledigen; book auslesen (*inf*), durchbekommen (*inf*); person fertig werden mit; **by the time I've got through with him** wenn ich mit ihm fertig bin; **I'll never get through with that** ich werde das nie schaffen

▶ **get to VI** +*prep obj* **a** (*lit, fig*, = *arrive at*) kommen zu; hotel, town etc ankommen in (+*dat*); **where did you get to last night?** (= *where were you*) wo bist du gestern Abend abgeblieben? (*inf*); **where have you got to in French/with that book?** wie weit seid ihr in Französisch/mit dem Buch?; **to get to a high position** auf einen hohen Posten kommen or gelangen

b (*inf*) **I got to thinking/wondering** ich hab mir überlegt/mich gefragt; **we got to talking about it** wir sind darauf zu sprechen gekommen

c (*inf*, = *annoy, upset*) aufregen; **don't let them/ their comments get to you** ärgere dich nicht über sie/ihre Kommentare; **don't let them get to you with their sarcasm** lass dich von ihrem Sarkasmus nicht rausbringen (*inf*)

▶ **get together VI** zusammenkommen; (*estranged couple*) sich versöhnen; (= *combine forces*) sich zusammenschließen; **to get together about sth** zusammenkommen or sich zusammensetzen und etw beraten; **she has got together with John** sie ist jetzt mit John zusammen; **let's get together and decide ...** wir sollten uns zusammensetzen und entscheiden ...; **why don't we get together later and have a drink?** warum treffen wir uns nicht später und trinken einen?

VT *sep* people, collection zusammenbringen; documents, papers zusammentun or -suchen; thoughts, ideas sammeln; band gründen; money zusammenbekommen; **to get one's things together** seine Sachen zusammenpacken; **once I've got my thoughts** or **head** (*inf*) **together** wenn ich meine Gedanken beisammenhabe (*inf*); **to get it together** (*inf*) es bringen (*sl*); **that's no good, come on, get it together** (*inf*) das taugt doch nichts, nun reiß dich mal am Riemen (*inf*)

▶ **get under VI** darunter kriechen; (*under umbrella etc*) darunter kriechen; (+*prep obj*) kriechen/kommen unter (+*acc*); (= *manage to get under*) darunter kommen; (+*prep obj*) kommen

unter (+*acc*) **VT** +*prep obj always separate* bringen unter (+*acc*)

▶ **get up VI** **a** (= *stand up, get out of bed*) aufstehen

b (= *climb up*) hinaufsteigen or -klettern (*prep obj* auf +*acc*); (*on horse*) aufsteigen (*prep obj, on* auf +*acc*); (= *manage to get up*) hinaufkommen (*prep obj, on* auf +*acc*); (*vehicle*) hinaufkommen (*prep obj* +*acc*); **to get up behind sb** hinter jdm aufsitzen; **he couldn't get up the stairs** er kam nicht die Treppe hinauf; **getting up is all right, coming down is much harder** hinauf or rauf (*inf*) kommt man leicht, nur hinunterzukommen ist schwieriger

c (= *get stronger, wind*) aufkommen; (*sea*) stürmisch werden

get: get-at-able [ˌgetˈætəbl] ADJ (*inf*) leicht erreichbar or zu erreichen *pred*; house, person also zugänglich; **it's not very ~** es ist schwer zu erreichen; **getaway N** Flucht *f*; **to make one's ~** sich davonmachen (*inf*); **to make a quick ~** schnell abhauen (*inf*) ADJ *attr* Flucht-; **~ car/ plans** Fluchtauto *nt*/-pläne *pl*; **the ~ driver** der Fahrer/die Fahrerin des Fluchtautos

Gethsemane [geθˈsemənɪ] N Gethsemane *no art*, Gethsemani *no art*

get: get-together N (*inf*) Treffen *nt*; **family ~** Familientreffen *nt*; **we have a ~ once a year** wir treffen uns einmal im Jahr; **get-tough** ADJ politics aggressiv, entschlossen; **get-up** N (*inf*) Aufzug *m* (*inf*), Aufmachung *f*; **get-up- -and-go** N (*inf*) Elan *m*; **get-well card** N Karte *f* mit Genesungswünschen

gewgaw [ˈgjuːgɔː] N protziges, wertloses Schmuckstück; (*fig*) Lappalie *f*, Kleinigkeit *f*

geyser [ˈgiːzəʳ] N **a** (*Geol*) Geiser *m*, Geysir *m* **b** (= *domestic geyser*) Durchlauferhitzer *m*

G-force [ˈdʒiːfɔːs] N g-Druck *m*, Andruck *m*

Ghana [ˈgɑːnə] N Ghana *nt*

Ghanaian [gɑːˈneɪən] ADJ ghanaisch N (= *person*) Ghanaer(in) *m(f)*

ghastliness [ˈgɑːstlɪnɪs] N Grässlichkeit *f*; (= *appearance*) grässliches Aussehen; (= *pallor*) Totenblässe *f*

ghastly [ˈgɑːstlɪ] ADJ (+*er*) **a** (*inf*, = *dreadful*) person grässlich (*inf*); object scheußlich (*inf*); situa-

tion, experience, mistake schrecklich, furchtbar; pain entsetzlich; **to look ~** entsetzlich aussehen; **I feel ~** mir gehts scheußlich (*inf*) **b** (= *frightening, spectral*) pallor gespenstisch; (= *grim, gruesome*) accident, injuries, war, battle, news schrecklich, entsetzlich; crime, murder grausig

ghat [gɑːt] N (*Indian*) **a** (= *mountain pass*) Gebirgspass *m* **b** (*at river*) Lande- und Badeplatz *m* mit Ufertreppe; **burning ~** Totenverbrennungsplatz *m* an einer Ufertreppe

Ghent [gent] N Gent *nt*

gherkin [ˈgɜːkɪn] N Gewürz- or Essiggurke *f*

ghetto [ˈgetəʊ] N (*lit, fig*) G(h)etto *nt*

ghetto blaster [ˈgetəʊblɑːstəʳ] N (*inf*) Ghettoblaster *m* (*inf*), großes Kofferradio

ghettoization [ˌgetəʊaɪˈzeɪʃən] N **the ~ of this district** die G(h)ettobildung in diesem Viertel

ghettoize [ˈgetəʊaɪz] VT zum G(h)etto machen

ghillie N = **gillie**

ghost [gəʊst] N **a** (= *apparition*) Geist *m*, Gespenst *nt*; (*of sb*) Geist *m*

b (*fig*) **with the ~ of a smile** mit dem Anflug eines Lächelns, **she gave the ~ of a smile** sie lächelte zaghaft; **I don't have** or **stand the ~ of a chance** ich habe nicht die geringste Chance

c **to give up the ~** (*dated inf*) seinen or den Geist aufgeben

d (*TV: also* **ghost image**) Geisterbild *nt*

e (= *writer*) Ghostwriter *m*

VI **to ~ for sb** jds Ghostwriter sein

VT **to be ~ed** von einem Ghostwriter geschrieben sein; **to have sth ~ed** sich (*dat*) etw von einem Ghostwriter schreiben lassen; **to ~ sb's books/speeches** für jdn Bücher/Reden (als Ghostwriter) schreiben

ghost driver N (*US, inf*) Geisterfahrer(in) *m(f)* (*inf*)

ghosting [ˈgəʊstɪŋ] N (*TV*) Geisterbilder *pl*

ghostly [ˈgəʊstlɪ] ADJ (+*er*) geisterhaft, gespenstisch; **a ~ presence** die Gegenwart eines Geistes

ghost in *cpds* Geister-; **ghost story** N Geister- or Gespenstergeschichte *f*; **ghost town** N Geisterstadt *f*; **ghost train** N (*Brit, at funfair*) Geisterbahn *f*; **ghostwriter** N Ghostwriter *m*

ghoul [guːl] N (= *evil spirit*) Ghul *m*; (*fig*) Mensch *m* mit schaurigen Gelüsten

ghoulish [ˈguːlɪʃ] ADJ makaber; description schaurig

ghoulishly [ˈguːlɪʃlɪ] ADV auf makabre Art

GHQ *abbr of* **General Headquarters**

GI (*US*) *abbr of* **government issue** N GI *m*, US- -Soldat *m* ADJ *attr* GI-; **GI uniform** GI-Uniform *f*

giant [ˈdʒaɪənt] N Riese *m*; (= *star also*) Riesenstern *m*; (*fig*) (*führende*) Größe; (= *company*) Gigant *m*; **a ~ of a man** ein Riese (von einem Mann); **football ~** Fußballass *nt*, (*führende*) Größe im Fußball; **insurance/publishing ~** Großversicherung *f*/-verlag *m*; **one of the ~s in his field** einer der Großen auf seinem Gebiet; **the ~ of opera, Luciano Pavarotti** der Gigant der Oper, Luciano Pavarotti ADJ (= *huge*) riesig, riesenhaft, Riesen-; hill enorm; (*in animal names*) Riesen-; **~(-size) packet** Riesenpackung *f*; **~ tortoise** Riesenschildkröte *f*

giantess [ˈdʒaɪəntes] N Riesin *f*

giant: giant killer N (*fig*) Goliathbezwinger(in) *m(f)*; **giant-killing** N Goliathbezwingung *f* ADJ *attr* **Spain's ~ French Open champion** der spanische Favoritenschreck und French-Open-Gewinner; **giant panda** N Großer Panda, Riesenpanda *m*

Gib [dʒɪb] N *abbr of* **Gibraltar**

gibber [ˈdʒɪbəʳ] VI (*ape*) schnattern; (*foreigner*) plappern; **he ~ed at me** er plapperte or schnatterte drauflos (*inf*); **to ~ with rage/fear** vor Wut/Angst stammeln; **a ~ing idiot** ein daherplappernder Idiot; **I was a ~ing wreck by this stage** da war ich schon so nervös, dass ich nur noch Kauderwelsch herausbrachte

gibberish [ˈdʒɪbərɪʃ] N Quatsch *m* (*inf*); (= *foreign language, baby's gibberish*) Kauderwelsch *nt*

gibbet [ˈdʒɪbɪt] N Galgen *m*

gibbon [ˈgɪbən] N Gibbon *m*

gibbous [ˈgɪbəs] ADJ *moon* Dreiviertel-

gibe [dʒaɪb] **N** Spöttelei *f*, Stichelei *f* **VI** spotten, stichen; **to ~ at sb/sth** sich über jdn/etw lustig machen, spöttische Bemerkungen über jdn/etw machen

giblets [ˈdʒɪblɪts] PL Geflügelinnereien *pl*

Gibraltar [dʒɪˈbrɔːltə] N Gibraltar *nt*

giddily [ˈgɪdɪlɪ] ADV **a** benommen **b** *climb etc* Schwindel erregend; *spin* in Schwindel erregendem Tempo **c** (*fig*) leichtfertig, unbesonnen

giddiness [ˈgɪdɪnɪs] N **a** (= *dizziness*) Schwindelgefühl *nt*; **wave of ~** Schwindelanfall *m* **b** (*fig*) Leichtfertigkeit *f*, Unbesonnenheit *f*

giddy [ˈgɪdɪ] ADJ (+er) (*lit*, = *dizzy*) schwind(e)lig; **~ spells** Schwindelanfälle *pl*; **I feel ~** mir ist schwind(e)lig; **it makes me feel ~** mir wird (davon) schwind(e)lig; **heights always make me ~** ich bin nicht schwindelfrei **b** (= *causing dizziness*) *climb, speed* Schwindel erregend; *heights* Schwindel erregend, schwindelnd (*also fig*); *spin* rasend schnell **c** (*fig*, = *heedless, not serious*) leichtfertig, flatterhaft; (= *excited*) ausgelassen; **their life was one ~ round of pleasure** ihr Leben bestand nur aus Jubel, Trubel, Heiterkeit; **she was ~ with excitement** sie war vor Aufregung ganz aus dem Häuschen (*inf*); **that's the ~ limit!** (*dated inf*) das ist wirklich der Gipfel or die Höhe!

gift [gɪft] ○ 16.4, 24.3 **N a** (= *thing given*) Geschenk *nt*, Gabe *f* (*liter*); (= *donation to charity*) Spende *f*; (*Jur*) Schenkung *f*; **to make a ~ of sth to sb, to make sb a ~ of sth** jdm etw zum Geschenk machen (*form*); **there is a free ~ with every purchase over £10** bei jedem Kauf im Wert von über £ 10 erhalten Sie ein Geschenk; **a free ~ of a tin of soup** eine Dose Suppe umsonst; **I wouldn't have it as a ~** ich möchte es nicht geschenkt haben; **that question/goal was a ~** (*inf*) die Frage/das Tor war ja geschenkt (*inf*); **he thinks he's God's ~ (to women)** (*inf*) er denkt, er ist der Traum aller Frauen **b** (*form*, = *right to give*) **this is in the ~ of the government** das liegt im Ermessen der Regierung **c** (= *talent*) Gabe *f*; **to have a ~ for sth** ein Talent *nt* für etw haben; **she has a ~ for teaching** sie hat eine Begabung zur Lehrerin; **he has a ~ for languages/music** er ist sprachbegabt/musikalisch begabt → **gab** **VT** als Schenkung überlassen

gifted [ˈgɪftɪd] ADJ begabt (*in* für); **he is very ~ in languages/music** er ist sehr sprachbegabt/musikalisch sehr begabt

gift: gift horse N **don't look a ~ in the mouth** (*Prov*) einem geschenkten Gaul schaut man nicht ins Maul (*Prov*); **gift tax** N Schenkungssteuer *f*; **gift token, gift voucher** N Geschenkgutschein *m*; **giftwrap** **VT** in or mit Geschenkpapier einwickeln **nt**; **gift-wrapping** N Geschenkpapier *nt*

gig [gɪg] **N a** (= *carriage, boat*) Gig *nt* **b** (*inf*, = *concert*) Konzert *nt*, Gig *m* (*inf*); (*of comedian, singer, group*) Auftritt *m*; **to do a ~** ein Konzert geben, auftreten **c** (*US*, = *temporary job*) Job *m* **VI** auftreten

giga- [ˈdʒɪgə-] PREF Giga-

gigabyte [ˈdʒɪgəbaɪt] N (*Comput*) Gigabyte *nt*

gigahertz [ˈdʒɪgəhɜːts] N Gigahertz *nt*

gigantic [dʒaɪˈgæntɪk] ADJ riesig, riesengroß; *building, man, task also* gigantisch; *appetite, mistake* riesig, gewaltig; *amount* riesenhaft, enorm; **of ~ proportions** von riesigen Ausmaßen

gigantically [dʒaɪˈgæntɪkəlɪ] ADV enorm

gigawatt [ˈdʒɪgəˌwɒt] N Gigawatt *nt*

giggle [ˈgɪgl] **N a** Gekicher *nt* no pl, Kichern *nt* no pl; **..., he said with a ~** ..., sagte er kichernd; **we had a good ~ about it** (*inf*) wir haben uns darüber gekringelt (*inf*); **it was a bit of a ~** (*inf*)

es war ganz lustig; **a fit of the ~s** ein Kicheranfall *m*; **to get the ~s** anfangen herumzukichern; **to do sth as a ~** etw aus Spaß tun **VI** kichern, gickeln (*inf*)

giggler [ˈgɪglə] N Kichernde(r) *mf*; **she's a ~** sie kichert viel

giggly [ˈgɪglɪ] ADJ (+er) albern, gickelig (*inf*)

GIGO [ˈgaɪgəʊ] (*Comput*) abbr of **garbage in, garbage out**

gigolo [ˈʒɪgələʊ] N Gigolo *m*

gigot [ˈdʒɪgət] N (*old*) Hammelkeule *f*; **~ chop** (*Scot*) Hammelkotelett *nt* (*mit Mark im Knochen*)

GI Joe [ˌdʒiːˈdʒəʊ] N (*inf*) GI *m*

gild [gɪld] pret **gilded**, ptp **gilded** or **gilt** VT vergolden; **to ~ the lily** des Guten zu viel tun

gilder [ˈgɪldə] N Vergolder(in) *m(f)*

gilding [ˈgɪldɪŋ] N Vergoldung *f*

gill[1] [gɪl] N (*of fish*) Kieme *f*; **green about the ~s** (*inf*) blass um die Nase (*inf*)

gill[2] [dʒɪl] N (= *measure*) Gill *nt* (*0,148 l*)

gillie [ˈgɪlɪ] N (*Scot*) Jagdaufseher(in) *m(f)*

gilt [gɪlt] ptp of **gild** **N a** (= *material*) Vergoldung *f*; **to take the ~ off the gingerbread** (*fig*) jdm die Freude verderben **b** (*Fin*) **~s** mündelsichere Wertpapiere *pl* **ADJ** vergoldet

gilt-edged [ˈgɪltˈedʒd] ADJ mit Goldrand, goldumrandet; (*Fin*) *securities, stocks* mündelsicher; (*fig*) solide

gimcrack [ˈdʒɪmkræk] ADJ billig; *furniture, toys* also minderwertig

gimcrackery [ˈdʒɪmˌkrækərɪ] N Plunder *m*, Firlefanz *m* (*both pej inf*)

gimlet [ˈgɪmlɪt] N Hand- or Vorbohrer *m*; **her ~ eyes** ihre Luchsaugen; **to have eyes like ~s** Augen wie ein Luchs haben; **~-eyed** luchsäugig

gimme [ˈgɪmɪ] (*inf*) = **give me**

gimmick [ˈgɪmɪk] N Gag *m* (*inf*); (*in film etc*) effekthaschender Gag, Spielerei *f*; (= *gadget*) Spielerei *f*; **an election ~** ein Wahltrick *m*; **changing the name and not the product is just a (sales) ~** den Namen, aber nicht das Produkt zu ändern, ist nur ein (Verkaufs)trick

gimmickry [ˈgɪmɪkrɪ] N Effekthascherei *f*; (*in advertising, sales*) Gags *pl*; (= *gadgetry*) Spielereien *pl*

gimmicky [ˈgɪmɪkɪ] ADJ effekthascherisch

gin[1] [dʒɪn] N (= *drink*) Gin *m*, Wacholder(schnaps) *m*; **~ and tonic** Gin Tonic *m*; **and it** Gin und (italienischer) Wermut

gin[2] **a** (*Hunt*) Falle *f*; (= *snare*) Schlinge *f* **b** (*Tex*, = *cotton gin*) (Baumwoll)entkernungsmaschine *f*

ginger [ˈdʒɪndʒə] **N a** Ingwer *m* **b** (*pej inf, address for person*) Rotkopf or -schopf *m* **ADJ a** (*Cook*) Ingwer-; **~ biscuits/wine** Ingwerplätzchen *pl*/-wein *m* **b** *hair* kupferrot; *cat* rötlich gelb

▸ **ginger up** VT sep (*inf*) in Schwung bringen; *person also* aufmöbeln (*inf*); *book* würzen

ginger: ginger ale N Gingerale *nt*; **ginger beer** N Ingwerlimonade *f*; (*alcoholic*) Ingwerbier *nt*; **gingerbread** N Lebkuchen *m*, Pfefferkuchen *m* (*mit Ingwergeschmack*) **ADJ** attr Lebkuchen-; **~ man/house** Lebkuchenmann *m*/-haus *nt*; **ginger group** N (*Parl*) Aktionsgruppe *f*

gingerly [ˈdʒɪndʒəlɪ] ADV (= *carefully*) *step, walk, touch* vorsichtig, behutsam; *pick up, handle* (*sth dirty*) mit spitzen Fingern; (*sth cold or hot*) zaghaft

ginger: ginger nut N Ingwerplätzchen *nt*; **ginger snap** N Ingwerwaffel *f*

gingery [ˈdʒɪndʒərɪ] ADJ *hair, colour* rötlich

gingham [ˈgɪŋəm] N Gingan *m*, Gingham *m*

gingivitis [ˌdʒɪndʒɪˈvaɪtɪs] N Zahnfleischentzündung *f*

gin mill N (*US inf*) (billige or verrufene) Kneipe

ginormous [dʒaɪˈnɔːməs] ADJ (*inf*, = *enormous*) riesig (*inf*)

gin: gin rummy N Rommé *nt* or Rommee *nt* mit Zehn; **gin sling** N Gin-Fizz *m*

gippy tummy [ˈdʒɪpɪˈtʌmɪ] N (*inf*) Durchfall *m*

gipsy, gypsy [ˈdʒɪpsɪ] **N** Zigeuner(in) *m(f)* **ADJ** attr Zigeuner-; **~ music** Zigeunermusik *f*

gipsy moth N Schwammspinner *m*

giraffe [dʒɪˈrɑːf] N Giraffe *f*

gird [gɜːd] pret, ptp **girded** or (*rare*) **girt** VT (*old*) gürten (*old*); (*fig*) umgeben; **to ~ oneself** sich gürten (*with* mit); (*fig*, = *prepare*) sich wappnen; (*for* für)

▸ **gird up** VT sep (*old*) *robe* gürten; **to gird (up) one's loins** (*esp Bibl*) seine Lenden gürten (*Bibl*); **to gird oneself up** (*fig*) sich wappnen; **he girded himself up for action** er machte sich bereit (zum Handeln)

girder [ˈgɜːdə] N Träger *m*

girdle[1] [ˈgɜːdl] **N a** (= *belt, also fig*) Gürtel *m* **b** (= *corset*) Hüftgürtel or -halter *m* **VT** (*lit*) gürten; (*fig*) umgeben

girdle[2] N (*Scot*) = **griddle**

girl [gɜːl] **N a** Mädchen *nt*; (= *daughter*) Tochter *f*; (= *girlfriend*) Freundin *f*; **an English ~** eine Engländerin; **they are hoping for a little ~** sie wünschen sich (*dat*) ein Töchterchen; **the Smith ~s** die Smith-Mädchen, die Mädchen von den Smiths; **my eldest ~** meine älteste Tochter, meine Älteste; **the ~s** (= *colleagues*) die Damen; **~s' night out** Damengesellschaft *f*; **I'm going out with the ~s tonight** ich gehe heute Abend mit meinen Freundinnen aus; **thank you, ~s** vielen Dank; **the old ~** die Alte (*inf*) or alte Frau; (*inf*, = *wife, mother*) meine/seine *etc* Alte (*inf*) → **big** **b** (= *employee*) Mädchen *nt*; (*in shop*) Verkäuferin *f*; (*in factory*) Arbeiterin *f*

girl: girl band N (*Mus*) Girlband *f*; **girl Friday** N Allroundsekretärin *f*; **girlfriend** N Freundin *f*; **Girl Guide** N (*Brit*) Pfadfinderin *f*; **girlhood** N Mädchenzeit *f*, Jugend *f*; **in her ~** in ihrer Jugend

girlie [ˈgɜːlɪ] **N** (*inf*) Mädchen *nt* **ADJ** attr *magazine* mit nackten Mädchen; *photos* von nackten Mädchen

girlish [ˈgɜːlɪʃ] ADJ mädchenhaft; **she still looked ~** sie sah immer noch wie ein Mädchen aus

girlishly [ˈgɜːlɪʃlɪ] ADV mädchenhaft

girlishness [ˈgɜːlɪʃnɪs] N Mädchenhaftigkeit *f*

Girl Scout N (*US*) Pfadfinderin *f*

giro [ˈdʒaɪrəʊ] N (*Brit*) (= *bank giro*) Giro(verkehr *m*) *nt*; (= *post-office giro*) Postscheckverkehr or -dienst *m*; **~ (cheque)** (*Social Security*) Sozialhilfeüberweisung *f*; **~ cheque** (*for paying*) Postscheck *m*; **to pay a bill by ~** eine Rechnung durch Überweisung bezahlen

Girobank [ˈdʒaɪrəʊbæŋk] N (*Brit*) Postbank *f*; **~ transfer** Postüberweisung *f*

girt [gɜːt] (*rare*) pret, ptp of **gird**

girth [gɜːθ] **N a** (= *circumference*) Umfang *m*; **in ~** im Umfang; **a man of ample ~** ein Mann mit beträchtlichem Umfang **b** (= *harness*) (Sattel)gurt *m*

gismo N (*inf*) = **gizmo**

gist [dʒɪst] N , no pl (*of report, conversation, argument*) Wesentliche(s) *nt*; **that was the ~ of what he said** das war im Wesentlichen, was er gesagt hat; **to give sb the ~ of sth** jdm sagen, worum es bei etw geht; **to get the ~ of sth/the conversation** im Wesentlichen verstehen, worum es sich bei etw handelt/wovon geredet wird; **I got the ~ of it** das Wesentliche habe ich verstanden

git [gɪt] N (*inf*, = *stupid person*) Schwachkopf *m*, Depp *m* (*dial*); **a miserable old ~** ein alter Miesepeter (*inf*)

> **give** [gɪv]
> vb: pret **gave**, ptp **given**

1 TRANSITIVE VERB	3 NOUN
2 INTRANSITIVE VERB	4 PHRASAL VERBS

1 – TRANSITIVE VERB

When **give** is part of a set combination, eg. **give evidence**, **give chase**, look up the other word.

a geben; **to give sb sth** or **sth to sb** jdm etw geben; **they gave us food and drink** sie gaben uns zu essen und zu trinken; **the teacher gave us three exercises** der Lehrer hat uns drei Übungen gegeben or (as homework) aufgegeben; **we were given three exercises** wir haben drei Übungen bekommen or (as homework) aufbekommen; **she was given a sedative** man hat ihr or ihr wurde ein Beruhigungsmittel gegeben; **they gave us roast beef for lunch** sie servierten uns Roastbeef zum (Mittag)essen; **I'd give a lot/the world/anything to know …** ich würde viel/sehr viel/alles darum geben, wenn ich wüsste, …; **what wouldn't I give to be like you** was würde ich nicht darum geben, so wie du zu sein; **to give sb one's cold** (inf) jdn mit seiner Erkältung anstecken; **to give as good as one gets** sich kräftig wehren; **he gave everything he had** (fig) er holte das Letzte aus sich heraus

♦ **to give sth for sth** (= pay) etw für etw ausgeben; (= sacrifice) etw für etw (her)geben; (= exchange) etw gegen etw tauschen; **what will you give me for it?** was gibst du mir dafür?; **how much did you give for it?** wie viel hast du dafür bezahlt?

♦ **give or take 11 o'clock, give or take a few minutes** so gegen 11 Uhr; **six foot, give or take a few inches** ungefähr sechs Fuß

b as present schenken; (= donate) spenden, geben; **to give sb sth** or **sth to sb** jdm etw schenken; **it was given to me by my uncle, I was given it by my uncle** ich habe es von meinem Onkel bekommen or geschenkt bekommen; **he gave me a book as a present** er schenkte mir ein Buch, er machte mir ein Buch zum Geschenk

c with abstract nouns trouble machen; one's love, attention schenken; hospitality gewähren; **he gave the impression he didn't care** er machte den Eindruck, als ob es ihm egal wäre; **to give sb help** jdm helfen or Hilfe leisten; **to give sb support** jdn unterstützen; **(God) give me strength to do it** Gott gebe mir die Kraft, es zu tun!; **give me strength/patience!** großer Gott! (inf); **to be given a choice** die Wahl haben; **I wasn't given any choice** ich hatte keine Wahl; **to give sb a look/smile** jdn ansehen/anlächeln; **to give sb a blow** jdn schlagen, jdm einen Schlag versetzen; **to give sb a push/kick** jdm einen Stoß/Tritt geben, jdn stoßen/treten; **to give sb's hand a squeeze** jdm die Hand drücken; **to give one's hair a brush/wash** sich (dat) die Haare bürsten/waschen; **this incident gave him the basic plot of the story** durch dieses Ereignis bekam er die Grundidee für die Handlung der Geschichte; **who gave you that idea?** wer hat dich denn auf die Idee gebracht?; **what gives you that idea?** wie kommst du denn auf die Idee?; **that will give you something to think about** da hast du etwas, worüber du nachdenken kannst; **I'll give you something to cry about** ich werde schon zusehen, dass du weißt, warum du weinst; **give me Shakespeare/Spain (every time)!** (inf) es geht doch nichts über Shakespeare/Spanien!; **give me Renoir and Rembrandt, not these surrealist artists** mir sind Renoir und Rembrandt viel lieber als diese Surrealisten

♦ **to give way** = yield nachgeben (to +dat); **I'm not going to give way on this** ich werde in dieser Sache nicht nachgeben; **to give way to pressure** unter Druck nachgeben; **don't give way to despair** überlass dich nicht der Verzweiflung; **she gave way to tears** sie ließ den Tränen freien Lauf = be superseded to give way to sth von etw abgelöst werden; **tears gave way to smiles** die Tränen machten einem Lächeln Platz; **radio has almost given way to television** das Radio ist vom Fernsehen fast verdrängt worden on road (Brit) **give way to oncoming traffic** der Gegenverkehr hat Vorfahrt; **who has to give way here?** wer hat hier Vorfahrt?; **I was expecting him to give way** ich nahm an, er würde mir die Vorfahrt lassen; **"give way"** „Vorfahrt (gewähren)"

d = cause, cause to feel pleasure, joy machen, bereiten; pain bereiten; **to give sb pain** jdm wehtun (also fig), jdm Schmerzen bereiten; **it gives me great pleasure to …** es ist mir eine große Freude …; **to give sb a shock** jdm einen Schock versetzen

♦ **to give sb to understand that …** jdm zu verstehen geben, dass …; **I was given to understand/believe that …** mir wurde zu verstehen gegeben, dass …

e = punish with erteilen; **he gave the child a smack** er gab dem Kind einen Klaps; **he gave her 100 lines** (Brit) or **sentences** (US) er gab ihr 100 Zeilen als Strafarbeit auf; **to give sb five years** jdn zu fünf Jahren verurteilen, jdm fünf Jahre aufbrummen (inf); **he was given a thrashing/five years** er hat eine Tracht Prügel/fünf Jahre bekommen

♦ **to give sb what for** (inf) jdm Saures geben (inf), es jdm geben (inf)

f = utter **to give a cry/groan/laugh/sigh** aufschreien/-stöhnen/-lachen/-seufzen

g = yield, produce milk, warmth, light etc geben; results (er)bringen; answer liefern; **our satellite dish gives a very good picture** unsere Parabolantenne gibt ein sehr gutes Bild

h = allow time geben; **they gave me a week to do it** sie gaben or ließen mir eine Woche Zeit, um es zu machen; **give yourself time to recover** lassen Sie sich Zeit, um sich zu erholen; **give yourself half an hour** rechnen Sie mit einer halben Stunde; **I always give myself an extra hour in bed** ich genehmige mir eine Extrastunde im Bett; **how long do you give that marriage?** (inf) wie lange gibst du dieser Ehe? (inf)

♦ **I'll give you that** (= concede) **it's an improvement, I'll give you that** es ist eine Verbesserung, das gestehe ich (dir) ein; **he's a good worker, I'll give you that** eines muss man ihm lassen, er arbeitet gut

i = report, tell information, details, description, answer, advice geben; one's name, particulars angeben; suggestion machen; (= let sb know by letter, phone etc) decision, opinion, results mitteilen; **the court hasn't given a decision yet** das Gericht hat noch kein Urteil gefällt; **he wouldn't give me his decision/opinion** er wollte mir seine Entscheidung/Meinung nicht sagen; **they interrupted the film to give the football results** sie unterbrachen den Film, um die Fußballergebnisse zu bringen; **give him my regards** bestellen Sie ihm (schöne) Grüße, richten Sie ihm (schöne) Grüße von mir aus; **give her my thanks** richten Sie ihr meinen Dank aus; **to give no/the right answer** nicht/richtig antworten; **to give sb a warning** jdn warnen; **his letter gave us the latest news** in seinem Brief stand das Neueste; **she was given the news by John** John hat ihr das mitgeteilt; **he forgot to give us the date** er hat vergessen, uns das Datum anzugeben or (verbally also) zu sagen or (by letter, phone etc also) mitzuteilen; **who gave you that information?** wer hat Ihnen das gesagt or die Auskunft gegeben or erteilt?

j = hold, perform party, dinner, play geben; speech halten; song singen; toast ausbringen (to sb or jdn); **give us a song** sing uns was vor; **I give you Mary** (as toast) auf Mary!, auf Marys Wohl!; (as speaker) ich gebe Mary das Wort

k = do **the child gave a little jump of excitement** das Kind machte vor Aufregung einen kleinen Luftsprung; **he gave a shrug of his shoulders** er zuckte mit den Schultern

l = devote widmen (to +dat); **he has given himself entirely to medicine** er hat sich ganz der Medizin verschrieben; **he gave himself/his life to God** er weihte sich/sein Leben Gott

2 – INTRANSITIVE VERB

a = give way (lit, fig) (= collapse, yield) nachgeben; (strength, health, nerve, voice) versagen; (= break, rope, cable) reißen; (cold weather) nachlassen; **when you're under as much strain as that, something is bound to give** (inf) wenn man unter so viel Druck steht, muss es ja irgendwo aushaken (inf)

b = bend, be flexible nachgeben; (bed) federn; (dress) sich dehnen or weiten

c = give money etc geben, spenden; **it is more blessed to give than to receive** (Bibl) Geben ist seliger denn Nehmen; **you have to be prepared to give and take** (fig) man muss zu Kompromissen bereit sein, man muss auch mal zurückstecken können

d = be the matter (esp US inf) **what gives?** was gibts? (inf), was ist los? (inf); **what gives with him?** was ist los mit ihm? (inf); **what gives in this town?** was ist hier (in der Stadt) los? (inf)

e = tell (US inf) **OK, now give!** also, raus mit der Sprache! (inf)

3 – NOUN

Nachgiebigkeit f, Elastizität f; (of floor, bed, chair) Federung f; **this elastic hasn't got much give left** dieses Gummiband ist nicht mehr sehr elastisch; **it has a lot of give** es gibt sehr stark nach

4 – PHRASAL VERBS

▶ **give away** VT sep **a** (= give without charge) weggeben; (as present) verschenken; **at £5 I'm practically giving it away** ich will 5 £ dafür, das ist fast geschenkt **b** advantage, goal verschenken **c** bride zum Altar führen (als Brautvater etc) **d** (= hand out) prizes etc vergeben, verteilen **e** (fig, = betray) verraten (to sb an jdn); **to give the game** or **show away** (inf) alles verraten; **to give oneself away** sich verraten

▶ **give back** VT sep zurück- or wiedergeben; (mirror) image reflektieren

▶ **give in** VI (= surrender) sich ergeben (to sb jdm); (in guessing game etc) aufgeben; (= accede, back down) nachgeben (to +dat); **to give in to the majority** sich der Mehrheit beugen; **to give in to blackmail** auf Erpressung eingehen; **to give in to temptation** der Versuchung erliegen or nicht widerstehen VT sep document, essay einreichen; **to give in sb's/one's name** jdn/sich anmelden

▶ **give off** VT insep heat, gas abgeben; smell verbreiten, ausströmen; rays ausstrahlen

▶ **give on to** VI +prep obj (window) hinausgehen auf (+acc); (door) hinausführen auf (+acc); garden hinausführen in (+acc)

▶ **give out** VI (supplies, patience, strength) zu Ende gehen or (in past tense) sein; (engine, feet) versagen; (inspiration) versiegen; **my voice gave out** mir versagte die Stimme VT sep **a** (= distribute) aus- or verteilen **b** (= announce) bekannt geben; **to give oneself out as sth** or **to be sth** sich als etw ausgeben VT insep = **give off**

▶ **give over** VT sep **a** (= hand over) übergeben (to +dat) **b** (= set aside, use for) **to be given over to sth** für etw beansprucht werden **c** **to give oneself over to pleasure/despair** etc sich ganz dem Vergnügen/der Verzweiflung etc hingeben; **to be given over to pleasure** (life) ganz dem Vergnügen gewidmet sein VI (dial inf, = stop) aufhören; **give over!** hör auf! VI +prep obj aufhören; **give over tickling me!** hör auf, mich zu kitzeln!

▶ **give up** VI aufgeben; **I give up** ich gebe auf, ich gebs auf (inf) VT sep **a** habit, job, idea, hope aufgeben; claim verzichten auf (+acc), aufgeben; **to give up doing sth** aufhören or es aufgeben, etw zu tun; **I'm trying to give up smoking** ich versuche, das Rauchen aufzugeben; **I gave it/him up as a bad job** ich habe ihn/es abgeschrieben; **to give sb/sth up as lost** jdn/etw verloren geben; **to give sb up for dead** jdn für tot halten

b (= *surrender*) *land, territory* abgeben, abtreten (*to* +*dat*); *authority* abgeben, abtreten (*to an* +*acc*); *seat, place* freimachen (*to für*), abtreten (*to* +*dat*); *ticket* abgeben (*to bei*); **to give up one's life for one's country** sein Leben für sein Land opfern **c** (= *hand over to authorities*) übergeben (*to dat*); **to give oneself up** sich stellen; (*after siege etc*) sich ergeben **d** (= *devote*) widmen; **to give one's life up to music** sein Leben der Musik widmen *or* verschreiben **e** (= *disclose, yield up*) *secret, treasure* enthüllen (*geh*)

▶ **give up on** ⟨VI⟩ +*prep obj person, project* abschreiben; **to give up on life** am Leben verzweifeln

give: give-and-take N Entgegenkommen *nt*; (*in personal relationships*) (gegenseitiges) Geben und Nehmen; **giveaway** N **a** **the expression on her face was a (dead) ~** ihr Gesichtsausdruck verriet (wirklich) alles; **it was a real ~ when he said ...** er verriet sich, als er sagte ... **b** (*inf*) **that exam question was a ~** diese Prüfungsfrage war geschenkt **c** (*US, Comm,* = *gift*) Geschenk *nt* **d** (*US: Rad, TV*) Preisraten *nt*; **giveaway price** N Schleuderpreis *m*

given ['gɪvn] *ptp of* **give** ADJ **a** (*with indef art*) bestimmt; (*with def art*) angegeben; **in a ~ period** in einem bestimmten Zeitraum; **within the ~ period** im angegebenen Zeitraum **b** **~ name** (*esp US*) Vorname *m* **c** (= *having inclination*) **to be ~ to sth** zu etw neigen; **I'm ~ to doing that** ich tue das gern; **I'm not ~ to doing that** es ist nicht meine Art, das zu tun; **I'm not ~ to drinking on my own** ich habe nicht die Angewohnheit, allein zu trinken ⟨CONJ⟩ **~ sth** (= *with*) vorausgesetzt, man/er etc hat etw, wenn man/er etc etw hat; (= *in view of*) angesichts einer Sache (*gen*); **~ that he ...** (= *in view of the fact*) angesichts der Tatsache, dass er ...; (= *assuming*) vorausgesetzt *or* angenommen, (dass) er ...; **~ time, we can do it** vorausgesetzt, wir haben genug Zeit *or* wenn wir genug Zeit haben, können wir es schaffen; **~ the chance, I would ...** wenn ich die Gelegenheit hätte, würde ich ...; **~ these circumstances/conditions** unter diesen Umständen/Voraussetzungen; **~ these premises you can work out the answer** anhand dieser Voraussetzungen kannst du die Lösung finden; **~ the triangle ABC** (*Math*) gegeben ist *or* sei das Dreieck ABC

giver ['gɪvə'] N Spender(in) *m(f)*; **he was a generous ~ to church funds** er hat großzügig für die Kirche gespendet

give-way sign [gɪv'weɪˌsaɪn] N (*Brit*) Vorfahrtsschild *nt*

giving ['gɪvɪŋ] ADJ großzügig

gizmo ['gɪzməʊ] N (*inf*) Ding *nt* (*inf*)

gizzard ['gɪzəd] N Muskelmagen *m*

Gk *abbr of* **Greek** griech.

glabrous ['gleɪbrəs] ADJ (*Zool*) unbehaart; (*liter*) *youth* bartlos

glacé ['glæseɪ] ADJ *bun* mit Zuckerguss, glasiert; *cherry, fruit* kandiert; **~ icing** Zuckerguss *m*; **~ leather** Glacee- *or* Glacéleder *nt*

glacial ['gleɪsɪəl] ADJ **a** (*Geol*) Gletscher-, glazial (*spec*); **~ landscape** Gletscherlandschaft *f*; **at a ~ pace** (*fig*) im Schneckentempo **b** (= *cold*) *look, wind* eisig; (*fig*) *person, atmosphere, smile* frostig

glacial period N Eiszeit *f*, Glazial *nt* (*form*)

glaciated ['gleɪsɪeɪtɪd] ADJ (= *covered with glaciers*) gletscherbedeckt, vergletschert; (= *eroded by glaciers*) durch Gletschertätigkeit entstanden

glacier ['glæsɪə'] N Gletscher *m*

glaciology [ˌgleɪsɪ'ɒlədʒɪ] N Gletscherkunde *f*, Glaziologie *f* (*form*)

glad [glæd] ✪ 3.1, 25.2 ADJ (+*er*) **a** *pred* (= *pleased*) froh; **to be ~ about sth** sich über etw (*acc*) freuen; **I'm ~ (about that)** das freut mich, da bin ich froh; **to be ~ of sth** froh über etw

(*acc*) sein; **he was ~ of a chance to change the subject** er freute sich über die Gelegenheit, das Thema zu wechseln; **I'd be ~ of an opportunity to show you the house** ich würde dir gerne das Haus zeigen; **you'll be ~ of an umbrella** du wirst einen Schirm gut gebrauchen können; **we'd be ~ of your help** wir wären froh, wenn Sie uns helfen könnten; **I'd be ~ of your opinion on this** ich würde gerne Ihre Meinung dazu hören; **to be ~ (that)...** sich freuen, dass ...; (= *relieved*) froh sein, dass ...; **I'm ~ you like it** ich freue mich, dass es Ihnen gefällt; **I'm ~ I relented in the end** ich bin froh, dass ich schließlich nachgegeben habe; **to be ~ to do sth** sich freuen, etw zu tun; (= *relieved*) froh sein, etw zu tun; **~ to be of service** gern geschehen; **he is always ~ to come with us** er kommt immer gern mit (uns mit); **we should be ~ to answer any questions** eventuelle Fragen beantworten wir gerne; **I'll be ~ to show you everything** ich zeige Ihnen gerne alles; **to be only too ~ to do sth** etw sehr gern tun; **I was only too ~ to get away** ich war heilfroh, da wegzukommen (*inf*) **b** *attr* **the ~ tidings** die frohe Botschaft (*geh*), die gute *or* freudige Nachricht; **to give sb the ~ tidings** jdm die frohe Botschaft (*geh*) *or* freudige Nachricht überbringen → **glad eye, glad hand, glad rags**

gladden ['glædn] VT *person, heart* erfreuen

glade [gleɪd] N Lichtung *f*

glad: glad eye N **to give sb the ~** jdm schöne Augen machen (*inf*); **glad hand** N **to give sb the ~** jdn überschwänglich begrüßen

gladiator ['glædɪeɪtə'] N Gladiator *m*

gladiatorial [ˌglædɪə'tɔːrɪəl] ADJ Gladiatoren-; **~ combat** Gladiatorenkampf *m*

gladiolus [ˌglædɪ'əʊləs] N *pl* **gladioli** [ˌglædɪ'əʊlaɪ] Gladiole *f*

gladly ['glædlɪ] ADV (= *willingly, happily*) gern(e); **I'd ~ give her £5 to go away** ich gäbe ihr gern(e) £ 5, wenn sie nur wegginge

gladness ['glædnɪs] N (= *joy*) Freude *f*; (= *relief*) Erleichterung *f*; **an occasion of great ~** ein sehr freudiger Anlass

glad rags PL (*inf*) beste Klamotten *pl* (*inf*), Sonntagsstaat *m* (*inf*); **go and put your ~ on!** wirf dich in Schale! (*inf*)

gladsome ['glædsəm] ADJ (*old*) freudenreich (*liter*)

glam [glæm] ADJ (*inf*) schick

glamor N (*US*) = **glamour**

glamorize ['glæməraɪz] VT idealisieren, einen glamourösen Anstrich geben (+*dat*); *job, lifestyle also* einen besonderen Glanz *or* Reiz verleihen (+*dat*); (*author*) *war, violence* glorifizieren, verherrlichen

glamorous ['glæmərəs] ADJ (= *attractive*) *person, job, life* glamourös; *place, clothes* mondän, schick; *occasion* glanzvoll; **there's nothing ~ about the job** der Job ist überhaupt nicht reizvoll

glamorously ['glæmərəslɪ] ADV glamourös; **a ~ exciting life** ein fabelhaft aufregendes Leben

glamour, (*US*) **glamor** ['glæmə'] N Glamour *m*; (*of occasion, situation*) Glanz *m*; **she/the job doesn't have much ~** sie/dieser Beruf hat keinen besonderen Reiz; **she has ~ as well as prettiness** sie ist nicht nur hübsch, sondern besitzt auch noch einen besonderen Reiz

glamour, (*US*) **glamor**: **glamour boy** N (*inf*) Schönling *m* (*inf*); **glamour girl** N (*inf*) Glamourgirl *nt*; **glamour model** N Pin-up-Girl *nt*; **glamourpuss** N (*esp Brit inf,* = *female*) Glamourkätzchen *nt* (*inf*); (= *male*) Schönling *m* (*inf*)

glam rock N (*Mus inf*) Glam-Rock *m*

glance [glɑːns] ⟨N⟩ Blick *m*; **at a ~** auf einen Blick; **at first ~** auf den ersten Blick; **she gave him a warning/quick ~** sie warf ihm einen warnenden/kurzen Blick zu; **to take a quick ~ at sth** einen kurzen Blick auf etw (*acc*) werfen; **he cast** *or* **had a quick ~ round the room** er sah

sich kurz im Zimmer um; **we exchanged ~s** wir sahen uns kurz an ⟨VI⟩ sehen, blicken, schauen (*esp S Ger*); **to ~ at sb/sth** jdn/etw kurz ansehen, einen kurzen Blick auf etw (*acc*) werfen; **to ~ at** *or* **through a newspaper/report** einen kurzen Blick in eine Zeitung/einen Bericht werfen, eine Zeitung/einen Bericht überfliegen *or* kurz durchsehen; **to ~ over sth** etw überfliegen; **to ~ across to sb** jdm einen Blick zuwerfen; **to ~ down/in** einen Blick hinunter-/hineinwerfen, kurz hinunter-/hineinsehen; **to ~ up** aufsehen *or* -blicken (*from von*); **to ~ round** sich umblicken; **he ~d round the room** er sah sich im Zimmer um

▶ **glance off** VI (*prep obj von*) (*bullet etc*) abprallen; (*sword*) abgeleitet; (*light*) reflektiert werden

glancing ['glɑːnsɪŋ] ADJ **to strike sth a ~ blow** etw streifen; **she struck him a ~ blow** ihr Schlag streifte ihn; **it was only a ~ blow** ich/er *etc* wurde nur gestreift

gland [glænd] N Drüse *f*; (= *lymph gland*) Lymphdrüse *f or* -knoten *m*

glandular ['glændjʊlə'] ADJ **~ fever** Drüsenfieber *nt*

glans penis ['glænz'piːnɪs] N Glans *f*, Eichel *f*

glare [gleə'] ⟨N⟩ **a** greller Schein; (*from sun, bulb, lamp*) grelles Licht, greller Schein; **the ~ of the sun** das grelle Sonnenlicht; **to escape the ~ of publicity** dem grellen Licht der Öffentlichkeit entkommen **b** (= *stare*) wütender *or* stechender Blick; **a ~ of hatred/anger** ein hasserfüllter/ zorniger Blick ⟨VI⟩ **a** (*light, sun*) grell scheinen; (*headlights*) grell leuchten; (*bulb*) grell brennen **b** (= *stare*) (*zornig*) starren; **to ~ at sb/sth** jdn/ etw zornig anstarren ⟨VT⟩ **to ~ defiance/hatred at sb** jdn trotzig *or* voller Trotz/hasserfüllt *or* voll von Hass anstarren

glaring ['gleərɪŋ] ADJ **a** *look* stechend; (= *furious*) wütend; **her ~ eyes** ihr stechender Blick **b** *sun, light* grell, gleißend (*geh*) **c** (= *blatant*) *example, omission* eklatant; *error* offensichtlich, grob; *weakness* offensichtlich; *contradiction, inconsistency* krass; *injustice* (himmel)schreiend

glaringly ['gleərɪŋlɪ] ADV *a shine* grell; **~ bright** grell **b** (= *blatantly*) **~ obvious** (*fact, statement*) überdeutlich; **it was ~ obvious that he had no idea** es war nur zu ersichtlich, dass er keine Ahnung hatte; **a ~ obvious error** ein Fehler, der einem geradezu ins Auge springt; **it's ~ wrong** das ist ein eklatanter Fehler

glasnost ['glæznɒst] N Glasnost *f*

glass [glɑːs] ⟨N⟩ **a** (= *substance*) Glas *nt*; **a pane of ~** eine Glasscheibe; **to be grown under ~** (*Hort*) unter Glas gezogen werden **b** (= *object, vessel, contents, glassware*) Glas *nt*; (*dated,* = *mirror*) Spiegel *m*; **a ~ of wine** ein Glas Wein; **he's quite friendly when he's had a ~** (*inf*) er ist recht freundlich, wenn er ein Gläschen getrunken hat (*inf*) **c** (= *spectacles*) **~es** *pl*, **pair of ~es** Brille *f*; **he wears thick ~es** er trägt eine starke Brille *or* starke Gläser **d** (= *instrument*) (= *magnifying glass*) (Vergrößerungs)glas *nt*, Lupe *f*; (= *telescope*) Teleskop *nt*, Fernrohr *nt*; (= *barometer*) Barometer *nt*; **~es** *pl* (= *binoculars*) (Fern)glas *nt* ⟨VT⟩ verglasen ⟨ADJ⟩ *attr* Glas-; **~ bottle** Glasflasche *f*; **people who live in ~ houses shouldn't throw stones** (*Prov*) wer im Glashaus sitzt, soll nicht mit Steinen werfen (*Prov*)

glass *in cpds* Glas-; **glass block** N Glasbaustein *m*; **glass-blower** N Glasbläser(in) *m(f)*; **glass-blowing** N Glasbläserei *f*; **glass brick** N Glasziegel *m*; **glass case** N Glaskasten *m*, Vitrine *f*; **glass ceiling** N (*fig*) gläserne Decke; **she hit the ~** sie kam als Frau beruflich nicht mehr weiter; **glass cloth** N Gläsertuch *nt*; **glass-cutter** N (= *tool*) Glasschneider *m*; (= *person*) Glasschleifer(in) *m(f)*

glassed-in ['glɑːst'ɪn] ADJ verglast

glass: glass eye N Glasauge *nt*; **glass fibre**, (*US*) **glass fiber** N Glasfaser *f*; **glassful** N =

glass N b; **glasshouse** N (Brit) **a** (Hort) Gewächshaus nt **b** (Mil sl) Bau m, Bunker m (sl); **glasspaper** N Glaspapier nt; **glassware** N Glaswaren pl; **glass wool** N Glaswolle f; **glassworks** N sing or pl Glashütte f

glassy ['glɑːsɪ] ADJ (+er) surface, sea etc spiegelglatt; eye, look glasig; ~-eyed (look) glasig; to be ~-eyed einen glasigen Blick haben; to stare at sb ~-eyed jdn mit glasigem Blick anstarren

Glaswegian [glæz'wiːdʒən] **N** **a** Glasgower(in) m(f) **b** (= dialect) Glasgower Dialekt m **ADJ** Glasgower, von Glasgow

glaucoma [glɔːˈkəʊmə] N grüner Star, Glaukom nt (form)

glaucous ['glɔːkəs] ADJ leaves mit einer weißlichen Schicht überzogen; ~ blue/green gräulich blau/grün

glaze [gleɪz] **N** (on pottery, tiles, Cook) Glasur f; (on paper, fabric) Appretur f; (on painting) Lasur f **VT** a door, window verglasen **b** pottery, tiles glasieren; fabric, paper appretieren; painting lasieren; ~d tile Kachel f **c** (Cook) cake glasieren; meat mit Gelee überziehen; fruit kandieren; ~d ham Schinken m in Aspik **VI** (eyes: also **glaze over**) glasig werden; she had a ~d look in her eyes sie hatte einen glasigen Blick

glazier ['gleɪzɪə'] N Glaser(in) m(f)

glazing ['gleɪzɪŋ] N **a** (= act) Verglasen nt; (= glass) Verglasung f; (= trade) Glaserei f **b** = glaze N

GLC abbr of **Greater London Council**

gleam [gliːm] **N** **a** Schein m, Schimmer m; (of metal, water) Schimmern nt; **a ~ of light** ein Lichtschimmer m; **a ~ of white** ein weißer Schimmer; **the ~ from his torch** der Schein seiner Taschenlampe; **~s of moonlight came through the curtains** das Mondlicht schimmerte durch die Vorhänge **b** (fig) **a ~ of hope** ein Hoffnungsschimmer m; **a ~ of pride/curiosity** ein Funke m von Stolz/Neugier; **a ~ of sense** ein Hauch m von Vernunft; **not a ~ of hope/pride** kein Funke m Hoffnung/Stolz; **he had a (dangerous) ~ in his eye** seine Augen funkelten (gefährlich) **VI** schimmern; (hair, skin also) glänzen; (eyes) funkeln

gleaming ['gliːmɪŋ] ADJ schimmernd; car, hair, silver, water also glänzend; smile strahlend; eyes funkelnd; ~ **white teeth** blendend weiße Zähne

glean [gliːn] VT (lit) corn, field nachlesen; (fig) facts, news herausbekommen, ausfindig machen, erkunden (geh); **to ~ sth from sb/sth** etw von jdm erfahren/einer Sache (dat) entnehmen

gleaner ['gliːnə'] N Ährenleser(in) m(f)

gleanings ['gliːnɪŋz] PL (lit) Nachlese f, aufgelesene Ähren pl; **the ~ of twenty years of study** die Ausbeute eines zwanzigjährigen Studiums; **a few ~ from the press conference** ein paar Informationen von der Pressekonferenz

glebe [gliːb] N (Eccl) Pfarrland nt; ~ **house** pfarreieigenes Haus; (= vicarage) Pfarrhaus nt

glee [gliː] **N** **a** Freude f; (malicious) Schadenfreude f; **he shouted with ~** er stieß einen Freudenschrei aus; **he told the story with great ~** er erzählte die Geschichte mit großem Vergnügen; **his victory was greeted with ~** sein Sieg löste Begeisterung aus; **they were full of ~** sie waren (hell) begeistert; **they were full of malicious ~** sie freuten sich hämisch or diebisch; **they were rubbing their hands in ~** (also fig) sie rieben sich (dat) schadenfroh die Hände; **his defeat caused great ~ among his enemies** seine Feinde freuten sich diebisch or hämisch über seine Niederlage **b** (Mus) mehrstimmiges Lied

glee club N (esp US) Chor m

gleeful ['gliːfʊl] ADJ fröhlich, vergnügt; (maliciously) hämisch, schadenfroh; **they were all ~ about his failure** sie freuten sich alle diebisch über sein Versagen

gleefully ['gliːfəlɪ] ADV (= exultantly) fröhlich, vergnügt; (= maliciously) hämisch, schadenfroh

glen [glen] N Tal nt

glib [glɪb] ADJ (+er) person zungenfertig; excuse, reply glatt, leichtzüngig; attitude, ideas leichtfertig; promise, generalization vorschnell; ~ **talk** leichtfertiges Gerede; ~ **phrases** schön klingende Phrasen pl; **I don't want to sound ~** ich möchte nicht den Eindruck erwecken, das so leichthin zu sagen; **to have a ~ tongue** zungenfertig sein, eine glatte Zunge haben

glibly ['glɪblɪ] ADV talk leichthin; promise, generalize vorschnell; reply glatt; lie geschickt; **he ~ produced a couple of excuses** er war schnell mit ein paar glatten Ausreden bei der Hand

glibness ['glɪbnɪs] N (of person) Zungenfertigkeit f; (of reply, excuse, lie) Leichtzüngigkeit f; **a remark of such ~** eine so leichtzüngige Bemerkung

glide [glaɪd] **VI** **a** (person) gleiten; (through the air) schweben, gleiten; **to ~ into a room** in ein Zimmer schweben; **to ~ in** hereinschweben; **to ~ off** or **away** davongleiten; (person, ghost) davonschweben **b** (bird) gleiten; (plane) im Gleitflug fliegen; (glider) gleiten, schweben; (= fly in a glider) segelfliegen; **I would like to learn to ~** ich möchte Segelfliegen lernen; **to ~ down to land** zur Landung ansetzen **VT** gleiten lassen; plane im Gleitflug fliegen (lassen) **N** **a** (Dancing) Gleit- or Schleifschritt m **b** (Mus) Portamento nt; (Phon) Gleitlaut m **c** (Aviat) Gleitflug m

glider ['glaɪdə'] N (Aviat) Segelflugzeug nt; ~ **pilot** Segelflieger(in) m(f)

gliding ['glaɪdɪŋ] N (Aviat) Segelfliegen nt; ~ **club** Segelfliegerklub m

glimmer ['glɪmə'] **N** **a** (of light, candle etc) Schimmer m; (of fire) Glimmen nt; **the ~ of the distant river** das Schimmern des Flusses in der Ferne; **the faint ~ of dawn** der schwache Schein der Morgendämmerung **b** (fig: also **glimmering**) = gleam N b **VI** (light, water) schimmern; (flame, fire) glimmen

glimpse [glɪmps] **N** Blick m; **it was our last ~ of home** das war der letzte Blick auf unser Zuhause; **a ~ of life in 18th-century London** ein (Ein)blick in das Leben im London des 18. Jahrhunderts; **to catch a ~ of sb/sth** einen flüchtigen Blick auf jdn/etw werfen können or von jdm/etw erhaschen; (fig) eine Ahnung von etw bekommen; **a ~ into the future** ein Blick m in die Zukunft **VT** kurz sehen, einen Blick erhaschen von **VI to ~ at sth** einen Blick auf etw (acc) werfen; **to ~ through a window** einen Blick durch ein Fenster werfen

glint [glɪnt] **N** (of light, metal) Glitzern nt no pl, Blinken nt no pl; (of eyes) Funkeln nt no pl; **a ~ of light** ein glitzernder Lichtstrahl; **brown hair with golden ~s in it** braunes Haar mit einem goldenen Schimmer; **he has a wicked/merry ~ in his eyes** seine Augen funkeln böse/lustig; **a ~ of triumph/amusement** ein triumphierendes/amüsiertes Augenfunkeln **VI** glitzern, blinken; (eyes) funkeln

glissade [glɪˈseɪd] N (in dancing) Glissade f

glisten ['glɪsn] **VI** glänzen; (dewdrops, tears) glitzern **N** Glänzen nt, Glitzern nt

glister ['glɪstə'] N, VI (old) = glitter

glitch [glɪtʃ] N (Comput) Funktionsstörung f; **a technical ~** eine technische Panne

glitter ['glɪtə'] **N** Glitzern nt; (of eyes, diamonds) Funkeln nt; (for decoration) Glitzerstaub m; (fig) Glanz m, Prunk m; **the ~ of life in London** das glanzvolle Leben in London **VI** glitzern; (eyes, diamonds) funkeln; **all that ~s is not gold** (Prov) es ist nicht alles Gold, was glänzt (Prov)

glitterati [glɪtəˈrɑːtɪ] PL (inf) Hautevolee f

glittering ['glɪtərɪŋ] ADJ glitzernd; eyes, diamonds funkelnd; occasion glanzvoll; career glänzend; prizes verlockend; **a ~ array of celebrities** ein glanzvolles Aufgebot an Stars

glittery ['glɪtərɪ] ADJ (inf) glitzernd

glitz [glɪts] N (inf) Glanz m

glitzy ['glɪtsɪ] ADJ (+er) (inf) occasion glanzvoll, schillernd; dress schick

gloaming ['gləʊmɪŋ] N (liter) Dämmer- or Zwielicht nt (geh)

gloat [gləʊt] VI (with pride at oneself) sich großtun (over, about mit); (verbally also) sich brüsten (over, about mit); (over sb's misfortune or failure) sich hämisch freuen (over, about über +acc); **to ~ over sb's misfortune** sich an jds Unglück weiden; **to ~ over one's successes** sich in seinen Erfolgen sonnen; **there's no need to ~ (over me)!** das ist kein Grund zur Schadenfreude!

gloating ['gləʊtɪŋ] **N** Selbstgefälligkeit f; (over sb's misfortune or failure) Schadenfreude f; **it wasn't pleasant to listen to their ~** es war kein Vergnügen, ihren selbstgefälligen Reden/schadenfrohen Bemerkungen zuzuhören; **their ~ over their own success** ihre selbstgefällige Freude über ihren Erfolg **ADJ** (= self-satisfied) selbstgefällig; (= malicious) hämisch, schadenfroh; **he cast a ~ look at the money** er weidete sich genüsslich am Anblick des Geldes

gloatingly ['gləʊtɪŋlɪ] ADV say, smile, laugh selbstgefällig

glob [glɒb] N (inf) Klacks m (inf); (of mud) Klümpchen nt

global ['gləʊbl] ADJ global; recession, problem weltweit; **taking a ~ view of the matter ...** global gesehen ...; **a ~ figure of £2 million** eine Gesamtsumme von £ 2 Millionen; ~ **peace/war** Weltfrieden/-krieg m

global: global climate N Erdklima nt, Weltklima nt; **global economy** N Weltwirtschaft f

globalize ['gləʊbəlaɪz] **VI** globalisieren, weltweit zusammenarbeiten **VT** economy globalisieren

globally ['gləʊbəlɪ] ADV **a** (= worldwide) global, weltweit; think global; ~, **the risks are huge** global gesehen sind die Risiken enorm **b** (= universally) accepted, recognized allgemein

global: global trade N Welthandel m; **global village** N Weltdorf nt; **the world is considered as a ~** die Welt wird als Dorf angesehen; **global warming** N Erwärmung f der Erdatmosphäre

globe [gləʊb] N (= sphere) Kugel f; (= map) Globus m; (= fish bowl) Glaskugel f; **the ~** (= the world) der Globus, der Erdball; **all over the ~** auf der ganzen Erde or Welt; **terrestrial/celestial ~** Erd-/Himmelskugel f

globe: globe artichoke N Artischocke f; **globefish** N Kugelfisch m; **globeflower** N (Bot) Trollblume f; **globe lightning** N Kugelblitz m; **globetrotter** N Globetrotter(in) m(f), Weltenbummler(in) m(f); **globetrotting** **N** Globetrotten nt **ATTR** reporter etc globetrottend

globular ['glɒbjʊlə'] ADJ kugelförmig

globule ['glɒbjuːl] N Klümpchen nt, Kügelchen nt; (of oil, water) Tröpfchen nt; ~**s of grease floating on the soup** Fettaugen pl auf der Suppe

glockenspiel ['glɒkənʃpiːl] N Glockenspiel nt

gloom [gluːm] N **a** (= darkness) Düsterkeit f; (= sadness) düstere or gedrückte Stimmung; **economic ~** depressive Wirtschaftslage; **an air or atmosphere of ~** eine düstere or gedrückte Atmosphäre; **to cast a ~ over sth** einen Schatten auf etw (acc) werfen; **a ~ descended on us** eine düstere Stimmung überkam uns; **he was filled with ~** er war sehr bedrückt or niedergeschlagen

gloomily ['gluːmɪlɪ] ADV **a** ~ lit schlecht beleuchtet **b** ask, think, say niedergeschlagen, bedrückt; (= pessimistically) view, predict pessimistisch

gloominess ['gluːmɪnɪs] N **a** (= darkness, of place, sky) Düsterkeit f; (of day, weather, light) Trübheit f **b** (= despondency: of person) Niedergeschlagenheit f, Bedrücktheit f; (= melancholy) Trübsinn m; (= pessimism) Pessimismus m; (of thoughts, expression) Düsterkeit f; (of forecast, fu-

ture, news) bedrückende Art; (*of outlook*) Trübheit *f*; (*of assessment, view*) pessimistische Art

gloomster ['gluːmstə'] N (*inf*) Pessimist(in) *m(f)*, Schwarzmaler(in) *m(f)* (*inf*)

gloomy ['gluːmɪ] ADJ (+er) **a** (= *dark*) *place, sky* düster; *day, weather, light* trüb

b (= *dismal, despondent*) *person, mood* niedergeschlagen, bedrückt; *voice* traurig; (= *pessimistic*) pessimistisch (*about* über +acc); *thought, expression* düster; (= *dispiriting*) *picture, forecast, future* düster, bedrückend; *news* bedrückend; *outlook, prospects* trübe; *assessment, view* pessimistisch; **there is a ~ future ahead** die Zukunft sieht düster aus; **to feel/look ~** niedergeschlagen *or* bedrückt sein/aussehen; **to take a ~ view of things** schwarz sehen; **just thinking about the situation makes me feel ~** es bedrückt mich, wenn ich nur über die Lage nachdenke; **he is very ~ about his chances of success** er beurteilt seine Erfolgschancen sehr pessimistisch

glorification [ˌɡlɔːrɪfɪˈkeɪʃən] N Verherrlichung *f*; (*of God also*) Lobpreis *m*; (= *beautification*) Verschönerung *f*

glorified ['ɡlɔːrɪfaɪd] ADJ **this restaurant is just a ~ snack bar** dieses Restaurant ist nur eine bessere Imbissstube; **I'm just a ~ secretary** ich bin nur eine bessere Sekretärin

glorify ['ɡlɔːrɪfaɪ] VT verherrlichen; (= *praise*) *God* lobpreisen

gloriole ['ɡlɔːrɪəʊl] N Gloriole *f*, Heiligenschein *m*

glorious ['ɡlɔːrɪəs] ADJ **a** (= *splendid*) herrlich, wunderbar; **a ~ mess** (*iro*) ein schönes *or* herrliches Durcheinander **b** (= *illustrious*) *career, future* glanzvoll; *years, days, era, victory, history* ruhmreich

gloriously ['ɡlɔːrɪəslɪ] ADV **a** (= *marvellously*) herrlich; **~ happy** überglücklich **b** (= *illustriously*) glanzvoll; *die* ruhmreich

glory ['ɡlɔːrɪ] **N a** (= *honour, fame*) Ruhm *m*; **moment of ~** Ruhmesstunde *f*; **covered in ~** ruhmbedeckt; **she led her team to Olympic ~** sie führte ihre Mannschaft zu olympischen Ehren

b (= *praise*) Ehre *f*; **~ to God in the highest** Ehre sei Gott in der Höhe; **~ be!** (*dated inf*) du lieber Himmel! (*inf*)

c (= *beauty, magnificence*) Herrlichkeit *f*; **the glories of the past, past glories** vergangene Herrlichkeiten *pl*; **the glories of the desert** die Schönheiten *pl* der Wüste; **the rose in all its ~** die Rose in ihrer ganzen Pracht *or* Herrlichkeit; **Rome at the height of its ~** Rom in seiner Blütezeit; **they restored the car to its former ~** sie restaurierten das Auto, bis es seine frühere Schönheit wiedererlangt hatte

d (= *source of pride*) Stolz *m*

e (= *celestial bliss*) **the saints in ~** die Heiligen in der himmlischen Herrlichkeit; **Christ in ~** Christus in seiner himmlischen Herrlichkeit; **to go to ~** (*euph liter*) ins ewige Leben *or* in die Ewigkeit eingehen (*euph liter*)

VI to ~ in sb's attention jds Aufmerksamkeit genießen; **to ~ in one's/sb's success** sich in seinem/jds Erfolg sonnen; **to ~ in the knowledge/fact that ...** das Wissen/die Tatsache, dass ..., voll auskosten; **they gloried in showing me my mistakes** sie genossen es *or* kosteten es voll aus, mir meine Fehler zu zeigen; **to ~ in the name/title of ...** den stolzen Namen/Titel ... führen

glory hole N **a** (*inf*) Rumpel- *or* Kramecke *f*; (= *room*) Rumpelkammer *f*; (= *box*) Rumpelkiste *f*; (= *drawer*) Kramschublade *f* **b** (*Naut*) Logis *nt*

gloss[1] [ɡlɒs] N (= *shine, lip gloss*) Glanz *m*; (*fig, of respectability etc*) Schein *m*; **to take the ~ off sth** (*lit*) etw stumpf werden lassen; (*fig*) einer Sache (*dat*) den Glanz nehmen; **to lose its ~** (*lit, fig*) seinen Glanz verlieren; **~ finish** (*Phot: on paper*) Glanz(beschichtung *f*) *m*; (*of paint*) Lackanstrich *m*; **the photos had a ~ finish** es waren Glanzabzüge → *also* **gloss (paint)**

▶ **gloss over** VT *sep* (= *try to conceal*) vertuschen; (= *make light of*) beschönigen; **he**

glossed over the various points raised by the critics er hat die verschiedenen Punkte der Kritiker einfach vom Tisch gewischt

gloss[2] **N** (= *explanation*) Erläuterung *f*; (= *note also*) Anmerkung *f*, Glosse *f* (*geh*); **to put a ~ on sth** etw interpretieren **VT** erläutern

glossary ['ɡlɒsərɪ] N Glossar *nt*

glossily ['ɡlɒsɪlɪ] ADV effektvoll

glossiness ['ɡlɒsɪnɪs] N Glanz *m*

gloss (paint) N Glanzlack(farbe *f*) *m*; **high ~** Hochglanzlackfarbe *f*

glossy ['ɡlɒsɪ] ADJ (+er) glänzend; **to be ~** glänzen; **~ brochure** Hochglanzbroschüre *f*; **~ magazine** (Hochglanz)magazin *nt*; **~ paper/print** Glanzpapier *nt*/-lack *m*; **~ print** (*Phot*) Hochglanzbild *or* -foto *nt* **N** (*inf*) (Hochglanz)magazin *nt*

glottal ['ɡlɒtl] ADJ *sound* in der Stimmritze gebildet, glottal (*spec*)

glottal stop N (*Phon*) Knacklaut *m*, Stimmritzenverschlusslaut *m*

glottis ['ɡlɒtɪs] N Stimmritze *f*, Glottis *f* (*spec*)

Gloucs (*Brit*) *abbr of* **Gloucestershire**

glove [ɡlʌv] N (Finger)handschuh *m*; (*Sport*) Handschuh *m*; **to fit (sb) like a ~** (jdm) wie angegossen passen; **with the ~s off** (*fig*) schonungslos, ohne Rücksicht auf Verluste (*inf*); **the ~s are off** (*fig*) mit der Rücksichtnahme ist es vorbei, die Schonzeit ist vorbei

glove box N **a** (*Tech*) Handschuhschutzkasten *m* **b** (*Aut: also* **glove compartment**) Handschuhfach *nt*

gloved [ɡlʌvd] ADJ behandschuht

glove puppet N (*Brit*) Handpuppe *f*

glover ['ɡlʌvə'] N Handschuhmacher(in) *m(f)*

glow [ɡləʊ] **VI** glühen; (*colour, hands of clock*) leuchten; (*lamp, candle*) scheinen; **her cheeks ~ed** ihre Wangen glühten; **she/her cheeks ~ed with health** sie hatte ein blühendes Aussehen; **to ~ with pride** vor Stolz glühen; **to ~ with pleasure** vor Freude strahlen; **she ~ed with confidence** sie strahlte Selbstvertrauen vor; **to ~ red** rot leuchten

N Glühen *nt*; (*of colour, clock hands*) Leuchten *nt*; (*of lamp, candle*) Schein *m*; (*of fire, sunset, passion*) Glut *f*; **her face had a healthy ~** ihr Gesicht hatte eine blühende Farbe; **she felt a ~ of satisfaction/affection** sie empfand eine tiefe Befriedigung/Zuneigung; **there was a ~ about her** sie strahlte

glower ['ɡlaʊə'] **VI** ein finsteres Gesicht machen; **to ~ at sb** jdn finster ansehen **N** finsterer Blick; **surly ~** mürrischer Blick; **there was a ~ on his face** ein finsterer Ausdruck lag auf seinem Gesicht

glowering ['ɡlaʊərɪŋ] ADJ finster

gloweringly ['ɡlaʊərɪŋlɪ] ADV finster

glowing ['ɡləʊɪŋ] ADJ **a** glühend; *candle, colour, eyes* leuchtend; *cheeks, complexion* blühend; **to be ~ with health** blühend aussehen **b** (*fig, = enthusiastic*) *account, description* begeistert; *words* leidenschaftlich, begeistert; *praise, report* überschwänglich; *pride, admiration, enthusiasm* glühend; **to speak of sb/sth in ~ terms** voller Begeisterung von jdm/etw sprechen; **to paint sth in ~ colours** (*fig*) etw in den leuchtendsten Farben schildern

glowingly ['ɡləʊɪŋlɪ] ADV (*fig*) begeistert; *describe* in glühenden Farben; *praise* überschwänglich

glow-worm ['ɡləʊˌwɜːm] N Glühwürmchen *nt*

glucose ['ɡluːkəʊs] N Glucose *f*, Glukose *f*, Traubenzucker *m*

glue [ɡluː] **N** Klebstoff *m*, Leim *m*; **to stick to sb/sth like ~** an jdm/etw kleben (*inf*) **VT** kleben, leimen; **to ~ sth together** etw zusammenkleben *or* -leimen; **to ~ sth down/on** etw fest-/ankleben; **to ~ sth to sth** etw an etw (*acc*) kleben, etw an etw (*dat*) festkleben; **her ear was ~d to the keyhole** ihr Ohr klebte am Schlüsselloch; **to keep one's eyes ~d to sb/sth** jdn/etw nicht aus den Augen lassen; **his eyes**

were ~d to the screen seine Augen hingen an der Leinwand; **he's been ~d to the TV all evening** er hängt schon den ganzen Abend vorm Fernseher (*inf*); **he stood there as if ~d to the spot** er stand wie angewurzelt da; **we were ~d to our seats** wir saßen wie gebannt auf unseren Plätzen

glue: glue pot N Leimtopf *m*; **glue-sniffer** ['ɡluːsnɪfə'] N (Klebstoff)schnüffler(in) *m(f)*; **glue-sniffing** ['ɡluːsnɪfɪŋ] N (Klebstoff)schnüffeln *nt*

gluey ['ɡluːɪ] ADJ klebrig

glum [ɡlʌm] ADJ (+er) niedergeschlagen, bedrückt; *atmosphere* gedrückt; *thoughts* schwarz; **to feel/look ~** bedrückt sein/aussehen

glumly ['ɡlʌmlɪ] ADV niedergeschlagen, bedrückt

glumness ['ɡlʌmnɪs] N Bedrücktheit *f*, Niedergeschlagenheit *f*

glut [ɡlʌt] **VT a** (*Comm*) *market* (*manufacturer etc*) überschwemmen; **sugar is ~ting the world market** der Weltmarkt wird mit Zucker überschwemmt **b to ~ oneself** (*with food*) schlemmen; **to be ~ted with sth** mit etw voll gestopft sein **N** Schwemme *f*; (*of manufactured goods also*) Überangebot *nt* (*of an +dat*); **a ~ of oil** ein Überangebot an Öl

glutamate ['ɡluːtəmeɪt] N = **monosodium glutamate**

glute ['ɡluːt] N *usu pl* (*inf:* = *gluteus*) Hintern *m* (*inf*), Gesäß *nt*, Gesäßmuskel *m*

gluteal ['ɡluːtɪəl] ADJ Gesäß-; **~ muscles** Gesäßmuskeln *pl*

gluten ['ɡluːtən] N Kleber *m*, Gluten *nt*

glutinous ['ɡluːtɪnəs] ADJ klebrig

glutton ['ɡlʌtn] N Vielfraß *m* (*also Zool*); **to be a ~ for work** ein Arbeitstier *nt* sein (*inf*); **she's a ~ for punishment** sie ist die reinste Masochistin (*inf*)

gluttonous ['ɡlʌtənəs] ADJ (*lit, fig*) unersättlich; *person* gefräßig

gluttony ['ɡlʌtənɪ] N Völlerei *f*, Fresserei *f* (*inf*)

glycerin(e) ['ɡlɪsəriːn] N Glyzerin *nt*, Glycerin *nt* (*spec*)

glycerol ['ɡlɪsərɒl] N Glyzerin *nt*

glycol ['ɡlaɪkɒl] N Glykol *nt*

GM a *abbr of* **genetically modified b** (*Brit*) *abbr of* **George Medal** Tapferkeitsmedaille *f*

gm *abbr of* **gram(s)** *of* **gramme(s)** g

G-man ['dʒiːmæn] N *pl* **-men** [-men] (*US, inf*) FBI-Mann *m*

GMAT (*US Univ*) *abbr of* **Graduate Management Admission Test** Zulassungstest *für das post-graduale Studium der Betriebswirtschaft*

GMC (*Brit*) *abbr of* **General Medical Council**

GMO N ABBR *of* **genetically modified organism**

gms *abbr of* **gram(me)s** g

GMT *abbr of* **Greenwich Mean Time** WEZ

gnarled [nɑːld] ADJ *tree, roots, branch, trunk* knorrig; *hands, fingers* knotig; *person* verhutzelt; (= *bent*) krumm

gnash [næʃ] VT **to ~ one's teeth** mit den Zähnen knirschen

gnat [næt] N (Stech)mücke *f* → **strain**[1]

gnat's piss ['nætspɪs] N (*sl*) Gesöff *nt* (*inf*)

gnaw [nɔː] **VT** nagen an (+dat); *fingernails also* kauen an (+dat); (*rust, disease*) fressen an (+dat); *hole* nagen; (*fig*) *person* (*hunger, anxiety*) quälen; (*remorse*) verzehren; **to ~ sth off** etw abnagen; **the box had been ~ed by the rats** die Ratten hatten die Kiste angenagt **VI** nagen; **to ~ at sth** an etw (*dat*) nagen; (*rust, disease*) sich durch etw fressen; **to ~ at sb** (*fig*) jdn quälen; **to ~ on sth** an etw (*dat*) nagen; **to ~ through sth** etw durchnagen

▶ **gnaw away VI** nagen (*at, on* an +dat) **VT** *sep* wegnagen

gnawer ['nɔːə'] N (*Zool*) Nager *m*, Nagetier *nt*

gnawing ['nɔːɪŋ] ADJ *doubt, hunger, pain* nagend; *fear, guilt, remorse, anxiety* quälend

gneiss [naɪs] N Gneis m

gnocchi ['nɒkɪ] PL Gnocchi pl

gnome [nəʊm] N Gnom m; (in garden) Gartenzwerg m; **the ~s of Zurich** die Zürcher Gnome pl

GNP abbr of **gross national product**

gnu [nu:] N Gnu nt

GNVQ (Brit, Sch) abbr of **General National Vocational Qualification** ≈ Berufsschulabschluss m

go [gəʊ]
vb: pret **went**, ptp **gone**

1 INTRANSITIVE VERB	4 NOUN
2 AUXILIARY VERB	5 ADJECTIVE
3 TRANSITIVE VERB	6 PHRASAL VERBS

When **go** is part of a set combination, eg. **go crazy, go unheard, go ballistic, going cheap**, look up the other word.

1 – INTRANSITIVE VERB

a = proceed (= move) gehen; (vehicle, person in vehicle) fahren; (plane) fliegen; (= travel) reisen; (road) führen; **we can talk as we go** wir können uns unterwegs unterhalten; **the doll goes everywhere with her** sie nimmt die Puppe überallhin mit; **Sunny Boy is going well** Sunny Boy liegt gut im Rennen; **you go first** geh du zuerst!; **you go next** du bist der Nächste; **to go and** or **to get sth to go get sth** (US) etw holen gehen; **who goes there?** (guard) wer da?; **there he goes!** da ist er ja!; **there you go** (giving sth) bitte; (= I told you so) na bitte; **there you go again!** (inf) du fängst ja schon wieder an!; **here we go again!** (inf) jetzt geht das schon wieder los! (inf); **where do we go from here?** (lit) wo gehen wir anschließend hin?; (fig) und was (wird) jetzt?; **you're going too fast for me** (lit, fig) du bist mir zu schnell

♦ **to go to ... to go to France** nach Frankreich fahren; **I have to go to the doctor/to London** ich muss zum Arzt (gehen)/nach London; **to go to sb for sth** (= ask sb) jdn wegen etw fragen; (= fetch from sb) bei jdm etw holen

♦ **to go on ... to go on a journey** verreisen, eine Reise machen; **to go on a course** einen Kurs machen; **to go on holiday** (Brit) or **vacation** (US) in Urlaub gehen

♦ **to go for ... to go for a walk/swim** spazieren/schwimmen gehen; **to go for a doctor/newspaper** einen Arzt/eine Zeitung holen gehen

♦ **to go and ... go and shut the door** mach mal die Tür zu; **go and tell him** sags ihm; **he's gone and lost his new watch** (inf) er hat seine neue Uhr verloren; **now you've gone and done it!** (inf) na, jetzt hast du es geschafft!; **don't go and tell him** geh jetzt bitte nicht hin und erzähl ihm das (inf)

♦ **to go + -ing to go fishing/shopping/shooting** angeln/einkaufen/auf die Jagd gehen; **to go looking for sb/sth** nach jdm/etw suchen; **don't go telling him** geh jetzt bitte nicht hin und erzähl ihm das (inf); **don't go doing that!** mach das bloß nicht!

b = attend gehen; **to go to church** in die Kirche gehen; **to go to evening classes** Abendkurse besuchen; **to go to work** zur Arbeit gehen; **he's going as a pirate** er geht als Pirat; **what shall I go as?** wie soll ich mich verkleiden?; **what shall I go in?** was soll ich anziehen?

c = depart gehen; (vehicle, person in vehicle) (ab-)fahren; (plane, person in plane) (ab)fliegen; (= die) sterben; **has he gone yet?** ist er schon weg?; **I must go now** ich muss jetzt gehen or weg; **when I go** or **have gone** or **am gone** (= leave) wenn ich weg bin; (= die) wenn ich (einmal) nicht mehr (da) bin; **we must go** or **be going** or **get going** (inf) wir müssen gehen or uns langsam auf den Weg machen (inf); **time I was going** Zeit, dass ich gehe; **be gone!** (old) hinweg mit dir (old)!; **go!** (Sport) los!; **here goes!** jetzt gehts los! (inf)

d = no longer exist (= disappear, vanish) verschwinden; (= be used up) aufgebraucht wer-

den; (time) vergehen; **it is** or **has gone** (= disappeared) es ist weg; (= used up, eaten etc) es ist alle (inf); **where has it gone?** wo ist es hin or geblieben?; **the trees have been gone for years** die Bäume sind schon seit Jahren nicht mehr da; **gone are the days when ...** die Zeiten sind vorbei, wo ...; **I don't know where the money goes** ich weiß nicht, wo all das Geld bleibt; **all his money goes on computer games** er gibt sein ganzes Geld für Computerspiele aus, sein ganzes Geld geht für Computerspiele drauf (inf); **£75 a week goes in** or **on rent** £ 75 die Woche sind für die Miete (weg); **how is the time going?** wie stehts mit der Zeit?; **it's just gone three** es ist gerade drei vorbei, es ist kurz nach drei; **there goes another one!** und noch eine(r, s) weniger!

♦ **... to go two days to go till ...** noch zwei Tage bis ...; **only two more exams to go** nur noch zwei Prüfungen; **two exams down and one to go** zwei Prüfungen geschafft und eine kommt noch

e = be discarded (= be dismissed) gehen; (= be got rid of) verschwinden; (= be abolished) abgeschafft werden; **that minister will have to go** der Minister wird gehen müssen; **that old settee will have to go** das alte Sofa muss weg; **once that table has gone** wenn der Tisch erst einmal weg ist; **racial discrimination must go!** weg mit der Rassendiskriminierung!; **hundreds of jobs will go** hunderte or Hunderte von Stellen werden verloren gehen

f = be sold **the hats aren't going very well** die Hüte gehen nicht sehr gut (weg); **to go for next to nothing** so gut wie umsonst sein; **it went for £5** es ging für £ 5 weg; **they are going at 20p each** sie werden zu 20 Pence das Stück verkauft; **I won't let it go for less than that** billiger gebe ich es nicht her; **how much did the house go for?** für wie viel wurde das Haus verkauft?; **going, going, gone!** zum Ersten, zum Zweiten, und zum Dritten!

g = have recourse to gehen; **to go to the country** (Brit, Parl) Wahlen ausrufen; **to go to law** vor Gericht gehen; (over wegen); **to go to war** Krieg führen (over wegen); **he has gone so far as to accuse me** er ist so weit gegangen, mich zu beschuldigen

h = be awarded (prize, first place etc) gehen (to an +acc); (inheritance) zufallen (to sb jdm)

i = extend gehen; **the garden goes down to the river** der Garten geht bis zum Fluss hinunter; **the difference between them goes deep** der Unterschied zwischen ihnen geht tief; **I'll go to £100** ich gehe bis £ 100

j = function (watch) gehen; (car, machine) laufen, gehen; (workers) arbeiten; **to make sth go** etw in Gang bringen; **to go slow** (workers) im Bummelstreik sein; (watch) nachgehen

♦ **to get going** in Schwung or Fahrt kommen

♦ **to get going on** or **with sth** etw in Angriff nehmen; **once you get going on it** wenn man erst mal damit angefangen hat

♦ **to get sth going** etw in Gang bringen; party etw in Fahrt bringen; business etw auf Vordermann bringen

♦ **to get sb going** jdn in Fahrt bringen

♦ **to keep going** (person) weitermachen; (business, machine, engine etc) weiterlaufen; (car) weiterfahren; **keep going!** weiter!

♦ **to keep sth/sb going** to keep a factory going eine Fabrik in Betrieb halten; **to keep the fire going** das Feuer anbehalten; **she needs these pills/his friendship to keep her going** sie braucht diese Pillen/seine Freundschaft, um durchzuhalten; **this medicine/prospect kept her going** dieses Medikament/diese Aussicht hat sie durchhalten lassen; **here's £50/some work to keep you going** hier hast du erst mal £ 50/etwas Arbeit; **to keep sb going in food** jdn mit Essen versorgen

k = turn out (project, things) gehen; (event, evening) verlaufen; (voting, election) ausgehen; **I've forgotten how the words go** ich habe den Text vergessen; **how does the story/tune go?** wie war die Geschichte/Melodie noch mal?; **how does his theory go?** welche Theorie hat

er?, was ist seine Theorie?; **the story goes that ...** es geht das Gerücht, dass ...; **the election/decision went in his favour** (Brit) or **favor** (US) die Wahl/Entscheidung fiel zu seinen Gunsten aus; **we'll see how things go** (inf) wir werden sehen, wie es läuft (inf) or geht; **you know the way things go** Sie wissen ja, wie das so ist or geht; **the way things are going I'll ...** so wie es aussieht, werde ich ...; **nothing went unnoticed** nichts blieb unbemerkt; **she has a lot going for her** sie ist gut dran; **how's it going?, how goes it?** (inf) wie gehts (denn so)? (inf); **how did it go?** wie wars?; **how did the exam go?** wie gings in der Prüfung?; **how did your holiday go?** wie war der Urlaub?; **how's the essay going?** was macht der Aufsatz?

♦ **to go well/badly things have gone well/badly** es ist gut/schlecht gelaufen; **everything is going well (with us)** alles läuft gut, bei uns läuft alles gut; **if everything goes well** wenn alles gut geht; **all went well for him until ...** alles ging gut bei ihm, bis ...

l = fail, wear out (material, mechanism, bulb, zip etc) kaputtgehen; (health, strength, eyesight etc) nachlassen; (brakes, steering) versagen; (button) abgehen; **the sweater has gone at the elbows** der Pullover ist an den Ärmeln durch (inf); **his mind is going** er lässt geistig sehr nach

m = be accepted (behaviour, dress etc) gehen (inf); **anything goes!** alles ist erlaubt; **what I say goes!** was ich sage, gilt or wird gemacht!; **that goes for me too** (= that applies to me) das gilt auch für mich; (= I agree with that) das meine ich auch

n = be available **there are several houses/jobs going** es sind mehrere Häuser/Stellen zu haben; **is there any tea going?** gibt es Tee?; **I'll have whatever is going** ich nehme, was es gibt; **what do you want? – anything that's going** was möchtest du? – was da gibt; **the best beer going** das beste Bier, das es gibt

o = become werden; **to go deaf/mad/grey** (Brit) or **gray** (US) taub/verrückt/grau werden; **to go hungry** hungern; **I went cold** mir wurde kalt; **to go to sleep** einschlafen; **to go to ruin** zerfallen; **to go Japanese/ethnic** auf japanisch/auf Folklore machen (inf); **to go Labour** Labour wählen

p = be placed (= be contained, fit) gehen, passen; (= belong) hingehören; (in drawer, cupboard etc) (hin)kommen; **it won't go in the box** es geht or passt nicht in die Kiste; **the books go in that cupboard** die Bücher kommen or gehören in den Schrank dort; **4 into 12 goes 3** 4 geht in 12 dreimal; **4 into 3 won't go** 3 durch 4 geht nicht

q = match dazu passen; **to go with sth** zu etw passen; **these earrings don't go with that sweater** diese Ohrringe passen nicht zu dem Pullover

r = contribute **the money goes to help the poor** das Geld soll den Armen helfen; **the money will go toward(s) a new car** das ist Geld für ein neues Auto; **the qualities that go to make a great man** die Eigenschaften, die einen großen Mann ausmachen

s = make a sound or movement machen; **to go bang/shh/ticktock** peng/pst/ticktack machen; **how does a dog go?** wie macht der Hund?; **go like that (with your left foot)** mach so (mit deinem linken Fuß); **there goes the bell** es klingelt

t = take away (US) **large fries to go** eine große Portion Fritten zum Mitnehmen

u = comparison

♦ **as ... go as things go today** that's not very expensive für heutige Verhältnisse ist das nicht teuer; **he's not bad as boys/bosses go** verglichen mit anderen Jungen/Chefs ist er nicht übel

2 – AUXILIARY VERB

forming future tense

♦ **to be going to ... I'm/I was going to do it** ich werde/wollte es tun; **I had been going to**

do it ich habe es tun wollen; **I wasn't going to do it (anyway)** ich hätte es sowieso nicht gemacht; **it's going to rain** es wird wohl regnen; he knew that he wasn't going to see her again er wusste, dass er sie nicht wiedersehen würde; **there's going to be trouble** es wird Ärger geben

3 – TRANSITIVE VERB

a ⊡ route, way gehen; (vehicle, person in vehicle) fahren

♦ **to go it** (inf = go fast) ein tolles Tempo draufhaben (inf); (= live hard) es toll treiben (inf); (= work hard) sich hineinknien (inf); **to go it alone** sich selbstständig machen

b ⊡ Cards, Gambling setzen; **he went £50 on the red** er setzte £ 50 auf Rot

c ⊡ become **my mind went a complete blank** ich hatte ein Brett vor dem Kopf (inf)

d ⊡ say (inf) sagen; **he goes to me: "what do you want?"** er sagt zu mir: „was willst du?"

e ⊡ fancy **I could go a beer** ich könnte ein Bier vertragen

4 – NOUN pl **goes**

a ⊡ energy (inf) Schwung m; **to be full of go** unternehmungslustig sein

♦ **on the go to be on the go** auf Trab sein (inf); **to keep sb on the go** jdn auf Trab halten; **he's got two women/books on the go** er hat zwei Frauen/schreibt an zwei Büchern gleichzeitig

♦ **it's all go** es ist immer was los (inf)

b ⊡ attempt Versuch m; **at the first go** auf Anhieb (inf); **at the second go** beim zweiten Mal or Versuch

♦ **at** or **in one go** auf einen Schlag (inf); (drink) in einem Zug (inf)

♦ **to have a go** (Brit) es versuchen, es probieren; **to have a go at doing sth** versuchen or probieren, etw zu tun; **have a go!** versuchs or probiers (inf) doch mal!; **he's had several goes at the exam** er hat schon mehrere Anläufe auf das Examen genommen

♦ **to have a go at sb** (inf = criticize) jdn runterputzen (inf); (= fight) es mit jdm aufnehmen; **the public were warned not to have a go** (Brit) die Öffentlichkeit wurde gewarnt, nichts zu unternehmen

c ⊡ turn **it's your go** du bist dran (inf) or an der Reihe; **you've had your go** du warst schon dran (inf) or an der Reihe; **miss one go** (Brit) einmal aussetzen; **can I have a go?** darf ich mal?; **she asked for a go on his bike** sie wollte mal sein Fahrrad ausprobieren

d ⊡ bout (of illness etc) Anfall m

e ⊡ other set structures

♦ **(it's) no go** (inf) das ist nicht drin (inf), da ist nichts zu machen

♦ **to make a go of sth** in etw (dat) Erfolg haben

♦ **from the word go** von Anfang an

5 – ADJECTIVE

(esp Space) **you are go for takeoff/landing** alles klar zum Start/zur Landung; **all systems (are) go** (es ist) alles klar

6 – PHRASAL VERBS

▶ **go about** ⊡ **a** (Brit: = move from place to place) herumgehen, herumlaufen (inf); (by vehicle) herumfahren; (in old clothes etc) herumlaufen; **to go about in gangs** in Banden durch die Gegend ziehen; **to go about with sb** mit jdm zusammen sein or herumziehen (pej inf); **she's going about with John** sie geht mit John (inf); **you shouldn't go about doing that kind of thing** solche Sachen solltest du nicht machen

b (Brit) (= be current: rumour, flu etc) umgehen

c (Naut, = change direction) wenden

⊡ +prep obj **a** (= set to work at) task, problem anpacken; **we must go about it carefully** wir müssen vorsichtig vorgehen; **how does one go about getting seats/finding a job?** wie bekommt man Plätze/eine Stelle?

b (= be occupied with) work, jobs erledigen; **to go about one's business** sich um seine eigenen Geschäfte kümmern

▶ **go across** ⊡ +prep obj überqueren; street etc also gehen über (+acc); river also fahren über (+acc); **to go across the sea to Ireland** übers Meer nach Irland fahren

⊡ hinübergehen; (by vehicle) hinüberfahren; (by plane) hinüberfliegen; (to the enemy etc) überlaufen (to zu); **to go across to the other side** auf die andere Seite hinübergehen/-fahren; (to the enemy etc) zur anderen Seite überlaufen or -wechseln; **to go across to our neighbour/the pub** zum Nachbarn/in die Kneipe hinübergehen

▶ **go after** ⊡ +prep obj **a** (= follow) nachgehen (+dat), nachlaufen (+dat); (in vehicle) nachfahren (+dat); **the police went after the escaped criminal** die Polizei hat den entkommenen Verbrecher gejagt

b (= try to win or obtain) anstreben, es abgesehen haben auf (+acc) (inf); job sich bemühen um, aus sein auf (+acc) (inf); goal verfolgen, anstreben; (Sport) record einstellen wollen; personal best anstreben; girl sich bemühen um, nachstellen (+dat) (pej); **when he decides what he wants he really goes after it** wenn er weiß, was er will, tut er alles, um es zu bekommen

▶ **go against** ⊡ +prep obj **a** (= be unfavourable to, luck) sein gegen; (events) ungünstig verlaufen für; (evidence, appearance) sprechen gegen; **the verdict/decision went against her** das Urteil/die Entscheidung fiel zu ihren Ungunsten aus; **the vote went against her** sie verlor die Abstimmung; **the first round went against him** er hat die erste Runde verloren

b (= be contrary to) im Widerspruch stehen zu; principles, conscience, trend gehen gegen; (= oppose) person handeln gegen, sich widersetzen (+dat); wishes, orders zuwiderhandeln (+dat)

▶ **go ahead** ⊡ **a** (= go in front) vorangehen; (in race) sich an die Spitze setzen; (= go earlier) vorausgehen; (in vehicle) vorausfahren; **to go ahead of sb** vor jdm sein; sich vor jdn setzen; jdm vorausgehen/-fahren **b** (= proceed, person) es machen; (work, project) vorangehen; (event) stattfinden; **he just went ahead and did it** er hat es einfach gemacht; **go ahead!** nur zu!; **to go ahead with sth** etw durchführen

▶ **go along** ⊡ **a** (= walk along) entlanggehen, entlangspazieren (inf); (to an event) hingehen; **to go along to sth** zu etw gehen; **as one goes along** (= while walking) unterwegs; (= bit by bit) nach und nach; (= at the same time) nebenbei, nebenher; **I made the story up as I went along** ich habe mir die Geschichte beim Erzählen ausgedacht; **go along with you!** (inf) jetzt hör aber auf! (inf)

b (= accompany) mitgehen, mitkommen (with mit); **the furniture goes along with the apartment** die Möbel gehören zur Wohnung

c (= agree) zustimmen (with +dat); (= not object) sich anschließen (with +dat); **he went along with all my suggestions** er schloss sich allen meinen Vorschlägen an

d (= proceed) **things are going along very smoothly** es läuft alles sehr gut

▶ **go around** ⊡ = **go about** VI **a, b, go round**

▶ **go at** ⊡ +prep obj (inf, = attack) person losgehen auf (+acc) (inf); task sich machen an (+acc); **to go at it** es loslegen (inf)

▶ **go away** ⊡ (weg)gehen; (for a holiday) wegfahren; (from wedding) abreisen, wegfahren; **they went away together** (illicitly) sie sind miteinander durchgebrannt (inf); **"gone away"** (on letter) „verzogen"; **the smell still hasn't gone away** der Geruch ist immer noch nicht weg

▶ **go back** ⊡ **a** (= return) zurückgehen; (to a subject) zurückkommen (to auf +acc); (= revert: to habits, methods etc) zurückkehren (to zu); **they have to go back to Germany/school next week** nächste Woche müssen sie wieder nach Deutschland zurück/wieder zur Schule; **when do the schools go back?** wann fängt die Schule wieder an?; **to go back to the beginning** wieder von vorn anfangen; **you can't go back**

now du kannst jetzt nicht zurück; **there's no going back now** jetzt gibt es kein Zurück mehr; **I'll go back there next year** da gehe or fahre ich nächstes Jahr wieder hin

b (= be returned, faulty goods) zurückgehen; (library books) zurückgebracht werden

c (= date back) zurückgehen, zurückreichen (to bis zu); **we go back a long way** wir kennen uns schon ewig; **our friendship goes back to our student days** wir sind schon seit unserer Studienzeit befreundet; **this practice goes back to medieval times** dieser Brauch geht auf das Mittelalter zurück

d (clock: = be put back) zurückgestellt werden

e (= extend back: cave, garden etc) zurückgehen, zurückreichen (to bis zu)

▶ **go back on** ⊡ +prep obj zurücknehmen; decision rückgängig machen; **I never go back on my word** was ich versprochen habe, halte ich auch

▶ **go before** ⊡ (= live before) in früheren Zeiten leben; (= happen before) vorangehen; **those who have gone before (us)** unsere Vorfahren; **everything that had gone before** alles Vorhergehende ⊡ +prep obj **to go before the court** vor Gericht erscheinen; **to go before the headmaster/committee** zum Rektor/vor den Ausschuss kommen

▶ **go below** ⊡ (Naut) unter Deck gehen

▶ **go beyond** ⊡ +prep obj (= exceed) hinausgehen über (+acc); orders, instructions also überschreiten; hopes, expectations also übertreffen; **he went beyond the bounds of decency** er hat den Anstand nicht gewahrt

▶ **go by** ⊡ (person, opportunity) vorbeigehen (prep obj an +dat); (procession) vorbeiziehen (prep obj an +dat); (vehicle) vorbeifahren (prep obj an +dat); (time) vergehen; **as time went by** mit der Zeit; **in days gone by** in längst vergangenen Tagen

⊡ +prep obj **a** (= base judgement or decision on) gehen nach; (= be guided by) compass, stars, watch etc, sb's example sich richten nach; (= stick to) rules sich halten an (+acc); **if that's anything to go by** wenn man danach gehen kann; **going by what he said** nach dem, was er sagte; **that's not much to go by** das will nicht viel heißen

b **to go by the name of Smith** Smith heißen

▶ **go down** ⊡ **a** (= descend) hinuntergehen (prep obj +acc); (by vehicle, lift) hinunterfahren (prep obj +acc); (sun, moon: = set) untergehen; (Theat: curtain) fallen; (= fall, boxer etc) zu Boden gehen; (horse) stürzen; **to go down on one's knees** sich hinknien; (to apologize) auf die Knie fallen; **to go down on one knee** (to propose) auf die Knie fallen; **this wine/cake goes down rather well** dieser Wein/der Kuchen schmeckt gut; **it will help the tablet go down** dann rutscht die Tablette besser (hinunter); **to go down on sb** (sl: = have oral sex with) es jdm mit dem Mund machen

b (ship, person: = sink) untergehen; (plane) abstürzen; (= be defeated) geschlagen werden (to von); (= fail examination) durchfallen → **fight** VI

c (Brit Univ) die Universität verlassen; (for vacation) in die Semesterferien gehen

d (inf, = go to prison) eingelocht werden (inf)

e (= be accepted, approved) ankommen (with bei); **that won't go down well with him** das wird er nicht gut finden; **he went down big in the States** (inf) in den Staaten kam er ganz groß heraus (inf)

f (= be reduced, lessen, floods, temperature, fever, supplies, swelling) zurückgehen; (taxes, value) sich verringern, weniger werden; (prices) sinken, runtergehen (inf); (barometer) fallen; (wind) nachlassen; (sea) sich beruhigen; (balloon, tyre) Luft verlieren; (= deteriorate: neighbourhood) heruntergehen; **he has gone down in my estimation** er ist in meiner Achtung gesunken → **world**

g (= go as far as) gehen (to bis); **I'll go down to the bottom of the page** ich werde die Seite noch fertig machen

h (= be noted, remembered) vermerkt werden; **to go down to posterity** der Nachwelt überliefert werden; **to go down in history** in die Geschichte eingehen; **it went down as a significant event in British history** es ging als ein bedeutendes Ereignis in die britische Geschichte ein

i (*Bridge*) den Kontrakt nicht erfüllen; **she went five down** sie blieb fünf unter dem gebotenen Kontrakt

j (= *become ill*) **to go down with a cold** eine Erkältung bekommen

k (*Mus inf*, = *lower pitch*) heruntergehen (*inf*), tiefer singen/spielen

l (*Comput*) ausfallen

m (*Sport*) (= *be relegated*) absteigen; (= *be defeated*) verlieren; **they went down 2-1 to Rangers** sie verloren 2:1 gegen Rangers

▶ **go for** **VI** +*prep obj* **a** (*inf*, = *attack*) person losgehen auf (+*acc*) (*inf*); (*verbally*) herziehen über (+*acc*); **the fumes went for my throat** ich habe die Abgase im Hals gespürt; **go for him!** (*to dog*) fass!

b (*inf*, = *admire, like*) gut finden, stehen auf (+*acc*) (*inf*); (= *choose*) nehmen

c (= *aim at*) zielen auf (+*acc*); (*fig*) aus sein auf (+*acc*) (*inf*); (*in claim etc*) fordern; **go for it!** nichts wie ran! (*inf*); **if I were you I'd go for it** an deiner Stelle würde ich zugreifen; **he was obviously going for the ball** er hatte es offensichtlich auf den Ball abgesehen

▶ **go forth** **VI** (*old, liter, person*) hingehen; (*order*) ergehen (*liter*); **to go forth into battle** in den Kampf ziehen

▶ **go forward** **VI** **a** (= *make progress: work etc*) vorangehen **b** (= *proceed, go ahead*) **to go forward with sth** etw durchführen, etw in die Tat umsetzen **c** (= *be put forward: suggestion etc*) vorgelegt werden (*to dat*)

▶ **go in** **VI** **a** (= *enter*) hineingehen; (*Cricket*) nach „innen" gehen; **I must go in now** ich muss jetzt hinein(gehen); **go in and win!** (*inf*) jetzt zeigs ihnen aber! (*inf*) **b** (*sun, moon: = go behind clouds*) weggehen, verschwinden **c** (= *fit in*) hineingehen, hineinpassen **d** (= *sink in, be assimilated*) jdm eingehen

▶ **go in for** **VI** +*prep obj* **a** (= *enter for*) teilnehmen an (+*dat*)

b (= *approve of, be interested in, practise*) zu haben sein für; (*as career*) sich entschieden haben für, gewählt haben; **to go in for sports/tennis** (= *play oneself*) Sport treiben/Tennis spielen; (= *be interested in*) sich für Sport/Tennis interessieren; **he's gone in for growing vegetables/breeding rabbits** *etc* er hat sich auf den Gemüseanbau/die Kaninchenzucht *etc* verlegt; **he goes in for big words** große Worte haben es ihm angetan

▶ **go into** **VI** +*prep obj* **a** drawer, desk *etc* kramen in (+*dat*); *a house, hospital, politics, the grocery trade* gehen in (+*acc*); *the army, navy etc* gehen zu; **to go into publishing** ins Verlagswesen gehen; **to go into teaching/parliament/the Church** Lehrer(in)/Abgeordnete(r)/Geistliche(r) werden; **it's going into its second year** das geht jetzt schon ins zweite Jahr

b (= *crash into*) car (hinein)fahren in (+*acc*); *wall* fahren gegen

c (= *embark on*) *explanation, description etc* von sich (*dat*) geben, vom Stapel lassen (*inf*); *routine* verfallen in (+*acc*)

d ⟨trance, coma⟩ fallen in (+*acc*); *convulsions, fit* bekommen; **to go into hysterics** hysterisch werden; **to go into fits of laughter** einen Lachanfall bekommen; **to go into mourning** (*emotionally*) trauern

e (= *start to wear*) *long trousers etc* tragen

f (= *look into*) sich befassen mit; (= *treat, explain at length*) abhandeln; **I don't want to go into that now** darauf möchte ich jetzt nicht (näher) eingehen; **this matter is being gone into** man befasst sich im Moment mit dieser Angelegenheit; **to go into detail** auf Einzelheiten eingehen

g (= *be invested*) **a lot of time/money/effort has gone into it** da steckt viel Zeit/Geld/Mühe drin

▶ **go in with** **VI** +*prep obj* sich zusammentun *or* zusammenschließen mit

▶ **go off** **VI** **a** (= *leave*) weggehen; (*by vehicle*) abfahren, wegfahren (*on* mit); (*Theat*) abgehen; **he went off to the States** er fuhr in die Staaten; **to go off with sb/sth** mit jdm/etw weggehen; (*illicitly*) mit jdm/etw auf und davon gehen (*inf*)

b (= *stop operating, light*) ausgehen; (*water, electricity, gas*) wegbleiben; (*telephones*) nicht funktionieren

c (*gun, bomb, alarm*) losgehen; (*alarm clock*) klingeln

d **to go off into fits of laughter** einen Lachanfall bekommen

e (*Brit* = *go bad, food*) schlecht werden; (*milk*) sauer *or* schlecht werden; (*butter*) ranzig *or* schlecht werden; (*fig, person, work, performance*) nachlassen, sich verschlechtern; (*sportsman, writer, actor*) abbauen (*inf*), schlechter werden

f (*inf*, = *go to sleep*) einschlafen; (*into trance*) in Trance verfallen

g (= *take place*) verlaufen; **to go off well/badly** gut/schlecht gehen

VI +*prep obj* **a** (*Brit* = *lose liking for*) nicht mehr mögen; *hobby* das Interesse verlieren an (+*dat*); **I've gone off him/that** ich mache mir nichts mehr aus ihm/daraus, ich mag ihn/es nicht mehr; **it's funny how you go off people** so schnell kann einem jemand unsympathisch werden

b **to go off the gold standard** vom Goldstandard abgehen

▶ **go on** **VI** **a** (= *fit*) passen (*prep obj* auf +*acc*)

b (= *begin to operate*: *light, power*) angehen

c (= *walk on etc*) weitergehen; (*by vehicle*) weiterfahren; (*ahead of others*) vorausgehen

d (= *carry on, continue, talks, problems, war etc*) weitergehen; (*person*) weitermachen; **it goes on and on** es hört nicht mehr auf; **to go on with sth** etw fortsetzen, mit etw weitermachen; **to go on working/coughing** weiterarbeiten/-husten; **to go on hoping** weiter hoffen; **to go on trying** es weiter(hin) versuchen; **go on with your work** arbeitet *or* macht weiter; **I want to go on being a teacher** *etc* ich möchte Lehrer *etc* bleiben; **to go on speaking** weitersprechen; (*after a pause*) fortfahren; **go on, tell me!** na, sag schon!; **go on, give it a try!** na, versuchs doch!; **go on (with you)!** (*iro inf*) na komm, komm! (*iro inf*); **to have enough/something to be going on with** fürs Erste genug haben/ schon mal etwas haben; **to go on to another matter** zu einer anderen Sache übergehen; **he went on to say that ...** dann sagte er, dass ...; **she went on to become a doctor** sie wurde später Ärztin; **I can't go on** ich kann nicht mehr; (= *I'm stuck*) ich weiß nicht mehr weiter

e (= *talk incessantly*) wie ein Buch (*inf*) *or* unaufhörlich reden; (= *nag, harp on*) darauf herumhacken (*inf*); **she just goes on and on** sie redet und redet; **don't go on (about it)** nun hör aber (damit) auf; **you do go on a bit** du weißt manchmal nicht, wann du aufhören solltest; **to go on about sb/sth** (= *talk a lot*) stundenlang von jdm/etw erzählen; (= *complain*) dauernd über jdn/etw klagen; **to go on at sb** jdm herumnörgeln, auf jdm herumhacken (*inf*)

f (= *happen*) passieren, vor sich gehen; (*party, argument etc*) im Gange sein; **this has been going on for a long time** das geht schon lange so; **what's going on here?** was geht hier vor?

g (*time*: = *pass*) vergehen; **as time goes on** im Laufe der Zeit

h (*pej*, = *behave*) sich aufführen; **what a way to go on!** wie kann man sich nur so aufführen!

i (= *appear, Theat*) auftreten; (*Sport*) dran sein (*inf*), an der Reihe sein

VI +*prep obj* **a** (= *ride on*) *bus, bike, roundabout etc* fahren mit; *tour* machen; *horse, donkey etc* reiten auf (+*dat*); **to go on the swings/slide** auf die Schaukel/Rutschbahn gehen

b (= *be guided by*) gehen nach, sich verlassen auf (+*acc*); *evidence* sich stützen auf (+*acc*); **what have you got to go on?** worauf stützt du dich dabei?, wovon gehst du dabei aus?; **we've got nothing to go on** wir haben keine Anhaltspunkte

c **to go on short time** kurzarbeiten; **to go on the dole** (*Brit*) stempeln gehen (*inf*); **to go on a diet** eine Schlankheitskur machen; **to go on the pill** die Pille nehmen

d (*inf*, = *like*) stehen auf (+*acc*) (*inf*) → **gone**

e (= *approach*) fifty etc zugehen auf (+*acc*)

f (= *appear on*) **to go on television** im Fernsehen auftreten

▶ **go on for** **VI** +*prep obj* fifty, one o'clock zugehen auf (+*acc*); **there were going on for twenty people there** es waren fast zwanzig Leute da

▶ **go out** **VI** **a** (= *leave*) hinausgehen; **to go out of a room** aus einem Zimmer gehen

b (*shopping etc*) weggehen; (*socially, to theatre etc*) ausgehen; (*with girl-/boyfriend*) gehen; **to go out riding** ausreiten; **to go out for a meal** essen gehen; **John has been going out with Susan for months** John geht schon seit Monaten mit Susan

c (= *be extinguished: fire, light*) ausgehen

d (= *become unconscious*) das Bewusstsein verlieren, weg sein (*inf*); (= *fall asleep*) einschlafen, weg sein (*inf*)

e (= *become outmoded, fashion*) unmodern werden; (*custom*) überholt sein

f **to go out to work** arbeiten gehen

g (*Pol*, = *leave office*) abgelöst werden

h (*Brit* = *emigrate, go overseas*) **the family went out to Australia** die Familie ging nach Australien

i (= *strike*) streiken; **to go out on strike** in den Streik treten

j (*tide*) zurückgehen

k **my heart went out to him** ich fühlte mit ihm mit; **all our sympathy goes out to you** wir teilen Ihr Leid

l (*Sport*, = *be defeated*) ausscheiden, herausfliegen (*inf*)

m (= *strive*) **to go all out** sich ins Zeug legen (*for* für)

n (= *be issued: pamphlet, circular*) (hinaus)gehen; (*Rad, TV: programme*) ausgestrahlt werden; (*message*) verbreitet werden

o (*year, month*: = *end*) enden, zu Ende gehen

p **to go out for** (*US*: = *be a candidate for*) antreten für; (*Ftbl etc also*) spielen für

q (= *disappear, be lost*) **the fun had gone out of it** es machte keinen Spaß mehr; **the love had gone out of their marriage** ihre Ehe war lieblos geworden; **all the fight had gone out of him** sein Kampfgeist war erloschen

▶ **go over** **VI** **a** (= *cross*) hinübergehen, rübergehen (*inf*); (*by vehicle*) hinüberfahren, rüberfahren (*inf*)

b (= *change allegiance, habit, diet etc*) übergehen (*to* zu); (*to another party*) überwechseln (*to* zu); **to go over to the other side** zur anderen Seite überwechseln

c (*TV, Rad, to news desk, another studio*) umschalten

d (*vehicle etc*: = *be overturned*) umkippen

e (= *be received: play, remarks etc*) ankommen

VI +*prep obj* **a** (= *examine, check over*) accounts, report durchgehen; house, luggage durchsuchen; person, car untersuchen; (= *see over*) house etc sich (*dat*) ansehen, besichtigen

b (= *repeat, rehearse, review*) lesson, role, facts durchgehen; **to go over sth in one's mind** etw durchdenken *or* überdenken; **to go over the ground** es durchsprechen

c (= *wash, dust etc*) windows, room schnell sauber machen

d (= *redraw*) outlines etc nachzeichnen

▶ **go past** **VI** vorbeigehen (*prep obj* an +*dat*); (*vehicle*) vorbeifahren (*prep obj* an +*dat*); (*procession*) vorbeiziehen (*prep obj* an +*dat*); (*time*) vergehen, verfließen

▶ **go round** **VI** (*esp Brit*) **a** (= *turn, spin*) sich drehen; **my head is going round** mir dreht sich alles

b (= *make a detour*) außen herumgehen; (*by vehicle*) außen herumfahren; **to go round sth** um etw herumgehen/-fahren; **to go round the long way** außen herumgehen/-fahren; **we went round by Winchester** wir fuhren bei Winchester herum

c (= *visit, call round*) vorbeigehen (*to* bei)

d (= *tour: round museum etc*) herumgehen (*prep obj* in +*dat*)

e (= *be sufficient*) langen, (aus)reichen; **there's enough food to go round (all these people)** es ist (für all diese Leute) genügend zu essen da; **to make the money go round** mit dem Geld auskommen

f +*prep obj* (= *encircle, reach round*) herumgehen um

g = **go about** VI a, b

▶ **go through** VI (*lit, fig*) durchgehen; (*business deal*) abgeschlossen werden; (*divorce, law, bill*) durchkommen

VI +*prep obj* **a** *hole, door, customs etc* gehen durch

b (= *suffer, endure*) durchmachen

c (= *examine, discuss, rehearse*) *list, subject, play, mail, lesson* durchgehen

d (= *search*) *pocket, suitcase* durchsuchen

e (= *use up*) aufbrauchen; *money* ausgeben, durchbringen (*inf*); *shoes* durchlaufen (*inf*); *food* aufessen; **he has gone through the seat of his trousers** (*Brit*) **or pants** (*esp US*) er hat seine Hose durchgesessen; **this book has already gone through 13 editions** das Buch hat schon 13 Auflagen erlebt

f *formalities, apprenticeship, initiation* durchmachen; *course* absolvieren; *funeral, matriculation* mitmachen; *routine* abziehen (*inf*); **they went through the agenda very quickly** sie haben die Tagesordnung sehr schnell abgearbeitet; **to go through the marriage ceremony** sich trauen lassen

▶ **go through with** VI +*prep obj* *plan* durchziehen (*inf*); *crime* ausführen; **she realized that she had to go through with it** sie sah, dass es kein Zurück gab *or* dass sich das nicht mehr vermeiden ließ; **she couldn't go through with it** sie brachte es nicht fertig

▶ **go to** VI +*prep obj* **a** **to go to sb** (*credit, job*) an jdn gehen **b** (= *make an effort*) **to go to it** sich ranhalten (*inf*); **go to it!** los, ran! (*inf*), auf geht's! (*inf*)

▶ **go together** VI **a** (= *harmonize: colours, ideas, people*) zusammenpassen **b** (= *go hand in hand: events, conditions*) zusammen auftreten **c** (= *go out together*) miteinander gehen

▶ **go under** VI (= *sink: ship, person*) untergehen; (= *fail, businessman*) scheitern (*because of an* +*dat*); (*company*) eingehen (*inf*) VI +*prep obj* (= *pass under*) durchgehen unter (+*dat*); (= *fit under*) gehen *or* passen unter (+*acc*) **b** **to go under the name of Jones** als Jones bekannt sein

▶ **go up** VI **a** (= *rise: price, temperature etc*) steigen; **to go up (and up) in price** (immer) teurer werden

b (= *climb, up stairs, hill*) hinaufgehen, hinaufsteigen (*prep obj* +*acc*); (*up ladder*) hinaufsteigen (*prep obj* +*acc*); (*up tree*) hinaufklettern (*prep obj* auf +*acc*); **to go up to bed** nach oben gehen

c (*lift*) hochfahren; (*balloon*) aufsteigen; (*Theat: curtain*) hochgehen; (= *be built: new flats etc*) gebaut werden

d (= *travel, to the north*) hochfahren; (*to London*) fahren; **to go up (to university)** (*Brit*) auf die Universität gehen

e (= *explode, be destroyed*) hochgehen (*inf*), in die Luft gehen; **to go up in flames** in Flammen aufgehen

f (*cheer, shout*) ertönen

g (*Sport: = be promoted*) aufsteigen

▶ **go with** VI +*prep obj* **a** *sb* mitgehen mit **b** (= *go hand in hand with*) Hand in Hand gehen mit **c** (= *be included or sold with*) gehören zu **d** (= *harmonize with*) passen zu

▶ **go without** VI +*prep obj* nicht haben; **to go without food** nicht essen; **to go without breakfast** nicht frühstücken; **to have to go without sth** ohne etw auskommen müssen, auf etw (*acc*) verzichten müssen; **to manage to go without sth** ohne etw auskommen; **he doesn't like to go without the luxuries of life** er verzichtet nicht gern auf den Luxus im Leben VI darauf verzichten

goad [gəʊd] N (= *stick*) Stachelstock *m*; (*fig, = spur*) Ansporn *m*; (= *taunt*) aufstachelnde Bemerkung VT (= *taunt*) aufreizen; **to ~ sb into sth** jdn zu etw anstacheln *or* treiben

▶ **goad on** VT *sep cattle* antreiben; (*fig*) anstacheln, aufstacheln

go-ahead [ˈgəʊəhed] ADJ fortschrittlich, progressiv N **to give sb/sth the ~** jdm/für etw grünes Licht *or* freie Fahrt geben

goal [gəʊl] N **a** (*Sport*) Tor *nt*; **to keep ~, to play in ~** im Tor stehen, im Tor spielen, das Tor hüten; **to score/kick a ~** ein Tor erzielen/schießen **b** (= *aim, objective*) Ziel *nt*; **to set (oneself) a ~** (sich *dat*) ein Ziel setzen

goal: goal area N Torraum *m*; **goal average** N (*Brit, Ftbl*) Tordifferenz *f*, Torverhältnis *nt*; **goal crease** N (*Ice hockey*) Torraum *m*; **goalgetter** [ˈgəʊlˌgetə] N (*Sport*) Torjäger(in) *m(f)*

goalie [ˈgəʊlɪ] N (*inf*) Tormann *m*/-frau *f*, Goalie *m* (*inf*)

goal: goal judge N (*Ice hockey*) Torrichter(in) *m(f)*; **goalkeeper** N Torwart *m*, Torhüter(in) *m(f)*; **goalkeeping** N Torhüten *nt*; **his excellent ~ saved the game** seine hervorragende Leistung als Torwart rettete das Spiel; **goal kick** N Abstoß *m* (vom Tor); **goalless** [ˈgəʊllɪs] ADJ *draw, half* torlos; **goal line** N Torlinie *f*; **goalmouth** N unmittelbarer Torbereich; **goal poacher** N (*Sport*) Abstauber(in) *m(f)*; **goalpost** N Torpfosten *m*; **to move the ~s** (*fig inf*) die Spielregeln (ver)ändern

goanna [gəʊˈænə] N (*Zool*) Waran *m*

go-as-you-please ADJ ungezwungen, ungebunden; **~ ticket** *or* **pass** (*Rail*) Netzkarte *f*

goat [gəʊt] N Ziege *f*; (*inf, = silly person*) (= *man*) Esel *m* (*inf*); (= *woman*) Ziege *f* (*inf*); (= *lecher*) Bock *m* (*inf*); **to act the ~** (*inf*) herumalbern; **to get sb's ~** (*inf*) jdn auf die Palme bringen (*inf*)

goat cheese N Ziegenkäse *m*

goatee (beard) [gəʊˈtiː(ˌbɪəd)] N Spitzbart *m*

goat: goatfish N (*US*) Meerbarbe *f*; **goatherd** N Ziegenhirt(in) *m(f)*; **goat's cheese** N = **goat cheese**; **goatskin** N Ziegenleder *nt*; **goat's milk** N Ziegenmilch *f*; **~ yoghurt** Jo-g(h)urt *m or nt* aus Ziegenmilch; **goatsucker** N (*US, Orn*) Ziegenmelker *m*, Nachtschwalbe *f*

gob[1] [gɒb] N (= *lump*) Klumpen *m*; **a ~ of spit** (*inf*) eine Ladung Spucke (*inf*) VI (*Brit inf*) spucken; **to ~ at sb** jdn anspucken

gob[2] N (*Brit, inf, = mouth*) Schnauze *f* (*inf*); **shut your ~!** halt die Schnauze! (*inf*)

gob[3] N (*dated US, sl, = sailor*) blauer Junge (*inf*), Blaujacke *f* (*inf*)

gobbet [ˈgɒbɪt] N Brocken *m*

gobble [ˈgɒbl] VT verschlingen VI **a** (= *eat noisily*) schmatzen **b** (*turkey*) kollern N (*of turkey*) Kollern *nt*

▶ **gobble down** VT *sep* hinunterschlingen

▶ **gobble up** VT *sep* (*lit, fig*) verschlingen; (*company*) schlucken

gobbledegook, gobbledygook [ˈgɒbldɪˌguːk] N (*inf*) Kauderwelsch *nt*

gobbler [ˈgɒblə] N Truthahn *m*

go-between [ˈgəʊbɪˌtwiːn] N *pl* **-s** Vermittler(in) *m(f)*, Mittelsmann *m*

Gobi Desert [ˈgəʊbɪˈdezət] N Wüste *f* Gobi

goblet [ˈgɒblɪt] N Pokal *m*; (*esp of glass*) Kelchglas *nt*

goblin [ˈgɒblɪn] N Kobold *m*

gobo [ˈgəʊbəʊ] N *pl* **gobos** *or* **goboes** (*TV, Film*) Linsenschirm *m*; (*for microphones*) Schallschirm *m*

gobsmacked [ˈgɒbsmækt] ADJ (*inf, = amazed*) platt (*inf*)

gobstopper [ˈgɒbˌstɒpə] N Riesenbonbon *m or nt* (*mit verschiedenen Farbschichten*)

goby [ˈgəʊbɪ] N (= *fish*) Meergrundel *f*

go-by [ˈgəʊbaɪ] N (*inf*) **to give sb the ~** jdn schneiden, jdn links liegen lassen (*inf*)

GOC *abbr of* **General Officer Commanding**

go-cart [ˈgəʊkɑːt] N (*child's cart*) Seifenkiste *f*; (*Sport: = kart*) Gokart *m*; (*US, = walker*) Laufstuhl *m*; (= *pushchair*) Sportwagen *m*

god [gɒd] N **a** **God** Gott *m*; **now he lies in God's (green) acre** (*euph*) nun deckt ihn der grüne Rasen (*euph*), nun liegt er auf dem Gottesacker (*old*); **God willing** so Gott will; **God forbid** (*inf*) Gott behüte *or* bewahre; **please God, let him be all right** lieber Gott, bitte mach, dass er durchkommt; **would to God that** (*form*) ich hoffe zu Gott, dass (*geh*); **I wish to God I hadn't told him** ich wünschte (bei Gott), ich hätte es ihm nicht gesagt; **God (only) knows** (*inf*) wer weiß; **do you think he'll succeed? – God knows!** glaubst du, dass er Erfolg haben wird? – das wissen die Götter!; **(my) God!, good God!** (*all inf*) O Gott! (*inf*), großer Gott! (*inf*); **be quiet, for God's sake!** sei still, verdammt noch mal *or* Herrgott noch mal! (*inf*); **for God's sake!** (*inf*) um Gottes *or* Himmels willen (*inf*); **what/why in God's name …?** um Himmels willen, was/warum …?; **God help you if …** der Himmel steh euch bei, wenn …; **he thinks he's God** er hält sich für Gott *or* den Herrgott; **to play God** Gott *or* den Herrgott spielen

b (*non-Christian*) Gott *m*; **Mars, the ~ of war** Mars, der Gott des Krieges; **the commander was a ~ to his men** der Kommandant wurde von seinen Leuten wie ein (Ab)gott verehrt; **money is his ~** das Geld ist sein Gott *or* Götze

c (*Brit Theat inf*) **the ~s** die Galerie, der Olymp (*inf*)

god: god-awful ADJ (*inf*) beschissen (*inf*); **god-botherer** [ˈgɒdˌbɒðərə] N (*pej*) Religionsfanatiker(in) *m(f)* (*inf*), Proselytenmacher(in) *m(f)* (*pej geh*); **godchild** N Patenkind *nt*; **goddamn, goddam** (*esp US, inf*) INTERJ verdammt! (*inf*); **I don't give a ~** es ist mir scheißegal! (*inf*) ADJ (*emph*) gottverdammt (*inf*); **it's no ~ use!** es hat überhaupt keinen Zweck, verdammt noch mal! (*inf*); **you're ~ right** du hast, verdammt noch mal, Recht (*inf*); **you don't belong here and you ~ well know it** du gehörst hier nicht hierher und du weißt es auch, verdammt noch mal (*inf*); **goddamned** ADJ, ADV = **goddamn**; **goddaughter** N Patentochter *f*

goddess [ˈgɒdɪs] N Göttin *f*

god: godfather N (*lit, fig*) Pate *m*; **my ~** mein Patenonkel *m*; **God-fearing** [ˈgɒdˌfɪərɪŋ] ADJ gottesfürchtig; **godforsaken** (*inf*) gottverlassen; **godhead** N Gottheit *f*; **the Godhead** Gott *m*; **godless** ADJ gottlos; **godlessness** [ˈgɒdlɪsnɪs] N Gottlosigkeit *f*; **godlike** ADJ göttergleich; *characteristics* gottähnlich

godliness [ˈgɒdlɪnɪs] N Frömmigkeit *f*, Gottesfürchtigkeit *f*

godly [ˈgɒdlɪ] ADJ (+*er*) fromm, gottesfürchtig

god: godmother N Patin *f*; **my ~** meine Patentante *f* → **fairy godmother**; **godparent** N Pate *m*, Patin *f*; **godsend** N Geschenk *nt* des Himmels; **God slot** N (*Brit TV inf*) religiöse Sendungen *pl*, ≈ Wort *nt* zum Sonntag; **godson** N Patensohn *m*; **Godspeed** INTERJ (*old*) behüt dich/euch Gott (*old*), geh/geht mit Gott (*old*); **to wish sb ~** jdn mit den besten Segenswünschen auf die Reise schicken

goer [ˈgəʊə] N **a** **to be a good ~** gut laufen **b** (*Austral, inf, = good idea*) **to be a ~** was taugen (*inf*)

-goer N *suf* -besucher(in), -gänger(in) *m(f)*; **cinemagoer** Kinogänger(in) *or* -besucher(in) *m(f)*

goes [gəʊz] *3rd pers sing present of* **go**

gofer [ˈgəʊfə] N (*inf*) Mädchen *nt* für alles (*inf*)

go-getter [ˈgəʊgetə] N (*inf*) Tatmensch *m*, Ellbogentyp *m* (*pej inf*)

go-getting [ˈgəʊgetɪŋ] ADJ (*inf*) *person* aufstrebend

goggle [ˈgɒgl] VI (*person*) staunen, starren, glotzen (*pej inf*); (*eyes*) weit aufgerissen sein; **to ~ at sb/sth** jdn/etw anglotzen (*pej inf*) *or* anstarren, auf jdn/etw glotzen (*pej inf*) *or* starren

goggle: gogglebox N (*Brit, inf*) Glotzkiste *f* (*inf*), Glotze *f* (*inf*); **goggle-eyed** ADJ mit Kulleraugen, kulleräugig; **he stared at him/it** ~ er starrte *or* glotzte (*pej inf*) ihn/es an; **they were ~ from watching TV** sie hatten Glotzaugen vom Fernsehen (*inf*)

goggles ['gɒglz] PL Schutzbrille *f*; (*inf, = glasses*) Brille *f*

go-go ['gəʊgəʊ] ADJ **a** Go-go-Girl *nt*; **~ girl** Go-go-Girl *nt* **b** (*US Comm inf*) **~ years** Hochkonjunktur- *or* Boomjahre *pl*; **the ~ days of the late 1960s** die Zeit der Hochkonjunktur Ende der 60er Jahre; **the ~ 1980s** die vom Boom geprägten 80er Jahre

go-go: go-go dancer N Go-go-Tänzerin *f*; **go-go dancing** N Go-go *nt*

going ['gəʊɪŋ] PRP of **go** N **a** (= *departure*) Weggang *m*, (Weg)gehen *nt*
b (= *pace, conditions*) **it's slow ~** es geht nur langsam voran; **that's good ~** das ist ein flottes Tempo; **that's not bad ~ for you** das ist gar nicht schlecht für deine Verhältnisse; **the ~ is good/soft/hard** (*Horse-racing*) die Bahn ist gut/weich/hart; **the road was rough** ~ man kam auf der Straße nur mit Mühe voran; **it's heavy ~ talking to him** es ist sehr mühsam, sich mit ihm zu unterhalten; **to get out while the ~ is good** sich rechtzeitig absetzen; **when the ~ gets tough** wenn es hart auf hart kommt; **when the ~ gets tough, the tough get** ~ wenn es hart auf hart kommt zeigt sich, wer wirklich was kann
ADJ **a** (= *customary*) rate, price gängig, üblich
b (*after superl: inf*) **the best thing** ~ das Beste überhaupt; **the biggest fool** ~ der allergrößte Idiot
c a **~ concern** (*Comm*) ein gut gehendes Unternehmen; **to sell a business as a ~ concern** ein bestehendes Unternehmen verkaufen; **to be a ~ concern** (*fig, = successful*) ein Erfolg *m* sein; (= *working*) in Betrieb sein; (= *in existence*) bestehen; **he sold me the car as a ~ concern** (*hum*) als er mir das Auto verkaufte, lief es angeblich noch

going-away outfit [ˌgəʊɪŋəˈweɪˌaʊtfɪt] N *Kleidung, die die Braut trägt, wenn sie den Hochzeitsempfang verlässt*

going-over [ˌgəʊɪŋˈəʊvə'] N **a** (= *examination*) Untersuchung *f*; **to give sth a good ~** (*contract*) etw gründlich prüfen; *house* wie bestellt durchsuchen; **she gave the patient a good ~** sie untersuchte den Patienten gründlich **b** (*inf, = beating-up*) Abreibung *f* (*inf*); **to give sb a good ~** jdm eine tüchtige Abreibung verpassen (*inf*)

goings-on [ˌgəʊɪŋˈzɒn] PL (*inf, = happenings*) Dinge *pl*; **there have been strange ~** da sind seltsame Dinge passiert; **the ~ in parliament** die Sachen, die im Parlament passieren

goitre, (*US*) **goiter** ['gɔɪtə'] N Kropf *m*

go-kart ['gəʊˌkɑːt] N Gokart *m*

gold [gəʊld] N **a** (= *metal, currency, objects*) Gold *nt* → *also* **glitter** VI, **good 1 e, heart b, weight N a**
b (*Sport inf*: = *gold medal*) Goldmedaille *f*; **four swimming ~s** vier Goldmedaillen im Schwimmen; **she won (the) ~ at 100 and 200 metres** sie gewann die Goldmedaille im 100- und 200-Meter-Lauf
c (= *colour*) Gold *nt*
ADJ **a** (= *made of gold*) bracelet, chain, ring, earring etc golden; **~ jewellery** (*Brit*) *or* **jewelry** (*US*) Goldschmuck *m*; **~ coin** Goldmünze *f*; **~ bullion** *or* **bars** Goldbarren *pl*; **~ tooth** Goldzahn *m*
b (= *gold-coloured*) fabric, paint, frame, lettering etc golden; **~ braid** Goldtressen *pl*; **a green-and-gold flag** eine grün-goldene Fahne

gold: goldbrick (*US*) N **a** (*inf, = gilded metal bar*) falscher Goldbarren; (= *worthless object*) schöner Schund; **to sell sb a ~** jdm etwas andrehen (*inf*) **b** (*sl, = shirker*) Drückeberger *m* (*inf*) VI (*sl*) sich drücken (*inf*); **goldbricker** ['gəʊldbrɪkə'] N (*US, sl*) = **goldbrick** N **b**; **Gold Card®** N Goldkarte *f*; **Gold Coast** N Gold-

küste *f*; **gold-coloured**, (*US*) **gold-colored** ADJ goldfarben; **goldcrest** N Goldhähnchen *nt*; **gold-digger** N Goldgräber(in) *m(f)*; **she's really just a ~** (*inf*) sie ist eigentlich nur aufs Geld aus (*inf*); **gold disc** N goldene Schallplatte; **gold dust** N Goldstaub *m*; **to be (like) ~** (*fig*) sehr schwer zu finden sein, (selten wie) ein weißer Rabe sein

golden ['gəʊldən] ADJ **a** (*in colour*) golden; hair golden, goldblond; suntan goldbraun; sand goldgelb; (*Cook*) goldbraun; **fry until ~** anbräunen; **~ yellow/brown** goldgelb/-braun **b** (*liter, = made of gold*) golden → *also* **goose c** (*fig, = excellent*) future, years, era golden; **a ~ opportunity/chance** eine einmalige Gelegenheit/Chance

golden: golden age N (*Myth*) goldenes Zeitalter; (*fig*) Blütezeit *f*; **golden boy** N (*inf*) Goldjunge *m*; **golden buck** N (*US Cook*) überbackene Käseschnitte mit pochiertem Ei; **golden calf** N **the ~** das Goldene Kalb; **golden chain** N Goldkette *f*; **Golden Delicious** N Golden Delicious *m*; **golden eagle** N Steinadler *m*; **Golden Fleece** N **the ~** das Goldene Vlies; **Golden Gate** N **the ~ (Bridge)** die Golden-Gate-Brücke; **golden girl** N (*inf*) Goldmädchen *nt*; **golden goal** N (*Ftbl*) Golden Goal *nt*; **golden goose** N (*fig*) Huhn, das goldene Eier legt, Goldgrube *f*; **golden hamster** N (*Zool*) Goldhamster *m*; **golden handcuffs** PL (*inf*) Vergünstigungen *pl* (*für leitende Angestellte, um diese längerfristig an ein Unternehmen zu binden*); **golden handshake** N (*inf*) goldener Handschlag (*inf*), Abstandssumme *f*; **the director got a ~ of £50,000** der Direktor hat bei seinem Ausscheiden £ 50.000 bekommen; **golden hello** N (*inf*) Einstellungsprämie *f*; **golden jubilee** N goldenes Jubiläum *f*; **golden labrador** N Goldener Labrador; **golden mean** N **the ~** (*form*) der goldene Mittelweg; **to follow** *or* **pursue the ~** die goldene Mitte wählen; **golden oldie** N (*inf, = tune, record*) (Golden) Oldie *m* (*inf*); **golden oriole** N Pirol *m*; **golden parachute** N (*inf*) *Schutzklausel für leitende Angestellte für den Fall einer Übernahme oder Fusion*, goldener Fallschirm (*inf*); **golden pheasant** N Goldfasan *m*; **golden retriever** N Golden Retriever *m*; **goldenrod** N Goldrute *f*; **golden rule** N goldene Regel; **my ~ is never to ...** ich mache es mir zu Regel, niemals zu ...; **golden section** N (*Math, Phot*) goldener Schnitt; **golden syrup** N (*Brit*) (gelber) Sirup; **Golden Temple** N **the ~** (*Rel*) der goldene Tempel; **golden thread** N (*fig liter*) roter Faden; **Golden Triangle** N **the ~** (*Geog*) das goldene Dreieck; **golden wedding (anniversary)** N goldene Hochzeit

gold: gold fever N Goldfieber *nt*; **gold field** N Goldfeld *nt*; **goldfinch** N (*European*) Stieglitz *m*, Distelfink *m*; (*US*) Amerikanischer Fink; **goldfish** N Goldfisch *m*; **goldfish bowl** N Goldfischglas *nt*; **it's like living in a ~** da ist man wie auf dem Präsentierteller; **gold foil** N Goldfolie *f*; **gold leaf** N Blattgold *nt*; **gold medal** N Goldmedaille *f*; **gold medallist**, (*US*) **gold medalist** N (*Sport*) Goldmedaillengewinner(in) *m(f)*; **gold mine** N Goldbergwerk *nt*, Goldgrube *f* (*also fig*); **gold plate** N (= *plating*) Goldüberzug *m*; (= *plated articles*) vergoldetes Gerät; (= *gold articles*) goldenes Gerät; **gold-plate** VT vergolden; **gold record** N = **gold disc**; **gold reserves** PL Goldreserven *pl*; **gold rush** N Goldrausch *m*; **goldsmith** N Goldschmied(in) *m(f)*; **gold standard** N Goldstandard *m*

golf [gɒlf] N Golf *nt* VI Golf spielen

golf: golf bag N Golftasche *f*; **golf ball** N **a** Golfball *m* **b** (*on typewriter*) Kugelkopf *m*; **golf-ball printer** N Kugelkopfdrucker *m*; **golf club** N (*instrument*) Golfschläger *m*; (= *association*) Golfklub *m*; **golf course** N Golfplatz *m*

golfer ['gɒlfə'] N Golfer(in) *m(f)*, Golfspieler(in) *m(f)*

golf links PL Golfplatz *m*

Goliath [gəˈlaɪəθ] N (*lit, fig*) Goliath *m*

golliwog ['gɒlɪwɒg] N Negerpuppe *f*; **to look like a ~** = eine Negerkrause haben

golly¹ ['gɒlɪ] N (*Brit, inf*) = **golliwog**

golly² INTERJ (*inf*) Menschenskind (*inf*)

goloshes [gəˈlɒʃəz] PL = **galoshes**

Gomorrah, Gomorrha [gəˈmɒrə] N Gomorr(h)a *nt*

gonad ['gəʊnæd] N Gonade *f*

gondola ['gɒndələ] N **a** (*in Venice, of balloon, cable car etc*) Gondel *f* **b** (*US, Rail: also* **gondola car**) offener Güterwagen **c** (*in supermarket*) Gondel *f*

gondolier [ˌgɒndəˈlɪə'] N Gondoliere *m*

gone [gɒn] PTP of **go** ADJ PRED **a** (*inf, = enthusiastic*) to be on sb/sth von jdm/etw (ganz) weg sein (*inf*); **I'm not ~ on ...** ich bin nicht verrückt auf (+acc)... (*inf*) **b** (*inf, = pregnant*) **she was 6 months ~** sie war im 7. Monat **c** ~ **if far** ADV **d** PREP **it's just ~ three** es ist gerade drei Uhr vorbei

goner ['gɒnə'] N (*inf*) **to be a ~** (*patient*) es nicht mehr lange machen; (*socially, professionally: person, company*) weg vom Fenster sein (*inf*); **if you pull out the whole plan's a ~** wenn du nicht mitmachst, wird aus der ganzen Sache nichts

gong [gɒŋ] N **a** Gong *m* **b** (*Brit, inf, = medal*) Blech *nt* (*inf*); **~s** Lametta *nt* (*inf*)

gonk [gɒŋk] N (= *toy*) Stoffpuppe *f*

gonna ['gɒnə] (*incorrect*) = **going to I'm not ~ tell you** das sage ich dir nicht

gonorrhoea, (*US*) **gonorrhea** [ˌgɒnəˈrɪə] N Gonorrhö(e) *f*, Tripper *m*

goo [guː] N (*inf, = sticky stuff*) Papp *m* (*inf*), Schmiere *f* (*inf*); (*fig, = sentimentality*) Schmalz *m* (*inf*)

goober ['guːbə'] N (*US inf*) (= *peanut*) Erdnuss *f*; (= *idiot*) Blödmann *m* (*inf*)

---

good [gʊd]
🗣 11.2, 16.4, 23.5, 24.3

1 ADJECTIVE	3 NOUN
2 ADVERB	

1 – ADJECTIVE
comp **better**, *superl* **best**

a gut; **good weather** gutes Wetter; **that's a good one!** (*joke*) das ist ein guter Witz; (*usu iro: excuse*) wers glaubt, wird selig! (*inf*); **you've done a good day's work** du hast gute Arbeit (für einen Tag) geleistet; **all I need is a good meal** ich brauche nur eine ordentliche *or* anständige Mahlzeit; **this is a good firm to work for** in dieser Firma lässt es sich gut arbeiten; **he tells a good story** er erzählt gut; **it must be good for something** das muss doch zu *or* für etwas gut sein; **she looks good enough to eat** sie sieht zum Anbeißen aus (*inf*); **to be good with people** gut mit Menschen umgehen können; **good fortune** Glück *nt*; **you've never had it so good!** es ist euch noch nie so gut gegangen, ihr habt es noch nie so gut gehabt; **it's too good to be true** es ist so schön, um wahr zu sein; **to come in a good third** einen guten dritten Platz belegen; **this is as good as it gets** besser wirds nicht mehr
◆ **to be good at sth** gut in etw (*dat*) sein; **to be good at sport/languages** gut im Sport/in Sprachen sein; **to be good at sewing/typing** gut nähen/tippen können; **I'm not very good at it** ich kann es nicht besonders gut; **he's good at telling stories** er kann gut Geschichten erzählen
◆ **good enough that's (not) good enough** das reicht (nicht); **that's not good enough, you'll have to do better than that** das geht so nicht, du musst dich schon etwas mehr anstrengen; **if he gives his word, that's good enough for me** wenn er sein Wort gibt, reicht mir das; **it's just not good enough!** so geht das nicht; **his attitude is just not good enough** er hat einfach nicht die richtige Einstellung; **her work/conduct is just not good enough** ihre Arbeit/

ihr Benehmen ist einfach nicht gut genug *or* nicht akzeptabel; **they felt he wasn't good enough for her** sie waren der Meinung, dass er nicht gut genug für sie war

♦ **to feel good** sich wohl fühlen; **I don't feel too good** mir ist nicht gut, ich fühle mich nicht wohl; **I don't feel too good about it** mir ist nicht ganz wohl dabei

♦ **to look good** **you look good in that** du siehst gut darin aus, das steht dir gut

♦ **to make good** *mistake, damage* wieder gutmachen; *threat* wahr machen; *promise* erfüllen; **to make good one's losses** seine Verluste wettmachen; **to make good sb's losses** jdm seine Verluste ausgleichen *or* ersetzen

♦ **as good as** (= *practically*) so gut wie; **as good as new** so gut wie neu; **as good as dead** so gut wie tot; **he was as good as his word** er hat sein Wort gehalten; **he as good as called me a liar/invited me to come** er nannte mich praktisch einen Lügner/hat mich praktisch eingeladen

b = beneficial gut; **to be good for sb** gut für jdn sein; (= *be healthy*) gesund für jdn sein; **milk is good for children** Milch ist gut *or* gesund für Kinder; **to be good for toothache/one's health** gut gegen Zahnschmerzen/für die Gesundheit sein; **to drink more than is good for one** mehr trinken, als einem gut tut

♦ **what's good for what's good for consumers isn't always good for the economy** was gut für den Verbraucher ist, ist nicht immer gut für die Wirtschaft

c = favourable *moment, chance, opportunity* günstig, gut; **a good day for a picnic** ein günstiger *or* guter Tag für ein Picknick; **it's a good thing** *or* **job I was there** (nur) gut, dass ich dort war

d = enjoyable *holiday, evening* schön; **the good life** das süße Leben; **did you have a good day?** wie wars heute?, wie gings (dir) heute?

♦ **a good time** **to have a good time** sich gut amüsieren; **have a good time!** viel Spaß *or* Vergnügen!

e = kind gut, lieb; **good nature** Gutmütigkeit *f*; **to be good to sb** gut zu jdm sein; **that's very good of you** das ist sehr lieb *or* nett von Ihnen; **(it was) good of you to come** nett, dass Sie gekommen sind; **would you be good enough to tell me ...** wären Sie so nett, mir zu sagen ... (*also iro*); **with every good wish** mit den besten Wünschen

f = virtuous *name, manners, behaviour* gut; **the Good Shepherd** der Gute Hirte; **all good men and true** alle wackeren und aufrechten Männer (*old*); **if you can't be good, be careful** wenn du es schon tun musst, sei wenigstens vorsichtig

g = well-behaved artig, brav (*inf*); **(as) good as gold** mustergültig; **be a good girl/boy** sei artig *or* lieb *or* brav (*inf*); **be a good girl/boy and ...** sei so lieb und ...; **good girl/boy!** (= *well done*) gut!; **that's a good dog!** guter Hund!

h = admirable **your good lady** (*dated*) Ihre werte Gemahlin (*geh*); **my good man** (*dated*) mein Guter (*old*); **good man!** sehr löblich!, gut gemacht!; **good old Charles!** der gute alte Charles!; **the Good Book** das Buch der Bücher; **the good ship Santa Maria** die Santa Maria

i = valid *advice, excuse* gut; *reason* gut, triftig; *ticket* gültig; **is his credit good?** ist er kreditfähig?

♦ **good for** **he's good for £10,000** (= *will give us*) bei ihm kannst du mit £ 10.000 rechnen; (= *has got*) er hat gut und gern £ 10.000; **he is good for another few years** mit ihm kann man noch ein paar Jahre rechnen; **the car is good for another few years** das Auto hält *or* tuts (*inf*) noch ein paar Jahre; **she's good for nothing** sie ist ein Nichtsnutz *or* Taugenichts; **that's always good for a laugh** darüber kann man immer lachen

j = handsome *looks, figure, features* gut; *legs, body* schön; **a good appearance** (*of person*) ein gepflegtes Äußeres

k = uninjured *eye, leg* gesund

l = thorough gut, gründlich, tüchtig (*inf*); **to give sb a good scolding** jdn gründlich *or* tüch-

tig (*inf*) ausschimpfen; **to give sth a good clean** etw gut *or* gründlich reinigen; **to have a good cry** sich ausweinen; **to have a good laugh** ordentlich *or* so richtig lachen (*inf*); **to take a good look at sth** sich (*dat*) etw gut ansehen; **to have a good grounding in sth** gute Grundkenntnisse in etw (*dat*) haben

m = considerable *hour, while* gut; *amount, distance, way* gut, schön; **it's a good distance** es ist eine ganz schöne Strecke; **it's a good 8 km** es sind gute 8 km; **he ate a good half of the cake** er hat gut und gern den halben Kuchen gegessen; **a good many/few people** ziemlich viele/ nicht gerade wenig Leute

n = in greetings gut; **good morning** guten Morgen

o = in exclamations gut, prima; **that's good!** gut!, prima!; **(it's) good to see you/to be here** (es ist) schön, dich zu sehen/hier zu sein; **good enough!** (= *OK*) schön!; **good heavens** *or* **Lord** *or* **God!** um Himmels willen! (*inf*); **good grief** *or* **gracious!** ach du liebe *or* meine Güte! (*inf*); **very good, sir** sehr wohl (*old*); **good for** *or* (*esp Austral*) **on you/him** *etc*! gut!, prima!; (*iro also*) das ist ja toll!

p = emphatic use schön; **a good strong stick** ein schön(er) starker Stock; **a good old age** ein schön(es) hohes Alter

♦ **good and ...** ganz; **good and hard/strong** (*inf*) ganz schön fest/stark (*inf*); **good and proper** (*inf*) ganz anständig (*inf*)

2 – ADVERB

a = fine gut; **how are you? – good!** wie gehts? – gut!

b = well (*strictly incorrect*) gut

3 – NOUN

a = what is morally right Gute(s) *nt*; **good and evil** Gut und Böse; **to do good** Gutes tun; **there's some good in everybody** in jedem steckt etwas Gutes; **to be up to no good** (*inf*) nichts Gutes im Schilde führen (*inf*)

b = advantage, benefit Wohl *nt*; **the common good** das Gemeinwohl; **for the good of the nation** zum Wohl(e) der Nation; **this affects us, for good or ill** das wirkt sich auf uns aus, positiv oder negativ; **it's done now, for good or ill** es ist nun einmal geschehen; **I did it for your own good** ich meine es nur gut mit dir, es war nur zu deinem Besten; **for the good of one's health** *etc* seiner Gesundheit *etc* zuliebe; **he'll come to no good** mit ihm wird es noch ein böses Ende nehmen

♦ **to do good** **to do (some) good** (etwas) helfen *or* nützen; **to do sb good** jdm helfen; (*rest, drink, medicine etc*) jdm gut tun; **what good will that do you?** was hast du davon?; **much good may it do you** (*iro inf*) na, dann viel Vergnügen! (*iro inf*); **that won't do much/any good** das hilft auch nicht viel/auch nichts; **that won't do you much/any good** das hilft dir auch nicht viel/auch nichts; (= *will be unhealthy etc*) das ist nicht gut für dich; **a (fat) lot of good that will do!** (*iro inf*) als ob das viel helfen würde! (*iro*); **a (fat) lot of good that will do you!** (*iro inf*) und wie dir das gut tun wird! (*iro inf*)

c = use **what's the good of hurrying?** wozu eigentlich die Eile?; **it would be some good es** wäre ganz nützlich; **if that is any good to you** wenn es dir hilft

♦ **no/not any good** **that's no good** das ist nichts; **he's no good to us** er nützt uns (*dat*) nichts; **it's no good complaining to me** es ist sinnlos *or* es nützt nichts, sich bei mir zu beklagen; **it's no good doing it like that** es hat keinen Sinn, das so zu machen; **he's no good at it** er kann es nicht; **I'm no good at things like that** ich bin nicht gut in solchen Dingen; **the applicant was no good** der Bewerber war nicht gut; **he wasn't any good for the job** er eignete sich nicht für die Arbeit; **he wasn't any good at the job** er machte die Arbeit nicht gut

d = set structures

♦ **for good** (= *for ever*) **for good (and all)** für immer (und ewig)

♦ **to the good** **we were 5 points/£5 to the good** wir hatten 5 Punkte zu viel/£ 5 plus; **that's all to the good** auch gut!

♦ **the good** (= *good people*) die Guten *pl*

goodbye [ɡʊdˈbaɪ] **N** Abschied *m*, Lebewohl *nt* (*geh*); **to say ~, to say ~s** sich verabschieden, Lebewohl sagen (*geh*); **to wish sb ~, to say ~ to sb** sich von jdm verabschieden, von jdm Abschied nehmen; **to say ~ to sth** einer Sache (*dat*) Lebewohl sagen; **well, it's ~ to all that** damit ist es jetzt vorbei; **when all the ~s were over** als das Abschiednehmen vorbei war (*geh*) **INTER** auf Wiedersehen, lebe wohl (*geh*) **ADJ** *attr* Abschieds-; **~ party** Abschiedsparty *f*

good: good-for-nothing N Nichtsnutz *m*, Taugenichts *m* **ADJ** nichtsnutzig; **his ~ brother** sein Nichtsnutz von Bruder; **Good Friday N** Karfreitag *m*; **good-hearted ADJ** gutherzig; **good-humoured**, (*US*) **good-humored ADJ** *person* (*by nature*) gutmütig; (*on a certain occasion*) gut gelaunt; *crowd* gut gelaunt; *atmosphere* freundlich; *rivalry* gutmütig; *event, demonstration* friedlich; **it was a ~ conference** bei der Konferenz herrschte eine freundliche Atmosphäre

goodish [ˈɡʊdɪʃ] **ADJ** (= *quite good*) ganz gut, anständig; (= *considerable*) ganz schön

good: good-looker N (*inf*) **to be a real ~** wirklich gut *or* klasse (*inf*) aussehen; **good-looking ADJ** gut aussehend

goodly [ˈɡʊdlɪ] **ADJ** ansehnlich, stattlich (*geh*)

good: good-natured ADJ *person* (*by nature*) gutmütig; (*on a certain occasion*) gut gelaunt; *face, smile, attitude* gutmütig; *crowd, demonstration* friedlich; *atmosphere, conversation, laughter* freundlich; *fun* harmlos; **good-naturedly ADV** gutmütig

goodness [ˈɡʊdnɪs] **N** **a** Güte *f*; (*of food*) Güte *f*, Nährgehalt *m*; **out of the ~ of his/her heart** aus reiner Herzensgüte; **would you have the ~ to ...** (*form*) hätten Sie bitte die Güte, zu ... (*geh*) **b** (*in exclamations etc*) **~ knows** weiß der Himmel (*inf*); **for ~' sake** um Himmels willen (*inf*); **I wish to ~ I had never met him** wenn ich ihm doch bloß nie begegnet wäre!; **(my) ~!** meine Güte! (*inf*); **~ gracious** *or* **me!** ach du liebe *or* meine Güte! (*inf*)

goodnight [ɡʊdˈnaɪt] **ADJ** *attr* Gutenacht-; **~ kiss** Gutenachtkuss *m*

goods [ɡʊdz] ✿ 20.5 **PL** Güter *pl* (*also Comm*); (= *merchandise also*) Waren *pl*; (= *possessions also*) Gut *nt* (*geh*), Habe *f* (*geh, liter*); **leather/manufactured ~** Leder-/Fertigwaren *pl*; **canned ~** Konserven *pl*; **stolen ~** gestohlene Waren *pl*, Diebesgut *nt*; **~ depot/train/yard** Güterdepot *nt*/-zug *m*/-bahnhof *m*; **one's ~ and chattels** (*Brit*) sein Hab und Gut (*also Jur*), seine Siebensachen (*inf*); **to send sth ~** etw als Frachtgut schicken; **it's the ~** (*esp US, inf*) das ist große Klasse (*inf*); **to get/have the ~ on sb** (*esp US, inf*) gegen jdn etwas in die Hand bekommen/in der Hand haben; **if we don't come up with the ~ on time** (*inf*) wenn wir es nicht rechtzeitig schaffen

good: good-sized ADJ ziemlich groß; *building, room also* geräumig; **good-tempered ADJ** *person* verträglich; *animal* gutartig; *behaviour* gutmütig; **good-time Charlie N** (*US, inf*) Luftikus *m*, (Bruder) Leichtfuß *m*; **good-time girl N** Playgirl *nt*; (= *prostitute*) Freudenmädchen *nt*; **goodwill N** Wohlwollen *nt*; (*between nations, Comm*) Goodwill *m*; **a gesture of ~** ein Zeichen seines/ihres *etc* guten Willens; **to gain sb's ~** jds Gunst gewinnen; **~ ambassador** (*for UNICEF etc*) Botschafter(in) *m(f)* des guten Willens; **~ mission/tour** Goodwillreise *f*/-tour *f*

goody [ˈɡʊdɪ] (*inf*) **INTER** toll, prima; **~, ~ gum- drops!** (*hum*) juchhei, juchhe! **N** **a** (= *person*) Gute(r) *m*; **b** (= *delicacy*) gute Sache (*inf*), Leckerbissen *m*; (= *sweet*) Süßigkeit *f*, **c** (*inf, of joke, story etc*) guter Witz/gute Geschichte *etc*

goody: goody bag N (*inf*) Tüte *f* mit Leckereien; (*Comm*) (*with gifts*) Tüte *f* mit Geschenken; (*with free samples*) Tüte *f* mit Probepackungen; **goody-goody** (*inf*) N Tugendlamm *nt*, Musterkind *nt* (*inf*) ADJ tugendhaft, superbrav (*pej inf*); *attitude, behaviour also* musterhaft; (*pretending*) scheinheilig; **goody two-shoes** N (*pej inf*) Tugendlamm *nt* (*pej*)

gooey ['guːɪ] ADJ (*+er*) (*inf*) **a** (= *sticky*) klebrig; (= *slushy*) breiig **b** (*pej*) *behaviour, song, letter* rührselig, schnulzig (*pej inf*); **to go (all) ~** vor Rührung zerfließen; **he makes her go all ~** bei seinem Anblick gerät sie ins Schwärmen; **to go ~ over sb** für jdn schwärmen

goof [guːf] (*inf*) N **a** (*esp US,* = *idiot*) Dussel *m* (*inf*), Doofie *m* (*inf*) **b** (= *mistake*) Schnitzer *m* (*inf*), dicker Hund (*dated inf*) VI **a** (= *blunder*) sich (*dat*) etwas leisten (*inf*), danebenhauen (*inf*) **b** (*US,* = *loiter: also* **goof around**) (herum)trödeln, bummeln; **to ~ off** abzwitschern (*inf*)

▶ **goof up** VT *sep* (*inf*) vermasseln (*inf*), vermurksen (*inf*)

goofball ['guːfbɔːl] N (*esp US, inf*) Doofkopp *m* (*sl*)

go-off N (*inf*) Anfang *m*, Start *m*; **at the first ~** (gleich) beim ersten Mal, auf Anhieb

goofy ['guːfɪ] ADJ (*+er*) (*inf*) dämlich (*inf*), doof (*inf*)

google ['guːgl] VI (*Internet*) googeln (*im Internet mit einer Suchmaschine nach Informationen suchen*)

googler ['guːglə] N (*Internet*) jd, der im Internet mit einer Suchmaschine nach Informationen sucht

googly ['guːglɪ] N (*Cricket*) gedrehter Ball

goo-goo eyes [ˌguːguːˈaɪz] N (*hum inf*) **to make ~ at sb** jdn anhimmeln (*inf*)

goolies ['guːlɪz] N (*Brit vulg sl:* = *testicles*) Eier *pl* (*vulg*)

goon [guːn] N **a** (*inf,* = *idiot*) Idiot *m*, Dussel *m* (*inf*) **b** (*US, inf,* = *hired thug*) Schlägertyp *m* (*inf*)

goop [guːp] N (*esp US, inf*) klebriger Schleim

goose [guːs] N pl **geese** (*lit, inf*) Gans *f*; **silly little ~!** (*inf*) dummes Gänschen! (*inf*); **all his geese are swans** bei ihm ist immer alles besser; **to kill the ~ that lays the golden eggs** das Huhn schlachten, das die goldenen Eier legt VT (*inf*) einen Klaps auf den Hintern geben (*+dat*) (*inf*)

gooseberry ['gʊzbərɪ] N (= *plant, fruit*) Stachelbeere *f*; **~ bush** Stachelbeerstrauch *m*; **to play ~** (*Brit inf*) Anstandswauwau spielen (*inf*), das fünfte Rad am Wagen sein

goose: goose bumps PL , **goose flesh** N Gänsehaut *f*; **gooseneck lamp** N Bogenleuchte *f*; **goose pimples** PL (*Brit*) Gänsehaut *f*; **goose step** N Stechschritt *m*; **goose-step** VI im Stechschritt marschieren

goosey ['guːsɪ] ADJ (*+er*) (*inf*) (= *foolish*) dumm; (*US:* = *ticklish*) kitz(e)lig; (= *nervous*) nervös; **to get ~** eine Gänsehaut bekommen

GOP (*US, Pol*) abbr of **Grand Old Party**

Gopher ['gəʊfə] N (*Comput*) Gopher *m*

gopher ['gəʊfə] N Taschenratte *f*; (= *squirrel*) Ziesel *m*

gorblimey [ˌgɔːˈblaɪmɪ] INTERJ (*Brit, inf*) ach du grüne Neune (*inf*), ich denk mich laust der Affe (*inf*)

Gordian ['gɔːdɪən] ADJ gordisch; **to cut the ~ knot** den gordischen Knoten durchhauen

gore¹ [gɔːʳ] N (*liter,* = *blood*) Blut *nt*

gore² VT aufspießen, durchbohren; **~d to death by a bull** durch die Hörner eines Stiers tödlich verletzt

gore³ N (= *panel*) Bahn *f*; (*in sail*) Gehren *m*

gored [gɔːd] ADJ mit Bahnen; **~ skirt** Bahnenrock *m*

gorge [gɔːdʒ] N **a** (*Geog*) Schlucht *f* **b** (*old,* = *gullet*) Schlund *m*; **it stuck in my ~ to ...** (*fig*) es war mir zuwider, zu ...; **it makes my ~ rise** (*fig,*

= *makes me angry*) dabei kommt mir die Galle hoch VR schlemmen, sich voll essen; (*animal*) gierig fressen, schlingen; **to ~ (oneself) on sth** (*also fig*) etw in sich (*acc*) hineinschlingen, etw verschlingen VT **they were ~d** sie hatten sich reichlich gesättigt (on an *+dat*); (*animals*) sie hatten sich voll gefressen (on an *+dat*)

gorgeous ['gɔːdʒəs] ADJ **a** (= *lovely*) *weather, scenery, sunset, colours, food, wine, melody* herrlich, fantastisch, phantastisch; **to look ~** fantastisch *or* phantastisch aussehen; **to taste/ smell ~** herrlich schmecken/duften **b** (*inf,* = *beautiful*) *woman, man, eyes, hair* hinreißend; *clothes* hinreißend, toll (*inf*); *present* toll (*inf*); **a ~ blonde** eine sagenhafte Blondine (*inf*); **a ~ hunk** ein toller Typ (*inf*); **hi, ~!** hallo, Süßer/ Süße! **c** (= *sumptuous, magnificent*) *clothes, fabric, jewellery, flowers, building* prächtig

gorgeously ['gɔːdʒəslɪ] ADV herrlich; **~ dressed women** hinreißend angezogene Frauen; **~ embroidered clothing** prächtig bestickte Kleidung

gorgeousness ['gɔːdʒəsnɪs] N Herrlichkeit *f*; (= *splendour*) Pracht *f*; (= *beauty*) hinreißende Schönheit

Gorgon ['gɔːgən] N (*Myth*) Gorgo *f*; (*inf*) Drachen *m* (*inf*)

Gorgonzola [ˌgɔːgənˈzəʊlə] N Gorgonzola *m*

gorilla [gəˈrɪlə] N Gorilla *m*

gormless ['gɔːmlɪs] ADJ (*Brit, inf*) doof (*inf*)

gorse [gɔːs] N Stechginster *m*; **~ bush** Stechginsterstrauch *m*

gory ['gɔːrɪ] ADJ *scene, story, violence* blutrünstig; *murder, wound* blutig

gosh [gɒʃ] INTERJ Mensch (*inf*), Mann (*inf*)

goshawk ['gɒshɔːk] N (*Hühner*)habicht *m*

gosling ['gɒzlɪŋ] N junge Gans, Gänschen *nt*

go-slow ['gəʊsləʊ] N (*Brit*) Bummelstreik *m*

gospel ['gɒspəl] N **a** (*Bibl*) Evangelium *nt*; **the Gospels** das Evangelium, die Evangelien *pl*; **the Gospel according to St John** das Evangelium nach Johannes; **St John's Gospel** das Johannesevangelium; **the Gospel for today** das heutige Evangelium
b (*fig:* = *doctrine*) Grundsätze *pl*, Prinzipien *pl*; (*of ideology, religion*) Lehre *f*; **to preach the ~ of abstinence** Abstinenz predigen; **she's a firm believer in the ~ of free enterprise** sie ist eine überzeugte Anhängerin des freien Unternehmertums; **to take sth for** *or* **as ~** etw für bare Münze nehmen (*inf*); **whatever he said was ~ to her** alles, was er auch sagte, war für sie (ein) Evangelium
c (*Mus*) Gospel *m*

gospeller ['gɒspələ] N → **hot gospeller**

gospel: gospel song N Gospel(lied) *nt*; **gospel truth** N (*inf*) reine Wahrheit

gossamer ['gɒsəmə] N **a** Spinnfäden *pl*, Marienfäden *pl* **b** (*Tex*) hauchdünne Gaze ADJ hauchdünn

gossip ['gɒsɪp] N **a** Klatsch *m*, Tratsch *m* (*inf*); (= *chat*) Schwatz *m*; **to have a ~ with sb** mit jdm schwatzen *or* plauschen (*inf*) *or* klönen (*N Ger*); **it started a lot of ~** es gab Anlass zu vielem Gerede *or* Tratsch (*inf*) *or* Klatsch; **office ~** Bürotratsch *m* (*inf*) **b** (= *person*) Klatschbase *f* VI schwatzen, plauschen (*inf*), klönen (*N Ger*); (*maliciously*) klatschen, tratschen (*inf*)

gossip: gossip column N Klatschkolumne *or* -spalte *f*; **gossip columnist** N Klatschkolumnist(in) *m(f)*

gossiping ['gɒsɪpɪŋ] ADJ geschwätzig, schwatzhaft; (*malicious*) klatschsüchtig; **to have a ~ tongue** ein Klatschmaul sein (*inf*); **her ~ tongue will get her into trouble** ihre Klatschsucht wird ihr noch einmal Unannehmlichkeiten einbringen N Geschwätz *nt*; (*malicious*) Geklatsche *nt*, Getratsche *nt* (*inf*); **there's too much ~ and not enough work done in this office** in diesem Büro wird zu viel geschwatzt und zu wenig gearbeitet

gossip: gossipmonger ['gɒsɪpˌmʌŋgə] N Klatschmaul *nt* (*inf*); **gossipmongering** ['gɒ-

sɪpˌmʌŋgərɪŋ] N Klatscherei *f*, Tratscherei *f* (*inf*)

gossipy ['gɒsɪpɪ] ADJ *person* geschwätzig; *book, letter* im Plauderton geschrieben; **the ~ world of publishing** die klatschsüchtige Welt des Verlagswesens; **a long ~ phone call** ein langer Schwatz *or* Tratsch am Telefon (*inf*); **~ style** Plauderton *m*

got [gɒt] pret, ptp of **get**

gotcha ['gɒtʃə] INTERJ (*inf*) **a** (= *I see*) kapiert! (*inf*) **b** (*when catching, hitting, killing sb*) erwischt! (*inf*)

Goth [gɒθ] N **a** (*Hist*) Gote *m*, Gotin *f* **b** (*Mus, Fashion*) = **goth** ADJ (*Mus, Fashion*) = **goth**

goth [gɒθ] (*esp Brit*) N **a** (= *person*) Grufti *m* **b** (*Mus*) Gruftimusik *f* **c** (= *fashion*) Gruftistil *m* ADJ (*Mus, Fashion*) Grufti-; **~ band** Gruftiband *f*

Gothic ['gɒθɪk] ADJ **a** *people, language, script, lettering* gotisch **b** (*Art*) gotisch; **the ~ age** das Zeitalter der Gotik; **~ Revival** (*Archit*) Neugotik *f*; **~ Revival architecture** neugotische Architektur **c** (*Liter,* = *horror*) schaurig; **a ~ story** eine Schauergeschichte; **~ (horror) novel** Schauerroman *m* N **a** (*Archit*) Gotik *f* **b** (= *language*) Gotisch *nt* **c** (*Typ*) Gotisch *nt*; (*US*) Grotesk *f*

gotten ['gɒtn] (*esp US*) ptp of **get**

gouache [gʊˈɑːʃ] N Guasch *f*, Gouache *f*

gouge [gaʊdʒ] N (= *tool*) Hohlmeißel *or* -beitel *m*; (= *groove*) Rille *f*, Furche *f* VT bohren; **the river ~d a channel in the mountainside** der Fluss grub sich (*dat*) sein Bett in den Berg

▶ **gouge out** VT *sep* herausbohren; **to gouge sb's eyes out** jdm die Augen ausstechen

goulash ['guːlæʃ] N Gulasch *nt*

gourd [gʊəd] N Flaschenkürbis *m*; (*dried*) Kürbisflasche *f*

gourmand ['gʊəmənd] N Schlemmer *m*, Gourmand *m*

gourmet ['gʊəmeɪ] N Feinschmecker(in) *m(f)*, Gourmet *m*

gout [gaʊt] N (*Med*) Gicht *f*

gouty ['gaʊtɪ] ADJ (*+er*) *person* gichtkrank; *limb, joint also* gichtisch; **~ condition** Gichtleiden *nt*

gov abbr of **government**

Gov abbr of **governor**

govern ['gʌvən] VT **a** (= *rule*) *country* regieren; *province, colony, school etc* verwalten **b** (= *control: rules, laws etc*) bestimmen; (*legislation*) regeln; (= *determine, influence*) *choice, decision* bestimmen, beeinflussen; *development, person, actions* beeinflussen; *life* beherrschen; **regulations ~ing the sale of spirits** Bestimmungen über den Verkauf von Spirituosen; **strict rules ~ing how much they can earn** strenge Vorschriften darüber, wie viel sie verdienen dürfen; **to be ~ed by sb's wishes** sich nach jds Wünschen richten
c (= *hold in check*) *passions etc* beherrschen; (*Mech*) *speed, engine* regulieren; **to ~ one's temper** sich beherrschen
d (*Gram*) *case* regieren; **the number of the verb is ~ed by the subject** das Verb richtet sich in der Zahl nach dem Subjekt
VI (*Pol*) regieren, an der Regierung sein

governable ['gʌvənəbl] ADJ regierbar

governance ['gʌvənəns] N (*action*) Regierungsgewalt *f*; (*manner*) Regierungsform *f*; (*fig:* = *control*) Gewalt *f*, Kontrolle *f* (of über)

governess ['gʌvənɪs] N Gouvernante *f*, Hauslehrerin *f*

governing ['gʌvənɪŋ] N (*of country*) Regierung *f*; (*of town, province etc*) Verwaltung *f* ADJ **a** (*Pol*) *coalition* regierend **b** (*Admin*) *committee* leitend; **~ authority** Regierungsbehörde *f*; **the ~ class** die herrschende Klasse; **~ council/board** Vorstand *m*; **the ~ party** die Regierungspartei

governing body N (*of sport, professional association*) leitendes Gremium; (*of school*) ≈ Schulbeirat *m*; (*of university*) Senat *m*

government ['gʌvənmənt] N **a** (= *action of governing, body of administrators*) Regierung *f*; **strong ~ is difficult in a democracy** es ist schwierig, in einer Demokratie mit fester Hand zu regieren; **to form a ~** eine Regierung bilden **b** (= *system*) Regierungsform *f attr* Regierungs-, der Regierung; *agency* staatlich; **~ official** Regierungsbeamter *m*/-beamtin *f*; **~ action** Maßnahmen *pl* der Regierung; (= *intervention*) staatlicher Eingriff; **~ backing** staatliche Unterstützung; **~ intervention** staatlicher Eingriff

governmental [ɡʌvən'mentl] ADJ Regierungs-; **~ system/crisis/policy** Regierungssystem *nt*/-krise *f*/-politik *f*

government: government department N Ministerium *nt*; **government grant** N (staatliche) Subvention; **Government House** N Gouverneursresidenz *f*; **government loan** N Staatsanleihe *f*; **government monopoly** N Staatsmonopol *nt*, staatliches Monopol; **government-run** ADJ *television, newspaper etc* staatlich; **government securities** PL Staatsanleihen *pl*; **government spending** N öffentliche Ausgaben *pl*; **government stocks** PL (*Fin*) Staatspapiere *or* -anleihen *pl*

governor ['ɡʌvənə] N **a** (*of colony, state etc*) Gouverneur(in) *m(f)* **b** (*esp Brit, of bank, prison*) Direktor(in) *m(f)*; (*of school*) ≈ Mitglied *nt* des Schulbeirats; **the (board of) ~s** der Vorstand; (*of bank also*) das Direktorium; (*of school*) ≈ der Schulbeirat **c** (*Brit inf, = boss*) Chef *m* (*inf*); (= *father*) alter Herr (*inf*) **d** (*Mech*) Regler *m*

governor general N Generalgouverneur(in) *m(f)*

governorship ['ɡʌvənəʃɪp] N (= *office*) Gouverneursamt *nt*; (= *period*) Amtszeit *f* als Gouverneur

govt *abbr of* **government** Reg.

gown [ɡaʊn] N **a** Kleid *nt*; (= *evening gown*) Robe *f*, Abendkleid *nt*; (= *dressing gown*) Morgenmantel *m*; (*in hospital*) Kittel *m*; **wedding ~** Hochzeitskleid **b** (= *academic gown*) Robe *f*; (*of clergyman, judge*) Talar *m* → **town** VT kleiden

GP (*Brit*) *abbr of* **general practitioner** praktischer Arzt, praktische Ärztin; **to go to one's GP** zu seinem Hausarzt/seiner Hausärztin gehen

GPMU (*Brit*) *abbr of* **Graphical, Paper and Media Union** ≈ IG Medien

GPO *abbr of* **General Post Office**

GPS *abbr of* **Global Positioning System** GPS *nt*

gr N *abbr of* **gross**[1] Gr ADJ *abbr of* **gross**[2] btto.

grab [ɡræb] N **a** Griff *m*; **to make a ~ at** *or* **for sth** nach etw greifen *or* schnappen (*inf*) **b** (*Mech*) Greifer *m* **c** (*inf*) **to be up for ~s** zu haben sein (*inf*); **there are big prizes up for ~s** es gibt tolle Preise zu gewinnen; **~ bag** (*US*) Glücksbeutel *m*, Grabbelsack *m*

VT **a** (= *seize*) packen; (*greedily*) packen, sich (*dat*) schnappen (*inf*); (= *take, obtain*) wegschnappen (*inf*); *money* raffen; (= *catch*) *person* schnappen (*inf*); *chance* beim Schopf ergreifen (*inf*); *attention* auf sich (*acc*) ziehen; **he ~bed (hold of) my sleeve** er packte mich am Ärmel; **to ~ sth away from sb** jdm etw wegreißen; **I'll just ~ a sandwich** (*inf*) ich esse nur schnell ein Sandwich; **I'll just ~ a nap** (*inf*) ich mache nur schnell ein Nickerchen (*inf*); **to ~ the headlines** Schlagzeilen machen

b (*inf, = appeal to*) anmachen (*inf*); **it didn't ~ me** das hat mich nicht angemacht (*inf*); **how does that ~ you?** wie findest du das?, was meinst du dazu?

VI (*hastig*) zugreifen *or* zupacken; **to ~ at** greifen *or* grapschen (*inf*) nach, packen (+*acc*); **he ~bed at the chance of promotion** er ließ sich die Chance, befördert zu werden, nicht entgehen; **help yourselves, children, but don't ~** greift zu, Kinder, aber nicht so hastig

grabby ['ɡræbɪ] ADJ (*inf, = wanting possessions*) raffgierig, raffsüchtig; (= *wanting more*) gierig

grace [ɡreɪs] N **a** *no pl* (= *gracefulness, graciousness*) Anmut *f*; (*of movement*) Anmut *f*, Grazie *f*; (*of monarch etc*) Würde *f*; **with ~** anmutig; **he performs his office with ~ and charm** er übt sein Amt würdevoll und charmant aus; **to do sth with (a) good/bad ~** etw anstandslos/wider-

willig *or* unwillig tun; **he bore his defeat with good ~** er nahm seine Niederlage mit Fassung *or* anstandslos hin; **he took it with good ~** er machte gute Miene zum bösen Spiel; **he took it with bad ~** er war sehr ungehalten darüber; **he had/didn't even have the (good) ~ to apologize** er war so anständig/brachte es nicht einmal fertig, sich zu entschuldigen

b (= *pleasing quality*) (angenehme) Eigenschaft; **social ~s** (gesellschaftliche) Umgangsformen *pl*; **a young woman with many ~s** eine sehr kultivierte junge Dame

c (= *favour*) **to be in sb's good ~s** bei jdm gut angeschrieben sein

d (= *respite*: *for payment*) Zahlungsfrist *f*; **a day's ~** ein Tag *m* Aufschub; **to give sb a few days' ~** jdm ein paar Tage Zeit lassen; **days of ~** (*Comm*) Respekttage *pl*

e (= *prayer*) Tischgebet *nt*; **to say ~** das Tischgebet sprechen

f (= *mercy*) Gnade *f*; **act of ~** Gnadenakt *m*; **by the ~ of God** durch die Gnade Gottes; **by the ~ of God Queen ...** Königin ... von Gottes Gnaden; **there but for the ~ of God go I** es hätte genauso gut auch mich treffen können; **in this year of ~ 1998** im Jahre des Heils 1998; **in a state of ~** (*Eccl*) im Zustand der Gnade; **to fall from ~** in Ungnade fallen

g (= *title*) (*duke, duchess*) Hoheit *f*; (*archbishop*) Exzellenz *f*; **Your Grace** Euer Gnaden

h (*Myth*) **the Graces** die Grazien *pl*

i (*Mus*) Verzierung *f*, Ornament *nt*; **~ note** Verzierung *f*

VT **a** (= *adorn*) zieren (*geh*)

b (= *honour*) beehren (*with* mit); *event etc* zieren (*geh*), sich (*dat*) die Ehre geben bei (+*dat*); **to ~ the occasion with one's presence** sich (*dat*) die Ehre geben

graceful ['ɡreɪsfʊl] ADJ *person, animal, movement* anmutig, graziös; *appearance, outline, shape* anmutig, elegant; *building, bow, manner, way of doing sth* elegant

gracefully ['ɡreɪsfəlɪ] ADV **a** *move, dance* anmutig, graziös; *curved, shaped* anmutig, elegant **b** (= *without a fuss*) *retire, accept, withdraw* anstandslos; **he gave in ~** er gab großzügig(erweise) nach; **to grow old ~** in Würde alt werden

gracefulness ['ɡreɪsfʊlnɪs] N **a** Anmut(igkeit) *f*; (*of movement also*) Grazie *f*; (*of building, handwriting, bow, manner*) Eleganz *f*

graceless ['ɡreɪslɪs] ADJ **a** (*Eccl*) ruchlos, gottlos **b** (= *unattractive*) *building* reizlos **c** (= *rude*) *person, behaviour* ungehobelt, schroff; (= *lacking charm*) *teenager* linkisch

gracious ['ɡreɪʃəs] ADJ **a** (*form*) *person, manner, character* (= *courteous, kind*) liebenswürdig; (*condescendingly*) gnädig; **by ~ permission of ...** mit der gütigen Erlaubnis (+*gen*) ...; **she was so ~ as to give her blessing** sie war so gnädig *or* gütig, ihren Segen dazu zu geben; **to be ~ to sb** jdn liebenswürdig behandeln

b (= *elegant*) *lifestyle, era* kultiviert, elegant; *district* vornehm, elegant; **~ living** ein kultivierter Lebensstil

INTERJ (*dated*) **good** *or* **goodness ~ (me)!** (*expressing surprise or interest*) ach du meine Güte!; (*expressing annoyance*) um Gottes willen!; **good ~ yes/no** aber natürlich/nein

graciously ['ɡreɪʃəslɪ] ADV liebenswürdig; (= *condescendingly*) gnädigerweise

graciousness ['ɡreɪʃəsnɪs] N **a** Liebenswürdigkeit *f* (*towards* gegenüber); (*condescending*) Gnädigkeit *f* **b** (= *elegance*: *of lifestyle*) Kultiviertheit *f*

grad N (*inf*) *abbr of* **graduate**[1]

gradate [ɡrə'deɪt] VT abstufen

gradation [ɡrə'deɪʃən] N **a** (= *step, degree*) Abstufung *f*; (= *mark on thermometer etc*) Gradeinteilung *f*; **the ~s of public opinion ran from sympathy to anger** die Skala der öffentlichen Meinung reichte von Sympathie bis zu Zorn **b** (= *gradual change*) Abstufung *f*

grade [ɡreɪd] N **a** (= *level, standard*) Niveau *nt*; (*of goods*) (Güte)klasse *f*; **high-/low-grade goods** hoch-/minderwertige Ware; **small-/large-grade eggs** kleine/große Eier; **this is ~ A** (*inf*) das ist I

a (*inf*); **to make the ~** (*fig inf*) es schaffen (*inf*) **b** (= *job grade*) Position *f*, Stellung *f*; (*Mil*) Rang *m*, (Dienst)grad *m* (*auch von Beamten*); (= *salary grade*) Gehaltsgruppe *f*, Gehaltsstufe *f*; **she's on (salary) ~ 3** sie ist in Gehaltsgruppe 3; **to go up a ~** (*in salary*) in die nächste Gehaltsgruppe *or* Gehaltsstufe vorrücken

c (*Sch*, = *mark*) Note *f*; (*esp US*, = *class*) Klasse *f*; **to get good/poor ~s** gute/schlechte Noten bekommen

d (*esp US*) = **gradient**

e (*US*) **at ~** auf gleicher Ebene; **an apartment at ~ (level)** eine Wohnung zu ebener Erde

VT **a** *goods, animals* klassifizieren; *colours* abstufen; *students etc* einstufen

b (*US Sch*, = *mark*) benoten

c (= *level*) *road, slope* ebnen

▸ **grade down** VT *sep* (= *put in lower grade*) niedriger einstufen; *exam paper* schlechter benoten

▸ **grade up** VT *sep* höher einstufen; *exam paper* höher benoten

┌──────────────────────────────────┐
GRADE

In den USA und Kanada werden die Schuljahre als **grades** bezeichnet, beginnend mit dem **first grade** in der Grundschule bis hin zum **twelfth grade** in der Highschool. In den Highschools der USA werden die Schüler der 9. bis 12. Klasse mit folgenden Spitznamen belegt: **freshmen (ninth grade)**, **sophomores (tenth grade)**, **juniors (eleventh grade)** und **seniors (twelfth grade)**.
└──────────────────────────────────┘

grade crossing N (*US*) Bahnübergang *m*

-grader [-ɡreɪdə] N *suf* (*US Sch*) -klässler(in) *m(f)*; **sixth-grader** Sechstklässler(in) *m(f)*

grade school N (*US*) ≈ Grundschule *f*

gradient ['ɡreɪdɪənt] N (*esp Brit*) Neigung *f*; (*upward also*) Steigung *f*; (*downward also*) Gefälle *nt*; **a ~ of 1 in 10** eine Steigung/ein Gefälle von 10%; **what is the ~?** wie groß ist die Steigung/das Gefälle?; **what is the ~ of the hill?** welche Steigung/welches Gefälle hat der Berg?

gradual ['ɡrædjʊəl] ADJ allmählich; *decline, recovery, progress* langsam; *slope* sanft

gradually ['ɡrædjʊəlɪ] ADV nach und nach, allmählich; *slope* sanft

graduate[1] ['ɡrædjʊɪt] N (*Brit Univ*) (Hochschul-)Absolvent(in) *m(f)*; (= *person with degree*) Akademiker(in) *m(f)*; (*US Sch*) Schulabgänger(in) *m(f)*; **high-school ~** (*US*) ≈ Abiturient(in) *m(f)*

graduate[2] ['ɡrædjʊeɪt] VT **a** (= *mark*) einteilen, graduieren (*form*) **b** *colours* abstufen **c** (*US: Sch, Univ*) als Absolventen haben VI **a** (*Univ*) graduieren; (*US, Sch*) die Abschlussprüfung bestehen (*from an* +*dat*); **to ~ in English** einen Hochschulabschluss in Englisch machen; **she ~d to television from radio** sie arbeitete sich vom Radio zum Fernsehen hoch; **to ~ from the school of hard knocks** (*fig*) eine harte Lehre durchmachen **b** (= *change by degrees*) allmählich übergehen

graduate ['ɡrædʊɪt-] *in cpds* (*Brit*) für Akademiker; *unemployment* unter den Akademikern; **graduate course** N *Kurs für Studenten mit abgeschlossenem Studium*

graduated ['ɡrædʊeɪtɪd] ADJ **a** (= *rising*) stufenweise zunehmend; *increase* stufenweise; (*Fin*) gestaffelt **b** (= *calibrated*) mit Maßeinteilung, graduiert (*form*); **~ tube/measure/flask** Messglas *nt*

graduate ['ɡrædʊɪt]: **graduate school** N (*US*) *Hochschulabteilung für Studenten mit abgeschlossenem Studium*; **graduate student** N (*US*) Student(in) *mit abgeschlossenem Studium*, Jungakademiker(in) *m(f)*

graduation [ɡrædjʊ'eɪʃən] N **a** (= *mark*) (Maß)einteilung *f* **b** (*Univ, US, Sch*, = *ceremony*) (Ab)schlussfeier *f* (*mit feierlicher Überreichung der Zeugnisse*); **his ~ was delayed by illness** wegen Krankheit wurde ihm sein Zeugnis erst später überreicht

---

GRADUATION

Der erfolgreiche Studienabschluss wird traditionell in Form einer offiziellen Zeremonie, der **graduation**, gefeiert. Dabei bekommen die Absolventen ihre Diplome oder Zeugnisse öffentlich vor den versammelten Angehörigen und Gästen vom Leiter des jeweiligen Instituts überreicht. Doktorhüte und -roben werden auch heute noch mit Stolz getragen, und das offizielle Foto des Absolventen in komplettem Outfit bekommt häufig einen Ehrenplatz auf dem Kaminsims der Eltern und Großeltern.
In den USA versteht man unter **graduation** auch eine ähnliche Feier zum Abschluss der Highschool.

---

graduation day N Tag *m* der Abschlussfeier (und Überreichung der Zeugnisse)

Graeco- (*Brit*), **Greco-** (*esp US*) ['gri:kəʊ-] PREF griechisch-

Graeco-Roman (*Brit*), **Greco-Roman** (*esp US*) [,gri:kəʊ'rəʊmən] ADJ *art, sculpture* griechisch-römisch; ~ **wrestling** Ringen *nt* im griechisch-römischen Stil

graffiti [grə'fi:tɪ] PL Graffiti *pl*, Wandschmierereien *pl* (*pej*); **a piece of** ~ eine Wandschmiererei, ein Graffito *nt*

graffiti artist N Graffitikünstler(in) *m(f)*

graft [grɑːft] **N a** (*Bot*) (Pfropf)reis *nt*; (*Med*) Transplantat *nt* **b** (*esp US inf*, = *corruption*) Mauschelei *f* (*inf*), Schiebung *f* **c** (*Brit inf*, = *hard work*) Schufterei *f* (*inf*), Plackerei *f* (*inf*) **VT** (*Bot*) (auf)pfropfen (*on* auf +*acc*), (ein)pfropfen (*in* in +*acc*); (*Med*) übertragen (*on* auf +*acc*), einpflanzen (*in* in +*acc*); (*fig*: = *incorporate*) einbauen (*onto* in +*acc*); (*artificially* =) aufpfropfen (*onto* +*dat*) **VI** (*inf*, = *work hard*) schuften (*at* an +*dat*) (*inf*)

▶ **graft on** VT *sep* = **graft** VT

grafter ['grɑːftə] N (*inf*) **a** (*Brit* = *hard worker*) Arbeitstier *nt* (*inf*), Malocher(in) *m(f)* (*inf*) **b** (*esp US*) Gauner(in) *m(f)*

graham ['greɪəm] ADJ (*US*) ~ **flour** Weizenschrot(mehl) *nt*

grail [greɪl] N Gral *m*

grain [greɪn] **N a** *no pl* Getreide *nt*, Korn *nt* **b** (*of corn, salt, sand etc*) Korn *nt*; (*fig, of sense, malice*) Spur *f*; (*of truth*) Körnchen *nt*; (*of hope*) Funke *m*; **that's a ~ of comfort** das ist wenigstens ein kleiner Trost **c** (*of leather*) Narben *m*; (*of cloth*) Strich *m*; (*of meat*) Faser *f*; (*of wood, marble*) Maserung *f*; (*of stone*) Korn *nt*, Gefüge *nt*; (*Phot*) Korn *nt*; **it goes against the** (*Brit*) or **my** (*US*) ~ (*fig*) es geht einem gegen den Strich **d** (= *weight*) Gran *nt* **VT** *wood* masern; *leather, paper* narben

grain: grain alcohol N Äthylalkohol *m*; **grain elevator** *nt* Getreideheber *m*

grainy ['greɪnɪ] ADJ (+*er*) **a** (= *granular*) *texture* körnig; *surface* gekörnt **b** *leather* genarbt; *wood* maserig, gemasert **c** *photograph, video* unscharf

gram, gramme [græm] N Gramm *nt*

gram flour N Kichererbsenmehl *nt*

grammar ['græmə] **N a** (= *subject, book*) Grammatik *f*, Sprachlehre *f*; **your ~ is terrible** von Grammatik hast du keine Ahnung; **his ~ is excellent** seine Grammatik ist fehlerfrei; **that is bad** ~ das ist grammat(ikal)isch falsch **b** (*inf*) = **grammar school**

grammar book N Grammatik(buch *nt*) *f*, Sprachlehrbuch *nt*

grammarian [grə'mɛərɪən] N Grammatiker(in) *m(f)*

grammar school N (*Brit*) ≈ Gymnasium *nt*; (*US*) ≈ Mittelschule *f* (*Stufe zwischen Grundschule und Höherer Schule*)

grammatical [grə'mætɪkəl] ADJ **a** (= *relating to grammar*) grammatisch; ~ **error/rule** Grammatikfehler *m/*-regel *f* **b** (= *correct*) grammat(ikal)isch richtig or korrekt; **his English is not** ~ sein Englisch ist grammatikalisch falsch

grammaticality [grə,mætɪ'kælɪtɪ] N Grammatikalität *f*

grammatically [grə'mætɪkəlɪ] ADV *write, speak* grammat(ikal)isch richtig or korrekt; ~ **correct** grammat(ikal)isch richtig; ~, **this sentence is wrong** dieser Satz ist grammat(ikal)isch falsch; ~, **his work is poor** von der Grammatik her ist seine Arbeit schlecht

gramme N = **gram**

Grammy ['græmɪ] N (= *award*) Grammy *m* (*Schallplattenpreis*)

gramophone ['græməfəʊn] N (*Brit, old*) Grammophon® *nt* (*dated*), Grammofon *nt*; ~ **record** Schallplatte *f*

gramps [græmps] N (*US, inf*) Opa *m* (*inf*), Opapa *m* (*inf*)

grampus ['græmpəs] N Rundkopf- or Rissosdelphin *m* or -delfin *m*, Grampus *m* (*spec*); **to puff/snort like a** ~ (*inf*) wie eine Lokomotive schnaufen (*inf*)

gran [græn] N (*inf*) Oma *f* (*inf*), Omi *f* (*inf*)

granary ['grænərɪ] N Kornkammer *f* (*also fig*), Kornspeicher *m*

grand [grænd] **ADJ** (+*er*) **a** (= *imposing*) grandios; *architecture, building* prachtvoll, grandios; *scheme, strategy* groß angelegt; *gesture* großartig; *ideas* hochfliegend; *person, clothes, manner* vornehm; *job* bedeutend; ~ **design** groß angelegter (Gesamt)plan; **on a ~ scale** im großen Rahmen; **to make a ~ entrance** einen großen Auftritt inszenieren; **to do sth the ~ manner** im großen Stil tun; **to give oneself ~ airs** den großen Herrn/die große Dame spielen; ~ **occasion** großer or feierlicher Anlass; **the ~ opening** die große Eröffnung; **the ~ old man of English politics** der große Alte or der Grand Old Man der englischen Politik
b (*dated*, = *great, wonderful*) *activity, experience, success, idea* fabelhaft, großartig; (*inf*) *person* fantastisch (*inf*), phantastisch (*inf*), toll (*inf*); **to have a ~ (old) time** sich glänzend or großartig amüsieren
N a (*Fin inf*: = *thousand pounds or dollars*) Riese *m* (*inf*); **ten ~** zehn Riesen (*inf*)
b (*Mus inf*: = *grand piano*) Flügel *m* → *also* **baby grand**

grand: grandaunt N Großtante *f*; **Grand Canary** N Gran Canaria *nt*; **Grand Canyon** N Grand Canyon *m*; **grandchild** N Enkel(kind *nt*) *m*; **grand(d)ad** N (*inf*) Opa *m* (*inf*), Opi *m* (*inf*); **granddaughter** N Enkelin *f*; **grand duchess** N Großherzogin *f*; **grand duchy** N Großherzogtum *nt*; **grand duke** N Großherzog *m*

grandee [græn'di:] N (*of Spain*) Grande *m*; (*fig*) Fürst *m* (*inf*); **the ~s of broadcasting/business** die Größen des Fernsehens/der Geschäftswelt

grandeur ['grændjə] N Größe *f*; (*of scenery, music also*) Erhabenheit *f*; (*of manner also*) Würde *f*, Vornehmheit *f*

grandfather ['grændfɑːðə] N Großvater *m*

grandfather clock N Standuhr *f*, Großvateruhr *f*

grandfatherly ADJ großväterlich

grand finale N großes Finale

grandiloquence [græn'dɪləkwəns] N (*form, of language, speech, style*) hochtrabende Art; **his ~** seine hochtrabende Art; (= *words*) seine großtönenden Worte

grandiloquent [græn'dɪləkwənt] ADJ (*form*) *language, style, speech* hochtrabend; *gesture* übertrieben; *description* grandios

grandiloquently [græn'dɪləkwəntlɪ] ADV *speak* hochtrabend; *announce* großspurig; *expressed, phrased, described* hochtrabend, grandios

grandiose ['grændɪəʊz] ADJ (= *impressive*) *house, speech, ambition* grandios (*also pej*), großartig; (*pej*, = *pompous*) *person, style* schwülstig, bombastisch (*inf*); *idea, plan* grandios, hochfliegend; *claim* großspurig

grandiosely ['grændɪəʊzlɪ] ADV *remark* grandios (*also pej*); *name* schwülstig

grand jury N (*US, Jur*) Großes Geschworenengericht

GRAND JURY

Im US-Rechtssystem entscheidet die **grand jury** darüber, ob jemand wegen einer Straftat angeklagt und der Fall vor Gericht behandelt werden soll. Eine **grand jury** setzt sich aus zwölf bis dreiundzwanzig Personen zusammen. Das Verfahren findet normalerweise nicht öffentlich statt. Die **grand jury** ist ermächtigt, Zeugen vorzuladen und sie zu einer Aussage zu zwingen. Die Jury aus zwölf Geschworenen, die bei einer Gerichtsverhandlung über die Schuld oder Unschuld eines Angeklagten zu entscheiden hat, wird **trial jury** oder **petit jury** genannt.

---

grand larceny N schwerer Diebstahl

grandly ['grændlɪ] ADV **a** (= *impressively*) eindrucksvoll; *named* grandios; *situated, built* prachtvoll; **it is ~ described as/called/titled ...** es trägt die grandiose Bezeichnung ... **b** (= *pompously*) *announce, proclaim, declare* großspurig; *say* hochtrabend

grand: grandma N (*inf*) Oma *f* (*inf*), Omi *f* (*inf*); **grand mal** [,grɒn'mæl] N (*Med*) Grand Mal *nt*; **grand master, grandmaster** N (*Chess*) Großmeister(in) *m(f)*; **grandmother** N Großmutter *f*; **grandmotherly** ADJ großmütterlich; **Grand National** N Grand National *nt* (*bedeutendes Pferderennen in Großbritannien*)

grandness ['grændnɪs] N grandiose Art; (*of architecture, building also*) Pracht *f*; (*of scheme*) groß angelegte Art; (*of person, clothes, manner*) Vornehmheit *f*; (*of occasion*) Größe *f*; (*of gesture*) Großartigkeit *f*

grand: Grand Old Party N **the ~** (*US Pol*) die Republikanische Partei; **grand opera** N große Oper; **grandpa** N (*inf*) Opa *m* (*inf*), Opi *m* (*inf*); **grandparent** N Großelternteil *m* (*form*), Großvater *m/*-mutter *f*; **grandparents** PL Großeltern *pl*; **grand piano** N Flügel *m*; **Grand Prix** N Grand Prix *m*; **grand slam** N (*Bridge*) Großschlemm *m*; **to win the ~** (*Sport*) alle Wettbewerbe gewinnen; **grandson** N Enkel(sohn) *m*; **grandstand** N Haupttribüne *f*; **a ~ finish** eine Entscheidung auf den letzten Metern; **to have a ~ view of sth** (direkten) Blick auf etw (*acc*) haben; **grand total** N Gesamtsumme *f*; **a ~ of £50** insgesamt £ 50; **grand tour** N **a the Grand Tour** (*Hist*) die Kavalierstour **b** (*fig, of a place*) große Besichtigungstour; **to give sb a ~ of sth** jdm etw in allen Einzelheiten zeigen; **grand vizier** N (*Hist*) Großwesir *m*

grange [greɪndʒ] N Bauernhof *m*, (kleiner) Gutshof

granger [greɪndʒə] N Bauer *m*, Farmer *m*

granite ['grænɪt] N Granit *m*

granny, grannie ['grænɪ] N **a** (*inf*) Oma *f* (*inf*), Omi *f* (*inf*) **b** (*also* **granny knot**) Altweiberknoten *m*

granny: granny bonds PL (*Brit Fin inf*) *index-gebundene staatliche Sparbriefe*; **granny flat** N (*Brit*) Einliegerwohnung *f*; **granny glasses** PL randlose Brille; **Granny Smith** N (= *apple*) Granny Smith *m*

grant [grɑːnt] **VT a** (= *accord*) gewähren (*sb* jdm); *period of grace, privilege, right* gewähren, zugestehen (*sb* jdm); *prayer* erhören; *honour* erweisen (*sb* jdm); *permission, licence, visa* erteilen (*sb* jdm); *request* stattgeben (+*dat*) (*form*); *land, pension* zusprechen, bewilligen (*sb* jdm); *wish* (= *give*) gewähren, freistellen (*sb* jdm); (= *fulfil*) erfüllen; **to ~ recognition to sb/sth** jdn/etw anerkennen; **to ~ an amnesty to sb** jdm amnestieren; **I beg your pardon – ~ed** ich bitte (vielmals) um Entschuldigung – sie sei dir gewährt (*hum, form*)
b (= *admit, agree*) zugeben, zugestehen; **~ed that this is true ...** angenommen, das ist wahr ...; **~ed, he looks good for his age** man muss

zugeben, dass er für sein Alter gut aussieht; **I ~ you that** da gebe ich dir Recht, das gebe ich zu; **to take sb/sth for ~ed** jdn/etw als selbstverständlich hinnehmen; **to take it for ~ed that ...** es selbstverständlich finden or als selbstverständlich betrachten, dass ...; **you take too much for ~ed** für dich ist (zu) vieles (einfach) selbstverständlich

N (of money) Subvention f; (for studying etc) Stipendium nt

grantable ['grɑːntəbl] ADJ **a** (= transferable) verleihbar (to dat), übertragbar (to auf +acc) **b** (= approvable) zu bewilligen(d)

grant-aided ADJ student gefördert; group, school, programme subventioniert

grantee [grɑːn'tiː] N Begünstigte(r) mf; (Jur) Zessionar(in) m(f), Rechtsnachfolger(in) m(f)

grant: grant-in-aid N Zuschuss m, Beihilfe f; **grant-maintained** ADJ school staatlich finanziert; **to have ~ status** staatlich finanziert sein

---

GRANT-MAINTAINED SCHOOL

Eine **grant-maintained school** ist eine staatliche Schule in Großbritannien, die nicht durch einer lokalen Schulbehörde, sondern durch Subventionen, **grants**, der Zentralregierung finanziert wird. Das System wurde ins Leben gerufen, um einzelnen Schulen größere Autonomie zu gewähren und den Einfluss der kommunalen Behörden auf das Bildungswesen zu begrenzen, auch wenn es viele Schulen vorgezogen haben, weiterhin der lokalen Schulbehörde zu unterstehen. Jede Schule, die sich für den Status einer **grant-maintained school** entscheidet, wird von einem eigenen Verwaltungsausschuss geleitet, in dem Vertreter des Personals, der Eltern und andere gewählte Mitglieder viele der schulischen Entscheidungen übernehmen, die sonst der Schulbehörde vorbehalten waren, wie die Einstellung neuen Personals, die Zuteilung des Schulbudgets und der Unterhalt des Schulgebäudes.

---

grantor [grɑːn'tɔː, 'grɑːntə] N Verleiher(in) m(f), Erteiler(in) m(f); (Jur) Zedent(in) m(f)

granular ['grænjʊlə] ADJ körnig, gekörnt, granular (spec); leather genarbt, narbig

granulate ['grænjʊleɪt] VT granulieren, körnen; leather rauen VI körnig werden

granulated sugar ['grænjʊleɪtɪd'ʃʊgə] N Zuckerraffinade f

granule ['grænjuːl] N Körnchen nt

grape [greɪp] N (Wein)traube f, Weinbeere f; **a pound of ~s** ein Pfund (Wein)trauben; **a bunch of ~s** eine (ganze) Weintraube

grape: grapefruit N Grapefruit f, Pampelmuse f; **grapefruit juice** N Grapefruitsaft m; **grape harvest** N Weinlese f; **grape hyacinth** N Traubenhyazinthe f; **grape juice** N Traubensaft m; **grapeshot** N (Hist) Kartätsche f; **grapestone** N Traubenkern m; **grape sugar** N Traubenzucker m; **grape type** N Rebsorte f; **grapevine** N Weinstock m; (inf) Nachrichtendienst m (inf); **I heard it on** or **through the ~** es ist mir zu Ohren gekommen

graph [grɑːf] N Diagramm nt, Schaubild nt; (Math, of a function) Graph m, Schaubild nt

grapheme ['græfiːm] N Graphem nt

graphic ['græfɪk] ADJ **a** (= vivid) account, description anschaulich; (= unpleasantly realistic) drastisch; **to describe sth in ~ detail** etw in allen Einzelheiten anschaulich darstellen **b** (Art) grafisch; ~ **work** Grafiken pl → also **graphics**

graphical ['græfɪkəl] ADJ grafisch

graphically ['græfɪkəlɪ] ADV **a** (= clearly) describe, portray anschaulich, in allen Einzelheiten; (= in unpleasantly realistic way) illustrate, demonstrate, display auf drastische Art; ~ **clear** sonnenklar (inf) **b** (= using illustrations) display, illustrate grafisch

graphical user interface N (Comput) grafische Benutzeroberfläche

---

graphic: graphic artist N Grafiker(in) m(f); **graphic arts** PL , **graphic design** N Grafik f; **graphic designer** N Grafiker(in) m(f); **graphic display** N (Comput) grafische Anzeige; **graphic equalizer** N (Graphic) Equalizer m; **graphic novel** N Roman in Cartoonform

graphics ['græfɪks] **N a** sing (= subject) Zeichnen nt, zeichnerische or grafische Darstellung **b** pl (= drawings) Zeichnungen pl, (grafische) Darstellungen pl **c** pl (Comput) Grafik f; **can your computer do ~?** ist Ihr Computer grafikfähig? ADJ attr (Comput) Grafik-; ~ **card** Grafikkarte f; ~ **mode** Grafikmodus m; ~ **printer** Grafikdrucker m; ~ **software** Grafiksoftware f

graphite ['græfaɪt] N Graphit m, Grafit m

graphologist [græ'fɒlədʒɪst] N Grafologe m, Grafologin f

graphology [græ'fɒlədʒɪ] N Grafologie f, Handschriftendeutung f

graph paper N Millimeterpapier nt

-graphy [-grəfɪ] N suf -grafie f

grapnel ['græpnəl] N **a** (= anchor) (Dregg)anker m, Draggen m (spec) **b** = **grappling iron**

grapple ['græpl] **N** = **grappling iron** VI (lit) ringen, kämpfen; **to ~ with a problem/situation** sich mit einem Problem/einer Situation herumschlagen; **the wrestlers ~d with each other** die Ringer hielten sich in enger Umklammerung VT festhalten; enemy boat die Enterhaken verwenden bei; **the boats were ~d together** die Boote waren durch Haken verbunden

grappling ['græplɪŋ] N (Sport inf) Ringen nt

grappling hook, **grappling iron** N Haken m, Greifer m; (Naut) Enterhaken m

grasp [grɑːsp] **N a** (= hold) Griff m; **he held my arm firmly in his ~** er hielt meinen Arm mit festem Griff; **the knife slipped from her ~** das Messer rutschte ihr aus der Hand; **just when peace/fame was within their ~** gerade als Frieden/Ruhm greifbar nahe war or in greifbare Nähe gerückt war

b (fig, = understanding) Verständnis nt; **to have a good ~ of sth** etw gut beherrschen; **her ~ of the language/subject is not very good** sie beherrscht die Sprache/das Gebiet nicht sehr gut; **it is beyond his ~** das geht über seinen Verstand; **it's within his ~** das kann er verstehen or begreifen

VT **a** (= catch hold of) ergreifen, greifen nach; (= hold tightly) festhalten; **he ~ed the bundle in his arms** er hielt das Bündel in den Armen; **to ~ a chance** eine Gelegenheit ergreifen; **to ~ sb's hand** nach jds Hand greifen

b (fig, = understand) begreifen, erfassen

VI **to ~ at sth** (lit) nach etw greifen; (fig) sich an etw (acc) stürzen; hope sich klammern an (+dat); **to ~ at an opportunity** eine Gelegenheit ergreifen or beim Schopfe packen → also **straw**

grasping ['grɑːspɪŋ] ADJ (fig) habgierig

grass [grɑːs] **N a** (= plant) Gras nt; **wheat is a ~** der Weizen gehört zu den Gräsern; **blade of ~** Grashalm m; ~ **seed** Grassamen m; **to let the ~ grow under one's feet** die Sache auf die lange Bank schieben; **the ~ is always greener (on the other side of the fence** or **hill)** (Prov) auf des Nachbars Feld steht das Korn besser (Prov), die Kirschen in Nachbars Garten ... (Prov)

b no pl (= lawn) Rasen m; (= pasture) Weide(land nt) f; **to play on ~** (Sport) auf (dem) Rasen spielen; **the cattle are out at ~** (Brit) das Vieh ist auf der Weide; **to put** or **turn out to ~** (Brit, cattle) auf die Weide führen or treiben; old horses das Gnadenbrot geben (+dat); (inf) employee aufs Abstellgleis schieben (inf)

c (inf, = marijuana) Gras(s) nt (inf)

d (Brit, inf, = informer) Spitzel m (sl)

VT (also **grass over**) ground mit Gras bepflanzen

VI (Brit, inf) singen (inf) (to bei); **to ~ on sb** jdn verpfeifen (inf)

grass: grass blade N Grashalm m; **grass box** N Grasfangkorb m; **grass-green** ADJ gras-

---

grün; **grass-grown** ADJ mit Gras bewachsen; **grasshopper** N Heuschrecke f, Grashüpfer m (inf); **grassland** N Grasland nt; **grass roots** PL Volk nt; (of a party) Basis f, Fußvolk nt (hum inf); **grass-roots** ADJ attr Basis-, an der Basis; ~ **democracy** Basisdemokratie f; **at ~ level** an der Basis; **a ~ movement** eine Bürgerinitiative; **grass skirt** N Bastrock m; **grass snake** N Ringelnatter f; **grass widow** N Strohwitwe f; (dated US, divorced) geschiedene Frau; (separated) (von ihrem Mann) getrennt lebende Frau; **grass widower N** Strohwitwer m; (dated US, divorced) geschiedener Mann; (separated) (von seiner Frau) getrennt lebender Mann

grassy ['grɑːsɪ] ADJ (+er) grasig; ~ **slope** Grashang m

grate¹ [greɪt] N (= grid) Gitter nt; (in fire) (Feuer)rost m; (= fireplace) Kamin m

grate² VT **a** (Cook) reiben; vegetables raspeln, reiben **b** (bottom of car, boat etc = scrape) streifen; (person: = make a grating noise with) kratzen mit; one's teeth knirschen mit VI (= scrape) streifen (against +acc); (= make a noise) kratzen; (rusty door) quietschen; (feet on gravel) knirschen; (fig) wehtun (on sb jdm), krank machen (on sb jdn); **to ~ on sb's nerves** jdm auf die Nerven gehen; **this phrase ~s on the ear** dieser Ausdruck hört sich schlimm an

grateful ['greɪtfʊl] ❍ 2.1, 4, 20.1, 22 ADJ dankbar; **he was ~ for her support** er war dankbar für ihre Unterstützung; **I'm ~ to you for believing me** ich bin dir dankbar (dafür), dass du mir glaubst; **I'm ~ to you for buying** or **having bought the tickets** ich bin dir dankbar (dafür), dass du die Karten gekauft hast; **he was ~ to be home/that he was still alive** er war froh or dankbar, zu Hause zu sein/noch am Leben zu sein; **to express one's ~ thanks (to sb)** (jdm) seine aufrichtige Dankbarkeit aussprechen

gratefully ['greɪtfəlɪ] ADV dankbar; acknowledged also in Dankbarkeit

grater ['greɪtə] N Reibe f

gratification [grætɪfɪ'keɪʃən] N **a** (= pleasure) Genugtuung f; **it is a source of great ~ to me** ich empfinde große Genugtuung darüber **b** (= satisfying: of desires etc) Befriedigung f

gratify ['grætɪfaɪ] VT **a** (= give pleasure) erfreuen; **to be gratified at** or **by** or **with sth** über etw (acc) hocherfreut sein; **I was gratified to hear that ...** ich habe mit Genugtuung gehört, dass ... **b** (= satisfy) befriedigen, zufrieden stellen

gratifying ['grætɪfaɪɪŋ] ADJ (sehr) erfreulich; **it is ~ to learn that ...** es ist erfreulich zu erfahren, dass ...

gratifyingly ['grætɪfaɪɪŋlɪ] ADV erfreulich; **he was ~ pleased** es war erfreulich zu sehen, wie er sich freute

grating¹ ['greɪtɪŋ] N Gitter nt

grating² ADJ kratzend; sound quietschend; (= rasping) knirschend; (on nerves) auf die Nerven gehend; voice schrill **N** Kratzen nt; (of rusty door) Quietschen nt; (of teeth, feet on gravel) Knirschen nt

gratis ['grætɪs] ADJ, ADV gratis, umsonst

gratitude ['grætɪtjuːd] ❍ 22, 24.4 N Dankbarkeit f (to gegenüber)

gratuitous [grə'tjuːɪtəs] ADJ überflüssig, unnötig; (= unasked-for) unerwünscht

gratuitously [grə'tjuːɪtəslɪ] ADV unnötigerweise

gratuity [grə'tjuːɪtɪ] N Gratifikation f, (Sonder)zuwendung f; (form. = tip) Trinkgeld nt

grave¹ [greɪv] N (lit, fig) Grab nt; **silent as the ~** totenstill; **the house was like the ~** es herrschte Totenstille im Haus; **to turn in one's ~** sich im Grabe herumdrehen; **from beyond the ~** aus dem Jenseits; **to go to an early ~** einen frühen Tod finden; **to rise from the ~** von den Toten auferstehen; **to dig one's own ~** (fig) sein eigenes Grab graben or schaufeln

grave² ADJ (+er) **a** (= serious, considerable) concern, danger, problem, difficulty groß; consequences schwerwiegend; threat, situation, matter ernst; mistake schwer, gravierend; illness, crime schwer;

news schlimm; *suspicion, doubt* stark **b** (= *solemn*) *person, face, expression* ernst

grave³ [grɑːv] **ADJ** ~ **accent** Gravis *m*, Accent grave *m*; (*in Greek*) Gravis *m*; **e** ~, ~ **e** e Accent grave **N** Gravis *m*

grave: graveclothes PL Totengewand *nt*; **grave digger** N Totengräber(in) *m(f)*; **grave goods** PL (*Archeol*) Grabbeigaben *pl*

gravel ['grævəl] **N a** Kies *m*; (= *large chippings*) Schotter *m* **b** (*Med*) Nierensand or -grieß *m*; (*in bladder*) Harngrieß *m* **ADJ** *attr* Kies-; *road, drive* mit Kies bedeckt; ~ **path** Kiesweg *m*; ~ **pit** Kiesgrube *f* **VT** *path, lane* mit Kies bestreuen, schottern

gravelled, (*US*) **graveled** ['grævəld] ADJ mit Kies bedeckt; ~ **path** Kiesweg *m*

gravelly ['grævəlɪ] ADJ **a** (*liter*, = *stony*) *shore, drive* kiesbedeckt; *soil* steinig **b** (*fig*) *voice* tief und rau; (= *hoarse*) heiser

gravely ['greɪvlɪ] ADV **a** (= *severely, seriously*) *ill, wounded* schwer; ~ **ill patients** schwer kranke Patienten; ~ **concerned** ernstlich besorgt **b** (= *solemnly*) *say, nod* ernst

grave mound N Grabhügel *m*

graven ['greɪvən] ADJ (*old, liter*) gehauen (*on, in* +*acc*); ~ **image** Götzenbild *nt*; **to be** ~ **in one's heart** *or* **on one's memory** sich in jds Gedächtnis (*acc*) eingegraben haben (*geh*)

grave: grave robber N Grabräuber(in) *m(f)*; **graveside** N **at the** ~ am Grabe; **a** ~ **service** ein Gottesdienst am Grabe; **gravestone** N Grabstein *m*; **graveyard** N Friedhof *m*; **that ministry is a** ~ **of political careers** in diesem Ministerium hat schon manche politische Laufbahn ein vorzeitiges Ende genommen; **graveyard shift** N (*esp US*) Nachtschicht *f*

graving dock ['greɪvɪŋdɒk] N Trockendock *nt*

gravitate ['grævɪteɪt] VI (*lit*) gravitieren (*form*) (*to(wards)* zu, auf +*acc*), angezogen werden (*to(wards)* von); (*fig*) hingezogen werden (*to(wards)* zu), angezogen werden (*to(wards)* von)

gravitation [ˌgrævɪ'teɪʃən] N (*Phys*) Gravitation *f*, Schwerkraft *f*; (*fig*) Hinneigung *f* (*to* zu); **the hippies'** ~ **to San Francisco** die Anziehungskraft, die San Francisco auf die Hippies ausübt

gravitational [ˌgrævɪ'teɪʃənl] ADJ Gravitations-

gravitational: gravitational field N Gravitations- or Schwerefeld *nt*; **gravitational force** N Schwerkraft *f*; (*Space*) Andruck *m*; **gravitational pull** N Anziehungskraft *f*

gravity ['grævɪtɪ] N **a** (*Phys*) Schwere *f*, Schwerkraft *f*; **the law(s) of** ~ das Gravitationsgesetz; **centre** (*Brit*) *or* **center** (*US*) **of** ~ Schwerpunkt *m*; **force of** ~ Schwerkraft *f*; ~ **feed** Fall- or Schwerkraftspeisung *f* **b** (= *seriousness, of person, expression, situation, matter, threat*) Ernst *m*; (*of mistake, illness, crime*) Schwere *f*; (*of danger, problem, difficulty*) Größe *f*; (*of consequences*) schwerwiegende Art; **the** ~ **of the news** die schlimmen Nachrichten

gravlax ['grævlæks] N *Art Räucherlachs*

gravy ['greɪvɪ] N **a** (*Cook*, = *juice*) Fleisch- or Bratensaft *m*; (= *sauce*) Soße *f* **b** (*inf*, = *perks*) Spesen *pl*; (= *corrupt money*) Schmiergelder *pl* (*inf*); **to get on the** ~ **train** auch ein Stück vom Kuchen abbekommen (*inf*); **to ride on the** ~ **train** locker Geld machen (*inf*)

gravy: gravy boat N Sauciere *f*, Soßenschüssel *f*; **gravy train** N (*inf*) **to climb** *or* **get on the** ~ leicht ans große Geld kommen

gray N, ADJ, VI (*US*) = **grey**

graze¹ [greɪz] **VI** (*cattle etc*) grasen, weiden **VT** *meadow, field* abgrasen, abweiden; *cattle* weiden lassen

graze² **VT** (= *touch lightly*) streifen; (= *scrape skin off*) aufschürfen; **to** ~ **one's knees** sich (*dat*) die Knie aufschürfen; **to** ~ **oneself** sich (*dat*) die Haut aufschürfen, sich aufschürfen **VI** streifen; **the car** ~**d along the wall** das Auto ist an der Mauer entlanggestreift **N** Abschürfung *f*, Schürfwunde *f*

grazier ['greɪzɪə'] N (*esp Brit*) Viehzüchter(in) *m(f)*

grazing ['greɪzɪŋ] N Weideland *nt*; **this land offers good** ~ dies ist gutes Weideland; ~ **land** Weideland *nt*; ~ **rights** Weiderechte *pl*

GRE (*US, Univ*) *abbr of* **Graduate Record Examination** *Zulassungsprüfung für ein weiterführendes Studium*

grease [griːs] **N a** Fett *nt*; (= *lubricant*) (Schmier)fett *nt*, Schmiere *f*; **his hair was thick with** ~ seine Haare starrten vor Fett **b** (*also* **grease wool**) Schweißwolle *f* **VT** fetten; *skin* einfetten, einschmieren, (*inf*), (*Aut, Tech*) schmieren; **to** ~ **back one's hair** sich (*dat*) die Haare mit Pomade nach hinten frisieren; **to** ~ **sb's palm** (*inf*) jdm etwas zustecken (*inf*), jdn schmieren (*inf*); **like** ~**d lightning** (*inf*) wie ein geölter Blitz

grease: grease gun N Fettspritze *or* -presse *f*; **grease mark** N Fettfleck *m*; **grease monkey** N (*inf*) Mechanikerlehrling *m*; **grease nipple** N Schmiernippel *m*; **greasepaint** N (*Theat*) (Fett)schminke *f*; **greaseproof** ADJ fettdicht; ~ **paper** Pergamentpapier *nt*

greaser ['griːsə'] N **a** (*inf*, = *motorcyclist*) Motorradfahrer(in) *m(f)*; (= *gang member*) Rocker *m* **b** (*US, pej* = *Latin American*) Latino *m* (*inf*) **c** (*inf*, = *motor mechanic*) Automechaniker(in) *m(f)*

grease remover N Fettlösungsmittel *nt*, Entfetter *m*

greasiness ['griːsɪnɪs] N **a** (= *oiliness*) Fettigkeit *f* **b** (= *dirtiness: of hands, clothes etc*) Schmierigkeit *f*; (= *slipperiness*) Glätte *f* **c** (*pej*, = *smarminess*) Schmierigkeit *f* (*pej inf*)

greasy ['griːsɪ] ADJ (+*er*) **a** (= *oily*) *food* fett; *hair, skin, complexion* fettig **b** (= *dirty*) *clothes* schmierig; (= *slippery*) *surface* rutschig, glatt **c** (*pej*, = *smarmy*) schmierig (*pej inf*)

greasy spoon (café) N (*pej inf*) billiges Fresslokal (*pej inf*)

great [greɪt] ☉ 3.2, 13, 24.4, 26.1 **ADJ** (+*er*) **a** (*in size*) groß; (= *very large*) sehr groß; (= *huge*) riesig; (*in extent*) *effort, variety, shock, need, success, help etc* groß; **with a** ~ **effort** mit großer Mühe *or* Anstrengung; **a** ~ **variety of opinions** viele ganz unterschiedliche Ansichten; **there is a** ~ **need for economic development** wirtschaftliche Entwicklung ist dringend nötig; **of no** ~ **importance** ziemlich unwichtig; **at a** ~ **pace** in *or* mit schnellem Tempo; ~ **good fortune** großes Glück; **with** ~ **good humour** sehr gut gelaunt; **in** ~ **detail** ganz ausführlich; **with** ~ **care** mit großer Vorsicht; **I'll take** ~ **care of it** ich werde sehr gut darauf aufpassen; **to take a** ~ **interest in sth** sich sehr für etw interessieren; **he did not live to a** ~ **age** er erreichte kein hohes Alter; **with** ~ **difficulty** mit großen Schwierigkeiten; **a player of** ~ **ability** ein sehr *or* ausgesprochen fähiger Spieler; **to a** ~ **extent** in hohem Maße; **it was** ~ **fun** es hat großen Spaß gemacht; **a** ~ **many, a** ~ **number of** sehr viele; **a** ~ **many people** sehr viele *or* eine Menge (*inf*) Leute → *also* **deal**

b (= *important, famous*) *person, achievement, work, event, city etc* groß; **his** ~**est work** sein Hauptwerk *nt*; **to think** ~ **thoughts** geniale Gedanken haben; **the** ~ **thing is to ...** das Wichtigste ist zu ...; ~ **minds think alike** große Geister denken gleich; **Alexander the Great** Alexander der Große

c (= *strong, enthusiastic*) **he was a** ~ **friend of my father** er war mit meinem Vater sehr gut befreundet; **he is a** ~ **admirer of British orchestras** er bewundert britische Orchester sehr; **I'm a** ~ **lover of** *or* **a** ~ **one for cakes** ich esse für mein Leben gern Kuchen; **she's a** ~ **one for punctuality** sie legt großen Wert auf Pünktlichkeit; **he's a** ~ **one for criticizing others** im Kritisieren anderer ist er (ganz) groß; **to be a** ~ **believer in sth** sehr viel von etw halten; **to be a** ~ **believer in doing sth** grundsätzlich dafür sein, etw zu tun; **he was a** ~ **womanizer** er stellte ständig den Frauen nach

d (*inf*, = *terrific*) *person, idea* toll (*inf*), prima

(*inf*); **I think she's** ~ ich finde sie toll (*inf*) *or* prima (*inf*); **this cookbook is** ~ **for desserts** in diesem Kochbuch findet man besonders gute Nachspeisen; **this whisk is** ~ **for sauces** dieser Schneebesen eignet sich besonders gut für Soßen; **to be** ~ **at football/at singing** ein großer Fußballspieler/Sänger sein; **to be** ~ **on jazz** ein großer Jazzkenner sein; **to feel** ~ sich toll *or* prima fühlen (*inf*); **my wife isn't feeling so** ~ meiner Frau geht es nicht besonders gut; **Great Scott** *or* **Heavens!** (*dated*) (ach du) großer Gott *or* lieber Himmel!

e (= *excellent, outstanding*) ausgezeichnet, großartig; **one of the** ~ **footballers of our generation** einer der großen Fußballspieler unserer Generation

INTERJ (*inf*) toll (*inf*), super (*inf*); **oh** ~ (*iro*) na wunderbar; **if that's what they want to believe,** ~ wenn sie das glauben wollen, dann sollen sie doch

ADV a (*inf*, = *well*) **she's doing** ~ (*in job*) sie macht sich hervorragend; (*healthwise*) sie macht große Fortschritte; **everything's going** ~ alles läuft nach Plan

b ~ **big** (*emph inf*) riesengroß; **I want to give you a** ~ **big kiss** ich möchte dir einen ganz dicken Kuss geben; **a** ~ **big wedding** eine Hochzeit im großen Stil; **he's a** ~ **big softie** er ist ein ganz großer Softie

N a *pl* **the** ~ die Großen *pl*; **the** ~ **and the good** die Prominenz

b *usu pl* (= *person*) Größe *f*; **the** ~**s** (= *stars*) die Großen *pl*; **one of the all-time** ~**s** einer der Größten aller Zeiten; **the golfing/literary** ~**s** die Golfgrößen/literarischen Größen

great: great ape N Menschenaffe *m*; **great assize** [ˌgreɪtə'saɪz] N (*Rel*) Jüngstes Gericht; **great auk** N Toralk *m*; **great-aunt** N Großtante *f*; **Great Australian Bight** N die Große Australische Bucht; **Great Barrier Reef** N **the** ~ das Große Barriereriff; **Great Bear** N **the** ~ der Große Bär; **Great Britain** N Großbritannien *nt*; **great calorie** N Kilokalorie *f*; **greatcoat** N Überzieher *m*, Paletot *m*; **Great Dane** N Deutsche Dogge; **Great Depression** N (*Hist*) Weltwirtschaftskrise *f*; **Great Divide** N (*US*) **the** ~ die Rocky Mountains *pl*; (*fig*, = *death*) die Schwelle des Todes (*liter*); **the great divide between ...** der Abgrund zwischen ... (*dat*); **Great Dividing Range** N **the** ~ die Ostaustralischen Kordilleren *pl*

greater ['greɪtə'] ADJ *comp of* **great** größer; **to pay** ~ **attention** besser aufpassen; **of** ~ **importance is ...** noch wichtiger ist ...; **one of the** ~ **painters** einer der bedeutenden Maler; **and** ~ immer größer

Greater London N Groß-London *nt*

greatest ['greɪtɪst] **ADJ** *superl of* **great** größte(r, s); **with the** ~ **(of) pleasure** mit dem größten Vergnügen **N** **he's the** ~ (*inf*) er ist der Größte; **it's the** ~ (*inf*) das ist das Größte (*sl*), das ist einsame Klasse (*inf*)

great: great-grandchild N Urenkel(in) *m(f)*; **great-grandparents** PL Urgroßeltern *pl*; **great-great-grandchild** N Ururenkel(in) *m(f)*; **great-great-grandparents** PL Ururgroßeltern *pl*; **great-hearted** ADJ (= *brave*) beherzt; (= *generous*) hochherzig; **Great Lakes** PL **the** ~ die Großen Seen *pl*

greatly ['greɪtlɪ] ADV *increase, influence, exaggerated, diminished* stark; *admire, surprise* sehr; **he was not** ~ **surprised** er war nicht besonders überrascht

great-nephew ['greɪtˌnefjuː] N Großneffe *m*

greatness ['greɪtnɪs] N Größe *f*; (*of size, height, degree etc also*) Ausmaß *nt*; (= *importance also*) Bedeutung *f*; ~ **of heart** Hochherzigkeit *f*, Großmut *f*; ~ **of mind** Geistesgröße *f*

great: great-niece N Großnichte *f*; **Great Plains** PL **the** ~ die Great Plains *pl*, die Großen Ebenen *pl*; **Great Powers** PL (*Pol*) **the** ~ die Großmächte *pl*; **great tit** N Kohlmeise *f*; **great-uncle** N Großonkel *m*; **Great Wall of China** N Chinesische Mauer; **Great War** N the ~ der Erste Weltkrieg; **Great Week** N (Rel) Karwoche f; **Great White Way** N the ~ (esp US, inf) das Theaterviertel am Broadway

greaves [gri:vz] PL (Cook) Grieben pl

grebe [gri:b] N (See)taucher m

Grecian ['gri:ʃən] ADJ griechisch

Greco- ['gri:kəʊ-] PREF (esp US) = Graeco-

Greece [gri:s] N Griechenland nt

greed [gri:d] N Gier f (for nach +dat); (for material wealth also) Habsucht f, Habgier f; (for gluttony) Gefräßigkeit f; ~ **for money/power** Geld-/Machtgier f

greedily ['gri:dɪlɪ] ADV gierig

greediness ['gri:dɪnɪs] N Gierigkeit f; (= gluttony) Gefräßigkeit f

greedy ['gri:dɪ] ADJ (+er) gierig (for auf +acc, nach); (for material wealth also) habgierig; (= gluttonous) gefräßig; ~ **for power/money** macht-/geldgierig; **to be** ~ **for approval** nach Anerkennung gieren; **don't be so** ~! sei nicht so unbescheiden; **you** ~ **thing!** du Nimmersatt! (inf)

greedy guts ['gri:dɪgʌts] N sing (Brit inf) Fresssack m (inf)

Greek [gri:k] ADJ griechisch; **he is** ~ er ist Grieche; ~ **letter society** (US, Univ) Studentenverbindung, deren Name aus drei griechischen Buchstaben besteht the ~ **Orthodox Church** die griechisch-orthodoxe Kirche N a (Ling) Griechisch nt; **Modern** ~ Neugriechisch nt; **Ancient** ~ Altgriechisch nt; **it's all** ~ **to me** (inf) das sind böhmische Dörfer für mich (inf) b (= person) Grieche m, Griechin f

Greek gift N (fig) Danaergeschenk nt

Greek tragedy N (Theat) (= genre) die griechische Tragödie; (= play) griechische Tragödie

green [gri:n] ADJ (+er) a grün; ~ **space** Grünfläche f; **to go** ~ (person) grün im Gesicht werden; **to be/turn** ~ **with envy** blass or grün or gelb vor Neid sein/werden; **to make sb** ~ **with envy** jdn vor Neid erblassen lassen; **the** ~ **shoots of recovery** die ersten Anzeichen für einen Aufschwung; ~ **salad** grüner Salat b (Pol) movement, party, issues grün; person, company grün, umweltbewusst; policy, measures, product, technology grün, umweltfreundlich; **he stressed his** ~ **credentials** er betonte, was er alles schon für die Umwelt getan habe c (= unripe) fruit, tomatoes grün d (= inexperienced) grün; (= naive) naiv; **I'm not as** ~ **as I look** (inf) ich bin nicht so dumm, wie ich aussehe (inf) N a (= colour) Grün nt b (= area of grass) Grünfläche f; (Golf) Grün nt; (**village**) ~ Dorfwiese f, Dorfanger m (dated) → also **bowling green** c (greens PL = vegetables) Grüngemüse nt d (Pol) **the Greens** die Grünen pl ADV (Pol) vote, think grün

green: green algae PL (Bot) Grünalgen pl; **greenback** N (US, inf) Lappen m (sl), Geldschein m; **green bean** N grüne Bohne; **green belt** N Grüngürtel m; **Green Berets** PL (US, Mil) Kommandotruppe f der US-Streitkräfte; **green card** N a (US, = residence permit) Aufenthaltsgenehmigung f b (Brit, Insur) grüne Versicherungskarte; **green cloth** N (esp US) (for gambling) Spieltisch m; (for billiards) Billardtisch m (Brit) Regeln für Kinder zur Sicherheit im Straßenverkehr

greenery ['gri:nərɪ] N Grün nt; (= foliage) grünes Laub, grüne Zweige pl

green: green-eyed ADJ (lit) grünäugig; (fig) scheel(äugig), missgünstig; (fig) **the** ~ **monster** (fig) der blasse Neid; **greenfield** ADJ land etc unerschlossen; ~ **site** Bauplatz m im Grünen; **many universities are on** ~ **sites** viele Universitäten befinden sich im Grünen; **greenfinch** N Grünfink m; **green fingers** PL (Brit) gärtnerisches Geschick; **to have** ~ eine Hand für Pflanzen haben; **greenfly** N Blattlaus f; **greengage** N Reneklode f, Reineclaude f; **green goddess** N (Brit inf) meist vom Militär eingesetztes Feuerwehrauto; **greengrocer** N

(esp Brit) (Obst- und) Gemüsehändler(in) m(f); **at the** ~**'s** (shop) im Gemüseladen; **greengrocery** N (esp Brit, = shop) Obst- und Gemüsehandlung f; (= trade) Obst- und Gemüsehandel m; (= articles) Obst und Gemüse nt; **greenhorn** N (inf, inexperienced) Greenhorn nt; (gullible) Einfaltspinsel m; **greenhouse** N Gewächshaus nt, Treibhaus nt; **greenhouse effect** N Treibhauseffekt m; **greenhouse gas** N Treibhausgas nt

greening ['gri:nɪŋ] N (Pol) **the** ~ **of Japan/politics** das zunehmende Umweltbewusstsein in Japan/in der Politik

greenish ['gri:nɪʃ] ADJ grünlich

green keeper N (Sport) Platzwart(in) m(f)

Greenland ['gri:nlənd] N Grönland nt

Greenlander ['gri:nləndə'] N Grönländer(in) m(f)

Greenlandic [gri:n'lændɪk] ADJ grönländisch N (Ling) Grönländisch nt

green: green light N grünes Licht; **to give sb/sth the** ~ jdm/einer Sache grünes Licht or freie Fahrt geben; **green lung** N (fig) grüne Lunge, Grünfläche f; **green man** N (at street crossing) grünes Licht; (as said to children) grünes Männchen; **little green men** kleine grüne Männchen; **green monkey disease** N (Med) Marburg-Krankheit f; **Green Mountain State** N the ~ der US-Bundesstaat Vermont

greenness ['gri:nnɪs] N a (= colour) Grün nt b (Pol, of policies) Umweltfreundlichkeit f; (of person) Umweltbewusstsein nt c (= unripeness) Grünheit f, Unreife f d (= lack of experience) Grünheit f; (= naivety) Naivität f

green: green onion N (US) Frühlingszwiebel f; **Green Paper** N (Brit, Pol) Vorlage f für eine Parlamentsdebatte; **Green Party** N **the** ~ die Grünen pl; **green pea** N (grüne) Erbse f; **Greenpeace** N Greenpeace nt; **green pepper** N (grüne) Paprikaschote; **green pound** N (Econ) **the** ~ das grüne Pfund; **green revolution** N (Econ, Agr) **the** ~ die grüne Revolution; **greenroom** N (Theat) Garderobe f; **greenstick fracture** N Grünholzbruch m; **greenstuff** N a (for cattle) Grünfutter nt b (= vegetable) grünes Gemüse; **green table** N Sitzungstisch m; **green tea** N grüner Tee; **green thumb** N (US) = **green fingers**; **green vegetables** PL Grüngemüse nt

---

GREEN-WELLIE BRIGADE

Green wellingtons, grüne Gummistiefel von hoher Qualität, werden in Großbritannien von all jenen getragen, die auf dem Land ausreiten, zum Jagen oder Angeln gehen, also den „klassischen" Freizeitaktivitäten der reichen Oberschicht nachgehen. Daher werden die **green wellingtons** zwangsläufig mit der gesellschaftlichen Oberschicht assoziiert. Der Ausdruck **green-wellie brigade** wird als Verallgemeinerung für all die Reichen und Adeligen benutzt, die manchmal ein recht elitäres Gruppenverhalten an den Tag legen.

Greenwich (Mean) Time ['grenɪtʃ('mi:n)taɪm] N westeuropäische Zeit, Greenwicher Zeit f

greenwood ['gri:nwʊd] N grüner Wald

green woodpecker N (Orn) Grünspecht m

greet [gri:t] VT (= welcome) begrüßen; (= receive, meet) empfangen; (= say hello to) grüßen; news, decision aufnehmen; **a terrible sight** ~**ed him** ihm bot sich ein fürchterlicher Anblick

greeting ['gri:tɪŋ] N Gruß m; (act, = welcoming) Begrüßung f; (= receiving, meeting) Empfang m; **we received a friendly** ~ **from the crowd** die Menge bereitete uns einen freundlichen Empfang; ~**s** Grüße pl; (= congratulations) Glückwünsche pl; **to send** ~**s to sb** jdn grüßen lassen; (through sb else) jdn grüßen lassen; **please give my** ~**s to them** bitte grüße sie von mir

greetings card N Grußkarte f

gregarious [grɪ'gɛərɪəs] ADJ person gesellig; ~ **animal/instinct** Herdentier nt/-trieb or -instinkt m

Gregorian [grɪ'gɔ:rɪən] ADJ gregorianisch

Gregorian calendar N gregorianischer Kalender

Gregorian chant N gregorianischer Choral or Gesang

greige [greɪʒ] ADJ textiles naturfarben

gremlin ['gremlɪn] N (hum) böser Geist, Maschinenteufel m (hum)

Grenada [gre'neɪdə] N Grenada nt

grenade [grɪ'neɪd] N Granate f

Grenadian [gre'neɪdɪən] ADJ grenadisch N Grenader(in) m(f)

grenadier [grenə'dɪə'] N Grenadier m

grenadine ['grenədi:n] N Grenadine f

grew [gru:] pret of **grow**

grey, (US) **gray** [greɪ] ADJ (+er) a (in colour) grau; (= ashen) person, face grau, fahl; weather, sky, day grau, trüb; **to go** or **turn** ~ (person, hair) grau werden, ergrauen (geh); **their faces were** ~ **with fatigue** sie or ihre Gesichter waren ganz blass vor Müdigkeit; **men in** ~ **suits** anonyme, aber mächtige Hintermänner b (= bleak) world, year, days, outlook grau, trostlos, öde c (= anonymous) person grau, gesichtslos; place grau, anonym N (= colour) Grau nt; **subtle** ~**s** zarte Grautöne pl VI (person, hair) grau werden, ergrauen (geh); **he was** ~**ing at the temples** seine Schläfen wurden grau, seine Schläfen ergrauten

grey, (US) **gray: grey area** N (fig) Grauzone f; **greybeard**, (US) **graybeard** N Graubart m; **grey cells** PL (inf) (**little**) ~ (kleine) graue Zellen pl (inf); **grey eminence** N graue Eminenz; **grey-haired** ADJ grauhaarig

greyhound ['greɪhaʊnd] N Windhund m, Windspiel nt

GREYHOUND

Die Greyhound-Gesellschaft betreibt ein Netz von Langstreckenbussen in den gesamten Vereinigten Staaten. Auch wenn eine Reise mit dem Greyhound wesentlich länger dauert als ein Flug, bietet sie doch einige Vorteile: Busse sind billig und zuverlässig und sind nun einmal für Touristen der beste Weg, Amerika mit einem schmalen Geldbeutel zu bereisen und dabei viele interessante Menschen kennen zu lernen. Die Gesellschaft bietet auch ein Ticket an, mit dem man unbegrenzt durch die USA reisen kann, den so genannten „Ameripass".
Die Amerikaner betrachten die Greyhound-Busse als einen nostalgischen Teil ihrer Tradition, immer unterwegs zu sein, der auch ins Liedgut Eingang gefunden hat: so gibt es einen Song mit dem Titel „Thank God and Greyhound she's gone".

---

greyhound racing N Windhundrennen nt

greyish, (US) **grayish** ['greɪʃ] ADJ gräulich

grey, (US) **gray: greylag (goose)** N Graugans f, Wildgans f; **grey market** N (Comm) grauer Markt; **grey matter** N (Med inf) graue Zellen pl; **grey mullet** N Meeräsche f

greyness, (US) **grayness** ['greɪnɪs] N a (= colour) Grau nt; (of face) Fahlheit f; (of weather, day) Trübheit f b (= bleakness: of life, world, outlook) Trostlosigkeit f, Öde f c (= anonymity, of person) Gesichtslosigkeit f; (of place) Anonymität f

grey, (US) **gray: grey parrot** N Graupapagei m; **grey seal** N Kegelrobbe f; **grey squirrel** N Grauhörnchen nt; **grey wolf** N Timberwolf f

grid [grɪd] N a (= grating) Gitter nt; (in fireplace, on barbecue) Rost m; ~ **system** (in road-building) Rechteckschema nt b (on map) Gitter nt, Netz nt c (= electricity, gas network) Verteilernetz nt; **the (national) ~** (Elec) das Überland(leitungs)netz **d** (Motor-racing: = starting grid) Start(platz) m; (US, Ftbl) Spielfeld nt; **they're on the ~** sie sind auf den Startplätzen **e** (Elec, = electrode) Gitter nt **f** (Theat) Schnürboden m

griddle ['grɪdl] N (Cook) gusseiserne Platte zum Pfannkuchenbacken

griddlecake ['grɪdlkeɪk] N kleiner Pfannkuchen

gridiron ['grɪdˌaɪən] N **a** (Cook) (Brat)rost m **b** (US, Ftbl) Spielfeld nt

gridlock ['grɪdlɒk] N (Mot) totaler Stau; (fig) festgefahrene Situation; **total ~** (Mot) Verkehrskollaps m

gridlocked ['grɪdlɒkt] ADJ **a** road völlig verstopft; **traffic is ~ in the cities** der Verkehr in den Städten ist zum völligen Stillstand gekommen **b** (fig) talks, negotiations festgefahren

grid: grid reference N Planquadratangabe f; **grid square** N Planquadrat nt

grief [gri:f] N Leid nt, Kummer m, Gram m (geh); (because of loss) große Trauer, Schmerz m, Gram m (geh); **to cause ~ to sb** jdn zutiefst betrüben; (death, loss also) jdm großen Schmerz bereiten; (failure, sb's behaviour also) jdm großen Kummer bereiten; **to come to ~** Schaden erleiden; (= be hurt, damaged) zu Schaden kommen; (= fail) scheitern

grief-stricken ['gri:fˌstrɪkən] ADJ untröstlich, tieftraurig; look, voice schmerzerfüllt, gramgebeugt (geh)

grievance ['gri:vəns] N Klage f; (= resentment) Groll m; **~ procedure** Beschwerdeweg m; **I've no ~ against him** (= no cause for complaint) ich habe an ihm nichts auszusetzen; (= no resentment) ich nehme ihm nichts übel; **to have a ~ against sb for sth** jdm etw übel nehmen; **to air one's ~s** seine Beschwerden vorbringen, sich offen beschweren, sich beklagen

grieve [gri:v] **VT** Kummer bereiten (+dat), betrüben; **it ~s me to see that ...** ich sehe mit Schmerz u Kummer, dass ...; **I was deeply ~d to hear of his death** die Nachricht von seinem Tod hat mich tief betrübt **VI** sich grämen (geh), trauern (at, about über +acc); **to ~ for sb/sth** um jdn/etw trauern; **to ~ for sb** (= sympathize with) zutiefst mit jdm mitfühlen, jds Schmerz teilen; **my heart ~s for you** mir blutet das Herz; **to ~ over sb/sth** sich über jdn/etw grämen (geh), über jdn/etw zutiefst bekümmert sein; **I didn't have any time to ~** ich hatte keine Zeit zum Trauern; **the grieving process** das Trauern

grievous ['gri:vəs] ADJ (form) damage, injury, suffering, blow, setback, crime, neglect schwer; news schmerzlich; error schwerwiegend, schwer wiegend; injustice, wrong schreiend; **his death is a ~ loss** sein Tod ist ein schwerer or schmerzlicher Verlust; **~ bodily harm** (Jur) schwere Körperverletzung

grievously ['gri:vəslɪ] ADV (form) injure, wound, disappoint, offend, neglect schwer; **he had been ~ wronged** man hatte ihm sehr großes Unrecht zugefügt

griffin ['grɪfɪn] N (Myth) (Vogel) Greif m

griffon ['grɪfən] N **a** (= bird) (Gänse)geier m **b** (= dog) Griffon m, Affenpinscher m **c** (Myth) = **griffin**

grift [grɪft] (dated US, sl) **N** (= money) ergaunertes or erschwindeltes Geld **VI** krumme Dinger drehen (sl)

grifter ['grɪftə'] N (dated US, sl, = swindler) Gauner(in) m(f), Schwindler(in) m(f)

grig [grɪg] N **merry as a ~** lustig und fidel

grill [grɪl] **N a** (Cook, on cooker etc) Grill m; (= gridiron) Grill m, (Brat)rost m; (= food) Grillgericht nt, Grillade f; (= restaurant) Grill(room) m **b** = **grille VT a** (Cook) grillen **b** (inf, = interrogate) in die Zange nehmen (inf); **to ~ sb about sth** jdn über etw (acc) ausquetschen (inf) or ins Verhör nehmen **VI a** (food) auf dem Grill liegen, gegrillt werden **b** (inf, in sun) schmoren (inf)

grille [grɪl] N Gitter nt; (on window) Fenstergitter nt; (to speak through) Sprechgitter nt; (Aut) Kühlergrill m

grilling ['grɪlɪŋ] N **a** (Cook) Grillen nt **b** (= interrogation) strenges Verhör; **to give sb a ~** jdn in die Zange nehmen (inf); **to give sb a ~ about sth** jdn über etw (acc) ausquetschen (inf) or ins Verhör nehmen

grill: grill pan N (Brit) Grillpfanne f; **grillroom** N Grillroom m

grilse [grɪls] N junger Lachs

grim [grɪm] ADJ (+er) **a** (= terrible) discovery, scene, task, news, story grauenvoll; joke, warning, reminder grauenhaft; situation ernst, trostlos; necessity, truth bitter; (= depressing) building, place, news, story trostlos; prospect trübe, düster; (= stern) person, face, smile, humour, silence, determination grimmig; voice ernst; battle, struggle verbissen, unerbittlich; **the ~ reality of hospital work** die harte Realität der Arbeit in einem Krankenhaus; **a ~ picture of life in the war zone** ein trostloses Bild vom Leben im Kriegsgebiet; **to paint a ~ picture of sth** etw in düsteren Farben schildern; **to look ~** (situation, future) trostlos aussehen; (person) ein grimmiges Gesicht machen; **~ (sense of) humour** (Brit) or **humor** (US) Galgenhumor m; **to cling or hang on to sth like ~ death** sich verzweifelt an etw (dat) festklammern; **the Grim Reaper** der Sensenmann **b** (inf, = lousy) fürchterlich (inf); **the side effects are pretty ~** die Nebenwirkungen sind ziemlich schlimm; **to feel ~** (= unwell) sich elend or mies (inf) fühlen; **you're looking pretty ~** du siehst ziemlich elend or schlecht aus

grimace ['grɪməs] **N** Grimasse f; **to make a ~** eine Grimasse machen or schneiden; (with disgust, pain also) das Gesicht verziehen **VI** Grimassen machen or schneiden; (with disgust, pain etc also) das Gesicht verziehen

grime [graɪm] N Dreck m, Schmutz m; (sooty) Ruß m

grimly ['grɪmlɪ] ADV fight, struggle, hold on verbissen; (= sternly) look, nod, say mit grimmiger Miene; smile, silent grimmig; bleak, barren trostlos; depressing grauenhaft; **~ determined** verbissen

Grimm's law [ˌgrɪmz'lɔː] N (Ling) Lautverschiebungsgesetz nt, erste Lautverschiebung

grimness ['grɪmnɪs] N (= terribleness) Grauenhaftigkeit f; (of situation) Ernst m; (= depressing nature, of building, place, news, story) Trostlosigkeit f; (of prospects) Trübheit f; (= sternness, of person, face, expression, smile, humour, determination) Grimmigkeit f; (of voice) Ernst m; (of battle, struggle) Verbissenheit f, Unerbittlichkeit f

grimy ['graɪmɪ] ADJ schmutzig, dreckig; clothes also verdreckt; (= greasy) schmierig; (= blackened with soot) city, building verrußt

grin [grɪn] **N** (showing pleasure) Lächeln nt, Strahlen nt; (showing scorn, stupidity, impudence) Grinsen nt; **to give a huge ~** (with pleasure) über das ganze Gesicht strahlen; (in scorn etc) breit grinsen; **to give a wry ~** ironisch lächeln **VI** (with pleasure) lächeln, strahlen; (in scorn, stupidly, cheekily) grinsen; **to ~ and bear it** gute Miene zum bösen Spiel machen; (= tolerate pain) die Zähne zusammenbeißen; **to ~ at sb** jdn anlächeln/angrinsen; **to ~ from ear to ear** über das ganze Gesicht strahlen; **to ~ like a Cheshire cat** wie ein Honigkuchenpferd grinsen

grind [graɪnd] vb: pret, ptp **ground VT a** (= crush) zerkleinern, zermahlen; corn, coffee, pepper, flour mahlen; (in mortar) zerstoßen; **to ~ sth to a powder** etw fein zermahlen/zerstoßen; **to ~ one's teeth** mit den Zähnen knirschen **b** (= polish, sharpen) gem, lens, knife schleifen **c** (= turn) handle, barrel organ drehen; **to ~ one's heel into the earth** den Absatz in die Erde bohren **d** **the tyrant ground the people into the dust** der Tyrann hat das Volk zu Tode geschunden **VI a** (mill) mahlen; (brakes, teeth, gears) knirschen; **the metal ground against the stone** das

Metall knirschte auf dem Stein; **the ship ground against the rocks** das Schiff lief knirschend auf die Felsen auf; **to ~ to a halt** or **standstill** (lit) quietschend zum Stehen kommen; (fig) stocken; (production etc) zum Erliegen kommen; (negotiations) sich festfahren; **the tanks were ~ing south** die Panzer rollten langsam nach Süden **b** (inf, = study) büffeln (inf) **N a** (= sound) Knirschen nt → **bump b** (fig inf: = drudgery) Schufterei f (inf); (US, inf, = swot) Streber(in) m(f) (inf); **the daily ~** der tägliche Trott; **it's a real ~** das ist ganz schön mühsam (inf); **she found housework a ~** sie empfand Hausarbeit als Plackerei (inf)

▶ **grind away** VI schuften (inf); **to grind away at sth** an etw (dat) schuften (inf)

▶ **grind down** VT sep (lit) (mill) pepper etc zermahlen; (sea) rocks abschleifen; (fig) people, resistance zermürben; **ground down by poverty** von Armut niedergedrückt

▶ **grind on** VI (enemy, invasion) unaufhaltsam vorrücken; (fig, bureaucracy etc) unaufhaltsam sein; **to grind on toward(s) sth** einer Sache (dat) unaufhaltsam entgegengehen; **the process grinds slowly on** das Verfahren schleppt sich hin

▶ **grind out** VT sep **a** article, essay sich (dat) abquälen; propaganda ausspucken (inf); victory sich (dat) mühsam erkämpfen; tune orgeln (inf) **b** (= extinguish by crushing) cigarette (with hand) ausdrücken; (with foot) austreten

▶ **grind up** VT sep zermahlen

grinder ['graɪndə'] N **a** (= meat grinder) Fleischwolf m; (= coffee grinder) Kaffeemühle f; (for sharpening) Schleifmaschine f; (= stone) Schleifstein m **b** (= person) Schleifer(in) m(f) **c** (= tooth) Backenzahn m; (of animals) Mahlzahn m

grinding ['graɪndɪŋ] ADJ **a** (= grating) noise knirschend; **to come to a ~ halt** (lit, fig) völlig zum Stillstand kommen; (vehicle) plötzlich stehen bleiben; **to bring sth to a ~ halt** (lit, fig) etw völlig zum Stillstand bringen **b** (= relentless) poverty (er)drückend; tedium, work zermürbend

grindingly ['graɪndɪŋlɪ] ADV erdrückend; **~ hard work** zermürbende Knochenarbeit; **~ slow** zermürbend langsam

grinding wheel N Schleifscheibe f, Schleifstein m

grindstone ['graɪndstəʊn] N **to keep one's nose to the ~** hart arbeiten; **to keep sb's nose to the ~** jdn hart arbeiten lassen; **back to the ~** wieder in die Tretmühle (hum)

gringo ['grɪŋgəʊ] N (esp US pej) Gringo m

grip [grɪp] **N a** Griff m; (on rope, on road) Halt m; **to get a ~ on the road/rope** auf der Straße/am Seil Halt finden; **these shoes/tyres** (Brit) or **tires** (US) **have got a good ~** diese Schuhe/Reifen greifen gut; **I can't get a ~ with these shoes** ich finde mit diesen Schuhen keinen Halt; **cold weather had a firm ~ on the capital** das kalte Wetter hatte die Hauptstadt fest im Griff; **to get a ~ on sth** (on situation, inflation etc) etw in den Griff bekommen; **to get a ~ on oneself** (inf) sich zusammenreißen (inf); **he had a good ~ on himself** er hatte sich gut im Griff or in der Gewalt; **to have a good ~ of a subject** ein Thema im Griff haben; **to let go or release one's ~** loslassen (on sth etw); **to lose one's ~** (lit) den Halt verlieren; (fig) nachlassen; **the chairman is losing his ~ (on the company)** der Vorsitzende hat die Firma nicht mehr richtig im Griff; **the President was losing his ~ on power** dem Präsidenten entglitt die Macht; **I must be losing my ~** mit mir gehts bergab; **to lose one's ~ on reality** den Bezug zur Wirklichkeit verlieren; **to lose one's ~ on a situation** eine Situation nicht mehr im Griff haben; **to have sb in one's ~** jdn in seiner Gewalt haben; **to be in the ~ of fear/passion** von Angst/Leidenschaft erfasst sein; **the country is in the ~ of a general strike** das Land ist von einem Generalstreik lahm gelegt; **the country is in the ~ of winter** der Winter hat im Land seinen Einzug gehalten; **to get** or **come to ~s with sth** mit etw klarkommen (*inf*), etw in den Griff bekommen; **to get** or **come to ~s with sb** jdm zu Leibe rücken, zum Angriff gegen jdn übergehen **b** (= *handle*) Griff *m* **c** (*esp Brit*: = *hair grip*) Klemmchen *nt* **d** (= *travelling-bag*) Reisetasche *f* **VT** packen; *hand* also ergreifen; (*fig, fear etc* also) ergreifen; (*film, story etc* also) fesseln; **the car ~s the road well** der Wagen liegt gut auf der Straße; **the tyre** (*Brit*) or **tire** (*US*) **~s the road well** der Reifen greift gut; **fear ~ped his heart** Furcht ergriff or packte ihn **VI** greifen

gripe [graɪp] **VT** (*US, inf,* = *annoy*) aufregen, fuchsen (*inf*) **VI** (*inf,* = *grumble*) meckern (*inf*), nörgeln; **to ~ at sb** jdn anmeckern (*inf*), jdn anmotzen (*inf*) **N a the gripes** PL Kolik *f*, Bauchschmerzen *pl*; **~ water** Kolikmittel *nt* **b** (*inf,* = *complaint*) Meckerei *f* (*inf*); **have you any more ~s?** sonst hast du nichts zu meckern? (*inf*)

grippe [grɪp] N (*dated US*) Grippe *f*

gripping ['grɪpɪŋ] ADJ *story, book, film* packend, fesselnd; **the Olympics have made ~ television** die Olympiade war ein fesselndes Fernseherlebnis; **it's ~ stuff** (*inf*) es packt or fesselt einen total (*inf*)

gripsack N (*US*) Reisetasche *f*

grisly ['grɪzlɪ] ADJ (*+er*) grausig, grässlich

grist [grɪst] N **it's all ~ to his/the mill** das kann er/man alles verwerten; (*for complaint*) das ist Wasser auf seine Mühle

gristle ['grɪsl] N Knorpel *m*

gristly ['grɪslɪ] ADJ (*+er*) knorpelig

grit [grɪt] **N a** (= *dust, in eye*) Staub *m*; (= *gravel*) Splitt *m*, feiner Schotter; (*for roads in winter*) Streusand *m* **b** (= *courage*) Mut *m*, Mumm *m* (*inf*) **c grits** PL (*US*) Grütze *f* **VT a** *road etc* streuen **b to ~ one's teeth** (*lit, fig*) die Zähne zusammenbeißen

gritter ['grɪtə'] N Streuwagen *m*

gritty ['grɪtɪ] ADJ (*+er*) **a** (*lit*) (= *sandy*) *soil, path* sandig; (= *grainy*) *texture, food* körnig **b** (*fig,* = *courageous*) *person* mutig, tapfer; *determination* zäh; **the team's ~ display** das tapfere Spiel der Mannschaft **c** (*fig, = unsentimental*) *realism* hart; *drama, film* wirklichkeitsnah; *portrayal, account* ungeschminkt

grizzle ['grɪzl] VI (*Brit, inf*) quengeln

grizzled ['grɪzld] ADJ *person* grauhaarig; *hair, beard* (= *grey*) grau; (= *streaked with grey*) grau meliert

grizzly ['grɪzlɪ] N (*also* **grizzly bear**) Grisli(bär) *m*, Grizzly(bär) *m* ADJ (*Brit, inf*) *baby* quengelig

groan [grəʊn] **N** Stöhnen *nt no pl*; (*of gate, planks etc*) Ächzen *nt no pl*; **to let out** or **give a ~** (auf)stöhnen; **moans and ~s** Jammern und Stöhnen *m* **VI** stöhnen (*with* vor *+dat*); (*gate, planks*) ächzen (*with* vor *+dat*); **the table ~ed under the weight** der Tisch ächzte unter der Last; **the country ~ed under** or **beneath its burdens** das Land ächzte unter seiner Last; **to ~ about sb/sth** über jdn/etw stöhnen

groat [grəʊt] N (*Brit, Hist*) *Silbermünze im Wert von 4 alten Pence*

groats [grəʊts] PL Schrot *nt* or *m*; (= *porridge*) Grütze *f*

grocer ['grəʊsə'] N Lebensmittelhändler(in) *m(f)*, Kaufmann *m*/-frau *f*; **at the ~'s** im Lebensmittelladen, beim Kaufmann

grocery ['grəʊsərɪ] N **a** (= *business, shop*) Lebensmittelgeschäft *nt* **b groceries** PL (= *goods*) Lebensmittel *pl*

grog [grɒg] N Grog *m*

groggily ['grɒgɪlɪ] ADV (*inf*) groggy (*inf*); **shake one's head, answer** schwach; **move** benommen

groggy ['grɒgɪ] ADJ (*+er*) (*inf*) angeschlagen (*inf*), groggy *pred inv* (*inf*)

groin [grɔɪn] N **a** (*Anat*) Leiste *f*; **to kick sb in the ~** jdn in den Unterleib or die Leistengegend treten **b** (*Archit*) Grat *m* **c** = **groyne**

grommet ['grɒmɪt] N Öse *f*; (*Naut*) Taukranz *m*

groom [gru:m] **N a** (*in stables*) Stallbursche *m*, Pferde- or Reitknecht *m* **b** (= *bridegroom*) Bräutigam *m* **VT a** *horse* striegeln, putzen; **to ~ oneself** (*birds, animals*) sich putzen; (*people*) sich pflegen; **well ~ed** gepflegt; **badly ~ed** ungepflegt **b** (= *prepare*) **he's being ~ed for the job of chairman/for the Presidency** er wird als zukünftiger Vorsitzender/Präsidentschaftskandidat aufgebaut; **to ~ sb for stardom** jdn als Star lancieren; **he is ~ing him as his successor** er zieht sich (*dat*) ihn als Nachfolger heran

grooming ['gru:mɪŋ] N ein gepflegtes Äußeres

groove [gru:v] **N** Rille *f*; (*in rock also*) Rinne *f*, Furche *f*; (*in face*) Furche *f*; (*fig*) altes Gleis; **to get into the ~** (*inf*) in Fahrt kommen; **he's (stuck) in a ~** (*inf*) er kommt aus seinem alten Trott nicht heraus **VT** Rillen machen in (*+acc*), rillen; (*water*) *stone* aushöhlen, Rinnen or Furchen machen in (*+acc*); *face* furchen **VI** (*dated sl*) einen losmachen (*dated sl*); **to ~ to the music** mit der Musik mitgehen

groover ['gru:və'] N (*dated sl,* = *man*) irrer or starker Typ (*sl*); (= *woman*) irre or starke Frau (*sl*)

groovy ['gru:vɪ] ADJ (*+er*) (*inf*) irr (*sl*), stark (*sl*)

grope [grəʊp] **VI** (*also* **grope around** or **a-bout**) (herum)tasten (*for* nach); (*for words, solution*) suchen (*for* nach); **to be groping in the dark** im Dunkeln tappen; (= *try things at random*) vor sich (*acc*) hin wursteln (*inf*); **groping hands** tastende Hände *pl* **VT** tasten nach; (*inf*) *girlfriend* befummeln (*inf*); **to ~ one's way** sich vorwärts tasten; **to ~ (one's way) in/out** sich hinein-/hinaustasten; **they are groping (their way) toward(s) a cure** sie bemühen sich darum, ein Heilmittel zu finden **N** (*inf*) **to have a ~** fummeln (*inf*); **a quick ~** eine schnelle Fummelei (*inf*)

gropingly ['grəʊpɪŋlɪ] ADV tastend

grosgrain ['grəʊgreɪn] N grob geripptes Seidentuch

gross¹ [grəʊs] N , *no pl* Gros *nt*

gross² ADJ (*+er*) **a** (= *serious*) *mismanagement, exaggeration, simplification, error, insult* grob; *inequality, violation* krass; *injustice* schreiend; **that is a ~ understatement** das ist stark untertrieben **b** (= *fat*) fett **c** (*inf*) *person, remarks, jokes* (= *disgusting*) abstoßend; (= *tasteless*) ordinär; **he is the ~est thing alive** er ist total ekelhaft **d** (= *total*) Gesamt-; (= *before deductions*) Brutto-; **~ amount** Gesamtbetrag *m*, Gesamtsumme *f*; **~ income** Bruttoeinkommen *nt*; **~ output** Gesamtproduktion *f*; **~ register(ed) ton** (*Naut*) Bruttoregistertonne *f* ADV *earn, pay, weigh* brutto; **she earns £30,000 ~ per annum** sie verdient £ 30 000 brutto im Jahr, ihr Bruttoverdienst ist £ 30 000 im Jahr; **the yield is 10% ~** der Bruttoertrag ist 10% **VT** (= *earn*) brutto verdienen **N the ~** (= *amount*) die Gesamtsumme

gross: gross domestic product N (*Econ*) Bruttoinlandsprodukt *nt*; **gross indecency** N (*Jur*) grob unsittliches Verhalten

grossly ['grəʊslɪ] ADV **a** (= *very*) *unfair, misleading, inadequate, inaccurate, inefficient, irresponsible* äußerst; *overweight, exaggerate, underestimate, o-verestimate* stark; *mislead* grob; *underpaid, underfunded, overpaid* extrem; **to be ~ negligent** grob fahrlässig handeln **b** (= *crassly*) *express, put* krass; *classify* grob; **~ comic** urkomisch **c** (*inf,* = *coarsely*) *behave, talk* derb, rüde; **to eat ~** essen wie ein Schwein

gross: gross misconduct N (*Jur*) grobes Fehlverhalten; **gross national product** N (*Econ*) Bruttosozialprodukt *nt*; **gross negligence** N grobe Fahrlässigkeit

grossness ['grəʊsnɪs] N **a** (= *seriousness, of error, insult, exaggeration, simplification*) Grobheit *f*; (*of inequality, violation*) Krassheit *f*; (*of negligence, in-*

justice) ungeheures Ausmaß **b** (= *fatness*) Körperfülle *f*, Fettheit *f* **c** (*inf*) (= *disgusting nature*) abstoßende Art; (= *tastelessness*) ordinäre Art

gross: gross profit N Gesamtgewinn *m*; (*before deductions*) Bruttogewinn *m*; **gross salary** N Bruttogehalt *nt*; **gross turnover** N Gesamtumsatz *m*; **gross weight** N Bruttogewicht *nt*; **gross yield** N Gesamt-/Bruttoertrag *m*

grotesque [grəʊ'tesk] **ADJ a** (= *outlandish, ridiculous*) *sight, spectacle, shape* grotesk; *idea, proposal, allegation* absurd **b** (= *distorted*) *grimace* verzerrt; **the body was in a ~ position** der Körper lag völlig verzerrt da; **he was rather ~ to look at** seine Erscheinung wirkte grotesk **c** (*Art*) grotesk **N a** (*Art*) **the ~** die Groteske **b** (*Typ*) Grotesk *f*

grotesquely [grəʊ'tesklɪ] ADV auf groteske Art; *swollen, deformed* grauenhaft; **~ exaggerated** bis ins Groteske übertrieben; **the image in the mirror was ~ distorted** das Spiegelbild war so verzerrt, dass es schon grotesk war

grotesqueness [grəʊ'tesknɪs] N **a** (= *outlandishness of idea, proposal, allegation*) Absurdität *f*; **the ~ of the shape/this answer/his appearance** das Groteske an der Form/dieser Antwort/seiner Erscheinung **b** (= *distortion*) Verzerrtheit *f*

grotto ['grɒtəʊ] N *pl* **-(e)s** Grotte *f*, Höhle *f*; **fairy ~** Märchenhöhle *f*; **Santa's ~** *Raum, in dem der Weihnachtsmann in Kaufhäusern etc auftritt*

grotty ['grɒtɪ] ADJ (*+er*) (*inf*) **a** (= *foul*) grausig (*inf*); (= *filthy*) dreckig, verdreckt (*inf*) **b** (= *awful, lousy*) mies (*inf*); (= *dilapidated*) heruntergekommen; (= *tacky*) geschmacklos; **to feel ~** sich mies fühlen (*inf*)

grouch [graʊtʃ] **N a** (= *complaint*) Klage *f*; **to have a ~** (= *grumble*) schimpfen (*about* über *+acc*) **b** (*inf,* = *person*) Miesepeter *m* (*inf*), Muffel *m* (*inf*) **VI** schimpfen, meckern (*inf*)

grouchiness ['graʊtʃɪnɪs] N schlechte Laune, Miesepetrigkeit (*inf*) *f*

grouchy ['graʊtʃɪ] ADJ (*+er*) griesgrämig, miesepetrig (*inf*)

ground¹ [graʊnd] **⊙** 15.2, 26.1 **N a** (= *soil, terrain, fig*) Boden *m*; **snow on high ~** Schnee in höheren Lagen; **hilly ~** hügeliges Gelände; **how much ~ do you own?** wie viel Grund und Boden or wie viel Land besitzen Sie?; **the middle ~ of politics** die politische Mitte; **there is common ~ between us** uns verbindet einiges; **they found common ~ in the fact that ...** die Tatsache, dass ..., verband sie; **to be on dangerous ~** (*fig*) sich auf gefährlichem Boden bewegen; **to be on firm** or **sure ~** festen or sicheren Boden unter den Füßen haben; (*fig*) sich auf sicherem Boden bewegen; **on familiar ~** auf vertrautem Boden; **to meet sb on his own ~** zu jdm kommen; **to be beaten on one's own ~** auf dem eigenen Gebiet geschlagen werden; **to cut the ~ from under sb** or **sb's feet** jdm den Boden unter den Füßen wegziehen; **to gain/lose ~** Boden gewinnen/verlieren; (*disease, rumour*) um sich greifen/im Schwinden begriffen sein; **to lose ~ to sb/sth** gegenüber jdm/etw an Boden verlieren; **to give ~ to sb/sth** vor jdm/etw zurückweichen; **to regain the ~ lost to sb** seine Position jdm gegenüber zurückerobern; **to break new ~** (*lit, fig*) neue Gebiete erschließen; (*person*) sich auf ein neues or unbekanntes Gebiet begeben; **to prepare the ~ for sth** den Boden für etw vorbereiten; **to go over the ~** (*fig*) alles durchgehen; **to cover the/a lot of ~** (*lit*) die Strecke/eine weite Strecke zurücklegen; (*fig*) das Thema/eine Menge Dinge behandeln; **that covers the ~** das umreißt das Thema; **to hold** or **stand one's ~** (*lit*) nicht von der Stelle weichen; (*fig*) seinen Mann stehen, sich nicht unterkriegen lassen; **to shift** or **change one's ~** (*fig*) seine Haltung ändern → **foot** N **b**
b (= *surface*) Boden *m*; **above/below ~** über/unter der Erde; (*Min*) über/unter Tage; (*fig*) unter den Lebenden/unter der Erde; **to fall to the ~** (*lit*) zu Boden fallen; (*fig, plans*) ins Wasser fallen, sich zerschlagen; **to sit on the ~** auf

der Erde or dem Boden sitzen; **our hopes were dashed to the ~** unsere Hoffnungen wurden am Boden zerstört; **to burn sth to the ~** etw niederbrennen; **to raze sth to the ~** etw dem Erdboden gleichmachen; **it suits me down to the ~** das ist ideal für mich; **to get off the ~** (*plane etc*) abheben; (*fig: plans, project etc*) sich realisieren; **to go to ~** (*fox*) im Bau verschwinden; (*person*) untertauchen (*inf*); **to run a fox to ~** einen Fuchs aufstöbern; **to run sb/sth to ~** jdn/etw aufstöbern, jdn/etw ausfindig machen; **to run sb/oneself into the ~** (*inf*) jdn/sich selbst fertig machen (*inf*); **to run a car into the ~** (*inf*) ein Auto schrottreif fahren

c (= *pitch*) Feld *nt*, Platz *m*; (= *parade ground, drill ground*) Platz *m*; **hunting ~s** Jagdgebiete *pl*; **fishing ~s** Fischgründe *pl*

d grounds PL (= *premises, land*) Gelände *nt*; (= *gardens*) Anlagen *pl*; **a house standing in its own ~s** ein von Anlagen umgebenes Haus

e grounds PL (= *sediment*) Satz *m*; **let the coffee ~s settle** warten Sie, bis sich der Kaffee gesetzt hat

f (= *background*) Grund *m*; **on a blue ~** auf blauem Grund

g (*US, Elec*) Erde *f*

h (= *sea-bed*) Grund *m*

i (= *reason*) Grund *m*; **to have ~(s) for sth** Grund zu etw haben; **to be ~(s) for sth** Grund für or zu etw sein; **to give sb ~(s) for sth** jdm Grund zu etw geben; **~s for divorce** Scheidungsgrund *m*; **~s for dismissal** Entlassungsgrund *m*/-gründe *pl*; **~s for suspicion** Verdachtsmomente *pl*; **on the ~s of...** aufgrund ... (*gen*), auf Grund ... (*gen*), aufgrund or auf Grund von ...; **on the ~s that ...** mit der Begründung, dass ...; **on health ~s** aus gesundheitlichen Gründen

VT *a* **ship** auflaufen lassen, auf Grund setzen; **to be ~ed** aufgelaufen sein

b (*Aviat*) *plane* (*for mechanical reasons*) aus dem Verkehr ziehen; *pilot* sperren, nicht fliegen lassen; **to be ~ed by bad weather/a strike** wegen schlechten Wetters/eines Streiks nicht starten or fliegen können

c (= *punish*) *child* Hausarrest erteilen (+*dat*); **she was ~ed for a week** sie hatte eine Woche Hausarrest

d (*US, Elec*) erden

e (= *base*) **to be ~ed on sth** sich auf etw (*acc*) gründen, auf etw (*dat*) basieren; **the story wasn't ~ed in reality** die Geschichte hatte keinen Bezug zur Wirklichkeit

f to ~ sb in a subject jdm die Grundlagen eines Faches beibringen; **to be well ~ed in English** gute Grundkenntnisse im Englischen haben

VI (*Naut*) auflaufen

ground² *pret, ptp of* **grind** ADJ *glass* matt; *coffee* gemahlen; **~ rice** Reismehl *nt*; **freshly ~ black pepper** frisch gemahlener schwarzer Pfeffer; **~ meat** (*US*) Hackfleisch *nt*

ground: ground advantage N (*Sport*) Platzvorteil *m*; **ground alert** N (*Mil*) Alarmbereitschaft *f*; (*Aviat*) Startbereitschaft *f*; **ground attack** N Bodenangriff *m*; **groundbait** N Grundköder *m*; **ground bass** N Grundbass *m*; **ground-breaking** ADJ umwälzend; *research etc* bahnbrechend; **ground coat** N Grundanstrich *m*; **ground colour**, (*US*) **ground color** N Untergrund *m*; (= *undercoat*) Grundierfarbe *f*; **ground conditions** PL (*Sport*) Platzverhältnisse *pl*; **ground control** N (*Aviat*) Bodenkontrolle *f*; **ground cover** N (*Hort*) Bodenvegetation *f*; **ground crew** N Bodenpersonal *nt*

grounder ['graʊndə'] N (*US, Sport*) Bodenball *m*

ground: ground floor N Erdgeschoss *nt*, Erdgeschoß *nt* (*Aus*); **to get in on the ~** (*fig*) gleich zu Anfang einsteigen (*inf*); **ground fog** N Bodennebel *m*; **ground forces** PL (*Mil*) Bodentruppen *pl*, Landstreitkräfte *pl*; **ground frost** N Bodenfrost *m*; **groundhog** N (*US*) Waldmurmeltier *nt*

GROUNDHOG DAY

Am **Groundhog Day** wird in den USA ein nicht ganz ernst gemeinter Brauch gepflegt, den Frühlingsbeginn vorherzusagen. Am 2. Februar, dem **Groundhog Day**, soll der **groundhog**, auch bekannt als **woodchuck**, eine Art Murmeltier, aus seinem Winterschlaf erwachen und aus seinem Bau hervorkommen. Wenn nun die Sonne scheint und das Tier seinen eigenen Schatten erblickt, erschrickt es so sehr, dass es wieder in seinen Bau zurückkehrt und weitere sechs Wochen Winterschlaf einlegt – es wird also weitere sechs Wochen Winter geben. Das Ereignis wird landesweit aus Punxsutawney, Pennsylvania, übertragen, wo sich der bekannteste Groundhog-Bau befindet, dessen Bewohner immer Phil genannt wird. Manchmal weigert sich das Tier jedoch aufzutauchen. 1993 wurde eine Komödie über einen Meteorologen gedreht, der auf das Punxsutawney-Fest wartet: „Groundhog Day - Und täglich grüßt das Murmeltier".

---

grounding ['graʊndɪŋ] N *a* (= *basic knowledge*) Grundwissen *nt*; **to give sb a ~ in English** jdm die Grundlagen *pl* des Englischen beibringen *b* (*Aviat, of plane*) Startverbot *nt* (*of* für); (*due to strike, bad weather*) Hinderung *f* am Start; (*of pilot*) Sperren *nt*

ground: ground ivy N Gundelrebe *f*, Gundermann *m*; **groundkeeper** N (*US*) = **groundsman**; **ground-launched** ADJ *missile* bodengestützt; **groundless** ADJ grundlos, unbegründet; **ground level** N Boden *m*; **below ~** unter dem Boden; **ground note** N (*Mus*) Grundton *m*; **groundnut** N Erdnuss *f*; **ground pass** N (*Sport*) Flachpass *m*; **ground plan** N Grundriss *m*; **ground rent** N Grundrente *f*; **ground rules** PL Grundregeln *pl*

groundsel ['graʊnsl] N Kreuzkraut *nt*

groundsheet ['graʊndʃiːt] N Zeltboden(plane *f*) *m*

groundsman ['graʊndzmən] N *pl* **-men** [-mən] (*esp Brit*) Platzwart *m*

ground: groundspeed N Bodengeschwindigkeit *f*; **ground squirrel** N Erdhörnchen *nt*; **ground staff** N (*Aviat*) Bodenpersonal *nt*; (*Sport*) Platzwarte *pl*; **ground stroke** N (*Tennis*) nicht aus der Luft gespielter Ball; **groundswell** N Dünung *f*; (*fig*) Anschwellen *nt*, Zunahme *f*; **there was a growing ~ of public opinion against him** die Öffentlichkeit wandte sich zunehmend gegen ihn; **ground-to-air missile** N Boden-Luft-Rakete *f*; **ground-to-ground missile** N Boden-Boden-Flugkörper *m*; **ground troops** PL (*Mil*) Bodentruppen *pl*; **ground water** N Grundwasser *nt*; **groundwire** N (*US, Elec*) Erdleitung *f*; **groundwork** N Vorarbeit *f*; **to do the ~ for sth** die Vorarbeit für etw leisten; **ground zero** N *a* (*of atomic bomb*) Bodennullpunkt *m* *b* (*fig*) absoluter Nullpunkt *m* (*Hist*) **Ground Zero** Gelände, auf dem am 11. September 2001 das World Trade Center in New York City einstürzte

group [gruːp] N Gruppe *f*; (*Comm also*) Konzern *m*; (= *theatre group also*) Ensemble *nt*; **a ~ of people** eine Gruppe Menschen; **a ~ of houses/trees** eine Häuser-/Baumgruppe; **to form a ~ around sb/sth** sich um jdn/etw gruppieren

ATTR Gruppen-; *living, activities* in der Gruppe or Gemeinschaft; **~ discussion** Gruppendiskussion *f*

VT gruppieren; **to ~ together** (*in one group*) zusammentun; (*in several groups*) in Gruppen einteilen or anordnen; **pupils are ~ed according to age and ability** die Schüler werden nach Alter und Fähigkeiten in Gruppen eingeteilt; **it's wrong to ~ all criminals together** es ist nicht richtig, alle Verbrecher über einen Kamm zu scheren or in einen Topf zu werfen (*inf*); **~ the blue ones with the red ones** ordnen Sie die Blauen bei den Roten ein, tun Sie die Blauen mit den Roten zusammen; **they ~ed them-**

selves round him sie stellten sich um ihn (herum) auf, sie gruppierten sich um ihn; **the books were ~ed on the shelf according to subject** die Bücher standen nach Sachgruppen geordnet im Regal

group: group booking N Gruppenbuchung or -reservierung *f*; **group captain** N (*Aviat*) Oberst *m*; **group dynamics** N *a pl* (= *relationships*) Gruppendynamik *f* *b* **sing** (= *subject*) Gruppendynamik *f*

groupie ['gruːpɪ] N Groupie *nt*

grouping ['gruːpɪŋ] N Gruppierung *f*; (= *group of things also*) Anordnung *f*

group: group insurance N Gruppenversicherung *f*; **group practice** N Gemeinschaftspraxis *f*; **to be in a ~** in einem Ärztekollektiv arbeiten; **group therapy** N Gruppentherapie *f*; **groupware** N (*Comput*) Groupware *f*

grouse¹ [graʊs] N *pl* **-** Waldhuhn *nt*, Raufußhuhn *nt*; (= *red grouse*) Schottisches Moor(schnee)huhn; **~ shooting** Moorhuhnjagd *f*

grouse² (*Brit inf*) N (= *complaint*) Klage *f*; **to have a good ~** sich ausschimpfen (*inf*) VI schimpfen, meckern (*inf*) (*about über +acc*)

grouser ['graʊsə'] N (*inf*) Meckerfritze *m*/-liese *f* (*inf*)

grout [graʊt] VT *tiles* verfugen, verkitten; *bricks* mit Mörtel ausgießen N Vergussmaterial *nt*, Fugenkitt *m*; (*for bricks*) Mörtel *m*

grove [grəʊv] N Hain *m*, Wäldchen *nt*

grovel ['grɒvl] VI kriechen; **to ~ at sb's feet** vor jdm kriechen; (*dog*) sich um jdn herumdrücken; **to ~ to** or **before sb** (*fig*) vor jdm kriechen; (*in apology*) vor jdm zu Kreuze kriechen

groveller ['grɒvələ'] N Kriecher(in) *m(f)* (*inf*), Speichellecker(in) *m(f)* (*inf*)

grovelling, (*US*) **groveling** ['grɒvəlɪŋ] ADJ kriecherisch (*inf*), unterwürfig N Kriecherei *f* (*inf*), Speichelleckerei *f* (*inf*)

grow [grəʊ] *pret* **grew**, *ptp* **grown** VT *a plants* ziehen; (*commercially*) *potatoes, wheat, tea etc* anbauen, anpflanzen; (= *cultivate*) *flowers* züchten *b* **to ~ a beard/one's hair** sich (*dat*) einen Bart/die Haare wachsen lassen

VI *a* (= *get bigger, longer etc*) wachsen; (*person, baby*) wachsen, größer werden; (*hair*) wachsen, länger werden; (*in numbers*) zunehmen; (*in size*) sich vergrößern; (*fig, = become more mature*) sich weiterentwickeln; **to ~ in stature/wisdom** an Ansehen/Weisheit zunehmen; **to ~ in popularity** immer beliebter werden; **to ~ in beauty** schöner werden; **my, how you've** or **haven't you ~n!** du bist aber groß geworden!; **fears were ~ing for her safety** man machte sich zunehmend Sorgen um ihre Sicherheit; **the economy/market/population is ~ing by 2% a year** die Wirtschaft/der Markt/die Bevölkerung wächst um 2% pro Jahr; **pressure is ~ing for him to resign** er gerät zunehmend unter Druck zurückzutreten

b (= *become*) werden; **to ~ to do/be sth** allmählich etw tun/sein; **to ~ to hate/love sb** jdn hassen/lieben lernen; **to ~ to enjoy sth** langsam Gefallen an etw (*dat*) finden; **I've ~n to like him** ich habe ihn mit der Zeit lieb gewonnen; **to ~ used to sth** sich an etw (*acc*) gewöhnen; **to ~ like sb** jdm immer ähnlicher werden

▶ **grow apart** VI (*fig*) sich auseinander entwickeln

▶ **grow away** VI (*fig*) **to grow away from sb** sich jdm entfremden

▶ **grow from** VI +*prep obj* = **grow out of b**

▶ **grow in** VI (*hair*) nachwachsen; (*teeth*) kommen; (*toenail*) einwachsen

▶ **grow into** VI +*prep obj* *a clothes, job* hineinwachsen in (+*acc*) *b* (= *become*) sich entwickeln zu, werden zu; **to grow into a man/woman** zum Mann/zur Frau heranwachsen; **to grow into a crisis** sich zur Krise auswachsen or entwickeln

▶ **grow on** VI +*prep obj* **it'll grow on you** das wird dir mit der Zeit gefallen, du wirst schon noch Geschmack daran finden

▶ **grow out** VI (*perm, colour*) herauswachsen

▶ **grow out of** VI +*prep obj* **a** *clothes* herauswachsen aus; **to grow out of a habit** eine Angewohnheit ablegen; **to grow out of one's friends** seinen Freunden entwachsen (*geh*), sich von seinen Freunden entfernen **b** (= *arise from*) entstehen aus, erwachsen aus (*geh*)

▶ **grow together** VI (*lit, fig*) zusammenwachsen

▶ **grow up** VI (= *spend childhood*) aufwachsen; (= *become adult*) erwachsen werden; (*fig, custom, hatred*) aufkommen; (*city*) entstehen; **what are you going to do when you grow up?** was willst du mal werden, wenn du groß bist?; **she's grown up into an attractive young woman/an alcoholic** sie hat sich zu einer attraktiven jungen Frau/Alkoholikerin entwickelt; **grow up!, when are you going to grow up?** werde endlich erwachsen!

grow bag N Tüte *f* mit Komposterde

grower ['grəʊə'] N **a** (= *plant*) **to be a fast ~** schnell wachsen **b** (= *person, of fruit, vegetables*) Anbauer(in) *m(f)*; (*of flowers*) Züchter(in) *m(f)*; (*of tobacco, tea*) Pflanzer(in) *m(f)*

growing ['grəʊɪŋ] ADJ (*lit, fig*) wachsend; *child* heranwachsend, im Wachstum befindlich (*form*); *importance, interest, number etc* wachsend, zunehmend; **he's still a ~ boy** er steckt noch (*inf*) or befindet sich noch im Wachstum **N** Wachstum *nt*, Wachsen *nt*

growing pains PL (*Med*) Wachstumsschmerzen *pl*; (*fig*) Kinderkrankheiten *pl*, Anfangsschwierigkeiten *pl*

growing season N Zeit *f* des Wachstums, Vegetationszeit *f* (*spec*)

growl [graʊl] **N** Knurren *nt no pl*; (*of bear*) (böses) Brummen *no pl* **VI** knurren; (*bear*) böse brummen; **to ~ at sb** jdn anknurren/anbrummen **VT** *answer* knurren

grown [grəʊn] *ptp of* **grow** ADJ erwachsen; **fully ~** ausgewachsen

grown: grown-over ADJ überwachsen; *garden also* überwuchert; **grown-up** ADJ erwachsen; *clothes, book* für Erwachsene, für Große (*inf*); **they have a ~ family** sie haben schon erwachsene Kinder **N** Erwachsene(r) *mf*

growth [grəʊθ] N **a** Wachstum *nt*; (= *increase in quantity, fig: of love, interest etc*) Zunahme *f*, Anwachsen *nt*; (= *increase in size*) Vergrößerung *f*, Wachstum *nt*; (*of capital etc*) Zuwachs *m*; **to reach full ~** seine/ihre volle Größe erreichen; **~ industry/stock** Wachstumsindustrie *f*/-aktien *pl*; **rate of export ~** Wachstums- or Zuwachsrate *f* im Export **b** (= *plants*) Vegetation *f*; (*of one plant*) Triebe *pl*; **~ ring** (*of tree*) Jahresring *m*; **covered with a thick ~ of ivy** von Efeu überwuchert or überwachsen; **cut away the old ~** schneiden Sie die alten Blätter und Zweige aus; **with two days' ~ (of beard) on his face** mit zwei Tage alten Bartstoppeln **c** (*Med*) Gewächs *nt*, Wucherung *f*

groyne [grɔɪn] N Buhne *f*

grub [grʌb] **N a** (= *larva*) Larve *f* **b** (*inf*, = *food*) Fressalien *pl* (*hum inf*), Futterage *f* (*inf*); **~('s) up!** antreten zum Essenfassen (*inf*) **VT** (*animal*) *ground, soil* aufwühlen, wühlen in (+*dat*) **VI** (*also* grub about or around, *pig*) wühlen (*in* in +*dat*); (*person*) (herum)kramen, (herum)wühlen (*in* in +*dat, for* nach)

▶ **grub out** VT *sep* ausgraben

▶ **grub up** VT *sep weeds* jäten; *potatoes, bush etc* ausgraben; *soil* wühlen in (+*dat*); (*bird*) *worms* aus dem Boden ziehen; (*fig*) *information, people* auftreiben, zusammensammeln

grubbily ['grʌbɪlɪ] ADV schmuddelig (*inf*)

grubbiness ['grʌbɪnɪs] N **a** (= *dirtiness*) Dreckigkeit *f*; (*of person, clothes, house*) Schmuddeligkeit *f* **b** (*fig, = sordidness*) Schmutzigkeit *f*

grubby ['grʌbɪ] ADJ (+*er*) **a** (= *dirty*) dreckig; *person, clothes, house* schmuddelig (*inf*) **b** (*fig, = sordid*) *business, corruption, politics* schmutzig; *aspect* zwielichtig

grudge [grʌdʒ] **N** Groll *m* (*against* gegen); **to bear sb a ~, to have a ~ against sb** jdm böse sein, jdm grollen, einen Groll gegen jdn hegen (*geh*); **I bear him no ~** ich trage ihm das nicht nach, ich nehme ihm das nicht übel; **to bear ~s** nachtragend sein; **to settle a ~** eine alte Rechnung begleichen

VT to ~ sb sth jdm etw nicht gönnen, jdm etw neiden (*geh*); **I don't ~ you your success** ich gönne Ihnen Ihren Erfolg; **to ~ doing sth** etw äußerst ungern tun, etw mit Widerwillen tun; **I don't ~ it es** macht mir nichts aus, das zu tun; **I ~ spending money/time on it** es widerstrebt mir or es geht mir gegen den Strich, dafür Geld auszugeben/Zeit aufzuwenden; **I don't ~ the money/time** es geht mir nichts ums Geld/um die Zeit; **I do ~ the money/time for things like that** das Geld/meine Zeit für solche Dinge tut mir Leid

grudge match N (*inf: Sport, fig*) erbitterter Zweikampf (*von Mannschaften oder Persönlichkeiten, zwischen denen eine offene Feindschaft besteht*)

grudging ['grʌdʒɪŋ] ADJ *respect, admiration, consent, approval, support* widerwillig; *attitude* unwillig; *applause* sparsam; *apology* widerwillig gegeben; **we have a ~ attitude to spending money** es widerstrebt uns, Geld auszugeben; **to do sth in a ~ way** etw nur widerwillig tun; **he was ~ about her talent** er nahm ihr Talent nur widerwillig zur Kenntnis; **to be ~ in one's support for sth** etw nur widerwillig unterstützen

grudgingly ['grʌdʒɪŋlɪ] ADV widerwillig, **albeit ~** wenn auch nur widerwillig; **he ~ accepted the offer** er nahm das Angebot widerwillig an

gruel [grʊəl] N Haferschleim *m*, Schleimsuppe *f*

gruelling, (*US*) **grueling** ['grʊəlɪŋ] ADJ *schedule, journey, day, week* (äußerst) anstrengend; *pace, conditions* mörderisch (*inf*); *race, match, event* (äußerst) strapaziös; *talks, negotiations* aufreibend; **200 ~ miles** 200 mörderische Meilen (*inf*); **the most ~ part of my trip** der anstrengendste Teil meiner Reise

gruesome ['gruːsəm] ADJ grausig, schauerlich; *laugh* schaurig, makaber

gruesomely ['gruːsəmlɪ] ADV (+*vb*) auf grausame Weise; (+*adj*) grausam, schauerlich

gruff [grʌf] ADJ *voice* barsch; (= *brusque*) *person, manner* barsch, schroff; *exterior* bärbeißig

gruffly ['grʌflɪ] ADV barsch, schroff

gruffness ['grʌfnɪs] N (*of voice*) Barschheit *f*; (*of person, manner*) Barschheit *f*, Schroffheit *f*

grumble ['grʌmbl] **N** (= *complaint*) Murren *nt no pl*; Schimpfen *nt no pl*; (= *noise: of thunder, guns*) Grollen *nt*; **his only ~ is that ...** das Einzige, was er auszusetzen hat, ist, dass ...; **all his ~s** sein ständiges Schimpfen or Gemecker (*inf*) **VI** murren, schimpfen (*about, over* über +*acc*); (*thunder, gunfire*) grollen; **to ~ at sb** jdm gegenüber schimpfen or klagen; **grumbling appendix** (*inf*) gereizter Blinddarm

grumbler ['grʌmblə'] N Nörgler(in) *m(f)*, Brummbär *m* (*inf*)

grummet ['grʌmɪt] N = **grommet**

grump [grʌmp] N (*inf*) **a** (= *person*) **to be a ~** ein alter Brummbär sein (*inf*) **b** (= *bad mood*) **to have the ~s** brummig sein (*inf*)

grumpily ['grʌmpɪlɪ] ADV (*inf*) brummig (*inf*), mürrisch

grumpy ['grʌmpɪ] ADJ (+*er*) (*inf*) brummig (*inf*), mürrisch, grantig; *child* quengelig (*inf*)

grunge [grʌndʒ] N Grunge *nt*

grungy ['grʌndʒɪ] ADJ (*inf*) mies (*inf*)

grunt [grʌnt] **N** (*of animal, person*) Grunzen *nt no pl*; (*of pain, in exertion*) Ächzen *nt no pl*, Ächzer *m* (*inf*); **to give a ~** grunzen (*of vor* +*dat*), ächzen (*of vor* +*dat*) **VI** (*animal, person*) grunzen; (*with pain, exertion*) ächzen, aufseufzen; (*in irritation*) knurren **VT** *reply* brummen, knurren

gryphon ['grɪfən] N = **griffin**

GS *abbr of* **General Staff**

GSM (*Telec*) *abbr of* **Global System for Mobile Communications** GSM

gsm *abbr of* **gram(me)s per square metre** g/m^2

GSOH (*inf*) *abbr of* **good sense of humour** guter Sinn für Humor

g-spot ['dʒiːspɒt] N G-Punkt *m*

G-string ['dʒiːstrɪŋ] N **a** (*Mus*) G-Saite *f*; **Bach's Air on a ~** Bachs Air *nt* **b** (= *clothing*) Minislip *m*, Tangahöschen *nt*

GT *abbr of* **gran turismo** GT

Gt *abbr of* **Great**

Guadeloupe [ˌgwɑːdə'luːp] N Guadalupe *nt*, Guadelupe *nt*

guano ['gwɑːnəʊ] N Guano *m*

guarantee [ˌgærən'tiː] **N a** (*Comm*) Garantie *f*; (= *guarantee slip*) Garantie(schein *m*) *f*; **to have or carry a 6-month ~** 6 Monate Garantie haben; **there is a year's ~ on this watch** auf der Uhr ist ein Jahr Garantie; **while it is still under ~** solange noch Garantie darauf ist; **to sell sth with a money-back ~** volles Rückgaberecht beim Verkauf von etw garantieren

b (= *promise*) Garantie *f* (*of* für); **that's no ~ that ...** das heißt noch lange nicht, dass ...; **it will be sent today, I give you my ~** or **you have my ~** es wird heute noch abgeschickt, das garantiere ich Ihnen

c (*Jur*) = **guaranty**

VT a (*Comm*) garantieren

b (= *promise, ensure*) garantieren (*sb sth* jdm etw); (= *take responsibility for*) garantieren für; **I can't ~ (that) he will be any good** ich kann nicht dafür garantieren, dass er gut ist; **I ~ to come tomorrow** ich komme garantiert morgen

c (*Jur*) garantieren, gewährleisten; *loan, debt* bürgen für

guaranteed [ˌgærən'tiːd] ADJ garantiert; **to be ~ for three months** (*goods*) drei Monate Garantie haben; (*prices*) für drei Monate garantiert sein; **to be ~ not to rust** garantiert nicht rostend sein; **~ price** Garantiepreis *m*; **that's a ~ success** das wird garantiert ein Erfolg; **such reports are ~ to cause anxiety** solche Berichte machen den Leuten garantiert Angst

guarantor [ˌgærən'tɔː'] N Garant(in) *m(f)*; (*Jur also*) Bürge *m*, Bürgin *f*; **to stand ~ for sb** für jdn eine Bürgschaft übernehmen

guaranty ['gærəntɪ] N (*Jur*) Garantie *f*; (= *pledge of obligation*) Bürgschaft *f*; (= *security*) Sicherheit *f*

guard [gɑːd] **N a** (*Mil*) Wache *f*; (= *single soldier*) Wachtposten *m*, Wache *f*; (*no pl*: = *squad*) Wachmannschaft *f*; **the Guards** (*Brit*) die Garde, das Garderegiment; **~ of honour** (*Brit*) honour ~ (*US*) Ehrenwache *f*; **to change ~** Wachablösung machen

b (= *security guard*) Sicherheitsbeamte(r) *m*/-beamtin *f*; (*at factory gates, in park etc*) Wächter(in) *m(f)*; (*esp US*: = *prison guard*) Gefängniswärter(in) *m(f)*; (*Brit, Rail*) Schaffner(in) *m(f)*, Zugbegleiter(in) *m(f)*

c (= *watch: also Mil*) Wache *f*; **under ~** unter Bewachung; **to be under ~** bewacht werden; (*person also*) unter Bewachung or Aufsicht stehen; **to keep sb/sth under ~** jdn/etw bewachen; **to be on ~, to stand or keep ~** Wache halten or stehen; **to keep or stand ~ over sth** etw bewachen; **to put a ~ on sb/sth** jdn/etw bewachen lassen

d (*Boxing, Fencing*) Deckung *f*; **on ~!** (*Fencing*) en garde!; **to take ~** in Verteidigungsstellung gehen; (*Cricket*) in Schlagstellung gehen; **to drop** or **lower one's ~** (*fig*) seine Deckung vernachlässigen; (*fig*) seine Reserve aufgeben; **to have one's ~ down** (*lit*) nicht gedeckt sein; (*fig*) nicht auf der Hut sein; **he caught his opponent off (his) ~** er hat seinen Gegner mit einem Schlag erwischt, auf den er nicht vorbereitet or gefasst war; **the invitation caught me off ~** ich war auf die Einladung nicht vorbereitet; **I was off (my) ~ when he mentioned that** ich war nicht darauf gefasst or vorbereitet, dass er das erwähnen würde; **to be on/off one's ~ (against sth)** (*fig*) (vor etw *dat*) auf der/nicht auf der

Hut sein; **to put sb on his ~ (against sth)** jdn (vor etw *dat*) warnen; **to throw** or **put sb off his ~** (*lit*) jdn seine Deckung vernachlässigen lassen; (*fig*) jdn einlullen

e (= *safety device, for protection*) Schutz *m* (*against* gegen); (*on machinery*) Schutz(vorrichtung *f*) *m*; (= *fire guard*) Schutzgitter *nt*; (*on foil*) Glocke *f*; (*on sword etc*) Korb *m*

f (*in basketball*) Verteidigungsspieler(in) *m(f)*

VT *prisoner, place, valuables* bewachen; *treasure, secret, tongue* hüten; *machinery* beaufsichtigen; *luggage* aufpassen auf (+*acc*); (= *protect*) (*ill*) *person, place* schützen (*from, against* vor +*dat*), abschirmen (*from, against* gegen); *one's life* schützen; *one's reputation* achten auf (+*acc*), (*fig*) *child etc* behüten, beschützen (*from, against* vor +*dat*); **a closely ~ed secret** ein gut or streng gehütetes Geheimnis

▶ **guard against** VI +*prep obj* (= *take care to avoid*) *suspicion, being cheated etc* sich in Acht nehmen vor (+*dat*); *hasty reaction, bad habit, scandal also* sich hüten vor (+*dat*); (= *take precautions against*) *illness, attack, danger, misunderstandings* vorbeugen (+*dat*); *accidents* verhüten; **you must guard against catching cold** Sie müssen aufpassen or sich in Acht nehmen, dass Sie sich nicht erkälten; **in order to guard against this** um (dem) vorzubeugen

guard: guard chain N Sicherheitskette *f*; **guard dog** N Wachhund *m*; **guard duty** N Wachdienst *m*; **to be on ~** auf Wache sein, Wache haben (*inf*)

guarded ['gɑːdɪd] ADJ *person, smile* zurückhaltend, reserviert; *response, support, optimism* vorsichtig; **I'm being a bit ~, I suppose** ich bin wohl ein bisschen zu vorsichtig; **to give sth a ~ welcome** etw vorsichtig begrüßen; **to be ~ about sth** sich über etw (*acc*) zurückhalten; **he is ~ about his intentions** er hält sich mit seinen Absichten zurück

guardedly ['gɑːdɪdlɪ] ADV vorsichtig; *smile* zurückhaltend; **~ optimistic** vorsichtig optimistisch

guardedness ['gɑːdɪdnɪs] N Vorsichtigkeit *f*; (*of smile*) Reserviertheit *f*

guardhouse ['gɑːdhaʊs] N (*Mil, for soldiers*) Wachlokal *nt*, Wachstube *f*; (*for prisoners*) Arrestlokal *nt*, Bunker *m* (*sl*)

guardian ['gɑːdɪən] N Hüter(in), Wächter(in) *m(f)*; (*Jur*) Vormund *m*; **~ of tradition** Hüter(in) *m(f)* der Tradition

guardian angel N Schutzengel *m*

GUARDIAN READER

„Sage mir, welche Zeitung du liest und ich sage dir, wer du bist!" Dieser Spruch hat nirgendwo mehr Gültigkeit als in Großbritannien, wo sich recht ausgeprägte Klischees vom typischen Leser der größten und bekanntesten Tageszeitungen entwickelt haben. Der **Guardian reader** ist demnach linksorientiert, bürgerlich, sieht sich Politmagazine an und interessiert sich für ausländische Kunst und Filme. Lehrer und Sozialarbeiter gelten als typische Vertreter dieses Leserkreises. Ihnen gegenübergestellt werden die **Sun readers**. Die **Sun** ist ein Boulevardblatt, dessen Leser als sexistische Proletarier eingestuft werden, die Ausländer und Homosexuelle hassen.

---

guardianship ['gɑːdɪənʃɪp] N Wachen *nt* (*of* über +*acc*); (*Jur*) Vormundschaft *f* (*of* über +*acc*)

guard: guardrail N Schutzgeländer *nt*; (*around machinery*) Schutzleiste *f*; (*Rail*) Schutzschiene *f*, Zwangsschiene *f*; (= *US: Mot*) Leitplanke *f*; **guardroom** N (*used by guard*) Wachstube *f*; **guard rope** N Absperrseil *nt*

guardsman ['gɑːdzmən] N *pl* **-men** [-mən] Wache *f*, Wachtposten *m*; (= *member of guards regiment*) Gardist *m*; (*US, in National Guard*) Nationalgardist *m*

---

guard's van ['gɑːdzvæn] N (*Brit, Rail*) Schaffnerabteil *nt*, Dienstwagen *m*

Guatemala [ˌgwɑːtɪˈmɑːlə] N Guatemala *nt*

Guatemalan [ˌgwɑːtɪˈmɑːlən] ADJ guatemaltekisch, aus Guatemala **N** Guatemalteke *m*, Guatemaltekin *f*

guava ['gwɑːvə] N Guave *f*; (= *tree also*) Guavenbaum *m*

gubbins ['gʌbɪnz] N (*Brit dated inf, things*) Zeug *nt* (*inf*); (*person*) Dussel *m* (*inf*)

gubernatorial [ˌguːbənəˈtɔːrɪəl] ADJ (*esp US, Pol*) Gouverneurs-; *candidate, campaign* für das Gouverneursamt; **~ election** Gouverneurswahl *f*

guddle ['gʌdl] (*Scot*) **VT** *fish* mit den Händen fangen **N** (*inf, = mess*) Durcheinander *nt*; **this room's (in) a ~** in diesem Zimmer herrscht das reinste Durcheinander (*inf*)

gudgeon ['gʌdʒən] N Gründling *m*

guelder-rose ['geldəˌrəʊz] N (*Bot*) Schneeball *m*

Guernsey ['gɜːnzɪ] N **a** Guernsey *nt* **b** (= *sweater*) dicker Pullover (*von Fischern getragen*)

guer(r)illa [gəˈrɪlə] **N** Guerillero *m*, Guerillera *f*, Guerillakämpfer(in) *m(f)*; **Palestinian ~s** palästinensische Freischärler or Guerillas *pl* ATTR Guerilla-

guer(r)illa fighter N Guerillakämpfer(in) *m(f)*

guer(r)illa war, **guer(r)illa warfare** N Guerillakrieg *m*

guess [ges] **N** Vermutung *f*, Annahme *f*; (= *estimate*) Schätzung *f*; **to have** or **make a ~ (at sth)** (etw) raten; (= *estimate*) (etw) schätzen; **his ~ was nearly right** er hat es fast erraten/hat es gut geschätzt; **it's a good ~** gut geraten or geschätzt or getippt; **it was just a lucky ~** das war nur gut geraten, das war ein Zufallstreffer *m*; **I'll give you three ~es** dreimal darfst du raten; **50 people, at a ~** schätzungsweise 50 Leute; **at a rough ~** grob geschätzt, über den Daumen gepeilt (*inf*); **my ~ is that ...** ich tippe darauf (*inf*) or schätze mal, dass ...; **your ~ is as good as mine!** (*inf*) da kann ich auch nur raten!; **it's anybody's ~** (*inf*) das wissen die Götter (*inf*)

VI **a** (= *surmise*) raten; **how did you ~?** wie hast du das bloß erraten?; (*iro*) du merkst auch alles!; **to keep sb ~ing** jdn im Ungewissen lassen; **he's only ~ing when he says they'll come** das ist eine reine Vermutung von ihm, dass sie kommen; **you'll never ~!** das wirst du nie erraten; **to ~ at sth** etw raten

b (*esp US*) **I ~ not** wohl nicht; **he's right, I ~** er hat wohl Recht; **I think he's right – I ~ so** ich glaube, er hat Recht – ja, das hat er wohl; **shall we go? – I ~ (so)** sollen wir gehen? – na gut or (*inf*) schätze ja (*inf*); **that's all, I ~** das ist wohl alles, (ich) schätze, das ist alles (*inf*)

VT **a** (= *surmise*) raten; (= *surmise correctly*) erraten; (= *estimate*) *weight, numbers, amount* schätzen; **I ~ed as much** das habe ich mir schon gedacht; **to ~ sb to be 20 years old/sth to be 10 lbs** jdn auf 20 Jahre/etw auf 10 Pfund schätzen; **I ~ed (that) she was about 40** ich schätzte sie auf etwa 40; **you'll never ~ who/what ...** das errätst du nie, wer/was ...; **~ who!** (*inf*) rat mal, wer!; **~ what!** (*inf*) stell dir vor! (*inf*), denk nur! (*inf*)

b (*esp US, = suppose*) **I ~ we'll just have to wait and see** wir werden wohl abwarten müssen, ich schätze, wir werden abwarten müssen

guessable ['gesəbl] ADJ *answer* erratbar, zu erraten *pred*; *number* schätzbar, zu schätzen *pred*

guesser ['gesəʳ] N **to be a good ~** gut schätzen können

guessing game ['gesɪŋgeɪm] N (*lit, fig*) Ratespiel *nt*

guesstimate ['gestɪmɪt] N grobe Schätzung

guesswork ['geswɜːk] N (reine) Vermutung; **there's too much ~ in historical essays** in historischen Aufsätzen wird zu viel vermutet; **they**

---

did it by ~ sie haben nur geraten; **it's all ~** sind doch nur Vermutungen, das ist alles nur geraten

guest [gest] **N** Gast *m*; **~ of honour** (*Brit*) or **honor** (*US*) Ehrengast *m*; **be my ~!** (*inf*) nur zu! (*inf*) **to ~ on sth** einen Gastauftritt in etw (*dat*) haben; **he ~ed for several clubs** er hatte in mehreren Klubs Gastauftritte

guest in *cpds* Gast-; **guest appearance** N Gastauftritt *m*; **to make a ~** als Gast auftreten; **guest artist** N Gast(star) *m*, Gastkünstler(in) *m(f)*; (*Theat*) Gastspieler(in) *m(f)*; **guesthouse** N Gästehaus *nt*; (= *boarding house*) (Fremden)pension *f*; **guest list** N Gästeliste *f*; **guest night** N Gästeabend *m*; **guest room** N Gästezimmer *nt*; **guest speaker** N Gastredner(in) *m(f)*

guff [gʌf] N (*inf*) Quark *m* (*inf*), Käse *m* (*inf*)

guffaw [gʌˈfɔː] **N** schallendes Lachen *no pl*; **~s of laughter** Lachsalven *pl*; **to let out a ~** schallend lachen **VI** schallend (los)lachen

GUI (*Comput*) *abbr of* **graphical user interface** GUI *nt*

Guiana [gaɪˈænə] N Guayana *nt*

guidance ['gaɪdns] N (= *direction*) Führung *f*, Leitung *f*; (= *counselling*) Beratung *f* (*on* über +*acc*); (*from superior, parents, teacher etc*) Anleitung *f*; **spiritual ~** geistiger Rat; **for your ~** zu Ihrer Orientierung or Hilfe; **to give sb ~ on sth** jdn bei etw beraten; **to pray for ~** um Erleuchtung bitten

guidance: guidance system N (*on rocket*) Steuerungssystem *nt*; **guidance teacher** N (*Scot*) Verbindungslehrer(in) *m(f)*

guide [gaɪd] **N a** (= *person*) Führer(in) *m(f)*; (*fig, = indication, pointer*) Anhaltspunkt *m* (*to* für); (= *model*) Leitbild *nt*; **let reason/your conscience be your ~** lassen Sie sich von der Vernunft/Ihrem Gewissen leiten; **they used the star as their ~** sie ließen sich von dem Stern leiten; **he is my spiritual ~** er ist mein geistiger Berater

b (*Tech*) Leitvorrichtung *f*

c (*Brit, = Girl Guide*) Pfadfinderin *f*

d (= *instructions*) Anleitung *f*; (= *manual*) Leitfaden *m*, Handbuch *nt* (*to* +*gen*); (= *travel guide*) Führer *m*; **let this piece of work be your ~** orientieren Sie sich an dieser Arbeit; **as a rough ~** als Faustregel

VT *people, blind man etc* führen; *discussion also* leiten; *missile, rocket, sb's behaviour, studies, reading* lenken; **to ~ a plane in** ein Flugzeug einweisen; **to be ~d by sb/sth** (*person*) sich von jdm/etw leiten lassen; **to ~ sb to victory** jdn zum Sieg führen; **this will ~ you through difficult times** das wird dich in schweren Zeiten begleiten; **his life was ~d by his beliefs** sein Leben war von seinen Überzeugungen bestimmt; **to ~ sb on his way** jdm den Weg zeigen or weisen

guidebook ['gaɪdbʊk] N (Reise)führer *m* (*to* von)

guided missile [ˌgaɪdɪdˈmɪsaɪl] N ferngelenktes Geschoss, Lenkwaffe *f*

guide dog N Blindenhund *m*

guided tour [ˌgaɪdɪdˈtʊəʳ] N Führung *f* (*of* durch); **to give sb a ~** jdn herumführen

guide: guideline N Richtlinie *f*, Richtschnur *f* *no pl*; (*Typ, for writing*) Leitlinie *f*; **safety ~s** Sicherheitshinweise *pl*; **I gave her a few ~s on looking after a kitten** ich gab ihr ein paar Hinweise, wie man eine junge Katze versorgt; **guide price** N (*Comm*) Richtpreis *m*; **guidepost** N Wegweiser *m*

Guider ['gaɪdəʳ] N (*Brit*) Pfadfinderinnenführerin *f*

guide rope N Schlepptau *nt*

guiding ['gaɪdɪŋ] ATTR **he took on a ~ role in his nephew's life** er wurde ein Leitbild im Leben seines Neffen; **~ force** leitende Kraft; **~ hand** leitende Hand; **~ principle** Leitmotiv *nt*; **~ star** Leitstern *m*

guild [gɪld] N (Hist) Zunft f, Gilde f; (= association) Verein m

guilder ['gɪldə'] N Gulden m

guildhall ['gɪldhɔ:l] N **a** (Hist) Zunfthaus nt **b** (Brit) Rathaus nt; **the Guildhall** das Rathaus der City of London

guile [gaɪl] N Tücke f, (Arg)list f; **to have ~** sehr tückisch or arglistig sein; **without ~** ohne Arg, ohne Falsch (liter)

guileful ['gaɪlfʊl] ADJ hinterhältig, tückisch, arglistig

guileless ['gaɪllɪs] ADJ arglos, harmlos, unschuldsvoll

guillemot ['gɪlɪmɒt] N Lumme f

guillotine [ˌgɪlə'ti:n] **N a** Guillotine f, Fallbeil nt **b** (for paper) (Papier)schneidemaschine f **c** (Parl) Beschränkung f der Diskussionszeit **VT a** person mit der Guillotine or dem Fallbeil hinrichten **b** paper schneiden **c** (Parl) bill die Diskussionszeit einschränken für

guilt [gɪlt] N Schuld f (for, of an +dat); **to feel ~ (about sth)** sich (wegen etw) schuldig fühlen, (wegen etw) Schuldgefühle haben; **feelings of ~** Schuldgefühle pl; **~ complex** Schuldkomplex m

guiltily ['gɪltɪlɪ] ADV schuldbewusst

guiltiness ['gɪltɪnɪs] N Schuld f; (of look, smile, silence) Schuldbewusstsein nt

guiltless ['gɪltlɪs] ADJ schuldlos, unschuldig (of an +dat); **he is ~ of any crime** er ist keines Verbrechens schuldig

guilty ['gɪltɪ] ADJ (+er) **a** smile, look, silence schuldbewusst; secret, pleasure mit Schuldgefühlen verbunden; **~ conscience** schlechtes Gewissen; **~ feelings** Schuldgefühle pl; **to feel ~ (about sth)** ein schlechtes Gewissen haben(, weil man etw tut/getan hat); **she felt ~ about or because of her rudeness** sie hatte wegen ihrer Unhöflichkeit ein schlechtes Gewissen; **I never stop feeling ~ about having let you down** ich habe immer ein schlechtes Gewissen, weil ich dich im Stich gelassen habe; **to make sb feel ~** jdm ein schlechtes Gewissen einreden; **to look ~** schuldbewusst aussehen **b** (= to blame) person schuldig (of sth einer Sache gen); **the ~ person** der/die Schuldige; **the ~ party** die schuldige Partei; **to find sb ~/not ~ (of sth)** jdn (einer Sache gen) für schuldig/ nicht schuldig befinden; **they were found not ~ of murder** sie wurden des Mordes für nicht schuldig befunden; **they were found not ~ of killing him** sie wurden für nicht schuldig befunden, ihn getötet zu haben; **to plead (not) ~ to a crime** sich eines Verbrechens (nicht) schuldig bekennen; **do you plead ~ or not ~?** plädieren Sie auf schuldig oder nicht schuldig?; **a ~ verdict, a verdict of ~** ein Schuldspruch m; **a not ~ verdict, a verdict of not ~** ein Freispruch m; **they returned a verdict of not ~ on him** sie sprachen ihn frei; **a ~ plea, a plea of ~** ein Geständnis nt; **a not ~ plea, a plea of not ~** ein Unschuldsbekenntnis nt; **their parents are ~ of gross neglect** ihre Eltern haben sich grobe Fahrlässigkeit zuschulden or zu Schulden kommen lassen; **we're all ~ of neglecting the problem** uns trifft alle die Schuld, dass das Problem vernachlässigt wurde; **I've been ~ of that too** ich muss zugeben, dass ich das auch schon gemacht habe

Guinea ['gɪnɪ] N Guinea nt

guinea ['gɪnɪ] N (Brit, old) Guinee f, Guinea f (21 Shilling)

guinea: guinea fowl N Perlhuhn nt; **guinea pig** N Meerschweinchen nt; (fig) Versuchskaninchen nt

guise [gaɪz] N (= disguise) Gestalt f; (= pretence) Vorwand m; **in the ~ of a clown** als Clown verkleidet; **under the ~ of friendship/scientific research** unter dem Deckmantel der Freundschaft/der wissenschaftlichen Forschung; **under the ~ of doing sth** unter dem Vorwand, etw zu tun

guitar [gɪ'tɑ:'] N Gitarre f

guitarist [gɪ'tɑ:rɪst] N Gitarrist(in) m(f)

gulch [gʌltʃ] N (US) Schlucht f

gulf [gʌlf] N **a** (= bay) Golf m, Meerbusen m; **the Gulf of Mexico** der Golf von Mexiko; **the Gulf of Bothnia** der Bottnische Meerbusen; **the (Persian) Gulf** der (Persische) Golf **b** (lit, fig, = chasm) tiefe Kluft

Gulf States PL **the ~** die Golfstaaten pl

Gulf Stream N Golfstrom m

gull¹ [gʌl] N (= seagull) Möwe f

gull² (liter) **N** Spielball m (of +gen) **VT** übertölpeln; **to ~ sb out of his money** jdm sein Geld ablisten; **to be ~ed into sth** dazu gebracht werden, etw zu tun; **to be ~ed into doing sth** durch eine üble List dazu gebracht werden, etw zu tun

gullet ['gʌlɪt] N Speiseröhre f, Kehle f; **that really stuck in my ~** (fig) das ging mir sehr gegen den Strich (inf)

gullibility [ˌgʌlɪ'bɪlɪtɪ] N Leichtgläubigkeit f

gullible ADJ , **gullibly** ADV ['gʌlɪbl, -ɪ] leichtgläubig

gull: gull wing door N (Aut) Flügeltür f; **gull-winged** ADJ car mit Flügeltüren

gully ['gʌlɪ] N (= ravine) Schlucht f; (= narrow channel) Rinne f

gulp [gʌlp] **N** Schluck m; **at a ~, in one ~** auf einen Schluck; **..., he said with a ~** ..., sagte er und schluckte **VT** (also **gulp down**) drink runterstürzen; food runterschlingen; medicine hinunterschlucken; **to ~ back one's tears** die Tränen hinunterschlucken; **to ~ back a sob** einen Schluchzer unterdrücken; **what?, he ~ed** was?, presste er hervor **VI** (= try to swallow) würgen; (= eat fast) schlingen; (= drink fast) hastig trinken; (from emotion) trocken schlucken; **to make loud ~ing noises** gluckernd trinken

gum¹ [gʌm] N (Anat) Zahnfleisch nt no pl

gum² **N a** Gummi nt; (= gumtree) Gummibaum m; (= glue) Klebstoff m **b** (= chewing gum) Kaugummi m; (= sweet) Weingummi m **c** (US, inf) = **gumshoe** **VT** (= stick together) kleben; (= spread gum on) gummieren

▶ **gum down** VT sep label aufkleben; envelope zukleben

▶ **gum up** VT sep verkleben; **to gum up the works** (inf) alles verkleben; (fig) die Sache vermasseln (inf); **to get gummed up** verkleben

gum³ N (dated inf) **by ~!** Teufel noch mal! (dated sl)

gum arabic N Gummiarabikum nt

gumbo ['gʌmbəʊ] N Gumbo m

gum: gumboil N Zahnfleischabszess m; **gumboot** N Gummistiefel m; **gumdrop** N Weingummi m

gummy ['gʌmɪ] ADJ (+er) substance, surface, food klebrig; eyes verklebt

gumption ['gʌmpʃən] N (inf) Grips m (inf); **to have the ~ to do sth** geistesgegenwärtig genug sein, etw zu tun

gum: gumshield N Zahnschutz m; **gumshoe** (US) **N a** (= overshoe) Überschuh m, Galosche f; (= gym shoe) Turnschuh m **b** (sl, = detective) Schnüffler(in) m(f) (inf) **VI** (sl, = move stealthily) schleichen; **gumtree** N Gummibaum m; (Austral) Eukalyptusbaum m, Eukalyptus m; **to be up a ~** (Brit, inf) aufgeschmissen sein (inf)

gun [gʌn] **N a** (= cannon etc) Kanone f, Geschütz nt; (= rifle) Gewehr nt; (= pistol etc) Pistole f, Kanone f (sl), Schießeisen nt (hum inf); **to carry a ~** (mit einer Schusswaffe) bewaffnet sein, eine Schusswaffe tragen (form); **to draw a ~** eine (Schuss)waffe ziehen; **to draw a ~ on sb** jdn mit einer Schusswaffe bedrohen; **to fire a 21-gun salute** 21 Salutschüsse abgeben; **the big ~s** die schweren Geschütze; **big ~** (fig inf) hohes or großes Tier (inf) (in in +dat); **to hold or put a ~ to sb's head** (fig) jdm die Pistole auf die Brust setzen; **to stick to one's ~s** nicht nachgeben, bei etw festbleiben; **to jump the ~** (Sport) Frühstart machen; (fig) voreilig sein or handeln; **to be going great ~s** (Brit inf, team, person) toll in Schwung or Fahrt sein (inf); (car) wie ge-

schmiert laufen (inf); (business) gut in Schuss sein (inf)
   b (= spray gun) Pistole f
   c (= person) Schütze m, Schützin f; (Hunt) Jäger(in) m(f); (esp US inf: = gunman) Pistolenheld m (inf); **he's the fastest ~ in the West** (inf) er zieht am schnellsten im ganzen Westen (inf)
   VT a (= kill: also **gun down**) person erschießen, zusammenschießen; pilot, plane abschießen
   b (inf, = rev) engine aufheulen lassen **VI a** (inf) **to be ~ning for sb** (lit) Jagd auf jdn machen; (fig) jdn auf dem Kieker haben (inf); for opponent jdn auf die Abschussliste gesetzt haben
   b (inf, = speed) schießen (inf)

gun: gun barrel N (on cannon) Kanonen- or Geschützrohr nt; (on rifle) Gewehrlauf m; (on pistol) Pistolenlauf m; **gunboat** N Kanonenboot nt; **gunboat diplomacy** N Kanonenbootdiplomatie f; **gun carriage** N Lafette f

---

GUN CONTROL

In den USA ist **gun control**, also die Frage, ob und wie der Schusswaffenverkauf kontrolliert werden soll, ein kontrovers diskutiertes Thema. Das Recht aller Bürger, eine Waffe zu tragen, ist in der US-Verfassung festgeschrieben, und die Lobbyisten der Schusswaffenbefürworter, wie zum Beispiel die mächtige **National Rifle Association**, sorgen dafür, dass die Bürger weiterhin, sich zur Selbstverteidigung legal zu bewaffnen. Dennoch ist man besorgt über eine alarmierend hohe Zahl von Unfällen mit Schusswaffen - vor allen Dingen in den Großstädten - über den weit verbreiteten illegalen Waffengebrauch sowie eine ständig steigende Zahl von Verletzten und Todesopfern. Durch eine strengere Gesetzgebung wurden daher Verkauf und Besitz von Schusswaffen eingeschränkt und viele Typen halbautomatischer Waffen wurden verboten.

---

gun: guncotton N Schießbaumwolle f; **gun crew** N Geschützbedienung f; **gun dog** N Jagdhund m; **gunfight** N Schießerei f; (Mil) Feuergefecht nt, Schusswechsel m; **gunfighter** N Revolverheld m; **gunfire** N Schießerei f, Schüsse pl; (Mil) Geschützfeuer nt, Artilleriefeuer nt

gunge [gʌndʒ] N (Brit, inf) klebriges or schmieriges Zeug (inf)

gung ho ['gʌŋ'həʊ] ADJ (inf) übereifrig

gungy ['gʌndʒɪ] ADJ (+er) (inf) schmierig

gunk [gʌŋk] N (esp US, inf) = **gunge**

gun: gunmaker N Waffenhersteller(in) m(f); **gunman** N (mit einer Schusswaffe) Bewaffnete(r) m (inf); **they saw the ~** sie haben den Schützen gesehen; **gunmetal** N Geschützmetall nt, Geschützbronze f; (= colour) metallisches Blaugrau nt **ADJ** attr aus Geschützmetall or -bronze; grey, colour metallisch; **gun permit** N Waffenschein m

gunnel ['gʌnəl] N = **gunwale**

gunner ['gʌnə'] N (Mil) Artillerist m; (= title) Kanonier m; (Naut) Geschützführer m; (in plane) Bordschütze m; **to be in the ~s** (Mil) bei der Artillerie sein

gunnery ['gʌnərɪ] N Schießkunst f; **~ officer** Artillerieoffizier m

gunny ['gʌnɪ] N Sackleinen nt

gun: gunpoint N **to hold sb at ~** jdn mit einer Schusswaffe bedrohen; **to force sb to do sth at ~** jdn mit vorgehaltener Waffe zwingen, etw zu tun; **to kidnap sb at ~** jdn mit Waffengewalt entführen; **gunpowder** N Schießpulver nt; **Gunpowder Plot** N (Brit Hist) Pulververschwörung f; **gun room** N Waffenkammer f; (Naut) Kadettenmesse f; **gunrunner** N Waffenschmuggler(in) or -schieber(in) m(f); **gunrunning** N Waffenschmuggel m, Waffenschieberei f (inf); **gunshot** N Schuss m; (= range) Schussweite f; **~ wound** Schusswunde f; **gunslinger** ['gʌnslɪŋə'] N (inf) Pistolenheld m (inf); **gun-**

smith N Büchsenmacher(in) *m(f)*; **gun turret** N Geschützturm *m*; **gunwale** ['gʌnl] N Dollbord *nt*

guppy ['gʌpɪ] N Guppy *m*, Millionenfisch *m*

gurgle ['gɜːgl] N (*of liquid*) Gluckern *nt no pl*; (*of brook also*) Plätschern *nt no pl*; (*of baby*) Glucksen *nt no pl*; **to give a ~ of pleasure/laughter** vor Vergnügen/Lachen glucksen VI (*liquid*) gluckern; (*brook also*) plätschern; (*person*) glucksen (*with* vor +*dat*)

Gurkha ['gɜːkə] N Gurkha *mf*

gurney ['gɜːnɪ] N (*US*) (Trag)bahre *f*

guru ['goru:] N (*lit, fig*) Guru *m*

gush [gʌʃ] N a (*of liquid*) Strahl *m*, Schwall *m*; (*of words*) Schwall *m*; (*of emotion, enthusiasm*) Ausbruch *m* b (*inf, = gushing talk*) Geschwärme *nt* (*inf*) VI a (*also* **gush out**, *water*) herausschießen, heraussprudeln; (*smoke, blood, tears*) hervorquellen; (*flames*) herausschlagen b (*inf: = talk*) schwärmen (*inf*) (*about, over* von); (*insincerely*) sich ergehen (*about, over* über +*acc*) VT (*liter, volcano*) ausstoßen; **the wound ~ed blood** aus der Wunde schoss *or* quoll Blut; **what a delightful hat, she ~ed** welch entzückender Hut, sagte sie überschwänglich

gusher ['gʌʃə'] N (*= oil well*) (natürlich sprudelnde) Ölquelle

gushing ['gʌʃɪŋ] ADJ a *water* sprudelnd, (heraus)schießend b (*fig*) überschwänglich; *talk* schwärmerisch, überschwänglich

gushingly ['gʌʃɪŋlɪ] ADV überschwänglich

gushy ['gʌʃɪ] ADJ (*pej inf*) schwärmerisch

gusset ['gʌsɪt] N (*in garment*) Keil *m*, Zwickel *m*

gust [gʌst] N a (*of wind*) Stoß *m*, Bö(e) *f*; (*of rain*) Böe *f*; (*fig, of emotion*) Anfall *m*; **a ~ of cold/hot air** ein Schwall *m* kalte/heiße Luft; **a ~ of laughter** eine Lachsalve; **~s of up to 100 km/h** Böen von bis zu 100 km/h; **the wind was blowing in ~s** der Wind wehte böig *or* stürmisch VI böig *or* stürmisch wehen

gustatory ['gʌstətərɪ] ADJ (*form*) **~ sense** Geschmackssinn *m*

gustily ['gʌstɪlɪ] ADV böig, stürmisch

gusto ['gʌstəu] N Begeisterung *f*; **to do sth with ~** etw mit Genuss tun

gusty ['gʌstɪ] ADJ (+er) *wind, day, rain* böig, stürmisch

gut [gʌt] N a (*= alimentary canal*) Darm *m*; (*= stomach, paunch*) Bauch *m* b *usu pl* (*inf: = stomach*) Eingeweide *nt*; (*fig*) (*= essence: of problem, matter*) Kern *m*; (*= contents*) Substanz *f*; **to slog** *or* **work one's ~s out** (*inf*) wie blöd schuften (*inf*); **to spill one's ~s (to sb)** (*inf*) (jdm) sein Herz ausschütten; **to hate sb's ~s** (*inf*) jdn auf den Tod nicht ausstehen können (*inf*); **I'll have his ~s for garters!** (*Brit inf*) den mache ich zur Minna (*inf*) *or* zur Schnecke (*inf*); **~ reaction** rein gefühlsmäßige Reaktion; **my ~ feeling is that …** rein gefühlsmäßig *or* so aus dem Bauch heraus (*inf*) würde ich sagen, dass …

c **guts** PL (*inf, = courage*) Mumm *m* (*inf*), Schneid *m* (*inf*)

d (*= catgut*) Darm *m*; (*for racket, violin*) Darmsaiten *pl*

VT a *animal, chicken, fish* ausnehmen b (*fire*) ausbrennen; (*= remove contents*) ausräumen; **it was completely ~ted by the fire** es war völlig ausgebrannt → *also* **gutted**

gutless ['gʌtlɪs] ADJ (*fig inf*) feige

gutsy ['gʌtsɪ] ADJ (*inf*) a (*= plucky*) *person, action, effort* mutig, tapfer; *performance*, *approach* kämpferisch; **he is a ~ performer** er ist eine richtige Kämpfernatur b (*= powerful*) *food, wine* kräftig; *music* feurig; *lyrics* kraftvoll; *car, engine* kraftstrotzend

gutta-percha [ˌgʌtə'pɜːtʃə] N Guttapercha *f or nt*

gutted ['gʌtɪd] ADJ (*esp Brit, inf, = disappointed*) am Boden (zerstört) (*inf*); **I was ~ total** am Boden (*inf*); **he was ~ by the news** die Nachricht machte ihn völlig fertig (*inf*)

gutter ['gʌtə'] N (*on roof*) Dachrinne *f*; (*in street*) Gosse *f* (*also fig*), Rinnstein *m*; **to be born in the ~** aus der Gosse kommen; **the language of the ~** die Gassensprache VI (*candle, flame*) flackern

guttering ['gʌtərɪŋ] N Regenrinnen *pl* ADJ flackernd

gutter: gutter press N (*Brit pej*) Boulevardpresse *f*; **guttersnipe** N Gassenkind *nt*

guttural ['gʌtərəl] N Guttural(laut) *m*, Kehllaut *m* ADJ *voice, accent* guttural, kehlig; (*Phon*) *sound* guttural

guv [gʌv], **guv'nor** ['gʌvnə'] N (*Brit, inf*) Chef *m* (*inf*)

guy¹ [gaɪ] N a (*inf, = man*) Typ *m* (*inf*), Kerl *m* (*inf*); **hey, you ~s** he Leute (*inf*); **great ~s** dufte Typen *pl* (*inf*); **I'll ask the ~ next door** ich werde (den Typ von) nebenan fragen (*inf*); **are you ~s ready?** seid ihr fertig? b (*Brit, = effigy*) (Guy-Fawkes-)Puppe *f*; (*inf: = sight*) Schießbudenfigur *f* (*inf*); **a penny for the ~** Geld *nt* für das (Guy Fawkes) Feuerwerk VT (*= ridicule*) sich lustig machen über (+*acc*)

guy² N (*also* **guy-rope**) Halteтau *or* -seil *nt*; (*for tent*) Zeltschnur *f*

Guyana [gaɪ'ænə] N Guyana *nt* (*form*), Guayana *nt*

Guyanese [ˌgaɪə'niːz] N Guayaner(in) *m(f)*

guzzle ['gʌzl] (*inf*) VI (*= eat*) futtern (*inf*); (*= drink*) schlürfen VT (*= eat*) futtern (*inf*); (*= drink*) schlürfen; *fuel* saufen (*inf*)

guzzler ['gʌzlə'] N (*inf, = eater*) Fresser(in) *m(f)* (*inf pej*); (*= drinker*) Säufer(in) *m(f)* (*inf pej*)

gym [dʒɪm] N (*= gymnasium*) Turnhalle *f*; (*for working out*) Fitnesscenter *nt*; (*= gymnastics*) Turnen *nt*

gymkhana [dʒɪm'kɑːnə] N Reiterfest *nt*

gymnasium [dʒɪm'neɪzɪəm] N *pl* **-s** *or* (*form*) **gymnasia** [dʒɪm'neɪzɪə] Turnhalle *f*

gymnast ['dʒɪmnæst] N Turner(in) *m(f)*

gymnastic [dʒɪm'næstɪk] ADJ *ability, training* turnerisch; **~ exercises** Turnübungen

gymnastics [dʒɪm'næstɪks] N a *sing* (*= discipline*) Gymnastik *f no pl*; (*with apparatus*) Turnen *nt no pl* b *pl* (*= exercises*) Übungen *pl*; **verbal ~** Wortakrobatik *f*

gym: gym shoe N (*Brit*) Turnschuh *m*; **gymslip** N (*Brit*) Schulträgerrock *m*; **gym teacher** N Turnlehrer(in) *m(f)*

gynaecological, (*US*) **gynecological** [ˌgaɪnɪkə'lɒdʒɪkəl] ADJ gynäkologisch; **~ illness** Frauenleiden *nt*, gynäkologisches Leiden

gynaecologist, (*US*) **gynecologist** [ˌgaɪnɪ'kɒlədʒɪst] N Gynäkologe *m*, Gynäkologin *f*, Frauenarzt *m*/-ärztin *f*

gynaecology, (*US*) **gynecology** [ˌgaɪnɪ'kɒlədʒɪ] N Gynäkologie *f*, Frauenheilkunde *f*

gyp [dʒɪp] N a (*Brit inf, = swindle*) Gaunerei *f* (*inf*) b (*inf, = swindler*) Gauner(in) *m(f)* c (*Brit Univ inf*) Putzfrau *f* d (*Brit inf*) **to give sb ~** jdn plagen (*inf*)

gyppo ['dʒɪpəu] N (*pej inf*) Zigeuner *m*, Zigeunerin *f*

gypsum ['dʒɪpsəm] N Gips *m*

gypsy ['dʒɪpsɪ] N Zigeuner(in) *m(f)* ADJ a (*= Romany*) Zigeuner-; **~ child** Zigeunerkind *nt*; **~ woman** Zigeunerin *f*; **~ camp** Zigeunerlager *nt*; **~ music** Zigeunermusik *f* b (*US, pej, = unofficial*) *cab, driver* illegal

gyrate [ˌdʒaɪə'reɪt] VI (*= whirl*) (herum)wirbeln; (*= rotate*) sich drehen, kreisen; (*dancer*) sich drehen und winden

gyration [ˌdʒaɪə'reɪʃən] N (*= whirling*) Wirbeln *nt no pl*; (*= rotation*) Drehung *f*, Kreisen *nt no pl*; (*of dancer*) Drehung und Windung *f usu pl*

gyratory [ˌdʒaɪə'reɪtərɪ] ADJ (*= whirling*) wirbelnd; (*= revolving*) kreisend

gyrocompass ['dʒaɪərəu'kʌmpəs] N Kreiselmagnetkompass *m*

gyroscope ['dʒaɪərə,skəup] N Gyroskop *nt*

gyroscopic [ˌdʒaɪərəu'skɒpɪk] ADJ gyroskopisch

H

H, h [eɪtʃ] N H *nt*, h *nt* → **drop**

H *abbr of* **hard** (*on pencil*) H

h *abbr of* **hour(s)** h

ha [hɑː] INTERJ ha

habeas corpus ['heɪbɪəs'kɔːpəs] N (*Jur*) Habeaskorpusakte *f*; **to file a writ of ~** einen Vorführungsbefehl erteilen; **the lawyer applied for a writ of ~** der Rechtsanwalt verlangte, dass sein Klient einem Untersuchungsrichter vorgeführt wurde

haberdasher ['hæbədæʃə'] N (*Brit*) Kurzwarenhändler(in) *m(f)*; (*US*) Herrenausstatter *m*; **to go to the ~'s** (*Brit*) zum Kurzwarengeschäft gehen; (*US*) zum Herrenmodengeschäft gehen

haberdashery [ˌhæbə'dæʃərɪ] N (*Brit*, = *articles*) Kurzwaren *pl*; (= *shop*) Kurzwarengeschäft *nt* or -handlung *f*; (*US*, = *articles*) Herrenbekleidung *f*, Herrenartikel *pl*; (= *shop*) Herrenmodengeschäft *nt*

habiliments [hə'bɪlɪmənts] PL (*form*) Ornat *nt* (*form*)

habit ['hæbɪt] N **a** Gewohnheit *f*; (*esp undesirable*) (An)gewohnheit *f*; **~ of mind** Denkweise *f*; **to be in the ~ of doing sth** die Angewohnheit haben, etw zu tun, etw gewöhnlich tun; **... as was his ~** ... wie es seine Gewohnheit war; **it became a ~** es wurde zur Gewohnheit; **out of (sheer) ~** aus (reiner) Gewohnheit, (rein) gewohnheitsmäßig; **his life was ruled by ~** sein Leben war von seinen Gewohnheiten bestimmt; **from (force of) ~** aus Gewohnheit; **she was a creature of ~** sie war ein Gewohnheitstier (*inf*) or Gewohnheitsmensch; **I don't make a ~ of inviting strangers in** (für) gewöhnlich bitte ich Fremde nicht herein; **don't make a ~ of it** lassen Sie (sich *dat*) das nicht zur Gewohnheit werden; **to get into/to get sb into the ~ of doing sth** sich/jdm angewöhnen, etw zu tun; **you must get out of the ~ of biting your nails** du musst dir das Nägelkauen abgewöhnen; **to have a ~ of doing sth** die Angewohnheit haben, etw zu tun; **he has a strange ~ of staring at you** er hat die merkwürdige Art, einen anzustarren; **history has a ~ of repeating itself** es kommt oft vor, dass die Geschichte sich wiederholt

b (= *addiction*) Sucht *f*; **to have a cocaine ~** kokainsüchtig sein

c (= *costume*) Gewand *nt*; (*esp monk's*) Habit *nt* or *m*; (*riding*) **~** Reitkleid *nt*

habitable ['hæbɪtəbl] ADJ bewohnbar

habitat ['hæbɪtæt] N Heimat *f*; (*of animals also*) Lebensraum *m*

habitation [ˌhæbɪ'teɪʃən] N (Be)wohnen *nt*; (= *place*) Wohnstätte *f*, Behausung *f*; **to show signs of ~** bewohnt aussehen; **unfit for human ~** menschenunwürdig, für Wohnzwecke nicht geeignet

habit-forming ['hæbɪtˌfɔːmɪŋ] ADJ **to be ~** zur Gewohnheit werden; **are those ~ drugs?** wird man davon abhängig?

habitual [hə'bɪtjʊəl] ADJ **a** (= *customary*) smile, expression, behaviour, way, position gewohnt; **he was smiling his ~ smile** er lächelte wie üblich;

his **~ guilty grin** das schuldbewusste Grinsen, das er sich angewöhnt hatte; **to become ~** zur Gewohnheit werden **b** (= *regular*) smoker, drug user, drug use gewohnheitsmäßig; liar notorisch; joker, gossip ewig; **~ criminal** Gewohnheitsverbrecher(in) *m(f)*; **~ offender** Gewohnheitstäter(in) *m(f)*; **~ drinker** Gewohnheitstrinker(in) *m(f)*

habitually [hə'bɪtjʊəlɪ] ADV ständig; (= *regularly*) regelmäßig; drink, smoke gewohnheitsmäßig

habituate [hə'bɪtjʊeɪt] VT gewöhnen (*sb to sth* jdn an etw (*acc*), *sb to doing sth* jdn daran, etw zu tun); **to be ~d to sth** an etw (*acc*) gewöhnt sein

habitué [hə'bɪtjʊeɪ] N regelmäßiger Besucher, regelmäßige Besucherin, Habitué *m* (*geh*, *Aus*); (*in pubs etc*) Stammgast *m*

hacienda ['hæsɪəndə] N Hazienda *f*

hack¹ [hæk] N **a** (= *cut*) (Ein)schnitt *m*, Kerbe *f*; (= *action*) Hieb *m*; **to take a ~ at sth** mit der Axt etc auf etw (*acc*) schlagen; (*in rage*) auf etw (*acc*) einhacken

b (= *kick*) Tritt *m*; **he had a ~ at his opponent's ankle** er versetzte seinem Gegner einen Tritt gegen den Knöchel

c (= *cough*) trockener Husten

VT **a** (= *cut*) schlagen, hacken; **don't ~ your meat, cut it** du musst das Fleisch nicht hacken, sondern schneiden; **to ~ sb/sth to pieces** (*lit*) jdn/etw zerstückeln; (*fig*) jdn/etw zerfetzen; **he was brutally ~ed to death** er ist brutal (mit einem Beil *etc*) erschlagen worden; **to ~ one's way out** sich einen Weg frei schlagen; **to ~ one's way through (sth)** sich (*dat*) einen Weg (durch etw) schlagen, sich (durch etw) durchhauen

b (*Sport*) ball treten gegen, einen Tritt versetzen (+*dat*); **to ~ sb on the shin** jdn vors or gegen das Schienbein treten

c (*inf*: = *cope*) **to ~ it** es bringen (*sl*)

VI **a** (= *chop*) hacken; **he ~ed (away) at the branch** er schlug auf den Ast; **don't ~ at it** hack nicht daran herum

b (= *cough*) trocken husten

c (*Sport*) **he was booked for ~ing** er wurde wegen Holzerei verwarnt

d (*Comput*) hacken; **to ~ into the system** in das System eindringen

►**hack about** VT *sep* (*esp Brit fig*) text etc zerstückeln

►**hack down** VT *sep* bushes etc abhacken; people also niedermetzeln; tree umhauen

►**hack off** VT *sep* **a** abhacken, abschlagen; **to hack sth off sth** etw von etw abhacken or abschlagen **b** (*inf*, = *annoy*) ankotzen (*sl*); **I'm really hacked off with her** sie kotzt mich echt an (*sl*)

►**hack out** VT *sep* clearing schlagen; hole heraushacken

►**hack up** VT *sep* zerhacken; meat, wood, furniture also klein hacken; bodies zerstückeln

hack² N **a** (= *hired horse*) Mietpferd *nt*; (= *worn-out horse*) Gaul *m*, Klepper *m*; (= *ride*) Ritt *m* **b** (*pej*, = *literary hack*) Schreiberling *m*; **the newspaper ~s** die Zeitungsschreiber *pl*; **paid ~** Lohn- or Soldschreiber(in) *m(f)* **c** (*pej inf*) **(party) ~** (Partei)heini *m* (*inf*) or -typ *m* (*inf*) **d** (*US*, = *taxi*) Taxi *nt* ADJ attr (*pej*) writing

stumpfsinnig; **~ writer** Schreiberling *m* VI einen Spazierritt machen; **to go ~ing** ausreiten

hacker ['hækə'] N (*Comput*) Hacker(in) *m(f)*

hackie ['hækɪ] N (*US*, *inf*) Taxifahrer(in) *m(f)*

hacking ['hækɪŋ] ADJ **~ cough** trockener Husten N (*Comput*) Hacken *nt*

hacking jacket N Sportsakko *m* or *nt*; (*for riding*) Reitjacke *f*

hackle ['hækl] N (*Orn*) lange Nackenfeder; (= *plumage also*) Nackengefieder *nt*; (*pl*: *of dog etc*) Fell *nt* im Nacken; **the dog's ~s rose** dem Hund sträubte sich das Fell; **his ~s rose at the very idea** bei dem bloßen Gedanken sträubte sich alles in ihm; **to get sb's ~s up, to raise sb's ~s** jdn reizen, jdn auf die Palme bringen (*inf*)

hackney carriage ['hæknɪˌkærɪdʒ] N (*horse-drawn*) (Pferde)droschke *f*; (*form*, = *taxi*) (Kraft)droschke *f* (*form*)

hackneyed ['hæknɪd] ADJ (*Brit*) phrase, word, metaphor, theme abgenutzt, abgedroschen (*inf*); photograph, image stereotyp; **~ idea** Klischee *nt*, Klischeevorstellung *f*

hack: hack pack ['hækpæk] N (*pej*) Journalistenzunft *f*; **hacksaw** ['hæksɔː] N Metallsäge *f*; **hackwork** N (= *trivial writing*) Schmiererei *f* (*inf*); (= *mindless editing*) Routinearbeit *f*

had [hæd] pret, ptp of **have**

haddock ['hædək] N Schellfisch *m*

Hades ['heɪdiːz] N (*Myth*) Hades *m*

hadn't ['hædnt] contr of **had not**

Hadrian ['heɪdrɪən] N **~'s Wall** Hadrianswall *m*

haematologist, (*US*) **hematologist** [ˌhiːmə'tɒlədʒɪst] N Hämatologe *m*, Hämatologin *f*

haematology, (*US*) **hematology** [ˌhiːmə'tɒlədʒɪ] N Hämatologie *f*

haematoma, (*US*) **hematoma** [ˌhiːmə'təʊmə] N *pl* **-mas** or **-mata** Hämatom *nt* (*spec*), Bluterguss *m*

haemoglobin, (*US*) **hemoglobin** [ˌhiːməʊ'gləʊbɪn] N Hämoglobin *nt*, roter Blutfarbstoff

haemophilia, (*US*) **hemophilia** [ˌhiːməʊ'fɪlɪə] N Bluterkrankheit *f*, Hämophilie *f* (*spec*)

haemophiliac, (*US*) **hemophiliac** [ˌhiːməʊ'fɪlɪæk] N Bluter *m*

haemorrhage, (*US*) **hemorrhage** ['hemərɪdʒ] N Blutung *f*, Hämorrhagie *f* (*spec*); (*fig*, *of talent, young people etc*) Exodus *m*, Abwanderung *f* VI bluten

haemorrhoids, (*US*) **hemorrhoids** ['hemərɔɪdz] PL Hämorr(ho)iden *pl*

hafnium ['hæfnɪəm] N (*Chem*) Hafnium *nt*

haft [hɑːft] N (*of knife*) Heft *nt*; (*of sword*) Griff *m*

hag [hæg] N Hexe *f*

haggard ['hægəd] ADJ ausgezehrt; (*from tiredness*) abgespannt; (*from worry*) abgehärmt, verhärmt; **he had a very ~ expression throughout the trial** er wirkte während der ganzen Verhandlung sehr mitgenommen

haggis ['hægɪs] N *schottisches Gericht aus gehackten Schafsinnereien und Hafer im Schafsmagen*

haggish ['hægɪʃ] ADJ zänkisch, garstig

haggle ['hægl] VI (= *bargain*) feilschen (*about or over um*); (= *argue also*) sich (herum)streiten (over um or wegen); **let's stop haggling over who's going to pay** hören wir doch auf mit dem Hin und Her (darüber), wer nun bezahlt

haggling [ˈhæglɪŋ] N Feilschen nt, Gefeilsche nt, Feilscherei f

hagiographer [ˌhægɪˈɒɡrəfə'] N (lit, fig) Hagiograf(in) m(f)

hagiography [ˌhægɪˈɒɡrəfɪ] N (lit, fig) Hagiografie f; (lit also) Heiligengeschichte f

hagiology [ˌhægɪˈɒlədʒɪ] N (form) Hagiologie f (spec)

hag-ridden [ˈhægrɪdn] ADJ (= worried) vergrämt, verhärmt; **to be ~** (hum, = tormented by women) unter Weiberherrschaft stehen

Hague [heɪɡ] N **the ~** Den Haag nt; **in the ~** in Den Haag; **the ~ Conventions** (Pol) die Haager Abkommen; **the ~ Tribunal** (Pol) der Internationale Gerichtshof

ha-ha [ˈhɑːˈhɑː] INTERJ ha, ha N (= fence) versenkter Grenzzaun

hail¹ [heɪl] N Hagel m; **a ~ of stones** ein Steinhagel m, ein Hagel von Steinen; **a ~ of blows** ein Hagel von Schlägen; **in a ~ of bullets** im Kugel- or Geschosshagel VI hageln

▸**hail down** VI (stones etc) niederprasseln, niederhagelln (on sb/sth auf jdn/etw); **blows hailed down (on him)** es hagelte Schläge (auf ihn nieder) VT sep blows niederprasseln lassen

hail² [heɪl] **a** (= acclaim) zujubeln (+dat), bejubeln; **to ~ sb/sth as sth** jdn/etw als etw feiern **b** (= call loudly) zurufen (+dat); ship anrufen, preien (spec); taxi (by calling) rufen; (by making sign) anhalten, (herbei)winken; **within ~ing distance** in Rufweite VI a ship ~ing from London ein Schiff nt mit (dem) Heimathafen London; **where does that boat ~ from?** was ist der Heimathafen dieses Schiffs?; **they ~ from all parts of the world** sie kommen or stammen aus allen Teilen der Welt; **where do you ~ from?** wo stammen Sie her? INTERJ (obs, liter) **(to) ...** sei gegrüßt, ... (liter); **~ Caesar** heil dir Cäsar; **the Hail Mary** das Ave Maria N (Zu)ruf m; **within ~** in Rufweite

hail-fellow-well-met [ˈheɪlfeləʊˈwelˈmet] ADJ plumpvertraulich; **he tries to be ~ with everyone** er versucht, sich bei allen anzubiedern

hail: hailstone N Hagelkorn nt; **hailstorm** N Hagel(schauer) m

hair [heə'] N a (collective: on head) Haare pl, Haar nt; **a fine head of ~** schönes volles Haar, schöne volle Haare; **to do one's ~** sich frisieren, sich (dat) die Haare (zurecht)machen (inf); **to have one's ~ cut/done** sich (dat) die Haare schneiden/frisieren lassen; **her ~ always looks nice** sie ist immer sehr gut frisiert; **she usually wears her ~ up** (in pony tail/bun) sie trägt ihr Haar normalerweise in einem Pferdeschwanz/Knoten; **to let one's ~ down** (lit) sein Haar aufmachen or lösen (geh); (fig) aus sich (dat) herausgehen; **keep your ~ on!** (Brit inf) ruhig Blut!; **to get in sb's ~** (inf) jdm auf den Wecker or auf die Nerven gehen (inf); **I wish you'd get out of my ~ while I'm working** (inf) kannst du mich vielleicht in Ruhe lassen, während ich arbeite; **that film really made my ~ stand on end** bei dem Film lief es mir eiskalt den Rücken herunter **b** (= single hair) Haar nt; **not a ~ on his head was harmed** (fig) ihm wurde kein Haar gekrümmt; **not a ~ out of place** (fig) wie aus dem Ei gepellt; **to win/lose by a ~** ganz knapp gewinnen/verlieren → **turn, split c** (= on body) Haar nt, Haare pl; (= total body hair) Behaarung f; **body ~** Körperbehaarung f **d** (of animal, plant) Haar nt; (of pig) Borste f; **I'm allergic to cat ~** ich bin gegen Katzenhaare allergisch; **the best cure for a hangover is the ~ of the dog (that bit you)** einen Kater kuriert man am besten, wenn man mit dem anfängt, womit man aufgehört hat ATTR Haar-; (= horsehair) Rosshaar-; **~ growth** Haarwuchs m

hair: hairball N Haarknäuel nt; **hairband** N Haarband nt; **hairbrush** N Haarbürste f; **hair care** N Haarpflege f; **hair clip** N Clip m, Klipp m; (for ponytail etc) Haarspange f; **hair clippers** PL elektrische Haarschneidemaschine; **hair conditioner** N Pflegespülung f; **hair cream** N Haarcreme f, Pomade f; **hair curler** N Lockenwickler m; **haircut** N Haarschnitt m; (= act also) Haarschneiden nt; (= hairdo) Frisur f; **to have** or **get a ~** sich (dat) die Haare schneiden lassen; **I need a ~** ich muss zum Friseur, ich muss mir die Haare schneiden lassen; **hairdo** N (inf) Frisur f; **hairdresser** N Friseur m, Friseuse f; **the ~'s** der Friseur; **hairdressing** N Frisieren nt; (= tonic) Haarwasser nt; **hairdressing salon** N Friseursalon m; **hairdrier** N Haartrockner m; (hand-held also) Fön® m, Föhn m; (over head also) Trockenhaube f

-haired [ˈheəd] ADJ suf -haarig; **dark-/long-haired** dunkel-/langhaarig

hair: hair extension N Haarverlängerung f; **hair follicle** N Haarfollikel nt, Haarbalg m; **hair gel** N (Haar)gel nt; **hairgrip** N (Brit) Haarklemme f, Klemmchen nt

hairiness [ˈheərɪnɪs] N Behaartheit f; **is ~ a sign of virility?** ist starker Haarwuchs ein Zeichen von Männlichkeit?

hair: hair lacquer N Haarspray m or nt; **hairless** ADJ unbehaart; plant haarlos; **hairline** N a Haaransatz m b (= thin line) haarfeine Linie; (in telescope, on sight) Faden m; (Typ) senkrechter Strich; **~s** Fadenkreuz nt; **hairline crack** N Haarriss m; **hairline fracture** N Haarriss m; **hair loss** N Haarausfall m; **hairnet** N Haarnetz nt; **hair oil** N Haaröl nt; **hairpiece** N Haarteil nt; (for men) Toupet nt; **hairpin** N Haarnadel f; **hairpin (bend)** N Haarnadelkurve f; **hair-raiser** N (inf, experience) haarsträubendes or entsetzliches Erlebnis; (= film) Horror- or Gruselfilm m, Schocker m (inf); (= story) Grusel- or Horrorgeschichte f; **hair-raising** ADJ haarsträubend; **hair remover** N Haarentferner m, Haarentfernungsmittel nt; **hair restorer** N Haarwuchsmittel nt; **hair roller** N Lockenwickler m; **hair's breadth** N Haaresbreite f; **by a ~** um Haaresbreite; **to be within a ~ of ruin** am Rande des Ruins stehen; **he was within a ~ of winning** er hätte um ein Haar gewonnen; **to escape by a ~** mit knapper Not entkommen; **hair shirt** N härenes Gewand (old, liter); (fig) Büßerhemd nt; **hair slide** N (Brit) Haarspange f; **hair space** N (Typ) Haarspatium nt; **hairsplitter** N Haarspalter m; **hairsplitting** N Haarspalterei f ADJ haarspalterisch; **hairspray** N Haarspray m or nt; **hairspring** N Spiralfeder f; **hairstyle** N Frisur f; **hair stylist** N Coiffeur m, Coiffeuse f, Haarkünstler(in) m(f); **hair transplant** N Haartransplantation f; **hair trigger** N Stecher m

hairy [ˈheərɪ] ADJ (+er) **a** person, body, plant, spider behaart; leg, arm, chest, armpits haarig, behaart; animal, coat haarig; **she has very ~ armpits** sie hat viele Achselhaare **b** (inf, = scary, risky) haarig (inf); situation brenzlig (inf); adventure riskant; driving rasant (inf)

Haiti [ˈheɪtɪ] N Haiti nt

Haitian [ˈheɪʃɪən] ADJ haitianisch, haitisch N **a** Haitianer(in) m(f) **b** (Ling) Haitisch nt

hake [heɪk] N See- or Meerhecht m, Hechtdorsch m

halberd [ˈhælbəd] N Hellebarde f

halberdier [ˌhælbəˈdɪə'] N Hellebardier m

halcyon [ˈhælsɪən] ADJ **~ days** glückliche Tage pl

hale [heɪl] ADJ (+er) kräftig; old man rüstig; **~ and hearty** gesund und munter

half [hɑːf] N pl **halves** **a** Hälfte f; **two halves make a whole** zwei Halbe machen ein Ganzes; **the first ~ of the year** die erste Jahreshälfte; **to cut sth in ~** etw halbieren; (with knife also) etw in zwei Hälften or Teile schneiden; salary etc etw um or auf die Hälfte kürzen; **to break/tear sth in ~** etw durchbrechen/durchreißen; **~ of**

it/them die Hälfte davon/von ihnen; **~ the book/money** die Hälfte des Buches/Geldes, das halbe Buch/Geld; **~ my life** die Hälfte meines Lebens, mein halbes Leben; **~ a million dollars** eine halbe Million Dollar; **he gave me ~** er gab mir die Hälfte; **a cup/an hour** eine halbe Tasse/Stunde; **~ a lifetime** ein halbes Leben; **he's not ~ the man he used to be** er ist längst nicht mehr das, was er einmal war; **~ a second!** (einen) Augenblick mal!; **I'll be round in ~ a second** (inf) ich komme gleich (mal) hin; **to listen with ~ an ear** nur mit halbem Ohr zuhören; **to take ~ of sth** die Hälfte von etw nehmen; **to go halves (with sb on sth)** (mit jdm mit etw) halbe-halbe machen (inf); **that's only ~ the story** das ist nur die halbe Geschichte; **have ~ of my apple** willst du einen halben Apfel von mir haben?; **bigger by ~** anderthalbmal so groß; **to increase sth by ~** etw um die Hälfte vergrößern; **he is too clever by ~** (Brit inf) das ist ein richtiger Schlaumeier; **he's too cocky by ~** (Brit inf) er hält sich für wer weiß was (inf); **one and a ~** eineinhalb, anderthalb; **an hour and a ~** eineinhalb or anderthalb Stunden; **he's two and a ~** er ist zweieinhalb; **he doesn't do things by halves** er macht keine halben Sachen; **~ and ~** halb und halb; **that's a hill and a ~!** (inf) das ist vielleicht ein Berg!; **that's not the ~ of it** (inf) **I haven't told you the ~ of it yet** (inf) und das ist noch nicht einmal die Hälfte (inf) **b** (Sport, of match) (Spiel)hälfte f, Halbzeit f; (= player) Läufer(in) m(f) **c** (of ticket) Abschnitt m der Fahrkarte; (= travel, admission fee) halbe Karte (inf); **return ~** (Brit) Abschnitt m für die Rückfahrt; **two adults and one ~, please** zwei Erwachsene und ein Kind, bitte; **two and a ~ (to London)** zweieinhalb(mal London) **d** (= beer) kleines Bier, Halbe f (dial), Halbe(s) nt, Kleine(s) nt; (Scot, = whisky) einfacher Whisky, Einfache(r) m **e** (= husband etc) **my better** (hum) or **other ~** meine bessere Hälfte ADJ halb; **a ~ cup** eine halbe Tasse; **with ~ his usual strength** nur mit halber Kraft; **at** or **for ~ price** zum halben Preis; **~ one thing ~ another** halb und halb, halb das eine und halb das andere; **~ man ~ beast** halb Mensch, halb Tier; **it's neither opera nor operetta but sort of ~ and ~** es ist so ein Zwischending nt zwischen Oper und Operette ADV **a** halb; **I ~ thought ...** ich hätte fast gedacht ...; **I was ~ afraid that ...** ich habe fast befürchtet, dass ...; **~ melted** halb geschmolzen; **the work is only ~ done** die Arbeit ist erst halb or zur Hälfte erledigt; **that's ~ right** das ist zur Hälfte richtig; **to be ~ asleep** (= almost asleep) schon fast schlafen; (= very tired) todmüde sein (inf); **to be ~ awake** halb wach sein; **~ laughing, ~ crying** halb lachend, halb weinend; **~ laughing, ~ crying he told me ...** mit einem lachenden und einem weinenden Auge erzählte er mir ...; **he ~ rose to his feet** er erhob sich halb; **I ~ think that ...** ich habe beinahe den Eindruck, dass ...; **he only ~ understands** or **versteht** nur die Hälfte; **the book was ~ in German, ~ in English** das Buch war zur Hälfte auf Deutsch und zur Hälfte auf Englisch; **she's ~ German and ~ Russian** sie ist zur Hälfte Deutsche und zur Hälfte Russin **b** (Brit, inf) **he's not ~ stupid/rich** etc er ist vielleicht or unheimlich dumm/reich etc; **it didn't ~ rain** es HAT vielleicht geregnet; **not ~ bad** gar nicht schlecht; **not ~!** und wie! und ob! **c** it's ~ past three or ~ three es ist halb vier **d** **he is ~ as big as his sister** er ist halb so groß wie seine Schwester; **~ as big again** anderthalbmal so groß; **he earns ~ as much as you** er verdient halb so viel wie Sie; **he earns ~ as much again as you** er verdient die Hälfte mehr als du or anderthalbmal so viel wie du; **give me ~ as much again** gib mir noch die Hälfte dazu

half: half-a-crown N = half-crown; **half-a-dozen** N = half-dozen; **half-arsed**, (US) **half-as-**

sed ADJ (*vulgar*) bescheuert (*inf*); (= *incompetent*) unfähig; **halfback** N (*Sport*) Läufer(in) *m(f)*; **half-baked** ADJ (*fig*) person, plan, idea unausgegoren; **half-binding** N (*of book*) Halbband *m*; **half board** N Halbpension *f*; **half bottle** N kleine Flasche; **a ~ of wine** eine kleine Flasche Wein; **half-bred** ADJ = **half-breed** ADJ; **half-breed** N a (*dated*, = *person*) Mischling *m*; (*esp Red Indian*) Halbblut nt b (= *animal*) Rassenmischung *f*; (= *horse*) Halbblut nt, Halbblüter *m* ADJ a *animal* gekreuzt; **~ horse** Halbblut nt; **a ~ dog** eine Mischrasse, eine Rassenmischung *f*; **a ~ child** (*dated*) ein Mischlingskind nt; (*Red Indian*) ein Halbblutindianer *m*; **a ~ Indian** (*dated*) ein Halbblut nt; **a ~ American** ein amerikanischer Mischling; **half-circle** N Halbkreis *m*; **half-closed** ADJ halb geschlossen; **half-cock** N **to go off at ~** (*inf*) ein Reinfall sein (*inf*), ein Schuss in den Ofen sein (*inf*); **half-cocked** ADJ *pistol* in Vorderraststellung; **to go off ~** (*fig inf*: *person*) voreilig handeln, einfach drauflosmachen (*inf*); **half-cooked** ADJ halb gar; **half-cracked** ADJ (*esp Brit*, *inf*, = *crazy*) bekloppt (*sl*), bescheuert (*inf*); **half-crown** N (*in old Brit system*) Half Crown *f*, Zweieinhalbschillingstück nt; **half-cup brassière** N Büstenhalter *m* mit Halbschalen; **half-cut** ADJ (*Brit*, *inf*, = *drunk*) besoffen (*inf*); **half-day** N (= *holiday*) halber freier Tag; **we've got a ~** wir haben einen halben Tag frei; **half-dead** ADJ (*lit*, *fig*) halb tot (*with* vor +*dat*); **half-dollar** N halber Dollar; **half-dozen** N halbes Dutzend; **half-dressed** ADJ halb bekleidet; **half-empty** ADJ halb leer VT zur Hälfte leeren or leer machen; **half face** N (*in painting*, *photography*) Profil nt; **half-fare** N halber Fahrpreis ADV zum halben Preis; **half-fill** VT halb füllen; **half-forgotten** ADJ fast vergessen; **half-frame camera** N Halbformatkamera *f*; **half-full** ADJ halb voll; **half-hearted** ADJ halbherzig; *attempt also* lustlos; *manner* lustlos, lau; **he was rather ~ about accepting** er nahm es ohne rechte Lust an; **he seems ~ about it** er scheint sich dafür nicht so recht begeistern zu können; **half-heartedly** ADV *agree* ohne rechten Herzens, mit halbem Herzen; **to do sth ~** etw ohne rechte Überzeugung or Lust tun; **half-heartedness** N Halbherzigkeit *f*, Lustlosigkeit *f*; **the ~ of his attempts** seine halbherzigen or lustlosen Versuche *pl*; **half holiday** N (*Brit*) halber Urlaubstag; (= *public holiday*) halber Feiertag; **we've got a ~ tomorrow morning** wir haben morgen Vormittag frei; **half-hour** N halbe Stunde; **half-an-hour's** or **a ~ interval** eine halbstündige Pause, eine halbe Stunde Pause; **it strikes (on) the ~** sie schlägt die halben Stunden; **half-hourly** ADV jede or alle halbe Stunde, halbstündlich ADJ halbstündlich; **half landing** N Treppenabsatz *m*; **half-length** ADJ ~ *portrait* Brustbild nt; **half-life** N (*Phys*) Halbwertszeit *f*; **half-light** N Dämmerlicht nt, Halbdunkel nt; **half-mast** N **at ~** (*also hum*) (auf) halbmast; **with his trousers at ~** (*Brit*: = *too short*) mit Hochwasserhosen; **half measure** N halbe Maßnahme, Stehenbleiben nt no pl auf halbem Weg; **we don't do things by ~s** wir machen keine halben Sachen, wir begnügen uns nicht mit Halbheiten; **half-monthly** ADJ zweiwöchentlich, vierzehntäglich; *publication* zweimal im Monat erscheinend ADV zweimal im Monat; **half-moon** N a Halbmond *m* b (*of fingernails*) Mond *m*; **half-naked** ADJ halb nackt; **half nelson** N (*Wrestling*) Nelson *m*, einfacher Nackenheber; **to have sb in a ~** einen Nelson bei jdm ansetzen; **half-note** N (*US*, *Mus*) halbe Note; **half-open** ADJ halb offen VT halb öffnen or aufmachen; **half-pay** N (*of salaried employee*) halbes Gehalt; **to be on ~** den halben Lohn/das halbe Gehalt bekommen; **to go on ~** auf halben Lohn/halbes

Gehalt gesetzt werden; **halfpence** ['hɑːfˌpəns] N halber Penny; **halfpenny** ['heɪpnɪ] (*Brit*, *old*) N halber Penny, Halfpenny *m* ATTR Halfpenny-; **~ stamp/coin** Halfpennymarke/-münze *f*; **half-pint** N a = Viertelliter *m* or nt; (*of beer*) kleines Bier b (*inf*, = *person*) halbe Portion (*inf*), Knirps *m* (*inf*); **half-pipe** N (*Sport*) Halfpipe *f*; **half-price** ADJ zum halben Preis; **to be ~** die Hälfte kosten, um die Hälfte reduziert sein; **~ electricity** Strom *m* zum halben Preis ADV *drink*, *stay* zum halben Preis; **half-rest** N (*US*, *Mus*) halbe Pause; **half seas over** ADJ (*dated inf*) bezecht, leicht hinüber (*inf*); **half-serious** ADJ **I was only ~ about it** ich habe das nicht ganz ernst gemeint; **actually, I was ~ about it** ich habe das nicht im Scherz gesagt; **half-sister** N Halbschwester *f*; **half-size** N Zwischengröße *f* ADJ halb so groß; **~ desk** kleiner Schreibtisch; **a ~ model of sth** ein Modell nt von etw in halber Größe; **half term** N (*Brit*) Ferien pl in der Mitte des Trimesters; **we get three days at ~** wir haben drei Tage Ferien in der Mitte des Trimesters; **half-timbered** ADJ Fachwerk-; **half-timbered house** Fachwerkbau *m*/-haus nt; **half-timbering** N Fachwerkbauweise *f*; **half-time** N a (*Sport*) Halbzeit *f*; **at ~** bei or zur Halbzeit b (*Ind*) **to be on/to be put on ~** auf Kurzarbeit sein/gesetzt werden ATTR Halbzeit-, zur Halbzeit; **~ whistle/score** Halbzeitpfiff *m*/-stand *m* ADV **to work** ~ halbtags arbeiten or beschäftigt sein; **half-title** N Schmutztitel *m*; **halftone** N (*Art*, *Phot*, *US Mus*) Halbton *m*; (*Phot*, = *process*) Halbtonverfahren nt; (= *picture*) Halbtonbild nt; **halftone screen** N Raster *m*; **half-track** N (= *vehicle*) Halbkettenfahrzeug nt; **half-truth** N Halbwahrheit *f*; **half volley** N (*Tennis*) Halfvolley *m*, Halbflugball *m*; **half-volley** VT (*Tennis*) *ball* als Halfvolley schlagen

halfway ['hɑːfˌweɪ] ADJ *attr measures* halb; **at the ~ stage of the Tour de France** in der Mitte der Tour de France; **when we reached the ~ stage** or **point on our journey** as wir die Hälfte der Reise hinter uns (*dat*) hatten; **he was at the ~ stage in his musical career** er befand sich in der Mitte seiner musikalischen Karriere; **we're past the ~ stage** wir haben die Hälfte geschafft ADV *her hair reached ~ down her back* die Haare gingen ihr bis weit über die Schultern; **~ to** auf halbem Weg nach; **we drove ~ to London** wir fuhren die halbe Strecke or den halben Weg nach London; **~ between two points** (in der Mitte or genau) zwischen zwei Punkten; **I live ~ up the hill** ich wohne auf halber Höhe des Berges; **we went ~ up the hill** wir gingen den Berg halb hinauf; **~ through a book** halb durch ein Buch (durch); **she dropped out ~ through the race** nach der Hälfte des Rennens gab sie auf; **to go ~** (*lit*) die halbe Strecke or die Hälfte des Weges zurücklegen; **he went ~ round the world to find her** er reiste um die halbe Welt, um sie zu finden; **this money will go ~ toward(s) the cost of the car** diese Summe wird die Hälfte der Kosten für das Auto decken; **to meet sb ~** (*lit*, *fig*) jdm (auf halbem Weg) entgegenkommen; **~ decent** halbwegs anständig

halfway house N Gasthaus nt auf halbem Weg; (= *hostel*) offene Anstalt; (*fig*) Zwischending nt; **we could stop off at the King's Head, that's a ~** wir können im „King's Head" einkehren, das liegt auf halbem Wege; **it is a ~ between democracy and ...** das ist ein Zwischending zwischen Demokratie und ...; (*non-temporal*) es nimmt eine Zwischenstellung zwischen Demokratie und ... ein

half: **halfwit** N Schwachsinnige(r) *mf*; (*fig*) Schwachkopf *m*; **halfwitted** ADJ schwachsinnig; **half-year** N Halbjahr nt; **half-yearly** ADJ halbjährlich ADV halbjährlich, jedes halbe Jahr

halibut ['hælɪbət] N Heilbutt *m*

halitosis [ˌhælɪ'təʊsɪs] N schlechter Mundgeruch

hall [hɔːl] N a (= *entrance hall of house*) Diele *f*, Korridor *m*
b (= *large building*) Halle *f*; (= *large room*) Saal

m; (*Brit*: *of college*) Speisesaal *m*; (*Brit*: = *college mealtime*) Essen nt; (= *dance hall*) Tanzdiele *f*; (= *village hall*) Gemeindehalle *f*, Gemeindehaus nt; (= *school assembly hall*) Aula *f*; **he will join the ~ of fame of ...** (*fig*) er wird in die Geschichte des ... eingehen, er wird in die Ruhmeshalle des ... aufgenommen (*liter*)
c (= *mansion*) Herrensitz *m*, Herrenhaus nt; (*Brit*: = *students' residence*: also **hall of residence**) Studenten(wohn)heim nt; **to live** or **be in ~** (*Brit*) im Wohnheim wohnen; **Ruskin ~** Haus Ruskin nt
d (*US*: = *corridor*) Korridor *m*, Gang *m*

hallelujah [ˌhælɪ'luːjə] INTERJ halleluja N Halleluja nt

hallmark ['hɔːlmɑːk] N a (*on gold, silver*) (Feingehalts)stempel *m*, Repunze *f* b (*fig*) Kennzeichen nt (*of* +gen, für); **it is of good quality** ein Gütesiegel nt; **this is the ~ of a true genius** daran erkennt man das wahre Genie VT *gold*, *silver* stempeln; **to be ~ed by sth** (*fig*) durch etw gekennzeichnet sein

hallo [hə'ləʊ] INTERJ, N = hello

halloo [hə'luː] INTERJ hallo; (*Hunt*) horrido, hallo N Halloruf *m*; (*Hunt*) Horrido nt, Hallo nt VI (hallo) rufen; (*Hunt*) die Hunde hetzen

hallow ['hæləʊ] VT heiligen; (= *consecrate*) weihen

hallowed ['hæləʊd] ADJ geheiligt; **~ traditions** geheiligte Traditionen pl; **on ~ ground** auf heiligem Boden; **~ be Thy name** (*Bibl*) geheiligt werde Dein Name

Halloween, Hallowe'en [ˌhæləʊˈiːn] N der Tag vor Allerheiligen, Halloween nt

HALLOWEEN

Halloween wird in der Nacht vor Allerheiligen, am 31. Oktober, gefeiert. Früher glaubte man, dass in dieser Nacht die Seelen der Toten in ihre ehemaligen Häuser zurückkehrten, doch heutzutage ist **Halloween** ein willkommener Anlass zu feiern und Schabernack zu treiben. Kinder verkleiden sich (traditionellerweise als Hexen und Gespenster) und basteln sich Laternen aus ausgehöhlten Rüben und Kürbissen, in die Kerzen gestellt werden. Sie ziehen dann von Tür zu Tür und sammeln bei Freunden und Nachbarn Süßigkeiten und Geld ein. Der Spruch dabei ist **trick or treat**, d. h., die Kinder drohen damit, dem Hausbesitzer einen Streich (**trick**) zu spielen, wenn sie kein Geschenk (**treat**), normalerweise Süßigkeiten, bekommen. Außerdem werden jede Menge Halloween-Parties – auch für Erwachsene – veranstaltet, bei denen man kostümiert erscheint.

hall: **hall porter** N Portier *m*; **hall stand** N (Flur)garderobe *f*; (*tree-like*) Garderobenständer *m*

hallucinate [hə'luːsɪneɪt] VI halluzinieren, Wahnvorstellungen haben

hallucination [həˌluːsɪ'neɪʃən] N a Halluzination *f*, Wahnvorstellung *f* b (*inf*, = *false idea*) Wahnvorstellung *f*

hallucinatory [həˌluːsɪnətərɪ] ADJ *drug* Halluzinationen hervorrufend attr, halluzinogen (*spec*); *state, effect, vision, experience* halluzinatorisch

hallucinogenic [həˌluːsɪnə'dʒenɪk] ADJ Halluzinationen hervorrufend attr, halluzinogen (*spec*); **LSD is ~** LSD ist ein Halluzinogen nt

hallway ['hɔːlweɪ] N Flur *m*, Korridor *m*

halo ['heɪləʊ] N pl -(e)s (*of saint*, *fig iro*) Heiligenschein *m*; (*Astron*) Hof *m*, Halo *m* (*spec*); **his ~ slipped** er büßte seinen Heiligenschein ein VT (*fig*) umrahmen

halogen ['hæləʊdʒɪn] N Halogen nt

halogen lamp N Halogenlampe *f*; (*Aut*) Halogenscheinwerfer *m*

halt[1] [hɔːlt] N a (= *stop*) Pause *f*; (*Mil*) Halt *m*; (*in production*) Stopp *m*; **to come to a ~** zum Stillstand kommen; **to bring sth to a ~** etw zum Stillstand bringen; **the officer called a ~**

der Offizier ließ Halt machen; **the referee called a ~** der Schiedsrichter pfiff ab; **shall we call a ~ now, gentlemen?** wollen wir jetzt Schluss machen, meine Herren?; **to call a ~ to sth** einer Sache (dat) ein Ende machen or bereiten; **he called a ~ to the discussion** er beendete die Diskussion; **the government called for a ~ to the fighting** die Regierung verlangte die Einstellung der Kämpfe

b (= small station) Haltepunkt m

VI zum Stillstand kommen; (person) anhalten, stehen bleiben; (Mil) Halt machen; **he was going to call her back but then ~ed** er wollte sie zurückrufen, aber hielt dann inne; **we ~ed briefly before attempting the summit** wir hielten kurz an or machten kurz Halt, bevor wir den Gipfel in Angriff nahmen

VT zum Stillstand bringen; fighting einstellen; arms race, war beenden; troops Halt machen lassen; **bad light ~ed play** das Spiel wurde wegen der schlechten Lichtverhältnisse abgebrochen

INTERJ halt; (traffic sign) stop

halt² **VI** (obs) hinken; (in speech) stockend sprechen **N** (Bibl) **the ~ and the lame** die Krummen und die Lahmen

halter ['hɔːltə'] **N a** (horse's) Halfter nt **b** (for hanging) Schlinge f

halterneck ['hɒltənek] **N** rückenfreies Kleid mit Nackenband **ADJ** rückenfrei mit Nackenverschluss

halting ['hɔːltɪŋ] **ADJ** voice, efforts, steps, answer zögernd; speech, performance, progress stockend; French, German, verse holprig; **their steps toward(s) reform are ~** sie machen nur zögernde Schritte zur Reform

haltingly ['hɔːltɪŋlɪ] **ADV** zögernd; speak, progress stockend

halt sign **N** (Aut) Stoppschild nt

halve [hɑːv] **VT a** (= separate in two) halbieren **b** (= reduce by one half) auf die Hälfte reduzieren, halbieren

halves [hɑːvz] pl of half

halyard ['hæljəd] **N** (Naut) Fall nt; (for flag) Flaggleine f

ham [hæm] **N a** (Cook) Schinken m; **~ sandwich** Schinkenbrot nt **b** (Anat) **~s** (hintere) Oberschenkel pl; (of animal) (Hinter)keulen pl; **to squat on one's ~s** hocken, in der Hocke sitzen **c** (Theat) Schmierenkomödiant(in) m(f) **d** (Rad inf) Funkamateur(in) m(f) **ADJ** attr acting übertrieben, zu dick aufgetragen; **~ actor** Schmierenkomödiant(in) m(f) **VI** (Theat) chargieren, übertrieben spielen

▶ **ham up** **VT** sep (inf) übertreiben; **to ham it up** zu dick auftragen

hamburger ['hæmbɜːgə'] **N** Hamburger m

ham-fisted [ˌhæm'fɪstɪd], **ham-handed** [ˌhæm'hændɪd] **ADJ** ungeschickt; efforts, person also tollpatschig (inf)

Hamitic [hæ'mɪtɪk] **ADJ** hamitisch

hamlet ['hæmlɪt] **N** Weiler m, kleines Dorf

hammer ['hæmə'] **N** (generally) Hammer m; (of gun) Hahn m; **to go at it ~ and tongs** (inf) sich ins Zeug legen (inf), sich reinhängen (sl); (= work also) schuften, dass die Fetzen fliegen (inf); (= quarrel) sich in die Wolle kriegen (inf), sich streiten, dass die Fetzen fliegen (inf); (= have sex) es miteinander machen (inf); **to go/come under the ~** (at auction) unter den Hammer kommen; **throwing the ~** (Sport) Hammerwerfen nt; **in the ~** (Sport) im Hammerwurf

VT a nail, metal hämmern; **to ~ a nail into a wall** einen Nagel in die Wand schlagen; **to ~ sth into shape** (metal) etw zurechthämmern; (fig) agreement etw ausarbeiten; **to ~ sth into sb** or **into sb's head** (inf) jdm etw einbläuen (inf) **b** (inf, = defeat badly) eine Schlappe beibringen +dat (inf); **Chelsea were ~ed 6-1** Chelsea musste eine 6:1-Schlappe einstecken (inf) **c** (St Ex sl) stockbroker für zahlungsunfähig erklären **d** (inf: = criticize) kritisieren, attackieren **e** (inf: = harm) **small businesses have been ~ed by the recession** kleine Firmen sind von der Rezession schwer in Mitleidenschaft gezogen worden

VI hämmern; **to ~ on the door** an die Tür hämmern; **my heart was ~ing** mein Herz pochte wild

▶ **hammer away** **VI** (darauflos)hämmern; **to hammer away at an issue** sich (dat) über eine Frage den Kopf zerbrechen; **the politicians were hammering away at each other** die Politiker hackten aufeinander herum; **his heart was hammering away** sein Herz pochte wild; **the pianist hammered away at the keys** der Pianist hämmerte auf die Tasten

▶ **hammer down** **VT** sep festhämmern; nail, door einschlagen; bump flach hämmern

▶ **hammer home** **VT** sep **a** nail fest hineinschlagen **b** argument, point etc Nachdruck verleihen (+dat), untermauern; **he tried to hammer it home to the pupils that ...** er versuchte, den Schülern einzubläuen or einzuhämmern, dass...

▶ **hammer in** **VT** sep **a** nail etc einschlagen, einhämmern **b** (fig) fact einhämmern, einbläuen (inf)

▶ **hammer out** **VT** sep **a** metal hämmern; nail, bricks (her)ausschlagen or -klopfen; dent ausbeulen **b** (fig) plan, agreement, solution ausarbeiten, aushandeln; difficulties beseitigen, bereinigen; verse schmieden; tune hämmern

hammer and sickle **N** sing Hammer und Sichel pl

hammer: hammer beam **N** Stichbalken m; **hammer drill** **N** Schlagbohrmaschine f; **hammerhead** ['hæməhed] **N** (= shark) Hammerhai m; (of hammer) Hammerkopf m

hammering ['hæmərɪŋ] **N** (esp Brit) **a** Hämmern nt, Klopfen nt **b** (inf, = defeat) Schlappe f (inf); **our team took a ~** unsere Mannschaft musste eine Schlappe einstecken (inf) **c** (inf, = criticism) scharfe Kritik; **doctors took a terrible ~ in the report** die Ärzteschaft wurden in dem Bericht scharf unter Beschuss genommen (inf)

hammertoe ['hæmə.təʊ] **N** Hammerzehe f or -zeh m

hammock ['hæmək] **N** Hängematte f

hammy ['hæmɪ] **ADJ** (+er) (inf) actor übertrieben spielend; acting übertrieben

hamper¹ ['hæmpə'] **N** (esp Brit) (= basket) Korb m; (as present) Geschenkkorb m

hamper² **VT** behindern; movement also erschweren; person also Schwierigkeiten bereiten (+dat); **to be ~ed (by sth)** (durch etw) gehandikapt sein; **the police were ~ed in their search by the shortage of clues** der Mangel an Hinweisen erschwerte der Polizei die Suche

hamster ['hæmstə'] **N** Hamster m

hamstring ['hæmstrɪŋ] vb: pret, ptp **hamstrung** ['hæmstrʌŋ] **N** (Anat) Kniesehne f; (of animal) Achillessehne f **VT a** (lit) person, animal die Kniesehne/Achillessehne durchschneiden (+dat) **b** (fig) attempt etc vereiteln, unterbinden; person handlungsunfähig machen; **to be hamstrung** aufgeschmissen sein (inf); (project) lahm gelegt sein, lahm liegen

---

hand [hænd]

⊙ 26.2, 26.3

1 NOUN	3 PHRASAL VERBS
2 TRANSITIVE VERB	

1 – NOUN

a Hand f; (of clock) Zeiger m; **on (one's) hands and knees** auf allen vieren; **to take/lead sb by the hand** jdn an die or bei der Hand nehmen/ an der Hand führen; **hand in hand** Hand in Hand; **to go hand in hand with sth** mit etw einhergehen or Hand in Hand gehen; **these symptoms often go hand in hand** diese Symptome treten oft gleichzeitig auf; **hands up!** Hände hoch!; (Sch) meldet euch!; **hands up who knows the answer/who wants to go** Hand hoch, wer es weiß/wer gehen will; **hands off!**

(inf) Hände weg!; **keep your hands off my wife** lass die Finger or Pfoten (inf) von meiner Frau!; **done** or **made by hand** handgearbeitet; **this sweater was knitted by hand** dieser Pullover ist handgestrickt; **to deliver a letter by hand** einen Brief persönlich überbringen; **"by hand"** „durch Boten"; **to raise an animal by hand** ein Tier von Hand or mit der Flasche aufziehen; **pistol in hand** mit vorgehaltener Pistole, mit der Pistole in der Hand; **to climb hand over hand** Hand über Hand klettern; **to live (from) hand to mouth** von der Hand in den Mund leben; **with a heavy/firm hand** (fig) mit harter/fester or starker Hand; **to get one's hands dirty** (fig) sich (dat) die Hände schmutzig machen; **to give with one hand and take away with the other** mit einer Hand geben, mit der anderen nehmen; **it's a case of the right hand not knowing what the left hand's doing** das ist so ein Fall, wo die rechte Hand nicht weiß, was die linke tut; **we're forced to do it with one hand** or **both hands** or **our hands tied behind our back** (fig) wir sind gezwungen, es zu tun, während uns die Hände gebunden sind → **hold, shake**

b = side Seite f; **on the right hand** auf der rechten Seite, rechts, rechter Hand; **on my right hand** rechts von mir, zu meiner Rechten (geh); **on every hand, on all hands** auf allen Seiten, ringsum(her); **on the one hand ... on the other hand ...** einerseits or auf der einen Seite ..., andererseits or auf der anderen Seite ...

c = agency, possession **it's the hand of God/fate** das ist die Hand Gottes/des Schicksals; **your future is in your own hands** Sie haben Ihre Zukunft (selbst) in der Hand; **to take one's life in one's hands** sein Leben selbst in die Hand nehmen; **to put sth in sb's hands** jdm etw in die Hand geben, etw in jds Hände legen; **he put the matter in the hands of his lawyer** er übergab die Sache seinem Anwalt; **to leave sb in sb's hands** jdn in jds Obhut lassen; **to leave sth in sb's hands** jdm etw überlassen; **to put oneself in(to) sb's hands** sich jdm anvertrauen, sich in jds Hände begeben (geh); **my life is in your hands** mein Leben ist or liegt in Ihren Händen; **to fall into the hands of sb** jdm in die Hände fallen; **to fall into the wrong hands** in die falschen Hände geraten; **to be in good hands** in guten Händen sein; **to change hands** den Besitzer wechseln; **I received some pretty rough treatment at her hands** ich bin von ihr ganz schön grob behandelt worden; **he suffered terribly at the hands of the enemy** er machte in den Händen des Feindes Schreckliches durch; **he has too much time on his hands** er hat zu viel Zeit zur Verfügung; **he has a problem/five children on his hands** er hat ein Problem/fünf Kinder am Hals (inf); **it's no fun having three noisy children on your hands** es macht keinen Spaß, drei laute Kinder am Hals zu haben (inf); **we've got a fight on our hands** wir haben einen harten Kampf vor uns; **I've got enough on my hands already** ich habe ohnehin schon alle Hände voll zu tun, ich habe schon genug um die Ohren (inf) or am Hals (inf); **she read everything she could get her hands on** sie las alles, was sie in die Finger bekommen konnte; **just wait till I get my hands on him!** warte nur, bis ich ihn zwischen die Finger kriege! (inf); **to get sb/sth off one's hands** jdn/etw loswerden; **to take sb/sth off sb's hands** jdm jdn/etw abnehmen; **goods left on our hands** (Comm) nicht abgesetzte Waren → die¹ **VI a**, change **VT a**, free **ADJ a**

d = applause **it's the hand of God/fate** Applaus m, Beifall m; **they gave him a big hand** sie gaben ihm großen Applaus, sie klatschten ihm großen Beifall; **let's give our guest a big hand** und nun geben wir Beifall für unseren Gast

e = worker Arbeitskraft f, Arbeiter(in) m(f); (Naut) Besatzungsmitglied nt; **to take on hands** Leute einstellen; (Naut) Leute anheuern; **hands** Leute pl, Belegschaft f; **(ship's) hands** Besatzung f, Mannschaft f; **all hands on deck!** alle Mann an Deck!; **lost with all hands** mit der ganzen Besatzung untergegangen

f = expert **to be an old hand (at sth)** ein alter Hase f sein; **he is an experienced hand at that** er hat viel Erfahrung darin → **dab³**

g = handwriting Handschrift f; **it is written in his own hand** es ist in seiner Handschrift geschrieben

h = measure (of horse) ≈ 10 cm

i Cards Blatt nt; (= person) Mann m; (= game) Runde f; **3 hands** (= people) 3 Mann; **a hand of bridge** eine Runde Bridge; **to show one's hand** seine Karten aufdecken; (fig) sich (dat) in die Karten sehen lassen

j other phrases **to ask for a lady's hand (in marriage)** um die Hand einer Dame anhalten; **to have one's hands full with sb/sth** mit jdm/etw alle Hände voll zu tun haben; **to wait on sb hand and foot** jdn von vorne und hinten bedienen; **to have a hand in sth** (in decision) an etw (dat) beteiligt sein; (in crime) die Hand bei etw im Spiel haben; **I had no hand in it** ich hatte damit nichts zu tun; **to take a hand in sth** an etw (dat) teilnehmen, sich an etw (dat) beteiligen; **to keep one's hand in** in Übung bleiben; **to lend** or **give sb a hand** jdm behilflich sein, jdm zur Hand gehen; **give me a hand!** hilf mir mal!; **to give sb a hand up** jdm hochhelfen; **give me a hand down** helfen Sie mir mal herunter; **to force sb's hand** jdn zwingen, auf jdn Druck ausüben; **he never does a hand's turn** er rührt keinen Finger, er macht keinen Finger krumm; **to be hand in glove with sb** mit jdm unter einer Decke stecken, mit jdm gemeinsame Sache machen; **to win hands down** mühelos or spielend gewinnen; **to stay one's hand** abwarten; **to have the upper hand** die Oberhand behalten; **to get** or **gain the upper hand (of sb)** (über jdn) die Oberhand gewinnen; **he is making money hand over fist** er scheffelt das Geld nur so; **we're losing money hand over fist** wir verlieren massenweise Geld; **the inflation rate is rising hand over fist** die Inflationsrate steigt rasend schnell

◆ **at + hand to keep sth at hand** etw in Reichweite haben; **according to the information at hand** gemäß or laut der vorhandenen or vorliegenden Informationen; **it's quite close at hand** es ist ganz in der Nähe; **summer/Christmas is (close) at hand** der Sommer/Weihnachten steht vor der Tür, es ist bald Sommer/Weihnachten; **at first/second hand** aus erster/zweiter Hand → also (**c**)

◆ **in + hand he had the situation well in hand** er hatte die Situation im Griff; **she took the child in hand** sie nahm die Erziehung des Kindes in die Hand; **to take sb in hand** (= discipline) jdn in Obhut nehmen, nach jdm sehen; (= look after) jdn in Obhut nehmen, nach jdm sehen; **stock in hand** (Comm) Warenlager nt; **what stock have you in hand?** welche Waren haben Sie am Lager?; **he still had £600/a couple of hours in hand** er hatte £ 600 übrig/noch zwei Stunden Zeit; **the matter in hand** die vorliegende or (in discussion) die zur Debatte stehende Angelegenheit; **work in hand** Arbeit, die zur Zeit erledigt wird; **we've got a lot of work in hand** wir haben viel Arbeit anstehen or zu erledigen; **a matter/project is in hand** eine Sache/ein Projekt ist in Bearbeitung; **we still have a game in hand** wir haben noch ein Spiel ausstehen; **to put sth in hand** zusehen, dass etw erledigt wird → also (**a, c, g**)

◆ **on + hand according to the information on hand** gemäß or laut der vorhandenen or vorliegenden Informationen; **we have little information on hand** wir haben kaum Informationen pl (zur Verfügung) → also (**a, b, c**)

◆ **out + hand to eat out of sb's hand** (lit, fig) jdm aus der Hand fressen; **the children got out of hand** die Kinder waren nicht mehr zu bändigen or gerieten außer Rand und Band; **the horse got out of hand** er hat/ich habe etc die Kontrolle über das Pferd verloren; **the party got out of hand** die Party ist ausgeartet; **things got out of hand** die Dinge sind außer

Kontrolle geraten; **I dismissed the idea out of hand** ich verwarf die Idee sofort

◆ **to + hand I don't have the letter to hand** ich habe den Brief gerade nicht zur Hand; **your letter has come to hand** (Comm) wir haben Ihren Brief erhalten; **he seized the first weapon to hand** er ergriff die erstbeste Waffe; **we have little information to hand** wir haben kaum Informationen pl (zur Verfügung) → **palm²**, **cash**

2 – TRANSITIVE VERB

(= give) reichen, geben (sth to sb, sb sth jdm etw); **he handed the lady into/out of the carriage** er half der Dame in die/aus der Kutsche; **you've got to hand it to him** (fig inf) das muss man ihm lassen (inf)

3 – PHRASAL VERBS

▶ **hand (a)round** VT sep herumreichen; bottle also herumgehen lassen; (= distribute) papers austeilen, verteilen

▶ **hand back** VT sep zurückgeben

▶ **hand down** VT sep **a** (lit) herunterreichen or -geben (to sb jdm)
b (fig) weitergeben; tradition, belief überliefern, weitergeben; heirloom etc vererben (to +dat); clothes vererben (inf) (to +dat); story (from sb to sb) überliefern (to an +acc), weitergeben (to an +acc); **the farm's been handed down from generation to generation** der Hof ist durch die Generationen weitervererbt worden; **all his clothes were handed down from his elder brothers** er musste die Kleidung seiner älteren Brüder auftragen
c (Jur) sentence fällen

▶ **hand in** VT sep abgeben; forms, thesis also, resignation einreichen

▶ **hand off** VT sep (Rugby) (mit der Hand) wegstoßen

▶ **hand on** VT sep weitergeben (to an +acc)

▶ **hand out** VT sep austeilen, verteilen (to sb an jdm); advice geben, erteilen (to sb jdm); heavy sentence verhängen, austeilen; **the Spanish boxer was really handing it out** (inf) der spanische Boxer hat wirklich ganz schön zugeschlagen or ausgeteilt (inf)

▶ **hand over** VT sep (= pass over) (herüber)reichen (to dat); (= hand on) weitergeben (to an +acc); (= give up) (her)geben (to dat); (to third party) (ab)geben (to dat); criminal, prisoner übergeben (to dat); (from one state to another) ausliefern; leadership, authority, powers abgeben, abtreten (to an +acc); the controls, property, business übergeben (to dat); **hand over that gun!** Waffe her!; **I now hand you over to our political correspondent** ich gebe nun weiter or übergebe nun an unseren (politischen) Korrespondenten; **to hand oneself over to the police/authorities** sich der Polizei/den Behörden ergeben
VI **when the Conservatives handed over to Labour** als die Konservativen die Regierung an Labour abgaben; **when the chairman handed over to his successor** als der Vorsitzende das Amt an seinen Nachfolger abgab; **I now hand over to our sports correspondent** ich übergebe nun an unseren Sportberichterstatter; **he handed over to the co-pilot** er übergab an den Kopiloten

▶ **hand up** VT sep hinaufreichen

hand: handbag N Handtasche f; **hand baggage** N Handgepäck nt; **handball** N **a** (= game) Handball m **b** (Ftbl, = foul) Handspiel nt, Hand f INTERJ (Ftbl) Hand!; **handbarrow** N Schubkarre f; **hand basin** N Handwaschbecken nt; **handbell** N Schelle f, Glocke f (mit Stiel); **handbill** N Flugblatt nt, Handzettel m; **handbook** N Handbuch nt; (tourist's) Reiseführer m; **handbrake** N (esp Brit) Handbremse f; **handbrake turn** N (Aut) **to do a ~** durch Anziehen der Handbremse wenden; **handbreadth** N Handbreit f

h & c abbr of **hot and cold (water)** k.u.w., kalt und warm

hand: handcar N (Rail) Draisine f, Dräsine f; **handcart** N Handwagen m; **handclasp** N (US) Händedruck m; **hand controls** PL (Aut) Handbedienung f; **handcuff** VT Handschellen anlegen (+dat); **he ~ed himself to the railings** er machte sich mit Handschellen am Geländer fest; **to be ~ed** Handschellen angelegt bekommen; **the accused was ~ed to a police officer** der Angeklagte war (mit Handschellen) an einen Polizisten gefesselt; **handcuffs** PL Handschellen pl; **handdrier** N Händetrockner m

-hander [-hændə] SUFF (esp Brit: Theat, TV) **a two-/three-hander** ein Zwei-/Dreipersonenstück nt

hand-eye coordination [ˈhændaɪkəʊˌɔːdɪˈneɪʃən] N visuell-motorische Koordination f

handfeed [ˈhændˌfiːd] pret, ptp **handfed** [ˈhændˌfed] VT animal mit der Flasche aufziehen

handful [ˈhændfʊl] N **a** Hand f voll; (of hair, fur) Büschel nt; **a ~ of soil** eine Hand voll Erde; **by the ~, in ~s** händeweise; (hair, fur) büschelweise **b** (= small number) Hand f voll **c** (fig) **those children are a ~** die Kinder können einen ganz schön in Trab halten; **his new girl's quite a ~** (hum) an seiner neuen Freundin ist ganz hübsch was dran (inf)

hand: hand grenade N Handgranate f; **handgrip** N (Hand)griff m; (= handshake) Händedruck m; **handgun** N Handfeuerwaffe f; **hand-held** ADJ device, computer im Taschenformat; **taken with a ~ camera** aus der (freien) Hand aufgenommen; **handhold** N Halt m

handicap [ˈhændɪkæp] N **a** (Sport) Handicap nt, Handikap nt, Vorgabe f; (= race) Handicaprennen nt; **a ~ of 5lbs** eine (Gewichts)vorgabe or ein Handikap von 5 Pfund **b** (= disadvantage) Handikap nt; (physical, mental) Behinderung f; **to be under a great ~** sehr im Nachteil sein, stark gehandikapt sein VT ein Handikap nt darstellen für; chances beeinträchtigen; (fig) person benachteiligen; **he has always been ~ped by his accent** sein Akzent war immer ein Nachteil m für ihn; **to be (physically/mentally) ~ped** (körperlich/geistig) behindert sein; **~ped children** behinderte Kinder pl

handicraft [ˈhændɪkrɑːft] N **a** (= work) Kunsthandwerk nt; (= needlework etc) Handarbeit f; (= woodwork, modelling etc) Werken nt, Bastelarbeit f; **~s** (= products) Kunstgewerbe nt **b** (= skill) Geschick nt, Handfertigkeit f, Geschicklichkeit f

handily [ˈhændɪlɪ] ADV **a** situated günstig **b** (US, = easily) win mit Leichtigkeit

handiness [ˈhændɪnɪs] N **a** (= skill) Geschick nt, Geschicklichkeit f **b** (= nearness, accessibility: of shops etc) günstige Lage **c** (= convenience, usefulness: of tool, car etc) Nützlichkeit f; (= easiness to handle) Handlichkeit f

handiwork [ˈhændɪwɜːk] N , no pl **a** (lit) Arbeit f; (Sch: = subject) Werken nt; (= needlework etc) Handarbeit f; **examples of the children's ~** Werkarbeiten/Handarbeiten pl der Kinder; **to do ~** werken, handarbeiten; (at home) basteln **b** (fig) Werk nt; (pej) Machwerk nt; **that looks like the ~ of the Gillies gang** das sieht ganz nach der Gillies-Bande aus

handjob [ˈhændʒɒb] N (vulg sl) **to give sb a ~** jdm einen runterholen (vulg sl)

handkerchief [ˈhæŋkətʃɪf] N Taschentuch nt

hand-knitted [ˈhændˌnɪtɪd] ADJ handgestrickt

handle [ˈhændl] N **a** Griff m; (of door) Klinke f, Griff m; (esp of broom, saucepan) Stiel m; (esp of basket, bucket, casserole, cup, jug etc) Henkel m; (of handbag) Griff m, Bügel m; (of pump) Schwengel m; (of car: = starting handle) (Anlass- or Start)kurbel f; **to fly off the ~** (inf) an die Decke gehen (inf); **to have/get a ~ on sth** (inf) etw im Griff haben/in den Griff bekommen
b (fig, = pretext) Handhabe f
c (inf) Titel m; **to have a ~ to one's name** ein „von und zu" sein (inf)
VT **a** (= touch, use hands on) anfassen, berühren; (Ftbl) ball mit der Hand berühren; **be careful how you ~ that** gehen Sie vorsichtig damit

um; **please do not ~ the goods** Waren bitte nicht berühren; **"handle with care"** „Vorsicht - zerbrechlich"; „Vorsicht Glas/Blumen" *etc*

b (= *deal with*) *person, animal, plant, tool, weapon, machine, words, numbers, money etc* umgehen mit; *economy* handhaben; *legal or financial matters* erledigen; *legal case* handhaben, bearbeiten; *applicant, matter, problem* sich befassen mit; *material for essay etc* bearbeiten, verarbeiten; (= *tackle*) *problem, interview etc* anfassen, anpacken; (= *succeed in coping with*) *child, drunk, situation, problem, emergency* fertig werden mit; (= *resolve*) *matter* erledigen; (= *control*) *vehicle, plane, ship* steuern; **how would you ~ the situation?** wie würden Sie sich in der Situation verhalten?; **you have to ~ this situation very carefully** in dieser Situation müssen Sie sehr behutsam vorgehen; **you didn't ~ the situation very well** du bist mit der Situation nicht gut fertig geworden; **you have to ~ these people very carefully** Sie müssen mit diesen Leuten sehr vorsichtig umgehen; **a car that is easy to ~** ein Auto, das leicht zu fahren *or* zu steuern ist; **I can't ~ pressure** ich komme unter Druck nicht zurecht; **six children are too much for one woman to ~** mit sechs Kindern kann eine Frau allein nicht fertig werden; **there's a salesman at the door – I'll ~ him** ein Vertreter ist an der Tür – ich werde ihn abfertigen; **you keep quiet, I'll ~ this** sei still, lass mich mal machen; **the accused decided to ~ his own defence** (*Brit*) *or* **defense** (*US*) der Angeklagte beschloss, seine eigene Verteidigung zu übernehmen; **who's handling the publicity for this?** wer macht die Öffentlichkeitsarbeit dafür?; **could you ~ these interviews for me?** könnten Sie diese Interviews für mich machen?

c (*Comm*) *types of goods, items* handeln mit *or* in (+*dat*); *orders* bearbeiten; *prescriptions* ausführen; *shares, securities* handeln; *financial affairs* besorgen; **airport workers refused to ~ goods for Uganda** die Flughafenarbeiter weigerten sich, Waren nach Uganda abzufertigen; **we ~ tax problems for several big companies** wir bearbeiten die Steuerangelegenheiten mehrerer großer Firmen; **the millionaire has several secretaries to ~ his business** der Millionär hat mehrere Sekretäre, die seine Geschäfte für ihn führen; **this department ~s all the export business** diese Abteilung bearbeitet den gesamten Export

VI (*ship, plane*) sich steuern lassen; (*car, motorbike*) sich fahren *or* lenken lassen; (*gun*) sich handhaben lassen; **how does the car ~?** wie fährt sich der Wagen?

VR he ~s himself well in a fight er kann sich in einer Schlägerei behaupten; **they observed how the applicant ~d himself** sie beobachteten, wie der Bewerber sich verhielt

handlebar moustache N Schnauzbart *m*, Schnäuzer *m* (*inf*)

handlebar(s) ['hændlbɑːʳ, -bɑːz] N(PL) Lenkstange *f*

handler ['hændləʳ] N (= *dog-handler*) Hundeführer(in) *m(f)*; **baggage ~** Gepäckmann *m*

handling ['hændlɪŋ] N **a** (= *touching*) Berühren *nt*

b (*of plant, animal, matter, problem*) Behandlung *f* (*of* +*gen*); (*of person, patient etc*) Umgang *m* (*of* mit), Behandlung *f* (*of* +*gen*); (*of vehicle, plane, ship, drug, explosive*) Umgang *m* (*of* mit); (*of tool, weapon, machine*) Umgang *m* (*of* mit), Handhabung *f*; (*of writer's material*) Verarbeitung *f*, Bearbeitung *f*; (*of legal or financial matters*) Erledigung *f*; (= *official handling of matters, of legal case*) Bearbeitung *f*; **his adroit ~ of the car/troops** sein geschickter Umgang mit dem Auto/den Truppen; **her adroit ~ of the economy** ihre geschickte Handhabung der Wirtschaft; **the policeman's tactful ~ of the drunk/crowd** das taktvolle Verhalten des Polizisten gegenüber dem Betrunkenen/der Menge; **his ~ of the matter/situation** die Art, wie er die Angelegenheit/die Situation angefasst hat; **his successful ~ of the crisis/task** seine Bewältigung der Krise/der Aufgabe; **his expert ~ of the deal** sein Ge-

schick beim Abschluss des Geschäfts; **toxic waste requires very careful ~** mit Giftmüll muss sehr vorsichtig umgegangen werden; **this package needs careful ~** dieses Paket muss vorsichtig behandelt werden; **these goods were damaged in ~** (*Comm*) diese Waren wurden beschädigt

c (*of vehicle*) **what's its ~ like?** wie fährt es sich?; **a car not renowned for its easy ~** ein Auto, das sich nicht gerade durch leichte Lenkung auszeichnet

handling charge N (= *management fee*) Bearbeitungsgebühr *f*; (*in warehouse*) Umladekosten *pl*; (*in banking*) Kontoführungsgebühren *pl*

hand: hand loom N Handwebstuhl *m*; **hand-loom weaver** Handweber(in) *m(f)*; **hand-loom weaving** Handweben *nt*; **hand lotion** N Handlotion *f*; **hand luggage** N (*Brit*) Handgepäck *nt*; **handmade** ADJ handgearbeitet; **this is ~** das ist Handarbeit; **handmaid** N (*obs*) Zofe *f* (*old*); (*Bibl*) Magd *f*; **hand-me-down** (*inf*) **N** abgelegtes Kleidungsstück **ADJ** *clothes* abgelegt; *piano, books* geerbt (*hum*); **hand mirror** N Handspiegel *m*; **hand-off** N (*Rugby*) Wegstoß(en *nt*) *m* (mit der Hand); **hand-operated** ADJ von Hand bedient *or* betätigt, handbedient, handbetrieben; **hand-out** N (= *money*) Unterstützung *f*, (Geld)zuwendung *f*; (= *food*) Essensspende *f*; (= *leaflet*) Flugblatt *nt*; (*with several pages*) Broschüre *f*; (*in school*) Arbeitsblatt *nt*; (= *publicity hand-out*) Reklamezettel *m*; **budget ~** Zuwendung *f or* Geschenk *nt* aus dem Etat; **handover** N (*Pol*) Übergabe *f*; **~ of power** Machtübergabe *f*; **hand-picked** ADJ (*lit*) von Hand geerntet, handverlesen; (*fig*) *successor, team, staff* sorgfältig ausgewählt, handverlesen (*hum*); **hand puppet** N (*US*) = **glove puppet**; **handrail** N (*of stairs etc*) Geländer *nt*; (*of ship*) Reling *f*; (*for bath etc*) Haltegriff *m*; **handsaw** N Handsäge *f*, Fuchsschwanz *m*; **handset** **N** (*Telec*) Hörer *m* **VT** (*Typ*) (von Hand) setzen

hands-free ['hændz'friː] ADJ *telephone etc* handfrei, Freisprech-; **~ kit** Freisprechset *nt or* -anlage *f*

handshake ['hændʃeɪk] N **a** Händedruck *m*

b (*Comput*) Handshake *m*, Quittungsaustausch *m*

handshaking ['hændʃeɪkɪŋ] N Händeschütteln *nt*

hands-off ['hændz'ɒf] ADJ *approach etc* passiv; **a ~ manager** ein Geschäftsführer, der die Zügel gern locker lässt; **they have a ~ policy/attitude** sie lassen die Zügel gern locker

handsome ['hænsəm] ADJ **a** (= *good-looking*) *man, woman* gut aussehend; (= *well-built*) stattlich; *face, features* attraktiv; *animal, building, place, furniture* schön; (= *elegant*) elegant; (= *imposing*) stattlich, imposant; **he is ~/has a ~ face** er sieht gut aus; **~ is as ~ does** (*Prov*) edel ist, wer edel handelt **b** (= *large*) *profit, return, increase, salary* ansehnlich; *reward* großzügig; *sum* stolz, stattlich; *win, victory* deutlich, entscheidend; **a ~ 57 per cent** ansehnliche 57 Prozent; **to win a ~ victory** überlegen gewinnen

handsomely ['hænsəmlɪ] ADV **a** (= *attractively*) *produced, bound, printed, dressed* schön **b** (= *generously*) *pay* großzügig; *reward, profit* reichlich; (= *convincingly*) *win* überlegen; **this strategy has paid off ~** diese Strategie hat sich voll ausgezahlt

handsomeness ['hænsəmnɪs] N **a** (= *good looks*) gutes Aussehen; (*of animal, thing*) Schönheit *f*; (= *elegance*) Eleganz *f*; (= *imposing nature*) Stattlichkeit *f* **b** (= *generosity, of profit, return, increase, salary*) Ansehnlichkeit *f*; (*of reward*) Großzügigkeit *f*

hands-on ['hændz'ɒn] ADJ *experience, approach etc* aktiv; *exhibit* interaktiv; **a ~ manager** ein Geschäftsführer, der die Zügel gern fest in der Hand hält; **they have a ~ policy/attitude** sie halten die Zügel fest in der Hand

hand: handspring N (Handstand)überschlag *m*; **handstand** N Handstand *m*; **to do a ~** (ei-

nen) Handstand machen; **hand-stitched** ADJ handgenäht; **hand-to-hand** ADV im Nahkampf, Mann gegen Mann **ADJ** **~ fight/fighting** Nahkampf *m*; **hand-to-mouth** ADJ *existence* kümmerlich, armselig; **to lead a ~ existence, to exist on a ~ basis** von der Hand in den Mund leben; **hand towel** N Händehandtuch *nt*; **handwork** N Handarbeit *f*; **hand-woven** ADJ handgewebt; **handwriting** N Handschrift *f*; **handwritten** ADJ handgeschrieben, von Hand geschrieben

handy ['hændɪ] ADJ (+*er*) **a** (= *useful, convenient*) *tool, device* praktisch; *hint, tip* nützlich, praktisch; *car, size* handlich; **to come in ~** sich als nützlich erweisen; **that key will come in ~** den Schlüssel wirst du noch gut gebrauchen können; **the salary increase comes in ~** die Gehaltserhöhung kommt sehr gelegen; **my experience as a teacher comes in ~** meine Lehrerfahrung kommt mir zugute; **a ~ way to do sth** eine praktische Art, etw zu tun; **this is a ~ way to take notes** auf diese Art kann man leicht *or* gut Notizen machen

b (= *skilful*) geschickt; **he's ~ around the home** *or* **house** er ist ein geschickter Heimwerker; **to be ~ with a tool** mit einem Werkzeug gut umgehen können

c (= *conveniently close*) in der Nähe; **the house is (very) ~ for the shops** das Haus liegt (ganz) in der Nähe der Geschäfte; **to keep** *or* **have sth ~** etw griffbereit *or* zur Hand haben

handyman ['hændɪmæn] N *pl* **-men** [-mən] (= *servant*) Hausknecht *m*, Mädchen *nt* für alles (*inf*); (= *in DIY*) Bastler *m*, Heimwerker *m*; (*as job*) Hilfskraft *f*; **I'm not much of a ~** ich bin kein großer Bastler, Basteln ist nicht gerade meine Stärke

handywoman ['hændɪwʊmən] N *pl* **-women** [-wɪmɪn] (*in DIY*) Bastlerin *f*, Heimwerkerin *f*; (*as job*) Hilfskraft *f*

hang [hæŋ] *vb*: pret, ptp **hung** **VT** **a** hängen; *painting, curtains, decorations, clothes* aufhängen; *door, gate* einhängen; (*Cook*) *game* abhängen lassen; **to ~ wallpaper** tapezieren; **to ~ sth from sth** etw an etw (*dat*) aufhängen; **to ~ sth on a hook** etw an einen Haken hängen; **to ~ clothes on the line** Wäsche auf die Leine hängen

b **the rooms of the castle were hung with priceless pictures** kostbare Gemälde hingen in den Räumen des Schlosses; **the walls were hung with tapestries** die Wände waren mit Gobelins behängt; **they hung the windows/streets with bunting** sie schmückten die Fenster/Straßen mit Fahnen

c **to ~ one's head** den Kopf hängen lassen

d **to ~ fire** (*lit: guns*) das Feuer einstellen; (*fig, people*) zögern; **I think we should ~ fire a little longer** (*fig*) ich glaube, wir sollten noch etwas (zu)warten

e pret, ptp **hanged** *criminal* hängen, aufhängen, henken (*form*); **hung, drawn and quartered** gehängt, gestreckt und geviertelt; **to ~ oneself** sich erhängen *or* aufhängen

f (*inf*) **~ him!** zum Kuckuck mit ihm (*inf*); **(I'm) ~ed if I will …** den Teufel werd ich … (*inf*); **(I'm) ~ed if I know** weiß der Henker (*inf*); **~ it!** so ein Mist (*inf*), verflixt (noch mal) (*inf*); **~ the cost!** ist doch piepegal, was es kostet (*inf*)

VI **a** (*curtains, painting*) hängen (*on an* +*dat*, *from* von); (*drapery, clothes, hair*) fallen; (*inelegantly*) (herunter)hängen; (*pheasant etc*) abhängen

b (*gloom, fog etc*) hängen (*over* über +*dat*); **to ~ in the air** (*fig*) in der Schwebe sein; **the question was left ~ing in the air** die Frage blieb im Raum stehen; **the hawk hung motionless in the sky** der Falke stand bewegungslos in der Luft; **time ~s heavy on my hands** die Zeit wird mir sehr lang; **the constant threat of unemployment ~s over us** *or* **our heads** über uns hängt die ständige Angst vor der Arbeitslosigkeit › *also* **balance** N **a**

c (*criminal*) gehängt werden, hängen; **to be sentenced to ~** zum Tod durch Erhängen verurteilt werden

d it/he can go ~! (*inf*) es/er kann mir gestohlen bleiben (*inf*)

N a (*of drapery*) Fall *m*; (*of suit*) Sitz *m*

b no pl (*inf*) **to get the ~ of sth** den (richtigen) Dreh bei etw herauskriegen *or* -finden (*inf*); **to get the ~ of doing sth** den Dreh herausbekommen, wie man etw macht (*inf*)

▶ **hang about** (*Brit*) *or* **around** **VI a** (*inf*, = *wait*) warten; (= *loiter*) sich herumtreiben (*inf*), herumlungern; **to keep sb hanging about** jdn warten lassen; **to hang around with sb** sich mit jdm herumtreiben (*inf*); **he got sick of hanging around waiting for me** er hatte die Nase voll davon, auf mich zu warten (*inf*)

b (*Brit, inf*, = *hold on*) warten; **hang about, I'm just coming** wart mal, ich komm ja schon; **now hang about, I didn't say that** Moment mal, das habe ich nicht gesagt (*inf*)

c (*inf*) **this car doesn't hang around** das Auto zieht ganz schön ab (*inf*); **he doesn't hang around** (= *move quickly*) er ist einer von der schnellen Truppe (*inf*)

VI +*prep obj* **to hang around sb** um jdn herumstreichen; **to hang around a place** sich an einem Ort herumtreiben (*inf*), an einem Ort herumlungern

▶ **hang back** VI (*lit*) sich zurückhalten; (*fig*, = *hesitate*) zögern; **one little boy was hanging back** ein kleiner Junge hielt sich immer im Hintergrund; **don't hang back, go and ask her** worauf wartest du denn, frag sie doch; **they hung back on closing the deal** sie zögerten, das Geschäft abzuschließen

▶ **hang behind** VI zurückbleiben; (= *dawdle*) (hinter)herbummeln *or* -trödeln

▶ **hang down** **VI** herunterhängen; **VT** *sep* herunterhängen lassen

▶ **hang in** VI (*inf*) **just hang in there!** bleib am Ball (*inf*)

▶ **hang on** **VI a** (= *hold*) sich festhalten, sich festklammern (*to sth* an etw *dat*); **to hang on by one's fingernails** *or* **fingertips (to sth)** (an etw *dat*) festkrallen

b (= *hold out*) durchhalten; (*Telec*) am Apparat bleiben; (*inf*, = *wait*) warten; **hang on (a minute)** wart mal, einen Augenblick (mal); **hang on tight, we're off!** festhalten, es geht los!; **Liverpool hung on to win the match** Liverpool konnte seine Führung verteidigen und gewann das Spiel

VI +*prep obj* **a** **to hang on sb's arm** an jds Arm (*dat*) hängen; **he hangs on her every word** er hängt an ihren Lippen

b (= *depend on*) **everything hangs on his decision/getting the cash** alles hängt von seiner Entscheidung ab/davon ab, ob man das Geld bekommt

▶ **hang on to** VI +*prep obj* **a** (*lit*, = *hold on to*) festhalten; (*fig*) hope sich klammern an (+*acc*); *ideas* festhalten an (+*dat*); **b** (= *keep*) behalten; **to hang on to power** sich an die Macht klammern; **to hang on to one's lead** seine Führung verteidigen; **could you hang on to my seat until I get back?** können Sie mir den Platz so lange freihalten, bis ich zurück bin?

▶ **hang out** **VI a** (*tongue, shirt tails etc*) heraushängen **b** (*inf*) sich aufhalten; (= *live*) hausen, wohnen; (= *usually be found also*) sich herumtreiben (*inf*), zu finden sein **c** (= *resist, endure*) nicht aufgeben; **they hung out for more pay** sie hielten an ihrer Lohnforderung fest **d** (*inf*) **to let it all hang out** die Sau rauslassen (*inf*); **come on now, let it all hang out** lass jucken (*sl*), und ab geht die Post (*inf*) **VT** *sep* hinaushängen; *washing also* (draußen) aufhängen; **to hang sb out to dry** (*inf*) jdn seinem Schicksal überlassen

▶ **hang over** VI (= *continue*) andauern

▶ **hang together** VI (*people*) zusammenhalten; (*argument, ideas*) folgerichtig *or* zusammenhängend sein; (*alibi*) keinen Widerspruch aufweisen *or* enthalten; (*story, report etc*) zusammenhängen; (*statements*) zusammenpassen, keine Widersprüche *pl* aufweisen

▶ **hang up** **VI** (*Telec*) auflegen, aufhängen; **he hung up on me** er legte einfach auf **VT** *sep hat*, *picture* aufhängen; *telephone receiver* auflegen, aufhängen; **Keegan announced he was hanging up his boots for good** Keegan erklärte, dass er die Fußballschuhe an den Nagel hängen würde → **hung-up**

▶ **hang upon** VI +*prep obj* = **hang on** VI +*prep obj* **b**

hangar ['hæŋə'] N Hangar *m*, Flugzeughalle *f*

hangdog ['hæŋdɒg] ADJ look, expression (= *abject*) niedergeschlagen, trübsinnig; (= *ashamed*) zerknirscht

hanger ['hæŋə'] N (*for clothes*) (Kleider)bügel *m*; (= *loop on garment*) Aufhänger *m*

hanger-on [ˌhæŋər'ɒn] N *pl* **hangers-on** (*to celebrity*) Trabant *m*, Satellit *m*; **the film crew turned up with all its hangers-on** die Filmmannschaft erschien mit ihrem ganzen Anhang; **the celebrity was accompanied by his usual crowd of hangers-on** die Berühmtheit kam mit den üblichen Schwarm von Gefolgsleuten

hang: hang-glide VI Drachen fliegen; **hang-glider** N (= *device*) Drachen *m*; (= *person*) Drachenflieger(in) *m(f)*; **hang-gliding** N Drachenfliegen *nt*

hanging ['hæŋɪŋ] **N a** (*of criminal*) Tod *m* durch den Strang, Erhängen *nt*; (= *event*) Hinrichtung *f* (durch den Strang); **he deserves ~** er sollte aufgehängt werden; **to bring back ~** die Todesstrafe wieder einführen **b** (*of wallpaper*) Anbringen *nt*, Kleben *nt*; (*of door*) Einhängen *nt*; (*of pictures*) (Auf)hängen *nt*; **wallpaper ~** Tapezieren *nt* **c** **hangings** PL (= *curtains etc*) Vorhänge *pl*; (*on wall*) Tapete *f*; (= *tapestry*) Wandbehang *m or* -behänge *pl*; **bed ~s** Vorhänge *pl* des Himmelbetts **ADJ** *attr* **a** hängend; **the ~ gardens of Babylon** die Hängenden Gärten der Semiramis **b** **it's a ~ matter** darauf steht der Galgen

hanging: hanging basket N Blumen- *or* Hängeampel *f*; **hanging bridge** N Hängebrücke *f*; **hanging committee** N (*Art*) Hängekommission *f*; **hanging judge** N Richter, der (zu) leicht das Todesurteil fällt

hang: hangman N Henker *m*; (= *game*) Galgen *m*; **hangnail** N Niednagel *m*; **hang-out** N (*inf*, = *place where one lives*) Bude *f* (*inf*); (= *pub*, *café etc*) Stammlokal *nt*; (= *group*) Treff *m* (*inf*); **this club is his usual ~** er hängt für gewöhnlich in diesem Klub herum (*inf*); **hangover** N **a** Kater *m* (*inf*) **b** (= *sth left over*) Überbleibsel *nt*

Hang Seng Index [ˌhæŋsen'ɪndeks] N Hang-Seng-Index *m*

hang-up ['hæŋʌp] N (*inf*) Komplex *m* (*about* wegen); (= *obsession*) Fimmel *m* (*inf*); **he has a ~ about people smoking** er stellt sich furchtbar an, wenn Leute rauchen (*inf*)

hank [hæŋk] N (*of wool etc*) Strang *m*; (*of hair*, *fur*) Büschel *nt*

hanker ['hæŋkə'] VI sich sehnen, Verlangen haben (*for or after sth* nach etw)

hankering ['hæŋkərɪŋ] N Verlangen *nt*, Sehnsucht *f*; **to have a ~ for sth** Verlangen *or* Sehnsucht nach etw haben; **I've always had a ~ to be an actress** ich wollte schon immer Schauspielerin werden

hankie, hanky ['hæŋkɪ] N (*inf*) Taschentuch *nt*

hanky-panky [ˌhæŋkɪ'pæŋkɪ] N (*inf*) **a** (*esp US*: = *dishonest dealings*) Mauscheleien *pl* (*inf*), Tricks *pl* (*inf*); **there's some ~ going on** hier ist was faul (*inf*) **b** (= *love affair*) Techtelmechtel *nt* (*inf*); **c** (*esp Brit*: = *intimate behaviour*) Gefummel *nt* (*inf*); **they were having a bit of ~ on the settee** sie haben auf dem Sofa ein bisschen gefummelt (*inf*)

Hanover ['hænəʊvə'] N Hannover *nt*

Hanoverian [ˌhænəʊ'vɪərɪən] **ADJ** hannover(i)sch; **the ~ dynasty** das Haus Hannover **N** Hannoveraner(in) *m(f)*

Hansard ['hænsɑːd] N der Hansard, die britischen Parlamentsberichte

Hanseatic [ˌhænzɪ'ætɪk] ADJ hanseatisch; **~ town/port** Hansestadt *f*

Hanseatic League N Hanse *f*, Hansebund *m*

hansom ['hænsəm] N (zweirädriger) Einspänner, Hansom *m*

Hants [hænts] *abbr of* **Hampshire**

hap [hæp] VI (*obs*) = **happen**[1]

ha'pence ['heɪpəns] N (*Brit, old*) halber Penny

haphazard [ˌhæp'hæzəd] ADJ willkürlich, planlos; **the whole thing was very ~** das Ganze war ziemlich zufällig *or* planlos; **nothing is ~ in the universe** im Universum bleibt nichts dem Zufall überlassen; **in a ~ way** *or* **fashion** planlos, wahllos

haphazardly [hæp'hæzədlɪ] ADV wahllos, (ganz) willkürlich, planlos; **decisions are made ~** Entscheidungen werden willkürlich *or* aufs Geratewohl *or* auf gut Glück getroffen; **a ~ organized reception** ein völlig ungeplanter Empfang

hapless ['hæplɪs] ADJ glücklos; **yet another misfortune in the life of this ~ man** noch ein Unglück im Leben dieses vom Pech verfolgten Menschen

ha'p'orth ['heɪpəθ] N *contr of* **halfpennyworth a ~ of sweets** Bonbons für einen halben Penny; **to spoil the ship for a ~ of tar** (*Prov*) am falschen Ende sparen

happen[1] ['hæpən] **VI a** (= *occur*) geschehen; (*somewhat special or important event*) sich ereignen; (*esp unexpected, unintentional or unpleasant event*) passieren, geschehen; (*process also*) vor sich gehen, geschehen; **it ~ed like this ...** es geschah *or* war so ...; **nothing ever ~s here** hier ereignet sich *or* geschieht *or* passiert (doch) überhaupt nie etwas; **this interview/conversation never ~ed** dieses Interview/Gespräch hat nicht stattgefunden; **it's all ~ing here today** heute ist hier ganz schön was los (*inf*); **what's ~ing?** was läuft? (*inf*); **you can't just let things ~** du kannst die Dinge nicht einfach laufen lassen; **it's broken, how did it ~?** es ist kaputt, wie ist denn das passiert?; **it just ~ed** es ist (ganz) von allein passiert *or* gekommen; **as if nothing had ~ed** als ob nichts geschehen *or* gewesen wäre; **worse things have ~ed** es ist schon Schlimmeres passiert *or* vorgekommen; **don't let it ~ again** dass das nicht noch mal vorkommt *or* passiert!; **these things ~ so** was kommt (schon mal) vor; **what has ~ed to him?** (= *what have they done to him*) was ist mit ihm passiert *or* geschehen?; (= *what's wrong with him*) was ist mit ihm los?; (= *what has become of him*) was ist aus ihm geworden?; **what's ~ed to your leg?** was ist mit deinem Bein los *or* passiert?; **if anything should ~ to me** wenn mir etwas zustoßen *or* passieren sollte; **you're the best thing that's ever ~ed to me** du bist der größte Glücksfall in meinem Leben; **it all ~ed so quickly** es ging alles so schnell

b (= *chance*) **how does it ~ that ...?** (*cause*) wie kommt es, dass ...?; (*possibility*) wie ist es möglich, dass ...?; **it might ~ that you will be asked such a question** es könnte passieren *or* sein, dass Ihnen solch eine Frage gestellt wird; **to ~ to do sth** zufällig(erweise) etw tun; **we ~ed to discover we had a friend in common** wir stellten durch Zufall fest, dass wir einen gemeinsamen Bekannten hatten; **do you ~ to know whether ...?** wissen Sie vielleicht *or* zufällig, ob ...?; **I ~ to know it's true** ich weiß zufällig(erweise), dass es stimmt; **I just ~ed to come along when ...** ich kam zufällig (gerade) vorbei, als ...; **he ~ed to see me just as I ...** muss er mich doch gerade in dem Augenblick sehen, als ich ...; **I picked up the nearest paper, which ~ed to be the Daily Mail** ich nahm die erstbeste Zeitung zur Hand, es war zufällig die Daily Mail; **it so ~s** *or* **as it ~s I (don't) like that kind of thing** so etwas mag ich nun einmal (nicht); **as it ~s I've been there too/I'm going there today** zufällig(erweise) bin ich auch dort gewesen/gehe ich heute (dort)hin; **you don't want to come, do you? – it so ~s, I do** du möchtest doch sicher nicht kommen, oder? – doch, natürlich

▶ **happen along** VI zufällig (an)kommen

▶ **happen (up)on** VI +prep obj zufällig stoßen auf (+acc); person zufällig treffen or sehen

happen² ['æpn] ADV (N Engl, inf: = perhaps) vielleicht

happening ['hæpnɪŋ] N **a** Ereignis nt; (not planned) Vorfall m; **there have been some strange ~s in that house** in dem Haus sind sonderbare Dinge vorgegangen **b** (Theat) Happening nt

happenstance ['hæpənstæns] N (inf) Zufall m; **by ~** durch Zufall, zufällig

happily ['hæpɪlɪ] ADV **a** glücklich; say, play vergnügt, fröhlich; **it all ended ~** es ging alles gut or glücklich aus; **a ~ married man** ein glücklich verheirateter Mann; **they lived ~ ever after** (in fairy tales) und wenn sie nicht gestorben sind, dann leben sie noch heute; **his dream was to get married and live ~ ever after** sein Wunschtraum war, zu heiraten und dann glücklich und zufrieden zu leben **b** (= harmoniously) live together, combine harmonisch; **these plants grow ~ in any good soil** diese Pflanzen wachsen gut or problemlos in allen guten Böden **c** (= gladly) gern; **I would ~ have lent her the money** ich hätte ihr das Geld ohne weiteres geliehen **d** (= fortunately) glücklicherweise, zum Glück; **~ for him, he can afford it** zu seinem Glück kann er es sich leisten **e** (= felicitously) glücklich, treffend; **~ worded/chosen** glücklich formuliert/gewählt

happiness ['hæpɪnɪs] N Glück nt; (= feeling of contentment) Zufriedenheit f; (= cheerfulness) Heiterkeit f, Fröhlichkeit f; **the ~ of his expression** sein glücklicher or freudiger Gesichtsausdruck

happy ['hæpɪ] ✿ 3.1, 3.2, 14, 23.2, 23.3, 24.1, 24.2, 24.3, 25.2 ADJ (+er) **a** (= joyful, glad) person, smile, expression, time, life, home, marriage glücklich; atmosphere harmonisch; **the ~ couple** (= newlyweds) das Brautpaar; **a ~ feeling** ein Glücksgefühl nt; **that gives me a ~ feeling** das macht mich glücklich; **to make sb ~** jdn glücklich machen; **they were having such a ~ time** sie hatten so viel Spaß; **the school is a ~ place, it's a ~ school** an der Schule sind die Kinder glücklich; **a ~ atmosphere for their children** eine glückliche Umgebung für ihre Kinder; **a ~ ending** ein guter or glücklicher Ausgang, ein Happyend nt, ein Happy End nt; **~ birthday (to you)** herzlichen Glückwunsch zum Geburtstag; **Happy Easter/Christmas** frohe Ostern/Weihnachten → **return** N **a** **b** (= content, satisfied) (not) **to be ~ about** or **with sth** mit etw (nicht) zufrieden sein; **to be ~ to do sth** (= willing) etw gern tun; (= pleased) sich freuen, etw zu tun; (= relieved) froh sein, etw zu tun; **that's a risk I'm ~ to take** dieses Risiko gehe ich gern ein; **I was ~ to hear that you passed your exam** es hat mich gefreut zu hören, dass du die Prüfung bestanden hast; **I'm just ~ to be back** ich bin einfach nur froh, wieder da zu sein; **to be ~ to let sb do sth** damit einverstanden sein, dass jd etw tut; **he's ~ to leave it to me** er überlässt es mir gern **c** (= fortunate, felicitous) chance, coincidence, solution, choice glücklich; **by ~ chance** durch einen glücklichen Zufall **d** (inf, = tipsy) angeheitert, beschwipst (inf)

-happy ADJ suf (inf) **trigger-/strike-happy** schieß-/streikfreudig (inf); **snap-happy** fotowütig (inf)

happy: **happy-clappy** ['hæpɪ'klæpɪ] ADJ (pej inf Rel) service mit Händeklatschen und moderner Musik; **happy event** N (inf) frohes or freudiges Ereignis; **happy families** N sing (Cards) ≈ Quartett nt; **happy-go-lucky** ADJ unbekümmert, sorglos; **I wish you wouldn't be so ~ about things** ich wollte, du wärst bei allem so sorglos or würdest nicht alles so lässig nehmen (inf); **happy hour** N (in pubs etc)

Zeit, in der Getränke zu ermäßigten Preisen angeboten werden; **happy hunting ground** N **a** (Myth) ewige Jagdgründe pl **b** (fig) Paradies nt; **happy medium** N goldener Mittelweg; **to strike a ~** den goldenen Mittelweg finden

hara-kiri [ˌhærə'kɪrɪ] N Harakiri nt

harangue [hə'ræŋ] **N** (= scolding) (Straf)predigt f, Sermon m; (lengthy also) Tirade f; **to give sb a ~** jdm eine (Straf)predigt etc halten **VT** person eine (Straf)predigt or einen Sermon halten (+dat); (at length also) eine Tirade loslassen auf (+acc) (inf); **I don't like being ~d** ich kann es nicht leiden, wenn mir jemand lange Reden hält; **stop haranguing me about how lucky other men's wives are** hör auf, mir dauernd vorzuhalten or mir damit in den Ohren zu liegen (inf), wie gut es die Frauen anderer Männer haben; **he tried to ~ the mob into direct action** er versuchte, den Mob zum direkten Handeln aufzustacheln

harass ['hærəs] VT belästigen; (= mess around) schikanieren; (Mil) the enemy Anschläge verüben auf (+acc), immer wieder überfallen; **don't ~ me** dräng or hetz (inf) mich doch nicht so!; **he sexually ~ed her** er belästigte sie (sexuell); **they eventually ~ed him into resigning** sie setzten ihm so lange zu, bis er schließlich zurücktrat; **the landlord was ~ing me about the rent** der Hauswirt belästigte mich ständig wegen der Miete; **a lot of these people are ~ed by the police** viele dieser Leute werden ständig von der Polizei schikaniert; **a salesman should never seem to ~ a potential customer** ein Vertreter sollte einem potenziellen or potentiellen Kunden gegenüber niemals aufdringlich werden

harassed ['hærəst] ADJ abgespannt, angegriffen, mitgenommen; (= worried) von Sorgen gequält; **a ~ father** ein (viel) geplagter Vater; **she was very ~ that day** an dem Tag wusste sie nicht, wo ihr der Kopf stand; **he wiped his brow in a ~ manner** er wischte sich (dat) gequält die Stirn

harassment ['hærəsmənt] N (= act) Belästigung f, Bedrängung f; (= messing around) Schikanierung f; (= state) Bedrängnis f; (Mil) Kleinkrieg m; **constant ~ of the enemy** ständiger Kleinkrieg gegen den Feind; police **~** Schikane f vonseiten or von Seiten der Polizei; **racial ~** rassistisch motivierte Schikanierung; **sexual ~** sexuelle Belästigung

harbinger ['hɑːbɪndʒə'] N (liter) Herold m (liter), (Vor)bote m/-botin f

harbour, (US) **harbor** ['hɑːbə'] **N** Hafen m **VT** **a** criminal etc beherbergen, Unterschlupf gewähren (+dat); goods (bei sich) aufbewahren **b** suspicions, grudge, doubts, resentment hegen; ambitions, feelings haben; regrets empfinden; **to ~ thoughts of revenge** Rachegedanken hegen **c** (= conceal, contain) dirt **~s germs** Schmutz ist eine Brutstätte für Krankheitserreger; **some sufferers continue to ~ the virus** in manchen Kranken lebt der Virus weiter

harbour, (US) **harbor**: **harbour bar** N Sandbank f vor dem Hafen; **harbour dues** PL Hafengebühr(en) f(pl); **harbour master** N Hafenmeister(in) m(f)

hard [hɑːd] **ADJ** (+er) **a** (= not soft) hart; **as ~ as rocks** or **iron** steinhart; **the ground was baked ~** der Boden war völlig ausgedörrt **b** (= difficult) schwer, schwierig; **this is ~ to do, it is ~ to do** es ist schwer, das zu tun; **stories that are ~ to understand** Geschichten, die schwer verständlich sind; **that is a very ~ question to answer** diese Frage lässt sich nur schwer beantworten; **their prices are ~ to beat** ihre Preise sind kaum zu unterbieten; **she is ~ to please** man kann ihr kaum etwas recht machen; **it's ~ to tell** es lässt sich schwer sagen, es ist schwer zu sagen; **it was ~ to believe** es war kaum zu glauben; **I find it ~ to believe** ich kann es kaum glauben; **she found it ~ to make friends** es fiel ihr schwer, Freunde zu finden; **to do sth the ~ way** etw auf die schwere Art

machen; **I don't see the point in doing it the ~ way** warum soll man es sich schwer machen?; **to play ~ to get** so tun, als sei man nicht interessiert

c (= strenuous, demanding) work, day, week hart, anstrengend; **he leaves all the ~ work to me** die ganze Schwerarbeit überlässt er mir; **it was very ~ work in the shop** die Arbeit in dem Geschäft war sehr anstrengend; **he's ~ work** (inf) er ist ziemlich anstrengend (inf); (= difficult to know or persuade) er ist ein harter Brocken (inf); **getting on with him is ~ work** (inf) es gehört schon etwas dazu, mit ihm auszukommen (inf); **it was ~ work for me not to swear at him** es hat mich große Mühe gekostet, ihn nicht zu beschimpfen; **a ~ worker** ein fleißiger Arbeiter; **to be a ~ worker** sehr fleißig sein; **it was ~ going** man kam nur mühsam voran; **learning Japanese is ~ going** Japanisch zu lernen ist sehr schwierig; **this novel is ~ going** durch diesen Roman muss man sich mühsam durchbeißen; **chatting her up is ~ going** (inf) es ist gar nicht so einfach, sie anzumachen (inf)

d (= forceful) pull, tug, kick kräftig; blow, punch heftig; **to give sb/sth a ~ push** jdm/etw einen harten Stoß versetzen; **to give sth a ~ pull** or **tug** kräftig an etw (dat) ziehen; **it was a ~ blow** or **knock (for** or **to her)** (fig) es war ein schwerer Schlag (für sie); **to take a ~ knock** (fig) schwer angeschlagen werden; **he took a ~ knock** (fig) er musste einen schweren Schlag einstecken

e (= severe, tough) person, look, eyes, smile, voice, life hart; winter, frost streng, hart; **to be ~ on sb** (= cause strain or wear) jdn strapazieren; (person) hart zu or streng mit jdm sein; **to be ~ on sth** (= cause strain or wear) etw strapazieren; (person) etw kritisieren; **the job's a bit ~ on the nerves** die Arbeit ist ziemlich nervenaufreibend; **don't be so ~ on the children** sei nicht so streng mit den Kindern; **to have a ~ time** es schwer or nicht leicht haben; **I had a ~ time finding a job** ich hatte Schwierigkeiten, eine Stelle zu finden; **he had a ~ time of it** er hat es nicht leicht gehabt; (in negotiations, boxing match etc) es hat ihn einen harten Kampf gekostet; (with illness, operation etc) es war eine schwere Zeit für ihn; **to give sb a ~ time** jdm das Leben schwer machen; **~ times** schwere Zeiten pl; **to fall on ~ times** in finanzielle Schwierigkeiten geraten; **there are no ~ feelings between them** sie sind einander nicht böse; **no ~ feelings?** nimm es mir nicht übel; **to be as ~ as nails** knallhart sein (inf) → also **nut a, bargain f**

f (= harsh) light grell; sound hart

g (= real, unquestionable) facts, information gesichert; **~ evidence** schlüssige Beweise pl

ADV **a** (= with effort) work hart, schwer; run, drive sehr schnell; breathe schwer; study, play eifrig; (= carefully) listen, look genau, gut; think scharf, angestrengt; (= strongly, forcefully) push, pull kräftig, fest; laugh, scream, cry, beg sehr; rain, snow stark; blow kräftig; **I've been ~ at work** or **(going) ~ at it** (inf) since 7 this morning ich bin seit heute Morgen um 7 schwer am Werk or schwer dabei (inf); **she works ~ at keeping herself fit** sie gibt sich viel Mühe, sich fit zu halten; **to try ~** sich wirklich Mühe geben; **no matter how ~ I try** ... wie sehr ich mich auch anstrenge, ...; **if you try ~ you can do it** wenn du dich richtig bemühst or anstrengst, kannst du es tun; **you're not trying ~ enough** du strengst dich nicht genügend an; **he tried as ~ as he could** er hat sein Bestes getan or sich nach Kräften bemüht; **he listened ~** (straining to hear) er horchte angestrengt; **you're not thinking ~ enough** du denkst nicht angestrengt genug nach; **think ~er** denk mal ein bisschen besser nach; **she slammed the door ~ behind us** sie knallte die Tür fest hinter uns zu; **it was freezing ~** es herrschte strenger Frost

b (= severely) **to be ~ pushed** or put to do sth es sehr schwer finden, etw zu tun; **to clamp down ~** hart durchgreifen; **it'll go ~ for** or **with him if** ... er wird Schwierigkeiten bekommen, wenn ...; (= it will cost him dear) es kann ihn teuer zu stehen kommen, wenn ...; **to be ~ done**

by übel dran sein; (= *unfairly treated*) ungerecht behandelt sein; **he reckons he's ~ done by having to work on Saturdays** er findet es ungerecht, dass er samstags arbeiten muss; **they are ~ hit by the cuts** sie sind von den Kürzungen schwer getroffen; **she took it very ~** es traf sie sehr *or* schwer, es ging ihr sehr nahe → *also* **hard-pressed**

c (= *as far as possible*) **~ right/left** scharf rechts/ links; **to turn/go ~ round** eine scharfe Kehrtwendung machen; **bear ~ round to your left** halten Sie sich scharf links; **to lock ~ over** voll einschlagen; **~ a-port/a-starboard/astern** *etc* (*Naut*) hart backbord/steuerbord/nach achtern *etc*

d (= *close*) **to follow ~ behind/upon sth** unmittelbar auf etw (*acc*) folgen; **my sister was ~ behind me** meine Schwester war direkt hinter mir; **following ~ upon the opening of the new cinema** kurz nach der Öffnung des neuen Kinos; **~ by (sth)** (*dated*) ganz in der Nähe (von etw) → *also* **heel**[1] **N a**

hard: **hard and fast** ADJ fest; *rules also* bindend, verbindlich; **hardback** ADJ (*also* **hardbacked**) **a** *book* gebunden **b** *chair* mit einer harten Rückenlehne N gebundene Ausgabe; **hardball** N (*US*) **a** (*Baseball*) Hardball *m* **b** (*fig*) **to play ~** rücksichtslos sein *or* vorgehen; **hard-bitten** ADJ *person* abgebrüht; *manager* knallhart (*inf*); **hardboard** N Hartfaser- *or* Pressspanplatte *f*; **hard-boiled** ADJ **a** *egg* hart gekocht **b** (*fig, = shrewd*) gerissen, ausgekocht (*inf*), mit allen Wassern gewaschen (*inf*) **c** (*fig, = unsentimental*) kaltschnäuzig (*inf*) **d** (*fig, = realistic*) *approach, appraisal etc* nüchtern, sachlich; **hard case** N **a** (= *difficult person*) schwieriger Mensch **b** (= *criminal*) Gewohnheitsverbrecher(in) *m(f)* **c** (= *hardship*) Härtefall *m*; **~ Nut** Bargeld *nt*, Bares(nt) *nt* (*inf*); **hard cheese** INTERJ (*Brit, inf*) **= hard lines**; **hard copy** N Ausdruck *m*, Hardcopy *f*; **hard core** N **a** (*for road*) Schotter *m* **b** (*fig*) harter Kern; (= *pornography*) harter Porno (*inf*); **hard-core** ADJ *pornography* hart; **~ film** harter Pornofilm, Hardcoreporno *m* **b** (= *committed*) *members* zum harten Kern gehörend; *support* des harten Kerns; **he's a ~ heroin addict** er kommt vom Heroin nicht mehr los; **hardcore** N (*Mus*) Hardcore *m*; **hard court** N Hartplatz *m*; **hardcover** ADJ, N (*US*) **= hardback** ADJ a N; **hard currency** N harte Währung; **hard disk** N (*Comput*) Festplatte *f*; **hard disk computer** N Festplattencomputer *m*; **hard disk drive** N Festplattenlaufwerk *nt*; **hard drink** N hartes Getränk; **hard-drinking** ADJ stark trinkend; **hard drug** N harte Droge; **hard-earned** ADJ *wages, cash* sauer verdient; *savings* mühsam erspart; *reward* redlich verdient; *victory* hart erkämpft; **hard-edged** ADJ (*fig*) hart, kompromisslos; *reality* hart

harden ['hɑːdn] VT *steel* härten; *body, muscles* kräftigen, stählen (*geh*); *person* (*physically*) abhärten; (*emotionally*) verhärten (*pej*), abstumpfen (*pej*); *clay* hart werden lassen; **this ~ed his attitude** dadurch hat sich seine Haltung verhärtet; **to ~ oneself to sth** (*physically*) sich gegen etw abhärten; (*emotionally*) gegen etw unempfindlich werden; **war had ~ed the soldiers to death and killing** der Krieg hatte die Soldaten gegen den Tod und das Töten abgestumpft; **to ~ one's heart against sb** sein Herz gegen jdn verhärten (*geh*) → **hardened**

VI (*substance*) hart werden; (*fig, attitude*) sich verhärten; (*St Ex, = cease to fluctuate*) sich festigen, sich stabilisieren; (= *rise*) anziehen; **his voice ~ed** seine Stimme wurde hart *or* bekam einen harten Klang; **his eyes/face ~ed** seine Augen bekamen/sein Gesicht bekam einen harten Ausdruck

▶ **harden off** VT sep *plants* widerstandsfähig machen

▶ **harden up** VI (*concrete, glue etc*) hart werden VT sep (= *make hard*) härten, hart machen; (*fig, = toughen*) abhärten

hardened ['hɑːdnd] ADJ *steel* gehärtet; *troops* zäh, abgehärtet; *sinner* verstockt; *attitude* ver-

härtet; *arteries* verkalkt; **~ criminal** Gewohnheitsverbrecher(in) *m(f)*; **to be ~ to the cold/ the climate** gegen die Kälte/das Klima abgehärtet sein; **to be ~ to sb's charms** unempfänglich für jds Charme sein; **to be ~ to death** an den Tod gewöhnt sein; **you become ~ to it after a while** daran gewöhnt man sich mit der Zeit

hardening ['hɑːdnɪŋ] N (*of steel*) (Er)härten *nt*, Härtung *f*; (*fig*) Verhärten *nt*, Verhärtung *f*; (*St Ex*) Versteifung *f*, Festigung *f*; (= *rise*) Anziehen *nt*; **I noticed a ~ of his attitude** ich habe bemerkt, dass sich seine Einstellung verhärtet; **~ of the arteries** Arterienverkalkung *f*

hard: **hard-featured** ADJ *person* mit harten Gesichtszügen; **hard-fought** ADJ *battle, campaign* erbittert; *victory* hart erkämpft; *boxing match, competition, game* hart; **a ~ election** eine (erbitterte) Wahlschlacht; **hard hat** N Schutzhelm *m*; (= *construction worker*) Bauarbeiter(in) *m(f)*; **hard-headed** ADJ nüchtern; **hardhearted** ADJ hartherzig; (*towards sb* jdm gegenüber); **hardheartedness** N Hartherzigkeit *f*; **hard-hitting** ADJ *speech, report* äußerst kritisch

hardihood ['hɑːdɪhʊd] N Kühnheit *f*; (= *courage also*) Mut *m*; (= *audacity also*) Dreistigkeit *f*

hardiness ['hɑːdɪnɪs] N **a** (= *toughness*) Zähigkeit *f*; (= *hardened nature*) Abgehärtetsein *nt*; (*Bot*) Winterhärte *f* **b** (= *courage*) Unerschrockenheit *f*

hard: **hard labour**, (*US*) **hard labor** N Zwangsarbeit *f*; **hard left** N (*Pol*) **the ~** die extreme Linke; **hard lens** N (*Opt*) harte Kontaktlinse *f*; **hard line** N harte Haltung, harte Linie; **to take a ~** eine harte Haltung einnehmen, eine harte Linie verfolgen; **hardline** ADJ kompromisslos; **hardliner** N Vertreter(in) *m(f)* der harten Linie, Hardliner(in) *m(f)* (*esp Pol*); **hard lines** INTERJ (*Brit, inf*) Pech (gehabt)!; **hard liquor** N Schnaps *m*; **hard luck** N (*inf*) Pech *nt* (on für); **~!** Pech gehabt!; **it was very ~ on him** da hat er aber wirklich Pech gehabt; **that's just his ~** das ist sein Pech; **hard-luck story** N Leidensgeschichte *f*

hardly ['hɑːdlɪ] ADV **a** (= *barely*) kaum; **I ~ knew him** ich kannte ihn kaum; **the boy was ~ seventeen** der Junge war kaum *or* keine siebzehn; **I could understand ~ a word** ich konnte kaum ein Wort *or* fast kein Wort verstehen; **~ ever** fast nie; **~ any money** fast kein Geld; **it's worth ~ anything** es ist fast nichts wert; **you've ~ eaten anything** du hast (ja) kaum etwas gegessen; **I ~ know any French** ich kann kaum Französisch *or* fast kein Französisch; **there was ~ anywhere to go** man konnte fast nirgends hingehen; **~ a day goes by when we don't read about murder in the newspaper** es vergeht kaum ein Tag, an dem wir nicht von Mordfällen in der Zeitung lesen; **I can still ~ believe it** ich kann es immer noch kaum glauben; **~ had he uttered the words when he began laughing** er hatte die Worte kaum ausgesprochen, als er anfing zu lachen

b (= *certainly not*) wohl kaum; **I will ~ need to remind you to be polite to your grandmother** ich muss euch wohl kaum daran erinnern, höflich zu eurer Großmutter zu sein; **will she remember? – ~!** wird sie daran denken? – bestimmt nicht!

hardness ['hɑːdnɪs] N **a** Härte *f* **b** (= *difficulty*) Schwere *f*, Schwierigkeit *f*; **~ of hearing** Schwerhörigkeit *f* **c** (= *severity*) Härte *f*; (*of winter, frost*) Strenge *f*; (*of light*) Grelle *f*, Grellheit *f*; **the ~ of his heart** seine Hartherzigkeit

hard: **hard-nosed** ADJ (*inf, = down-to-earth*) nüchtern; (= *tough*) *person, government* abgebrüht (*inf*); *approach, attitude, leadership* rücksichtslos; **hard on** N (*sl*) Ständer *m* (*inf*); **to have a ~** einen stehen *or* einen Ständer haben (*inf*); **hard-packed** ADJ *snow* festgetreten; *sand, earth* festgedrückt; **hardpad** N (*Vet*) Hartballenkrankheit *f*; **hard palate** N (*Anat*) harter Gaumen, Vordergaumen *m*; **hardpan** N (*Geol*) Ortstein *nt*; **hard-pressed** ADJ *consumer, firm, family, troops etc* hart bedrängt; (*with*

work) stark beansprucht; **to be ~ to do sth** es sehr schwer finden, etw zu tun; **to be ~ (for money)** in Geldnot sein, knapp bei Kasse sein (*inf*); **hard right** N (*Pol*) **the ~** die extreme Rechte; **hardrock** N (*Mus*) Hardrock *m*; **hardscrabble** ADJ **a** *circumstances, situation* ärmlich, bescheiden **b** *soil* karg; **hard sell** N aggressive Verkaufstaktik, Hardselling *nt* ATTR aggressiv

hardship ['hɑːdʃɪp] N (= *condition*) Not *f*, Elend *nt*; (= *instance*) Härte *f*; (= *deprivation*) Entbehrung *f*; **economic/financial ~** wirtschaftliche/finanzielle Not; **to suffer great ~s** große Not leiden; **the ~s of war** das Elend/die Entbehrungen des Kriegs; **is that such a great ~?** ist das wirklich ein solches Unglück?; **it was no ~ at all** es hat überhaupt keine Mühe gemacht; **if it's not too much (of a) ~ for you ...** (*also iro*) wenn es dir nichts ausmacht *or* nicht zu viel Mühe macht ...; **the ~(s) of life in the country** die Entbehrungen *pl* des Landlebens

hard: **hard shoulder** N (*Brit*) Seitenstreifen *m*; **hardstanding** N (*Brit: for vehicle*) befestigter Abstellplatz *m*; **hardtack** N Schiffszwieback *m*; **hardtop** N Hardtop *nt or m*

hardware ['hɑːdwɛə'] N **a** Eisenwaren *pl*; (= *household goods*) Haushaltswaren *pl* **b** (*Comput*) Hardware *f* **c** (*Mil*) (Wehr)material *nt* **d** (*US, inf, = gun*) Schießeisen *nt* (*num inf*), Kanone *f* (*sl*) ATTR **a** **~ dealer** Eisenwarenhändler(in) *m(f)*; (*including household goods*) Haushalts- und Eisenwarenhändler(in) *m(f)*; **~ shop** *or* **store** Eisenwarenhandlung *f*; (*including household goods*) Haushalts- und Eisenwarengeschäft *nt* **b** (*Comput*) Hardware-; **~ manufacturer** Hardwarehersteller *m*

hard: **hard-wearing** ADJ widerstandsfähig; *cloth, clothes* strapazierfähig; **hard-wired** ADJ (*Comput*) fest verdrahtet; **hard-won** ADJ hart *or* schwer erkämpft; *expertise* schwer erarbeitet; **hardwood** N Hartholz *nt*; **hard-working** ADJ *person* fleißig; *engine* leistungsfähig

hardy ['hɑːdɪ] ADJ (*+er*) **a** (= *tough, robust*) *person, animal* robust, zäh; (= *hardened*) abgehärtet; (*Bot*) *plant* winterhart **b** (= *bold*) *person* unerschrocken

hardy annual N einjährige winterharte Pflanze

hardy perennial N mehrjährige winterharte Pflanze

hare [hɛə'] N (Feld)hase *m*; **~ and hounds** (= *game*) Schnitzeljagd *f*; **to run with the ~ and hunt with the hounds** (*prov*) es mit niemandem verderben wollen; **to start a ~** (*fig*) vom Thema ablenken → **mad** VI (*Brit inf*) sausen, flitzen (*inf*); **~ off** lossausen *or* -flitzen (*inf*)

hare: **harebell** N Glockenblume *f*; **harebrained** ADJ *person, plan* verrückt, behämmert (*inf*); **harelip** N Hasenscharte *f*

harem [hɑː'riːm] N Harem *m*

haricot ['hærɪkəʊ] N **~ (bean)** Gartenbohne *f*

hark [hɑːk] VI **to ~ to sb** (*liter*) einer Sache (*dat*) lauschen (*liter*); **~!** (*liter*) horch(t)! (*liter*); hört!; **~ at him!** (*inf*) hör ihn dir nur an!, hör sich einer den an! (*inf*)

▶ **hark back** VI +*prep obj* zurückkommen; **this custom harks back to the days when ...** dieser Brauch geht auf die Zeit zurück, als ...; **he's always harking back to the good old days** er fängt immer wieder von der guten alten Zeit an; **the author is harking back to former times** der Autor geht auf vergangene Zeiten zurück

Harlequin ['hɑːlɪkwɪn] N (*Theat*) Harlekin *m*, Hanswurst *m* ADJ Harlekin(s)-; **~ costume** Harlekin(s)kostüm *nt*

harlequin ['hɑːlɪkwɪn] N (= *colourful*) bunt; **~ glasses** buntes Brillengestell

harlot ['hɑːlət] N (*old*) Metze *f* (*old*), Hure *f*

harm [hɑːm] N (*bodily*) Verletzung *f*; (= *material damage, to relations, psychological*) Schaden *m*; **to do ~ to sb** jdm eine Verletzung/jdm Schaden zufügen; **to do ~ to sth** einer Sache (*dat*) schaden; **you could do somebody/yourself ~ with that knife** mit dem Messer können Sie jemanden/sich verletzen; **the blow didn't do him any** ~ der Schlag hat ihm nichts getan *or* ihn nicht verletzt; **a bit of exercise never did anyone any** ~ ein bisschen Sport hat noch niemandem geschadet; **he never did anyone any** ~ er hat keiner Fliege jemals etwas zuleide *or* zu Leide getan; **he did his reputation quite a lot of** ~ **with his TV appearance** er hat seinem Ruf mit diesem Fernsehauftritt ziemlich geschadet; **you will come to no** ~ es wird Ihnen nichts geschehen; **I'll make sure no** ~ **comes to him** ich werde dafür sorgen, dass ihm nichts passiert *or* geschieht; **it will do more** ~ **than good** es wird mehr schaden als nützen; **it won't do you any** ~ es wird dir nicht schaden; **I see no** ~ **in the odd cigarette** ich finde nichts dabei, wenn man ab und zu eine Zigarette raucht; **to mean no** ~ es nicht böse meinen; **I don't mean him any** ~ ich meine es nicht böse mit ihm; (*bodily, = not offend*) ich will ihm nicht wehtun; **no** ~ **done** es ist nichts Schlimmes passiert; **there's no** ~ **in asking/trying** es kann nicht schaden, zu fragen/es zu versuchen; **there's no** ~ **in me putting a word in for him, is there?** es kann doch nichts schaden, wenn ich ein gutes Wort für ihn einlege, oder?; **where's** *or* **what's the** ~ **in that?** was kann denn das schaden?; **to keep** *or* **stay out of** ~**'s way** die Gefahr meiden, der Gefahr (*dat*) aus dem Weg gehen; **you stay here out of** ~**'s way** du bleibst schön hier, in Sicherheit; **I've put those tablets in the cupboard out of** ~**'s way** ich habe die Tabletten im Schrank in Sicherheit gebracht

VT *person* verletzen; *thing, environment* schaden (+*dat*); *sb's interests, relations, reputation* etc schaden (+*dat*), abträglich sein (+*dat*); **don't** ~ **the children** tu den Kindern nichts (an); **it wouldn't** ~ **you to be a little more polite** es würde nicht(s) schaden, wenn du ein bisschen höflicher wärst

harmful ['hɑːmfʊl] ADJ schädlich (*to* für); *remarks* verletzend; ~ **to one's health** gesundheitsschädlich

harmless ['hɑːmlɪs] ADJ (= *safe*) *substance, animal* harmlos, ungefährlich; (*fig, = inoffensive*) *person, pleasure, question* harmlos; **the bomb was rendered** ~ die Bombe wurde entschärft; **this experiment was** ~ **to the animals** dieses Experiment war für die Tiere ungefährlich; **it's just a bit of** ~ **fun** es ist nur ein harmloser Spaß

harmlessly ['hɑːmlɪslɪ] ADV **a** (= *without causing damage*) harmlos; **the missile exploded** ~ **outside the town** die Rakete explodierte außerhalb der Stadt, ohne Schaden anzurichten **b** (= *inoffensively*) harmlos, arglos; **they lived** ~ **in their seaside paradise** sie lebten arglos in ihrem Paradies am Meer

harmlessness ['hɑːmlɪsnɪs] N (*lit, fig*) Harmlosigkeit *f*; (*of substance, animal also*) Ungefährlichkeit *f*

harmonic [hɑːˈmɒnɪk] **N** (*Mus*) Oberton *m* **ADJ** (*Mus, Phys*) harmonisch

harmonica [hɑːˈmɒnɪkə] N Harmonika *f*

harmonics [hɑːˈmɒnɪks] N *sing* Harmonik *f*

harmonious ADJ , **harmoniously** ADV [hɑːˈməʊnɪəs, -lɪ] (*Mus, fig*) harmonisch

harmonium [hɑːˈməʊnɪəm] N Harmonium *nt*

harmonization [ˌhɑːmənaɪˈzeɪʃən] N (*Mus, fig*) Harmonisierung *f*

harmonize ['hɑːmənaɪz] **VT** (*Mus, fig*) harmonisieren; *ideas etc* miteinander in Einklang bringen; *plans, colours* aufeinander abstimmen (*sth with sth* etw auf etw *acc*) **VI a** (*notes, colours, people etc*) harmonieren; (*facts*) übereinstimmen **b** (= *sing in harmony*) mehrstimmig singen

harmony ['hɑːmənɪ] N Harmonie *f*; (*of colours also*) harmonisches Zusammenspiel; (*fig, = harmonious relations*) Eintracht *f*; **to live/work in perfect** ~ **with sb** in Harmonie *or* Eintracht mit jdm leben/zusammenarbeiten; **to be in/out of** ~ **with** (*lit*) harmonieren/nicht harmonieren mit; (*fig also*) in Einklang/nicht in Einklang stehen *or* sein mit; **to live in** ~ **with nature** im Einklang mit der Natur leben; **to sing in** ~

mehrstimmig singen; (= *in tune*) rein singen; **his ideas are out of** ~ **with the age** seine Vorstellungen sind nicht zeitgemäß *or* passen nicht in die Zeit

harness ['hɑːnɪs] **N a** Geschirr *nt*; **to be back in** ~ (*fig*) wieder bei der Arbeit *or* im gewohnten Trott sein; **to work in** ~ (*fig*) zusammenarbeiten; **to die in** ~ (*fig: often hum*) in den Sielen sterben **b** (*of parachute*) Gurtwerk *nt*; (*for baby*) Laufgurt *m* **c** (*Elec*) Kabelbaum *m* **VT a** *horse* anschirren, aufzäumen; **a horse that has never been** ~**ed** ein Pferd, das nie im Geschirr gegangen ist; **to** ~ **a horse to a carriage** ein Pferd vor einen Wagen spannen **b** (= *utilize*) nutzen; *river etc also* nutzbar machen; *anger etc* nutzen, sich (*dat*) zunutze *or* zu Nutze machen

harp [hɑːp] N Harfe *f*

▶ **harp on** VI (*inf*) **to harp on sth** auf etw (*dat*) herumreiten; **he's always harping on about the need for …** er spricht ständig von der Notwendigkeit (+*gen* …); **she's always harping on about her problems** sie lamentiert ständig über ihre Probleme, sie jammert einem dauernd die Ohren voll mit ihren Problemen (*inf*); **she is always harping on the same theme** es ist immer die alte Leier *or* das alte Lied bei ihr

harpist ['hɑːpɪst] N Harfenspieler(in) *m(f)*, Harfenist(in) *m(f)*

harpoon [hɑːˈpuːn] **N** Harpune *f*; ~ **gun** Harpunenkanone *f* **VT** harpunieren

harpsichord ['hɑːpsɪkɔːd] N Cembalo *nt*

harpy ['hɑːpɪ] N Harpyie *f*; (= *shrewish woman*) Hexe *f*; (= *grasping person*) Hyäne *f*

harpy eagle N Harpyie *f*

harridan ['hærɪdən] N Vettel *f*, Drache *m*

harrier ['hærɪə'] N **a** (*Sport*) Querfeldeinläufer(in) *m(f)*, Geländeläufer(in) *m(f)* **b** (*Orn*) Weih *m* **c** (= *dog*) Hund für die Hasenjagd

harrow ['hærəʊ] **N** (*Agr*) Egge *f* **VT a** (*Agr*) eggen **b** (*fig, usu pass*) **to** ~ **sb** jdn quälen *or* peinigen (+*dat*)

harrowed ['hærəʊd] ADJ *look* gequält

harrowing ['hærəʊɪŋ] ADJ *story, picture etc* entsetzlich, erschütternd, grauenhaft; *experience* qualvoll, grauenhaft; *time* entsetzlich

harrumph [həˈrʌmf] VI sich (laut) räuspern

Harry ['hærɪ] N *dim of* **Henry**

harry ['hærɪ] VT **a** (= *hassle*) *sb, government* bedrängen, zusetzen (+*dat*) **b** (*old*) *country* plündern

harsh [hɑːʃ] ADJ (+*er*) **a** (= *inclement*) *winter* hart, streng; *weather, climate, environment* rau, unwirtlich; *conditions* hart

b (= *severe*) *words, remarks, criticism* scharf; *verdict, sentence, punishment, treatment* hart; *discipline* streng; ~ **justice** ein strenges Urteil; **to be** ~ **with** *or* **on sb** jdn hart anfassen; **don't be too** ~ **with him** sei nicht zu streng mit *or* hart zu ihm

c (= *abrasive, grating*) *sound, voice* rau, kratzig; *breathing* rasselnd; *cleaner, detergent* scharf; *wool, fabric* rau; *taste, wine, whisky* herb; *light, glare, colours* grell; **the** ~ **glare of the sun** das grelle Sonnenlicht; **the** ~ **cries of the seagulls** das Kreischen der Möwen

d (= *unpleasant, unwelcome*) *reality, facts, truth* bitter

harshly ['hɑːʃlɪ] ADV **a** (= *severely*) *judge, treat* streng; *criticize* scharf; **he was** ~ **treated by the referee** (= *too severely*) der Schiedsrichter behandelte ihn streng; **to be** ~ **critical of sth** etw scharf kritisieren; **a** ~ **worded attack** ein scharf formulierter Angriff **b** (= *in a harsh voice*) *say* scharf, schroff; *laugh* kratzig; **he never once spoke** ~ **to her** (= *unkindly*) er sprach sie nie in einem scharfen Ton an

harshness ['hɑːʃnɪs] N **a** (*of winter, conditions*) Härte *f*; (*of weather, climate, environment*) Rauheit *f*, Unwirtlichkeit *f* **b** (= *severity, of words, remarks, criticism*) Schärfe *f*; (*of verdict, sentence, punishment, treatment*) Härte *f*; (*of discipline*) Strenge *f* **c** (= *roughness, of sound, voice, wool,*

fabric) Rauheit *f*; (*of breathing*) rasselnde Art; (*of cleaner, detergent*) Schärfe *f*; (*of taste, wine, whisky*) Herbheit *f*; (*of light, colours*) Grelle *f*

hart [hɑːt] N Hirsch *m*

harum-scarum [ˈhɛərəmˈskɛərəm] **ADJ** unbesonnen, unbedacht **N** unbedachter Tollkopf

harvest ['hɑːvɪst] **N** Ernte *f*; (*of wines, berries also*) Lese *f*; (*of the sea*) Ausbeute *f*, Ertrag *m*; (*fig*) Frucht *f*, Ertrag *m*; **the** ~ **of ideas** die Ausbeute an Ideen; **a bumper potato** ~ eine Rekordkartoffelernte; **to reap the** ~ **of sth** (= *benefit*) die Früchte einer Sache (*gen*) ernten; (= *suffer*) die Konsequenzen einer Sache (*gen*) tragen **VT** (= *reap: also fig*) ernten; *vines also* lesen; *trees, timber* schlagen; *fish* fangen; (= *bring in*) einbringen **VI** ernten

harvester ['hɑːvɪstə'] N (= *person*) Erntearbeiter(in) *m(f)*; (= *machine*) Mähmaschine *f*; (*cuts and binds*) Mähbinder *m*, Bindemäher *m*; (= *combine harvester*) Mähdrescher *m*

harvest: harvest festival N Erntedankfest *nt*; **harvest fly** N (*Zool*) Zikade *f*; **harvest home** N (Einbringen *nt* der) Ernte *f*; (= *festival*) Erntedankfest *nt*; **harvest moon** N Herbstmond *m*, heller Vollmond im September; **harvest time** N Erntezeit *f*

has [hæz] *3rd pers sing present of* **have**

has-been ['hæzbiːn] N (*pej*) vergangene *or* vergessene Größe; **every comedian must dread becoming a** ~ jeder Komiker hat Angst davor, in Vergessenheit zu geraten

hash [hæʃ] **N a** (*Cook*) Haschee *nt* **b** (*fig, = mess*) Durcheinander *nt*, Kuddelmuddel *m* (*inf*); (= *bad work*) Pfusch *m* (*inf*), Pfuscherei *f* (*inf*); **to make a** ~ **of sth** etw verpfuschen *or* vermasseln (*inf*) **c** (*inf, = hashish*) Hasch *nt* (*inf*) **VT** (*Cook*) hacken

▶ **hash over** VI +*prep obj strategy etc* ändern

▶ **hash up** VT *sep* **a** (*Cook*) hacken, zerkleinern **b** (*inf, = mess up*) verpfuschen, vermasseln (*inf*)

hash: hash browns [ˌhæʃˈbraʊnz] PL ≈ Kartoffelpuffer *pl*; **hash head** N (*inf*) Kiffer(in) *m(f)*, Hascher(in) *m(f)*; **hash house** N (*esp US inf*) billiges Lokal

hashish ['hæʃɪʃ] N Haschisch *nt*

hasn't ['hæznt] *contr of* **has not**

hasp [hɑːsp] N (*for chest, door etc*) Überfall *m*; (*for book covers*) (Verschluss)spange *f*, Schließe *f*

Hassidic [hæˈsɪdɪk] ADJ chassidisch; ~ **Jews** Hassidim *pl*, Chassidim *pl*

hassle ['hæsl] (*inf*) **N** Auseinandersetzung *f*; (= *bother, trouble*) Mühe *f*, Theater *nt* (*inf*); **we had a real** ~ **getting these tickets for tonight** es war ein richtiges Theater (*inf*) *or* es hat uns (*dat*) viel Mühe gemacht, diese Karten für heute Abend zu bekommen; **getting there is such a** ~ es ist so umständlich, dorthin zu kommen; **commuting is a bit of a** ~ Pendeln ist etwas lästig; **it's too much** ~ **cooking for myself** es ist mir zu umständlich *or* mühsam, für mich allein zu kochen; **don't worry, it's no** ~! keine Sorge, es macht keine Mühe *or* Umstände!; **legal** ~**s** Anwaltskram *m* (*inf*); **don't give me any** ~ mach kein Theater (*inf*); **it's not worth the** ~ es ist die ganze Mühe *or* das ganze Theater (*inf*) nicht wert

VT a (= *mess around*) schikanieren **b** (= *keep on at*) bedrängen; **keep hassling them till they pay** bleib ihnen auf den Fersen, bis sie bezahlen; **stop hassling me** lass mich in Ruhe!; **I'm feeling a bit** ~**d** ich fühle mich etwas im Stress (*inf*) *or* unter Druck; **she gets easily** ~**d** sie lässt sich leicht unter Druck setzen; **he was always being** ~**d for money** man wollte ständig Geld von ihm

VI keep hassling him/ihnen *etc* auf den Fersen, **in a job like this you have to be prepared to** ~ in diesem Job muss man (anderen) Dampf machen können

hassler ['hæslə'] N aufdringlicher Typ; **we need someone who is a bit of a ~** wir brauchen einen, der Dampf machen kann

hassock ['hæsək] N Betkissen *nt*, Kniekissen *nt*

hast [hæst] (*obs*) *2nd pers sing present of* **have**

haste [heɪst] N Eile *f*; (*nervous*) Hast *f*; **to do sth in ~** etw in Eile tun; **in great ~** in großer Eile; **to make ~** to do sth sich beeilen, etw zu tun; **make ~!** (*old*) spute dich (*old*); **more ~ less speed** (*Prov*) eile mit Weile (*Prov*)

hasten ['heɪsn] VI sich beeilen; **he ~ed to add that ...** er fügte schnell hinzu dass ..., er beeilte sich hinzuzufügen, dass ...; **I ~ to add that ...** ich muss allerdings hinzufügen, dass ...; **she ~ed down the stairs** sie eilte or hastete die Treppe hinunter VT beschleunigen; **the strain of office ~ed his death** die Belastung seines Amtes trug zu seinem vorzeitigen Tod bei; **to ~ sb's departure** jdn zum Aufbruch drängen
► **hasten away** VI forteilen or -hasten, eilig weggehen
► **hasten back** VI eilig or schnell zurückkehren, zurückeilen
► **hasten off** VI weg- or forteilen

hastily ['heɪstɪlɪ] ADV **a** (= *hurriedly*) arranged eilig; examine, glance flüchtig; dress, dash, eat, drink hastig; (= *quickly*) say, add schnell, eilig **b** (= *too quickly*) act, decide, thought out überstürzt, übereilt; speak, speak vorschnell; **the decision was ~ made** die Entscheidung war übereilt

hastiness ['heɪstɪnɪs] N **a** (= *hurriedness*) Eile *f*; (*of meal, movement, goodbye*) Hastigkeit *f*; (*of glance, examination, kiss*) Flüchtigkeit *f*; (*of departure*) Plötzlichkeit *f* **b** (= *rashness, excessive haste*) Übereile *f*; (*of marriage, decision, reaction*) Überstürzung *f*; (*of action, judgement*) Voreiligkeit *f*; **he regretted his ~ in resorting to violence** er bedauerte, dass er so schnell gewalttätig geworden war

hasty ['heɪstɪ] ADJ (+er) **a** (= *hurried*) meal, movement, goodbye hastig; kiss, glance, examination flüchtig; departure plötzlich; **to beat a ~ retreat**, **to make a ~ escape** sich schnellstens aus dem Staub machen (*inf*); **we ate a ~ breakfast** wir frühstückten hastig or in aller Eile; **I bade a ~ goodbye** (*dated*) ich verabschiedete mich hastig or in aller Eile **b** (= *rash, too quick*) marriage, decision, reaction überstürzt, übereilt; action voreilig; judgement vorschnell; **don't be ~!** nicht so schnell or hastig!; **I had been too ~** ich hatte voreilig gehandelt; **to take a ~ decision** eine Entscheidung überstürzen

hasty pudding N (*US*) Maismehlbrei *m*

hat [hæt] N **a** Hut *m*; (*of cook*) Mütze *f*; **to put on one's ~** den or seinen Hut aufsetzen; **to take one's ~ off** den Hut abnehmen; (*for greeting also*) den Hut ziehen (*to sb* vor jdm); **~s off!** Hut ab!; **my ~!** (*dated inf*) dass ich nicht lache! (*inf*) **b** (*fig*) **he's a bad ~** (*dated inf*) er ist ein übler Patron (*dated inf*); **I'll eat my ~ if ...** ich fresse einen Besen, wenn ... (*inf*); **I take my ~ off to him** Hut ab vor ihm!; **~s off to them for supporting us** Hut ab vor ihnen, dass sie uns unterstützt haben; **to talk through one's ~** (*inf*) dummes Zeug reden; **to keep sth under one's ~** (*inf*) etw für sich behalten; **at the drop of a ~** auf der Stelle, ohne weiteres; **to toss one's ~ in the ring** sich am politischen Reigen beteiligen; (*non-political*) sich einschalten; **that's old ~** (*inf*) das ist ein alter Hut (*inf*); **they're all pretty old ~** (*inf*) das sind doch alles olle Kamellen (*inf*); **to pass round the ~ for sb** für jdn sammeln or den Hut rumgehen lassen (*inf*); **with my accountant's ~ on I would say ...** (*inf*) als Buchhalter würde ich sagen ...; **he wears several different ~s** (*inf*) er übt mehrere Funktionen aus

hatable ['heɪtəbl] ADJ hassenswert, abscheulich

hat: **hatband** N Hutband *nt*; **hatbox** N Hutschachtel *f*

hatch[1] [hætʃ] VT (*also* **hatch out**) ausbrüten; (*fig*) plot, scheme *also* aushecken; compromise aushandeln VI (*also* **hatch out:** bird) aus-

schlüpfen; **when will the eggs ~?** wann schlüpfen die Jungen aus? N (= *act of hatching*) Ausbrüten *nt*; (= *brood*) Brut *f*

hatch[2] N **a** (*Naut*) Luke *f*; (*in floor, ceiling*) Bodenluke *f*; (= *half-door*) Halbtür *f*, Niedertür *f*; (= *turret hatch*) Ausstiegsluke *f* (*in Turm*) → **batten down** **b** (**service**) ~ Durchreiche *f* **c** **down the ~!** (*inf*) hoch die Tassen! (*inf*)

hatch[3] VT (*Art*) schraffieren

hatchback ['hætʃbæk] N Hecktürmodell *nt*; (= *door*) Hecktür *f*

hatchery ['hætʃərɪ] N Brutplatz *m* or -stätte *f*

hatchet ['hætʃɪt] N Beil *nt*; (= *tomahawk*) Kriegsbeil *nt*; **to bury the ~** (*fig*) das Kriegsbeil begraben

hatchet: **hatchet face** N scharf geschnittenes Gesicht; (*inf, = person*) Raubvogelgesicht *nt*; **hatchet-faced** ADJ mit scharfen Gesichtszügen; **hatchet job** N (*inf*) **to do a ~ on sb** jdn fertig machen (*inf*); **hatchet man** N (= *hired killer*) gedungener Mörder; (*fig*) Vollstreckungsbeamte(r) *m*

hatching ['hætʃɪŋ] N (*Art*) Schraffur *f*, Schraffierung *f*

hatchway ['hætʃweɪ] N = **hatch**[2] a

hate [heɪt] ⊗ 7.3 VT hassen; (= *detest also*) verabscheuen, nicht ausstehen können; (= *dislike also*) nicht leiden können; **to ~ the sound of sth** etw nicht hören können; **to ~ to do sth** or **doing sth** hassen, etw zu tun; (*weaker*) etw äußerst ungern tun; **I ~ being late** ich hasse es, zu spät zu kommen, ich komme äußerst ungern zu spät; **I ~ seeing** or **to see her in pain** ich kann es nicht ertragen, sie leiden zu sehen; **I ~ the idea of leaving** der Gedanke, weggehen zu müssen, ist mir äußerst zuwider; **I ~ it when people accuse me of lying** ich kann es nicht ausstehen, wenn man mich als Lügner bezeichnet; **I ~ to bother/rush you** es ist mir sehr unangenehm, dass ich Sie belästigen/zur Eile drängen muss; **I ~ to say/admit it but ...** es fällt mir schwer, das sagen/zugeben zu müssen, aber ...; **I ~d myself for writing that letter** ich konnte es mir nicht verzeihen, dass ich diesen Brief geschrieben hatte; **she ~s me having any fun** sie kann es nicht haben, wenn ich Spaß habe; **you'll ~ me for this but ...** du wirst es mir vielleicht übel nehmen, aber ...; **don't ~ me for telling you the truth** nimm es mir nicht übel or sei mir nicht böse, dass ich dir die Wahrheit sage; **I should ~ to keep you waiting** ich möchte Sie auf keinen Fall warten lassen; **I'd ~ to think I'd never see him again** ich könnte den Gedanken, ihn nie wiederzusehen, nicht ertragen N **a** (= *hatred*) Hass *m* (*for, of* auf +acc) **b** (= *object of hatred*) **one of his pet ~s is plastic cutlery/having to wait** Plastikbesteck/Warten ist ihm ein Gräuel, Plastikbesteck/Warten gehört zu den Dingen, die er am meisten hasst or verabscheut; **celery is/spiders are my pet ~** ich kann Sellerie/Spinnen auf den Tod nicht ausstehen or leiden (*inf*)

hate campaign N Hasskampagne *f*

hated ['heɪtɪd] ADJ verhasst

hateful ['heɪtfʊl] ADJ **a** abscheulich; remarks also hässlich; person unausstehlich; **sth is ~ to sb** etw ist jdm verhasst; **it was a ~ thing to say/do** das war abscheulich **b** (= *full of hate*) hasserfüllt

hatefully ['heɪtfʊlɪ] ADV abscheulich

hate mail N beleidigende Briefe *pl*

hatemonger ['heɪtˌmʌŋgə'] N Aufhetzer(in) *m(f)*, Aufwiegler(in) *m(f)*

hath [hæθ] (*obs*) = **has**

hat: **hatless** ADJ ohne Hut; **hatpin** N Hutnadel *f*; **hat rack** N Hutablage *f*

hatred ['heɪtrɪd] N Hass *m* (*for, of* auf +acc); (*of spinach, spiders etc*) Abscheu *m* (*of* vor +dat); **racial ~** Rassenhass *m*

hat stand, (*US*) **hat tree** N Garderobenständer *m*; (*for hats only*) Hutständer *m*

hatter ['hætə'] N Hutmacher(in) *m(f)*; (= *seller*) Hutverkäufer(in) *m(f)* → **mad**

hat trick N Hattrick *m*; **to score a ~** einen Hattrick erzielen; **with two husbands already behind her she looks like making it a ~** nachdem sie nun schon zweimal geschieden ist, denkt sie wohl, aller guten Dinge sind drei

haughtily ['hɔːtɪlɪ] ADV say hochmütig, überheblich; dismiss, ignore arrogant; look geringschätzig

haughtiness ['hɔːtɪnɪs] N Hochmut *m*, Überheblichkeit *f*; (*of look*) Geringschätzigkeit *f*

haughty ['hɔːtɪ] ADJ (+er) manner, attitude, voice, expression hochmütig, überheblich; disdain, person also arrogant; look geringschätzig

haul [hɔːl] N **a** (= *hauling*) **a truck gave us a ~** ein Lastwagen schleppte uns ab or (*out of mud etc*) zog uns heraus **b** (= *journey*) Strecke *f*; **it's a long ~ to recovery** es ist ein weiter Weg bis zum Aufschwung; **short/long/medium ~ aircraft** Kurz-/Lang-/Mittelstreckenflugzeug *nt*; **the project has been a long ~** das Projekt hat sich lang hingezogen; **the long ~ through the courts** der lange Weg durch die Instanzen; **revitalizing the economy will be a long ~** es wird lange dauern, die Wirtschaft wieder anzukurbeln; **over the long ~** (*esp US*) langfristig **c** (*Fishing*) (Fisch)fang *m*; (*fig, = booty: from robbery*) Beute *f*; (*of cocaine etc*) Fund *m*; (*inf, of presents*) Ausbeute *f* (*inf*); **our ~ on the last trawl was 500 kg of herring** bei unserer letzten Fahrt hatten wir eine Ausbeute von 500 kg Hering; **drugs ~** Drogenfund *m* VT **a** (= *pull*) ziehen; heavy objects ziehen, schleppen; **he ~ed himself/Paul to his feet** er wuchtete sich/Paul wieder auf die Beine → **coal** **b** (= *transport*) befördern, transportieren **c** (*Naut*) den Kurs (+gen) ändern; **to ~ a boat into the wind** an den Wind segeln VI (*Naut: also* **haul round**) den Kurs ändern; **the yacht ~ed into the wind** die Jacht segelte an den Wind
► **haul away** VI (= *pull*) mit aller Kraft ziehen (*at, on* an +dat); (*rowers*) sich in die Riemen legen; **haul away!** hau ruck!
► **haul down** VT sep **a** flag, sail einholen, niederholen **b** (*with effort*) herunterschleppen; (= *pull down*) herunterzerren
► **haul in** VT sep einholen; rope einziehen; (*police*) festnehmen
► **haul off** VI (*Naut*) (ab)drehen, den Kurs ändern
► **haul round** VI (*Naut, ship*) den Kurs ändern; (*wind*) drehen
► **haul up** VT sep **a** (= *carry*) hinauf- or hochschleppen; (= *pull up*) hochzerren, hochziehen; flag, sail hissen; (*aboard ship*) (an Bord) hieven, hochziehen; (*onto beach*) schleppen, ziehen; **the dinghies were lying hauled up on the beach for the winter** man hatte die Jollen für den Winter an Land gezogen **b** (*fig inf*) **to haul sb up before the magistrate/headmaster** jdn vor den Kadi/Schulleiter schleppen (*inf*); **he's been hauled up on a drugs charge** er wurde wegen einer Rauschgiftsache vor den Kadi gebracht (*inf*); **he was hauled up for speeding** er wurde wegen Geschwindigkeitsüberschreitung vor Gericht gebracht

haulage ['hɔːlɪdʒ] N (*Brit*) **a** (= *road transport*) Transport *m* **b** (= *transport charges*) Speditions- or Transportkosten *pl*

haulage business N (*esp Brit*) (= *firm*) Transport- or Fuhrunternehmen *nt*, Spedition(sfirma) *f*; (= *trade*) Speditionsbranche *f*, Fuhrwesen *nt*

haulage contractor N (*esp Brit*) (= *firm*) Transportunternehmen *nt*, Spedition(sfirma) *f*; (= *person*) Transport- or Fuhrunternehmer(in) *m(f)*, Spediteur(in) *m(f)*

haulier ['hɔːlɪə'], (*US*) **hauler** ['hɔːlə'] N Spediteur(in) *m(f)*, Fuhrunternehmer(in) *m(f)*; (=

company) Spedition *f*; **firm of ~s** Spedition(sfirma) *f*, Transportunternehmen *nt*

haulm [hɔːm] N (*single*) Stängel *m*; (*grain, grass also*) Halm *m*; (*collectively*) Stroh *nt*

haunch [hɔːntʃ] N (*of person*) Hüfte *f*; (= *hip area*) Hüftpartie *f*; (*of animal*, = *hindquarters*) Hinterbacke *f*; (= *top of leg*) Keule *f*; (*Cook*) Keule *f*, Lendenstück *nt*; **~es** Gesäß *nt*; (*of animal*) Hinterbacken *pl*; **to go down on one's ~es** in die Hocke gehen; **to squat on one's ~es** in der Hocke sitzen; **the dog was sitting on its ~es** der Hund saß auf den Hinterbeinen; **~ of venison** (*Cook*) Rehkeule *f*

haunt [hɔːnt] VT **a** (*ghost*) *house, place* spuken in (+*dat*), umgehen in (+*dat*)
b *person* verfolgen; (*memory*) nicht loslassen, verfolgen; (*fear, decision*) quälen; **the nightmares which ~ed him** die Albträume *or* Alpträume, die ihn heimsuchten; **lack of money ~ed successive projects** mehrere aufeinander folgende Projekte waren vom Geldmangel verfolgt
c (= *frequent*) verkehren in (+*dat*), frequentieren, häufig besuchen; (*animal*) vorkommen, auftreten
N (*of person*, = *pub etc*) Stammlokal *nt*; (= *favourite resort*) Lieblingsort *or* -platz *m*; (*of criminals*) Treff(punkt) *m*; (*of animal*) Heimat *f*; **the riverbank is the ~ of a variety of animals** eine Vielzahl von Tieren lebt an Flussufern; **to revisit the ~s of one's youth** die Stätten seiner Jugend wieder aufsuchen; **her usual childhood ~s** Stätten, die sie in ihrer Kindheit oft aufsuchte; **a ~ of literary exiles** ein Treffpunkt *m* für Exilliteraten

haunted [ˈhɔːntɪd] ADJ **a** Spuk-; **~ castle** Spukschloss *nt*; **a ~ house** ein Spukhaus *nt*, ein Haus *nt*, in dem es spukt; **this place is ~** hier spukt es; **is it ~?** spukt es da? **b** *look* gehetzt, gequält; *person* ruhelos

haunting [ˈhɔːntɪŋ] ADJ *doubt* quälend, nagend; *tune, visions, poetry, cry, eyes* eindringlich; *memory* lastend; *music* schwermütig; **these ~ final chords** diese Schlussakkorde, die einen nicht loslassen

hauntingly [ˈhɔːntɪŋlɪ] ADV ergreifend; *melodious, tuneful* eindringlich

haute couture [ˌəʊtkuːˈtʊəʳ] N Haute Couture *f* ADJ *attr* der Haute Couture

hauteur [əʊˈtɜːʳ] N (*liter*) Hochmütigkeit *f*

Havana [həˈvænə] N **a** Havanna *nt* **b** (= *cigar*) Havanna(zigarre) *f*

---

have [hæv]
pret, ptp **had**, *3rd pers sing present* **has**
✪ 10.2, 10.3

1 AUXILIARY VERB	3 TRANSITIVE VERB
2 MODAL AUXILIARY VERB	4 PHRASAL VERBS

When **have** is part of a set combination, eg **have a look**, **have a dream**, **have a good time**, look up the noun.

1 – AUXILIARY VERB

a haben

The verb **haben** is the auxiliary used with most verbs to form past tenses in German. For important exceptions see (**b**).

to have seen/heard/eaten gesehen/gehört/gegessen haben; **I have/had seen** ich habe/hatte gesehen; **I have not/had not** *or* **I haven't/I hadn't seen him** ich habe/hatte ihn nicht gesehen; **had I seen him, if I had seen him** hätte ich ihn gesehen, wenn ich ihn gesehen hätte; **having seen him** (= *after I had*) als ich ihn gesehen hatte; **having realized this** (= *since I had*) nachdem ich das erkannt hatte; **having said that he left** nachdem *or* als er das gesagt hatte, ging er

Note the tenses used in the following:

I have lived *or* **have been living here for 10 years/since January** ich wohne *or* lebe schon 10 Jahre/seit Januar hier

b sein

The verb **sein** is used with verbs of motion, eg. **gehen, fahren**, or verbs implying development, eg. **wachsen**, and to form past tenses.

to have gone/run gegangen/gelaufen sein; **you HAVE grown!** du bist aber gewachsen!; **to have been** gewesen sein; **I have been to London** ich bin in London gewesen; **I have been against this for years** ich bin schon seit Jahren dagegen

c in tag questions etc **you've seen her, haven't you?** du hast sie gesehen, oder nicht?; **you haven't seen her, have you?** du hast sie nicht gesehen, oder?; **you haven't seen her – yes, I have** du hast sie nicht gesehen – doch *or* wohl (*inf*); **you've made a mistake – no, I haven't** du hast einen Fehler gemacht – nein(, hab ich nicht); **you've dropped your book – so I have** dir ist dein Buch hingefallen – stimmt *or* tatsächlich; **have you been there? if you have/haven't...** sind Sie schon mal da gewesen? wenn ja/nein *or* nicht, ...; **I have seen a ghost – have you?** ich habe ein Gespenst gesehen – wahrhaftig *or* tatsächlich?; **I've lost it – you haven't!** (*disbelieving*) ich habe es verloren – nein!

2 – MODAL AUXILIARY VERB

♦ **to have to do sth** (= *to be obliged*) etw tun müssen; **I have (got** *esp Brit*) **to do it** ich muss es tun *or* machen; **have you got to go now?** (*Brit*) **do you have to go now?** müssen Sie jetzt (wirklich) unbedingt gehen?; **do you have to make such a noise?** müssen Sie (unbedingt) so viel Lärm machen?; **she was having to get up at 6 o'clock each morning** sie musste jeden Morgen um 6 Uhr aufstehen; **we've had to go and see her twice this week** wir mussten diese Woche schon zweimal zu ihr (hin); **the letter will have to be written tomorrow** der Brief muss morgen unbedingt geschrieben werden; **I'm afraid it has to be** das muss leider sein; **it's got to be** *or* **it has to be the biggest scandal this year** das ist todsicher der (größte) Skandal des Jahres
♦ **don't/doesn't have to** *or* (*esp Brit*) **haven't/hasn't got to I haven't got to do it** (*esp Brit*) **I don't have to do it** ich muss es nicht tun, ich brauche es nicht zu tun; **you didn't have to tell her** das musst Sie ihr nicht unbedingt sagen, das hätten Sie ihr nicht unbedingt sagen müssen *or* brauchen; **he hasn't got to work** (*esp Brit*) **he doesn't have to work** er braucht nicht zu arbeiten, er muss nicht arbeiten

3 – TRANSITIVE VERB

a = possess haben; **have you (got** *esp Brit*) **or do you have a car?** hast du ein Auto?; **I haven't (got** *esp Brit*) **or I don't have a pen** ich habe keinen Kugelschreiber; **to have something/nothing to do** etwas/nichts zu tun haben; **I (got** *esp Brit*) **work/a translation to do** ich habe zu arbeiten/eine Übersetzung zu erledigen; **I must have more time** ich brauche mehr Zeit; **have you (got** *esp Brit*) **or do you have a cigarette?** hast du (mal) eine Zigarette?; **I don't have any German** (*Brit*) ich kann kein (Wort) Deutsch; **she has (got** *esp Brit*) **blue eyes** sie hat blaue Augen; **I have it!** ich habs!; **what time do you have?** (*US*) wie viel Uhr hast du? (*inf*), wie spät hast du es?

b = receive, obtain, get haben; **to have news from sb** von jdm hören; **I have it on good authority that ...** ich habe aus zuverlässiger Quelle gehört *or* erfahren, dass ...; **I must have something to eat** ich brauche etwas zu essen, ich muss dringend etwas zu essen haben; **there are no newspapers to be had** es sind keine Zeitungen zu haben; **it's nowhere to be had** es ist nirgends zu haben *or* kriegen (*inf*); **there are some great bargains to be had in the shops** in den Geschäften gibt es tolle Angebote; **I'll have the bed in this room** das Bett möchte *or* werde ich in dieses Zimmer stellen; **thanks for having me** vielen Dank für Ihre Gastfreundschaft

♦ **to let sb have sth** jdm etw geben; **please let me have your address** geben Sie mir bitte Ihre Adresse; **I'll let you have it for £50** ich gebe es dir für £ 50

c = eat, drink, take **to have breakfast** frühstücken; **to have lunch/dinner** zu Mittag/Abend essen; **to have tea with sb** mit jdm (zusammen) Tee trinken; **will you have tea or coffee?** möchten Sie lieber Tee oder Kaffee?; **will you have a drink/cigarette?** möchten Sie etwas zu trinken/eine Zigarette?; **what will you have?** – **I'll have the steak** was möchten *or* hätten Sie gern(e)? – ich hätte *or* möchte gern das Steak; **he had a cigarette/drink/steak** er rauchte eine Zigarette/trank etwas/aß ein Steak; **will you have some more?** möchten Sie *or* hätten Sie gern(e) (noch etwas) mehr?; **have another one** nimm noch eine/einen/eines; (*drink*) trink noch einen; (*cigarette*) rauch noch eine

d = catch, hold (gepackt) haben; **he had (got** *esp Brit*) **me by the throat/the hair** er hatte *or* hielt mich am Hals/bei den Haaren gepackt; **I have (got** *esp Brit*) **him where I want him** ich habe ihn endlich so weit, ich habe ihn endlich (da), wo ich ihn will; **the champion had him now** der Meister hatte ihn jetzt fest im Griff *or* in der Tasche (*inf*); **I'll have you** (*inf*) dich krieg ich (beim Kragen); **you have me there** da bin ich überfragt

e = suffer from **he has diabetes** er ist zuckerkrank, er hat Zucker (*inf*); **to have a heart attack** einen Herzinfarkt bekommen; **I've (got** *esp Brit*) **a headache** ich habe Kopfschmerzen

f = experience **to have a pleasant evening** einen netten Abend verbringen; **to have a good time** Spaß haben, sich amüsieren; **have a good time!** viel Spaß!

g = hold, organize *party* geben, machen; *meeting* abhalten; **are you having a reception?** gibt es einen Empfang?; **we decided not to have a reception** wir haben uns gegen einen Empfang entschieden

h = go for **to have a walk** einen Spaziergang machen, spazieren gehen; **to have a swim** schwimmen gehen

i = give birth to **to have a child** *or* **baby** ein Kind *or* Baby bekommen; **she is having a baby in April** sie bekommt *or* kriegt (*inf*) im April ein Kind; **she had twins** sie hat Zwillinge bekommen *or* geboren *or* gekriegt (*inf*); **our cat has had kittens** unsere Katze hat Junge gekriegt (*inf*) *or* bekommen

j = cause to be **I had him in such a state that ...** er war in einer solchen Verfassung, dass ...; **he had the audience in hysterics** das Publikum kugelte sich vor Lachen; **he had the police baffled** die Polizei stand vor einem Rätsel; **she nearly had the table over** (*Brit*) sie hätte den Tisch beinahe umgekippt *or* zum Umkippen gebracht

k = maintain, insist **he will have it that Paul is guilty** (*Brit*) **as he has it, Paul is guilty** er besteht darauf, dass Paul schuldig ist; **he wouldn't have it that Paul is guilty** (*Brit*) **as he had it, Paul isn't guilty** er wollte nichts davon hören, dass Paul schuldig ist; **as rumour** (*Brit*) *or* **rumor** (*US*) **has it** Gerüchten zufolge; **as the Bible/Shakespeare has it** wie es in der Bibel/bei Shakespeare steht

l = refuse to allow (*in negative sentences*) **I won't have this nonsense** dieser Unsinn kommt (mir) nicht infrage *or* in Frage!; **I won't have this sort of rudeness!** diese Unhöflichkeit lasse ich mir ganz einfach nicht bieten; **I won't have it!** das lasse ich mir nicht bieten!; **I won't have him insulted** ich lasse es nicht zu *or* dulde es nicht, dass man ihn beleidigt; **I won't have him insult his mother** ich lasse es nicht zu, dass er seine Mutter beleidigt; **we won't have women in our club** in unserem Klub sind Frauen nicht zugelassen; **I'm not having any of that!** (*inf*) mit mir nicht! (*inf*); **but she wasn't having any** (*inf*) aber sie wollte nichts davon wissen

m = wish mögen; **which one will you have?** welche(n, s) möchten Sie haben *or* hätten Sie gern?; **as fate would have it, ...** wie es das

Schicksal so wollte, ...; **what would you have me do?** was wollen Sie, dass ich mache?

n set structures

♦ **to have sth done**
= request, order etw tun lassen; **to have one's hair cut** sich (*dat*) die Haare schneiden lassen; **to have a suit made** sich (*dat*) einen Anzug machen lassen; **I had my cases brought up** ich habe (mir) meine Koffer nach oben bringen lassen; **have it mended** geben Sie es in Reparatur, lassen Sie es reparieren; **they had him shot** sie ließen ihn erschießen
= suffer, experience **he had his car stolen** man hat ihm sein Auto gestohlen; **he had his arm broken** er hat/hatte einen gebrochenen Arm; **I've had three windows broken** (bei) mir sind drei Fenster eingeworfen worden

♦ **to have sb do sth**
= make them do jdn etw tun lassen; **I had him wash the car** ich ließ ihn den Wagen waschen; **I'll have you know ...** Sie müssen nämlich wissen ...
= experience **I had my friends turn against me** ich musste es erleben, wie *or* dass sich meine Freunde gegen mich wandten

♦ **to have sb doing sth she had us all helping with the dinner** nach ihrer Ermunterung halfen wir alle mit beim Abendessen; **she soon had them all reading and writing** dank ihres Engagements konnten alle schon bald lesen und schreiben

♦ **to have had it** (*inf*) **he has had it with politics** er hat von der Politik die Nase voll (*inf*); **that coat has had it** der Mantel ist im Eimer (*inf*); **if I miss the last bus, I've had it** wenn ich den letzten Bus verpasse, bin ich geliefert (*inf*) *or* ist der Ofen aus (*inf*)

♦ **let him have it!** (*inf*) gibs ihm! (*inf*)

♦ **have it your own way** machen Sie es *or* halten Sie es, wie Sie wollen

♦ **to be had** (*inf, = tricked*) übers Ohr gehauen werden (*inf*); **you've been had!** da hat man dich übers Ohr gehauen (*inf*)

4 – PHRASAL VERBS

▶ **have around** VT *always separate* **a** (bei sich) zu Besuch haben; (= *invite*) einladen **b** **he's a useful man to have around** es ist ganz praktisch, ihn zur Hand zu haben

▶ **have at** VI +*prep obj* (*old*) angreifen; **she had at me with her umbrella** sie ging mit ihrem Regenschirm auf mich los

▶ **have away** VT *always separate* **to have it away with sb** (*inf*) es mit jdm treiben (*inf*)

▶ **have back** *sep* zurückhaben

▶ **have down** VT *sep people, guests* (bei sich) zu Besuch haben VT *always separate* (= *take down*) scaffolding abbauen; (= *knock down*) buildings abreißen; *vase* herunterwerfen; (= *put down*) carpets verlegen

▶ **have in** VT *always separate* **a** (*in the house*) im Haus haben; **we've got** *esp Brit* **the decorators in all week** wir haben die ganze Woche (über) die Anstreicher im Haus
b **to have it in for sb** (*inf*) jdn auf dem Kieker haben (*inf*)
c (= *make come in*) hereinrufen; **can we have the next interviewee in?** können wir den nächsten Kandidaten haben?
d (= *put in*) **he had the new engine in by lunchtime** er hatte den neuen Motor bis mittags drin (*inf*)
e **I didn't know he had it in him** ich hätte ihm das nicht zugetraut; **he's got it in him to succeed** er hat das Zeug dazu, erfolgreich zu sein

▶ **have off** VT *always separate* **a** **to have it off with sb** (*Brit*) es mit jdm treiben (*inf*) **b** (= *take off*) **he had the top off in a second** er hatte den Deckel in Sekundenschnelle (he)runter; **he had to have his leg off** ihm musste das Bein abgenommen werden

▶ **have on** VT *sep* (= *wear*) anhaben; *radio, TV* anhaben
VT *always separate* **a** (= *have arranged*) vorhaben; (= *be busy with*) zu tun haben; **we've (got**

esp Brit) **a big job on** wir haben ein großes Projekt in Arbeit
b (*inf, = deceive, trick*) übers Ohr hauen (*inf*); (= *tease*) auf den Arm nehmen (*inf*)
c **to have nothing on sb** nichts gegen jdn in der Hand haben; **they've got nothing on me!** mir kann keiner! (*inf*)
d (= *put on*) **they had new tyres** (*Brit*) *or* **tires** (*US*) **on in no time** sie hatten die neuen Reifen im Nu drauf (*inf*); **they still haven't got the roof on** das Dach ist immer noch nicht drauf

▶ **have out** VT *always separate* **a** (= *have taken out*) herausgenommen bekommen; **he had his tonsils/appendix out** ihm wurden die Mandeln/wurde der Blinddarm herausgenommen
b (= *discuss*) ausdiskutieren; **to have it out with sb** etw mit jdm ausdiskutieren; **I'll have it out with him** ich werde mit ihm reden, ich werde mich mit ihm aussprechen

▶ **have over** *or* (*esp Brit*) **round** VT *always separate* (bei sich) zu Besuch haben; (= *invite*) (zu sich) einladen

▶ **have up** VT *always separate* **a** (*inf, = cause to appear in court*) drankriegen (*inf*); **that's the second time he's been had up for drunken driving** jetzt haben sie ihn schon zum zweiten Mal wegen Trunkenheit am Steuer drangekriegt (*inf*); **he's been had up again** er war schon wieder vor dem Kadi (*inf*) **b** (= *put up*) **as soon as we had the tent/shelves up** sobald wir das Zelt aufgestellt/die Regale an der Wand hatten

---

have-a-go [ˌhævəˈɡəʊ] ADJ ATTR (*Brit, inf*) **~-hero** heldenmütiger Kämpfer

haven [ˈheɪvən] N (*fig*) Zufluchtsstätte f

haven't [ˈhævnt] *contr of* **have not**

haves [hævz] PL (*inf*) **the ~** die Betuchten *pl* (*inf*), die Begüterten *pl*; **the ~ and the have-nots** die Betuchten und die Habenichtse

havoc [ˈhævək] N verheerender Schaden, (= *devastation also*) Verwüstung f; (= *chaos*) Chaos *nt*; **to cause** *or* **create ~** ein Chaos verursachen; **to wreak ~ in** *or* **on** *or* **with sth, to play ~ with sth** bei etw verheerenden Schaden anrichten; (*physical damage also*) etw verwüsten, etw verheerend zurichten; **with health, part of the body** für etw üble *or* schlimme Folgen haben, sich übel auf (*acc*) auswirken; **with life, career** etw ruinieren; **the tornado wreaked ~ all along the coast** der Tornado richtete entlang der ganzen Küste große Verwüstungen an; **this wreaked ~ with their plans** das brachte ihre Pläne völlig durcheinander; **the sudden rise in oil prices played ~ with India's five-year plan** der plötzliche Anstieg der Ölpreise hat Indiens Fünfjahresplan vollständig über den Haufen geworfen (*inf*)

haw¹ [hɔː] N (*Bot*) Mehlfässchen *nt*, Mehlbeere f

haw² → **hum**

Hawaii [həˈwaɪiː] N Hawaii *nt*

Hawaiian [həˈwaɪjən] ADJ hawaii(ani)sch, Hawaii-; **~ island** Hawaii-Insel f; **~ Standard Time** (*US*) hawaiische Zeit **a** N Hawaiianer(in) *m(f)* **b** (*Ling*) Hawaiisch *nt*

Hawaiian guitar N Hawaiigitarre f

Hawaiian shirt N grellbuntes Hemd

hawfinch [ˈhɔːfɪntʃ] N (*Orn*) Kernbeißer *m*

hawk¹ [hɔːk] N **a** (*Orn*) Habicht *m*; (= *sparrow hawk*) Sperber *m*; (= *falcon*) Falke *m*; **to watch sb like a ~** jdn ganz genau beobachten **b** (*fig, = politician*) Falke *m*; **the ~s and the doves** die Falken und die Tauben **VI** mit Falken jagen

hawk² VI (*with phlegm*) sich räuspern

hawk³ VT hausieren (gehen) mit; (*in street*) verkaufen, feilhalten, feilbieten; (*by shouting out*) ausschreien

▶ **hawk about** VT *sep* (*Brit*) term etc benutzen

▶ **hawk around** VT *sep* (*lit, fig*) hausieren (gehen) mit

▶ **hawk up** VT *sep phlegm* aushusten

hawker [ˈhɔːkə] N **a** (= *hunter*) Falkner(in) *m(f)* **b** (= *pedlar, door-to-door*) Hausierer(in) *m(f)*; (*in*

street) Straßenhändler(in) *m(f)*; (*at market*) Marktschreier(in) *m(f)*

hawk-eyed [ˈhɔːkaɪd] ADJ scharfsichtig, adleräugig; **to be ~** Adleraugen haben

hawking [ˈhɔːkɪŋ] N (Falken)beize f, Falkenjagd f

hawk moth N Schwärmer *m*

hawser [ˈhɔːzə] N (*Naut*) Trosse f

hawthorn [ˈhɔːθɔːn] N (*also* **hawthorn bush/ tree**) Weiß- *or* Rot- *or* Hagedorn *m*; **~ hedge** Weiß- *or* Rotdornhecke f

hay [heɪ] N Heu *nt*; **to make ~** Heu machen; heuen; (*fig*) profitieren; **to hit the ~** (*inf*) sich aufs Ohr hauen (*inf*); **to make ~ while the sun shines** (*Prov*) das Eisen schmieden, solange es heiß ist (*Prov*)

hay: **haycock** N Heuhaufen *m*; **hay fever** N Heuschnupfen *m*; **hayfork** N Heugabel f; (*motor-driven*) Heuwender *m*; **hayloft** N Heuboden *m*; **haymaker** N **a** Heumacher(in) *m(f)* **b** (*Boxing only*) knallharter Schlag, Schwinger *m*; **haymaking** N Heuen *nt*, Heuernte f; **hayrack** N (*for fodder*) (Heu)raufe f; (*US, on wagon*) Heuwagenaufbau *m*; **hayrick, haystack** N Heuhaufen *m*

haywire [ˈheɪwaɪə] ADJ *pred* (*inf*) **to be (all) ~** (vollständig) durcheinander *or* ein Wirrwarr (*inf*) sein; **the local economy is all ~ again** die örtliche Wirtschaft ist wieder im Chaos versunken (*inf*); **to go ~** (= *go crazy*) durchdrehen (*inf*); (*plans, arrangements*) durcheinander geraten, über den Haufen geworfen werden (*inf*); (*machinery*) verrückt spielen (*inf*)

hazard [ˈhæzəd] N **a** (= *danger*) Gefahr f; (= *risk*) Risiko *nt*; **the ~s of war** die Gefahren des Krieges; **a safety ~** ein Sicherheitsrisiko *nt*; **it's a fire ~** es ist feuergefährlich, es stellt eine Feuergefahr dar; **to pose a ~ (to sb/sth)** eine Gefahr (für jdn/etw) darstellen
b (= *chance*) by ~ durch Zufall
c (*Sport, Golf, Showjumping*) Hindernis *nt*
d **hazards** PL (*Aut: also* **hazard (warning) lights**) Warnblinklicht *nt* VT **a** (= *risk*) *life, health, reputation* riskieren, aufs Spiel setzen; (= *endanger*) *person* in Gefahr bringen
b (= *venture to make*) wagen, riskieren; **if I might ~ a remark/suggestion** wenn ich mir eine Bemerkung/einen Vorschlag erlauben darf; **to ~ a guess** (es) wagen, eine Vermutung anzustellen; **to ~ a guess that ...** zu vermuten wagen, dass ...

hazardous [ˈhæzədəs] ADJ (= *dangerous*) gefährlich; (= *risky*) riskant; **~ to health** gesundheitsgefährdend; **bungee jumping is a ~ business** Bungeespringen ist eine gefährliche *or* riskante Angelegenheit; **such jobs are ~ to one's health** solche Arbeiten gefährden die Gesundheit

hazardous: hazardous material N Gefahrstoff *m*; (*Mot*) Gefahrgut *nt*; **hazardous waste** N Sondermüll *m*

haze [heɪz] N **a** Dunst *m*; **a ~ of exhaust fumes** ein Dunstschleier *m* von Abgasen **b** (*fig*) **he/ his mind was in a ~** (= *confused*) er war völlig verwirrt; **in a ~ of alcohol** vom Alkohol benebelt (*inf*)

hazel [ˈheɪzl] N (*Bot*) Haselnussstrauch *m*, Haselbusch *m* ADJ (*colour*) haselnuss- *or* hellbraun

hazelnut [ˈheɪzlnʌt] N Haselnuss f

hazily [ˈheɪzɪlɪ] ADV **a** **the island/hills loomed ~ through the mist** die Insel zeichnete/die Berge zeichneten sich verschwommen im Dunst ab **b** (= *vaguely*) remember, say vage

haziness [ˈheɪzɪnɪs] N **a** (of *sunshine*) Trübheit f; (of *view, outline, vision, surroundings*) Verschwommenheit f; **due to the ~ of the weather** wegen des dunstigen *or* diesigen Wetters **b** (of *ideas, memory, details*) Unklarheit f, Vagheit f

HAZMAT [ˈhæzˌmæt] N (*inf*) of *hazardous material* Gefahrstoff *m*; (*Mot*) Gefahrgut *nt*

hazy [ˈheɪzɪ] ADJ (+*er*) **a** *day, morning, weather* dunstig, diesig; *sunshine, sky* trübe; *view* verschwommen; **the ~ horizon** der im Dunst liegende Horizont; **~ blue** blassblau

b (= *blurred*) *outline, vision, surroundings* verschwommen

c (= *confused*) *notion, details, memory* unklar, vage; **to have only a ~ notion/idea of sth** nur unklare *or* vage Vorstellungen von etw haben; **I have only a ~ memory of her** ich erinnere mich nur dunkel *or* vage an sie; **I'm a bit ~ about that** ich bin mir nicht ganz im Klaren darüber; **I'm ~ about what really happened** ich weiß nicht so genau, was wirklich passiert ist; **my memory's a little ~ on this** ich kann mich nur dunkel *or* vage daran erinnern; **she's still (feeling) ~ (from the anaesthetic** (*Brit*) *or* **anesthetic** (*US*)**)** sie ist (von der Narkose) noch benommen

HB ADJ (*on pencil*) HB

H-bomb [ˈeɪtʃbɒm] N H-Bombe *f*

HDD (*Comput*) *abbr of* **hard disk drive** Festplattenlaufwerk *nt*

HDTV *abbr of* **high-definition television** HDTV *nt*

HE *abbr of* **His Excellency** *of* **His Eminence** S. E.

he [hiː] PERS PRON **a** er; **it is he** (*form*) er ist es, es ist er; **if I were he** (*form*) wenn ich er wäre; **he didn't do it, I did it** nicht er hat das getan, sondern ich; **so he's the one** (*inf*) er *or* es ist es also!; **Harry Rigg? who's he?** Harry Rigg? wer ist das denn? **b** **he who** *or* **that ...** (*liter*) derjenige, der ...; (*in proverbs*) wer ... **N** (*of animal*) Männchen *nt*; **it's a he** (*inf: of newborn baby*) es ist ein Er PREF männlich

---

head [hed]

1 NOUN	3 INTRANSITIVE VERB
2 TRANSITIVE VERB	4 PHRASAL VERBS

1 – NOUN

a Anat Kopf *m*, Haupt *nt* (*geh*); **from head to foot** von Kopf bis Fuß; **covered from head to foot** *or* **toe in mud** von oben bis unten mit Schlamm bedeckt; **head down(wards)** mit dem Kopf nach unten; **he can hold his head high in any company** er kann sich in jeder Gesellschaft sehen lassen; **the condemned man held his head high as he went to the scaffold** der Verurteilte ging erhobenen Hauptes zum Schafott; **to keep one's head above water** (*lit*) den Kopf über Wasser halten; (*fig*) sich über Wasser halten; **I've got a really bad head this morning** (*inf*) ich habe einen ziemlichen Brummschädel heute Morgen (*inf*); **to give a horse its head** einem Pferd die Zügel schießen lassen; **to give sb his head** jdn machen lassen; **to go to one's head** (*whisky, power*) einem in den *or* zu Kopf steigen; **I can't make head nor tail of it** daraus werde ich nicht schlau

♦ **a** *or* **per head** pro Kopf; **to pay 10 euros a** *or* **per head** 10 Euro pro Kopf bezahlen

♦ **head and shoulders** *or* **be head and shoulders above sb** (*lit*) jdn um Haupteslänge überragen; (*fig*) jdm haushoch überlegen sein

♦ **head over heels to fall head over heels in love with sb** sich bis über beide Ohren in jdn verlieben; **to fall head over heels down the stairs** kopfüber die Treppe herunterfallen

♦ **on one's/its head to stand on one's head** auf dem Kopf stehen; **to stand** *or* **turn sth on its head** etw auf den Kopf stellen; (*fig*) etw umkehren; **you could do it standing on your head** (*inf*) das kann man ja im Schlaf machen

♦ **on one's (own) head on your (own) head be it** auf Ihre eigene Kappe (*inf*) *or* Verantwortung

♦ **over sb's head to go over sb's head** über jds Kopf hinweg handeln; **he gave orders over my head** er hat über meinen Kopf (hin)weg Anordnungen gegeben; **to be promoted over sb's head** vor jdm bevorzugt befördert werden

♦ **one's head off to talk one's head off** (*inf*) reden wie ein Wasserfall (*inf*) *or* wie ein Buch (*inf*); **to laugh one's head off** (*inf*) sich fast totlachen (*inf*); **to shout one's head off** (*inf*) sich (*dat*) die Lunge aus dem Leib schreien (*inf*);

♦ **to scream one's head off** (*inf*) aus vollem Halse schreien

b = *measure of length* Kopf *m*; (*Racing*) Kopflänge *f*; **taller by a head** (um) einen Kopf größer; **by a short head** (*Horse Racing, fig*) um Nasenlänge

c = *intellect* Kopf *m*, Verstand *m*; **use your head** streng deinen Kopf an; **it never entered his head that ...** es kam ihm nie in den Sinn, dass ...; **we put our heads together** wir haben unsere Köpfe zusammengesteckt; **he has an old head on young shoulders** er ist sehr reif für sein Alter; **two heads are better than one** (*prov*) besser zwei als einer allein; **to be above** *or* **over sb's head** über jds Horizont (*acc*) gehen; **the joke went** *or* **was over his head** er verstand *or* kapierte (*inf*) den Witz nicht; **he talked over their heads** er hat über ihre Köpfe hinweg geredet; **to keep one's head** den Kopf nicht verlieren; **to lose one's head** den Kopf verlieren; **to be weak** *or* **soft in the head** (*inf*) einen (kleinen) Dachschaden haben (*inf*)

♦ **into one's/sb's head to get sth into one's head** etw begreifen; **he can't get it into his head that ...** es will ihm nicht in den Kopf, dass ...; **I can't get it into his head that ...** ich kann es ihm nicht begreiflich machen, dass ...; **to take it into one's head to do sth** sich (*dat*) in den Kopf setzen, etw zu tun; **don't put ideas into his head** bring ihn bloß nicht auf dumme Gedanken!; (= *unrealistic wish*) setz ihm bloß keinen Floh ins Ohr! (*inf*); **what/who put that idea into his head?** wie kommt er denn darauf?; (= *unrealistic wish also*) was/wer hat ihm denn den Floh ins Ohr gesetzt? (*inf*)

♦ **out of one's head to put** *or* **get sb/sth out of one's head** sich (*dat*) jdn/etw aus dem Kopf schlagen; **he couldn't get her out of his head** er konnte sie sich nicht aus dem Kopf schlagen

♦ **off one's head he is off his head** (*Brit inf*) er ist (ja) nicht (ganz) bei Trost (*inf*), er hat ja den Verstand verloren; (*with drugs*) er ist auf dem Trip (*inf*)

♦ **a (good) head (for) he has a good head for figures** er ist ein guter Rechner; **you need a good head for heights** Sie müssen schwindelfrei sein; **she has no head for heights** sie ist nicht schwindelfrei; **he has a good business head** er hat einen ausgeprägten Geschäftssinn; **he has a good head on his shoulders** er ist ein heller *or* kluger Kopf

d of cattle **twenty head of cattle** zwanzig Stück Vieh

e of vegetable (*of lettuce, cabbage, asparagus*) Kopf *m*; (*of celery*) Staude *f*

f = *top part* (*of flower, hammer, nail, page, pier*) Kopf *m*; (*of arrow, spear*) Spitze *f*; (*of bed*) Kopf(ende *nt*) *m*; (*on beer*) Blume *f*; (*of cane*) Knauf *m*, Griff *m*; (*of corn*) Ähre *f*; (*Archit: of column*) Kapitell *nt*; (*of stream, = upper area*) Oberlauf *m*; (= *source*) Ursprung *m*; (*of abscess etc*) Eiterpfropf *m*; **head of steam/water** (= *pressure*) Dampf-/Wasserdruck *m*; **at the head of the lake** am Zufluss des Sees; **at the head of the page/stairs** oben auf der Seite/an der Treppe; **at the head of the list** oben auf der Liste; **at the head of the table** oben am Tisch, am Kopf(ende) des Tisches; **at the head of the queue** (*Brit*)**/army** an der Spitze der Schlange/des Heeres; **at the head of the field** (*in race*) an der Spitze des Feldes

g = *crisis*

♦ **to a head to come to a head** sich zuspitzen; **the problem has come to a head** das Problem hat sich zugespitzt; **if things come to a head** wenn sich die Sache zuspitzt; **to bring matters to a head** die Sache auf die Spitze treiben

h = *leader* (*of family*) Oberhaupt *nt*; (*of business, organization*) Chef(in) *m(f)*, Boss *m* (*inf*); (*of department*) Leiter(in) *m(f)*; (*of office, sub-department*) Vorsteher(in) *m(f)*; (*Sch*) Schulleiter(in) *m(f)*; **head of department** (*in business*) Abteilungsleiter(in) *m(f)*; (*Sch, Univ*) Fachbereichsleiter(in) *m(f)*; **head of state** Staatsoberhaupt *nt*

i = *heading* Rubrik *f*; **listed under three main heads** in drei Rubriken eingetragen

j of coin Kopfseite *f*; **heads or tails?** Kopf oder Zahl?; **heads you win** bei Kopf gewinnst du

k Naut (= *bow*) Bug *m*; (*of mast*) Topp *m*; (= *toilet*) Pütz *f*

l Tech (*on tape recorder*) Tonkopf *m*; (*Comput, = read/write head*) Kopf *m*

m Drugs (*inf*) Junkie *m* (*inf*)

2 – TRANSITIVE VERB

a = *lead* (= *be at the head of*) anführen; (= *be in charge of*) führen; *team* leiten; **they headed the procession/list** sie führten den Umzug/die Liste an; **a coalition government headed by Mr Schröder** eine Koalitionsregierung unter der Führung von Herrn Schröder

b = *direct* steuern, lenken (*towards, for* in Richtung +*gen*)

c = *give a heading* überschreiben, eine Überschrift geben (+*dat*); **in the chapter headed ...** in dem Kapitel mit der Überschrift ...; **he heads each chapter with a quotation** er stellt jedem Kapitel ein Zitat voran

d Ftbl köpfen

3 – INTRANSITIVE VERB

gehen; (*vehicle*) fahren; **where are you heading** *or* **headed?** (*inf*) wo gehen/fahren Sie hin?; **are you heading my way?** gehen/fahren Sie in der gleichen Richtung wie ich?; **and the tornado was heading our way** und der Tornado kam auf uns zu

4 – PHRASAL VERBS

▶ **head back** VI zurückgehen/-fahren; **to be heading back** auf dem Rückweg sein; **it's time we were heading back now** es ist Zeit, umzukehren *or* sich auf den Rückweg zu machen

▶ **head for** VI +*prep obj* **a** *place, person* zugehen/zufahren auf (+*acc*); *town, country, direction* gehen/fahren in Richtung (+*gen*); *door, pub, bargain counter, prettiest girl* zusteuern auf (+*acc*) (*inf*); (*ship*) zufahren *or* Kurs halten auf (+*acc*); **where are you heading** *or* **headed for?** wo gehen/fahren *or* steuern (*inf*) Sie hin?; **to head for home** sich auf den Heimweg machen **b** (*fig*) zusteuern auf (+*acc*), auf dem Weg sein zu; **you're heading for trouble** du bist auf dem besten Weg, Ärger zu bekommen; **he is heading for a fall/the rocks** er rennt in sein Verderben; **to head for victory/defeat** auf einen Sieg/eine Niederlage zusteuern

▶ **head in** VT *sep ball* hineinköpfen; **to head the ball into the net** den Ball ins Netz köpfen VI köpfen

▶ **head off** VT *sep* **a** (= *divert*) umdirigieren **b** (= *avert*) *quarrel, war, strike* abwenden; *person* ablenken; *questions* abbiegen VI (= *set off*) sich aufmachen

▶ **head up** VT *sep committee, delegation* führen, leiten

---

head *in cpds* (= *top, senior*) Ober-; **headache** N Kopfweh *nt*, Kopfschmerzen *pl*; (*inf, = problem*) Problem *nt*; **to have a ~** Kopfschmerzen haben; **this is a bit of a ~ (for us)** das macht *or* bereitet uns ziemliches Kopfzerbrechen; **his teenage daughter was a real ~** mit seiner heranwachsenden Tochter hatte er große Schwierigkeiten; **headachy** [ˈhedɪkɪ] ADJ (*inf*) () **to be ~** (= *to suffer from headache*) an (leichten) Kopfschmerzen leiden; (= *to cause a headache*) Kopfschmerzen verursachen; **headband** N Stirnband *nt*; **head-banger** N (*inf, = crazy person*) Bekloppte(r) *mf* (*inf*); **headboard** N Kopfteil *nt*; **head boy** N *vom Schulleiter bestimmter Schulsprecher*; **headbutt** N Kopfstoß *m* VT mit dem Kopf stoßen; **headcase** N (*inf*) Spinner(in) *m(f)* (*inf*); **headcheese** N (*US*) Schweinskopfsülze *f*; **head clerk** N (*Comm*) Bürovorsteher(in) *m(f)*; (*Jur*) Kanzleivorsteher(in) *m(f)*; **head cold** N Kopfgrippe *f*; **head count** N **to have** *or* **take a ~** abzählen; **headcrash** N (*Comput*) Headcrash *m*; **headdress** N Kopfschmuck *m*

-headed [-hedɪd] ADJ *suf* -köpfig; **bald-headed** kahlköpfig; **a curly-headed child** ein lockiges Kind, ein Kind *nt* mit lockigen Haaren

headed notepaper N Schreibpapier *nt* mit Briefkopf

header ['hedə'] N **a** (*Brit*: = *dive*) Kopfsprung *m*, Köpfer *m* (*inf*); **to take a ~ into the water** einen Kopfsprung ins Wasser machen; (= *fall*) kopfüber ins Wasser fallen; **the dollar took a ~** der Dollarkurs fiel, der Dollar machte eine Talfahrt (*inf*) **b** (*Ftbl*) Kopfstoß *m*, Kopfball *m*; **he's a good ~ of the ball** er köpft gut **c** (*Typ*) Kopfzeile *f*

head: headfirst ADV (*lit, fig*) kopfüber; **head gate** N (*oberes*) Schleusentor; **headgear** N Kopfbedeckung *f*; (*of horse*: = *bridle*) Zaumzeug *nt*; **head girl** N *vom Schulleiter bestimmte Schulsprecherin*; **headguard** N Kopfschutz *m*; **head-hunt** VT abwerben; **I've been ~ed** ich bin abgeworben worden; (= *have been approached*) man hat versucht, mich abzuwerben; **VI** **we'll have to go out and ~** wir werden Mitarbeiter von anderen Firmen abwerben müssen; **head-hunter** N (*lit*) Kopfjäger *m*; (*fig*) Kopfjäger(in) *m(f)*, Headhunter(in) *m(f)*

headiness ['hedɪnɪs] N **a** berauschende Art; (*of experience*) Aufregung *f*; **the ~ of success** der Erfolgsrausch; **this wine is known for its ~** dieser Wein ist dafür bekannt, dass er schnell zu Kopf(e) steigt; **the ~ of this intellectual atmosphere** das Berauschende dieser geistesgeladenen Atmosphäre **b** (= *impetuosity*) Unbesonnenheit *f*

heading ['hedɪŋ] N **a** Überschrift *f*; (*on letter, document*) Kopf *m*; (*in encyclopedia*) Stichwort *nt*; **under the ~ of anthropology** unter dem Stichwort Anthropologie **b** (*Ftbl*) Köpfen *nt*

head: head lad N (*Horse Racing*) erster Stallbursche; **headlamp, headlight** N Scheinwerfer *m*; **headland** N Landspitze *f*; **headless** ADJ ohne Kopf; (*fig old*) kopflos; **to run around like a ~ chicken** (*Brit*) or **like a chicken with its head cut off** (*US*) wie ein aufgescheuchtes or kopfloses Huhn herumlaufen (*inf*); **headlight** N = **headlamp**; **headline** **N** (*Press*) Schlagzeile *f*; **he is always in the ~s** er macht immer Schlagzeilen; **the ~s were full of the story** die Geschichte beherrschte die Schlagzeilen; **to grab** or **hit** or **make the ~s** Schlagzeilen machen; **the news ~s** Kurznachrichten *pl*, das Wichtigste in Kürze **VT** **to be ~d ...** die Überschrift ... haben; **an article ~d ...** ein Artikel mit der Überschrift ...; **headline news** N , *no pl* **to be ~** in den Schlagzeilen sein; **headliner** N (*US, Mus, Theat inf*) Headliner(in) *m(f)*; **headline rate** N (*Brit, Econ*) **~ of inflation** Inflationsrate *f* (*unter Einbeziehung von Variablen wie Hypothekenzinssätzen etc*); **headlock** N **to get/have sb in a ~** jdn in den Schwitzkasten nehmen/im Schwitzkasten haben; **headlong** ADV **a** (= *very fast*) flee, run überstürzt, Hals über Kopf (*inf*); (= *with head forward*) fall vornüber; **he ran ~ down the stairs** er rannte in Windeseile die Treppe hinunter **b** (*fig, without careful thought*) rush, plunge überstürzt, Hals über Kopf (*inf*); **to rush** or **plunge ~ into sth** sich Hals über Kopf in etw (*acc*) stürzen (*inf*); **ADJ** flight, dash, rush überstürzt; **the army was in ~ flight** die Armee hatte Hals über Kopf die Flucht ergriffen (*inf*); **they made a ~ dash for the door** sie stürzten blindlings auf die Tür zu; **the dollar's ~ fall** der unaufhaltsame Sturz des Dollars; **headman** N (*of tribe*) Häuptling *m*, Stammesoberhaupt *nt*; **headmaster** N (*esp Brit*) Schulleiter *m*; (*of secondary school also*) Direktor *m*; (*of primary school also*) Rektor *m*; **headmistress** N (*esp Brit*) Schulleiterin *f*; (*of secondary school also*) Direktorin *f*; (*of primary school also*) Rektorin *f*; **headnote** N (*at the beginning of chapter, article*) kurze (Inhalts)angabe; **head office** N Zentrale *f*; **head-on** ADV **a** collide, crash frontal **b** (*fig, directly*) meet, confront, tackle direkt; **to meet tough issues ~** schwierige Fragen direkt angehen; **to confront sb/sth ~** jdm/einer Sache

ohne Umschweife entgegentreten **ADJ** **a** **~ collision** or **smash** Frontalzusammenstoß *m* **b** (*fig*) conflict, confrontation offen, direkt; **headphones** PL Kopfhörer *pl*; **head post office** N Hauptpostamt *nt*; **headquarter** VT **to be ~ed in** (*Mil*) sein Hauptquartier haben in (+*dat*); (*business*) seine Hauptstelle or Zentrale haben in (+*dat*); (*political party*) seine Parteizentrale haben in (+*dat*); **headquarters** N *sing* or *pl* (*Mil*) Hauptquartier *nt*; (*of business*) Hauptstelle *f*, Zentrale *f*; (*of political party*) Parteizentrale *f*, Hauptquartier *nt*; **headrace** N Gerinne *nt*; **headrest** N Kopfstütze *f*; **head restraint** N Kopfstütze *f*; **headroom** N lichte Höhe; (*in car*) Kopfraum *m*; **15 ft ~** (lichte) Höhe 15 Fuß; **headscarf** N Kopftuch *nt*; **headset** N Kopfhörer *pl*; **headship** N Schulleiterstelle *f*, Direktoren-/Rektorenstelle *f*; **headshrinker** ['hedʃrɪŋkə'] N (*lit*) Schrumpfkopfindianer *m*; (*inf*, = *psychiatrist*) Seelenklempner(in) *m(f)* (*inf*); **headsquare** N Kopftuch *nt*; **head start** N Vorsprung *m* (*on sb* jdm gegenüber); **headstone** N (*on grave*) Grabstein *m*; **headstrong** ADJ eigensinnig, dickköpfig; **head teacher** N (*Brit*) = **headmaster, headmistress**; **head-to-head** **ADV** **to compete ~ with sb** sich direkt mit jdm messen **ADJ** contest, competition direkt; (*with mit*); **head voice** N (*Mus*) Kopfstimme *f*; **head waiter** N Oberkellner *m*; **head waitress** N Oberkellnerin *f*; **headwaters** PL Quellflüsse *pl*; **headway** N **to make ~** (*lit, fig*) vorankommen; **did you make any ~ with the unions?** haben Sie bei den Gewerkschaften etwas erreicht?; **headwind** N Gegenwind *m*; **headword** N Anfangswort *nt*; (*in dictionary*) Stichwort *nt*; **headwork** N **a** (= *mental work*) Kopfarbeit *f*, geistige Arbeit **b** (*Ftbl*) Kopfballspiel *nt* **c** (*Tech*) Wasserkontrollanlage

heady ['hedɪ] ADJ (+*er*) **a** wine, scent, mixture, speed, atmosphere, sensation, success berauschend; experience aufregend; **the air is ~ with scent/spices** ein berauschender Duft/der berauschende Duft von Gewürzen hängt in der Luft; **to feel ~** berauscht sein; **the ~ heights of the Premier League** die Schwindel erregenden Höhen der Bundesliga; **to be ~ with success** im Erfolgsrausch sein; **~ with victory** siegestrunken; **~ stuff** (*fig inf*) eine aufregende Sache **b** (= *impetuous*) unbesonnen, impulsiv

heal [hiːl] **VI** (*Med, fig*) heilen **VT** heilen; **time ~s all wounds** (*Prov*) die Zeit heilt alle Wunden (*Prov*) **b** (*fig*) differences etc beilegen; (*third party*) schlichten; **they succeeded in ~ing the rift between them** es gelang ihnen, die Kluft zwischen ihnen zu überbrücken

▶ **heal over** VI zuheilen

▶ **heal up** VI zuheilen VT *sep* zuheilen lassen

healer ['hiːlə'] N Heiler(in) *m(f)* (*geh*); (= *herb etc*) Heilmittel *nt*; **time is a great ~** (*prov*) die Zeit heilt alle Wunden (*Prov*)

healing ['hiːlɪŋ] N Heilung *f*; (*of wound*) (Zu)heilen *nt* **ADJ** (*Med*) Heil-, heilend; (*fig*) besänftigend; **~ process** Heilprozess *m*; **~ powers** Heilkräfte *pl*, heilende Kräfte *pl*

health [helθ] N **a** Gesundheit *f*; (= *state of health*) Gesundheitszustand *m*; **in good ~** gesund, bei guter Gesundheit; **in poor ~** nicht gesund, bei schlechter Gesundheit; **state of ~** Gesundheitszustand *m*, Befinden *nt*; **how is his ~?** wie geht es ihm gesundheitlich?; **to regain one's ~** wieder gesund werden; **at least we still have our ~** wenigstens sind wir immer noch gesund; **to enjoy good ~** sich guter Gesundheit (*gen*) erfreuen; **to suffer from poor** or **bad ~** kränklich sein; **to be good/bad for one's ~** gesund/ungesund or gesundheitsschädlich sein, der Gesundheit (*dat*) zuträglich/nicht zuträglich sein; **poverty can cause poor ~** Armut kann zu schlechter Gesundheit führen; **~ and safety regulations** Arbeitsschutzvorschriften *pl*; **Ministry of Health** Gesundheitsministerium *nt*; **I'm not just doing it for the good of my ~** (*inf*) ich mache das doch nicht bloß aus Spaß (*inf*); **he stressed the ~ benefits of regular ex-**

ercise er betonte, wie gut regelmäßige Bewegung für die Gesundheit sei
b (*fig*) Gesundheit *f*
c **to drink (to) sb's ~** auf jds Wohl (*acc*) or Gesundheit (*acc*) trinken; **your ~!, good ~!** zum Wohl!, auf Ihre Gesundheit!

health: Health and Safety Executive N (*Brit*) Arbeitsschutzbehörde *f*; **Health and Social Services** PL (*US*) das amerikanische Gesundheits- und Sozialministerium; **health authority** N Gesundheitsbehörde *f*; **health care** N Gesundheitsfürsorge *f*; **health centre** (*Brit*) **a** (*Med*) Ärztezentrum *nt* **b** (*keep-fit*) Fitness-Center *nt*; **health certificate** N Gesundheitszeugnis *nt*; **health check** N Check-up *m*; **health club** N (= *place*) Fitnesscenter *nt*; **health education** N Hygiene *f*; **health farm** N Gesundheitsfarm *f*; **health food** N Reformkost *f*; **health food shop** (*Brit*), **health food store** (*esp US*) N Reformhaus *nt*, Bioladen *m*, Naturkostladen *m*

healthful ['helθfʊl], **healthgiving** ['helθgɪvɪŋ] ADJ gesund

health hazard N Gefahr *f* für die Gesundheit

healthily ['helθɪlɪ] ADV **a** (= *sensibly*) eat, live gesund; (= *robustly*) grow kräftig; **the recipe is ~ low in fat** das Rezept ist fettarm und daher gesund; **we felt ~ tired** wir fühlten eine gesunde Müdigkeit; **her face was glowing ~** ihr Gesicht hatte eine blühende Farbe **b** (*fig, = refreshingly*) **~ cynical/irreverent/independent** erfrischend zynisch/respektlos/unabhängig

healthiness ['helθɪnɪs] N (*lit, fig*) Gesundheit *f*; (*of bank balance*) gesunder Zustand

health: health inspector N Hygieneinspektor(in) *m(f)*; **health insurance** N Krankenversicherung *f*

HEALTH MAINTENANCE ORGANIZATION

Eine **health maintenance organization** (oder auch **HMO**) ist eine Gesellschaft, die in den Vereinigten Staaten ihren Mitgliedern medizinische Dienste anbietet. Die Mitglieder müssen einen monatlichen oder jährlichen Beitrag entrichten, im Gegenzug stellt die Gesellschaft medizinisches Personal an, das sich um alle gesundheitlichen Belange kümmert, auch bei stationären Krankenhausaufenthalten. Obwohl **HMOs** ähnlich eingestuft werden wie private Krankenversicherungen, gibt es doch einige wichtige Unterschiede. So haben die Mitglieder keine freie Arztwahl. Aus Kostendämpfungsgründen wird besonderer Wert auf Prävention gelegt, und unnötige Untersuchungen und Operationen werden nach Möglichkeit vermieden.

health: health problem N **to have ~s** gesundheitliche Probleme haben; **he retired because of ~s** er trat aus gesundheitlichen Gründen in den Ruhestand; **health resort** N Kurort *m*; (= *spa also*) Kurbad *nt*, Heilbad *nt*; **Health Service** N (*Brit*) **the ~** das Gesundheitswesen; **~ doctor** Kassenarzt *m*/-ärztin *f*; **health studio** N Fitnessstudio *nt*; **health visitor** N (*Brit*) Sozialarbeiter(in) *m(f)* (*in der Gesundheitsfürsorge*); **health warning** N (*on cigarette packet*) (gesundheitlicher) Warnhinweis

healthy ['helθɪ] ADJ (+*er*) (*lit, fig*) gesund; **a ~ mind in a ~ body** ein gesunder Geist in einem gesunden Körper; **to earn a ~ profit** einen ansehnlichen Gewinn machen; **he has a ~ bank balance** sein Kontostand ist gesund; **a ~ dose of sth** ein gesundes Maß an etw (*dat*); **that's not a ~ idea/attitude** das ist keine vernünftige Idee/gesunde Haltung; **to have a ~ respect for sb/sth** einen gesunden Respekt vor jdm/etw haben; **a ~ interest in sth** ein gesundes Interesse an etw (*dat*)

heap [hiːp] **N** Haufen *m*; (*inf*, = *old car*) Klapperkiste *f* (*inf*); **(to leave sth) in a ~** (etw) auf einem Haufen (liegen lassen); **the building was reduced to a ~ of rubble** das Haus sank in Schutt und Asche; **he fell in a ~ on the floor** er sackte zu Boden; **at the bottom/top of the ~** (fig) ganz unten/oben

b ~s of (inf) ein(en) Haufen (inf); **it's happened ~s of times** es ist schon zigmal vorgekommen (inf); **do you have any glasses? – yes, ~s** haben Sie Gläser? – (ja), jede Menge (inf); **she has ~s of enthusiasm/time** sie hat jede Menge Enthusiasmus/Zeit (inf); **to be in a whole ~ of trouble** tief in Schwierigkeiten stecken; **they got ~s of criticism** sie wurden massiv kritisiert

ADV ~s (inf) (unheimlich) viel

VT häufen; **he ~ed his clothes together** er warf seine Kleider auf einen Haufen; **to ~ praise on sb/sth** über jdn/etw voll des Lobes sein (geh), jdn/etw über den grünen Klee loben (inf); (in addressing) jdn mit Lob überschütten; **to ~ scorn on sb/sth** jdn/etw mit Spott übergießen; **to ~ abuse on sb** jdm Beleidigungen an den Kopf werfen; (cursing) jdn mit einer Flut von Schimpfwörtern überschütten; **a ~ed spoonful** ein gehäufter Löffel; **an armchair ~ed with cushions** ein Sessel, auf dem sich Kissen türmen

▶**heap up** **VT** sep aufhäufen; **he heaped up the litter into piles/a pile** er machte aus dem Abfall Haufen/einen Haufen **VI** sich häufen

hear [hɪə] ✆ 11.1, 12.2, 21.1, 24.3, 26.1 pret, ptp **heard** **VT** **a** (= also learn) hören; **I ~d him say that ...** ich habe ihn sagen hören, dass ...; **I ~d somebody come in** ich habe jemanden (herein)kommen hören; **there wasn't a sound to be ~d** es war kein Laut zu hören, man hörte keinen Laut; **he was ~d to say that ...** man hat ihn sagen hören, dass ...; **to make oneself ~d** sich (dat) Gehör verschaffen; **you're not going, do you ~ me!** du gehst nicht, hörst du (mich)!; **to ~ him speak you'd think ...** wenn man ihn so reden hört, könnte man meinen, ...; **I've often ~d say** or **it said that ...** ich habe oft gehört or sagen hören, dass ...; **I ~ you play chess** ich höre, Sie spielen Schach; **have you ~d the one about ...?** (haben Sie) den schon gehört von ...?; **I ~ tell you're going away** ich höre, Sie gehen weg; **I've ~d tell of a monster in the lake** ich habe von einem Ungeheuer in dem See gehört; **I've ~d it all before** ich habe das schon hundertmal gehört; **I've been ~ing things about you** von dir hört man ja schöne Dinge; **I must be ~ing things** ich glaube, ich höre nicht richtig

b (= listen to) lecture, programme etc hören; **to ~ a case** (Jur) einen Fall verhandeln; **to ~ evidence** (Jur) Zeugen vernehmen; **Lord, ~ our prayer** Herr, (er)höre unser Gebet; **Lord, ~ us** Herr, erhöre uns; **let's ~ your prayers before you go to sleep** wir wollen beten, bevor du schläfst

VI **a** (physically) hören; **he does not** or **cannot ~ very well** er hört nicht sehr gut; **~, ~!** (sehr) richtig!; (Parl) hört!, hört!

b (= get news) hören; **he's left his wife – yes, so I ~** er hat seine Frau verlassen – ja, ich habe es gehört; **I ~ from my daughter every week** ich höre jede Woche von meiner Tochter; **you'll be ~ing from me!** (threatening) Sie werden noch von mir hören!; **to ~ about sth** von etw hören or erfahren; **have you ~d about John? he's getting married** haben Sie gehört? John heiratet; **I've ~d a lot about you** ich habe schon viel von Ihnen gehört; **never ~d of him/it** nie (von ihm/davon) gehört; **I've ~d of him** ich habe schon von ihm gehört; **he wasn't ~d of for a long time** man hat lange Zeit nichts von ihm gehört; **he was never ~d of again** man hat nie wieder etwas von ihm gehört; **I've never ~d of such a thing!** das ist ja unerhört!; **I ~ about nothing else but that)!** ich höre überhaupt nichts anderes mehr!

▶**hear of** **VI** +prep obj (fig, = allow) hören wollen von; **I won't hear of it** ich will davon (gar) nichts hören

▶**hear out** **VT** sep person ausreden lassen; story zu Ende hören

heard [hɜːd] pret, ptp of **hear**

hearer ['hɪərə] **N** Hörer(in) m(f)

hearing ['hɪərɪŋ] **N** **a** Gehör nt; **to have a keen sense of ~** ein gutes Gehör haben

b within/out of ~ (distance) in/außer Hörweite; **he said that in/out of my ~** ich war in Hörweite/nicht in Hörweite, als er das sagte

c (Pol) Hearing nt, Anhörung f; (Jur) Verhandlung f; **disciplinary ~** Disziplinarverfahren nt; **~ of witnesses** (Jur) Zeugenvernehmung f; **he was refused a ~** er wurde nicht angehört; **he didn't get a fair ~** man hörte ihn nicht richtig an; (Jur) er bekam keinen fairen Prozess; **he got a sympathetic ~** er wurde wohlwollend angehört; **the Minister gave the petitioners a ~** der Minister hörte die Überbringer der Petition an; **to condemn sb without a ~** jdn verurteilen, ohne ihn (an)gehört zu haben; (Jur) jdn ohne Anhörung verurteilen

hearing: hearing aid **N** Hörgerät nt, Hörhilfe f; **hearing-impaired** ['hɪərɪŋɪm,peəd] **ADJ** (= deaf) gehörlos; (= partially deaf) hörgeschädigt **N** the ~ (= deaf) Gehörlose pl; (= partially deaf) Hörgeschädigte pl

hearken ['hɑːkn] **VI** (old, liter) horchen (to auf +acc)

hearsay ['hɪəseɪ] **N** Gerüchte pl; **to know sth from** or **by ~** etw vom Hörensagen wissen or haben; **~ rule** (Jur) Regel über den grundsätzlichen Ausschluss aller Beweise vom Hörensagen

hearsay: hearsay account **N** Bericht m aus zweiter Hand; **hearsay evidence** **N** Zeugenaussage, die auf Hörensagen beruht

hearse [hɜːs] **N** Leichenwagen m

heart [hɑːt] **N** **a** (Anat) Herz nt

b (fig, for emotion, courage etc) Herz nt; **to break sb's ~** jdm das Herz brechen; **it breaks my ~ to see her so upset** es bricht mir das Herz, sie so betrübt zu sehen; **it breaks my ~ to think that ...** mir bricht das Herz, wenn ich daran denke, dass ...; **she thought her ~ would break** sie meinte, ihr würde das Herz brechen; **you're breaking my ~** (iro) ich fang gleich an zu weinen (iro); **a man after my own ~** ein Mann ganz nach meinem Herzen; **to have a change of ~** sich anders besinnen, seine Meinung ändern; **to be close** or **dear to one's ~** (cause, subject) jdm am Herzen liegen; **to learn/know/recite sth (off) by ~** etw auswendig lernen/kennen/aufsagen; **I know the route by ~** ich kenne die Strecke (in- und) auswendig; **she was right in his ~ – she was right** im Grunde seines Herzens, dass sie Recht hatte; **in my ~ of ~s** im Grunde meines Herzens; **with all my ~** von ganzem Herzen; **from the bottom of one's ~** aus tiefstem Herzen; **to be the ~ and soul of sth** das Herz und die Seele einer Sache (gen) sein; **to put (one's) ~ and soul into sth** sich mit Leib und Seele einer Sache (dat) widmen; **to take sth to ~** sich (dat) etw zu Herzen nehmen; **we (only) have your interests at ~** uns liegen doch nur Ihre Interessen am Herzen; **to set one's ~ on sth** sein Herz an etw (acc) hängen (geh); **it did my ~ good** es wurde mir warm ums Herz; **to one's ~'s content** nach Herzenslust; **most men are boys at ~** die meisten Männer sind im Grunde (ihres Herzens) noch richtige Kinder; **I couldn't find it in my ~ to forgive him** ich konnte es nicht über mich bringen, ihm zu verzeihen; **his ~ isn't in his work/in it** er ist nicht mit dem Herzen bei der Sache/dabei; **he's putting/not putting his ~ into his work** er ist mit ganzem Herzen/nur mit halbem Herzen bei seiner Arbeit; **to give sb ~** jdm Mut machen; **to lose ~** den Mut verlieren; **to lose one's ~ (to sb/sth)** sein Herz (an jdn/etw) verlieren; **to take ~** Mut fassen; **to take ~ from his brother's example** das Beispiel seines Bruders machte ihm Mut; **they've taken him to their ~s** sie haben ihn ins Herz geschlossen; **to put new** or **fresh ~ into sb** jdm mit neuem Mut erfüllen; **to put new ~ into sth** etw mit neuem Leben erfüllen; **to be in good ~** (liter) guten Mutes sein (geh); **her ~ is in the right place** (inf) sie hat das Herz auf dem rechten Fleck

(inf); **to have a ~ of stone** ein Herz aus Stein haben; **to wear one's ~ on one's sleeve** (prov) das Herz auf der Zunge tragen (prov); **my ~ was in my mouth** (inf) mir schlug das Herz bis zum Hals; **his ~ was in his boots** (inf) ihm ist das Herz in die Hose(n) gerutscht (inf); **have a ~!** (inf) gib deinem Herzen einen Stoß! (inf); **I didn't have the ~ to say no** ich brachte es nicht übers Herz, nein or Nein zu sagen; **she has a ~ of gold** sie hat ein goldenes Herz; **my ~ sank** (with apprehension) mir wurde bang ums Herz (liter), mir rutschte das Herz in die Hose(n) (inf) (with sadness) das Herz wurde mir schwer; (= I was discouraged) mein Mut sank

c (= centre: of town, country, cabbage etc) Herz nt; **in the ~ of the forest** im tiefsten or mitten im Wald; **the ~ of the matter** der Kern der Sache; **the ~ of the tree** das Mark des Baumes; **artichoke ~** Artischockenherz nt

d yes, my ~ (liter) ja, mein Herz (liter); **dear ~** (old, liter) liebes Herz (liter)

e hearts **PL** (Cards) Herz nt; (Bridge) Coeur nt; **queen of ~s** Herz-/Coeurdame f

heart: heartache **N** Kummer m, Herzeleid nt (old liter), Herzweh nt (geh); **heart attack** **N** Herzanfall m; (= thrombosis) Herzinfarkt m; **I nearly had a ~** (fig inf, from shock) ich habe fast einen Herzschlag gekriegt (inf); (from surprise also) da hat mich doch fast der Schlag getroffen (inf); **heartbeat** **N** Herzschlag m; **heartbreak** **N** großer Kummer, Leid nt; **I've had my share of ~s** ich habe meinen Teil an Kummer gehabt; **it caused ~ for him** es brach ihm (beinahe) das Herz; **heartbreaker** **N** Herzensbrecher m; **heartbreaking** **ADJ** herzzerreißend; **it was ~ to see him with crutches** es brach einem das Herz, ihn an Krücken zu sehen; **it's a ~ situation** es bricht einem das Herz; **heartbroken** **ADJ** untröstlich, todunglücklich; **she was ~ about it** sie war darüber todunglücklich; (because of love, death etc also) es hat ihr das Herz gebrochen; **don't look so ~** schau (doch) nicht so unglücklich drein; **heartburn** **N** Sodbrennen nt; **heart case** **N** Herzpatient(in) m(f); **heart complaint** **N** Herzbeschwerden pl; **heart condition** **N** Herzleiden nt; **he has a ~** er ist herzleidend, er hats am Herzen (inf); **heart disease** **N** Herzkrankheit f

-hearted [-hɑːtɪd] **ADJ** suf -herzig; **kind-/cold-hearted** gut-/kaltherzig

hearten ['hɑːtn] **VT** ermutigen

heartening ['hɑːtnɪŋ] **ADJ** news ermutigend

heart: heart failure **N** Herzversagen nt; **he suffered ~** sein Herz hat versagt; **heartfelt** **ADJ** thanks, apology aufrichtig; sympathy, tribute, appeal, plea tief empfunden; **~ thanks to you all** Ihnen allen danke ich von ganzem Herzen; **her apology did not seem to be ~** ihre Entschuldigung schien nicht von Herzen zu kommen; **my ~ sympathy** or **condolences** mein tief empfundenes or herzliches Beileid

hearth [hɑːθ] **N** Feuerstelle f; (= whole fireplace) Kamin m; (fig, = home) (häuslicher) Herd; **the kettle was keeping warm on the ~** der Kessel wurde auf dem Herd warm gehalten; **~ and home** Haus und Herd

hearth: hearth brush **N** Kaminbesen m; **hearthrug** **N** Kaminvorleger m

heartily ['hɑːtɪlɪ] **ADV** **a** (= enthusiastically) laugh, say herzlich; sing aus voller Kehle; eat tüchtig

b (= thoroughly) recommend uneingeschränkt; agree voll und ganz; endorse, welcome von Herzen; **~ dislike doing sth** etw äußerst ungern tun; **to be ~ sick of sth** etw herzlich leid sein; **to be ~ fed up with sth** (inf) die Nase von etw gestrichen voll haben (inf); **I'm ~ glad he isn't coming** ich bin ausgesprochen froh, dass er nicht kommt

heartland ['hɑːtlænd] **N** Herzland nt, Herz des Landes; **in the Tory ~s** in den Hochburgen der Konservativen

heart: heartless **ADJ** herzlos; (= cruel also) grausam; **heartlessly** **ADV** grausam; **she ~ abandoned the child** sie verließ das Kind auf herzlose Weise; **how can you be so ~ cruel!**

wie kannst du nur so schrecklich grausam sein?; **heartlessness** N Herzlosigkeit f; (= cruelty) Grausamkeit f; **heart-lung machine** N Herz-Lungen-Maschine f; **heart murmur** N Herzgeräusche pl; **heart-rending** ADJ herzzerreißend; **heart-searching** f; **heart-shaped** ADJ herzförmig; **heartsick** ADJ (liter) **to be ~** Herzeleid haben (old liter); **heartstrings** PL **to pull** or **tug at sb's ~** jdn zu Tränen rühren, bei jdm auf die Tränendrüsen drücken (inf); **he plucked the ~ of rich old women** er nutzte die Gefühle von reichen alten Frauen aus; **heart-throb** N (inf) Schwarm m (inf); **heart-to-heart** ADJ ganz offen; **to have a ~ talk with sb** sich mit jdm ganz offen aussprechen N offene Aussprache; **it's time we had a ~** es ist Zeit, dass wir uns einmal offen aussprechen; **heart transplant** N Herztransplantation f, Herzverpflanzung f; **heart trouble** N Herzbeschwerden pl; **heart-warming** ADJ herzerfreuend

hearty ['hɑːtɪ] ADJ (+er) **a** (= loud and friendly) laugh, voice, greeting herzlich; person, manner (= boisterous) raubeinig; (= over-familiar) plumpvertraulich; **he gave a ~ laugh** er lachte herzlich or herzhaft
  b slap, blow kräftig
  c (= wholehearted) endorsement, condemnation uneingeschränkt; agreement ungeteilt; hatred, dislike tief; **~ congratulations** herzliche Glückwünsche pl; **~ welcome** herzlicher Empfang; **we bid you a ~ welcome** wir heißen Sie herzlich willkommen
  d food herzhaft, kräftig; meal herzhaft, deftig (inf); appetite gesund; helping kräftig, ordentlich; **to be a ~ eater** einen gesunden Appetit haben, kräftig zulangen (inf) → also **hale**
N **a** (Naut inf) **me hearties!** Jungs! (inf), Leute!
  b (inf, = sporting man/woman) Sportfreund(in) m(f); **a rugby ~** ein Rugbyfan m

heat [hiːt] N **a** Hitze f; (pleasant, Phys) Wärme f; (of curry etc) Schärfe f; (= heating) Heizung f; **I don't mind the ~** mir macht (die) Hitze nichts aus; **in the ~ of the day** wenn es heiß ist; **on** or **over (a) low ~** bei schwacher Hitze; **to regulate the ~** (in oven) die Hitze regulieren; (on fire) die Wärme regulieren
  b (fig, of argument, discussion) Hitze f; **in the ~ of the moment** in der Hitze des Gefechts; (when upset) in der Erregung; **the discussion generated quite a lot of ~** die Diskussion erhitzte die Gemüter; **to take the ~ out of the situation/an argument** die Situation/Diskussion entschärfen; **with some ~** (say, debate) hitzig; **in the ~ of the election campaign** in der Aufregung des Wahlkampfs
  c (inf, = pressure) Druck m; **to put the ~ on** Druck machen (inf); **to turn up the ~ on sb** jdm die Hölle heiß machen (inf); **the ~ is on now** wir/sie etc stehen jetzt unter enormem Druck; **the ~ is off** der Druck ist weg (inf); (= danger is past) die Gefahr ist vorbei
  d (Sport) Vorlauf m; (Boxing etc) Vorkampf m; **final ~** Finale nt
  e (Zool) Brunst f; (Hunt) Brunft f; (of dogs, cats) Läufigkeit f; **on** (Brit) or **in** (esp US) **~** brünstig; (Hunt) brunftig; (dog, cat) läufig, heiß; (inf: person) heiß (inf)
VT erhitzen; food also aufwärmen, heiß or warm machen; house, room heizen; pool beheizen; (= provide with heat) house, town beheizen
VI (room etc) sich erwärmen, warm werden; (get very hot) sich erhitzen, heiß werden; **your dinner is ~ing in the oven** dein Essen steht (im Backofen) warm

▶ **heat up** VI sich erwärmen, warm werden; (= get very hot) sich erhitzen; (engine) heißlaufen; (fig, situation) sich zuspitzen VT sep erwärmen; food aufwärmen, warm or heiß machen; (fig) discussion anheizen

heat death N Wärmetod m

heated ['hiːtɪd] ADJ **a** (lit) swimming pool, greenhouse etc beheizt; room geheizt; rear window, towel rail heizbar; **~ air** Warmluft f **b** (fig, = angry) debate, discussion, dispute, meeting hitzig, erregt;

---

argument, exchange, row heftig; words erregt; **to grow** or **become ~** (person) sich aufregen; (debate) hitzig or erregt werden; **things got very ~** die Gemüter erhitzten sich

heatedly ['hiːtɪdlɪ] ADV hitzig; argue heftig

heater ['hiːtə'] N Ofen m; (electrical also) Heizgerät nt; (in car) Heizung f; (for fondue) Rechaud m; **what sort of ~s do you have?** was für eine Heizung haben Sie?; **turn the ~ on** stell die Heizung an

heat: heat exchanger N Wärme(aus)tauscher m; **heat exhaustion** N Hitzeschäden pl; **heat flash** N Hitzeblitz m

heath [hiːθ] N **a** (= moorland) Heide f; (= type of country) Heide f, Heideland nt **b** (= plant) Heidekraut nt, Erika f

heat haze N Hitzeflimmern nt

heathen ['hiːðən] ADJ heidnisch; (fig) unkultiviert, unzivilisiert N Heide m, Heidin f; (fig) unkultivierter or unzivilisierter Mensch; **the ~** (collectively, lit) die Heiden; (fig) die Barbaren

heathenism ['hiːðənɪzəm] N Heidentum nt

heather ['heðə'] N Heidekraut nt, Erika f, Heide f

Heath Robinson [ˌhiːθ'rɒbɪnsən] ADJ (inf) device, machine wunderlich

heating ['hiːtɪŋ] N Heizung f; (= act, of room, house) (Be)heizen nt; (of substances) Erwärmen nt, Erhitzen nt; **what sort of ~ do you have?** was für eine Heizung haben Sie?

heating: heating apparatus N Heizapparat m; **heating element** N Heizelement nt; **heating engineer** N Heizungsinstallateur(in) m(f); **heating pad** N Heizkissen nt; **heating system** N Heizungssystem nt; (= apparatus) Heizungsanlage f

heat: heat lightning N Wetterleuchten nt; **heat loss** N Wärmeverlust m; **heatproof** ADJ hitzebeständig; **heat pump** N Wärmepumpe f; **heat rash** N Hitzeausschlag m, Hitzepocken pl; **heat-resistant**, **heat-resisting** ADJ hitzebeständig; **heat-seeking** ADJ Wärme suchend; **heat-sensitive** ADJ wärmeempfindlich; **heat shield** N (for protection) Hitzeschild m; (to retain heat) Wärmeschutz m; **heat spot** N (Brit) Hitzebläschen nt; **heatstroke** N Hitzschlag m; **heat treatment** N (Metal, Med) Wärmebehandlung f; **heat wave** N Hitzewelle f

heave [hiːv] VT **a** (= lift) (hoch)hieven, (hoch)heben, wuchten (onto or +acc); (= drag) schleppen; **he ~d himself out of bed** er hievte sich aus dem Bett (inf); **she ~d him to his feet** sie wuchtete ihn auf die Beine
  b (= throw) werfen, schmeißen (inf)
  c sigh, sob ausstoßen
  d pret, ptp hove (Naut) wenden; **to ~ anchor** den Anker lichten
VI **a** (= pull) ziehen, hieven
  b (= move: ground) sich heben und senken; (sea, waves, bosom) wogen (geh); (stomach) sich umdrehen; (body) sich krümmen; **the earthquake made the ground ~** bei dem Beben hob sich die Erde
  c pret, ptp hove (Naut) **to ~ into sight** or **view** in Sicht kommen; **to ~ alongside** längsseits gehen
N (of sea, waves) Auf und Ab nt, Wogen nt (geh); (of bosom, chest) Wogen nt (geh); **to lift/throw sth with a great ~** etw mit großer Anstrengung hochhieven or hochwuchten/mit großer Wucht werfen

▶ **heave to** (Naut) VI beidrehen VT sep ship stoppen

▶ **heave up** VI (inf, = vomit) brechen VT sep **a** (= pull up) hochhieven, hochwuchten; (= push up) hochstemmen **b** (inf, = vomit) ausbrechen, von sich geben (inf)

heave ho INTERJ hau ruck

heaven ['hevn] N **a** (lit, fig inf) Himmel m; **the ~s** (liter) der Himmel; **in ~** im Himmel; **to go to ~** in den Himmel kommen; **he is in (seventh) ~** er ist im siebten Himmel; **to move ~ and earth**

Himmel und Hölle in Bewegung setzen; **it was ~** es war einfach himmlisch; **the shop was a chocolate lover's ~!** das Geschäft war ein Paradies für Schokoladenfans!; **the ~s opened** der Himmel öffnete seine Schleusen
  b (inf) **(good) ~s!** (du) lieber Himmel! (inf), du liebe Zeit! (inf); **would you like to? – (good) ~s no!** möchten Sie? – um Gottes or Himmels willen, bloß nicht!; **I wish to ~ (that) ...** ich wünschte mir wirklich, dass ...; **~ knows what ...** weiß Gott or der Himmel, was ... (inf); **~ knows I need some good luck** ich brauche weiß Gott ein bisschen Glück; **~ forbid!** bloß nicht, um Himmels willen! (inf); **~ forbid that I should end up like him** dass ich um Himmels willen nicht auch so wie er werde! (inf); **~ help the man she marries** der arme Mann, den sie mal heiratet (inf); **for ~'s sake!** um Himmels or Gottes willen!; **what in ~'s name ...?** was um Himmels or Gottes willen ...?

heavenly ['hevnlɪ] ADJ **a** himmlisch, Himmels-; **~ body** Himmelskörper m; **~ host** himmlische Heerscharen pl; **~ peace** himmlischer Frieden **b** (inf, = delightful) himmlisch, traumhaft

heaven-sent ['hevn,sent] ADJ opportunity ideal; **it was ~** das kam wie gerufen

heavenward(s) ['hevnwəd(z)] ADV zum Himmel, gen Himmel (liter); **to raise one's eyes heavenward** den Augen zum Himmel erheben

heaves [hiːvz] N sing (Vet) Dämpfigkeit f; **to have the ~** dämpfig sein; (sl, = vomit) reihern (sl)

heavily ['hevɪlɪ] ADV **a** (= a lot) stark; populated, wooded dicht; armed, fortified schwer; guarded streng; **~ underlined** (word, passage) dick unterstrichen; **~ accented** (English, German etc) mit starkem Akzent; **to borrow ~** hohe Kredite aufnehmen; (fig) viele Anleihen machen (from bei); **to gamble ~** ein leidenschaftlicher Spieler sein; **to gamble ~ on sth** viel Geld auf etw (acc) wetten; (fig) sehr auf etw (acc) bauen; **his face was ~ bruised** sein Gesicht war voller blauer Flecken; **their feet are ~ bandaged** ihre Füße sind dick verbunden; **~ disguised** (lit, fig) völlig unkenntlich gemacht; **to lose ~** (in gambling, sport, election) hoch verlieren; **to be ~ reliant on sb/sth** stark auf jdn/etw angewiesen sein; **to depend** or **rely ~ on sb/sth** stark von jdm/etw abhängen; **to draw ~ on sth** sich zum großen Teil auf etw (acc) stützen; **to be ~ involved in** or **with sth** sehr viel mit etw zu tun haben; **to be ~ involved in a party/movement** in einer Partei/Bewegung stark engagiert sein; **to be ~ into sth** (inf) voll auf etw (acc) abfahren (inf); **to be ~ in debt** stark verschuldet sein; **to be ~ weighted in sb's favour** (Brit) or **favor** (US)/**against sb** jdn stark begünstigen/benachteiligen; **to be ~ fined** zu einer hohen Geldstrafe verurteilt werden; **to be ~ outnumbered** zahlenmäßig stark unterlegen sein; **to be ~ defeated** eine schwere Niederlage erleiden; **to be ~ booked** fast ganz ausgebucht sein; **~ pregnant** hochschwanger
  b (= deeply) breathe schwer; sigh tief; pant stark
  c (lit) land, lean, fall schwer; (= clumsily) move, walk schwerfällig; **~ laden** schwer beladen; **~ built** kräftig gebaut; **she sat down ~ on the bed** sie setzte sich schwerfällig aufs Bett
  d (= slowly) say schleppend
  e (= richly) carved, encrusted, embroidered, gilded reich

heaviness ['hevɪnɪs] N **a** (of person, object, load) Schwere f; (of features) Grobheit f; **~ of heart** schweres Herz; **~ of spirit** gedrückte Stimmung, Niedergeschlagenheit f **b** (of tread, blow, gunfire, casualties etc) Stärke f; (of traffic) Stärke f; (of defeat, losses, taxes) Höhe f; (of buying) Umfang m; (of line) Dicke f; (of sleep) Tiefe f
  c (= heavy-handedness: of manner, style) Schwerfälligkeit f **d** (= oppressiveness, of air) Schwüle f; (of sky) Bedecktheit f

heavy ['hevɪ] ADJ (+er) **a** (= of great weight, Phys, fig) schwer; features grob; **with a ~ heart** schweren Herzens, mit schwerem Herzen; **~ with**

pollen mit Pollen geschwängert (*geh*); **~ with sleep** (*person*) schläfrig; **~ also** schwer; **the air was ~ with smoke/the smell of cooking** der Rauch/Essensgeruch hing schwer in der Luft; **his voice was ~ with sarcasm** seine Stimme triefte von *or* vor Sarkasmus

b *blow, gunfire, casualties, fog, book, meal, defeat, losses* schwer; *rain, traffic, drinker, smoker, period* stark; *expenses, taxes* hoch; *buying* groß; *line* dick; *sleep* tief; *landing, fall* hart; **~ buyer** Großabnehmer *m*; **~ type** (*Typ*) Fettdruck *m*; **~ breathing** schweres Atmen; **to be ~ on petrol** (*Brit*) *or* **gas** (*US*) viel Benzin brauchen; **to be ~ on the stomach** schwer im Magen liegen; **to be ~ with child** (*liter*) schweren Leibes sein (*geh*)

c (= *heavy-handed*) *manner, style, sense of humour* schwerfällig

d (= *oppressive*) *silence* bedrückend; *weather, air* drückend, schwül; *sky* bedeckt

e (= *difficult*) *task, work, day* schwer; **the going was ~** wir kamen nur schwer voran; **she can be ~ going** sie kann ziemlich anstrengend sein; **the conversation was ~ going** die Unterhaltung war mühsam; **this book is very ~ going** das Buch liest sich schwer

f (*Theat*) *part* schwer, ernst

g (*inf*, = *strict*) streng (*on* mit); **to play the ~ father/husband** den gestrengen Vater/Ehemann spielen

h (*dated US sl*) prima (*inf*), dufte (*dated inf*)

ADV schwer; **his guilt weighs** *or* **lies ~ on him** seine Schuld lastet schwer auf ihm

N a (*Brit inf*: = *thug*) Schlägertyp *m*

b (*Theat*, = *villain*) Schurke *m*

c (*Scot*, = *beer*) dunkleres, obergäriges Bier

heavy: heavy artillery N (*Mil*) schwere Artillerie; **heavy-duty** ADJ *clothes, tyres etc* strapazierfähig; *plastic, flex* dick; **~ machine** Hochleistungsmaschine *f*; **heavy-footed** ADJ schwerfällig; **heavy goods vehicle** N Lastkraftwagen *m*; **heavy-handed** ADJ schwerfällig, ungeschickt; **heavy-hearted** ADJ mit schwerem Herzen, bedrückt; **heavy hitter** N (*US*) sehr wichtige *or* einflussreiche Persönlichkeit; **heavy industry** N Schwerindustrie *f*; **heavy-laden** ADJ schwer beladen (*also Bibl*); **heavy metal** N **a** Schwermetall *nt* **b** (*Mus*) Heavymetal *m*; **heavy water** N schweres Wasser; **heavy water reactor** N Schwerwasserreaktor *m*

heavyweight ['hevɪweɪt] **N a** (*Sport*) Schwergewicht *nt*, Schwergewichtler(in) *m(f)* **b** (*fig inf*: = *influential person*) großes Tier (*inf*); **the literary ~s** die literarischen Größen *pl* **ADJ a** (*Sport*) **~ champion** Meister(in) *m(f)* im Schwergewicht; **~ boxer** (Boxer(in) *m(f)*) im Schwergewicht *nt*, Schwergewichtler(in) *m(f)*; **~ class** Schwergewicht *nt* **b** (*fig inf*: = *serious*) *issue, subject* gewichtig; *writer, commentator, interviewer* ernst zu nehmend; *position* bedeutend; *newspaper* seriös **c** (= *thick, heavy*) *cloth, plastic, paper* schwer

hebdomadal [heb'dɒmədl] ADJ (*form*) wöchentlich

Hebrew ['hiːbruː] **ADJ** hebräisch **N a** Hebräer(in) *m(f)* **b** (*Ling*) Hebräisch *nt* → *also* **English**

Hebridean [ˌhebrɪ'diːən] ADJ Hebriden-, der Hebriden; **~ island** Hebrideninsel *f*

Hebrides ['hebrɪdiːz] PL Hebriden *pl*

heck [hek] INTERJ (*inf*) oh **~!** zum Kuckuck! (*inf*); **ah, what the ~!** ach, was solls! (*inf*); **what the ~ do you mean?** was zum Kuckuck soll das heißen? (*inf*); **I've a ~ of a lot to do** ich habe irrsinnig viel zu tun (*inf*); **I'm in one ~ of a mess** ich stecke bis zum Hals im Schlamassel (*inf*)

heckle ['hekl] **VT** *speaker* (durch Zwischenrufe) stören **VI** stören, Zwischenrufe machen

heckler ['heklə'] N Zwischenrufer(in) *m(f)*, Störer(in) *m(f)* (*pej*)

heckling ['heklɪŋ] N Zwischenrufe *pl*

hectare ['hektɑː'] N Hektar *m or nt*

hectic ['hektɪk] ADJ (*also Med*) hektisch; **~ colour** (*Med*) hektische Röte

hectogramme, (*US*) **hectogram** ['hektəʊgræm] N Hektogramm *nt*

hectolitre, (*US*) **hectoliter** ['hektəʊˌliːtə'] N Hektoliter *m*

hector ['hektə'] VT (*liter*, = *bully*) tyrannisieren

hectoring ['hektərɪŋ] ADJ herrisch, tyrannisch

he'd [hiːd] contr of **he would** of **he had**

hedge [hedʒ] **N** Hecke *f*; (*fig*, = *protection*) Schutz *m*; **to be a ~ against sth** ein Schutz(-wall) *m* gegen etw sein **VI** ausweichen, kneifen (*inf*) (*at* bei); **to ~ on a question** einer Frage ausweichen; **to ~ on a promise** nichts versprechen wollen; **the president continues to ~ on whether to …** der Präsident lässt es weiterhin offen, ob …; **stop hedging and say what you think** weich nicht immer aus, sag, was du denkst!; **to ~ against sth** sich vor etw (*dat*) schützen **VT a** *investment* absichern; **to ~ one's bets** (*lit, fig*) sich absichern, auf Nummer sicher gehen (*inf*) **b** *field, garden* (mit einer Hecke) umgeben

▶**hedge about** (*Brit*) *or* **around** VT sep **a** (*with restrictions etc*) *procedure* erschweren, behindern; *offer, reform* einschränken (*with* durch) **b** (*rare: lit*) (mit einer Hecke) einfassen

▶**hedge in** *or* (*esp Brit*) **round** VT sep **a** *field* mit einer Hecke umgeben *or* einfassen **b** (*fig*) *procedure* behindern, erschweren; **to hedge sb in** jdn in seiner Freiheit einengen *or* beschränken

▶**hedge off** VT sep mit einer Hecke abgrenzen *or* abtrennen

hedgehog ['hedʒhɒg] N Igel *m*

hedge: hedgehop VI tief fliegen; **hedgerow** N Hecke *f*, Knick *m* (*N Ger*); **hedge sparrow** N Heckenbraunelle *f*; **hedge trimmer** N Elektroheckenschere *f*

hedonism ['hiːdənɪzəm] N Hedonismus *m*

hedonist ['hiːdənɪst] **N** Hedonist(in) *m(f)* **ADJ** hedonistisch

hedonistic ['hiːdənɪstɪk] ADJ hedonistisch

heebie-jeebies ['hiːbɪ'dʒiːbɪz] PL (*inf*) Gänsehaut *f* (*inf*); **it/he gives me the ~** dabei/wenn ich ihn sehe, bekomm ich eine Gänsehaut (*inf*)

heed [hiːd] **N** Beachtung *f*; **to take ~** Acht geben, aufpassen; **to pay ~ to sb/sth**, **to take ~ of sb/sth** jdn/etw beachten, jdm/einer Sache Beachtung schenken; **to pay no ~ to sb/sth**, **to take no ~ of sb/sth** jdn/etw nicht beachten, jdm/einer Sache keine Beachtung schenken; **to take ~ to do sth** darauf achten, etw zu tun **VT** beachten, Beachtung schenken (+*dat*); **just ~ what your father says** hör auf deinen Vater; **he never ~s my advice** er hört nie auf meinen Rat

heedful ['hiːdfʊl] ADJ **to be ~ of sb's warning/advice** auf jds Warnung (*acc*)/Rat (*acc*) hören

heedless ['hiːdlɪs] ADJ rücksichtslos; *extravagance* leichtsinnig; **to be ~ of sth** etw nicht beachten, auf etw (*acc*) nicht achten; **~ of their complaints** ohne sich um ihre Beschwerden zu kümmern, ohne Rücksicht auf ihre Beschwerden

heedlessly ['hiːdlɪslɪ] ADV rücksichtslos

heehaw ['hiːhɔː] **N** Iah *nt* **VI** iahen

heel¹ [hiːl] **N a** Ferse *f*; (*of shoe*) Absatz *m*; **the ~ of the hand** der Handballen; **I like to wear ~s** ich trage gerne Schuhe mit hohen Absätzen; **with his dog/the children at his ~s** gefolgt von seinem Hund/den Kindern; **to be right on sb's ~s** jdm auf den Fersen folgen; (*fig*: = *chase*) jdm auf den Fersen sein; **to follow hard upon sb's ~s** jdm dicht auf den Fersen sein, sich an jds Fersen (*acc*) heften (*geh*); **panic buying came hard on the ~s of the government's announcement** Hamsterkäufe folgten der Erklärung der Regierung auf dem Fuße; **the police were hot on our ~s** die Polizei war uns dicht auf den Fersen; **to be snapping at sb's ~s** (*fig inf*) jdm dicht auf den Fersen sein; **to be down at ~** (*person*) abgerissen *or* heruntergekommen sein; (*shoes*) schiefe Absätze haben,

abgelaufen sein; (*building*) heruntergekommen sein; **to take to one's ~s** sich aus dem Staub(e) machen, Fersengeld geben (*dated, hum*); **to show sb a clean pair of ~s** (= *escape*) vor jdm davonlaufen, jdm die Fersen zeigen (*geh*); (= *leave behind*) jdm weit voraus sein, jdn weit hinter sich lassen; **~!** (*to dog*) (bei) Fuß!; **he brought the dog to ~** er befahl dem Hund, bei Fuß zu gehen; **to bring sb to ~** jdn an die Kandare nehmen (*inf*); **to turn** *or* **spin on one's ~** auf dem Absatz kehrtmachen; **to cool** *or* **kick one's ~s** (*inf*, = *wait*) warten; (= *do nothing*) Däumchen drehen; **to set** *or* **rock sb back on his/her** *etc* **~s** (*fig inf*) jdm einen Schock versetzen

b (*of golf club*) Ferse *f*; (*of loaf*) Kanten *m*; (*of mast*) Fuß *m*

c (*dated pej sl*, = *person*) Saukerl *m* (*sl*)

VT a to ~ shoes auf Schuhe neue Absätze machen; **these shoes need ~ing** diese Schuhe brauchen neue Absätze

b (*Rugby*) *ball* hakeln

heel² (*Naut*) VI (*ship: also* **heel over**) krängen **a** (*spec*), sich (auf die Seite) legen *or* neigen; **to ~ hard over** sich stark auf die Seite legen, stark krängen (*spec*) **VT** krängen lassen (*spec*), sich seitlich überlegen lassen **N** (*seitliches*) Überlegen, Seitenneigung *f*

heel bar N Absatzbar *f*

heft [heft] **VT** (*US inf*, = *lift*) (hoch)heben; (= *assess weight*) abwägen, das Gewicht (ab)schätzen von **N** Gewicht *nt*; (= *strength*) (Muskel-)kraft *f*

hefty ['heftɪ] ADJ (+*er*) (*inf*) **a** (= *large*) *person* kräftig (gebaut); *object* massiv; *meal* kräftig, deftig (*inf*); *fine, bill, increase, fees, payment* saftig (*inf*); *profit* anständig (*inf*); *debt* hoch; **a ~ tome** ein Schmöker *m* (*inf*) **b** (= *powerful*) *kick, punch, slap* kräftig, saftig (*inf*)

Hegelian [heɪ'geɪlɪən] **ADJ** Hegelsch; (= *in Hegelian tradition*) hegelianisch **N** Hegelianer(in) *m(f)*

hegemony [hɪ'gemənɪ] N Hegemonie *f*

hegira [he'dʒaɪrə] N Hedschra *f*

Heidelberg man ['haɪdlbɜːg'mæn] N Homo heidelbergensis *m*

heifer ['hefə'] N Färse *f*

heigh [heɪ] INTERJ **~-ho!** nun ja!

height [haɪt] **N a** (*of building, mountain etc*, = *altitude*) Höhe *f*; (*of person*) Größe *f*; **to be six feet in ~** sechs Fuß groß *or* (*wall etc*) hoch sein; **what ~ are you?** wie groß sind Sie?; **he pulled himself up to his full ~** er richtete sich zu voller Größe auf; **you can raise the ~ of the saddle** du kannst den Sattel höher stellen; **at shoulder/head ~** in Schulter-/Kopfhöhe **b heights** PL (= *high place*) Höhen *pl*; **to scale the ~s of** Everest den Mount Everest besteigen; **fear of ~s** Höhenangst *f*; **to be afraid of ~s** nicht schwindelfrei sein **c** (*fig*) Höhe *f*; (*of stupidity*) Gipfel *m*; **at the ~ of his power** auf der Höhe seiner Macht; **the speculation has reached new ~s** die Spekulationen haben einen neuen Höhepunkt erreicht; **the ~ of luxury** das Nonplusultra an Luxus; **that is the ~ of arrogance/folly** das ist der Gipfel der Arroganz/der Torheit; **that is the ~ of bad manners!** das ist doch die Höhe!, das ist der Gipfel der Unverschämtheit!; **it is the ~ of bad manners to …** es verstößt gegen jede Etikette, zu …; **at the ~ of the season** in der Hauptsaison; **at the ~ of the storm** als der Sturm am heftigsten war; **at the ~ of summer** im Hochsommer; **at its ~ the company employed 12,000 people** in ihrer Glanzzeit hatte die Firma 12.000 Angestellte; **during the war emigration was at its ~** im Krieg erreichte die Auswanderungswelle ihren Höhepunkt; **to be the ~ of fashion** große Mode *or* der letzte Schrei sein

height-adjustable ADJ höhenverstellbar

heighten ['haɪtn] **VT** (= *raise*) höher stellen *or* machen; (= *emphasize*) *colour etc* hervorheben; (*Med*) *fever* steigen lassen, erhöhen; *intensity* steigern; *colour, feelings, anger, love, ambition* verstärken; *passions, fear, fitness, effect, tension* verstärken, erhöhen; **with ~ed colour** (*Brit*) or **colour** (*US*) mit (hoch)rotem Gesicht; **~ed awareness** erhöhte Aufmerksamkeit ▣ (*fig, = increase*) wachsen, größer or stärker werden

heinous ['heɪnəs] **ADJ** abscheulich, verabscheuungswürdig

heinously ['heɪnəslɪ] **ADV** auf abscheuliche Weise

heinousness ['heɪnəsnɪs] **N** Abscheulichkeit *f*

heir [ɛə] **N** Erbe *m*, Erbin *f* (*to +gen*); **~ to the throne** Thronfolger(in) *m(f)*

heir apparent **N** gesetzlicher Erbe, gesetzliche Erbin

heiress ['ɛərɛs] **N** Erbin *f*

heirloom ['ɛəluːm] **N** Erbstück *nt*

heist [haɪst] (*esp US, inf*) **N** Raubüberfall *m* **VT** rauben

held [held] *pret, ptp of* **hold**

Helen ['helɪn] **N** Helene *f*; (*Myth*) Helena *f*; **~ of Troy** die Schöne Helena

helical ['helɪkəl] **ADJ** spiralförmig, helikal (*spec*); *gear* schräg verzahnt

helicopter ['helɪkɒptə] **N** Hubschrauber *m* **VT** **he was ~ed out of the area** er wurde per Hubschrauber aus dem Gebiet abtransportiert

helicopter gunship **N** Kampfhubschrauber *m*

Heligoland ['helɪɡəʊlænd] **N** Helgoland *nt*

heliocentric [ˌhiːlɪəʊ'sentrɪk] **ADJ** heliozentrisch

heliograph ['hiːlɪəɡrɑːf] **N** Heliograf *m* **VT** heliografisch übermitteln

heliotrope ['hiːlɪətrəʊp] **N** (*Bot, = colour*) Heliotrop *nt* **ADJ** heliotrop(isch)

heliotropic [ˌhiːlɪəʊ'trəʊpɪk] **ADJ** heliotrop(isch)

helipad ['helɪpæd] **N** Hubschrauberlandeplatz *m*

heliport ['helɪpɔːt] **N** Heliport *m*, Hubschrauberflugplatz *m*

heliskiing ['helɪˌskiːɪŋ] **N** Heliskiing *nt* (*Skifahren mit einem Hubschrauber, der den Skifahrer auf den Gipfel fliegt*)

helispot ['helɪspɒt] **N** provisorischer Hubschrauberlandeplatz

helium ['hiːlɪəm] **N** Helium *nt*

helix ['hiːlɪks] **N** (räumliche) Spirale, Helix *f*

hell [hel] **N** **a** Hölle *f*; **to go to ~** (*lit*) in die Hölle kommen, zur Hölle fahren (*liter*); **the road to Hell is paved with good intentions** (*prov*) der Weg zur Hölle ist mit guten Vorsätzen gepflastert (*Prov*); **~ hath no fury like a woman scorned** (*liter*) es gibt nichts Schlimmeres als die Rache einer geschmähten Frau **b** (*fig uses*) **all ~ broke loose** die Hölle war los; **it's ~ working there** es ist die reine Hölle, dort zu arbeiten; **it was ~ in the trenches** es war die reine Hölle in den Schützengräben; **their life together was ~ on earth** ihr gemeinsames Leben war die reinste Hölle or die Hölle auf Erden; **a living ~** die Hölle auf Erden; **life became ~** das Leben wurde zur Hölle; **to go through ~** Höllenqualen ausstehen; **I put her through ~** ich machte ihr das Leben zur Hölle; **she made his life ~** sie machte ihm das Leben zur Hölle; **we've been to ~ and back** (*inf*) es war die reinste Hölle; **to give sb ~** (*tell off*) jdm die Hölle heiß machen; (*= make life unpleasant*) jdm das Leben zur Hölle machen; **you'll get ~ if he finds out** (*inf*) der macht dich zur Schnecke or Sau, wenn er das erfährt (*inf*); **there'll be ~ to pay when he finds out** wenn er das erfährt, ist der Teufel los (*inf*); **to play ~ with sth** etw total durcheinander bringen; **I did it (just) for the ~ of it** (*inf*) ich habe es nur zum Spaß or aus Jux gemacht; **come ~ or high water** egal, was passiert; **you can wait until ~ freezes over** da kannst du warten, bis du schwarz wirst; **~ for leather** was das Zeug hält; *run also* was die Beine hergeben; **the mother-in-law from ~** die böse Schwiegermutter, wie sie im

Buche steht; **the holiday from ~** der absolut katastrophale Urlaub **c** (*inf, intensifier*) **a ~ of a noise** ein Höllen- or Heidenlärm *m* (*inf*); **it's (as) hot as ~** es ist höllisch heiß (*inf*); **I was angry as ~** ich war stinksauer (*inf*); **to work like ~** arbeiten, was das Zeug hält, wie wild arbeiten (*inf*); **to run like ~** laufen, was die Beine hergeben (*inf*); **it hurts like ~** es tut wahnsinnig weh (*inf*); **we had a or one ~ of a time** (*= bad, difficult*) es war grauenhaft; (*= good*) wir haben uns prima amüsiert (*inf*); **a ~ of a lot** verdammt viel (*inf*); **she's a or one ~ of a girl** die ist wahnsinnig in Ordnung (*inf*), das ist ein klasse Mädchen (*inf*); **that's one or a ~ of a problem/difference/climb** das ist ein verdammt or wahnsinnig schwieriges Problem (*inf*)/ein wahnsinniger Unterschied (*inf*)/eine wahnsinnige Kletterei (*inf*); **I hope to ~ he's right** ich hoffe ja nur, dass er Recht hat; **to ~ with you/him** hol dich/ihn der Teufel (*inf*), du kannst/ der kann mich mal (*inf*); **to ~ with it!** verdammt noch mal (*inf*); **to ~ with your problems!** deine Probleme können mir gestohlen bleiben (*inf*); **~ out of my house!** mach, dass du aus meinem Haus kommst!; **go to ~!** scher dich or geh zum Teufel! (*inf*); **he can go to ~ for all I care** meinetwegen soll er sich zum Teufel scheren (*inf*); **what the ~ do you want?** was willst du denn, verdammt noch mal? (*inf*); **where the ~ is it?** wo ist es denn, verdammt noch mal? (*inf*); **you scared the ~ out of me** du hast mich zu Tode erschreckt; **like ~ he will!** den Teufel wird er tun (*inf*); **pay that much for a meal? like ~** so viel für ein Essen bezahlen? ich bin doch nicht verrückt! (*inf*); **he knows the Queen? – like ~!** er und die Königin kennen? – wers glaubt!; **~! so'n Mist!** (*inf*), verdammt noch mal! (*inf*); **~'s bells!, ~'s teeth!** (*euph, expressing surprise*) heiliger Strohsack or Bimbam! (*inf*); (*expressing anger*) zum Kuckuck noch mal! (*inf*); **what the ~, I've nothing to lose** zum Teufel, ich habe nichts zu verlieren (*inf*)

he'll [hiːl] *contr of* **he shall** *of* **he will**

hellacious [he'leɪʃəs] **ADJ** (*US, inf*) **a** (*= terrible*) *fighting, car crash* höllisch (*inf*) **b** (*= wild*) *party* wild **c** (*= excellent*) *vacation* fantastisch, phantastisch

hell: hellbender **N** (*US*) **a** (*Zool*) Schlammteufel *m*, Riesensalamander *m* **b** (*inf, = hell-raiser*) ausschweifender Mensch; **hellbent** **ADJ** versessen (*on* auf +*acc*); **to be ~ on vengeance** unerbittlich auf Rache sinnen; **hellcat** **N** Giftziege *f* (*inf*)

hellebore ['helɪbɔː] **N** (*Bot*) Nieswurz *f*

Hellenic [he'liːnɪk] **ADJ** hellenisch; **a ~ cruise** eine Hellas-Kreuzfahrt

hell: hellfire **N** Höllenfeuer *nt*; (*= punishment*) Höllenqualen *pl*; **hellhole** **N** grässliches Loch; **the trenches were a real ~** die (Schützen)gräben waren die reine Hölle; **hellhound** **N** Höllenhund *m*; (*fig*) Teufel *m*

hellish ['helɪʃ] (*inf*) **ADJ** **a** (*fig = diabolical*) höllisch (*inf*); *traffic, heat, cold* mörderisch (*inf*); **it's ~** es ist die reinste Hölle (*inf*); **the exams were ~** die Prüfungen waren verteufelt schwer (*inf*) **b** (*= wicked*) *plan, actions* höllisch, teuflisch **ADV** (*= awfully*) höllisch (*inf*), mörderisch (*inf*); **he felt ~ guilty** er hatte schreckliche Schuldgefühle

hellishly ['helɪʃlɪ] **ADV** (*inf*) *hot, cold* höllisch (*inf*), mörderisch (*inf*); *difficult, complicated* verteufelt (*inf*), busy, tired fürchterlich

hello [hə'ləʊ] ✪ 21.2 **INTERJ** hallo; **say ~ to your aunt** sag deiner Tante mal schön „Guten or guten Tag!"; **say ~ to your parents (from me)** grüß deine Eltern (von mir); **~, ~, ~! what's going on here?** nanu or he! was ist denn hier los? **N** Hallo *nt*

hell-raiser ['helreɪzə] **N** (*inf*) ausschweifender Mensch

Hell's Angels [ˌhelz'eɪndʒəlz] **PL** Hell's Angels *pl*

helluva ['heləvə] **ADJ, ADV** (*inf*) = **hell of a** → **hell** **c**

hell week **N** (*US Univ inf*) Woche, in der die angehende Mitglieder einer Studentenverbindung durch Demütigungen „getestet" werden

helm [helm] **N** **a** (*Naut*) Ruder *nt*, Steuer *nt*; **to be at the ~** (*lit, fig*) am Ruder sein **b** (*obs, = helmet*) Helm *m*

helmet ['helmɪt] **N** Helm *m*; (*Fencing*) Maske *f*

helmeted ['helmɪtɪd] **ADJ** behelmt

helmsman ['helmzmən] **N** *pl* **-men** [-mən] Steuermann *m*

helo ['heləʊ] **N** (*inf: = helicopter*) Hubschrauber *m*

help [help] ✪ 6.2 **N** , *no pl* Hilfe *f*; (*= person: with pl*) Hilfe *f*; **with his brother's ~** mithilfe or mit (der) Hilfe seines Bruders; **his ~ with the project** seine Mithilfe an dem Projekt; **with the ~ of a knife** mithilfe or mit Hilfe eines Messers; **we need all the ~ we can get** wir brauchen jede nur mögliche Hilfe; **~ was at hand** Hilfe war zur Stelle; **he is beyond ~** ihm ist nicht mehr zu helfen; **he is beyond medical ~** ihm kann kein Arzt mehr helfen; **to ask sb for ~** jdn um Hilfe bitten; **to give ~** Hilfe leisten; **to come to sb's ~** jdm zu Hilfe kommen; **to be of ~ to sb** jdm helfen; (*person also*) jdm behilflich sein; (*thing also*) jdm nützen; **he isn't much ~ to me** er ist mir keine große Hilfe; **you're a great ~!** (*iro*) du bist mir eine schöne Hilfe!; **we are short of ~ in the shop** wir haben nicht genügend (Hilfs)kräfte im Geschäft; **there's no ~ for it** da ist nichts zu machen

VT **a** helfen (+*dat*); **to ~ sb (to) do sth** jdm (dabei) helfen, etw zu tun; **to ~ sb with the cooking/his bags** jdm beim Kochen/mit seinen Taschen helfen; **~!** Hilfe!, zu Hilfe! (*old*); **so ~ me God!** so wahr mir Gott helfe!; **can I ~ you?** kann ich (Ihnen) helfen or behilflich sein?; **that won't ~ you** das wird Ihnen nichts nützen; **this will ~ the pain/your headache** das wird gegen die Schmerzen/gegen Ihr Kopfweh helfen; **it will ~ the wound to heal** das wird die Heilung (der Wunde) fördern; **it will ~ the crops to grow** es wird das Wachstum des Getreides fördern; **God ~s those who ~ themselves** (*Prov*) hilf dir selbst, so hilft dir Gott (*Prov*); **a man is ~ing the police with their inquiries** (*form euph*) ein Mann wird zur Zeit von der Polizei vernommen

b (*with particle*) **to ~ sb down** jdm hinunterhelfen; **take some water to ~ the pill down** trinken Sie etwas Wasser, damit die Tablette besser rutscht; **to ~ sb on/off with his/her etc coat** jdm in den/aus dem Mantel helfen; **to ~ed him out of the car** er half ihr aus dem Auto; **to ~ sb over the street** jdm über die Straße helfen; **to ~ sb through a difficult time** (*belief, hope, pills etc*) jdm in einer schwierigen Zeit durchhelfen; (*person also*) jdm in einer schwierigen Zeit beistehen; **to ~ sb up** (*from floor, chair etc*) jdm aufhelfen or (*up stairs etc*) hinaufhelfen; **I ~ed him in with his cases** ich half ihm mit seinem Gepäck

c she ~ed him to potatoes/meat sie gab ihm Kartoffeln/Fleisch; **to ~ oneself to sth** sich (*dat*) etw nehmen; (*inf, = steal*) etw mitgehen lassen; **~ yourself!** nehmen Sie sich doch!; **I'll ~ the children first** (*inf*) ich gebe den Kindern zuerst

d (*with can or cannot*) **he can't ~ it, he's only a baby** er kann nichts dafür, er ist doch noch ein Baby; **he can't ~ it!** (*hum inf, = he's stupid*) (d)er ist nun mal so (doof)!; **I can't ~ being clever** (ich kann nichts dafür,) ich bin nun mal ein Genie or so schlau (*inf*); **he can't ~ the way he is** das ist nun mal (so) seine Art; **don't say more than you can ~** sagen Sie nicht mehr als unbedingt nötig; **not if I can ~ it** nicht, wenn es nach mir geht; **I couldn't ~ laughing** ich konnte nicht helfen, ich musste (einfach) lachen; **I had to do it, I couldn't ~ it** or *myself* ich konnte mir nicht helfen, ich musste es einfach tun; **I couldn't ~ thinking** or **but think ...** ich konnte nicht umhin zu denken ...; **one**

cannot ~ wondering whether ... man muss sich wirklich fragen, ob ...; **it can't be ~ed** das lässt sich nicht ändern, das ist nun mal so; **I can't ~ it if he's always late** ich kann nichts dafür, dass er immer zu spät kommt

VI helfen; **and your attitude didn't ~ either** und Ihre Einstellung war auch nicht gerade hilfreich; **it ~s (to) fight pollution** es trägt zur Bekämpfung der Umweltverschmutzung bei

▶ **help out** ☉ 2.1 **VI** aushelfen (*with* bei) **sep** helfen (+*dat*) (*with* mit); (*in crisis also*) aufhelfen (+*dat*) (*with* bei); **will £3 help you out?** helfen Ihnen £ 3 weiter?

help desk N *telefonischer Informationsdienst*, Support *m*

helper ['helpə'] N Helfer(in) *m(f)*; (= *assistant*) Gehilfe *m*, Gehilfin *f*

helpful ['helpfʊl] ☉ 4 ADJ **a** *person* (= *willing to help*) hilfsbereit; (= *giving help*) hilfreich; **to be ~ to sb** jdm helfen *or* behilflich sein; **they were very ~ with the move** sie haben beim Umzug viel geholfen **b** (= *useful*) *advice, information, theory, book, tool* nützlich; *remedy* hilfreich; **meditation is often ~ at these times** in solchen Zeiten hilft es oft zu meditieren; **you'll find these tablets most ~** diese Tabletten werden Ihnen sehr helfen *or* gut tun; **she finds it ~ to pray** sie findet, es hilft ihr zu beten

helpfully ['helpfəlɪ] ADV (= *willing to help*) hilfsbereit; (= *giving help*) hilfreich; (= *thoughtfully*) *provide, include* liebenswürdigerweise; **he ~ showed us the best beach** er war so hilfsbereit, uns den besten Strand zu zeigen

helpfulness ['helpfʊlnɪs] N **a** (*of person*) Hilfsbereitschaft *f* **b** (= *usefulness: of suggestion, advice, information, theory, book, tool*) Nützlichkeit *f*

help function N (*Comput*) Hilfefunktion *f*

helping ['helpɪŋ] **N** (*at table, fig*) Portion *f*; **to take a second ~ of sth** sich (*dat*) noch einmal von etw nehmen; **he even had a third ~** er nahm sich (*dat*) sogar eine dritte Portion; **the public appetite for huge ~s of nostalgia** das Bedürfnis der Öffentlichkeit nach großen Portionen Nostalgie **ADJ** *attr* **to give** *or* **lend a ~ hand to sb** jdm helfen, jdm behilflich sein; **if you want a ~ hand ...** wenn Sie Hilfe brauchen, ...

helpless ['helplɪs] ADJ (= *powerless*) *person* machtlos (*against* gegen); (= *vulnerable*) *child, victim, invalid, gesture* hilflos; **a ~ feeling** ein Gefühl *nt* der Hilflosigkeit; **he was ~ to prevent it** er konnte es nicht verhindern; **he was ~ to resist** er konnte nicht widerstehen; **to feel ~** sich hilflos fühlen; **she was ~ with laughter** sie konnte sich vor Lachen kaum halten; **~ state** Hilflosigkeit *f*; **he is reduced to a ~ state** er ist zur Hilflosigkeit verurteilt

helplessly ['helplɪslɪ] ADV *look, stand, shrug, sob, drift, lie* hilflos; (*lit, fig*: = *impotently*) *watch* machtlos; **~ confused** völlig verwirrt; **~ drunk** sinnlos betrunken

helplessness ['helplɪsnɪs] N Hilflosigkeit *f*; (= *powerlessness*) Machtlosigkeit *f*

help: helpline N (*for emergencies*) Notruf *m*; (*for information*) Informationsdienst *m*; **helpmate** (*old*), **helpmeet** (*obs*) N Gefährte *m* (*geh*), Gefährtin *f* (*geh*); (= *helper*) Gehilfe *m* (*old*), Gehilfin *f* (*old*); **help screen** N (*Comput*) Hilfsbildschirm *m*

helter-skelter ['heltə'skeltə'] ADJ wild; *account* chaotisch; **the last minute ~ rush for the bus** die wilde Hetze in letzter Minute, um den Bus zu erwischen ADV *run, rush* Hals über Kopf (*inf*) **N a** (*Brit, in fairground*) spiralförmige Rutschbahn **b** (= *disorder*) wildes Durcheinander; (= *haste*) wilde Hetze

hem¹ [hem] INTERJ = **hum VI c**

hem² **N** Saum *m* **VT** säumen

▶ **hem about** (*Brit*) *or* **around** VT *sep* umgeben

▶ **hem in** VT *sep troops etc* einschließen, umgeben; (*fig*) einengen

---

he-man ['hi:mæn] N *pl* **-men** [-men] (*inf*) sehr männlicher Typ, echter *or* richtiger Mann; **he fancies himself as a ~** er kommt sich unheimlich männlich vor (*inf*)

hematite ['hi:mətaɪt] N Hämatit *m*

hematology N (*US*) = **haematology**

hemidemisemiquaver [ˌhemɪdemɪˈsemɪˌkweɪvə'] N (*Mus*) Vierundsechzigstel(note *f*) *nt*

hemiplegia [ˌhemɪˈpliːdʒɪə] N halbseitige Lähmung

hemiplegic [ˌhemɪˈpliːdʒɪk] ADJ halbseitig gelähmt

hemisphere ['hemɪsfɪə'] N Halbkugel *f*, Hemisphäre *f*; (*of brain*) Hemisphäre *f*, Gehirnhälfte *f*; **in the northern ~** auf der nördlichen Halbkugel, in der nördlichen Hemisphäre

hemispheric [ˌhemɪˈsferɪk] ADJ **a** (*Geog*) **Northern ~ summers** die Sommer in der nördlichen Hemisphäre *or* auf der nördlichen Halbkugel **b** (*Med, Psych*) *asymmetry, specialization, activity* hemisphärisch **c** (*Pol*) **Western ~ nations** die Länder *pl* der westlichen Hemisphäre **d** (*US, Pol*) *relations, solidarity* zwischen den Nord- und Südstaaten der USA; **a sense of ~ identity** ein Gefühl der Identität in den Nord- und Südstaaten der USA

hemline ['hemlaɪn] N Saum *m*; **~s are lower this year** der Rocksaum ist dieses Jahr etwas tiefer gerutscht

hemlock ['hemlɒk] N (*Bot*, = *poisonous plant*) Schierling *m*; (= *tree*) Schierlings- *or* Hemlocktanne *f*; (= *poison*) Schierling(saft) *m*; **Socrates drank the ~** Sokrates trank den Schierlingsbecher

hemo- *in cpds* (*US*) = **haemo-**

hemp [hemp] N **a** (*Bot*) Hanf *m*; **~ seed** Hanfsamen *pl* **b** (= *drug*) Hanf *m* **c** (= *fibre*) Hanf(faser *f*) *m*

hemstitch ['hemstɪtʃ] **VT** in Hohlsaum nähen **N** Hohlsaum *m*

hen [hen] N **a** Huhn *nt*, Henne *f*; **as scarce** *or* **rare as ~'s teeth** (*dated inf*) so selten wie ein weißer Rabe **b** (= *female bird, lobster*) Weibchen *nt* **c** (*inf: also* **mother hen**) Glucke *f* (*inf*)

hen: henbane N Bilsenkraut *nt*; **hen bird** N (*Vogel*)weibchen *nt*

hence [hens] ADV **a** (= *for this reason*) also; **~ the name** daher der Name **b** (= *from now*) **two years ~** in zwei Jahren **c** (*obs, liter*, = *from here*) von hier; **(get thee) ~!** hinweg (mit dir)! (*liter*); **get thee ~, Satan!** weiche, Satan! (*liter*)

henceforth [ˌhensˈfɔːθ], **henceforward** [ˌhensˈfɔːwəd] ADV (= *from that time on*) von da an, (*liter*); (= *from this time on*) von nun an, künftig

henchman ['hentʃmən] N *pl* **-men** [-mən] (*pej*) Spießgeselle *m*, Kumpan *m*

hencoop ['henku:p] N Hühnerstall *m*

henhouse ['henhaʊs] N Hühnerhaus *nt*, Hühnerstall *m*

henna ['henə] **N** Henna *f* **VT** mit Henna färben

hen: hen night N *für die Braut vor der Hochzeit arrangierte Damengesellschaft*; **hen party** N (*inf*) Damenkränzchen *nt*, = Kaffeeklatsch *m* (*inf*), reine Weibergesellschaft (*pej, inf*); (*before wedding*) *für die Braut vor der Hochzeit arrangierte Damengesellschaft*; **henpeck** VT unterm Pantoffel haben (*inf*); **a ~ed husband** ein Pantoffelheld *m* (*inf*); **he is ~ed** er steht unterm Pantoffel (*inf*); **hen run** N Hühnerhof *m*

Henry ['henrɪ] N Heinrich *m*

hep [hep] ADJ (*dated US, sl*) = **hip⁴**

hepatitis [ˌhepəˈtaɪtɪs] N Hepatitis *f*

heptagon ['heptəgən] N Siebeneck *nt*, Heptagon *nt*

heptathlon [hepˈtæθlɒn] N Siebenkampf *m*

her [hɜː'] PERS PRON **a** (*dir obj, with prep +acc*) sie; (*indir obj, with prep +dat*) ihr; (*when she is previously mentioned in clause*) sich; **with ~ books about ~** mit ihren Büchern um sich **b** (*emph*)

---

sie; **it's ~** sie ists; **who, ~?** wer, sie? POSS ADJ ihr → *also* **my**

Heraclitean [ˌherəˈklaɪtɪən] ADJ heraklitisch

Heraclitus [ˌherəˈklaɪtəs] N Heraklit *m*

herald ['herəld] **N a** (*Hist*) Herold *m*; (*in newspaper titles*) Bote *m* **b** (*fig*) (Vor)bote *m* (*geh*); **~ of spring** Frühlingsbote *m* **c** (*Her*) **College of Heralds** Heroldsamt *nt* **VT** *arrival of summer* ankündigen, Vorbote(n) sein für; **to ~ (in) a new age** den Beginn eines neuen Zeitalters ankündigen; **tonight's game is being ~ed as the match of the season** das Spiel heute Abend wird als die Begegnung der Saison groß herausgebracht

heraldic [heˈrældɪk] ADJ heraldisch; **~ arms** Wappen *pl*

heraldry ['herəldrɪ] N **a** (= *science*) Wappenkunde *f*, Heraldik *f* **b** (= *heraldic signs*) Wappen *pl* **c** (= *ceremonial*) traditioneller höfischer Prunk

herb [hɜːb] N Kraut *nt*

herbaceous [hɜːˈbeɪʃəs] ADJ krautig

herbaceous border N Staudenrabatte *f*

herbage ['hɜːbɪdʒ] N Grünpflanzen *pl*; (= *leaves and stems*) Grünzeug *nt*; (= *pasturage*) Weide(-land *nt*) *f*

herbal ['hɜːbəl] ADJ Kräuter-; **~ tea** Kräutertee *m*; **~ remedies** Kräuterheilmittel *pl* **N** Kräuterbuch *nt*

herbalism ['hɜːbəlɪzəm] N Kräuterheilkunde *f*

herbalist ['hɜːbəlɪst] N Kräutersammler(in) *m(f)*; (= *healer*) Naturheilkundige(r) *mf*

herbarium [hɜːˈbeərɪəm] N Herbarium *nt*

herb garden N Kräutergarten *m*

herbicide ['hɜːbɪsaɪd] N Herbizid *nt*

herbivore ['hɜːbɪvɔː'] N (*Zool*) Pflanzenfresser *m*, Herbivore *m* (*spec*)

herbivorous [hɜːˈbɪvərəs] ADJ (*form*) Pflanzen fressend

herculean [ˌhɜːkjʊˈliːən] ADJ herkulisch; *proportions* riesenhaft; *effort* übermenschlich; **~ strength** Bären- *or* Riesenkräfte *pl*; **a ~ task** eine Herkulesarbeit

Hercules ['hɜːkjuliːz] N (*lit, fig*) Herkules *m*

herd [hɜːd] **N** (*of cattle etc*) Herde *f*; (*of deer*) Rudel *nt*; (*fig pej: of people*) Herde *f*, Schar *f*; **the common ~** die breite Masse; **to follow the ~** (*fig*) der Herde folgen, mit der Herde laufen **VT a** (= *drive*) *sheep, cattle, prisoners* treiben **b** (= *tend*) *cattle* hüten

▶ **herd together** **VI** sich zusammendrängen **VT** *sep* zusammentreiben

herd instinct N Herdentrieb *m*

herdsman ['hɜːdzmən] N Hirt *m*, Hirte *m*

here [hɪə'] ADV **a** hier; (*with motion*) hierher, hierhin; **~!** (*at roll call*) hier!; (*to dog*) hierher!; **come ~!** komm her!; **~ I am** da *or* hier bin ich; **~'s the taxi** das Taxi ist da; **~ he comes** da kommt *or* ist er ja; **spring is ~** der Frühling ist da; **this one ~** der/die/das hier *or* da; **this man ~** dieser Mann (hier) ...; **John ~ reckons ...** John hier meint ...; **this ~ notice** (*incorrect*) dieser Anschlag da (*inf*); **~ and now** auf der Stelle, jetzt sofort; **I won't be ~ for lunch** ich bin zum Mittagessen nicht da; **she's not ~ yet** sie ist noch nicht da; **shall we wait till he gets ~?** sollen wir warten, bis er hier *or* da ist?; **~ and there** hier und da; **~, there and everywhere** überall; **around/about ~** hierherum, ungefähr hier; **near ~** (hier) in der Nähe; **I've read down to ~** ich habe bis hierher *or* hierhin gelesen; **it's in/over ~** es ist hier (drin)/hier drüben; **put it in/over ~** stellen Sie es hierherein/hierherüber *or* hierher; **come in/over ~** kommen Sie hierherein/hierherüber *or* hierher; **from ~ on in** (*esp US*) von jetzt *or* nun an; **~ I would like to draw your attention to ...** an dieser Stelle möchte ich Sie auf ... aufmerksam machen **b** (*in phrases*) **~ you are** (*giving sth*) hier (, bitte); (*on finding sb*) da bist du ja!, ach, hier bist du!; (*on finding sth*) da *or* hier ist es ja; **~ we are, home again** so, da wären wir also wieder zu

Hause; **~ we go again, another crisis** da hätten wir also wieder eine Krise; **look out, ~ he comes** Vorsicht, er kommt!; **~ comes trouble** jetzt gehts los (*inf*); **~ goes!** (*before attempting sth*) dann mal los; **~, try this one** hier, versuchs mal damit; **~, let me do that** komm, lass mich das mal machen; **~!** he!; **~'s to you!** (*in toast*) auf Ihr Wohl!; **~'s to the success of the venture!** auf den Erfolg des Vorhabens!; **it's neither ~ nor there** es spielt keine Rolle, tut nichts zur Sache; **I've had it up to ~ (with him/ it)** (*inf*) ich habe die Nase voll (von ihm/davon) (*inf*); **I'm up to ~ with paperwork** (*inf*) der Papierkram steht mir bis zum Hals (*inf*)
N **the ~ and now** das Hier und Heute; (*Rel, Philos*) das Diesseits

here: hereabouts ['hɪərəbaʊts] ADV hier (in der Gegend), in dieser Gegend; **hereafter** (*form*) **N** **the/a ~** das/ein Jenseits ADV **a** (*Jur etc*) im Folgenden **b** (= *from now on*) künftig, in Zukunft **c** (= *later*) **I shall say more of this ~** ich werde später darauf zurückkommen; **hereby** ADV (*form*) hiermit

hereditable [hə'redɪtəbl] ADJ (*Jur*) vererbbar; (*Med also*) (ver)erblich

hereditary [hɪ'redɪtərɪ] ADJ *factor, characteristic* erblich, angeboren; *ruler, title, position, right* erblich; **~ disease** or **illness** Erbkrankheit *f*, erbliche Krankheit; **~ peer** *Peer, der seine Peerswürde geerbt hat* **~ monarch** Erbmonarch(in) *m(f)*

heredity [hɪ'redɪtɪ] N Vererbung *f*; **the title is his by ~** er hat den Titel geerbt/wird den Titel erben

here: herein ADV (*form*) hierin; **and ~ lies the problem** und das ist or hier liegt das Problem; **hereinafter** ADV (*form*) im Folgenden; **hereof** ADV (*form*) hiervon (*form*); **the house and the inhabitants** ~ das Haus und die Bewohner desselben (*form*)

heresy ['herəsɪ] N Ketzerei *f*, Häresie *f* (*spec*); **heresies** Ketzereien *pl*, ketzerische Lehren *pl*

heretic ['herətɪk] N Ketzer(in) *m(f)*, Häretiker(in) *m(f)* (*spec*)

heretical [hɪ'retɪkəl] ADJ ketzerisch, häretisch (*spec*)

here: hereto ADV (*form*) **the documents attached** ~ die beigefügten Dokumente; **additions ~ can only be made with his permission** Zusätze können hierzu nur mit seiner Erlaubnis gemacht werden; **he gave his signature** ~ er setzte seine Unterschrift hinzu; **heretofore** ADV (*form*, = *up to this time*) bisher; (= *up to that time*) bis dahin; **hereunto** ADV (*form*) = **hereto**; **hereupon** ADV daraufhin; **herewith** ADV (*form*) hiermit

heritable ['herɪtəbl] ADJ **a** erblich **b** (*Jur*) *person* erbfähig

heritage ['herɪtɪdʒ] N (*lit, fig*) Erbe *nt*, Erbschaft *f*

heritage centre N (*Brit*) *auf ein bestimmtes Gebiet spezialisiertes (Heimat)museum*

hermaphrodite [hɜː'mæfrədaɪt] **N** Zwitter *m*, Hermaphrodit *m* (*geh*) ADJ zwittrig, hermaphroditisch (*geh*); *plants also* gemischtgeschlechtig

hermaphroditic [hɜː'mæfrə'dɪtɪk] ADJ hermaphroditisch

hermetic [hɜː'metɪk] ADJ hermetisch

hermetically [hɜː'metɪkəlɪ] ADV hermetisch; **~ sealed** (*jar, container*) hermetisch verschlossen; (*fig*) *world, existence* hermetisch abgeriegelt

hermit ['hɜːmɪt] N Einsiedler(in) *m(f)* (*also fig*), Eremit(in) *m(f)*

hermitage ['hɜːmɪtɪdʒ] N (*lit, fig*) Einsiedelei *f*, Klause *f*

hermit crab N Einsiedlerkrebs *m*

hernia ['hɜːnɪə] N (Eingeweide)bruch *m*, Hernie *f* (*spec*)

hero ['hɪərəʊ] N *pl* **-es** Held *m*, Heros *m* (*geh*); (*fig: = object of hero-worship also*) Idol *nt*; (*Liter, of novel etc*) Held *m*; **the ~ of the hour** der Held des Tages

Herod ['herəd] N Herodes *m*

heroic [hɪ'rəʊɪk] ADJ **a** *person* heldenhaft; (= *brave*) mutig; *behaviour, action* heroisch; *struggle, resistance, match* heldenhaft, heroisch; **~ action** or **deed** Heldentat *f*; **~ efforts** gewaltige Anstrengungen *pl*; **~ attempt** tapferer Versuch **b** (*Liter*) Helden-; **~ poem/epic** Heldengedicht *nt*/-epos *nt*; **~ character** or **figure** heroische Gestalt, Heldengestalt *f*; (= *hero/heroine*) Held *m*, Heldin *f*; **a novel of ~ proportions** ein groß angelegter Roman
N **heroics** *pl* (= *heroic deeds*) Heldentaten *pl*; **the actor's ~s** das übertriebene Pathos des Schauspielers; **it is recorded without ~s** es wird ohne hochtrabende or große Worte beschrieben

heroic age N Heldenzeitalter *nt*

heroically [hɪ'rəʊɪkəlɪ] ADV **a** heldenhaft; (= *bravely*) mutig **b** (= *with great effort*) *work, struggle, play* mit heroischem or heldenhaftem Einsatz; *sacrifice, try* heldenhafterweise **c** (= *grandly*) **his brow furrows** ~ er runzelt dramatisch or pathetisch die Stirn; **a ~ delivered speech** eine mit viel Pathos vorgetragene Rede

heroic couplet N (*Poet*) Heroic Couplet *nt*, Reimpaar aus fünffüßigen Jamben

heroic verse N (*Poet*) heroischer Vers

heroin ['herəʊɪn] N Heroin *nt*; **~ addict** Heroinsüchtige(r) *mf*

heroine ['herəʊɪn] N Heldin *f*; (*esp Theat also*) Heroine *f*

heroism ['herəʊɪzəm] N Heldentum *nt*, Heroismus *m*; (= *daring*) Kühnheit *f*; **I'm not one for ~** ich bin kein Held

heroize ['hɪərəʊaɪz] VT heroisieren, zum Helden/zur Heldin machen

heron ['herən] N Reiher *m*

hero worship N Verehrung *f* (*of* +*gen*); (*in ancient tribe etc*) Heldenverehrung *f*; (*of pop star etc*) Schwärmerei *f* (*of* für); **the ~ of a boy for his older brother** die blinde Bewunderung eines Jungen für seinen älteren Bruder

hero-worship ['hɪərəʊˌwɜːʃɪp] VT anbeten, verehren; *popstar etc* schwärmen für

herpes ['hɜːpiːz] N (*Med*) Herpes *m*; **~ labialis** Herpes *m* labialis, Lippen-/Gesichtsherpes *m*

herring ['herɪŋ] N Hering *m* → **red herring**

herring: herringbone **N** **a** (= *pattern*) Fischgrät *m* **b** (*Ski*) Grätenschritt *m* ADJ *attr* **~ pattern** Fischgrät(en)muster *nt*; **~ suit** Anzug *m* mit Fischgrätmuster; **herringbone stitch** N Hexenstich *m*; **herring gull** N Silbermöwe *f*; **herring pond** N (*hum inf*) großer Teich (*hum*)

hers [hɜːz] POSS PRON ihre(r, s); **~** (*on towels etc*) sie → *also* **mine¹**

herself [hɜː'self] PERS PRON **a** (*dir and indir obj, with prep*) sich → *also* **myself** **b** (*emph*) (sie) selbst **N** (*Ir, inf*) **it was ~ who told me** sie selbst hat es mir gesagt

herstory ['hɜːstərɪ] N (*inf*) *feministische Geschichtsbetrachtung*

Herts [hɑːts] *abbr* of **Hertfordshire**

he's [hiːz] *contr* of **he is** of **he has**

hesitancy ['hezɪtənsɪ] N Zögern *nt*; (= *indecision*) Unschlüssigkeit *f*; (*of voice*) Unsicherheit *f*

hesitant ['hezɪtənt] ADJ zögernd; *person* = *undecided* unschlüssig, unsicher; *voice* unsicher; **to be ~ to do sth** or **about doing sth** zögern, etw zu tun; (= *reluctant*) etw nicht tun wollen; (= *doubtful*) Bedenken haben, etw zu tun

hesitantly ['hezɪtəntlɪ] ADV zögernd

hesitate ['hezɪteɪt] VI zögern, zaudern (*geh*); (*in speech*) stocken; **he who ~s is lost** (*Prov*) dem Feigen kehrt das Glück den Rücken (*Prov*); **I ~ to ask him round** ich bin mir nicht schlüssig, ob ich ihn einladen soll; **I'd ~ to take** or **at taking on such a task** ich würde es mir gut überlegen, ob ich so eine Aufgabe übernehmen würde; **I ~d about having another baby** ich hatte Bedenken, noch ein Kind zu bekommen; **he didn't ~ at the idea of leaving home** er zögerte keinen Augenblick, von zu Hause wegzuge-

hen; **even he would ~ at murder** selbst er hätte bei einem Mord Bedenken; **he ~s at nothing** er macht vor nichts Halt, er schreckt vor nichts zurück; **the President is hesitating over whether to attend the conference** der Präsident ist sich unschlüssig, ob er an der Konferenz teilnehmen soll; **I am still hesitating about what I should do** ich bin mir immer noch nicht schlüssig, was ich tun soll; **I ~ to say it, but ...** es widerstrebt mir, das zu sagen, aber ...; **if I did think that, I wouldn't ~ to say so** wenn ich wirklich der Meinung (*gen*) wäre, hätte ich keine Hemmungen, es zu sagen; **don't ~ to ask/contact me** fragen Sie mich ruhig/wenden Sie sich ruhig an mich; (*more formally*) zögern Sie nicht, mich zu fragen/sich an mich zu wenden

hesitation [ˌhezɪ'teɪʃən] N Zögern *nt*, Zaudern *nt* (*geh*); **after some/a moment's ~** nach einigem/kurzem Zögern; **without the slightest ~** ohne auch nur einen Augenblick zu zögern; **I have no ~ in saying that ...** ich kann ohne weiteres sagen, dass ...; **I had no ~ about taking the job** ich zögerte keinen Augenblick, die Stelle anzunehmen

hessian ['hesɪən] **N** Sackleinen *nt*, Rupfen *m* **ATTR** sackleinen, aus Sackleinen or Rupfen

hetaera [hɪ'taɪərə] N *pl* **-rae** or **-ras** Hetäre *f*

hetero ['hetərəʊ] N (*inf*) Hetero *m* (*inf*), Heterosexuelle(r) *mf*

heterodox ['hetərədɒks] ADJ heterodox, andersgläubig

heterodoxy ['hetərədɒksɪ] N Heterodoxie *f*, Andersgläubigkeit *f*

heterogeneity [ˌhetərəʊdʒɪ'neɪtɪ] N Heterogenität *f*

heterogeneous [ˌhetərəʊ'dʒiːnɪəs] ADJ heterogen

heterosexism ['hetərəʊ'seksɪzm] N Heterosexismus *m*

heterosexual [ˌhetərəʊ'seksjʊəl] ADJ heterosexuell **N** Heterosexuelle(r) *mf*

heterosexuality [ˌhetərəʊseksjʊ'ælɪtɪ] N Heterosexualität *f*

het up [ˌhet'ʌp] ADJ (*Brit inf*) aufgeregt; **to get ~ about/over sth** sich über etw (*acc*)/wegen einer Sache (*gen*) aufregen

heuristic [hjʊə'rɪstɪk] ADJ heuristisch **N** **~s** *sing* Heuristik *f*

hew [hjuː] *pret* **hewed**, *ptp* **hewn** or **hewed** VT hauen; (= *shape*) behauen; **to ~ sth (in)to pieces** etw in Stücke hauen; **to be ~n into logs** zu Klötzen gehackt werden; **they ~ed their captives to pieces** sie zerstückelten ihre Gefangenen

▶ **hew down** VT *sep trees* fällen, umhauen; *persons* niederhauen; (*with machine gun*) niedermähen

▶ **hew off** VT *sep* abhauen, abhacken, abschlagen

▶ **hew out** VT *sep* heraushauen, herausschlagen (*of* aus); **he's hewn out a career for himself** er hat sich (*dat*) seine Karriere erkämpft

▶ **hew up** VT *sep* zerstückeln; *wood* zerhacken

hewer ['hjuːə] N (*Min*) Hauer *m*

hex [heks] (*esp US, inf*) **N** Fluch *m*; **there must be a ~ on this project** dieses Projekt muss verhext sein (*inf*); (*more serious*) auf dem Projekt muss ein Fluch liegen; **to put a ~ on sb/sth** jdn/etw verhexen **VT** verhexen

hexadecimal [ˌheksə'desɪməl] ADJ hexadezimal

hexagon ['heksəgən] N Sechseck *nt*, Hexagon *nt*

hexagonal [hek'sægənəl] ADJ sechseckig, hexagonal

hexameter [hek'sæmɪtə] N Hexameter *m*

hex code N (*Comput*) Hexadezimalcode *m*

hey [heɪ] INTERJ (*to attract attention*) he (Sie/du); (*in surprise*) he, Mensch (*inf*); **~ presto** Hokuspokus (Fidibus)

heyday ['heɪdeɪ] N Glanzzeit *f*, Blütezeit *f*; **in the ~ of his power** auf dem Höhepunkt seiner

Macht; **in the ~ of glam rock** als Glam-Rock groß in Mode war; **in his ~** in seiner Glanzzeit

Hezbollah ['hezbə'lɑː] N = Hizbollah

HGV (*Brit*) *abbr of* **heavy goods vehicle** LKW *m*

HH ADJ (*on pencil*) HH, 2H

H-hour N (*Mil*) Stunde *f* X (*für militärische Operationen*)

hi [haɪ] INTERJ hallo

hiatus [haɪ'eɪtəs] N Lücke *f*; (*Gram, Poet*) Hiatus *m*; **after a two-week ~** nach einer Unterbrechung von zwei Wochen

hibernate ['haɪbəneɪt] VI Winterschlaf halten *or* machen

hibernation [ˌhaɪbə'neɪʃən] N (*lit, fig*) Winterschlaf *m*

hibernator ['haɪbəneɪtə'] N *Tier, das Winterschlaf hält*

Hibernian [hɪ'bɜːnɪən] (*poet*) ADJ hibernisch N Hibernier(in) *m(f)*

hibiscus [hɪ'bɪskəs] N Hibiskus *m*, Eibisch *m*

hic [hɪk] INTERJ hick

hiccough, hiccup ['hɪkʌp] N Schluckauf *m*; (*fig inf: = problem*) Problemchen *nt* (*inf*); **to have the ~s** den Schluckauf haben; **to give a ~** hick machen (*inf*), hicksen (*dial*); **without any ~s** ohne Störungen; **the recent sales ~** die jüngsten Verkaufsprobleme VI hicksen (*dial*); **he started ~ing** er bekam den Schluckauf

hick [hɪk] N (*US inf*) Hinterwäldler(in) *m(f)* (*inf*); (*female also*) Landpomeranze *f* (*inf*)

hickey ['hɪkɪ] N (*inf*) **a** (= *thingummy*) Dingsbums *nt* (*inf*) **b** (= *love bite*) Knutschfleck *m* (*inf*)

hickory ['hɪkərɪ] N (= *tree*) Hickory(nussbaum) *m*; (= *wood*) Hickory(holz) *nt*

hide¹ [haɪd] *vb: pret* **hid** [hɪd] *ptp* **hid** *or* **hidden** ['hɪdn] VT verstecken (*from* vor +*dat*); *truth, tears, grief, feelings, face* verbergen (*from* vor +*dat*); (= *obstruct from view*) *moon, rust* verdecken; **hidden from view** nicht zu sehen, dem Blick *or* den Blicken entzogen; **the building was hidden by trees** das Gebäude war hinter Bäumen versteckt; **he's hiding something in his pocket** er hat etwas in seiner Tasche versteckt; **I have nothing to ~** ich habe nichts zu verbergen; **his words had a hidden meaning** seine Worte hatten eine verborgene *or* versteckte Bedeutung; **they have a hidden agenda** sie führen etwas im Schilde; **there is a hidden agenda** da steckt noch etwas anderes dahinter; **you're hiding something from me** (*truth etc*) Sie verheimlichen mir etwas, Sie verbergen etwas vor mir; **he tried to ~ his excitement** er versuchte, seine Aufregung nicht zu zeigen

VI sich verstecken, sich verbergen (*from sb* vor jdm); **quick! ~ in the cupboard** schnell, versteck dich im Schrank!; **he was hiding in the cupboard** er hielt sich im Schrank versteckt *or* verborgen; **he's hiding behind a pseudonym** er verbirgt sich hinter einem Pseudonym; **he's hiding behind his office** (*fig*) er benutzt sein Amt als Vorwand

N Versteck *nt*

▸ **hide away** VI sich verstecken, sich verbergen VT *sep* verstecken

▸ **hide out** *or* **up** VI sich verstecken; (= *to be hiding also*) sich versteckt *or* verborgen halten

hide² N (*of animal*) Haut *f*; (*on furry animal*) Fell *nt*; (*processed*) Leder *nt*; (*fig, of person*) Haut *f*, Fell *nt*; **the bags are made out of rhino ~** die Taschen sind aus Nashornleder; **to save one's own ~** die eigene Haut retten; **I haven't seen ~ nor hair of him for weeks** (*inf*) den habe ich in den letzten Wochen nicht mal von weitem gesehen

hide: **hide-and-seek**, (*US*) **hide-and-go-seek** N Versteckspiel *nt*; **to play ~** Verstecken spielen; **hideaway** N Versteck *nt*; (= *refuge*) Zufluchtsort *m*; **hidebound** ADJ *person, views* engstirnig; **an officer of the old school, ~ by convention** ein Offizier der alten Schule, der den Konventionen verhaftet ist

hideous ['hɪdɪəs] ADJ **a** (= *very ugly*) grauenhaft, scheußlich; *colour* scheußlich, schrecklich **b** (= *appalling*) *embarrassment, disappointment, expense, price* fürchterlich

hideously ['hɪdɪəslɪ] ADV **a** *painted, designed, deformed, scream* grauenhaft; **~ ugly** potthässlich (*inf*); **to grimace ~** scheußliche Grimassen ziehen **b** (*emph*) *expensive, slow, loud* schrecklich, fürchterlich; **she'd probably be ~ embarrassed** es wäre ihr sicher schrecklich *or* fürchterlich peinlich

hideousness ['hɪdɪəsnɪs] N Grauenhaftigkeit *f*, Scheußlichkeit *f*

hideout ['haɪdaʊt] N Versteck *nt*

hidey-hole ['haɪdɪhəʊl] N (*inf*) Versteck *nt*

hiding¹ ['haɪdɪŋ] N **to be in ~** sich versteckt halten; **to go into ~** untertauchen, sich verstecken; **he came out of ~** er tauchte wieder auf, er kam aus seinem Versteck

hiding² N **a** (= *beating*) Tracht *f* Prügel; **to give sb a good ~** jdm eine Tracht Prügel geben **b** (*inf, = defeat*) Schlappe *f* (*inf*); **the team took *or* got a real ~** die Mannschaft musste eine schwere Schlappe einstecken (*inf*); **to be on a ~ to nothing** keine Aussicht auf Erfolg haben

hiding place N Versteck *nt*

hidy-hole ['haɪdɪhəʊl] N (*inf*) Versteck *nt*

hie [haɪ] VR (*old, hum*) eilends laufen; **~ thee hence!** hebe dich hinweg (*old, hum*)

hierarchic(al) [ˌhaɪə'rɑːkɪk(əl)] ADJ , **hierarchically** [ˌhaɪə'rɑːkɪklɪ] ADV hierarchisch

hierarchy ['haɪərɑːkɪ] N Hierarchie *f*

hieratic [haɪə'rætɪk] ADJ (*Rel*) hieratisch

hieroglyph ['haɪərəglɪf] N Hieroglyphe *f*

hieroglyphic [ˌhaɪərə'glɪfɪk] ADJ hieroglyphisch N **hieroglyphics** PL Hieroglyphen *pl*, Hieroglyphenschrift *f*

hi-fi ['haɪfaɪ] N **a** Hi-Fi *nt* **b** (= *system*) Hi-Fi-Anlage *f* ADJ Hi-Fi-; **~ equipment** Hi-Fi-Geräte *pl*

higgledy-piggledy ['hɪgldɪ'pɪgldɪ] ADV durcheinander, wie Kraut und Rüben (*inf*) ADJ durcheinander, (= *confused*) wirr

high [haɪ] ADJ (+er) **a** *mountain, wall, forehead, building* hoch *pred*, hohe(r, s) *attr*; **a building 80 metres** (*Brit*) *or* **meters** (*US*) **~, an 80-metre** (*Brit*) *or* **80-meter** (*US*) **~ building** ein 80 Meter hohes Gebäude; **the building is 80 metres** (*Brit*) *or* **meters** (*US*) **~** das Gebäude ist 80 Meter hoch; **a ~ dive** ein Kopfsprung *m* aus großer Höhe; **on one of the ~er floors** in einem der oberen Stockwerke; **he lives on a ~er floor** er wohnt weiter oben; **the ~er floor** die oberste Etage; **at ~ tide** *or* **water** bei Flut *or* Hochwasser; **the river is quite ~** der Fluss führt ziemlich viel Wasser; **~ and dry** (*boat*) auf dem Trockenen; **to be left ~ and dry** auf dem Trockenen sitzen (*inf*); **he left her ~ and dry with four young children** er hat sie mit vier kleinen Kindern sitzen lassen; **I knew him when he was only so ~** ich kannte ihn, als er nur SO groß war *or* noch so klein war → *also* **high ground**

b (= *important, superior*) hoch *pred*, hohe(r, s) *attr*; **~ office** hohes Amt; **on the ~est authority** von höchster Stelle; **to be ~ and mighty** erhaben tun; **to be on one's ~ horse** (*fig*) auf den hohen Ross sitzen; **O Lord most ~** (*Bibl*) erhabener Gott

c (= *considerable, extreme, great*) *opinion, speed, temperature, fever, pressure, salary, price, rate, density, sea* hoch *pred*, hohe(r, s) *attr*; *reputation* ausgezeichnet, hervorragend; *altitude* groß; *wind* stark; *complexion, colour* (hoch)rot; **of the ~est calibre** (*Brit*) *or* **caliber** (*US*)/**quality** von bestem Format/bester Qualität; **casualties were ~** es gab viele Opfer; (*Mil*) es gab hohe Verluste; **the temperature was in the ~ twenties** die Temperatur lag bei fast 30 Grad; **to pay a ~ price for sth** (*lit, fig*) etw teuer bezahlen; **to put a ~ value on sth** etw hoch einschätzen; **the ~est common factor** der größte gemeinsame Teiler; **to the ~est degree** im höchsten Grad *or* Maß; **to have ~ expectations of sb/sth** hohe Erwartun-

gen an jdn/etw stellen; **in (very) ~ spirits** in Hochstimmung, in äußerst guter Laune; **in fat** fettreich; **to have a ~ old time** (*inf*) sich prächtig amüsieren, mächtig Spaß haben (*inf*); **it was ~ drama** es war hochdramatisch

d (= *good, admirable*) *ideals, principles* hoch; **a man of ~ character** ein Mann von Charakter

e (*of time*) **~ noon** zwölf Uhr mittags; **it's ~ time you went home** es ist *or* wird höchste Zeit, dass du nach Hause gehst

f *sound, note* hoch; (= *shrill*) schrill

g (*inf, on drugs*) high (*inf*); (*on drink*) blau (*inf*); **to get ~ on alcohol** sich (mit Alkohol) besaufen (*inf*); **to get ~ on cocaine** sich mit Kokain anturnen (*sl*)

h *meat* angegangen

i (*Cards*) hoch *pred*, hohe(r, s) *attr*; **aces ~** Ass ist die höchste (Stich)karte

ADV (+er) **a** hoch; **~ up** (*position*) hoch oben; (*motion*) hoch hinauf; **birds circling very ~ up** Vögel, die ganz weit oben kreisen; **~er up the hill was a small farm** etwas weiter oben am Berg lag ein kleiner Bauernhof; **~ (up) on the agenda** ganz oben auf der Tagesordnung; **~ up in the organization** weit oben in der Organisationsstruktur; **one floor ~er** ein Stockwerk höher; **to throw sth ~ in(to) the air** etw hoch in die Luft werfen

b **to go as ~ as £200** bis zu £ 200 (hoch) gehen; **inflation is climbing ~er and ~er** die Inflationsrate steigt immer mehr *or* wird immer höher; **the sea is running ~** das Meer ist sehr stürmisch; **feelings ran ~** die Gemüter erhitzten sich; **to search ~ and low** überall suchen

N **a** God on ~ Gott in der Höhe *or* im Himmel; **the orders have come from on ~** (*hum inf*) der Befehl kommt von oben

b **unemployment/the pound has reached a new ~** die Arbeitslosenzahlen haben/das Pfund hat einen neuen Höchststand erreicht; **sales have reached an all-time ~** die Verkaufszahlen sind so hoch wie nie zuvor; **the ~s and lows of my career** die Höhen und Tiefen *pl* meiner Laufbahn

c (*Met*) Hoch *nt*

d **he's still on a ~** (*inf: = on drugs*) er ist immer noch high (*inf*); **I was on a ~ after the concert** (*inf: = excited*) nach dem Konzert war ich ganz high (*inf*)

e (*US, Aut, = top gear*) **in ~** im höchsten Gang; **he moved into ~** er schaltete hoch *or* in den höchsten Gang

f (*US, inf, = high school*) Penne *f* (*inf*)

high: high altar N Hochaltar *m*; **highball** N (*US*) Highball *m*; **high beam** N (*Aut*) Fernlicht *nt*; **highboard** N (*for diving*) Turm *m*; **highborn** ADJ von hoher Geburt, von edler Abkunft (*liter*); **highboy** N (*US*) hohe Kommode; **highbrow** N Intellektuelle(r) *mf* ADJ *interests* intellektuell, hochgestochen (*pej*); *tastes, music, author* anspruchsvoll; **high-calorie** ADJ kalorienreich; **highchair** N Hochstuhl *m*; **High Church** N Hochkirche *f* ADJ der Hochkirche; **to be very ~** streng hochkirchlich eingestellt sein; **high-circulation** ADJ *newspaper* auflagenstark; **high-class** ADJ erstklassig; **~ prostitute** Edelnutte *f* (*inf*); **high-coloured**, (*US*) **high-colored** ADJ *complexion, skin* rot; **high comedy** N Gesellschaftskomödie *f*; **high commission** N Hochkommissariat *nt*; **high commissioner** N Hochkommissar(in) *m(f)*; **high court** N oberstes *or* höchstes Gericht; (= *institution also*) oberster Gerichtshof; **high court judge** N Richter(in) *m(f)* am obersten Gerichtshof; **high day** N (*Brit*) Festtag *m*; **~s and holidays** Fest- und Feiertage; **high-density** ADJ **a** *housing, population* dicht **b** (*Comput*) *disk* mit hoher Schreibdichte; **high diving** N Turmspringen *nt*; **high-energy** ADJ *particle, food* energiereich

higher ['haɪə'] ADJ **a** *comp of* **high** **b** *mathematics* höher; *animals, life-forms* höher (entwickelt) N **Higher** (*Scot*) ≈ Abiturabschluss *m*; **to take one's Highers** ≈ das Abitur machen; **three Highers** ≈ das Abitur in drei Fächern

higher: higher education N Hochschulbildung f; **Higher National Certificate** N (Brit) ≈ Berufsschulabschluss m; **Higher National Diploma** N (Brit) Qualifikationsnachweis in technischen Fächern; **higher-up** N (inf) höheres Tier (inf)

high: high explosive N hochexplosiver Sprengstoff; **high-explosive shell** N Sprenggranate f, Brisanzgeschoss nt; **highfalutin** [ˌhaɪfəˈluːtɪn], **highfaluting** [ˌhaɪfəˈluːtɪŋ] ADJ (inf) language, behaviour hochtrabend, geschwollen; scheme großkotzig (inf); idea hochgestochen; people aufgeblasen, hochgestochen; **high farming** N (Agr) intensive Bodenbewirtschaftung; **high-fibre**, (US) **high-fiber** ADJ diet ballaststoffreich; **high fidelity** N Highfidelity f, Tontreue f; **high-fidelity** ADJ Hi-Fi-~; **sound** Hi-Fi-Sound m; **high-five** N (inf) Highfive nt; **to give sb a ~** jdn mit Highfive begrüßen; **high-flier** N (inf, = successful person) Senkrechtstarter(in) m(f); (= ambitious person) Ehrgeizling m (pej); **he's a ~** er ist ein Erfolgstyp (inf); **high-flown** ADJ style, speech hochtrabend, geschwollen; ambitions hoch gesteckt; ideas, plans hochfliegend; **high-flyer** N = high-flier; **high-flying** ADJ aircraft mit großer Flughöhe; (fig) businessman etc erfolgreich; lifestyle exklusiv; **high frequency** N Hochfrequenz f ADJ hochfrequent, Hochfrequenz-; **~ signal** Hochfrequenzsignal nt; **High German** N Hochdeutsch nt; **high-grade** ADJ hochwertig; ore gediegen; **high ground** N a hoch liegendes Land; snow on **~** b Schnee in hoch liegenden Gebieten; b (fig) **to regain the ~** seine überlegene Position zurückerobern; **to take the political/intellectual ~** sich politisch/intellektuell aufs hohe Ross setzen; **to lose/claim the moral ~** die moralische Überlegenheit verlieren/für sich beanspruchen; **high-handed** ADJ character überheblich; manner, behaviour, attitude selbstherrlich; treatment arrogant; **high hat** N (US, inf) hochnäsiger Typ (inf); **high-hat** (US, inf) ADJ hochnäsig (inf) VT herablassend behandeln, von oben herab behandeln; **high-heeled** ADJ mit hohen Absätzen, hochhackig; **high heels** PL hohe Absätze pl; **high-income** ADJ einkommensstark; **high-interest** ADJ (Fin) shares, account hoch verzinslich; loan hoch verzinst; purchase mit hohen Zinsen; **highjack** VT, N = hijack; **highjacker** N = hijacker; **high jinks** PL (inf) ausgelassene Späße pl; **the ~ over this bill** das Theater um diesen Gesetzesentwurf (inf); **there wasn't much substance behind the verbal ~** hinter den Worten steckte nicht viel; **high jump** N (Sport) Hochsprung m; **to be for the ~** (fig inf) dran sein (inf); **high jumper** N (Sport) Hochspringer(in) m(f); **highland** ADJ hochländisch; area, town also im Hochland; **Highlander** N Bewohner(in) m(f) des schottischen Hochlands or der schottischen Highlands; **Highland fling** N schottischer Volkstanz; **Highland Games** PL schottisches Volksfest mit traditionellen Wettkämpfen; **Highlands** PL schottisches Hochland, (schottische) Highlands pl; (generally) Berg- or Hochland nt; **high-level** ADJ talks, discussion auf höchster Ebene; (Comput) language höher; **~ official** Spitzenfunktionär(in) m(f); **high life** N Highlife nt, Leben nt in großem Stil; **highlight** ✿ 26.3 N a (Art, Phot) Glanzlicht nt; (in hair) Strähne f; (in hair) Strähnchen pl b (fig) Höhepunkt m; I **watched the ~s of the match** ich sah mir die Höhepunkte des Spiels an VT a need, issue, problem, dangers ein Schlaglicht werfen auf (+acc); **this ~s the fact that ...** das verdeutlicht die Tatsache, dass ... b text (with highlighter) hervorheben, markieren; (on computer screen) markieren; hair Strähnen machen in (+acc); **highlighter** N a (= pen) Leuchtstift m, Textmarker m b (for hair) Aufheller m; (= cosmetic) Töner m; **high living** N flottes or (pej) ausschweifendes Leben

highly [ˈhaɪlɪ] ADV a (emph, = extremely) successful, sensitive, competitive, controversial, critical äußerst; inflammable leicht; spiced stark; individual,

unusual, significant, efficient äußerst, höchst; **~ charged** (atmosphere) aufgeladen; debate hitzig; **~ coloured** (Brit) or **colored** (US) (lit) farbenfroh, sehr bunt; (fig) report, description (= one-sided) stark gefärbt; (= detailed) ausgeschmückt; **to be ~ critical of sb/sth** jdn/etw scharf kritisieren; **~ trained** äußerst gut ausgebildet; skilled worker hoch qualifiziert; sportsperson durchtrainiert; **~ skilled** äußerst geschickt; worker, workforce hoch qualifiziert; **~ placed** (in organization, society) hoch gestellt; (Sport, in league) führend; **~ respected/gifted/educated/paid/developed** hoch geachtet/begabt/gebildet/bezahlt/entwickelt; **~ intelligent/topical** hochintelligent/-aktuell; **~ polished** (= shiny) auf Hochglanz poliert; shoes, brass blank geputzt; (= accomplished) performance, style, manners, language perfekt ausgefeilt; **~ sophisticated** (person, audience) höchst anspruchsvoll; technology, equipment hoch entwickelt; **~ toxic** hochgiftig; **~ unlikely** or **improbable** äußerst or höchst unwahrscheinlich

b regard, rate, prize hoch; **he is a ~ regarded writer** er ist ein hoch angesehener Autor; **they were ~ praised** sie wurden hoch gelobt; **I don't rate him very ~ at all** ich halte überhaupt nicht viel von ihm; **she rates ~ among world class athletes** sie zählt zu den Weltklassesportlern; **to be ~ prized for its flavour** wegen seines Geschmacks hoch geschätzt werden; **to speak ~ of sb/sth** sich sehr positiv über jdn/etw äußern; **to think ~ of sb/sth** eine hohe Meinung von jdm/etw haben; **~ recommended** sehr empfehlenswert; **I can ~ recommend it** ich kann es sehr empfehlen; **she came ~ recommended** sie kam mit einer sehr guten Empfehlung

highly strung ADJ (Brit) nervös

high: High Mass N Hochamt nt; **high-minded** ADJ ideals hoch; intentions hochgesinnt; critics anspruchsvoll; **high muck-a-muck** [ˌhaɪˈmʌkəmʌk] N (sl) arrogantes, hohes Tier (pej); **high-necked** ADJ hochgeschlossen

highness [ˈhaɪnɪs] N a Höhe f; **~ of ideals** hohe Ideale pl b Her/Your Highness Ihre/Eure Hoheit; **yes, Your Highness** ja, Hoheit

high: high-octane ADJ mit einer hohen Oktanzahl; **high-performance** ADJ Hochleistungs-; **computer** Hochleistungscomputer m; **high-pitched** ADJ a sound, voice hoch; scream, squeak schrill b (Archit) roof steil; **high point** N Höhepunkt m; **high-powered** ADJ a (= powerful) machine, engine, computer leistungsfähig; rifle, gun leistungsstark; car stark (-motorig); laser stark b person hoch gestellt, hochkarätig (inf); (= dynamic) dynamisch; academic etc äußerst fähig; job, career, course anspruchsvoll; conversation hochintellektuell; delegation hochkarätig (inf); **high-pressure** ADJ a (using air or liquid) Hochdruck-; **~ pump** Hochdruckpumpe f; **~ cylinder** Hochdruckzylinder m; **~ air** Druckluft f; **~ hose** Druckleitung f b (Met) **~ area** Hochdruckgebiet nt; a **~ area over the Atlantic** ein Hoch(druckgebiet) nt über dem Atlantik, ein atlantisches Hoch c (fig) sales technique aggressiv; salesman also aufdringlich d (= stressful) job sehr stressig; atmosphere sehr (an)gespannt VT (US) **~ sb into doing sth** jdn so unter Druck setzen, dass er etw tut; **high-priced** ADJ teuer; **high priest** N (lit, fig) Hohepriester m; a **~** ein Hoher Priester m; **of the ~** des Hohen Priesters; **high priestess** N (lit, fig) Hohepriesterin f; **of the ~** der Hohen Priesterin; **high-principled** ADJ mit strengen Grundsätzen; **high-profile** ADJ profiliert; **high-protein** ADJ eiweißreich; **high-ranking** ADJ hoch(rangig), von hohem Rang; **high relief** N Hochrelief nt; **high-resolution** ADJ screen, graphics hoch auflösend; **high-rise** ADJ **~ building** Hochhaus nt; **~ office (block)** Bürohochhaus nt; **~ flats** (Brit) (Wohn)hochhaus nt; **high-risk** ADJ risikoreich; **~ group** Risikogruppe f; **~ victim** einer Risikogruppe angehörendes Opfer; **highroad** N (old) Landstraße f; **the ~ to success** der sichere Weg zum Erfolg; **high school** N (Brit) ≈

Oberschule f (für 11 bis 18-Jährige); (US) ≈ Oberschule f (für 15 bis 18-Jährige)

high: high-scoring ADJ game (Ftbl, Hockey, Handball) torreich; (Basketball) punktreich; **high seas** PL the **~** die Meere pl; **on the ~** auf hoher See, auf offenem Meer; **high season** N Hochsaison f; **during (the) ~** während der Hochsaison; **high seat** N (Hunt) Hochsitz m; **high-security** ADJ **~ prison** Hochsicherheitsgefängnis nt; **~ wing** Hochsicherheitstrakt m; **high-sided** ADJ **~ vehicle** hohes Fahrzeug; **high sign** N (US, inf) vereinbartes Signal; **to give sb a ~** jdm ein vereinbartes Signal geben; **high society** N Highsociety f; **high-sounding** ADJ klangvoll; **high-speed** ADJ schnell; drill mit hoher Umdrehungszahl; **~ car chase** wilde Verfolgungsjagd im Auto; **~ crash** Zusammenstoß m bei hoher Geschwindigkeit; **~ train** Hochgeschwindigkeitszug m; **~ rail link** Hochgeschwindigkeitszugverbindung f; **~ printer** Schnelldrucker m; **~ lens** hoch lichtstarkes Objektiv, lichtstarke Linse; **~ film** hoch (licht)empfindlicher Film; **high-spirited** ADJ temperamentvoll, lebhaft; **high spirits** PL Hochstimmung f; **youthful ~** jugendlicher Übermut; **high spot** N Höhepunkt m; **to hit the ~s** (inf) auf den Putz hauen (inf); **high street** N (Brit) Hauptstraße f; **~ banks** Geschäftsbanken pl; **~ shops** Geschäfte pl in der Innenstadt; **high-strung** ADJ (US) nervös; **high summer** N Hochsommer m; **high table** N (Sch) Lehrertisch m; (Univ) Tisch m für Professoren und Dozenten

hightail [ˈhaɪteɪl] VI (US, inf) **to ~ (it) out of a place** (aus einem Ort) abhauen (inf), (von or aus einem Ort) verduften (inf)

high: high tea N (frühes) Abendessen; **high-tech** N, ADJ = hi-tech; **high technology** N Hochtechnologie f, Spitzentechnologie f; **high-tension** ADJ (Elec) Hochspannungs-; **~ cable** Hochspannungskabel nt; **high treason** N Hochverrat m; **high-up** ADJ person hoch gestellt N (inf) hohes Tier (inf); **high-velocity** ADJ Hochgeschwindigkeits-; **~ rifle** Hochgeschwindigkeitsgewehr nt; **high-water mark** N (lit) Hochwasserstandsmarke f; (fig) höchster Stand; **highway** N a (US) Highway m, ≈ Autobahn f b (Brit) Landstraße f; public ~ öffentliche Straße f; **the ~s and byways** die Straßen und Wege pl; (fig, of life, music) alle Aspekte; **he knows all the ~s and byways of Dorset** er kennt Weg und Steg in Dorset; **Highway Code** N (Brit) Straßenverkehrsordnung f; **highwayman** N Räuber m, Wegelagerer m, Strauchdieb m; **highway robbery** N Straßenraub m; (fig) Nepp m (inf); **Highways Department** N Tiefbauamt nt; **high wire** N Drahtseil nt; **high-yield** ADJ (Agr) ertragsreich; (Fin) investment, bond ertragsstark

hijack [ˈhaɪdʒæk] VT aircraft etc entführen; (fig) für sich beanspruchen N (of aircraft etc) Entführung f

hijacker [ˈhaɪdʒækə˙] N Entführer(in) m(f), Hijacker(in) m(f)

hike [haɪk] **VI** wandern **VT** *prices, rates* erhöhen **N** **a** (*lit*) Wanderung *f* **b** (*fig: in interest rates*) Erhöhung *f*

▶ **hike up** VT *sep* **a** *trousers, skirt* hochziehen **b** *prices, rates* erhöhen

hiker ['haɪkə'] N Wanderer *m*, Wanderin *f*

hiking ['haɪkɪŋ] N Wandern *nt*

hiking boots PL Wanderstiefel *pl*

hilarious [hɪ'leərɪəs] ADJ irrsinnig komisch (*inf*), urkomisch (*inf*); (= *loud and happy*) *mood* ausgelassen, übermütig

hilariously [hɪ'leərɪəslɪ] ADV *talk* sehr amüsant; *juxtaposed, mixed up* auf komische Weise; *disguised, dressed up* urkomisch (*inf*); ~ **funny** zum Schreien (*inf*), irrsinnig komisch (*inf*); ~ **old-fashioned** so altmodisch, dass es zum Schreien ist

hilarity [hɪ'lærɪtɪ] N Heiterkeit *f*; (= *gaiety*) Fröhlichkeit *f*; (= *laughter*) Gelächter *nt*; **his statement caused some** ~ seine Behauptung löste einige Heiterkeit aus

Hilary ['hɪlərɪ] N (*Oxford Univ*) Frühjahrstrimester *nt*; (*Jur*) Frühjahrssitzungsperiode *f*

hill [hɪl] N **a** Hügel *m*; (*higher*) Berg *m*; (= *incline*) Hang *m*; **the castle stands on a** ~ das Schloss steht auf einem Berg; **the houses on the** ~ **beneath the castle** die Häuser am Schlossberg; **these flats are built on a** ~ diese Wohnungen sind am Hang *or* Berg gebaut; **to park on a** ~ am Berg parken; **you hardly feel the** ~**s in this car** in diesem Auto spürt man die Steigungen kaum; **up** ~ **and down dale** bergauf und bergab; **as old as the** ~**s** steinalt, uralt; **that joke's as old as the** ~**s** der Witz hat ja so einen langen Bart; **to take to the** ~**s** sich in die Berge flüchten; **to be over the** ~ (*fig inf*) seine beste Zeit *or* die besten Jahre hinter sich (*dat*) haben

b → **anthill, molehill** etc

hillbilly ['hɪlbɪlɪ] (*US, inf*) N Hinterwäldler(in) *m(f)* (*pej*); (*female also*) Landpomeranze *f* (*inf*) **ADJ** hinterwäldlerisch (*pej*); ~ **music** Hillbilly *no art*, Hillbillymusik *f*

hill farmer N Bergbauer *m*, Bergbäuerin *f*

hilliness ['hɪlɪnɪs] N Hügeligkeit *f*; (*higher*) Bergigkeit *f*; **the** ~ **of the terrain** das hügelige *or* (*higher*) bergige Gelände

hillock ['hɪlək] N Hügel *m*, Anhöhe *f*

hill: hillside N Hang *m*; **hilltop** N Gipfel *m*; **hill-walker** N Bergwanderer *m*, Bergwanderin *f*; **hill-walking** N Bergwandern *nt*

hilly ['hɪlɪ] ADJ (*+er*) hüg(e)lig; (*higher*) bergig

hilt [hɪlt] N Heft *nt*; (*of dagger*) Griff *m*; (**up**) **to the** ~ (*fig*) voll und ganz; (*involved, in debt also*) bis über beide Ohren (*inf*); **I'll back you (up) to the** ~ ich stehe voll und ganz hinter Ihnen

him [hɪm] PERS PRON **a** (*dir obj, with prep +acc*) ihn; (*indir obj, with prep +dat*) ihm; (*when he is previously mentioned in clause*) sich; **with his things around** ~ mit seinen Sachen um sich **b** (*emph*) er; **it's** ~ er ists; **who,** ~**?** wer, er?

Himalayan [,hɪmə'leɪən] ADJ Himalaya-, des Himalaya; ~ **state** Himalayastaat *m*

Himalayas [,hɪmə'leɪəz] PL Himalaya *m*

himbo ['hɪmbəʊ] N (*inf pej*) gut aussehender aber wenig intelligenter Mann

himself [hɪm'self] PERS PRON **a** (*dir and indir obj, with prep*) sich → *also* **myself** **b** (*emph*) (er) selbst **N** (*Ir, inf*) **it was** ~ **who told me** er selbst hat es mir gesagt

hind¹ [haɪnd] N (*Zool*) Hirschkuh *f*, Hindin *f* (*poet*)

hind² ADJ Hinter-; ~ **legs** Hinterbeine *pl*; ~ **feet** Hinterfüße *pl*; ~ **paws** Hinterpfoten *pl*; **the horse reared up on its** ~ **legs** das Pferd bäumte sich auf; **he can** *or* **could talk the** ~ **leg(s) off a donkey** (*inf*) er kann einem ein Ohr *or* die Ohren abreden (*inf*)

hinder ['hɪndə'] VT **a** (= *obstruct, impede*) behindern; (= *delay*) *person* aufhalten; *arrival* verzögern; **b** (= *stop, prevent from happening*) verhindern; **to** ~ **sb from doing sth** jdn daran hindern

or davon abhalten, etw zu tun; **he doesn't let his disability** ~ **him** *or* lässt sich nicht durch seine Behinderung abhalten

Hindi ['hɪndiː] N Hindi *nt*

hind: hindmost ADJ *superl of* **hind²** hinterste(r, s); **hindquarters** PL Hinterteil *nt*; (*of carcass*) Hinterviertel *nt*; (*of horse*) Hinterhand *f*

hindrance ['hɪndrəns] N Behinderung *f*; (= *obstacle*) Hindernis *nt* (*to* für); **the rules/children are a** ~ die Regeln/Kinder sind hinderlich; **it was a serious** ~ **to progress** es behinderte den Fortschritt sehr; **he/it is more of a** ~ **than a help** er/es hindert mehr, als dass er/es hilft; **without** ~ unbehindert → **let¹**

hindsight ['haɪndsaɪt] N **now with the benefit** *or* **wisdom of** ~ hinterher *or* im Nachhinein ist man ja immer schlauer; **with** ~ **it's easy to criticize** hinterher *or* im Nachhinein ist es leicht zu kritisieren; **it was, in** ~**, a mistaken judgement** es war, rückblickend betrachtet, ein Fehlurteil

Hindu ['hɪnduː] **ADJ** hinduistisch; ~ **people** Hindu(s) *pl* **N** Hindu *m*

Hinduism ['hɪnduːɪzəm] N Hinduismus *m*

Hindustan [,hɪndʊ'staːn] N Hindustan *nt*, Hindostan *nt*

Hindustani [,hɪndʊ'staːnɪ] **ADJ** hindustanisch **N** **a** Bewohner(in) *m(f)* Hindustans **b** (*Ling*) Hindustani *nt*

hinge [hɪndʒ] **N** **a** (*of door*) Angel *f*; (*of box etc*) Scharnier *nt*; (*of limb, shell*) Gelenk *nt*; (*fig*) Angelpunkt *m*; **the door is off its** ~**s** die Tür ist aus den Angeln; **the lid is off its** ~**s** das Scharnier des Deckels ist ab; **take the door off its** ~**s** häng die Tür aus! **b** (*also* **stamp hinge**) (Klebe)falz *m* **VT to** ~ **sth (to sth)** etw mit einem Scharnier/mit Scharnieren (an etw *dat*) befestigen **VI** (*fig*) abhängen (*on* von), ankommen (*on* auf *+acc*)

hinged [hɪndʒd] ADJ mit Scharnier/mit Scharnieren (versehen); *door* eingehängt; ~ **lid** Klappdeckel *m*

hint [hɪnt] **N** **a** (= *intimation, suggestion*) Andeutung *f*, Hinweis *m*; **a strong** ~ ein deutlicher Hinweis; **a subtle** ~ ein zarter Wink; **to give a/no** ~ **of sth** etw ahnen lassen *or* andeuten/ nicht ahnen lassen *or* andeuten; **to give** *or* **drop sb a** ~ jdm einen Wink geben, jdm gegenüber eine Andeutung machen; **he was given a gentle** ~ **about attention to detail** man hat ihm leise angedeutet *or* den leisen Wink gegeben, auf Details zu achten; **to throw out** *or* **drop a** ~ eine Andeutung machen, eine Bemerkung fallen lassen; **to know how to take a** ~ einen Wink verstehen; **OK, I can take a** ~ schon recht, ich verstehe *or* ich habe den Wink mit dem Zaunpfahl verstanden (*inf*); **I've almost run out of this perfume,** ~**,** ~ ich habe fast nichts mehr von dem Parfüm, hörst du?

b (= *trace*) Spur *f*; **a** ~ **of garlic** eine Spur Knoblauch; **a** ~ **of irony** ein Hauch *m* von Spott; **with just a** ~ **of sadness in his smile** mit einem leichten Anflug von Traurigkeit in seinem Lächeln; **with the** ~ **of a smile** mit dem Anflug eines Lächelns; **not a** ~ **of emotion** keinerlei Gefühl; **a** ~ **of desperation** ein Anflug *m* von Verzweiflung; **at the first** ~ **of trouble** beim ersten Zeichen von Ärger; **there was no** ~ **of apology in his voice** seine Stimme klang überhaupt nicht entschuldigend

c (= *tip, piece of advice*) Tipp *m*; ~**s for travellers** (*Brit*) *or* **travelers** (*US*) Reisetipps *pl*; **I'll give you a** ~**, the answer has two words** ich gebe dir einen Tipp *or* Hinweis, die Antwort besteht aus zwei Wörtern

VT andeuten (*to* gegenüber); **what are you** ~**ing?** wollen Sie damit sagen *or* andeuten?; **he** ~**ed strongly that ...** er gab deutlich zu verstehen, dass ...

▶ **hint at** VI *+prep obj* **he hinted at changes in the cabinet** er deutete an, dass im Kabinett Umbesetzungen geben würde; **he hinted at my involvement in the affair** er spielte auf meine Rolle in der Affäre an

hinterland ['hɪntəlænd] N Hinterland *nt*

hip¹ [hɪp] N Hüfte *f*; **with one's hands on one's** ~**s** die Arme in die Hüften gestemmt

hip² N (*Bot*) Hagebutte *f*

hip³ INTERJ ~! ~!, **hurrah!** hipp hipp, hurra!

hip⁴ ADJ (*inf*) hip (*inf*); **to be** ~ **to sth** in etw (*dat*) voll drin sein (*inf*); **to get** ~ **to sth** sich in etw (*acc*) voll reinhängen (*sl*)

hip *in cpds* Hüft-; **hip bath** N Sitzbad *nt*; **hip bone** N (*Anat*) Hüftbein *nt*, Hüftknochen *m*; **hip flask** N Taschenflasche *f*, Flachmann *m* (*inf*); **hip-huggers** ['hɪphʌgəz] PL (*US*) Hüfthose(n) *f(pl)*; **hip joint** N (*Anat*) Hüftgelenk *nt*; **hip measurement** N Hüftweite *f*, Hüftumfang *m*

-hipped [-hɪpt] ADJ *suf* mit ... Hüften; **a big-hipped woman** eine Frau mit breiten Hüften, eine breithüftige Frau

hippie N = **hippy**

hippo ['hɪpəʊ] N (*inf*) Nilpferd *nt*

hip pocket N Gesäßtasche *f*

Hippocratic oath [,hɪpəʊˌkrætɪk'əʊθ] N hippokratischer Eid, Eid *m* des Hippokrates

hippodrome ['hɪpədrəʊm] N Hippodrom *m or nt*; (*dated, = music hall*) Varietee- *or* Varieté(theater) *nt*

hippopotamus [,hɪpə'pɒtəməs] N *pl* **-es** *or* **hippopotami** [,hɪpə'pɒtəmaɪ] Nilpferd *nt*, Flusspferd *nt*

hippy, hippie ['hɪpɪ] N Hippie *m*

hip

hip replacement N Hüftoperation *f*; (= *device*) Hüftprothese *f*

hip roof N (*Archit*) Walmdach *nt*

hipster ['hɪpstə'] **N** **a** (*dated inf, = one who is hip*) hipper Typ (*sl*) **b** **hipsters** PL (= *trousers*) Hüfthose(n) *f(pl)* **ADJ** Hüft-; ~ **pants** Hüfthose(n) *f(pl)*

hire [haɪə'] **N** **a** (= *rental*) Mieten *nt*; (*of car also, of suit*) Leihen *nt*; (= *employment: of servant*) Einstellen *nt*; **to have sth for** ~ etw vermieten/verleihen; **the hall is available for** ~ man kann den Saal mieten; **for** ~ (*taxi*) frei; **it's on** ~ (= *is a hired item*) es ist gemietet/geliehen; **to be (out) on** ~ vermietet sein **b** (= *wages*) Lohn *m*; (*of sailor*) Heuer *f* **VT** **a** (= *rent*) mieten; *car* mieten, leihen; *suit* leihen; ~**d car** Mietwagen *m*, Leihwagen *m* **b** (= *employ*) *staff, person* einstellen; ~**d assassin** gedungener Mörder **c** = **hire out** VT

▶ **hire out** **VT** *sep* (*esp Brit*) vermieten, verleihen **VI** (*US*) sich verdingen

hired gun [,haɪəd'gʌn] N gedungener Mörder, bezahlter Killer (*inf*)

hired hand [,haɪəd'hænd] N Lohnarbeiter(in) *m(f)*

hireling ['haɪəlɪŋ] N (*pej*) Mietling *m* (*old pej*)

hire-purchase [,haɪə'pɜːtʃəs] N (*Brit*) Ratenkauf *m*, Teilzahlungskauf *m*; **on** ~ auf Raten *or* Teilzahlung; ~ **agreement** Teilzahlungs(kauf)vertrag *m*

hirsute ['hɜːsjuːt] ADJ stark behaart

his [hɪz] POSS ADJ sein → *also* **my** POSS PRON seine(r, s); ~ (*on towels etc*) er → *also* **mine¹**

Hispanic [hɪs'pænɪk] **ADJ** hispanisch; *community* spanisch **N** Hispanoamerikaner(in) *m(f)*

hiss [hɪs] **VI** zischen; (*cat*) fauchen **VT** **a** zischen; **come here, he** ~**ed** komm her, zischte er **b** *actor, speaker* auszischen **N** Zischen *nt*; (*of cat*) Fauchen *nt*

histamine ['hɪstəmiːn] N (*Med*) Histamin *nt*

histology [hɪs'tɒlədʒɪ] N Histologie *f*

historian [hɪs'tɔːrɪən] N Historiker(in) *m(f)*; (*in ancient times*) Geschichtsschreiber(in) *m(f)*

historic [hɪs'tɒrɪk] ADJ (*also Gram*) historisch

historical [hɪs'tɒrɪkəl] ADJ historisch; *studies, background, investigation, method also* geschichtlich; ~ **research** Geschichtsforschung *f*; **places of** ~ **interest** historisch *or* geschichtlich interessante Stätten *pl*

historically [hɪs'tɒrɪkəlɪ] ADV (= *traditionally*) traditionellerweise; **the country has** ~ **been ve-**

ry **dependent on agriculture** das Land war immer schon stark von der Landwirtschaft abhängig **b** (= *relating to history*) important, accurate, consider historisch; **~ unique** einmalig in der Geschichte; **as ~ significant as ...** von gleicher historischer Bedeutung wie ...; **~ (speaking)** historisch gesehen, aus historischer Sicht **c** (= *uniquely*) important, high etc einmalig, beispiellos

historicism [hɪsˈtɒrɪsɪzəm] N Historizismus *m*

historicity [hɪstəˈrɪsɪtɪ] N Geschichtlichkeit *f*, Historizität *f*

historiography [ˌhɪstɒrɪˈɒɡrəfɪ] N Geschichtsschreibung *f*, Historiografie *f*

history [ˈhɪstərɪ] N **a** Geschichte *f*; (= *study of history*) Geschichtswissenschaft *f*; **~ will judge** die Geschichte wird ihr Urteil fällen; **~ has taught us that ...** die Geschichte lehrt uns, dass ...; **the highest salary in television** – das höchste Gehalt in der Geschichte des Fernsehens; **to make ~** Geschichte machen; **... and the rest is ~** ... und der Rest ist Geschichte; **that's all ~ now** (fig) das gehört jetzt alles der Vergangenheit an; **he's ~** er ist schon lange vergessen *or* passé (inf) **b** (= *personal record*) Geschichte *f*; **he has a ~ of violence** er hat eine Vorgeschichte als Gewalttäter; **the family has a ~ of heart disease** Herzleiden liegen in der Familie; **he has a ~ of heart disease** er hat schon lange ein Herzleiden **c** (= *background*) Vorgeschichte *f*; **to know the ~ of an affair** den Hintergrund einer Affäre kennen

histrionic [hɪstrɪˈɒnɪk] ADJ **a** (= *overdone, affected*) theatralisch **b** (= *relating to acting*) schauspielerisch

histrionically [hɪstrɪˈɒnɪkəlɪ] ADV theatralisch

histrionics [hɪstrɪˈɒnɪks] PL **a** theatralisches Getue; **to put on a display of ~** sich theatralisch aufführen **b** (*Theat*) Schauspielkunst *f*

hit [hɪt] vb: pret, ptp **hit** N **a** (= *blow*) Schlag *m*; (on target, Fencing) Treffer *m*; (Baseball) Schlag *m* → **score**
b (= *success, also Theat*) Erfolg *m*, Knüller *m* (inf); (= *song*) Hit *m*; **to be** *or* **make a (big) ~ with sb** bei jdm (ausgesprochen) gut ankommen **c** (*of sarcasm etc*) Spitze *f*; **that's a ~ at me** das ist eine Spitze gegen mich; (indirect also) das ist auf mich gemünzt **d** (*Comput*) Hit *m* **e** (*Drugs inf*) (= *injection*) Schuss *m*; (= *drag*) Zug *m* **d** (inf, = *murder*) Mord *m*
VT **a** (= *strike*) schlagen; (*Comput*) key drücken; **to ~ sb a blow** jdm einen Schlag versetzen; **he ~ him a blow over the head** er gab ihm einen Schlag auf den Kopf; **to ~ one's head against sth** (*dat*) den Kopf an etw (*dat*) stoßen; **he ~ his head on the table** er schlug mit dem Kopf auf dem Tisch auf; **the car ~ a tree** das Auto fuhr gegen einen Baum; **he was ~ by a stone** er wurde von einem Stein getroffen, ihn traf ein Stein; **the house was ~ by a shell** das Haus wurde von einer Granate getroffen; **the tree was ~ by lightning** der Baum wurde vom Blitz getroffen; **to ~ one's way out of trouble** sich freischlagen; (*Tennis*) sich freispielen; (*Boxing*) sich freiboxen; **we're going to ~ the enemy as hard as we can** wir werden so hart wie möglich gegen den Feind vorgehen; **the commandos ~ the town at dawn** die Kommandos griffen die Stadt im Morgengrauen an; **the hurricane ~ Miami last night** der Hurrikan erreichte gestern Abend Miami; **the courts will ~ drug pushers hard** die Gerichte werden hart gegen Dealer vorgehen; **the smell ~ me as I entered the room** der Geruch schlug mir entgegen, als ich ins Zimmer kam; **he didn't know what had ~ him** (inf) er wusste nicht, wie ihm geschah; **you won't know what has ~ you** (inf) du wirst dein blaues Wunder erleben (inf)
b (= *wound*) treffen; **he's been ~ in the leg** es hat ihn am Bein getroffen, er ist am Bein ge-

troffen worden; **I've been ~!** ich bin getroffen worden, mich hats erwischt (inf) **c** mark, target treffen; (*Fencing*) treffen; **that ~ home** (fig) das hat getroffen, das saß (inf); **you've ~ it (on the head)** (fig) du hast es (genau) getroffen **d** (= *affect adversely*) betreffen; **the crops were ~ by the rain** der Regen hat die Ernte geschadet; **to be hard ~ by sth** von etw schwer getroffen werden; **how will this tax ~ you?** wie wird sich diese Steuer auf Sie auswirken? **e** (= *achieve, reach*) likeness, top C treffen; speed, level, top form etc erreichen **f** (*news, story*) **to ~ the papers** in die Zeitungen kommen; **the news ~ us/Wall Street like a bombshell** die Nachricht schlug bei uns/in Wall Street wie eine Bombe ein **g** (= *occur to*) **to ~ sb** jdm aufgehen; **has it ever ~ you how alike they are?** ist dir schon mal aufgefallen, wie ähnlich sie sich sind? **h** (= *come to, arrive at*) beaches etc erreichen; **to ~ town** (inf) die Stadt erreichen; **we eventually ~ the right road** schließlich haben wir den richtigen Weg gefunden *or* erwischt (inf); **we're going to ~ the rush hour** wir geraten *or* kommen direkt in den Stoßverkehr; **the driver ~ a patch of ice** der Fahrer geriet auf eine vereiste Stelle; **to ~ trouble/a problem** auf Schwierigkeiten/ein Problem stoßen **i** (= *score*) schlagen; **to ~ a century** hundert Läufe machen **j** (inf, = *murder*) killen (inf), umlegen (inf) **k** (*US, inf*) **to ~ sb for 50 dollars** jdn um 50 Dollar anhauen (inf) **l** (*fig inf phrases*) **to ~ the bottle** zur Flasche greifen; **to ~ the roof** an die Decke *or* in die Luft gehen (inf); **to ~ the deck** sich zu Boden werfen, sich hinwerfen; **the vase ~ the deck and shattered** die Vase schlug *or* knallte (inf) auf den Boden und zerschellte; **to ~ the dance floor** tanzen; **let's ~ the floor** lass uns tanzen; **to ~ the road** sich auf den Weg *or* die Socken (inf) machen; **in April the candidates will ~ the campaign trail** im April werden sich die Kandidaten in den Wahlkampf stürzen; **to ~ the ground running** (person) sofort alles im Griff haben
VI **a** (= *strike*) schlagen; **he ~s hard** er schlägt hart zu
b (= *collide*) zusammenstoßen
c (= *attack, go in*) losschlagen

▶**hit back** **VI** (*lit, fig*) zurückschlagen; **to hit back at the enemy** zurückschlagen; **he hit back at his critics** er gab seinen Kritikern Kontra; **he hit back at the accusations** er wehrte sich gegen die Anschuldigungen **VT** sep zurückschlagen

▶**hit off** **VT** sep **a** **he hit him off beautifully** er hat ihn ausgezeichnet getroffen **b** **to hit it off with sb** (inf) sich gut mit jdm verstehen, prima mit jdm auskommen (inf); **they hit it off straight away** sie haben sich von Anfang an gut verstanden

▶**hit on** **VI** +prep obj **a** stoßen auf (+acc), finden **b** (*esp US inf:* = *chat up*) anmachen (inf)

▶**hit out** **VI** **a** (*lit*) einschlagen, losschlagen (*at sb* auf jdn) **b** (*fig*) **to hit out at** *or* **against sb/sth** jdn/etw attackieren *or* scharf angreifen; **he hit out angrily when I suggested it was his fault** er griff mich scharf an, als ich ihm die Schuld geben wollte

▶**hit up** **VT** sep (*US inf*) **to hit sb up for 50 dollars** jdn um 50 Dollar anhauen (inf)

▶**hit upon** **VI** +prep obj = **hit on a**

hit-and-run [ˈhɪtənˈrʌn] N **there was a ~ here last night** hier hat heute Nacht jemand einen Unfall gebaut und Fahrerflucht begangen **ADJ** **~ raid** (*Mil*) Blitzüberfall *m*; **~ accident/incident** Unfall *m* mit Fahrerflucht; **~ cases** Fälle *pl* von Fahrerflucht; **~ driver** unfallflüchtiger Fahrer, unfallflüchtige Fahrerin, Unfallflüchtige(r) *mf*

hitch [hɪtʃ] N **a** (= *snag*) Haken *m*; (in plan, proceedings, programme) Schwierigkeit *f*, Problem *nt*; **a technical ~** eine technische Panne;

without a ~ reibungslos, ohne Schwierigkeiten; **but there is a ~** aber die Sache hat einen Haken; **there's been a ~** es haben sich Schwierigkeiten ergeben, da ist ein Problem aufgetaucht **b** (= *quick pull*) Ruck *m*; **she gave her skirt a quick ~** sie zog schnell ihren Rock am Bund zurecht **c** (= *knot*) Knoten *m*; (*Naut*) Stek *m* **d** (inf, = *lift*) **I got a ~ all the way to London** ich bin in einem Rutsch bis London (durch-) getrampt (inf)
VT **a** (= *fasten*) festmachen, anbinden (*sth to sth* etw an etw *dat*); **to ~ one's wagon to a star** (*dated US*) sich (*dat*) ein hohes Ziel setzen, nach den Sternen greifen (geh); **to ~ one's wagon to sb** (*dated US*) sich mit jdm zusammentun **b** (inf) **to get ~ed** heiraten, vor Anker gehen (hum); **why don't we get ~ed?** warum heiraten wir (eigentlich) nicht? **c** **to ~ a lift** *or* **ride** trampen, per Anhalter fahren; **she ~ed a lift** *or* **ride with a truck driver** ein Lastwagenfahrer nahm sie mit **VI** (*esp Brit*) trampen, per Anhalter fahren → also **hitchhike**

▶**hitch up** **VT** sep **a** horses, oxen anschirren, anspannen; trailer etc anhängen; **we hitched up the horses to the wagon** wir spannten die Pferde vor den Wagen **b** trousers, skirt hochziehen

hitcher [ˈhɪtʃə] N (*esp Brit inf*) Anhalter(in) *m(f)*, Tramper(in) *m(f)*

hitch: hitchhike **VI** per Anhalter fahren, trampen; **he's been away hitchhiking around Europe** er ist durch Europa getrampt; **hitchhiker** N Anhalter(in) *m(f)*, Tramper(in) *m(f)*; **hitchhiking** N Trampen *nt*

hitching post [ˈhɪtʃɪŋpəʊst] N Pfosten *m* (*zum Anbinden von Pferden*)

hi tech [ˈhaɪˌtek] N Spitzentechnologie *f*, Hitech *nt*, Computertechnik *f*

hi-tech [ˈhaɪˌtek] ADJ Hitech-; **~ equipment** Hi-techgeräte *pl*

hither [ˈhɪðə] ADV **a** (old, = *to this place*) hierher → also **come-hither** **b** **~ and thither** (liter, = *to and fro*) hierhin und dorthin

hitherto [ˌhɪðəˈtuː] ADV bisher, bis jetzt

hit: hit list N (*lit, fig*) Abschussliste *f*; **hitman** N (inf) Killer *m* (inf); **hit-or-miss** ADJ auf gut Glück pred, aufs Geratewohl pred; methods, planning schlampig, schludrig (inf); **it was a rather ~ affair** das ging alles aufs Geratewohl; **hit parade** N Hitparade *f*; **hit record** N Hit *m*; **hit show** N erfolgreiche Show, Publikumserfolg *m*; **hit single** N Hitsingle *f*; **hit song** N Hit *m*; **hit squad**, **hit team** N Killerkommando *nt*

hitter [ˈhɪtə] N (*Boxing, inf*) Schlager *m*, Puncher *m*

hit: hit tune N Schlagermelodie *f*; **hitwoman** N (inf) Killerin *f* (inf)

HIV abbr of **human immunodeficiency virus** HIV *nt*; **~ positive/negative** HIV-positiv/-negativ

hive [haɪv] N **a** (= *beehive*) Bienenkorb *m*, Bienenstock *m*; (= *bees in a hive*) (Bienen)schwarm *m*, (Bienen)volk *nt* **b** (fig) **to be a ~ of industry** das reinste Bienenhaus sein; **the office was a ~ of activity** das Büro glich einem Bienenhaus **VT** bees, swarm einfangen, in den Stock bringen **VI** (= *swarm*) in den (Bienen)stock (ein)fliegen, einen Stock beziehen

▶**hive off** **VT** sep department, company ausgliedern; staff abbauen; work vergeben (*to an* +acc); **the branch could be hived off into a separate company** die Filiale könnte als eigene Firma verselbstständigt werden **VI** **a** (= *branch out*) sich absetzen **b** (inf, = *slip away*) abschwirren (inf)

hives [haɪvz] PL (*Med*) Nesselausschlag *m*, Nesselsucht *f*

hiya [ˈhaɪjə] INTERJ hallo

Hizbollah [ˈhɪzbəˈlɑː] N Hisb Allah *f*, Hisbollah *f*

HM abbr of **His/Her Majesty** S. M./I. M.

HMG *abbr of* **His/Her Majesty's Government**

HMI (*Brit*) *abbr of* **His/Her Majesty's Inspector** ≈ Schulrat *m*, Schulrätin *f*

HMS (*Brit*) *abbr of* **His/Her Majesty's Ship** HMS *f*

HMSO (*Brit*) *abbr of* **His/Her Majesty's Stationery Office** Druckerei *für staatliche Drucksachen*

HNC (*Brit*) *abbr of* **Higher National Certificate**

HND (*Brit*) *abbr of* **Higher National Diploma**

hoagie, hoagy ['həʊgɪ] N (*US*) *großes, reichlich belegtes Sandwich*, Jumbo-Sandwich *nt* (*inf*)

hoar [hɔː'] N Reif *m*

hoard [hɔːd] **N** Vorrat *m*; (= *treasure*) Schatz *m*; **a ~ of weapons** ein Waffenlager *nt*; **~ of money** Schatz *m*, gehortetes Geld **VT** (*also* **hoard up**) *food etc* hamstern; *money, supplies, weapons* horten; *information* zusammentragen; **a squirrel ~s nuts for the winter** ein Eichhörnchen hortet Nüsse für den Winter

hoarder ['hɔːdə'] N (= *animal*) *Tier, das Vorräte anlegt* (= *person*) Hamsterer *m*, Hamsterin *f*

hoarding¹ ['hɔːdɪŋ] N (*of food etc*) Hamstern *nt*; (*of capital*) Anhäufen *nt*, Anhäufung *f*

hoarding² N (*Brit*, = *fence, board*) Bretterzaun *m*; (*at building sites also*) Bauzaun *m*; (**advertising**) ~ Plakatwand *f*

hoarfrost ['hɔːfrɒst] N (Rau)reif *m*

hoarse [hɔːs] ADJ (+*er*) heiser; **he shouted himself ~** er schrie sich heiser; **you sound rather ~** deine Stimme klingt heiser

hoarsely ['hɔːslɪ] ADV heiser, mit heiserer Stimme

hoarseness ['hɔːsnɪs] N (*of person*) Heiserkeit *f*; **the ~ of his voice** seine heisere Stimme

hoary ['hɔːrɪ] ADJ (+*er*) **a** *hair, old man etc* ergraut **b** (*fig*: = *old*) uralt, altehrwürdig; **a ~ old joke** ein alter Hut, ein Witz mit (einem langen) Bart

hoax [həʊks] **N** (= *practical joke*) Streich *m*; (= *trick etc*) Trick *m*; (= *false alarm*) blinder Alarm; **to play a ~ on sb** jdm einen Streich spielen **VT** anführen, hereinlegen (*inf*); **to ~ sb into believing sth** jdm etw weismachen; **we were completely ~ed** wir ließen uns anführen, wir fielen darauf herein

hoax: hoax call N a ~ ein blinder Alarm; **hoax caller, hoaxer** ['həʊksə'] N (*in bomb scares etc*) *jd, der einen blinden Alarm auslöst*; **hoax story** N Zeitungsente *f*

hob [hɒb] N Kamineinsatz *m* (zum Warmhalten); (*on modern cooker*) Kochfeld *nt*

hobble ['hɒbl] **VI** humpeln, hinken; **to ~ in/out** herein-/hinaushumpeln **VT** a *horse* Fußfesseln anlegen (+*dat*), die Vorderbeine fesseln (+*dat*) **b** (*fig*) *person, company* einschränken, behindern; *economy* lahm legen **N** (*for horses*) Fußfessel *f*

hobbledehoy ['hɒbldɪ'hɔɪ] N (*old*) Tollpatsch *m*

hobby ['hɒbɪ] N Hobby *nt*, Steckenpferd *nt* (*dated*)

hobbyhorse ['hɒbɪhɔːs] N (*lit, fig*) Steckenpferd *nt*; (*lit*, = *rocking horse*) Schaukelpferd *nt*; **this is my personal ~** (*fig*) das ist mein Lieblingsthema

hobgoblin ['hɒbgɒblɪn] N Kobold *m*, Butzemann *m*; (= *bogey*) schwarzer Mann, Butzemann *m*

hobnail ['hɒbneɪl] N Schuhnagel *m*, Schuhzwecke *f*

hobnailed ['hɒbneɪld] ADJ genagelt; **~ boots** genagelte Schuhe *pl*, Nagelschuhe *pl*; **~ liver** Säuferleber *f* (*inf*), Alkoholleber *f*

hobnob ['hɒbnɒb] VI **of course I'm not used to ~bing with the aristocracy** ich stehe *or* bin natürlich nicht mit dem Adel auf Du und Du; **she's been seen ~bing with the chairman and his wife** sie ist viel mit dem Vorsitzenden und seiner Frau zusammen gesehen worden; **who was that you were ~bing with last night?** mit wem hast du da gestern zusammengesessen?

hobo ['həʊbəʊ] N (*US*) **a** (= *tramp*) Penner *m* (*inf*) **b** (= *worker*) Wanderarbeiter *m*

Hobson's choice ['hɒbsəns'tʃɔɪs] N **it's ~** da habe ich (wohl) keine andere Wahl

hock¹ [hɒk] N (*Anat, of animal*) Sprunggelenk *nt*

hock² N (= *wine*) weißer Rheinwein

hock³ (*inf*) **VT** (= *pawn*) versetzen, verpfänden **N** = verpfändet, versetzt, im Leihhaus; **to be in ~ to sb** in jds Schuld stehen

hockey ['hɒkɪ] N Hockey *nt*; (*US*) Eishockey *nt*

hockey: hockey pitch N Hockeyfeld *nt*; **hockey player** N Hockeyspieler(in) *m(f)*; (*US*) Eishockeyspieler(in) *m(f)*; **hockey stick** N Hockeyschläger *m*

hocus-pocus ['həʊkəs'pəʊkəs] N **a** (*inf*, = *trickery*) faule Tricks *pl* (*inf*), Hokuspokus *m* **b** (= *formula*) Hokuspokus *m*

hod [hɒd] N (*for bricks, mortar etc*) Tragmulde *f* **b** (= *also coal hod*) Kohlenschütte(r *m*) *f*

hodgepodge ['hɒdʒpɒdʒ] N (*US*) = **hotchpotch**

hoe [həʊ] **N** Hacke *f* **VTI** hacken

hoedown ['həʊdaʊn] N (*US*) Schwof *m* (*inf*)

hog [hɒg] **N** **a** (Mast)schwein *nt*; (*US*, = *pig*) Schwein *nt* **b** (*pej inf*, = *person*) Schwein *nt* (*inf*); (*greedy*) Vielfraß *m* (*inf*); (*selfish*) Sau *f* (*inf*); (*dirty*) Sau *f* (*inf*), Ferkel *nt* (*inf*) → **road hog, whole hog** **VT** (*inf*) sich (*dat*) aneignen, in Beschlag nehmen; **he always ~s the bathroom** er nimmt immer das Badezimmer in Beschlag; **she ~ged his attention all evening** sie belegte ihn den ganzen Abend lang mit Beschlag; **a lot of drivers ~ the middle of the road** viele Fahrer meinen, sie hätten die Straßenmitte gepachtet (*inf*); **to ~ the limelight** alle Aufmerksamkeit für sich beanspruchen

Hogmanay [ˌhɒgməˈneɪ] N (*Scot*) Silvester *nt*

> **HOGMANAY**
>
> **Hogmanay** ist der schottische Name für den Silvesterabend, der dort ein wichtiger Feiertag ist. Der Silvesterabend wird mit Parties gefeiert. Um Mitternacht stoßen die Menschen dann auf das neue Jahr an und singen das traditionsreiche Lied „Auld Lang Syne", was so viel wie „Längst vergangene Zeiten" heißt und auf sentimentale Weise an die Vergangenheit erinnern soll. Dann wird zum **first footing** aufgebrochen: man besucht Freunde, um zusammen mit ihnen das neue Jahr mit einem Drink willkommen zu heißen. Nach alter Tradition bringt es besonders viel Glück, wenn der erste, der nach Mitternacht die Schwelle überschreitet, ein dunkelhaariger Mann ist, der etwas zu essen, zu trinken oder zum Verbrennen (normalerweise einen Brocken Kohle) mitbringt, was als Zeichen für Wohlstand im neuen Jahr gilt.

hogshead ['hɒgzhed] N großes Fass; (= *measure*) Oxhoft *nt* (*obs*), *Flüssigkeitsmaß zwischen 200-250 l*

hog: hogtie VT (*US*) an allen vieren fesseln; (*fig inf*) handlungsunfähig machen; **we're ~d** uns (*dat*) sind Hände und Füße gebunden; **hogwash** N **a** (= *swill*) Schweinefutter *nt* **b** (*inf*, = *nonsense*) Quatsch *m*, Quark *m* (*inf*), blödes Zeug (*inf*); **hog wild** ADJ (*US inf*) **to go ~** total ausflippen (*inf*)

ho hum ['həʊ'hʌm] INTERJ (*hum*) na und?

hoick [hɔɪk] VT (*Brit, inf*) **a** (= *lift*) **to ~ one's trousers up** sich (*dat*) schnell die Hose hochziehen; **to ~ sb out of bed** jdn aus dem Bett reißen **b** (*Sport*, = *hit*) *shot, ball* schießen

hoi polloi [ˌhɔɪpəˈlɔɪ] N (*pej*) Volk *nt*, Pöbel *m*, Plebs *m*

hoist [hɔɪst] **VT** hochheben, hieven (*inf*); (= *pull up*) hochziehen, hieven (*inf*); *flag* hissen; *sails* aufziehen, hissen; **to be ~ with** *or* **by** *or* **on one's own petard** (*prov*) in die eigene Falle gehen **N** Hebezeug *nt*, Hebevorrichtung *f*; (*in ships*) Hebewerk *nt*; (= *lift*) (Lasten)aufzug *m*;

(= *block and tackle*) Flaschenzug *m*; (= *winch*) Winde *f*; (= *crane*) Kran *m*

hoity-toity ['hɔɪtɪ'tɔɪtɪ] (*inf*) **ADJ** hochnäsig, eingebildet; **she's gone all ~** sie markiert die feine Dame (*inf*); **oh ~, are we?** wohl zu fein für unsereins? **INTERJ** sieh mal einer an (*inf*)

hokey ['həʊkɪ] ADJ (*US, inf*) **a** (= *phoney*) künstlich; *excuse* faul (*inf*); **it's ~** das ist Quatsch **b** (= *corny*) *excuse* abgedroschen; *story, song* kitschig

hokum ['həʊkəm] N (*US, inf*) **a** (= *nonsense*) Quatsch *m* (*inf*), Mumpitz *m* **b** (= *cheap sentiment*) Gefühlsduselei *f* (*inf*)

> **hold** [həʊld]
> *vb: pret, ptp* **held**
> ✪ 5.3, 27.3
>
> | 1 NOUN | 3 INTRANSITIVE VERB |
> | 2 TRANSITIVE VERB | 4 PHRASAL VERBS |

1 – NOUN

a = grip, clutch Griff *m*; (*Mountaineering*) Halt *m no pl*; (*Wrestling*) Griff *m*; **I tried to break free from his hold** ich versuchte, mich aus seinem Griff zu befreien; **the rock face offers few holds to climbers** die Felswand bietet dem Bergsteiger wenig Halt; **to release/ loosen one's hold on sb/sth** jdn/etw loslassen; **to have a firm hold on sb** (*lit*) jdn festhalten

♦ **to have/get/keep** *etc* **(a) hold of** to have/ catch hold of sth (*lit*) etw festhalten/fassen *or* packen; **to keep hold of sth** etw nicht loslassen; (= *keep*) etw behalten; **to seize** *or* **grab hold of sb/sth** jdn/etw fassen *or* packen; **grab hold of my hand** fass mich bei der Hand; **to get** *or* **take (a) hold of sth** sich an etw (*dat*) festhalten; **to get** *or* **lay hold of sth** (*fig*, = *obtain*) etw finden *or* auftreiben (*inf*); *guns, drugs* etw in die Finger bekommen; *information, story, facts* etw in Erfahrung bringen; **where did you get hold of that idea?** wie kommst du denn auf die Idee?; **to get hold of sb** (*fig*) jdn finden *or* auftreiben (*inf*); (*on phone etc*) jdn erreichen; **to get (a) hold of oneself** (*fig*) sich in den Griff bekommen; **get (a) hold of yourself!** reiß dich zusammen!

♦ **to lose one's hold** den Halt verlieren; **he lost his hold and fell** er verlor den Halt und stürzte ab; **to lose one's hold on life** mit dem Leben nicht mehr fertig werden; **he's lost his hold on reality** er hat den Sinn für die Realität verloren

♦ **to take hold** (*person: of rope, support*) sich festhalten; (*fig, custom, practice, fashion, idea*) sich durchsetzen; (*fire, epidemic*) sich ausbreiten; (*disease*) sich verschlimmern; (*recession*) sich breit machen; (*truce, ceasefire*) andauern

♦ **on hold to be on hold** warten; (*fig*) auf Eis liegen; **to put sb on hold** (*Telec*) jdn auf Wartestellung schalten; (*in larger organizations*) jdn auf die Warteschlange legen; **to put sth on hold** (*fig, decision, plan, career*) etw auf Eis legen; **can we put this discussion on hold?** können wir diese Diskussion unterbrechen?

♦ **no holds barred** (*lit*) alle Griffe (sind) erlaubt; **when those two have a row, there are no holds barred** (*fig*) wenn die beiden sich streiten, dann kennen sie nichts mehr (*inf*) *or* kein Pardon (*inf*)

b = influence Einfluss *m* (*over* auf +*acc*)

♦ **hold on** *or* **over sb/sth to have a hold over** *or* **on sb** (*großen*) Einfluss auf jdn ausüben; *audience, followers* jdn in seiner Gewalt haben; **to have a firm hold on sb** (*fig*) jdn fest im Griff haben; **he hasn't got any hold on** *or* **over me** er kann mir nichts anhaben; **she still has a hold on him** sie hat ihn immer noch in der Hand; **the president has consolidated his hold on power** der Präsident hat seine Macht gefestigt

c of hairspray, mousse Halt *m*; **firm/extra hold** fester/zusätzlicher Halt

d Naut, Aviat Laderaum *m*, Frachtraum *m*

2 – TRANSITIVE VERB

a = grasp, grip halten; **to hold one's sides with laughter** sich (*dat*) den Bauch vor Lachen halten; **to hold sb/sth tight** jdn/etw (ganz) festhalten; **the frightened children held each other tight** die verängstigten Kinder klammerten sich aneinander; **this car holds the road well** dieses Auto hat eine gute Straßenlage; **to hold sth in place** etw (fest)halten

♦ **to hold hands** sich an der Hand halten, sich anfassen; (*lovers, children etc*) Händchen halten; **to walk along holding hands** angefasst gehen

b = carry, maintain halten; **to hold oneself upright** sich gerade *or* aufrecht halten; **to hold oneself/sth ready** *or* **in readiness** sich/etw bereithalten

c = contain enthalten; (= have capacity etc of: *bottle, tank etc*) fassen; (= have room for: *bus, plane, hall etc*) Platz haben für; **this room holds twenty people** in diesem Raum haben zwanzig Personen Platz; **this CD rack holds 20 CDs** in diesem CD-Ständer haben 20 CDs Platz; **this holds the radar equipment** dies enthält die Radarausrüstung; **my brain can't hold so much information at one time** so viel kann ich nicht auf einmal behalten; **what does the future hold (for us)?** was bringt *or* birgt (*geh*) (uns) die Zukunft?; **death holds no fears for them** der Tod hat *or* birgt (*geh*) nichts Beängstigendes für sie

d = believe meinen; (= maintain) behaupten; **it was universally held that Andy was an excellent teacher** alle meinten, dass Andy ein hervorragender Lehrer sei; **I have always held that ...** ich habe schon immer behauptet, dass ...; **to hold sth to be true/false/immoral** *etc* etw für wahr/falsch/unmoralisch *etc* halten; **to hold the belief that ...** glauben, dass ...; **to hold the view** *or* **opinion that ...** die Meinung vertreten, dass ...; **the court held that ...** das Gericht entschied, dass...

e = consider **to hold sb responsible (for sth)** jdn (für etw) verantwortlich machen; **she held the memory of her late husband dear** sie hielt das Andenken an ihren verstorbenen Mann hoch; **she held her youngest grandchild dear** ihr jüngstes Enkelkind bedeutete ihr sehr viel *or* war ihr teuer (*liter*)

f = restrain, retain, keep back *train* aufhalten; *one's breath* anhalten; *suspect, hostages etc* festhalten; *parcel, confiscated goods etc* zurückhalten; **to hold sb (prisoner)** jdn gefangen halten; **to hold sb hostage** jdn als Geisel festhalten; **there's no holding him** er ist nicht zu bremsen (*inf*); **hold everything!** (*inf*) stop!; **hold the line!** bleiben Sie am Apparat!; **hold hard, hold your horses!** (*inf*) immer mit der Ruhe, immer sachte mit den jungen Pferden! (*inf*)

♦ **to hold one's fire** (= not shoot) nicht schießen; (*fig* = delay action) sich zurückhalten

♦ **to hold one's breath** (*lit*) den Atem anhalten; **don't hold your breath!** (*iro*) erwarte nicht zu viel!

♦ **hold it!** (*inf*) Momentchen (*inf*), Moment mal (*inf*); **hold it there!** (when taking photograph) so ist gut; **hold it right there, buster** (*inf*) keine Bewegung, Freundchen (*inf*)

g = possess, occupy *post, position* innehaben, bekleiden (*form*); *passport, permit, degree* haben; *power* haben, besitzen; (*Fin*) *shares* besitzen; (= have) *records* führen; *file* haben; (= store: *on computer, disk*) speichern; (*Sport*) *record* halten; (*Mil*) *position* halten; (*against attack*) behaupten, halten; (*Eccl*) *living* innehaben; **the family holds most of the shares** die meisten Aktien sind *or* befinden sich in den Händen *or* im Besitz der Familie; **when Spain held vast territories in South America** als Spanien riesige Besitzungen in Südamerika hatte; **she holds the key to the mystery** sie hat den Schlüssel zu dem Geheimnis; **to hold office** im Amt sein

h = keep, not let go **to hold its value** seinen Wert behalten (können); **to hold one's own** sich behaupten (können); **to hold course for** (*Naut*) Kurs halten auf (+*acc*); **to hold one's course** die Richtung beibehalten; **to hold one's serve** (*Ten-*

nis) den Aufschlag behalten; **to hold sb's attention** jds Aufmerksamkeit fesseln; **to hold sb's interest** jds Interesse wach halten; **to hold a note** (*Mus*) einen Ton halten

♦ **to hold sb to sth** I'll hold you to your promise *or* to that! ich werde Sie beim Wort nehmen

i = organize, have *meeting, session, debate, election* abhalten; *talks* führen; *party* geben; (*Eccl*) *service* (ab)halten; **services are held every Sunday at 11 am** Gottesdienst findet jeden Sonntag um 11 Uhr statt; **to hold a check on sb/sth** jdn/etw kontrollieren; **to hold a conversation** eine Unterhaltung führen *or* haben, sich unterhalten

j = cope with **he can't hold his liquor** er verträgt nichts; **she can hold her drink** (*esp Brit*) sie verträgt was

3 – INTRANSITIVE VERB

a rope, nail, roof etc halten; **to hold firm** *or* **fast** halten

b person **to hold still** still halten; **to hold tight** festhalten; **he held tight to his assertion** er hielt an seiner Behauptung fest

c Telec **please hold!** bitte bleiben Sie am Apparat!; **I've been holding for five minutes** ich warte schon fünf Minuten

d = continue **will the weather hold?** wird sich das Wetter wohl halten?; **if his luck holds** wenn ihm das Glück treu bleibt

e = be valid, apply gelten; *theory* stimmen; **to hold good** (*rule, promise etc*) gelten; **it holds for all these cases** es gilt in allen diesen Fällen *or* für alle diese Fälle

4 – PHRASAL VERBS

▶ **hold against** ⓥⓣ always separate **to hold sth against sb** jdm etw übel nehmen *or* verübeln; *criminal record, past failings* jdm etw anlasten *or* zur Last legen

▶ **hold back** ⓥⓘ (= stay back, hesitate, not perform fully) sich zurückhalten; (= fail to act) zögern; **I think he's holding back, he knows more** ich glaube, er weiß mehr und rückt nur nicht mit der Sprache heraus; **I held back from telling him just what I thought of him** ich unterließ es, ihm meine Meinung zu sagen ⓥⓣ sep **a** *crowd* zurückhalten; *river, floods* (auf)stauen; *tears* zurückhalten, unterdrücken; *emotions* verbergen, unterdrücken; **to hold sb back from doing sth** jdn daran hindern, etw zu tun **b** (= prevent from making progress) daran hindern, voranzukommen; **he would let nothing hold him back from getting his way** nichts kann ihn daran hindern, seinen Willen durchzusetzen; **nothing could hold him back now** jetzt ist er nicht mehr aufzuhalten **c** (= withhold) verheimlichen, verbergen; *information, report* geheim halten; *pay increase* verzögern; **he was holding something back from me** er verheimlichte *or* verbarg mir etwas

▶ **hold down** ⓥⓣ sep **a** (= keep on the ground) niederhalten, unten halten; (= keep in its place) (fest)halten; (= oppress) *country, people* unterdrücken; (= keep in check) unter Kontrolle haben; (= keep low) *prices, costs, numbers, pressure* niedrig halten; **to hold one's head down** den Kopf senken **b** *job* haben; **he can't hold any job down for long** er kann sich in keiner Stellung lange halten

▶ **hold forth** ⓥⓘ sich ergehen (*geh*), sich auslassen (on über +*acc*) ⓥⓣ sep (form, = offer) bieten

▶ **hold in** ⓥⓣ sep *stomach* einziehen; *emotions* zurückhalten; *horse* zurückhalten, zügeln; **to hold in one's anger** seinen Ärger unterdrücken; **to hold oneself in** (emotionally) sich beherrschen, an sich halten

▶ **hold off** ⓥⓘ **a** (= keep away) sich fern halten (from von); (= not act) warten; (enemy) nicht angreifen; **they held off where they should have intervened** sie hätten eingreifen sollen, haben sich aber zurückgehalten; **they held off eating until she arrived** sie warteten mit dem Essen, bis sie kam

b (rain, storm) ausbleiben; **I hope the rain holds off** ich hoffe, dass es nicht regnet ⓥⓣ sep (= keep back, resist) *enemy, attack, challenge* abwehren; *inflation* eindämmen; **how much longer can she go on holding him off?** wie lange kann sie ihn wohl noch hinhalten?

▶ **hold on** ⓥⓘ (*lit*: = maintain grip) sich festhalten; (= endure, resist) durchhalten, aushalten; (= wait) warten; **hold on (a minute)!** Moment!; (*Telec*) einen Moment bitte!; **now hold on a minute!** Moment mal! ⓥⓣ sep (fest)halten; **to be held on by sth** mit etw befestigt sein; **this Sellotape won't hold it on** mit dem Tesafilm hält das nicht

▶ **hold on to** ⓥⓣ +prep obj **a** (*lit*) festhalten; **here, hold on to this!** halt das mal (fest)!; **he was holding on to the ledge** er hielt *or* klammerte sich am Felsvorsprung fest; **they held on to each other** sie hielten sich aneinander fest, sie klammerten sich aneinander

b (*fig*) hope nicht aufgeben; *idea, belief* festhalten an (+*dat*)

c (= keep) behalten; *position* beibehalten; *staff* halten; **to hold on to the lead** in Führung bleiben; **to hold on to power** sich an der Macht halten

▶ **hold out** ⓥⓘ **a** (supplies etc) reichen

b (= endure, resist) aushalten, durchhalten; (= refuse to yield) nicht nachgeben; **to hold out against sb/sth** sich gegen jdn/etw behaupten; **to hold out for sth** auf etw (+*dat*) bestehen ⓥⓣ sep **a** (*lit*) vorstrecken, ausstrecken; **to hold out sth to sb** jdm etw hinhalten; **to hold out one's hand** halt die Hand auf; **hold your hand out** halt die Hand auf; **she held out her arms** sie breitete die Arme aus

b (*fig*) prospects bieten; *offer* machen; **I held out little hope of seeing him again** ich machte mir nur wenig Hoffnung, ihn wiederzusehen

▶ **hold out on** ⓥⓘ +prep obj (*inf*) **you've been holding out on me** du verheimlichst mir doch was (*inf*)

▶ **hold over** ⓥⓣ sep **a** *question, matter* vertagen; *meeting also, decision* verschieben (until auf +*acc*) **b** **to hold sth over sb** (= threaten) jdn etw nicht vergessen lassen; **he held it over me as a threat** er bedrohte mich damit

▶ **hold to** ⓥⓣ +prep obj festhalten an (+*dat*), bleiben bei; **I hold to my belief that ...** ich bleibe dabei, dass ...; **you should hold to the assurance** you should hold to the assurance Sie sollten Ihr Wort ihnen gegenüber einhalten

▶ **hold together** ⓥⓣ sep zusammenhalten ⓥⓘ zusammenhalten

▶ **hold under** ⓥⓣ sep *country, race* unterdrücken, knechten

▶ **hold up** ⓥⓘ **a** (tent, wall etc) stehen bleiben; (light fitting, tile etc) halten

b (belief) standhalten; (theory) sich halten lassen; **their support held up well in the election** ihre Anhänger blieben ihnen bei der Wahl treu ⓥⓣ sep **a** (= raise) hochheben, hochhalten; *face* nach oben wenden; **hold up your hand** heb die Hand; **to hold sth up to the light** etw gegen das Licht halten

b (= support, from above) halten; (from the side) stützen; (from beneath) tragen

c **to hold sb/sth up to ridicule/scorn** jdn/etw lächerlich/verächtlich machen; **to hold sb up as an example** jdn als Beispiel hinstellen; **I don't want to hold him up as the perfect statesman/goalkeeper** *etc* **but ...** ich möchte ihn nicht als den perfekten Politiker/Torwart etc hinstellen, aber ...

d (= stop) anhalten; (= delay) people aufhalten; *traffic, production* ins Stocken bringen; *talks, delivery* verzögern; **my application was held up by the postal strike** durch den Poststreik hat sich meine Bewerbung verspätet

e (robbers) bank, person, vehicle überfallen

▶ **hold with** ⓥⓣ +prep obj (*inf*) **I don't hold with that** ich bin gegen so was (*inf*)

holdall [ˈhəʊldɔːl] N Reisetasche f

holdback ['həʊldbæk] N **a** (= *obstacle*) Hindernis *nt* **b** (= *thing held back*) Einbehaltung *f* (*form*); **~ pay** einbehaltener Lohn

holder ['həʊldə'] N **a** (= *person*) Besitzer(in) *m(f)*, Inhaber(in) *m(f)*; (*of title, office, record, passport*) Inhaber(in) *m(f)*; (*of farm*) Pächter(in) *m(f)* **b** (= *object*) Halter *m*; (= *cigarette-holder*) Spitze *f*; (= *flowerpot-holder*) Übertopf *m*

holding ['həʊldɪŋ] N **a** (*Fin, of shares*) Anteil *m* (*in an +dat*); **the maximum ~** der maximal zulässige Anteil **b** (*of books, paintings*) Sammlung *f* (*of von*) **c** (*of land*) Landgut *nt*; **a ~ of 10 hectares** ein Landgut von 10 Hektar

holding: holding company N Holding(gesellschaft) *f*; **holding operation** N provisorische Maßnahme; (= *damage limitation*) Schadensbegrenzungsaktion *f*; **holding pattern** N (*Aviat*) Warteschleife *f*; (*fig*) Warteposition *f*

hold: holdout N (*US*) Verweigerer *m*; **Britain was the only ~ on this agreement** Großbritannien war das einzige Land, das sich dieser Vereinbarung widersetzte; **hold-up** N **a** (= *delay*) Verzögerung *f*; (*of traffic*) Stockung *f*; **what's the ~?** warum dauert das so lange?; **the strike caused a two-week ~ in production** der Streik brachte die Produktion zwei Wochen lang ins Stocken **b** (= *armed robbery*) bewaffneter Raubüberfall; **(hands up,) this is a ~!** Hände hoch, das ist ein Überfall!

hole [həʊl] **N a** (*in clothes, bucket, ground etc*) Loch *nt*; **to make or blow a ~ in sb's savings** ein Loch in jds Ersparnisse reißen; **to blow a ~ in sb's plans** jds Pläne über den Haufen werfen (*inf*); **to be full of ~s** (*fig, plot, story*) viele Schwächen aufweisen; (*argument, theory*) unhaltbar sein; **I need that like I need a ~ in the head** (*inf*) das ist das Letzte, was ich gebrauchen kann **b** (*inf, = awkward situation*) Klemme *f* (*inf*), Patsche *f* (*inf*); **to be in a ~** in der Patsche or Klemme sitzen (*inf*); **to get sb out of a ~** jdm aus der Patsche or Klemme helfen (*inf*) **c** (*rabbit's, fox's*) Bau *m*, Höhle *f*; (*mouse's*) Loch *nt* **d** (*pej inf*) Loch *nt* (*inf*); (= *town*) Kaff *nt* (*inf*), Nest *nt* (*inf*) **e** (*Golf*) Loch *nt*; **an 18-hole course** ein 18-Loch-Platz *m* **f** (*vulg: = vagina*) Loch *nt* (*vulg*) **VT a** (= *make a hole in*) ein Loch machen in (+*acc*); **to be ~d** ein Loch bekommen; **the ship was ~d by an iceberg** der Eisberg schlug das Schiff leck **b** ball (*Golf*) einlochen, versenken; (*Billiards*) versenken; **to ~ a putt** einen Putt einlochen **VI a** (*socks etc*) Löcher bekommen **b** (*Golf*) einlochen

▶**hole out** VI (*Golf*) ein Loch spielen; **to hole out in one** ein Hole-in-One spielen

▶**hole up** VI (*animal*) sich verkriechen; (*inf: gang etc, = hide*) sich verkriechen (*inf*) or verstecken; (= *barricade themselves in*) sich verschanzen

hole: hole-and-corner ADJ obskur, zwielichtig; **hole in one** N (*Golf*) Hole-in-One *nt*; **hole in the heart** N (*Med*) Loch *nt* in der Herzscheidewand; **hole-in-the-heart** ADJ attr **~ baby** Baby *nt* mit (angeborenem) Herzfehler; **hole-in-the-wall** N (in die Wand eingebauter) Geldautomat *m* ATTR machine in die Wand eingebaut

holey ['həʊlɪ] ADJ (*inf*) löchrig

holiday ['hɒlədɪ] **N a** (= *day off*) freier Tag; (= *public holiday*) Feiertag *m*; **to take a ~** einen Tag frei nehmen **b** (*esp Brit, = period*) often *pl* Ferien *pl*, Urlaub *m*; (*Sch*) Ferien *pl*; **the school/Christmas ~s** die Schul-/Weihnachtsferien *pl*; **on ~** in den Ferien, auf or im Urlaub; **to go on ~** Ferien/Urlaub machen; **where are you going for your ~(s)?** wo fahren Sie in den Ferien/im Urlaub hin?, wo machen Sie Ferien/Urlaub?; **to take a ~** Urlaub nehmen or machen; **to take one's ~s** seinen Urlaub nehmen; **I need a ~** ich bin ferienreif; **to take a month's ~** einen Monat Urlaub

nehmen; **~ with pay, paid ~s** bezahlter Urlaub; **it was no ~, I can tell you** ich kann dir sagen, das war alles andere als eine Erholung **VI** (*esp Brit*) Ferien or Urlaub machen

holiday in cpds (*esp Brit*) Ferien-, Urlaubs-; **holiday camp** N Feriendorf *nt*; **holiday clothes** PL Urlaubskleidung *f*; **holiday destination** N Urlaubs- or Ferienziel *nt*; **holiday entitlement** N Urlaubsanspruch *m*; **holiday feeling** N Urlaubsstimmung *f*; **holiday guest** N (*esp Brit*) Feriengast *m*; **holiday home** N Ferienhaus *nt*/-wohnung *f*; **holiday job** N Ferienjob *m*; **holiday-maker** N Urlauber(in) *m(f)*; **holiday mood** N Urlaubsstimmung *f*; **holiday resort** N Ferienort *m*; **holiday season** N Urlaubszeit *f*; **holiday traffic** N Reiseverkehr *m*

holier-than-thou ['həʊlɪəðən'ðaʊ] ADJ attitude, person selbstgerecht, selbstgefällig

holiness ['həʊlɪnɪs] N Heiligkeit *f*; **His/Your Holiness** (*Eccl*) Seine/Eure Heiligkeit

holism ['həʊlɪzəm] N Holismus *m*

holistic [həʊ'lɪstɪk] ADJ holistisch

Holland ['hɒlənd] N Holland *nt*

Hollander ['hɒləndə'] N (*Typ*) Holländer *m*

holler ['hɒlə'] (*inf*) **N** Schrei *m* **VTI** (*also* **holler out**) brüllen

hollow ['hɒləʊ] **ADJ a** hohl; (= *concave*) surface, cheeks hohl, eingefallen; eyes tief liegend; (= *empty*) feeling hohl, leer; **I feel ~ (inside)** (= *hungry*) ich habe ein Loch im Bauch (*inf*); (*after a bad shock*) ich fühle mich innerlich leer **b** (= *meaningless*) gesture, threat, sham, words, promise leer; victory geschenkt; (= *insincere*) person unaufrichtig; laugh hohl; (= *forced*) gequält; **to sound ~, to have a ~ ring (to it)** (*fig*) hohl klingen; **this claim rings ~** diese Behauptung klingt hohl or falsch **c** sound hohl, dumpf; voice hohl; **with a (deep,) ~ voice** mit Grabesstimme **N a** (= *cavity*) Höhlung *f*; (*in larger structure*) Hohlraum *m*; **the ~ in the tree's trunk** die Höhlung im Baum **b** (= *depression*) Vertiefung *f*; (= *small valley*) (Boden)senke *f*; **a wooded ~** eine bewaldete Niederung; **in the ~ between two waves** im Wellental; **to hold sth in the ~ of one's hand** etw in der hohlen Hand halten; **the ~ of the back** das Kreuz **ADV** (*Brit*) **to beat sb ~** (*inf*) jdn haushoch schlagen, jdn fertig machen (*inf*)

▶**hollow out** VT sep aushöhlen

hollow-eyed ['hɒləʊaɪd] ADJ hohläugig

hollowly ['hɒləʊlɪ] ADV hohl; laugh also gequält; say also mit hohler Stimme; sound, echo hohl, dumpf

hollowness ['hɒləʊnɪs] N (*fig*) (of promise) Leere *f*; (of guarantee) Wertlosigkeit *f*

holly ['hɒlɪ] N **a** (= *tree*) Stechpalme *f*, Ilex *m*; **~ berry** Stechpalmenfrucht *f* **b** (= *foliage*) Stechpalme(nzweige *pl*) *f*

hollyhock ['hɒlɪhɒk] N Malve *f*

Hollywood ['hɒlɪwʊd] N Hollywood *nt*

holmium ['hɒlmɪəm] N (*Chem*) Holmium *nt*

holm oak ['həʊm'əʊk] N Steineiche *f*

holocaust ['hɒləkɔːst] N **a** Inferno *nt*; **nuclear ~** Atominferno *nt* **b** (= *mass extermination*) Massenvernichtung *f*; (*in Third Reich*) Holocaust *m*

hologram ['hɒləgræm] N Hologramm *nt*

holograph ['hɒləgrɑːf] **N** handschriftliches Dokument **ADJ** eigenhändig geschrieben, holografisch (*form*)

holography [hɒ'lɒgrəfɪ] N Holografie *f*

hols [hɒlz] (*Brit inf*) abbr of **holidays**

holster ['həʊlstə'] N (Pistolen)halfter *nt or f*

holy ['həʊlɪ] **ADJ a** (*Rel*) holy; oil, bread, ground geweiht **b** **~ cow** or **mackerel!** (*inf*) (ach du) heiliger Strohsack or Bimbam! (*inf*); **~ smoke!** (*inf*) großer Gott! (*inf*); **~ shit!** (*sl*) du liebe Scheiße! (*inf*); **~ terror** Nervensäge *f* (*inf*),

Landplage *f* (*hum*) **N the Holy of Holies** (*lit*) das Allerheiligste; (*fig*) ein Heiligtum *nt*

holy: Holy Ark N (*Eccl*) Thoraschrein *m*; **Holy Bible** N the ~ die Bibel, die Heilige Schrift; **Holy City** N the ~ die heilige Stadt; **Holy Communion** N die heilige Kommunion, das heilige Abendmahl; **Holy Father** N the ~ (= *the Pope*) der Heilige Vater; **Holy Ghost** N = Holy Spirit; **Holy Grail** N the ~ der heilige Gral; **Holy Land** N the ~ das Heilige Land; **holy orders** PL Priesterweihe *f*; **to be in ~** dem geistlichen Stand angehören; **to take ~** die Priesterweihe empfangen; **Holy Roman Empire** N the ~ (*Hist*) das Heilige Römische Reich; **Holy Rood** N (heiliges) Kruzifix *nt*; **Holy Saturday** N Karsamstag *m*; **Holy Scripture** N die Heilige Schrift; **Holy See** N the ~ der Heilige Stuhl; **Holy Sepulchre** N the ~ das Heilige Grab; **Holy Spirit** N the ~ der Heilige Geist; **Holy Thursday** N **a** (*in Roman Catholic Church*) Gründonnerstag *m* **b** (*in Anglican Church*) Himmelfahrtstag *m*; **Holy Trinity** N the ~ die Heilige Dreifaltigkeit or Dreieinigkeit; **holy war** N heiliger Krieg; **holy water** N heiliges Wasser; (*in Catholic Church*) Weihwasser *nt*; **Holy Week** N Karwoche *f*; **Holy Writ** N (*dated*) the ~ die Heilige Schrift

homage ['hɒmɪdʒ] N Huldigung *f*; (*for elders*) Ehrerbietung *f*; **to pay or do ~ to sb** jdm huldigen; jdm seine Ehrerbietung erweisen; **in order to pay ~ to the dead king** um dem König die letzte Ehre zu erweisen; **a speech in ~ to the president/the victims of the disaster** eine Rede als Hommage für den Präsidenten/als Ehrerbietung für die Opfer der Katastrophe; **they stood there in silent ~** sie standen in stummer Ehrerbietung da

homburg ['hɒmbɜːg] N Homburg *m*

home [həʊm] **N a** (= *where one lives*) Zuhause *nt*, Heim *nt*; (= *house*) Haus *nt*; (= *country, area etc*) Heimat *f*; **a loving/good ~** ein liebevolles/gutes Zuhause; **gifts for the ~** Geschenke *pl* für das Haus or die Wohnung; **a useful gadget to have in your ~** ein sehr praktisches Gerät für den Haushalt; **his ~ is in Brussels** er ist in Brüssel zu Hause; **Bournemouth is his second ~** Bournemouth ist seine zweite Heimat (geworden); **haven't you got a ~ to go to?** hast du kein Zuhause?; **he invited us round to his ~** er hat uns zu sich (nach Hause) eingeladen; **away from ~** von zu Hause weg; **a long way from ~** weit von zu Hause weg or entfernt; (*in different country also*) weit von der Heimat entfernt; **to live away from ~** nicht zu Hause wohnen; **he worked away from ~** er hat auswärts gearbeitet; **let's concentrate on problems closer to ~** wir sollten uns auf unsere eigenen Probleme konzentrieren; **to have a ~ of one's own** ein eigenes Heim or Zuhause haben; **to find a ~ for sb/an animal** ein Zuhause für jdn/ein Tier finden; **does this hammer have a ~?** (*hum*) gehört dieser Hammer an einen bestimmten Platz?; **I'll give that picture a ~** bei mir wird das Bild einen guten Platz finden or haben; **it's a ~ from ~** es ist wie zu Hause; **at ~** zu Hause; (*Comm*) im Inland; (*Sport*) auf eigenem Platz; **the next match will be at ~** das nächste Spiel ist ein Heimspiel; **Miss Hooper is not at ~ today** Frau Hooper ist heute nicht zu Hause or nicht da; **Miss Hooper is not at ~ to anyone today** Frau Hooper ist heute für niemanden zu Hause or zu sprechen; **who's he when he's at ~?** (*inf*) wer in aller Welt ist er?; **to be or feel at ~ with sb** sich in jds Gegenwart (*dat*) wohl fühlen; **he doesn't feel at ~ with English** er fühlt sich im Englischen nicht sicher or zu Hause; **I don't feel at ~ with this new theory yet** ich komme mit dieser neuen Theorie noch nicht ganz zurecht; **to make oneself at ~** es sich (*dat*) gemütlich or bequem machen; **to make sb feel at ~** es jdm gemütlich machen; **to leave ~** von zu Hause weggehen; **Scotland is the ~ of the haggis** Schottland ist die Heimat des Haggis, das Haggis ist in Schottland zu Hause; **the city/this building is ~ to some 1,500 students** in dieser Stadt/diesem Gebäude wohnen etwa 1.500

Studenten or sind etwa 1.500 Studenten zu Hause; **there's no place like ~** (Prov) daheim ist daheim (prov), eigener Herd ist Goldes wert (Prov); **~ sweet ~** (Prov) trautes Heim, Glück allein (Prov)
b (= institution) Heim nt; (for orphans) Waisenhaus nt, Heim nt; (for blind) Heim nt, Anstalt f → **nursing home**
c (Zool, Bot) Heimat f
d (Sport) (= base) Mal nt; (Racing) Ziel nt
ADV **a** (position) zu Hause, zuhause (Aus, Sw), daheim; (with verb of motion) nach Hause, nachhause (Aus, Sw), heim; **to go ~** (to house) nach Hause or (Aus, Sw) nachhause gehen/fahren; (to country) heimfahren; **on the way ~** auf dem Heim- or Nachhauseweg; **the first runner ~** der Erste, der durchs Ziel geht; **the first runner ~ was Fred** Fred ging als Erster durchs Ziel; **to get ~** nach Hause or (Aus, Sw) nachhause kommen, heimkommen; (in race) durchs Ziel gehen; **I have to get ~ before ten** ich muss vor zehn zu Hause or (Aus, Sw) zuhause or daheim sein; **to return ~ from abroad** aus dem Ausland zurückkommen
b (= to the mark) **to drive a nail ~** einen Nagel einschlagen; **he nudged the ball ~** (Ftbl) er schob den Ball ins Tor; **to bring** or **get sth ~ to sb** jdm etw klarmachen or beibringen; **it came ~ to him that ...** es wurde ihm klar, dass ...; **to strike ~** (torpedo etc) treffen; (fig: remark) ins Schwarze treffen, sitzen (inf) → **drive home, hammer home, hit, press, push**
VI (pigeons) heimkehren

▶ **home in** VI (missiles) sich ausrichten (on sth auf etw acc); **the missile will home in** das Geschoss findet sein Ziel; **to home in on a target** ein Ziel finden or selbstständig ansteuern; **he immediately homed in on the essential point** er hat sofort den wichtigsten Punkt herausgegriffen

home: home address N Heimatadresse or -anschrift f; (as opposed to business address) Privatanschrift f; **home-baked** ADJ selbst gebacken; **home banking** N Homebanking nt; **home base** N (Baseball) Homebase nt, Schlagmal nt; **home birth** N Hausgeburt f; **homebody** N (inf) Heimchen nt; **homeboy** N (dated US inf) Einheimische(r) m; (US sl: = close friend) Kumpel m; **homebred** ADJ (= indigenous) einheimisch; **home-brew** N selbst gebrautes Bier, Selbstgebraute(s) nt; **home-brewed** ADJ selbst gebraut; **home comforts** PL heimeliger Komfort; **homecoming** N Heimkehr f; **home computer** N Homecomputer m, Heimcomputer m; **home computing** N Computern nt; **home contents** PL Hausrat m; **~ insurance** Hausratsversicherung f; **home cooking** N häusliche Küche, Hausmannskost f; **Home Counties** PL Grafschaften, die an London angrenzen; **home-cured** ADJ selbst gebeizt; **home economics** N sing Hauswirtschaft(slehre) f; **home entertainment system** N Home-Entertainment-System nt; **home exercise machine** N Hometrainer m; **home front** N on the **~** (Mil, Pol) im eigenen Land; (in business contexts) im eigenen Betrieb; (in personal, family contexts) zu Hause; **home game** N (Sport) Heimspiel nt; **homegirl** N (dated US inf) Einheimische f; (US sl: = close friend) Kumpel m; **home ground** N (Sport) eigener Platz; **to be on ~** (fig) sich auf vertrautem Terrain bewegen; **home-grown** ADJ vegetables selbst gezogen; (= not imported) einheimisch; (fig) talent, player heimisch; **Home Guard** N Bürgerwehr f; **home help** N Haushaltshilfe f; **home improvements** N Renovierungsarbeiten pl (am Haus oder in der Wohnung); **home improvements loan** N Modernisierungsdarlehen nt; **home key** N (Comput) Hometaste f; **homeland** N Heimat(land nt) f, Vaterland nt; **homeless** ADJ obdachlos; **PL the ~** die Obdachlosen pl; **homelessness** N Obdachlosigkeit f; **home life** N Familienleben nt; **homelike** ADJ heimelig, wie daheim; **home loan** N Hypothek f; **home-loving** ADJ häuslich

homely ['həʊmlɪ] ADJ (+er) **a** person (Brit: = home-loving) häuslich, hausbacken (pej); atmosphere, restaurant heimelig, gemütlich, behaglich; style anspruchslos, hausbacken (pej); advice einfach **b** food bürgerlich **c** (US, = plain) person unscheinbar, reizlos

home: home-made ADJ selbst gemacht; **homemaker** N (US, = housewife) Hausfrau f, Hausmutter f; (= social worker) Familienfürsorger(in) m(f); **home market** N Inlandsmarkt m, inländischer Markt; **home match** N (Sport) Heimspiel nt; **home movie** N Amateurfilm m; **home news** N Meldungen pl aus dem Inland; **Home Office** N (Brit) Innenministerium nt; (with relation to aliens) Einwanderungsbehörde f

homeopath etc (US) = **homoeopath** etc

home: homeowner N (of house) Hauseigentümer(in) m(f); (of flat) Wohnungseigentümer(in) m(f); **homeownership** N Eigenbesitz m von Häusern/Wohnungen; **home page** N (Comput) Homepage f; **home plate** N (Baseball) Ausgangsbase nt; **home port** N Heimathafen m

Homer ['həʊmə'] N Homer m

homer ['həʊmə'] N **a** (= homing pigeon) Brieftaube f **b** (Brit, inf, = job) Nebenjob m (inf); **to do sth as a ~** etw privat or nebenher machen

Homeric [həʊ'merɪk] ADJ homerisch

home: home rule N Selbstbestimmung f, Selbstverwaltung f; **home run** N (Baseball) Homerun m zu alle vier Male laufen; (US fig) das große Los ziehen; **home sales** PL Inlandsumsatz m; **Home Secretary** N (Brit) Innenminister(in) m(f); **home shopping** N Homeshopping nt; (on TV also) Teleshopping nt; **homesick** ADJ heimwehkrank; **to be ~** Heimweh haben (for nach); **homesickness** N Heimweh nt (for nach); **home side** N (Sport) Gastgeber pl, Heimmannschaft f; **homespun** ADJ **a** cloth selbst gesponnen, handgesponnen **b** (fig: = simple) einfach; (pej) hausbacken; **~ philosophy** Lebensweisheiten pl; **~ advice** altbewährter Rat **N** (= cloth) Homespun nt (grober, genoppter Wollstoff); **homestead** N **a** Heimstätte f **b** (US) Heimstätte f für Siedler; **homesteader** ['həʊmstedə'] N **a** Heimstättenbesitzer(in) m(f) **b** (US) Heimstättensiedler(in) m(f); **home straight, home stretch** N (Sport) Zielgerade f; **we're in the ~ now** (fig inf) das Ende ist in Sicht; **home team** N (Sport) Gastgeber pl, Heimmannschaft f, Platzherren pl (inf); **home town**, (US) **hometown** N Heimatstadt f; **home truth** N (Brit) bittere Wahrheit; **to tell sb a few ~s** jdm die Augen öffnen; **home video** N Amateurvideo nt

homeward ['həʊmwəd] ADJ **~ journey/flight** Heimreise f/-flug m; **to be on the ~ stretch** bald zu Hause sein; **we are ~ bound** es geht Richtung Heimat

homeward(s) ['həʊmwəd(z)] ADV nach Hause or (Aus, Sw) nachhause, heim; (= to country also) in Richtung Heimat

home: home waters PL (Naut) heimatliche Gewässer pl; **homework** N (Sch) Hausaufgaben pl, Schulaufgaben pl; **to give sb sth as ~** jdm etw aufgeben; **what ~ have you got?** was hast du auf?; **the minister had not done his ~** (inf) der Minister hatte sich mit der Materie nicht vertraut gemacht; **homeworker** N Heimarbeiter(in) m(f); **homeworking** N Heimarbeit f

homey ['həʊmɪ] ADJ (+er) (US, inf) gemütlich; atmosphere also heimelig, behaglich

homicidal [ˌhɒmɪˈsaɪdl] ADJ (= murderous) person gemeingefährlich; **that man is a ~ maniac** dieser Mann ist ein mordgieriger Verrückter; **he is potentially ~, he has ~ tendencies** er könnte zum Mörder werden; **~ fury** or **rage** Mordrausch m

homicide ['hɒmɪsaɪd] N **a** Totschlag m; **~ (squad)** Mordkommission f **b** (= person) Mörder(in) m(f); Totschläger(in) m(f)

homie ['həʊmiː] N (US, inf) Homie m

homily ['hɒmɪlɪ] N Predigt f; (fig also) Sermon m (pej)

homing ['həʊmɪŋ] ADJ missile mit Zielsucheinrichtung; **~ device** Zielfluggerät nt, Zielsucheinrichtung f

homing instinct N Heimfindevermögen nt

homing pigeon N Brieftaube f

homo ['həʊməʊ] N (pej inf) Homo m (dated inf)

homoeopath, (US) **homeopath** ['həʊmɪəʊpæθ] N Homöopath(in) m(f)

homoeopathic, (US) **homeopathic** [ˌhəʊmɪəʊ'pæθɪk] ADJ homöopathisch

homoeopathy, (US) **homeopathy** [ˌhəʊmɪ'ɒpəθɪ] N Homöopathie f

homoerotic [ˌhəʊməʊ'rɒtɪk] ADJ image, fantasy, subtext homoerotisch

homogeneity [ˌhɒmədʒə'niːɪtɪ] N Homogenität f

homogeneous [ˌhɒmə'dʒiːnɪəs] ADJ homogen

homogenize [hə'mɒdʒənaɪz] VT homogenisieren; **~d milk** homogenisierte Milch

homogenous [hə'mɒdʒɪnəs] ADJ homogen

homograph ['hɒməʊɡrɑːf] N Homograf nt

homologous [hə'mɒləɡəs] ADJ homolog

homonym ['hɒmənɪm] N Homonym nt

homonymous [hə'mɒnɪməs] ADJ homonym

homophobe ['həʊməʊfəʊb] N Homophobe(r) mf

homophobia [ˌhəʊməʊ'fəʊbɪə] N Homophobie f

homophobic [ˌhəʊməʊ'fəʊbɪk] ADJ homophob

homophone ['hɒməfəʊn] N Homophon nt

Homo sapiens [ˌhəʊməʊ'sæpɪəns] N Homo sapiens m

homosexual [ˌhɒməʊ'seksjʊəl] ADJ homosexuell **N** Homosexuelle(r) mf

homosexuality [ˌhɒməʊseksjʊ'ælɪtɪ] N Homosexualität f

homunculus [hɒ'mʌŋkjʊləs] N Homunkulus m

homy ADJ (+er) (US, inf) = **homey**

Hon a abbr of **honorary b** abbr of **Honourable**

hon [hʌn] N (US inf) abbr of **honey hi, ~!** hallo, Schatz!

Honduran [hɒn'djʊərən] ADJ honduranisch **N** Honduraner(in) m(f)

Honduras [hɒn'djʊərəs] N Honduras nt

hone [həʊn] N Schleifstein m, Wetzstein m **VT** blade schleifen; (fig) person aufbauen; (as a successor) heranziehen; skills vervollkommnen

▶ **hone down** VT sep (fig) (zurecht)feilen (to auf +acc)

honest ['ɒnɪst] ADJ **a** (= truthful) ehrlich; **to be ~ with sb** jdm die Wahrheit sagen, jdm nichts vormachen (inf); **you must be brutally ~ with yourself** du darfst dir absolut nichts vormachen (inf); **I don't think you've been quite ~ with us** ich glaube, du hast uns nicht die ganze Wahrheit gesagt; **to be ~ about sth** etw ehrlich darstellen; **to be perfectly ~ (with you), I don't really know** um (ganz) ehrlich zu sein, ich weiß es nicht genau, (ganz) offen or ehrlich gesagt, ich weiß es nicht genau; **I'd like your ~ opinion of it** ich möchte wissen, was Sie wirklich davon halten; **what do you think of the school, in your ~ opinion?** was hältst du von der Schule, ganz ehrlich gesagt?; **the ~ truth** die reine Wahrheit
b (= law-abiding, decent) person redlich; money, profit ehrlich or redlich erworben; **they are good ~ people** sie sind gute, rechtschaffene Leute; **to make an ~ living** or **penny** sein Geld ehrlich or redlich verdienen; **he made an ~ woman of her** (dated hum) er machte sie zu seiner Angetrauten (hum); **after an ~ day's work** nach einem ordentlichen Tagewerk; **he's never done an ~ day's work in his life** er ist in seinem ganzen Leben noch keiner ordentlichen Arbeit nachgegangen; **(as) ~ as the day is long** grundehrlich
c (= straightforward, real) material, cooking einfach, echt; mistake echt; **good ~ cooking** gutbürgerliche Küche

ADV (inf) **I didn't know about it, ~** ich wusste nichts davon, ehrlich or Ehrenwort!; **it's true, ~ it is** es stimmt, ganz ehrlich; **~ to God** or **to goodness** (emph) ehrlich; **~ injun** (emph inf) ganz ehrlich

honest broker N (esp Pol) Vermittler(in) m(f)

honestly ['ɒnɪstlɪ] ADV **a** (= truthfully) answer ehrlich, aufrichtig; (= legally) earn money ehrlich, auf ehrliche or redliche Weise; **to talk about** or **discuss sth openly and ~** offen und ehrlich über etw (acc) reden **b** (emph) say, believe ehrlich, wirklich; call, think, expect wirklich; **I ~ thought you'd be pleased** ich dachte wirklich, dass du dich freuen würdest; **no, ~, I'm fine** nein, wirklich or (ganz) ehrlich, mir gehts gut; **I don't mind, ~** es ist mir wirklich or ehrlich egal; **~, it's terrible** das ist wirklich furchtbar; **quite ~ I don't remember it** ehrlich gesagt or um ehrlich zu sein, ich kann mich daran nicht erinnern; **~!** (showing exasperation) also ehrlich or wirklich!

honest-to-goodness ['ɒnɪstə'gʊdnɪs] ADJ (inf, = genuine) echt; person, expression waschecht

honesty ['ɒnɪstɪ] N **a** (= truthfulness) Ehrlichkeit f; (= being law-abiding, decent) Redlichkeit f; **in all ~** ganz ehrlich; **one must admit, in all ~, ...** man muss ehrlicherweise zugeben, ...; **~ is the best policy** (Prov) ehrlich währt am längsten (Prov) **b** (Bot) Mondviole f, Silberblatt nt, Judassilberling m (inf)

honesty box N Büchse, in der man Geld hinterlässt, wenn niemand da ist, um es zu kassieren, Kasse f des Vertrauens (esp E Ger)

honey ['hʌnɪ] N **a** Honig m **b** (inf, = dear) Schätzchen nt; **she is an absolute ~** (= she's gorgeous) sie ist einfach süß (inf); **my mum's a real ~** meine Mutter ist ein (Gold)schatz (inf)

honey: honeybee N (Honig)biene f; **honeybunch** N (inf) Schätzchen nt; **honeycomb** N (Bienen)wabe f; (filled with honey also) Honigwabe f **VT** usu pass durchlöchern; **the mountain was ~ed with caves** der Berg war von Höhlen durchsetzt; **honeydew** N Honigtau m; **honeydew melon** N Honigmelone f; **honey eater** N (Orn) Honigfresser m

honeyed ['hʌnɪd] ADJ words, voice honigsüß

honey extractor N Honigschleuder f

honeymoon ['hʌnɪmuːn] N **a** Flitterwochen pl; (= trip) Hochzeitsreise f; **to be on one's ~** in den Flitterwochen/auf Hochzeitsreise sein; **where did you go for your ~?** wo habt ihr eure Flitterwochen verbracht?, wohin seid ihr auf Hochzeitsreise gemacht?; **the ~ is over** (fig inf) jetzt werden andere Saiten aufgezogen (inf), die Schonzeit ist vorbei **VI** seine Hochzeitsreise machen; **they are ~ing in Spain** sie sind in Spanien auf Hochzeitsreise

honeymoon couple N Flitterwöchner pl

honeymooner ['hʌnɪmuːnə'] N Hochzeitsreisende(r) mf, Flitterwöchner(in) m(f)

honeymoon period N (fig) Schonzeit f

honeymoon suite N Suite f für Hochzeitsreisende

honeysuckle ['hʌnɪsʌkəl] N Geißblatt nt

Hong Kong ['hɒŋ'kɒŋ] N Hongkong nt

honk [hɒŋk] N (of car) Hupen nt; (of goose etc) Schrei m **INTERJ ~ ~** tut, tut, tüt, tüt **VI a** (car) hupen, tuten **b** (geese) schreien **c** (inf, = stink) stinken **VT** horn drücken auf (+acc)

honky ['hɒŋkɪ] N (pej inf) Weiße(r) mf

honky-tonk [ˌhɒŋkɪ'tɒŋk] N (US, inf, = country-music bar) Schuppen m (inf) **ADJ** music, piano schräg; **~ bar** Schuppen m (inf)

Honolulu [ˌhɒnə'luːluː] N Honolulu nt

honor etc (US) = **honour** etc

honorarium [ˌɒnə'rɛərɪəm] N pl **honoraria** [ˌɒnə'rɛərɪə] Honorar nt

honorary ['ɒnərərɪ] ADJ Ehren-; **~ member/president/title/citizen** Ehrenmitglied nt/-präsident/-titel/-bürger m

honorary degree N ehrenhalber verliehener akademischer Grad

Honorary Secretary N ehrenamtlicher Sekretär, ehrenamtliche Sekretärin

honor guard N (US) Ehrenwache f

honour, (US) **honor** ['ɒnə'] N **a** Ehre f; **sense of ~** Ehrgefühl nt; **he made it a point of ~** er betrachtete es als Ehrensache; **he decided to make it a point of ~, never to ...** er schwor sich (dat), nie zu ...; **there is ~ among thieves** es gibt so etwas wie Ganovenehre; **~ where ~ is due** Ehre, wem Ehre gebührt; **on my ~!** (old) bei meiner Ehre (old); **I promise on my ~** ich gebe mein Ehrenwort; **you're on your ~ not to leave** Sie haben Ihr Ehrenwort gegeben, dass Sie bleiben; **to put sb on his ~** jdm vertrauen; **he's put me on my ~ not to tell** ich habe ihm mein Ehrenwort gegeben, dass ich nichts sage; **man of ~** Ehrenmann m; **to lose one's ~** (old) seine Ehre verlieren (old); **to do ~ to sb** (at funeral) jdm die letzte Ehre erweisen; (action, thought etc) jdm zur Ehre gereichen; **to do ~ to sth** einer Sache (dat) Ehre machen; **in ~ of sb** zu Ehren von jdm, zu jds Ehren; of dead person in ehrendem Andenken an jdn; **in ~ of sth** zu Ehren von etw; of past thing in ehrendem Andenken an etw; **may I have the ~ of accompanying you?** (form) ich bitte um die Ehre, Sie begleiten zu dürfen (geh); **may I have the ~ (of the next dance)?** (form) darf ich (um den nächsten Tanz) bitten?; **if you would do me the ~ of accepting** (form) wenn Sie mir die Ehre erweisen würden anzunehmen (geh); **to whom do I have the ~ of speaking?** (form, hum) mit wem habe ich die Ehre? (geh, hum); **he is ~ bound to do it** es ist Ehrensache für ihn, das zu tun **b** (= title) **Your Honour** Hohes Gericht; **His Honour** das Gericht; **the case was up before His Honour, Sir Charles** der Fall wurde unter dem Vorsitz des vorsitzenden Richters Sir Charles verhandelt **c** (= distinction, award) **~s** Ehren pl, Auszeichnung(en) f(pl); **with full military ~s** mit militärischen Ehren; **New Year's Honour** Titelverleihung f am Neujahrstag **d** **to do the ~s** (inf) die Honneurs machen; (on private occasions) den Gastgeber spielen **e** (Univ) **~s** (also **honours degree**) akademischer Grad mit Prüfung im Spezialfach **to do** or **take ~s in English** Englisch belegen, um den „Honours Degree" zu erwerben; **to get first-class ~s** das Examen mit Auszeichnung or „sehr gut" bestehen **f** (Golf) **it's his ~** er hat die Ehre **g** (Cards) eine der (beim Bridge) 5 bzw. (beim Whist) 4 höchsten Karten einer Farbe **the ~s** die Honneurs pl **VT** jdm ehren; **to ~ sb with a title** jdm einen Titel verleihen; **I would be ~ed** es wäre mir eine Ehre; **I should be (deeply) ~ed if you ...** ich würde mich (zutiefst) geehrt fühlen, wenn Sie ...; **we are ~ed by your visit** (also iro) wir fühlen uns durch Ihren Besuch geehrt; **he ~ed us with his presence** (also iro) er beehrte uns mit seiner Gegenwart; **it's Angelika, we ARE ~ed** (iro) es ist Angelika, welche Ehre; **would you ~ me by dining with me tonight?** würden Sie mir die Ehre erweisen, heute Abend mit mir zu speisen? (geh) **b** cheque annehmen, einlösen; debt begleichen; bill of exchange respektieren; obligation nachkommen (+dat); commitment stehen zu; credit card anerkennen; pledge, promise halten, einlösen; agreement, contract sich halten an (+acc), erfüllen

honourable, (US) **honorable** ['ɒnərəbl] ADJ **a** ehrenhaft; person ehrenhaft, ehrenwert; peace, discharge ehrenvoll; exception rühmlich; **to get an ~ mention** rühmend or lobend erwähnt werden **b** (Brit Parl) Anrede von Abgeordneten innerhalb des Parlaments **the Honourable member for X** der (Herr)/die (Frau) Abgeordnete für X; **the Honourable member** or **gentleman is wrong** der geschätzte or ehrenwerte (Herr) Kollege täuscht sich; **I agree with my right ~ friend** ich stimme meinem geschätzten Herrn Kollegen/ meiner geschätzten Frau Kollegin zu

c (= title) Titel der jüngeren Söhne von Grafen und der Kinder von Freiherrn und Baronen **I didn't know he was an Honourable** ich wusste nicht, dass er adlig or ein „von" (inf) ist

honourably, (US) **honorably** ['ɒnərəblɪ] ADV in Ehren; behave, act ehrenhaft, wie ein Ehrenmann; settle peace ehrenvoll; mention rühmend, lobend

honours, (US) **honors** ['ɒnəz-]: **honours board** N Ehrentafel f; **honours degree** N = **honour** N **e**; **honours list** N (Brit) Liste f der Titel- und Rangverleihungen (die zweimal im Jahr veröffentlicht wird); (Univ) Liste der Kandidaten, die den „Honours Degree" verliehen bekommen

---

HONOURS LIST

Die **honours list** ist eine vom britischen Premierminister zusammen mit dem Monarchen gebilligte Liste, auf der Personen aufgeführt werden, die eine besondere Auszeichnung erhalten sollen und daher mit einem bestimmten Titel geehrt werden. Ein Großteil der Auszeichnungen geht an herausragende Persönlichkeiten des öffentlichen Lebens, aber auch an Leute, die einen bedeutenden Beitrag zum Gemeinwohl geleistet haben. Zweimal im Jahr wird eine solche Liste veröffentlicht, die **New Year's Honours List** im Januar und die **Queen's Birthday Honours List** im Juni. Die meisten der vergebenen Auszeichnungen sind **MBE (Member of the British Empire)** oder **OBE (Order of the British Empire)**.

Hon. Sec. abbr of **Honorary Secretary**

hooch [huːtʃ] N (esp US, inf) Stoff m (sl)

hood [hʊd] N **a** Kapuze f; (thief's) Maske f; (hawk's) Kappe f **b** (Aut) (= roof) Verdeck nt; (US: = bonnet) (Motor)haube f; (on fireplace etc) Abzug m; (on cooker) Abzugshaube f **c** (of cobra) Brillenzeichnung f **d** (esp US inf) (= gangster) Gangster m (inf), Ganove m (inf); (= young ruffian) Rowdy m, Rüpel m **e** (esp US sl: = ghetto) G(h)etto nt **VT** eine Kapuze aufsetzen (+dat); hawk eine Kappe aufsetzen (+dat)

hooded ['hʊdɪd] ADJ **~ executioner/monk** der Scharfrichter/Mönch mit seiner Kapuze; **the ~ robber/gunman** der maskierte Räuber/ Schütze; **~ anorak/sweatshirt** Anorak m/Sweatshirt m mit Kapuze; **~ eyes** Augen mit schweren Lidern

hoodlum ['huːdləm] N Rowdy m; (= member of gang) Ganove m (inf), Gangster m (inf); **you young ~** du Rowdy, du Rüpel

hoodoo ['huːduː] N Unglück nt; (= person, thing) Unglücksbote m

hoodwink ['hʊdwɪŋk] VT (inf) (he)reinlegen (inf); **to ~ sb into doing sth** jdn dazu verleiten, etw zu tun; **they ~ed him into signing the contract** er ließ sich von ihnen (dazu) verleiten, den Vertrag zu unterschreiben; **I was ~ed into buying an imitation** man hat mir eine Imitation angedreht (inf)

hooey ['huːɪ] N (dated inf) Gelabere nt (inf), Quatsch m (inf)

hoof [huːf] N pl **-s** or **hooves** Huf m; **hooves** (hum inf: = feet) Quadratlatschen pl (inf); **cattle on the ~** Vieh nt; **to eat on the ~** (inf) unterwegs essen; **they tend to make policy on the ~** (inf) sie legen ihre Politik oft aus dem Stegreif fest **VT to ~ it** (inf, = go on foot) latschen (inf); (= dance on stage) tingeln (inf)

hoofbeat ['huːfbiːt] N Hufschlag m

hoofed [huːft] ADJ Huf-; **~ animal** Huftier nt

hook [hʊk] N **a** Haken m **b** (Boxing) Haken m; (Golf) Kurvball m (nach links) **c** (Geog) (gekrümmte) Landzunge f **d** (fig uses) **he swallowed the story ~, line and sinker** er hat die Geschichte tatsächlich mit Stumpf und Stiel geschluckt (inf); **he fell for it ~, line and sinker** er ging auf den Leim; **he fell for her ~, line and sinker** er war ihr mit Haut und Haaren verfallen; **by ~ or by crook** auf Biegen und Brechen; **to get sb off the ~** (*inf*) jdn herausreißen (*inf*); (= *out of trouble also*) jdn herauspauken (*inf*); **it gets him off the ~ every time** damit kommt er jedes Mal wieder davon; **that lets me off the ~** (*inf*) damit bin ich aus dem Schneider (*inf*); **to leave the phone off the ~** den Hörer neben das Telefon legen; (*unintentionally*) nicht auflegen; **the phone was ringing off the ~** (*US inf*) das Telefon klingelte pausenlos; **to do sth on one's own ~** (*US inf*) etw auf eigene Faust machen; **to get one's ~s into sb/sth** (*pej inf*) jdn/etw in die Finger kriegen (*inf*)

VT **a** (= *fasten with hook*) **he ~ed the door back** er hakte die Tür fest; **the old man ~s the rowing boats and pulls them in** der alte Mann zieht die Ruderboote mit einem Haken ans Ufer; **to ~ a trailer to a car** einen Anhänger an ein Auto hängen

b **to ~ one's arm/feet around sth** seinen Arm/seine Füße um etw schlingen; **the trapeze artist ~s his legs over the bar** der Trapezkünstler hängt sich mit den Beinen an der Stange ein **c** *fish* an die Angel bekommen; (*fig*) *husband, wife* sich (*dat*) angeln; **to be ~ed** an der Angel hängen; **the helicopter ~ed him out of the water** der Hubschrauber zog or angelte (*inf*) ihn aus dem Wasser **d** (*Boxing*) einen Haken versetzen (+*dat*) or geben (+*dat*) **e** (*inf:* = *addicted, on drugs*) von etw abhängig sein/werden; *on film, food, place etc* auf etw (*acc*) stehen (*inf*); **he's ~ed on the idea** er ist von der Idee besessen; **he's become ~ed on power and money** er ist jetzt auf Macht und Geld versessen **f** (*Rugby*) hakeln **g** (*Sport*) *ball* einen Linksdrall geben (+*dat*) **h** (*inf:* = *clear off*) **to ~ it** die Fliege machen (*sl*) **VI** (*dress etc*) zugehakt werden

▸ **hook on** **VI** (an)gehakt werden (*to* an +*acc*); (*with towbar*) angekoppelt or angehängt werden (*to* an +*acc*); (*burrs etc*) sich festhaken (*to* an +*dat*) **VT** *sep* anhaken (*to* an +*acc*), mit einem Haken befestigen (*to* an +*dat*); (*with towbar*) ankoppeln, anhängen; **to hook sth onto sth** etw an etw (*acc*) (an)haken; **the gliders were hooked on behind the towplane** die Segelflugzeuge waren hinten an das Schleppflugzeug angehängt or angekoppelt

▸ **hook up** **VI** **a** (*dress*) mit Haken zugemacht werden **b** (*Rad, TV*) gemeinsam ausstrahlen; **to hook up with sb** sich jdm anschließen **VT** *sep* **a** *dress etc* zuhaken; **hook me or the dress up, please** mach mir bitte die Haken zu **b** *trailer, caravan* ankoppeln, anhängen; *broken-down car* abschleppen; (*recovery vehicle*) auf den Haken nehmen **c** (= *connect*) *computer etc* anschließen (*to* an +*acc*); (*Rad, TV*) anschließen (*with* an +*acc*); **the doctor hooked her up to a drip** der Arzt hängte sie an den Tropf (*inf*)

hookah ['hʊkə] N (*Brit*) Wasserpfeife *f*, Huka *f*

hook and eye N Haken und Öse *no art, pl vb*

hooked [hʊkt] ADJ **a** (= *hook-shaped*) gebogen; **~ beak/nose** Hakenschnabel *m*/-nase *f* **b** (= *equipped with hooks*) mit Haken versehen

hooker[1] ['hʊkə'] N (*esp US, inf*) Nutte *f* (*inf*)

hooker[2] N (*Rugby*) Hakler *m*

hook: hooknosed ADJ mit einer Hakennase, hakennasig; **hook-up** N **a** (*Rad, TV*) gemeinsame Ausstrahlung; **a telephone ~** eine Konferenzschaltung **b** (= *connection*) Anschluss *m*; **hookworm** N Hakenwurm *m*; (= *disease*) Hakenwurmkrankheit *f*

hooky ['hʊkɪ] N (*US, inf*) Schuleschwänzen *nt* (*inf*); **to play ~** (die) Schule schwänzen (*inf*)

hooligan ['huːlɪɡən] N Rowdy *m*

hooliganism ['huːlɪɡənɪzəm] N Rowdytum *nt*

hoop [huːp] **N** Reifen *m*; (*in croquet*) Tor *nt*; (*in basketball*) Korb *m*; (*on bird's plumage*) Kranz *m*; (*on animal*) Ring *m*; (= *earring*) Creole *f*; **to jump**

through ~s (*fig inf*) sich (*dat*) ein Bein ausreißen (*inf*); **they put him through** or **made him jump through ~s** (*fig*) sie haben ihn auf Herz und Nieren geprüft **VT** *barrel* bereifen

hoop(ed) skirt ['huːp(t)skɜːt] N Reifrock *m*

hoopla ['huːplɑː] N Ringwerfen *nt*

hoopoe ['huːpuː] N Wiedehopf *m*

hooray [huːˈreɪ] INTERJ = hurrah

Hooray Henry N *junger Angehöriger der Oberschicht mit auffälligem Gehabe*

hoosegow ['huːsɡaʊ] N (*dated US, sl:* = *jail*) Knast *m* (*inf*)

hoot [huːt] **N** **a** (*of owl*) Ruf *m*, Schrei *m*; **~s of derision** verächtliches Gejohle; **~s of laughter** johlendes Gelächter; **I don't care** or **give a ~** or **two ~s** (*inf*) das ist mir piepegal (*inf*) or völlig schnuppe (*inf*); **to be a ~** (*inf, person, event etc*) zum Schießen (komisch) sein, zum Schießen sein (*inf*) **b** (*Aut*) Hupen *nt no pl*; (*of train, hooter*) Pfeifen *nt no pl* **VI** **a** (*owl*) schreien, rufen; (*person: derisively*) johlen, buhen; **to ~ with derision/delight** verächtlich/begeistert johlen; **to ~ with laughter** in johlendes Gelächter ausbrechen **b** (*Aut*) hupen; (*train, factory hooter*) pfeifen **VT** **a** *actor, speaker* auspfeifen, ausbuhen; **he was ~ed off the stage** er wurde mit Buhrufen von der Bühne verjagt **b** (*esp Brit Aut*) **to ~ one's/the horn** hupen, auf die Hupe drücken (*inf*)

▸ **hoot down** VT *sep* niederschreien

hootchy-kootchy ['huːtʃɪ'kuːtʃɪ] N (*dated US, inf*) Bauchtanz *m*

hootenanny ['huːtənænɪ] N Hootenanny *f*

hooter ['huːtə'] N (*Brit*) **a** (*Aut*) Hupe *f*; (*at factory*) Sirene *f* **b** (*inf:* = *nose*) Zinken *m* (*inf*)

Hoover® ['huːvə'] N (*Brit*) Staubsauger *m*

hoover ['huːvə'] (*Brit*) **VT** (staub)saugen, Staub saugen; *carpet also* absaugen **VI** (*also* **hoover up**) (staub)saugen

▸ **hoover up** VI +*prep obj* (staub)saugen; (*fig*) *food* verputzen (*inf*)

hovering ['hʊvərɪŋ] N **to do the ~** (staub)saugen, Staub saugen

hooves [huːvz] *pl of* **hoof**

hop[1] [hɒp] **N** **a** (kleiner) Sprung; (*of deer, rabbit*) Satz *m*, Sprung *m*; **to catch sb on the ~** (*fig inf*) jdn überraschen or überrumpeln; **to keep sb on the ~** (*fig inf*) jdn in Trab halten **b** (*inf,* = *dance*) Tanz *m*, Hopserei *f* (*pej inf*) **c** (*Aviat inf*) Sprung *m*, Satz *m*; **a short ~** ein kleiner Satz (*inf*), ein Katzensprung *m* (*inf*) **VI** (*animal*) hüpfen, springen; (*rabbit*) hoppeln; (*person*) (auf einem Bein) hüpfen, hopsen (*inf*); **~ in, said the driver** steigen Sie ein, sagte der Fahrer; **he'd ~ into bed with anyone** der steigt mit jeder ins Bett (*inf*); **to ~ off (the train)** (aus dem Zug) aussteigen; (*while moving*) vom Zug abspringen; **he ~ped off his bicycle** er sprang vom Fahrrad; **to ~ on** aufsteigen; **to ~ on a train** in einen Zug einsteigen; (*while moving*) auf einen Zug aufspringen; **he ~ped on his bicycle** er schwang sich auf sein Fahrrad; **to ~ out** heraushüpfen; **he ~ped over the wall** er sprang über die Mauer **VT** **a** *ditch* springen über (+*acc*); *bus etc* schwarzfahren in (+*dat*) or mit **b** (*Brit inf*) **~ it!** verschwinde, zieh Leine (*inf*); **I ~ped it quick** ich habe mich schnell aus dem Staub gemacht (*inf*)

▸ **hop off** VI (*inf*) sich verdrücken (*inf*), sich aus dem Staub machen (*inf*) (*with sth* mit etw)

hop[2] N (*Bot*) Hopfen *m*

hope [həʊp] ✪ 8.4 **N** (*also person*) Hoffnung *f*; **she is our best ~** sie ist unsere größte Hoffnung; **past** or **beyond ~** hoffnungslos, aussichtslos; **the patient is beyond ~** für den Patienten besteht keine Hoffnung mehr; **to be full of ~** hoffnungsvoll or voller Hoffnung sein; **my ~ is that ...** ich hoffe nur, dass ...; **in the ~ that ...** in der Hoffnung, dass ...; **in the ~ of**

doing sth in der Hoffnung, etw zu tun; **to have (high** or **great) ~s of doing sth** hoffen, etw zu tun; **her family has high** or **great ~s of her** ihre Familie setzt große Hoffnungen in sie; **to live in ~ of sth** in der Hoffnung auf etw (*acc*) leben; **well, we live in ~** nun, wir hoffen eben (weiter); **to place one's ~ in sb/sth** seine Hoffnungen in or auf jdn/etw setzen; **don't get** or **build your ~s up too much** mach dir keine allzu großen Hoffnungen; **there is no ~ of him having survived** es besteht keine Hoffnung, dass er überlebt hat; **we have some ~ of success** es besteht die Hoffnung, dass wir Erfolg haben; **there's no ~ of that** da braucht man sich gar keine Hoffnungen zu machen; **where there's life there's ~** es ist noch nicht aller Tage Abend; (*said of invalid*) solange er/sie sich noch regt, besteht auch noch Hoffnung; **to give up/ lose ~ of doing sth** die Hoffnung aufgeben, etw zu tun; **what a ~!** (*inf*) schön wärs! (*inf*); **some ~(s)!** (*inf*) schön wärs! (*inf*); **she hasn't got a ~ in hell of passing her exams** (*inf*) es besteht nicht die geringste Chance, dass sie ihre Prüfung besteht; **~ springs eternal** (*prov*) wenn die Hoffnung nicht wäre!

VI hoffen (*for* auf +*acc*); **to ~ for the best** das Beste hoffen; **you can't ~ for anything else from him** man kann sich doch von ihm nichts anderes erhoffen; **one might have ~d for something better** man hätte (eigentlich) auf etwas Besseres hoffen dürfen, man hätte sich eigentlich Besseres erhoffen dürfen; **a pay rise would be too much to ~ for** auf eine Gehaltserhöhung braucht man sich (*dat*) gar keine Hoffnungen zu machen; **I ~ so** hoffentlich, ich hoffe es; **I ~ not** hoffentlich nicht, ich hoffe nicht **VT** hoffen; **I ~ to see you** hoffentlich sehe ich Sie, ich hoffe, dass ich Sie sehe; **the party cannot ~ to win** für die Partei besteht keine Hoffnung zu gewinnen; **I ~ I'm not disturbing you** ich hoffe, dass ich Sie nicht störe; **to ~ against ~ that ...** trotz allem die Hoffnung nicht aufgeben, dass ..., wider alle Hoffnung hoffen, dass ...; **hoping to hear from you** ich hoffe, von Ihnen zu hören, in der Hoffnung (*form*), von Ihnen zu hören

hope chest N (*US*) Aussteuertruhe *f*

hoped-for ['həʊptfɔː'] ADJ erhofft

hopeful ['həʊpfʊl] **ADJ** **a** *person, face, action* hoffnungsvoll; **he was still ~ (that ...)** er machte sich (*dat*) immer noch Hoffnungen(, dass ...); **I am ~ (that) this misunderstanding will be rectified** ich habe die Hoffnung, dass dieses Missverständnis aufgeklärt wird; **people ~ of obtaining the few tickets available were all disappointed** Leute, die auf die wenigen erhältlichen Karten Hoffnungen machten, wurden alle enttäuscht; **they weren't very ~** sie hatten keine große Hoffnung; **the doctor was not very ~** der Arzt war nicht sehr zuversichtlich; **they are ~ about the negotiations** sie setzen Hoffnungen in die Verhandlungen; **he was feeling more ~** er war optimistischer; **don't be too ~** machen Sie sich (*dat*) keine zu großen Hoffnungen; **they continue to be ~** sie hoffen weiter, sie geben die Hoffnung nicht auf; **you're (being) ~!** (*iro*) du bist vielleicht ein Optimist! (*inf*) **b** (= *promising*) *future* viel versprechend; *news* positiv; *forecast* optimistisch; **it is not a ~ sign for the future** es ist kein gutes Zeichen für die Zukunft **N** (= *aspirant*) Anwärter(in) *m(f)*; (= *applicant*) Bewerber(in) *m(f)*; (= *candidate*) Kandidat(in) *m(f)*; **presidential ~s** Anwärter *pl* auf die Präsidentschaft; **our Olympic ~s** unsere olympischen Hoffnungen; **a young ~** (*seems likely to succeed*) eine junge Hoffnung; (*hopes to succeed*) ein hoffnungsvoller junger Mensch

hopefully ['həʊpfəlɪ] ADV **a** *ask, look, say* hoffnungsvoll; **I looked ~ around for a glimpse of my luggage** ich sah mich um, in der Hoffnung, mein Gepäck zu erspähen **b** (*inf: introducing sentence or as answer:* = *with any luck*) hoffentlich

hopeless ['həʊplɪs] ADJ **a** (= *impossible*) *love, attempt, task, cause* aussichtslos; *situation, case* hoffnungslos; (= *despairing*) *person, cry, sigh, gesture, look* verzweifelt; **to feel ~** keine Hoffnung haben; **pupils feel ~ about job prospects** Schüler haben keine Hoffnung auf eine Stelle **b** (*inf*) (= *useless, terrible*) hoffnungslos; (= *incorrigible*) *drunk, liar, romantic* unverbesserlich; **she's a ~ manager/organizer** als Managerin/im Organisieren ist sie ein hoffnungsloser Fall; **I'm ~ at maths/sport** in Mathe/Sport bin ich hoffnungslos *or* ein hoffnungsloser Fall; **to be ~ at doing sth** etw absolut *or* überhaupt nicht können; **her room is in a ~ muddle** *or* **mess** in ihrem Zimmer herrscht ein hoffnungsloses *or* heilloses Durcheinander; **the buses are quite ~** die Busse kann man vergessen (*inf*); **the weather/food was ~** das Wetter/Essen war unmöglich

hopelessly ['həʊplɪslɪ] ADV **a** (= *despairingly*) *sigh, shrug, cry* verzweifelt **b** (*emph*: = *utterly*) ~ **confused** völlig verwirrt; **the service was ~ inadequate** der Service war völlig unmöglich; **I feel ~ inadequate** ich komme mir völlig minderwertig vor; **he got ~ lost in the fog** er hat sich im Nebel hoffnungslos verirrt; **I was ~ in love with Louise** ich hatte mich rettungslos in Louise verliebt; **I'm ~ bad at maths** in Mathe bin ich ein hoffnungsloser Fall

hopelessness ['həʊplɪsnɪs] N (*of love, attempt, cause, task*) Aussichtslosigkeit *f*; (*of situation*) Hoffnungslosigkeit *f*; **a sense of ~** ein Gefühl *nt* der Verzweiflung *or* Hoffnungslosigkeit

hop garden N Hopfengarten *m*

hophead ['hɒphed] N (*US pej inf*) Junkie *m* (*inf*)

hoplite ['hɒplaɪt] N Hoplit *m*

hop-o'-my-thumb ['hɒpəmaɪ'θʌm] N Knirps *m*, Stöpsel *m* (*inf*)

hopper ['hɒpə'] N **a** (*Tech*) Einfülltrichter *m*; (*for coal*) Einfüll- *or* Speisetrichter *m* **b** (= *young locust*) junge Heuschrecke

hop-picker ['hɒpɪkə'] N Hopfenpflücker(in) *m(f)*

hop-picking ['hɒpɪkɪŋ] N Hopfenernte *f*, Hopfenpflücken *nt*; ~ **season** Hopfenernte *f*

hopping mad ['hɒpɪŋ'mæd] ADJ (*inf*) fuchsteufelswild (*inf*)

hop: hopscotch N Himmel-und-Hölle(-Spiel) *nt*, Hopse *f* (*inf*); **hop, skip and jump** N, **hop, step and jump** N Dreisprung *m*; **it's a ~ from here** es ist nur ein Katzensprung von hier

hopvine ['hɒpvaɪn] N (= *vine*) Hopfenranke *f*; (= *plant*) Hopfenpflanze *f*

Horace ['hɒrɪs] N Horaz *m*

Horatian [hə'reɪʃən] ADJ horazisch

horde [hɔːd] N **a** (*of wild animals*) Horde *f*; (*of insects*) Schwarm *m* **b** (*inf*) Masse *f*; (*of football fans, children etc*) Horde *f* (*pej*)

horizon [hə'raɪzn] N Horizont *m*; (*fig also*) Gesichtskreis *m no pl*; (*fig*) **new ~s** neue Horizonte; **a limited ~** ein enger *or* begrenzter Horizont; **on the ~** am Horizont; (*fig*) in Sicht; **the ship went over the ~** das Schiff verschwand am Horizont; **the sun was below the ~** die Sonne war hinter dem Horizont

horizontal [ˌhɒrɪ'zɒntl] ADJ waag(e)recht, horizontal; ~ **line** Waag(e)rechte *f*, Horizontale *f*

horizontal: horizontal bar N Reck *nt*; **horizontal hold** N (*TV*) Zeilenfang *m*, Bildfang *m*

horizontally [ˌhɒrɪ'zɒntəlɪ] ADV horizontal

hormonal [hɔː'məʊnəl] ADJ hormonal, hormonell

hormone ['hɔːməʊn] N Hormon *nt*

hormone replacement therapy N Hormonersatztherapie *f*

hormone treatment N Hormonbehandlung *f*

horn [hɔːn] N **a** (*of cattle, substance, container, Mus*) Horn *nt*; (*inf*, = *trumpet, saxophone etc*) Kanne (*sl*), Tüte (*sl*) *f*; ~**s** (*of deer*) Geweih *nt*; (*fig, of cuckold*) Hörner *pl*; **caught on the ~s of a dilemma** in einer Zwickmühle; ~ **of plenty** Füllhorn *nt*; **to lock ~s** (*lit*) beim Kampf die Geweihe verhaken; (*fig*) die Klingen kreuzen **b** (*Aut*) Hupe *f*; (*Naut*) (Signal)horn *nt*; **to**

sound *or* **blow the ~** (*Aut*) hupen, auf die Hupe drücken (*inf*); (*Naut*) tuten, das Horn ertönen lassen **c** (*of snail, insect*) Fühler *m*; **to draw** *or* **pull in one's ~s** (*fig*) einen Rückzieher machen; (= *spend less*) den Gürtel enger schnallen **d** (*of crescent moon*) Spitze *f* (der Mondsichel) **VT** (= *gore*) mit den Hörnern aufspießen; (= *butt*) auf die Hörner nehmen

▶ **horn in** VI (*inf*) (= *interfere*) mitmischen (*inf*) (**on** bei); (= *muscle in*) sich hineindrängen (**on** in +*acc*); **dozens of entrepreneurs started horning in** zig Unternehmer versuchten, auch ein Stück vom Kuchen zu bekommen

horn in *cpds* Horn-; **hornbeam** N (*Bot*) Hain- *or* Weißbuche *f*; **hornbill** N (*Orn*) (Nas)hornvogel *m*; **horn bug** N (*Zool*) Hirschkäfer *m*

horned [hɔːnd] ADJ gehörnt, mit Hörnern

horned owl N Ohreule *f*

horned toad N Krötenechse *f*

hornet ['hɔːnɪt] N Hornisse *f*; **to stir up a ~'s nest** (*fig*) in ein Wespennest stechen

hornist ['hɔːnɪst] N (*Mus*) Hornist (in)*m(f)*

hornless ['hɔːnlɪs] ADJ ohne Hörner, hornlos

horn: hornpipe N englischer Seemannstanz; **horn-rimmed** ADJ ~ **glasses** *or* **spectacles** Hornbrille *f*

horny ['hɔːnɪ] ADJ (+*er*) **a** (= *like horn*) hornartig; *hands etc* schwielig; *soles* hornig **b** (*inf*) (= *sexually aroused*) scharf (*inf*), geil (*inf*); (*Brit* = *sexually attractive*) scharf (*inf*)

horology [hɒ'rɒlədʒɪ] N (*measuring time*) Zeitmessung *f*; (= *watchmaking*) Uhrmacherkunst *f*

horoscope ['hɒrəskəʊp] N Horoskop *nt*

horrendous [hɒ'rendəs] ADJ **a** (= *horrific*) *accident, injury, war, experience* entsetzlich, grauenhaft; *crime, attack, violence* entsetzlich, abscheulich **b** (*inf*: = *dreadful*) *conditions, traffic* fürchterlich (*inf*); *loss, cost, price, stupidity* horrend; **children's shoes are a ~ price** Kinderschuhe sind horrend teuer

horrendously [hɒ'rendəslɪ] ADV **a** (= *horrifically*) entsetzlich **b** (*inf*: = *dreadfully*) fürchterlich (*inf*); *expensive* horrend

horrible ['hɒrɪbl] ADJ **a** (*inf*: = *awful*) schrecklich (*inf*); (= *ghastly*) *food* grauenhaft (*inf*); *clothes, colour, sight, smell, taste* scheußlich, abscheulich; *person* gemein, fies (*inf*); **what a ~ thought!** was für eine schreckliche Vorstellung!; **to look ~** scheußlich aussehen; **that jumper looks ~ on you** in dem Pullover siehst du schrecklich aus; **to be ~ to sb** fies (*inf*) *or* gemein zu jdm sein **b** (= *horrific*) *death, crime, sound, war, accident, injury* grauenhaft

horribly ['hɒrɪblɪ] ADV **a** (= *in a horrible manner*) grauenhaft; *murdered* auf grauenhafte Art; **they died ~** sie starben einen grauenhaften Tod; **the man had been ~ injured** der Mann hatte grauenhafte Verletzungen davongetragen **b** (*inf*: = *dreadfully*) *drunk, expensive, embarrassed* schrecklich (*inf*), fürchterlich (*inf*)

horrid ['hɒrɪd] ADJ entsetzlich, fürchterlich, schrecklich; **don't be so ~** sei nicht so gemein (*inf*)

horridly ['hɒrɪdlɪ] ADV *behave* schrecklich

horrific [hɒ'rɪfɪk] ADJ entsetzlich, schrecklich; *documentary* erschreckend; *price increase* horrend

horrifically [hɒ'rɪfɪkəlɪ] ADV grauenhaft; **he was ~ injured in the crash** bei dem Unfall trug er grauenhafte Verletzungen davon; ~ **expensive** horrend teuer

horrify ['hɒrɪfaɪ] VT entsetzen; **he was horrified by** *or* **at the suggestion** er war über den Vorschlag entsetzt; **it horrifies me to think what ...** ich denke (nur) mit Entsetzen daran, was ...

horrifying ['hɒrɪfaɪɪŋ] ADJ schrecklich, fürchterlich, entsetzlich; *mutilation* grauenhaft; *crash* entsetzlich

horrifyingly ['hɒrɪfaɪɪŋlɪ] ADV *high, low, violent, fast* entsetzlich, fürchterlich; *mutilated, disfigured* grauenhaft; *crash, die* auf entsetzliche Weise;

and, perhaps most ~, this is only the beginning und, was vielleicht am erschreckendsten ist, dies ist nur der Anfang

horror ['hɒrə'] **N** **a** Entsetzen *nt*, Grauen *nt*; (= *strong dislike*) Horror *m* (*of vor* +*dat*); **to have a ~ of sth** einen Horror vor etw (*dat*) haben; **to have a ~ of doing sth** einen Horror davor haben, etw zu tun; **he has a ~ of growing old** er hat eine panische Angst vor dem Altwerden, ihm graut vor dem Altwerden; **she shrank back in ~** sie fuhr entsetzt zurück; **they watched in ~** sie sahen entsetzt zu; **a scene of ~** ein Bild *nt* des Grauens **b** *usu pl* (= *horrifying thing, of war etc*) Schrecken *m*, Gräuel *m* **c** (*inf*) **to be a real ~** furchtbar sein (*inf*); **you little ~!** du kleines Ungeheuer! (*inf*) **d** (*inf usages*) **to have the ~s** (*in delirium tremens*) weiße Mäuse sehen (*inf*); ~ **of ~s** (*referring to an actual event*) oh Schreck (*inf*); **if, ~ of ~s, ...** wenn, Gott behüte, ... **ATTR** Horror-; ~ **film/story** Horrorfilm *m*/-geschichte *f*; **most people have a ~ story about holidays** fast jeder kann eine Horrorgeschichte aus dem Urlaub erzählen; ~ **trip** (*inf*) Horrortrip *m*

horror-stricken ['hɒrəˌstrɪkən], **horror-struck** ['hɒrəˌstrʌk] ADJ von Entsetzen *or* Grauen gepackt; **I was ~ when he told me** mir grauste es *or* ich war hell entsetzt, als er es mir erzählte

hors de combat [ˌɔːdə'kɒmbɑː] ADJ (*lit, fig*) außer Gefecht gesetzt, kampfunfähig

hors d'oeuvre [ɔː'dɜːv] N Hors d'oeuvre *nt*, Vorspeise *f*

horse [hɔːs] N **a** Pferd *nt*, Ross *nt* (*liter, pej*); **he lost a lot of money on the ~s** (*betting*) er hat beim Pferderennen *or* bei der Pferdewette viel Geld verloren **b** (*fig usages*) **wild ~s would not drag me there** keine zehn Pferde würden mich dahin bringen; **to eat like a ~** wie ein Scheunendrescher *m* essen *or* fressen (*inf*); **I could eat a ~** ich könnte ein ganzes Pferd essen; **to work like a ~** wie ein Pferd arbeiten; **information straight from the ~'s mouth** Informationen *pl* aus erster Hand; **to back the wrong ~** aufs falsche Pferd setzen; **to change** *or* **switch ~s in midstream** mitten im Strom die Pferde wechseln; **it's a case of ~s for courses** (*Brit*) man muss den Richtigen/die Richtige/das Richtige dafür finden **c** (*Gymnastics*) Pferd *nt*; (= *sawhorse*) Sägebock *m* **d** (*Mil*) *collective sing* Reiterei *f*, Kavallerie *f*; **light ~** leichte Kavallerie; **a thousand ~** tausend Reiter *or* Berittene

▶ **horse about** (*Brit*) *or* **around** VI (*inf*) herumalbern (*inf*)

horse: horse-and-buggy ADJ (*US*) *approach, system* vorsintflutlich (*inf*); **horse artillery** N berittene Artillerie; **horseback** **ADV** **to ride ~** (zu Pferd) reiten **N** **on ~** zu Pferd; **to travel by** *or* **on ~** zu Pferd reisen; **to go/set off on ~** (zu Pferd) reiten/wegreiten; **policemen on ~** berittene Polizisten; **horsebean** N Saubohne *f*; **horsebox** N (= *van*) Pferdetransporter *m*; (= *trailer*) Pferdetransportwagen *m*; (*in stable*) Box *f*; ~ **horse brass** N Zaumzeugbeschlag *m*; **horse breeder** N Pferdezüchter(in) *m(f)*; **horse chestnut** N (= *tree, fruit*) Rosskastanie *f*; **horse doctor** N (*inf*) Viehdoktor(in) *m(f)* (*inf*); **horse-drawn** ADJ von Pferden gezogen; *hearse, milk cart* pferdebespannt *attr*; ~ **carriage** Pferdewagen *m*; ~ **carriage** Kutsche *f*; **horseflesh** N (= *meat of horse*) Pferdefleisch *nt*; (= *horses collectively*) Pferde *pl*; **a good judge of ~** ein guter Pferdekenner; **horsefly** N (Pferde)bremse *f*; **Horse Guards** PL berittene Garde, Gardekavallerie *f*; **horsehair** **N** Rosshaar *nt* **ADJ** *attr* Rosshaar-; ~ **mattress** Rosshaarmatratze *f*; **horse latitudes** PL Rossbreiten *pl*; **horse laugh** N wieherndes Lachen *or* Gelächter; **horseless** ADJ ohne Pferd; ~ **carriage** (*old, = motorcar*) selbstfahrender Wagen; **horseman** N Reiter *m*; **horsemanship** N Reitkunst *f*;

horse meat N Pferdefleisch nt; **horse opera** N (hum inf: Film) Western m; **horseplay** N Alberei f, Balgerei f; **horse pond** N Pferdeschwemme f; **horsepower** N Pferdestärke f; **a 200 ~ car/engine** ein Auto/Motor mit 200 PS or Pferdestärken; **horse race** N Pferderennen nt; **horse racing** N Pferderennsport m; (= races) Pferderennen pl; **horseradish** N Meerrettich m; **horse-riding** N Reiten nt; **horse sense** N gesunder Menschenverstand; **horseshit** N (fig sl, = nonsense) Scheiß m (inf); **horseshoe** N Hufeisen nt ATTR hufeisenförmig, Hufeisen-; **~ shape** Hufeisenform f; **~ throwing** Hufeisenwerfen nt; **horse show** N Pferdeschau f; **horse trading** N (fig) Kuhhandel m; **horsewhip** N Reitpeitsche f VT auspeitschen; **horsewoman** N Reiterin f

horsey, horsy ['hɔːsɪ] ADJ (+er) a (= keen on horses) person, family pferdenärrisch; **~ people** Pferdenarren pl; **she's a bit ~** sie ist ein ziemlicher Pferdenarr or -fan b (pej: = horse-like) person pferdeähnlich; **~ face** Pferdegesicht nt

hortative ['hɔːtətɪv] ADJ anspornend

horticultural [ˌhɔːtɪˈkʌltʃərəl] ADJ Garten(bau)-; **~ show** Gartenschau f, Gartenbauausstellung f

horticulturalist [ˌhɔːtɪˈkʌltʃərəlɪst] N Gärtner(in) m(f)

horticulture ['hɔːtɪkʌltʃə] N Gartenbau(kunst f) m

horticulturist [ˌhɔːtɪˈkʌltʃərɪst] N Gärtner(in) m(f)

hosanna [həʊˈzænə] INTERJ hos(i)anna N Hos(i)anna nt

hose¹ [həʊz] N Schlauch m VT (also **hose down**) abspritzen

▶ **hose out** VT sep ausspritzen

hose² N, no pl a (Comm, = stockings) Strümpfe pl, Strumpfwaren pl b (Hist, for men) (Knie)hose f

hosepipe ['həʊzpaɪp] N (esp Brit) Schlauch m

hosepipe ban N durch Wasserknappheit bedingtes Verbot, den Rasen zu sprengen oder das Auto mit dem Gartenschlauch zu waschen

hosier ['həʊʒə] N Strumpfwarenhändler(in) m(f)

hosiery ['həʊʒərɪ] N Strumpfwaren pl

hosp abbr of hospital

hospice ['hɒspɪs] N a (for terminally ill) Pflegeheim nt (für unheilbar Kranke) b (for travellers) Hospiz nt

hospitable [hɒsˈpɪtəbl] ADJ a (= friendly, sociable) person gastfreundlich, gastlich; **welcome** gastlich; **to be ~ to sb** jdn gastfreundlich or gastlich aufnehmen b (= favourable) place, climate gastlich; **environment** freundlich; **~ to sth** (soil, environment) günstig für etw

hospitably [hɒsˈpɪtəblɪ] ADV gastfreundlich, gastlich

hospital ['hɒspɪtl] N Krankenhaus nt, Klinik f, Hospital nt (old, Sw); **in ~** im Krankenhaus; **he's got to go (in)to ~** or (US) **(in)to the ~** er muss ins Krankenhaus (gehen)

hospital in cpds Krankenhaus-; **hospital administration** N Krankenhausverwaltung f; **hospital administrator** N Krankenhausverwalter(in) m(f); **hospital bed** N Krankenhausbett nt; **hospital case** N Fall, der im Krankenhaus behandelt werden muss; **hospital facilities** PL (= equipment) Krankenhauseinrichtung(en) f(pl); (= hospitals) Kranken(heil)anstalten pl

hospitalism ['hɒspɪtlɪzəm] N (Med) Hospitalismus m

hospitality [ˌhɒspɪˈtælɪtɪ] N Gastfreundschaft f, Gastlichkeit f; (Comm: = refreshments etc for clients) Bewirtung f

hospitalization [ˌhɒspɪtəlaɪˈzeɪʃən] N a Einweisung f ins Krankenhaus; (= stay in hospital) Krankenhausaufenthalt m b (US: = hospitalization insurance) Versicherung f für Krankenhauspflege

hospitalize ['hɒspɪtəlaɪz] VT ins Krankenhaus einweisen; **he was ~d for three months** er lag drei Monate lang im Krankenhaus

hospital: hospital nurse N Krankenschwester f (im Krankenhaus); **hospital porter** N Pfleger(in) m(f); (= doorman) Pförtner(in) m(f) (im Krankenhaus); **hospital ship** N Lazarettor Krankenschiff nt; **hospital train** N Lazarettzug m

Host [həʊst] N (Eccl) Hostie f

host¹ [həʊst] N a Gastgeber(in) m(f); (in own home) Hausherr(in) m(f), Gastgeber(in) m(f); **to be** or **play ~ to sb** jds Gastgeber(in) m(f) sein; (in own home also) jdn zu Besuch or Gast haben; **to play ~ to an event** eine Veranstaltung ausrichten

b (in hotel etc) Wirt(in) m(f); **your ~s are Mr and Mrs X** Ihre Wirtsleute sind Herr und Frau X; **mine ~** (obs, hum) der Herr Wirt

c (Bot) Wirt(spflanze f) m; (Zool) Wirt(stier nt) m

d (on TV programme etc) Gastgeber(in) m(f)

e (also **host computer**) Host(-Rechner) m VT banquet, ball, TV programme Gastgeber(in) sein bei; (country, city) event, conference, Olympics ausrichten

host² N a Menge f, Masse f (inf); **he has a ~ of friends** er hat massenweise (inf) or eine Menge Freunde; **a whole ~ of reasons** eine ganze Menge or Anzahl von Gründen b (obs, liter) Heerschar f (obs, liter); **a ~ of angels** eine Engelschar; **the Lord of Hosts** der Herr der Heerscharen

hostage ['hɒstɪdʒ] N Geisel f; **to take/hold sb ~** jdn als Geisel nehmen/halten; **to take ~s** Geiseln nehmen

hostage: hostage-taker N Geiselnehmer(in) m(f); **hostage-taking** N Geiselnahme f

host country N Gastland nt

hostel ['hɒstəl] N (for students, workers etc) (Wohn)heim nt VI **to go ~ling** in Jugendherbergen übernachten

hosteller ['hɒstələ] N Heimbewohner(in) m(f); (in youth hostel) Herbergsgast m

hostelry ['hɒstəlrɪ] N (obs) Herberge f (liter)

hostess ['həʊstɪs] N a (person) Gastgeberin f; (in own home) Hausherrin f, Gastgeberin f; **to be** or **play ~ to sb** jds Gastgeberin sein; (in own home also) jdn zu Besuch or Gast haben b (in hotel etc) Wirtin f c (in nightclub) Hostess f d (= air hostess) Stewardess f; (at exhibition etc) Hostess f e (on TV programme etc) Gastgeberin f

hostess trolley N Servierwagen m

hostile ['hɒstaɪl] ADJ a (= antagonistic) person (in attitude, feelings) feindselig; (= opposed in principle) person, society, press, government feindlich (gesinnt); question, attitude, reception, atmosphere feindselig; (Mil) fire, forces, aircraft feindlich; **to feel ~** feindselig (gesinnt) sein; **to be ~ to sb** sich jdm gegenüber feindselig verhalten; **to be ~ to** or **toward(s) sth** einer Sache (dat) feindlich gegenüberstehen; **a church ~ to any form of birth control** eine Kirche, die jede Art von Geburtenkontrolle ablehnt

b (= unfavourable) conditions, environment, weather unwirtlich

c (Econ, Fin) bid, takeover, bidder feindlich

hostility [hɒsˈtɪlɪtɪ] N a Feindseligkeit f; (between people) Feindschaft f; **to show ~ to sb** sich jdm gegenüber feindselig verhalten; **to show ~ to sth** einer Sache (dat) feindlich gegenüberstehen; **feelings of ~** feindselige Gefühle pl; **he feels no ~ toward(s) anybody** er ist niemandem feindlich gesinnt; **there is some ~ among them to the idea** sie sind teilweise gegen den Gedanken; **~ to foreigners** Ausländerfeindlichkeit f b **hostilities** PL (= warfare) Feindseligkeiten pl

hostler ['ɒslə] N = ostler

hot [hɒt] ADJ (+er) a heiß; meal, tap, drink warm; **I am** or **feel ~** mir ist (es) heiß; **with ~ and cold water** mit warm und kalt Wasser; **it was a ~ and tiring climb** der Aufstieg machte

warm und müde; **the weather is ~** es ist heißes Wetter; **in the ~ weather** bei dem heißen Wetter, wenn es so heiß ist; **the room was ~** in dem Zimmer war es heiß; **Africa is a ~ country** in Afrika ist es heiß; **to get ~** (things) heiß werden; **I'm getting ~** mir wird (es) warm

b (to taste) curry, spices etc scharf

c (inf) radioactive material radioaktiv, heiß (inf)

d (inf) stolen goods heiß (inf); **it's too ~ to sell** so heiße Ware lässt sich nicht verkaufen (inf)

e (inf, = in demand) product zugkräftig; **she's the ~test property in show business** sie ist die heißeste Nummer im Showbusiness

f (inf, = good, competent) stark (inf); **the ~test show in town** die stärkste Show in der Stadt (inf); **he's pretty ~ at maths** in Mathe ist er ganz schön stark (inf); **I'm not feeling too ~** mir gehts nicht besonders (inf); **she's so ~** (inf) sie ist eine starke Frau (inf)

g (fig) **to be (a) ~ favourite** (Brit) or **favorite** (US) hoch favorisiert sein, der große Favorit sein; **~ tip** heißer Tipp; **a ~ issue** eine umstrittene Frage; **a ~ topic of conversation** ein kontroverses Gesprächsthema; **the ~ news** das Neuste vom Neuen; **~ off the press** gerade erschienen; **the latest designs ~ from Milan** die neuesten Entwürfe, gerade aus Mailand eingetroffen; **the competition was very ~** der Wettbewerb war äußerst scharf; **she has a ~ temper** sie braust leicht auf, sie hat ein hitziges Wesen; **she's too ~ to handle** (inf) mit der wird keiner fertig (inf); **it's too ~ to handle** (political issue, in journalism) das ist ein heißes Eisen; **that's a ~ button, that hits a ~ button** (US) das ist ein heißes Eisen; **to get into ~ water** in (des) Teufels Küche kommen (inf), in Schwulitäten kommen (inf); **to be/get (all) ~ and bothered** (inf) ganz aufgeregt sein/werden (about wegen); **to feel ~ and bothered** (inf) ins Schwitzen kommen (inf); **to get ~ under the collar about sth** wegen etw in Rage geraten; (= embarrassed) wegen etw verlegen werden; **I went ~ and cold all over** (inf) (because of illness) mir wurde abwechselnd heiß und kalt; (with emotion) mir wurde es ganz anders (inf); **things started getting ~ in the tenth round** (inf) in der zehnten Runde wurde es langsam spannend or gings los (inf); **to make things too ~ for sb** (inf) jdm die Hölle heiß machen (inf), jdm einheizen (inf); **it's getting too ~ for me here** (inf) hier wird mir der Boden unter den Füßen zu heiß → **trail N** b

ADV (+er) **the engine's running ~** der Motor läuft heiß; **he keeps blowing ~ and cold** er sagt einmal hü und einmal hott

N **to have the ~s for sb** (inf) auf jdn scharf sein (inf)

▶ **hot up** (inf) VI **the pace is hotting up** das Tempo wird schneller; **things are hotting up in the Middle East** die Lage im Nahen Osten spitzt sich zu or verschärft sich; **things are hotting up** es geht langsam los; (party also) die Sache kommt in Schwung; **the bars rarely hot up before midnight** in den Bars geht es selten vor Mitternacht richtig los VT sep (fig) music verpoppen (inf); pace steigern; surveillance verschärfen; engine frisieren

hot: hot air N (fig) leeres Gerede, Gewäsch nt; **hot-air balloon** N Heißluftballon m; **hot-air drier** N Heißlufttrockner m; **hotbed** N a (fig) Brutstätte f, Nährboden m (of für) b (Hort) Mist- or Frühbeet nt; **hot-blooded** ADJ heißblütig; **hotcake** N (US) = pancake

hotchpotch ['hɒtʃpɒtʃ] N (Brit) Durcheinander nt, Mischmasch m

hot: hot cross bun N Rosinenbrötchen mit kleinem Teigkreuz, wird in der Karwoche gegessen; **hot-desking** N Desksharing nt; **hot dog** N Hot dog m or nt; **hot-dogging** N (Ski) Freestyle nt

hotel [həʊˈtel] N Hotel nt

hotelier [həʊˈtelɪə] N Hotelier m

hotel: hotel industry N Hotelgewerbe nt, Hotellerie f; **hotel keeper** N Hotelier m, Hotelbesitzer(in) m(f); **hotel manager** N Hoteldirektor(in) m(f); **hotel porter** N Haus- or

Hoteldiener(in) *m(f)*; **hotel room** N Hotelzimmer *nt*

hot: hot flushes PL (*Med*) fliegende Hitze; **hotfoot** (*inf*) ADV *arrive* stehenden Fußes VT he ~ed it back home/out of town er ging schleunigst nach Hause/verließ schleunigst die Stadt; **hot gospeller** N Erweckungsprediger(in) *m(f)*; **hothead** N Hitzkopf *m*; **hot-headed** ADJ hitzköpfig, unbeherrscht; **hothouse** N (*lit, fig*) Treibhaus *nt* ADJ *attr* (*lit*) Treibhaus-; (*fig*) spannungsgeladen, angespannt; ~ **plant/vegetables** Treibhauspflanze *f*/-gemüse *nt*; **hot-housing** N Intensivunterricht für besonders begabte Kleinkinder; **hot jazz** N Hotjazz *m*, Hot Jazz *m*; **hot line** N (*Pol*) heißer Draht; (*TV etc*) Hotline *f*; to get on the ~ (*Pol*) sich an den heißen Draht hängen (*inf*)

hotly [ˈhɒtlɪ] ADV **a** (= *fiercely*) *debate, deny, say, protest* heftig; *contest, dispute* heiß; **a ~ contested final** ein heiß umkämpftes Finale; **a ~ contested** or **disputed move** eine heiß umstrittene Maßnahme; **this claim is ~ disputed** diese Behauptung ist heiß umstritten or wird heftig bestritten

b he was ~ **pursued by two policemen** zwei Polizisten waren ihm dicht auf den Fersen (*inf*); **he has been ~ pursued by the media** die Medien haben ihn auf Schritt und Tritt verfolgt

c to be ~ **tipped for sth** als heißer Favorit für etw gelten; **the ~ tipped new band** die neue Band, der eine große Zukunft vorausgesagt wird

hot: hot metal (*Typ*) N Blei *nt*; (= *setting*) Bleisatz *m*; **hot-metal** ADJ *attr* ~ **setting** Bleisatz *m*; **hot pants** PL heiße Höschen, Hotpants *pl*, Hot Pants *pl*; **hot pepper** N Peperoni *f*; **hotplate** N (*of stove*) Koch- or Heizplatte *f* **b** (= *plate warmer*) Warmhalteplatte *f*, Wärmplatte *f*; **hotpot** N (*esp Brit Cook*) Fleischeintopf *m* mit Kartoffeleinlage; **hot potato** N (*fig inf*) heißes Eisen; **hot rod** N (*Aut*) hoch frisiertes Auto; **hot seat** N Schleudersitz *m*; (*US, inf*, = *electric chair*) elektrischer Stuhl; **to be in the ~** auf dem Schleudersitz sein; (*in quiz etc*) auf dem Armsünderbänkchen sitzen (*hum*); **to step into the ~** auf den Schleudersitz kommen; **hot shoe** N (*Phot*) Steckschuh *m*; **hotshot** (*inf*) N Kanone *f* (*inf*), Ass *nt* (*inf*) ADJ *attr* Spitzen- (*inf*), erstklassig; **hot spot** N (*Pol*) Krisenherd *m*; (*inf*: = *club etc*) heißer Schuppen (*inf*); **hot spring** N heiße Quelle, Thermalquelle *f*; **hot stuff** N (*inf*) **this is ~** (= *very good*) das ist große Klasse (*inf*); (= *provocative*) das ist Zündstoff; **she's/he's ~** (= *very good*) sie/er ist große Klasse (*inf*) or eine Kanone (*inf*); (= *very sexy*) das ist eine Klassefrau (*inf*) or scharfe Braut (*sl*)/ein scharfer Typ (*inf*); **hot-tempered** ADJ leicht aufbrausend, jähzornig

Hottentot [ˈhɒtntɒt] N **a** Hottentotte *m*, Hottentottin *f* **b** (*Ling*) Hottentottisch *nt* ADJ hottentottisch

hottie [ˈhɒtɪ] N (*Austral inf*) Wärmflasche *f*

hot-water bottle [ˌhɒtˈwɔːtəˌbɒtl] N Wärmflasche *f*

hommos, houm(o)us [ˈhuːməs] N orientalische Creme aus Kichererbsen, Sesam und Knoblauch

hound [haʊnd] N **a** (*Hunt*) (Jagd)hund *m*; **the ~s lost the scent** die Meute verlor die Spur; **to ride to ~s** (*person*) mit der Meute jagen **b** (*any dog*) Hund *m*, Tier *nt* VT hetzen, jagen; **to be ~ed** gehetzt sein; **to be ~ed by the press** von der Presse verfolgt werden

▸**hound down** VT *sep* Jagd machen auf (+*acc*), niederhetzen (*form*); *criminal also* zur Strecke bringen

▸**hound out** VT *sep* verjagen, vertreiben (*of* aus)

hound's-tooth (check) [ˈhaʊndztuːθ(ˌtʃek)] N Hahnentritt(muster *nt*) *m*

hour [ˈaʊə'] N **a** Stunde *f*; (= *time of day*) Zeit *f*; **half an ~, a half ~** eine halbe Stunde; **three-quarters of an ~** eine Dreiviertelstunde, drei viertel Stunden; **a quarter of an ~** eine Viertelstunde, eine viertel Stunde; **an ~ and a half** anderthalb or eineinhalb Stunden; **it's two ~s' walk from here** von hier geht man zwei Stunden, von hier sind es zu Fuß zwei Stunden; **two ~s' walk from here there is an old castle** nach einem Weg von zwei Stunden kommt man an ein altes Schloss or zu einem alten Schloss; **at 1500/1530 ~s** um 15.00/15.30 Uhr; **at fifteen hundred/fifteen thirty ~s** (*spoken*) um fünfzehn Uhr/fünfzehn Uhr dreißig; ~ **by** ~ mit jeder Stunde, stündlich; ~ **after** ~ Stunde um Stunde; **on the ~** zur vollen Stunde; **every** ~ **on the ~** jede volle Stunde; **20 minutes past the ~** 20 Minuten nach; **at the ~ of his death** in der Stunde seines Todes, in seiner Todesstunde; **at an early ~** früh, zu früher Stunde (*geh*); **at a late ~** spät, zu später Stunde (*geh*); **at all ~s (of the day and night)** zu jeder (Tages- und Nacht)zeit; **what! at this ~ of the night!** was! zu dieser nachtschlafenden Zeit!; **what is the ~?** (*old*) wie viel Uhr ist es?; **to drive at 50 kilometres an ~** 50 Kilometer in der Stunde or 50 Stundenkilometer fahren; **a 30 mile(s) an ~ limit** eine Geschwindigkeitsbegrenzung von 30 Meilen in der Stunde; **to be paid by the ~** stundenweise bezahlt werden; **she is paid £6 an ~** sie bekommt £6 pro Stunde **b** **hours** PL (*inf*, = *a long time*) Stunden *pl*; **for ~s** stundenlang; ~**s and ~s** Stunden und aber Stunden; **I was ~s late** ich war sehr spät dran (*inf*), ich hatte mich um Stunden verspätet; **the train was ~s late** der Zug hatte Stunden Verspätung; **he took ~s to do it** er brauchte ewig lang (*inf*) or stundenlang dazu **c** **hours** PL (*of banks, shops etc*) Geschäftszeit(en) *f(pl)*; (*of pubs, park etc*) Öffnungszeiten *pl*; (*of post office*) Schalterstunden *pl*; (= *office hours*) Dienststunden *pl*; (= *working hours etc*) Arbeitszeit *f*; (*of doctor etc*) Sprechstunde *f*; **out of/after** ~**s** (*of shops etc*) außerhalb der gesetzlich erlaubten Zeit/ nach der Polizeistunde; (*of school*) außerhalb der Unterrichtszeit/nach Schulschluss; (*in shops etc*) außerhalb der Geschäftszeit(en)/ nach Laden- or Geschäftsschluss; (*in office etc*) außerhalb der Arbeitszeit/nach Dienstschluss; (*of doctor etc*) außerhalb/nach der Sprechstunde; **what are your ~s?** (*shops, pubs etc*) wann haben Sie geöffnet or offen?; (*employee*) wie ist Ihre Arbeitszeit?; **the ~s are good** die Arbeitszeit ist günstig; **to work long ~s** einen langen Arbeitstag haben; (*doctors, nurse, policeman etc*) lange Dienststunden haben **d** (*fig*) **his ~ has come** seine Stunde ist gekommen; (= *death also*) sein (letztes) Stündchen hat geschlagen; **in the ~ of danger** in der Stunde der Gefahr; **the man/hero of the ~** der Mann/Held der Stunde; **the issue of the ~** die aktuelle Frage

hour: hourglass N Sanduhr *f*, Stundenglas *nt* (*old*) ADJ *figure* kurvenreich; **hour hand** N Stundenzeiger *m*, kleiner Zeiger

houri [ˈhuːrɪ] N (*Rel*) Huri *f*; (*fig*) orientalische Schönheit

hourly [ˈaʊəlɪ] ADJ **a** (= *every hour*) stündlich; **an ~ bus service** ein stündlich verkehrender Bus; **at ~ intervals** stündlich, jede Stunde; **at two-hourly intervals** alle zwei Stunden

b (= *per hour*) *earnings* pro Stunde; *worker, job* stundenweise bezahlt; *wage* or *pay* Stundenlohn *m*; ~ **rate** Stundensatz *m*; **they are engaged on an ~ rate** sie werden stundenweise engagiert; **an ~ fee** stundenweise Bezahlung; **on an ~ basis** stundenweise

ADV **a** (*lit*: = *every hour*) stündlich, jede Stunde; (*fig*) (= *constantly*) ständig; *diminish, grow* mit jeder Stunde; (= *at any moment*) *expect* stündlich, jeden Augenblick

b *pay* stundenweise; ~ **paid work/worker** stundenweise bezahlte Arbeit/Arbeitskraft

house [haʊs] N *pl* **houses** [ˈhaʊzɪz] **a** Haus *nt*; (= *household*) Haushalt *m*; **at my** ~ bei mir (zu Hause or zuhause (*Aus, Sw*)); **to my** ~ zu mir (nach Hause or nachhause (*Aus, Sw*)); **to keep**

~ **(for sb)** (jdm) den Haushalt führen; **to set up** ~ einen eigenen Hausstand gründen; (*in particular area*) sich niederlassen; **they set up** ~ **together** sie gründeten einen gemeinsamen Hausstand; **to play at** ~**s** Vater und Mutter spielen; **to put** or **set one's** ~ **in order** (*fig*) seine Angelegenheiten in Ordnung bringen; **he gets on like a** ~ **on fire with her** (*inf*) er kommt ausgezeichnet or prima (*inf*) mit ihr aus; **they get on like a** ~ **on fire** (*inf*) sie kommen ausgezeichnet miteinander aus; **as safe as** ~**s** (*Brit*) bombensicher (*inf*); **a steak** ~ ein Steakhaus *nt*; **a coffee** ~ ein Café *nt*; **House of God** or **the Lord** Haus *nt* Gottes, Gotteshaus *nt*; **a** ~ **of worship** ein Ort *m* des Gebets, ein Haus *nt* der Andacht

b (*Pol*) **the upper/lower** ~ das Ober-/Unterhaus; **House of Commons/Lords** (*Brit*) (britisches) Unter-/Oberhaus; **the House** (*Brit, inf*) das Parlament; (*as address also*) das Hohe Haus; **House of Representatives** (*US*) Repräsentantenhaus *nt*; **the Houses of Parliament** das Parlament(sgebäude)

c (= *family, line*) Haus *nt*, Geschlecht *nt*; **the House of Bourbon** das Haus Bourbon, das Geschlecht der Bourbonen

d (= *firm*) Haus *nt*; **on the** ~ auf Kosten des Hauses; (*on the company*) auf Kosten der Firma; **we ordered a bottle of** ~ **red** wir bestellten eine Flasche von dem roten Hauswein

e (*Theat*) Haus *nt*; (= *performance*) Vorstellung *f*; **to bring the** ~ **down** (*inf*) ein Bombenerfolg (beim Publikum) sein (*inf*)

f (*in boarding school*) Gruppenhaus *nt*; (*in day school*) *eine von mehreren Gruppen verschiedenaltriger Schüler, die z. B. in Wettkämpfen gegeneinander antreten*

g (*in debate*) House Versammlung *f*; **the motion before the House** das Diskussionsthema, das zur Debatte or Diskussion stehende Thema; **this House believes capital punishment should be reintroduced** wir stellen die Frage zur Diskussion, ob die Todesstrafe wieder eingeführt werden sollte; (*in conclusion*) die Anwesenden sind der Meinung, dass die Todesstrafe wieder eingeführt werden sollte

h full ~ (*Cards*) Full House *nt*; (= *bingo*) volle Karte

i (*Astrol*) Haus *nt*

VT [haʊz] *people, goods, collection* unterbringen; (*Tech also*) einbauen; **this building ~s three offices/ten families** in diesem Gebäude sind drei Büros/zehn Familien untergebracht, dieses Gebäude beherbergt drei Büros/zehn Familien; **the sauna is ~d in their garage** die Sauna befindet sich in ihrer Garage

---

HOUSE

Britisches und amerikanisches Englisch haben für Häuser und Wohnungen häufig verschiedene Ausdrücke. Mit **flat** (Brit) oder **apartment** (US) wird allgemein eine Wohnung innerhalb eines größeren Gebäudes bezeichnet. Bei einem **condominium** (US) handelt es sich um einen Wohnblock mit Eigentumswohnungen, dessen Gemeinschaftseinrichtungen allen Bewohnern gemeinsam gehören. **Terraced** (Brit) oder **row** (US) **houses** heißen die Reihenhäuser. Doppelhäuser heißen **semi-detached** (Brit) oder **duplex** (US) **houses**. **Detached houses** (Brit) sind frei stehende Eigenheime, die normalerweise von einem Garten umgeben sind. Für die USA typisch sind die **ranch houses** (US), lang gezogene, einstöckige Gebäude, und **colonials** (US), zweigeschossige Schindel- oder Backsteinhäuser im traditionellen Stil, denen eine überdachte Veranda vorgebaut ist.

---

house *in cpds* Haus-; **house arrest** N Hausarrest *m*; **houseboat** N Hausboot *nt*; **housebound** ADJ ans Haus gefesselt; **houseboy** N (*dated*) Hausdiener *m*; **housebreaker** N Einbrecher(in) *m(f)*; **housebreaking** N Einbruch(sdiebstahl) *m*; **house-broken** ADJ (*US*: = *house-trained*) stubenrein; **house call** N (*of* *doctor*) Hausbesuch *m*; **house captain** N (*Brit Sch*) (*in boarding school*) Haussprecher(in) *m(f)*, Hausälteste(r) *mf*; (*in day school*) Gruppensprecher(in) *m(f)*, Gruppenälteste(r) *mf*; **house cleaning** N **a** (= *cleaning*) Hausputz *m*, Großreinemachen *nt* **b** (*fig*) Säuberungsaktion *f*; **housecoat** N Morgenrock *or* -mantel *m*; **house detective** N (*in hotel, shop etc*) Hausdetektiv *m*; **house dog** N Haushund *m*; **housedress** N (*US*) Schürzenkleid *nt*; **housefly** N Stubenfliege *f*; **houseguest** N (Haus)gast *m*

household ['haʊshəʊld] **N** Haushalt *m*; **a male-only** ~ ein Haushalt, der nur aus Männern besteht **ATTR** Haushalts-; ~ **appliance** Haushaltsgerät *nt*; ~ **furniture** Wohnmöbel *pl*; ~ **chores** häusliche Pflichten *pl*, Hausarbeit *f*; ~ **goods** Hausrat *m*

Household Cavalry N (*Brit*) Gardekavallerie *f*

householder ['haʊshəʊldəʳ] N Haus-/Wohnungsinhaber(in) *m(f)*

household: household god N Hausgott *m*; **the telly has become the** ~ **in many homes** der Fernseher ist in vielen Familien zum Götzen geworden; **household insurance** N Hausratversicherung *f*; **household linen** N Tisch- und Bettwäsche *f*, Weißwäsche *f* (*dated*); **household name** N **to be a** ~ ein Begriff sein; **to become a** ~ zu einem Begriff werden; **household word** N Begriff *m*; **to become a** ~ zu einem Begriff werden

house: house-hunt VI auf Haussuche sein; **they have started** ~**ing** sie haben angefangen, nach einem Haus zu suchen; **house-hunting** N Haussuche *f*; **househusband** N Hausmann *m*; **house journal** N Hausnachrichten *pl*; **housekeeper** N Haushälterin *f*, Wirtschafterin *f*; (*in institution also*) Wirtschaftsleiterin *f*; **his wife is a good** ~ seine Frau ist eine gute Hausfrau; **housekeeping** N **a** Haushalten *nt* **b** (*Brit: also* **housekeeping money**) Haushalts- *or* Wirtschaftsgeld *nt*; **houseless** ['haʊslɪs] ADJ *person* obdachlos; *area* ohne Häuser, unbebaut; **house lights** PL Lichter *pl* im Saal; **house magazine** N = **house journal**; **housemaid** N Dienstmädchen *nt*; **housemaid's knee** N Schleimbeutelentzündung *f*; **houseman** N (*Brit*) Assistenzarzt *m*; **house martin** N Mehlschwalbe *f*; **housemaster** N (*Brit*) Erzieher *m*; (*on teaching staff*) Lehrer *m*, der für ein Gruppenhaus zuständig ist; **housemate** N **my** ~**s** meine Mitbewohner; **four young** ~**s** vier junge Mieter in einer Wohngemeinschaft; **housemistress** N (*Brit*) Erzieherin *f*; (*on teaching staff*) Lehrerin *f*, die für ein Gruppenhaus zuständig ist; **House music** N Hausmusik *f*; **house parent** N Hausvater *m/*-mutter *f*; ~**s** Hauseltern *pl*; **house party** N mehrtägige Einladung; (= *group invited*) Gesellschaft *f*; **house physician** N im (Kranken)haus wohnender Arzt *m*; (*in private clinic etc*) Haus- *or* Anstaltsarzt *m/*-ärztin *f*; **house plant** N Zimmerpflanze *f*; **house-proud** ADJ **she is** ~ sie ist eine penible Hausfrau; **houseroom** N **I wouldn't give it** ~ das wollte ich nicht geschenkt haben; **I wouldn't give him** ~ (*fig*) mit ihm möchte ich nichts zu tun haben; **house rule** N (*Bestimmung der*) Hausordnung *f*; **house-sit** VI **to** ~ **for sb** *während jds Abwesenheit in dessen Haus/Wohnung einziehen, um darauf aufzupassen*; **house-sitter** N Housesitter(in) *m(f)* (*jd, der während der Abwesenheit der Bewohner in ein Haus/eine Wohnung zieht, um darauf aufzupassen*); **house sparrow** N Haussperling *m*; **house style** N Stil *m* des Hauses; **house surgeon** N Chirurg(in) *m(f)* (*der/die im Krankenhaus selbst wohnt*); (*in private clinic*) Haus- *or* Anstaltschirurg(in) *m(f)*; **house-to-house** ADJ von Haus zu Haus; **a** ~ **search** eine Suche *or* Fahndung von Haus zu Haus; **to conduct** ~ **inquiries** von Haus zu Haus gehen und fragen; ~ **collection** Haussammlung *f*; **housetop** N (Haus)dach *nt*; **house-train** VT stubenrein machen; **house-trained** ADJ stubenrein; **House Un-American Activities Commit-**

tee N (*US Hist*) Senatsausschuss *m* zur Untersuchung unamerikanischer Umtriebe; **housewarming (party)** N Einzugsparty *f*; **to have a** ~ Einzug feiern; **housewife** N **a** (= *person*) Hausfrau *f* **b** ['hʌzɪf] (*dated:* = *sewing case*) Nähetui *nt*, Nähzeug *nt*; **housewifely** ADJ hausfraulich; **house wine** N Hauswein *m*; **housework** N Hausarbeit *f*

housey-housey ['haʊsɪ'haʊsɪ] N (*dated*) Lotto *nt*

housing ['haʊzɪŋ] N **a** (*act*) Unterbringung *f* **b** (= *houses*) Wohnungen *pl*; (*temporary*) Unterkunft *f* **c** (= *provision of houses*) Wohnungsbeschaffung *f*; (= *building of houses*) Wohnungsbau *m* **d** (*Tech*) Gehäuse *nt*

housing in cpds Wohnungs-; **housing association** N Wohnungsbaugesellschaft *f*; **housing benefit** N (*Brit*) Wohngeld *nt*; **housing complex** N Wohnungskomplex *m*; **housing conditions** PL Wohnbedingungen *or* -verhältnisse *pl*; **housing development**, (*Brit also*) **housing estate** N Wohnsiedlung *f*; **housing list** N Warteliste *f* für Sozialwohnungen; **housing market** N Wohnungsmarkt *m*; **housing programme**, (US) **housing program** N Wohnungsbeschaffungsprogramm *nt*; **housing scheme** N (= *estate*) Siedlung *f*; (= *project*) Siedlungsbauvorhaben *nt*; **housing stock** N Bestand *m* an Häusern und Wohnungen

hove [həʊv] *pret, ptp of* **heave** VT **d** VI **c**

hovel ['hɒvəl] N armselige Hütte; (*fig pej*) Bruchbude *f*, Loch *nt* (*inf*)

hover ['hɒvəʳ] VI **a** (*helicopter, insect*) schweben; (*bird*) schweben, stehen **b** (*fig*) **a smile** ~**ed on her lips** ein Lächeln lag auf ihren Lippen; **she** ~**ed on the verge of death** sie war dem Tode nahe; **to** ~ **on the brink of disaster** am Rande des Ruins stehen; **danger was** ~**ing all around them** ringsum lauerte Gefahr; **he** ~**ed between two alternatives** er schwankte zwischen zwei Alternativen; **he was** ~**ing between life and death** er schwebte zwischen Leben und Tod; **the exchange rate is** ~**ing around 110 yen to the dollar** der Wechselkurs bewegt sich um die 110 Yen für den Dollar **c** (*fig:* = *stand around*) herumstehen; **to** ~ **over sb** jdm nicht von der Seite weichen; **don't** ~ **over me** geh endlich weg; **a waiter** ~**ed at his elbow, waiting to refill his glass** ein Kellner schwebte herum und wartete nur darauf, nachzuschenken

▶ **hover about** (*Brit*) *or* **around** VI (*person*) herumlungern, herumhängen; (*helicopter, bird etc*) (in der Luft) kreisen; **he was hovering around, waiting to speak to us** er strich um uns herum und wartete auf eine Gelegenheit, mit uns zu sprechen VI +prep obj **to hover around sb/sth** um jdn/etw herumschleichen *or* -streichen, sich um jdn/etw herumdrücken; **the hostess hovered around her guests** die Gastgeberin umsorgte ihre Gäste mit (über)großer Aufmerksamkeit

hover: hovercraft N Luftkissenboot *nt*; **hoverport** N Anlegestelle *f* für Luftkissenboote; **hovertrain** N Luftkissenzug *m*

how¹ [haʊ] ADV **a** (*in what way*) wie; ~ **will we ever survive?** wie sollen wir nur *or* bloß überleben?; ~ **so?**, ~**'s that?**, ~ **come?** (*all inf*) wieso (denn das)?, wie kommt (denn) das?; ~ **do you mean?** (*inf*) wie meinst du das?; ~ **is that we** *or* ~ **come** (*inf*) **we earn less?** wieso *or* warum verdienen wir denn weniger?; ~ **is it that ...?** wie kommt es, dass ...?; ~ **I see** ~ **it is** ich verstehe (schon); ~**'s that for luck?** ist das nicht ein Glück?; ~ **do you know that?** woher wissen Sie das?; **to learn/know** ~ **to do sth** lernen/wissen, wie man etw macht; **I'd like to learn** ~ **to swim/drive** *etc* ich würde gerne schwimmen/Auto fahren *etc* lernen

    b (*in degree, quantity etc*) wie; ~ **nice!** wie nett!; ~ **much** (+*n, adj, adv*) wie viel; (+*vb*) wie viel; ~ **often do you visit them/go out?** wie oft besuchen Sie sie/gehen Sie aus?; ~ **many** wie viel, wie viele; **I can't**

tell you ~ **glad I was to leave** ich kann Ihnen gar nicht sagen, wie froh ich war, dort wegzukommen; ~ **would you like to ...?** hätten Sie Lust, ... zu ...?

    c (*regarding health, general situation etc*) ~ **do you do?** (*on introduction*) Guten Tag/Abend!, angenehm! (*form*); ~ **are you?** wie geht es Ihnen?; ~**'s life?** wie gehts?; ~**'s work/the new job?** *etc* was macht die Arbeit/die neue Stelle? *etc* (*inf*); ~ **are things at school/in the office?** *etc* wie gehts in der Schule/im Büro? *etc*; ~ **did the job interview go?** wie ist das Bewerbungsgespräch gelaufen?

    d ~ **about ...?** wie wäre es mit ...?; ~ **about it?** (*about suggestion*) wie wäre es damit?; ~ **about going for a walk?** wie wärs mit einem Spaziergang?; ~ **about we meet for lunch tomorrow?** wie wäre es, wenn wir uns morgen zum Mittagessen treffen?; **I've had enough,** ~ **about you?** mir reichts, wie siehts bei dir aus?

    e **and** ~! und ob *or* wie!; ~ **he's grown!** er ist aber *or* vielleicht groß geworden; **look** ~ **he's grown!** sieh mal, wie groß er geworden ist

    f (= *that*) dass; **she told me** ~ **she had seen him there** sie sagte mir, dass sie ihn dort gesehen hat

how² INTERJ (*Indian greeting*) hugh

howdah ['haʊdə] N Sänfte *f* (*auf Elefanten*)

howdy ['haʊdɪ] INTERJ (*US, inf*) Tag (*inf*)

how-d'ye-do ['haʊdjədu:] **INTERJ** Tag (*inf*), Tagchen (*inf*) **N** (= *palaver, fuss*) Theater *nt*; (= *argument also*) Krach *m*; **a fine** *or* **pretty** ~ eine schöne Bescherung (*inf*)

howe'er [haʊ'ɛəʳ] CONJ, ADV (*poet*) contr of **however**

however [haʊ'ɛvəʳ] ✪ 26.1, 26.2, 26.3 **CONJ** **a** jedoch, aber; ~**, we finally succeeded** wir haben es schließlich doch noch geschafft **b** (*inf,* = *oh well*) na ja (*inf*), nun ja (*inf*) **ADV** **a** (= *no matter how*) wie ... auch, egal wie (*inf*); (= *in whatever way*) wie; ~ **strong he is** wie stark er auch ist, egal wie stark er ist (*inf*); ~ **you do it** wie immer du es machst, wie du es auch machst; **do it** ~ **you like** machs, wie du willst; **buy it** ~ **expensive it is** kaufen Sie es, egal, was es kostet; ~ **much you** und wenn du noch so weinst, wie sehr du auch weinst; **wait 30 minutes or** ~ **long it takes** warte eine halbe Stunde oder so lange, wie es dauert; ~ **that may be** wie dem auch sei **b** (*in question*) wie ... bloß *or* nur; ~ **did you manage it?** wie hast du das bloß *or* nur geschafft?

howitzer ['haʊɪtsəʳ] N Haubitze *f*

howl [haʊl] **N** **a** Schrei *m*; (*of animal, wind*) Heulen *nt no pl*; **the dog let out a** ~ der Hund heulte auf *or* jaulte; **a** ~ **of pain** ein Schmerzensschrei *m*; ~**s of derision/rage** höhnisches/wütendes Geschrei *or* Gebrüll; ~**s of laughter** brüllendes Gelächter; ~**s (of protest)** Protestgeschrei *nt* **b** (*from loudspeaker*) Pfeifen *nt no pl*, Rückkopp(e)lung *f* **VI** **a** (*person*) brüllen, schreien; (*animal*) heulen, jaulen; (*wind*) heulen; **to** ~ **with laughter** in brüllendes Gelächter ausbrechen; **to** ~ **with delight** vor Freude schreien **b** (= *weep noisily*) heulen; (*baby*) schreien, brüllen (*inf*) **c** (*Elec, loudspeaker etc*) rückkoppeln, pfeifen **VT** hinausbrüllen, hinausschreien; **they** ~**ed their disapproval** sie äußerten lautstark ihr Missfallen

▶ **howl down** VT sep niederbrüllen, niederschreien

howler ['haʊləʳ] N (*Brit inf*) Hammer *m* (*inf*), Schnitzer *m* (*inf*); **he made a real** ~ da hat er sich (*dat*) einen Hammer geleistet (*inf*); **stylistic** ~ Stilblüte *f* (*hum*)

howling ['haʊlɪŋ] **N** (*of person*) Gebrüll *nt*, Geschrei *nt*; (= *noisy crying, of animal*) Heulen *nt*, Geheul *nt*; (*of wind*) Heulen *nt*; **stop that child's** ~! bring das Kind zum Schweigen! **ADJ** **a** (*lit*) heulend **b** (*inf,* = *tremendous*) enorm; **a** ~ **success** ein Riesenerfolg *m*

howsoever [ˌhaʊsəʊˈevəʳ] (*old, form*) **ADV** wie auch (immer); **~ bad the situation may seem** wie schlecht die Lage auch (immer) aussehen mag **CONJ** **~ that may be** wie dem auch sei

hoy [hɔɪ] **INTERJ** he

hoyden [ˈhɔɪdn] **N** wilde Range (*dated*), Wildfang *m* (*dated*)

hoydenish [ˈhɔɪdənɪʃ] **ADJ** rangenhaft (*dated*), wild, ungestüm

HP, hp **a** *abbr of* **hire purchase** **b** *abbr of* **horse power** PS

HQ *abbr of* **headquarters**

hr *abbr of* **hour** Std.

HR abbr *of* **human resources**

HRH *abbr of* **His/Her Royal Highness** S. M./I. M.

HRT *abbr of* **hormone replacement therapy**

HSS (*US*) *abbr of* **Health and Social Services** *das amerikanische Gesundheits- und Sozialministerium*

HST **a** (*Brit*) *abbr of* **high speed train** Hochgeschwindigkeitszug *m* **b** (*US*) *abbr of* **Hawaiian Standard Time** hawaiische Zeit

ht *abbr of* **height**

HTML (*Comput*) *abbr of* **hypertext mark-up language** HTML

HTTP, http (*Comput*) *abbr of* **hypertext transfer protocol** http

HUAC (*US Hist*) *abbr of* **House Un-American Activities Committee**

hub [hʌb] **N** **a** (*of wheel*) (Rad)nabe *f* **b** (*fig*) Zentrum *nt*, Mittelpunkt *m*; **a ~ of finance** ein finanzielles Zentrum; **the ~ of the universe** der Nabel der Welt; **a ~ of activity** das reinste Bienenhaus; **the island's social ~** der gesellschaftliche Mittelpunkt der Insel

hub airport **N** (*US*) Großflughafen *m*

hubble-bubble [ˈhʌblˈbʌbl] **N** **a** (*Brit*: = *pipe*) Wasserpfeife *f* **b** (= *noise*) Brodeln *nt*

hubbub [ˈhʌbʌb] **N** Tumult *m*; **a ~ (of noise)** ein Radau *m*; **a ~ of voices** ein Stimmengewirr *nt*

hubby [ˈhʌbɪ] **N** (*inf*) Mann *m*

hubcap [ˈhʌbkæp] **N** Radkappe *f*

hubris [ˈhjuːbrɪs] **N** (*liter*) Anmaßung *f*; (*esp in Greek drama*) Hybris *f*

huckleberry [ˈhʌklbərɪ] **N** amerikanische Heidelbeere

huckster [ˈhʌkstəʳ] **N** **a** (= *hawker*) Straßenhändler(in) *m(f)* **b** (*US, inf*) Reklamefritze *m* (*inf*)

huddle [ˈhʌdl] **N** (wirrer) Haufen *m*; (*of people*) Gruppe *f*; **in a ~** dicht zusammengedrängt; **to go into a ~** (*inf*) die Köpfe zusammenstecken **VI** (*also* **to be huddled**) (sich) kauern; **they ~d under the umbrella** sie drängten sich unter dem Schirm zusammen; **we ~d around the fire** wir saßen eng zusammengedrängt um das Feuer herum; **small sheds, ~d under the trees** kleine Hütten, die sich unter die Bäume kauerten; **the president was ~d with his aides** der Präsident und seine Berater steckten die Köpfe zusammen

▶ **huddle down** **VI** sich kuscheln

▶ **huddle together** **VI** sich aneinander kauern; **to be huddled together** aneinander kauern

▶ **huddle up** **VI** sich zusammenkauern; **to be huddled up** zusammenkauern; **to huddle up against sb/sth** sich an jdn/etw kauern

hue¹ [hjuː] **N** (= *colour*) Farbe *f*; (= *shade*) Schattierung *f*; (*fig*: = *political leaning*) Schattierung *f*, Färbung *f*, Couleur *f* (*geh*)

hue² **N** **~ and cry** Zeter und Mordio (*against* gegen); **to set up** *or* **raise a ~ and cry** Zeter und Mordio schreien

huff [hʌf] **N** **to be/go off in a ~** beleidigt *or* eingeschnappt sein/abziehen (*inf*); **to get into a ~** einschnappen (*inf*), den Beleidigten spielen **VI** **to ~ and puff** (*inf*) schnaufen und keuchen

huffily [ˈhʌfɪlɪ] **ADV** beleidigt

huffiness [ˈhʌfɪnɪs] **N** Beleidigtsein *nt*; (= *touchiness*) Empfindlichkeit *f*; **the ~ in his voice** sein beleidigter Ton

huffy [ˈhʌfɪ] **ADJ** (*+er*) (= *in a huff*) beleidigt; (= *touchy*) empfindlich; **to get/be ~ about sth** wegen etw eingeschnappt (*inf*) *or* beleidigt sein; **he's quite a ~ person** er ist leicht beleidigt *or* eingeschnappt (*inf*)

hug [hʌg] **N** Umarmung *f*; **to give sb a ~** jdn umarmen **VT** **a** (= *hold close*) umarmen; (*bear etc*) umklammern; (*fig*) *hope, belief* sich klammern an (*+acc*); **to ~ sb/sth to oneself** jdn/etw an sich (*acc*) pressen *or* drücken; **she ~ged her legs tight to her** sie schlang die Arme eng um die Beine

b (= *keep close to*) sich dicht halten an (*+acc*); (*car, ship etc also*) dicht entlangfahren an (*+dat*) **VI** umarmen; **we ~ged and kissed** wir umarmten und küssten uns **VR** **a** **to ~ oneself to keep warm** die Arme verschränken, damit einem warm ist; **she stood ~ging herself** sie stand mit verschränkten Armen da

b **he ~ged himself with pleasure** er war sehr zufrieden mit sich selbst

huge [hjuːdʒ] **ADJ** (*+er*) riesig; *appetite, thirst, disappointment, deficit, selection* Riesen- (*inf*); *effort* gewaltig; *problem, difference, increase* riesig, enorm; **a ~ success** ein Riesenerfolg (*inf*); **a ~ city** eine Riesenstadt (*inf*); **a ~ job** eine Riesenarbeit (*inf*); **~ numbers of these children** ungeheuer viele von diesen Kindern; **human suffering on a ~ scale** unermessliches menschliches Leiden

hugely [ˈhjuːdʒlɪ] **ADV** (*emph*) *successful, expensive, important, entertaining, talented* außerordentlich, ungeheuer; *enjoy oneself* riesig; *vary, increase* ungemein; **the whole thing is ~ enjoyable** das Ganze macht ungeheuer viel Spaß; **I enjoyed the play ~** das Stück hat mir ausgesprochen gut gefallen

hugeness [ˈhjuːdʒnɪs] **N** gewaltiges *or* riesiges Ausmaß

Huguenot [ˈhjuːgənəʊ] **ADJ** hugenottisch **N** Hugenotte *m*, Hugenottin *f*

huh [hʌ] **INTERJ** was; (*derision*) haha

hula [ˈhuːlə] **N** Hula-(Hula) *m or f*; **to do the ~(-hula)** Hula-(Hula) tanzen

Hula Hoop® **N** Hula-Hoop-Reifen *m*

hula skirt **N** Bastrock *m*

hulk [hʌlk] **N** **a** (*Naut*: = *body of ship*) (Schiffs)rumpf *m* **b** (*inf*: = *person*) Hüne *m* (*inf*); **I followed his big ~ into the room** ich folgte seiner hünenhaften Gestalt ins Zimmer **c** (= *wrecked vehicle*) Wrack *nt*; (= *wrecked building etc*) Ruine *f*

hulking [ˈhʌlkɪŋ] **ADJ** **~ great, great ~** massig; **a great ~ wardrobe** ein Ungetüm *nt* von einem Kleiderschrank; **a ~ great brute of a man** ein grobschlächtiger, brutaler Kerl; **a ~ great brute of a dog** ein scheußliches Ungetüm von einem Hund

hull¹ [hʌl] **N** (*Naut*) Schiffskörper *m*; (*Aviat*) Rumpf *m*; **ship ~ down on the horizon** Schiff in Sicht am Horizont

hull² **N** Hülse *f*; (*of peas also*) Schote *f*; (*of barley, oats also*) Spelze *f*; (*of strawberries etc*) Blättchen *nt* **VT** schälen; *beans, peas* enthülsen; *strawberries etc* entstielen

hullabaloo [ˌhʌləbəˈluː] **N** (*Brit inf*) Spektakel *nt*; (= *noise also*) Radau *m*; **I don't know what all the ~ is about** ich verstehe nicht, was das ganze Theater eigentlich soll (*inf*)

hullo [hʌˈləʊ] **INTERJ** (*Brit*) = **hello**

hum [hʌm] **N** **a** (*of insect, person*) Summen *nt*; (*of traffic*) Brausen *nt*; (*of engine, electric tool, radio, top etc*) Brummen *nt*; (*of small machine, camera etc*) Surren *nt*; (*of voices*) Gemurmel *nt*

b (*inf*: = *smell*) Gestank *m* (*inf*) **VI** **a** (*insect, person*) summen; (*traffic*) brausen; (*engine, electric tool, radio, top etc*) brummen; (*small machine, camera etc*) surren; **the lines were**

~ming with the news (*fig*) die Drähte liefen heiß

b (*fig inf*: *party, concert etc*) in Schwung kommen; **to make things/the party ~** die Sache/die Party in Schwung bringen; **the headquarters was ~ming with activity** im Hauptquartier ging es zu wie in einem Bienenstock

c **to ~ and haw** (*inf*) herumdrucksen (*inf*) (*over, about* um)

d (*inf*, = *smell*) stinken (*inf*) **VT** *music, tune* summen **INTERJ** hm

human [ˈhjuːmən] **ADJ** menschlich; *health, brain, part of the body* des Menschen; **~ dignity** Menschenwürde; **~ sacrifice** Menschenopfer *nt*; **not fit for ~ consumption** zum Verzehr (durch den Menschen) ungeeignet; **~ error** menschliches Versagen; **~ capital** Menschenkapital *nt*; **~ chain** Menschenkette *f*; **~ shield** menschlicher Schutzschild; **I'm only ~** ich bin auch nur ein Mensch; **that's only ~** das ist doch nur menschlich; **these footprints certainly aren't ~** diese Fußspuren sind *or* stammen sicher nicht von Menschen **N** Mensch *m*

human being **N** Mensch *m*

humane [hjuːˈmeɪn] **ADJ** **a** (= *considerate*) *person, society, decision, treatment, prison* human; *treatment of people* menschenwürdig, human; *rearing of animals* unter humanen Bedingungen; **a ~ method of killing animals** eine möglichst schmerzlose Methode, Tiere zu töten **b** (*form*: = *civilizing*) *education* humanistisch

humanely [hjuːˈmeɪnlɪ] **ADV** *treat human*; *treat people also* menschenwürdig; *rear animals* unter humanen Bedingungen; *destroy, slaughter, kill* (möglichst) schmerzlos; **to destroy an animal ~** (= *put to sleep*) ein Tier einschläfern

human interest **N** (*in newspaper story etc*) Emotionalität *f*; **a ~ story** eine ergreifende Story; **the film's main ~ is centred on this relationship** auf der menschlichen Ebene dreht sich der Film hauptsächlich um diese Beziehung

humanism [ˈhjuːmənɪzəm] **N** Humanismus *m*

humanist [ˈhjuːmənɪst] **N** Humanist(in) *m(f)* **ADJ** humanistisch

humanistic [ˌhjuːməˈnɪstɪk] **ADJ** humanistisch

humanitarian [hjuːˌmænɪˈtɛərɪən] **N** Vertreter(in) *m(f)* des Humanitätsgedankens **ADJ** humanitär

humanitarianism [ˌhjuːmænɪˈtɛərɪənɪzəm] **N** Humanitarismus *m*; (*of individual*) humanitäre Gesinnung

humanity [hjuːˈmænɪtɪ] **N** **a** (= *mankind*) die Menschheit **b** (= *humaneness*) Menschlichkeit *f*, Menschenhaftigkeit *f* **c** (= *humaneness*) Humanität *f*, Menschlichkeit *f*; **to treat sb with ~** jdn human behandeln **d** **humanities** PL Geisteswissenschaften *pl*; (= *Latin and Greek*) Altphilologie *f*

humanize [ˈhjuːmənaɪz] **VT** humanisieren

humankind [ˌhjuːmənˈkaɪnd] **N** die Menschheit

humanly [ˈhjuːmənlɪ] **ADV** menschlich; **~ comprehensible** für den Menschen verständlich; **the ~ constructed world** die vom Menschen gebaute Welt; **as far as ~ possible** soweit es überhaupt möglich ist, soweit überhaupt möglich; **as safe as ~ possible** so sicher wie überhaupt möglich; **to do all that is** *or* **everything ~ possible** alles Menschenmögliche tun

human nature **N** die menschliche Natur; **it's ~ to do that** es liegt (nun einmal) in der Natur des Menschen, das zu tun

humanoid [ˈhjuːmənɔɪd] **ADJ** menschenähnlich **N** (*esp in science fiction*) (= *robot*) menschenähnlicher Roboter; (= *creature*) menschenähnliches Lebewesen

human: human race **N the ~** die Menschheit, das Menschengeschlecht (*geh*); **human resources** PL (= *people*) Personal *nt*, Arbeitskräfte *pl*; **human-resources** ADJ ATTR Personal-; **~ department** Personalabteilung *f*; **~ manager** Personalleiter(in) *m(f)*; **human rights** PL Menschenrechte *pl*; **~ organization** Menschenrechtsorganisation f; ~ **activist** Menschenrecht-ler(in) m(f); **human touch** N **the** ~ die menschliche Wärme; **to lack the** ~ nichts Menschliches haben

humble ['hʌmbl] **ADJ** (+er) **a** (= modest) person bescheiden, demütig (esp Rel); apology demütig; **my** ~ **apologies!** ich bitte inständig um Verzeihung!; **to be** ~ **about one's origins** mit seiner Herkunft nicht angeben; **to eat** ~ **pie** klein beigeben; **in my** ~ **opinion** meiner bescheidenen Meinung nach → **servant**

b (= lowly) curate, clerk, beginner einfach; origins niedrig, einfach; background, beginnings bescheiden; **of** ~ **origins/birth** von niedriger Herkunft/Geburt

c (= insignificant) abode, restaurant, potato, maggot bescheiden

VT (= crush) demütigen; **to** ~ **oneself** sich demütigen or erniedrigen; **to be/feel** ~**d** sich (dat) klein vorkommen, sich gedemütigt fühlen

humblebee ['hʌmbl,biː] N Hummel f

humbleness ['hʌmblnɪs] N (= modesty, insignificance) Bescheidenheit f; (= lowliness) Einfachheit f; (esp Rel: = meekness, humility) Demut f

humbly ['hʌmblɪ] **ADV** (= unassumingly, with deference) bescheiden, demütig (esp Rel); (= in a lowly way) einfach, bescheiden; ~ **born** von niedriger Geburt; **I** ~ **submit this little work** in aller Bescheidenheit überreiche ich diese kleine Arbeit; **he** ~ **apologized** sie entschuldigte sich kleinlaut or zerknirscht; **he** ~ **agreed that he was wrong** er gab kleinlaut zu, dass er Unrecht hatte; **I most** ~ **beg your pardon** ich bitte ergebenst um Verzeihung

humbug ['hʌmbʌg] N **a** (Brit: = sweet) Pfefferminzbonbon m or nt **b** (inf: = talk) Humbug m, Mumpitz m (inf) **c** (inf: = person) Halunke m, Gauner(in) m(f)

humdinger ['hʌmdɪŋəʳ] N (inf, = person, thing) **to be a** ~ Spitze or große Klasse sein (inf); **a** ~ **of a job/girl** etc ein klasse Job/Mädchen etc (inf); **a** ~ **of a hangover** ein Kater, der sich gewaschen hat (inf); **he hit him with a real** ~ **of a left hook** er landete einen erstklassigen linken Haken bei ihm (inf)

humdrum ['hʌmdrʌm] **ADJ** stumpfsinnig

humerus ['hjuːmərəs] N Oberarmknochen m

humid ['hjuːmɪd] **ADJ** feucht; **it's (hot and)** ~ **today** es ist schwül heute

humidifier [hjuːˈmɪdɪfaɪəʳ] N Luftbefeuchter m; (= humidification system) Luftbefeuchtungsanlage f

humidify [hjuːˈmɪdɪfaɪ] **VT** air befeuchten; **to** ~ **a room** die Luft in einem Zimmer befeuchten

humidity [hjuːˈmɪdɪtɪ] N (Luft)feuchtigkeit f

humidor ['hjuːmɪdɔːʳ] N Feuchtraum m

humiliate [hjuːˈmɪlɪeɪt] **VT** demütigen, erniedrigen; **to** ~ **oneself** sich beschämen

humiliating [hjuːˈmɪlɪeɪtɪŋ] **ADJ** defeat, experience demütigend; blow, conditions beschämend

humiliatingly [hjuːˈmɪlɪeɪtɪŋlɪ] **ADV** beschämend; lose, be defeated, concede beschämenderweise; (introducing sentence) zu seiner/ihrer etc Beschämung

humiliation [hjuːˌmɪlɪˈeɪʃən] N Demütigung f, Erniedrigung f; (because of one's own actions) Beschämung f no pl; **much to my** ~ sehr zu meiner Schande or Beschämung; **she couldn't hide her** ~ sie konnte das Gefühl der Demütigung/Beschämung nicht verbergen; **the result is a** ~ **for the prime minister** das Ergebnis ist eine demütigende Niederlage für den Premierminister

humility [hjuːˈmɪlɪtɪ] N Demut f; (= unassumingness) Bescheidenheit f

humming ['hʌmɪŋ] N (of insect, person) Summen nt; (of traffic) Brausen nt; (of engine, electric tool, radio, top etc) Brummen nt; (of small machine, camera etc) Surren nt; (of voices) Murmeln nt, Gemurmel nt

humming: hummingbird N Kolibri m; **humming top** N Brummkreisel m

hummock ['hʌmək] N (kleiner) Hügel m

hummus ['hʊməs] N = **hoummos**

humongous [hjuːˈmɒŋgəs] **ADJ** (inf) wahnsinnig groß (inf), Riesen- (inf); **she's a** ~ **star** sie ist ein Riesenstar (inf); **we had a** ~ **row** wir hatten einen Riesenkrach (inf)

humor etc (US) = **humour** etc

humorist ['hjuːmərɪst] N Humorist(in) m(f)

humorous ['hjuːmərəs] **ADJ** person, speech, comment humorvoll; book, story etc also, situation lustig, komisch; idea, thought witzig; smile, programme lustig, heiter; **to see the** ~ **side of sth** die lustige or komische Seite an etw (dat) sehen

humorously ['hjuːmərəslɪ] **ADV** humorvoll, witzig; reflect, smile, say heiter

humour, (US) **humor** ['hjuːməʳ] **N** **a** Humor m; **a sense of** ~ (Sinn m für) Humor m; **their own inimitable brand of** ~ ihre eigene unnachahmliche Art von Humor; **a story full of** ~ eine humorvolle Geschichte; **I don't see the** ~ **in that** ich finde das gar nicht komisch; **there was little room for** ~ es war nicht die Zeit für Witze

b (= mood) Stimmung f, Laune f; **to be in a good** ~ in guter Stimmung sein, gute Laune haben; **with good** ~ gut gelaunt; **to be out of** ~, **to be in a bad** ~ schlechte Laune haben, schlecht gelaunt sein

c (old Med) Körpersaft m

VT **to** ~ **sb** jdm seinen Willen lassen or tun; **do it just to** ~ **him** tus doch, damit er seinen Willen hat

-humoured, (US) **-humored** ['hjuːməd] **ADJ** suf gelaunt; **good-/ill-humoured** gut/schlecht gelaunt

humourless, (US) **humorless** ['hjuːməlɪs] **ADJ** humorlos, ohne jeden Humor; speech, laugh, book etc also trocken

humourlessly, (US) **humorlessly** ['hjuːməlɪslɪ] **ADV** humorlos, ohne jeden Humor

hump [hʌmp] **N** **a** (Anat) Buckel m; (of camel) Höcker m **b** (= hillock) Hügel m, Buckel m (esp S Ger); **we're over the** ~ **now** (fig) wir sind jetzt über den Berg **c** (Brit inf) **he's got the** ~ er ist sauer (inf); **he/that gives me the** ~ er/das fällt mir auf den Wecker (inf) **VT** **a** **to** ~ **one's back** einen Buckel machen **b** (inf: = carry) schleppen; (on back, shoulders) auf dem Rücken/den Schultern tragen or schleppen **c** (inf: = have sex with) bumsen (inf)

humpback ['hʌmpbæk] N (= person) Buck(e)lige(r) mf; (= back) Buckel m

humpbacked ['hʌmpbækt] **ADJ** person buck(e)lig; bridge gewölbt

humpbacked whale N Buckelwal m

humped [hʌmpt] **ADJ** buck(e)lig

humph [mm] **INTERJ** hm

humpy ['hʌmpɪ] **ADJ** (+er) country hügelig, buckelig (esp S Ger)

humungous [hjuːˈmʌŋgəs] **ADJ** (inf) = **humongous**

humus ['hjuːməs] N Humus m

Hun [hʌn] N **a** (Hist) Hunne m, Hunnin f **b** (pej inf) Teutone m (pej), Teutonin f (pej), Boche m (pej)

hunch [hʌntʃ] **N** **a** (= hump on sb's back) Buckel m **b** (= premonition) Gefühl nt, Ahnung f; **to act on a** ~ einem inneren Gefühl zufolge handeln; **to have a** ~ **that ...** den (leisen (inf)) Verdacht or das (leise) Gefühl haben, dass ...; **your** ~ **paid off** du hattest die richtige Ahnung, es hat sich gelohnt **VT** (also **hunch up**) **to** ~ **one's back** einen Buckel machen, den Rücken krümmen; **to** ~ **one's shoulders** die Schultern hochziehen; **to** ~ **oneself over sth** sich über etw (acc) beugen; **he was** ~**ed over his desk** er saß über seinen Schreibtisch gebeugt; ~**ed up in pain** vor Schmerzen gekrümmt

hunch: hunchback N (= person) Buck(e)lige(r) mf; (= back) Buckel m; **The Hunchback of Notre Dame** der Glöckner von Notre-Dame; **hunchbacked** **ADJ** buck(e)lig

hundred ['hʌndrɪd] **ADJ** hundert; **a** or **one** ~ **years** (ein)hundert Jahre; **two/several** ~ **years** zweihundert/mehrere hundert or Hundert Jahre; **a** or **one** ~ **and one** (lit) (ein)hundert(und)-eins; (fig) tausend; **a** or **one** ~ **and two/ten** (ein)hundert(und)zwei/-zehn; (**one**) ~ **and first/second** etc hundert(und)erste(r, s)/-zweite(r, s) etc; **a** or **one** ~ **thousand** (ein)hundert-tausend; **a** ~**-mile walk** ein Hundertmeilenmarsch; **a** or **one** ~ **per cent** hundert Prozent; **a (one)** ~ **per cent increase** eine hundertprozentige Erhöhung, eine Erhöhung von or um hundert Prozent; **a** or **one** ~ **per cent inflation** eine Inflationsrate von hundert Prozent; **I'm not a** or **one** ~ **per cent fit/sure** ich bin nicht hundertprozentig fit/sicher; **I agree with you one** ~ **per cent** ich stimme hundertprozentig mit Ihnen überein; **the Hundred Years' War** (Hist) der Hundertjährige Krieg; **never in a** ~ **years!** nie im Leben!

N hundert num; (written figure) Hundert f; ~**s** (lit, fig) hunderte or Hunderte pl; (Math: figures in column) Hunderter pl; **to count in** ~**s** in hunderten or Hunderten zählen; **to count up to a** or **one** ~ bis hundert zählen; **the** ~**s column** (Math) die Hunderterspalte; **one in a** ~ einer unter hundert; **eighty out of a** ~ achtzig von hundert; **an audience of a** or **one/two** ~ hundert/zweihundert Zuschauer; ~**s of times** hundertmal, hunderte or Hunderte von Malen; ~**s and** ~**s** Hunderte und Aberhunderte, hunderte und aberhunderte; ~**s of** or **and thousands** hunderttausende or Hunderttausende pl; ~**s and thousands** (Cook) Liebesperlen pl; **he earns nine** ~ **a month** er verdient neunhundert im Monat; **I'll lay (you) a** ~ **to one** ich wette hundert gegen eins; **to sell sth by the** ~ (lit, fig) etw im Hundert verkaufen; **it'll cost you a** ~ das wird dich einen Hunderter kosten; **to live to be a** ~ hundert Jahre alt werden; **they came in (their)** ~**s** or **by the** ~ sie kamen zu hunderten or Hunderten

hundredfold ['hʌndrɪdfəʊld] **ADJ, ADV** hundertfach; **to increase a** ~ um das Hundertfache steigern

hundredth ['hʌndrɪdθ] **ADJ** (in series) hunderts-te(r, s); (of fraction) hundertstel **N** Hundertste(r, s) decl as adj; (= fraction) Hundertstel nt → also **sixth**

hundredweight ['hʌndrɪdweɪt] N Zentner m; (Brit) 50,8 kg; (US) 45,4 kg

hung [hʌŋ] pret, ptp of **hang** **ADJ** (inf: sexually) **the way he's** ~ wie er ausgestattet ist (inf); **to be** ~ **like a mule** ein Riesengehänge haben (inf)

Hungarian [hʌŋˈgeərɪən] **ADJ** ungarisch **N** **a** (= person) Ungar(in) m(f) **b** (Ling) Ungarisch nt

Hungary ['hʌŋgərɪ] N Ungarn nt

hunger ['hʌŋgəʳ] **N** **a** (lit) Hunger m; **to die of** ~ verhungern **b** (fig) Hunger m (for nach) **VI** (old, liter) hungern; **to** ~ **to do sth** danach hungern, etw zu tun

▶ **hunger after** or **for** VI +prep obj (liter) hungern nach; news sehnsüchtig warten auf (+acc)

hunger march N Hungermarsch m

hunger strike N **to be on (a)** ~ sich im Hungerstreik befinden; **to go on (a)** ~ in (den) Hungerstreik treten

hung over **ADJ** **to be** ~ einen Kater haben (inf); **to look** ~ verkatert aussehen (inf)

hung parliament N Parlament nt ohne klare Mehrheitsverhältnisse; **the election resulted in a** ~ die Wahl führte zu einem parlamentarischen Patt

hungrily ['hʌŋgrɪlɪ] **ADV** (lit, fig) hungrig

hungry ['hʌŋgrɪ] **ADJ** (+er) **a** (lit) hungrig; **to be** or **feel/get** ~ Hunger haben/bekommen; **to go** ~ hungern **b** (fig) hungrig; ~ **for knowledge/love/power** bildungs-/liebes-/machthungrig; **to be** ~ **for news** sehnsüchtig auf Nachricht warten; **to be** ~ **for fame/riches/company** sich nach Ruhm/Reichtum/Gesellschaft sehnen; **this is** ~ **work** das macht hungrig

hung up **ADJ** (inf) **to be/get** ~ **about sth** (= be neurotic) wegen etw einen Knacks weghaben (inf)/durchdrehen (inf); (= have complex) Komplexe wegen etw haben/kriegen; **he's really ~ about things like that** wenn es darum geht, hat er einen richtigen Knacks weg (*inf*); **to be ~ about being old/single** *etc* einen Komplex haben, weil man alt/nicht verheiratet *etc* ist; **he's ~ on her** (*inf*) er steht auf sie (*sl*)

hunk [hʌŋk] N **a** Stück *nt* **b** (*sl inf*, = *man*) **a gorgeous ~ (of a man)** ein Mann! (*inf*)

hunky-dory [ˈhʌŋkɪˈdɔːrɪ] ADJ (*inf*) **that's ~** das ist in Ordnung

hunt [hʌnt] **N** Jagd *f*; (= *huntsmen*) Jagd(gesellschaft) *f*; (*fig*: = *search*) Suche *f*; **tiger ~** Tigerjagd *f*; **the ~ is on** die Suche hat begonnen; **to have a ~ for sth** nach etw fahnden (*inf*), eine Suche nach etw veranstalten; **to be on the ~ for sth** (*for animal*) etw jagen, auf etw (*acc*) Jagd machen; (*fig*) auf der Suche *or* Jagd nach etw sein (*inf*)

VT **a** (*Hunt*) jagen; (= *search for*) *criminal* jagen, fahnden nach; *missing article etc* suchen; *missing person* suchen, fahnden nach; **~ the slipper/ thimble** Pantoffel-/Fingerhutverstecken *nt* **b** **to ~ a horse/hounds** zu Pferd/mit Hunden jagen

VI **a** (*Hunt*) jagen; **to go ~ing** jagen, auf die Jagd gehen **b** (= *search*) suchen (*for, after* nach); **to ~ for an animal** auf ein Tier Jagd machen; **he is ~ing for a job** er sucht eine Stelle

▶ **hunt about** *or* **around** VI herumsuchen *or* -kramen (*for* nach)

▶ **hunt down** VT *sep animal, person* (unerbittlich) Jagd machen auf (+*acc*); (= *capture*) zur Strecke bringen

▶ **hunt out** VT *sep* heraussuchen, hervorkramen (*inf*); *person, facts* ausfindig machen, aufstöbern (*inf*)

▶ **hunt up** VT *sep person* Nachforschungen anstellen über (+*acc*); *facts* ausfindig machen; *old clothes, records etc* kramen nach (+*dat*), hervorkramen; **hunt him up for me, would you?** sieh mal bitte nach, ob du ihn irgendwo auftreiben kannst

hunt-and-peck method N (*inf hum: typing*) Adlersuchsystem *nt*, Zweifingersystem *nt*

hunt ball N Jagdball *m*

hunter [ˈhʌntə'] N **a** (= *person*) Jäger(in) *m(f)*; (= *horse*) Jagdpferd *nt*; (= *dog*) Jagdhund *m* **b** (= *watch*) Sprungdeckeluhr *f* **c** (*Astron*) **the Hunter** Orion *m*

hunter-gatherer [ˌhʌntəˈgæðərə'] N Jäger und Sammler *m*; **they were hunters-gatherers** sie waren Jäger und Sammler

hunter-killer [ˌhʌntə'ˈkɪlə'] N Jagd-U-Boot *nt*

hunting [ˈhʌntɪŋ] N **a** die Jagd, das Jagen; **the ~ in these woods is excellent** diese Wälder sind ein gutes Jagdgebiet **b** (*fig*: = *search*) Suche *f* (*for* nach); **after a lot of ~ ...** nach langer Suche ...

hunting *in cpds* Jagd-; **hunting box** N Jagdhütte *f*, **hunting ground** N (*lit, fig*) Jagdrevier *nt*, Jagdgebiet *nt*; **to go to the happy ~s** in die ewigen Jagdgründe eingehen; **a happy ~** (*fig*) ein beliebtes *or* einträgliches Jagdrevier (*for* für); **hunting horn** N Jagdhorn *nt*; **hunting licence**, (*US*) **hunting license** N Jagdschein *m*; **hunting lodge** N Jagdhütte *f*; (*larger*) Jagdschloss *nt*; **hunting pink** N (= *colour*) Rot *nt* (*des Reitrockes*); (= *clothes*) roter (Jagd)rock

Huntington's chorea [ˌhʌntɪŋtənzkɔːˈrɪə], **Huntington's disease** [ˌhʌntɪŋtənzdɪˈziːz] N Chorea Huntington *f* (*spec*), huntingtonsche Krankheit

huntress [ˈhʌntrɪs] N Jägerin *f*

hunt saboteur N (*Brit*) *jd, der versucht, die Fuchsjagd durch Sabotageakte zu verhindern*, Jagdsaboteur(in) *m(f)*

huntsman [ˈhʌntsmən] N *pl* **-men** [-mən] Jagdreiter *m*

huntswoman [ˈhʌntswʊmən] N *pl* **-women** [-wɪmɪn] Jagdreiterin *f*

hurdle [ˈhɜːdl] **N** (*Sport, fig*) Hürde *f*; **~s** *sing* (= *race*) Hürdenlauf *m*; (*Horse Racing*) Hürdenren-

nen *nt*; **the 100m ~s** (die) 100 m Hürden, (der) 100-m-Hürdenlauf; **to fall at the first ~** (*fig*) (schon) über die erste *or* bei der ersten Hürde stolpern **VT** *fence* nehmen **VI** Hürdenlauf machen; **hurdling** der Hürdenlauf

hurdler [ˈhɜːdlə'] N (*Sport*) Hürdenläufer(in) *m(f)*

hurdle race N Hindernislauf *m*; (*Sport*) Hürdenlauf *m*; (*for horses*) Hindernisrennen *nt*

hurdy-gurdy [ˈhɜːdɪ,gɜːdɪ] N Leierkasten *m*, Drehorgel *f*

hurl [hɜːl] VT schleudern; **to ~ oneself at sb/into a chair** sich auf jdn stürzen/in einen Sessel werfen; **she ~ed herself from the roof** sie stürzte sich vom Dach; **they ~ed back their attackers** sie warfen ihre Angreifer zurück; **to ~ insults at sb** jdm Beleidigungen entgegenschleudern

hurly-burly [ˈhɜːlɪˈbɜːlɪ] N Getümmel *nt*, Rummel *m* (*inf*); **the ~ of politics** der Rummel der Politik

hurrah [hʊˈrɑː], **hurray** [hʊˈreɪ] INTERJ hurra; **~ for the king!** ein Hoch dem König!

hurricane [ˈhʌrɪkən] N Orkan *m*; (*tropical*) Hurrikan *m*; **~ force** Orkanstärke *f*

hurricane-force [ˈhʌrɪkən,fɔːs] ADJ **~ wind** Wind *m or* Orkanstärke

hurricane lamp N Sturmlaterne *f*

hurried [ˈhʌrɪd] ADJ *eilig; letter, essay* eilig *or* hastig geschrieben; *ceremony, meeting* hastig durchgeführt; *work* in Eile gemacht; (= *with little preparation*) *departure, wedding etc* überstürzt; **to have a ~ breakfast** hastig frühstücken; **a ~ goodbye** ein hastiger Abschied; **to pay sb a ~ visit** jdm einen hastigen Besuch abstatten

hurriedly [ˈhʌrɪdlɪ] ADV (= *rapidly*) eilig, hastig; *say* hastig; *leave* in großer Eile; **a ~ arranged press conference** eine hastig einberufene Pressekonferenz

hurry [ˈhʌrɪ] **N** Eile *f*; **in my ~ to get it finished ...** vor lauter Eile, damit fertig zu werden ...; **to do sth in a ~** etw schnell *or* (*too fast*) hastig tun; **I need it in a ~** ich brauche es schnell *or* eilig *or* dringend; **to be in a ~** es eilig haben, in Eile sein; **I'm in no particular ~** ich habe es nicht besonders eilig; **I'm in no ~ to leave home** ich will nicht so schnell von zu Hause ausziehen; **I won't do that again in a ~!** (*inf*) das mache ich so schnell nicht wieder!; **what's the ~?** was soll die Eile *or* Hast?; **what's your ~?** warum (hast dus) so eilig?; **is there any ~ for it?** eilt es damit?, eilt das?; **there's no ~** es eilt nicht, es hat Zeit

VI sich beeilen; (= *run/go quickly*) laufen, eilen (*geh*); **there's no need to ~** kein Grund zur Eile; **can't you make her ~?** kannst du sie nicht zur Eile antreiben?; **don't ~!** lass dir Zeit!, immer mit der Ruhe! (*inf*); **I must ~ back** ich muss schnell zurück

VT *person* (= *make act quickly*) (zur Eile) antreiben; (= *make move quickly*) scheuchen (*inf*); *work etc* beschleunigen, schneller machen; (= *do too quickly*) überstürzen; **troops were hurried to the spot** es wurden schleunigst Truppen dorthin gebracht; **don't ~ me** hetz mich nicht so!; **don't ~ your meals** schling das Essen nicht so runter!; **I won't be hurried into a decision** ich lasse mich nicht zu einer schnellen Entscheidung drängen

▶ **hurry along** **VI** sich beeilen; **hurry along there, please!** schnell weitergehen, bitte!; **she hurried along to where her friend was waiting** sie lief schnell zu ihrer wartenden Freundin; **to hurry along the road** die Straße entlanglaufen **VT** *sep person* weiterdrängen; (*with work etc*) zur Eile antreiben; *things, work etc* vorantreiben, beschleunigen

▶ **hurry away** *or* **off** **VI** schnell weggehen, forteilen (*geh*) **VT** *sep* schnell wegbringen; **they hurried him off to the waiting car** sie brachten ihn schnell zum wartenden Wagen

▶ **hurry on** **VI** weiterlaufen; (*verbally, with work*) weitermachen; **she hurried on ahead** sie lief *or*

eilte (*geh*) voraus **VT** *sep person* weitertreiben; (*with work*) antreiben

▶ **hurry out** **VI** hinauslaufen *or* -eilen **VT** *sep* schnell hinausbringen *or* -treiben

▶ **hurry up** **VI** sich beeilen; **hurry up!** Beeilung!, beeil dich!; **hurry up and put your coat on!** jetzt zieh dir schnell deinen Mantel an!, mach schon und zieh dir deinen Mantel an!; **can't you make him hurry up?** kannst du nicht dafür sorgen, dass er sich beeilt?; **hurry up with that coffee, will you!** beeilen Sie sich mit dem Kaffee! **VT** *sep person* zur Eile antreiben; *work, process etc* vorantreiben, beschleunigen; **hurry it up!** Beeilung!

hurry-scurry [ˈhʌrɪ'skʌrɪ] **N** Gewühl *nt*, Gewimmel *nt* **VI** (hin und her) hasten, herumschwirren; (*children, insects*) wuseln

hurt [hɜːt] *vb*: *pret, ptp* **hurt** **VT** **a** (*lit, fig*) (= *cause pain*) *person, animal* wehtun (+*dat*); (= *injure*) verletzen; **to ~ oneself** sich (*dat*) wehtun; **to ~ one's arm** sich (*dat*) am Arm wehtun; (= *injure*) sich (*dat*) den Arm verletzen; **my arm is ~ing me** mein Arm tut mir weh, mir tut der Arm weh; **if you go on like that someone is bound to get ~** wenn ihr so weitermacht, verletzt sich bestimmt noch jemand

b (= *harm*) schaden (+*dat*); **it won't ~ him to wait** es schadet ihm gar nicht(s), wenn er etwas wartet *or* warten muss; **it never ~s to talk to somebody** es kann nie schaden, mit jemandem zu sprechen; **walking on the grass doesn't ~ it** es schadet dem Gras nicht, wenn man darauf (herum)läuft; **those most ~ by this measure** die von dieser Maßnahme am stärksten Betroffenen

VI **a** (= *be painful*) wehtun; (*fig*) wehtun, verletzend sein; **that ~s!** (*lit, fig*) das tut weh!; **nothing ~s like the truth** nichts schmerzt mehr *or* tut mehr weh als die Wahrheit; **I love him so much it ~s** ich liebe ihn so sehr, dass es wehtut

b (= *do harm*) schaden; **but surely one drink won't ~** aber ein Gläschen kann doch wohl nicht schaden

N Schmerz *m*; (*baby-talk*) Wehweh *nt*; (*to feelings*) Verletzung *f* (*to* +*gen*); (*to reputation etc*) Schädigung *f* (*to* +*gen*)

ADJ *limb, feelings* verletzt; *tone, look* gekränkt

hurtful [ˈhɜːtfʊl] ADJ *words, action* verletzend; **it was very ~ to him** es verletzte ihn sehr; **to say/ do ~ things** Verletzendes sagen/tun

hurtfully [ˈhɜːtfʊlɪ] ADV verletzend; *say* in verletzendem Ton

hurtle [ˈhɜːtl] **VI** rasen; **the car was hurtling along** das Auto sauste *or* brauste dahin; **it ~d into the wall** es sauste gegen die Mauer; **he came hurtling round the corner** er kam um die Ecke gerast

husband [ˈhʌzbənd] **N** Ehemann *m*; **my/her** *etc* **~** mein/ihr *etc* Mann; **give my best wishes to your ~** grüßen Sie Ihren Mann *or* Gatten (*form*) von mir; **~ and wife** Mann und Frau; **they are ~ and wife** sie sind Eheleute *or* verheiratet **VT** *strength, resources* haushalten *or* Haus halten mit, sparsam umgehen mit

husbandry [ˈhʌzbəndrɪ] N **a** (= *management*) Haushalten *nt*, Wirtschaften *nt* **b** (= *farming*) Landwirtschaft *f*

husband-to-be N *pl* **husbands-to-be** her **~** ihr zukünftiger Mann

hush [hʌʃ] **VT** *person* zum Schweigen bringen; (= *soothe*) *fears etc* beschwichtigen **VI** still sein **N** Stille *f*; **a ~ fell over the crowd** die Menge verstummte plötzlich **INTERJ** pst; **~, ~, it's all right** sch, sch, es ist ja gut

▶ **hush up** VT *sep* vertuschen

hushed [hʌʃt] ADJ *voices* gedämpft; *words* leise; *crowd* schweigend; *courtroom* still; **in ~ tones** mit gedämpfter Stimme; **in ~ whispers** im gedämpften Flüsterton

hush-hush [ˈhʌʃˈhʌʃ] ADJ (*inf*) streng geheim

hush money [ˈhʌʃmʌnɪ] N Schweigegeld *nt*

husk [hʌsk] **N** Schale *f*; (*of wheat, rice*) Spelze *f*; (*of maize*) Hüllblatt *nt* **VT** schälen

huskily ['hʌskɪlɪ] ADV mit rauer Stimme; (= *hoarsely*) heiser, mit heiserer Stimme

huskiness ['hʌskɪnɪs] N Rauheit f; (= *hoarseness*) Heiserkeit f

husky¹ ['hʌskɪ] ADJ (+er) **a** rau, belegt; *singer's voice* rau, rauchig; (= *hoarse*) heiser; **his voice was ~ with emotion** seine Stimme war heiser vor Erregung **b** (= *sturdy*) *person* stämmig

husky² N (= *dog*) Schlittenhund m

hussar [hʊˈzɑː'] N Husar m

hussy ['hʌsɪ] N (= *pert girl*) Fratz m (*inf*), (freche) Göre (*inf*); (= *whorish woman*) Flittchen nt (*pej*); **a brazen or wanton ~** ein schamloses Flittchen

hustings ['hʌstɪŋz] PL (*Brit*) (= *campaign*) Wahlkampf m; (= *meeting*) Wahlveranstaltung f; **on the ~** im Wahlkampf; (= *at election meeting*) in or bei einer Wahlveranstaltung

hustle ['hʌsl] **N** (= *jostling*) Gedränge nt; (= *hurry*) Hetze f, Eile f; **the ~ (and bustle) of the city centre** das geschäftige Treiben or das Gewühl (*inf*) in der Innenstadt
VT **a** (= *hurry*) **to ~ sb into a room/out of a building** jdn schnell in einen Raum/aus einem Gebäude bringen or befördern (*inf*); **she ~d her way through the crowd** sie drängelte sich durch die Menge
b (*fig inf*) drängen; **I won't be ~d into a decision** ich lasse mich nicht zu einer Entscheidung drängen; **I won't be ~d into selling my shares** ich lasse mich nicht dazu drängen, meine Aktien zu verkaufen; **to ~ things (on or along)** die Dinge vorantreiben or beschleunigen
VI **a** hasten, eilen; (*through crowd etc*) sich (durch)drängeln
b (= *solicit*) auf den Strich gehen (*inf*); **to ~ for business** (*entrepreneur etc*) Aufträgen nachjagen **c** (*US inf*: = *work quickly*) sich ins Zeug legen (*inf*)

hustler ['hʌslə'] N **a** (*male*) Strichjunge m (*inf*) **b** (*US*, *inf*: = *hard worker*) Arbeitstier nt (*inf*)

hustling ['hʌslɪŋ] N (Straßen)prostitution f, der Strich (*inf*)

hut [hʌt] N Hütte f; (*Mil*) Baracke f

hutch [hʌtʃ] N Verschlag m, Stall m

HWM *abbr of* **high-water mark**

hyacinth ['haɪəsɪnθ] N Hyazinthe f

hyaena, hyena [haɪˈiːnə] N Hyäne f; **to laugh like a ~** wiehernd lachen

hybrid ['haɪbrɪd] **N** (*Ling*) hybride Bildung or Form; (*Bot, Zool*) Kreuzung f, Hybride m/f (*form*); (*fig*) Mischform f **ADJ** (*Ling*) hybrid (*spec*); (*Bot, Zool*) Misch-; **~ plant** Mischpflanze f

hybridism ['haɪbrɪdɪzəm] N (*lit, fig*) Hybridismus m

hybridization [ˌhaɪbrɪdaɪˈzeɪʃən] N (*Ling*) Hybridisation f (*spec*); (*Bot, Zool also*) Kreuzung f; (*fig*) Mischung f, Zwitter m

hybridize ['haɪbrɪdaɪz] VT (*Ling*) hybridisieren (*spec*); (*Bot, Zool also*) kreuzen; (*fig*) mischen, kreuzen

hydra ['haɪdrə] N (*Zool, Myth*) Hydra f

hydrangea [haɪˈdreɪndʒə] N Hortensie f

hydrant ['haɪdrənt] N Hydrant m

hydrate ['haɪdreɪt] **N** Hydrat nt [haɪˈdreɪt] **VT** hydratisieren

hydrated [haɪˈdreɪtɪd] ADJ wasserhaltig

hydraulic [haɪˈdrɒlɪk] ADJ hydraulisch; **~ dock** (*Naut*) Schwimmdock nt

hydraulics [haɪˈdrɒlɪks] N *sing* Hydraulik f

hydro ['haɪdrəʊ] N Kurhotel nt (*mit Hydrotherapie*)

hydro- ['haɪdrəʊ-] PREF (= *concerning water*) Hydro-, hydro-, Wasser-, wasser-; (*Chem*, +n) -wasserstoff m; **hydrocarbon** N Kohlenwasserstoff m; **hydrocephalic** [ˌhaɪdrəʊsəˈfælɪk] ADJ wasserköpfig, mit einem Wasserkopf; **hydrocephalus** [ˌhaɪdrəʊˈsefələs] N Wasserkopf m; **hydrochloric acid** N Salzsäure f; **hydrodynamics** N *sing or pl* Hydrodynamik f; **hydroelectric** ADJ hydroelektrisch; **hydroelec-**

tricity N durch Wasserkraft erzeugte Energie; **hydroelectric power** N durch Wasserkraft erzeugte Energie; **hydroelectric power station** N Wasserkraftwerk nt; **hydrofoil** N (= *boat*) Tragflächen- or Tragflügelboot nt; (= *fin*) Tragfläche f or -flügel m

hydrogen ['haɪdrɪdʒən] N Wasserstoff m, Hydrogenium nt (*spec*)

hydrogen: hydrogen bomb N Wasserstoffbombe f; **hydrogen bond** N Wasserstoffbrücke(nbindung) f; **hydrogen sulphide** N (= *gas*) Schwefelwasserstoff m

hydrography [haɪˈdrɒgrəfɪ] N Gewässerkunde f

hydrology [haɪˈdrɒlədʒɪ] N Hydrologie f

hydrolysis [haɪˈdrɒlɪsɪs] N Hydrolyse f

hydrometer [haɪˈdrɒmɪtə'] N Hydrometer nt

hydro-: hydropathic [ˌhaɪdrəʊˈpæθɪk] ADJ hydrotherapeutisch; **hydrophobia** N Hydrophobie f (*spec*), Wasserscheu f; (= *rabies*) Tollwut f; **hydrophobic** ADJ hydrophob (*spec*), wasserscheu; **hydroplane** N **a** (*Aviat*) (= *aircraft*) Wasserflugzeug nt, Flugboot nt; (= *float*) Schwimmer m **b** (*Naut*) (= *boat*) Gleitboot nt; (*of submarine*) Tiefenruder nt; **hydroponics** [ˌhaɪdrəʊˈpɒnɪks] N *sing* Hydrokultur f; **hydropower** N Wasserkraft f; **hydrotherapeutics** N *sing* Wasserheilkunde f, Hydrotherapeutik f (*spec*); **hydrotherapy** N Wasserbehandlung f, Hydrotherapie f (*spec*)

hydroxide [haɪˈdrɒksaɪd] N Hydroxid nt

hyena [haɪˈiːnə] N = **hyaena**

hygiene ['haɪdʒiːn] N Hygiene f; **personal ~** Körperpflege f

hygienic [haɪˈdʒiːnɪk] ADJ hygienisch

hygienically [haɪˈdʒiːnɪkəlɪ] ADV hygienisch

hygienics [haɪˈdʒiːnɪks] N *sing* Hygiene f, Gesundheitslehre f

hygro- ['haɪgrəʊ-] PREF Hygro-, hygro-, (Luft)feuchtigkeits-; **hygrometer** ['haɪˈgrɒmɪtə'] N Hygrometer nt, (Luft)feuchtigkeitsmesser m

hymen ['haɪmen] N Hymen nt (*spec*), Jungfernhäutchen nt

hymenopterous [ˌhaɪməˈnɒptərəs] ADJ **~ insect** Hautflügler m

hymn [hɪm] **N** Kirchenlied nt; **~ of praise** (*fig*) Lobeshymne f **VT** (*old*) besingen; (*Eccl*) (lob)preisen

hymnal ['hɪmnəl] N Gesangbuch nt

hymn book N Gesangbuch nt

hymnic ['hɪmnɪk] ADJ hymnenartig, hymnisch

hymn-singing ['hɪmˌsɪŋɪŋ] N Singen nt (von Chorälen); **we had ~ once a week** wir hatten einmal in der Woche Choralsingen

hype [haɪp] (*inf*) **N** Publicity f; **media ~** Medienrummel m (*inf*); **the concept is mainly ~** das Konzept beruht hauptsächlich auf Publicity; **all this ~ about …** dieser ganze Rummel um … (*inf*) **VT** (*also* **hype up**) *product etc* Publicity machen für; **the film was ~d up too much** um den Film wurde zu viel Rummel gemacht (*inf*)

hyped up ['haɪpt'ʌp] ADJ (*inf*) aufgeputscht; (= *excited*) aufgedreht (*inf*)

hyper- ['haɪpə'] PREF Hyper-, hyper-, Über-, über-; **hyperacidity** N Übersäuerung f, Hyperazidität f (*spec*); **hyperactive** ADJ überaktiv, sehr or äußerst aktiv; **a ~ thyroid** eine Überfunktion der Schilddrüse

hyperbola [haɪˈpɜːbələ] N (*Math*) Hyperbel f

hyperbole [haɪˈpɜːbəlɪ] N (*Liter*) Hyperbel f

hyperbolic(al) [ˌhaɪpəˈbɒlɪk(əl)] ADJ (*Liter, Math*) hyperbolisch; (*Math also*) Hyperbel-; **hyperbolic function** Hyperbelfunktion f

hyper-: hypercard N (*Comput*) Hypercard f; **hypercritical** ADJ übertrieben kritisch

hyperglycaemia, (*US*) **hyperglycemia** [ˌhaɪpəglaɪˈsiːmɪə] N Hyperglykämie f (*spec*), Überzuckerung f

hyperglycaemic, (*US*) **hyperglycemic** [ˌhaɪpəglaɪˈsiːmɪk] ADJ *symptoms* hyperglykämisch (*spec*); *person* hyperglykämisch (*spec*), an Überzuckerung leidend

hyper-: hyperlink N (*Comput*) Hyperlink f; **hypermarket** N (*Brit*) Verbrauchermarkt m, Hypermarkt m; **hypersensitive** ADJ überempfindlich; **hypertension** N Hypertonie f, erhöhter Blutdruck; **hypertext** N (*Comput*) Hypertext m; **hyperthyroidism** [ˌhaɪpəˈθaɪrɔɪdɪzəm] N Überfunktion f der Schilddrüse; **hypertrophy** [haɪˈpɜːtrəfɪ] N Hypertrophie f; **hyperventilate** [ˌhaɪpəˈventɪleɪt] VI hyperventilieren; **hyperventilation** ['haɪpəˌventɪˈleɪʃən] N Hyperventilation f

hyphen ['haɪfən] N Bindestrich m; (*at end of line*) Trenn(ungs)strich m; (*Typ*) Divis nt

hyphenate ['haɪfəneɪt] VT mit Bindestrich schreiben; (*Typ*) koppeln (*spec*); **~d word** Bindestrich- or (*Typ*) Koppelwort nt

hyphenation [ˌhaɪfəˈneɪʃən] N Silbentrennung f

hypnosis [hɪpˈnəʊsɪs] N Hypnose f; **under ~** unter or in Hypnose, in hypnotisiertem Zustand

hypnotherapist [ˌhɪpnəʊˈθerəpɪst] N Hypnotherapeut(in) m(f)

hypnotherapy [ˌhɪpnəʊˈθerəpɪ] N Hypnotherapie f

hypnotic [hɪpˈnɒtɪk] **ADJ** **a** (= *hypnotized*) *regression, trance* hypnotisch; **~ state** Hypnose f, Hypnosezustand m **b** (= *mesmerizing*) *effect, rhythm, music, power, voice, eyes* hypnotisch, hypnotisierend **N** **a** (= *drug*) Hypnotikum nt (*spec*), Schlafmittel nt **b** (= *person*) (*easily hypnotized*) leicht hypnotisierbarer Mensch; (*under hypnosis*) Hypnotisierte(r) mf

hypnotism ['hɪpnətɪzəm] N Hypnotismus m; (= *act*) Hypnotisierung f

hypnotist ['hɪpnətɪst] N Hypnotiseur(in) m(f)

hypnotize ['hɪpnətaɪz] VT hypnotisieren; **to be ~d by sb/sth** (= *fascinated*) von jdm/etw wie hypnotisiert sein

hypo ['haɪpəʊ] N (*Med inf*) Hypo m (*inf*)

hypo- [haɪpəʊ-] PREF Hypo-, hypo-; **hypoallergenic** ADJ hypoallergen

hypochondria [ˌhaɪpəʊˈkɒndrɪə] N Hypochondrie f

hypochondriac [ˌhaɪpəʊˈkɒndrɪæk] **N** Hypochonder m **ADJ** (*also* **hypochondriacal**) [ˌhaɪpəʊkɒnˈdraɪəkəl] hypochondrisch

hypocrisy [hɪˈpɒkrɪsɪ] N (= *hypocritical behaviour*) Heuchelei f; (= *sanctimony*) Scheinheiligkeit f

hypocrite ['hɪpəkrɪt] N Heuchler(in) m(f), Scheinheilige(r) mf

hypocritical ADJ , **hypocritically** ADV [ˌhɪpəˈkrɪtɪkəl, -ɪ] heuchlerisch, scheinheilig

hypodermic [ˌhaɪpəˈdɜːmɪk] **ADJ** *injection* subkutan **N** **a** (= *syringe*) subkutane Spritze **b** (= *injection*) subkutane Injektion

hypodermic needle N (Injektions)nadel f

hypodermic syringe N (Injektions)spritze f

hypoglycaemia, (*US*) **hypoglycemia** [ˌhaɪpəʊglaɪˈsiːmɪə] N (*Med*) Hypoglykämie f (*spec*), Unterzuckerung f

hypoglycaemic, (*US*) **hypoglycemic** [ˌhaɪpəʊglaɪˈsiːmɪk] ADJ (*Med*) *symptoms* hypoglykämisch (*spec*), Unterzuckerungs-; *person* hypoglykämisch (*spec*), an Unterzuckerung leidend

hypotenuse [haɪˈpɒtɪnjuːz] N Hypotenuse f; **the square on the ~** das Quadrat über der Hypotenuse

hypothalamus [ˌhaɪpəʊˈθæləməs] N *pl* **-mi** [-maɪ] (*Anat*) Hypothalamus m

hypothermia [ˌhaɪpəʊˈθɜːmɪə] N Unterkühlung f, Kältetod m

hypothesis [haɪˈpɒθɪsɪs] N *pl* **hypotheses** [haɪˈpɒθɪsiːz] Hypothese f, Annahme f; **working ~** Arbeitshypothese f

hypothesize [haɪˈpɒθɪsaɪz] VI Hypothesen aufstellen VT annehmen

hypothetical [ˌhaɪpəʊˈθetɪkəl] ADJ hypothetisch, angenommen; **purely ~** reine Hypothese

hypothetically [ˌhaɪpəʊˈθetɪkəlɪ] ADV **a** (= *as a hypothesis*) hypothetisch, als Hypothese **b** (= *in theory*) theoretisch

hysterectomy [ˌhɪstəˈrektəmɪ] N Hysterektomie f (spec), Totaloperation f

hysteria [hɪˈstɪərɪə] N Hysterie f; **completely overcome with** ~ völlig hysterisch

hysterical [hɪˈsterɪkəl] ADJ **a** (also Psych) hysterisch; **I was nearly** ~ ich war der Hysterie nahe **b** (inf, = hilarious) wahnsinnig komisch (inf)

hysterically [hɪˈsterɪkəlɪ] ADV **a** scream, cry, sob, laugh hysterisch **b** (inf) ~ **funny** wahnsinnig komisch (inf) **c** (= frantically) wie wahnsinnig (inf)

hysterics [hɪˈsterɪks] PL Hysterie f, hysterischer Anfall; **to go into** or **have** ~ hysterisch werden, einen hysterischen Anfall bekommen; (fig inf: = laugh) sich totlachen, sich nicht mehr halten können vor Lachen; **to be in** ~ hysterisch sein, einen hysterischen Anfall haben; (fig inf: = be laughing) sich (halb) totlachen (inf); **we were in** ~ **about it** (fig inf) wir haben uns darüber (halb) totgelacht (inf); **he had us all in** ~ (fig inf) wir haben uns über ihn (halb) totgelacht (inf)

Hz abbr of **hertz** Hz

I

I¹, i [aɪ] N I *nt*, i *nt* → **dot**

I² *abbr of* **Island** *of* **Isle**

I³ PERS PRON ich; **it is I** (*form*) ich bin es

IAAF *abbr of* **International Amateur Athletic Federation** IAAF *f*, Leichtathletik-Weltverband *m*

IAEA *abbr of* **International Atomic Energy Agency**

iambic [aɪˈæmbɪk] ADJ jambisch; **~ pentameter** fünffüßiger Jambus N Jambus *m*

IATA [aɪˈɑːtə] *abbr of* **International Air Transport Association** IATA *f*

iatrogenic [ˌjætrəʊˈdʒɛnɪk, aɪˌætrəʊ-] ADJ iatrogen

IBA (*Brit*) *abbr of* **Independent Broadcasting Authority** Aufsichtsgremium der Fernsehanstalt ITV

Iberia [aɪˈbɪərɪə] N Iberien *nt*

Iberian [aɪˈbɪərɪən] ADJ iberisch N a Iberer(in) *m(f)* b (*Ling*) Iberisch *nt*

Iberian Peninsula N Iberische Halbinsel

ibex [ˈaɪbɛks] N Steinbock *m*

ib(id) *abbr of* **ibidem** ib., ibd

ibis [ˈaɪbɪs] N Ibis *m*

IBRD *abbr of* **International Bank of Reconstruction and Development**

IBS *abbr of* **irritable bowel syndrome** Reizdarm *m*

IC *abbr of* **intellectual capital** geistiges Kapital

i/c, I/C *abbr of* **in charge** v. D., vom Dienst

ICBM *abbr of* **intercontinental ballistic missile** Interkontinentalrakete *f*

ice [aɪs] N a Eis *nt*; (*on roads*) (Glatt)eis *nt*; **to be as cold as ~** eiskalt sein; **my hands are like ~** ich habe eiskalte Hände; **"Cinderella on Ice"** „Aschenputtel auf dem Eis"; **to keep** *or* **put sth on ~** (*lit*) etw kalt stellen; (*fig*) etw auf Eis legen; **to break the ~** (*fig*) das Eis brechen; **to be** *or* **be treading** *or* **be skating on thin ~** (*fig*) sich aufs Glatteis begeben/begeben haben; **you are (skating) on thin ~ there** (*fig*) da begibst du dich aufs Glatteis; **to cut no ~ with sb** (*inf*) auf jdn keinen Eindruck machen; **that cuts no ~ with me** (*inf*) das kommt bei mir nicht an b (*Brit*: = *ice cream*) (Speise)eis *nt*, Eiskrem *f* c *no pl* (*US, sl*, = *diamond*) Klunker *m* (*inf*) VT a (= *make cold*) (mit Eis) kühlen; (= *freeze*) tiefkühlen b *cake* glasieren, mit Zuckerguss überziehen

▶ **ice over** VI zufrieren; (*windscreen*) vereisen

▶ **ice up** VI (*aircraft wings, rail points, windscreen*) vereisen; (*pipes etc*) einfrieren

ice *in cpds* Eis-; **ice age** N Eiszeit *f*; **ice axe**, (*US*) **ice ax** N Eispickel *m*; **ice bag** N Eisbeutel *m*; **iceberg** N (*lit, fig*) Eisberg *m*; **ice-blue** ADJ eisblau; **iceboat** N a (*Sport*) Segelschlitten *m* b = **icebreaker**; **icebound** ADJ *port, lake* zugefroren, vereist; *ship, place* vom Eis eingeschlossen; *road* vereist; *ground* zu Eis gefroren; **icebox** N (*Brit*: *in refrigerator*) Eisfach *nt*; (*US*) Eisschrank *m*; (= *insulated box*) Eisbox *f*, Kühltasche *f*; **this room is like an ~** dieses Zimmer ist der reinste Eiskeller; **icebreaker** N Eisbrecher *m*; **ice bucket** N Eiskühler *m*; **icecap** N Eisdecke *f*, Eisschicht *f*; (*polar*) Eiskappe *f*; **ice-cold** ADJ eiskalt; **ice cream** N Eis *nt*, Eiskrem *f*; **ice-cream cone**, **ice-cream cornet** N Eistüte *f*; **ice-cream parlour**, (*US*) **ice-cream parlor** N Eisdiele *f*; **ice-cream soda** N *Eisbecher mit Sirup, Marmelade, Früchten, Milch und Ingwerlimonade*; **ice-cream van** N (*Brit*) Eiswagen *m*; **ice crusher** N Eiszerkleinerer *m*; **ice cube** N Eiswürfel *m*

iced [aɪst] ADJ a (= *cooled*) *drink* eisgekühlt; **~ tea** Eistee *m*; **~ coffee** Eiskaffee *m* b (= *covered in icing*) *cake, bun* glasiert, mit Zuckerguss überzogen

ice: **ice dancing** N Eistanz *m*; **ice floe** N Eisscholle *f*; **ice hockey** N Eishockey *nt*; **ice house** N Eiskeller *m*

Iceland [ˈaɪslənd] N Island *nt*

Icelander [ˈaɪsləndə] N Isländer(in) *m(f)*

Icelandic [aɪsˈlændɪk] ADJ isländisch N (*Ling*) Isländisch *nt*

ice: **ice lolly** N (*Brit*) Eis *nt* am Stiel; **ice maiden** N (*inf*) eiskalte Schönheit; **ice man** N (*US*) Eisverkäufer *m*; **ice pack** N Packeis *nt*; (*on head*) Eisbeutel *m*; **ice pick** N Eispickel *m*; **ice point** N (*Phys*) Gefrierpunkt *m*; **ice rink** N (Kunst)eisbahn *f*, Schlittschuhbahn *f*; **ice sheet** N Eisschicht *f*; **ice-skate** VI Schlittschuh laufen *or* fahren; **ice skate** N Schlittschuh *m*; **ice-skater** N Schlittschuhläufer(in) *m(f)*; (= *figure-skater*) Eiskunstläufer(in) *m(f)*; **ice-skating** N Eislauf *m*, Schlittschuhlaufen *nt*; (= *figure-skating*) Eiskunstlauf *m*; **ice storm** N (*US*) Eissturm *m*; **ice tray** N Eisschale *f*; **ice water** N Eiswasser *nt*

ichneumon fly [ɪkˈnjuːmənˌflaɪ] N Schlupfwespe *f*

ichthyology [ˌɪkθɪˈɒlədʒɪ] N Fischkunde *f*, Ichthyologie *f* (*spec*)

icicle [ˈaɪsɪkl] N Eiszapfen *m*

icily [ˈaɪsɪlɪ] ADV a *blow* eisig; **a north-east wind blew ~** es wehte ein eisiger Nordostwind; **~ cold** eisig kalt, eiskalt b (*fig*) *say, stare* eisig, frostig; *smile* kalt; *calm, polite, cold* eisig; **to look ~ at sb** jdm einen eisigen Blick zuwerfen

iciness [ˈaɪsɪnɪs] N a (*of windows etc*) Vereisung *f*; **the ~ of the roads** das Glatteis auf den Straßen b (= *freezing cold*) Eiseskälte *f*, eisige Kälte c (*fig*) (*of stare*) eisige Kälte; (*of tone, reception, silence*) Frostigkeit *f*

icing [ˈaɪsɪŋ] N a (*Cook*) Zuckerguss *m*; **this is the ~ on the cake** (*fig*) das ist die Krönung des Ganzen b (*on aircraft, rail points*) Eisbildung *f*, Vereisung *f*

icing sugar N (*Brit*) Puderzucker *m*

icky [ˈɪkɪ] ADJ (*inf*) a (= *yucky*) ekelhaft, eklig (*inf*) b (= *sentimental*) kitschig (*pej*)

icon [ˈaɪkɒn] N a (*Art*) Ikone *f* b (= *cultural symbol*) Ikone *f* c (*Comput*) Ikon *nt*, ikonisches Zeichen

iconic [aɪˈkɒnɪk] ADJ a (*Ling, Comput, Psych*) ikonisch b (*Art*) *portrait* ikonisch c (*culturally*) **an ~ figure** eine Ikone; **to achieve ~ status** zur Ikone werden

iconoclasm [aɪˈkɒnəklæzəm] N (*lit, fig*) Bildersturm *m*

iconoclast [aɪˈkɒnəklæst] N (*lit*) Bilderstürmer *m*, Ikonoklast *m* (*liter*); (*fig*) Bilderstürmer(in) *m(f)*

iconoclastic [aɪˌkɒnəˈklæstɪk] ADJ (*fig*) bilderstürmerisch

iconographic [aɪˌkɒnəˈgræfɪk] ADJ ikonografisch

ictus [ˈɪktəs] N *pl* **ictuses** *or* **ictus** (*Liter*) Iktus *m*, Versakzent *m*

ICU *abbr of* **intensive care unit**

icy [ˈaɪsɪ] ADJ (+*er*) a (= *ice-covered*) *road, pavement* vereist; **the ~ conditions on the roads** das Glatteis auf den Straßen; **when it's ~** bei Glatteis b (= *freezing cold*) *air, wind, river, hands, feet* eiskalt, eisig; **~ cold** (*water, weather*) eiskalt, eisig; *drink* eiskalt, eisgekühlt c (*fig*) *stare* eisig; *tone, reception, silence* frostig

ID N *abbr of* **identification** *of* **identity** **I don't have any ID on me** ich habe keinen Ausweis dabei; **he showed them his ID** er zeigte ihnen seinen Ausweis; **you need ID to get in** man braucht einen Ausweis, um hineinzukommen VT *person* identifizieren; **we've ID'd the girl** wir haben das Mädchen identifiziert

I'd [aɪd] *contr of* **I would** *of* **I had**

id [ɪd] N (*Psych*) Es *nt*

ID card [aɪˈdiːkɑːd] N Ausweis *m*; (*state-issued*) Personalausweis *m*

idea [aɪˈdɪə] ✪ 1.1, 6.2, 6.3, 8.2, 8.3, 26.2 N a Idee *f* (*also Philos*); (*esp sudden*) Einfall *m*; **good ~!** gute Idee!; **that's not a bad ~** das ist keine schlechte Idee; **what an ~!** so eine *or* was für eine Idee!; **who thought of that ~?** wer hat sich (*dat*) denn das einfallen lassen?; **whose bright ~ was that?** (*iro*) wer hat denn diese glänzende Idee gehabt?; **he's our new ~s man** (*inf*) er ist hier der Mann mit den neuen Ideen; **history of ~s** Geistesgeschichte *f*; **man of ~s** Denker *m*; **the very ~!** (nein,) so was!; **the very ~ of eating horse meat revolts me** der bloße Gedanke an Pferdefleisch ekelt mich; **the ~ never entered my head!** auf den Gedanken bin ich überhaupt nicht gekommen; **he is full of (bright) ~s** ihm fehlt es nie an (guten) Ideen; **to hit upon the ~ of doing sth** den plötzlichen Einfall haben, etw zu tun; **that gives me an ~, we could ...** da fällt mir ein, wir könnten ...; **he got the ~ for his novel while he was having a bath** die Idee zu seinem Roman kam ihm in der Badewanne; **to lack ~s** phantasielos *or* fantasielos *or* einfallslos sein; **somehow he's got the ~ into his head that ...** er bildet sich (*dat*) irgendwie ein, dass ...; **where did you get that ~ that I was ill?** wie kommst du auf den Gedanken, dass ich krank war?; **don't get ~s** *or* **don't you go getting ~s about promotion** machen Sie sich (*dat*) nur keine falschen Hoffnungen auf eine Beförderung; **don't get** *or* **go getting any ~s about that fur coat** bilde dir nur nicht ein, du würdest den Pelzmantel bekommen; **to put ~s into sb's head** jdm einen Floh ins Ohr setzen, jdn auf dumme Gedanken bringen b (= *purpose*) **the ~ was to meet at 6** wir wollten uns um 6 treffen; **what's the ~ of keeping him waiting?** was soll denn das, ihn warten zu lassen?; **what's the big ~?** (*inf*) was soll das denn?; **the ~ is to reduce expenditure** es geht darum, die Ausgaben zu senken; **he sat down with the ~ of writing a letter** er setzte sich mit der Absicht, einen Brief zu schreiben; **that's the ~** so ist es richtig, genau (das ists)!; **you're**

getting the ~ Sie verstehen langsam, worum es geht **c** (= *opinion*) Meinung *f*, Ansicht *f*; (= *conception*) Vorstellung *f*; **if that's your ~ of fun** wenn Sie das lustig finden, wenn das Ihre Vorstellung von Spaß ist; **this isn't my ~ of a holiday** so stelle ich mir den Urlaub nicht vor; **he has some very strange ~s** er hat manchmal merkwürdige Vorstellungen; **according to his ~** seiner Meinung *or* Ansicht nach; **he has no ~ of right and wrong** er kann zwischen Gut und Böse nicht unterscheiden; **his ~ of a pleasant evening is ...** seine Vorstellung von einem angenehmen Abend ist ... **d** (= *knowledge*) Ahnung *f*; **you've no ~ how worried I've been** du kannst dir nicht vorstellen, welche Sorgen ich mir gemacht habe; **(I've) no ~** (ich habe) keine Ahnung; **I've got some ~ (of)** ich weiß so ungefähr, worum es hier geht; **I haven't the least** *or* **slightest** *or* **faintest ~** ich habe nicht die leiseste *or* geringste Ahnung; **I have an ~ that ...** ich habe so das Gefühl, dass ...; **I had no ~ that ...** ich hatte ja keine Ahnung, dass ...; **just to give me an ~ of how long it will take** damit ich so ungefähr weiß, wie lange es dauert; **could you give me an ~ of how long ...?** könnten Sie mir ungefähr sagen, wie lange ...?; **to give you an ~ of how difficult it is** um Ihnen eine Vorstellung davon zu vermitteln, wie schwierig es ist

ideal [aɪ'dɪəl] **N** Ideal *nt* (of +*gen*); (= *model*) Ideal(bild) *nt* (of +*gen*) **ADJ** ideal; **~ solution** Ideallösung *f*; **~ weight** Idealgewicht *nt*; **he is ~** *or* **the ~ person for the job** er ist für den Job ideal geeignet; **the plants are ~ for growing in the home** die Pflanzen eignen sich ideal als Zimmerpflanzen; **in an ~ world** im Idealfall; (*philosophical statement*) in einer vollkommenen *or* idealen Welt

idealism [aɪ'dɪəlɪzəm] **N** Idealismus *m*

idealist [aɪ'dɪəlɪst] **N** Idealist(in) *m(f)*

idealistic [aɪ,dɪə'lɪstɪk] **ADJ** idealistisch

idealize [aɪ'dɪəlaɪz] **VT** idealisieren

idealized [aɪ'dɪəlaɪzd] **ADJ** *person, version, landscape* idealisiert; *image, view* idealisierend

ideally [aɪ'dɪəlɪ] **ADV a** (*introducing sentence*) idealerweise, im Idealfall **b** (= *perfectly*) *suited, placed, situated, located* ideal; **they were ~ suited** sie passten ideal zusammen; **I'm not ~ placed to give you advice** ich bin nicht gerade der Richtige/die Richtige, um dir Ratschläge zu geben; **the hotel is ~ located** das Hotel liegt ideal; **I'm ~ situated in this neighbourhood** diese Gegend liegt für mich ideal

ideation [,aɪdɪ'eɪʃən] **N** Ideenbildung *f*; (= *imagination*) Vorstellungsvermögen *nt*

idée fixe [i:deɪ'fiːks] **N** *pl* **idées fixes** fixe Idee

idem ['ɪdem] **PRON, ADJ** idem, derselbe

ident [aɪ'dent] **N** (*TV inf: also* **station ident**) Logo *nt* des Senders; **the MTV station ~s** die Logos des Senders MTV

identical [aɪ'dentɪkəl] **ADJ** (= *exactly alike*) identisch, (völlig) gleich; (= *same*) der-/die-/dasselbe; **~ twins** eineiige Zwillinge *pl*; **we have ~ views** wir haben die gleichen Ansichten

identically [aɪ'dentɪkəlɪ] **ADV** identisch, gleich

identifiable [aɪ'dentɪ,faɪəbl] **ADJ** erkennbar; (*esp in scientific contexts*) identifizierbar; **he is ~ by his red hair** er ist an seinem roten Haar zu erkennen; **that makes him/it ~** daran kann man ihn/es erkennen

identification [aɪ,dentɪfɪ'keɪʃən] **N a** (*of criminal, dead person etc*) Identifizierung *f*, Feststellung *f* der Identität; (*of genes*) Identifizierung *f*; (*fig*) (*of goals*) Setzen *nt*; (*of problems*) Erkennen *nt*; **a system of ~ using fingerprints** ein erkennungsdienstliches System auf der Basis von Fingerabdrücken **b** (= *papers*) Ausweispapiere *pl*, Legitimation *f*; **because he had no (means of) ~** weil er sich nicht ausweisen konnte **c** (= *considering as identical, equation*) Gleichsetzung *f*, Identifizierung *f*

d (= *association*) Identifikation *f*; **a politician who has a strong ~ with a criminal group** ein Politiker, der mit einer kriminellen Gruppe in Verbindung gebracht wird **e** (= *sympathy, support*) Identifikation *f*

identification: identification parade N Gegenüberstellung *f* (zur Identifikation des Täters); **identification tag** N (*US*) Erkennungsmarke *f*

identifier [aɪ'dentɪfaɪə'] **N** (*Comput*) Kennzeichnung *f*

identify [aɪ'dentɪfaɪ] **VT a** (= *establish identity of*) identifizieren, die Identität (+*gen*) feststellen; *gene, virus etc* identifizieren; *plant, species etc* bestimmen; (= *mark identity of*) kennzeichnen; (= *recognize, pick out*) erkennen; **to ~ one's goals** sich (*dat*) Ziele setzen; **to ~ sb/sth by sth** jdn/etw an etw (*dat*) erkennen **b** (= *consider as the same*) gleichsetzen (*with* mit) **c** (= *associate with*) assoziieren (*with* mit) **VR a to ~ oneself** sich ausweisen **b to ~ oneself with sb/sth** sich mit jdm/etw identifizieren **VI** (*with film hero etc*) sich identifizieren (*with* mit)

Identikit® [aɪ'dentɪkɪt] **N ~ (picture)** Phantombild *nt*

identity [aɪ'dentɪtɪ] **N a** Identität *f*; **to prove one's ~** sich ausweisen; **a driving licence will be accepted as proof of ~** ein Führerschein genügt, um sich auszuweisen; **proof of ~** (= *permit*) Legitimation *f*; **a sense of ~** ein Bewusstsein *nt* der eigenen Identität → **mistaken b** (= *identicalness*) Gleichheit *f*, Übereinstimmung *f*, Identität *f*; **~ of interest** Interessengleichheit *f*

identity: identity bracelet N Identitätsarmband *nt*; **identity card** N Ausweis *m*; (*state-issued*) Personalausweis *m*; **identity crisis** N Identitätskrise *f*; **identity disc** N (*Brit Mil*) Erkennungsmarke *f*; (*for dogs*) Hundemarke *f*; **identity papers** PL Ausweispapiere *pl*; **identity parade** N Gegenüberstellung *f*; **identity theft** N (*Internet*) Identitätsraub *m* (*Straftat, bei der die Identität einer anderen Person vorgegeben wird, auf deren Kosten im Internet eingekauft wird*)

ideogram ['ɪdɪəʊɡræm], **ideograph** ['ɪdɪəʊɡrɑːf] N Ideogramm *nt*

ideological [,aɪdɪə'lɒdʒɪkəl] **ADJ** ideologisch

ideologically [,aɪdɪə'lɒdʒɪkəlɪ] **ADV** ideologisch; **to be ~ opposed to sth** etw vom ideologischen Standpunkt aus ablehnen; **~, there was nothing in common between them** in ideologischer Hinsicht hatten sie nichts gemeinsam

ideologist [,aɪdɪ'ɒlədʒɪst] **N** Ideologe *m*, Ideologin *f*

ideologue ['aɪdɪəlɒɡ] **N** (*form*) = **ideologist**

ideology [,aɪdɪ'ɒlədʒɪ] **N** Weltanschauung *f*, Ideologie *f*

ides [aɪdz] **PL** Iden *pl*; **the ~ of March** die Iden *pl* des März

idiocy ['ɪdɪəsɪ] **N a** *no pl* Idiotie *f*, Schwachsinn *m* **b** (= *stupid act, words*) Dummheit *f*, Blödheit *f*

idiolect ['ɪdɪəʊlekt] **N** Idiolekt *m*

idiom ['ɪdɪəm] **N a** (= *special phrase, group of words*) idiomatische Wendung, Redewendung *f* **b** (= *language*) Sprache *f*, Idiom *nt*; (*of region*) Mundart *f*, Dialekt *m*; (*of author*) Ausdrucksweise *f*, Diktion *f*; **... to use the modern ~ ...** um es modern auszudrücken **c** (*in music, art*) Ausdrucksform *f*

idiomatic [,ɪdɪə'mætɪk] **ADJ** idiomatisch; **to speak ~ German** idiomatisch richtiges Deutsch sprechen; **an ~ expression** eine Redensart, eine idiomatische Redewendung

idiomatically [,ɪdɪə'mætɪkəlɪ] **ADV** idiomatisch

idiomaticity [,ɪdɪəʊmə'tɪsɪtɪ] **N** Idiomatik *f*; **his language lacked ~** er drückte sich nicht sehr idiomatisch aus

idiosyncrasy [,ɪdɪəʊ'sɪŋkrəsɪ] **N** Eigenheit *f*, Eigenart *f*, Besonderheit *f*; (*Ling, Med*) Idiosynkrasie *f*

idiosyncratic [,ɪdɪəsɪŋ'krætɪk] **ADJ** eigenartig; (*Ling, Med*) idiosynkratisch; **in his own ~ way** in der ihm eigenen Art

idiot ['ɪdɪət] **N** Idiot *m*, Dummkopf *m*, Schwachkopf *m*; (*old Med*) Idiot(in) *m(f)*, Schwachsinnige(r) *mf*; **what an ~!** so ein Idiot *or* Dummkopf!; **you (stupid) ~!** du Idiot!; **where's that ~ waiter?** wo ist dieser blöde Ober?, wo ist dieser Idiot von Ober?; **this ~ brother of mine** dieser Schwachkopf *or* Dummkopf *or* Idiot von meinem Bruder; **what an ~ I am/was!** ich Idiot!; **to feel like an ~** sich dumm vorkommen; **to look like an ~** dumm aussehen

idiot: idiot board N (*inf*) Teleprompter *m*; **idiot box** N (*inf*) Glotze *f* (*inf*); **idiot card** N (*TV*) Neger *m*

idiotic [,ɪdɪ'ɒtɪk] **ADJ** blöd(sinnig), idiotisch; **don't be ~!** sei nicht so blöd!; **what an ~ mistake to make!** so ein blöder Fehler!

idiotically [,ɪdɪ'ɒtɪkəlɪ] **ADV** blödsinnig, idiotisch; *fast* schwachsinnig; **~, I had/said ...** blödsinniger- *or* idiotischerweise hatte/sagte ich ...

idiot-proof ['ɪdɪət,pruːf] **ADJ** (*inf*) idiotensicher (*inf*)

idle ['aɪdl] **ADJ a** (= *not working*) *person* müßig, untätig; *moment* ruhig; **the ~ rich** die reichen Müßiggänger; **in my ~ moments** in ruhigen *or* stillen Augenblicken; **~ life** faules Leben; **~ money, money lying ~** totes *or* brachliegendes Kapital; **we don't want to let the money lie ~** wir wollen das Geld nicht ungenutzt liegen lassen; **his car was lying ~ most of the time** sein Auto stand meistens unbenutzt herum **b** (= *lazy*) faul, träge **c** (*in industry*) *person* unbeschäftigt; *machine* stillstehend *attr*, stillliegend *attr*, außer Betrieb; **500 men have been made ~ by the strike** durch den Streik mussten 500 Leute ihre Arbeit einstellen; **the whole factory stood ~** die ganze Fabrik hatte die Arbeit eingestellt; **the machine stood ~** die Maschine stand still *or* arbeitete nicht *or* war außer Betrieb; **~ capacity** freie *or* brachliegende Kapazität **d** *promise, threat, words* leer; *speculation, talk* müßig; *remark* beiläufig; **~ boast** bloße Angeberei; **~ curiosity** pure *or* bloße Neugier; **~ fear** grundlose *or* unbegründete Angst; **~ wish** Wunschtraum *m*; **the ~ pleasures of this worldly life** die eitlen Vergnügungen dieses Erdenlebens **e** (= *useless*) **it would be ~ to go on trying** es wäre nutzlos *or* zwecklos, (es) weiter zu versuchen **VI a** (*person*) untätig sein, faulenzen, nichts tun; **a day spent idling on the river** ein Tag, den man untätig auf dem Wasser verbringt **b** (*engine*) leer laufen; **when the engine is idling** wenn der Motor im Leerlauf ist

▶ **idle about** (*Brit*) *or* **around VI** herumtrödeln, bummeln; (= *loiter*) herumlungern; **we were idling about** *or* **around on the beach** wir faulenzten am Strand herum; **don't idle about** *or* **around** trödle nicht herum!, bummle nicht!

▶ **idle away VT** *sep one's time etc* vertrödeln, verbummeln

idleness ['aɪdlnɪs] **N a** (= *state of not working*) Untätigkeit *f*; (*pleasurable*) Muße *f*, Müßiggang (*liter*) *m*; **to live in ~** ein untätiges Leben führen, ein Leben der Muße führen (*liter*); **a life of blissful ~** ein Leben voller köstlicher Muße **b** (= *laziness*) Faulheit *f*, Trägheit *f* **c** (*of promise, threat, words*) Leere *f*; (*of speculation, talk*) Müßigkeit *f*; (*of remark*) Beiläufigkeit *f*; (= *uselessness*) Nutzlosigkeit *f*, Vergeblichkeit *f*, Eitelkeit *f* (*old*)

idler ['aɪdlə'] **N a** (*Brit* = *person not working*) Müßiggänger(in) *m(f)*; (= *lazy person*) Faulenzer(in) *m(f)*, Faulpelz *m* **b** (*Tech*, = *wheel*) Zwischenrad *nt*; (= *pulley*) Spannrolle *f*

idle time N Brachzeit *f*, Leerzeit *f*

idly ['aɪdlɪ] **ADV a** (= *without working*) untätig; (= *pleasurably*) müßig; **to stand ~ by** untätig herumstehen **b** (= *lazily*) faul, träge **c** (= *ab-*

stractedly) watch, toy with sth gedankenverloren; (= without thinking) say, suggest ohne sich/mir etc etwas dabei zu denken; **I was ~ curious** ich war irgendwie neugierig **d** (= vainly) speculate müßig

idol ['aɪdl] N (lit) Götze m, Götzenbild nt; (fig) Idol nt, Abgott m; (Film, TV etc) Idol nt; **a teen ~** ein Teenageridol nt; **a fallen ~** ein gefallenes Idol

idolater [aɪ'dɒlətə'] N Götzendiener m

idolatress [aɪ'dɒlətrɪs] N Götzendienerin f

idolatrous [aɪ'dɒlətrəs] ADJ (lit) Götzen-; (fig) abgöttisch

idolatry [aɪ'dɒlətrɪ] N (lit) Götzendienst m, Götzenverehrung f; (fig) Vergötterung f, abgöttische Verehrung

idolize ['aɪdəlaɪz] VT abgöttisch lieben or verehren, vergöttern; **to ~ sth** etw anbeten

I'd've ['aɪdəv] contr of **I would have**

idyll ['ɪdɪl] N **a** (Liter) Idylle f **b** (fig) Idyll nt

idyllic ADJ , **idyllically** ADV [ɪ'dɪlɪk, -lɪ] idyllisch

i.e. abbr of **id est** i.e., d.h.

if [ɪf] ✪ 1.1, 2.2, 17.1 **CONJ** wenn; (= in case also) falls, für den Fall, dass ...; (= whether, in direct clause) ob; **I would be really pleased if you could do it** wenn Sie das tun könnten, wäre ich sehr froh; **if it rains tomorrow** wenn es or falls es morgen regnet; **if I may say so** wenn ich das sagen darf; **I wonder if he'll come** ich bin gespannt, ob er kommt; **do you know if they have gone?** wissen Sie, ob sie gegangen sind?; **what if something happens to him?** was ist, wenn ihm etwas passiert?; **I'll let you know if and when I come to a decision** ich werde Ihnen mitteilen, ob und wenn ich mich entschieden habe; **where will you live when you get married? – if we get married?** wo wollt ihr wohnen, wenn ihr heiratet? – wenn wir überhaupt heiraten!; **if I ask him he does help me** wenn ich ihn darum bitte, hilft er mir auch; **(even)** if auch wenn; **it's a good film (even) if I rather long** es ist ein guter Film, auch wenn er etwas lang ist; **even if they are poor, at least they are happy** sie sind zwar arm, aber wenigstens glücklich; **if only** wenn (doch) nur; **if only I had known!** wenn ich das nur gewusst hätte!; **I would like to see him, if only for a few hours** ich würde ihn gerne sehen, wenn auch nur für ein paar Stunden; **as if** als ob; **he acts as if he were** or **was** (inf) **rich** er tut so, als ob er reich wäre; **it's not as if I meant to hurt her** es ist nicht so, dass ich ihr hätte wehtun wollen; **as if by chance** wie zufällig; **he stood there as if he were dumb** er stand wie stumm da; **meat was available once a week, if at all** Fleisch gab es einmal in der Woche, wenn überhaupt; **if necessary** falls nötig, im Bedarfsfall; **if so** wenn ja; **if not** falls nicht; **if not, why not?** falls nicht, warum?; **this is difficult, if not impossible, to do** das ist schwer, wenn nicht sogar unmöglich; **if I were you/him** wenn ich Sie/er wäre, an Ihrer/seiner Stelle; **if anything this one is bigger** wenn überhaupt, dann ist dieses hier größer; **if I know Pete, he'll ...** so wie ich Pete kenne, wird er ...; **well, if he didn't try to steal my bag!** (inf) wollte der doch tatsächlich meine Tasche klauen (inf); **well, if it isn't old Jim!** (inf) ich werd verrückt, das ist doch der Jim (inf)

N Wenn nt; **it's a big if** das ist noch sehr fraglich, das ist die große Frage; **ifs and buts** Wenn und Aber nt

iffy ['ɪfɪ] ADJ (+er) (inf) strittig, fraglich; neighbourhood etc zweifelhaft; **he was a bit ~** er hat sich sehr vage ausgedrückt; **I was feeling a bit ~** ich fühlte mich nicht wohl

igloo ['ɪɡluː] N Iglu m or nt

igneous ['ɪɡnɪəs] ADJ (Geol) **~ rock** Eruptivgestein nt

ignite [ɪɡ'naɪt] **VT** entzünden, anzünden; (Aut) zünden; (fig) passions, interest erwecken **VI** sich entzünden, Feuer fangen; (Aut) zünden

ignition [ɪɡ'nɪʃən] N **a** Entzünden nt, Anzünden nt **b** (Aut) Zündung f; **we have ~** (of rocket) „Zündung"

ignition (Aut) in cpds Zünd-; **ignition coil** N Zündspule f; **ignition key** N Zündschlüssel m; **ignition lock** N Zündschloss nt; **ignition switch** N Zündschalter m

ignoble [ɪɡ'nəʊbl] ADJ schändlich, unwürdig, unehrenhaft

ignominious [,ɪɡnə'mɪnɪəs] ADJ schmachvoll; (= humiliating) entwürdigend; defeat schmachvoll, schmählich; behaviour schändlich, unehrenhaft; **to come to an ~ end** ein schmachvolles Ende finden

ignominiously [,ɪɡnə'mɪnɪəslɪ] ADV schmachvoll; (= humiliatingly) entwürdigend

ignominy ['ɪɡnəmɪnɪ] N Schmach f, Schande f, Schimpf m (old)

ignoramus [,ɪɡnə'reɪməs] N Nichtswisser(in) m(f), Ignorant(in) m(f)

ignorance ['ɪɡnərəns] N (= general lack of knowledge, education) Unwissenheit f, Mangel m an Bildung, Ignoranz f; (of particular subject, language, plan) Unkenntnis f; **to keep sb in ~ of sth** jdn in Unkenntnis über etw (acc) lassen, jdn etw nicht wissen lassen; **to be in ~ of sth** etw nicht wissen; **~ (of the law) is no excuse** Unkenntnis schützt vor Strafe nicht

ignorant ['ɪɡnərənt] ADJ **a** (= generally uneducated) unwissend, ungebildet, ignorant; (of particular subject) unwissend; (of plan, requirements etc) nicht informiert (of sth +acc); **to be ~ of geography** sich in Geografie nicht auskennen; **to be ~ of the facts** die Tatsachen nicht kennen; **I am not exactly ~ of what has been going on** es ist nicht so, als wüsste ich nicht, was los ist; **they are ~ of** or **about what happened** sie wissen nicht, was geschehen ist **b** (= ill-mannered) unhöflich, ungeschliffen, ungehobelt; **you ~ fool** du ungehobelter Patron

ignorantly ['ɪɡnərəntlɪ] ADV unwissentlich; behave unhöflich, ungeschliffen, ungehobelt

ignore [ɪɡ'nɔː'] VT ignorieren, (= deliberately overlook also) hinwegsehen über (+acc); (= pass over, pay no attention to) nicht beachten, unbeachtet lassen; remark überhören, übergehen; person übersehen, nicht beachten; **I'll ~ that** (remark) ich habe nichts gehört; **but I can't ~ the fact that ...** ich kann mich der Tatsache nicht verschließen, dass ...

iguana [ɪ'ɡwɑːnə] N Leguan m

ikon ['aɪkɒn] N = icon

ILEA ['ɪlɪə] abbr of **Inner London Education Authority** Londoner Schulaufsichtsbehörde

ilex ['aɪleks] N **a** (= holm oak) Steineiche f, Immergrüneiche f **b** (= holly) Ilex f, Stechpalme f

Iliad ['ɪlɪæd] N Ilias f, Iliade f

ilk [ɪlk] N **people of that ~** solche Leute; **all things of that ~** dergleichen Dinge; **and others of that ~** und dergleichen, und ihresgleichen

ill [ɪl] **ADJ** **a** pred (= sick) krank; **to fall** or **take** (inf) or **be taken ~** erkranken (with sth an etw dat), krank werden; **to feel ~** sich unwohl or krank fühlen; **I feel (terribly) ~** mir ist (ganz und gar) nicht gut; **he is ~ with fever/a cold** er hat Fieber/eine Erkältung; **to be ~ with chicken pox** an Windpocken erkrankt sein; **~ with anxiety/jealousy** krank vor Angst/Eifersucht; **she is making herself ~ with worry** sie macht sich ganz krank vor lauter Sorgen

b comp **worse**, superl **worst** (= bad) schlecht, übel; (= adverse) effects unerwünscht; **~ will** böses Blut; **I don't bear them any ~ will** ich trage ihnen nichts nach; **~ health** schlechter Gesundheitszustand; **to suffer ~ health** gesundheitlich angeschlagen sein; **due to ~ health** aus Gesundheitsgründen; **~ humour** or (US) **humor** schlechte Laune; **~ luck** Pech nt; **as ~ luck would have it** wie es der Teufel so will; **~ nature** Übellaunigkeit f; **it's an ~ wind (that blows nobody any good)** (Prov) so hat alles seine guten Seiten

N **a** (liter: = evil) **to bode** or **augur ~** Böses ah-

nen lassen; **to think ~ of sb** schlecht or Schlechtes von jdm or über jdn denken; **to speak ~ of sb** schlecht über jdn reden

b **ills** PL (= misfortunes) Missstände pl, Übel pl; **to do ~** (old) Böses or Unrecht tun

ADV schlecht; **to take sth ~** (liter) etw übel nehmen; **things went ~ with him** (liter) es erging ihm nicht gut, es ward ihm kein Glück beschieden (liter); **he can ~ afford to refuse** er kann es sich (dat) schlecht leisten abzulehnen; **it ~ becomes you** (form) es steht Ihnen nicht an (form)

ill. abbr of **illustrated** of **illustration** Abb., Abbildung f

I'll [aɪl] contr of **I will** of **I shall**

ill: **ill-advised** ADJ person, attempt unklug; action also unratsam; **you would be ~ to trust her** Sie wären schlecht beraten, wenn Sie ihr trauten; **ill-assorted** ADJ group, bunch schlecht zusammenpassend; **ill-at-ease** ADJ unbehaglich; **I always felt ~ in his presence** ich habe mich in seiner Gegenwart nie wohl gefühlt; **ill-bred** ADJ ungezogen, schlecht erzogen; **ill-breeding** N schlechte Erziehung, Unerzogenheit f; **it's a sign of ~ to ...** es ist ein Zeichen für eine schlechte Kinderstube, wenn man ...; **ill-conceived** ADJ plan, policy schlecht durchdacht; **ill-conditioned** ADJ übellaunig; **ill-considered** ADJ action, words unüberlegt, unbedacht; **ill-defined** ADJ goals, task, powers unklar definiert; **ill-disposed** ADJ **to be ~ to(wards) sb** jdm übel gesinnt sein

illegal [ɪ'liːɡəl] ADJ unrechtmäßig, ungesetzlich; (= against a law) gesetzwidrig; trade, immigration, possession, drugs, profits illegal; (= prohibited) substance, organization verboten, illegal; (Sport) regelwidrig

illegality [,ɪliː'ɡælɪtɪ] N Unrechtmäßigkeit f, Ungesetzlichkeit f; (against a specific law) Gesetzwidrigkeit f; (of trade, possession, drug, organization, profits) Illegalität f; (Sport) Regelwidrigkeit f

illegally [ɪ'liːɡəlɪ] ADV (= against the law) unrechtmäßig, ungesetzlich; (= against a specific law) gesetzwidrig; **~ imported** illegal eingeführt; **you're ~ parked** Sie stehen im Parkverbot; **to act ~** sich gesetzwidrig verhalten; (against international law) gegen das Völkerrecht verstoßen; **they were convicted of ~ possessing a handgun** sie wurden wegen unerlaubten Besitzes einer Handfeuerwaffe verurteilt

illegibility [ɪ,ledʒɪ'bɪlɪtɪ] N Unleserlichkeit f

illegible ADJ , **illegibly** ADV [ɪ'ledʒəbl, -ɪ] unleserlich

illegitimacy [,ɪlɪ'dʒɪtɪməsɪ] N **a** (of child) Unehelichkeit f **b** (= unlawfulness) Unzulässigkeit f; (of government) Unrechtmäßigkeit f **c** (of argument, conclusion) Unzulässigkeit f

illegitimate [,ɪlɪ'dʒɪtɪmɪt] ADJ **a** child, birth unehelich **b** (= contrary to law) unzulässig, unerlaubt; government unrechtmäßig; **the ~ use of drugs** (der) Drogenmissbrauch **c** argument, conclusion, inference unzulässig, nicht folgerichtig, illegitim

illegitimately [,ɪlɪ'dʒɪtɪmɪtlɪ] ADV **a** born unehelich **b** (= contrary to law) unzulässig, unerlaubt; use unrechtmäßigerweise, unzulässigerweise **c** argue, conclude unzulässig, nicht folgerichtig

ill: **ill-fated** ADJ **a** (= unfortunate, unlucky) person vom Unglück verfolgt, unglücklich **b** (= doomed, destined to fail) unglückselig, verhängnisvoll; **the ~ Titanic** die unglückselige Titanic; **ill-favoured** ADJ (liter: = ugly) ungestalt (liter), hässlich, unschön; **ill feeling** N böses Blut; **no ~?** ist es wieder gut?; **no ~!** ist schon vergessen; **ill-fitting** ADJ clothes, dentures schlecht sitzend; shoes schlecht passend; **ill-founded** ADJ unbegründet, unerwiesen, fragwürdig; **ill-gotten gains** PL unrechtmäßiger Gewinn, Sündengeld nt (hum); **ill-humoured**, (US) **ill-humored** ADJ schlecht or übel gelaunt, schlecht aufgelegt, verstimmt

illiberal [ɪ'lɪbərəl] ADJ **a** (= narrow-minded) engstirnig, intolerant, engherzig; (= reactionary) reaktionär; (*Pol, Jur:* = *strict, repressive*) *law* restriktiv; *rule* antiliberal; *system, regime* autoritär **b** (= *niggardly*) knauserig, geizig

illicit [ɪ'lɪsɪt] ADJ illegal; *affair, relationship* verboten; *spirits* schwarz hergestellt *or* gebrannt; **~ trade** *or* **sale** Schwarzhandel *m*

illicitly [ɪ'lɪsɪtlɪ] ADV verbotenerweise; (= *illegally*) illegal(erweise); **~ acquired** unrechtmäßig erworben

illimitable [ɪ'lɪmɪtəbl] ADJ grenzenlos, unbegrenzt; **the ~ ocean** der unendliche Ozean

ill-informed [ɪlɪnˌfɔː'mɪd] ADJ *person* schlecht informiert *or* unterrichtet (*about* über); *attack, criticism, speech* wenig sachkundig

illiteracy [ɪ'lɪtərəsɪ] N Analphabetentum *nt*; **~ rate** Analphabetismus *m*

illiterate [ɪ'lɪtərət] **ADJ** des Schreibens und Lesens unkundig; *country, population* analphabetisch; (= *badly-educated, uncultured*) *person* ungebildet, unwissend; *letter* voller Fehler; **he's ~** er ist Analphabet; **to be functionally ~** praktisch nicht lesen und schreiben können; **economically/musically ~** völlig unwissend, wenn es um Wirtschaft/Musik geht; **many people are computer-illiterate** viele Menschen kennen sich nicht mit Computern aus **N** Analphabet(in) *m(f)*

ill: ill-judged ADJ unklug, wenig bedacht; **ill-mannered** ADJ unhöflich; **ill-matched** ADJ nicht zusammenpassend; **they're ~** sie passen nicht zueinander; **ill-natured** ADJ , **ill-naturedly** ADV bösartig

illness ['ɪlnɪs] N Krankheit *f*

illogical [ɪ'lɒdʒɪkəl] ADJ unlogisch

illogicality [ɪˌlɒdʒɪ'kælɪtɪ] N mangelnde Logik, Unlogik *f*; **the illogicalities in his argument** die logischen Fehler in seiner Argumentation

illogically [ɪ'lɒdʒɪkəlɪ] ADV *behave, argue* unlogisch; **~, I felt guilty** entgegen jeder Logik hatte ich Schuldgefühle

ill: ill-omened ADJ unter einem unglücklichen Stern *or* unter einem Unstern stehend; **ill-prepared** ADJ schlecht vorbereitet; **ill-starred** ADJ *person* vom Unglück *or* Pech verfolgt; *undertaking etc* unter einem ungünstigen Stern (stehend); **~ day** Unglückstag *m*; **ill-suited** ADJ (*to one another*) nicht zusammenpassend; (*to sth*) ungeeignet (*to* für); **they are ~** sie passen nicht zueinander; **ill-tempered** ADJ (*habitually*) missmutig, übellaunig; (*on particular occasion*) schlecht gelaunt *pred*; (*violently*) schlecht gelaunt *attr*; **ill-timed** ADJ ungelegen, unpassend; *move, speech* zeitlich schlecht abgestimmt; **ill-treat** VT schlecht behandeln, misshandeln; **ill-treatment** N Misshandlung *f*, schlechte Behandlung

illuminate [ɪ'luːmɪneɪt] VT **a** (= *light up*) *room, building* erhellen, erleuchten, beleuchten; *sky* erleuchten; (*spotlight etc*) anstrahlen; (= *decorate with lights*) festlich beleuchten, illuminieren; **~d sign** Leuchtzeichen *nt* **b** (*Art*) *manuscript* illuminieren; **~d letters** (verzierte) Initialen *pl* **c** (*fig*) *subject* erhellen, erläutern

illuminating [ɪ'luːmɪneɪtɪŋ] ADJ (= *instructive*) aufschlussreich

illumination [ɪˌluːmɪ'neɪʃən] N **a** (*of street, room, building*) Beleuchtung *f*; **source of ~** Lichtquelle *f* **b illuminations** PL (= *decorative lights*) festliche Beleuchtung, Illumination *f* **c** (*Art*) (*of manuscript*) Illumination *f*; (= *subject*) Buchmalerei *f* **d** (*fig*) Erläuterung *f*

illuminator [ɪ'luːmɪneɪtə'] N (*Art, of manuscript*) Buchmaler(in) *m(f)*, Illuminator(in) *m(f)*

illumine [ɪ'luːmɪn] VT (*liter fig*) erhellen

illus. *abbr of* **illustrated** *of* **illustration** Abb., Abbildung *f*

ill-use [ˌɪl'juːz] VT schlecht behandeln, schlecht umgehen mit; (*physically*) misshandeln

illusion [ɪ'luːʒən] N Illusion *f*; (= *hope also*) trügerische Hoffnung; (= *misperception*) Täuschung *f*; **to be under an ~** einer Täuschung (*dat*) unterliegen, sich (*dat*) Illusionen machen; **to be under the ~ that …** sich (*dat*) einbilden, dass

...; **to be under** *or* **have no ~s** sich (*dat*) keine Illusionen machen, sich (*dat*) nichts vormachen (*about* über +*acc*); **no one has any ~s about winning the war** niemand macht sich Illusionen, dass der Krieg gewonnen werden kann; **it gives the ~ of space** es vermittelt die Illusion von räumlicher Weite; **a tan can give the ~ of being slimmer** wenn man braun ist, kann das den Eindruck erwecken, dass man schlanker ist → **optical illusion**

illusionary [ɪ'luːʒənərɪ] ADJ illusorisch

illusionist [ɪ'luːʒənɪst] N Illusionist(in) *m(f)*

illusive [ɪ'luːsɪv], **illusory** [ɪ'luːsərɪ] ADJ illusorisch, trügerisch

illustrate ['ɪləstreɪt] **◎** 26.2 VT **a** *book, story* illustrieren, bebildern; **his lecture was ~d by** coloured slides er veranschaulichte seinen Vortrag mit Farbdias; **~d (magazine)** Illustrierte *f* **b** (*fig*) veranschaulichen, illustrieren

illustration [ˌɪləs'treɪʃən] N **a** (= *picture*) Abbildung *f*, Bild *nt*, Illustration *f* **b** (*fig*) (*of problem, subject*) Erklärung *f*, Erläuterung *f*; (*of rule*) (= *act*) Veranschaulichung *f*; (= *thing*) Beispiel *nt*; **by way of ~** als Beispiel

illustrative ['ɪləstrətɪv] ADJ veranschaulichend, verdeutlichend; **~ of** bezeichnend *or* beispielhaft für; **for ~ purposes** zur Veranschaulichung

illustrator ['ɪləstreɪtə'] N Illustrator(in) *m(f)*

illustrious [ɪ'lʌstrɪəs] ADJ glanzvoll; *person* berühmt; *deeds, past* glorreich

ILO *abbr of* **International Labour Organization**

I'm [aɪm] *contr of* **I am**

image ['ɪmɪdʒ] N **a** (= *carved, sculpted figure*) Standbild *nt*, Figur *f*; (= *painted figure*) Bild *nt*, Bildnis *nt* (*geh*) **b** (= *likeness*) Ebenbild *nt*, Abbild *nt*; **he is the (spitting** (*inf*) *or* **living) ~ of his father** er ist sein Vater, wie er leibt und lebt, er ist seinem Vater wie aus dem Gesicht geschnitten; **God created man in his own ~** Gott (er)schuf den Menschen nach seinem Bilde **c** (*Opt*) Bild *nt*; **~ processing** Bildverarbeitung *f* **d** (= *mental picture*) Vorstellung *f*, Bild *nt* **e** (= *public face*) Image *nt*; **brand ~** Markenimage *nt*; **~ maker** Imagemacher(in) *m(f)* **f** (*Liter*) **to think in ~s** in Bildern *or* Metaphern denken

image-building N Imagepflege *f*

image converter N (*Elec*) Bildwandler *m*

image enhancement ['ɪmɪdʒɪnˌhɑː'nsmənt] N Bildoptimierung *f*

imagery ['ɪmɪdʒərɪ] N Metaphorik *f*; **visual ~** Bildersymbolik *f*

imaginable [ɪ'mædʒnəbl] ADJ vorstellbar, denkbar, erdenklich; **the best excuse ~** die beste Ausrede, die man sich vorstellen kann; **the easiest/fastest way ~** der denkbar einfachste/schnellste Weg; **parents encourage every activity ~** Eltern fördern alle erdenklichen Aktivitäten; **this is of no ~ value** das hat keinen erdenklichen Wert

imaginary [ɪ'mædʒɪnərɪ] ADJ *danger* eingebildet, imaginär; *characters* frei ersonnen, erfunden; *friend* erfunden; *line* vorgestellt; **~ world** Fantasiewelt *f*; **an ~ case** ein konstruierter Fall

imagination [ɪˌmædʒɪ'neɪʃən] N (*creative*) Fantasie *f*, Phantasie *f*, Vorstellungskraft *f*, Einbildungskraft *f*; (*self-deceptive*) Einbildung *f*; **to have (a lively** *or* **vivid) ~** (eine lebhafte *or* rege) Fantasie haben; **he has little ~** er hat wenig Fantasie; **use your ~** lassen Sie Ihrer Fantasie spielen; **in order to encourage children to use their ~(s)** um die Fantasie von Kindern anzuregen; **to lack ~** fantasielos *or* einfallslos sein; **it's just your ~!** das bilden Sie sich (*dat*) nur ein!; **it's all in your ~** das ist alles Einbildung; **to capture** *or* **catch sb's ~** jdn in seinen Bann ziehen; **it captures the ~** es ist faszinierend; **to stretch the ~** große Vorstellungskraft erfordern

imaginative ADJ , **imaginatively** ADV [ɪ'mædʒnətɪv, -lɪ] fantasievoll

imaginativeness [ɪ'mædʒnətɪvnɪs] N Fantasiereichtum *m*, Phantasiereichtum *m*; (*of person also*) Fantasie *f*, Phantasie *f*

imagine [ɪ'mædʒɪn] VT **a** (= *picture to oneself*) sich (*dat*) vorstellen, sich (*dat*) denken; **~ you're rich/lying on a beach** stellen Sie sich mal vor, Sie wären reich/lägen am Strand; **he ~d himself kissing her** er stellte sich vor, sie zu küssen; **you can ~ how I felt** Sie können sich vorstellen, wie mir zumute *or* zu Mute war; **you can't ~ how …** Sie machen sich kein Bild *or* Sie können sich nicht vorstellen wie …; **I can't ~ living there** ich kann mir nicht vorstellen, dort zu leben; **just ~ my surprise** stellen Sie sich nur meine Überraschung vor; **you can't ~ it!** Sie machen sich keine Vorstellungen!; **as may (well) be ~d** wie man sich (leicht) denken *or* vorstellen kann **b** (= *be under the illusion that*) sich (*dat*) einbilden; **don't ~ that …** bilden Sie sich nur nicht ein, dass …, denken Sie nur nicht, dass …; **he is always imagining things** (*inf*) er leidet ständig an Einbildungen; **you're (just) imagining things** (*inf*) Sie bilden sich das alles nur ein **c** (= *suppose, conjecture*) annehmen, vermuten; **is that her father? – I would ~ so** ist das ihr Vater? – ich denke schon; **I would never have ~d he could have done that** ich hätte nie gedacht, dass er das tun würde; **I ~d her to be dark-haired** ich habe sie mir dunkelhaarig vorgestellt

imbalance [ɪm'bæləns] N Unausgeglichenheit *f*

imbalanced [ɪm'bælənst] ADJ *distribution* ungleichmäßig; *structure* unausgewogen

imbecile [ɪ'mbəsiːl] **N** **a** Dummkopf *m*, Idiot *m*, Schwachkopf *m*; **to behave like an ~** sich völlig blödsinnig *or* wie ein Idiot benehmen **b** (*Med*) Schwachsinnige(r) *mf* **ADJ** **a** *person* beschränkt, schwachsinnig, geistig minderbemittelt (*inf*); *laugh* schwachsinnig, dumm, blöd(e); *idea* dumm, töricht **b** (*Med*) schwachsinnig, geistesschwach, imbezil (*spec*)

imbecilic [ˌɪmbə'sɪlɪk] ADJ = **imbecile** ADJ a

imbecility [ˌɪmbə'sɪlɪtɪ] N **a** Beschränktheit *f*, Idiotie *f*, Schwachsinn *m* **b** (*Med*) Schwachsinn *m*

imbed [ɪm'bed] VT = **embed**

imbibe [ɪm'baɪb] **VT** **a** (*form, hum*) trinken, bechern (*hum*) **b** (*fig*) *ideas, information* in sich (*acc*) aufnehmen **VI** (*hum*: = *drink*) viel trinken

imbroglio [ɪm'brəʊlɪəʊ] N (*liter*) verwickelte Lage, Verwirrung *f*

imbue [ɪm'bjuː] VT (*fig*) durchdringen, erfüllen (*with* mit)

IMF *abbr of* **International Monetary Fund** IWF *m*

imitable ['ɪmɪtəbl] ADJ nachahmbar, imitierbar

imitate ['ɪmɪteɪt] VT **a** (= *copy*) *person, accent etc* imitieren, nachmachen, nachahmen; **children learn by imitating their parents** Kinder lernen dadurch, dass sie ihre Eltern nachahmen **b** (= *counterfeit*) nachmachen, imitieren

imitation [ˌɪmɪ'teɪʃən] **N** Imitation *f*, Nachahmung *f*; **to do an ~ of sb** jdn imitieren *or* nachmachen *or* nachahmen; **~ is the sincerest form of flattery** (*prov*) Nachahmung ist das beste Kompliment **ADJ** unecht, künstlich, falsch; **~ gold/pearl** Gold-/Perlenimitation *f*; **~ leather** Lederimitation *f*, Kunstleder *nt*; **~ jewellery** unechter Schmuck; **~ fur** Webpelz *m*

imitative ['ɪmɪtətɪv] ADJ nachahmend, imitierend; **children are naturally ~** Kinder machen von Natur aus alles nach

imitator ['ɪmɪteɪtə'] N Nachahmer(in) *m(f)*, Imitator(in) *m(f)*

immaculate [ɪ'mækjʊlɪt] ADJ **a** untadelig, tadellos, picobello *inv* (*inf*); *behaviour* tadellos, mustergültig; *manuscript etc* fehlerfrei, einwandfrei **b** (*Eccl*) **the Immaculate Conception** die Unbefleckte Empfängnis

immaculately [ɪ'mækjʊlɪtlɪ] ADV tadellos; *behave also* untadelig

immanence ['ɪmənəns] N Immanenz *f*

immanent ['ɪmənənt] ADJ innewohnend, immanent (*also Philos*); **to be ~ in sth** einer Sache (*dat*) eigen sein or innewohnen

immaterial [ˌɪmə'tɪərɪəl] ADJ **a** (= *unimportant*) *objection, question* nebensächlich, unwesentlich, bedeutungslos; **it is quite ~ to me (whether)** ... es ist für mich ohne Bedeutung or unwichtig, (ob) ...; **that's (quite) ~** das spielt keine Rolle, das ist egal **b** (*Philos etc*) immateriell

immature [ˌɪmə'tjʊəʳ] ADJ (*lit, fig*) unreif; *plans, ideas etc also* unausgegoren; *wine* nicht ausreichend gelagert; **don't be so ~** sei nicht so kindisch!

immaturely [ˌɪmə'tjʊəlɪ] ADV *react, behave* unreif

immaturity [ˌɪmə'tjʊərɪtɪ] N Unreife *f*

immeasurable [ɪ'meʒərəbl] ADJ unermesslich, grenzenlos; *amount, distances* unmessbar, riesig

immeasurably [ɪ'meʒərəblɪ] ADV unermesslich, grenzenlos; **it has helped ~ that** ... es hat ungeheuer geholfen, dass ...

immediacy [ɪ'mi:dɪəsɪ] N Unmittelbarkeit *f*, Direktheit *f*; (= *urgency*) Dringlichkeit *f*

immediate [ɪ'mi:dɪət] ADJ **a** *knowledge, future, object, danger, threat, need, neighbour* unmittelbar; *vicinity, neighbourhood* unmittelbar, nächste(r, s); *cause, impact, successor* direkt, unmittelbar; **only the ~ family were invited** nur die engste Familie wurde eingeladen; **in the ~ aftermath of the war** unmittelbar nach dem Krieg; **our ~ plan is to go to France** wir fahren zuerst einmal nach Frankreich; **he has no ~ plans to retire** er hat derzeit or im Moment nicht die Absicht, sich zur Ruhe zu setzen **b** (= *instant*) *reply, reaction* sofortig, umgehend, prompt; *thought, conclusion* unmittelbar; *access* direkt; **to take ~ action** sofort handeln; **with ~ effect** mit sofortiger Wirkung; **to come into ~ effect** sofort in Kraft treten; **this had the ~ effect of** ... das hatte prompt zur Folge, dass ...; **for ~ delivery** zur sofortigen Lieferung; **the matter requires your ~ attention** die Sache bedarf sofort Ihrer Aufmerksamkeit **c** (= *most urgent*) *problem, concern* dringendste(r, s); **my ~ concern was for the children** mein erster Gedanke galt den Kindern

immediately [ɪ'mi:dɪətlɪ] ADV **a** (= *at once*) sofort, gleich; *reply, return, depart* umgehend, sofort; **~ after/before that** unmittelbar danach/davor; **that's not ~ obvious** das ist nicht sofort or unmittelbar klar **b** (= *directly*) direkt, unmittelbar; **~ below/above sth** direkt unter/über etw (*dat*) CONJ (*Brit*) sobald, sofort als ...

immemorial [ˌɪmɪ'mɔːrɪəl] ADJ uralt; **from time ~** seit undenklichen Zeiten, seit Urzeiten

immense [ɪ'mens] ADJ *difficulty, fortune, sum of money, possibilities* riesig, enorm, immens; *problem, difference also, ocean, heat* gewaltig; *self-confidence, success* ungeheuer, enorm; *achievement* großartig

immensely [ɪ'menslɪ] ADV unheimlich (*inf*), enorm; **to enjoy oneself ~** sich ausgezeichnet or köstlich amüsieren (*inf*); **~ grateful** äußerst dankbar

immensity [ɪ'mensɪtɪ] N ungeheure Größe, Unermesslichkeit *f*; **the ~ of this task** das gewaltige Ausmaß dieser Aufgabe; **the ~ of space** die Unendlichkeit des (Welt)alls

immerse [ɪ'mɜːs] VT **a** (*lit*) eintauchen (*in in* +*acc*); **to ~ sth in water** etw in Wasser tauchen; **to be ~d in water** unter Wasser sein **b** (*fig*) **to ~ oneself in one's work** sich in seine Arbeit vertiefen or stürzen (*inf*); **to ~ oneself in a language** sich vollkommen in eine Sprache vertiefen; **to be ~d in one's work** in seine Arbeit vertieft sein **c** (*Eccl*) untertauchen

immerser [ɪ'mɜːsəʳ] N Boiler *m*, Heißwasserbereiter *m*

immersion [ɪ'mɜːʃən] N **a** (*lit*) Eintauchen *nt*, Untertauchen *nt*; **after two hours' ~ in this solution** nach zwei Stunden in dieser Flüssigkeit **b** (*fig*) Vertieftsein *nt*, Versunkensein *nt* **c** (*Eccl*) Taufe *f* durch Untertauchen

immersion course N Intensivkurs *m*

immersion heater N (*Brit*) Boiler *m*, Heißwasserbereiter *m*; (*for jug etc*) Tauchsieder *m*

immigrant ['ɪmɪgrənt] N Einwanderer *m*, Einwanderin *f*, Immigrant(in) *m(f)* ATTR **the ~ population/community** die Einwanderer *pl*; ... **has an ~ population of 50,000** ... hat einen ausländischen Bevölkerungsanteil von 50.000

immigrant labour N , **immigrant workers** PL ausländische Arbeitnehmer *pl*; (*esp in Germany*) Gastarbeiter *pl*; (*in Switzerland*) Fremdarbeiter *pl*

immigrate ['ɪmɪgreɪt] VI einwandern, immigrieren (*to in* +*dat*)

immigration [ˌɪmɪ'greɪʃən] N Einwanderung *f*, Immigration *f*; (*also* **immigration control**: *at airport etc*) Einwanderungsstelle *f*

immigration authorities PL , **immigration department** N Einwanderungsbehörde *f*

immigration officer N Beamte(r) *m*/Beamtin *f* der Einwanderungsbehörde; (*at customs*) Grenzbeamte(r) *m*/-beamtin *f*

imminence ['ɪmɪnəns] N nahes Bevorstehen; **he hadn't appreciated the ~ of the danger/of war** er war sich (*dat*) nicht bewusst, dass die Gefahr/der Krieg so unmittelbar bevorstand

imminent ['ɪmɪnənt] ADJ nahe bevorstehend; **to be ~** nahe bevorstehen; **I think an announcement is ~** ich glaube, es steht eine Ankündigung bevor

immobile [ɪ'məʊbaɪl] ADJ (= *not moving*) unbeweglich; (= *not able to move*) *person* (*through injury etc*) bewegungslos; (*through lack of transport*) unbeweglich, immobil; **to render sb ~** jdn bewegungsunfähig machen

immobiliser [ɪ'məʊbɪlaɪzəʳ] N (*Aut*) Wegfahrsperre *f*

immobility [ˌɪməʊ'bɪlɪtɪ] N (= *inability to move*) (*through injury etc*) Unbeweglichkeit *f*, Bewegungslosigkeit *f*; (*through lack of transport*) Immobilität *f*

immobilize [ɪ'məʊbɪlaɪz] VT *car, broken limb* stilllegen; *army* bewegungsunfähig machen; *enemy tanks* außer Gefecht setzen; (*Fin*) *capital* festlegen; **to be ~d by fear/pain** sich vor Angst/Schmerzen nicht bewegen können

immoderate [ɪ'mɒdərɪt] ADJ *desire* übermäßig, unmäßig; *views* übertrieben, extrem; *person* extrem

immoderately [ɪ'mɒdərɪtlɪ] ADV *eat, drink* unmäßig; *hate* maßlos

immodest [ɪ'mɒdɪst] ADJ unbescheiden; (= *indecent*) unanständig

immodestly [ɪ'mɒdɪstlɪ] ADV *say, claim* unbescheiden; (= *indecently*) unanständig

immodesty [ɪ'mɒdɪstɪ] N Unbescheidenheit *f*; (= *indecency*) Unanständigkeit *f*

immolate ['ɪməʊleɪt] VT (*liter*) opfern, zum Opfer bringen

immolation [ˌɪməʊ'leɪʃən] N (*liter*) **a** (= *sacrifice*) Opfer *nt* **b** (*action*) Opfern *nt*, Opferung *f*

immoral [ɪ'mɒrəl] ADJ *action, life* unmoralisch; *behaviour also* unsittlich; *person also* sittenlos; **~ earnings** (*Jur*) Einkünfte *pl* aus gewerbsmäßiger Unzucht

immorality [ˌɪmə'rælɪtɪ] N Unmoral *f*; (*of behaviour also*) Unsittlichkeit *f*; (*of person also*) Sittenlosigkeit *f*; (= *immoral act*) Unsittlichkeit *f*

immorally [ɪ'mɒrəlɪ] ADV *act, live* unmoralisch; *behave also* unsittlich

immortal [ɪ'mɔːtl] ADJ *person, soul, God, phrase* unsterblich; *fame also* unvergänglich, ewig; *life* ewig; **in the ~ words of** ... in den unsterblichen Worten +*gen* ... N Unsterbliche(r) *mf*

immortality [ˌɪmɔː'tælɪtɪ] N (*of person, God*) Unsterblichkeit *f*; (*of fame*) Unvergänglichkeit *f*; (*of life*) Ewigkeit *f*

immortalize [ɪ'mɔːtəlaɪz] VT verewigen; **the film which ~d her** der Film, der sie unsterblich machte

immovable [ɪ'mu:vəbl] ADJ **a** (*lit*) unbeweglich; (*fig*) *obstacle* unüberwindlich, unbezwinglich **b** (*fig*: = *steadfast*) fest; **John was ~ in his**

decision John war von seiner Entscheidung nicht abzubringen

immovably [ɪ'mu:vəblɪ] ADV unbeweglich; **each picture was nailed ~ in place** alle Bilder waren fest angenagelt

immune [ɪ'mju:n] ADJ **a** (*Med*) immun (*from, to* gegen); **~ deficiency syndrome** Immunschwächekrankheit *f* **b** (*fig*) sicher (*from, to* vor +*dat*); (*from temptation etc*) geschützt, gefeit (*from, to* gegen); (= *not susceptible*: *to criticism etc*) unempfindlich, immun (*to* gegen); **~ from prosecution** vor Strafverfolgung geschützt, immun (*spec*)

immune system N Immunsystem *nt*

immunity [ɪ'mju:nɪtɪ] N **a** (*Med*) Immunität *f* (*to, against* gegen) **b** (*fig*) Sicherheit *f* (*from* vor +*dat*); (*diplomatic*) Immunität *f*; (*to temptation etc*) Geschütztheit *f*, Gefeitheit *f* (*to* gegen); (= *imperviousness to criticism etc*) Unempfindlichkeit *f*, Immunität *f* (*to* gegen); **~ from prosecution** Schutz *m* vor Strafverfolgung

immunization [ˌɪmjʊnaɪ'zeɪʃən] N Immunisierung *f*

immunize ['ɪmjʊnaɪz] VT immunisieren, immun machen

immunocompromised [ˌɪmjuːnəʊ'kɒmprəmaɪzd] ADJ (*Med*) immungeschwächt

immunodeficiency [ˌɪmjʊnəʊdɪ'fɪʃənsɪ] N (*Med*) Immunschwäche *f*

immunoglobulin [ˌɪmjʊnəʊ'glɒbjʊlɪn] N Immunglobulin *nt*

immunological [ˌɪmjʊnəʊ'lɒdʒɪkəl] ADJ (*Med*) immunologisch

immunologist [ˌɪmjʊ'nɒlədʒɪst] N (*Med*) Immunologe *m*, Immunologin *f*

immunology [ˌɪmjʊ'nɒlədʒɪ] N (*Med*) Immunologie *f*

immunosuppressive [ˌɪmjʊnəʊsʌ'presɪv] ADJ immunosuppressiv, das Immunsystem unterdrückend

immure [ɪ'mjʊəʳ] VT einkerkern

immutability [ɪˌmju:tə'bɪlɪtɪ] N Unveränderlichkeit *f*, Unwandelbarkeit *f*

immutable [ɪ'mju:təbl] ADJ unveränderlich, unwandelbar

imp [ɪmp] N Kobold *m*; (*inf*: = *child*) Racker *m* (*inf*)

impact ['ɪmpækt] N Aufprall *m* (*on, against* auf +*acc*); (*of two moving objects*) Zusammenprall *m*, Aufeinanderprallen *nt*; (*of bomb*) (*on house, factory*) Einschlag *m* (*on* in +*acc*); (*on roof, ground*) Aufschlag *m* (*on* auf +*dat*); (*of light, rays*) Auftreffen *nt* (*on* auf +*acc*); (= *force*) Wucht *f*; (*fig*) (Aus)wirkung *f* (*on* auf +*acc*); **on ~ (with)** beim Aufprall (auf +*acc*)/Zusammenprall (mit) *etc*; **he staggered under the ~ of the blow** er taumelte unter der Wucht des Schlages; **his speech had a great ~ on his audience** seine Rede machte großen Eindruck auf seine Zuhörer; **you can imagine the ~ of this on a four-year-old** Sie können sich vorstellen, wie sich das auf einen Vierjährigen auswirkt VI **to ~ on sb/sth** (*fig*) auf jdn/etw einwirken VT aufschlagen auf (+*acc*); **two things** zusammendrücken; (*fig*: = *have an effect on*) einwirken auf (+*acc*)

impacted [ɪm'pæktɪd] ADJ eingeklemmt, eingekeilt; *tooth also* impaktiert (*spec*); **to be ~ by sth** (*fig*) von etw getroffen werden

impact printer N Impactdrucker *m*

impair [ɪm'peəʳ] VT beeinträchtigen; *hearing, sight also* verschlechtern; *relations also, health* schaden (+*dat*)

impairment [ɪm'peəmənt] N **a** no pl (= *weakening*: *of judgement, mental functions*) Beeinträchtigung *f* **b** (= *defect*) Schaden *m*; **hearing/visual ~** Hör-/Sehschaden *m*; **speech** or **language ~** Sprachfehler *m*

impala [ɪm'pɑːlə] N Impala *f*

impale [ɪm'peɪl] VT aufspießen (*on auf* +*dat*)

impalpable [ɪm'pælpəbl] ADJ (*lit*) nicht fühlbar; (*fig*) nicht greifbar, vage

impanel [ɪmˈpænl] VT als Geschworenen einsetzen

imparity [ɪmˈpærɪtɪ] N Ungleichheit f

impart [ɪmˈpɑːt] VT **a** (= make known) information, news mitteilen, übermitteln; knowledge vermitteln; secret preisgeben **b** (= bestow) verleihen, geben (to +dat)

impartial [ɪmˈpɑːʃəl] ADJ unparteiisch, unvoreingenommen

impartiality [ɪmˌpɑːʃɪˈælɪtɪ], **impartialness** [ɪmˈpɑːʃəlnɪs] N Unparteilichkeit f, Unvoreingenommenheit f

impartially [ɪmˈpɑːʃəlɪ] ADV act unparteiisch; judge unvoreingenommen

impassable [ɪmˈpɑːsəbl] ADJ unpassierbar

impasse [ɪmˈpɑːs] N (fig) Sackgasse f; **to have reached an ~** sich festgefahren haben, einen toten Punkt erreicht haben

impassioned [ɪmˈpæʃnd] ADJ leidenschaftlich

impassive ADJ , **impassively** ADV [ɪmˈpæsɪv, -lɪ] gelassen

impassiveness [ɪmˈpæsɪvnɪs], **impassivity** [ɪmpæˈsɪvɪtɪ] N Gelassenheit f

impatience [ɪmˈpeɪʃəns] N Ungeduld f; (= intolerance) Unduldsamkeit f

impatient [ɪmˈpeɪʃənt] ADJ ungeduldig; (= intolerant) unduldsam (of gegenüber); **to be ~ to do sth** unbedingt etw tun wollen

impatiently [ɪmˈpeɪʃəntlɪ] ADV ungeduldig; **he looked forward ~ to her next visit** er konnte ihren nächsten Besuch kaum erwarten

impeach [ɪmˈpiːtʃ] VT **a** (Jur: = accuse) public official (eines Amtsvergehens) anklagen; (US) president ein Amtsenthebungsverfahren or Impeachment einleiten gegen; **to ~ sb for sth** jdn wegen einer Sache anklagen; **to ~ sb for doing sth** jdn anklagen, etw getan zu haben **b** (= challenge) sb's character, motives infrage or in Frage stellen, anzweifeln; witness's testimony also anfechten; **to ~ a witness** die Glaubwürdigkeit eines Zeugen anzweifeln or anfechten

impeachable [ɪmˈpiːtʃəbl] ADJ person (eines Amtsvergehens) anzuklagen; action als Amtsvergehen verfolgbar

impeachment [ɪmˈpiːtʃmənt] N **a** (Jur: = accusation) Anklage f (wegen eines Amtsvergehens); (US: of president) Amtsenthebungsverfahren nt, Impeachment nt **b** (= questioning) (of sb's character, motives) Infragestellung f, Anzweiflung f; (of testimony also) Anfechtung f

impeccably [ɪmˈpekəblɪ] ADV tadellos; **high standards** kompromisslos hohe Ansprüche

impeccable [ɪmˈpekəbl] ADJ untadelig, tadellos

impecunious [ˌɪmpɪˈkjuːnɪəs] ADJ mittellos, unbemittelt

impede [ɪmˈpiːd] VT person hindern; action, progress, work behindern, erschweren; movement, traffic, process behindern

impediment [ɪmˈpedɪmənt] N **a** Hindernis nt **b** (Med) Behinderung f; **speech ~** Sprachfehler m, Sprachstörung f

impedimenta [ɪmˌpedɪˈmentə] PL **a** (inf) (unnötiges) Gepäck **b** (Mil) Tross m

impel [ɪmˈpel] VT **a** (= force) nötigen; **to ~ sb to do sth** jdn (dazu) nötigen, etw zu tun; **to ~ sb (in)to action** jdn zum Handeln nötigen **b** (= drive on) (voran)treiben

impend [ɪmˈpend] VI bevorstehen; (= threaten) drohen

impending [ɪmˈpendɪŋ] ADJ bevorstehend; death, disaster also nahe; storm also heraufziehend; (= threatening) drohend; **a sense of ~ doom** eine Ahnung von unmittelbar drohendem Unheil

impenetrability [ɪmˌpenɪtrəˈbɪlɪtɪ] N Undurchdringlichkeit f; (of fortress) Uneinnehmbarkeit f; (of enemy lines) Undurchlässigkeit f; (of mind, character, mystery) Unergründlichkeit f; (of theory) Undurchschaubarkeit f, Undurchsichtigkeit f

impenetrable [ɪmˈpenɪtrəbl] ADJ undurchdringlich; fortress uneinnehmbar; enemy lines undurchlässig; mind, character, mystery unergründlich; theory undurchschaubar, undurchsichtig; accent völlig unverständlich (to sb für jdn)

impenetrably [ɪmˈpenɪtrəblɪ] ADV **a** thick, dark undurchdringlich **b** (= incomprehensibly) unergründlich, undurchschaubar; **his pictures can appear, at first sight, ~ obscure** auf den ersten Blick kann die Obskurität seiner Bilder unverständlich erscheinen

impenitence [ɪmˈpenɪtəns] N Reuelosigkeit f

impenitent [ɪmˈpenɪtənt] ADJ reuelos; **he remained quite ~** er zeigte keine Reue, er bereute es gar nicht; **to die ~** sterben, ohne bereut zu haben

impenitently [ɪmˈpenɪtəntlɪ] ADV ohne Reue

imperative [ɪmˈperətɪv] ADJ **a** need, desire dringend; **immediate action is ~** sofortiges Handeln ist dringend geboten **b** manner gebieterisch, befehlend, herrisch; order strikt **c** (Gram) imperativisch, Imperativ-, befehlend, Befehls-; **~ form** Imperativ- or Befehlsform f N **a** the political/moral/economic ~ die politische/moralische/wirtschaftliche Notwendigkeit; **there is a moral ~ to help the poor** es ist moralisch geboten, den Armen zu helfen **b** (Gram) Imperativ m; **in the ~** im Imperativ, in der Befehlsform

imperceptible [ˌɪmpəˈseptəbl] ADJ (to sb für jdn) nicht wahrnehmbar; difference, movement also unmerklich; sight also unsichtbar; sound also unhörbar

imperceptibly [ˌɪmpəˈseptəblɪ] ADV kaum wahrnehmbar; move, differ also unmerklich; (= invisibly) unsichtbar; (= inaudibly) unhörbar

imperfect [ɪmˈpɜːfɪkt] ADJ **a** (= faulty) unvollkommen, mangelhaft; (Comm) goods fehlerhaft **b** (= incomplete) unvollständig, unvollkommen **c** (Gram) Imperfekt-, Vergangenheits-; **~ form** Imperfekt- or Vergangenheitsform f N (Gram) Imperfekt nt, Vergangenheit f

imperfect competition N (Econ) unvollständige Konkurrenz

imperfection [ˌɪmpəˈfekʃən] N **a** no pl (= faultiness) Unvollkommenheit f, Mangelhaftigkeit f; (= incompleteness) Unvollständigkeit f **b** (= fault, defect) Mangel m

imperfectly [ɪmˈpɜːfɪktlɪ] ADV unvollkommen; (= incompletely) unvollständig

imperfect market N (Econ) unvollkommener Markt

imperial [ɪmˈpɪərɪəl] ADJ **a** (= of empire) Reichs-; (= of emperor) kaiserlich; **~ Rome** das Rom der Kaiserzeit; **His Imperial Highness** Seine Kaiserliche Majestät; **~ eagle** Kaiseradler m **b** (= of British Empire) Empire-, des Empire **c** (= lordly, majestic) majestätisch, gebieterisch **d** weights, measures englisch

---

IMPERIAL SYSTEM

In Großbritannien ist für Maß- und Gewichtsangaben zum Teil noch das **imperial system** in Gebrauch, auch wenn das metrische System offiziell bereits 1971 eingeführt wurde. Die Kinder rechnen in der Schule im metrischen Dezimalsystem, doch Lebensmittel werden oft immer noch in **pounds** verkauft, Bier wird nach **pints** abgezapft und viele Leute denken noch in **stones** und **pounds**, wenn es um das eigene Gewicht, bzw. in **feet** und **inches**, wenn es um die persönliche Größe geht. Entfernungen werden in **miles** angegeben. In den USA ist das **imperial system** sowieso noch für alle Gewichts- und Maßangaben gültig, wobei es bei den Flüssigkeiten einen kleinen Unterschied zu den britischen Maßen gibt: die amerikanischen Mengen von **liquid ounce**, **pint** und **gallon** sind etwas kleiner als die britischen Entsprechungen. Und über ihr persönliches Gewicht sprechen die Amerikaner nur in **pounds**.

---

imperialism [ɪmˈpɪərɪəlɪzəm] N Imperialismus m (often pej), Weltmachtpolitik f

imperialist [ɪmˈpɪərɪəlɪst] N Imperialist(in) m(f)

imperialistic [ɪmˌpɪərɪəˈlɪstɪk] ADJ imperialistisch

imperially [ɪmˈpɪərɪəlɪ] ADV majestätisch, gebieterisch

imperil [ɪmˈperɪl] VT gefährden, in Gefahr bringen

imperious ADJ , **imperiously** ADV [ɪmˈpɪərɪəs, -lɪ] herrisch, gebieterisch

imperishable [ɪmˈperɪʃəbl] ADJ (lit) unverderblich; (fig) unvergänglich

impermanence [ɪmˈpɜːmənəns] N Unbeständigkeit f

impermanent [ɪmˈpɜːmənənt] ADJ unbeständig

impermeable [ɪmˈpɜːmɪəbl] ADJ undurchlässig, impermeabel (spec)

impermissible [ˌɪmpəˈmɪsɪbl] ADJ unzulässig, unstatthaft

impers. abbr of **impersonal**

impersonal [ɪmˈpɜːsənl] ADJ unpersönlich (also Gram)

impersonality [ɪmˌpɜːsəˈnælɪtɪ] N Unpersönlichkeit f

impersonally [ɪmˈpɜːsənəlɪ] ADV unpersönlich

impersonate [ɪmˈpɜːsəneɪt] VT **a** (= pretend to be) sich ausgeben als **b** (= take off) imitieren, nachahmen

impersonation [ɪmˌpɜːsəˈneɪʃən] N **a** (= passing oneself off) Verkörperung f; **his ~ of an officer** sein Auftreten nt als Offizier **b** (= impression, takeoff) Imitation f, Nachahmung f; **he does ~s of politicians** er imitiert Politiker; **his Elvis ~** seine Elvis-Imitation

impersonator [ɪmˈpɜːsəneɪtə] N (Theat) Imitator(in) m(f)

impertinence [ɪmˈpɜːtɪnəns] N Unverschämtheit f, Impertinenz f (dated); **what ~!, the ~ of it!** so eine Unverschämtheit!; **to ask would be an ~** es wäre unverschämt zu fragen

impertinent [ɪmˈpɜːtɪnənt] ADJ **a** (= impudent) unverschämt (to zu, gegenüber), impertinent (dated) (to gegenüber) **b** (form: = irrelevant) irrelevant

impertinently [ɪmˈpɜːtɪnəntlɪ] ADV unverschämt

imperturbability [ˈɪmpəˌtɜːbəˈbɪlɪtɪ] N Unerschütterlichkeit f

imperturbable [ˌɪmpəˈtɜːbəbl] ADJ unerschütterlich; **he is completely ~** er ist durch nichts zu erschüttern

impervious [ɪmˈpɜːvɪəs] ADJ **a** substance, rock undurchlässig; **~ to rain/water** regen-/wasserundurchlässig; coat, material regen-/wasserdicht **b** (fig) unzugänglich (to für); (to criticism) unberührt (to von); **he is ~ to logic** ihm ist mit Logik nicht beizukommen; **she is ~ to pressure** sie lässt sich nicht unter Druck setzen

impetigo [ˌɪmpɪˈtaɪɡəʊ] N (Med) Eiterflechte f, Impetigo f

impetuosity [ɪmˌpetjʊˈɒsɪtɪ] N **a** (of action, person) Ungestüm nt; (of decision) Impulsivität f; (of attack) Stürmische(s) nt **b** (= impetuous behaviour) ungestümes Handeln

impetuous [ɪmˈpetjʊəs] ADJ act, person ungestüm, stürmisch; decision impulsiv; (liter) attack, wind stürmisch

impetuously [ɪmˈpetjʊəslɪ] ADV ungestüm

impetuousness [ɪmˈpetjʊəsnɪs] N = **impetuosity**

impetus [ˈɪmpɪtəs] N (lit, fig) Impuls m; (= force) Kraft f; (= momentum) Schwung m, Impetus m (geh); **the ~ behind this increase in activity** die treibende Kraft hinter dieser zunehmenden Aktivität; **to give (an) ~ to sth** (fig) einer Sache (dat) Impulse geben

impiety [ɪmˈpaɪətɪ] N **a** Gottlosigkeit f, Ungläubigkeit f; (= irreverence) Pietätlosigkeit f; (to God) Ehrfurchtslosigkeit f; (to superior etc) Respektlosigkeit f **b** (= act) Pietätlosigkeit f; (to reverence) Respektlosigkeit f

impinge [ɪmˈpɪndʒ] VI **a** (= have effect: on sb's life, habits) sich auswirken (on auf +acc), beeinflussen (on +acc); (= infringe: on sb's rights etc) einschränken (on +acc); **to ~ on sb/sb's consciousness** jdm zu Bewusstsein kommen **b** (= strike) (auf)treffen, fallen (on auf +acc)

impingement [ɪmˈpɪndʒmənt] N **a** Auswirkung f, Einfluss m (on auf +acc) **b** (= striking) Auftreffen nt (on auf +dat)

impious [ˈɪmpɪəs] ADJ (= not pious) gottlos, ungläubig; (= irreverent) pietätlos; (to God) ehrfurchtslos; (to superior etc) respektlos

impish [ˈɪmpɪʃ] ADJ remark schelmisch; smile, look also verschmitzt; child also lausbübisch

impishly [ˈɪmpɪʃlɪ] ADV schelmisch; smile, look also verschmitzt

impishness [ˈɪmpɪʃnɪs] N (of remark) Schelmische(s) nt; (of smile, look also) Verschmitztheit f; (of child also) Lausbubenhaftigkeit f

implacable [ɪmˈplækəbl] ADJ opponent, enemy, hatred, logic unerbittlich; fate unausweichlich; face unnachgiebig

implacably [ɪmˈplækəblɪ] ADV unerbittlich; **he was ~ opposed to capital punishment** er war ein unerbittlicher Gegner der Todesstrafe

implant [ɪmˈplɑːnt] VT **a** (fig) einimpfen (in sb jdm); **to be deeply ~ed in sb** (tief) in jdm verwurzelt sein **b** (Med) implantieren, einpflanzen VI (Med: in womb) sich einnisten N [ˈɪmplɑːnt](Med) Implantat nt; **breast ~** Brustimplantat nt

implantation [ɪmplɑːnˈteɪʃən] N **a** (fig) Einimpfung f (in sb jdm) **b** (Med) Implantation f, Einpflanzung f; (in womb) Einnisten nt

implausibility [ɪmplɔːzəˈbɪlɪtɪ] N mangelnde Plausibilität f; (of story, tale, excuse also) Unglaubhaftigkeit f, Unglaubwürdigkeit f; (of lie) Ungeschicktheit f

implausible [ɪmˈplɔːzəbl] ADJ nicht plausibel; story, tale, excuse also unglaubhaft, unglaubwürdig; lie wenig überzeugend, ungeschickt; combination unwahrscheinlich

implement [ˈɪmplɪmənt] N **a** Gerät nt; (= tool) Werkzeug nt **b** (fig: = agent) Werkzeug nt ▶ [ˈɪmplɪment] law vollziehen; contract, promise erfüllen; (= carry out, put into effect) plan, reform, measure etc durchführen, ausführen; decisions, ceasefire in die Tat umsetzen, durchführen

implementary [ˈɪmplɪmentərɪ], **implementing** [ˈɪmplɪmentɪŋ] ADJ ausführend; **~ regulations** pl Ausführungsbestimmungen pl

implementation [ɪmplɪmenˈteɪʃən] N (of law) Vollzug m; (of contract, promise) Erfüllung f; (= carrying out) (of plan etc) Ausführung f, Durchführung f; (of decisions, ceasefire) Durchführung f

implicate [ˈɪmplɪkeɪt] VT **to ~ sb in sth** jdn in etw verwickeln

implication [ɪmplɪˈkeɪʃən] N **a** (of statement, situation) Implikation f; (of law, agreement etc) Auswirkung f; (of events) Bedeutung f no pl, Implikation f; **the ~ of your statement is that ...** Ihre Behauptung impliziert, dass ...; **the possible ~s of his decision** die ganze Tragweite seiner Entscheidung; **by ~** implizit; **what are the political ~s?** was sind die politischen Auswirkungen?, was bedeutet das politisch gesehen? **b** (in crime) Verwicklung f (in in +acc)

implicit [ɪmˈplɪsɪt] ADJ **a** (= implied) implizit; threat indirekt, implizit; agreement, recognition stillschweigend; **to be ~ in sth** durch etw impliziert werden; in contract etc in etw (dat) impliziert sein; **a threat was ~ in his action** in seiner Handlungsweise lag eine indirekte Drohung **b** (= unquestioning) belief, confidence absolut, unbedingt

implicitly [ɪmˈplɪsɪtlɪ] ADV **a** (= by implication) implizit; accept, recognize stillschweigend; criticize indirekt **b** (= unquestioningly) **to trust/believe sb ~** jdm blind vertrauen/vorbehaltlos glauben

implied [ɪmˈplaɪd] ADJ impliziert; threat also indirekt

implied reader N (Liter) fiktiver Leser (als Bestandteil der literarischen Fiktion)

implied warranty N (US, Jur) konkludente Zusicherung (spec) (stillschweigende Zusage der Freiheit von Mängeln)

implode [ɪmˈpləʊd] VI implodieren ▶ (Ling) als Verschlusslaut or Explosivlaut sprechen VT

implore [ɪmˈplɔː] VT person anflehen, inständig bitten; forgiveness etc erbitten, erflehen; **do it, I ~ you!** ich flehe Sie an, tun Sie es!

imploring ADJ, **imploringly** ADV [ɪmˈplɔːrɪŋ, -lɪ] flehentlich, flehend

implosion [ɪmˈpləʊʒən] N Implosion f

imply [ɪmˈplaɪ] VT **a** (= suggest) andeuten, implizieren; **are you ~ing** or **do you mean to ~ that ...?** wollen Sie damit vielleicht sagen or andeuten, dass ...?; **this implies that he has changed his mind** das deutet darauf hin, dass er es sich (dat) anders überlegt hat **b** (= indicate, lead to conclusion) schließen lassen auf (+acc) **c** (= involve) bedeuten

impolite [ɪmpəˈlaɪt] ADJ unhöflich (to sb jdm gegenüber)

impolitely [ɪmpəˈlaɪtlɪ] ADV unhöflich

impoliteness [ɪmpəˈlaɪtnɪs] N Unhöflichkeit f

impolitic [ɪmˈpɒlɪtɪk] ADJ unklug

imponderable [ɪmˈpɒndərəbl] ADJ unberechenbar, unwägbar N unberechenbare or unwägbare Größe; **~s** Unwägbarkeiten pl, Imponderabilien pl (geh)

import [ɪmˈpɔːt] N **a** (Comm) Import m, Einfuhr f **b** (of speech, document etc) (= meaning) Bedeutung f; (= significance) Wichtigkeit f, Bedeutung f; **to be of (great) ~ to sb** für jdn von (großer) Bedeutung sein VT [ɪmˈpɔːt] **a** (Comm) goods einführen, importieren; population, workforce importieren **b** (= mean, imply) bedeuten, beinhalten **c** (Comput) importieren

importable [ɪmˈpɔːtəbl] ADJ einführbar

importance [ɪmˈpɔːtəns] ✪ 7.5 N Wichtigkeit f; (= significance also) Bedeutung f; (= influence also) Einfluss m; **I don't see the ~ of this** ich verstehe nicht, warum das wichtig sein soll; **to be of great ~** äußerst wichtig sein; **to be of no (great) ~** nicht (besonders) wichtig sein; **to be without ~** unwichtig sein; **to attach the greatest ~ to sth** einer Sache (dat) größten Wert or größte Wichtigkeit beimessen; **a man of ~** ein wichtiger or einflussreicher Mann; **to be full of one's own ~** ganz von seiner eigenen Wichtigkeit erfüllt sein

important [ɪmˈpɔːtənt] ADJ wichtig; (= significant also) bedeutend; (= influential) einflussreich, bedeutend; **that's not ~** das ist unwichtig; **it's not ~** (= doesn't matter) das macht nichts; **the (most) ~ thing is to stay fit** das Wichtigste or die Hauptsache ist, fit zu bleiben; **to try to look ~** sich (dat) ein gewichtiges Aussehen geben; **that letter looks ~** dieser Brief scheint wichtig zu sein; **it sounds ~** es hört sich an, als ob es wichtig sei; **he's trying to sound ~** er spielt sich (dat) wichtig auf; **to make sb feel ~** jdm das Gefühl geben, er/sie sei wichtig ADV = **importantly c**

importantly [ɪmˈpɔːtəntlɪ] ADV **a** (usu pej: = self-importantly) wichtigtuerisch (pej) **b** (= significantly) bedeutend, wesentlich; **to figure ~ in sth** eine bedeutende Rolle in etw (dat) spielen; **it is ~ different** das ist entscheidend anders **c** (qualifying sentence) **I was hungry and, more/most ~, my children were hungry** ich hatte Hunger, und was noch wichtiger/am allerwichtigsten war, meine Kinder hatten Hunger

importation [ɪmpɔːˈteɪʃən] N Einfuhr f, Import m

import duty N Einfuhrzoll m, Importzoll m

imported [ɪmˈpɔːtɪd] ADJ importiert, eingeführt, Import-; **~ goods/cars** importierte Waren/Autos, Importwaren/-autos pl

importer [ɪmˈpɔːtə] N Importeur(in) m(f) (of von); (= country also) Importland nt (of für)

import: import-export trade N Import-Export-Handel m, Ein- und Ausfuhr f; **import**

licence N Einfuhrlizenz f, Importlizenz f; **import permit** N Einfuhr- or Importerlaubnis f

importunate [ɪmˈpɔːtjʊnɪt] ADJ aufdringlich; salesman also, creditor, demand hartnäckig, beharrlich

importunately [ɪmˈpɔːtjʊnɪtlɪ] ADV aufdringlich

importunateness [ɪmˈpɔːtjʊnɪtnɪs] N Aufdringlichkeit f; (of salesman also, creditor, demand) Hartnäckigkeit f, Beharrlichkeit f

importune [ɪmpɔːˈtjuːn] VT belästigen; (creditor, with questions) zusetzen (+dat); (visitor) zur Last fallen (+dat)

importunity [ɪmpɔːˈtjuːnɪtɪ] N **a** = importunateness **b** (= demand, request) unverschämte Bitte

impose [ɪmˈpəʊz] VT **a** task, conditions aufzwingen, auferlegen (on sb jdm); sanctions, fine, sentence verhängen (on gegen); tax erheben; opinions, taste aufzwingen (on sb jdm); **to ~ a tax on sth** etw mit einer Steuer belegen, etw besteuern; **the pressures ~d upon teachers** der Druck, dem Lehrer ausgesetzt sind **b to ~ oneself** or **one's presence on sb** sich jdm aufdrängen; **he ~d himself on them for three months** er ließ sich einfach drei Monate bei ihnen nieder VI zur Last fallen (on sb jdm); **I don't wish to ~** ich möchte Ihnen nicht zur Last fallen

imposing [ɪmˈpəʊzɪŋ] ADJ beeindruckend, imponierend; person, appearance, building also stattlich, imposant

imposition [ɪmpəˈzɪʃən] N **a** no pl (of task, conditions) Aufzwingen nt, Auferlegung f (on sb jdm); (of sanctions, fine, sentence) Verhängung f (on gegen); (of tax) Erhebung f **b** (= tax) Steuer f (on für, auf +dat) **c** (= taking advantage) Zumutung f (on für); **I'd love to stay if it's not too much of an ~ (on you)** ich würde liebend gern bleiben, wenn ich Ihnen nicht zur Last falle

impossibility [ɪmpɒsəˈbɪlɪtɪ] N Unmöglichkeit f; **that's an ~** das ist unmöglich or ein Ding der Unmöglichkeit

impossible [ɪmˈpɒsəbl] ✪ 16.1 ADJ **a** unmöglich; dream unerfüllbar; **~!** ausgeschlossen!, unmöglich!; **it is ~ for him to leave/do that** er kann unmöglich gehen/das unmöglich tun; **this cooker is ~ to clean** es ist unmöglich, diesen Herd sauber zu kriegen; **I find it ~ to understand why she resigned** ich finde es unverständlich or unbegreiflich or ich kann nicht begreifen, warum sie gekündigt hat; **to make it ~ for sb to do sth** es jdm unmöglich machen, etw zu tun **b** (= hopeless) situation, position aussichtslos; **I am faced with an ~ choice/decision** ich stehe vor einer unmöglichen Wahl/Entscheidung; **you put me in an ~ position** du bringst mich in eine unmögliche Lage **c** (inf: = intolerable) person unerträglich, unmöglich (inf); **you're ~!** du bist unmöglich! (inf) N Unmögliche(s) nt; **to ask for the ~** Unmögliches verlangen; **to do the ~** (in general) Unmögliches tun; (in particular case) das Unmögliche tun

impossibly [ɪmˈpɒsəblɪ] ADV unmöglich; **an ~ high standard** ein unerreichbar hohes Niveau

impostor [ɪmˈpɒstə] N Betrüger(in) m(f), Schwindler(in) m(f); (assuming higher position also) Hochstapler(in) m(f)

imposture [ɪmˈpɒstʃə] N Betrug m, Schwindelei f

impotence [ˈɪmpətəns] N **a** (sexual) Impotenz f **b** (fig) Schwäche f, Machtlosigkeit f **c** (physical) Schwäche f, Kraftlosigkeit f

impotent [ˈɪmpətənt] ADJ **a** (sexually) impotent **b** (fig) schwach, machtlos; grief, rage ohnmächtig **c** (physically) schwach, kraftlos

impound [ɪmˈpaʊnd] VT **a** (= seize) goods, assets, contraband beschlagnahmen **b** cattle einsperren; car abschleppen (lassen)

impoverish [ɪmˈpɒvərɪʃ] VT person, country in Armut bringen, verarmen lassen; soil auslaugen, erschöpfen; *(fig) culture* verkümmern *or* verarmen lassen

impoverished [ɪmˈpɒvərɪʃt] ADJ arm; *person, conditions also* ärmlich; (= *having become poor*) verarmt; *soil* ausgelaugt, erschöpft; *supplies* erschöpft; *(fig)* dürftig

impoverishment [ɪmˈpɒvərɪʃmənt] N Verarmung *f*; *(of soil)* Auslaugung *f*, Erschöpfung *f*; *(fig: of culture)* Verkümmerung *f*

impracticability [ɪmˌpræktɪkəˈbɪlɪtɪ] N Impraktikabilität *f*; *(of design, size)* Unbrauchbarkeit *f*; *(of road)* schlechte Befahrbarkeit

impracticable [ɪmˈpræktɪkəbl] ADJ impraktikabel; *plan also* in der Praxis nicht anwendbar, praktisch unmöglich; *design, size* unbrauchbar; *road* schwer befahrbar

impractical [ɪmˈpræktɪkəl] ADJ unpraktisch; *scheme also* unbrauchbar

impracticality [ɪmˌpræktɪˈkælɪtɪ] N *(of person)* unpraktische Art; *(of scheme, idea)* Unbrauchbarkeit *f*

imprecate [ˈɪmprɪkeɪt] VT verfluchen, verwünschen; **to ~ curses on sb** jdn verfluchen

imprecation [ˌɪmprɪˈkeɪʃən] N Verwünschung *f*, Fluch *m*

imprecise ADJ , **imprecisely** ADV [ˌɪmprɪˈsaɪs, -lɪ] ungenau, unpräzis(e)

imprecision [ˌɪmprɪˈsɪʒən] N Ungenauigkeit *f*

impregnable [ɪmˈprɛgnəbl] ADJ *(Mil)* fortress, defences uneinnehmbar; *(fig)* position unerschütterlich; *argument* unwiderlegbar, unumstößlich

impregnate [ˈɪmprɛgneɪt] VT **a** (= *saturate*) tränken **b** *(fig)* erfüllen; *person* durchdringen, erfüllen **c** *(Biol* = *fertilize)* befruchten; *humans also* schwängern

impregnation [ˌɪmprɛgˈneɪʃən] N **a** (= *saturation*) Tränkung *f* **b** *(fig)* Erfüllung *f* **c** *(Biol:* = *fertilization)* Befruchtung *f*; *(of humans also)* Schwängerung *f*

impresario [ˌɪmprɛˈsɑːrɪəʊ] N Impresario *m*, Theater-/Operndirektor(in) *m(f)*

impress [ɪmˈprɛs] ⚙ 13 **a** *person* beeindrucken, (= *arouse admiration in*) imponieren (+*dat*); **how did it/he ~ you?** wie fanden Sie das/ihn?; **he/it ~ed me favourably** er/das hat einen guten *or* günstigen Eindruck auf mich gemacht; **I am not ~ed** das beeindruckt mich nicht, das imponiert mir gar nicht; **she is not easily ~ed** sie lässt sich nicht so leicht beeindrucken; **he doesn't ~ me as a politician** als Politiker macht er keinen Eindruck auf mich **b** (= *fix in mind*) einschärfen *(on sb* jdm); *idea, danger, possibility* (deutlich) klarmachen *(on sb* jdm) **c** (= *press to make mark*) **to ~ sth onto/into sth** etw auf etw (*acc*) aufdrücken *or* aufprägen/in etw (*acc*) eindrücken *or* einprägen; **his parting words ~ed themselves on my mind** seine Abschiedsworte haben sich mir eingeprägt; **that day has remained ~ed in my memory** diesen Tag werde ich nie vergessen

VI Eindruck machen; *(person: deliberately)* Eindruck schinden *(inf)*

N [ˈɪmprɛs] Abdruck *m*

impressible [ɪmˈprɛsɪbl] ADJ beeinflussbar, leicht zu beeindrucken *(to* durch), empfänglich *(to* für)

impression [ɪmˈprɛʃən] ⚙ 6.2 N **a** Eindruck *m*; **to make a good/bad ~ on sb** einen guten/schlechten Eindruck auf jdn machen; **the theatre made a lasting ~ on me** das Theater beeindruckte mich tief; **his words made an ~** seine Worte machten Eindruck; **I haven't made any ~ on this job** ich bin mit dieser Arbeit noch nicht weit gekommen; **he made quite an ~ on the pile of ironing** er hat den Stapel Bügelwäsche fast ganz weggebügelt; **he created an ~ of power** er erweckte den Eindruck von Macht; **first ~s are usually right** der erste Eindruck ist gewöhnlich richtig

b (= *idea*) Eindruck *m*; (= *feeling*) Gefühl *nt*; **to give sb the ~ that ...** jdm den Eindruck vermitteln, dass ...; **he gave the ~ of being unhap-**

py/self-confident er wirkte unglücklich/selbstsicher; **I was under the ~ that ...** ich hatte den Eindruck, dass ...; **that gives an ~ of light** das vermittelt den Eindruck von Licht; **he had the ~ of falling** er hatte das Gefühl, zu fallen

c *(on wax etc)* Abdruck *m*; *(of engraving)* Prägung *f*

d *(of book etc)* Nachdruck *m*; **first ~** Erstdruck *m*

e (= *take-off*) Nachahmung *f*, Imitation *f*; **to do an ~ of sb** jdn imitieren *or* nachahmen

impressionable [ɪmˈprɛʃnəbl] ADJ für Eindrücke empfänglich, leicht zu beeindrucken *pred (pej)*; **at an ~ age** in einem Alter, in dem man für Eindrücke besonders empfänglich ist

impressionism [ɪmˈprɛʃənɪzəm] N Impressionismus *m*

impressionist [ɪmˈprɛʃənɪst] N Impressionist(in) *m(f)*

impressionistic [ɪmˌprɛʃəˈnɪstɪk] ADJ impressionistisch; *(fig)* story, account also in groben Zügen (geschildert)

impressive [ɪmˈprɛsɪv] ADJ beeindruckend; *performance, speech, ceremony, personality also* eindrucksvoll; *(in size)* building, person also imposant

impressively [ɪmˈprɛsɪvlɪ] ADV eindrucksvoll; **he was ~ brave** sein Mut war beeindruckend; **she won both tournaments ~** sie gewann beide Turniere auf eindrucksvolle Weise

imprimatur [ˌɪmprɪˈmɑːtəʳ] N *(form)* Imprimatur *nt*

imprint [ɪmˈprɪnt] **VT a** (= *mark*) leather prägen; *paper* bedrucken; *seal etc* aufprägen *(on auf* +*acc)*; *(on paper)* aufdrucken *(on auf* +*acc)* **b** *(fig)* einprägen *(on sb* jdm); **to be ~ed on sb's mind** sich jdm eingeprägt haben; **to be ~ed on sb's memory** sich in jds Gedächtnis (*acc*) eingeprägt haben **N** [ˈɪmprɪnt] **a** *(lit)* *(on leather, wax etc)* Abdruck *m*; *(on paper)* (Auf)druck *m*; *(fig)* Spuren *pl*, Zeichen *pl*, bleibender Eindruck **b** *(Typ)* Impressum *nt*; **under the Collins ~** mit dem Collins-Impressum

imprison [ɪmˈprɪzn] VT *(lit)* inhaftieren, einsperren *(inf)*; *(fig)* gefangen halten; **to be ~ed** *(lit, fig)* gefangen sein; **to keep sb ~ed** jdn gefangen halten

imprisonment [ɪmˈprɪznmənt] N (= *action*) Einsperren *nt (inf)*, Inhaftierung *f*; (= *state*) Gefangenschaft *f*; **the prospect of ~** die Aussicht auf eine Freiheitsstrafe; **to sentence sb to one month's/life ~** jdn zu einem Monat Gefängnis *or* Freiheitsstrafe/zu lebenslänglicher Freiheitsstrafe verurteilen; **to serve a term of ~** eine Freiheitsstrafe verbüßen

impro [ˈɪmprəʊ] N *(inf)* Impro *f (inf)*, Improvisation *f*

improbability [ɪmˌprɒbəˈbɪlɪtɪ] N Unwahrscheinlichkeit *f*

improbable [ɪmˈprɒbl] ADJ unwahrscheinlich

improbably [ɪmˈprɒbəlɪ] ADV unwahrscheinlich; **he works, ~, for the World Bank** er arbeitet, kaum zu glauben, für die Weltbank

impromptu [ɪmˈprɒmptjuː] ADJ improvisiert; **an ~ speech** eine Stegreifrede ADV improvisiert; *perform* aus dem Stegreif; **to speak/sing ~** improvisieren **N** *(Mus)* Impromptu *nt*

improper [ɪmˈprɒpəʳ] ADJ (= *unsuitable*) unpassend, unangebracht; (= *unseemly*) unschicklich; (= *indecent*) unanständig; (= *wrong*) diagnosis, interpretation unzutreffend; *use* unsachgemäß; (= *dishonest*) practice unlauter; (= *not professional*) conduct unehrenhaft; **it is ~ to do that** es gehört sich nicht, das zu tun; **~ use of tools** Zweckentfremdung *f* von Geräten; **~ use of drugs/one's position** Drogen-/Amtsmissbrauch *m*

improperly [ɪmˈprɒpəlɪ] ADV *act, dress* unpassend; *use, install* unsachgemäß; *diagnose* unzutreffend; *behave* unangemessen; (= *indecently*) unanständig

impropriety [ˌɪmprəˈpraɪətɪ] N Unschicklichkeit *f*; *(of behaviour etc, language, remark)* Ungehörigkeit *f*; (= *indecency: of jokes etc*) Unanständigkeit *f*; **sexual/financial ~** sexuelles/finanzielles Fehlverhalten

improv [ˈɪmprɒv] N *(inf)* improvisierter Sketch

improve [ɪmˈpruːv] **VT a** (= *make better*) verbessern; *knowledge* erweitern; *salaries* aufbessern; *area, appearance* verschönern; *sauce, food etc* verfeinern; *production, value* erhöhen, steigern; **to ~ one's mind** sich weiterbilden **b** **to ~ the shining hour** *(liter)* die Gelegenheit beim Schopfe packen

VI sich verbessern, sich bessern; *(area, appearance)* schöner werden; *(production, value)* sich erhöhen, steigen; **he has ~d in maths** er hat sich in Mathematik gebessert; **to ~ with practice** durch Übung besser werden; **wine ~s with age** je älter der Wein desto besser; **the invalid is improving** dem Kranken geht es besser; **I'll try to ~** ich werde versuchen, mich zu bessern; **things are improving** es sieht schon besser aus, die Lage bessert sich

VR **to ~ oneself** an sich (*dat*) arbeiten

▸ **improve (up)on** VI +prep obj **a** (= *improve*) übertreffen, besser machen; *nature, performance* verbessern; **that can't be improved upon** das kann man nicht übertreffen **b** *(Comm, Fin)* offer überbieten, gehen über (+*acc*)

improved [ɪmˈpruːvd] ADJ besser, verbessert; *offer also* höher

improvement [ɪmˈpruːvmənt] N Verbesserung *f*, Besserung *f*; *(of area, appearance)* Verschönerung *f*; *(of sauce, food etc)* Verfeinerung *f*; *(increase)* *(in production, value)* Erhöhung *f*, Steigerung *f*; *(of knowledge)* Erweiterung *f*; *(of salaries)* Aufbesserung *f*; *(in health)* Besserung *f*; *(in studies)* Verbesserung *f*, Fortschritte *pl*; **an ~ in performance** eine Leistungssteigerung; **to be open to ~** verbesserungsfähig sein; **an ~ on the previous one** eine Verbesserung gegenüber dem Früheren; **to make ~s** Verbesserungen machen *or* durchführen *(to* an +*dat)*; **to carry out ~s to a house** Ausbesserungs- *or* *(to appearance)* Verschönerungsarbeiten an einem Haus vornehmen

improvidence [ɪmˈprɒvɪdəns] N mangelnde Vorsorge *(of* für), Sorglosigkeit *f (of in* Bezug auf +*acc)*

improvident [ɪmˈprɒvɪdənt] ADJ sorglos

improving [ɪmˈpruːvɪŋ] ADJ informativ, lehrreich; *book also* bildend; (= *morally improving*) erbaulich

improvisation [ˌɪmprəvaɪˈzeɪʃən] N Improvisation *f*, Improvisierung *f*; *(object improvised)* Provisorium *nt*

improvise [ˈɪmprəvaɪz] **VT** improvisieren **VI** improvisieren; **to ~ on a tune** *(Mus)* über eine Melodie improvisieren; **to ~ on a story** eine Geschichte abändern

imprudence [ɪmˈpruːdəns] N Unklugheit *f*

imprudent ADJ , **imprudently** ADV [ɪmˈpruːdənt, -lɪ] unklug

impudence [ˈɪmpjʊdəns] N Unverschämtheit *f*, Frechheit *f*; **what ~!** so eine Unverschämtheit *or* Frechheit!; **he had the ~ to ask me** er hatte die Stirn *or* er besaß die Frechheit, mich zu fragen

impudent ADJ , **impudently** ADV [ˈɪmpjʊdənt, -lɪ] unverschämt, dreist

impugn [ɪmˈpjuːn] VT *person* angreifen; *sb's behaviour etc also* scharfe Kritik üben an (+*dat*); *sb's honesty, motives* in Zweifel ziehen, Zweifel hegen an (+*dat*); *statement, evidence, veracity of witness* bestreiten, anfechten

impulse [ˈɪmpʌls] N Impuls *m*; (= *driving force*) (Stoß- *or* Trieb)kraft *f*; **nerve ~** nervöser Reiz *or* Impuls; **to give a new ~ to the peace process** dem Friedensprozess einen neuen Impuls geben; **man of ~** impulsiver Mensch; **she resisted an ~ to smile** sie widerstand dem Impuls zu lächeln; **to yield to a sudden ~** einem Impuls nachgeben *or* folgen; **on ~** aus einem Impuls heraus, impulsiv; **I had an ~ to hit him** ich hatte den unwiderstehlichen Drang or das plötzliche Verlangen, ihn zu schlagen; **he is ruled by his ~** er lässt sich von seinen spontanen Regungen leiten

impulse buying [ˌɪmpʌls'baɪɪŋ] N impulsives or spontanes Kaufen; **an impulse buy** or **purchase** ein Impulskauf m

impulsion [ɪm'pʌlʃən] N (lit: = act of impelling) Antrieb m; (lit, fig: = driving force also) Antriebskraft f; (fig) (= impetus) Impuls m; (= compulsion) Trieb m, Drang m

impulsive [ɪm'pʌlsɪv] ADJ **a** impulsiv; (= spontaneous) spontan **b** (Phys, Tech) (an)treibend; **~ force** Triebkraft f

impulsively [ɪm'pʌlsɪvlɪ] ADV impulsiv; (= spontaneously) spontan

impulsiveness [ɪm'pʌlsɪvnɪs] N Impulsivität f; (= spontaneity) Spontaneität f

impunity [ɪm'pjuːnɪtɪ] N Straflosigkeit f; **with ~** ungestraft

impure [ɪm'pjʊəʳ] ADJ water, drugs, thoughts, mind unrein; food verunreinigt; motives unsauber

impurity [ɪm'pjʊərɪtɪ] N Unreinheit f; (of food) Verunreinigung f; (of motives) Unsauberkeit f; **the impurities in the liquid** die Verunreinigungen in der Flüssigkeit

imputation [ˌɪmpjʊ'teɪʃən] N (of crime) Bezichtigung f; (of lie also) Unterstellung f

impute [ɪm'pjuːt] VT zuschreiben (to sb/sth jdm/ einer Sache); **to ~ a crime to sb** jdn eines Verbrechens bezichtigen

---

in [ɪn]

1 PREPOSITION	3 ADJECTIVE
2 ADVERB	4 PLURAL NOUN

1 – PREPOSITION

When **in** is the second element of a phrasal verb, eg **ask in**, **fill in**, **hand in**, look up the verb. When it is part of a set combination, eg in **danger**, **in the end**, **weak in**, **wrapped up in**, look up the other word.

a position in (+dat); (with motion) in (+acc); **it was in the lorry/bag/car** es war auf dem Lastwagen/in der Tasche/im Auto; **he put it in the lorry/car/bag** er legte es auf den Lastwagen/ins Auto/steckte es in die Tasche; **in here/there** hierin, hier/da drin (inf); **go in that direction** gehen Sie in diese or dieser Richtung; **in the street** auf der/die Straße; **in Thompson Street** in der Thompsonstraße; **he lives in a little village** er wohnt auf or in einem kleinen Dorf; **sitting in the window** am Fenster sitzend; **a flag hung in the window** eine Flagge hing im Fenster; **in (the) church** in der Kirche; **to stay in the house** im Haus or (at home) zu Hause or zuhause (Aus, Sw) bleiben; **in bed/ prison** im Bett/Gefängnis; **in Germany/Switzerland/the United States** in Deutschland/der Schweiz/den Vereinigten Staaten

after the superlative, **in** is sometimes untranslated and the genitive case used instead.

the highest mountain in Scotland der höchste Berg Schottlands or in Schottland; **the best in the class** der Beste der Klasse, der Klassenbeste

b people bei; **you can find examples of this in Dickens** man findet Beispiele dafür bei Dickens or in Dickens' Werken; **rare in a child of that age** selten bei einem Kind in diesem Alter; **you have a great leader in him** ihr habt ihr einen großen Führer; **he hasn't got it in him** er hat nicht das Zeug dazu; **he doesn't have it in him to ...** er bringt es nicht fertig, ... zu ...

c dates, seasons, time of day in (+dat); **in 1999** (im Jahre) 1999; **in May 1999** im Mai 1999; **in the sixties** in den sechziger Jahren or Sechzigerjahren; **in June** im Juni; **in (the) spring** im Frühling; **in the morning(s)** morgens, am Morgen, am Vormittag; **in the afternoon** nachmittags, am Nachmittag; **in the daytime** tagsüber,

während des Tages; **in the evening** abends, am Abend; **three o'clock in the afternoon** drei Uhr nachmittags; **in those days** damals, zu jener Zeit

d time of life in (+dat); **she is in her thirties** sie ist in den Dreißigern, in den mittleren Alter; **in old age** im Alter; **in childhood** in der Kindheit, im Kindesalter; **in my childhood** in meiner Kindheit

e interval of time in (+dat); **she did it in three hours** sie machte es in drei Stunden or innerhalb von drei Stunden; **in a short time** in kurzer Zeit; **in a week('s time)** in einer Woche; **I haven't seen him in years** ich habe ihn jahrelang or seit Jahren nicht mehr gesehen; **in a moment** or **minute** sofort, gleich

f numbers, quantities zu; **packed in hundreds** zu Hunderten abgepackt; **to walk in twos** zu zweit gehen; **to count in fives** in Fünfern zählen; **to die in hundreds** zu hunderten or Hunderten sterben; **in large/small quantities** in großen/kleinen Mengen; **in some measure** in gewisser Weise, zu einem gewissen Grad; **in part** teilweise, zum Teil

g ratios **he has a one in 500 chance of winning** er hat eine Gewinnchance von eins zu 500; **one (man) in ten** einer von zehn, jeder Zehnte; **one book/child in ten** jedes zehnte Buch/ Kind, ein Buch/Kind von zehn; **one in five children** ein Kind von fünf; **a tax of twenty pence in the pound** ein Steuersatz von zwanzig Prozent; **there are 12 inches in a foot** ein Fuß hat 12 Zoll

h manner, state, condition **to speak in a loud/ soft voice** mit lauter/leiser Stimme sprechen, laut/leise sprechen; **to speak in a whisper** flüstern, flüsternd sprechen; **to speak in German** Deutsch reden; **the background is painted in red** der Hintergrund ist rot (gemalt) or in Rot gehalten; **to pay in dollars** mit or in Dollar bezahlen; **to stand in a row/in groups** in einer Reihe/in Gruppen stehen; **in this way** so, auf diese Weise; **she squealed in delight** sie quietschte vor Vergnügen; **in anger** im Zorn; **in surprise** überrascht; **to be in a rage** wütend or zornig sein; **in good condition** in gutem Zustand; **to live in luxury/poverty** im Luxus/in Armut leben

i clothes in (+dat); **in one's best clothes** in Sonntagskleidung; **in his shirt** im Hemd; **in his shirt sleeves** in Hemdsärmeln, hemdsärmelig; **in his slippers** in Hausschuhen; **dressed in white** weiß gekleidet; **she was dressed in silk** sie war in Seide gekleidet; **the lady in green** die Dame in Grün

j substance, material **upholstered in silk** mit Seide bezogen; **to paint in oils** in Öl malen; **to write in ink/pencil** mit Tinte/Bleistift schreiben; **in marble** in Marmor, marmorn; **a sculptor who works in marble** ein Bildhauer, der mit Marmor arbeitet

k in respect of **blind in the left eye** auf dem linken Auge blind, links blind; **a rise in prices** ein Preisanstieg m, ein Anstieg m der Preise; **ten feet in height by thirty in length** zehn Fuß hoch auf dreißig Fuß lang; **the trousers are too long in the leg** die (Hosen)beine sind zu lang; **five in number** fünf an der Zahl; **the latest thing in hats** der letzte Schrei bei Hüten

l occupation, activity **he is in the army** er ist beim Militär; **he is in banking/the motor business** er ist im Bankwesen/in der Autobranche (tätig)

m set structures

♦ **in + -ing in saying this, I ...** wenn ich das sage, ... ich; **in trying to escape** beim Versuch zu fliehen, beim Fluchtversuch; **in trying to save him** she fell into the water herself beim Versuch or als sie versuchte, ihn zu retten, fiel sie selbst ins Wasser; **but in saying this** aber indem ich dies sage; **he made a mistake in saying that** es war ein Fehler von ihm, das zu sagen

♦ **in that** (= seeing that) insofern als; **the plan was unrealistic in that it didn't take account of the fact that ...** der Plan war unrealistisch, da or weil ich nicht berücksichtige, dass ...

2 – ADVERB

When **in** is the second element in a phrasal verb, eg **come in**, **live in**, **sleep in**, look up the verb.

da; (at home also) zu Hause, zuhause (Aus, Sw); **there is nobody in** es ist niemand da/zu Hause

to be in may require a more specific translation.

the train is in der Zug ist da or angekommen; **the harvest is in** die Ernte ist eingebracht; **the tide is in** (Cricket) unsere Mannschaft ist am Schlag; **the Socialists are in** (= in power) die Sozialisten sind an der Regierung; **our candidate is in** unser Kandidat wurde gewählt or ist reingekommen (inf); **my luck is in** ich habe einen Glückstag

♦ **to be in for sth he's in for a surprise/ disappointment** ihm steht eine Überraschung/ Enttäuschung bevor, er kann sich auf eine Überraschung/Enttäuschung gefasst machen; **we are in for rain/a cold spell** uns (dat) steht Regen/eine Kältewelle bevor; **he is in for the job of manager** (= applying for) er hat sich um die Stelle des Managers beworben; **he's in for it!** der kann sich auf was gefasst machen (inf), der kann sich freuen (iro)

♦ **to have it in for sb** (inf) es auf jdn abgesehen haben (inf)

♦ **to be in on sth** an einer Sache beteiligt sein; on secret etc über etw (acc) Bescheid wissen; **he likes to be in on things** er mischt gern (überall) mit (inf)

♦ **to be (well) in with sb** sich gut mit jdm verstehen

3 – ADJECTIVE

(inf) in inv (inf); **long skirts are in** lange Röcke sind in (inf) or sind in Mode; **the in thing** das, was zur Zeit in ist (inf) or Mode ist; **the in thing to is to ...** es ist zur Zeit in (inf) or Mode, zu ...; **it's the in place to go** da gehen jetzt alle hin; **the in thing to do** groß in Mode

4 – the ins PLURAL NOUN

a = details

♦ **the ins and outs** die Einzelheiten pl; **to know the ins and outs of sth** bei einer Sache genau Bescheid wissen; **I don't know the ins and outs of the situation** über die Einzelheiten der Sache weiß ich nicht Bescheid

b Pol (US) **the ins** die Regierungspartei

---

inability [ˌɪnə'bɪlɪtɪ] N Unfähigkeit f, Unvermögen nt; **~ to pay** Zahlungsunfähigkeit f

inaccessibility ['ɪnæk,sesə'bɪlɪtɪ] N Unzugänglichkeit f; (of place also) Unerreichbarkeit f; (fig: of idea, music, painting, novel) Unverständlichkeit f

inaccessible [ˌɪnæk'sesəbl] ADJ **a** (= impossible to reach) unzugänglich (to sb/sth für jdn/etw); place also unerreichbar; **to be ~ by land/sea** auf dem Landweg/Seeweg nicht erreichbar sein **b** (fig: = difficult to understand) idea, music, painting, novel unverständlich

inaccuracy [ɪn'ækjʊrəsɪ] N Ungenauigkeit f; (= incorrectness) Unrichtigkeit f

inaccurate [ɪn'ækjʊrɪt] ADJ (= lacking accuracy) ungenau; (= not correct) unrichtig; **she was ~ in her judgement of the situation** ihre Beurteilung der Lage traf nicht zu; **it is ~ to say that ...** es ist nicht richtig zu sagen, dass ...

inaccurately [ɪn'ækjʊrɪtlɪ] ADV ungenau; (= incorrectly) unrichtig

inaction [ɪn'ækʃən] N Untätigkeit f, Tatenlosigkeit f

inactive [ɪn'æktɪv] ADJ untätig; person, life, hands also müßig (geh); mind träge, müßig (geh); volcano erloschen, untätig; (Fin) account umsatzlos; **don't have money lying ~ in the bank** lassen Sie (Ihr) Geld nicht auf der Bank brachliegen

inactivity [ˌɪnæk'tɪvɪtɪ] N Untätigkeit f, (of mind) Trägheit f; (Comm) Stille f, Flaute f

inadequacy [ɪn'ædɪkwəsɪ] N Unzulänglichkeit f; (of measures) Unangemessenheit f

inadequate [ɪnˈædɪkwɪt] ADJ unzulänglich, inadäquat (*geh*); *supplies, resources, punishment, reasons, proposals also* unzureichend; *measures* unangemessen; **he is ~ for such a job/responsibility** er ist für eine solche Stelle nicht geeignet/einer solchen Verantwortung nicht gewachsen; **she makes him feel ~** sie gibt ihm das Gefühl der Unzulänglichkeit

inadequately [ɪnˈædɪkwɪtlɪ] ADV unzulänglich, inadäquat (*geh*); *equipped, explained, documented also* unzureichend

inadmissibility [ˈɪnədˌmɪsəˈbɪlɪtɪ] N Unzulässigkeit *f*

inadmissible [ˌɪnədˈmɪsəbl] ADJ unzulässig

inadvertence [ˌɪnədˈvɜːtəns] N Ungewolltheit *f*; **it resulted from ~** es geschah versehentlich *or* aus Versehen

inadvertent [ˌɪnədˈvɜːtənt] ADJ unbeabsichtigt, ungewollt

inadvertently [ˌɪnədˈvɜːtəntlɪ] ADV versehentlich

inadvisability [ˈɪnədˌvaɪzəˈbɪlɪtɪ] N Unratsamkeit *f* (*of doing sth* etw zu tun)

inadvisable [ˌɪnədˈvaɪzəbl] ✪ 2.2 ADJ unratsam, nicht zu empfehlen *pred*, nicht zu empfehlend *attr*

inalienable [ɪnˈeɪlɪənəbl] ADJ *rights* unveräußerlich

inalterable [ɪnˈɔːltərəbl] ADJ unveränderlich, unabänderlich; **it is ~** es lässt sich nicht ändern

inane [ɪˈneɪn] ADJ dumm; *suggestion also* hirnverbrannt

inanely [ɪˈneɪnlɪ] ADV dumm; **they chatted on ~** sie plauderten albern weiter; **he suggested ~ that ...** er machte den hirnverbrannten Vorschlag, zu ...

inanimate [ɪnˈænɪmɪt] ADJ leblos, tot; *nature, world* unbelebt

inanition [ˌɪnəˈnɪʃən] N Auszehrung *f*

inanity [ɪˈnænɪtɪ] N Dummheit *f*; (*of suggestion also*) Hirnverbranntheit *f*

inappetency [ɪnˈæpɪtənsɪ] N (*fig liter*) Lustlosigkeit *f*, Unlust *f*

inapplicable [ɪnˈæplɪkəbl] ADJ *answer* unzutreffend; *laws, rules* nicht anwendbar (*to sb* auf jdn)

inapposite [ɪnˈæpəzɪt] ADJ unpassend, unangebracht

inappropriate [ˌɪnəˈprəʊprɪɪt] ADJ unpassend, unangebracht; *action also* unangemessen; *time* unpassend, ungelegen, ungünstig; **this translation is rather ~** das ist keine angemessene Übersetzung; **you have come at a most ~ time** Sie kommen sehr ungelegen

inappropriately [ˌɪnəˈprəʊprɪɪtlɪ] ADV unpassend; **she was ~ treated** sie wurde nicht richtig behandelt

inappropriateness [ˌɪnəˈprəʊprɪɪtnɪs] N Unpassende(s) *nt*, Unangebrachtheit *f*; (*of action also*) Unangemessenheit *f*; (*of time*) Ungünstigkeit *f*

inapt [ɪnˈæpt] ADJ ungeschickt; *comparison* unpassend

inaptitude [ɪnˈæptɪtjuːd] N (*of person*) Unfähigkeit *f*; (*for work etc*) Untauglichkeit *f*; (*of remark*) Ungeschicktheit *f*

inarticulacy [ˌɪnɑːˈtɪkjʊləsɪ] N (*form*) Inartikuliertheit *f* (*geh*), mangelnde Wortgewandtheit *f*; **he was reduced to ~** er konnte keine Worte mehr finden

inarticulate [ˌɪnɑːˈtɪkjʊlɪt] ADJ **a** *essay* schlecht *or* unklar ausgedrückt, inartikuliert (*geh*); *speech also* schwerfällig; **she's very ~** sie kann sich kaum *or* nur schlecht ausdrücken; **a brilliant but ~ scientist** ein glänzender, aber wenig wortgewandter Wissenschaftler; **~ with rage** sprachlos vor Zorn; **just a string of ~ grunts** nur eine Reihe unverständlicher Grunzlaute **b** (*Zool*) nicht gegliedert

inarticulately [ˌɪnɑːˈtɪkjʊlɪtlɪ] ADV (= *incomprehensibly*) unverständlich

inartistic ADJ , **inartistically** ADV [ˌɪnɑːˈtɪstɪk, -əlɪ] unkünstlerisch; *work also* kunstlos

inasmuch [ˌɪnəzˈmʌtʃ] ADV **~ as** da, weil; (= *to the extent that*) insofern als

inattention [ˌɪnəˈtenʃən] N Unaufmerksamkeit *f*; **~ to detail** Ungenauigkeit *f* im Detail

inattentive [ˌɪnəˈtentɪv] ADJ unaufmerksam; **he was ~ to her requests** er beachtete ihre Wünsche nicht

inattentively [ˌɪnəˈtentɪvlɪ] ADV unaufmerksam

inattentiveness [ˌɪnəˈtentɪvnɪs] N Unaufmerksamkeit *f*

inaudibility [ɪnˌɔːdəˈbɪlɪtɪ] N Unhörbarkeit *f*

inaudible ADJ , **inaudibly** ADV [ɪnˈɔːdəbl, -ɪ] unhörbar (*to* für)

inaugural [ɪˈnɔːɡjʊrəl] **ADJ** *lecture* Antritts-; *meeting, address, speech* Eröffnungs- **N** (= *speech*) Antritts-/Eröffnungsrede *f*

inaugurate [ɪˈnɔːɡjʊreɪt] VT **a** *president, pope, king, official etc* (feierlich) in sein/ihr Amt einsetzen *or* einführen, inaugurieren (*geh*) **b** *policy* einführen; *building* einweihen; *exhibition* eröffnen; *era* einleiten

inauguration [ɪˌnɔːɡjʊˈreɪʃən] N **a** (*of president, pope, king, official etc*) Amtseinführung *f*, Inauguration *f* (*geh*) **b** (*of policy*) Einführung *f*; (*of building*) Einweihung *f*; (*of exhibition*) Eröffnung *f*; (*of era*) Beginn *m*, Anfang *m*

INAUGURATION DAY

Inauguration Day ist der Tag der feierlichen Amtseinführung des frisch gewählten Präsidenten der Vereinigten Staaten von Amerika. Die Zeremonie wird am 20. Januar abgehalten, auch wenn die Präsidentschaftswahlen schon im vorhergehenden November stattgefunden haben. Gewöhnlich wird in der Hauptstadt Washington DC eine Parade abgehalten, und der Präsident erklärt in einer Ansprache die Ziele und Pläne für seine Amtszeit. Bei dieser Zeremonie wird auch der Vizepräsident in sein Amt eingeführt.

---

inauspicious [ˌɪnɔːsˈpɪʃəs] ADJ Unheil verheißend; *circumstances, omen also* unheilträchtig; **to get off to an ~ start** (*career, campaign*) sich nicht gerade viel versprechend anlassen; (*person*) keinen viel versprechenden Anfang machen

inauspiciously [ˌɪnɔːsˈpɪʃəslɪ] ADV Unheil verheißend

in-between [ɪnbɪˈtwiːn] (*inf*) **N** **the ~s** wer/was dazwischenliegt *or* -kommt **ADJ** Mittel-, Zwischen-; **it is sort of ~** es ist so ein Mittelding; **~ stage** Zwischenstadium *nt*; **~ times** adv zwischendurch, dazwischen

inboard [ˈɪnbɔːd] (*Naut*) **ADJ** Innenbord-; **~ motor** Innenbordmotor *m* **ADV** binnenbords **N** Innenbordmotor *m*

inborn [ˈɪnˈbɔːn] ADJ angeboren

inbound [ˈɪnˌbaʊnd] ADJ *flight* ankommend; **a special ~ flight from Honduras** eine ankommende Sondermaschine aus Honduras

inbred [ˈɪnˈbred] ADJ **a** **an ~ family** eine Familie, in der Inzucht herrscht; **they look very ~** sie sehen nach Inzucht aus; **to stop them becoming ~** um die Inzucht bei ihnen aufzuhalten; **the royal family became very ~** in der Königsfamilie herrschte Inzucht **b** *quality* angeboren (*in sb* jdm)

inbreed [ˈɪnˈbriːd] VT *animals* durch Inzucht züchten

inbreeding [ˈɪnˈbriːdɪŋ] N Inzucht *f*

inbuilt [ˈɪnˈbɪlt] ADJ *safety features, error detection etc* integriert; *dislike, fear, awareness* angeboren, instinktiv; *majority* automatisch; *predisposition, fondness, resistance* natürlich

Inc (*US*) abbr of *Incorporated*

Inca [ˈɪŋkə] **N** Inka *mf* **ADJ** (*also* **Incan**) Inka-, inkaisch; **~(n) empire** Inkareich *nt*

incalculable [ɪnˈkælkjʊləbl] ADJ **a** *amount* unschätzbar, unermesslich; *damage, harm* uner-

messlich, unabsehbar; *consequences* unabsehbar **b** (*Math*) nicht berechenbar **c** *character, mood* unberechenbar, unvorhersehbar

incandescence [ˌɪnkænˈdesns] N (Weiß)glühen *nt*, (Weiß)glut *f*; (*fig*) Leuchten *nt*, Strahlen *nt*

incandescent [ˌɪnkænˈdesnt] ADJ (*lit*) (weiß) glühend; (*fig liter*) hell leuchtend, strahlend; **~ light** Glühlampe *f*, Glühbirne *f*; **~ with rage** *or* **fury** bis zur Weißglut gereizt

incantation [ˌɪnkænˈteɪʃən] N Zauber(spruch) *m*, Zauberformel *f*; (= *act*) Beschwörung *f*

incapability [ɪnˌkeɪpəˈbɪlɪtɪ] N Unfähigkeit *f*, Unvermögen *nt* (*of doing sth* etw zu tun)

incapable [ɪnˈkeɪpəbl] ✪ 16.4 ADJ **a** *person* unfähig; (*physically*) hilflos; **to be ~ of doing sth** außerstande *or* nicht imstande *or* nicht im Stande sein, etw zu tun, etw nicht tun können; **she is physically ~ of lifting it** sie ist körperlich nicht in der Lage, es zu heben; **drunk and ~** volltrunken; **he was completely ~** (*because drunk*) er war volltrunken; **~ of working** arbeitsunfähig; **~ of tenderness** zu Zärtlichkeit nicht fähig; **do it yourself, you're not ~** (*inf*) mach es doch selbst, du bist nicht so hilflos **b** (*form*) **~ of proof** nicht beweisbar; **~ of measurement** nicht messbar; **~ of improvement** nicht verbesserungsfähig; **~ of solution** unlösbar

incapacitate [ˌɪnkəˈpæsɪteɪt] VT **a** (= *immobilize*) unfähig machen (*for* für, *from doing sth* etw zu tun); **to ~ sb for work** jdn arbeitsunfähig machen; **physically ~d** körperlich behindert; **somewhat ~d by his broken ankle** durch seinen gebrochenen Knöchel ziemlich behindert **b** (*Jur*) entmündigen

incapacity [ˌɪnkəˈpæsɪtɪ] N **a** Unfähigkeit *f* (*for* für); **~ for work** Arbeitsunfähigkeit *f* **b** (*Jur*) mangelnde Berechtigung (*for* zu); **~ to inherit** Erbunfähigkeit *f*; **~ of a minor** Geschäftsunfähigkeit *f* eines Minderjährigen

in-car [ˈɪnkɑː] ADJ *attr* Auto-; *entertainment, stereo* im Auto; **~ computer** Autocomputer *m*

incarcerate [ɪnˈkɑːsəreɪt] VT einkerkern

incarceration [ɪnkɑːsəˈreɪʃən] N (= *act*) Einkerkerung *f*; (= *period*) Kerkerhaft *f*

incarnate [ɪnˈkɑːnɪt] **ADJ** (*Rel*) Fleisch geworden, Mensch geworden; (= *personified*) leibhaftig *attr*, in Person; **to become ~** Fleisch werden, Mensch werden; **the word incarnate** das Fleisch gewordene Wort; **he's the devil ~** er ist der leibhaftige Teufel *or* der Teufel in Person; **she is cynicism ~** sie ist der Zynismus in Person **VT** [ˈɪnkɑːneɪt] (= *make real*) Gestalt *or* Form geben (+*dat*); (= *be embodiment of*) verkörpern

incarnation [ˌɪnkɑːˈneɪʃən] N (*Rel*) Inkarnation *f* (*geh*), Menschwerdung *f*, Fleischwerdung *f*; (*fig*) Inbegriff *m*, Verkörperung *f*, Inkarnation *f* (*geh*)

incautious ADJ , **incautiously** ADV [ɪnˈkɔːʃəs, -lɪ] unvorsichtig, unbedacht

incendiary [ɪnˈsendɪərɪ] **ADJ** **a** (*lit*) Brand-; **~ attack** Brandanschlag *m*; **~ bomb** Brandbombe *f* **b** (*fig*) *speech* aufwiegelnd, aufhetzend **N** **a** (= *bomb*) Brandbombe *f* **b** (= *person*) (*lit*) Brandstifter(in) *m(f)*; (*fig*) Aufrührer(in) *m(f)*, Unruhestifter(in) *m(f)*

incendiary device N Brandsatz *m*

incense¹ [ɪnˈsens] VT wütend machen, erbosen, erzürnen; **~d** wütend, erbost (*at, by* über +*acc*)

incense² [ˈɪnsens] N (*Eccl*) Weihrauch *m*; (*fig*) Duft *m*

incense: incense bearer N Weihrauchschwenker *m or* -träger *m*; **incense burner** N Weihrauchschwenker *m*, Räucherpfanne *f*

incentive [ɪnˈsentɪv] N Anreiz *m*; **this will give them a bit of an ~** das wird ihnen einen gewissen Anreiz *or* Ansporn geben; **they have little ~ to keep going** ihnen fehlt der Anreiz durchzuhalten; **financial/economic ~s** finanzielle/wirtschaftliche Anreize *pl*; **~ bonus payment** Leistungszulage *f*; **~ scheme** (*Ind*) Anreizsystem *nt*

inception [ɪn'sepʃən] N Beginn m, Anfang m; **from its ~** von Anbeginn an; **at its ~** zu Anbeginn

incertitude [ɪn'sɜːtɪtjuːd] N Ungewissheit f, Unsicherheit f

incessant [ɪn'sesnt] ADJ unaufhörlich, unablässig; *complaints also* nicht abreißend; *noise* ununterbrochen

incessantly [ɪn'sesntlɪ] ADV unaufhörlich

incest ['ɪnsest] N Inzest m, Blutschande f

incestuous [ɪn'sestjʊəs] ADJ blutschänderisch, inzestuös (geh)

inch [ɪntʃ] Ⓝ Zoll m, Inch m; **3.5 ~ disk** 3,5-Zoll-Diskette f; **because of his lack of ~es** weil er ein bisschen klein ist; **she's grown a few ~es** sie ist ein paar Zentimeter gewachsen; **by ~** Zentimeter um Zentimeter; **an ~-by-inch search** eine gründliche Durchsuchung; **he came within an ~ of winning/victory** er hätte um ein Haar or beinahe gewonnen; **he came within an ~ of being killed** er ist dem Tod um Haaresbreite entgangen; **they beat/thrashed him (to) within an ~ of his life** sie haben ihn so geschlagen/verprügelt, dass er fast gestorben wäre; **the lorry missed me by ~es** der Lastwagen hat mich um Haaresbreite verfehlt; **he knows every ~ of the area** er kennt die Gegend wie seine Westentasche; **he is every ~ a soldier** er ist jeder Zoll ein Soldat; **we will not surrender one ~ of our territory** wir werden keinen Zentimeter unseres Gebiets abtreten; **they searched every ~ of the room** sie durchsuchten das Zimmer Zentimeter für Zentimeter; **he couldn't see an ~ in front of him** er konnte die Hand nicht vor den Augen sehen; **give him an ~ and he'll take a mile** (prov) wenn man ihm den kleinen Finger gibt, nimmt er die ganze Hand (prov)

Ⓥ **to ~ forward/out/in** sich millimeterweise or stückchenweise vorwärts schieben/hinausschieben/hineinschieben; **because prices are ~ing up** weil die Preise allmählich ansteigen; **the Dutch swimmer is ~ing ahead** der holländische Schwimmer schiebt sich langsam an die Spitze

Ⓥⓣ langsam manövrieren; **he ~ed his way forward/through** er schob sich langsam vorwärts/durch

inchoate ['ɪnkəʊeɪt] ADJ (liter) unausgeformt

incidence ['ɪnsɪdəns] N Ⓐ (Opt) Einfall m; **angle of ~** Einfallswinkel m Ⓑ (of crime, disease) Häufigkeit f; **a high ~ of crime** eine hohe Verbrechensquote Ⓒ (= occurrence) Vorkommen nt; **isolated ~s** vereinzelte Fälle pl

incident ['ɪnsɪdənt] N Ⓐ (= event) Ereignis nt, Begebenheit f, Vorfall m; **a day/book full of ~** ein ereignisreicher Tag/ereignisreiches Buch; **an ~ from his childhood** ein Kindheitserlebnis nt Ⓑ (diplomatic etc) Zwischenfall m; (= disturbance in bar etc) Vorfall m; **without ~** ohne Zwischenfälle; **there were several ~s of violence** es kam mehrmals zu Gewalttätigkeiten; (during demonstration etc) es kam mehrmals zu gewalttätigen Ausschreitungen Ⓒ (in book, play) Episode f ADJ Ⓐ **~ to** (form) verbunden mit Ⓑ (Opt) ray

incidental [ˌɪnsɪ'dentl] ADJ Ⓐ **dangers ~ to foreign travel** (liter) mit Auslandsreisen verbundene Gefahren Ⓑ (= unplanned) event zufällig Ⓒ (= secondary etc) remark beiläufig N Nebensächlichkeit f, Nebensache f; **~s** (= expenses) Nebenausgaben pl

incidental expenses PL Nebenkosten pl

incidentally [ˌɪnsɪ'dentlɪ] ✪ 26.2 ADV Ⓐ (= by the way) übrigens Ⓑ (= casually) **to mention sth ~** etw beiläufig erwähnen Ⓒ (= secondarily) **it's only ~ important** das ist nur von nebensächlicher Bedeutung

incidental music N Begleitmusik f

incident room N (Police) Einsatzzentrale f

incinerate [ɪn'sɪnəreɪt] VT verbrennen; (= cremate) einäschern

incineration [ɪnsɪnə'reɪʃən] N Verbrennung f; (= cremation) Einäscherung f

incinerator [ɪn'sɪnəreɪtə'] N (Müll)verbrennungsanlage f; (= garden incinerator) Verbrennungsofen m; (in crematorium) Feuerbestattungsofen m, Verbrennungsofen m

incipience [ɪn'sɪpɪəns] N Anfang m, Beginn m

incipient [ɪn'sɪpɪənt] ADJ anfangend, beginnend; disease, difficulties also einsetzend; panic aufkommend; democracy jung

incise [ɪn'saɪz] VT Ⓐ (= cut) (ein)schneiden (into in +acc) Ⓑ (Art, in wood) (ein)schnitzen; (in metal, stone) eingravieren, einritzen

incision [ɪn'sɪʒən] N Schnitt m; (Med) Einschnitt m

incisive [ɪn'saɪsɪv] ADJ style, tone, words prägnant; criticism treffend, scharfsinnig; mind scharf; person scharfsinnig

incisively [ɪn'saɪsɪvlɪ] ADV speak, formulate, put prägnant; argue, criticize, reason treffend, scharfsinnig

incisiveness [ɪn'saɪsɪvnɪs] N (of style, tone, words) Prägnanz f; (of criticism) Scharfsinnigkeit f; (of mind) Schärfe f; (of person) Scharfsinn m

incisor [ɪn'saɪzə'] N Schneidezahn m

incite [ɪn'saɪt] VT aufhetzen; masses also aufwiegeln; racial hatred, violence, riot aufhetzen zu; **to ~ the masses/sb to violence** die Massen/jdn zu Gewalttätigkeiten aufhetzen

incitement [ɪn'saɪtmənt] N Ⓐ no pl Aufhetzung f; (of masses also) Aufwieg(e)lung f (to zu) Ⓑ (= incentive) Anreiz m (to zu), Ansporn m (to zu)

incivility [ˌɪnsɪ'vɪlɪtɪ] N Unhöflichkeit f

incl abbr of inclusive(ly) of including incl., inkl.

inclemency [ɪn'klemənsɪ] N (of weather) Rauheit f, Unfreundlichkeit f

inclement [ɪn'klemənt] ADJ weather rau, unfreundlich

inclinable [ɪn'klaɪnəbl] ADJ Ⓐ (= with a tendency to) tendierend, (hin)neigend; **to be ~ to** tendieren zu, neigen zu Ⓑ (= in favour of) wohlwollend gegenüberstehend (geh) dat, günstig gesinnt (geh) dat

inclination [ɪnklɪ'neɪʃən] N Ⓐ (= tendency, wish etc) Neigung f; **he follows his (own) ~s** er tut das, wozu er Lust hat; **what are his natural ~s?** welches sind seine Neigungen?; **my (natural) ~ is to carry on** ich neige dazu, weiterzumachen; **~ to stoutness** Anlage f or Neigung f zu Korpulenz; **to have an ~ toward(s) rudeness** zur Unhöflichkeit neigen; **I have no ~ to see him again** ich habe keinerlei Bedürfnis, ihn wiederzusehen; **my immediate ~ was to refuse** mein erster Gedanke war abzulehnen; **he showed no ~ to leave** er schien nicht gehen zu wollen Ⓑ (of head, body) Neigung f Ⓒ (of hill, slope etc) Neigung f, Gefälle nt

incline [ɪn'klaɪn] Ⓥⓣ Ⓐ head, body, roof neigen Ⓑ (= dispose) veranlassen, bewegen; **this ~s me to think that he must be lying** das lässt mich vermuten, dass er lügt; **the news ~s me to stay** aufgrund or auf Grund der Nachricht würde ich gern bleiben → **inclined** Ⓥ Ⓐ (= slope) sich neigen; (ground) abfallen Ⓑ (= be disposed, tend towards) neigen; **to ~ to a point of view** zu einer Ansicht neigen or tendieren; **he's beginning to ~ toward(s) our point of view** er beginnt unserer Ansicht zuzuneigen N ['ɪnklaɪn] Neigung f; (of hill) Abhang m; (= gradient: Rail etc) Gefälle nt

inclined [ɪn'klaɪnd] ADJ Ⓐ **to be ~ to do sth** (= feel that one wishes to) Lust haben, etw zu tun, etw tun wollen; (= have tendency to) dazu neigen, etw zu tun; **they are ~ to be late** sie kommen gern zu spät, sie neigen zum Zuspätkommen; **I am ~ to think that ...** ich neige zu der Ansicht, dass ...; **I'm ~ to disagree** ich möchte da doch widersprechen; **I am not ~ to approve of this** ich bin nicht geneigt, das gutzuheißen; **I'm ~ to believe you** ich möchte Ihnen gern glauben; **it's ~ to break** das bricht leicht; **if you feel ~** wenn Sie Lust haben or dazu aufgelegt sind; **to be well or favourably** (Brit) or **favorably** (US) **~ toward(s) sb** jdm geneigt or gewogen sein; **he is ~ towards our viewpoint** er ist unse-

rer Ansicht zugeneigt; **if you're that way ~** wenn Ihnen so etwas liegt; **mathematically/artistically ~** mathematisch/künstlerisch veranlagt; **to be romantically ~** eine romantische Ader haben

Ⓑ (= at an angle) geneigt; plane geneigt, schräg; **~ towards the sun** (hemisphere) der Sonne zugewandt

inclose [ɪn'kləʊz] VT **= enclose**

include [ɪn'kluːd] VT einschließen, enthalten; (on list, in group etc) aufnehmen, einbeziehen; **your name is not ~d on the list** Ihr Name ist nicht auf der Liste; **service not ~d** Bedienung nicht inbegriffen; **all ~d** alles inklusive or inbegriffen; **everyone, children ~d** alle einschließlich der Kinder; **the invitation ~s everybody** die Einladung betrifft alle; **the hostages ~d three Britons** unter den Geiseln befanden sich drei Briten; **does that ~ me?** gilt das auch für mich?; **shut up! you ~d or that ~s you** Ruhe! Sie sind auch gemeint; **to ~ sb in one's prayers** jdn in sein Gebet einschließen; **I worked hard to be ~d in the project** ich habe mich sehr angestrengt, um an dem Projekt teilnehmen zu können; **in which category would you ~ this?** in welche Kategorie würden Sie das aufnehmen?; **I think we should ~ a chapter on ...** ich finde, wir sollten auch ein Kapitel über ... dazunehmen; **the book ~s two chapters on grammar** das Buch enthält auch zwei Grammatikkapitel

▶ **include out** VT sep (hum inf) auslassen; **include me out** ohne mich

including [ɪn'kluːdɪŋ] PREP einschließlich, inklusive, inbegriffen, mit; **that makes seven ~ you** mit Ihnen sind das sieben; **that comes to 100 euros ~ postage and packing** das kommt auf 100 EUR inklusive or einschließlich Porto und Verpackung; **there were six rooms ~ kitchen** mit Küche waren es sechs Zimmer, es waren sechs Zimmer einschließlich Küche; **many people, ~ my father, had been invited** viele Leute, darunter mein Vater, waren eingeladen; **~ the service charge, ~ service** inklusive Bedienung, Bedienung (mit) inbegriffen; **up to and ~ chapter V** bis inklusive or einschließlich Kapitel V; **up to and ~ March 4th** bis einschließlich 4. März

inclusion [ɪn'kluːʒən] N Aufnahme f; **the team was revamped with the ~ of John** das Team wurde neu zusammengestellt und John gehörte dazu

inclusive [ɪn'kluːsɪv] ADJ inklusive, einschließlich; **~ price** Inklusiv- or Pauschalpreis m; **~ sum** Pauschale f, Pauschalsumme f; **~ terms** Pauschalpreis m; **it's a fully ~ price** im Preis ist alles inbegriffen; **to be ~ of all charges** alle Gebühren einschließen, einschließlich aller Gebühren (gen) sein; **the course fee is fully ~ of all costs** in den Kursgebühren sind alle Kosten enthalten; **to the fifth page ~** bis einschließlich der fünften Seite, bis Seite fünf einschließlich; **from 1st to 6th May ~** vom 1. bis einschließlich 6. Mai, vom 1. bis 6. Mai inklusive

inclusively [ɪn'kluːsɪvlɪ] ADV inklusive, einschließlich; **from 7 to 10 ~** von 7 bis einschließlich or inklusive 10

incognito [ˌɪnkɒg'niːtəʊ] ADV inkognito N Inkognito nt ADJ traveller unter fremdem Namen; **to remain ~** inkognito bleiben

incoherence [ˌɪnkəʊ'hɪərəns] N (of style, prose) Zusammenhanglosigkeit f, mangelnder Zusammenhang; **with each drink his ~ grew** seine Worte wurden mit jedem Glas wirrer or zusammenhangloser

incoherent [ˌɪnkəʊ'hɪərənt] ADJ style, argument, speech zusammenhanglos, unzusammenhängend, inkohärent (geh); person sich unklar or undeutlich ausdrückend; drunk etc schwer verständlich; **he was ~ with rage** seine wütenden Worte waren kaum zu verstehen; **the patient is still ~** der Kranke ist noch nicht ansprechbar; **an ~ set of objectives** in sich widersprüchliche Ziele pl

incoherently [ˌɪnkəʊ'hɪərəntlɪ] ADV *talk, write* zusammenhanglos, unzusammenhängend, wirr

incombustible [ˌɪnkəm'bʌstəbl] ADJ unbrennbar

income ['ɪnkʌm] N Einkommen *nt*; (= *receipts*) Einkünfte *pl*; **an annual ~ of £45,000** ein Jahreseinkommen von £ 45.000; **families on low ~s, low-income families** einkommensschwache Familien *pl*; **to live within one's ~** seinen Verhältnissen entsprechend leben

income: income account N Ertragskonto *nt*; **income bond** N Schuldverschreibung *f* (*mit vom Gewinn der Gesellschaft abgängiger Verzinsung*); **income bracket** N Einkommensklasse *f*; **income group** N Einkommensgruppe *f*

incomer ['ɪnˌkʌmə'] N (= *new arrival*) Neuankömmling *m*; (= *successor*) Nachfolger(in) *m(f)*

income: incomes policy N Lohnpolitik *f*; **income statement** N (*US*) Gewinn- und Verlustrechnung *f*; **income support** N (*Brit*) ≈ Sozialhilfe *f*; **income tax** N Lohnsteuer *f*; (*on private income*) Einkommensteuer *f*; **income tax return** N Steuererklärung *f*

incoming ['ɪnˌkʌmɪŋ] ADJ **a** ankommend; *train also* einfahrend; *ship also* einlaufend; *missile* anfliegend; *mail, orders* eingehend; (*Phys*) *light, radiation* einfallend; **~ tide** Flut *f*; **to receive ~ (phone) calls** (Telefon)anrufe entgegennehmen **b** (= *succeeding*) *president etc* nachfolgend, neu

incomings ['ɪnˌkʌmɪŋz] PL Einkünfte *pl*, Einnahmen *pl*

incommensurable [ˌɪnkə'menʃərəbl] ADJ nicht zu vergleichend *attr*, nicht vergleichbar; (*Math*) inkommensurabel

incommensurate [ˌɪnkə'menʃərɪt] ADJ **a** **to be ~ with sth** in keinem Verhältnis zu etw stehen **b** (= *inadequate*) unzureichend (*to* für)

incommode [ˌɪnkə'məʊd] VT (*form*) lästig sein (+*dat*); **I don't wish to ~ you but could you ...** ich möchte Sie nicht behelligen, aber könnten Sie vielleicht ...

incommodious [ˌɪnkə'məʊdɪəs] ADJ (*form*) lästig, unbequem; (= *cramped*) beengt

incommunicado [ˌɪnkəmjʊnɪ'kɑːdəʊ] ADJ *pred* ohne jede Verbindung zur Außenwelt, abgesondert; **he was held** ≈ er hatte keinerlei Verbindung zur Außenwelt; **to be ~** (*fig*) für niemanden zu sprechen sein

in-company ADJ firmenintern

incomparable [ɪn'kɒmpərəbl] ADJ nicht vergleichbar (*with* mit); *beauty, skill* unvergleichlich

incomparably [ɪn'kɒmpərəblɪ] ADV unvergleichlich

incompatibility ['ɪnkəmˌpætə'bɪlɪtɪ] N (*of characters, temperaments, ideas, propositions*) Unvereinbarkeit *f*; (*of drugs, blood groups, colours*) Unverträglichkeit *f*; (*of technical systems*) Inkompatibilität *f*; **divorce on grounds of ~** Scheidung aufgrund *or* auf Grund der Unvereinbarkeit der Charaktere der Ehepartner

incompatible [ˌɪnkəm'pætəbl] ADJ *characters, ideas, propositions, temperaments* unvereinbar; *technical systems* nicht kompatibel; *drugs, blood groups, colours* nicht miteinander verträglich; **the drugs are ~** die Arzneimittel vertragen sich nicht miteinander; **we are ~, she said** wir passen überhaupt nicht zusammen *or* zueinander, sagte sie; **to be ~ with sb/sth** sich nicht mit jdm/etw vertragen; (= *not suit*) nicht zu jdm/etw passen; **the possession of great wealth is surely ~ with genuine Marxist beliefs** der Besitz großer Reichtümer lässt sich wohl kaum mit echtem Marxismus vereinbaren

incompetence [ɪn'kɒmpɪtəns], **incompetency** [ɪn'kɒmpɪtənsɪ] N **a** Unfähigkeit *f*; (*for job*) Untauglichkeit *f* **b** (*Jur*) Unzuständigkeit *f*, Inkompetenz *f*

incompetent [ɪn'kɒmpɪtənt] ADJ **a** *person, institution* unfähig; (*for sth*) untauglich; *management* stümperhaft, inkompetent; *piece of work* stümperhaft, unzulänglich; **to be ~ in business** nicht geschäftstüchtig sein; **to be ~ to teach**

music unfähig sein, Musik zu unterrichten, zum Musiklehrer untauglich sein; **I was ~ at playing the piano** *or* **an ~ pianist** ich konnte nur sehr schlecht Klavier spielen **b** (*Jur*) *court, authority etc* unzuständig, nicht zuständig; (**legally/mentally**) **~** (= *not capable of contracting*) geschäftsunfähig **c** (*Med*) **~ cervix** isthmozervikale Insuffizienz, Zervixinsuffizienz *f* **N** Nichtskönner(in) *m(f)*

incompetently [ɪn'kɒmpɪtəntlɪ] ADV schlecht, stümperhaft

incomplete [ˌɪnkəm'pliːt] ADJ *collection, series* unvollkommen, unvollständig; *knowledge, information* lückenhaft; (= *not finished also*) *painting, novel* unfertig; (*referring to numbers*) unvollständig, nicht vollzählig

incompletely [ˌɪnkəm'pliːtlɪ] ADV unvollständig

incompleteness [ˌɪnkəm'pliːtnɪs] N (*of collection, series*) Unvollkommenheit *f*, Unvollständigkeit *f*; (*of knowledge, information*) Lückenhaftigkeit *f*; (= *unfinished state: of painting, novel*) Unfertigkeit *f*

incomprehensible [ɪnˌkɒmprɪ'hensəbl] ADJ unverständlich (*to sb* jdm); *act also* unbegreiflich, unfassbar (*to sb* jdm); **people like that are just ~** solche Leute kann ich einfach nicht begreifen

incomprehensibly [ɪnˌkɒmprɪ'hensəblɪ] ADV unverständlich; **~, their offer was turned down** unverständlicherweise wurde ihr Angebot abgelehnt

inconceivable [ˌɪnkən'siːvəbl] ADJ unvorstellbar, undenkbar; (= *hard to believe also*) unfassbar, unbegreiflich; **it was ~ to her that ...** sie konnte sich (*dat*) nicht vorstellen, dass ...

inconceivably [ˌɪnkən'siːvəblɪ] ADV unvorstellbar; **almost ~, she ...** es war fast nicht zu fassen, aber sie ...

inconclusive [ˌɪnkən'kluːsɪv] ADJ (= *not decisive*) *result* unbestimmt, zu keiner Entscheidung führend; *election* ohne eindeutiges Ergebnis; *action, discussion, investigation* ohne (schlüssiges) Ergebnis, ergebnislos; *war* erfolglos; (= *not convincing*) *evidence, argument* nicht überzeugend, nicht schlüssig, nicht zwingend

inconclusively [ˌɪnkən'kluːsɪvlɪ] ADV (= *without result*) ergebnislos; *argue* nicht überzeugend, nicht schlüssig, nicht zwingend; **his speech ended rather ~** seine Rede kam zu keinem überzeugenden Schluss

incongruent [ɪn'kɒŋgrʊənt] ADJ (= *incompatible*) nicht übereinstimmend (*to, with* mit); (= *incongruous*) unpassend, unangebracht; (*Math, Ling*) inkongruent; (*fig*) *story* ungereimt, widersinnig

incongruity [ˌɪnkɒŋ'gruːɪtɪ] N **a** *no pl* (*of remark, sb's presence*) Unpassende(s), Unangebrachtsein *nt*; (*of juxtaposition, mixture*) Missklang *m*; (*of situation*) Absurdität *f*; (*of behaviour*) Unangebrachtheit *f*; **such was the ~ of his remark** seine Bemerkung war so unangebracht *or* unpassend; **the ~ between what is said and what is left unsaid** das Missverhältnis zwischen dem, was gesagt wird, und dem, was ungesagt bleibt; **the film relies on the ~ of these images** der Film lebt von der inneren Widersprüchlichkeit dieser Bilder; **he commented on the ~ of it all** er bemerkte, wie absurd das alles war **b** (= *incongruous thing*) Unstimmigkeit *f*

incongruous [ɪn'kɒŋgrʊəs] ADJ *couple, juxtaposition, mixture* wenig zusammenpassend *attr*; *thing to do, remark* unpassend; *behaviour* unangebracht; **he uses these ~ images** er benutzt diese unstimmigen Bilder; **it seems ~ that ... es** scheint abwegig *or* widersinnig, dass ...; **how ~ it seemed that he should have been chosen** es schien eigenartig, dass ausgerechnet er ausgewählt wurde; **he was an ~ figure among the tourists** unter den Touristen wirkte er fehl am Platz

incongruously [ɪn'kɒŋgrʊəslɪ] ADV unpassend

inconsequence [ɪn'kɒnsɪkwəns] N (*in logic*) Inkonsequenz *f*, Unlogik *f*; (*irrelevance*) Belanglosigkeit *f*

inconsequent [ɪn'kɒnsɪkwənt] ADJ unlogisch, nicht folgerichtig; *remark* nicht zur Sache gehörend *attr*, beziehungslos

inconsequential [ɪnˌkɒnsɪ'kwenʃəl] ADJ beziehungslos, irrelevant; (= *not logical*) unlogisch, nicht folgerichtig; (= *unimportant*) unbedeutend, unwichtig

inconsequentially [ɪnˌkɒnsɪ'kwenʃəlɪ] ADV unlogisch

inconsiderable [ˌɪnkən'sɪdərəbl] ADJ unbedeutend, unerheblich; **a not ~ amount** ein nicht unbedeutender Betrag

inconsiderate [ˌɪnkən'sɪdərɪt] ADJ rücksichtslos; (*in less critical sense*: = *not thinking*) unaufmerksam

inconsiderately [ˌɪnkən'sɪdərɪtlɪ] ADV rücksichtslos

inconsiderateness [ˌɪnkən'sɪdərɪtnɪs]

inconsideration ['ɪnkənˌsɪdə'reɪʃən] N Rücksichtslosigkeit *f*

inconsistency [ˌɪnkən'sɪstənsɪ] N **a** (= *contradictoriness*) Widersprüchlichkeit *f*, Ungereimtheit *f*; **the inconsistencies in his evidence** die Widersprüche in seiner Aussage **b** (= *unevenness: of work, in quality etc*) Unbeständigkeit *f*

inconsistent [ˌɪnkən'sɪstənt] ADJ **a** (= *contradictory*) *action, speech* widersprüchlich, ungereimt; **to be ~ with sth** zu etw im Widerspruch stehen, mit etw nicht übereinstimmen **b** (= *uneven, irregular*) *work* unbeständig, ungleich; *person* inkonsequent; **but you're ~, sometimes you say ...** aber da sind Sie nicht konsequent, manchmal sagen Sie ...; **recently we** *or* **our performances have been ~** in letzter Zeit schwanken unsere Leistungen

inconsistently [ˌɪnkən'sɪstəntlɪ] ADV **a** *argue, behave* widersprüchlich; **he is behaving ~ with his beliefs** sein Verhalten steht im Widerspruch zu seinen Auffassungen **b** *work, perform* unbeständig, ungleichmäßig

inconsolable [ˌɪnkən'səʊləbl] ADJ untröstlich

inconsolably [ˌɪnkən'səʊləblɪ] ADV untröstlich; **she wept ~** sie weinte und war nicht zu trösten

inconspicuous [ˌɪnkən'spɪkjʊəs] ADJ unauffällig; **to make oneself ~** so wenig Aufsehen wie möglich erregen, sich klein machen (*inf*)

inconspicuously [ˌɪnkən'spɪkjʊəslɪ] ADV unauffällig

inconstancy [ɪn'kɒnstənsɪ] N (*of friend*) Unbeständigkeit *f*, Wankelmut *m*; (*of lover*) Unstetigkeit *f*, Wankelmut *m*; (*of weather, quality*) Veränderlichkeit *f*

inconstant [ɪn'kɒnstənt] ADJ *person* (*in friendship*) unbeständig, wankelmütig; (*in love*) unstet, wankelmütig; (= *variable*) *weather, quality* veränderlich, unbeständig

incontestable [ˌɪnkən'testəbl] ADJ unbestreitbar, unanfechtbar; **it is ~ that ...** es ist unbestritten, dass ...

incontestably [ˌɪnkən'testəblɪ] ADV unbestreitbar

incontinence [ɪn'kɒntɪnəns] N (*Med*) Inkontinenz *f*; (*of desires*) Zügellosigkeit *f*, Hemmungslosigkeit *f*

incontinence: incontinence pad N Einlage *f* für Inkontinente; **incontinence sheet** N Unterlage *f* für Inkontinente

incontinent [ɪn'kɒntɪnənt] ADJ (*Med*) inkontinent; *desires* zügellos, hemmungslos

incontrovertible [ɪnˌkɒntrə'vɜːtəbl] ADJ unbestreitbar, unwiderlegbar; *evidence* unwiderlegbar; *argument* unanfechtbar

incontrovertibly [ɪnˌkɒntrə'vɜːtəblɪ] ADV unbestreitbar

inconvenience [ˌɪnkən'viːnɪəns] **N a** (= *inconvenient thing*) Unannehmlichkeit *f*; **it's one of the ~s of getting old** es ist einer der Nachteile, wenn man älter wird; **it was something of an ~ not having a car** es war eine ziemlich lästige *or* leidige Angelegenheit, kein Auto zu haben **b** *no pl* (= *trouble, awkwardness*) Unannehmlichkeit(en) *f(pl)* (*to sb* für jdn); **the ~ of a delayed flight** die Unannehmlichkeiten, die durch einen verspäteten Flug verursacht werden; **she complained about the ~ of having no shops nearby** sie beklagte sich darüber, wie unbequem *or* beschwerlich es sei, keine Geschäfte in der Nähe zu haben; **I don't want to cause you any ~** ich möchte Ihnen keine Umstände bereiten *or* machen; **to put sb to great ~** jdm große Umstände bereiten; **he went to a great deal of ~ to help** er machte sich viele Unannehmlichkeiten, um zu helfen; **at considerable personal ~** trotz beträchtlicher persönlicher Unannehmlichkeiten; **because of the ~ of the time/date** weil die Uhrzeit/der Termin ungelegen war

VT Unannehmlichkeiten *or* Umstände bereiten (+*dat*); (*with reference to time*) ungelegen kommen (+*dat*); **don't ~ yourself** machen Sie keine Umstände

inconvenient [ˌɪnkən'viːnɪənt] ✪ 14 ADJ **a** *time* ungelegen, ungünstig; *house, design* unbequem, unpraktisch; *location* ungünstig; *shops* ungünstig *or* ungeschickt gelegen; *journey* beschwerlich, lästig; **3 o'clock is very ~ for me** 3 Uhr kommt mir sehr ungelegen *or* ist sehr ungünstig für mich; **if it's ~, I can come later** wenn es Ihnen ungelegen ist, kann ich später kommen; **you couldn't have chosen a more ~ time** einen ungünstigeren Zeitpunkt hätten Sie kaum wählen können; **it's very ~ of you to come so early** es kommt mir wirklich sehr ungelegen, dass Sie so früh kommen; **it's very ~ of you to live so far out** es ist wenig rücksichtsvoll von Ihnen, so weit außerhalb zu wohnen; **it is ~ to have to wait** es ist lästig, warten zu müssen **b** (= *embarrassing*) *fact, information* unbequem

inconveniently [ˌɪnkən'viːnɪəntlɪ] ADV *situated* ungünstig; *laid out, designed* unpraktisch; **it was ~ timed** es fand zu einer ungünstigen Zeit statt; **he ~ decided to leave** er beschloss zu gehen, was sehr ungünstig war *or* was sehr ungelegen kam

inconvertibility [ˈɪnkənˌvɜːtɪ'bɪlɪtɪ] N (*Fin*) Uneinlösbarkeit *f*, Inkonvertibilität *f*

inconvertible [ˌɪnkən'vɜːtəbl] ADJ (*Fin*) uneinlösbar, inkonvertibel

incorporate [ɪn'kɔːpəreɪt] VT **a** (= *integrate*) aufnehmen, einbauen, integrieren (*into* in +*acc*); **his proposals were ~d into the project** ihre Vorschläge gingen in das Projekt ein; **Hanover was ~d into Prussia in 1886** Hannover wurde 1886 Preußen angegliedert *or* mit Preußen vereinigt **b** (= *contain*) (in sich *dat*) vereinigen, enthalten; **the tax is ~d in the price** (die) Steuer ist im Preis enthalten; **a new James Bond film incorporating all the standard ingredients** ein neuer James-Bond-Film, der alle Standardelemente enthält; **all the tribes are now ~d in one state** die Stämme sind jetzt zu einem Staat zusammengeschlossen **c** (*Jur, Comm*) gesellschaftlich organisieren; (*US*) (amtlich) als Aktiengesellschaft eintragen, registrieren; **to ~ a company** eine Gesellschaft gründen; **~d company** (*US*) (als Kapitalgesellschaft) eingetragenes Unternehmen

incorporation [ɪnˌkɔːpə'reɪʃən] N **a** (= *integration*) Aufnahme *f*, Integration *f* (*into*, *in* in +*acc*) **b** (= *containing*) Verbindung *f*, Vereinigung *f* **c** (*Jur, Comm: of company*) Gründung *f*

incorporeal [ˌɪnkɔː'pɔːrɪəl] ADJ nicht körperlich, körperlos

incorrect [ˌɪnkə'rekt] ADJ **a** (= *wrong*) falsch; *calculation* falsch, fehlerhaft; *statement, assessment* falsch, unzutreffend, unrichtig; *opinion* falsch, irrig; *text* ungenau, fehlerhaft; **~ diet** Fehlernährung *f*, falsche Ernährung; **that is ~** das stimmt nicht, das ist nicht richtig *or* wahr; **you are ~** Sie irren sich, Sie haben Unrecht; **you are ~ in your assumption** Sie irren sich in

Ihrer Annahme; **you are ~ in thinking that ...** Sie haben Unrecht, wenn Sie denken, dass ... **b** (= *improper*) *behaviour* inkorrekt, nicht einwandfrei; *dress* inkorrekt, falsch; **it is ~ to ...** es ist nicht korrekt, zu ...

incorrectly [ˌɪnkə'rektlɪ] ADV (= *wrongly*) falsch; *state also* unzutreffend; (= *improperly*) inkorrekt, nicht korrekt; **I had ~ assumed that ...** ich hatte fälschlich(erweise) angenommen, dass ...

incorrigible [ɪn'kɒrɪdʒəbl] ADJ unverbesserlich

incorrigibly [ɪn'kɒrɪdʒəblɪ] ADV unverbesserlich; **to be ~ romantic/optimistic** ein unverbesserlicher Romantiker/Optimist sein

incorruptible [ˌɪnkə'rʌptəbl] ADJ **a** *person* charakterstark; (= *not bribable*) unbestechlich; **she's ~** man kann sie nicht verderben **b** *material, substance* unzerstörbar

increase [ɪn'kriːs] VI zunehmen; (*taxes*) erhöht werden; (*pain also*) stärker werden; (*amount, number, noise, population also*) anwachsen; (*possessions, trade, riches also*) sich vermehren, (an-)wachsen; (*pride also, strength*) wachsen; (*price, sales, demand*) steigen; (*supply, joy, rage*) sich vergrößern, größer werden; (*business, institution, town*) sich vergrößern, wachsen; (*rain, wind*) stärker werden; **to ~ in volume/weight** umfangreicher/schwerer werden, an Umfang/Gewicht zunehmen; **to ~ in breadth/size/number** sich verbreitern/vergrößern/vermehren, breiter/größer/mehr werden; (*in height* höher werden; **industrial output ~d by 2% last year** die Industrieproduktion wuchs im letzten Jahr um 2%

VT vergrößern; *rage, sorrow, joy, possessions, riches also* vermehren; *darkness, noise, love, resentment also, effort* verstärken; *trade, sales* erweitern; *numbers, taxes, price, speed, demand, tension* erhöhen; *chances* verbessern; **he ~d his efforts** er strengte sich mehr an, er machte größere Anstrengungen; **then to ~ our difficulties** was die Dinge noch schwieriger machte, was unsere Schwierigkeiten noch vergrößerte; **~d demand** erhöhte *or* verstärkte Nachfrage; **~d efficiency** Leistungssteigerung *f*; **his hours were ~d to 25 per week** seine Stundenzahl wurde auf 25 Wochenstunden erhöht; **we ~d output to ...** wir erhöhten den Ausstoß auf ...; **they ~d her salary by £2,000 to £20,000 a year** sie erhöhten ihr Jahresgehalt um £ 2.000 auf £ 20.000

N ['ɪnkriːs] Zunahme *f*, Erhöhung *f*, Steigerung *f*; (*in size*) Vergrößerung *f*, Erweiterung *f*; (*in number*) Vermehrung *f*, Zuwachs *m*, Zunahme *f*; (*in speed, spending*) Erhöhung *f* (*in* +*gen*), Steigerung *f* (*in* +*gen*); (*of business*) Erweiterung *f*, Vergrößerung *f*; (*in sales*) Zuwachs *m*; (*in expenses*) Vermehrung *f* (*in* +*gen*), Steigerung *f* (*in* +*gen*); (*of effort etc*) Vermehrung *f*, Steigerung *f*, Verstärkung *f*; (*of demand*) Verstärkung *f*, Steigen *nt*; (*of work*) Mehr *nt* (*of* an +*dat*), Zunahme *f*; (*of violence*) Zunahme *f*, Anwachsen *nt*; (*of salary*) Gehaltserhöhung *f* *or* -aufbesserung *f*; (*of noise*) Zunahme *f*, Verstärkung *f*; **an ~ in the population of 10% per year** eine jährliche Bevölkerungszunahme *or* ein jährlicher Bevölkerungszuwachs von 10%; **to get an ~ of £5 per week** £ 5 pro Woche mehr bekommen, eine Lohnerhöhung von £ 5 pro Woche bekommen; **to be on the ~** ständig zunehmen; **~ in value** Wertzuwachs *m*, Wertsteigerung *f*; **rent ~** Mieterhöhung *f*

increasing [ɪn'kriːsɪŋ] ADJ zunehmend, steigend, (an)wachsend; **an ~ number of people are changing to ...** mehr und mehr Leute steigen auf (+*acc*) ... um; **there is ~ pressure on her to resign** sie gerät zunehmend unter Druck zurückzutreten; **there are ~ signs that ...** es gibt immer mehr Anzeichen dafür, dass ...

increasingly [ɪn'kriːsɪŋlɪ] ADV zunehmend, immer mehr; **he became ~ angry** er wurde immer *or* zunehmend ärgerlicher; **~, people are finding that ...** man findet in zunehmendem Maße, dass ...; **this is ~ the case** dies ist immer häufiger der Fall

incredible [ɪn'kredəbl] ADJ unglaublich; (*inf*, = *amazing also*) unwahrscheinlich (*inf*); *scenery* sagenhaft; **it seems ~ to me that ...** ich kann es nicht fassen, dass ...; **~ though it may seem, ...** so unglaublich es auch scheinen mag, ...; **this music is ~** (*inf*) diese Musik ist sagenhaft (*inf*); **you're ~** (*inf*) du bist wirklich unschlagbar

incredibly [ɪn'kredəblɪ] ADV unglaublich, unwahrscheinlich; **~, he wasn't there** unglaublicherweise war er nicht da

incredulity [ˌɪnkrɪ'djuːlɪtɪ] N Ungläubigkeit *f*, Skepsis *f*

incredulous [ɪn'kredjʊləs] ADJ ungläubig, skeptisch; *look also* zweifelnd; **his voice was ~** seine Stimme klang ungläubig

incredulously [ɪn'kredjʊləslɪ] ADV ungläubig, skeptisch; *look also* zweifelnd

increment ['ɪnkrəmənt] N Zuwachs *m*, Steigerung *f*; (*in salary*) Gehaltserhöhung *f* *or* -zulage *f*; (*on scale*) Stufe *f*

incriminate [ɪn'krɪmɪneɪt] VT belasten; **he is afraid of incriminating himself** er hat Angst, dass er sich belasten könnte

incriminating [ɪn'krɪmɪneɪtɪŋ], **incriminatory** [ɪn'krɪmɪneɪtərɪ] ADJ belastend

incrimination [ɪnˌkrɪmɪ'neɪʃən] N Belastung *f*

incriminator [ɪn'krɪmɪneɪtəʳ] N Beschuldiger(in) *m(f)*

in-crowd ['ɪnkraʊd] N (*inf*) Schickeria *f* (*inf*); **to be in with the ~** zur Schickeria gehören (*inf*)

incrust [ɪn'krʌst] = **encrust**

incubate ['ɪnkjʊbeɪt] VT *egg* ausbrüten; *bacteria* züchten; *plan, idea* ausbrüten (*inf*), ausreifen lassen VI (*lit*) ausgebrütet *or* bebrütet werden; (*fig*) (aus)reifen, sich formen; **the virus can ~ for up to 10 days** das Virus hat eine Inkubationszeit von bis zu 10 Tagen

incubation [ˌɪnkjʊ'beɪʃən] N (*of egg, fig: of plan*) Ausbrüten *nt*; (*of bacteria*) Züchten *nt*

incubation period N (*Med*) Inkubationszeit *f*

incubator ['ɪnkjʊbeɪtəʳ] N (*for babies*) Brutkasten *m*, Inkubator *m*; (*for chicks*) Brutapparat *m*; (*for bacteria*) Brutschrank *m*

incubus ['ɪnkjʊbəs] N **a** (= *demon*) Alp *m* **b** (= *burden*) Albtraum *m*, Alptraum *m*, drückende Last

inculcate ['ɪnkʌlkeɪt] VT einimpfen, einprägen (*in sb* jdm)

inculcation [ˌɪnkʌl'keɪʃən] N Einimpfen *nt*, Einimpfung *f*

incumbency [ɪn'kʌmbənsɪ] N **a** (*Eccl*) Pfründe *f* **b** (*form, = tenure of office*) Amtszeit *f* **c** (*form, = obligation*) Obliegenheit *f* (*form*), Verpflichtung *f*

incumbent [ɪn'kʌmbənt] (*form*) ADJ **a** **to be ~ upon sb** jdm obliegen (*form*), jds Pflicht sein (*to do sth* etw zu tun) **b** **the ~ mayor** der amtierende Bürgermeister, die amtierende Bürgermeisterin N Amtsinhaber(in) *m(f)*; (*Eccl*) Inhaber(in) *m(f)* einer Pfarrstelle

incunabula [ˌɪnkjʊ'næbjʊlə] PL Inkunabeln *pl*, Wiegendrucke *pl*

incur [ɪn'kɜːʳ] VT *anger, injury, displeasure* sich (*dat*) zuziehen, auf sich (*acc*) ziehen; *penalty* belegt werden mit; *risk* eingehen, laufen; **to ~ the wrath of sb** jds Zorn auf sich (*acc*) ziehen **b** (*Fin*) *loss* erleiden; *debts, expenses* machen; *costs* haben; **other expenses ~red** weitere Auslagen *or* Ausgaben *pl*

incurable [ɪn'kjʊərəbl] ADJ (*Med*) unheilbar; (*fig*) unverbesserlich N (*Med*) unheilbar Kranke(r) *mf*

incurably [ɪn'kjʊərəblɪ] ADV (*Med*) unheilbar; (*fig*) unverbesserlich

incurious [ɪn'kjʊərɪəs] ADJ (= *not curious*) nicht wissbegierig, nicht neugierig; (= *uninterested*) gleichgültig, uninteressiert

incuriously [ɪn'kjʊərɪəslɪ] ADV (= *uninterestedly*) gleichgültig

incursion [ɪn'kɜːʃən] N Einfall *m*, Eindringen *nt* (*into* in +*acc*); (*fig*) Ausflug *m* (*into* in +*acc*)

indebted [ɪnˈdetɪd] ADJ a (fig) verpflichtet; **to be ~ to sb for sth** jdm für etw (zu Dank) verpflichtet sein, für etw in jds Schuld (dat) stehen; **he's obviously greatly ~ to Matisse/Steinbeck** er hat offensichtlich Matisse/Steinbeck viel zu verdanken; **thank you very much, I am most ~ to you** vielen Dank, ich stehe zutiefst in Ihrer Schuld (geh) b (Fin) verschuldet (to sb bei jdm); **I was ~ to them for £3,000** ich schuldete ihnen £ 3000, ich war bei ihnen mit £ 3000 verschuldet

indebtedness [ɪnˈdetɪdnɪs] N (fig) Verpflichtung f (to gegenüber); (Fin) Verschuldung f; **we can see his obvious ~ to Matisse** wir können sehen, dass er Matisse viel zu verdanken hat

indecency [ɪnˈdiːsnsɪ] N Unanständigkeit f, Anstößigkeit f; **act of ~** (Jur) unsittliches Verhalten

indecent [ɪnˈdiːsnt] ADJ unanständig, anstößig; (Jur) act unsittlich, unzüchtig; joke schmutzig, unanständig, zotig; (= excessive) amount unerhört; **with ~ haste** mit ungebührlicher Eile or Hast

indecent assault N Notzucht f

indecent exposure N Erregung f öffentlichen Ärgernisses

indecently [ɪnˈdiːsntlɪ] ADV unanständig; **to be ~ assaulted** sexuell missbraucht werden

indecipherable [ˌɪndɪˈsaɪfərəbl] ADJ nicht zu entziffern pred, nicht zu entziffernd attr; handwriting unleserlich

indecision [ˌɪndɪˈsɪʒən] N Unentschlossenheit f, Unschlüssigkeit f

indecisive [ˌɪndɪˈsaɪsɪv] ADJ a person, manner unschlüssig, unentschlossen (in or about or over sth in Bezug auf etw acc) b (= inconclusive) discussion, vote ergebnislos; argument, battle nicht(s) entscheidend attr; result nicht eindeutig

indecisively [ˌɪndɪˈsaɪsɪvlɪ] ADV unentschlossen; (= inconclusively) unentschieden, ergebnislos

indeclinable [ˌɪndɪˈklaɪnəbl] ADJ (Gram) nicht deklinierbar, unbeugbar, beugungsunfähig

indecorous [ɪnˈdekərəs] ADJ unschicklich, ungehörig

indecorously [ɪnˈdekərəslɪ] ADV unschicklich, ungehörig

indecorum [ˌɪndɪˈkɔːrəm] N Unschicklichkeit f, Ungehörigkeit f

indeed [ɪnˈdiːd] ADV a (= really, in reality, in fact) tatsächlich, wirklich, in der Tat; **I am ~ quite tired** ich bin wirklich or tatsächlich or in der Tat recht müde; **I feel, ~ I know he is right** ich habe das Gefühl, ja ich weiß (sogar), dass er recht hat; **who else? – ~, who else?** wer sonst? – in der Tat or ganz recht, wer sonst? b (confirming) **isn't that strange? – ~ (it is)** ist das nicht seltsam? – allerdings; **are you coming? – ~ I am!** kommst du? – aber sicher or natürlich; **may I open the window? – you may ~/~ you may not** darf ich das Fenster öffnen? – ja bitte, aber gern doch!/nein, das dürfen Sie nicht!; **are you pleased? – yes, ~ or ~, yes!** bist du zufrieden? – oh ja, das kann man wohl sagen!; **is that Charles? – ~ it is** ist das Charles? – ganz recht c (as intensifier) wirklich; **very ... ~** wirklich sehr ...; **thank you very much ~** vielen herzlichen Dank d (showing interest, irony, surprise) wirklich, tatsächlich; **did you/is it/has she etc ~?** nein wirklich?, tatsächlich?; **his wife, ~!** seine Frau ..., dass ich nicht lache!; **who is she ~!** na, wer wohl or wer schon!; **what ~!** was wohl!; **~?** ach so?, ach wirklich?; **where ~?** ja, wo?; **what ~?** ja, was? e (= admittedly) zwar; **there are ~ mistakes in it, but ...** es sind zwar Fehler darin, aber ... f (expressing possibility) **if ~ ...** falls ... wirklich; **if ~ he were wrong** falls er wirklich Unrecht haben sollte; **I may ~ come** es kann gut sein, dass ich komme

indefatigable ADJ , **indefatigably** ADV [ˌɪndɪˈfætɪgəbl, -lɪ] unermüdlich, rastlos

indefensible [ˌɪndɪˈfensəbl] ADJ a behaviour, remark etc unentschuldbar, nicht zu rechtfertigen attr or rechtfertigen pred; cause, theory unhaltbar, unvertretbar; policy unhaltbar; **morally ~** moralisch nicht vertretbar b town etc nicht zu verteidigen attr or verteidigen pred, unhaltbar

indefinable [ˌɪndɪˈfaɪnəbl] ADJ word, colour, charm unbestimmbar, undefinierbar; feeling, impression unbestimmt; **she has a certain ~ something** sie hat das gewisse Etwas

indefinably [ˌɪndɪˈfaɪnəblɪ] ADV undefinierbar

indefinite [ɪnˈdefɪnɪt] ADJ a number, length unbestimmt; (Gram) article, pronoun unbestimmt; **for the ~ future** auf unbestimmte Zeit; **at some ~ time** irgendwann einmal; **~ leave** unbeschränkter or unbegrenzter Urlaub, Urlaub m auf unbestimmte Zeit b (= vague) unklar, undeutlich; **he was very ~ about it** er war sehr unbestimmt or vage in dieser Sache

indefinite article N (Gram) unbestimmter Artikel

indefinitely [ɪnˈdefɪnɪtlɪ] ADV a wait etc unbegrenzt (lange), unendlich lange, endlos; postpone, continue, close auf unbestimmte Zeit; **we can't go on like this ~** wir können nicht endlos so weitermachen; **to be extended ~** auf unbestimmte Zeit verlängert werden b (= vaguely) unklar, undeutlich

indeliberate [ˌɪndɪˈlɪbərɪt] ADJ (form, = inconsiderate) unüberlegt; (= unintentional) unabsichtlich

indelible [ɪnˈdelɪbl] ADJ stain nicht zu entfernen; ink also wasserunlöslich; (fig) impression unauslöschlich; **~ pencil** Kopierstift m, Tintenstift m; **to leave an ~ mark on sb/sth** (fig) jdn/etw für immer zeichnen

indelibly [ɪnˈdelɪblɪ] ADV (fig) unauslöschlich

indelicacy [ɪnˈdelɪkəsɪ] N Taktlosigkeit f, Ungehörigkeit f; (of person) Mangel m an Feingefühl, Taktlosigkeit f; (= crudity) Geschmacklosigkeit f

indelicate [ɪnˈdelɪkət] ADJ person taktlos; act, remark also ungehörig; subject peinlich; (= crude) geschmacklos

indelicately [ɪnˈdelɪkətlɪ] ADV (= tactlessly) taktlos; (= rudely) ungehörig; (= crudely) geschmacklos

indemnification [ɪnˌdemnɪfɪˈkeɪʃən] N a (= compensation) Schadensersatz m, Entschädigung f (for für); (= sum received) Schadensersatz(summe f) m, Entschädigung(ssumme) f; (for expenses) Erstattung f (for +gen) b (for, against gegen) (= safeguard) Absicherung f; (= insurance) Versicherung f

indemnify [ɪnˈdemnɪfaɪ] VT a (= compensate) entschädigen (for für); (for expenses) erstatten (sb for sth jdm etw) b (= safeguard) absichern (from, against gegen); (= insure) versichern (against, from gegen)

indemnitee [ɪnˌdemnɪˈtiː] N Entschädigungsberechtigte(r) mf

indemnity [ɪnˈdemnɪtɪ] N a (= compensation) (for damage, loss etc) Schadensersatz m, Entschädigung f, Abfindung f; (after war) Wiedergutmachung f b (= insurance) Versicherung (-sschutz m) f; **deed of ~** (Jur) ≈ Versicherungspolice f

indent [ɪnˈdent] VT border, edge einkerben; coast zerklüften, einbuchten; (Typ) word, line einrücken, einziehen; (= leave dent in) metal etc einbeulen VI **to ~ on sb for sth** (Brit Comm) etw bei jdm ordern N [ˈɪndent](in border etc) Einkerbung f, Kerbe f; (in coast) Einbuchtung f; (Typ, of line) Einrückung f, Einzug m; (= dent: in metal etc) Beule f, Delle f

indentation [ˌɪndenˈteɪʃən] N (= notch, dent) (in border, edge) Kerbe f, Einschnitt m; (in coast) Einbuchtung f; (Typ) Einrückung f, Einzug m; (in metal etc) Delle f, Vertiefung f; (= print: of foot, shoe) Abdruck m

indenture [ɪnˈdentʃə] N a **indentures** PL (of apprentice) Ausbildungs- or Lehrvertrag m b (Jur) Vertrag in zwei or mehreren Ausführungen mit bestimmter Kanteneinkerbung zur Identifizierung VT apprentice in die Lehre nehmen

independence [ˌɪndɪˈpendəns] N Unabhängigkeit f (of von); (of person: in attitude, spirit also) Selbstständigkeit f; **to gain** or **achieve/declare ~** die Unabhängigkeit erlangen/erklären

Independence Day N (US) der Unabhängigkeitstag

independent [ˌɪndɪˈpendənt] ADJ a (= autonomous) unabhängig (of sb/sth von jdm/etw) (also Pol: country); person (in attitude, spirit) selbstständig, unabhängig; income eigen, privat; **she is a very ~ young lady** sie ist eine sehr selbstständige junge Dame; **a man of ~ means** eine Person mit Privateinkommen, ein Privatmann m; **to become ~** (country) die Unabhängigkeit erlangen b (= unconnected) report, research, thinker etc unabhängig; **~ confirmation** Bestätigung f aus unabhängiger Quelle; **they reached the summit by ~ routes** sie erreichten den Gipfel auf getrennten or gesonderten Wegen; **the two explosions were ~ of each other** die beiden Explosionen hatten nichts miteinander zu tun or hatten keine gemeinsame Ursache N (Pol) Unabhängige(r) mf

independent clause N (Gram) übergeordneter Satz, Hauptsatz m

independently [ˌɪndɪˈpendəntlɪ] ADV unabhängig (of sb/sth von jdm/etw); (in attitude, spirit also) selbstständig; (on own initiative also) von allein(e); live ohne fremde Hilfe; work selbstständig; **quite ~ he offered to help** er bot von sich aus seine Hilfe an; **they each came ~ to the same conclusion** sie kamen unabhängig voneinander zur gleichen Schlussfolgerung; **she is ~ wealthy** sie hat ein Privatvermögen

independent school N freie or unabhängige Schule

independent suspension N (Aut) Einzel(rad)aufhängung f

in-depth [ˈɪndepθ] ADJ eingehend, gründlich; interview ausführlich

indescribable [ˌɪndɪˈskraɪbəbl] ADJ unbeschreiblich; (inf: = terrible) fürchterlich, schrecklich

indescribably [ˌɪndɪˈskraɪbəblɪ] ADV unbeschreiblich; (inf: = terribly also) schrecklich, fürchterlich

indestructibility [ˈɪndɪˌstrʌktəˈbɪlɪtɪ] N Unzerstörbarkeit f

indestructible ADJ , **indestructibly** ADV [ˌɪndɪˈstrʌktəbl, -lɪ] unzerstörbar

indeterminable [ˌɪndɪˈtɜːmɪnəbl] ADJ unbestimmbar, nicht zu bestimmen attr or bestimmen pred

indeterminate [ˌɪndɪˈtɜːmɪnɪt] ADJ amount, length unbestimmt; duration also ungewiss; meaning, concept unklar, vage; **of ~ sex/age** von unbestimmbarem or nicht bestimmbarem Geschlecht/Alter

indeterminately [ˌɪndɪˈtɜːmɪnɪtlɪ] ADV unbestimmt; **it continued ~** es ging auf unbestimmte Zeit weiter

indetermination [ˈɪndɪˌtɜːmɪˈneɪʃən] N (= indecisiveness) Entschlusslosigkeit f, Unschlüssigkeit f, Unentschiedenheit f

index [ˈɪndeks] N a pl **-es** (in book) Register nt, Index m; (of sources) Quellenverzeichnis nt; (in library) (of topics) (Schlagwort)katalog m; (of authors) (Verfasser)katalog m; (= card index) Kartei f; **Index** (Eccl) Index m b pl **indices** (= pointer, = Typ) Hinweiszeichen nt, Handzeichen nt; (on scale) (An)zeiger m, Zunge f; **this is a good ~ of his character** das zeigt deutlich seinen Charakter, das lässt deutlich auf seinen Charakter schließen; **to provide a reliable ~ to** or **of the true state of affairs** zuverlässigen Aufschluss über den wahren Stand der Dinge geben c pl **-es** or **indices** (= number showing ratio) Index m, Messzahl f, Indexziffer f; **cost-of-living ~** Lebenshaltungskostenindex m

d *pl* **indices** (*Math*) Index *m*; (= *exponent*) Wurzelexponent *m*

VT a mit einem Register *or* Index versehen; *word* in das Register *or* in den Index aufnehmen; **the book is clearly ~ed** das Buch hat ein klares Register *or* einen klaren Index **b** **to ~ sth to inflation** etw an den Index binden, etw indexieren; *pension* etw dynamisieren

index card N Karteikarte *f*

indexed ['ɪndekst] ADJ (*Econ*) dynamisch

index: index finger N Zeigefinger *m*; **index-linked** ADJ *rate, salaries, trading, gilts* indexgebunden; *pensions* dynamisch; **index-tracker (fund)**, **index-tracking fund** N (*Fin*) indexorientierter Fonds

India ['ɪndɪə] N Indien *nt*; **~man** Indienfahrer *m*

India ink N (*US*) Tusche *f*

Indian ['ɪndɪən] ADJ **a** indisch; **the ~ rope-trick** der indische Seiltrick **b** (= *American Indian*) indianisch, Indianer- **a** Inder(in) *m(f)* **b** (= *American Indian*) Indianer(in) *m(f)*; **too many chiefs and not enough ~s** (*fig*) zu viele Köpfe und nicht genug Hände

Indian: Indian club N Keule *f*; **Indian corn** N Mais *m*; **Indian cress** N (*Bot*) Kapuzinerkresse *f*; **Indian elephant** N Indischer Elefant; **Indian file** N Gänsemarsch *m*; **in ~** im Gänsemarsch; **Indian giver** N (*US, inf*) jd, der etwas Geschenktes zurückfordert; **Indian ink** N Tusche *f*; **Indian meal** N **a** (*US, of corn*) Maismehl *nt* **b** (*Cook: = dish*) indisches Gericht; **Indian Ocean** N Indischer Ozean; **Indian reservation** N Indianerreservat *nt*; **Indian sign** N (*US*) Zauber *m*; **to put an ~ on sb** jdn verzaubern *or* verhexen; **Indian summer** N Altweibersommer *m*, Spät- *or* Nachsommer *m*; (*esp Brit fig: = success late in life*) späte Blüte; **Indian wrestling** N Armdrücken *nt*

India: India paper N Dünndruckpapier *nt*; **India rubber** N Gummi *m*, Kautschuk *m*; (= *eraser*) Radiergummi *m* **ATTR** Gummi-; **~ ball** Gummiball *m*

indicate ['ɪndɪkeɪt] **VT a** (= *point out, mark*) zeigen, deuten auf (+*acc*); (= *point to*) zeigen *or* deuten auf (+*acc*); **large towns are ~d in red** Großstädte sind rot eingezeichnet *or* gekennzeichnet; **sit down, he said, indicating a chair** setzen Sie sich, sagte er und zeigte *or* deutete auf einen Stuhl

b (*person: = gesture, express*) andeuten, zeigen, zu verstehen geben; **to ~ one's feelings** seine Gefühle zeigen *or* zum Ausdruck bringen; **to ~ one's intention to do sth** seine Absicht anzeigen, etw zu tun

c (= *be a sign of, suggest*) erkennen lassen, schließen lassen auf (+*acc*), (hin)deuten auf (+*acc*); **what does it ~ to you?** was erkennen Sie daraus?, welche Schlüsse ziehen Sie daraus?; **opinion polls ~ that ...** die Meinungsumfragen deuten darauf hin, dass ...

d (= *register and display*) *temperature, speed* (an)zeigen

e (*Med*) *treatment* indizieren; *illness* Anzeichen sein für, anzeigen

VI (*esp Brit Aut*) (Richtungswechsel) anzeigen (*form*), blinken, den Blinker setzen; **to ~ right** rechts blinken, Richtungswechsel nach rechts anzeigen (*form*)

indication [,ɪndɪˈkeɪʃən] ✪ 26.3 N **a** (= *sign*) (An)zeichen *nt* (*also Med*) (*of* für), Hinweis *m* (*of* auf +*acc*); **there is every/no ~ that he is right** alles/nichts weist darauf hin *or* lässt darauf schließen, dass er Recht hat; **there are few ~s that they are ready to come to an agreement** es gibt kaum Anzeichen dafür, dass sie zu einer Einigung bereit sind; **he gave a clear ~ of his intentions** er zeigte seine Absichten deutlich, er ließ seine Absichten deutlich erkennen; **he gave no ~ that he was ready to compromise** nichts wies darauf hin, dass er zu einem Kompromiss bereit war; **what are the ~s that it will happen?** was deutet darauf hin *or* spricht dafür *or* welchen Hinweis gibt es dafür, dass es geschieht?; **we had no ~ that ...** es gab kein Anzeichen dafür, dass ...; **that is some ~**

of what we can expect das gibt uns einen Vorgeschmack auf das, was wir zu erwarten haben; **if you could give me a rough ~ of ...** wenn Sie mir eine ungefähre Vorstellung davon geben könnten ...

b (= *showing, marking*) (*by gesturing, facial expression*) Anzeigen *nt*, Erkennenlassen *nt*; (*by pointing, drawing*) Anzeigen *nt*, Bezeichnen *nt*; **~ of the boundaries on this map is very poor** die Grenzen sind auf dieser Karte sehr undeutlich bezeichnet

c (*on gauge*) Anzeige *f*

indicative [ɪnˈdɪkətɪv] **ADJ a** bezeichnend (*of* für); **to be ~ of sth** auf etw (*acc*) schließen lassen, auf etw (*acc*) hindeuten; *of sb's character* für etw bezeichnend sein **b** (*Gram*) indikativisch; **~ mood** Indikativ *m*, Wirklichkeitsform *f* **N** (*Gram*) Indikativ *m*, Wirklichkeitsform *f*; **in the ~** im Indikativ, in der Wirklichkeitsform

indicator ['ɪndɪkeɪtə'] N (= *instrument, gauge*) Anzeiger *m*; (= *needle*) Zeiger *m*; (*esp Brit Aut*) Richtungsanzeiger *m* (*form*); (*flashing*) Blinker *m*; (*Chem*) Indikator *m*; (*fig: of economic position etc*) Messlatte *f*; **altitude/pressure ~** Höhen-/Druckmesser *m*; **~ board** Anzeigetafel *f*; **arrival/departure ~ board** (*Rail*) Ankunfts-/Abfahrts(-anzeige)tafel *f*; (*Aviat*) Anzeige(tafel) *f* für Ankünfte/Abflüge, Fluginformationsanzeige *f*; **this is an ~ of economic recovery** dies ist ein Indikator für den Aufschwung

indices ['ɪndɪsiːz] *pl of* **index**

indict [ɪnˈdaɪt] VT (= *charge*) anklagen, beschuldigen (*on a charge of sth* einer Sache *gen*), unter Anklage stellen; (*US Jur*) Anklage erheben gegen (*for wegen* +*gen*); **to ~ sb as a murderer** jdn unter Mordanklage stellen, jdn des Mordes anklagen

indictable [ɪnˈdaɪtəbl] ADJ *offence* strafbar; *person* strafrechtlich verfolgbar

indictment [ɪnˈdaɪtmənt] N (*of person*) (= *accusation*) Beschuldigung *f*, Anschuldigung *f*; (= *charge sheet*) Anklage *f* (*for, on a charge of wegen*); (*US: by grand jury*) Anklageerhebung *f*; **to bring an ~ against sb** gegen jdn Anklage erheben, jdn unter Anklage stellen; **bill of ~** Anklageschrift *f*; **to be an ~ of sth** (*fig*) ein Armutszeugnis *nt* für etw sein; **the speech was a damning ~ of government policy** die Rede war eine vernichtende Anklage gegen die Regierungspolitik

indifference [ɪnˈdɪfrəns] N Gleichgültigkeit *f* (*to, towards* gegenüber), Indifferenz *f* (*geh*) (*to, towards* gegenüber); **it's a matter of complete ~ to me** das ist mir völlig egal *or* gleichgültig

indifferent [ɪnˈdɪfrənt] ADJ **a** (= *lacking interest*) gleichgültig, indifferent (*geh*) (*to, towards* gegenüber); **he is quite ~ about it/to her** es/sie ist ihm ziemlich gleichgültig; **~ to her despair** ungerührt von ihrer Verzweiflung; **his ~ attitude to the killings** seine Gleichgültigkeit gegenüber den Morden **b** (= *mediocre*) mittelmäßig, durchschnittlich

indifferently [ɪnˈdɪfrəntlɪ] ADV **a** (= *without interest*) gleichgültig **b** (= *poorly*) (mittel)mäßig (*gut*), nicht besonders (*gut*)

indigence ['ɪndɪdʒəns] N Bedürftigkeit *f*, Armut *f*

indigenous [ɪnˈdɪdʒɪnəs] ADJ einheimisch (*to* in +*dat*); *customs* landeseigen; **~ language** Landessprache *f*; **plants ~ to Canada** in Kanada heimische *or* beheimatete Pflanzen; **~ tribes** einheimische *or* eingeborene Volksstämme

indigent ['ɪndɪdʒənt] ADJ bedürftig, arm, ärmlich

indigestible [,ɪndɪˈdʒestɪbl] ADJ (*Med*) unverdaulich; (*fig*) Stärke verdaulich, schwer zu ertragen *attr* or ertragen *pred*; **fried food is very ~** Gebratenes ist sehr schwer verdaulich

indigestion [,ɪndɪˈdʒestʃən] N Verdauungsbeschwerden *pl*; **acid ~** Sodbrennen *nt*

indignant [ɪnˈdɪgnənt] ADJ entrüstet, empört (*at, about, with* über +*acc*), unwillig (*at, about* wegen); **to be ~ with sb** über jdn empört sein; **to make sb ~** jds Unwillen *or* Entrüstung erre-

gen; **it's no good getting ~** es hat keinen Zweck, sich zu entrüsten *or* sich aufzuregen

indignantly [ɪnˈdɪgnəntlɪ] ADV entrüstet, empört

indignation [,ɪndɪgˈneɪʃən] N Entrüstung *f* (*at, about, with* über +*acc*), Unwillen *m* (*at, about* wegen)

indignity [ɪnˈdɪgnɪtɪ] N Demütigung *f*, Schmach *f* (*liter*); **oh, the ~ of it!** also, das ist doch der Gipfel!

indigo ['ɪndɪgəʊ] **N** Indigo *nt or m* **ADJ** indigofarben

indigo blue ADJ indigoblau

indirect [,ɪndɪˈrekt] ADJ **a** indirekt; *consequence, result* indirekt, mittelbar; **in an ~ way, by ~ means** auf indirekte Weise, auf Umwegen; **by an ~ route/path/road** auf Umwegen *or* einem Umweg; **to make an ~ reference to sb/sth** auf jdn/etw anspielen *or* indirekt Bezug nehmen **b** (*Gram*) indirekt

indirect discourse (*US*) N (*Gram*) indirekte Rede

indirectly [,ɪndɪˈrektlɪ] ADV indirekt

indirectness [,ɪndɪˈrektnɪs] N Indirektheit *f*

indirect object N (*Gram*) Dativobjekt *nt*

indirect speech N (*Gram*) indirekte Rede

indiscernible [,ɪndɪˈsɜːnəbl] ADJ nicht erkennbar *or* sichtbar; *improvement, change etc* also unmerklich; *noise* nicht wahrnehmbar; **to be almost ~** kaum zu erkennen sein; (*noise*) kaum wahrzunehmen sein

indiscipline [ɪnˈdɪsɪplɪn] N Mangel *m* an Disziplin, Undiszipliniertheit *f*, Disziplinlosigkeit *f*

indiscreet [,ɪndɪˈskriːt] ADJ indiskret; (= *tactless*) taktlos, ohne Feingefühl; **to be ~ about sth** in Bezug auf etw (*acc*) indiskret sein; **he is too ~ ever to be a successful diplomat** wegen seiner Neigung zu Indiskretionen wird er nie ein erfolgreicher Diplomat werden

indiscreetly [,ɪndɪˈskriːtlɪ] ADV indiskret; (= *tactlessly*) taktlos

indiscreetness [,ɪndɪˈskriːtnɪs] N = **indiscretion**

indiscrete [,ɪndɪˈskriːt] ADJ kompakt, zusammenhängend, homogen

indiscretion [,ɪndɪˈskreʃən] N Indiskretion *f*; (= *tactlessness*) Taktlosigkeit *f*, Mangel *m* an Feingefühl; (= *affair*) Abenteuer *nt*, Affäre *f*; **his youthful ~s** seine jugendliche Unvernunft, sein jugendlicher Leichtsinn

indiscriminate [,ɪndɪˈskrɪmɪnɪt] ADJ wahllos; *spending* also unüberlegt; *reading* also kritiklos, unkritisch; *mixture* also kunterbunt; *choice* willkürlich; *reader, shopper* kritiklos, unkritisch; *tastes* unausgeprägt; **you shouldn't be so ~ in the friends you make** du solltest dir deine Freunde etwas sorgfältiger aussuchen; **he was completely ~ in whom he punished** er verteilte seine Strafen völlig wahllos *or* willkürlich

indiscriminately [,ɪndɪˈskrɪmɪnɪtlɪ] ADV wahllos; *choose* willkürlich

indiscriminating [,ɪndɪˈskrɪmɪneɪtɪŋ] ADJ unkritisch, kritiklos

indispensability ['ɪndɪ,spensɪˈbɪlɪtɪ] N Unentbehrlichkeit *f*, unbedingte Notwendigkeit (*to* für)

indispensable [,ɪndɪˈspensəbl] ADJ unentbehrlich, unbedingt notwendig *or* erforderlich (*to* für); **nobody's ~** niemand ist unentbehrlich; **to make oneself ~ to sb** sich für jdn unentbehrlich machen

indispensably [,ɪndɪˈspensəblɪ] ADV **it is ~ necessary to them** es ist unbedingt notwendig *or* erforderlich für sie; **that is necessarily and ~ a part of our system** das ist notwendiger und unverzichtbarer Bestandteil unseres Systems

indisposed [,ɪndɪˈspəʊzd] ADJ **a** (= *unwell*) unwohl, indisponiert (*geh*), unpässlich (*geh*) **b** (= *disinclined*) **to be ~ to do sth** nicht gewillt *or* geneigt sein, etw zu tun

indisposition [,ɪndɪspəˈzɪʃən] N **a** (= *illness*) Unwohlsein *nt*, Indisposition *f* (*geh*), Unpässlichkeit f (geh) **b** (= disinclination) Unwilligkeit f

indisputability [ˌɪndɪˌspjuːtəˈbɪlɪtɪ] N Unbestreitbarkeit f, Unstrittigkeit f

indisputable [ˌɪndɪˈspjuːtəbl] ADJ unbestreitbar; evidence unanfechtbar

indisputably [ˌɪndɪˈspjuːtəblɪ] ✪ 26.3 ADV unbestreitbar

indissolubility [ˈɪndɪˌsɒljʊˈbɪlɪtɪ] N (Chem) Unlöslichkeit f, Unlösbarkeit f; (fig) Unauflöslichkeit f, Unauflösbarkeit f

indissoluble ADJ , **indissolubly** ADV [ˌɪndɪˈsɒljʊbl, -lɪ] (Chem) unlöslich, unlösbar f; (fig) unauflöslich, unauflösbar, unlöslich

indistinct [ˌɪndɪˈstɪŋkt] ADJ object, shape, words verschwommen, unklar, undeutlich; noise schwach, unklar; memory undeutlich; voice undeutlich, unklar; line unscharf

indistinctly [ˌɪndɪˈstɪŋktlɪ] ADV see nicht deutlich, verschwommen; speak undeutlich; remember schwach, dunkel

indistinguishable [ˌɪndɪˈstɪŋgwɪʃəbl] ADJ **a** nicht unterscheidbar, nicht zu unterscheidend attr or unterscheiden pred (from von); **the twins are ~ (from one another)** man kann die Zwillinge nicht (voneinander) unterscheiden **b** (= indiscernible) nicht erkennbar or sichtbar; improvement, change, difference etc unmerklich, nicht erkennbar; noise nicht wahrnehmbar

individual [ˌɪndɪˈvɪdjʊəl] ADJ **a** (= separate) einzeln; **~ cases** Einzelfälle pl; **to give ~ help** jedem Einzeln helfen, Einzelhilfe leisten; **~ tastes differ** jeder hat einen eigenen or individuellen Geschmack, die Geschmäcker sind verschieden
b (= own) eigen; (= for one person) einzeln; **serve on ~ plates** auf einzelnen Tellern servieren; **~ portions cost 95p** eine Einzelportion kostet 95 Pence
c (= distinctive, characteristic) eigen, individuell
N Individuum nt, Einzelne(r) mf, Einzelperson f; (inf) Individuum nt, Mensch m, Person f; **the freedom of the ~** die Freiheit des Einzelnen, die individuelle Freiheit → private

individualism [ˌɪndɪˈvɪdjʊəlɪzəm] N Individualismus m

individualist [ˌɪndɪˈvɪdjʊəlɪst] **N** Individualist(in) m(f) **ADJ** individualistisch

individualistic [ˌɪndɪˈvɪdjʊəlɪstɪk] ADJ individualistisch

individuality [ˈɪndɪˌvɪdjʊˈælɪtɪ] N Individualität f, (eigene) Persönlichkeit f

individualize [ˌɪndɪˈvɪdjʊəlaɪz] VT individualisieren; (= treat separately) einzeln behandeln; (= give individuality to) book, author's style, performance eine persönliche or individuelle or eigene Note verleihen (+dat); **each patient has ~d treatment/an ~d exercise plan** jeder Patient bekommt eine individuelle Behandlung/seinen eigenen Trainingsplan

individually [ˌɪndɪˈvɪdjʊəlɪ] ADV individuell; (= separately) numbered, wrapped einzeln; **~ styled suit** Modellanzug m; **to be ~ responsible for sth** persönlich für etw verantwortlich sein

indivisible ADJ , **indivisibly** ADV [ˌɪndɪˈvɪzəbl, -lɪ] unteilbar (also Math), untrennbar

Indo- [ˈɪndəʊ-] PREF Indo-; **Indo-China** N Indochina nt

indocile [ɪnˈdəʊsaɪl] ADJ (form) (difficult to teach) ungelehrig; (= insubordinate) unfügsam

indoctrinate [ɪnˈdɒktrɪneɪt] VT indoktrinieren

indoctrination [ɪnˌdɒktrɪˈneɪʃən] N Indoktrination f

Indo: Indo-European **ADJ** indogermanisch, indoeuropäisch **N** **a** Indogermane m, Indogermanin f, Indoeuropäer(in) m(f) **b** (Ling) Indogermanisch nt, Indoeuropäisch nt; **Indo-Germanic** (old) ADJ, N = **Indo-European ADJ, N b**

indolence [ˈɪndələns] N Trägheit f, Indolenz f (rare)

indolent ADJ , **indolently** ADV [ˈɪndələnt, -lɪ] träge, indolent (rare)

indomitable [ɪnˈdɒmɪtəbl] ADJ person, courage unbezähmbar, unbezwingbar; will unbeugsam, eisern, unerschütterlich; **his ~ pride** sein nicht zu brechender Stolz

Indonesia [ˌɪndəʊˈniːzɪə] N Indonesien nt

Indonesian [ˌɪndəʊˈniːzɪən] **ADJ** indonesisch **N** **a** Indonesier(in) m(f) **b** (Ling) Indonesisch nt

indoor [ˈɪndɔː'] ADJ Innen-; clothes für zu Hause or zuhause (Aus, Sw); **~ activity** Beschäftigung f für drinnen; **~ aerial** Zimmerantenne f; **~ market** überdachter Markt; **~ plant** Zimmerpflanze f; **~ sport** Hallensport m; **~ swimming pool** (public) Hallenbad nt; (private) überdachter Swimmingpool; **~ tennis court** Tennishalle f; **~ cycle track** Radsporthalle f; **~ work** Arbeit, die nicht im Freien ausgeführt wird; **~ air pollution** Innenraumluftverschmutzung f; **~ games** Spiele pl fürs Haus, Haus- or Zimmerspiele pl; (Sport) Hallenspiele pl

indoors [ɪnˈdɔːz] ADV drin(nen) (inf), innen; (= at home) zu Hause, zuhause (Aus, Sw); (= into house) ins Haus; **what's the house like ~?** wie sieht das Haus innen aus?; **to stay ~** im Haus bleiben, drin bleiben (inf); **go and play ~** geh ins Haus or nach drinnen spielen; **to go ~** ins Haus gehen, nach drinnen gehen; **~ and outdoors** im und außer Haus, drinnen und draußen, im Haus und im Freien

indrawn [ˈɪnˈdrɔːn] ADJ **a** breath eingezogen **b** (form) person zurückhaltend

indubitable ADJ , **indubitably** ADV [ɪnˈdjuːbɪtəbl, -lɪ] zweifellos, unzweifelhaft

induce [ɪnˈdjuːs] VT **a** (= persuade) **to ~ sb to do sth** jdn dazu bewegen or bringen or veranlassen, etw zu tun **b** reaction, change, hypnosis herbeiführen; relaxation bewirken; sleep herbeiführen; illness, vomiting verursachen, führen zu; labour, birth einleiten; **this drug ~s sleep** dieses Mittel hat eine einschläfernde Wirkung; **she had to be ~d** die Geburt musste eingeleitet werden; **(artificially) ~d sleep** künstlicher Schlaf; **a stress-/drug-induced condition** ein durch Stress/Drogen ausgelöstes Leiden **c** (Philos) induktiv or durch Induktion erarbeiten **d** (Elec) current, magnetic effect induzieren

inducement [ɪnˈdjuːsmənt] N **a** (no pl: = persuasion) Überredung f; (= motive, incentive) Anreiz m, Ansporn m no pl; **to offer ~s** Anreize bieten; **cash/financial ~s** finanzielle Anreize pl **b** = **induction b**

induct [ɪnˈdʌkt] VT **a** bishop, president etc in sein Amt einsetzen or einführen **b** (US Mil) einziehen, einberufen

inductee [ɪndʌkˈtiː] N (US Mil) (zum Wehrdienst) Eingezogene(r) or Einberufene(r) mf

induction [ɪnˈdʌkʃən] N **a** (of bishop, president etc) Amtseinführung f; (US Mil) Einberufung f, Einziehung f **b** (of sleep, reaction etc) Herbeiführen nt; (of labour, birth) Einleitung f **c** (Philos, Math, Elec) Induktion f

induction: induction coil N (Elec) Induktionsspule f; **induction course** N Einführungskurs m; **induction loop** N (Elec) Induktionsschleife f

inductive ADJ , **inductively** ADV [ɪnˈdʌktɪv, -lɪ] induktiv

indulge [ɪnˈdʌldʒ] **VT** **a** appetite, desires etc, person nachgeben (+dat); (= overindulge) children verwöhnen, verhätscheln; one's imagination frönen (+dat); **he ~s her every whim** er erfüllt ihr jeden Wunsch; **to ~ oneself in sth** sich (dat) etw gönnen, in etw (dat) schwelgen; **she ~d herself with a glass of wine** sie gönnte sich (dat) ein Glas Wein; **go on, ~ yourself!** nun komm schon, gönn dir mal was (inf)
b debtor Zahlungsaufschub gewähren (+dat)
VI **to ~ in sth** sich (dat) etw gönnen or genehmigen (inf); in vice, drink, daydreams einer Sache (dat) frönen, sich einer Sache (dat) hingeben; **to ~ in sth to excess** etw bis zum Exzess treiben; **dessert came, but I didn't ~** (inf) der

Nachtisch kam, aber ich konnte mich beherrschen; **I don't ~** ich trinke/rauche etc nicht; **we don't ~ in such underhand tactics** wir geben uns mit solchen hinterhältigen Taktiken nicht ab

indulgence [ɪnˈdʌldʒəns] N **a** Nachsicht f; (of appetite etc) Nachgiebigkeit f (of gegenüber); (= overindulgence) Verwöhnung f, Verhätschelung f **b** (in activity, drink etc) **~ in drink/food/sport** übermäßiges Trinken/Essen/Sporttreiben **c** (= thing indulged in) Luxus m; (= food, drink, pleasure) Genuss m; **he allowed himself the ~ of a day off work** er gönnte sich (dat) den Luxus eines freien Tages; **smoking/the car is one of my few ~s** Rauchen/das Auto ist fast das Einzige, was ich mir gönne **d** (form: = permission) Einwilligung f, Zustimmung f **e** (Eccl) Ablass m

indulgent [ɪnˈdʌldʒənt] ADJ nachsichtig (to gegenüber); mother etc also nachgiebig; (to one's own desires etc) zu nachgiebig

indulgently [ɪnˈdʌldʒəntlɪ] ADV nachsichtig

industrial [ɪnˈdʌstrɪəl] **ADJ** industriell, Industrie-; **~ country** Industriestaat m; **~ fabric** Industriefasern pl; **~ growth** Industriewachstum nt; **~ nation** Industriestaat m; **~ production** Industrieproduktion f; **~ research** Arbeits- or Betriebsforschung f; **the Industrial Revolution** die industrielle Revolution; **~ robot** Industrieroboter m; **~ state** Industriestaat m; **~ training** betriebliche Ausbildung f **N** **industrials** PL (St Ex) Industrieaktien pl

industrial: industrial accident N Betriebs- or Arbeitsunfall m; **industrial action** N Arbeitskampfmaßnahmen pl; **to take ~** in den Ausstand treten; **industrial archaeology**, (US) **industrial archeology** N Industriearchäologie f; **industrial democracy** N Demokratie f im Betrieb; **industrial design** N Konstruktionslehre f; **industrial designer** N Industriedesigner(in) m(f); **industrial diamond** N Industriediamant m; **industrial disease** N Berufskrankheit f; **industrial dispute** N Auseinandersetzungen pl zwischen Arbeitgebern und Arbeitnehmern; (about pay also) Tarifkonflikt m; (= strike) Streik m; **industrial engineering** N Fertigungstechnik f; **industrial espionage** N Industriespionage f; **industrial estate** N (Brit) Industriegebiet nt; **industrial injury** N Arbeitsunfall m; **industrial insurance** N Unfallversicherung f

industrialism [ɪnˈdʌstrɪəlɪzəm] N Industrie f

industrialist [ɪnˈdʌstrɪəlɪst] N Industrielle(r) m f

industrialization [ɪnˌdʌstrɪəlaɪˈzeɪʃən] N Industrialisierung f

industrialize [ɪnˈdʌstrɪəlaɪz] VTI industrialisieren

industrial: industrial medicine N Arbeits- or Betriebsmedizin f; **industrial park** N (US) Industriegelände nt; **industrial psychology** N Arbeits- or Betriebspsychologie f; **industrial relations** PL Beziehungen pl zwischen Arbeitgebern und Gewerkschaften; **industrial-strength** ADJ (usu hum) extrastark; **~ claret** vollmundiger Bordeaux; **industrial tribunal** N Arbeitsgericht nt; **industrial trouble**, **industrial unrest** N Arbeitsunruhen pl; **industrial waste** N Industrieabfälle pl, Industriemüll m; **industrial worker** N Industriearbeiter(in) m(f)

industrious ADJ , **industriously** ADV [ɪnˈdʌstrɪəs, -lɪ] arbeitsam, fleißig

industriousness [ɪnˈdʌstrɪəsnɪs] N Arbeitsamkeit f, Fleiß m

industry [ˈɪndəstrɪ] N **a** (= trade, branch of industry) Industrie f; **heavy/light ~** Schwer-/Leichtindustrie f; **hotel ~** Hotelgewerbe nt; **tourist ~** Tourismusbranche or -industrie f; **in certain industries** in einigen Branchen **b** (= industriousness) Fleiß m

industry standard **N** Industrienorm f **ADJ** **industry-standard** der Industrienorm entsprechend

inebriate [ɪˈniːbrɪɪt] **N** (form) Trinker(in) m(f) **ADJ** = **inebriated a** [ɪˈniːbrɪeɪt] **VT** (lit) betrunken machen; (fig) trunken machen; (success, popularity etc) berauschen

inebriated [ɪ'ni:brɪeɪtɪd] ADJ **a** (form) betrunken, unter Alkoholeinfluss (form) **b** (fig) berauscht, trunken (liter)

inebriation [ɪ,ni:brɪ'eɪʃən], **inebriety** [,ɪni:'braɪətɪ] N (form) betrunkener Zustand

inedible [ɪn'edɪbl] ADJ nicht essbar; (= unpleasant) meal etc ungenießbar

ineducable [ɪn'edjʊkəbl] ADJ bildungsunfähig

ineffable [ɪn'efəbl] ADJ (form) unsäglich (geh), unsagbar, unaussprechlich

ineffably [ɪn'efəblɪ] ADV (form, = indescribably) unsäglich (geh), unaussprechlich; **Walters is ~ entertaining** Walters ist unbeschreiblich unterhaltsam

ineffective [,ɪnɪ'fektɪv] ADJ unwirksam, ineffektiv; attempt also fruchtlos, nutzlos; person unfähig, untauglich; government, management unfähig; **to be ~ against sth** nicht wirksam gegen etw sein; **to render sth ~** etw unwirksam machen

ineffectively [,ɪnɪ'fektɪvlɪ] ADV ineffektiv

ineffectiveness [,ɪnɪ'fektɪvnɪs] N Unwirksamkeit f, Ineffektivität f; (of attempt) Fruchtlosigkeit f, Nutzlosigkeit f; (of person) Unfähigkeit f

ineffectual [,ɪnɪ'fektjʊəl] ADJ ineffektiv; (= half-hearted) halbherzig

ineffectually [,ɪnɪ'fektjʊəlɪ] ADV ohne Wirkung; (= half-heartedly) halbherzig

inefficacious [,ɪnefɪ'keɪʃəs] ADJ unwirksam, wirkungslos, ohne Wirkung; policy erfolglos, fruchtlos

inefficacy [ɪn'efɪkəsɪ] N Unwirksamkeit f, Wirkungslosigkeit f; (of policy) Erfolglosigkeit f, Fruchtlosigkeit f

inefficiency [,ɪnɪ'fɪʃənsɪ] N (of person) Unfähigkeit f, Ineffizienz f (geh); (of machine, engine) geringe Leistung; (of factory, company) Unproduktivität f; **the ~ of this method** diese unrationelle Methode

inefficient [,ɪnɪ'fɪʃənt] ADJ person unfähig, ineffizient (geh); machine, engine leistungsschwach; method unrationell; use unwirtschaftlich; factory, company unproduktiv, ineffizient (geh); **to be ~ at doing sth** etw schlecht machen; **the ~ working of a mechanism** das schlechte Funktionieren eines Mechanismus; **~ combustion of fuel** unwirtschaftliche Verbrennung des Treibstoffs

inefficiently [,ɪnɪ'fɪʃəntlɪ] ADV schlecht; **to work ~** (person) unrationell arbeiten; (machine) unwirtschaftlich arbeiten

inelastic [,ɪnɪ'læstɪk] ADJ (lit) unelastisch; (fig) starr, nicht flexibel

inelasticity [,ɪnɪlæs'tɪsɪtɪ] N (lit) Mangel m an Elastizität; (fig) Mangel m an Flexibilität, Starrheit f

inelegance [ɪn'elɪgəns] N Uneleganz f; (of clothes, person also) Mangel m an Schick or Eleganz; (of style also) Schwerfälligkeit f, Unausgewogenheit f; (of prose, phrase also) Ungeschliffenheit f, Plumpheit f, Schwerfälligkeit f; (of dialect) Derbheit f, Schwerfälligkeit f

inelegant [ɪn'elɪgənt] ADJ unelegant; clothes, person also ohne Schick or Eleganz; style also schwerfällig, unausgewogen; prose, phrase also ungeschliffen, plump, schwerfällig; dialect derb, schwerfällig

inelegantly [ɪn'elɪgəntlɪ] ADV unelegant; **she walks very ~** ihr Gang ist ohne Eleganz, sie hat einen wenig eleganten Gang

ineligibility [ɪn,elɪdʒə'bɪlɪtɪ] N (for benefits, grant) Nichtberechtigung nt; (for election) Unwählbarkeit f; (for job, office, as husband) mangelnde Eignung, Untauglichkeit f

ineligible [ɪn'elɪdʒəbl] ADJ (for benefits, grant) nicht berechtigt (for zu Leistungen +gen); (for election) nicht wählbar; (for job, office, as husband) ungeeignet, untauglich; **~ for military service** wehruntauglich; **you are ~ for social security benefits** Sie sind nicht zu Leistungen

der Sozialversicherung berechtigt; **to be ~ for a pension** nicht pensionsberechtigt sein

ineloquent [ɪn'eləkwənt] ADJ nicht wortgewandt

ineluctable [,ɪnɪ'lʌktəbl] ADJ (liter) unausweichlich, unabwendbar (liter)

inept [ɪ'nept] ADJ behaviour ungeschickt, linkisch, unbeholfen; remark unpassend, unangebracht, ungeschickt; performance, display ungeschickt, stümperhaft (pej); compliment, refusal, attempt plump; comparison ungeeignet, unpassend; person (= clumsy) ungeschickt, unbeholfen; (= slow at learning) begriffsstutzig, ungelehrig, unverständig

ineptitude [ɪ'neptɪtju:d], **ineptness** [ɪ'neptnɪs] N (of behaviour) Ungeschicktheit f, Unbeholfenheit f; (of remark) Unangebrachtheit f, Ungeschicktheit f; (of performance, display) Ungeschicklichkeit f, Stümperhaftigkeit f (pej); (of compliment, refusal, attempt) Plumpheit f; (of comparison) Ungeeignetheit f; (of person) (= clumsiness) Ungeschick nt, Unbeholfenheit f; (= slowness at learning) Begriffsstutzigkeit f, Ungelehrigkeit f

inequality [,ɪnɪ'kwɒlɪtɪ] N (= lack of equality) Ungleichheit f; (= instance of inequality) Unterschied m; **great inequalities in wealth** große Unterschiede pl in der Verteilung von Reichtum; **~ of opportunity** Chancenungleichheit f; **~ of opportunity in education** Ungleichheit f der Bildungschancen

inequitable [ɪn'ekwɪtəbl] ADJ ungerecht

inequity [ɪn'ekwɪtɪ] N Ungerechtigkeit f

ineradicable [,ɪnɪ'rædɪkəbl] ADJ mistake, failing unabänderlich, unwiderruflich; feeling of guilt, hatred tief sitzend, unauslöschlich; disease, prejudice unausrottbar

inerrancy [ɪn'erənsɪ] N (form: of scriptures) Unfehlbarkeit f

inert [ɪ'nɜ:t] ADJ unbeweglich; (Phys) matter träge; (Chem) substance inaktiv

inert gas N (Chem) Edelgas nt

inertia [ɪ'nɜ:ʃə] N (lit, fig) Trägheit f; **~-reel seat belt** Automatikgurt m

inescapable [,ɪnɪs'keɪpəbl] ADJ unvermeidlich; fact, reality unausweichlich; consequence, logic, conclusion zwangsläufig, unausweichlich

inescapably [,ɪnɪs'keɪpəblɪ] ADV unvermeidlich; **~, this means that ...** dies bedeutet unvermeidlicherweise, dass ...

inessential [,ɪnɪ'senʃəl] **ADJ** unwesentlich, unerheblich, unwichtig **N** Unwesentliche(s) nt no pl, Nebensächlichkeit f

inestimable [ɪn'estɪməbl] ADJ unschätzbar

inevitability [ɪn,evɪtə'bɪlɪtɪ] N Unvermeidlichkeit f

inevitable [ɪn'evɪtəbl] ◑ 15.1 **ADJ** unvermeidlich, unvermeidbar; result also zwangsläufig; **victory/defeat seemed ~** der Sieg/die Niederlage schien unabwendbar; **a tourist with his ~ camera** ein Tourist mit dem unvermeidlichen Fotoapparat **N** **the ~** das Unvermeidliche

inevitably [ɪn'evɪtəblɪ] ADV zwangsläufig; **if it's ~ the case that ...** wenn es notgedrungenerweise or zwangsläufig so sein muss, dass ...; **~ rising prices** zwangsläufig steigende Preise; **one question ~ leads to another** eine Frage zieht unweigerlich weitere nach sich; **talk ~ turned to politics** das Gespräch kam unweigerlich or zwangsläufig auf Politik; **~, he got drunk/was late** es konnte ja nicht ausbleiben, dass er sich betrank/zu spät kam; **as ~ happens on these occasions** wie es bei solchen Anlässen immer ist

inexact ADJ , **inexactly** ADV [,ɪnɪg'zækt, -lɪ] ungenau

inexactitude [,ɪnɪg,zæktɪtju:d] N Ungenauigkeit f

inexcusable [,ɪnɪks'kju:zəbl] ADJ unverzeihlich, unverzeihbar, unentschuldbar; failure unverzeihlich; **it would be ~ for him to leave now** es wäre unverzeihlich, wenn er jetzt gehen würde

inexcusably [,ɪnɪks'kju:zəblɪ] ADV unverzeihlich; **she had been ~ careless/lazy** ihre Nachlässigkeit/Faulheit war unverzeihlich gewesen

inexhaustible [,ɪnɪg'zɔ:stəbl] ADJ unerschöpflich; source, spring also nie versiegend; curiosity unstillbar, unendlich; person, talker unermüdlich

inexorable [ɪn'eksərəbl] ADJ (= relentless) erbarmungslos, unerbittlich; (= not to be stopped) unaufhaltsam; truth, facts unumstößlich

inexorably [ɪn'eksərəblɪ] ADV erbarmungslos, unerbittlich; (= unstoppably) unaufhaltsam

inexpediency [,ɪnɪks'pi:dɪənsɪ] N (of plan, measures, action, decision) Ungeeignetheit f, Unzweckmäßigkeit f; (of policy) Unratsamkeit f, Unklugheit f

inexpedient [,ɪnɪks'pi:dɪənt] ADJ plan, measures, action, decision ungeeignet, unzweckmäßig; policy unratsam, unklug; **it would be ~ to do that** es wäre unklug, das zu tun

inexpensive [,ɪnɪk'spensɪv] ADJ billig, preisgünstig

inexpensively [,ɪnɪk'spensɪvlɪ] ADV billig; live also ohne große Kosten; buy also günstig

inexperience [,ɪnɪk'spɪərɪəns] N Unerfahrenheit f, Mangel m an Erfahrung; **his ~ with our system** seine mangelnde Vertrautheit mit unserem System

inexperienced [,ɪnɪk'spɪərɪənst] ADJ unerfahren; woodworker, skier etc ungeübt, nicht so versiert; **to be ~ in doing sth** wenig Erfahrung darin haben, etw zu tun

inexpert [ɪn'ekspɜ:t] ADJ unfachmännisch, laienhaft; treatment also unsachgemäß; (= untrained) ungeübt; **to be ~ in sth** in etw (dat) ungeübt sein

inexpertly [ɪn'ekspɜ:tlɪ] ADV unfachmännisch, laienhaft

inexpertness [ɪn'ekspɜ:tnɪs] N Laienhaftigkeit f; (of treatment also) Unsachgemäßheit f; (= lack of training) Ungeübtheit f

inexplicability [,ɪnɪksplɪkə'bɪlɪtɪ] N Unerklärlichkeit f, Unerklärbarkeit f

inexplicable [,ɪnɪk'splɪkəbl] ADJ unerklärlich, unerklärbar

inexplicably [,ɪnɪk'splɪkəblɪ] ADV (+adj) unerklärlich; (+vb) unerklärlicherweise

inexplicit [ɪnɪk'splɪsɪt] ADJ unklar, ungenau

inexpressible [,ɪnɪk'spresəbl] ADJ thoughts, feelings unbeschreiblich, unbeschreibbar; pain, joy also unsagbar

inexpressive [,ɪnɪk'spresɪv] ADJ face ausdruckslos; word blass, nichts sagend; style blass, ohne Ausdruckskraft

in extenso [,ɪnɪk'stensəʊ] ADV in extenso; (= at length) ausführlich; (= in full) vollständig, ungekürzt

inextinguishable [,ɪnɪk'stɪŋgwɪʃəbl] ADJ fire unlöschbar; love, hope unerschütterlich, beständig; passion unbezwinglich

in extremis [,ɪnek'stri:mɪs] ADV **to be ~** (= dying) im Sterben liegen; (= in difficulties) sich in äußerster Not befinden; **to help a friend ~** einem Freund in der Not helfen

inextricable [,ɪnɪk'strɪkəbl] ADJ tangle unentwirrbar; confusion unüberschaubar; link, relationship untrennbar

inextricably [,ɪnɪk'strɪkəblɪ] ADV entangled unentwirrbar; linked untrennbar; **he has become ~ involved with her** er kommt nicht mehr von ihr los

infallibility [ɪn,fælə'bɪlɪtɪ] N Unfehlbarkeit f (also Eccl)

infallible [ɪn'fæləbl] ADJ unfehlbar (also Eccl)

infallibly [ɪn'fæləblɪ] ADV unfehlbar; work fehlerfrei

infamous ['ɪnfəməs] ADJ (= notorious) berüchtigt (for wegen); area, bar berüchtigt, verrufen; (= shameful) person niederträchtig, gemein, ruchlos (old, liter); deed, conduct niederträchtig, infam, schändlich (geh)

infamy ['ɪnfəmɪ] N **a** (= notoriousness) Verrufenheit f; (= shamefulness) Niedertracht f, Gemeinheit f; (of deed, conduct) Niedertracht f, Infamie f, Schändlichkeit f (geh) **b** (= public disgrace) Schande f

infancy ['ɪnfənsɪ] N frühe Kindheit, Kindesalter nt; (Jur) Minderjährigkeit f; (fig) Anfangsstadium nt; **in early ~** in frühester Kindheit; **when radio was still in its ~** als das Radio noch in den Kinderschuhen steckte; **data processing is no longer in its ~** die Datenverarbeitung steckt nicht mehr in den Kinderschuhen or ist den Kinderschuhen entwachsen

infant ['ɪnfənt] **N** (= baby) Säugling m; (= young child) Kleinkind nt; (Jur) Minderjährige(r) mf; **she teaches ~s** sie unterrichtet Grundschulkinder; **~ care** Säuglingspflege f; **~ class** (Brit) erste und zweite Grundschulklasse ~ **death** Säuglingstod m, Tod m im ersten Lebensjahr; **~ formula** Säuglingsnahrung f; **~ seat** Kindersitz m **ADJ** (= new) democracy, industry etc jung

infanta [ɪn'fæntə] N Infantin f

infante [ɪn'fæntɪ] N Infant m

infanticide [ɪn'fæntɪsaɪd] N Kindesmord m, Kindestötung f; (= person) Kindesmörder(in) m(f)

infantile ['ɪnfəntaɪl] ADJ **a** (= childish) kindisch, infantil **b** (Med) Kinder-

infantile paralysis N (dated Med) Kinderlähmung f

infantilize [ɪn'fæntɪˌlaɪz] VT infantilisieren; (= decide for) bevormunden

infant mortality N Säuglingssterblichkeit f

infantry ['ɪnfəntrɪ] N (Mil) Infanterie f, Fußtruppe f (Hist)

infantryman ['ɪnfəntrɪmən] N pl **-men** [-mən] Infanterist m, Fußsoldat m (Hist)

infant school N (Brit) Grundschule für die ersten beiden Jahrgänge

infarct ['ɪnfɑːkt] N (Med) Infarkt m

infarction [ɪn'fɑːkʃən] N (Med) **a** (= dead tissue) Infarkt m **b** (= forming of dead tissue) Infarktbildung f

infatuated [ɪn'fætjʊeɪtɪd] ADJ vernarrt, verknallt (inf) (with in +acc); **to become ~ with sb** sich in jdn vernarren; **he's ~ with himself** er ist in sich selbst vernarrt

infatuation [ɪnˌfætjʊ'eɪʃən] N **a** (= state) Vernarrtheit f (with in +acc) **b** (= object of infatuation) Angebetete(r) mf

infect [ɪn'fekt] VT **a** wound, blood infizieren; (lit) person anstecken, infizieren; water verseuchen, verunreinigen; meat verderben; **to be ~ed with** or **by an illness** sich mit einer Krankheit infiziert or angesteckt haben; **his wound became ~ed** seine Wunde entzündete sich; **her cold ~ed all her friends** sie steckte alle ihre Freunde mit ihrer Erkältung an; **this is likely to ~ the rest of the economy** das breitet sich wahrscheinlich auf den Rest der Wirtschaft aus **b** (fig: with enthusiasm etc) anstecken; **for a moment I was ~ed by her fear** für einen Augenblick ließ ich mich von ihrer Angst anstecken

infected [ɪn'fektɪd] ADJ infiziert; water, place verseucht; meat verdorben

infection [ɪn'fekʃən] N **a** (= illness) Infektion f, Entzündung f **b** (= act of infecting) Infektion f; (of water) Verseuchung f, Verunreinigung f

infectious [ɪn'fekʃəs] ADJ **a** (Med) disease ansteckend, infektiös; **are you still ~?** besteht bei dir noch Ansteckungsgefahr? **b** (fig) enthusiasm, laugh anstecknd; idea zündend; rhythm mitreißend

infectious hepatitis N epidemische Hepatitis, Hepatitis f A

infectiousness [ɪn'fekʃəsnɪs] N **a** (Med) **the ~ of this disease** die Ansteckungs- or Infektionsgefahr bei dieser Krankheit **b** (fig) **the ~ of the rhythm** der zündende Rhythmus; **the ~ of his laughter** sein ansteckendes Lachen; **the ~ of her enthusiasm** ihre mitreißende Begeisterung

infective [ɪn'fektɪv] ADJ (Med) agent infektiös; **~ disease** Infektionskrankheit f

infeed ['ɪnfiːd] **N** (mechanism) Vorschub m; (action) Zuführung f, Aufgabe f **VT** zuführen, aufgeben

infelicitous [ˌɪnfɪ'lɪsɪtəs] ADJ unglücklich; remark etc unangebracht, unpassend

infelicity [ˌɪnfɪ'lɪsɪtɪ] N (form) **the ~ of the expression** der unglücklich or ungeschickt gewählte Ausdruck

infer [ɪn'fɜː] VT **a** (= deduce) schließen, folgern (from aus); **nothing can be ~red from this** daraus kann man nichts schließen or folgern **b** (= imply) andeuten, zu verstehen geben

inferable [ɪn'fɜːrəbl] ADJ ableitbar, zu folgern pred, zu schließen pred

inference ['ɪnfərəns] N Schluss(folgerung f) m; **it has a tiny head and, by ~, a tiny brain** es hat einen winzigen Kopf und demzufolge ein winziges Gehirn; **he said, by ~, that ...** implizit sagte er, dass ...

inferential [ˌɪnfə'renʃəl] ADJ statistics, thinking auf Schlussfolgerungen beruhend

inferior [ɪn'fɪərɪə] **ADJ** **a** (in quality) minderwertig; person unterlegen; (in rank) untergeordnet, niedriger; quality geringer, minderwertig; (Jur) court untergeordnet; **an ~ workman** ein weniger guter Handwerker; **to be ~ to sth** (in quality) von minderer or geringerer Qualität sein als etw, gegen etw abfallen or nicht ankommen; **to be ~ to sb** jdm unterlegen sein; (in rank) jdm untergeordnet or nachgestellt sein; **he feels ~** er kommt sich (dat) unterlegen or minderwertig vor
b (Typ) **~ letter** tiefstehender Buchstabe **c** (Biol) order, species niedriger **N** one's **~s** (in social standing) Leute or Personen pl aus einer niedrigeren Schicht; (in rank) seine Untergebenen pl

inferiority [ɪnˌfɪərɪ'ɒrɪtɪ] N (in quality) Minderwertigkeit f; (of person) Unterlegenheit f (to gegenüber); (in rank) untergeordnete Stellung, niedrigere Stellung, niedrigerer Rang (to als)

inferiority complex N Minderwertigkeitskomplex m

infernal [ɪn'fɜːnl] ADJ **a** (lit) Höllen-; **~ fire** Höllenfeuer nt **b** (fig) cruelty, scheme teuflisch; weather grässlich; (inf) impudence, nuisance verteufelt; noise höllisch; **this ~ machine** diese Höllenmaschine

infernally [ɪn'fɜːnəlɪ] ADV (inf) teuflisch, verdammt (inf)

inferno [ɪn'fɜːnəʊ] N (= hell) Hölle f, Inferno nt; (= blazing house etc) Flammenmeer nt; **a blazing ~** ein flammendes Inferno; **it's like an ~ in here** (fig) hier ist es wie in einem Brutofen

infertile [ɪn'fɜːtaɪl] ADJ soil, womb, person unfruchtbar; animal fortpflanzungsunfähig; mind unergiebig, ideenlos

infertility [ˌɪnfə'tɪlɪtɪ] N (of soil, womb, person) Unfruchtbarkeit f; (of animal) Fortpflanzungsunfähigkeit f; (of mind) Unergiebigkeit f, Ideenlosigkeit f

infertility clinic N Zentrum nt für Sterilitätsbehandlung

infertility treatment N Sterilitätsbehandlung f

infest [ɪn'fest] VT (rats, lice) herfallen über (+acc); (plague also) befallen; (fig: unwanted people) heimsuchen, verseuchen; (crime, drugs etc) verseuchen; **to be ~ed with rats** mit Ratten verseucht sein; **to be ~ed** (with lice etc) mit Ungeziefer verseucht sein

infestation [ˌɪnfes'teɪʃən] N Verseuchung f; **an ~ of rats** eine Rattenplage

infidel ['ɪnfɪdəl] N (Hist, Rel) Ungläubige(r) mf

infidelity [ˌɪnfɪ'delɪtɪ] N Untreue f

in-fighting ['ɪnfaɪtɪŋ] N (Boxing) Nahkampf m; (fig) interner Machtkampf

infill ['ɪnfɪl] N (Build) Füllmaterial nt, Ausfüllung f

infiltrate ['ɪnfɪltreɪt] **VT** **a** (troops) infiltrieren; enemy lines eindringen in (+acc); (Pol) organization unterwandern; spies, informer einschleusen **b** (liquid) einsickern in (+acc), durchsickern in (+acc), durchdringen; **to ~ a liquid into a substance** eine Flüssigkeit in eine Substanz einsickern or eindringen lassen
VI **a** (Mil) eindringen (into in +acc); (spy, informer) eindringen, sich einschleusen (into in +acc), unterwandern (into in +acc); (fig: ideas) infiltrieren, eindringen (into in +acc)
b (liquid) **to ~ into a substance** in eine Substanz eindringen or einsickern; **to ~ through sth** durch etw durchsickern

infiltration [ˌɪnfɪl'treɪʃən] N **a** (Mil) Infiltration f; (Pol) Unterwanderung f; **the ~ of spies** das Einschleusen von Spionen; **by ~ of the enemy's lines** durch Eindringen in die feindlichen Linien, durch Infiltration der feindlichen Linien **b** (of liquid) Eindringen nt, Durchsickern nt, Einsickern nt

infiltrator ['ɪnfɪlˌtreɪtə] N (Mil) Eindringling m; (Pol) Unterwanderer m; **~s** (Mil) Sickertruppe f

infinite ['ɪnfɪnɪt] **ADJ** (lit) unendlich; (fig also) care, trouble, joy, pleasure grenzenlos; possibilities unendlich viele; choice unendlich groß, riesig; knowledge grenzenlos, unendlich groß; **an ~ amount of time/money** unendlich viel Zeit/Geld; **the organizers, in their ~ wisdom, planned the two events for the same day** die Organisatoren, klug wie sie waren, legten die beiden Veranstaltungen auf den gleichen Tag **N** the **~** (= space) das Unendliche; (= God) der Unendliche

infinitely ['ɪnfɪnɪtlɪ] ADV unendlich; (fig also) grenzenlos; improved ungeheuer; better, worse unendlich viel

infinitesimal [ˌɪnfɪnɪ'tesɪməl] ADJ unendlich klein, winzig; (Math) infinitesimal, unendlich klein

infinitesimal calculus N (Math) Infinitesimalrechnung f

infinitesimally [ˌɪnfɪnɪ'tesɪməlɪ] ADV smaller, better, slower nur ganz geringfügig; small zum Verschwinden

infinitive [ɪn'fɪnɪtɪv] (Gram) **ADJ** Infinitiv-, infinitivisch; **~ form** Infinitivform f **N** Infinitiv m, Grundform f; **in the ~** im Infinitiv

infinitude [ɪn'fɪnɪtjuːd] N (= infinite number) unbegrenztes Maß (of an +dat); (of facts, possibilities etc) unendliches Maß (of an +dat); (of space) unendliche Weite (of +gen)

infinity [ɪn'fɪnɪtɪ] N (lit) Unendlichkeit f; (fig also) Grenzenlosigkeit f; (Math) das Unendliche; **to ~** (bis) ins Unendliche; **in ~** in der Unendlichkeit/im Unendlichen; **to focus on ~** (Phot) (auf) Unendlich einstellen; **an ~ of reasons/details/possibilities** unendlich viele Gründe/Einzelheiten/Möglichkeiten; **I have an ~ of things to do** ich habe unendlich viel zu tun

infirm [ɪn'fɜːm] ADJ gebrechlich, schwach; **~ of purpose** (liter) willensschwach, wenig zielstrebig

infirmary [ɪn'fɜːmərɪ] N (= hospital) Krankenhaus nt; (in school etc) Krankenzimmer nt or -stube f; (in prison, barracks) (Kranken)revier nt, Krankenstation f

infirmity [ɪn'fɜːmɪtɪ] N Gebrechlichkeit f; **the infirmities of (old) age** die Altersgebrechen pl; **his ~ of purpose** seine Willensschwäche, sein Mangel m an Zielstrebigkeit

infix [ɪn'fɪks] **VT** idea einprägen; (Ling) einfügen; **the idea is ~ed in his mind** diese Idee hat sich bei ihm festgesetzt **N** ['ɪnfɪks](Ling) Infix nt, Einfügung f

infixation [ˌɪnfɪk'seɪʃən] N (of idea) Einprägen nt, Festsetzen nt; (Ling) Einfügung f

in flagrante delicto [ˌɪnfləˈgræntɪdɪ'lɪktəʊ] ADV in flagranti

inflame [ɪn'fleɪm] VT **a** (Med) entzünden; **her eyes were ~d from crying** ihre Augen waren vom Weinen gerötet; **to become ~d** (wound, eyes etc) sich entzünden **b** person erzürnen, aufbringen; *feelings* entflammen, entfachen; *situation, public opinion* anheizen; **his speech ~d the people** seine Rede brachte die Menge auf; **they were ~d by the news** die Nachricht brachte sie auf; **~d with passion he ...** von glühender Leidenschaft erfasst, er ...; **he was ~d with rage/ jealousy** *etc* er glühte vor Zorn/Eifersucht *etc*

inflammable [ɪnˈflæməbl] **ADJ** (*lit*) feuergefährlich, (leicht) entzündbar; *fabric* leicht entflammbar; (*fig*) *temperament* explosiv, leicht reizbar; *situation* brisant, gereizt; **"highly ~"** „Vorsicht Feuergefahr", „feuergefährlich" **N** feuergefährlicher *or* leicht brennbarer Stoff

inflammation [ˌɪnfləˈmeɪʃən] **N** **a** (*Med*) Entzündung f **b** (*fig, of passion, anger etc*) Aufstacheln *nt*, Aufstachelung f

inflammatory [ɪnˈflæmətərɪ] **ADJ** **a** *rhetoric, statement* aufrührerisch, aufwieglerisch; **speech/pamphlet** Hetzrede/-schrift f **b** (*Med*) entzündlich; **~ reaction** Entzündungsreaktion f

inflatable [ɪnˈfleɪtəbl] **ADJ** aufblasbar; **~ dinghy** Schlauchboot *nt* **N** (= *boat*) Gummiboot *nt*

inflate [ɪnˈfleɪt] **VT** **a** (*lit*) aufpumpen; (*by mouth*) aufblasen **b** (*Econ*) *prices, bill* hoch treiben; **to ~ the currency** die Inflation anheizen, den Geldumlauf steigern; **to ~ the budget** (*for a project etc*) den Etat aufblähen; (*Econ*) inflationäre Haushaltspolitik betreiben **c** (*fig*) steigern, erhöhen; *sb's ego* aufblähen, steigern **VI** **a** (*lit*) sich mit Luft füllen **b** (*fig: price*) rapide steigen

inflated [ɪnˈfleɪtɪd] **ADJ** **a** (*lit*) (*with pump*) aufgepumpt; (*by mouth*) aufgeblasen **b** (*fig*) *price, salary* überhöht; *pride* übersteigert, übertrieben; *ego* übersteigert; *style, rhetoric* geschwollen, hochtrabend; **to have an ~ opinion of oneself** ein übertriebenes Selbstbewusstsein haben

inflation [ɪnˈfleɪʃən] **N** **a** (*Econ*) Inflation f; **~ rate** Inflationsrate f; **to fight ~** die Inflation bekämpfen **b** (= *act of inflating*) (*with pump*) Aufpumpen *nt*; (*by mouth*) Aufblasen *nt*; (*Econ: of prices*) Steigern *nt*, Hochtreiben *nt*; (*fig*) Steigern *nt*, Erhöhen *nt*; (*of ego*) Aufblähen *nt*

inflationary [ɪnˈfleɪʃənərɪ] **ADJ** *impact, consequences* inflationär; **~ pressures/spiral/politics** Inflationsdruck *m*/-spirale f/-politik f

inflationism [ɪnˈfleɪʃənɪzəm] **N** Inflationspolitik f

inflation-proof [ɪnˈfleɪʃən,pruːf] **ADJ** inflationssicher, inflationsgeschützt

inflect [ɪnˈflekt] **VT** **a** (*Gram*) flektieren, beugen **b** *voice* modulieren **VI** (*Gram*) flektierbar *or* veränderlich sein, gebeugt werden

inflected [ɪnˈflektɪd] **ADJ** (*Gram*) *form, ending* flektiert, gebeugt; *language* flektierend

inflection [ɪnˈflekʃən] **N = inflexion**

inflexibility [ɪnˌfleksɪˈbɪlɪtɪ] **N** (*lit*) Unbiegsamkeit f, Starrheit f; (*fig*) Unbeugsamkeit f, Sturheit f (*pej*)

inflexible [ɪnˈfleksəbl] **ADJ** (*lit*) *substance, object* unbiegsam, starr; (*fig*) *person, attitude, opinion* unbeugsam, inflexibel, stur (*pej*)

inflexion [ɪnˈflekʃən] **N** **a** (*Gram, of word, language*) Flexion f, Beugung f **b** (*of voice*) Tonfall *m*

inflexional [ɪnˈflekʃənl] **ADJ** (*Gram*) Flexions-; **~ ending** Flexionsendung f

inflict [ɪnˈflɪkt] **VT** *punishment, fine* verhängen (*on, upon* gegen), auferlegen (*on or upon sb* jdm); *suffering, damage, pain* zufügen (*on or upon sb* jdm), *wound, defeat* zufügen, beibringen (*on or upon sb* jdm); **to ~ oneself on sb** sich jdm aufdrängen; **the enemy ~ed heavy casualties on us** der Feind fügte uns hohe Verluste zu

infliction [ɪnˈflɪkʃən] **N** **a** (= *act*) (*of punishment, fine*) Verhängung f (*on, upon* gegen), Auferlegung f; (*of suffering, damage, pain*) Zufügen *nt*; (*of wound*) Zufügen *nt*, Beibringen *nt* **b** (= *misfortune*) Plage f, Kreuz *nt*

in-flight [ˈɪnflaɪt] **ADJ** *entertainment, refuelling* während des Fluges; *service* an Bord; **~ magazine** Bordmagazin *nt*

inflorescence [ˌɪnfləˈresəns] **N** Blütenstand *m*

inflow [ˈɪnfləʊ] **N** **a** (*of water, air*) (= *action*) Zustrom *m*, Einfließen *nt*, Zufließen *nt*; (= *quantity*) Zuflussmenge f; (= *place*) Zufluss *m*; **~ pipe** Zuflussrohr *nt* **b** (*fig*) (*of foreign currency, goods*) Zustrom *m*; (*of people*) Zustrom *m*, Andrang *m*; (*of ideas etc*) Eindringen *nt*

influence [ˈɪnfluəns] **N** Einfluss *m* (*over* auf +*acc*); **to have an ~ on sb/sth** (*person*) Einfluss auf jdn/etw haben; (*fact, weather etc also*) Auswirkungen *pl* auf jdn/etw haben; **the weather had a great ~ on the number of voters** das Wetter beeinflusste die Zahl der Wähler stark; **the book had** *or* **was a great ~ on him** das Buch hat ihn stark beeinflusst; **to have a great deal of ~ with sb** großen Einfluss bei jdm haben; **he was a great ~ in ...** er war ein bedeutender Faktor bei ...; **he's been a bad ~ on you** er war ein schlechter Einfluss für Sie; **to bring ~ to bear on sb, to exert an ~ on sb** Einfluss auf jdn ausüben; **to use one's ~** seinen Einfluss einsetzen; **you have to have ~ to get a job here** Sie müssen schon einigen Einfluss haben, wenn Sie hier eine Stelle haben wollen; **a man of ~** eine einflussreiche Person; **under the ~ of sb/sth** unter jds Einfluss/dem Einfluss einer Sache; **under the ~ of drink/drugs** unter Alkohol-/Drogeneinfluss, unter Alkohol-/Drogeneinwirkung; **under the ~** (*inf*) betrunken; **the changes were due to American ~** die Veränderungen sind auf amerikanische Einflüsse zurückzuführen; **one of my early ~s was Beckett** einer der Schriftsteller, die mich schon früh beeinflusst haben, war Beckett **VT** beeinflussen; **to be easily ~d** leicht beeinflussbar *or* zu beeinflussen sein

influential [ˌɪnfluˈenʃəl] **ADJ** einflussreich; **these factors were ~ in my decision** diese Faktoren haben meine Entscheidung beeinflusst

influenza [ˌɪnfluˈenzə] **N** Grippe f

influx [ˈɪnflʌks] **N** **a** (*of capital, shares, foreign goods*) Zufuhr f; (*of people*) Zustrom *m*, Andrang *m*; (*of ideas etc*) Zufluss *m* **b = inflow a**

info [ˈɪnfəʊ] **N** (*inf*) = **information**

infobahn [ˈɪnfəʊbaːn] **N the ~** die Datenautobahn

infomercial [ˈɪnfəʊmɜːʃəl] **N** *als Informationssendung getarntes Werbevideo*, Infomercial *nt*

inform [ɪnˈfɔːm] **O** 12.3, 24.4 **VT** **a** *person* informieren (*about* über +*acc*), unterrichten; **to ~ sb of sth** jdn von etw unterrichten, jdn über etw informieren; **to ~ sb (that) ...** jdn informieren, dass ...; **I am pleased to ~ you that ...** ich freue mich, Ihnen mitteilen zu können *or* Sie davon in Kenntnis setzen zu können (*form*), dass ...; **to ~ the police** die Polizei verständigen *or* benachrichtigen *or* informieren; **to keep sb/oneself ~ed** jdn/sich auf dem Laufenden halten (*of* über +*acc*); **to ~ oneself about sth** sich über etw (*acc*) informieren; **until we are better ~ed** bis wir Näheres wissen *or* besser Bescheid wissen *or* genauer informiert sind; **she is better ~ed than most of her colleagues** sie ist besser informiert als die meisten ihrer Kollegen; **why was I not ~ed?** warum wurde mir das nicht mitgeteilt?, warum wurde ich nicht (darüber) informiert?; **I should like to be ~ed just as soon as he arrives** unterrichten Sie mich bitte sofort von seiner Ankunft, informieren Sie mich bitte sofort über seine Ankunft **b** (*liter, = permeate*) durchdringen, erfüllen **VI** **to ~ against** *or* **on sb** jdn anzeigen *or* denunzieren (*pej*)

informal [ɪnˈfɔːml] **ADJ** **a** (*esp Pol: = not official*) *meeting, talks* inoffiziell, nicht formell, nicht förmlich; *visit* inoffiziell, nicht förmlich; *arrangement* inoffiziell **b** (= *simple, without ceremony*) *meeting, gathering, party, conversation, atmosphere* zwanglos, ungezwungen; *manner, clothes, tone also* leger; *language, speech* ungezwungen, informell; *restaurant* gemütlich; **the ~ use of "du"** die vertraute Anrede „du"; **"dress ~"** „zwanglose Kleidung"; **he is very ~** er ist sehr leger

informality [ˌɪnfɔːˈmælɪtɪ] **N** **a** (*esp Pol: = unofficial nature*) (*of meeting, talks*) nicht formeller *or* förmlicher Charakter; (*of visit, arrangement*) in-

offizieller Charakter **b** (= *simplicity, lack of ceremony*) (*of meeting, party, conversation, atmosphere*) Zwanglosigkeit f, Ungezwungenheit f; (*of manner, tone also*) legere Art; (*of language, speech*) informeller Charakter *or* Ton; (*of restaurant*) Gemütlichkeit f

informally [ɪnˈfɔːmlɪ] **ADV** (= *unofficially*) inoffiziell; (= *casually, without ceremony*) zwanglos, ungezwungen

informant [ɪnˈfɔːmənt] **N** **a** Informant(in) *m(f)*; **according to my ~ the book is out of print** wie man mir mitteilt *or* berichtet, ist das Buch vergriffen **b** (*police*) ~ Polizeispitzel *m*

informatics [ˌɪnfəˈmætɪks] **N** *sing* Informatik f

information [ˌɪnfəˈmeɪʃən] **N** **a** Auskunft f, Informationen *pl*; **a piece of ~** eine Auskunft *or* Information; **for your ~** zu Ihrer Information *or* Kenntnisnahme (*form*); (*indignantly*) damit Sie es wissen; **his ~ on the subject is most extensive** sein Wissen auf diesem Gebiet ist äußerst umfassend; **to give sb ~ about** *or* **on sb/sth** jdm Auskunft *or* Informationen über jdn/etw geben; **to get ~ about** *or* **on sb/sth** sich über jdn/etw informieren, über jdn/etw Erkundigungen einziehen; **to ask for ~ on** *or* **about sb/sth** um Auskunft *or* Informationen über jdn/etw bitten; **"information"** „Auskunft"; **I have ~ that they will be arriving today** mir liegen Informationen darüber vor, dass sie heute ankommen; **we have no ~ about that** wir wissen darüber nicht Bescheid; **my ~ is that he is unreliable** soweit ich informiert bin, ist er unzuverlässig; **until further ~ is available** bevor wir nichts Näheres wissen; **for further ~ please contact this number ...** Näheres erfahren Sie unter Telefonnummer ...; **what ~ do we have on Kowalsky?** welche Informationen besitzen wir über Kowalsky?; **where did you get your ~?** woher haben Sie diese Kenntnisse *or* Informationen?; **detailed ~** Einzelheiten *pl* **b** (*Comput, = information content*) Information f

informational [ˌɪnfəˈmeɪʃənl] **ADJ** informationell; **~ needs** Informationsbedürfnisse *pl*; **~ programme** (*TV*) Informationssendung f

information: information bulletin N Mitteilungsblatt *nt*; **information bureau** N Auskunft(sbüro *nt*) f, Verkehrsbüro *nt*; **information content** N Informationsgehalt *m*; **information desk** N Information f, Informationsschalter *m*; **information exchange** N Informationsaustausch *m*; **information officer** N Auskunftsbeamte(r) *m*/-beamtin f; **information pack** N Informationsmaterial *nt*; **information processing** N Informationsverarbeitung f; **information question** N (*Ling*) Ergänzungsfrage f; **information retrieval** N Informations- *or* Datenabruf *m*; **information sciences** PL Informatik f; **information scientist** N Informatiker(in) *m(f)*; **information storage** N Datenspeicherung f; **information superhighway** N Datenautobahn f; **information technology** N Informationstechnik f; **information theory** N Informationstheorie f

informative [ɪnˈfɔːmətɪv] **ADJ** aufschlussreich, informativ (*geh*); *book, lecture also* lehrreich; **he's not very ~ about his plans** er ist nicht sehr mitteilsam, was seine Pläne betrifft

informed [ɪnˈfɔːmd] **ADJ** (= *having information*) *observer, source* informiert, (gut) unterrichtet; *guess, choice* fundiert; (= *educated*) gebildet

informer [ɪnˈfɔːmə] **N** Informant(in) *m(f)*, Denunziant(in) *m(f)* (*pej*); **police ~** Polizeispitzel *m*; **to turn ~** seine Mittäter verraten

infotainment [ˌɪnfəʊˈteɪnmənt] **N** (*Brit TV*) Infotainment *nt*

infraction [ɪnˈfrækʃən] **N** **a** (= *infringement*) Verletzung f, Verstoß *m* **b** (*Med*) Infraktion f (*spec*), Knickbruch *m*

infra dig [ˈɪnfrəˈdɪg] **ADJ** (*inf*) unter meiner/seiner *etc* Würde

infrangible [ɪnˈfrændʒɪbl] **ADJ** (*form*) (= *unbreakable*) unzerbrechlich; (*fig: = inviolable*) unverletzlich

infrared [ˈɪnfrəˈred] **ADJ** infrarot

infrastructure ['ɪnfrə,strʌktʃə'] N Infrastruktur f

infrequency [ɪn'fri:kwənsɪ] N Seltenheit f

infrequent [ɪn'fri:kwənt] ADJ selten; **at ~ intervals** in großen Abständen; **her mistakes are so ~** sie macht so selten Fehler

infrequently [ɪn'fri:kwəntlɪ] ADV selten

infringe [ɪn'frɪndʒ] VT verstoßen gegen; law also verletzen, übertreten; copyright also verletzen; rights verletzen, eingreifen in (+acc) VI **to ~ (up)on sb's rights** in jds Rechte (acc) eingreifen, jds Rechte verletzen

infringement [ɪn'frɪndʒmənt] N **a** **an ~ (of a rule)** ein Regelverstoß m; **~ of the law** Gesetzesverletzung or -übertretung f; **~ of a patent** Patentverletzung f; **~ of copyright** Verletzung f des Urheberrechts; **~ of sb's rights** die Verletzung von jds Rechten, Übergriffe pl auf jds Rechte (acc) **b** (of privacy) Eingriff m (of in +acc)

infuriate [ɪn'fjʊərɪeɪt] VT wütend or rasend machen, zur Raserei bringen; **to be/get ~d** wütend or rasend sein/werden

infuriating [ɪn'fjʊərɪeɪtɪŋ] ADJ (äußerst) ärgerlich; **an ~ habit** eine Unsitte; **an ~ person** ein Mensch, der einen zur Raserei bringen kann or der einen rasend or wütend machen kann

infuriatingly [ɪn'fjʊərɪeɪtɪŋlɪ] ADV aufreizend; **she's ~ slow/clumsy** sie ist zum Verzweifeln langsam/so unbeholfen, dass es zum Verzweifeln ist; **~, she couldn't say a word against him** es machte sie rasend, dass sie kein Wort gegen ihn sagen konnte

infuse [ɪn'fju:z] VT **a** courage, enthusiasm etc einflößen, geben (into sb jdm); **~d with excitement** von Aufregung erfüllt **b** (Cook) tea, herbs aufbrühen, aufgießen VI ziehen

infuser [ɪn'fju:zə'] N Tee-Ei nt

infusion [ɪn'fju:ʒən] N **a** (of hope etc) Einflößen nt; **an ~ of cash/capital** eine Finanzspritze **b** (Cook) Aufguss m; (tea-like) Tee m; **an ~ of rosehip tea** Hagebuttentee m **c** (Med) Infusion f

ingenious [ɪn'dʒi:nɪəs] ADJ genial; person also erfinderisch, geschickt, findig; idea, method also glänzend, ingeniös (geh); device, instrument also raffiniert, geschickt

ingeniously [ɪn'dʒi:nɪəslɪ] ADV genial, glänzend

ingeniousness [ɪn'dʒi:nɪəsnɪs] N = **ingenuity**

ingénue [,ænʒeɪ'nju:] N naives Mädchen; (Theat) Naive f

ingenuity [,ɪndʒɪ'nju:ɪtɪ] N Genialität f; (of person also) Einfallsreichtum m, Findigkeit f; (of idea, method also) Brillanz f; (of device, instrument also) Raffiniertheit f

ingenuous [ɪn'dʒenjʊəs] ADJ **a** (= candid) offen, aufrichtig, unbefangen **b** (= naïve) naiv

ingenuously [ɪn'dʒenjʊəslɪ] ADV offen, unbefangen; (= naïvely) naiv

ingenuousness [ɪn'dʒenjʊəsnɪs] N **a** (= candour) Offenheit f, Aufrichtigkeit f, Unbefangenheit f **b** (= naïveté) Naivität f

ingest [ɪn'dʒest] VT (Biol) zu sich nehmen, aufnehmen

ingesta [ɪn'dʒestə] PL (Biol, Med) Ingesta pl (spec), aufgenommene Nahrung

ingestion [ɪn'dʒestʃən] N (Biol) Nahrungsaufnahme f

inglenook ['ɪŋɡəlnʊk] N Kaminecke f

inglorious [ɪn'ɡlɔ:rɪəs] ADJ unrühmlich, unehrenhaft; defeat schmählich, ruhmlos

ingloriously [ɪn'ɡlɔ:rɪəslɪ] ADV unrühmlich

ingoing ['ɪnɡəʊɪŋ] ADJ mail eingehend, einlaufend; **~ tenant** neuer Mieter, neue Mieterin

ingot ['ɪŋɡət] N Barren m; **steel ~** Stahlblock m

ingrained [,ɪn'ɡreɪnd] ADJ **a** (fig) habit fest, eingefleischt; prejudice tief verwurzelt or eingewurzelt; belief fest verankert, unerschütterlich; **to be (deeply) ~** fest verwurzelt sein **b** dirt tief eingedrungen, tief sitzend (attr); **the dirt was deeply ~ in the carpet** der Schmutz hatte sich tief im Teppich festgesetzt; **hands ~ with dirt**

Hände, bei denen sich der Schmutz in den Poren festgesetzt hat

ingrate ['ɪnɡreɪt] N undankbarer Mensch, Undankbare(r) mf (old, liter)

ingratiate [ɪn'ɡreɪʃɪeɪt] VR **to ~ oneself with sb** sich bei jdm einschmeicheln

ingratiating [ɪn'ɡreɪʃɪeɪtɪŋ] ADJ person, speech, manner schmeichlerisch, schöntuerisch; smile süßlich

ingratiatingly [ɪn'ɡreɪʃɪeɪtɪŋlɪ] ADV schmeichlerisch; smile süßlich

ingratitude [ɪn'ɡrætɪtju:d] N Undank m; **sb's ~** jds Undankbarkeit f

ingredient [ɪn'ɡri:dɪənt] N Bestandteil m, Ingredienz f (spec); (for recipe) Zutat f; **all the ~s for success** alles, was man zum Erfolg braucht; **the ~s of a man's character** alles, was den Charakter eines Menschen ausmacht

ingress ['ɪnɡres] N (form) Zutritt m, Eintritt m; **no right of ~** Zutritt verboten; **to have free ~** Recht auf freien Zugang haben

in-group ['ɪnɡru:p] N maßgebliche Leute pl, Spitze f; (Sociol) In-Group f

ingrowing ['ɪnɡrəʊɪŋ] ADJ (Med) toenail eingewachsen

ingrown ['ɪnɡrəʊn] ADJ toenail eingewachsen; (= innate) angeboren; (= self-contained) (in sich selbst) zurückgezogen

inguinal ['ɪŋɡwɪnəl] ADJ (Med) Leisten-, inguinal (spec); **~ hernia** Leistenbruch m

inhabit [ɪn'hæbɪt] VT bewohnen; (animals) leben in (+dat)

inhabitable [ɪn'hæbɪtəbl] ADJ bewohnbar

inhabitant [ɪn'hæbɪtənt] N (of house, burrow etc) Bewohner(in) m(f); (of island, town also) Einwohner(in) m(f)

inhalation [,ɪnhə'leɪʃən] N (Med) Inhalation f; smoke ~ Einatmen nt von Rauch

inhalator ['ɪnhəleɪtə'] N Inhalationsapparat m

inhale [ɪn'heɪl] VT einatmen; (Med) inhalieren VI (in smoking) Lungenzüge machen, inhalieren; **do you ~?** rauchen Sie auf Lunge?

inhaler [ɪn'heɪlə'] N Inhalationsapparat m

inharmonious [,ɪnhɑ:'məʊnɪəs] ADJ unharmonisch

inhere [ɪn'hɪə'] VI **to ~ in sth** einer Sache (dat) innewohnen

inherent [ɪn'hɪərənt] ADJ innewohnend, eigen, inhärent (esp Philos) (to, in +dat); **the ~ hardness of diamonds** die den Diamanten eigene Härte; **instincts ~ in all animals** allen Tieren inhärente or eigene Instinkte

inherently [ɪn'hɪərəntlɪ] ADV von Natur aus

inherit [ɪn'herɪt] VT (lit, fig) erben; **the problems which we ~ed from the last government** die Probleme, die uns die letzte Regierung hinterlassen or vererbt hat VI erben; **to ~ from sb** jdn beerben

inheritable [ɪn'herɪtəbl] ADJ (lit, fig) erblich; goods vererbbar

inheritance [ɪn'herɪtəns] N Erbe nt (also fig), Erbschaft f; **it passed to him through** or **by ~** er hat es durch eine Erbschaft bekommen; **~ tax** Erbschaftssteuer f

inherited [ɪn'herɪtɪd] ADJ wealth, property geerbt, ererbt; qualities, disease ererbt

inhibit [ɪn'hɪbɪt] VT hemmen (also Psych, Sci); ability, performance beeinträchtigen; **to ~ sb from doing sth** jdn daran hindern, etw zu tun; **don't let me ~ you** haben Sie meinetwegen keine Hemmungen; **don't let my presence ~ the discussion** lassen Sie sich durch meine Anwesenheit in Ihrer Diskussion nicht stören

inhibited [ɪn'hɪbɪtɪd] ADJ gehemmt; **to be ~** Hemmungen haben, gehemmt sein

inhibition [,ɪnhɪ'bɪʃən] N Hemmung f (also Psych, Sci); **he has no ~s about speaking French** er hat keine Hemmungen, Französisch zu sprechen; **to lose one's ~s** seine Hemmungen verlieren; **~ threshold** Hemmschwelle f

inhibitory [ɪn'hɪbɪtərɪ] ADJ (Psych) hemmend; (Physiol also) behindernd

inhospitable [,ɪnhɒ'spɪtəbl] ADJ ungastlich; climate, terrain, region unwirtlich

inhospitably [,ɪnhɒ'spɪtəblɪ] ADV ungastlich

inhospitality ['ɪn,hɒspɪ'tælɪtɪ] N Ungastlichkeit f, mangelnde Gastfreundschaft; (of climate) Unwirtlichkeit f

in-house ['ɪnhaʊs] ADJ hausintern; staff im Haus; jobs, work im Hause zu erledigend attr or zu erledigen pred ADV [ɪn'haʊs] hausintern

inhuman [ɪn'hju:mən] ADJ (lit) monster, shape nicht menschlich; (fig) conditions, treatment unmenschlich

inhumane [,ɪnhju:'meɪn] ADJ inhuman; treatment, housing menschenunwürdig

inhumaneness [,ɪnhju:'meɪnnɪs] N Inhumanität f; (of treatment, housing) Menschenunwürdigkeit f

inhumanity [,ɪnhju:'mænɪtɪ] N Unmenschlichkeit f; **man's ~ to man** die Unmenschlichkeit der Menschen untereinander

inhumation [,ɪnhju:'meɪʃən] N (form) Beisetzung f (form)

inhume [ɪn'hju:m] VT (form) beisetzen (form)

inimical [ɪ'nɪmɪkəl] ADJ (form) (= hostile) feindselig (to gegen); (= injurious) abträglich (to +dat)

inimitable [ɪ'nɪmɪtəbl] ADJ unnachahmlich

iniquitous [ɪ'nɪkwɪtəs] ADJ ungeheuerlich

iniquity [ɪ'nɪkwɪtɪ] N (no pl: = wickedness) Ungeheuerlichkeit f; (= sin) Missetat f; (= crime) Gräueltat f → **den**

initial [ɪ'nɪʃəl] ADJ **a** anfänglich, Anfangs-; **my ~ reaction** meine anfängliche Reaktion; **in the ~ stages** im Anfangsstadium; **according to ~ reports** ersten Berichten zufolge; **~ cost** Startkosten pl **b** (Ling) anlautend; **~ sound** Anlaut m **c** (Typ) **~ letter** Anfangsbuchstabe m, Initiale f **N** Initiale f; (Typ also) Anfangsbuchstabe m; **to sign a letter with one's ~s** seine Initialen or (Pol) Paraphe unter einen Brief setzen; (Comm) einen Brief abzeichnen or mit seinem Namenszeichen versehen VT letter, document mit seinen Initialen unterzeichnen; (Comm) abzeichnen; (Pol) paraphieren

initialization [ɪ,nɪʃəlaɪ'zeɪʃən] N (Comput) Initialisierung f

initialize [ɪ'nɪʃəlaɪz] VT (Comput) initialisieren

initially [ɪ'nɪʃəlɪ] ADV anfangs, zu or am Anfang; (Ling) im Anlaut

initial public offering N (St Ex) erstes öffentliches Zeichnungsangebot

initiate [ɪ'nɪʃɪeɪt] VT **a** (= set in motion) den Anstoß geben zu, initiieren (geh); negotiations einleiten; discussion eröffnen; project in die Wege leiten; legislation einbringen; **to ~ proceedings against sb** (Jur) gegen jdn einen Prozess anstrengen **b** (= formally admit) (into club etc) feierlich aufnehmen; (in tribal society) adolescents initiieren **c** (= instruct: in knowledge, skill) einweihen; **to ~ sb into sth** jdn in etw (acc) einführen **N** (in club etc) Neuaufgenommene(r) mf; (in tribal society) Initiierte(r) mf; (in knowledge) Eingeweihte(r) mf

initiation [ɪ,nɪʃɪ'eɪʃən] N **a** (of project, fashion etc) Initiierung f (geh); (of negotiations) Einleitung f; (of discussions) Eröffnung f **b** (into society) Aufnahme f; (as tribal member) Initiation f **c** (into branch of knowledge) Einweihung f

initiation ceremony N Aufnahmezeremonie f

initiation rite N Initiationsritus m

initiative [ɪ'nɪʃətɪv] N Initiative f; **to take the ~** die Initiative ergreifen; **on one's own ~** aus eigener Initiative; **to have ~** Initiative haben; **to have the ~** überlegen sein; **to lose the ~** seine Überlegenheit verlieren; **it was an ~ test for me** das hat meine Initiative auf die Probe gestellt

initiator [ɪ'nɪʃɪeɪtə'] N Initiator(in) m(f)

initiatory [ɪ'nɪʃɪətərɪ] ADJ (= introductory) einleitend, einführend

inject [ɪnˈdʒekt] VT (ein)spritzen; *drugs, heroin* spritzen; *gas* einblasen; *(fig)* comment einwerfen; *money into economy* pumpen; **to ~ sb with sth** *(Med)* jdm etw spritzen *or* injizieren; **I wanted to ~ some humour into my speech** ich wollte etwas Humor in meine Rede bringen; **they are trying to ~ some life into the economy** sie versuchen, die Wirtschaft neu zu beleben; **he ~ed new life into the team** er brachte neues Leben in das Team

injection [ɪnˈdʒekʃən] N (= *act*) Einspritzung *f*; *(of gas)* Einblasen *nt*; (= *substance injected*) Injektion *f*, Spritze *f*; **to give sb an ~** jdm eine Injektion *or* Spritze geben; **to give sth by ~** etw spritzen; **the ~ of more money into the economy** eine größere Finanzspritze für die Wirtschaft; **a £250 million cash ~** eine Finanzspritze von 250 Millionen Pfund; **the team needed an ~ of new life** die Mannschaft brauchte frisches Blut; **~ moulding** Spritzguss *m*; **~ syringe** Injektionsspritze *f*

injector [ɪnˈdʒektə'] N Einspritzpumpe *f*

injudicious ADJ , **injudiciously** ADV [ˌɪndʒʊˈdɪʃəs, -lɪ] unklug

injunction [ɪnˈdʒʌŋkʃən] N Anordnung *f*; *(Jur)* gerichtliche Verfügung; **to take out a court ~** eine gerichtliche Verfügung erwirken

injure [ˈɪndʒə'] VT **a** *(lit)* verletzen; **to ~ one's leg** sich *(dat)* das Bein verletzen, sich *(acc)* am Bein verletzen; **the horse was ~d** das Pferd verletzte sich; **how many were ~d?, how many ~d were there?** wie viele Verletzte gab es? **the ~d** die Verletzten *pl* **b** *(fig)* (= *offend*) sb, sb's *feelings* verletzen, kränken; (= *damage*) *reputation* schaden (+*dat*); **his ~d reputation** sein geschädigter Ruf; **the ~d party** *(Jur)* der/die Geschädigte; **~d innocence** gekränkte Unschuld

injurious [ɪnˈdʒʊərɪəs] ADJ schädlich; **to be ~ to sb/sth** jdm/einer Sache schaden *or* schädlich sein; **~ to health** gesundheitsschädigend *or* -schädlich

injury [ˈɪndʒərɪ] N Verletzung *f* (to +*gen*); *(fig also)* Kränkung *f* (to +*gen*); **to do sb/oneself an ~** jdn/sich verletzen; **to play ~ time** *(Brit Sport)* *or* **~ overtime** *(US Sport)* nachspielen, Nachspielzeit haben; **they are into ~ time** *(Brit Sport)* *or* **overtime** *(US Sport)* das ist Nachspielzeit; **~ benefit** *(Brit)* Unfall- *or* Krankengeld *nt*

injury-prone [ˈɪndʒərɪ,prəʊn] ADJ verletzungsanfällig

injustice [ɪnˈdʒʌstɪs] N (= *unfairness, inequality*) Ungerechtigkeit *f*; (= *violation of sb's rights*) Unrecht *nt no pl*; **to do sb an ~** jdm unrecht tun; **if a real ~ has been done to you ...** wenn Ihnen wirklich Unrecht geschehen ist ...

ink [ɪŋk] **N** Tinte *(also Zool) f*; *(Art)* Tusche *f*; *(Typ)* Druckfarbe *f*; *(for newsprint)* Druckerschwärze *f*; **written in ~** mit Tinte geschrieben; **a sketch in ~** eine Tuschzeichnung VT mit Tinte beschmieren; *(Typ)* einfärben

▶ **ink in** VT *sep outline, writing* mit Tinte *or* *(Art)* Tusche nachziehen; (= *fill in*) *shape* mit Tinte *or* *(Art)* Tusche ausmalen *or* ausfüllen

▶ **ink out** VT *sep* mit Tinte übermalen

▶ **ink over** VT *sep* mit Tinte *or* *(Art)* Tusche nachzeichnen

ink *in cpds* Tinten-; *(Art)* Tusch-; **ink bag** N *(Zool)* Tintenbeutel *m*; **inkblot** N Tintenklecks *m*; **~ test** *(Psych)* Rorschachtest *m*; **ink bottle** N Tintenfass *nt*; **ink drawing** N Tuschzeichnung *f*; **ink eraser** N Tintenradiergummi *m*, Tintenradierer *m* *(inf)*; **ink-jet (printer)** N Tintenstrahldrucker *m*

inkling [ˈɪŋklɪŋ] N (= *vague idea*) dunkle Ahnung; **he didn't have an ~** er hatte nicht die leiseste Ahnung *or* keinen blassen Schimmer *(inf)*; **to give sb an ~** jdm eine andeutungsweise Vorstellung geben; **there was no ~ of the disaster to come** nichts deutete auf die bevorstehende Katastrophe hin

ink: ink pad N Stempelkissen *nt*; **inkpot** N Tintenfass *nt*; **inkstain** N Tintenfleck *m*; **inkstained** ADJ tintenbeschmiert; **inkstand** N Tintenfass *nt* *(mit Halter für Federn etc)*; **ink-**

well N Tintenfass *nt* *(in eine Tischplatte eingelassen)*

inky [ˈɪŋkɪ] ADJ *(+er)* **a** *(lit)* tintenbeschmiert, voller Tinte; **~ fingers** Tintenfinger *pl*; **~ newspaper** von Druckerschwärze strotzende Zeitung; **~ smell** Geruch *m* von Druckerschwärze **b** *(fig)* *darkness, night* tintenschwarz; *blue, black* tintig

inky cap N *(Bot)* Tintling *m*, Tintenpilz *m*

inlaid [ɪnˈleɪd] *ptp of* inlay ADJ eingelegt *(with* mit)*; **~ table** Tisch *m* mit Einlegearbeit; **~ work** Einlegearbeit *f*

inland [ˈɪnlænd] **ADJ** **a** *waterway* binnenländisch; **~ navigation** Binnenschifffahrt *f*; **~ town** Stadt *f* im Landesinneren **b** (= *domestic*) *produce* inländisch; **~ mail** Inlandspost *f*; **~ trade** Binnenhandel *m* **ADV** landeinwärts

inland: inland lake N Binnensee *m*; **Inland Revenue** N *(Brit)* ≈ Finanzamt *nt*; **inland sea** N Binnenmeer *nt*

inlaw [ˈɪnlɔ:] N angeheirateter Verwandter, angeheiratete Verwandte; **~s** (= *parents-in-law*) Schwiegereltern *pl*

inlay [ɪnˈleɪ] *vb: pret, ptp* **inlaid** **N** *(in table, box)* Einlegearbeit *f*, Intarsien *pl*; *(Dentistry)* Plombe *f*, Füllung *f* VT einlegen *(with* mit)*

inlet [ˈɪnlet] **N** **a** *(of sea)* Meeresarm *m*; *(of river)* Flussarm *m* **b** *(Tech)* Zuleitung *f*; *(of ventilator)* Öffnung *f*

inlet: inlet pipe N Zuleitung(srohr *nt*) *f*; **inlet valve** N Einlassventil *nt*

in-line skates [ˈɪnlaɪn,skeɪts] PL Inline-Skates *pl*

in loco parentis [ɪnˈləʊkəʊpəˈrentɪs] ADV an Eltern statt

inmate [ˈɪnmeɪt] N Insasse *m*, Insassin *f*

inmost [ˈɪnməʊst] ADJ = innermost

inn [ɪn] N **a** Gasthaus *nt*; *(old)* (= *hotel*) Herberge *f (old)*; (= *tavern*) Schenke *f*, Schänke *f* **b** *(Jur)* **the Inns of Court** die vier englischen Juristenverbände

innards [ˈɪnədz] PL Innereien *pl (also fig)*, Eingeweide *pl*

innate [ɪˈneɪt] ADJ angeboren; **man's ~ desire for happiness** das dem Menschen angeborene Verlangen nach Glück

innately [ɪˈneɪtlɪ] ADV (= *naturally*) von Natur aus

inner [ˈɪnə'] **ADJ** **a** innere(r, s); **~ side/door** Innenseite/-tür *f*; **~ court/city** Innenhof *m*/-stadt *f*; **~ sole** Innensohle *f* **b** *(fig)* *emotions, beauty, voice* innere(r, s); *meaning* verborgen; **his ~ circle of friends** sein engster Freundeskreis; **he wasn't one of the ~ circle** er gehörte nicht zum engeren Kreise; **~ life** Seelenleben *nt*; **~ self** wahres Ich; **the ~ man** (= *soul*) das Innere; **the needs of the ~ man** die inneren Bedürfnisse **N** *(Archery)* Schwarze(s) *nt*

inner-city [ˈɪnə'sɪtɪ] ADJ *attr* Innenstadt-; *traffic* innenstädtisch; *housing* in der Innenstadt; (= *of cities generally*) in den Innenstädten; *decay, renewal, problem* der Innenstadt/der Innenstädte; **~ area** Innenstadtbereich *m*; **deprived ~ children** heruntergekommene Stadtkinder

---

INNER CITY

Inner city ist ein ursprünglich amerikanischer Begriff, mit dem die vernachlässigte und heruntergekommene Stadtteile beschrieben werden. Eine typische **inner city** ist gekennzeichnet von Armut, Arbeitslosigkeit, unzulänglichen Wohnbedingungen und Spannungen zwischen den Rassen. Der Ausdruck hat sich mittlerweile für jedes heruntergekommene Stadtgebiet etabliert, ganz egal, ob dieses wirklich in der Stadtmitte liegt oder nicht. In den letzten Jahren hat es sowohl in den USA als auch in Großbritannien Versuche gegeben, der Verelendung der **inner cities** Einhalt zu gebieten und die Wohnqualität in diesen Gegenden zu verbessern.

---

inner: inner ear N Innenohr *nt*; **inner harbour** N Innenbecken *nt*; **innermost** ADJ innerste(r, s); **~ in sb** zuinnerst in jdm; **in the ~ recesses of the mind** in den hintersten Winkeln des Gehirns; **his ~ being/heart** sein Innerstes; **in the ~ depths of the forest** im tiefsten Wald; **inner part** N *(Mus)* Mittelstimme *f*; **inner tube** N Schlauch *m*

inning [ˈɪnɪŋ] N *(Baseball)* Inning *nt*

innings [ˈɪnɪŋz] N *(Cricket)* Innenrunde *f*; **to have one's ~** *(fig)* länger an der Reihe sein; **he has had a good ~** *(fig inf)* er war lange an der Reihe; (= *life*) er hatte ein langes, ausgefülltes Leben

innit [ˈɪnɪt] INTERJ *(Brit inf)* **~?** oder? *(inf)*

innkeeper [ˈɪn,ki:pə'] N (Gast)wirt(in) *m(f)*

innocence [ˈɪnəsəns] N **a** Unschuld *f*; **to feign ~** vorgeben, unschuldig zu sein, unschuldig tun; **in all ~** in aller Unschuld **b** *(liter, = ignorance)* Unkenntnis *f*

innocent [ˈɪnəsənt] **ADJ** **a** unschuldig; *mistake, misrepresentation* unabsichtlich; **she is ~ of the crime** sie ist an dem Verbrechen unschuldig; **a defendant is ~ until proved guilty** ein Angeklagter gilt als unschuldig, bis ihm seine Schuld nachgewiesen wird; **to put on an ~ air** eine Unschuldsmiene aufsetzen; **as ~ as a newborn babe** unschuldig wie ein Lamm; **he is ~ about night life in a big city** er ist die reine Unschuld, was das Nachtleben in einer Großstadt angeht **b** (= *innocuous*) *question* naiv; *remark* arglos; *amusement* harmlos **c** **~ of** *(liter)* (= *ignorant*) nicht vertraut mit; (= *devoid of*) frei von, ohne **N** Unschuld *f*; **he's a bit of an ~** er ist eine rechte Unschuld; **the massacre of the Holy Innocents** *(Rel)* der Kindermord zu Bethlehem; **Holy Innocents' Day** das Fest der Unschuldigen Kinder

innocently [ˈɪnəsəntlɪ] ADV unschuldig; (= *in all innocence*) in aller Unschuld; **the quarrel began ~ enough** der Streit begann ganz harmlos

innocuous ADJ , **innocuously** ADV [ɪˈnɒkjʊəs, -lɪ] harmlos

innovate [ˈɪnəʊveɪt] **VT** neu einführen; **the new techniques which he ~d** die neuen Techniken, die er einführte **VI** Neuerungen einführen

innovation [ˌɪnəʊˈveɪʃən] N Innovation *f*; (= *introduction also*) Neueinführung *f* (of +*gen*); (= *thing introduced also*) Neuerung *f*

innovative [ɪnəˈveɪtɪv] ADJ innovativ; *idea* originell, neu

innovator [ˈɪnəʊveɪtə'] N Neuerer *m*, Neuerin *f*; *(of reform)* Begründer(in) *m(f)*

innuendo [ˌɪnjʊˈendəʊ] N *pl* **-es** versteckte Andeutung; **sexual ~** sexuelle Anspielung

innumerable [ɪˈnju:mərəbl] ADJ unzählig

innumeracy [ɪˈnju:mərəsɪ] N Nicht-Rechnen-Können *nt*

innumerate [ɪˈnju:mərɪt] ADJ **to be ~** nicht rechnen können

innutrition [ˌɪnju:ˈtrɪʃən] N *(spec)* Nahrungsmangel *m*

inoculant [ɪˈnɒkjʊlənt] N *(Med)* Impfstoff *m*

inoculate [ɪˈnɒkjʊleɪt] VT *person* impfen *(against* gegen)*; **to ~ sb with a virus** jdm einen Virus einimpfen

inoculation [ɪˌnɒkjʊˈleɪʃən] N Impfung *f*; **to give sb an ~ (against smallpox)** jdn (gegen Pocken) impfen

inoculum [ɪˈnɒkjʊləm] N *pl* **inocula** *(Med)* Impfstoff *m*

inodorous [ɪnˈəʊdərəs] ADJ *(geh)* geruchlos

in-off [ˈɪnɒf] N *(inf)* **a** *(Ftbl)* Abprallertor *nt* **b** *(Billiards etc)* Kugel, die von einer anderen abprallt und dann in ein Loch geht

inoffensive [ˌɪnəˈfensɪv] ADJ harmlos

inofficious [ˌɪnəˈfɪʃəs] ADJ *(Jur)* pflichtwidrig; **~ testament** *or* **will** gegen die natürlichen Pflichten des Erblassers verstoßendes Testament

inoperable [ɪnˈɒpərəbl] ADJ *disease, tumour* inoperabel, nicht operierbar; *policy* undurchführbar

inoperative [ɪnˈɒpərətɪv] ADJ **a** (= *ineffective*) *law, rule* außer Kraft, ungültig **b** (= *not working*) **to be ~** (*machine, radio*) nicht funktionieren; **to render sth ~** etw außer Betrieb setzen

inopportune [ɪnˈɒpətjuːn] ADJ inopportun; *demand, visit, resignation, moment also* ungelegen; *words* unpassend, nicht angebracht; **to be ~** ungelegen *or* zur Unzeit kommen; **it's very ~ that ...** es kommt sehr ungelegen, dass ...

inopportunely [ɪnˈɒpətjuːnlɪ] ADV zur Unzeit

inordinate [ɪˈnɔːdɪnɪt] ADJ unmäßig; *number, size, sum of money* übermäßig; *demand, claim, fondness* übertrieben

inordinately [ɪˈnɔːdɪnɪtlɪ] ADV unmäßig; *large, high, long* übermäßig; **to be ~ fond of sth** etw allzu gern mögen

inorganic [ɪnɔːˈɡænɪk] ADJ anorganisch; (*fig*) unorganisch

inpatient [ˈɪnpeɪʃnt] N stationär behandelter Patient/behandelte Patientin

inpouring [ˈɪnpɔːrɪŋ] **N** (Her)einströmen *nt* **ADJ** (her)einströmend

input [ˈɪnpʊt] **N** **a** (*into computer*) Eingabe *f*, Input *m or nt*; (*of capital*) Investition *f*; (*of manpower*) (Arbeits)aufwand *m*; (= *power input*) Energiezufuhr *f*; (*of project etc*) Beitrag *m*; **artistic/creative ~** künstlerische/kreative Beiträge *pl*; **their ~ into the project** ihr Beitrag *m* zum Projekt; **~ port** (*Comput*) Eingabeport *m* **b** (= *point of input, input terminal*) Eingang *m* **VT** (*Comput*) *data, text, information* eingeben

inquest [ˈɪnkwest] N (*Jur: into death*) gerichtliche Untersuchung der Todesursache; (*fig*) Manöverkritik *f*

inquietude [ɪnˈkwaɪətjuːd] N (*liter*) Unruhe *f*

inquire, enquire [ɪnˈkwaɪə] **VT** *the time, a name, the way* sich erkundigen nach, fragen nach; **to ~ sth of sb** sich bei jdm nach etw erkundigen; **he ~d what/whether/when** *etc* **...** er erkundigte sich *or* fragte, was/ob/wann *etc* ...; **VI** sich erkundigen (*about* nach), fragen (*about* nach, wegen); **"inquire within"** „Näheres im Geschäft"

▶ **inquire about** *or* **after** VI +prep obj *person, sb's health* sich erkundigen nach

▶ **inquire for** VI +prep obj *person* fragen nach; *information, details* erfragen

▶ **inquire into** VI +prep obj untersuchen

inquirer, enquirer [ɪnˈkwaɪərə] N Fragende(r) *mf*

inquiring, enquiring [ɪnˈkwaɪərɪŋ] ADJ fragend; *mind* forschend

inquiringly, enquiringly [ɪnˈkwaɪərɪŋlɪ] ADV *look* fragend

inquiry [ɪnˈkwaɪrɪ, (*US*) ˈɪnkwɪrɪ], **enquiry** [ɪnˈkwaɪrɪ] N **a** (= *question*) Anfrage *f* (*about* über +*acc*); (*for tourist information, direction etc*) Erkundigung *f* (*about* über +*acc*, nach); **to make inquiries** Erkundigungen einziehen; (*police etc*) Nachforschungen anstellen (*about sb* über jdn, *about sth* nach etw); **all inquiries to ...** alle Anfragen an (+*acc*) ...; **Inquiries** (*office*) Auskunft *f*; **he is helping the police with their inquiries** (*euph*) er wird von der Polizei vernommen

b (= *investigation*) Untersuchung *f*; **to hold an ~ into the cause of the accident** eine Untersuchung der Unfallursache durchführen; **court of ~** Untersuchungskommission *f*

inquisition [ɪnkwɪˈzɪʃən] N (*Hist Eccl*) **the Inquisition** die Inquisition **b** (*Jur*) Untersuchung *f* **c** (*fig*) Inquisition *f*, Verhör *nt*

inquisitive [ɪnˈkwɪzɪtɪv] ADJ neugierig; (*for knowledge*) wissbegierig; **he's very ~ about my friends** er will alles über meine Freunde wissen

inquisitively [ɪnˈkwɪzɪtɪvlɪ] ADV neugierig

inquisitiveness [ɪnˈkwɪzɪtɪvnɪs] N (*of person*) Neugier *f*; (*for knowledge*) Wissbegier(de) *f*; **the ~ of her look** ihr neugieriger Blick

inquisitor [ɪnˈkwɪzɪtə] N (*Hist Eccl*) Inquisitor *m*; (*fig*) Inquisitor(in) *m(f)*

inquisitorial [ɪnˌkwɪzɪˈtɔːrɪəl] ADJ inquisitorisch; **after an ~ meeting with the headmaster** nachdem ihn der Rektor streng verhört hatte *or* ins Verhör genommen hatte

inquorate [ɪnˈkwɔːreɪt, -rət] ADJ (*Brit*) beschlussunfähig

inroad [ˈɪnrəʊd] N **a** (*Mil*) Einfall *m* (*into* in +*acc*) **b** (*fig*) **the Japanese are making ~s into the British market** die Japaner dringen in den britischen Markt ein; **these expenses are making great ~s into my bank account** diese Ausgaben greifen mein Bankkonto stark an

inrush [ˈɪnrʌʃ] N Zustrom *m*; (*of water*) Einbruch *m*; **there was a sudden ~ of tourists** die Touristen kamen plötzlich in Strömen

ins **a** abbr of **insurance** Vers. **b** abbr of **inches**

insalubrious [ɪnsəˈluːbrɪəs] ADJ unzuträglich

insane [ɪnˈseɪn] **ADJ** **a** (*lit*) geisteskrank; (*fig inf*) wahnsinnig, irrsinnig; **to drive sb ~** (*lit*) jdn um den Verstand bringen; (*fig inf*) jdn wahnsinnig machen; **to go ~** (*lit*) den Verstand verlieren; (*fig inf*) wahnsinnig werden; **you must be ~!** (*inf*) du bist wohl wahnsinnig!; **that's ~!** (*inf*) das ist Wahnsinn *or* Irrsinn!; **~ jealousy** rasende Eifersucht; **he was judged criminally ~** er wurde als psychisch kranker Straftäter eingeschätzt **b** (*esp US*) **~ asylum/ward** Anstalt *f*/Abteilung *f* für Geisteskranke **PL** **the ~** die Geisteskranken *pl*

insanely [ɪnˈseɪnlɪ] ADV irr; (*fig inf*) verrückt; *jealous* irrsinnig; *laugh* wie ein Geisteskranker/eine Geisteskranke

insanitary [ɪnˈsænɪtərɪ] ADJ unhygienisch

insanity [ɪnˈsænɪtɪ] N Geisteskrankheit *f*, Wahnsinn *m*; (*fig inf*) Irrsinn *m*, Wahnsinn *m*

insatiability [ɪnseɪʃəˈbɪlɪtɪ] N Unersättlichkeit *f*; (*of thirst, curiosity, desire*) Unstillbarkeit *f*

insatiable [ɪnˈseɪʃəbl], **insatiate** [ɪnˈseɪʃɪt] (*liter*) ADJ unersättlich; *curiosity, desire also* unstillbar; **an ~ hunger/thirst for sth** ein unersättlicher Hunger/unstillbarer Durst nach etw; **he/his mind is ~ for knowledge** er hat einen unersättlichen Wissensdurst

insatiably [ɪnˈseɪʃəblɪ] ADV **he is ~ hungry/curious** er hat einen unersättlichen Hunger/eine unstillbare Neugier

inscribe [ɪnˈskraɪb] VT **a** (*sth on sth* etw in etw *acc*) *words, symbols etc* (= *engrave*) (*on ring, watch etc*) eingravieren; (*on rock, stone, wood*) einmeißeln; (*on tree*) einritzen **b** *book* eine Widmung schreiben in (+*acc*); **a watch, ~d ...** eine Uhr mit der Widmung ... **c** **to ~ sth in sb's mind** etw in jds Gedächtnis (*dat*) verankern **d** (*Math*) einbeschreiben (*in a circle etc* einem Kreis *etc*) **e** (*Fin*) **~d stock** Namensaktien *pl*

inscription [ɪnˈskrɪpʃən] N **a** (*on monument etc*) Inschrift *f*; (*on coin*) Aufschrift *f* **b** (*in book*) Widmung *f*

inscrutability [ɪnˌskruːtəˈbɪlɪtɪ] N Unergründlichkeit *f*

inscrutable [ɪnˈskruːtəbl] ADJ unergründlich (*to* für); **~ face** undurchdringlicher Gesichtsausdruck; **don't pretend to be so ~** tu nicht so geheimnisvoll; **she remained ~ to him** sie blieb für ihn undurchschaubar

insect [ˈɪnsekt] N Insekt *nt*

insect: insect bite N Insektenstich *m*; **insect eater** N Insektenfresser *m*; **insect-eating plant** N Fleisch fressende Pflanze

insecticide [ɪnˈsektɪsaɪd] N Insektengift *nt*, Insektizid *nt* (*form*)

insectivorous [ɪnsekˈtɪvərəs] ADJ Insekten fressend

insect: insect powder N Insektenpulver *nt*; **insect repellent** N Insektenbekämpfungsmittel *nt*; **insect-repellent** ADJ Insekten vertreibend

insecure [ɪnsɪˈkjʊə] ADJ **a** (= *uncertain, unsafe*) unsicher; **~ future** ungesicherte Zukunft; **if they feel ~ in their jobs** wenn sie sich in ihrem

Arbeitsplatz nicht sicher fühlen **b** (= *loose*) *load, ladder* ungesichert

insecurely [ɪnsɪˈkjʊəlɪ] ADV *fastened* nicht sicher

insecurity [ɪnsɪˈkjʊərɪtɪ] N Unsicherheit *f*

inseminate [ɪnˈsemɪneɪt] VT inseminieren (*spec*), befruchten; *cattle* besamen; (*fig*) *beliefs* einimpfen

insemination [ɪnsemɪˈneɪʃən] N Insemination *f* (*spec*), Befruchtung *f*; (*of cattle*) Besamung *f*; (*fig*) (*of beliefs*) Einimpfung *f*; (*of knowledge*) Vermittlung *f*

insensate [ɪnˈsenseɪt] ADJ (*liter*) **a** *matter, stone* leblos, tot **b** (*fig,* = *unfeeling*) gefühllos; **she flew into an ~ fury** ein unmäßiger Zorn bemächtigte sich ihrer (*liter*)

insensibility [ɪnsensəˈbɪlɪtɪ] N **a** (*bodily*) Unempfindlichkeit *f* (*to* gegenüber); (= *unconsciousness*) Bewusstlosigkeit *f* **b** (= *lack of feeling*) Gefühllosigkeit *f* (*to* gegenüber); **~ to art** Unempfänglichkeit *f* für Kunst

insensible [ɪnˈsensəbl] ADJ **a** (*bodily*) unempfindlich (*to* gegen); (= *unconscious*) bewusstlos; **he seems to be ~ to the cold** er scheint kälteunempfindlich zu sein; **his hands became ~ to any feeling** seine Hände verloren jegliches Gefühl **b** (*liter, of beauty, music*) unempfänglich (*of, to* für) **c** (*liter: = unaware*) **~ of** *or* **to sth** einer Sache (*gen*) nicht bewusst **d** (*form: = imperceptible*) unmerklich, nicht wahrnehmbar

insensitive [ɪnˈsensɪtɪv] ADJ **a** (= *unfeeling, uncaring*) gefühllos; *remark* taktlos; *policy, action* rücksichtslos; **to be ~ to** *or* **about sb's problems/fears/feelings** auf jds Probleme/Ängste/Gefühle keine Rücksicht nehmen **b** (= *unappreciative*) unempfänglich; **to be ~ to the beauties of nature** *etc* für Schönheiten der Natur *etc* unempfänglich sein **c** (*physically*) unempfindlich (*to* gegen); **~ to pain/light** schmerz-/lichtunempfindlich **d** (*Econ*) **they are relatively ~ to price** für sie spielt der Preis eine relativ untergeordnete Rolle

insensitivity [ɪnsensɪˈtɪvɪtɪ] N **a** (= *unfeeling/uncaring attitude*) Gefühllosigkeit *f* (*towards* gegenüber); (*of remark*) Taktlosigkeit *f*; (*of policy, action*) Rücksichtslosigkeit *f* **b** (= *unappreciativeness*) Unempfänglichkeit *f* (*to* für); **his ~ to the reasons behind the demands** seine Verständnislosigkeit *or* sein Unverständnis für die Gründe, die hinter den Forderungen stehen **c** (*physical*) Unempfindlichkeit *f* (*to* gegen)

inseparability [ɪnsepərəˈbɪlɪtɪ] N Untrennbarkeit *f*; (*of friends*) Unzertrennlichkeit *f*

inseparable [ɪnˈsepərəbl] ADJ untrennbar; *friends* unzertrennlich; **these two issues are ~** diese beiden Fragen sind untrennbar miteinander verbunden

inseparably [ɪnˈsepərəblɪ] ADV untrennbar

insert [ɪnˈsɜːt] **VT** (= *stick into*) hineinstecken; (= *place in*) hineinlegen; (= *place between*) einfügen; *zip, pocket* einsetzen; *thermometer, suppository* einführen; *coin* einwerfen; *injection needle* einstechen; *text, clause* einfügen; (*Comput*) *disk* einlegen; **to ~ sth in(to) sth** (= *stick into*) etw in etw (*acc*) stecken; (= *place in*) etw in etw (*acc*) hineinlegen; (= *place between*) etw in etw (*acc*) einfügen; **to ~ an extra paragraph in(to) a chapter** einen weiteren Absatz in ein Kapitel einfügen; **to ~ an advert in a newspaper** eine Anzeige in die Zeitung setzen, in einer Zeitung inserieren; **he managed to ~ himself between two other students on the crowded benches** es gelang ihm, sich auf den gefüllten Bänken zwischen zwei andere Studenten zu zwängen; **~ mode** (*Comput*) Einfügemodus *m*
N [ˈɪnsɜːt] (*in book*) Einlage *f*; (= *word*) Beifügung *f*, Einfügung *f*; (*in magazine*) Beilage *f*; (= *advertisement*) Inserat *nt*

insertion [ɪnˈsɜːʃən] N **a** (= *sticking into*) Hineinstecken *nt*; (= *placing in*) Hineinlegen *nt*; (= *placing between*) Einfügen *nt*; (*of pocket*) Einsetzen *nt*; (*of thermometer, suppository*) Einführen *nt*; (*of coin*) Einwerfen *nt*; (*of injection needle*) Einstechen *nt*; (*of advert*) Aufgeben *nt*; (*by print-*

er) Einrücken *nt*; (*of text, clause*) Einfügen *nt*; (*Comput: of disk*) Einlegen *nt* **b** = **insert N** **c** (*Sew*) Einsatz *m*

in-service ['ɪn,sɜːvɪs] ADJ *attr* ~ **training** (berufsbegleitende) Fortbildung; (*in firm also*) innerbetriebliche Fortbildung; (*course also*) Fortbildungslehrgang *m*

inset [ɪn'set] *vb: pret, ptp* **inset** **VT** *map, illustration* einfügen; (*Sew*) einsetzen; **the text is ~ with illustrations** in den Text sind Illustrationen eingefügt ['ɪnset] **N** **a** (= *pages*) Einlage *f*, Beilage *f*; (*also* **inset map**) Nebenkarte *f*; (*on diagram*) Nebenbild *nt* **b** (*Sew*) Einsatz *m*

inshore ['ɪn'ʃɔː] **a** Küsten-; ~ **fishing/waters** Küstenfischerei *f*/-gewässer *pl* ADV *fish, be* in Küstennähe; *blow, flow* auf die Küste zu; **to be close ~** dicht an der Küste sein; **to go close ~** dicht an die Küste heranfahren

inside [ɪn'saɪd] **N** **a** Innere(s) *nt*; (*of pavement*) Innenseite *f*; **the car overtook on the ~** das Auto überholte innen; **it's painted on the ~** es ist innen bemalt; **you'll have to ask someone on the ~** Sie müssen einen Insider or Eingeweihten fragen; **to know a company from the ~** interne Kenntnisse über eine Firma haben; **he's seen politics from the ~** er kennt die Politik von innen; **locked from** or **on the ~** von innen verschlossen **b** **the wind blew the umbrella ~ out** der Wind hat den Schirm umgestülpt; **her umbrella blew ~ out** ihr Schirm hat sich umgestülpt; **your sweater's ~ out** du hast deinen Pullover links or verkehrt herum an; **to turn sth ~ out** etw umdrehen; (*fig*) *flat etc* etw auf den Kopf stellen; **war turns morality ~ out** im Krieg wird die Moral auf den Kopf gestellt; **to know sth ~ out** etw in- und auswendig kennen; **we know each other ~ out** wir kennen einander in- und auswendig **c** (*inf:* = *stomach: also* **insides**) Eingeweide *nt*, Innere(s) *nt*; **he felt the excitement grip his ~s** er spürte, wie die Aufregung ihn im Innersten packte ADJ Innen-, innere(r, s); **it looks like an ~ job** (*crime*) es sieht nach dem Werk von Insidern aus (*inf*); ~ **leg measurement** innere Beinlänge; ~ **pocket** Innentasche *f*; ~ **seat** Platz *m* an der Wand/am Fenster, Fensterplatz *m*; ~ **story** (*Press*) Insidestory *f*; ~ **left** Halblinke(r) *mf*; ~ **right** Halbrechte(r) *mf* ADV innen; (= *indoors*) drin(nen); (*direction*) nach innen, herein; **look ~** sehen Sie hinein; (= *search*) sehen Sie innen nach; **come ~!** kommen Sie herein!; **let's go ~** gehen wir hinein; **he played the ball ~** er spielte nach innen ab; **I heard music coming from ~** ich hörte von innen Musik; **there is something/nothing ~** es ist etwas/nichts (innen) drin; **to be ~** (*inf: = in prison*) sitzen (*inf*) **b** (*time*) innerhalb; **he's well ~ the record time** er liegt noch gut unter der Rekordzeit; **he was 5 seconds ~ the record** er ist 5 Sekunden unter dem Rekord geblieben PREP (*esp US: also* **inside of**) **a** (*place*) innen in (+*dat*); (*direction*) in (+*acc*) ... (hinein); **don't let him come ~ the house** lassen Sie ihn nicht ins Haus (herein); **he was waiting ~ the house** er wartete im Haus; **something ~ me snapped** bei mir hakte etwas aus (*inf*)

inside: inside forward N Halbstürmer(in) *m(f)*; **inside information** N Insiderinformationen *pl*, interne Informationen *pl*; **inside lane** N (*Sport*) Innenbahn *f*; (*Aut*) Innenspur *f*

insider [ɪn'saɪdə'] N Insider(in) *m(f)*, Eingeweihte(r) *mf*

insider dealing, **insider trading** N (*Fin*) Insiderhandel *m*

inside track N Innenbahn *f*

insidious ADJ, **insidiously** ADV [ɪn'sɪdɪəs, -lɪ] heimtückisch

insight ['ɪnsaɪt] N **a** *no pl* Verständnis *nt*; **he lacks ~** ihm fehlt das Verständnis; **his ~ into my problems** sein Verständnis für meine Probleme; ~ **into human nature** Menschenkenntnis *f* **b** Einblick *m* (*into* in +*acc*); **to gain (an) ~**

into sth (einen) Einblick in etw gewinnen or bekommen; **to give sb (an) ~ into sth** jdm (einen) Einblick in etw (*acc*) geben

insightful ['ɪnsaɪtfʊl] ADJ *questions, analysis* einsichtsvoll

insignia [ɪn'sɪɡnɪə] PL Insignien *pl*

insignificance [,ɪnsɪɡ'nɪfɪkəns] N Bedeutungslosigkeit *f*, Belanglosigkeit *f*; (*of wound, alteration*) Geringfügigkeit *f*; (*of person, appearance*) Unscheinbarkeit *f*

insignificant [,ɪnsɪɡ'nɪfɪkənt] ADJ unbedeutend; *sum also, wound, alteration* geringfügig; *little man, person, appearance* unscheinbar; (= *inconsequential*) *remark* belanglos; **her not ~ talents** ihre nicht unbeträchtlichen Talente; **statistically ~** statistisch vernachlässigbar

insincere [,ɪnsɪn'sɪə'] ADJ unaufrichtig; *person, smile also* falsch

insincerely [,ɪnsɪn'sɪəlɪ] ADV unaufrichtig; *smile* falsch

insincerity [,ɪnsɪn'serɪtɪ] N Unaufrichtigkeit *f*; (*of person, smile also*) Falschheit *f*

insinuate [ɪn'sɪnjʊeɪt] VT **a** (= *hint, suggest*) andeuten (*sth to sb* etw jdm gegenüber); **what are you insinuating?** was wollen Sie damit sagen?; **are you insinuating that I am lying?** willst du damit sagen, dass ich lüge? **b** **to ~ oneself into sb's favour** (*Brit*) or **favor** (*US*)/**the smart set** sich bei jdm/bei der Schickeria einschmeicheln

insinuating [ɪn'sɪnjʊeɪtɪŋ] ADJ *remark* anzüglich; *article also* voller Anzüglichkeiten; *tone of voice* spitz, bedeutungsvoll

insinuation [ɪn,sɪnjʊ'eɪʃən] N Anspielung *f* (*about* auf +*acc*); **he objected strongly to any ~ that ...** er wehrte sich heftig gegen jede Andeutung, dass ...

insipid [ɪn'sɪpɪd] ADJ fade; *colour* langweilig; (= *vapid*) *person, novel, lyrics* geistlos

insipidity [,ɪnsɪ'pɪdɪtɪ] N Fadheit *f*; (= *vapidity*) Geistlosigkeit *f*

insist [ɪn'sɪst] **VI** **I ~!** ich bestehe darauf!; **if you ~** wenn Sie darauf bestehen; (= *if you like*) wenns unbedingt sein muss; **he ~s on his innocence** or **that he is innocent** er behauptet beharrlich, unschuldig zu sein; **to ~ on a point** auf einem Punkt beharren; **to ~ on silence** auf absoluter Ruhe bestehen; **I ~ on the best** ich bestehe auf bester Qualität; **to ~ on doing sth/on sb doing sth** darauf bestehen, etw zu tun/dass jd etw tut; **he will ~ on calling her by the wrong name** er redet sie beharrlich beim falschen Namen an; **if you will ~ on smoking that foul tobacco** wenn Sie schon unbedingt diesen scheußlichen Tabak rauchen müssen **VT** **to ~ that ...** darauf beharren or bestehen, dass ...; **he ~s that he is innocent** er behauptet beharrlich, unschuldig zu sein; **"it wasn't me", she ~ed** "ich wars nicht!" sagte sie beharrlich; **but he still ~ed that ...** aber er beharrte or bestand trotzdem darauf, dass ...; **I must ~ that you stop** ich muss darauf bestehen, dass Sie aufhören; **she ~s that she is right** sie besteht darauf, dass sie Recht hat

insistence [ɪn'sɪstəns] N Bestehen *nt* (*on auf* +*dat*); **the accused's ~ on his innocence** die Unschuldsbeteuerungen des Angeklagten; **in spite of his ~ that he was right** trotz seiner beharrlichen Behauptung, Recht zu haben; **I did it at his ~** ich tat es auf sein Drängen, ich tat es, weil er darauf bestand; **I can't understand his ~ on using** or **the use of oil** ich kann nicht verstehen, warum er darauf besteht, dass Öl benutzt wird

insistent [ɪn'sɪstənt] ADJ **a** *person* beharrlich, hartnäckig; *salesman etc* aufdringlich; **I didn't want to but he was ~ (that ...)** ich wollte eigentlich nicht, aber er bestand or beharrte darauf (, dass ...); **he was most ~ about it** or beharrte or bestand hartnäckig darauf **b** (= *urgent*) *demand, tone* nachdrücklich, penetrant (*pej*); *rhythm* aufdringlich; *ringing* penetrant (*pej*); (= *constant*) unaufhörlich

insistently [ɪn'sɪstəntlɪ] ADV mit Nachdruck; **the telephone rang ~** das Telefon klingelte penetrant und unaufhörlich; **this question will be put more and more ~** diese Frage wird immer beharrlicher gestellt werden

in situ [ɪn'sɪtjuː] ADV in situ (*esp Med, Archeol*); **this part can be repaired ~** man braucht das Teil nicht auszubauen, um es zu reparieren ADJ ~ **investigator** Ermittler(in) *m(f)* vor Ort

insofar [,ɪnsəʊ'fɑː] ADV ~ **as** soweit

insole ['ɪnsəʊl] N Einlegesohle *f*; (= *part of shoe*) Brandsohle *f*

insolence ['ɪnsələns] N Unverschämtheit *f*, Frechheit *f*; **the ~ of it!** so eine Unverschämtheit or Frechheit!

insolent ADJ, **insolently** ADV ['ɪnsələnt, -lɪ] unverschämt, frech

insolubility [ɪn,sɒljʊ'bɪlɪt] N **a** (*of substance*) Unlöslichkeit *f* **b** (*of problem*) Unlösbarkeit *f*

insoluble [ɪn'sɒljʊbl] ADJ **a** *substance* unlöslich **b** *problem* unlösbar

insolvency [ɪn'sɒlvənsɪ] N Zahlungsunfähigkeit *f*, Insolvenz *f* (*geh*)

insolvent [ɪn'sɒlvənt] ADJ zahlungsunfähig, insolvent (*geh*)

insomnia [ɪn'sɒmnɪə] N Schlaflosigkeit *f*

insomniac [ɪn'sɒmnɪæk] N **to be an ~** an Schlaflosigkeit leiden

insomuch [,ɪnsəʊ'mʌtʃ] ADV = **inasmuch**

insouciance [ɪn'suːsɪəns] N (*liter*) Unbekümmertheit *f*, Sorglosigkeit *f*

insouciant [ɪn'suːsɪənt] ADJ (*liter.* = *careless*) unbekümmert; **to be ~ about sth** sich nicht um etw kümmern

inspect [ɪn'spekt] VT **a** (= *examine*) kontrollieren, prüfen; *school, hotel etc* inspizieren; **to ~ sth for sth** etw auf etw (*acc*) (hin) prüfen or kontrollieren **b** (*Mil etc:* = *review*) inspizieren

inspection [ɪn'spekʃən] N **a** Kontrolle *f*, Prüfung *f*; (*medical*) Untersuchung *f*; (*of school, hotel etc*) Inspektion *f*; **to make an ~ of sth** etw kontrollieren or prüfen; *of school etc* etw inspizieren; **on ~** bei näherer Betrachtung or Prüfung; **customs ~** Zollkontrolle *f*; **for your ~** zur Prüfung; (*documents also*) zur Einsicht; ~ **copy** Ansichtsexemplar *nt* **b** (*Mil*) Inspektion *f*

inspector [ɪn'spektə'] N (= *factory inspector, on buses, trains*) Kontrolleur(in) *m(f)*; (*of schools*) Schulrat *m*, Schulrätin *f*; (*of police*) Polizeiinspektor(in) *m(f)*; (*higher*) Kommissar(in) *m(f)*; (*of taxes*) Steuerinspektor(in) *m(f)*; **customs ~** Zollinspektor(in) *m(f)*

inspectorate [ɪn'spektərɪt] N Inspektion *f*

inspiration [,ɪnspə'reɪʃən] N Inspiration *f* (*for* zu or für), Eingebung *f* (*for* zu); **he gets his ~ from ...** er lässt sich von ... inspirieren; **you give me ~** Sie inspirieren mich; **I haven't had any ~ for months** seit Monaten habe ich keine Inspirationen mehr; **to find (one's) ~ in sth** von etw inspiriert werden; **to have a sudden ~** eine plötzliche Inspiration or Erleuchtung haben; **you are my ~** du inspirierst mich; **his courage has been an ~ to us all** sein Mut hat uns alle inspiriert

inspirational [,ɪnspə'reɪʃənl] ADJ inspirativ

inspire [ɪn'spaɪə'] VT **a** *respect, trust, awe* einflößen (*in sb* jdm); *hope, confidence etc* (er)wecken (*in* in +*dat*); *hate, fear* hervorrufen (*in* in); **to ~ sb with hope/confidence** jdn mit Hoffnung/Vertrauen erfüllen **b** (= *be inspiration to*) *person* inspirieren; **to ~ sb with an idea** jdn zu einer Idee inspirieren; **I was ~d by his example/courage** sein Vorbild/Mut hat mich inspiriert; **the book was ~d by a real person** die Inspiration zu dem Buch kommt von einer wirklichen Person; **whatever ~d you to change it?** (*iro*) was hat dich bloß dazu inspiriert, es zu ändern?

inspired [ɪn'spaɪəd] ADJ genial; *work, performance also* voller Inspiration; *author, performer, athlete etc* inspiriert; **in an ~ moment** in einem Augenblick der Inspiration; (*iro*) in einem lichten Moment; **it was an ~ guess/choice** das war genial geraten/gewählt; **the strike was politically**

~ der Streik war politisch motiviert; **the divinely ~ word of the Bible** der göttlich geoffenbarte Bibeltext

inspiring [ɪnˈspaɪərɪŋ] ADJ *speech, teacher, leader, speaker, example* inspirierend; **this subject/translation isn't particularly** ~ dieses Thema/diese Übersetzung begeistert einen nicht gerade; **she is an ~ teacher** als Lehrerin ist sie eine Inspiration

Inst. *abbr of* **Institute** Inst.

inst. *abbr of* **instant** d. M.

instability [ˌɪnstəˈbɪlɪtɪ] N Instabilität *f*; *(of character also)* Labilität *f*

install [ɪnˈstɔːl] VT installieren; *telephone also* anschließen; *bathroom, fireplace* einbauen; *person (in ein Amt)* einsetzen *or* einführen; *government* einsetzen; *priest* investieren; **to have electricity ~ed** ans Elektrizitätsnetz angeschlossen werden; **when you've ~ed yourself in your new office** wenn Sie sich in Ihrem neuen Büro installiert *or* eingerichtet haben; **he ~ed himself in the best armchair** *(inf)* er pflanzte sich auf den besten Sessel *(inf)*

installation [ˌɪnstəˈleɪʃən] N **a** *(= action)* Installation *f*; *(of telephone)* Anschluss *m*; *(of bath, kitchen, engine etc)* Einbau *m*; *(of person in office)* Amtseinsetzung *f or* -einführung *f*; *(of government)* Einsetzung *f*; *(of priest)* Investitur *f*; **~ program** *(Comput)* Installationsprogramm *nt* **b** *(= machine etc)* Anlage *f*, Einrichtung *f* **c** **military ~** militärische Anlage

installment plan N *(US)* Ratenzahlung *f*; **to buy on the ~** auf Raten kaufen

instalment, *(US)* **installment** [ɪnˈstɔːlmənt] N **a** *(of story, serial)* Fortsetzung *f*; *(Rad, TV)* (Sende)folge *f* **b** *(Fin, Comm)* Rate *f*; **monthly ~** Monatsrate *f*; **to pay in** *or* **by ~s** in Raten *or* ratenweise bezahlen

instalment credit, *(US)* **installment credit** N Teilzahlungs- *or* Abzahlungskredit *m*

instance [ˈɪnstəns] N **a** *(= example)* Beispiel *nt*; *(= case)* Fall *m*; **for ~** zum Beispiel; **as an ~ of** als (ein) Beispiel für; **in many ~s** in vielen Fällen; **there have been many ~s of people refusing to go** es hat viele Fälle gegeben, in denen Leute es abgelehnt haben zu gehen; **in the first ~** zuerst *or* zunächst (einmal); **the appointment will be for two years in the first ~** die Anstellung ist zunächst auf zwei Jahre befristet; **this is a good ~ of the way …** das ist ein gutes Beispiel dafür, wie … **b at the ~ of** *(form)* auf Ersuchen *or* Betreiben (+*gen*) *(form)*, auf Veranlassung von **c** *(Jur)* **court of first ~** erste Instanz ▸ **VT a** *(= exemplify)* Beispiele anführen für **b** *(= cite)* cost, example anführen

instant [ˈɪnstənt] ▸ **ADJ a** unmittelbar; *relief, result, reply, success* sofortig *attr*, unmittelbar; **sweets give ~ energy** Süßigkeiten sind sofortige Energielieferanten; **~ photography** Sofortbildfotografie *f* **b** *(Cook)* Instant-; **~ milk** Trockenmilch *f*; **~ food** Schnellgerichte *pl*; **~ mashed potatoes** fertiger Kartoffelbrei **c** *(Comm)* dieses Monats; **your letter of the 10th inst(ant)** Ihr Schreiben vom 10. dieses Monats **d** *(Jur)* **in the ~ case** im vorliegenden Fall ▸ **N** Augenblick *m*; **this (very) ~** sofort, auf der Stelle; **I'll be ready in an ~** ich bin sofort fertig; **it was all over in an ~** in einem Augenblick *or* im Nu *(inf)* war alles vorbei; **he left the ~ he heard the news** er ging sofort, als er die Nachricht hörte; **at that very ~ …** genau in dem Augenblick …; **the next ~, an ~ later** im nächsten Augenblick; **in the same ~** im gleichen Augenblick

instant access N *(Fin, Comput)* sofortiger Zugriff *(to* auf); **~ account** Sparkonto ohne Zugriffsbeschränkungen

instantaneous [ˌɪnstənˈteɪnɪəs] ADJ unmittelbar; **death was ~** der Tod trat sofort *or* unmittelbar ein; **the reaction was almost ~** die Reaktion erfolgte fast sofort

instantaneously [ˌɪnstənˈteɪnɪəslɪ] ADV sofort, unverzüglich

instant camera N Sofortbildkamera *f*

instant coffee N Pulver- *or* Instantkaffee *m*

instanter [ɪnˈstæntə] ADV stante pede, stehenden Fußes *(geh)*

instantly [ˈɪnstəntlɪ] ADV sofort; **the game was ~ forgettable** das Spiel konnte man total vergessen *(inf)*

instant replay N *(TV)* Wiederholung *f*

instead [ɪnˈsted] ▸ **PREP** **~ of** statt (+*gen or (inf)* +*dat)*, anstelle *or* an Stelle von; **~ of going to school** (an)statt zur Schule zu gehen; **~ of that** statt dessen; **his brother came ~ of him** sein Bruder kam an seiner Stelle *or* statt ihm *(inf)*; **he accidentally hit Jim ~ of John** er traf aus Versehen Jim (an)statt John; **this is ~ of a Christmas present** das ist anstelle *or* an Stelle eines Weihnachtsgeschenks ▸ **ADV** stattdessen, dafür; **if he doesn't want to go, I'll go ~** wenn er nicht gehen will, gehe ich (stattdessen); **if he doesn't come here, I shall go there ~** wenn er nicht herkommt, gehe ich stattdessen hin

instep [ˈɪnstep] N **a** *(Anat)* Spann *m*, Rist *m* **b** *(of shoe)* Blatt *nt*

instigate [ˈɪnstɪgeɪt] VT anstiften; *rebellion, strike also* anzetteln; *violence* aufrufen zu; *new idea, reform etc* initiieren

instigation [ˌɪnstɪˈgeɪʃən] N Anstiftung *f*; *(of rebellion, strike also)* Anzettelung *f*, Aufruf *m*; *(of new idea, reform)* Initiierung *f*; **~ of violence** Aufruf *f* zur Gewalt; **at sb's ~** auf jds Betreiben *or* Veranlassung

instigator [ˈɪnstɪgeɪtə] N *(of crime etc)* Anstifter(in) *m(f)*; *(of new idea, reform etc)* Initiator(in) *m(f)*

instil, *(US)* **instill** [ɪnˈstɪl] VT einflößen *(into sb* jdm); *knowledge, attitudes, discipline* beibringen *(into sb* jdm)

instinct [ˈɪnstɪŋkt] ▸ **N** Instinkt *m*; **the sex/survival ~** der Geschlechts-/Überlebenstrieb; **by** *or* **from ~** instinktiv; **to have an ~ for business, to have a good business ~** einen ausgeprägten Geschäftssinn *or* -instinkt haben; **to follow one's ~s** sich auf seinen Instinkt verlassen ▸ [ɪnˈstɪŋkt] **ADJ** *(liter)* **~ with** erfüllt von

instinctive [ɪnˈstɪŋktɪv] ADJ instinktiv; *behaviour also* instinktgesteuert

instinctively [ɪnˈstɪŋktɪvlɪ] ADV instinktiv

institute [ˈɪnstɪtjuːt] ▸ **VT a** *new laws, tax, custom, reforms, policy* einführen; *(= found) organization etc* einrichten; *search* einleiten; **a newly ~d post** eine neu eingerichtete Stelle **b** *(Jur) inquiry* einleiten; *an action* einleiten *(against sb* gegen jdn); *proceedings* anstrengen *(against* gegen); **to ~ divorce proceedings** die Scheidung einreichen ▸ **N a** Institut *nt*; *(= home)* Anstalt *f*; **Institute of Technology/Education** technische/pädagogische Hochschule; **educational ~** pädagogische Einrichtung; **women's ~** Frauenverein *m*

institution [ˌɪnstɪˈtjuːʃən] N **a** *(of new laws, customs, reforms)* Einführung *f*; *(of organization)* Einrichtung *f* **b** *(Jur, of inquiry, action)* Einleitung *f*; *(of proceedings)* Anstrengung *f*; **~ of divorce proceedings** Einreichung *f* der Scheidung **c** *(= organization)* Institution *f*, Einrichtung *f* **d** *(= building, home etc)* Anstalt *f* **e** *(= custom)* Institution *f*; **the ~ of marriage** die Institution der Ehe; **he's been here so long he's become an ~** er ist schon so lange hier, dass er zur Institution geworden ist

institutional [ˌɪnstɪˈtjuːʃənl] ADJ **a** *(= of institutions) reform, structure, arrangement* institutionell **b** *(= in an institution) food, atmosphere* Anstalts-; **~ life/care** Anstaltsleben *nt*/-pflege *f*; **~ care in hospital/an old folk's home** stationäre Versorgung *or* Pflege im Krankenhaus/in einem Altenheim **c** *(US)* **~ advertising** Prestigewerbung *f* **d** *(Fin) support, funds* institutionell; **~ buying** Käufe *pl* durch institutionelle Anleger; **~ investors** institutionelle Anleger *pl*

institutionalize [ˌɪnstɪˈtjuːʃənəlaɪz] VT institutionalisieren

institutionalized [ˌɪnstɪˈtjuːʃənəlaɪzd] ADJ **a** *person* in einer Anstalt untergebracht; **to become ~** *(Psych)* sich an das Anstaltsleben gewöhnen **b** *(= organized, established) religion, racism, system* institutionalisiert; **homelessness and destitution are becoming ~ here** Obdachlosigkeit und Elend werden hier zur Norm

in-store [ˈɪnstɔː] ADJ *attr* im Laden; **~ surveillance system** geschäftsinternes Überwachungssystem

instruct [ɪnˈstrʌkt] VT **a** *(= teach) person* unterrichten; **to ~ sb in the use of a machine** jdn in der Handhabung einer Maschine unterweisen **b** *(= tell, direct) person* anweisen; *(= command)* die Anweisung erteilen (+*dat)*; *(Brit Jur) solicitor (= give information to)* unterrichten, instruieren; *(= appoint) lawyer* beauftragen; *jury* instruieren, belehren; **I've been ~ed to report to you** ich habe (An)weisung, Ihnen Meldung zu erstatten; **what were you ~ed to do?** welche Instruktionen *or* Anweisungen haben Sie bekommen? **c** *(form: = inform)* in Kenntnis setzen

instruction [ɪnˈstrʌkʃən] N **a** *(= teaching)* Unterricht *m*; **course of ~** Lehrgang *m*; **to give sb ~ in fencing** jdm Fechtunterricht erteilen **b** *(= order, command)* Anweisung *f*, Instruktion *f*; *(of jury)* Belehrung *f*, Instruktion *f*; **what were your ~s?** welche Instruktionen *or* Anweisungen hatten Sie?; **on whose ~s did you do that?** auf wessen Anweisung *or* Anordnung haben Sie das getan?; **~s for use** Gebrauchsanweisung *f*, Gebrauchsanleitung *f*; **~ manual** *(Tech)* Bedienungsanleitung *f*

instructive [ɪnˈstrʌktɪv] ADJ instruktiv, aufschlussreich; *(= of educational value)* lehrreich

instructor [ɪnˈstrʌktə] N *(also Sport)* Lehrer *m*; *(US)* Dozent *m*; *(Mil)* Ausbilder *m*

instructress [ɪnˈstrʌktrɪs] N *(also Sport)* Lehrerin *f*; *(US)* Dozentin *f*; *(Mil)* Ausbilderin *f*

instrument [ˈɪnstrʊmənt] ▸ **N a** *(Mus, Med, Tech)* Instrument *nt*; *(domestic)* Gerät *nt*; **to fly an aircraft on ~s** ein Flugzeug nach den (Bord)instrumenten fliegen **b** *(fig: = person)* Werkzeug *nt* **c** *(Jur)* Urkunde *f*, Dokument *nt* [ˈɪnstrʊˌment] ▸ **VT a** *(Mus)* instrumentieren **b** *(= put into effect)* durchführen, ausführen

instrument *in cpds (Aviat)* Instrumenten-; **~ panel** *or* **board** *(Aviat)* Instrumententafel *f*; *(Aut)* Armaturenbrett *nt*

instrumental [ˌɪnstrʊˈmentl] ▸ **ADJ a** *role* entscheidend; **she was ~ in my release** sie hat bei meiner Freilassung eine entscheidende Rolle gespielt; **he was ~ in getting her the job** er hat ihr zu dieser Stelle verholfen; **he was ~ in bringing about the downfall of the government** er war maßgeblich am Sturz der Regierung beteiligt **b** *(Mus)* Instrumental-; **~ music/version** Instrumentalmusik *f*/-version *f*; **~ performer** Instrumentalist(in) *m(f)* ▸ **N** *(Mus)* Instrumentalstück *nt*

instrumentalist [ˌɪnstrʊˈmentəlɪst] N Instrumentalist(in) *m(f)*

instrumentality [ˌɪnstrʊmenˈtælɪtɪ] N **through** *or* **by the ~ of sb** durch jds Vermittlung *or* Eingreifen

instrumentation [ˌɪnstrʊmenˈteɪʃən] N Instrumentation *f*

insubordinate [ˌɪnsəˈbɔːdənɪt] ADJ aufsässig

insubordination [ˈɪnsəˌbɔːdɪˈneɪʃən] N Aufsässigkeit *f*; *(Mil)* Gehorsamsverweigerung *f*, Insubordination *f* *(dated)*

insubstantial [ˌɪnsəbˈstænʃəl] ADJ wenig substanziell *or* substantiell; *fear, hopes, accusation, rumour* gegenstandslos; *argument* haltlos; *amount* gering(fügig); *meal, plot, evidence* dürftig

insufferable ADJ , **insufferably** ADV [ɪnˈsʌfərəbl, -lɪ] unerträglich

insufficiency [ˌɪnsəˈfɪʃənsɪ] N *(of supplies)* Knappheit *f*, unzureichende Menge; *(of sb's work)* Unzulänglichkeit *f*

insufficient [ˌɪnsəˈfɪʃənt] ADJ nicht genügend; ~ **evidence** Mangel *m* an Beweisen; **to take ~ account of sth** etw nicht genug in Betracht ziehen

insufficiently [ˌɪnsəˈfɪʃəntlɪ] ADV ungenügend, unzulänglich

insulant [ˈɪnsjələnt] N Isolierstoff *m*, Dämmmaterial *nt*; (*for rooms*) Dämmstoff *m*

insular [ˈɪnsjələ] ADJ **a** (= *narrow-minded*) engstirnig **b** (= *of an island*) Insel-, insular

insularity [ˌɪnsjʊˈlærɪtɪ] N (= *narrow-mindedness*) Engstirnigkeit *f*

insulate [ˈɪnsjʊleɪt] VT **a** (*lit*) isolieren; **in this a-norak you're well ~d against the cold** in diesem Anorak sind Sie gut gegen Kälte geschützt; **to ~ sth from noise** etw schallisolieren; **~d pliers** Isolierzange *f* **b** (*fig: from unpleasantness etc*) abschirmen (*from* gegen)

insulating [ˈɪnsjʊleɪtɪŋ]: **insulating material** N Isoliermaterial *nt*; **insulating tape** N Isolierband *nt*

insulation [ˌɪnsjʊˈleɪʃən] N **a** (*lit*) Isolierung *f*; (= *material*) Isoliermaterial *nt* **b** (*fig*) Geschütztheit *f* (*from* gegen)

insulator [ˈɪnsjʊleɪtə] N (*Elec*: = *device*) Isolator *m*; (= *material*) Isolierstoff *m*; (*for heat*) Wärmeschutzisolierung *f*

insulin [ˈɪnsjʊlɪn] N Insulin *nt*

insult [ɪnˈsʌlt] VT beleidigen; (*by words also*) beschimpfen **N** [ˈɪnsʌlt] Beleidigung *f*; (*with words also*) Beschimpfung *f*; **an ~ to the profession** eine Beleidigung für den ganzen Berufsstand; **an ~ to my intelligence** eine Beleidigung meiner Intelligenz; **that's not a salary, it's an ~!** das ist doch kein Gehalt, das ist blanker Hohn *or* das ist eine Beleidigung!; **to add ~ to injury** das Ganze noch schlimmer machen

insulting [ɪnˈsʌltɪŋ] ADJ beleidigend; *question* unverschämt; **to use ~ language to sb** jdm gegenüber beleidigende Äußerungen machen, jdn beschimpfen; **he was very ~ to her** er hat sich ihr gegenüber sehr beleidigend geäußert

insultingly [ɪnˈsʌltɪŋlɪ] ADV beleidigend; *behave* in beleidigender *or* unverschämter Weise

insuperable [ɪnˈsuːpərəbl] ADJ unüberwindlich

insuperably [ɪnˈsuːpərəblɪ] ADV **it was ~ difficult** es hat unüberwindliche Schwierigkeiten bereitet; **this could affect its development ~** das könnte seiner Entwicklung einen bleibenden Schaden zufügen

insupportable [ˌɪnsəˈpɔːtəbl] ADJ unerträglich

insurable [ɪnˈʃʊərəbl] N versicherbar

insurance [ɪnˈʃʊərəns] N Versicherung *f*; (= *amount paid out*) Versicherungssumme *f* or -betrag *m*; **the ~ on a building** die Versicherung für ein Gebäude; **to take out ~** eine Versicherung abschließen (*against* gegen)

insurance: insurance adjuster N (*US*) Schadenssachverständige(r) *mf*; **insurance agent** N Versicherungsvertreter(in) *m(f)*; **insurance broker** N Versicherungsmakler(in) *m(f)*; **insurance company** N Versicherungsgesellschaft *f*; **insurance cover** N Versicherungsschutz *m*; **insurance office** N Versicherungsanstalt *f*/-büro *nt*; **insurance policy** N Versicherungspolice *f*; (*fig*) Sicherheitsvorkehrung *f*; **to take out an ~** eine Versicherung abschließen; (*fig*) Sicherheitsvorkehrungen treffen; **as an ~** (*fig*) für alle Fälle, sicherheitshalber; **as an ~ against sth** (*fig*) als Sicherheitsvorkehrung gegen etw; **insurance premium** N Versicherungsprämie *f*; **insurance scheme** N Versicherung(smöglichkeit) *f*; **insurance stamp** N (*Brit*) Versicherungsmarke *f*

insure [ɪnˈʃʊə] VT *a car, house* versichern (lassen) (*against* gegen); **he ~d his house contents for £10,000** er schloss eine Hausratsversicherung über £ 10.000 ab; **to ~ one's life** eine Lebensversicherung abschließen; **to ~ oneself against poverty/failure** *etc* (*fig*) sich gegen Armut/einen Fehlschlag *etc* (ab)sichern **b** = **ensure**

insured [ɪnˈʃʊəd] ADJ versichert (*by, with* bei); **~ against fire** feuerversichert **N** **the ~** (party) der Versicherungsnehmer, die Versicherungsnehmerin, der/die Versicherte

insurer [ɪnˈʃʊərə] N Versicherer *m*, Versicherungsgeber *m*

insurgence [ɪnˈsɜːdʒəns], **insurgency** N Aufruhr *m*, Aufstand *m*

insurgent [ɪnˈsɜːdʒənt] ADJ aufständisch **N** Aufständische(r) *mf*

insurmountable [ˌɪnsəˈmaʊntəbl] ADJ unüberwindlich

insurrection [ˌɪnsəˈrekʃən] N Aufstand *m*

insurrectionary [ˌɪnsəˈrekʃənərɪ] ADJ aufständisch **N** Aufständische(r) *mf*

insurrectionist [ˌɪnsəˈrekʃənɪst] N Aufständische(r) *mf*

insusceptible [ˌɪnsəˈseptɪbl] ADJ nicht anfällig (*to* für), unempfindlich (*to* gegen); (*fig: = immune*) unempfänglich (*to* für); **~ to pain** schmerzunempfindlich

int. *abbr of* **international** int.

intact [ɪnˈtækt] ADJ (= *not damaged*) unversehrt, intakt; (= *whole, in one piece*) intakt; **not one window was left ~** kein einziges Fenster blieb ganz *or* heil; **his confidence remained ~** sein Vertrauen blieb ungebrochen *or* unerschüttert

intake [ˈɪnteɪk] N **a** (= *act*) (*of water, electric current*) Aufnahme *f*; (*of steam*) Ansaugen *nt*; (= *amount*) (*of water, electricity*) Aufnahme *f*, aufgenommene Menge; (*of steam*) angesaugte *or* einströmende Menge; (= *pipe*) (*for water*) Zuflussrohr *nt*, Einführungsrohr *nt*; (*for steam*) Einströmungsöffnung *f*, Ansaugöffnung *f*, Einführungsrohr *nt*; *food* ~ Nahrungsaufnahme *f*; **(sharp) ~ of breath** (plötzlicher) Atemzug **b** (*Sch, of immigrants*) Aufnahme *f*; (*Mil*) Rekrutierung *f*; **what is your annual ~?** (*Sch*) wie viele neue Schüler nehmen Sie im Jahr auf?; (*Mil*) wie viele Soldaten rekrutieren Sie im Jahr?; **the latest ~ of graduates into our company** die Hochschulabsolventen, die kürzlich in unserer Firma eingestellt worden sind

intake: intake class N (*Sch*) Anfängerklasse *f*; **intake valve** N Einlassventil *nt*; (= *suction valve*) Ansaugventil *nt*

intangible [ɪnˈtændʒəbl] ADJ **a** nicht greifbar **b** *fears, longings* unbestimmt **c** (*Jur, Comm*) ~ **property** immaterielle Güter *pl*; ~ **capital** immaterielles Kapital

intangible assets PL (*Jur, Comm*) immaterielle Werte *pl*

intarsia [ɪnˈtɑːsɪə] PL Intarsien *pl*, Einlegearbeiten *pl*

integer [ˈɪntɪdʒə] N ganze Zahl

integral [ˈɪntɪɡrəl] ADJ **a** *part* wesentlich, integral (*geh*); **to be ~ to sth** ein wesentlicher Bestandteil einer Sache (*gen*) sein; **to play an ~ role in sth** eine wesentliche Rolle bei etw spielen **b** (= *whole*) vollständig, vollkommen **c** (*Math*) Integral- **N** (*Math*) Integral *nt*

integral calculus N (*Math*) Integralrechnung *f*

integrate [ˈɪntɪɡreɪt] VT integrieren; **to ~ sb into** *or* **with sth** jdn in etw (*acc*) integrieren; **to ~ sth into sth** etw in etw (*acc*) integrieren; **to ~ sth with sth** etw auf etw (*acc*) abstimmen; **to ~ a school/college** (*US*) eine Schule/ein College auch für Schwarze *etc* zugänglich machen **VI** (*US: schools etc*) auch für Schwarze *etc* zugänglich werden

integrated [ˈɪntɪɡreɪtɪd] ADJ integriert; *plan* einheitlich; *piece of work* einheitlich, ein organisches Ganzes bildend; *school, town* ohne Rassentrennung; **an ~ whole** ein integriertes Ganzes; **a fully ~ personality** eine in sich ausgewogene Persönlichkeit

integrated circuit N integrierter Schaltkreis

integration [ˌɪntɪˈɡreɪʃən] N Integration *f* (*into* in +*acc*); **(racial) ~** Rassenintegration *f*

integrationist [ˌɪntɪˈɡreɪʃənɪst] N (*US*) Vertreter(in) *m(f)* der Rassenintegration

integrity [ɪnˈteɡrɪtɪ] N **a** (= *honesty*) Integrität *f* **b** (= *wholeness*) Einheit *f*

integument [ɪnˈteɡjʊmənt] N Integument *nt* (*spec*)

intellect [ˈɪntɪlekt] N **a** Intellekt *m*; **a man of keen ~** ein Mensch *m* mit einem scharfen Intellekt; **his powers of ~** seine intellektuellen Fähigkeiten **b** (= *person*) großer Geist

intellectual [ˌɪntɪˈlektjʊəl] ADJ intellektuell; *freedom, climate, property, activity, interests* geistig; **something a little more ~** etwas geistig Anspruchsvolleres **N** Intellektuelle(r) *mf*

intellectualism [ˌɪntɪˈlektjʊəlɪzəm] N Intellektualismus *m*

intellectualize [ˌɪntɪˈlektjʊəlaɪz] VT intellektualisieren **VI** **you always have to ~** du musst immer alles verstandesgemäß angehen, bei dir muss immer alles über den Kopf gehen (*inf*)

intellectually [ˌɪntɪˈlektjʊəlɪ] ADV intellektuell; **~ demanding work** intellektuell anspruchsvolle Arbeit; **he always approaches emotional problems much too ~** er geht an Gefühlsprobleme immer viel zu verstandesmäßig heran

intellectual: intellectual power N Verstandes- *or* Geisteskraft *f*; **intellectual property rights** PL (*Jur*) Urheberrecht *nt*; **intellectual worker** N Kopfarbeiter(in) *m(f)*

intelligence [ɪnˈtelɪdʒəns] N **a** Intelligenz *f*; **a man of little ~** ein Mensch von geringer Intelligenz; **if he hasn't got the ~ to wear a coat** wenn er nicht gescheit genug ist, einen Mantel anzuziehen **b** (= *news, information*) Informationen *pl*; **according to our latest ~** unseren letzten Meldungen *or* Informationen zufolge **c** (*Mil etc*) Geheim- *or* Nachrichtendienst *m*

intelligence: intelligence corps N (*Mil*) Geheim- *or* Nachrichtendienst *m*; **intelligence officer** N (*Mil*) Nachrichtenoffizier(in) *m(f)*; **intelligence quotient** N Intelligenzquotient *m*; **intelligence service** N (*Pol*) Geheim- *or* Nachrichtendienst *m*; **intelligence test** N Intelligenztest *m*

intelligent [ɪnˈtelɪdʒənt] ADJ intelligent; **are there ~ beings on Mars?** gibt es auf dem Mars vernunftbegabte *or* intelligente Lebewesen?

intelligently [ɪnˈtelɪdʒəntlɪ] ADV intelligent

intelligentsia [ɪnˌtelɪˈdʒentsɪə] N Intelligenz *f*, Intelligenzija *f*

intelligibility [ɪnˌtelɪdʒəˈbɪlɪtɪ] N Verständlichkeit *f*; (*of handwriting*) Leserlichkeit *f*

intelligible [ɪnˈtelɪdʒəbl] ADJ zu verstehen *pred*, verständlich (*to sb* für jdn); **in (an) ~ form** in verständlicher Form

intelligibly [ɪnˈtelɪdʒəblɪ] ADV deutlich

intemperance [ɪnˈtempərəns] N (= *lack of moderation*) Maßlosigkeit *f*, Unmäßigkeit *f*; (= *drunkenness*) Trunksucht *f*

intemperate [ɪnˈtempərɪt] ADJ **a** *person* (= *lacking moderation*) unmäßig, maßlos; (= *addicted to drink*) trunksüchtig **b** *climate* extrem; *wind* heftig; *zeal, haste* übermäßig **c** *language, comment* ausfallend, unbeherrscht

intend [ɪnˈtend] ◎ 8.1, 8.2, 8.3 VT **a** (+*n*) beabsichtigen, wollen; **I ~ him to go with me, I ~ that he should go with me** ich beabsichtige *or* habe vor, ihn mitzunehmen; (= *insist*) er soll mit mir mitkommen; **I ~ed no harm** es war (von mir) nicht böse gemeint; (*with action*) ich hatte nichts Böses beabsichtigt; **did you ~ that?** hatten Sie das beabsichtigt?, war das Ihre Absicht?; **I didn't ~ it as an insult** das sollte keine Beleidigung sein; **it was ~ed as a compliment** das sollte ein Kompliment sein; **I wondered what he ~ed by that remark** ich fragte mich, was er mit dieser Bemerkung beabsichtigte; **he is ~ed for the diplomatic service** er soll einmal in den diplomatischen Dienst; **this park is ~ed for the general public** dieser Park ist für die Öffentlichkeit gedacht *or* bestimmt; **that remark was ~ed for you** diese Bemerkung war auf Sie gemünzt, mit dieser Bemerkung waren Sie gemeint; **games ~ed for young children** Spiele, die für kleine Kinder gedacht sind; **it was ~ed that he should become an accountant** er sollte eigentlich Buchhalter werden

b (+vb) beabsichtigen, fest vorhaben; **he ~s to win** er hat fest vor zu gewinnen; **I ~ to leave next year** ich beabsichtige or habe vor, nächstes Jahr zu gehen; **if you don't change your mind I ~ to leave you!** wenn du es dir nicht anders überlegst, verlasse ich dich!; **what do you ~ to do about it?** was beabsichtigen Sie, dagegen zu tun?; **I fully ~ to punish him** ich habe fest vor or bin fest entschlossen, ihn zu bestrafen; **this is ~ed to help me** das soll mir helfen; **did you ~ that to happen?** hatten Sie das beabsichtigt?

intendant [ɪn'tendənt] N Intendant(in) m(f)

intended [ɪn'tendɪd] **ADJ a** effect beabsichtigt, geplant; victim ausgeguckt; target anvisiert; **what is the ~ meaning of that remark?** was ist mit dieser Bemerkung gemeint? **b** husband, wife zukünftig, in spe pred **N** my ~ (inf) mein Zukünftiger (inf), meine Zukünftige (inf)

intendment [ɪn'tendmənt] N (Jur) wahre Bedeutung; **~ of the law** gesetzgeberische Absicht

intense [ɪn'tens] ADJ **a** pain, colour, activity intensiv; disappointment bitter, schmerzlich; pressure, interest, enthusiasm enorm; joy, effort riesig; heat, cold ungeheuer; desire brennend; competition, fighting, debate, speculation heftig; hatred, jealousy, anger rasend **b** person ernsthaft; conversation, relationship, feeling, study, life intensiv; **he suddenly looked very ~** er sah plötzlich ganz ernst aus

intensely [ɪn'tenslɪ] ADV **a** (= extremely) cold, hot, disappointed, irritated, difficult äußerst; ~ **flavoured** intensiv gewürzt; **an ~ competitive business** eine Branche mit äußerst scharfer Konkurrenz; **I dislike it ~** ich kann es absolut nicht ausstehen **b** (= with strong emotion, hard) feel, live, stare, work, study intensiv; **he spoke so ~ that none could doubt his sincerity** er sprach mit einer solchen Intensität, dass niemand an seiner Aufrichtigkeit zweifeln konnte

intenseness [ɪn'tensnɪs] N = **intensity**

intensification [ɪn,tensɪfɪ'keɪʃən] N Intensivierung f; (Phot) Verstärkung f

intensifier [ɪn'tensɪfaɪə'] N (Gram) Verstärkungspartikel f; **image ~** (Phys) Bildverstärker m

intensify [ɪn'tensɪfaɪ] **VT** intensivieren; meaning, fears verstärken; conflict, competition verschärfen **VI** zunehmen; (pain, heat also) stärker werden; (fighting also) sich verschärfen

intension [ɪn'tenʃən] N (Philos: of a concept) Intension f, Inhalt m

intensity [ɪn'tensɪtɪ] N Intensität f; (of feeling, storm also) Heftigkeit f; **~ of a negative** (Phot) Dichte f eines Negativs

intensive [ɪn'tensɪv] ADJ intensiv, Intensiv-; **to be in ~ care** (Med) auf der Intensivstation sein; **~ care unit** Intensivstation f; **they came under ~ fire** sie kamen unter heftigen Beschuss

intensively [ɪn'tensɪvlɪ] ADV intensiv; **~ reared beef** aus Intensivhaltung stammendes Rindfleisch

intent [ɪn'tent] **N** Absicht f; **with good ~** in guter Absicht; **to all ~s and purposes** im Grunde; **with ~ to** (esp Jur) in der Absicht or mit dem Vorsatz zu; **to do sth with ~** etw vorsätzlich tun; **letter of ~** (schriftliche) Willenserklärung → **loiter**

ADJ a look durchdringend, forschend **b** **to be ~ on achieving sth** fest entschlossen sein, etw zu erreichen; **they were ~ on winning** sie wollten unbedingt gewinnen; **she is ~ on a comeback** sie hat die feste Absicht, ein Comeback zu machen; **he was so ~ on catching the bus that he didn't notice the lorry coming** er war so darauf bedacht, den Bus zu erreichen, dass er den Lastwagen nicht kommen sah; **to be ~ on one's work** auf seine Arbeit konzentriert sein

intention [ɪn'tenʃən] ✪ 8.2, 8.3 N **a** Absicht f, Intention f; **what was your ~ in publishing the article?** mit welcher Absicht haben Sie den Artikel veröffentlicht?; **it is my ~ to punish you severely** ich beabsichtige, Sie streng zu bestrafen; **I have every ~ of doing it** ich habe die feste Absicht, das zu tun; **to have no ~ of doing sth** nicht die Absicht haben, etw zu tun; **I have no or I haven't the least or the slightest ~ of staying!** ich habe nicht die geringste Absicht hier zu bleiben, ich denke nicht daran hier zu bleiben; **with good ~s** mit guten Vorsätzen; **with the best of ~s** in der besten Absicht; **with the ~ of ...** in der Absicht zu ..., mit dem Vorsatz zu ...; **his ~s are good, but he seldom carries them out** er hat immer gute Vorsätze pl, aber er führt sie selten aus

b ~s (inf) (Heirats)absichten pl; **his ~s are honourable** er hat ehrliche Absichten

intentional [ɪn'tenʃənl] ADJ absichtlich, vorsätzlich (esp Jur); **it wasn't ~** das war keine Absicht, es war unabsichtlich

intentionally [ɪn'tenʃnəlɪ] ADV absichtlich

intently [ɪn'tentlɪ] ADV listen, gaze, talk konzentriert

inter [ɪn'tɜː'] VT (form) bestatten

inter- ['ɪntə-] PREF zwischen-, Zwischen-; (esp with foreign words) inter-, Inter-; **interpersonal** zwischenmenschlich; **interdisciplinary** interdisziplinär

interact [,ɪntər'ækt] VI aufeinander wirken; (Phys) wechselwirken; (Psych, Sociol) interagieren

interaction [,ɪntər'ækʃən] N gegenseitige Einwirkung; (Phys) Wechselwirkung f; (Psych, Sociol) Interaktion f

interactive [,ɪntər'æktɪv] ADJ interaktiv; **~ television** ineraktives Fernsehen

inter alia ['ɪntər'eɪlɪə] ADV unter anderem

interbank ['ɪntə'bæŋk] ADJ (Fin) **~ deposits** Bank-bei-Bank-Einlagen pl; **~ loan** Bank-an--Bank-Kredit m

interbreed ['ɪntə'briːd] **VT** kreuzen **VI** (= inbreed) sich untereinander vermehren; (= crossbreed) sich kreuzen

intercalary [ɪn'tɜːkələrɪ] ADJ Schalt-; **~ day** Schalttag m

intercede [,ɪntə'siːd] VI sich einsetzen, sich verwenden (with bei, for, on behalf of für); (in argument) vermitteln

intercellular [,ɪntə'seljʊlə'] ADJ interzellular

intercept [,ɪntə'sept] VT message, person, plane, pass abfangen; (Math) abschneiden; **they ~ed the enemy** sie schnitten dem Feind den Weg ab

interception [,ɪntə'sepʃən] N (of message, person, plane etc) Abfangen nt; (Math) Abschneiden nt; **point of ~** (Math) Schnittpunkt m

interceptor [,ɪntə'septə'] N (Aviat) Abfangjäger m

intercession [,ɪntə'seʃən] N Fürsprache f; (in argument) Vermittlung f

interchange ['ɪntə'tʃeɪndʒ] **N a** (of roads) Kreuzung f; (of motorways) (Autobahn)kreuz nt **b** (= exchange) Austausch m **VT** [,ɪntə'tʃeɪndʒ] **a** (= switch round) (miteinander) vertauschen, (aus)tauschen **b** ideas etc austauschen (with mit)

interchangeable [,ɪntə'tʃeɪndʒəbl] ADJ austauschbar; **the front wheels are ~ with the back ones** Vorder- und Hinterräder sind austauschbar

interchangeably [,ɪntə'tʃeɪndʒəblɪ] ADV austauschbar; **they are used ~** sie können ausgetauscht werden

intercity [,ɪntə'sɪtɪ] ADJ Intercity-; **~ train** Intercityzug m

intercollegiate ['ɪntəkə'liːdʒɪɪt] ADJ zwischen Colleges

intercom ['ɪntəkɒm] N (Gegen)sprechanlage f; (in ship, plane) Bordverständigungsanlage f; (in schools etc) Lautsprecheranlage f

intercommunicate [,ɪntəkə'mjuːnɪkeɪt] VI (departments, people) miteinander in Verbindung stehen; (rooms) miteinander verbunden sein

intercommunication ['ɪntəkə,mjuːnɪ'keɪʃən] N gegenseitige Verbindung, Verbindung f untereinander

intercommunion [,ɪntəkə'mjuːnɪən] N Beziehungen pl

interconnect [,ɪntəkə'nekt] **VT** miteinander verbinden; loudspeakers, circuits also zusammenschalten; **~ed problems/events etc** zusammenhängende Probleme/Ereignisse etc; **are these events ~ed in any way?** besteht irgendein Zusammenhang zwischen diesen Vorfällen?; **to be ~ed by sth** durch etw (miteinander) verbunden sein **VI** miteinander verbunden sein; (facts, events) in Zusammenhang stehen; **to ~ with sth** mit etw verbunden sein/in Zusammenhang stehen; **~ing rooms** miteinander verbundene Zimmer pl

interconnection [,ɪntəkə'nekʃən] N Verbindung f; (of circuits etc) Zusammenschaltung f; (of facts, events etc) Verbindung f, Zusammenhang m

intercontinental ['ɪntə,kɒntɪ'nentl] ADJ interkontinental, Interkontinental-; **~ ballistic missile** ballistische Interkontinentalrakete f

intercourse ['ɪntəkɔːs] N **a** Verkehr m; **commercial ~** Handelsbeziehungen pl; **human ~** Verkehr m mit Menschen; **social ~** gesellschaftlicher Verkehr **b** (sexual) ~ (Geschlechts)verkehr m; **anal ~** Analverkehr m; **did ~ take place?** hat (Geschlechts)verkehr or Beischlaf stattgefunden?

intercross [,ɪntə'krɒs] (Biol) **VT** animals, plants kreuzen **VI** sich kreuzen **N** ['ɪntəkrɒs] (crossbreeding) Kreuzen nt; (hybrid) Kreuzung

intercut [,ɪntə'kʌt] VT **to be ~ with** (film) zwischengeschnitten sein mit, mit Zwischenschnitten von ... versehen sein

interdenominational ['ɪntədɪ,nɒmɪ'neɪʃənl] ADJ interkonfessionell

interdepartmental ['ɪntə,diːpɑːt'mentl] ADJ relations, quarrel zwischen den Abteilungen; conference, projects mehrere Abteilungen betreffend; committee abteilungsübergreifend

interdependence [,ɪntədɪ'pendəns] N wechselseitige Abhängigkeit, Interdependenz f (geh)

interdependent [,ɪntədɪ'pendənt] ADJ wechselseitig voneinander abhängig, interdependent (geh)

interdict ['ɪntədɪkt] **VT a** (Jur) untersagen, verbieten **b** (Eccl) person, place mit dem Interdikt belegen; priest suspendieren **c** (Mil, = intercept) plane, supplies abfangen **N a** (Jur) Verbot nt **b** (Eccl) Interdikt nt

interdiction [,ɪntə'dɪkʃən] N (Jur) Verbot nt, Untersagung f; (Eccl) Interdikt nt

interest ['ɪntrɪst] ✪ 2.2, 7.5 N **a** Interesse nt; **do you have any ~ in chess?** interessieren Sie sich für Schach?, haben Sie Interesse an Schach (dat)?; **to take/feel an ~ in sb/sth** sich für jdn/etw interessieren; **after that he took no further ~ in us/it** danach war er nicht mehr an uns (dat)/daran interessiert; **to show (an) ~ in sb/sth** Interesse für jdn/etw zeigen; **is it of ~ to you?** (= do you want it?) sind Sie daran interessiert?; **just for ~** nur aus Interesse, nur interessehalber; **he has lost ~** er hat das Interesse verloren; **what are your ~s?** was sind Ihre Interessen(gebiete)?; **his ~s are ...** er interessiert sich für ...

b (= importance) Interesse nt (to für); **matters of vital ~ to the economy** Dinge pl von lebenswichtiger Bedeutung or lebenswichtigem Interesse für die Wirtschaft

c (= advantage, welfare) Interesse nt; **to act in sb's/one's own (best) ~(s)** in jds/im eigenen Interesse handeln; **in the ~(s) of sb** in jds Interesse (dat); **in the ~(s) of sth** im Interesse einer Sache (gen); **the public ~** das öffentliche Wohl; **in the public ~** im öffentlichen Interesse

d (Fin) Zinsen pl; **~ on an investment** Zinsen aus einer Kapitalanlage; **rate of ~** Zinssatz m;

to bear ~ at 4% 4% Zinsen tragen, mit 4% verzinst sein; **to repay a loan with ~** ein Darlehen mit Zins und Zinseszins zurückzahlen; **to return sb's kindness with ~** (fig) jds Freundlichkeit vielfach erwidern; **I'll pay him back with ~** (fig) ich werde es ihm mit Zinsen heimzahlen **e** (Comm, = share, stake) Anteil m; (= interest group) Kreise pl, Interessentengruppe f; **shipping/oil ~s** (= shares) Reederei-/Ölanteile pl; (= people) Reedereikreise pl/Vertreter pl von Ölinteressen; **the landed ~(s)** die Landbesitzer pl, die Gutsbesitzer pl; **he has a financial ~ in the company** er ist finanziell an der Firma beteiligt; **British trading ~s** britische Handelsinteressen pl; **German ~s in Africa** deutsche Interessen pl in Afrika; **America has an ~ in helping Russia with its economy** Amerika hat ein Interesse daran, Russland Wirtschaftshilfe zu geben **VT** interessieren (in für, an +dat); **to ~ sb in doing sth** jdn dafür interessieren, etw zu tun; **can I ~ you in a drink?** kann ich Sie zu etwas Alkoholischem überreden?; **to ~ sb in politics** etc jds Interesse an or für Politik etc wecken, jdn für Politik etc interessieren; **to ~ oneself in sb/sth** sich für jdn/etw interessieren

interest: interest account N Zinsenkonto nt; **interest-bearing** ['ɪntrɪst,bɛərɪŋ] ADJ loan verzinslich; account, investment mit Zinsertrag, zinsbringend; **interest coupon** N Zinsabschnitt m, Zinsschein m

interested ['ɪntrɪstɪd] ADJ **a** interessiert (in an +dat); **I'm not ~** das interessiert mich nicht; **... and I'm not even ~ either** ... und es interessiert mich auch gar nicht; **to be ~ in sb/sth** sich für jdn/etw interessieren, an jdm/etw interessiert sein; **would you be ~ in a game of cards?** hätten Sie Interesse, Karten zu spielen?; **I'm going to the cinema, are you ~ (in coming)?** ich gehe ins Kino, haben Sie Interesse daran or Lust mitzukommen?; **I'm selling my car, are you ~?** ich verkaufe meinen Wagen, sind Sie interessiert?; **the company is ~ in expanding its sales** die Firma hat Interesse daran or ist daran interessiert, ihren Absatz zu vergrößern; **I'd be ~ to know how ...** es würde mich ja schon interessieren, wie ...; **she was ~ to see what he would do** sie war gespannt, was er wohl tun würde; **I was ~ to hear that** es interessierte mich, das zu hören; **to get sb ~ (in sth)** jdn (für etw) interessieren **b** (= having personal or financial interest) befangen; (= involved) beteiligt; **he is an ~ party** er ist befangen, er ist daran beteiligt

interest: interest-free ADJ, ADV zinslos, zinsfrei; **interest group** N Interessengruppe f

interesting ['ɪntrɪstɪŋ] ADJ interessant; **the ~ thing about it is that ...** das Interessante daran ist, dass ...; **she's in an ~ condition** (euph) sie ist in anderen Umständen

interestingly ['ɪntrɪstɪŋlɪ] ADV auf interessante Weise; **~ enough, I saw him yesterday** interessanterweise habe ich ihn gestern gesehen

interest: interest instalment, (US) **interest installment** N Zinsrate f; **interest rate** N (Fin) Zinssatz m; **interest statement** N Zinsaufstellung f

interface ['ɪntəfeɪs] **N a** Grenzfläche f, Grenzschicht f; **there's a bigger ~ between these two fields than I thought** diese beiden Gebiete haben mehr Berührungspunkte, als ich gedacht hätte **b** (Comput) Schnittstelle f, Interface nt **VT** [ɪntə'feɪs] koppeln **VI** [ɪntə'feɪs] **to ~ with sth** Berührungspunkte mit etw haben

interfacing ['ɪntəfeɪsɪŋ] N (Sew) Einlage f

interfere [ˌɪntə'fɪə] VI **a** (= meddle) (in argument, sb's affairs) sich einmischen (in in +acc); (with machinery, sb's property) sich zu schaffen machen (with an +dat); (euph: sexually) sich vergehen (with an +dat); **don't ~ with the machine** lass die Finger von der Maschine; **who's been interfering with my books?** wer war an meinen Büchern?; **the body has been ~d with** jemand hatte sich an der Leiche zu schaffen gemacht; (sexually) die Leiche zeigte Spuren eines Sexualverbrechens

b (thing, event: = disrupt, obstruct) **to ~ with sth** etw stören (also Rad); with work, ability to do sth etw beeinträchtigen; **to ~ with sb's plans** jds Pläne durchkreuzen

interference [ˌɪntə'fɪərəns] N **a** (= meddling) Einmischung f; **I don't want any ~ with my books/papers** ich will nicht, dass jemand an meine Bücher/Papiere geht **b** (= disruption, Rad, TV) Störung f (with +gen)

interfering [ˌɪntə'fɪərɪŋ] ADJ person sich ständig einmischend; **his ~ ways annoy me** es ärgert or stört mich, wie er sich immer einmischt; **don't be so ~** misch dich nicht immer ein

interferon [ˌɪntə'fɪərɒn] N (Chem) Interferon nt

interfuse [ˌɪntə'fjuːz] **VT** (poet, liter) (= pervade) durchdringen, durchsetzen; (= mix) (ver)mischen **VI** sich (ver)mischen, sich (miteinander) vermischen

intergalactic [ˌɪntəgə'læktɪk] ADJ intergalaktisch

interim ['ɪntərɪm] **N** Zwischenzeit f, Interim nt (geh); **in the ~** in der Zwischenzeit **ADJ** vorläufig; **~ agreement/solution** Übergangsabkommen nt/-lösung f; **~ report** Zwischenbericht m; **~ government/president** Interims- or Übergangsregierung f/-präsident(in) m(f); **~ period** Zwischenzeit f; (= transitional) Übergangszeit f; **~ payment** Interimszahlung f

interim dividend N Abschlagsdividende f, Zwischendividende f

interim financing N Zwischenfinanzierung f

interior [ɪn'tɪərɪə] **ADJ a** (= inside) Innen-; **~ wall** Innenwand f; **~ space** Innenraum m; **~ light** (Aut) Innenraumbeleuchtung f **b** (Pol) **~ minister** Innenminister(in) m(f); **~ ministry** Innenministerium nt **c** the ~ **region(s)** of a country) das Landesinnere **N** (of country) Innere(s) nt; (Art) Interieur nt; (of house) Innenausstattung f, Interieur nt (geh); (Phot) Innenaufnahme f; **deep in the ~** tief im Landesinneren; **Department of the Interior** (US) Innenministerium nt; **the ~ of the house has been newly decorated** das Haus ist innen neu gemacht

interior: interior angle N Innenwinkel m; **interior decoration** N Innenausstattung f; (= decor also) Interieur nt; **interior decorator** N Innenausstatter(in) m(f); **interior design** N Innenarchitektur f; **interior designer** N Innenarchitekt(in) m(f); **interior monologue** N innerer Monolog; **interior-sprung** ADJ Federkern-; **~ mattress** Federkernmatratze f

interject [ˌɪntə'dʒekt] VT remark, question einwerfen; **..., he ~ed** ..., rief er dazwischen

interjection [ˌɪntə'dʒekʃən] N (= exclamation) Ausruf m; (Ling also) Interjektion f; (= remark) Einwurf m

interlace [ˌɪntə'leɪs] **VT** threads etc verflechten; (in cloth also) verweben; cloth (with thread) durchwirken; fingers verschlingen; (fig) scenes, styles verflechten **VI** sich ineinander verflechten; (twigs) verschlungen sein

interlacing [ˌɪntə'leɪsɪŋ] **ADJ** verflochten; branches also verschlungen **N** Flechtwerk nt

interlanguage ['ɪntə,læŋgwɪdʒ] N Verkehrssprache f

interlard [ˌɪntə'lɑːd] VT **to ~ a speech with facetious comments** witzige Kommentare in eine Rede einflechten; **a speech ~ed with jokes** eine mit Witzen gespickte Rede

interleaf [ˌɪntə'liːf] N leeres Zwischenblatt

interleave [ˌɪntə'liːv] VT mit Zwischenblättern versehen, durchschießen (spec)

interlibrary loan ['ɪntə,laɪbrəri'ləʊn] N Fernleihe f; **to have a book on ~** ein Buch über die Fernleihe (ausgeliehen) haben

interline [ˌɪntə'laɪn] VT **a** (Typ) corrections, translation interlinear einfügen **b** (Sew) mit einer Einlage versehen

interlinear [ˌɪntə'lɪnɪə] ADJ Interlinear-, interlinear; **~ version** Interlinearversion f

interlink [ˌɪntə'lɪŋk] **VT** ineinander hängen; (fig) theories etc miteinander verknüpfen or verbinden **VI** ineinander hängen; (fig: theories etc) zu-

sammenhängen; **a transport network with bus and rail services ~ing** ein Verkehrsnetz nt, in dem Bus und Bahn im Verbund fahren

interlock [ˌɪntə'lɒk] **VT** (fest) zusammenstecken, (fest) ineinander stecken **VI** ineinander greifen; (one piece) fest stecken or sitzen (with in +dat); (chariot wheels etc) sich verfangen; (antlers) sich verhaken, sich verfangen; (fig: destinies) verkettet sein

interlocutor [ˌɪntə'lɒkjʊtə] N Gesprächspartner(in) m(f); (asking questions) Fragesteller(in) m(f)

interloper ['ɪntələʊpə] N Eindringling m

interlude ['ɪntəluːd] N **a** Periode f; (Theat) (= interval) Pause f; (= performance) Zwischenspiel nt; (Mus) Interludium nt; (= episode) Intermezzo nt, Episode f; **a peaceful ~ in his busy life** eine friedliche Unterbrechung seines geschäftigen Lebens

intermarriage [ˌɪntə'mærɪdʒ] N (between groups) Mischehen pl; (within the group) Heirat f untereinander

intermarry [ˌɪntə'mærɪ] VI (= marry within the group) untereinander heiraten; (two groups: = marry with each other) sich durch Heirat vermischen, Mischehen eingehen; **they were not allowed to ~ with another tribe** sie durften keine Mischehen mit einem anderen Stamm eingehen

intermediary [ˌɪntə'miːdɪərɪ] **N** (Ver)mittler(in) m(f), Mittelsperson f, Mittelsmann m **ADJ** (= intermediate) mittlere(r, s); (= mediating) vermittelnd; **~ role** Vermittlerrolle f

intermediate [ˌɪntə'miːdɪət] **ADJ** Zwischen-; French, maths etc für fortgeschrittene Anfänger; **~ position** Zwischenposition f; **~ stage** Zwischenstadium nt; **the ~ stations** die dazwischenliegenden Bahnhöfe; **~ step** Zwischenstufe f; **an ~ student** ein fortgeschrittener Anfänger, eine fortgeschrittene Anfängerin; **~ range ballistic missile** ballistische Mittelstreckenrakete f; **~ goods** (Econ, = semi-finished) Halbfabrikate pl; **~ treatment** (Brit) Sozialprogramm für jugendliche Straftäter und sozial gefährdete Jugendliche, das weder Inhaftierung noch Bestrafung beinhaltet **N** fortgeschrittener Anfänger, fortgeschrittene Anfängerin

interment [ɪn'tɜːmənt] N Beerdigung f, Bestattung f

intermezzo [ˌɪntə'metsəʊ] N Intermezzo nt

interminable [ɪn'tɜːmɪnəbl] ADJ endlos; **after what seemed an ~ journey** nach einer Reise, die nicht enden zu wollen schien

interminably [ɪn'tɜːmɪnəblɪ] ADV endlos, ewig

intermingle [ˌɪntə'mɪŋgl] **VT** vermischen **VI** sich mischen (with unter +acc); **people from many countries ~d at the conference** Menschen aus vielen Ländern bekamen bei der Konferenz Kontakt miteinander

intermission [ˌɪntə'mɪʃən] N **a** Unterbrechung f, Pause f **b** (Theat, Film) Pause f

intermittent [ˌɪntə'mɪtənt] ADJ periodisch auftretend; (Tech) intermittierend

intermittent fever N Wechselfieber nt

intermittently [ˌɪntə'mɪtntlɪ] ADV periodisch; (Tech) intermittierend; **the patient was only ~ conscious** der Patient war nur zeitweise bei Bewusstsein

intermix [ˌɪntə'mɪks] **VT** vermischen **VI** sich vermischen

intern[1] [ɪn'tɜːn] VT person internieren; ship etc festhalten

intern[2] ['ɪntɜːn] (US) **N a** (= junior doctor) Assistenzarzt m/-ärztin f **b** (= trainee) Praktikant(in) m(f) **VI** das Medizinalpraktikum absolvieren

internal [ɪn'tɜːnl] ADJ (= inner) innere(r, s); (Math) angle, diameter Innen-; (= within country) Binnen-, im Inland; (= within organization) policy, debate, investigation, mail, examination intern; **~ examiner** (Univ) interner Prüfer, interne Prüferin; **~ flight** Inlandsflug m; **Internal Revenue**

Service (*US*) Steueramt *nt*, Finanzamt *nt*; ~ **trade** Binnenhandel *m*; ~ **telephone** Haustelefon *nt*; ~ **wall** Innenwand *f*

internal: internal affairs PL innere Angelegenheiten *pl*, Inneres *nt*; **internal bleeding** N innere Blutungen *pl*; **internal combustion engine** N Verbrennungsmotor *m*

internalize [ɪnˈtɜːnəlaɪz] VT verinnerlichen, internalisieren (*spec*)

internally [ɪnˈtɜːnəlɪ] ADV innen, im Inneren; (= *in body*) innerlich; (= *in country*) landesintern; (= *in organization*) intern; **he is bleeding** ~ er hat innere Blutungen; **"not to be taken ~"** „nicht zur inneren Anwendung", „nicht zum Einnehmen"

internal: internal market N (*Econ*) Binnenmarkt *m*; (*in health service etc, within organization*) marktwirtschaftliche Struktur; **internal medicine** N innere Medizin; **internal revenue** N (*Econ*) Staatseinkünfte *pl*

international [ˌɪntəˈnæʃnəl] ADJ international; ~ **money order** Auslandsanweisung *f*; **International Olympic Committee** Internationales Olympisches Komitee; ~ **relations** internationale Beziehungen *pl* **N** **a** (*Sport*) (= *match*) Länderspiel *nt*; (= *player*) Nationalspieler(in) *m(f)* **b** (*Pol*) **International** Internationale *f*

International: International Bank for Reconstruction and Development N Internationale Bank für Wiederaufbau und Entwicklung; **International Court of Justice** N Internationaler Gerichtshof; **International Date Line** N Datumsgrenze *f*

Internationale [ˌɪntəˌnæʃəˈnɑːl] N Internationale *f*

internationalism [ˌɪntəˈnæʃnəlɪzəm] N Internationalismus *m*

internationalist [ˌɪntəˈnæʃnəlɪst] N Internationalist(in) *m(f)*

internationalize [ˌɪntəˈnæʃnəlaɪz] VT internationalisieren

International Labour Organization N Internationale Arbeitsorganisation

international law N Völkerrecht *nt*, internationales Recht

international lending N (*Fin*) internationaler Kreditverkehr

internationally [ˌɪntəˈnæʃnəlɪ] ADV international; *compete* auf internationaler Ebene

International Monetary Fund N (*Econ*) Internationaler Währungsfonds

International Phonetic Alphabet N internationale Lautschrift

International Standards Organization N Internationaler Normenausschuss

interne N, VI = **intern²**

internecine [ˌɪntəˈniːsaɪn] ADJ **a** (= *mutually destructive*) für beide Seiten verlustreich; (= *bloody*) mörderisch; ~ **war** gegenseitiger Vernichtungskrieg **b** (= *internal*) *quarrel, conflict* intern; ~ **strife** innere Zerrissenheit

internee [ˌɪntɜːˈniː] N Internierte(r) *mf*

Internet [ˈɪntənet] N **the** ~ das Internet; **to surf the** ~ im Internet surfen

Internet: Internet banking N Internetbanking *nt*; **Internet café** N Internet-Café *nt*; **Internet service provider** N Internet-Anbieter *m*

internist [ɪnˈtɜːnɪst] N (*US*) Internist(in) *m(f)*

internment [ɪnˈtɜːnmənt] N Internierung *f*; ~ **camp** Internierungslager *nt*

internship [ˈɪntɜːnʃɪp] N (*US*) **a** (*Med*) Medizinalpraktikum *nt* **b** (*as trainee*) Praktikum *nt*

internuncio [ˌɪntəˈnʌnsɪəʊ] N Internuntius *m*

interoperability [ˈɪntərˌɒpərəˈbɪlɪtɪ] N (*Comput*) Interoperabilität *f*

interparty [ˈɪntəˈpɑːtɪ] ADJ parteiübergreifend

interpenetrate [ˌɪntəˈpenɪtreɪt] VT durchdringen VI einander durchdringen

interplanetary [ˌɪntəˈplænɪtərɪ] ADJ interplanetar

interplay [ˈɪntəpleɪ] N Zusammenspiel *nt*

Interpol [ˈɪntəpɒl] N Interpol *f*

interpolate [ɪnˈtɜːpəleɪt] VT *remark* einwerfen; *matter into book etc* interpolieren, einfügen; (*Math*) interpolieren

interpolation [ɪnˌtɜːpəˈleɪʃən] N (*of remark*) Einwerfen *nt*; (= *remark made*) Einwurf *m*; (*in text*) Interpolation *f*, Einfügung *f*; (*Math*) Interpolation *f*

interpose [ˌɪntəˈpəʊz] VT **a** *object* dazwischenstellen/-legen; **to** ~ **sth between two things** etw zwischen zwei Dinge stellen/legen; **to be** ~**d between two things** zwischen zwei Dingen stehen/liegen; **to** ~ **oneself between two people** sich zwischen zwei Leute stellen **b** (= *interject*) *remark, question* einwerfen; *objection* vorbringen (*into* in +*dat*) VI (= *intervene*) eingreifen

interpret [ɪnˈtɜːprɪt] VT **a** (= *translate orally*) dolmetschen **b** (= *explain, understand*) auslegen, interpretieren; *omen, dream* deuten; *world* verstehen; (*Theat, Mus*) interpretieren; **this could be ~ed as meaning** *or* **to mean that ...** das könnte man so auslegen *or* interpretieren, dass ...; **how would you ~ what he said?** wie würden Sie seine Worte verstehen *or* auffassen? VI dolmetschen

interpretation [ɪnˌtɜːprɪˈteɪʃən] N **a** (= *explanation*) Auslegung *f*, Interpretation *f*; (*of omen, dream*) Deutung *f*; (*of world*) Verständnis *nt*; (*Theat, Mus*) Interpretation *f*; **she put quite a different ~ on the figures** sie legte die Zahlen ganz anders aus, sie interpretierte die Zahlen ganz anders; **the speech can be given several ~s** die Rede kann verschieden ausgelegt *or* interpretiert werden; **an ~ of a poem** eine Gedichtinterpretation **b** (*Admin*: = *interpreting*) Dolmetschen *nt*

interpretative [ɪnˈtɜːprɪtətɪv] ADJ interpretierend

interpreter [ɪnˈtɜːprɪtə˙] N **a** Dolmetscher(in) *m(f)*; (*Theat, Mus*) Interpret(in) *m(f)*; (*of dreams*) Traumdeuter(in) *m(f)* **b** (*Comput*) Interpreter *m*

interpreting [ɪnˈtɜːprɪtɪŋ] N (= *profession*) Dolmetschen *nt*

interpretive [ɪnˈtɜːprɪtɪv] ADJ = **interpretative**

interracial [ˌɪntəˈreɪʃəl] ADJ (= *between races*) zwischen den *or* verschiedenen Rassen; (= *multiracial*) gemischtrassig

interregnum [ˌɪntəˈregnəm] N *pl* **-s** *or* **interregna** [ˌɪntəˈregnə] Interregnum *nt*

interrelate [ˌɪntərɪˈleɪt] VT *two things* zueinander in Beziehung bringen, eine Beziehung herstellen zwischen (+*dat*); **to** ~ **one thing with another** eine Sache in Beziehung zu einer anderen bringen; **to be** ~**d** zueinander in Beziehung stehen, zusammenhängen; ~**d factors** zusammenhängende Faktoren *pl* VI zueinander in Beziehung stehen, zusammenhängen; **this influences the way in which we** ~ **with others** das beeinflusst unsere Beziehungen zu anderen

interrelation [ˌɪntərɪˈleɪʃən] N Beziehung *f* (*between* zwischen +*dat*); (*between factors, events*) Zusammenhang *m* (*between* zwischen +*dat*)

interrogate [ɪnˈterəgeɪt] VT verhören; (*father, headmaster etc*) regelrecht verhören

interrogation [ɪnˌterəˈgeɪʃən] N Verhör *nt*; **to submit to** ~ sich verhören lassen; ~ **room** Vernehmungsraum *m or* -zimmer *nt*

interrogative [ˌɪntəˈrɒgətɪv] ADJ *look, tone* fragend; (*Gram*) Interrogativ-; ~ **pronoun/clause** Interrogativpronomen *nt*/-satz *m* **N** **a** (*Gram*) (= *pronoun*) Interrogativpronomen *nt*, Fragefürwort *nt*; (= *mood*) Interrogativ *m*, Frageform *f*; **in the** ~ in der Frageform

interrogatively [ˌɪntəˈrɒgətɪvlɪ] ADV fragend; (*Gram also*) interrogativ

interrogator [ɪnˈterəgeɪtə˙] N Vernehmungsbeamte(r) *mf* (*form*); **my/his ~s** die, die mich/ihn verhören

interrogatory [ˌɪntəˈrɒgətərɪ] ADJ fragend

interrupt [ˌɪntəˈrʌpt] VT (= *break the continuity of*) unterbrechen (*also Elec*); (*in conversation: rudely also*) ins Wort fallen (+*dat*); *activity, work also* stören; *traffic flow also* unterbrechen, stören; (= *obstruct*) *view* versperren; ~ **function** (*Comput*) Unterbrechungsfunktion *f* VI (*in conversation*) unterbrechen, (= *interrupt sb's work etc*) stören; **stop ~ing!** fall mir/ihm *etc* nicht dauernd ins Wort!

interrupter [ˌɪntəˈrʌptə˙] N (*Elec*) Unterbrecher *m*

interruption [ˌɪntəˈrʌpʃən] N Unterbrechung *f*; (*of work, activity, traffic flow also*) Störung *f*; (*of view*) Versperrung *f*; **without** ~ ohne Unterbrechung, ununterbrochen; **an** ~ **to her career** eine Unterbrechung ihrer Karriere

intersect [ˌɪntəˈsekt] VT durchschneiden; (*Geometry*) schneiden VI sich kreuzen; (*Geometry, in set theory*) sich schneiden; ~**ing sets** Schnittmengen *pl*

intersection [ˌɪntəˈsekʃən] N (= *crossroads*) Kreuzung *f*; (*Geometry*) Schnittpunkt *m*; **point of** ~ Schnittpunkt *m*

intersperse [ˌɪntəˈspɜːs] VT (= *scatter*) verteilen; ~**d with sth** mit etw dazwischen; **a speech** ~**d with quotations** eine mit Zitaten gespickte Rede; **periods of sunshine** ~**d with showers** von Schauern unterbrochener Sonnenschein; **boredom** ~**d with periods of ...** Langeweile und dazwischen *or* zwischendurch ...

interstate [ˌɪntəˈsteɪt] ADJ (*US*) zwischen den (US-Bundes)staaten, zwischenstaatlich; ~ **highway** (Bundes)autobahn *f*, Interstate Highway *m* **N** (*US*) (Bundes)autobahn *f*, Interstate (Highway) *m*

interstellar [ˌɪntəˈstelə˙] ADJ interstellar

interstice [ɪnˈtɜːstɪs] N Zwischenraum *m*; (*in wall etc also*) Sprung *m*, Riss *m*; (*between panels also*) Fuge *f*

intertextuality [ˈɪntəˌtekstjuːˈælɪtɪ] N (*Liter*) Intertextualität *f*

intertribal [ˌɪntəˈtraɪbl] ADJ zwischen den *or* verschiedenen Stämmen; ~ **war** Stammeskrieg *m*

intertwine [ˌɪntəˈtwaɪn] VT verschlingen; (*fig*) *destinies also* verknüpfen; *stories* verweben VI (*branches, arms etc*) sich ineinander verschlingen; (*threads*) verschlungen sein; (*fig: destinies*) sich verbinden

interurban [ˌɪntəˈɜːbən] ADJ (*US*) *railroad* städteverbindend

interval [ˈɪntəvəl] N **a** (*in space, time*) Abstand *m*, Intervall *nt* (*form*); **at** ~**s** in Abständen; **at two-weekly** ~**s** in Abständen von zwei Wochen; **at** ~**s of two metres** (*Brit*) *or* **meters** (*US*) in Abständen von zwei Metern; **sunny** ~**s** (*Met*) Aufheiterungen *pl* **b** (*Sch, Theat etc*) Pause *f* **c** (*Mus*) Intervall *nt*

intervene [ˌɪntəˈviːn] VI (*person*) einschreiten (*in* bei), intervenieren; (= *interrupt*) unterbrechen; (*event, fate*) dazwischenkommen; **if nothing ~s** wenn nichts dazwischenkommt

intervener [ˌɪntəˈviːnə˙] N Vermittler(in) *m(f)*; (*Jur*) Nebenintervenient(in) *m(f)*

intervening [ˌɪntəˈviːnɪŋ] ADJ *period of time, space* dazwischenliegend; **in the** ~ **weeks** in den Wochen dazwischen, in den dazwischenliegenden Wochen; **in the** ~ **period** in der Zwischenzeit

intervention [ˌɪntəˈvenʃən] N Eingreifen *nt*, Eingriff *m*, Intervention *f*

interventionist [ˌɪntəˈvenʃənɪst] N Interventionist(in) *m(f)* ADJ interventionistisch

intervertebral disc [ˈɪntəˌvɜːtɪbrəlˈdɪsk] N Bandscheibe *f*

interview [ˈɪntəvjuː] ✪ 19.3, 19.5 **N** **a** (*for job*) Vorstellungsgespräch *nt*; (*with authorities, employer etc*) Gespräch *nt*; (*for grant*) Auswahlgespräch *nt* **b** (*Press, TV etc*) Interview *nt*; **to give an** ~ ein Interview *nt* geben **c** (= *formal talk*) Gespräch *nt*, Unterredung *f* VT **a** *job applicant* ein/das Vorstellungsgespräch führen mit; *applicant for grant etc* Fragen stellen (+*dat*);

he is being ~ed on Monday for the job er hat am Montag sein Vorstellungsgespräch **b** (*Press, TV etc*) interviewen **VI** **a** (*for job*) das Vorstellungsgespräch/die Vorstellungsgespräche führen **b** (*Press, TV etc*) interviewen

interviewee [ˌɪntəvjuˈiː] N (*for job*) Kandidat(in) *m(f)* (für die Stelle); (*Press, TV etc*) Interviewte(r) *mf*

interviewer [ˈɪntəvjuːə] N (*for job*) Leiter(in) *m(f)* des Vorstellungsgesprächs; (*Press, TV etc*) Interviewer(in) *m(f)*

interwar [ˈɪntəˈwɔː] ADJ *years, period* zwischen den Weltkriegen; **~ Britain** Großbritannien in der Zeit zwischen den Weltkriegen

interweave [ˌɪntəˈwiːv] **VT** (*lit, fig*) verweben; *branches, fingers* verschlingen, ineinander schlingen **VI** sich verweben; (*branches*) sich ineinander schlingen

intestate [ɪnˈtestɪt] ADJ (*Jur*) nicht testamentarisch vermacht; **to die ~** ohne Testament sterben

intestinal [ɪnˈtestɪnl] ADJ Darm-, intestinal (*form*); **~ cancer** Darmkrebs *m*

intestine [ɪnˈtestɪn] N Darm *m*; **small/large ~** Dünn-/Dickdarm *m*

intimacy [ˈɪntɪməsɪ] N Vertrautheit *f*, Intimität *f*; (*euph*: = *sexual intimacy*) Intimität *f*; **~ took place** (*form euph*) es kam zu Intimitäten

intimate¹ [ˈɪntɪmɪt] **ADJ** **a** *friend* eng, vertraut, intim; (*sexually*) intim; **we're friends but we are not ~** wir sind befreundet, stehen aber nicht auf so vertraulichem Fuß; **to be on ~ terms with sb** mit jdm auf vertraulichem Fuß stehen; **he was a bit too ~ with my wife** er war ein bisschen zu vertraulich mit meiner Frau; **to be/become ~ with sb** mit jdm vertraut sein/werden; (*sexually*) mit jdm intim sein/werden **b** (*fig*) intim (*geh*); *feelings, thoughts* geheim, intim; *connection* eng; *knowledge* gründlich; **to have an ~ knowledge of sth** über etw (*acc*) in allen Einzelheiten Bescheid wissen **c** *freshness* im Intimbereich; **~ deodorant** Intimspray *m or nt* **N** Vertraute(r) *mf*

intimate² [ˈɪntɪmeɪt] VT andeuten; **he ~d to them that they should stop** er gab ihnen zu verstehen, dass sie aufhören sollten

intimately [ˈɪntɪmɪtlɪ] ADV *acquainted* bestens; *behave, speak* vertraulich; *related, connected* eng; *know* genau, gründlich; **we know each other but not ~** wir kennen uns, aber nicht besonders gut; **he is ~ involved in local politics** er ist tief in Lokalpolitik verwickelt

intimation [ˌɪntɪˈmeɪʃən] N Andeutung *f*; **he gave no ~ that he was going to resign** er deutete durch nichts an or machte keinerlei Andeutungen, dass er zurücktreten würde

intimidate [ɪnˈtɪmɪdeɪt] VT einschüchtern; **they ~d him into not telling the police** sie schüchterten ihn so ein, dass er der Polizei nichts erzählte; **we won't be ~d** wir lassen uns nicht einschüchtern

intimidation [ɪnˌtɪmɪˈdeɪʃən] N Einschüchterung *f*

intimidatory [ɪnˌtɪmɪˈdeɪtərɪ] ADJ *telephone call, behaviour* einschüchternd; **~ tactics** Einschüchterungstaktik *f*

into [ˈɪntʊ] PREP **a** in (+*acc*); (= *against*) *crash, drive* gegen; **to translate sth ~ French** etw ins Französische übersetzen; **to change euros ~ pounds** Euro in Pfund umtauschen; **to divide 3 ~ 9** 9 durch 3 teilen *or* dividieren; **3 ~ 9 goes 3** 3 geht dreimal in 9; **to get ~ trouble** in Schwierigkeiten kommen; **to go ~ politics** in die Politik gehen; **they worked far ~ the night** sie arbeiteten bis tief in die Nacht hinein; **he's well ~ his sixties** er ist in den späten Sechzigern; **it turned ~ a nice day** es wurde ein schöner Tag; **I can't get ~ my jeans any more** ich komme nicht mehr in meine Jeans; **research ~ AIDS/cancer** Aids-/Krebsforschung *f*
b (*inf*) **to be ~ sb/sth** (= *like*) auf jdn/etw (*acc*) stehen (*inf*); (= *be interested in*) sich für jdn/etw interessieren; **to be ~ sth** (= *use, drugs etc*) etw

nehmen; **I'm not really ~ the job yet** ich bin noch nicht ganz drin im Job (*inf*); **he's ~ local politics in a big way** (= *actively involved*) er ist schwer in der Lokalpolitik aktiv (*inf*); **she's ~ getting up early** sie ist passionierte Frühaufsteherin; **she's ~ health food** sie steht auf Gesundheitskost (*inf*); **he's ~ wine** (= *likes*) er ist Weinliebhaber; (= *is expert*) er ist Weinkenner; **he's ~ computers** er ist Computerfan (*inf*); **well if that's what you're ~ ...** also, wenn das dein Fall ist ...; **I'm not ~ that** darauf stehe ich nicht (*inf*)

intolerable ADJ , **intolerably** ADV [ɪnˈtɒlərəbl, -lɪ] unerträglich

intolerance [ɪnˈtɒlərəns] N **a** Intoleranz *f* (*of* gegenüber) **b** (*esp Med*) Überempfindlichkeit *f* (*to, of* gegen)

intolerant [ɪnˈtɒlərənt] ADJ intolerant (*of* genüber); (*Med*) überempfindlich (*to, of* gegen)

intolerantly [ɪnˈtɒlərəntlɪ] ADV intolerant; *refuse* intoleranterweise

intonate [ˈɪntəneɪt] VT (*Ling*) intonieren

intonation [ˌɪntəˈneɪʃən] N Intonation *f*; (*Ling also*) Satzmelodie *f*

intonation pattern N (*Ling*) Intonationsmuster *nt*

intone [ɪnˈtəʊn] VT intonieren

in toto [ɪnˈtəʊtəʊ] ADV im Ganzen, in toto (*geh*)

intoxicant [ɪnˈtɒksɪkənt] N Rauschmittel *nt*

intoxicate [ɪnˈtɒksɪkeɪt] VT (*lit, fig*) berauschen

intoxicated [ɪnˈtɒksɪkeɪtɪd] ADJ betrunken, berauscht (*also fig*), im Rausch (*also fig*); **to become ~** sich berauschen (*also fig*) (*by, with* an +*dat*, von); **~ by drugs** im Drogenrausch; **~ by** *or* **with success** vom Erfolg berauscht

intoxication [ɪnˌtɒksɪˈkeɪʃən] N Rausch *m* (*also fig*), (Be)trunkenheit *f*; (*Med:* = *poisoning*) Vergiftung *f*; **in a state of ~** (*form*) in (be)trunkenem Zustand, im Rausch

intra- [ˌɪntrə-] PREF intra-; **intramuscular** intramuskulär

intractable [ɪnˈtræktəbl] ADJ *metal* unnachgiebig; *nature, problem, illness, pain* hartnäckig; *conflict* unlösbar; *issue* äußerst schwierig

intracutaneous [ˌɪntrəkjuːˈteɪnɪəs] ADJ (*Med*) intrakutan (*spec*), in der Haut (gelegen); **~ injection** Injektion *f* in die Haut

intramural [ˌɪntrəˈmjʊərəl] ADJ (*esp Univ*) *course* innerhalb der Universität; *activities* studienspezifisch

intranet [ˈɪntrənet] N (*Comput*) Intranet *nt*

intransigence [ɪnˈtrænsɪdʒəns] N Unnachgiebigkeit *f*

intransigent [ɪnˈtrænsɪdʒənt] ADJ unnachgiebig

intransitive [ɪnˈtrænsɪtɪv] **ADJ** *verb* intransitiv **N** Intransitiv *nt*

intraparty [ˈɪntrəˈpɑːtɪ] ADJ parteiintern, innerparteilich

intrastate [ˌɪntrəˈsteɪt] ADJ (*US*) innerhalb des (Bundes)staates

intrauterine device [ˌɪntrəˈjuːtəraɪndɪˌvaɪs] N Intrauterinpessar *nt*

intravenous [ˌɪntrəˈviːnəs] ADJ intravenös; **~ drip** (*Med*) intravenöse Infusion; **~ drug user** Drogenabhängige(r) *mf*, der/die intravenös spritzt

intravenously [ˌɪntrəˈviːnəslɪ] ADV *feed, give, administer* intravenös

in-tray [ˈɪntreɪ] N Ablage *f* für Eingänge

intrepid ADJ , **intrepidly** ADV [ɪnˈtrepɪd, -lɪ] unerschrocken, kühn

intrepidity [ˌɪntrɪˈpɪdɪtɪ] N Unerschrockenheit *f*, Kühnheit *f*

intricacy [ˈɪntrɪkəsɪ] N Kompliziertheit *f*; (= *intricate part: of law, chess etc*) Feinheit *f*; **the intricacies of the job** die Feinheiten der Arbeit

intricate [ˈɪntrɪkɪt] ADJ kompliziert; (= *involved also*) verwickelt

intricately [ˈɪntrɪkɪtlɪ] ADV kompliziert; **these issues are ~ connected** diese Fragen sind auf komplizierte Weise miteinander verknüpft

intrigue [ɪnˈtriːg] **VI** intrigieren **VT** (= *arouse interest of*) faszinieren; (= *arouse curiosity of*) neugierig machen; **to be ~d with** *or* **by sth** von etw fasziniert sein; **I would be ~d to know why ...** es würde mich schon interessieren, warum ...; **I'm ~d to hear what she's been saying** ich würde wirklich gerne hören, was sie gesagt hat **N** [ˈɪntriːg] **a** (= *plot*) Intrige *f*; (*no pl:* = *plotting*) Intrigen(spiel *nt*) *pl* **b** (*dated:* = *love affair*) Liaison *f*, Liebschaft *f*

intriguer [ɪnˈtriːgə] N Intrigant(in) *m(f)*, Ränkeschmied *m*

intriguing [ɪnˈtriːgɪn] **ADJ** faszinierend, interessant **N** Intrigen(spiel *nt*) *pl*

intriguingly [ɪnˈtriːgɪnlɪ] ADV auf faszinierende Weise; **her questions were ~ different** ihre Fragen faszinierten durch ihre Andersartigkeit; **most ~, no fingerprints could be found** höchst interessant war die Tatsache, dass man keine Fingerabdrücke finden konnte

intrinsic [ɪnˈtrɪnsɪk] ADJ *merit, value* immanent; (= *essential*) wesenhaft, wesentlich; **~ evidence** (*Jur*) reiner Urkundenbeweis; **is this form ~ to the poem?** ist dies eine dem Gedicht innewohnende Form? (*geh*); **financial insecurity is ~ to capitalism** finanzielle Unsicherheit gehört zum Wesen des Kapitalismus

intrinsically [ɪnˈtrɪnsɪkəlɪ] ADV an sich; **these instruments are ~ dangerous** diese Instrumente sind an sich äußerst gefährlich; **~ linked** *or* **connected** untrennbar miteinander verbunden

intro [ˈɪntrəʊ] N (*inf*) abbr of **introduction** Intro *nt* (*inf*)

introduce [ˌɪntrəˈdjuːs] VT **a** (= *make acquainted*) (*to person*) vorstellen (*to sb* jdm), bekannt machen (*to* mit); (*butler*) ankündigen; (*to subject*) einführen (*to* in +*acc*); **have you two been ~d?** hat man Sie bekannt gemacht?; **I don't think we've been ~d** ich glaube nicht, dass wir uns kennen; **to ~ oneself** sich vorstellen; **allow me to** *or* **let me ~ myself** darf ich mich vorstellen?; **he was ~d to drink at an early age** er hat schon früh Bekanntschaft mit dem Alkohol gemacht; **who ~d him to heroin?** durch wen ist er ans Heroin geraten?; **he ~d me to flying by a friend** er ist durch einen Freund zum Fliegen gekommen; **I ~d him to the firm** ich habe ihn in die Firma eingeführt
b *fashion, practice, reform, invention* einführen; (*Parl*) *bill* einbringen; *mood, competition* bringen (*into* in +*acc*); *book, subject, era* einleiten; (= *announce*) *speaker* vorstellen, ankündigen; *programme* ankündigen; **to ~ sth onto the market** etw auf den Markt bringen, etw auf dem Markt einführen
c (= *insert*) einführen (*into* in +*acc*)

introduction [ˌɪntrəˈdʌkʃən] N **a** (*to person*) Vorstellung *f*; **since his ~ to Lord X** seit er Lord X vorgestellt worden ist; **to make** *or* **perform the ~s** die Vorstellung übernehmen; **letter of ~** Einführungsbrief *m or* -schreiben *nt*; **~ agency** Partnervermittlung *f*
b (= *introductory part: to book, music*) Einleitung *f* (*to* zu)
c (= *elementary course, book*) Einführung *f*; **an ~ to French** eine Einführung ins Französische
d (= *introducing, being introduced*) (*to subject*) Einführung *f* (*to* in +*acc*); (*to habit, hobby*) Bekanntschaft *f* (*to* mit); (*of fashion, practice, reform etc*) Einführung *f*; (*of bill, competition*) Einbringen *nt*; (= *announcing*) (*of speaker*) Vorstellung *f*, Ankündigung *f*; (*of programme*) Ankündigung *f*; (= *bringing or carrying in*) Einführung *f* (*into* in +*dat*); (= *insertion*) Einführung *f* (*into* in +*acc*); **our next guest needs no ~** unser nächster Gast braucht nicht vorgestellt zu werden

introductory [ˌɪntrəˈdʌktərɪ] ADJ *page, paragraph, chapter* einleitend; *words, remarks* einführend; *course, fee, offer* Einführungs-; **~ speech** Einführungsrede *f*; **~ price** Einführungspreis *m*

introit [ˈɪntrɔɪt] N Introitus *m*

introspect [ˌɪntrəʊˈspekt] VI sich selbst beobachten

introspection [ˌɪntrəʊˈspekʃən] N Selbstbeobachtung f, Introspektion f (geh)

introspective [ˌɪntrəʊˈspektɪv] ADJ person selbstbeobachtend, introspektiv (geh); novel, remarks introspektiv

introspectiveness [ˌɪntrəʊˈspektɪvnɪs] N (of novel, remarks) introspektiver Charakter; (of person) Neigung f zur Selbstbeobachtung or Introspektion (geh)

introversion [ˌɪntrəʊˈvɜːʃən] N (Psych) Introversion f

introvert [ˈɪntrəʊvɜːt] N (Psych) Introvertierte(r) mf; **to be an ~** introvertiert sein VT (Psych) nach innen wenden; (Biol) nach innen stülpen

introverted [ˈɪntrəʊvɜːtɪd] ADJ introvertiert, in sich gekehrt

intrude [ɪnˈtruːd] VI stören; **to ~ on sb** jdn stören; **his mother ~d on our relationship** seine Mutter mischte sich in unsere Beziehung ein; **am I intruding?** störe ich?; **to ~ on sb's privacy** jds Privatsphäre verletzen; **my family has been ~d upon by the press** meine Familie ist von der Presse belästigt worden; **to ~ on sb's grief** jdn in seinem Kummer stören; **to ~ on a meeting** eine Besprechung stören; **to ~ into sb's thoughts** jdn in seinen Gedanken stören; **personal feelings cannot be allowed to ~** für persönliche Gefühle ist kein Platz VT remark einwerfen; **to ~ oneself upon sb** sich jdm aufdrängen; **to ~ oneself into sb's affairs** sich in jds Angelegenheiten (acc) mischen

intruder [ɪnˈtruːdə] N Eindringling m

intrusion [ɪnˈtruːʒən] N a Störung f; **forgive the ~, I just wanted to ask ...** entschuldigen Sie, wenn ich hier so eindringe, ich wollte nur fragen ...; **the ~ of** or **on his privacy** die Verletzung seiner Privatsphäre; **the sudden ~ of the outside world** das plötzliche Eindringen der Außenwelt; **they regarded her presence as an ~** sie betrachteten ihre Anwesenheit als störend b (= forcing: of opinions, advice, one's presence) Aufdrängen nt

intrusive [ɪnˈtruːsɪv] ADJ person aufdringlich; presence störend; government, legislation einmischend; (Phon) intrusiv

intubate [ˈɪntjʊbeɪt] VT (Med) intubieren

intubation [ˌɪntjʊˈbeɪʃən] N (Med) Intubation f

intuit [ɪnˈtjuːɪt] VT (form) thought intuitiv erahnen

intuition [ˌɪntjuːˈɪʃən] N Intuition f; (of future events etc) (Vor)ahnung f (of von); **to know sth by ~** etw intuitiv wissen

intuitive [ɪnˈtjuːɪtɪv] ADJ intuitiv; guess, feeling, assessment instinktiv; **~ powers** Intuition f

intuitively [ɪnˈtjuːɪtɪvlɪ] ADV intuitiv; **~ I'd say 50** ich hätte instinktiv 50 gesagt

inundate [ˈɪnʌndeɪt] VT (lit, fig) überschwemmen, überfluten; (with work) überhäufen; **have you a lot of work on? – I'm ~d** haben Sie viel Arbeit? – ich ersticke darin

inundation [ˌɪnʌnˈdeɪʃən] N (lit, fig) (with invitations, offers etc) Überschwemmung f; (with work) Überhäufung f

inure [ɪnˈjʊə] VT gewöhnen (to an +acc); (physically) abhärten (to gegen); (to danger) stählen (to gegen); **to become ~d to sth** an etw (acc) gewöhnen; (physically) to danger sich gegen etw abhärten/stählen

invade [ɪnˈveɪd] VT (Mil) country einmarschieren in (+acc); (fig) überfallen, heimsuchen; privacy eindringen in (+acc), stören; (Med) cell etc befallen

invader [ɪnˈveɪdə] N (Mil) Invasor m; (fig) Eindringling m (of in +acc); (of privacy) Eindringling (of in +acc), Störer m (of +acc)

invading [ɪnˈveɪdɪŋ] ADJ einmarschierend; Huns, Vikings etc einfallend; virus, organism eindringend; **~ army/troops** Invasionsarmee f/-truppen pl

---

invalid¹ [ˈɪnvəlɪd] ADJ a krank; (= disabled) invalide, körperbehindert b (= for invalids) Kranken-, Invaliden- N Kranke(r) mf; (= disabled person) Invalide m, Invalidin f, Körperbehinderte(r) mf; **he's been an ~ all his life** er hat sein ganzes Leben lang ein körperliches Leiden gehabt; **to treat sb like an ~** jdn wie einen Invaliden behandeln

▶ **invalid out** VT sep dienstunfähig schreiben or erklären; **to be invalided out of the army** wegen Dienstunfähigkeit aus der Armee entlassen werden

invalid² [ɪnˈvælɪd] ADJ (esp Jur) ungültig; deduction, argument nicht schlüssig or stichhaltig; assumption nicht zulässig; **it makes the argument ~** es entkräftet das Argument; **to declare sth ~** etw für ungültig erklären

invalidate [ɪnˈvælɪdeɪt] VT ungültig machen; theory, feelings entkräften

invalidation [ɪnˌvælɪˈdeɪʃən] N (of document) Ungültigmachung f; (of theory) Entkräftung f

invalid car N Invaliden(kraft)fahrzeug nt

invalid chair N Roll- or Krankenstuhl m

invalidism [ˈɪnvəlɪdɪzəm] N körperliches Leiden; (= disability) Körperbehinderung f, Invalidität f

invalidity [ˌɪnvəˈlɪdɪtɪ] N a (esp Jur) Ungültigkeit f; (of deduction, argument) mangelnde Schlüssigkeit or Stichhaltigkeit; (of assumption) Unzulässigkeit f b (= disability) Körperbehinderung f, Invalidität f

invaluable [ɪnˈvæljʊəbl] ADJ unbezahlbar; service, role, help, contribution unschätzbar; advice, experience, jewel, treasure von unschätzbarem Wert; **to be ~ (to sb)** (für jdn) von unschätzbarem Wert sein; **to be an ~ source of sth** eine ausgezeichnete Quelle für etw sein

invariable [ɪnˈvɛərɪəbl] ADJ (also Math) unveränderlich; reply, characteristic gleich bleibend; bad luck konstant, ständig N (Math) Konstante f

invariably [ɪnˈvɛərɪəblɪ] ADV ständig, unweigerlich; (= not changing) unveränderlich; **do you trust his judgement? – ~!** trauen Sie seinem Urteil? – ausnahmslos!

invariant [ɪnˈvɛərɪənt] ADJ (also Math) unveränderlich N (Math) Konstante f

invasion [ɪnˈveɪʒən] N (lit, fig) Invasion f; (of privacy etc) Eingriff m (of in +acc); **the Viking ~** der Einfall der Wikinger; **the German ~ of Poland** der Einmarsch or Einfall der Deutschen in Polen

invasive¹ [ɪnˈveɪsɪv] ADJ a (Med) invasiv b (Mil) Invasions-; **~ war** Invasionskrieg m

invective [ɪnˈvektɪv] N Beschimpfungen pl (against +gen), Schmähungen pl (geh) (against gegen), Invektiven pl (liter)

inveigh [ɪnˈveɪ] VI **to ~ against sb/sth** (liter) jdn/ etw schmähen (liter), sich in Schimpfreden gegen jdn/etw ergehen (geh)

inveigle [ɪnˈviːgl] VT (liter) verleiten (into zu); (= lure) locken; **to ~ sb into doing sth** jdn dazu verleiten or verlocken, etw zu tun

invent [ɪnˈvent] VT erfinden

invention [ɪnˈvenʃən] N a Erfindung f; **of one's own** ~ selbsterfunden b (= inventiveness) Fantasie f

inventive [ɪnˈventɪv] ADJ (= creative) powers, skills, mind schöpferisch; novel, design, menu einfallsreich; (= resourceful) erfinderisch; **~ genius** schöpferisches Genie; **games which encourage a child to be ~** Spiele, die die Fantasie or Phantasie des Kindes anregen

inventiveness [ɪnˈventɪvnɪs] N Einfallsreichtum m

inventor [ɪnˈventə] N Erfinder(in) m(f)

inventory [ˈɪnvəntrɪ] N Inventar nt, Bestandsaufnahme f; **to make** or **take an ~ of sth** Inventar von etw or den Bestand einer Sache (gen) aufnehmen VT (Comm) inventarisieren

inventory control N Bestandskontrolle f

---

inverse [ˈɪnvɜːs] ADJ umgekehrt, entgegengesetzt; **in ~ order** in umgekehrter Reihenfolge N Gegenteil nt

inversion [ɪnˈvɜːʃən] N Umkehrung f; (Mus also, Gram) Inversion f; (fig: of roles, values) Verkehrung f, Umkehrung f

invert [ɪnˈvɜːt] VT umkehren; object also auf den Kopf stellen; order also umdrehen; (Gram) subject and object umstellen; word order umkehren; **~ed nipples** Hohlwarzen pl

invertebrate [ɪnˈvɜːtɪbrɪt] N Wirbellose(r) m, Invertebrat m (spec) ADJ wirbellos

inverted [ɪnˈvɜːtɪd] **inverted commas** PL (Brit) Anführungszeichen pl; **his new job, in ~** sein so genannter neuer Job; **inverted snobbery** N **that's just ~** das ist die umgekehrte Variante von Snobismus

invert sugar [ˈɪnvɜːtˌʃʊgə] N Invertzucker m

invest [ɪnˈvest] VT a (Fin) investieren (in in +acc or dat), anlegen (in in +dat); (fig) investieren (in in +acc) b (form: with rank or authority) president etc einsetzen, investieren (old); **to ~ sb/sth with sth** jdm/einer Sache etw verleihen; **this number is ~ed with magical qualities** diese Zahl besitzt Zauberkräfte c (Mil: = besiege) belagern VI investieren, Geld anlegen (in in +acc or dat, with bei); **to ~ in shares** in Aktien investieren, sein Geld in Aktien anlegen; **to ~ in a new car** sich (dat) ein neues Auto anschaffen

investigate [ɪnˈvestɪgeɪt] VT untersuchen; (doing scientific research also) erforschen; sb's political beliefs, an insurance claim, business affairs überprüfen; complaint nachgehen (+dat); motive, reason, cause erforschen; crime untersuchen; **to ~ a case** in einem Fall ermitteln or Ermittlungen anstellen VI nachforschen; (police) ermitteln, Ermittlungen anstellen

investigation [ɪnˌvestɪˈgeɪʃən] N a (to determine cause) Untersuchung f (into +gen); (= official inquiry) Ermittlung f, Untersuchung f; **to call for an immediate ~ into sth** die sofortige Untersuchung einer Sache (gen) fordern; **to order an ~ into** or **of sth** anordnen, dass in einer Sache (dat) ermittelt wird; **on ~ it turned out that ...** bei näherer Untersuchung stellte (es) sich heraus, dass ... b (= looking for sth) Nachforschung f; (by police) Ermittlungen pl; (of affairs, applicants, political beliefs etc) Überprüfung f; **to be under ~** überprüft werden; **he is under ~** (by police) gegen ihn wird ermittelt; **new methods of criminal ~** neue polizeiliche Ermittlungsmethoden; (**private**) ~ **agency** Detektei f, Detektivbüro nt c (= scientific research) (in field) Forschung f; (of bacteria, object etc) Erforschung f (into +gen); **recent scientific ~ has shown ...** die neuesten wissenschaftlichen Untersuchungen haben gezeigt ...

investigative [ɪnˈvestɪgətɪv] ADJ journalist, series, programme investigativ; **~ journalism** Enthüllungsjournalismus m; **~ mind** Forschergeist m; **~ technique/work** Forschungstechnik/-arbeit f; **~ report** Untersuchungsbericht m; **~ custody** (Jur) Untersuchungshaft f

investigator [ɪnˈvestɪgeɪtə] N Ermittler(in) m(f); (= private investigator) (Privat)detektiv m(f); (= insurance investigator) (Schadens)ermittler(in) m(f); (from government department) Untersuchungs- or Ermittlungsbeamte(r) m/-beamtin f; **a team of ~s** ein Untersuchungsausschuss m, eine Untersuchungskommission

investiture [ɪnˈvestɪtʃə] N (of president etc) (feierliche) Einsetzung f, Amtseinführung f; (of royalty) Investitur f; (of honour) Verleihung f; (= occasion) Auszeichnungsfeier f; **after his ~ with the VC,** ~ nachdem ihm das Viktoriakreuz verliehen worden war, ...

investment [ɪnˈvestmənt] N a (Fin) Investition f; (= act also) Anlage f; **we need more ~ in industry** in die Industrie muss mehr investiert werden, die Industrie braucht mehr Investitionen; **to make an ~** investieren (of sth etw); **foreign ~** Auslandsinvestition(en pl) f; **return on**

one's ~s Anlageertrag *m*; **oil/this company is a good** ~ Öl/diese Firma ist eine gute (Kapital)anlage; **a portable TV is a good** ~ ein tragbarer Fernseher macht sich bezahlt **b** (= *investiture*) (*as sth*) (Amts)einsetzung *f*; (*with sth*) Verleihung *f* (+*gen*) **c** (*Mil*: = *blockade*) Belagerung *f*

investment: investment allowance N Investitionsabschreibung *f*; **investment bonds** PL festverzinsliche Anlagepapiere *pl*; **investment capital** N Anlagekapital *nt*; **investment company** N Investmentgesellschaft *f*; **investment failure** N Fehlinvestition *f*; **investment incentive** N Investitionsanreiz *m*; **investment income** N Kapitalerträge *pl*; **investment management** N Vermögensverwaltung *f*; **investment manager** N Vermögensverwalter(in) *m(f)*, Investmentmanager(in) *m(f)*; **investment trust** N Investmenttrust *m*

investor [ɪn'vestə'] N Kapitalanleger(in) *m(f)*, Investor(in) *m(f)*; **the small** ~ die Kleinanleger *pl*

inveterate [ɪn'vetərɪt] ADJ *dislike, hatred* tief verwurzelt, abgrundtief; *laziness* chronisch; *opposition, prejudice, habit* hartnäckig; *enemies* unversöhnlich; *liar, gambler* unverbesserlich; *collector, traveller* passioniert; ~ **smoker/criminal** Gewohnheitsraucher(in) *m(f)*/-verbrecher(in) *m(f)*

invidious [ɪn'vɪdɪəs] ADJ *remark* gehässig, boshaft; *task, position* unerfreulich, unangenehm; *behaviour, conduct* gemein; *distinctions, comparison, discrimination* ungerecht; **it would be** ~ **to ...** es wäre ungerecht, zu ...

invigilate [ɪn'vɪdʒɪleɪt] (*Brit*) VT *exam* Aufsicht führen bei VI Aufsicht führen

invigilation [ɪn,vɪdʒɪ'leɪʃən] N (*Brit*) Aufsicht *f*; **to do (the)** ~ Aufsicht führen

invigilator [ɪn'vɪdʒɪleɪtə'] N (*Brit*) Aufsicht *f*, Aufsichtführende(r) *mf*, Aufsichtsperson *f*

invigorate [ɪn'vɪgəreɪt] VT beleben, (*tonic, cure*) kräftigen

invigorating [ɪn'vɪgəreɪtɪŋ] ADJ *climate* gesund, *sea air, shower* erfrischend, belebend; *tonic, cure* kräftigend, stärkend; (*fig*) *attitude, frankness* (herz)erfrischend; **he found the American business world very** ~ die amerikanische Geschäftswelt stimulierte ihn

invincibility [ɪn,vɪnsɪ'bɪlɪtɪ] N Unbesiegbarkeit *f*

invincible [ɪn'vɪnsəbl] ADJ *army etc* unbesiegbar, unschlagbar; *courage, determination* unerschütterlich

invincibly [ɪn'vɪnsəblɪ] ADV ~ **strong** unbesiegbar; **he is** ~ **placed** er hat eine unschlagbare Position

inviolability [ɪn,vaɪələ'bɪlɪtɪ] N Unantastbarkeit *f*; (*of frontiers*) Unverletzlichkeit *f*; (*of law, oath*) Heiligkeit *f*

inviolable [ɪn'vaɪələbl] ADJ unantastbar; *frontiers also* unverletzlich; *law, oath* heilig

inviolate [ɪn'vaɪəlɪt] ADJ (*form*) *honour* unbeschadet; *rights* unangetastet

invisibility [ɪn,vɪzə'bɪlɪtɪ] N Unsichtbarkeit *f*

invisible [ɪn'vɪzəbl] ADJ unsichtbar; **to feel** ~ sich (*dat*) unsichtbar vorkommen; ~ **thread** Nylonfaden *m*; ~ **to the naked eye** mit dem bloßen Auge nicht erkennbar N ~s (*Comm*) unsichtbarer Handel

invisible: invisible earnings PL (*Econ*) unsichtbare Einkünfte *pl*; **invisible exports** PL (*Econ*) unsichtbare Exporte *pl*; **invisible ink** N Geheimtinte *f*; **invisible mending** N Kunststopfen *nt*

invisibly [ɪn'vɪzəblɪ] ADV unsichtbar; **you should have it** ~ **mended** du solltest es kunststopfen lassen

invitation [,ɪnvɪ'teɪʃən] ✪ 25.1, 25.2 N Einladung *f*; **by** ~ **(only)** nur auf Einladung; **at sb's** ~ auf jds Aufforderung (*acc*) (hin); **an** ~ **to burglars** eine Aufforderung zum Diebstahl; ~ **card** Einladungskarte *f*

invitational [,ɪnvɪ'teɪʃənl] ADJ (*Sport*) *nur für eingeladene Teilnehmer zugänglich* ~ **tournament** Einladungsturnier *nt*

invite [ɪn'vaɪt] VT **a** *person* einladen; **to** ~ **sb to do sth** jdn auffordern *or* bitten, etw zu tun; **he ~d me to try for myself** er bot mir an, es doch selbst zu versuchen **b** (= *ask for, attract*) *suggestions, questions* bitten um; (*behaviour*) *ridicule, contempt, trouble* auslösen, führen zu; **written in such a way as to** ~ **further discussion** so geschrieben, dass es zu weiteren Diskussionen auffordert; **it** ~**s comparison with another theory** der Vergleich mit einer anderen Theorie drängt sich auf; **you're inviting defeat by ...** das muss ja zu einer Niederlage führen, wenn du ...; **you're inviting ridicule/criticism** du machst dich lächerlich/setzt dich der Kritik aus; **he just seems to** ~ **trouble** wo er auftaucht, gibt es meistens Unannehmlichkeiten; **it** ~**s thieves** es lädt geradezu zum Diebstahl ein N ['ɪnvaɪt](*inf*) Einladung *f*

▶ **invite (a)round** VT *sep* (zu sich) einladen

▶ **invite in** VT *sep* hereinbitten, ins Haus bitten; **could I invite you in for (a) coffee?** möchten Sie auf eine Tasse Kaffee hereinkommen?

▶ **invite out** VT *sep* einladen; **I invited her out** ich habe sie gefragt, ob sie mit mir ausgehen möchte; **to invite sb out for a meal** jdn in ein Restaurant einladen

▶ **invite up** VT *sep* heraufbitten

inviting [ɪn'vaɪtɪŋ] ADJ einladend; *prospect, idea, meal, sea, water* verlockend; *room* heimelig

invitingly [ɪn'vaɪtɪŋlɪ] ADV einladend; (= *temptingly*) verlockend

in vitro [ɪn'vi:trəʊ] (*Biol*) ADJ künstlich, In-vitro-(*spec*); ~ **fertilization** künstliche Befruchtung, In-vitro-Fertilisation *f* (*spec*) ADV *fertilize* künstlich, in vitro (*spec*)

invocation [,ɪnvə'keɪʃən] N Beschwörung *f*; (*Eccl*) Invokation *f*; **an** ~ **to the muses** (*Liter*) eine Anrufung der Musen

invoice ['ɪnvɔɪs] ✪ 20.7 N (= *bill*) (Waren)rechnung *f*; (= *list*) Lieferschein *m* VT *goods* in Rechnung stellen, berechnen; **to** ~ **sb for sth** jdm für etw eine Rechnung ausstellen; **has he been** ~**d for these yet?** hat er dafür schon eine Rechnung bekommen?; **we'll** ~ **you** wir senden Ihnen die Rechnung

invoice clerk N Fakturist(in) *m(f)*

invoicing ['ɪnvɔɪsɪŋ] N Fakturierung *f*; (*of goods also*) Berechnung *f*, Inrechnungstellung *f*; (= *invoiced sales*) Fakturierungen *pl*

invoke [ɪn'vəʊk] VT **a** (= *appeal to, call for*) *God, the law, muse* anrufen; *evil spirits* beschwören; *memories* heraufbeschwören; **to** ~ **the name of Marx** Marx ins Feld führen; **to** ~ **God's blessing** Gottes Segen erbitten; **to** ~ **sb's help** an jds Hilfsbereitschaft (*acc*) appellieren **b** (= *call into operation*) *treaty etc* sich berufen auf (+*acc*)

involuntarily [ɪn'vɒləntərɪlɪ] ADV unbeabsichtigt, unabsichtlich; (= *automatically*) unwillkürlich; **he found himself** ~ **involved** er sah sich unfreiwilligerweise verwickelt

involuntary [ɪn'vɒləntərɪ] ADJ unbeabsichtigt, ungewollt; *repatriation* unfreiwillig; *shudder, muscle movement etc* unwillkürlich; **I found myself an** ~ **listener/guest** ich wurde zum unfreiwilligen Zuhörer/Gast; ~ **manslaughter** (*Jur*) fahrlässige Tötung

involute ['ɪnvəlu:t] ADJ (*liter*: = *complex*) verwickelt

involuted [,ɪnvə'lu:tɪd] ADJ verwickelt, kompliziert

involve [ɪn'vɒlv] VT **a** (= *entangle*) verwickeln (*sb in sth* jdn in etw *acc*); (= *include*) beteiligen (*sb in sth* jdn an etw *dat*); (= *concern*) betreffen; **to** ~ **sb in a quarrel** jdn in einen Streit verwickeln *or* hineinziehen; **to** ~ **sb in expense** jdm Kosten verursachen; **the book doesn't** ~ **the reader** das Buch fesselt *or* packt den Leser nicht; **it wouldn't** ~ **you at all** du hättest damit gar nichts zu tun; **to be** ~**d in sth** etwas mit etw zu tun haben; (= *have part in also*) an etw (*dat*) beteiligt sein; (*in sth bad also*) in etw (*acc*) verwickelt sein; **to get** ~**d in sth** in etw (*acc*) verwickelt werden; *in quarrel, crime etc also* in etw (*acc*) hineingezogen werden; **to** ~ **oneself in sth** sich in etw (*dat*) engagieren; **to** ~ **oneself in politics** sich politisch engagieren; **I didn't want to get** ~**d** ich wollte damit/mit ihm etc nichts zu tun haben; **I didn't want to get too** ~**d** ich wollte mich nicht zu sehr engagieren; **a matter of principle is** ~**d** es ist eine Frage des Prinzips, es geht ums Prinzip; **the person** ~**d** die betreffende Person; **we are all** ~**d in the battle against inflation** der Kampf gegen die Inflation geht uns alle an; **to be/get** ~**d with sth** etwas mit etw zu tun haben; (= *have part in*) an etw (*dat*) beteiligt sein; *with work etc* mit etw beschäftigt sein; **he got** ~**d with local politics** er hat sich lokalpolitisch engagiert; **to be** ~**d with sb** mit jdm zu tun haben; (*sexually*) mit jdm ein Verhältnis haben; **to be romantically** ~**d (with sb)** eine Liebesbeziehung (zu jdm) haben; **he's** ~**d with some shady characters** er hat Umgang mit einigen zwielichtigen Gestalten; **to get** ~**d with sb** mit jdm Kontakt bekommen, sich mit jdm einlassen (*pej*); **I don't want to get** ~**d with them** ich will mit ihnen nichts zu tun haben; **he got** ~**d with a girl** er hat eine Beziehung mit einem Mädchen angefangen **b** (= *entail*) mit sich bringen, zur Folge haben; (= *encompass*) umfassen; (= *mean*) bedeuten; **what does the** ~? worin besteht die Arbeit?; **this problem** ~**s many separate issues** dieses Problem umfasst viele verschiedene Punkte *or* schließt viele verschiedene Punkte ein; **to** ~ **considerable expense/a lot of hard work** beträchtliche Kosten/viel Arbeit mit sich bringen *or* zur Folge haben; **such a project** ~**s considerable planning** zu so einem Projekt gehört eine umfangreiche Planung; **will the post** ~ **much foreign travel?** ist der Posten mit vielen Auslandsreisen verbunden?; **he doesn't understand what's** ~**d in this sort of work** er weiß nicht, worum es bei dieser Arbeit geht; **do you realize what's** ~**d in raising a family?** weißt du denn, was es bedeutet, eine Familie großzuziehen?; **about £1,000 was** ~**d** es ging dabei um etwa £ 1.000; **the job** ~**d 50 workmen** für die Arbeit wurden 50 Arbeiter gebraucht; **it would** ~ **moving to Germany** das würde bedeuten, nach Deutschland umzuziehen; **finding the oil** ~**d the use of a special drill** um das Öl zu finden, brauchte man einen Spezialbohrer

involved [ɪn'vɒlvd] ADJ kompliziert; *regulations also* verwirrend; *story also* verwickelt; *style* komplex, umständlich (*pej*); **a long** ~ **sentence** ein umständlicher Schachtelsatz; **a long** ~ **explanation** eine lange und komplizierte Erklärung

involvement [ɪn'vɒlvmənt] N (= *being concerned with*) Beteiligung *f* (*in an* +*dat*); (*in quarrel, crime etc*) Verwicklung *f* (*in* +*acc*); (= *commitment*) Engagement *nt*; (*sexually*) Verhältnis *nt*; (= *complexity*) Kompliziertheit *f*, Verworrenheit *f* (*pej*); **his** ~ **with shady characters** sein Umgang *m* mit zwielichtigen Gestalten; **she denied any** ~ **in** *or* **with drugs** sie leugnete, dass sie etwas mit Drogen zu tun hatte; **the extent of his** ~ **with her** das Maß, in dem er sich bei ihr engagiert hat; **we don't know the extent of his** ~ **in the plot/plan** wir wissen nicht, wie weit er an dem Komplott/Plan beteiligt ist; **there is no** ~ **of the reader in the novel** der Leser fühlt sich von dem Roman nicht angesprochen; **a romantic** ~ **(with sb)** eine Liebesbeziehung (zu jdm)

invulnerability [ɪn,vʌlnərə'bɪlɪtɪ] N Unverwundbarkeit *f*, Unverletzbarkeit *f*; (*of fortress*) Uneinnehmbarkeit *f*; (*lit, fig*: *of position*) Unangreifbarkeit *f*

invulnerable [ɪn'vʌlnərəbl] ADJ unverwundbar, unverletzbar; *fortress* uneinnehmbar; (*lit, fig*) *position* unangreifbar; ~ **to attack** unbezwingbar

inward ['ɪnwəd] ADJ **a** (= *inner*) innere(r, s); *smile, life* innerlich; *thoughts* innerste(r, s) **b** (= *incoming*) *movement* nach innen; *curve* nach innen gehend; *mail* eintreffend; ~ **breath** Einatmen *nt*; ~ **flow** Zustrom *m* **c** (*Fin*) ~ **invest-**

ment Investitionen *pl* aus dem Ausland; **~ investor** ausländischer Investor **ADV** = **inwards**

inward-looking ['ɪnwəd'lʊkɪŋ] ADJ in sich gekehrt, beschaulich

inwardly ['ɪnwədlɪ] ADV innerlich, im Inneren; **to ~ digest sth** etw geistig verarbeiten

inwardness ['ɪnwədnɪs] N Innerlichkeit *f*

inwards ['ɪnwədz] ADV nach innen; **his thoughts turned ~** er versank in Selbstbetrachtung

in-your-face, **in-yer-face** [,ɪnjə'feɪs] ADJ (*inf*) *attitude etc* provokativ

I/O *abbr of* **input/output**

IOC *abbr of* **International Olympic Committee** IOK *nt*

iodic [aɪ'ɒdɪk] ADJ (*spec*) jodhaltig, Jod-

iodide ['aɪədaɪd] N Jodid *nt*

iodine ['aɪədiːn] N Jod *nt*

ion ['aɪən] N Ion *nt*

Ionian [aɪ'əʊnɪən] ADJ **~ Sea** Ionisches Meer

Ionic [aɪ'ɒnɪk] ADJ ionisch

ionic [aɪ'ɒnɪk] ADJ Ionen-; **~ bond** Ionenbindung *f*

ionization [,aɪənaɪ'zeɪʃən] N Ionisierung *f*

ionize ['aɪənaɪz] VTI ionisieren

ionosphere [aɪ'ɒnəsfɪə] N Ionosphäre *f*

iota [aɪ'əʊtə] N Jota *nt*; **not an** *or* **one ~** nicht ein Jota; **not an ~ of truth** kein Funke *m* *or* Körnchen *nt* Wahrheit; **it won't make an ~ of difference** es wird nicht den geringsten Unterschied machen

IOU [,aɪəʊ'juː] *abbr of* **I owe you** Schuldschein *m*; **to give sb an ~** jdm einen Schuldschein ausschreiben

IPA *abbr of* **International Phonetic Alphabet**

ipso facto ['ɪpsəʊ'fæktəʊ] ADV eo ipso

ipso jure ['ɪpsəʊ'dʒʊərɪ] ADV ipso jure, durch das Recht selbst

IQ *abbr of* **intelligence quotient** IQ *m*, Intelligenzquotient *m*; **IQ test** Intelligenztest *m*, IQ-Test *m*

IRA *abbr of* **Irish Republican Army** IRA *f*

Iran [ɪ'rɑːn] N (der) Iran

Irangate [ɪ'rɑːngeɪt] N (*Pol*) Iran-Contra-Affäre *f*, Irangate *nt* (*inf*)

Iranian [ɪ'reɪnɪən] ADJ iranisch N a Iraner(in) *m(f)* b (*Ling*) Iranisch *nt*

Iraq [ɪ'rɑːk] N (der) Irak

Iraqi [ɪ'rɑːkɪ] ADJ irakisch N Iraker(in) *m(f)*

irascibility [ɪ,ræsɪ'bɪlɪtɪ] N Reizbarkeit *f*, Jähzorn *m*

irascible [ɪ'ræsɪbl] ADJ reizbar, erregbar, jähzornig; *temperament also* jähzornig, heftig, aufbrausend

irascibly [ɪ'ræsɪblɪ] ADV gereizt

irate [aɪ'reɪt] ADJ zornig; *crowd* wütend

irately [aɪ'reɪtlɪ] ADV zornig

ire [aɪə] N (*liter*) Zorn *m*

Ireland ['aɪələnd] N Irland *nt*; **Northern ~** Nordirland *nt*; **Republic of ~** Republik *f* Irland

iridescence [,ɪrɪ'desəns] N (*liter*) Irisieren *nt*; (*of plumage also, of water*) Schillern *nt*; (*of opals, silk*) Schimmern *nt*

iridescent [,ɪrɪ'desənt] ADJ (*liter*) irisierend; *plumage also, water, bubble* schillernd; *opals, silk* schimmernd

iris ['aɪərɪs] N a (*of eye*) Regenbogenhaut *f*, Iris *f* b (*Bot*) Iris *f*, Schwertlilie *f*

Irish ['aɪərɪʃ] ADJ a irisch; **~ Free State** irischer Freistaat; **~ joke** Irenwitz *m*, ≈ Ostfriesenwitz *m*; **~man** Ire *m*, Irländer *m*; **≈ Republican Army** Irisch-Republikanische Armee; **~woman** Irin *f*, Irländerin *f* b (*hum inf*: = *illogical*) unlogisch, blödsinnig N *pl* **the ~** die Iren *pl*, die Irländer *pl* b (*Ling*) Irisch *nt*, irisches Gälisch

Irish: Irish coffee N Irishcoffee *m*; **Irish Sea** N Irische See; **Irish setter** N Irischer Setter; **Irish stew** N Irishstew *nt*

irk [ɜːk] VT verdrießen (*geh*), ärgern

irksome ['ɜːksəm] ADJ lästig

---

iron ['aɪən] N a Eisen *nt*; **old ~** Alteisen *nt*; **~ tablets** *pl* Eisentabletten *pl*; **a man of ~** ein stahlharter Mann; **a will of ~** ein eiserner Wille; **to rule with a rod of ~** (*Brit*) mit eiserner Rute *or* Hand herrschen; **to pump ~** (*inf*) Krafttraining machen

b (= *electric iron*) Bügeleisen *nt*; **to have other ~s in the fire** (*fig*) noch andere Eisen im Feuer haben; **he has too many ~s in the fire** er macht zu viel auf einmal; **to strike while the ~ is hot** (*Prov*) das Eisen schmieden, solange es heiß ist (*Prov*)

c (*Golf*) Eisen *nt*

d **irons** PL (= *fetters*) Hand- und Fußschellen *pl*; **to put a man in ~s** jdn in Eisen legen

ADJ a (*Chem*) Eisen-; (= *made of iron*) Eisen-, eisern, aus Eisen; **~ bar** Eisenstange *f*; **~ deficiency** Eisenmangel *m*; **~ pyrites** Eisenkies *m*, Pyrit *m*

b (*fig*) *constitution, hand* eisern; *will* eisern, stählern; *rule* streng, unbarmherzig; **to rule with an ~ hand** mit eiserner Faust regieren; **they soon discovered that here was an ~ fist in a velvet glove** es wurde ihnen bald klar, dass mit ihm *etc* nicht zu spaßen war, obwohl er *etc* so sanft wirkte

VT *clothes* bügeln

VI (*person*) bügeln; (*cloth*) sich bügeln lassen

▸ **iron out** VT *sep* (*lit, fig*) ausbügeln; *differences also* ausgleichen; *problems, difficulties also* aus dem Weg räumen

iron: Iron Age N Eisenzeit *f*; **Iron Chancellor** N Eiserne(r) Kanzler; **ironclad** ADJ gepanzert N (*obs*) Panzerschiff *nt*; **Iron Curtain** N Eiserne(r) Vorhang; **the ~ countries** die Länder hinter dem Eisernen Vorhang; **Iron Duke** N Wellington *m*; **iron horse** N (*old*: = *train*) Dampfross *nt* (*old hum*)

ironic(al) [aɪ'rɒnɪk(əl)] ADJ ironisch; *smile also* spöttisch; *position* paradox; **it's really ~** das ist wirklich witzig (*inf*); **it's really ~ that now he's got a car he's not allowed to drive** es ist doch paradox *or* wirklich witzig (*inf*), dass er jetzt, wo er ein Auto hat, nicht fahren darf

ironically [aɪ'rɒnɪkəlɪ] ADV ironisch; **and then, ~ enough, he turned up** komischerweise *or* witzigerweise (*inf*) tauchte er dann auf; **and then, ~, it was he himself who had to do it** und dann hat ausgerechnet er *or* und dann hat paradoxerweise er es tun müssen

ironing ['aɪənɪŋ] N (= *process*) Bügeln *nt*; (= *clothes*) Bügelwäsche *f*; **to do the ~** (die Wäsche) bügeln

ironing board N Bügelbrett *nt*

ironist ['aɪərənɪst] N Ironiker(in) *m(f)*

ironize ['aɪərənaɪz] VTI ironisieren

iron: Iron Lady N (*Brit Pol*) eiserne Lady; **iron lung** N eiserne Lunge; **ironmonger** ['aɪənmʌŋgə] N (*Brit*) Eisen(waren)händler(in) *m(f)*; **ironmonger's (shop)** N (*Brit*) Eisen- und Haushaltswarenhandlung *f*; **ironmongery** ['aɪən,mʌŋgərɪ] N (*Brit*: = *shop*) Eisen- und Haushaltswarenhandlung *f*; (= *goods*) Eisenwaren *pl*; **iron mould,** (*US*) **iron mold** N Rostfleck *m*; **iron ore** N Eisenerz *nt*; **ironware** ['aɪənwɛə] N Eisenwaren *pl*; (= *household goods*) Haushaltswaren *pl*; **ironwork** N Eisen *nt*; (*on chest, cart etc*) Eisenbeschläge *pl*; **ornamental ~** Eisenverzierungen *pl*; **ironworks** N *sing or pl* Eisenhütte *f*

irony ['aɪərənɪ] N Ironie *f* *no pl*; **the ~ of the situation** das Ironische an der Situation; **the ~ of it is that ...** das Ironische daran ist, dass ..., die Ironie liegt darin, dass ...; **one of the great ironies of history** eine der ironischsten Fügungen der Geschichte; **life's ironies** die Ironie des Lebens; **by some ~ of fate, he ...** durch eine ironische Wendung des Schicksals geschah es, dass er ...

irradiate [ɪ'reɪdɪeɪt] VT a (= *emit*) *heat, light rays* ausstrahlen b (*liter*: = *illumine*) erhellen (*liter*) c (= *treat by irradiating*) bestrahlen; **~d food** strahlungsbehandelte Lebensmittel *pl*

---

irradiation [ɪ,reɪdɪ'eɪʃən] N a (= *emission*) Ausstrahlung *f* b (*Med*: *treatment; of food*) Bestrahlung *f*; (*of pain*) Ausstrahlung *f*, Irradiation *f* (*spec*) c (*fig, geh*: = *enlightenment*) Erleuchtung *f* (*fig*), Aufklärung *f*

irrational [ɪ'ræʃənl] ADJ a (= *illogical, also Math, Psych*) irrational; *fear, belief* unsinnig, irrational; (= *not sensible*) unvernünftig; **he had become quite ~ about it** er hatte eine irrationale Einstellung dazu entwickelt; **if you maintain X, then it is ~ to deny Y** wenn Sie X behaupten, ist es widersinnig *or* unlogisch, Y zu leugnen b (= *not having reason*) *animal* vernunftlos

irrationality [ɪ,ræʃə'nælɪtɪ] N (= *illogicality, Math, Psych*) Irrationalität *f*; (*of fear, belief*) Unsinnigkeit *f*, Irrationalität *f*; (= *lack of good sense*) Unvernünftigkeit *f*

irrationally [ɪ'ræʃnəlɪ] ADV irrational; (= *not sensibly*) unvernünftig; **quite ~, he believed ...** er glaubte gegen jede Vernunft *or* völlig unsinnigerweise ...; **he's ~ angry with you** er ist grundlos böse auf dich

irreal [ɪ'rɪəl] ADJ (*geh*) irreal, unwirklich

irrebuttable [,ɪrɪ'bʌtəbl] ADJ (*form*) unwiderlegbar; **~ presumption** (*Jur*) unwiderlegbare Rechtsvermutung

irreconcilable [ɪ,rekən'saɪləbl] ADJ a *enemy, hatred* unversöhnlich b *belief, opinion, differences* unvereinbar

irreconcilably [ɪ,rekən'saɪləblɪ] ADV *fight* unversöhnlich; **~ different** völlig unvereinbar; **to be ~ opposed to sth** absolut gegen etw sein; **they clashed ~** sie konnten ihre Meinungsverschiedenheiten nicht beseitigen

irrecoverable [,ɪrɪ'kʌvərəbl] ADJ endgültig *or* für immer verloren, unwiederbringlich verloren; *loss* unersetzlich, unersetzbar; *debt* nicht eintreibbar, uneinbringlich; **the company's losses are ~** die Verluste der Firma können nicht mehr wettgemacht werden

irrecoverably [,ɪrɪ'kʌvrəblɪ] ADV *broken* irreparabel; **~ lost** für immer verloren

irredeemable [,ɪrɪ'diːməbl] ADJ a *currency, pawned object* nicht einlösbar; *bonds* unkündbar, untilgbar; *annuity, debt* nicht ablösbar b (*fig*) *sinner* (rettungslos) verloren; *loss* unwiederbringlich; *transgression* unverzeihlich

irredeemably [,ɪrɪ'diːməblɪ] ADV *lost* rettungslos; *confused* hoffnungslos; **he's an ~ wicked man** er ist ein von Grund auf böser *or* ein abgrundtief böser Mensch; **democracy was ~ damaged** die Demokratie hatte irreparablen Schaden genommen

irreducible [,ɪrɪ'djuːsəbl] ADJ (*Chem, Math*) nicht reduzierbar; **the ~ minimum** das Allermindeste

irrefragable [ɪ'refrəgəbl] ADJ (*form*) unwiderlegbar

irrefutability [,ɪrɪfjuːtə'bɪlɪtɪ] N Unwiderlegbarkeit *f*

irrefutable [,ɪrɪ'fjuːtəbl] ADJ unwiderlegbar, unbestreitbar

irrefutably [,ɪrɪ'fjuːtɪblɪ] ADV unwiderlegbar; *demonstrate also* eindeutig

irregular [ɪ'regjʊlə] ADJ a (= *uneven*) unregelmäßig; *teeth, shape, coastline* ungleichmäßig; *surface* uneben; **at ~ intervals** in unregelmäßigen Abständen; **to be ~ in one's attendance** unregelmäßig erscheinen; **the windows are deliberately ~** die Fenster sind bewusst uneinheitlich; **to keep ~ hours** ein ungeregeltes Leben führen, keine festen Zeiten haben; **he's been a bit ~ recently** (*inf*) er hat in letzter Zeit ziemlich unregelmäßigen Stuhlgang

b (= *not conforming*) unstatthaft; (= *contrary to rules*) unvorschriftsmäßig; (= *contrary to law*) ungesetzlich; *marriage* ungültig; *behaviour* ungebührlich, ungehörig; **well, it's a bit ~, but I'll ...** eigentlich dürfte ich das nicht tun, aber ich ...; **it's a most ~ request, but ...** das ist ein höchst unübliches Ersuchen, aber ...; **this is most ~!** das ist äußerst ungewöhnlich!; **because of ~ procedures, the contract was not valid** wegen einiger Formfehler war der Vertrag ungültig;

she led a somewhat ~ private life ihr Privatleben war ziemlich turbulent **c** (*Gram*) unregelmäßig **d** *troops* irregulär **N** (*Mil*) Irreguläre(r) *mf*; **the ~s** die irreguläre Truppe

irregularity [ˌɪregjʊˈlærɪtɪ] N **a** (= *unevenness*) Unregelmäßigkeit *f*; (*of teeth, shape, coastline*) Ungleichmäßigkeit *f*; (*of surface*) Unebenheit *f*; (= *lack of uniformity*) Uneinheitlichkeit *f*; (*of sb's life*) Ungeregeltheit *f* **b** (= *failure to conform*) Unstatthaftigkeit *f*; (= *non-observation of rules*) Unvorschriftsmäßigkeit *f*; (= *unlawfulness*) Ungesetzlichkeit *f*; (*of marriage*) unvorschriftsmäßige Durchführung; (= *impropriety: of behaviour*) Ungebührlichkeit *f*, Ungehörigkeit *f*; **a slight ~ in the proceedings** ein kleiner Formfehler **c** (*Gram*) Unregelmäßigkeit *f*

irregularly [ɪˈregjʊlǝlɪ] ADV **a** (= *unevenly*) unregelmäßig; *shaped* ungleichmäßig; (= *at random intervals*) *eat, occur, go etc* in unregelmäßigen Abständen **b** (= *inadmissibly*) unstatthaft; (= *against the rules*) unvorschriftsmäßig; (= *against the law*) ungesetzlich; (= *improperly*) *behave* ungebührlich, ungehörig

irrelevance [ɪˈreləvǝns], **irrelevancy** [ɪˈreləvǝnsɪ] N Irrelevanz *f no pl*; (*of details also*) Unwesentlichkeit *f*, Nebensächlichkeit *f*; (*of titles, individuals*) Bedeutungslosigkeit *f*; **his speech was full of irrelevancies** vieles in seiner Rede war irrelevant *or* nebensächlich *or* unwesentlich; **it's become something of an ~** es ist ziemlich irrelevant geworden; **she dismissed his opinions as an ~** sie tat seine Ansichten als irrelevant *or* belanglos ab

irrelevant [ɪˈreləvǝnt] ADJ irrelevant; *details also, information* unwesentlich, nebensächlich; *titles etc* bedeutungslos; **it is ~ whether he agrees or not** es ist irrelevant *or* belanglos, ob er zustimmt; **these issues are ~ to the younger generation** diese Fragen sind für die jüngere Generation irrelevant *or* belanglos; **it's ~ to the subject** das ist für das Thema irrelevant; **his novels are largely ~ to the concerns of today** seine Romane haben wenig Bezug auf die Probleme von heute; **don't be ~** (*in discussion*) bleib bei der Sache; (*in essay writing*) bleiben Sie beim Thema

irrelevantly [ɪˈreləvǝntlɪ] ADV belanglos; **..., he said ~** ..., sagte er, obwohl das gar nicht zur Sache gehörte; **he rambled on ~** er schwafelte irrelevantes *or* belangloses Zeug

irreligious [ˌɪrɪˈlɪdʒǝs] ADJ unreligiös, irreligiös; *youth* gottlos; (= *lacking respect*) pietätlos

irremediable [ˌɪrɪˈmiːdɪǝbl] ADJ *character defects, errors* nicht behebbar; *damage* nicht wieder gutzumachen *pred*, nicht wieder gutzumachend *attr*; *situation* nicht mehr zu retten *pred or* rettend *attr*

irremediably [ˌɪrɪˈmiːdɪǝblɪ] ADV hoffnungslos

irreparable [ɪˈrepǝrǝbl] ADJ *damage* irreparabel, nicht wieder gutzumachen *pred*, nicht wieder gutzumachend *attr*; *harm also* bleibend; *loss* unersetzlich; *injury* irreparabel

irreparably [ɪˈrepǝrǝblɪ] ADV irreparabel; **his reputation was ~ damaged** sein Ruf war unwiderruflich geschädigt

irreplaceable [ˌɪrɪˈpleɪsǝbl] ADJ unersetzlich

irrepressible [ˌɪrɪˈpresǝbl] ADJ *urge, curiosity, energy, spirit* unbezähmbar; *optimism, sense of humour* unerschütterlich, unverwüstlich; *person* nicht kleinzukriegen; *child* sonnig; *delight* unbändig; **his ~ high spirits** sein sonniges Gemüt; **the ~ Susan** Susan, die sich nicht unterkriegen lässt

irrepressibly [ˌɪrɪˈpresǝblɪ] ADV *laugh, high-spirited* unbändig; **he was ~ optimistic** sein Optimismus war nicht kleinzukriegen

irreproachable [ˌɪrɪˈprǝʊtʃǝbl] ADJ *manners* tadellos, einwandfrei; *conduct also* untadelig

irreproachably [ˌɪrɪˈprǝʊtʃǝblɪ] ADV tadellos

irresistible [ˌɪrɪˈzɪstǝbl] ADJ unwiderstehlich (*to* für); **he is ~ to women** er wirkt auf Frauen unwiderstehlich; **he was in ~ form** (*Sport*) er war

in unschlagbarer Form; **the truth is ~** (*form*) die Wahrheit kommt immer ans Licht

irresistibly [ˌɪrɪˈzɪstǝblɪ] ADV unwiderstehlich; **it's ~ funny** es ist von unwiderstehlicher Komik

irresolute [ɪˈrezǝluːt] ADJ unentschlossen, unentschieden

irresolutely [ɪˈrezǝluːtlɪ] ADV unentschlossen, unschlüssig

irresoluteness [ɪˈrezǝluːtnɪs], **irresolution** [ɪˌrezǝˈluːʃǝn] N Unentschiedenheit *f*, Unentschlossenheit *f*

irrespective [ˌɪrɪˈspektɪv] ADJ **~ of** ungeachtet (+*gen*), unabhängig von; **candidates should be chosen ~ of sex/race** bei der Auswahl der Kandidaten sollte das Geschlecht/die Rasse keine Rolle spielen; **~ of whether they want to or not** egal *or* gleichgültig, ob sie wollen oder nicht

irresponsibility [ˈɪrɪˌspɒnsǝˈbɪlɪtɪ] N (*of action, behaviour*) Unverantwortlichkeit *f*; (*of person*) Verantwortungslosigkeit *f*

irresponsible [ˌɪrɪˈspɒnsǝbl] ADJ *action, behaviour* unverantwortlich; *person* verantwortungslos; **she was ~ to say that** es war unverantwortlich von ihr, das zu sagen

irresponsibly [ˌɪrɪˈspɒnsǝblɪ] ADV unverantwortlich; *behave also* verantwortungslos; **he was ~ extravagant with money** es war unverantwortlich, wie verschwenderisch er mit Geld umging

irretrievable [ˌɪrɪˈtriːvǝbl] ADJ **a** (= *unrecoverable*) nicht mehr wiederzubekommen; *past, happiness etc* unwiederbringlich; *loss* unersetzlich; *debt* nicht eintreibbar; **the erased information is ~** die gelöschte Information kann nicht mehr abgerufen werden **b** (= *irreparable*) *damage, harm* irreparabel; **~ breakdown of marriage** (*unheilbare*) Zerrüttung der Ehe

irretrievably [ˌɪrɪˈtriːvǝblɪ] ADV **~ lost** für immer verloren; **~ damaged** irreparabel; **her marriage broke down ~** ihre Ehe war (unheilbar) zerrüttet

irreverence [ɪˈrevǝrǝns] N (*of behaviour*) Unehrerbietigkeit *f*; (*of remark, attitude*) Respektlosigkeit *f*, Despektierlichkeit *f* (*geh*); (*of book, author*) Respektlosigkeit *f*; (*towards religion, the dead*) Pietätlosigkeit *f*

irreverent [ɪˈrevǝrǝnt] ADJ *behaviour* unehrerbietig; *remark, attitude* respektlos, despektierlich (*geh*); *book, author* respektlos; (*towards religion, the dead*) pietätlos

irreverently [ɪˈrevǝrǝntlɪ] ADV *behave* unehrerbietig; *say, speak, name* respektlos, despektierlich (*geh*); *write* respektlos; (*towards religion, the dead*) pietätlos

irreversible [ˌɪrɪˈvɜːsǝbl] ADJ nicht rückgängig zu machen; *decision, judgement* unwiderruflich; (*Med, Phys, Chem*) irreversibel; *damage* bleibend; *decision* unumstößlich; **to be in ~ decline** sich in einem unaufhaltsamen Abwärtstrend befinden

irreversibly [ˌɪrɪˈvɜːsǝblɪ] ADV *change* für immer; **the peace process has been ~ damaged** der Friedensprozess hat einen nicht wiedergutzumachenden Schaden davongetragen

irrevocable ADJ , **irrevocably** ADV [ɪˈrevǝkǝbl, -lɪ] unwiderruflich

irrigate [ˈɪrɪgeɪt] VT **a** *land, crop* bewässern **b** (*Med*) spülen

irrigation [ˌɪrɪˈgeɪʃǝn] N **a** (*Agr*) Bewässerung *f*; **~ canal** Bewässerungskanal *m* **b** (*Med*) Spülung *f*, Irrigation *f*; **colonic ~** Darmspülung *f*

irrigator [ˈɪrɪgeɪtǝʳ] N **a** (*Agr*) Bewässerungsanlage *f* **b** (*Med*) Spülapparat *m*, Irrigator *m*

irritability [ˌɪrɪtǝˈbɪlɪtɪ] N Reizbarkeit *f*; (*on occasion*) Gereiztheit *f*

irritable [ˈɪrɪtǝbl] ADJ (*as characteristic*) reizbar; (*on occasion*) gereizt; **don't be so ~** sei doch nicht so gereizt

irritable bowel syndrome N Reizdarm *m*

irritably [ˈɪrɪtǝblɪ] ADV gereizt

irritant [ˈɪrɪtǝnt] N (*Med*) Reizerreger *m*; (= *person*) Nervensäge *f* (*inf*); (= *noise etc*) Ärgernis *nt*

irritate [ˈɪrɪteɪt] VT **a** (= *annoy*) ärgern, aufregen; (*deliberately*) reizen; (= *get on nerves of*) irritieren; **to get ~d** ärgerlich werden; **she's easily ~d** sie ist sehr reizbar *or* schnell verärgert; **I get ~d at** *or* **with him** er reizt *or* ärgert mich, er regt mich auf **b** (*Med*) reizen

irritating [ˈɪrɪteɪtɪŋ] ADJ ärgerlich; *cough* lästig; **I find his jokes most ~** seine Witze regen mich wirklich auf; **you really are the most ~ person** du kannst einem wirklich auf die Nerven gehen; **how ~ for you!** wie ärgerlich!; **the ~ thing is that ...** das Ärgerliche ist, dass ...; **she has an ~ habit of snapping her fingers** sie hat die ärgerliche Angewohnheit, mit den Fingern zu schnipsen

irritatingly [ˈɪrɪteɪtɪŋlɪ] ADV ärgerlich; **he very ~ changed his mind** ärgerlicherweise hat er seine Meinung geändert

irritation [ˌɪrɪˈteɪʃǝn] N **a** (= *state*) Ärger *m*, Verärgerung *f*; (= *act*) Ärgern *nt*; (*deliberate*) Reizen *nt*; (= *thing that irritates*) Ärgernis *nt*, Unannehmlichkeit *f*; **the noise is a source of ~** der Lärm irritiert einen; **to avoid the ~ of a long delay** um eine ärgerliche *or* lästige Verzögerung zu vermeiden **b** (*Med*) Reizung *f*

irrupt [ɪˈrʌpt] VI eindringen, hereinstürzen; (*water also*) hereinbrechen

irruption [ɪˈrʌpʃǝn] N Eindringen *nt*, Hereinstürzen *nt*; (*of water also*) Hereinbrechen *nt*

IRS (*US*) *abbr* of **Internal Revenue Service** Finanzamt *nt*

Is *abbr* of **Island(s)** of **Isle(s)**

is [ɪz] *3rd pers sing present of* **be**

ISA [ˈaɪsǝ] N ABBR of **Individual Savings Account** (*Brit, Fin*) *von Zinsabschlagsteuer befreites Sparkonto*

Isaiah [aɪˈzaɪǝ] N Jesaja *m*

ISBN *abbr* of **International Standard Book Number** ISBN-Nummer *f*

ISDN *abbr* of **Integrated Services Digital Network** ISDN *nt*

-ise [-aɪz] VB *suf* → **-ize**

ish [ɪʃ] ADV (*inf*) ein bisschen; **hungry? – ~** Hunger? – ein bisschen

-ish [-ɪʃ] ADJ *suf* (+*adj*) -lich; (+*n*) -haft; (= *approximately*) um ... herum, zirka; **greenish** grünlich; **coldish** ziemlich kalt; **smallish** ziemlich klein; **youngish** ziemlich jung; **boyish** jungenhaft; **fortyish** um vierzig herum, zirka vierzig

isinglass [ˈaɪzɪŋglɑːs] N Fischleim *m*

Islam [ˈɪzlɑːm] N (= *religion*) der Islam; (= *Moslems collectively*) die Moslems *pl*

Islamic [ɪzˈlæmɪk] ADJ islamisch

Islamicist [ɪzˈlæmɪsɪst] N Islamist(in) *m(f)*

Islamist [ˈɪzlǝmɪst] N Islamist(in) *m(f)* ADJ islamistisch

island [ˈaɪlǝnd] N (*lit, fig*) Insel *f*

islander [ˈaɪlǝndǝʳ] N Insulaner(in) *m(f)*, Inselbewohner(in) *m(f)*

island-hopping [ˈaɪlǝndˌhɒpɪŋ] (*inf*) N Inselhüpfen *nt* (*inf*); **to go ~** von Insel zu Insel reisen ADJ **~ holiday** Urlaub *m* mit Inselhüpfen (*inf*)

isle [aɪl] N (*poet*) Eiland *nt* (*poet*); **the Isle of Man** die Insel Man

islet [ˈaɪlɪt] N kleines Eiland (*poet*), Inselchen *nt*

ism [ˈɪzǝm] N (*inf*) Ismus *m* (*inf*); **Marxism or any other ~** Marxismus oder jeder andere Ismus (*inf*)

isn't [ˈɪznt] *contr of* **is not**

ISO *abbr* of **International Standards Organization**

isobar [ˈaɪsǝʊbɑːʳ] N Isobare *f*

isolate [ˈaɪsǝʊleɪt] VT **a** (= *separate*) absondern, isolieren; (*Med, Chem*) isolieren; **the causes of crime cannot be ~d from social conditions** man kann die Gründe für kriminelles Verhalten nicht von den gesellschaftlichen Verhältnissen gesondert *or* isoliert betrachten **b** (= *cut off*) abschneiden, isolieren; **to ~ oneself**

from other people sich (von anderen) abkapseln; **to ~ oneself from the outside world** sich isolieren, sich von der Außenwelt zurückziehen **c** (= *pinpoint*) herausfinden; *essential factor* herauskristallisieren

isolated [ˈaɪsəʊleɪtɪd] ADJ **a** (= *cut off, marginalized*) abgeschnitten, isoliert; (= *remote*) abgelegen; *existence* zurückgezogen; (*Med*) isoliert; **the islanders feel ~** die Inselbewohner fühlen sich von der Außenwelt abgeschnitten; **she kept her sons ~ from other children** sie hielt ihre Söhne von anderen Kindern fern **b** (= *single*) einzeln; **~ instances** Einzelfälle *pl*

isolating [ˈaɪsəʊleɪtɪŋ] ADJ **~ language** isolierende Sprache

isolation [ˌaɪsəʊˈleɪʃən] N **a** (= *act*) (= *separation, cutting-off*) Absonderung *f*, Isolierung *f* (*esp Med, Chem*); (= *pinpointing*) Herausfinden *nt*; (*of essential factor*) Herauskristallisierung *f* **b** (= *state*) Isoliertheit *f*, Abgeschnittenheit *f*; (= *remoteness*) Abgelegenheit *f*, Abgeschiedenheit *f*; **his ~ from the outside world** seine Abgeschiedenheit von der Außenwelt; **this deliberate and self-imposed social ~** diese absichtliche und selbst auferlegte gesellschaftliche Isolation; **spiritual ~** geistige Isolation; **he felt a sense of ~** er fühlte sich isoliert; **Splendid Isolation** (*Hist*) Splendid Isolation *f*; **he lived in splendid ~ in a bedsitter in the suburbs** (*iro*) er wohnte weitab vom Schuss in einem möblierten Zimmer am Stadtrand (*inf*); **he was in ~ for three months** er war drei Monate lang isoliert; (*in hospital*) er war drei Monate auf der Isolierstation; **to keep a patient in ~** einen Patienten isolieren; **to live in ~** zurückgezogen leben; **to consider sth in ~** etw gesondert *or* isoliert betrachten; **it doesn't make much sense (when taken) in ~** für sich genommen *or* ohne Zusammenhang ist es ziemlich unverständlich

isolation hospital N Isolierspital *nt*

isolationism [ˌaɪsəʊˈleɪʃənɪzəm] N Isolationismus *m*

isolationist [ˌaɪsəʊˈleɪʃənɪst] ADJ isolationistisch **N** Isolationist(in) *m(f)*

isolation ward N Isolierstation *f*

isomer [ˈaɪsəʊməʳ] N (*Chem*) Isomer(e) *nt*

isomeric [ˌaɪsəʊˈmerɪk] ADJ (*Chem*) isomer

isometrics [ˌaɪsəʊˈmetrɪks] N *sing* Isometrie *f*

isomorphic [ˌaɪsəʊˈmɔːfɪk] ADJ (*form*) isomorph

isosceles [aɪˈsɒsɪliːz] ADJ **~ triangle** gleichschenkliges Dreieck

isotherm [ˈaɪsəʊθɜːm] N (*Met*) Isotherme *f*

isotope [ˈaɪsəʊtəʊp] N Isotop *nt*

ISP (*Comput*) abbr of **Internet service provider** Provider *m*

I-spy [ˈaɪˈspaɪ] N (*Brit*) → **spy**

Israel [ˈɪzreɪl] N Israel *nt*

Israeli [ɪzˈreɪlɪ] ADJ israelisch **N** Israeli *mf*

Israelite [ˈɪzrɪəlaɪt] N (*Bibl*) Israelit(in) *m(f)*

issei [ˈiːseɪ] N *pl* **issei** (*US*) *japanischer Einwanderer in den USA*

ISSN abbr of **International Standard Serial Number** ISSN *f*

issue [ˈɪʃuː] **VT** **a** (= *give, send out*) *passport, documents, certificate, driving licence* ausstellen; *tickets, library books* ausgeben; *shares, banknotes* ausgeben, emittieren; *stamps* herausgeben; *coins* ausgeben; *order* erteilen (*to* +*dat*); *warning, declaration, statement* abgeben, aussprechen; *proclamation* erlassen; *details* bekanntgeben; *ultimatum* stellen; **the issuing authorities** die ausstellende Behörde; **to ~ sb with a visa, to ~ a visa to sb** jdm ein Visum ausstellen; **a warrant for his arrest was ~d** gegen ihn wurde Haftbefehl erlassen; **~d capital** (*Fin*) ausgegebenes Kapital **b** (= *publish*) *book, newspaper* herausgeben **c** (= *supply*) *rations, rifles, ammunition* ausgeben; **to ~ sth to sb/sb with sth** etw an jdn ausgeben; **all troops are ~d with ...** alle Truppen sind mit ... ausgerüstet

VI (*from* aus) (*liquid, gas*) austreten; (*smoke, blood, water*) quellen, austreten; (*sound*) (hervoror heraus)dringen; (*people etc*) (heraus)strömen;

his actions ~ from a desire to help seine Handlungen entsprangen dem Wunsch zu helfen; **the sewage/river ~s into the sea** das Abwasser fließt/der Fluss mündet ins Meer

N **a** (= *question*) Frage *f*; (= *matter*) Angelegenheit *f*; (*problematic*) Problem *nt*; **the main** *or* **key ~ is reducing unemployment** das Wichtigste ist es, die Arbeitslosigkeit zu verringern; **the factual ~** die Tatsachen *pl*; **to raise an ~** eine Frage aufwerfen; **she raised the ~ of human rights** sie brachte die Frage der Menschenrechte zur Sprache; **the ~ is whether ...** es geht darum *or* die Frage ist, ob ...; **the whole future of the country is at ~** es geht um die Zukunft des Landes; **what is at ~?** worum geht es?; **this matter/question is not at ~** diese Angelegenheit/Frage steht nicht zur Debatte; **to take ~ with sb over sth** jdm in etw (*dat*) widersprechen; **this has become something of an ~** das ist zu einem Problem geworden; **to make an ~ of sth** etw aufbauschen; **do you want to make an ~ of it?** (*inf*) du willst dich wohl mit mir anlegen?; **to avoid the ~** ausweichen; (*in reply also*) ausweichend antworten **b** (= *outcome, result*) Ergebnis *nt*; **that decided the ~** das war entscheidend *or* ausschlaggebend; **to force the ~** eine Entscheidung erzwingen **c** (= *giving out, that given out*) (*of banknotes, shares, coins, stamps etc*) Ausgabe *f*; (*of shares*) Emission *f*, Ausgabe *f*; **place of ~** (*of tickets*) Ausgabestelle *f*; (*of passports*) Ausstellungsort *m*; **date of ~** (*of tickets*) Ausstellungsdatum *nt*; (*of stamps*) Ausgabetag *m*; **~ desk** Ausgabe (-schalter *m*) *f*; **~ price** (*of shares*) Zeichnungsor Emissionspreis *m* **d** (= *handing-out*) Ausgabe *f*; (= *supplying, thing supplied*) Lieferung *f*; **the ~ of guns to the troops** die Ausrüstung der Truppen mit Gewehren; **it's part of the clothing ~** es ist Teil der Ausstattung **e** (*of book etc*) Herausgabe *f*; (= *book etc*) Ausgabe *f* **f** (*of liquid, gas*) Ausströmen *nt*; **~ of pus** Eiterabsonderung *f*; **an ~ of blood from the cut** eine Blutung der Wunde **g** (*Jur: = offspring*) Nachkommenschaft *f*

issuer [ˈɪʃuːəʳ] N (*of shares*) Emittent(in) *m(f)*, Ausgeber(in) *m(f)*

issue-related [ˈɪʃuːrɪˈleɪtɪd] ADJ sachbezogen

Istanbul [ˌɪstænˈbuːl] N Istanbul *nt*

isthmus [ˈɪsməs] N Landenge *f*, Isthmus *m*

IT abbr of **information technology**

it¹ [ɪt] PRON **a** (*when replacing German noun*) (*subj*) er/sie/es; (*dir obj*) ihn/sie/es; (*indir obj*) ihm/ihr/ihm; **of it** davon; **behind/over/under** etc **it** dahinter/darüber/darunter *etc*; **who is it? – it's me** *or* (*form*) **I** wer ist da? – ich (bins); **who is it? – it's the Browns!** wer ist da? – die Browns!; **once the baby had been fed, it stopped crying** als das Baby gefüttert worden war, hörte es auf zu weinen; **what is it?** was ist es *or* das?; (= *what's the matter?*) was ist los?; **that's not it** (= *not the trouble*) das ist es (gar) nicht; (= *not the point*) darum gehts gar nicht; **the cheek of it!** so eine Frechheit!; **the worst of it is that ...** das Schlimmste daran ist, dass ...; **I like it here** mir gefällt es hier **b** (*indef subject*) es; **it's raining** es regnet; **yes, it is a problem** ja, das ist ein Problem; **it seems simple to me** mir scheint das ganz einfach; **if it hadn't been for her, we would have come** wenn sie nicht gewesen wäre, wären wir gekommen; **it's not that I don't want to go** es ist nicht so, dass ich nicht gehen will; **why is it always me who has to ...?** warum muss (ausgerechnet) immer ich ...?; **why is it always him who can't ...?** warum ist es immer er, der nicht ... kann?; **it wasn't me** ICH wars nicht; **it was the Italians who won** es waren die Italiener, die gewannen; **it was ten miles to the station** bis zum Bahnhof waren es zehn Meilen; **I don't think it (is) wise of you ...** ich halte es für unklug, wenn du ...; **it is said that ...** es wird gesagt, dass ..., man sagt, dass ...

c (*emph*) **it was him** *or* **he** (*form*) **who asked her** ER hat sie gefragt; **it was a cup that he dropped and not ...** er hat eine TASSE fallen lassen und nicht ...; **it's his appearance I object to** ich habe nur etwas gegen sein Äußeres; **it was for his sake that she lied** nur um seinetwillen hat sie gelogen; **it's the OTHER one I like** ich mag den ANDEREN/das ANDERE *etc* **d** (*inf phrases*) **that's it!** (*agreement*) ja, genau!; (*annoyed*) jetzt reichts mir!; **that's it (then)!** (*achievement*) (so,) das wärs!, geschafft!; (*disappointment*) ja, das wars dann wohl; **this is it!** (*before action*) jetzt gehts los! → **at, in, with-it** **N** (*inf*) **a** (*in children's games*) **you're it!** du bist! **b** **this is really it!** das ist genau das richtige, DAS ist es; **he really thinks he's it** er bildet sich (*dat*) ein, er sei sonst wer **c** **my cat's an it** meine Katze ist ein Neutrum **d** (*dated: = sex appeal*) Sexappeal *m*

it² N (*dated sl*) **gin and it** Gin mit italienischem Wermut

ITA (*dated Brit*) abbr of **Independent Television Authority**

ita abbr of **initial teaching alphabet** *Lautschrift für den Anfangsunterricht im Lesen*

Italian [ɪˈtæljən] ADJ italienisch **N** **a** Italiener(in) *m(f)* **b** (*Ling*) Italienisch *nt*

Italianate [ɪˈtæljəneɪt] ADJ nach italienischer Art; **the ~ style of the church** der von der italienischen Schule beeinflusste Stil der Kirche

italic [ɪˈtælɪk] ADJ kursiv; **~ type** Kursivdruck *m*; **~ script** Kurrentschrift *f* **italics** PL Kursivschrift *f*, Kursive *f*; **in ~s** kursiv (gedruckt)

italicize [ɪˈtælɪsaɪz] VT kursiv schreiben

Italo- [ɪˈtæləʊ-] PREF Italo-, italo-; **~American** italo-amerikanisch

Italy [ˈɪtəlɪ] N Italien *nt*

ITC (*Brit*) abbr of **Independent Television Commission**

itch [ɪtʃ] **N** **a** (*lit*) Jucken *nt*, Juckreiz *m*; **I have an ~** mich juckt es, ich habe einen Juckreiz **b** (*fig inf: = urge*) Lust *f*; **I have the ~ to do sth** es reizt *or* juckt (*inf*) mich, etw zu tun; **the seven-year ~** das verflixte siebte Jahr **VI** **a** (*lit*) jucken; **my back is ~ing** mein Rücken juckt (mich), mir *or* mich juckt der Rücken; **that rash made me ~ all over** der Ausschlag juckte am ganzen Körper **b** (*fig inf*) **he is ~ing to ...** es reizt *or* juckt (*inf*) ihn, zu ...; **he's ~ing for a fight** er ist auf Streit aus

itching [ˈɪtʃɪŋ] **ADJ** juckend **N** Jucken *nt*, Juckreiz *m*; **~ powder** Juckpulver *nt*

itchy [ˈɪtʃɪ] ADJ (+*er*) (= *itching*) juckend; **my back is ~** mein Rücken juckt; **I've got an ~ leg** mir juckt das Bein; **to become ~** anfangen zu jucken; **I've got ~ feet** (*inf*) ich will hier weg (*inf*); (= *want to travel also*) mich packt das Fernweh; **he's got ~ fingers** (*inf*) er macht lange Finger (*inf*); **he's got an ~ (trigger) finger** er hat einen lockeren Finger am Abzug **b** (= *causing itching*) *cloth* kratzig

it'd [ˈɪtəd] *contr* of **it would** *of* **it had**

-ite [-aɪt] N *suf* (= *follower of*) -anhänger(in) *m(f)*; **Blairite** Blair-Anhänger(in) *m(f)*

item [ˈaɪtəm] ◑ **20.3** N **a** (*in programme, on agenda etc*) Punkt *m*; (*Comm: in account book*) (Rechnungs)posten *m*; (= *article*) Stück *nt*, Ding *nt*, Gegenstand *m*; (*in catalogue etc*) Artikel *m*; (*Brit: in variety show*) Nummer *f*; **~s of furniture/clothing/jewellery** Möbel-/Kleidungs-/Schmuckstücke *pl*; **~s of food** Lebensmittel *pl*; **he went through it ~ by ~** er ging die Sache Punkt für Punkt durch; **heating oil is one of the most expensive ~s I have to buy** Heizöl gehört zu den teuersten Dingen, die ich kaufe **b** (*of news*) Bericht *m*; (*short: Rad, TV*) Meldung *f*; **a short news ~** (*in newspaper*) eine Zeitungsnotiz; (*Rad, TV*) eine Kurzmeldung; **the main news ~** die wichtigste Nachricht **c** (*inf*) **Lynn and Craig are an ~** zwischen Lynn und Craig spielt sich was ab (*inf*)

itemization [ˌaɪtəmaɪˈzeɪʃən] N detaillierte Aufstellung, Einzelaufführung *f*

itemize ['aɪtəmaɪz] VT spezifizieren, einzeln aufführen; **to ~ a bill** die Rechnungsposten einzeln aufführen, die Rechnung spezifizieren

iterate ['ɪtəreɪt] VT (form) wiederholen

iteration [ɪtə'reɪʃən] N (form) Wiederholung f

iterative ['ɪtərətɪv] ADJ (Gram) iterativ

itinerant [ɪ'tɪnərənt] **ADJ** umherziehend, wandernd; minstrel fahrend; **an ~ lifestyle** ein Wanderleben nt; **~ preacher** Wanderprediger(in) m(f); **~ worker** Saison- or Wanderarbeiter(in) m(f); **~ theatre** (Brit) or **theater** (US) **group** Wandertruppe f **N** (= worker) Wanderarbeiter(in) m(f)

itinerary [aɪ'tɪnərərɪ] N (= route) (Reise)route f; (= map) Straßenkarte f, Wegeverzeichnis nt

it'll ['ɪtl] contr of **it will** of **it shall**

ITN (Brit) abbr of **Independent Television News** Nachrichtendienst der Fernsehanstalt ITV

ITO abbr of **International Trade Organization**

its [ɪts] POSS ADJ sein(e)/ihr(e)/sein(e)

it's [ɪts] contr of **it is** of **it has** as aux

itself [ɪt'self] PRON **a** (reflexive) sich **b** (emph) selbst; **and now we come to the text ~** und jetzt kommen wir zum Text selbst; **the frame ~ is worth £1,000** der Rahmen allein or schon der Rahmen ist £ 1.000 wert; **she has been**

kindness **~** sie war die Freundlichkeit in Person; **in ~, the actual amount is not important** der Betrag an sich ist unwichtig; **enthusiasm is not enough in ~** Begeisterung allein genügt nicht **c by ~** (= alone) allein; (= automatically) von selbst, selbsttätig; **seen by ~** einzeln betrachtet; **the bomb went off by ~** die Bombe ging von selbst los

itsy-bitsy ['ɪtsɪ'bɪtsɪ], **itty-bitty** ['ɪtɪ'bɪtɪ] ADJ (inf: = tiny) klitzeklein (inf), winzig

ITV (Brit) abbr of **Independent Television** britische Fernsehanstalt

IUD abbr of **intra-uterine device**

I've [aɪv] contr of **I have**

ivied ['aɪvɪd] ADJ efeuumrankt

ivory ['aɪvərɪ] **N a** (also colour) Elfenbein nt; **the ~ trade** der Elfenbeinhandel **b** (Art) Elfenbeinschnitzerei f **c** (inf) **ivories** (= piano keys) Tasten pl; (= billiard balls) Billardkugeln pl; (= dice) Würfel pl; (dated: = teeth) Beißer pl (inf) **ADJ a** elfenbeinern **b** (colour) elfenbeinfarben

Ivory Coast N Elfenbeinküste f

ivory tower N (fig) Elfenbeinturm m **ADJ** attr weltfremd

ivy ['aɪvɪ] N Efeu m

Ivy League N (US) Eliteuniversitäten pl der USA

IVY LEAGUE

Als **Ivy League** bezeichnet man acht Universitäten im Nordosten der Vereinigten Staaten von Amerika, Harvard, Yale, Pennsylvania, Princeton, Columbia, Brown, Dartmouth und Cornell, die neben einem ausgezeichneten akademischen Ruf ein großartiges Renommee haben, das mit dem von Oxford und Cambridge in England verglichen werden kann. **Ivy League** heißen sie deshalb, weil viele der Institutsgemäuer efeubedeckt sind. Der Ausdruck kam erstmals auf, als sich diese Universitäten 1956 zu einer gemeinsamen American Football Liga zusammenschlossen, um den sportlichen Wettkampf unter den Universitäten zu fördern. Studenten dieser ehrwürdigen Universitäten werden „Ivy Leaguer" genannt, eine Bezeichnung, die auch für solche Leute benutzt wird, die Haltung und Moden der Ivy League-Universitäten annehmen.

-ize [-aɪz] VB suf -isieren; **authorize** autorisieren; **rationalize** rationalisieren

J

J, j [dʒeɪ] N J nt, j nt

jab [dʒæb] **VT** **a** (with stick, elbow etc) stoßen; (with knife) stechen, stoßen; **she ~bed the jellyfish with a stick** sie pik(s)te mit einem Stock in die Qualle (hinein) (inf); **he ~bed his finger at the map** er tippte mit dem Finger auf die Karte; **a sharp ~bing pain** ein scharfer, stechender Schmerz
b (Brit inf: = give injection to) eine Spritze geben (+dat) or verpassen (+dat) (inf)
VI stoßen (at sb with sth mit etw nach jdm); (Boxing) eine (kurze) Gerade schlagen (at auf +acc)
N **a** (with stick, elbow) Stoß m; (with needle, knife) Stich m; **he gave the jellyfish a ~ with a stick** er stieß or pik(s)te (inf) mit einem Stock in die Qualle (hinein); **he got a nasty ~ in the eye when she opened her umbrella** sie stach ihn ins Auge, als sie den Regenschirm öffnete
b (Brit inf: = injection) Spritze f
c (Boxing) (kurze) Gerade

jabber ['dʒæbə'] **VT** (daher)plappern (inf); poem, prayers herunterrasseln, abhaspeln (inf) **VI** (also jabber away) plappern, schwätzen, quasseln (inf); **they sat there ~ing away in Spanish** sie saßen da und quasselten spanisch (inf) **N** Geplapper nt, Gequassel nt (inf), Geschnatter nt

jabbering ['dʒæbərɪŋ] N Geplapper nt, Plappern nt, Geschnatter nt

jacaranda [,dʒækə'rændə] N Jakaranda(baum) m; (= wood) Jakarandaholz nt, Palisander(holz nt) m

Jack [dʒæk] N dim of **John** Hans m; **I'm all right ~** das kann mich überhaupt nicht jucken (inf); **his attitude of I'm all right ~** seine Einstellung „das kann mich überhaupt nicht jucken"

jack [dʒæk] N **a** Hebevorrichtung f; (Aut) Wagenheber m **b** (Cards) Bube m **c** (Naut: = flag) Gösch f, Bugflagge f → **Union Jack** **d** (Bowling) Zielkugel f **e** (= bootjack) Stiefelknecht m **f** (inf) **every man ~ (of them)** alle ohne Ausnahme, (alle) geschlossen; **every man ~ of them voted against it** sie stimmten alle ohne Ausnahme or ohne Ausnahme dagegen

▶ **jack in** VT sep (Brit inf) university, job etc stecken (sl), aufgeben; **jack it in!** (= stop it) hör auf damit!, stecks (sl)

▶ **jack up** VT sep **a** car aufbocken **b** (inf) prices, wages, interest rates (in die Höhe) treiben

jackal ['dʒækɔ:l] N Schakal m

jackanapes ['dʒækəneɪps] N pl - (old) (= man) Fant m (old), (eingebildeter) Laffe (old); (= child) Racker m (old)

jackass ['dʒækæs] N (= donkey) Eselshengst m; (inf: = person) Esel (inf), Dummkopf (inf) m

jackboot ['dʒækbu:t] N Schaftstiefel m; **to be under the ~ (of)** unter dem Stiefel (+gen) stehen

jackdaw ['dʒækdɔ:] N Dohle f

jacket ['dʒækɪt] N **a** (= garment) Jacke f; (= man's tailored jacket) Jackett nt; (= life jacket) Schwimmweste f **b** (of book) Schutzumschlag m, Buchhülle f; (US: of record) Plattenhülle f (esp US: for papers etc) Umschlag m **d** **~ potatoes, potatoes (baked) in their ~s** (in der Schale) gebackene Kartoffeln pl **e** (Tech: of boiler etc) Mantel m, Ummantelung f

jack: Jack Frost N der Frost, der Reif (personifiziert); **~ has been, ~ has painted the window** es sind Eisblumen am Fenster; **jackhammer** N (US) Presslufthammer m; **jack-in-office** N Beamtenseele f; **jack-in-the-box** N Schachtel- or Kastenteufel m; **he was up and down like a ~** er sprang immer wieder auf, der reinste Hampelmann

jackknife ['dʒæknaɪf] N **a** (großes) Taschenmesser **b** (also **jackknife dive**) gehechteter Sprung **VI** **the lorry ~d** der Lastwagenanhänger hat sich quer gestellt

jack: jack of all trades N Alleskönner m; **to be (a) ~ (and master of none)** (prov) ein Hansdampf in allen Gassen sein; **jack-o'-lantern** N Kürbislaterne f; (= will-o'-the-wisp) Irrlicht nt; **jack plane** N (Tech) Schropp- or Doppelhobel m; **jack plug** N Bananenstecker m; (for telephone) Klinkenstecker m

jackpot ['dʒækpɒt] N Pott m (inf); (Cards also) Jackpot m; (in lottery etc) Hauptgewinn m; **the ~ this week stands at £10 million** diese Woche ist der Höchstgewinn zehn Millionen Pfund; **to hit the ~** (lit) einen Treffer haben; (in lottery) den Hauptgewinn bekommen; (fig) das große Los ziehen

jack: jack rabbit N Eselhase m; **Jack Robinson** [,dʒæk'rɒbɪnsən] N **before you could say ~** (inf) im Nu, im Handumdrehen; **Jack Russell** [,dʒæk'rʌsl] N Jack Russell m

jacks [dʒæks] N sing (= game) Kinderspiel mit kleinem Gummiball und Metallsternchen

jackstraws ['dʒækstrɔ:z] N sing Mikado m

jack: Jack Tar N (Naut inf) Seebär m (inf); **Jack-the-lad** N (Brit inf) Großmaul nt (inf)

Jacob ['dʒeɪkəb] N Jakob m

Jacobean [,dʒækə'bi:ən] ADJ aus der Zeit Jakobs I.

Jacobite ['dʒækəbaɪt] N Jakobit(in) m(f)

Jacuzzi® [dʒə'ku:zɪ] N Whirlpool m

jade¹ [dʒeɪd] **N** (= stone) Jade m or f; (= colour) Jadegrün nt **ADJ** Jade-; (colour) jadegrün; **a ~ necklace** eine Jadekette, eine Kette aus Jade

jade² N (old) **a** (= horse) Schindmähre f (old), Klepper m (old) **b** (= loose woman) Weibsbild nt, Weibsstück nt; (= pert girl) freches or keckes Weibsbild

jaded ['dʒeɪdɪd] ADJ (physically) matt, abgespannt; (permanently) verbraucht, abgelebt; (= mentally dulled) stumpfsinnig, abgestumpft; (from overindulgence etc) übersättigt; appearance verlebt, verbraucht; palate abgestumpft

jade-green ADJ jadegrün

Jag [dʒæg] N (inf: = car) Jaguar® m

jag [dʒæg] N **a** (of rock) Zacke f, Spitze f; (of saw) Zacke f **b** **to go on a ~** (inf) einen draufmachen (inf) **c** (Scot, inf, = injection) Spritze f

jagged ['dʒægɪd] ADJ zackig; edge, hole also schartig, (aus)gezackt; teeth gezackt; wound, tear ausgefranst; coastline, rocks zerklüftet; mountains, peaks spitz

jaguar ['dʒægjʊə'] N Jaguar m

jail [dʒeɪl] **N** Gefängnis nt; **in ~** im Gefängnis; **after two years in ~** nach zwei Jahren Gefängnis, nach zweijähriger Haft; **to go to ~** eingesperrt werden, ins Gefängnis kommen **VT** einsperren, ins Gefängnis sperren

jail: jailbait N (inf) **she's ~** die ist noch minderjährig, lass lieber die Finger von ihr (inf); **jailbird** N (inf) Knastbruder m/-schwester f (inf); **jailbreak** N Ausbruch m (aus dem Gefängnis); **jailbreaker** N Ausbrecher(in) m(f)

jailer ['dʒeɪlə'] N Gefängniswärter(in) m(f), Gefängnisaufseher(in) m(f)

jail: jailhouse N (US) Gefängnis nt; **jail sentence** N Gefängnisstrafe f

jalop(p)y [dʒə'lɒpɪ] N (inf) alte (Klapper)kiste or Mühle (inf)

jalousie ['ʒælu(:)zi:] N Jalousie f

jam¹ [dʒæm] N (Brit) Marmelade f, Konfitüre f; **you want ~ on it too, do you?** (Brit inf) du kriegst wohl nie genug or den Hals voll? (inf); **the company has promised (us) ~ tomorrow** die Firma hat uns auf die Zukunft vertröstet

jam² **N** **a** (= crowd) Gedränge nt, Gewühl nt
b (= traffic jam) (Verkehrs)stau m, Stauung f
c (= blockage: in machine, of logs etc) Stockung f, Stauung f
d (inf: = tight spot) Klemme f (inf), Patsche f (inf); **to be in a ~** in der Klemme or Patsche sitzen (inf); **to get oneself into a ~** ins Gedränge kommen (inf); **to get sb/oneself out of a ~** jdn/sich aus der Patsche ziehen (inf)
VT **a** (= make stick) window, drawer etc verklemmen, verkanten; gun, brakes etc blockieren; (= wedge) (to stop rattling etc) festklemmen; (between two things) einklemmen; **to ~ a door open/shut** eine Tür festklemmen(, so dass sie auf/zu bleibt); **be careful not to ~ the lock** pass auf, dass sich das Schloss nicht verklemmt; **they had him ~med up against the wall** sie hatten ihn gegen die Wand gedrängt; **it's ~med** es klemmt; **he got his finger ~med** or **he ~med his finger in the door** er hat sich (dat) den Finger in der Tür eingeklemmt
b (= cram, squeeze) (into in +acc) things stopfen, hineinzwängen, quetschen; people quetschen, pferchen; **to be ~med together** (things) zusammengezwängt sein; (people) zusammengedrängt sein; (in train etc also) zusammengepfercht sein; **why ~ all the facts into one article?** warum zwängen or quetschen (inf) Sie alle Fakten in einen Artikel?
c (= crowd, block) street, town etc verstopfen, blockieren; phone lines blockieren; **spectators ~med the stadium** das Stadion war mit Zuschauern voll gestopft; **a street ~med with cars** eine verstopfte Straße; **the drain was ~med with rubbish** der Abfluss war durch Abfall verstopft; **the passage was ~med with people** Menschen verstopften or versperrten den Durchgang; **the switchboard has been ~med all day** sämtliche Leitungen der Telefonzentrale waren den ganzen Tag blockiert
d (= move suddenly) **to ~ one's foot on the brake** eine Vollbremsung machen, auf die Bremse steigen (inf) or latschen (inf); **he ~med his hands into his pockets** er steckte die Hände fest in die Taschen → also **jam on**
e (Rad) station, broadcast stören
VI **a** **the crowd ~med into the bus** die Menschenmenge zwängte sich in den Bus
b (= become stuck) (brake) sich verklemmen;

(*gun*) Ladehemmung haben; (*door, window etc*) klemmen; **the key ~med in the lock** der Schlüssel blieb im Schloss stecken **c** (*Mus*) eine Jamsession machen

▶ **jam in** VT *sep* **a** (= *wedge in*) einkeilen; **he was jammed in by the crowd** er war in der Menge eingekeilt **b** (= *press in*) (herein)stopfen in (+*acc*) VI (= *crowd in*) sich hineindrängen

▶ **jam on** VT *sep* **a** **to jam on the brakes** eine Vollbremsung machen, voll auf die Bremse latschen (*inf*) **b** **to jam on one's hat** sich (*dat*) den Hut aufstülpen VI (*brakes*) klemmen

▶ **jam up** VT *sep* **a** = **jam²** VT **a** **b** (= *block*) *roads, entrance etc* blockieren, versperren; *drain, pipe* verstopfen, blockieren

Jamaica [dʒəˈmeɪkə] N Jamaika *nt*

Jamaican [dʒəˈmeɪkən] ADJ jamaikanisch N Jamaikaner(in) *m(f)*

Jamaica rum N Jamaikarum *m*

jamb [dʒæm] N (*of door/window*) (Tür-/Fenster)pfosten *m*

jambalaya [ˌdʒʌmbəˈlaɪə] N *aus Louisiana stammendes Gericht aus Reis, Schinken und Meeresfrüchten*

jamboree [ˌdʒæmbəˈriː] N (*Scouts'*) Pfadfindertreffen *nt*; (*dated*: = *party*) Rummel *m* (*inf*); **village ~** Dorffest *nt*

James [dʒeɪmz] N Jakob *m*

jam: jam-full ADJ *container* voll gestopft, gepfropft voll; *room, bus* überfüllt, überfüllt (*inf*), proppenvoll (*inf*); **~ of people** voll gestopft mit Leuten; **jam jar** N (*Brit*) Marmeladenglas *nt*

jammer [ˈdʒæmə] N (*Rad*) Störsender *m*

jamming [ˈdʒæmɪŋ] N (*Rad*) Störung *f*; **~ station** Störsender *m*

jammy [ˈdʒæmɪ] ADJ (+*er*) (*Brit inf*: = *lucky*) Glücks-; **a ~ shot** ein Glückstreffer *m*; **the ~ bugger won three in a row** der verdammte Glückspilz hat dreimal nacheinander gewonnen (*inf*)

jam: jam nut N (*Tech*) Gegenmutter *f*; **jam-packed** ADJ überfüllt, proppenvoll (*inf*); **~ with tourists** voller Touristen; **jam pot** N Marmeladentöpfchen *nt*; **jam puff** N Blätterteigteilchen *nt* mit Marmelade; **jam roll** N Biskuitrolle *f*; **jam session** N Jamsession *f*; **jam tart** N Marmeladenkuchen *m*, Marmeladentörtchen *nt*

Jan *abbr of* **January** Jan.

Jane [dʒeɪn] N **a** → **plain b** **jane** (*US sl*: = *woman*) Frau *f*

Jane Doe N (*US Jur*) *Frau, deren Name nicht bekannt ist*

jangle [ˈdʒæŋgl] VI (*keys, money*) klimpern (*inf*); (*bells*) bimmeln (*inf*); (*chains, harness*) klirren, rasseln; **my nerves are jangling** ich bin genervt (*inf*) VT *money* klimpern mit; *bell* bimmeln lassen; *keys, chains* rasseln mit; **it ~d my nerves** das ist mir durch Mark und Bein gegangen N (*of keys, money*) Klimpern *nt*, Geklimper *nt* (*inf*); (*of bells*) Bimmeln *nt* (*inf*); (*of chains, harness*) Klirren *nt*, Rasseln *nt*

jangling [ˈdʒæŋglɪŋ] ADJ *keys, money* klimpernd; *bells* bimmelnd; *chains, harness* klirrend, rasselnd N = **jangle** N

janitor [ˈdʒænɪtə] N Hausmeister(in) *m(f)*; (*of block of flats also*) Hauswart(in) *m(f)*

janitress [ˈdʒænɪtrɪs] N Hausmeisterin *f*

jankers [ˈdʒæŋkəz] PL (*Mil sl*: = *prison*) Bau *m* (*Mil sl*)

January [ˈdʒænjʊərɪ] N Januar *m* → *also* **September**

Janus [ˈdʒeɪnəs] N Janus *m*

Jap [dʒæp] N (*pej inf*) Japse *m* (*pej*)

Japan [dʒəˈpæn] N Japan *nt*

japan [dʒəˈpæn] N schwarzer Lack, Japanlack *m* VT mit Japanlack überziehen

Japanese [ˌdʒæpəˈniːz] ADJ japanisch N **a** Japaner(in) *m(f)* **b** (*Ling*) Japanisch *nt*

jape [dʒeɪp] N (*old*) Spaß *m*, Scherz *m*; (= *trick*) Streich *m* VI spaßen, scherzen

japonica [dʒəˈpɒnɪkə] N Japanische Quitte

jar¹ [dʒɑː] N **a** (*for jam etc*) Glas *nt*; (*without handle*) Topf *m*, Gefäß *nt* **b** (*Brit inf*: = *drink*) Bierchen *nt* (*inf*); **fancy a ~?** kommst du (mit) auf ein Bierchen? (*inf*)

jar² N **a** (= *jolt*) Ruck *m*; **he/his neck got quite a ~ in the accident** er/sein Hals hat bei dem Autounfall einen schweren Stoß abbekommen **b** (*fig*) Schock *m* VI **a** (= *grate: metal etc*) kreischen, quietschen; **to ~ against sth** auf etw (*dat*) quietschen *or* kreischen **b** (= *be out of harmony*) (*note*) schauerlich klingen; (*colours, patterns*) sich beißen (*inf*), nicht harmonieren (*with* mit); (*ideas, opinions*) sich nicht vertragen, nicht harmonieren (*with* mit) VT *building etc, brain* erschüttern; *back, knee* sich (*dat*) stauchen; (= *jolt continuously*) durchrütteln; (*fig*) einen Schock versetzen (+*dat*); **he must have ~red the camera** er muss mit dem Fotoapparat gewackelt haben; **someone ~red my elbow** jemand hat mir an den *or* mich am Ellbogen gestoßen; **the sight of this ~red my memory** dieser Anblick rüttelte alte Erinnerungen wach

▶ **jar on** VI +*prep obj* Schauer über den Rücken jagen (+*dat*); **this noise jars on my nerves** dieser Lärm geht mir auf die Nerven; **her voice jars on my ears** ihre Stimme geht mir durch und durch

jardinière [ˌdʒɑːdɪnɪˈeə] N Blumenbank *f*

jargon [ˈdʒɑːgən] N Jargon *m* (*pej*), Fachsprache *f*

jarring [ˈdʒɑːrɪŋ] ADJ *sound* gellend, kreischend; *colours* sich beißend *attr* (*inf*), nicht zusammenpassend *attr*; **to strike a ~ note** einen Misston anschlagen

jasmin(e) [ˈdʒæzmɪn] N Jasmin *m*

Jason [ˈdʒeɪsən] N Jason *m*

jasper [ˈdʒæspə] N Jaspis *m*

jaundice [ˈdʒɔːndɪs] N Gelbsucht *f*

jaundiced [ˈdʒɔːndɪst] ADJ **a** (*lit*) gelbsüchtig **b** *attitude* verbittert, zynisch; **to take a ~ view of sth** in Bezug auf etw (*acc*) zynisch sein; **to regard sth with a ~ eye** eine zynische Einstellung zu etw haben

jaunt [dʒɔːnt] N Trip *m*, Spritztour *f*; **to go for a ~** einen Ausflug *or* eine Spritztour machen; **on his last ~ through Europe** auf seiner letzten Europatour, auf seinem letzten Trip durch Europa

jauntily [ˈdʒɔːntɪlɪ] ADV munter, fröhlich, unbeschwert; *walk also* schwungvoll; **with his hat perched ~ over one ear** den Hut keck aufgesetzt, den Hut keck auf einem Ohr; **she remains ~ confident** sie bewahrt sich ihr unbeschwertes Selbstbewusstsein

jauntiness [ˈdʒɔːntɪnɪs] N Unbeschwertheit *f*, Sorglosigkeit *f*; (*of singing*) Munterkeit *f*, Fröhlichkeit *f*, Heiterkeit *f*; **the ~ of his step** sein schwungvoller *or* munterer Gang

jaunty [ˈdʒɔːntɪ] ADJ (+*er*) munter, fröhlich; *tune also, hat* flott; *steps also* schwungvoll; *attitude* unbeschwert, sorglos; **with a ~ air** unbeschwert; **he wore his hat at a ~ angle** er hatte den Hut keck aufgesetzt

Java [ˈdʒɑːvə] N Java *nt*

Javanese [ˌdʒɑːvəˈniːz] ADJ (*also* **Javan**) javanisch N **a** Javaner(in) *m(f)* **b** (*Ling*) Javanisch *nt*

javelin [ˈdʒævlɪn] N Speer *m*; **in the ~** (*Sport*) beim Speerwerfen; **throwing the ~, ~ throwing** Speerwerfen *nt*; **~ thrower** Speerwerfer(in) *m(f)*

jaw [dʒɔː] N **a** Kiefer *m*, Kinnlade *f*; **the lion opened its ~s** der Löwe riss seinen Rachen auf; **with its prey between its ~s** mit der Beute im Maul; **his ~ dropped** sein Unterkiefer fiel *or* klappte herunter; **his ~ was set** (in concentration) er spannte sein Gesicht (konzentriert) an **b jaws** PL (*fig: of valley etc*) Mündung *f*, Öffnung *f*; **the horsemen rode into the ~s of death** die Reiter gingen in den sicheren Tod;

snatched from the ~s of death den Klauen des Todes entrissen **c** (*of pincer, vice*) (Klemm)backe *f* **d** (*inf*) (= *chatting*) Gerede *nt*, Geschwätz *nt*; (= *chat*) Schwatz *m*, Schwätzchen *nt* **e** (*inf*) (= *sermonizing*) (Moral)predigen *nt* (*inf*); (= *sermon*) Moralpredigt *f* (*inf*) VI **a** (*inf*: = *chat*) quatschen (*inf*), quasseln (*inf*) **b** (*inf*: = *moralize*) predigen (*inf*)

jaw: jawbone N Kieferknochen *m*, Kinnbacke *f*; **jawboning** N (*US Pol inf*) *Appelle eines Regierungschefs an Wirtschafts- und Gewerkschaftsführer zur Mäßigung bei Preiserhöhungen und Lohnforderungen*; **jawbreaker** N (*inf*) Zungenbrecher *m*

jay [dʒeɪ] N Eichelhäher *m*

jay: jaywalk VI sich als Fußgänger unachtsam verhalten; **jaywalker** N unachtsamer Fußgänger, unachtsame Fußgängerin; **jaywalking** N Unachtsamkeit *f* (eines Fußgängers) im Straßenverkehr

jazz [dʒæz] N **a** (*Mus*) Jazz *m* **b** (*inf*: = *talk*) Getön *nt* (*inf*), Gewäsch *nt* (*pej*); **... and all that ~** ... und all so 'n Zeug (*inf*), ... und das ganze Drum und Dran (*inf*) *attr* Jazz-; **~ band** Jazzband *f*; **~ music** Jazzmusik *f*, Jazz *m* VI (*dated*: = *play jazz*) jazzen, Jazz machen

▶ **jazz up** VT *sep* aufmöbeln (*inf*), aufpeppen (*inf*); **to jazz up the classics** klassische Musik verjazzen

jazz: jazz ballet N Jazzballett *nt*; **jazzman** N *pl* **-men** [-men] Jazzer *m*; **jazz rock** N Jazz-Rock *m*

jazzy [ˈdʒæzɪ] ADJ (+*er*) **a** *colour* knallig (*inf*), auffallend, schreiend (*pej*); *pattern* wild, stark gemustert, auffallend; *dress, tie* poppig (*inf*), knallig (*inf*) **b** *music* verjazzt

JC *abbr of* **Jesus Christ** J. Chr.

JCB® [dʒeɪsiːˈbiː] N Erdräummaschine *f*

JCR (*Brit Univ*) *abbr of* **Junior Common Room** Gemeinschaftsraum *m* für Studenten

jealous [ˈdʒeləs] ADJ **a** *husband, lover, child etc* eifersüchtig; (= *envious of sb's possessions, success etc*) neidisch, missgünstig; **to be ~ of sb** auf jdn eifersüchtig sein; (= *envious*) jdn beneiden; **I'm not at all ~ of his success** ich bin nicht neidisch auf seinen Erfolg, ich beneide ihn nicht um seinen Erfolg; **in a (fit of) ~ rage** in einem Anfall von rasender Eifersucht **b** (= *watchful, careful*) sehr besorgt (*of* um), bedacht (*of* auf +*acc*); **~ guardian** strenger Wächter *or* Hüter; **to keep a ~ watch over** *or* **a ~ eye on sb** jdn mit Argusaugen bewachen **c** (*Bibl*) **a ~ God** ein eifersüchtiger Gott

jealously [ˈdʒeləslɪ] ADV **a** eifersüchtig; (= *enviously*) neidisch; **she's ~ possessive of him** sie stellt eifersüchtige Besitzansprüche an ihn **b** (= *watchfully, carefully*) *guard* eifersüchtig

jealousy [ˈdʒeləsɪ] N Eifersucht *f* (*of* auf +*acc*); (= *envy: of sb's possessions, success etc*) Neid *m*, Missgunst *f*; **their small-minded, petty jealousies** ihre engstirnigen, kleinlichen Eifersüchteleien *pl*

jeans [dʒiːnz] PL Jeans *pl*; **a pair of ~** (ein Paar) Jeans *pl*

Jeep® [dʒiːp] N Jeep *m*

jeepers (creepers) [ˈdʒiːpəz(ˈkriːpəz)] INTERJ (*US inf*) Mensch (*inf*)

jeer [dʒɪə] N (= *remark*) höhnische Bemerkung; (= *shout, boo*) Buhruf *m*; **~s** Johlen *nt* *no pl*; (= *laughter*) Hohngelächter *nt* VI höhnische Bemerkungen machen, höhnen (*old, geh*); (= *shout, boo*) johlen, buhen; (= *laugh*) höhnisch lachen; **to ~ at sb** jdn (laut) verhöhnen; **he's doing his best, don't ~** er versucht sein Bestes, also spotte nicht VT verhöhnen

jeering [ˈdʒɪərɪŋ] ADJ höhnisch; (= *shouting, booing*) johlend; (= *laughing*) höhnisch lachend N (= *shouting, booing*) Johlen *nt*, Gejohle *nt*; (= *laughing*) Hohngelächter *nt*

jeeringly ['dʒɪərɪŋlɪ] ADV *laugh, remark, smile* höhnisch

Jehovah [dʒɪˈhəʊvə] N Jehova *m*, Jahwe *m*

Jehovah's Witness N Zeuge *m*/Zeugin *f* Jehovas

jejune [dʒɪˈdʒuːn] ADJ (*liter,* = *dull*) fade, langweilig; (= *naive, simple*) simpel

Jekyll and Hyde ['dʒekələnd'haɪd] N a ~ (**character**) eine Art Jekyll und Hyde

jell [dʒel] VI = **gel**

jellied eels [ˌdʒelɪd'iːlz] PL Aal *m* in Aspik, Sülzaale *pl*

Jell-O® ['dʒeləʊ] N (*US*) Wackelpeter *m* (*inf*)

jelly ['dʒelɪ] N a Gelee *nt*; (*esp Brit:* = *dessert*) Götterspeise *f*, Wackelpeter *m* (*inf*); (*esp US:* = *jam*) Marmelade *f*; (*round meat etc*) Aspik *m or nt*, Gallert(e) *m(f)*; **it forms a kind of** ~ es bildet eine gelee- *or* gallertartige Masse; **my legs were like** ~ ich hatte Pudding in den Beinen (*inf*); **I** *or* **my legs turned to** ~ ich wurde ganz weich in den Knien b (*sl:* = *gelignite*) Dynamit *nt* VT in Aspik einlegen

jelly: jelly baby N (*Brit*) ≈ Gummibärchen *nt*; **jellybean** N Geleebonbon *m or nt*; **jellyfish** N Qualle *f*; **jelly jar** N (*US*) = **jam jar**; **jelly roll** N (*US*) Biskuitrolle *f*

jemmy ['dʒemɪ], (*US*) **jimmy** N Brecheisen *nt*, Stemmeisen *nt*

jenny ['dʒenɪ] N (= *donkey*) Eselin *f*; (= *mule*) weibliches Maultier; (= *spinning jenny*) (frühe) Feinspinnmaschine

jenny wren N Zaunkönigweibchen *nt*; (*in children's stories*) Frau Zaunkönig

jeopardize ['dʒepədaɪz] VT gefährden, in Gefahr bringen

jeopardy ['dʒepədɪ] N Gefahr *f*; **in** ~ in Gefahr, gefährdet; **to put sb/sth in** ~ jdn/etw gefährden *or* in Gefahr bringen; **to be in** ~ **of life and limb** in Lebensgefahr schweben *or* sein

jerbil N = **gerbil**

jeremiad [ˌdʒerɪˈmaɪəd] N (*liter*) Jeremiade *f* (*liter*), Klagelied *nt*

Jeremiah [ˌdʒerɪˈmaɪə] N Jeremia(s) *m*

Jericho ['dʒerɪkəʊ] N Jericho *nt*

jerk [dʒɜːk] N a Ruck *m*; (= *jump*) Satz *m*; (= *spasm, twitch*) Zuckung *f*, Zucken *nt no pl*; **to give sth a** ~ einer Sache (*dat*) einen Ruck geben; *rope, fishing line* an etw (*dat*) ruckartig ziehen; **to give a** ~ (*car*) rucken, einen Satz machen; (= *twitch*) (*person*) zusammenzucken; (*knee etc*) zucken; (*head*) zurückzucken; **the train stopped with a** ~ der Zug hielt mit einem Ruck an; **to move in short ~s** sich ruckartig bewegen b → **physical jerks** c (*inf:* = *person*) Dumpfbacke *f* (*sl*), Trottel *m* (*inf*)
VT rucken *or* ruckeln (*inf*) an (+*dat*); **the impact ~ed his head forward/back** beim Aufprall wurde sein Kopf nach vorn/hinten geschleudert; **she ~ed her thumb toward(s) the car** sie streckte schnell ihren Daumen dem Auto entgegen; **he ~ed the fish out of the water** er zog den Fisch mit einem Ruck aus dem Wasser; **he ~ed his head back to avoid the punch** er riss den Kopf zurück, um dem Schlag auszuweichen; **he ~ed the book away/out of my hand** er riss das Buch weg/mir das Buch aus der Hand; **he ~ed himself free** er riss sich los; **to** ~ **out one's words** die Worte hervorstoßen
VI (*rope, fishing line*) rucken; (= *move jerkily*) ruckeln (*inf*); (*body, muscle*) zucken, zusammenzucken; (*head*) zurückzucken; **he ~ed away from me** er sprang mit einem Satz von mir weg; **his head ~ed forward** sein Kopf wurde nach vorne geschleudert; **the car ~ed forward** der Wagen machte einen Satz *or* Ruck nach vorn; **the car ~ed to a stop** das Auto hielt ruckweise an; **to** ~ **open** aufspringen

▶ **jerk around** VT *sep* (*inf:* = *mess around*) an der Nase herumführen (*inf*)

▶ **jerk off** VI (*sl:* = *masturbate*) sich (*dat*) einen runterholen (*inf*)

jerkily ['dʒɜːkɪlɪ] ADV ruckartig; (*over cobbles etc*) holpernd, rüttelnd; *speak* holprig

jerkin ['dʒɜːkɪn] N Jacke *f*; (*Hist*) (Leder)wams *nt*

jerkwater ['dʒɜːkˌwɔːtə] ADJ *attr* (*US inf*) Provinz-; **a** ~ **town** ein Kaff *nt* (*inf*), ein Provinznest *nt* (*inf*)

jerky ['dʒɜːkɪ] ADJ (+*er*) a ruckartig; *way of speaking* abgehackt; **a** ~ **ride over cobbles/in an old bus** eine holprige Fahrt über Kopfsteinpflaster/in einem alten Bus b (*inf:* = *foolish*) bekloppt (*inf*)

jeroboam [ˌdʒerɪˈbəʊəm] N Doppelmagnum(flasche) *f*

Jerome [dʒeˈrəʊm] N Hieronymus *m*

Jerry ['dʒerɪ] N (*esp Mil sl*) (= *German soldier*) deutscher Soldat, Deutsche(r) *m*; (= *the Germans*) die Deutschen *pl*

jerry ['dʒerɪ] N (*dated Brit inf:* = *chamber pot*) Pott *m* (*inf*), Thron *m* (*inf*)

jerry: jerry-builder N schlampiger Bauunternehmer; **jerry-building** N schlampige Bauweise; **jerry-built** ADJ schlampig gebaut; **jerry can** N großer (Blech)kanister

Jersey ['dʒɜːzɪ] N a Jersey *nt* b (= *cow*) Jersey(rind) *nt*

jersey ['dʒɜːzɪ] N Pullover *m*; (*Cycling, Ftbl etc*) Trikot *nt*; (*cloth*) Jersey *m*; ~ **wool** Welljersey *m*

Jerusalem [dʒəˈruːsələm] N Jerusalem *nt*

Jerusalem artichoke N Jerusalem- *or* Erdartischocke *f*, Topinambur *m*

jessamine ['dʒesəmɪn] N Jasmin *m*

jest [dʒest] N (*no pl*) (= *fun*) Spaß *m*; (= *joke also*) Scherz *m*, Witz *m*; **in** ~ im Spaß VI scherzen, spaßen; **you ~, sir!** (*old*) Sie belieben zu scherzen, mein Herr! (*old*); **to** ~ **with sb** mit jdm spaßen; **to** ~ **about sth** über etw (*acc*) Scherze *or* Witze machen

jester ['dʒestə] N a (*Hist*) Narr *m*; **the King's** ~ der Hofnarr b (= *joker*) Spaßvogel *m*, Witzbold *m* (*inf*)

jesting ['dʒestɪŋ] ADJ spaßend, scherzhaft N Spaßen *nt*, Scherzen *nt*

jestingly ['dʒestɪŋlɪ] ADV im Spaß, scherzhaft

Jesuit ['dʒezjʊɪt] N Jesuit *m*

Jesuitic(al) [ˌdʒezjʊˈɪtɪk(əl)] ADJ jesuitisch

Jesus ['dʒiːzəs] N Jesus *m*; ~ **Christ** Jesus Christus INTERJ (*sl*) Mensch (*inf*); ~ **Christ!** Herr Gott, (noch mal)! (*inf*); (*surprised*) Menschenskind! (*inf*)

jet¹ [dʒet] N a (*of water, vapour*) Strahl *m*; **a thin** ~ **of water** ein dünner Wasserstrahl; **a** ~ **of gas** (aus einer Düse) austretendes Gas b (= *nozzle*) Düse *f* c (= *engine*) Düsentriebwerk *nt*; (*also* jet plane) Düsenflugzeug *nt*, Jet *m* VI (*water etc*) schießen *attr* (*Aviat*) Düsen-, Jet-; ~ **pilot** Jetpilot(in) *m(f)*

▶ **jet off** VI düsen (*inf*) (*to* nach), jetten (*inf*) (*to* nach); **she's jetting off to Spain next week** nächste Woche düst *or* jettet sie nach Spanien (*inf*)

jet² N (*Miner*) Jet(t) *m or nt*, Gagat *m*

jet: jet airliner N Jet *m*, Düsenflugzeug *nt*; **jet-black** ADJ kohl(pech)rabenschwarz, pechschwarz; **jet boat** N Jetboot *nt*; **jet engine** N Düsentriebwerk *nt*; **jet-engined** ADJ mit Düsenantrieb; **jet fighter** N Düsenjäger *m*; **jet foil** N Tragflügelboot *nt*; **jet fuel** N Düsentreibstoff *m*; **jet lag** N Jetlag *nt*, Schwierigkeiten *pl* durch den Zeitunterschied; **he's suffering from** ~ er hat Jetlag, er ist durch den Zeitunterschied völlig aus dem Rhythmus gekommen; **jetlagged** ADJ **to be** ~ an Jetlag leiden; **jetliner** N Jet *m*; **jet plane** N Düsenflugzeug *nt*; **jet-powered**, **jet-propelled** ADJ mit Düsenantrieb; **jet propulsion** N Düsenantrieb *m*

jetsam ['dʒetsəm] N über Bord geworfenes Gut; (*on beach*) Strandgut *nt* → **flotsam**

jet: jet set N Jetset *m*; **jet-set** VI **he ~ted off to Rio** er ist im Jet nach Rio gedüst; **jet-setter** N Jetsetter(in) *m(f)*; **he has become a real** ~ der ist voll im Jetset eingestiegen (*inf*); **jet-**

-setting ADJ ~ **person** Jetsetter(in) *m(f)*; ~ **lifestyle** Jetsetleben *nt*; **jet ski** N Wassermotorrad *nt*; **jet-ski** VI Wassermotorrad fahren; **jet stream** N a (= *air current*) Jetstream *m* b (*of jet engine*) Düsenstrahl *m*

jettison ['dʒetɪsn] VT a (*Naut, Aviat*) (als Ballast) abwerfen *or* über Bord werfen b (*fig*) *plan, view, policy* über Bord werfen; *person* abhängen, aufgeben; *unwanted articles* wegwerfen

jetty ['dʒetɪ] N (= *breakwater*) Mole *f*, Hafendamm *m*; (= *landing pier*) Landesteg *m*, Pier *m*, Landungsbrücke *f*

Jew [dʒuː] N a Jude *m*, Jüdin *f* b (*pej inf*) Geizkragen *m*, Geizhals *m* (*inf*)

Jew-baiting ['dʒuːˌbeɪtɪŋ] N Judenverfolgung *f*, Judenhetze *f*

jewel ['dʒuːəl] N a (= *gem*) Edelstein *m*, Juwel *nt* (*geh*); (= *piece of jewellery*) Schmuckstück *nt*; **a case full of ~s** ein Koffer voll Juwelen *or* wertvoller Schmuckstücke b (*of watch*) Stein *m* c (*fig:* = *person*) Juwel *nt*, Goldstück *nt* (*inf*); **this new book is the** ~ **in her crown** dieses neue Buch ist ihr Meisterwerk

jewel box, jewel case N Schmuckkästchen *nt*, Schmuckkasten *m*

jewelled, (*US*) **jeweled** ['dʒuːəld] ADJ mit Juwelen (*geh*) *or* Edelsteinen besetzt; *watch* mit Steinen; *fingers* mit Juwelen geschmückt

jeweller, (*US*) **jeweler** ['dʒuːələ] N Juwelier(in) *m(f)*, Schmuckhändler(in) *m(f)*; (*making jewellery*) Goldschmied(in) *m(f)*; **at the ~'s (shop)** beim Juwelier, im Juwelierladen

jewellery, (*US*) **jewelry** ['dʒuːəlrɪ] N Schmuck *m no pl*; **a piece of** ~ ein Schmuckstück *nt*

Jewess ['dʒuːɪs] N Jüdin *f*

Jewish ['dʒuːɪʃ] ADJ jüdisch; (*pej inf:* = *mean*) knickerig (*inf*)

Jewry ['dʒʊərɪ] N die Juden *pl*, das jüdische Volk

jew's-harp [ˌdʒuːzˈhɑːp] N Maultrommel *f*, Brummeisen *nt*

Jezebel ['dʒezəbel] N (*Bibl*) Isebel *f*; (*fig*) verruchtes Weib

jib [dʒɪb] N a (*of crane*) Ausleger *m*, Dreharm *m* b (*Naut*) Klüver *m* c (*dated inf*) **I don't like the cut of his** ~ seine Nase gefällt mir nicht VI (*horse*) scheuen, bocken (*at* vor +*dat*); **to** ~ **at sth** (*person*) sich gegen etw sträuben

jib boom N (*Naut*) Klüverbaum *m*

jibe [dʒaɪb] N, VI = **gibe**

jiffy ['dʒɪfɪ], **jiff** [dʒɪf] N (*inf*) Minütchen *nt* (*inf*); **I won't be a** ~ ich komme sofort *or* gleich; (= *back soon*) ich bin sofort *or* gleich wieder da; **wait a ~!** Augenblick (mal)! (*inf*); **in a** ~ sofort, gleich

Jiffy bag® N (*Brit*) (gepolsterte) Versandtasche; (*smaller*) gefütterter Briefumschlag

jig [dʒɪg] N a (= *dance*) lebhafter Volkstanz; **she did a little** ~ sie vollführte eine Freudentanz b (*Tech*) Spannvorrichtung *f* VI (= *dance*) tanzen; (*fig: also* **jig about**) herumhüpfen; **to** ~ **up and down** herumspringen VT **to** ~ **a baby up and down on one's knee** ein Kind auf seinen Knien reiten lassen

jigger ['dʒɪgə] N a (= *sieve*) Schüttelsieb *nt* b (*US:* = *measure*) Messbecher für Alkohol: 1½ Unzen c (= *sandflea*) Sandfloh *m*

jiggered ['dʒɪgəd] ADJ (*inf*) **well, I'll be ~!** da bin ich aber platt (*inf*) *or* baff (*inf*); **I'm ~ if I'll do it** den Teufel werde ich tun (*inf*); **to be** ~ (= *tired*) kaputt sein (*inf*)

jiggery-pokery ['dʒɪgərɪ'pəʊkərɪ] N (*inf*) Schmu *m* (*inf*); **I think there's been some** ~ **going on here** ich glaube, hier geht es nicht ganz hasenrein zu (*inf*) *or* hier ist was faul (*inf*)

jiggle ['dʒɪgl] VT wackeln mit; *door handle* rütteln an (+*dat*) VI (*also* **jiggle about**) herumzappeln

jigsaw ['dʒɪgsɔː] N a (*Tech*) Tischlerbandsäge *f* b (*also* **jigsaw puzzle**) Puzzle(spiel) *nt*

jihad [dʒɪ'hæd] N (Rel) Dschihad m, Heiliger Krieg

jillion ['dʒɪljən] N (inf) Unmenge f, Unzahl f; **~s of …** jede Menge …

jilt [dʒɪlt] VT lover den Laufpass geben (+dat); girl sitzen lassen; **~ed** verschmäht

Jim [dʒɪm] N dim of **James**

Jim Crow N (pej) (= negro) Nigger (pej), Schwarze(r) m; (= discrimination) Rassendiskriminierung f attr law, policy (gegen Schwarze) diskriminierend; saloon etc für Schwarze

jim-dandy ['dʒɪm'dændɪ] ADJ (US inf) prima (inf), klasse (inf)

jiminy (cricket) ['dʒɪmɪnɪ('krɪkɪt)] INTERJ (US) Menschenskind (inf)

jimjams ['dʒɪmdʒæmz] PL (Brit inf) **a** (inf, = pyjamas) Pyjama m **b** (sl, = nervousness) **it gives me the ~** da kriege ich Muffensausen (inf) **c** (sl, = the creeps) **he gives me the ~** bei dem kriege ich das große Grausen (inf)

Jimmy ['dʒɪmɪ] N dim of **James**

jimmy ['dʒɪmɪ] N (US) = **jemmy**

jingle ['dʒɪŋgl] **N a** (of keys, bracelets, coins etc) Geklimper nt, Klimpern nt; (of bells) Bimmeln nt **b** (= catchy verse) Spruch m; (for remembering) Merkvers m; (advertising) Jingle m **VI** (keys, bracelets, coins etc) klimpern; (bells) bimmeln **VT** keys, bracelets, coins klimpern mit; bells bimmeln lassen

jingly ['dʒɪŋglɪ] ADJ klingelnd, bimmelnd

jingo ['dʒɪŋgəʊ] N pl **-es a** Hurrapatriot(in), Chauvinist(in) m(f) **b** (dated inf) **by ~!** Tod und Teufel! (old), Teufel, Teufel! (inf)

jingoism ['dʒɪŋgəʊɪzəm] N Hurrapatriotismus m, Chauvinismus m

jingoistic [,dʒɪŋgəʊ'ɪstɪk] ADJ hurrapatriotisch, chauvinistisch

jinks [dʒɪŋks] PL (inf) → **high jinks**

jinn [dʒɪn] N Dschinn m

jinx [dʒɪŋks] N **there must be or there's a ~ on it** das ist verhext; **there must be or there's a ~ on us** wir sind vom Unglück verfolgt; **to put a ~ on sth** etw verhexen

jinxed [dʒɪŋkst] ADJ verhext

jitney ['dʒɪtnɪ] N (US inf) Fünfcentmünze f; (= bus) billiger Bus

jitterbug ['dʒɪtəbʌg] **N a** (= dance) Jitterbug m **b** (inf: = panicky person) Nervenbündel nt (inf) **VI** Jitterbug tanzen

jitters ['dʒɪtəz] PL (inf) **the ~** das große Zittern (inf) or Bibbern (inf); **his ~** sein Bammel m (inf); **he had (a bad case of) the ~ about the exam** er hatte wegen der Prüfung das große Zittern (inf); **to give sb the ~** jdn ganz rappelig machen (inf)

jittery ['dʒɪtərɪ] ADJ (inf) nervös, rappelig (inf)

jiujitsu [dʒuː'dʒɪtsuː] N Jiu-Jitsu nt

jive [dʒaɪv] **N a** (= dance) Swing m **b** (US inf: = nonsense) **don't give me that ~** hör bloß mit dem Quatsch auf (inf) **VI** swingen, Swing tanzen

Joan [dʒəʊn] N Johanna f; **~ of Arc** Johanna von Orléans, Jeanne d'Arc

Job [dʒəʊb] N (Bibl) Hiob m, Job m; **the Book of ~** das Buch Hiob; **he has the patience of ~** er hat eine Engelsgeduld

job [dʒɒb] ⊗ 19.1, 19.2 **N a** (= piece of work) Arbeit f; (Comput) Job m; **I have a ~ to do** ich habe zu tun; **I have several ~s to do** ich habe verschiedene Sachen zu erledigen; **a ~ of work** eine Arbeit, eine Arbeit; **I have a little ~ for you** ich habe da eine kleine Arbeit or Aufgabe für Sie; **it's quite a ~ to paint the house** das ist vielleicht eine Arbeit or eine Heidenarbeit (inf), das Haus zu streichen; **the car's in for a paint ~** (inf) der Wagen ist zum Lackieren in der Werkstatt; **the plumbers have a lot of ~s on just now** die Klempner haben zurzeit viele Aufträge; **to be paid by the ~** für (die) geleistete Arbeit bezahlt werden, pro Auftrag bezahlt werden; **he's on the ~** (inf: = at work) er ist bei or an der Arbeit; (inf: = having sex) er ist zu

Gange (inf); **to make a good/bad ~ of sth** bei etw gute/schlechte Arbeit leisten; **the decorators made a terrible ~ of the kitchen** die Maler haben in der Küche schrecklich gepfuscht; **we could do a far better ~ of running the company** wir könnten die Firma viel besser leiten; **he knows his ~** er versteht sein Handwerk → **odd** f
b (= employment) Stelle f, Job m (inf); **to look for/get/have a ~** eine Stelle suchen/bekommen/haben; **to lose one's ~** seine Stelle verlieren; **the nice thing about a teaching ~ is …** das Schöne am Lehrberuf or an einer Anstellung als Lehrer ist …; **he had a holiday ~** er hatte eine Ferienarbeit or einen Ferienjob (inf); **I've got a Saturday ~** ich habe einen Samstagsjob (inf); **500 ~s lost** 500 Arbeitsplätze verloren gegangen; **to bring new ~s to a region** in einer Gegend neue Arbeitsplätze schaffen
c (= duty) Aufgabe f; **that's not my ~** dafür bin ich nicht zuständig; **it's not my ~ to tell him** es ist nicht meine Aufgabe, ihm das zu sagen; **I'll do my ~ and you do yours** ich mache meine Arbeit, und Sie Ihre; **I had the ~ of breaking the news to her** es fiel mir zu, ihr die Nachricht beizubringen; **he's not doing his ~** er erfüllt seine Aufgabe(n) nicht; **I'm only doing my ~** ich tue nur meine Pflicht; **drinking a lot of water helps the kidneys do their ~** viel Wasser zu trinken hilft den Nieren bei ihrer Arbeit
d (= good thing) **that's a good ~!** so ein Glück; **what a good ~ or it's a good ~ I brought my cheque book** nur gut, dass ich mein Scheckbuch mitgenommen habe; **to give sb/sth up as a bad ~** jdn/ etw aufgeben; **to make the best of a bad ~** das Beste daraus machen; **that should do the ~** das müsste hinhauen (inf); **this is just the ~** das ist goldrichtig or genau das Richtige; **a holiday in the sun would be just the ~** Ferien in der Sonne, das wäre jetzt genau das Richtige; **double whisky? – just the ~** einen doppelten Whisky? – prima Idee (inf)
e (= difficulty) **I had a ~ convincing him or to convince him** es war gar nicht so einfach, ihn zu überzeugen; **you'll have a ~** das wird gar nicht so einfach sein; **she has a ~ getting up the stairs** es ist gar nicht einfach für sie, die Treppe raufzukommen; **it was quite a ~** das war ganz schön schwer (inf) or schwierig
f (inf: = crime) Ding nt (sl); **we're going to do a ~ next week** wir drehen nächste Woche ein Ding (sl); **remember that bank ~?** erinnerst du dich an das große Ding in der Bank? (sl)
g (inf: = person, thing) Ding nt; **his new car's a lovely little ~** sein neues Auto ist wirklich große Klasse (inf) or eine Wucht (inf); **that blonde's a gorgeous little ~** die Blondine (da) sieht wirklich klasse aus (inf)
h (baby-talk) **to do a (big/little) ~** ein (großes/ kleines) Geschäft machen (inf), Aa/Pipi machen (baby-talk)
i (inf: = operation) Korrektur f; **to have a nose/ chin ~ (done)** eine Nasen-/Kinnkorrektur machen lassen
j **to do a ~ on sb** (inf, = defeat) jdn in die Pfanne hauen (inf); (= beat up) jdn vermöbeln (inf)
VI a (= do casual work) Gelegenheitsarbeiten tun or verrichten, jobben (inf); **a graphic designer who ~s for various advertising firms** ein Grafiker, der für verschiedene Werbeagenturen Aufträge or Arbeiten ausführt
b (St Ex) als Makler tätig sein, Maklergeschäfte betreiben
c (= profit from public position) sein Amt (zu privatem Nutzen) missbrauchen
VT (also **job out**) work in Auftrag geben, auf Kontrakt or auf feste Rechnung vergeben

job advertisement N Stellenanzeige f

jobber ['dʒɒbə] **N a** (St Ex) Makler(in) m(f), Börsenhändler(in) m(f) **b** (= casual worker) Gelegenheitsarbeiter(in) m(f)

jobbery ['dʒɒbərɪ] N Schiebung f, Amtsmissbrauch m

jobbing ['dʒɒbɪŋ] ADJ Gelegenheits-; **~ worker/ actor** Gelegenheitsarbeiter(in) m(f)/-schauspie-

ler m **N a** (= casual work) Gelegenheitsarbeit f **b** (St Ex) Börsen- or Effektenhandel m

jobbing printer N Akzidenzdrucker m

job: Jobcentre N (Brit) Arbeitsamt nt; **job creation** N Arbeitsbeschaffung f; **~ scheme** Arbeitsbeschaffungsmaßnahme f; **job cuts** PL Arbeitsplatzabbau m; **job description** N Tätigkeitsbeschreibung f; **job evaluation** N Arbeitsplatzbewertung f; **job holder** N Arbeitnehmer(in) m(f); **job hopper** N (inf) jd, der häufig seine Arbeitsstelle wechselt; **job-hunter** N Arbeitsuchende(r) mf; **job-hunting** N Arbeitsuche f, Stellenjagd f (inf); **to be ~** auf Arbeitsuche or Stellenjagd (inf) sein; **jobless** ADJ arbeitslos, stellungslos **N the ~** pl die Arbeitslosen pl; **job loss** N **there were 1,000 ~s** 1 000 Arbeitsplätze gingen verloren; **job lot** N (Comm) (Waren)posten m; **job printer** N Akzidenzdrucker m; **job profile** N Stellenbeschreibung f, Stellenprofil nt; **job satisfaction** N Zufriedenheit f am Arbeitsplatz; **I've got ~** ich bin mit meiner Arbeit zufrieden

Job's comforter N jd, der durch seinen Trost die Situation nur verschlimmert **you're a real ~** du bist vielleicht ein schöner or schwacher Trost

job: job security N Sicherheit f des Arbeitsplatzes; **we can offer no ~ guarantees** wir können die Sicherheit des Arbeitsplatzes/der Arbeitsplätze nicht garantieren; **jobseeker** N Arbeitsuchende(r) mf; **~'s allowance** (Brit) Arbeitslosengeld nt; **job sharer** N jd, der seinen Arbeitsplatz mit anderen teilt; **job sharing** N Arbeitsplatzteilung f, Jobsharing nt attr scheme zur Arbeitsplatzteilung

jobsworth ['dʒɒbzwɜːθ] N (inf pej) Paragraphenreiter(in) m(f)

Jock [dʒɒk] N (inf) Schotte m, Schottin f

jockey ['dʒɒkɪ] **N** Jockey m, Jockei m, Rennreiter(in) m(f) **VI to ~ for position** (lit) sich in eine gute Position zu drängeln versuchen, sich gut platzieren wollen; (fig) rangeln; **they were all ~ing for office in the new government** sie rangelten alle um ein Amt in der neuen Regierung **VT** (= force by crafty manoeuvres) **to ~ sb into doing sth** jdn dazu bringen, etw zu tun; **he felt he had been ~ed into it** er hatte das Gefühl, dass man ihn da reinbugsiert hatte (inf)

jockey shorts PL Jockeyshorts pl

jockstrap ['dʒɒkstræp] N Suspensorium nt

jocose [dʒə'kəʊs] ADJ (dated) scherzend, launig (geh)

jocosely [dʒə'kəʊslɪ] ADV (dated) scherzhaft; (= as a joke) say im Scherz

jocular ['dʒɒkjʊlə] ADJ lustig, spaßig, witzig; **to be in a ~ mood** zu Scherzen or Späßen aufgelegt sein

jocularity [,dʒɒkjʊ'lærɪtɪ] N Spaßigkeit f, Witzigkeit f, Scherzhaftigkeit f

jocularly ['dʒɒkjʊləlɪ] ADV scherzhaft; (= as a joke) im Scherz

jocund ['dʒɒkənd] ADJ heiter, fröhlich, frohsinnig (geh)

jodhpurs ['dʒɒdpəz] PL Reithose(n) f(pl)

Joe [dʒəʊ] N dim of **Joseph** Sepp (S Ger), Jupp (dial) m

Joe Bloggs [,dʒəʊ'blɒgz], **Joe Public** N (inf: = ordinary person) Otto Normalverbraucher m (inf)

joey ['dʒəʊɪ] N (Austral inf) junges Känguru

jog [dʒɒg] **VT** stoßen an (+acc) or gegen; person anstoßen; **he ~ged the child up and down on his knee** er ließ das Kind auf seinen Knien reiten; **he was being ~ged up and down on the horse** das Pferd schüttelte ihn durch; **to ~ sb's memory** jds Gedächtnis (dat) nachhelfen or auf die Sprünge helfen; **to ~ sb's conscience** jdm Gewissensbisse bereiten
VI trotten, zuckeln (inf); (Sport) Dauerlauf machen, joggen; **to ~ up and down** auf und ab hüpfen

N **a** (= *push, nudge*) Stoß *m*, Schubs *m*, Stups *m*; **to give sb's memory a ~** jds Gedächtnis (*dat*) nachhelfen
　b (= *run*) trabender Lauf, Trott *m*; (*Sport*) Dauerlauf *m*; **he broke into a ~** er fing an zu traben; **she starts the day with a gentle ~ around the park** für sie fängt der Tag mit einem langsamen Lauf durch den Park an; **to go for a ~** (*Sport*) einen Dauerlauf machen, joggen (gehen); **to set off at a ~** lostraben

▶ **jog about** (*Brit*) *or* **around** **VI** hin und her gerüttelt werden **VT** *sep* durchschütteln, durchrütteln

▶ **jog along** VI **a** (= *go along: person, vehicle*) entlangzuckeln **b** (*fig*) (*person, worker, industry*) vor sich (*acc*) hin wursteln (*inf*); (*work*) seinen Gang gehen

jogger ['dʒɒɡə'] **N** **a** (= *person*) Jogger(in) *m(f)*; **~'s nipple** besonders bei Joggern auftretende Entzündung der Brustwarzen **b** (= *shoe*) Joggingschuh *m*, Freizeitstiefel *m*

jogging ['dʒɒɡɪŋ] **N** Jogging *nt*, Joggen *nt*

jogging: jogging pants PL Jogginghose *f*; **jogging shoes** PL Joggingschuhe *pl*; **jogging suit** **N** Jogginganzug *m*

joggle ['dʒɒɡl] **VT** schütteln, rütteln **N** Schütteln *nt*, Rütteln *nt*

jog trot **N** Trott *m*

John [dʒɒn] **N** Johannes *m*; **~ the Baptist** Johannes der Täufer

john [dʒɒn] **N** (*esp US inf*) (= *toilet*) Klo *nt* (*inf*); (= *prostitute's customer*) Freier *m* (*inf*)

John: John Barleycorn [ˌdʒɒn'baːlɪkɔːn] **N** der Gerstensaft; **John Bull** **N** ein typischer Engländer, John Bull *m*; (= *the English*) die Engländer *pl*; **John Doe** **N** (*US*) (= *average man*) Otto Normalverbraucher *m* (*inf*); (*Jur*) Mann, dessen Name nicht bekannt ist; **John Hancock** [ˌdʒɒn'hænkɒk], **John Henry** [ˌdʒɒn'henrɪ] (*inf*: = *signature*) Friedrich Wilhelm *m* (*inf*); **to put one's ~ on sth** seinen Friedrich Wilhelm auf etw setzen

Johnny ['dʒɒnɪ] **N** *dim of* **John** Hänschen *nt*, Hänsel *m* (*old*)

johnny ['dʒɒnɪ] **N** (*Brit inf*) (= *man*) Typ *m* (*inf*); (= *condom*) Pariser *m* (*inf*)

Johnny-come-lately [ˌdʒɒnɪkʌm'leɪtlɪ] **N** (*inf*) (= *newcomer*) Neuankömmling *m*; (= *late starter*) Nachzügler(in) *m*

joie de vivre [ˌʒwɑːdə'viːvr] **N** Lebensfreude *f*, Lebenslust *f*

join [dʒɔɪn] ✪ 25.1 **VT** **a** (*lit, fig: = connect, unite*) verbinden (*to* mit); **to ~ two things together** zwei Dinge (miteinander) verbinden; (= *attach also*) zwei Dinge zusammenfügen or aneinander fügen; **~ the dots (together)** verbinden Sie die Punkt; **to ~ battle (with the enemy)** den Kampf mit dem Feind aufnehmen; **to ~ hands** (*lit, fig*) sich (*dat*) or einander die Hände reichen; **~ed in marriage** durch das heilige Band der Ehe verbunden or vereinigt; **they are ~ed at the hip** (*fig inf*) sie sind völlig unzertrennlich, sie hängen wie Kletten aneinander (*inf*)
　b (= *become member of*) army gehen zu; **one's regiment** sich anschließen (+*dat*), sich begeben zu; **NATO, the EU** beitreten (+*dat*); **political party, club** beitreten (+*dat*), Mitglied werden von or bei or in (+*dat*), eintreten in (+*acc*); **religious order** eintreten in (+*acc*), beitreten (+*dat*); **university** (*as student*) anfangen an (+*dat*); (*as staff*) firm anfangen bei; **group of people, procession** sich anschließen (+*dat*); **to ~ the queue** sich in die Schlange stellen or einreihen; **he has been ordered to ~ his ship at Liverpool** er hat Order bekommen, sich in Liverpool auf seinem Schiff einzufinden or zu seinem Schiff zu begeben; **Dr Morris will be ~ing us for a year as guest professor** Dr. Morris wird ein Jahr bei uns Gastprofessor sein
　c **he ~ed us in France** er stieß in Frankreich zu uns; **I ~ed him at the station** wir trafen uns am Bahnhof, ich traf mich mit ihm am Bahnhof; **I'll ~ you in five minutes** ich bin in fünf

Minuten bei Ihnen; (= *follow you*) ich komme in fünf Minuten nach; **may I ~ you?** kann ich mich Ihnen anschließen?; (= *sit with you*) darf ich Ihnen Gesellschaft leisten?, darf ich mich zu Ihnen setzen?; (*in game, plan etc*) kann ich mitmachen?; **will you ~ us?** machen Sie mit?, sind Sie dabei?; (= *sit with us*) wollen Sie uns nicht Gesellschaft leisten?, wollen Sie sich (nicht) zu uns setzen?; (= *come with us*) kommen Sie mit?; **do ~ us for lunch** wollen Sie nicht mit uns essen?; **will you ~ me in a drink?** trinken Sie ein Glas mit mir?; **Paul ~s me in wishing you ...** Paul schließt sich meinen Wünschen für ... an; **they ~ed us in singing ...** sie sangen mit uns zusammen ...; **Moscow has ~ed Washington in condemning these actions** Moskau hat sich Washington angeschlossen und diese Handlungen verurteilt
　d (*river*) another river, the sea einmünden or fließen in (+*acc*); (*road*) another road (ein)münden in (+*acc*); **his estates ~ ours** seine Ländereien grenzen an unsere (an)

VI **a** (*also* **join together**: *two parts*) (= *be attached*) (miteinander) verbunden sein; (= *be attachable*) sich (miteinander) verbinden lassen; (= *grow together*) zusammenwachsen; (= *meet, be adjacent*) zusammenstoßen, zusammentreffen; (*estates*) aneinander (an)grenzen; (*rivers*) zusammenfließen, sich vereinigen; (*roads*) sich treffen; **let us all ~ together in the Lord's Prayer** wir wollen alle zusammen das Vaterunser beten; **he ~s with me in wishing you ...** er schließt sich meinen Wünschen für ... an; **to ~ together in doing sth** etw zusammen or gemeinsam tun; **Moscow and Washington have ~ed in condemning these actions** Moskau und Washington haben diese Handlungen gemeinsam verurteilt; **they all ~ed together to get her a present** sie taten sich alle zusammen, um ihr ein Geschenk zu kaufen
　b (*club member*) beitreten, Mitglied werden **N** Naht(stelle) *f*; (*in pipe, knitting*) Verbindungsstelle *f*

▶ **join in** VI (*in activity*) mitmachen (*prep obj* bei); (*in game also*) mitspielen (*prep obj* bei); (*in demonstration also, in protest*) sich anschließen (*prep obj* +*dat*); (*in conversation*) sich beteiligen (*prep obj* an +*dat*); **join in, everybody!** (*in song etc*) alle (mitmachen)!; **everybody joined in the chorus** sie sangen alle zusammen den Refrain, alle fielen in den Refrain ein; **he didn't want to join in the fun** er wollte nicht mitmachen

▶ **join on** **VI** (= *be attachable*) sich verbinden lassen (*prep obj, -to* mit), sich anfügen lassen (*prep obj, -to* an +*acc*); (= *be attached*) verbunden sein (*prep obj, -to* mit); (*people: in procession etc*) sich anschließen (*prep obj, -to* +*dat*, an +*acc*) **VT** *sep* verbinden (*prep obj, -to* mit); (= *extend with*) ansetzen (*prep obj, -to* an +*acc*)

▶ **join up** **VI** **a** (*Brit Mil*) Soldat werden, zum Militär gehen **b** (= *meet: roads etc*) sich treffen, aufeinander stoßen; (= *join forces*) sich zusammenschließen, sich zusammentun (*inf*) **VT** *sep* (miteinander) verbinden

joiner ['dʒɔɪnə'] **N** Tischler(in) *m(f)*, Schreiner(in) *m(f)*

joinery ['dʒɔɪnərɪ] **N** (= *trade*) Tischlerei *f*, Tischlerhandwerk *nt*; (= *piece of joinery*) Tischlerarbeit *f*

joining fee ['dʒɔɪnɪŋfiː] **N** Aufnahmegebühr *f*

joint [dʒɔɪnt] **N** **a** (*Anat, tool, in armour etc*) Gelenk *nt*; **ankle ~** Knöchel *m*; **knee ~** Kniegelenk *nt*; **~ pains** Gelenkschmerzen *pl*; **he's a bit stiff in the ~s** (*inf*) er ist ein bisschen steif (in den Knochen); **the times are out of ~** (*fig liter*) die Zeit or Welt ist aus den Fugen → **nose**
　b (= *join*) (*in woodwork*) Fuge *f*; (*in pipe etc*) Verbindung(sstelle) *f*; (*welded etc*) Naht(stelle) *f*; (= *junction piece*) Verbindungsstück *nt*
　c (*Brit Cook*) Braten *m*; **a ~ of beef** ein Rindsbraten *m*
　d (*inf*) (= *place*) Laden *m* (*inf*); (*for gambling*) Spielhölle *f*
　e (*inf: of marijuana*) Joint *m* (*inf*)
　VT **a** (*Cook*) (in Stücke) zerlegen or zerteilen

　b boards, pipes etc verbinden
　ADJ *attr* gemeinsam; (*in connection with possessions also*) gemeinschaftlich; (= *total, combined*) influence, strength vereint; **he finished ~ second** or **in ~ second place** (*Brit*) er belegte gemeinsam mit einem anderen den zweiten Platz; **~ action** gemeinsame Aktion, Gemeinschaftsaktion *f*; **~ committee** gemeinsamer or gemischter Ausschuss; **it was a ~ effort** das ist in Gemeinschaftsarbeit entstanden; **it took the ~ efforts of six strong men to move it** es waren die vereinten Anstrengungen or Kräfte von sechs starken Männern nötig, um es von der Stelle zu bewegen

joint account N gemeinsames Konto

joint agreement N *Lohnabkommen mehrerer Firmen mit einer Gewerkschaft*

joint capital N Gesellschaftskapital *nt*

> ### JOINT CHIEFS OF STAFF
>
> **Joint Chiefs of Staff** ist eine Behörde innerhalb des US-Verteidigungsministeriums, deren fünf Mitglieder die wichtigsten militärischen Berater des Präsidenten, des Nationalen Sicherheitsrates und des Verteidigungsministers sind. Diese 1942 eingerichtete Gruppe setzt sich aus einem Vorsitzenden, einem Vizepräsidenten, den Stabschefs der Armee, Luftwaffe und Marine und dem Kommandanten des Marine Corps zusammen. Der wohl bekannteste Vorsitzende als letzter Zeit ist General Colin Powell, der erste Schwarze auf diesem Posten, der dieses Amt von 1989 bis 1993 innehatte.

joint: joint custody N (*Jur*) gemeinsames Sorgerecht (*getrennt lebender Eltern*); **joint debt** N (*Jur*) gemeinsame Verbindlichkeit

jointed ['dʒɔɪntɪd] **ADJ** (= *articulated*) mit Gelenken versehen, gegliedert; **a ~ doll** eine Gliederpuppe; **a ~ fishing rod** eine zerlegbare Angel

joint estate N Gemeinschaftsbesitz *m*

joint family N Großfamilie *f*

join-the-dots puzzle [dʒɔɪnðə'dɒts 'pʌzl] **N** (*esp Brit*) Spiel, bei dem man eine Figur zeichnet, indem man einzelne Punkte verbindet

joint heir N Miterbe *m*, Miterbin *f*; **they were ~s** sie waren gemeinsame Erben

joint life insurance N wechselseitige (Über-)lebensversicherung

jointly ['dʒɔɪntlɪ] **ADV** **a** gemeinsam; decide, work, rule also zusammen, miteinander; **to be owned by ...** im gemeinsamen Besitz von ... sein **b** (*Jur*) **to be ~ and severally liable** gesamtschuldnerisch or als Gesamtschuldner haften

joint: joint owner N Mitbesitzer(in) *m(f)*; **joint ownership** N Miteigentum *nt*, Mitbesitz *m*; **joint partner** N Teilhaber(in) *m(f)*; **joint plaintiff** N Nebenkläger(in) *m(f)*; **~s** gemeinsame Kläger *pl*; **joint production** N (*TV, Film*) Koproduktion *f*; **joint resolution** N (*US Pol*) gemeinsamer Beschluss (beider gesetzgebender Versammlungen); **joint stock** N Aktienkapital *nt*; **joint stock bank** N ≈ Aktienbank *f*; **joint stock company** N ≈ Kapitalgesellschaft *f*

jointure ['dʒɔɪntʃə'] **N** (*Jur*) Wittum *nt*

joint venture N Gemeinschaftsunternehmen *nt*, Joint-venture *nt* (*Comm*)

joist [dʒɔɪst] **N** Balken *m*; (*of metal, concrete*) Träger *m*

joke [dʒəʊk] **N** Witz *m*; (= *hoax*) Scherz *m*; (= *prank*) Streich *m*; (*inf*) (= *pathetic person or thing*) Witz *m*; (= *laughing stock*) Gespött *nt*, Gelächter *nt*; **for a ~** zum Spaß, zum or aus Jux (*inf*); **I don't see the ~** ich möchte wissen, was daran so lustig is or sein soll; **he treats the school rules as a big ~** er sieht die Schulregeln als einen Witz; **he can/can't take a ~** er versteht Spaß/keinen Spaß; **what a ~!** zum Totlachen! (*inf*), zum Schießen! (*inf*); **it's no ~** das ist nicht witzig; **the ~ is that ...** das Witzige or

Lustige daran ist, dass ...; **it's beyond a ~** (*Brit*) das ist kein Spaß *or* Witz mehr, das ist nicht mehr lustig; **this is getting beyond a ~** (*Brit*) das geht (langsam) zu weit; **the ~ was on me** der Spaß ging *auf* meine Kosten; **why do you have to turn everything into a ~?** warum müssen Sie über alles Ihre Witze machen?, warum müssen Sie alles ins Lächerliche ziehen?; **I'm not in the mood for ~s** ich bin nicht zu(m) Scherzen aufgelegt; **to play a ~ on sb** jdm einen Streich spielen; **to make a ~ of sth** Witze über etw (*acc*) machen; **to make ~s about sb/sth** sich über jdn/etw lustig machen, über jdn/etw Witze machen *or* reißen (*inf*) **VI** Witze machen, scherzen (*geh*) (*about* über +*acc*); (= *pull sb's leg*) Spaß machen; **I'm not joking** ich scherze nicht; **you must be joking!** das ist ja wohl nicht Ihr Ernst, das soll wohl ein Witz sein; **you're joking!** mach keine Sachen (*inf*) *or* Witze!; **...**, he ~d ..., sagte er scherzhaft

joker ['dʒəʊkə] N **a** (= *person*) Witzbold *m*, Spaßvogel *m* **b** (*inf*) Typ *m* (*inf*), Kerl *m* (*inf*) **c** (*Cards*) Joker *m*; **he's/it's the ~ in the pack** (*esp Brit*) er/es ist ein Unsicherheitsfaktor, er/es ist eine unbekannte Größe

jokey ADJ = **joky**

jokily ['dʒəʊkɪlɪ] ADV lustig; *say* scherzhaft, im Scherz(e)/im Scherz

joking ['dʒəʊkɪŋ] ADJ *tone* scherzhaft, spaßend; **in a ~ manner** spaßend; **it's no ~ matter** darüber macht man keine Witze **N** Witze *pl*; **I'm in no mood for ~** ich bin nicht zu Scherzen *or* Späßen aufgelegt; **~ apart** *or* **aside** Spaß *or* Scherz beiseite

jokingly ['dʒəʊkɪŋlɪ] ADV im Spaß; *say*, *call also* scherzhaft

joky ['dʒəʊkɪ] ADJ lustig

jollification [ˌdʒɒlɪfɪ'keɪʃən] N (*hum*) Festivität *f* (*hum*); (= *merrymaking*: *also* **jollifications**) Festlichkeiten *pl*

jollity ['dʒɒlɪtɪ] N Fröhlichkeit *f*, Ausgelassenheit *f*

jolly ['dʒɒlɪ] ADJ (+*er*) **a** (*esp Brit*: = *merry*) fröhlich, vergnügt; **everyone had a very ~ time** alle haben sich köstlich amüsiert **b** (*inf*: = *tipsy*) angeheitert (*inf*) ADV (*dated Brit inf*) ganz schön (*inf*), vielleicht (*inf*); *nice*, *warm*, *happy*, *pleased* mächtig (*inf*); **you are ~ lucky** Sie haben vielleicht Glück *or* ein Mordsglück (*inf*); **~ good** prima (*inf*), famos (*dated inf*); **a ~ good idea** eine tolle Idee; **that's ~ kind of you** das ist furchtbar *or* unheimlich nett von Ihnen; **it's getting ~ late** es wird langsam spät; **he took the news ~ well** er hat die Nachricht wirklich gut verkraftet; **you ~ well will go!** und ob du gehst!; **so you ~ well should be!** das will ich schwer meinen! (*inf*); **I should ~ well hope/think so!** das will ich auch hoffen/gemeint haben! **VT** (*Brit*) **to ~ sb into doing sth** jdn bereden, etw zu tun; **to ~ sb along** jdm aufmunternd zureden; **to ~ sb up** jdn aufmuntern **N a** (*Brit inf*) (= *party*) Fete *f* (*inf*); (= *trip*) Vergnügungsreise *f* **b** (*Brit inf*) **to get one's jollies (from sth)** (von etw) einen Kick bekommen (*sl*)

jolly: jolly boat N Beiboot *nt*; **Jolly Roger** N Totenkopfflagge *f*, Piratenflagge *f*

jolt [dʒəʊlt] **VI** (*vehicle*) holpern, rüttelnd fahren; (= *give one jolt*) einen Ruck machen; **to ~ a-long** rüttelnd entlangfahren; **to ~ to a halt** ruckweise anhalten **VT** (*lit*) durchschütteln, durchrütteln; (*once*) einen Ruck geben *or* versetzen (+*dat*); (*fig*) aufrütteln; **she was ~ed awake** sie wurde wachgerüttelt; **she was ~ed back to reality** sie wurde mit einem Ruck wieder in die Wirklichkeit zurückgeholt; **to ~ sb out of his complacency** jdn aus seiner Zufriedenheit aufrütteln *or* reißen; **to ~ sb into doing sth** jdn so aufrütteln, dass er/sie etw tut; **it ~ed him into action** das hat ihn aufgerüttelt **N a** (= *jerk*) Ruck *m* **b** (*fig inf*) Schock *m*; **he realized with a ~ ...**

mit einem Schlag wurde ihm klar, ...; **it gave me a ~** das hat mir einen Schock versetzt

jolting ['dʒəʊltɪŋ] N Rütteln *nt*, Schütteln *nt*, Holpern *nt*

jolty ['dʒəʊltɪ] ADJ (+*er*) *cart etc* holp(e)rig, rüttelnd; *road* holp(e)rig, uneben

Jonah ['dʒəʊnə] N Jona(s) *m*

jonquil ['dʒɒŋkwɪl] N Jonquille *f* (*Art von Narzisse*)

Jordan ['dʒɔːdn] N (= *country*) Jordanien *nt*; (= *river*) Jordan *m*

Joseph ['dʒəʊzɪf] N Joseph *m*, Josef *m*

Josephine ['dʒəʊzɪfiːn] N Josephine *f*

josh [dʒɒʃ] (*esp US*, *inf*) **VT** aufziehen, veräppeln, verulken (*all inf*) **VI** Spaß machen (*inf*) **N** Neckerei *f*, Hänselei *f*

Joshua ['dʒɒʃjʊə] N Josua *m*

joss stick ['dʒɒsstɪk] N Räucherstäbchen *nt*

jostle ['dʒɒsl] **VI** drängeln; **he ~d against me** er rempelte mich an; **the people jostling round the stalls** die Leute, die sich vor den Buden drängelten; **they are jostling for the top job** sie streiten *or* rangeln um den Spitzenjob → **position** N **a** **VT** anrempeln, schubsen; **they ~d him out of the room** sie drängten *or* schubsten ihn aus dem Zimmer; **he was ~d along with the crowd** die Menge schob ihn mit sich; **to ~ one's way through** sich durchschubsen **N** Gedränge *nt*, Rempelei *f*

jot [dʒɒt] N (*inf*, *of truth*, *sense*) Funken *m*, Fünkchen *nt*, Körnchen *nt*; **it won't do a ~ of good** das nützt gar nichts *or* kein bisschen; **this won't affect my decision one ~** das wird meine Entscheidung nicht im Geringsten beeinflussen; **not one ~ or tittle** (*inf*) aber auch nicht das kleinste bisschen (*inf*), keinen Deut

▶ **jot down** VT *sep* sich (*dat*) notieren, sich (*dat*) eine Notiz machen von; **to jot down notes** Notizen machen

jotter ['dʒɒtə] N (*Brit*, = *note pad*) Notizblock *m*; (= *notebook*) Notizheft(chen) *nt*

jottings ['dʒɒtɪŋz] PL Notizen *pl*

joule [dʒuːl] N (*Phys*) Joule *nt*

journal ['dʒɜːnl] N **a** (= *magazine*) Zeitschrift *f*; (= *newspaper*) Zeitung *f* **b** (= *diary*) Tagebuch *nt*; **to keep a ~** Tagebuch führen **c** (*Naut*) Logbuch *nt*, Bordbuch *nt*; (*Comm*) Journal *nt*; (= *daybook*) Tagebuch *nt*; (*Jur*) Gerichtsakten *pl* **d** (*Mech*) Achszapfen *m*, Achsschenkel *m*

journalese [ˌdʒɜːnə'liːz] N Zeitungs- *or* Pressejargon *m*

journalism ['dʒɜːnəlɪzəm] N Journalismus *m*

journalist ['dʒɜːnəlɪst] N Journalist(in) *m(f)*

journalistic [ˌdʒɜːnə'lɪstɪk] ADJ journalistisch

journalistically [ˌdʒɜːnə'lɪstɪkəlɪ] ADV im Zeitungsstil

journey ['dʒɜːnɪ] **N** Reise *f*; (*by car*, *train etc also*) Fahrt *f*; **to go on a ~** eine Reise machen, verreisen; **they have gone on a ~** sie sind verreist; **to set out on one's ~** abreisen; **to set out on a ~** eine Reise antreten; **it's a ~ of 50 miles** *or* **a 50-mile ~** es ist 50 Meilen entfernt; **from X to Y is a ~ of 50 miles/two hours** es sind 50 Meilen/zwei Stunden (Fahrt) von X nach Y; **a two-day ~** eine Zweitagereise; **it's a two-day ~ to get to ... from here** man braucht zwei Tage, um von hier nach ... zu kommen; **a bus/train ~** eine Bus-/Zugfahrt; **the ~ home** die Heimreise, die Heimfahrt; **he has quite a ~ to get to work** er muss ziemlich weit fahren, um zur Arbeit zu kommen; **to reach one's ~'s end** (*liter*) am Ziel der Reise angelangt sein; **his ~ through life** sein Lebensweg *m*; **a ~ of discovery** eine Entdeckungsreise **VI** reisen; **to ~ on** weiterreisen

journeyman ['dʒɜːnɪmən] N *pl* **-men** [-mən] Geselle *m*; **~ baker** Bäckergeselle *m*; **~ actor/artist** *etc* (*of average talent*) durchschnittlicher Schauspieler/Künstler *etc*

joust [dʒaʊst] **VI** im Turnier kämpfen, turnieren (*obs*); (*fig*) sich rangeln **N** Zweikampf *m* im Turnier

jousting ['dʒaʊstɪŋ] N Turnier(kämpfe *pl*) *nt*; (*fig*) Rangeleien *pl*

Jove [dʒəʊv] N Jupiter *m*; **by ~!** (*dated*) Donnerwetter!; **have you/did he etc, by ~!** tatsächlich!

jovial ['dʒəʊvɪəl] ADJ fröhlich, jovial (*esp pej*); *welcome* freundlich, herzlich; **in (a) ~ mood** gut gelaunt

joviality [ˌdʒəʊvɪ'ælɪtɪ] N Fröhlichkeit *f*, Jovialität *f* (*esp pej*); (*of welcome*) Herzlichkeit *f*

jovially ['dʒəʊvɪəlɪ] ADV fröhlich, jovial; *welcome* freundlich, herzlich

jowl [dʒaʊl] N (= *jaw*) (Unter)kiefer *m*; (*often pl*) (= *cheek*) Backe *f*; (= *fold of flesh*) Hängebacke *f* → **cheek**

jowly ['dʒaʊlɪ] ADJ **to be ~** Hängebacken haben

joy [dʒɔɪ] N **a** Freude *f*; **to my great ~** zu meiner großen Freude; **to be full of the ~s of spring** froh und munter sein; **she/the garden is a ~ to behold** sie/der Garten ist eine Augenweide; **it's a ~ to hear him** es ist eine wahre Freude *or* ein Genuss, ihn zu hören; **this car is a ~ to drive** es ist eine Freude, dieses Auto zu fahren; **to wish sb ~** jdm Glück *or* Zufriedenheit wünschen; **I wish you ~ (of it)!** (*iro*) na dann viel Spaß *or* viel Vergnügen!; **one of the ~s of this job is ...** eine der erfreulichen Seiten dieses Berufs ist ...; **that's the ~ of this system** das ist das Schöne an diesem System → **jump** **b** *no pl* (*Brit inf*: = *success*) Erfolg *m*; **I didn't get much/any ~** ich hatte nicht viel/keinen Erfolg; **any ~?** hat es geklappt? (*inf*); **you won't get any ~ out of him** bei ihm werden Sie keinen Erfolg haben

joyful ['dʒɔɪfʊl] ADJ freudig, froh

joyfully ['dʒɔɪfəlɪ] ADV freudig

joyfulness ['dʒɔɪfʊlnɪs] N Fröhlichkeit *f*; (*of person also*) Frohsinn *m*, Heiterkeit *f*

joyless ['dʒɔɪlɪs] ADJ freudlos; *person also* griesgrämig

joyous ['dʒɔɪəs] ADJ (*liter*) freudig, froh

joyously ['dʒɔɪəslɪ] ADV (*liter*) freudig

joy: joyride N Spritztour *f* (*in einem gestohlenen Auto*); **to take a car for a ~** (ein Auto stehlen und damit) eine Spritztour machen; **joyrider** N Autodieb, *der den Wagen nur für eine Spritztour will*, Joyrider(in) *m(f)*; **joyriding** N Joyriding *nt*; **joystick** N (*Aviat*) Steuerknüppel *m*; (*Comput*) Joystick *m*

JP (*Brit*) abbr of **Justice of the Peace**

Jr abbr of **junior** jr., jun.

JSA (*Brit Admin*) abbr of **job seeker's allowance** ≈ Arbeitslosengeld *nt*

jubilant ['dʒuːbɪlənt] ADJ überglücklich; (= *expressing joy*) jubelnd *attr*; *voice* jubelnd *attr*, frohlockend *attr*; *face* strahlend *attr*; (*at sb's failure etc*) triumphierend *attr*; **they gave him a ~ welcome** sie empfingen ihn mit Jubel; **to be ~** überglücklich sein, jubeln, strahlen, triumphieren

jubilation [ˌdʒuːbɪ'leɪʃən] N Jubel *m*; **a cause for ~** ein Grund zum Jubel; **a mood of ~** eine triumphale Stimmung

jubilee ['dʒuːbɪliː] N Jubiläum *nt*

Judaea [dʒuː'diːə] N Judäa *nt*

Judaeo-Christian, (*US*) **Judeo-Christian** [dʒuːˌdeɪəʊ'krɪstɪən] ADJ jüdisch-christlich

Judah ['dʒuːdə] N Juda *m*

Judaic [dʒuː'deɪk] ADJ judaisch

Judaism ['dʒuːdeɪɪzəm] N Judaismus *m*

Judas ['dʒuːdəs] N (*Bibl*, *fig*) Judas *m*

judas (hole) N Guckloch *nt*

judder ['dʒʌdə] N (*Brit*) **a** (*Mech*) Erschütterung *f*; (*in car etc*) Ruckeln *nt*; **to give a ~** (*car etc*) ruckeln **VI** erzittern; (*car etc*) ruckeln; **the train ~ed to a halt** der Zug kam ruckartig zum Stehen

Judea N = **Judaea**

judge [dʒʌdʒ] ☼ 6.3 **N a** (*Jur*) Richter(in) *m(f)*; (*of competition*) Preisrichter(in) *m(f)*; (*Sport*) Punktrichter(in) *m(f)*, Kampfrichter(in) *m(f)* **b** (*fig*) Kenner(in) *m(f)*; **he's a good/bad ~ of**

character er ist ein guter/schlechter Menschenkenner; **to be a good ~ of wine** ein(e) Weinkenner(in) sein; **I'll be the ~ of that** das müssen Sie mich schon selbst beurteilen lassen

c (Bibl) **(the Book of) Judges** (das Buch der) Richter

VT a (Jur) person die Verhandlung führen über (+acc); case verhandeln; (God) richten

b competition beurteilen, bewerten; (Sport) Punktrichter or Kampfrichter sein bei

c (fig: = pass judgement on) ein Urteil fällen über (+acc); **you shouldn't ~ people by appearances** Sie sollten Menschen nicht nach ihrem Äußeren beurteilen; **don't ~ a book by its cover** (prov) man sollte nicht nach dem ersten Eindruck urteilen

d (= consider, assess, deem) halten für, erachten für (geh); **this was ~d to be the best way** dies wurde für die beste Methode gehalten or erachtet (geh); **you can ~ for yourself which is better** Sie können selbst beurteilen, was besser ist; **you can ~ for yourself how upset I was** Sie können sich (dat) denken, wie bestürzt ich war; **I can't ~ whether he was right or wrong** ich kann nicht beurteilen, ob er Recht hatte or Unrecht hatte; **I ~d from his manner that he was guilty** ich schloss aus seinem Verhalten, dass er schuldig war; **how would you ~ him?** wie würden Sie ihn beurteilen or einschätzen?

e (= estimate) speed, width, distance etc einschätzen; **he ~d the moment well** er hat den richtigen Augenblick abgepasst

VI a (Jur) Richter sein; (God) richten; (at competition) Preisrichter sein; (Sport) Kampfrichter or Punktrichter sein

b (fig) (= pass judgement) ein Urteil fällen; (= form an opinion) (be)urteilen; **who am I to ~?** ich kann mir dazu kein Urteil erlauben; **as or so far as one can ~** soweit man (es) beurteilen kann; **judging by** or **from sth** nach etw zu urteilen; **judging by appearances** dem Aussehen nach; **to ~ by appearances** nach dem Äußeren urteilen; **(you can) ~ for yourself** beurteilen Sie das selbst; **he let me ~ for myself** er überließ es meinem Urteil

judge advocate N (Mil) Beisitzer(in) m(f) bei einem Kriegsgericht, Kriegsgerichtsrat m, Kriegsgerichtsrätin f

judg(e)ment ['dʒʌdʒmənt] N **a** (Jur) (Gerichts)urteil nt; (Eccl) Gericht nt, Richterspruch m; (= divine punishment) Strafe f Gottes; **to await ~** (Jur) auf sein or das Urteil warten; (Eccl) auf das Gericht or den Richterspruch (Gottes) warten; **the Day of Judg(e)ment** der Tag des Jüngsten Gerichtes; **to pass** or **give ~** (also fig) ein Urteil fällen, das Urteil sprechen (on über +acc); **to sit in ~ on a case** Richter in einem Fall sein; **to sit in ~ on sb** über jdn zu Gericht sitzen; (Jur also) die Verhandlung über jdn führen; **I don't want to sit in ~ on you** ich möchte mich nicht zu Ihrem Richter aufspielen; **it's a ~ from above** das ist die Strafe Gottes; **it's a ~ on him for being so lazy** das ist die Strafe Gottes dafür, dass er so faul ist

b (= opinion) Meinung f, Ansicht f, Urteil nt; (= moral judg(e)ment, value judg(e)ment) Werturteil nt; (= estimation: of distance, speed etc) Einschätzung f; **to give one's ~ on sth** sein Urteil über etw (acc) abgeben, seine Meinung zu etw äußern; **an error of ~** eine falsche Einschätzung, eine Fehleinschätzung; **in my ~** meines Erachtens, meiner Meinung nach; **against one's better ~** gegen (sein) besseres Wissen, wider besseres Wissen

c (= discernment) Urteilsvermögen nt; **to show ~** ein gutes Urteilsvermögen beweisen or zeigen; **it's all a question of ~** das ist Ansichtssache

judg(e)mental [dʒʌdʒ'mentl] ADJ wertend; **don't be so ~** nimm nicht immer gleich Wertungen vor, bewerte nicht immer gleich alles

judg(e)ment: judg(e)ment call N (esp US) Gewissensentscheidung f; **to make a ~** eine Gewissensentscheidung treffen; **Judg(e)ment Day** N Tag m des Jüngsten Gerichts; **judg(e)ment seat** N Gottes Richterstuhl m

judicable ['dʒuːdɪkəbl] ADJ justiziabel; case verhandlungsfähig; person rechtsfähig

judicature ['dʒuːdɪkətʃə] N (= judges) Richterstand m; (= judicial system) Gerichtswesen nt, Gerichtsbarkeit f

judicial [dʒuː'dɪʃəl] ADJ **a** (Jur) inquiry, review gerichtlich; power richterlich; **~ function** Richteramt nt; **to take ~ proceedings against sb** ein Gerichtsverfahren nt gegen jdn anstrengen or einleiten; **~ system** Justizsystem nt **b** (= critical) mind klar urteilend attr, kritisch

judicially [dʒuː'dɪʃəlɪ] ADV defeat, approve gerichtlich; **to apportion blame ~** eine gerichtliche Schuldzuweisung erteilen; **the country is ~ corrupt** das Justizsystem des Landes ist korrupt

judicial murder N Justizmord m

judicial separation N Gerichtsbeschluss m zur Aufhebung der ehelichen Gemeinschaft

judiciary [dʒuː'dɪʃərɪ] N (= branch of administration) Gerichtsbehörden pl; (= legal system) Gerichtswesen nt; (= judges) Richterstand m

judicious ADJ , **judiciously** ADV [dʒuː'dɪʃəs, -lɪ] klug, umsichtig

judo ['dʒuːdəʊ] N Judo nt

Judy ['dʒuːdɪ] N abbr of Judith (in Punch and Judy) Gretel f

jug¹ [dʒʌg] N **a** (for milk, coffee etc) (with lid) Kanne f; (without lid) Krug m; (small) Kännchen nt **b** (Brit inf: = prison) Kittchen nt (inf), Knast m (inf); **in ~** hinter schwedischen Gardinen (inf), im Kittchen (inf) or Knast (inf) **VT** (Cook) schmoren

jug² N (of nightingale) Flöten nt

jugged hare ['dʒʌgd'hɛə] N (Brit Cook) ≈ Hasenpfeffer m

juggernaut ['dʒʌgənɔːt] N **a** (Brit: = lorry) Schwerlaster m **b** (Rel) **Juggernaut** Dschagannath m, Jagannath m **c** (fig: = destructive force) verheerende Gewalt; **a media ~** ein Medienkonglomerat nt; **the military ~** der Militärapparat; **the ~ of British government** die unaufhaltsame britische Regierungsmaschinerie; **Puritanism, like some huge ~, swept across the country** der Puritanismus rollte mit unaufhaltsamer Gewalt über das Land

juggins ['dʒʌgɪnz] N (Brit inf) Depp m (S Ger), Trottel m (inf)

juggle ['dʒʌgl] **VI** jonglieren; **to ~ with the figures** die Zahlen so hindrehen, dass sie passen **VT** balls jonglieren (mit); figures so hindrehen, dass sie passen; debts umverteilen; **many women have to ~ (the demands of) family and career** viele Frauen müssen (die Anforderungen von) Familie und Beruf miteinander vereinbaren; **they ~d the schedules to show the final** die Programmfolge wurde so umgeändert, dass das Endspiel gezeigt werden konnte

juggler ['dʒʌglə] N **a** (lit) Jongleur(in) m(f) **b** (fig: = trickster) Schwindler(in) m(f); **~ with words** Wortverdreher(in) m(f)

jugglery ['dʒʌglərɪ] N = **juggling**

juggling ['dʒʌglɪŋ] N **a** (lit) Jonglieren nt **b** (fig) Verdrehen nt (with von); **~ with words/figures** Wort-/Zahlenakrobatik f; **there has been a bit of ~ here** das ist doch so hingedreht worden, dass es passt, das ist doch nicht ganz hasenrein (inf)

juggling act N (fig) Balanceakt m

jughead ['dʒʌghed] N (US pej sl) Knallkopf m (inf)

Jugoslav ['juːgəʊslɑːv] ADJ jugoslawisch N Jugoslawe m, Jugoslawin f

Jugoslavia [juːgəʊ'slɑːvɪə] N Jugoslawien nt

jugular ['dʒʌgjʊlə] N **~ (vein)** Drosselvene f, Jugularvene f; **to go for the ~** (fig) zum entscheidenden Schlag ausholen (fig)

juice [dʒuːs] N **a** (of fruit, meat) Saft m **b** usu pl (of body) Körpersäfte pl **c** (inf: = electricity, petrol) Saft m (inf)

juice up VT SEP (US inf) **a** car frisieren (inf) **b** (= spice up) party aufpeppen (inf); image, brand aufmöbeln (inf)

juicer ['dʒuːsə] N Entsafter m

juiciness ['dʒuːsɪnɪs] N (lit) Saftigkeit f; (fig) Pikanterie f, Schlüpfrigkeit f, gewisser Reiz; (of scandal) Saftigkeit f (inf)

juicy ['dʒuːsɪ] ADJ (+er) fruit saftig, (inf) profit saftig (inf); squelch schmatzend, quatschend; story pikant, schlüpfrig; scandal gepfeffert (inf), saftig (inf); **a big ~ kiss** ein dicker Schmatz (inf)

jujitsu [ˌdʒuː'dʒɪtsuː] N Jiu-Jitsu nt

jujube ['dʒuːdʒuːb] N (Bot) Jujube f; (= berry also) Brustbeere f

jukebox ['dʒuːkbɒks] N Jukebox f, Musikbox f, Musikautomat m; **my favourite song is playing on the ~** die Jukebox spielt mein Lieblingslied

juke joint ['dʒuːkdʒɔɪnt] N (inf) Bumslokal nt (inf pej)

Jul abbr of **July**

julep ['dʒuːlep] N **a** ≈ Sirup m, ≈ Saft m **b** → mint²

Julian ['dʒuːlɪən] N Julian m ADJ **~ calendar** julianischer Kalender

Julius Caesar ['dʒuːlɪəs'siːzə] N Julius Caesar m

July [dʒuː'laɪ] N Juli m → also **September**

jumble ['dʒʌmbl] **VT** (also **jumble up**) **a** (lit) durcheinander werfen, kunterbunt vermischen; **~d up** durcheinander, kunterbunt vermischt; **a ~d mass of wires** ein Wirrwarr m von Kabeln; **to ~ everything up** alles durcheinander bringen or in Unordnung bringen; **his clothes are ~d together on the bed** seine Kleider liegen in einem unordentlichen Haufen auf dem Bett **b** (fig) facts durcheinander bringen; **~d thoughts/memories** verworrene Gedanken/Erinnerungen pl N **a** (of objects) Durcheinander nt; (of ideas, words, memories) Wirrwarr m **b** no pl (for jumble sale) gebrauchte Sachen pl

jumble sale N (Brit) ≈ Flohmarkt m (von Vereinen veranstalteter Verkauf von gebrauchten Sachen); (for charity) Wohltätigkeitsbasar m

jumbly ['dʒʌmblɪ] ADJ wirr, durcheinander

jumbo ['dʒʌmbəʊ] N **a** (inf) Jumbo m (inf) **b** (= jumbo jet) Jumbo(jet) m

jump [dʒʌmp] N **a** (lit) Sprung m; (with parachute) Absprung m; (on race-course) Hindernis nt; **this horse is no good over the ~s** dieses Pferd taugt bei den Hindernissen nichts **b** (fig: of prices) (plötzlicher or sprunghafter) Anstieg m; (in narrative) Sprung m, abrupter Übergang; **to take a sudden ~** (prices, temperature) ruckartig or sprunghaft ansteigen (to auf +acc), in die Höhe schnellen; **a 5% ~ in the number of unemployed people** ein 5%iger Anstieg der Arbeitslosenziffern; **it's a big ~ from medical student to doctor** es ist ein großer Sprung vom Medizinstudenten zum Arzt; **he's always one ~ ahead** er ist immer einen Schritt voraus; **you can take a running ~** (Brit inf) das kannst du vergessen

c (= start) **to give a ~** zusammenfahren; **my heart gave a ~** mein Herz machte einen Sprung

d (esp US inf) **to get a** or **the ~ on sb/sth** jdm/etw gegenüber im Vorteil sein; **to give sb a** or **the ~ on sb/sth** jdm einen Vorsprung vor jdm/etw verschaffen

VI a (= leap) springen, einen Satz machen; (Sport) springen; (parachutist) (ab)springen; **to ~ into a river** in einen Fluss springen; **this horse ~s well** dieses Pferd springt gut or nimmt die Hindernisse gut; **to ~ for joy** einen Freudensprung machen; (heart) vor Freude hüpfen; **to ~ to one's feet** aufspringen; **to ~ up and down on the spot** auf der Stelle hüpfen; **they ~ed up and down on his stomach** sie hüpften auf seinem Bauch herum; **they're ~ing up and down about it** (fig) sie regen sich furchtbar darüber auf; **to ~ to conclusions** vorschnelle Schlüsse ziehen

b (typewriter) Buchstaben überspringen or auslassen

c (*fig*) springen, unvermittelt übergehen; (*prices, shares*) in die Höhe schnellen, sprunghaft ansteigen; **~ to it!** los schon!, mach schon!; **the film suddenly ~s from the 18th into the 20th century** der Film macht plötzlich einen Sprung von 18. ins 20. Jahrhundert; **her salary ~ed from £15,000 to £22,000** ihr Gehalt schnellte von £ 15.000 auf £ 22.000; **if you keep ~ing from one thing to another** wenn Sie nie an einer Sache bleiben; **she ~ed from kitchen assistant to chef** sie stieg plötzlich von der Küchenhilfe zur Köchin auf; **let's offer £200 and see which way they ~** (*inf*) machen wir ihnen doch (einfach) ein Angebot von £ 200 und sehen dann, wie sie darauf reagieren

d (= *start*) zusammenfahren, zusammenzucken; **the shout made him ~** er zuckte or fuhr bei dem Schrei zusammen; **you made me ~** du hast mich (aber) erschreckt; **his heart ~ed when ...** sein Herz machte einen Satz, als ...

VT a ditch, fence etc überspringen, hinüberspringen über (+*acc*); **the horse ~ed a clear round** das Pferd sprang eine fehlerfreie Runde; **he ~ed two metres** er hat zwei Meter übersprungen

b *horse* springen lassen; **he ~ed his horse over the fence** er setzte mit seinem Pferd über den Zaun

c (= *skip*) überspringen, auslassen

d (*pick-up*) *groove* überspringen; **to ~ the rails** (*train*) entgleisen; **to ~ a man** (*Draughts*) einen überspringen

e (*inf usages*) **to ~ bail** (*Jur*) abhauen (*inf*) (*während man auf Kaution freigelassen ist*); **to ~ a claim** einen schon bestehenden Anspruch (auf Land or Rechte) übergehen; **to ~ the lights** or **a red light** bei Rot rüberfahren (*inf*) or über die Kreuzung fahren; **to ~ the queue** (*Brit*) sich vordrängeln; **to ~ ship** (*Naut, passenger*) das Schiff vorzeitig verlassen; (*sailor*) heimlich abheuern; (*fig, = leave failing organization etc*) das sinkende Schiff verlassen; (= *join rival organization etc*) abspringen (und zur Konkurrenz gehen); **to ~ a train** (= *get on*) auf einen Zug aufspringen; (= *get off*) von einem Zug abspringen; **they ~ed a train to Acapulco** sie fuhren schwarz nach Acapulco; **to ~ sb** jdn überfallen

▶ **jump about** (*Brit*) or **around** VI herumhüpfen or -springen

▶ **jump at** VI +prep obj person (*lit*) anspringen; (*fig*) anfahren; object zuspringen auf (+*acc*); offer sofort zugreifen bei, sofort ergreifen; suggestion sofort aufgreifen; chance sofort beim Schopf ergreifen

▶ **jump down** VI herunterhüpfen or -springen (*from* von); **to jump down sb's throat** jdn anfahren, jdm dazwischenfahren (*inf*); **jump down!** spring or hüpf (runter)!

▶ **jump in** VI hineinspringen; (*fig*) eingreifen; **jump in!** (*to car*) steig ein!; (*at swimming pool etc*) spring rein!

▶ **jump off** VI **a** (= *leap off*) herunterspringen (*prep obj* von); (*from train, bus*) aussteigen (*prep obj* aus); (*when moving*) abspringen (*prep obj* von); (*from bicycle, horse*) absteigen (*prep obj* von) **b** (*Showjumping*) den Wettbewerb durch ein Stechen entscheiden; **they had to jump off to decide the winner** der Sieger musste durch ein Stechen ermittelt werden

▶ **jump on** VI (*lit, onto vehicle*) einsteigen (*prep obj, -to in* +acc); (*onto moving train, bus*) aufspringen (*prep obj, -to auf* +acc); (*onto bicycle, horse*) aufsteigen (*prep obj, -to auf* +acc); **to jump on(to) sb/sth** auf jdn/etw springen; **he jumped on(to) his bicycle** er schwang sich auf sein Fahrrad VI +prep obj (*inf*) person (= *criticize*) anfahren; (= *attack*) überfallen; suggestion kritisieren, heruntermachen (*inf*)

▶ **jump out** VI hinausspringen; (*from vehicle*) aussteigen (*of* aus); (*when moving*) abspringen (*of* von); **to jump out of bed** aus dem Bett springen; **to jump out of the window** aus dem Fenster springen, zum Fenster hinausspringen;

the caption jumps out at you die Überschrift springt einem ins Auge

▶ **jump up** VI hochspringen; (*from sitting or lying position also*) aufspringen; (*onto sth*) hinaufspringen (*onto auf* +acc)

jump ball N Schiedsrichterball m

jumped-up ['dʒʌmpt'ʌp] ADJ (*inf*) **this new ~ manageress** dieser kleine Emporkömmling von einer Abteilungsleiterin

jumper ['dʒʌmpə'] N **a** (= *garment*) (*Brit*) Pullover m; (*US*: = *dress*) Trägerkleid nt **b** (= *person*) Springer(in) m(f); (= *animal*) Springer m **c** (*Comput*) (Steck)brücke f

jumper cables N (*US Aut*) = jump leads

jumpiness ['dʒʌmpɪnɪs] N (*inf*) Nervosität f; (*of easily startled person*) Schreckhaftigkeit f

jumping jack ['dʒʌmpɪŋ'dʒæk] N Hampelmann m

jumping-off place [dʒʌmpɪŋ'ɒfpleɪs] N (*fig*) (*for negotiations*) Ausgangsbasis f; (*for job*) Sprungbrett nt

jump: jump jet N Senkrechtstarter m; **jump jockey** N (*Brit, Horse Racing*) Springreiter(in) m(f); **jump leads** PL (*Brit, Aut*) Starthilfekabel nt; **jump-off** N (*Showjumping*) Stechen nt; **jump pass** N (*Basketball*) Sprungpass m; **jump rope** N (*US*) = skipping rope; **jump seat** N Notsitz m, Klappsitz m; **jump shot** N (*Basketball*) Sprungwurf m; **jump-start** N (*Mot*) Starthilfe f; **to give sb a ~** (*lit, fig*) jdm Starthilfe geben VT (*Mot*) Starthilfe geben; (*fig: = start*) in Gang setzen or bringen, anschieben (*fig*); **jump suit** N Overall m

jumpy ['dʒʌmpɪ] ADJ (+er) **a** (*inf*) person nervös; (= *easily startled*) schreckhaft; market unsicher **b** motion ruckartig

Jun abbr **a** of **June b** of **junior** jr., jun.

junction ['dʒʌŋkʃən] N **a** (*Rail*) Gleisanschluss m; (*of roads*) Kreuzung f; (*of rivers*) Zusammenfluss m; **Clapham Junction** Claphamer Kreuz nt; **Hamm is a big railway ~** Hamm ist ein großer Eisenbahnknotenpunkt **b** (*Elec*) Anschlussstelle f **c** (*act*) Verbindung f

junction box N (*Elec*) Verteilerkasten m, Kabelkasten m

juncture ['dʒʌŋktʃə'] N **at this ~** zu diesem Zeitpunkt

June [dʒuːn] N Juni m → also **September**

jungle ['dʒʌŋgl] N Dschungel m (*also fig*), Urwald m; **concrete ~** Betonwüste f; **the law of the ~** das Gesetz des Dschungels

jungle: jungle gym N (*US*) Klettergerüst nt; **jungle juice** N (*hum inf*: = *alcohol*) Feuerwasser nt (*inf*)

junior ['dʒuːnɪə'] ADJ **a** (= *younger*) jünger; **he is ~ to me** er ist jünger als ich; **Hiram Schwarz, ~** Hiram Schwarz junior; **Smith, ~** (*at school*) Smith II, der kleine Smith; **the ~ miss** die kleine Dame **b** (= *subordinate*) employee untergeordnet; officer rangniedriger; **to be ~ to sb** unter jdm stehen **c** (*Sport*) Junioren-, der Junioren; **~ team** Juniorenmannschaft f

N **a** Jüngere(r) mf; **he is my ~ by two years, he is two years my ~** er ist zwei Jahre jünger als ich; **where's ~?** wo ist der Junior? **b** (*Brit Sch*) (*at primary school*) Grundschüler(in) m(f); (*at secondary school*) Unterstufenschüler(in) m(f) **c** (*US Univ*) Student(in) im vorletzten Studienjahr **d** (*Sport*) Junior(in) m(f); **the ~s** die Junioren/Juniorinnen pl

junior: junior classes PL (*Sch*) Unterstufe f; **junior clerk** N zweiter Buchhalter; **he's just some ~** er ist bloß ein kleiner Angestellter; **junior college** N (*US Univ*) College, an dem man die ersten zwei Jahre eines 4-jährigen Studiums absolviert; **junior common room** N (*Brit Univ*) Gemeinschaftsraum m für Studenten; **junior high (school)** N (*US*) = Mittelschule f; **Junior League** N **a** (*Brit Sport*) Amateurliga f **b** (*US: for voluntary work*) Wohltätigkeitsverband von Frauen, die sich im Sozial-

bereich engagieren; **junior minister** N Staatssekretär(in) m(f); **junior partner** N jüngerer Teilhaber; (*in coalition*) kleinerer (Koalitions)partner; **junior school** N (*Brit*) Grundschule f

juniper ['dʒuːnɪpə'] N Wacholder m; **~ berry** Wacholderbeere f

junk[1] [dʒʌŋk] N **a** (= *discarded objects*) Trödel m, altes Zeug, Gerümpel nt **b** (*inf*: = *trash*) Ramsch m, Plunder m, Schund m **c** (*inf*: = *drugs*) Stoff m (*inf*) VT (*inf*: = *get rid of*) object wegschmeißen (*inf*); idea, attempt aufgeben

junk[2] N (*boat*) Dschunke f

junk: junk bond N (*Fin*) niedrig eingestuftes Wertpapier mit hohen Ertragschancen bei erhöhtem Risiko; **junk car** N Schrottauto nt; **junk dealer** N Trödler(in) m(f), Altwarenhändler(in) m(f); **junk e-mail** N unerbetene E-Mail mit Werbung

junket ['dʒʌŋkɪt] N **a** (*Cook*) Dickmilch f **b** (*old, hum*: = *merrymaking*) Gelage nt, Fest nt, Lustbarkeit f (*old, hum*) **c** (= *trip at public expense*) (Vergnügungs)reise f auf Staatskosten VI (*old, hum*) ein Gelage abhalten

junketing ['dʒʌŋkɪtɪŋ] N **a** (*old, hum, = merrymaking*) Festivitäten pl (*esp hum*), Lustbarkeit f (*old, hum*) **b** (= *trips at public expense*) (Vergnügungs)reisen pl auf Staatskosten

junk: junk fax N unerbetenes Fax mit Werbung; **junk food** N Junk food nt (*inf*), ungesundes Essen; **junk heap** N (*also inf*: = *car*) Schrotthaufen m (*inf*); **you'll end up on the ~** du wirst in der Gosse landen

junkie ['dʒʌŋkɪ] N (*inf*) Fixer(in) m(f) (*inf*), Junkie m (*inf*); **fast food ~** Fan m von Fastfood; **computer ~** Computerfreak m (*sl*)

junk: junk mail N (Post)wurfsendungen pl, Reklame f; **junk room** N Rumpelkammer f; **junk shop** N Trödelladen m; **junk yard** N (*for metal*) Schrottplatz m; (*for discarded objects*) Schuttabladeplatz m; (*of rag and bone merchant*) Trödellager(platz m) nt

junta ['dʒʌntə] N Junta f

Jupiter ['dʒuːpɪtə'] N Jupiter m

juridical [dʒʊə'rɪdɪkəl] ADJ (*of law*) juristisch; (*of court*) gerichtlich

jurisdiction [dʒʊərɪs'dɪkʃən] N Gerichtsbarkeit f; (= *range of authority*) Zuständigkeit(sbereich m) f; **matters that fall outside the ~ of this court** Fälle, für die dieses Gericht nicht zuständig ist; **this court has no ~ over him** er untersteht diesem Gericht nicht; **that's not within my ~** dafür bin ich nicht zuständig

jurisprudence [dʒʊərɪs'pruːdəns] N Jura nt, Rechtswissenschaft f, Jurisprudenz f (*old*) → **medical**

jurist ['dʒʊərɪst] N Jurist(in) m(f), Rechtswissenschaftler(in) m(f)

juror ['dʒʊərə'] N Schöffe m, Schöffin f; (*for capital crimes*) Geschworene(r) mf; (*in competition*) Preisrichter(in) m(f), Jurymitglied nt

jury ['dʒʊərɪ] N **a** (*Jur*) **the ~** die Schöffen pl, die Jury; (*for capital crimes*) die Geschworenen pl; **they don't have juries there** dort gibt es keine Schöffengerichte or keine Jury or (*for capital crimes*) keine Schwurgerichte; **to sit** or **be on the ~** Schöffe/Geschworener sein; **Ladies and Gentlemen of the Jury** meine Damen und Herren Schöffen/Geschworenen; **the ~ is (still) out** (*lit*) die Schöffen/Geschworenen beraten noch; (*fig*) es ist noch nichts entschieden; **the ~ is out on whether this is true** es ist noch nicht heraus, ob das stimmt

b (*for examination*) Prüfungsausschuss m; (*for exhibition, competition*) Jury f, Preisgericht nt

jury: jury box N Schöffenbank f; (*for capital crimes*) Geschworenenbank f; **juryman** N Schöffe m; (*for capital crimes*) Geschworene(r) m; **jury rig** N (*Naut*) Hilfstakelage f, Nottakelage f; **jury service** N Schöffenamt nt; (*for capital crimes*) Amt nt des Geschworenen; **to do ~** Schöffe/Geschworener sein; **he's never been called for ~** er wurde nie als Schöffe/Geschworener berufen; **jury system** N Jurysystem *nt*, Schöffengerichte *pl*; (*for capital crimes*) Schwurgerichte *pl*; **jurywoman** N Schöffin *f*; (*for capital crimes*) Geschworene *f*

just¹ [dʒʌst] ✪ 5.4 ADV **a** (*immediate past*) gerade, (so)eben, (so)eben gegangen; **she left ~ before I came** sie war, gerade *or* kurz bevor ich kam, weggegangen; **he's ~ been appointed** er ist gerade *or* eben erst ernannt worden; **I met him ~ after lunch** ich habe ihn direkt *or* gleich nach dem Mittagessen getroffen

b (= *at this/that very moment*) gerade; **hurry up, he's ~ going** beeilen Sie sich, er geht gerade; **he's ~ coming** er kommt gerade *or* eben; **I'm ~ coming** ich komme ja schon; **I was ~ going to ...** ich wollte gerade ...; **as I was going** genau in dem Moment *or* gerade, als ich gehen wollte

c (= *barely, almost not*) gerade noch, mit knapper Not; **he (only) ~ escaped being run over** er wäre um ein Haar überfahren worden; **it ~ missed** es hat fast *or* beinahe getroffen; **I've got only ~ enough to live on** mir reicht es gerade so *or* so eben noch zum Leben; **I arrived ~ in time** ich bin gerade (noch) rechtzeitig gekommen

d (= *exactly*) genau, gerade; **it is ~ five o'clock** es ist genau fünf Uhr; **that's ~ like you** das sieht dir ähnlich; **it's ~ on nine o'clock** es ist gerade neun Uhr; **it happened ~ as I expected** es passierte genau so, wie ich es erwartet hatte; **it's ~ because of that that he insists** gerade *or* eben deshalb besteht er darauf; **that's ~ it!** das ists ja gerade *or* eben!; **that's ~ what I was going to say** genau das wollte ich (auch) sagen; **~ what do you mean by that?** was wollen Sie damit sagen?; **~ what does this symbol mean?** was bedeutet dieses Zeichen genau?; **it was ~ there** genau da war es; **~ so!** (*old*) genau, ganz recht; **everything has to be ~ so** es muss alles seine Ordnung haben

e (= *only, simply*) nur, bloß; **I can stay ~ a minute** ich kann nur *or* bloß eine Minute bleiben; **~ you and me** nur wir beide, wir beide allein; **this is ~ to show you how it works** dies soll Ihnen lediglich zeigen, wie es funktioniert; **this is ~ to confirm ...** hiermit bestätigen wir, dass ...; **he's ~ a boy** er ist doch noch ein Junge; **why don't you want to/like it? – I ~ don't** warum willst du nicht/magst du es nicht? – ich will/mags eben *or* halt (*inf*) nicht; **~ like that** (ganz) einfach so; **I don't know, I ~ don't** ich weiß (es) nicht, beim besten Willen nicht; **you can't ~ assume ...** Sie können doch nicht ohne weiteres annehmen ...; **it's ~ not good enough** es ist einfach nicht gut genug; **I ~ prefer it this way** ich finds eben *or* einfach besser so

f (= *a small distance: with position*) gleich; **~ round the corner** gleich um die Ecke; **~ above the trees** direkt über den Bäumen; **put it ~ over there** stells mal da drüben hin; **~ here** (genau) hier

g (= *absolutely*) einfach, wirklich; **it was ~ fantastic** es war einfach prima; **it's ~ terrible** das ist ja schrecklich!

h **~ as** genauso, ebenso; **the blue hat is ~ as nice as the red one** der blaue Hut ist genauso hübsch wie der rote; **she didn't understand you – it's ~ as well!** sie hat Sie nicht verstanden – das ist vielleicht auch besser so; **it's ~ as well you stayed at home, you didn't miss anything** es macht nichts, dass Sie zu Hause geblieben sind, Sie haben nichts verpasst; **it's ~**

as well you didn't go out nur gut, dass Sie nicht weggegangen sind; **it would be ~ as well if you came** es wäre doch besser, wenn Sie kämen; **come ~ as you are** kommen Sie so, wie Sie sind; **it's ~ as you please** wie Sie wollen; **~ as I thought!** ich habe es mir doch gedacht!

i **~ about** in etwa, so etwa; **I am ~ about ready** ich bin so gut wie fertig; **it's ~ about here** es ist (so) ungefähr hier; **did he make it in time? – ~ about** hat ers (rechtzeitig) geschafft? – so gerade; **will this do? – ~ about** ist das recht so? – so in etwa; **I am ~ about fed up with it!** (*inf*) so langsam aber sicher hängt es mir zum Hals raus (*inf*); **that's ~ about the limit!** das ist doch die Höhe!

j **~ now** (*in past*) soeben (erst), gerade erst; **not ~ now** im Moment nicht; **~ now?** jetzt gleich?; **you can go, but not ~ now** Sie können gehen, aber nicht gerade jetzt

k (*other uses*) **~ think** denk bloß; **~ listen** hör mal; **~ try** versuchs doch mal; **~ taste this** probier das mal; (*it's awful*) probier bloß das mal; **~ let me try** lassen Sies mich doch mal versuchen; **~ shut up!** sei bloß still!; **~ wait here a moment** warten Sie hier mal (für) einen Augenblick; **~ a moment** *or* **minute!** Moment mal!; **I can ~ see him as a soldier** ich kann ihn mir gut als Soldat vorstellen; **~ see you getting up so early** (*iro*) du - und so früh aufstehen!; **can I ~ finish this?** kann ich das eben noch fertig machen?; **the possibilities ~ go on for ever** die Möglichkeiten sind ja unerschöpflich; **don't I ~!** und ob (ich ...); **~ watch it** nimm dich bloß in Acht; **~ you dare** wehe, wenn du das wagst

just² ADJ (+*er*) **a** *person, decision* gerecht (*to* gegenüber) **b** *punishment, reward* gerecht; *anger* berechtigt; *suspicion* gerechtfertigt, begründet; **a ~ cause** eine gerechte Sache; **I had ~ cause to be alarmed** ich hatte guten Grund, beunruhigt zu sein; **as (it) is only ~** wie es recht und billig ist

justice ['dʒʌstɪs] N **a** (*Jur*) (= *quality*) Gerechtigkeit *f*; (*system*) Gerichtsbarkeit *f*, Justiz *f*; **British ~** britisches Recht; **is this the famous British ~?** ist das die berühmte britische Gerechtigkeit?; **to bring sb to ~** jdn vor Gericht bringen; **court of ~** Gerichtshof *m*, Gericht *nt*; **to administer ~** Recht sprechen → **poetic justice**

b (= *fairness*) Gerechtigkeit *f*; (*of claims*) Rechtmäßigkeit *f*; **to do him ~** um ihm gegenüber gerecht zu sein, um fair zu sein (*inf*); **this photograph doesn't do her ~** auf diesem Foto ist sie nicht gut getroffen; **she never does herself ~** sie kommt nie richtig zur Geltung; **that's not true, you're not doing yourself ~** stimmt nicht, Sie unterschätzen sich; **you didn't do yourself ~ in the exams** Sie haben im Examen nicht gezeigt, was Sie können; **they did ~ to the wine** sie wussten den Wein zu würdigen; **and with ~** und (zwar) zu Recht; **there's no ~, is there?** das ist doch nicht gerecht

c (= *judge*) Richter(in) *m(f)*; **Lord Chief Justice** oberster Richter in Großbritannien **Justice of the Peace** Friedensrichter(in) *m(f)*; **Mr Justice Buchanan** Richter Buchanan

justifiable [ˌdʒʌstɪ'faɪəbl] ADJ gerechtfertigt, berechtigt

justifiably [ˌdʒʌstɪ'faɪəblɪ] ADV mit *or* zu Recht, berechtigterweise; **and ~ so** und das mit *or* zu Recht

justification [ˌdʒʌstɪfɪ'keɪʃən] N **a** Rechtfertigung *f* (*of* +gen, *for* für); **it can be said in his ~ that ...** zu seiner Verteidigung *or* Entschuldigung kann gesagt werden, dass ...; **as (a) ~ for his action** zur Rechtfertigung *or* Verteidigung seiner Handlungsweise; **he had no ~ for lying** er hatte keine Rechtfertigung *or* Entschuldigung für seine Lüge **b** (*Typ*) Justieren *nt*; (*Comput*) Randausgleich *m*

justify ['dʒʌstɪfaɪ] ✪ 26.1 VT **a** (= *show to be right*) rechtfertigen, verteidigen (*sth to sb* etw vor jdm *or* jdm gegenüber); **you don't need to ~ yourself** Sie brauchen sich nicht zu rechtfertigen *or* verteidigen; **don't try to ~ your action** versuchen Sie nicht, Ihre Tat zu entschuldigen *or* zu verteidigen; **am I justified in believing that ...?** glaube ich zu Recht, dass ...?

b (= *be good reason for*) rechtfertigen, ein Grund sein für; **the future could hardly be said to ~ great optimism** die Zukunft berechtigt wohl kaum zu großem Optimismus; **this does not ~ his being late** das ist kein Grund für sein Zuspätkommen; **he was justified in doing that** es war gerechtfertigt, dass er das tat; **you're not justified in talking to her like that** Sie haben kein Recht, so mit ihr zu reden

c (*Typ*) justieren; (*Comput*) ausrichten; **right/left justified** rechts-/linksbündig

justly ['dʒʌstlɪ] ADV zu Recht, mit Recht; *treat, try* gerecht; *condemn* gerechterweise

justness ['dʒʌstnɪs] N (*of cause*) Gerechtigkeit *f*, Billigkeit *f* (*liter*); (*of character*) Gerechtigkeit *f*

jut [dʒʌt] VI (*also* **jut out**) hervorstehen, hervorragen, herausragen; (*chin, jaw*) vorspringen; **he saw a gun ~ting (out) from behind the wall** er sah ein Gewehr hinter der Mauer (her)vorragen; **the peninsula ~s out into the sea** die Halbinsel ragt ins Meer hinaus; **to ~ out over the street** über die Straße vorstehen *or* hinausragen VT **to ~ one's chin/jaw forward** sein Kinn/seinen Kiefer vorstrecken

jute [dʒuːt] N Jute *f*

Jutland ['dʒʌtlənd] N Jütland *nt*

juvenile ['dʒuːvənaɪl] N (*Admin*) Jugendliche(r) *mf*; (= *animal*) Jungtier *nt* ADJ (= *youthful*) jugendlich; (= *for young people*) für Jugendliche; (*pej*) kindisch, unreif; **~ crime** Jugendkriminalität *f*

juvenile: juvenile center N (*US*) Heim *nt* für jugendliche Straftäter; **juvenile court** N Jugendgericht *nt*; **juvenile delinquency** N Jugendkriminalität *f*, Kriminalität *f* bei Jugendlichen; **juvenile delinquent** N jugendlicher Straftäter, jugendliche Straftäterin; **juvenile home** N (*US*) Heim *nt* für jugendliche Straftäter; **juvenile lead** N (*Theat*) Rolle *f* des jugendlichen Hauptdarstellers; (*actor*) jugendlicher Hauptdarsteller; **juvenile offender** N (*Jur*) jugendlicher Straftäter, jugendliche Straftäterin

juvenilia [ˌdʒuːvɪ'nɪlɪə] PL (*form*) Jugendwerke *pl*

juxtapose ['dʒʌkstəˌpəʊz] VT nebeneinander stellen; *ideas also* gegeneinander halten; *colours* nebeneinander setzen

juxtaposition [ˌdʒʌkstəpə'zɪʃən] N (= *act*) Nebeneinanderstellung *f*; **in ~ (with each other)** (direkt) nebeneinander

K

K, k [keɪ] N K *nt*, k *nt*

k N (Comput) *abbr of* **kilobyte** KB

K *abbr* (*in salaries etc*) -tausend; **15 K** 15.000

Kaffir ['kæfə'] N (*also pej*) Kaffer *m*

Kafkaesque [,kæfkə'esk] ADJ kafkaesk

kagoul(e) [kə'guːl] N = **cagoule**

kagul [kə'guːl] N = **cagoule**

kalashnikov [kə'læʃnɪkɒf] N Kalaschnikow *f*

kale, kail [keɪl] N Grünkohl *m*

kaleidoscope [kə'laɪdəskəʊp] N Kaleidoskop *nt*; **a ~ of emotion** ein Wechselspiel *nt* der Gefühle

kaleidoscopic [kə,laɪdə'skɒpɪk] ADJ kaleidoskopisch

kamikaze [kæmɪ'kɑːzɪ] N Kamikaze *nt*; **~ pilot** Kamikazeflieger *m*; **~ mission** Kamikaze-Mission *f*

Kampuchea [,kæmpʊ'tʃɪə] N Kampuchea *nt*

kangaroo [,kæŋgə'ruː] N Känguru *nt*; **to have ~s in one's top paddock** (*Austral inf*) nicht alle Tassen im Schrank haben (*inf*)

kangaroo court N inoffizielles Gericht, Femegericht *nt*

kaolin ['keɪəlɪn] N Kaolin *m or nt*, Porzellanerde *f*

kapok ['keɪpɒk] N Kapok *m*

Kaposi's sarcoma [kæ'pəʊsɪzsɑː'kəʊmə] N (*Med*) Kaposisarkom *nt*

kaput [kə'pʊt] ADJ (*inf*) kaputt (*inf*)

karaoke [,kærə'əʊkɪ] N Karaoke *nt*

karaoke machine N Karaoke-Gerät *nt*

karat ['kærət] N = **carat**

karate [kə'rɑːtɪ] N Karate *nt*

karate chop N Karateschlag *or* -hieb *m*

karma ['kɑːmə] N Karma *nt*

kart [kɑːt] N Gokart *m*

karting ['kɑːtɪŋ] N Gokartfahren *nt*

Kashmir [kæʃ'mɪə'] N Kaschmir *nt*

Kate [keɪt] N *dim of* **Catherine** Kät(h)e *f*

katydid ['keɪtɪdɪd] N Laubheuschrecke *f*

kayak ['kaɪæk] N Kajak *m or nt*

KBE (*Brit*) *abbr of* **Knight of the British Empire** *britischer Verdienstorden*

KC (*Brit*) *abbr of* **King's Counsel**

kc *abbr of* **kilocycle**

kcal ['keɪkæl] *abbr of* **kilocalorie** kcal

KCB (*Brit*) *abbr of* **Knight Commander of the Bath** *britischer Verdienstorden*

kebab [kə'bæb] N Kebab *m*

kedge [kedʒ] N (*Naut*) Warpanker *m*

kedgeree [,kedʒə'riː] N *Reisgericht mit Fisch und Eiern*

keel [kiːl] N (*Naut*) Kiel *m*; **to be back on an even ~** (*lit*) sich wieder aufgerichtet haben; **he put the business back on an even ~** er brachte das Geschäft wieder ins Lot *or* wieder auf die Beine (*inf*); **when things are on a more even ~** wenn sich alles besser eingespielt hat

▶ **keel over** VI (*ship*) kentern; (*fig inf*) umkippen; **she keeled over in a faint** sie klappte zusammen (*inf*), sie kippte um (*inf*)

keelhaul ['kiːlhɔːl] VT kielholen

keen¹ [kiːn] ⊙ 8.3 ADJ (+er) **a** (= *acute, intense*) *appetite* kräftig; *interest* groß, stark; *pleasure* groß; *anticipation* gespannt; *feeling* stark, tief; *desire, pain* heftig, stark; *mind, intelligence, sense of humour, wit* scharf; *sight, eye, hearing, ear* gut, scharf; *awareness* geschärft; *competition* scharf; **to keep a ~ eye on sth** ein wachsames Auge auf etw (*acc*) haben; **to have a ~ nose for sth** eine gute *or* feine Nase für etw haben; **they have a ~ awareness** *or* **appreciation of the dangers** sie sind sich der Gefahren deutlich bewusst; **he has a ~ sense of history** er hat ein ausgeprägtes Gefühl für Geschichte

b (= *enthusiastic*) begeistert; *football fan, golfer, supporter* leidenschaftlich, begeistert; (= *eager, interested*) *applicant, learner* stark interessiert; (= *hardworking*) eifrig; **~ to learn** lernbegierig; **~ to know** begierig zu wissen; **try not to seem too ~** versuchen Sie, Ihr Interesse nicht zu sehr zu zeigen; **if he's ~ we can teach him** wenn er wirklich interessiert ist *or* Interesse hat, können wir es ihm beibringen; **he is terribly ~** seine Begeisterung/sein Interesse/sein Eifer kennt kaum Grenzen; **to be ~ on sb** von jdm sehr angetan sein; (= *sexually attracted*) scharf auf jdn sein (*inf*); *on pop group, actor, author* von jdm begeistert sein; **to be ~ on sth** etw sehr gern mögen; (*on classical music, Italian cooking also, football*) sehr viel für etw übrig haben; **to be ~ on doing sth** (= *like to do*) etw gern *or* mit Begeisterung tun; **to be ~ to do sth** (= *want to do*) sehr darauf erpicht sein *or* scharf darauf sein (*inf*), etw zu tun; **to be ~ on mountaineering/dancing** begeisterter *or* leidenschaftlicher Bergsteiger/Tänzer sein, leidenschaftlich gern bergsteigen/tanzen; **he is very ~ on golf/tennis** *etc* er ist ein Golf-/Tennisfan *m etc*; **to become ~ on sb/sth** sich für jdn/etw erwärmen; **I'm not very ~ on him/that idea** ich bin von ihm/dieser Idee nicht gerade begeistert; **he's very ~ on getting the job finished** ihm liegt sehr viel daran, dass die Arbeit fertig wird; **he's not ~ on her coming** er legt keinen (gesteigerten) Wert darauf, dass sie kommt; **he's very ~ that we should go/for us to go** er legt sehr großen Wert darauf *or* ihm ist sehr daran gelegen, dass wir gehen; **they are ~ for revenge** sie sind auf Rache aus

c (= *sharp*) *blade, wind* scharf; *frost* scharf, klirrend

d (*esp Brit*: = *competitive*) *prices* günstig

e (*US inf*: = *very good*) spitzenmäßig (*inf*)

keen² (*Ir*) N Totenklage *f* VI die Totenklage halten

keenly ['kiːnlɪ] ADV **a** (= *intensely, acutely*) *feel* leidenschaftlich, tief, stark; *interested, wish, desire* stark, sehr, leidenschaftlich; *listen* aufmerksam; *observe* scharf; **I am ~ aware that ...** ich bin mir deutlich bewusst, dass ...; **the match was ~ contested** in dem Spiel wurde hart gekämpft **b** (= *enthusiastically*) mit Begeisterung; **~ awaited** mit Ungeduld erwartet **c** (*esp Brit*: = *competitively*) **~ priced goods** Waren *pl* zu scharf kalkulierten Preisen

keenness ['kiːnnɪs] N **a** (*of blade, mind, wind, sight*) Schärfe *f* **b** (= *enthusiasm*) Begeisterung *f*; (*of fan, supporter, golfer*) Leidenschaftlichkeit *f*; (*of applicant, learner*) starkes Interesse; (= *hardworking nature*) Eifer *m*; **his ~ to go is suspi-**

cious dass er so unbedingt gehen will, ist verdächtig

keep [kiːp]
vb: pret, ptp **kept**
1 TRANSITIVE VERB   3 NOUN
2 INTRANSITIVE VERB 4 PHRASAL VERBS

When **keep** is part of a set combination, e.g. **keep in mind, keep house, keep goal** etc, look up the noun. For combinations of **keep** with adverbs and prepositions, e.g. **keep in, keep on, keep up** etc, see also the phrasal verbs section.

1 – TRANSITIVE VERB

a = retain behalten; **you can keep this book** du kannst dieses Buch behalten; **I can't keep that number in my head** ich kann die Nummer nicht behalten, ich kann mir die Nummer nicht merken; **he wanted to keep the dog for another week** er wollte den Hund noch eine Woche (bei sich) behalten; **to keep a place for sb** einen Platz für jdn freihalten; **to keep one's place in a book** sich (*dat*) die Stelle im Buch markieren; **to keep a note of sth** sich (*dat*) etw notieren; **to keep one's temper** sich beherrschen; **to keep a grip on sth** (*fig*) etw unter Kontrolle halten; **you can keep it!** (*inf*) das kannst du behalten *or* dir an den Hut stecken (*inf*)

b = maintain in a certain state, place etc halten; **to keep sb at work** jdn bei der Arbeit halten; **he kept his hands in his pockets** er hat die Hände in der Tasche gelassen; **to keep good health** sich guter Gesundheit erfreuen; **the garden was well kept** der Garten war (gut) gepflegt

◆ **to keep sb/sth doing sth to keep sb waiting** jdn warten lassen; **keep her thinking that ...** lassen Sie sie in dem Glauben, dass ...; **can't you keep him talking?** können Sie ihn nicht in ein Gespräch verwickeln?; **to keep the traffic moving** den Verkehr in Fluss *or* am Fließen halten; **to keep a machine running** eine Maschine laufen lassen; **to keep the conversation going** das Gespräch in Gang halten

◆ **to keep sb/sth + ADJ to keep one's dress clean** sein Kleid nicht schmutzig machen; **to keep sb quiet** zusehen *or* dafür sorgen, dass jd still ist; **that'll keep them quiet for a while** das wird für eine Weile Ruhe schaffen; **just to keep her happy** damit sie zufrieden ist; **to keep sb alive** jdn am Leben halten; **to keep oneself busy** sich selbst beschäftigen; **to keep oneself warm** sich warm halten

c = have in a certain place, look after aufbewahren; **where does he keep his money?** wo bewahrt er sein Geld auf?; **where do you keep your spoons?** wo sind die Löffel?

d = put aside aufheben; **I've been keeping it for you** ich habe es für Sie aufgehoben; **I'm keeping the best ones for Christmas** die besten hebe ich für Weihnachten auf

e = detain aufhalten, zurückhalten; **I mustn't keep you** ich will Sie nicht aufhalten; **what kept you?** wo waren Sie denn so lang?; **what's keeping him?** wo bleibt er denn?; **to keep sb prisoner** jdn gefangen halten; **to keep sb in prison** jdn in Haft halten; **they kept h**

hospital **over night** sie haben ihn über Nacht im Krankenhaus behalten; **it kept her in bed for a week** sie musste deswegen eine Woche im Bett bleiben

f = have, look after shop, hotel, restaurant haben, unterhalten, führen; bees, pigs etc halten; **to keep servants** sich (dat) Diener halten; **he keeps an excellent cellar** er hat einen ausgezeichneten Weinkeller

♦ **to keep sb in sth to keep sb in clothes** (person) für jds Kleidung sorgen; **I couldn't afford to keep you in drink** ich könnte deine Getränke nicht bezahlen

g = support versorgen, unterhalten; **I earn enough to keep myself** ich verdiene genug für mich (selbst) zum Leben; **I have six children to keep** ich habe sechs Kinder zu unterhalten; **he keeps a mistress** er hält sich (dat) eine Geliebte

h = be faithful to, observe promise halten; law, rule einhalten, befolgen; treaty einhalten; obligations nachkommen (+dat), erfüllen; appointment einhalten; **to keep a vow** einen Schwur halten, ein Gelübde erfüllen; **to keep Lent/the Sabbath** das Fasten/die Sonntagsruhe or den Sabbat (ein)halten; **to keep late hours** lange aufbleiben

i = guard, protect (be)hüten; sheep etc hüten, aufpassen auf (+acc); **God keep you!** (old) Gott befohlen! (old) → keep from VT b

j accounts, diary etc führen (of über +acc)

k Comm (= stock) führen, (zu verkaufen) haben

l US (= continue to follow) road, path weitergehen or -fahren, folgen (+dat); direction einhalten; **to keep one's course** (den) Kurs (ein)halten

m US (= remain in) **to keep one's room** auf seinem Zimmer bleiben; **to keep one's seat** sitzen bleiben

2 – INTRANSITIVE VERB

a = continue in a specified direction **to keep (to the) left/right** sich links/rechts halten; **to keep to the left** (Aut) auf der linken Seite bleiben, links fahren; **to keep to the middle of the road** immer in der Mitte der Straße fahren; **keep on this road** bleiben Sie auf dieser Straße; **keep north** gehen/fahren Sie immer Richtung Norden

b = remain in a certain state, position bleiben

♦ **to keep +** ADJ **to keep fit** fit bleiben, sich in Form halten; **to keep quiet** still sein; **to keep silent** schweigen; **to keep calm** ruhig bleiben, Ruhe bewahren

♦ **to keep doing sth** (= not stop) etw weiter tun; (repeatedly) etw immer wieder tun; (constantly) etw dauernd tun; **to keep walking** weitergehen; **he kept lying to her** er hat sie immer wieder belogen; **if you keep complaining** wenn Sie sich weiter beschweren; **she keeps talking about you all the time** sie redet dauernd von Ihnen; **keep going** machen Sie weiter; **I keep hoping she's still alive** ich hoffe immer noch, dass sie noch lebt; **I keep thinking ...** ich denke immer ...

c food etc sich halten; **that meat won't keep** dieses Fleisch hält sich nicht or bleibt nicht gut

d = be in a certain state of health **how are you keeping?** wie geht es Ihnen so?; **he's not keeping too well** es geht ihm nicht besonders gut; **he's keeping better now** es geht ihm wieder besser

e = wait **that business can keep** das kann warten; **will it keep?** kann das warten?

3 – NOUN

a = livelihood, food Unterhalt m; **I got £300 a week and my keep** ich bekam £ 300 pro Woche und freie Kost und Logis; **to earn one's keep** seinen Lebensunterhalt verdienen; **in a poem every word must earn its keep** in einem Gedicht muss jedes Wort seine Daseinsberechtigung haben

b in castle Bergfried m; (as prison) Burgverlies nt

c

♦ **for keeps** (inf) für immer; **he's playing for keeps** ihm ists ernst; **it's yours for keeps** das darfst du behalten

4 – PHRASAL VERBS

▶ **keep ahead** VI vorne bleiben; **to keep ahead of one's rivals** seinen Konkurrenten vorausbleiben VT sep **to keep one step ahead of the others** den anderen einen Schritt voraus sein

▶ **keep at** VI +prep obj **a** (= continue with) weitermachen mit; **keep at it** machen Sie weiter so **b** (= nag) herumnörgeln an (+dat); **keep at him until he says yes** lass ihm so lange keine Ruhe, bis er ja sagt VT +prep obj **to keep sb at a task** jdn nicht mit einer Arbeit aufhören lassen; **to keep sb (hard) at it** jdn hart rannehmen (inf), jdn an der Kandare haben; **they kept him at it all day** sie haben ihn den ganzen Tag hart rangenommen (inf)

▶ **keep away** VI (lit) wegbleiben; (= not approach) nicht näher herankommen (from an +acc); **keep away!** nicht näher kommen!; **keep away from that place** gehen Sie da nicht hin; **he just can't keep away from the pub** es zieht ihn immer wieder in die Wirtschaft; **I just can't keep away** es zieht mich immer wieder hin; **keep away from him** lassen Sie die Finger von ihm; **he just can't keep away from her** er kann einfach nicht von ihr lassen VT (always separate) person, children, pet etc fern halten (from von); **to keep sth away from sth** etw nicht an etw (acc) kommen lassen; **keep your hand away from the cutting edge** kommen Sie mit Ihrer Hand nicht an die Schneide; **keep them away from each other** halten Sie sie auseinander; **to keep sb away from school** jdn nicht in die Schule (gehen) lassen; **business kept him away for three months** er war aus geschäftlichen Gründen drei Monate weg; **what's been keeping you away?** wo waren Sie denn so lange?

▶ **keep back** VI zurückbleiben, nicht näher kommen; **keep back!** bleiben Sie, wo Sie sind!, treten Sie zurück!; **please keep back from the edge** bitte gehen Sie nicht zu nahe an den Rand VT sep **a** (= hold back) person, hair, crowds, enemy zurückhalten; water stauen; tears unterdrücken; **to keep sb/sth back from sb** jdn/etw von jdm abhalten

b (= withhold) money, taxes einbehalten; information, facts etc verschweigen (from sb jdm); (from parent, husband etc) verheimlichen; verschweigen (from sb jdm); **I know you're keeping something back** ich weiß, dass du mir etwas verheimlichst or verschweigst; **they are keeping back the names of the victims** die Namen der Opfer werden nicht bekannt gegeben; **keep some cheese back to sprinkle over the top** behalten Sie etwas Käse zum Darüberstreuen zurück

c (= make late) aufhalten; pupil dabehalten; **I don't want to keep you back** ich möchte Sie nicht aufhalten

d (= hold up, slow down) behindern; **being with the slower learners is keeping him back** weil er mit schwächeren Schülern zusammen ist, kommt er nicht so schnell voran

▶ **keep down** VI unten bleiben; **keep down!** duck dich!, bleib unten! VT sep **a** (lit) unten lassen; (= hold down) unten halten; head ducken; eyes gesenkt halten; **keep your voices down** reden Sie leise or nicht so laut

b people, revolt unterdrücken; dog bändigen; rebellious person im Zaum or unter Kontrolle halten; rabbits, weeds etc in Grenzen or unter Kontrolle halten; **you can't keep a good man down** der Tüchtige lässt sich nicht unterkriegen

c taxes, rates, prices niedrig halten; spending einschränken; costs, wages drücken; **to keep numbers down** die Zahlen gering halten; **keep one's weight down** nicht zunehmen

d food, drink bei sich behalten; **she can't keep anything down** sie kann nichts bei sich behalten

e (Sch) wiederholen lassen; **he was kept down** er musste wiederholen

▶ **keep from** VT +prep obj **a** sb hindern an (+dat); (from going, doing sth) abhalten von, hindern an (+dat); **I couldn't keep him from doing it/going there** ich konnte ihn nicht daran hindern or davon abhalten, das zu tun/ dort hinzugehen; **to keep sb from falling** jdn am Fallen hindern; **to keep oneself from doing sth** sich (davor) hüten, etw zu tun; **shyness keeps him from making new friends** er ist zu schüchtern, um neue Freunde zu gewinnen; **what can we do to keep it from happening again?** was können wir tun, damit es nicht noch einmal passiert?; **the bells keep me from sleeping** die Glocken lassen mich nicht schlafen; **keep them from getting wet** verhindern Sie es, dass sie nass werden; **this will keep the water from freezing** das verhindert, dass das Wasser gefriert; **you shouldn't keep them from their work** Sie sollten sie nicht von der Arbeit abhalten

b (= protect) **to keep sb from sth** jdn vor etw (dat) bewahren; **to keep sb from harm** jdn vor Schaden (dat) bewahren

c (= withhold) **to keep sth from sb** jdm etw verschweigen; piece of news also jdm etw vorenthalten; **can you keep this from your mother?** können Sie das vor Ihrer Mutter geheim halten or verbergen? VI +prep obj **to keep from doing sth** etw nicht tun; (= avoid doing also) es vermeiden, etw zu tun; **she bit her lip to keep from crying** sie biss sich (dat) auf die Lippe, um nicht zu weinen; **she couldn't keep from laughing** sie musste einfach lachen

▶ **keep in** VT sep **a** schoolboy nachsitzen lassen; **I've been kept in!** ich musste nachsitzen!; **his parents have kept him in** seine Eltern haben ihn nicht weggelassen or gehen lassen **b** feelings zügeln **c** stomach einziehen VI (= stay indoors) drinnen bleiben

▶ **keep in with** VI +prep obj sich gut stellen mit; **he's just trying to keep in with her** er will sich nur bei ihr lieb Kind machen

▶ **keep off** VI (person) wegbleiben; **if the rain keeps off** wenn es nicht regnet; **"keep off!"** „Betreten verboten!" VT sep **a** dog, person fern halten (prep obj von); one's hands wegnehmen, weglassen (prep obj von); **to keep one's mind off sth** nicht an etw (acc) denken; **keep him off me** halten Sie ihn mir vom Leib; **keep your hands off** Hände weg!; **keep the dog off the couch** lassen Sie den Hund nicht aufs Sofa; **to keep sb off drugs** jdn von Drogen fern halten; **to keep sb off the streets** (fig) jdn davon abhalten, auf der Straße zu landen **b** jacket etc ausbehalten; hat abbehalten VI +prep obj vermeiden; **"keep off the grass"** „Betreten des Rasens verboten"; **keep off the whisky** lassen Sie das Whiskytrinken

▶ **keep on** VI **a** (= continue) weitermachen, nicht aufhören; **to keep on doing sth** etw weiter tun; (repeatedly) etw immer wieder tun; (incessantly) etw dauernd tun; **he keeps on swearing** er flucht dauernd; **keep on talking!** reden Sie weiter!; **if you keep on like this** wenn du so weitermachst; **keep on trying** versuchen Sie es weiter; **I keep on telling you** ich sage dir ja immer; **the rain kept on all night** es regnete die ganze Nacht durch; **he kept on crying the whole night** er hat die ganze Nacht unaufhörlich geweint

b (= keep going) weitergehen/-fahren; **keep on past the church** fahren Sie immer weiter an der Kirche vorbei; **keep straight on** immer geradeaus

c **to keep on at sb** (inf) dauernd an jdm herummeckern (inf); **they kept on at him until he agreed** sie haben ihm so lange keine Ruhe gelassen, bis er zustimmte

d **to keep on about sth** (inf) unaufhörlich von etw reden; **there's no need to keep on a-**

bout it (*inf*) es ist wirklich nicht nötig, ewig darauf herumzuhacken (*inf*); **don't keep on so!** (*inf*) hören Sie doch endlich auf damit! **VT** *sep* **a** *servant, employee* weiterbeschäftigen, behalten **b** *coat etc* anbehalten; *hat* aufbehalten

▶ **keep out** **VI** (*of room, building*) draußen bleiben; (*of property, land, area*) etw nicht betreten; **keep out of my room!** geh/komm nicht in mein Zimmer; **"keep out"** „Zutritt verboten"; **to keep out of the rain/sun** nicht in den Regen/die Sonne gehen; **to keep out of sight** sich nicht zeigen; (*hiding*) in Deckung bleiben; **to keep out of danger** Gefahr meiden; **to keep out of debt** keine Schulden machen; **that child can't keep out of trouble** das Kind kommt immer in Schwierigkeiten; **to keep out of sb's affairs** sich nicht in jds Angelegenheiten einmischen, sich aus jds Angelegenheiten heraushalten; **you keep out of this!** halten Sie sich da or hier raus! **VT** *sep* **a** *person* nicht hereinlassen (*of in +acc*); *light, cold, rain, enemy etc* abhalten; **this screen keeps the sun out of your eyes** diese Blende schützt Ihre Augen vor Sonne; **how can I keep the rabbits out/out of my garden?** was kann ich tun, dass die Kaninchen nicht hereinkommen/nicht in meinen Garten kommen? **b** **to keep sb out of danger/harm's way** jdn vor Gefahr/Gefahren schützen; **I wanted to keep him out of this** ich wollte nicht, dass er da mit hereingezogen wurde; **to keep sb's name out of the papers** jds Namen nicht in der Zeitung erwähnen; **keep him out of my way** halte ihn mir vom Leib; **they kept him out of their plans** sie haben ihn von ihren Plänen ausgeschlossen

▶ **keep to** **VI** +*prep obj* **a** **to keep to one's promise** sein Versprechen halten, zu seinem Wort stehen; **to keep to one's bed/one's room** im Bett/in seinem Zimmer bleiben; **to keep to the main road** bleiben Sie auf der Hauptstraße; **to keep to the schedule/plan** den Zeitplan einhalten, sich an den Zeitplan/Plan halten; **to keep to the speed limit** sich an die Geschwindigkeitsbegrenzung halten; **to keep to the subject/point** bei der Sache or beim Thema bleiben; **to keep to the script** sich am Text halten, am Text bleiben **b** **to keep (oneself) to oneself** nicht sehr gesellig sein, ein Einzelgänger sein; **they keep (themselves) to themselves** (*as a group*) sie bleiben unter sich **VT** +*prep obj* **to keep sb to his word/promise** jdn beim Wort nehmen; **to keep sth to a minimum** etw auf ein Minimum beschränken; **to keep sth to oneself** etw für sich behalten; **keep it to yourself** behalten Sie das für sich; **keep your hands to yourself!** nehmen Sie Ihre Hände weg!

▶ **keep together** **VI** (= *stay together*) zusammenbleiben; (*as friends, community etc*) zusammenhalten; (*singers, oarsmen etc*) im Einklang or Takt sein **VT** *sep* zusammen aufbewahren; (= *fix together, unite*) *things, people* zusammenhalten; (*conductor*) *orchestra* im Takt halten

▶ **keep under** **VI** *sep people, race* unterdrücken; *subordinates* streng behandeln, an der Kandare haben; (= *keep under anaesthetic*) unter Narkose halten **VI** (*under water etc*) unter Wasser bleiben

▶ **keep up** **VI** **a** (*tent, pole*) stehen bleiben **b** (*rain*) (an)dauern; (*weather, hurricane etc*) anhalten; (*prices, output, standard*) gleich hoch bleiben; (*morale, strength, determination*) nicht nachlassen **c** **to keep up (with sb/sth)** (*in race, work, with prices*) (mit jdm/etw) Schritt halten, (mit jdm/etw) mithalten können (*inf*); (*in comprehension*) (jdm/einer Sache) folgen können; **they bought it just to keep up with the Joneses** sie kauften es nur, um den Nachbarn nicht nachzustehen; **to keep up with the times** mit der Zeit gehen; **to keep up with the news** sich auf dem Laufenden halten; **I haven't kept up with my**

French ich bin mit meinem Französisch ganz aus der Übung gekommen **d** (= *stay in touch*) **to keep up with sb** mit jdm in Kontakt bleiben; **we haven't kept up at all since she went abroad** wir haben nichts mehr voneinander gehört, seit sie im Ausland ist **VT** *sep* **a** *pole, tent* aufrecht halten; **the life belt kept him up** der Rettungsring hielt ihn über Wasser; **to keep his trousers up** damit die Hose nicht herunterrutscht **b** (= *not stop*) nicht aufhören mit; *study etc* fortsetzen, weitermachen; *quality, prices, output, friendship, tradition, custom* aufrechterhalten; *subscription* beibehalten; *payments etc* weiterbezahlen; *workrate, speed* (= *maintain*) halten; (= *endure*) durchhalten; **I try to keep up my Spanish** ich versuche, mit meinem Spanisch nicht aus der Übung zu kommen; **to keep up a correspondence** in Briefwechsel bleiben; **to keep one's morale up** den Mut nicht verlieren; **he kept their morale up** er hat ihnen Mut gemacht; **keep it up!** (machen Sie) weiter so!; **he couldn't keep it up** er hat schlappgemacht (*inf*); (*sexually*) er ist ihm weggeslafft (*sl*) **c** (= *maintain*) *house* unterhalten; *road* instand or in Stand halten **d** (= *prevent from going to bed*) am Schlafengehen hindern; **that child kept me up all night** das Kind hat mich die ganze Nacht nicht schlafen lassen; **I was kept up pretty late last night** ich bin gestern Abend ziemlich spät ins Bett gekommen

keeper ['kiːpə] N (*in asylum, zoo*) Wärter(in) *m(f)*, Pfleger(in) *m(f)*, Betreuer(in) *m(f)*; (*of museum*) Kustos *m*, Kustode *m*, Kustodin *f*; (= *guard*) Wächter(in) *m(f)*, Aufseher(in) *m(f)*, Aufpasser(in) *m(f)*; (*Brit inf*, = *goalkeeper*) Torhüter(in) *m(f)*; **I'm not my brother's ~** ich bin nicht der Hüter meines Bruders

keep fit N Fitnessübungen *pl*

keeping ['kiːpɪŋ] N **a** (= *care*) **to put sth in sb's ~** jdm etw zur Aufbewahrung übergeben → **safe-keeping** **b** (*of rule*) Beachten *nt*, Einhalten *nt* **c** **in ~ with** in Übereinstimmung or Einklang mit; **her behaviour was out of ~ with the dignity of the occasion** ihr Benehmen entsprach nicht der Feierlichkeit des Anlasses

keepsake ['kiːpseɪk] N Andenken *nt*

keg [keg] N **a** (= *barrel*) kleines Fass, Fässchen *nt* **b** (*also* **keg beer**) Bier *nt* vom Fass

kegger ['kegə] N (*US inf*) Bierparty *f*

keister ['kiːstə] N (*US inf*) **a** (= *buttocks*) Hintern *m* (*inf*) **b** (*rare*, = *case*) Koffer *m*

keks [keks] PL (*Brit inf*) Hose *f*, Buxe *f* (*N Ger inf*)

kelly-green ['kelɪ'griːn] (*US*) **ADJ** leuchtend gelbgrün **N** leuchtendes Gelbgrün

kelp [kelp] N Seetang *m*

kempt [kempt] ADJ *person, place* gepflegt; *hair* gekämmt

ken [ken] **N** **that is beyond my ~** das entzieht sich meiner Kenntnis **VT** (*Scot*) = **know 1 2**

kennel ['kenl] N **a** Hundehütte *f* **b** **~s** (= *cage*) Hundezwinger *m*; (*for breeding*) Hundezucht *f*; (*boarding*) (Hunde)heim *nt*, Tierheim *nt*; **to put a dog in ~s** einen Hund in Pflege geben

Kenya ['kenjə] N Kenia *nt*

Kenyan ['kenjən] **N** Kenianer(in) *m(f)* **ADJ** kenianisch

kepi ['keɪpi] N Käppi *nt*

kept [kept] *pret, ptp of* **keep** ADJ **~ woman** Mätresse *f*; **she's a ~ woman** sie lässt sich aushalten

kerb [kɜːb] N (*Brit*) Bordkante *f*, Randstein *m*

kerb: kerb crawler N Freier *m* im Autostrich (*inf*); **kerb crawling** N Autostrich *m*; **kerb crawling area** N Autostrich *m*; **kerb drill** N Verkehrserziehung *f*; **kerb market** N (*St Ex*) Freiverkehr *m*; **kerbstone** N Bordstein *m*, Randstein *m*; **kerb weight** N (*of a car*) Leergewicht *nt*

kerchief ['kɜːtʃɪf] N (*old*) Hals- or Kopftuch *nt*

kerf [kɜːf] N Kerbe *f*, Einschnitt *m*

kerfuffle [kə'fʌfl] N (*Brit inf*) (= *noise*) Lärm *m*, Gedöns *nt* (*inf*); (= *fight*) Balgerei *f* (*inf*); (= *trouble*) Theater *nt* (*inf*)

kernel ['kɜːnl] N (*lit, fig*) Kern *m*

kerning ['kɜːnɪŋ] N (*Comput*) Kerning *nt*

kerosene ['kerəsiːn] N Kerosin *nt*

kerosene lamp N Petroleum- or Paraffinlampe *f*

kestrel ['kestrəl] N Turmfalke *m*

ketch [ketʃ] N Ketsch *f*

ketchup ['ketʃəp] N Ket(s)chup *nt or m*

kettle ['ketl] N Kessel *m*; **I'll put the ~ on** ich stelle mal eben (Kaffee-/Tee)wasser auf; **the ~'s boiling** das Wasser kocht; **this is a different ~ of fish** (*Brit inf*) das ist doch was ganz anderes

kettledrum ['ketldrʌm] N (Kessel)pauke *f*

key [kiː] **N** **a** Schlüssel *m* **b** (*fig*: = *solution*) Schlüssel *m*; **education is the ~ to success** Bildung ist der Schlüssel zum Erfolg; **the ~ to the mystery** der Schlüssel zum Geheimnis, des Rätsels Lösung; **this was the ~ to the murderer's identity** das gab Aufschluss darüber or das gab den Hinweis, wer der Mörder war **c** (= *answers*) Lösungen *pl*, Schlüssel *m*; (*Sch*) Schlüssel *m*, Lehrerheft *nt*; (*Math etc*) Lösungsheft *nt*; (*for maps etc*) Zeichenerklärung *f* **d** (*of piano, typewriter, Comput*) Taste *f* **e** (*Mus*) Tonart *f*; **to sing off ~** falsch singen; **change of ~** Tonartwechsel *m*, Modulation *f*; **in the ~ of C** in C-Dur/c-Moll **f** (*Build*) Untergrund *m* **ADJ** *attr* (= *vital*) Schlüssel-, wichtigste(r, s); *witness* wichtigste(r, s); **~ area** Schlüsselbereich *m*; **~ factor** Schlüsselfaktor *m* (*in sth* bei etw); **education is a ~ issue** Bildung ist eines der entscheidenden Themen; **~ industry** Schlüsselindustrie *f*; **~ man** Schlüsselfigur *f*; **~ point** springender Punkt *m*; **~ position** Schlüsselposition or -stellung *f*; **~ question** Schlüsselfrage *f*; **~ role** Schlüsselrolle *f* **VT** **a** *speech etc* (*to or for one's audience*) (auf jdn) abstimmen or zuschneiden (*to, for* auf +*acc*), anpassen (*to, for* +*dat*) **b** (*Comput*) (= *input*) *text, data* eingeben; (= *hit*) *character, F7 etc* drücken **VI** (*Comput*) Text/Daten eingeben

▶ **key in** VT *sep* (*Comput*) eingeben

▶ **key up** VT *sep* **a** **she was (all) keyed up about the interview** sie war wegen des Interviews ganz aufgedreht (*inf*); **he was all keyed up for the big race** er hatte sich schon ganz auf das große Rennen eingestellt **b** (*Comput*) eingeben

keyboard ['kiːbɔːd] **N** (*of piano*) Klaviatur *f*, Tastatur *f*; (*of organ*) Manual *nt*; (*of typewriter, Comput*) Tastatur *f*; **~ skills** (*Comput*) Fertigkeiten *pl* in der Texterfassung; **a genius on the ~** (*Mus*) ein Klaviergenie *nt* **VTI** (*Typ, Comput*) eingeben

keyboarder ['kiːbɔːdə] N (*Typ, Comput*) Texterfasser(in) *m(f)*; **what's she like as a ~?** wie ist sie bei der Texterfassung?

keyboarding ['kiːbɔːdɪŋ] N (*Comput*) Texteingabe *f*; **~ skills** Fertigkeiten *pl* in der Texterfassung

keyboard instrument N (*Mus*) Tasteninstrument *nt*

keyboardist ['kiːbɔːdɪst] N (*Mus*) Keyboardspieler(in) *m(f)*, Keyboarder(in) *m(f)*

keyboard operator N Texterfasser(in) *m(f)*

keyboard template N Tastaturschablone *f*

key: key card N Schlüsselkarte *f*; **key case** N Schlüsseletui *nt*; **key chord** N (*Mus*) Grunddreiklang *m*; **keyhole** N Schlüsselloch *nt*; **keyhole surgery** N minimal invasive Chirurgie, Schlüssellochchirurgie *f*

keying ['kiːɪŋ] N (*Comput*) Texteingabe *f*

key: key money N Provision *f*, Schlüsselgeld *nt*; **keynote** **N** (*Mus*) Grundton *m*; (*of a speech*) Leitgedanke *m*, Tenor *m* **ADJ ATTR** **~**

speech (*Pol etc*) programmatische Rede; **keynoter** [ˈkiːnəʊtəʳ] N (*Pol*) jd, der eine programmatische Rede hält; **keypad** N (*Comput*) Tastenfeld *nt*; **keyring** N Schlüsselring *m*; **key signature** N (*Mus*) Tonartbezeichnung *f*; **keystone** N (*Archit*) Schlussstein *m*; (*fig*) Grundpfeiler *m*; **keystroke** N Anschlag *m*; **keyword** N **a** (= *significant word*) Schlüsselwort *nt*; (*in index*) Stichwort *nt*, Schlagwort *nt* **b** (= *code*) Passwort *nt*, Kennwort *nt*

KG (*Brit*) abbr of **Knight of the Garter**

kg abbr of **kilogramme(s)** of **kilogram(s)** kg

KGB N KGB *m*

khaki [ˈkɑːkɪ] **N** Khaki *nt* **ADJ** khaki(braun or -farben)

Khmer Rouge [kˈmɛəˈruːʒ] PL Rote Khmer *pl*

kHz abbr of **kilohertz** kHz

kibbutz [kɪˈbʊts] N pl **-im** [ˌkɪbʊtˈsiːm] Kibbuz *m*

kibitz [ˈkɪbɪts] VI (*US inf*) **a** (*Cards*) kibitzen (*inf*) **b** (= *chat*) plaudern, quatschen (*inf*)

kibosh [ˈkaɪbɒʃ] N (*inf*) **to put the ~ on sth** etw vermasseln (*inf*)

kick [kɪk] **N** **a** (= *act of kicking*) Tritt *m*, Stoß *m*, Kick *m* (*inf*); **to take a ~ at sb/sth** nach jdm/ etw treten; **to give sth a ~** einer Sache (*dat*) einen Tritt versetzen; **he gave the ball a tremendous ~** er trat mit Wucht gegen den Ball; **a tremendous ~ by Beckenbauer** ein toller Schuss von Beckenbauer; **to get a ~ on the leg** einen Tritt ans Bein bekommen, gegen das or ans Bein getreten werden; **what he needs is a good ~ up the backside** or **in the pants** (*inf*) er braucht mal einen kräftigen Tritt in den Hintern (*inf*)
b (*inf*: = *thrill*) **she gets a ~ out of it** es macht ihr einen Riesenspaß (*inf*); (*physically*) sie verspürt einen Kitzel dabei; **to do sth for ~s** etw zum Spaß or Jux (*inf*) or Fez (*inf*) tun; **just for ~s** nur aus Jux und Tollerei (*inf*); **how do you get your ~s?** was machen Sie zu ihrem Vergnügen?
c no pl (*inf*: = *power to stimulate*) Feuer *nt*, Pep *m* (*inf*); **this drink hasn't much ~ in it** dieses Getränk ist ziemlich zahm (*inf*); **he has plenty of ~ left in him** er hat immer noch viel Pep (*inf*)
d (*of gun*) Rückstoß *m*
VI (*person*) treten; (= *struggle*) um sich treten; (*baby, while sleeping*) strampeln; (*animal*) austreten, ausschlagen; (*dancer*) das Bein hochwerfen; (*gun*) zurückstoßen or -schlagen, Rückstoß haben; (*inf*: *engine*) stottern (*inf*); **~ing and screaming** (*fig*) unter großem Protest; **he ~ed into third** (*inf*) er ging in den dritten (Gang)
VT **a** (*person, horse*) sb treten, einen Tritt versetzen (+*dat*); *door* treten gegen; *football* kicken (*inf*); *object* einen Tritt versetzen (+*dat*), mit dem Fuß stoßen; **to ~ sb's backside** jdn in den Hintern treten; **to ~ sb in the head/stomach** jdm gegen den Kopf/in den Bauch treten; **to ~ sb in the teeth** (*fig*) jdn vor den Kopf stoßen (*inf*); **to ~ a goal** ein Tor schießen; **to ~ one's legs in the air** die Beine in die Luft werfen; **to ~ the bucket** (*inf*) abkratzen, ins Gras beißen (*inf*); **I could have ~ed myself** (*inf*) ich hätte mir ohrfeigen können, ich hätte mir in den Hintern beißen können (*inf*)
b (*inf*: = *stop*) **to ~ heroin** vom Heroin runterkommen (*inf*); **to ~ the habit** es sich (*dat*) abgewöhnen

▶ **kick about** (*Brit*) or **around** **VI** (*inf*) () *person* rumhängen (*inf*) (*prep obj* in +*dat*); (*thing*) rumliegen (*inf*) (*prep obj* in +*dat*) **VT** sep **to kick a ball about** or **around** (*herum*)bolzen (*inf*), den Ball herumkicken (*inf*); **you shouldn't let them kick you about** or **around** Sie sollten sich nicht so herumschubsen lassen; **don't kick that book about** or **around** werfen Sie das Buch nicht so herum; **to kick an idea about** or **around** (*inf*) eine Idee durchdiskutieren

▶ **kick against** VI +prep obj treten gegen

▶ **kick at** VI +prep obj treten nach

▶ **kick away** VT sep wegstoßen; (= *knock down*) niedertreten

▶ **kick back** **VI** **a** (*person*) zurücktreten; **if you annoy him he'll kick back** (*fig*) wenn Sie ihn ärgern, gibt er es Ihnen zurück **b** (*gun*) zurückstoßen, einen Rückstoß haben **VT** sep *blanket* wegstrampeln; *ball* zurückspielen or -schieben

▶ **kick down** VT SEP *door* eintreten

▶ **kick in** **VT** sep *door* eintreten; **to kick sb's teeth in** jdm die Zähne einschlagen **VI** (= *take effect*) (*system, fear*) ausgelöst werden; (*drug etc*) wirken

▶ **kick off** **VI** (*Ftbl*) anstoßen; (*player also*) den Anstoß ausführen; (*fig inf*) losgehen (*inf*), beginnen; **who's going to kick off?** (*fig inf*) wer fängt an? **VT** sep *wegtreten*; *shoes* von sich schleudern; **they kicked him off the committee** (*inf*) sie warfen ihn aus dem Ausschuss

▶ **kick out** **VI** (*horse*) ausschlagen; (*person*) um sich treten; **to kick out at sb** nach jdm treten **VT** sep hinauswerfen (*of* aus); **he was kicked out of the club** er ist aus dem Verein hinausgeworfen worden or geflogen (*inf*)

▶ **kick over** VI +prep obj **to kick over the traces** über die Stränge schlagen

▶ **kick up** VT sep *dust* aufwirbeln **b** (*fig inf*) **to kick up a row** or **a din** Krach machen (*inf*); **to kick up a fuss** or **a stink** Krach schlagen (*inf*); **to kick up one's heels** (*at a party etc*) einen draufmachen (*inf*)

kick: kickback N (*inf*) (= *reaction*) Auswirkung *f*; (*as bribe*) Provision *f*; (= *perk*) Nebeneinnahme *f*; **kickboxing** N Kickboxen *nt*; **kickdown** N Kick-down *m*

kicker [ˈkɪkəʳ] N *Spieler, der Strafstöße etc ausführt*, Strafstoßexperte *m*/-expertin *f*

kick: kickoff N **a** (*Sport*) Anpfiff *m*, Anstoß *m*; **the kick-off is at 3 o'clock** Anpfiff ist um 3 Uhr **b** (*inf*: *of ceremony etc*) Start *m*, Anfang *m*; **the kick-off is at 3 o'clock** um 3 gehts los (*inf*); **for a kick-off** (= *to begin with*) erst mal, zunächst; **kickout** N (*Ftbl*) Abschlag *m* **b** (*fig inf*: = *dismissal*) Rausschmiss *m*; **kick-start(er)** N Kickstarter *m*; **kickturn** N (*Ski*) Kehre *f*

kid [kɪd] **N** **a** (= *young goat*) Kitz *nt*, Zicklein *nt* (*liter*)
b (= *leather*) Ziegen- or Glacéleder *nt*
c (*inf*, = *child*) Kind *nt*; **when I was a ~** als ich klein war; **to get the ~s to bed** die Kleinen ins Bett bringen; **it's ~'s stuff** (= *for children*) das ist was für kleine Kinder (*inf*); (= *easy*) das ist doch ein Kinderspiel; **to be like a ~ in a candy store** (*US*) sich wie ein verwöhntes Kind aufführen
d (*inf*) (= *man*) Junge *m*, Bursche *m* (*inf*); (= *woman*) Kleine *f* (*inf*); **listen ~, I didn't mean it** nun hör mir mal gut zu, ich habs doch nicht so gemeint; **listen ~, you keep out of this** hör mal Kleiner, du hältst dich hier raus (*inf*); **come on ~s!** los Jungs! (*inf*); **she's some ~** die ist nicht ohne (*inf*); (= *clever*) die ist ganz schön clever (*inf*); **he's done it already? some ~!** was, er hat das schon gemacht? tolle Leistung (*inf*)
ADJ attr **a** (*inf*: = *younger*) **~ brother** kleiner Bruder, Brüderchen *nt*; **~ sister** kleine Schwester, Schwesterchen *nt*
b (= *of goat leather*) *boots* aus Glacéleder
VT (*inf*) **to ~ sb (on)** (= *tease*) jdn aufziehen (*inf*); (= *deceive*) jdm etw vormachen, jdn an der Nase rumführen (*inf*); **you can't ~ me** mir kannst du doch nichts vormachen; **don't ~ yourself!** machen Sie sich doch nichts vor!; **I ~ you not** das ist mein Ernst, ganz ehrlich (*inf*); **who is she trying to ~?, who is she ~ding?** wem will sie was weismachen?
VI (*inf*) Jux machen (*inf*); **no ~ding** im Ernst, ehrlich (*inf*); **you've got to** or **you must be ~ding!** das ist doch wohl nicht dein Ernst!

▶ **kid on** VT sep = **kid** VT

kidder [ˈkɪdəʳ] N (*inf*) Spaßvogel *m*

kiddo [ˈkɪdəʊ] N (*inf*) = **kid** N d

kiddy [ˈkɪdɪ] N (*inf*) Kleinchen *nt* (*inf*), Kindchen *nt* (*inf*)

kid gloves [kɪdˈɡlʌvz] PL Glacéhandschuhe *pl*; **to handle** or **treat sb with ~** (*fig*) jdn mit Samthandschuhen or Glacéhandschuhen anfassen

kidnap [ˈkɪdnæp] **VT** entführen, kidnappen **N** Entführung *f*, Kidnapping *nt*

kidnapper [ˈkɪdnæpəʳ] N Entführer(in) *m(f)*, Kidnapper(in) *m(f)*

kidnapping [ˈkɪdnæpɪŋ] N Entführung *f*, Kidnapping *nt*

kidney [ˈkɪdnɪ] **N** **a** (*Anat, Cook*) Niere *f* **b** (*fig*: = *type, temperament*) **of the same ~** vom gleichen Schlag or Typ

kidney: kidney bean N rote Bohne, Kidneybohne *f*; **kidney dish** N Nierenschale *f*; **kidney failure** N (*Med*) Nierenversagen *nt*; **kidney machine** N künstliche Niere; **kidney-shaped** ADJ nierenförmig; **kidney stone** N (*Med*) Nierenstein *m*

kidology [kɪˈdɒlədʒɪ] N (*inf*: = *bluffing*) Bluff *m* (*inf*)

kill [kɪl] **VT** **a** (*lit*) töten, umbringen; (*by beating*) totschlagen, erschlagen; (*by shooting*) erschießen, totschießen; (*by stabbing*) erstechen, erdolchen; *animals* töten; (*Hunt*) erlegen; (= *slaughter*) schlachten; (*shock*) umbringen; *pain* beseitigen; *weeds* vernichten; **to be ~ed in action** fallen; **to be ~ed in battle/in the war** im Kampf/Krieg fallen; **too many people are ~ed on the roads** zu viele Menschen sterben auf der Straße or kommen auf der Straße um; **last year's drought ~ed thousands of animals** bei der letztjährigen Trockenheit kamen tausende or Tausende von Tieren um; **her brother was ~ed in a car accident** ihr Bruder ist bei einem Autounfall ums Leben gekommen; **how many were ~ed?** wie viel Todesopfer gab es?; **smoking will ~ you** das Rauchen wird Sie (noch) das Leben kosten; **the frost has ~ed my geraniums** meine Geranien sind erfroren; **she ~ed herself** sie brachte sich um, sie nahm sich (*dat*) das Leben; **he was ~ed with this weapon** dies ist die Mord- or Tatwaffe; **please, don't ~ me** bitte, lassen Sie mich leben; **he was ~ed by cancer** er starb an Krebs; **many people were ~ed by the plague** viele Menschen sind der Pest zum Opfer gefallen; **he was ~ed with poison gas** er wurde vergast; **she was ~ed with a knife** sie wurde (mit einem Messer) erstochen; **he was ~ed with an axe** er wurde mit einer Axt erschlagen; **he was ~ed by a stray bullet** er wurde von einer verirrten Kugel getötet; **each man ~s the thing he loves** jeder zerstört das, was er liebt; **I'll ~ him!** (*also fig*) den bring ich um (*inf*); **the bullet ~ed him** die Kugel traf ihn tödlich, die Kugel tötete ihn
b (*fig*) *feelings, love etc* töten, zerstören; **to ~ time** die Zeit totschlagen; **we have two hours to ~** wir haben noch zwei Stunden übrig; **to ~ two birds with one stone** (*Prov*) zwei Fliegen mit einer Klappe schlagen; **these stairs are ~ing me** (*inf*) diese Treppe bringt mich (noch mal) um (*inf*); **she was ~ing herself (laughing)** (*inf*) sie hat sich totgelacht or kaputtgelacht (*inf*); **this one'll ~ you** (*inf*) da lachst du dich tot (*inf*); **a few more weeks won't ~ you** (*inf*) noch ein paar Wochen bringen dich nicht um (*inf*); **my feet are ~ing me** (*inf*) mir brennen die Füße; **I'll do it (even) if it ~s me** (*inf*) ich mache es, und wenn es mich umbringt (*inf*); **they're not exactly ~ing themselves** (*inf*: = *overworking*) sie bringen sich nicht gerade um (*inf*), sie reißen sich (*dat*) kein Bein aus; **don't ~ yourself** (*iro*) übernehmen Sie sich nicht; **to ~ sb with kindness** es allzu gut mit jdm meinen
c (= *spoil the effect of*) *taste, performance* verderben, überdecken; *hopes* vernichten, zunichte machen; **this red ~s the other colours** dieses Rot übertönt or erschlägt die anderen Farben
d (= *defeat*) *parliamentary bill, proposal* zu Fall bringen; *project* zum Scheitern bringen
e *sound* schlucken; **to ~ a ball** eine Bombe schlagen (*inf*); **~ that light!** (*inf*) Licht aus!
f (*Press etc*) *paragraph, story* streichen, abwürgen (*inf*)
g (*Tech*) *engine etc* abschalten, ausschalten; (*Elec*) *circuit* unterbrechen
h (*inf*) *bottle* leer machen, auf den Kopf stellen (*inf*)

VI töten; **cigarettes can ~** Zigaretten können tödlich sein *or* tödliche Folgen haben; **she was dressed to ~** sie hatte sich in Schale geworfen (*inf*)
N a (*Hunt*) Erlegen *nt*, Abschuss *m*; (*at bullfight*) Todesstoß *m*; **the wolves gathered round for the ~** die Wölfe kreisten die Beute ein, um sie zu erlegen; **the tiger has made a ~** der Tiger hat ein Opfer erlegt *or* geschlagen; **to be in at the ~** (*lit*) beim Abschuss dabei sein; (*fig*) den Schlussakt miterleben; **to move** *or* **close in for the ~** (*lit*) sich an die Beute anschleichen; (*fig*) zum entscheidenden Schlag ausholen
b (*Hunt etc* = *animals killed*) Beute *f no pl*

▶ **kill off** VT SEP **a** vernichten, töten; *whole race* ausrotten, vernichten; *cows, pigs, elephants* abschlachten; *infection* abtöten; *weeds* vertilgen; *character in TV series* sterben lassen **b** (*fig*) *hopes* zerstören; *speculation* ein Ende machen (+*dat*); *jobs* streichen; *company* zugrunde *or* zu Grunde richten

killer ['kɪlə'] N (*person*) Mörder(in) *m(f)*, Killer(in) *m(f)* (*inf*); **this disease is a ~** diese Krankheit ist tödlich; **it's a ~** (*inf, race, job etc*) das ist der glatte Mord (*inf*) → **lady-killer**, **weedkiller**

killer: killer instinct N **the ~** (*lit*) der Tötungsinstinkt; **a boxer with the ~** ein Boxer, in dem der Killer wach wird (*inf*); **a successful businessman needs the ~** ein erfolgreicher Geschäftsmann muss über Leichen gehen können; **killer satellite** N Killersatellit *m*; **killer whale** N Schwertwal *m*, Mordwal *m*

killing ['kɪlɪŋ] **N a** (*of animals*) (*Hunt*) Erlegen *nt*; (*at abattoir*) (Ab)schlachten *nt* **b** (*of person*) Töten *nt*, Tötung *f*; **three more ~s in Belfast** drei weitere Morde *or* Todesopfer in Belfast **c** (*fig*) **to make a ~** einen Riesengewinn machen **ADJ a** *blow etc* tödlich (*inf*) **b** (= *exhausting*) *work* mörderisch (*inf*) **c** (= *funny*) urkomisch (*inf*)

killingly ['kɪlɪŋlɪ] ADV **~ funny** zum Totlachen (*inf*)

killjoy ['kɪldʒɔɪ] N Spielverderber(in) *m(f)*, Miesmacher(in) *m(f)*

kill-time **N** Zeitvertreib *m* **ADJ** als Zeitvertreib, zum Zeitvertreib

kiln [kɪln] N (*for baking, burning*) (Brenn)ofen *m*; (*for minerals*) Röst- *or* Kiesofen *m*; (*for drying bricks etc*) Trockenofen *m*; (*for hops etc*) Darre *f*, Darrofen *m*

kilo ['kiːləʊ] N Kilo *nt*

kilobyte ['kiːləʊbaɪt] N Kilobyte *nt*

kilocalorie ['kɪləʊˌkælərɪ] N Kilokalorie *f*

kilocycle ['kɪləʊˌsaɪkl] N Kilohertz *nt*

kilogramme, (US) **kilogram** ['kɪləʊgræm] N Kilogramm *nt*

kilohertz ['kɪləʊhɜːts] N Kilohertz *nt*

kilolitre, (US) **kiloliter** ['kɪləʊˌliːtə'] N Kiloliter *m*

kilometre, (US) **kilometer** [kɪ'lɒmɪtə'] N Kilometer *m*

kilovolt ['kɪləʊˌvəʊlt] N Kilovolt *nt*

kilowatt ['kɪləʊwɒt] N Kilowatt *nt*; **~-hour** Kilowattstunde *f*

kilt [kɪlt] N Kilt *m*, Schottenrock *m*

kimono [kɪ'məʊnəʊ] N Kimono *m*

kin [kɪn] **N** Familie *f*, Verwandte *pl*, Verwandtschaft *f*; **has he any ~?** hat er Verwandte *or* Familie? → **kith**, **next of kin** **ADJ** verwandt (*to* mit)

kind¹ [kaɪnd] N **a** (= *class, variety, nature*) Art *f*; (*of coffee, sugar, paint etc*) Sorte *f*; **they differ in ~** sie sind verschiedenartig; **several ~s of flour** mehrere Mehlsorten; **this ~ of book** diese Art Buch; **all ~s of ...** alle möglichen ...; **what ~ of ...?** was für ein(e) ...?; **what ~ of people does he think we are?** für wen hält er uns denn?; **the only one of its ~** das Einzige seiner Art; **a funny ~ of name** ein komischer Name; **he is not the ~ of man to refuse** er ist nicht der Typ, der Nein *or* nein sagt; **he's not that ~ of person** so ist er nicht; **I'm not that ~ of girl** so eine bin ich nicht; **they're two of a ~** die beiden sind vom gleichen Typ *or* von der gleichen Art;

(*people*) sie sind vom gleichen Schlag; **she's one of a ~** sie ist wirklich einzigartig, jemanden wie sie gibt es nur einmal; **I know your ~** deinen Typ kenne ich; **your ~ never do any good** Leute Ihres Schlags *or* Leute wie Sie sind für nichts gut; **this ~ of thing** so etwas; **you know the ~ of thing I mean** Sie wissen, was ich meine; **... of all ~s** alle möglichen ...; **something of the ~** so etwas Ähnliches; **nothing of the ~** nichts dergleichen; **you'll do nothing of the ~** du wirst dich schwer hüten, du wirst schön bleiben lassen!; **it was beef of a ~** (*pej*) es war Rindfleisch oder so was Ähnliches (*inf*); **it's not my ~ of holiday** solche Ferien sind nicht mein Fall (*inf*) *or* nach meinem Geschmack; **she's my ~ of woman** sie ist mein Typ **b a ~ of ...** eine Art ..., so ein(e) ...; **a ~ of box** so (etwas wie) eine Schachtel, eine Art Schachtel; **in a ~ of way I'm disappointed** (*inf*) ich bin irgendwie enttäuscht; **he was ~ of worried-looking** (*inf*) er sah irgendwie bedrückt aus; **I ~ of thought that he ...** (*inf*) (*and he didn't*) ich habe eigentlich gedacht, dass er ...; (*and he did*) ich habe es mir beinahe gedacht, dass er ...; **are you nervous? – ~ of** (*inf*) bist du nervös? – ja, schon (*inf*)
c (= *goods, as opposed to money*) Naturalien *pl*, Ware *f*; **payment in ~** Bezahlung *f* in Naturalien; **I shall pay you back in ~** (*fig*) ich werde es Ihnen in gleicher Münze heimzahlen; **the police responded in ~** die Polizei reagierte, indem sie das Gleiche tat

kind² ◇ 4, 21.2 ADJ (+*er*) **a** (= *caring*) *person* liebenswürdig, nett, freundlich (*to* zu); *voice, smile, face* freundlich; **he's ~ to animals** er ist gut zu Tieren; **the ~est thing to do would be to shoot the wounded animal** das Humanste wäre, das verletzte Tier zu erschießen; **would you be ~ enough to open the door** wären Sie (vielleicht) so nett *or* freundlich *or* lieb, die Tür zu öffnen; **he was so ~ as to show me the way** er war so nett *or* freundlich *or* lieb und zeigte mir den Weg; **it was very ~ of you to help me** es war wirklich nett *or* lieb von Ihnen, mir zu helfen; **you're too ~!** (*also iro*) Sie sind zu liebenswürdig!
b (= *charitable*) *description, words* freundlich; (= *flattering*) *description, photograph, lighting* schmeichelhaft; **this dress is ~ to the figure** dieses Kleid schmeichelt der Figur (*dat*)
c (= *gentle*) **to be ~ to your hands/skin** sanft zu den Händen/zur Haut sein; **the years have been ~ to her** die Jahre sind fast spurlos an ihr vorübergegangen

kinda ['kaɪndə] ADV (*incorrect*) = **kind of** → **kind¹** **b**

kindergarten ['kɪndəˌgɑːtn] N Kindergarten *m*

kind-hearted ['kaɪnd'hɑːtɪd] ADJ gutherzig, gütig

kind-heartedness ['kaɪnd'hɑːtɪdnɪs] N Gutherzigkeit *f*, Güte *f*

kindle ['kɪndl] **VT** *fire* entfachen, anzünden, entzünden; *imagination* anregen; *interest* wecken; *enthusiasm* entfachen **VI** (*fire, wood etc*) brennen; (*passions, enthusiasm etc*) entbrennen, aufflammen

kindliness ['kaɪndlɪnɪs] N Freundlichkeit *f*, Güte *f*, Liebenswürdigkeit *f*

kindling ['kɪndlɪŋ] N (= *wood*) Anzündholz *nt*, Anmachholz *nt*

kindly ['kaɪndlɪ] **ADV a** *speak, act* freundlich, nett; *treat* liebenswürdig, freundlich; (= *generously*) *give, donate, offer* großzügig, freundlicherweise; *invite* freundlicherweise; **to look ~ (up-)on sb** jdm gewogen sein; **to look ~ (up)on sth** etw positiv betrachten; **to think ~ of sb** nicht schlecht von jdm denken; **they ~ put me up for a night** sie nahmen mich freundlicherweise für eine Nacht auf
b (*with request*) bitte; **~ shut the door** machen Sie doch bitte die Tür zu; **will you ~ do as you are told** werden Sie jetzt bitte tun, was ich sage; **will you ~ shut up!** halten Sie doch endlich den Mund
c I don't take ~ to his smoking sein Rauchen

ist mir gar nicht angenehm; **he won't take at all ~ to that** das wird ihm gar nicht gefallen; **I don't take ~ to not being asked** es ärgert mich, wenn ich nicht gefragt werde; **she didn't take ~ to the idea of going abroad** sie konnte sich gar nicht mit dem Gedanken anfreunden, ins Ausland zu gehen; **she didn't take it ~ when I said ...** sie hat es nicht gut aufgenommen, als ich sagte ...
ADJ (+*er*) *person* lieb, nett, freundlich; *face, eyes, smile* freundlich; *advice* gut gemeint, freundlich; *voice* sanft, gütig; **a ~ soul** ein guter Mensch

kindness ['kaɪndnɪs] N **a** *no pl* Freundlichkeit *f* (*towards* gegenüber), Liebenswürdigkeit *f* (*towards* gegenüber); (= *goodness of heart*) Güte *f* (*towards* gegenüber); **thank you very much for all your ~** vielen Dank, dass Sie so freundlich *or* liebenswürdig waren; **to treat sb with ~, to show sb ~** freundlich *or* liebenswürdig zu jdm sein; **out of the ~ of one's heart** aus reiner Nächstenliebe; **would you have the ~ to ...?** hätten Sie die Freundlichkeit *or* Güte, zu ...?
b (= *act of kindness*) Gefälligkeit *f*, Aufmerksamkeit *f*; **to do sb a ~** jdm eine Gefälligkeit erweisen; **it would be a ~ to tell him** man würde ihm einen Gefallen tun, wenn man es ihm sagen würde; **thank you for all your many ~es** vielen Dank für alles, was Sie für mich getan haben

kindred ['kɪndrɪd] **N** , *no pl* (= *relatives*) Verwandtschaft *f* **ADJ** (= *related*) verwandt; **~ spirit** Gleichgesinnte(r) *mf*

kinesiology [ˌkɪniːsɪ'bləʒɪ] N (*Med*) Kinesiologie *f*

kinetic [kɪ'netɪk] ADJ kinetisch

kinfolk ['kɪnfəʊk] N = **kinsfolk**

king [kɪŋ] N **a** (*lit*) König *m*; **the ~'s highway** (*old, form*) *eine öffentliche Straße* **it must have cost a ~'s ransom** das muss eine stolze Summe *or* ein Vermögen gekostet haben; **to live like a ~** leben wie ein Fürst **b** (*fig*) König *m*; **an oil ~** ein Ölkönig *or* -magnat *m* **c** (*Chess, Cards*) König *m*; (*Draughts*) Dame *f*

king: kingbolt N (*US*) = **kingpin**; **king crab** N Königskrabbe *f*; **kingcup** N (= *buttercup*) Hahnenfuß *m*, Butterblume *f*; (= *marsh marigold*) Sumpfdotterblume *f*

kingdom ['kɪŋdəm] N **a** (*lit*) Königreich *nt* **b** (*Rel*) **~ of heaven** Himmelreich *nt*; **to blow sth to ~ come** (*inf*) etw in die Luft jagen (*inf*); **you can go on doing that till ~ come** (*inf*) Sie können (so) bis in alle Ewigkeit weitermachen; **he's gone to ~ come** (*inf*) er hat das Zeitliche gesegnet (*hum inf*) **c** (*Zool, Bot*) Reich *nt*; **the animal/plant ~** das Tier-/Pflanzenreich, das Reich der Tiere/Pflanzen

kingfisher ['kɪŋˌfɪʃə'] N Eisvogel *m*

kingfisher-blue [ˌkɪŋfɪʃə'bluː] ADJ eisblau, gletscherblau

kinglet ['kɪŋlɪt] N **a** (*US: Orn*) Goldhähnchen *nt* **b** (= *king*) König *m* eines kleinen oder unbedeutenden Landes

kingly ['kɪŋlɪ] ADJ königlich, majestätisch

king: kingmaker N (*lit, fig*) Königsmacher(in) *m(f)*; **kingpin** N (*Tech*) Königsbolzen *m*, Drehzapfen *m*; (*Aut*) Achsschenkelbolzen *m*; (*fig*: = *person*) Stütze *f*; **he's the ~ of the whole organization** mit ihm steht und fällt die ganze Organisation; **king prawn** N Königskrabbe *f*; **King's Bench** N (*Jur*) erste Kammer des Obersten Gerichts in Großbritannien; **King's Counsel** N (*Jur*) Kronanwalt *m*/-anwältin *f* (*Staatsanwalt, der in höheren Strafsachen die Krone vertritt*); **King's English** N englische Hochsprache; **kingship** N Königtum *nt*; **King's highway** N (*Brit*) öffentliche Straße; **king-size(d)** ADJ (*inf*) in Großformat, großformatig; *cigarettes* King-size; *bed* extra groß; **I've got a ~ headache** (*hum*) ich hab vielleicht einen Brummschädel (*inf*) *or* einen dicken Kopf (*inf*); **king's messenger** N (*Diplomacy*) königlicher Gesandter; **King's speech** N Thronrede *f*

kink [kɪŋk] **N** **a** (*in rope etc*) Knick *m*, Schlaufe *f*; (*in hair*) Welle *f*; **to work out** *or* **iron out the ~s** (*fig*) die Sache geradebiegen (*inf*) **b** (= *mental peculiarity*) Schrulle *f*, Tick *m* (*inf*); (*sexual*) abartige Veranlagung **VI** (*rope*) Schlaufen bilden, sich verdrehen; (*hair*) sich wellen

kinky [ˈkɪŋkɪ] **ADJ** (+*er*) **a** hair wellig **b** (*inf*) person, ideas, mind verdreht (*inf*), schrullig, spleenig (*inf*); boots, fashion verrückt (*inf*); (*sexually*) abartig; underwear, leather gear sexy inv; **~!** nein, so was! (*inf*), lustig, lustig! (*inf*)

kinsfolk [ˈkɪnzfəʊk] **N** Verwandtschaft *f*, Verwandte(n) *pl*

kinship [ˈkɪnʃɪp] **N** Verwandtschaft *f*; **to feel ~ with sb** sich jdm verwandt fühlen

kinsman [ˈkɪnzmən] **N** *pl* **-men** [-mən] Verwandte(r) *m*

kinswoman [ˈkɪnzwʊmən] **N** *pl* **-women** [-wɪmɪn] Verwandte *f*

kiosk [ˈkiːɒsk] **N** **a** Kiosk *m*, Verkaufsstand *m*, Bude *f* **b** (*Brit, Telec*) (Telefon)zelle *f*

kip [kɪp] (*Brit, inf*) **N** (= *sleep*) Schläfchen *nt*; **I've got to get some ~** ich muss mal 'ne Runde pennen (*inf*); **I need a good ~** ich muss mal (wieder) richtig pennen (*inf*) *or* ratzen (*inf*); **I'm going for a ~** ich geh mal 'ne Runde pennen (*inf*) **VI** (*also* **kip down**) pennen (*inf*)

kipper [ˈkɪpəʳ] **N** Räucherhering *m*, Bückling *m*

kipper tie **N** breite Krawatte

kir [kiːəʳ] **N** Kir *m*

Kirghiz [ˈkɜːgɪz] **N** Kirgise *m*, Kirgisin *f* **ADJ** kirgisisch

Kirghizia [kɜːˈgɪzɪə] **N** Kirgisien *nt*

Kirghizstan, Kirgizstan [ˌkɜːgɪzˈstaːn] **N** Kirgistan *nt*, Kirgisien *nt*

kirk [kɜːk] **N** (*Scot*) Kirche *f*; **the Kirk** die Presbyterianische Kirche Schottlands

kiss [kɪs] **N** Kuss *m*; **~ of life** Mund-zu-Mund-Beatmung *f*; **that will be the ~ of death for them** das wird ihnen den Todesstoß versetzen **VT** küssen; (*fig*: = *touch gently*) sanft berühren; **to ~ sb's cheek** jdn auf die Wange küssen; **to ~ sb's hand** jdm die Hand küssen; *woman's hand* (*in greeting*) jdm einen Handkuss geben; **they ~ed each other** sie gaben sich einen Kuss, sie küssten sich; **to ~ sb back** jds Kuss (*acc*) erwidern, jdn wiederküssen; **to ~ sb good night/ goodbye** jdm einen Gutenachtkuss/Abschiedskuss geben; **to ~ sth goodbye** (*fig inf*) sich (*dat*) etw abschminken (*inf*); **come here and I'll ~ it better** komm her, ich werde mal blasen, dann tuts nicht mehr weh **VI** küssen; (= *kiss each other*) sich küssen; **to ~ and make up** sich mit einem Kuss versöhnen; **to ~ and tell** Informationen über eine Affäre an die Medien verkaufen

▶ **kiss away** **VT** *sep* **she kissed away the child's tears** sie küsste dem Kind die Tränen fort

kissable [ˈkɪsəbl] **ADJ** mouth zum Küssen einladend *attr*; **a ~ girl** ein Mädchen, das man küssen möchte

---

---

kiss-and-tell [ˌkɪsənˈtel] **ADJ** **~ story** Enthüllungsstory *f* (*mit Details einer Affäre mit einer prominenten Person*)

kiss curl **N** Schmachtlocke *f*

kisser [ˈkɪsəʳ] **N** **a** **to be a good ~** gut küssen (können) **b** (*inf*: = *mouth, face*) Fresse *f* (*vulg*), Schnauze *f* (*inf*)

kissing: kissing disease [ˈkɪsɪŋdɪˌziːz] **N** Kusskrankheit *f* (*inf*), Pfeiffersches Drüsenfieber; **kissing gate** [ˈkɪsɪŋˌgeɪt] **N** Schwinggatter *nt* (*an Weidenzäunen und Hecken, das nur je eine Person durchlässt*)

kiss-off [ˈkɪsɒf] **N** (*US inf*) **to give sb the ~** jdn in die Wüste schicken (*inf*); boyfriend etc jdm den Laufpass geben (*inf*)

kissogram [ˈkɪsəgræm] **N** *Glückwunsch, der von einer Agentur mit einem Kuss überbracht wird*

kissproof [ˈkɪspruːf] **ADJ** kussecht

kit [kɪt] **N** **a** (= *equipment*) (*for fishing, photography etc*) Ausrüstung *f*; (*Mil*) Ausrüstung *f*, Montur *f* (*old*); **~ inspection** (*Mil*) Bekleidungs- or Ausrüstungsappell *m* **b** (*Sport*: *clothes*) Ausrüstung *f*, Zeug *nt* (*inf*), Sachen *pl* (*inf*); **gym ~** Sportzeug *nt*, Sportsachen *pl*; **get your ~ off!** (*inf*: = *undress*) zieh dich aus! **c** (= *belongings, luggage etc*) Sachen *pl* → **caboodle** **d** (= *set of items*) (*tools*) Werkzeug *nt*; (*in box*) Werkzeugkasten *m*; (= *puncture repair kit*) Flickzeug *nt* **e** (*for self-assembly*) Bastelsatz *m* **f** (*Brit sl*: = *heroin*) H *nt* (*sl*), Sugar *nt* (*sl*)

▶ **kit out** *or* **up** **VT** *sep* (*Brit*) ausrüsten (*esp Mil*), ausstatten; (= *clothe*) einkleiden; **he arrived kitted out in oilskins** er erschien in Ölzeug

kit: kitbag **N** Seesack *m*; **kit car** **N** *aus einem Bausatz zusammengebautes Kraftfahrzeug*

kitchen [ˈkɪtʃɪn] **N** Küche *f*

kitchenette [ˌkɪtʃɪˈnet] **N** (= *separate room*) kleine Küche; (= *part of one room*) Kochnische *f*

kitchen: kitchen foil **N** Alufolie *f*; **kitchen garden** **N** Gemüsegarten *m*, Küchengarten *m*; **kitchen knife** **N** Küchenmesser *nt*; **kitchenmaid** **N** Küchenmagd *f*; **kitchen range** **N** Küchenherd *m*; **kitchen roll** **N** Küchenrolle *f*; **kitchen scales** **PL** Küchenwaage *f*, Haushaltswaage *f*; **kitchen scissors** **PL** Küchenschere *f*, Haushaltsschere *f*; **kitchen sink** **N** Spüle *f*, Ausguss *m*, Spülstein *m*; **I've packed everything but the ~** (*inf*) ich habe den ganzen Hausrat eingepackt; **kitchen-sink drama** **N** Alltagsdrama *nt*, Wohnküchendrama *nt*; **kitchen timer** **N** Kurzzeitwecker *m*; **kitchen unit** **N** Küchenschrank *m*; **kitchenware** **N** Küchengeräte *pl*

kite [kaɪt] **N** **a** (*Orn*) Milan *m* **b** (= *toy*) Drachen *m*; **to fly a ~** (*lit*) einen Drachen steigen lassen; (*fig*) einen Versuchsballon steigen lassen; **she's as high as a ~** (*inf*) (= *excited*) sie ist völlig aufgedreht (*inf*); (= *on drugs*) sie ist total high (*inf*) **c** (*Aviat sl*) Vogel *m* (*sl*)

kite flying **N** Steigenlassen *nt* eines Drachens; (*Econ*) Wechselstreiterei *f*

Kite mark **N** (*Brit*) dreieckiges Gütezeichen

kith [kɪθ] **N** **~ and kin** Blutsverwandte *pl*; **they came with ~ and kin** sie kamen mit Kind und Kegel

kitsch [kɪtʃ] **N** Kitsch *m*

kitschy [ˈkɪtʃɪ] **ADJ** (+*er*) kitschig

kitten [ˈkɪtn] **N** kleine Katze, Kätzchen *nt*; **to have ~s** (*fig inf*) Zustände kriegen (*inf*)

kittenish [ˈkɪtənɪʃ] **ADJ** verspielt; (*fig*) woman kokett

kittiwake [ˈkɪtɪweɪk] **N** Dreizehenmöwe *f*

kitty [ˈkɪtɪ] **N** **a** (= *shared money*) (gemeinsame) Kasse; (*Cards etc*) (Spiel)kasse *f*; **we'll have a ~ for the drinks** wir legen für die Getränke zusammen; **there's nothing left in the ~** die Kasse ist leer; **the total prize ~ is now £9 million** in der Gewinnkasse sind jetzt neun Millionen Pfund **b** (*inf*: = *cat*) Mieze *f*

kiwi [ˈkiːwiː] **N** **a** Kiwi *m* **b** (*also* **kiwi fruit**) Kiwi(frucht) *f* **c** (*inf*: = *New Zealander*) Neuseeländer(in) *m(f)*, Kiwi *m* (*inf*)

KKK *abbr of* **Ku Klux Klan**

Klansman [ˈklænzmən] **N** *pl* **-men** [-mən] (*US*) Mitglied *nt* des Ku-Klux-Klan

klaxon [ˈklæksn] **N** Horn *nt*, Hupe *f*

Kleenex® [ˈkliːneks] **N** Tempo(taschentuch)® *nt*

kleptomania [ˌkleptəʊˈmeɪnɪə] **N** Kleptomanie *f*

kleptomaniac [ˌkleptəʊˈmeɪnɪæk] **N** Kleptomane *m*, Kleptomanin *f* **ADJ** kleptomanisch

klieg light [ˈkliːglaɪt] **N** (*esp US*) vor allem in Filmstudios verwendete Bogenlampe

km *abbr of* **kilometre(s)** km

km/h, kmph *abbr of* **kilometres per hour** km/h

knack [næk] **N** Trick *m*, Kniff *m*; (= *talent*) Talent *nt*, Geschick *nt*; **there's a (special) ~ (to it)** da ist ein (gewisser) Trick *or* Kniff dabei; **there's a (special) ~ to opening it** da ist ein Trick *or* Kniff dabei, wie man das aufbekommt; **to get the ~ of doing sth** (es) herausbekommen, wie man etw macht; **you'll soon get the ~ of it** Sie werden den Dreh bald rausbekommen *or* raushaben; **I never really got the ~ of it** ich habe den Trick nie richtig herausbekommen; **I've lost the ~** ich bekomme *or* kriege (*inf*) das nicht mehr hin *or* fertig; **she's got a ~ of saying the wrong thing** sie hat ein Geschick *or* Talent, immer das Falsche zu sagen

knacker [ˈnækəʳ] **N** (*Brit inf*, *of horses*) Abdecker(in) *m(f)*, Schinder(in) *m(f)*; (*of boats, houses*) Abbruchunternehmer(in) *m(f)*; **to send a horse to the ~'s (yard)** ein Pferd zum Abdecker *or* auf den Schindanger (*old*) bringen

knackered [ˈnækəd] **ADJ** (*Brit inf*) (= *exhausted*) geschafft (*inf*); (= *broken*) kaputt (*inf*)

knapsack [ˈnæpsæk] **N** Proviantbeutel *m*, Tornister *m* (*esp Mil*), Knappsack *m* (*old*)

knave [neɪv] **N** **a** (*old*) Bube *m* (*old*), Schurke *m* **b** (*Brit Cards*) Bube *m*, Unter *m* (*old*)

knavery [ˈneɪvərɪ] **N** (*old*) Bubenstück *nt* (*old*), Büberei *f* (*old*)

knavish [ˈneɪvɪʃ] **ADJ** (*Brit old*) bübisch (*old*), schurkisch

knead [niːd] **VT** dough kneten; (= *massage*) muscles massieren, durchkneten (*inf*)

knee [niː] **N** Knie *nt*; **to be on one's ~s** (*lit, fig*) auf den Knien liegen; **on one's ~s, on bended ~(s)** (*liter, hum*) kniefällig; **to go (down) on one's ~s** (*lit*) niederknien, (sich) hinknien; (*fig*) sich auf die Knie werfen; **to go down on one's ~s to sb** (*lit, fig*) sich vor jdm auf die Knie werfen, vor jdm einen Kniefall machen; **to bow** *or* **bend the ~ (to sb)** (vor jdm) die Knie beugen; **to bring sb to his/her** etc **~s** (*lit, fig*) jdn in die Knie zwingen; **to bring a country/a government to its ~s** einen Land/eine Regierung in die Knie zwingen; **he sank in up to the** *or* **his ~s** er sank knietief *or* bis zu den Knien ein; **I'll put you over my ~ in a minute** ich lege dich gleich übers Knie **VT** mit dem Knie stoßen; **to ~ sb in the groin** jdm das Knie zwischen die Beine stoßen; **he ~d his opponent in the chest** er hat seinem Gegner mit dem Knie eins gegen den Brustkasten gegeben (*inf*)

knee: knee bend **N** Kniebeuge *f*; **to do a ~** eine Kniebeuge machen; **knee breeches** **PL** Kniehose *f*, Bundhose *f*; **kneecap** **N** Kniescheibe *f* **VT** die Kniescheibe(n) durchschießen (+*dat*); **knee-deep** **ADJ** knietief; **the water was ~** das Wasser ging mir etc bis zum Knie *or* war knietief; **he was ~ in mud** er steckte knietief im Schlamm; **knee-high** **ADJ** kniehoch, in Kniehöhe; **knee jerk** **N** (*Med*) Kniesehnenreflex *m*; **kneejerk reaction** **N** Kurzschlussreaktion *f*; **knee joint** **N** (*Med, Tech*) Kniegelenk *nt*

kneel [niːl] pret, ptp **knelt** *or* **kneeled** **VI** (*before* vor +*dat*) knien; (*also* **kneel down**) niederknien, sich hinknien

knee-length [ˈniːleŋθ] **ADJ** skirt knielang; boots kniehoch; **~ socks** Kniestrümpfe *pl*

kneeler [ˈniːləʳ] **N** Kniepolster *nt*; (= *stool*) Kniebank *f*

knee: kneepad **N** Knieschützer *m*, Knieleder *nt*; **knee reflex** **N** Kniesehnenreflex *m*; **knee**

shot N (TV, Film) Halbtotale f; **knee-slapper** N (inf) Witz m zum Totlachen (inf)

knees-up ['niːzʌp] N (Brit inf, = dance) Tanz m; (= party) Fete f, Party f

knell [nel] N Geläut nt, (Toten)glocke f; **to sound the ~** die (Toten)glocke läuten; **to sound the (death) ~ for sb/sth** (fig) jdm/etw den Todesstoß geben or versetzen

knelt [nelt] pret, ptp of **kneel**

Knesset ['knesɪt] N **the ~** die Knesset

knew [njuː] pret of **know**

knickerbocker glory [ˌnɪkəbɒkəˈglɔːrɪ] N (Brit) Eisbecher mit Gelee, Sahne und Obst

knickerbockers ['nɪkəbɒkəz] PL Knickerbocker pl

knickers ['nɪkəz] PL **a** (Brit) Schlüpfer m; **to get one's ~ in a twist (over sth)** (inf) sich (dat) (wegen etw) ins Hemd machen (sl); **don't get your ~ in a twist!** (inf) dreh nicht gleich durch! (inf); **~ to you!** (inf: = rubbish!) Quatsch! (inf) **b** (old) = **knickerbockers**

knick-knack ['nɪknæk] N nette Kleinigkeit, Kinkerlitzchen nt; **~s** Krimskrams m; (= figurines) Nippes pl, Nippsachen pl

knife [naɪf] **N** pl **knives** Messer nt; **~, fork and spoon** Besteck nt; **like a (hot) ~ through butter** (fig) völlig mühelos; **to be under the ~** (Med inf) unterm Messer sein (inf); **to go under the ~** (Med inf) unters Messer kommen (inf); **to turn** or **twist the ~ (in the wound)** (fig) Salz in die Wunde streuen; **to put** or **stick the ~ in** (inf) böse zuschlagen (inf); **the knives are out for him** (esp Brit inf) für ihn wird schon das Messer gewetzt; **before you could say ~** (inf) eh man sichs versah, im Nu; **it's war to the ~ between them** sie bekämpfen sich bis aufs Messer; **you could have cut the atmosphere with a ~** die Stimmung war zum Zerreißen gespannt **VT** einstechen auf (+acc); (fatally) erstechen, erdolchen

knife: knife blade N Messerklinge f; **knife box** N Besteckkasten m; **knife edge** N (lit) (Messer)schneide f; **to be balanced on a ~** (fig) auf Messers Schneide stehen; **knife grinder** N (= person) Scherenschleifer(in) m(f); (= thing) Schleifrad nt or -stein m; **knifeman** N (Brit) Messerstecher m; **knife pleat** N einfache Falte; **knife-point** N **to hold sb at ~** jdn mit einem Messer bedrohen; **to force sb to do sth at ~** jdn mit vorgehaltenem Messer zwingen, etw zu tun; **knifer** ['naɪfə'] N Messerstecher m

knife: kniferest N Messerbänkchen nt; **knife sharpener** N Messerschärfer m

knifing ['naɪfɪŋ] N Messerstecherei f

knight [naɪt] **N** (= title, Hist) Ritter m; (Chess) Springer m, Pferd(chen) nt, Rössel nt; **Knight of the Garter** Träger(in) m(f) des Hosenbandordens; **~ of the road** (Brit hum) Kapitän m der Landstraße (hum); **a ~ in shining armour** (fig) ein Märchenprinz m **VT** adeln, zum Ritter schlagen

knight: knight errant N pl **knights errant** fahrender Ritter; **knight errantry** [naɪtˈerəntrɪ] N fahrendes Rittertum; (fig) Ritterlichkeit f

knighthood ['naɪthʊd] N **a** (= knights collectively) Ritterschaft f; **b** (= rank) Ritterstand m; **to receive a ~** in den Adelsstand erhoben werden; **he's hoping for a ~** er hofft, in den Adelsstand erhoben zu werden

knightly ['naɪtlɪ] ADJ (+er) ritterlich

knit [nɪt] pret, ptp **knitted** or **knit** **VT** **a** blanket, scarf etc stricken; **to ~ sth for sb, to ~ sb sth** jdm etw stricken; **the wool is then ~ted into ...** aus der Wolle wird dann ... gestrickt; **~ three, purl two** drei rechts, zwei links **b** **to ~ one's brows** die Stirn runzeln **VI** **a** (= person) stricken **b** (bones: also **knit together, knit up**) verwachsen, zusammenwachsen

▶ **knit together** **VT** **a** stitches zusammenstricken; (= unite) threads of story (miteinander) verknüpfen; people eng verbinden **VI** **a** = **knit VI b** **b** (= unite) miteinander verwachsen; **they knit well together** sie harmonieren gut;

▶ **knit up** **VI** **a** (wool) sich stricken **b** = **knit VI b** **VT** sep jersey stricken

knitted ['nɪtɪd] ADJ gestrickt; cardigan, dress etc Strick-; **~ goods** Strickwaren or -sachen pl

knitter ['nɪtə'] N Stricker(in) m(f)

knitting ['nɪtɪŋ] N **a** Stricken nt; (= material being knitted) Strickzeug nt, Strickarbeit f; (= knitted goods) Gestrickte(s) nt, Stricksachen pl; **she was doing her ~** sie strickte **b** (of bones etc) Verwachsen nt, Zusammenwachsen nt

knitting: knitting machine N Strickmaschine f; **knitting needle** N Stricknadel f; **knitting wool** N (Strick)wolle f, Strickgarn nt

knitwear ['nɪtwɛə'] N Strickwaren pl, Strick- or Wollsachen pl

knives [naɪvz] pl of **knife**

knob [nɒb] N **a** (on walking stick) Knauf m; (on door) Griff m, Knauf m; (on instrument etc) Knopf m; **and the same to you with (brass) ~s on** (Brit, inf) das beruht auf Gegenseitigkeit **b** (= swelling) Beule f, Knubbel m (inf); (on tree) Knoten m, Auswuchs m **c** (= small piece) Stückchen nt; **a ~ of butter** ein Stich m Butter **d** (sl: = penis) Prügel m (sl), Lanze f (sl)

knobbly ['nɒblɪ] ADJ (+er) wood knorrig, verwachsen; surface uneben, höckrig, knubbelig (inf); **~ knees** Knubbelknie pl (inf)

knobby ['nɒbɪ] ADJ (+er) wood, trunk knorrig

knock [nɒk] **N** **a** (esp Brit) (= blow) Stoß m; (esp with hand, tool etc) Schlag m; **to get a ~** einen Stoß/Schlag abbekommen; **I got a ~ on the head** (= was hit) ich habe einen Schlag auf den Kopf bekommen, (= hit myself) ich habe mir den Kopf angeschlagen or angestoßen; **he got a ~ from the swing** ich habe von der Schaukel hat ihn getroffen; **he took a bit of a ~** er hat einiges abbekommen (inf); **the car took a few ~s** mit dem Auto hat es ein paar Mal gebumst (inf); **the furniture has had a few ~s** die Möbel haben ein paar Schrammen abbekommen; **he gave himself a nasty ~** er hat sich böse angeschlagen or angestoßen **b** (= noise) Klopfen nt no pl, Pochen nt no pl (liter); (in engine) Klopfen nt no pl, Klopfgeräusch nt; **there was a ~ at the door** es hat (an der Tür) geklopft; **I heard a ~** ich habe es klopfen hören; **I'll give you a ~ at 7 o'clock** (Brit) ich klopfe um 7 Uhr (an deine Tür) **c** (esp Brit) (fig: = setback) (Tief)schlag m; **~s** (inf: = criticism) Kritik f; **to (have to) take a lot of ~s** viele Tiefschläge einstecken (müssen); (= be criticized) unter starken Beschuss kommen; **to take a ~** (self-confidence, pride etc) erschüttert werden; (reputation) geschädigt werden; (person) einen Tiefschlag erleben; **the company took a bit of a ~ as a result of the tax changes** die Steuerreform hat der Firma einen Schlag versetzt **VT** **a** (= hit, strike) stoßen; (with hand, tool, racket etc) schlagen; one's knee, head etc anschlagen, anstoßen (on an +dat); (= nudge, jolt) stoßen gegen; (= collide with: car, driver) rammen; **to ~ one's head/elbow** etc sich (dat) den Kopf/Ellbogen etc anschlagen or anstoßen; **he ~ed his foot against the table** er stieß mit dem Fuß gegen den Tisch; **to ~ sb on the head** jdn an or auf den Kopf schlagen; **that ~ed his idea on the head** (Brit inf) damit konnte er sich die Idee aus dem Kopf schlagen (inf); **I decided to ~ it on the head** (Brit inf) ich beschloss, der Sache (dat) ein Ende zu machen; **the plan wasn't working so we ~ed it on the head** (Brit inf) der Plan klappte nicht, also ließen wir ihn fallen; **to ~ sb to the ground** jdn zu Boden werfen; **to ~ sb unconscious** jdn bewusstlos werden lassen; (person) jdn bewusstlos schlagen; **to ~ sb dead** (fig inf) jdn umhauen (inf); **go out there and ~ 'em dead** (inf) jetzt zeigs denen aber mal! (inf); **he ~ed some holes in the side of the box** er machte ein paar Löcher in die Seite der Kiste; **we ~ed the two rooms into one** wir verbanden die beiden Zimmer indem wir die Verbindungswand abrissen; **to ~ holes in an argument**

ein Argument zerpflücken; **to ~ sb/sth out of the way** jdn/etw beiseite stoßen; **he ~ed it as he went past** er ist beim Vorbeigehen dagegengestoßen; (deliberately) er hat ihm/ihr etc beim Vorbeigehen einen Stoß versetzt or gegeben; **she ~ed the glass to the ground** sie stieß gegen das Glas und es fiel zu Boden; **watch you don't ~ your glass off the table** pass auf, dass du dein Glas nicht vom Tisch stößt; **to ~ the nonsense out of sb** jdm den Unsinn austreiben; **to ~ some sense into sb** jdn zur Vernunft bringen; **to ~ sb's confidence** jds Selbstbewusstsein erschüttern; **he was ~ed sideways by it** (fig inf) es haute ihn um (inf); **confidence in the legal system has been ~ed sideways** (inf) das Vertrauen in das Rechtssystem hat schwer gelitten **b** (inf: = criticize) (he)runtermachen (inf); **if you haven't tried it, don't ~ it** verurteile es doch nicht, wenn du es noch nie versucht hast **VI** **a** (on door etc) klopfen, pochen (liter); (engine etc) klopfen; **to ~ at** or **on the door** an die Tür klopfen, anklopfen; **opportunity was** or **came ~ing at his door** ihm bot sich eine Gelegenheit; **he is ~ing on the door of the England team** er wird als Anwärter für die englische Nationalmannschaft gehandelt; **to ~ at** or **on the window** gegen das Fenster klopfen; **~ before entering** bitte anklopfen; **he ~ed on the table** er schlug or klopfte auf den Tisch **b** (= bump, collide) stoßen (into, against gegen); **he ~ed into** or **against the gatepost** er rammte den Türpfosten **c** his knees were ~ing (together) ihm zitterten or schlotterten (inf) die Knie **INTERJ** **~!** klopf, klopf

▶ **knock about** (Brit) or **around** **VI** (inf) **a** (person) herumziehen (prep obj in +dat); **to knock around the house** im Haus rumgammeln (inf); **he has knocked about** or **around a bit** er ist schon (ganz schön) (he)rumgekommen (inf); **who's he knocking about** or **around with these days?** mit wem hängt er denn jetzt so herum? (inf) **b** (object) herumliegen (prep obj in +dat); (boxes etc) herumstehen **VT** sep **a** (= ill-treat) verprügeln, schlagen; **he was badly knocked about in the accident** er ist bei dem Unfall ziemlich zugerichtet worden; **he knocks her about** or **around** er (ver)prügelt sie ständig **b** (= damage) ramponieren (inf), beschädigen **c** **to knock a ball about** or **around** ein paar Bälle schlagen

▶ **knock back** VT sep (inf) **a** he knocked back his whisky er kippte sich (dat) den Whisky hinter die Binde (inf); **come on, knock it back** nun trink schon (aus) (inf) **b** (= cost) this watch knocked me back £20 ich habe für die Uhr £ 20 hingelegt, die Uhr hat mich £ 20 gekostet; **what did they knock you back for it?** was mussten Sie dafür hinlegen or blechen? (inf) **c** (= shock) schocken, erschüttern **d** (= reject) zurückweisen

▶ **knock down** VT sep **a** person, thing umwerfen, zu Boden werfen; opponent (by hitting) niederschlagen; (car, driver) anfahren; (completely) umfahren; (fatally) überfahren; building abreißen, niederreißen; tree fällen, umhauen; door einschlagen; obstacle, fence niederreißen; **she was knocked down and killed** sie wurde überfahren; **he knocked him down with one blow** er schlug or streckte (geh) ihn mit einem Schlag zu Boden **b** price (buyer) herunterhandeln (to auf +acc); (seller) heruntergehen mit; **I managed to knock him down a pound** ich konnte ein Pfund herunterhandeln; **I knocked him down to £15** ich habe es auf £ 15 heruntergehandelt; **he knocked the price down by £5 for me** er hat mir £ 5 nachgelassen **c** (at auction) zuschlagen (to sb jdm); **to be knocked down at £1** für ein Pfund versteigert werden **d** machine, furniture zerlegen, auseinander nehmen

▶ **knock in** VT sep nail einschlagen

▶ **knock off** Ⓥ (*inf*) aufhören, Feierabend *or* Schluss machen (*inf*); **let's knock off now** Schluss für heute (*inf*); **to knock off for lunch** Mittag machen

Ⓥ *sep* **a** (*lit*) *vase, cup, person etc* hinunterstoßen; *nose off statue etc* abschlagen; *insect* abschütteln; *high jump bar* reißen; (*off list etc*) streichen; **the branch knocked the rider off (his horse)** der Ast riss den Reiter vom Pferd; **somebody knocked the nose off the statue** jemand hat der Statue (*dat*) die Nase abgeschlagen **b** (*inf*: = *reduce price by*) nachlassen (*for sb* jdm), runtergehen (*inf*); **he knocked £5 off the bill/price** er hat £ 5 von der Rechnung/vom Preis nachgelassen; **I got something knocked off** ich habe es billiger bekommen **c** (*inf*: = *do quickly*) *essay, painting* hinhauen (*inf*); (*with good result*) aus dem Ärmel schütteln (*inf*) **d** (*Brit inf*: = *steal*) klauen (*inf*) **e** (*inf*: = *kill*) umlegen (*inf*) **f** (*inf*: = *stop*) aufhören mit; *smoking, criticizing* stecken (*sl*); **to knock off work** Feierabend machen; **knock it off!** nun hör schon auf!

▶ **knock on** Ⓥ (*Brit inf*) **he's knocking on for fifty** er geht auf die fünfzig zu

▶ **knock out** Ⓥ *sep* **a** *tooth* ausschlagen; *nail* herausschlagen (*aus*); *pipe* ausklopfen; *contents* herausklopfen (*aus*) **b** (= *stun*) bewusstlos werden lassen; (*by hitting*) bewusstlos schlagen, k. o. schlagen; (*Boxing*) k. o. schlagen; (*drink*) umhauen (*inf*); **he was knocked out** er wurde bewusstlos; (*Boxing*) er wurde k. o. geschlagen; (*by drink*) ihn hats umgehauen (*inf*); **to knock oneself out** sich so stoßen, dass man bewusstlos wird **c** (*from competition*) besiegen (*of* in +*dat*); **to be knocked out** ausscheiden, rausfliegen (*inf*) (*of* aus) **d** (*inf*: = *stun, shock*) (*good news*) umwerfen, umhauen (*inf*); (*bad news, sb's death etc*) schocken **e** (*inf*: = *bowl over*) hinreißen (*inf*), umhauen (*inf*) **f** (*inf*: = *exhaust*) schaffen (*inf*), kaputtmachen (*inf*)

▶ **knock over** Ⓥ *sep* umwerfen, umstoßen; (*car*) anfahren; (*fatally*) überfahren

▶ **knock together** Ⓥ **his knees were knocking together** seine Knie zitterten *or* schlotterten (*inf*) Ⓥ *sep* **a** (= *make hurriedly*) *shelter, object* zusammenzimmern; *meal, snack* auf die Beine stellen (*inf*) **b** (*lit*) aneinander stoßen; **I'd like to knock their heads together** man sollte die beiden zur Räson bringen

▶ **knock up** Ⓥ **a** (*Brit Sport*) sich einspielen, ein paar Bälle schlagen **b** (*US sl*) bumsen (*inf*) Ⓥ *sep* **a** (= *hit upwards*) hochschlagen **b** (*Brit*: = *wake*) (auf)wecken **c** (= *make hurriedly*) *meal* auf die Beine stellen (*inf*); *building* hochziehen, hinstellen; *shelter* zusammenzimmern **d** (*Brit sl*: = *exhaust*) kaputtmachen (*inf*), schaffen (*inf*); (*experience, shock*) schaffen (*inf*) **e** (*inf*: = *make pregnant*) ein Kind anhängen (+*dat*) (*inf*), ein Kind machen (+*dat*) (*inf*); (*US sl*: = *have sex with*) bumsen mit (*inf*); **she's knocked up** (*inf*) die hat 'nen dicken Bauch (*sl*) **f** (*Cricket*) **to knock up 20 runs** 20 Läufe machen **g** (*inf*: = *do*) *mileage* fahren; *overtime* machen

knock: knockabout ADJ **a** ~ **comedy** (*Theat*) Klamaukstück *nt* **b** ~ **clothes** gammelige Kleidung Ⓝ (*Naut*) kleiner Einmaster; **knockback** N (*inf*: = *setback*) Rückschlag *m*; **he wasn't used to getting a ~ from a woman** er war es nicht gewöhnt, von einer Frau zurückgewiesen zu werden *or* einen Korb zu bekommen (*inf*); **knockdown** ADJ *attr* **a** ~ **price** Schleuderpreis *m*; (*at auction*) Mindestpreis *m* **b** *furniture etc* zerlegbar; ~ **blow** (*Boxing*) Niederschlag *m*; **a** ~ **drag-out fight** (*US inf*) (= *fisti-*

cuffs) eine handfeste Schlägerei; (= *argument*) ein handfester Streit; (= *difficult procedure*) ein langwieriger Kampf Ⓝ (*Boxing*) Niederschlag *m*

knocker ['nɒkə'] N **a** (= *door knocker*) (Tür)klopfer *m* **b** (*inf*: = *breasts*) **(pair of) ~s** Titten *pl* (*sl*); **what a pair of ~s!** toller Vorbau (*inf*), geile Titten (*sl*) **c** (*inf*: = *critic*) Nörgler(in) *m(f)*

knock-for-knock ['nɒkfə'nɒk] ADJ (*Insur*) ~ **agreement** Vereinbarung, bei der jede Versicherungsgesellschaft den Schaden des von ihr versicherten Fahrzeugs übernimmt

knocking ['nɒkɪŋ] N **a** Klopfen *nt*, Pochen *nt* (*liter*); (*in engine*) Klopfen *nt* **b** (*inf*) Kritik *f* (*of* an +*dat*); **he has taken a ~** er ist unter Beschuss gekommen

knocking: knocking copy N (*in advertising*) Negativwerbung *f*; **knocking-off time** N (*inf*) Feierabend *m*; **knocking-shop** N (*Brit inf*) Puff *m* (*inf*)

knock: knock-kneed [nɒk'niːd] ADJ x-beinig, X-beinig; **to be ~** X-Beine haben; **knock-me-down** ADJ (*US inf*) überwältigend; **knock-on effect** N (*Brit*) Folgewirkungen *pl* (*on* auf +*acc*)

knockout ['nɒkaʊt] Ⓝ **a** (*Boxing*) Knockout *m*, K. o. *m*; **he won by a ~** er gewann durch K. o. *or* errang einen K.-o.-Sieg **b** (*inf*: = *person, thing*) Wucht *f* (*inf*); **she looked a ~ in her new dress** sie sah in ihrem neuen Kleid umwerfend aus ATTR **a** (*Boxing, fig*) ~ **blow** K.-o.-Schlag *m*; **to deliver a ~ blow** *or* **punch** einen K.-o.-Schlag landen **b** ~ **competition** Ausscheidungskampf *m*

knock-up ['nɒkʌp] N (*Brit Sport*) **to have a ~** ein paar Bälle schlagen

knoll [nəʊl] N Hügel *m*, Kuppe *f*

knot [nɒt] Ⓝ **a** (*in string, tie, fig*) Knoten *m*; (*in muscle*) Verspannung *f*; **to tie/undo** *or* **untie a ~** einen Knoten machen/aufmachen *or* lösen; **to tie the ~** (*fig*) den Bund fürs Leben schließen; **to tie oneself (up) in ~s** (*fig*) sich immer mehr verwickeln, sich immer tiefer verstricken; **to tie sb (up) in ~s** jdn völlig verwirren; **there was a ~ in his stomach** sein Magen krampfte sich zusammen; **a ~ of muscles** ein Muskelbündel *nt*; **the whole matter is full of legal ~s** die ganze Sache ist rechtlich äußerst verwickelt **b** (*Naut*: = *speed*) Knoten *m*; **to make 20 ~s** 20 Knoten machen → **rate** ¹ N **a** **c** (*in wood*) Ast *m*, Verwachsung *f* **d** (= *group*) Knäuel *m*; **a ~ of tourists** ein Touristenknäuel *m* Ⓥ einen Knoten machen in (+*acc*); (= *knot together*) verknoten, verknüpfen; *stomach* verkrampfen; **to ~ sth to sth** etw mit etw verknoten; **to ~ sth around sth** etw um etw knoten; **get ~ted!** verdammt nochmal! (*inf*), rutsch mir den Buckel runter! (*inf*); **I told him to get ~ted** (*inf*) ich hab ihm gesagt, er kann mich mal (*inf*) *or* er kann mir den Buckel runterrutschen (*inf*) Ⓥ sich verknoten, Knoten bilden; (*stomach, muscles*) sich verkrampfen; (*forehead*) sich runzeln

▶ **knot together** VT *sep* verknoten

knotgrass ['nɒtgrɑːs] N (*Bot*) Knöterich *m*

knothole ['nɒthəʊl] N (*in timber*) Astloch *nt*

knotty ['nɒtɪ] ADJ (+*er*) *wood* astreich, knorrig; *veins, rope* knotig; *problem* verwickelt, verzwickt (*inf*)

knout [naʊt] N Knute *f*

know [nəʊ]
vb: pret **knew**, *ptp* **known**
✪ 15.1, 15.4, 16.1, 16.4, 26.3

1 TRANSITIVE VERB	4 NOUN
2 INTRANSITIVE VERB	5 PHRASAL VERBS
3 SET STRUCTURES	

1 – TRANSITIVE VERB

a = have knowledge about wissen; *answer, facts, dates, details, results etc* kennen, wissen; *French, English etc* können; **he knew her to be guilty** er

wusste, dass sie schuldig war; **to know what one is talking about** wissen, wovon man redet; **to know one's own mind** wissen, was man will; **she knows all the answers** sie weiß Bescheid, sie kennt sich aus; (*pej*) sie weiß immer alles besser; **he might even be dead for all I know** vielleicht ist er sogar tot, was weiß ich; **he thinks he knows all the answers** *or* **everything** er meint, er wüsste alles; **that's what I'd like to know (too)** das möchte ich auch wissen; **THAT'S what I'd like to know** das möchte ich wirklich wissen; **that's worth knowing** das ist ja interessant; **that might be worth knowing** es könnte interessant sein, das zu wissen; **before you know where you are** ehe man sichs versieht; **I've been a fool and don't I know it!** (*inf*) ich sehs ja ein, ich war doof (*inf*), ich war vielleicht doof (*inf*); **she's angry! – don't I know it!** (*inf*) sie ist wütend! – wem sagst du das! (*inf*)

b = be acquainted with *people, places, book, author* kennen; **I know Bavaria well** ich kenne Bayern gut, ich kenne mich gut in Bayern aus; **do you know him to speak to?** kennen Sie ihn näher?; **we all know her as the headmistress/a generous person** wir kennen Sie alle als die Schulleiterin/einen großzügigen Menschen; **if I know John, he'll already be there** wie ich John kenne, ist er schon da; **he didn't want to know me** er wollte nichts mit mir zu tun haben; **know thyself!** erkenne dich selbst! → **name** N **a**, **sight** N **b**

c = recognize erkennen; **to know sb by his voice/walk** *etc* jdn an der Stimme/am Gang *etc* erkennen; **would you know him again?** würden Sie ihn wieder erkennen?; **he knows a good thing when he sees it** er weiß, was gut ist; **he knows a bargain/good manuscript when he sees one** er weiß, was ein guter Kauf/ein gutes Manuskript ist; **this is the end of the welfare system as we know it** das ist das Ende des uns bekannten Wohlfahrtssystems

d = be able to distinguish unterscheiden können; **don't you know your right from your left?** können Sie rechts und links nicht unterscheiden?; **you wouldn't know him from his brother** Sie könnten ihn nicht von seinem Bruder unterscheiden; **do you know the difference between...?** wissen Sie, was der Unterschied zwischen ... ist?; **to know the difference between right and wrong, to know right from wrong** den Unterschied zwischen Gut und Böse kennen, Gut und Böse unterscheiden können; **he wouldn't know the difference** das merkt er nicht; **he doesn't know one end of a horse/hammer from the other** er hat keine Ahnung von Pferden/keine Ahnung, was ein Hammer ist (*inf*)

e = experience erleben; **I've never known it to rain so heavily** so einen starken Regen habe ich noch nie erlebt; **I've never known him (to) smile** ich habe ihn noch nie lächeln sehen, ich habe es noch nie erlebt, dass er lächelt; **have you ever known me (to) tell a lie?** haben Sie mich jemals lügen hören?; **have you ever known such a thing to happen before?** haben Sie je schon so etwas erlebt?, ist Ihnen so etwas schon einmal vorgekommen?

f Bibl (*obs: sexually*) erkennen

2 – INTRANSITIVE VERB

wissen; **who knows?** wer weiß?, weiß ichs?; **I know!** ich weiß!, weiß ich (doch)!; (*having a good idea*) ich weiß was!, ich habe eine Idee!; **I don't know** (das) weiß ich nicht; **as far as I know** soviel ich weiß, meines Wissens; **he just didn't want to know** er wollte einfach nicht hören; **afterwards they just didn't want to know** nachher wollten sie einfach nichts mehr davon wissen; **I wouldn't know** (*inf*) weiß ich (doch) nicht (*inf*); **don't you know?** weißt du das denn nicht?; **how should I know?** wie soll ich das wissen?; **how was I to know?** wie sollte ich das wissen?; **I'm damned if I know** (*inf*) ich habe echt keinen Schimmer (*inf*); **the channel was rough, as I well know** *or* **as well I know!** die Überfahrt war stürmisch, das kann ich dir sagen

3 – SET STRUCTURES

♦ **to know that ...** wissen, dass ...

> Note that while in English **that** can be omitted, in German **dass** must be used to introduce the next sentence.

when I saw the ambulance, I knew (that) something was wrong als ich den Krankenwagen sah, wusste ich, dass etwas nicht stimmte
♦ **to know why...** wissen, warum ...; **he didn't know why** er wusste nicht, warum; **I don't know why you think it's so funny** ich weiß nicht, was du daran so komisch findest
♦ **to know how to know how to do sth** (*in theory*) wissen, wie man etw macht; (*in practice*) etw tun können; **I know how you feel** ich weiß, wie Sie sich fühlen; **I don't know how you can say that!** wie kannst du das nur sagen!; **you don't know how good it is to see you again** Sie wissen gar nicht, wie sehr ich mich freue, Sie wiederzusehen
♦ **to know better I know better than that** ich bin ja nicht ganz dumm; **I know better than to say something like that** ich werde mich hüten, so etwas zu sagen; **he knows better than to eat into the profits** er ist nicht so dumm, den Gewinn anzugreifen; **he/you ought to have known better** das war dumm (von ihm/dir); **he ought to have or should have known better than to do that** es war dumm von ihm, das zu tun; **you ought to know better at your age** in deinem Alter müsste man das aber (besser) wissen; **they don't know any better** sie kennens nicht anders; **he says he didn't do it, but I know better** er sagt, er war es nicht, aber ich weiß, dass dies nicht stimmt
♦ **to know best OK, you know best** o.k., Sie müssens wissen; **mother always knows best** Mutter weiß es am besten
♦ **to get to know to get to know sb** jdn kennen lernen; **to get to know sth** (*methods, techniques, style, pronunciation etc*) etw lernen; (*habits, faults, shortcuts etc*) etw herausfinden; **to get to know a place** einen Ort kennen lernen
♦ **to let sb know to let sb know sth** (= *not keep back*) jdn etw wissen lassen; (= *tell, inform*) jdm von etw Bescheid sagen or geben; **he soon let me know what he thought of it** er hat mich schnell wissen lassen, was er davon hielt; **when can you let me know?** wann können Sie es mich wissen lassen?, wann können Sie mir Bescheid sagen?
♦ **you know... you know, we could/there is ...** weißt du, wir könnten/da ist ...; **he gave it away, you know** er hat es nämlich weggegeben; **it's raining, you know** es regnet; **then there was this man, you know, and ...** und da war dieser Mann, nicht (wahr), und ...; **wear the black dress, you know, the one with the red belt** zieh das schwarze Kleid an, du weißt schon, das mit dem roten Gürtel; **it's long and purple and, you know, sort of crinkly** es ist lang und lila und, na ja, so kraus; **(if you) know what I mean** du weißt schon
♦ **you never know** man kann nie wissen
♦ **I'll have you know it was nothing to do with me, I'll have you know!** es hatte nichts mit mir zu tun, damit du es weißt!
♦ **there's no knowing** (*inf*) das kann keiner sagen, das weiß niemand; **there's no knowing what he'll do** man weiß nie, was er noch tut
♦ **what do you know!** (*inf*) sieh mal einer an!; **what do you know! I've just seen her!** (*inf*) stellen Sie sich vor, ich habe sie eben gesehen
♦ **to be known** → *also* **known to be known (to sb)** (jdm) bekannt sein; **it is (well) known that ...** es ist (allgemein) bekannt, dass ...; **is he/it known here?** ist er/das hier bekannt?, kennt man ihn/das hier?; **to be known for sth** für etw bekannt sein; **he is known to have been here** man weiß, dass er hier war; **he is known as Mr Smith** man kennt ihn als Herrn Smith; **she wishes to be known as Mrs White** sie möchte Frau White genannt werden → *also* **known**
♦ **to make sb/sth known** jdn/etw bekannt machen; **to make it known that ...** bekannt ge-

ben, dass ...; **to make oneself known** sich melden (*to sb* bei jdm); (= *introduce oneself*) sich vorstellen (*to sb* jdm); (= *become well-known*) sich (*dat*) einen Namen machen; **to make one's presence known** sich melden (*to* bei)
♦ **to become known** bekannt werden; (= *famous*) berühmt werden
♦ **to let it be known that ...** bekannt geben, dass ...

4 – NOUN

♦ **to be in the know** (*inf*) eingeweiht sein, im Bild sein (*inf*), Bescheid wissen (*inf*); **the people in the know say ...** Leute, die darüber Bescheid wissen, sagen ..., die Fachleute sagen ...

5 – PHRASAL VERBS

▶ **know about** **VI** +*prep obj* (= *have factual knowledge, experience of*) *history, maths, politics* sich auskennen in (+*dat*); *Africa* Bescheid wissen (+*acc*); *women, men, cars, horses* sich auskennen mit; (= *be aware of, have been told about*) wissen von; **I know about that** das weiß ich; **I didn't know about that** das wusste ich nicht; **I only knew about it yesterday** ich habe erst gestern davon gehört; **I'd rather not know about it** das möchte ich lieber nicht wissen; **did you know about Maggie?** weißt du über Maggie Bescheid?; **I know about John, but is anyone else absent?** John, das weiß ich, aber fehlt sonst noch jemand?; **to get to know about sb/sth** von jdm/etw hören; **I don't know about that** davon weiß ich nichts; (= *don't agree*) da bin ich aber nicht so sicher; **I don't know about you, but I'm hungry** ich weiß nicht, wie es Ihnen geht, aber ich habe Hunger; **she's very clever, isn't she? – I don't know about clever, but she certainly knows how to use people** sie ist sehr klug, nicht wahr? – klug, na ich weiß nicht, aber sie weiß Leute auszunutzen

VT *sep* +*prep obj* **to know a lot/nothing/something about sth** (= *have factual knowledge*) viel/nichts/einiges über etw (*acc*) wissen; (*in history, maths etc*) in etw (*dat*) gut/nicht/ein bisschen Bescheid wissen; (*about cars, horses etc*) viel/nichts/einiges von etw verstehen; (= *be aware of, have been told about*) viel/nichts/einiges von etw wissen; **we don't know anything about him** wir wissen nichts über ihn; **that was the first I knew about it** davon hatte ich nichts gewusst; **not much is known about that** darüber weiß man nicht viel; **I know all about that** da kenne ich mich aus; (= *I'm aware of that*) das weiß ich; (= *I've been told about it*) ich weiß Bescheid; **I know all about you** ich weiß über Sie Bescheid; **that's all you know about it!** (*iro*) das meinst auch nur du!; **I don't know about that!** da bin ich mir nicht so sicher!

▶ **know of** **VI** +*prep obj café, better method* kennen; (= *have heard of*) *sb, sb's death* gehört haben; **I soon got to know of all the facts/all his problems** ich war bald über alle Fakten/all seine Probleme informiert; **I know of him, although I've never met him** ich habe von ihm gehört, aber ich habe ihn noch nie getroffen; **not that I know of** nicht, dass ich wüsste

knowable ['nəʊəbl] **ADJ** den/die/das man wissen kann; **it's not ~** das kann man nicht wissen

know: know-all **N** (*Brit inf*) Alleswisser(in) *m(f)*, Besserwisser(in) *m(f)*; **know-how** **N** praktische Kenntnis, Know-how *nt*; **he hasn't got the ~ for or to do the job** er hat nicht die nötige Sachkenntnis für diese Arbeit

knowing ['nəʊɪŋ] **ADJ** *look, smile* wissend; *person* verständnisvoll

knowingly ['nəʊɪŋlɪ] **ADV** **a** (= *consciously*) bewusst, absichtlich, wissentlich **b** *look, smile* wissend

know-it-all ['nəʊɪtɔːl] **N** (*US inf*) = **know-all**

knowledge ['nɒlɪdʒ] ✿ 19.2 **N** **a** (= *understanding, awareness*) Wissen *nt*, Kenntnis *f*;

to have ~ of Kenntnis haben or besitzen von, wissen von; **to have no ~ of** keine Kenntnis haben von, nichts wissen von; **to (the best of) my ~** soviel ich weiß, meines Wissens; **to the best of my ~ and belief** nach bestem Wissen und Gewissen; **not to my ~** nicht, dass ich wüsste; **without his ~** ohne sein Wissen; **without the ~ of her mother** ohne Wissen ihrer Mutter, ohne dass ihre Mutter es weiß; **it has come to my ~ that ...** ich habe erfahren, dass ...; **safe in the ~ that ...** in der Gewissheit, dass ...

b (= *learning, facts learned*) Kenntnisse *pl*, Wissen *nt*; **my ~ of English** meine Englischkenntnisse *pl*; **my ~ of D.H. Lawrence** was ich von D. H. Lawrence kenne; **I have a thorough ~ of this subject** auf diesem Gebiet ich ich gründlich Bescheid or besitze ich umfassende Kenntnisse; **the police have no ~ of him/his activities** die Polizei weiß nichts über ihn/seine Aktivitäten

knowledgeable ['nɒlɪdʒəbl] **ADJ** *person* kenntnisreich, bewandert; *report* gut fundiert; **to be ~** viel wissen (*about* über +*acc*)

knowledgeably ['nɒlɪdʒəblɪ] **ADV** *speak, write* kenntnisreich

known [nəʊn] *ptp of* **know** **ADJ** bekannt; *expert also* anerkannt; **it is a ~ fact that ...** es ist (allgemein) bekannt, dass ...; **~ quantity** bekannte Größe

knuckle ['nʌkl] **N** (*Finger*)knöchel *m*; (*of meat*) Hachse *f*, Haxe *f* → **near 2 a, rap**

▶ **knuckle down** **VI** (*inf*) sich dahinter klemmen (*inf*), sich dranmachen (*inf*); **to knuckle down to work** sich hinter die Arbeit klemmen (*inf*), sich an die Arbeit machen

▶ **knuckle under** **VI** (*inf*) spuren (*inf*), sich fügen (*to* +*dat*); (*to demands*) sich beugen (*to* +*dat*)

knuckle: knucklebone **N** Knöchelbein *nt*; **knucklebones** PL → **jacks**; **knuckle-duster** **N** (*esp Brit*) Schlagring *m*; **knucklehead** **N** (*inf*) Holzkopf *m* (*inf*); **knuckle joint** **N** (*Anat*) Knöchel- or Fingergelenk *nt*; (*Tech*) Kardan- or Kreuzgelenk *nt*; **knuckle sandwich** **N** (*Brit inf*) Keile *pl* (*inf*), Prügel *pl* (*inf*)

knurl [nɜːl] **N** Einkerbung *f*, Riffelung *f*; (*Tech*) Rändelrad *nt* **VT** rändeln, kordieren

KO **N** K. o. *m*, K.-o.-Schlag *m* **VT** (*Boxing*) k. o. schlagen

koala [kəʊˈɑːlə] **N** (*also* **koala bear**) Koala(bär) *m*

kookaburra ['kʊkəˌbʌrə] **N** Rieseneisvogel *m*, Lachender Hans

kooky ['kuːkɪ] **ADJ** (+*er*) (*US inf*) komisch (*inf*), verrückt (*inf*)

kopeck ['kəʊpek] **N** Kopeke *f*

Koran [kɒˈrɑːn] **N** Koran *m*

Korea [kəˈrɪə] **N** Korea *nt*

Korean [kəˈrɪən] **ADJ** koreanisch; **~ war** Koreakrieg *m* **N** **a** Koreaner(in) *m(f)* **b** (*Ling*) Koreanisch *nt*

kosher ['kəʊʃəʳ] **ADJ** **a** koscher **b** (*inf*) in Ordnung; **to make everything ~** alles in Ordnung bringen; **there's something not quite ~ about the deal** an dem Geschäft ist etwas faul (*inf*)

Kosovan ['kɒsəvən], **Kosovar** ['kɒsəvɑːʳ] **ADJ** kosovarisch; **the ~ Albanians** die Kosovo-Albaner **N** Kosovare *m*, Kosovarin *f*

Kosovo ['kɒsəvəʊ] **N** Kosovo *nt*

kowtow ['kaʊtaʊ] **VI** einen Kotau machen, dienern; **to ~ to sb** vor jdm dienern or katzbuckeln (*inf*) or einen Kotau machen

KP **a** (*US Mil*) *abbr of* **kitchen police** (= *work*) Küchendienst *m*; (= *soldiers*) Soldaten, die Küchendienst haben **b** (*Med*) *abbr of* **Kaposi's sarcoma** Kaposisarkom *nt*

kph *abbr of* **kilometres per hour** kph

kraal [krɑːl] **N** Kral *m*

kraft [krɑːft], **kraft paper** **N** starkes Packpapier

kraken ['krɑːkən] **N** Krake *m*

Kraut [kraʊt] N, ADJ *als Schimpfwort ge-brauchte Bezeichnung für Deutsche und Deutsches*

Kremlin [ˈkremlɪn] N **the** ~ der Kreml

kremlinologist [ˌkremlɪˈnɒlədʒɪst] N Kremlfor-scher(in) *m(f)*

kremlinology [ˌkremlɪˈnɒlədʒɪ] N Kremlfor-schung *f*

krona [ˈkrəʊnə] N schwedische Krone

krone [ˈkrəʊnə] N (*Danish*) dänische Krone; (*Norwegian*) norwegische Krone

krypton [ˈkrɪptɒn] N Krypton *nt*

Kt (*Brit*) abbr of **Knight**

kudos [ˈkjuːdɒs] N Ansehen *nt*, Ehre *f*; **he only did it for the** ~ er tat es nur der Ehre wegen

Ku Klux Klan [ˌkjuːklʌksˈklæn] N Ku-Klux-Klan *m*

kumquat [ˈkʌmkwɒt] N Kumquat *f*, *kleine Orange*

kung fu [ˈkʌŋˈfuː] N Kung-Fu *nt*

Kurd [kɜːd] N Kurde *m*, Kurdin *f*

Kurdish [ˈkɜːdɪʃ] ADJ kurdisch N Kurdisch *nt*

Kuwait [kʊˈweɪt] N Kuwait *nt*

Kuwaiti [kʊˈweɪtɪ] ADJ kuwaitisch N Kuwai-ter(in) *m(f)*

kV abbr of **kilovolt(s)** kV

kvetch [kvetʃ] (*pej*) N **a** (= *person*) Nörgler(in) *m(f)* (*pej*) **b** (= *complaint*) Nörgelei *f* (*pej*) VI nörgeln

kW abbr of **kilowatt(s)** kW

kWh, **kwh** abbr of **kilowatt hour(s)** kWh

KWIC (*Comput*) abbr of **keyword in context** KWIC

Kyrgyzstan [ˌkɜːgɪsˈtɑːn] N = **Kirghizstan**

L

L, l [el] N L *nt*, l *nt*

L **a** (*Brit Mot*) *abbr of* **Learner** **b** *abbr of* **Lake** **c** *abbr of* **large**

l **a** *abbr of* **litre(s)** l. **b** *abbr of* **left** l

LA *abbr of* **Los Angeles**

Lab (*Brit Pol*) *abbr of* **Labour**

lab [læb] *abbr of* **laboratory**

label ['leɪbl] **N** **a** (*lit*) Etikett *nt*, Label *nt*; (*showing contents, instructions etc*) Aufschrift *f*, Beschriftung *f*; (*on specimen, cage*) Schild *nt*; (*tied on*) Anhänger *m*; (*adhesive*) Aufkleber *m*, Aufklebeetikett *nt*; (*on parcel*) Paketadresse *f*; (*of record company*) Label *nt*, Plattenfirma *f*; **on the Pye** ~ unter dem Pye-Label **b** (*fig*) Etikett *nt* (*usu pej*)

VT **a** (*lit*) etikettieren, mit einem Schild/Anhänger/Aufkleber versehen; (= *write on*) beschriften; **the bottle was ~led** (*Brit*) *or* ~**ed** (*US*) **"poison"** die Flasche trug die Aufschrift „Gift" **b** (*fig*) *ideas* bezeichnen; (*pej*) abstempeln; **to ~ sb (as) sth** jdn als etw abstempeln; **he got himself ~led** (*Brit*) *or* ~**ed** (*US*) **as a troublemaker** er brachte sich (*dat*) den Ruf eines Unruhestifters ein

labia ['leɪbɪə] *pl of* **labium**

labial ['leɪbɪəl] **ADJ** (*Anat, Phon*) labial, Lippen-; ~ **sound** Labial- *or* Lippenlaut **N** (*Phon*) Labial- *or* Lippenlaut *m*

labiodental [ˌleɪbɪəʊ'dentəl] (*Phon*) **ADJ** labiodental **N** Labiodental *m*

labium ['leɪbɪəm] N *pl* **labia** (*Anat*) Schamlippe *f*, Labium *nt* (*spec*)

labor *etc* (*US*) = **labour** *etc* **labor union** (*US*) Gewerkschaft *f*

LABOR DAY

Labor Day ist ein gesetzlicher Feiertag in den USA und Kanada, der jeweils am ersten Montag im September begangen wird. 1894 führte der US-Kongress diesen nationalen Tag der Arbeit zu Ehren der Werktätigen ein, nachdem Arbeiter zwölf Jahre lang einen solchen Tag eingefordert hatten. Heute hat **Labor Day** kaum noch politische Bedeutung, sondern gilt als eine schöne Gelegenheit, zum Abschluss des Sommers und vor Beginn der Schulzeit mit der ganzen Familie noch einmal einen Ausflug oder ein Picknick zu machen - das Verkehrschaos am **Labor Day** ist dementsprechend gefürchtet. Mitunter finden auch noch Paraden und Reden statt.

---

laboratory [lə'bɒrətəri, (*US*) 'læbrətɔːri] N Labor(atorium) *nt*; ~ **assistant** Laborant(in) *m(f)*; ~ **results** Laborwerte *pl*; **the project was abandoned at the** ~ **stage** das Projekt wurde im Versuchsstadium abgebrochen

laborious [lə'bɔːrɪəs] ADJ *task, undertaking* mühsam, mühselig; *style* schwerfällig, umständlich

laboriously [lə'bɔːrɪəslɪ] ADV mühsam; *speak* umständlich

labour, (*US*) **labor** ['leɪbə'] **N** **a** (= *work in general*) Arbeit *f*; (= *toil*) Anstrengung *f*, Mühe *f*; **after much** ~ **the job was at last completed** nach langen Mühen war die Arbeit endlich vollendet

b (= *task*) Aufgabe *f*; **it was a** ~ **of love** ich/er *etc* tat es aus Liebe zur Sache; **this biography is clearly a** ~ **of love** diese Biografie ist eindeutig mit viel Liebe zur Sache entstanden; **the** ~**s of Hercules** die Arbeiten *pl* des Herkules

c (*Jur*) → **hard labour**

d (= *persons*) Arbeiter *pl*, Arbeitskräfte *pl*; **to withdraw one's** ~ die Arbeit verweigern

e (*Brit Pol*) **Labour** die Labour Party; **this district is Labour** dies ist ein Labourbezirk

f (*Med*) Wehen *pl*; **to be in** ~ in den Wehen liegen, die Wehen haben; **to go into** ~ die Wehen bekommen

VT *point, subject* auswalzen, breittreten (*inf*); **I won't** ~ **the point** ich will nicht darauf herumreiten

VI **a** (*in fields etc*) arbeiten; (= *work hard*) sich abmühen (*at, with* mit); **they** ~**ed hard to get the house finished on time** sie gaben sich die größte Mühe, das Haus rechtzeitig fertig zu stellen; **to** ~ **for a cause** sich für eine Sache einsetzen; **to** ~ **under a misapprehension** sich einer Illusion (*dat*) hingeben; **to** ~ **under difficulties** mit Schwierigkeiten zu kämpfen haben **b** (= *move etc with effort or difficulty*) sich quälen; **the engine is** ~**ing** der Motor hört sich gequält an; (*in wrong gear*) der Motor läuft untertourig; **to** ~ **up a hill** sich einen Hügel hinaufquälen, mühsam den Berg hochkriechen; **his breathing became** ~**ed** er begann, schwer zu atmen

labour camp, (*US*) **labor camp** N Arbeitslager *nt*

Labour Day N der Tag der Arbeit

laboured, (*US*) **labored** ['leɪbəd] ADJ schwerfällig; *breathing* schwer

labourer, (*US*) **laborer** ['leɪbərə'] N (Hilfs)arbeiter(in) *m(f)*; (= *farm labourer*) Landarbeiter(in) *m(f)*; (= *day-labourer*) Tagelöhner(in) *m(f)*

labour exchange N (*dated Brit*) Arbeitsamt *nt*

labour force, (*US*) **labor force** N Arbeiterschaft *f*; (*of company*) Belegschaft *f*

labouring, (*US*) **laboring** ['leɪbərɪŋ] ADJ ~ **class** Arbeiterklasse *f*; ~ **job** Aushilfsjob *m*

labour-intensive, (*US*) **labor-intensive** [ˌleɪbərɪn'tensɪv] ADJ arbeitsintensiv

labourite ['leɪbəraɪt] N (*pej*) Labour-Anhänger *m*

labour, (*US*) **labor**: **labour market** N Arbeitsmarkt *m*; **labour movement** N Arbeiterbewegung *f*; **labour pains** PL Wehen *pl*

Labour Party N (*Brit*) Labour Party *f*

labour, (*US*) **labor**: **labour relations** PL die Beziehungen *pl* zwischen Unternehmern und Arbeitern *or* Gewerkschaften; **labour-saving** ADJ arbeitssparend; **labour shortage** N Arbeitskräftemangel *m*; **labour supply** N Angebot *nt* an Arbeitskräften; **labour ward** N (*Brit*) Kreißsaal *m*

Labrador ['læbrədɔː'] N Labradorhund *m*

laburnum [lə'bɜːnəm] N Goldregen *m*

labyrinth ['læbɪrɪnθ] N (*lit, fig*) Labyrinth *nt*

labyrinthine [ˌlæbɪ'rɪnθaɪn] ADJ labyrinthisch (*also fig*), labyrinthähnlich

lace [leɪs] **N** **a** (= *fabric*) Spitze *f*; (*as trimming*) Spitzenborte *f or* -besatz *m*; (*of gold, silver*) Tresse *f*, Litze *f*

b (*of shoe*) (Schuh)band *nt*, Schnürsenkel *m*

VT **a** *corset* schnüren; (*also* **lace up**) *shoe* zubinden; (*fig: also* **lace together**) *fingers* ineinander verschlingen

b **to** ~ **a drink** einen Schuss Alkohol in ein Getränk geben; **to** ~ **a drink with drugs/poison** Drogen/Gift in ein Getränk mischen; ~**d with brandy** mit einem Schuss Weinbrand; **a** ~**d drink** ein Getränk mit Schuss; **coffee** ~**d with cyanide** Kaffee, dem Zyanid beigemischt wurde

c (*fig*) *speech, conversation* würzen; **her comments were** ~**d with sarcasm/humour** (*Brit*) *or* **humor** (*US*) ihre Bemerkungen waren mit Sarkasmus/Humor gewürzt

VI (*shoes etc*) (zu)geschnürt werden

▶ **lace into** VI +*prep obj* **to lace into sb** (*verbally*) jdm eine Standpauke halten, jdn anschnauzen (*inf*); (*physically*) auf jdn losgehen, jdn verprügeln

▶ **lace up** **VT** *sep* (zu)schnüren **VI** geschnürt werden

lace: **lace-curtain** ADJ der Mittelklasse *or* Mittelschicht; **lace paper** N Papierspitzen *pl*, Spitzenpapier *nt*

lacerate ['læsəreɪt] VT **a** (*lit*) *hand, skin* verletzen; *clothes* aufreißen; (*by glass etc*) zerschneiden; (*by thorns*) zerkratzen, aufreißen; (*by claws, whip*) zerfetzen; **he** ~**d his arm** er zog sich (*dat*) tiefe Wunden am Arm zu; **she** ~**d her wrist with a razor-blade** sie schlitzte sich (*dat*) die Pulsadern mit einer Rasierklinge auf; **her knee was badly** ~**d** sie hatte tiefe Wunden am Knie **b** (*fig*) zutiefst verletzen

laceration [ˌlæsə'reɪʃən] N Verletzung *f*, Fleischwunde *f*; (= *tear*) Risswunde *f*; (*from blow*) Platzwunde *f*; (*from whip*) Striemen *m*; (*from glass*) Schnittwunde *f*; (*from claws etc*) Kratzwunde *f*

lace-up (shoe) ['leɪsʌp(ʃuː)] N Schnürschuh *m*

lacework ['leɪswɜːk] N (= *fabric*) Spitzenarbeit *f*, Spitzenmuster *nt*; (*of gold and silver*) Filigranmuster *nt*

lachrymose ['lækrɪməʊs] ADJ (*liter*) *person* weinerlich; *story, film etc* rührselig, ergreifend

lacing ['leɪsɪŋ] N (*of shoe*) Schnürsenkel *pl*, Schuhbänder *pl*; (*of corset*) Schnürung *f*; **uniforms with gold** ~ goldbetresste Uniformen *pl*; **tea with a** ~ **of rum** Tee *m* mit einem Schuss Rum

lack [læk] ⊙ 17.1 **N** Mangel *m*; **for** *or* **through** ~ **of sth** aus Mangel an etw (*dat*); **they failed for** *or* **through** ~ **of support** sie scheiterten, weil es ihnen an Unterstützung fehlte *or* mangelte; **though it wasn't for** *or* **of trying** nicht, dass er sich/ich mich *etc* nicht bemüht hätte; **there was a complete** ~ **of interest** es bestand überhaupt kein Interesse; **such was their** ~ **of confidence that ...** sie hatten so wenig Selbstbewusstsein, dass ...; ~ **of water/time** Wasser-/Zeitmangel *m*; **there is no** ~ **of money in that family** in dieser Familie fehlt es nicht an Geld; **there was no** ~ **of applicants** es bestand kein Mangel an Bewerbern, es fehlte nicht an Bewerbern

VT **they** ~ **the necessary equipment/talent** es fehlt ihnen an der notwendigen Ausrüstung/ am richtigen Talent; **we** ~ **time** uns fehlt die nötige Zeit

VI **a** **to be** ~**ing** fehlen; **his sense of humour**

lackadaisical – lamely

(*Brit*) *or* **humor** (*US*) **is sadly ~ing** mit seinem Sinn für Humor ist es nicht weit her; **innovation has been sadly ~ing throughout the project** es fehlte leider während des ganzen Projektes an Innovationen

b **he is ~ing in confidence** ihm fehlt es an Selbstvertrauen; **he is completely ~ing in any sort of decency** er besitzt überhaupt keinen Anstand; **I find her ~ing in humour** (*Brit*) *or* **humor** (*US*) ich vermisse an ihr den Humor; **I find him ~ing in intelligence** ich finde, er ist nicht besonders intelligent

c **he ~ed for nothing** es fehlte ihm an nichts

lackadaisical [ˌlækəˈdeɪzɪkəl] ADJ (= *lacking energy*) lustlos, desinteressiert; (= *careless*) nachlässig, lasch

lackey [ˈlækɪ] N (*lit, fig*) Lakai *m*

lacking [ˈlækɪŋ] ADJ **a** **to be found ~** sich nicht bewähren, der Sache (*dat*) nicht gewachsen sein; **they were not found ~** sie waren der Sache (*dat*) gewachsen **b** (*inf*) geistig minderbemittelt (*inf*), beschränkt

lacklustre, (*US*) **lackluster** [ˈlækˌlʌstə] ADJ *surface* stumpf, glanzlos; *eyes also* trübe; *style* farblos, langweilig

laconic [ləˈkɒnɪk] ADJ lakonisch; *prose, style* knapp

laconically [ləˈkɒnɪkəlɪ] ADV lakonisch; *write* knapp

lacquer [ˈlækə] N Lack *m*; (= *hair lacquer*) Haarspray *nt*; (= *nail lacquer*) Nagellack *m* VT lackieren; *hair* sprayen

lacquered [ˈlækəd] ADJ lackiert; *hair* gesprayt; **table** Lacktisch *m*

lacrimal gland [ˈlækrɪməlˈglænd] N Tränendrüse *f*

lacrosse [ləˈkrɒs] N Lacrosse *nt*

lactate [lækˈteɪt] VI Milch absondern, laktieren (*spec*)

lactation [lækˈteɪʃən] N Milchabsonderung *f*, Laktation *f* (*spec*); (= *period*) Stillzeit *f*, Laktationsperiode *f* (*spec*)

lactic acid [ˈlæktɪkˈæsɪd] N Milchsäure *f*

lacto-ovo-vegetarian [ˌlæktəʊˌəʊvəʊˌvedʒɪ-ˈtɛərɪən] N Lacto-ovo-Vegetarier(in) *m(f)*

lactose [ˈlæktəʊs] N Milchzucker *m*, Laktose *f*

lacuna [ləˈkjuːnə] N *pl* **-e** [ləˈkjuːniː] Lakune *f*

lacy [ˈleɪsɪ] ADJ (+*er*) Spitzen-; (= *like lace*) spitzenartig; **~ underwear** Spitzenunterwäsche *f*

lad [læd] N Junge *m*; (*in stable etc*) Bursche *m*; **young ~** junger Mann; **listen, ~** hör mir mal zu, mein Junge!; **when I was a ~** als ich ein junger Bursche war; **he's only a ~** er ist (doch) noch jung, er ist (doch) noch ein Junge; **a simple country ~** ein einfacher Bauernjunge, ein einfacher Junge vom Land; **all together, ~s, push!** alle Mann anschieben!, alle zusammen, Jungs, anschieben!; **he's a bit of a ~** (*inf*) er ist ein ziemlicher Draufgänger; **he's one of the ~s** (*Brit inf*) er gehört dazu; **he likes a night out with the ~s** (*Brit inf*) er geht gern mal mit seinen Kumpels weg (*inf*)

ladder [ˈlædə] N **a** Leiter *f* **b** (*fig*) (Stufen)leiter *f*; **to be at the top/bottom of the ~** ganz oben/unten auf der Leiter stehen; **evolutionary ~** Leiter *f* der Evolution; **social ~** Leiter *f* des gesellschaftlichen Erfolges; **to move up the social/career ~** gesellschaftlich/beruflich aufsteigen; **to move up the housing ~** ein anspruchsvolleres Haus kaufen; **it's a first step up the ~** das ist ein Anfang; **a big step up the ~** ein großer Schritt nach vorn → **top** **c** (*Brit: in stocking*) Laufmasche *f* VT (*Brit*) *stocking* zerreißen; **I've ~ed my tights** ich habe mir eine Laufmasche (in meiner Strumpfhose) geholt VI (*Brit: stocking*) Laufmaschen bekommen

ladderproof [ˈlædəpruːf] ADJ maschenfest, laufmaschensicher

ladder tournament N (*Sport*) Ranglistenturnier *nt*

laddie [ˈlædɪ] N (*esp Scot inf*) Junge *m*, Bub *m* (*S Ger, Aus, Sw*)

laddish [ˈlædɪʃ] ADJ (*Brit inf*) machohaft (*inf*)

lade [leɪd] *pret* **laded**, *ptp* **laden** VT *ship* beladen; *cargo* verladen VI Ladung übernehmen *or* an Bord nehmen

laden [ˈleɪdn] ADJ (*lit, fig*) beladen (**with** mit); **bushes ~ with flowers** blütenschwere Büsche *pl*

la-di-da [ˌlɑːdiːˈdɑː] ADJ, ADV (*inf*) affektiert, affig (*inf*)

ladies' fingers [ˈleɪdɪzˌfɪŋgəz] PL Okra *f*

ladies' man [ˈleɪdɪzmæn] N Charmeur *m*, Frauenheld *m*; **he's a bit of a ~** er wirkt auf Frauen

lading [ˈleɪdɪŋ] N (= *act*) Verladen *nt*; (= *cargo*) Ladung *f*

ladle [ˈleɪdl] N (Schöpf- *or* Suppen)kelle *f*, Schöpflöffel *m* VT schöpfen; **he's ladling money into the business** er steckt *or* pumpt massenhaft Geld in das Geschäft

▶ **ladle out** VT *sep soup etc, money* austeilen

ladleful [ˈleɪdlfʊl] N **one ~** eine Kelle (voll); **each pan holds ten ~s** in jeden Topf passt der Inhalt von zehn Schöpfkellen

lady [ˈleɪdɪ] N **a** Dame *f*; **"Ladies"** (= *lavatory*) „Damen"; **where is the ladies** *or* **the ladies' room?** wo ist die Damentoilette?; **ladies and gentlemen!** sehr geehrte Damen und Herren!, meine Damen und Herren!; **ladies, ...** meine Damen, ...; **~ of the house** Dame *f* des Hauses; **the minister and his ~** der Minister und seine Gattin; **your good ~** (*hum, form*) Ihre Frau Gemahlin (*hum, form*); **the old ~** (*inf, = mother*) die alte Dame (*inf*); (= *wife*) meine/deine/seine Alte (*inf*) *or* Olle (*N Ger inf*); **a little old ~** eine alte Dame (*inf*); **young ~** junge Dame; (*scoldingly*) mein Fräulein; **his young ~** seine Freundin; **she's no ~** sie ist keine Dame; **ladies' bicycle** Damen(fahr)rad *nt* **b** (= *noble*) Adlige *f*; **Lady** (*as a title*) Lady *f*; **dinner is served, my ~** es ist angerichtet, Mylady *or* gnädige Frau; **to live like a ~** wie eine große Dame leben **c** **Our Lady** die Jungfrau Maria, Unsere Liebe Frau; **Church of Our Lady** (Lieb)frauenkirche *f*

lady: ladybird, (*US*) **ladybug** N Marienkäfer *m*; **Lady Chapel** N Marienkapelle *f*; **Lady Day** N (*Brit*) Mariä Verkündigung *no art*; **lady doctor** N Ärztin *f*; **ladyfinger** N (*US*) Löffelbiskuit *nt*; **lady friend** N Dame *f*; **lady-in-waiting** N Ehrendame *f*, Hofdame *f*; **lady-killer** N (*inf*) Herzensbrecher *m*; **ladylike** ADJ **it's not ~** es ist nicht ladylike, es gehört sich nicht für eine Dame; **ladylove** N (*old*) Geliebte *f*, Feinsliebchen *nt* (*old*); **lady mayoress** N *Titel der Frau des Lord Mayor*, Frau *f* (Ober)bürgermeister (*dated*); **ladyship** N **Her/Your Ladyship** Ihre Ladyschaft; **certainly, Your Ladyship** gewiss, Euer Gnaden; **lady's maid** N (Kammer)zofe *f*

lag¹ [læg] N (= *time-lag*) Zeitabstand *m*, Zeitdifferenz *f*; (= *delay*) Verzögerung *f*; **there is too much of a ~** es vergeht zu viel Zeit; **after a ~ of six months** nach sechs Monaten, nachdem sechs Monate vergangen *or* verstrichen waren; **there was a ~ of six months between buying the house and moving in** das Haus konnte erst sechs Monate nach dem Kauf bezogen werden; **the cultural ~ is very apparent** der kulturelle Rückstand ist offensichtlich VI (*time*) langsam vergehen, dahinkriechen; (*in pace*) zurückbleiben

▶ **lag behind** VI zurückbleiben; **we lag behind in space exploration** in der Raumforschung liegen wir (weit) zurück *or* hinken wir hinterher (*inf*); **the government is lagging behind in the polls** die Regierung liegt in den Meinungsumfragen zurück; **why don't you walk beside me instead of always lagging behind?** warum läufst du nicht neben mir, anstatt immer hinterherzutrödeln?; **they are lagging ten points behind** sie liegen zehn Punkte zurück

lag² VT *boiler, pipe* umwickeln, isolieren

lag³ N (*inf: also* **old lag**) (ehemaliger) Knacki (*inf*)

lager [ˈlɑːgə] N helles Bier; **a glass of ~** ein (Glas) Helles

lager lout N (*Brit, inf*) betrunkener Rowdy; (*causing damage also*) betrunkener Randalierer

laggard [ˈlægəd] N (= *sb who has fallen behind*) Nachzügler(in) *m(f)*; (= *idler*) Trödler(in) *m(f)*; **he is a ~ in love** (*liter, hum*) er ist nicht so stürmisch ADJ *student, worker* faul

lagging [ˈlægɪŋ] N Isolierschicht *f*; (= *material*) Isoliermaterial *nt*

lagoon [ləˈguːn] N Lagune *f*

lah-di-dah [ˌlɑːdiːˈdɑː] ADJ, ADV (*inf*) = **la-di-da**

laid [leɪd] *pret, ptp of* **lay⁴**

laid-back [ˌleɪdˈbæk] ADJ (*inf*) gelassen, cool (*inf*)

lain [leɪn] *ptp* → **lie²**

lair [lɛə] N Lager *nt*; (= *cave*) Höhle *f*; (= *den*) Bau *m*

laird [lɛəd] N (*Scot*) Gutsherr(in) *m(f)*

laissez faire [ˈleɪseɪˈfɛə] N Laisser-faire *nt*; **there's too much ~ here** hier geht es zu leger zu

laissez-faire [ˈleɪseɪˈfɛə] ADJ (*Econ*) Laisser-faire-; (*fig*) leger, lax; **~ economics** Laisser-faire-Wirtschaftspolitik *f*

laity [ˈleɪɪtɪ] N **a** (= *laymen*) Laienstand *m*, Laien *pl* **b** (= *those outside a profession*) Laien *pl*

lake¹ [leɪk] N See *m*

lake² N (*colour*) Karm(es)inrot *nt*

lake: Lake District N Lake District *m* (*Seengebiet im NW Englands*); **lake dweller** N Pfahlbaubewohner(in) *m(f)*; **lake dwelling** N Pfahlbau *m*; **Lake Poets** PL *Dichter des Lake District*: Wordsworth, Coleridge, Southey; **lakeside** N Seeufer *nt* ATTR am See

la-la land [ˈlɑːlɑːlænd] N (*esp US inf*) Bezeichnung für Los Angeles, insbesondere Hollywood **to be in ~** (*inf*) ganz weit weg sein

lallygag [ˈlælɪgæg] VI (*dated US sl*) = **lollygag**

lam¹ [læm] (*sl*) VT vermöbeln (*inf*) VI **to ~ into sb** jdn zur Schnecke machen (*inf*); (*physically*) auf jdn eindreschen (*inf*)

lam² N (*US sl*) **he's on the ~** hinter dem sind sie her (*inf*); **to go on the ~** türmen (*inf*), die Fliege machen (*sl*); **he took it on the ~** er türmte (*inf*), er machte die Fliege (*sl*)

lama [ˈlɑːmə] N (*Rel*) Lama *m*

lamb [læm] N **a** (= *young sheep*) Lamm *nt* **b** (= *meat*) Lamm(fleisch) *nt* **c** (= *person*) Engel *m*; **the little ~s** (*children*) die lieben Kleinen; **you poor ~!** du armes Lämmchen!; **she took it like a ~** sie ertrug es geduldig wie ein Lamm; **he followed her like a ~** er folgte ihr wie ein Lamm; **like a ~ to the slaughter** wie das Lamm zur Schlachtbank, wie ein Opferlamm **d** **the Lamb of God** das Lamm Gottes VI lammen; **the ~ing season** die Lammungszeit

lambast [læmˈbæst], **lambaste** [læmˈbeɪst] VT fertig machen (*inf*); **to ~ sb for sth** es jdm wegen etw tüchtig geben (*inf*)

lamb: lamb chop N Lammkotelett *nt*; **lamblike** ADJ lammfromm, sanft wie ein Lamm; **lambskin** N Lammfell *nt*; **lamb's lettuce** N Feldsalat *m*; **lamb's tail** N (*Bot*) Haselkätzchen *nt*; **lambswool** N Lammwolle *f*

lame [leɪm] ADJ (+*er*) **a** lahm; (*as result of stroke etc*) gelähmt; **to be ~ in one leg** auf einem Bein lahm sein; **the animal was ~** das Tier war lahm; **the horse went ~** das Pferd fing an zu lahmen **b** (*fig*) *excuse* lahm, faul; *argument* schwach, wenig überzeugend; *metre* holprig VT lähmen; *horse* lahm machen

lamé [ˈlɑːmeɪ] N Lamé *nt*

lame duck N Niete *f* (*inf*); **~ company** unwirtschaftliche Firma

lamella [ləˈmelə] N *pl* **-lae** *or* **-las** Lamelle *f*

lamely [ˈleɪmlɪ] ADV *argue, say etc* lahm; **to walk ~** lahmen; (*horse*) lahmen; **he limped ~ into the room** er humpelte ins Zimmer; **~ he mumbled an excuse** er murmelte eine lahme Entschuldigung vor sich hin

lameness ['leɪmnɪs] N **a** Lähmung f (*in, of* +*gen*); **his ~** sein Gelähmtsein *nt* **b** (*fig*) (*of excuse*) Lahmheit f; (*of argument*) Schwäche f, mangelnde Überzeugungskraft

lament [lə'ment] N **a** Klagen *pl*, (Weh)klage f; **in ~** (weh)klagend **b** (*Liter, Mus*) Klagelied *nt* ▶VT beklagen; *misfortune etc also* bejammern; **to ~ sb** jds Tod beklagen, um jdn trauern; **it is much to be ~ed that ...** es ist sehr zu beklagen, dass ...; **to ~ the fact that ...** die Tatsache bedauern, dass ...; **what will become of me now?, he ~ed** was soll nun aus mir werden?, klagte *or* jammerte er ▶VI (weh)klagen; **to ~ for sb** um jdn trauern; **to ~ over sth** über etw (*acc*) jammern, etw bejammern *or* beklagen; **to ~ over one's lost youth** über seine verlorene Jugend trauern; **she ~ed over his dead body** sie wehklagte über seinem Leichnam

lamentable ['læməntəbl] ADJ beklagenswert; *piece of work* jämmerlich schlecht, erbärmlich

lamentably ['læməntəblɪ] ADV erbärmlich, beklagenswert; **he failed ~** er scheiterte kläglich; **~, this idea is not practicable** bedauerlicherweise lässt sich diese Idee nicht verwirklichen; **she was ~ ignorant of politics** es war traurig *or* zum Weinen, wie wenig sie von Politik wusste; **the level of their commitment is ~ low** es ist jämmerlich, wie wenig sie sich engagieren; **there are ~ few female surgeons** es gibt immer noch beklagenswert wenige Chirurginnen

lamentation [,læmən'teɪʃən] N (Weh)klage f; (= *act*) Klagen *nt*, Jammern *nt*; (= *poem, song*) Klagelied *nt*; **he cried out with ~** er brach in lautes Wehklagen aus

laminated ['læmɪneɪtɪd] ADJ geschichtet; *card, book cover* laminiert; **~ glass** Verbundglas *nt*; **~ wood** Sperrholz *nt*; **~ plastic** Resopal® *nt*; **~ working surfaces** Arbeitsflächen aus Resopal®

lamp [læmp] N Lampe f; (*in street*) Laterne f; (*Aut, Rail*) Scheinwerfer *m*; (= *rear lamp*) Rücklicht *nt*; (= *torch*) Taschenlampe f; (= *sun lamp*) Höhensonne f

lamp: lampblack N Farbruß *m*; **lamp bracket** N Lampenhalterung f; **lamp chimney, lamp glass** N Zylinder *m*; **lamplight** N Lampenlicht *nt*, Schein *m* der Lampe(n); (*in street*) Licht *nt* der Laterne(n); **by ~** bei Lampenlicht; **in the ~** im Schein der Lampe(n); **lamplighter** N Laternenanzünder *m*

lampoon [læm'puːn] N Spott- *or* Schmähschrift f ▶VT verspotten, verhöhnen

lamppost ['læmppəʊst] N Laternenpfahl *m*

lamprey ['læmprɪ] N Neunauge *nt*, Bricke f; (= *sea lamprey*) Lamprete f

lamp: lampshade N Lampenschirm *m*; **lamp standard** N = lamppost

LAN [læn] (*Comput*) abbr of **local area network** LAN *nt*

lance [lɑːns] N Lanze f ▶VT (*Med*) öffnen, aufschneiden

lance corporal N Obergefreite(r) *mf*

lancer ['lɑːnsə'] N (*Mil Hist*) Lanzenreiter, Ulan *m*

lancers ['lɑːnsəz] PL *sing* (= *dance*) Lancier *m*, Quadrille f

lancet ['lɑːnsɪt] N (*Med*) Lanzette f

lancet arch N (*Archit*) Spitzbogen *m*

lancet window N (*Archit*) Spitzbogenfenster *nt*

Lancs [læŋks] abbr of **Lancashire**

land [lænd] N **a** (= *not sea*) Land *nt*; **by ~** auf dem Landwege; **by ~ and sea** zu Land und zu Wasser; **as they approached ~** als sie sich dem Land näherten; **to see how the ~ lies** (*lit*) das Gelände erkunden *or* auskundschaften; (*fig*) die Lage sondieren *or* peilen; **the lay *or* lie of the ~** (*lit*) die Beschaffenheit des Geländes; **until I've seen the lay *or* lie of the ~** (*fig*) bis ich die Lage sondiert habe; **for ~'s sake** (*US, inf*) um Himmels willen → **dry land** **b** (= *nation, region: also fig*) Land *nt*; **to be in the ~ of the living** unter den Lebenden sein;

the ~ of opportunity (= *USA*) das Land der unbegrenzten Möglichkeiten **c** (*as property*) Grund und Boden *m*; (= *estates*) Ländereien *pl*; **to own ~** Land besitzen; **she's bought a piece of ~** sie hat ein Stück Land *or* (*for building*) ein Grundstück gekauft; **get off my ~!** verschwinden Sie von meinem Grundstück *or* von meinem Grund und Boden! **d** (*Agr*) Land *nt*; (= *soil*) Boden *m*; **to return to the ~** zur Scholle zurückkehren; **to work on the ~** das Land bebauen; **the drift from the ~** die Landflucht; **to live off the ~** (= *grow own food*) sich vom Lande ernähren, von den Früchten des Landes leben (*liter*); (= *forage*) sich aus der Natur ernähren ▶VT **a** (*Naut*) *passengers* absetzen, von Bord gehen lassen; *troops* landen; *goods* an Land bringen, löschen; *fish at port* anlanden; *boat* an Land ziehen; **he ~ed the boat on the beach** er zog das Boot an den Strand **b** (*Aviat*) *passengers* absetzen, von Bord gehen lassen; *troops* landen; *goods* abladen; **to ~ a plane** (mit einem Flugzeug) landen; **the helicopter ~ed a doctor on the ship** der Hubschrauber setzte einen Arzt auf dem Schiff ab; **scientists will ~ a space probe on the moon** Wissenschaftler werden eine Raumsonde auf dem Mond landen **c** *fish on hook* an Land ziehen **d** (*inf*: = *obtain*) kriegen (*inf*); *contract* sich (*dat*) verschaffen; *prize* (sich *dat*) holen (*inf*); *job* an Land ziehen (*inf*); **she finally ~ed him** sie hat sich (*dat*) ihn schließlich geangelt (*inf*) **e** (*Brit inf*) *blow* landen (*inf*); **he ~ed him one, he ~ed him a punch on the jaw** er versetzte ihm *or* landete bei ihm einen Kinnhaken **f** (*inf*: = *place*) bringen; *behaviour* (*Brit*) *or* *behavior* (*US*) **like that will ~ you in trouble/jail** bei einem solchen Betragen wirst du noch mal Ärger bekommen/im Gefängnis landen; **it ~ed me in a mess** dadurch bin ich in einen ganz schönen Schlamassel (*inf*) geraten *or* gekommen; **I've ~ed myself in a real mess** ich bin (ganz schön) in die Klemme geraten (*inf*); **his attitude ~ed him in trouble** durch seine Einstellung handelte er sich (*dat*) Ärger ein; **buying the house ~ed him in debt** durch den Kauf des Hauses verschuldete er sich; **being overdrawn could ~ you with big bank charges** wenn man sein Konto überzieht, kann einen das hohe Bankgebühren kosten **g** (*inf*, = *lumber*) **to ~ sb with sth** jdm etw aufhalsen (*inf*) *or* andrehen (*inf*); **I got ~ed with the job** man hat mir die Arbeit aufgehalst (*inf*); **I got ~ed with him for two hours** ich hatte ihn zwei Stunden lang auf dem Hals ▶VI **a** (*from ship*) an Land gehen **b** (*Aviat*) (*bird, insect*) landen, sich setzen; **as it ~ed** (*Aviat*) bei der Landung; **we're coming in to ~** wir setzen zur Landung an **c** (= *fall, be placed, strike*) landen; **the bomb ~ed on the building** die Bombe fiel auf das Gebäude; **to ~ on one's feet** (*lit*) auf den Füßen landen; (*fig*) auf die Füße fallen; **to ~ on one's head** auf dem Kopf fallen; **he ~ed awkwardly** er ist ungeschickt aufgekommen *or* gelandet (*inf*)

▶ **land up** VI (*inf*) landen (*inf*); **you'll land up in trouble** du wirst noch mal Ärger bekommen; **I landed up with nothing** ich hatte schließlich nichts mehr

land agent N Gutsverwalter(in) *m(f)*

land army N Landstreitkräfte *pl*

landau ['lændɔ:] N Landauer *m*

land: land-based ADJ *missiles, aircraft* landgestützt; **land breeze** N Landwind *m*; **land defences,** (*US*) **land defenses** PL Landwehr f; **land development** N Erschließung f von Bauland

landed ['lændɪd] ADJ **the ~ class** die Großgrundbesitzer *pl*; **~ gentry** Landadel *m*; **~ property** Grundbesitz *m*

land: landfall N Sichten *nt* von Land; (= *land sighted*) gesichtetes Land; **to make ~** Land sichten; **landfill (site)** N Mülldeponie f; **land forces** PL Landstreitkräfte *pl*; **landholder** N

(= *land-owner*) Grundbesitzer(in) *m(f)*; (= *tenant*) Pächter(in) *m(f)*

landing ['lændɪŋ] N **a** (*Naut*) (*of person*) Landung f; (*of ship*) Anlegen *nt*, Landung f; (*of goods*) Löschen *nt* **b** (*Aviat*) Landung f **c** (*on stairs, inside house*) Flur *m*, Gang *m*; (*outside flat door*) Treppenabsatz *m*; (*corridor outside flat doors*) Gang *m*, Etagenabsatz *m*

landing: landing approach N (*Aviat*) Landeanflug *m*; **landing card** N Einreisekarte f; **landing craft** N Landungsboot *nt*; **landing field** N Landeplatz *m*; **landing gear** N Fahrgestell *nt*; **landing net** N Käscher *m*, Kescher *m*; **landing party** N Landetrupp *m*; **landing place** N (*Naut*) Anlegeplatz *m*; **landing stage** N (*Naut*) Landesteg *m*, Landungsbrücke f; **landing strip** N Landebahn f; **landing wheels** PL (*Lauf*)räder *pl*

land: landlady N (*of land*) Grundbesitzerin f; (*of flat etc*) Vermieterin f, Hauswirtin f; (*of pub*) Wirtin f; **~!** Frau Wirtin!; **land law** N Bodenrecht *nt*; **landless** ADJ landlos; **land line** N (*Telec*) Landkabel *nt*; **landlocked** ADJ von Land eingeschlossen; **a ~ country** ein Land *nt* ohne Zugang zum Meer, ein Binnenstaat *m*; **landlord** N (*of land*) Grundbesitzer *m*; (*of flat etc*) Vermieter *m*, Hauswirt *m*; (*of pub*) Wirt *m*; **~!** Herr Wirt!; **landlubber** ['lændlʌbə'] N Landratte f (*inf*); **landmark** N (*Naut*) Landmarke f; (= *boundary mark*) Grenzstein *m*, Grenzpfahl *m*; (= *well-known thing*) Wahrzeichen *nt*; (*fig*) Meilenstein *m*, Markstein *m*; **landmass** N Landmasse f; **land mine** N Landmine f; **land office** N (*US*) Grundbuchamt *nt*; **to do a land-office business** (*inf*) ein Bombengeschäft machen (*inf*); **landowner** N Grundbesitzer(in) *m(f)*; **landowning** ADJ attr mit Grundbesitz; **the ~ class** die Grundbesitzer *pl*; **land reform** N Boden(rechts)reform f; **land register** N (*Brit*) Grundbuch *nt*; **land route** N Landweg *m*; **by ~** auf dem Landweg; **landscape** ['lændskeɪp] N Landschaft f; (*Art also*) Landschaftsbild *nt* ▶VT *big area, natural park* landschaftlich gestalten; *garden, grounds* gärtnerisch gestalten, anlegen; **landscape architect** N Landschaftsarchitekt(in) *m(f)*; **landscape gardener** N (*for big areas etc*) Landschaftsgärtner(in) *m(f)*; (*for gardens etc*) Gartengestalter(in) *m(f)*; **landscape gardening** N Landschaftsgärtnerei *or* -gestaltung f, Gartengestaltung f; **landslide** N (*lit, fig*) Erdrutsch *m*; **a ~ victory** ein überwältigender Sieg, ein Erdrutschsieg *m*; **landslip** N Erdrutsch *m*; **land tax** N Grundsteuer f; **landward** ADJ *view* zum (Fest)land; **they were sailing in a ~ direction** sie fuhren in Richtung Land *or* auf das Land zu; **on the ~ side** auf der Landseite, auf der dem Land zugekehrten Seite; **landward(s)** ADV landwärts; **to landward** in Richtung Land

lane [leɪn] N (*in country*) (*for walking*) (Feld)weg *m*; (*for driving*) Sträßchen *nt*; (*in town*) Gasse f, Weg *m*; (*Sport*) Bahn f; (*on road*) Spur f; (= *shipping lane*) Schifffahrtsweg *m* *or* -linie f; (= *air lane*) (Flug)route f, Luftstraße f; **in the left-hand ~** (*Aut*) in *or* auf der linken Spur; **~ markings** (*on road*) Spurmarkierungen *pl*; **"get in ~"** „einordnen"

language ['læŋgwɪdʒ] N Sprache f; **the English ~** Englisch *nt*, die englische Sprache; **a book on ~** ein Buch über die Sprache; **philosophy of ~** Sprachphilosophie f; **the ~ of business/diplomacy** die Sprache der Geschäftswelt/Diplomatie; **the ~ of flowers** die Blumensprache; **to study ~s** Sprachen studieren; **your ~ is appalling** deine Ausdrucksweise ist entsetzlich, du drückst dich entsetzlich aus; **that's no ~ to use to your mother!** so spricht man nicht mit seiner Mutter!; **it's a bloody nuisance! – ~!** verfluchter Mist! – na, so was sagt man doch nicht!; **bad ~** Kraftausdrücke *pl*; **strong ~** Schimpfwörter *pl*, derbe Ausdrücke *pl*; (= *forceful language*) starke Worte *pl*; **he used strong ~, calling them fascist pigs** er beschimpfte sie als Faschistenschweine; **the request/complaint was put in rather strong ~** die Aufforderung/Beschwerde hörte sich ziemlich krass an; **putting it in plain ~ ...** (= *simply*) einfach ausgedrückt ...; (= *bluntly*) um es ganz direkt *or* ohne Umschweife zu sagen, ...; **to talk sb's ~** jds Sprache sprechen; **to talk the same ~ (as sb)** die gleiche Sprache (wie jd) sprechen

language: language barrier N Sprachbarriere *f*; **language course** N Sprachkurs(us) *m*; **language lab(oratory)** N Sprachlabor *nt*; **language learning** N Sprachenlernen *nt*; **language-learning** ADJ *facilities, skills* zum Sprachenlernen; **language teacher** N Sprachlehrer(in) *m(f)*

languid ['læŋgwɪd] ADJ träge; *gesture* müde, matt; *manner* lässig, gelangweilt; *walk* lässig, schlendernd; *voice* müde

languidly ['læŋgwɪdlɪ] ADV träge, lässig; **is that all? she said ~** ist das alles?, sagte sie gelangweilt; **the model posed ~ against the sofa** das Modell lehnte sich in einer lässigen Pose gegen das Sofa; **~ she waved to the crowd** mit einer müden *or* matten Geste winkte sie der Menge zu; **the chords build up slowly and ~** die Akkorde bauen sich langsam und schleppend auf

languidness ['læŋgwɪdnɪs] N Trägheit *f*; (*of gesture*) Mattigkeit *f*; (*of manner*) Lässigkeit *f*; **the ~ of her voice** ihre müde Stimme

languish ['læŋgwɪʃ] VI schmachten; (*flowers*) dahinwelken; (= *pine*) sich sehnen (*for* nach); **he ~ed in prison for months** er schmachtete monatelang im Gefängnis; **the panda merely ~ed in its new home** der Panda wurde in seiner neuen Heimat immer apathischer *or* stumpfer; **the child ~ed during his mother's absence** das Kind verzehrte sich nach seiner Mutter (*geh*); **the products ~ on the shelves** die Waren bleiben in den Regalen liegen; **I ~ without you, he wrote** ich verzehre mich vor Sehnsucht nach dir, schrieb er

languishing ['læŋgwɪʃɪŋ] ADJ schmachtend

languor ['læŋgə'] N (= *indolence*) Trägheit *f*, Schläfrigkeit *f*; (= *weakness*) Mattigkeit *f*, Schlappheit *f*; (*emotional*) Stumpfheit *f*, Apathie *f*

languorous ['læŋgərəs] ADJ träge, schläfrig; *heat* schläfrig, wohlig; *feeling* wohlig; *music* schmelzend; *rhythm, metre* gleitend, getragen; *tone, voice* schläfrig; **a ~ beauty** eine schwüle Schönheit

languorously ['læŋgərəslɪ] ADV träge; *speak* mit schläfriger Stimme; **the soft, ~ sentimental mood of the poem** die weiche, schwül-sentimentale Stimmung des Gedichts; **she stretched out ~** sie räkelte *or* rekelte sich verführerisch

langur [l(ae)ŋ'guə'] N (*Zool*) Langur *m*

lank [læŋk] ADJ *person, body* dürr, hager; *hair* strähnig, kraftlos; *grass* dürr, mager

lanky ['læŋkɪ] ADJ (+*er*) schlaksig N (*inf*) Lange(r) *mf* (*inf*)

lanolin(e) ['lænəʊlɪn] N Lanolin *nt*

lantern ['læntən] N (*also Archit*) Laterne *f* → **Chinese lantern**

lantern: lantern-jawed ADJ hohlwangig; **lantern slide** N Glasdiapositiv *nt*, Lichtbild *nt*

lanyard ['lænjəd] N (= *cord*) Kordel *f* (*an der Pfeife oder Messer getragen wird*); (*Naut*) Taljereep *nt*

Laos [laʊs] N Laos *nt*

Laotian ['laʊʃən] ADJ laotisch N Laote *m*, Laotin *f*

lap¹ [læp] N Schoß *m*; **in** *or* **on her ~** auf dem/ihrem Schoß; **his opponent's mistake dropped victory into his ~** durch den Fehler seines Gegners fiel ihm der Sieg in den Schoß; **it's in the ~ of the gods** es liegt im Schoß der Götter; **to live in the ~ of luxury** ein Luxusleben führen

lap² N Überlappung *f* VT (= *overlap*) überlappen VI sich überlappen

lap³ VT (= *wrap*) wickeln

lap⁴ (*Sport*) N (= *round*) Runde *f*; (*fig*: = *stage*) Etappe *f*, Strecke *f*, Abschnitt *m*; **his time for the first ~** seine Zeit in der ersten Runde; **on the second ~** in der zweiten Runde; **~ of hon-**

our (*esp Brit*) Ehrenrunde *f*; **we're on the last ~ now** (*fig*) wir haben es bald geschafft VT überrunden VI to ~ **at 90 mph** mit einer Geschwindigkeit von 90 Meilen pro Stunde seine Runden drehen; **he's ~ping at 58 seconds** (*athlete*) er läuft die Runde in einer Zeit von 58 Sekunden

lap⁵ N (= *lick*) Schlecken *nt*, Lecken *nt*; (*of waves*) Klatschen *nt*, Schlagen *nt*, Plätschern *nt* VT a (= *lick*) lecken, schlecken b **the waves ~ped the shore** die Wellen rollten *or* plätscherten an das Ufer VI (*waves, water*) plätschern (*against an* +*acc*), klatschen (*against* gegen); **to ~ over sth** schwappen über etw (*acc*)

▶ **lap up** VT *sep* a *liquid* auflecken, aufschlecken, aufschlabbern (*inf*); **the children hungrily lapped up their soup** die Kinder löffelten hungrig ihre Suppe b *praise, compliments, sunshine* genießen; **she lapped it up** das ging ihr runter wie Honig (*inf*); **he lapped up the compliments** die Komplimente gingen ihm wie Honig runter (*inf*); **the media are lapping up this latest scandal** die Medien haben sich gierig auf diesen neuesten Skandal gestürzt

laparoscopy [‚læpə'rɒskəpɪ] N Laparoskopie *f*

laparotomy [‚læpə'rɒtəmɪ] N Laparotomie *f*

lap: lap belt N Beckengurt *m*; **lap dancer** N Tänzerin, die über dem Schoß einen Zuschauers einen provokativen Striptease aufführt; **lap dancing** N *provokativer Striptease, bei dem die Tänzerin über dem Schoß eines Zuschauers tanzt*; **lapdog** N Schoßhund *m*

lapel [lə'pel] N Aufschlag *m*, Revers *nt* or *m*

lapidary ['læpɪdərɪ] ADJ ~ **art** (Edel)steinschneidekunst *f*; ~ **inscription** in Stein gehauene Inschrift N Steinschneider(in) *m(f)*

lapis lazuli ['læpɪs'læzjʊlaɪ] N Lapislazuli *m*

Lapland ['læplænd] N Lappland *nt*

Laplander ['læplændə'], **Lapp** [læp] N Lappländer(in) *m(f)*, Lappe *m*, Lappin *f*

Lapp [læp] N a = **Laplander** b = **Lappish**

lapping ['læpɪŋ] N (*of water*) Plätschern *nt*, Schlagen *nt*

Lappish ['læpɪʃ] N Lappländisch *nt*, Lappisch *nt*

lap robe N (*US*) Reisedecke *f*

lapse [læps] N a (= *error*) Fehler *m*; (*moral*) Fehltritt *m*, Verfehlung *f*; ~ **of judgement** Fehlurteil *nt*; **he had a momentary ~ of concentration** seine Konzentration ließ einen Augenblick nach; **to suffer from ~s of memory** *or* **memory ~s** an Gedächtnisschwäche leiden; ~ **of taste** Geschmacksverirrung *f*; **a serious security** = an schwerer Verstoß gegen die Sicherheitsvorkehrungen

b (= *decline*) Absinken *nt no pl*, Abgleiten *nt no pl*; **a ~ in confidence** ein Vertrauensschwund *m*; ~ **in standards** Niveauabfall *m*; **he noticed her ~ into German** ihm fiel auf, dass sie ins Deutsche verfiel

c (= *expiry*) Ablauf *m*; (*of claim*) Verfall *m*, Erlöschen *nt*; (= *cessation*) Aussterben *nt*, Schwinden *nt*

d (*of time*) Zeitspanne *f*, Zeitraum *m*; **time ~** Zeitspanne *f*, Zeitraum *m*; **after a ~ of 4 months** nach (einem Zeitraum von) 4 Monaten; **there was a ~ in the conversation** es gab eine Gesprächspause

VI a (= *make mistake*) einen Fehler begehen, etwas falsch machen; (*morally*) fehlen (*liter*), einen Fehltritt begehen, Unrecht tun; **to ~ from one's faith** von seinem Glauben abfallen, seinem Glauben abtrünnig werden

b (= *decline*) verfallen (*into* in +*acc*), abgleiten (*from sth into sth* von etw in etw *acc*); **to ~ into one's old ways** wieder in seine alten Gewohnheiten verfallen; **he ~d into German/legal jargon** er verfiel ins Deutsche/in den Anwaltsjargon; **he ~d into silence** er versank in Schweigen; **he ~d into a coma** er sank in ein Koma; **he/his work is lapsing** er/seine Arbeit lässt nach, mit ihm/seiner Arbeit geht es bergab

c (= *expire*) ablaufen; (*claims*) verfallen, erlö-

schen; (= *cease to exist*) aussterben; (*friendship, correspondence*) einschlafen; **after two months have ~d** nach (Ablauf von) zwei Monaten

lapsed [læpst] ADJ *Catholic* abtrünnig, vom Glauben abgefallen; *insurance policy* abgelaufen, verfallen

lap time N (*Sport*) Rundenzeit *f*

laptop ['læptɒp] (*Comput*) N Laptop *m* ATTR Laptop-; ~ **PC/computer** Laptop(-PC/Computer) *m*

lapwing ['læpwɪŋ] N Kiebitz *m*

larboard ['lɑːbəd] (*old*) ADJ Backbord-; ~ **side** Backbordseite *f* N Backbord *nt*

larceny ['lɑːsənɪ] N (*Jur*) Diebstahl *m*

larch [lɑːtʃ] N (*also* **larch tree**) Lärche *f*; (= *wood*) Lärche(nholz *nt*) *f*

lard [lɑːd] N Schweineschmalz *nt* VT (*esp Brit*) mit Schweineschmalz bestreichen; (*with strips of bacon, fig*) spicken

larder ['lɑːdə'] N (*esp Brit*) (= *room*) Speisekammer *f*; (= *cupboard*) Speiseschrank *m*

lardy cake ['lɑːdɪkeɪk] N *Schmalzkuchen aus Brotteig mit Rosinen*

large [lɑːdʒ] ADJ (+*er*) a (= *big*) groß; *person* stark, korpulent; *meal* reichlich, groß; *list* lang; ~ **print** Großdruck *m*; **"large"** (*on clothing label*) „Large"; **I need a ~r size** ich brauche eine größere Größe; **he's a ~ landowner** er ist ein Großgrundbesitzer; **she looks as ~ as life in that photograph** sie sieht auf dem Foto aus, wie sie leibt und lebt; **there he/it was as ~ as life** da war er/es in voller Lebensgröße

b (= *extensive*) *interests, power* weitreichend, weit reichend, bedeutend; **his interests were on a ~ scale** er hatte weitreichende *or* breit gestreute Interessen; **taking the ~ view** global betrachtet

c (*old:* = *generous, tolerant*) großzügig; **a ~ understanding** ein großes Verständnis

ADV groß; **guilt was written ~ all over his face** die Schuld stand ihm deutlich im Gesicht geschrieben

N a **at ~** (= *in general*) im Großen und Ganzen, im Allgemeinen; **people** *or* **the world at ~** die Allgemeinheit; **he wanted to tell his story to the world at ~** er wollte der ganzen Welt seine Geschichte erzählen

b **to be at ~** (= *free*) frei herumlaufen

c **at ~** (= *in detail, at length*) ausführlich, lang und breit

d **strewn at ~** (= *at random*) kreuz und quer verstreut; **scattering accusations at ~** mit Anschuldigungen um sich werfend

e **ambassador at ~** Sonderbotschafter(in) *m(f)*

large-hearted ['lɑːdʒ,hɑːtɪd] ADJ großherzig

largely ['lɑːdʒlɪ] ADV (= *mainly*) zum größten Teil

large-minded ['lɑːdʒ,maɪndɪd] ADJ aufgeschlossen

largeness ['lɑːdʒnɪs] N a (= *big size*) Größe *f*, Umfang *m*; (*of meal*) Reichlichkeit *f*; (*of list*) Länge *f* b (= *extent: of interests, power*) Bedeutung *f*, Umfang *m* c (*old:* = *generosity*) Großzügigkeit *f*

large: large-print ADJ *book* in Großdruck; ~ **edition** Großdruckausgabe *f*; **large-scale** ADJ groß angelegt; *reception, party, changes* in großem Rahmen; **a ~ producer of food** ein Großhersteller *m* von Nahrungsmitteln; ~ **production** (*Ind*) Massenproduktion *f*; ~ **unrest** Massenaufruhr *m*, Massenunruhen *pl*; **a ~ map** eine (Land)karte in großem Maßstab; ~ **integration** (*Comput*) Großintegration *f*; **large-sized** ADJ groß

largesse [lɑː'ʒes] N Großzügigkeit *f*, Freigebigkeit *f*; (= *gift*) (großzügige) Gabe

largish ['lɑːdʒɪʃ] ADJ ziemlich groß

largo ['lɑːgəʊ] N Largo *nt*

lariat ['lærɪət] N Lasso *nt* or *m*

lark¹ [lɑːk] N (*Orn*) Lerche *f*; **to be up with the ~** mit den Hühnern aufstehen; **as happy as a ~** quietschfidel

lark² N (inf) **a** (esp Brit: = joke, fun, frolic) Jux m (inf), Spaß m; **let's go to the party, it'll be a bit of a ~** gehen wir zu der Party, das wird bestimmt lustig; **that's the best ~ we've had for a long time!** so viel Spaß haben wir schon lange nicht mehr gehabt!; **what a ~!** das ist (ja) zum Schreien or Schießen!; **to do sth for a ~** etw (nur) zum Spaß or aus Jux machen; **to have a ~** with jdm zusammen Spaß haben **b** (Brit inf: = business, affair) **this whole agency ~ is ...** die ganze Geschichte mit der Agentur ist ... (inf); **I wouldn't get involved in that ~** auf so was or so 'ne Sache würde ich mich nicht einlassen (inf); **politics and all that ~** Politik und der ganze Kram (inf); **I don't believe in all this horoscopes ~** ich glaube nicht an diesen Blödsinn mit den Horoskopen (inf)

▶ **lark about** or **around** VI (Brit inf) herumblödeln, herumalbern; **to lark about with sth** mit etw herumspielen

larkspur ['lɑːkspɜː] N Rittersporn m

larrikin ['lærɪkɪn] N (Austral inf) Rowdy m

Larry ['lærɪ] N **a** dim of **Laurence** of **Lawrence** **b** (dated Brit inf) **as happy as ~** quietschvergnügt (inf)

larva ['lɑːvə] N pl **-e** [-viː] Larve f

larval ['lɑːvəl] ADJ Larven-, larvenähnlich; **~ stage** Larvenzustand m

laryngeal [lə'rɪndʒəl] ADJ Kehlkopf-; **~ reflex** Kehlkopfreflex m

laryngitis [ˌlærɪn'dʒaɪtɪs] N Kehlkopfentzündung f, Laryngitis f (spec)

larynx ['lærɪŋks] N Kehlkopf m, Larynx m (spec)

lasagne, lasagna [lə'zænjə] N Lasagne pl

lascivious [lə'sɪvɪəs] ADJ lasziv (geh); movements, person, look, behaviour also lüstern; book schlüpfrig

lasciviously [lə'sɪvɪəslɪ] ADV lüstern; **the dancer moved ~** die Bewegungen der Tänzerin waren lasziv

lasciviousness [lə'sɪvɪəsnɪs] N Laszivität f (geh); (of movement, person, look, behaviour also) Lüsternheit f; (of book) Schlüpfrigkeit f

laser ['leɪzə] N Laser m; (Comput: = printer) Laserdrucker m

laser in cpds Laser-; **laser beam** N Laserstrahl m; **laser disc** N Laserdisc f, Laserdisk f; **laser gun** N Laserkanone f; **laser printer** N Laserdrucker m; **laser show** N Lasershow f; **laser surgery** N Laserchirurgie f; **laser technology** N Lasertechnik f; **laser weapon** N Laserwaffe f

lash¹ [læʃ] N (= eyelash) Wimper f; **she fluttered her ~es at him** sie machte ihm schöne Augen

lash² N **a** (= whip) Peitsche f; (= thong) Schnur f **b** (= stroke: as punishment) (Peitschen)schlag m **c** (= lashing, of tail) Schlagen nt; (of waves, rain) Peitschen nt **d** (fig) Schärfe f; **the ~ of her tongue** ihre scharfe Zunge **VT a** (= beat) peitschen; (as punishment) auspeitschen; (hail, rain, waves) peitschen gegen; tail schlagen mit; **the wind ~ed the sea into a fury** wütend peitschte der Wind die See; **the cow ~ed the flies with its tail** die Kuh schlug mit ihrem Schwanz nach den Fliegen; **to ~ the crowd into a fury** die Menge aufpeitschen **b** (fig: = criticize) heruntermachen (inf), abkanzeln **c** (= tie) festbinden (to an +dat); **to ~ sth together** etw zusammenbinden **VI to ~ against** peitschen gegen

▶ **lash about** (Brit) or **around** VI (wild) um sich schlagen

▶ **lash along** VT sep = **lash on**

▶ **lash around** VI = **lash about**

▶ **lash back** VT sep festbinden

▶ **lash down** **VT** sep (= tie down) festbinden or -zurren **VI** (rain etc) niederprasseln

▶ **lash into** VI +prep obj **to lash into sb** (physically) auf jdn einschlagen; (with words) jdn anfahren or anbrüllen (inf)

▶ **lash on** or **along** VT sep horse, slaves mit der Peitsche antreiben

▶ **lash out** **VI** **a** (physically) (wild) um sich schlagen or hauen; (horse) ausschlagen; **to lash out at sb** auf jdn losgehen; **she lashed out with a knife** sie stieß mit einem Messer; **he lashed out with his fists** er schlug mit den Fäusten zu **b** (in words) von Leder ziehen (inf); **to lash out against** or **at sb/sth** gegen jdn/etw wettern; **"TUC boss lashes out"** „Gewerkschaftsboss holt zum Schlag aus" **c** (inf: with money) sich in Unkosten stürzen; **to lash out on sth** sich (dat) etw was kosten lassen (inf); **I'm going to lash out on a new car** ich werde mir ein neues Auto leisten; **now we can really lash out** jetzt können wir uns wirklich mal etwas leisten **VT** insep sum of money springen lassen

▶ **lash up** VT sep verschnüren

lashing ['læʃɪŋ] N **a** (= beating) Prügel pl; (= punishment) Auspeitschung f **b** (fig, = criticism) scharfe Kritik **c** (= tying) Verschnürung f; (of prisoner) Fesseln pl; (Naut) Tau nt, Zurring m **d lashings** PL (inf) eine Unmenge (inf); **~s of money/cream** eine Unmenge or massenhaft Geld/Schlagsahne (inf)

lass [læs] N (junges) Mädchen, Mädel nt (dial); (= country lass) Mädchen nt vom Land; (= sweetheart) Freundin f, Schatz m

lassie ['læsɪ] N (inf: esp Scot, N Engl) = **lass**

lassitude [læsɪtjuːd] N Mattigkeit f, Trägheit f

lasso [læˈsuː] N pl **-(e)s** Lasso m or nt **VT** mit dem Lasso einfangen

last¹ [lɑːst] ADJ **a** letzte(r, s); **he was ~ to arrive** er kam als Letzter an; **the ~ person** der Letzte; **the ~ but one, the second ~ (one)** der/die/das Vorletzte; **the third ~ house** das drittletzte Haus; **(the) ~ one there buys the drinks!** der Letzte or wer als Letzter ankommt, zahlt die Getränke; **~ Monday, on Monday ~** letzten Montag; **~ year** letztes Jahr, im vorigen Jahr; **during the ~ 20 years, these ~ 20 years** in den letzten 20 Jahren; **~ but not least** nicht zuletzt, last not least **b** (= most unlikely, unsuitable etc) **that's the ~ thing I worry about** das ist das Letzte, worüber ich mir Sorgen machen würde; **that was the ~ thing I expected** damit hatte ich am wenigsten gerechnet; **that's the ~ thing I wanted to happen** das habe ich am wenigsten gewollt; **he's the ~ person I want to see** er ist der Letzte, den ich sehen möchte; **you're the ~ person to be entrusted with it** du bist der Letzte, dem man das anvertrauen kann **N a** (= final one or part, one before) der/die/das Letzte; **he was the ~ of the visitors to leave** er ging als Letzter der Besucher; **I'm always the ~ to know** ich erfahre immer alles als Letzter; **he withdrew the ~ of his money from the bank** er hob sein letztes Geld von der Bank ab; **each one is better than the ~** eins ist besser als das andere; **this is the ~ of the cake** das ist der Rest des Kuchens; **that's the ~ of the fighting** jetzt ist der Kampf ein Ende; **that was the ~ we saw of him** danach haben wir ihn nicht mehr gesehen; **the ~ we heard of him was ...** das Letzte, was wir von ihm hörten, war ...; **that was the ~ we heard of it/him** seitdem haben wir nichts mehr darüber/von ihm gehört; **I hope this is the ~ we'll hear of it** ich hoffe, damit ist die Sache erledigt; **the ~ I heard, they were getting married** das Letzte, was ich gehört habe, war, dass sie heiraten; **I shall be glad to see the ~ of this/him** ich bin froh, wenn ich das hinter mir habe/wenn ich den los bin (inf) or wenn ich den nicht mehr sehe; **we shall never hear the ~ of it** das werden wir noch lange zu hören kriegen; **to look one's ~ on sth** den letzten Blick auf etw (acc) werfen; **my ~** (Comm) mein letztes Schreiben **b at ~** endlich; **at long ~** schließlich und endlich; **so you're ready at long ~!** du bist also

endlich fertig geworden!; **to the ~** bis zum Schluss

ADV when did you ~ have a bath or **have a bath ~?** wann hast du das letzte Mal gebadet?; **I ~ heard from him a month ago** vor einem Monat habe ich das letzte Mal von ihm gehört; **he spoke ~** er sprach als Letzter; **the horse came in ~** das Pferd ging als letztes durchs Ziel

last² **VT** **it will ~ me/a careful user a lifetime** das hält/bei vernünftiger Benutzung hält es ein Leben lang; **the car has ~ed me eight years** das Auto hat acht Jahre (lang) gehalten; **these cigarettes will ~ me a week** diese Zigaretten reichen mir eine Woche; **I didn't think he'd ~ the week** ich hätte nicht gedacht, dass er die Woche durchhält **VI** (= continue) dauern; (= remain intact: cloth, flowers, marriage) halten; **it can't ~** es hält nicht an; **it won't ~** es wird nicht lange anhalten or so bleiben; **it's too good to ~** das ist zu schön, um wahr zu sein; **he'll stay as long as the beer ~s** er bleibt, solange Bier da ist; **will this material ~?** ist dieses Material haltbar or dauerhaft?; **none of his girlfriends ~s for long** bei ihm hält sich keine Freundin lange; **he won't ~ long in this job** er wird in dieser Stelle nicht alt werden (inf); **the previous boss only ~ed a week** der letzte Chef blieb nur eine Woche

▶ **last out** **VT** sep ausreichen für; (people) durchhalten **VI** (money, resources) ausreichen; (person) durchhalten

last³ N Leisten m; **cobbler, stick to your ~!** Schuster, bleib bei deinem Leisten!

last: last-chance saloon N (Brit inf) **they are drinking in the ~** es ist ihre letzte Chance; **Last Day** N **the ~** der Jüngste Tag; **last-ditch** ADJ allerletzte(r, s); attempt, proposals, talks etc in letzter Minute

lasting ['lɑːstɪŋ] ADJ relationship dauerhaft; material also haltbar; shame etc anhaltend

Last Judgement N **the ~** das Jüngste or Letzte Gericht

lastly ['lɑːstlɪ] ADV schließlich, zum Schluss

last: last-minute ADJ in letzter Minute; **last number redial** N (Telec) Wahlwiederholung f; **last post** N Zapfenstreich m; **last rites** PL Letzte Ölung; **Last Supper** N **the ~** das (Letzte) Abendmahl; **last word** N **the ~** (in fashion) der letzte Schrei; **to have the ~ (on sth)** das letzte Wort (zu etw) haben; **the ~ on biochemistry/on this subject** das maßgebende Werk über Biochemie/auf diesem Gebiet

Lat abbr of **Latin** lat., Lat.

lat abbr of **latitude** Br.

latch [lætʃ] **N** Riegel m; **to be on the ~** nicht verschlossen sein, nur eingeklinkt sein; **to leave the door on the ~** die Tür nur einklinken **VT** verriegeln

▶ **latch on** VI (inf) **a** (= get hold) sich festhalten; (with teeth) sich festbeißen (to sth an etw dat); **he latched on to the idea of coming with us** er hat es sich (dat) in den Kopf gesetzt, mitzukommen **b** (= attach o.s.) sich anschließen (to +dat); **she latched on to me at the party** sie hängte sich auf der Party an mich (inf) **c** (= understand) kapieren (inf)

latchkey ['lætʃkiː] N Hausschlüssel m

latchkey child N Schlüsselkind nt

late [leɪt] **ADJ** (+er) **a** spät; **to be ~ (for sth)** (zu etw) zu spät kommen; **the train/bus is (five minutes) ~** der Zug/Bus hat (fünf Minuten) Verspätung; **dinner will be ~ tonight** wir essen heute Abend später; (in hotels) es wird heute Abend später serviert; **I was ~ in getting up this morning** ich bin heute Morgen zu spät aufgestanden; **he is ~ with his rent** er hat seine Miete noch nicht bezahlt; **he is always ~ with his rent** er bezahlt seine Miete immer zu spät; **my period is ~, I am ~** meine Periode ist noch nicht da; **I don't want to make you ~** ich möchte Sie nicht aufhalten; **you'll make me ~** Ihretwegen werde ich mich verspäten; **that made me ~ for work** dadurch bin ich zu spät zur Arbeit gekommen; **I don't want to make you ~ for**

work ich möchte nicht, dass du zu spät zur Arbeit kommst; **that made the coach ~** dadurch hatte der Bus Verspätung; **that made the harvest ~** dadurch verzögerte sich die Ernte; **due to the ~ arrival of ...** wegen der verspäteten Ankunft ... (+*gen*); **it's too ~ (in the day) for that** dafür ist es jetzt zu spät; **it's too ~ in the day (for you) to do that** es ist zu spät (für dich), das noch zu tun; **it's not too ~ to change your mind** es ist noch nicht zu spät, um es sich anders zu überlegen; **it's never too ~ to learn** zum Lernen ist es nie zu spät

b **it's ~** es ist spät; **it's getting ~** es ist schon spät; **is it as ~ as that?** ist es schon so spät?

c *hour* spät; *opening hours* lang; **~ train/bus** Spätzug/-bus *m*; **at this ~ hour** zu so später Stunde, so spät; **at a ~ hour** zu später *or* vorgerückter Stunde; **he keeps very ~ hours** er geht sehr spät ins Bett; **they work ~ hours** sie arbeiten bis spät (am Abend); **the night was cold and the hour ~** die Nacht war kalt und es war sehr spät; **they had a ~ dinner yesterday** sie haben gestern spät zu Abend gegessen; **there is no ~ delivery of post on Saturdays** sonnabends gibt es keine zweite Zustellung; **~ night club** Nachtbar *f*; **~ potato/summer/edition/programme** Spätkartoffel *f*/-sommer *m*/-ausgabe *f*/-programm *nt*; **"late opening until 7pm on Fridays"** „freitags verlängerte Öffnungszeiten bis 19 Uhr"; **he's a ~ developer** er ist ein Spätentwickler; **both my babies were ~** meine Kinder sind beide nach dem Termin gekommen; **~ entrants to the examination will be charged £10 extra** für Nachmeldungen zur Prüfung wird eine Gebühr von £ 10 erhoben; **this essay was a ~ entry for the competition** dieser Aufsatz wurde verspätet für den Wettbewerb eingereicht; (= *last-minute*) dieser Aufsatz wurde in letzter Minute eingereicht; **they scored two ~ goals** sie erzielten zwei Tore in den letzten Spielminuten; **it happened in the ~ eighties** es geschah Ende der achtziger Jahre; **a man in his ~ eighties** ein Mann hoch in den Achtzigern, ein Endachtziger; **in the ~ morning** am späten Vormittag; **a ~ 18th-century building** ein Gebäude aus dem späten 18. Jahrhundert; **he came in ~ June** er war Ende Juni; **Late Stone Age** Jungsteinzeit *f*; **Easter is ~ this year** Ostern liegt *or* ist dieses Jahr spät; **spring is ~ this year** wir haben dieses Jahr einen späten Frühling

d (= *deceased*) verstorben; **the ~ John F. Kennedy** John F. Kennedy

e (= *former*) **the ~ Prime Minister** der frühere *or* vorige Premierminister

f (= *recent*) jüngst; **in the ~ war** im letzten Krieg

g **~ of No 13 White St** ehemals White St Nr. 13; **~ of the Diplomatic Service** ehemals *or* bis vor kurzem im diplomatischen Dienst tätig

ADV spät; **to come** *or* **arrive ~** (= *after the arranged/scheduled time*) (*person*) zu spät kommen; (*bus, train*) Verspätung haben; **I'll be home ~ today** ich komme heute spät nach Hause, es wird heute spät; **the train arrived/was running eight minutes ~** der Zug hatte acht Minuten Verspätung; **the baby was born two weeks ~** das Baby kam zwei Wochen nach dem Termin; **we're running ~ today** wir sind heute spät dran; **better ~ than never** lieber *or* besser spät als gar nicht; **to sit** *or* **stay up ~** lange aufbleiben; **don't wait up ~ for me** warte nicht zu lange auf mich; **the chemist is open ~ on Thursdays** die Apotheke hat donnerstags länger geöffnet; **to work ~ at the office** länger im Büro arbeiten; **~ at night** spät abends; **~ last night** spät gestern Abend; **~ in the night** spät in der Nacht; **~ into the night** bis spät in die Nacht; **~ in the afternoon** am späten Nachmittag; **~ last century/ in the year** (gegen) Ende des letzten Jahrhunderts/Jahres; **they scored ~ in the second half** gegen Ende der zweiten Halbzeit gelang ihnen ein Treffer; **he took up the piano rather ~ in life** er begann ziemlich spät mit dem Klavierspielen; **Goethe was still active even ~ in life** Goethe war auch im hohen Alter noch aktiv; **we decided rather ~ in the day to come too** wir haben uns ziemlich spät entschlossen,

auch zu kommen; **he left it very ~ in the day (to decide)** er hat (mit seiner Entscheidung) bis zum letzten Augenblick gewartet; **of ~ in letzter Zeit; until as ~ as 1900** noch bis 1900; **it was as ~ as 1900 before child labour** (*Brit*) *or* **labor** (*US*) **was abolished** erst 1900 wurde die Kinderarbeit abgeschafft

latecomer ['leɪtkʌmə'] N Zuspätkommende(r) *mf*, Nachzügler(in) *m(f)* (*inf*); **the product is a ~ to the market** das Produkt ist neu auf dem Markt

lateen sail [lə'tiːn'seɪl] N Lateinsegel *nt*

late lamented ADJ kürzlich verstorben *or* verschieden (*geh*); **my ~ boss** (*iro*) mein heiß geliebter ehemaliger Chef (*iro*)

Late Latin N Spätlatein *nt*

lately ['leɪtlɪ] ADV in letzter Zeit; **till ~** bis vor kurzem

latency ['leɪtənsɪ] N Latenz *f*

lateness ['leɪtnɪs] N (= *arriving late at work etc*) Zuspätkommen *nt*; (*of train, payments*) Verspätung *f*; (*of meal*) späte Zeit; (*of harvest, seasons*) spätes Eintreten; **the ~ of the hour** die so späte Stunde

late-night ['leɪt,naɪt] ADJ *period* spät am Abend; **~ movie** Spätfilm *m*; **~ shopping** Einkauf *m* am (späten) Abend, Dämmershopping *nt* (*inf*); **~ losses** (*St Ex*) späte Verluste *pl*

latent ['leɪtənt] ADJ latent; *strength also* verborgen; *artistic talent, ability also* verborgen, versteckt; *heat also* gebunden; *energy* ungenutzt; **the evil which is ~ in all men** das in jedem Menschen latent vorhandene Böse; **~ period/ phase** (*Med, Psych*) Latenzperiode/-phase *f*

later ['leɪtə'] ADJ später; **at a ~ hour, at a ~ time** später, zu einer späteren Zeit; **this version is ~ than that one** diese Version ist neuer als die andere; **in (his) ~ years** *or* **life** in späteren Jahren, in seinem späteren Leben

ADV später; **Mr Smith, ~ to become Sir John** Mr Smith, der spätere Sir John; **the weather cleared up ~ (on) in the day** das Wetter klärte sich im Laufe des Tages auf; **~ (on) that night/ week/day** später in der Nacht/Woche/an dem Tag; **~ (on) in life** später im Leben, in späteren Jahren; **~ (on) in the play** im weiteren Verlauf des Stückes; **I'll tell you ~ (on)** ich erzähle es dir später; **a moment ~** einen Augenblick später, im nächsten Augenblick; **see you ~!** bis nachher, bis später; **I saw him no ~ than yesterday** ich habe ihn (erst) gestern noch gesehen; **come at 7 o'clock and no ~** komm um 7 Uhr und nicht *or* keine Minute später; **not ~ than 1995** spätestens 1995; **they must be handed in no ~ than Monday** sie müssen bis spätestens Montag abgegeben werden

lateral ['lætərəl] ADJ seitlich; **~ view/window** Seitenansicht *f*/-fenster *nt*

lateral line N (*of fish*) Seitenlinie *f*

laterally ['lætərəlɪ] ADV seitlich

lateral thinking N unkonventionelles Denken, Querdenken *nt*

latest ['leɪtɪst] ADJ **a** (= *most recent*) *fashion, version* neu(e)ste(r, s); (= *most modern*) *technology* modernste(r, s); **the ~ news** das Neu(e)ste; **the ~ attempt to rescue them** der jüngste Versuch, sie zu retten

b späteste(r, s); **what is the ~ date you can come?** wann kannst du spätestens kommen?; **the ~ possible moment** der letztmögliche *or* allerletzte Augenblick

c *people* letzte(r, s); **the ~ men to resign** die Letzten, die zurückgetreten sind

ADV am spätesten; **he came ~** er kam zuletzt *or* als Letzter

N **a** he was the ~ **to arrive** er kam als Letzter; **the ~ in a series of attacks** der jüngste in einer Reihe von Anschlägen; **what's the ~ (about John)?** was gibts Neues (über John)?; **wait till you hear the ~!** warte, bis du das Neueste gehört hast!; **have you seen John's ~?** (= *girl*) hast du Johns Neu(e)ste schon gesehen?; **have you heard John's ~?** (= *joke*) hast du Johns Neuesten schon gehört?; **it's the ~ in computer**

games/in technology es ist das neueste Computerspiel/die neueste Technik

b **at the (very) ~** spätestens

latex ['leɪteks] N Latex *m*

lath [læθ] N Latte *f*; **~s** *pl* (= *structure*) Lattenwerk *nt*

lathe [leɪð] N Drehbank *f*; **~ operator** Dreher(in) *m(f)*

lather ['lɑːðə'] **N** (Seifen)schaum *m*; (= *sweat*) Schweiß *m*; **work the soap into a rich ~** die Seife zum Schäumen bringen; **to get** *or* **work oneself up into a ~ (about sth)** (*inf*) sich (über etw *acc*) aufregen, (wegen etw *dat*) durchdrehen (*inf*) **VT** einschäumen **VI** schäumen

Latin ['lætɪn] **ADJ a** (= *Roman*) *civilization, world* römisch; *poets, literature* römisch, lateinisch; **~ language** lateinische Sprache **b** (= *of Roman origin*) romanisch; *temperament, charm* südländisch **c** (*Rel*) römisch-katholisch **N a** (= *inhabitant of ancient Latium*) Latiner(in) *m(f)*; (= *Roman*) Römer(in) *m(f)*; (= *a member of any Latin race*) Südländer(in) *m(f)*, Romane *m*, Romanin *f* **b** (*Ling*) Latein(isch) *nt*

Latin America N Lateinamerika *nt*

Latin American ['lætɪnə'merɪkən] **ADJ** lateinamerikanisch **N** Lateinamerikaner(in) *m(f)*

latinism ['lætɪnɪzəm] N Latinismus *m*

latinist ['lætɪnɪst] N Latinist(in) *m(f)*

latinity [lə'tɪnɪtɪ] N (*geh*) Latinität *f*

latinize ['lætɪnaɪz] VT latinisieren

Latin lover N Latin Lover *m*

Latin Quarter N Quartier Latin *nt*

latish ['leɪtɪʃ] **ADJ** ziemlich spät; *applicant, letter* verspätet; *amendment* neuer, später **ADV** ziemlich spät

latitude ['lætɪtjuːd] N Breite *f*; (*fig*) Freiheit *f*, Spielraum *m*

latitudinal [,lætɪ'tjuːdɪnl] ADJ Breiten-; **~ lines** Breitengrade *pl*

latrine [lə'triːn] N Latrine *f*

latte ['lætɪ] N Caffè latte *m*

latter ['lætə'] ✪ 26.2 **ADJ a** (= *second of two*) letztere(r, s) **b** (= *at the end*) **the ~ part of the book/story is better** gegen Ende wird das Buch/die Geschichte besser; **the ~ half of the week/year/century** die zweite Hälfte der Woche/des Jahres/des Jahrhunderts; **in the ~ years** in den letzten Jahren; **in his ~ years** in späteren Jahren **N** **the ~** der/die/das/Letztere; (*more than one*) die Letzteren *pl*; **I don't agree with the ~** ich bin mit Letzterem nicht einverstanden; **of these two theories I prefer the ~** von diesen beiden Theorien ziehe ich (die) letztere vor

latter-day ['lætə,deɪ] ADJ modern; **the Latter-day Saints** die Heiligen der Letzten Tage

latterly ['lætəlɪ] ADV (= *recently*) in letzter Zeit; (= *towards end of period*) zuletzt; (= *towards end of life*) in späteren Jahren; **she worked there for 30 years, ~ as manager** sie hat 30 Jahre dort gearbeitet, zuletzt als Geschäftsführerin

lattice ['lætɪs] N Gitter *nt*

latticed ['lætɪst] ADJ vergittert

latticework ['lætɪswɜːk] N Gitterwerk *nt*

Latvia ['lætvɪə] N Lettland *nt*

Latvian ['lætvɪən] **ADJ** lettisch **N a** Lette *m*, Lettin *f* **b** (*Ling*) Lettisch *nt*

laud [lɔːd] VT (*old*) preisen (*geh*)

laudable ['lɔːdəbl] ADJ lobenswert

laudably ['lɔːdəblɪ] ADV lobenswerterweise; **~ unselfish remarks** lobenswert selbstlose Worte *pl*

laudanum ['lɔːdnəm] N Laudanum *nt*

laudatory ['lɔːdətərɪ] ADJ lobend; **a ~ speech** eine Lobrede *or* Laudatio (*geh*)

laugh [lɑːf] **N a** Lachen *nt*; **no, she said, with a ~** nein, sagte sie lachend; **she let out** *or* **gave a loud ~** sie lachte laut auf; **that woman has a ~ like a hyena** die Frau gackert wie ein Huhn; **what a ~ (she's got)!** die hat vielleicht 'ne Lache! (inf); **to have a good ~ over** or **about sth** sich köstlich über etw (acc) amüsieren; **to have a good ~ at sb** jdn gründlich auslachen; **you'll have a good ~ about it one day** eines Tages wirst du darüber lachen können; **give us a ~!** (inf) bring uns mal zum Lachen!; **it'll give us a ~** (inf) das wird lustig; **the ~ was on me** der Witz ging auf meine Kosten; **to have the last ~** (**over** or **on sb**) es jdm zeigen (inf); **I'll have the last ~** ich werds dir schon noch zeigen (inf); **to get a ~** einen Lacherfolg verbuchen; **to play for ~s** Lacherfolge haben wollen; **he played Hamlet for ~s** er machte aus Hamlet eine komische Figur; **they played "Othello" for ~s** sie machten aus „Othello" eine Komödie

b (inf. = fun) **what a ~** (das ist ja) zum Totlachen or zum Schreien (inf)!; **just for a ~** or **for ~s** nur (so) aus Spaß; **it'll be a good ~** es wird bestimmt lustig; **we didn't achieve much, but we had a good ~** wir haben nicht viel geschafft, aber es war trotzdem lustig; **he's a (good) ~** er ist urkomisch or zum Schreien (inf); **to be good for a ~** ganz lustig sein; **it was a ~ a minute!** es war zum Schreien! (inf)

VI lachen (about, at, over über +acc); **to ~ at sb** sich über jdn lustig machen; **to ~ up one's sleeve** sich (dat) ins Fäustchen lachen; **she's ~ing up her sleeve at us** sie macht sich heimlich über uns lustig; **it's nothing to ~ about** das ist nicht zum Lachen; **it's all very well for you to ~** du hast gut lachen; **you'll be ~ing on the other side of your face** (Brit) or **mouth** (US) **soon** dir wird das Lachen noch vergehen; **to ~ out loud** laut auflachen; **to ~ in sb's face** jdm ins Gesicht lachen; **he who ~s last ~s longest** (Prov) wer zuletzt lacht, lacht am besten (Prov); **you've got to ~** es ist eigentlich zum Lachen; **don't make me ~!** (iro inf) dass ich nicht lache! (inf); **if you've got your own house, you're ~ing** (inf) wenn man ein eigenes Haus hat, hat man es gut; **he'll be ~ing all the way to the bank** er wird das Geld nur so scheffeln (inf) → **drain N a**

VT **to ~ oneself silly** sich tot- or kaputtlachen (inf); **he was ~ed out of court** er wurde ausgelacht; **the idea was ~ed out of court** die Idee wurde verlacht; **don't be silly, he ~ed** red keinen Unsinn, sagte er lachend

▶ **laugh away VT** sep mit Humor tragen, sich lachend hinwegsetzen über (+acc); **my father laughed away my fears** mein Vater nahm mir mit einem Lachen die Angst **VI** **he sat there laughing away** er saß da und lachte und lachte

▶ **laugh down VT** sep auslachen, mit Gelächter übertönen; **the audience laughed him/his reply down** er/seine Antwort ging im Gelächter des Publikums unter

▶ **laugh off VT a** always separate **to laugh one's head off** sich tot- or kaputtlachen (inf) **b** sep (= dismiss) lachen über (+acc), mit einem Lachen abtun

laughable ['lɑːfəbl] ADJ lachhaft, lächerlich; **if it wasn't so serious, it would be almost ~** wenn es nicht so ernst wäre, könnte man fast darüber lachen

laughably ['lɑːfəblɪ] ADV lächerlich; **we got what was ~ called a double room** wir bekamen ein so genanntes Doppelzimmer

laughing ['lɑːfɪŋ] ADJ lachend; **it's no ~ matter** das ist nicht zum Lachen, das ist gar nicht komisch **N** Lachen nt; **hysterical ~** hysterisches Gelächter

laughing: laughing gas N Lachgas nt; **laughing hy(a)ena** N Tüpfel- or Fleckenhyäne f; **laughing jackass** N Rieseneisvogel m

laughingly ['lɑːfɪŋlɪ] ADV (= with a laugh) lachend; (= ridiculously) lächerlicherweise; **what the government ~ calls its economic policy** das, was die Regierung als Wirtschaftspolitik bezeichnet, obwohl das eigentlich ein Witz ist

laughing stock N Witzfigur f; **his visionary ideas made him a ~** mit seinen fantastischen or phantastischen Ideen machte er sich lächerlich or zum allgemeinen Gespött

laughter ['lɑːftə] N Gelächter nt; **~ broke out among the audience** das Publikum brach in Gelächter aus; **children's ~** Kinderlachen nt; **he shook with silent ~** er schüttelte sich vor Lachen; **at this there was loud ~** das rief lautes Gelächter hervor; **there was a little nervous ~** ein nervöses Lachen war zu hören

launch [lɔːntʃ] **N a** (= vessel) Barkasse f **b** (= launching) (of ship) Stapellauf m; (of lifeboat) Aussetzen nt; (of rocket) Abschuss m **c** (= launching) (of company) Gründung f, Eröffnung f; (of new product) Einführung f; (with party, publicity: of film, play, book) Lancierung f; (bringing out, of film, play) Premiere f; (of book) Herausgabe f; (of shares) Emission f

VT a new vessel vom Stapel lassen; (= christen) taufen; lifeboat zu Wasser lassen, aussetzen; rocket abschießen; plane katapultieren; **Lady X ~ed the new boat** der Stapellauf fand in Anwesenheit von Lady X statt; **the rocket was ~ed into space** die Rakete wurde in den Weltraum geschossen

b company, newspaper, initiative gründen; new product einführen, auf den Markt bringen; (with party, publicity) film, play, book lancieren; (= bring out) film anlaufen lassen; play auf die Bühne bringen; book, series herausbringen; plan, investigation in die Wege leiten; programme, trend einführen; career starten; policy in Angriff nehmen; shares emittieren, ausgeben; **to ~ an offensive** or **an attack against the enemy** zum Angriff gegen den Feind übergehen; **the attack was ~ed at 15.00 hours** der Angriff fand um 15.00 Uhr statt; **to ~ sb into society** jdn in die Gesellschaft einführen; **this film ~ed him as a comic actor** mit diesem Film machte er sich (dat) als Komiker einen Namen; **to ~ sb on his way** jdm einen guten Start geben; **once he is ~ed on this subject ...** wenn er einmal mit diesem Thema angefangen hat or bei diesem Thema gelandet ist, ...; **now that he's ~ed himself on the road to success** jetzt, wo er auf Erfolgskurs ist **c** (= hurl) schleudern; **he ~ed himself into the crowd** er stürzte sich in die Menge

▶ **launch forth VI** = **launch out** (a, d)

▶ **launch into VI** +prep obj (= question, attack etc vigorously) angreifen; **the author launches straight into his main theme** der Autor kommt gleich zum Hauptthema; **he launched into a description of his new house** er legte mit einer Beschreibung seines neuen Hauses los (inf)

▶ **launch out VI a** (also **launch forth**) **the astronauts launched out into the unknown** die Astronauten starteten ins Unbekannte **b** (= diversify) sich verlegen (in auf +acc); **the company launched out in several new directions** die Firma stieg in einige neue Branchen ein **c** (inf: = spend a lot) **to launch out** sich in Unkosten stürzen; **now we can afford to launch out a bit** jetzt können wir es uns leisten, etwas mehr auszugeben (on für) **d** (= start: also **launch forth**) anfangen (into sth mit etw, etw acc); **to launch out into a new career** eine neue Karriere starten

launcher ['lɔːntʃə] N **a** (Mil) Werfer m; (for rockets) Abschussvorrichtung f **b** (Aviat) Katapult nt, Startschleuder f

launching ['lɔːntʃɪŋ] N = **launch** N b, c

launching: launching pad N Start- or Abschussrampe f; (fig) Sprungbrett nt; **launching site** N Abschussbasis f

launch: launch pad N = **launching pad**; **launch party** N (for book) Buchpremiere f; (for film, play) Premierenfeier f; **launch vehicle** N (Space) Booster m, Startrakete f

launder ['lɔːndə] **VT** waschen und bügeln; (fig) money waschen **VI** waschen und bügeln; **modern fabrics ~ easily** moderne Gewebe lassen sich leicht reinigen or sind pflegeleicht

Launderette® [ˌlɔːndəˈret] N (Brit) Waschsalon m

laundress ['lɔːndrɪs] N Waschfrau f, Wäscherin f

laundrette [ˌlɔːnˈdret] N (Brit) Waschsalon m

Laundromat® ['lɔːndrəʊmæt] N (US) Waschsalon m

laundry ['lɔːndrɪ] N (= establishment) Wäscherei f; (= clothes) (dirty) schmutzige Wäsche; (washed) Wäsche f; **to do the ~** (Wäsche) waschen

laundry: laundry bag N Wäschesack m; **laundry basket** N Wäschekorb m; **laundry list** N (fig) lange Liste f; (of wants) Wunschzettel m; **laundryman** N Wäschemann m (inf)

laurel ['lɒrəl] N Lorbeer m; **to look to one's ~s** sich behaupten (müssen); **to rest on one's ~s** sich auf seinen Lorbeeren ausruhen; **to win** or **gain one's ~s** Lorbeeren ernten

lav [læv] N (esp Brit inf) Klo nt (inf)

lava ['lɑːvə] N Lava f; **~ bed** Lavadecke f

lavatory ['lævətrɪ] N Toilette f

lavatory: lavatory attendant N Toilettenfrau f/-mann m; **lavatory paper** N Toilettenpapier nt; **lavatory seat** N Toilettensitz m, Klobrille f (inf)

lavender ['lævɪndə] **N** (= flower) Lavendel m; (= colour) Lavendel nt **ADJ** (colour) lavendelfarben; **~ blue eyes** lavendelblaue Augen

lavender: lavender bag N Lavendelsäckchen nt; **lavender water** N Lavendelwasser nt

lavish ['lævɪʃ] **ADJ** gifts großzügig, üppig; praise, affection überschwänglich; banquet üppig; party feudal; (pej) verschwenderisch; expenditure verschwenderisch; **to be ~ in** or **with sth** mit etw verschwenderisch sein or umgehen; **he was ~ in his help to others** er half anderen großzügig; **he's ~ in giving money to good causes** für gute Zwecke spendet er großzügig Geld; **you were very ~ with the cream** du hast ja mit der Sahne nicht gespart; **to be ~ with one's money** das Geld mit vollen Händen ausgeben **VT** **to ~ sth on sb** jdn mit etw überhäufen; praise, attention jdn mit etw überschütten; **they ~ed food and drink on them** sie bewirtete sie fürstlich; **to ~ attention on sth** viel Aufmerksamkeit auf etw (acc) richten

lavishly ['lævɪʃlɪ] ADV give, equipped großzügig; praise überschwänglich; put paint on, spread reichlich; entertain üppig, reichlich; illustrated reich, aufwändig, aufwendig; **they entertain ~** sie geben feudale Feste; **~ furnished** luxuriös or aufwändig or aufwendig eingerichtet; **to spend (money) ~** das Geld mit vollen Händen ausgeben (on für); **he is ~ extravagant in his hospitality** seine Gastfreundschaft kennt keine Grenzen

lavishness ['lævɪʃnɪs] N (of gifts) Großzügigkeit f, Üppigkeit f; (of praise, affection) Überschwänglichkeit f; (of banquet) Üppigkeit f; (of person) Großzügigkeit f; (pej) Verschwendungssucht f; **the ~ of the party** die feudale Party

law [lɔː] N **a** (= rule, also Jewish, Sci) Gesetz nt; **~ of nature** Naturgesetz nt; **it's the ~** das ist Gesetz; **his word is ~** sein Wort ist Gesetz; **to become ~** rechtskräftig werden; **to pass a ~** ein Gesetz verabschieden; **is there a ~ against it?** ist das verboten?; **there is no ~ against asking, is there?** (inf) man darf doch wohl noch fragen, oder?; **he is a ~ unto himself** er macht, was er will

b (= body of laws) Gesetz nt no pl; (= system) Recht nt; **according to** or **in** or **by** or **under French ~** nach französischem Recht; **by ~** gesetzlich; **by ~ all restaurants must display their prices outside** alle Restaurants sind gesetzlich dazu verpflichtet, ihre Preise draußen auszuhängen; **he is above/outside the ~** er steht über dem Gesetz/außerhalb des Gesetzes; **what is the ~ on drugs?** wie sind die Drogengesetze?; **to keep within the ~** sich im Rahmen des Gesetzes bewegen; **in ~** vor dem Gesetz; **ignorance is no defence** (Brit) or **defense** (US) **in ~** Unwissenheit schützt vor Strafe nicht; **a change in the ~** eine Gesetzesänderung; **the ~ as it relates to property** die gesetzlichen Bestimmungen über das Eigentum; **civil/criminal ~** Zivil-/Strafrecht nt

c (as study) Jura no art, Recht(swissenschaft f) nt

d (*Sport*) Regel *f*; (*Art*) Gesetz *nt*; **the ~s of harmony** die Harmonielehre; **one of the basic ~s of harmony** eins der grundlegenden Prinzipien der Harmonielehre

e (= *operation of law*) **to practise** (*Brit*) *or* **practice** (*US*) ~ eine Anwaltspraxis haben; **to go to ~** vor Gericht gehen, den Rechtsweg beschreiten; **to take sb to ~** gegen jdn gerichtlich vorgehen, jdn vor Gericht bringen; **to take a case to ~** in einer Sache gerichtlich vorgehen, einen Fall vor Gericht bringen; **to take the ~ into one's own hands** das Recht selbst in die Hand nehmen; **~ and order** Ruhe *or* Recht und Ordnung, Law and Order; **the forces of ~ and order** die Ordnungskräfte *pl*

f **the ~** (*inf*) die Polente (*dated inf*), die Bullen (*sl*); **I'll get the ~ on you** (*Brit inf*) ich hole die Polizei; **he got the ~ on to me** (*Brit inf*) er hat mir die Polizei auf den Hals gehetzt (*inf*)

law: **law-abiding** ADJ gesetzestreu; **lawbreaker** N Rechtsbrecher(in) *m(f)*; **lawbreaking** ADJ gesetzesübertretend, rechtsbrecherisch N Rechtsbruch *m*, Gesetzesübertretung *f*; **law centre**, (*US*) **law center** N *kostenlose Rechtsberatungsstelle*; **law court** N Gerichtshof *m*, Gericht *nt*; **law enforcement** N **the duty of the police is ~** Aufgabe der Polizei ist es, dem Gesetz Geltung zu verschaffen; **law enforcement authorities** PL Vollstreckungsbehörden *pl*; **law enforcement officer** N Polizeibeamte(r) *m*/-beamtin *f*

lawful ['lɔ:fʊl] ADJ rechtmäßig; **~ wedded wife** rechtmäßig angetraute Frau; **will you take this man to be your ~ wedded husband?** willst du mit diesem Mann den Bund der Ehe eingehen?

lawfully ['lɔ:fəlɪ] ADV rechtmäßig; **he is ~ entitled to compensation** er hat einen Rechtsanspruch *or* rechtmäßigen Anspruch auf Entschädigung; **he was careful to carry on his activities ~** er achtete darauf, dass seine Handlungen im Rahmen des Gesetzes blieben

lawfulness ['lɔ:fʊlnɪs] N Rechtsgültigkeit *f*; (= *permission by law*) Gesetzlichkeit *f*, Gesetzmäßigkeit *f*; (= *recognition by law*) Rechtmäßigkeit *f*, Legitimität *f*

lawgiver ['lɔ:gɪvə] N Gesetzgeber *m*

lawgiving ['lɔ:gɪvɪŋ] N Gesetzgebung *f* ADJ gesetzgebend; **~ power** gesetzgebende Gewalt

lawless ['lɔ:lɪs] ADJ *act* gesetzwidrig; *person, society* gesetzlos; *country* ohne Gesetzgebung; *violence* ungezügelt

lawlessness ['lɔ:lɪsnɪs] N (*of act*) Gesetzwidrigkeit *f*; (*of person, society, country*) Gesetzlosigkeit *f*; **~ among young people** gesetzwidriges Verhalten unter Jugendlichen; **after the coup, the country reverted to ~** nach dem Staatsstreich fiel das Land in einen Zustand der Gesetzlosigkeit zurück

Law Lord N (*Brit*) Lordrichter *m*

lawman ['lɔ:mən] N *pl* **-men** (*US*) Polizist *m*, Sheriff *m*

lawn[1] [lɔ:n] N (= *grass*) Rasen *m no pl*; **the ~s in front of the houses** der Rasen vor den Häusern

lawn[2] N (*Tex*) Batist *m*, Linon *m*

lawn: **lawn chair** N Liegestuhl *m*; **lawn mower** N Rasenmäher *m*; **lawn party** N (*US*) Gartenfest *nt*, Gartenparty *f*; (*for charity*) Wohltätigkeitsveranstaltung *f* im Freien; **lawn tennis** N Rasentennis *nt*

law office N (*US*) Rechtsanwaltsbüro *nt*, Rechtsanwaltspraxis *f*

lawrencium [lɔ:'rensɪəm] N (*Chem*) Lawrencium *nt*

law: **law reports** PL Entscheidungs- *or* Fallsammlung *f*; (= *journal*) Gerichtszeitung *f*; **law school** N (*US*) juristische Fakultät; **law student** N Jurastudent(in) *m(f)*, Student(in) *m(f)* der Rechte (*form*); **lawsuit** N Prozess *m*, Klage *f*; **he filed a ~ for damages** er strengte eine Schadensersatzklage an; **to bring a ~ against sb** gegen jdn einen Prozess anstrengen

lawyer ['lɔ:jə] N (Rechts)anwalt *m*, (Rechts)anwältin *f*

lax [læks] ADJ (*+er*) **a** lax; *discipline* lasch, lax; *morals* locker, lose; **she is rather ~ in her relations with men** sie hat ein recht lockeres Verhältnis zu Männern; **to be ~ about sth** etw vernachlässigen; **he's ~ about washing/imposing discipline** er nimmts mit dem Waschen/der Disziplin nicht so genau; **I've been rather ~ about replying to your letters** ich habe mir mit der Beantwortung Ihrer Briefe reichlich viel Zeit gelassen; **things are very ~ at the school** in der Schule gehts es sehr lax *or* undiszipliniert zu **b** **~ bowels** dünner Stuhl(gang)

laxative ['læksətɪv] ADJ abführend, laxativ (*spec*) N Abführmittel *nt*, Laxativ(um) *nt* (*spec*)

laxity ['læksɪtɪ], **laxness** ['læksnɪs] N (= *lack of vigour, discipline*) Laxheit *f*; (= *carelessness also*) Nachlässigkeit *f*; **his moral ~** seine lockeren *or* laxen moralischen Einstellungen; **sexual ~** lockere Sitten *pl*, sexuelle Freizügigkeit

lay[1] [leɪ] N (*Liter, Mus*) Ballade *f*, Lied *nt*

lay[2] ADJ Laien-; **~ opinion** die öffentliche Meinung, die Öffentlichkeit; **a ~ opinion** die Meinung eines Laien

lay[3] *pret of* **lie**[2]

lay[4] *vb*: pret, ptp **laid** N **a** Lage *f* → **land** N **a**
b (*sl*) **he's an easy ~** er lässt jeden ran (*inf*); **she's a good ~** sie ist gut im Bett (*inf*); **that's the best ~ I ever had** das war die beste Nummer, die ich je gemacht habe (*inf*)
VT **a** (= *place, put*) legen (*sth on sth* etw auf etw *acc*); *wreath* niederlegen; **to ~ (one's) hands on** (= *get hold of*) erwischen, fassen; (= *find*) finden; **to ~ a hand on sb** jdm etwas tun, Hand an jdn legen (*geh*); **I never laid a hand on him** ich habe ihn überhaupt nicht angefasst, ich habe ihm überhaupt nichts getan; **he took all the money he could ~ his hands on** er nahm alles Geld, das ihm in die Finger kam (*inf*)
b *bricks, foundations, track* legen; *concrete* gießen; *cable, mains, pipes* verlegen; *road* bauen, anlegen; *carpet, lino* (ver)legen
c (= *prepare*) *fire* herrichten; (*esp Brit*) *table* decken; *mines, ambush* legen; *trap* aufstellen; *plans* schmieden; **to ~ the table for breakfast/lunch** (*esp Brit*) den Frühstücks-/Mittagstisch decken;

to ~ a trap for sb jdm eine Falle stellen; **even the best-laid plans can go wrong** selbst die ausgeklügeltsten Pläne können schief gehen
d (*non-material things*) *burden* auferlegen (*on sb* jdm); **to ~ the blame for sth on sb/sth** jdm/einer Sache die Schuld an etw (*dat*) geben; **to ~ responsibility for sth on sb** jdn für etw verantwortlich machen; **the stress which he ~s on it** der Nachdruck, den er darauf legt
e (= *bring forward*) *complaint* vorbringen (*before* bei); *accusation* erheben; **the police laid a charge of murder against him** die Polizei erstattete gegen ihn Anzeige wegen Mordes; **he laid out his case before them** er trug ihnen seinen Fall vor
f *dust* binden; *ghost* austreiben; *fear* zerstreuen; *doubts* beseitigen; **to ~ waste** verwüsten; **to ~ the ghost of sth** (*fig*) etw endgültig begraben → **low**[1], **open** etc
g *eggs* (*hen*) legen; (*fish, insects*) ablegen
h *bet* ablegen; *money* setzen; **to ~ bets on sth** auf etw (*acc*) wetten; **I ~ you a fiver on it!** ich wette mit dir um 5 Pfund!; **I'll ~ you that ...** ich wette mit dir, dass ...; **I'll ~ you anything ...** ich gehe mit dir jede Wette ein ...
i (*sl*) **to ~ a woman** eine Frau flachlegen (*sl*); **he just wants to get laid** er will nur bumsen (*inf*)
VI (*hen*) legen

► **lay about** VI um sich schlagen VT *sep* losschlagen gegen

► **lay aside** *or* **away** VT *sep* *work etc* weglegen, zur Seite legen; (= *keep in reserve, save*) beiseite *or* auf die Seite legen; (= *cast away*) ablegen; *doubts* aufgeben; *plans etc* auf Eis legen; **to lay sb away** (= *bury*) jdn zu Grabe tragen

► **lay back** VT *sep* *ears* anlegen; *person* zurücklegen

► **lay before** VT +*prep obj* **to lay sth before sb** (*plan*) jdm etw vorlegen; *ideas also* jdm etw unterbreiten; *claim, complaint* etw bei jdm vorbringen

► **lay by** VT *sep* beiseite *or* auf die Seite legen

► **lay down** VT *sep* **a** *book, pen etc* hinlegen; **he laid his bag down on the table** er legte seine Tasche auf den Tisch; **she laid herself down to sleep** (*liter*) sie begab sich zur Ruhe
b (= *give up*) *burden* ablegen; *office* niederlegen; **to lay down one's arms** die Waffen niederlegen; **to lay down one's life** sein Leben geben *or* opfern
c (= *impose, establish*) *condition* festsetzen *or* -legen; *policy* festsetzen, bestimmen; *rules* aufstellen, festlegen; *price* festsetzen, vorschreiben; **it is laid down that** es wurde festgelegt, dass; **to lay down the law** (*inf*) Vorschriften machen (*to sb* jdm)
d (= *store*) lagern
e *ship* auf Stapel legen
f *deposit* hinterlegen

► **lay in** VT *sep* *food etc* einlagern; *supplies also* anlegen; **they have laid in plenty of water** sie haben (sich *dat*) einen großen Wasservorrat angelegt

► **lay into** VI +*prep obj* (*inf*) **to lay into sb** auf jdn losgehen; (*verbally*) jdn fertig machen (*inf*) *or* runterputzen (*inf*)

► **lay off** VI (*inf*: = *stop*) aufhören (*prep obj* mit); **lay off, will you?** hör (mal) auf, ja?; **you'll have to lay off smoking** du wirst das Rauchen aufgeben müssen (*inf*); **I wish you'd lay off coming here every day** ich wünschte, du würdest nicht mehr jeden Tag hierher kommen; **lay off my little brother, will you!** lass bloß meinen kleinen Bruder in Ruhe! VT *sep* *workers* Feierschichten machen lassen; (*permanently*) entlassen; **to be laid off** Feierschichten einlegen müssen; (*permanently*) entlassen werden

► **lay on** VT *sep* **a** (= *apply*) *paint* auftragen → **thick**
b (= *prepare, offer*) *hospitality* bieten (*for sb* jdm); (= *supply*) *entertainment* sorgen für; *excursion* veranstalten; *extra buses* einsetzen; *water, electricity* anschließen; **if you lay on the drinks I'll get the food** wenn du die Getränke stellst,

besorge ich das Essen; **she had laid on a lot of food** sie hatte sehr viel zu essen aufgetischt; **an extra flight was laid on** eine Sondermaschine wurde eingesetzt or bereitgestellt

c (= *impose*) **to lay a tax on sth** etw mit einer Steuer belegen, etw besteuern

d (*esp US inf*: = *tell off*) **he laid it on me** er hat mich zur Sau gemacht (*inf*)

▶**lay out** VT *sep* **a** (= *spread out*) ausbreiten; **the vast plain laid out before us** die weite Ebene, die sich vor uns ausbreitete

b (= *present*) darlegen; **he laid out his plans for the country** er legte seine Pläne für das Land dar

c (= *prepare*) *clothes* zurechtlegen; *corpse* (waschen und) aufbahren

d (= *design, arrange*) anlegen, planen; *garden* anlegen, gestalten; *room* aufteilen; *rooms in house* verteilen, anordnen; *office* aufteilen, anordnen; *book* gestalten; *page* umbrechen; (*in magazines*) das Lay-out (+*gen*) machen

e *money* (= *spend*) ausgeben; (= *invest*) investieren

f (= *knock out*) **to lay sb out** jdn k. o. schlagen; **three whiskies were enough to lay him out** nach drei Whiskys war er erledigt (*inf*); **he was laid out cold when he fell downstairs** er verlor das Bewusstsein, als er die Treppe hinunterfiel VR (*dated*, = *take trouble*) sich bemühen, sich (*dat*) Mühe geben; **to lay oneself out to please** sich Mühe geben zu gefallen

▶**lay over** VI (*US*) Aufenthalt haben

▶**lay to** VI (*Naut*) beidrehen

▶**lay up** VT *sep* **a** (= *store*) lagern; *supply* anlegen; (= *amass, save*) anhäufen, ansammeln; **he's laying up trouble for himself in the future** er wird später noch (viel) Ärger bekommen **b** (= *immobilize*) *ship* auflegen; *boat* aufbocken; *car* stilllegen, einmotten (*inf*); **to be laid up** (*in bed*) auf der Nase (*inf*) or im Bett liegen; **you'd better take it easy or you'll lay yourself up** Sie müssen etwas langsamer treten, sonst liegen Sie nachher flach or auf der Nase (*inf*)

lay: layabout N (*Brit*) Nichtstuer(in) *m(f)*, Arbeitsscheue(r) *mf*; **layaway** N (*US Comm*) angezahlte und zurückgelegte Ware; **lay brother** N Laienbruder *m*; **lay-by** N (*Brit*) (*in town*) Parkbucht *f*; (*in country*) Parkplatz *m*; (*big*) Rastplatz *m*

layer ['leɪə'] N **a** Schicht *f* (*also Geol*), Lage *f*; **to arrange the vegetables in ~s** das Gemüse schichten; **we climbed through ~ upon ~ of cloud** wir stiegen durch eine Wolkenschicht nach der anderen auf; **the cake was covered with ~ upon ~ of chocolate** der Kuchen war mit vielen Schokoladenschichten überzogen; **several ~s of clothing** mehrere Kleidungsstücke übereinander **b** (*Hort*) Ableger *m* **c** (= *hen*) Legehenne *f* VT **a** (*Hort*) absenken **b** *hair* abstufen **c** *vegetables etc* schichten

layer cake N Schichttorte *f*

layette [leɪˈet] N Babyausstattung *f*

lay figure N Gliederpuppe *f*; (*fig*) Marionette *f*

laying ['leɪɪŋ] N **~ on of hands** Handauflegen *nt*

lay: layman N Laie *m*; **lay-off** N *further* **~s were unavoidable** weitere Arbeiter mussten Feierschichten einlegen or (*permanent*) mussten entlassen werden; **he is playing again after a lengthy ~** er spielt wieder nach einer längeren Pause; **layout** N Anordnung *f*, Anlage *f*; (*Typ*) Lay-out *nt*; **the standard ~ of German stations** wie deutsche Bahnhöfe normalerweise angelegt sind; **we have changed the ~ of this office** wir haben dieses Büro anders aufgeteilt; **our house has a different ~** unser Haus hat eine andere Zimmerverteilung or ist anders angelegt; **layover** N (*US*) Aufenthalt *m*; **layperson** N Laie *m*; **lay reader** N Hilfsdiakon *m*; **lay sister** N Laienschwester *f*; **laywoman** N Laie *m*

laze [leɪz] N **to have a long ~ in bed** lange faul im Bett (liegen) bleiben VI faulenzen

▶**laze about** (*Brit*) or **around** VI faulenzen, auf der faulen Haut liegen; **stop lazing about** or **around** steh/sitz *etc* nicht so faul herum!

▶**laze away** VT *sep* verbummeln

lazily ['leɪzɪlɪ] ADV faul; (= *languidly, unhurriedly*) träge; *drift, float* gemächlich

laziness ['leɪzɪnɪs] N Faulheit *f*; (= *languor*) Trägheit *f*

lazy ['leɪzɪ] ADJ (+*er*) **a** (= *not inclined to work*) faul; **to be ~ about doing sth** zu faul sein, etw zu tun; **~ about writing** schreibfaul; **I'm feeling ~ today** ich habe heute einfach keine Lust (, etw zu tun); **he's getting ~ in his old age** (*hum*) er wird auf seine alten Tage faul

b (= *slow-moving*) langsam, träge; (= *lacking activity*) träge; (= *relaxed*) *lunch, dinner, evening* gemütlich; *smile* träge; **his ~ drawl** seine träge, schleppende Sprache; **~ little streams** träge fließende kleine Bäche *pl*; **the long, ~ days of summer** die langen, trägen Sommertage; **we had a ~ holiday** (*esp Brit*) or **vacation** (*US*) wir haben im Urlaub nur gefaulenzt; **I enjoy a ~ day at home** ich mache mir gerne einen faulen or gemütlichen Tag zu Hause

c (*pej*: = *sloppy*) *work, writing, style, attitude* schluderig (*inf*)

lazy: lazybones N *sing* (*inf*) Faulpelz *m*, Faultier *nt*; **lazy eye** N (*Med*) zeitweilig schielendes Auge, das weniger belastet wird und daher in der Sehkraft nachlässt, Amblyopia ex anopsia *f* (*spec*); **lazy Susan** N drehbare Tischmenage

lb N (*weight*) ≈ Pfd.

LBO (*Fin*) *abbr of* **leveraged buyout**

lbw *abbr of* **leg before wicket**

lc (*Typ*) *abbr of* **lower case**

LCD *abbr of* **liquid crystal display** LCD *nt*; **~ screen** LCD-Bildschirm *m*

L-driver ['el,draɪvə'] N (*Brit inf*) Fahrschüler(in) *m(f)*

LEA (*Brit*) *abbr of* **Local Education Authority**

lea [liː] N (*poet*) Au(e) *f* (*poet*), Wiesengrund *m* (*liter*)

leach [liːtʃ] VT (*durch*)filtern; (= *extract*) auslaugen

lead¹ [led] N **a** (= *metal*) Blei *nt*; **they pumped him full of ~** (*inf*) sie pumpten ihn mit Blei voll (*inf*) **b** (*in pencil*) Graphit *nt*, Grafit *nt*; (= *single lead*) Mine *f*; **that'll put ~ in your pencil** (*inf*) das wird dir die Glieder stärken (*inf*) **c** (*Naut*) Lot *nt* **d** **leads** PL (*on roof*) Bleiplatten *pl*; (*in window*) Bleifassung *f* VT (= *weight with lead*) mit Blei beschweren

lead² [liːd] ✪ 26.1 *vb: pret, ptp* **led** N **a** (= *front position*) Spitzenposition *f*; (= *leading position, Sport*) Führung *f*, Spitze *f*; (*in league etc*) Tabellenspitze *f*; **to be in the ~** führend sein, in Führung liegen; (*Sport*) in Führung or vorn liegen, führen; **to take the ~, to move into the ~** in Führung gehen, die Führung übernehmen; (*in league*) Tabellenführer werden; **this set gives him the ~** mit diesem Satz liegt er in Führung; **this match gives them the ~ in the league** mit diesem Spiel gehen sie in der Liga in Führung; **he took the ~ from the German runner** er übernahm die Führung vor dem deutschen Läufer; **Japan took the ~ from Germany in exports** Japan verdrängte Deutschland auf dem Exportmarkt von der Spitze

b (= *distance, time ahead*) Vorsprung *m*; **to have two minutes' ~ over sb** zwei Minuten Vorsprung vor jdm haben

c (= *example*) Beispiel *nt*; **to give sb a ~** jdm etw vormachen; **to take the ~, to show a ~** mit gutem Beispiel vorangehen

d (= *clue*) Indiz *nt*, Anhaltspunkt *m*; (*in guessing etc*) Hinweis *m*, Tipp *m*; **the police have a ~** die Polizei hat eine Spur; **it gave the police a ~** das brachte die Polizei auf die Spur

e (*Cards*) **it's my ~** ich fange an

f (*Theat*) (= *part*) Hauptrolle *f*; (= *person*) Hauptdarsteller(in) *m(f)*; **to sing the ~** die Titelpartie or die tragende Partie singen

g (= *leash*) Leine *f*; **on a ~** an der Leine

h (*Elec*) Leitung(skabel *nt*) *f*, Kabel *nt*; (*from separate source*) Zuleitung *f* (*form*)

VT **a** (= *conduct*) *person, animal* führen; *water* leiten; **to ~ sb in/out** *etc* jdn hinein-/hinaus- *etc* führen; **that road will ~ you back to the station** auf dieser Straße kommen Sie zum Bahnhof zurück; **to ~ the way** (*lit, fig*) vorangehen; (*fig*: = *be superior*) führend sein; **all this talk is ~ing us nowhere** dieses ganze Gerede bringt uns nicht weiter; **the argument led us round in circles** unsere Argumentation drehte sich im Kreis

b (= *be the leader of, direct*) (an)führen; *expedition, team* leiten; *regiment* führen; *movement, revolution* anführen; *conversation* bestimmen; *orchestra* (*conductor*) leiten; (*first violin*) führen; **to ~ a government** an der Spitze einer Regierung stehen, Regierungschef sein; **to ~ a party** Parteivorsitzender sein, den Parteivorsitz führen

c (= *be first in*) anführen; **they led us by 30 seconds** sie lagen mit 30 Sekunden vor uns (*dat*); **Britain ~s the world in textiles** Großbritannien ist auf dem Gebiet der Textilproduktion führend in der Welt

d *card* ausspielen

e *life* führen; **to ~ a life of luxury/deception** ein Luxusleben/betrügerisches Leben führen

f (= *influence*) beeinflussen; **to ~ sb to do sth** jdn dazu bringen, etw zu tun; **to ~ a witness** einen Zeugen/eine Zeugin beeinflussen; **what led him to change his mind?** wie kam er dazu, seine Meinung zu ändern?; **to ~ sb to believe that ...** jdm den Eindruck vermitteln, dass ..., jdn glauben machen, dass ... (*geh*); **I am led to believe that ...** ich habe Grund zu der Annahme, dass ...; **to ~ sb into error** jdn irreleiten or fehlleiten; **to ~ sb into trouble** jdn in Schwierigkeiten bringen; **he is easily led** er lässt sich leicht beeinflussen; (= *deceived*) er lässt sich leicht täuschen or sich (*dat*) leicht etwas weismachen; **this led me to the conclusion that ...** daraus schloss ich, dass ...; **I am led to the conclusion that ...** ich komme zu dem Schluss, dass ...; **what ~s you to think that?** woraus schließen Sie das?

g *wire, flex* legen, entlangführen

VI **a** (= *go in front*) vorangehen; (*in race*) in Führung liegen; **to ~ by 10 metres** einen Vorsprung von 10 Metern haben, mit 10 Metern in Führung liegen; **he easily ~s** er liegt klar in Führung; **he always follows where his brother ~s** er macht alles nach, was sein Bruder macht; **the "Times" led with a story about the financial crisis** die „Times" berichtete auf der ersten Seite ausführlich über die Finanzkrise; **he ~s with his right** (*Boxing*) er ist Rechtsausleger

b (= *be a leader, also in dancing*) führen; **he had shown the ability to ~** er hat gezeigt, dass er Führungsqualitäten besitzt

c (*Cards*) ausspielen; (*with sth*) etw; **who ~s?** wer spielt aus?, wer fängt an?

d (*street etc*) führen, gehen; **it ~s into that room** es führt zu diesem Raum; **this road ~s nowhere** diese Straße führt nirgendwohin or geht nicht weiter

e (= *result in, cause*) führen (*to* zu); **all this talk is ~ing nowhere** dieses ganze Gerede führt zu nichts; **remarks like that could ~ to trouble** solche Bemerkungen können unangenehme Folgen haben; **what will all these strikes ~ to?** wo sollen all diese Streiks hinführen?

▶**lead along** VT *sep* führen; **he led him along the street** er führte ihn die Straße entlang

▶**lead aside** VT *sep* auf die Seite or beiseite nehmen

▶**lead away** VT *sep* wegführen or -bringen; *criminal, prisoner* abführen; **we must not allow this argument to lead us away from the matter in hand** wir dürfen uns durch dieses Argument nicht vom eigentlichen Thema abbringen lassen; **this is leading away from the subject** das führt vom Thema ab

▶**lead off** VT *sep* abführen; **a policeman led the drunk man off the pitch** ein Polizist führte den Betrunkenen vom Platz VI **a** (= *go off* *from*) abgehen; **several streets led off the square** mehrere Straßen gingen von dem Platz ab **b** (= *start*) beginnen; **my partner led off with the ten of hearts** mein Partner spielte die Herzzehn aus

▶ **lead on** vi *usu imper* **lead on, sergeant!** führen Sie an, Feldwebel!; **lead on, John!** geh vor, John! vt *sep* (= *deceive*) anführen (*inf*), hinters Licht führen; (= *tease*) aufziehen, auf den Arm nehmen (*inf*); **she's just leading him on** sie hält ihn nur zum Narren *or* führt ihn nur an der Nase herum

▶ **lead on to** vi +*prep obj* führen zu

▶ **lead out** vt *sep* hinausführen; **he led his wife out onto the dance floor** er führte seine Frau auf die Tanzfläche vi hinausgehen

▶ **lead up** vt *sep* hinaufführen (*to* auf +*acc*); (= *lead across*) führen (*to* zu); **to lead sb up the garden path** (*fig*) jdm etwas vormachen, jdn an der Nase herumführen

vi **a** (= *come before*) **the events/years that led up to the war** die Ereignisse/Jahre, die dem Krieg voran- *or* vorausgingen

b (= *introduce*) **he was obviously leading up to an important announcement** er schickte sich offensichtlich an, etwas Wichtiges anzukündigen; **his speech was obviously leading up to an important announcement** seine Rede war offensichtlich die Einleitung zu einer wichtigen Ankündigung; **what are you leading up to?** worauf willst du hinaus?; **what's all this leading up to?** was soll das Ganze?

lead [led]: **lead acetate** N Bleiacetat *nt*, Bleiazetat *nt*; **lead content** N Bleigehalt *m*; **lead crystal** N Bleikristall *nt*; **lead-crystal** ADJ aus Bleikristall; **~ bowl** Bleikristallschale *f*

leaded ['ledɪd] ADJ *petrol* verbleit; **~ glass** Bleiglas *nt*; **~ window** Bleiglasfenster *nt*

leaden ['ledn] ADJ **a** *sky, colour, clouds* bleiern (*geh*); *heart, limbs, steps* bleischwer; *silence* bedrückend **b** (*pej*) (= *tedious*) *translation, dialogue* schwerfällig; (= *stodgy*) *food* sehr schwer **c** (*old*: = *of lead*) bleiern (*geh*)

leader ['liːdə] N **a** Führer(in) *m(f)*; (*of union, party*) Vorsitzende(r) *mf*, Führer(in) *m(f)*; (*military*) Befehlshaber(in) *m(f)*; (*of gang, rebels*) Anführer(in) *m(f)*; (*of expedition, project*) Leiter(in) *m(f)*; (*Sport*) (*in league*) Tabellenführer *m*; (*in race*) der/die Erste; (*Mus, of orchestra*) Konzertmeister(in) *m(f)*; (*of choir*) Leiter(in) *m(f)*; (*of brass band*) erster Bläser, erste Bläserin; (*of jazz band, pop group*) Leader(in) *m(f)*; **to be the ~** (*in race, competition*) in Führung liegen; **the ~s** (*in race, competition*) die Spitzengruppe; **~ of the opposition** Oppositionsführer(in) *m(f)*; **the ~s of fashion** die Modemacher *pl*; **the product is a ~/the world** in its field dieses Produkt ist auf diesem Gebiet führend/weltweit führend; **we are still the ~s in biochemical research** wir sind auf dem Gebiet der biochemischen Forschung immer noch führend; **has he the qualities to be a ~ of men?** hat er Führungsqualitäten?

b (*Brit Press*) Leitartikel *m*; **~ writer** Leitartikler(in) *m(f)*

leaderless ['liːdəlɪs] ADJ führerlos, ohne Führer; *party, union* führungslos

---

LEADER OF THE HOUSE

Leader of the House werden die Führer sowohl des Unterhauses (Leader of the House of Commons) als auch des Oberhauses (Leader of the House of Lords) genannt. Sie sind hohe Mitglieder der britischen Regierung und verantwortlich für die Gestaltung und Verlesung der wöchentlichen Geschäftsordnung ihres jeweiligen Hauses, wobei sie Rücksprache mit ihren Kollegen aus der Opposition halten.

---

leadership ['liːdəʃɪp] N **a** Führung *f*, Leitung *f*; (= *office*) Vorsitz *m*, Leitung *f*; **under the ~ of** unter (der) Führung von; **a crisis in the ~, a ~ crisis** eine Führungskrise **b** (= *quality*) Füh-

rungsqualitäten *pl*; **the country is looking for firm ~** das Land ruft nach einer straffen Führung; **he has ~ potential** er besitzt Führungsqualitäten

lead-free ['ledfriː] ADJ bleifrei; *petrol also* unverbleit N (= *petrol*) unverbleites *or* bleifreies Benzin

lead guitar ['liːd-] N Leadgitarre *f*

lead-in ['liːdɪn] N Einführung *f* (*to* in +*acc*), Einleitung *f* (*to* in +*acc*)

leading[1] ['ledɪŋ] N (*Typ*) Durchschuss *m*

leading[2] ['liːdɪŋ] ADJ **a** (= *first*) vorderste(r, s); *runner, horse, car also* führend; **the ~ car in the procession** das die Kolonne anführende Auto **b** (= *most important*) *person, writer, politician, company* führend; **~ product/sportsman** Spitzenprodukt *nt*/-sportler *m*; **~ part** *or* **role** (*Theat*) Hauptrolle *f*; (*fig*) führende Rolle (*in* bei); **the ~ issue** das Hauptthema, das wichtigste Thema; **we are a ~ company in ...** unsere Firma ist führend auf dem Gebiet ... (+*gen*)

leading ['liːdɪŋ]: **leading article** N Leitartikel *m*; **leading case** N (*Jur*) wichtiger Präzedenzfall; **leading counsel** N (*Brit Jur, for the defence*) Hauptverteidiger(in) *m(f)*; (*for the prosecution*) Kronanwalt *m*/-anwältin *f*; **leading edge** N **a** (*Aviat*) (Flügel)vorderkante *f* **b** **the ~ of technology** die Spitzentechnologie; **to be at** *or* **on the ~ of technology** (*machine etc*) zur Spitzentechnologie gehören; (*country etc*) in der Technologie führend sein; **leading-edge** ADJ *company* führend; **~ technology** Spitzentechnologie *f*; **leading lady** N Hauptdarstellerin *f*; **she was Mel Gibson's ~** sie spielte an der Seite von Mel Gibson die weibliche Hauptrolle; **leading light** N Nummer eins *f*; (= *person also*) großes Licht, Leuchte *f*; **leading man** N Hauptdarsteller *m*; **he was Sharon Stone's ~** er spielte an der Seite von Sharon Stone die männliche Hauptrolle; **leading note** N (*Mus*) Leitton *m*; **leading question** N Suggestivfrage *f*; **leading reins** PL (*for child*) Laufgeschirr *nt*; **leading role** N Hauptrolle *f*

lead [led-]: **lead paint** N Bleifarbe *f*; **lead pencil** N Bleistift *m*; **lead poisoning** N Bleivergiftung *f*; **lead shot** N Schrot *m or nt*

lead ['liːd-]: **lead singer** N Leadsänger(in) *m(f)*; **lead story** N Hauptartikel *m*; **lead time** N (*for production*) Produktionszeit *f*; (*for delivery*) Lieferzeit *f*

leaf [liːf] N *pl* **leaves** **a** Blatt *nt*; **to be in ~** grün sein; **to come into ~** grün werden, ausschlagen (*poet*); **he swept the leaves into a pile** er fegte das Laub auf einen Haufen

b (*of paper*) Blatt *nt*; **to take a ~ out of** *or* **from sb's book** sich (*dat*) von jdm eine Scheibe abschneiden; **to turn over a new ~** einen neuen Anfang machen; **it's time you turned over a new ~, said the teacher** es wird Zeit, dass du dich änderst, sagte der Lehrer

c (*of table*) Ausziehplatte *f*; **pull the leaves out** zieh den Tisch aus!

d (*of metal*) Folie *f*; **gold/silver ~** Blattgold-/-silber *nt*

vi **to ~ through a book** ein Buch durchblättern

leaf bud N Blattknospe *f*

leafed [liːft] ADJ belaubt; **four-leafed** vierblättrig

leaf green N Blattgrün *nt*

leafless ADJ blattlos, kahl

leaflet ['liːflət] N **a** Prospekt *m*; (= *single page*) Handzettel *m*, Reklamezettel *m*; (*with instructions*) Merkblatt *nt*; (= *handout*) Flugblatt *nt*; (= *brochure for information*) Broschüre *f*, Informationsblatt *nt* **b** (= *young leaf*) Blättchen *nt* vt **~ area** Flugblätter verteilen in (+*dat*); (*Comm*) Werbematerial verteilen in (+*dat*)

leafleting ['liːflətɪŋ] N Flugblattaktionen *pl*; (*Comm*) Verteilen *nt* von Werbematerial; **~ campaign** Flugblattaktion *f*

leaf: **leaf mould**, (*US*) **leaf mold** N (Laub-)kompost *m*; **leaf spring** N Blattfeder *f*; **leaf tobacco** N Rohtabak *m*, Blättertabak *m*

leafy ['liːfɪ] ADJ *branch, tree* grün, belaubt; *bower, lane* grün

league[1] [liːg] N (*Measure*) Wegstunde *f*

league[2] N **a** (= *treaty*) Bündnis *nt*, Bund *m*; (= *organization*) Verband *m*, Liga *f*; **League of Nations** Völkerbund *m*; **to enter into a ~** einen Bund schließen; **to be in ~ with sb** mit jdm gemeinsame Sache machen; **to be in ~ with the devil** mit dem Teufel im Bunde sein; **these two boys must be in ~ with each other** diese beiden Jungen stecken sicher unter einer Decke (*inf*); **to be in ~ against sb** sich gegen jdn verbündet haben

b (*Sport*) Liga *f*; **the club is top of the ~** der Klub ist Tabellen- *or* Ligaführer; **he was not in the same ~** (*fig*) er hatte nicht das gleiche Format; **Peter's car is not in the same ~ as Wendy's** Peters Auto ist eine Nummer kleiner als Wendys; **this is way out of your ~!** das ist einige Nummern zu groß für dich!

league: **league game** N Ligaspiel *nt*; **league leaders** PL Tabellenführer *m*; **league match** N (*Brit*) Ligaspiel *nt*; **league table** N Tabelle *f*

leak [liːk] N **a** (= *hole*) undichte Stelle; (*in container*) Loch *nt*; (*Naut*) Leck *nt*; **to have a ~** undicht sein; (*bucket etc*) laufen, lecken; **my pen has a ~** mein Kugelschreiber läuft aus *or* ist nicht dicht; **there's a ~ in the gas pipe** die Gasleitung ist undicht; **the rain is coming in through a ~ in the roof** es regnet durchs Dach herein

b (= *escape of liquid*) Leck *nt*; **a gas ~** eine undichte Stelle in der Gasleitung; **the tunnel was flooded because of the ~** der Tunnel wurde vom eindringenden Wasser überflutet; **a faulty joint caused a gas ~** durch die fehlerhafte Verbindung strömte Gas aus

c (*fig*) undichte Stelle; **there was a ~ of information** es sind Informationen durchgesickert; **a security/news ~** eine undichte Stelle; **the news ~ may have been the result of carelessness** die Nachricht kann aufgrund *or* auf Grund einer Unachtsamkeit durchgesickert sein; **a ~ to the press** eine Indiskretion der Presse gegenüber; **they wanted to break the news gently by a series of ~s to the press** sie wollten die Nachricht langsam an die Presse durchsickern lassen

d (*inf*) **to go for a ~, to have a ~** pissen gehen (*vulg*)

vt **a** (*lit*) durchlassen; *fuel* verlieren; **that tank is ~ing acid** aus diesem Tank läuft Säure aus; **the tanker had ~ed its contents into the river** der Tankerinhalt war in den Fluss gelaufen

b (*fig*) *information, story, plans* zuspielen (*to sb* jdm); *secret* verraten (*to sb* jdm)

vi **a** (*ship, receptacle, pipe*) lecken; (*roof*) undicht *or* nicht dicht sein; (*pen*) auslaufen, undicht sein

b (*gas*) ausströmen, entweichen; (*liquid*) auslaufen; (= *ooze out*) tropfen (*from* aus); **water is ~ing (in) through the roof** Wasser tropft *or* sickert durch das Dach, es regnet durch (das Dach durch); **to ~ away** auslaufen

▶ **leak out** vt *sep news* zuspielen (*to sb* jdm) vi **a** (*liquid*) auslaufen, durchsickern **b** (*news*) durchsickern

leakage ['liːkɪdʒ] N **a** (= *act*) Auslaufen *nt*; (*of body fluids*) Austreten *nt*; **there's a ~ of water into the oil** da läuft *or* tropft Wasser ins Öl; **there's still a slight ~** es ist immer noch etwas undicht; **the ground was polluted by a ~ of chemicals** der Boden war durch auslaufende Chemikalien verunreinigt **b** (*fig*) **~ of information** (= *act*) Durchsickern *nt* von Informationen; **the government was worried by repeated security ~s** die Regierung war besorgt, weil wiederholt Informationen durchgesickert waren

leakproof ['liːkpruːf] ADJ dicht, lecksicher (*spec*); **we'll have to make the department ~** (*fig*) wir müssen undichte Stellen in der Abteilung beseitigen

leaky ['liːkɪ] ADJ (+er) undicht; *boat also* leck; **the ministry has become rather ~** (*fig inf*) aus dem Ministerium sickert inzwischen einiges durch

lean¹ [liːn] ADJ (+er) **a** (= *thin*) mager, dünn; *face, person* schmal; (*through lack of food*) hager; (= *fatless*) *meat* mager; **to grow ~** schlank *or* schmal werden; **to have a ~ build** schlank gebaut sein **b** (= *poor*) *year, times, harvest* mager; **to go through a ~ patch** eine Durststrecke durchlaufen **c** (*Comm*) schlank; **~er companies** verschlankte Firmen *pl* **N** mageres Fleisch

lean² *vb*: pret, ptp **leant** (*esp Brit*) *or* **leaned** **N** Neigung *f*
VT **a** (= *put in sloping position*) lehnen (*against* gegen, an +*acc*); **to ~ one's head on sb's shoulder** seinen Kopf an jds Schulter (*acc*) lehnen **b** (= *rest*) aufstützen (*on* auf +*dat or acc*); **to ~ one's elbow on sth** sich mit dem Ellbogen auf etw (*acc*) stützen; **she ~ed her weight on the door** sie lehnte sich mit ihrem Gewicht gegen die Tür
VI **a** (= *be off vertical*) sich neigen (*to* nach); (*trees*) sich biegen; **the box was ~ing dangerously to the side** die Kiste neigte sich gefährlich auf die Seite; **he ~ed across the counter** beugte sich über den Ladentisch; **a motorcyclist should ~ into the corner** ein Motorradfahrer sollte sich in die Kurve legen **b** (= *rest*) sich lehnen; **to ~ against sth** sich gegen etw lehnen; **~ing against the bar** an die Bar gelehnt; **she ~ed on my arm** sie stützte sich auf meinen Arm; **to ~ on the edge of the table** er stützte sich auf die Tischkante; **to ~ on one's elbow** sich mit dem Ellbogen aufstützen **c** (= *tend in opinion etc*) **to ~ toward(s) the left/socialism** nach links/zum Sozialismus tendieren; **to ~ toward(s) sb's opinion** zu jds Ansicht neigen *or* tendieren; **which way does he ~?** in welche Richtung tendiert er?; **he started to ~ away from the party line** er entfernte sich allmählich von der Parteilinie; **at least they're ~ing in the direction of reform** sie neigen immerhin Reformen (*dat*) zu

▶ **lean back** VI sich zurücklehnen

▶ **lean forward** VI sich vorbeugen

▶ **lean on** VI **a** (= *depend on*) **to lean on sb** sich auf jdn verlassen **b** (*inf*: = *put pressure on*) **to lean on sb** jdn bearbeiten (*inf*) *or* beknien (*inf*); **they leaned on him too hard** sie haben ihn zu sehr unter Druck gesetzt (*inf*)

▶ **lean out** VI sich hinauslehnen (*of* aus)

▶ **lean over** VI **a** (= *be off vertical*: *object, tree*) sich (vor)neigen **b** (*person*) sich vorbeugen; **they leaned over the side of the bridge** sie beugten sich über das Brückengeländer; **he leaned over her shoulder** er beugte sich über ihre Schulter → **backwards**

lean-burn ['liːnbɜːn] ADJ **~ engine** Magermotor *m*

leaning ['liːnɪŋ] ADJ schräg, schief; **the Leaning Tower of Pisa** der Schiefe Turm von Pisa **N** Hang *m*, Neigung *f*; **he had a ~ toward(s) the left** er hatte einen Hang nach links; **what are his ~s?** was sind seine Neigungen?; **artistic ~s** künstlerische Neigungen *pl*

leanness ['liːnnɪs] N Magerkeit *f*; **the ~ of his face** sein schmales Gesicht; (*through lack of food*) sein hageres Gesicht

lean production N (*Comm*) Lean Production *f* (*spec*)

leant [lent] (*esp Brit*) pret, ptp of **lean²**

lean-to ['liːntuː] **N** Anbau *m*; (= *shelter*) Wetterschutz *or* -schirm *m* ADJ angebaut

leap [liːp] *vb*: pret, ptp **leapt** (*esp Brit*) *or* **leaped** **N** Sprung *m*, Satz *m* (*inf*); (*fig*: *in profits, unemployment etc*) sprunghafter Anstieg; **in one ~** mit einem Satz; **to take a ~** einen Satz machen; **a great ~ forward** (*fig*) ein großer Sprung nach vorn; **a ~ into the unknown, a ~ in the dark** (*fig*) ein Sprung ins Ungewisse; **a ~ of imagination is needed** man braucht viel Fantasie *or* Phantasie; **by** *or* **in ~s and bounds** (*fig*) sprunghaft

VT springen *or* setzen über (+*acc*); **he ~t the horse across the ditch** er ließ das Pferd über den Graben springen
VI springen; **my heart ~ed (with joy)** mein Herz hüpfte vor Freude (*geh*), mein Herz machte vor Freude einen Sprung; **to ~ about** herumspringen; **to ~ for joy** vor Freude hüpfen, Freudensprünge machen; **try to ~ over to the other side** versuch mal, auf die andere Seite zu springen; **to ~ to one's feet** aufspringen; **he ~t to her assistance** er sprang ihr zu Hilfe; **the shares ~t by 21p** die Aktien stiegen mit einem Sprung um 21 Pence → *also* **look**

▶ **leap at** VI +prep obj **to leap at a chance** eine Gelegenheit beim Schopf packen, sofort zugreifen; **to leap at an offer** sich (förmlich) auf ein Angebot stürzen

▶ **leap out** VI **a** (= *jump out*) hinausspringen (*of* aus +*dat*); **he leapt out of the car** er sprang aus dem Auto **b** (*colours*) ins Auge springen, hervorstechen; **the bright colours leap out at you** die hellen Farben springen einem ins Auge

▶ **leap up** VI (*person, animals*) aufspringen; (*flames*) hoch schlagen; (*prices*) sprunghaft ansteigen, emporschnellen; **he leapt up from behind the wall** er sprang hinter der Mauer hervor; **to leap up into the air** in die Höhe springen

leap day N Schalttag *m*

leapfrog ['liːpfrɒg] **N** Bockspringen *nt*; **to play ~** Bockspringen spielen *or* machen (*inf*) **VI** bockspringen; **the children ~ged over one another** die Kinder spielten *or* machten (*inf*) Bockspringen **VT** **to leap sb** er machte einen Bocksprung über ihn; **he ~ged his way to the top of the company** er machte in der Firma eine Blitzkarriere

leap of faith N Vertrauensvorschuss *m*; **to take** *or* **make a ~** einen Vertrauensvorschuss gewähren; **it takes a considerable ~ to believe that ...** man muss schon eine Menge Vertrauen aufbringen, um zu glauben, dass ...

leapt [lept] (*esp Brit*) pret, ptp of **leap**

leap year N Schaltjahr *nt*

learn [lɜːn] pret, ptp **learnt** (*Brit*) *or* **learned** **VT** **a** (= *gain knowledge, skill etc*) lernen; (= *memorize*) *poem etc* auswendig lernen; **where did you ~ that habit?** wo hast du dir das angewöhnt?; **I ~ed (how) to swim** ich habe schwimmen gelernt **b** (= *be informed*) erfahren **VI** **a** (= *gain knowledge, skill*) lernen; **I can't play the piano, but I'm hoping to ~** ich kann nicht Klavier spielen, aber ich hoffe, es zu lernen; **he'll never ~!** er lernt es nie!; **some people never ~!** manche lernen nie!; **to ~ from experience** aus der Erfahrung *or* durch Erfahrung lernen **b** (= *find out*) hören, erfahren (*about, of* von)

▶ **learn off** VT sep lernen

▶ **learn up** VT sep (= *learn by study*) lernen, pauken (*inf*); (= *memorize*) auswendig lernen

learned¹ ['lɜːnɪd] ADJ gelehrt; *book also, journal* wissenschaftlich; *society also, profession* akademisch; **a ~ man** ein Gelehrter *m*; **my ~ colleague** *or* **friend** (*Jur*) mein verehrter Herr Kollege, meine verehrte Frau Kollegin

learned² [lɜːnd] pret, ptp of **learn** ADJ (*Psych*) *behaviour* angelernt; *reaction* antrainiert

learnedly ['lɜːnɪdlɪ] ADV gelehrt

learner ['lɜːnə] N Anfänger(in) *m(f)*, Lerner(in) *m(f)* (*esp Ling*); (= *learner driver*) Fahrschüler(in) *m(f)*; **~s of languages** Sprachschüler *or* -studenten *pl*; **special classes for slow ~s** Sonderklassen *pl* für lernschwache Schüler

learner-centred, (*US*) **learner-centered** ['lɜːnəˌsentəd] ADJ auf den Lernenden ausgerichtet

learning ['lɜːnɪŋ] N **a** (= *act*) Lernen *nt*; **difficulties encountered during the ~ of geometry/English** Schwierigkeiten beim Erlernen der Geometrie/beim Englischlernen **b** (= *erudition*) Gelehrsamkeit *f*, Gelehrtheit *f*; **a man of ~** ein Gelehrter *m*; **the ~ contained in these volumes** das in diesen Bänden enthaltene Wissen; **seat of ~** Stätte *f* der Gelehrsamkeit

learning: learning curve N Lernkurve *f*; **to be on a steep ~** viel dazulernen; **life is a constant ~** man lernt immer noch dazu; **learning disability** N Lernbehinderung *f*; **learning-disabled** ADJ lernbehindert

learnt [lɜːnt] (*Brit*) pret, ptp of **learn**

lease [liːs] **N** (*of land, farm, business premises etc*) Pacht *f*; (= *contract*) Pachtvertrag *m*; (*of house, flat, equipment*) Leasing *nt*; (= *contract*) Leasingvertrag *m*; **the ~ was prematurely terminated** die Pacht *or* das Pachtverhältnis/das Mietverhältnis wurde vorzeitig beendet; **to take a ~ on a house** ein Haus mieten; **to take a ~ on business premises** ein Geschäft(sgrundstück) *nt* pachten; **to take a house on a 99-year ~** ein Haus auf 99 Jahre pachten; **you can buy the ~ for a period of 99 years** Sie können einen Pachtvertrag für 99 Jahre abschließen; **we rented the house/farm on a ~** wir haben das Haus gemietet/den Bauernhof gepachtet; **to let sth on a ~** etw verpachten/vermieten; **to be on ~** so ... verpachtet/vermietet sein an (+*acc*) ...; **to give sb a new ~ of life** jdm (neuen) Aufschwung geben; **the renovations have given the old farmhouse a new ~ of life** durch die Renovierung ist der alte Bauernhof wieder in Schuss gekommen
VT (= *take*) pachten (*from* von), in Pacht nehmen (*from* bei); *house, flat, office* mieten (*from* von); *equipment* mieten, leasen (*from* von); (= *give*: *also* **lease out**) verpachten (*to* an +*acc*), in Pacht geben (*to sb* jdm); *house, flat, office* vermieten (*to* an +*acc*); *equipment* vermieten, leasen (*to* an +*acc*)

lease: leaseback **N** Verkauf und Rückmiete *pl* ATTR *arrangement* mit Rückvermietung an den Verkäufer; **leasehold** **N** (= *property*) Pachtbesitz *m*; (= *land also*) Pachtgrundstück *nt*; (= *building also*) gepachtetes Gebäude; (= *contract, tenure*) Pachtvertrag *m*; **who has the ~ on the property?** wer hat das Land/Gebäude gepachtet?; **we own the house on ~** wir haben das Haus langfristig gepachtet; **~ reform** Mietrechtsreform *f* ADJ gepachtet; **~ property** (*generally*) Pachtbesitz *m*; (= *land*) Pachtgrund *m*, Pachtland *nt*; (= *building*) Pachtobjekt *nt* ADJ **to buy a property** ~ ein Objekt *nt* mit Pachtvertrag kaufen; **leaseholder** N Pächter(in) *m(f)*

leash [liːʃ] N Leine *f*; **on a ~** an der Leine; **to give sb a longer ~** (*esp US fig*) jdm mehr Freiheit geben → *also* **strain¹**

leasing ['liːsɪŋ] N **a** (= *renting*) Mieten *nt*; (*of land*) Pachten *nt* **b** (= *hiring out*) Vermieten *nt*; (*of land*) Verpachten *nt*; (*of car, computer*) Leasing *nt*

least [liːst] ⊘ 26.3 ADJ **a** (= *slightest, smallest*) geringste(r, s) **b** (*with uncountable nouns*) wenigste(r, s); **he has the ~ money** er hat am wenigsten Geld
ADV **a** (+*vb*) am wenigsten; **~ of all would I wish to offend him** auf gar keinen Fall möchte ich ihn beleidigen **b** (+*adj*) **~ possible expenditure** möglichst geringe Kosten; **the ~ expensive car** das billigste *or* preiswerteste Auto; **the ~ important matter** das Unwichtigste; **of all my worries that's the ~ important** das ist meine geringste Sorge; **the ~ talented player** der am wenigsten talentierte Spieler; **the ~ known** der/die/das Unbekannteste; **the ~ interesting** der/die/das Uninteressanteste; **he's the ~ aggressive of men** er ist nicht im mindesten *or* Mindesten aggressiv; **not the ~ bit drunk** kein bisschen *or* nicht im Geringsten betrunken
N **the ~** der/die/das Geringste *or* wenigste; **that's the ~ of my worries** darüber mache ich mir die wenigsten Sorgen; **I have many worries, and money is the ~ of them** ich habe viele Sorgen, und Geld kümmert mich am wenigsten; **it's the ~ I can do** es ist das wenigste, was ich

tun kann; **you gave yourself the ~** du hast dir (selbst) am wenigsten gegeben; **at ~, I think so** ich glaube wenigstens; **at ~ it's not raining** wenigstens or zumindest regnet es nicht; **we can at ~ try** wir können es wenigstens versuchen; **there were at ~ eight** es waren mindestens acht da; **we need at ~ three** wir brauchen wenigstens or mindestens drei; **we need three at the very ~** allermindestens brauchen wir drei; **there must have been twenty at the very ~** es waren mindestens zwanzig da; **at the very ~ you could apologize** du könntest dich wenigstens or zumindest entschuldigen; **all nations love football, not ~ the British** alle Völker lieben Fußball, nicht zuletzt die Briten; **and that's the ~ of it** und das ist noch das wenigste; **not in the ~!** nicht im Geringsten!, ganz und gar nicht!; **he was not in the ~ upset** er war kein bisschen or nicht im Geringsten verärgert; **to say the ~** um es milde zu sagen; **the ~ said, the better, ~ said, soonest mended** (Prov) je weniger man darüber spricht, desto besser

leastways ['liːstweɪz] ADV (inf) zumindest, wenigstens

leather ['leðə'] N Leder nt; ~s (for motorbike) Lederzeug nt ADJ Leder-, ledern; **~ goods** Lederwaren pl; **~ shoes** Lederschuhe pl VT (inf) versohlen (inf), ein paar überziehen (+dat) (inf)

leatherette [ˌleðə'ret] N Kunstleder nt

leathering ['leðərɪŋ] N (Brit inf) Tracht f Prügel

leatherneck ['leðənek] N (US inf) Ledernacken m

leathery ['leðərɪ] ADJ material lederartig; skin ledern; meat zäh; **a ~ smell** ein Ledergeruch m

leave [liːv] vb: pret, ptp **left** N a (= permission) Erlaubnis f; **by your ~** (form) mit Ihrer (gütigen) Erlaubnis (form); **to ask sb's ~ to do sth** jdn um Erlaubnis bitten, etw zu tun; **he borrowed my car without so much as a by your ~** er hat sich (dat) einfach so mein Auto geliehen

b (= permission to be absent, Mil) Urlaub m; **to be on ~** auf Urlaub sein, Urlaub haben; **to be on ~ from sth** von etw beurlaubt sein; **I've got ~ to attend the conference** ich habe freibekommen, um an der Konferenz teilzunehmen; **a two-day ~** zwei Tage Urlaub; **~ of absence** Beurlaubung f; **to be on ~ of absence** beurlaubt sein

c **to take one's ~** sich verabschieden; **to take ~ of sb** sich von jdm verabschieden; **to take ~ of one's senses** den Verstand verlieren

VT a (= depart from, quit) place, person verlassen; **the train left the station** der Zug fuhr aus dem Bahnhof; **when the plane left Rome** als das Flugzeug von Rom abflog; **when he left Rome** als er von Rom wegging/wegfuhr/abflog etc; **would you ~ us, please?** würden Sie uns bitte allein lassen?; **please sir, may I ~ the room?** Herr X, darf ich mal raus?; **to ~ the country** das Land verlassen, (permanently) auswandern; **to ~ home** von zu Hause weggehen/wegfahren; (permanently) von zu Hause weggehen; **she left her parents' home** sie verließ ihr Elternhaus; **to ~ school** die Schule verlassen, (prematurely also) (von der Schule) abgehen; **to ~ the table** vom Tisch aufstehen; **to ~ one's job** seine Stelle aufgeben; **to ~ the road** (= crash) von der Straße abkommen, (= turn off) von der Straße abbiegen; **to ~ the rails** entgleisen; **the rocket left the ground** die Rakete hob (vom Boden) ab; **I'll ~ you at the station** am Bahnhof trennen wir uns dann; (in car) ich setze dich am Bahnhof ab; **he left her for another woman** er verließ sie wegen einer anderen

b (= allow or cause to remain) lassen; bad taste, dirty mark, message, scar, impression hinterlassen; **I'll ~ my address with you** ich lasse Ihnen meine Adresse da; **I'll ~ the key with the neighbours** (Brit) or **neighbors** (US) ich hinterlege or lasse den Schlüssel bei den Nachbarn; **to ~ one's supper** sein Abendessen stehen lassen; **the postman** (Brit) or **mailman** (US) **left three letters for you** der Briefträger hat drei Briefe für dich gebracht; **they were left to die** man ließ sie sterben

c (= leave in a certain condition) lassen; **who left the window open?** wer hat das Fenster offen gelassen?; **to ~ two pages blank** zwei Seiten frei lassen; **this ~s me free for the afternoon/free to go shopping** dadurch habe ich den Nachmittag frei/Zeit zum Einkaufen; **this new development ~s us with a problem** diese neue Entwicklung stellt uns vor ein Problem; **the death of her uncle left her with no financial worries** nach dem Tod ihres Onkels hatte sie keine finanziellen Probleme mehr; **~ the dog alone** lass den Hund in Ruhe; **~ me alone!** lass mich (in Ruhe)!; **~ well alone** die Finger davonlassen (inf); **to ~ sb to do sth** es jdm überlassen, etw zu tun; **I'll ~ you to it** ich lasse Sie jetzt allein weitermachen; **to ~ sb to himself** jdn allein lassen; **to ~ go of sb/sth** jdn/etw loslassen; **let's ~ it at that** lassen wir es dabei (bewenden); **if we ~ it so that he'll contact us** wenn wir dabei verbleiben, dass er sich mit uns in Verbindung setzt; **how did he ~ things at the last meeting?** wobei hat er es beim letzten Treffen belassen?; **to ~ sth to the last minute** mit etw bis zur letzten Minute warten

d (= forget) liegen lassen, stehen lassen

e (after death) person, money hinterlassen; **he left his wife very badly off** er ließ seine Frau fast mittellos zurück

f **to be left** (= remain, be over) übrig bleiben; **all I have left** alles, was ich noch habe; **I've (got) £6 left** ich habe noch 6 Pfund (übrig); **how many are there left?** wie viele sind noch da or übrig?; **3 from 10 ~s 7** 10 minus 3 ist or (ist) gleich 7; **what does that ~?** wie viel bleibt übrig?; (Math) wie viel gibt or ist das?; **there was nothing left for me to do but to sell it** mir blieb nichts anderes übrig, als es zu verkaufen

g (= entrust) überlassen (up to sb jdm); **~ it to me** lass mich nur machen; **I ~ it to you to judge** es bleibt dir überlassen, zu urteilen; **to ~ sth to chance** etw dem Zufall überlassen

h (= stop) **let's ~ this now** lassen wir das jetzt mal

VI (person) (weg)gehen, (in vehicle) abfahren; (in plane) abfliegen, (train, bus, ship) abfahren; **we ~ for Sweden tomorrow** wir fahren morgen nach Schweden; **which flight did he ~ on?** welchen Flug hat er genommen?; **his girlfriend has already left** seine Freundin ist schon gegangen

▶ **leave about** (Brit) or **around** VT sep herumliegen lassen

▶ **leave aside** VT sep beiseite lassen; **leaving aside the fact that …** wenn man die Tatsache außer Acht lässt, dass …

▶ **leave behind** VT sep a the car, the children dalassen, zurücklassen; fingerprints, chaos hinterlassen; the past hinter sich (dat) lassen; **we've left all behind us** das alles liegt hinter uns; **we've left all our worries behind us** (= settled) wir sind alle Sorgen los; (= forgotten) wir haben all unsere Sorgen vergessen b (= outstrip) hinter sich (dat) lassen; **he left all his fellow students behind** er stellte alle seine Kommilitonen in den Schatten c (= forget) liegen lassen, stehen lassen

▶ **leave in** VT sep sentence, scene in play etc lassen, nicht herausnehmen, drinlassen (inf); **don't leave the dog in all day** lassen Sie den Hund nicht den ganzen Tag im Haus; **how long should the meat be left in?** wie lange muss das Fleisch im Ofen bleiben or im Ofen gelassen werden?

▶ **leave off** VT sep clothes nicht anziehen; lid nicht darauf tun, ablassen (inf); radio, lights auslassen; umlaut weglassen; **you can leave your coat off** du brauchst deinen Mantel nicht anzuziehen; **don't leave the top off your pen** lass den Füllhalter nicht offen or ohne Kappe liegen; **you left her name off the list** Sie haben ihren Namen nicht in die Liste aufgenommen VI +prep obj (inf) aufhören; **we left off work after lunch** wir haben nach dem Mittagessen Feierabend gemacht; **leave off doing that, will you!** hör auf damit, ja? VI (inf) aufhören; **leave off!** lass das!; **he**

picked up where he left off last year er machte weiter, wo er letztes Jahr aufgehört hatte

▶ **leave on** VT sep clothes anbehalten, anlassen (inf); lights, fire etc anlassen; **we left the wallpaper on and painted over it** wir haben die Tapete drangelassen (inf) or nicht entfernt und sie überstrichen

▶ **leave out** VT sep a (= not bring in) draußen lassen

b (= omit) auslassen; (= exclude) people ausschließen (of von); **he was instructed to leave out all references to politics** er bekam Anweisung, alle Hinweise auf Politik wegzulassen; **he had been left out in the restructuring** er wurde bei der Neugliederung nicht berücksichtigt; **you leave my wife/politics out of this** lassen Sie meine Frau/die Politik aus dem Spiel; **he got left out at school** er wurde in der Schule nie mit einbezogen; **she felt left out** sie fühlte sich ausgeschlossen

c (= leave available) dalassen; **I'll leave the books out on my desk** ich lasse die Bücher auf meinem Schreibtisch; **will you leave the tools out ready?** legen Sie bitte das Werkzeug zurecht

d (= not put away) nicht wegräumen, liegen lassen

▶ **leave over** VT sep a (= leave surplus) übrig lassen; **to be left over** übrig (geblieben) sein b (= postpone) verschieben, vertagen

leaven ['levn] N (also **leavening**) - [-ɪŋ] Treibmittel nt; (= fermenting dough) Sauerteig m; (fig) Auflockerung f; **even his most serious speeches had a ~ of humour** auch seine ernstesten Reden waren mit Humor gewürzt VT (auf)gehen lassen, treiben; (fig) auflockern

leaves [liːvz] pl of leaf

leave-taking ['liːvteɪkɪŋ] N Abschied m; (= act) Abschiednehmen m

leaving ['liːvɪŋ] N Fortgang m, Weggang m; **~ was very difficult (for him)** das Weggehen fiel ihm schwer

leaving: leaving certificate N (Brit) Abgangszeugnis nt; **leaving day** N (Sch) Schuljahrsabschluss m, letzter Schultag; **leaving party** N Abschiedsfeier or -party f; **leaving present** N Abschiedsgeschenk nt

leavings ['liːvɪŋz] PL (= food) (Über)reste pl; (= rubbish) Abfälle pl

Lebanese [ˌlebə'niːz] ADJ libanesisch N Libanese m, Libanesin f

Lebanon ['lebənən] N the ~ der Libanon

lech [letʃ] VI (esp Brit inf) **to ~ after sb** (= chase) jdm nachstellen; (in mind) sich (dat) lüsterne Vorstellungen über jdn machen

lecher ['letʃə'] N Lüstling m, Wüstling m; (hum) Lustmolch m VI lüstern sein

lecherous ['letʃərəs] ADJ lüstern; man, behaviour also geil

lecherously ['letʃərəslɪ] ADV lüstern

lechery ['letʃərɪ] N Lüsternheit f, Geilheit f; **his reputation for ~** sein Ruf m als Wüstling

lectern ['lektɜːn] N Pult nt

lector ['lektɔː] N (Univ, = foreign language assistant) Lektor(in) m(f)

lecture ['lektʃə'] N a Vortrag m; (Univ) Vorlesung f; **to give a ~** einen Vortrag/eine Vorlesung halten (to für, on sth über etw acc); **I asked for a short explanation and got a ~** ich wollte nur eine kurze Erklärung und bekam einen Vortrag zu hören

b (= scolding) (Straf)predigt f; **to give sb a ~** jdm eine Strafpredigt or Standpauke (inf) halten (about wegen)

VT a (= give a lecture) **to ~ sb on sth** jdm einen Vortrag/eine Vorlesung über etw (acc) halten; **he ~s us in French** wir hören bei ihm (Vorlesungen in) Französisch

b (= scold) tadeln, abkanzeln; **to ~ sb** jdm eine Strafpredigt halten (on wegen)

VI einen Vortrag halten; (Univ) (= give lecture) eine Vorlesung halten; (= give lecture course) lesen, Vorlesungen halten (on über +acc); **he ~s**

in English er ist Dozent für Anglistik; **he ~s on Victorian poetry** er liest über viktorianische Dichtung; **have you ever heard him ~?** hast du schon mal eine Vorlesung bei ihm gehört?; **he ~s at Princeton** er lehrt in Princeton; **he ~s well** seine Vorlesungen sind gut

lecture: lecture course N Vorlesungs-/Vortragsreihe f; **lecture hall** N Hörsaal m; **lecture notes** PL (*professor's*) Manuskript nt; (*student's*) Aufzeichnungen pl; (= *handout*) Vorlesungsskript nt

lecturer ['lɛktʃərəʳ] N Dozent(in) m(f); (= *speaker*) Redner(in) m(f); **assistant ~** ≈ Assistent(in) m(f); **senior ~** Dozent(in) in höherer Position

lecture room N Hörsaal m

lectureship ['lɛktʃəʃɪp] N Stelle f als Dozent, Lehrauftrag m

lecture: lecture theatre, (*US*) **lecture theater** N Hörsaal m; **lecture tour** N Vortragsreise f

LED abbr of **light-emitting diode**

led [led] pret, ptp of **lead²**

LED display N Leuchtanzeige f

ledge [lɛdʒ] N **a** Leiste f, Kante f; (*along wall*) Leiste f; (*of window*) (*inside*) Fensterbrett nt; (*outside*) (Fenster)sims nt or m; (= *shelf*) Ablage f, Bord nt; (= *mountain ledge*) (Fels)vorsprung m **b** (= *ridge of rocks*) Riff nt

ledger ['lɛdʒəʳ] N Hauptbuch nt

ledger line N (*Mus*) Hilfslinie f

lee [liː] N **a** Lee-; **~ side** Leeseite f N **a** (*Naut*) Lee f **b** (= *shelter*) Schutz m, Windschatten m

leech [liːtʃ] N Blutegel m; (*fig*) Blutsauger(in) m(f)

leek [liːk] N Porree m, Lauch m

leer [lɪəʳ] N (*knowing, sexual*) anzügliches Grinsen; (*evil*) heimtückischer Blick VI anzüglich grinsen; einen heimtückischen Blick haben; **he ~ed at the girl** er warf dem Mädchen lüsterne Blicke zu

leery ['lɪərɪ] ADJ (*inf*) misstrauisch; **I'm a bit ~ of him** ich traue ihm nicht so recht

lees [liːz] PL Bodensatz m

leeward ['liːwəd] ADJ Lee-; **~ side** Leeseite f ADV leewärts; **the ship was anchored ~ of the island** das Schiff ankerte an der Leeseite der Insel N Lee(seite) f; **to ~** an der Leeseite; **steer to ~** nach der Leeseite steuern, leewärts steuern

Leeward Islands ['liːwəd,aɪləndz] PL **the ~** die Inseln pl über dem Winde (*von den Jungferninseln bis Trinidad*)

leeway ['liːweɪ] N **a** (*Naut*) Abtrift f, Leeweg m **b** (*fig, = flexibility*) Spielraum m; (*in a decision*) Freiheit f; (= *time lost*) Zeitverlust m; **he has given them too much ~** er hat ihnen zu viel Freiheit or Spielraum gelassen; **to make up the ~** den Zeitverlust aufholen; **there's a lot of ~ to make up** es gibt viel nachzuarbeiten, ein großer Rückstand muss aufgeholt werden

left¹ [left] pret, ptp of **leave**

left² [left] ADJ (*also Pol*) linke(r, s); **no ~ turn** Linksabbiegen verboten; **he's got two ~ hands** (*inf*) er hat zwei linke Hände (*inf*); **he's got two ~ feet** (*inf*) er ist sehr ungelenk; **to come out of ~ field** (*esp US*) überraschend kommen ADV links (*of von*); **turn ~** (*Aut*) links abbiegen; **keep ~** sich links halten, links fahren; **move ~ a little** rücken Sie ein bisschen nach links; **~, right, ~,** right links, rechts, links, rechts; **~ turn!** (*Mil*) links um! N **a** Linke(r, s); **on the ~** links (*of von*), auf der linken Seite (*of +gen*); **on or to sb's ~** links von jdm, zu jds Linken (*form*); **his wife sat on my ~** seine Frau saß links von mir or zu meiner Linken (*form*); **take the first (on the) ~ after the church** biegen Sie hinter der Kirche die erste (Straße) links ab; **the third/fourth** etc **... from the ~** der/die/das dritte/vierte etc ... von links; **to keep to the ~** sich links halten; **to drive on the ~** links fahren; **to fall to the ~** nach links fallen **b** (*Pol*) Linke f; **the parties of the ~** die linken

Parteien, die Parteien der Linken; **to be on the ~** links stehen; **to move to the ~** nach links rücken; **he's further to the ~ than I am** er steht weiter links als ich; **to be on the ~ of the party** dem linken Flügel der Partei angehören **c** (*Boxing*) Linke f

left: left back N linker Verteidiger; **left-click** (*Comput*) VI links klicken VT links klicken auf (+acc); **left-footed** [,left'futɪd] (*Ftbl*) ADJ shot mit dem linken Fuß; **~ player** Linksfüßer(in) m(f); **he is a ~ player** er ist Linksfüßer, er spielt mit dem linken Fuß ADV **to shoot ~** mit links schießen; **left half** N linker Vorstopper; **left-hand** ADJ **~ drive** Linkssteuerung f; **~ side** linke Seite; **he stood on the ~ side of the king** er stand zur Linken des Königs; **~ turn** linke Abzweigung; **take the ~ turn** bieg links ab; **left-handed** ADJ linkshändig; tool für Linkshänder; (*fig*) compliment zweifelhaft; **both the children are ~** beide Kinder sind Linkshänder; **a ~ blow** ein linker Treffer ADV write, bat, bowl etc mit links; **left-hander** N (= *punch*) Linke f; (= *person*) Linkshänder(in) m(f)

leftie ['leftɪ] N (*pej*) linker Typ (*pej*), Rote(r) mf (*pej inf*)

leftish ['leftɪʃ] ADJ linksliberal, links angehaucht (*inf*); **his views are ~** er ist links angehaucht

leftist ['leftɪst] ADJ linke(r, s), linksgerichtet; **his views are ~** er ist linksgerichtet, er steht links N Linke(r) mf

left: left-luggage locker N (*Brit*) Gepäckschließfach nt; **left-luggage (office)** N (*Brit*) Gepäckaufbewahrung f; **is there a ~ in this station?** kann man auf diesem Bahnhof irgendwo sein Gepäck zur Aufbewahrung geben?; **left-of-centre**, (*US*) **left-of-center** ADJ politician links von der Mitte stehend; **~ party** Mitte-Links-Partei f; **leftover** ADJ übrig geblieben N **a** ~s (Über)reste pl **b** (*fig*) **to be a ~ from the past** ein Überbleibsel nt aus der Vergangenheit sein; **left property** N Hinterlassenschaft f, Nachlass m

leftward(s) ['leftwəd(z)] ADJ nach links; **leftward bend** Linkskurve f; **a leftward shift** (*Pol*) ein Linksruck m ADV (*Pol*) move, shift nach links

left: left wing N linker Flügel (*also Sport*); (= *player*) Linksaußen m; **on the ~** (*Pol, Sport*) auf dem linken Flügel; **left-wing** ADJ linke(r, s); politician also linksgerichtet; **left-winger** N (*Pol*) Linke(r) mf; (*Sport*) Linksaußen m

lefty ['leftɪ] (*inf*) N **a** (*Pol*) Linke(r) mf **b** (*person*) Linkshänder(in) m(f) → **leftie**

leg [leg] N **a** (*also of trousers*) Bein nt; **the newborn calf seemed to be all ~s** das neugeborene Kalb schien nur aus Beinen zu bestehen; **to be on one's last ~s** (= *dying*) in den letzten Zügen liegen (*inf*); (= *exhausted*) auf dem letzten Loch pfeifen (*inf*); **this carpet is on its last ~s** dieser Teppich hält or machts (*inf*) nicht mehr lange; **he hasn't (got) a ~ to stand on** (*fig, = no excuse*) er kann sich nicht herausreden; (= *no proof*) das kann er nicht belegen; **to have ~s** (*esp US inf*) (*idea, plan*) klappen; (*story*) laufen (*inf*); **to walk one's ~s off** sich (*dat*) die Füße wund laufen; **to walk sb's ~s off** jdn (ganz schön) scheuchen (*inf*), jdm davonlaufen; **you've walked my ~s off** du bist mir zu schnell gelaufen; **to run sb's ~s off** (*fig*) jdn herumscheuchen (*inf*); **he ran the other athletes' ~s off** er rannte den anderen Läufern davon; **I'll take the children to the park and run their ~s off** ich gehe mit den Kindern in den Park, da können sie sich austoben; **to be out ~ before wicket** (*Cricket*) aus sein, weil sein vor dem Mal stehendes Bein von einem Wurf getroffen wurde; **to get one's ~ over** (*Brit inf*) bumsen (*inf*) **b** (*as food*) Keule f, Hachse f; **~ of lamb** Lammkeule f **c** (*of furniture*) Bein nt; (*of bed*) Fuß m, Bein nt **d** (= *stage*) Etappe f VT **to ~ it** (*inf*: = *go on foot*) laufen, zu Fuß gehen

legacy ['legəsɪ] N (*lit, fig*) Erbschaft f, Vermächtnis nt; (*fig also*) Erbe nt; (*fig pej*) Hinterlassenschaft f; **to leave sb a ~ of sth** (*fig*) jdm etw hinterlassen; **our ~ to future generations must not be a polluted world** wir dürfen den zukünftigen Generationen keine verschmutzte Welt hinterlassen; **the tragedy left a ~ of bitterness** die Tragödie hinterließ Bitterkeit

legal ['liːgl] ADJ **a** (= *lawful*) legal, rechtlich zulässig; (= *according to the law*) restrictions, obligation, limit gesetzlich; (= *allowed by law*) fare, speed zulässig; (= *valid before law*) will, purchase rechtsgültig; **to become ~** rechtskräftig werden; **to make sth ~** etw legalisieren; **the ~ age for marriage** das gesetzliche Heiratsalter, die Ehemündigkeit; **it is not ~ to sell drink to children** es ist gesetzlich verboten, Alkohol an Kinder zu verkaufen; **~ limit** (*of blood alcohol when driving*) Promillegrenze f; **~ claim** rechtmäßiger Anspruch, Rechtsanspruch m; **~ document** or **instrument** (rechtskräftige) Urkunde; **~ rights** gesetzlich verankerte Rechte pl; **they don't know what their ~ rights are** sie kennen ihre eigenen Rechte nicht; **the ~ custody of the children** das Sorgerecht für die Kinder; **women had no ~ status** Frauen waren nicht rechtsfähig; **he made ~ provision for his ex-wife** er hat die Versorgung seiner geschiedenen Frau rechtlich geregelt **b** (= *relating to the law*) Rechts-; matters, affairs juristisch, rechtlich; advice, services, journal, mind juristisch; decision richterlich; inquiry, investigation gerichtlich; **from a ~ point of view** aus juristischer Sicht, rechtlich gesehen; **for ~ reasons** aus rechtlichen Gründen; **what's his ~ position?** wie ist seine rechtliche Stellung?; **~ charges** or **fees** or **costs** (*solicitor's*) Anwaltskosten pl; (*court's*) Gerichtskosten pl; **to take ~ advice on** or **over** or **about sth** in Bezug auf etw (acc) juristischen Rat einholen; **to start ~ proceedings against sb** gegen jdn Klage erheben, jdn verklagen; **~ opinion is that ...** die Anwälte sind der Meinung, dass ...; **~ loophole** Gesetzeslücke f; **the British ~ system** das britische Rechtssystem; **the ~ profession** der Anwaltsstand, die Anwaltschaft; (*including judges*) die Juristenschaft; **~ representation** Rechtsvertretung f; **~ representative** gesetzlicher Vertreter; (= *counsel*) (Rechts)anwalt m, (Rechts)anwältin f, Verteidiger(in) m(f)

legal: legal action N Klage f; **to take ~ against sb** gegen jdn Klage erheben, jdn verklagen; **legal adviser** N Rechtsberater(in) m(f); **legal aid** N Rechtshilfe f; **legal department** N Rechtsabteilung f, juristische Abteilung; **legal eagle** N (*hum inf*) Rechtsverdreher(in) m(f) (*hum inf*); **legal entity** N juristische Person

legalese [,liːgə'liːz] N (*pej*) Juristensprache f or -jargon m, Juristendeutsch nt

legal fiction N juristische Fiktion

legalistic [,liːgə'lɪstɪk] ADJ legalistisch

legalistically [,liːgə'lɪstɪkəlɪ] ADV legalistisch; **to examine the issues ~** die Fragen nach dem Wortlaut des Gesetzes betrachten

legality [liː'gælɪtɪ] N Legalität f; (*of claim*) Rechtmäßigkeit f; (*of tender*) Gesetzlichkeit f; (*of restrictions, obligation*) Gesetzmäßigkeit f; (*of fare, speed*) Zulässigkeit f; (*of contract, will, marriage, purchase, decision, limit*) rechtliche Gültigkeit, Rechtsgültigkeit f

legalization [,liːgəlaɪ'zeɪʃən] N Legalisierung f

legalize ['liːgəlaɪz] VT legalisieren

legally ['liːgəlɪ] ADV (= *lawfully*) transacted, acquire, trade legal; married rechtmäßig; guaranteed, obliged, set down gesetzlich; (= *relating to the law*) advise juristisch; indefensible rechtlich; **what's the position ~?** wie ist die Lage rechtlich gesehen?; **~, there was no objection** gab es juristisch (gesehen) keine Einwände; **~ speaking** vom rechtlichen Standpunkt aus, juristisch gesehen; **it's wrong ~ – or morally?** es ist nicht richtig – aus rechtlicher oder moralischer Sicht?; **~ responsible** vor dem Gesetz verantwortlich; **to be ~ entitled to sth** einen

Rechtsanspruch auf etw (acc) haben; **~ binding** rechtsverbindlich; **~, he can only stay for 3 months** legal(erweise) kann er nur 3 Monate bleiben; **~ valid** rechtsgültig; **this herbicide can still be ~ sold** dieses Herbizid kann immer noch legal gehandelt werden

legal: legal offence, (US) **legal offense** N strafbare Handlung; **drug-peddling is a ~** der Handel mit Drogen ist strafbar; **legal protection** N Rechtsschutz m; **legal separation** N gesetzliche Trennung; **legal successor** N Rechtsnachfolger(in) m(f); **legal tender** N gesetzliches Zahlungsmittel

legate ['lɛgɪt] N Legat m

legatee [ˌlɛgə'tiː] N Vermächtnisnehmer(in) m(f)

legation [lɪ'geɪʃən] N (= diplomats) Gesandtschaft f, Vertretung f; (= building) Gesandtschaftsgebäude nt

legend ['lɛdʒənd] N **a** Legende f; (fictitious) Sage f; **heroes of Greek ~** griechische Sagenhelden pl; **to become a ~ in one's lifetime** schon zu Lebzeiten zur Legende werden **b** (= inscription, caption) Legende f

legendary ['lɛdʒəndərɪ] ADJ **a** legendär; person legendär, sagenumwoben; **~ proportions** legendäre Ausmaße pl; **to achieve ~ status** zur Legende werden **b** (= famous) berühmt

legerdemain [ˌlɛdʒədə'meɪn] N Taschenspielerei f

-legged [-'lɛgd, -'lɛgɪd] ADJ suf -beinig; **two-/four-legged** zwei-/vierbeinig; **long-legged** langbeinig; **bare-legged** ohne Strümpfe

leggings ['lɛgɪŋz] PL (hohe or lange) Gamaschen pl; (fireman's, yachtsman's) Beinlinge f; (= trousers) Leggings pl; (baby's) Gamaschenhose f

leggy ['lɛgɪ] ADJ (+er) langbeinig; (= gawky) staksig

Leghorn ['lɛghɔːn] N (Geog) Livorno nt

legibility [ˌlɛdʒɪ'bɪlɪtɪ] N Lesbarkeit f, Leserlichkeit f

legible ['lɛdʒɪbl] ADJ lesbar; handwriting also leserlich

legibly ['lɛdʒɪblɪ] ADV lesbar; write leserlich

legion ['liːdʒən] N **a** Armee f; (= Foreign Legion) Legion f **b** (Roman) Legion f **c** (= organization) **Legion** Legion f; **American/British Legion** American/British Legion f (Verband der Kriegsveteranen); **Legion of Honour** Ehrenlegion f **d** (fig: = large number) Legion f; **they are ~** ihre Zahl ist Legion; **his supporters are ~** seine Anhänger sind Legion

---

LEGION

In Großbritannien ist die **Legion** eine Organisation, die die Veteranen der Streitkräfte und ihre Familien unterstützt und für diese Vereinsheime betreibt. Jeden November ruft die **Legion** mit dem **Poppy Day Appeal** zu Spenden für die Wohlfahrtseinrichtungen der Streitkräfte auf. Die amerikanische **Legion** ist eine ähnliche Einrichtung, die Militärveteranen und ihren Familien finanzielle Unterstützung und Hilfe zur Wiedereingliederung anbietet. Zudem setzt sie sich im Kongress für die Interessen der Veteranen ein und wirbt für eine starke nationale Verteidigung. Für ihre Mitglieder betreibt die **Legion** soziale Einrichtungen auf kommunaler Ebene.

---

legionary ['liːdʒənərɪ] ADJ Legions-; **~ cohort** Legionskohorte f **N** (also **legionnaire**) Legionär m

legionnaire [ˌliːdʒə'nɛə] N Legionär m

legionnaire's disease [ˌliːdʒə'nɛədɪˌziːz] N Legionärskrankheit f

legislate ['lɛdʒɪsleɪt] **VI a** (= make laws) Gesetze/ein Gesetz erlassen; **parliament's job is to ~** die Aufgabe des Parlaments ist die Gesetzgebung **b** (fig) (= give ruling on) für etw Regeln aufstellen **VT to ~ sth out of existence** etw durch Gesetz aus der Welt schaffen

legislation [ˌlɛdʒɪs'leɪʃən] N (= making laws) Gesetzgebung f, Legislatur f (geh); (= laws) Gesetze pl

legislative ['lɛdʒɪslətɪv] ADJ gesetzgebend, legislativ (geh); **~ reforms** Gesetzesreformen pl; **~ programme** (Brit) or **program** (US) (of government) Gesetzgebungsprogramm nt

legislator ['lɛdʒɪsleɪtə] N Gesetzgeber m

legislature ['lɛdʒɪsleɪtʃə] N Legislative f

legit [lɪ'dʒɪt] ADJ (inf) O.K. (inf)

legitimacy [lɪ'dʒɪtɪməsɪ] N Rechtmäßigkeit f, Legitimität f; (of birth) Ehelichkeit f; (of conclusion) Berechtigung f; **I don't doubt the ~ of your excuse/reason** ich bezweifle nicht, dass Ihre Entschuldigung/Ihr Grund gerechtfertigt ist

legitimate [lɪ'dʒɪtɪmət] ADJ **a** (= lawful) rechtmäßig, legitim; rights, claim legitim **b** (= reasonable) berechtigt; excuse begründet; reason zulässig; target, purpose legitim; **his use of the company car was not ~** er war nicht berechtigt, den Firmenwagen zu benutzen; **it's perfectly ~ to ask questions** es ist vollkommen in Ordnung, Fragen zu stellen; **it's ~ for them to behave like that** sie dürfen sich so benehmen **c** (= born in wedlock) ehelich **d** (Theat) **the ~ theatre** das traditionelle Sprechtheater

legitimately [lɪ'dʒɪtɪmətlɪ] ADV (= lawfully) legitim; (= with reason) berechtigterweise, mit Recht; **he argues, quite ~, that ...** er führt das berechtigte Argument an, dass ...; **it can ~ be expected of people that ...** man kann mit Recht von den Leuten erwarten, dass ...

legitimation [lɪˌdʒɪtɪ'meɪʃən] N Legitimation f; (= action) Legitimierung f

legitimatize [lɪ'dʒɪtɪmətaɪz], **legitimize** [lɪ'dʒɪtɪmaɪz] VT legitimieren; children für ehelich erklären

leg: legless ADJ (= without legs) ohne Beine; (Brit inf: = drunk) sternhagelvoll (inf); **legman** N (US) kleiner Reporter, der Informationsquellen abklappert (who runs errands) Laufbursche m, Bote m; **leg-of-mutton** ADJ sleeve keulenförmig; **leg-pull** N (inf) Scherz m, Bluff m (inf); **what he said to us was only a ~** damit wollte er uns nur auf den Arm nehmen; **legroom** N Platz m für die Beine, Beinfreiheit f; **leg show** N (inf) Revue f; **leg warmers** PL Stulpen pl, Legwarmer pl

legume ['lɛgjuːm] N (= species) Hülsenfrüchtler m; (= fruit) Hülsenfrucht f

leguminous [le'gjuːmɪnəs] ADJ Hülsenfrucht-, Leguminosen- (spec); **~ plant** Hülsenfrüchtler m, Leguminose f (spec)

leg: leg-up N **to give sb a ~** jdm hochhelfen; **legwarmer** N Legwarmer m; **legwork** N Lauferei f

Leics abbr of **Leicestershire**

leisure ['lɛʒə] N Freizeit f; **a gentleman of ~** ein Privatier m (dated); **she decided to give up her job and become a lady of ~** sie entschloss sich, ihren Beruf aufzugeben und in Muße zu leben; **to lead a life of ~** ein Leben in or der Muße führen (geh), sich dem (süßen) Nichtstun ergeben; **the problem of what to do with one's ~** das Problem der Freizeitgestaltung; **a park where the public can stroll at ~** ein Park, in dem die Öffentlichkeit in aller Ruhe spazieren gehen kann; **the Prime Minister is seldom at ~** der Premierminister hat selten Zeit für sich or hat selten freie Zeit; **do it at your ~** (= in own time) tun Sie es, wenn Sie Zeit or Ruhe dazu haben; (= at own speed) lassen Sie sich (dat) Zeit damit; **to have the ~ to do sth** die Zeit or Muße haben, etw zu tun

leisure: leisure activities PL Hobbys pl, Freizeitbeschäftigungen pl; **leisure centre** N (Brit) Freizeitzentrum nt; **leisure clothes** PL Freizeitkleidung f

leisured ['lɛʒəd] ADJ **a** ~ **life** ein Leben nt der Muße (geh); **the ~ classes** die feinen Leute

leisure hours PL Freizeit f

leisurely ['lɛʒəlɪ] **ADJ** geruhsam; **to go at a ~ pace** (person) gemächlich gehen; (vehicle) in gemächlichem Tempo fahren; **the train's pace was so ~ that ...** der Zug fuhr so langsam, dass ...; **to have a ~ bath/breakfast** in aller Ruhe baden/frühstücken; **to adopt a more ~ approach** sich mehr Zeit lassen; **to do sth in a ~ way** etw ohne Hast und Eile machen **ADV** walk, stroll gemächlich

leisure: leisure suit N Jogginganzug m; **leisure time** N Freizeit f; **leisurewear** N Freizeitbekleidung f

leitmotif, leitmotiv ['laɪtməʊˌtiːf] N (Mus, fig) Leitmotiv nt

lemma ['lɛmə] pl **-s** or **-ta** ['lɛmətə] N (Ling) Lemma nt

lemmatization [ˌlɛmətaɪ'zeɪʃən] N (Ling) Lemmatisierung f

lemming ['lɛmɪŋ] N Lemming m

lemon ['lɛmən] **N a** Zitrone f; (= colour) Zitronengelb nt; (= tree) Zitrone(nbaum m) f **b** (inf: = fool) Dussel m (inf) **c** (inf: = poor-quality product) schlechte Ware; **I bought a ~** sie haben mir was angedreht (inf) **ADJ** Zitronen-; **~ paint** zitronengelbe Farbe; **~ yellow** Zitronengelb nt

lemonade [ˌlɛmə'neɪd] N Limonade f; (with lemon flavour) Zitronenlimonade f

lemon: lemon cheese, lemon curd N zähflüssiger Brotaufstrich mit Zitronengeschmack; **lemon juice** N Zitronensaft m; **lemon law** N (US) Schutzgesetz für Autokäufer; **lemon meringue pie** N mit Baisermasse gedeckter Mürbeteig mit einer Zitronencremefüllung; **lemon sole** N Rotzunge f; **lemon squash** N Zitronensaft m; (in bottle) Zitronensirup m; **lemon squeezer** N Zitronenpresse f; **lemon tea** N Zitronentee m; **lemon zest** N (geriebene) Zitronenschale

lemony ['lɛmənɪ] ADJ Zitronen-; **~ flavour** (Brit) or **flavor** (US) Zitronengeschmack m

lemur ['liːmə] N Lemur m, Maki m

lend [lɛnd] pret, ptp **lent** **VT a** (= loan) leihen (to sb jdm); (banks) money verleihen (to an +acc)
b (fig: = give) verleihen (to +dat); name geben; **I am not going to ~ my name to this** dafür gebe ich meinen (guten) Namen nicht her; **to ~ (one's) support to sb/sth** jdn/etw unterstützen; **to ~ a hand** helfen, mit anfassen
VR to ~ oneself to sth sich für etw hergeben; (= be suitable) sich für etw eignen; **the programme** (Brit) or **program** (US) **doesn't really ~ itself to radio** die Sendung ist eigentlich für den Hörfunk ungeeignet; **these problems don't ~ themselves to quick solutions** für diese Probleme gibt es keine schnelle Lösung

▶ **lend out** VT sep verleihen; books also ausleihen

lender ['lɛndə] N (professional) Geldverleiher(in) m(f); **he paid the £100 back to the ~** er zahlte die £ 100 an den zurück, der sie ihm geliehen hatte

lending ['lɛndɪŋ] ADJ **~ bank** kreditierende Bank; **~ business** Kreditgeschäft nt; **~ country** Gläubigerland nt; **~ policy** (of bank etc) Kreditpolitik f

lending: lending library N Leihbücherei f; **lending rate** N (Darlehens)zinssatz m; **lending rights** PL Verleihrecht nt; (for author) Anspruch m auf Leihbücherei-Tantiemen

lend-lease ['lɛnd'liːs] N **~ agreement** Leih-Pacht-Abkommen nt

length [lɛŋθ] **N a** Länge f; **a journey of considerable ~** eine ziemlich lange or weite Reise; **to be 4 feet in ~** 4 Fuß lang sein; **what ~ is it?** wie lang ist es?; **what ~ do you want it?** wie lang hätten Sie es gerne?; **of such ~** so lang; **the river, for most of its ~, meanders through meadows** der Fluss schlängelt sich in seinem Verlauf größtenteils durch Wiesen; **the pipe, for most of its ~, ...** fast das ganze Rohr ...; **along the whole ~ of the river/lane** den ganzen Fluss/Weg entlang; **it turns in its own ~** es kann sich um die eigene Achse drehen; **(through) the ~ and breadth of England** in ganz England; *travel* kreuz und quer durch ganz England; **the ~ of skirts** die Rocklänge; **at full ~** in voller Länge

b (= *section, of cloth, rope, pipe*) Stück *nt*; (of *wallpaper*) Bahn *f*; (of *road*) Abschnitt *m*; (of *pool*) Bahn *f*, Länge *f*

c (*of time*) Dauer *f*; (= *great length*) lange Dauer; **at such ~** so lange; **we didn't stay any (great) ~ of time** wir sind nicht lange geblieben; **the ~ of time needed** die Zeit, die man dazu braucht; **in that ~ of time I could have ...** in dieser Zeit hätte ich ...; **for any ~ of time** für längere Zeit; **for what ~ of time?** für wie lange?; **~ of life** (of *people*) Lebenserwartung *f*; (of *animals*) Lebensalter *nt*; (of *machine*) Lebensdauer *f*; **~ of service with a company** Betriebszugehörigkeit *f*; **~ of service with the army** Dienstjahre *pl* bei der Armee; **at ~** (= *finally*) schließlich; (= *for a long time*) lange, ausführlich, lang und breit (*pej*)

d (*Phon, Poet, Sport*) Länge *f*; **to win by half a ~** mit einer halben Länge siegen

e **to go to any ~s to do sth** vor nichts zurückschrecken, um etw zu tun; **to go to great ~s to do sth** sich (*dat*) sehr viel Mühe geben *or* alles Mögliche versuchen, um etw zu tun; **to go to the ~ of ...** so weit gehen, dass ...

lengthen ['leŋθən] **VT** verlängern; *clothes, queues* länger machen; **to ~ one's stride** größere Schritte machen **VI** länger werden

lengthily ['leŋθɪlɪ] **ADV** ausführlich, langatmig (*pej*)

length mark N (*Phon, Poet*) Längenzeichen *nt*

lengthways ['leŋθweɪz], **lengthwise** ['leŋθwaɪz] **ADJ** Längen-, Längs-; **~ measurement** Längenmessung *f*; **~ cut** Längsschnitt *m* **ADV** der Länge nach

lengthy ['leŋθɪ] **ADJ** (+*er*) sehr lang; (= *dragging on*) langwierig; *speech* ausführlich, langatmig (*pej*); *meeting, war* lang andauernd; (= *extensive*) *article, report, statement* sehr umfangreich; *interview, explanation* sehr ausführlich; **a ~ prison sentence** eine lange *or* hohe Gefängnisstrafe; **to have a ~ wait for sth** sehr lange auf etw (*acc*) warten müssen

lenience ['liːnɪəns], **leniency** ['liːnɪənsɪ] N Nachsicht *f* (*towards* gegenüber); (of *judge, attitude, treatment, sentence*) Milde *f*

lenient ['liːnɪənt] **ADJ** nachsichtig (*towards* gegenüber); *judge, attitude, treatment, sentence* milde; **to be ~ with sb** mit jdm milde umgehen; **to be ~ in one's assessment** milde urteilen

leniently ['liːnɪəntlɪ] **ADV** nachsichtig; *judge* milde

Leninism ['lenɪnɪzəm] N Leninismus *m*

Leninist ['lenɪnɪst] **ADJ** leninistisch **N** Leninist(in) *m(f)*

lenity ['lenɪtɪ] N Nachsicht *f*, Milde *f*

lens [lenz] N (*Anat, Opt, Phot*) Linse *f*; (in *spectacles*) Glas *nt*; (= *camera part containing lens*) Objektiv *nt*; (= *eyeglass*) Klemmlupe *f*; (for *stamps etc*) Vergrößerungsglas *nt*, Lupe *f*

lens: lens cap N Schutzkappe *f*; **lens hood** N Sonnenblende *f*, Gegenlichtblende *f*

Lent [lent] N Fastenzeit *f*

lent [lent] *pret, ptp of* **lend**

Lenten ['lentən] **ADJ** Fasten-; **~ season** Fastenzeit *f*; **~ fast** Fasten *nt* (zur Fastenzeit)

lentil ['lentl] N Linse *f*; **~ soup** Linsensuppe *f*

Leo ['liːəʊ] N (*Astrol*) Löwe *m*; **he's (a) ~** er ist Löwe

leonine ['liːənaɪn] **ADJ** Löwen-, löwenartig; **~ courage** (*liter*) Löwenmut *m*; **the ~ bust of Karl Marx** die Büste von Karl Marx mit seiner Löwenmähne

leopard ['lepəd] N Leopard *m*; **a ~ never changes its spots** (*Prov*) die Katze lässt das Mausen nicht (*Prov*)

leotard ['liːətɑːd] N Trikot *nt*; (*Gymnastics*) Gymnastikanzug *m*

leper ['lepə'] N Leprakranke(r) *mf*, Lepröse(r) *mf* (*spec*), Aussätzige(r) *mf* (*old, fig*)

leper colony N Leprasiedlung *f*, Lepradorf *nt*

lepidoptera [lepɪ'dɒptərə] **PL** Falter *pl*, Lepidopteren *pl* (*spec*)

leprechaun ['leprəkɔːn] N Gnom *m*, Kobold *m*

leprosy ['leprəsɪ] N Lepra *f*, Aussatz *m* (*old*)

leprous ['leprəs] **ADJ** leprös, aussätzig (*old*)

lesbian ['lezbɪən] **ADJ** lesbisch; **~ and gay rights/issues** Rechte *pl*/Probleme *pl* der Lesben und Schwulen; **the ~ and gay community** die Lesben und Schwulen; **~ and gay people** Lesben und Schwule *pl*; **the ~ and gay movement** die Lesben- und Schwulenbewegung **N** Lesbierin *f*, Lesbe *f* (*inf*)

lesbianism ['lezbɪənɪzəm] N (in *general*) lesbische Liebe; (of *one person*) Lesbiertum *nt*

lesbo ['lezbəʊ] N *pl* **-bos** (*inf pej*) Lesbe *f* (*inf*)

lèse-majesté, **lese majesty** ['leɪz'mæʒəsteɪ] N (= *high treason*) Hochverrat *m*; (= *insult to dignity*) (Majestäts)beleidigung *f*

lesion ['liːʒən] N Verletzung *f*; (= *structural change*) krankhafte Gewebsveränderung; **~s in the brain** Gehirnverletzungen *pl*

Lesotho [lɪ'səʊtəʊ] N Lesotho *nt*

less [les] ✪ 5.1, 5.3, 7.5, 26.3 **ADJ, ADV, N** weniger; **of ~ importance** von geringerer Bedeutung, weniger bedeutend; **~ noise, please!** nicht so laut, bitte!; **no ~ a person than the bishop** kein Geringerer als der Bischof; **he did it in ~ time** er hat es in kürzerer Zeit *or* schneller getan; **to grow ~** weniger werden; (= *grow at slow rate*) langsamer wachsen; (= *decrease*) abnehmen; **his problem is ~ one of money than of enthusiasm** sein Problem ist weniger das Geld als vielmehr mangelnde Begeisterung; **~ and ~** immer weniger; **she saw him ~ and ~** (often) sie sah ihn immer seltener; **a sum ~ than £1** eine Summe unter £ 1; **it's nothing ~ than disgraceful/than a disaster** es ist wirklich eine Schande/ein Unglück *nt*; **this is nothing ~ than blackmail** das ist ja direkt Erpressung; **it was little ~ than blackmail** das war schon fast Erpressung, das war so gut wie Erpressung; **he was ~ frightened than angry** er war nicht so sehr ängstlich, sondern eher ärgerlich; **~ beautiful** nicht so schön; **~ quickly** nicht so schnell; **he works ~ than I (do)** er arbeitet weniger als ich; **still** *or* **even ~** noch weniger; **none the ~** trotzdem, nichtsdestoweniger; **I didn't find the film any the ~ interesting** ich fand den Film nicht weniger interessant; **I don't love her any the ~** ich liebe sie nicht weniger; **their apology did not make him any the ~ angry** ihre Entschuldigung konnte seinen Ärger nicht besänftigen; **can't you let me have it for ~?** können Sie es mir nicht etwas billiger lassen?; **I hope you won't think (any the) ~ of me** ich hoffe, du denkst nicht schlecht von mir; **~ of that!** komm mir nicht so!

PREP weniger; (*Comm*) abzüglich; **a year ~ 4 days** ein Jahr weniger 4 Tage; **6 ~ 4 is 2** 6 weniger *or* minus 4 ist 2

-less [-lɪs] **ADJ** *suf* -los; **hopeless** hoffnungslos; **heartless** herzlos; **hatless** ohne Hut; **sunless** ohne Sonne

lessee [le'siː] N Pächter(in) *m(f)*; (of *house, flat*) Mieter(in) *m(f)*; (of *equipment*) Leasingnehmer(in) *m(f)*

lessen ['lesn] **VT** (= *make less*) verringern; *cost* senken, vermindern; *effect, impact* vermindern, abschwächen; *pain* lindern **b** (= *make seem less important etc*) herabsetzen, herabwürdigen **VI** nachlassen; (*danger, wind, enthusiasm, difficulty also*) abnehmen; (*value of money*) sich verringern, abnehmen

lessening ['lesnɪŋ] N Nachlassen *nt* (in *sth* +*gen*); **~ of value** Wertabnahme *f*; **a ~ in the rate of inflation** ein Rückgang *m or* eine Verringerung der Inflationsrate

lesser ['lesə'] **ADJ** geringer; (in *names*) klein; **to a ~ extent** in geringerem Maße; **a ~ amount** ein kleinerer Betrag; **the ~ weight** das leichtere

Gewicht; **~ offence** (*Brit*) *or* **offense** (*US*) (*Jur*) Vergehen *nt*, Übertretung *f*; **which is the ~ crime?** welches Verbrechen ist weniger schlimm?; **he is a ~ man than his brother** (= *less good*) er ist kein so guter Mensch wie sein Bruder; (= *less great*) er ist weniger bedeutend als sein Bruder

lesson ['lesn] N **a** (*Sch etc*) Stunde *f*; (= *unit of study*) Lektion *f*; **~s** Unterricht *m*; (= *homework*) (Haus)aufgaben *pl*; **his ~s are boring** sein Unterricht ist *or* seine Stunden sind langweilig; **~s begin at 9** der Unterricht *or* die Schule beginnt um 9; **he's not very good at his ~s** er ist kein besonders guter Schüler; **a French ~** eine Französischstunde; **a driving ~** eine Fahrstunde; **to give** *or* **teach a ~** eine Stunde geben, unterrichten; **we're having a French ~ now** wir haben jetzt Französisch

b (*fig*) Lehre *f*; **to be a ~ to sb** jdm eine Lehre sein; **he has learned his ~** er hat seine Lektion gelernt; **to teach sb a ~** jdm eine Lektion erteilen; **what ~ can we learn from this story?** was können wir von dieser Geschichte lernen?; **it was an important ~ of life for me** das war mir eine wichtige Lehre im Leben

c (*Eccl*) Lesung *f*; **to read the ~** die Lesung halten

lessor [le'sɔː'] N (*form*) Verpächter(in) *m(f)*; (of *flat etc*) Vermieter(in) *m(f)*; (of *equipment*) Leasinggeber(in) *m(f)*

lest [lest] **CONJ** (*form*) **a** (= *for fear that*) aus Furcht, dass; (= *in order that ... not*) damit ... nicht; (= *in case*) für den Fall, dass; **I didn't do it ~ somebody should object** ich habe es aus Furcht, dass jemand dagegen sein könnte, nicht getan; **~ we forget** damit wir nicht vergessen **b** (*after fear, be afraid etc*) dass; **I was frightened ~ he should fall** ich hatte Angst, dass er fallen könnte

let[1] [let] N **a** (*Tennis*) Netz(ball *m*) *nt* **b** **without ~ or hindrance** (*Jur*) ungehindert

let[2] N **they are looking for a ~ in this area** sie wollen eine Wohnung/ein Haus in dieser Gegend mieten; **I have this house on a long ~** ich habe dieses Haus für längere Zeit gemietet

let[3] ✪ 9.3, 26.1 *pret, ptp* **let VT a** (= *permit*) lassen; **to ~ sb do sth** jdn etw tun lassen; **she ~ me borrow the car** sie lieh mir das Auto, ich durfte ihr Auto nehmen; **we can't ~ that happen** wir dürfen das nicht zulassen; **he wants to but I won't ~ him** er möchte gern, aber ich lasse ihn nicht *or* erlaube es ihm nicht; **the particle wants to escape but the magnetic force won't ~ it** das Teilchen möchte sich freimachen, aber die magnetische Kraft verhindert es; **oh please ~ me** bitte, bitte, lass mich doch (mal)!; **~ me help you** darf ich Ihnen helfen *or* behilflich sein?; **~ me know what you think** sagen Sie mir (Bescheid) *or* lassen Sie mich wissen (*form*), was Sie davon halten; **to ~ oneself be seen** sich sehen lassen; **to ~ sb be** jdn (in Ruhe) lassen; **to ~ sb/sth go, to ~ go of sb/sth** jdn/etw loslassen; **to ~ sb go** (= *depart*) jdn gehen lassen; **~ me go!** lassen Sie mich los!, loslassen!; **I'm afraid we'll have to ~ you go** (*euph*: = *dismiss*) wir müssen uns leider von Ihnen trennen; **to ~ oneself go** (= *neglect oneself*) sich gehen lassen; (= *relax*) aus sich herausgehen; **to ~ sth go** (= *neglect*) etw vernachlässigen; **to ~ it go at that** es dabei bewenden lassen; **to ~ sb pass** jdn vorbeilassen; **we'll ~ it pass** *or* **go this once** (= *disregard, error*) wir wollen es mal durchgehen lassen → **drop, fly**[2]**, slip**

b (*old: causative*) lassen; **the bells be rung** lasset die Glocken ertönen (*liter*); **~ it be known by all citizens that ...** allen Bürgern sei kundgetan, dass ... (*old*); **~ it be known that ...** alle sollen wissen, dass ...

c **to ~ sb/sth alone** jdn/etw in Ruhe lassen; **we can't improve it any more, we'd better ~ it alone** wir können es nicht mehr verbessern, also lassen wir es besser sein; **~ me by/past** bitte, lassen Sie mich vorbei/durch; **to ~ sb/sth through** jdn/etw durchlassen

d **~ alone** (= *much less*) geschweige denn

e ~'s **go home** komm, wir gehen nach Hause; ~'s **go!** gehen wir!; ~'s **get out of here** bloß weg von hier!; **yes**, ~'s oh ja!; **it's late, but yes** ~'s es ist spät, aber na ja, einverstanden; ~'s **not** lieber nicht; **don't** ~'s or ~'s **not fight** wir wollen uns doch nicht streiten; ~'s **be happy** lass uns glücklich sein; ~'s **be friends** wir wollen Freunde sein; ~'s **all be a bit more friendly** seien wir doch alle ein bisschen freundlicher; ~'s **look at this in more detail** wir wollen es einmal genauer betrachten; ~ **him try (it)!** das soll er nur or mal versuchen!; ~ **me think** or **see, where did I put it?** warte mal or Moment mal, wo habe ich das nur hingetan?; ~ **their need be never so great** mag ihre Not auch noch so groß sein; ~ **there be music** lasst Musik erklingen; ~ **there be peace** es soll Friede sein; ~ **there be light** es werde Licht; ~ **us pray** lasst uns beten; ~ **us suppose ...** nehmen wir (mal) an, dass ... → **equal VI**

f (esp Brit, = hire out) vermieten; **"to ~"** „zu vermieten"; **we can't find a house to ~** wir können kein Haus finden, das zu mieten ist

g **to ~ blood** einen Aderlass machen; **they ~ so much of his blood** sie nahmen ihm so viel Blut ab

▶ **let away** VT sep **to let sb (get) away with sth** jdm etw durchgehen lassen; **I'll let you (get) a-way with it just this once** diesmal drücke ich noch ein Auge zu (inf)

▶ **let down** VT sep **a** (= lower) rope, person herunterlassen; seat herunterklappen; hair, window herunterlassen; **I tried to let him down gently** (fig) ich versuchte, ihm das schonend beizubringen; **to let one's guard down** (lit) seine Deckung vernachlässigen; (fig) sich aus der Reserve locken lassen

b (= lengthen) dress länger machen; hem auslassen

c (= deflate) **to let a tyre** (Brit) or **tire** (US) **down** die Luft aus einem Reifen lassen

d (= fail to help) **to let sb down** jdn im Stich lassen (over mit); **the weather let us down** das Wetter machte uns einen Strich durch die Rechnung; **to let the side down** die anderen im Stich lassen

e (= disappoint) enttäuschen; **to feel let down** enttäuscht sein

f **to let the school/oneself down** die Schule/ sich blamieren or in Verruf bringen; **you'd be letting yourself down if you only got 5 out of 10** es wäre unter deinem Niveau, nur 5 von 10 Punkten zu bekommen

▶ **let in** VT sep **a** water durchlassen

b (= admit) air, cat, visitor hereinlassen; (to club etc) zulassen (to zu); **he let himself in (with his key)** er schloss die Tür auf und ging hinein; **he let her/himself into the apartment** er ließ sie/er ging in die Wohnung hinein; **just let yourself in** geh einfach hinein; **I was just letting myself in** ich schloss gerade die Tür auf

c (= involve in) **to let sb in for a lot of work** jdm eine Menge Arbeit aufhalsen; **see what you've let me in for now** da hast du mir aber was eingebrockt! (inf); **to let oneself in for sth** sich auf etw (acc) einlassen; **I got let in for £50** ich bin £ 50 losgeworden (inf)

d (= allow to know) **to let sb in on sth, to let sb into sth** jdn in etw (acc) einweihen; **she let me in on the secret** sie hat es mir verraten

e (Sew) **to let in a panel** eine Bahn einsetzen **VI** (shoes, tent) Wasser durchlassen, undicht sein

▶ **let off** VT sep **a** (= fire) arrow abschießen; gun, shot abfeuern

b (= explode) firework, bomb hochgehen lassen

c (= emit) vapour von sich geben; gases absondern; smell verbreiten; **to let off steam** (lit) Dampf ablassen; (fig also) sich abreagieren

VT always separate **a** (= forgive) **to let sb off** jdm etw durchgehen lassen; **I'll let you off this time** diesmal drücke ich noch ein Auge zu; **OK, I'll let you off, you're quite right** gut, ich will dir mal ausnahmsweise Recht geben; **to let sb off sth** jdm etw erlassen; **to let sb off with a warning/fine** jdn mit einer Verwarnung/Geld-

strafe davonkommen lassen; **to let sb off lightly** mit jdm glimpflich verfahren; **to be let off lightly** glimpflich davonkommen; **he's been let off** man hat ihn laufen lassen

b (= allow to go) gehen lassen; **we were let off early** wir durften früher gehen; **I let the dog off (the leash)** ich machte den Hund (von der Leine) los

c (from car etc) herauslassen (inf), aussteigen lassen

VI (inf: = fart) einen fahren lassen (inf)

▶ **let on** VI **a** (inf: = tell, give away) verraten; **don't let on you know** lass dir bloß nicht anmerken, dass du das weißt; **he let on that he had known all the time** er kam damit heraus (inf), dass er es schon die ganze Zeit gewusst hatte; **don't let on about our meeting with John** verrate nichts von unserem Treffen mit John **b** (= pretend) **to let on that ...** vorgeben, dass ...

▶ **let out** VT sep **a** (= allow to go out) cat, smell, air herauslassen; (from car) absetzen; **to let oneself out** (dat) die Tür aufmachen; **I'll let myself out** ich finde alleine hinaus

b prisoner entlassen, rauslassen (inf); (= divulge) news bekannt geben, bekannt machen; secret verraten, ausplaudern (inf); feelings freien Lauf lassen (+dat)

c (= emit) **to let out a long sigh** tief seufzen; **to let out a scream** einen Schrei ausstoßen; **to let out a groan** (auf)stöhnen; **to let one's breath out** ausatmen

d (= make larger) dress weiter machen, auslassen; seam auslassen

e fire ausgehen lassen

f (= free from responsibility) **that lets me out (of it)** da komme ich (schon mal) nicht in Frage

g (esp Brit: = rent) vermieten

▶ **let up** VI **a** (= cease) aufhören; **he never lets up about his money** er redet unaufhörlich or pausenlos von seinem Geld **b** (= ease up) nachlassen **c** **to let up on sb** jdn in Ruhe lassen; **the trainer didn't let up on them until they were perfect** der Trainer hat so lange nicht locker gelassen, bis sie perfekt waren

-let [-lɪt] SUF -lein, -chen; **booklet** Büchlein nt; **starlet** Sternchen nt

letdown ['letdaʊn] N (inf: = disappointment) Enttäuschung f

lethal ['liːθəl] ADJ **a** (= fatal) tödlich; **a ~-looking knife** ein nach einer tödlichen Waffe aussehendes Messer; **to be ~ to rats/fish** Ratten/Fische töten; **to die/be executed by ~ injection** durch die Todesspritze sterben/hingerichtet werden; **a ~ cocktail of drugs** ein tödlicher Drogencocktail **b** (fig) (= dangerous) opponent äußerst gefährlich; (inf: = strong) drink tödlich stark (inf); curry höllisch scharf (inf); ~ **striker** (Ftbl) todsicherer Torschütze; **this coffee is pretty ~** (inf) dieser Kaffee hats in sich (inf), in diesem Kaffee steht der Löffel (inf)

lethargic [lɪ'θɑːdʒɪk] ADJ **a** appearance, person, atmosphere träge, lethargisch; animal träge; pace of music schleppend; (= uninterested) lethargisch, teilnahmslos, lustlos; **a ~-looking child** ein teilnahmslos aussehendes Kind; **to feel ~** sich träge fühlen **b** (Med) schlafsüchtig, lethargisch **c** (Comm, St Ex) sales, trading stagnierend; market lustlos

lethargically [lɪ'θɑːdʒɪkəlɪ] ADV träge; (= without interest) teilnahmslos, lustlos

lethargy ['leθədʒɪ] N **a** Lethargie f, Trägheit f **b** (Med) Schlafsucht f, Lethargie f

Letraset® ['letrəˌset] N Letraset® nt

let's [lets] contr of **let us**

Lett [let] ADJ, N = **Latvian**

letter ['letə'] ✪ 21.1 **N** **a** (of alphabet) Buchstabe m; **the ~ of the law** der Buchstabe des Gesetzes; **to the ~** buchstabengetreu, genau; **did he do it? – to the ~** hat er es getan? – ganz nach Vorschrift

b (= written message) Brief m; (Comm etc) Schreiben nt (form) (to an +acc); **by ~** schriftlich, brieflich; **to write a ~ of complaint/apology** sich schriftlich beschweren/entschuldigen

c (Liter) ~s Literatur f; **man of ~s** Belletrist m; (= writer) Literat m

d (US, = award) als Auszeichnung verliehenes Schulabzeichen

VT sign, label beschriften; **he ~ed the invitations in gold** er ließ die Einladungen in Gold (-buchstaben) drucken

letter: letter bomb N Briefbombe f; **letter box** N (Brit) Briefkasten m; **letter card** N Briefkarte f; **letter carrier** N (US) Briefträger(in) m/f, Postbote m/-botin f; **letter drop** N Briefeinwurf m

lettered ['letəd] ADJ **a** (rare) person gelehrt **b** object beschriftet; ~ **in gold** in Goldschrift

letterhead ['letəhed] N Briefkopf m; (= writing paper) Geschäfts(brief)papier nt

lettering ['letərɪŋ] N Beschriftung f

letter: letter jacket N (US: Univ) Jacke, auf die die Initialen des besuchten Colleges gestickt sind; **letter of credit** N Kreditbrief m, Akkreditiv nt; **letter opener** N Brieföffner m; **letter-perfect** ADJ textsicher, sicher im Text; **to be ~** den Text perfekt beherrschen, den Text bis aufs Wort beherrschen; **letterpress** N Hochdruck m; **letter quality** N Korrespondenz- or Briefqualität f, Schönschrift f; **letter-quality** ADJ script korrespondenzfähig; printout in Korrespondenz- or Briefqualität; ~ **printer** Schönschriftdrucker m; **letter rack** N Briefablage f

letters page ['letəz'peɪdʒ] N (Press) Leserbriefseite f

letters patent ['letəz'peɪtənt] PL Patent(urkunde f) nt

letting ['letɪŋ] N (esp Brit) Vermieten nt; **he's in the ~ business** er ist in der Wohnungsbranche

Lettish ['letɪʃ] ADJ = **Latvian**

lettuce ['letɪs] N Kopfsalat m; (genus) Lattich m

let-up ['letʌp] N (inf) Pause f; (= easing up) Nachlassen nt; **if there is a ~ in the rain** wenn der Regen aufhört/nachlässt

leucocyte, **leukocyte** ['luːkəʊsaɪt] N (form) Leukozyt m

leukaemia, (US) **leukemia** [luː'kiːmɪə] N Leukämie f

Levant [lɪ'vænt] N Levante f

Levantine ['levəntaɪn] ADJ levantinisch **N** (= person) Levantiner(in) m(f)

levee¹ ['levɪ] N (Hist) (on awakening) Lever nt; (at British court) Nachmittagsempfang m

levee² ['levɪ] N Damm m, Deich m

level ['levl] ADJ **a** (= flat) ground, surface, floor eben; spoonful gestrichen; **try to keep the boat ~** versuchen Sie, das Boot waagerecht zu halten; **the glider maintained a ~ course** das Segelflugzeug behielt die gleiche Flughöhe bei

b (= at the same height) auf gleicher Höhe (with mit); (= parallel) parallel (with zu); **the bedroom is ~ with the ground** das Schlafzimmer liegt ebenerdig or zu ebener Erde

c (= equal) gleichauf; (fig) gleich gut; **the two runners are absolutely ~ or dead ~** die beiden Läufer liegen or sind genau auf gleicher Höhe; **Jones was almost ~ with the winner** Jones kam fast auf gleiche Höhe mit dem Sieger; **the two teams are ~ in the league** die beiden Mannschaften haben den gleichen Tabellenstand; ~ **race** Kopf-an-Kopf-Rennen nt

d (= steady) tone of voice ruhig; (= well-balanced) judgement abgewogen, ausgewogen; head kühl; **to have/keep a ~ head** einen kühlen Kopf haben/bewahren

e **I'll do my ~ best** (Brit) ich werde mein Möglichstes tun

ADV ~ **with** in Höhe (+gen); **it should lie ~ with ...** es sollte gleich hoch sein wie ...; **the pipe runs ~ with the ground** das Rohr verläuft zu ebener Erde; (= parallel) das Rohr verläuft parallel zum Boden; **they're running absolutely ~** sie laufen auf genau gleicher Höhe; **the value of the shares stayed ~ for some time** der Wert der Aktien blieb für einige Zeit gleich; **to draw ~ with sb** jdn einholen, mit jdm gleichziehen;

(*in league etc*) punktegleich mit jdm sein; **the two runners drew ~ on the last lap** in der letzten Runde zogen die beiden Läufer gleich **N** **a** (= *instrument*) Wasserwaage *f* **b** (= *altitude*) Höhe *f*; **on a ~ (with)** auf gleicher Höhe (mit); **water always finds its own ~** Wasser kehrt immer in die Waagerechte zurück; **at eye ~** in Augenhöhe; **the trees were very tall, almost at roof ~** die Bäume waren sehr hoch, sie reichten fast bis zum Dach; **to be on a ~ with the roof** in Dachhöhe sein **c** (= *flat place*) ebene Fläche, ebenes Stück **d** (= *storey*) Etage *f*, Stockwerk *nt*; **the house is on four ~s** das Haus hat vier Etagen **e** (= *position on scale*) Ebene *f*; (*social, intellectual etc*) Niveau *nt*; **they're on a different ~** sie haben ein unterschiedliches Niveau; **to descend** *or* **come down to that ~** auf ein so tiefes Niveau absinken; **he expects everyone to come down to his ~** er erwartet von jedem, dass er sich auf sein Niveau herabbegibt; **she tried to go beyond her natural ~ of ability** sie versuchte, ihre natürlichen Grenzen zu überschreiten; **to be on a ~ with** auf gleichem Niveau sein wie; **they are on a ~ as far as salaries are concerned** sie bekommen das gleiche Gehalt; **he tried to raise the ~ of the conversation** er versuchte, der Unterhaltung etwas mehr Niveau zu geben; **if profit stays at the same ~** wenn sich der Gewinn auf dem gleichen Stand hält; **the pound has been left to find its own ~** der Pfundkurs wurde freigegeben, um seinen natürlichen Stand zu erreichen; **the rising ~ of inflation** die steigende Inflationsrate; **he maintains his high ~ of excellence** er hält sein äußerst hohes Niveau; **a high ~ of intelligence** ein hoher Intelligenzgrad; **a high ~ of interest** sehr großes Interesse; **a high ~ of support** sehr viel Unterstützung; **a high ~ of civilization** eine hohe Kulturstufe; **the very high ~ of production** das hohe Produktionsniveau; **the higher ~s of academic research** die höheren Stufen der wissenschaftlichen Forschung; **the talks were held at a very high ~** die Gespräche fanden auf hoher Ebene statt; **a low ~ of sales** ein sehr geringer Absatz; **he reduces everything to the commercial ~** er reduziert alles auf eine rein kommerzielle Basis; **on an intellectual ~** auf intellektueller Ebene; **on the moral ~** aus moralischer Sicht; **on a purely personal ~** rein persönlich, auf rein persönlicher Ebene **f** (= *amount, degree*) **a high ~ of hydrogen** ein hoher Wasserstoffanteil; **the ~ of alcohol in the blood** der Alkoholspiegel im Blut; **~ of consciousness** Bewusstseinsebene *f*; **cholesterol ~** Cholesterinspiegel *m*; **the ~ of violence** das Ausmaß der Gewalttätigkeit **g** **it's on the ~** (*inf*: = *straightforward, honest*) (*business*) es ist reell; (*proposition*) es ist ehrlich gemeint; **I guess you're on the ~** du bist wohl schon in Ordnung (*inf*); **is he on the ~?** meint er es ehrlich?; **to be on the ~ with sb** jdm gegenüber ehrlich *or* aufrichtig sein

VT **a** *ground, site etc* einebnen, planieren; *building* abreißen; *town* dem Erdboden gleichmachen; **to ~ sth to the ground** etw dem Erdboden gleichmachen **b** *blow* versetzen, verpassen (*inf*) (*at sb* jdm); *weapon* richten (*at sb* +*acc*) *accusation* erheben (*at* gegen); *remark* richten (*at* gegen); *criticism* üben (*at* an +*dat*); **to ~ a charge against sb** Anklage gegen jdn erheben, jdn anklagen **c** (*Sport*) **to ~ the match** den Ausgleich erzielen; **to ~ the score** gleichziehen **VI** (*inf*) **to ~ with sb** jdm keinen Quatsch *or* Scheiß erzählen (*inf*); **I'll ~ with you** ich werd ehrlich mit dir sein

▸ **level down** VT *sep* (*lit*) einebnen; (*fig*) auf ein tieferes Niveau bringen *or* herabsetzen; *salaries* nach unten angleichen

▸ **level out** VI (*also* **level off**) **a** (*ground*) eben *or* flach werden; (*fig*) sich ausgleichen, sich einpendeln; (*output, growth*) sich stabilisieren **b** (*Aviat, pilot*) das Flugzeug abfangen; (*plane*) sich fangen; (*after rising*) horizontal fliegen **VT** *sep site* planieren, einebnen; (*fig*) *differences* ausgleichen

▸ **level up** VT *sep* (*lit*) ausgleichen; *salaries* angleichen; (*fig*) auf ein höheres Niveau bringen; **you sit on the other side of the boat and that'll level it up** du setzt dich auf die andere Seite des Bootes, dann ist das Gleichgewicht (wieder) hergestellt

level: **level crossing** N (*Brit*) (beschrankter) Bahnübergang; **level-headed** ADJ *person* ausgeglichen; *attitude* ausgewogen; *reply, decision* ausgewogen, überlegt

leveller, (US) **leveler** ['levlə'] N Gleichmacher *m*; **death is a great ~** der Tod macht alle (Menschen) gleich

levelly ['levəlɪ] ADV (= *calmly*) ruhig; *gaze* gerade

level pegging ['levl'pegɪŋ] ADJ (*Brit*) punktgleich; **with 30 votes each they are ~** mit jeweils 30 Stimmen liegen sie auf gleicher Höhe; **it's ~ as they go round the final bend** sie liegen in der letzten Kurve auf gleicher Höhe

lever ['liːvə', (US) 'levə'] **N** Hebel *m*; (= *crowbar*) Brechstange *f*; (*fig*) Druckmittel *nt*; **that should give us a ~** (*fig*) das können wir als Druckmittel benutzen **VT** (hoch)stemmen, mit einem Hebel/einer Brechstange (an)heben; **he ~ed the machine-part into place** er hob das Maschinenteil durch Hebelwirkung an seinen Platz; **he ~ed the box open** er stemmte die Kiste auf; **he ~ed himself onto the ledge** er hievte sich auf den Felsvorsprung (hoch); **he seems to have ~ed himself into a position of power** er scheint sich in eine Machtposition manövriert zu haben

▸ **lever out** VT *sep* herausstemmen *or* -brechen; **we'll never lever him out of such a comfortable job** wir werden ihn nie aus dem bequemen Job werden wir ihn nie herausholen *or* -lotsen können (*inf*); **he levered himself out of the armchair** er hievte sich aus dem Sessel (hoch)

▸ **lever up** VT *sep* mit einem Hebel/einer Brechstange hochheben, aufstemmen

leverage ['liːvərɪdʒ, (US) 'liːvərɪdʒ] **N** Hebelkraft *f*; (*fig*) Einfluss *m*; **this spanner can exert considerable ~** dieser Schraubenschlüssel kann eine beträchtliche Hebelwirkung ausüben; **to use sth as ~** (*fig*) etw als Druckmittel benutzen; (= *to one's own advantage*) etw zu seinem Vorteil ausnützen; **this gave us a bit of ~ with the authorities** dadurch konnten wir etwas Druck auf die Behörden ausüben; **his approval gives us a bit of ~ with them** seine Zustimmung verstärkt unsere Position ihnen gegenüber

leveraged buyout [ˌliːvərɪdʒd'baɪaʊt, (US) ˌliːvərɪdʒd'baɪaʊt] N (*Comm*) Aufkauf einer Kapitalgesellschaft durch das eigene Management mit Hilfe externer Finanzierung

lever-arch file ['liːvərɑːtʃfaɪl] N Leitz-Ordner® *m*

leveret ['levərɪt] N junger Hase, Häschen *nt*

leviathan [lɪ'vaɪəθən] N Leviathan *m*, Meerungeheuer *nt*; (*fig*) Gigant *m*; (= *state*) Leviathan *m*

Levis, levis® ['liːvaɪz] PL Levis® *f*, Jeans *pl*

levitate ['levɪteɪt] **VT** schweben lassen **VI** schweben

levitation [ˌlevɪ'teɪʃən] N Levitation *f*, freies Schweben

Levite ['liːvaɪt] N Levit(e) *m*

levity ['levɪtɪ] N Leichtfertigkeit *f*

levy ['levɪ] **N** (= *act*) (Steuer)einziehung *f* *or* -eintreibung *f*; (= *tax*) Steuer *f*, Abgaben *pl*; (*Mil*) Aushebung *f*; (*of supplies*) Einziehung *f*, Beschlagnahme *f*; **there were 100 men in the first ~** 100 Männer wurden bei der ersten Aushebung eingezogen; **political ~** (*Brit Pol*) zur Unterstützung der Labour Party verwendeter Teil des Gewerkschaftsbeitrags **VT** **a** (= *raise*) *tax* einziehen, erheben; *charge* erheben; *fine* auferlegen (*on sb* jdm); *sanctions* verhängen; (*Mil*) *army, troops* ausheben; *supplies* einziehen, beschlagnahmen; **to ~ a tax on beer** Bier mit einer Steuer belegen, Steuern *pl* auf Bier erheben **b** (= *wage*) *war* führen (*against, on* gegen)

lewd [luːd] ADJ (+*er*) unanständig; (= *lustful*) lüstern; *remark* anzüglich; *joke, song* unanständig, anstößig, anzüglich; *imagination* schmutzig; **don't be ~** werd nicht anzüglich

lewdly ['luːdlɪ] ADV anzüglich; **he spoke ~ about his amorous adventures** er erzählte lüstern *or* in anzüglicher Weise von seinen amourösen Abenteuern

lewdness ['luːdnɪs] N (= *being indecent*) Anstößigkeit *f*, Unanständigkeit *f*; (= *being lustful*) Lüsternheit *f*; (*of remark*) Anzüglichkeit *f*; (*of imagination*) Schmutzigkeit *f*

lexical ['leksɪkəl] ADJ lexikalisch

lexicalize ['leksɪkəlaɪz] VT lexikalisieren

lexicographer [ˌleksɪ'kɒgrəfə'] N Lexikograf(in) *m(f)*

lexicographic(al) [ˌleksɪkəʊ'græfɪk(əl)] ADJ lexikografisch

lexicography [ˌleksɪ'kɒgrəfɪ] N Lexikografie *f*

lexicology [ˌleksɪ'kɒlədʒɪ] N Lexikologie *f*

lexicon ['leksɪkən] N Wörterbuch *nt*, Lexikon *nt*; (*in linguistics*) Lexikon *nt*

lexis ['leksɪs] N (*Ling*) Lexik *f*

Leyden jar ['laɪdn'dʒɑː'] N Leidener Flasche *f*

l.h.d. *abbr of* left-hand drive

liability [ˌlaɪə'bɪlɪtɪ] **N** **a** (= *burden*) Belastung *f* **b** (= *being subject to*) **one's ~ for tax** jds Steuerpflicht *f*; **he has a tax ~ of £1,000** er muss £ 1000 Steuern bezahlen; **~ to pay damages** Schadensersatzpflicht *f* **c** (= *proneness*) Anfälligkeit *f* (*to* für); **his ~ to digestive disorders** seine Anfälligkeit für Verdauungsstörungen **d** (= *responsibility*) Haftung *f*; **we accept no ~ for …** wir übernehmen keine Haftung für …; **his ~ for his wife's debts** seine Haftung *or* Haftbarkeit für die Schulden seiner Frau **e** (*Fin*) **liabilities** Verbindlichkeiten *pl*, Verpflichtungen *pl*

liable ['laɪəbl] ADJ **a** (= *subject to*) **to be ~ for** *or* **to sth** einer Sache (*dat*) unterliegen; **to be ~ for tax** (*things*) besteuert werden; (*income, person*) steuerpflichtig sein; **people earning over £X are ~ for surtax** wer mehr als £ X verdient, unterliegt einer Zusatzsteuer *or* ist zusatzsteuerpflichtig; **~ to penalty** strafbar; **to be ~ to prosecution** der Strafverfolgung unterliegen; **you'll make yourself ~ to a heavy fine** Sie können zu einer hohen Geldstrafe verurteilt werden **b** (= *prone to*) anfällig; **he's always been ~ to bronchitis** er war schon immer anfällig für Bronchitis; **~ to inflation** inflationsanfällig **c** (= *responsible*) **to be ~** haften, haftbar sein; **to be ~ for sth** für etw haftbar sein *or* haften, für etw aufkommen müssen; **he is not legally ~ to pay** er ist nicht gesetzlich verpflichtet zu zahlen **d** (= *likely to*) **to be ~ to do sth** (*in future*) wahrscheinlich etw tun (werden); (*habitually*) dazu neigen, etw zu tun; **we are ~ to get shot here** wir können hier leicht beschossen werden; **the pond is ~ to freeze** der Teich friert leicht zu; **is he ~ to come?** ist anzunehmen, dass er kommt?; **he's ~ to tell the police** es wäre ihm zuzutrauen, dass er es der Polizei meldet; **if you don't write it down I'm ~ to forget it** wenn Sie das nicht aufschreiben, kann es durchaus sein, dass ich es vergesse; **the plan is ~ to changes** der Plan wird möglicherweise geändert; **I don't think it's ~ to happen tonight** ich halte es für nicht wahrscheinlich, dass es heute Nacht passiert; **the car is ~ to run out of petrol** (*Brit*) *or* **gas** (*US*) **any minute** dem Auto kann jede Minute das Benzin ausgehen; **if you tell him that, he's ~ to lose his temper** wenn Sie ihm das sagen, wird er wahrscheinlich wütend

liaise [lɪ'eɪz] VI (= *be the contact person*) als Verbindungsperson fungieren; (= *get in contact*) sich in Verbindung setzen (*with* mit); (= *be in contact*) in Verbindung stehen (*with* mit); **social services and health workers ~ closely** das Sozialamt und der Gesundheitsdienst arbeiten eng zusammen

liaison [lɪ'eɪzɒn] **N** **a** (= *coordination*) Verbindung *f*, Zusammenarbeit *f*; (= *person*) Verbindungsmann *m*/-frau *f*, V-Mann *m*/-Frau *f* (*inf*);

(*Mil*) Verbindung *f*; (*person*) Verbindungsoffizier *m* **b** (= *affair*) Liaison *f*

liaison officer N Verbindungsmann *m*/-frau *f*; (*Mil*) Verbindungsoffizier *m*; **the firm's ~** der/die Firmensprecher(in)

liar ['laɪə'] N Lügner(in) *m(f)*

Lib (*Brit Pol*) abbr of **Liberal**

lib [lɪb] N abbr of **liberation**

libation [laɪˈbeɪʃən] N **a** (= *offering*) Trankopfer *nt* **b** (*inf*: = *drink*) **we had a few small ~s** wir hatten ein paar getrunken (*inf*)

Lib Dem [ˌlɪbˈdem] (*Brit Pol*) abbr of **Liberal Democrat** **N** Liberaldemokrat(in) *m(f)* **ADJ** liberaldemokratisch; *gain, loss, policy* der Liberaldemokraten

libel ['laɪbəl] **N** (schriftlich geäußerte) Verleumdung (*on +gen*); **to begin a ~ action against sb** jdn wegen Verleumdung verklagen; **it's a ~ on all of us** das ist eine Verleumdung, die uns alle trifft **VT** verleumden

libellous, (*US*) **libelous** ['laɪbələs] ADJ verleumderisch

liberal ['lɪbərəl] **ADJ** **a** (= *generous*) *offer, supply* großzügig; *helping of food* reichlich; **to be ~ with one's praise/comments** mit Lob/seinen Kommentaren freigebig sein; **to be ~ with one's money** mit seinem Geld großzügig umgehen **b** (= *broad-minded*) liberal **c** (*Pol*) liberal; **the Liberal Party** (*Brit Hist, in Canada*) die Liberale Partei **N** **a** (*Pol*) Liberale(r) *mf* **b** (= *liberal-minded person*) Liberalbesinnte(r) *mf*; **he's a ~ in social matters** er hat eine liberale Einstellung in sozialen Angelegenheiten

liberal: liberal arts PL **the ~** (*esp US*) die geisteswissenschaftlichen Fächer; **liberal democracy** N (*Pol*) freiheitliche Demokratie; **Liberal Democrat** (*Brit Pol*) **N** Liberaldemokrat(in) *m(f)* **ADJ** liberaldemokratisch; *gain, loss, policy* der Liberaldemokraten; **the ~ Party** die liberaldemokratische Partei; **liberal education** N Allgemeinbildung *f*

liberalism ['lɪbərəlɪzəm] N Liberalität *f*; **Liberalism** (*Pol*) der Liberalismus

liberality [ˌlɪbəˈrælɪtɪ] N **a** (= *generosity*) Großzügigkeit *f* **b** = **liberal-mindedness**

liberalization [ˌlɪbərəlaɪˈzeɪʃən] N Liberalisierung *f*

liberalize ['lɪbərəlaɪz] VT liberalisieren

liberally ['lɪbərəlɪ] ADV (= *broad-mindedly*) liberal; (= *generously*) großzügig; (= *in large quantities*) reichlich; **he applies the paint very ~** er trägt die Farbe dick or reichlich auf

liberal: liberal-minded ADJ *person* liberal (eingestellt); *views, country* liberal; **liberal-mindedness** N (*of person*) liberale Einstellung or Gesinnung; (*of views*) Liberalität *f*; **liberal studies** PL (*esp US*) Geisteswissenschaften *pl*

liberate ['lɪbəreɪt] VT **a** (= *free*) *prisoner, country, city* befreien; **to ~ sb from sth** jdn von etw befreien **b** *gas etc* freisetzen

liberated ['lɪbəreɪtɪd] ADJ *women, times* emanzipiert

liberation [lɪbəˈreɪʃən] N Befreiung *f*; (*of gases*) Freisetzung *f*

liberator ['lɪbəreɪtə'] N Befreier(in) *m(f)*

Liberia [laɪˈbɪərɪə] N Liberia *nt*

Liberian [laɪˈbɪərɪən] **ADJ** liberianisch, liberisch **N** Liberianer(in) *m(f)*, Liberier(in) *m(f)*

libertarian [lɪbəˈtɛərɪən] **ADJ** (= *freedom-loving*) freiheitsliebend; (= *opposed to authority*) antiautoritär, libertär; *policy, politics* liberalistisch; **attitude** freiheitliche/antiautoritäre or libertäre Gesinnung **N** Verfechter(in) *m(f)* des freien Willens, Liberalist(in) *m(f)* (*esp Pol*)

libertine ['lɪbətiːn] N Wüstling *m*, Libertin *m* (*geh*)

liberty ['lɪbətɪ] N **a** Freiheit *f*; **individual ~** die Freiheit des Einzelnen; **basic liberties** Grundrechte *pl*; **to set sb at ~** jdn auf freien Fuß setzen; **to be at ~** (*criminal etc*) frei herumlaufen; (= *not busy*) Zeit haben; **to be at ~ to do sth** (= *be permitted*) etw tun dürfen; **I am not at ~ to**

comment es ist mir nicht gestattet, darüber zu sprechen; **you are at ~ to go** es steht Ihnen frei zu gehen; **is he at ~ to come?** darf er kommen?
b (= *presumptuous action, behaviour*) **I have taken the ~ of giving your name** ich habe mir erlaubt, Ihren Namen anzugeben; **to take liberties with the truth** es mit der Wahrheit nicht so genau nehmen; **to take liberties with sb** sich jdm gegenüber Freiheiten herausnehmen; **what a ~!** (*inf*) so eine Frechheit!

liberty bodice N Leibchen *nt*

libidinous [lɪˈbɪdɪnəs] ADJ lüstern; *person, behaviour also* triebhaft; (*Psych*) *urge, effect* libidinös

libido [lɪˈbiːdəʊ] N Libido *f*

Lib-Lab ['lɪbˌlæb] ADJ abbr of **Liberal-Labour** (*Brit Pol inf*) **~ pact** Pakt *m* zwischen den Liberalen und der Labour Party

LIBOR ['liːbɔː'] N abbr of **London Inter-Bank Offer Rate** bankeninterner Wechselkurs

Libra ['liːbrə] N Waage *f*; **she's (a) ~** sie ist Waage

Libran ['liːbrən] N Waage *f*, Waagemensch *m*

librarian [laɪˈbrɛərɪən] N Bibliothekar(in) *m(f)*

librarianship [laɪˈbrɛərɪənʃɪp] N **a** (= *subject*) Bibliothekswesen *nt* or -lehre *f* **b** (= *job*) Bibliothekarsstelle *f*

library ['laɪbrərɪ] N **a** (*public*) Bibliothek *f*, Bücherei *f* **b** (*private*) Bibliothek *f* **c** (= *collection of books/records*) (Bücher-/Schallplatten)sammlung *f* **d** (= *series of books*) Buchreihe *f*, Bibliothek *f*

library: library book N Leihbuch *nt*; **library card** N Benutzerausweis *m*; **library edition** N Leihbuchausgabe *f*; **library pictures** PL (*TV*) Archivbilder *pl*; **library science** N Bibliothekswissenschaften *pl*; **library ticket** N Leserausweis *m*

librettist [lɪˈbretɪst] N Librettist(in) *m(f)*

libretto [lɪˈbretəʊ] N Libretto *nt*

Libya ['lɪbɪə] N Libyen *nt*

Libyan ['lɪbɪən] **ADJ** libysch **N** Libyer(in) *m(f)*

lice [laɪs] pl of **louse**

licence, (*US*) **license** ['laɪsəns] N **a** (= *permit*) Genehmigung *f*, Erlaubnis *f*; (*by authority*) behördliche Genehmigung, Konzession *f*; (*Comm*) Lizenz *f*; (= *driving licence*) Führerschein *m*; (= *road licence*) Kfz-Steuer *f*; (= *gun licence*) Waffenschein *m*; (= *hunting licence*) Jagdschein *m*; (= *marriage licence*) Eheerlaubnis *f*; (= *radio/television licence*) (Rundfunk-/Fernseh)genehmigung *f*; (= *dog licence*) Hundemarke *f*; **he hasn't paid his (dog) ~** er hat seine Hundesteuer nicht bezahlt; **you have to have a (television) ~** man muss Fernsehgebühren bezahlen; **a ~ to practise medicine** (*Brit*), **a license to practice medicine** (*US*) die Approbation, die staatliche Zulassung als Arzt; **the restaurant has lost its ~ (to sell drinks)** das Restaurant hat seine Schankerlaubnis or Konzession verloren; **we'll get a late ~ for the reception** für den Empfang bekommen wir eine Genehmigung für verlängerte Ausschankzeiten; **a ~ to kill** ein Freibrief *m* zum Töten; **it is just a ~ to print money** (*fig*) es ist ein sehr lukratives Geschäft; **to manufacture sth under ~** etw in Lizenz herstellen; **to give sb ~ to do sth** jdm erlauben, etw zu tun

b (= *freedom*) Freiheit *f*; **translated with considerable ~** sehr frei übersetzt
c (= *excessive freedom*) Zügellosigkeit *f*; **there is too much ~ in sexual matters/the cinema nowadays** in sexuellen Dingen/im Kino geht es heutzutage zu freizügig zu

licence: licence fee N (*Brit TV*) ≈ Fernsehgebühr *f*; **licence number**, (*US*) **license number** N (*Aut*) Kraftfahrzeug- or Kfz-Kennzeichen *nt*; **licence plate**, (*US*) **license plate** N (*Aut*) Nummernschild *nt*

license ['laɪsəns] **N** (*US*) = **licence** **VT** eine Lizenz/Konzession vergeben an (+*acc*); **to ~ a pub** einer Gaststätte Schankerlaubnis or eine Schankkonzession erteilen; **to be ~d to do sth** die Genehmigung haben, etw zu tun; **he is ~d to practise** (*Brit*) or **practice** (*US*) **medicine** er ist approbierter Arzt, er ist als Arzt zugelassen; **we are not ~d to sell alcohol** wir haben keine Schankerlaubnis or Konzession; **secret agents are ~d to kill** Geheimagenten dürfen Leute umbringen

licensed ['laɪsənst] ADJ **a** *pilot* mit Pilotenschein; *taxi driver* mit Taxischein; *physician* approbiert; **he's a ~ pilot** er hat einen Pilotenschein **b** (= *selling alcohol*) **~ bar/premises** Lokal *nt* mit Schankerlaubnis; **fully ~** mit voller Schankkonzession or -erlaubnis; **~ trade** (konzessionierter) Alkoholhandel; **I used to be in the ~ trade** ich war früher Gastwirt; **~ victualler** *Lebensmittelhändler mit einer Konzession für den Verkauf von Alkohol* **he won't stay at a hotel unless it's ~** er übernachtet nur in Hotels mit Alkoholausschank

licensee [ˌlaɪsənˈsiː] N → **licence** Konzessions-/Lizenzinhaber(in) *m(f)*/Inhaber(in) *m(f)* eines Waffenscheins *etc*; (*of bar*) Inhaber(in) *m(f)* einer Schankerlaubnis; **the ~ of our local pub** (*Brit*) or **bar** der Wirt unserer Stammkneipe

licenser, licensor ['laɪsənsə'] N Lizenzgeber(in) *m(f)*, Konzessionserteiler(in) *m(f)*

licensing ['laɪsənsɪŋ] ADJ **~ agreement** Lizenzabkommen *nt*; **~ hours** Ausschankzeiten *pl*; **~ laws** Schankgesetze *pl*, Gesetz *nt* über den Ausschank und Verkauf alkoholischer Getränke

licensor ['laɪsənsə'] N → **licenser**

licentiate [laɪˈsenʃɪɪt] N Lizenziat(in) *m(f)*, Lizentiat(in) *m(f)*; (= *degree*) Lizenziat *nt*, Lizentiat *nt*

licentious [laɪˈsenʃəs] ADJ ausschweifend, lasterhaft; *behaviour* unzüchtig; *book* sehr freizügig; *look* lüstern

licentiousness [laɪˈsenʃəsnɪs] N Unmoral *f*, Unzüchtigkeit *f*; (*of book*) Freizügigkeit *f*; (*of look*) Lüsternheit *f*

lichen [ˈlaɪkən] N Flechte *f*

lichgate, lychgate [ˈlɪtʃɡeɪt] N überdachter Kirchhofseingang

licit [ˈlɪsɪt] ADJ erlaubt, gesetzlich

lick [lɪk] **N a** (*with tongue*) Lecken *nt*, Schlecken *nt* (*dial*); **to give sth a ~** an etw (*dat*) lecken; **the cat gave me/my hand a ~** die Katze leckte mich ab/mir die Hand

b (= *salt lick*) (Salz)lecke *f*; (*artificial*) Leckstein *m*

c (*inf*: = *small quantity*) **it's time we gave the kitchen a ~ of paint** die Küche könnte auch mal wieder etwas Farbe vertragen (*inf*); **he doesn't do a ~ of work** er tut keinen Schlag

d (*Brit inf*: = *pace*) **the project is coming along at a good ~** das Projekt geht ganz gut voran (*inf*); **to go/drive at a fair old ~** einen ganz schönen Zahn draufhaben (*inf*); **he rushed to the station at full ~** er raste mit Vollgas zum Bahnhof (*inf*)

VT a (*with tongue*) lecken; **he ~ed the stamp** er leckte an der Briefmarke; **the cat ~ed the ice cream** er leckte an Eis; **to ~ one's lips** sich (*dat*) die Lippen lecken; (*fig*) sich (*dat*) die Finger lecken; **the cat ~ed its paws** die Katze leckte sich (*dat*) die Pfoten; **to ~ the bowl out** die Schüssel auslecken; **to ~ one's wounds** (*fig*) seine Wunden lecken; **to ~ sb's boots** (*fig*) vor jdm kriechen (*inf*), jds Stiefel lecken; **to ~ sb into shape** (*fig*) jdn auf Vordermann bringen (*inf*)

b (*waves*) plätschern an (+*acc*); (*flames*) züngeln an (+*dat*)

c (*inf*: = *beat, defeat*) in die Pfanne hauen (*inf*); **I think we've got it ~ed** ich glaube, wir haben die Sache jetzt im Griff

VI a **to ~ at sth** an etw (*dat*) lecken; **flames ~ed around the building** Flammen züngelten an dem Gebäude empor

▶ **lick off** VT *sep* ablecken; **to lick sth off sth** etw von etw ablecken

▶ **lick up** VT *sep* auflecken

lickety-split [ˈlɪkɪtɪˈsplɪt] ADV (*US inf*) blitzschnell, mit Volldampf (*inf*)

licking [ˈlɪkɪŋ] N (*inf*) (= *beating*) Tracht *f* Prügel; (= *defeat*) Niederlage *f*; **to give sb a ~** (= *beating*) jdm eine Abreibung geben (*inf*); (= *defeat*) jdn in die Pfanne hauen (*inf*)

licorice [ˈlɪkərɪs] N = **liquorice**

lid [lɪd] N **a** Deckel *m*; **that puts the (tin) ~ on it** (*inf*) das ist doch die Höhe, das schlägt dem Fass den Boden aus; **a documentary that really takes the ~ off Hollywood** ein Dokumentarfilm, der das wahre Gesicht Hollywoods zeigt; **the press took the ~ off the whole plan** die Presse hat den Plan enthüllt *or* aufgedeckt; **to keep a ~ on sth** etw unter Kontrolle halten; *on information* etw geheim halten; **to put the ~ on sth** (*on scandal, affair*) etw vertuschen; **to put the ~ on sb** jdn zum Schweigen bringen **b** (= *eyelid*) Lid *nt*

lidless [ˈlɪdlɪs] ADJ **a** ohne Deckel **b** *eyes* ohne Lider

lido [ˈliːdəʊ] N Freibad *nt*

lie¹ [laɪ] **N a** Lüge *f*; **it's a ~!** das ist eine Lüge!, das ist gelogen!; **to tell a ~** lügen; **I tell a ~, it's actually tomorrow** das stimmt ja gar nicht *or* ich hab mich vertan, es ist morgen; **to give the ~ to sb** jdn der Lüge bezichtigen *or* beschuldigen; **to give the ~ to a claim** die Unwahrheit einer Behauptung (*gen*) zeigen *or* beweisen; **a Behauptung Lügen strafen** (*geh*) **b** lügen; **to ~ to sb** jdn belügen *or* anlügen; **the camera never ~s** die Kamera lügt nie **VT to ~ one's way out of sth** sich aus etw herauslügen

lie² *vb: pret* **lay**, *ptp* **lain** **N** (= *position*) Lage *f*, Position *f*

VI a (*in horizontal or resting position*) liegen; (= *lie down*) sich legen; **he lay where he had fallen** er blieb liegen, wo er hingefallen war; **~ on your back** leg dich auf den Rücken; **obstacles ~ in the way of our success** unser Weg zum Erfolg ist mit Hindernissen verstellt; **the snow didn't ~ on the Schnee blieb nicht liegen; to ~ with sb** (*Bibl, old*) bei jdm liegen (*Bibl, old*)

b (= *be buried*) ruhen; **to ~ at rest** zur letzten Ruhe gebettet sein (*geh*)

c (= *be situated*) liegen; **the runner who is lying third** (*esp Brit*) der Läufer, der auf dem dritten Platz liegt; **Uganda ~s far from the coast** Uganda liegt weit von der Küste ab *or* entfernt; **our road lay along the river** unsere Straße führte am Fluss entlang; **our futures ~ in quite different directions** unsere zukünftigen Wege führen in verschiedene Richtungen; **you are young and your life ~s before you** du bist jung, und das Leben liegt noch vor dir

d (= *be, remain in a certain condition*) liegen; **to ~ asleep** (daliegen und) schlafen; **to ~ helpless** hilflos daliegen; **to ~ dying** im Sterben liegen; **he lay resting on the sofa** er ruhte sich auf dem Sofa aus; **the snow lay deep** es lag tiefer Schnee; **the book lay unopened** das Buch lag ungeöffnet da; **to ~ low** untertauchen, sich nicht mehr sehen lassen; **to ~ heavy on the stomach** schwer im Magen liegen; **to ~ heavy on the conscience** schwer auf dem Gewissen lasten

e (*immaterial things*) liegen; **where does the difficulty ~?** wo liegt die Schwierigkeit?; **it ~s with you to solve the problem** es liegt bei dir, das Problem zu lösen; **his interests ~ in music** seine Interessen liegen auf dem Gebiet der Musik *or* gelten der Musik; **he did everything that lay in his power to help us** er tat alles in seiner Macht Stehende, um uns zu helfen; **that responsibility ~s with your department** dafür ist Ihre Abteilung verantwortlich; **the real solution ~s in education** Bildung ist die wahre Lösung

▶ **lie about** (*Brit*) *or* **around** VI herumliegen

▶ **lie back** VI **a** (= *recline*) sich zurücklehnen **b** (*fig*: = *take no action*) es sich gemütlich machen, sich ausruhen; **we can't afford to lie back and relax until the job's finished** wir können uns (*dat*) keine Ruhe gönnen, bis die Arbeit erledigt ist

▶ **lie behind** VI +*prep obj decision, remarks* stehen hinter (+*dat*); **I don't know what lies behind it** ich weiß nicht, was dahintersteht

▶ **lie down** VI **a** (*lit*) sich hinlegen; **he lay down on the bed** er legte sich aufs Bett; **lie down!** (*to a dog*) leg dich!, hinlegen! **b** (*fig*: = *accept, submit*) **to lie down under sth** sich (*dat*) etw gefallen *or* bieten lassen; **he won't take that lying down!** das lässt er sich nicht gefallen *or* bieten!; **he didn't take defeat lying down** er nahm die Niederlage nicht tatenlos hin

▶ **lie in** VI **a** (= *stay in bed*) im Bett bleiben **b** (*old: in childbirth*) im Wochenbett liegen

▶ **lie off** VI (*Naut,* = *be anchored nearby*) vor Anker liegen; **the ship lay off Aberdeen** das Schiff lag vor Aberdeen vor Anker

▶ **lie over** VI *vtag* *or* zurückgestellt werden

▶ **lie to** VI (*Naut,* = *be anchored*) vor Anker liegen, ankern **b** (= *come into a position for anchoring*) beidrehen

▶ **lie up** VI **a** (= *rest after illness etc*) im Bett bleiben **b** (= *hide*) untertauchen; **the robbers are lying up** die Räuber sind untergetaucht **c** (= *be out of use*) nicht benutzt werden, unbenutzt stehen; (*car*) abgestellt sein

lie-abed [ˈlaɪəbed] N Langschläfer(in) *m(f)*

Liechtenstein [ˈliːxtənʃtaɪn] N Liechtenstein *nt*

lie detector N Lügendetektor *m*

lie-down [ˈlaɪdaʊn] N (*inf*) Schläfchen *nt* (*inf*), Nickerchen *nt* (*inf*); **to have a ~** ein Schläfchen *or* Nickerchen machen (*inf*)

lief [liːf] ADV (*old*) **I would as ~** ich würde ebenso gern; **I would as ~ ... as anything** ich würde nichts lieber tun als ...

liege [liːdʒ] N (*old*) **a** (*also* **liege lord**) Lehnsherr *m*; **my ~** Euer Gnaden **b** (*also* **liege man**) Lehnsmann *m*, Vasall *m*

lie-in [ˈlaɪɪn] N (*Brit inf*) **to have a ~** (sich) ausschlafen

lien [lɪən] N Zurückbehaltungsrecht *nt*, Pfandrecht *nt*

lieu [luː] N (*form*) **money in ~** stattdessen Geld; **in ~ of X** an Stelle von X; **in ~ of that** stattdessen; **I work weekends and get time off in ~** (*esp Brit*) ich arbeite an Wochenenden und kann mir dafür (an anderen Tagen) frei nehmen

Lieut. (*Mil*) *abbr* of **lieutenant** Lt

lieutenancy [leftˈenənsɪ, (*US*) luːˈtenənsɪ] N Leutnantsrang *m*; **he gained his ~** er ist zum Leutnant befördert worden

lieutenant [leftˈenənt, (*US*) luːˈtenənt] N **a** Leutnant *m*; (*Brit*) Oberleutnant *m*; **first ~** (*US*) Oberleutnant *m*; **second ~** Leutnant *m* **b** (= *governor*) Statthalter(in) *m(f)*, Gouverneur(in) *m(f)*

lieutenant: lieutenant colonel N Oberstleutnant *m*; **lieutenant commander** N Korvettenkapitän *m*; **lieutenant general** N (*Brit*) Generalleutnant *m*; **lieutenant governor** N (*US*) Vizegouverneur(in) *m(f)*

life [laɪf] N *pl* **lives a** Leben *nt*; **bird/plant ~** die Vogel-/Pflanzenwelt; **there is not much insect ~ here** hier gibt es nicht viele Insekten; **drawn from ~** lebensnah; **to draw from ~** (*Art*) nach dem Leben zeichnen; **to ~ lebensecht; the battle resulted in great loss of ~** bei der Schlacht kamen viele ums Leben; **this is a matter of ~ and death** hier geht es um Leben und Tod; **a ~ and death struggle** ein Kampf auf Leben und Tod; **~ after death** das Leben nach dem Tod; **~ begins at 40** das Leben fängt mit 40 (erst richtig) an; **to be tired of ~** des Lebens überdrüssig sein; **~ goes on** das Leben geht weiter; **to bring sb back to ~** jdn wieder beleben, jdn ins Leben zurückrufen; **his book brings history to ~** sein Buch lässt die Geschichte lebendig werden; **to come to ~** (*fig*) lebendig werden; **I'm the sort of person who comes to ~ in the evenings** ich bin ein Typ, der erst abends munter wird; **after half an hour the discussion came to ~** nach einer halben Stunde kam Leben in die Diskussion; **to put new ~ into sb** jdm wieder Auftrieb geben; **for dear ~** verzweifelt; **they swam for dear ~** sie schwammen um ihr Leben; **they looked at him in the oxygen tent fighting for dear ~** sie sahen, wie er im Sauerstoffzelt um sein Leben kämpfte; **at my time of ~** in meinem Alter; **marriage should be for ~** eine Ehe sollte fürs Leben geschlossen werden; **he's got a job for ~** er hat eine Stelle auf Lebenszeit; **the murderer was imprisoned for ~** der Mörder wurde zu lebenslänglicher Freiheitsstrafe verurteilt; **he's doing ~ (for murder)** (*inf*) er sitzt lebenslänglich (wegen Mord) (*inf*); **he got ~** (*inf*) er hat lebenslänglich gekriegt (*inf*)

b (= *individual life*) **how many lives were lost?** wie viele (Menschen) sind ums Leben gekommen?; **the lives of the prisoners** das Leben der Gefangenen; **I've got a new man in my ~** in meinem Leben gibt es einen neuen Mann; **to take sb's ~** jdn umbringen; **to take one's own ~** sich (*dat*) das Leben nehmen; **to save sb's ~** (*lit*) jdm das Leben retten; (*fig*) jdn retten; **I couldn't do it to save my ~** ich kann es beim besten Willen nicht; **the church is my ~** die Kirche ist mein ganzes Leben; **to rule sb's ~** jds Leben bestimmen; **the suspected murderer is on trial for his ~** für den Mordverdächtigen geht es bei dem Prozess um Leben und Tod; **in the next ~** im nächsten Leben; **early in ~, in early ~** in frühen Jahren; **later in ~, in later ~** in späteren Jahren, später im Leben; **she leads a busy ~** bei ihr ist immer etwas los; **she began (her working) ~ as a teacher** sie begann ihr Berufsleben als Lehrerin; **the book started ~ as a**

screenplay das Buch war ursprünglich ein Drehbuch; **all his ~** sein ganzes Leben lang; **I've never been to London in my ~** ich war in meinem ganzen Leben noch nicht in London; **to fight for one's ~** um sein Leben kämpfen; **run for your lives!** rennt um euer Leben!; **it gave me the fright of my ~** es hat mich zu Tode erschreckt; **I can't for the ~ of me ...** (inf) ich kann beim besten Willen nicht ...; **never in my ~ have I heard such nonsense** ich habe mein Lebtag noch nicht or noch nie im Leben so einen Unsinn gehört; **not on your ~!** (inf) ich bin doch nicht verrückt! (inf); **would you ever disobey him? – not on your ~!** (inf) würdest du je seine Befehle missachten? – nie im Leben!; **get a ~!** (inf) sonst hast du keine Probleme? (inf); **to have a ~** etwas von Leben haben; **to have a ~ of one's own** sein eigenes Leben führen; **it seemed to have a ~ of its own** es scheint seinen eigenen Willen zu haben; **he is a good/bad ~** (Insur) er ist ein niedriges/hohes Risiko **c** (= the world, social activity) **to see ~** die Welt sehen; **there isn't much ~ here in the evenings** hier ist abends nicht viel Leben or nicht viel los **d** (= liveliness) Leben nt; **those children are full of ~!** diese Kinder stecken voller Leben or sind sehr lebhaft!; **the city centre** (Brit) or **center** (US) **was full of ~** im Stadtzentrum ging es sehr lebhaft zu; **he's still got so much ~ in him** er ist noch so vital or steckt noch voller Leben; **there's ~ in the old girl yet** (inf) sie ist noch schwer aktiv (inf); (of car) die Kiste bringts noch (sl); **he is the ~ and soul** (Brit) or **~** (US) **of every party** er bringt Leben in jede Party; **wherever John goes, he wants to be the ~ and soul** (Brit) or **~** (US) **of the party** John will überall im Mittelpunkt stehen **e** (= way of life) Leben nt; **village ~** das Leben auf dem Dorf; **this is the ~!** ja, ist das ein Leben!; **what a ~!** was für ein Leben!; **such is ~, that's ~** so ist das Leben; **it's a good ~** es ist ein schönes Leben; **the good ~** das süße Leben **f** (= useful or active life) Lebensdauer f; **during the ~ of the present Parliament** während der Legislaturperiode des gegenwärtigen Parlaments; **there's not much ~ left in the battery, the battery's nearing the end of its ~** die Batterie machts nicht mehr lange (inf) **g** (= biography) Biografie f; (of saint, king etc) Lebensbeschreibung f

life: **life annuity** N Leib- or Lebensrente f; **life assurance** N (Brit) Lebensversicherung f; **lifebelt** N Rettungsgürtel m; **lifeblood** N Blut nt; (fig) Lebensnerv m; **to drain sb's ~** (fig) jdn ausbluten lassen; **lifeboat** N (from shore) Rettungsboot nt; (from ship also) Beiboot nt; **lifebuoy** N Rettungsring m; **life class** N (Art) Kurs m im Modellzeichnen; **life cycle** N Lebenszyklus m; **life-enhancing** ['laɪfɪn,hɑːnsɪŋ] ADJ bereichernd; **life expectancy** N Lebenserwartung f; **life force** N Lebenskraft f; **life-giving** ADJ Leben spendend; **~ aid to poor countries** lebensnotwendige Hilfe für arme Länder; **lifeguard** N **a** (on beach) Rettungsschwimmer(in) m(f); (in baths) Bademeister(in) m(f) **b** (Mil) Leibwache f; **life history** N Lebensgeschichte f; (Biol) Entwicklungsgeschichte f; **the ~ of the salmon** der Lebenskreislauf des Lachses; **life imprisonment** N lebenslängliche Freiheitsstrafe; **life instinct** N (Psych) Lebenstrieb m; **life insurance** N = **life assurance**; **life interest** N (Jur) lebenslänglicher Nießbrauch f; **life jacket** N Schwimmweste f

lifeless ['laɪflɪs] ADJ **a** (= dead, as if dead) leblos **b** (= inanimate) leblos, tot; planet unbelebt, ohne Leben **c** (fig: = listless, dull) lahm (inf), langweilig

lifelessly ['laɪflɪslɪ] ADV leblos; (fig) teilnahmslos

lifelessness ['laɪflɪsnɪs] N Leblosigkeit f; (fig) Teilnahmslosigkeit f

life: **lifelike** ADJ lebensecht; imitation also naturgetreu; **lifeline** N **a** Rettungsleine f; (of diver) Signalleine f; (fig) Rettungsanker m; **the tele-**

phone is a ~ for many old people das Telefon ist für viele alte Leute lebenswichtig; **in doing this they risked severing their financial ~** dadurch haben sie riskiert, dass ihnen der Geldhahn zugedreht wird **b** (Palmistry) Lebenslinie f; **lifelong** ADJ lebenslang; **they are ~ friends** sie sind schon ihr Leben lang Freunde; **he's my ~ friend** er war schon immer mein Freund; **we became ~ friends** wir wurden Freunde fürs Leben; **his ~ devotion to the cause** die Sache, in deren Dienst er sein Leben gestellt hat; **her ~ fear of water** ihre angeborene Angst vor Wasser; **life membership** N Mitgliedschaft f auf Lebenszeit; **life net** N Sprungtuch nt; **life-or-death** ADJ **~ struggle** Kampf m auf Leben und Tod; **life peer** N Peer m auf Lebenszeit; **life preserver** N **a** (Brit) Totschläger m **b** (US) Schwimmweste f

lifer ['laɪfə'] N (inf) Lebenslängliche(r) mf (inf)

life: **life raft** N Rettungsfloß nt; **life-saver** N **a** Lebensretter(in) m(f); (= lifeguard) Rettungsschwimmer(in) m(f) **b** (fig) Retter m in der Not; **it was a real ~!** das hat mich gerettet; **life-saving** N Lebensrettung f; (= saving people from drowning) Rettungsschwimmen nt **ADJ** techniques, apparatus zur Lebensrettung; phone call, drug, operation, treatment lebensrettend; drop of whisky rettend; **~ certificate** Rettungsschwimmabzeichen nt; **life science** N Medizin, Biologie etc; **life sentence** N lebenslängliche Freiheitsstrafe; **life-size(d)** ADJ in Lebensgröße, lebensgroß; **lifespan** N (of people) Lebenserwartung f; (of animals, plants) Leben(sdauer f) nt; **life story** N Lebensgeschichte f; **lifestyle** N Lebensstil m; **life support machine** N Herz-Lungen-Maschine f; **life support system** N Lebenserhaltungssystem nt; **life table** N Sterblichkeitstabelle f; **life-threatening** ADJ lebensbedrohend; **lifetime** N **a** Lebenszeit f; (of battery, machine, animal) Lebensdauer f; **once in a ~** einmal im Leben; **during** or **in my ~** während meines Lebens; **in his ~ there were no buses** zu seiner Zeit gab es keine Busse; **the chance of a ~** eine einmalige Chance, DIE Chance (inf); **a ~'s devotion to charity** ein Leben, das der Wohltätigkeit gewidmet ist; **the work of a ~** ein Lebenswerk nt **b** (fig) Ewigkeit f; **life vest** N Rettungs- or Schwimmweste f; **lifework** N Lebenswerk nt

lift [lɪft] N **a** (= lifting) Heben nt; **the haughty ~ of her head** ihre hochmütige Kopfhaltung; **give me a ~ up** heb mich mal hoch; **give me a ~ with this trunk** hilf mir, den Koffer hochzuheben **b** (Weightlifting) **that was a good ~** das war eine gute Leistung; **his next ~ is 100 kg** beim nächsten Versuch will er 100 kg stemmen; **different types of ~** mehrere verschiedene Hebearten pl **c** (= emotional uplift) **to give sb a ~** jdn aufmuntern; (drug) jdn aufputschen; (prospect) jdm Auftrieb geben **d** (in car etc) Mitfahrgelegenheit f; **to give sb a ~** (take along) jdn mitnehmen; (as special journey) jdn fahren; **to get a ~ from sb** von jdm mitgenommen werden/von jdm gefahren werden; **want a ~?** möchten Sie mitkommen?, soll ich dich fahren?; **don't take ~s from strangers** lass dich nicht von Fremden mitnehmen **e** (Brit: = elevator) Fahrstuhl m, Aufzug m, Lift m; (for goods) Aufzug m; **he took the ~** er fuhr mit dem Fahrstuhl etc **f** (Aviat) Auftrieb m **VT a** (also **lift up**) hochheben; window hochschieben; feet, head heben; eyes aufschlagen; hat lüften, ziehen; potatoes etc ernten; child etc hochheben; **to ~ the baby out of his playpen** das Baby aus dem Laufgitter heben; **to ~ one's hand to sb** die Hand gegen jdn erheben; **to ~ the phone** den Hörer abnehmen **b** (fig: also **lift up**) heben; voice erheben; **to ~ the spirits/mood** die Stimmung heben; **the news ~ed him out of his depression** durch die Nachricht verflog seine Niedergeschlagenheit; **the excellence of his style ~s him far above his contemporaries** sein ausgezeichneter Stil stellt

ihn weit über seine Zeitgenossen **c** (= remove) restrictions etc aufheben; **to ~ the siege of a city** die Belagerung einer Stadt beenden **d** (inf: = steal) mitgehen lassen (inf), klauen (inf); (= plagiarize) abkupfern (inf) **e** **to have one's face ~ed** sich (dat) das Gesicht straffen or liften lassen **f** (Brit inf: = arrest) schnappen (inf) **VI a** (= be lifted) sich hochheben lassen; **that chair is too heavy (for you) to ~** dieser Stuhl ist zu schwer zum Hochheben **b** (mist) sich lichten; (mood, spirits) sich heben **c** (rocket, plane) abheben; **it ~ed slowly into the sky** es stieg langsam zum Himmel auf

▸ **lift down** VT sep herunterheben

▸ **lift off** **VT** sep abheben **VI** abheben

▸ **lift up** **VT** sep = **lift VT a, b to lift up one's head** (fig) den Kopf hoch halten; **I'll never lift up my head again** (fig) ich kann niemandem mehr in die Augen blicken **VI** hochgeklappt werden

lift: **lift attendant** N (Brit) Fahrstuhlführer(in) m(f); **liftboy** N (Brit) Liftboy m; **lift cage** N (Brit) Fahrstuhl m; **liftman** N (Brit) = **lift attendant**; **liftoff** N (Space) Abheben nt, Start m; **we have ~** der Start ist erfolgt; **lift-off correction tape** N (for typewriter) (Lift-off-)-Korrekturband nt; **lift operator** N = **lift attendant**; **lift pass** N Skipass m; **liftshaft** N (Brit) Aufzugsschacht m

lig [lɪg] VI (Brit inf) (at party) sich selbst einladen, schmarotzen; (at concert, etc) ohne Eintrittskarte reingehen (inf)

ligament ['lɪgəmənt] N Band nt, Ligament nt; **he's torn a ~ in his shoulder** er hat einen Bänderriss in der Schulter

ligature ['lɪgətʃə'] N (Med, Mus, Typ) Ligatur f; (= bandage) Binde f; (Med: = thread/cord) Abbindungsschnur f/-draht m

ligger ['lɪgə'] N (Brit inf) (at party) jd, der sich selbst einlädt, Schmarotzer(in) m(f); (at concert etc) jd, der ohne Eintrittskarte hereinkommt

light¹ [laɪt] vb: pret, ptp **lit** or **lighted** N **a** (in general) Licht nt; **by the ~ of a candle/the fire** im Schein einer Kerze/des Feuers; **~ and shade** Licht und Schatten; **at first ~** bei Tagesanbruch; **hang the picture in a good ~** häng das Bild ins richtige Licht; **to cast** or **throw** or **shed ~ on sth** (lit) etw beleuchten; (fig also) Licht in etw (acc) bringen; **the moon cast its silvery ~ on ...** der Mond beleuchtete ... silbern or warf sein silbernes Licht auf (+acc) ...; **to cast a new** or **fresh ~ on sth** neues Licht auf etw (acc) werfen; **to be in sb's ~** (lit) jdm im Licht stehen; **in the cold ~ of day** (fig) bei Licht besehen; **the harsh ~ of reality** die raue Wirklichkeit; **this story shows his character in a bad ~** diese Geschichte wirft ein schlechtes Licht auf seinen Charakter; **to see sb/sth in a different ~** jdn/etw in einem anderen Licht sehen; **it showed him in a different ~** es zeigte ihn in einem anderen Licht; **I don't see things in that ~** ich sehe die Dinge anders or in einem anderen Licht; **to see sth in a new ~** etw mit anderen Augen betrachten; **in the ~ of** angesichts (+gen); **the theory, seen in the ~ of recent discoveries** die Theorie im Licht(e) der neuesten Entdeckungen betrachtet; **in the ~ of what you say** in Anbetracht dessen, was Sie sagen; **to bring sth to ~** etw ans Tageslicht bringen; **to come to ~** ans Tageslicht kommen; **to see the ~** (liter) (= be born) das Licht der Welt erblicken (liter); (= be made public) veröffentlicht werden; **finally I saw the ~** (inf) endlich ging mir ein Licht auf (inf); (morally) endlich wurden mir die Augen geöffnet; **to see the ~ of day** (report) veröffentlicht werden; (project) verwirklicht werden; **the ~ dawned** (fig) mir ging ein Licht auf (inf); **to go out like a ~** sofort weg sein (inf) **b** Licht nt; (= lamp) Lampe f; (= fluorescent light) Neonröhre f; **put out the ~s before you go to bed** mach das Licht aus, bevor du ins Bett gehst; **all the ~s went out during the storm**

während des Sturms gingen alle Lichter aus; **(traffic)** ~ Ampel *f*; **the ~s** (*of a car*) die Beleuchtung; **all ships must show a ~ while at sea** alle Schiffe müssen auf See Lichter führen; **~s out** (*Mil*) Zapfenstreich *m*; **~s out for the boys was at 8 pm** um 20 Uhr mussten die Jungen das Licht ausmachen; **~s out!** Licht aus(machen)!; **to hide one's ~ under a bushel** (*prov*) sein Licht unter den Scheffel stellen (*prov*); **the ~s are on but nobody's (at) home** (*fig inf*) er/sie ist geistig weggetreten (*inf*)

c (= *flame*) **have you (got) a ~?** haben Sie Feuer?; **to put a ~ to sth, to set ~ to sth** etw anzünden

d (*Archit*) (Dach)fenster *nt*; (= *skylight*) Oberlicht *nt*; **leaded ~s** in Blei gefasste Fensterscheiben

e (*in eyes*) Leuchten *nt*; **the ~ went out of her eyes** das Strahlen erlosch in ihren Augen

f (= *standards*) **according to his ~s** nach bestem Wissen und Gewissen

ADJ (+*er*) hell; **a ~ green dress** ein hellgrünes Kleid; **it's getting** *or* **growing ~** es wird hell; **it is ~ now** es ist jetzt hell *or* Tag

VT a (= *illuminate*) beleuchten; *lamp, light* anmachen; **a smile lit her face** ein Lächeln erhellte ihr Gesicht; **to ~ the way for sb** jdm leuchten; (*fig*) jdm den Weg weisen; **his pioneering work lit the way for a whole generation of scholars** seine Pionierarbeit war wegweisend für eine ganze Gelehrtengeneration

b (= *ignite*) anzünden; *cigarette* anstecken, anzünden; *fire, candle* anzünden, anmachen; **to ~ a fire under sb** (*esp US fig*) jdm Feuer unter dem Hintern machen (*inf*)

VI (= *begin to burn*) brennen; **this fire won't ~** das Feuer geht nicht an

▶ **light up VI a** (= *be lit*) aufleuchten; **the shop signs light up after dark** die Leuchtreklamen werden nach Einbruch der Dunkelheit eingeschaltet; **the room suddenly lit up** plötzlich ging das Licht im Zimmer an

b (*face*) sich erhellen; (*eyes*) aufleuchten; **his face lit up with joy** sein Gesicht strahlte vor Freude

c (= *start to smoke*) **the men took out their pipes and lit up** die Männer holten ihre Pfeifen hervor und zündeten sie an

VT sep a (= *illuminate*) beleuchten; *lights* anmachen; **a smile lit up his face** ein Lächeln erhellte sein Gesicht; **Piccadilly Circus was all lit up** der Piccadilly Circus war hell erleuchtet; **flames lit up the night sky** Flammen erleuchteten den Nachthimmel

b *cigarette etc* anzünden

c (*fig inf*) **to be lit up** angesäuselt sein (*inf*)

light² **ADJ** (+*er*) leicht; *taxes* niedrig; *punishment* milde; **to give sb ~ weight** jdm zu wenig abwiegen; **she has a very ~ touch on the piano** sie hat einen sehr weichen Anschlag; **to be a ~-eater** wenig essen, kein großer Esser sein; **~ comedy** Lustspiel *nt*, Schwank *m*; **~ opera** Operette *f*; **~ reading** Unterhaltungslektüre *f*; **a ~ and cheerful approach to life** eine unbeschwerte, fröhliche Einstellung zum Leben; **with a ~ heart** leichten Herzens; **as ~ as air** *or* **a feather** federleicht; **to be ~ in the head** (= *crazy*) nicht ganz richtig im Kopf; (= *tipsy*) angeheitert; (= *dizzy*) benommen; **to be ~ on one's feet** sich leichtfüßig bewegen; **you shouldn't make ~ of her problems** du solltest dich über ihre Probleme nicht lustig machen; **to make ~ of one's difficulties** seine Schwierigkeiten auf die leichte Schulter nehmen; **to make ~ work of sth** spielend fertig werden mit

ADV **to travel ~** mit wenig *or* leichtem Gepäck reisen

light³ **VI** *pret, ptp* **lighted** *or* **lit** (*liter*) sich niederlassen

▶ **light (up)on** **VI** +*prep obj* (*inf*) entdecken, stoßen auf (+*acc*)

light: light barrier N Lichtschranke *f*; **light bulb** N Glühlampe *or* -birne *f*; **light-coloured**, (*US*) **light-colored** ADJ *comp* **lighter-colo(u)red**, *superl* **lightest-colo(u)red** hell; **light**

cream N (*US*) = **single cream**; **light-emitting diode** N Leuchtdiode *f*

lighten¹ ['laɪtn] **VT** erhellen; *colour, hair* aufhellen; *gloom* aufheitern **VI** hell werden, sich aufhellen; (*mood*) sich heben; (*atmosphere*) sich entspannen; **to thunder and ~** (*Met*) donnern und blitzen

lighten² **VT** *load* leichter machen; **to ~ a ship's cargo** ein Schiff leichtern; **to ~ sb's burden** *or* **load** (*fig*) jds Lage erleichtern; **to ~ sb's workload** jdm etwas Arbeit abnehmen; **the good news ~ed her heart** die gute Nachricht machte ihr das Herz leichter **VI** (*load*) leichter werden; **her heart ~ed** ihr wurde leichter ums Herz

▶ **lighten up** **VI** (*inf*) die Dinge leichter nehmen; **lighten up!** nimms leicht!

lighter¹ ['laɪtə] N Feuerzeug *nt*

lighter² N (*Naut*) Leichter *m*

lighter fuel N Feuerzeugbenzin *nt*

light: lightfast ['laɪtfɑːst] ADJ lichtecht; **light-fingered** [ˌlaɪt'fɪŋɡəd] ADJ *comp* **lighter-fingered**, *superl* **lightest-fingered** langfingerig; **light fitting, light fixture** N (= *lightbulb holder*) Fassung *f*; (= *bracket*) (Lampen)halterung *f*; **light-footed** ADJ *comp* **lighter-footed**, *superl* **lightest-footed** leichtfüßig; **light-haired** ADJ *comp* **lighter-haired**, *superl* **lightest-haired** hellhaarig; *animals also* mit hellem Fell; **light-handed** ADJ , **light-handedly** ADV geschickt; **light-headed** ADJ *comp* **lighter-headed**, *superl* **lightest-headed** benebelt (*inf*); (= *dizzy also*) benommen; (= *tipsy also*) angeheitert; (*with fever*) wirr (im Kopf); (= *frivolous*) oberflächlich, leichtfertig; **I felt quite ~ when I heard I'd passed the exam** mir wurde ganz ausgelassen *or* übermütig, als ich hörte, dass ich die Prüfung bestanden hatte; **wine makes me ~** Wein steigt mir in den Kopf; **light-headedness** N benebelter Zustand; (= *dizziness*) Benommenheit *f*; (= *tipsy state*) angeheiterter Zustand; (*with fever*) Verwirrtsein *nt*; (= *frivolity*) Oberflächlichkeit *f*, Leichtfertigkeit *f*; (= *elation*) Ausgelassenheit *f*, Übermut *m*; **light-hearted** ADJ unbeschwert, unbekümmert; *chat* zwanglos; *reply* scherzhaft; *book, film* fröhlich; *look at life* heiter, unbekümmert; *comedy* leicht; **light-heartedly** ADV unbekümmert, leichten Herzens; (= *jokingly*) reply scherzhaft; **light-heartedness** N Unbeschwertheit *f*, Unbekümmertheit *f*; (*of chat*) Zwanglosigkeit *f*; (*of reply*) Scherzhaftigkeit *f*; (*of book, film*) Fröhlichkeit *f*, Vergnüglichkeit *f*; (= *amusing nature*) Heiterkeit *f*; **light heavyweight** N Halbschwergewicht *nt*; (= *person*) Halbschwergewichtler(in) *m(f)*; **lighthouse** N Leuchtturm *m*; **lighthouse keeper** N Leuchtturmwärter(in) *m(f)*

lighting ['laɪtɪŋ] N Beleuchtung *f*

lighting-up time [ˌlaɪtɪŋ'ʌptaɪm] N *Zeitpunkt, zu dem Straßen- und Fahrzeugbeleuchtung eingeschaltet werden muss* **when is ~?** wann wird die Beleuchtung angemacht?

lightish ['laɪtɪʃ] ADJ *colour* hell; **a ~ brown** ein helleres Braun

lightless ['laɪtlɪs] ADJ dunkel, lichtlos

light lorry N Kleinlastwagen *m*

lightly ['laɪtlɪ] ADV **a** *touch, rain, eat, wounded, armed, stressed* leicht; *walk, tread* leise; **to sleep ~** einen leichten Schlaf haben; **~ clad (in sth)** leicht (mit etw) bekleidet; **they are ~ taxed** sie haben niedrige Steuern; **to get off ~** glimpflich davonkommen; **to touch ~ on a subject** ein Thema nur berühren *or* streifen

b (= *casually*) *say* leichthin; **to speak ~ of sb/sth** sich abfällig *or* geringschätzig über jdn/etw äußern; **he spoke ~ of his illness** er nahm seine Krankheit auf die leichte Schulter; **don't take her problems so ~** nimm ihre Probleme etwas ernster; **to treat sth too ~** etw nicht ernst genug nehmen; **she referred ~ to the fact that ...** sie erwähnte leichthin, dass ...; **a responsibility not to be ~ undertaken** eine Verantwortung, die man nicht unbedacht auf sich

nehmen sollte; **it's not a job I'd ~ do again** die Arbeit würde ich so leicht nicht wieder tun

light: light meter N Belichtungsmesser *m*; **light-minded** ADJ oberflächlich, leichtfertig

lightness¹ ['laɪtnɪs] N Helligkeit *f*

lightness² N **a** geringes Gewicht, Leichtheit *f*; (*of task, step, movements*) Leichtigkeit *f*; (*of taxes*) Niedrigkeit *f*; (*of punishment*) Milde *f*; (*of soil, cake*) Lockerheit *f*; **~ of touch** (*of pianist*) weicher *or* leichter Anschlag; **the ~ of the breeze/music** die leichte Brise/Musik; **a feeling of ~ came over him** ein Gefühl der Erleichterung überkam ihn **b** (= *lack of seriousness*) mangelnder Ernst; **a certain ~ in your attitude toward(s) the authorities** eine gewisse Leichtfertigkeit den Behörden gegenüber

lightning ['laɪtnɪŋ] **N** Blitz *m*; **a flash of ~** ein Blitz *m*; (*doing damage*) ein Blitzschlag *m*; **struck by ~** vom Blitz getroffen; **what causes ~?** wie entstehen Blitze?; **we had some ~ an hour ago** vor einer Stunde hat es geblitzt; **as quick as ~, like (greased) ~** wie der Blitz, wie ein geölter Blitz; **~ never strikes twice in the same place** (*lit, fig*) der Blitz schlägt nie zweimal am gleichen Ort ein **ATTR** blitzschnell, Blitz-; **~ attack** Überraschungs- *or* Blitzangriff *m*; **~ strike** spontaner Streik; **with ~ speed** blitzschnell, mit Blitzesschnelle; **~ visit** Blitzbesuch *m*

lightning conductor, (*US*) **lightning rod** N Blitzableiter *m*; **he is a lightning rod for controversy** (*US fig*) er gibt immer Anlass zu Kontroversen

light: light pen N (*Comput*) Lichtgriffel *m*, Lichtstift *m*; **light pollution** N **a** (*in a city*) Lichtüberflutung *f* **b** (*Astrol*) Lichtverschmutzung *f*; **lightproof** ADJ lichtundurchlässig; **light railway** N Leichteisenbahn *f*; **Docklands Light Railway** *Schnellbahn in den Londoner Docklands*

lights [laɪts] PL (*Anat*) Tierlunge *f*

light: lightship N Feuerschiff *nt*; **light show** N Lightshow *f*; **light-skinned** ADJ *comp* **lighter-skinned**, *superl* **lightest-skinned** hellhäutig; **lights out** N **~ is at 10 p.m.** um 10 Uhr heißt es „Licht aus"; **light switch** N Lichtschalter *m*; **light water reactor** N Leichtwasserreaktor *m*; **light wave** N (Licht)welle *f*; **lightweight** ADJ leicht; (*fig*) schwach; **~ boxer** Leichtgewichtsboxer(in) *m(f)*; **the ~ boxing championship** die Boxmeisterschaft im Leichtgewicht ■ N Leichtgewicht *nt*; (= *person*) Leichtgewichtler(in) *m(f)*; (*fig*) Leichtgewicht *nt*; **he is regarded as a ~ in academic circles** er wird in akademischen Kreisen für voll genommen; **light year** N Lichtjahr *nt*; **to be ~s ahead of sb** jdm um Lichtjahre voraus sein

ligneous ['lɪɡnɪəs] ADJ hölzern, holzartig

lignite ['lɪɡnaɪt] N Lignit *m*

likable ADJ = **likeable**

like¹ [laɪk] **◯** 5.1, 17.2 **a** (= *similar*) ähnlich; **the two boys are very ~** die beiden Jungen sind sich (*dat*) sehr ähnlich

b (= *same*) **of ~ origin** gleicher Herkunft

PREP wie; **to be ~ sb** jdm ähnlich sein; **they are very ~ each other** sie sind sich (*dat*) sehr ähnlich; **to look ~ sb** jdm ähnlich sehen; **who(m) is he ~?** wem sieht er ähnlich?, wem gleicht er?; **what's he ~?** wie ist er?; **he's just bought a new car - what is it ~?** er hat sich gerade ein neues Auto gekauft - wie sieht es aus?; **what's your new coat ~?** wie sieht dein neuer Mantel aus?; **she was ~ a sister to me** sie war mir wie eine Schwester zu mir; **that's just ~ him!** das sieht ihm ähnlich!, das ist typisch!; **it's not ~ him** es ist nicht seine Art; **I never saw anything ~ it** so (et)was habe ich noch nie gesehen; **that's just ~ a woman!** typisch Frau!; **that's more ~ it!** so ist es schon besser!; **it's on company advice - orders, more ~** (*inf*) es ist auf Anraten der Firma - besser gesagt auf Anordnung; **that hat's nothing ~ as nice as this one** der Hut ist bei weitem nicht so hübsch wie dieser; **there's nothing ~ a nice**

cup of tea! es geht nichts über eine schöne Tasse Tee!; **there's nothing ~ it** das ist einmalig; **is this what you had in mind? – it's something/nothing ~ it** hattest du dir so etwas vorgestellt? – ja, so ähnlich/nein, überhaupt nicht; **that's something ~ a steak!** das ist vielleicht ein Steak!, das nenne ich ein Steak!; **the Americans are ~ that** so sind die Amerikaner; **people ~ that** solche Leute; **a car ~ that** so ein Auto, ein solches Auto; **I found one ~ it** ich habe ein Ähnliches gefunden; **one exactly ~ it** eines, das genau gleich ist; **it will cost something ~ £10** es wird etwa or so ungefähr £ 10 kosten; **I was thinking of something ~ a doll** ich habe an so etwas wie eine Puppe gedacht; **that sounds ~ a good idea** das hört sich gut an; **~ a man** wie ein Mann; **~ mad** (Brit inf) **~ anything** (inf) wie verrückt (inf) or wild (inf); **~ that** so; **it wasn't ~ that at all** so wars doch gar nicht; **he thinks ~ us** er denkt wie wir; **A, ~ B, thinks that ...** A wie (auch) B meinen, dass ...

ADV (inf) **it's nothing ~** es ist nichts dergleichen; **(as) ~ as not, very ~, ~ enough** höchstwahrscheinlich, sehr wahrscheinlich; **I found this money, ~** (dial) ich hab da das Geld gefunden, nich (sl) or wa (dial) or gell (S Ger)

CONJ (strictly incorrect) **~ I said** wie ich schon sagte, wie gesagt; **it's just ~ I say** das sage ich ja immer; **~ we used to (do)** wie früher; **do it ~ I do** mach es so wie ich

N (= equal etc) **we shall not see his ~ again** einen Mann or so etwas (inf) wie ihn bekommen wir nicht wieder; **did you ever see the ~?** (inf) hast du so was schon gesehen?; **and the ~, and such ~** und dergleichen; **the ~(s) of which** dergleichen; **I've met the ~s of you before** solche wie dich kenne ich schon; **I've no time for the ~s of him** (inf) mit solchen Leuten gebe ich mich nicht ab (inf); **~ attracts ~** Gleich und Gleich gesellt sich gern (prov)

like² ✪ 3.1, 3.3, 7.2, 7.3, 7.4, 8.4, 13, 25.2 **N** usu pl (= taste) Geschmack m; **she tried to find out his ~s and dislikes** sie wollte herausbekommen, was er mochte und was nicht; **when it comes to food he has far too many ~s and dislikes** beim Essen ist er viel zu wählerisch

VT a person mögen, gern haben; **don't you ~ me a little bit?** magst du mich nicht ein kleines bisschen?; **how do you ~ him?** wie gefällt er dir?; **I don't ~ him** ich kann ihn nicht leiden, ich mag ihn nicht; **he is well ~d here** er ist hier sehr beliebt

b (= find pleasure in) **I ~ black shoes** ich mag schwarze Schuhe, mir gefallen schwarze Schuhe; **I ~ it** das gefällt mir; **I ~ chocolate** ich mag Schokolade, ich esse gern Schokolade; **I ~ football** (= playing) ich spiele gerne Fußball, (= watching) ich finde Fußball gut; **I ~ dancing** ich tanze gern; **I ~ this translation** ich finde diese Übersetzung gut; **we ~ it here** es gefällt uns hier; **that's one of the things I ~ about you** das ist eines der Dinge, die ich an dir mag; **how do you ~ your coffee?** wie trinken Sie Ihren Kaffee?; **I ~ wine but wine doesn't ~ me** (inf) ich trinke gern Wein, aber er bekommt mir nicht; **how do you ~ Cádiz?** wie gefällt Ihnen Cádiz?; **how would you ~ to go for a walk?** was hältst du von einem Spaziergang?; **how would you ~ a black eye?** du willst dir wohl ein blaues Auge holen!; **your father won't ~ it** deinem Vater wird das nicht gefallen; **well, I ~ that!** (inf) das ist ein starkes Stück! (inf); **(well) how do you ~ that?** (inf) wie findest du denn das? (inf)

c (= wish, wish for) **I'd ~ an explanation** ich hätte gerne eine Erklärung; **I should ~ more time** ich würde mir gerne noch etwas Zeit lassen; **they would have ~d to come** sie wären gern gekommen; **I should ~ to know why** ich wüsste gern(e), warum; **I should ~ you to do it** ich möchte, dass du es tust; **I ~ to be obeyed** ich erwarte Gehorsam; **whether he ~s it or not** ob es ihm passt oder nicht, ob er

will oder nicht; **I didn't ~ to disturb him** ich wollte ihn nicht stören; **what would you ~?** was hätten or möchten Sie gern?, was darf es sein?; **would you ~ a drink?** möchten Sie etwas trinken?; **would you ~ to go to Seville?** würden Sie gern nach Sevilla fahren?; **I would ~ to take this opportunity to welcome Dr Allan** ich möchte diese Gelegenheit ergreifen, um Dr. Allan willkommen zu heißen

VI **he is free to act as he ~s** es steht ihm frei, zu tun, was er will; **as you ~** wie Sie wollen; **if you ~** wenn Sie wollen

-like ADJ suf -ähnlich, -artig; **cement-like** zementartig or -ähnlich

likeable (Brit), **likable** ['laɪkəbl] ADJ sympathisch, liebenswert

likeableness (Brit), **likableness** ['laɪkəblnɪs] N liebenswertes Wesen; **there's a certain lik(e)-ableness about him** er hat etwas Sympathisches or Liebenswertes an sich

likelihood ['laɪklɪhʊd] N Wahrscheinlichkeit f; **in all ~** aller Wahrscheinlichkeit nach; **the ~ is that ...** es ist wahrscheinlich, dass ...; **there is no ~ of that** das ist nicht wahrscheinlich; **there is little/every ~ that ...** es ist kaum/durchaus anzunehmen, dass ...; **is there any ~ of him coming?** besteht die Möglichkeit, dass er kommt?; **what's the ~ of their getting married?** wie wahrscheinlich ist es or wie groß ist die Wahrscheinlichkeit, dass die beiden heiraten?; **what's the ~ of you coming out with me tonight?** wie sind die Chancen, dass du heute Abend mit mir ausgehst?

likely ['laɪklɪ] ADJ (+er) **a** (= probable) wahrscheinlich; **he is not ~ to come** es ist unwahrscheinlich, dass er kommt; **they are ~ to accept/refuse** sie werden wahrscheinlich zusagen/ablehnen; **she is hardly ~ to come now** sie wird jetzt kaum kommen; **is it ~ that I would do that?** trauen Sie mir das zu?; **the plan most ~ to succeed** der erfolgversprechendste Plan; **an incident ~ to cause trouble** ein Zwischenfall, der möglicherweise Ärger nach sich zieht; **a ~ explanation** eine mögliche or wahrscheinliche Erklärung; (iro) wers glaubt, wird selig! (inf); **this is a ~ place for him to stay** es ist gut möglich, dass er sich hier aufhält; **a ~ story** or **tale!** (iro) das soll mal einer glauben!

b (inf: = suitable) geeignet; **a ~ spot for a picnic** ein geeignetes or prima (inf) Plätzchen für ein Picknick; **he is a ~ person for the job** er kommt für die Stelle infrage or in Frage; **~ candidates** aussichtsreiche Kandidaten; **a ~(-looking) lad** ein viel versprechender junger Mann; **a ~-looking target** ein geeignetes Ziel

ADV wahrscheinlich; **as ~ as not** höchstwahrscheinlich; **very ~ they've lost it** höchstwahrscheinlich haben sie es verloren; **they'll ~ be late** (dial) sie kommen wahrscheinlich zu spät; **it's more ~ to be early than late** es wird eher früh als spät werden; **not ~!** (inf iro) wohl kaum (inf)

like-minded ['laɪk'maɪndɪd] ADJ gleich gesinnt; **~ people** Gleichgesinnte pl

liken ['laɪkən] VT vergleichen (to mit)

like-named ['laɪk'neɪmd] ADJ gleichnamig

likeness ['laɪknɪs] ✪ 5.5 N (= resemblance) Ähnlichkeit f; (= portrait) Bild(nis) nt; **to have a ~ to sb/one another** jdm/einander ähnlich sehen; **the ghost appeared in the ~ of a monk** der Geist erschien in der Gestalt eines Mönchs; **the god took on the ~ of a bull** der Gott nahm die Form eines Stiers an; **the painting is a good ~ of him** er ist auf dem Gemälde gut getroffen

likewise ['laɪkwaɪz] ADV ebenso, gleichermaßen; **he did ~** er machte es ebenso, er tat das Gleiche; **in Italy there is a national dish, ~ in France** in Italien gibt es, ebenso wie in Frankreich, ein Nationalgericht; **my wife is well, the children ~** meiner Frau geht es gut und den Kindern auch; **have a nice weekend – ~** schönes Wochenende! – danke gleichfalls!; **I'm going to**

the cinema tonight – ~ ich gehe heute Abend ins Kino – ich auch

liking ['laɪkɪŋ] N **a** (for particular person) Zuneigung f; (for types) Vorliebe f; **to have a ~ for sb** Zuneigung für jdn empfinden, jdn gern haben; **she took a ~ to him** sie mochte ihn (gut) leiden), er war ihr sympathisch **b** (for thing) Vorliebe f; **to have a ~ for sth** eine Vorliebe für etw haben; **to take a ~ to sth** nach jds Geschmack sein; **to be to sb's ~** nach jds Geschmack sein; **she asks too many questions for my ~** für meinen Geschmack stellt sie zu viele Fragen

lilac ['laɪlək] **N a** (= plant) Flieder m **b** (= colour) (Zart)lila nt **ADJ** fliederfarben, (zart)lila

Lilliput ['lɪlɪpət] N Liliput nt

Lilliputian [lɪlɪ'pjuːʃɪən] ADJ winzig, liliputanerhaft **N** Liliputaner(in) m(f)

Lilo® ['laɪləʊ] N (Brit) Luftmatratze f

lilt [lɪlt] **N a** (of song) munterer Rhythmus; (of voice) singender Tonfall; **she spoke with a Welsh ~** sie sprach mit dem singenden Tonfall der Waliser **b** (= song) fröhliches or munteres Lied **VT** song trällern **VI** **I love the way her voice ~s** ich mag ihren singenden Tonfall; **the tune ~s merrily along** die Melodie plätschert munter dahin

lilting ['lɪltɪŋ] ADJ accent singend; ballad, tune, melody beschwingt, munter

liltingly ['lɪltɪŋlɪ] ADV sing, play mit beschwingtem Rhythmus

lily ['lɪlɪ] N Lilie f; (= water lily) Seerose f; **~ of the valley** Maiglöckchen nt

lily: lily-livered ['lɪlɪ'lɪvəd] ADJ feige; **lily pad** N Seerosenblatt nt; **lily-white** ADJ **a** schnee-or blütenweiß; (fig) tugendhaft **b** (US, inf: racially) club, suburb streng weiß

limb [lɪm] N **a** (Anat) Glied nt; **~s** pl Glieder pl, Gliedmaßen pl; **the lower ~s** die unteren Gliedmaßen; **to rest one's tired ~s** seine müden Glieder or Knochen (inf) ausruhen; **to tear sb ~ from ~** jdn in Stücke reißen; **to risk life and ~** Leib und Leben riskieren or aufs Spiel setzen **b** (of tree) Ast m; **to be out on a ~** (fig) exponiert sein; **to go out on a ~** (fig) sich exponieren; **John's ideas put him out on a ~** John steht mit seinen Ideen allein auf weiter Flur; **he had left himself out on a ~** er hatte sich in eine prekäre Lage gebracht **c** (of cross) Balken m; (of organization etc) Glied nt

-limbed [-lɪmd] ADJ suf -gliedrig; **short-/long- -limbed** kurz-/langgliedrig

limber¹ ['lɪmbə] N (Mil) Protze f

limber² ADJ beweglich, gelenkig

▶**limber up** VI Lockerungsübungen machen; (fig) sich vorbereiten; **limber up with a few easy exercises** machen Sie sich mit ein paar einfachen Übungen warm

limbless ['lɪmlɪs] ADJ tree astlos; **a ~ person** (= with no limbs) ein Mensch m ohne Gliedmaßen

limbo¹ ['lɪmbəʊ] N **a** (Rel) Vorhölle f, Limbus m (spec) **b** (fig) Übergangs- or Zwischenstadium nt; **our expansion plans are in ~ because of lack of money** unsere Erweiterungspläne sind wegen Geldmangels in der Schwebe; **I'm in a sort of ~** ich hänge in der Luft (inf)

limbo² N (= dance) Limbo m

lime¹ [laɪm] **N a** (Geol) Kalk m **b** (= bird lime) (Vogel)leim m **VT** mit Kalk düngen

lime² N (Bot: = linden, also **lime tree**) Linde(nbaum m) f

lime³ **N a** (Bot: = citrus fruit) Limone(lle) f; (= tree) Limonenbaum m **ADJ** (colour) hellgrün

lime: lime-green ADJ hellgrün; **lime juice** N Limonensaft m; **limekiln** N Kalkofen m

limelight ['laɪmlaɪt] N Rampenlicht nt; **to be in the ~** im Rampenlicht or im Licht der Öffentlichkeit stehen; **he never sought the ~** er stand nie gern im Rampenlicht or im Licht der Öffentlichkeit

limerick ['lɪmərɪk] N Limerick m

LIMERICK

Ein **limerick** ist ein kurzes komisches Gedicht in fünf Zeilen, in dem das Reimschema „aabba" verwendet wird. Es handelt normalerweise von einer bestimmten Person, und die Aussage ist oft surreal oder vulgär. **Limericks** beginnen häufig mit „There was a …". Auf zwei längere Zeilen folgen dann zwei kürzere. Das Ganze endet mit einer Pointe, wobei der letzte Reim nicht unbedingt lupenrein sein muss.

---

limestone ['laɪmstəʊn] N Kalkstein m

limewash ['laɪmwɒʃ] **VT** kalken, weißen, tünchen **N** (Kalk)tünche f

limey ['laɪmɪ] N (dated US, inf) Engländer(in) m(f)

limit ['lɪmɪt] **N a** Grenze f; (= limitation) Beschränkung f, Begrenzung f; (= speed limit) Geschwindigkeitsbegrenzung f; (Comm) Limit nt; **the city ~s** die Stadtgrenzen pl; **a 40-mile ~** eine Vierzigmeilengrenze; **the 50 km/h ~** die Geschwindigkeitsbegrenzung von 50 Stundenkilometern; **is there any ~ on the size?** gibt es irgendwelche Größenbeschränkungen?, ist die Größe begrenzt or beschränkt?; **to put a ~ on sth, to set a ~ to** or **on sth** etw begrenzen, etw beschränken; **that's beyond my financial ~s** das übersteigt meine finanziellen Möglichkeiten; **I am at the ~ of my patience** meine Geduld ist am Ende; **we're constantly working at the ~s of our abilities** unsere Arbeit bringt uns ständig an die Grenzen unserer Leistungsfähigkeit; **there's a ~!** alles hat seine Grenzen!; **there is a ~ to what one person can do** ein Mensch kann nur so viel tun und nicht mehr; **there's a ~ to the time you should spend** Sie sollten nicht allzu viel Zeit darauf verwenden; **there is no ~ to his stupidity** seine Dummheit kennt keine Grenzen; **there's a ~ to the amount of money we can spend** unseren Ausgaben sind Grenzen gesetzt, wir können nicht unbegrenzt Geld ausgeben; **there are ~s!** es gibt (schließlich) Grenzen!; **it is true within ~s** es ist bis zu einem gewissen Grade richtig; **I'll tell you what I can, within ~s** ich sage Ihnen, was ich kann, innerhalb gewisser Grenzen; **off ~s to military personnel** Zutritt für Militär verboten, für Militär gesperrt; **smoking is off ~s** Rauchen ist nicht erlaubt; **to know no ~s** keine Grenzen kennen; **over the ~** zu viel; (in time) zu lange; **you are or your baggage is over the ~** Ihr Gepäck hat Übergewicht; **you shouldn't drive, you're over the ~** du solltest dich nicht ans Steuer setzen, du hast zu viel getrunken; **he was three times over the ~** er hatte dreimal so viel Promille wie gesetzlich erlaubt; **he had more than the legal ~ (of alcohol) in his blood** er hatte mehr Promille als gesetzlich erlaubt; **top C is my ~** höher als bis zum hohen C komme ich nicht; **I'll offer £400, that's my ~** ich biete £ 400, das ist mein Limit or höher kann ich nicht gehen; **50 pages per week is my ~** 50 Seiten pro Woche sind mein Limit

b (inf) **that's (just) the ~!** das ist die Höhe (inf) or das Letzte (inf); **that child is the ~!** dieses Kind ist eine Zumutung! (inf); **he's the ~!, isn't he the ~?** das ist 'ne Type! (inf)

VT begrenzen, beschränken; freedom, spending, possibilities einschränken; imagination hemmen; **to ~ sb/sth to sth** jdn/etw auf etw (acc) beschränken; **to ~ oneself to a few remarks** sich auf einige (wenige) Bemerkungen beschränken; **time is the ~ing factor** wir sind zeitlich gebunden; **what are the ~ing factors?** wodurch sind uns (dat) Grenzen gesetzt?

limitation [ˌlɪmɪ'teɪʃən] N Beschränkung f; (of freedom, spending) Einschränkung f; **damage ~** Schadensbegrenzung f; **poor education is a great ~** eine schlechte Schulbildung ist ein großes Handikap; **there is no ~ on exports of coal** es gibt keine Beschränkungen für den Kohleexport; **the ~s of a bilingual dictionary** die beschränkten Möglichkeiten eines zweispra-

chigen Wörterbuchs; **to have one's/its ~s** seine Grenzen haben

limited ['lɪmɪtɪd] ADJ **a** improvement, number, amount, resources, range begrenzt, beschränkt; intelligence, knowledge also mäßig; person beschränkt; **this offer is for a ~ period only** dieses Angebot ist (zeitlich) befristet or gilt nur für kurze Zeit; **in a more ~ sense** in engerem Sinn; **this is only true in a ~ sense** or **to a ~ extent** das ist nur in gewissem Maße wahr; **he can only get about/look after himself to a ~ extent** er kann sich nur eingeschränkt bewegen/sich nur teilweise selber versorgen; **they are getting together again to a ~ extent** sie haben sich bis zu einem gewissen Punkt versöhnt

b (esp Brit, Comm) liability, right, authority beschränkt; **ABC Travel Limited** ≈ ABC-Reisen GmbH

limited: limited company N (esp Brit Comm) ≈ Gesellschaft f mit beschränkter Haftung; **limited edition** N limitierte Auflage; (of car) limitierte Serie; **limited liability company** N (esp Brit) = **limited company**; **limited parking zone** N Kurzparkzone f; **limited partner** N (esp Brit) Kommanditist(in) m(f); **limited partnership** N (esp Brit) ≈ Kommandgesellschaft f

limiter ['lɪmɪtə'] N **a** (= limitation) einschränkender Faktor **b** (Elec) (Amplituden)begrenzer m

limitless ['lɪmɪtlɪs] ADJ grenzenlos

limo ['lɪməʊ] N (inf: = limousine) Limousine f

limousine ['lɪməzɪːn] N Limousine f

limp¹ [lɪmp] **N** Hinken nt, Humpeln nt; **to walk with a ~** hinken, humpeln; **the accident left him with a ~** seit dem Unfall hinkt er; **he has a bad ~** er hinkt or humpelt sehr stark **VI** hinken, humpeln; **the ship managed to ~ into port** das Schiff kam gerade noch or mit Müh und Not in den Hafen

limp² ADJ (+er) schlapp, schlaff; handshake schlaff, schlaff; flowers welk; material, cloth weich; voice matt, müde; (= effeminate) süßlich; **to hang ~** (arms, flag) schlaff herunterhängen; **he's a ~ sort of character** er hat einen schwachen Charakter; **let your body go ~** alle Muskeln entspannen, alles locker lassen

limpet ['lɪmpɪt] N Napfschnecke f; **to stick to sb like a ~** (inf) wie eine Klette an jdm hängen

limpet mine N Haftmine f

limpid ['lɪmpɪd] ADJ klar; liquid also durchsichtig; style klar

limply ['lɪmplɪ] ADV schlapp, schlaff; **~ bound in calfskin** in weiches Kalbsleder gebunden; **..., he said ~** ..., sagte er mit matter Stimme; (= effeminately) ..., flötete er (inf)

limpness ['lɪmpnɪs] N Schlaffheit f, Schlappheit f; (of flower) Welkheit f; (of cloth, material) Weichheit f; (of voice) Mattigkeit f

limp-wristed ['lɪmp'rɪstɪd] ADJ (inf: = gay) schwul (inf), warm (inf)

limy ['laɪmɪ] ADJ (+er) kalkhaltig

linage ['laɪnɪdʒ] N (Press) Zeilenzahl f; **advertising ~** Anzeigenzeilenzahl f; **~ advertisement** Kleinanzeige f

linchpin ['lɪntʃpɪn] N Achs(en)nagel m, Lünse f; (fig) Stütze f; **accurate timing is the ~ of the entire operation** das ganze Unternehmen steht und fällt mit genauer Zeiteinteilung

linden ['lɪndən] N (also **linden tree**) Linde f, Lindenbaum m

---

line¹ [laɪn]

✿ 27.3, 27.5, 27.7

1 NOUN	3 PHRASAL VERB
2 TRANSITIVE VERB	

1 – NOUN

a [for washing, fishing] Leine f

b [= mark] (on paper, on tennis court etc, on palm) Linie f; **drawn in a few bold lines** mit wenigen kühnen Strichen gezeichnet

c [= wrinkle] Falte f

d [= boundary] Grenze f; **the state line** die Staatsgrenze; **the snow/tree line** die Schnee-/Baumgrenze; **the line** (= the equator) die Linie, der Äquator; **the (fine** or **thin) line between right and wrong** der (feine) Unterschied zwischen Recht und Unrecht; **to draw a line between** (fig) einen Unterschied machen zwischen → also **draw¹**

e [= shape] **the ship's graceful lines** die schnittigen Linien des Schiffes

f [= row] (of people, cars) (side by side) Reihe f; (one behind the other) Schlange f; (of hills) Kette f; (Sport) Linie f; **in (a) line** in einer Reihe; **in a straight line** geradlinig; **a line of soldiers** eine Reihe Soldaten; **a line of traffic** eine Autoschlange; **a single line of traffic** einspuriger Verkehr

◆ **to be in line** (buildings etc) geradlinig sein; **to be in line (with)** (fig) in Einklang stehen (mit), übereinstimmen (mit)

◆ **to keep sb/sth in line** (fig) dafür sorgen, dass jd nicht aus der Reihe tanzt; **to keep the party in line** die Einheit der Partei wahren

◆ **into line to bring sb/sth into line (with sth)** (fig) jdn/etw auf die gleiche Linie (wie etw) bringen; **it's time these rebels were brought into line** es wird Zeit, dass die Rebellen zurückgepfiffen werden; **to fall** or **get into line** (= abreast) sich in Reih und Glied aufstellen; (= behind one another) sich hintereinander or in einer Reihe aufstellen; **the policemen fell into line six abreast** die Polizisten stellten sich in Sechserreihen auf; **he refused to fall into line with the new proposals** er weigerte sich, mit den neuen Vorschlägen konform zu gehen; **it's time these rebels fell into line** es ist Zeit, dass sich diese Rebellen anpassen or dass diese Rebellen spuren (inf); **to move into line** sich einreihen; (fig) sich anpassen, die gleiche Linie einschlagen

◆ **out of line to be out of line** nicht geradlinig sein; **to be out of line with sth** (fig) mit etw nicht übereinstimmen or in Einklang stehen; **to step out of line** (lit) aus der Reihe treten; (fig) aus der Reihe tanzen; **he was stepping out of line telling the director what to do** es war anmaßend von ihm, dem Direktor zu sagen, was er zu tun hätte; **if he steps out of line again** wenn er sich noch einmal etwas zuschulden or zu Schulden kommen lässt

g [= queue] (US) Schlange f; **to stand in line** Schlange stehen

h [= assembly line] Band nt

i [= company] (of aircraft, liners, buses) Gesellschaft f, Linie f; (= shipping company) Reederei f

j [indicating succession] **through the male line** durch die männliche Linie; **he was descended from a long line of farmers** er stammte aus einem alten Bauerngeschlecht; **it's the latest in a long line of tragedies** es ist die neueste Tragödie in einer ganzen Serie; **royal line** königliche Familie; **in an unbroken line** in ununterbrochener Folge; **to be next in line** als Nächste(r) an der Reihe sein; **John is next in line for promotion** John ist als Nächster mit der Beförderung an der Reihe; **who is fourth in line to the throne?** wer steht an vierter Stelle der Thronfolge?

k [Rail] (in general) Strecke f, Bahnlinie f; (= section of track) Strecke f; **lines** pl Gleise pl; **to reach the end of the line** (fig) am Ende sein

l [Telec] (= cable) Leitung f; **the firm has 52 lines** die Firma hat 52 Anschlüsse; **this is a very bad line** die Verbindung ist sehr schlecht; **to be on the line to sb** mit jdm telefonieren; **get off the line!** gehen Sie aus der Leitung!; **hold the line** bleiben Sie am Apparat!; **can you get me a line to Chicago?** können Sie mir eine Verbindung nach Chicago geben?; **an information line** ein Infotelefon nt

m [written] Zeile f; **lines** (Brit Sch) Strafarbeit f; **the teacher gave me 200 lines** der Lehrer ließ mich 200 mal … schreiben; **lines** (Theat) Text m; **to learn one's lines** seinen Text auswendig lernen; **I don't get any good lines in this part**

der Text für diese Rolle or diese Partie ist sehr dürftig; **he gets all the funny lines** er bekommt immer die lustigen Stellen; **to drop sb a line** jdm ein paar Zeilen or Worte schreiben; **to read between the lines** zwischen den Zeilen lesen

n = direction **we tried a new line of approach to the problem** wir versuchten, an das Problem anders heranzugehen; **line of argument** Argumentation f; **line of attack** (fig) Taktik f; **what's your line of attack?** wie wollen Sie an die Sache herangehen?; **the police refused to reveal their lines of inquiry** die Polizei weigerte sich zu sagen, in welcher Richtung sie ermittelte; **line of thought** Denkrichtung f; **line of vision** Blickrichtung f; **I can't see if you stand in my line of vision** ich kann nichts sehen, wenn du mir die Sicht versperrst; **to be on the right lines** (fig) auf dem richtigen Weg sein, richtig liegen (inf); **a possible line of development** eine mögliche Entwicklungsrichtung; **the line of least resistance** der Weg des geringsten Widerstandes

♦ **to take + line we must take a firm or strong line with these people** wir müssen diesen Leuten gegenüber sehr bestimmt auftreten; **the government will take a strong line on inflation** die Regierung wird gegen die Inflation energisch vorgehen; **he took a strong/moderate line in the discussion** er vertrat in der Diskussion einen festen/gemäßigten Standpunkt; **what sort of line do you think I should take when I see him?** wie meinen Sie, soll ich mich verhalten, wenn ich ihn sehe?; **he took the line that ...** er vertrat den Standpunkt, dass ...; **what line is your thesis going to take?** in welcher Richtung wollen Sie in Ihrer Doktorarbeit argumentieren?

o Mil **line of battle** Kampflinie f; **to draw up the battle lines or the lines of battle** (fig) (Kampf)stellung beziehen; **enemy lines** feindliche Stellungen or Linien pl; **lines of communication** Verbindungswege pl; **line of retreat** Rückzugslinie f; **to keep one's lines of retreat open** sich (dat) den Rückzug offen halten; **the first line of defence** (Brit) or **defense** (US) (fig) die zuerst gebrauchte Verteidigung → **fire**

p = field Branche f; **what line (of work) is he in?, what's his line (of work)?** was ist er von Beruf?, was macht er beruflich?; **that's not in my line of business** damit habe ich nichts zu tun; **we're in the same line of business** wir sind in der gleichen Berufssparte or Branche tätig; **that's not in my line** das liegt mir nicht

q = course **it's all in the line of duty** das gehört zu meinen/seinen etc Pflichten; **some of the things you do in the line of duty** einige der dienstlichen Pflichten

r in shop = item Modell nt; (= range) Kollektion f; **we have a new line in spring hats** wir haben eine neue Kollektion Frühjahrshüte; **that line did not sell at all** dieses Modell ließ sich überhaupt nicht verkaufen

s = talk (inf) **I've heard that line before** die Platte kenn ich schon (inf); **he has a good line in patter** das ist eine gute Masche, wie er die Leute anquatscht (inf); **to give sb a line about sth** jdm flotte Sprüche über etw (acc) erzählen (inf); **chat-up line** (Brit) Anmacherspruch m

t = clue, information **to give sb a line on sth** jdm einen Hinweis auf etw (acc) geben; **can you give me a line on it?** können Sie mir darüber etwas sagen?; **the police eventually managed to get a line on him** die Polizei konnte ihm schließlich etwas nachweisen; **once a journalist has got a line on a story ...** wenn ein Journalist einer Geschichte erst einmal auf der Spur ist ...

u of cocaine etc Dosis f, Linie f (sl)

v set structures

♦ **along the line somewhere along the line** (= at some time) irgendwann; (= somewhere) irgendwo; **all along the line** (fig) auf der ganzen Linie

♦ **along the lines of to be along the lines of ...** ungefähr so etwas wie ... sein; **the essay is**

written along the lines of the traditional theory der Aufsatz ist in Richtung der herkömmlichen Lehre verfasst

♦ **along these/the same lines along these lines** ungefähr so; **something along these lines** etwas in dieser Richtung or Art; **the story developed along these lines** die Geschichte hat sich so or folgendermaßen entwickelt; **I was thinking along the same lines** ich hatte etwas Ähnliches gedacht; **to be on the same lines as** in der gleichen Richtung liegen wie

♦ **to lay it on the line** (inf) die Karten auf den Tisch legen (inf); **they laid it on the line to the government, that ...** sie erklärten der Regierung klipp und klar, dass ... (inf)

♦ **to put one's life/job etc on the line** (inf) sein Leben/seine Stelle etc riskieren; **to put oneself on the line** sich in die Schusslinie begeben

2 – TRANSITIVE VERB

a = cross with lines linieren, liniieren; **worry had lined his face** sein Gesicht war von Sorgen gezeichnet

b = border säumen; **an avenue lined with trees** eine von Bäumen gesäumte Straße; **the streets were lined with cheering crowds** eine jubelnde Menge säumte die Straßen; **the crew lined the sides of the ship** die Mannschaft hatte sich auf beiden Seiten des Schiffes aufgestellt; **portraits lined the walls** an den Wänden hing ein Porträt neben dem andern

3 – PHRASAL VERB

▶ **line up** VI (= stand in line) sich aufstellen, antreten; (= queue) sich anstellen; **the teams lined up like this** die Mannschaften hatten folgende Aufstellung; **the party lined up behind/against their leader** (fig) die Partei stellte sich hinter/gegen ihren Vorsitzenden

VT **a** troops, pupils, prisoners antreten lassen; boxes, books etc in einer Reihe or nebeneinander aufstellen; **the police lined the gang up with their backs to the wall** die Polizei befahl der Bande, sich mit dem Rücken zur Wand aufzustellen; **they lined the prisoners up along the wall** die Gefangenen mussten sich an der Wand entlang aufstellen

b (= prepare, arrange) entertainment sorgen für, auf die Beine stellen (inf); speakers bekommen, verpflichten; support mobilisieren; **what have you got lined up for me today?** was haben Sie heute für mich geplant?; **I've lined up a meeting with the directors** ich habe ein Treffen mit den Direktoren arrangiert; **I've got a meeting with John lined up for 10 o'clock** um 10 Uhr steht ein Treffen mit John auf dem Programm; **I've got a nice little date lined up for this evening** ich habe für heute Abend eine nette Verabredung arrangiert

line² VT clothes füttern; pipe auskleiden, innen beziehen; floor of attic auslegen; **~ the box with paper** den Karton mit Papier auskleiden or ausschlagen; **to ~ brakes** Bremsbeläge pl erneuern (lassen); **the membranes which ~ the stomach** die Schleimhäute, die den Magen auskleiden or innen überziehen; **to ~ one's own pockets** (fig) sich bereichern, in die eigene Tasche arbeiten or wirtschaften (inf)

lineage¹ ['lɪnɪɪdʒ] N (= descent) Abstammung f; (= descendants) Geschlecht nt

lineage² ['laɪnɪdʒ] N = linage

lineal ['lɪnɪəl] ADJ descent direkt

lineament ['lɪnɪəmənt] N (form) Lineament nt (rare); **~s** pl (of face) Gesichtszüge pl

linear ['lɪnɪə'] ADJ **a** (Math, Phys) linear; motion linear, geradlinig; **~ foot/metre** Längenfuß m/ -meter m or nt **b** (form: = sequential) sequence, narrative, thinking linear; time linear fortlaufend; view eindimensional

linear: linear accelerator N Linearbeschleuniger m; **Linear B** N (Ling) Linear B f; **linear equation** N (Math) lineare Gleichung, Gleichung f ersten Grades; **linear measure** N

Längenmaß nt; **linear perspective** N Linearperspektive f

line: linebacker N (US Sport) ≈ Linebacker m; **line break** N (Comput, Typ) Zeilenumbruch m; **line command** N (Comput) Zeilenbefehl m

lined [laɪnd] ADJ face etc (of old people) faltig; (through worry, tiredness etc) gezeichnet; paper liniert, liniiert; **to become ~ with age** Altersfalten bekommen

line: line dancing N Line-Country-Dance m; **line drawing** N Zeichnung f; **line editor** N (Comput) Zeileneditor m; **line feed** N (Comput) Zeilenvorschub m; **line judge** N (Tennis) Linienrichter(in) m(f); **line manager** N Vorgesetzte(r) mf

linen ['lɪnɪn] N Leinen nt; (= table linen) Tischwäsche f; (= sheets, garments etc) Wäsche f ADJ Leinen-; **~ blouse** Leinenbluse f

linen closet, linen cupboard N Wäscheschrank m

line: line-out N (Rugby) Gasse f; **line printer** N (Comput) Zeilendrucker m; **line print-out** N (Comput) Zeilenausdruck m

liner ['laɪnə'] N (= ship) Passagierschiff nt, Liniendampfer m; (= plane) Verkehrsflugzeug nt

liner note N usu pl (US) Covertext m

linesman ['laɪnzmən] N pl **-men** [-mən] (Sport) Linienrichter m; (Rail) Streckenwärter m; (Elec, Telec) Leitungsmann m; (for faults) Störungssucher m

line spacing N Zeilenabstand m

lineswoman ['laɪnzwʊmən] N pl **-women** [-wɪmɪn] (Sport) Linienrichterin f

line-up ['laɪnʌp] N (Sport) Aufstellung f; (= cast) Besetzung f; (= alignment) Gruppierung f; (US, = queue) Schlange f; **she picked the thief out of the ~** sie erkannte den Dieb bei der Gegenüberstellung

line width N Zeilenlänge f

ling¹ [lɪŋ] N (Zool) Leng(fisch) m

ling² N (Bot) Heidekraut nt

linger ['lɪŋgə'] VI **a** (also **linger on**) (zurück-) bleiben, verweilen (liter); (in dying) zwischen Leben und Tod schweben; (custom) fortbestehen, sich halten; (doubts, suspicions) zurückbleiben; (feeling, emotion, pain) anhalten, bleiben; (memory) fortbestehen, bleiben; (chords) nachklingen; (scent) sich halten; **the party was over, but many of the guests ~ed in the hall** die Party war vorbei, aber viele Gäste standen noch im Flur herum; **it was incredible how Franco ~ed on** es war erstaunlich, wie Franco sich an der Macht festkrallte

b (= delay) sich aufhalten, verweilen (liter); **I mustn't ~ or I'll miss the bus** ich darf mich nicht lange aufhalten, sonst verpasse ich den Bus

c (= dwell) **to ~ on a subject** bei einem Thema verweilen (geh); **I let my eyes ~ on the scene** ich ließ meinen Blick auf der Szene ruhen; **to ~ over a meal** sich (dat) bei einer Mahlzeit Zeit lassen, bei einer Mahlzeit lange aufhalten; **we ~ed over a glass of wine** wir tranken gemächlich ein Glas Wein

lingerie ['lænʒəriː] N (Damen)unterwäsche f

lingering ['lɪŋgərɪŋ] ADJ lang, ausgedehnt; death langsam; illness langwierig, schleppend; doubt zurückbleibend; look sehnsüchtig; chords lange (nach)klingend; kiss innig; **the lovers took a ~ farewell of each other** der Abschied der Liebenden wollte kein Ende nehmen; **I've still got one ~ doubt** es bleibt noch ein Zweifel (zurück); **the customs officer gave him a long ~ look** der Zollbeamte sah ihn lange prüfend an

lingo ['lɪŋgəʊ] N (inf) Sprache f; (= specialist jargon) Jargon m, Kauderwelsch m (inf); **I don't speak the ~** ich kann die Sprache (hier/dort) nicht (inf)

lingua franca ['lɪŋgwə'fræŋkə] N Verkehrssprache f, Lingua franca f; (= official language) Amtssprache f

lingual ['lɪŋgwəl] ADJ Zungen-; **~ sound** Zungenlaut m

linguist ['lɪŋgwɪst] N **a** (= *speaker of languages*) Sprachkundige(r) *mf*; **he's a good** ~ er ist sehr sprachbegabt; **I'm no** ~ ich bin nicht sprachbegabt **b** (= *specialist in linguistics*) Linguist(in) *m(f)*, Sprachforscher(in) *m(f)*

linguistic [lɪŋ'gwɪstɪk] ADJ **a** (= *concerning language*) sprachlich; ~ **competence** or **ability** Sprachfähigkeit *f*; ~ **knowledge** Sprachkenntnisse *pl* **b** (= *concerning language science*) linguistisch, sprachwissenschaftlich

linguistically [lɪŋ'gwɪstɪkəlɪ] ADV sprachlich, linguistisch; ~ **aware** sprachbewusst; ~ **speaking** vom linguistischen Standpunkt aus (gesehen)

linguistic philosophy N Sprachphilosophie *f*

linguistics [lɪŋ'gwɪstɪks] N *sing* Linguistik *f*, Sprachwissenschaft *f*

liniment ['lɪnɪmənt] N Einreibemittel *nt*, Liniment *nt* (*spec*)

lining ['laɪnɪŋ] N (*of clothes etc*) Futter *nt*; (= *lining material*) Futterstoff *m*; (*of brake*) (Brems)belag *m*; (*of pipe*) Auskleidung *f*; (*of attic floor*) Belag *m*; **the** ~ **of the stomach** die Magenschleimhaut

link [lɪŋk] N **a** (*of chain, fig*) Glied *nt*; (*person*) Verbindungsmann *m*/-frau *f*, Bindeglied *nt* **b** (= *connection*) Verbindung *f*; **a new rail** ~ **for the village** eine neue Zug- or Bahnverbindung zum Dorf; **photographs give you a** ~ **with the past** Fotos verbinden einen mit der Vergangenheit; **cultural** ~**s** kulturelle Beziehungen *pl*; **this is the first cultural** ~ **between our two countries** das ist der Anfang der kulturellen Beziehungen zwischen unseren beiden Ländern; **the strong** ~**s between Britain and Australia** die starken Bindungen or engen Beziehungen zwischen Großbritannien und Australien; **are there any** ~**s between the two phenomena?** besteht zwischen diesen beiden Phänomenen ein Zusammenhang or eine Beziehung or eine Verbindung? **c** (*Measure*) Link *nt* **VT** verbinden; *spaceships also* aneinander koppeln; **to** ~ **arms** sich unterhaken (*with* bei); **the police** ~**ed arms** die Polizisten bildeten einen Kordon; **we are** ~**ed by telephone to ...** wir sind telefonisch verbunden mit ...; **the two companies are now** ~**ed** die beiden Firmen haben sich zusammengeschlossen; **do you think these two murders are** ~**ed?** glauben Sie, dass zwischen den beiden Morden eine Verbindung besteht?; **police are not** ~**ing him with the crime** die Polizei bringt ihn nicht mit dem Verbrechen in Verbindung; **success in business is closely** ~**ed with self-confidence** Erfolg im Beruf hängt eng mit Selbstvertrauen zusammen; **his name has been** ~**ed with several famous women** sein Name ist mit mehreren berühmten Frauen in Verbindung gebracht worden **VI to** ~ **(together)** (*parts of story*) sich zusammenfügen lassen; (*parts of machine*) verbunden werden; (*railway lines*) sich vereinigen, zusammenlaufen

▶ **link up VI** zusammenkommen; (*people*) sich zusammentun; (*facts*) übereinstimmen, zusammenpassen; (*companies*) sich zusammenschließen; **to link up in space** ein Kopplungsmanöver im Weltraum durchführen; **how does that link up with what Freud says?** wie hängt das mit dem zusammen, was Freud sagt? **VT** *sep* miteinander verbinden; *bits of evidence* miteinander in Verbindung bringen; *spaceships* koppeln

linkage ['lɪŋkɪdʒ] N Verbindung *f*

linkman ['lɪŋkmən] N *pl* **-men** [-men] Verbindungsmann *m*; (*Rad, TV*) Moderator *m*

link road N (*Brit*) Verbindungsstraße *f*

links [lɪŋks] PL **a** Dünen *pl* **b** (= *golf course*) Golfplatz *m*

linkup ['lɪŋkʌp] N (*Telec, general*) Verbindung *f*; (*of spaceships*) Kopplung(smanöver *nt*) *f*

link verb N (*Ling*) Kopula *f*

linnet ['lɪnɪt] N (Blut)hänfling *m*

lino ['laɪnəʊ] N (*esp Brit*) Linoleum *nt*

linocut ['laɪnəʊkʌt] N Linolschnitt *m*

linoleum [lɪ'nəʊlɪəm] N Linoleum *nt*

Linotype® ['laɪnəʊtaɪp] N Linotype® *f*, Zeilensetzmaschine *f*

linseed ['lɪnsiːd] N Leinsamen *m*

linseed oil N Leinöl *nt*

lint [lɪnt] N Scharpie *f*, Mull *m*

lintel ['lɪntl] N (*Archit*) Sturz *m*

lint-free ['lɪnt,friː] ADJ flusenfrei

lion ['laɪən] N Löwe *m*; **he was one of the literary** ~**s of his day** er war einer der bedeutendsten or größten Schriftsteller seiner Zeit; **to fight** or **battle like a** ~ kämpfen wie ein Löwe; **to throw sb to the** ~**s** (*fig*) jdn den Löwen zum Fraß vorwerfen; **the** ~**'s share** der Löwenanteil

lioness ['laɪənɪs] N Löwin *f*

lionhearted ['laɪən,hɑːtɪd] ADJ unerschrocken, furchtlos

lionize ['laɪənaɪz] VT **to** ~ **sb** jdn feiern, jdn zum Helden machen

lip [lɪp] N **a** (*Anat*) Lippe *f*; **he wouldn't open his** ~**s** er wollte den Mund nicht aufmachen; **to keep a stiff upper** ~ Haltung bewahren; **to lick** or **smack one's** ~**s** sich (*dat*) die Lippen lecken; **the question on everyone's** ~**s** die Frage, die sich (*dat*) jeder stellt **b** (*of jug*) Schnabel *m*; (*of cup, crater*) Rand *m* **c** (*inf*: = *cheek*) Frechheit(en) *f(pl)*; **to give sb a lot of** ~ jdm gegenüber eine (dicke or freche) Lippe riskieren (*inf*); **any more of your** ~ **and there'll be trouble** wenn du weiterhin so eine (dicke or freche) Lippe riskierst, gibts Ärger (*inf*); **none of your** ~! sei nicht so frech

lip: **lip balm** N = **lip salve; lip gloss** N Lipgloss *m*

liposuction ['lɪpəʊ,sʌkʃən] N Fettabsaugung *f*

-lipped [-lɪpt] ADJ *suf* -lippig; **thin-lipped** dünnlippig

lip pencil N Lippencil *m*

lippy ['lɪpɪ] N (*Brit, inf*) Lippenstift *m*

lip: **lip-read VT** I could ~ what he said ich konnte ihm von den Lippen or vom Mund ablesen, was er sagte **VI** von den Lippen or vom Mund ablesen; **lip-reading** N deaf people use/learn ~ Taube lesen vom Mund ab/lernen, vom Mund abzulesen; **lip salve** N Lippenfettstift *m*, Lippenpflegestift *m*; **lip service** N **to pay** ~ **to an idea** ein Lippenbekenntnis zu einer Idee ablegen; **lip-smacking** ADJ (*inf*) pleasure unbändig; satisfaction, relish ungemein; **lipstick** N Lippenstift *m*; **lip-sync(h)** ['lɪp,sɪŋk] **VI** (= *talk*) lippensynchron sprechen; (= *sing*) lippensynchron singen **VT** *song* lippensynchron singen; **to** ~ **sb's words** jdn lippensynchron synchronisieren

liquefaction [,lɪkwɪ'fækʃən] N Verflüssigung *f*

liquefy ['lɪkwɪfaɪ] **VT** verflüssigen **VI** sich verflüssigen

liqueur [lɪ'kjʊə] N Likör *m*

liquid ['lɪkwɪd] ADJ **a** flüssig; (*fig*) eyes blank, glänzend; (*fig*) notes, song perlend **b** (*Comm*) asset (frei) verfügbar, flüssig **c** (*Phon*) consonant Liquida *f*, Fließlaut *m* **N a** Flüssigkeit *f*; **she can only take** ~**s** sie kann nur Flüssiges zu sich nehmen **b** (*Phon*) Liquida *f*, Fließlaut *m*

liquidate ['lɪkwɪdeɪt] VT **a** (*Comm*) liquidieren; assets liquidieren, flüssig machen; company auflösen, liquidieren; **to** ~ **a debt** eine Schuld tilgen **b** enemy etc liquidieren

liquidation [,lɪkwɪ'deɪʃən] N **a** (*Comm*) Liquidation *f*, Liquidierung *f*; (*of company*) Auflösung *f*, Liquidation *f*; (*of debts*) Tilgung *f*; **to go into** ~ in Liquidation gehen **b** (*of enemy etc*) Liquidierung *f*

liquidator ['lɪkwɪdeɪtə] N Liquidator *m*, Abwickler *m*

liquid-crystal ['lɪkwɪd'krɪstəl] ADJ Flüssigkristall-; ~ **display** Flüssigkristallanzeige *f*

liquidity [lɪ'kwɪdɪtɪ] N Liquidität *f*

liquidize ['lɪkwɪdaɪz] VT (im Mixer) pürieren or zerkleinern

liquidizer ['lɪkwɪdaɪzə] N Mixgerät *nt*

liquid measure N Flüssigkeitsmaß *nt*

liquor ['lɪkə] N **a** (*esp US*, = *whisky, brandy etc*) Spirituosen *pl*; (= *alcohol*) Alkohol *m*; **people who drink hard** ~ Leute, die scharfe Sachen trinken, Schnapstrinker *pl*; **a strong** ~ ein hochprozentiges Getränk; **the local** ~ der am Ort hergestellte Schnaps; **he can't take his** ~ er verträgt nichts **b** (= *juice*) Flüssigkeit *f*; **potato** ~ Kartoffelwasser *nt*

▶ **liquor up** VT *sep* (*US, inf*) **to get liquored up** sich besaufen (*inf*); **to be liquored up** besoffen sein (*inf*)

liquorice, licorice ['lɪkərɪs] N (= *plant*) Süßholz *nt*; (= *root*) Süßholzwurzel *f*; (= *flavouring, sweetmeat*) Lakritze *f*

liquor store N (*US*) ≈ Wein- und Spirituosengeschäft *nt*

lira ['lɪərə] N Lira *f*; **500** ~**(s)** 500 Lire

L iron ['el,aɪən] N (*Tech*) Winkeleisen *nt*

Lisbon ['lɪzbən] N Lissabon *nt*

lisle [laɪl] N (*also* **lisle thread**) Florgarn *nt*; ~ **stockings** Baumwollstrümpfe *pl*

lisp [lɪsp] N Lispeln *nt*; **to speak with a** ~, **to have a** ~ lispeln **VT** lispeln

lissom(e) ['lɪsəm] ADJ geschmeidig; person also gelenkig

list¹ [lɪst] N **a** Liste *f*; (= *shopping list*) Einkaufszettel *m*; **it's not on the** ~ es steht nicht auf der Liste; ~ **of names** Namensliste *f*; (*esp in book*) Namensregister *nt*, Namensverzeichnis *nt*; ~ **of prices** Preisliste *f*, Preisverzeichnis *nt*; ~ **of applicants** Bewerberliste *f*; **there's a long** ~ **of people waiting for houses** für Häuser besteht eine lange Warteliste; **it's on my** ~ **for tomorrow** es steht für morgen auf dem Programm **b** (= *publisher's list*) Programm *nt*; **we'd like to start an educational** ~ wir würden gern Lehrbücher in unser Programm aufnehmen **VT** aufschreiben, notieren; *single item* in die Liste aufnehmen; (*verbally*) aufzählen; **it is not** ~**ed** es ist nicht aufgeführt

list² (*Naut*) **N** Schlagseite *f*, Krängung *f* (*spec*); **to have a bad** ~ schwere Schlagseite haben; **to have a** ~ **of 20°** sich um 20° auf die Seite neigen; **a** ~ **to port** Schlagseite nach Backbord **VI** Schlagseite haben, krängen (*spec*); **to** ~ **badly** schwere Schlagseite haben

list³ VI (*obs*) lauschen (*old*)

list⁴ VI (*obs, poet*) **the wind bloweth where it** ~**eth** der Wind bläst, wo er will

listed ['lɪstɪd] ADJ (*Brit*) building unter Denkmalschutz (stehend *attr*); **it's a** ~ **building** es steht unter Denkmalschutz

listen ['lɪsn] VI **a** (= *hear*) hören (*to sth* etw *acc*); **to** ~ **to the radio** Radio hören; **if you** ~ **hard, you can hear the sea** wenn du genau horchst or hinhörst, kannst du das Meer hören; **she** ~**ed carefully to everything he said** sie hörte ihm genau zu; **to** ~ **for sth** auf etw (*acc*) horchen; **the boys are** ~**ing for the bell at the end of the lesson** die Jungen warten auf das Klingeln am Ende der Stunde; **we** ~**ed for footsteps approaching** wir horchten, ob sich Schritte näherten; **to** ~ **for sb** horchen or hören, ob jd kommt **b** (= *heed*) zuhören; ~ **to me!** hör mir zu!; ~, **I know what we'll do** pass auf, ich weiß, was wir machen; **now** ~ **here!** nun hör mir mal zu!; **don't** ~ **to him** hör nicht auf ihn; **if he suggests anything, don't** ~ hör nicht darauf, wenn er etwas vorschlägt; **he wouldn't** ~ er wollte nicht hören

▶ **listen in** VI (im Radio) hören (*to sth* etw *acc*); (= *listen secretly*) mithören (*on sth* etw *acc*); **I'd like to listen in on** or **to your discussion** ich möchte mir Ihre Diskussion mit anhören

listener ['lɪsnə] N Zuhörer(in) *m(f)*; (*Rad*) Hörer(in) *m(f)*; **to be a good** ~ gut zuhören können

listening [ˈlɪsnɪŋ] N he did all the talking, I did all the ~ er redete die ganze Zeit, und ich hörte die ganze Zeit zu; ~ device Abhörgerät nt

listening: listening post N (Mil, fig) Horchposten m; **listening service** N (Mil) Abhördienst m

listeria [lɪsˈtɪərɪə] N Listeriose f

listing [ˈlɪstɪŋ] N **a** Auflistung f, Verzeichnis nt **b** **listings** (TV, Rad, Film) Programm nt; **~s magazine** Programmzeitschrift f

listing paper N (Comput) Endlospapier nt

listless [ˈlɪstlɪs] ADJ lustlos; patient teilnahmslos

listlessly [ˈlɪstlɪslɪ] ADV lustlos; **to watch ~** teilnahmslos or apathisch zusehen

listlessness [ˈlɪstlɪsnɪs] N Lustlosigkeit f; (of patient) Teilnahmslosigkeit f, Apathie f

list price N Listenpreis m

lists [lɪsts] PL (Hist) Schranken pl; **to enter the ~** (fig) in die Schranken treten (liter), zum Kampf antreten; **he entered the ~ after the first ballot** er trat nach dem ersten Wahlgang in den Wahlkampf ein

lit [lɪt] pret, ptp of light¹ of light³

litany [ˈlɪtənɪ] N Litanei f

lit crit [ˈlɪtˈkrɪt] N (Brit inf) abbr of literary criticism

lite [laɪt] ADJ (inf: Cook, fig) Light-, light pred; **~ beer** Light-Bier nt

liter N (US) = litre

literacy [ˈlɪtərəsɪ] N Fähigkeit f lesen und schreiben zu können; **many adults have problems with ~** viele Erwachsene haben Probleme mit dem Lesen und Schreiben; **~ campaign** Kampagne f gegen das Analphabetentum, Alphabetisierungskampagne f; **the ~ rate in this region is only 30%** die Analphabetenquote in dieser Region beträgt 70%; **~ is high here** die Analphabetenquote hier ist niedrig; **~ test** Lese- und Schreibtest m

literal [ˈlɪtərəl] ADJ **a** (esp Typ) **~ error** Schreib-/Tipp-/Druckfehler m **b** translation, meaning, sense wörtlich; **in the ~ sense (of the word)** im wörtlichen Sinne **c** (= real) **that is the ~ truth** das ist die reine Wahrheit; **it was a ~ disaster** es war im wahrsten Sinne des Wortes eine Katastrophe; **the ~ impossibility of working there** die völlige or buchstäbliche Unmöglichkeit, dort zu arbeiten; **d** (= prosaic) nüchtern, prosaisch; **he has a very ~ mind** or **is very ~-minded** er denkt sehr nüchtern, er ist sehr prosaisch **N** Schreib-/Tipp-/Druckfehler m

literally [ˈlɪtərəlɪ] ADV **a** (= word for word, exactly) (wort)wörtlich; **to take sb/sth ~** jdn/etw wörtlich nehmen; **to be ~ true** wortwörtlich stimmen **b** (= really) buchstäblich, wirklich; **the best meal I've ever had, ~** wirklich das Beste, was ich je gegessen habe; **it was ~ impossible to work there** es war wirklich or einfach unmöglich, dort zu arbeiten; **I was ~ shaking with fear** ich zitterte regelrecht vor Angst; **he was quite ~ a giant** er war im wahrsten Sinne des Wortes ein Riese

literariness [ˈlɪtərərɪnɪs] N literarische Stilebene

literary [ˈlɪtərərɪ] ADJ literarisch; **he has ~ tastes** er interessiert sich für Literatur; **a ~ man** ein Literaturkenner m; (= author) ein Literat or Autor m; **the ~ scene** die Literaturszene

literary: literary agent N Literaturagent(in) m(f); **literary critic** N Literaturkritiker(in) m(f); **literary criticism** N (as subject) Literaturwissenschaft f; (= reviews) Literaturkritik f; **literary historian** N Literaturhistoriker(in) m(f); **literary theory** N Literaturtheorie f

literate [ˈlɪtərɪt] ADJ **a** **to be ~** lesen und schreiben können; **they aim to achieve a ~ population in one generation** sie wollen die Bevölkerung in einer Generation alphabetisieren **b** (= well-educated) gebildet; **his style is not very ~** er schreibt einen ungeschliffenen Stil

literati [ˌlɪtəˈrɑːtiː] PL Literaten pl

literatim [ˌlɪtəˈrɑːtɪm] ADV (form) Buchstabe für Buchstabe

literature [ˈlɪtərɪtʃəˀ] N Literatur f; (inf: = brochures etc) Informationsmaterial nt; (= specialist literature) (Fach)literatur f

lithe [laɪð] ADJ (+er) geschmeidig; person, body also gelenkig

lithium [ˈlɪθɪəm] N Lithium nt

litho [ˈlaɪθəʊ] N (inf) Litho nt

lithograph [ˈlɪθəʊgrɑːf] **N** Lithografie f, Steindruck m **VT** lithografieren

lithographer [lɪˈθɒgrəfəˀ] N Lithograf(in) m(f)

lithographic [ˌlɪθəʊˈgræfɪk] ADJ lithografisch

lithography [lɪˈθɒgrəfɪ] N Lithografie f, Steindruck m

Lithuania [ˌlɪθjʊˈeɪnɪə] N Litauen nt

Lithuanian [ˌlɪθjʊˈeɪnɪən] **ADJ** litauisch **N** **a** Litauer(in) m(f) **b** (Ling) Litauisch nt

litigable [ˈlɪtɪgəbl] ADJ (Jur) streitig, strittig

litigant [ˈlɪtɪgənt] N prozessführende Partei; **the ~s** die Prozessgegner pl, die prozessführenden Parteien

litigate [ˈlɪtɪgeɪt] VI einen Prozess führen or anstrengen

litigation [ˌlɪtɪˈgeɪʃən] N Prozess m, Rechtsstreit m; **he threatened them with ~** er drohte ihnen mit einem Prozess

litigator [ˈlɪtɪgeɪtəˀ] N (Jur) Prozessanwalt m/-anwältin f

litigious [lɪˈtɪdʒəs] ADJ prozesssüchtig; **a ~ person** jd, der ständig Prozesse führt, ein Prozesshansel m (inf)

litmus [ˈlɪtməs] N Lackmus m or nt

litmus paper N Lackmuspapier nt

litmus test N (lit) Lackmustest m; (fig) entscheidender Test

litotes [laɪˈtəʊtiːz] N Litotes f

litre, (US) **liter** N [ˈliːtəˀ] N Liter m or nt

litter [ˈlɪtəˀ] **N** **a** Abfälle pl; (= papers, wrappings) Papier nt; **the park was strewn with ~** der Park war mit Papier und Abfällen übersät; **don't leave** or **drop ~** (on notice) bitte keinen Abfall zurücklassen; **a ~ of books** ein Haufen m Bücher **b** (Zool) Wurf m **c** (= vehicle) Sänfte f; (Med) Tragbahre f, Trage f **d** (= bedding for animals) Streu f, Stroh nt; (for plants) Stroh nt; (= cat litter) Katzenstreu f **VT** **a** **to be ~ed with sth** (lit, fig) mit etw übersät sein; **old cans ~ed the countryside** alte Dosen verschandelten die Landschaft; **glass from broken bottles ~ed the streets** Glasscherben lagen überall auf den Straßen herum; **to ~ a room with papers** Papier(e) im Zimmer verstreuen **b** (= give birth to) werfen **c** plant abdecken; animal Streu geben (+dat) **VI** **a** (= have young) werfen **b** (esp US) Abfall wegwerfen

litter: litterbag N (US) Abfalltüte f; **litter basket** N Abfallkorb m; **litter bin** N (Brit) Abfalleimer m; (hooked on) Abfallkorb m; (bigger) Abfalltonne f; **litter box** N (US) = **litter tray**; **litter bug**, **litter lout** N (inf) Dreckspatz m (inf), Schmutzfink m (inf); **litter tray** N Katzenklo nt

little [ˈlɪtl] **ADJ** **a** klein; **a ~ house** ein Häuschen nt, ein kleines Haus; **a funny ~ nose** ein lustiges (kleines) Näschen; **the ~ ones** die Kleinen pl; **a nice ~ profit** ein hübscher Gewinn; **the ~ people** or **folk** die Elfen; **~ green men** (inf) kleine grüne Männchen pl (inf); **he will have his ~ joke** er will auch einmal ein Witzchen machen; **to worry about ~ things** sich (dat) über Kleinigkeiten Gedanken machen; **he has a ~ mind** er ist ein Kleingeist; **~ things please ~ minds** so kann man auch mit kleinen Sachen Kindern eine Freude machen; **a ~ while ago** vor kurzem, vor kurzer Zeit; **it's only a ~ while till I ...** es ist nicht mehr lange, bis ich ...; **in a ~ while** bald

ADV, N **a** wenig; **of ~ importance/interest** von geringer Bedeutung/geringem Interesse; **he knows ~ Latin and less Greek** er kann (nur) wenig Latein und noch weniger Griechisch; **~ better than** kaum besser als; **~ more than a month ago** vor kaum einem Monat; **~ short of** fast schon, beinahe; **~ did I think that ...** ich hätte kaum gedacht, dass ...; **~ does he know that ...** er hat keine Ahnung, dass ...; **they ~ realize what will happen to them** sie sind sich (dat) wohl kaum darüber im Klaren, was mit ihnen geschehen wird; **to think ~ of sb/sth** nicht viel von jdm/etw halten; **I walk as ~ as possible** ich laufe so wenig wie möglich; **to spend ~ or nothing** so gut wie (gar) nichts ausgeben; **every ~ helps** Kleinvieh macht auch Mist (Prov); **please donate, every ~ helps** auch die kleinste Spende hilft; **he had ~ to say** er hatte nicht viel zu sagen; **I see very ~ of her nowadays** ich sehe sie in letzter Zeit sehr selten; **there was ~ we could do** wir konnten nicht viel tun; **the ~ of his book that I have read** das wenige or bisschen, was ich von seinem Buch gelesen habe; **she did what ~ she could** sie tat das wenige, das sie tun konnte; **~ by ~** nach und nach; **~ by ~, he dragged himself across the room** Stückchen für Stückchen schleppte er sich durch das Zimmer; **to make ~ of sth** etw herunterspielen or bagatellisieren; **I could make ~ of this book** ich konnte mit diesem Buch nicht viel anfangen

b **a ~** ein wenig, ein bisschen; **a ~ (bit) hot** etwas or ein bisschen heiß; **a ~ (bit) better** etwas or ein wenig besser; **with a ~ effort** mit etwas Anstrengung; **I'll give you a ~ advice** ich gebe dir einen kleinen Tipp; **a ~ after five** kurz nach fünf; **we were not a ~ worried** wir waren recht besorgt; **I was not a ~ surprised** ich war einigermaßen überrascht; **we walked on for a ~** wir liefen noch ein bisschen or Stück or Weilchen weiter; **after a ~** nach einer Weile; **for a ~** für ein Weilchen

little: **little auk** N Krabbentaucher m; **Little Englander** N (Brit: = anti-European) europafeindlich eingestellter Engländer (Hist) Gegner des Imperialismus im 19. Jahrhundert, Isolationist(in) m(f); **Little League** N (US Sport) Baseball-Liga für Kinder unter 12 Jahren

littleness [ˈlɪtlnɪs] N Kleinheit f, geringe Größe; (of contribution) Geringfügigkeit f; (of mind) Beschränktheit f

Little Red Ridinghood [ˌlɪtlredˈraɪdɪŋhʊd] N (fairy tale) Rotkäppchen nt

little theatre, (US) **little theater** N Kleinbühne f, Kammerspiele pl; (for experimental theatre) Experimentierbühne f

littoral [ˈlɪtərəl] (form) **ADJ** litoral (spec), Litoral- (spec); (of lake also) in Ufernähe; (of sea also) in Küstennähe; **~ fauna/flora** Litoralfauna/-flora f (spec) **N** Litorale nt; Uferland nt; Küstenstrich m or -region f

liturgical [lɪˈtɜːdʒɪkəl] ADJ liturgisch

liturgy [ˈlɪtədʒɪ] N Liturgie f

livable, liveable [ˈlɪvəbl] ADJ life erträglich; **the house is ~ (in)** (inf) in dem Haus kann man wohnen, in dem Haus lässt es sich wohnen; **arthritis can't be cured, but it can be made ~ (with)** (inf) Arthritis ist unheilbar, kann aber erträglich gemacht werden

live¹ [lɪv] **VT** life führen; **to ~ a part** in einer Rolle aufgehen; **he had been living a lie** sein Leben war eine Lüge; **to ~ one's own life** sein eigenes Leben leben; **he ~s and breathes golf** er lebt nur für Golf

VI **a** (= be alive, survive) leben; **there is no man living who can equal him** es gibt niemanden, der es ihm gleichtun könnte; **will he ~, doctor?** wird er (über)leben, Herr Doktor?; **don't worry, you'll ~, it's only a broken ankle** reg dich nicht auf, du stirbst schon nicht, du hast nur ein gebrochenes Knöchel; **long ~ Queen Anne!** lang lebe Königin Anne!; **we ~ and learn** man lernt nie aus; **to ~ and let ~** leben und leben lassen; **to ~ like a king** or **lord** fürstlich or wie Gott in Frankreich leben; **not many people - to be a hundred** nicht viele Menschen werden hundert (Jahre alt); **to ~ to a ripe old age** ein hohes Alter erreichen; **his name will ~ for ever** sein Ruhm wird nie vergehen; **his music will ~ for ever** seine Musik ist unvergänglich; **his spirit still ~s in his work** sein Geist lebt in seinem Werk weiter; **if the spirit of the Renaissance should ever ~ again** wenn der Geist der Renaissance je wieder erwachen sollte; **it was as though the father were living again in the son** es war, als lebte der Vater im Sohn weiter; **to ~ by one's wits** sich (so) durchschlagen; **to ~ by one's pen** von seinen Büchern or vom Schreiben leben; **to ~ by crime** von Verbrechen leben; **they ~d in fear of losing their jobs** sie lebten in ständiger Angst, ihre Stelle zu verlieren; **he ~d through two wars** er hat zwei Kriege miterlebt; **to ~ through an experience** eine Erfahrung durchmachen; **the patient was not expected to ~ through the night** man rechnete nicht damit, dass der Patient die Nacht überstehen or überleben würde; **people living with HIV and AIDS** Menschen mit HIV und Aids; **I would rather like to ~ to the end of the century** ich möchte die Jahrhundertwende noch miterleben; **to ~ within one's income** nicht über seine Verhältnisse leben; **you'll ~ to regret it** das wirst du noch bereuen; **he ~s for his work/children** er lebt für seine Arbeit/Kinder

b (= *experience real living*) **I want to ~** ich will leben *or* was erleben (*inf*); **that's existing, not living** das ist doch kein Leben; **you've never skied? you haven't ~d!** du bist noch nie Ski gefahren? du weißt gar nicht, was du versäumt hast!; **you've never ~d until you've discovered Crete** wer Kreta nicht kennt, hat noch nicht gelebt; **before she met him she hadn't ~d** sie begann erst zu leben, als sie ihn kennen lernte

c (= *reside*) wohnen, leben; (*animals*) leben; **he ~s at 19 Marktstraße** er wohnt in der Marktstraße Nr. 19; **he ~s in Gardner St/on the High Street** er wohnt in der Gardner St/auf der *or* in der Hauptstraße; **who ~s in that big house?** wer bewohnt das große Haus?, wer wohnt in dem großen Haus?; **he ~s with his parents** er wohnt bei seinen Eltern; **a house not fit to ~ in** ein unbewohnbares Haus, ein Haus, in dem man nicht wohnen kann; **this house is not fit for a human being to ~ in** dies ist eine menschenunwürdige Behausung

d (*inf*: = *belong*) **where does this jug ~?** wo gehört der Krug hin?; **the knives ~ in this drawer** die Messer gehören in diese Schublade

e **the other athletes couldn't ~ with him/the pace** die anderen Läufer konnten mit ihm/mit dem Tempo nicht mithalten

▶ **live down** VT *sep scandal, humiliation* hinwegkommen über (+*acc*), verwinden; (*actively*) *scandal, mistake* Gras wachsen lassen über (+*acc*); **he'll never live it down** das wird man ihm nie vergessen

▶ **live in** VI im Haus/im Wohnheim *etc* wohnen, nicht außerhalb wohnen

▶ **live off** VI +*prep obj* **a** **to live off the land** sich vom Lande ernähren; (= *forage*) sich aus der Natur ernähren; **to live off one's relations** auf Kosten seiner Verwandten leben **b** = **live on** VI +*prep obj*

▶ **live on** VI (= *continue to live*) weiterleben VI +*prep obj* **to live on eggs** sich von Eiern ernähren, von Eiern leben; **he doesn't earn enough to live on** er verdient nicht genug, um davon zu leben; **to live on hope** (nur noch) von der Hoffnung leben; **to live on one's reputation** von seinem Ruf zehren

▶ **live out** VI außerhalb (des Hauses/des Wohnheims *etc*) wohnen VT *sep life* verbringen; *winter* überleben; **he lived out a life of poverty in the country** er lebte bis an sein Ende in Armut auf dem Land

▶ **live together** VI (= *cohabit*) zusammenleben; (= *share a room, flat etc*) zusammen wohnen

▶ **live up** VT *always separate* **to live it up** (*inf*) die Puppen tanzen lassen (*inf*); (*extravagantly*) in Saus und Braus leben (*inf*); **in my young days we really knew how to live it up** in meiner Jugend wussten wir noch, wie man sich so richtig auslebt

▶ **live up to** VI +*prep obj* **the holiday** (*esp Brit*) *or* **vacation** (*US*) **lived up to (my) expectations/the advertiser's claims** der Urlaub hielt, was ich mir davon versprochen hatte/was die Werbung versprochen hatte; **sales have not lived up to expectations** die Verkaufszahlen entsprachen nicht den Erwartungen; **to live up to standards/one's reputation** den Anforderungen/seinem Ruf gerecht werden; **the reality never lives up to the anticipation** die Wirklichkeit kommt nie an die Erwartungen heran; **the holiday didn't live up to our hopes** der Urlaub entsprach nicht dem, was wir uns (*dat*) erhofft hatten; **he's got a lot to live up to** in ihn werden große Erwartungen gesetzt; **if he wants to emulate his father he's got a lot to live up to** er hat sich (*dat*) ein hohes Ziel gesteckt, wenn er seinem Vater nacheifern will; **you should live up to your father's principles** du solltest die Grundsätze deines Vaters anstreben; **I doubt whether he can live up to his brother's success** ich bezweifle, dass er so erfolgreich wie sein Bruder wird

live² [laɪv] ADJ **a** (= *alive*) lebend; *issue, question* aktuell; **a real ~ duke** ein waschechter Herzog; **~ births** Lebendgeburten *pl* **b** (= *having power or energy*) *coal* glühend; *match* ungebraucht; *cartridge, shell* scharf; (*Elec*) geladen; **"danger, ~ wires!"** „Vorsicht Hochspannung!"; **she's a real ~ wire** (*fig*) sie ist ein richtiges Energiebündel **c** (*Rad, TV*) live; **a ~ programme** (*Brit*) *or* **program** (*US*) eine Livesendung ADV (*Rad, TV*) live, direkt

liveable ['lɪvəbl] ADJ = **livable**

live-cell therapy [ˌlaɪvsel'θerəpɪ] N Frischzellentherapie *f*

lived-in ['lɪvdɪn] ADJ *feel* gemütlich, behaglich

live-in ['lɪvɪn] ADJ *cook, maid* in Haus wohnend; **her ~ partner** ihr Partner, mit dem sie zusammen wohnt

livelihood ['laɪvlɪhʊd] N Lebensunterhalt *m*; **fishing is their ~** sie verdienen ihren Lebensunterhalt mit Fischfang; **to earn a ~** sich (*dat*) seinen Lebensunterhalt verdienen; **they earned a ~ from farming** sie lebten von der Landwirtschaft

liveliness ['laɪvlɪnɪs] N Lebhaftigkeit *f*; (*of scene, account, sense of humour, imagination*) Lebendigkeit *f*; (*of tune*) Beschwingtheit *f*; (*of campaign*) Dynamik *f*; (= *rapidity*) Schnelligkeit *f*; (*of mind*) Aufgewecktheit *f*

livelong ['lɪvlɒŋ] ADJ **all the ~ day** den lieben langen Tag, den ganzen Tag über; **all the ~ night** die ganze Nacht durch

lively ['laɪvlɪ] ADJ (+*er*) lebhaft; *scene, account, sense of humour* lebendig; *campaign* dynamisch; *pace* flott; *mind* wach, aufgeweckt; *imagination* lebendig, blühend; *tune* schwungvoll; **things are getting ~** es geht hoch her (*inf*); **at 8 things will start to get ~** um 8 wird es dann lebhafter; **we had a ~ time** es war viel los (*inf*); **he's having a ~ time of it in his new job** in seiner neuen Stelle kann er sich über Langeweile nicht beklagen; **look ~!** (= *speed up*) mach schnell!, ein bisschen lebhaft, bitte!

liven up ['laɪvn'ʌp] VT *sep* beleben, Leben bringen in (+*acc*) (*inf*) VI in Schwung kommen; (*person*) aufleben

liver¹ ['lɪvə'] N **clean ~** solider Mensch; **he's a fast ~** er führt ein flottes Leben (*inf*)

liver² N (*Anat, Cook*) Leber *f*

liveried ['lɪvərɪd] ADJ livriert

liverish ['lɪvərɪʃ] ADJ **a** **to be ~** etwas mit der Leber haben; **I felt a bit ~ after the party** mir ging es nach der Party ziemlich mies (*inf*) **b** (= *bad-tempered*) mürrisch

liver pâté N Leberpastete *f*

Liverpudlian [ˌlɪvə'pʌdlɪən] N Liverpooler(in) *m(f)* ADJ Liverpooler

liver: liver salts PL *salzhaltiges Mittel gegen Magenverstimmung*; **liver sausage** N Leberwurst *f*; **liver spot** N (*Med*) Leberfleck *m*

liverwort ['lɪvəwɜːt] N (*Bot*) Lebermoos *nt*; (= *hepatica*) Leberblümchen *nt*

liverwurst ['lɪvəwɜːst] N (*esp US*) Leberwurst *f*

livery ['lɪvərɪ] N Livree *f*; (*fig liter*) Kleid *nt*

livery: livery company N Zunft *f*; **livery stable** N Mietstall *m*

lives [laɪvz] *pl of* **life**

livestock ['laɪvstɒk] N Vieh *nt*; (= *number of animals*) Viehbestand *m*

liveware ['laɪvweə'] N (*inf*) Personal *f*, Belegschaft *f*

live wire N (*Elec*) Strom führender Draht; (*fig inf*: *person*) Energiebündel *nt* (*inf*)

livid ['lɪvɪd] ADJ **a** (*inf*: = *furious*) wütend, fuchsteufelswild (*inf*) (*about, at* über +*acc*); **he was ~ about having to do it himself** er war höchst empört darüber, dass er es selbst machen musste; **to be ~ with rage** eine Stinkwut haben (*inf*), fuchsteufelswild sein (*inf*); **he got ~ with us** er hatte eine Stinkwut auf uns (*inf*) **b** (= *dark purple*) dunkelviolett; (= *greyish*) purpurgrau; **~ red** purpurrot; **the sky was a ~ blue** der Himmel war purpurblau

living ['lɪvɪŋ] ADJ lebend; *example, faith* lebendig; **the greatest ~ playwright** der bedeutendste noch lebende Dramatiker; **I have no ~ relatives** ich habe keine Verwandten mehr; **a ~ creature** ein Lebewesen *nt*; **not a ~ soul** keine Menschenseele; **(with)in ~ memory** seit Menschengedenken; **he is ~ proof of ...** er ist der lebende Beweis für ...; **her existence was a ~ death** ihr Leben war eine einzige Qual; **~ or dead** tot oder lebendig

N **a** **the living** PL die Lebenden *pl*

b (= *way of living*) **the art of ~** Lebenskunst *f*; **he is fond of good ~** er lebt gern *gut*; **gracious ~** die vornehme Lebensart; **loose ~** lockerer Lebenswandel; **healthy ~** gesundes Leben → standard N **b**

c (= *livelihood*) Lebensunterhalt *m*; **to earn** *or* **make a ~** sich (*dat*) seinen Lebensunterhalt verdienen; **what does he do for a ~?** womit verdient er sich (*dat*) seinen Lebensunterhalt?; **he sells brushes for a ~** er verkauft Bürsten, um sich (*dat*) seinen Lebensunterhalt zu verdienen; **they made a bare ~ out of the soil** sie hatten mit dem Ertrag des Bodens ihr Auskommen; **it is possible to make a very good ~ from modelling** (*Brit*) *or* **modeling** (*US*) von der Arbeit als Model kann man sehr gut leben; **to work for one's ~** arbeiten, um sich (*dat*) seinen Lebensunterhalt zu verdienen; **some of us have to work for a ~** es gibt auch Leute, die arbeiten müssen

d (*Eccl*) Pfründe *f*

living: living cell N (*Med*) Frischzelle *f*; **living conditions** PL Wohnverhältnisse *pl*; **living dead** PL Untote *pl*; (*fig*) Scheintote *pl*; **living expenses** PL Lebenskosten *pl*; **living quarters** PL Wohnräume *pl*; (*for soldiers, sailors*) Quartier *nt*; **living room** N Wohnzimmer *nt*; **living space** N (*in house*) Wohnraum *m*; (*for a nation*) Lebensraum *m*; **living wage** N ausreichender Lohn; **£65 a week is not a ~** von £ 65 pro Woche kann man nicht leben; **living will** N testamentartige Erklärung, dass jd im Falle einer tödlichen Erkrankung nicht künstlich am Leben gehalten werden will

Livy ['lɪvɪ] N Livius *m*

lizard ['lɪzəd] N Eidechse *f*; (*including larger forms also*) Echse *f*

ll *abbr of* **lines** Z

llama ['lɑːmə] N Lama *nt*

LLB *abbr of* **Bachelor of Laws**

LLD *abbr of* **Doctor of Laws** Dr. jur.

LMT (*US*) *abbr of* **local mean time** Ortszeit *f*

LNG *abbr of* **liquefied natural gas** LNG *nt*, Flüssiggas *nt*

lo [ləʊ] INTERJ (old) siehe (old); **lo and behold!** und siehe da

loach [ləʊtʃ] N Schmerle f

load [ləʊd] **N a** (= sth carried, burden) Last f; (= cargo) Ladung f; (on girder, axle etc, fig) Belastung f, Last f; **what sort of ~ was the ship/truck carrying?** was hatte das Schiff/der Lastwagen geladen?; **to put a ~ on sth** etw belasten; **to put too heavy a ~ on sth** etw überlasten; **the maximum ~ for that bridge is 10 tons** die maximale Tragkraft or -fähigkeit dieser Brücke beträgt 10 Tonnen; **an arm-load of shopping** ein Arm voll Einkäufe; **a train-load of passengers** ein Zug voll Reisender; **(work) ~ (Arbeits)pensum** nt; **he has a heavy teaching ~ this term** er hat in diesem Semester eine hohe Stundenzahl; **he carries a heavy ~ of responsibility** er trägt eine schwere Verantwortung; **I put a ~ in the washing machine** ich habe die Maschine mit Wäsche gefüllt; **that's a ~ off my mind!** da fällt mir ein Stein vom Herzen!; **to take a ~ off sb's mind** jdm eine Last von der Seele nehmen **b** (Elec) (supplied) Leistung f; (carried) Spannung f **c** (inf usages) ~s of, a ~ of massenhaft (inf), jede Menge (inf); **thanks, we have ~s** danke, wir haben jede Menge (inf); **it's a ~ of old rubbish** (Brit) das ist alles Blödsinn (inf) or Quatsch (inf); (film, book, translation) das ist alles Mist! (inf); **to take one a ~** (= ganz schön) einen heben (inf); **get a ~ of this!** (= listen) hör dir das mal an!; (= look) guck dir das mal an! (inf) **VT a** goods laden; lorry etc beladen; **the ship was ~ed with bananas** das Schiff hatte Bananen geladen **b** (= burden, weigh down) beladen; **the branch was ~ed with pears** der Ast war mit Birnen überladen **c** (fig) überhäufen; **to ~ sb with honours** (Brit) or **honors** (US) jdn mit Ehrungen überschütten or -häufen; **the whole matter is ~ed with problems** die Angelegenheit steckt voller Probleme; **they were ~ed with debt** sie steckten tief in Schulden **d** gun laden; **to ~ a camera** einen Film (in einen Fotoapparat) einlegen; **is this camera ~ed?** ist ein Film im Apparat? **e** dice fälschen, präparieren; **to ~ the dice** (fig) mit gezinkten Karten spielen; **to ~ the dice against sb** (fig) jdn übervorteilen; (= be a disadvantage) ein Nachteil m für jdn sein; **the dice had been ~ed against him** (fig) alles sprach gegen ihn **f** (Comput) laden **VI a** (= load goods, truck) laden; **"loading and unloading"** "Be- und Entladen" **b** (= load gun) laden; (= load camera) einen Film einlegen; **~!** Gewehr(e) laden!; **how does this gun ~?** wie lädt man dieses Gewehr?; **how does this camera ~?** wie legt man einen Film in diesen Apparat ein? **c** (Comput) laden

▶ **load down** VT sep (schwer) beladen; (fig) überladen; **the poor animal was loaded down with luggage** das arme Tier war schwer mit Gepäck beladen; **he is loaded down with guilt** Schuldgefühle lasten schwer auf ihm

▶ **load up VI** aufladen **VT** sep **a** lorry beladen; goods aufladen **b** (Comput) laden

loadable [ləʊdəbl] ADJ (Comput) ladbar

load: load-bearing ADJ wall tragend; **load capacity** N (Elec) Belastung(sfähigkeit) f; (of lorry) maximale Nutzlast; **load centre**, (US) **load center** N Lastschwerpunkt m; **load displacement** N (Naut) Ladeverdrängung f

loaded [ləʊdɪd] ADJ beladen; dice falsch, präpariert; camera mit eingelegtem Film; gun, software geladen; **the dice are ~ in their favour** (Brit) or **favor** (US)/**against them** (fig) alles spricht für/gegen sie; **a ~ question** eine Fangfrage; **that's a ~ word/term** das ist kein neutrales Wort/kein neutraler Ausdruck; **emotionally ~** (word, speech) emotional aufgeladen; **he's ~** (inf) (= rich) er ist stink- or steinreich (inf), er

schwimmt im Geld (inf); (= drunk) der hat einen in der Krone (inf)

loading: loading bay [ləʊdɪŋbeɪ] N Ladeplatz m; **loading bridge** [ləʊdɪŋbrɪdʒ] N Verladebrücke f; (Aviat) Fluggastbrücke f

load: load line N Ladelinie f; **load space** N (Aut etc) Ladefläche f; **loadstar** N = lodestar; **loadstone** N = lodestone

loaf [ləʊf] N pl **loaves** Brot nt; (unsliced) (Brot-)laib m; (= meat loaf) Hackbraten m; **a ~ of bread** ein (Laib) Brot; **a small white ~** ein kleines Weißbrot; **half a ~ is better than none** or **than no bread** (Prov) (wenig ist) besser als gar nichts; **use your ~!** (inf) streng deinen Grips an (inf)

▶ **loaf about** (Brit) or **around** VI (inf) faulenzen; **he loafed about** or **around the house all day** er hing den ganzen Tag zu Hause herum

loafer [ləʊfə] N **a** (inf: = idler) Faulenzer(in) m(f), Nichtstuer(in) m(f) **b** (esp US: = casual shoe) Halbschuh m, Trotteur m

loaf tin, (US) **loaf pan** N Kastenform f

loam [ləʊm] N Lehmerde f

loamy [ləʊmɪ] ADJ (+er) lehmig; **~ soil** Lehmboden m

loan [ləʊn] **N a** (= thing lent) Leihgabe f; (from bank etc) Darlehen nt; (= public loan) Anleihe f; **my friend let me have the money as a ~** mein Freund hat mir das Geld geliehen; **it's not a gift, it's a ~** es ist nicht geschenkt, sondern nur geliehen; **government ~s** Regierungsdarlehen nt; (= borrowings) Staatsanleihen pl **b** I asked for the ~ of a bicycle ich bat darum, ein Fahrrad ausleihen zu dürfen; **he gave me the ~ of his bicycle** er hat mir sein Fahrrad geliehen; **conditions governing the ~ of this book** Leihbedingungen pl für dieses Buch; **it's on ~** es ist geliehen; (= out on loan) es ist verliehen or ausgeliehen; **the machinery is on ~ from the American government** die Maschinen sind eine Leihgabe der amerikanischen Regierung; **she's on ~ to us from the CIA** sie ist vom CIA an uns abgestellt worden; **to have sth on ~** etw geliehen haben (from von) **VT** leihen (to sb jdm)

loan: loan account N Darlehenskonto nt, Kreditkonto nt; **loanback facility** N (Insur) Beleihungsmöglichkeit f; **loan bank** N (Brit) Darlehensbank f, Kreditanstalt f; **loan capital** N Anleihekapital nt; **loan collection** N Leihgaben pl; **loan shark** N (inf) Kredithai m (inf); **loan word** N Lehnwort nt

loath, loth [ləʊθ] ADJ **to be ~ to do sth** etw ungern tun; **~ as I am to leave** so ungern ich auch gehe; **he was ~ for us to go** er ließ uns ungern gehen; **nothing ~** (old) bereitwillig(st)

loathe [ləʊð] VT thing, person verabscheuen; modern art, spinach, jazz etc nicht ausstehen können; **I ~ the idea** die Vorstellung ist mir zuwider; **I ~ doing it** (in general) ich hasse es, das zu tun; (on particular occasion) es ist mir zuwider, das zu tun

loathing [ləʊðɪŋ] N Abscheu m

loathly [ləʊðlɪ] ADJ (sehr) ungern or widerwillig

loathsome [ləʊðsəm] ADJ thing, person abscheulich, widerlich; task verhasst; deformity abstoßend; wound Ekel erregend

loathsomeness [ləʊðsəmnɪs] N Abscheulichkeit f, Widerlichkeit f; (of task) Verhasstheit f; (of deformity) abstoßender Anblick

loaves [ləʊvz] pl of **loaf**

lob [lɒb] **N** (Tennis) Lob m **VT** ball im Lob spielen, lobben; **he ~bed the grenade over the wall** er warf die Granate im hohen Bogen über die Mauer; **to ~ sth over to sb** jdm etw zuwerfen; **~ it over!** wirf es herüber! **VI** (Tennis) lobben

lobby [lɒbɪ] **N** (= entrance hall) Vor- or Eingangshalle f; (of hotel, theatre) Foyer nt; (= corridor) Flur m, Korridor m; (= anteroom, waiting room) Vorzimmer nt; (= place in Parliament) Lobby f; (Pol) Lobby f, Interessengruppe f or -verband m; **the gun ~** die Waffenlobby

VT to ~ one's Member of Parliament auf seinen Abgeordneten Einfluss nehmen; **to ~ a bill through parliament** als Interessengruppe ein Gesetz durchs Parlament bringen
VI auf die Abgeordneten Einfluss nehmen, Lobbyist(in) m(f) sein; **they are ~ing for this reform** die Lobbyisten versuchen, diese Reform durchzubringen; **the farmers are ~ing for higher subsidies** die Bauernlobby will höhere Subventionen durchsetzen

lobbying [lɒbɪɪŋ] N Beeinflussung f von Abgeordneten (durch Lobbys); **the Prime Minister refused to be influenced by ~** der Premierminister wollte sich nicht von Lobbys or Interessenverbänden beeinflussen lassen

lobbyist [lɒbɪɪst] N Lobbyist(in) m(f)

lobe [ləʊb] N **a** (Anat) (of ear) Ohrläppchen nt; (of lungs, brain) Lappen m, Lobus m (spec); (of leaf) Ausbuchtung f

lobed [ləʊbd] ADJ gelappt

lobelia [ləʊbiːlɪə] N Lobelie f

lobotomize [ləʊbɒtəmaɪz] VT **to ~ sb** an jdm eine Lobotomie durchführen

lobotomy [ləʊbɒtəmɪ] N (Med) Lobotomie f

lobster [lɒbstə] N Hummer m

lobster pot N Hummer(fang)korb m

local [ləʊkəl] ADJ örtlich; (= in this area) hiesig; (= in that area) dortig; anaesthetic lokal, örtlich; **~ radio** Lokalradio nt; **~ radio station** Regionalsender m; **~ news** Lokalnachrichten pl; **~ newspaper** Lokalzeitung f; **~ politician** Kommunalpolitiker(in) m(f); **all the ~ residents** alle Ortsansässigen pl; **he's a ~ man** er ist ein Ortsansässiger, er ist von hier (inf); **~ community** Kommune f; **~ taxes** Kommunalabgaben pl; **~ currency** Landeswährung f; **at ~ level** auf lokaler Ebene; **it's only of ~ interest** es ist nur für die Einheimischen interessant; **~ opinion is against the change** die öffentliche Meinung am Ort ist gegen die Änderung; **the latest ~ gossip** der neueste Klatsch (hier/dort); **~ bus** Stadtbus m; (serving the immediate locality) Nahverkehrsbus m; **~ train** Nahverkehrszug m; **~ traffic** Ortsverkehr m; **~ time** Ortszeit f; **go into your ~ branch** gehen Sie zu Ihrer Zweigstelle; **vote for your ~ candidate** wählen Sie den Kandidaten Ihres Wahlkreises; **accents with the usual ~ variations** Dialekte mit den üblichen regionalen Unterschieden; **one of our ~ sons** einer der Söhne unserer Gemeinde/Stadt; **we used the ~ shops when we were in Spain** wir haben in den Läden der Einheimischen eingekauft, als wir in Spanien waren; **our village hasn't got a ~ butcher** unser Dorf hat keinen eigenen Schlachter; **there are two ~ grocers** (esp Brit) es gibt zwei Lebensmittelhändler am Ort; **the ~ shops aren't very good** die dortigen/hiesigen Geschäfte sind nicht sehr gut; **our ~ doctor back home in Canada** unser Arzt zu Hause in Kanada; **what are their main ~ products there?** was wird dort (in der Gegend) hauptsächlich erzeugt?; **the best ~ wine** der beste Wein der Gegend; **the ~ wine over there will make you sick** von dem dortigen Wein wird es einem schlecht
N a (Brit inf: = pub) **the ~** (in village) der Dorfkrug, die Dorfkneipe (inf); (in community) das Stammlokal; **our ~** unsere Stammkneipe (inf), unser Stammlokal nt **b** (born in) Einheimische(r) mf; (living in) Einwohner(in) m(f) **c** (Med inf: = local anaesthetic) örtliche Betäubung **d** (US) (= branch) Zweigstelle f; (= train) Nahverkehrszug m

local: local area network N (Comput) lokales Rechnernetz, LAN nt; **local authority** N Kommunalbehörde f; **local call** N (Telec) Ortsgespräch nt; **local colour**, (US) **local color** N Lokalkolorit nt; **local council** N Gemeindeverwaltung f; (= councillors) Gemeinderat m; (in town) Stadtverwaltung f; (= councillors) Gemeinderat m; (in town) Stadtrat m

locale [ləʊkɑːl] N Schauplatz m

local education authority N örtliche Schulbehörde

local government N Kommunal- or Gemeindeverwaltung f; **~ expenditure** ≈ der kommunale Haushalt; **~ elections** Kommunalwahlen pl; **he is in ~** er ist im Gemeinderat or (in town) Stadtrat; **reform of ~** Gemeindereform f

locality [ləʊˈkælɪtɪ] N Gegend f; **a house in the immediate ~ of shops and schools** ein Haus nt in nächster Nähe von Geschäften und Schulen

localize [ˈləʊkəlaɪz] VT **a** (= detect) lokalisieren **b this custom, once widespread, has now become very ~d** die einst weit verbreitete Sitte ist jetzt auf wenige Orte begrenzt

locally [ˈləʊkəlɪ] ADV am Ort; (Med) örtlich; **houses are dear ~** Häuser sind hier teuer; **I prefer to shop ~** ich kaufe lieber im Ort ein; **the shops are situated ~** die Geschäfte befinden den sich in der Nähe; **do you live ~?** wohnen Sie am Ort?; **I work in Glasgow but I don't live ~** ich arbeite in Glasgow, wohne aber nicht hier/da; **it is known ~ as Tarzan** es wird von den Einheimischen Tarzan genannt; **was she well-known ~?** war sie in dieser Gegend sehr bekannt?; **it was organized both nationally and ~** es wurde sowohl auf nationaler als auch auf lokaler Ebene organisiert; **if each district is ~ governed** wenn jeder Bezirk regional regiert wird; **the plant grows ~** die Pflanze wächst in dieser Gegend; **~ grown** or **produced** in der Region angebaut

locate [ləʊˈkeɪt] VT **a** (= position) legen; headquarters einrichten; (including act of building) bauen, errichten; sportsground, playground anlegen; road bauen, anlegen; **to be ~d at** or **in** sich befinden in (+dat); **the hotel is centrally ~d** das Hotel liegt zentral; **where shall we ~ the new branch?** wohin sollen wir die neue Zweigstelle legen? **b** (= find) ausfindig machen; submarine, plane orten

location [ləʊˈkeɪʃən] N **a** (= position, site) Lage f; (of building) Standort m, Lage f; (of road) Führung f; (of ship) Position f; **this would be an ideal ~ for the road/airport** das wäre ein ideales Gelände für die Straße/den Flughafen; **they moved the ~ of the rig** sie verlegten die Bohrinsel; **the precise ~ of the accident** der genaue Unfallort; **the doctors haven't determined the precise ~ of the tumour** (Brit) or **tumor** (US) die Ärzte haben den Tumor noch nicht genau lokalisiert; **that shop is in a good ~** dieses Geschäft hat eine gute Lage **b** (= positioning, siting) (of building, road) Bau m; (of park) Anlage f; (of headquarters) (= removal) Einrichtung f; (= building) Errichtung f; **they discussed the ~ of the proposed road/airport** sie diskutierten, wo die geplante Straße/der geplante Flughafen gebaut werden sollte **c** (= finding) Auffinden nt; (of tumour) Lokalisierung f; (of star, ship) Ortung f, Positionsbestimmung f; **the ~ of oil in the North Sea** die Entdeckung von Erdöl in der Nordsee **d** (Film) Drehort m; **to be on ~ in Mexico** (person) bei Außenaufnahmen in Mexiko sein; **part of the film was shot on ~ in Mexico** ein Teil der Außenaufnahmen für den Film wurde in Mexiko gedreht; **we had a lot of ~ work** wir mussten viele Außenaufnahmen machen

locative [ˈlɒkətɪv] N Lokativ m

loc cit [ˈlɒkˈsɪt] abbr of **loco citato** l. c., a. a. O.

loch [lɒx] N (Scot) See m; (= sea loch) Meeresarm m

loci [ˈləʊkiː] pl of **locus**

lock¹ [lɒk] N (of hair) Locke f; **her wavy ~s** ihr gewelltes Haar

lock² N **a** (on door, box, gun) Schloss nt; **to put/keep sb under ~ and key** jdn hinter Schloss und Riegel bringen/verwahren; **to put sth under ~ and key** etw wegschließen; **to keep money under ~ and key** Geld unter Verschluss halten; **he offered me the house ~, stock and barrel** er bot mir das Haus mit allem Drum und Dran an (inf); **they destroyed it ~, stock and barrel** sie haben es total zerstört; **to own sth ~, stock and barrel** etw ganz besitzen **b** (= canal lock) Schleuse f **c** (= hold) Fesselgriff m **d** (Aut) Wendekreis m; **the steering wheel was on full ~** das Lenkrad war voll eingeschlagen ▊VT door etc ab- or zuschließen; steering wheel sperren, arretieren; wheel blockieren; (Comput) keyboard verriegeln; **to ~ sb in a room** jdn in einem Zimmer einschließen; **the armies were ~ed in combat** die Armeen waren in Kämpfe verwickelt; **they were ~ed in each other's arms** sie hielten sich fest umschlungen; **he ~ed my arm in a firm grip** er umklammerte meinen Arm mit festem Griff; **this bar ~s the wheel in position** diese Stange hält das Rad fest; **the handcuffs were ~ed round his wrists** die Handschellen waren an seinen Handgelenken festgemacht → **stable²** N ▊VI schließen; (wheel) blockieren; **a suitcase that ~s** ein verschließbarer Koffer, ein Koffer, der sich abschließen lässt; **his jaw had ~ed fast** er hatte Mundsperre; **the lion's jaws ~ed round his arm** der Kiefer des Löwen schloss sich fest um seinen Arm

▸ **lock away** VT sep wegschließen; person einsperren; **he locked the money away in his safe** er schloss das Geld in seinem Safe ein

▸ **lock in** VT sep **a** (= shut in) person, animal einschließen; **to be locked in** eingesperrt sein **b we're locked into this supplier** wir sind an diesen Lieferanten gebunden; **I don't want to get myself locked in** ich will mich nicht zu sehr binden; **to lock in on an idea** sich in eine Idee verbeißen

▸ **lock on** VI (spaceship etc) gekoppelt werden (to mit); **the radio automatically locks onto a channel** das Radio hat automatische Feineinstellung; **the missile locks onto its target** das Geschoss richtet sich auf das Ziel ▊VT sep radio, scanner einstellen (to auf +acc); **with a padlock he locked the extra piece on** er befestigte das zusätzliche Stück mit einem Anhängeschloss

▸ **lock out** VT sep workers aussperren; **I've locked myself out** ich habe mich ausgesperrt

▸ **lock together** VI (rockets) (miteinander) gekoppelt werden; (pieces of jigsaw) sich zusammenstecken lassen ▊VT sep rockets (miteinander) koppeln; currencies (aneinander) koppeln; pieces of jigsaw zusammenstecken; **locked together in a passionate embrace** in einer leidenschaftlichen Umarmung fest umschlungen

▸ **lock up** ▊VT sep **a** thing, house abschließen; person einsperren; **to lock sth up in sth** etw in etw (dat) einschließen; **he ought to be locked up!** den müsste man einsperren! **b** (Comm) capital fest anlegen ▊VI abschließen

lockable [ˈlɒkəbl] ADJ abschließbar, verschließbar

lockage [ˈlɒkɪdʒ] N **a** (= canal lock) Schleusensystem nt, Schleusenanlage f **b** (= toll) Schleusengeld nt **c** (= passage of ship) (Durch)schleusen nt

locker [ˈlɒkə'] N Schließfach nt; (Naut, Mil) Spind m

locker room N Umkleideraum m

locket [ˈlɒkɪt] N Medaillon nt

lock: lock gate N Schleusentor nt; **lockjaw** N Wundstarrkrampf m; **lock keeper** N Schleusenwärter(in) m(f); **locknut** N Gegenmutter f; **lockout** N Aussperrung f; **locksmith** N Schlosser(in) m(f); **lockstitch** N Steppstich m; **lock-up** N **a** (= shop) Laden m, Geschäft nt; (= garage) Garage f **b** (= prison) Gefängnis nt

loco¹ [ˈləʊkəʊ] N (Rail inf) Lok f (inf)

loco² ADJ (esp US inf) bekloppt (inf); **he's gone ~** der spinnt (inf)

loco citato [ˌlɒkəʊsɪˈtɑːtəʊ] = **loc cit**

locomotion [ˌləʊkəˈməʊʃən] N Fortbewegung f; **means of ~** Fortbewegungsmittel nt

locomotive [ˌləʊkəˈməʊtɪv] ▊ADJ Fortbewegungs-; **~ power** Fortbewegungsfähigkeit f ▊N Lokomotive f

locum (tenens) [ˈləʊkəm(ˈtenenz)] N (Brit) Vertreter(in) m(f)

locus [ˈlɒkəs] N pl **loci** geometrischer Ort

locust [ˈləʊkəst] N Heuschrecke f

locust tree N Robinie f

locution [ləˈkjuːʃən] N Ausdrucksweise f; (= expression) Ausdruck m; **a set ~** eine feste or feststehende Redewendung

lode [ləʊd] N Ader f

lode: lodestar N Leitstern m, Polarstern m; (fig) (= person) Leitbild nt; (= principle) Leitstern m; **lodestone** N Magnetit m, Magneteisenstein m

lodge [lɒdʒ] ▊N (in grounds) Pförtnerhaus nt; (of Red Indian) Wigwam m; (= shooting lodge, skiing lodge etc) Hütte f; (= porter's lodge) Pförtnerloge f; (Sch, Univ) Pedellzimmer nt; (= masonic lodge) Loge f; (of beaver) Bau m ▊VT **a** (Brit) person unterbringen **b** (with bei) complaint einlegen; protest erheben; claim geltend machen; charge, petition, application einreichen; **to ~ an appeal** Einspruch erheben; (Jur) Berufung einlegen **c** (= insert) spear stoßen; **to be ~d** (fest)stecken **d** jewellery, money deponieren, hinterlegen ▊VI **a** (Brit: = live) (zur or in Untermiete) wohnen (with sb, at sb's bei jdm); (at boarding house) wohnen (in in +dat) **b** (object, bullet) stecken bleiben; **to ~ in sb's mind** jdm in Erinnerung bleiben

lodger [ˈlɒdʒə'] N Untermieter(in) m(f); **I was a ~ there once** ich habe dort einmal zur or in Untermiete gewohnt; **she takes ~s** sie vermietet (Zimmer), sie nimmt Untermieter auf

lodging [ˈlɒdʒɪŋ] N **a** Unterkunft f; **they gave me a night's ~** sie gaben mir Unterkunft or ein Zimmer für die Nacht **b lodgings** PL ein möbliertes Zimmer, möblierte Zimmer pl; **where are your ~s?** wo wohnen Sie?; **we took ~s with Mrs B** wir mieteten uns bei Frau B ein

lodging house N Pension f

loess [ˈləʊɪs] N Löss m, Löß m

loft [lɒft] ▊N **a** Boden m, Speicher m; (= hay loft) Heuboden m; **in the ~** auf dem Boden or Speicher **b** (= organ loft, choir loft) Empore f ▊VT (Sport) hochschlagen; **he ~ed the ball over the fence** er schlug den Ball im hohen Bogen über den Zaun

loft conversion N Dachausbau m

loftily [ˈlɒftɪlɪ] ADV hoch; say, speak stolz, hochmütig; gaze hochmütig

loftiness [ˈlɒftɪnɪs] N **a** (of tree, mountain) Höhe f **b** (of sentiments) Erhabenheit f; (of prose) erlesener or gehobener or hochtrabender (pej) Stil; **the ~ of his ambitions/ideals** seine hochfliegenden Ambitionen/Ideale **c** (= haughtiness) Hochmütigkeit f

lofty [ˈlɒftɪ] ▊ADJ (+er) **a** (= high) hoch; **he rose to a ~ position** er stieg in eine gehobene Position auf **b** (= noble) ideals hoch(fliegend); ambitions hochfliegend; sentiments erhaben; prose, style erlesen, gehoben, hochtrabend (pej) **c** (= haughty) stolz, hochmütig ▊N (inf) Lange(r) mf (inf)

log¹ [lɒg] N Baumstamm m; (= short length of tree trunk) Block m, Klotz m; (for a fire) Scheit m; **to sleep like a ~** wie ein Stein schlafen

log² ▊N **a** (Naut: = apparatus) Log nt **b** (= record) Aufzeichnungen pl; (Naut) Logbuch nt; **to keep a ~ of sth** über etw (acc) Buch führen ▊VT **a** (= record) Buch führen über (+acc); (Naut) (ins Logbuch) eintragen; **details are ~ged in the computer** Einzelheiten sind im Computer gespeichert **b** (= travel) zurücklegen

▸ **log in** VI (Comput) einloggen

▸ **log off** (Comput) ▊VI ausloggen ▊VT ausloggen, abmelden

▸ **log on** (Comput) ▊VI einloggen ▊VT einloggen, anmelden

▸ **log out** VI (Comput) ausloggen

▶ **log up** VT sep (Naut) (ins Logbuch) eintragen; (= clock up) distance zurücklegen; (fig) successes einheimsen (inf)

log³ abbr of **logarithm** log; ~ **tables** Logarithmentafel f

loganberry ['ləʊgənbəri] N (= fruit) Loganbeere f; (= bush) Loganbeerbusch m

logarithm ['lɒgərɪθəm] N Logarithmus m

logarithmic [ˌlɒgə'rɪθmɪk] ADJ logarithmisch

logbook ['lɒgbʊk] N (Naut) Logbuch nt; (Aviat) Bordbuch nt; (of lorries) Fahrtenbuch nt; (Aut: = registration book) Kraftfahrzeug- or Kfz-Brief m; (in hospitals, police stations etc) Dienstbuch nt

log cabin N Blockhaus nt, Blockhütte f

loggerheads ['lɒgəhedz] PL **to be at ~ (with sb)** (esp Brit) Streit (mit jdm) haben, sich (dat) (mit jdm) in den Haaren liegen (inf); **they were constantly at ~ with the authorities** sie standen mit den Behörden dauernd auf Kriegsfuß

loggia ['lɒdʒɪə] N Loggia f

logging ['lɒgɪŋ] N Holzfällen nt

logic ['lɒdʒɪk] N Logik f; **there's no ~ in that** das ist völlig unlogisch

logical ['lɒdʒɪkəl] ADJ logisch; conclusion also folgerichtig; **he has a ~ mind** er denkt logisch; **they are incapable of ~ thinking** sie können nicht logisch denken; **to take sth to its ~ conclusion** etw bis zur logischen Konsequenz führen

logically ['lɒdʒɪkəlɪ] ADV think, argue logisch; **~, he may be right** logisch gesehen könnte er Recht haben; **it follows ~ from this that ...** daraus lässt sich die logische Schlussfolgerung ziehen, dass ...

logic: logic analyzer N (Comput) Logikanalysator m; **logic bomb** N (Comput) Langzeitvirus m, Virus-Zeitbombe f

logician [lɒ'dʒɪʃən] N Logiker(in) m(f)

logic circuit N (Comput) logische Schaltung

logistic [lɒ'dʒɪstɪk] ADJ logistisch

logistically [lɒ'dʒɪstɪkəlɪ] ADV logistisch

logistics [lɒ'dʒɪstɪks] N sing Logistik f

logo ['ləʊgəʊ, 'lɒgəʊ] N Logo nt, Emblem nt

logrolling ['lɒgrəʊlɪŋ] N (Pol) Kuhhandel m (inf); (Sport) Wettkampf bei dem zwei Gegner auf einem im Wasser schwimmenden Baumstamm stehen und sich durch Drehen desselben zum Fallen bringen

loin [lɔɪn] N Lende f → **gird up**

loincloth ['lɔɪnklɒθ] N Lendenschurz m

loiter ['lɔɪtə'] VI **a** (= waste time) trödeln, bummeln **b** (= hang around suspiciously) sich herumtreiben, herumlungern; "**no ~ing**" „unberechtigter Aufenthalt verboten"; **to ~ with intent** sich verdächtig machen, sich auffällig verhalten

▶ **loiter about** (Brit) or **around** VI herumlungern

loiterer ['lɔɪtərə'] N Herumtreiber(in) m(f), Herumlungerer m; (= straggler) Nachzügler(in) m(f), Bummelant(in) m(f) (inf)

loll [lɒl] VI **a** sich lümmeln; **he was ~ing in an easy chair** er hing (inf) or räkelte sich or rekelte sich im Sessel; **to ~ against sth** sich (lässig) gegen or an etw (acc) lehnen **b** (= flop) (head) hängen; (tongue) heraushängen

▶ **loll about** (Brit) or **around** VI herumlümmeln, herumhängen (inf)

▶ **loll back** VI sich zurücklehnen

▶ **loll out** VI heraushängen; **the dog's tongue was lolling out** dem Hund hing die Zunge heraus

lollapalooza [ˌlɒləpə'luːzə'], **lollapaloosa** [ˌlɒləpə'luːsə'] N (dated US sl, = amazing thing) Wahnsinnsding nt (inf); (= large thing) Riesending nt (inf)

lollipop ['lɒlɪpɒp] N Lutscher m; (= iced lollipop) Eis nt am Stiel

lollipop lady N (Brit inf) ≈ Schülerlotsin f

lollipop man N (Brit inf) ≈ Schülerlotse m

lollop ['lɒləp] VI (also **lollop along**, animal) trotten, zotteln; (puppy, rabbit) hoppeln; (person) zockeln

lolly ['lɒlɪ] N (esp Brit) **a** (inf: = lollipop) Lutscher m; **an ice ~** ein Eis nt am Stiel **b** (inf: = money) Kohle f (inf)

lollygag ['lɒlɪgæg], **lallygag** ['lælɪgæg] VI (dated US sl) **a** (= waste time) seine Zeit verplempern (inf) **b** (= kiss and cuddle) schmusen (inf)

Lombard ['lɒmbɑːd] ADJ lombardisch N Lombarde m, Lombardin f

Lombardy ['lɒmbədɪ] N Lombardei f

London ['lʌndən] N London nt ADJ Londoner

Londoner ['lʌndənə'] N Londoner(in) m(f)

lone [ləʊn] ADJ (= single) einzeln; (= isolated) einsam; (= only) survivor, success einzig; **~ traveller** (Brit) or **traveler** (US) Alleinreisende(r) mf; **he prefers to play a ~ hand** er macht lieber alles im Alleingang; **to be a ~ voice** ein einsamer Rufer sein; **to fight a ~ battle** einen einsamen Kampf führen; **~ mother** allein erziehende Mutter; **~ father** allein erziehender Vater; **~ parent** Alleinerziehende(r) mf, allein erziehender Elternteil; **~ parent family** Einelternfamilie f, Alleinerziehendenhaushalt m

loneliness ['ləʊnlɪnɪs] N Einsamkeit f

lonely ['ləʊnlɪ] ADJ (+er) einsam; **it's ~ at the top** an der Spitze lebt es sich einsam; **~ hearts ad** Kontaktanzeige f; **~ hearts column** Kontaktanzeigen pl; **~ hearts club** Singletreff m, Singleklub m

loner ['ləʊnə'] N Einzelgänger(in) m(f)

lonesome ['ləʊnsəm] ADJ (esp US) einsam

Lone Star State N (US) **the ~** Texas nt

lone wolf N (fig) Einzelgänger m

long¹ abbr of **longitude** L

long² [lɒŋ] ADJ (+er) **a** (in size) lang; glass hoch; journey weit; **it is 6 feet ~** es ist 6 Fuß lang; **to be ~ in the leg** lange Beine haben; **to pull a ~ face** ein langes Gesicht machen; **it's a ~ way** das ist weit; **it's a ~ way to Hamburg** nach Hamburg ist es weit; **to have a ~ memory** ein gutes Gedächtnis haben; **to be ~ in the tooth** (inf) nicht mehr der/die Jüngste sein; **surely he is a bit ~ in the tooth to be climbing Everest** ist er nicht schon ein bisschen (zu) alt, um den Everest zu besteigen? **b** (in time) lang; job langwierig; **it's a ~ time since I saw her** ich habe sie schon lange nicht mehr gesehen; **will you need it for a ~ time?** brauchen Sie es lange?; **he's been here (for) a ~ time** er ist schon lange hier; **she was abroad for a ~ time** sie war (eine) lange Zeit im Ausland; **well hullo, it's been a ~ time** hallo, schon lange nicht mehr gesehen; **~ time no see** (inf) sieht man dich auch mal wieder? (inf); **to take a ~ look at sth** etw lange or ausgiebig betrachten; **how ~ is the film?** wie lange dauert der Film?; **a year is 12 months** ~ ein Jahr hat 12 Monate; **how ~ are your holidays?** (Brit), **how ~ is your vacation?** (US) wie lange haben Sie Urlaub?; **to take the ~ view** etw auf lange Sicht betrachten

c (Poet, Phon) vowel, syllable lang

d **a ~ drink** (mixed) ein Longdrink m; (= beer) ein Bier nt; **a ~ gin** ein Gin mit Tonic und Eis etc; **I'd like something ~ and cool** ich möchte einen kühlen Longdrink

ADV **a** lang(e); **to be ~ in** or **about doing sth** lange zu etw brauchen; **don't be ~!** beeil dich!; **don't be too ~ about it** lass dir nicht zu viel Zeit, mach nicht zu lange (inf); **don't be too ~ about phoning me** ruf mich bald (mal) an; **I shan't be ~** (in finishing) ich bin gleich fertig; (in returning) ich bin gleich wieder da; **two months without you, it's been too ~** zwei Monate ohne dich, das war zu lang(e); **he drank ~ and deep** er nahm einen langen, tiefen Schluck; **all night ~** die ganze Nacht; **~ ago** vor langer Zeit; **not ~ ago** vor kurzem; **~ before** lange vorher; **~ before now** viel früher; **~ before they arrived** lange bevor sie ankamen; **not ~ before I met you** kurz bevor ich dich kennen lernte; **not ~ before that** kurz davor; **those days are ~**

(since) past diese Tage sind schon lange vorbei; **at the ~est** höchstens; **as ~ as** so lange wie; **we waited as ~ as we could** wir haben gewartet, solange wir konnten; **as ~ as, so ~ as** (= provided that) solange → also **ago**, **since**

b (in comp) **how much ~er can you stay?** wie lange können Sie noch bleiben?; **I can't wait any ~er** (from then) länger kann ich nicht warten; (from now) ich kann nicht mehr länger warten; **if that noise goes on any ~er** wenn der Lärm weitergeht; **no ~er** (= not any more) nicht mehr; **I'll wait no ~er** ich warte nicht länger; **I'll insist no ~er** ich werde nicht weiter darauf bestehen

c **so ~!** (inf) tschüs(s)! (inf), bis später!

N **a** **the ~ and the short of it is that ...** kurz gesagt ..., der langen Rede kurzer Sinn ...; **that's the ~ and the short of it** und damit hat sichs (inf); **before ~** bald; **are you going for ~?** werden Sie länger weg sein?; **I won't stay for ~** ich bleibe nicht lange; **it won't take ~** das dauert nicht lange; **it didn't take ~ before ...** es dauerte nicht lange, bis ...; **I won't take ~** ich brauche nicht lange (dazu)

b (Poet) lange Silbe

long³ VI sich sehnen (for nach); (less passionately) herbeisehnen, kaum erwarten können (for sth etw acc); **he ~ed for his wife to return** er wartete sehnsüchtig auf die Rückkehr seiner Frau; **I'm ~ing for him to resign** ich warte ungeduldig auf seinen Rücktritt; **the children were ~ing for the bell to ring** die Kinder warteten sehnsüchtig auf das Klingeln or konnten das Klingeln kaum erwarten; **he is ~ing for me to make a mistake** er möchte zu gern, dass ich einen Fehler mache; **I am ~ing to go abroad** ich brenne darauf, ins Ausland zu gehen; **he ~ed to know what was happening** er hätte zu gerne gewusst, was vorging; **I'm ~ing to see my cat again** ich möchte meine Katze so gern wiedersehen; **I'm ~ing to see that film** ich will den Film unbedingt sehen; **I'm ~ing to hear his reaction** ich bin sehr auf seine Reaktion gespannt; **how I ~ for a cup of tea/a shower** wie ich mich nach einer Tasse Tee/einer Dusche sehne

long: long-acting ADJ (Pharm) mit Langzeitwirkung; **~ medicine** Depotpräparat nt; **longboat** N großes Beiboot; (of Vikings) Wikingerboot nt; **longbow** N (Lang)bogen m; **longcase clock** N Großvateruhr f; **long-chain** ADJ (Chem) langkettig; **long-distance** ADJ **call** Ferngespräch nt; (Brit) **driver** Fernfahrer(in) m(f); **~ flight/race** Langstreckenflug m/-rennen nt; **~ runner** Langstreckenläufer(in) m(f); **~ running** Langstreckenlauf m; **journey/travel** Fernreise f/-reisen pl; **~ train** Fernverkehrszug m; **~ bus** (Fern)reisebus m, Überlandbus m ADV **to call ~** ein Ferngespräch führen; **long division** N schriftliche Division; **long-drawn-out** ADJ speech, argument langatmig; meeting ausgedehnt, in die Länge gezogen; affair, war sich lange hinziehend; process langwierig

longed-for ['lɒŋdfɔː'] ADJ ersehnt; **the much ~ cup of tea** die heiß ersehnte Tasse Tee

longevity [lɒn'dʒevɪtɪ] N Langlebigkeit f

long: long-forgotten ADJ längst vergessen; **long-grain** ADJ **~ rice** Langkornreis m; **longhaired** ADJ person, animal langhaarig; **~ cow** Kuh f mit langhaarigem Fell; **longhand** N Langschrift f ADV in Langschrift; **long-haul** ADJ **~ truck driver** Fernfahrer(in) m(f); **longheaded** ADJ (fig) klug, weitblickend, weit blickend; **long hill** N (Ski) Großschanze f; **longhorn** N Longhorn nt

longing ['lɒŋɪŋ] ADJ look sehnsüchtig; eyes sehnsuchtsvoll N Sehnsucht f (for nach); **this sense of ~** diese Sehnsucht; **to have a (great) ~ to do sth** sich (sehr) danach sehnen, etw zu tun

longingly ['lɒŋɪŋlɪ] ADV sehnsüchtig

longish ['lɒŋɪʃ] ADJ ziemlich lang

longitude ['lɒŋgɪtjuːd] N Länge f; **lines of ~** Längengrade pl

longitudinal [ˌlɒŋgɪˈtjuːdɪnəl] ADJ Längs-; **~ direction** Längsrichtung f

longitudinally [ˌlɒŋgɪˈtjuːdɪnəlɪ] ADV der Länge nach

long: long johns PL (inf) lange Unterhosen pl; **long jump** N Weitsprung m; **long jumper** N Weitspringer(in) m(f); **long-legged** ADJ langbeinig; **long-life** ADJ battery etc mit langer Lebensdauer; **long-life milk** N H-Milch f; **long-limbed** ADJ langglied(e)rig; **long-lived** [ˈlɒŋlɪvd] ADJ langlebig; success dauerhaft, von Dauer; **~ trees** Bäume, die lange leben; **long-lost** ADJ person verloren geglaubt; ideals, enthusiasm etc verloren gegangen; **long-playing** ADJ Langspiel-; **~ record** Langspielplatte f; **long-range** ADJ gun mit hoher Reichweite; forecast, plan langfristig; **~ aircraft** Langstreckenflugzeug nt; **~ missile** Langstreckenrakete f; **~ study** Langzeitstudie f; **long-running** ADJ series lange laufend; affair langjährig; feud lange andauernd; **longship** N Wikingerboot nt; **longshoreman** N (US) Hafenarbeiter m; **long shot** N **a** (Phot) Fernaufnahme f **b** (inf) **it's a ~, but it may pay off** es ist gewagt, aber es könnte sich auszahlen; **it was a ~, but it proved to be true** die Vermutung war weit hergeholt, hat sich aber als wahr erwiesen; **that horse is a ~** auf das Pferd zu setzen, ist gewagt; **not by a ~** bei weitem nicht, noch lange nicht; **long sight** N = long-sightedness; **long-sighted** ADJ (Brit lit, fig) weitsichtig; **long-sightedness** N (Brit) Weitsichtigkeit f; (fig) Weitsicht f; **long-standing** ADJ alt; friendship langjährig, alt; interest, invitation schon lange bestehend → **standing**; **long-stay** ADJ (Brit) hospital, patient Langzeit-; car park Dauer-; **long-suffering** ADJ schwer geprüft; **long suit** N (Cards) lange Reihe; (fig) Trumpf m; **long-tailed** ADJ langschwänzig; **long term** N **in the ~** auf lange Sicht gesehen; **to plan for the ~** auf lange Sicht planen; **long-term** ADJ plans, investment, loan, effect, future langfristig; relationship dauerhaft; **~ care insurance** (US) ≈ Pflegeversicherung f; **~ car park** Langzeitparkplatz m; **~ memory** Langzeitgedächtnis nt; **the ~ unemployed** die Langzeitarbeitslosen pl

longueur [lɔ̃ˈgɜːʳ] N (in novel, play etc) Länge f, langweilige Stelle

long: long vacation N (Univ) (Sommer)semesterferien pl; (Sch) große Ferien pl; **long wave** N Langwelle f; **long-wave** ADJ Langwellen-; **~ frequency** Langwellenfrequenz f

longways [ˈlɒŋweɪz] ADV der Länge nach, längs

long: long-winded ADJ umständlich; story, speech langatmig; affair langwierig; **long-windedness** N Langatmigkeit f

loo [luː] N (Brit inf) Klo nt (inf); **to go to the ~** aufs Klo gehen (inf); **in the ~** auf dem Klo (inf)

loofah [ˈluːfə] N Luffa f; (as sponge) Luffa (-schwamm) m

look [lʊk] ✿ 15.2, 15.3 **N a** (= glance) Blick m; **she gave me a dirty ~, I got a dirty ~ from her** sie warf mir einen vernichtenden Blick zu; **she gave me a ~ of disbelief** sie sah mich ungläubig an; **he gave me such a ~!** er hat mir (vielleicht) einen Blick zugeworfen!; **we got some very odd ~s** wir wurden komisch angesehen; **to have** or **take a ~ at sth** sich (dat) etw ansehen; **he had a quick ~ at his watch** er sah kurz auf die Uhr; **can I have a ~?** darf ich mal sehen or gucken (inf)?; **have a ~ at this!** sieh or guck (inf) dir das mal an!; **is it in the dictionary? – have a ~ (and see)** steht das im Wörterbuch? – sieh or guck (inf) mal nach; **let's have a ~** lass mal sehen, zeig mal her; **let's have a ~ at it** lass mal sehen; **let's have a ~ at you** lass dich mal ansehen; **do you want a ~?** willst du mal sehen?; (at the paper) willst du mal hineinsehen or einen Blick hineinwerfen?; **to take a good ~ at sth** sich (dat) etw genau ansehen; **take** or **have a good ~** sehen or gucken (inf) Sie genau hin; **to have a ~ for sth** nach etw umsehen; **I can't find it – have another ~** ich finde es nicht – sieh or guck (inf) noch mal nach; **to have a ~ (a)round** sich umsehen; **shall**

we have a ~ (a)round the town? sollen wir uns (dat) die Stadt ansehen?

b (= air, appearance) Aussehen nt; **there was a ~ of despair in his eyes** ein verzweifelter Blick war in seinen Augen; **he put on a serious ~** er machte ein ernstes Gesicht; **he had the ~ of a sailor** er sah wie ein Seeman aus; **I don't like the ~ of him/this wound** er/die Wunde gefällt mir gar nicht; **by the ~ of him** so, wie er aussieht; **judging by the ~ of the sky** wenn man sich (dat) den Himmel ansieht, so, wie der Himmel aussieht; **to give sth a new ~** einer Sache (dat) ein neues Aussehen verleihen or Gesicht geben; **the town has now taken on a new ~** die Stadt hat ein neues Gesicht bekommen **c looks** PL Aussehen nt; **good ~s** gutes Aussehen; **~s aren't everything** auf das Aussehen allein kommt es nicht an; **you can't judge by ~s alone** man kann nicht nur nach dem Aussehen or Äußeren urteilen; **she began to lose her ~s** sie verlor allmählich ihr gutes Aussehen

VT he ~s his age man sieht ihm sein Alter an; **he's not ~ing himself these days** er sieht in letzter Zeit ganz verändert aus; **he's ~ing his old self again** er ist wieder ganz der Alte; **to ~ one's best** sehr vorteilhaft aussehen; **I want to ~ my best tonight** ich möchte heute Abend besonders gut aussehen; **she ~s best in red** Rot steht ihr am besten; **he ~ed death in the face** er sah dem Tod ins Angesicht (geh) or Auge; **~ what you've done!** sieh or guck (inf) dir mal an, was du da angestellt hast!; **~ what you've done, now she's offended** jetzt hast dus geschafft, nun ist sie beleidigt; **~ what you've made me do** (sieh or schau (dial) or guck (inf) mal,) daran bist du schuld; **can't you ~ what you're doing?** kannst du nicht aufpassen, was du machst?; **~ where you're going!** pass auf, wo du hintrittst!; **just ~ where he's put the car!** sieh or schau (dial) or guck (inf) dir bloß mal an, wo er das Auto abgestellt hat!; **~ who's here!** guck (inf) or schau (dial) mal or sieh doch, wer da ist!

VI a (= see, glance) gucken (inf), schauen (liter, dial); **to ~ (a)round** sich umsehen; **he ~ed in(to) the box** er sah or schaute (dial) or guckte (inf) in die Kiste (hinein); **to ~ carefully** genau hinsehen etc; **to ~ and see** nachsehen etc; **~ here!** hör (mal) zu!; **now ~ here, it wasn't my fault** Moment mal, das war aber nicht meine Schuld; **~, I know you're tired, but …** ich weiß ja, dass du müde bist, aber …; **~, there's a much better solution** da gibt es doch eine wesentlich bessere Lösung; **just ~!** guck mal!; **to ~ the other way** (fig) die Augen verschließen; **to ~ over sb's shoulder** jdm über die Schulter sehen; **to ~ over sb's shoulder** nach hinten sehen; **~ before you leap** (Prov) erst wägen, dann wagen (Prov)

b (= search) suchen, nachsehen

c (= seem) aussehen; **it ~s all right to me** es scheint mir in Ordnung zu sein; **it ~s suspicious to me** es kommt mir verdächtig vor, es sieht verdächtig aus; **how does it ~ to you?** was meinst du dazu?; **I think the cake is done, how does it ~ to you?** ich glaube, der Kuchen ist fertig, was meinst du?; **the car ~s about 10 years old** das Auto sieht so aus, als ob es 10 Jahre alt wäre; **the trophy ~s well on your mantelpiece** die Trophäe macht sich gut auf deinem Kaminsims

d (to ~ like) aussehen wie; **the picture doesn't ~ like him** das Bild sieht ihm nicht ähnlich; **it ~s like rain, it ~s as if it will rain** es sieht nach Regen aus; **it ~s like cheese to me** (I can find,) das sieht wie Käse aus; **it ~s as if we'll be late** es sieht (so) aus, als würden wir zu spät kommen; **the festival ~s like being busy** auf dem Festival wird es wahrscheinlich sehr voll (werden)

e (= face) gehen nach; **this window ~s (toward(s) the) north** dieses Fenster geht nach Norden; **the village ~s toward(s) the forest** das Dorf liegt dem Wald zugewendet

▶ **look about** VI (Brit) sich umsehen (for sth nach etw); **to look about one** sich umsehen; **if**

we look about we might find some more examples wenn wir suchen, finden wir vielleicht noch ein paar Beispiele

▶ **look after** VI +prep obj **a** (= take care of) sich kümmern um; **to look after oneself** (= cook etc) für sich selbst sorgen, sich selbst versorgen; (= be capable, strong etc) auf sich (acc) aufpassen; **he's only looking after his own interests** er handelt nur im eigenen Interesse **b** (temporarily) sehen nach; children aufpassen auf (+acc) **c** (= follow with eyes) nachsehen (+dat)

▶ **look ahead** VI **a** (lit) nach vorne sehen or gucken (inf) **b** (fig) vorausschauen; **when we look ahead to the next 30 years/the future of this country** wenn wir die nächsten 30 Jahre/die Zukunft dieses Landes betrachten; **a good manager is one who can look ahead** ein guter Manager muss Weitblick haben

▶ **look around** VI **a** (generally) sich umsehen **b** (in shop etc) sich umsehen; (+prep obj) sich (dat) ansehen or angucken (inf); **I wanted to look around the exhibition** ich wollte mir die Ausstellung ansehen

▶ **look at** VI +prep obj **a** (= observe) person, object ansehen, anschauen (dial), angucken (inf); **just look at him!** sieh etc dir den mal an!; **look at the time, I'd better go!** so spät ist es schon, ich muss los!; **he looked at his watch** er sah etc auf die Uhr; **look at the blackboard** schau(t) an or auf die Tafel; **don't look directly at the sun** sehen etc Sie nicht direkt in die Sonne; **I can't look at him without feeling …** wenn ich ihn ansehe etc, habe ich immer das Gefühl, dass …; **he/it isn't much to look at** (= not attractive) er/es sieht nicht besonders (gut) aus; (= nothing special) er/es sieht nach nichts aus; **to look at him …** wenn man ihn sieht …

b (= examine) sich (dat) ansehen or -schauen (dial) or -gucken (inf); offer prüfen; **we'll have to look at the financial aspect** wir müssen die finanzielle Seite betrachten; **has the manuscript been looked at yet?** ist das Manuskript schon durchgesehen worden?

c (= view) betrachten, sehen; **they look at life in a different way** sie haben eine andere Einstellung zum Leben, sie sehen das Leben von einer anderen Warte aus

d (= consider) possibilities sich (dat) überlegen; suggestions, offer in Betracht ziehen

▶ **look away** VI **a** (person) wegsehen **b** the house looks away from the sea das Haus liegt vom Meer abgewendet

▶ **look back** VI sich umsehen; (fig) zurückblicken (on sth, to sth auf etw acc); **he's never looked back** (fig inf) es ist ständig mit ihm bergauf gegangen

▶ **look down** VI hinunter-/heruntersehen or -schauen (dial) or -gucken (inf); **we looked down the hole** wir sahen etc ins Loch hinunter; **look down on the valley below** sieh etc ins Tal hinunter

▶ **look down on** VI +prep obj herabsehen auf (+acc); **you shouldn't look down on his attempts to help** du solltest ihn nicht belächeln, wenn er versucht zu helfen

▶ **look for** VI +prep obj **a** (= seek) suchen; **he's looking for trouble** er wird sich (dat) Ärger einhandeln; (actively) er sucht Streit **b** (= expect) erwarten

▶ **look forward to** ✿ 21.2 VI +prep obj sich freuen auf (+acc); **I'm so looking forward to seeing you again** ich freue mich so darauf, dich wiederzusehen; **I look forward to hearing from you** ich hoffe, bald von Ihnen zu hören

▶ **look in** VI **a** (in window etc) hinein-/hereinsehen or -schauen (dial) or -gucken (inf) **b** (= visit) vorbeikommen (on sb bei jdm); **would you look in at Smith's and collect my dress?** kannst du bei Smith vorbeigehen und mein Kleid abholen? **c** (= watch TV) fernsehen

▶ **look into** VI +prep obj **a** to look into sb's face jdm ins Gesicht sehen; **to look into the future** in die Zukunft sehen or blicken **b** (= in-

vestigate) untersuchen; *matter, complaint etc* prüfen

▶ **look on** VI **a** (= *watch*) zusehen, zugucken *(inf)* **b to look onto** *(window)* (hinaus)gehen auf (+*acc*); *(building)* liegen an (+*dat*) **c** +*prep obj (also* **look upon**) betrachten, ansehen; **to look on sb as a friend** jdn als Freund betrachten; **I look on him as a good doctor** ich halte ihn für einen guten Arzt; **to look on sb with respect** Achtung *or* Respekt vor jdm haben; **employers look favourably** *(Brit) or* **favorably** *(US)* **on people with experience** Arbeitgeber bevorzugen Leute mit Erfahrung

▶ **look out** VI **a** (*of window etc*) hinaus-/heraussehen *or* -schauen *(dial) or* -gucken *(inf)*; **to look out (of) the window** zum Fenster hinaussehen *etc*, aus dem Fenster sehen *etc* **b** *(building etc)* **to look out on** *or* **over sth** einen Blick auf etw *(acc)* haben **c** (= *take care*) aufpassen; **look out!** pass auf!, Vorsicht! **VT** *sep* heraussuchen

▶ **look out for** VI +*prep obj* **a** (= *keep watch for*) **we'll look out for you at the station/after the meeting** wir werden auf dem Bahnhof/nach der Versammlung nach dir Ausschau halten; **look out for pickpockets/his left hook** nimm dich vor Taschendieben/seinem linken Haken in Acht, pass auf Taschendiebe/auf seinen linken Haken auf; **the bouncers were told to look out for troublemakers** die Rausschmeißer sollten auf Unruhestifter achten *or* Acht geben; **you must look out for spelling mistakes/snakes** Sie müssen auf Rechtschreibfehler/Schlangen achten

b (= *seek*) *new job* sich umsehen nach; *new staff, ideas* suchen

c (= *take care of*) sich kümmern um

▶ **look over** VT *sep papers, notes etc* durchsehen; *house* sich *(dat)* ansehen

▶ **look round** VI *(esp Brit)* = **look around**

▶ **look through** **VI** durchsehen *or* -schauen *(dial) or* -gucken *(inf) (prep obj* durch); **he stopped at the window and looked through** er blieb am Fenster stehen und sah *etc* hinein/herein; **he looked through the window** er sah *etc* zum Fenster hinein/herein/hinaus/heraus; **to look straight through sb** durch jdn hindurchgucken **VT** *sep* (= *examine*) durchsehen; (= *read*) durchlesen

▶ **look to** VI +*prep obj* **a** (= *rely on*) sich verlassen auf (+*acc*); **they looked to him to solve the problem** sie verließen sich darauf, dass er das Problem lösen würde; **we look to you for support** wir rechnen auf Ihre *or* mit Ihrer Hilfe; **we look to you to lead the country** wir rechnen damit *or* zählen darauf, dass Sie das Land führen; **there's no point in looking to him for help** es ist sinnlos, von ihm Hilfe zu erwarten; **we look to you for guidance** wir wenden uns an Sie um Rat

b to look to the future in die Zukunft sehen *or* blicken

c (= *look after*) sich kümmern um; **look to it that ...** sieh zu, dass ...

▶ **look up** **VI** **a** *(lit)* aufsehen *or* -blicken; **don't look up** guck nicht hoch *(inf)* **b** (= *improve*) besser werden; *(shares, prices)* steigen; **things are looking up** es geht bergauf **VT** *sep* **a to look sb up and down** jdn von oben bis unten ansehen *or* mustern **b** (= *visit*) **to look sb up** bei jdm vorbeischauen, jdn besuchen **c** (= *seek*) *word* nachschlagen; *phone number, address* heraussuchen

▶ **look upon** VI +*prep obj* = **look on c**

▶ **look up to** VI +*prep obj* **to look up to sb** zu jdm aufsehen; **he was always looked up to** andere haben immer zu ihm aufgesehen

look: lookalike N Doppelgänger(in) *m(f)*; **a Rupert Murdoch ~** ein Doppelgänger von Rupert Murdoch; **it's not just another ~** es sieht nicht wie all die anderen aus; **look-around** N **to have** *or* **take a ~** sich umsehen

looked-for ['lʊktfɔːʳ] ADJ (= *expected*) (lang) ersehnt

looker ['lʊkəʳ] N *(inf)* **to be a (good** *or* **real) ~ klasse** aussehen *(inf)*

looker-on ['lʊkərɒn] N Zuschauer(in) *m(f)*, Schaulustige(r) *mf (pej)*

look-in ['lʊkɪn] N *(inf)* Chance *f*; **he didn't get a ~** er hatte keine Chance

-looking [-ˈlʊkɪŋ] ADJ *suf* aussehend; **good--looking** gut aussehend; **she/it is not bad-looking** sie/es sieht nicht schlecht aus

looking glass N Spiegel *m*

lookism ['lʊkɪzəm] N *Bevorzugung von gut aussehenden Menschen*

look: lookout N **a** (= *tower etc*) *(Mil)* Ausguck *m*; **~ post/station/tower** Beobachtungsposten *m*/-station *f*/-turm *m* **b** (= *person*) *(Mil)* Wacht- *or* Beobachtungsposten *m*; **the thieves had a ~ on the building opposite** einer der Diebe stand auf dem gegenüberliegenden Gebäude Wache *or* Schmiere *(inf)* **c** (= *keep*) **to keep a ~** Ausschau halten; **to be on the ~ for, to keep a ~ for →** **look out for d** (= *prospect*) Aussichten *pl*; **it's a grim ~ for us** es sieht schlecht aus für uns **e** *(inf:* = *worry)* **that's his ~** das ist sein Problem! **look--over** N **to give sth a ~** (sich *dat*) etw flüchtig ansehen; (= *check*) etw flüchtig (über)prüfen; **look-see** N *(inf)* **to have a ~** nachgucken *(inf) or* -sehen *(dial) or* -sehen; **look-through** N *(inf)* Durchsicht *f*; **would you have a ~?** können Sie sich das mal durchsehen?; **to give sth a quick ~** etw kurz durchsehen

loom[1] [luːm] N Webstuhl *m*

loom[2] VI *(also* **loom ahead** *or* **up**) *(lit, fig)* sich abzeichnen; *(storm)* heraufziehen; *(disaster)* sich zusammenbrauen; *(danger)* drohen; *(difficulties)* sich auftürmen; *(exams)* bedrohlich näherrücken; **the ship ~ed (up) out of the mist** das Schiff tauchte bedrohlich aus dem Nebel (auf); **the threat of unemployment was ~ing on the horizon** Arbeitslosigkeit zeichnete sich bedrohlich am Horizont ab; **the threat of war ~s a-head** ein Krieg zeichnet sich bedrohlich ab; **the fear of a sudden attack ~ed in his mind** er hatte große Angst vor einem plötzlichen Angriff; **to ~ large** eine große Rolle spielen; **the skyscraper ~s over the city** der Wolkenkratzer ragt über die Stadt

loon[1] [luːn] N *(Orn)* Seetaucher *m*

loon[2] N *(inf)* Blödmann *m (inf)*

loon pants, loons [luːnz] PL *enge Hüfthose mit Schlag*

loony ['luːnɪ] *(inf)* **ADJ** (+*er*) bekloppt *(inf)* **N** Verrückte(r) *mf (inf)*, Irre(r) *mf*

loony: loony bin N *(inf)* Klapsmühle *f (inf)*; **loony left** *(Brit, Pol) (pej inf)* **the ~** die radikale Linke **ADJ ATTR** linksradikal

loop [luːp] N **a** (= *curved shape*) Schlaufe *f*; *(of wire)* Schlinge *f*; *(of river, Rail)* Schleife *f*; *(Med)* Spirale *f*; **to knock** *or* **throw sb for a ~** *(esp US inf)* jdn völlig umhauen *(inf)* **b** *(Aviat)* Looping *m*; **to ~ the ~** einen Looping machen **c** *(Comput)* Schleife *f* **VT** *rope etc* schlingen *(round* um); **to ~ a rope through a ring** ein Seil durch einen Ring ziehen; **she ~ed her arm through his** sie hängte sich bei ihm ein **VI** *(rope etc)* sich schlingen; *(line, road etc)* eine Schleife machen; **the road ~s (a)round the fields** die Straße schlängelt sich um die Felder

▶ **loop back** **VT** *sep* **loop the wire back around the lid** biegen Sie den Draht zurück um den Deckel **VI** **a** *(road)* eine Schleife machen **b** *(per-son)* in einem Bogen zurückkehren; **this wire has to loop back** dieser Draht muss zurückgebogen werden **b** *(Comput)* **the program then loops back to ...** die Programmschleife wird dann ab ... nochmals durchlaufen

loop: loophole N *(Mil)* Schießscharte *f*; *(fig)* Hintertürchen *nt*; **a ~ in the law** eine Lücke im Gesetz; **loopline** N *(Rail)* Schleife *f*

loopy ['luːpɪ] ADJ (+*er*) *(Brit inf)* bekloppt *(inf)*; **to go ~** durchdrehen *(inf)*

loose [luːs] **ADJ** (+*er*) **a** (= *not tight, movable*) *board, button* lose; *dress, collar* weit; *tooth, bandage, knot, screw, soil, weave* locker; *limbs* beweg-

lich, locker; **he kept his change ~ in his pocket** er hatte sein Kleingeld lose in der Tasche; **a ~ connection** *(Elec)* ein Wackelkontakt *m*; **to come** *or* **work ~** *(screw, handle etc)* sich lockern; *(sole, cover etc)* sich (los)lösen; *(button)* abgehen; **to hang ~** lose herunterhängen; **her hair hung ~** sie trug ihr Haar offen; **to have ~ bowels** Durchfall haben; **just stay** *or* **hang ~** *(inf)* bleib cool *(inf)*; **to sell sth ~** (= *not pre-packed*) etw lose verkaufen

b (= *free*) **to break** *or* **get ~** *(person, animal)* sich losreißen *(from* von); *(ship)* sich (von der Vertäuung) losreißen; *(from group of players etc)* sich trennen, sich lösen; (= *break out*) ausbrechen; *(from commitment, parental home etc)* sich freimachen *(from* von); **to run ~** frei herumlaufen; *(children)* unbeaufsichtigt herumlaufen; **to turn** *or* **let** *or* **set ~** *(animal)* frei herumlaufen lassen; *prisoner* freilassen; *imagination* freien Lauf lassen; **to let ~ political forces that will be difficult to control** politische Kräfte entfesseln *or* freisetzen, die nur schwer unter Kontrolle zu bringen sind; **I let him ~ on the garden** ich ließ ihn auf den Garten los; **to be at a ~ end** *(fig)* nichts mit sich anzufangen wissen; **to tie up the ~ ends** *(fig)* ein paar offene *or* offen stehende Probleme lösen

c (= *not exact, vague*) *translation* frei; *account, thinking, planning* ungenau; *connection* lose; **in a ~ sense** im weiteren Sinne; (= *approximately*) grob gesagt

d (= *informal*) *group, alliance, organization, arrangement* lose, locker

e (= *too free, immoral*) *conduct* lose; *morals* locker; *person* unmoralisch, lose; **a ~ life** ein lockerer Lebenswandel; **a ~ woman** eine Frau mit lockerem Lebenswandel; **in that bar you get ~ women** in der Bar findest du lose Mädchen; **do you think that's being ~?** meinst du, das ist unmoralisch?; **to have a ~ tongue** nichts für sich behalten können; **~ talk** leichtfertiges Gerede

N *(inf)* **to be on the ~** *(prisoners, dangerous animals)* frei herumlaufen; **he was on the ~ in Paris** er machte Paris unsicher; **the troops were on the ~ in the city** die Truppen wüteten in der Stadt; **oh dear, when these two are on the ~** wehe, wenn sie losgelassen!

VT **a** (= *free*) befreien

b (= *untie*) losmachen

c (= *slacken*) lockern

d *(also* **loose off**) *bullet, missile* abfeuern; *arrow* schießen; *gun* feuern; *(fig)* tirade, curse loslassen; **to ~ off a volley** *or* **stream of abuse at sb** eine Schimpfkanonade auf jdn loslassen

loose: loosebox N Box *f*; **loose cannon** N **to be a ~** (= *uncontrollable*) unkontrollierbar sein; (= *dangerous*) gemeingefährlich sein; **loose change** N Kleingeld *nt*; **loose chippings** PL *(on roadway)* Rollsplitt *m*; **loose covers** PL Überzüge *pl*; **loose-fitting** ADJ weit; **loose-leaf** N Ringbuch *nt*; **~ book** Loseblattausgabe *f*; **~ pad** Ringbucheinlage *f*; **loose-limbed** ADJ (= *lithe*) gelenkig, beweglich; (= *gangling*) schlaksig; **loose-living** ADJ verkommen, lose

loosely ['luːslɪ] ADV **a** lose, locker; *knit, weave* locker; **in hot countries it's better to be ~ dressed in robes** in warmen Ländern trägt man besser weit geschnittene *or* lose hängende Kleider; **his hands dangled ~ from his wrists** er ließ seine Hände locker baumeln; **he held her hand ~ in his** er hielt ihre Hand locker in der seinen

b (= *imprecisely*) **~ speaking** grob gesagt; **~ translated** frei übersetzt; **~ based on Shakespeare** frei nach Shakespeare; **the character is ~ based on X** die Figur ist frei nach X gestaltet; **what is ~ termed socialist realism** das, was man ganz allgemein als sozialistischen Realismus bezeichnet; **I was using the word rather ~** ich habe das Wort ziemlich frei gebraucht; **they are ~ connected** sie hängen lose zusammen

c (= *informally*) *organized, structured* lose; **a ~ knit group** eine lose Gruppe

d *behave* unmoralisch; **he lives ~** er führt ein loses *or* lockeres Leben

loosen ['luːsn] **VT a** (= *free*) befreien; *tongue* lösen **b** (= *untie*) losmachen, lösen **c** (= *slacken*) lockern; *belt* lockern, weiter machen; *soil* auflockern; *collar* aufmachen; *reins* locker lassen; **to ~ one's grip on sth** (*lit*) seinen Griff um etw lockern; (*fig*) *on the party, on power* etw nicht mehr so fest im Griff haben **VI** sich lockern

▶ **loosen up** **VT** *sep muscles* lockern; *soil* auflockern **VI** (*muscles*) locker werden; (*athlete*) sich (auf)lockern; (= *relax*) auftauen

looseness ['luːsnɪs] N Lockerheit *f*; (*of clothes*) Weite *f*; (*of translation*) Ungenauigkeit *f*; (*of translation*) Freiheit *f*; **~ of the bowels** zu rege Darmtätigkeit; **the ~ of her conduct** ihr loses *or* unmoralisches Benehmen; **the ~ of the book's structure** die lockere Struktur des Buches

loot [luːt] **N** Beute *f*; (*dated inf*: = *money*) Zaster *m* (*dated sl*) **VTI** plündern

looter ['luːtə'] N Plünderer *m*

lop [lɒp] VT (*also* **lop off**) abhacken

lope [ləʊp] VI in großen Sätzen springen; (*hare*) hoppeln; **he ~d along beside her** er lief mit großen Schritten neben ihr her; **to ~ off** davonspringen

lop-eared ['lɒp‚ɪəd] ADJ mit Hängeohren

lop ears PL Hänge- *or* Schlappohren (*inf*) *pl*

lopsided ['lɒp'saɪdɪd] ADJ schief; (*fig*) einseitig

loquacious [lə'kweɪʃəs] ADJ redselig

loquacity [lə'kwæsɪtɪ] N Redseligkeit *f*

lord [lɔːd] **N a** (= *master, ruler*) Herr *m*; **~ and master** Herr und Meister *m*; (*hum*: = *husband*) Herr und Gebieter *m*; **tobacco ~s** Tabakkönige *pl*

b (*Brit*: = *nobleman*) Lord *m*; **the (House of) Lords** das Oberhaus; **my ~** (*to bishop*) Exzellenz; (*to noble, in English contexts*) Mylord; (*to baron*) Herr Baron; (*to earl, viscount*) Euer Erlaucht; (*to judge*) Euer Ehren

c (*Brit*: = *important official*) **First Lord of the Admiralty** Stabschef *m* der Marine

d (*Rel*) Lord Herr *m*; **the Lord (our) God** Gott, der Herr; **(good) Lord!** (*inf*) ach, du lieber Himmel! (*inf*), (ach,) du meine Güte! (*inf*); (*annoyed*) mein Gott! (*inf*); **Lord help him!** (*inf*) (dann) Gnade ihm Gott!; **Lord knows** (*inf*) wer weiß; **Lord knows I've tried often enough** ich habs weiß Gott oft genug versucht

VT to ~ it das Zepter schwingen; **to ~ it over sb** jdn herumkommandieren

Lord Chancellor N (*Brit*) Lordsiegelbewahrer *m*, Lordkanzler *m*

Lord Justice N (*Brit*) Richter an einem Berufungsgericht

lordliness ['lɔːdlɪnɪs] N Vornehmheit *f*; (= *haughtiness*) Überheblichkeit *f*, Arroganz *f*

lordly ['lɔːdlɪ] ADJ (+*er*) **a** (= *magnificent*) vornehm; *house* (hoch)herrschaftlich **b** (= *proud, haughty*) hochmütig, arrogant; *tone of voice* herrisch, gebieterisch

Lord Mayor N (*Brit*) ≈ Oberbürgermeister *m*

Lord's Day ['lɔːdzdeɪ] N (*Rel*) **the ~** der Tag des Herrn

Lordship ['lɔːdʃɪp] N (*Brit*: = *title*) Lordschaft *f*; **His/Your ~** Seine/Eure Lordschaft; (*to bishop*) Seine/Eure Exzellenz; (*to judge*) Seine/Euer Ehren *or* Gnaden

Lord's Prayer ['lɔːdz'prɛə'] N (*Rel*) **the ~** das Vaterunser

Lord's Supper ['lɔːdz'sʌpə'] N (*Rel*) **the ~** das (Heilige) Abendmahl

lore [lɔː'] N Überlieferungen *pl*; **in local ~** nach hiesiger Überlieferung; **plant ~** Pflanzenkunde *f*

lorgnette [lɔː'njet] N Lorgnette *f*

lorry ['lɒrɪ] N (*Brit*) Last(kraft)wagen *m*, Lkw *m*, Laster *m* (*inf*); **it fell off the back of a ~** (*hum inf*) ich hab/er hat etc das „gefunden" (*hum inf*)

lorry driver N (*Brit*) Last(kraft)wagenfahrer(in) *m(f)*, Lkw-Fahrer(in) *m(f)*

lose [luːz] *pret, ptp* **lost** **VT a** (*generally*) verlieren; *pursuer* abschütteln; *one's French* vergessen,

verlernen; *prize* nicht bekommen; **to ~ one's job/(driving) licence** (*Brit*) *or* **(driver's) license** (*US*) die Stelle/den Führerschein verlieren; **many men ~ their hair** vielen Männern gehen die Haare aus; **the cat has lost a lot of hair** die Katze hat viel Haar verloren; **they lost 100 planes in one battle** sie haben in einer Schlacht 100 Flugzeuge verloren; **the shares have lost 15% in a month** die Aktien sind in einem Monat um 15% gefallen; **to ~ one's way** (*lit*) sich verirren; (*fig*) die Richtung verlieren; **you will ~ nothing by helping them** es kann dir nicht schaden, wenn du ihnen hilfst; **they have nothing/a lot to ~** sie haben nichts/viel zu verlieren; **that mistake lost him his job/her friendship/the game** dieser Fehler kostete ihn die Stellung/ihre Freundschaft/den Sieg; **she lost her brother in the war** sie hat ihren Bruder im Krieg verloren; **he lost the use of his legs in the accident** seit dem Unfall kann er seine Beine nicht mehr bewegen; **he lost himself in his work** er ging ganz in seiner Arbeit auf; **he likes to ~ himself in his memories** er verliert sich gern in Erinnerungen; **he's lost the desire to live** er hat keinen Lebenswillen mehr; **to ~ no time in doing sth** etw sofort tun; **we lost valuable time just talking** wir haben beim Reden wertvolle Zeit verloren

b **my watch lost three hours** meine Uhr ist drei Stunden nachgegangen

c **you've lost me now with all this abstract argument** bei dieser abstrakten Argumentation komme ich nicht mehr mit

d (= *not catch*) *opportunity* verpassen; *words* nicht mitbekommen; **to ~ no opportunity to do sth** keine Gelegenheit verpassen, etw zu tun

e (*inf*: = *go crazy*) **to ~ it** durchdrehen (*inf*); **he's finally lost it** jetzt ist er völlig durchgedreht (*inf*)

f (*passive usages*) **to be lost** (*things*) verschwunden sein; (*people*) verloren haben; (*fig*) verloren sein; (*words*) untergehen; **I can't follow the reasoning, I'm lost** ich kann der Argumentation nicht folgen, ich verstehe nichts mehr; **he was soon lost in the crowd** er hatte sich bald in der Menge verloren; **to be lost at sea** auf See geblieben sein; (*ship*) auf See vermisst sein; **the ship was lost with all hands** das Schiff war mit der ganzen Besatzung untergegangen; **all is (not) lost!** (noch ist nicht) alles verloren!; **to get lost** sich verlaufen *or* verirren; (*boxes etc*) verloren gehen; **I got lost after the second chapter** nach dem zweiten Kapitel kam ich nicht mehr mit; **to get lost in the post/move** in der Post/beim Umzug verloren gehen; **get lost!** (*inf*) verschwinde! (*inf*); **to look lost** (ganz) verloren aussehen; (*fig*) ratlos *or* hilflos aussehen; **you look (as though you're) lost, can I help you?** haben Sie sich verlaufen *or* verirrt, kann ich Ihnen behilflich sein?; **to give sb up for lost** jdn verloren geben; **to give sth up for lost** etw abschreiben; **he was lost to science** er war für die Wissenschaft verloren; **to be lost to all finer feelings** er hat keinen Sinn für höhere Gefühle; **I'm lost without my watch** ohne meine Uhr bin ich verloren *or* aufgeschmissen (*inf*); **classical music is lost on him** er hat keinen Sinn für klassische Musik; **the joke/remark was lost on her** der Witz/die Bemerkung kam bei ihr nicht an; **the irony was not lost on me** ich verstand die Ironie durchaus; **to be lost for words** sprachlos sein; **to be lost in thought** in Gedanken versunken sein; **to be lost in one's reading/playing** in seine Lektüre/sein Spiel versunken sein; **to be lost to the world** für die Welt verloren sein

VI verlieren; (*watch*) nachgehen; **you can't ~** du kannst nichts verlieren; **the novel ~s a lot in the film** der Roman verliert in der Verfilmung sehr; **you will not ~ by helping him** es kann dir nicht schaden, wenn du ihm hilfst

▶ **lose out** VI (*inf*) schlecht wegkommen (*inf*), den Kürzeren ziehen (*on* bei); **to lose out to sb/sth** von jdm/etw verdrängt werden

loser ['luːzə'] N Verlierer(in) *m(f)*; **he is a good/bad ~** er ist ein guter/schlechter Verlierer; **he's a born ~** er ist der geborene Verlierer; **what a ~!** (*inf*) was für eine Null! (*inf*)

losing ['luːzɪŋ] ADJ **the ~ team** die unterlegene Mannschaft; **to fight a ~ battle** einen aussichtslosen Kampf führen; **the ~ side/party** die Verliererseite; **to be on the ~ side** verlieren **N ~s** Verluste *pl*

loss [lɒs] **a** Verlust *m*; *hair* ~ Haarausfall *m*; *weight* ~ Gewichtsverlust *m*; **~ of memory, memory ~** Gedächtnisverlust *m*; **progressive ~ of memory** Gedächtnisschwund *m*; **the ~ of the last three games upset the team** die letzten drei Niederlagen brachten die Mannschaft aus der Fassung; **the factory closed with the ~ of 300 jobs** bei der Schließung der Fabrik gingen 300 Stellen verloren; **~ of speed/time** *etc* Geschwindigkeits-/Zeitverlust *m etc*; **~ of picture/sound** (*TV*) Bild-/Tonausfall *m*; **to feel a sense of ~** ein Gefühl *nt* des Verlusts haben; **he felt her ~ very deeply** ihr Tod war ein schwerer Verlust für ihn; **there was a heavy ~ of life** viele kamen ums Leben

b (= *amount, sth lost*) Verlust *m*; *job* ~**es** Stellenkürzungen *pl*; **how many ~es has the team had so far?** wie viele Spiele hat die Mannschaft bis jetzt verloren?; **the army suffered heavy ~es** die Armee erlitt schwere Verluste; **Conservative ~es in the North** Verluste *pl* der Konservativen im Norden; **his business is running at a ~** er arbeitet mit Verlust; **to sell sth at a ~** etw mit Verlust verkaufen; **it's your ~** es ist deine Sache; **he's no ~** er ist kein (großer) Verlust; **you're a great ~ to the civil service** (= *should have been a civil servant*) an dir ist ein Beamter verloren gegangen; **a dead ~** (*Brit inf*) ein böser Reinfall (*inf*); (= *person*) ein hoffnungsloser Fall (*inf*); **total ~** Totalverlust *m*; **to cut one's ~es** (*fig*) Schluss machen, ehe der Schaden (noch) größer wird, Schadensbegrenzung *f* betreiben

c **to be at a ~** nicht mehr weiterwissen; **we are at a ~ with this problem** wir stehen dem Problem ratlos gegenüber; **we are at a ~ for what to do** wir wissen nicht mehr aus noch ein; **to be at a ~ to explain sth** etw nicht erklären können; **we are at a ~ to say why** wir haben keine Ahnung, warum; **to be at a ~ for words** nicht wissen, was man sagen soll; **he's never at a ~ for words/an excuse** er ist nie um Worte/eine Ausrede verlegen

loss: **loss adjuster** N (*Brit Insur*) Schadenssachverständige(r) *mf*; **loss leader** N Lockvogelangebot *nt*; **lossmaker** N (= *company*) mit Verlust arbeitender Betrieb; (= *transaction*) Verlustgeschäft *nt*; (= *product*) Verlustbringer *m*; **lossmaking** ADJ **a** **~ company** ein Unternehmen, das mit Verlust arbeitet; **loss ratio** N (= *Insur*) Schadensquote *f*

lost [lɒst] *pret, ptp of* **lose** ADJ *attr* verloren; *support* verloren gegangen; *art* ausgestorben; *civilization* untergegangen, versunken; *cause* aussichtslos; (= *missing*) *person* vermisst; *dog, cat* entlaufen; (= *mislaid*) *book, glasses etc* verlegt; (= *missed*) *opportunity* verpasst; **I was groping on the floor for a ~ contact lens** ich tastete auf dem Fußboden nach einer heruntergefallenen Kontaktlinse; **he is mourning his ~ wife** er betrauert den Verlust seiner Frau

lost: **lost-and-found (department)** N (*US*) Fundbüro *nt*; **lost property** N (*Brit*) **a** (= *items*) Fundstücke *pl* **b** = **lost property office**; **lost property office** N (*Brit*) Fundbüro *nt*

lot[1] [lɒt] **N a** (*for deciding*) Los *nt*; **by ~** durch Losentscheid, durch das Los; **to cast** *or* **draw ~s** losen, Lose ziehen; **to draw ~s for sth** etw verlosen; **to draw ~s for a task** eine Aufgabe auslosen; **they drew ~s to see who would begin** sie losten aus, wer anfangen sollte

b (= *destiny*) Los *nt*; **failure was his ~ in life** es war sein Los, immer zu versagen; **it falls to my ~ to tell him** mir fällt die Aufgabe zu, es ihm zu sagen; **to throw in one's ~ with sb** sich mit jdm zusammentun; **to improve one's ~** seine Lage verbessern

c (= *plot*) Parzelle *f*; (*Film*) Filmgelände *nt*; **building ~** Bauplatz *m*; **parking ~** (*US*) Parkplatz *m*; **all over the ~** (*US inf*) (= *everywhere*) überall; (= *in confusion*) völlig durcheinander **d** (= *articles of same kind*) Posten *m*; (*at auction*) Los *nt* **e** (*esp Brit*: = *group of things*) **where shall I put this ~?** wo soll ich das hier or das Zeug (*inf*) hintun?; **can you carry that ~ by yourself?** kannst du das (alles) alleine tragen?; **divide the books up into three ~s** teile die Bücher in drei Teile or Stapel ein; **we moved the furniture in two ~s** wir haben die Möbel in zwei Fuhren befördert; **I'd just finished marking the papers when he gave me another ~** ich war gerade mit dem Korrigieren fertig, da gab er mir einen neuen Packen or Stoß or noch eine Ladung (*inf*); **we bought a new ~ of cutlery** wir haben uns (ein) neues Besteck gekauft **f** (*esp Brit*) **he/she is a bad ~** (*inf*) er/sie taugt nichts, er/sie ist eine miese Type (*inf*); **they are a bad ~** (*inf*) das ist ein übles Pack **g** (*esp Brit inf*: = *group*) Haufen *m*; **that ~ in the next office** die Typen vom Büro nebenan (*inf*); **I'm fed up with you ~** ich hab die Nase voll von euch allen (*inf*) or von euch Bande (*inf*); **are you ~ coming to the pub?** kommt ihr (alle) in die Kneipe?; **us ~ should stick together** wir sollten alle zusammenhalten; **bring your ~ with you** bring die ganze Mannschaft mit **h** the ~ (*inf*) alle; alles; **that's the ~** das ist alles, das wärs (*inf*); **the whole ~ of them** sie alle; **he's eaten the ~** er hat alles aufgegessen; **big ones, little ones, the ~!** Große, Kleine, alle!

lot² **N** a ~, ~s viel; **a ~ of money** viel or eine Menge Geld; **a ~ of books, ~s of books** viele or eine Menge Bücher; **such a ~** so viel; **what a ~!** was für eine Menge!; **what a ~ of time you take to get ready** wie lange du nur brauchst, um dich fertig zu machen; **what a ~ you've got** du hast aber viel; **how much has he got? – ~s or a ~** wie viel hat er? – jede Menge (*inf*) or viel; **quite a ~ of books** ziemlich viele or eine ganze Menge Bücher; **such a ~ of books** so viele Bücher; **an awful ~ of things to do** furchtbar viel zu tun; **he made ~s and ~s of mistakes** er hat eine Unmenge Fehler gemacht; **I want ~s and ~s** ich will jede Menge (*inf*); **we see a ~ of John these days** wir sehen John in letzter Zeit sehr oft; **I'd give a ~ to know ...** ich würde viel drum geben, wenn ich wüsste ... **ADV** a ~, ~s viel; **things have changed a ~** es hat sich vieles geändert; **I like him a ~** ich mag ihn sehr; **I feel ~s** or **a ~ better** es geht mir sehr viel besser; **a ~ you care!** dich interessiert das überhaupt nicht!

loth ADJ = **loath**

Lothario [ləʊˈθɑːrɪˌəʊ] N (*hum*) Don Juan *m*

lotion [ˈləʊʃən] N Lotion *f*

lottery [ˈlɒtərɪ] N Lotterie *f*; **life is a ~** das Leben ist ein Glücksspiel

lotus [ˈləʊtəs] N Lotos *m*

lotus-eater [ˈləʊtəsˌiːtəʳ] N Lotophage *m*, Lotosesser(in) *m(f)*; (*fig*) Müßiggänger(in) *m(f)*

lotus position N Lotossitz *m*

louche [luːʃ] ADJ (= *disreputable*) *person, place* verrufen, berüchtigt

loud [laʊd] **ADJ** (*+er*) **a** laut; *protest, criticism, complaint* lautstark; **he was ~ in his praise of the concert** er lobte das Konzert überschwänglich; **to be ~ in one's condemnation of/opposition to sth** etw lautstark verurteilen/ablehnen **b** (= *obtrusive*) *behaviour* aufdringlich; (= *garish*) *colour* grell, schreiend; *tie, clothes* knallbunt **ADV** laut; **~ and clear** laut und deutlich; **to say/read sth out ~** etw laut sagen/lesen; **to laugh/think out ~** laut lachen/denken

loud-hailer [ˌlaʊdˈheɪləʳ] N Megafon *nt*, Megaphon *nt*, Flüstertüte *f* (*inf*); (*not hand-held*) Lautsprecher *m*

loudly [ˈlaʊdlɪ] ADV **a** laut; *complain, condemn, oppose, criticize* lautstark **b** (= *garishly*) *clothed* knallbunt; *coloured* grell; **he was ~ dressed in blue** er war in ein grelles Blau gekleidet

loud: loudmouth N (*inf*) Großmaul *nt* (*inf*); **loudmouthed** [ˈlaʊdˌmaʊðd] ADJ (*inf*) großmäulig (*inf*)

loudness [ˈlaʊdnɪs] N **a** (= *volume*) Lautstärke *f*; **the ~ of his voice** seine laute Stimme **b** (= *obtrusiveness*) Aufdringlichkeit *f*; (*of colour*) Grellheit *f*; (*of clothes*) Buntheit *f*

loudspeaker [ˌlaʊdˈspiːkəʳ] N Lautsprecher *m*; (*of hi-fi also*) Box *f*

lough [lɒx] N (*Ir*) See *m*; (= *sea lough*) Meeresarm *m*

lounge [laʊndʒ] **N** (*in house*) Wohnzimmer *nt*; (*in hotel*) Gesellschaftsraum *m*; (= *lounge bar: on liner etc*) Salon *m*; (*at airport*) Warteraum *m*; **TV ~** Fernsehraum *m* **VI** faulenzen; (= *sit about*) (*Brit*) or **around** herumliegen/-sitzen; **to ~ against a wall** sich lässig gegen eine Mauer lehnen; **to ~ back in a chair** sich in einem Stuhl zurücklehnen

lounge: lounge bar N Salon *m* (*vornehmerer Teil einer Gaststätte*); **lounge chair** N Klubsessel *m*; **lounge lizard** N Salonlöwe *m*

lounger [ˈlaʊndʒəʳ] N **a** Nichtstuer(in) *m(f)*, Faulenzer(in) *m(f)* **b** (*Brit*: = *reclining chair*) Ruhesessel *m*

lounge: lounge suit N Straßenanzug *m*; **lounge suite** N Couch- or Polstergarnitur *f*

loupe [luːp] N (*for jewellers and watchmakers*) Lupe *f*

lour, lower [ˈlaʊəʳ] VI (*person*) ein finsteres Gesicht machen; (*clouds*) sich türmen; **a threatening sky ~ed** der Himmel war bedrohlich dunkel or überzogen

louring [ˈlaʊərɪŋ] ADJ finster

louse [laʊs] **N** *pl* **lice** **a** (*Zool*) Laus *f* **b** (*inf*) fieser Kerl (*inf*); **he behaved like a real ~ to her** er war richtig fies zu ihr (*inf*), er hat sich richtig fies benommen (*inf*) **VT** (*sl*) **to ~ sth up** etw vermasseln (*inf*); *friendship* etw kaputtmachen (*inf*)

lousy [ˈlaʊzɪ] ADJ **a** verlaust; **he is ~ with money** (*inf*) er ist stinkreich (*inf*); **this place is ~ with cops** (*inf*) hier wimmelt es nur so von Polizei (*inf*) **b** (*inf*: = *very bad*) mies (*inf*); *trick etc* fies (*inf*); **I'm ~ at arithmetic** in Mathe bin ich mies or miserabel (*inf*); **he is ~ at (playing) golf** or **a ~ golfer** er spielt miserabel Golf (*inf*); **you've done a ~ job** du hast saumäßig gearbeitet (*sl*); **to have ~ luck** saumäßiges Pech haben (*inf*); **to feel ~** sich mies fühlen (*inf*); **I feel ~ about it** mir ist gar nicht wohl bei dem Gedanken daran **c** (*inf*: = *meagre*) *offer* lausig (*inf*), mies (*inf*); **a ~ £3** popelige or lausige drei Pfund (*inf*)

lout [laʊt] N Rüpel *m*, Flegel *m*

loutish [ˈlaʊtɪʃ] ADJ rüpelhaft, flegelhaft

louvre, (*US*) **louver** [ˈluːvəʳ] N Jalousie *f*; **~ door** Lamellentür *f*

louvred, (*US*) **louvered** [ˈluːvəd] ADJ Jalousie-; **~ door** Jalousietür *f*; **~ blinds** Jalousie *f*

lovable [ˈlʌvəbl] ADJ liebenswert

lovage [ˈlʌvɪdʒ] N (*Bot*) Liebstöckel *nt* or *m*

love [lʌv] ⊕ 8.4, 21.2, 23.1 **N** a (= *affection*) Liebe *f*; **~ is ...** die Liebe ist ...; **the ~ he has for his wife** die Liebe, die er für seine Frau empfindet; **to have a ~ for** or **of sb/sth** jdn/etw sehr lieben; **he has a great ~ of soccer/music** er ist ein großer Fußballanhänger/Musikliebhaber; **~ of learning** Freude *f* am Lernen; **~ of adventure** Abenteuerlust *f*; **~ of books** Liebe *f* zu Büchern; **~ of God for his creatures** die Liebe Gottes zu seinen Geschöpfen; **~ of (one's) country** Vaterlandsliebe *f*; **for ~** aus Liebe; (= *free*) umsonst; (= *without stakes*) nur zum Vergnügen; **for ~ nor money** nicht für Geld und gute Worte; **for the ~ of** aus Liebe zu; **for the ~ of God!** um Himmels willen!; **he studies history for the ~ of it** er studiert Geschichte aus Liebe zur Sache; **to be in ~ (with sb)** (in jdn) verliebt sein; **to fall in ~ (with sb)** sich (in jdn) verlieben; **there is no ~ lost between them** sie können sich nicht ausstehen; **to make ~ (sexu-**

ally) sich lieben, miteinander schlafen; (*dated*) (= *flirt*) flirten (*to sb* mit jdm); (= *court*) den Hof machen (*dated*) (*to sb* jdm); **to make ~ to sb** (*sexually*) mit jdm schlafen; **I've never made ~** ich habe noch mit keinem/keiner geschlafen; **make ~ to me** liebe mich; **he's good at making ~** er ist gut in der Liebe; **make ~ not war** Liebe, nicht Krieg **b** (= *greetings: in letters etc*) **with all my ~** mit herzlichen Grüßen; **~ from Anna** herzliche Grüße von Anna; **give him my ~** grüß ihn von mir; **to send one's ~** to sb jdn grüßen lassen; **he sends his ~** er lässt grüßen **c** (= *sb/sth causing fondness*) Liebe *f*; **yes, (my) ~** ja, Liebling or Schatz; **she's the ~ of my life** sie ist die große Liebe meines Lebens; **sport is the ~ of her life** Sport ist ihre große Liebe; **he sent some roses to his ~** (*dated*) er schickte seiner Liebsten (*dated*) ein paar Rosen; **the child is a little ~** das Kind ist ein richtiger Schatz **d** (*inf: form of address*) mein Lieber/meine Liebe; **I'm afraid the bus is full, ~** der Bus ist leider voll **e** (*Tennis*) null; **fifteen ~** fünfzehn null **VT** lieben; (= *like*) *thing* gern mögen; **they ~ each other** sie lieben sich; **I ~ tennis** ich mag Tennis sehr gern; (*to play*) ich spiele sehr gern Tennis; **he ~s swimming, he ~s to swim** er schwimmt sehr gern or für sein Leben gern; **don't be sad, you know we all ~ you** sei nicht traurig, du weißt doch, dass wir dich alle sehr gern haben; **I'd ~ to be with you all the time** ich wäre so gerne die ganze Zeit mit dir zusammen; **I'd ~ a cup of tea** ich hätte (liebend) gern(e) eine Tasse Tee; **I'd ~ to come** ich würde sehr or liebend gern(e) kommen; **I should ~ to!** sehr or liebend gerne!; **we'd all ~ you to come with us** wir würden uns alle sehr freuen, wenn du mitkommen würdest; **I ~ the way she smiles** ich mag es, wie sie lächelt; **I ~ the way he leaves us to do all the work** (*iro*) ist es nicht toll, wie er uns die ganze Arbeit überlässt (*iro*); **she's going to ~ you for this** (*iro*) das wird sie dir nie vergessen (*iro*); **she's going to ~ that** (*iro*) na, da wird sie sich aber freuen (*iro*) **VI** lieben

love: love affair N Liebschaft *f*, Verhältnis *nt*; **the Americans' ~ with firearms** das innige Verhältnis der Amerikaner zu Schusswaffen; **lovebird** N (*Orn*) Unzertrennliche(r) *m*; (*fig inf*) Turteltaube *f*; **lovebite** N Knutschfleck *m* (*inf*); **love child** N (*dated*) Kind *nt* der Liebe (*dated*)

-loved [-lʌvd] ADJ *suf* -geliebt; **much-loved** viel geliebt; **best-loved** beliebteste(r, s)

love: love game N (*Tennis*) Zunullspiel *nt*; **Rosewall lost 3 ~s** Rosewall verlor 3 Spiele zu null; **love handles** PL (*inf*) Rettungsring *m* (*hum inf*); **love-hate relationship** N Hassliebe *f*; **they have a ~** zwischen ihnen besteht eine Hassliebe; **loveless** ADJ *life, marriage* ohne Liebe; *home, family, environment* lieblos; **love letter** N Liebesbrief *m*; **love life** N Liebesleben *nt*

loveliness [ˈlʌvlɪnɪs] N Schönheit *f*; (*of weather, view also*) Herrlichkeit *f*

lovelorn [ˈlʌvlɔːn] ADJ (*liter*) *person* liebeskrank (*liter*); *song, poem* liebesweh (*liter*)

lovely [ˈlʌvlɪ] **ADJ** (*+er*) (= *beautiful*) wunderschön; *baby* niedlich, reizend; (= *delightful*) herrlich, wunderschön; *joke* herrlich; (= *charming, likeable*) liebenswürdig, nett; *personality* einnehmend; *smile* gewinnend; **the dress looks ~ on you** dieses Kleid steht dir sehr gut; **we had a ~ time** es war sehr schön; **it's ~ and warm in this room** es ist schön warm in diesem Zimmer; **all this ~ money** das ganze schöne Geld; **he made a ~ job of it** er hat das wunderbar gemacht; **have a ~ holiday** (*esp Brit*) or **vacation** (*US*)! schöne Ferien!; **it's been ~ to see you** es war schön, dich zu sehen; **how ~ of you to remember!** wie nett or lieb, dass Sie daran gedacht haben; **what a ~ thing to say!** wie nett, so was zu sagen!

N (*inf*: = *person*) Schöne *f*; **yes, my ~** ja, mein schönes Kind

love: lovemaking N (*sexual*) Liebe *f*; (*dated*: = *flirtation*) Flirt *m*; (*dated*: = *courting*) Liebeswerben *nt* (*dated*); **his expert ~** sein gekonntes Liebesspiel; **love match** N Liebesheirat *f*; **love nest** N Liebesnest *nt*; **love philtre** (*old*), **love potion** N Liebestrank *m*

lover ['lʌvə'] N **a** Liebhaber *m*, Geliebte(r) *m* (*old*, *liter*), Geliebte *f*; **the ~s** die Liebenden *pl*, das Liebespaar; **we were ~s for two years** wir waren zwei Jahre lang zusammen; **Romeo and Juliet were ~s** Romeo und Julia liebten sich; **so she took a ~** da nahm sie sich (*dat*) einen Liebhaber **b a ~ of books** ein(e) Bücherfreund(in) *m(f)*, ein(e) Liebhaber(in) *m(f)* von Büchern; **a ~ of good food** ein(e) Freund(in) *or* Liebhaber(in) *m(f)* von gutem Essen; **music-lover** Musikliebhaber(in) *m(f)* *or* -freund(in) *m(f)*; **soccer ~s** Fußballanhänger *or* -begeisterte *pl*

loverboy ['lʌvəbɔɪ] N (*inf*) unser Freund hier (*inf*); (= *boyfriend*) Freund *m*; **listen, ~** hör mal zu, mein Freund(chen) (*inf*)

love: love rival N Nebenbuhler(in) *m(f)* (*geh*); **love seat** N S-förmiges Sofa, Tete-a-tete *nt*, Tête-à-tête *nt*; **love set** N (*Tennis*) Zunullsatz *m*; **lovesick** ADJ liebeskrank; **to be ~** Liebeskummer *m* haben; **love song** N Liebeslied *nt*; **love story** N Liebesgeschichte *f*; **lovestruck** ADJ liebestoll; **love token** N Liebespfand *nt*; **love triangle** N Dreiecksverhältnis *nt*; **love truncheon** N (*Brit hum sl*: = *penis*) Feuerlöscher *m* (*sl*)

lovey ['lʌvɪ] N (*Brit inf: address*) Schatz *m* (*inf*)

lovey-dovey ['lʌvɪ'dʌvɪ] ADJ (*inf*) turtelig, wie die Turteltauben; **to be all ~** völlig vernarrt ineinander sein (*inf*); **~ couple** (schmusendes) Liebespaar

loving ['lʌvɪŋ] ADJ liebend; *look, disposition, relationship, marriage* liebevoll; **~ kindness** Herzensgüte *f*; (*of God*) Barmherzigkeit *f*; **your ~ son ...** in Liebe euer Sohn ...; **they are such a couple/family** sie gehen so liebevoll miteinander um

loving cup N Pokal *m*

lovingly ['lʌvɪŋlɪ] ADV liebevoll

low¹ [ləʊ] ADJ (+*er*) **a** niedrig; *form of life, musical key* nieder; *bow, note* tief; *density, intelligence* gering; *food supplies* knapp; *pulse* schwach; *quality* gering; *light* gedämpft, schwach; (*pej*) minderwertig (*pej*); (*Ling*) *vowel* offen; (*Math*) *denominator* klein; **the lamp was ~** die Lampe brannte schwach; **the sun was ~ in the sky** die Sonne stand tief am Himmel; **her dress was ~ at the neck** ihr Kleid hatte einen tiefen Ausschnitt; **~ blow** *or* **punch** Tiefschlag *m*; **that punch was a bit ~** der Schlag war etwas tief; **the river is ~** der Fluss hat *or* führt wenig Wasser; **a ridge of ~ pressure** ein Tiefdruckkeil *m*; **~ density housing** aufgelockerte Bauweise; **activity on the stock exchange is at its ~** die Börsentätigkeit hat ihren Tiefstand erreicht; **to be ~ in funds** knapp bei Kasse sein (*inf*)

b (= *not loud or shrill*) **to speak in a ~ voice** leise sprechen

c (= *socially inferior, vulgar*) *birth* nieder, niedrig; *rank, position* untergeordnet, niedrig; *tastes, manners* gewöhnlich, ordinär (*pej*); *character, company* schlecht; *joke, song* geschmacklos, gemein; **I really felt ~ having to tell him that** ich kam mir richtig gemein vor, dass ich ihm das sagen musste; **how ~ can you get!** wie kann man nur so tief sinken!; **~ cunning** Gerissenheit *f*

d (= *weak in health or spirits*) *resistance* schwach, gering; *morale* schlecht; **the patient is rather ~ today** der Patient ist heute nicht auf der Höhe; **to be in ~ health** bei schlechter Gesundheit sein; **to be in ~ spirits** in gedrückter Stimmung sein, bedrückt *or* niedergeschlagen sein; **to feel ~** sich nicht wohl *or* gut fühlen; (*emotionally*) niedergeschlagen sein; **to make sb feel ~** (*events*) jdn mitnehmen, jdm zu schaffen machen; (*people*) jdn niederdrücken *or* bedrücken

ADV *aim* nach unten; *speak, sing* leise; *fly, bow* tief; **they turned the lamps down ~** sie drehten die Lampen herunter; **a dress cut ~ in the back** ein Kleid mit tiefem Rückenausschnitt; **to fall ~** (*morally*) tief sinken; **I would never sink so ~ as to ...** so tief würde ich nie sinken, dass ich ...; **share prices went so ~ that ...** die Aktienkurse fielen so sehr, dass ...; **to buy ~ and sell high** billig kaufen und teuer verkaufen; **to lay sb ~** (*Brit*) (*punch*) jdn zu Boden strecken; (*disease*) jdn befallen; **he's been laid ~ with the flu** (*Brit*) er liegt mit Grippe im Bett; **to play ~** (*Cards*) um einen niedrigen *or* geringen Einsatz spielen; **to run** *or* **get ~** knapp werden; **we are getting ~ on petrol** (*Brit*) *or* **gas** (*US*) uns (*dat*) geht das Benzin aus

N a (*Met*) Tief *nt*; (*fig also*) Tiefpunkt *m*, Tiefstand *m*; **to reach a new ~** einen neuen Tiefstand erreichen; **this represents a new ~ in advertising** so tief ist die Werbung noch nie zuvor gesunken

b (*Aut*, = *low gear*) niedriger Gang

low² N (*of cow*) Muh *nt* **VI** muhen

low: low-alcohol ADJ alkoholarm; **lowball** ADJ (*US inf*) *costs* bewusst zu niedrig veranschlagt; **lowborn** ADJ von niedriger Geburt; **lowboy** N (*US*) niedrige Kommode; **lowbred** ADJ gewöhnlich, ordinär (*pej*); **lowbrow** ADJ (geistig) anspruchslos **N** Anspruchslose(r) *m/f*; (*pej*: = *philistine*) Kulturbanause *m* (*inf*); **low-cal** (*inf*), **low-calorie** ADJ kalorienarm; **a ~orie diet** eine kalorienarme Diät; **Low Church** N reformierter, puritanischer Teil der anglikanischen Kirche; **low comedy** N Schwank *m*, Klamotte *f* (*pej*); **low-cost** ADJ preiswert; **~ airline** Billigfluglinie *f*; **Low Countries** PL **the ~** die Niederlande *pl*; **low-cut** ADJ *dress* tief ausgeschnitten; **low-down** ADJ (*esp US inf*) gemein, fies (*inf*); **lowdown** N (*inf*) Informationen *pl*; **what's the ~ on Kowalski?** was wissen *or* haben (*inf*) wir über Kowalski?; **he gave me the ~ on it** er hat mich darüber aufgeklärt; **to get the ~ on sth** über etw (*acc*) aufgeklärt werden; **low-emission** ADJ *car* schadstoffarm, abgasarm

lower¹ ['ləʊə'] ADJ **a** (*in height*) niedriger; *part, half, limb, storey, latitude* untere(r, s); *note* tiefer; (*Geog*) Nieder-; **the Lower Rhine** der Niederrhein; **~ leg/arm** Unterschenkel *m*/-arm *m*; **~ abdomen** Unterleib *m*; **the ~ back** das Kreuz; **~ jaw/lip** Unterkiefer *m*/-lippe *f*; **the ~ reaches of the river** der Unterlauf des Flusses; **the ~ parts of the hill** die tiefer gelegenen Teile des Berges; **the ~ of the two holes** das untere der beiden Löcher; **hemlines are ~ this year** die Röcke sind dieses Jahr länger; **the ~ deck** (*of bus*) das untere Deck; (*of ship*) das Unterdeck; (*men*) die Unteroffiziere und Mannschaft

b (*in hierarchy*) *rank, level* niedere(r, s); (*Zool*) *animals* niedere(r, s); **the ~ classes** (*Sociol*) die unteren Schichten; **a ~ middle-class family** eine Familie aus der unteren Mittelschicht; **the ~ school** die unteren Klassen, die Unter- und Mittelstufe → **lower sixth (form)**

ADV tiefer, leiser; **~ down the mountain** weiter unten am Berg; **~ down the list** weiter unten auf der Liste

VT a (= *let down*) *boat, injured man, load* herunterlassen; *eyes, gun* senken; *mast* umlegen; *sail, flag* einholen; *bicycle saddle* niedriger machen; **to ~ oneself** sich herunterlassen; **he ~ed himself into an armchair** er ließ sich in einen Sessel nieder; **"lower the lifeboats!"** „Rettungsboote aussetzen!"; **"lower away!"** „holt ein!"

b (= *reduce*) *pressure, risk* verringern; *price, interest rate, cost, tone, temperature* senken; *morale, resistance* schwächen; *standard* herabsetzen; **~ your voice** sprich leiser; **that is no excuse for ~ing the standards of service** das ist keine Entschuldigung dafür, den Service zu verschlechtern; **to ~ oneself** sich hinunterlassen; (*socially*) sich unter sein Niveau begeben; **to ~ oneself to do sth** sich herablassen, etw zu tun

VI sinken, fallen

lower² ['laʊə'] VI = **lour**

lower: Lower Austria N Niederösterreich *nt*; **lower case N** Kleinbuchstaben *pl*, Gemeine *pl* (*spec*) ADJ klein, gemein (*spec*); **Lower Chamber** N Unterhaus *nt*, zweite Kammer; **lower-class** ADJ der Unterschicht; *habit, vocabulary* der unteren *or* niederen Schichten; **~ people** Leute *pl* der Unterschicht *or* unteren Schicht(en); (*fig*) **a ~ neighbourhood** (*Brit*) *or* **neighborhood** (*US*) eine sozial schwache Gegend; **lower court** N (*Jur*) untergeordnete Instanz; **Lower Egypt** N Unterägypten *nt*; **lower-income** ADJ *people* gering verdienend *attr*; *household* mit niedrigem Einkommen; **the ~ group** die Gruppe der Geringverdiener; **in the ~ bracket** in der Steuerklasse für Niedrigeinkommen

lowering ['laʊərɪŋ] ADJ = **louring**

lower: Lower Saxony N Niedersachsen *nt*; **lower sixth (form)** N (*Brit Sch*) *vorletztes Schuljahr*; **lower world** N Unterwelt *f*, Hölle *f*

low: low-fat ADJ *milk, cheese* fettarm, Mager-; **low-flying** ADJ tief fliegend; **~ plane** Tiefflieger *m*; **low frequency** N Niederfrequenz *f*; **Low German** N Platt(deutsch) *nt*; (*Ling*) Niederdeutsch *nt*; **low-grade** ADJ minderwertig; **low-grade petrol** N Benzin *nt* mit niedriger Oktanzahl; **low-heeled** ADJ *shoes* mit flachem *or* niedrigem Absatz; **low-impact** ADJ *aerobics, workout* leicht; **low-income** ADJ einkommensschwach

lowing ['ləʊɪŋ] N Muhen *nt*

low: low-interest ADJ *credit, loan* zinsgünstig; **low-key** ADJ *approach* gelassen; *handling* besonnen; *production, film's treatment* einfach gehalten, unaufdringlich; *reception* reserviert; *colours* gedämpft; **lowland** N Flachland *nt*; **the Lowlands of Scotland** das schottische Tiefland; **the ~s of Central Europe** die Tiefebenen *pl* Mitteleuropas ADJ des Flachlands; (*of Scotland*) des Tieflands; **lowlander** N Flachlandbewohner(in) *m(f)*; **Lowlander** N (*in Scotland*) Bewohner(in) *m(f)* des schottischen Tieflandes; **Low Latin** N nichtklassisches *or* nicht klassisches Latein; **low-level** ADJ *radioactivity* mit niedrigem Strahlungswert; *exposure* schwach; *radiation* niedrig; *attacks, warfare* begrenzt; (*Comput*) *language* nieder; **~ flying** Tiefflüge *pl*; **low-life** ['ləʊlaɪf] N niederes Milieu *nt*; **lowlights** ['ləʊlaɪts] PL **a** (*Hairdressing*) dunkle Strähnchen *pl* **b** (*usu hum*) **one of the season's television ~** ein Tiefpunkt *m* im Fernsehangebot dieser Saison

lowliness ['ləʊlɪnɪs] N Bescheidenheit *f*; (*of position, birth also*) Niedrigkeit *f*

low-loader ['ləʊˌləʊdə'] N Tieflader *m*

lowly ['ləʊlɪ] ADJ (+*er*) bescheiden; *position, birth also* niedrig

low: low-lying ADJ tief gelegen; **Low Mass** N (einfache) Messe; **low-minded** ADJ gemein; **low-necked** ADJ tief ausgeschnitten

lowness ['ləʊnɪs] N **a** Niedrigkeit *f*; (*of bow, note*) Tiefe *f*; (*of food, supplies*) Knappheit *f*; (*of light*) Gedämpftheit *f*; (*of sun, shares*) niedriger Stand; (*pej*) Niedrigkeit *f*; **~ of a river** niedriger Wasserstand eines Flusses **b the ~ of her voice** ihre leise Stimme **c** (*of birth, rank*) Niedrigkeit *f*; (*of taste, manners*) Gewöhnlichkeit *f*; (*of character*) Schlechtheit *f*, Schlechtigkeit *f*; (*of joke*) Geschmacklosigkeit *f*; (*of trick*) Gemeinheit *f* **d** (*of resistance, morale*) Schwäche *f*; **the present ~ of his spirits** seine gegenwärtige Niedergeschlagenheit

low: low pass N (*Sport*) Flachpass *m*; **low-pitched** ADJ tief; **low-powered** ADJ (= *requiring little power*) sparsam im Stromverbrauch; **low-pressure** ADJ **a** (*Tech*) Niederdruck-; **~ system** Niederdrucksystem *nt* **b** (*Met*) Tiefdruck-; **a ~ zone** ein Tiefdruckgebiet *nt*; **low-priced** ADJ günstig; **low-profile** ADJ wenig profiliert; *politician* medienscheu; **a ~ campaign** (*Pol*) eine Kampagne, die in den Medien kaum Beachtung findet; **low-rent** ADJ *housing, flat* mit niedriger Miete; (*fig*) zweitklassig; **low-rise** ATTR niedrig (gebaut); **low-scoring** ADJ *game,* *match* mit wenigen Punkten/Toren; **low sea-son** N Nebensaison *f*; **low-slung** ADJ *chair, sports car* niedrig; **to have ~ hips** kurze Beine haben; **low-spirited** ADJ , **low-spiritedly** ADV niedergeschlagen; **low-start** ADJ **~ mort-gage** (*Brit*) Hypothek, bei der die Rückzahlun-gen zu Anfang niedrig sind und dann steigen; **low-tar** ADJ *cigarette* teerarm; **low-tech** ADJ nicht mit Hi-Tech ausgestattet; **it's pretty ~** es ist nicht gerade hi-tech; **low-tension** ADJ (*Elec*) Niederspannungs-; **~ cable** Niederspan-nungskabel *nt*; **low tide**, **low water** N Niedrigwasser *nt*; **at ~** bei Niedrigwasser; **low- -wage country** N Niedrig- *or* Billiglohnland *nt*; **low-water mark** N Niedrigwassergrenze *f*

loyal ['lɔɪəl] ADJ (*+er*) **a** (= *faithful*) treu; **he was very ~ to his friends/country** er hielt (treu) zu seinen Freunden/seinem Land; **he remained ~ to his wife/the king** er blieb seiner Frau/dem König treu; **~ toast** (*Brit*) Toast *m* auf die Köni-gin/den König **b** (= *without emotional involve-ment*) loyal (*to a party* einer Partei gegenüber); **he's too ~ to say anything against the party/his colleague** er ist zu loyal, um etwas gegen seine Partei/seinen Kollegen zu sagen

loyalist ['lɔɪəlɪst] **N** Loyalist(in) *m(f)*; **the ~s in the army** die regierungstreuen Teile der Armee **ADJ** loyal; *army, troops* regierungstreu

loyally ['lɔɪəlɪ] ADV **a** (= *faithfully*) serve treu **b** (= *without emotional involvement*) loyal; **he ~ re-fused to give the names** er war zu loyal, um die Namen zu verraten

loyalty ['lɔɪəltɪ] N **a** Treue *f*; **conflicting loyal-ties** nicht zu vereinbarende Treuepflichten; **torn between ~ to X and ~ to Y** hin- und her-gerissen in der Treue zu X und der zu Y **b** (*non-emotional*) Loyalität *f*; **his changing politi-cal loyalties** seine wechselnden politischen Be-kenntnisse

loyalty card N (*Brit Comm*) Kundenkarte *f*

lozenge ['lɒzɪndʒ] N **a** (*Med*) Pastille *f* **b** (= *shape*) Raute *f*, Rhombus *m*

LP N *abbr of* **long player, long-playing record** LP *f*

LPF *abbr of* **light protection factor** SF

L-plate ['elpleɪt] N *Schild mit der Aufschrift „L" (für Fahrschüler)*

LRAM (*Brit*) *abbr of* **Licentiate of the Royal Acad-emy of Music**

LRP (*Brit*) N ABBR *of* **lead replacement petrol** *Benzin mit integriertem Bleiersatz-Additiv*

LSD *abbr of* **lysergic acid diethylamide** LSD *nt*

lsd N (*old Brit inf:* = *money*) Geld *nt*, Pinke *f* (*inf*)

LSE (*Brit*) *abbr of* **London School of Economics**

Lt *abbr of* **Lieutenant** Lt

LTA (*Brit*) *abbr of* **Lawn Tennis Association**

Ltd *abbr of* **Limited** GmbH

lube [luːb] (*US inf*) **N** Schmieröl *nt*; (*Med*) Gleit-mittel *nt* **VT** schmieren, ölen

lubricant ['luːbrɪkənt] **ADJ** Schmier-; **~ oil** Schmieröl *nt* **N** Schmiermittel *nt*; (*Med*) Gleit-mittel *nt*

lubricate ['luːbrɪkeɪt] VT (*lit, fig*) schmieren, ölen; **~d sheath** Kondom *m* mit Gleitsubstanz; **well-lubricated** (*hum*) bezecht; **to ~ the wheels of commerce** den Handel reibungslos gestalten

lubrication [ˌluːbrɪˈkeɪʃən] N Schmieren *nt*, Ölen *nt*; (*fig*) reibungslose Gestaltung

lubricator ['luːbrɪkeɪtə] N Schmiervorrichtung *f*

lubricity [luːˈbrɪsɪtɪ] N (*liter*, = *lewdness*) Schlüpf-rigkeit *f*

lucent ['luːsnt] ADJ (*liter, poet*) glänzend, strah-lend; (= *transparent*) durchsichtig, klar

Lucerne [luːˈsɜːn] N Luzern *nt*; **Lake ~** Vier-waldstätter See *m*

lucid ['luːsɪd] ADJ (*+er*) **a** (= *clear*) klar; *account* klar, präzise; *explanation* einleuchtend, an-schaulich **b** (= *sane*) **~ intervals** lichte Augen-blicke; **he was ~ for a few minutes** ein paar Mi-nuten lang war er bei klarem Verstand

lucidity [luːˈsɪdɪtɪ] N Klarheit *f*; (*of explanation*) Anschaulichkeit *f*

lucidly ['luːsɪdlɪ] ADV klar; *explain* einleuchtend, anschaulich; *write* verständlich

Lucifer ['luːsɪfə'] N Luzifer *m*

luck [lʌk] **✪** 23.5 N Glück *nt*; **by ~** durch einen glücklichen Zufall; **bad ~** Unglück *nt*, Pech *nt*; **bad *or* hard *or* tough ~!** so ein Pech!; **bad ~, but it's your own fault** Pech, da bist du selbst schuld; **good ~** Glück *nt*; **good ~!** viel Glück!; **good ~ to them!** (*iro*) **and the best of (British) ~!** (*iro*) na dann viel Glück!; **it was his good ~ to be chosen** er hatte das Glück, gewählt zu werden; **here's ~ to you/us!** (*toast*) auf glückliche Zeiten!; **no such ~!** schön wärs! (*inf*); **just my ~!** Pech (gehabt), wie immer!; **it's just his ~ to miss the train** es musste ihm na-türlich wieder passieren, dass er den Zug ver-passt hat; **it's the ~ of the draw** man muss es eben nehmen, wies kommt; **with any ~** mit et-was Glück; **any ~?** (= *did it work?*) hats ge-klappt?; (= *did you find it?*) hast du es gefun-den?; **worse ~!** leider, wie schade; **better ~ next time!** vielleicht klappts beim nächsten Mal!; **to be in ~** Glück haben; **to be out of ~** kein Glück haben; **he was a bit down on his ~** er hatte eine Pechsträhne; **tramps and others who are down on their ~** Landstreicher und an-dere, die kein Glück im Leben haben; **to bring sb good/bad ~** jdm Glück/Unglück bringen; **as ~ would have it** wie es der Zufall wollte; **to have ~ on one's side** das Glück auf seiner Seite haben; **for ~** als Glücksbringer *or* Talisman; **Bernstein kisses his cuff links for ~** Bernstein küsst seine Manschettenknöpfe, damit sie ihm Glück bringen; **to keep sth for ~** etw als Glücksbringer aufheben; **one for ~** und noch eine(n, s); **to try one's ~** sein Glück versuchen

▶ **luck out** VI (*US, inf*) Schwein haben (*inf*)

luckily ['lʌkɪlɪ] ADV glücklicherweise; **~ for me** zu meinem Glück

luckless ['lʌklɪs] ADJ glücklos; *attempt also* er-folglos

lucky ['lʌkɪ] ADJ (*+er*) **a** (= *having luck*) Glücks-; **a ~ shot** ein Glückstreffer *m*; **that was a ~ move** der Zug war Glück; **you ~ thing!**, **~ you!** du Glückliche(r) *mf*; **who's the ~ man?** wer ist der Glückliche?; **the ~ winner** der glückliche Gewinner, die glückliche Gewinnerin; **to be ~** Glück haben; **I was ~ enough to meet him** ich hatte das (große) Glück, ihn kennen zu ler-nen; **you are ~ to be alive** du kannst von Glück sagen, dass du noch lebst; **you were ~ to catch him** du hast Glück gehabt, dass du ihn erwischt hast; **to strike (it) ~ (with sb), to get ~ (with sb)** (*inf*) (bei jdm) Glück haben; **he's a ~ man to have a wife like that** mit dieser Frau hat er das große Los gezogen (*inf*); **you're a ~ man** du bist ein Glückspilz; **you'll be ~ to make it in time** wenn du das noch schaffst, hast du (aber) Glück; **I want another £ 500 – you'll be ~!** ich will nochmal £ 500 haben – viel Glück!; **I should be so ~!** (*iro*) schön wärs! (*inf*); **to be ~ at cards/in love** Glück im Spiel/ in der Liebe haben; **to be born ~** ein Glücks- *or* Sonntagskind sein; **to be ~ (in) that ...** Glück haben, dass ...; **we are ~ in having (such) a great teacher** wir haben Glück, dass wir so einen großartigen Lehrer haben; **I am luckier than most: I have a job** ich bin besser dran als die meisten, ich habe (wenigstens) einen Job **b** (= *bringing luck*) *star, day* Glücks-; **~ number** Glückszahl *f*; **~ charm** Glücksbringer *m*, Talis-man *m*; **it must be my ~ day** ich habe wohl heute meinen Glückstag; **to be ~ (charm, num-ber etc)** Glück bringen
c (= *happening fortunately*) *coincidence* glücklich; **it was ~ I stopped him in time** ein Glück, dass ich ihn rechtzeitig aufgehalten habe, zum Glück habe ich ihn rechtzeitig aufgehalten; **it's ~ for you I remembered the number** dein Glück, dass ich die Nummer noch wusste; **that was very ~ for you** das tut du aber Glück ge-habt; **they had a ~ escape from the fire** sie wa-ren dem Feuer glücklich entkommen; **he had a ~ escape in the accident** bei dem Unfall ist er glücklich davongekommen; **that was a ~ es-**

cape da habe ich/hast du *etc* noch mal Glück gehabt

lucky dip N ≈ Glückstopf *m*; **it's something of a ~** (*fig*) es ist Glückssache

lucrative ['luːkrətɪv] ADJ einträglich, lukrativ

lucrativeness ['luːkrətɪvnɪs] N Einträglichkeit *f*

lucre ['luːkə'] N **filthy ~** schnöder Mammon

Lucretius [luːˈkriːʃəs] N Lukrez *m*

lucubration [ˌluːkjʊˈbreɪʃən] N (*form*) geistige Arbeit

Lucullan [luːˈkʌlən] ADJ (*geh*) *food* lukullisch

Luddite ['lʌdaɪt] (*Hist, fig*) **N** Maschinenstürmer *m* **ADJ** maschinenstürmerisch

ludic ['lʌdɪk] ADJ (*liter*) spielerisch

ludicrous ['luːdɪkrəs] ADJ grotesk; *sight, words* lächerlich; *idea, suggestion* haarsträubend; (= *low*) *prices, wages, speed* lächerlich, lachhaft; (= *high*) *prices, wages, speed* unerhört, haarsträu-bend; **don't be ~, I can't do it that fast** das is ja grotesk, so schnell kann ich das nicht (ma-chen); **I've done the most ~ thing!** mir ist et-was Haarsträubendes passiert!

ludicrously ['luːdɪkrəslɪ] ADV grotesk; *small, lit-tle, low* lächerlich; (= *appallingly*) *high, fast* haar-sträubend; **it takes me a ~ long time to ...** ich brauche lachhaft lange dazu, zu ...; **~ expen-sive** absurd teuer; **prices are ~ high/low** die Preise sind haarsträubend *or* absurd hoch/lä-cherlich *or* grotesk niedrig; **the description is ~ inadequate** die Beschreibung ist hoffnungslos unzulänglich

ludicrousness ['luːdɪkrəsnɪs] N Groteskheit *f*; (*of sight, words, low prices, slow speed*) Lächerlich-keit *f*; (*of high prices, high speed*) Absurdität *f*

ludo ['luːdəʊ] N Mensch, ärgere dich nicht *nt*

luff [lʌf] (*Naut*) **N** Vorliek *nt* **VTI** (an)luven

lug¹ [lʌg] N **a** (= *earflap*) Klappe *f*; (*Tech*) Halte-vorrichtung *f* **b** (*esp Brit inf*: = *ear*) Ohr *nt*

lug² N = **lugsail**

lug³ VT schleppen; (*towards one*) zerren; **to ~ sth around with one** etw mit sich herumschleppen; **to ~ sth along behind one** etw hinter sich (*dat*) herschleppen

luge [luːʒ] **N** Rodelschlitten *m* **VI** rodeln

luggage ['lʌgɪdʒ] N Gepäck *nt*

luggage: luggage carrier N Gepäckträger(in) *m(f)*; **luggage compartment** N (*Rail*) Ge-päckraum *m*; (*Brit Aut*) Kofferraum *m*; **luggage insurance** N (Reise)gepäckversicherung *f*; **luggage locker** N Gepäckschließfach *nt*; **luggage office** N Gepäckschalter *m*; **lug-gage rack** N (*Rail etc*) Gepäcknetz *nt or* -abla-ge *f*; (*Aut*) Gepäckträger *m*; **luggage trolley** N Kofferkuli *m*; **luggage van** N (*Brit Rail*) Ge-päckwagen *m*

lugger ['lʌgə'] N Logger *m*

lughole ['lʌghəʊl] N (*Brit inf*) Ohr *nt*, Löffel *pl* (*inf*)

lugsail ['lʌgsl] N Loggersegel *nt*

lugubrious [luːˈguːbrɪəs] ADJ *person, song* schwermütig; *smile, tune* wehmütig; *face, expres-sion* kummervoll

lugubriously [luːˈguːbrɪəslɪ] ADV traurig, kum-mervoll

lugworm ['lʌgwɜːm] N Köderwurm *m*

Luke [luːk] N Lukas *m*

lukewarm ['luːkwɔːm] ADJ (*lit, fig*) lauwarm; *ap-plause, support* lauwarm, mäßig; *friendship* lau, oberflächlich; **he's ~ about *or* on the idea/a-bout her** er ist von der Idee/von ihr nur mäßig begeistert

lull [lʌl] **N** Pause *f*; (*Comm*) Flaute *f*; **a ~ in the wind** eine Windstille; **we heard the scream dur-ing a ~ in the storm** wir hörten den Schrei, als der Sturm für einen Augenblick nachließ; **a ~ in the conversation/fighting** eine Gesprächs-/ Gefechtspause; **the ~ before the storm** (*fig*) die Ruhe vor dem Sturm **VT** *baby* beruhigen; (*fig*) einlullen; *fears etc* zerstreuen, beseitigen; **to ~ a baby to sleep** ein Baby in den Schlaf wiegen;

he ~ed them into a false sense of security er wiegte sie in trügerische Sicherheit

lullaby [ˈlʌləbaɪ] N Schlaflied nt, Wiegenlied nt

lulu [ˈluːluː] N (inf) (object) tolles Ding (inf); (person) toller Typ (inf); **a ~ of a story** eine tolle Geschichte (inf); **a ~ of a mistake** ein dicker Hund (inf)

lumbago [lʌmˈbeɪɡəʊ] N Hexenschuss m, Lumbago f (spec)

lumbar [ˈlʌmbə] ADJ Lenden-, lumbal (spec); **the ~ region** die Lendengegend; **~ puncture** Lumbalpunktion f

lumber¹ [ˈlʌmbə] N a (esp US: = timber) (Bau-)holz nt b (= junk) Gerümpel nt VT a (also **lumber up**) space, room voll stopfen, voll pfropfen b (Brit, inf) **to ~ sb with sth** jdm etw aufhalsen (inf); **he got ~ed with the job** man hat ihm die Arbeit aufgehalst (inf); **I got ~ed with her for the evening** ich hatte sie den ganzen Abend auf dem Hals (inf); **what a job! you've really been ~ed!** was für eine Arbeit! da hat man dir aber was aufgehalst! (inf) c (US) hillside, forest abholzen VI (US) Holz fällen, holzen

lumber² VI (cart) rumpeln; (tank) walzen; (elephant, person) trampeln; (bear) tapsen; **a big fat man came ~ing into the room** ein dicker, fetter Mann kam ins Zimmer gewalzt; **she went ~ing about the room** sie trampelte im Zimmer herum

lumbering¹ [ˈlʌmbərɪŋ] ADJ cart rumpelnd; elephant, person trampelnd; bear tapsig; tank schwer, klobig; gait schwerfällig

lumbering² N (US) Holzfällen nt, Holzfällerei f

lumber: lumberjack [ˈlʌmbədʒæk] N Holzfäller m; **lumberjacket** N Lumberjack m; **lumberjack shirt** N bunt kariertes Hemd, Holzfällerhemd nt; **lumberman** N (US) Holzfäller m; **lumbermill** N (US) Sägemühle f or -werk nt; **lumber room** N Rumpelkammer f; **lumber trade** N (Bau)holzhandel m; **lumberyard** N (US) Holzlager nt

luminary [ˈluːmɪnərɪ] N a (form) Himmelskörper m, Gestirn nt b (fig) Koryphäe f, Leuchte f (inf)

luminescence [ˌluːmɪˈnesns] N Lumineszenz f (spec), Leuchten nt

luminescent [ˌluːmɪˈnesnt] ADJ lumineszierend (spec), leuchtend

luminosity [ˌluːmɪˈnɒsɪtɪ] N (form) Helligkeit f; (= emission of light) Leuchtkraft f; (fig) Brillanz f

luminous [ˈluːmɪnəs] ADJ a leuchtend; glow fluoreszierend; **~ paint/colour** (Brit) or **color** (US) Leuchtfarbe f; **~ dial** Leuchtzifferblatt nt; **my watch is ~** meine Uhr leuchtet im Dunkeln b (fig, liter) writings brillant, luzid (liter)

lummox [ˈlʌməks] N (US, inf) Trottel m (inf)

lummy, lumme [ˈlʌmɪ] INTERJ (Brit) ach, du Schreck!

lump [lʌmp] N a Klumpen m; (of sugar) Stück nt b (= swelling) Beule f; (inside the body) Geschwulst f; (in breast) Knoten m; (on surface) Huppel m (inf), kleine Erhebung; **with a ~ in one's throat** (fig) mit einem Kloß im Hals, mit zugeschnürter Kehle; **I get a ~ in my throat when I hear that song** wenn ich dieses Lied höre, ist mir die Kehle wie zugeschnürt; **it brings a ~ to my throat** dabei schnürt sich mir die Kehle zu c (inf, = person) Klotz m, Trampel m or nt (inf); **a big** or **great fat ~ (of a man)** ein Fettkloß m (inf) d **you can't judge them in the ~ like that** du kannst sie doch nicht so pauschal beurteilen or nicht alle über einen Kamm scheren; **to pay money in a ~** (= at once) auf einmal bezahlen; (= covering different items) pauschal bezahlen VT (esp Brit inf: = put up with) **to ~ it** sich damit abfinden; **like it or ~ it** you'll have to go **to work** (inf) du musst zur Arbeit, ob es dir passt oder nicht; **if he doesn't like it he can**

~ **it** wenns ihm nicht passt, hat er eben Pech gehabt (inf) VI (sauce, flour) klumpen

▶ **lump together** VT sep a (= put together) zusammentun; books zusammenstellen; expenses, money zusammenlegen b (= judge together) persons, topics in einen Topf werfen, über einen Kamm scheren; **he lumped all the soldiers together as traitors** er urteilte all die Soldaten pauschal als Verräter ab

lumpen [ˈlʌmpən] ADJ (= bulky) building etc klobig; (inf: = stupid) blöd (inf)

lumpish [ˈlʌmpɪʃ] ADJ person klobig, plump

lump: lump payment N (at once) einmalige Bezahlung; (covering different items) Pauschalbezahlung f; **lump sugar** N Würfelzucker m; **lump sum** N Pauschalbetrag m or -summe f; **to pay sth in a ~** etw pauschal bezahlen

lumpy [ˈlʌmpɪ] ADJ (+er) liquid etc, mattress, cushion klumpig; figure pummelig, plump; **to go ~** (sauce, rice) klumpen

lunacy [ˈluːnəsɪ] N Wahnsinn m; **it's sheer ~!** das ist reiner Wahnsinn!; **lunacies** pl Verrücktheiten pl

lunar [ˈluːnə] ADJ Mond-, lunar (spec); **~ landscape** Mondlandschaft f

lunar: lunar eclipse N Mondfinsternis f; **lunar module** N Mondlandefähre f or -fahrzeug nt; **lunar orbit** N Mondumlaufbahn f

lunatic [ˈluːnətɪk] ADJ verrückt, wahnsinnig N Wahnsinnige(r) mf, Irre(r) mf

lunatic asylum N Irrenanstalt f

lunatic fringe N Extremisten pl, radikale or extremistische Randgruppe

lunch [lʌntʃ] N Mittagessen nt; **to have** or **take ~ (zu) Mittag essen; let's do ~** (inf) wir sollten uns zum Mittagessen treffen; **to give sb ~** jdn zum Mittagessen einladen; **how long do you get for ~?** wie lange haben Sie Mittagspause?; **when do you have ~ in the office?** wann haben or machen Sie im Büro Mittag?; **he's at ~** er ist beim Mittagessen; **to have ~ out** auswärts or im Restaurant (zu Mittag) essen; **out to ~** (inf, = crazy) weggetreten (inf); **there's no such thing as a free ~** (fig) man bekommt im Leben nichts geschenkt VT zum Mittagessen einladen VI (zu) Mittag essen; **we ~ed on a salad** zum (Mittag)essen gab es einen Salat

▶ **lunch out** VI auswärts or im Restaurant (zu) Mittag essen

lunch: lunchbox N a Vesperbox f, Lunchbox f b (Brit hum inf) Gemächte nt (old, hum); **lunch break** N Mittagspause f; **lunch counter** N (US = café) Imbiss m; (= counter) Imbisstheke f

luncheon [ˈlʌntʃən] N (form) Lunch nt or m, Mittagessen nt

luncheonette [ˌlʌntʃəˈnet] N (US) Imbissstube f

luncheon: luncheon meat N Frühstücksfleisch nt; **luncheon voucher** N Essen(s)bon m or -marke f

lunch: lunch hour N Mittagsstunde f; (= lunch break) Mittagspause f; **lunch meeting** N Geschäftsessen nt (über Mittag); **lunch money** N (US Sch) Essensgeld nt; **lunchpail** N (US) (= lunchbox; **lunchroom** N (US) Imbissstube f; (= canteen) Kantine f; **lunchtime** N Mittagspause f; **they arrived at ~** sie kamen um die Mittagszeit an, sie kamen gegen Mittag an

lung [lʌŋ] N Lunge f; (= iron lung) eiserne Lunge; **that baby has plenty of ~ power** das Baby hat eine kräftige Lunge; **he has weak ~s** er hat keine gute Lunge

lung cancer N Lungenkrebs m

lunge [lʌndʒ] N Satz m nach vorn; (esp Fencing) Ausfall m; **he made a ~ at his opponent** er stürzte sich auf seinen Gegner; (Fencing) er machte einen Ausfall VI (sich) stürzen; (esp Fencing) einen Ausfall machen; **to ~ at sb** sich auf jdn stürzen; **the exhausted boxer could on-**

ly ~ **at his opponent** der erschöpfte Boxer schlug nur noch wahllos nach seinem Gegner

▶ **lunge out** VI ausholen; **to lunge out at sb** sich auf jdn stürzen

lunula [ˈluːnjʊlə] N pl **-e** Lunula f (spec), Nagelmöndchen nt

lupin, (US) **lupine** [ˈluːpɪn] N Lupine f

lupine [ˈluːpaɪn] ADJ wölfisch

lurch¹ [lɜːtʃ] N **to leave sb in the ~** (inf) jdn im Stich lassen, jdn hängen lassen (inf)

lurch² N Ruck m; (of boat) Schlingern nt; **with a drunken ~ he started off down the road** betrunken taumelte er die Straße hinunter; **to give a ~** einen Ruck machen; (boat) schlingern; **my heart gave a ~** mein Herz stand still; **the party's ~ to the right** der Rechtsruck der Partei; **a ~ into recession** ein Schlittern nt in die Rezession VI a einen Ruck machen b (= move with lurches) ruckeln, sich ruckartig bewegen; (boat) schlingern; (person) taumeln, torkeln; **the train ~ed to a standstill** der Zug kam mit einem Ruck zum Stehen; **he ~ed to his feet** er stand schwankend auf; **to ~ about** hin und her schlingern/taumeln or torkeln; **the bus ~ed off down the bumpy track** der Bus ruckelte den holprigen Weg hinunter; **to ~ in/out** (person) herein-/hinaustaumeln; **my heart ~ed** mein Herz stand still; **my stomach ~ed** mir drehte sich der Magen um (inf); **to ~ along** dahinruckeln/entlangtorkeln or -taumeln; **the economy still manages to ~ along** die Wirtschaft schlittert gerade so eben dahin; **the government ~es from one crisis to the next** die Regierung schlittert von einer Krise in die andere

lure [ljʊə] N (= bait) Köder m; (= person, for hawk) Lockvogel m; (general) Lockmittel nt; (fig: of city, sea etc) Verlockungen pl; **the ~ of the wild** der lockende Ruf der Wildnis VT anlocken; **to ~ sb away from sth** jdn von etw weg- or fortlocken; **to ~ sb/an animal into a trap** jdn/ein Tier in eine Falle locken; **to ~ sb/ an animal out** jdn/ein Tier herauslocken

▶ **lure on** VT sep (inf) spielen mit

lurgy [ˈlɜːgɪ] N (Brit inf) **to have the ~** (= flu, cold) die Schnieferei haben (inf); **to pick up the ~** sich (dat) was holen; **to give sb the dreaded ~** jdn anstecken

lurid [ˈljʊərɪd] ADJ a colour, sky grell; dress grellfarben, in grellen Farben; posters schreiend; **a ~ sunset of pinks and oranges** ein Sonnenuntergang in grellen Rosa- und Orangetönen; **her taste in clothes is rather ~** sie mag Kleider in ziemlich grellen or schreienden Farben; **she was painting her toenails a ~ red** sie lackierte sich die Fußnägel grellrot b (fig) language, headline, novel, imagination reißerisch; (= bloodthirsty) blutrünstig; account, description reißerisch, sensationslüstern; (= sordid) detail, crime widerlich; photo, image schaurig; (= prurient) anzüglich; **~ tale** Schauergeschichte f; **all the love scenes are presented in ~ detail** die Liebesszenen werden in allen widerlichen Einzelheiten dargestellt; **~ details of their quarrels** peinliche Einzelheiten ihrer Streitereien; **he has a ~ imagination** er kann sich (dat) die schaurigsten Dinge vorstellen

luridly [ˈljʊərɪdlɪ] ADV a coloured grell, knallig (inf); **the sky glowed ~** der Himmel leuchtete in grellen Farben; **he sat down on the ~-coloured** (Brit) or **~-colored** (US) **settee** er setzte sich auf das knallige Sofa b (fig) reißerisch; report reißerisch, sensationslüstern; **~ written/presented** reißerisch aufgemacht; **... his ~ reported private life** ... sein Privatleben, über das reißerisch berichtet wird; **Reggie swore briefly and ~** Reggie fluchte kurz und derb

luridness [ˈljʊərɪdnɪs] N a (of colour, sky, dress) Grellheit f; (of posters) schreiende Art b (of account) reißerische or sensationslüsterne Aufmachung; (of details) grausige Darstellung; **the ~ of his language** seine reißerische Sprache; **the ~ of this tale** diese blutrünstige or grausige Geschichte

lurk [lɜːk] VI lauern; **a nasty suspicion ~ed at the back of his mind** er hegte einen fürchterlichen Verdacht; **the fears which still ~ in the unconscious** Ängste, die noch im Unterbewusstsein lauern; **a doubt/the thought still ~ed in his mind** ein Zweifel/der Gedanke plagte ihn noch

▶ **lurk about** (Brit) or **around** VI herumschleichen

lurking [ˈlɜːkɪŋ] ADJ heimlich; doubt also nagend; danger lauernd

luscious [ˈlʌʃəs] ADJ **a** (= delicious) köstlich, lecker **b** (= gorgeous) colour satt; girl, boy zum Anbeißen (inf); figure (= full) üppig; (= pleasing) fantastisch, phantastisch; lips üppig **c** (= lush) pasture, vegetation üppig

lusciously [ˈlʌʃəslɪ] ADV köstlich; **~ coated in thick cream** mit einer köstlich dicken Sahneschicht

lusciousness [ˈlʌʃəsnɪs] N Köstlichkeit f; (of fruit also) Saftigkeit f; (of colour) Sattheit f; (of girl) knuspriges or appetitliches Aussehen (inf); (of figure) Üppigkeit f

lush [lʌʃ] ADJ **a** grass, meadows saftig, satt; vegetation üppig **b** (inf: = opulent) hotel, house feudal; lifestyle üppig; (Mus) harmonies, sound üppig **N** (sl) Säufer(in) m(f) (inf)

lushness [ˈlʌʃnɪs] N **a** (of grass, meadow) Saftigkeit f; (of vegetation) Üppigkeit f **b** (inf: = opulence) (of hotel, house) Feudalität f; (of lifestyle, Mus: of harmonies, sound) Üppigkeit f

lust [lʌst] **N** (= inner sensation) Wollust f, Sinneslust f; (= wanting to acquire) Begierde f (for nach); (= greed) Gier f (for nach); **rape is an act of ~** Vergewaltigungen entspringen triebhafter Gier; **the ~s of the flesh** die fleischlichen (Ge-)lüste, die Fleischeslust; **~ for power** Machtgier f; **his uncontrollable ~** seine ungezügelte Gier; (sexual) seine fleischliche Begierde **VI** **to ~ after, to ~ for** (old, hum, sexually) begehren (+acc); (greedily) gieren nach

luster N (US) = lustre

lustful ADJ , **lustfully** ADV [ˈlʌstfʊl, -fəlɪ] lüstern

lustfulness [ˈlʌstfʊlnɪs] N Lüsternheit f, Begierde f

lustily [ˈlʌstɪlɪ] ADV kräftig; work mit Schwung und Energie; eat herzhaft; sing aus voller Kehle; cry, cheer aus vollem Hals(e)

lustre, (US) **luster** [ˈlʌstə] N **a** Schimmer m, schimmernder Glanz; (in eyes) Glanz m **b** (fig) Glanz m, Ruhm m

lustreless [ˈlʌstəlɪs] ADJ glanzlos; eyes, hair also stumpf

lustrous [ˈlʌstrəs] ADJ schimmernd, glänzend

lusty [ˈlʌstɪ] ADJ (+er) person gesund und munter, voller Leben; life urwüchsig; appetite herzhaft, kräftig; cheer, cry laut, kräftig; push, kick etc kräftig, kraftvoll

lute [luːt] N Laute f

lutenist [ˈluːtənɪst] N Lautenist(in) m(f), Lautenspieler(in) m(f)

lutetium [lʊˈtiːʃɪəm] N (Chem) Lutetium nt

Luther [ˈluːθə] N Luther m

Lutheran [ˈluːθərən] ADJ lutherisch **N** Lutheraner(in) m(f)

Lutheranism [ˈluːθərənɪzəm] N Luthertum nt

luvvie, **luvvy** [ˈlʌvɪ] N (Brit inf) **a** (address) Schatz m (inf) **b** (= actor) Akteur(in) m(f)

lux abbr of **luxury**

luxation [lʌkˈseɪʃən] N (Med) Luxation f (spec), Verrenkung f (eines Gelenks)

Luxembourg [ˈlʌksəmbɜːg] **N** Luxemburg nt **ADJ** attr Luxemburger

Luxembourger [ˈlʌksəmbɜːgə] N Luxemburger(in) m(f)

luxuriance [lʌgˈzjʊərɪəns] N Üppigkeit f; (of hair also) Fülle f, Pracht f

luxuriant [lʌgˈzjʊərɪənt] ADJ üppig; flowers, plants üppig, prächtig; forest dicht; (= thick) beard, hair üppig, dicht; (= elaborate) furnishings, style prunkvoll, prächtig

luxuriantly [lʌgˈzjʊərɪəntlɪ] ADV üppig; (= thickly) dicht

luxuriate [lʌgˈzjʊərɪeɪt] VI **to ~ in sth** (people) sich in etw (dat) aalen

luxurious [lʌgˈzjʊərɪəs] ADJ luxuriös; food üppig; **a ~ hotel** ein Luxushotel nt; **~ travel** Luxusreisen pl; **~ car** Luxusauto nt; **he is a man of ~ habits/tastes** er hat einen luxuriösen Lebensstil/einen Hang zum Luxus; **with a ~ sigh** mit einem wohligen Seufzer

luxuriously [lʌgˈzjʊərɪəslɪ] ADV luxuriös; **to live ~** ein Luxusleben or ein Leben im Luxus führen; **he sank back ~ into the cushions** er ließ sich genüsslich in die Kissen sinken

luxury [ˈlʌkʃərɪ] **N** **a** (in general) Luxus m; (of car, house etc) luxuriöse or feudale Ausstattung, Komfort m; **to live a life of ~** ein Luxusleben or ein Leben im Luxus führen **b** (= article) Luxus m no pl; **we can't allow ourselves many luxuries** wir können uns (dat) nicht viel Luxus leisten; **little luxuries** Luxus m; (to eat) kleine Genüsse pl **ADJ** attr Luxus-; **~ car** Luxusauto nt; **~ goods** Luxusgüter pl; **~ liner** Luxusdampfer m; **~ tax** Luxussteuer f

LV (Brit) abbr of **luncheon voucher**

LW abbr of **long wave** LW

lychee [ˈlaɪtʃiː] N Litschi f

lychgate N = lichgate

Lycra® [ˈlaɪkrə] N Lycra® nt

lye [laɪ] N Lauge f

lying [ˈlaɪɪŋ] **ADJ** lügnerisch, verlogen **N** Lügen nt; **that would be ~** das wäre gelogen

lying-in [ˈlaɪɪŋˈɪn] N (old Med) Wochenbett nt (dated); **during her ~** im Wochenbett (dated); **~ ward** Wöchnerinnenstation f (dated)

lymph [lɪmf] N Lymphe f, Gewebsflüssigkeit f

lymphatic [lɪmˈfætɪk] **ADJ** lymphatisch, Lymph-; **~ tissue** Lymphgewebe nt **N** Lymphgefäß nt

lymph gland N Lymphdrüse f

lymph node N Lymphknoten m

lymphocyte [ˈlɪmfəʊˌsaɪt] N Lymphozyt m

lymph vessel N Lymphgefäß nt

lynch [lɪntʃ] VT lynchen

lynching [ˈlɪntʃɪŋ] N Lynchen nt; **there'll be a ~** soon er etc wird bestimmt gelyncht werden

lynch law N Lynchjustiz f

lynx [lɪŋks] N Luchs m

lynx-eyed [ˈlɪŋksˌaɪd] ADJ mit Luchsaugen; **the ~ teacher** der Lehrer, der Augen wie ein Luchs hatte

lyre [laɪə] N Leier f, Lyra f (geh)

lyrebird [ˈlaɪəbɜːd] N Leierschwanz m

lyric [ˈlɪrɪk] **ADJ** lyrisch **N** (= poem) lyrisches Gedicht; (= genre) Lyrik f; (= often pl: words of pop song) Text m

lyrical [ˈlɪrɪkəl] ADJ lyrisch; (fig: = enthusiastic) schwärmerisch; **to wax ~ about sth** über etw (acc) ins Schwärmen geraten

lyrically [ˈlɪrɪkəlɪ] ADV **a** lyrisch; (fig: = enthusiastically) schwärmerisch; sing, play, speak melodisch **b** (Mus, referring to the text) textlich; **~, it is full of clichés** der Text ist voller Klischees

lyricism [ˈlɪrɪsɪzəm] N Lyrik f

lyricist [ˈlɪrɪsɪst] N **a** (= poet) Lyriker(in) m(f) **b** (Mus) Texter(in) m(f)

lysergic acid diethylamide [laɪˈsɜːdʒɪkˌæsɪdˌdaɪəˈθɪləmaɪd] N Lysergsäurediäthylamid nt

Lysol® [ˈlaɪsɒl] N Lysol® nt

M

M, m [em] N M *nt*, m *nt*

M *abbr of* **medium**

m **a** *abbr of* **million(s)** Mill., Mio. **b** *abbr of* **metre(s)** m **c** *abbr of* **mile(s)** **d** *abbr of* **minute(s)** min **e** *abbr of* **married** verh. **f** *abbr of* **masculine** m

MA *abbr of* **Master of Arts** M. A.

ma [mɑː] N (*inf*) Mama *f* (*inf*), Mutti *f* (*inf*)

ma'am [mæm] N gnä' Frau *f* (*form*) → *also* **madam a**

mac¹ [mæk] N (*Brit, inf*) Regenmantel *m*

mac² N (*esp US, inf*) Kumpel *m* (*inf*)

macabre [məˈkɑːbrə] ADJ makaber

macadam [məˈkædəm] N Schotter *m*, Splitt *m*, Makadam *m or nt*; **~ road** Schotterstraße *f*

macadamize [məˈkædəmaɪz] VT schottern, makadamisieren (*spec*)

macaque [məˈkɑːk] N (*monkey*) Makak *m*

macaroni [ˌmækəˈrəʊnɪ] N Makkaroni *pl*

macaronic [ˌmækəˈrɒnɪk] ADJ makkaronisch

macaroni cheese N Käsemakkaroni *pl*

macaroon [ˌmækəˈruːn] N Makrone *f*

macaw [məˈkɔː] N Ara *m*

Mace® [meɪs] N (= *gas*) ≈ Tränengas *nt*

mace¹ [meɪs] N (= *weapon*) Streitkolben *m*, Keule *f*; (*mayor's*) Amtsstab *m*

mace² N (= *spice*) Muskatblüte *f*, Mazis *m*

macebearer [ˈmeɪsbɛərə'] N Träger(in) *m(f)* des Amtsstabes

Macedonia [ˌmæsɪˈdəʊnɪə] N Makedonien *nt*, Mazedonien *nt*

Macedonian [ˌmæsɪˈdəʊnɪən] N Makedonier(in) *m(f)*, Mazedonier(in) *m(f)* ADJ makedonisch, mazedonisch

macerate [ˈmæsəreɪt] VT aufweichen, einweichen VI aufweichen, weich werden

Mach [mæk] N Mach *nt*; **~ number** Machzahl *f*; **the jet was approaching ~ 2** das Flugzeug näherte sich (einer Geschwindigkeit von) 2 Mach

machete [məˈtʃeɪtɪ] N Machete *f*, Buschmesser *nt*

Machiavelli [ˌmækɪəˈvelɪ] N Machiavelli *m*

Machiavellian [ˌmækɪəˈvelɪən] ADJ machiavellistisch

machination [ˌmækɪˈneɪʃən] N *usu pl* Machenschaften *pl*

machine [məˈʃiːn] N Maschine *f*, Apparat *m*; (= *vending machine*) Automat *m*; (= *car*) Wagen *m*; (= *cycle, plane*) Maschine *f*; (*fig*: = *person*) Maschine *f*, Roboter *m*; **by ~** maschinell; **the party ~** (*Pol*) der Parteiapparat; **the political ~** die politischen Drahtzieher *pl*; **the publicity/propaganda ~** die Publicity-/Propagandamaschine *or* -maschinerie; **to be a money-making ~** (*fig*) am laufenden Band Geld machen VT (*Tech*) maschinell herstellen; (= *treat with machine*) maschinell bearbeiten; (*Sew*) mit der Maschine nähen

machine: machine age N **the ~** das Maschinenzeitalter; **machine code** N Maschinenkode *m*; **machine gun** N Maschinengewehr *nt*; **machine-gun** VT mit dem Maschinengewehr beschießen *or* (*kill*) erschießen; **machine gunner** N (*Mil*) Maschinengewehr-

schütze *m*; **machine intelligence** N künstliche Intelligenz; **machine language** N (*Comput*) Maschinensprache *f*; **machine-made** ADJ maschinell hergestellt; **machine operator** N Maschinenarbeiter(in) *m(f)*; (*skilled*) Maschinist(in) *m(f)*; **machine-readable** ADJ ATTR , **machine readable** ADJ PRED (*Comput*) maschinenlesbar; **~ data** maschinenlesbaren Daten

machinery [məˈʃiːnərɪ] N (= *machines*) Maschinen *pl*, Maschinerie *f*; (= *mechanism*) Mechanismus *m*; (*fig*) Maschinerie *f*; **the ~ of government** der Regierungsapparat

machine: machine shop N Maschinensaal *m*; **machine-stitch** VT maschinell *or* mit der Maschine nähen; **machine time** N Betriebszeit *f*; (= *computing time*) Rechenzeit *f*; **the relationship between cost and ~** das Verhältnis der Kosten zur Betriebszeit der Maschine(n); **machine tool** N Werkzeugmaschine *f*; **machine translation** N maschinelle Übersetzung; **machine-washable** ADJ waschmaschinenfest

machinist [məˈʃiːnɪst] N (*Tech*, = *operator*) Maschinist(in) *m(f)*; (= *constructor, repairer*) Maschinenschlosser(in) *m(f)*; (*Sew*) Näherin *f*

machismo [mæˈkɪzməʊ, mæˈtʃɪzməʊ] N Machismo *m*

macho [ˈmætʃəʊ] ADJ macho *pred*, Macho-; *management* machomäßig; **~ image** Macho-Image *nt*; **a ~ type** ein Macho-Typ *m*; **a ~ man** ein Macho *m* VT Macho *m*

mackerel [ˈmækrəl] N Makrele *f*

mackerel sky N (Himmel *m* mit) Schäfchenwolken

mackintosh [ˈmækɪntɒʃ] N Regenmantel *m*

macramé [məˈkrɑːmɪ] N Makramee *nt*

macro [ˈmækrəʊ] N (*Comput*) Makro *nt*

macro- PREF makro-, Makro-; **macrolanguage** Makrosprache *f*

macrobiotic [ˈmækrəʊbaɪˈɒtɪk] ADJ makrobiotisch; **~ restaurant** *Restaurant, in dem makrobiotische Kost serviert wird*

macrocosm [ˈmækrəʊˌkɒzəm] N Makrokosmos *m*; **the ~ of Italian society** die italienische Gesellschaft als ganzes *or* in ihrer Gesamtheit

macroeconomics [ˈmækrəʊˌiːkəˈnɒmɪks] N *sing or pl* Makroökonomie *f*

macron [ˈmækrɒn] N (*Typ*) Querbalken *m*, Längezeichen *nt*

macroscopic [ˈmækrəʊˈskɒpɪk] ADJ makroskopisch, mit bloßem Auge erkennbar

MAD N (*US Mil*) *abbr of* **mutual(ly) assured destruction** Gleichgewicht *nt* des nuklearen Zerstörungspotenzials

mad [mæd] ADJ (*+er*) **a** wahnsinnig; (= *genuinely insane*) geisteskrank; (*inf*: = *crazy*) verrückt; (= *with rabies*) *animal* tollwütig; **to go ~** wahnsinnig werden; (= *go insane*) den Verstand verlieren; **to drive sb ~** jdn wahnsinnig machen; (*lit*: = *drive sb insane*) jdn um den Verstand bringen; **it's enough to drive you ~** es ist zum Verrücktwerden; **he has a ~ look in his eye** er hat einen irren Blick; **he's as ~ as a hatter** *or* a **March hare** (*prov*) er hat einen Dachschaden (*inf*); **are you raving ~?** bist du total verrückt

geworden?; **you must be ~!** du bist wohl wahnsinnig!; **I must have been ~ to believe him** ich war wohl von Sinnen, ihm zu glauben; **~ dog** tollwütiger Hund; (*fig*: = *person*) verrückter Typ

b (*inf*: = *angry*) böse, sauer (*inf*); **to be ~ at sb** auf jdn böse *or* sauer (*inf*) sein; **to be ~ about** *or* **at sth** über etw (*acc*) wütend *or* sauer (*inf*) sein; **this makes** *or* **drives me ~** das bringt mich auf die Palme (*inf*); **he makes me so ~** er macht mich so wütend; **don't get ~ at** *or* **with me** sei nicht böse *or* sauer (*inf*) auf mich; **(as) ~ as a hornet** (*US*) fuchsteufelswild (*inf*)

c (*esp Brit*: = *stupid, rash*) verrückt; **you ~ fool!** du bist ja wahnsinnig *or* verrückt!; **she's ~ doing something like that** sie ist verrückt, so etwas zu tun; **it's a ~ hope** es ist verrückt, darauf zu hoffen; **that was a ~ thing to do** das war Wahnsinn (*inf*)

d (*esp Brit inf*: = *very keen*) **to be ~ about** *or* **on sth** auf etw (*acc*) verrückt sein; **I'm not exactly ~ about this job** ich bin nicht gerade versessen auf diesen Job; **I'm (just) ~ about you** ich bin (ganz) verrückt nach dir!; **the audience went ~** das Publikum tobte vor Begeisterung; **don't go ~!** (= *don't overdo it*) übertreib es nicht

e (= *wild, frantic*) wahnsinnig (*with* vor +*dat*); **they ~e a ~ rush** *or* **dash for the door** sie stürzten wie wild zur Tür; **why the ~ rush?** warum diese Hektik?; **the ~ rush toward(s) federalism** die überstürzte Entwicklung zum Föderalismus; **the prisoner ~e a ~ dash for freedom** der Gefangene unternahm einen verzweifelten Ausbruchsversuch; **to be ~ with joy** sich wahnsinnig freuen; **after the news came through the phones went ~** nach der Bekanntgabe der Nachricht standen die Telefone nicht mehr still; **this is bureaucracy gone ~** das ist Bürokratie hoch drei

ADV (*inf*) **to be ~ keen on sb/sth** ganz scharf auf jdn/etw sein (*inf*); **to be ~ keen to do sth** ganz versessen darauf sein, etw zu tun; **like ~** wie verrückt; **he ran like ~** er rannte wie wild

Madagascan [ˌmædəˈɡæskən] ADJ madegassisch N Madegasse *m*, Madegassin *f*

Madagascar [ˌmædəˈɡæskə'] N Madagaskar *nt*

madam [ˈmædəm] N **a** gnädige Frau (*old, form*); **~, would you kindly desist!** würden Sie das bitte unterlassen! (*form*); **yes, ~** sehr wohl, gnädige Frau (*old, form*), ja (wohl); **can I help you, ~?** kann ich Ihnen behilflich sein?; **dear ~** (*esp Brit*) sehr geehrte gnädige Frau; **Dear Sir or Madam** (*esp Brit*) Sehr geehrte Damen und Herren **b** (*Brit inf*: = *girl*) kleine Prinzessin; **she's a spoiled little ~** sie ist eine verwöhnte kleine Prinzessin **c** (*of brothel*) Bordellwirtin *f*, Puffmutter *f* (*inf*)

madcap [ˈmædkæp] ADJ *idea* versponnen; *youth* stürmisch; *tricks* toll; *scheme* hirnverbrannt N impulsiver Mensch

mad cow disease N Rinderwahnsinn *m*

MADD *abbr of* **mothers against drunk driving**

madden [ˈmædn] VT (= *make mad*) verrückt machen; (= *make angry*) ärgern, fuchsen (*inf*); **it ~s me to think of the opportunity we missed** ich könnte mich schwarz ärgern, wenn ich daran denke, was für eine Chance wir vertan haben (*inf*)

maddening ['mædnɪŋ] ADJ unerträglich, zum Verrücktwerden; *delay* unerträglich, lästig; *habit* aufreizend; **the ~ thing is that ...** das Verrückte daran ist, dass ...; **isn't it ~?** ist das nicht ärgerlich?; **this is ~!** das ist (ja) zum Verrücktwerden!

maddeningly ['mædnɪŋlɪ] ADV unerträglich; **the train ride was ~ slow** es war zum Verrücktwerden, wie langsam der Zug fuhr; **his work is ~ inconsistent** seine Arbeit ist so ungleichmäßig, dass es zum Verrücktwerden ist; **he grinned ~** er grinste, dass es zum Verrücktwerden war

madder ['mædə] N (= *plant*) Krapp *m*, Färberröte *f*; (= *dye*) Krapprot *nt*, Krappfarbstoff *m*

made [meɪd] *pret, ptp of* **make**

Madeira [mə'dɪərə] N Madeira *nt*; (= *wine*) Madeira *m*

Madeira cake N Sandkuchen *m*

made-to-measure ['meɪdtə'meʒə] ADJ (*Brit*) maßgeschneidert; *curtains* nach Maß; *furniture etc* spezialangefertigt; **~ suit** Maßanzug *m*; **~ clothes** Maßkonfektion *f*; **~ service** (*Sew*) Maßschneiderei *f*

made up ADJ (*Brit, inf*: = *pleased*) erfreut; **I'm ~ for you** ich freue mich für dich

made-up ['meɪd'ʌp] ADJ **a** (= *invented*) *story, name, word, character* erfunden **b** (= *wearing make-up*) *face* geschminkt; **she was over ~** *or* **too heavily ~** sie hatte zu viel Make-up aufgelegt, sie war zu stark geschminkt **c** (= *ready-made*) *curtains* fertig genäht; **~ meat products** fertige Fleischprodukte **d** (= *surfaced*) *road* asphaltiert

madhouse ['mædhaʊs] N (*lit, fig*) Irrenhaus *nt*

madly ['mædlɪ] ADV **a** wie verrückt; **he worked ~ for weeks on end** er arbeitete wochenlang wie besessen *or* verrückt **b** (*inf, = extremely*) wahnsinnig; **to be ~ in love (with sb)** bis über beide Ohren (in jdn) verliebt sein, total (in jdn) verschossen sein (*inf*); **I'm not ~ keen to go** ich bin nicht wahnsinnig scharf (*inf*) *or* erpicht darauf (zu gehen)

madman ['mædmən] N *pl* **-men** [-mən] Irre(r) *m*, Verrückte(r) *m*

madness ['mædnɪs] ◷ 2.3 N Wahnsinn *m*; **it's sheer ~!** das ist heller *or* reiner Wahnsinn!; **what ~!** das ist doch Wahnsinn!

Madonna [mə'dɒnə] N Madonna *f*; (= *picture*) Madonnenbild *nt*, Madonna *f*; (= *statue also*) Madonnenfigur *f*

Madrid [mə'drɪd] N Madrid *nt*

madrigal ['mædrɪgəl] N Madrigal *nt*

madwoman ['mædwʊmən] N Verrückte *f*

Maecenas [miː'siːnəs] N Maecenas *m*; (*fig*) Mäzen *m*

maelstrom ['meɪlstrəʊm] N (*lit rare*) Malstrom *m*; (*fig*) Malstrom *m* (*liter*), Sog *m*; **he returned to the ~ of public life** er kehrte in den Trubel des öffentlichen Lebens zurück

maestro ['maɪstrəʊ] N Maestro *m*

mae west ['meɪ'west] N (*hum*) Schwimmweste *f*

Mafia ['mæfɪə] N **a** Mafia *f* **b** (*fig*) **the literary/ medical mafia** die Literatur-/Medizinmafia

mafioso [ˌmæfɪ'əʊsəʊ] N *pl* **-sos** *or* **-si** Mafioso *m*

mag [mæg] N (*inf*) Magazin *nt*; (*glossy also*) Illustrierte *f*; *porn ~* Pornoheft *nt*

magalog ['mægəlɒg] N Bestellkatalog, *der wie eine Illustrierte aufgemacht ist*

magazine [ˌmægə'ziːn] N **a** (= *journal*) Zeitschrift *f*, Magazin *nt* **b** (*in gun*) Magazin *nt* **c** (*Mil, = store*) Magazin *nt* (*Hist*), Depot *nt*

magazine rack N Zeitungsständer *m*

mag card N ['mægkɑːd] (*inf*) Magnetkarte *f*

magenta [mə'dʒentə] N Fuchsin *nt* ADJ tiefrot

maggot ['mægət] N Made *f*

maggoty ['mægətɪ] ADJ madig; **the cheese has gone all ~** der Käse wimmelt von Maden

Magi ['meɪdʒaɪ] PL **the ~** die Heiligen Drei Könige, die drei Weisen aus dem Morgenland

magic ['mædʒɪk] N **a** Magie *f*, Zauberei *f*, Zauberkunst *f*; **the witch doctor tried ~ to cure the woman** der Medizinmann versuchte, die Frau durch Magie zu heilen; **he entertained them with a display of ~** er unterhielt sie mit ein paar Zauberkunststücken; **he made the spoon disappear by ~** er zauberte den Löffel weg; **you don't expect the essay to write itself by ~?** glaubst du, dass der Aufsatz sich von alleine schreibt?; **as if by ~** wie durch Zauberei *or* Zauberhand, wie durch ein Wunder; **it worked like ~** (*inf*) es klappte *or* lief wie am Schnürchen (*inf*) **b** (= *mysterious charm*) Zauber *m* ADJ **a** Zauber-; *powers, square* magisch; *moment* zauberhaft; **~ formula** Zauberformel *f*; (*fig*) Patentrezept *nt*; **the ~ word** (*having special effect*) das Stichwort; (*making sth possible*) das Zauberwort; **a pianist with the ~ touch** ein begnadeter Pianist; **he gave it his ~ touch and it worked** er hat es nur angefasst und schon funktionierte es; **he hasn't lost his ~ touch** er hat nichts von seiner Genialität verloren; **"The Magic Flute"** „Die Zauberflöte" **b** (*inf, = fantastic*) toll (*inf*), super (*inf*)

▶ **magic away** VT SEP wegzaubern

▶ **magic up** VT SEP heraufbeschwören

magical ['mædʒɪkəl] ADJ *powers, attraction, light* magisch; *atmosphere* unwirklich; **the effect was ~** das wirkte (wahre) Wunder; (*visually*) die Wirkung war zauberhaft; **~ formula** Zauberformel *f*

magically ['mædʒɪkəlɪ] ADV wunderbar; **~ transformed** auf wunderbare Weise verwandelt; **her headache ~ disappeared** ihre Kopfschmerzen waren auf einmal wie weggeblasen

magic: magic bullet N (*inf, Med: for cancer*) selektiv wirksames Krebsmedikament, *das nur die kranken Zellen zerstört* (*US fig*) Patentlösung *f*; **magic carpet** N fliegender Teppich; **magic circle** N **a** Zauberkreis *m* **b** (*fig, = cabal*) Clique *f* **c Magic Circle** (= *organization*) Gilde *f* der Zauberkünstler; **magic eye** N magisches Auge

magician [mə'dʒɪʃən] N Magier *m*, Zauberer *m*, Zauberin *f*; (= *conjuror*) Zauberkünstler(in) *m(f)*; **I'm not a ~!** ich kann doch nicht hexen!

magic: magic lantern N Laterna magica *f*; **magic mushroom** N (*inf*) Magic Mushroom *m*; **magic realism** N (*Liter*) magischer Realismus; **magic spell** N Zauber *m*; (= *words*) Zauberspruch *m*; **the witch cast a ~ on her** die Hexe verzauberte sie; **magic wand** N Zauberstab *m*; **to wave a ~** (*lit, fig*) den Zauberstab schwingen; **there is no ~ to bring about political change** ein politischer Wandel lässt sich nicht herbeizaubern

magisterial [ˌmædʒɪ'stɪərɪəl] ADJ **a** (*lit*) *powers, office, robes* eines Friedensrichters; **b** (= *imperious*) gebieterisch

magisterially [ˌmædʒɪs'tɪərɪəlɪ] ADV majestätisch, gebieterisch; **Johnson waves his hand ~** Johnson winkt majestätisch

magistracy ['mædʒɪstrəsɪ] N (= *position*) Amt *nt* des Friedensrichters; (= *judges*) Friedensrichter *pl*

magistrate ['mædʒɪstreɪt] N Friedensrichter(in) *m(f)*, Schiedsmann *m*/-frau *f*

magistrates' court ['mædʒɪstreɪts'kɔːt] N (*Brit*) Friedensgericht *nt*, Schiedsgericht *nt*

maglev ['mæglev] N (*Rail*) Magnet(schwebe)bahn *f*

magma ['mægmə] N (*Geol*) Magma *nt*

magna cum laude ['mægnəkʌm'laʊdeɪ] ADV (*US*) magna cum laude, sehr gut

magnanimity [ˌmægnə'nɪmɪtɪ] N Großherzigkeit *f*, Großmut *f*; **he acted with great ~** er handelte sehr großherzig

magnanimous [mæg'nænɪməs] ADJ großmütig, großherzig; (= *generous*) großzügig; **to be ~ to sb** sich jdm gegenüber großherzig verhalten; **he was ~ in victory/defeat** er zeigte Großmut im Sieg/in der Niederlage

magnanimously [mæg'nænɪməslɪ] ADV großmütig; (= *generously*) großzügig

magnate ['mægneɪt] N Magnat *m*

magnesia [mæg'niːʃə] N Magnesia *f*

magnesium [mæg'niːzɪəm] N Magnesium *nt*

magnet ['mægnɪt] N (*lit, fig*) Magnet *m*

magnetic [mæg'netɪk] ADJ (*lit*) magnetisch; (*fig*) *charms* unwiderstehlich; **he has a ~ personality** er hat eine große Ausstrahlung *or* ein sehr anziehendes Wesen; **this perfume has a ~ effect on men** dieses Parfüm übt eine magnetische Wirkung auf Männer aus; **~ attraction** magnetische Anziehungskraft

magnetically [mæg'netɪkəlɪ] ADV (*lit, fig*) magnetisch; **she is ~ attractive/sensual** sie/ihre Sinnlichkeit übt eine magnetische Anziehungskraft aus; **to be ~ drawn to sb/sth** von jdm/etw magnetisch angezogen werden

magnetic: magnetic card N Magnetkarte *f*; **magnetic card reader** N Magnetkartenleser *m*; **magnetic compass** N Magnetkompass *m*; **magnetic disk** N (*Comput*) Magnetplatte *f*; **magnetic field** N Magnetfeld *nt*; **magnetic mine** N Magnetmine *f*; **magnetic needle** N Magnetnadel *f*; **magnetic north** N nördlicher Magnetpol *m*; **magnetic pole** N Magnetpol *m*; **magnetic resonance** N (*Med*) Magnetresonanz *f*, Kernspinresonanz *f*; **~ imager** Kernspintomograf *m*; **magnetic resonance imaging** N (*Med*) Magnetresonanzspektroskopie *f*; **magnetic storm** N (*erd*)magnetischer Sturm; **magnetic strip, magnetic stripe** N Magnetstreifen *m*; **magnetic tape** N Magnetband *nt*

magnetism ['mægnɪtɪzəm] N Magnetismus *m*; (*fig: of person*) Anziehungskraft *f*, Ausstrahlung *f*

magnetize ['mægnɪtaɪz] VT magnetisieren; **the audience was ~d by this incredible performance** das Publikum folgte dieser unglaublichen Darstellung wie gebannt

magneto [mæg'niːtəʊ] N Magnetzünder *m*

magnification [ˌmægnɪfɪ'keɪʃən] N Vergrößerung *f*; **high/low ~** starke/geringe Vergrößerung; **seen at 300 ~s** in 300facher Vergrößerung, 300fach vergrößert

magnificence [mæg'nɪfɪsəns] N **a** (= *excellence*) Großartigkeit *f*, Größe *f* **b** (= *splendid appearance*) Pracht *f*, Glanz *m* **c** **his Magnificence** Seine Magnifizenz

magnificent [mæg'nɪfɪsənt] ADJ **a** (= *wonderful, excellent*) großartig; *food, meal* hervorragend, ausgezeichnet; **he has done a ~ job** er hat das ganz hervorragend gemacht; **a ~ folly** eine Torheit grandiosen Ausmaßes **b** (= *of splendid appearance*) prachtvoll, prächtig

magnificently [mæg'nɪfɪsəntlɪ] ADV (= *excellently*) großartig; **you did ~** das hast du großartig gemacht; **a ~ rousing finale** ein glanzvolles (und) mitreißendes Finale; **the islands are ~ pure and unspoilt** die Inseln sind herrlich rein und unberührt **b** (*in appearance*) prachtvoll, prächtig

magnifier ['mægnɪfaɪə] N **a** (= *magnifying glass*) Vergrößerungsglas *nt*, Lupe *f* **b** (*Elec*) Verstärker *m*

magnify ['mægnɪfaɪ] VT **a** (= *make bigger*) *image* vergrößern; **to ~ sth 7 times** etw 7fach vergrößern **b** (= *exaggerate*) aufbauschen **c** (*obs, liter, = praise*) **the Lord** lobpreisen (*old, liter*)

magnifying glass ['mægnɪfaɪɪŋ'glɑːs] N Vergrößerungsglas *nt*, Lupe *f*

magniloquence [mæg'nɪləkwəns] N (*liter*) Wortgewalt *f* (*liter*)

magniloquent [mæg'nɪləkwənt] ADJ (*liter*) wortgewaltig (*liter*)

magnitude ['mægnɪtjuːd] N **a** Ausmaß *nt*, Größe *f*; (= *importance*) Bedeutung *f*; **I didn't appreciate the ~ of the task** ich war mir über den Umfang der Aufgabe im Klaren; **in operations of this ~** bei Vorhaben dieser Größenordnung; **a matter of the first ~** eine Angelegenheit von äußerster Wichtigkeit; **a mistake**

of the first ~ ein Fehler ersten Ranges; **order of** ~ Größenordnung f **b** (*Astron*) Größenklasse f

magnolia [mæg'nəʊlɪə] N Magnolie f; (*also* **magnolia tree**) Magnolienbaum m

magnum ['mægnəm] N ≈ Anderthalbliterflasche f (*esp von Sekt*)

magnum opus N Hauptwerk nt

magpie ['mægpaɪ] N Elster f

Magyar ['mægjɑː'] ADJ madjarisch, magyarisch N Madjar(in) m(f), Magyar(in) m(f)

maharajah [ˌmɑːhə'rɑːdʒə] N Maharadscha m

maharani [ˌmɑːhə'rɑːnɪ] N Maharani f

maharishi [ˌmɑːhɑː'rɪʃɪ] N Maharischi m

mahogany [mə'hɒgənɪ] N Mahagoni nt; (= *tree*) Mahagonibaum m ADJ Mahagoni-; (*colour*) mahagoni(farben); ~ **furniture** Mahagonimöbel pl

Mahomet [mə'hɒmɪt] N Mohammed m, Mahomet m (*liter*)

Mahometan [mə'hɒmɪtən] ADJ mohammedanisch N Mohammedaner(in) m(f)

mahout [mə'haʊt] N Mahaut m, Elefantenführer m

maid [meɪd] N **a** (= *servant*) (Dienst)mädchen nt, Hausangestellte f; (*in hotel*) Zimmermädchen nt; (= *lady's maid*) Zofe f **b** (*old*, = *maiden*) Jungfer f (*obs*), Maid f (*old*, *poet*); (= *young girl*) Mägdelein nt (*poet*); **the Maid of Orleans** die Jungfrau von Orleans

maidan [maɪ'dɑːn] N (*India*) (Markt)platz m, Esplanade f

maiden ['meɪdn] N (*liter*) Maid f (*old*, *poet*), Mädchen nt ADJ attr Jungfern-; ~ **flight** Jungfernflug m; ~ **voyage** Jungfernfahrt f

maiden: **maiden aunt** N unverheiratete, ältere Tante; **maidenhair** N Frauenhaar nt; **maidenhead** N (*Anat*) Jungfernhäutchen nt; **she lost her** ~ (*liter*) sie hat ihre Unschuld verloren; **maidenhood** N Jungfräulichkeit f, Unschuld f; (= *time*) Jungmädchenzeit f

maidenly ['meɪdnlɪ] ADJ jungfräulich; (= *modest*) mädchenhaft

maiden: **maiden name** N Mädchenname m; **maiden over** N (*Cricket*) 6 Würfe ohne einen Lauf; **maiden speech** N Jungfernrede f

maid: **maid of all work** N (= *person*) Mädchen nt für alles; (= *machine*) Allzweckgerät nt; **maid of honour** (US) **maid of honor** N Brautjungfer f; **maidservant** N Hausangestellte f, Hausmädchen nt

mail¹ [meɪl] N Post f; **to send sth by** ~ etw mit der Post versenden or schicken; **is there any** ~ **for me?** ist Post für mich da? VT aufgeben; (= *put in letter box*) einwerfen; (= *send by mail*) mit der Post schicken; (= *send by e-mail*) per E-Mail senden, mailen (*inf*); **to** ~ **sb** jdm ein E-Mail senden

mail² N (*Mil*) Kettenpanzer m VT **the ~ed fist of imperialism** die gepanzerte Faust des Imperialismus

mailable ['meɪləbl] ADJ (*esp US*) postversandfähig

mail: **mailbag** N Postsack m; **mailboat** N Postdampfer m; **mail bomb** N (*US*) Briefbombe f; **mailbox** N **a** (*US*) Briefkasten m **b** (*Comput*) Mailbox f, (elektronischer) Briefkasten; **mailcar** N (*US Rail*) Postwagen m; **mail carrier** N (*US*) = mailman; **mailcoach** N (*Brit*) (*Hist*) Postkutsche f; (*Rail*) Postwagen m; **mail drop** N (*US*) Briefeinwurf m (*form*), Briefschlitz m; **mailer** ['meɪlə'] N (*US*) **a** (= *machine*) Adressiermaschine f; (*for stamps*) Frankiermaschine f **b** (= *advertisement*) Postwurfsendung f; **Mailgram**® N (*US*) *auf elektronischem Wege an ein Postamt im Bezirk des Empfängers übermittelte Nachricht, die dann als normale Briefsendung zugestellt wird*

mailing ['meɪlɪŋ] N Rundschreiben nt

mailing address N (*US*) Postanschrift f

mailing list N Adressenliste f; (*e-mail*) Mailingliste f

mail: **mailman** N (*US*) Briefträger m, Postbote m; **mail merge** N (*Comput*) Mailmerge nt; **program** Dateimischprogramm nt; **mail-order** ADJ Versand-; ~ **catalogue** (*Brit*) or **catalog** (*US*) Versandhauskatalog m; ~ **firm**, ~ **house** Versandhaus nt, Versandgeschäft nt; **mailroom** N (*esp US*) Poststelle f; **mailshot** (*Brit*) N Direktwerbung f (per Post); **to send out a** ~ Werbebriefe verschicken VT Werbebriefe verschicken an (+*acc*); **mail train** N Postzug m; **mail van** N (*on roads*) Postauto nt; (*Brit Rail*) Postwagen m; **mailwoman** N (*US*) Briefträgerin f, Postbotin f

maim [meɪm] VT (= *mutilate*) verstümmeln; (= *cripple*) zum Krüppel machen; **the wounded and the ~ed** die Verletzten und Versehrten; **he will be ~ed for life** er wird sein Leben lang ein Krüppel bleiben; **he was ~ed in the bomb attack** der Bombenanschlag machte ihn zum Krüppel

main [meɪn] ADJ attr Haupt-; **the ~ reason** der Hauptgrund; **the ~ idea in this book** der Haupt- or Leitgedanke in diesem Buch; **what is the ~ thing in life?** was ist die Hauptsache im Leben?; **the ~ thing is to ...** die Hauptsache ist, dass ...; **the ~ thing is you're still alive** Hauptsache, du lebst noch N **a** (= *pipe*) Hauptleitung f; **the ~s** (*of town*) das öffentliche Versorgungsnetz; (*for electricity*) das Stromnetz; (*of house*) der Haupthahn; (*for electricity*) der Hauptschalter; **the machine is run directly off the ~s** das Gerät wird direkt ans Stromnetz angeschlossen; **the water/gas/electricity was switched off at the ~s** der Haupthahn/Hauptschalter für Wasser/Gas/Elektrizität wurde abgeschaltet **b** (*poet*) **the** ~ das offene Meer, die hohe See **c in the** ~ im Großen und Ganzen **d** → might²

main: **mainbrace** N Großbrasse f; **to splice the** ~ Rum an die Mannschaft ausgeben; **main clause** N (*Gram*) Hauptsatz m; **main course** N Hauptgericht nt; **main deck** N Hauptdeck nt; **main drag** N (*US*, *inf*: = *main street*) Hauptstraße f; **main drain** N Hauptrohr nt; (*for sewage*) Hauptkanal m; **main establishment** N (*Comm*) Hauptniederlassung f; **main force** N rohe Gewalt; **mainframe (computer)** N Großrechner m, Mainframe m; **mainland** N Festland nt; **on the** ~ **of Europe** auf dem europäischen Festland; **main line** N (*Rail*) Hauptstrecke f; ~ **train** Schnellzug m; **mainline** VI (*sl*) fixen (*inf*)

mainly ['meɪnlɪ] ADV hauptsächlich, in erster Linie; **the meetings are held** ~ **on Tuesdays** die Besprechungen werden meistens dienstags statt; **the climate is** ~ **wet** das Klima ist vorwiegend or überwiegend feucht

main: **main man** N (*US inf*) **a** (*in film*) Hauptdarsteller m **b** (= *best friend*) bester Freund; **mainmast** N Haupt- or Großmast m; **main memory** N (*Comput*) Hauptspeicher m; **main office** N (= *headquarters*) Zentrale f; **main road** N Hauptstraße f; **mainsail** N Haupt- or Großsegel nt; **mainsheet** N (*Naut*) Großschot f

mains-operated ['meɪnzˌɒpəreɪtɪd], **mains-powered** ['meɪnzˌpaʊəd] ADJ für Netzbetrieb, mit Netzanschluss

main: **mainspring** N (*Mech*, *fig*) Triebfeder f; **mainstay** N (*Naut*) Haupt- or Großstag nt; (*fig*) Stütze f

mainstream N **a** Hauptrichtung f; **to be in the** ~ **of sth** der Hauptrichtung einer Sache (*gen*) angehören **b** (*Jazz*) Mainstream m ADJ **a** politician, party, politics der Mitte; philosophy, opinion nt vorherrschend; schools, education regulär; ~ **society** die Mitte der Gesellschaft; **the ~ press/media** die Hauptvertreter pl der Presse/Medien **b** ~ **cinema** Mainstreamkino nt; ~ **jazz** Mainstreamjazz m VT (*US Sch*) in die reguläre Schule schicken

maintain [meɪn'teɪn] ⊘ 26.2 VT **a** (= *keep up*) aufrechterhalten; law and order, peace etc wahren; speed, attitude beibehalten; prices halten; life

erhalten; **he wants to** ~ **his weight at 75 kilos** er möchte sein Gewicht von 75 Kilo beibehalten; **to** ~ **the status quo** den Status quo (aufrecht)erhalten; **to** ~ **sth at a constant temperature** etw bei gleich bleibender Temperatur halten **b** (= *support*) family unterhalten **c** (= *keep in good condition*) machine warten; roads, building instand or in Stand halten; car pflegen; **this old car is too expensive to** ~ dieses alte Auto ist im Unterhalt zu teuer; **products which help to** ~ **healthy skin** Produkte, die die Haut gesund erhalten **d** (= *claim*) behaupten; **he still ~ed he was innocent, he still ~ed his innocence** er beteuerte immer noch seine Unschuld **e** (= *defend*) theory vertreten; rights verteidigen

maintained school [meɪn'teɪndskuːl] N (*Brit*) staatliche Schule

maintenance ['meɪntɪnəns] N **a** (= *keeping up*) Aufrechterhaltung f; (*of law and order, peace etc*) Wahrung f; (*of speed, attitude*) Beibehaltung f; (*of life*) Erhaltung f **b** (*Brit*) (*of family*) Unterhalt m; (= *social security*) Unterstützung f; **he has to pay** ~ er ist unterhaltspflichtig **c** (= *servicing*: *of machine, car*) Wartung f; (= *upkeep*) (*of road, building etc*) Instandhaltung f; (*of gardens*) Pflege f; (= *cost*) Unterhalt m

maintenance: **maintenance contract** N Wartungsvertrag m; **maintenance costs** PL Unterhaltskosten pl; **maintenance crew** N Wartungsmannschaft f

maintop ['meɪntɒp] N Großmars m

maisonette [ˌmeɪzə'net] N (= *small flat*) Appartement nt; (= *small house*) Häuschen nt

maître d' [ˌmetrə'diː] N (*US*: = *head waiter*) Oberkellner m

maize [meɪz] N Mais m

Maj abbr of **major**

majestic [mə'dʒestɪk] ADJ majestätisch; proportions stattlich; music getragen; (= *not slow*) erhaben

majestically [mə'dʒestɪkəlɪ] ADV move, rise majestätisch; ~ **proportioned buildings** Gebäude von stattlichen Ausmaßen; **the music ends** ~ die Musik kommt zu einem erhabenen or grandiosen Schluss

majesty ['mædʒɪstɪ] N (= *stateliness*) Majestät f; (*of movements etc*) Würde f; **the ~ of the mountains** die Majestät or Erhabenheit der Bergwelt; **His/Her Majesty** Seine/Ihre Majestät; **Your Majesty** Eure Majestät

Maj Gen abbr of **major general**

major ['meɪdʒə'] ADJ **a** Haupt-; (= *of great importance*) bedeutend; cause, factor wesentlich; incident schwerwiegend, schwer wiegend; part, role groß, führend; (*Pol*) party groß, führend; (= *of great extent*) groß; **a** ~ **road** eine Hauptverkehrsstraße; **a** ~ **factor in our decision/his defeat** ein wesentlicher Faktor in unserem Entschluss/seiner Niederlage; **a** ~ **poet** ein bedeutender Dichter; **Sapporo, the** ~ **city on Hokkaido** Sapporo, die wichtigste Stadt auf Hokkaido; **matters of** ~ **interest** Angelegenheiten pl von großem or größerem Interesse; **of** ~ **importance** von großer or größerer Bedeutung; **a** ~ **operation** eine größere Operation; **a** ~ **work of art** ein bedeutendes Kunstwerk **b** (*Mus*) Dur-; ~ **chord** Durakkord m; ~ **key** Durtonart f; ~ **scale** Durtonleiter f; **A** ~ A-Dur nt; **A flat** ~ As-Dur nt; **G sharp** ~ Gis-Dur nt; ~ **third** große Terz **c Jenkins Major** Jenkins der Ältere N **a** (*Mil*) Major(in) m(f) **b** (*Mus*) Dur nt; **in the** ~ in Dur **c** (*Jur*) **to become a** ~ volljährig or mündig werden **d** (*US*: = *subject*) Hauptfach nt; **he's a psychology** ~ Psychologie ist/war sein Hauptfach VI (*US*) **to** ~ **in French** Französisch als Hauptfach studieren, das Examen mit Französisch im Hauptfach ablegen

Majorca [mə'jɔːkə] N Mallorca nt

Majorcan [mə'jɔːkən] **ADJ** mallorquinisch **N** Mallorquiner(in) *m(f)*

major-domo [,meidzə'dəuməu] N Haushofmeister *m*, Majordomus *m*

majorette [,meidzə'ret] N Majorette *f*

major general N Generalmajor(in) *m(f)*

majority [mə'dʒɒrɪtɪ] N **a** Mehrheit *f*; **the ~ of cases** die Mehrheit *or* Mehrzahl der Fälle; **to be in a** *or* **the ~** in der Mehrzahl sein; **to be in a ~ of 3** eine Mehrheit von 3 Stimmen haben; **to have/get a ~** die Mehrheit haben/bekommen; **to have a ~ of 10** eine Mehrheit von 10 Stimmen haben; **what was his ~?** wie groß war seine Mehrheit?; **a two-thirds ~** die Zweidrittelmehrheit; **by a small** *or* **narrow ~** mit knapper Mehrheit **b** *(Jur)* Volljährigkeit *f*, Mündigkeit *f*; **to reach the age of ~** volljährig *or* mündig werden

majority: majority decision N Mehrheitsbeschluss *m*; **majority holding** N *(Fin)* Mehrheitsbeteiligung *f*; **majority rule** N Mehrheitsregierung *f*

major: major league N (= *US Sport*) oberste Spielklasse; **major-league** ADJ *attr* (= *US Sport*) *football, baseball etc* der obersten Spielklasse; **major premise** N erste Prämisse, Obersatz *m*

---

make [meik]
vb: pret, ptp **made**

1 TRANSITIVE VERB	4 NOUN
2 INTRANSITIVE VERB	5 PHRASAL VERBS
3 REFLEXIVE VERB	

1 – TRANSITIVE VERB

a = produce, prepare machen; *bread* backen; *cars* herstellen; *dress* nähen; *coffee* kochen; *peace* stiften; **she made it into a suit** sie machte einen Anzug daraus; **God made the world** Gott erschuf die Welt; **he's as clever as they make 'em** *(inf)* der ist ein ganz gerissener Hund *(inf)*

made in/of/for/to made in Germany in Deutschland hergestellt, made in Germany; **it's made of gold** es ist aus Gold; **to show what one is made of** zeigen, was in einem steckt; **the job is made for him** die Arbeit ist wie für ihn geschaffen; **I'm not made for running** ich bin nicht zum Laufen *or* zum Läufer geschaffen; **they're made for each other** sie sind wie geschaffen füreinander; **this car wasn't made to carry eight people** dieses Auto ist nicht dazu gedacht, acht Leute zu transportieren

b = do, execute *bow, journey, mistake, attempt, plan, remarks, suggestions etc* machen; *speech* halten; *choice, arrangements* treffen; *decision* fällen, treffen; **to make an application** sich bewerben; **to make a guess** raten; **to make sb a present of sth** jdm etw schenken, jdm etw zum Geschenk machen *(geh)*

c = cause to be or become machen
to make sb/sth + ADJ to make sb happy/angry *etc* jdn glücklich/wütend *etc* machen; **does that make you happy?** bist du jetzt endlich zufrieden?; **I'll make it easy for you** ich mache dir leicht *or* es leicht für dich; **to make one's voice heard** mit seiner Stimme durchdringen; **he makes Macbeth very evil** er lässt Macbeth sehr böse erscheinen

to make sb/sth + NOUN to make sb one's wife jdn zu seiner Frau machen; **he was made a judge** man ernannte ihn zum Richter; **to make a success of sth, to make sth a success** etw erfolgreich erledigen; **Shearer made it 1-0** Shearer erzielte das 1:0; **they'll never make a soldier of him** *or* **out of him** aus ihm wird nie ein Soldat

to make a day/night of it we decided to make a day/night of it wir beschlossen, den ganzen Tag dafür zu nehmen/(die Nacht) durchzumachen

to make something of oneself/one's life etwas aus sich/seinem Leben machen

to make something of it *(inf)* do you want **to make something of it?** hast du was dagegen? *(inf)*, störts dich etwa? *(inf)*

d = cause to do or happen lassen, (dazu) bringen; (= compel to do) zwingen

to make sb do sth (= *cause to do*) jdn dazu bringen *or* veranlassen *(geh)*, etw zu tun; (= *compel to do*) jdn zwingen, etw zu tun; **to make sb laugh** jdn zum Lachen bringen; **what made you come to this town?** was hat Sie dazu veranlasst, in diese Stadt zu kommen?; **what makes you say that?** warum sagst du das?; **what makes you think you can do it?** was macht Sie glauben, dass Sie es schaffen können?; **it all makes me think that ...** das alles lässt mich denken, dass ...; **how can I make you understand?** wie kann ich es Ihnen verständlich machen?; **that certainly made him think again** das hat ihm bestimmt zu denken gegeben; **what will make you change your mind?** was wird Sie dazu bringen, Ihre Meinung zu ändern?; **what finally made me drop the idea was ...** was mich am Ende dazu veranlasst hat, den Gedanken fallen zu lassen, war ...; **he makes his heroine die** er lässt seine Heldin sterben; **her conduct made him seem polite by comparison** im Vergleich zu ihrem Verhalten machte er einen höflichen Eindruck; **I'll make him suffer for this** dafür soll er mir büßen!; **you can't make me!** mich kann keiner zwingen!; **make me!** *(challenging)* versuch mal, mich zu zwingen!; **I'll make him!** den zwing ich!

to make sth do sth what makes the engine go? was treibt den Motor an?, wie wird der Motor angetrieben?; **what made it explode?** was hat die Explosion bewirkt?; **onions make your eyes water** von Zwiebeln tränen einem die Augen; **it makes the room look smaller** es lässt den Raum kleiner wirken; **the chemical makes the plant grow faster** die Chemikalie bewirkt, dass die Pflanze schneller wächst; **that made the cloth shrink** dadurch ging der Stoff ein; **that will make the pain go** das wird den Schmerz vertreiben; **I wish I could make the rain stop** wenn ich nur machen *(inf)* *or* bewirken könnte, dass der Regen aufhört; **if I could make your problems disappear** wenn ich (nur) Ihre Probleme beseitigen könnte; **you can't make things happen** man kann den Lauf der Dinge nicht erzwingen

to make do to make do with sth sich mit etw begnügen; **to make do with less money/on a small income** mit weniger Geld/einem niedrigen Gehalt auskommen

e = earn *money* verdienen; *profit, loss, fortune* machen (on bei); *reputation* sich *(dat)* verschaffen; **to make a name for oneself** sich *(dat)* einen Namen machen; **how much do you stand to make?** wie viel verdienst du (dabei)?, was bringt dir das ein? *(inf)*

f = reach, achieve schaffen, erreichen; *train, plane etc* erwischen; (= *catch*) schaffen; *connection* schaffen; *summit, top, shore etc* es schaffen zu; *(ship)* 20 knots machen; **to make land** *(Naut)* anlegen; **to make port** *(Naut)* in den Hafen einlaufen; **we made good time** wir kamen schnell voran; **sorry I couldn't make your party last night** tut mir Leid, ich habe es gestern Abend einfach nicht zu deiner Party geschafft; **his first record didn't make the charts** seine erste Platte schaffte es nicht bis in die Hitparade; **we'll never make the airport in time** wir kommen garantiert nicht rechtzeitig zum Flughafen; **he made colonel in one year** er brachte es in einem Jahr zum Obersten; **he made university/the first team** er schaffte es, an die Universität/in die erste Mannschaft zu kommen; **the story made the front page** die Geschichte kam auf die Titelseite

to make it (= *succeed*) es schaffen, es zu etwas bringen; **he just made it** er hat es gerade noch geschafft; **we've made it!** wir haben es geschafft!; **he'll never make it through the winter** (= *survive*) er wird den Winter nie überstehen

to make it (with sb) *(inf, = have sex)* mit jdm schlafen; **they were making it all night** sie liebten sich die ganze Nacht

to make good to make good as a writer es als Schriftsteller(in) schaffen *or* zu etwas bringen; **he is a poor boy made good** er ist ein armer Junge, der es zu etwas gebracht hat

g = cause to succeed berühmt machen, zum Erfolg verhelfen (+*dat*); **this film made her** mit diesem Film schaffte sie es *or* schaffte sie den Durchbruch; **his performance makes the play** das Stück lebt von seiner schauspielerischen Leistung; **you'll be made for life** Sie werden ausgesorgt haben; **he's got it made** *(inf)* er hat ausgesorgt; **he's a made man** er ist ein gemachter Mann; **but what really made the evening was ...** die eigentliche Krönung des Abends war ...

to make sb's day that makes my day! das freut mich ungemein!; *(iro)* das hat mir gerade noch gefehlt!; **seeing the Queen made her day** sie war selig, als sie die Königin gesehen hatte; **you've made my day** ich könnte dir um den Hals fallen! *(inf)*

to make or break sth/sb the weather will make or break the parade der Festzug steht und fällt mit dem Wetter; **he can make or break you** er hat dein Schicksal in der Hand

h = be, constitute sein, machen, (ab)geben; **he made a good father** er gab einen guten Vater ab; **he'll never make a soldier/an actor** aus dem wird nie ein Soldat/Schauspieler; **you'd make someone a good wife** Sie würden eine gute Ehefrau abgeben; **she made him a good wife** sie war ihm eine gute Frau; **he'd make a fantastic Hamlet/a good teacher** er wäre ein fantastischer *or* phantastischer Hamlet/ein guter Lehrer, er gäbe einen fantastischen *or* phantastischen Hamlet/einen guten Lehrer ab; **they make a good/an odd couple** sie sind ein gutes/ungleiches Paar; **it makes good television/publicity** es ist sehr fernsehwirksam/werbewirksam; **it made a very strange sight** es war ein sehr merkwürdiger Anblick; **to make a fourth at bridge** den vierten Mann beim Bridge machen

i = equal sein, (er)geben; **2 plus 2 makes 4** 2 und 2 ist 4; **1760 yards make 1 mile** 1760 Yards sind eine Meile; **this makes the fifth time** das ist nun das fünfte Mal; **that makes £55 you owe me** Sie schulden mir damit (nun) £ 55; **how much does that make altogether?** was macht das insgesamt?

j = reckon *distance, total* schätzen auf (+*acc*); **I make the total 107** ich komme auf 107

to make it + *time, date, figure* **what time do you make it?** wie spät hast du es?, wie spät ist es bei dir?; **I make it 3.15** ich habe 3.15 Uhr, auf meiner Uhr ist es 3.15 Uhr; **I make it 3 miles** ich schätze 3 Meilen; **how many do you make it?** wie viele sind es nach deiner Zählung?; **let's make it 7 o'clock** (= *agree*) sagen wir 7 Uhr?; **let's make it Monday** sagen wir Montag

k Cards (= *fulfil contract*) erfüllen; (= *win*) *trick* machen; *(shuffle)* pack mischen → **bid**

l Elec *circuit* schließen; *contact* herstellen

m Naut (= *signal*) senden, funken; **make (the following message) to HMS Victor** machen Sie die folgende Meldung an HMS Victor

2 – INTRANSITIVE VERB

a = go **to make toward(s) a place** auf einen Ort zuhalten; *(ship)* Kurs auf einen Ort nehmen; **to make after sb** jdm nachsetzen → **make for**

b = profit **to make on a deal** bei einem Geschäft verdienen

c = act
to make as if to do sth Anstalten machen, etw zu tun; *(as deception)* so tun, als wolle man etw tun

to make to... (= *try*) **I made to speak** ich setzte zur Rede an

to make like... *(inf)* so tun, als ob...; **he made like he was dying** er tat so, als ob er am Sterben wäre, er markierte *(inf)* *or* spielte den Sterbenden; **he's started making like a big-shot** er hat angefangen, den starken Mann zu spielen *or* zu markieren *(inf)*

3 – REFLEXIVE VERB

♦ **to make oneself +** *ADJ or NOUN* (= *cause oneself to be*) **to make oneself useful** sich nützlich machen; **to make oneself comfortable** es sich (*dat*) bequem machen; **make yourself small** mach dich klein; **to make oneself conspicuous** auffallen; **you'll make yourself ill!** du machst dich damit krank!; **to make oneself heard** sich (*dat*) Gehör verschaffen; **to make oneself understood** sich verständlich machen; **he made himself Emperor for life** er krönte *or* machte sich selbst zum Kaiser auf Lebenszeit

♦ **to make oneself sth** (= *to make sth for oneself*) sich (*dat*) etw machen; **he made himself a cup of tea/a sandwich** er machte sich (*dat*) eine Tasse Tee/ein Butterbrot; **she made herself a lot of money on the deal** sie hat bei dem Geschäft eine Menge Geld verdient

♦ **to make oneself do sth** (= *force oneself*) sich dazu zwingen, etw zu tun; **I made myself apologize to him** ich zwang mich dazu, mich bei ihm zu entschuldigen; **he's just made himself look ridiculous** er hat sich nur lächerlich gemacht

4 – NOUN

a = brand Marke *f*, Fabrikat *nt*; **what make of car do you have?** welche (Auto)marke fahren Sie?; **it's a good make** das ist eine gute Marke; **these are my own make** die sind selbst gemacht, die sind Eigenfabrikat (*hum*)

b

♦ **on the make** (*pej inf, for profit*) profitgierig (*inf*), auf Profit aus; (= *ambitious*) karrieresüchtig (*inf*), auf Karriere aus; (*sexually*) sexhungrig (*inf*), auf sexuelle Abenteuer aus

5 – PHRASAL VERBS

▶ **make away** `VI` = make off

▶ **make away with** `VI` +*prep obj* **to make away with sb** jdn beseitigen *or* umbringen; **to make away with oneself** sich umbringen

▶ **make for** `VI` +*prep obj* **a** (= *head for*) zuhalten auf (+*acc*); (*crowd*) zuströmen (+*dat*, auf +*acc*); (= *attack*) losgehen auf (+*acc*); (*vehicle*) losfahren auf (+*acc*); **where are you making for?** wo willst du hin?; **we are making for London** wir wollen nach London; (*by vehicle*) wir fahren *or* wollen Richtung London; (*by ship*) wir halten Kurs auf London

b (= *promote*) führen zu; **happy marriage, successful parties** den Grund legen für; **such tactics don't make for good industrial relations** solche Praktiken wirken sich nicht gerade günstig auf das Arbeitsklima aus; **the trade figures make for optimism** die Handelsziffern geben Anlass zum Optimismus

▶ **make of** `VI` +*prep obj* halten von; **I didn't make much of it** ich konnte nicht viel dabei finden; **well, what do you make of that?** nun, was halten Sie davon?, was sagen Sie dazu?; **don't make too much of it** überbewerten Sie es nicht

▶ **make off** `VI` sich davonmachen (*with sth* mit etw)

▶ **make out** `VT` *sep* **a** (= *write out*) *cheque, receipt* ausstellen (*to* auf +*acc*); *list, bill* aufstellen, zusammenstellen; (= *fill out*) *form* ausfüllen; **to make out a case for sth** für etw argumentieren

b (= *see, discern*) ausmachen; (= *decipher*) entziffern; (= *understand*) verstehen; *person, actions* schlau werden aus; **I can't make out what he wants** ich komme nicht dahinter, was er will; **how do you make that out?** wie kommst du darauf?

c (= *claim*) behaupten

d (= *imply*) **to make out that ...** es so hinstellen, als ob ...; **he made out that he was hurt** er tat, als sei er verletzt; **to make sb out to be clever/a genius** jdn als klug/Genie hinstellen; **she's not as rich as he makes out** sie ist nicht so reich, wie er es hinstellt; **he tried to make out it was my fault** er versuchte, es so hinzustellen, als wäre ich daran schuld; **Jesus is made out to be a Communist** Jesus wird zum Kommunisten gemacht `VI` **a** (*inf*) (= *get on*)

zurechtkommen; (*with people*) auskommen; (= *succeed*) es schaffen; **he didn't make out with her** er ist bei ihr nicht gelandet (*inf*)

b (*US, inf,* = *pet*) knutschen (*inf*), fummeln (*inf*)

▶ **make over** `VT` *sep* **a** (= *assign*) überschreiben (*to sb* jdm); (= *bequeath*) *property, money* vermachen (*to sb* jdm) **b** (= *convert*) umändern, umarbeiten; *house* umbauen; **the gardens have been made over into a parking lot** man hat die Anlagen in einen Parkplatz umgewandelt

▶ **make up** `VT` *sep* **a** (= *constitute*) bilden; **to be made up of** bestehen aus, sich zusammensetzen aus

b (= *put together*) *food, medicine, bed* zurechtmachen; *parcel* packen; *list, accounts* zusammenstellen, aufstellen; *team* zusammenstellen; (*Typ*) *page* umbrechen; (= *design*) *layout* aufmachen; **to make material up into sth** Material zu etw verarbeiten; **they made the daffodils up into bunches** sie banden die Osterglocken zu Sträußen

c *quarrel* beilegen, begraben; **to make it up (with sb)** sich (mit jdm) wieder vertragen, sich (mit jdm) aussöhnen; **come on, let's make it up** komm, wir wollen uns wieder vertragen

d *face, eyes* schminken; **to make sb/oneself up** jdn/sich schminken; **the way she's made up** wie sie geschminkt ist

e **to make up one's mind (to do sth)** sich (dazu) entschließen(, etw zu tun); **make up your mind!** entschließ dich!; **my mind is quite made up** mein Entschluss steht fest; **once his mind is made up, that's it** wenn er einmal einen Entschluss gefasst hat, bleibt es dabei; **I can't make up your mind for you** ich kann das nicht für dich entscheiden; **to make up one's mind about sb/sth** sich (*dat*) eine Meinung über jdn/etw bilden; **I can't make up my mind about him** ich weiß nicht, was ich von ihm halten soll

f (= *invent*) erfinden, sich (*dat*) ausdenken; **you're making that up!** jetzt schwindelst du aber! (*inf*); **he makes it up as he goes along** (*storyteller*) er macht das aus dem Stegreif; (*child playing*) er macht das, wie es ihm gerade einfällt; (*making excuses, telling lies*) er saugt sich (*dat*) das nur so aus den Fingern; **it was all made up** das war alles nur erfunden

g (= *complete*) *crew* vollständig *or* komplett (*inf*) machen; **I'll make up the other £20** ich komme für die restlichen £ 20 auf; **he made the gift up to £50** er rundete das Geschenk auf £ 50 auf; **add water to make it up to one pint** mit Wasser auf 0,57 Liter auffüllen; **he made up the four at bridge** er war der vierte Mann zum *or* beim Bridge

h (= *compensate for*) *loss* ausgleichen; *time* einholen, aufholen; *sleep* nachholen; **to make it up to sb (for sth)** (= *compensate*) jdn (für etw) entschädigen; (*emotionally, return favour etc*) jdm etw wieder gutmachen

i *fire* (wieder) anschüren *or* anfachen `VI` **a** (= *after quarrelling*) sich versöhnen, sich wieder vertragen; **let's kiss and make up** komm, gib mir einen Kuss und wir vertragen uns wieder

b (*material*) **this material will make up into a nice coat** dieser Stoff wird sich als Mantel gut machen

c (= *catch up*) aufholen; **to make up on sb** jdn einholen, an jdn herankommen; **you've a lot of making up to do** du hast viel nachzuholen *or* aufzuarbeiten

▶ **make up for** `VI` +*prep obj* **to make up for sth** etw ausgleichen; **to make up for lost time** verlorene Zeit aufholen; **to make up for the loss of sb/lack of sth** jdn/etw ersetzen; **that still doesn't make up for the fact that you were very rude** das macht noch lange nicht ungeschehen, dass du sehr unhöflich warst

▶ **make up to** `VI` +*prep obj* (*inf*) sich heranmachen an (+*acc*)

▶ **make with** `VI` +*prep obj* (*US, inf*) **he started making with his trumpet** er legte mit seiner Trompete los (*inf*); **OK, let's make with the**

paint brushes na dann, schnappen wir uns die Pinsel (*inf*); **just make with the scissors** mach schon los mit der Schere (*inf*)

makebelieve ['meɪkbɪliːv] `VT` sich (*dat*) vorstellen

make-believe ['meɪkbɪliːv] `ADJ` *attr* Fantasie-, Phantasie-, imaginär; **a ~ world** eine Fantasie- *or* Phantasie- *or* Scheinwelt `N` Fantasie *f*, Phantasie *f*; **a world of ~** eine Fantasie- *or* Phantasie- *or* Scheinwelt; **don't be afraid, it's only ~** hab keine Angst, das ist doch nur eine Geschichte

make-or-break ['meɪkɔː'breɪk] `ADJ` *attr* (*inf*) kritisch, entscheidend

makeover ['meɪkəʊvə] `N` (= *beauty treatment*) Schönheitskur *f*; (*of car, building*) Verschönerung *f*; **to give sb a complete ~** (= *give new clothes, hairstyle etc*) jdm einen neuen Look verpassen (*inf*)

maker ['meɪkə] `N` (= *manufacturer*) Hersteller(in) *m(f)*; **our Maker** unser Schöpfer *m*; **to go to meet one's Maker** zum Herrn eingehen (*geh*)

-maker ['meɪkə] `N` *suf* (*hat-maker, clockmaker*) -macher(in) *m(f)*

make-ready ['meɪkredɪ] `N` (*Typ*) Zurichtung *f*

make-ready time `N` (*Ind*) Vorbereitungszeit *f*

makeshift ['meɪkʃɪft] `ADJ` improvisiert; *office* provisorisch; *weapon, tool, repairs* behelfsmäßig; **~ accommodation** Notunterkunft *f*; **~ hospital** Notkrankenhaus *nt* `N` Übergangslösung *f*, Notbehelf *m* → shift `N` d

make-up ['meɪkʌp] `N` **a** Make-up *nt*; (*Theat*) Maske *f*, Schminke *f*; **the star does his own ~** der Star schminkt sich selbst *or* macht seine Maske selbst; **she spends hours on her ~** sie braucht Stunden zum Schminken **b** (= *composition: of team, party etc*) Zusammenstellung *f*; (= *character*) Veranlagung *f*; **psychological ~** Psyche *f*; **loyalty is part of his ~** er ist loyal veranlagt; **it's part of their national ~** das gehört zu ihrem Nationalcharakter **c** (*Typ*) Umbruch *m*; (= *layout*) Aufmachung *f*

make-up artist `N` Maskenbildner(in) *m(f)*

make-up bag `N` Kosmetiktasche *f*

make-up girl `N` Maskenbildnerin *f*

make-up kit `N` Schminkset *nt*

make-up man `N` Maskenbildner *m*

make-up mirror `N` Schminkspiegel *m*

make-up woman `N` Maskenbildnerin *f*

makeweight ['meɪkweɪt] `N` **a** (*lit*) **he added a few more as ~s** er gab noch ein paar dazu, um das Gewicht voll zu machen **b** (*fig*) Lückenbüßer *m*; (= *person*) Lückenbüßer(in) *m(f)*; **to use sth as a ~** etw in die Waagschale werfen

making ['meɪkɪŋ] `N` **a** (= *production*) Herstellung *f*; (*of food*) Zubereitung *f*; **in the ~** im Werden, im Entstehen; **the film was three months in the ~** der Film wurde in drei Monaten gedreht; **here you can see history in the ~** hier hat man den Finger am Puls der Geschichte (*liter*); **a star/dictator in the ~** ein werdender Star/Diktator; **it's a civil war/a disaster in the ~** es bahnt sich ein Bürgerkrieg/eine Katastrophe an; **the mistake was not of my ~** der Fehler war nicht mein Werk; **many of her problems are of her own ~** an vielen ihrer Probleme ist sie selbst schuld; **it was the ~ of him** das hat ihn zum Mann gemacht; (= *made him successful*) das hat ihn zu dem gemacht, was er (*heute*) ist **b** **makings** PL Voraussetzungen *pl* (*of* zu); **he has the ~s of an actor/a general** *etc* er hat das Zeug zu einem Schauspieler/General *etc*; **the situation has all the ~s of a strike** die Situation bietet alle Voraussetzungen für einen Streik

maladjusted [ˌmælə'dʒʌstɪd] `ADJ` (*Psych, Sociol*) verhaltensgestört; **psychologically ~** verhaltensgestört; **emotionally ~** emotional gestört; **~ youths** fehlangepasste *or* nicht angepasste Jugendliche *pl*

maladjustment [ˌmælə'dʒʌstmənt] `N` (*Psych, Sociol*) Verhaltensstörung *f*

maladministration ['mæləd͵mɪnɪs'treɪʃən] N schlechte Verwaltung

maladroit ADJ , **maladroitly** ADV [͵mælə'drɔɪt, -lɪ] ungeschickt

maladroitness [͵mælə'drɔɪtnɪs] N Ungeschicklichkeit f

malady ['mælədɪ] N Leiden nt, Krankheit f; **social ~** gesellschaftliches Übel

malaise [mæ'leɪz] N Unwohlsein nt; (fig) Unbehagen nt; **I have a vague feeling of ~ about the future** mich überkommt ein leises Unbehagen, wenn ich an die Zukunft denke

malapropism ['mæləprɒpɪzəm] N Malapropismus m

malaria [mə'lɛərɪə] N Malaria f

malarial [mə'lɛərɪəl] ADJ Malaria-

malarkey [mə'lɑːkɪ] N (inf) (= messing about) Blödelei f (inf); (= nonsense) Hokuspokus m (sl); (= goings-on) Gedöns nt (inf)

Malawi [mə'lɑːwɪ] N Malawi nt

Malay [mə'leɪ] ADJ malaiisch; **the ~ Archipelago** der Malaiische Archipel; **the ~ Peninsula** die Malaiische Halbinsel, die Halbinsel Malakka █ a Malaie m, Malaiin f █ b (Ling) Malaiisch nt

Malaya [mə'leɪə] N Malaya nt

Malayan [mə'leɪən] ADJ malaiisch █ Malaie m, Malaiin f

Malaysia [mə'leɪzɪə] N Malaysia nt

Malaysian [mə'leɪzɪən] ADJ malaysisch █ Malaysier(in) m(f)

malcontent ['mælkən͵tent] ADJ unzufrieden █ Unzufriedene(r) mf

Maldive Islands ['mɔːldaɪv'aɪləndz], **Maldives** ['mɔːldaɪvz] PL Malediven pl

male [meɪl] ADJ █ a männlich; **~ child** Junge m; **a ~ doctor** ein Arzt m; **~ nurse** Krankenpfleger m; **~ sparrow/crocodile** Spatzen-/Krokodilmännchen nt; **~ violence** männliche Gewalt █ b choir, voice Männer-; **an all-male club** ein reiner Männerverein; **that's a typical ~ attitude** das ist typisch männlich █ c (= manly) männlich; **~ bonding** Verbundenheit f unter Männern █ d (Mech) **~ screw** Schraube f; **~ thread** Außengewinde nt; **~ plug** (Elec) Stecker m; **~ connector** Stiftstecker m █ N (= animal) Männchen nt; (inf, = man) Mann m, männliches Wesen; **the ~ of the species** das männliche Tier, das Männchen; **that's typical of a ~** (inf) das ist typisch Mann (inf)

male: **male chauvinism** N Chauvinismus m; **male chauvinist** N Chauvi m (inf); **~ attitude** chauvihafte Haltung (inf); **~ remark** chauvihafte Bemerkung (inf); **male chauvinist pig** N (pej inf) Chauvi m (inf), Chauvinistenschwein nt (pej)

malediction [͵mælɪ'dɪkʃən] N Fluch m, Verwünschung f

male-dominated [meɪl'dɒmɪneɪtɪd] ADJ von Männern beherrscht; **~ society** Männergesellschaft f

malefactor ['mælɪfæktə'] N Übeltäter(in) m(f), Missetäter(in) m(f)

male menopause N (hum) Wechseljahre pl (des Mannes)

maleness ['meɪlnɪs] N Männlichkeit f

malevolence [mə'levələns] N Boshaftigkeit f; (of action) Böswilligkeit f; **to feel ~ toward(s) sb** einen Groll gegen jdn hegen

malevolent [mə'levələnt] ADJ boshaft; gods übel wollend; action böswillig; power, force böse; fate grausam; presence unheilvoll

malfeasance [mæl'fiːzəns] N (Jur) strafbare Handlung, (Amts)vergehen nt

malformation [͵mælfɔː'meɪʃən] N Missbildung f

malformed [mæl'fɔːmd] ADJ missgebildet; characters verzerrt

malfunction [͵mæl'fʌŋkʃən] █ N (of liver etc) Funktionsstörung f; (of machine) Defekt m; **a ~ of the carburettor** ein Defekt m im Vergaser,

ein defekter Vergaser █ VI (liver etc) nicht richtig arbeiten; (machine etc) defekt sein, nicht richtig funktionieren; (system) versagen, nicht richtig funktionieren; **the ~ing part** das defekte Teil

malice ['mælɪs] N █ a Bosheit f, Bösartigkeit f; (of action) Böswilligkeit f; **a look of ~** ein boshafter Blick; **out of ~** aus Bosheit; **to bear sb ~** einen Groll gegen jdn hegen; **I bear him no ~** ich bin ihm nicht böse █ b (Jur) **with ~ aforethought** in böswilliger Absicht, vorsätzlich

malicious [mə'lɪʃəs] ADJ █ a person, words boshaft; behaviour bösartig, böswillig; letter, phone call bedrohend; crime gemein, arglistig; action böswillig █ b (Jur) damage mutwillig, böswillig; **with ~ intent** in böswilliger Absicht

malicious falsehood N (Jur) böswillige Verleumdung

maliciously [mə'lɪʃəslɪ] ADV act böswillig; say, smile boshaft

malicious slander N (Jur) böswillige Verleumdung

malicious wounding N (Jur) vorsätzliche Körperverletzung

malign [mə'laɪn] ADJ (liter) person boshaft; force, intent böse; influence, effect unheilvoll → also **malignant** VT verleumden; (= run down) schlecht machen; **without wishing in any way to ~ her ...** ich will ihr ja nichts (Schlechtes) nachsagen, aber ...

malignancy [mə'lɪgnənsɪ] N Bösartigkeit f; (Med) Malignität f (spec), Bösartigkeit f; (fig: = evil thing) Übel nt

malignant [mə'lɪgnənt] ADJ bösartig; (Med also) maligne (spec); effect negativ; **he took a ~ delight in our misfortunes** unser Unglück bereitete ihm ein hämisches Vergnügen; **a ~ growth** (Med, fig) ein bösartiges Geschwür; **~ melanoma** (Med) malignes Melanom

malignantly [mə'lɪgnəntlɪ] ADV look, say boshaft; **his eyes looked ~ at me** seine Augen schauten mich mit boshaftem Blick an

malignity [mə'lɪgnɪtɪ] N Bösartigkeit f; (Med also) Malignität f (spec)

malinger [mə'lɪŋgə'] VI simulieren, krank spielen

malingerer [mə'lɪŋgərə'] N Simulant(in) m(f)

mall [mɔːl, mæl] N (US: also **shopping mall**) Einkaufszentrum nt

mallard ['mælɑːd] N Stockente f

malleability [͵mælɪə'bɪlɪtɪ] N Formbarkeit f; (of clay, wax also) Geschmeidigkeit f

malleable ['mælɪəbl] ADJ formbar (also fig), weich; (of clay, wax also) geschmeidig

mallet ['mælɪt] N Holzhammer m; (Croquet) (Krocket)hammer m; (Polo) (Polo)schläger m

mallow ['mæləʊ] N Malve f

mallrats ['mɔːlræts] PL (US sl) Jugendliche, die sich zum Zeitvertreib ständig in Einkaufszentren aufhalten

malmsey ['mɑːmzɪ] N Malvasier(wein) m

malnourished [͵mæl'nʌrɪʃt] ADJ (form) person unterernährt; **severely ~** stark unterernährt

malnutrition [͵mælnjuː'trɪʃən] N Unterernährung f

malodorous [mæl'əʊdərəs] ADJ (form) übel riechend

malpractice [͵mæl'præktɪs] N Berufsvergehen nt, Verstoß m gegen das Berufsethos, Amtsvergehen nt (eines Beamten)

malpractice suit N (US: Jur, Med) Strafverfolgung wegen Verletzung der Berufspflichten **to bring a ~ against a surgeon** einen Chirurg wegen eines Kunstfehlers vor Gericht bringen

malt [mɔːlt] █ N Malz nt █ VT barley malzen, mälzen; drink etc mit Malz versetzen or mischen; **~ed barley** gemälzte Gerste

Malta ['mɔːltə] N Malta nt

malted milk ['mɔːltɪd'mɪlk] N Malzmilch f

Maltese [͵mɔːl'tiːz] ADJ maltesisch █ a Malteser(in) m(f) █ b (Ling) Maltesisch nt

Maltese cross N Malteserkreuz nt

malt: **malt extract** N Malzextrakt m; **malt liquor** N aus Malz gebrautes alkoholisches Getränk (US: = beer) Starkbier nt; **malt loaf** N ≈ Rosinenbrot nt

maltreat [͵mæl'triːt] VT schlecht behandeln; (using violence) misshandeln

maltreatment [͵mæl'triːtmənt] N schlechte Behandlung; (violent) Misshandlung f

malt whisky N Malt Whisky m

mamba ['mæmbə] N Mamba f

mambo ['mæmbəʊ] N Mambo m

mam(m)a [mə'mɑː] N (inf) Mama f (inf)

mammal ['mæml] N Säugetier nt, Säuger m

mammalian [mæ'meɪlɪən] ADJ der Säugetiere

mammary ['mæmərɪ] ADJ Brust-; **~ gland** Brustdrüse f

mammogram ['mæməgræm] N (Med) Mammogramm nt

mammography [mæ'mɒgrəfɪ] N Mammografie f

mammon ['mæmən] N Mammon m, Reichtum m; **Mammon** der Mammon

mammoth ['mæməθ] █ N Mammut nt █ ADJ Mammut-; cost, enterprise kolossal; change gewaltig; proportions riesig; **a ~ task** eine Mammutaufgabe, eine kolossale Aufgabe

mammy ['mæmɪ] N (inf) Mami f (inf); (dated US) (schwarze) Kinderfrau, schwarze Mami (inf)

man [mæn] █ N pl **men** █ a (= adult male) Mann m; **be a ~!** sei ein Mann!; **to make a ~ out of sb** einen Mann aus jdm machen; **this incident made a ~ out of him** dieses Ereignis hat ihn zum Mann gemacht; **we'll never make a ~ out of him** aus ihm wird nie ein Mann; **he's only half a ~** er ist kein richtiger Mann; **I'm only half a ~ without you** ohne dich bin ich nur ein halber Mensch; **he took it like a ~** er hat es wie ein Mann or mannhaft ertragen; **that's just like a ~** das ist typisch Mann (inf); **her ~** (inf) ihr Mann; **~ and boy** von Kindheit/Jugend an; **they are ~ and wife** sie sind Mann und Frau; **the ~ in the street** der Mann auf der Straße; **the ~ on the Clapham omnibus** (Brit) der Mann auf der Straße; **~ of God** Mann m Gottes; **~ of letters** (= writer) Schriftsteller m, Literat m; (= scholar) Gelehrter m; **~ of property** vermögender Mann; **you're a ~ about town, you know where ...** (Brit) du kennst dich aus, du weißt, wo ...; **he used to be something of a ~ about town** (Brit) er hatte früher ein reges gesellschaftliches Leben; **a suit for the ~ about town** (Brit) ein Anzug für den feinen Herrn; **a ~ of the world** ein Mann m von Welt; **as one ~ to another** von Mann zu Mann; **well done, that ~!** gut gemacht, alter Junge! (inf); **to be ~ enough (to do sth)** Manns genug sein(, etw zu tun); **~'s bicycle/jacket** Herrenfahrrad nt/-jacke f; **old ~** (dated) alter Junge (dated) or Knabe (dated) → **good** █ b (= human race: also **Man**) der Mensch, die Menschen; **that's no use or good to ~ or beast** das nützt niemandem etwas █ c (= person) man; **no ~** keiner, niemand; **any ~** jeder; **any ~ who believes that ...** wer das glaubt, ...; **sometimes a ~ needs a change** (inf) manchmal braucht man einfach etwas Abwechslung; **that ~!** dieser Mensch!; **that Jones ~** dieser or der Jones!; **our ~ in Beirut** unser Mann in Beirut; **the strong ~ of the government** der starke Mann (in) der Regierung; **as one ~** geschlossen, wie ein Mann; **they are communists to a ~** sie sind allesamt Kommunisten █ d (= type) **the right/wrong ~** der Richtige/Falsche; **you've come to the right ~** da sind or liegen (inf) Sie bei mir richtig; **then I am your ~** dann bin ich genau der Richtige (für Sie); **he's not the ~ for the job** er ist nicht der Richtige für diese Aufgabe; **he's not the ~ to make a mistake like that** so etwas würde ihm bestimmt nicht passieren; **he's not a ~ to ...** er ist nicht der Typ, der ...; **he's not a ~ to meddle with** mit ihm ist nicht gut Kirschen essen; **he is a Cambridge ~** er hat in Cambridge studiert; **family ~**

Familienvater *m*; **he's a family ~** (= *home-loving*) er ist sehr häuslich; **it's got to be a local ~** es muss jemand von hier *or* aus dieser Gegend sein; **I'm not a drinking ~** ich bin kein großer Trinker; **I'm a whisky ~ myself** ich bin mehr für Whisky; **he's a leg/tit ~** (*inf*) er steht bei Frauen vor allem auf Beine/Titten (*inf*); **I'm not a football ~** ich mache mir nicht viel aus Fußball; **he's a ~'s ~** er bevorzugt Männergesellschaft **e** (*inf: interj*) Mensch (*inf*), Mann (*inf*); **you can't do that, ~** Mensch *or* Mann, das kannst du doch nicht machen! (*inf*); **fantastic, ~!** klasse, Mann! (*inf*); **see you, ~!** bis später; **are you coming with us, ~?** du, kommst du noch mit? **f** (= *employee, soldier etc*) Mann *m*; (= *servant*) Bedienstete(r) *m*; **she has a ~ to do the garden** sie hat jemanden, der den Garten macht; **officers and men** Offiziere und Mannschaften; **follow me, men!** mir nach, Leute! **g** (*Chess*) Figur *f*; (*in draughts*) Stein *m* **h the Man** (*US inf* = *boss*) der Boss (*inf*), der Alte (*inf*); (= *police*) die Bullen *pl* (*sl*); (= *white man*) die Weißen *pl* **VT** *ship* bemannen; *fortress, barricades, checkpoint* besetzen; *power station, pump, gun, telephone etc* bedienen; *pickets* bewachen; **the ship is ~ned by a crew of 30** das Schiff hat 30 Mann Besatzung; **a fully ~ned ship** ein voll bemanntes Schiff; **he left 10 soldiers behind to ~ the fortress** er ließ 10 Soldaten als Besatzung für die Festung zurück; **~ the guns/pumps!** an die Geschütze/Pumpen!; **the captain gave the signal to ~ the guns** der Kapitän gab das Zeichen zur Besetzung der Geschütze

manacle ['mænəkl] **N** *usu pl* Handfesseln *pl*, Ketten *pl* **VT** *person* in Ketten legen; *hands* (mit Ketten) fesseln; **they were ~d together** sie waren aneinander gekettet; **he was ~d to the wall** er war an die Wand gekettet

manage ['mænɪdʒ] **VT a** *company, organization, economy* leiten; *property* verwalten; *affairs* in Ordnung halten, regeln; *time, money, resources* einteilen; *football team, pop group* managen; **he ~d the election** er war Wahlleiter; **the election was ~d** (*pej*) die Wahl war manipuliert **b** (= *handle, control*) *person, child, animal* zurechtkommen mit, fertig werden mit; *car, ship* zurechtkommen mit, handhaben; **the car is too big for her to ~** sie kommt mit dem großen Auto nicht zurecht; **she can't ~ children** sie kann nicht mit Kindern umgehen; **I can ~ him** mit dem werde ich schon fertig **c** *task* bewältigen, zurechtkommen mit; *another portion* bewältigen, schaffen; **£50/two hours is the most I can ~** ich kann mir höchstens £ 50 leisten/zwei Stunden erlauben; **I'll ~ it** das werde ich schon schaffen; **he ~d it very well** er hat das sehr gut gemacht; **you'll ~ it next time** nächstes Mal schaffst du's; **I'll do that as soon as I can ~ it** ich mache das, sobald ich kann *or* sobald ich es schaffe; **he should take some exercise as soon as he can ~ it** er sollte sich so bald wie möglich Bewegung verschaffen; **can you ~ the cases?** kannst du die Koffer (allein) tragen?; **thanks, I can ~ them** danke, das geht schon; **she can't ~ the stairs** sie schafft die Treppe nicht; **can you ~ two more in the car?** kriegst du noch zwei Leute in dein Auto? (*inf*); **can you ~ 8 o'clock?** 8 Uhr, ginge *or* geht das?; **could you ~ (to be ready by) 8 o'clock?** kannst du um 8 Uhr fertig sein?; **can you ~ another cup?** darfs noch eine Tasse sein?; **could you ~ another whisky?** schaffst du noch einen Whisky?; **I think I could ~ another piece of cake** ich glaube, ich könnte noch ein Stück Kuchen vertragen; **I couldn't ~ another thing** ich könnte keinen Bissen mehr runterbringen; **she ~d a weak smile** sie brachte ein schwaches Lächeln über (*acc*); **he ~d a few words about his visit** er verlor nur ein paar Worte über seinen Besuch **d to ~ to do sth** es schaffen, etw zu tun; **we have ~d to reduce our costs** es ist uns gelungen, die Kosten zu senken; **do you think you'll ~ to do it?** meinen Sie, Sie können *or* schaffen das?; **I hope you'll ~ to come** ich hoffe, Sie

können kommen; **how did you ~ to get a salary increase?** wie hast du es geschafft *or* angestellt, eine Gehaltserhöhung zu bekommen?; **he ~d to control himself** es gelang ihm, sich zu beherrschen; **he ~d not to get his feet wet** es ist ihm gelungen, keine nassen Füße zu bekommen; **how did you ~ to miss that?** wie konnte Ihnen das nur entgehen?; **how could you possibly ~ to do that?** wie hast du das denn fertig gebracht?; **how could anybody possibly ~ to be so stupid?** wie kann ein Mensch nur so dumm sein?; **could you possibly ~ to close the door?** (*iro*) wäre es vielleicht möglich, die Tür zuzumachen? **VI** zurechtkommen, es schaffen; **can you ~?** geht es?; **thanks, I can ~** danke, es geht schon *or* ich komme schon zurecht; **I thought I could cope with things, but I can't ~** ich dachte, ich käme zurecht, aber ich schaffe es nicht *or* ich bringe es nicht fertig; **she ~s well enough** sie kommt ganz gut zurecht; **how do you ~?** wie schaffen *or* machen Sie das bloß?; **to ~ without sth** ohne etw auskommen, sich (*dat*) ohne etw behelfen; **we'll just have to ~ without** dann müssen wir uns (*dat*) eben so behelfen, dann müssen wir eben so auskommen; **to ~ without sb** ohne jdn auskommen *or* zurechtkommen; **I can ~ by myself** ich komme (schon) allein zurecht; **how do you ~ on £20 a week?** wie kommen Sie mit £ 20 pro Woche aus?

manageable ['mænɪdʒəbl] **ADJ** *child* folgsam, fügsam; *horse* fügsam; *amount, job, task* zu bewältigen; *hair* leicht frisierbar, geschmeidig; *number, proportions* überschaubar; *car* leicht zu handhaben; **since the treatment he's been less violent, more ~** seit der Behandlung ist er nicht mehr so gewalttätig, man kann besser mit ihm umgehen *or* zurechtkommen; **the children are no longer ~ for her** sie wird mit den Kindern nicht mehr fertig; **is that ~ for you?** schaffen Sie das?; **the situation is ~** die Situation lässt sich in den Griff bekommen; **this company is just not ~** es ist unmöglich, dieses Unternehmen (erfolgreich) zu leiten; **to keep sth to a ~ level** etw im überschaubaren Rahmen halten; **you should try and keep the book within ~ limits** Sie sollten versuchen, das Buch in überschaubaren Grenzen zu halten; **pieces of a more ~ size** Stücke, die leichter zu handhaben sind, Stücke in handlicher Größe; **a job of ~ size** eine überschaubare Aufgabe; **the staircase isn't ~ for an old lady** die Treppe ist für eine alte Dame zu beschwerlich

managed: managed economy N Planwirtschaft *f*; **managed fund** ['mænɪdʒd'fʌnd] **N** Investmentfonds *m* (*mit gelegentlicher Umschichtung des Aktienbestandes*)

management ['mænɪdʒmənt] **N a** (= *act*) (*of company*) Leitung *f*, Führung *f*, Management *nt*; (*of non-commercial organization*) Leitung *f*; (*of estate, assets, money*) Verwaltung *f*; (*of affairs*) Regelung *f*; **losses due to bad ~** Verluste, die auf schlechtes Management zurückzuführen sind; **crisis/time/people ~** Krisen-/Zeit-/Personalmanagement *nt* **b** (= *persons*) Unternehmensleitung *f*; (*of single unit or smaller factory*) Betriebsleitung *f*; (*non-commercial*) Leitung *f*; (*Theat*) Intendanz *f*; **"under new ~"** „neuer Inhaber"; (*shop*) „neu eröffnet"; (*pub*) „unter neuer Bewirtschaftung"

management: management accounting N Kosten- und Leistungsrechnung *f*; **management accounts** PL Geschäftsbilanz *pl*; **management buyout** N Aufkauf eines Unternehmens durch Mitglieder der Geschäftsleitung, Management-Buy-out *nt*; **management consultancy** N Unternehmensberatung *f*; **management consultant** N Unternehmensberater(in) *m(f)*; **management course** N Managerkurs *m*; **management fee** N Verwaltungsgebühr *f*; **management skills** PL Führungsqualitäten *pl*; **management studies** N Betriebswirtschaft *f*; **management style** N Führungsstil *m*

manager ['mænɪdʒə'] **N** (*Comm etc*) Geschäftsführer(in) *m(f)*, Manager(in) *m(f)*; (*of restau-*

rant) Geschäftsführer(in) *m(f)*; (*of smaller firm or factory*) Betriebsleiter(in) *m(f)*; (*of bank, chain store*) Filialleiter(in) *m(f)*; (*of department*) Abteilungsleiter(in) *m(f)*; (*of estate etc*) Verwalter(in) *m(f)*; (*Theat*) Intendant(in) *m(f)*; (*of hotel*) Direktor(in) *m(f)*; (*of pop group, boxer etc*) Manager(in) *m(f)*; (*of team*) Trainer(in) *m(f)*; **sales ~** Verkaufsleiter(in) *m(f)*; **publicity ~** Werbeleiter(in) *m(f)*; **business ~** (*for theatre*) Verwaltungsdirektor(in) *m(f)*; (*of pop star etc*) Manager(in) *m(f)*

manageress [,mænɪdʒə'res] **N** (*Comm etc*) Geschäftsführerin *f*, Managerin *f*; (*of restaurant*) Geschäftsführerin *f*; (*of chain store*) Filialleiterin *f*; (*of hotel*) Direktorin *f*

managerial [,mænə'dʒɪərɪəl] **ADJ** geschäftlich; (= *executive*) Management-; *post, staff* leitend; **the ~ team** das Management(team); **at ~ level** auf der Führungsebene; **he has no ~ skills** er ist für leitende Funktionen ungeeignet; **proven ~ skills** nachgewiesene Führungs- *or* Leitungsfähigkeit *f*; **career ~** Karriere *f* als Manager; (*Ftbl*) Trainerkarriere *f*; **~ responsibilities** Führungs- *or* Leitungsaufgaben *pl*; **~ style** Führungsstil *m*; **~ class** Führungsklasse *f*

managing board ['mænɪdʒɪŋ,bɔːd] **N** Direktorium *nt*, geschäftsführender Vorstand

managing director ['mænɪdʒɪŋdɪ'rektə'] **N** Geschäftsführer(in) *m(f)*

managing partner N geschäftsführende(r) Gesellschafter(in) *m(f)* or Teilhaber(in) *m(f)*

man-at-arms [,mænət'ɑːmz] **N** *pl* **men-at-arms** [,menət'ɑːmz] Soldat *m*, Krieger *m* (*old*)

manatee [,mænə'tiː] **N** (Rundschwanz)seekuh *f*

Manchuria [mæn'tʃʊərɪə] **N** die Mandschurei

Manchurian [mæn'tʃʊərɪən] **N a** Mandschu *m* **b** (*Ling*) Mandschu *nt*

Mancunian [mæn'kjuːnɪ ən] **N** Bewohner(in) *m(f)* Manchesters; **he's a ~** er kommt *or* ist aus Manchester **ADJ** aus Manchester

mandarin ['mændərɪn] **N a** (= *Chinese official*) Mandarin *m*; (= *official*) hoher Funktionär, Bonze *m* (*pej*) **b** (*Ling*) **Mandarin** Hochchinesisch *nt* **c** (= *fruit*) Mandarine *f*

mandate ['mændeɪt] **N** Auftrag *m*; (*Pol*) Mandat *nt*; (= *territory*) Mandat(sgebiet) *nt*; **to give sb a ~ to do sth** jdm den Auftrag geben *or* jdn damit beauftragen, etw zu tun; **we have a clear ~ from the country to ...** wir haben den eindeutigen Wählerauftrag, zu ... **VT to ~ a territory to sb** ein Gebiet jds Verwaltung (*dat*) unterstellen, ein Gebiet als Mandat an jdn vergeben

mandated ['mændeɪtɪd] **ADJ ~ territory** Mandatsgebiet *nt*

mandatory ['mændətərɪ] **ADJ a** obligatorisch; **~ retirement age** vorgeschriebenes Rentenalter; **the ~ nature of this ruling** der Zwangscharakter dieser Regelung; **union membership is ~** Mitgliedschaft in der Gewerkschaft ist Pflicht; **it is ~ for him to do this** er ist dazu verpflichtet, das zu tun **b** (*Jur*) *sentence, ban, fine* vorgeschrieben; **murder carries a ~ death sentence** bei Mord ist die Todesstrafe vorgeschrieben; **Singapore has a ~ death penalty for drug offences** (*Brit*) *or* **offenses** (*US*) auf Drogendelikte steht in Singapur die Todesstrafe **c** (*Pol*) **~ state** (= *having a mandate*) Mandatarstaat *m*; (= *being a mandate*) Mandat *nt*; **Mandatory Palestine** das Mandat(sgebiet) Palästina; **to be a ~ power** Mandatarstaat *or* Mandatsherr sein; **to have ~ powers** über Vollmachten verfügen

man-day ['mæn'deɪ] **N** Manntag *m*

Mandelbrot set ['mændlbrɒt,set] **N** (*Math*) Mandelbrotmenge *f*

mandible ['mændɪbl] **N** (*of vertebrates*) Unterkiefer(knochen) *m*, Mandibel *f* (*spec*); **~s** (*of insects*) Mundwerkzeuge *pl*, Mundgliedmaßen *pl*, Mandibel *f* (*spec*); (*of birds*) Schnabel *m*

mandolin(e) ['mændəlɪn] **N** Mandoline *f*

mandrake ['mændreɪk] **N** Mandragore *f*; **~ root** Alraune *f*

mandrill ['mændrɪl] N Mandrill *m*

mane [meɪn] N (*lit, fig*) Mähne *f*

man-eater ['mænˌiːtəʳ] N Menschenfresser *m*; (= *shark*) Menschenhai *m*; (*inf*, = *woman*) männermordendes Weib (*inf*)

man-eating ['mænˌiːtɪŋ] ADJ Menschen fressend; **~ shark** Menschenhai *m*

maneuver N, VTI (*US*) = **manoeuvre**

man Friday N (= *male helper*) rechte Hand (*fig*), Mädchen *nt* für alles (*inf iro*)

manful ADJ , **manfully** ADV ['mænfʊl, -fəlɪ] mannhaft (*geh*), mutig, beherzt

manganese [ˌmæŋgə'niːz] N Mangan *nt*

mange [meɪndʒ] N Räude *f*; (*of man*) Krätze *f*

mangel(wurzel) ['mæŋgl(ˌwɜːzl)] N Runkel- or Futterrübe *f*

manger ['meɪndʒəʳ] N Krippe *f*

mangetout ['mɑ̃ːʒ'tuː] N (*Brit: also* **mangetout pea**) Zuckererbse *f*

mangle[1] ['mæŋgl] N Mangel *f* VT clothes mangeln

mangle[2] VT (*also* **mangle up**) (übel) zurichten

mangler ['mæŋgləʳ] N Hackmaschine *f*, Fleischwolf *m*; (*fig: person*) Verstümmler(in) *m(f)*

mango ['mæŋgəʊ] N (= *fruit*) Mango *f*; (= *tree*) Mangobaum *m*

mangold(wurzel) ['mæŋgəld(ˌwɜːzl)] N = **mangel(wurzel)**

mangrove ['mæŋgrəʊv] N Mangrove(n)baum *m*; **~ swamp** Mangrove *f*

mangy ['meɪndʒɪ] ADJ (+*er*) *dog* räudig; *carpet* schäbig; *hotel* schäbig, heruntergekommen

manhandle ['mænhændl] VT [a] *person* grob or unsanft behandeln; **he was ~d into the back of the van** er wurde recht unsanft or gewaltsam in den Laderaum des Wagens verfrachtet [b] *piano etc* hieven

manhole ['mænhəʊl] N Kanal- or Straßenschacht *m*; (*in boiler etc*) Mannloch *nt*, Einsteigeöffnung *f*

manhood ['mænhʊd] N [a] (= *state*) Mannesalter *nt* [b] (= *manliness*) Männlichkeit *f* [c] (= *men*) Männer *pl*; **a fine example of American ~** ein gutes Beispiel für den amerikanischen Mann [d] (*euph* = *penis*) Männlichkeit *f* (*inf*)

man: man-hour N Arbeitsstunde *f*; **manhunt** N Fahndung *f*; (*hum, of woman*) Männerfang *m*

mania ['meɪnɪə] N [a] (= *madness*) Manie *f*; **persecution ~** Verfolgungswahn *m* [b] (*inf*, = *enthusiasm*) Manie *f*, Tick *m* (*inf*), Fimmel *m* (*inf*); **this ~ for nationalization** diese Verstaatlichungsmanie; **Gazza ~** Gazza-Manie *f*, Gazza-Rummel *m*; **this current ~ for the 1920's** die derzeitige Manie für die 20er Jahre; **he has a ~ for collecting old matchboxes** er hat den Tick or Fimmel, alte Streichholzschachteln zu sammeln (*inf*); **he has a ~ for collecting things** er hat einen Sammeltick (*inf*) or -fimmel (*inf*); **~ for cleanliness** Sauberkeitstick *m* (*inf*), Reinlichkeitsfimmel *m* (*inf*); **tennis has become a ~ with him** Tennis ist bei ihm zur Manie geworden

maniac ['meɪnɪæk] ADJ wahnsinnig N [a] Wahnsinnige(r) *mf*, Irre(r) *mf* [b] (*fig*) **these sports ~s** diese Sportfanatiker *pl*; **you ~** du bist ja wahnsinnig!

maniacal [mə'naɪəkəl] ADJ wahnsinnig

maniacally [mə'naɪəkəlɪ] ADV *grin, laugh* wie ein Irrer/eine Irre; **they were laughing ~** sie lachten wie die Irren

manic ['mænɪk] ADJ [a] (= *frenzied*) *activity, excitement* fieberhaft; *energy, person* rasend [b] (= *insane*) *grin, laughter, sense of humour* wahnsinnig, irre; *jealousy* rasend [c] (*Psych*) *state, depression* manisch

manic-depressive ['mænɪkdɪ'presɪv] ADJ manisch-depressiv N Manisch-Depressive(r) *mf*; **he is a ~** er ist manisch-depressiv

manicure ['mænɪkjʊəʳ] N Maniküre *f*; **to have a ~** sich (*dat*) (die Hände) maniküren lassen; **to**

give sb a ~ jdm die Hände maniküren, jdn maniküren VT maniküren

manicured ['mænɪkjʊəd] ADJ *nails, hands* manikürt; *lawn, garden* gepflegt; **his well-manicured hands** seine gepflegten Hände, seine sorgfältig manikürten Hände

manicure set N Nagelnecessaire *nt*, Nagel- or Maniküreetui *nt*

manicurist ['mænɪˌkjʊərɪst] N Handpflegerin *f*

manifest ['mænɪfest] ADJ offenkundig, offenbar; (= *definite*) eindeutig; **I think it's ~ that ...** es liegt doch wohl auf der Hand, dass ...; **to make sth ~** etw klar or deutlich machen; **he made it ~ that ...** er machte klar or deutlich, dass ... N (*Naut*) Manifest *nt* VT zeigen, bekunden VR sich zeigen; (*Sci, Psych etc*) sich manifestieren; (*ghost*) erscheinen; (*guilt etc*) sich offenbaren, offenbar werden

---

MANIFEST DESTINY

Manifest Destiny war eine gängige Auffassung im Amerika des 19. Jahrhunderts, gemäß der es göttlicher Wille sei, dass die Vereinigten Staaten die Pflicht und die Bestimmung hätten, ihr Territorium und ihren Einfluss auf dem nordamerikanischen Kontinent auszubreiten. Mit diesem Konzept wurde die Siedlerbewegung nach Westen und in Richtung Mexiko gerechtfertigt und ebenso der spanisch-amerikanische Krieg 1898, durch den Puerto Rico und die Philippinen dazugewonnen wurden. Auch wenn das **Manifest Destiny** in der heutigen Zeit nicht mehr angeführt wird, ist es doch immer noch eine unterschwellige Grundeinstellung vieler Amerikaner, wenn es um die Vorrangstellung ihres Landes in der Neuen Welt und rund um den Pazifischen Ozean geht und wird als Legitimation für interventionistische Politik bemüht.

---

manifestation [ˌmænɪfe'steɪʃən] N (= *act of showing*) Ausdruck *m*, Manifestierung *f*, Bekundung *f*; (= *sign*) Anzeichen *nt*, Manifestation *f*; (*of spirit*) Erscheinung *f*

manifestly ['mænɪfestlɪ] ADV eindeutig, offensichtlich; **it's so ~ obvious** es ist so völlig offensichtlich; **the policy ~ failed to work** die Politik funktionierte offenkundig nicht

manifesto [ˌmænɪ'festəʊ] N *pl* -(e)s Manifest *nt*

manifold ['mænɪfəʊld] ADJ mannigfaltig (*geh*), vielfältig; **~ uses** vielseitige Anwendung; **there are ~ problems/dangers** es gibt vielfache Probleme/Gefahren N (*Aut*) (= *inlet manifold*) Ansaugrohr *nt*; (= *exhaust manifold*) Auspuffrohr *nt*

manikin ['mænɪkɪn] N (= *dwarf*) Männchen *nt*, Knirps *m*; (*Art*) Modell *nt*, Gliederpuppe *f*

manila, manilla [mə'nɪlə] N [a] (= *manila paper*) Hartpapier *nt*; **~ envelopes** braune Umschläge [b] (= *manila hemp*) Manilahanf *m*

manioc ['mænɪɒk] N Maniok *m*

manipulate [mə'nɪpjʊleɪt] VT [a] *public opinion, person, prices, data, media* manipulieren; *accounts, figures* manipulieren, frisieren (*inf*); **to ~ sb into doing sth** jdn so manipulieren, dass er/sie etw tut [b] *machine etc* handhaben, bedienen; *bones* einrenken; (*after fracture*) zurechtrücken

manipulation [məˌnɪpjʊ'leɪʃən] N Manipulation *f*

manipulative [mə'nɪpjʊlətɪv] ADJ [a] (*pej*) *behaviour, skill* manipulativ; *film, article, speech* manipulierend; **~ person** Manipulant(in) *m(f)*; **he was very ~** er konnte andere gut manipulieren [b] (*Med*) **~ therapy** Manipulationstherapie *f*; **~ technique** Manipulationstechnik *f*; **~ treatment** Manipulation *f*; **~ operation** manipulativer Eingriff

manipulator [mə'nɪpjʊleɪtəʳ] N Manipulator(in) *m(f)*, Manipulant(in) *m(f)*; **he's a skilled ~ of public opinion** er versteht es, die öffentliche Meinung geschickt zu manipulieren

mankind [mæn'kaɪnd] N die Menschheit

manky ['mæŋkɪ] ADJ (*Brit inf*) dreckig (*inf*)

manlike ['mænlaɪk] ADJ menschlich; (= *like a male*) männlich; *robot* menschenähnlich

manliness ['mænlɪnɪs] N Männlichkeit *f*

manly ['mænlɪ] ADJ (+*er*) männlich; **to behave in a ~ fashion** sich als Mann erweisen

man-made ['mæn'meɪd] ADJ [a] (= *artificial*) künstlich; **~ fibres** (*Brit*) or **fibers** (*US*) Kunstfasern *pl*, synthetische Fasern *pl*; **~ leather/silk** Kunstleder *nt*/-seide *f* [b] (= *caused by man*) *disaster, pollution* vom Menschen verursacht; *world, environment, laws* vom Menschen geschaffen

man-mark ['mænmɑːk] VT (*Sport*) *player, opponent* in Manndeckung nehmen

man-marker ['mænˌmɑːkəʳ] N (*Sport Ftbl*) Manndecker(in) *m(f)*

man-marking ['mænˌmɑːkɪŋ] N (*Sport Ftbl*) Manndeckung *f*

manna ['mænə] N Manna *nt*

manned [mænd] ADJ *satellite etc* bemannt

mannequin ['mænɪkɪn] N (*Fashion*) Mannequin *nt*; (*Art*) (= *dummy*) Gliederpuppe *f*

manner ['mænəʳ] N [a] (= *mode*) Art *f*, (Art und) Weise *f*; **in** or **after this ~** auf diese Art und Weise; **in** or **after the ~ of Petrarch** im Stile Petrarcas; **in the Spanish ~** im spanischen Stil; **in like ~** (*form*) auf die gleiche Weise, ebenso; **in such a ~ that ...** so ..., dass ...; **a painter in the grand ~** ein Maler der alten Schule; **a ball in the grand ~** ein Ball alten Stils or im alten Stil; **in a ~ of speaking** sozusagen, gewissermaßen; **in a ~ of speaking, the job's finished** die Arbeit ist sozusagen or gewissermaßen fertig; **it's just a ~ of speaking** (*of idiom*) das ist nur so eine Redensart; **I didn't mean to insult him, it was just a ~ of speaking** das sollte keine Beleidigung sein, ich habe das nur so gesagt; **as to the ~ born** als sei er/sie dafür geschaffen; **a horseman as to the ~ born** ein geborener Reiter [b] (= *behaviour etc*) Art *f*; **he has a very kind ~** er hat ein sehr freundliches Wesen; **his ~ to his parents** sein Verhalten gegenüber seinen Eltern; **I don't like his ~** ich mag seine Art nicht; **there's something odd about his ~** er benimmt sich irgendwie komisch [c] **manners** PL (*good, bad etc*) Manieren *pl*, Benehmen *nt*, Umgangsformen *pl*; **road ~s** Verhalten *nt* im Straßenverkehr; **he hasn't got any road ~s** er ist ein sehr unhöflicher or rücksichtsloser Fahrer; **that's bad ~s** das or so etwas gehört sich nicht, das ist unanständig; **~s!** benimm dich!; **it's bad ~s to ...** es gehört sich nicht or es ist unanständig, zu ...; **to have bad ~s** schlechte Manieren haben; **he has no ~s** er hat keine Manieren, er kann sich nicht benehmen; **have you forgotten your ~s?** wo hast du denn deine Manieren gelassen?; **now, don't forget your ~s!** du weißt doch, was sich gehört!; **to teach sb some ~s** jdm Manieren beibringen [d] **manners** PL (*of society*) Sitten (und Gebräuche) *pl*; **a novel of ~s** ein Sittenroman *m*; **a comedy of ~s** eine Sittenkomödie [e] (= *class, type*) Art *f*; **all ~ of birds** die verschiedensten Arten von Vögeln; **we saw all ~ of interesting things** wir sahen allerlei Interessantes or so manches Interessante; **I've got all ~ of things to do yet** ich habe noch allerlei or tausenderlei zu tun; **by no ~ of means** keineswegs, in keinster Weise (*inf*); **what ~ of man is he?** (*liter*) was ist er für ein Mensch?

mannered ['mænəd] ADJ [a] (= *affected, fussy*) *style, work of art, gestures* manieriert; *friendliness, subservience etc* betont, prononciert (*geh*) [b] (*with adv*) **to be well-/ill-/impeccably ~** gute/ schlechte/tadellose Manieren haben; **a well-/ ill-/impeccably ~ man** ein Mann mit guten/ schlechten/tadellosen Manieren

mannerism ['mænərɪzəm] N [a] (*in behaviour, speech*) Angewohnheit *f*, Eigenheit *f* [b] (*of style*) Manieriertheit *f*; **his ~s** seine Manierismen

mannerliness ['mænəlɪnɪs] N Wohlerzogenheit *f*

mannerly ['mænəlɪ] ADJ wohlerzogen

mannish ['mænɪʃ] ADJ *woman, clothes* männlich wirkend

mannishly ['mænɪʃlɪ] ADV *dress* maskulin; *walk, behave* wie Männer/ein Mann

manoeuvrability, (US) **maneuverability** [mə,nu:vrə'bɪlɪtɪ] N Manövrierfähigkeit *f*, Wendigkeit *f*

manoeuvrable, (US) **maneuverable** [mə'nu:vrəbl] ADJ manövrierfähig, wendig; **easily ~** leicht zu manövrieren

manoeuvre, (US) **maneuver** [mə'nu:və'] **N a** (*Mil*) Feldzug *m*; **in a well-planned ~** durch einen geschickt geplanten Feldzug
b manoeuvres PL (*Mil*) Manöver *nt* or *pl*, Truppenübung *f*; **the troops were out on ~s** die Truppen befanden sich im Manöver
c (= *clever plan*) Manöver *nt*, Winkelzug *m*, Schachzug *m*; **rather an obvious ~** ein ziemlich auffälliges Manöver
VT manövrieren; **he ~d his troops out onto the plain** er dirigierte or führte seine Truppen hinaus auf die Ebene; **to ~ a gun into position** ein Geschütz in Stellung bringen; **to ~ sb into doing sth** jdn dazu bringen, etw zu tun; **he ~d his brother into a top job** er manövrierte or lancierte seinen Bruder in eine Spitzenposition
VI manövrieren; (*Mil*) (ein) Manöver durchführen; **to ~ for position** (*lit, fig*) sich in eine günstige Position manövrieren; **room to ~** Spielraum *m*, Manövrierfähigkeit *f*

man-of-war [,mænəv'wɔ:'] N *pl* **men-of-war** [,menə'wɔ:'] (*old*) → **Portuguese man-of-war**

manometer [mə'nɒmɪtə'] N (*Tech*) Manometer *nt*

manor ['mænə'] N Gutshof *m*, (Land)gut *nt*; **lord/lady of the ~** Gutsherr *m*/-herrin *f*

manor house N Herrenhaus *nt*

manpower ['mæn,paʊə'] N Leistungspotential *nt* or -potenzial *nt*; (*Mil*) Stärke *f*; **we haven't got the ~** wir haben dazu nicht genügend Personal or Arbeitskräfte *pl*; **Manpower Services Commission** (*Brit*) *Behörde für Arbeitsbeschaffung, Arbeitsvermittlung und Berufsausbildung*

manqué ['mɒŋkeɪ] ADJ *pred* (= *failed*) gescheitert; (= *unrecognized*) verkannt; **he's a novelist ~** (= *unfulfilled*) an ihm ist ein Schriftsteller verloren gegangen

mansard ['mænsɑ:d] N , **mansard roof** N Mansardendach *nt*

manse [mæns] N Pfarrhaus *nt*

manservant ['mænsɜ:vənt] N *pl* **menservants** ['mensɜ:vənts] Diener *m*

mansion ['mænʃən] N Villa *f*; (*of ancient family*) Herrenhaus *nt*

man: man-sized ADJ Riesen-; **~ portion/steak** Riesenportion *f*/-steak *nt*; **manslaughter** N Totschlag *m*

manta (ray) ['mæntə(reɪ)] N Teufelsrochen *m*, Manta *m*

mantelpiece ['mæntlpi:s] N (*above fireplace*) Kaminsims *nt* or *m*; (*around fireplace*) Kaminverkleidung or -einfassung *f*

mantelshelf ['mæntlʃelf] N *pl* **-shelves** [-ʃelvz] = **mantelpiece**

mantilla [mæn'tɪlə] N Mantille *f*, Mantilla *f*

mantis ['mæntɪs] N = **praying mantis**

mantle ['mæntl] **N a** Umhang *m*; (*fig*) Deckmantel *m*; **a ~ of snow** eine Schneedecke **b** (= *gas mantle*) Glühstrumpf *m* **VT** (*liter*) bedecken

man: man-to-man ADJ, ADV **a** (= *frank*) von Mann zu Mann; **a ~ talk** ein Gespräch *nt* von Mann zu Mann **b** (*Sport*) **~ marking** Manndeckung *f*; **~ marker** Manndecker *m*; **man--trained** ['mæntreɪnd] ADJ *dog* auf den Mann dressiert; **mantrap** N Fußangel *f*

manual ['mænjʊəl] **ADJ** manuell; *labour* körperlich; **~ work** manuelle Arbeit, Handarbeit *f*; **~ labourer** (*Brit*) or **laborer** (*US*) Schwerarbeiter(in) *m(f)*; **~ worker** Handarbeiter(in) *m(f)*; **~ skill** Handwerk *nt*; **he was trained in several ~ skills** er hatte verschiedene Handwerksberufe *pl* erlernt; **~ gear change** (*Brit*) or **shift** (*US*) Schaltung *f* von Hand; **~ control** Handsteuerung *f*; **~ operation** Handbetrieb *m* **N a** (= *book*) Handbuch *nt* **b** (*Mus*) Manual *nt* **c** (= *manual operation*) Handbetrieb *m*, manueller Betrieb; **to run on ~** im Handbetrieb laufen; **to put a machine on ~** eine Maschine auf Handbetrieb stellen

manual gearbox ['mænjʊəl'gɪəbɒks] N (*Brit*) Schaltgetriebe *nt*

manually ['mænjʊəlɪ] ADV von Hand, manuell; **~ operated** handbetrieben; **~ controlled** handgesteuert

manual strangulation N Erwürgen *nt* mit bloßen Händen

manual transmission N Schaltgetriebe *nt*

manufacture [,mænjʊ'fæktʃə'] **N** (= *act*) Herstellung *f*; (*pl*: = *products*) Waren *pl*, Erzeugnisse *pl*; **articles of foreign ~** ausländische Erzeugnisse *pl* **VT a** (*lit*) herstellen; **~d goods** Fertigware *f*, Fertigerzeugnisse *pl* **b** (*fig*) *excuse* erfinden **VI** **we started manufacturing ...** wir begannen mit der Herstellung ...

manufacturer [,mænjʊ'fæktʃərə'] N (= *person*) Hersteller(in) *m(f)*; (= *company*) Hersteller *m*; **this country/firm has always been a big ~ of ...** dieses Land/Unternehmen hat schon immer eine bedeutende Rolle bei der Herstellung von ... gespielt

manufacturing [,mænjʊ'fæktʃərɪŋ] **ADJ** Herstellungs-, Produktions-; *industry* verarbeitend; **~ techniques/costs/process** Herstellungs- or Produktionstechniken *pl*/-kosten *pl*/-verfahren *nt*; **~ company** Herstellerfirma *f*; **~ town/city** Industriestadt *f*; **~ output** Produktionsmenge *f*; **the ~ sector** das verarbeitende Gewerbe **N** Erzeugung *f*, Herstellung *f*

manure [mə'njʊə'] **N** Dung *m*, Mist *m*; (*esp artificial*) Dünger *m*; **liquid ~** Jauche *f*; **artificial ~** Kunstdünger *m* **VT** *field* düngen

manuscript ['mænjʊskrɪpt] N Manuskript *nt*; (*ancient still in*) Handschrift *f*; **the novel is still in ~** der Roman ist noch in Manuskriptform; **I read it first in ~ form** ich habe es zuerst als Manuskript gelesen

Manx [mæŋks] **ADJ** der Insel Man **N** (*Ling*) Manx *nt*

Manx: Manx cat N Manx-Katze *f* (*stummelschwänzige Katze*); **Manxman** ['mæŋksmən] N *pl* **-men** [-mən] Bewohner *m* der Insel Man; **Manxwoman** ['mæŋkswʊmən] N *pl* **-women** [-wɪmɪn] Bewohnerin *f* der Insel Man

many ['menɪ] **ADJ, PRON** viele; **~ people** viele (Menschen or Leute); **she has ~** sie hat viele (davon); **he hasn't got ~** er hat nicht viele (davon); **there were as ~ as 20** es waren sogar 20 da; **fifty went to France and as ~ to Germany** fünfzig gingen nach Frankreich und ebenso viele nach Deutschland; **as ~ again** noch einmal so viele; **they are just so ~ cowards** das sind lauter Feiglinge; **there's one too ~** einer ist zu viel; **he's had one too ~** (*inf*) er hat einen zu viel or einen über den Durst getrunken (*inf*); **they were too ~ for us** sie waren zu viele or zu zahlreich für uns; **he made one mistake too ~** er hat einen Fehler zu viel gemacht; **a good/great ~ houses** eine (ganze) Reihe or Anzahl Häuser; **~ a good soldier** so mancher gute Soldat; **~ a time** so manches Mal; **she waited ~ a long year** (*liter*) sie wartete gar manches lange Jahr (*liter*); **~'s the time I've heard that old story** ich habe diese alte Geschichte so manches Mal gehört **N** **the ~** die (große) Masse

many: many-coloured, (*US*) **many-colored** ADJ bunt, vielfarbig; **many-sided** ADJ vielseitig; *figure also* vieleckig; **it's a ~ problem** das Problem hat sehr viele verschiedene Aspekte

Maoist ['maʊɪst] N Maoist(in) *m(f)*

Maori ['maʊrɪ] **ADJ** Maori-; **~ chief** Maorihäuptling *m* **N a** Maori *mf* **b** (*Ling*) Maori *nt*

map [mæp] **N** (Land)karte *f*; (*of streets, town*) Stadtplan *m*; (*showing specific item*) Karte *f*; **a ~ of the stars/rivers** eine Stern-/Flusskarte; **is it on the ~?** ist das auf der Karte (eingezeichnet)?; **this will put Cheam on the ~** (*fig*) das wird Cheam zu einem Namen verhelfen; **it's right off the ~** (*fig*) das liegt (ja) am Ende der Welt or hinter dem Mond (*inf*); **entire cities were wiped off the ~** ganze Städte wurden ausradiert **VT** (= *measure*) vermessen; (= *make a map of*) eine Karte anfertigen von; **the history of her suffering was ~ped on her face** ihr Gesicht war von Leid gezeichnet

▶ **map out** VT *sep* **a** (*lit*) = **map** VT **b** (*fig*: = *plan*) entwerfen; **the essay is well mapped out** der Aufsatz ist gut angelegt; **the conference schedule was all mapped out in advance** der Zeitplan für die Konferenz war schon im Voraus genau festgelegt; **he has mapped out what he will do** er hat bereits geplant, was er tun wird

maple ['meɪpl] N (= *wood, tree*) Ahorn *m*

maple: maple leaf N Ahornblatt *nt*; **maple sugar** N Ahornzucker *m*; **maple syrup** N Ahornsirup *m*

map: mapmaker N Kartograf(in) *m(f)*; **mapmaking** N Kartografie *f*

mapping ['mæpɪŋ] N (*Comput*) Abbildung *f*, Mapping *nt*

map: mapreader N Kartenleser(in) *m(f)*; **mapreading** N Kartenlesen *nt*

maquis [mæ'ki:] N **a the Maquis** der Maquis (*französische Widerstandsbewegung im Zweiten Weltkrieg*) **b** (*Bot*) Macchia *f*

Mar *abbr of* **March** Mrz

mar [mɑ:'] VT verderben; *happiness* trüben; *beauty* mindern; **not a cloud to ~ the sky** kein Wölkchen trübte den Himmel; **his essay was ~red by careless mistakes** durch seine Flüchtigkeitsfehler verdarb er (sich) den ganzen Aufsatz

marabou ['mærəbu:] N Marabu *m*

maracas [mə'rækəz] PL Rassel *f*, Maracá *f*

maraschino [,mærə'ski:nəʊ] N (= *drink*) Maraschino *m*; (= *maraschino cherry*) Maraschinokirsche *f*

marathon ['mærəθən] **N a** (*lit*) Marathon(lauf) *m*; **~ runner** Marathonläufer(in) *m(f)* **b** (*fig*) Marathon *nt*; **this film is a real ~** das ist wirklich ein Marathonfilm **ADJ** Marathon-; *negotiations* endlos (lang); **~ speech/film** Marathonrede *f*/-film *m*

maraud [mə'rɔ:d] **VI** plündern; **they went ~ing about the countryside** sie zogen plündernd durch die Lande **VT** plündern

marauder [mə'rɔ:də'] N Plünderer *m*, Plünderin *f*; (= *animal*) Räuber *m*

marauding [mə'rɔ:dɪŋ] ADJ plündernd; **the deer fled from the ~ wolf** das Reh floh vor dem Beute suchenden Wolf

marble ['mɑ:bl] **N a** Marmor *m* **b** (= *work in marble*) Marmorplastik *f* **c** (= *glass ball*) Murmel *f*, Klicker *m* (*inf*); **he's lost his ~s** (*inf*) er hat nicht mehr alle Tassen im Schrank (*inf*); **to pick up one's ~s and go home** (*US*) die Koffer packen und nach Hause gehen **ADJ** Marmor-; **~ pillar/staircase** Marmorsäule *f*/-treppe *f*

marble cake N Marmorkuchen *m*

marbled ['mɑ:bld] ADJ *surface, paper, wall, soap, colour* marmoriert; **~ effect/finish** Marmoreffekt *m*; **meat ~ with fat** durchwachsenes Fleisch

March [mɑ:tʃ] N März *m* → *also* **September**

march[1] [mɑ:tʃ] **N a** (*Mil, Mus*) Marsch *m*; (= *demonstration*) Demonstration *f*; (*fig: = long walk*) Weg *m*; **to move at a good stiff ~** mit strammen Schritten or stramm marschieren; **we had been five days on the ~** wir waren fünf Tage lang marschiert; **it's two days' ~** es ist ein Zwei-Tage-Marsch; **he went for a good ~ across the moors** er ist durchs Moorland marschiert
b (*of time, history, events*) Lauf *m*
c **to steal a ~ on sb** jdm zuvorkommen
VT *soldiers* marschieren lassen; *distance* marschieren; **to ~ sb off** jdn abführen
VI marschieren; **forward ~!** vorwärts

(,marsch)!; **quick ~!** im Laufschritt, marsch!; **to ~ in** einmarschieren; **she just ~ed into the room** sie marschierte einfach (ins Zimmer) hinein; **time ~es on** die Zeit bleibt nicht stehen; **to ~ out** abmarschieren, ausrücken; **to ~ past sb** an jdm vorbeimarschieren; **she ~ed straight up to him** sie marschierte schnurstracks auf ihn zu

march² N (*Hist*) Grenzmark *f*; **the Welsh ~es** das Grenzland zwischen England und Wales

marcher ['mɑːtʃə] N (*in demo*) Demonstrant(in) *m(f)*

marching ['mɑːtʃɪŋ]: **marching orders** PL (*Brit*) (*Mil*) Marschbefehl *m*; (*inf*) Entlassung *f*; **the new manager got his ~** der neue Manager ist gegangen worden (*inf*); **she gave him his ~** sie hat ihm den Laufpass gegeben; **marching song** N Marschlied *nt*

marchioness ['mɑːʃənɪs] N Marquise *f*

march past N Vorbeimarsch *m*, Aufmarsch *m*, Defilee *nt*

Mardi Gras ['mɑːdɪ'grɑː] N Karneval *m*

mare [mɛə'] N (= *horse*) Stute *f*; (= *donkey*) Eselin *f*

mare's-nest ['mɛəznest] N Windei *nt*, Reinfall *m*

Margaret ['mɑːgərɪt] N Margarete *f*

margarine [,mɑːdʒə'riːn], **marge** [mɑːdʒ] (*inf*) N Margarine *f*

margarita [,mɑːgə'riːtə] N , **marguerita** [,mɑːgə'riːtə] N Margarita *m* (*Tequila mit Zitronensaft*)

margin ['mɑːdʒɪn] N **a** (*on page*) Rand *m*; **a note (written) in the ~** eine Randbemerkung, eine Bemerkung am Rand **b** (= *extra amount*) Spielraum *m*; **~ of error** Fehlerspielraum *m*; **to allow for a ~ of error** etwaige Fehler mit einkulieren; **he left a safety ~ of one hour** sicherheitshalber kalkulierte er einen Spielraum von einer Stunde ein; **by a narrow ~** knapp; **it's within the safety ~** das ist noch sicher **c** (*Comm: also* **profit margin**) Gewinnspanne *f*, Verdienstspanne *f* **d** (*liter, = edge*) Rand *m*, Saum *m* (*liter*); **the grassy ~ of the lake** das grüne Seeufer

marginal ['mɑːdʒɪnl] ADJ **a** (= *slight*) *improvement, difference* geringfügig, unwesentlich; *issue* nebensächlich; **to be of ~ importance** nebensächlich sein; **~ figure** Randfigur *f* **b** (*Sociol*) *people, groups* randständig **c** (= *borderline*) (*Brit Parl*) *constituency, seat* mit knapper Mehrheit; **this is a ~ constituency for the Tories** die Tories haben in diesem Wahlkreis nur eine knappe Mehrheit; **~ case** Grenzfall *m* **d** (= *barely profitable*) *business* kaum rentabel; *land* ertragsarm; **~ cost** Grenzkosten *pl* **e** **~ note** Randbemerkung *f*

MARGINAL SEAT

In Großbritannien spricht man dann von einem **marginal seat** oder einer **marginal constituency**, wenn eine bestimmte politische Partei nur mit einer knappen Mehrheit die Macht in einem Wahlbezirk behaupten kann. Bei einer Neuwahl bestehen dann gute Chancen, dass dieser Sitz von einer Oppositionspartei erobert wird. Wenn es für einen **marginal seat** zu einer **by-election**, einer Nachwahl aufgrund des Todes oder des Rücktritts eines Parlamentsmitgliedes kommt, wird das Wahlergebnis häufig von den Medien genauestens analysiert, um eventuelle Rückschlüsse auf die landesweite Beliebtheit der Regierung zu ziehen. Wenn ein Sitz von einer Partei stets mit großer Mehrheit gewonnen wird, spricht man von einem **safe seat**.

---

marginalization [,mɑːdʒɪnəlaɪ'zeɪʃən] N Marginalisierung *f* (*geh*)

marginalize ['mɑːdʒɪnəlaɪz] VT marginalisieren (*geh*)

---

marginally ['mɑːdʒɪnəlɪ] ADV geringfügig; *higher, lower, faster etc* etwas; **is that better? – ~** ist das besser? – etwas *or* ein wenig; **he failed, but only just ~** es gelang ihm nicht, aber nur ganz knapp; **it's only ~ useful** es hat nur sehr begrenzte Anwendungsmöglichkeiten

margin: margin release N Randlöser *m*; **margin stop** N Randsteller *m*

marguerite [,mɑːgə'riːt] N Margerite *f*

marigold ['mærɪgəʊld] N (= *African or French marigold*) Tagetes *f*, Studentenblume *f*; (= *common or pot marigold*) Ringelblume *f*

marihuana, marijuana [,mærɪ'hwɑːnə] N Marihuana *nt*

marimba [mə'rɪmbə] N Marimba *f*

marina [mə'riːnə] N Yacht- *or* Jachthafen *m*

marinade [,mærɪ'neɪd] N Marinade *f*

marinate ['mærɪneɪt] VT marinieren

marine [mə'riːn] ADJ Meeres-, See-; **~ life** Meeresfauna und -flora *f*; **~ animal** Meerestier *nt*; **~ bird** Seevogel *m*; **~ plant** Meerespflanze *f*; **~ pollution** Meeresverschmutzung *f*; **~ environment** Meeresumwelt *f* N **a** (= *fleet*) Marine *f* **b** (= *person*) Marineinfanterist(in) *m(f)*; **the ~s** die Marineinfanterie *pl*, die Marinetruppen *pl*; **tell that to the ~s!** (*Brit inf*) das kannst du mir nicht weismachen, das kannst du deiner Großmutter erzählen! (*inf*)

marine: marine biologist N Meeresbiologe *m*, Meeresbiologin *f*; **marine biology** N Meeresbiologie *f*; **marine dumping** N Verklappung *f*; **marine engineer** N Marineingenieur(in) *m(f)*; **marine insurance** N Seeversicherung *f*

mariner ['mærɪnə'] N Seefahrer *m*, Seemann *m*

marine science N Meereskunde *f*

marine underwriter N (*Insur*) Seeversicherer *m*

marionette [,mærɪə'net] N Marionette *f*

marital ['mærɪtl] ADJ ehelich

marital: marital bed N Ehebett *nt*; **marital bliss** N Eheglück *nt*; **they lived together in ~** sie genossen ein glückliches Eheleben; **marital rape** N Vergewaltigung *f* in der Ehe; **marital status** N Familienstand *m*; **marital vows** PL Ehegelübde *nt*

maritime ['mærɪtaɪm] ADJ See-; **~ warfare** Seekrieg *m*; **~ regions** Küstenregionen *pl*; **~ museum** (*for seafaring*) Schifffahrtsmuseum *nt*; (*for marine science*) Meereskundemuseum *nt*

maritime: maritime law N Seerecht *nt*; **maritime nation** N Seefahrernation *f*; **maritime power** N Seemacht *f*; **Maritime Provinces** PL (*Canada*) **the ~** die (kanadischen) Ostprovinzen

marjoram ['mɑːdʒərəm] N Majoran *m*

Mark [mɑːk] N Markus *m*; **~ Antony** Mark Anton

mark¹ [mɑːk] N (*Hist Fin*) Mark *f*

mark² N **a** (= *stain, spot etc*) Fleck *m*; (= *scratch*) Kratzer *m*, Schramme *f*; **to make a ~ on sth** einen Fleck/Kratzer auf etw (*acc*) machen; **dirty ~s** Schmutzflecken *pl*; **with not a ~ on it** in makellosem Zustand; **will the operation leave a ~?** wird die Operation Spuren *or* Narben hinterlassen?; **the ~s of violence** die Spuren der Gewalt; **he left the ring without a ~ on him/his body** er verließ den Ring, ohne auch nur eine Schramme abbekommen zu haben; **the corpse didn't have a ~ on it** die Leiche wies keine Verletzungen auf

b (= *marking*) (*on animal*) Fleck *m*; (*on person*) Mal *nt*; (*on plane, football pitch etc*) Markierung *f*; (= *sign: on monument etc*) Zeichen *nt*

c (*in exam*) Note *f*; **high** *or* **good ~s** gute Noten *pl*; **the ~s are out of 100** insgesamt kann man 100 Punkte erreichen; **you get no ~s at all for your cooking** (*fig*) in puncto Kochen bist du ja nicht gerade eine Eins (*inf*); **there are no ~s for guessing** (*fig*) das ist ja wohl nicht schwer zu zu erraten; **he gets full ~s for punctuality** (*fig*) in Pünktlichkeit verdient er eine Eins

d (= *sign, indication*) Zeichen *nt*; **he had the ~s**

---

of old age er war vom Alter gezeichnet; **it bears the ~s of genius** das trägt geniale Züge; **it's the ~ of a gentleman** daran erkennt man den Gentleman

e (*instead of signature*) **to make one's ~** drei Kreuze (als Unterschrift) machen

f (= *level*) **expenses have reached the £100 ~** die Ausgaben haben die 100-Pfund-Grenze erreicht; **the temperature reached the 35° ~** die Temperatur stieg bis auf 35° an

g **Cooper Mark II** Cooper, II; **the new secretary, a sort of Miss Jones ~ 2** die neue Sekretärin, eine zweite Ausführung von Fräulein Jones

h (*phrases*) **to be quick off the ~** (*Sport*) einen guten Start haben; (*fig*) blitzschnell handeln *or* reagieren; **you were quick off the ~** (*fig*) du warst aber fix!; **he was quickest off the ~** er war der Schnellste; **to be slow off the ~** (*Sport*) einen schlechten Start haben; (*fig*) nicht schnell genug schalten *or* reagieren; (*as characteristic*) eine lange Leitung haben (*inf*); **to be up to the ~** den Anforderungen entsprechen; **his work is not up to the ~** seine Arbeit ist unter dem Strich; **I'm not feeling quite up to the ~** ich bin *or* fühle mich nicht ganz auf dem Posten; **to leave one's ~ (on sth)** seine Spuren (an etw *dat*) hinterlassen; **to make one's ~** sich (*dat*) einen Namen machen; **on your ~s!** auf die Plätze!; **to be wide of the ~** (*shooting*) danebentreffen, danebenschießen; (*fig: in guessing, calculating*) sich verhauen (*inf*); **your calculations were wide of the ~** mit deiner Kalkulation hast du dich ganz schön verhauen (*inf*); **to hit the ~** (*fig*) ins Schwarze treffen

i (*Rugby*) Freifang *m*; "**mark!**" „Marke!"

VT **a** (*adversely*) beschädigen; (= *stain*) schmutzig machen, Flecken machen auf (+*acc*); (= *scratch*) zerkratzen; **the other boxer was not ~ed at all** der andere Boxer hatte nicht eine Schramme abbekommen *or* überhaupt nichts abbekommen; **her face was ~ed for life** sie hat bleibende Narben im Gesicht zurückbehalten; **the experience ~ed him for life** das Erlebnis hat ihn für sein Leben gezeichnet

b (*for recognition, identity*) markieren, bezeichnen; (= *label*) beschriften; (= *price*) auszeichnen; *playing cards* zinken; **~ed with the name and age of the exhibitor** mit Namen und Alter des Ausstellers versehen; **the bottle was ~ed "poison"** die Flasche trug die Aufschrift „Gift"; **the chair is ~ed at £2** der Stuhl ist mit £ 2 ausgezeichnet; **the picture isn't ~ed** das Bild ist ohne Angaben; **the cage isn't ~ed** der Käfig hat keine Aufschrift; **~ where you have stopped in your reading** mach dir ein Zeichen, bis wohin du gelesen hast; **to ~ sth with an asterisk** etw mit einem Sternchen versehen; **X ~s the spot** X markiert *or* bezeichnet die Stelle; **the teacher ~ed him absent** der Lehrer trug ihn als fehlend ein; **it's not ~ed on the map** es ist nicht auf der Karte eingezeichnet; **it's ~ed with a blue dot** es ist mit einem blauen Punkt gekennzeichnet; **he ~ed his own books with a secret sign** er kennzeichnete seine eigenen Bücher mit einem Geheimzeichen

c (= *characterize*) kennzeichnen; **a decade ~ed by violence** ein Jahrzehnt, das im Zeichen der Gewalt stand; **the new bill ~s a change of policy** das neue Gesetz deutet auf einen politischen Kurswechsel hin; **it ~ed the end of an era** damit ging eine Ära zu Ende; **it ~s him as a future star** daran zeigt sich, dass er eine große Karriere vor sich (*dat*) hat; **a month ~ed by inactivity** ein Monat, der sich durch Untätigkeit auszeichnete

d (*usu pass*) zeichnen; **~ed with grief** von Schmerz gezeichnet; **a beautifully ~ed bird** ein schön gezeichneter Vogel

e *exam, paper* korrigieren (und benoten); **to ~ a paper A** eine Arbeit mit (einer) Eins benoten; **to ~ a candidate** einem Kandidaten eine Note geben; **the candidate was ~ed ...** der Kandidat erhielt die Note ...; **we ~ed him A** wir haben ihm eine Eins gegeben; **to ~ sth wrong** etw anstreichen

f (= *heed*) hören auf (+*acc*); **~ my words** eins

kann ich dir sagen; (*threatening, warning also*) lassen Sie sich das gesagt sein!; **~ you, he may have been right** er könnte gar nicht so Unrecht gehabt haben; **~ you, I didn't believe him** ich habe ihm natürlich nicht geglaubt

g (*old, = notice*) bemerken; **did you ~ where it fell?** hast du dir gemerkt, wo es hingefallen ist?

h (*Sport*) *player, opponent* decken

i to ~ time (*Mil, fig*) auf der Stelle treten

VI a (*= get dirty*) schmutzen, schmutzig werden; (*= scratch*) Kratzer bekommen

b her skin **~s easily** sie bekommt leicht blaue Flecken

c (*Sport*) decken

▶ **mark down** VT *sep* **a** (*= note down*) (sich *dat*) notieren **b** *prices* herab- *or* heruntersetzen

▶ **mark off** VT *sep* kennzeichnen; *boundary* markieren; *football pitch etc* abgrenzen; *danger area etc* absperren; **these characteristics mark him off from the others** durch diese Eigenschaften unterscheidet er sich von den anderen

▶ **mark out** VT *sep* **a** *tennis court etc* abstecken **b** (*= note*) bestimmen (*for* für); **he's been marked out for promotion** er ist zur Beförderung vorgesehen; **the area has been marked out for special government grants** für das Gebiet sind besondere staatliche Zuschüsse vorgesehen **c** (*= identify*) **his speeches have marked him out as a communist** aus seinen Reden kann man schließen, dass er Kommunist ist; **what marks this example out as being different?** worin unterscheidet sich dieses Beispiel?

▶ **mark up** VT *sep* **a** (*= write up*) notieren (*on* auf +*dat*) (*Typ*) auszeichnen **b** *price* heraufsetzen, erhöhen

markdown ['mɑːkdaʊn] N (*Comm*) Preissenkung *f* (*of* um); **~ price** herabgesetzter Preis

marked [mɑːkt] ADJ **a** *contrast* merklich, deutlich; *accent* stark, deutlich; *change* spürbar, merklich; **in ~ contrast (to sb/sth)** in scharfem Gegensatz (zu jdm/etw); **it is becoming more ~** es wird immer deutlicher, es tritt immer deutlicher zutage *or* zu Tage **b** **he's a ~ man** er steht auf der schwarzen Liste **c** (*= signposted*) *path, trail* ausgezeichnet

markedly ['mɑːkɪdlɪ] ADV *improve, increase, differ, change* merklich; *quicker, slower, more, less* wesentlich; **it is ~ better** es ist wesentlich *or* bedeutend besser; **not ~ so** nicht, dass es auffallen würde; **they are not ~ different** es besteht kein wesentlicher *or* großer Unterschied zwischen ihnen

marker ['mɑːkə'] N **a** Marke *f*; (*to turn at*) Wendemarke *f*, Wendepunkt *m*; (*on road*) Schild *nt*, Wegweiser *m*; (*in book*) Lesezeichen *nt* **b** (*= indication*) **a ~ for sth** eine Kennzeichnung für etw **c** (*for exams*) Korrektor(in) *m(f)*; (*= scorekeeper in games*) Punktezähler(in) *m(f)*; **will you be the ~?** schreibst du (die Punkte) auf? **d** (*Ftbl*) Beschatter(in) *m(f)* **e** (*= pen*) Markierstift *m*, Marker *m*

market ['mɑːkɪt] **N** **a** Markt *m*; **when is the next ~?** wann ist wieder Markt(tag)?; **he took his sheep to ~** er brachte seine Schafe zum Markt; **at the ~** auf dem Markt; **to go to ~** auf den Markt gehen

b (*= trade*) Markt *m*; **world ~** Weltmarkt *m*; **open ~** offener Markt; **to be in the ~ for sth** an etw (*dat*) interessiert sein; **to be on the ~** auf dem Markt sein; **to come on(to) the ~** auf den Markt kommen; **to put on the ~** auf den Markt bringen; *house* zum Verkauf anbieten

c (*= demand*) (Absatz)markt *m*; (*= area*) Absatzgebiet *nt* *or* -markt *m*; **to create a ~** Nachfrage erzeugen; **to find a ready ~** guten Absatz finden

d (*= stock market*) Börse *f*; **to play the ~** (an der Börse) spekulieren

VT vertreiben; **to ~ a (new) product** ein (neues) Produkt auf den Markt bringen; **it's a nice idea, but we can't ~ it** das ist eine gute Idee, sie lässt sich nur nicht verkaufen *or* vermark-

ten; **the reason it didn't sell was simply that it wasn't properly ~ed** es fand wegen unzureichenden Marketings keinen Absatz

VI sich verkaufen, Absatz finden, gehen (*inf*)

marketability [,mɑːkɪtə'bɪlɪtɪ] N Marktfähigkeit *f*

marketable ['mɑːkɪtəbl] ADJ absetzbar, marktfähig; (*fig*) *actor, sportsperson* vermarktbar

market: market analysis N Marktanalyse *f*; **market behaviour** N Marktverhalten *nt*; **market condition** N *usu pl* Marktlage *f*, Konjunktur *f*; **market day** N Markttag *m*; **market dealings** PL (*Brit St Ex*) Börsenhandel *m*; **market dominance** N (*Econ*) Marktbeherrschung *f*; **market-driven**, **market-led** ADJ *product, decision, change, company* marktbestimmt, marktgesteuert; **market economy** N Marktwirtschaft *f*; **market forces** PL Marktkräfte *pl*; **market garden** N Gemüseanbaubetrieb *m*, Gärtnerei *f*; **market gardener** N Gärtner(in) *m(f)*; **market gardening** N (gewerbsmäßiger) Anbau von Gemüse

marketing ['mɑːkɪtɪŋ] N Marketing *nt*; **~ manager** Marketingmanager(in) *m(f)*

market: market leader N Marktführer *m*; **market niche** N Marktnische *f*; **marketplace** N **a** Marktplatz *m*; **on the ~** auf dem Marktplatz **b** (*= world of trade*) Markt *m*; **in the ~** auf dem Markt; **market price** N Marktpreis *m*; **market research** N Marktforschung *f*; **market researcher** N Marktforscher(in) *m(f)*; **market share** N Marktanteil *m*; **market square** N Marktplatz *m*; **market survey** N Marktuntersuchung *f*; **market swing** N (*US*) Konjunkturumschwung *m*; **market town** N Marktstädtchen *nt*; **market trader** N (*Brit*) Markthändler(in) *m(f)*; **market trends** PL Markttendenzen *pl*; **market value** N Marktwert *m*

marking ['mɑːkɪŋ] N **a** Markierung *f*; (*on animal*) Zeichnung *f* **b** (*of exams*) (*= correcting*) Korrektur *f*; (*= grading*) Benotung *f* **c** (*Sport*) Decken *nt*, Deckung *f*

marking ink N Wäschetinte *f*

marksman ['mɑːksmən] N *pl* **-men** [-mən] Schütze *m*; (*police etc*) Scharfschütze *m*

marksmanship ['mɑːksmənʃɪp] N Treffsicherheit *f*

markswoman ['mɑːks,wʊmən] N *pl* **-women** [-,wɪmɪn] Schützin *f*; (*police etc*) Scharfschützin *f*

mark-up ['mɑːkʌp] N **a** Handelsspanne *f*; (*= amount added*) Preiserhöhung *f* *or* -aufschlag *m*; **~ price** Verkaufspreis *m* **b** (*Typ*) Auszeichnung *f*

marl [mɑːl] N Mergel *m*

marlin ['mɑːlɪn] N Fächerfisch *m*, Marlin *m*

marlinspike ['mɑːlɪnspaɪk] N Marlspieker *m*, Splisseisen *nt*

marmalade ['mɑːmələɪd] N Marmelade *f* aus Zitrusfrüchten; (**orange**) **~** Orangenmarmelade *f*

marmoreal [mɑː'mɔːrɪəl] ADJ marmorn, aus Marmor; (*= resembling marble*) marmorartig

marmoset ['mɑːməʊzet] N Krallenaffe *m*, Pinseläffchen *nt*

marmot ['mɑːmət] N Murmeltier *nt*

maroon¹ [mə'ruːn] ADJ kastanienbraun, rötlich braun **N** (*= colour*) Kastanienbraun *nt*; (*= firework*) Leuchtkugel *f*

maroon² VT aussetzen; **~ed** von der Außenwelt abgeschnitten; **~ed by floods** vom Hochwasser eingeschlossen

marque [mɑːk] N (*= brand*) Marke *f*

marquee [mɑː'kiː] N **a** Festzelt *nt* **b** (*US: of theatre etc*) Vordach *nt*, Canopy *nt*; **his name's on all the ~s** sein Name ist auf allen Anzeigetafeln zu sehen

marquess ['mɑːkwɪs] N Marquis *m*

marquetry ['mɑːkɪtrɪ] N Marketerie *f*, Einlegearbeit *f*

marquis ['mɑːkwɪs] N = **marquess**

marram grass ['mærəm,grɑːs] N Strandhafer *m*, Dünengras *nt*

marriage ['mærɪdʒ] ✪ 24.3 N **a** (*state*) die Ehe; (*= wedding*) Hochzeit *f*, Heirat *f*; (*= marriage ceremony*) Trauung *f*; **~ of convenience** Vernunftehe *f*; **relations by ~** angeheiratete Verwandte; **to be related by ~** (*in-laws*) miteinander verschwägert sein; (*others*) miteinander verwandt sein; **to give sb in ~ to sb** jdn jdm zur Frau geben; **to give sb in ~** jdn verheiraten; **an offer of ~** ein Heiratsantrag *m* **b** (*fig*) Verbindung *f*; **a ~ of two minds** eine geistige Ehe

marriageable ['mærɪdʒəbl] ADJ heiratsfähig; **of ~ age** im heiratsfähigen Alter

marriage: marriage bed N Ehebett *nt*; **marriage broker** N Heiratsvermittler(in) *m(f)*; (*Jur*) Ehemakler(in) *m(f)*; **marriage bureau** N Heiratsinstitut *nt*; **marriage ceremony** N Trauzeremonie *f*; **marriage certificate** N Heiratsurkunde *f*; **marriage contract** N (*Jur*) Ehevertrag *m*; **marriage counselling**, (*US*) **marriage counseling** N Eheberatung *f*; **marriage counsellor** N, (*US*) **marriage counselor** N Eheberater(in) *m(f)*; **marriage guidance** N Eheberatung *f*; **marriage guidance centre**, **marriage guidance center** (*US*) N Eheberatungsstelle *f*; **marriage guidance counsellor**, **marriage guidance counselor** (*US*) N Eheberater(in) *m(f)*; **marriage licence**, (*US*) **marriage license** N Eheerlaubnis *f*; **marriage lines** PL Trauschein *m*; **marriage portion** N (*old*) Mitgift *f*; **marriage settlement** N Ehevertrag *m*; **marriage vow** N Ehegelübde *nt*

married ['mærɪd] ADJ *man, woman* verheiratet (*to sb* mit jdm); **just** *or* **newly ~** frisch vermählt; **~ couple** Ehepaar *nt*; **~ life** das Eheleben; **he/she is a ~ man/woman** er/sie ist verheiratet

married: married name N Ehename *m*; **married quarters** PL Unterkünfte *pl* für Eheleute

marrow ['mærəʊ] N **a** (*Anat*) (Knochen)mark *nt*; **he's a Scot to the ~** er ist durch und durch Schotte; **to be frozen to the ~** völlig durchgefroren sein **b** (*fig: of statement etc*) Kern *m*, Wesentliche(s) *nt* **c** (*Brit Bot: also* **vegetable marrow**) Gartenkürbis *m*

marrowbone ['mærəʊbəʊn] N Markknochen *m*

marrowfat ['mærəʊfæt] N , **marrowfat pea** N Markerbse *f*

marry ['mærɪ] ✪ 24.3 **VT** **a** (*= get married to*) heiraten; **to ~ money** reich heiraten; **will you ~ me?** willst du mich heiraten?

b (*priest*) trauen

c (*father*) verheiraten; **he married all his daughters into very rich families** er hat zugesehen, dass alle seine Töchter in reiche Familien einheirateten

VI **a** (*also* **get married**) heiraten, sich verheiraten; (*couple*) heiraten, sich vermählen (*geh*); **to ~ into a rich family** in eine reiche Familie einheiraten; **to ~ into money** reich heiraten; **he married into a small fortune** durch die Heirat ist er an ein kleines Vermögen gekommen; **he's not the ~ing kind** er ist nicht der Typ, der heiratet; **~ in haste, repent at leisure** (*prov*) Heiraten in Eile bereut man in Weile (*prov*)

b (*fig: two pieces of wood etc*) ineinander passen

▶ **marry off** VT *sep* an den Mann/die Frau bringen (*inf*); *girl also* unter die Haube bringen (*inf*); **he has married off his daughter to a rich young lawyer** er hat dafür gesorgt, dass seine Tochter einen reichen jungen Anwalt heiratet

Mars [mɑːz] N Mars *m*

Marseillaise [,mɑːseɪ'leɪz] N **the ~** die Marseillaise

Marseilles [mɑː'seɪlz] N Marseille *nt*

marsh [mɑːʃ] N Sumpf *m*

marshal ['mɑːʃəl] **N** (*Mil, of royal household*) Marschall *m*; (*at sports meeting etc*) Platzwärter(in) *m(f)*; (*at demo etc*) Ordner(in) *m(f)*; (*US*) Bezirkspolizeichef(in) *m(f)* **VT** *facts, arguments* ordnen; *soldiers* antreten lassen; (*= lead*) geleiten, führen

marshalling yard, (US) **marshaling yard** ['mɑːʃəlɪŋ'jɑːd] N Rangier- or Verschiebebahnhof m

marsh: marsh gas N Methangas nt, Sumpf- or Grubengas nt; **marshland** N Marschland nt; **marshmallow** N (= sweet) Marshmallow nt; (Bot) Eibisch m; **marsh marigold** N Sumpfdotterblume f

marshy ['mɑːʃɪ] ADJ (+er) sumpfig; **a ~ district** ein Sumpfgebiet nt

marsupial [mɑːˈsuːpɪəl] ADJ **~ animal** Beuteltier nt N Beuteltier nt

mart [mɑːt] N (old) Markt m

marten ['mɑːtɪn] N Marder m

martial ['mɑːʃəl] ADJ music kriegerisch; bearing stramm, soldatisch

martial art N **the ~s** die Kampfkunst; **the ~ of judo** der Kampfsport Judo

martial law N Kriegsrecht nt; **the state was put under ~** über den Staat wurde (das) Kriegsrecht verhängt

Martian ['mɑːʃən] ADJ atmosphere, exploration des Mars; invaders vom Mars N Marsbewohner(in) m(f), Marsmensch m

martin ['mɑːtɪn] N Schwalbe f

martinet [ˌmɑːtɪˈnet] N (strenger) Zuchtmeister; **he's a real ~** er führt ein strenges Regiment

martingale ['mɑːtɪŋɡeɪl] N (Horseriding) Martingal nt

martini [mɑːˈtiːnɪ] N Martini m

Martinique [ˌmɑːtɪˈniːk] N Martinique nt

Martinmas ['mɑːtɪnməs] N Martinstag m, Martini nt

martyr ['mɑːtə'] N Märtyrer(in) m(f); **he was a ~ to the cause of civil rights** er wurde zum Märtyrer für die Sache der Bürgerrechtsbewegung; **to be a ~ to arthritis** entsetzlich unter Arthritis zu leiden haben; **there's no need to make a ~ of yourself** (inf) du brauchst hier nicht den Märtyrer zu spielen (inf) VT martern, (zu Tode) quälen; **thousands of Christians were ~ed** tausende or Tausende von Christen starben den Märtyrertod

martyrdom ['mɑːtədəm] N (= suffering) Martyrium nt; (= death) Märtyrertod m

marvel ['mɑːvəl] N Wunder nt; **the ~s of modern science** die Wunder der modernen Wissenschaft; **this medicine is a ~** diese Medizin wirkt Wunder; **if he ever gets there it will be a ~** (inf) wenn er jemals dort ankommt, ist das ein Wunder; **it's a ~ to me that he escaped unhurt** es kommt mir wie ein Wunder vor, dass er ohne Verletzungen davonkam; **it's a ~ to me how he does it** (inf) es ist mir einfach unerklärlich or schleierhaft, wie er das macht; **her desk is a ~ of tidiness** ihr Schreibtisch ist ein Muster an Ordnung; **you're a ~!** (inf) du bist ein Engel!; (= clever) du bist ein Genie!
VI staunen (at über +acc); **to ~ at a sight** einen Anblick bestaunen; **they ~led** (Brit) or **~ed** (US) **at her beauty** (liter) sie bewunderten ihre Schönheit

marvellous, (US) **marvelous** ['mɑːvələs] ADJ wunderbar, fantastisch, phantastisch, fabelhaft; **isn't it ~?** ist das nicht herrlich?; (iro) gut, nicht! (iro); **they've done a ~ job** das haben sie hervorragend gemacht

marvellously, (US) **marvelously** ['mɑːvələslɪ] ADV (with adj) herrlich; (with vb) großartig, fabelhaft

marvy ['mɑːvɪ] ADJ (+er) (US sl) prima, klasse (inf)

Marxian ['mɑːksɪən] ADJ Marxisch

Marxism ['mɑːksɪzəm] N der Marxismus

Marxist ['mɑːksɪst] ADJ marxistisch N Marxist(in) m(f)

Mary ['mɛərɪ] N Maria f

marzipan [ˌmɑːzɪˈpæn] N Marzipan nt or m

mascara [mæˈskɑːrə] N Wimperntusche f, Maskara f VT tuschen

mascaraed [mæsˈkɑːrəd] ADJ getuscht

mascot ['mæskət] N Maskottchen nt

masculine ['mæskjʊlɪn] ADJ männlich; woman, room, decor maskulin; (Gram) maskulin, männlich N (Gram) Maskulinum nt

masculinist ['mæskjʊlɪnɪst] ADJ maskulinistisch

masculinity [ˌmæskjʊˈlɪnɪtɪ] N Männlichkeit f

MASH N (US) abbr of **Mobile Army Surgical Hospital** mobiles Lazarett

mash [mæʃ] N Brei m; (for animals) Futterbrei m, Schlempe f; (= potatoes) Püree nt; (in brewing) Maische f VT zerstampfen

mashed [mæʃt] ADJ **~ potatoes** Kartoffelbrei m or -püree nt

masher ['mæʃə'] N Stampfer m; (for potatoes) Kartoffelstampfer m

mashy ['mæʃɪ] ADJ (+er) (= pulpy) breiig

mask [mɑːsk] N (lit, fig, Comput) Maske f; **the ~ slipped** (fig) er/sie etc ließ die Maske fallen; **surgeon's ~** Mundschutz m VT maskieren; (clouds, trees etc) verdecken; feelings verbergen; intentions verschleiern

masked [mɑːskt] ADJ maskiert

masked ball N Maskenball m

masking tape N (= adhesive tape) Kreppband m

masochism ['mæsəʊkɪzəm] N Masochismus m

masochist ['mæsəʊkɪst] N Masochist(in) m(f)

masochistic [ˌmæsəʊˈkɪstɪk] ADJ masochistisch

masochistically [ˌmæsəʊˈkɪstɪkəlɪ] ADV masochistisch

mason ['meɪsn] N a (= builder) Steinmetz(in) m(f); (in quarry) Steinhauer(in) m(f) → **monumental mason** b (= freemason) Freimaurer m

---

MASON-DIXON LINE

Die **Mason-Dixon line** ist die symbolische Linie, die den Norden der Vereinigten Staaten von Amerika vom Süden abtrennt. Die 233 Meilen lange Linie wurde im 18. Jahrhundert zunächst festgelegt, um die Grenzstreitigkeiten zwischen Maryland und Pennsylvania ein Ende zu setzen, danach wurde sie auf die Grenzlinie zwischen Pennsylvannia und Virginia ausgedehnt. Bis zum Ende des Bürgerkriegs trennte diese Grenze die Sklavenstaaten von den freien Staaten. Heute wird die **Mason-Dixon line** immer noch herangezogen, um einen Südstaatler und den Süden im Allgemeinen zu definieren: "Sie wurde auf einer Farm geboren, die zu ihrem größten Bedauern ein paar Meilen nördlich der Mason-Dixon-Linie lag." Country-Sänger träumen in ihren Lieder häufig von "crossing that Mason-Dixon line", der Heimkehr in den Süden.

---

masonic [məˈsɒnɪk] ADJ Freimaurer-; handshake unter Freimaurern; **~ lodge/order** Freimaurerloge f/-orden m

masonry ['meɪsnrɪ] N a (= stonework) Mauerwerk nt b (= free masonry) Freimaurerei f, Freimaurertum nt

masque [mɑːsk] N Maskenspiel nt

masquerade [ˌmæskəˈreɪd] N Maskerade f; **that's just a ~, she's not really like that at all** (fig) das ist alles nur Theater, in Wirklichkeit ist sie gar nicht so VI **to ~ as ...** sich verkleiden als ...; (fig) sich ausgeben als ..., vorgeben, ... zu sein; **this cheap trash masquerading as literature** dieser Schund, der als Literatur ausgegeben wird

mass¹ [mæs] N (Eccl) Messe f; **High Mass** Hochamt nt; **to go to ~** zur Messe gehen; **to hear ~** die Messe feiern; **to say ~** die Messe lesen

mass² N a (general, Phys) Masse f; (of people) Menge f; **a ~ of snow** eine Schneemasse; **a ~ of rubble** ein Schutthaufen m; **the ~ of rubble** der Haufen Schutt; **a ~ of cold air** eine kalte Luftmasse; **a ~ of red hair** ein Wust m roter Haare; **a ~ of flames** ein einziges Flammenmeer; **this confused ~ of thoughts** dieser wirre Gedankenwust; **the essay is one great ~ of**

spelling mistakes der Aufsatz wimmelt nur so von Schreibfehlern; **he's a ~ of bruises** er ist voller blauer Flecken; **the garden is a ~ of yellow/colour** (Brit) or **color** (US) der Garten ist ein Meer nt von Gelb/ein Farbenmeer nt; **the ~es** die Masse(n pl); **the great ~ of the population** die (breite) Masse der Bevölkerung; **the nation in the ~** die breite(n) Volksmasse(n); **people, in the ~, prefer ...** die breite Masse (der Menschen) zieht es vor, ...

b (= bulk) **the great ~ of the mountains** das riesige Bergmassiv; **the huge ~ of the ship loomed up out of the night** die riesige Form des Schiffes tauchte aus der Nacht auf

c **masses** PL (inf) massenhaft, eine Masse (inf); **he has ~es of money/time** er hat massenhaft or massig (inf) or eine Masse (inf) Geld/Zeit; **the factory is producing ~es of cars** die Fabrik produziert Unmengen von Autos; **I've got ~es (of things) to do** ich habe noch massig (inf) zu tun

VT troops massieren, zusammenziehen
VI (Mil) sich massieren; (Red Indians etc) sich versammeln; (clouds) sich (zusammen)ballen; **they're ~ing for an attack** sie sammeln sich zum Angriff

massacre ['mæsəkə'] N Massaker nt VT niedermetzeln, massakrieren; **last Saturday they ~d us 6-0** (inf) letzten Samstag haben sie uns mit 6:0 fertig gemacht (inf)

massage ['mæsɑːʒ] N Massage f VT massieren

massage parlour, (US) **massage parlor** N Massagesalon m

mass: mass culture N Massenkultur f; **mass destruction** N Massenvernichtung f; **weapons of ~** Massenvernichtungswaffen pl

massed [mæst] ADJ troops, tanks zusammengezogen; people, plants dicht gedrängt; **~ ranks** dicht gedrängte Reihen; **~ sprint** (Cycling) Massensprint m; **the ~ bands of the Royal Navy** die vereinigten Militärkapellen der königlichen Marine; **sung by ~ choirs** von den Stimmen mehrerer Chöre gesungen; **the ~ weight of medical opinion** das ganze Gewicht der ärztlichen Meinung

mass education N Massenerziehung f

masseur [mæˈsɜː'] N Masseur m

masseuse [mæˈsɜːz] N Masseuse f

mass: mass funeral N Massenbegräbnis nt; **mass grave** N Massengrab nt; **mass hysteria** N Massenhysterie f

massif [mæˈsiːf] N (Geog) (Gebirgs)massiv nt

massive ['mæsɪv] ADJ (= huge) riesig, enorm; task gewaltig; attack, pressure, support, heart attack, stroke massiv; (= bulky, weighty) structure, wall massiv, wuchtig; forehead breit, wuchtig; boxer wuchtig, massig; **he weighs in at a ~ 17 stone** er wiegt beachtliche 108 Kilo; **~ furniture** Massivholzmöbel pl; **on a ~ scale** in riesigem Umfang; **the ship was designed on a ~ scale** das Schiff hatte riesenhafte Ausmaße; **the symphony is conceived on a ~ scale** die Sinfonie or Symphonie ist grandios konzipiert; **space research is financed on a ~ scale** Raumforschung wird mit riesigen Summen finanziert

massively ['mæsɪvlɪ] ADV (= hugely) popular, expensive, increase enorm; (= bulkily) made massiv; **a ~ built man** ein Schrank m von einem Mann; **~ in debt** enorm verschuldet; **to invest/borrow ~** riesige Summen investieren/aufnehmen

massiveness ['mæsɪvnɪs] N (of expanse of land, plane, ship, hotel etc) riesige or gewaltige Ausmaße pl; (of fortune, expenditure, orchestra) enorme Größe; (of structure, wall) Wuchtigkeit f, Massivität f; (of boxer, forehead) Wuchtigkeit f; **the ~ of the task** die gewaltige Aufgabe

mass: mass killing N Massenmord m; **mass market** N Massenmarkt m; **mass-market** ADJ **~ paperbacks** Taschenbücher pl für den Massenmarkt; **mass marketing** N massenweise Vermarktung; **mass media** PL Massenmedien pl; **mass meeting** N Massenveranstaltung f; (in company) Betriebsversammlung f;

(*of trade union*) Vollversammlung *f*; (*Pol*) Massenkundgebung *f*; **mass murderer** N Massenmörder(in) *m(f)*; **mass murders** PL Massenmord *m*; **mass number** N (*Phys*) Massenzahl *f*; **mass-produce** VT in Massenproduktion herstellen; *cars, engines etc* serienweise herstellen; **mass-produced** ADJ ~ **items** Massenartikel *pl*; **it looks as though it was** ~ das sieht sehr nach Massenware aus; **mass production** N Massenproduktion *f*; **mass protests** PL Massenproteste *pl*; **mass psychology** N Massenpsychologie *f*; **mass rally** N Massenkundgebung *f*; **mass storage (device)** N (*Comput*) Massenspeicher *m*; **mass survey** N (*Med*) Reihenuntersuchung *f*; **mass tourism** N Massentourismus *m*; **mass unemployment** N Massenarbeitslosigkeit *f*

mast[1] [mɑ:st] N (*Naut*) Mast(baum) *m*; (*Rad etc*) Sendeturm *m*; **10 years before the** ~ 10 Jahre auf See

mast[2] N (*Bot*) Mast *f*

mastectomy [mæ'stektəmɪ] N Brustamputation *f*

-masted [-mɑ:stɪd] ADJ *suf* -mastig; **two-masted** zweimastig; **a three-masted vessel** ein Dreimaster *m*

master ['mɑ:stə'] N **a** (*of the house, dog, servants*) Herr *m*; **Master** (= *Christ*) der Herr; (*in address*) Meister; **I am (the)** ~ **now** jetzt bin ich der Herr; **to be** ~ **in one's own house** (*also fig*) Herr im Hause sein; **to be one's own** ~ sein eigener Herr sein
   b (*Naut*) Kapitän *m*; ~**'s certificate** Kapitänspatent *nt*
   c (= *musician, painter etc*) Meister(in) *m(f)*
   d (= *teacher*) Lehrer *m*; (*of apprentice*) Meister *m*
   e **to be** ~ **of sth** etw beherrschen; **to be** ~ **of the situation** Herr *m* der Lage sein; **to be the** ~ **of one's fate** sein Schicksal in der Hand haben → **grand master, past master**
   f (= *boy's title*) Master *m*, Meister *m* (*old*)
   g (*of college*) Leiter *m*, Rektor *m*
   h (= *master copy*) Original *nt*
   i (*Univ*, = *Master of Arts etc*) **to do a** ~**'s** seinen Magister machen (*in* in +*dat*)
   VT meistern; *one's emotions* unter Kontrolle bringen; *technique, method* beherrschen; **to** ~ **the violin** das Geigenspiel beherrschen; **to** ~ **one's temper** sich beherrschen, sein Temperament zügeln

master *in cpds* (*with trades*) -meister(in) *m(f)*; **master-at-arms** N Bootsmann *m* mit Polizeibefugnis; **master baker** N Bäckermeister(in) *m(f)*; **master bedroom** N großes Schlafzimmer; **master builder** N Baumeister *m*; **master card** N (*fig*) Trumpf *m*; **to play one's** ~ seinen Trumpf ausspielen; **master chef** N Meisterkoch *m*/-köchin *f*; **master copy** N Original *nt*; **master craftsman** N Handwerksmeister *m*; **master criminal** N Meister(in) *m(f)* des Verbrechens; **master disk** N Hauptplatte *f*; **master file** N (*Comput*) Stammdatei *f*

masterful ['mɑ:stəfʊl] ADJ meisterhaft; *ball control* gekonnt; (= *dominating*) gebieterisch; **he's got a** ~, **yet polite attitude** er hat eine bestimmte, aber trotzdem höfliche Art; **he said in a** ~ **tone** sagte er in bestimmtem Ton; **we were amazed at his** ~ **control of the meeting** wir staunten darüber, wie überlegen *or* souverän er die Sitzung in der Hand hatte

masterfully ['mɑ:stəfəlɪ] ADV meisterhaft; *control* souverän; *play, kick etc* gekonnt

master key N Haupt- *or* Generalschlüssel *m*

masterly ['mɑ:stəlɪ] ADJ meisterhaft, gekonnt; **in a** ~ **fashion** meisterhaft, gekonnt; **..., he said with** ~ **understatement** ..., sagte er, meisterhaft untertreibend

master: **master magician** N Zaubermeister(in) *m(f)*; **master mariner** N Kapitän *m*; **master mason** N Steinmetzmeister *m*; **mastermind** N (*führender*) Kopf; **who's the** ~ **who planned all these operations?** wer ist der Kopf, der hinter der Planung dieser Unternehmungen steckte? VT **who** ~**ed the robbery?** wer

---

steckt hinter dem Raubüberfall?; **Master of Arts/Science** N ≈ Magister *m* (*der philosophischen/naturwissenschaftlichen* Fakultät); **master of ceremonies** N (*at function*) Zeremonienmeister(in) *m(f)*; (*on stage*) Conférencier *m*; (*on TV*) Showmaster(in) *m(f)*; **master of (fox)hounds** N Master *m*; **masterpiece** N Meisterwerk *nt*; **master plan** N (*overall*) Gesamtplan *m*; (*masterly*) Meisterplan *m*; **master race** N Herrenvolk *nt*; **master sergeant** N (*US*) Oberfeldwebel *m*; **master spy** N Meisterspion(in) *m(f)*; **masterstroke** N Meister- *or* Glanzstück *nt*; **master switch** N Hauptschalter *m*; **master tape** N Originalband *nt*; (*Comput*) Stammband *nt*; **master thief** N Meisterdieb(in) *m(f)*; **masterwork** N Meisterwerk *nt*

mastery ['mɑ:stərɪ] N (= *control: of language, technique, instrument etc*) Beherrschung *f*; (= *skill*) Können *nt*; (*over competitors etc*) Oberhand *f*; ~ **of the seas** Herrschaft *f* über die Meere; **the painter's** ~ **of form** des Malers meisterhafter Gebrauch von Form; **to gain the** ~ **of sth** etw beherrschen

masthead ['mɑ:sthed] N **a** (*Naut*) Mars *m*, Mastkorb *m* **b** (*Press: in newspaper, magazine*) Impressum *nt*

mastic ['mæstɪk] N (*Build*) Mastix *m*

masticate ['mæstɪkeɪt] VTI kauen; (*for young*) vorkauen

mastication [ˌmæstɪ'keɪʃən] N Kauen *nt*; (*for young*) Vorkauen *nt*

mastiff ['mæstɪf] N Dogge *f*

mastitis [mæ'staɪtɪs] N Brust(drüsen)entzündung *f*, Mastitis *f*

mastodon ['mæstədɒn] N Mastodon *nt*

mastoid ['mæstɔɪd] ADJ warzenförmig, mastoid (*spec*) N Warzenfortsatz *m*, Mastoid *nt* (*spec*)

masturbate ['mæstəbeɪt] VI masturbieren, onanieren

masturbation [ˌmæstə'beɪʃən] N Masturbation *f*, Onanie *f*

masturbatory [ˌmæstə'beɪtərɪ] ADJ masturbatorisch

mat[1] [mæt] N Matte *f*; (= *door mat*) Fußmatte *f*; (*on table*) Untersetzer *m*; (*of cloth*) Deckchen *nt*; (*of hair*) Gewirr *nt*; **to go to the** ~ **for sb** (*US*) sich für jdn auf einen Streit einlassen; **to go to the** ~ **to do sth** (*US*) einen Streit riskieren, um etw zu tun VT **the sea-water had** ~**ted his hair** durch das Salzwasser waren seine Haare filzig geworden VI verfilzen

mat[2] ADJ = **matt**

matador ['mætədɔ:'] N Matador *m*

match[1] [mætʃ] N Streichholz *nt*, Zündholz *nt*

match[2] ⚙ 5.3 N **a** (= *sb/sth similar, suitable etc*) **to be** *or* **make a good** ~ gut zusammenpassen; **the skirt is a good** ~ **for the sweater** der Rock passt gut zum Pullover; **I want a** ~ **for this yellow paint** ich möchte Farbe in diesem Gelbton; **this chair is a** ~ **for that one** dieser Stuhl ist das Gegenstück zu
   b **to be a/no** ~ **for sb** (= *be able to compete with*) sich mit jdm messen/nicht messen können; (= *be able to handle*) jdm gewachsen/nicht gewachsen sein; **he's a** ~ **for anybody** er kann es mit jedem aufnehmen; **A was more than a** ~ **for B** A war B weit überlegen; **to meet one's** ~ seinen Meister finden
   c (= *marriage*) Heirat *f*; **who thought up this** ~? wer hat die beiden zusammengebracht?; **she made a good** ~ sie hat eine gute Partie gemacht; **he's a good** ~ er ist eine gute Partie
   d (*Sport*) (*general*) Wettkampf *m*; (= *team game*) Spiel *nt*; (*Tennis*) Match *nt*, Partie *f*; (*Boxing, Fencing*) Kampf *m*; (= *quiz*) Wettkampf *m*, Wettbewerb *m*; **athletics** ~ Leichtathletikkampf *m*; **I'll give you a** ~ ich werde einmal gegen Sie spielen; **we must have another** ~ **some time** wir müssen wieder einmal gegeneinander spielen; **that's** ~ (*Tennis*) Match!, damit ist das Match entschieden
   VT **a** (= *pair off*) (einander) anpassen; ~ **each diagram with its counterpart** ordnen Sie die

---

Schaubilder einander zu
   b (= *equal*) gleichkommen (+*dat*) (*in an* +*dat*); **A doesn't quite** ~ **B in originality** A kann es an Originalität nicht mit B aufnehmen; **nobody can** ~ **him in argument** niemand kann so gut argumentieren wie er; **a quality that has never been** ~**ed since** eine Qualität, die bislang unerreicht ist *or* noch ihresgleichen sucht (*geh*); **no knight could** ~ **him in battle** kein Ritter konnte sich mit ihm messen; **I can't** ~ **him in chess** im Schach kann ich es mit ihm nicht aufnehmen; **that sort of easy self-confidence which is not** ~**ed by any great degree of intelligence** jene Selbstsicherheit, die nicht mit der entsprechenden Intelligenz gepaart ist; ~ **that if you can!** das soll erst mal einer nachmachen, das macht so leicht keiner nach!; **three kings!** ~ **that!** drei Könige! kannst du da noch mithalten?; **this climate/whisky can't be** ~**ed anywhere in the world** so ein Klima/so einen Whisky gibt es nicht noch einmal
   c (= *correspond to*) entsprechen (+*dat*); **the results did not** ~ **our hopes** die Ergebnisse entsprachen nicht unseren Hoffnungen
   d (*clothes, colours*) passen zu; **she** ~**ed the carpet with a nice rug** sie fand einen hübschen, zum Teppich passenden Läufer; **can you** ~ **this fabric?** haben Sie etwas, das zu diesem Stoff passt?; **to** ~ **textures and fabrics so that ...** Strukturen und Stoffe so aufeinander abstimmen, dass ...; **his face** ~**ed the red of his sweater** sein Gesicht war so rot wie sein Pullover
   e (= *pit*) **he decided to** ~ **his team against** *or* **with the champions** er beschloss, seine Mannschaft gegen die Meister antreten zu lassen; **to be** ~**ed against sb** gegen jdn antreten; **to** ~ **one's wits against sb** sich geistig mit jdm messen; **to** ~ **one's strength against sb** seine Kräfte mit jdm messen
   VI zusammenpassen; **it doesn't** ~ das passt nicht (zusammen); **with a skirt to** ~ mit (dazu) passendem Rock

▸ **match up** VI **a** (= *correspond*) zusammenpassen **b** (= *be equal*) **he matched up to the situation** er war der Situation gewachsen VT *sep colours* aufeinander abstimmen; **I matched the lampshade up with the wallpaper** ich fand den passenden Lampenschirm zu der Tapete

match: **matchbook** N (*esp US*) Streichholzheftchen *nt*; **matchbox** N Streichholzschachtel *f*; **match day** N (*Brit Sport*) Spieltag *m*

matched [mætʃt] ADJ (= *well matched*) zusammenpassend; **they're well** ~ (*couple*) die beiden passen gut zusammen; (*colours*) sie sind gut aufeinander abgestimmt; **the two boxers were well** ~ die beiden Boxer waren einander ebenbürtig; **the teams are closely** *or* **evenly** ~ die Mannschaften sind gleichwertig

match-fit ['mætʃfɪt] ADJ (*Brit Sport*) in guter Spielform

match-fitness [ˌmætʃ'fɪtnɪs] N (*Brit Sport*) **to regain** ~ wieder in gute Spielform kommen

matching ['mætʃɪŋ] ADJ (*dazu*) passend; **they form a** ~ **pair** sie passen *or* gehören zusammen; **a** ~ **set of wine glasses** ein Satz *m* Weingläser

matching: **matching funds** PL *Geldmittel, die von der Regierung oder einem Unternehmen zur Verfügung gestellt werden, um von privater Seite aufgebrachte Spenden etc zu verdoppeln*; **matching test** N Vergleichsprobe *f*

matchless ['mætʃlɪs] ADJ einzigartig, unvergleichlich

match: **matchlock** N Luntenschloss *nt*; **matchmaker** N Ehestifter(in) *m(f)*, Kuppler(in) *m(f)* (*pej*); **matchmaking** N **she loves** ~ sie verkuppelt die Leute gern (*inf*); **match penalty** N (*Ice hockey*) Matchstrafe *f*; **match point** N (*Tennis*) Matchball *m*; **matchstick** N Streichholz *nt*; **matchwood** N Holz zur Herstellung von Streichhölzern **reduced to** ~ (*fig*) zu Kleinholz gemacht (*inf*)

mate[1] [meɪt] (*Chess*) N Matt *nt* VT matt setzen VI **white** ~**s in two** Weiß setzt den Gegner in zwei Zügen matt

mate² N **a** (= *fellow worker*) Arbeitskollege *m*/-kollegin *f*, Kumpel *m* **b** (= *helper*) Gehilfe *m*, Gehilfin *f* **c** (*Naut*) Maat *m* **d** (*of animal*) (*male*) Männchen *nt*; (*female*) Weibchen *nt*; **his ~** das Weibchen **e** (*inf*, = *friend*) Freund(in) *m(f)*, Kamerad(in) *m(f)*; **listen, ~** hör mal, Freundchen! (*inf*); **got a light, ~?** hast du Feuer, Kumpel? (*inf*) **f** (*hum inf*) (= *husband*) Mann *m*; (= *wife*) Frau *f*; (*of animal, male*) Partner *m*; (*female*) Partnerin *f* **g** (*of pair*) **here's one sock, where's its ~?** hier ist eine Socke, wo ist die andere *or* zweite? ▪ VT *animals* paaren; *female animal* decken lassen; (*fig hum*) verkuppeln; **they ~d their mare with our stallion** sie haben ihre Stute von unserem Hengst decken lassen ▪ VI (*Zool*) sich paaren

mater ['meɪtə'] N (*Brit, inf*) Mama *f*

material [mə'tɪərɪəl] ADJ **a** (= *of matter, things*) materiell; **~ damage** Sachschaden *m* **b** (= *physical*) *needs, comforts* materiell **c** (*esp Jur*: = *important*) *evidence, witness* wesentlich; *difference* grundlegend, wesentlich; *fact, information* relevant; **that's not ~** das ist nicht relevant ▪ N **a** Material *nt*; (*for report, novel etc*) Stoff *m*; **he's good editorial ~** er hat das Zeug zum Redakteur; **this group would be good ~ for our show** diese Band wäre für unsere Show ganz brauchbar **b** **materials** PL Material *nt*; **building ~s** Baustoffe *pl*, Baumaterial *nt*; **raw ~s** Rohstoffe *pl*; **writing ~s** Schreibzeug *nt* **c** (= *cloth*) Stoff *m*, Material *nt*

materialism [mə'tɪərɪəlɪzəm] N der Materialismus

materialist [mə'tɪərɪəlɪst] N Materialist(in) *m(f)*

materialistic ADJ , **materialistically** ADV [mə,tɪərɪə'lɪstɪk, -əlɪ] materialistisch

materialization [mə,tɪərɪəlaɪ'zeɪʃən] N Verkörperung *f*; (*of ghosts*) Materialisation *f*

materialize [mə'tɪərɪəlaɪz] VI **a** (*idea, plan*) sich verwirklichen; (*promises, hopes etc*) wahr werden; **this idea will never ~** aus dieser Idee wird nie etwas; **the meeting never ~d** das Treffen kam nie zustande *or* zu Stande; **if this deal ever ~s** wenn aus diesem Geschäft je etwas wird, wenn dieses Geschäft je zustande *or* zu Stande kommt; **the money he'd promised me never ~d** von dem Geld, das er mir versprochen hatte, habe ich nie etwas gesehen **b** (*ghost*) erscheinen; (*indistinct object*) auftauchen

materially [mə'tɪərɪəlɪ] ADV grundlegend, wesentlich; **they are not ~ different** sie unterscheiden sich nicht wesentlich

matériel [mə,tɪərɪ'el] N (*US*) Ausrüstung *f*

maternal [mə'tɜːnl] ADJ mütterlich; **~ grandfather** Großvater mütterlicherseits; **~ affection** *or* **love** Mutterliebe *f*; **~ instincts** Mutterinstinkte *pl*, mütterliche Instinkte *pl*; **to be ~ to sb** sich jdm gegenüber mütterlich *or* wie eine Mutter verhalten; **~ health care** medizinische Betreuung für Mütter; **~ death rate** Müttersterblichkeit *f*

maternal deprivation N (*Psych*) Verlust *m* der Mutter

maternity [mə'tɜːnɪtɪ] N Mutterschaft *f*; **the idea of ~ never appealed to her** sie konnte sich nicht mit dem Gedanken befreunden, Mutter zu werden

maternity: maternity allowance, **maternity benefit** N (*Brit*) Mutterschaftshilfe *f*, Mutterschaftsgeld *nt*; **maternity dress** N Umstandskleid *nt*; **maternity home**, **maternity hospital** N Entbindungsheim *nt*; **maternity leave** N Mutterschaftsurlaub *m*; **maternity pay** N (*Brit*) Mutterschaftsgeld *nt* (*als Lohnfortzahlung*); **maternity unit** N Entbindungsstation *f*; **maternity ward** N Entbindungsstation *f*

matey ['meɪtɪ] (*Brit, inf*) ADJ (+*er*) *person* freundlich, kollegial; (*pej*) vertraulich; *atmosphere* freundschaftlich, kollegial; *gathering* vertraulich; **careful what you say, he's ~ with the director** sei vorsichtig mit dem, was du sagst, er steht mit dem Direktor auf Du und Du; **he was getting just a bit too ~ with my wife** er wurde ein wenig zu vertraulich mit meiner Frau ▪ N Kumpel *m*; (*warningly*) Freundchen *nt* (*inf*)

math [mæθ] N (*US, inf*) Mathe *f* (*inf*)

mathematical [,mæθə'mætɪkəl] ADJ mathematisch

mathematically [,mæθə'mætɪkəlɪ] ADV mathematisch; *possible, impossible, complicated* rechnerisch; **~ speaking** (= *numerically speaking*) rein zahlenmäßig

mathematician [,mæθəmə'tɪʃən] N Mathematiker(in) *m(f)*

mathematics [,mæθə'mætɪks] N **a** *sing* Mathematik *f* **b** *pl* **the ~ of this are complicated** das ist mathematisch kompliziert

maths [mæθs] N *sing* (*Brit, inf*) Mathe *f* (*inf*)

matinée ['mætɪneɪ] N Matinee *f*; (*in the afternoon*) Frühvorstellung *f*; **~ coat**, **~ jacket** (*for baby*) Ausfahrjäckchen *nt*

mating ['meɪtɪŋ] N Paarung *f*

mating: mating call N Lockruf *m*; (*of birds also*) Balzlaut *m*; (*of deer also*) Brunstschrei *m*; **mating dance** N Paarungstanz *m*; **mating season** N Paarungszeit *f*

matins ['mætɪnz] N *sing* (*Catholic*) Matutin *f*, Morgenlob *nt*; (*Anglican*) Morgenandacht *f*

matriarch ['meɪtrɪɑːk] N Matriarchin *f*

matriarchal [,meɪtrɪ'ɑːkl] ADJ matriarchalisch

matriarchy ['meɪtrɪɑːkɪ] N Matriarchat *nt*

matric [mə'trɪk] N (*inf*) = **matriculation**

matrices ['meɪtrɪsiːz] *pl of* **matrix**

matricide ['meɪtrɪsaɪd] N (= *act*) Muttermord *m*; (= *person*) Muttermörder(in) *m(f)*

matriculate [mə'trɪkjʊleɪt] VI sich immatrikulieren ▪ VT immatrikulieren

matriculation [mə,trɪkjʊ'leɪʃən] N Immatrikulation *f*; (= *ceremony*) Immatrikulationsfeier *f*

matrimonial [,mætrɪ'məʊnɪəl] ADJ ehelich

matrimonial: matrimonial bed N Ehebett *nt*; **matrimonial law** N Eherecht *nt*; **matrimonial vow** N Ehegelübde *nt*

matrimony ['mætrɪmənɪ] N (*form*) Ehe *f*; **to enter into holy ~** in den heiligen Stand der Ehe treten

matrix ['meɪtrɪks] N *pl* **matrices** *or* **-es** **a** (= *mould*) Matrize *f*, Mater *f* **b** (*Geol, Math*) Matrix *f*

matrix printer N Matrixdrucker *m*

matron ['meɪtrən] N **a** (*in hospital*) Oberin *f*, Oberschwester *f*; (*in school*) Schwester *f* **b** (= *married woman*) Matrone *f*

matronly ['meɪtrənlɪ] ADJ matronenhaft

matron of honour ['meɪtrənəv'ɒnə'] N *pl* **matrons of honour** *verheiratete Frau, die als Brautjungfer fungiert*

matt [mæt] ADJ matt, mattiert; **a paint with a ~ finish** ein Mattlack *m*

matted ['mætɪd] ADJ verfilzt; **hair ~ with blood/mud** mit Blut/Schlamm verkrustetes Haar

matter ['mætə'] N **a** (= *substance, not mind*) die Materie; **organic/inorganic ~** organische/anorganische Stoffe *pl* **b** (*particular kind*) Stoff *m*; **advertising ~** Reklame *f*, Werbung *f*; **printed ~** Büchersendung *f*; **colouring ~** Farbstoff(e) *m(pl)*; **vegetable ~** pflanzliche Stoffe *pl* **c** (*Med*, = *pus*) Eiter *m* **d** (*Typ*) (= *copy*) Manuskript *nt*; (= *type set up*) Satz *m* **e** (= *content*) Inhalt *m*; **the main ~ of his speech was ...** (der) Hauptgegenstand seiner Rede war ... **f** (= *question, affair*) Sache *f*, Angelegenheit *f*; (= *topic*) Thema *nt*, Stoff *m*; **can I talk to you on a ~ of great urgency?** kann ich Sie in einer äußerst wichtigen Angelegenheit sprechen?; **this is a ~ I know little about** darüber weiß ich wenig; **in the ~ of ...** was ... (+*acc*) anbelangt, hinsichtlich ... (+*gen*); **in the ~ of clothes** *etc* in puncto Kleidung *etc*; **there's the ~ of my expenses** da ist (noch) die Sache *or* Frage mit meinen Ausgaben; **it's no great ~** das macht nichts, das ist nicht so wichtig; **that's quite another ~** das ist etwas (ganz) anderes; **that's another ~ altogether, that's a very different ~** das ist etwas völlig anderes; **it will be no easy ~ (to) ...** es wird nicht einfach sein, zu ...; **it's a serious ~** das ist eine ernste Angelegenheit, die Sache ist ernst; **the ~ is closed** die Sache *or* der Fall ist erledigt **g** **matters** PL Angelegenheiten *pl*; **business ~s** geschäftliche Angelegenheiten *or* Dinge *pl*, Geschäftliche(s) *nt*; **as ~s stand** wie die Dinge liegen; **to make ~s worse** zu allem Unglück (noch) **h** **for that ~** eigentlich; **I haven't seen him for weeks, nor for that ~ has anybody else** ich habe ihn seit Wochen nicht mehr gesehen, und eigentlich hat ihn sonst auch niemand gesehen; **he wants to complain about it and for that ~, so do I** er will sich darüber beschweren und ich eigentlich auch **i** **a ~ of** eine Frage (+*gen*), eine Sache von; **it's a ~ of form/time** das ist eine Formsache/Zeitfrage *or* Frage der Zeit; **it's a ~ of taste/opinion** das ist Geschmacks-/Ansichtssache; **it's a ~ of adjusting this part exactly** es geht darum, dieses Teil genau einzustellen; **it will be a ~ of a few weeks** es wird ein paar Wochen dauern; **it's a ~ of 10 miles from ...** es sind 10 Meilen von ...; **it's a ~ of a couple of hours** das ist eine Sache von ein paar Stunden; **if it's just a ~ of another 10 minutes, then I'll wait** wenn es sich nur noch um 10 Minuten handelt, dann warte ich solange; **in a ~ of minutes** innerhalb von Minuten; **it's a ~ of great concern to us** die Sache ist für uns von großer Bedeutung; **it's not just a ~ of increasing the money supply** es ist nicht damit getan, die Geldzufuhr zu erhöhen; **it's just a ~ of trying harder** man muss sich ganz einfach etwas mehr anstrengen; **as a ~ of course** selbstverständlich; **it's a ~ of course with us** für uns ist das eine Selbstverständlichkeit; **you should always take your passport with you as a ~ of course** es sollte für Sie eine Selbstverständlichkeit sein, stets Ihren Pass bei sich zu haben; **earthquakes happen as a ~ of course in that part of the world** Erdbeben sind in der Gegend an der Tagesordnung **j** **no ~!** macht nichts; **I've decided to leave tomorrow, no ~ what** ich gehe morgen, egal was passiert; **no ~ how/what/when/where** *etc* ... egal, wie/was/wann/wo *etc* ...; **no ~ how you do it** wie du es auch machst, egal, wie du es machst; **no ~ how hot it was** auch *or* selbst bei der größten Hitze; **no ~ how hard he tried** so sehr er sich auch anstrengte **k** **sth is the ~ with sb/sth** etw ist mit jdm/etw los; (*ill*) etw fehlt jdm; **what's the ~?** was ist (denn) los?, was ist (denn)?; **what's the ~ with you this morning? – nothing's the ~** was hast du denn heute Morgen? – gar nichts; **what's the ~ with having a little fun?** was ist denn schon dabei, wenn man ein bisschen Spaß hat?; **something's the ~ with the lights** mit dem Licht ist irgendetwas nicht in Ordnung; **as if nothing was the ~** als ob nichts (los) wäre ▪ VI **it doesn't ~** (es *or* das) macht nichts, ist schon gut; **what does it ~?** was macht das schon?; **I forgot it, does it ~? – yes, it does** – ich habs vergessen, ist das schlimm? – ja, das ist schlimm; **does it ~ to you if I go?** macht es dir etwas aus, wenn ich gehe?; **doesn't it ~ to you at all if I leave you?** macht es dir denn gar nichts aus, wenn ich dich verlasse?; **why should it ~ to me?** warum sollte mir das etwas ausmachen?; **why should it ~ to me if people are starving?** was geht es mich an, wenn Menschen verhungern?; **it doesn't ~ to me what you do** es ist mir (ganz) egal, was du machst; **some things ~ more than others** es ist aber nicht alles gleich wichtig; **the things which ~ in life** was im Leben wichtig ist *or* zählt; **poverty ~s** Armut geht jeden etwas an

matter-of-course [ˌmætərəvˈkɔːs] ADJ *attr* selbstverständlich, natürlich

matter-of-fact [ˌmætərəvˈfækt] ADJ *attr* sachlich, nüchtern; **he was very ~ about it** er blieb sehr sachlich *or* nüchtern

matter-of-factly [ˌmætərəvˈfæktlɪ] ADV *say, answer* nüchtern, sachlich; *explain* sachlich; **I hated her, he said ~** ich habe sie gehasst, sagte er nüchtern

Matthew [ˈmæθjuː] N Matthias *m*; (*Bibl*) Matthäus *m*

matting [ˈmætɪŋ] N Matten *pl*; (= *material*) Mattenmaterial *nt*

mattock [ˈmætək] N Breithacke *f*

mattress [ˈmætrɪs] N Matratze *f*

maturate [məˈtjʊəreɪt] VI **a** (*lit, fig*) reifen **b** (*Med, abscess etc*) reifen, zum Reifen kommen

maturation [ˌmætjʊˈreɪʃən] N Reifeprozess *m*, Reifung *f*

mature [məˈtjʊə] ADJ (+er) **a** *person, mind* reif; *child* verständig, vernünftig; (*euph, = middle-aged*) gereift; **~ skin** reifere Haut; **his mind is very ~** geistig ist er schon sehr reif; **of ~ years, in his/her ~ years** im reiferen *or* vorgerückten Alter
b *wine* ausgereift; *sherry, port, cheese* reif; *fruit* reif, ausgereift; *plant* ausgewachsen; *plans* ausgereift; **after ~ deliberation** nach reiflicher Überlegung; **his ~r poems** seine reiferen Gedichte
c (*Comm*) bill, debt fällig
VI a (*person*) heranreifen (geh), reifer werden; (*animal*) auswachsen; **his character ~d during the war years** der Krieg ließ ihn reifer werden *or* machte ihn reifer
b (*wine, cheese*) reifen, reif werden
c (*Comm*) fällig werden
VT a *person* reifer machen
b *wine, cheese* reifen lassen

maturely [məˈtjʊəlɪ] ADV *behave* verständig, vernünftig; **a more ~ conceived novel** ein ausgereifterer Roman

mature student N Spätstudierende(r) *mf*

maturity [məˈtjʊərɪtɪ] N **a** Reife *f*; **to reach ~** (*person*) erwachsen werden; (*legally*) volljährig werden; (*animal*) ausgewachsen sein; **poems of his ~** Gedichte *pl* seiner reiferen Jahre; **he's somewhat lacking in ~** ihm fehlt die nötige Reife **b** (*Comm*) Fälligkeit *f*; (= *date*) Fälligkeitsdatum *nt*

maty [ˈmeɪtɪ] ADJ, N (*Brit, inf*) = **matey**

matzo [ˈmɒtsə] N Matze *f*, Matzen *m*

maudlin [ˈmɔːdlɪn] ADJ *story, play, sentimentality* rührselig; *person* sentimental, gefühlsselig; **don't get ~ about it** werden Sie deswegen nicht gleich sentimental

maul [mɔːl] VT übel zurichten; (*fig*) writer, play etc verreißen

mauling [ˈmɔːlɪŋ] N **to get a ~** (*player, team*) vernichtend geschlagen werden; (*author, book*) von der Kritik verrissen werden

Maundy money [ˈmɔːndɪˌmʌnɪ] N *speziell geprägte Münzen, die am Gründonnerstag vom britischen Monarchen als Almosen verteilt werden*

Maundy Thursday N Gründonnerstag *m*

Mauritius [məˈrɪʃəs] N Mauritius *nt*

mausoleum [ˌmɔːsəˈlɪəm] N Mausoleum *nt*

mauve [məʊv] ADJ mauve, malvenfarben **N** Mauvein *nt*

maverick [ˈmævərɪk] N **a** (*US Agr*) herrenloses Kalb *nt* ohne Brandzeichen **b** (= *dissenter*) Abtrünnige(r) *mf* **c** (= *independent person*) Alleingänger(in) *m(f)*, Einzelgänger(in) *m(f)*

maw [mɔː] N **a** (*Anat*) Magen *m*; (*of cow*) (Lab-)magen *m*; (*of bird*) Hals *m* **b** (*liter*) Maul *nt*; (*fig*) Rachen *m*, Schlund *m*

mawkish [ˈmɔːkɪʃ] ADJ rührselig, sentimental

mawkishness [ˈmɔːkɪʃnɪs] N Rührseligkeit *f*, Sentimentalität *f*

max **N** *abbr of* **maximum** max.; **to the ~** (*inf, run up debts, fill up tank*) bis zum Maximum; *enjoy*

---

life, live in vollen Zügen; **to go to the ~** (*in partying*) die Sau rauslassen (*inf*); **stressed to the ~** total gestresst (*inf*) **VT** **to ~ out sth, to ~ sth out** (*US inf*) etw ausschöpfen; **to ~ out one's credit card** seinen Kredit (auf der Kreditkarte) voll ausschöpfen

maxi [ˈmæksɪ] N (*Tex*) Maxirock *m*/-kleid *nt*/-mantel *m*

maxim [ˈmæksɪm] N Maxime *f*

maximal [ˈmæksɪməl] ADJ maximal

maximization [ˌmæksɪmaɪˈzeɪʃən] N Maximierung *f*

maximize [ˈmæksɪmaɪz] VT maximieren

maximum [ˈmæksɪməm] **ADJ** *attr* Höchst-; *size, height, costs, length* maximal; **~ amount** (= *money*) Höchstbetrag *m*; **~ penalty/sentence** Höchststrafe *f*; **~ fine** maximale Geldstrafe; **~ credible accident** größter anzunehmender Unfall, GAU *m*; **for ~ effect** um die größte Wirkung zu erzielen; **they capitalized on our mistakes to ~ effect** sie haben unsere Fehler maximal ausgenutzt; **he scored ~ points** er hat die höchste Punktzahl erreicht; **a ~ speed of ...** eine Höchstgeschwindigkeit von ...; **we are producing at ~ speed** wir produzieren mit maximaler Geschwindigkeit; **five is the ~ number allowed in a taxi** maximal *or* höchstens fünf Leute dürfen in ein Taxi; **~ security wing/prison** Hochsicherheitstrakt *m*/-gefängnis *nt*
N *pl* **-s** *or* **maxima** [ˈmæksɪmə] Maximum *nt*; **up to a ~ of £8** bis zu maximal *or* höchstens £ 8; **temperatures reached a ~ of 34°** die Höchsttemperatur betrug 34°; **is that the ~ you can offer?** ist das Ihr höchstes Angebot?; **£20 at the ~ maximal** 20 Pfund; **my salary is now at its ~** ich bin jetzt in der höchsten *or* obersten Gehaltsstufe; **to exploit sth to the ~** etw maximal ausnutzen
ADV (= *at the most*) maximal; **drink two cups of coffee a day ~** trinken Sie maximal zwei Tassen Kaffee pro Tag

maxiskirt [ˈmæksɪˌskɜːt] N Maxirock *m*

May [meɪ] **N** Mai *m* **VI** **to go maying** den Mai feiern

may [meɪ] ❖ 3.3, 9.1, 15.2, 26.3 VI *pret* **might** → *also* **might** [1] **a** (*possibility: also* **might**) können; **it ~ rain** es könnte regnen, vielleicht regnet es; **it ~ be that ...** vielleicht..., es könnte sein, dass ...; **although it ~ have been useful** obwohl es hätte nützlich sein können; **he ~ not be hungry** vielleicht hat er keinen Hunger; **I ~ have said so** es kann *or* könnte sein, dass ich das gesagt habe; **you ~ be right** Sie könnten Recht haben; **there ~ not be a next time** vielleicht gibts gar kein nächstes Mal; **they ~ be brothers for all I know** es kann *or* könnte sein, dass sie Brüder sind; **yes, I ~** ja, das ist möglich *or* das kann sein; **I ~ just do that** vielleicht tue ich das wirklich; **that's as ~ be** (*not might*) das mag ja sein(, aber ...); **one ~ well wonder why ...** die Frage wäre wohl berechtigt, warum ...; **you ~ well ask** das kann man wohl fragen
b (*permission*) dürfen; **~ I go now?** darf ich jetzt gehen?; **yes, you ~** ja, Sie dürfen
c **I hope he ~ succeed** ich hoffe, dass es ihm gelingt; **I had hoped he might succeed this time** ich hatte gehofft, es würde ihm diesmal gelingen; **such a policy as ~** *or* **might bring peace** eine Politik, die zum Frieden führen könnte; **we ~** *or* **might as well go** ich glaube, wir können (ruhig) gehen; **you ~** *or* **might as well go now** du kannst jetzt ruhig gehen; **if they don't have it we ~** *or* **might as well go to another firm** wenn es sie nicht haben, gehen wir am besten zu einer anderen Firma; **if they won't help we ~** *or* **might just as well give up** wenn sie uns nicht helfen, können wir (ja) gleich aufgeben
d (*in wishes*) **~ you be successful!** (ich wünsche Ihnen) viel Erfolg!; **~ your days be full of joy** mögen Ihnen glückliche Tage beschieden sein; **~ you be very happy together** ich wünsche euch, dass ihr sehr glücklich miteinander werdet; **~ the Lord have mercy on your soul** der Herr sei deiner Seele gnädig; **~ you be forgiven**

(*inf*) so was tut man doch nicht!; **~ I be struck dead if I lie!** ich will auf der Stelle tot umfallen, wenn das nicht stimmt
e (*in questions*) **who ~** *or* **might you be?** und wer sind Sie?, wer sind Sie denn?

Maya [ˈmeɪjə] **N** **a** Maya *mf* **b** (*Ling*) Maya *nt*, Mayasprache *f*

Mayan [ˈmeɪjən] **ADJ** Maya-; **~ ruins** Mayaruinen *pl* **N** **a** Maya *mf* **b** (*Ling*) Maya(sprache *f*) *nt*

maybe [ˈmeɪbɪ] ❖ 2.2, 4 ADV vielleicht, kann sein(, dass ...); **that's as ~** kann schon sein; **~, ~ not** vielleicht, vielleicht auch nicht

May: May beetle, May bug N (*Zool*) Maikäfer *m*; **May Day** N der 1. Mai, der Maifeiertag; **Mayday** N (= *distress call*) Maydaysignal *nt*, SOS-Ruf *m*; (*said*) Mayday

mayest [ˈmeɪəst] (*obs*), **mayst** (*obs*) 2nd pers sing of **may**

mayfly [ˈmeɪflaɪ] N Eintagsfliege *f*

mayhem [ˈmeɪhem] N **a** (*US Jur*) (schwere) Körperverletzung **b** (= *havoc*) Chaos *nt*

mayn't [meɪnt] *contr of* **may not**

mayo [ˈmeɪəʊ] N (*US, inf*) Mayonnaise *f*, Majonäse *f*, Mayo *f* (*inf*)

mayonnaise [ˌmeɪəˈneɪz] N Mayonnaise *f*, Majonäse *f*

mayor [mɛə] N Bürgermeister(in) *m(f)*

mayoral [ˈmɛərəl] ADJ des Bürgermeisters

mayoralty [ˈmɛərəltɪ] N (= *office*) Bürgermeisteramt *nt*, Amt *nt* des Bürgermeisters; **during his ~ ...** als er Bürgermeister war ..., während seiner Zeit als Bürgermeister ...

mayoress [ˈmɛəres] N Frau *f* Bürgermeister; (= *lady mayor*) Bürgermeisterin *f*

may: maypole N Maibaum *m*; **May queen** N Maikönigin *f*

mayst [meɪst] (*obs*) = **mayest**

maze [meɪz] N Irrgarten *m*; (= *puzzle*) Labyrinth *nt*; (*fig*) Wirrwarr *m*, Gewirr *nt*; **the ~ of streets** das Gewirr der Straßen

mazurka [məˈzɜːkə] N Mazurka *f*

MB[1] *abbr of* **Bachelor of Medicine**

MB[2] *abbr of* **megabyte**

MBA *abbr of* **Master of Business Administration** **he's doing an ~** er studiert Betriebswirtschaft; **he has an ~** er ist Betriebswirt

MBE *abbr of* **Member of the Order of the British Empire** *britischer Verdienstorden*

MBO N (*Fin*) *abbr of* **management buyout**

MC **a** *abbr of* **Master of Ceremonies** **b** *abbr of* **Military Cross**

MCAT N (*US Univ*) *abbr of* **Medical College Admissions Test**

MCC *abbr of* **Marylebone Cricket Club**

McCoy [məˈkɔɪ] N → **real**

MCP (*Brit inf*) *abbr of* **male chauvinist pig**

MD **a** *abbr of* **Doctor of Medicine** Dr. med. **b** *abbr of* **managing director** **c** *abbr of* **Minidisc** MD *f*; **MD-player** MD-Spieler *m*

m.d. *abbr of* **mentally deficient**

me [miː] PRON **a** (*dir obj, with prep +acc*) mich; (*indir obj, with prep +dat*) mir; **with my books about me** mit meinen Büchern um mich herum; **he's older than me** er ist älter als ich **b** (*emph*) ich; **who, me?** wer, ich?; **it's me** ich bins

mead[1] [miːd] N (= *drink*) Met *m*

mead[2] [miːd] N (*old, poet*) Aue *f*

meadow [ˈmedəʊ] N Wiese *f*, Weide *f*; **in the ~** auf der Wiese *or* Weide

meadow: meadowland N Weideland *nt*; **meadowlark** N Wiesenstärling *m*; **meadowsweet** N Mädesüß *nt*

meagre, (*US*) **meager** [ˈmiːgə] ADJ **a** spärlich; *amount, crowd* kläglich; *meal* dürftig, kärglich; **to eke out a ~ existence** ein kümmerliches Dasein fristen; **he earns a ~ £500 a month** er verdient magere *or* mickrige (*inf*) £ 500 im Monat **b** (*liter, = lean*) hager

meagrely, (*US*) **meagerly** [ˈmiːgəlɪ] ADV spärlich; *live* kärglich

meagreness, (US) **meagerness** ['miːɡənɪs] N Spärlichkeit f; (of amount, crowd) Kläglichkeit f; (of meal) Dürftigkeit f, Kärglichkeit f

meal¹ [miːl] N Schrot(mehl nt) m

meal² N Mahlzeit f; (= food) Essen nt; **come round for a ~** komm zum Essen (zu uns); **to go for a ~** essen gehen; **to have a (good) ~** (gut) essen; **hot ~s** warme Mahlzeiten pl, warmes Essen; **I haven't had a ~ for two days** ich habe seit zwei Tagen nichts Richtiges mehr gegessen; **to make a ~ of sth** (inf) etw auf sehr umständliche Art machen; **don't make a ~ of it** (inf) nun übertreib mal nicht (inf)

mealie meal ['miːlɪmiːl] N Maismehl nt

meal: meals on wheels N Essen nt auf Rädern; **meal ticket** N **a** (US: lit) Essensbon m or -marke f **b** (fig) **that letter of introduction was his ~ for the next few months** dank des Empfehlungsschreibens konnte er sich die nächsten paar Monate über Wasser halten; **a boyfriend is just a ~ to a lot of girls** viele Mädchen haben nur einen Freund, um sich von ihm aushalten zu lassen; **mealtime** N Essenszeit f; **you shouldn't smoke at ~s** Sie sollten während des Essens nicht rauchen

mealworm ['miːlwɜːm] N Mehlwurm m

mealy ['miːlɪ] ADJ mehlig

mealy-mouthed ['miːlɪˈmaʊðd] ADJ unaufrichtig; politician schönfärberisch; **let's not be ~ about it** wir wollen doch mal nicht so um den heißen Brei herumreden

mean¹ [miːn] ADJ (+er) **a** (esp Brit: = miserly) geizig, knauserig; **don't be ~!** sei doch nicht so geizig or knauserig!; **you ~ thing!** du Geizhals or Geizkragen!
b (= unkind, spiteful) gemein; **don't be ~!** sei nicht so gemein or fies! (inf); **you ~ thing!** du gemeines or fieses Stück! (inf), du Miststück! (inf); **it made me feel ~** ich kam mir richtig schäbig or gemein vor
c (= base, inferior) birth, motives niedrig; **the ~est citizen** der Geringste unter den Bürgern (old)
d (= shabby, unimpressive) shack, house schäbig, armselig
e (= vicious) bösartig; look gehässig, hinterhältig; criminal niederträchtig, abscheulich
f **he is no ~ player** er ist ein beachtlicher Spieler; **he plays a ~ game of poker** er ist ein ausgefuchster Pokerspieler (inf); **that's no ~ feat** diese Aufgabe ist nicht zu unterschätzen or nicht von Pappe (inf); **a sportsman/politician of no ~ ability** ein sehr fähiger Sportler/Politiker

mean² N (= middle term) Durchschnitt m; (Math) Durchschnitt m, Mittelwert m, Mittel nt; **the golden** or **happy ~** die goldene Mitte ADJ mittlere(r, s); **~ sea level** Normalnull nt

mean³ ✪ 6.3, 8.2, 16.1, 26.3 pret, ptp **meant** VT **a** (= signify) bedeuten; (person: = refer to, have in mind) meinen; **what do you ~ by that?** was willst du damit sagen?; **the name ~s nothing to me** der Name sagt mir nichts; **it ~s starting all over again** das bedeutet or das heißt, dass wir wieder ganz von vorne anfangen müssen; **this will ~ great changes** dies wird bedeutende Veränderungen zur Folge haben; **a pound ~s a lot to her** für sie ist ein Pfund eine Menge Geld; **your friendship/he ~s a lot to me** deine Freundschaft/er bedeutet mir viel; **you ~ everything to me** du bist alles für mich
b (= intend) beabsichtigen; **to ~ to do sth** etw tun wollen; (= do on purpose) etw absichtlich tun; **to be ~t for sb/sth** für jdn/etw bestimmt sein; **to ~ sb to do sth** wollen, dass jd etw tut; **sth is ~t to be sth** etw soll etw sein; **what do you ~ to do?** was wirst du tun?, was hast du vor?; **I only ~t to help** ich wollte nur helfen; **of course it hurt, I ~t it to** or **it was ~t to** natürlich tat das weh, das war Absicht; **without ~ing to sound rude** ich möchte nicht unverschämt klingen(, aber ...); **I ~t it as a joke** das sollte ein Witz sein; **I ~t you to have it** das solltest du haben; **I was ~t to do that** ich hätte das tun sollen; **you are ~t to be on time** du solltest

pünktlich sein; **he wasn't ~t to be a leader** er war nicht zum Führer bestimmt; **I thought it was ~t to be hot in the south** ich dachte immer, dass es im Süden so heiß sei; **I ~ to be obeyed** ich verlange, dass man mir gehorcht; **I ~ to have it** ich bin fest entschlossen, es zu bekommen; **this pad is ~t for drawing** dieser Block ist zum Zeichnen gedacht or da (inf); **if he ~s to be awkward ...** wenn er vorhat, Schwierigkeiten zu machen ...; **this present was ~t for you** dieses Geschenk sollte für dich sein or war für dich gedacht → **business, mischief**
c (= be serious about) ernst meinen; **I ~ it!** das ist mein Ernst!, ich meine das ernst!; **do you ~ to say you're not coming?** willst du damit sagen or soll das heißen, dass du nicht kommst?; **I ~ what I say** ich sage das im Ernst; **do you really ~ it this time?** ist es dir diesmal ernst or Ernst damit?
d **he ~s well/no harm** er meint es gut/nicht böse; **to ~ well by sb** es gut mit jdm meinen; **to ~ sb no harm** es gut mit jdm meinen, jdm nichts Böses wollen; (physically) jdm nichts tun; (in past tense) jdm nichts tun wollen; **I ~t no harm by what I said** was ich da gesagt habe, war nicht böse gemeint

meander [mɪˈændə] VI (river) sich (dahin-) schlängeln, mäandern; (person) wirr sein; (= go off subject) (vom Thema) abschweifen; (walking) schlendern

meanderings [mɪˈændərɪŋz] PL (of river) Windungen pl, Mäander m; (= talk) Gefasel nt; (off subject) Abschweifungen pl, Exkurse pl; **the ~ of his mind** seine verworrenen Gedankengänge

meanie ['miːnɪ] N (esp Brit, inf: = miserly person) Geizhals or -kragen m; (= nasty person) Miststück nt (inf)

meaning ['miːnɪŋ] ADJ look etc viel sagend, bedeutsam N Bedeutung f; (= sense: of words, poem etc also) Sinn m; **a look full of ~** ein bedeutungsvoller or bedeutsamer Blick; **what's the ~ of (the word) "hick"?** was soll das Wort „hick" heißen or bedeuten?; **to mistake sb's ~** jdn missverstehen; **do you get my ~?** haben Sie mich (richtig) verstanden?; **you don't know the ~ of love/hunger** du weißt ja gar nicht, was Liebe/Hunger ist or bedeutet; **what's the ~ of this?** was hat denn das zu bedeuten?, was soll denn das (heißen)?

meaningful ['miːnɪŋfʊl] ADJ **a** (= having meaning) word, statement, symbol mit Bedeutung; (Ling) unit bedeutungstragend; poem, film bedeutungsvoll; (= expressive) look, glance bedeutungsvoll; **to be ~** eine Bedeutung haben **b** (= comprehensible) advice, information, question, answer, results sinnvoll; **the statistics only become ~ when ...** die Zahlen ergeben nur dann einen Sinn, wenn ... **c** (= purposeful) job, negotiations sinnvoll; relationship tiefer gehend

meaningfully ['miːnɪŋfʊlɪ] ADV **a** (= pointedly) look bedeutungsvoll; say, add vielsagend **b** (= comprehensibly) explain, answer sinnvoll **c** (= purposefully) spend one's time, participate, negotiate sinnvoll

meaningless ['miːnɪŋlɪs] ADJ **a** (semantically) word, symbol etc ohne Bedeutung, bedeutungslos **b** (= aimless) **my life is ~** mein Leben hat keinen Sinn

meanly ['miːnlɪ] ADV **a** (esp Brit: = ungenerously) geizig, knauserig **b** (= unkindly) behave, treat gemein; **~, he took her last cigarette** er war so gemein, ihre letzte Zigarette zu nehmen

meanness ['miːnnɪs] N **a** (esp Brit: = miserliness) Geiz m, Knauserigkeit f **b** (= unkindness, spite) Gemeinheit f **c** (= baseness: of birth, motives) Niedrigkeit f **d** (= shabbiness) Schäbigkeit f, Armseligkeit f **e** (= viciousness) Bösartigkeit f; (of look) Gehässigkeit f, Hinterhältigkeit f; (of criminal) Niedertracht f

means [miːnz] ✪ 17.1 N **a** sing (= method) Möglichkeit f; (= instrument) Mittel nt; **a ~ of transport** ein Beförderungsmittel nt; **a ~ of escape** eine Fluchtmöglichkeit f; **a ~ to an end** ein Mittel nt zum Zweck; **I have/there is no ~ of**

doing it es ist mir/es ist unmöglich, das zu tun; **is there any ~ of doing it?** ist es irgendwie möglich, das zu tun?; **there must be a ~ of doing it** es muss doch irgendwie or auf irgendeine Art zu machen sein; **we've no ~ of knowing** wir können nicht wissen; **he was the ~ of sending it** man ließ es durch ihn überbringen; **they used him as the ~ of getting the heroin across the border** sie benutzten ihn, um das Heroin über die Grenze zu bringen; **all known ~ have been tried** man hat alles Mögliche versucht; **by ~ of sth** mittels einer Sache (gen) (form); **by ~ of doing sth** dadurch, dass man etw tut; **by this ~** dadurch, auf diese Weise; **by some ~ or other** auf irgendeine Art und Weise, irgendwie
b sing by all ~! (aber) selbstverständlich or natürlich!; **by all ~ take one** nehmen Sie sich ruhig (eins); **by no ~, not by any ~** keineswegs, durchaus nicht; (= under no circumstances) auf keinen Fall
c pl (= wherewithal) Mittel pl; (= financial means) Gelder pl, Mittel pl; **a man of ~** ein vermögender Mann; **private ~** private Mittel pl; **that is within/beyond my ~** das kann ich mir leisten/nicht leisten; **to live beyond one's ~** über seine Verhältnisse leben; **to live within one's ~** seinen Verhältnissen entsprechend leben

mean-spirited [miːnˈspɪrɪtɪd] ADJ geizig, knauserig

means test N Einkommens- or Vermögensverhältnisse

meant [ment] pret, ptp of **mean**³

meantime ['miːntaɪm] ADV inzwischen N for the ~ vorerst, im Augenblick, einstweilen; **in the ~** in der Zwischenzeit, inzwischen

meanwhile ['miːnwaɪl] ADV **a** (= in the meantime) inzwischen **b** (= in contrast) währenddessen; **every packet carries a warning, ~ many continue to smoke** auf jeder Packung steht eine Warnung, trotzdem rauchen viele auch weiterhin

measles ['miːzlz] N sing Masern pl

measly ['miːzlɪ] ADJ (+er) (inf) mick(e)rig (inf), poplig (inf)

measurable ['meʒərəbl] ADJ messbar; (= perceptible) erkennbar

measurably ['meʒərəblɪ] ADV messbar; (= perceptibly) deutlich

measure ['meʒə] N **a** (= unit of measurement) Maß(einheit f) nt; **a ~ of length** ein Längenmaß nt; **to have sth made to ~** etw nach Maß anfertigen lassen; **the furniture has been made to ~** die Möbel sind Maßarbeit; **beyond ~** grenzenlos; **her joy was beyond** or **knew no ~** ihre Freude kannte keine Grenzen → **weight**
b (= object for measuring) Maß nt; (graduated for length) Maßstab m; (graduated for volume) Messbecher m
c (= amount measured) Menge f; **a small ~ of flour** ein wenig Mehl; **wine is sold in ~s of 1/4 litre** (Brit) or **liter** (US) Wein wird in Vierteln ausgeschenkt; **to give sb full/short ~** (barman) richtig/zu wenig ausschenken; (grocer) richtig/zu wenig abwiegen; **in full ~** in höchstem Maße; **for good ~** zur Sicherheit, sicherheitshalber; **... and another one for good ~** und noch eines obendrein
d (fig: = yardstick) Maßstab m (of für); **can we regard this exam as a ~ of intelligence?** kann diese Prüfung als Intelligenzmaßstab gelten?; **MacLeod's approval is the ~ of a good whisky** MacLeods Urteil in Bezug auf Whisky ist (für mich) maßgebend or ausschlaggebend; **please consider this as a ~ of my esteem for ...** bitte betrachten Sie dies als Ausdruck meiner Anerkennung für ...; **it gave us some ~ of the difficulty** es gab uns einen Begriff von der Schwierigkeit; **it's a ~ of his skill as a writer that ...** seine schriftstellerischen Fähigkeiten lassen sich daran beurteilen, dass ...; **words cannot always give the ~ of one's feelings** Worte können nicht immer Gefühle angemessen ausdrücken
e (= extent) **in some ~** in gewisser Hinsicht or Beziehung; **some ~ of** ein gewisses Maß an; **to**

a large ~, in large ~ in hohem Maße; **to get the ~ of sb/sth** jdn/etw (richtig) einschätzen **f** (= *step*) Maßnahme *f*; **to take ~s to do sth** Maßnahmen ergreifen, um etw zu tun **g** (*Poet*) Versmaß *nt* **h** (*US Mus*) Takt *m* **i** (*old*, = *dance*) Tanz *m*; **to tread a ~ with sb** mit jdm ein Tänzchen wagen █ **VT** messen; *length also* abmessen; *room also* ausmessen; (= *take sb's measurements*) Maß nehmen bei; (*fig*) beurteilen, abschätzen; *words* abwägen; **a ~d mile** genau eine Meile; **to ~ one's length** (*fig*) der Länge nach hinfallen █ **VI** messen; **what does it ~?** wie viel misst es?, wie groß ist es?

▶ **measure off** VT *sep* *area*, *length of cloth* abmessen

▶ **measure out** VT *sep* abmessen; *weights also* abwiegen

▶ **measure up** █ **VT** *sep* **a** (= *take measurements of*) *wood*, *room etc* abmessen; *person for suit etc* Maß nehmen bei **b** (*fig*: = *assess*) *situation* abschätzen; *person* einschätzen █ **VI** **a** (= *be good enough*, *compare well*) **he didn't measure up** er hat enttäuscht; **to measure up to sth** an etw (*acc*) herankommen; **visually he measured up (to the description)** vom Aussehen her passte er (auf die Beschreibung); **it's a hard job, but he should measure up** das ist eine schwierige Aufgabe, aber er sollte ihr gewachsen sein **b** (= *take measurements*) Maß nehmen, messen

measured ['meʒəd] ADJ *tread* gemessen (*liter*); *tone* bedacht, bedächtig; *words* wohl überlegt, durchdacht; *approach*, *response* maßvoll; **he walked with ~ steps** er ging gemessenen Schrittes (*liter*); **at a ~ pace** in gemäßigtem Tempo; **he is becoming calmer and more ~** er wird ruhiger und bedächtiger

measureless ['meʒəlɪs] ADJ unermesslich

measurement ['meʒəmənt] N **a** (= *act*) Messung *f*; **the metric system of ~** das metrische Maßsystem **b** (= *measure*) Maß *nt*; (= *figure*) Messwert *m*; (*fig*) Maßstab *m*; **to take sb's ~s** an jdm *or* bei jdm Maß nehmen

measuring ['meʒərɪŋ] N Messen *nt*; **to take ~s of sth** etw messen

measuring *in cpds* Mess-; **measuring device** N Messgerät *nt*; **measuring equipment** N Messvorrichtungen *pl*; **measuring instrument** N Messinstrument *nt*; **measuring jug** N Messbecher *m*; **measuring range** N (*Phys*) Messbereich *m*; **measuring tape** N Bandmaß *nt*, Metermaß *nt*

meat [miːt] N **a** Fleisch *nt*; **cold ~** kalter Braten; (= *sausage*) Wurst *f*; **assorted cold ~s** Aufschnitt *m* **b** (*old*: = *food*) Essen *nt*, Speise *f* (*liter*); **food and drink** Speise und Trank; **one man's ~ is another man's poison** (*Prov*) des einen Freud, des andern Leid (*Prov*) **c** (*fig*: of *argument*, *book*) Substanz *f*; **a book with some ~ in it** ein aussagestarkes Buch

meat *in cpds* Fleisch-; **meatball** N Fleischkloß *m*; **meat-chopper** N **a** (= *knife*) Hackmesser *nt* **b** (= *mincer*) Fleischhackmaschine *f*, Fleischwolf *m*; **meat-grinder** N (*US*) Fleischwolf *m*; **meathead** N (*US*, *inf*) Dummkopf *m*; **meat loaf** N ≈ Fleischkäse *m*; **meat market** N **a** (*for animals*) Viehmarkt *m* **b** (*pej inf*) (*for people*) Aufreißschuppen *m* (*inf*); (= *beauty contest etc*) Fleischbeschau *f* (*inf*); **meatpacker** N (*US Comm*) Arbeiter(in) *m(f)* in der Fleischverarbeitung; **meatpacking** N (*US Comm*) Fleischverarbeitung *f*; (= *industry*) Fleischverarbeitungsindustrie *f*; **meat products** PL Fleisch- und Wurstwaren *pl*; **meat safe** N Fliegenschrank *m*

meaty ['miːtɪ] ADJ (+er) *soup*, *sauce*, *meal*, *dish* mit viel Fleisch; **~ chunks** Fleischbrocken *pl*; **~ texture** Fleischstruktur *f*; **this is a ~ fish** dieser Fisch hat Fleischcharakter **b** (= *fleshy*) *arms*, *hands* fleischig **c** (*fig*) *book* aussagestark, gehaltvoll; *role*, *part* anspruchsvoll

Mecca ['mekə] N (*lit*, *fig*) Mekka *nt*

mechanic [mɪ'kænɪk] N Mechaniker(in) *m(f)*

mechanical [mɪ'kænɪkəl] ADJ (*lit*, *fig*) mechanisch; *toy* technisch; **a ~ device** ein Mechanismus *m*

mechanical: mechanical digger N Bagger *m*; (*also* **mechanical shovel**) Löffelbagger *m*; **mechanical engineer** N Maschinenbauer(in) *or* -bauingenieur(in) *m(f)*; **mechanical engineering** N Maschinenbau *m*

mechanically [mɪ'kænɪkəlɪ] ADV (*lit*, *fig*) mechanisch; **~-minded** technisch begabt

mechanical shovel N Löffelbagger *m*

mechanician [mekə'nɪʃən] N → **mechanic**

mechanics [mɪ'kænɪks] N **a** *sing* (= *subject*) (= *engineering*) Maschinenbau *m*; (*Phys*) Mechanik *f*; **home ~ for the car-owner** kleine Maschinenkunde für den Autobesitzer **b** *pl* (= *technical aspects*) Mechanik *f*, Mechanismus *m*; (*fig*: of *writing etc*) Technik *f*; **there is something wrong with the ~ of the car** das Auto ist mechanisch nicht in Ordnung; **I don't understand the ~ of parliamentary procedure** ich verstehe den Mechanismus parlamentarischer Abläufe nicht

mechanism ['mekənɪzəm] N Mechanismus *m*

mechanistic [mekə'nɪstɪk, -əlɪ] , **mechanistically** ADV mechanistisch

mechanization [mekənaɪ'zeɪʃən] N Mechanisierung *f*

mechanize ['mekənaɪz] VT mechanisieren

mechanized ['mekənaɪzd] ADJ mechanisiert; **highly ~ production** stark automatisierte Produktion

med *abbr of* **medium**

medal ['medl] N Medaille *f*; (= *decoration*) Orden *m*

medalist N (*US*) = **medallist**

medallion [mɪ'dæljən] N Medaillon *nt*; (= *medal*) Medaille *f*

medallist, (*US*) **medalist** ['medəlɪst] N Medaillengewinner(in) *m(f)*

meddle ['medl] VI **a** (= *interfere*) sich einmischen (*in* in +*acc*) **b** (= *tamper*) sich zu schaffen machen, herumfummeln (*inf*) (*with* an +*dat*); **to ~ with sb** sich mit jdm einlassen; **he's not a man to ~ with** mit ihm ist nicht gut Kirschen essen; **he's always meddling** er mischt sich in alles ein

meddler ['medlə] N **he's a terrible ~** er muss sich immer in alles einmischen

meddlesome ['medlsəm] ADJ , **meddling** ['medlɪŋ] ADJ *attr* **she's a ~ old busybody** sie mischt sich dauernd in alles ein

media ['miːdɪə] N *pl of* **medium** Medien *pl*; **he works in the ~** er ist im Mediensektor tätig *or* beschäftigt; **~ coverage** Berichterstattung *f* in den Medien; **to get too much ~ coverage** zu viel Publicity bekommen

mediaeval ADJ = **medieval**

mediaevalist N = **medievalist**

media: media environment N (*fig*) Medienlandschaft *f*; **media event** N Medienereignis *nt*

medial ['miːdɪəl] ADJ (= *in the middle*) mittlere(r, s); **in (word) ~ position** (*Ling*) im Inlaut

media landscape N (*fig*) Medienlandschaft *f*

median ['miːdɪən] **ADJ** mittlere(r, s) **N** (*Math*) Zentralwert *m*

median strip N (*US*) Mittelstreifen *m*

mediaperson ['miːdɪəpɜːsn] N *pl* **mediapeople** ['miːdɪəpiːpl] (*well-known*) Medienstar *m*

media studies PL Medienwissenschaft *f*

mediate¹ ['miːdɪət] ADJ (*rare*) mittelbar

mediate² ['miːdɪeɪt] **VI** vermitteln **VT** *settlement* aushandeln, herbeiführen

mediation [miːdɪ'eɪʃən] N Vermittlung *f*

mediator ['miːdɪeɪtə] N Vermittler(in) *m(f)*, Mittelsmann *m*, Mittelsperson *f*

mediatorship ['miːdɪeɪtəʃɪp] N **a** (= *role of mediator*) Vermittleramt *nt*, Vermittlerrolle *f* **b** (= *help*, *arrangement*) Vermittlung *f*

mediatory ['miːdɪətərɪ] ADJ vermittelnd, des Vermittlers; **in a ~ capacity** als Vermittler

medic ['medɪk] N (*inf*) Mediziner(in) *m(f)* (*inf*)

Medicaid ['medɪkeɪd] N (*US*) *staatliche Krankenversicherung und Gesundheitsfürsorge für Einkommensschwache unter 65 in den USA* → *also* **Medicare**

MEDICAID, MEDICARE

Medicaid ist ein gemeinsames Programm der US-Bundesregierung und der Bundesstaaten, mit dem die stationäre Krankenhausbehandlung und medizinische Versorgung für all diejenigen Personen unter 65 Jahren finanziert wird, die an oder unterhalb der offiziellen staatlichen Armutsgrenze leben. Die Berechtigungskriterien wie auch die Leistungspalette variieren von Staat zu Staat und können auch Kosten beinhalten, die nicht von **Medicare** getragen werden.

Medicare ist das staatlich finanzierte US--Krankenversicherungsprogramm, das speziell die Kosten für Krankenhausbehandlung und medizinische Versorgung für über 65-jährige, Nierenpatienten und einige Behinderte übernimmt. Die Mitglieder zahlen einen monatlichen Beitrag. Die Behandlung erfolgt durch bestimmte Krankenhäuser und Ärzte, die am Programm teilnehmen. Parallel dazu gibt es ein Privatversicherungsprogramm, **Medigap**, das als Zusatzversicherung zu **Medicare** fungiert.

Alle, die nicht durch **Medicare** oder **Medicaid** abgedeckt sind, müssen ihre medizinische Versorgung durch private Krankenversicherungen absichern.

---

medical ['medɪkəl] **ADJ** (= *related to science*) *research*, *study*, *journal*, *faculty*, *training* medizinisch; (*in military contexts*) Sanitäts-; (= *relating to doctors*) *test*, *examination*, *treatment*, *attention*, *advice*, *expertise*, *care*, *staff* ärztlich; **~ advances** Fortschritte *pl* in der Medizin; **the ~ profession** die Ärzteschaft; (= *doctors*) die Ärzteschaft; **I'm not a ~ man** ich bin kein Arzt; **~ condition** *or* **disorder** Erkrankung *f*; **~ opinion** ärztliches Gutachten █ **N** (*ärztliche*) Untersuchung *f*; **have you had your ~?** bist du zur Untersuchung gewesen?, hast du dich untersuchen lassen?

medical: medical authority N Gesundheitsbehörde *f*; **medical card** (*Brit*) Krankenversicherungsausweis *m*; **medical centre**, (*US*) **medical center** N (*Brit*) Ärztehaus *nt*; (*US*) Krankenhaus *nt*, Klinik *f*; **medical certificate** N ärztliches Attest; **Medical College Admissions Test** N (*US Univ*) Zulassungsprüfung *f* zum Medizinstudium; **medical corps** N (*Mil*) Sanitätstruppe *f*; **medical doctor** N Arzt *m*, Ärztin *f*; **medical examiner** N (*US Jur*) Gerichtsmediziner(in) *m(f)*; **medical history** N **a** (= *medical background*) **her ~** ihre Krankengeschichte **b** (= *history of medicine*) die Geschichte der Medizin; **that made ~** das hat in der Medizin Geschichte gemacht; **medical insurance** N Krankenversicherung *f*; **medical jurisprudence** N Gerichtsmedizin *f*

medically ['medɪkəlɪ] ADV medizinisch; *examine* ärztlich; **to be ~ qualified/trained** eine medizinische Ausbildung absolviert/gemacht haben

medical: medical officer N (*Mil*) Stabsarzt *m*; (= *official*) Amtsarzt *m*; **medical practice** N (= *business*) Arztpraxis *f*; (= *procedure*) medizinisches Verfahren; **in western ~** in der westlichen Medizin; **medical practitioner** N Arzt *m*, Ärztin *f*; **medical profession** N (= *doctor's job*) Arztberuf *m* **b** (= *doctors as a whole*) Ärzteschaft *f* *no pl*; **medical record** N (= *medical background*) Krankengeschichte *f*; **~s** (= *detailed notes*) Krankenblatt *nt*; **Medical Register** N (*Brit*) Ärzteregister *nt*; **to strike sb off the ~** jdm die Approbation entziehen; **Medical Research Council** N (*Brit*) Organisation *zur Förderung der medizinischen Forschung*; **medical school** N ≈ medizinische Fakultät; **medical science** N die ärztliche Wissenschaft; **medical student** N Medizinstudent(in) *m(f)*; **medical unit** N (*Mil*) Sanitätsbataillon *nt*; **medical ward** N Innere Abteilung

medicament [me'dɪkəmənt] N Medikament *nt*, Mittel *nt*

Medicare ['medɪˌkeə'] N (*US*) staatliche Krankenversicherung und Gesundheitsfürsorge für ältere Bürger in den USA → also **Medicaid**

medicate ['medɪkeɪt] VT (medizinisch) behandeln

medicated ['medɪkeɪtɪd] ADJ medizinisch

medication [medɪ'keɪʃən] N (*act*) (medizinische) Behandlung *f*; (= *drugs etc*) Verordnung *f*, Medikamente *pl*

medicinal [me'dɪsɪnl] ADJ Heil-, heilend; **for ~ purposes** zu medizinischen Zwecken; **I need a whisky - for ~ purposes** (*hum*) ich brauche einen Whisky, aus medizinischen Gründen; **the ~ properties of various herbs** die Heilkraft verschiedener Kräuter

medicinally [me'dɪsɪnəlɪ] ADV *use, take* zu Heilzwecken, zu medizinischen Zwecken; *valuable* medizinisch; **~, it aids digestion** medizinisch gesehen fördert es die Verdauung

medicine ['medsɪn, 'medsɪn] N **a** Arznei *f*, Medizin *f* (*inf*); (= *one particular preparation*) Medikament *nt*; **to take one's ~** (*lit*) seine Arznei einnehmen; (*fig*) die bittere Pille schlucken, in den sauren Apfel beißen; **to give sb a taste of his own ~** (*fig*) es jdm mit gleicher Münze heimzahlen *or* zurückzahlen; **now we'll see how you like a taste of your own ~** jetzt werden wir sehen, wie es dir schmeckt, wenn dir das passiert **b** (= *science*) Medizin *f*; **to practise** (*Brit*) *or* **practice** (*US*) **~** den Arztberuf ausüben

medicine: medicine ball N Medizinball *m*; **medicine chest** N Hausapotheke *f*, Arzneischränkchen *nt*; **medicine man** N Medizinmann *m*; **medicine show** N (*US Hist*) Schau eines reisenden Wunderdoktors

medico ['medɪkəʊ] N (*dated inf*) Medikus *m* (*dated, hum*)

medieval [medɪ'iːvəl] ADJ (*lit, fig*) mittelalterlich; **in ~ times** im Mittelalter; **it's positively ~** (*practice, attitude*) es ist wie im Mittelalter

medieval history N die Geschichte des Mittelalters

medievalist [medɪ'iːvəlɪst] N Mediävist(in) *m(f)*

Medigap ['medɪgæp] N (*US*) Zusatzkrankenversicherung *f*

mediocre [miːdɪ'əʊkə'] ADJ mittelmäßig

mediocrity [miːdɪ'ɒkrɪtɪ] N **a** (= *quality*) Mittelmäßigkeit *f* **b** (= *person*) kleines Licht

meditate ['medɪteɪt] VT **to ~ revenge** auf Rache sinnen (*liter*) VI nachdenken (*upon, on* über +*acc*); (*Rel, Philos*) meditieren

meditation [medɪ'teɪʃən] N Nachdenken *nt*; (*Rel, Philos*) Meditation *f*; **"A Meditation on Life"** „Betrachtungen über das Leben"

meditative ['medɪtətɪv] ADJ nachdenklich; (*Rel, Philos*) Meditations-; **~ techniques** Meditationstechniken *pl*

meditatively ['medɪtətɪvlɪ] ADV nachdenklich; *sit, look* meditierend

Mediterranean [medɪtə'reɪnɪən] N Mittelmeer *nt*; **in the ~** (= *in sea*) im Mittelmeer; (= *in region*) am Mittelmeer, im Mittelmeerraum ADJ Mittelmeer-; *scenery, character, person* südländisch; **~ climate/nations** Mittelmeerklima *nt*/-länder *pl*; **~ island** Mittelmeerinsel *f*; **~ fruit** Südfrüchte *pl*; **~ types** Südländer *pl*; **~ cruise** Kreuzfahrt *f* im Mittelmeer; **~ holiday** (*Brit*) *or* **vacation** (*US*) Urlaub *m* im Mittelmeerraum

Mediterranean Sea N **the ~** das Mittelmeer

medium ['miːdɪəm] ADJ *quality, size, height, length etc* mittlere(r, s); *steak* halbdurch, medium; (= *medium-sized*) mittelgroß; **~ brown** mittelbraun; **of ~ height/build/size** mittelgroß; **of ~ difficulty** mittelschwer; **cook over a ~ heat** bei mittlerer Hitze kochen; **in/over the ~ term** mittelfristig

N *pl* **media** *or* **-s** **a** (= *means*) Mittel *nt*; (*TV, Rad, Press*) Medium *nt*; (*Art, Liter*) Ausdrucksmittel *nt*; **~ of exchange** Tauschmittel *nt*; **through the ~ of the press** durch die Presse; **advertising ~** Werbeträger *m* **b** (= *surrounding substance*) (*Phys*) Medium *nt*; (= *environment*) Umgebung *f*; (*air, water etc*) Element *nt* **c** (= *midpoint*) Mitte *f*; **happy ~** goldener Mittelweg; **to strike a happy ~** den goldenen Mittelweg finden **d** (= *spiritualist*) Medium *nt*

medium in *cpds* mittel-; **medium-dry** ADJ *wine, sherry* halbtrocken; **medium-priced** ADJ **a ~ hotel/whisky** ein Hotel *nt*/ein Whisky *m* mittlerer Preislage; **in the ~ range** in der mittleren Preislage; **medium-range** ADJ Mittelstrecken-; **~ aircraft/missile** Mittelstreckenflugzeug *nt*/-rakete *f*; **medium-rare** ADJ rosa, englisch; **mediumship** N Tätigkeit *f* als Medium; **medium-size, medium-sized** ADJ mittelgroß; **medium-sweet** ADJ *wine* fruchtig; *sherry, cider* halbsüß; **medium-term** ADJ mittelfristig; **medium wave** N Mittelwelle *f*; **medium-wave** ADJ **~ transmission** Mittelwellenübertragung *f*; **~ transmitter** Mittelwellensender *m*

medley ['medlɪ] N Gemisch *nt*; (*Mus*) Potpourri *nt*, Medley *f*

medley relay N *Staffellauf, bei dem die einzelnen Teilnehmer über verschieden lange Strecken laufen, z. B.* Schwedenstaffel; *olympische Staffel* (*Swimming*) Lagenstaffel *f*

medulla [me'dʌlə] N Mark *nt*; (*of spine*) Rückenmark *nt*; (= *renal medulla*) Nierenmark *nt*

meek [miːk] ADJ (+*er*) sanft(mütig), lammfromm (*inf*); (*pej*) duckmäuserisch; (= *uncomplaining*) duldsam, geduldig; *voice* schüchtern; *acceptance* widerstandslos; **as ~ as a lamb** sanft wie ein Lamm; **don't be so ~ and mild** lass dir doch nicht (immer) alles gefallen! N (*Bibl*) **the ~** *pl* die Sanftmütigen *pl*

meekly ['miːklɪ] ADV sanft, lammfromm (*inf*); (*pej*) duckmäuserisch; *agree* widerspruchslos; *submit, accept* widerstandslos; *listen, sit, stand* geduldig

meekness ['miːknɪs] N Sanftmut *f*; (*pej*) Duckmäuserei *f*; (= *tolerance*) Duldsamkeit *f*

meerschaum ['mɪəʃəm] N Meerschaum *m*; (= *pipe*) Meerschaumpfeife *f*

meet[1] [miːt] ADJ (*obs*) geziemend (*liter*); **it is ~ that ...** es ist billig *or* (ge)ziemt sich (*liter, old*), dass ...; **to be ~ for** sich (ge)ziemen für (*liter, old*)

meet[2] *vb*: *pret, ptp* **met** VT **a** (= *encounter*) *person* treffen, begegnen (+*dat*); (*by arrangement*) treffen, sich treffen mit; *difficulty* stoßen auf (+*acc*); (*Sport*) treffen auf (+*acc*); **I'll ~ you outside** ich treffe euch draußen; **he met his guests at the door** er empfing seine Gäste an der Tür; **he met him in a duel** er duellierte sich mit ihm; **he met his death in 1800** im Jahre 1800 fand er den Tod; **to ~ death calmly** dem Tod gefasst entgegentreten; **to arrange to ~ sb** sich mit jdm verabreden; **to ~ a challenge** sich einer Herausforderung (*dat*) stellen; **the last time the two teams met there was a riot** bei der letzten Begegnung zwischen beiden Teams kam es zu heftigen Auseinandersetzungen; **his eyes** *or* **gaze met mine** unsere Blicke trafen sich; **she refused to ~ his eyes** *or* **gaze** sie wich seinem Blick aus; **I could not ~ his eyes** ich konnte ihm nicht in die Augen sehen; **there's more to it than ~s the eye** da steckt mehr dahinter, als man auf den ersten Blick meint **b** (= *get to know*) kennenlernen; (= *be introduced to*) bekannt gemacht werden mit; **you don't know him? come and ~ him** du kennst ihn nicht? komm, ich mache dich mit ihm bekannt; **pleased to ~ you!** guten Tag/Abend, sehr angenehm! (*form*) **c** (= *await arrival, collect*) abholen (*at an* +*dat*, *von*); (= *connect with*) *train, boat etc* Anschluss haben an (+*acc*); **I'll ~ your train** ich hole dich vom Zug ab; **the car will ~ the train** der Wagen wartet am Bahnhof *or* steht am Bahnhof bereit

d (= *join, run into*) treffen *or* stoßen auf (+*acc*); (= *converge with*) sich vereinigen mit; (*river*) münden *or* fließen in (+*acc*); (= *intersect*) schneiden; (= *touch*) berühren; **where East ~s West** (*fig*) wo Ost und West sich schneiden **e** *expectations, target, obligations, deadline* erfüllen; *requirement, demand, wish* entsprechen (+*dat*), gerecht werden (+*dat*); *deficit, expenses, needs* decken; *debt* bezahlen, begleichen; *charge, objection, criticism* begegnen (+*dat*) VI **a** (= *encounter*) (*people*) sich begegnen; (*by arrangement*) sich treffen; (*society, committee etc*) zusammenkommen, tagen; (*Sport*) aufeinander treffen; (*in duel*) sich duellieren; **keep it until we ~ again** behalten Sie es, bis wir uns mal wiedersehen; **until we ~ again!** bis zum nächsten Mal!; **to ~ halfway** einen Kompromiss schließen **b** (= *become acquainted*) sich kennen lernen; (= *be introduced*) bekannt gemacht werden; **we've met before** wir kennen uns bereits; **haven't we met before somewhere?** sind wir uns nicht schon mal begegnet?, kennen wir uns nicht irgendwoher? **c** (= *join*) sich treffen, aufeinander stoßen; (= *converge*) sich vereinigen; (*rivers*) ineinander fließen; (= *intersect*) sich schneiden; (= *touch*) sich berühren; (*fig*: = *come together*) sich treffen; **our eyes met** unsere Blicke trafen sich; **the skirt wouldn't ~ round her waist** der Rock ging an der Taille nicht zu N (*Brit Hunt*) Jagd(veranstaltung) *f*; (*US*) (*Athletics*) Sportfest *nt*; (*Swimming*) Schwimmfest *nt*

▶ **meet up** VI sich treffen

▶ **meet with** VI +*prep obj* **a** (= *encounter, experience*) *hostility, opposition, problems* stoßen auf (+*acc*); *success, accident* haben; *disaster, loss, shock* erleiden; *setback* erleben; *approval, encouragement, an untimely death* finden; **to meet with derision** verspottet werden; **to meet with kindness/a warm welcome** freundlich behandelt/herzlich empfangen werden; **I was met with a blank stare** sie/er *etc* starrte mich unwissend an **b** *person* treffen; (*esp US*: = *have a meeting with*) (zu einer Unterredung) zusammenkommen mit

meeting ['miːtɪŋ] N **a** Begegnung *f*, Zusammentreffen *nt*; (*arranged*) Treffen *nt*; (= *business meeting*) Besprechung *f*, Konferenz *f*; **the minister had a ~ with the ambassador** der Minister traf zu Gesprächen mit dem Botschafter zusammen **b** (*of committee, board of directors, council*) Sitzung *f*; (*of members, employees, citizens*) Versammlung *f*, Meeting *nt*; **at the last ~** bei der letzten Sitzung; **the committee has three ~s a year** der Ausschuss tagt dreimal im Jahr; **Mr Jones is at/in a ~** Herr Jones ist (gerade) in einer Sitzung; **~ of creditors** Gläubigerversammlung *f* **c** (*Sport*) Veranstaltung *f*; (*between teams, opponents*) Begegnung *f*, Treffen *nt* **d** (*of rivers*) Zusammenfluss *m*; **at the ~ of the X and the Y** wo X und Y zusammenfließen

meeting: meeting house N Gemeindehaus *nt* (der Quäker); **meeting place** N Treffpunkt *m*; **meeting point** N Treffpunkt *m*; (*of rivers*) Zusammenfluss *m*; (*of lines*) Berührungspunkt *m*; **at the ~ of the two roads** wo die beiden Straßen zusammentreffen; **at the ~ of the two cultures** wo sich die beiden Kulturen treffen; **meeting room** N Sitzungssaal *m*

meg [meg] N (*Comput inf*) Mega(byte) *nt*

mega- ['megə-] PREF Mega-; **megabucks** PL (*inf*) **he's making ~** er verdient ein Schweinegeld (*inf*), er macht einen Haufen Kohle (*inf*)

megabyte ['megəbaɪt] N (*Comput*) Megabyte *nt*; **a 40-megabyte memory** ein 40-Megabyte-Speicher *m*

megalith ['megəlɪθ] N Megalith *m*

megalithic [megə'lɪθɪk] ADJ megalithisch

megalomania [megələʊ'meɪnɪə] N Größenwahn *m*, Megalomanie *f* (*spec*)

megalomaniac [megələʊ'meɪnɪæk] N Größenwahnsinnige(r) *mf*; **he's a ~** er leidet an Größenwahn, er ist größenwahnsinnig **ADJ** *person, ambition* größenwahnsinnig; *(Psych)* delusions megaloman(isch); **~ frenzy** Anfall *m* von Megalomanie *or* Größenwahn

mega: megaphone N Megaphon *nt*, Megafon *nt*; **megastar** N Megastar *m*; **megastore** N Großmarkt *m*; **megaton** N *(Phys)* Megatonne *f*; **megavolt** N Megavolt *nt*; **megawatt** N Megawatt *nt*

meiosis [maɪˈəʊsɪs] N *pl* **-ses** [-siːz] *(Biol)* Meiose *f*

melamine [ˈmeləmiːn] N Melamin *nt*

melancholia [ˌmelənˈkəʊlɪə] N Schwermut *f*, Melancholie *f*

melancholic [ˌmelənˈkɒlɪk] **ADJ** melancholisch, schwermütig **N** *(liter)* Melancholiker(in) *m(f)*

melancholy [ˈmelənkəlɪ] **ADJ** melancholisch, schwermütig; *duty, sight, truth etc* traurig; *place* trist **N** Melancholie *f*, Schwermut *f*

melange, mélange [meɪˈlɑːnʒ] N Mischung *f*

Melba toast [ˈmelbəˈtəʊst] N dünner, harter Toast

mêlée [ˈmeleɪ] N (= *confused struggle*) Gedränge *nt*, Gewühl *nt*; (= *fighting*) Handgemenge *nt*

mellifluous [meˈlɪfluəs] **ADJ** wohltönend, wohlklingend

mellifluously [meˈlɪfluəslɪ] **ADV** klangvoll; **...**, **he said ~** ..., sagte er mit wohltönender *or* klangvoller Stimme

Mellotron® [ˈmelətrɒn] N Mellotron® *nt*

mellow [ˈmeləʊ] **ADJ** (+er) **a** *fruit* ausgereift, saftig; *wine* ausgereift; *brandy, whisky, flavour* mild; *colour, light, stone, brick* warm; *sound* voll, rund; (= *soft*) weich; *voice* weich, sanft; **a ~ instrument** ein Instrument mit einem vollen, weichen Klang
 b *person* (= *relaxed*) abgeklärt, gesetzt; (= *affable*) umgänglich; (= *in a good mood*) gut gelaunt; *(fig:* = *slightly drunk)* angeheitert; **in the ~ later years** im gesetzteren Alter; **in a ~ mood** guter Laune, stillvergnügt
 VT reifen, heranreifen lassen; (= *relax*) heiter stimmen; *sounds, colours* dämpfen, abschwächen; *taste* mildern; **the rum began to ~ her** der Rum versetzte sie allmählich in freundlichere Stimmung
 VI *(wine, fruit)* reif werden, (heran)reifen; *(colours, sounds)* weicher werden; *(person)* (= *become more relaxed*) abgeklärter *or* gesetzter werden; (= *become more affable*) umgänglicher werden

mellowness [ˈmeləʊnɪs] N **a** (of *fruit*) Ausgereiftheit *f*, Saftigkeit *f*; (of *wine*) Ausgereiftheit *f*; (of *brandy, whisky, flavour*) Milde *f*; (of *colour, light, stone, brick*) Wärme *f*; (= *softness*) Weichheit *f*; (= *mellow sound*) weicher *or* sanfter Klang **b** (of *person*) (= *relaxed attitude*) Abgeklärtheit *f*, Gesetztheit *f*; (= *affability*) Umgänglichkeit *f*; (= *good mood*) gute Laune *f*; (= *slight tipsiness*) angeheiterte Stimmung

melodic ADJ, **melodically** ADV [mɪˈlɒdɪk, -əlɪ] melodisch

melodious [mɪˈləʊdɪəs] **ADJ** melodiös, melodisch, wohlklingend; **a ~ tune** eine harmonische Melodie

melodiously [mɪˈləʊdɪəslɪ] **ADV** melodiös, melodisch

melodiousness [məˈləʊdɪəsnɪs] N Wohlklang *m*, Melodik *f*

melodrama [ˈmeləʊdrɑːmə] N Melodrama *nt*

melodramatic ADJ, **melodramatically** ADV [ˌmeləʊdrəˈmætɪk, -əlɪ] melodramatisch

melody [ˈmelədɪ] N Melodie *f*; *(fig: of poetry etc)* Melodik *f*

melon [ˈmelən] N Melone *f*

melt [melt] **VT** **a** *(lit)* schmelzen; *snow* schmelzen, zum Schmelzen bringen; *butter* zergehen lassen, zerlassen; *sugar, grease* auflösen **b** *(fig)* *heart etc* erweichen; **her tears ~ed my heart** der Anblick ihrer Tränen erweichte mein Herz **VI** **a** schmelzen; *(sugar, grease)* sich (auf)lösen; **it just ~s in the mouth** es zergeht einem nur so auf der Zunge **b** *(fig)* *(person)* dahinschmel-

zen; *(anger)* verfliegen; **... and then his heart ~ed** ... und dann ließ er sich erweichen

▶ **melt away** VI **a** *(lit)* (weg)schmelzen **b** *(fig)* sich auflösen; *(crowd)* dahinschmelzen; *(anger, anxiety)* verfliegen; *(suspicion, money)* zerrinnen

▶ **melt down** **VT** *sep* einschmelzen **VI** *(reactor core)* schmelzen

meltdown [ˈmeltdaʊn] N Kernschmelze *f*; *(fig)* (of *market, industry*) Crash *m*; (of *company*) Zusammenbruch *m*

melting [ˈmeltɪŋ]: **melting point** N Schmelzpunkt *m*; **what is the ~ of iron?** welchen Schmelzpunkt hat Eisen?; **melting pot** N *(lit, fig)* Schmelztiegel *m*; **to be in the ~** in der Schwebe sein

member [ˈmembə] **a** Mitglied *nt*; (of *tribe, species*) Angehörige(r) *mf*; **"members only"** „nur für Mitglieder"; **~ of the family** Familienmitglied *nt*; **if any ~ of the audience ...** falls einer der Zuschauer/Zuhörer ...; **you have to be a ~** Sie müssen Mitglied sein; **the ~ countries/ states** die Mitgliedsstaaten *pl* **b** *(Parl)* Abgeordnete(r) *mf*; **~ of parliament** Parlamentsmitglied *nt*; *(in GB)* Abgeordnete(r) *mf* des Unterhauses; *(Ger)* Bundestagsabgeordnete(r) *mf*; **the ~ for Woodford** der/die Abgeordnete für den Wahlkreis Woodford **c** *(Math, Logic)* Glied *nt*

membership [ˈmembəʃɪp] N Mitgliedschaft *f* (of *in* +*dat*); (= *number of members*) Mitgliederzahl *f*; **when I applied for ~ of the club** als ich mich um die Klubmitgliedschaft bewarb

membership: membership card N Mitgliedsausweis *m*; **membership fee** N Mitgliedsbeitrag *m*; **membership list** N Mitgliederkartei *f*

membrane [ˈmembreɪn] N Membran(e) *f*

membranous [memˈbreɪnəs] **ADJ** membranartig

memento [məˈmentəʊ] N *pl* **-(e)s** Andenken *nt* (of *an* +*acc*)

memo [ˈmeməʊ] N *abbr of* **memorandum** Mitteilung *f*, Notiz *f*, Memo *nt*

memoir [ˈmemwɑː] **a** Kurzbiografie *f* **b** **memoirs** PL Memoiren *pl*

memo pad N Notizblock *m*

memorable [ˈmemərəbl] **ADJ** unvergesslich; (= *important*) denkwürdig; **on one ~ occasion he/ she ...** unvergesslich bleibt, wie er/sie einmal ...; **the play was not at all ~** das Stück kann man vergessen

memorably [ˈmemərəblɪ] **ADV** bemerkenswert; **she sang ~** ihr Gesang war unvergesslich

memorandum [ˌmeməˈrændəm] N *pl* **memoranda** [ˌmeməˈrændə] **a** *(in business)* Mitteilung *f*, (= *personal reminder*) Notiz *f*, Vermerk *m* **b** *(Pol)* Memorandum *nt*

memorial [mɪˈmɔːrɪəl] **ADJ** Gedenk-; **~ plaque** Gedenktafel *f* **N** Denkmal *nt* (*to* für)

memorial: Memorial Day N *(US)* ≈ Volkstrauertag *m*; **memorial park** N *(US:* = *cemetery)* Friedhof *m*; **memorial service** N Gedenkgottesdienst *m*

memorize [ˈmeməraɪz] VT sich *(dat)* einprägen

memory [ˈmemərɪ] N **a** Gedächtnis *nt*; (= *faculty*) Erinnerungsvermögen *nt*; **from ~** aus dem Kopf; **to lose one's ~** sein Gedächtnis verlieren; **to commit sth to ~** sich *(dat)* etw einprägen; *poem* etw auswendig lernen; **to have a long ~** ein langes Gedächtnis haben; **I have a bad ~ for faces/names** ich habe ein schlechtes Personen/Namensgedächtnis; **if my ~ serves me right** wenn ich mich recht entsinne → **living**
 b (= *thing remembered*) Erinnerung *f* (of *an* +*acc*); **I have no ~ of it** ich kann mich nicht daran erinnern; **he had happy memories of his father** er verband angenehme Erinnerungen mit seinem Vater
 c *(Comput)* Speicher *m*
 d **to honour** *(Brit)* or **honor** *(US)* **sb's ~** jds Andenken *nt* ehren; **in ~ of** zur Erinnerung *or* zum Gedenken *(form)* an (+*acc*) → **blessed**

memory: memory bank N *(Comput)* Datenbank *f*; **memory card** N *(Comput)* Speicherkarte *f*; **memory chip** N *(Comput)* Speicherchip *m*; **memory expansion card** N *(Comput)* Speichererweiterungskarte *f*; **memory lane** N **to take a trip** or **to walk down ~** in Erinnerungen schwelgen; **memory management** N *(Comput)* Speicherverwaltung *f*; **memory-resident** ADJ *(Comput)* speicherresident

men [men] *pl of* **man**

menace [ˈmenɪs] **N a** Bedrohung *f* (*to* +*gen*); *(issued by a person)* Drohung *f*; (= *imminent danger*) drohende Gefahr; **to demand money with ~s** unter Androhung von Gewalt Geld fordern **b** *(inf,* = *nuisance)* (Land)plage *f*; **she's a ~ on the roads** sie gefährdet den ganzen Verkehr **VT** bedrohen

menacing [ˈmenɪsɪŋ] ADJ drohend; *threat* gefährlich; **to look ~** bedrohlich aussehen

menacingly [ˈmenɪsɪŋlɪ] ADV drohend; **...**, **he said ~** ..., sagte er mit drohender Stimme

ménage [meˈnɑːʒ] N Haushalt *m*; **~ à trois** Dreiecksverhältnis *nt*

menagerie [mɪˈnædʒərɪ] N Menagerie *f*

mend [mend] **N** (*in shoe*) reparierte Stelle; (*in piece of metal, cloth etc also*) Flickstelle *f*; (*in roof, fence etc also*) ausgebesserte Stelle; **the ~ is almost invisible** man sieht kaum, dass es repariert/geflickt/ausgebessert worden ist; **to be on the ~** *(fig, lit: person)* sich (langsam) erholen, sich auf dem Wege der Besserung befinden *(form)*; **the fracture is on the ~** der Bruch heilt schon wieder *or* ist am Verheilen *(inf)*
 VT a (= *repair*) reparieren; *roof, fence* ausbessern, reparieren; *hole, clothes* flicken; **my shoes need ~ing** ich muss meine Schuhe reparieren *or* machen *(inf)* lassen
 b (= *improve*) **to ~ relations with sb** die Beziehungen zu jdm verbessern; **to ~ one's ways** sich bessern; **you'd better ~ your ways** das muss aber anders werden mit dir!; **to ~ matters** eine Angelegenheit bereinigen; **that won't ~ matters** das macht die Sache auch nicht besser; **to ~ fences** *(fig)* Unstimmigkeiten ausbügeln; **to ~ one's marriage** seine Ehe kitten **VI** *(bone)* (ver)heilen; **make do and ~** *(prov)* aus Alt mach Neu *(prov)*

mendacious [menˈdeɪʃəs] **ADJ** lügnerisch, verlogen

mendaciously [menˈdeɪʃəslɪ] ADV unwahrheitsgemäß

mendacity [menˈdæsɪtɪ] N Verlogenheit *f*

Mendelian [menˈdiːlɪən] ADJ mendelsch

mendicant [ˈmendɪkənt] **ADJ** bettelnd; **~ monk** Bettelmönch *m*; **~ order** Bettelorden *nt* **N** (= *beggar*) Bettler(in) *m(f)*; (= *monk*) Bettelmönch *m*

mending [ˈmendɪŋ] N (= *articles to be mended*) Flickarbeit *f*

menfolk [ˈmenfəʊk] PL Männer *pl*, Mannsvolk *nt (old)*

menhir [ˈmenhɪə] N *(Archeol)* Menhir *m*

menial [ˈmiːnɪəl] **ADJ** niedrig, untergeordnet; **she regards no task as too ~ for her** sie betrachtet keine Arbeit für unter ihrer Würde; **the ~ staff** die (unteren) Dienstboten, das Gesinde *m (pej)* Dienstbote *m/*-botin *f*

meningitis [ˌmenɪnˈdʒaɪtɪs] N Hirnhautentzündung *f*, Meningitis *f*

meniscus [mɪˈnɪskəs] N *pl* **menisci** [mɪˈnɪsaɪ] Meniskus *m*

menopause [ˈmenəʊpɔːz] N Wechseljahre *pl*, Menopause *f (spec)*

menorrhagia [ˌmenɔːˈreɪdʒɪə] N *(Med)* überhöhte Menstruationsblutung *f*

Mensa [ˈmensə] N Mensa *no art*

menses [ˈmensiːz] PL *(rare)* Menses *pl (dated)*

men's room [ˈmenzruːm] N *(esp US)* Herrentoilette *f*

menstrual [ˈmenstrʊəl] **ADJ** Menstruations-, menstrual *(spec)*; **~ bleeding** Monatsblutung *f*; **~ cramps** Menstruationskrämpfe *pl*

menstrual: menstrual cycle N Menstruationszyklus *m*; **menstrual period** N Menstruation *f*

menstruate ['menstrʊeɪt] VI menstruieren *(spec)*, die Menstruation haben

menstruation [ˌmenstrʊ'eɪʃən] N die Menstruation *or* Periode

menswear ['menzweə'] N Herrenbekleidung *f*

mental ['mentl] ADJ **a** geistig; *strain* psychisch; *cruelty* seelisch; **to make a ~ note of sth** sich *(dat)* etw merken; **~ process** geistiger *or* gedanklicher Prozess, Denkvorgang *m*; **the causes are ~ not physical** die Ursachen sind eher psychischer als physischer Natur; **he still shows great ~ agility** er ist geistig noch immer sehr rege **b** *(inf: = mad)* übergeschnappt *(inf)*; **to go ~** verrückt werden, durchdrehen *(inf)*; (= *get furious)* ausrasten *(inf)*

mental: mental age N he has a ~ of ten er ist auf dem geistigen Entwicklungsstand eines Zehnjährigen; **mental arithmetic** N Kopfrechnen *nt*; **mental block** N Bewusstseinsstörung *f*; **to have a ~** eine Bewusstseinsstörung haben, geistig weggetreten sein *(inf)*; *(due to alcohol)* einen Filmriss haben *(inf)*; *(in exam)* ein Brett vor dem Kopf haben *(inf)*; **mental breakdown** N Nervenzusammenbruch *m*; **mental deficiency** N Geistesschwäche *f*, Geistesstörung *f*; **mental health** N Geisteszustand *m*; **mental home** N (Nerven)heilanstalt *f*; **mental hospital** N psychiatrische Klinik, Nervenklinik *f*; **mental illness** N Geisteskrankheit *f*; **mental institution** N (Nerven-)heilanstalt *f*

mentality [men'tælɪtɪ] N Mentalität *f*; **how can we change this class ~?** wie können wir dieses Klassendenken ändern?

mentally ['mentlɪ] ADV **a** geistig; **~ handicapped** geistig behindert; **~ deficient** geistesschwach; **he is ~ ill** er ist geisteskrank **b** (= *in one's head)* im Kopf

mental patient N Geisteskranke(r) *mf*

mental reservation N (stille) Bedenken *pl*, Vorbehalte *pl*

menthol ['menθɒl] N Menthol *nt*; **~ cigarettes** Mentholzigaretten *pl*

mentholated ['menθəleɪtɪd] ADJ mit Menthol

mention ['menʃən] ⊙ 19.4, 26.2, 26.3 N Erwähnung *f*; **to get** *or* **receive a ~** erwähnt werden; **he received a ~ for bravery** er erhielt eine Auszeichnung *or* Belobigung für seine Tapferkeit; **to give sb/sth a ~** jdn/etw erwähnen; **there is a/no ~ of it** es wird erwähnt/nicht erwähnt; **I can't find any ~ of his name** ich kann seinen Namen nirgendwo finden; **his contribution deserves special ~** sein Beitrag verdient es, besonders hervorgehoben zu werden; **~ should also be made of ...** ... sollte Erwähnung finden *(form)*; **it's hardly worth a ~** es ist kaum erwähnenswert, es lohnt sich kaum, das zu erwähnen; **at the ~ of his name/the police ...** als sein Name/das Wort Polizei fiel *or* erwähnt wurde ...

VT erwähnen *(to sb* jdm gegenüber); **he was ~ed in several dispatches** er wurde mehrfach lobend erwähnt; **not to ~ ...** nicht zu vergessen ..., geschweige denn ...; **France and Spain, not to ~ Holland** Frankreich und Spanien, von Holland ganz zu schweigen *or* ganz abgesehen von Holland; **too numerous to ~** zu zahlreich, um sie einzeln erwähnen zu können; **don't ~ it!** (das ist doch) nicht der Rede wert!, (bitte,) gern geschehen!; **if I may ~ it** wenn ich das einmal sagen darf; **it hardly needs ~ing that we're very grateful** es versteht sich wohl von selbst, dass wir sehr dankbar sind; **to ~ sb in one's will** jdn in seinem Testament berücksichtigen; **~ me to your parents!** empfehlen Sie mich Ihren Eltern! *(form)*, viele Grüße an Ihre Eltern!

mentor ['mentɔ:'] N Mentor(in) *m(f)*

menu ['menju:] N **a** (= *bill of fare)* Speisekarte *f*; (= *dishes served)* Menü *nt*; **may we see the ~?** können *or* würden Sie uns bitte die Karte brin-

gen?, können wir bitte die Karte sehen?; **what's on the ~?** was steht heute auf dem Speisezettel?, was gibt es heute (zu essen)?; **they have a very good ~ there** man kann dort ausgezeichnet essen; **the typical British ~ consists of ...** ein typisches britisches Essen besteht aus ... **b** *(Comput)* Menü *nt*

menu *(Comput)*: **menu-driven** ADJ menügesteuert; **menu line** N Menüzeile *f*

meow N, VI = miaow

MEP abbr of **Member of the European Parliament** Mitglied *nt* des Europäischen Parlaments

mercantile ['mɜ:kəntaɪl] ADJ Handels-; *nation also* Handel treibend; **the ~ marine** die Handelsmarine

mercantilism ['mɜ:kəntɪlɪzəm] N Merkantilismus *m*

mercenary ['mɜ:sɪnərɪ] ADJ **a** *person* geldgierig; **his motives were purely ~** er tat es nur des Geldes wegen; **don't be so ~** sei doch nicht so hinter dem Geld her *(inf)* **b** *(Mil)* Söldner-; **army** Söldnerarmee *f* N Söldner(in) *m(f)*

mercerized ['mɜ:səraɪzd] ADJ *thread* merzerisiert

merchandise ['mɜ:tʃəndaɪz] N (Handels)ware *f*; **"please do not handle the ~"** „das Berühren der Ware(n) ist verboten"

merchandiser ['mɜ:tʃəndaɪzə'] N Verkaufsförderungsexperte *m*/-expertin *f*

merchandising ['mɜ:tʃəndaɪzɪŋ] N Verkaufsförderung *f*

merchant ['mɜ:tʃənt] N **a** Kaufmann *m*/-frau *f*; **corn/fruit/diamond ~** Getreide-/Obst-/Diamantenhändler(in) *m(f)* **b** *(Brit, inf)* Typ *m* *(sl)*; **he's a real speed ~** der ist ein Raser *(inf)*, der fährt wie die gesengte Sau *(inf)*; **he is a rip-off ~** er zockt seine Kunden ganz schön ab *(inf)*

merchant in cpds Handels-; **merchant bank** N *(Brit)* Handelsbank *f*; **merchant banker** N *(Brit)* Handelsbankier *m*; **merchant fleet** N Handelsflotte *f*; **merchantman** N Handelsschiff *nt*; **merchant marine** N *(US)* Handelsmarine *f*; **merchant navy** N *(Brit)* Handelsmarine *f*; **merchant prince** N reicher Kaufmann, Handelsboss *m (inf)*; **merchant seaman** N Matrose *m* in der Handelsmarine; **merchant ship** N Handelsschiff *nt*

merciful ['mɜ:sɪfʊl] ADJ gnädig *(to sb* jdm gegenüber); **o ~ Lord** gütiger Gott; **O Lord be ~!** Gott, sei uns *(dat)* gnädig!; **I begged him to be ~** ich bat ihn um Gnade; **his death was a ~ release from pain** sein Tod war für ihn eine Erlösung; **~ heavens!** *(dated)* gütiger Himmel! *(dated)*

mercifully ['mɜ:sɪfʊlɪ] ADV *act* barmherzig; *treat sb* gnädig; (= *fortunately)* glücklicherweise; **his suffering was ~ short** es war eine Gnade, dass er nicht lange leiden musste; **the country is ~ free from ethnic tensions** das Land ist glücklicherweise frei von ethnischen Spannungen

merciless ['mɜ:sɪlɪs] ADJ unbarmherzig, erbarmungslos; *destruction* schonungslos; (= *unrelenting) treatment, scrutiny, competition, glare, sun* gnadenlos

mercilessly ['mɜ:sɪlɪslɪ] ADV erbarmungslos; *glare* gnadenlos

mercurial [mɜ:'kjʊərɪəl] ADJ **a** *(Chem: = containing mercury)* quecksilberhaltig **b** *(fig)* (= *volatile)* sprunghaft, wechselhaft; (= *lively)* quicklebendig

Mercury ['mɜ:kjʊrɪ] N Merkur *m*

mercury ['mɜ:kjʊrɪ] N Quecksilber *nt*

mercy ['mɜ:sɪ] N **a** *no pl* (= *feeling of compassion)* Erbarmen *nt*; (= *action, forbearance from punishment)* Gnade *f*; (= *God's mercy)* Barmherzigkeit *f*; **to beg for ~** um Gnade bitten *or* flehen; **to have ~/no ~ on sb** mit jdm Erbarmen/kein Erbarmen haben; **have ~!** Gnade!, Erbarmen!; **Lord have ~ upon us** Herr, erbarme dich unser; **to show sb ~/no ~** Erbarmen/kein Erbarmen mit jdm haben; **to throw oneself on sb's ~** sich jdm auf Gnade und Ungnade ausliefern; **to be**

at the ~ of sb jdm (auf Gedeih und Verderb) ausgeliefert sein; **to be at the ~ of sth** einer Sache *(dat)* ausgeliefert sein; **we're at your ~** wir sind in Ihrer Gewalt *or* Hand; **at the ~ of the elements** dem Spiel der Elemente preisgegeben; **a mission of ~** eine Hilfsaktion **b** *(inf: = blessing)* Segen *m*, Glück *nt*; **it's a ~ nobody was hurt** man kann von Glück sagen, dass niemand verletzt wurde; **we must be thankful for small mercies** man muss schon mit wenigem zufrieden *or* für weniges dankbar sein

mercy: mercy killing N Euthanasie *f*, Töten *nt* aus Mitleid; **mercy seat** N Gnadenthron *or* -stuhl *m*

mere¹ [mɪə'] N *(poet)* See *m*

mere² ADJ **a** bloß; *formality also, nonsense* rein; **a ~ mortal** ein gewöhnlicher Sterblicher, eine gewöhnliche Sterbliche; **he's a ~ clerk** er ist bloß ein kleiner Angestellter; **a ~ 3%/two hours** bloß *or* lediglich 3%/zwei Stunden; **a ~ nothing** eine (bloße) Lappalie; **but she's a ~ child** aber sie ist doch noch ein Kind!; **the ~ thought of food made me hungry** schon *or* allein beim Gedanken an Essen bekam ich Hunger; **the ~ sight of him makes me shiver** sein bloßer Anblick lässt es mir kalt über den Rücken laufen; **the ~ fact that we have won is enough** allein die Tatsache, dass wir gewonnen haben, genügt **b** **the ~st ...** (= *slightest)* der/die/das kleinste ...; *suspicion, sign* der/die/das geringste ...; **the ~st hint of any corruption** das geringste Zeichen von Korruption; **they giggle at the ~st mention of sex** sie kichern jedes Mal, wenn Sex auch nur erwähnt wird

merely ['mɪəlɪ] ADV lediglich, bloß; **it's not ~ broken, it's ruined** es ist nicht bloß kaputt, es ist völlig ruiniert

meretricious [ˌmerɪ'trɪʃəs] ADJ trivial; (= *kitschy)* kitschig

merge [mɜ:dʒ] VI **a** (= *come together)* zusammenkommen; *(colours)* ineinander übergehen; *(roads)* zusammenlaufen *or* -führen; *(US Aut)* sich einordnen; **to ~ with sth** mit etw verschmelzen, sich mit etw vereinen; *(colour)* in etw *(acc)* übergehen; *(road)* in etw *(acc)* einmünden; **to ~ (in) with/into the crowd** in der Menge untergehen/untertauchen; **to ~ into sth** in etw *(acc)* übergehen; **the bird ~d in with its background of leaves** der Vogel verschmolz mit dem Laubwerk im Hintergrund; **"motorways ~"** „Autobahneinmündung"; **to ~ to the left** *(US Aut)* sich links einordnen **b** *(Comm)* fusionieren, sich zusammenschließen

VT **a** (= *bring together)* miteinander vereinen *or* verbinden *or* verschmelzen; *colours* (miteinander) verschmelzen, ineinander übergehen lassen; *metals* legieren; *(Comput) files* mischen; **to ~ sth with sth** etw mit etw vereinen *or* verbinden *or* verschmelzen; etw in etw *(acc)* übergehen lassen **b** *(Comm)* zusammenschließen, fusionieren; **they were ~d into one company** sie wurden zu einer Firma zusammengeschlossen; **they were ~d with ...** sie haben mit ... fusioniert

merger ['mɜ:dʒə'] N *(Comm)* Fusion *f*

merging lane N *(US)* Spur *f* zum Einordnen, Abbiegespur *f*

meridian [mə'rɪdɪən] N *(Astron, Geog)* Meridian *m*; *(fig)* Höhepunkt *m*, Gipfel *m*

meringue [mə'ræŋ] N Meringe *f*, Baiser *nt*

merino [mə'ri:nəʊ] N **a** (= *sheep)* Merino *m*, Merinoschaf *nt* **b** (= *wool)* Merinowolle *f*

merit ['merɪt] N **a** (= *achievement)* Leistung *f*, Verdienst *nt*; (= *advantage)* Vorzug *m*; **to look** *or* **inquire into the ~s of sth** etw auf seine Vorteile *or* Vorzüge untersuchen; **a work of great literary ~** ein Werk von großem literarischem Wert; **what are the particular ~s of Greek drama?** wodurch zeichnet sich das griechische Drama besonders aus?; **she was elected on ~ alone** sie gewann die Wahl aufgrund *or* auf Grund persönlicher Fähigkeiten; **judged on one's own ~s** ausschließlich nach Leistung(en) *or* Verdiensten beurteilt; **judged on its own ~s** für sich selbst beurteilt; **to judge a case on its ~s** einen Fall für sich selbst or gesondert behandeln; **I don't see any ~ in being rich** ich betrachte Reichtum als kein besonderes Verdienst; **he sees little ~ in paying for research** er sieht nicht viel Sinn darin, für Forschungsvorhaben zu bezahlen; **there's no particular ~ in coming early** es ist keine besondere Leistung or kein besonderes Verdienst, früh zu kommen; **to pass an exam with ~** ein Examen mit Auszeichnung bestehen; **certificate of ~** (Sch, Univ) Urkunde für besonders gute Leistungen an Schule oder Universität

VT verdienen; **it ~s your consideration** das ist es wert, dass Sie sich damit beschäftigen

meritocracy [ˌmerɪˈtɒkrəsɪ] N Leistungsgesellschaft f, Meritokratie f (geh)

meritocratic [ˌmerɪtəˈkrætɪk] ADJ leistungsorientiert

meritorious ADJ , **meritoriously** ADV [ˌmerɪˈtɔːrɪəs, -lɪ] lobenswert

Merlin [ˈmɜːlɪn] N (Myth) Merlin m (Zauberer in der keltischen Sage)

mermaid [ˈmɜːmeɪd] N Nixe f, See- or Meerjungfrau f

merman [ˈmɜːmæn] N pl **-men** [-men] Nix m, Wassergeist m

merrily [ˈmerɪlɪ] ADV **a** (= happily) vergnügt; (fig) boil munter; **to burn ~** (fire in grate) munter vor sich hin brennen **b** (= blithely) continue, say munter

merriment [ˈmerɪmənt] N Heiterkeit f, Fröhlichkeit f; (= laughter) Gelächter nt; **at this there was much ~** das erregte allgemeine Heiterkeit, das rief großes Gelächter hervor

merry [ˈmerɪ] ✪ 23.2 ADJ (+er) **a** (= cheerful) fröhlich, vergnügt, lustig; song, tune fröhlich; **to make ~** lustig und vergnügt sein; **Merry Christmas!** fröhliche or frohe Weihnachten!; **a Merry Christmas to all our readers** allen unseren Lesern ein frohes Weihnachtsfest; **Merry England** das gute alte England

b (fig) **to lead sb a ~ dance** jdn ganz schön an der Nase herumführen; **to play ~ hell with sth** (inf) etw total durcheinander bringen; **to give sb ~ hell** (inf) jdm einheizen (inf); **to go one's ~ way** seiner Wege gehen

c (Brit inf, = tipsy) beschwipst, angeheitert (inf); **to get ~** sich (dat) einen anpicheln (inf)

merry: merry-go-round N Karussell nt; **merrymaker** N Festgast m, Feiernde(r) mf; **merrymaking** N Feiern nt, Belustigung f, Lustbarkeit f (liter); **after the ~ had finished** nach Beendigung des Festes or der Lustbarkeiten (liter)

mesa [ˈmeɪsə] N Tafelberg m

mescalin(e) [ˈmeskəlɪn] N Meskalin nt

mesh [meʃ] **N a** (= hole) Masche f; (= size of hole) Maschenweite f; **caught in the fine ~ of the net** in den feinen Maschen des Netzes gefangen; **fine ~ stockings** feinmaschige Strümpfe pl; **the big ~ of this material makes it ideal** die Grobmaschigkeit dieses Materials ist ideal; **a 5mm ~ screen** ein 5 mm Maschendraht; **the ~ is big enough to see through** es ist großmaschig genug, um durchzuschauen

b (material) (= wire mesh) Maschendraht m; (= network of wires) Drahtgeflecht nt; (Tex) Gittergewebe nt

c (Mech) **out of ~** nicht im Eingriff; **in ~** im Eingriff; **the tight ~ of the cogwheels** die enge Verzahnung der Räder

d (fig) **to catch** or **entangle sb in one's ~es** jdn umgarnen, jdn in sein Netz locken; **to be caught in sb's ~es** jdm ins Netz gegangen sein; **a ~ of lies** ein Lügengespinst nt

VI a (Mech) eingreifen (with in +acc); **the gears ~ (together)** die Zahnräder greifen ineinander

b (fig: views, approach) sich vereinen lassen; **he tried to make the departments ~ (together)** er versuchte, die einzelnen Abteilungen miteinander zu koordinieren

VT = enmesh

mesh stocking N Netzstrumpf m

meshugge [mɪˈʃʊɡə] ADJ (US sl) meschugge (inf)

mesmeric [mezˈmerɪk] ADJ hypnotisch; movement hypnotisierend

mesmerism [ˈmezmərɪzəm] N hypnotische Wirkung; (old) Mesmerismus m

mesmerize [ˈmezməraɪz] VT hypnotisieren; (fig) faszinieren, fesseln; **the audience sat ~d** die Zuschauer saßen wie gebannt

mesmerizing [ˈmezməraɪzɪŋ] ADJ effect hypnotisch; rhythm, phrase, experience hypnotisierend; smile, voice faszinierend

meson [ˈmiːzɒn] N (Phys) Meson nt

Mesopotamia [ˌmesəpəˈteɪmɪə] N Mesopotamien nt

mess¹ [mes] **N a** Durcheinander nt; (dirty) Schweinerei f; **to be (in) a ~** unordentlich sein, in einem fürchterlichen Zustand sein; (= disorganized) ein einziges Durcheinander sein; (fig: one's life, marriage, career etc) verkorkst sein (inf); **to be a ~ (piece of work)** eine Schweinerei sein (inf); (= disorganized) ein einziges or heilloses Durcheinander sein; (person) (in appearance) unordentlich aussehen; (psychologically) verkorkst sein (inf); **to look a ~** (person) unmöglich aussehen; (= untidy also) schlampig or unordentlich aussehen; (= dirty also) völlig verdreckt sein; (room, piece of work) unordentlich or schlimm aussehen; **to make a ~** (= be untidy) Unordnung machen; (= be dirty) eine Schweinerei machen; **to make a ~ of sth** (= make untidy) etw in Unordnung bringen, etw durcheinander bringen; (= make dirty) etw verdrecken; (= bungle, botch) etw verpfuschen, bei etw Mist bauen (inf); of one's life etw verkorksen (inf) or verpfuschen; **I made a ~ of sewing it on** ich habe beim Annähen Mist gebaut (inf); **you've really made a ~ of things** du hast alles total vermasselt (inf); **a fine ~ you've made of that** da hast du was Schönes angerichtet; **what a ~!** wie sieht das denn aus!, das sieht ja vielleicht aus!; (fig) ein schöner Schlamassel! (inf); **I'm not tidying up your ~** ich räume nicht für dich auf; **a ~ of beer cans/pots and pans** ein Haufen Bierdosen/Töpfe und Pfannen

b (= awkward predicament) Schwierigkeiten pl, Schlamassel m (inf); **cheating got him into a ~** durch seine Mogelei ist er in ziemliche Schwierigkeiten geraten; **he got into a ~ with the police** er hat Ärger mit der Polizei bekommen

c (euph: = excreta) Dreck m; **the cat/baby has made a ~ on the carpet** die Katze/das Baby hat auf den Teppich gemacht

VI = **mess about** VI c, d

▶ **mess about** (Brit) or **around** (inf) **VT** sep (= fiddle, tinker with) herumpfuschen an (+dat) (inf); person an der Nase herumführen (inf); (boss, person in authority) herumschikanieren; (by delaying decision) hinhalten

VI a (= play the fool) herumalbern or -blödeln (inf)

b (= do nothing in particular) herumgammeln (inf); **he enjoys messing about** or **around on the river** (in boat) er gondelt gern (im Boot) auf dem Fluss herum

c (= tinker, fiddle) herumfummeln (inf) or -spielen (with an +dat); (as hobby etc) herumbasteln (with an +dat) (inf); **that'll teach you to mess about** or **around with explosives** das soll dir eine Lehre sein, nicht mit Sprengkörpern herumzuspielen; **I don't like film directors messing about** or **around with my scripts** ich kann es nicht haben, wenn Regisseure an meinen Drehbüchern herumändern

d to mess around with sb (= associate with) sich mit jdm einlassen or abgeben; (= not take seriously) jdn zum Narren haben; **he was messing about** or **around with my wife** (= having affair) er trieb es mit meiner Frau

▶ **mess up** VT sep durcheinander bringen; (= make dirty) verdrecken; (= botch, bungle) verpfuschen, verhunzen (inf); marriage kaputtmachen

(inf), ruinieren; life, person verkorksen (inf); person (as regards looks) übel zurichten; **missing the connection messed up the whole journey** dadurch, dass wir den Anschluss verpassten, lief die ganze Reise schief; **her visit really messed me up** (inf) ihr Besuch hat mir wirklich alles vermasselt (inf); **that's really messed things up** das hat wirklich alles verdorben or vermasselt (inf)

mess² (Mil) **N** Kasino nt; (on ships) Messe f; (= food) Essen nt **VI** essen, das Essen einnehmen

message [ˈmesɪdʒ] ✪ 27.6 N **a** Mitteilung f, Nachricht f, Botschaft f (old, form); (= radio message) Funkspruch m or -meldung f; (= report, police message) Meldung f; **to take a ~ to sb** jdm eine Nachricht überbringen; **to give sb a ~** (verbal) jdm etwas ausrichten; jdm eine Nachricht geben; **would you give John a ~ (for me)?** könnten Sie John etwas (von mir) ausrichten?; **have you given him my ~ yet?** hast du es ihm schon ausgerichtet?; **to send a ~ to sb, to send sb a ~** jdn benachrichtigen; **to leave a ~ for sb** (written) jdm eine Nachricht hinterlassen; (verbal) jdm etwas ausrichten lassen; **can I take a ~ (for him)?** (on telephone) kann ich (ihm) etwas ausrichten?; **the Queen's ~** die (Fernseh)ansprache der Königin

b (= moral) Botschaft f; **the ~ of the play is ...** die Aussage des Stückes ist ..., das Stück will Folgendes sagen ...; **a pop song with a ~** ein Schlagertext, der einem etwas zu sagen hat; **to get the** or **one's ~ across to sb** es jdm verständlich machen

c (fig inf) **to get the ~** kapieren (inf); **I got the ~** ich habe schon verstanden or kapiert (inf)

d (Scot: = errand) Einkauf m; **to do** or **get one's ~s** einkaufen

message switching [ˈmesɪdʒˌswɪtʃɪŋ] N (Comput) Speichervermittlung f

messaging [ˈmesɪdʒɪŋ] N Datentransfer m

mess deck N Speisedeck nt

messenger [ˈmesɪndʒəˈ] N Bote m (old, form), Botin f (old, form), Überbringer(in) m(f), (einer Nachricht); (Mil) Kurier(in) m(f); **bank ~** Bankbote m/-botin f; **don't shoot the ~** (fig) lassen Sie Ihren Zorn an dem Verantwortlichen aus

messenger boy N Botenjunge m, Laufbursche m

mess hall N Kasino nt

Messiah [mɪˈsaɪə] N Messias m

messianic [ˌmesɪˈænɪk] ADJ messianisch

messily [ˈmesɪlɪ] ADV unordentlich; **they divorced ~** ihre Scheidung war eine unerfreuliche Angelegenheit

mess: mess jacket N Affenjäckchen nt (inf); **mess kit** **a** (Brit) Uniform für gesellschaftliche Anlässe **b** (US) Essgeschirr nt; **messmate** N **they were ~s** sie waren Kameraden bei der Armee

Messrs [ˈmesəz] PL of **Mr** abbr of **Messieurs to ~ ... ** an die Herren ...

mess tin N Ess- or Kochgeschirr nt

mess-up [ˈmesʌp] N Kuddelmuddel nt (inf); **it's a complete ~** da ist alles schief gelaufen (inf)

messy [ˈmesɪ] ADJ (+er) **a** (= dirty) dreckig, schmutzig; (= untidy) unordentlich; **~ writing** fürchterliche Klaue (inf); **he's a ~ eater** er kann nicht ordentlich essen, er isst wie ein Schwein

b (fig) situation verfahren; (= confused) durcheinander; (= unpleasant) unschön; process, relationship schwierig; dispute unschön; **their divorce was a ~ business, they had a ~ divorce** ihre Scheidung war eine unerfreuliche Angelegenheit

Met [met] N (inf) **a** (US) abbr of **Metropolitan Opera Company** Metropolitan (Oper) f **b** (US) abbr of **Metropolitan Museum of Art** Kunstmuseum in New York **c** (Brit) abbr of **Metropolitan Police**

met¹ [met] pret, ptp of **meet²**

met² abbr of **meteorological**

meta- [ˈmetə-] PREF meta-, Meta-

metabolic [ˌmetəˈbɒlɪk] ADJ Stoffwechsel-, metabolisch

metabolic disorder N Stoffwechselkrankheit f

metabolic rate N Stoffwechselrate f

metabolism [meˈtæbəlɪzəm] N Stoffwechsel m, Metabolismus m

metacarpal [ˌmetəˈkɑːpl] N Mittelhandknochen m

metal ['metl] **N** **a** Metall nt; (Brit: on road) Schotter m **b** **metals** PL (Rail) Schienen pl **VT** (Brit) road beschottern; **~led road** Asphaltstraße f (mit Schotterunterbau)

metalanguage ['metəlæŋgwɪdʒ] N Metasprache f

metal: metal-arc welding N (Tech) Metalllichtbogenschweißen nt; **metal detector** N Metallsuchgerät nt

metalled, (US) **metaled** ['metld] ADJ road Schotter-

metallic [mɪˈtælɪk] ADJ metallisch; **~ finish/paint** Metalliclackierung f/-lack m; **~ blue/green** blau-/grünmetallic; **a ~ blue car** ein Auto nt in Blaumetallic

metallurgic(al) [ˌmetəˈlɜːdʒɪk(əl)] ADJ metallurgisch

metallurgist [meˈtælədʒɪst] N Metallurg(e) m, Metallurgin f

metallurgy [meˈtælədʒɪ] N Hüttenkunde f, Metallurgie f

metal in cpds Metall-; **metal plating** N Metallschicht f; (= act) Plattierung f; **metal polish** N Metallpolitur f; **metal processing** N Metallverarbeitung f; **metalwork** N Metall nt; **we did ~ at school** wir haben in der Schule Metallarbeiten gemacht; **metalworker** N Metallarbeiter(in) m(f); **metalworking** N Metallbearbeitung f

metamorphose [ˌmetəˈmɔːfəʊz] **VT** verwandeln; (Sci) umwandeln **VI** sich verwandeln; (Sci) sich umwandeln

metamorphosis [ˌmetəˈmɔːfəsɪs] N pl **metamorphoses** [ˌmetəˈmɔːfəsiːz] Metamorphose f; (fig) Verwandlung f

metaphor ['metəfə] N Metapher f; **to mix one's ~s** unterschiedliche Metaphern zusammen verwenden

metaphorical [ˌmetəˈfɒrɪkəl] ADJ metaphorisch

metaphorically [ˌmetəˈfɒrɪkəlɪ] ADV metaphorisch; **~ speaking** metaphorisch ausgedrückt, bildlich gesprochen

metaphysical ADJ , **metaphysically** ADV [ˌmetəˈfɪzɪkəl, -ɪ] metaphysisch

metaphysician [ˌmetəfɪˈzɪʃn] N Metaphysiker(in) m(f)

metaphysics [ˌmetəˈfɪzɪks] N sing Metaphysik f

metastasis [mɪˈtæstəsɪs] N pl **metastases** [mɪˈtæstəsiːz] Metastasenbildung f, Metastasierung f

metatarsal [ˌmetəˈtɑːsl] ADJ Mittelfuß-, metatarsal (spec); **~ bone** Mittelfußknochen m

metathesis [meˈtæθəsɪs] N pl **metatheses** [meˈtæθəsiːz] Metathese f, Metathesis f

metazoan [metəˈzəʊən] **N** Metazoon nt (spec), Vielzeller m **ADJ** vielzellig, metazoisch (spec)

mete [miːt] VT **to ~ out** zuteil werden lassen (to sb jdm); praise austeilen; rewards verteilen; **to ~ out punishment to sb** jdn bestrafen; **the function of the courts is to ~ out justice** es ist Aufgabe der Gerichte zu richten; **justice was ~d out to them** es wurde über sie gerichtet

metempsychosis [ˌmetəmsaɪˈkəʊsɪs] N pl **metempsychoses** [ˌmetəmsaɪˈkəʊsiːz] Metempsychose f

meteor ['miːtɪə] N Meteor m

meteoric [ˌmiːtɪˈɒrɪk] ADJ meteorisch; (fig) kometenhaft

meteorite ['miːtɪəraɪt] N Meteorit m

meteoroid ['miːtɪərɔɪd] N Sternschnuppe f

meteorological [ˌmiːtɪərəˈlɒdʒɪkəl] ADJ Wetter-, meteorologisch; **~ station** Wetterstation f

Meteorological Office N **the ~** (Brit) das Wetteramt

meteorologist [ˌmiːtɪəˈrɒlədʒɪst] N Meteorologe m, Meteorologin f

meteorology [ˌmiːtɪəˈrɒlədʒɪ] N Meteorologie f, Wetterkunde f

meteor shower N Meteoritenschauer m

meter[1] ['miːtə] **N** Zähler m; (= gas meter also) Gasuhr f; (= water meter) Wasseruhr f; (= parking meter) Parkuhr f; (= exposure or light meter) Belichtungsmesser m; (= coin meter) Münzzähler m; **the ~ has run out** (parking meter) die Parkuhr ist abgelaufen; (coin meter) es ist kein Geld mehr im Zähler; **to turn the water/gas off at the ~** das Wasser/Gas am Hauptschalter abstellen; **to turn the electricity off at the ~** den Strom am Hauptschalter abschalten **VT** messen

meter[2] N (US) = metre

meter maid N (inf) Politesse f

methamphetamine [ˌmeθæmˈfetəmiːn] N Metamphetamin nt

methane ['miːθeɪn] N Methan nt

methanol ['meθənɒl] N Methanol nt

methinks [mɪˈθɪŋks] pret **methought** [mɪˈθɔːt] VI impers (obs) mich deucht (obs), mir or mich dünkt (old)

method ['meθəd] N Methode f; (= process) Verfahren nt; (Cook) Zubereitung f; (in experiment) Vorgehens- or Verfahrensweise f; **~ of payment/application** Zahlungs-/Anwendungsweise f; **there's ~ in his madness** sein Wahnsinn hat Methode

method acting N (Theat) Schauspielen nach dem System Stanislawski

methodical ADJ , **methodically** ADV [mɪˈθɒdɪkəl, -ɪ] methodisch

Methodism ['meθədɪzəm] N Methodismus m

Methodist ['meθədɪst] **ADJ** methodistisch **N** Methodist(in) m(f)

methodology [ˌmeθəˈdɒlədʒɪ] N Methodik f, Methodologie f

methought [mɪˈθɔːt] PRET of methinks

meths [meθs] N sing abbr of **methylated spirits** Spiritus m; **~ drinker** ≈ Fuseltrinker(in) m(f)

Methuselah [məˈθuːzələ] N Methusalem m; **as old as ~** so alt wie Methusalem

methyl alcohol ['miːθaɪlˈælkəhɒl] N Methylalkohol m

methylated spirits ['meθɪleɪtɪdˈspɪrɪts] N sing Äthylalkohol m, (Brenn)spiritus m

meticulous [mɪˈtɪkjʊləs] ADJ sorgfältig, genau, exakt; (= fastidious) peinlich genau; **to be ~ about sth** es mit etw sehr genau nehmen; **with ~ attention to detail** mit besonderer Sorgfalt für das Detail

meticulously [mɪˈtɪkjʊləslɪ] ADV sorgfältig; (= fastidiously) peinlich genau; **~ clean** peinlich sauber

métier ['meɪtɪeɪ] N Metier nt

met office ['metˌɒfɪs] N (Brit) Wetteramt nt

metonymy [məˈtɒnɪmɪ] N Metonymie f

me-too product N (Comm) Me-too-Produkt nt, Nachahmerprodukt nt

metre, (US) **meter** ['miːtə] **N** **a** (Measure) Meter m or nt **b** (Poet) Metrum nt

metric ['metrɪk] ADJ metrisch; **the ~ system** das metrische Maßsystem; **to go ~** auf das metrische Maßsystem umstellen

metrical ['metrɪkəl] ADJ (Poet) metrisch

metrication [ˌmetrɪˈkeɪʃən] N Umstellung f auf das metrische Maßsystem

metric ton N Metertonne f

metronome ['metrənəʊm] N Metronom nt

metronomic [ˌmetrəˈnɒmɪk] ADJ metronomartig; **variety is the charm of tennis, which could otherwise become a ~ bore** der Reiz von Tennis liegt in der Abwechslung, sonst könnte es leicht so eintönig wie ein Metronom werden

metropolis [mɪˈtrɒpəlɪs] N Metropole f, Weltstadt f; (= capital) Hauptstadt f

metropolitan [ˌmetrəˈpɒlɪtən] **ADJ** **a** weltstädtisch; (of a capital) hauptstädtisch; **~ diocese** Erzdiözese f; **~ bishop** Diözesanbischof m; **a ~ city** eine Weltstadt; **~ district/area** Stadtgebiet nt **b** (= mainland) **~ France** das französische Mutterland **N** **a** Weltbürger(in) m(f); (= citizen) Großstädter(in) m(f), Hauptstädter(in) m(f) **b** (Eccl) Metropolit m

Metropolitan Police N Londoner/New Yorker Polizei

mettle ['metl] N (= spirit) Courage f, Stehvermögen nt; (of horse) Zähigkeit f; (= temperament) Feuer nt; **a man of ~** ein Mann von echtem Schrot und Korn; **to show one's ~** zeigen, was in einem steckt; **to test sb's ~**, **to be a test of sb's ~** (thing) zeigen, was in jdm steckt; (person) herausfinden, was in jdm steckt; **to be on one's ~** auf dem Posten sein; **to put sb on his ~** jdn fordern

mettlesome ['metlsəm] ADJ person couragiert, schneidig; horse feurig

mew [mjuː] **N** Miau(en) nt **VI** miauen

mewl [mjuːl] VI (cat) maunzen, mauzen; (baby) wimmern

mews [mjuːz] N sing or pl (= houses) Siedlung ehemaliger zu modischen Wohnungen umgebauter Kutscherhäuschen (= street) Gasse f; (old, = stables) Stall m, Stallungen pl; **a ~ cottage** ein ehemaliges Kutscherhäuschen

Mexican ['meksɪkən] **ADJ** mexikanisch **N** Mexikaner(in) m(f)

Mexican wave N La-Ola-Welle f

Mexico ['meksɪkəʊ] N Mexiko nt

Mexico City N Mexiko City nt

mezzanine ['mezəniːn] N Mezzanin nt

mezzo-soprano [ˌmetsəʊsəˈprɑːnəʊ] N (= voice) Mezzosopran m; (= singer) Mezzosopranistin f

mezzotint ['metsəʊtɪnt] N Mezzotint nt

mfd abbr of **manufactured** hergest.

MG abbr of **machine gun** MG nt

mg abbr of **milligram(s), milligramme(s)** mg

MHz abbr of **megahertz** MHz

mi. abbr of **mile(s)**

MI abbr of **machine intelligence**

MI5 (Brit) abbr of **Military Intelligence, section 5** MI5 m, Spionageabwehrdienst der britischen Regierung

MI6 (Brit) abbr of **Military Intelligence, section 6** MI6 m, britischer Auslandsgeheimdienst

miaow [miːˈaʊ] (Brit) **N** Miau(en) nt **VI** miauen

miasma [mɪˈæzmə] N pl **miasmata** or **miasmas** [mɪˈæzmətə, mɪˈæzməz] Miasma nt

mica ['maɪkə] N Muskovit m

mice [maɪs] pl of **mouse**

Michaelmas ['mɪklməs] N Michaeli(s) nt

Michaelmas daisy N Herbstaster f

Michaelmas Day N Michaelis(tag m) nt

mickey ['mɪkɪ] N (Brit inf) **to take the ~ out of sb** jdn auf den Arm or auf die Schippe nehmen (inf), jdn veräppeln (inf); **are you taking the ~?** du willst mich/ihn etc wohl veräppeln etc (inf)

Mickey Finn ['mɪkɪ'fɪn] N (Brit inf) Betäubungsmittel nt; (= drink) präparierter Drink; **they slipped him a ~** sie haben ihm was in den Drink getan (inf)

Mickey Mouse **N** Mickymaus f **ADJ** attr (inf) company etc lachhaft; **~ ears** Mickymaus-Ohren pl; **~ money** Spielgeld nt

micro ['maɪkrəʊ] N (Comput) Mikro(computer) m

micro- PREF mikro-, Mikro-

microbe ['maɪkrəʊb] N Mikrobe f

micro: microbiology N Mikrobiologie f; **microchannel architecture** N (Comput) Microchannel-Architektur f; **microchip** N Mikrochip nt; **microcircuit** N Mikroschaltung f; **microcircuitry** N Mikroschaltung f; **microclimate** N Mikroklima nt; **microcomputer** N

Mikrorechner m, Mikrocomputer m; **microcosm** N Mikrokosmos m; **microdiskette** N Mikrofloppy f, Mikrodiskette f; **microdot** N Mikrobild nt; **microeconomics** N sing Mikroökonomie f; **microelectronics** N sing Mikroelektronik f; **microfiche** N Mikrofiche m or nt, Mikrokarte f; **microfilm** N Mikrofilm m **VT** auf Mikrofilm aufnehmen; **microgravity** N (Phys) Mikrogravitation f; **microlight** N Ultraleichtflugzeug nt; **micrological** ADJ , **micrologically** ADV pedantisch, kleinlich; **micromesh** ADJ stockings feinmaschig; **micrometer** [maɪˈkrɒmɪtə] N (= gauge) Mikrometerschraube f, Messschraube f; **micrometre**, (US) **micrometer** N Mikrometer m or nt

micron [ˈmaɪkrɒn] N Mikron nt, Mikrometer m or nt

micro: microorganism N Mikroorganismus m; **microphone** N Mikrophon nt, Mikrofon nt; **microprocessor** N Mikroprozessor m; **microscope** N Mikroskop nt

microscopic [ˌmaɪkrəˈskɒpɪk] ADJ (in size) mikroskopisch (klein); ~ **creature** mikroskopisch kleines Lebewesen; ~ **details** feinste Details; **in ~ detail** bis ins kleinste Detail

microscopically [ˌmaɪkrəˈskɒpɪkəlɪ] ADV mikroskopisch

micro: microsecond N Mikrosekunde f; **microspacing** N (Comput) Feinausgleich m; **microstructural** ADJ mikrostrukturell; **microsurgery** N Mikrochirurgie f; **microsurgical** ADJ mikrochirurgisch; **microtransmitter** N Mikrosender m; **microwave** N Mikrowelle f; **microwavable**, **microwaveable** ADJ food mikrowellen(herd)geeignet, -tauglich; **microwave oven** N Mikrowellenherd m

micturate [ˈmɪktjʊreɪt] VI (Med: = urinate) urinieren, harnen (form)

micturition [ˌmɪktjʊˈrɪʃən] N (Med: = urinating) Urinieren nt, Miktion f (spec)

mid [mɪd] **PREP** (poet) = amid(st)
ADJ **in ~ January/June** Mitte Januar/Juni; **in the ~ 1950s** Mitte der fünfziger Jahre; **in the ~ 20th century** Mitte des 20. Jahrhunderts; **temperatures in the ~ eighties** Temperaturen um 85° Fahrenheit; **to be in one's ~ forties** Mitte vierzig or Mittvierzige(r) mf sein; **in ~ morning/afternoon** am Vormittag/Nachmittag; **a ~-morning/-afternoon break** eine Frühstücks-/Nachmittagspause; **a ~-morning snack** ein zweites Frühstück; **a ~-afternoon snack** ein Imbiss m am Nachmittag; **in ~ channel** in der Mitte des Kanals; **in ~ ocean** mitten auf dem Meer; **in ~ air** in der Luft; **in ~ flight** während des Flugs

mid-air [ˌmɪdˈɛə] ADJ ~ **collision** Zusammenstoß m in der Luft

Midas [ˈmaɪdəs] N Midas m; **the ~ touch** eine glückliche Hand, Glück nt; **he has the ~ touch** er macht aus Dreck Geld (inf)

mid-Atlantic [ˌmɪdətˈlæntɪk] ADJ accent etc angloamerikanisch

midday [ˈmɪddeɪ] **N** Mittag m; **at ~** mittags, gegen Mittag, um die Mittagszeit **ADJ** attr mittäglich; ~ **meal** Mittagessen nt; ~ **sun/heat** Mittagssonne/-hitze f

midden [ˈmɪdn] N (Archeol) Muschelhaufen m; (dial) (= dustbin) Mülleimer m; (= rubbish dump) Müll m

middle [ˈmɪdl] **N** Mitte f; (= central section: of book, film etc) Mittelteil m, mittlerer Teil; (= inside: of fruit, nut etc) Innere(s) nt; (= stomach) Bauch m, Leib m; (= waist) Taille f; **in the ~ of the table** mitten auf dem Tisch; (in exact centre) in der Mitte des Tisches; **he passed the ball to the ~ of the field** er spielte den Ball zur (Feld)mitte; **in the ~ of the night** mitten in der Nacht; **in the ~ of the day** mitten am Tag; (= around midday) gegen Mittag; **in the ~ of nowhere** jwd (inf), am Ende der Welt; **in the ~ of summer** mitten im Sommer; (= height of summer season) im Hochsommer; **in or about the ~ of May** Mitte Mai; **in the ~ of the century** um die Jahrhundertmitte, mitten des Jahrhunderts; **we**

were in the ~ of lunch wir waren mitten beim Essen; **in the ~ of my back** im Kreuz; **to be in the ~ of doing sth** mitten dabei sein, etw zu tun; **I'm in the ~ of reading it** ich bin mittendrin; **in the ~** in der Mitte; **he parts his hair down the ~** er hat einen Mittelscheitel
ADJ mittlere(r, s); **the ~ house** das mittlere Haus, das Haus in der Mitte; **to be in one's ~ twenties/thirties** Mitte zwanzig/dreißig sein; **I'm the ~ child of three** ich bin das mittlere der drei Kinder

middle in cpds Mittel-, mittel-; **middle age** N mittleres Lebensalter; **middle-aged** ADJ in den mittleren Jahren, mittleren Alters; feeling, appearance alt; attitudes spießig (pej), altmodisch; **Middle Ages** PL Mittelalter nt; **Middle America** N a (Geog) Mittelamerika nt b (= class) die amerikanische Mittelschicht; **middlebrow** ADJ für den (geistigen) Normalverbraucher; ~ **tastes** Durchschnittsgeschmack m **N** (geistiger) Normalverbraucher; **middle C** N (eingestrichenes) C; **middle-class** ADJ bürgerlich, spießig (pej); (Sociol) mittelständisch; **he's so typically ~** er ist ein typischer Vertreter der Mittelklasse, er ist ein richtiger Spießer (pej); **middle class(es)** N(PL) Mittelstand m or -schicht f; **middle distance** N mittlere Entfernung; (Sport) Mittelstrecke f; (Art) Mittelgrund m; **middle-distance runner** N Mittelstreckenläufer(in) m(f); **middle-distance running** N Mittelstreckenlauf m; ~ **is ...** der Mittelstreckenlauf ist ...; **middle ear** N Mittelohr nt; **Middle East** N Naher Osten; (from Iran and Iraq to India) Mittlerer Osten; **Middle England** N (fig: = middle classes) die englische Mittelschicht; **Middle English** N Mittelenglisch nt; **middle finger** N Mittelfinger m; **Middle High German** N Mittelhochdeutsch nt; **middle-income** ADJ family mit mittlerem Einkommen; ~ **earner** Mittelverdiener(in) m(f); **Middle Low German** N Mittelniederdeutsch nt; **middleman** N Mittelsmann m, Mittelsperson f; (Comm) Zwischenhändler m; **middle management** N mittleres Management; **middle manager** N mittlerer Manager, mittlere Managerin, mittlere Führungskraft; **middle name** N zweiter (Vor)name; **modesty is my ~** (fig) ich bin die Bescheidenheit in Person; **middle-of-the-road** ADJ a (= moderate) gemäßigt; policy, politician der gemäßigten Mitte b (= conventional) style, person konventionell; music anspruchslos, für den Normalverbraucher; **middle-of-the-roader** N Vertreter(in) m(f) der gemäßigten Mitte; **middle-ranking** ADJ mittlere(r, s); army officers Armeeoffiziere pl mittleren Ranges; **middle school** N (Brit) Schule für 9-12-jährige; **middle watch** N Mittelwache f; **middleweight** (Sport) **N** Mittelgewicht nt; (= person also) Mittelgewichtler(in) m(f) **ADJ** Mittelgewichts-; ~ **champion** Mittelgewichtsmeister(in) m(f), Meister(in) m(f) im Mittelgewicht

middling [ˈmɪdlɪŋ] **ADJ** mittelmäßig; (of size) mittlere(r, s); **how are you? – ~** wie geht es dir? – mittelprächtig (inf) or einigermaßen; **what was the weather like? – ~** wie war das Wetter? – durchwachsen or so sala (inf) **ADV** (inf: = fairly) ~ **rich** ziemlich reich

Middx abbr of **Middlesex**

Mideast [mɪdˈiːst] (US) **N** **the ~** der Nahe Osten; (from Iran and Iraq to India) der Mittlere Osten **ADJ** Nahost-; (from Iran and Iraq to India) des Mittleren Ostens; **a ~ peace conference** eine Nahost-Friedenskonferenz/eine Friedenskonferenz des Mittleren Ostens

midfield [ˌmɪdˈfiːld] **N** Mittelfeld nt **ADJ** Mittelfeld-; ~ **player/position** Mittelfeldspieler(in) m(f)/-position f

midfielder [mɪdˈfiːldə] N (Ftbl) Mittelfeldspieler(in) m(f)

midge [mɪdʒ] N (Brit) Mücke f

midget [ˈmɪdʒɪt] **N** kleiner Mensch, Liliputaner(in) m(f); (= child) Knirps m **ADJ** winzig; ~ **submarine** Kleinst-U-Boot nt

MIDI [ˈmɪdɪ] abbr of **musical instrument digital interface** **N** Midi-System nt or -Anlage f **ADJ** Midi-

midi (system) [ˈmɪdɪˌsɪstəm] N Midi-System nt or -Anlage f

mid: midland **ADJ** attr im Landesinneren (gelegen) **N** Landesinnere(s) nt; **the Midlands** die Midlands; **midlife crisis** N Midlifecrisis f, Midlife-Crisis f, Krise f in der Mitte des Lebens; **he's having his ~** er befindet sich in der Midlifecrisis or Midlife-Crisis; **midnight** **N** Mitternacht f; **at ~** um Mitternacht **ADJ** attr mitternächtlich, Mitternachts-; ~ **mass** Mitternachtsmesse f; **the ~ hour** die Mitternachtsstunde, Mitternacht f; **the ~ sun** die Mitternachtssonne; **midnight-blue** ADJ nachtblau; **midpoint** N mittlerer Punkt; (Geometry) Mittelpunkt m; **to pass ~** die Hälfte hinter sich (dat) haben; **mid-price** **ADJ** im mittleren Preisbereich **N** mittlerer Preisbereich, Mittelpreislage f; **at ~** im mittleren Preisbereich; **mid-range** ADJ hotel, computer der Mittelklasse pred, im mittleren Bereich; **a ~ car** ein Mittelklassewagen m

midriff [ˈmɪdrɪf] N Taille f; **a punch to the ~** ein Schlag in die Magengegend or -grube

mid: midshipman N Fähnrich m zur See; **midships** ADV mittschiffs

midst [mɪdst] **N** Mitte f; **in the ~ of** mitten in; **we are in the ~ of an economic crisis** wir stecken mitten in einer Wirtschaftskrise; **and in the ~ of our troubles Grandpa died** und zu allem Unglück starb noch Großvater; **in our ~** unter uns, in unserer Mitte (geh); **in the ~ of life (we are in death)** (Bibl) mitten im Leben sind wir vom Tod umgeben **PREP** (old poet) = **amid(st)**

mid: midstream N **in ~** (lit) in der Mitte des Flusses; (fig) auf halber Strecke, mittendrin; **midsummer** **N** Hochsommer m **ADJ** days, nights, festival im Hochsommer; "A Midsummer Night's Dream" „Ein Sommernachtstraum"; **midsummer madness** N Sommerkoller m (inf); **that was ~** das war eine Schnapsidee (inf); **Midsummer's Day** N Sommersonnenwende f, Johannistag m; **midterm** N **in ~** (three-term year) mitten im Trimester; (two-term year) mitten im Schulhalbjahr or (Univ) Semester; **by ~** bis zur Trimesterhälfte/bis zur Mitte des Schulhalbjahres/Semesters; **it was ~ before ...** das halbe Trimester/Schulhalbjahr/Semester war schon vorbei, bevor ... **ADJ** ~ **elections** (Pol) Zwischenwahlen pl; ~ **examinations** Prüfungen in der Mitte eines Trimesters/Schulhalbjahres/Semesters; **midtown** (US) **N** Stadtzentrum nt **ADJ** im Stadtzentrum; **the ~ bus** der Bus ins Stadtzentrum; **a ~ Manhattan hotel** ein Hotel im Zentrum von Manhattan

midway **ADV** auf halbem Weg; **Düsseldorf is ~ between Krefeld and Cologne** Düsseldorf liegt auf halber Strecke zwischen Krefeld und Köln; ~ **through sth** mitten in etw (dat); **we are now ~** die Hälfte haben wir hinter uns (dat) **ADJ** **X is the ~ point between A and B** X liegt auf halbem Wege zwischen A und B; **we've now reached the ~ point** or **stage in the project** das Projekt ist jetzt zur Hälfte fertig **N** (US: at fair) Mittelweg eines Jahrmarkts, an dem sich die Hauptattraktionen befinden

mid: midweek **ADV** mitten in der Woche; **by ~** Mitte der Woche **ADJ** attr Mitte der Woche; **he booked a ~ flight** er buchte einen Flug für Mitte der Woche; **Midwest** N Mittelwesten m; **Midwestern** ADJ mittelwestlich; songs, dialect etc also des Mittelwestens; **Midwesterner** N (US) Bewohner(in) m(f) des Mittelwestens

midwife [ˈmɪdwaɪf] N pl **-wives** Hebamme f

midwifery [ˈmɪdˈwɪfərɪ] N Geburtshilfe f

midwife toad N (Zool) Geburtshelferkröte f

midwinter [ˌmɪdˈwɪntə] **N** Mitte f des Winters, Wintermitte f **ADJ** um die Mitte des Winters, mittwinterlich

midwives [ˈmɪdwaɪvz] pl of **midwife**

mien [miːn] N (liter) Miene f

miff [mɪf] VT (inf) **to be ~ed at** or **about sth** (= annoyed) über etw (acc) verärgert sein; (= offended) sich wegen etw auf den Schlips getreten fühlen (inf); **to get ~ed at sth** sich über etw (acc) erhitzen

miffy ['mɪfɪ] ADJ (+er) (inf: = easily annoyed) leicht beleidigt, mimosenhaft; plant empfindlich

might¹ [maɪt] ✪ 15.2, 15.3 pret of **may**; **they ~ be brothers, they look so alike** sie könnten Brüder sein, sie sehen sich so ähnlich; **as you ~ expect** wie zu erwarten war; **... I ~ add ...** möchte ich hinzufügen; **how old ~ he be?** wie alt er wohl ist?; **~ I smoke?** dürfte ich wohl rauchen?; **you ~ try Smith's** sie könnten es ja mal bei Smiths versuchen; **he ~ at least have apologized** er hätte sich wenigstens entschuldigen können; **I ~ have known** das hätte ich mir denken können; **she was thinking of what ~ have been** sie dachte an das, was hätte sein können

might² N Macht f; **with all one's ~** mit aller Kraft; **superior ~** Übermacht f, Überlegenheit f; **~ is right** (Prov) Macht geht vor Recht (Prov)

mightily ['maɪtɪlɪ] ADV **a** mit aller Macht; (fig: = majestically, imposingly) gewaltig **b** (inf: = extremely) mächtig (inf); **a ~ improved team** eine stark verbesserte Mannschaft; **~ impressive** höchst beeindruckend; **I was ~ impressed/relieved** ich war überaus beeindruckt/erleichtert

mightiness ['maɪtɪnɪs] N Macht f; (of wave, shout, scream) Gewalt f; (of warrior, noise, cheer) Stärke f; (of ship, tree etc) gewaltige Ausmaße pl

mightn't ['maɪtnt] contr of **might not**

mighty ['maɪtɪ] ADJ **a** (= wielding power) person, force, army mächtig; **the ~** die Mächtigen pl; **how are the ~ fallen** wie sind die Helden gefallen (Bibl), Hochmut kommt vor dem Fall (Prov); **a ~ warrior** ein großer Krieger **b** (= massive) building, noise, load, crowd, ship gewaltig; river, tree, wave, effect, blow mächtig, gewaltig; cheer lautstark ADV (esp US inf) mächtig (inf)

mignonette [ˌmɪnjə'net] N Reseda f, Resede f

migraine ['miːgreɪn] N Migräne f

migrant ['maɪgrənt] ADJ **~ bird** Zugvogel m; **~ butterfly** Wanderfalter m; **~ worker** Wanderbeiter(in) m(f); (esp in EC) Gastarbeiter(in) m(f); **~ labour** (Brit) or **labor** (US) Wanderarbeiter pl; (esp in EC) Gastarbeiter pl; **~ family** Migrantenfamilie f; **~ child** Migrantenkind nt N **a** (= bird) Zugvogel m **b** (= worker) Wanderarbeiter(in) m(f); (esp in EC) Gastarbeiter(in) m(f)

migrate [maɪ'greɪt] VI (animals, workers) (ab)wandern; (birds) nach Süden ziehen; (fig: townsfolk etc) ziehen; **do these birds ~?** sind das Zugvögel?

migration [maɪ'greɪʃən] N **a** Wanderung f; (of birds) (Vogel)zug m; (fig: of people) Abwanderung f; (seasonal) Zug m **b** (= number) Schwarm m

migratory [maɪ'greɪtərɪ] ADJ Wander-; population wandernd; **~ habits** Wanderungsgewohnheiten pl; **~ life** Wanderleben nt; **~ instinct** Wandertrieb m; **~ worker** Wanderarbeiter(in) m(f); **~ labour** (Brit) or **labor** (US) Wanderarbeiter pl; **~ birds** Zugvögel pl; **~ creatures** or **animals** Tiere, die auf Wanderung gehen, wandernde Tiere; **~ fish** Wanderfisch m; **sea turtles are ~** Meeresschildkröten sind wandernde Tiere

Mike [maɪk] N **a** dim of **Michael** **b** **for the love of ~!** (inf) um Himmels willen (inf)

mike [maɪk] N (inf) Mikro nt (inf), Mikrophon nt, Mikrofon nt

milady [mɪ'leɪdɪ] N Mylady f, gnädige Frau

milage N = **mileage**

Milan [mɪ'læn] N Mailand nt

mild [maɪld] ADJ (+er) **a** (= gentle) climate, weather, soap, punishment, spring day mild; breeze, criticism, rebuke leicht, sanft; medicine leicht; person, character, eyes sanft **b** (in flavour) taste, cigar, cheese, whisky mild; cigarettes mild, leicht; **this cheese has a very ~ taste** der Käse ist sehr mild (im Geschmack); **~ ale** leichtes dunkles Bier **c** (= slight) illness leicht; **a ~ form/case of**

meningitis eine leichte Gehirnhautentzündung N (Brit: = beer) leichtes dunkles Bier

mildew ['mɪldjuː] N Schimmel m; (on plants) Mehltau m VI verschimmeln, Schimmel ansetzen; (plants) von Mehltau befallen sein

mildewy ['mɪldjuːɪ] ADJ schimmelig, verschimmelt; plants von Mehltau befallen

mildly ['maɪldlɪ] ADV leicht; say, ask sanft; scold, rebuke, protest, curse, reply milde; **to put it ~** gelinde gesagt; **... and that's putting it ~** ... und das ist noch milde ausgedrückt; **they seemed ~ interested** sie machten einen leicht interessierten Eindruck; **to be ~ critical of sth** etw milde kritisieren

mildness ['maɪldnɪs] N **a** (= gentleness) (of climate, weather, day, soap, punishment) Milde f; (of breeze, criticism, rebuke) Sanftheit f; (of medicine) Leichtheit f; (of person, character) Sanftmütigkeit f **b** (in flavour) Milde f; (of cigarettes) Milde f, Leichtheit f **c** (= slightness: of illness) leichte Form

mile [maɪl] N Meile f; **how many ~s per gallon does your car do?** wie viel verbraucht Ihr Auto?; **a fifty-mile journey** eine Fahrt von fünfzig Meilen; **it's 12 ~s to Manchester** bis Manchester sind es 12 Meilen; **~s (and ~s)** (inf) meilenweit; **~ of sandy beaches** meilenweite Sandstrände pl; **to go the extra ~** (fig) besondere Anstrengungen unternehmen; **the President is willing to go the extra ~ for peace** der Präsident ist bereit, für den Frieden Zugeständnisse zu machen; **they live ~s away** sie wohnen meilenweit weg; **sorry, I was ~s away** (inf) tut mir Leid, ich war mit meinen Gedanken ganz woanders (inf); **you can tell it a ~ off, it stands** or **sticks out a ~** das sieht ja ein Blinder (mit Krückstock) (inf); **it smelled for ~s around** das roch 10 Kilometer gegen den Wind (inf); **you were ~s off the target** du hast meilenweit danebengetroffen; **he's ~s better at tennis than she is** er spielt hundertmal besser Tennis als sie (inf); **not a million ~s from here** (fig) in nächster Nähe, gar nicht weit weg; **if she invited me for dinner, I'd run a ~** (fig inf) wenn sie mich zum Abendessen einladen würde, würde mich das kalte Grausen packen (inf); **to talk a ~ a minute** (US inf) das Blaue vom Himmel (herunter)reden (inf)

mileage ['maɪlɪdʒ] N Meilen pl; (on odometer) Meilenstand m, Meilenzahl f; **what ~ did you do yesterday?** wie viele Meilen seid ihr gestern gefahren?; **~ per gallon** Benzinverbrauch m; **you get a much better ~ (per gallon) from this car if ...** dieser Wagen ist viel sparsamer im Verbrauch, wenn ...; **~ allowance** ≈ Kilometerpauschale f; **we got a lot of ~ out of it** (fig inf) das war uns (dat) sehr dienlich; **it's still got a lot of ~ left in it** (fig inf) da steckt noch einiges drin (inf); **he decided there was no ~ in provoking a row with his boss** er entschied, dass es nichts bringen würde, mit dem Chef einen Streit anzufangen (inf)

mileometer [maɪ'lɒmɪtə'] N (Brit) ≈ Kilometerzähler m

milepost ['maɪlpəʊst] N Meilenanzeiger m or -pfosten m

miler ['maɪlə'] N 1500-Meter-Läufer(in) m(f)

milestone ['maɪlstəʊn] N (lit, fig) Meilenstein m

milieu ['miːljɜː] N Milieu nt

militant ['mɪlɪtənt] ADJ militant; **to be in (a) ~ mood** in militanter Stimmung sein N militantes Element; **the ~s among the students** die militanten Studenten

militantly ['mɪlɪtəntlɪ] ADV (= fiercely) militant; **the army is ~ nationalist** die Armee ist militant-nationalistisch

Militant Tendency N (Brit, Pol) trotzkistische Splittergruppe innerhalb der Labour Party

militarily ['mɪlɪtrɪlɪ] ADV intervene, respond militärisch; (= from a military point of view) militärisch (gesehen), auf militärischem Gebiet; **to get involved ~** in Militäraktionen (acc) verwickelt werden

militarism ['mɪlɪtərɪzəm] N Militarismus m

militarist ['mɪlɪtərɪst] ADJ militaristisch N Militarist(in) m(f)

militaristic [ˌmɪlɪtə'rɪstɪk] ADJ militaristisch

militarize ['mɪlɪtəraɪz] VT militarisieren; **fully ~d** hoch militarisiert

military ['mɪlɪtərɪ] ADJ militärisch; **~ government** Militärregierung f; **~ personnel** Militär- or Armeeangehörige pl; **to do sth with ~ precision** etw mit militärischer Präzision tun; **the top ~ men** die führenden Militärs N **the ~** das Militär

military: military academy N Militärakademie f; **military band** N Militärkapelle f; **military base** N Militär- or Armeestützpunkt m; **military-industrial complex** N **the ~** (US) der militärisch-industrielle Komplex; **military police** N Militärpolizei f; **military policeman** N Militärpolizist m; **military policewoman** N Militärpolizistin f; **military school** N Militärschule f; **military service** N Militärdienst m, Wehrdienst m; **to do one's ~** seinen Wehr- or Militärdienst ableisten or machen (inf); **he's doing his ~** er ist gerade beim Militär; **military spending** N Militärausgaben pl

militate ['mɪlɪteɪt] VI **to ~ against/in favour** (Brit) or **favor** (US) **of sth** für/gegen etw sprechen

militia [mɪ'lɪʃə] N Miliz f, Bürgerwehr f

militiaman [mɪ'lɪʃəmən] N pl **-men** [-mən] Milizsoldat m

milk [mɪlk] N Milch f; **the land of** or **flowing with ~ and honey** das Land, wo Milch und Honig fließt; **the ~ of human kindness** die Milch der frommen Denk(ungs)art (liter); **she was not exactly flowing over with the ~ of human kindness** sie strömte nicht gerade über vor Freundlichkeit; **it's** or **there's no use crying over spilled ~** (prov) was passiert ist, ist passiert VT (lit, fig) melken; **the little old lady was ~ed dry by some heartless swindler** die alte Frau wurde von einem gewissenlosen Betrüger nach Strich und Faden ausgenommen (inf) VI Milch geben, milchen (dial)

milk in cpds Milch-; **milk-and-water** ADJ (fig) seicht, verwässert; **he described the report as milk and water** er tat den Bericht als nichtssagend ab; **milk bar** N Milchbar f; **milk carton** N Milchtüte f, Milchkarton m; **milk chocolate** N Vollmilchschokolade f; **milk churn** N Milchkanne f; **milk float** N Milchauto nt

milkiness ['mɪlkɪnɪs] N Milchigkeit f

milking ['mɪlkɪŋ] N Melken nt

milking machine N Melkmaschine f

milking stool N Melkschemel m

milk: milkmaid N Milchmädchen nt; **milkman** N Milchmann m; **milk of magnesia** N Magnesiamilch f; **milk powder** N Milchpulver nt; **milk product** N Milchprodukt nt; **milk pudding** N (Brit) Milchspeise f; **milk round** N (Brit) **a** (of milkman) Milchrunde f **b** (Univ) regelmäßige Besuche von Personalvertretern großer Firmen an Universitäten, um mögliche Mitarbeiter zu rekrutieren; **milk run** N (Aviat inf) Routineflug m; **milkshake** N Milchmixgetränk nt, Milchshake m; **milksop** N Milchbart m, Milchgesicht nt; **milk stout** N (Brit) ≈ Malzbier nt; **milk tooth** N Milchzahn m; **milkweed** N (US) Schwalbenwurzgewächs n, milk-white ADJ milchig-weiß, milchweiß

milky ['mɪlkɪ] ADJ (+er) milchig; **~ green/blue/white** milchig grün/blau/weiß; **~ drink** Milchgetränk nt; **~ coffee** Milchkaffee m; **rich ~ chocolate** sahnige Vollmilchschokolade

Milky Way [ˌmɪlkɪ'weɪ] N Milchstraße f

mill [mɪl] N **a** (= building) Mühle f **b** (= machine) Mühle f; **the poor man really went through the ~** (inf) der Arme hat wirklich viel durchmachen müssen; (= was questioned hard) der Arme wurde wirklich durch die Mangel gedreht (inf); **in training you're really put through the ~** (inf) im Training wird man ganz schön hart rangenommen (inf) **c** (= paper, steel mill etc) Fabrik f; (= cotton mill, for thread) Spinnerei *f*; (*for cloth*) Weberei *f* **VT** *flour, coffee etc* mahlen; *metal, paper* walzen; (*with milling machine*) *metal* fräsen; *coin* rändeln

▶ **mill about** (*Brit*) or **around** VI umherlaufen; **people were milling about** or **around the office** es herrschte ein Kommen und Gehen im Büro; **the crowds milling about** or **around the stalls in the marketplace** die Menschenmenge, die sich zwischen den Marktständen einherschob

millboard ['mɪlbɔːd] N (= *pasteboard*) starke Pappe, Pappdeckel *m*

milled [mɪld] ADJ *grain* gemahlen; *coin, edge* gerändelt; **freshly-milled pepper** frisch gemahlener Pfeffer

millenarian [ˌmɪləˈnɛərɪən] ADJ (*Rel*) millenaristisch, chiliastisch

millennial [mɪˈlɛnɪəl] ADJ tausendjährig

millennium [mɪˈlɛnɪəm] N *pl* **-s** or **millennia** [mɪˈlɛnɪə] (= *1,000 years*) Jahrtausend *nt*, Millennium *nt*; (= *state of perfection*) Tausendjähriges Reich, Millennium *nt*

millennium: millennium bug N (*Comput inf*) Jahrtausendfehler *m* or -problem *nt*; **Millennium Fund** N (*Brit*) Fonds für die Finanzierung von Projekten zur Feier der Jahrtausendwende

millepede ['mɪlɪpiːd] N = **millipede**

miller ['mɪlə'] N Müller(in) *m(f)*

millet ['mɪlɪt] N Hirse *f*

milli- ['mɪlɪ-] PREF Milli-; **millisecond** Millisekunde *f*

milliard ['mɪlɪɑːd] N (*Brit*) Milliarde *f*

milli: millibar N Millibar *nt*; **milligram(me)** N Milligramm *nt*; **millilitre**, (*US*) **milliliter** N Milliliter *m* or *nt*; **millimetre**, (*US*) **millimeter** N Millimeter *m* or *nt*

milliner ['mɪlɪnə'] N Hutmacher *m*, Hut- or Putzmacherin *f*, Modistin *f*; **at the ~'s (shop)** im Hutgeschäft or -laden

millinery ['mɪlɪnərɪ] N (= *trade*) Hut- or Putzmacherhandwerk *nt*; (= *articles*) Hüte *pl*

milling machine ['mɪlɪŋməʃiːn] N (*for coins*) Rändel(eisen) *nt*; (*for metal*) Fräse *f*, Fräsmaschine *f*

million ['mɪljən] N Million *f*; **4 ~ people** 4 Millionen Menschen; **for ~s and ~s of years** für millionen und abermillionen or Millionen und Abermillionen von Jahren; **the starving ~s** die Millionen, die Hunger leiden; **she's one in a ~** (*inf*) so jemanden wie sie findet man sobald nicht wieder, sie ist einmalige Klasse (*inf*); **it will sell a ~** (*inf*) das wird ein Millionenerfolg; **I've done it ~s of times** (*inf*) das habe ich schon tausendmal gemacht; **to feel (like) a ~ dollars** (*inf*) sich pudelwohl fühlen; **to look (like) a ~ dollars** (*inf*) umwerfend aussehen (*inf*)

millionaire [ˌmɪljəˈnɛə'] N Millionär *m*

millionairess [ˌmɪljəˈnɛərɪs] N Millionärin *f*

millionfold ['mɪljənfəʊld] (*liter*) ADJ millionenfach **ADV** **a ~** millionenfach, millionenfältig

millionth ['mɪljənθ] ADJ (= *fraction*) millionstel; (*in series*) millionste(r, s) **N** Millionstel *nt*

millipede ['mɪlɪpiːd] N Tausendfüß(l)er *m*

mill: millpond N Mühlteich *m*; **millrace** N Mühlbach or -graben *m*; **millstone** N Mühlstein *m*, Mahlstein *m*; **she's/it's a ~ around his neck** sie/das ist für ihn ein Klotz am Bein; **millstream** N Mühlbach *m*; **millwheel** N Mühlrad *nt*

milord [mɪˈlɔːd] N (= *person*) Mylord *m*, Lord *m*; (*as address*) Mylord *m*; **like some English ~** wie ein englischer Lord

milt [mɪlt] N (*Fishing*) Milch *f*

mime [maɪm] **N** (= *acting*) Pantomime *f*; (= *actor*) Pantomime *m*, Pantomimin *f*; (= *ancient play, actor*) Pantomime *m*; **the art of ~** die Pantomime, die Kunst der Pantomime; **to do a ~** eine Pantomime darstellen **VT** pantomimisch darstellen **VI** Pantomimen spielen

mime artist N Pantomime *m*, Pantomimin *f*

---

mimeograph ['mɪmɪəɡrɑːf] **N** Vervielfältigungsapparat *m* **VT** vervielfältigen, abziehen (*inf*)

mimic ['mɪmɪk] **N** Imitator(in) *m(f)*; **he's a very good ~** er kann sehr gut Geräusche/andere Leute nachahmen or -machen **VT** nachahmen or -machen; (= *ridicule*) nachäffen

mimicry ['mɪmɪkrɪ] N Nachahmung *f*; (*Biol*) Mimikry *f*; **protective ~** Schutzfärbung *f*, Tarnfarbe *f*; **his talent for ~** sein Talent dafür, andere nachzuahmen

mimosa [mɪˈməʊzə] **N** **a** (*Bot*) Mimose *f* **b** (*US: = drink*) Sekt *m* mit Orangensaft

Min **a** *abbr of* **Minister** Min. **b** *abbr of* **Ministry** Min.

min **a** *abbr of* **minute(s)** min **b** *abbr of* **minimum** min.

minaret [ˌmɪnəˈret] N Minarett *nt*

mince [mɪns] **N** (*esp Brit*) Hackfleisch *nt*, Gehackte(s) *nt* **VT** *meat* hacken, durch den Fleischwolf drehen; **he doesn't ~ his words** er nimmt kein Blatt vor den Mund; **he didn't ~ matters** er sagte es mal ganz deutlich or brutal (*inf*) **VI** (*Brit*) (= *walk*) tänzeln, trippeln, schwänzeln; (= *behave/speak*) sich geziert benehmen/ausdrücken

mince: mincemeat N *süße Gebäckfüllung aus Dörrobst und Sirup* **to make ~ of sb** (*inf*) (*physically*) Hackfleisch aus jdm machen (*inf*); (*verbally*) jdn zur Schnecke machen (*inf*); **to make ~ of sth** (*inf*) keinen guten Faden an etw (*dat*) lassen; **mince pie** N *mit Mincemeat gefülltes Gebäck*

mincer ['mɪnsə'] N (*esp Brit*) Fleischwolf *m*

mincing ['mɪnsɪŋ] ADJ (*Brit*) geziert; *steps* tänzelnd, trippelnd

mincingly ['mɪnsɪŋlɪ] ADV (*Brit*) gekünstelt; **he walked ~ away from her** er entfernte sich tänzelnd von ihr

mincing machine N (*esp Brit*) Fleischwolf *m*

---

mind [maɪnd]
✪ 4, 9.1

1 NOUN	3 INTRANSITIVE VERB
2 TRANSITIVE VERB	4 PHRASAL VERB

1 – NOUN

a = **intellect** Geist *m* (*also Philos*), Verstand *m*; **things of the mind** Geistiges *nt*; **the conscious and unconscious mind** das Bewusste und das Unbewusste; **to have a good mind** ein heller Kopf sein; **one of the finest minds of our times** einer der großen Geister unserer Zeit; **it's all in the mind** das ist alles Einbildung; **in one's mind's eye** vor seinem geistigen Auge, im Geiste; **to blow sb's mind** (*inf*) jdn umwerfen (*inf*); (*drugs*) jdn high machen (*inf*) → **boggle, great, improve**

♦ **mind over matter** it's a question of mind over matter es ist eine Willenssache or -frage; **a triumph of mind over matter** ein Triumph des Geistes or Willens über den Körper

b = **way of thinking** Denkweise *f*; (= *type of mind*) Geist *m*, Kopf *m*; **to the child's/Victorian mind** in der Denkweise des Kindes/der viktorianischen Zeit; **he has that kind of mind** er ist so veranlagt; **to have a literary/logical etc mind** literarisch/logisch *etc* veranlagt sein; **he has the mind of a five-year old** er verhält sich wie ein Fünfjähriger; **in the public mind prostitution is immoral** nach dem Empfinden der Öffentlichkeit ist Prostitution unmoralisch; **state** or **frame of mind** (seelische) Verfassung, (Geistes)zustand *m*

c = **thoughts** Gedanken *pl*; **to be clear in one's mind about sth** sich (*dat*) über etw im Klaren sein; **to put** or **set one's mind to sth** (= *try to do sth*) sich anstrengen, etw zu tun; (= *think about sth*) sich auf etw (*acc*) konzentrieren; **if you put** or **set your mind to it** wenn du dich anstrengst; **he had something on his mind** ihn beschäftigte etwas; **I've a lot on my mind** ich muss mich um (so) viele Dinge kümmern; **you are always on my mind** ich denke ständig an

---

dich; **keep your mind on the job** bleib mit den Gedanken *or* dem Kopf bei der Arbeit; **she couldn't get** or **put the song/him out of her mind** das Lied/er ging ihr nicht aus dem Kopf; **you can put that idea out of your mind!** den Gedanken kannst du dir aus dem Kopf schlagen!; **to take sb's mind off things** jdn auf andere Gedanken bringen; **to take sb's mind off sth** jdn etw vergessen lassen; **my mind isn't on my work** ich kann mich nicht auf meine Arbeit konzentrieren; **don't let your mind dwell on the problem** grüble nicht über dieses Problem nach; **he can't keep his mind off sex** er denkt nur an Sex *or* an nichts anderes als Sex; **the idea never entered my mind** daran hatte ich überhaupt nicht gedacht; **it's been going through my mind** es ging mir im Kopf herum; **nothing was further from my mind** nichts lag mir ferner; **his mind is set on that** er hat sich (*dat*) das in den Kopf gesetzt; **he guessed what is in my mind** er erriet meine Gedanken; **in my mind's eye** vor meinem inneren Auge → **cross** [1]

d = **memory** Gedächtnis *nt*; **it went right out of my mind** daran habe ich überhaupt nicht mehr gedacht; **that quite put it out of my mind** dadurch habe ich es vergessen; **to bring** or **call sth to mind** etw in Erinnerung rufen, an etw (*acc*) erinnern → **sight, slip**

e = **inclination** Lust *f*; (= *intention*) Sinn *m*, Absicht *f*; **I've half a mind/a good mind to ...** ich hätte Lust/große *or* gute Lust, zu ...; **to be of a mind to do sth** geneigt sein, etw zu tun (*geh*) → **read** [1]

f = **opinion** Meinung *f*, Ansicht *f*; **to change one's mind** seine Meinung ändern (*about* über +*acc*), es sich (*dat*) anders überlegen; **to be in two minds about sth** sich (*dat*) über etw (*acc*) nicht im Klaren sein; **to be of one** or **of the same mind** eines Sinnes (*geh*) *or* gleicher Meinung sein; **I'm of the same mind as you** ich denke wie du, ich bin deiner Meinung; **with one mind** wie ein Mann; **to my mind he's wrong** meiner Ansicht nach *or* nach meiner Meinung irrt er sich; **to have a mind of one's own** (*person, = think for oneself*) eine eigene Meinung haben; (= *not conform*) seinen eigenen Kopf haben; (*hum, machine etc*) seine Mucken haben (*inf*) → **close** [2], **know, make up, open, piece, speak**

g = **sanity** Verstand *m*, Sinne *pl*; **his mind was wandering** (*out of boredom etc*) seine Gedanken wanderten umher; **to lose one's mind** verrückt werden, den Verstand verlieren; **nobody in his right mind** kein normaler Mensch; **while the balance of his mind was disturbed** (*Jur*) wegen Verlusts des seelischen Gleichgewichts

h set structures

♦ **in mind to bear** or **keep sth in mind** etw nicht vergessen; *facts also, application* etw im Auge behalten; **to bear** or **keep sb in mind** an jdn denken; *applicant also* jdn im Auge behalten; **with this in mind...** mit diesem Gedanken im Hinterkopf...; **to have sb/sth in mind** an jdn/etw denken; **to have in mind to do sth** vorhaben *or* im Sinn haben, etw zu tun; **to have it in mind to do sth** beabsichtigen *or* sich (*dat*) vorgenommen haben, etw zu tun; **it puts me in mind of sb/sth** es weckt in mir Erinnerungen an jdn/etw

♦ **out of one's mind to go out of one's mind** verrückt werden, den Verstand verlieren; **to be out of one's mind** verrückt sein; **to go out of one's mind with worry/grief** vor Sorge/Trauer den Verstand verlieren; **to drive sb out of his mind** jdn um den Verstand bringen, jdn wahnsinnig machen; **I'm bored out of my mind** ich langweile mich zu Tode

2 – TRANSITIVE VERB

a = **look after** aufpassen auf (+*acc*); *sb's chair, seat* freihalten; **I'm minding the shop** (*fig*) ich sehe nach dem Rechten

b = **be careful of** aufpassen auf (+*acc*); (= *pay attention to*) achten auf (+*acc*); (= *act in accordance with*) beachten; **mind what you're doing!**

pass (doch) auf!; **mind what you're doing with that car** pass mit dem Auto auf; **mind what I say!** lass dir das gesagt sein; (= *do as I tell you*) hör auf das, was ich dir sage; **mind how you go** passen Sie auf, wo Sie hintreten; **mind your language!** drück dich anständig aus!; **mind the step!** (*Brit*) Vorsicht Stufe!; **mind your head!** (*Brit*) Kopf einziehen (*inf*), Vorsicht, niedrige Tür/Decke *etc*; **mind your feet!** (*Brit*) (*when sitting*) zieh die Füße ein!; (*when moving*) pass auf, wo du hintrittst!; **mind your own business** kümmern Sie sich um Ihre eigenen Angelegenheiten

c = care about sich kümmern um; (= *object to*) etwas haben gegen; **she minds/doesn't mind it** es macht ihr etwas/nichts aus; (= *is/is not bothered, annoyed by*) es stört sie/stört sie nicht; (= *is not/is indifferent to*) es ist ihr nicht egal/ist ihr egal; **I don't mind the cold** die Kälte macht mir nichts aus; **I don't mind what he does** es ist mir egal, was er macht; **I don't mind four but six is too many** ich habe nichts gegen vier, aber sechs sind zu viel; **do you mind coming with me?** würde es dir etwas ausmachen mitzukommen?; **would you mind opening the door?** wären Sie so freundlich, die Tür aufzumachen?; **do you mind my smoking?** macht es Ihnen etwas aus *or* stört es Sie *or* haben Sie etwas dagegen, wenn ich rauche?; **I don't mind telling you, I was shocked** ich war schockiert, das kannst du mir glauben; **I hope you don't mind my asking/sitting here** ich hoffe, Sie haben nichts dagegen, wenn ich Sie frage/dass ich hier sitze; **don't mind me** lass dich (durch mich) nicht stören; (*iro*) nimm auf mich keine Rücksicht; **I wouldn't mind a cup of tea** ich hätte nichts gegen eine Tasse Tee

♦ **never mind** + *sb/sth* **never mind the expense** (es ist) egal, was es kostet; **never mind that now** das ist jetzt nicht wichtig, lass das doch jetzt; **never mind your back, I'm worried about ...** dein Rücken ist mir doch egal, ich mache mir Sorgen um ...; **never mind him** kümmere dich nicht um ihn

3 – INTRANSITIVE VERB

a = care, worry sich kümmern, sich (*dat*) etwas daraus machen; (= *object*) etwas dagegen haben; **he doesn't seem to mind about anything** ihn scheint nichts zu kümmern; **I wish he minded a little** ich wünschte, es würde ihm etwas ausmachen *or* ihn ein bisschen kümmern; **nobody seemed to mind** es schien keinem etwas auszumachen, niemand schien etwas dagegen zu haben; **I'd prefer to stand, if you don't mind** ich würde lieber stehen, wenn es Ihnen recht ist; **do you mind?** macht es Ihnen etwas aus?; **do you mind!** (*iro*) na hör mal!, ich möchte doch sehr bitten!; **do you mind if I open** *or* **would you mind if I opened the window?** macht es Ihnen etwas aus, wenn ich das Fenster öffne?; **I don't mind if I do** ich hätte nichts dagegen

♦ **never mind** macht nichts, ist doch egal; (*in exasperation*) ist ja auch egal, schon gut; **never mind, you'll find another** mach dir nichts draus, du findest bestimmt einen anderen; **oh, never mind, I'll do it myself** ach, lass (es) *or* schon gut, ich mache es selbst; **never mind about that now!** lass das doch jetzt!, das ist doch jetzt nicht wichtig; **never mind about what you said to him, what did he say to you?** es ist doch egal *or* unwichtig, was du zu ihm gesagt hast, was hat er zu dir gesagt?; **never mind about that mistake** mach dir nichts aus dem Fehler; **never mind about your shoes** (*in exasperation*) deine Schuhe sind mir doch egal; **I'm not going to finish school, never mind go to university** ich werde die Schule nicht beenden und schon gar nicht zur Universität gehen

♦ **never you mind!** kümmere du dich mal nicht darum; (= *none of your business*) das geht dich überhaupt nichts an!

b = be sure aufpassen; **mind and see if ...** sieh zu, ob ...; **mind you get that done** sieh zu, dass du das fertig bekommst; **I'm not saying I'll**

do it, mind ich will damit aber nicht sagen, dass ich es tue; **he's not a bad lad, mind, just ...** er ist eigentlich kein schlechter Junge, nur ...; **he didn't do it, mind** er hat es (ja) nicht getan

♦ **mind you** allerdings; **mind you, I'd rather not go** ich würde eigentlich *or* allerdings lieber nicht gehen; **it was raining at the time, mind you** allerdings hat es da geregnet; **mind you, he did try/ask** er hat es immerhin versucht/hat immerhin gefragt; **he's quite good, mind you** er ist eigentlich ganz gut

4 – PHRASAL VERB

▶ **mind out** **VI** (*Brit*) aufpassen (*for* auf +*acc*); **mind out!** pass (doch) auf!

mind: mind-bending ADJ (*inf*) Wahnsinns- (*inf*); *drug, substances* bewusstseinsverändernd; **mind-blowing** ADJ (*inf*) Wahnsinns- (*inf*); *simplicity* atemberaubend; **mind-boggling** ADJ (*inf*) irrsinnig (*inf*), verrückt (*inf*); **it's ~ that ...** es ist kaum zu fassen, dass ...; **~ statistics** Schwindel erregende Statistiken

minded ['maɪndɪd] ADJ gesonnen (*geh*), gewillt; **if you are so ~** wenn Ihnen der Sinn danach steht (*geh*)

-minded ADJ *suf* **romantically-minded** romantisch veranlagt; **nasty-minded** übel gesinnt; **she's very politically-minded** sie interessiert sich sehr für Politik; **I'm not really opera-minded** ich mache mir nichts aus Opern

minder ['maɪndə'] N (*inf*) Aufpasser(in) *m(f)*

mind-expanding ['maɪndɪks,pændɪŋ] ADJ bewusstseinserweiternd

mindful ['maɪndfʊl] ADJ **to be ~ of sth** etw berücksichtigen *or* bedenken; **ever ~ of the risks, she ...** weil sie sich (*dat*) der Risiken bewusst war, ... sie ...; **ever ~ of her words** immer an ihre Worte denkend

mindfulness ['maɪndfʊlnɪs] N Achtsamkeit *f*, Aufmerksamkeit *f*

mind: mind game N psychologisches Spiel; **to play ~s with sb** jdn verunsichern; **mindless** ADJ **a** (= *senseless*) *destruction, crime, violence* sinnlos; (= *unchallenging*) *work, entertainment, routine* stumpfsinnig; *occupation* geistlos; (= *stupid*) hirnlos, ohne Verstand; **~ idiot** hirnloser Idiot; **~ thug** hirnloser Schlägertyp **b** **to be ~ of sth** nicht an etw (*acc*) denken; **mindlessly** ADV (= *tediously*) stumpfsinnig; (= *stupidly*) hirnlos; **mind-reader** N Gedankenleser(in) *m(f)*; **I'm not a ~** ich bin doch kein Gedankenleser; **mindset** N Mentalität *f*

mine¹ [maɪn] POSS PRON meine(r, s); **this car is ~** das ist MEIN Auto, dieses Auto gehört mir; **is this ~?** gehört das mir?, ist das meine(r, s)?; **his friends and ~** seine und meine Freunde; **a friend of ~** ein Freund von mir; **will you be ~?** (*old*) willst du die Meine werden? (*old*); **~ is a rather different job** meine Arbeit ist ziemlich anders; **that aunt of ~** diese Tante von mir; **no advice of ~ could ...** keiner meiner Ratschläge konnte ...; **a favourite** (*Brit*) *or* **favorite** (*US*) **expression of ~** einer meiner Lieblingsausdrücke **ADJ** (*obs*) mein(e)

mine² **N** **a** (*Min*) Bergwerk *nt*; (= *gold mine, silver mine*) Bergwerk *nt*, Mine *f*; (= *coal mine*) Zeche *f*, Bergwerk *nt*; **to work down the ~s** unter Tage arbeiten

b (*Mil, Naut etc*) Mine *f*; **to lay ~s** Minen legen **c** (*fig*) **the book is a ~ of information** das Buch ist eine wahre Fundgrube; **he is a ~ of information** er ist ein wandelndes Lexikon (*inf*); **he's a ~ of information about history** er besitzt ein schier unerschöpfliches Geschichtswissen

VT **a** *coal, metal* fördern, abbauen; *area* Bergbau betreiben *or* Bodenschätze abbauen in (+*dat*)

b (*Mil, Naut*) *channel, road* verminen; *ship* eine Mine befestigen an (+*dat*); (= *blow up*) (mit einer Mine) sprengen

VI Bergbau betreiben; **to ~ for sth** nach etw graben; **they ~d deep down into the mountain**

sie trieben einen Stollen bis tief in den Berg hinein

mine: mine detector N Minensuchgerät *nt*; **mine disaster** N Grubenunglück *nt*; **minefield** N Minenfeld *nt*; **to enter a (political) ~** sich auf (politisch) gefährliches Terrain begeben; **it's an absolute ~!** das ist Sprengstoff!; **mine gas** N Grubengas *nt*, schlagende Wetter *pl*; **minehunter** N Minensuchboot *nt*; **minelayer** N Minenleger *m*

miner ['maɪnə'] N Bergarbeiter(in) *m(f)*, Bergmann *m*

mineral ['mɪnərəl] **N** Mineral *nt* **ADJ** mineralisch; **~ deposits** Mineralbestände *pl*; **~ exploration** Mineraliensuche *f*

mineralogical [ˌmɪnərə'lɒdʒɪkəl] ADJ mineralogisch

mineralogist [ˌmɪnə'rælədʒɪst] N Mineraloge *m*, Mineralogin *f*

mineralogy [ˌmɪnə'rælədʒɪ] N Mineralogie *f*

mineral: mineral oil N Mineralöl *nt*; **mineral spring** N Mineralquelle *f*, Heilbrunnen *m*; **mineral water** N Mineralwasser *nt*

miner's lamp ['maɪnəzlæmp] N Grubenlampe *f*

mineshaft ['maɪnʃɑːft] N Schacht *m*

minestrone [ˌmɪnɪ'strəʊnɪ] N Minestrone *f*, Gemüsesuppe *f*

mine: minesweeper N Minenräumboot *nt or* -suchboot *nt or* -sucher *m*; **mine workings** PL Stollen *pl*

Ming [mɪŋ] ADJ Ming-; **~ Dynasty** Ming-Dynastie *f*; **~ vase** Mingvase *f*

mingle ['mɪŋgl] **VI** sich vermischen; (*people, groups*) sich untereinander vermischen; **he ~d with people of all classes** er hatte Umgang mit Menschen aller gesellschaftlichen Schichten; **to ~ with the crowd** sich unters Volk mischen; **she ~d for a while, then sat down with her husband** (*at party*) sie mischte sich eine Zeit lang unter die Gäste und setzte sich dann mit ihrem Mann hin **VT** mischen (*with* mit); (*liter*) *waters* vermischen; **love ~d with hate** mit Hass vermischte *or* gemischte Liebe

mingy ['mɪndʒɪ] ADJ (*+er*) (*Brit, inf*) knickerig (*inf*); *amount* lumpig (*inf*), mickerig (*inf*)

mini- ['mɪnɪ-] PREF Mini-

miniature ['mɪnɪtʃə'] **N** Miniatur- *or* Kleinausgabe *f*; (*Art*) Miniatur *f*; (= *bottle*) Miniflasche *f*; **in ~** en miniature, im kleinen **ADJ** *attr* Miniatur-; **~ world** Miniaturmodell *nt*

miniature: miniature camera N Kleinbildkamera *f*; **miniature golf** N Mini- *or* Kleingolf *nt*; **miniature poodle** N Zwergpudel *m*; **miniature railway** N Liliputbahn *f*; **miniature submarine** N Kleinst-U-Boot *nt*

miniaturist ['mɪnɪtʃərɪst] N Miniaturmaler(in) *m(f)*

miniaturize ['mɪnɪtʃəraɪz] VT verkleinern

mini: minibar N Minibar *f*; **minibreak** N Kurzurlaub *m*; **minibudget** N *Etat, der nur Teilbereiche bzw. nur einen Teil des Rechnungsjahres abdeckt*, Zwischenetat *m*; **minibus** N Kleinbus *m*; **minicab** N Minicar *m*, Kleintaxi *nt*; **minicassette** N Minikassette *f*; **minicomputer** N Minicomputer *m*, Kleinrechner *m*; **Minidisc®** ['mɪnɪdɪsk] N (*Mus*) Minidisc *f*; **~ player** Minidisc-Spieler *m*; **minidress** N Minikleid *nt*

minim ['mɪnɪm] N (*Brit Mus*) halbe Note

minimal ['mɪnɪml] ADJ minimal; **at ~ cost** zu minimalen Kosten; **with ~ effort** mit minimalem Aufwand

minimal artist N (*Art*) Minimalist(in) *m(f)*

minimalism ['mɪnɪməlɪzəm] N Minimalismus *m*

minimalist ['mɪnɪməlɪst] ADJ minimalistisch

minimally ['mɪnɪmlɪ] ADV (= *marginally*) minimal; **this album sold ~ in the UK** dieses Album verkaufte sich in Großbritannien nur minimal; **~ invasive surgery** (*Med*) minimal invasive Chirurgie

minimize ['mɪnɪmaɪz] VT **a** (= *reduce*) *expenditure, time lost etc* auf ein Minimum reduzieren,

minimieren (form) **b** (= belittle, underestimate) schlecht machen, herabsetzen

minimum ['mɪnɪməm] **N** Minimum nt; **the temperature fell to a ~ of 5 degrees** die Temperatur fiel auf Tiefstwerte von 5 Grad; **with a ~ of inconvenience** mit einem Minimum an Unannehmlichkeiten; **what is the ~ you will accept?** was ist für Sie das Minimum or der Mindestbetrag?; **a ~ of 2 hours/£50/10 people** mindestens 2 Stunden/£ 50/10 Leute; **to keep sth to a or the ~** etw auf ein Minimum beschränken; **to reduce sth to a ~** etw auf ein Minimum or Mindestmaß reduzieren; **at a** or **the ~** (= at least) mindestens

ADJ attr Mindest-; **~ age** Mindestalter nt; **~ charge** Mindestgebühr f; **to achieve maximum possible profits from ~ possible expenditure** möglichst hohe Gewinne mit möglichst geringen Ausgaben erzielen; **the ~ expenditure will be ...** das wird mindestens ... kosten; **~ temperature** Tiefsttemperatur f; **a ~ level of discontent** ein Mindestmaß nt an Unzufriedenheit; **the ~ level of aluminium in the body** die Mindestmenge von Aluminium im Körper

minimum lending rate N (Brit Fin) Diskontsatz m

minimum wage N Mindestlohn m

mining ['maɪnɪŋ] N **a** (Min) Bergbau m; (= work at the face) Arbeit f im Bergwerk **b** (Mil) (of area) Verminen nt; (of ship) Befestigung f einer Mine (of an +dat); (= blowing-up) Sprengung f (mit einer Mine)

mining: mining area N Bergbaugebiet nt, Revier nt; **mining disaster** N Grubenunglück nt; **mining engineer** N Berg(bau)ingenieur(in) m(f); **mining industry** N Bergbau m; **mining town** N Bergarbeiterstadt f

minion ['mɪnɪən] N (old) Günstling m; (fig) Trabant m; **she delegated the job to one of her ~s** sie beauftragte einen/eine ihrer Untergebenen, die Sache zu erledigen

mini: minipill N Minipille f; **miniski** N Kurzski m; **miniskirt** N Minirock m; **ministate** N Zwergstaat m

minister ['mɪnɪstə'] **N a** (Pol) Minister(in) m(f) **b** (Eccl) Pfarrer(in) m(f), Pastor(in) m(f); **good morning, ~** guten Morgen, Herr Pfarrer or Herr Pastor **VI ~ to** to sb sich um jdn kümmern; **to ~ to sb's needs/wants** jds Bedürfnisse/Wünsche (acc) befriedigen; **a ~ing angel** (liter) ein barmherziger Engel

ministerial [ˌmɪnɪˈstɪərɪəl] ADJ (Pol) ministeriell, Minister-; source ministeriell; **~ post** Ministerposten m; **his ~ duties** seine Pflichten als Minister; **at ~ level** auf Ministerebene; **those of ~ rank** diejenigen, die im Rang eines Ministers stehen (form) or die einen Ministerposten innehaben

ministration [ˌmɪnɪˈstreɪʃən] N usu pl Pflege f, Fürsorge f

ministry ['mɪnɪstrɪ] N **a** (Pol) Ministerium nt; **~ of education/agriculture** Bildungs-/Landwirtschaftsministerium nt; **during his ~** in or während seiner Amtszeit (als Minister); **during the ~ of X** als X Minister war **b** (Eccl) geistliches Amt; **to join** or **enter** or **go into the ~** Pfarrer(in) or Geistliche(r) werden; **to enter the ~** Theologie studieren, um Geistlicher zu werden **c** (= ministering) Sendungsbewusstsein nt; **Christ's ~ here on earth** das Wirken Christi auf Erden

miniver ['mɪnɪvə'] N Hermelin m

mink [mɪŋk] N Nerz m; **~ coat** Nerzmantel m

minnow ['mɪnəʊ] N Elritze f

Minoan [mɪˈnəʊən] ADJ minoisch

minor ['maɪnə'] **ADJ a** (= of lesser extent) kleiner; (= of lesser importance) unbedeutend, unwichtig; offence, illness, operation, injuries leicht; surgery klein; interest, importance geringer; poet, position unbedeutend; prophet, planet klein; **~ road** Nebenstraße f; **a ~ role** eine Nebenrolle, eine kleinere Rolle; **he only played a ~ role in the company** er spielte in der Firma nur eine untergeordnete Rolle; **I have one or two ~ criticisms of the hotel** ich habe an dem Hotel nur ein paar Kleinigkeiten auszusetzen

b (Mus) Moll-; **~ key** Molltonart f; **~ scale** Molltonleiter f; **G/E flat/C sharp ~** g-/es-/cis-Moll nt; **~ third** kleine Terz; **the novel ends in a ~ key** or **on a ~ note** der Roman endet mit einer traurigen Note

c (Brit Sch inf) **Smith ~** Smith der Jüngere

N a (Mus) **the ~** Moll nt; **the music shifts to the ~** die Musik wechselt nach Moll über or geht in die Molltonart über

b (Jur) Minderjährige(r) mf

c (US Univ) Nebenfach nt

VI (US Univ) im Nebenfach studieren (in +acc)

Minorca [mɪˈnɔːkə] N Menorca nt

Minorcan [mɪˈnɔːkən] **ADJ** menorkinisch **N** Menorkiner(in) m(f)

minority [maɪˈnɒrɪtɪ] **N a** Minderheit f, Minorität f; **to be in a or the ~** in der Minderheit sein; **the reforms will affect only a small ~ of the population** die Reformen werden sich nur auf eine kleine Minderheit in der Bevölkerung auswirken; **you are in a ~ of one** Sie stehen allein da

b (Jur) Minderjährigkeit f

ADJ attr Minderheits-; **~ group** Minderheit f, Minorität f; **~ community** Minderheit f; **(ethnic) ~ students** Studenten pl, die einer (ethnischen) Minderheit angehören; **~ opinion** Minderheitsmeinung f; **a ~ view** die Ansicht einer Minderheit; **~ rights** (Pol) Minderheitenrechte pl; **~ programme** (Brit) or **program** (US) (Rad/TV) Programm, das nur einen kleinen Hörerkreis/Zuschauerkreis anspricht

b (US Pol: = opposition) **House/Senate Minority Leader** Oppositionsführer(in) m(f) (im Repräsentantenhaus/Senat)

minority: minority government N Minderheitsregierung f; **minority holding, minority interest** N (Fin) Minderheitsbeteiligung f; **minority shareholder** N (Fin) Kleinaktionär(in) m(f)

minor league ADJ person zweitklassig; subject zweitrangig; **~ baseball** (US) Baseball m or nt in den unteren Ligen

minor premise N Untersatz m

Minotaur ['maɪnətɔː'] N Minotaur(us) m

minster ['mɪnstə'] N Münster nt

minstrel ['mɪnstrəl] N (medieval) Spielmann m; (wandering) (fahrender) Sänger; (= ballad-singer) Bänkelsänger m; (= singer of love songs) Minnesänger m; (esp US: modern) weißer, als Neger zurechtgemachter Sänger und Komiker

mint¹ [mɪnt] **N** Münzanstalt f, Munzstätte f, Münze f; **(Royal) Mint** (Königlich-)Britische Münzanstalt; **to be worth a ~** (inf) Gold wert sein, unbezahlbar sein; **he is making a ~ (of money)** (inf) er verdient ein Heidengeld (inf); **his father made a ~** (inf) sein Vater hat einen Haufen Geld gemacht (inf) **ADJ** stamp postfrisch, ungestempelt; **in ~ condition** in tadellosem Zustand **VT** coin, phrase prägen

mint² N (Bot) Minze f; (= sweet) Pfefferminz nt

-minted ['-mɪntɪd] ADJ suf newly-/freshly-minted nagelneu (inf); **a freshly-minted medical doctor** ein frischgebackener Arzt

mint: mint julep N Whisky mit Eis und frischer Minze; **mint sauce** N Minzsoße f; **mint tea** N Pfefferminztee m

minuet [ˌmɪnjʊˈet] N Menuett nt

minus ['maɪnəs] **PREP a** minus, weniger; **£100 ~ taxes** £ 100 abzüglich (der) Steuern **b** (= without, deprived of) ohne; **he returned from the war ~ an arm** er kam mit einem Arm weniger aus dem Krieg zurück **ADJ** Minus-; quantity, value negativ; **~ point** Minuspunkt m; **~ temperatures** Minustemperaturen pl, Temperaturen pl unter null; **~ three degrees centigrade** drei Grad minus; **an A ~** (in grading) eine Eins minus **N a** (= sign) Minus(zeichen) nt; **two ~es make a plus** minus mal minus gibt plus; **if the result is a ~ ...** wenn das Ergebnis negativ ist or eine negative Größe ist ... **b** (= disadvantage) Minus nt

minuscule ['mɪnɪskjuːl] ADJ winzig

minus sign N Minuszeichen nt

minute¹ ['mɪnɪt] **N a** (of time, degree) Minute f; **it's 23 ~s past 3** es ist 3 Uhr und 23 Minuten; **in a ~** gleich, sofort; **this (very) ~!** auf der Stelle!; **at this very ~** gerade jetzt or in diesem Augenblick; **I shan't be a ~** ich bin nicht lang; **just a ~!** einen Moment bitte!; **any ~ (now)** jeden Augenblick; **tell me the ~ he comes** sag mir sofort Bescheid, wenn er kommt; **let me know the ~ it stops** sagen Sie mir Bescheid, sobald es aufhört; **we timed it to the ~** wir haben die Zeit auf die Minute genau genommen; **have you got a ~?** hast du mal eine Minute or einen Augenblick Zeit?; **it won't take a ~/5 ~s** es dauert keine Minute/keine 5 Minuten; **I enjoyed every ~ of it** ich habe es von Anfang bis Ende genossen; **I don't believe for a or one ~ that ...** ich glaube nicht einen Augenblick, dass...; **at the last ~** in letzter Minute

b (= official note) Notiz f; **~s** Protokoll nt; **to take the ~s** das Protokoll führen **VT** meeting protokollieren; remark, fact zu Protokoll nehmen

minute² [maɪˈnjuːt] ADJ (= small) winzig; resemblance ganz entfernt; (= detailed, exact) minuziös; detail kleinste(r, s)

minute ['mɪnɪt]: **minute book** N Protokollbuch nt; **minute hand** N Minutenzeiger m

minutely [maɪˈnjuːtlɪ] ADV (= by a small amount) ganz geringfügig; (= in detail) genauestens; **anything ~ resembling a fish** alles, was auch nur annähernd nach Fisch aussieht; **a ~ detailed account** eine sehr detaillierte Schilderung; **a ~ folded piece of paper** ein klitzeklein gefaltetes Stück Papier

Minuteman ['mɪnɪtmæn] N pl **-men** [-men] (US) Freiwilliger im Unabhängigkeitskrieg, der auf Abruf bereitstand

minuteness [maɪˈnjuːtnɪs] N (= small size) Winzigkeit f; (of account, description) Ausführlichkeit f; (of detail) Genauigkeit f

minute steak ['mɪnɪt-] N Minutensteak nt

minutiae [mɪˈnjuːʃiː] PL genaue Einzelheiten pl; **the ~ of daily life** die tägliche Kleinarbeit

minx [mɪŋks] N Biest nt (inf)

miracle ['mɪrəkəl] N Wunder nt; **to work** or **perform ~s** (lit) Wunder tun or wirken or vollbringen; **I can't work ~s** ich kann nicht hexen or zaubern; **by a ~** (fig) **by some ~** (fig) wie durch ein Wunder; **it will be a ~ if ...** das wäre ein Wunder, wenn ...; **it's a ~ he ...** es ist ein Wunder, dass er ...; **her recovery/his victory was a ~** es war ein Wunder, dass sie wieder gesund geworden ist/dass er gewonnen hat; **it'll take a ~ for us** or **we'll need a ~ to be finished on time** da müsste schon ein Wunder geschehen, wenn wir noch rechtzeitig fertig werden sollen

miracle: miracle drug N Wunderdroge f; **miracle play** N Mirakelspiel nt, geistliches Drama; **miracle worker** N Wundertäter m; **I'm not a ~, you know** (inf) ich kann doch keine Wunder vollbringen

miraculous [mɪˈrækjʊləs] ADJ **a** escape, recovery wundersam; **~ powers** Wunderkräfte pl; **that is nothing/little short of ~** das grenzt an ein Wunder **b** (= unbelievable, wonderful) wunderbar; achievement, improvement, transformation erstaunlich; **there was a ~ change in her appearance** es war kaum zu fassen, wie sie sich verändert hatte

miraculously [mɪˈrækjʊləslɪ] ADV **a** escape auf wundersame Weise; **~ intact/unharmed** wie durch ein Wunder unbeschädigt; **~ the baby was unhurt** es war wie ein Wunder, dass das Baby unverletzt blieb **b** (= unbelievably, wonderfully) wunderbar; **she was somehow ~ changed** es war nicht zu fassen, wie verändert sie war

mirage ['mɪrɑːʒ] N Fata Morgana f, Luftspiegelung f; (fig) Trugbild nt, Illusion f

MIRAS ['maɪræs] N (Brit Fin) abbr of **mortgage interest relief at source** Steuervergünstigung bei der Zahlung von Hypothekenzinsen

mire ['maɪə'] N Morast *m* (*also fig*), Schlamm *m*; **the football pitch was an absolute ~** der Fußballplatz war ein einziges Schlammfeld; **to drag sb/sth through the ~** (*fig*) jdn/etw in den Schmutz ziehen

mired ['maɪəd] ADJ (*esp liter*) **a** (= *dirtied*) **~ in mud** (*vehicle*) im Schlamm versunken; *road* schlammbedeckt **b** (= *involved*) **~ in debt** tief verschuldet; **~ in scandal** von Skandalen umwittert *or* verfolgt

mirror ['mɪrə'] **N** Spiegel *m*; **a ~ of 19th century life** ein Spiegelbild *nt* des Lebens im 19. Jahrhundert; **to hold a ~ up to sth** etw widerspiegeln **VT** widerspiegeln, spiegeln; **the trees ~ed in the lake** die Bäume, die sich im See (wider-) spiegelten

mirror: mirror image N Spiegelbild *nt*; **mirror site** N (*Comput*) Mirrorsite *f*; **mirror writing** N Spiegelschrift *f*

mirth [mɜːθ] N Freude *f*, Frohsinn *m*; (= *laughter*) Heiterkeit *f*; **shrieks of ~ coming from the classroom** frohes *or* fröhliches Lachen, das aus dem Klassenzimmer drang

mirthful ['mɜːθfʊl] ADJ froh, heiter, fröhlich

mirthless ['mɜːθlɪs] ADJ freudlos; *laughter* unfroh, beklemmt

mirthlessly ['mɜːθlɪslɪ] ADV (*liter*) *smile* betrübt; *laugh* unfroh, beklemmt

miry ['maɪərɪ] ADJ morastig, schlammig

misadventure [,mɪsəd'ventʃə'] N Missgeschick *nt*; **death by ~** Tod *m* durch Unfall

misalliance [,mɪsə'laɪəns] N Mesalliance *f*

misanthrope ['mɪzənθrəʊp] N = **misanthropist**

misanthropic [,mɪzən'θrɒpɪk] ADJ misanthropisch, menschenfeindlich

misanthropist [mɪ'zænθrəpɪst] N Misanthrop(in) *m(f)*, Menschenfeind(in) *m(f)*

misanthropy [mɪ'zænθrəpɪ] N Misanthropie *f*, Menschenfeindlichkeit *f*

misapply ['mɪsə'plaɪ] VT falsch anwenden; *funds* falsch verwenden; *one's energy* verschwenden

misapprehend ['mɪs,æprɪ'hend] VT missverstehen

misapprehension ['mɪs,æprɪ'henʃən] N Missverständnis *nt*; **I think you are under a ~** ich glaube, bei Ihnen liegt (da) ein Missverständnis vor; **he was under the ~ that ...** er hatte fälschlicherweise *or* irrtümlicherweise angenommen, dass ...

misappropriate ['mɪsə'prəʊprɪeɪt] VT entwenden; *money* veruntreuen

misappropriation ['mɪsə,prəʊprɪ'eɪʃən] N Entwendung *f*; (*of money*) Veruntreuung *f*

misbegotten ['mɪsbɪ'gɒtn] ADJ (*liter*: = *illegitimate*) unehelich; (*fig*: = *ill-conceived*) schlecht konzipiert

misbehave ['mɪsbɪ'heɪv] VI sich schlecht *or* unanständig benehmen; (*child also*) ungezogen sein; **I saw him misbehaving with my wife** ich habe ihn in einer unmissverständlichen *or* eindeutigen Situation mit meiner Frau gesehen

misbehaviour, (*US*) **misbehavior** ['mɪsbɪ'heɪvjə'] N schlechtes Benehmen; (*of child also*) Ungezogenheit *f*; **sexual ~** sexuelles Fehlverhalten

misbelief ['mɪsbɪ'liːf] N irrige Annahme; (*Rel*) Irrglaube *m*

misc. *abbr of* **miscellaneous**

miscalculate ['mɪs'kælkjʊleɪt] **VT** falsch berechnen; (= *misjudge*) falsch einschätzen **VI** sich verrechnen; (= *estimate wrongly*) sich verkalkulieren; (= *misjudge*) sich verschätzen

miscalculation ['mɪs,kælkjʊ'leɪʃən] N Rechenfehler *m*; (= *wrong estimation*) Fehlkalkulation *f*; (= *misjudgement*) Fehleinschätzung *f*; **to make a ~ in sth** bei etw einen Rechenfehler machen/ etw falsch kalkulieren/etw falsch einschätzen

miscall ['mɪs'kɔːl] VT (*Sport*) *shot* falsch bewerten *or* aufrufen

miscarriage ['mɪs,kærɪdʒ] N **a** (*Med*) Fehlgeburt *f* **b** **~ of justice** Justizirrtum *m* **c** (*form, of letter*) Fehlleitung *f*

miscarry [,mɪs'kærɪ] VI **a** (*Med*) eine Fehlgeburt haben **b** (= *fail*: *plans*) fehllaufen, fehlschlagen **c** (*form, letter, goods*) fehlgeleitet werden

miscast ['mɪs'kɑːst] pret, ptp **miscast** VT *play* falsch *or* schlecht besetzen, fehlbesetzen; **the actor was clearly ~ in this role** mit diesem Schauspieler war die Rolle eindeutig fehlbesetzt

miscegenation [,mɪsɪdʒɪ'neɪʃən] N Rassenmischung *f*

miscellanea [,mɪsə'leɪnɪə] PL Verschiedenes *nt*; (*of literary compositions, objects*) (bunte) Sammlung

miscellaneous [,mɪsɪ'leɪnɪəs] ADJ verschieden; *poems* vermischt, verschiedenerlei; *collection, crowd* bunt; **~ expenses/costs/income** sonstige Aufwendungen/Kosten/Erträge; **~ items** verschiedene Artikel; (= *news items*) Verschiedenes; **a ~ collection of junk** buntgemischtes altes Zeug; **"miscellaneous"** (*on agenda, list*) „Sonstiges"; **a ~ section** Vermischtes

miscellaneously [,mɪsɪ'leɪnɪəslɪ] ADV verschieden; *grouped, collected* bunt, wahllos

miscellany [mɪ'selənɪ] N (= *collection*) (bunte) Sammlung, (buntes) Gemisch; (= *variety*) Vielfalt *f*; (*of writings*) vermischte Schriften *pl*; (*of poems, articles*) Sammelband *m*, Auswahl *f*

mischance [,mɪs'tʃɑːns] N unglücklicher Zufall; **by some ~** durch einen unglücklichen Zufall

mischief ['mɪstʃɪf] N **a** (= *roguery*) Schalk *m*, Verschmitztheit *f*; (= *naughty, foolish behaviour*) Unsinn *m*, Unfug *m*; **she's full of ~** sie hat nur Unfug im Kopf; **he's up to ~** er führt etwas im Schilde; **he's always getting into ~** er stellt dauernd etwas an; **to keep sb out of ~** aufpassen, dass jd keine Dummheiten macht; **to keep out of ~** keinen Unfug machen; **that'll keep you out of ~** dann kannst du wenigstens nichts anstellen, dann kommst du wenigstens auf keine dummen Gedanken **b** (= *trouble*) **to cause** *or* **make ~** Unfrieden stiften; **to make ~ for sb** jdm Unannehmlichkeiten bereiten, jdn in Schwierigkeiten bringen **c** (= *damage, physical injury*) Schaden *m*; **to do sb/oneself a ~** jdm/sich Schaden zufügen; (*physically*) jdm/sich etwas (an)tun; **to do ~ to sth** Schaden bei etw anrichten **d** (= *person*) Schlawiner *m*; (= *child, puppy*) Racker *m*

mischief-maker ['mɪstʃɪf,meɪkə'] N Unruhestifter(in) *m(f)*

mischievous ['mɪstʃɪvəs] ADJ **a** (= *roguish, playful*) *expression, smile* schelmisch, verschmitzt, spitzbübisch; **a ~ person** ein Schlawiner *m*; **a ~ child** ein Schlingel *or* Racker *m*; **her son is really ~** ihr Sohn ist ein Schlingel *or* hat nur Unfug im Sinn; **what ~ pranks are you up to now?** welche üblen Streiche heckst du jetzt aus?; **a ~ elf** eine Elfe, die Schabernack treibt **b** (= *malicious, troublemaking*) *rumour, suggestion* bösartig; *person* boshaft; *strike* schädlich; (= *physically disabling*) *blow* verletzend

mischievously ['mɪstʃɪvəslɪ] ADV **a** (= *roguishly*) *smile, say* schelmisch, verschmitzt, spitzbübisch; **to behave ~** Unfug anstellen, Schabernack treiben **b** (= *maliciously*) bösartig, boshaft

mischievousness ['mɪstʃɪvəsnɪs] N (= *roguery*) Verschmitztheit *f*

miscible ['mɪsɪbl] ADJ (*form*) mischbar

misconceive ['mɪskən'siːv] VT (= *understand wrongly*) verkennen, eine falsche Vorstellung haben von; (= *base on false assumption*) von einer falschen Voraussetzung ausgehen bei

misconceived ['mɪskən'siːvd] ADJ (= *mistaken*) *policy* verfehlt; *idea* irrig, falsch; *approach, action* falsch; **such fears are ~** solche Befürchtungen sind unbegründet

misconception ['mɪskən'sepʃən] N fälschliche *or* irrtümliche Annahme; (*no pl*: = *misunderstanding*) Verkennung *f*

misconduct [,mɪs'kɒndʌkt] **N a** (= *improper behaviour*) schlechtes Benehmen; (*professional*) Berufsvergehen *nt*, Verfehlung *f* im Amt; (*sexual*) Fehltritt *m*; **gross ~** grobes Fehlverhalten **b** (= *mismanagement*) schlechte Verwaltung **VT** [,mɪskən'dʌkt] schlecht verwalten **VR** [,mɪskən'dʌkt] **to ~ oneself** sich schlecht benehmen; (*professionally*) sich falsch verhalten

misconstruction ['mɪskən'strʌkʃən] N falsche Auslegung, Fehlinterpretation *f*, Missdeutung *f*

misconstrue [,mɪskən'struː] VT missverstehen, missdeuten, falsch auslegen; **you have ~d my meaning** Sie haben mich falsch verstanden; **to ~ sth as sth** etw irrtümlicherweise für etw halten

miscount ['mɪs'kaʊnt] **N** there was a ~ da hat sich jemand verzählt **VT** falsch (aus)zählen **VI** sich verzählen

miscreant ['mɪskrɪənt] N (*old*) Bösewicht *m* (*old*), Schurke *m*

misdate [,mɪs'deɪt] VT *letter* falsch datieren

misdeal ['mɪs'diːl] pret, ptp **misdealt** ['mɪs'delt] **VT** *cards* falsch (aus)geben **VI** sich vergeben, falsch geben

misdeed ['mɪs'diːd] N Missetat *f* (*old*)

misdemeanour, (*US*) **misdemeanor** [,mɪsdɪ'miːnə'] N schlechtes Betragen *or* Benehmen; (*Jur*) Vergehen *nt*, Übertretung *f*; **she was guilty of a slight ~ at the party** sie benahm sich auf der Party leicht daneben

misdiagnose ['mɪsdaɪəgnəʊz] VT **a** (*Med*) *illness* falsch diagnostizieren; *patient* eine falsche Diagnose stellen (+*dat*) **b** (= *analyse wrongly*) *problem, situation* falsch diagnostizieren *or* einschätzen

misdiagnosis [,mɪsdaɪəg'nəʊsɪs] N *pl* **misdiagnoses** [,mɪsdaɪəg'nəʊsiːz] **a** (*Med*: *of illness*) Fehldiagnose *f*, falsche Diagnose *f* **b** (= *wrong analysis*: *of problem, situation*) Fehleinschätzung *f*

misdial ['mɪs'daɪəl] VTI (*Telec*) **to ~ (the number)** sich verwählen

misdirect ['mɪsdɪ'rekt] VT **a** *letter* (= *send to wrong address*) fehlleiten; (= *address wrongly*) falsch adressieren; *energies* falsch einsetzen, vergeuden; *pass, volley* falsch platzieren; *person* (= *send astray*) in die falsche Richtung schicken; (= *misinform*) falsch informieren, eine falsche Auskunft geben (+*dat*); (*Jur*) *jury* falsch belehren **b** *campaign, operation* schlecht durchführen

misdirected ['mɪsdɪ'rektɪd] ADJ **a** (*lit*) *mail* fehlgeleitet; (= *wrongly addressed*) falsch adressiert; *shot, pass* unplatziert; **the shot was ~** der Schuss verfehlte sein Ziel **b** (*fig*) = *misapplied*) *energy, effort* vergeudet; *spending, feeling* fehlgeleitet; (= *misconceived*) *policy, campaign* verfehlt

misdirection ['mɪsdɪ'rekʃən] N **a** (*of letter*) (= *sending to wrong address*) Fehlleiten *nt*; (= *addressing wrongly*) falsche Adressierung; (*of energies*) falscher Einsatz, Vergeudung *f*; (*of person*) (= *sending astray*) falsche Richtungsweisung; (= *misinforming*) falsche Information, falsche Unterrichtung **b** (*of campaign, operation*) schlechte Durchführung

mise en scène [,miːz ɑ̃'seɪn] N (*Theat, fig*) Kulisse *f*

miser ['maɪzə'] N Geizhals *m*, Geizkragen *m*

miserable ['mɪzərəbl] ADJ **a** (= *unhappy*) *person* unglücklich, trostlos; *colour* trist; (= *ill-tempered*) griesgrämig; **I feel ~ today** ich fühle mich heute elend *or* (*ill*) miserabel; **~ with hunger/ cold** elend vor Hunger/Kälte; **a ~ old hag** eine missmutige alte Hexe; **to make sb ~** jdm Kummer machen *or* bereiten, jdn unglücklich machen; **to make life ~ for sb, to make sb's life ~** jdm das Leben zur Qual machen **b** (= *wretched, causing distress*) *headache, cold, weather* grässlich, fürchterlich; *life, existence, hovel, spectacle* erbärmlich, elend, jämmerlich; *place* öde, trostlos; **he died a ~ death** er ist elend *or* jämmerlich zugrunde *or* zu Grunde gegangen **c** (= *contemptible*) miserabel, jämmerlich, erbärmlich; *person* gemein, erbärmlich; *treatment,* *behaviour* gemein; *sum, failure* kläglich, jämmerlich; **a ~ £3** mickrige 3 Pfund (*inf*); **you ~ little wretch!** du mieses kleines Biest!, du Miststück! (*inf*); **to be a ~ failure** kläglich versagen

miserably ['mɪzərəblɪ] ADV **a** (= *unhappily*) unglücklich; *say also* kläglich **b** (= *wretchedly, distressingly*) hurt, ache, rain *schrecklich, fürchterlich; live, die* elend, jämmerlich; *poor* erbärmlich; **~ unhappy** todunglücklich (*inf*); **it was ~ cold** es war erbärmlich kalt **c** (= *contemptibly*) pay, feed, play *miserabel; fail* kläglich, jämmerlich; *treat, behave* gemein; **the wages were ~ low** die Löhne waren miserabel

misericord ['mɪzərɪkɔːd] N Miserikordie *f*

miserliness ['maɪzəlɪnɪs] N Geiz *m*

miserly ['maɪzəlɪ] ADJ geizig; *hoarding* kleinlich; *offer* knauserig; **a ~ £8** miese *or* mickrige £ 8 (*inf*); **to be ~ with sth** mit etw geizen

misery ['mɪzərɪ] N **a** (= *sadness*) Kummer *m*, Trauer *f*; **she looked the picture of ~** sie war ein Bild des Jammers **b** (= *suffering*) Qualen *pl*; (= *wretchedness*) Elend *nt*; **the ~ caused by war** das Elend des Krieges; **a life of ~** ein erbärmliches *or* jämmerliches *or* elendes Leben; **to make sb's life a ~** jdm das Leben zur Qual *or* zur Hölle machen; **to put an animal out of its ~** ein Tier von seinen Qualen erlösen; **to put sb out of his ~** (*fig*) jdn nicht länger auf die Folter spannen **c** (*Brit inf*: = *person*) Miesepeter *m* (*inf*)

misery-guts ['mɪzərɪɡʌts] N (*Brit inf*) Miesmacher(in) *m(f)* (*inf*)

misfire ['mɪsˈfaɪə'] VI (*engine*) fehlzünden, eine Fehlzündung haben; (*plan*) fehlschlagen; (*joke, trick*) danebengehen

misfit ['mɪsfɪt] N (= *person*) Außenseiter(in) *m(f)*; (= *social misfit also*) Nichtangepasste(r) *mf*; **society's ~s** die Außenseiter der Gesellschaft; **he's a real ~** er ist ein sehr schwieriger Fall; **he's always been a ~ here** er hat nie richtig hierher gepasst, er hat sich hier nie angepasst; **I felt (like) a ~** ich fühlte mich fehl am Platze

misfortune [mɪsˈfɔːtʃuːn] N (= *ill fortune, affliction*) (schweres) Schicksal *or* Los *nt*; (= *bad luck*) Pech *nt no pl*; (= *unlucky incident*) Missgeschick *nt*; **companion in ~** Leidensgenosse *m/*-genossin *f*; **it was my ~** *or* **I had the ~ to ...** ich hatte das Pech, zu ...; **a victim of ~** ein Unglücksrabe *or* Pechvogel *m*; **financial ~s** finanzielle Fehlschläge *pl*

misgiving [mɪsˈɡɪvɪŋ] ✿ 26.3 N Bedenken *pl*; **I had (certain) ~s about the scheme** bei dem Vorhaben war mir nicht ganz wohl; **I had (certain) ~s about lending him the money** bei dem Gedanken, ihm das Geld zu leihen, war mir nicht ganz wohl

misgovern ['mɪsˈɡʌvən] VT schlecht regieren, schlecht verwalten

misgovernment ['mɪsˈɡʌvənmənt] N Misswirtschaft *f* (*of in +dat*)

misguided ['mɪsˈɡaɪdɪd] ADJ töricht; *decision also, opinions* irrig; (= *misplaced*) *kindness, enthusiasm, solicitude* unangebracht, fehl am Platz; **to be ~ in sth** mit etw falsch liegen; **I think it was ~ of you** *or* **you were ~ to accept his proposal** meiner Ansicht nach waren Sie schlecht beraten, seinen Vorschlag anzunehmen

misguidedly ['mɪsˈɡaɪdɪdlɪ] ADV töricht; *believe* irrigerweise

mishandle ['mɪsˈhændl] VT *case* falsch *or* schlecht handhaben

mishap ['mɪshæp] N Missgeschick *nt*; **without (further) ~** ohne (weitere) Zwischenfälle; **he's had a slight ~** ihm ist ein kleines Missgeschick *or* Malheur passiert

mishear ['mɪsˈhɪə'] *pret, ptp* **misheard** ['mɪsˈhɜːd] VT falsch hören VI sich verhören

mishmash ['mɪʃmæʃ] N Mischmasch *m*

misinform [mɪsɪnˈfɔːm] VT falsch informieren *or* unterrichten; **you've been ~ed** man hat Sie *or* Sie sind falsch informiert; **does the press ~ the public?** verbreitet die Presse falsche Informationen?

misinformation [ˌmɪsɪnfəˈmeɪʃən] N Fehlinformation *f*, Fehlinformationen *pl*

misinterpret [ˌmɪsɪnˈtɜːprɪt] VT falsch auslegen *or* deuten; *play, novel* fehlinterpretieren, falsch auslegen; (*interpreter*) falsch wiedergeben; **it could easily be ~ed as implying ingratitude** es könnte leicht als Undankbarkeit ausgelegt werden; **he ~ed her silence as agreement** er deutete ihr Schweigen fälschlich als Zustimmung

misinterpretation [ˈmɪsɪnˌtɜːprɪˈteɪʃən] N Fehldeutung *f*, falsche Auslegung; (*of play, novel*) Fehlinterpretation *f*, falsche Auslegung; (*by interpreter*) falsche Wiedergabe

misjudge ['mɪsˈdʒʌdʒ] VT falsch einschätzen, sich verschätzen in (+*dat*); *person also* falsch beurteilen

misjudgement [ˌmɪsˈdʒʌdʒmənt] N Fehleinschätzung *f*; (*of person also*) falsche Beurteilung

miskick [ˌmɪsˈkɪk] VT **to ~ the ball** den Ball nicht richtig treffen N Fehlschuss *m*

mislay [ˌmɪsˈleɪ] *pret, ptp* **mislaid** ['mɪsˈleɪd] VT verlegen

mislead [ˌmɪsˈliːd] *pret, ptp* **misled** VT **a** (= *give wrong idea*) irreführen; **you have been misled** Sie irren *or* täuschen sich, Sie befinden sich im Irrtum (*form*); **don't be misled by appearances** lassen Sie sich nicht durch Äußerlichkeiten täuschen; **the ad misled me into thinking that ...** die Anzeige ließ mich irrtümlicherweise annehmen, dass ... **b** (= *lead into bad ways*) verleiten (*into* zu) **c** (*in guiding*) in die Irre *or* in die falsche Richtung führen

misleading [ˌmɪsˈliːdɪŋ] ADJ irreführend; **the ~ simplicity of his style** die täuschende Einfachheit seines Stils

misleadingly [ˌmɪsˈliːdɪŋlɪ] ADV *tell, say etc* irreführenderweise; *presented* irreführend; (= *deceptively*) trügerisch; **the film has a ~ violent trailer** die brutale Vorankündigung für diesen Film war irreführend; **they looked ~ angelic** sie machten einen trügerisch engelhaften Eindruck

misled [ˌmɪsˈled] *pret, ptp of* **mislead**

mismanage ['mɪsˈmænɪdʒ] VT *company, finances* schlecht verwalten; *affair, deal* schlecht abwickeln *or* handhaben

mismanagement ['mɪsˈmænɪdʒmənt] N Misswirtschaft *f*

mismatch ['mɪsˈmætʃ] N **to be a ~** nicht zusammenpassen VI nicht zusammenpassen

misname ['mɪsˈneɪm] VT unzutreffend benennen

misnomer ['mɪsˈnəʊmə'] N unzutreffende Bezeichnung

misogamist [mɪˈsɒɡəmɪst] N Misogam *m*

misogamy [mɪˈsɒɡəmɪ] N Misogamie *f*

misogynist [mɪˈsɒdʒɪnɪst] N Frauenfeind *m*, Misogyn *m* (*geh*)

misogynistic [mɪˌsɒdʒɪˈnɪstɪk] ADJ frauenfeindlich, misogyn (*geh*)

misogyny [mɪˈsɒdʒɪnɪ] N Frauenfeindlichkeit *f*, Misogynie *f* (*geh*)

misplace ['mɪsˈpleɪs] VT **a** *document, file etc* falsch einordnen; (= *mislay*) verlegen **b** **to be ~d** (*confidence, trust, affection*) fehl am Platz sein, unangebracht sein; **her ~d trust** ihr törichtes Vertrauen

misplay [ˌmɪsˈpleɪ] VT verschießen

misprint ['mɪsprɪnt] N Druckfehler *m* [ˌmɪsˈprɪnt] verdrucken

mispronounce [ˌmɪsprəˈnaʊns] VT falsch aussprechen

mispronunciation ['mɪsprəˌnʌnsɪˈeɪʃən] N falsche *or* fehlerhafte Aussprache

misquotation [ˌmɪskwəʊˈteɪʃən] N falsches Zitat; **his constant ~ of Shakespeare** dass er Shakespeare ständig falsch zitiert

misquote ['mɪsˈkwəʊt] VT falsch zitieren; **he was ~d as having said ...** man unterstellte ihm, gesagt zu haben ...

misread ['mɪsˈriːd] *pret, ptp* **misread** ['mɪsˈred] VT falsch *or* nicht richtig lesen; (= *misinterpret*) falsch verstehen

misrepresent ['mɪsˌreprɪˈzent] VT falsch darstellen; *facts also* verdrehen; *ideas* verfälschen; **he was ~ed in the papers** seine Worte etc wurden von der Presse verfälscht *or* entstellt wiedergegeben; **he was ~ed as being for the strike** er wurde zu Unrecht als Befürworter des Streiks hingestellt

misrepresentation ['mɪsˌreprɪzənˈteɪʃən] N falsche Darstellung; (*of facts also*) Verdrehung *f*; (*of theory*) Verfälschung *f*; **to be accused of ~** der Verdrehung (*gen*) von Tatsachen beschuldigt werden

misrule ['mɪsˈruːl] N schlechte Regierung; (*by government also*) Misswirtschaft *f* VT schlecht regieren

miss¹ [mɪs] N **a** (= *shot*) Fehltreffer *m or* -schuss *m*; (= *failure*) Misserfolg *m*, Pleite *f* (*inf*), Reinfall *m* (*inf*); **his first shot was a ~** sein erster Schuss ging daneben; **it was a near ~** das war eine knappe Sache; (*shot*) das war knapp daneben; **we had a near ~ with that car** wir wären fast mit diesem Auto zusammengestoßen; **the sales department voted it a ~** in der Verkaufsabteilung räumte man dem keine Chance ein; **a ~ is as good as a mile** (*prov*) knapp vorbei ist auch daneben

b **to give sb a ~** (*inf*) sich (*dat*) etw schenken VT **a** (= *fail to hit, catch, reach, find, attend etc: by accident*) verpassen; *chance, appointment, bus, concert* verpassen, versäumen; (= *deliberately not attend*) nicht gehen zu *or* in (+*acc*); (= *not hit, find*) *target, ball, way, step, vocation, place, house* verfehlen; (*shot, ball*) verfehlen, vorbeigehen an (+*dat*); **to ~ breakfast** nicht frühstücken; **to be too late for** das Frühstück verpassen; **they ~ed each other in the crowd** sie verpassten *or* verfehlten sich in der Menge; **to ~ the boat** *or* **bus** (*fig*) den Anschluss verpassen; **he ~ed school for a week** er hat eine Woche lang die Schule versäumt; **~ a turn** einmal aussetzen; **have I ~ed my turn?** bin ich übergangen worden?; **if you ~ a pill** wenn Sie vergessen, eine Pille zu nehmen

b (= *fail to experience*) verpassen; (*deliberately*) sich (*dat*) entgehen lassen; (= *fail to hear or perceive*) nicht mitbekommen, verpassen; (*deliberately*) überhören/-sehen; **I ~ed that** das ist mir entgangen; **he doesn't ~ much** (*inf*) ihm entgeht so schnell nichts; **you haven't ~ed much!** da hast du nicht viel verpasst *or* versäumt!; **I wouldn't have ~ed it for anything** das hätte ich mir nicht entgehen lassen wollen

c (= *fail to achieve*) *prize* nicht bekommen *or* schaffen (*inf*); **he narrowly ~ed being first/becoming president** er wäre beinahe auf den ersten Platz gekommen/Präsident geworden

d (= *avoid*) *obstacle* (noch) ausweichen können (+*dat*); (= *escape*) entgehen (+*dat*); **to ~ doing sth** etw fast *or* um ein Haar tun; **the car just ~ed the tree** das Auto wäre um ein Haar gegen den Baum gefahren; **we narrowly ~ed having an accident** wir hätten um ein Haar einen Unfall gehabt

e (= *leave out*) auslassen; (= *overlook, fail to deal with*) übersehen; **my heart ~ed a beat** mir stockte das Herz

f (= *notice or regret absence of*) vermissen; **I ~ him/my old car** er/mein altes Auto fehlt mir; **he won't be ~ed** keiner wird ihn vermissen; **he'll never ~ it** er wird es nie merken(, dass es ihm fehlt)

VI **a** (= *not hit*) nicht treffen; (*punching*) danebenschlagen; (*shooting*) danebenschießen; (= *not catch*) danebengreifen; (= *not be present, not attend*) fehlen; (*ball, shot, punch*) danebengehen; (*Aut, engine*) aussetzen

b (*inf*, = *fail*) **you can't ~** da kann nichts schief gehen; **he never ~es** er schafft es immer

▶ **miss out** VT *sep* auslassen; (= *accidentally not see*) übersehen; *last line or paragraph etc* weglassen; **my name was missed out from the list** mein Name fehlte auf der Liste VI (*inf*) zu kurz kommen; **to miss out on sth** etw verpassen; (= *get less*) bei etw zu kurz kommen; **he's been missing out on life** er ist im Leben zu kurz gekommen

miss² N **a** Miss Fräulein *nt*, Frl. *abbr*; **Miss Germany 1998** (die) Miss Germany von 1998 **b** (= *girl*) **a proper little ~** ein richtiges kleines Fräulein; **look here, you cheeky little ~!** hör mal, mein (kleines) Fräulein! **c** (= *term of address*) (*to waitress etc*) Bedienung, Fräulein (*dated*); (*to teacher*) Frau X

missal ['mɪsəl] N Messbuch *nt*, Missale *nt*

misshapen ['mɪs'ʃeɪpən] ADJ missgebildet; *plant, tree also* verwachsen; *vegetables* unförmig, missraten

missile ['mɪsaɪl] N **a** (= *stone, javelin etc*) (Wurf-)geschoss *nt* **b** (= *rocket*) Rakete *f*, Flugkörper *m* (*form*)

missile: missile base N Raketenbasis *f*; **missile defence system** (*Brit*), **missile defense system** (*US*) N Raketenabwehrsystem *nt*; **missile launcher** N Abschuss- or Startrampe *f*; (= *vehicle*) Raketenwerfer *m*; **missile site** N Raketenbasis *f*

missilry ['mɪsɪlrɪ] N (= *science*) Raketentechnik *f*; (= *missiles*) Raketen(waffen) *pl*

missing ['mɪsɪŋ] ADJ (= *not able to be found*) *person, soldier, aircraft, boat* vermisst; *object* verschwunden; (= *not there*) fehlend; **to be ~/have gone ~** fehlen; (*person, aircraft, boat etc*) vermisst werden; **to go ~** (*person, aircraft, boat etc*) vermisst werden; (*object*) verloren gehen; **the coat has two buttons ~, two buttons are ~ from the coat** an dem Mantel fehlen zwei Knöpfe; **my name is ~ from the list** mein Name fehlt auf der Liste; **he has a tooth ~** er hat eine Zahnlücke; **we are £50 ~** uns (*dat*) fehlen £ 50; **the ~ clue to his identity** der Schlüssel zu seiner Identität; **~ in action** vermisst; (*Biol*) Missing link *nt*, Übergangs- or Zwischenform *f*

missing link N fehlendes Glied

missing person N Vermisste(r) *mf*; **~s bureau/file** Vermisstenbüro *nt*/-liste *f*

mission ['mɪʃən] N **a** (= *business, task*) Auftrag *m*; (= *calling*) Aufgabe *f*, Berufung *f*; (*Mil*) Befehl *m*; (= *operation*) Einsatz *m*; **what is their ~?** welchen Auftrag haben sie?, wie lauten ihre Befehle?; **our ~ is to ...** wir sind damit beauftragt, zu ...; **the soldiers' ~ was to ...** die Soldaten hatten den Befehl erhalten, zu ...; **to send sb on a secret ~** jdn mit einer geheimen Mission beauftragen; **he's on a secret ~** er ist in geheimer Mission unterwegs; **sense of ~** Sendungsbewusstsein *nt*; **~ accomplished** (*Mil, fig*) Befehl ausgeführt; (*without military overtones*) Auftrag ausgeführt **b** (= *journey*) Mission *f*; **~ of inquiry** Erkundungsreise *f*; **Henry Kissinger's ~ to the Middle East** Kissingers Nahostmission **c** (= *people on mission*) Gesandtschaft *f*, Delegation *f*; (*Pol*) Mission *f*; **trade ~** Handelsreise *f* **d** (*Rel*) Mission *f*; **~ hut** Mission(sstation) *f*

missionary ['mɪʃənrɪ] N Missionar(in) *m(f)* ADJ missionarisch

missionary position N (*fig inf*) Missionarsstellung *f*

mission: mission control N (*Space*) Kontrollzentrum *nt*, Flugleitung *f*; **mission controller** N (*Space*) Flugleiter(in) *m(f)*; **mission statement** N (*of company*) (Kurzdarstellung der) Firmenphilosophie *f*

missis ['mɪsɪz] N (*Brit inf*) (= *wife*) bessere Hälfte (*hum inf*), Alte *f* (*pej inf*), Olle *f* (*inf*); (= *mistress of household*) Frau *f* des Hauses; **yes, ~** ja(wohl)

Mississippi [mɪsɪ'sɪpɪ] N Mississippi *m*

missive ['mɪsɪv] N (*form, old*) Missive *f* (*form*)

Missouri [mɪ'zuːrɪ] N (= *river*) Missouri *m*; (= *state*) Missouri *nt*

misspell ['mɪs'spel] *pret, ptp* misspelled *or* misspelt VT falsch schreiben

misspelling ['mɪs'spelɪŋ] N (= *act*) falsches Schreiben; (= *spelling mistake*) Rechtschreibfehler *m*

misspelt ['mɪs'spelt] *pret, ptp of* misspell

misspent [ˌmɪs'spent] ADJ vergeudet, verschwendet; **I regret my ~ youth** ich bedaure es, in meiner Jugend so ein liederliches Leben geführt zu haben; (= *wasted youth*) ich bedaure es, meine Jugend so vergeudet or vertan zu haben

misstate ['mɪs'steɪt] VT falsch darlegen or darstellen

misstatement ['mɪs'steɪtmənt] N falsche Darstellung

missus ['mɪsɪz] N (*inf*) = missis

missy ['mɪsɪ] N (*inf*) Fräuleinchen *nt* (*inf*), kleines Fräulein

mist [mɪst] N **a** Nebel *m*; (*in liquid*) Trübung *f*; (= *haze*) Dunst *m*; (*on glass etc*) Beschlag *m* **b** (*fig*) **through a ~ of tears** durch einen Tränenschleier; **it is lost in the ~s of time** das liegt im Dunkel der Vergangenheit; **the ~s of confusion surrounding the affair** das undurchsichtige Dunkel, in das die Angelegenheit gehüllt ist VI **a** (*window etc*) beschlagen **b** (*fig: eyes*) sich verschleiern (*geh*)

▶ **mist over** VI (= *become cloudy*) sich trüben; (*glass, mirror: also* **mist up**) (sich) beschlagen; **her eyes misted over with tears** Tränen verschleierten ihren Blick (*liter*) VT *sep* **the condensation is misting over the windows** durch den Dampf beschlagen die Fensterscheiben

mistakable [mɪ'steɪkəbl] ADJ **the twins are easily ~** man kann die Zwillinge leicht miteinander verwechseln

mistake [mɪ'steɪk] N Fehler *m*; **to make a ~** (*in writing, calculating etc*) einen Fehler machen; (= *be mistaken*) sich irren; **you're making a big ~ in marrying him** Sie machen or begehen (*form*) einen schweren Fehler, wenn Sie ihn heiraten; **to make the ~ of asking too much** den Fehler machen or begehen (*form*), zu viel zu verlangen; **my biggest ~ was to ...** mein größter Fehler war, zu ...; **what a ~ (to make)!** wie kann man nur (so einen Fehler machen)!; **by ~** aus Versehen, versehentlich; **she was shot in ~ for her sister** sie wurde irrtümlicherweise anstelle ihrer Schwester erschossen; **there must be some ~** da muss ein Fehler or Irrtum vorliegen; **the ~ is mine** der Fehler liegt bei mir; **there's no ~ about it, ...** (es besteht) kein Zweifel, ...; **let there be no ~ about it, make no ~ (about it)** ein(e)s steht fest: ...; **make no ~, I mean what I say** damit wir uns nicht falsch verstehen: mir ist es ernst or Ernst; **it's freezing and no ~!** (*inf*) (ich kann dir sagen,) das ist vielleicht eine Kälte! (*inf*) VT *pret* mistook, *ptp* mistaken **a** *words, meaning, remarks etc* falsch auffassen or verstehen; *seriousness, cause* verkennen, nicht erkennen; *house, road, time of train* sich irren or vertun (*inf*) in (+*dat*); **to ~ sb's meaning** jdn falsch verstehen; **I mistook you** or **what you meant** ich habe Sie falsch or nicht richtig verstanden; **to ~ sb's identity** jdn verwechseln; **there's no mistaking the urgency of the situation** die Dringlichkeit der Situation steht außer Frage; **there's no mistaking her writing** ihre Schrift ist unverkennbar; **there's no mistaking what he meant** er hat sich unmissverständlich ausgedrückt; **there was no mistaking his anger** er war eindeutig wütend **b** **to ~ A for B** A mit B verwechseln, A für B halten; **it cannot possibly be ~n for anything else** das ist doch unverkennbar!, das kann man doch gar nicht verwechseln! **c** **to be ~n** sich irren; **to be ~n about sth/sb** sich in etw/jdm irren; **to be ~n in thinking that ...** fälschlicherweise annehmen, dass ...; **you are badly ~n there** da irren Sie sich aber gewaltig!; **if I am not ~n ..., unless I am (very much) ~n ...** wenn mich nicht alles täuscht ..., wenn ich mich nicht irre ...

mistaken [mɪ'steɪkən] **♦** 12.1 ADJ (= *wrong*) *idea* falsch; (= *misplaced*) *loyalty, kindness* unangebracht, fehl am Platz; *affection, trust* töricht; **in**

the ~ belief that ... in der falschen or irrigen Annahme, dass ...; **to be under** or **have the ~ impression that ...** fälschlicherweise vermuten, dass ...; **a case of ~ identity** eine Verwechslung

mistakenly [mɪ'steɪkənlɪ] ADV fälschlicherweise, irrtümlicherweise; (= *by accident*) versehentlich

mister ['mɪstə] N **a** (*abbr* **Mr**) Herr *m*; (*on envelope*) Herrn; (*with politicians' names etc*) *not translated* **b** (*inf*, = *sir*) *not translated* **please, ~, can you tell me ...?** können Sie mir bitte sagen ...?; **now listen here, ~** hören Sie mal her

mistime ['mɪs'taɪm] VT **a** *act* einen ungünstigen Zeitpunkt wählen für; **a badly ~d political announcement** eine politische Erklärung, die zu einem denkbar ungünstigen Zeitpunkt kommt; **he ~d his entrance** (*actor*) er trat zum falschen Zeitpunkt auf **b** *race* falsch stoppen

mistle thrush ['mɪsl.θrʌʃ] N Misteldrossel *f*

mistletoe ['mɪsltəʊ] N Mistel *f*; (= *sprig*) Mistelzweig *m*

mistook [mɪ'stʊk] *pret of* mistake

mistral [mɪ'strɑːl] N Mistral *m*

mistranslate ['mɪstrænz'leɪt] VT falsch übersetzen

mistranslation ['mɪstrænz'leɪʃən] N (= *act*) falsche Übersetzung; (= *error also*) Übersetzungsfehler *m*

mistreat [mɪs'triːt] VT schlecht behandeln; (*violently*) misshandeln

mistreatment [ˌmɪs'triːtmənt] N schlechte Behandlung; (*violent*) Misshandlung *f*

mistress ['mɪstrɪs] N **a** (*of house, horse, dog*) Herrin *f*; **she is now ~ of the situation** sie ist jetzt Herr der Lage **b** (= *lover*) Geliebte *f*, Mätresse *f* (*old*) **c** (= *teacher*) Lehrerin *f* **d** (*old*, = *Mrs*) Frau *f*

mistrial [ˌmɪs'traɪəl] N **it was declared a ~** das Urteil wurde wegen Verfahrensmängeln aufgehoben

mistrust ['mɪs'trʌst] N Misstrauen *nt* (*of gegenüber*) VT misstrauen (+*dat*)

mistrustful [ˌmɪs'trʌstfʊl] ADJ misstrauisch; **to be ~ of sb/sth** jdm/einer Sache misstrauen

misty ['mɪstɪ] ADJ (+*er*) *day, morning* neblig; (= *hazy*) dunstig; *mountain peaks* in Nebel gehüllt; *colour* gedeckt; (= *fine*) *rain* fein; **~ weather** Nebelwetter *nt*, Nebel *m*; **a ~ view of the valley** ein Blick auf das (nebel)verhangene or dunstige Tal; **a ~ drizzle** ein feiner Regenschleier *m* (*fig*: = *blurred*) *form, figure, memory* verschwommen; **her eyes grew ~, a ~ look came into her eyes** ihr Blick verschleierte sich; **~-eyed, with ~ eyes** mit verschleiertem Blick **c** *glasses* (= *misted up*) beschlagen; (= *opaque*) milchig; *liquid* trübe; **the window is getting ~** das Fenster beschlägt

misunderstand ['mɪsʌndə'stænd] *pret, ptp* misunderstood VT falsch verstehen, missverstehen; **don't ~ me ...** verstehen Sie mich nicht falsch ... VI **I think you've misunderstood** ich glaube, Sie haben das missverstanden or falsch verstanden

misunderstanding ['mɪsʌndə'stændɪŋ] N **a** Missverständnis *nt*; **there must be some ~** da muss ein Missverständnis vorliegen; **so that no ~ is possible** um Missverständnissen vorzubeugen; **let there be no ~ (about it) ...** damit keine Missverständnisse entstehen: ..., damit wir uns nicht missverstehen: ... **b** (= *disagreement*) Meinungsverschiedenheit *f*

misunderstood ['mɪsʌndə'stʊd] *ptp of* misunderstand ADJ unverstanden; *artist, playwright* verkannt

misuse ['mɪs'juːs] N Missbrauch *m*; (*of words*) falscher Gebrauch; (*of funds*) Zweckentfremdung *f*; **~ of power/authority** Macht-/Amtsmissbrauch *m* VT ['mɪs'juːz] missbrauchen; *words* falsch gebrauchen; *funds* zweckentfremden

misword ['mɪs'wɜːd] VT *contract etc* falsch formulieren

MIT (US) abbr of **Massachusetts Institute of Technology**

mite[1] [maɪt] N (Zool) Milbe f

mite[2] N a (Hist, = coin) Scherf m, Heller m; **to contribute one's ~ to sth** sein Scherflein zu etw beitragen b (= small amount) bisschen nt; **well, just a ~ then** na gut, ein (ganz) kleines bisschen c (Brit = child) Würmchen nt (inf); **poor little ~!** armes Wurm! (inf) ADV (inf) **a ~ surprised/disappointed** etwas or ein bisschen überrascht/enttäuscht; **could you wait a ~ longer?** können Sie noch ein Momentchen warten? (inf)

miter N (US) = **mitre**

mitigate ['mɪtɪgeɪt] VT pain lindern; punishment mildern; **mitigating circumstances/factors** mildernde Umstände pl

mitigation [ˌmɪtɪ'geɪʃən] N (of pain) Linderung f; (of punishment) Milderung f; **to say something in ~** etwas zu jds/seiner Verteidigung anführen; **have you anything to say in ~ of sentence?** haben Sie zu dem Urteil noch irgendetwas Entlastendes vorzubringen?

mitre, (US) **miter** ['maɪtə'] N a (Eccl) Mitra f b (Tech: also **mitre joint**) Gehrung f, Gehrfuge f VT (Tech) gehren

mitt [mɪt] N a = **mitten a** b (= baseball glove) Baseballhandschuh m c (inf, = hand) Pfote f (inf)

mitten ['mɪtn] N a Fausthandschuh m, Fäustling m; (with bare fingers) Handschuh m ohne Finger or mit halben Fingern b **mittens** PL (Boxing) Boxhandschuhe pl

mix [mɪks] N Mischung f; **a real ~ of people** eine bunte Mischung von Menschen; **a good social ~ at the gala performance** ein gut gemischtes Publikum auf der Galavorstellung; **a broad racial ~** ein breites Spektrum verschiedener Rassen; **product ~** Produktspanne f; **cement ~** Zementmischung f; **a wool ~ pullover** ein Pullover m aus verschiedenen Fasern

VT a (= combine) (ver)mischen; drinks (= prepare) mischen, mixen; (Cook) ingredients verrühren; dough zubereiten; salad untermengen, wenden; **you shouldn't ~ your drinks** man sollte nicht mehrere Sachen durcheinander trinken; **to ~ sth into sth** etw unter etw (acc) mengen or mischen; **I never ~ business with or and pleasure** ich vermische nie Geschäftliches mit Privates b (= confuse) durcheinander bringen; **to ~ sb/ sth with sb/sth** jdn/etw mit jdm/etw verwechseln c **to ~ it** (dated inf) sich prügeln, sich kloppen (inf); **the gangs were really ~ing it** die Banden haben sich eine ganz schöne Schlägerei geliefert (inf)

VI a (= combine) sich mischen lassen; (chemical substances, races) sich vermischen b (= go together) zusammenpassen; **business and pleasure don't ~** Arbeit und Vergnügen lassen sich nicht verbinden c (people) (= get on) miteinander auskommen; (= mingle) sich vermischen; (= associate) miteinander verkehren; **to ~ with sb** mit jdm auskommen, sich unter jdn mischen, mit jdm verkehren; **he finds it hard to ~** er ist nicht sehr gesellig or kontaktfreudig; **to ~ well** kontaktfreudig or gesellig sein; **he ~es in high society** er verkehrt in den besseren Kreisen

▶ **mix in** VT sep egg, water unterrühren

▶ **mix up** VT sep a (= combine) vermischen; ingredients verrühren; (= prepare) medicine mischen b (= get in a muddle) durcheinander bringen; (= confuse with sth/sb else) verwechseln c (= involve) **to mix sb up in sth** jdn in etw (acc) hineinziehen; in crime etc also jdn in etw (acc) verwickeln; **to be mixed up in sth** in etw (acc) verwickelt sein; **he's got himself mixed up with the police** er hat Schereien mit der Polizei bekommen; **he's got himself mixed up with that gang** er hat sich mit dieser Bande eingelassen d **to mix it up** (US inf) sich prügeln (with mit); (non-physically) sich anlegen (with mit)

mixed [mɪkst] ADJ a (= assorted) gemischt; **~ nuts/biscuits** Nuss-/Keksmischung f b (= of both sexes) choir, bathing, school gemischt; **in ~ company** in gemischter Gesellschaft c (= varied) gemischt; (= both good and bad) unterschiedlich; **of ~ race** or **parentage** gemischtrassig; **a class of ~ ability** eine Klasse mit Schülern unterschiedlicher Leistungsstärke; **a ~ set of people** eine bunt zusammengewürfelte Gruppe; **I have ~ feelings about him** ich habe ihm gegenüber zwiespältige Gefühle; **to have ~ feelings about sth** etw mit gemischten Gefühlen betrachten; **with ~ results** mit wechselndem or geteiltem Erfolg

mixed: mixed-ability ADJ group, class mit unterschiedlicher Leistungsstärke; **~ teaching** gemeinsamer Unterricht für Schüler mit unterschiedlicher Leistungsstärke; **mixed bag** N bunte Mischung; **the students are a bit of a ~** die Studenten sind eine ziemlich bunt gemischte Truppe (inf); **a very ~ of activities** eine bunte Mischung unterschiedlichster Aktivitäten; **mixed blessing** N it's a ~ das ist ein zweischneidiges Schwert; **children are a ~** Kinder sind kein reines Vergnügen; **mixed bunch** N (lit) bunt gemischter Blumenstrauß; (fig: = people) eine bunt gemischte Truppe (inf); **a ~ of products** ein bunt gemischtes Angebot; **mixed cloth** N meliertes Tuch; **mixed doubles** PL (Sport) gemischtes Doppel; **mixed drink** N Mixgetränk nt; **mixed economy** N gemischte Wirtschaftsform; **mixed farming** N Ackerbau und Viehzucht (+pl vb); **mixed grill** N Grillteller m; **mixed marriage** N Mischehe f; **mixed-media** ADJ work mittelmedial; **mixed metaphor** N gemischte Metapher, Bildervermengung f; **mixed pickles** PL Mixedpickles pl, Mixed Pickles pl; **mixed-race** ADJ children gemischtrassig; **mixed school** N Koedukationsschule f; **mixed-up** ADJ ATTR , **mixed up** ADJ PRED durcheinander pred; (= muddled) person also, ideas konfus; **she's just a crazy ~ kid** (inf) sie ist total verdreht; **I'm all mixed up** ich bin völlig durcheinander; **he got all mixed up** er hat alles durcheinander gebracht; **I got mixed up about the times** ich habe die Zeiten verwechselt

mixer ['mɪksə'] N a (= food mixer) Mixer m, Mixgerät nt; (= cement mixer) Mischmaschine f b (for drink) Cola, Ginger Ale, Tonic etc zum Auffüllen von alkoholischen Mixgetränken c (Rad) (= person) Toningenieur(in) m(f), Mixer(in) m(f); (= thing) Mischpult nt d (= sociable person) **to be a good ~** kontaktfreudig sein; **David's not much of a ~** David ist ziemlich kontaktarm or verschlossen e (US inf) Party f zum Kennenlernen; (for new students) Erstsemesterfete f

mixer tap N (Brit) Mischbatterie f

mixture ['mɪkstʃə'] N Mischung f; (Med) Mixtur f; (Cook) Gemisch nt; (= cake mixture, dough) Teig m; **~ of teas** Teemischung f; **~ of gases** Gasgemisch nt; **they spoke to each other in a ~ of French and English** sie haben miteinander eine Mischung aus Französisch und Englisch gesprochen; **I've had quite a ~ of drinks tonight** ich habe heute Abend ziemlich viel durcheinander getrunken; **a ~ of comedy and tragedy** eine Mischung aus Komödie und Tragödie; **fold the eggs into the cheese ~** heben Sie die Eier ins Käsegemisch or in die Käsemischung unter

mix-up ['mɪksʌp] N Durcheinander nt; **there seemed to be some ~ about which train ...** es schien völlig unklar, welchen Zug ...; **there must have been a ~** da muss irgendetwas schief gelaufen sein (inf)

MLA (Brit, Pol) abbr of **Member of the Legislative Assembly** Mitglied nt der legislativen Versammlung Nordirlands

MLR (Brit) abbr of **minimum lending rate**

M'lud [məˈlʌd] (Brit Jur) abbr of **My Lord** Euer Ehren

mm abbr of **millimetre(s)** mm

MMR (Med) abbr of **measles, mumps, rubella**

MMS (Telec) abbr of **Multimedia Messaging Service** MMS m

mnemonic [nɪˈmɒnɪk] ADJ a Gedächtnis-; **~ trick** or **device** Gedächtnisstütze f; **~ rhyme** Eselsbrücke f (inf) b (Comput) mnemotechnisch N Gedächtnisstütze or -hilfe f, Eselsbrücke f (inf)

MO a abbr of **money order** b abbr of **medical officer** c abbr of **modus operandi**

mo [məʊ] N (inf) abbr of **moment**

moan [məʊn] N a (= groan) Stöhnen nt; (of wind) Seufzen nt, Raunen nt (geh); (of trees etc) Raunen nt (geh) b (= grumble) Gejammer nt no pl (inf); **to have a ~ about sth** über etw (acc) jammern or schimpfen VI a (= groan) stöhnen; (wind, trees) raunen (geh) b (= grumble) jammern, schimpfen (about über +acc); **~, ~, ~, that's all she does** sie ist ständig am Maulen (inf) VT **...**, **he ~ed ...** stöhnte er; **he ~ed a sigh of relief** er stöhnte erleichtert auf

moaner ['məʊnə'] N (inf) Miesepeter m (inf), Mäkelliese f (inf)

moaning ['məʊnɪŋ] N a Stöhnen nt; (of wind) Seufzen nt; (of trees etc) Raunen nt (geh) b (= grumbling) Gestöhn(e) nt

moat [məʊt] N Wassergraben m; (of castle also) Burggraben m

moated ['məʊtɪd] ADJ von einem Wassergraben umgeben

mob [mɒb] N a (= crowd) Horde f, Schar f; (riotous, violent) Mob m no pl; **an undisciplined ~** ein undisziplinierter Haufen; **a ~ gathered to burn the houses** der Mob or Pöbel lief zusammen, um die Häuser zu verbrennen; **the crowd became a ~** das Volk wurde zur wütenden Menge; **they went in a ~ to the town hall** sie stürmten zum Rathaus b (inf) (= criminal gang) Bande f; (fig: = clique) Haufen m, Bande f; **which ~ were you in?** (Mil) bei welchem Haufen warst du denn? (inf); **the Mob** (= the Mafia) die Maf(f)ia c **the ~** (pej, = the masses) die Masse(n pl) VT herfallen über (+acc), sich stürzen auf (+acc); actor, pop star also belagern; **the prisoner was ~bed** die Menge fiel über den Gefangenen her

mobcap ['mɒbkæp] N (Hist) (Spitzen)haube f

mobile ['məʊbaɪl] ADJ a person beweglich, mobil; (= having means of transport) beweglich, motorisiert; (Sociol) mobil; **the patient is ~ already** der Patient kann schon aufstehen b X-ray unit etc fahrbar; missile launcher, laboratory mobil c mind wendig, beweglich; face, expression, features lebhaft, beweglich N a (= mobile phone) Handy nt b (= decoration) Mobile nt

mobile: mobile canteen N Kantine f auf Rädern, mobile Küche; (Mil) Feldküche f; **mobile home** N Wohnwagen m; **mobile library** N Fahrbücherei f; **mobile phone** N Mobiltelefon nt, Handy nt; **mobile shop** N (Brit) Verkaufswagen m; **mobile walkway** N (US) Rollsteg m

mobility [məʊˈbɪlɪtɪ] N (of person) Beweglichkeit f; (of mind also) Wendigkeit f; (of features, face etc also) Lebhaftigkeit f; (of work force, Sociol) Mobilität f; **a car gives you ~** ein Auto macht Sie beweglicher

mobilization [ˌməʊbɪlaɪˈzeɪʃən] N Mobilisierung f; (Mil also) Mobilmachung f

mobilize ['məʊbɪlaɪz] VT mobilisieren; (Mil also) mobil machen VI mobil machen

mob rule N Herrschaft f des Pöbels

mobster ['mɒbstə'] N (esp US) Gangster(in) m(f), Bandit(in) m(f)

mob violence N Massenausschreitungen pl

moccasin ['mɒkəsɪn] N Mokassin m

mocha ['mɒkə] N Mokka m

mock [mɒk] N a **to make a ~ of sth** etw ad absurdum führen b (= put an end to) etw vereiteln or zunichte machen b **mocks** (Brit Sch inf) Probeprüfungen pl ADJ attr emotions gespielt; crash, examination si-

muliert; *execution, trial* gestellt; **~ leather/fur** Kunstleder *nt*/-pelz *m*; **the house is ~ Tudor** das Haus ist nachgemachtes Tudor; **~ attack/ fight** Scheinangriff/-kampf *m*
VT a (= *ridicule*) sich lustig machen über (+*acc*), verspotten
b (= *mimic*) nachmachen, nachäffen
c (= *defy*) trotzen (+*dat*); *law* sich hinwegsetzen über (+*acc*); (= *set at nought*) *plans, efforts* vereiteln, zunichte machen
VI to ~ at sb/sth sich über jdn/etw lustig machen; **don't ~** mokier dich nicht!, spotte nicht! (*geh*)

mocker ['mɒkə'] N **a** Spötter(in) *m(f)*, spöttischer Mensch **b to put the ~s on sth** (*Brit, inf*) etw vermasseln (*inf*)

mockery ['mɒkərɪ] N **a** (= *derision*) Spott *m* **b** (= *object of ridicule*) Gespött *nt*; **they made a ~ of him** sie machten ihn zum Gespött der Leute; **to make a ~ of sth** etw lächerlich machen; (= *prove its futility*) etw ad absurdum führen; **inflation will make a ~ of our budget** durch die Inflation wird unser Haushaltsplan zur Farce **c this is a ~ of justice** das spricht jeglicher Gerechtigkeit Hohn; **it was a ~ of a trial** der Prozess war eine einzige Farce; **what a ~ (this is)!** das ist doch glatter Hohn *or* der reinste Hohn!

mock: mock-heroic ADJ (*Liter*) heroisch-komisch; **~ poem** komisches Epos; **mock-heroics** PL (*Liter*) heroisch-komische Passage(n) *f(pl)*

mocking ['mɒkɪŋ] ADJ spöttisch N Spott *m*

mockingbird ['mɒkɪŋˌbɜːd] N Spottdrossel *f*

mockingly ['mɒkɪŋlɪ] ADV spöttisch, voller Spott; **she ~ repeated his words** sie äffte seine Worte nach

mock: mock moon N (*Astron*) Nebenmond *m*; **mock orange** N Falscher Jasmin, Pfeifenstrauch *m*; **mock trial** N (*Jur*) Scheinprozess *m*; **mock turtle soup** N Mockturtlesuppe *f*; **mock-up** N Modell *nt* in Originalgröße

MOD (*Brit*) *abbr of* **Ministry of Defence**

mod [mɒd] **ADJ** (*dated sl*) modern, poppig (*inf*) N modisch gekleideter Halbstarker in den 60er Jahren

modal ['məʊdl] ADJ modal; **~ verb** Modalverb *nt*

modality [məʊ'dælɪtɪ] N Modalität *f*

mod cons ['mɒd'kɒnz] (*Brit inf*) *pl abbr of* **modern conveniences** mod. Komf., (moderner) Komfort

mode [məʊd] N **a** (*Gram*) Modus *m*; (*Mus*) Tonart *f*; (*Philos*) Modalität *f* (= *way*) Art *f* (und Weise); (= *form*) Form *f*; **~ of transport** Transportmittel *nt*; **~ of life** Lebensweise *f*; (*Biol*) Lebensform *f* **c** (*Fashion*) Mode *f*; **to be the ~** in Mode sein **d** (*Comput*) Modus *m*, Mode *m*

model ['mɒdl] N **a** Modell *nt*; **to make sth on the ~ of sth** etw (*acc*) einer Sache (*dat*) nachbilden; **it is built on the ~ of the Doge's Palace** es ist eine Nachbildung des Dogenpalastes; **our democracy is based on the ~ of Greece** unsere Demokratie ist nach dem Vorbild Griechenlands aufgebaut
b (= *perfect example*) Muster *nt* (of an +*dat*); **this book is a ~ of objectivity** dieses Buch ist ein Muster an Objektivität; **to hold sb up as a ~** jdn als Vorbild hinstellen
c (*artist's, photographer's*) Modell *nt*; (= *fashion model*) Mannequin *nt*; (= *male model*) Dressman *m*
d (*of car, dress, machine etc*) Modell *nt*
ADJ a Modell-; **~ railway** (*Brit*) *or* **railroad** (*US*) Modelleisenbahn *f*; **~ house** Puppenhaus *nt* **b** (= *perfect*) vorbildlich, mustergültig; **~ pupil** Musterschüler(in) *m(f)*
VT a to ~ X on Y Y als Vorlage *or* Muster für X benutzen; **X is** (*acc*) *or* **~ed** (*US*) **on Y** Y dient als Vorlage *or* Muster für X; **this building is ~led** (*Brit*) *or* **~ed** (*US*) **on the Parthenon** dieses Gebäude ist dem Parthenon nachgebildet; **the system was ~led** (*Brit*) *or* **~ed** (*US*) **on the A-**

merican one das System war nach amerikanischem Muster aufgebaut; **this poem is ~led** (*Brit*) *or* **~ed** (*US*) **on Shakespeare's sonnets** dieses Gedicht ist Shakespeares Sonetten nachempfunden; **it's not ~led** (*Brit*) *or* **~ed** (*US*) **on anything** es ist frei entstanden, dafür gibt es keine Vorlage; **to ~ oneself/one's life on sb** sich (*dat*) jdn zum Vorbild nehmen
b (= *make a model*) modellieren, formen; **her finely ~led** (*Brit*) *or* **~ed features** (*US, fig*) ihre fein geschnittenen Gesichtszüge
c *dress etc* vorführen
VI a (= *make models*) modellieren
b (*Art, Phot*) als Modell arbeiten *or* beschäftigt sein; (*Fashion*) als Mannequin/Dressman arbeiten; **to ~ for sb** (*Art, Phot*) jdm Modell stehen; (*Fashion*) jds Kreationen vorführen

modelling, (*US*) **modeling** ['mɒdlɪŋ] N **a** (*of statue etc*) Modellieren *nt*; (*fig: of features*) Schnitt *m* **b to do some ~** (*Phot, Art*) als Modell arbeiten; (*Fashion*) als Mannequin/Dressman arbeiten

modem ['məʊdem] N Modem *nt*

modem card N Modemkarte *f*

moderate ['mɒdərɪt] **ADJ** gemäßigt (*also Pol*); *appetite, enjoyment, lifestyle, speed, increase* mäßig; *gain, improvement* leicht; *demands, price* vernünftig, angemessen; *drinker, eater* maßvoll; *income, success* (mittel)mäßig, bescheiden; *punishment, winter* mild; **a ~ amount** einigermaßen viel; **~-sized, of ~ size** mittelgroß; **over a ~ heat** bei mittlerer Hitze; **in a ~ oven** im Backofen bei mittlerer Hitze; **~ drinking** Alkoholgenuss *m* in Maßen
N (*Pol*) Gemäßigte(r) *mf*
VT ['mɒdəreɪt] **a** (= *attenuate*) *demands, position, behaviour* mäßigen; **the climate is ~d by the Gulf Stream** das Klima wird durch den Golfstrom gemäßigter; **to have a moderating influence on sb** mäßigend auf jdn wirken
b *meeting, discussion* den Vorsitz führen bei; (*TV, Rad*) moderieren
VI ['mɒdəreɪt] **a** nachlassen, sich mäßigen; (*wind etc*) nachlassen, sich abschwächen; (*demands*) gemäßigter werden
b (*in meeting, discussion*) den Vorsitz führen; (*TV, Rad*) moderieren

moderately ['mɒdərɪtlɪ] ADV **a** (*with adj/adv*) einigermaßen; *increase, decline* mäßig; **a ~-priced suit** ein nicht allzu *or* übermäßig teurer Anzug; **the house was ~ large** das Haus war mäßig groß **b** (= *in moderation*) *drink, eat, exercise* in Maßen; *act* maßvoll

moderation [ˌmɒdə'reɪʃən] N Mäßigung *f*; **in ~** mit Maß(en)

moderator ['mɒdəreɪtə'] N (*Eccl*) Synodalpräsident *m*

modern ['mɒdən] **ADJ** modern (*also Art, Liter*); *times, world also* heutig; *history* neuere und neueste; **Modern Greek** *etc* Neugriechisch *nt etc* N Anhänger(in) *m(f)* der Moderne

modern-day [ˌmɒdən'deɪ] ADJ modern; **~ America** das heutige Amerika

modernism ['mɒdənɪzəm] N Modernismus *m*

modernist ['mɒdənɪst] **ADJ** modernistisch N Modernist(in) *m(f)*

modernistic [ˌmɒdə'nɪstɪk] ADJ modernistisch

modernity [mɒ'dɜːnɪtɪ] N Modernität *f*

modernization [ˌmɒdənaɪ'zeɪʃən] N Modernisierung *f*

modernize ['mɒdənaɪz] VT modernisieren

modern languages PL neuere Sprachen *pl*, moderne Fremdsprachen *pl*; (*Univ*) Neuphilologie *f*

modernly ['mɒdənlɪ] ADV (= *fashionably*) modern; **more ~ known as ...** in neuerer Zeit als ... bekannt

modernness ['mɒdənnɪs] N = **modernity**

modern studies PL Gegenwartskunde *f* und Kulturwissenschaft *f*

modest ['mɒdɪst] ADJ **a** (= *not boastful, humble*) bescheiden; **to be ~ about one's successes** nicht mit seinen Erfolgen prahlen **b** (= *moder-*

ate) bescheiden; *requirements also* gering; *price* mäßig; **a man of ~ means** ein Mann mit bescheidenen Mitteln; **on a ~ scale** in bescheidenem Rahmen; **a ~ crowd turned out for the occasion** die Veranstaltung war (nur) mäßig besucht **c** (= *chaste, proper*) schamhaft; (*in one's behaviour*) anständig, sittsam (*geh*), züchtig (*old*); **to be ~ in one's dress** sich anständig kleiden

modestly ['mɒdɪstlɪ] ADV **a** (= *unassumingly, moderately*) bescheiden; **~ successful** in bescheidenem Maße erfolgreich; **~ priced goods** Waren zu gemäßigten Preisen; **he still gambled ~** er spielte immer noch in Maßen **b** (= *chastely, properly*) schamhaft; *behave* anständig, züchtig (*old*); *dress* anständig

modesty ['mɒdɪstɪ] N **a** (= *humbleness*) Bescheidenheit *f*; **in all ~** bei aller Bescheidenheit; **the ~ of the man!** (*iro*) der ist ja überhaupt nicht von sich eingenommen! (*iro inf*) **b** (= *moderation*) Bescheidenheit *f*, Genügsamkeit *f*; (*of price*) Mäßigkeit *f* **c** (= *chasteness*) Schamgefühl *nt*; (*in behaviour*) Anstand *m*, Sittsamkeit *f* (*geh*), Züchtigkeit *f* (*old*); (*in dress*) Unauffälligkeit *f*, Dezentheit *f*

modicum ['mɒdɪkəm] N **a** (= *of*) ein wenig, ein bisschen; **with a ~ of luck** mit ein wenig *or* mit einem Quäntchen Glück; **a ~ of hope/intelligence** ein Funke *m* (von) Hoffnung/Intelligenz; **a ~ of truth** ein Körnchen *nt* Wahrheit

modifiable ['mɒdɪfaɪəbl] ADJ modifizierbar

modification [ˌmɒdɪfɪ'keɪʃən] N (Ver)änderung *f*; (*of design*) Abänderung *f*; (*of terms, contract, wording*) Modifizierung *f*, Modifikation *f*; **to make ~s to sth** (Ver)änderungen an etw (*dat*) vornehmen; etw abändern; etw modifizieren; **the suggested ~s to his design** die Änderungsvorschläge *pl* zu seinem Entwurf

modifier ['mɒdɪfaɪə'] N (*Gram*) Bestimmungswort *nt*, nähere Bestimmung

modify ['mɒdɪfaɪ] VT **a** (= *change*) (ver)ändern; *design* abändern; *terms, contract, wording* modifizieren **b** (= *moderate*) mäßigen **c** (*Gram*) näher bestimmen

modish ['məʊdɪʃ] ADJ (= *fashionable*) modisch; (= *stylish*) schick; **it is very ~** es ist große Mode

modishly ['məʊdɪʃlɪ] ADV (= *fashionably*) modisch; (= *stylishly*) schick; **he ~ professed his solidarity with the working classes** er folgte dem herrschenden Trend und bekannte sich mit der Arbeiterklasse solidarisch

modiste [məʊ'diːst] N Modistin *f*

modular ['mɒdjʊlə'] ADJ aus Elementen zusammengesetzt; (*Comput*) modular; (*esp Brit, Sch, Univ*) *course, degree etc* modular aufgebaut; **the ~ design of their furniture** ihre als Bauelemente konzipierten Möbel

modulate ['mɒdjʊleɪt] (*Mus, Rad*) **VI** modulieren; **the key ~d from major to minor** die Tonart wechselte von Dur nach Moll **VT** modulieren

modulated ['mɒdjʊleɪtɪd] ADJ **(beautifully) ~** (*voice*) (harmonisch) ausgewogen

modulation [ˌmɒdjʊ'leɪʃən] N (*Mus, Rad*) Modulation *f*

module ['mɒdjuːl] N (Bau)element *nt*; (*in education*) Kurs *m*; (*Comput*) Modul *nt*; (*Space*) Raumkapsel *f*

modus operandi ['məʊdəsˌɒpə'rændɪ] N Modus Operandi *m*

modus vivendi ['məʊdəsˌvɪ'vendɪ] N Modus Vivendi *m*; (= *way of life*) Lebensstil *m*, Lebensweise *f*

moggy ['mɒgɪ] N (*Brit, inf*) Mieze *f* (*inf*)

mogul ['məʊgəl] N **a** (*lit, fig*) Mogul *m* **b** (*Hist*) **Mogul emperor** Mogulkaiser *m*; **Mogul empire** Mogulreich *nt*; **Mogul invasion** Invasion *f* durch die Moguln; **Mogul city** mogulische Stadt

MOH *abbr of* **Medical Officer of Health**

mohair ['məʊheə'] N Mohair *m*, Mohär *m*

Mohammed [məʊ'hæmed] N Mohammed *m*

Mohammedan [məʊˈhæmɪdən] **ADJ** mohammedanisch **N** Mohammedaner(in) *m(f)*

Mohammedanism [məˈhæmədənɪzəm] N Islam *m*

Mohican [məʊˈhiːkən] N **a** Mohikaner(in) *m(f)* **b** **mohican** (*Brit: = haircut*) Irokesenschnitt *m*

moiety [ˈmɔɪɪtɪ] N (*Jur: = half*) Hälfte *f*; (*liter*) (= *small amount*) Hauch *m* (*geh*) (*of an +dat*); (= *small share*) Bruchteil *m*

moist [mɔɪst] **ADJ** (+*er*) feucht (*from, with* vor +*dat*); ~ **with tears** feucht von Tränen, tränenfeucht; ~ **with dew** taufeucht

moisten [ˈmɔɪsn] **VT** anfeuchten; **to ~ sth with sth** etw mit etw anfeuchten **VI** feucht werden

moistness [ˈmɔɪstnɪs] N Feuchtigkeit *f*

moisture [ˈmɔɪstʃə'] N Feuchtigkeit *f*; **drops of ~** (= *water*) Wassertropfen *pl*; (= *sweat*) Schweißtropfen *pl*

moisturize [ˈmɔɪstʃəraɪz] **VT** *skin* mit einer Feuchtigkeitscreme behandeln; (*cosmetic*) geschmeidig machen, Feuchtigkeit verleihen (+*dat*); *air* befeuchten

moisturizer [ˈmɔɪstʃəraɪzə'], **moisturizing cream** [ˈmɔɪstʃəraɪzɪŋˈkriːm] N Feuchtigkeitscreme *f*

molar (tooth) [ˈməʊlə'(ˌtuːθ)] N Backenzahn *m*

molasses [məʊˈlæsɪz] N Melasse *f*; **to be as slow as ~ (in winter)** (*US, inf*) eine (fürchterliche) Transuse sein (*inf*)

mold *etc* (*US*) = **mould** *etc*

Moldavia [mɒlˈdeɪvɪə] N = **Moldova**

Moldavian [mɒlˈdeɪvɪən] N, ADJ = **Moldovan**

Moldova [mɒlˈdəʊvə] N Moldawien *nt*

Moldovan [mɒlˈdəʊvən] **N** (*Ling*) Moldawisch **ADJ** moldawisch; **he is ~** er ist Moldawier

mole¹ [məʊl] N (*Anat*) Pigmentmal *nt* (*form*), Leberfleck *m*

mole² N (*Zool*) Maulwurf *m*; (*inf, = secret agent*) Spion(in) *m(f)*

mole³ N (*Naut*) Mole *f*

molecular [məʊˈlekjʊlə'] **ADJ** molekular, Molekular-

molecular biology N Molekularbiologie *f*

molecule [ˈmɒlɪkjuːl] N Molekül *nt*

mole: molehill N Maulwurfshaufen *or* -hügel *m*; **moleskin** N (= *fur*) Maulwurfsfell *nt*; (= *coat/jacket etc*) Mantel/Jacke *etc* aus Maulwurfsfell; (= *fabric*) Moleskin *m or nt*

molest [məʊˈlest] VT belästigen

molestation [ˌməʊlesˈteɪʃən] N Belästigung *f*

moll [mɒl] N (*inf*) Gangsterbraut *f* (*inf*)

mollify [ˈmɒlɪfaɪ] VT besänftigen, beschwichtigen; **he was somewhat mollified by this** daraufhin beruhigte er sich etwas

mollusc [ˈmɒləsk] N Molluske *f* (*spec*), Weichtier *nt*

mollycoddle [ˈmɒlɪˌkɒdl] **VT** verhätscheln, verpäppeln, verzärteln **N** Weichling *m*

Moloch [ˈməʊlɒk] N Moloch *m*

Molotov cocktail [ˈmɒlətɒfˈkɒkteɪl] N Molotowcocktail *m*

molt N, VTI (*US*) = **moult**

molten [ˈməʊltən] **ADJ** geschmolzen; *glass, lava* flüssig

Molucca [məʊˈlʌkə] N **the ~ Islands**, **the ~s** die Molukken *pl*

mom [mɒm] N (*US, inf*) = **mum²**

mom-and-pop store [ˈmɒmənˈpɒpˌstɔː'] N (*US, inf*) Tante-Emma-Laden *m* (*inf*)

moment [ˈməʊmənt] N **a** Augenblick *m*, Moment *m*; **there were one or two ~s when I thought ...** ein paar Mal dachte ich ...; **from ~ to ~** zusehends, von Minute zu Minute; **any ~ now**, **(at) any ~** jeden Augenblick; **at any ~** (= *any time*) jederzeit; **at the ~** im Augenblick, momentan; **at the ~ when ...** zu dem Zeitpunkt, als ...; **not at the or this ~** im Augenblick *or* zurzeit nicht; **at the ~ of impact** beim

Aufprall, im Augenblick des Aufpralls; **at the last ~** im letzten Augenblick; **at this (particular) ~ in time** momentan, augenblicklich; **for the ~** im Augenblick, vorläufig; **for a ~** (für) einen Moment; **for one ~ it seemed to have stopped** einen Augenblick lang schien es aufgehört zu haben; **not for a or one ~ ...** nie(mals) ...; **I didn't hesitate for a ~** ich habe keinen Augenblick gezögert; **in a ~** gleich; **in a ~ of madness** in einem Anflug von geistiger Umnachtung; **it was all over in a ~** *or* **in a few ~s** das ganze dauerte nur wenige Augenblicke; **to leave things until the last ~** alles erst im letzten Moment erledigen *or* machen (*inf*); **half a ~!**, **one ~!** einen Moment!; **just a ~!**, **wait a ~!** Moment mal!; **I shan't be a ~** ich bin gleich wieder da; (= *nearly ready*) ich bin gleich so weit; **do it this very ~!** tu das auf der Stelle!; **I have just this ~ heard about it** ich habe es eben *or* gerade erst erfahren; **we haven't a ~ to lose** wir haben keine Minute zu verlieren; **not a ~ too soon** keine Minute zu früh, in letzter Minute; **not a ~'s peace** *or* **rest** keine ruhige Minute; **one ~ she was laughing, the next she was crying** zuerst lachte sie, einen Moment später weinte sie; **the ~ it happened** (in dem Augenblick,) als es passierte; **the ~ I saw him I knew ...** als ich ihn sah, wusste ich sofort ...; **the ~ he arrives there's trouble** sobald er auftaucht, gibt es Ärger; **tell me the ~ he comes** sagen Sie mir sofort Bescheid, wenn er kommt; **the ~ of truth** die Stunde der Wahrheit; **he is the man of the ~** er ist der Mann des Tages; **the film has its ~s** streckenweise hat der Film was (*inf*) **b** (*Phys*) Moment *nt*; ~ **of acceleration/inertia** Beschleunigungs-/Trägheitsmoment *nt* **c** (= *importance*) Bedeutung *f*; **of little ~** bedeutungslos, unwichtig

momentarily [ˈməʊməntərɪlɪ] **ADV** **a** (für) einen Augenblick *or* Moment; **she shivered ~** sie zitterte einen Moment lang **b** (*US*) (= *very soon*) jeden Augenblick *or* Moment; (= *from moment to moment*) zusehends

momentary [ˈməʊməntərɪ] **ADJ** kurz; *glimpse also* flüchtig; *lapse of memory/concentration* momentan, vorübergehend; **a ~ feeling of nausea** eine momentane Übelkeit; **there was a ~ silence** einen Augenblick lang herrschte Stille

momentous [məʊˈmentəs] **ADJ** (= *memorable, important*) bedeutsam, bedeutungsvoll; (= *of great consequence*) von großer Tragweite; **of ~ significance** von entscheidender Bedeutung

momentousness [məʊˈmentəsnɪs] N Bedeutsamkeit *f*; (*of decision*) Tragweite *f*

momentum [məʊˈmentəm] N (*of moving object*) Schwung *m*; (*at moment of impact*) Wucht *f*; (*Phys*) Impuls *m*; (*fig*) Schwung *m*; **the rock's ~ carried it through the wall** der Felsbrocken hatte eine solche Wucht, dass er die Mauer durchschlug; **he let the car go under its own ~** er ließ das Auto von allein weiterrollen; **to gather or gain ~** (*lit*) sich beschleunigen, in Fahrt kommen (*inf*); (*fig, idea, movement, plan*) in Gang kommen; **the campaign is now gathering or gaining ~** die Kampagne kommt nun in Gang *or* in Schwung; **to keep going under its own ~** (*lit*) sich aus eigener Kraft weiterbewegen; (*fig*) eine Eigendynamik entwickelt haben; **to lose ~** (*lit, fig*) Schwung verlieren

Mon *abbr of* **Monday** Mo

Monaco [ˈmɒnəkəʊ] N Monaco *nt*

monad [ˈmɒnæd] N **a** (*Philos*) Monade *f* **b** (*Biol: dated*) Einzeller *m* **c** (*Chem*) einwertiges Element *or* Atom *or* Radikal

monarch [ˈmɒnək] N Monarch(in) *m(f)*, Herrscher(in) *m(f)*; (*fig*) König *m*; **absolute ~** Alleinherrscher(in) *m(f)*

monarchic(al) [mɒˈnɑːkɪk(əl)] **ADJ** monarchisch; (= *favouring monarchy*) monarchistisch

monarchism [ˈmɒnəkɪzəm] N (= *system*) Monarchie *f*; (= *advocacy of monarchy*) Monarchismus *m*

monarchist [ˈmɒnəkɪst] **ADJ** monarchistisch **N** Monarchist(in) *m(f)*, Anhänger(in) *m(f)* der Monarchie

monarchy [ˈmɒnəkɪ] N Monarchie *f*

monastery [ˈmɒnəstərɪ] N (Mönchs)kloster *nt*

monastic [məˈnæstɪk] **ADJ** mönchisch, klösterlich; ~ **life** Klosterleben *nt*; ~ **building** Klostergebäude *nt*; ~ **order** Mönchsorden *m*; ~ **vows** Ordensgelübde *nt*; **he leads a ~ existence** (*fig*) er lebt wie ein Mönch

monasticism [məˈnæstɪsɪzəm] N Mönch(s)tum *nt*

Monday [ˈmʌndɪ] N Montag *m* → *also* **Tuesday**

Monegasque [mɒnəˈgæsk] **N** Monegasse *m*, Monegassin *f* **ADJ** monegassisch

monetarism [ˈmʌnɪtərɪzəm] N Monetarismus *m*

monetarist [ˈmʌnɪtərɪst] **N** Monetarist(in) *m(f)* **ADJ** monetaristisch

monetary [ˈmʌnɪtərɪ] **ADJ** **a** (= *pertaining to finance or currency*) währungspolitisch, Währungs-; ~ **policy** Währungspolitik *f*; ~ **reform** Währungsreform *f*; ~ **reserves** Geldreserven *pl*; ~ **system** Währungssystem *nt*; ~ **union** Währungsunion *f* **b** (= *pecuniary*) *considerations etc* geldlich

monetary unit N Geld- *or* Währungseinheit *f*

money [ˈmʌnɪ] N Geld *nt*; (= *medium of exchange*) Zahlungsmittel *nt*; **monies** Zahlungsmittel *pl*; **they use these stones as ~** sie benutzen diese Steine als Zahlungsmittel, sie benutzen diese Steine anstelle *or* an Stelle von Geld; **to make ~** (*person*) (viel) Geld verdienen; (*business*) etwas einbringen, sich rentieren; **to lose ~** (*person*) Geld verlieren; (*business*) Verluste machen *or* haben; **he spends ~ like water** er wirft mit dem Geld nur so um sich; **there's ~ in it** das ist sehr lukrativ; **if you help me, there's ~ in it for you** wenn du mir hilfst, springt für dich auch etwas dabei heraus (*inf*); **it's a bargain for the ~** das ist eine günstige Anschaffung; **what can you expect for the ~?** was kann man da dem Preis schon verlangen?; **that's the one for my ~!** ich tippe auf ihn/sie *etc*; **the smart ~'s on him** er hat die besten Chancen; **it's ~ for jam** *or* **old rope** (*Brit inf*) da wird einem das Geld ja nachgeworfen (*inf*); **to be in the ~** (*inf*) Geld wie Heu haben; **what's the ~ like in this job?** wie wird der Job bezahlt?; **to earn good ~** gut verdienen; **to get one's ~'s worth** etwas für sein Geld bekommen; **I've really had my ~'s worth** *or* **my ~ out of that car** der Wagen hat sich wirklich bezahlt gemacht *or* war wirklich sein Geld wert; **do you think I'm made of ~?** (*inf*) ich bin doch kein Krösus!; **to throw ~ at sth** viel Geld in etw (*acc*) stecken; **to throw ~ at a problem** ein Problem dadurch zu lösen versuchen, dass man viel Geld dafür ausgibt; **to throw ~ at a solution** eine Lösung finden, indem man viel Geld dafür ausgibt; **that's throwing good ~ after bad** das ist rausgeschmissenes Geld (*inf*), das ist gutes Geld dem schlechten nachgeworfen; **your ~ or your life!** Geld oder Leben!; **to put one's ~ where one's mouth is** (*inf*) (nicht nur reden, sondern) Taten sprechen lassen; ~ **talks** (*inf*) mit Geld geht alles; ~ **isn't everything** (*prov*) Geld (allein) macht nicht glücklich (*prov*); **his analysis was right on the ~** (*US*) seine Analyse stimmte haargenau

money: money bag N Geldsack *m*; **moneybags** N *sing* (*inf*) Geldsack *m*; **money belt** N ≈ Gürteltasche *f* (*mit Geldfächern*); **moneybox** N Sparbüchse *f*; **moneychanger** N (= *person*) (Geld)wechsler(in) *m(f)*

moneyed [ˈmʌnɪd] **ADJ** begütert

money: money-grubber N (*Brit inf*) Raffke *m* (*inf*); **money-grubbing** (*Brit inf*) **ADJ** geld- *or* raffgierig **N** Geld- *or* Raffgier *f*; **money laundering** N Geldwäsche *f*; **moneylender** N Geldverleiher(in) *m(f)*; **moneylending** N Geldverleih *m*; **moneymaker** N (= *idea*) einträgliche Sache *f*; (= *product*) Verkaufserfolg *m*; (= *company*) gewinnbringendes *or* Gewinn bringendes Unternehmen, gutgehendes Unternehmen; **moneymaking** ADJ *idea, plan* gewinnbringend, Gewinn bringend, einträglich N Geldverdienen *nt*; **money market** N Geldmarkt *m*; **money matters** PL Geldangelegenheiten *or* -dinge *pl*; **money order** N Zahlungsanweisung *f*; **money prize** N Geldpreis *m*; **money spider** N *kleine Spinne*; **money-spinner** N (*inf*) Verkaufsschlager *m* (*inf*) *or* -hit *m* (*inf*); **money-spinning** ADJ (*Brit inf*) **a ~ idea** eine Idee, mit der sich viel Geld machen lässt; **money supply** N Geldvolumen *nt*

mongol ['mɒŋɡəl] ADJ **a** (*pej*) mongolisch **b** (*Med*) ~ mongoloid N **a** **Mongol = Mongolian b** (*Med*) **he's a ~** er ist mongoloid

Mongolia [mɒŋˈɡəʊlɪə] N Mongolei *f*

Mongolian [mɒŋˈɡəʊlɪən] N **a** Mongole *m*, Mongolin *f* **b** (= *language*) Mongolisch *nt*

mongolism ['mɒŋɡəlɪzəm] N (*Med*) Mongolismus *m*

mongoloid ['mɒŋɡəlɔɪd] ADJ **a** mongoloid **b** (*Med*) ~ mongoloid

mongoose ['mɒŋɡuːs] N *pl* **-s** Mungo *m*

mongrel ['mʌŋɡrəl] ADJ **~ race** Mischrasse *f* N (= *mongrel dog*) Promenadenmischung *f*; (*pej*) Köter *m*; (*pej*, = *person*) Mischling *m*

moni(c)ker ['mɒnɪkə*r*] N (*Brit, inf*, = *signature*) Name *m*, (Friedrich) Wilhelm *m* (*inf*)

monition [məˈnɪʃən] N **a** (*form*: = *reprimand*) (Er)mahnung *f* **b** (= *warning*) Warnung *f* **c** (*Jur*) Vorladung *f*

monitor ['mɒnɪtə*r*] N **a** (*Sch*) Schüler(in) *m(f)* mit besonderen Pflichten, **stationery/book ~** Schreibwaren-/Bücherwart(in) *m(f)* **b** (*TV, Tech*: = *screen*) Monitor *m* **c** (= *observer*) Überwacher(in) *m(f)*; (*of telephone conversations*) Abhörer(in) *m(f)*; (*Rad*) Mitarbeiter(in) *m(f)* am Monitordienst **d** (*also* **monitor lizard**) Waran *m*, Waranechse *f* VT **a** *foreign station, telephone conversation* abhören, *telephone conversation* mithören **b** (= *control, check*) überwachen; *TV programme* mithören **b** (= *control, check*) überwachen; *personal expenditure etc* kontrollieren

monitoring ['mɒnɪtərɪŋ] N **a** (*of foreign station, telephone conversation*) Abhören *nt*; (*of TV programme*) Mithören *nt* **b** (= *controlling, checking*) Überwachung *f*; (*of personal expenditure etc*) Kontrolle *f* ADJ *attr* Überwachungs-, Kontroll-; **~ body** Kontrollorgan *nt*; **~ function** Überwachungs- *or* Kontrollfunktion *f*

monk [mʌŋk] N Mönch *m*

monkey ['mʌŋkɪ] N Affe *m*; (*fig*: = *child*) Strolch *m*, Schlingel *m*; **to make a ~ out of sb** (*inf*) jdn verhohnepipeln (*inf*); **well, I'll be a ~'s uncle** (*inf*) (ich glaub,) mich laust der Affe (*inf*); **to have a ~ on one's back** (*US, inf*) an der Nadel hängen (*inf*); **I don't give a ~'s (about it)** (*Brit inf*) das ist mir scheißegal (*inf*) *or* schnurzpiepe (*hum inf*); **as clever as a cartload** *or* **barrel (load) of ~s** (*Brit inf*) ganz schön clever (*inf*) VI **to ~ around** (*inf*) herumalbern; **to ~ around with sth** an etw (*dat*) herumspielen *or* -fummeln (*inf*)

monkey: monkey bars PL Klettergerüst *nt*; **monkey business** N (*inf*) **no ~!** mach(t) mir keine Sachen!; **there's too much ~** da ist zu viel faul (*inf*); **what ~ have you been getting up to?** was hast du jetzt schon wieder angestellt?; **monkey engine** N (*Tech*: = *pile-driver*) Pfahlramme *f*; **monkey jacket** N Affenjäckchen *nt* (*inf*); **monkey nut** N Erdnuss *f*; **monkey puzzle (tree)** N Andentanne *f*, Araukarie *f* (*spec*); **monkeyshines** ['mʌŋkɪʃaɪnz] PL (*US inf*) Streiche *pl*; **monkey suit** N (*inf*, = *tails*) Frack *m*; **he was all done up in his ~** er hatte sich in volle Montur *or* in Schale geworfen (*inf*); **monkey tricks** PL Unfug *m*, dumme Streiche *pl*; **no ~!** mach(t) mir keinen Unfug!; **I bet he's been getting up to some ~ again!** der hat doch sicher wieder irgendwas ausgeheckt (*inf*); **monkey wrench** N verstellbarer Schraubenschlüssel, Engländer (*inf*) *m*; **to throw a ~ into the works** (*US, inf*) jdm einen Knüppel zwischen die Beine werfen (*inf*)

monkfish ['mʌŋkfɪʃ] N Seeteufel *m*

monkish ['mʌŋkɪʃ] ADJ mönchisch; (*fig pej*) pastorenhaft; **he leads a ~ life** er führt ein Leben wie ein Mönch

monk seal N (*Zool*) Mönchsrobbe *f*

mono ['mɒnəʊ] N Mono *nt* ADJ Mono-, mono-; *record also* in Mono *pred*; **~ recording** Monoaufnahme *f*

mono- PREF Mono-, mono-

monochrome ['mɒnəkrəʊm] ADJ monochrom, einfarbig; (*Comput*) monochrom, monochromatisch; **~ screen** Monochrombildschirm *m*; **~ television** Schwarzweißfernsehen *nt* **b** (*Art*) monochrome Malerei, in einer Farbe gehaltene Malerei; (*TV*) Schwarzweiß *nt*

monocle ['mɒnəkəl] N Monokel *nt*

monocled ['mɒnəkld] ADJ Monokel tragend

monocoque ['mɒnəkɒk] N **a** (*Aviat*) Schalenrumpf *m*; **~ construction** Schalenbau *m*, Schalenbauweise *f* **b** (*Aut, of racing car*) Monocoque *nt*

monogamous [mɒˈnɒɡəməs] ADJ monogam

monogamy [mɒˈnɒɡəmɪ] N Monogamie *f*

monogram ['mɒnəɡræm] N Monogramm *nt*

monogrammed ['mɒnəɡræmd] ADJ mit Monogramm

monograph ['mɒnəɡrɑːf] N Monografie *f*

monokini [ˌmɒnəˈkiːniː] N Monokini *m*

monolingual [ˌmɒnəˈlɪŋɡwəl] ADJ einsprachig

monolith ['mɒnəʊlɪθ] N Monolith *m*

monolithic [ˌmɒnəʊˈlɪθɪk] ADJ (*lit*) monolithisch; (*fig*) gigantisch, riesig

monologize [məˈnɒlədʒaɪz] VI (*geh*) monologisieren; (*to oneself*) ein Selbstgespräch führen

monologue, (*US*) **monolog** ['mɒnəlɒɡ] N Monolog *m*

mono: monomania N Monomanie *f*; **monoplane** N Eindecker *m*

monopolist [məˈnɒpəlɪst] N Monopolist(in) *m(f)*

monopolistic [məˈnɒpəlɪstɪk] ADJ monopolistisch

monopolization [məˌnɒpəlaɪˈzeɪʃən] N (*lit*) Monopolisierung *f*; (*fig*) (*of bathroom, best seat etc*) Beschlagnahme *f*; (*of person, sb's time etc*) völlige Inanspruchnahme *f*; (*of conversation etc*) Beherrschung *f*

monopolize [məˈnɒpəlaɪz] VT (*lit*) *market* monopolisieren, beherrschen; (*fig*) *person, place, sb's time etc* mit Beschlag belegen, in Beschlag nehmen; *conversation, discussion* beherrschen, an sich (*acc*) reißen; **to ~ the supply of ...** eine Monopolstellung für die Lieferung von ... haben; **she wants to ~ his attention** sie möchte seine Aufmerksamkeit ganz für sich haben

Monopoly® [məˈnɒpəlɪ] N (= *game*) Monopoly® *nt*; **~ money** (*inf*: = *large amount*) Wahnsinnssummen *pl* (*inf*); (*pej*: = *foreign currency*) ausländisches Geld, Spielgeld *nt* (*pej*)

monopoly [məˈnɒpəlɪ] N **a** (*lit*) Monopol *nt*; **~ position** Monopolstellung *f*; **coal is a government ~** der Staat hat das Kohlenmonopol *or* das Monopol für Kohle; **Monopolies and Mergers Commission** (*Brit*) *britisches Kartellamt* **b** (*fig*) **to have the** *or* **a ~ on** *or* **of sth** etw für sich gepachtet haben (*inf*); **you haven't got a ~ on me** ich bin doch nicht dein Eigentum

monorail ['mɒnəreɪl] N Einschienenbahn *f*

monosodium glutamate [ˌmɒnəʊˈsəʊdɪəmˈɡluːtəmeɪt] N Monosodiumglutamat *nt*

mono: monosyllabic ADJ (*lit*) einsilbig, monosyllabisch (*Ling*); (*fig*) *person* einsilbig; **his English was fairly ~** sein Englisch beschränkte sich größtenteils auf einsilbige Wörter; **monosyllable** N einsilbiges Wort, Einsilber *m*; **to speak/answer in ~s** einsilbig sein/antworten, einsilbige Antworten geben; **monotheism** N Monotheismus *m*; **monotheistic** ADJ monotheistisch

monotone ['mɒnətəʊn] N monotoner Klang; (= *voice*) monotone Stimme

monotonous [məˈnɒtənəs] ADJ (*lit, fig*) eintönig, monoton; **with ~ regularity** regelmäßig; **it's getting ~** es wird allmählich langweilig

monotonously [məˈnɒtənəslɪ] ADV monoton; **the days were ~ alike** die Tage waren eintönig in ihrer Ähnlichkeit

monotony [məˈnɒtənɪ] N (*lit, fig*) Eintönigkeit *f*, Monotonie *f*; **the sheer ~ of it!** dieses ewige Einerlei!; (*of work etc also*) dieser Stumpfsinn!

Monotype® ['mɒnəʊtaɪp] N Monotype-Verfahren® *nt*; **monotype machine** Monotype® *f*

monoxide [mɒˈnɒksaɪd] N Monoxid *nt*

Monsignor [mɒnˈsiːnjə*r*] N Monsignore *m*

monsoon [mɒnˈsuːn] N Monsun *m*; **the ~ rains** der Monsunregen; **the ~s, the ~ season** die Monsunzeit

monster ['mɒnstə*r*] N **a** (= *big animal, thing*) Ungetüm *nt*, Monstrum *nt*; (= *animal*) Ungeheuer *nt*, Ungetüm *nt*; **a real ~ of a fish** ein wahres Monstrum *or* Ungeheuer von (einem) Fisch; **a ~ of a book** ein richtiger Schinken (*inf*), ein Mammutwerk *nt*; **a ~ of greed** ein (hab)gieriges Monster **b** (= *abnormal animal*) Ungeheuer *nt*, Monster *nt*, Monstrum *nt*; (= *legendary animal*) (groteskes) Fabelwesen *nt*; **c** (= *cruel person*) Unmensch *m*, Ungeheuer *nt* ATTR **a** (= *enormous*) riesenhaft; **~ film** Monster- *or* Mammutfilm *m* **b** (= *to do with monsters*) Monster-; **~ hunt** Monsterjagd *f*

monstrance ['mɒnstrəns] N (*Eccl*) Monstranz *f*

monstrosity [mɒnˈstrɒsɪtɪ] N (= *quality*) Ungeheuerlichkeit *f*, Monstrosität *f*; (= *thing*) Monstrosität *f*; (= *cruel deed*) Gräueltat *f*; **it's a ~ that ...** es ist unmenschlich *or* schändlich, dass ...

monstrous ['mɒnstrəs] ADJ **a** (= *huge*) ungeheuer (groß), riesig **b** (= *shocking, horrible*) abscheulich; *crime, thought, colour* grässlich, abscheulich; *suggestion* ungeheuerlich; **it's ~ that ...** es ist einfach ungeheuerlich *or* schändlich, dass ...

monstrously ['mɒnstrəslɪ] ADV schrecklich, fürchterlich

mons veneris ['mɒnzˈvenərɪs] N *pl* **montes veneris** ['mɒntiːzˈvenərɪs] Venusberg *m*

montage [mɒnˈtɑːʒ] N Montage *f*

Montenegran [ˌmɒntrɪˈniːɡrən] N, ADJ = **Montenegrin**

Montenegrin [ˌmɒntrɪˈniːɡrɪn] ADJ montenegrinisch, montenegrisch; **he is ~** er ist Montenegriner N Montenegriner(in) *m(f)*

Montenegro [ˌmɒntrɪˈniːɡrəʊ] N Montenegro *nt*

month [mʌnθ] N Monat *m*; **in the ~ of October** im Oktober; **six ~s** ein halbes Jahr, sechs Monate; **in** *or* **for ~s** seit langem; **it went on for ~s** es hat sich monatelang hingezogen; **in the early ~s of the war** in den ersten Kriegsmonaten; **one ~'s salary** ein Monatsgehalt; **paid by the ~** monatlich bezahlt

monthly ['mʌnθlɪ] ADJ monatlich; **~ magazine** Monats(zeit)schrift *f*; **~ cycle** Monatszyklus *m*; **~ salary** Monatsgehalt *nt*; **~ ticket/payment** Monatskarte/-rate *f*; **they have ~ meetings** sie treffen sich einmal im Monat; **to pay on a ~ basis** monatlich zahlen ADV monatlich; **twice ~** zweimal im *or* pro Monat N Monats(zeit-)schrift *f*

monty, monte ['mɒntɪ] N (*inf*) **the full ~** absolut alles; **to go the full ~** (= *strip*) alle Hüllen fallen lassen (*hum*); (= *go the whole hog*) aufs Ganze gehen

monument ['mɒnjʊmənt] N Denkmal *nt*; (*big also*) Monument *nt*; (*small, on grave etc*) Gedenkstein *m*; (*fig*) Zeugnis *nt* (*to +gen*); **his great trilogy survives as a ~ to his talent** seine große Trilogie legt Zeugnis von seinem Talent ab

monumental [ˌmɒnjʊˈmentl] ADJ **a** (= *very great*) enorm, monumental (*geh*); *proportions, achievement* gewaltig; *ignorance, stupidity, error* kolossal, ungeheuerlich; **on a ~ scale, of ~ proportions** (*disaster, crisis*) von riesigem Ausmaß; *building, work of art* monumental **b** **~ inscrip-**

tion Grabinschrift f; ~ **sculptures** Steinfiguren pl

monumentally [ˌmɒnjʊ'mentəlɪ] ADV (inf, = immensely) stupid, incompetent, ugly ungeheuerlich; drink übermäßig; fail katastrophal

monumental mason N Steinmetz(in) m(f), Steinbildhauer(in) m(f)

moo [muː] N a Muhen nt; **the cow gave a ~** die Kuh muhte or machte „muh" (inf) b (inf, = woman) Kuh f (inf) VI muhen, „muh" machen (inf)

mooch [muːtʃ] (inf) VI tigern (inf); **I spent all day just ~ing out** (Brit) or **around the house** ich habe den ganzen Tag zu Hause herumgegammelt (inf) VT (US, inf) abstauben (inf)

moo-cow ['muːkaʊ] N (baby-talk) Muhkuh f (baby-talk)

mood¹ [muːd] N a (of party, town etc) Stimmung f; (of one person) Laune f, Stimmung f; **he was in a good/bad/foul ~** er hatte gute/schlechte/eine fürchterliche Laune, er war gut/schlecht/fürchterlich gelaunt; **to be in a cheerful ~** gut aufgelegt sein; **to be in a festive/forgiving ~** feierlich/versöhnlich gestimmt sein; **to be in a generous ~** in Geberlaune sein; **in one of his crazy** or **mad ~s** aus einer plötzlichen Laune heraus, in einer seiner Anwandlungen; **I'm in no ~ for laughing** mir ist nicht nach or zum Lachen zumute or zu Mute; **to be in the ~ for sth** zu etw aufgelegt sein; **to be in the ~ to do sth** dazu aufgelegt sein, etw zu tun; **to be in no ~ to do sth** nicht in der Stimmung sein, etw zu tun; **I'm not in the ~ for work** or **to work** ich habe keine Lust zum Arbeiten; **I'm not in the ~ for this type of music** ich bin nicht in der Stimmung für diese Musik; **I'm not in the ~** ich bin nicht dazu aufgelegt; (to do sth also) ich habe keine Lust; (for music etc also) ich bin nicht in der richtigen Stimmung; ~ **music** stimmungsvolle Musik b (= bad mood) schlechte Laune f; **he's in one of his ~s** er hat mal wieder eine seiner Launen; **he's in a ~** er hat schlechte Laune; **he has ~s** er ist sehr launisch

mood² N (Gram) Modus m; **indicative ~** Indikativ m; **imperative ~** Imperativ m; **subjunctive ~** Konjunktiv m

moodily ['muːdɪlɪ] ADV launisch, launenhaft; (= in a bad mood) schlecht gelaunt, übellaunig

moodiness ['muːdɪnɪs] N Launenhaftigkeit f; (= bad mood) schlechte Laune f; (of look, answer) Verdrossenheit f; **his ~** sein launisches Wesen

mood swing N Stimmungsschwankung f

moody ['muːdɪ] ADJ (+er) launisch, launenhaft; (= bad-tempered) schlecht gelaunt; look, answer verdrossen, übellaunig; picture, film, piece of music stimmungsvoll

moola(h) ['muːlɑː] N (dated US inf: = money) Kohle f (inf)

moon [muːn] N Mond m; **is there a ~ tonight?** scheint heute der Mond?; **when the ~ is full** bei Vollmond; **the man in the ~** der Mann im Mond; **you're asking for the ~!** du verlangst Unmögliches!; **to promise sb the ~** jdm das Blaue vom Himmel versprechen; **to be over the ~** (inf) überglücklich sein VI a (= mope) (vor sich acc hin) träumen b (inf, with backside) seinen nackten Hintern herausstrecken

▶ **moon about** (Brit) or **around** VI (vor sich acc hin) träumen; **to moon about** or **around (in) the house** zu Hause hocken

▶ **moon away** VT sep time verträumen

moon in cpds Mond-; **moonbeam** N Mondstrahl m; **moon blindness** N a (Vet) Mondblindheit f b (Med) Nachtblindheit f; **moonboots** PL Moonboots pl; **moonbuggy** N Mondauto or -fahrzeug nt; **mooncalf** N (dated) Schwachsinnige(r) mf; (inf) Mondkalb nt; **moon-faced** ['muːnˌfeɪst] ADJ mit rundem Mondgesicht, mondgesichtig

Moonie ['muːnɪ] N (inf) Anhänger(in) m(f) der Mun-Sekte, Moonie m (inf)

moon: **moon landing** N Mondlandung f; **moonless** ADJ night mondlos; **moonlight** N Mondlicht nt or -schein m; **it was ~** der Mond schien; **a ~ walk** ein Mondscheinspaziergang m → **flit** VI (inf) schwarzarbeiten; **moonlighter** N (inf) Schwarzarbeiter(in) m(f); **moonlighting** N (inf) Schwarzarbeit f; **moonlit** ADJ object mondbeschienen; night, landscape, lawn mondhell; **moonscape** ['muːnskeɪp] N Mondlandschaft f; **moonshine** N a (= moonlight) Mondschein m b (inf, = nonsense) Unsinn m c (inf, = illegal whisky) illegal gebrannter Whisky; **moonshiner** N (inf) Schwarzbrenner(in) m(f); **moonshot** N Mondflug m; **moonstone** N Mondstein m; **moonstruck** ADJ (= mad) mondsüchtig; (fig) vernarrt

moony ['muːnɪ] ADJ (+er) (inf, = dreamy) verträumt

Moor [mʊə] N Maure m; (old, = black man) Mohr m

moor¹ [mʊə] N (Hoch)moor nt; (Brit: for game) Moorjagd f; **a walk on the ~s** ein Spaziergang m übers Moor

moor² VT festmachen, vertäuen; (at permanent moorings) muren VI festmachen, anlegen

moorage ['mʊərɪdʒ] N (= place) Anlegeplatz m; (= charge) Anlegegebühren pl

moorhen ['mʊəhen] N Teichhuhn nt

mooring ['mʊərɪŋ] N (= act of mooring) Anlegen nt; (= place) Anlegeplatz m; ~**s** (= ropes, fixtures) Verankerung f

mooring buoy N Muringsboje f

Moorish ['mʊərɪʃ] ADJ maurisch; invasion der Mauren

moorland ['mʊələnd] N Moor- or Heideland nt

moose [muːs] N pl - Elch m

moot [muːt] ADJ a **a ~ point** or **question** eine fragliche Sache; **it's a ~ point** or **question whether ...** es ist noch fraglich or die Frage (inf), ob ... VT aufwerfen; suggestion vorbringen; **it has been ~ed that ...** es wurde zur Debatte gestellt, dass ...

mop [mɒp] N a (= floor mop) (Nass)mop m; (= dish mop) Spülbürste f; (= sponge mop) Schwammmopp m; (inf, = hair) Mähne f, Zotteln pl (inf); **her ~ of hair** ihre Mähne; **her ~ of curls** ihr Wuschelkopf m VT floor, kitchen wischen; **to ~ one's face/brow** sich (dat) den Schweiß vom Gesicht/von der Stirn wischen; **to ~ one's eyes** sich (dat) die Tränen abwischen

▶ **mop down** VT sep walls abwischen; floor wischen

▶ **mop up** VT sep a water etc aufwischen; **she mopped up the sauce with a piece of bread** sie tunkte die Soße mit einem Stück Brot auf b (Mil) säubern (inf); **mopping-up operations** Säuberungsaktion f (inf); (hum) Aufräumarbeiten pl VI (auf)wischen

mopboard ['mɒpbɔːd] N (US) Scheuerleiste f

mope [məʊp] VI Trübsal blasen (inf)

▶ **mope about** (Brit) or **around** VI mit einer Jammermiene herumlaufen; **to mope about** or **around the house** zu Hause hocken und Trübsal blasen (inf)

moped ['məʊped] N Moped nt; (very small) Mofa nt

mopes [məʊps] PL (inf) **to have a case of the ~** seinen or den Moralischen haben (inf)

mopy ['məʊpɪ] ADJ (+er) (inf) trübselig; **I'm feeling a bit ~ today** ich bin heute etwas in Tiefstimmung (inf)

MOR (Mus) abbr of **middle-of-the-road** für den Massenmarkt

moraine [mɒ'reɪn] N Moräne f

moral ['mɒrəl] ADJ a moralisch, sittlich; support, victory, obligation, principles moralisch; ~ **values** sittliche Werte pl, Moralvorstellungen pl; ~ **code** (of individual) Auffassung f von Moral; (of society) Sitten- or Moralkodex m; **a ~ imperative** ein Gebot nt der Moral; ~ **standards** Moral nt für Gut und Böse, moralisches Bewusstsein; ~ **support** moralische Unterstützung; **to give sb ~ support** jdn moralisch unterstützen; ~ **courage** Charakter m; ~ **lecture** Moralpredigt f b (= virtuous) integer, moralisch einwandfrei; (sexually) tugendhaft; (= moralizing) story, book moralisch c **it's a ~ certainty that ...** es ist mit Sicherheit anzunehmen, dass ...; **to have a ~ right to sth** jedes Recht auf etw (acc) haben N a (= lesson) Moral f; **to draw a ~ from sth** eine Lehre aus etw ziehen b **morals** PL (= principles) Moral f; **his ~s are different from mine** er hat ganz andere Moralvorstellungen als ich; **to have loose ~s** eine recht lockere Moral haben

morale [mɒ'rɑːl] N Moral f; **to boost sb's ~** jdm (moralischen) Auftrieb geben; **to destroy sb's ~** jdn entmutigen; **to be a ~ booster for sb** jdm (moralischen) Auftrieb geben

moralist ['mɒrəlɪst] N (Philos, fig) Moralist(in) m(f)

moralistic [ˌmɒrə'lɪstɪk] ADJ moralisierend; (Philos) moralistisch

morality [mə'rælɪtɪ] N Moralität f; (= moral system) Moral f, Ethik f

morality play N Moralität f

moralize ['mɒrəlaɪz] VI moralisieren; **to ~ about sb/sth** sich über jdn/etw moralisch entrüsten; **stop your moralizing!** hör mit deinen Moralpredigten auf!

morally ['mɒrəlɪ] ADV a (= ethically) moralisch; **I am ~ certain that ...** ich bin moralisch überzeugt, dass ... b (= virtuously) integer, moralisch einwandfrei; (sexually) tugendhaft

moral: **Moral Majority** N (US Pol) moralische Mehrheit; **moral philosopher** N Moralphilosoph(in) m(f); **moral philosophy** N Moralphilosophie f; **Moral Rearmament** N moralische Aufrüstung

morass [mə'ræs] N Morast m, Sumpf m (also fig); **to be sucked into the ~ (of vice)** sich immer tiefer (im Laster) verstricken; **a ~ of problems** ein Wust m von Problemen; **a ~ of emotions** ein Wirrwarr m der Gefühle

moratorium [ˌmɒrə'tɔːrɪəm] N Stopp m; (Mil) Stillhalteabkommen nt (on treaty etc) Moratorium nt; (Fin) Zahlungsaufschub m; **a ~ on nuclear armament** ein Atomwaffenstopp m; **to declare a ~ on sth** etw (vorläufig) mit einem Stopp belegen; **in der Frage einer Sache** (gen) ein Moratorium beschließen; **there's been a ~ on new transplant techniques** neue Transplantationstechniken wurden vorläufig gestoppt

Moravia [mə'reɪvɪə] N Mähren nt

morbid ['mɔːbɪd] ADJ a idea, thought, jealousy, curiosity etc krankhaft; interest, attitude unnatürlich, krankhaft; sense of humour, talk etc makaber; (= gloomy) outlook, thoughts düster; person trübsinnig, (= pessimistic) schwarzseherisch; poet, novel, music etc morbid; **that's ~!, that's a ~ thought** or **idea!** das ist ja makaber; **don't be so ~!** sieh doch nicht alles so schwarz!; **he's such a ~ little boy** er hat einen Hang zum Makaberen b (Med) morbid; growth krankhaft

morbid anatomy N (Med) Pathologie f

morbidity [mɔː'bɪdɪtɪ] N a (of idea, thought, jealousy, curiosity etc) Krankhaftigkeit f; (of interest, attitude) Unnatürlichkeit f; (of sense of humour, talk) Düsterkeit f; (of novel, music) Morbidität f; (of person) Trübsinn m; (of poet etc) Hang m zu düsteren Gedanken, Morbidität f; (= gloominess) Morbidität f b (Med) Morbidität f; (of growth) Krankhaftigkeit f

morbidly ['mɔːbɪdlɪ] ADV **to think ~** krankhafte or düstere or morbide (geh) Gedanken haben; **he is ~ interested in bad crashes** er hat ein krankhaftes Interesse an schweren Unfällen; **staring ~ out of the window** trübsinnig or düster aus dem Fenster schauend; **maybe I'll be dead then, he said ~** vielleicht bin ich dann schon tot, sagte er düster

mordacious [mɔː'deɪʃəs] ADJ = **mordant**

mordacity [mɔːˈdæsɪtɪ], **mordancy** [ˈmɔːdənsɪ] N beißender Humor; **the ~ of his wit** sein beißender Humor

mordant [ˈmɔːdənt] ADJ beißend, ätzend

more [mɔːʳ] ❂ 7.3, 12.2 [N, PRON] **a** (= greater amount) mehr; (= a further or additional amount) noch mehr; (of countable things) noch mehr or welche; **~ and ~** immer mehr; **I want a lot ~** ich will viel mehr; (in addition) ich will noch viel mehr; **three ~** noch drei; **a few ~** noch ein paar; **a little ~** etwas mehr; (in addition) noch etwas mehr; **many/much ~** viel mehr; **not many/much ~** nicht mehr viele/viel; **no ~** nichts mehr; (countable) keine mehr; **some ~** noch etwas; (countable) noch welche; **any ~?** noch mehr or etwas?; (countable) noch welche or welche?; **there isn't/aren't any ~** mehr gibt es nicht; (here, at the moment, left over) es ist nichts/es sind keine mehr da; **is/are there any ~?** gibt es noch mehr?; (left over) ist noch etwas/sind noch welche da?; **even ~** noch mehr; **I shall have ~ to say about this** dazu habe ich noch etwas zu sagen; **let's say no ~ about it** reden wir nicht mehr darüber; **we shall hear/see ~ of you** wir werden öfter von dir hören/dich öfter sehen; **there's ~ to come** da kommt noch etwas, das ist noch nicht alles; **what ~ do you want?** was willst du denn noch?; **what ~ could one want?** mehr kann man sich doch nicht wünschen; **there's ~ to it** da steckt (noch) mehr dahinter; **there's ~ to bringing up children than just ...** zum Kindererziehen gehört mehr als nur ...; **and what's ~, he ...** und außerdem or obendrein hat er ... (noch) ...; **they are ~ than we are** sie sind in der Mehrzahl; **there's ~ where that came from** davon gibts noch mehr

b (all) **the ~** umso mehr; **the ~ you give him, the ~ he wants** je mehr du ihm gibst, desto mehr verlangt er; **it makes me (all) the ~ ashamed** das beschämt mich umso mehr; **the ~ the merrier** je mehr, desto besser or umso besser

[ADJ] mehr; (in addition) noch mehr; **two/five ~ bottles** noch zwei/fünf Flaschen; **one ~ day, one day ~** noch ein Tag; **~ and ~ money/friends** immer mehr Geld/Freunde; **a lot/a little ~ money** viel/etwas mehr Geld; (in addition) noch viel/noch etwas mehr Geld; **a few ~ friends/ weeks** noch ein paar Freunde/Wochen; **you won't have many ~ friends/much ~ money left** du hast nicht mehr viele Freunde mehr/ viel Geld übrig; **no ~ money/friends** kein Geld/ keine Freunde mehr; **no ~ singing/squabbling!** Schluss mit der Singerei/mit dem Zanken!; **do you want some ~ tea/books?** möchten Sie noch etwas Tee/noch ein paar Bücher?; **is there any ~ wine in the bottle?** ist noch (etwas) Wein in der Flasche?; **there isn't any ~ wine** es ist kein Wein mehr da; **there aren't any ~ books** mehr Bücher gibt es nicht; (here, at the moment) es sind keine Bücher mehr da; **(the) ~ fool you!** du bist ja vielleicht ein Dummkopf!; **(the) ~ fool you for giving him the money** dass du auch so dumm bist und ihm das Geld gibst

[ADV] **a** mehr; **~ and ~** immer mehr; **it will weigh/grow a bit ~** es wird etwas mehr wiegen/ noch etwas wachsen; **will it weigh/grow any ~?** wird es mehr wiegen/noch etwas wachsen?; **it'll grow ~ if you ...** es wächst besser, wenn du ...; **to like/want sth ~** etw lieber mögen/wollen; **~ than** mehr als; **£5/2 hours ~ than I thought** £ 5 mehr/2 Stunden länger, als ich dachte; **it will ~ than meet the demand** das wird die Nachfrage mehr als genügend befriedigen; **he's ~ lazy than stupid** er ist eher faul als dumm; **no ~ than, not ~ than** nicht mehr als; **no ~ a duchess than I am** genauso wenig eine Herzogin wie ich (eine bin); **nothing ~ than a wild guess** eine reine Vermutung; **he's ~ like a brother to me** er ist eher wie ein Bruder (für mich); **no ~ do I** ich auch nicht; **he has resigned – that's no ~ than I expected** er hat gekündigt – das habe ich ja erwartet

b (= again) **once ~** noch einmal, noch mal

(inf); **never ~** nie mehr or wieder

c (= longer) mehr; **no ~, not any ~** nicht mehr; **to be no ~** (person) nicht mehr sein or leben; (thing) nicht mehr existieren; **if he comes here any ~ ...** wenn er noch weiter or länger hierher kommt ...

d (to form comp of adj, adv) -er (than als); **~ beautiful** schöner; **~ and ~ beautiful** immer schöner; **~ seriously** ernster; **no ~ stupid than I am** (auch) nicht dümmer als ich

e ~ or less mehr oder weniger; **neither ~ nor less, no ~, no less** nicht mehr und nicht weniger

moreish [ˈmɔːrɪʃ] ADJ (Brit inf) **these biscuits are very ~** diese Plätzchen schmecken nach mehr (inf)

morello [mɒˈreləʊ] N Sauerkirsche f, Morelle f

moreover [mɔːˈrəʊvəʳ] ❂ 26.1 ADV überdies, zudem, außerdem

mores [ˈmɔːreɪz] PL Sittenkodex m

morganatic [ˌmɔːɡəˈnætɪk] ADJ morganatisch

morgue [mɔːɡ] N **a** (= mortuary) Leichenschauhaus nt; **to be like a ~** wie ausgestorben sein **b** (Press) Archiv nt

MORI [ˈmɔːrɪ] (Brit) abbr of **Market and Opinion Research Institute** britisches Meinungsforschungsinstitut **~ poll** Meinungsumfrage f

moribund [ˈmɒrɪbʌnd] ADJ person todgeweiht (geh), moribund (spec); species im Aussterben begriffen; (fig) plan, policy zum Scheitern verurteilt; customs, way of life zum Aussterben verurteilt; **the empire was in a ~ state** das Weltreich stand vor dem Untergang or ging seinem Untergang entgegen

Mormon [ˈmɔːmən] [ADJ] mormonisch, Mormonen-; doctrine der Mormonen; **~ church** Mormonenkirche f [N] Mormone m, Mormonin f

Mormonism [ˈmɔːmənɪzəm] N Mormonentum nt

morn [mɔːn] N (poet) Morgen m

mornay [ˈmɔːneɪ] ADJ **~ sauce** Mornay- or Käsesoße f; **cauliflower/eggs ~** Blumenkohl/hart gekochte Eier in Käsesoße

morning [ˈmɔːnɪŋ] [N] Morgen m; (as opposed to afternoon also) Vormittag m; (fig) (of life) Frühling m (liter); (of an era) Anfänge pl, Beginn m; **~ dawned** es dämmerte; **in the ~** morgens, am Morgen, vormittags, am Vormittag; (= tomorrow) morgen früh; **early in the ~** früh(morgens), in der Frühe, am frühen Morgen; (= tomorrow) morgen früh; **very early in the ~** in aller Frühe, ganz früh (am Morgen); (= tomorrow) morgen ganz früh; **late (on) in the ~** am späten Vormittag, gegen Mittag; **(at) 7 in the ~** (um) 7 Uhr morgens or früh; (= tomorrow) morgen (früh) um 7; **I didn't get back until 2 in the ~** ich bin erst um 2 Uhr früh nach Hause gekommen; **this/yesterday ~** heute/gestern Morgen, heute/ gestern Vormittag; **tomorrow ~** morgen früh, morgen Vormittag; **on the ~ of November 28th** am Morgen des 28. November, am 28. November morgens; **it was the ~ after** es war am nächsten or anderen Tag or Morgen; **the ~ after the night before, the ~-after feeling** der Katzenjammer or die Katerstimmung am nächsten Morgen; **~, noon and night** morgens, mittags und nachts, Tag und Nacht [ATTR] am Morgen; (= regularly in the morning) morgendlich; **~ flight** Vormittagsflug m; **~ train** Frühzug m; **what time is ~ coffee?** (at work) wann ist morgens die Kaffeepause?; (in café) ab wann wird vormittags Kaffee serviert?

morning: morning-after pill N die Pille danach; **morning coat** N Cut(away) m; **morning dress** N , no pl Cut(away) m; (dark) Stresemann m; **morning-glory** N (Bot) Winde f; **morning gown** N Hauskleid nt; **Morning Prayer** N Morgenandacht f, Frühgottesdienst m; **morning room** N Frühstückszimmer nt; **morning sickness** N (Schwangerschafts-) übelkeit f; **morning star** N Morgenstern m; **morning suit** N Cut(away) m; (dark) Stresemann m

Moroccan [məˈrɒkən] [ADJ] marokkanisch [N] Marokkaner(in) m(f)

Morocco [məˈrɒkəʊ] N Marokko nt

morocco [məˈrɒkəʊ] N (also **morocco leather**) Maroquin m

moron [ˈmɔːrɒn] N (Med) Geistesschwache(r) mf, Debile(r) mf (spec); (inf) Trottel m (inf), Schwachkopf m (inf)

moronic [məˈrɒnɪk] ADJ (Med) geistesschwach, debil (spec); (inf) idiotisch (inf)

morose ADJ , **morosely** ADV [məˈrəʊs, -lɪ] verdrießlich, missmutig

moroseness [məˈrəʊsnɪs] N Verdrießlichkeit f, Missmut m

morpheme [ˈmɔːfiːm] N Morphem nt

morphia [ˈmɔːfɪə], **morphine** [ˈmɔːfiːn] N Morphium nt, Morphin nt (spec)

morphing [ˈmɔːfɪŋ] N Morphing nt

morphological [ˌmɔːfəˈlɒdʒɪkəl] ADJ morphologisch

morphology [mɔːˈfɒlədʒɪ] N Morphologie f

morris dance [ˈmɒrɪsˈdɑːns] N Moriskentanz m, alter englischer Volkstanz

morrow [ˈmɒrəʊ] N (old) **the ~** der kommende or folgende Tag; **on the ~** tags darauf; **good ~!** guten Morgen!

morse [mɔːs] N (also **Morse code**) Morsezeichen pl, Morseschrift f; **do you know ~ or (the) Morse code?** können Sie morsen?

morse alphabet N Morsealphabet nt

morsel [ˈmɔːsl] N (of food) Bissen m, Happen m; (fig) bisschen nt; (of information) Brocken m; **not a ~ of food** kein Bissen zu essen; **a ~ of comfort** ein kleiner Trost

mortal [ˈmɔːtl] [ADJ] **a** (= liable to die) sterblich; (= causing death) injury, combat tödlich; **to deal (sb/sth) a ~ blow** (jdm/einer Sache) einen tödlichen Schlag versetzen; **to be locked in ~ combat** auf Leben und Tod miteinander kämpfen

b (= extreme) tödlich, Todes-; (inf) hurry, embarrassment irrsinnig (inf); **~ fear** Todesangst f; **~ agony** Todesqualen pl; **to live in ~ fear or dread that ...** eine Todesangst haben, dass ...; **~ enemy** Todfeind(in) m(f)

c (inf, = conceivable) **no ~ use** überhaupt kein Nutzen

d (inf, = tedious) hours, boredom tödlich (inf) [N] Sterbliche(r) mf; **ordinary ~** (inf) Normalsterbliche(r) mf (inf); **a mere ~** ein bloßer Sterblicher

mortality [mɔːˈtælɪtɪ] N **a** (= mortal state) Sterblichkeit f **b** (= number of deaths) Todesfälle pl; (= rate) Sterblichkeit(sziffer) f, Mortalität f (form); **~ rate, rate of ~** Sterbeziffer f, Sterblichkeitsziffer f, Mortalität f (form)

mortally [ˈmɔːtəlɪ] ADV **a** (= fatally) tödlich; **~ ill** todkrank **b** (fig: = extremely) shocked etc zu Tode; wounded zutiefst; offended tödlich; **I was ~ afraid** ich habe Todesängste ausgestanden; **she is ~ embarrassed** es ist ihr höchst peinlich

mortal sin N Todsünde f

mortar¹ [ˈmɔːtəʳ] N **a** (= bowl) Mörser m **b** (= cannon) Minenwerfer m

mortar² [N] (= cement) Mörtel m [VT] mörteln

mortarboard [ˈmɔːtəbɔːd] N **a** (Univ) Doktorhut m **b** (Build) Mörtelbrett nt

mortgage [ˈmɔːɡɪdʒ] [N] Hypothek f (on auf +acc/dat); **a ~ for £50,000/for that amount** eine Hypothek über or von £ 50.000/über diesen Betrag [VT] house, land hypothekarisch belasten; **to ~ one's future** (fig) sich (dat) die or seine Zukunft verbauen

mortgage: mortgage bond N (Hypotheken)pfandbrief m; **mortgage deed** N (Jur) **a** Pfandbrief m **b** Hypothekenbrief m

mortgagee [ˌmɔːɡəˈdʒiː] N Hypothekar m

mortgage rate N Hypothekenzinssatz m

mortgage relief N Steuervergünstigung bei der Zahlung von Hypothekenzinsen

mortgagor [ˌmɔːɡəˈdʒɔː'] N Hypothekenschuldner(in) *m(f)*

mortice ['mɔːtɪs] N, VT = **mortise**

mortician [ˌmɔːˈtɪʃən] N (*US*) Bestattungsunternehmer(in) *m(f)*

mortification [ˌmɔːtɪfɪˈkeɪʃən] N **a** Beschämung *f*; (= *embarrassment*) äußerste Verlegenheit; (= *humiliation*) Demütigung *f*; **much to his ~, she ...** er empfand es als sehr beschämend, dass sie ...; (*embarrassment*) es war ihm äußerst peinlich, dass sie ...; (*humiliation*) er empfand es als eine Schmach, dass sie ...; **I discovered to my ~ that I had made a mistake** ich stellte zu meiner größten Verlegenheit fest, dass ich einen Fehler gemacht hatte; **because of her ~ at what had happened** weil ihr das, was geschehen war, so überaus peinlich war; **he felt great ~ at being rejected** er empfand es als eine Schmach *or* Schande, dass er nicht angenommen wurde **b** (*Rel*) Kasteiung *f* **c** (*Med*) Brand *m*

mortify ['mɔːtɪfaɪ] VT *usu pass* **a** (= *shame*) beschämen; (= *embarrass*) äußerst peinlich sein (+*dat*); **he was mortified** er empfand das als beschämend; (= *embarrassed*) es war ihm äußerst peinlich; **I was mortified!** peinlich? ich wäre am liebsten im Boden versunken!; **a mortified look** ein äußerst betretener Gesichtsausdruck **b** (*Rel*) kasteien **c** (*Med*) absterben lassen; **to be mortified** abgestorben sein **d** (*Med*) absterben

mortifying ADJ , **mortifyingly** ADV ['mɔːtɪfaɪɪŋ, -lɪ] beschämend; (= *embarrassing*) peinlich

mortise ['mɔːtɪs] **N** Zapfenloch *nt* **VT** verzapfen (*into* mit)

mortise and tenon joint N Zapfenverbindung *f*

mortise lock N (Ein)steckschloss *nt*

mortuary ['mɔːtjʊərɪ] N Leichenhalle *f*

Mosaic [məˈzeɪɪk] ADJ mosaisch

mosaic [məˈzeɪɪk] **N** Mosaik *nt* **ATTR** Mosaik-; **~ floor** Mosaikboden *m*

Moscow ['mɒskəʊ] N Moskau *nt*

Moselle [məˈzel] N Mosel *f*; (*also* **Moselle wine**) Mosel(wein) *m*

Moses ['məʊzɪz] N Mose(s) *m*

Moses basket N Körbchen *nt*

Moslem ['mɒzləm] ADJ mohammedanisch **N** Muslim(in) *m(f)*, Moslem(in) *m(f)*; (= *woman also*) Muslime *f*, Moslime *f*

mosque [mɒsk] N Moschee *f*

mosquito [mɒˈskiːtəʊ] N *pl* **-es** Stechmücke *f*; (*in tropics*) Moskito *m*

mosquito net N Moskitonetz *nt*

moss [mɒs] N Moos *nt*

Mossad ['mɒsæd] N Mossad *m* (*israelischer Geheimdienst*)

mossy ['mɒsɪ] ADJ (+*er*) (= *moss-covered*) moosbedeckt, bemoost; **lawn** vermoost; (= *mosslike*) moosig, moosartig

most [məʊst] ADJ *superl* **a** meiste(r, s); (= *greatest*) **satisfaction, pleasure etc** größte(r, s); (= *highest*) **speed etc** höchste(r, s); **who has (the) ~ money?** wer hat am meisten *or* das meiste Geld?; **that gave me (the) ~ pleasure** das hat mir am meisten Freude *or* die größte Freude gemacht; **for the ~ part** größtenteils, zum größten Teil; (= *by and large*) im Großen und Ganzen **b** (= *the majority of*) die meisten; **men/people** die meisten (Menschen/Leute); **he's better than ~ people** er ist besser als die meisten anderen

N, PRON (*uncountable*) das meiste; (*countable*) die meisten; **~ of it** das meiste; **~ of them** die meisten (von ihnen); **~ of the money** das meiste Geld; **~ of his friends** die meisten seiner Freunde; **~ of the winter/day** fast den ganzen Winter/Tag über; **~ of the time** die meiste Zeit, fast die ganze Zeit; (= *usually*) meist(ens); **at (the) ~** höchstens; **at (the) very ~** allerhöchs-

tens; **to make the ~ of sth** (= *make good use of*) etw voll ausnützen; (= *enjoy*) etw in vollen Zügen genießen; **to make the ~ of a story** so viel wie möglich aus einer Geschichte machen; **to make the ~ of one's looks or of oneself** das Beste aus sich machen; **the hostess with the ~est** (*inf*) die Supergastgeberin (*inf*); **it's the ~!** (*dated sl*) das ist dufte! (*dated sl*)

ADV **a** *superl* (+*vbs*) am meisten; (+*adj*) -ste(r, s); (+*adv*) -sten; **the ~ beautiful/difficult etc ...** der/die/das schönste/schwierigste *etc* ...; **who did it ~ easily?** wem ist es am leichtesten gefallen?; **what ~ displeased him ~ ...** was ihm am meisten missfiel ...; **~ of all** am allermeisten; **~ of all because ...** vor allem, weil ... **b** (= *very*) äußerst, überaus; **~ likely** höchstwahrscheinlich; **he added ~ unnecessarily ...** er sagte noch völlig unnötigerweise ...; **he had told you ~ explicitly** er hat Ihnen doch ganz eindeutig gesagt ... **c** (*old, dial, = almost*) fast, so ziemlich (*inf*), schier (*old, S Ger*)

most-favoured-nation clause, (*US*) **most-favored-nation clause** [ˌməʊstˈfeɪvədˈneɪʃnˌklɔːz] N (*Pol*) Meistbegünstigungsklausel *f*

mostly ['məʊstlɪ] ADV (= *principally*) hauptsächlich; (= *most of the time*) meistens; (= *by and large*) zum größten Teil; **they are ~ women/over fifty** die meisten sind Frauen/über fünfzig; **~ because ...** hauptsächlich, weil ...

MOT [ˌeməʊˈtiː] (*Brit*) **N** **a** *abbr of* Ministry of Transport **b** **~ (test)** ≈ TÜV *m*; **it failed its ~** ≈ es ist nicht durch den TÜV gekommen; **~ certificate** ≈ TÜV-Plakette *f* **VT** **to get one's car ~'d** ≈ sein Auto zum TÜV bringen; **I got my car ~'d** (*successfully*) ≈ mein Auto hat den TÜV bestanden; **the car is ~'d till June** ≈ das Auto hat noch TÜV bis Juni

mote [məʊt] N (*old*) Staubkorn *nt*, Stäubchen *nt*; **to see the ~ in one's neighbour's eye (and not the beam in one's own)** den Splitter im Auge des anderen (und nicht den Balken im eigenen Auge) sehen

motel [məʊˈtel] N Motel *nt*

motet [məʊˈtet] N Motette *f*

moth [mɒθ] N Nachtfalter *m*; (*wool-eating*) Motte *f*; **to be attracted like a ~ to a flame** wie die Motten vom Licht angezogen werden

moth: mothball **N** Mottenkugel *f*; **to put in ~s** (*lit, fig*) einmotten; **ship** stilllegen, außer Dienst stellen **VT** **plan, equipment etc** einmotten; **factory** stilllegen; **moth-eaten** ADJ (*lit*) mottenzerfressen; (*fig*) ausgedient, vermottet (*inf*)

mother ['mʌðə'] **N** **a** Mutter *f*; (= *animal*) Muttertier *nt*, Mutter *f*; (= *address to elderly lady*) Mütterchen; **Mother of God** Muttergottes *f*, Mutter *f* Gottes; **a ~'s love** Mutterliebe *f*; **she's a ~ of three** sie hat drei Kinder; **she's her ~'s daughter** sie ist wie ihre Mutter; **I had the ~ and father of a headache** (*inf*) ich hatte vielleicht Kopfschmerzen!; **the ~ of all battles/confrontations/traffic jams** die Mutter aller Kriege/Auseinandersetzungen/Staus; **shall I be ~?** (*inf*) (= *pour tea*) soll ich eingießen?; (= *serve food*) soll ich austeilen? **b** (*US, sl*) Arschloch *nt* (*vulg*), Saftsack *m* (*inf*); **a real ~ of a day** ein Scheißtag *m* (*inf*) **ATTR** Mutter-; **~ plant** Mutterpflanze *f*; **~ bird** Vogelmutter *f*; **hen** Glucke *f* **VT** (= *care for*) **young** auf- *or* großziehen; (= *give birth to*) zur Welt bringen; (= *cosset*) bemuttern

mother: motherboard N (*Comput*) Mutterplatine *f*, Hauptplatine *f*; **mother country** N (= *native country*) Vaterland *nt*, Heimat *f*; (= *head of empire*) Mutterland *nt*; **mothercraft** N Kinderpflege *f*; **mother earth** N Mutter *f* Erde; **mother figure** N Mutterfigur *f*; **motherfucker** N (*US, vulg*) Arschloch *nt* (*vulg*), Arschficker *m* (*vulg*); **motherfucking** ADJ (*US, vulg*) Scheiß- (*sl*); **motherhood** N Mutterschaft *f*

Mothering Sunday ['mʌðərɪŋ'sʌndɪ] N ≈ Muttertag *m*

mother: mother-in-law N *pl* **mothers-in-law** Schwiegermutter *f*; **motherland** N (= *native country*) Vaterland *nt*, Heimat *f*; (= *ancestral country*) Land *nt* der Väter *or* Vorfahren; **motherless** ADJ mutterlos; **he was left ~ at the age of 2** er verlor mit 2 Jahren seine Mutter; **mother lode** N (*Min*) Hauptader *f*; **mother love** N Mutterliebe *f*

motherly ['mʌðəlɪ] ADJ mütterlich

mother-naked ADJ *pred* [ˌmʌðə'neɪkɪd] splitternackt (*inf*)

mother nature N Mutter *f* Natur

mother-of-pearl [ˌmʌðərəv'pɜːl] **N** Perlmutt *nt*, Perlmutter *f* **ADJ** Perlmutt-; **~ button** Perlmuttknopf *m*

Mother's Day N Muttertag *m*

mother's help N Haus(halts)hilfe *f*

mother: mother ship N Mutterschiff *nt*; **mother superior** N Mutter Oberin *f*; **mother tie** N (*Psych*) Mutterbindung *f*; **mother-to-be** N *pl* **mothers-to-be** werdende Mutter; **mother tongue** N Muttersprache *f*; **mother wit** N Mutterwitz *m*

moth: mothhole N Mottenloch *nt*; **mothproof** **ADJ** mottenfest **VT** mottenfest machen

motif [məʊˈtiːf] N (*Art, Mus*) Motiv *nt*; (*Sew*) Muster *nt*

motion ['məʊʃən] **N** **a** *no pl* (= *movement*) Bewegung *f*; **to be in ~** sich bewegen; (*engine, machine etc*) laufen; (*train, bus etc*) fahren; **to set or put sth in ~** etw in Gang bringen *or* setzen; **to set the wheels in ~ (to do sth)** die Dinge ins Rollen bringen(, um etw zu tun) **b** (= *gesture*) Bewegung *f*; **to go through the ~s of doing sth** (*because protocol, etiquette etc demands it*) etw pro forma *or* der Form halber tun; (= *pretend*) so tun, als ob man etw täte, den Anschein erwecken, etw zu tun; (= *do mechanically*) etw völlig mechanisch tun **c** (= *proposal*) Antrag *m*; **to propose or make** (*US*) **a ~** einen Antrag stellen **d** (*in debate*) Thema *nt* **e** (*Brit*) (= *bowel motion*) Stuhlgang *m*; (= *faeces*) Stuhl *m*; **to have a ~** Stuhlgang haben **VT** **to ~ to sb to do sth** jdm bedeuten, etw zu tun (*geh*), jdm ein Zeichen geben, dass er etw tun solle; **he ~ed me to a chair** er wies mir einen Stuhl an; **he ~ed me in** er winkte mich herein; **she ~ed me away** sie gab mir ein Zeichen, wegzugehen **VI** **to ~ to sb to do sth** jdm bedeuten, etw zu tun (*geh*), jdm ein Zeichen geben, dass er etw tun solle

motion: motionless ADJ unbeweglich, reg(ungs)los; **to stand ~** bewegungslos dastehen; **motion picture** N (*esp US*) Film *m*; **motion sensor** N Bewegungsmelder *m*; **motion sickness** N (*Med*) Kinetose *f* (*spec*), Seekrankheit *f*; (*in the air*) Luftkrankheit *f*; (*in car*) Autokrankheit *f*; **motion study** N (*Econ*) Bewegungsstudie *f*

motivate ['məʊtɪveɪt] VT motivieren

motivated ['məʊtɪveɪtɪd] ADJ motiviert; **highly ~** hoch motiviert; **to keep sb ~** jds Motivation erhalten; **he's just not ~ enough** es fehlt ihm einfach die nötige Motivation

motivation [ˌməʊtɪˈveɪʃən] N Motivation *f*

motivational [ˌməʊtɪˈveɪʃənəl] ADJ motivational

motive ['məʊtɪv] **N** **a** (= *incentive, reason*) Motiv *nt*, Beweggrund *m*; (*for crime*) (Tat)motiv *nt*; **the profit ~** Gewinnstreben *nt*; **with the purest of ~s** mit den besten Absichten **b** = **motif** **ADJ** **~ power/force** Antriebs- *or* Triebkraft *f*

motiveless ['məʊtɪvlɪs] ADJ grundlos, ohne Motiv, unmotiviert

mot juste ['məʊ'ʒuːst] N passender *or* treffender Ausdruck

motley ['mɒtlɪ] **ADJ** kunterbunt; (= *varied also*) bunt (gemischt); (= *multicoloured also*) bunt (gescheckt) **N** Narrenkostüm *or* -kleid *nt*; **on with the ~!** lache, Bajazzo!

motocross ['məʊtəkrɒs] N Motocross *nt*

motor ['məʊtə] **N** **a** Motor *m* **b** (*Brit inf*: = *car*) Auto *nt* **VI** (*dated*) (mit dem Auto) fahren **ATTR** **a** (*Physiol*) motorisch **b** (= *motor-driven*) Motor-; **~ yacht** Motorjacht *f* **c** (= *relating to motor vehicles*) Kraftfahrzeug-, Kfz-; **~ manufacturer** Kraftfahrzeughersteller *m*; (*esp making cars*) Automobilhersteller *m*; **the ~ trade** die Kraftfahrzeugbranche, die Kfz-Branche

motor: motor-assisted ADJ mit Hilfsmotor; **motorbike** N Motorrad *nt*; **motorboat** N Motorboot *nt*

motorcade ['məʊtəkeɪd] N Fahrzeug- *or* Wagenkolonne *f*

motor: motorcar N (*dated, form*) Automobil *nt* (*dated*), Auto *nt*; **motor caravan** N (*Brit*) Wohnmobil *nt*; **motorcoach** N (*dated*) Autobus *m*; **motorcycle** N Motorrad *nt*, Kraftrad *nt* (*form*); **~ combination** Motorrad *nt* mit Beiwagen; **motorcycling** N Motorradfahren *nt*; (*Sport*) Motorradsport *m*; **motorcyclist** N Motorradfahrer(in) *m(f)*; **motor-driven** ADJ mit Motorantrieb

-motored [-'məʊtəd] ADJ *suf* -motorig; **tri-motored** dreimotorig

motor home N Wohnmobil *nt*

motor industry N Kraftfahrzeugindustrie *f*; (*esp making cars*) Automobilindustrie *f*

motoring ['məʊtərɪŋ] (*esp Brit*) **ADJ** *attr* Auto-; **~ accident** Autounfall *m*; **~ offence** Verkehrsdelikt *nt*; **the ~ public** die Autofahrer *pl* **N** Autofahren *nt*; **school of ~** Fahrschule *f*

motor inn N *US* = **motor lodge**

motor insurance N Kraftfahrzeugversicherung *f*, Kfz-Versicherung *f*

motorist ['məʊtərɪst] N Autofahrer(in) *m(f)*

motorization [ˌməʊtəraɪ'zeɪʃən] N Motorisierung *f*

motorize ['məʊtəraɪz] VT motorisieren; **to be ~d** motorisiert sein; (*private person also*) ein Auto haben

motor: motor lodge, motor inn N (*US*) Motel *nt*; **motorman** N (*of train*) Zugführer(in) *m(f)*; (*of tram*) Straßenbahnfahrer(in) *m(f)*; **motor mechanic** N Kraftfahrzeugmechaniker(in) *m(f)*, Kfz-Mechaniker(in) *m(f)*; **motor nerve** N motorischer Nerv; **motor neuron disease** N (*Med*) amyotrophe Lateralsklerose; **motor oil** Motorenöl *nt*, Motoröl *nt*; **motor race** N (Auto)rennen *nt*; **motor racing** N Rennsport *m*; **he did a lot of ~** er hat an vielen Autorennen teilgenommen; **motor road** N Fahrstraße *f*; **motor scooter** N (*form*) Motorroller *m*; **motor show** N Automobilausstellung *f*; **motor sport** N Motorsport *m*; (*with cars also*) Automobilsport *m*; **motor torpedo boat** N Torpedoboot *nt*; **motor truck** N (*dated US*) Lastwagen *m*; **motor vehicle** N (*form*) Kraftfahrzeug *nt*; **motor vessel** N Motorschiff *nt*; **motorway** N (*Brit*) Autobahn *f*; **~ driving** das Fahren auf der Autobahn, das Autobahnfahren; **~ junction** Autobahndreieck *nt*; **~ madness** Geschwindigkeitsrausch *m*

mottled ['mɒtld] ADJ gesprenkelt; *complexion* fleckig; **~ brown and white** braun und weiß gesprenkelt

motto ['mɒtəʊ] N *pl* **-es** Motto *nt*, Wahlspruch *m*; (*personal also*) Devise *f*; (*Her also*) Sinnspruch *m*; (*in cracker, on calendar*) Spruch *m*; **the school ~** das Motto der Schule

mould¹, (*US*) **mold** [məʊld] **N** **a** (= *hollow form*) (Guss)form *f*; (*Typ also*) Mater *f*; (= *shape, Cook*) Form *f* **b** (= *jelly, blancmange*) Pudding *m*, Wackelpeter *m* (*inf*) **c** (*fig*: = *character, style*) **to be cast in** *or* **from the same/a different ~** (*people*) vom gleichen/von einem anderen Schlag sein, aus dem gleichen/einem anderen Holz geschnitzt sein; (*novel characters*) nach demselben/einem anderen Muster geschaffen sein; **the two painters/novelists etc are cast in** *or* **from the same/a different ~** die beiden Maler/Schriftsteller *etc* verbindet viel/wenig miteinander; **to break the ~** (*fig*) mit der Tradition brechen; **they broke the**

~ when they made him er hat nicht seinesgleichen; **to fit sb/sth into a ~** jdn/etw in ein Schema zwängen **VT** **a** (*lit*) (= *fashion*) formen (*into* zu); (= *cast*) gießen **b** (*fig*) *character, person* formen; **to ~ sb into sth** etw aus jdm machen **VR to ~ oneself on sb** sich (*dat*) jdn zum Vorbild nehmen; **to ~ oneself on an ideal** sich an einem Ideal orientieren

mould², (*US*) **mold** N (= *fungus*) Schimmel *m*

mould³, (*US*) **mold** N (= *soil*) Humus(boden) *m*, Humuserde *f*

moulder¹, (*US*) **molder** ['məʊldə] N (*Tech*, = *person*) Former(in) *m(f)*, (Form)gießer(in) *m(f)*

moulder², (*US*) **molder** VI (*lit*) vermodern; (*leaves also*) verrotten; (*food*) verderben; (*carcass*) verwesen; (*fig*) (*mental faculties, building*) zerfallen; (*equipment*) vermodern, vergammeln (*inf*); (*person*) verkümmern

mouldiness, (*US*) **moldiness** ['məʊldɪnɪs] N Schimmel *m* (*of* auf +*dat*), Schimmligkeit *f*

moulding, (*US*) **molding** ['məʊldɪŋ] **N** **a** (= *act*) Formen *nt*; (*of metals*) Gießen *nt* **b** (= *cast*) Abdruck *m*; (*of metal*) (Ab)guss *m*; (= *ceiling moulding*) Deckenfries *m* or -stuck *m* **c** (*fig*) Formen *nt*

mouldy, (*US*) **moldy** ['məʊldɪ] ADJ (+*er*) **a** (= *covered with mould*) verschimmelt, schimmelig; (= *musty*) mod(e)rig; **to go ~** (*food*) verschimmeln **b** (*dated inf*) (= *pathetic, contemptible*) miserabel (*inf*); (= *mean*) *person* schäbig; *amount* lumpig (*inf*)

moult, (*US*) **molt** [məʊlt] **N** (*of birds*) Mauser *f* (*also Comput*); (*of mammals*) Haarwechsel *m*; (*of snakes*) Häutung *f* **VT** *hairs* verlieren; *feathers, skin* abstreifen **VI** (*bird*) sich mausern; (*mammals*) sich haaren; (*snake*) sich häuten

mound [maʊnd] **N** **a** (= *hill, burial mound*) Hügel *m*; (= *earthwork*) Wall *m*; (*Baseball*) Wurfmal *nt* **b** (= *pile*) Haufen *m*; (*of books, letters*) Stoß *m*, Stapel *m*

mount¹ [maʊnt] **N** **a** (*poet*, = *mountain, hill*) Berg *m* **b** (*in names*) **Mount Etna/Kilimanjaro** *etc* der Ätna/Kilimandscharo *etc*; **Mount Everest** Mount Everest *m*; **on Mount Sinai** auf dem Berg/Sinai

mount² **N** **a** (= *horse etc*) Reittier *nt*, Ross *nt* (*old, liter*) **b** (= *support, base*) (*of machine*) Sockel *m*, Untersatz *m*; (*of colour slide*) Rahmen *m*; (*of microscope slide*) Objektträger *m*; (*of jewel*) Fassung *f*; (*of photo, picture*) Passepartout *nt*; (= *backing*) Unterlage *f*, Rücken *m*; (= *stamp mount*) Falz *m* **VT** **a** (= *climb onto*) besteigen, steigen auf (+*acc*) **b** (= *place in/on mount*) montieren; *picture, photo* aufziehen; *colour slide* rahmen; *microscope slide, specimen, animal* präparieren; *jewel* (ein)fassen; *stamp* aufkleben **c** (= *organize*) *play* inszenieren; *attack, expedition, exhibition* organisieren, vorbereiten; *army* aufstellen **d to ~ a guard** eine Wache aufstellen (*on, over* vor +*dat*); **to ~ guard** Wache stehen *or* halten (*on, over* vor +*dat*) **e** (= *mate with*) bespringen; (*inf*: *person*) besteigen **f** (= *provide with horse*) mit Pferden/einem Pferd versorgen **VI** **a** (= *get on*) aufsteigen; (*on horse*) aufsitzen, aufsteigen **b** (*also* **mount up**) wachsen, zunehmen; (*evidence*) sich häufen; **the death toll has ~ed to 800** die Todesziffer ist auf 800 gestiegen; **pressure is ~ing on him to resign** er sieht sich wachsendem Druck ausgesetzt, zurückzutreten

mountain ['maʊntɪn] N (*lit, fig*) Berg *m*; **in the ~s** im Gebirge, in den Bergen; **to make a ~ out of a molehill** aus einer Mücke einen Elefant(en) machen (*inf*); **we have a ~ to climb** (*esp Brit fig*) wir haben eine riesige Aufgabe vor uns; **faith can move ~s** der Glaube kann Berge versetzen; **if Mohammed won't go to the ~, the**

~ must go to Mohammed (*prov*) wenn der Berg nicht zum Propheten kommen will, muss der Prophet zum Berge gehen (*prov*)

mountain in *cpds* Berg-; (*alpine, Himalayan etc*) Gebirgs-; **~ road** Berg-/Gebirgsstraße *f*; **~ air** Bergluft *f*; **mountain ash** N Eberesche *f*; **mountain bike** N Mountainbike *nt*; **mountain biker** N Mountainbiker(in) *m(f)*; **mountain chain** N Berg- *or* Gebirgskette *f*, Gebirgszug *m*; **mountain dew** N (*inf*) *illegal gebrannter Whisky*

mountaineer [ˌmaʊntɪ'nɪə] **N** Bergsteiger(in) *m(f)* **VI** bergsteigen

mountaineering [ˌmaʊntɪ'nɪərɪŋ] **N** Bergsteigen *nt* **ATTR** Bergsteiger-; **~ school** Bergsteigerschule *f*; **~ skill** bergsteigerisches Können; **learn ~ skills with ...** erlernen Sie das Bergsteigen mit ...; **in ~ circles** unter Bergsteigern

mountain goat N Bergziege *f*

mountain lion N Puma *m*, Silberlöwe *m*

mountainous ['maʊntɪnəs] ADJ bergig, gebirgig; (*fig*: = *huge*) riesig; *waves* meterhoch; **~ seas** stürmische See (mit meterhohen Wellen)

mountain: mountain pass N Gebirgspass *m*; **mountain range** N Gebirgszug *m* or -kette *f*

mountains classification N (*Cycling*) Bergwertung *f*

mountain: mountain sheep N Dickhornschaf *nt*; **mountain sickness** N Höhen- or Bergkrankheit *f*; **mountainside** N (Berg)hang *m*; **mountain slide** N Bergrutsch *m*

mountebank ['maʊntɪbæŋk] N Quacksalber *m*, Scharlatan *m*

mounted ['maʊntɪd] ADJ (= *on horseback*) beritten; (*Mil*, = *with motor vehicles*) motorisiert

Mountie ['maʊntɪ] N (*inf*) *berittener kanadischer Polizist*

mounting ['maʊntɪŋ] **ADJ** (= *increasing*) wachsend, zunehmend; **there is ~ evidence that ...** es häufen sich die Beweise dafür, dass ... **N** **a** (*of horse*) Besteigen *nt* **b** (*of picture, photo*) Aufziehen *nt*; (*of jewel*) (Ein)fassen *nt* **c** (= *frame etc*) = **mount²** B **b**

mourn [mɔːn] **VT** *person* trauern um, betrauern; *sb's death* beklagen, betrauern; (*with wailing*) beklagen; (*fig*) nachtrauern (+*dat*); **who is she ~ing?** um wen trauert sie?; (= *wear mourning for*) warum trägt sie Trauer?; **he is still ~ing the break-up of his relationship** er trauert noch immer über das Ende seiner Beziehung; **what is to become of us?, she ~ed** was soll aus uns werden?, klagte sie **VI** trauern; (= *wear mourning*) Trauer tragen, in Trauer gehen; **to ~ for** *or* **over sb** um jdn trauern, jds Tod (*acc*) betrauern; **to ~ for** *or* **over sth** einer Sache (*dat*) nachtrauern

mourner ['mɔːnə] N Trauernde(r) *mf*; (= *non-relative at funeral*) Trauergast *m*

mournful ['mɔːnfʊl] ADJ (= *sad*) *person, occasion, atmosphere, look* traurig, trauervoll; *person (as character trait), voice* weinerlich; *sigh, appearance* kläglich, jämmerlich; *sound, cry* klagend

mournfully ['mɔːnfʊlɪ] ADV (= *sadly*) traurig, trauervoll; *wail, cry* klagend

mournfulness ['mɔːnfʊlnɪs] N Traurigkeit *f*; (*of voice*) Weinerlichkeit *f*; (*of sigh, appearance*) Jämmerlichkeit *f*

mourning ['mɔːnɪŋ] N (= *act*) Trauer *f*, Trauern *nt* (*of* um); (*with wailing*) Wehklage *f*; (= *period etc*) Trauerzeit *f*; (= *dress*) Trauer(kleidung) *f*; **to be in ~ for sb** um jdn trauern; (= *wear mourning*) Trauer tragen; **to come out of ~** die Trauer ablegen; **to go into ~** trauern; (= *wear mourning*) Trauer anlegen; **next Tuesday has been declared a day of national ~** für den kommenden Dienstag wurde Staatstrauer angeordnet

mouse [maʊs] **N** *pl* **mice** **a** Maus *f* (*also Comput*) **b** (*inf*: = *person*) (*shy*) schüchternes Mäuschen; (*nondescript*) graue Maus **VI** Mäuse fangen, mausen; **to go mousing** auf Mäusejagd gehen

mouse in *cpds* Mause-; (*Comput*) Maus-; **mouse click** N (*Comput*) Mausklick *m*; **mouse-col-**

oured ADJ mausgrau; **mousehole** N Mauseloch *nt*; **mouse mat**, **mouse pad** N (*Comput*) Mausmatte *f*

mouser ['maʊsə] N Mäusefänger(in) *m(f)*, Mäusejäger(in) *m(f)*

mousetrap ['maʊstræp] N Mausefalle *f*

mousey ADJ = **mousy**

moussaka [muˈsɑːkə] N Moussaka *f*

mousse [muːs] N a Creme(speise) *f* b (*also* **styling mousse**) Schaumfestiger *m*

moustache, (US) **mustache** [məˈstɑːʃ] N Schnurrbart *m*

mousy, mousey ['maʊsɪ] ADJ (+*er*) (= *timid, shy*) schüchtern; (= *nondescript*) farblos, unscheinbar; *colour, hair* mausgrau

mouth [maʊθ] **N** (*of person*) Mund *m*; (*of animal*) Maul *nt*; (*of bird*) Rachen *m*; (*of bottle, cave, vice etc*) Öffnung *f*; (*of river*) Mündung *f*; (*of harbour*) Einfahrt *f*; **to be down in the ~** (*inf*) deprimiert *or* niedergeschlagen sein; **to keep one's (big) ~ shut (about sth)** (*inf*) (über etw *acc*) den Mund *or* die Klappe (*inf*) halten; **me and my big ~!** (*inf*) ich konnte wieder nicht den Mund *or* die Klappe (*inf*) halten; **he's all ~ and (no) trousers** (*Brit inf*) große Klappe, nichts dahinter (*inf*); **to have a foul ~** ein grobes *or* ungewaschenes Maul haben (*inf*); **watch your ~!** pass auf, was du sagst; **to speak** *or* **talk out of both sides of one's ~** (*US*) mit doppelter *or* gespaltener Zunge sprechen; **he has three ~s to feed** er hat drei Mäuler zu ernähren *or* stopfen (*inf*) → **word**

VT [maʊð] (= *say affectedly*) (über)deutlich artikulieren; (= *articulate soundlessly*) mit Lippensprache sagen

mouthful ['maʊθfʊl] N (*of drink*) Schluck *m*; (*of food*) Bissen *m*, Happen *m* (*inf*); (*fig*) (= *difficult word*) Zungenbrecher *m*; (= *long word*) Bandwurm *m*; **the diver gulped in great ~s of air** der Taucher machte ein paar tiefe Atemzüge; **I got a ~ of salt water** ich habe einen ganzen Schwall Salzwasser geschluckt; **you said a ~** (*US, inf*) das kann man wohl sagen

mouth in *cpds* Mund-; **mouth organ** N Mundharmonika *f*; **mouthpiece** N Mundstück *nt*; (*of telephone*) Sprechmuschel *f*; (*fig: = spokesman, publication*) Sprachrohr *nt*; **mouth-to-mouth** ADJ ~ **resuscitation** Mund-zu-Mund-Beatmung *f*; **mouthwash** N Mundwasser *nt*; **mouthwatering** ADJ lecker; (*fig*) *prospect, car etc* verlockend; **that smells/looks really ~** da läuft einem ja das Wasser im Mund(e) zusammen!; **a ~ sum** ein hübsches Sümmchen (*inf*); **to look ~** (*boy, girl*) appetitlich aussehen; **mouthwateringly** ADV appetitlich

mouthy ['maʊθɪ] ADJ (*inf*) **to be ~** eine große Klappe haben (*inf*)

movability [ˌmuːvəˈbɪlɪtɪ] N Beweglichkeit *f*; (= *transportability*) Transportfähigkeit *f*

movable ['muːvəbl] **ADJ** beweglich (*auch Jur, Eccl*); (= *transportable*) transportierbar, transportfähig; **not easily ~** schwer zu bewegen/transportieren **N** a (= *portable object*) bewegliches Gut; ~**s** *pl* Mobiliar *nt*, Mobilien *pl* b *usu pl* (*Jur*) bewegliches Vermögen, Mobiliarvermögen *nt*

move [muːv]	
1 TRANSITIVE VERB	3 NOUN
2 INTRANSITIVE VERB	4 PHRASAL VERBS

1 – TRANSITIVE VERB

a = **make sth move** bewegen; *wheel, windmill etc* (an)treiben; (= *shift*) *objects, furniture* woanders hinstellen; (= *move away*) wegstellen; (= *shift about*) umstellen, umräumen; *chest, chair* rücken; *vehicle (driver)* wegfahren; (*engine*) von der Stelle bewegen; (= *transport*) befördern; (= *remove*) *soil, dirt, rubble* wegschaffen; *obstacle* aus dem Weg räumen; *chess piece etc* ziehen mit, einen Zug machen mit; **to move sth to a different place** etw an einen anderen Platz stellen; **to be unable to**

move sth (= *lift*) etw nicht von der Stelle *or* vom Fleck (*inf*) bringen; *screw, nail* etw nicht losbekommen; **I can't move this lid/handle** der Deckel/Griff lässt sich nicht bewegen; **you'll have to move these books/your car (out of the way)** Sie müssen diese Bücher wegräumen/Ihr Auto wegfahren; **don't move anything, said the detective** verändern Sie nichts *or* lassen Sie alles so, wie es ist, sagte der Detektiv; **you must have moved the camera** da haben Sie wahrscheinlich gewackelt; **recent events have moved the share index upwards/downwards** infolge der jüngsten Ereignisse ist der Aktienindex gestiegen/gefallen

b parts of body bewegen; (= *take away*) *arm* wegnehmen; *one's foot, hand* wegziehen; **could you move your head a little to the side?** können Sie vielleicht Ihren Kopf ein wenig zur Seite drehen?; **he moved his face a little closer** er ging mit dem Gesicht etwas näher heran; **move your feet off the table!** nimm deine Füße vom Tisch!; **move yourself, can't you?** (= *make room*) können Sie nicht mal etwas Platz machen?

c people *enemy, demonstrators* vertreiben; *patient* bewegen; (= *transport*) transportieren; (= *transfer*) verlegen; *refugees* transportieren; (*out of area*) evakuieren; *employee* (*to different department*) versetzen; *pupil* (*by authorities*) versetzen; **move those people** schicken Sie die Leute da weg; **to move sb to a hospital** jdn ins Krankenhaus einliefern; **to move soldiers into a city** Soldaten in eine Stadt versetzen; **I'm going to move you to sales manager** ich werde Sie jetzt als Verkaufsleiter einsetzen; **his parents moved him to another school** seine Eltern haben ihn in eine andere Schule getan *or* gegeben

d = **change location of** *offices, troops, production* verlegen; (*Comput*) *text block* verschieben; **the removal men are moving us on Friday** die Spediteure machen am Freitag unseren Umzug; **we've been moved to a new office** wir mussten in ein anderes Büro umziehen

♦ **to move house** (*Brit*) umziehen

♦ **to move office** (in ein anderes Büro) umziehen

e = **change timing of** *event, date* verlegen; (= *put back*) verschieben; **they've moved the meeting to 3 o'clock on Tuesday** sie haben die Sitzung auf Dienstag 15 Uhr verlegt/verschoben

f = **cause emotion in** rühren, bewegen; (= *upset*) erschüttern, ergreifen; **to be moved** gerührt/erschüttert sein; **I'm not easily moved, but ...** ich bin ja sonst nicht so schnell gerührt/leicht zu erschüttern, aber ...; **his speech really moved them** sie waren von seiner Rede tief bewegt; **to move sb from an opinion** *etc* (= *sway*) jdn von einer Meinung *etc* abbringen; **I shall not be moved** ich bleibe hart *or* dabei

♦ **to move sb to... to move sb to tears** jdn zu Tränen rühren; **to move sb to anger/pity** jds Zorn/Mitleid erregen; **to move sb to action** jdn veranlassen, etw zu unternehmen

♦ **to move sb to do sth** jdn veranlassen *or* bewegen (*geh*) *or* dazu bringen, etw zu tun

g = **propose** (*form*) beantragen; **she moved an amendment to the motion** sie stellte einen Abänderungsantrag; **I move that we adjourn** ich beantrage eine Vertagung

h Med **to move the** *or* **one's bowels** Stuhlgang haben; **this mixture will help to move the bowels** dieses Mittel regt die Verdauung an *or* ist verdauungsfördernd

i Comm (= *sell*) absetzen

2 – INTRANSITIVE VERB

a sich bewegen; **the wheel/vehicle began to move** das Rad/Fahrzeug setzte sich in Bewegung; **how does a caterpillar move?** wie bewegt sich eine Raupe fort?; **she moves gracefully/like a cat** ihre Bewegungen sind anmutig/katzenhaft; **nothing/nobody moved** nichts/niemand rührte sich; **don't move!** stillhalten!; **don't move or I'll shoot!** keine Bewegung, oder ich schieße!

b = **not be stationary** (*vehicle, ship*) fahren; (*traffic*) vorankommen; **to keep moving** nicht stehen

bleiben; **to keep sb/sth moving** jdn/etw in Gang halten; **keep those people moving!** sorgen Sie dafür, dass die Leute weitergehen!

c = **move house** umziehen; **we moved to London/to a bigger house** wir sind nach London/in ein größeres Haus umgezogen; **they moved to Germany** sie sind nach Deutschland gezogen; **they moved from London** sie sind von London weggezogen

d = **change place** gehen; (*in vehicle*) fahren; **let's move into the garden** gehen wir in den Garten; **he has moved to room 52** er ist jetzt in Zimmer 52; **she has moved to another department/a different company** sie hat die Abteilung/Firma gewechselt; **he used to sit here, has he moved?** das war doch sein Platz, sitzt er nicht mehr da?; **he has moved to Brown's** er ist zu Brown gegangen *or* gewechselt; **have the troops moved?** sind die Truppen abgezogen?; **the troops moved to another base** die Truppen zogen zu einem anderen Stützpunkt weiter; **move!** weitergehen!; (= *go away*) verschwinden Sie!; **don't move** gehen Sie nicht weg; **I won't move from here** ich rühre mich nicht von der Stelle; **it's time we were moving** *or* **we moved** es wird Zeit, dass wir gehen

e = **change, progress** **to move (away) from sth** sich von etw entfernen; **to move (closer) to (-wards) sth** sich einer Sache (*dat*) nähern; **which way are events moving?** in welche Richtung entwickeln sich die Dinge?; **things are moving at last** endlich kommen die Dinge in Gang, endlich geschieht etwas; **technology moves at an ever faster rate** die Technik macht immer raschere Fortschritte; **to move with the times** mit der Zeit gehen; **let's move to another subject** wechseln wir das Thema

f = **go fast** (*inf*) einen Zahn *or* ein Tempo draufhaben (*inf*); (= *hurry up*) zumachen (*inf*), einen Zahn zulegen (*inf*); **he can really move** der ist unheimlich schnell (*inf*); **150? that's moving!** 150? das ist aber ein ganz schönes Tempo! (*inf*)

g = **be part of** **to move in high society/in royal circles** *etc* in der feinen Gesellschaft/in königlichen Kreisen *etc* verkehren

h in games (= *make a move*) einen Zug machen, ziehen; (= *have one's turn*) am Zug sein, ziehen

i = **act** (*fig*) etwas unternehmen, Maßnahmen ergreifen; **they must move first** sie müssen den ersten Schritt tun; **we'll have to move quickly (in order to avoid this)** wir müssen schnell handeln(um dies zu vermeiden); **the government won't move until ...** die Regierung wird nichts unternehmen, bis ...

j = **propose, request** (*form*) **to move for sth** etw beantragen

k Comm (= *sell*) sich absetzen lassen, gehen (*inf*)

3 – NOUN

a in game Zug *m*; (*fig*) (= *step, action*) Schritt *m*; (= *measure taken*) Maßnahme *f*; **it's my move** (*lit, fig*) ich bin am Zug, ich bin dran (*inf*); **that was a bad/good/clever move** (*lit, fig*) das war ein schlechter/guter/raffinierter Zug

♦ **to make a move** (*lit, fig*) einen Zug machen → *also* **(b)**

♦ **to make the first move** (*fig*) den ersten Zug machen, den ersten Schritt tun

b = **movement** Bewegung *f*; **to watch sb's every move** jdn nicht aus den Augen lassen

♦ **to make a move** (= *go, leave*) **nobody had made a move (toward(s) going)** keiner hatte Anstalten gemacht zu gehen; **it's time we made a move** es wird Zeit, dass wir gehen *or* dass wir uns auf den Weg machen → *also* **(a)**

♦ **to make a move to do sth** (*fig*) Anstalten machen, etw zu tun

♦ **to be on the move** (*things, people*) in Bewegung sein; (*fig: developments*) im Fluss sein; (*person: in different places*) unterwegs *or* auf Achse (*inf*) sein; (*vehicle*) fahren; (*country, institutions etc*) sich im Umbruch befinden

♦ **to get a move on (with sth)** (*inf*: = *hurry up*) sich beeilen (mit etw); (= *make quick pro-*

gress) (mit etw) vorankommen; **get a move on!** nun mach schon! (inf), mach mal zu! (inf)

c = change (of house etc) Umzug m; (to different job) Stellenwechsel m; (to different department) Wechsel m

4 – PHRASAL VERBS

▶ **move about** (Brit) **VT** sep (= place in different positions) umarrangieren; furniture, ornaments etc umstellen, umräumen; parts of body (hin und her) bewegen; (= fiddle with) herumspielen mit; employee versetzen; (= make travel) umher- or herumschicken; **the families of servicemen get moved about a lot** die Familien von Militärpersonal müssen oft umziehen

VI sich (hin und her) bewegen; (= fidget) herumzappeln; (= travel) unterwegs sein; (= move house) umziehen; **I can hear him moving about** ich höre ihn herumlaufen; **the car/stick will help her to move about** mit dem Auto/Stock ist sie beweglicher

▶ **move along** **VT** sep weiterrücken; car vorfahren; bystanders etc zum Weitergehen veranlassen; **they are trying to move things along** sie versuchen, die Dinge voranzutreiben **VI** (along seat etc) auf- or durchrücken; (along pavement, bus etc) weitergehen; (cars) weiterfahren

▶ **move around** **VTI** sep = **move about**

▶ **move aside** **VT** sep zur Seite or beiseite rücken or schieben; person beiseite drängen **VI** zur Seite gehen, Platz machen

▶ **move away** **VT** sep wegräumen; car wegfahren; person wegschicken; (to different town, job etc) versetzen; troops abziehen; (pupil) wegsetzen; **to move sb away from sb/sth** jdn von jdm/etw entfernen

VI **a** (= move aside) aus dem Weg gehen, weggehen; (= leave, people) weggehen; (vehicle) losfahren; (= move house) fort- or wegfahren (from aus, von); (firm) wegziehen (from von, aus), verziehen; (person, from department) verlassen (from +acc); (from job) wechseln (from +acc)

b (fig) sich entfernen (from von); **the country is moving away from communism** das Land entfernt sich vom Kommunismus

▶ **move back** **VT** sep **a** (to former place) zurückstellen; people zurückbringen; (into old house, town) wieder unterbringen (into in +dat); (to job) zurückversetzen; soldiers zurückbeordern; **they'll move you back when the danger is past** Sie werden zurückgeschickt, wenn die Gefahr vorbei ist

b (to the rear) things zurückschieben or -rücken; car zurückfahren; chess piece zurückschieben, zurückrücken mit; people zurückdrängen; troops zurückziehen

VI **a** (to former place) zurückkommen; (into one's house) wieder einziehen (into in +acc); (into old job) zurückgehen (to zu); (fig, to theory, ideology) zurückkehren (to zu)

b (to the rear) zurückweichen; (troops) sich zurückziehen; (car) zurückfahren; **move back, please!** bitte zurücktreten!

▶ **move down** **VT** sep (downwards) (weiter) nach unten stellen; (along) (weiter) nach hinten stellen; pupil zurückstufen; (Sport) absteigen lassen; **move that item further down the list** führen Sie diesen Punkt weiter unten auf der Liste auf; **he moved the cows/soldiers down to the plains** er trieb die Kühe/beorderte die Soldaten ins Flachland hinunter

VI (downwards) nach unten rücken or rutschen; (along) weiterrücken or -rutschen; (in bus etc) nach hinten aufrücken; (pupil) zurückgestuft werden; (team etc) absteigen, zurückfallen (to auf +acc); **move (right) down the bus, please!** rücken Sie bitte (ans hintere Ende des Busses) auf!; **he had to move down a year** (pupil) er musste eine Klasse zurück; **when the nomads/cows moved down to the plains** als die Nomaden/Kühe ins Flachland herunterkamen

▶ **move forward** **VT** sep **a** person vorgehen lassen; chair, table etc vorziehen, vorrücken; chess piece vorziehen, vorrücken mit; car vorfahren; troops vorrücken lassen

b (fig, = advance) event, date vorverlegen; **to move the clock forward** die Uhr vorstellen

VI (person) vorrücken; (crowd) sich vorwärts bewegen; (car) vorwärts fahren; (troops) vorrücken; **the clocks move forward tomorrow** morgen werden die Uhren vorgestellt

▶ **move in** **VT** sep **a** police, troops, extra staff einsetzen (-to in +dat); (= march/drive in) einrücken lassen (-to in +acc); (= take inside) luggage etc hineinstellen (-to in +acc); car hineinfahren (-to in +acc)

b **the council hasn't moved us in(to the house) yet** die Stadt hat uns noch nicht im Haus untergebracht; **when will the removal firm** (Brit) **or moving company** (US) **move our things in?** wann macht die Spedition unseren Umzug?

VI **a** (into accommodation) einziehen (-to in +acc)

b (= come closer) sich nähern (on dat), näher herankommen (on an +acc); (camera) näher herangehen (on an +acc); (police, troops) anrücken; (= start operations) (workers) (an)kommen, anfangen; (hooligans, firms) auf den Plan treten; **to move in on sb** (police, troops) gegen jdn vorrücken; (guests) jdm auf den Leib rücken; **the big concerns moved in on the market** die großen Konzerne etablierten sich auf dem Markt; **the troops moved into the town** die Truppen rückten in die Stadt ein

▶ **move off** **VT** sep people wegschicken; **move her off!** (inf: car, train etc) fahr los! **VI** **a** (= go away) (people) weggehen; (troops) abziehen **b** (= start moving) sich in Bewegung setzen

▶ **move on** **VT** sep **the policeman moved them on** der Polizist forderte sie auf weiterzugehen/weiterzufahren; **he moved the discussion on to the next point** er leitete die Diskussion zum nächsten Punkt über

VI (people) weitergehen; (vehicles) weiterfahren; **it's about time I was moving on** (fig, to new job etc) es wird Zeit, dass ich (mal) etwas anderes mache; **to move on to higher things** sich Höherem zuwenden; **to move on to a more responsible job** zu einem verantwortungsvolleren Posten aufsteigen; **they moved on to discuss the future of the company** als Nächstes besprachen sie die Zukunft der Firma; **let's move on to the next point** gehen wir zum nächsten Punkt über; **time is moving on** die Zeit vergeht

▶ **move out** **VT** sep **a** car herausfahren (of aus); **we had to move the furniture out** wir mussten die Möbel hinausräumen or -stellen; **move the table out of the corner** stellen or rücken Sie den Tisch von der Ecke weg; **she moved it out from under the bed** sie zog es unter dem Bett (her)vor

b (= withdraw) troops abziehen; **they are being moved out (of their house)** sie müssen (aus ihrem Haus) ausziehen; **they were moved out for non-payment of rent** wegen Nichtzahlung der Miete wurden sie gezwungen, ihre Wohnung zu räumen; **they moved everybody out of the danger zone** alle mussten die Gefahrenzone verlassen or räumen; **the removal men are moving us out tomorrow** die Spediteure machen morgen unseren Umzug

VI **a** (= leave accommodation) ausziehen; (= withdraw: troops) abziehen; **to move out of an area** ein Gebiet räumen

b (= leave: train etc) abfahren

▶ **move over** **VT** sep herüberschieben; **move your bottom over** (inf) rück or rutsch mal ein Stück zur Seite (inf); **he moved the car over to the side** er fuhr an die Seite heran

VI zur Seite rücken or rutschen; **move over, we all want to sit down** rück or rutsch mal ein Stück, wir wollen uns auch hinsetzen (inf); **move over to your side of the bed** leg dich in deine Hälfte des Betts; **he moved over to his own side of the bed** er rückte herüber in seine Betthälfte; **to move over to a new system** ein neues System einführen; **if he can't do the job he should move over and let someone else do it** wenn er die Arbeit nicht machen kann, sollte er einen anderen ranlassen (inf)

▶ **move up** **VT** sep **a** (= change to higher position) (weiter) nach oben stellen; (= promote) be-

fördern; pupil versetzen; (Sport) aufsteigen lassen; **move that up to the top of the list** stellen Sie das ganz oben an die Liste, führen Sie das ganz oben auf; **they moved him up two places** sie haben ihn zwei Plätze vorgerückt; **they moved the cows up to the pastures** sie trieben die Kühe auf die Alm (hinauf); **the general moved his men up onto the hill** der General beorderte seine Leute auf den Hügel hinauf; **to move sb up the line** jdn weiter vorn platzieren

b troops etc (into battle area) aufmarschieren lassen; (to front line) vorrücken lassen; guns, artillery auffahren

VI **a** (fig) aufsteigen; (shares, rates etc) steigen; (= be promoted) befördert werden; (Sch) versetzt werden; **the nomads moved up to the hills for the summer** die Nomaden zogen den Sommer über in die Berge hinauf; **to move up in the world** die gesellschaftliche Leiter hinaufklettern

b (= move along) auf- or weiterrücken; **move up the bus!** rücken Sie auf or weiter!

moveable ADJ, N = **movable**

movement ['muːvmənt] N **a** (= motion) Bewegung f; (of troops etc) Truppenbewegung f; (fig) (= trend) Trend m (towards zu); (of events) Entwicklung f; (of prices/rates) Preis-/Kursbewegung f; **a slight downward/upward ~** eine leichte Abwärts-/Aufwärtsbewegung; **the ~ of traffic** der Verkehrsfluss; **~ (of the bowels)** (Med) Stuhlgang m; **there was a ~ toward(s) the door** alles drängte zur Tür; **a marked ~ to the right** ein merklicher or deutlicher Rechtsruck; **the flowing ~ of the piece** (Mus) der fließende Rhythmus des Stückes; **the free ~ of capital and goods** der freie Kapital- und Warenverkehr

b (= political, artistic etc movement) Bewegung f

c (= transport: of goods etc) Beförderung f

d (Mus) Satz m

e (= mechanism) Antrieb(smechanismus) m, Getriebe nt; (of clock) Uhrwerk nt

mover ['muːvə'] N **a** (of proposition) Antragsteller(in) m(f) **b** (= remover) Möbelpacker(in) m(f) **c** (= walker, dancer etc) **he is a good/poor etc ~** seine Bewegungen sind schön/plump etc **d** **the ~s and shakers** (inf) die Leute pl mit Einfluss; **to be a fast ~** (inf) von der schnellen Truppe sein (inf)

movie ['muːvɪ] N (esp US) Film m; **(the) ~s** der Film; **to go to the ~s** ins Kino gehen

---

MOVIE RATING, FILM RATING

Es ist Aufgabe des „British Board of Film Classification", die in Großbritannien erscheinenden Filme und Videos einzustufen. Jeder Film erhält danach eine Klassifizierung: U (Universal) - für jedes Alter geeignet; PG (Parental Guidance) - einige Szenen könnten für jüngere Kinder ungeeignet sein; „12", „15" oder „18" - das ist das jeweilige Mindestalter der Zuschauer; „Restricted 18" - darf nur in bestimmten Lokalitäten, z. B. Kinoklubs, gezeigt werden.

In den USA erfüllt die „Motion Picture Association of America" eine ähnliche Aufgabe. Hier werden folgende Klassifizierungen vergeben: G (General) - für jedes Alter geeignet; PG (Parental Guidance) - einige Szenen könnten für jüngere Kinder ungeeignet sein; „PG13" - einige Szenen sind für Kinder unter 13 nicht geeignet sein; „R" (Restricted) - jeder unter 17 muss von einem Elternteil oder einer erwachsenen Aufsichtsperson begleitet werden; „NC-17" oder „X" - keine Jugendlichen unter 17.

---

movie (esp US) in cpds Film-; **movie camera** N Filmkamera f; **moviegoer** [inf] N Kinogänger(in) m(f); **movie house** N Kino nt, Filmtheater nt; **movie star** N Filmstar m; **movie theater** N Kino nt

moving ['muːvɪŋ] ADJ **a** (= *that moves*) beweglich **b** (= *causing emotion*) ergreifend; *tribute* rührend **c** (*Tech*, = *motive*) Antriebs-; ~ **power** Antriebskraft *f*; **the ~ spirit** or **force** (*fig*) die treibende Kraft (*behind sth* hinter etw *dat*) **d** (= *of removal*) ~ **costs/expenses** Umzugskosten *pl*

moving company N (*US*) Umzugsunternehmen *nt*

movingly ['muːvɪŋlɪ] ADV ergreifend

moving: moving pavement N (*esp Brit*) Rollband *nt*; **moving sidewalk** N (*US*) Rollband *nt*; **moving staircase** N , **moving stairs** PL Rolltreppe *f*; **moving van** N (*US*) Möbelwagen *m*

mow[1] [məʊ] pret **mowed**, ptp **mown** or **mowed** VTI mähen

▶ **mow down** VT sep abmähen; (*fig*: = *slaughter*) niedermähen

mow[2] N (*US*) Heuhaufen *m*; (= *storing place*) Heuboden *m*

mower ['məʊə'] N (= *person*) Mäher *m*, Schnitter *m* (*old*); (= *machine: on farm*) Mähmaschine *f*; (= *lawnmower*) Rasenmäher *m*

mowing ['məʊɪŋ] N Mähen *nt*; ~ **machine** Mähmaschine *f*

mown [məʊn] ptp of **mow**[1]

moxie ['mɒksɪ] N (*US sl*) (= *verve, determination*) Power *f* (*inf*); (= *courage*) Mumm *m* (*inf*); (= *skill, know-how*) Fachwissen *nt*, Sachkenntnis *f*

Mozambique [ˌməʊzəm'biːk] N Mosambik *nt*, Moçambique *nt*

MP **a** abbr of **Member of Parliament** **b** abbr of **Military Police** **c** abbr of **Metropolitan Police**

mpg abbr of **miles per gallon**

mph abbr of **miles per hour**

MPhil abbr of **Master of Philosophy**

MPV abbr of **multipurpose vehicle**

Mr ['mɪstə'] abbr of **Mister** Herr *m*

MRC N (*Brit*) abbr of **Medical Research Council** *Organisation zur Förderung der medizinischen Forschung*

MRI abbr of **magnetic resonance imaging**

MRP abbr of **manufacturer's recommended price** empf. Preis

Mrs ['mɪsɪz] abbr of **Mistress** Frau *f*

Mrs Mop ['mɪsɪz'mɒp] N (*dated Brit inf*) Putzfrau *f*

MS N abbr of **multiple sclerosis**

Ms [mɪz] N Frau *f* (*auch für Unverheiratete*)

Ms

Ms ist die schriftliche Anredeform für Frauen, mit der man die traditionelle Unterscheidung nach verheiratetem (**Mrs**) und unverheiratetem (**Miss**) Familienstand vermeidet. Es handelt sich dabei um die formale weibliche Entsprechung der männlichen Anrede **Mr**. Zunächst wurde **Ms** von vielen belächelt, doch heutzutage ist diese Anredeform weit verbreitet.

---

ms abbr of **manuscript** Ms, Mskr.

MSC (*Brit*) abbr of **Manpower Services Commission**

MSc abbr of **Master of Science**

MSF N (*Brit*) abbr of **Manufacturing, Science, Finance** *britische Angestelltengewerkschaft*

Msg abbr of **Monsignor** Msgr., Mgr.

MSP (*Brit, Pol*) abbr of **Member of the Scottish Parliament** Mitglied *nt* des schottischen Parlaments

MSS, **mss** abbr of **manuscripts**

MT abbr of **machine translation**

Mt abbr of **Mount**

much [mʌtʃ] **ADJ, ADV** **a** viel *inv*; **how** ~ wie viel *inv*; **not** ~ nicht viel; **that** ~ so viel; **but that ~ I do know** aber DAS weiß ich; **of this is true** viel or vieles daran ist wahr; **we don't see ~ of each other** wir sehen uns nicht oft or nur selten; **he's/it's not up to** ~ (*inf*) er/es ist nicht ge-

---

rade berühmt (*inf*); **I'm not ~ of a musician/ cook/player** ich bin nicht sehr musikalisch/ keine große Köchin/kein (besonders) guter Spieler; **not ~ of a choice** keine große Auswahl; **that wasn't ~ of a dinner/party** das Essen/die Party war nicht gerade besonders; **I find that a bit (too)** ~ **after all I've done for him** nach allem was ich für ihn getan habe, finde ich das ein ziemlich starkes Stück (*inf*)

b too ~ (*in quantity, money etc, inf*: = *more than one can take*) zu viel *inv*; (*with emphatic too*) zu viel; (*inf*) (= *marvellous, hilarious*) Spitze (*sl*); (= *ridiculous*) das Letzte (*sl*); **to be too** ~ **for sb** (*in quantity*) zu viel für jdn sein; (= *too expensive*) jdm zu viel or zu teuer sein; **that insult was too** ~ **for me** die Beleidigung ging mir zu weit; **the sight of her face was too** ~ **for me** (*inf*, = *outrageous*) ihr Gesicht war zum Schreien (*inf*); **he's just too** ~ (*inf*, = *hilarious*) er ist zum Schießen (*inf*); **these children are/this job is too** ~ **for me** ich bin den Kindern/der Arbeit nicht gewachsen; **he'd be too** ~ **for anybody** er wäre für jeden eine Zumutung; **he doesn't do too** ~ er tut nicht übermäßig viel; **far too** ~, **too** ~ **by half** viel zu viel

c (just) as ~ ebenso viel *inv*, genauso viel *inv*; **about/not as** ~ ungefähr/nicht so viel; **three times as** ~ dreimal so viel; **as** ~ **as you want/ can** *etc* so viel du willst/kannst *etc*; **as** ~ **as possible** so viel wie möglich; **he spends as** ~ **as he earns** er gibt (genau) so viel aus, wie er verdient; **they hope to raise as** ~ **as £2m** sie hoffen, nicht weniger als zwei Millionen Pfund aufzubringen; **as** ~ **again** noch einmal so viel; **I feared/thought** *etc* **as** ~ (= *genau*) das habe ich befürchtet/mir gedacht *etc*; **it's as** ~ **as I can do to stand up** es fällt mir schwer genug aufzustehen; **as** ~ **as to say ...** was so viel heißt or bedeutet wie ...

d so ~ so viel *inv*; (*emph so, with following that*) so viel; **it's not so** ~ **a problem of modernization as ...** es ist nicht so sehr ein Problem der Modernisierung als ...; **you know so** ~ du weißt so viel → *also* **so**

e to make ~ **of sb/sth** viel Wind um jdn/etw machen; **Glasgow makes** ~ **of its large number of parks** Glasgow rühmt sich seiner vielen Parks; **I couldn't make** ~ **of that chapter** mit dem Kapitel konnte ich nicht viel anfangen (*inf*)

ADV **a** (*with adj, adv*) viel; (*with vb*) sehr; (*with vb of physical action*) drive, sleep, think, talk, laugh *etc* viel; come, visit, go out *etc* oft, viel (*inf*); **a ~~admired/-married woman** eine ~ bewunderte/oft verheiratete Frau; **he was ~ dismayed/ embarrassed** *etc* er war sehr bestürzt/verlegen *etc*; **so** ~ so viel; **too** ~ zu viel, zu sehr; **I like it very/so** ~ es gefällt mir sehr gut/ so gut or so sehr; **I don't like him/it too** ~ ich kann es/ihn nicht besonders leiden; **thank you very** ~ vielen Dank; **thank you (ever) so** ~ vielen herzlichen Dank; **I don't** ~ **care** or **care** ~ es ist mir ziemlich egal; **however** ~ **he tries** sosehr or wie sehr er sich auch bemüht; ~ **to my astonishment** sehr zu meinem Erstaunen; **as I should like to** so gern ich möchte; ~ **as I like him** sosehr ich ihn mag; **there wasn't enough water to drink**, ~ **less wash in** es gab nicht genug Wasser zu trinken, ganz zu schweigen, um sich damit zu waschen → *also* **so**

b (= *by far*) weitaus, bei weitem; ~ **the biggest** weitaus or bei weitem der/die/das größte; **I would** ~ **prefer to** or ~ **rather stay** ich würde viel lieber bleiben

c (= *almost*) beinahe; **they are ~ of an age** or ~ **the same age** sie sind fast or beinahe gleichaltrig; **they're (fairly)** ~ **the same size** sie sind beinahe or so ziemlich gleich groß; **they are produced in** ~ **the same way** sie werden auf sehr ähnliche Art hergestellt

muchness ['mʌtʃnɪs] N (*Brit inf*) **they're much of a** ~ (*things*) das ist eins wie das andere; (*people*) sie sind einer wie der andere

mucilaginous [ˌmjuːsɪ'lædʒɪnəs] ADJ klebrig

muck [mʌk] N **a** (= *dirt*) Dreck *m*; (*euph*: = *cat's/dog's muck*) Kot *m*; (= *manure*) Dung *m*,

---

Mist *m*; (= *liquid manure*) Jauche *f*; **where there's ~, there's brass** or **money** (*Prov*) Dreck und Geld liegen nahe beisammen (*prov*) **b** (*fig*) (= *rubbish*) Mist *m*; (= *obscenities*) Schund *m*; (= *food etc*) Zeug *nt* (*inf*); **Lord Muck** (*Brit hum inf*) Graf Rotz (*inf*); **Lady Muck** (*Brit hum inf*) die feine Dame

▶ **muck about** or **around** (*Brit inf*) **VT** sep **a** **to muck sb about** mit jdm machen, was man will, jdn verarschen or money (*Prov*) b (fig) (= *not committing oneself*) jdn hinhalten; **the travel agents really mucked us about** das war ein ewiges Hin und Her mit dem Reisebüro (*inf*); **stop mucking me about!** sag mir endlich, woran ich bin or was los ist!

b (= *fiddle around with, spoil*) herumpfuschen an (+*dat*) (*inf*); **to muck things about** alles durcheinander bringen

VI **a** (= *lark about*) herumalbern or -blödeln (*inf*); (= *do nothing in particular*) herumgammeln (*inf*); **to muck about** or **around in boats** sich mit Booten beschäftigen; **to muck around (at) doing sth** Zeit damit vertrödeln, etw zu tun (*inf*)

b (= *tinker with*) herumfummeln (*with an* +*dat*) **c** **to muck about** or **around with sb** jdn an der Nase herumführen (*inf*)

▶ **muck in** VI (*Brit inf*) mit anpacken (*inf*)

▶ **muck out** (*Brit*) **VT** sep (aus)misten **VI** ausmisten

▶ **muck up** VT sep (*Brit inf*) **a** (= *dirty*) dreckig machen (*inf*); **you've really mucked up this place** ihr habt hier ja eine (ganz) schöne Schweinerei angerichtet! **b** (= *spoil*) vermasseln (*inf*); *person* (*emotionally*) verkorksen (*inf*); **that's really mucked me/my plans up** das hat mir alles/meine Pläne vermasselt (*inf*)

mucker ['mʌkə'] N **a** (*Brit inf*) Kumpel *m* (*inf*) **b** (*US inf*) ungehobelter Kerl, Bauer *m* (*inf*) **c** (*Min*: = *person who removes muck*) Lader *m*

muckiness ['mʌkɪnɪs] N Schmutzigkeit *f*

muck: muckrake VI (*fig inf*) im Schmutz wühlen; **muckraker** N (*fig inf*) Sensationshai *m* (*inf*); **muckraking** **N** (*fig inf*) Sensationsmache(rei) *f* (*inf*) ADJ (*fig inf*) *person* sensationslüstern; **a ~ newspaper** ein Skandalblatt *nt*; **muck-spread** VI (*fig inf*) Mist streuen; **muck- -spreading** N Miststreuen *nt*; **muck-up** N (*Brit inf*) Durcheinander *nt*; (= *fiasco*) Katastrophe *f*; **there's been a ~ with the invitations** bei den Einladungen hat jemand/habe ich *etc* Mist gemacht (*inf*)

mucky ['mʌkɪ] ADJ (+*er*) dreckig (*inf*), schmutzig; *soil etc* matschig; **to get oneself/sth all ~** sich/etw ganz dreckig (*inf*) or schmutzig machen (*inf*); **you ~ thing** or **pup!** (*Brit inf*) du Ferkel! (*inf*); **keep your ~ paws off!** (*hum inf*) nimm deine dreckigen Pfoten weg! (*inf*)

mucous ['mjuːkəs] ADJ schleimig, Schleim-; ~ **secretion** Schleimabsonderung *f*

mucous membrane N Schleimhaut *f*

mucoviscidosis [ˌmjuːkəʊvɪsɪ'dəʊsɪs] N (*Med*) Mukoviszidose *f*

mucus ['mjuːkəs] N Schleim *m*

mud [mʌd] N **a** Schlamm *m*; (*on roads etc*) Matsch *m*; **(here's) ~ in your eye!** (*dated*) zum Wohl!, prösterchen! (*hum*) **b** (*fig*) **his name is ~** (*inf*) er ist unten durch (*inf*); **to drag sb's/sb's name** or **reputation through the ~** jdn/jds guten Namen in den Schmutz zerren or ziehen; **to throw** or **sling ~** im Schmutz or Dreck (*inf*) wühlen; **to throw** or **sling ~ at sb** jdn mit Schmutz bewerfen; **to throw** or **sling ~ at sth** etw in den Dreck (*inf*) or Schmutz ziehen; **some of the ~ has stuck/is bound to stick** etwas ist hängen geblieben/bleibt immer hängen; ~ **sticks** etwas bleibt immer hängen

mud: mud bath N Schlammbad *nt*; (*Med*) Moorbad *nt*; **mud-coloured** ADJ schmutzig grau

muddle ['mʌdl] **N** Durcheinander *nt*; **to get in(to) a** ~ (*things*) durcheinander geraten; (*person*) konfus werden; **to get oneself in(to) a ~ over sth** mit etw nicht klarkommen (*inf*); **how**

did things get into such a ~? wie ist denn dieses Durcheinander entstanden?; **to be in a ~** völlig durcheinander sein; **this room is (in) a real ~** in diesem Zimmer herrscht ein einziges Durcheinander; **her office was a ~ of files and papers** in ihrem Büro lagen Akten und Papiere wild durcheinander; **to make a ~ of sth** etw völlig durcheinander bringen **VT** durcheinander bringen; *two things or people also* verwechseln; (= *make confused*) *person* verwirren, durcheinander bringen; **you're only muddling the issue** du machst die Sache nur verworrener

▶ **muddle along** *or* **on** VI vor sich (*acc*) hinwursteln (*inf*)

▶ **muddle through** VI durchkommen, sich (irgendwie) durchwursteln (*inf*) *or* durchschlagen

▶ **muddle up** VT *sep* = **muddle VT**

muddled ['mʌdld] ADJ konfus; *person also* durcheinander *pred*; *thoughts, ideas also* verworren, wirr; **to get ~ (up)** (*things*) durcheinander geraten; (*person*) konfus werden; **to be ~ about sth** verwirrt über etw (*acc*) sein; **to set in a ~ way** ziemlich konfus angelegt; **he has a rather ~ way of doing things** er macht alles ziemlich kompliziert; **in a ~ way it does make sense** es ist zwar verworren, ergibt aber doch einen Sinn

muddleheaded ['mʌdl,hedɪd] ADJ *person* zerstreut; *ideas* konfus, verworren

muddler ['mʌdlə'] N (= *person*) Tölpel *m*, Dussel *m* (*inf*)

muddy ['mʌdɪ] ADJ (+*er*) **a** *floor, shoes, hands etc* schmutzig, schlammbeschmiert; *road, ground etc* schlammig, matschig; *liquid* schlammig, trübe; **to get sb/oneself/sth ~** jdn/sich/etw schmutzig machen *or* mit Schlamm beschmieren; **I'm all ~** ich bin ganz voll Schlamm **b** (*fig*) *complexion* gräulich schimmernd; *style* verworren **VT** schmutzig machen, mit Schlamm beschmieren; *water, river* verschlammen; (*fig*: = *confuse*) *situation, issue* verwirren, in Verwirrung bringen; **his explanation only helped to ~ the waters** durch seine Erklärung ist die Sache nur noch verworrener geworden

mud: **mudflap** N (*Aut etc*) Schmutzfänger *m*; **mud flat** N Watt(enmeer) *nt no pl*; **mudguard** N (*Brit*) (*on cycles*) Schutzblech *nt*; (*on cars*) Kotflügel *m*; **mud hut** N Lehmhütte *f*; **mudpack** N Schlammpackung *f*; **mud pie** N Kuchen *m* (*aus Sand, Erde etc*); **mudslinger** N Dreckschleuder *f* (*inf*); **mudslinging** N Schlechtmacherei *f*; **all that ~ before every election** diese gegenseitige Verunglimpfung vor jeder Wahl; **we've had enough ~** es ist genug im Schmutz *or* Dreck (*inf*) gewühlt worden **ADJ** **a ~ election campaign** ein Wahlkampf, der darin besteht, sich gegenseitig mit Schmutz zu bewerfen; **the election turned into a ~ match** die Wahlen arteten zur reinsten Schlammschlacht aus; **mud wrestling** N Schlammringen *nt*

muesli ['mju:zlɪ] N Müsli *nt*, Müesli *nt* (*Sw*)

muezzin [mu:'ezɪn] N Muezzin *m*

muff¹ ['mʌf] N Muff *m*

muff² (*inf*) N **to make a ~ of** = **to muff VT** vermasseln (*inf*), verpatzen (*inf*); *exam also* verhauen (*inf*); *question* danebenhauen *or* sich verhauen bei (*inf*); *kick, shot, ball* danebensetzen (*inf*); *lines, text, passage* verpatzen (*inf*); **to ~ a catch** danebengreifen (*inf*), schlecht fangen

muffin ['mʌfɪn] N **a** Muffin *m*, kleiner, in Förmchen gebackener Kuchen **b** (*Brit*) weiches, flaches Milchbrötchen, meist warm gegessen

muffle ['mʌfl] VT **a** (= *wrap warmly: also* **muffle up**) *person* einmummen **b** (= *deaden*) *sound, shot etc* dämpfen; *noise* abschwächen; *shouts* ersticken; *bells, oars, drum* umwickeln

muffled ['mʌfld] ADJ *sound, voice etc* gedämpft; *shouts* erstickt; *drum, bells, oars* umwickelt; **a ~ conversation** eine Unterhaltung in gedämpftem Ton

muffler ['mʌflə'] N **a** (= *scarf*) (dicker) Schal **b** (*Tech*) Schalldämpfer *m*; (*US Aut*) Auspuff(topf) *m*

mufti ['mʌftɪ] N (= *clothing*) Zivil(kleidung *f*) *nt*; **in ~** in Zivil

mug [mʌg] N **a** (= *cup*) Becher *m*; (*for beer*) Krug *m* **b** (*esp Brit inf:* = *dupe*) Trottel *m* (*inf*); **have you found some ~ to do it?** hast du einen Dummen dafür gefunden? (*inf*); **I was left looking a real ~** ich stand dann blöd da (*inf*); **don't be such a ~** sei doch nicht so blöd (*inf*); **to take sb for a ~** jdn für blöd halten (*inf*); **that's a ~'s game** das ist doch schwachsinnig **c** (*inf:* = *face*) Visage *f* (*inf*) **VT a** (= *attack and rob*) überfallen **b** (*US, sl:* = *photograph*) fotografieren

▶ **mug up** VT *sep* **a** (*Brit inf: also* **mug up on**) **to mug sth/one's French up, to mug up on sth/one's French** etw/Französisch pauken (*inf*) **b** **to mug it up** (*US*) zu dick auftragen

mugger ['mʌgə'] N Straßenräuber(in) *m(f)*

mugging ['mʌgɪŋ] N Straßenraub *m no pl*; **a lot of ~s** viele Überfälle auf offener Straße

muggins ['mʌgɪnz] N *sing* (*Brit, inf*) Blödmann *m* (*inf*); **while ~ does all the work** und ich bin mal wieder der/die Dumme und kann die ganze Arbeit allein machen (*inf*); **and ~ here forgot ...** und ich Blödmann vergesse (*inf*) ..., und der Blödmann hier vergisst (*inf*) ...

muggy ['mʌgɪ] ADJ (+*er*) schwül; *heat* drückend

mug shot N (*inf*) Verbrecherfoto *nt* (*inf*)

mugwump ['mʌgwʌmp] N (*US, Pol*) Unabhängige(r) *mf*

Muhammad [mu:'hʌmʌd] N Mohammed *m*

Mujaheddin [,mu:dʒəhe'di:n] N Mudschaheddin *m*

mulatto [mju:'lætəʊ] ADJ Mulatten-; *features* eines Mulatten/einer Mulattin; **~ child** Mulattenkind *nt* N *pl* **-es** Mulatte *m*, Mulattin *f*

mulberry ['mʌlbərɪ] N (= *fruit*) Maulbeere *f*; (= *tree*) Maulbeerbaum *m*; (= *colour*) Aubergine *nt*, dunkles Violett

mulch [mʌltʃ] (*Hort*) N Krümelschicht *f*, Mulch *m* (*spec*) VT mulchen (*spec*), abdecken

mulct [mʌlkt] VT **a** (= *fine*) mit einer Geldstrafe belegen (*form*) **b** (= *defraud*) **to ~ sb of sth** jdm etw abschwindeln

mule¹ [mju:l] N **a** (*of donkey and mare*) Maultier *nt*; (*of stallion and donkey*) Maulesel *m* **b** (*inf*, = *person*) Maulesel *m*; **(as) stubborn as a ~** (so) störrisch wie ein Maulesel **c** (*Tech*) Selfaktor *m* **d** (*inf:* = *drugs courier*) Drogenkurier(in) *m(f)*

mule² N (= *slipper*) Schlappen *m* (*dial*), Pantoffel *m*

mule skinner N (*US, inf*) Maultiertreiber *m*

muleteer [,mju:lɪ'tɪə'] N Maultiertreiber(in) *m(f)*

mule track N Saumpfad *m*

mulish ['mju:lɪʃ] ADJ störrisch, stur

mulishly ['mju:lɪʃlɪ] ADV stur, starrsinnig

mulishness ['mju:lɪʃnɪs] N Starrsinn *m*, Sturheit *f*

mull [mʌl] VT *mit Zucker und Gewürzen ansetzen und erhitzen* **to ~ wine** Glühwein zubereiten

▶ **mull over** VT *sep* sich (*dat*) durch den Kopf gehen lassen

mullah ['mʌlə] N Mullah *m*

mulled wine [mʌld-] N Glühwein *m*

mullet ['mʌlɪt] N Meeräsche *f*

mulligatawny [,mʌlɪgə'tɔ:nɪ] N Currysuppe *f*

mullion ['mʌlɪən] N **a** Längs- *or* Zwischenpfosten *m* **b** **mullions** PL (*in Gothic Archit*) Stabwerk *nt*

mullioned ['mʌlɪənd] ADJ *window* längs unterteilt

multi ['mʌltɪ] N (*inf*, = *company*) Multi *m* (*inf*)

multi- PREF mehr-, Mehr-; (*with Latin stem in German*) Multi-, multi-; **multisyllabic** mehrsilbig; **multidisciplinary** multidisziplinär

multi: **multiaccess** ADJ (*Comput*) Mehrplatz-; **~ system** Mehrplatzsystem *nt*; **multiband** ADJ (*Telec*) Mehrband-; **~ radio** Mehrbandfunk *m*; **multicellular** ADJ viel- *or* mehrzellig; **multichannel** ADJ (*TV*) mehrkanalig, Mehrkanal-; **~ broadcasting** Mehrkanalfernsehen *nt*; **multicoloured**, (*US*) **multicolored** ADJ mehrfarbig; *material also, lights, decorations* bunt; *bird* bunt gefiedert; *fish* bunt schillernd; **multicultural** ADJ multikulturell; **multifaceted** ADJ vielseitig

multifarious [,mʌltɪ'fɛərɪəs] ADJ vielfältig, mannigfaltig

multi: **multifocals** ['mʌltɪ,fəʊkəlz] PL Gleitsichtgläser *pl*; (= *spectacles*) Gleitsichtbrille *f*; **multifold** ADJ vielfältig; **multiform** ADJ vielgestaltig; **multifunctional** ADJ multifunktional; (*Comput*) Multifunktions-; **~ keyboard** Multifunktionstastatur *f*; **multigrade** ADJ **~ oil** Mehrbereichsöl *nt*; **multihull** N (*Naut*) Mehrkörperschiff *nt*; **multilateral** ADJ (*Pol*) multilateral; (*Math*) mehrseitig; **multilateralist** (*Pol*) ADJ *campaigner* für die multilaterale atomare Abrüstung N Befürworter(in) *m(f)* der multilateralen atomaren Abrüstung; **multilevel** ADJ *shopping centre etc* mehrstöckig; (*fig*) *marketing etc* mehrschichtig; **multilingual** ADJ mehrsprachig; **multimedia** ADJ multimedial; (*Comput*) Multimedia-; **multimillionaire** N Multimillionär(in) *m(f)*; **multinational** N multinationaler Konzern, Multi *m* (*inf*) ADJ multinational; *aid, effort* international; **multipack** N Multipack *nt or m*; **multiparty** (*Pol*) Mehrparteien-; **~ system** Mehrparteiensystem *nt*; **multiplane** N (*Aviat*) Mehrdecker *m*, Vieldecker *m*

multiple ['mʌltɪpl] ADJ **a** (*with sing n: = of several parts*) mehrfach; **~ collision** *or* **crash** Massenkarambolage *f* **b** (*with pl n: = many*) mehrere; **he died of ~ injuries** er erlag seinen zahlreichen Verletzungen N **a** (*Math*) Vielfache(s) *nt*; **eggs are usually sold in ~s of six** Eier werden gewöhnlich in Einheiten zu je sechs verkauft **b** (*Brit: = store*) Ladenkette *f*

multiple: **multiple birth** N Mehrlingsgeburt *f*; **multiple choice** N Multiplechoice *nt*; **multiple cropping** N mehrfache Bebauung; **multiple-entry visa** N für wiederholte Einreisen gültiges Visum; **multiple personality** N (*Psych*) alternierende Persönlichkeit; **~ disorder** Persönlichkeitsspaltung *f*; **multiple sclerosis** N multiple Sklerose; **multiple star** N (*Astron*) Sternhaufen *m*; **multiple store** N Ladenkette *f*; **multiple unit** N (= *train*) Triebwagen *m*; **multiple voting** N mehrfache Stimmabgabe

multiplexer, **multiplexor** ['mʌltɪpleksə'] N (*Telec*) Multiplexer *m*

multiplicand [,mʌltɪplɪ'kænd] N Multiplikand *m*

multiplication [,mʌltɪplɪ'keɪʃən] N **a** (*Math*) Multiplikation *f* **b** (*fig*) Vervielfachung *f*, Vermehrung *f*

multiplication: **multiplication sign** N (*Math*) Multiplikationszeichen *nt*; **multiplication table** N (*Math*) Multiplikationstabelle *f*; **he knows all his ~s** er kann das Einmaleins

multiplicity [,mʌltɪ'plɪsɪtɪ] N Vielzahl *f*, Fülle *f*; **for a ~ of reasons** aus vielerlei Gründen

multiplier ['mʌltɪplaɪə'] N (*Math*) Multiplikator *m*

multiply ['mʌltɪplaɪ] VT **a** (*Math*) multiplizieren, malnehmen; **to ~ 8 by 7** 8 mit 7 multiplizieren *or* malnehmen; **4 multiplied by 6 is 24** 4 mal 6 ist 24 **b** (*fig*) vervielfachen, vermehren VI **a** (*Math*) (*person*) multiplizieren; (*numbers*) sich multiplizieren lassen **b** (*fig*) zunehmen, sich vermehren *or* vervielfachen **c** (= *breed*) sich vermehren

multi: **multipurpose** ADJ Mehrzweck-; **~ gadget** Mehrzweckgerät *nt*; **~ cleaner** Allzweckreiniger *m*; **multipurpose vehicle** N Mehrzweckfahrzeug *nt*; **multiracial** ADJ gemischtrassig; **~ policy** Politik *f* der Rassenintegration; **~ school** Schule f ohne Rassentrennung; **multistage** ADJ Mehrstufen-; **~ rocket** Mehrstufenrakete f; **multistorey**, (US) **multistory** ADJ mehrstöckig; **~ flats** (Brit), **multistory apartments** (US) (Wohn)hochhäuser pl; **~ car park** (Brit) Park(hoch)haus nt; **multistrike** ADJ (Mil) **~ capability** Fähigkeit f zum Angriff auf mehrere Ziele; **multitasking** N (Comput) Multitasking nt; **multitrack** ADJ mehrspurig; **~ recording** Mehrspuraufzeichnung f

multitude ['mʌltɪtjuːd] N Menge f; **a ~ of** eine Vielzahl von, eine Menge; (of people also) eine Schar (von); **for a ~ of reasons** aus vielerlei Gründen; **they came in their ~s** sie kamen scharenweise

multitudinous [ˌmʌltɪ'tjuːdɪnəs] ADJ zahlreich

multi-user [ˈmʌltɪ'juːzə'] ADJ (Comput) Mehrplatz-, Mehrbenutzer-; **~ system** Mehrplatz- or Mehrbenutzersystem nt

mum¹ [mʌm] N, ADJ (inf) **~ 's the word!** nichts verraten! (inf); **to keep** or **stay ~** den Mund halten (about über +acc) (inf)

mum² N (Brit inf) (= mother) Mutter f; (as address) Mutti f (inf)

mum³ N (US, inf: = chrysanthemum) Chrysantheme f

mumble ['mʌmbl] N Gemurmel nt, Murmeln nt VT murmeln; **he ~d the words** er nuschelte VI vor sich hin murmeln; (= speak indistinctly) nuscheln; **don't ~ (into your beard)** murm(e)le doch nicht so in deinen Bart

mumbler ['mʌmblə'] N **he's a real ~** er nuschelt so

mumblingly ['mʌmblɪŋlɪ] ADV undeutlich

mumbo jumbo ['mʌmbəʊ'dʒʌmbəʊ] N (= empty ritual, superstition) Hokuspokus m; (= gibberish) Kauderwelsch nt; (= idol) Abgott m

mummer ['mʌmə'] N (old) Mime m (old)

mummery ['mʌmərɪ] N (old) Pantomimenspiel nt; (fig) Mummenschanz m

mummification [ˌmʌmɪfɪ'keɪʃən] N Mumifizierung f

mummify ['mʌmɪfaɪ] VTI mumifizieren

mummy¹ ['mʌmɪ] N (= corpse) Mumie f

mummy² N (Brit, inf, = mother) Mami f (inf), Mama f (inf)

mumps [mʌmps] N sing Mumps m or f (inf) no art

mumsy ['mʌmzɪ] ADJ (inf) mütterlich

munch [mʌntʃ] VTI mampfen (inf)

► **munch away** VI vor sich hin mampfen (inf); **he was munching away on** or **at an apple** er mampfte einen Apfel or an einem Apfel

munchies ['mʌntʃɪz] PL (US, inf) Knabberei f (inf)

mundane [ˌmʌn'deɪn] ADJ (= worldly) weltlich, profan; (fig: = everyday) alltäglich; (pej: = humdrum) banal; (= boring) langweilig N **the ~** das Alltägliche

mundanely [ˌmʌn'deɪnlɪ] ADV weltlich; (= in a down-to-earth way) remark, describe nüchtern; **~ obvious** allzu offensichtlich

mundaneness [ˌmʌn'deɪnnɪs] N (= worldliness) Weltlichkeit f; (= everyday nature) Alltäglichkeit f; (= humdrum nature) Banalität f; (= tediousness) Langweiligkeit f

Munich ['mjuːnɪk] N München nt ADJ attr Münchner

municipal [mjuː'nɪsɪpəl] ADJ städtisch; **~ council** Stadt- or Gemeinderat m; **~ elections** Stadtrats- or Gemeinderatswahl f

municipality [mjuːˌnɪsɪ'pælɪtɪ] N (= place) Ort m, Gemeinde f; (= council) Stadt f, Gemeinde f

municipalization [ˌmjuːnɪsɪpəlaɪ'zeɪʃən] N Übernahme f durch die Stadt or durch die Gemeinde

municipalize [ˌmjuːˈnɪsɪpəlaɪz] VT bus service, baths etc unter städtische Verwaltung or Gemeindeverwaltung bringen

municipally [mjuːˈnɪsɪpəlɪ] ADV von der Stadt or Gemeinde; **~ owned** im Besitz der Stadt or Gemeinde

municipal rates PL (Brit), **municipal taxes** PL (US) Gemeindesteuern pl, Gemeindeabgaben pl

munificence [mjuːˈnɪfɪsns] N (form) Großzügigkeit f, Generosität f (geh)

munificent [mjuːˈnɪfɪsnt] ADJ (form) großzügig; person also generös (geh)

munificently [mjuːˈnɪfɪsntlɪ] ADV (form) großzügig, generös (geh); **~ donated by ...** großzügigerweise gespendet von ...

muniments ['mjuːnɪmənts] PL (Jur, form) Urkunde f

munition [mjuːˈnɪʃən] N usu pl Kriegsmaterial nt no pl, Waffen pl und Munition f

munitions dump [mjuːˈnɪʃənz'dʌmp] N (Waffen- und) Munitionslager or -depot nt

mural ['mjʊərəl] N Wandgemälde nt ADJ Wand-; **~ painting** Wandmalerei f

murder ['mɜːdə'] N a (lit) Mord m; **the ~ of John F. Kennedy** der Mord an John F. Kennedy, die Ermordung John F. Kennedys; **to stand accused of ~** unter Mordverdacht stehen

b (fig inf) **it was/it's ~** es war/ist mörderisch; **it'll be ~** es wird schrecklich werden; (= exhausting also) das ist glatter Mord (inf); **to scream blue** (Brit) or **bloody ~** Zeter und Mordio schreien, ein Mordsspektakel or -theater machen (inf); **to get away with ~** sich (dat) alles erlauben können

VT a (lit) ermorden, umbringen (inf); (= slaughter) morden; (fig inf) opponents haushoch schlagen

b (inf: = ruin) music, play etc verhunzen (inf)

murderer ['mɜːdərə'] N Mörder(in) m(f)

murderess ['mɜːdərɪs] N Mörderin f

murderous ['mɜːdərəs] ADJ a villain, soldiers etc mordgierig, blutrünstig; weapon mörderisch; **~ attack** Mordanschlag m; **~ intent** Mordabsicht f; **a ~ type** ein brutaler Typ; **there was a ~ look about him** er hatte etwas Brutales an sich; **he gave me a ~ look** er erdolchte mich mit Blicken; **once he had started on this ~ course** als er erst einmal den Weg der Gewalt eingeschlagen hatte b (inf: = hellish) heat, conditions, traffic mörderisch (inf)

murderously ['mɜːdərəslɪ] ADV mordgierig, blutdürstig; (fig) mörderisch; **a ~ cunning trap** eine teuflische Falle

murder: murder trial N Mordprozess m; **murder weapon** N Mordwaffe f

murk [mɜːk] N Düsternis f; (in water) trübes Wasser

murkily ['mɜːkɪlɪ] ADV trübe; **the wreck could be seen ~ through the muddy water** das Wrack zeichnete sich undeutlich im schlammigen Wasser ab

murkiness ['mɜːkɪnɪs] N a (= gloominess) Trübheit f; (of mist, street, sky) Düsterheit f; (of night) Finsternis f, Dunkelheit f b (= shady nature) (of character, deed) Finsterkeit f; (of past) Dunkel nt

murky ['mɜːkɪ] ADJ (+er) a (= gloomy) trüb; room, street düster, dunkel; night finster; sky verhangen, düster; water trüb, schmutzig; fog dicht; outline unscharf, unklar; **~ brown/green** trüb-braun/-grün; **it's really ~ outside** draußen ist es so düster b (= shady) character, deed finster; past dunkel; **the ~ waters of politics** der Sumpf der Politik; **that's a pretty ~ area** das ist eine ziemlich undurchsichtige Sache

murmur ['mɜːmə'] N a (= soft speech) Murmeln nt, Raunen nt (liter); (of discontent) Murren nt; (of water, wind, leaves, traffic) Rauschen nt; **there was a ~ of approval/discontent** ein beifälliges/ unzufriedenes Murmeln erhob sich; **a soft ~ of voices** gedämpftes Stimmengemurmel; **..., she said in a ~** ..., murmelte sie; **not a ~** kein Laut; **without a ~** ohne zu murren VT murmeln; (with discontent) murren VI murmeln; (with dis-

content) murren (about, against über +acc); (fig) rauschen

murmuring ['mɜːmərɪŋ] N Murmeln nt no pl; (of water, wind, leaves) Rauschen nt no pl; **~s (of discontent)** Unmutsäußerungen pl (from +gen); **do I hear ~?** asked the chairman irgendwelche Unstimmigkeiten? fragte der Vorsitzende

Murphy's Law ['mɜːfɪz'lɔː] N (hum inf) Murphys Gesetz nt, „Gesetz", demzufolge eine Sache, die schief gehen kann, auch bestimmt schief gehen wird

muscadel(le) [ˌmʌskə'del] N (= wine) Muskateller m

muscat ['mʌskət] N (= grape) Muskatellertraube f

muscatel [ˌmʌskə'tel] N (= wine) Muskateller m

muscle ['mʌsl] N Muskel m; (fig: = power) Macht f; **he's all ~** er besteht nur aus Muskeln, er ist sehr muskulös (gebaut); **to have financial ~** finanzstark or -kräftig sein; **he never moved a ~** er rührte sich nicht

► **muscle in** VI (inf) mitmischen (inf) (on bei); **to muscle in on sb's territory** jdm dazwischenfunken (inf)

muscle: muscle-bound ADJ (inf: = muscular) muskelbepackt (inf); **to be ~** ein Muskelpaket m sein (inf); **muscleman** N Muskelmann m, Muskelprotz m (pej)

muscl(e)y ['mʌsəlɪ] ADJ (inf) muskulös, muskelbepackt (inf)

Muscovite ['mʌskəvaɪt] ADJ Moskauer; (Hist) moskowitisch N Moskauer(in) m(f); (Hist) Moskowiter(in) m(f)

Muscovy ['mʌskəvɪ] N (Hist) Moskauer Staat m

Muscovy duck N (Zool) Moschusente f

muscular ['mʌskjʊlə'] ADJ a (= relating to muscles) Muskel-, muskulär (form); **~ cramp** or **spasm** Muskelkrampf m; **~ control** Muskelbeherrschung f; **~ pains** Muskelschmerzen pl b (= having strong muscles) muskulös; **to be of ~ build** muskulös gebaut sein

muscular atrophy N Muskelatrophie f, Muskelschwund m

muscular dystrophy N Muskeldystrophie f, Muskelschwund m

musculature ['mʌskjʊlətʃə'] N Muskulatur f

Muse [mjuːz] N (Myth) Muse f

muse [mjuːz] VI nachgrübeln, nachsinnen (liter) (about, on über +acc) VT grüblerisch or sinnierend (liter) sagen N Muse f

museum [mjuːˈzɪəm] N Museum nt

museum piece N (lit, hum) Museumsstück nt

mush¹ [mʌʃ] N a Brei m; (of fruit also) Mus nt b (inf) Schmalz m; **he always sings such ~** er singt immer solche Schnulzen

mush² [mʊʃ] N (Brit inf) a (= face) Visage f (inf) b (= person) hey, ~! he, du da!

mushroom ['mʌʃrʊm] N a (essbarer) Pilz; (= button mushroom) Champignon m; (= atomic mushroom) Pilz m; **a great ~ of smoke** ein großer Rauchpilz; **to spring up** or **sprout like ~s** wie die Pilze aus dem Boden schießen ATTR a (made of mushrooms) Pilz-, Champignon-; **~ soup** Pilz- or Champignonsuppe f; **~ farm** Pilzzuchtbetrieb m; **~-picker** Pilzsammler(in) m(f)

b (= mushroom-shaped) pilzförmig

c (= rapid and ephemeral) growth sprunghaft VI a (= go ~ing) in die Pilze gehen, Pilze sammeln (gehen)

b (= grow rapidly) wie die Pilze aus dem Boden schießen; **unemployment has ~ed** die Arbeitslosigkeit ist explosionsartig angestiegen; **to ~ into sth** sich rasch zu etw entwickeln

mushroom cloud N Atompilz m

mushroom town N Stadt, die aus dem Boden geschossen ist

mushy ['mʌʃɪ] ADJ (+er) a matschig; liquid, consistency breiig; (= puréed) food, vegetables püriert; **~ snow** Schneematsch m; **to go ~** zu Brei werden; (= go off: fruit) matschig werden b (inf: = maudlin) schmalzig

mushy peas PL Erbsenmus *nt*

music ['mjuːzɪk] N Musik *f*; (*of voice*) Musikalität *f*; (= *written score*) Noten *pl*; **do you use ~?** spielen/singen Sie nach Noten?; **to set** *or* **put sth to ~** etw vertonen; **~ of the spheres** Sphärenmusik *f*; **it was (like) ~ to my ears** das war Musik für mich *or* in meinen Ohren; **to face the ~** (*fig*) dafür gradestehen

musical ['mjuːzɪkəl] ADJ **a** (*of music*) musikalisch; **~ note** Note *f*; **~ evening** musikalischer Abend, Musikabend *m* **b** (= *tuneful*) melodisch **c** (= *musically-minded*) musikalisch **N** Musical *nt*

musical: musical box N Spieluhr *f or* -dose *f*; **musical chairs** N *sing* Reise *f* nach Jerusalem; **political ~** ein politisches Stühlerücken; **Labour and Tories play ~ in local government** Labour und die Konservativen wechseln sich in der Kommunalverwaltung ab; **musical director** N (*esp US*) (*of orchestra*) Chefdirigent(in) *m(f)*; (*of show*) musikalischer Leiter, musikalische Leiterin; **musical instrument** N Musikinstrument *nt*

musicality [ˌmjuːzɪ'kælɪtɪ] N Musikalität *f*

musically ['mjuːzɪkəlɪ] ADV **a** musikalisch; **I'm ~ trained** ich habe eine musikalische Ausbildung **b** (= *tunefully*) melodisch

musical score N (*written*) Partitur *f*; (*for film etc*) Musik *f*

music *in cpds* Musik-; **music box** N Spieldose *f or* -uhr *f*; **music centre** N Kompaktanlage *f*, Musikcenter *nt*; **music drama** N Musikdrama *nt*; **music hall** N Varietee *nt*, Varieté *nt*

musician [mjuː'zɪʃən] N Musiker(in) *m(f)*

musicianship [mjuː'zɪʃənʃɪp] N musikalisches Können

music lover N Musikliebhaber(in) *m(f)*

musicological [ˌmjuːzɪkə'lɒdʒɪkəl] ADJ musikwissenschaftlich

musicologist [ˌmjuːzɪ'kɒlədʒɪst] N Musikwissenschaftler(in) *m(f)*

musicology [ˌmjuːzɪ'kɒlədʒɪ] N Musikwissenschaft *f*

music: music paper N Notenpapier *nt*; **music shop** N Musikalienhandlung *f*; **music stand** N Notenständer *m*; **music stool** N Klavierstuhl *m or* -hocker *m*; **music video** N Musikvideo *nt*

musing ['mjuːzɪŋ] ADJ grüblerisch, nachdenklich, sinnierend (*liter*); *philosopher, book, article* gedankenvoll **N** Überlegungen *pl* (*on zu*)

musk [mʌsk] N **a** (= *secretion, smell*) Moschus *m* **b** (*Bot*) Moschuskraut *nt*

musk: musk deer N Moschustier *nt*, Moschushirsch *m*; **musk duck** N Moschusente *f*

musket ['mʌskɪt] N Muskete *f*

musketeer [ˌmʌskɪ'tɪə'] N Musketier *m*

musketry ['mʌskɪtrɪ] N (= *muskets*) Musketen *pl*; (= *troops*) Musketiere *pl*

musk: muskmelon N Zucker- *or* Gartenmelone *f*; **musk ox** N Moschusochse *m*; **muskrat** N Bisamratte *f*; **musk rose** N Moschusrose *f*

musky ['mʌskɪ] ADJ (+*er*) moschusartig *or* -ähnlich; **~ smell** *or* **scent** Moschusduft *m*

Muslim ['muzlɪm] ADJ, N = **Moslem**

muslin ['mʌzlɪn] **N** Musselin *m* ADJ aus Musselin

musquash ['mʌskwɒʃ] N Bisamratte *f*

muss [mʌs] N (*US, inf*) **N** Durcheinander *nt*; **to be in a ~** Durcheinander (*inf*) *or* unordentlich sein **VT** (*also* **muss up**) in Unordnung bringen; *hair, room also* durcheinander bringen (*inf*); **to get ~ed (up)** in Unordnung geraten

mussel ['mʌsl] N (*Mies*)muschel *f*; **~ bed** Muschelbank *f*

Mussulman ['mʌslmən] N *pl* **-mans** (*old*) Muselman(in) *m(f)*

mussy ['mʌsɪ] ADJ (+*er*) (*US, inf*) unordentlich, durcheinander *pred* (*inf*)

---

must¹ [mʌst] ✪ 4, 9.5, 10.1, 15.1, 15.2 VB AUX *present tense only* **a** müssen; **you ~ (go and) see this church** Sie müssen sich (*dat*) diese Kirche unbedingt ansehen; **do it if you ~** tu, was du nicht lassen kannst; **if you ~ know** wenn du es unbedingt wissen willst; **~ you/I** *etc*? (= *really?*) ja (wirklich)?; (= *do you/I have to?*) muss das sein?; **we ~ away** (*old*) wir müssen fort

b (*in neg sentences*) dürfen; **I ~n't forget that** ich darf das nicht vergessen

c (= *be certain to*) **he ~ be there by now** er ist wohl inzwischen da; (= *is bound to*) er ist inzwischen bestimmt da, er muss (wohl) inzwischen da sein; **he (surely) ~ be there by now** er MUSS doch inzwischen da sein; **I ~ have lost it** ich habe es wohl verloren, ich muss es wohl verloren haben; (*with stress on must*) ich muss es verloren haben; **you ~ have heard of him** Sie haben bestimmt schon von ihm gehört; (*with stress on must*) Sie müssen doch schon von ihm gehört haben; **there ~ have been five of them** es müssen fünf gewesen sein; (*about five*) es waren wohl etwa fünf; (*at least five*) es waren bestimmt fünf; **he ~ be older than that** er muss älter sein; **there ~ be a reason for it** es gibt bestimmt eine Erklärung dafür; (*with stress on must*) es muss doch eine Erklärung dafür geben; **it ~ be about 3 o'clock** es wird wohl (so) etwa 3 Uhr sein, es muss so gegen 3 Uhr sein; **I ~ have been dreaming** da habe ich wohl geträumt; **I ~ have been mad** ich muss (wohl) wahnsinnig gewesen sein; **you ~ be crazy!** du bist ja *or* wohl wahnsinnig!

d (*showing annoyance*) müssen; **he ~ come just now** natürlich muss er gerade jetzt kommen **N** (*inf*) Muss *nt*; **a sense of humour** (*Brit*) *or* **humor** (*US*)**/an umbrella is a ~** man braucht unbedingt Humor/einen Schirm, Humor/ein Schirm ist unerlässlich; **tighter security is a ~** bessere Sicherheitskontrollen sind unerlässlich; **this novel/film is a ~ for everyone** diesen Roman/diesen Film muss man einfach *or* unbedingt gelesen/gesehen haben

must² N (= *mustiness*) Muffigkeit *f*

must³ N (*Winemaking*) Most *m*

must- [mʌst] PREF (*inf*) **a ~see movie** ein Film, den man gesehen haben muss; **a ~read** ein Buch, das man gelesen haben muss; **it's a ~visit** dort muss man gewesen sein

mustache N (*US*) = **moustache**

mustachio [mʌ'stæʃɪəʊ] N *pl* **-s** Schnauzbart *m*

mustachioed [mʌ'stæʃɪəʊd] ADJ (*esp Brit*) schnauzbärtig

mustang ['mʌstæŋ] N Mustang *m*

mustard ['mʌstəd] N Senf *m*; (= *colour*) Senfgelb *nt*; **to be as keen as ~** Feuer und Flamme sein; **to cut the ~** (*inf*) es bringen (*sl*) ATTR Senf-; (= *yellow*) senffarben; **~ sauce** Senfsoße *f*

mustard *in cpds* Senf-; **mustard gas** N Senfgas *nt*; **mustard plaster** N Senfpackung *f*; **mustard powder** N Senfmehl *nt*; **mustard seeds** PL Senfkörner *pl*; **mustard yellow** N Senfgelb *nt*; **mustard-yellow** ADJ senfgelb

muster ['mʌstə'] N (*esp Mil*: = *assembly*) Appell *m*; (= *cattle muster*) Zusammentreiben *nt* der Herde; **to pass ~** (*fig*) den Anforderungen genügen; **~ station** (*on ship*) Sammelplatz *m* VT **a** (= *summon*) versammeln, zusammenrufen; (*esp Mil*) antreten lassen; *cattle* zusammentreiben; **the men were ~ed at 14.00** die Leute mussten um 14.00 Uhr zum Appell antreten **b** (= *manage to raise: also* **muster up**) zusammenbekommen, aufbringen; (*fig*) *intelligence* aufbieten; *strength, courage* aufbringen; **all one's strength, courage** zusammennehmen VI sich versammeln; (*esp Mil*) (zum Appell) antreten

▶ **muster in** VT *sep* (*US*) *troops, recruits* einziehen

▶ **muster out** VT *sep* (*US*) *troops* entlassen

mustiness ['mʌstɪnɪs] N Modergeruch *m*

mustn't ['mʌsnt] *contr of* **must not**

musty ['mʌstɪ] ADJ (+*er*) moderig; *air* muffig

mutability [ˌmjuːtə'bɪlɪtɪ] N Wandlungsfähigkeit *f*, Mutabilität *f* (*spec*)

---

mutable ['mjuːtəbl] ADJ variabel, veränderlich; (*Biol*) mutabel

mutant ['mjuːtənt] **N** Mutante *f* (*spec*), Mutation *f* ADJ mutierend

mutate [mjuː'teɪt] VI sich verändern; (*Biol*) mutieren (*to zu*); (*Ling*) sich verwandeln (*to in* +*acc*); **to ~ into sth** (*fig*) sich in etw (*acc*) verwandeln VT wandeln; (*Biol*) zu einer Mutation führen bei

mutation [mjuː'teɪʃən] N (= *process*) Veränderung *f*; (= *result*) Variante *f*; (*Biol*) Mutation *f*; (*Ling*) Wandel *m* (*to zu*)

mute [mjuːt] ADJ stumm (*also Ling*); *amazement, rage* sprachlos; **to be ~ about sth** über etw (*acc*) schweigen; **to sit ~** schweigend dasitzen; **he was ~ with rage** er brachte vor Wut kein Wort heraus **N a** (= *dumb person*) Stumme(r) *mf* **b** (= *hired mourner*) Totenkläger *m*; (= *woman*) Klageweib *nt* **c** (*Mus*) Dämpfer *m* VT dämpfen

muted ['mjuːtɪd] ADJ gedämpft; (*fig*) *criticism etc* leise, leicht

mute swan N Höckerschwan *m*

mutilate ['mjuːtɪleɪt] VT *person, animal, story, play* verstümmeln; *painting, building etc* verschandeln (*inf*)

mutilation [ˌmjuːtɪ'leɪʃən] N Verstümmelung *f*; (*of painting, building etc*) Verschandelung *f* (*inf*)

mutineer [ˌmjuːtɪ'nɪə'] N Meuterer *m*, Meuterin *f*

mutinous ['mjuːtɪnəs] ADJ (*Naut*) meuterisch, aufrührerisch; (*fig*) rebellisch

mutiny ['mjuːtɪnɪ] (*Naut, fig*) **N** Meuterei *f* VI meutern

mutism ['mjuːtɪzəm] N (*Psych*) Mutismus *m*

mutt [mʌt] N (*pej inf*) (= *dog*) Köter *m*; (= *idiot*) Dussel *m* (*inf*)

mutter ['mʌtə'] **N** Murmeln *nt*, Gemurmel *nt*; (*of discontent*) Murren *nt*; **a ~ of voices** ein Stimmengemurmel *nt*; **a ~ of discontent** ein unzufriedenes Murren VT murmeln, brummeln; **they ~ed their discontent** sie murrten unzufrieden; **are you ~ing threats at me?** höre ich Sie Drohungen (gegen mich) brummeln? VI murmeln; (*with discontent*) murren

muttering ['mʌtərɪŋ] N (= *act*) Gemurmel *nt*; (*with discontent*) Murren *nt*; (= *remark*) Gemurmel *nt no pl*, Meckerei *f* (*inf*)

mutton ['mʌtn] N Hammel(fleisch *nt*) *m*; **as dead as ~** mausetot (*inf*); **she's ~ dressed (up) as lamb** (*inf*) sie macht auf jung (*inf*)

mutton: muttonchops PL (= *whiskers*) Koteletten *pl*; **muttonhead** N (*fig inf*) Schafskopf *m* (*inf*)

mutual ['mjuːtjʊəl] ADJ (= *reciprocal*) *trust, respect, affection etc* gegenseitig; (= *bilateral*) *troop withdrawals, efforts, détente, satisfaction* beiderseitig; (= *shared, in common*) *interest, friends, dislikes etc* gemeinsam; **the divorce was by ~ consent** sie haben sich im gegenseitigen Einvernehmen scheiden lassen; **it would be for our ~ benefit** es wäre für uns beide von Vorteil *or* zu unser beider Nutzen (*form*); **the feeling is ~** das beruht (ganz) auf Gegenseitigkeit; **I hate you! – the feeling is ~** ich hasse dich! – ganz meinerseits (*inf*)

mutual: mutual fund N (*US, Fin*) Mutual Fund *m*, offener Investmentfonds; **mutual insurance** N Versicherung *f* auf Gegenseitigkeit

mutuality [ˌmjuːtjʊ'ælɪtɪ] N Gegenseitigkeit *f*

mutually ['mjuːtjʊəlɪ] ADV beide; (= *reciprocally*) *distrust* gegenseitig; *satisfactory, beneficial* für beide Seiten; *agreed, rejected* von beiden Seiten; **at a ~ convenient time** zu einem für beide Seiten annehmbaren Zeitpunkt; **~ contradictory** einander widersprechend; **a gentleman ~ known to us** ein Herr, den wir beide kennen; **~ assured destruction** (*Mil*) beiderseitige Bereitschaft zum nuklearen Gegenschlag

Muzak® ['mjuːzæk] N Berieselungsmusik *f* (*inf*)

muzziness ['mʌzɪnɪs] N (= *dizziness, dazed state*) Benommenheit *f*; (= *blurred state*) Verschwommenheit *f*; (*of noise*) Verzerrtheit *f*

muzzle ['mʌzl] **N a** (= *snout, mouth*) Maul *nt* **b** (*for dog etc*) Maulkorb *m* **c** (*of gun*) Mündung *f*; (= *barrel*) Lauf *m* **VT** *animal* einen Maulkorb um- *or* anlegen (+*dat*); (*fig*) *critics, the press* mundtot machen; *criticism, protest* ersticken

muzzle: muzzle-loader N Vorderlader *m*; **muzzle-loading** ADJ *gun* mit Vorderladung; **muzzle velocity** N Mündungs- *or* Auffangsgeschwindigkeit *f*

muzzy ['mʌzɪ] ADJ (+*er*) (= *dizzy, dazed*) benommen, benebelt; (= *blurred*) *view, memory etc* verschwommen; *noise* verzerrt

MVP N (*US Sport*) *abbr of* **most valuable player** bester Spieler, beste Spielerin

MW *abbr of* **medium wave** MW

my [maɪ] **POSS ADJ** mein; **I've hurt my leg/arm** ich habe mir das Bein/den Arm verletzt; **my father and mother** mein Vater und meine Mutter; **of course, my darling** natürlich, Liebling; **in my country** bei uns, in meinem Land (*form*); **my God!** mein Gott!; **my goodness!** (du) meine Güte! **INTERJ** (*surprise*) (du) meine Güte, du liebe Zeit; (*delight*) ach, oh; **my, my, hasn't she grown!** nein so was, die ist vielleicht groß geworden

Myanmar ['maɪænmɑː'] N Myanmar *nt*

mycosis [maɪ'kəʊsɪs] N (*Med*) Mykose *nt* (*spec*), Pilzkrankheit *f*

myna(h) bird ['maɪnəˌbɜːd] N Hirtenstar *m*

myocardial infarction ['maɪəʊˌkɑːdɪəlɪn'fɑːkʃən] N (*Med*) Myokardinfarkt *m*

myopia [maɪ'əʊpɪə] N Kurzsichtigkeit *f*, Myopie *f* (*spec*)

myopic [maɪ'ɒpɪk] ADJ kurzsichtig

myriad ['mɪrɪəd] **N** Myriade *f*; **a ~ of** Myriaden von **ADJ** (= *innumerable*) unzählige

myrrh [mɜː'] N Myrr(h)e *f*

myrtle ['mɜːtl] N Myrte *f*

myrtle-green ['mɜːtl'griːn] ADJ moosgrün

myself [maɪ'self] PERS PRON **a** (*dir obj, with prep +acc*) mich; (*indir obj, with prep +dat*) mir; **I said to ~** ich sagte mir; **singing to ~** vor mich hin singend; **I wanted to see (it) for ~** ich wollte es selbst *or* selber sehen; **I tried it out on ~** ich habe es an mir selbst *or* selber ausprobiert; **I addressed the letter to ~** ich habe den Brief an mich selbst adressiert **b** (*emph*) (ich) selbst; **my wife and ~** meine Frau und ich; **I did it ~** ich habe es selbst gemacht; **I thought so ~** das habe ich auch gedacht; **... if I say so or it ~** ... auch wenn ich es selbst sage; **(all) by ~** (ganz) allein(e); **I ~ believe that ...**, **~, I believe that ...** ich persönlich *or* ich selbst bin der Ansicht, dass ...; **~, I doubt it** ich persönlich *or* ich für meinen Teil bezweifle das **c** (= *one's normal self*) **I'm not (feeling) ~ today** mit mir ist heute etwas nicht in Ordnung; (*healthwise also*) ich bin heute nicht ganz auf der Höhe; **I just tried to be ~** ich versuchte, mich ganz natürlich zu benehmen

mysterious [mɪ'stɪərɪəs] ADJ (= *puzzling*) rätselhaft, mysteriös; (= *secretive*) geheimnisvoll; *atmosphere, stranger* geheimnisvoll; **she is being quite ~ about it/him** sie macht ein großes Geheimnis daraus/um ihn; **why are you being so ~?** warum tust du so geheimnisvoll?; **for some ~ reason** aus unerfindlichen Gründen; **the Lord moves in ~ ways** die Wege des Herrn sind unergründlich

mysteriously [mɪ'stɪərɪəslɪ] ADV *vague, unwilling, pleased* sonderbar; (= *puzzlingly*) *vanish, change, die* auf rätselhafte *or* geheimnisvolle *or* mysteriöse Weise; *disappointed, missing* unerklärlicherweise; (= *secretively*) geheimnisvoll

mystery ['mɪstərɪ] N (= *puzzle*) Rätsel *nt*; (= *secret*) Geheimnis *nt*; **to be shrouded** *or* **surrounded in ~** von einem Geheimnis umwittert *or* umgeben sein; **there's no ~ about it** da ist überhaupt nichts Geheimnisvolles dabei; **it's a ~ to me** das ist mir schleierhaft *or* ein Rätsel; **don't make a great ~ of it!** mach doch kein so großes Geheimnis daraus!; **why all the ~?** was soll denn die Geheimnistuerei?

mystery: mystery model N (*Aut*) Erlkönig *m* (*fig*); **mystery monger** ['mɪstərɪˌmʌŋgə'] N Geheimniskrämer(in) *m(f)*; **mystery novel** N = **mystery story**; **mystery play** N Mysterienspiel *nt*; **mystery story** N Kriminalgeschichte *f*, Krimi *m* (*inf*); **mystery tour** N Fahrt *f* ins Blaue; **a ~ of the Black Forest** eine Entdeckungsreise durch den Schwarzwald; **mystery writer** N Kriminalschriftsteller(in) *m(f)*

mystic ['mɪstɪk] **ADJ** mystisch; *writing, words, beauty also* geheimnisvoll **N** Mystiker(in) *m(f)*

mystical ['mɪstɪkəl] ADJ mystisch

mysticism ['mɪstɪsɪzəm] N Mystizismus *m*; (*of poetry etc*) Mystik *f*, Mystische(s) *nt*

mystification [ˌmɪstɪfɪ'keɪʃən] N (= *bafflement*) Verwunderung *f*, Verblüffung *f*; (= *act of bewildering*) Verwirrung *f*

mystified ['mɪstɪfaɪd] ADJ *person, look, frown* verblüfft; **she was ~ about it** es verblüffte sie, es war ihr rätselhaft *or* ein Rätsel; **I am ~ as to how this could happen** es ist mir ein Rätsel, wie das passieren konnte

mystify ['mɪstɪfaɪ] VT vor ein Rätsel stellen; **his explanation mystified us all** seine Erklärung blieb uns allen ein Rätsel; **the conjurer's tricks mystified the audience** die Kunststücke des Zauberers verblüfften das Publikum

mystifying ['mɪstɪfaɪɪŋ] ADJ unerklärlich, rätselhaft

mystique [mɪ'stiːk] N geheimnisvoller Nimbus; **modern women have little ~, there is little ~ about modern women** die moderne Frau hat wenig Geheimnisvolles an sich

myth [mɪθ] N Mythos *m*; (*fig*) Märchen *nt*; **it's a ~** (*fig*) das ist doch ein Gerücht *or* Märchen

mythic ['mɪθɪk] ADJ = **mythical a, b**

mythical ['mɪθɪkəl] ADJ **a** (*of myth*) mythisch; **the ~ figure/character of Arthur** die mythische Artusfigur, die Sagengestalt des Artus **b** (= *fantastic*) *proportions, status, figure* legendär; **their rivalry has taken on ~ proportions** ihre Rivalität ist zur Legende geworden **c** (= *unreal*) *figure, world* fantastisch, phantastisch; (= *invented*) erfunden

mythological [ˌmɪθə'lɒdʒɪkəl] ADJ mythologisch

mythology [mɪ'θɒlədʒɪ] N Mythologie *f*

myxomatosis [ˌmɪksəʊmə'təʊsɪs] N Myxomatose *f*

N

N, **n** [ɛn] N N nt, n nt

N abbr of **north** N

n a (Math) n b **'n** (inf) = **and** c (inf: = many) x (inf); **n times** x-mal (inf)

n a abbr of **noun** Subst. b abbr of **neuter** nt

n/a abbr of **not applicable** entf.

NAACP (US) abbr of **National Association for the Advancement of Colored People** Vereinigung zur Förderung Farbiger

Naafi ['næfɪ] abbr of **Navy, Army and Air Force Institutes** (= shop) Laden der britischen Armee (= canteen) Kantine der britischen Armee

nab [næb] VT (inf) a (= catch) erwischen; (police) schnappen (inf), erwischen (inf); **the police ~bed him when he ...** die Polizei hat ihn dabei erwischt, wie er ... (inf) b (= take for oneself) sich (dat) grapschen (inf); **somebody had ~bed my seat** mir hatte jemand den Platz geklaut (inf)

nabob ['neɪbɒb] N Nabob m; (fig also) Krösus m

nacelle [næ'sɛl] N a (on aeroplane) (Flugzeug-)rumpf m b (on gondola) (Luftschiff-)gondel f; (on balloon) (Ballon)korb m

nacre ['neɪkə] N Perlmutter f or nt, Perlmutt nt

nacreous ['neɪkrɪəs] ADJ perlmutterartig, Perlmutt(er)-

nadir ['neɪdɪə] N a (Astron) Nadir m, Fußpunkt m b (fig) Tiefstpunkt m; **the ~ of despair** tiefste Verzweiflung

naff [næf] ADJ (Brit inf) a (= stupid) idea, thing to do, suggestion blöd (inf) b (= not much use) management, company lahm (inf); computer, gadget etc nutzlos; **this new monitor's a bit ~** dieser neue Monitor bringts nicht (inf) or ist nicht das Wahre (inf) c (= not perceived as good style) colour, jacket, tie, design, book cover, car ordinär; **it looks a bit ~, doesn't it?** es sieht nicht gerade schick aus, oder?

▶ **naff off** VI (Brit inf) verschwinden (inf); **naff off!** (= go away) hau ab! (inf); (expressing refusal) du spinnst wohl!

naffing ['næfɪŋ] ADJ (Brit inf) verdammt (inf)

NAFTA ['næftə] N abbr of **North American Free Trade Agreement** NAFTA f

nag¹ [næg] VT (= find fault with) herumnörgeln an (+dat); (= pester) keine Ruhe lassen (+dat) (for wegen); **she's forever ~ging me** sie nörgelt immerzu an mir herum, sie hat dauernd etwas an mir auszusetzen; **don't ~ me** nun lass mich doch in Ruhe!; **to ~ sb about sth** jdm wegen etw keine Ruhe lassen; **to ~ sb to do sth** jdm schwer zusetzen or die Hölle heiß machen, damit er etw tut; **she kept on ~ging him until he did it** sie hat ihm solange zugesetzt or keine Ruhe gelassen, bis er es machte; **one thing that's been ~ging me for some time is ...** was mich schon seit einiger Zeit plagt or nicht in Ruhe lässt, ist ...

VI (= find fault) herumnörgeln, meckern (inf); (= be insistent) keine Ruhe geben; **to ~ at sb** an jdm herumnörgeln, jdm keine Ruhe lassen; **stop ~ging** hör auf zu meckern (inf)

N (= fault-finder) Nörgler m(f); (= woman also) Meckerliese f (inf), Meckerziege f (inf); (= man also) Meckerfritze m (inf); (pestering) Quälgeist m; **don't be a ~** nun meckre nicht immer (inf)

nag² N (= old horse) Klepper m, Mähre f; (inf: = horse) Gaul m

nagger ['nægə] N = **nag¹** N

nagging ['nægɪŋ] ADJ a wife, voice meckernd (inf), nörglerisch; (= pestering) ewig drängend b pain dumpf; worry, doubt quälend; question brennend; fear drückend N (= fault-finding) Meckern nt (inf), Nörgelei f; (= pestering) ewiges Drängen

NAHT (Brit) abbr of **National Association of Head Teachers**

naiad ['naɪæd] N Najade f, Wassernymphe f

nail [neɪl] N a (Anat) Nagel m b (Tech) Nagel m; **as hard as ~s** knallhart (inf), (unheimlich) hart; (physically) zäh wie Leder; **on the ~** (Brit fig inf) auf der Stelle, sofort; **cash on the ~** (Brit fig inf) Bargeld nt; **to hit the ~ (right) on the head** (fig) den Nagel auf den Kopf treffen; **to drive a ~ into sb's coffin** (fig) **to be a ~ in sb's coffin** (fig) ein Nagel zu jds Sarg sein

VT a (= fix with nails, put nails into) nageln; **to ~ sth to the floor/door/wall** etw an den Boden/an die Tür/Wand nageln, etw auf dem Boden/an der Tür/Wand festnageln; **~ this on here** nageln Sie das hier an or fest; **he ~ed his opponent to the canvas** er pinnte seinen Gegner auf die Matte (inf) b (fig) person festnageln; **fear ~ed him to the spot** er war vor Furcht wie auf der Stelle festgenagelt; **they ~ed the deal** sie haben den Handel unter Dach und Fach gebracht; **to ~ a lie** eine Lüge entlarven or entblößen c (inf) **to ~ sb** sich (dat) jdn schnappen (inf); (= charge) jdn drankriegen (inf)

▶ **nail down** VT sep a (lit) box zunageln; carpet, lid festnageln b (fig) person festnageln (to auf +acc); **I nailed him down to coming at 6 o'clock** ich nagelte ihn auf 6 Uhr fest

▶ **nail up** VT sep picture etc annageln; door, window vernageln; box zunageln

nail in cpds Nagel-; **nail-biting** N Nägelkauen nt ADJ (inf) suspense atemlos; match spannungsgeladen; **it's a ~ time for them** sie machen eine spannungsreiche Zeit durch; **nailbrush** f N Nagelbürste f; **nail clippers** PL Nagelzwicker m; **nailfile** N Nagelfeile f; **nail polish** N Nagellack m; **nail polish remover** N Nagellackentferner m; **nail scissors** PL Nagelschere f; **nail varnish** N (Brit) Nagellack m

naïve [naɪ'iːv] ADJ (+er) naiv (also Art); person, remark also einfältig

naïvely [naɪ'iːvlɪ] ADV naiv; **he ~ believed me** er war so naiv, mir zu glauben, in seiner Einfalt glaubte er mir; **I ~ thought that ...** naiverweise dachte ich, dass ...

naïveté [naɪ'iːvteɪ], **naïvety** [naɪ'iːvɪtɪ] N Naivität f; (of person also) Einfalt f

naked ['neɪkɪd] ADJ a person nackt, unbekleidet, bloß (liter); animal (= without fur) ohne Fell; bird (= without feathers) federlos; branch nackt, kahl; countryside kahl; earth nackt; sword bloß, blank, nackt; flame, light ungeschützt; wire blank; **to go ~** nackt gehen; **~ to the waist** mit freiem or nacktem Oberkörper; **I feel ~ without my wristwatch/make-up** ich fühle mich ohne meine Armbanduhr/ohne Make-up ganz nackt; **(as) ~ as nature intended** (hum, man) im Adamskostüm (hum); woman im Evaskostüm (hum); **(as) ~ as the day (that) he was born** splitterfasernackt (hum); **the ~ eye** das bloße Auge; **visible/invisible to the ~ eye** mit bloßem Auge erkennbar/nicht erkennbar; **a room with one ~ bulb** ein Zimmer, in dem nur eine Glühbirne hing b (= defenceless) schutzlos; **the President/army was left ~** der Präsident/das Heer stand schutzlos da c (= pure) truth, facts, aggression nackt; hatred, misery, anxiety blank, nackt

nakedly ['neɪkɪdlɪ] ADV a (= unashamedly) offen; **the new government is far more ~ military than the old** die neue Regierung zeigt ihren militärischen Charakter viel offener als die alte b (= without clothes) nackt; **a mass of bodies, writhing ~** eine Masse nackter, sich wälzender Körper

nakedness ['neɪkɪdnɪs] N Nacktheit f, Blöße f (liter)

NALGO ['nælgəʊ] (Brit) abbr of **National and Local Government Officers' Association** Gewerkschaft der staatlichen und kommunalen Verwaltungsangestellten

Nam [næm] N (US) abbr of **Vietnam**

namby-pamby ['næmbɪ'pæmbɪ] (esp Brit inf) N Mutterkind nt; (= boy also) Muttersöhnchen nt ADJ person verweichlicht, verzärtelt (inf); (= indecisive) unentschlossen

name [neɪm] N a Name m; **what's your ~?** wie heißen Sie?, wie ist Ihr Name? (form); **my ~ is ...** ich heiße ..., mein Name ist ... (form); **what's the ~ of this street?** wie heißt diese Straße?; **this man, Smith by ~** dieser Mann namens Smith; **a man (going) by the ~ of Gunn** ein Mann namens or mit Namen Gunn; **I know him only by ~** ich kenne ihn nur dem Namen nach; **he knows all his customers by ~** er kennt alle seine Kunden bei Namen; **to refer to sb/sth by ~** jdn/etw namentlich or mit Namen nennen; **in ~ alone** or **only** nur dem Namen nach; **a marriage in ~ only** eine nur auf dem Papier bestehende Ehe; **I won't mention any ~s** ich möchte keine Namen nennen; **he writes under the ~ of X** er schreibt unter dem Namen X; **fill in your ~(s) and address(es)** Namen und Adresse eintragen; **they married to give the child a ~** sie haben geheiratet, damit das Kind einen Namen hatte; **what ~ shall I say?** wie ist Ihr Name, bitte?; (on telephone) wer ist am Apparat?; (before showing sb in) wen darf ich melden?; **to have one's ~ taken** (Ftbl, Police etc) aufgeschrieben werden; **in the ~ of** im Namen (+gen); **stop in the ~ of the law** halt, im Namen des Gesetzes; **in the ~ of goodness/God** um Himmels/Gottes willen; **what in God's ~ ...** was in Gottes Namen ...; **all the big ~s were there** alle großen Namen waren da; **I'll put my/your ~ down** (on list, in register etc) ich trage mich/dich ein; (for school, class, excursion, competition etc) ich melde mich/dich an (for zu, for a school in einer Schule); (for tickets, goods etc) ich lasse mich/dich vormerken; (on waiting list) ich lasse mich or meinen Namen/dich or deinen Namen auf die Warteliste setzen; **I'll put your ~ down, Sir/Madam** ich werde Sie vormerken; **to call sb ~s** jdn beschimpfen; **you can call me all**

the **~s you like ...** du kannst mich nennen, was du willst ...; **not to have a penny/cent to one's** ~ völlig pleite sein (*inf*), keinen roten Heller haben (*dated*); **what's in a ~?** was ist *or* bedeutet schon ein Name?, Name ist Schall und Rauch (*Prov*); **in all but** ~ praktisch; **that's the ~ of the game** (*inf*) darum geht es; **for these people survival is the ~ of the game** diesen Leuten geht es ums Überleben; **I'll do it or my ~'s not Bob Brown** ich mache das, so wahr ich Bob Brown heiße

b (= *reputation*) Name *m*, Ruf *m*; **to have a good/bad** ~ einen guten/schlechten Ruf *or* Namen haben; **to get a bad** ~ in Verruf kommen; **to give sb a bad** ~ jdn in Verruf bringen; **to protect one's good** ~ seinen Ruf *or* guten Namen wahren; **to make one's** ~ as, **to make a** ~ **for oneself as** sich (*dat*) einen Namen machen als; **to make one's** ~ berühmt werden; **this book made his** ~ mit diesem Buch machte er sich einen Namen; **to have a** ~ **for sth** für etw bekannt sein

c (= *important person*) Persönlichkeit *f*

d (*Brit* = *Lloyd's investor*) Lloyd's-Gesellschafter(in) *m(f)*

VT a (= *call by a name, give a name to*) *person* nennen; *plant, new star etc* benennen, einen Namen geben (+*dat*); *ship* taufen, einen Namen geben (+*dat*); **I ~ this child/ship X** ich taufe dieses Kind/Schiff auf den Namen X; **a person ~d Smith** jemand namens *or* mit Namen Smith; **the child is ~d Peter** das Kind hat den *or* hört auf den Namen Peter; **to ~ a child after** *or* (*US*) **for sb** ein Kind nach jdm nennen; **to ~ sb as a witness** jdn als Zeugen/Zeugin nennen; **he was ~d as the thief/culprit/victim** er wurde als der Dieb/der Schuldige/das Opfer genannt *or* bezeichnet; **they refused to ~ the victim** sie hielten den Namen des Opfers geheim; **to ~ ~s** Namen nennen

b (= *appoint, nominate*) ernennen; **to ~ sb mayor/as leader** jdn zum Bürgermeister/Führer ernennen; **to ~ sb for the post of mayor** jdn für das Amt des Bürgermeisters vorschlagen; **he has been ~d as Nobel Prize winner** ihm wurde der Nobelpreis verliehen; **they ~d her as the winner of the award** sie haben ihr den Preis verliehen; **to ~ sb as one's heir** jdn zu seinem Erben bestimmen

c (= *describe, designate*) **to ~ sb (as) sth** jdn als etw bezeichnen

d (= *specify, list*) nennen; **~ the main plays by Shakespeare** nenne mir die wichtigsten Dramen Shakespeares; **~ your price** nennen Sie Ihren Preis; **to ~ the day** (*inf*) den Hochzeitstag festsetzen; **~ the date and I'll be there** bestimmen Sie den Tag, und ich werde da sein; **you ~ it, they have it/he's done it** es gibt nichts, was sie nicht haben/was er noch nicht gemacht hat

name-calling ['neɪmˌkɔːlɪŋ] N Beschimpfung(en) *f(pl)*, Schimpferei(en) *f(pl)*

-named [-neɪmd] ADJ *suf* genannt; **the first-/last-named** der Erst-/Letztgenannte, der zuerst/zuletzt Genannte

name: name day N Namenstag *m*; **name-drop** VI (*inf*) berühmte Bekannte in die Unterhaltung einfließen lassen; **she's always ~ping** sie muss dauernd erwähnen, wen sie alles kennt; **name-dropper** N (*inf*) **he's a terrible** ~ er muss dauernd erwähnen, wen er alles kennt; **name-dropping** N (*inf*) Angeberei *f* mit berühmten Bekannten; **his constant ~ is most tedious** es ist nicht auszuhalten, wie er ständig mit berühmten Namen um sich wirft; **nameless** ADJ **a** (= *unknown*) *person* unbekannt **b** (= *undesignated*) namenlos; *grave* anonym; **a person who shall be/remain** ~ jemand, der nicht genannt werden soll/der ungenannt bleiben soll **c** (= *undefined*) *sensation, emotion* unbeschreiblich; *longing, terror, suffering also* namenlos **d** (= *shocking*) *vice, crime* unaussprechlich

namely ['neɪmlɪ] ADV nämlich

name: namepart N Titelrolle *f*; **nameplate** N Namensschild *nt*; (*on door also*) Türschild *nt*;

(*on business premises*) Firmenschild *nt*; **namesake** N Namensvetter(in) *m(f)*; **name tag** N (= *badge*) Namensschild *nt*; **nametape** N Wäschezeichen *nt*

Namibia [næˈmɪbɪə] N Namibia *nt*

Namibian [næˈmɪbɪən] ADJ namibisch

naming ['neɪmɪŋ] N Namen(s)gebung *f*

nan(a) ['næn(ə)] N Oma *f* (*inf*)

nana ['nɑːnə] N (*inf*) Trottel *m* (*inf*)

nan bread ['nɑːnbred] N *warm serviertes, fladenförmiges Weißbrot als Beilage zu indischen Fleisch- und Gemüsegerichten*

nancy ['nænsɪ], **nancy-boy** N (*dated esp Brit inf*) **a** (= *homosexual*) Schwule(r) *m* **b** (= *softy*) Weichling *m* (*pej*)

nankeen [nænˈkiːn] N , *no pl* (= *cloth*) Nanking(-stoff) *m*

nanny ['nænɪ] N **a** Kindermädchen *nt* **b** (*inf: also* **nana**) Oma *f*, Omi *f* (*inf*) **c** (*also* **nanny goat**) Geiß *f*, Ziege *f*

nannying ['nænɪŋ] N **a** (= *job*) Arbeit *f* als Kindermädchen *nt* (*pej:* = *mollycoddling*) Bemutterung *f* **ADJ** (*pej*) bemutternd; **stupid, ~ legislation** dumme Gesetze, die die Bürger bevormunden wollen

nanny state N (*esp Brit pej*) Bevormundungsstaat *m*; (*all-providing*) Versorgungsstaat *m*

nanosecond ['nænəʊˌsekənd] N Nanosekunde *f*

nanotechnology [ˌnænəʊtekˈnɒlədʒɪ] N Nanotechnologie *f*

nap¹ [næp] N Schläfchen *nt*, Nickerchen *nt*; **afternoon** ~ Nachmittagsschläfchen *nt*; **to have** *or* **take a** ~ ein Schläfchen *or* ein Nickerchen machen; **he always has** *or* **takes a 20 minute ~ after lunch** nach dem Mittagessen legt er sich immer 20 Minuten aufs Ohr *or* hin **VI to catch sb ~ping** (*fig*) jdn überrumpeln

nap² N (*Tex*) Flor *m*; (*Sew*) Strich *m*

nap³ (*Racing*) N *winner, horse* setzen auf (+*acc*) **N** Tip *m*; **to select a** ~ auf ein bestimmtes Pferd setzen

napalm ['neɪpɑːm] N Napalm *nt* **VT** mit Napalm bewerfen

napalm: napalm bomb N Napalmbombe *f*; **napalm bombing** N Abwurf *m* von Napalmbomben

nape [neɪp] N **of the/one's neck** Nacken *m*, Genick *nt*

naphtha ['næfθə] N Naphtha *nt* or *f*

naphthalene ['næfθəliːn] N Naphthalin *nt*

napkin ['næpkɪn] N **a** (= *table napkin*) Serviette *f*, Mundtuch *nt* (*old*) **b** (*for baby*) Windel *f*; (*US* = *sanitary napkin*) (Damen)binde *f*

napkin ring N Serviettenring *m*

Naples ['neɪplz] N Neapel *nt*

Napoleon [nəˈpəʊlɪən] N Napoleon *m*

Napoleonic [nəˌpəʊlɪˈɒnɪk] ADJ napoleonisch

nappa ['næpə] N Nappa(leder) *nt*

napper ['næpə] N (*Brit inf:* = *a person's head*) Birne *f* (*inf*)

nappy ['næpɪ] N (*Brit*) Windel *f*

nappy rash N Wundsein *nt*, Windeldermatitis *f* (*spec*); **little Jonathan's got** ~ der kleine Jonathan ist wund

narc [nɑːk] N (*US sl*) Rauschgiftfahnder(in) *m(f)*

narcissi [nɑːˈsɪsaɪ] *pl of* **narcissus a**

narcissism [nɑːˈsɪsɪzəm] N Narzissmus *m*

narcissistic [ˌnɑːsɪˈsɪstɪk] ADJ narzisstisch

narcissus [nɑːˈsɪsəs] N **a** *pl* **narcissi** (*Bot*) Narzisse *f* **b** (*Myth*) **Narcissus** Narziss *m*

narcosis [nɑːˈkəʊsɪs] N Narkose *f*

narco-terrorism [ˌnɑːkəʊˈterəˌrɪzəm] N Narkoterrorismus *m*

narcotic [nɑːˈkɒtɪk] **ADJ a** ~ **substance/drug** Rauschgift *nt* **b** (*Med*) narkotisch **N a** Rauschgift *nt*; (= *illegal drugs also*) Drogen *pl*; **~s industry** Drogenindustrie *f*; **the ~s squad** das Rauschgiftdezernat; **~s offence** Drogendelikt *nt*; **to be on a ~s charge**

wegen eines Drogendelikts angeklagt sein **b** (*Med*) Narkotikum *nt*

narcotics [nɑːˈkɒtɪks]: **narcotics agent** N Rauschgiftfahnder(in) *m(f)*; **narcotics crime** N Drogenkriminalität *f*; **narcotics trade**, **narcotics traffic** N Drogenhandel *m*; **narcotics trafficker** N Drogendealer(in) *m(f)* (*inf*)

nark [nɑːk] **VT** (*inf*) ärgern; **to get ~ed wütend werden; to feel ~ed** sich ärgern **N** (*inf*) Spitzel *m*

narky ['nɑːkɪ] ADJ (+*er*) (*Brit inf*) gereizt

narrate [nəˈreɪt] VT erzählen; *events, journey etc* schildern

narration [nəˈreɪʃən] N Erzählung *f*; (*of events, journey*) Schilderung *f*

narrative ['nærətɪv] **N a** (= *story*) Erzählung *f*; (= *account*) Schilderung *f*; (= *text*) Text *m* **b** (= *act of narrating*) Erzählen *nt*; (*of events, journey*) Schilderung *f*; **he has a gift for** ~ er ist ein talentierter Erzähler **ADJ** erzählend; *ability etc* erzählerisch; **~ poem** Ballade *f*; (*modern*) Erzählgedicht *nt*; **~ structure** Erzählstruktur *f*

narrator [nəˈreɪtə] N Erzähler(in) *m(f)*; **first-person** ~ Icherzähler(in) *m(f)*; **third-person** ~ Ererzähler(in) *m(f)*

narrow ['nærəʊ] **ADJ** (+*er*) **a** *eng; road, path, passage, valley* eng, schmal; *shoulders, hips* schmal; **to become** ~ eng werden; (*road etc*) sich verengen

b (*fig*) *person, attitudes, ideas, views* engstirnig, beschränkt; *sense, meaning, interpretation* eng; *existence* beschränkt; *band, margin* schmal, eng; *range* eng, begrenzt; *majority, victory, defeat, lead* knapp; *scrutiny* peinlich genau; **to have a ~ mind** engstirnig sein; **to have a ~ escape** mit knapper Not davonkommen, gerade noch einmal davonkommen; **that was a ~ escape** (*inf*) das war knapp, das wäre beinahe ins Auge gegangen (*inf*)

c (*Ling*) *vowel* geschlossen

N narrows PL enge Stelle

VT *road etc* enger machen, verengen; (= *reduce*) *gap* verkleinern; **to ~ the field** (*fig*) die Auswahl reduzieren (*to auf* +*acc*); **they decided to ~ the focus of their investigation** sie beschlossen, ihre Untersuchung einzuengen; **with ~ed eyes** mit zusammengekniffenen Augen

VI enger werden, sich verengen; (*difference, majority*) geringer werden, sich verringern; **the field ~ed to two candidates** die Auswahl war auf zwei Kandidaten zusammengeschrumpft

▸ **narrow down** **VI** (*to auf* +*acc*) sich beschränken; (= *be concentrated*) sich konzentrieren; **the choice narrows down to this** die Auswahl reduziert sich hierauf **VT** *sep* (*to auf* +*acc*) (= *limit*) beschränken, einschränken; *possibilities etc* beschränken; (= *concentrate*) konzentrieren; **that narrows it down a bit** dadurch wird die Auswahl kleiner

narrow: narrow boat N (*esp Brit*) (langes, schmales) Kanalboot; **narrowcasting** N (*TV*) Spartenfernsehen *nt*; **narrow-gauge** ADJ schmalspurig; **~ railway** Schmalspurbahn *f*

narrowly ['nærəʊlɪ] ADV **a** (= *by a small margin*) *defeat, fail, avoid* knapp; *escape* mit knapper Not; **he ~ escaped being knocked down** er wäre um ein Haar *or* beinahe überfahren worden; **you ~ missed (seeing) him** du hast ihn gerade verpasst **b** *interpret, define, focus* eng; *examine* peinlich genau; *watch* genau, scharf; **to be ~ based** eine schmale Basis haben; **to focus too ~ on sth** sich zu sehr auf etw (*acc*) beschränken; **she looks at things/life much too ~** sie sieht die Dinge/das Leben viel zu eng

narrow: narrow-minded ADJ , **narrow-mindedly** ADV engstirnig; **narrow-mindedness** N Engstirnigkeit *f*; **narrowness** N Enge *f*; **narrow-shouldered** ADJ schmalschult(e)rig

narwhal ['nɑːwəl] N Narwal *m*

nary ['nɛərɪ] ADJ (*old*) **with ~ a word** ohne ein Wort zu sagen

NASA ['næsə] *abbr of* **National Aeronautics and Space Administration** NASA *f*

nasal ['neɪzəl] **ADJ** **a** (Anat, Med) Nasen-; ~ **cavities** Nasenhöhle f; ~ **membrane** Nasenschleimhaut f; ~ **congestion** Nasenverstopfung f; ~ **discharge** Ausfluss m aus der Nase **b** (Ling) nasal; accent, voice, intonation näselnd; **to speak in a ~ voice** durch die Nase sprechen, näseln; ~ **sound** Nasallaut m **N** (Ling) Nasal (-laut) m

nasalization [ˌneɪzəlaɪ'zeɪʃən] **N** Nasalierung f

nasalize ['neɪzəlaɪz] **VT** nasalieren

nasally ['neɪzəlɪ] **ADV** pronounce nasal; speak durch die Nase, näselnd

nasal: nasal passage N Nasengang m; **nasal spray N** Nasenspray nt

nascent ['næsnt] **ADJ** **a** (liter) republic, world, culture werdend, im Entstehen begriffen; doubt, hope, pride aufkommend **b** (Chem) naszierend

nastily ['nɑːstɪlɪ] **ADV** **a** (= unpleasantly) scheußlich; speak, say, laugh gehässig, gemein; behave gemein, scheußlich; **to speak ~ to sb** zu jdm gehässig sein, jdn angiften (inf) **b** (= awkwardly, dangerously) fall, cut oneself böse, schlimm; skid, veer gefährlich

nastiness ['nɑːstɪnɪs] **N** , no pl **a** (= unpleasantness) Scheußlichkeit f; (of medicine) Ekelhaftigkeit f; (of weather) Abscheulichkeit f; (= seriousness: of break, wound) schlimme Art; (= objectionableness: of crime, behaviour, language) Abscheulichkeit f; (= dirtiness) Schmutzigkeit f; (= dangerousness) Gefährlichkeit f **b** (= malice) (of behaviour etc) Gemeinheit f; (of person) Bosheit f, Gemeinheit f; (of remarks etc) Gehässigkeit f, Gemeinheit f; (= behaviour) gemeines or scheußliches Benehmen (to gegenüber); (= remarks) Gehässigkeit(en pl) f (to/wards) gegenüber) **c** (= offensiveness) Anstößigkeit f; (of film, book also) Ekelhaftigkeit f; **the ~ of his mind** seine üble/schmutzige Fantasie or Phantasie

nasturtium [nəs'tɜːʃəm] **N** (Kapuziner)kresse f, Kapuziner m

nasty ['nɑːstɪ] **ADJ** (+er) **a** (= unpleasant) scheußlich; smell, taste scheußlich, widerlich; medicine ekelhaft, widerlich; weather, habit abscheulich, scheußlich; surprise böse, unangenehm; (= serious) break, cough, wound, fall böse, schlimm; situation, problem, accident schlimm; moment böse; (= objectionable) crime, behaviour, language, word, names abscheulich; (= dirty) schmutzig; (= dangerous) virus, disease böse, gefährlich; corner, bend, fog böse, übel, gefährlich; **that's a ~-looking sky/cut** der Himmel/der Schnitt sieht böse aus; **she had a ~ fall** sie ist böse or schlimm gefallen; **history has a ~ habit of repeating itself** die Geschichte hat die unangenehme Gewohnheit, sich zu wiederholen; **he had a ~ time of it** es ging ihm sehr schlecht or ganz übel; **he has a ~ look in his eyes** sein Blick verheißt nichts Gutes; **don't touch that, that's ~** pfui, fass das nicht an; **they pulled all his teeth out – ~!** sie haben ihm alle Zähne gezogen – wie scheußlich or unangenehm!; **a ~ surprise or shock** eine böse or unangenehme Überraschung; **to turn ~** (situation, person) unangenehm werden; (animal) wild werden; (weather) schlecht werden, umschlagen; **events took a ~ turn** die Dinge nahmen eine Wendung zum Schlechten **b** (= malicious) person, behaviour gemein, gehässig, garstig (dated), fies (inf) (to sb jdm gegenüber); trick gemein, böse; remark, word gemein; rumour gehässig, übel; **he has a ~ temper** mit ihm ist nicht gut Kirschen essen; **don't say that, that's ~** pfui, so was sagt man doch nicht; **to be ~ about sb** gemein über jdn reden; **that was a ~ thing to say/do** das war gemein or fies (inf); **you ~ little boy (you)!** du böser Junge; **a ~ little man** ein Giftzwerg m (inf); **what a ~ man** was für ein ekelhafter Mensch; **he's a ~ bit or piece of work** (inf) er ist ein übler Kunde (inf) or Typ (inf) **c** (= offensive) anstößig; **to have a ~ mind** eine üble Fantasie or Phantasie haben; (= obsessed with sex) eine schmutzige Fantasie or Phantasie haben

N **nasties** pl (inf: = nasty things) ekelhafte Sachen pl; → also **video nasty**

Nat abbr of **national**

Natal [nə'tæl] **N** Natal nt

natal ['neɪtl] **ADJ** Geburts- → **antenatal, postnatal** etc

natality [nə'tælɪtɪ] **N** (esp US) Geburtenziffer f

natch [nætʃ] **INTERJ** (inf) natürlich!, klar!, logo! (inf)

NATFHE (Brit) abbr of **National Association of Teachers in Further and Higher Education**

nation ['neɪʃən] **N** Volk nt; (= people of one country) Nation f; **people of all ~s** Menschen aller Nationen; **the voice of the ~** die Stimme des Volkes; **in the service of the ~** im Dienste des Volkes; **to address the ~** zum Volk sprechen; **the whole ~ watched him do it** das ganze Land sah ihm dabei zu; **the Sioux ~** die Siouxindianer pl, das Volk der Sioux(indianer)

national ['næʃənl] **ADJ** national; problem, affairs also das (ganze) Land betreffend, des Landes, des Staates; election national, landesweit; strike, scandal landesweit; (= not local) agreement, radio station, press etc überregional; **the ~ average** der Landesdurchschnitt; ~ **character** Nationalcharakter m; ~ **defence** (Brit) or **defense** (US) Landesverteidigung f; ~ **economy** Volkswirtschaft f; ~ **language** Landessprache f; ~ **monument** nationales Denkmal, Nationaldenkmal nt; ~ **status** Landeszugehörigkeit f; ~ **team** Nationalmannschaft f

N **a** (= person) Staatsbürger(in) m(f); **foreign ~** Ausländer(in) m(f); **Commonwealth ~s** Angehörige pl des Commonwealth **b** (inf: = newspaper) überregionale Zeitung **c** (Sport) → **Grand National**

national: national anthem N Nationalhymne f; **national assistance N** Sozialhilfe f; **national bank N** National- or Staatsbank f; **national costume, national dress N** National- or Landestracht f

national: national debt N Staatsverschuldung f; **national flag N** National- or Landesflagge f; **National Front N** (Brit) rechtsradikale Partei; **national government N** nationale Regierung f; (in Germany) Bundesregierung f; (= coalition government) ≈ große Koalition; **National Guard N** (esp US) Nationalgarde f; **National Guardsman N** (US) Mitglied nt der Nationalgarde; **National Health ADJ** attr Kassen-; ~ **patient** ≈ Kassenpatient(in) m(f); **National Health (Service) N** (Brit) staatlicher Gesundheitsdienst; **I got it on the ~** ≈ das hat die Krankenkasse bezahlt; **national holiday N** gesetzlicher or staatlicher Feiertag; **National Hunt racing N** (Brit Horseracing) Hindernisrennen nt; **national income N** Volkseinkommen nt; **national insurance N** (Brit) Sozialversicherung f; ~ **contributions** Sozial-

versicherungsbeiträge pl; ~ **benefits** Arbeitslosen- und Krankengeld nt

nationalism ['næʃnəlɪzəm] **N** Nationalismus m; **feeling of ~** Nationalgefühl nt

nationalist ['næʃnəlɪst] **ADJ** nationalistisch **N** Nationalist(in) m(f)

nationalistic [ˌnæʃnə'lɪstɪk] **ADJ** nationalistisch

nationality [ˌnæʃə'nælɪtɪ] **N** Staatsangehörigkeit f, Nationalität f; **what ~ is he?** welche Staatsangehörigkeit hat er?; **she is of German ~** sie hat die deutsche Staatsangehörigkeit; **the many nationalities present** die Menschen verschiedener Nationalitäten, die anwesend sind

nationalization [ˌnæʃnəlaɪ'zeɪʃən] **N** Verstaatlichung f

nationalize ['næʃnəlaɪz] **VT** industries etc verstaatlichen

national: National League N (US Sport) eine der beiden bedeutendsten US-Baseballligen; **National Lottery N** (Brit) ≈ Lotto nt

nationally ['næʃnəlɪ] **ADV** (= as a nation) als Nation; (= nationwide) im ganzen Land, landesweit; recognized landesweit; ~ **televised** landesweit im Fernsehen übertragen

national: national park N Nationalpark m; **National Rifle Association N** (US) amerikanische Organisation, die das Recht der Bürger auf freien Kauf und Besitz von Waffen verteidigt; **National Savings PL** (Brit) ≈ Postsparkasse f; **national savings certificate N** (Brit) festverzinsliches öffentliches Sparpapier; **national security N** Staatssicherheit f; **National Security Council N** (US) Nationaler Sicherheitsrat; **national service N** Wehrdienst m; **National Socialism N** der Nationalsozialismus; **National Socialist N** Nationalsozialist(in) m(f) **ADJ** nationalsozialistisch; **National Trust N** (Brit) National Trust m, Natur- und Denkmalschutzverein in Großbritannien; ~ **property** (= building) Gebäude nt im Besitz des National Trust; (= estate) Gelände nt im Besitz des National Trust

nationhood ['neɪʃənhʊd] **N** nationale Einheit or Geschlossenheit

nationwide ['neɪʃən‚waɪd] **ADJ, ADV** landesweit; (in Germany also) bundesweit; **the speech was broadcast ~** die Rede wurde landesweit or (in Germany also) bundesweit übertragen; **the film opens ~ on Friday** der Film läuft am Freitag landesweit or im ganzen Land or (in Germany also) bundesweit an; **we have 300 branches ~** wir haben 300 Niederlassungen im ganzen Land

native ['neɪtɪv] **ADJ** **a** product, costume, customs, habits, plants einheimisch; (= associated with natives) der Eingeborenen; population eingeboren; ~ **country** Heimatland nt; ~ **town/city** Heimatstadt f; ~ **language** or **tongue** Muttersprache f; **the ~ inhabitants** or **people** die Einheimischen pl; (in colonial context) die Eingeborenen pl; (= original inhabitants) die Ureinwohner pl; ~ **tribe** Eingeborenenstamm m; **the ~ habitat of the tiger** die Heimat or der natürliche Lebensraum des Tigers; **my ~ Germany** mein Heimatland nt or meine Heimat Deutschland; **his ~ Berlin** seine Heimatstadt or Vaterstadt Berlin; **a ~ German** ein gebürtiger Deutscher, eine gebürtige

Deutsche; **California's most famous ~ son** der berühmteste Sohn Kaliforniens; **an animal/tree ~ to India** ein in Indien beheimatetes Tier/beheimateter Baum; **to go ~** wie die Eingeborenen leben

b (= *inborn*) *wit, quality* angeboren

c *metal* gediegen

N a (= *person*) Einheimische(r) *mf*; (*in colonial contexts*) Eingeborene(r) *mf*; (= *original inhabitant*) Ureinwohner(in) *m(f)*; **a ~ of Britain/Germany** ein gebürtiger Brite/Deutscher, eine gebürtige Britin/Deutsche

b to be a ~ of … (*plant, animal*) in … beheimatet sein

Native American ADJ indianisch **N** Indianer(in) *m(f)*

NATIVE AMERICAN

Native American ist der heutzutage gängige Begriff für die Urbevölkerung Amerikas, mit dem man diese von den Menschen europäischer, afrikanischer oder asiatischer Abstammung unterscheidet. Daneben kann man noch **American Indian** verwenden, doch **Red Indian** oder gar **Redskin** sollte man vermeiden, da dies als herablassend oder beleidigend empfunden wird. Es ist auch üblich, direkt den Namen des jeweiligen Volkes oder Stammes zu verwenden, wie zum Beispiel „Iroquois", „Navaho" oder „Mohawk", da sich diese durch ihre verschiedenen Kulturen und Sprachen unterscheiden → BUREAU OF INDIAN AFFAIRS

---

native: native-born ADJ *attr* gebürtig; **native country** N Heimatland *nt*, Vaterland *nt*; **native land** N Vaterland *nt*; **native speaker** N Muttersprachler(in) *m(f)*; **I'm not a ~** of English Englisch ist nicht meine Muttersprache; **he speaks English like a ~** er spricht Englisch, als wäre es seine Muttersprache

nativity [nə'tɪvɪtɪ] N Geburt *f*; **the Nativity** Christi Geburt *f*; (= *picture*) die Geburt Christi; **~ play** Krippenspiel *nt*

NATO ['neɪtəʊ] *abbr of* **North Atlantic Treaty Organization** NATO *f*

natter ['nætə] (*Brit, inf*) **VI** (= *gossip*) schwatzen (*inf*); (= *chatter also*) quasseln (*inf*); **to ~ away in German** deutsch quasseln (*inf*); **to ~ on about sth** über etw (*acc*) quasseln (*inf*) **N** Schwatz *m* (*inf*); **to have a ~** einen Schwatz halten (*inf*)

natty ['nætɪ] ADJ (+*er*) (*inf*) **a** (= *neat*) *dress* schick, schmuck (*dated*); *person* schick, adrett; **he's a ~ dresser** er zieht sich immer elegant *or* schmuck (*dated*) an **b** (= *handy*) *tool, gadget* handlich

natural ['nætʃrəl] ADJ **a** natürlich, Natur-; *rights* naturgegeben; (= *understandable*) *mistake* verständlich; **~ phenomenon** Naturphänomen *nt*; **it is (only) ~ for you/him to think …** es ist nur natürlich, dass Sie denken/er denkt …; **~ resources** Naturschätze *pl*; **the ~ world** die Natur; **in its ~ state** im Naturzustand; **to die a ~ death** *or* **of ~ causes** eines natürlichen Todes sterben; **death from ~ causes** (*Jur*) Tod durch natürliche Ursachen; **to be imprisoned for the rest of one's ~ life** (*Jur*) eine lebenslängliche Gefängnisstrafe verbüßen; **a ~ son of Utah** in Utah geboren

b (= *chemical-free*) *food, hair colour* natürlich; **~ cosmetics** Naturkosmetik *f*; **~ remedy** Naturheilmittel *nt*; **she is a ~ blonde** sie ist von Natur aus blond, blond ist ihre natürliche Haarfarbe

c (= *inborn*) *gift, ability, quality* angeboren; **to have a ~ talent for sth** eine natürliche Begabung für etw haben; **he is a ~ artist/comedian** er ist der geborene Künstler/Komiker; **it is ~ for birds to fly** Vögel können von Natur aus fliegen; **sth comes ~ to sb** etw fällt jdm leicht

d (= *unaffected*) *manner* natürlich, ungekünstelt; *person, charm* natürlich; **there was something not quite ~ about her way of speaking** ihre Sprechweise hatte etwas Gekünsteltes

e (*Math*) *number* natürlich

f *parents* leiblich; (*old*) *child* natürlich

N a (*Mus*) (= *symbol*) Auflösungszeichen *nt*; (= *note*) Note *f* ohne Vorzeichen; (= *note with a natural symbol*) Note *f* mit Auflösungszeichen; **B ~** H, h; **D ~** D, d; **you played F sharp instead of F ~** Sie haben fis statt f gespielt → *also* **major, minor**

b (*inf*: = *person*) Naturtalent *nt*; **he's a ~ for this part** diese Rolle ist ihm wie auf den Leib geschrieben

c (*inf*: = *life*) Leben *nt*; **I've never heard the like in all my ~** ich habe so was mein Lebtag noch nicht gehört (*inf*)

d (*old*: = *idiot*) Einfaltspinsel *m*

natural: natural-born ADJ *attr* geboren, von Natur aus begabt; **she'a a ~ teacher** sie ist die geborene Lehrerin; **natural childbirth** N natürliche Geburt; (= *method*) die schmerzlose Geburt; **natural disaster** N Naturkatastrophe *f*; **natural forces** PL Naturgewalten *pl*; **natural gas** N Erdgas *nt*; **natural history** N Naturkunde *f*; (*concerning evolution*) Naturgeschichte *f*

naturalism ['nætʃrəlɪzəm] N Naturalismus *m*

naturalist ['nætʃrəlɪst] N **a** Naturforscher(in) *m(f)*; (*Art, Liter*) Naturalist(in) *m(f)*

naturalistic [ˌnætʃrə'lɪstɪk] ADJ (*Art, Liter*) naturalistisch

naturalization [ˌnætʃrəlaɪ'zeɪʃən] N Naturalisierung *f*, Einbürgerung *f*; **~ papers** Einbürgerungsurkunde *f*

naturalize ['nætʃrəlaɪz] VT **a** *person* einbürgern, naturalisieren; **to become ~d** eingebürgert werden **b** *animal, plants* heimisch machen; *word* einbürgern; **to become ~d** heimisch werden/sich einbürgern

natural justice N Naturrecht *nt*

natural laws PL Naturgesetze *pl*

naturally ['nætʃrəlɪ] ADV **a** (= *of course*) natürlich; (= *understandably*) verständlicherweise **b** (= *unaffectedly*) *behave, speak* natürlich, ungekünstelt **c** (= *by nature*) von Natur aus; **he is ~ artistic/lazy** er ist künstlerisch veranlagt/von Natur aus faul **d** (= *not taught*) natürlich, instinktiv; **to do what comes ~** seiner Natur *or* seinem Trieb folgen; **it comes ~ to him** das fällt ihm leicht; **concern for the elderly comes ~ to him** die Sorge um ältere Menschen ist für ihn selbstverständlich

naturalness ['nætʃrəlnɪs] N Natürlichkeit *f*

natural: natural philosopher N Naturphilosoph(in) *m(f)*; **natural philosophy** N Naturwissenschaft *f*, Naturlehre *f* (*old*); **natural science** N Naturwissenschaft *f*; **the ~s** die Naturwissenschaften *pl*; **natural selection** N natürliche Auslese; **natural sign** N (*Mus*) Auflösungszeichen *nt*; **natural wastage** N natürliche Personalreduzierung; **to make job cuts through ~** Personal durch natürliche Fluktuation abbauen

nature ['neɪtʃə] **N a** Natur *f*; **Nature** die Natur; **laws of ~** Naturgesetze *pl*; **against ~** gegen die Natur; **in a state of ~** (= *uncivilized*, *inf*: = *naked*) im Naturzustand; **to return to ~** (*person*) zur Natur zurückkehren; (*garden*) in den Naturzustand zurückkehren; **to get back to ~** zur Natur zurückkehren; **to paint from ~** nach der Natur malen

b (*of person*) Wesen(sart *f*) *nt*, Natur *f*; **it is not in my ~ to say things like that** es entspricht nicht meiner Art *or* meinem Wesen, so etwas zu sagen; **it is in the ~ of young people to want to travel** es liegt im Wesen junger Menschen, reisen zu wollen; **cautious by ~** von Natur aus vorsichtig

c (*of object, material*) Beschaffenheit *f*; **it's in the ~ of things** das liegt in der Natur der Sache; **the ~ of the case is such …** der Fall liegt so …; **that's the ~ of the beast** (*fig*) das ist die Natur dieser Sache; **cash is, by its (very) ~, easy to steal** Geld ist aufgrund seiner Beschaffenheit leicht zu stehlen

d (= *type, sort*) Art *f*; **things of this ~** derartiges; **something in the ~ of an apology** so etwas

wie eine Entschuldigung; **… or something of that ~** … oder etwas in der Art

nature: nature conservancy N Naturschutz *m*; **nature cure** N Naturheilverfahren *nt*

-natured [-'neɪtʃəd] ADJ *suf things, animals* -artig; *person* mit einem … Wesen; **good-natured** (*person*) gutmütig; *animal, thing* gutartig; **ill-natured** bösartig

nature: nature lover N Naturfreund(in) *m(f)*; **nature poet** N Naturdichter(in) *m(f)*; **nature reserve** N Naturschutzgebiet *nt*; **nature study** N Naturkunde *f*; **nature trail** N Naturlehrpfad *m*; **nature worship** N Naturreligion *f*

naturism ['neɪtʃərɪzəm] N Freikörperkultur *f*, FKK *no art*

naturist ['neɪtʃərɪst] **N** Anhänger(in) *m(f)* der Freikörperkultur, FKK-Anhänger(in) *m(f)* ADJ FKK-; **~ beach** FKK-Strand *m*

naught [nɔːt] N (*old, form*) = **nought b**

naughtily ['nɔːtɪlɪ] ADV frech, dreist; (*esp of child*) *say, remark* ungezogen, frech; *behave* unartig, ungezogen; **I very ~ opened your letter** ich war so frech und habe deinen Brief aufgemacht; **but he very ~ did it all the same** aber frecherweise hat er es trotzdem getan

naughtiness ['nɔːtɪnɪs] N **a** Frechheit *f*, Dreistigkeit *f*; (*of child*) Unartigkeit *f*, Ungezogenheit *f*; (*of dog*) Unartigkeit *f*; (= *disobedience*) Ungehorsam *m* **b** (= *shocking nature*: *of joke, word, story*) Unanständigkeit *f*

naughty ['nɔːtɪ] ADJ (+*er*) **a** frech, dreist; *child* unartig, ungezogen; *dog* unartig; (= *disobedient*) ungehorsam; **you ~ boy/dog!** du böser *or* unartiger Junge/Hund!; **it was ~ of him to break it** das war aber gar nicht lieb von ihm, dass er das kaputtgemacht hat; **I was ~ and ate a whole bar of chocolate** ich habe schwer gesündigt und eine ganze Tafel Schokolade gegessen; **~, ~!** aber, aber!; **how ~ of me/him!** das war ja gar nicht lieb!; **the kitten's been ~ on the carpet** (*inf*) das Kätzchen hat auf den Teppich gemacht

b (= *fattening*: *of food*) **(it's) ~ but nice** es ist ungesund, dafür aber lecker

c (= *shocking*) *joke, word, story* unanständig; **~!** nein, wie unanständig!; **the ~ nineties** die frechen neunziger Jahre *or* Neunzigerjahre; **the ~ bits** (*hum*: = *genitals*) die Genitalien *pl*

nausea ['nɔːsɪə] N (*Med*) Übelkeit *f*; (*fig*) Ekel *m*; **a feeling of ~** Übelkeit *f*; (*fig*) ein Gefühl *nt* des Ekels; **the very thought fills me with ~** bei dem Gedanken allein wird mir schon übel

nauseate ['nɔːsɪeɪt] VT **to ~ sb** (*Med*) (bei) jdm Übelkeit verursachen, in jdm Übelkeit erregen; (*fig*) jdn anwidern

nauseating ['nɔːsɪeɪtɪŋ] ADJ *sight, smell, violence, food* Ekel erregend; *film, book, style* grässlich; *hypocrisy* widerlich; *person* ekelhaft, widerlich

nauseatingly ['nɔːsɪeɪtɪŋlɪ] ADV widerlich

nauseous ['nɔːsɪəs] ADJ **a** (*Med*) **that made me (feel) ~** dabei wurde mir übel **b** (*fig*) widerlich

nautical ['nɔːtɪkəl] ADJ nautisch; *prowess, superiority* zur See, seefahrerisch; *distance* zur See; *stories* von der Seefahrt; *language, tradition, appearance* seemännisch; **~ chart** Seekarte *f*; **a ~ nation** eine Seefahrernation; **he is interested in ~ matters, he's a very ~ person** er interessiert sich für die Seefahrt; **the music/play has a ~ flavour** die Musik/das Stück beschwört die See herauf

nautically ['nɔːtɪkəlɪ] ADV *superior* in Bezug auf die Seefahrt

nautical mile N Seemeile *f*

nautilus ['nɔːtɪləs] N Nautilus *m*, Schiffsboot *nt*

naval ['neɪvəl] ADJ der Marine; **his interests are ~ not military** er interessiert sich für die Marine und nicht für das Heer

naval: naval academy N Marineakademie *f*; **naval architect** N Schiffsbauingenieur(in) *m(f)*; **naval architecture** N Schiffsbau *m*; **naval aviation** N Seeflugwesen *nt*; **naval base** N Flottenbasis *f or* -stützpunkt *m*; **naval bat-**

tle N Seeschlacht f; **naval college** N Marineschule f; **naval forces** PL Seestreitkräfte pl; **naval officer** N Marineoffizier(in) m(f); **naval port** N Kriegshafen m, Flottenstützpunkt m; **naval power** N Seemacht f; **naval warfare** N Seekrieg m

nave [neɪv] N **a** (of church) Haupt- or Mittel- or Längsschiff nt **b** (of wheel) (Rad)nabe f

navel ['neɪvəl] N **a** (Anat) Nabel m **b** (also **navel orange**) Navelorange f

navel-gazing ['neɪvlˌgeɪzɪŋ] N (pej) Nabelschau f

navigable ['nævɪgəbl] ADJ **a** schiffbar; **in a ~ condition** (ship) seetüchtig **b** balloon, airship lenkbar

navigate ['nævɪgeɪt] **VI** (in plane, ship) navigieren; (in car) den Fahrer dirigieren; (in rally) der Beifahrer sein; **who was navigating?** (in plane, ship) wer war für die Navigation zuständig?; (in car) wer war der Beifahrer?; **I don't know the route, you'll have to ~** ich kenne die Strecke nicht, du musst mir sagen, wie ich fahren muss or du musst mich dirigieren
VT **a** aircraft, ship, spaceship navigieren; **to ~ sth through sth** etw durch etw (hindurch)navigieren; (fig) etw durch etw hindurchschleusen; **he ~d his way through the crowd** er bahnte sich (dat) einen Weg durch die Menge **b** (= journey through) durchfahren; (plane, pilot) durchfliegen; ocean durchqueren; river befahren

navigation [ˌnævɪ'geɪʃən] N **a** (= act of navigating) Navigation f **b** (= shipping) Schiffsverkehr m **c** (= skill: in ship, plane) Navigation f; **how's your ~?** (in car) bist du als Beifahrer gut zu gebrauchen?; **his ~ was lousy, we got lost** (in car) er hat mich so schlecht dirigiert, dass wir uns verirrt haben

navigation: navigation channel N (Naut) Fahrwasser nt; **navigation law** N Schifffahrtsregelung f; **navigation light** N Positionslicht nt or -lampe f; **navigation system** N (Tech, Aut) Navigationssystem nt

navigator ['nævɪgeɪtə'] N (Naut) Navigationsoffizier(in) m(f); (Aviat) Navigator(in) m(f); (Mot) Beifahrer(in) m(f)

navvy ['nævɪ] N (Brit) Bauarbeiter(in) m(f); (on road also) Straßenarbeiter(in) m(f)

navy ['neɪvɪ] N **a** (Kriegs)marine f; **to serve in the ~** in der Marine dienen **b** (also **navy blue**) Marineblau nt ADJ **a** attr Marine-; **~ ship** Marineschiff nt **b** (also **navy-blue**) marineblau

navy bean N (US) weiße Bohne

Navy Department N (US) Marineministerium nt

nawab [nə'wɒb] N = **nabob**

nay [neɪ] **ADV** **a** (obs, dial) nein **b** (liter) **surprised, ~ astonished** überrascht, mehr vielmehr verblüfft **N** Nein nt, Neinstimme f → **yea**

Nazarene ['næzəri:n] N Nazaräer(in) m(f)

Nazi ['nɑːtsɪ] **N** Nazi m; (fig pej) Faschist(in) m(f) **ADJ** Nazi-; **~ criminal** Naziverbrecher(in) m(f)

Nazism ['nɑːtsɪzəm] N Nazismus m

NB abbr of **nota bene** NB

NCB (Brit old) abbr of **National Coal Board** Verband der britischen Kohleindustrie

NCO abbr of **noncommissioned officer** Uffz. m

NE abbr of **north-east** NO

Neanderthal [nɪ'ændətɑːl] **ADJ** **a** (Hist) Neandertaler attr **b** (inf) (= brutish) person massig; appearance, grunt, conversation roh; (= reactionary) person, attitude, view rückständig; system, method vorsintflutlich **N** **a** (Hist) Neandertaler m **b** (inf) (= brute) Schlägertyp m (inf); (= reactionary) Neandertaler(in) m(f) (inf)

Neanderthal man N der Neandertaler

neap [ni:p] N (also **neap-tide**) Nippflut f, Nippzeit f, Nipptide f (N Ger)

Neapolitan [nɪə'pɒlɪtən] **ADJ** neapolitanisch; **~ ice cream** Fürst-Pückler-Eis nt **N** Neapolitaner(in) m(f)

---

near [nɪə'] (+er)

1 ADVERB	4 TRANSITIVE VERB
2 PREPOSITION	5 INTRANSITIVE VERB
3 ADJECTIVE	

1 – ADVERB

a = close in space or time nahe; **he lives quite near** er wohnt ganz in der Nähe; **don't sit/stand so near** setzen Sie sich/stehen Sie nicht so nahe (daran); **you live nearer/nearest** du wohnst näher/am nächsten; **to move/come nearer** näher kommen; **could you move nearer together?** könnten Sie näher or enger zusammenrücken?; **that was the nearest I ever got to seeing him** da hätte ich ihn fast gesehen; **this is the nearest I can get to solving the problem** besser kann ich das Problem nicht lösen; **that's the nearest I ever got to being fired** da hätte nicht viel gefehlt und ich wäre rausgeworfen worden; **the nearer it gets to the election, the more they look like losing** je näher die Wahl kommt or rückt, desto mehr sieht es danach aus, dass sie verlieren werden

♦ **to be near at hand** zur Hand sein; (shops) in der Nähe sein; (help) ganz nahe sein; (event) unmittelbar bevorstehen → **draw**

b = closely, accurately genau; **as near as I can tell** soweit ich es beurteilen kann; **the same size as near as dammit** (inf) fast genau die gleiche Größe

♦ **near enough (that's)** near enough so gehts ungefähr, das haut so ungefähr hin (inf); **... no, but near enough** ... nein, aber es ist nicht weit davon entfernt; **there were near enough 60 people at the party** es waren knapp 60 Leute auf der Party

♦ **as near as makes no difference** they're the same length or as near as makes no difference sie sind so gut wie gleich lang; **it's as near stopped as makes no difference** es hat so gut wie aufgehört

c = almost fast, beinahe; impossible nahezu, fast; dead nahezu; **he very near succeeded** fast or beinahe wäre es ihm gelungen

d in negative statements it's nowhere near enough das ist bei weitem nicht genug; **it's nowhere near right** das ist weit gefehlt; **we're not any nearer (to) solving the problem** wir sind der Lösung des Problems kein bisschen näher gekommen; **we're nowhere or not anywhere near finishing the book** wir haben das Buch noch lange nicht fertig; **nowhere near as much** lange or bei weitem nicht so viel; **you are nowhere or not anywhere near the truth** das ist weit gefehlt, du bist weit von der Wahrheit entfernt; **he is nowhere or not anywhere near as clever as you** er ist lange or bei weitem nicht so klug wie du

2 – PREPOSITION

(also ADV: **near to**)

a = close to (position) nahe an (+dat), nahe (+dat); (with motion) nahe an (+acc); (= in the vicinity of) in der Nähe von or +gen; (with motion) in die Nähe von or +gen; **to get near (to) the church** in die Nähe der Kirche kommen; **he lives near (to) the border** er wohnt in der Nähe der Grenze or nahe der Grenze; **the hotel is very near (to) the station** das Hotel liegt ganz in der Nähe des Bahnhofs; **move the chair near/nearer (to) the table** rücken Sie den Stuhl an den/näher an den Tisch; **to get near/nearer (to) sb/sth** nahe/näher an jdn/etw herankommen; **to stand near/nearer (to) the table** nahe/näher am Tisch stehen; **he won't go near anything illegal** mit Ungesetzlichem will er nichts zu tun haben; **when we got near (to) the house** als wir an das Haus herankamen or in die Nähe des Hauses kamen; **when we are nearer home** wenn wir nicht mehr so weit von zu Hause weg sind; **keep near me** bleib in meiner Nähe; **near here/there** hier/dort in der Nähe; **don't come near me** komm mir nicht zu nahe; **near (to) where I had seen him** nahe der Stelle, wo ich ihn gesehen hatte; **to be nearest to sth** einer Sache (dat) am nächsten sein;

---

take the chair nearest (to) you/the table nehmen Sie den Stuhl direkt neben Ihnen/dem Tisch; **that's nearer it** das trifft schon eher zu; **the adaptation is very near (to) the original** die Bearbeitung hält sich eng ans Original; **to be near (to) sb's heart** or **sb** jdm am Herzen liegen; **to be near (to) the knuckle** or **bone** (joke) gewagt sein; (remark) hart an der Grenze sein

b = close in time (with time stipulated) gegen; **near (to) death** dem Tode nahe; **she is near her time** es ist bald so weit (bei ihr); **near (to) the appointed time** um die ausgemachte Zeit herum; **phone again nearer (to) Christmas** rufen Sie vor Weihnachten noch einmal an; **come back nearer (to) 3 o'clock** kommen Sie gegen 3 Uhr wieder; **on the Wednesday nearest Easter** am Mittwoch (direkt) vor Ostern; **to be nearer/nearest (to) sth** einer Sache (dat) zeitlich näher liegen/am nächsten liegen; **near (to) the end of my stay/the play/the book** gegen Ende meines Aufenthalts/des Stücks/des Buchs; **I'm near (to) the end of the book** ich habe das Buch fast zu Ende gelesen; **she's near (to) the end of her stay** ihr Aufenthalt ist fast zu Ende or vorbei; **her birthday is near (to) mine** ihr und mein Geburtstag liegen nahe beieinander; **the sun was near (to) setting** die Sonne war am Untergehen; **it is drawing near (to) Christmas** es geht auf Weihnachten zu; **as it drew near/nearer (to) his departure** als seine Abreise heranrückte/näher heranrückte

c = on the point of **to be near (to) doing sth** nahe daran sein, etw zu tun; **to be near (to) tears/despair** etc den Tränen/der Verzweiflung etc nahe sein; **she was near (to) laughing out loud** sie hätte beinahe laut gelacht; **the project is near/nearer (to) completion** das Projekt steht vor seinem Abschluss/ist dem Abschluss näher gekommen; **he came near to ruining his chances** er hätte sich seine Chancen beinahe verdorben, es hätte nicht viel gefehlt, und er hätte sich seine Chancen verdorben; **we were near to being drowned** wir waren dem Ertrinken nahe, wir wären beinahe ertrunken

d = similar to ähnlich (+dat); **German is nearer (to) Dutch than English is** Deutsch ist dem Holländischen ähnlicher als Englisch; **it's the same thing or near it** es ist so ziemlich das Gleiche; **nobody comes anywhere near him at swimming** (inf) im Schwimmen kann es niemand mit ihm aufnehmen (inf)

3 – ADJECTIVE

a = close in space or time nahe; **to be near** (person, object) in der Nähe sein; (danger, end, help) nahe sein; (event, departure, festival) bevorstehen; **to be very near** ganz in der Nähe sein; (in time) or unmittelbar bevorstehen; (danger etc) ganz nahe sein; **to be nearer/nearest** näher/am nächsten sein; (event etc) zeitlich näher/am nächsten liegen; **it looks very near** es sieht so aus, als ob es ganz nah wäre; **our nearest neighbours are 5 miles away** unsere nächsten Nachbarn sind 5 Meilen entfernt; **these glasses make things look nearer** diese Brille lässt alles näher erscheinen; **his answer was nearer than mine/nearest** seine Antwort traf eher zu als meine/traf die Sachlage am ehesten; **when death is so near** wenn man dem Tod nahe ist; **these events are still very near** diese Ereignisse liegen noch nicht lange zurück; **the hour is near (when ...)** (old) die Stunde ist nahe(, da ...) (old); **her hour was near** (old) ihre Stunde war nahe (old)

b fig escape knapp; **a near disaster/accident** beinahe or fast ein Unglück nt/ein Unfall m; **his nearest rival** sein schärfster Rivale, seine schärfste Rivalin; **our nearest competition** unsere stärkste Konkurrenz; **to be in a state of near collapse/hysteria** am Rande eines Zusammenbruchs/der Hysterie sein; **round up the figure to the nearest pound** runden Sie die Zahl auf das nächste Pfund auf; **£50 or nearest offer** (Comm) Verhandlungsbasis £ 50; **we'll sell it for £50, or nearest offer** wir verkaufen es für £ 50 oder das nächstbeste Angebot; **the nearest in line to the throne** der unmittelbare

Thronfolger; **this is the nearest equivalent** das kommt dem am Nächsten; **this is the nearest translation you'll get** besser kann man es kaum übersetzen, diese Übersetzung trifft es noch am ehesten; **that's the nearest thing you'll get to a compliment/an answer** ein besseres Kompliment/eine bessere Antwort kannst du kaum erwarten **c** = *closely related, intimate* *relation* nah; *friend* nah, vertraut; **my nearest and dearest** meine Lieben *pl*; **a near and dear friend** ein lieber und teurer Freund

4 – TRANSITIVE VERB

sich nähern (+*dat*); **he was nearing his end** sein Leben neigte sich dem Ende zu; **to be nearing sth** (*fig*) auf etw (*acc*) zugehen; **she was nearing fifty** sie ging auf die Fünfzig zu; **to near completion** kurz vor dem Abschluss stehen

5 – INTRANSITIVE VERB

(*time, event*) näher rücken; **the time is nearing when ...** die Zeit rückt näher, da ...

near beer N alkoholarmes *or* -freies Bier

nearby [nɪəˈbaɪ] ADV (*also* **near by**) in der Nähe ADJ nahe gelegen

near: near-death experience N Nah-Todeserfahrung *f*; **Near East** N Naher Osten; **in the ~** im Nahen Osten; **near letter-quality** N Schönschrift *f*, Korrespondenz- *or* Briefqualität *f*

nearly [ˈnɪəlɪ] ADV **a** (= *almost*) beinahe, fast; **I ~ laughed** ich hätte fast *or* beinahe gelacht; **she was ~ crying** *or* **in tears** sie war den Tränen nahe; **we are ~ there** (*at a place*) wir sind fast da; (*with a job*) wir sind fast so weit; **he very ~ drowned** er wäre um ein Haar ertrunken **b** **not ~** bei weitem nicht, nicht annähernd; **not ~ enough** bei weitem nicht genug

nearly-new [ˌnɪəlɪˈnjuː] ADJ *clothes* fast neu; **~ shop** Second-Hand-Laden *m* (*der besonders gute Qualität anbietet*)

near miss N (*Aviat*) Beinahezusammenstoß *m* → *also* **miss** N **a**

nearness [ˈnɪənɪs] N Nähe *f*

near: nearside ADJ auf der Beifahrerseite; (*when driving on the left also*) linke(r, s); (*when driving on the right also*) rechte(r, s) **N** Beifahrerseite *f*; **near-sighted** ADJ kurzsichtig; **near-sightedness** N Kurzsichtigkeit *f*; **near thing** N **that was a ~** das war knapp

neat [niːt] ADJ (+*er*) **a** (= *tidy*) *person, house, hairstyle* ordentlich; *worker, work, handwriting, sewing* sauber, ordentlich; *hair, appearance* gepflegt; **he likes everything ~ and tidy** er will alles hübsch ordentlich haben; **to make a ~ job of sth** etw tadellos machen; **he made a very ~ job of repairing the window** er hat das Fenster tadellos repariert → **pin** **b** (= *precise*) *fit, category* genau; *division* sauber; *summary* prägnant; *explanation* prägnant formuliert; **it's a ~ fit in the corner** es passt genau in die Ecke **c** (= *pleasing*) nett; *clothes* nett, adrett; *person, figure* hübsch, nett; *ankles* schlank; **she has a ~ figure** sie hat ein nettes Figürchen; **~ little suit** schmucker *or* netter Anzug **d** (= *skilful*) *gadget, speech* gelungen; *style* gewandt; *solution* sauber, elegant; *plan* elegant; *trick* schlau; **that's very ~** das ist sehr schlau **e** (*esp Brit*: = *undiluted*) *spirits* pur; *wines* unverdünnt; **to drink one's whisky ~** Whisky pur trinken **f** (*US inf*: = *excellent*) prima (*inf*), klasse *inv* (*inf*); **a ~ guy** ein großartiger *or* toller Typ (*inf*)

neaten [ˈniːtn] VT (*also* **neaten up**) in Ordnung bringen; *phrasing* glätten

'neath [niːθ] PREP (*poet*) unter (+*dat*), unterhalb (+*gen*); (*with motion*) unter (+*acc*)

neatly [ˈniːtlɪ] ADV **a** (= *tidily*) ordentlich; *write, work, sew* ordentlich, sauber **b** (= *pleasingly*) nett, adrett, hübsch; **a ~ turned ankle** eine hüb-

sche schlanke Fessel **c** (= *skilfully*) gewandt; *solve* sauber, elegant; **that was ~ done** das hast du/hat er *etc* schlau gemacht; **~ put** prägnant formuliert; **~ turned phrases** prägnant formulierte Sätze *pl*

neatness [ˈniːtnɪs] N **a** (= *tidiness*) Ordentlichkeit *f*; (*of work, writing, sewing*) Ordentlichkeit *f*, Sauberkeit *f* **b** (= *precision*) (*of category*) Genauigkeit *f*; (*of division*) Sauberkeit *f*; (*of summary, explanation*) Prägnanz *f* **c** (= *pleasing nature*) Nettheit *f*; (*of clothes*) nettes Aussehen, Adrettheit *f*; (*of person, figure*) hübsches Aussehen; (*of ankles*) Schlankheit *f* **d** (= *successfulness*) Gelungenheit *f*; (= *skilfulness*) (*of speech, style*) Gewandtheit *f*; (*of solution*) Sauberkeit *f*, Eleganz *f*; (*of trick*) Schlauheit *f*

nebbish [ˈnebɪʃ] N (*sl*) Schlappschwanz *m* (*inf*)

nebula [ˈnebjʊlə] N *pl* **-e** [ˈnebjʊliː] **a** (*Astron*) Nebel *m*, Nebelfleck *m* **b** (*Med*) Trübung *f*

nebulous [ˈnebjʊləs] ADJ **a** (*Astron*) nebelartig **b** (*fig*) unklar, verworren, nebulös

necessarily [ˈnesɪsərɪlɪ] ✪ 16.1 ADV notwendigerweise (*also Logic*), unbedingt; **not ~** nicht unbedingt; **if that is true, then it is not ~ the case that ...** wenn das stimmt, muß es nicht unbedingt sein, dass ...

necessary [ˈnesɪsərɪ] ADJ **a** notwendig, nötig, erforderlich (*to, for* für); **it is ~ to ...** man muss ...; **is it really ~ for me to come too?** muss ich denn wirklich auch kommen?; **it's not ~ for you to come** Sie brauchen nicht zu kommen; **it is ~ for him to be there** es ist nötig *or* notwendig, dass er da ist, er muss da sein; **all the ~ qualifications** alle erforderlichen Qualifikationen; **~ condition** Voraussetzung *f*, (*Logic*) notwendige Voraussetzung; **to be/become ~ to sb** jdm unentbehrlich sein/werden; **to make it ~ for sb to do sth** es erforderlich machen, dass jd etw tut; **if/when ~** wenn nötig, nötigenfalls; **where ~** wo nötig; **you were rude to him, was that ~?** du warst grob zu ihm, war das denn notwendig *or* nötig?; **that won't be ~** das wird nicht nötig sein; **to make the ~ arrangements** die erforderlichen *or* notwendigen Maßnahmen treffen; **to do everything ~** das Nötige tun; **to do whatever is ~** alles Nötige tun; **to do no more than is (strictly) ~** nicht mehr tun, als unbedingt notwendig *or* nötig ist; **good food is ~ to health** gutes Essen ist für die Gesundheit notwendig **b** (= *unavoidable*) *conclusion, change, result* unausweichlich; **we drew the ~ conclusions** wir haben die entsprechenden Schlüsse daraus gezogen; **a ~ evil** ein notwendiges Übel **N a** (*inf*: = *what is needed*) **the ~** das Notwendige; **will you do the ~?** wirst du das Notwendige *or* Nötige erledigen? **b** (*inf*: = *money*) **the ~** das nötige Kleingeld **c** *usu pl* **the ~** *or* **necessaries** das Notwendige

necessitate [nɪˈsesɪteɪt] VT notwendig *or* erforderlich machen, erfordern (*form*); **the heat ~d our staying indoors** die Hitze zwang uns, im Haus zu bleiben

necessitous [nɪˈsesɪtəs] ADJ (*old, form*) dürftig, armselig

necessity [nɪˈsesɪtɪ] N **a** *no pl* Notwendigkeit *f*; **from** *or* **out of ~** aus Not; **of ~** notgedrungen, notwendigerweise; **to be born of ~** aus Notwendigkeit (heraus) geschehen; **he did not realize the ~ for a quick decision** er hat nicht erkannt, wie wichtig *or* notwendig eine schnelle Entscheidung war; **it is a case of absolute ~** es ist unbedingt notwendig; **there is no ~ for you to do that** es besteht nicht die geringste Notwendigkeit, dass Sie das tun; **~ is the mother of invention** (*Prov*) Not macht erfinderisch (*Prov*) **b** *no pl* (= *poverty*) Not *f*, Armut *f*; **to live in ~** Not leiden, in Armut leben **c** (= *necessary thing*) Notwendigkeit *f*; **the bare necessities (of life)** das Notwendigste (zum Leben)

neck [nek] N **a** Hals *m*; **to break one's ~** sich (*dat*) das Genick *or* den Hals brechen; **but don't break your ~** (*inf*) bring dich nicht um (*inf*); **to risk one's ~** Kopf und Kragen riskie-

ren; **to save one's ~** seinen Hals aus der Schlinge ziehen; **a stiff ~** ein steifer Hals *or* Nacken; **to win by a ~** um eine Kopflänge gewinnen; **to have sb round one's ~** (*fig inf*) jdn auf dem *or* am Halse haben; **to be up to one's ~ in work** bis über den Hals *or* über die Ohren in der Arbeit stecken; **he's in it up to his ~** (*inf*) er steckt bis über den Hals drin; **to get it in the ~** (*inf*) eins aufs Dach bekommen (*inf*); **to stick one's ~ out** seinen Kopf riskieren; **in this ~ of the woods** (*inf*) in diesen Breiten; **she's from your ~ of the woods** (*inf*) sie kommt aus der gleichen Ecke wie du (*inf*) → *also* **breathe** **VI** **b** (*Cook*) **~ of lamb** Halsstück *nt* vom Lamm **c** (*of bottle, vase, violin, bone*) Hals *m*; (*of land*) Landenge *f* **d** (*of dress etc*) Ausschnitt *m*; **it has a high ~** es ist hochgeschlossen **e** (*also* **neck measurement**) Halsweite *f* **VI** (*inf*) knutschen (*inf*), schmusen (*inf*)

neck: neck and neck (*lit, fig*) ADJ *attr* Kopf-an-Kopf-; **a ~ race** ein Kopf-an-Kopf-Rennen *nt* ADV Kopf an Kopf; **neckband** N Besatz *m*; (*of shirt*) Kragensteg *m*; (*of pullover*) Halsbündchen *nt*; **neckcloth** N (*obs*) Halstuch *nt*

neckerchief [ˈnekətʃiːf] N Halstuch *nt*

necklace [ˈneklɪs] N (Hals)kette *f*

necklet [ˈneklɪt] N Kettchen *nt*

neck: neckline N Ausschnitt *m*; **necktie** N (*esp US*) Krawatte *f*, Binder *m*, Schlips *m*

necrology [neˈkrɒlədʒɪ] N (*form*) Totenverzeichnis *nt*, Nekrologium *nt*; (= *obituary*) Nachruf *m*, Nekrolog *m*

necromancer [ˈnekrəʊˌmænsə] N Toten- *or* Geisterbeschwörer(in) *m(f)*, Nekromant(in) *m(f)*

necromancy [ˈnekrəʊˌmænsɪ] N Toten- *or* Geisterbeschwörung *f*, Nekromantie *f*

necrophilia [ˌnekrəʊˈfɪlɪə] N Leichenschändung *f*, Nekrophilie *f*

necrophiliac [ˌnekrəʊˈfɪlɪæk] ADJ nekrophil **N** Leichenschänder *m*, Nekrophile(r) *m*

necropolis [neˈkrɒpəlɪs] N Totenstadt *f*, Nekropole *f*, Nekropolis *f*

necrotising fasciitis [ˈnekrəʊtaɪzɪŋfæʃɪˈaɪtɪs] N (*Med*) nekrotisierende Fasciitis

nectar [ˈnektə] N (*lit, fig*) Nektar *m*

nectarine [ˈnektərɪn] N (= *fruit*) Nektarine *f*; (= *tree*) Nektarine(nbaum *m*) *f*

ned [ned] N (*inf*) Rowdy *m*; (= *criminal type*) Halunke *m*

NEDC (*Brit*) *abbr* of **National Economic Development Council** Rat für Wirtschaftsentwicklung

née [neɪ] ADJ **Mrs Smith, ~ Jones** Frau Smith, geborene Jones

need [niːd] ✪ 1.1, 9.4, 10.2 **N a** *no pl* (= *necessity*) Notwendigkeit *f* (*for* +*gen*); **if ~ be** nötigenfalls, wenn nötig; **in case of ~** notfalls, im Notfall; **(there is) no ~ for sth** etw ist nicht nötig; **(there is) no ~ to do sth** etw braucht nicht *or* muss nicht unbedingt getan werden; **there is no ~ for sb to do sth** jd braucht etw nicht zu tun; **there is no ~ for tears** du brauchst nicht zu weinen; **there was no ~ to send it immediately** es war nicht nötig, es sofort zu schicken; **there's no ~ to get angry** du brauchst nicht gleich wütend zu werden; **to be (badly) in ~ of sth** (*person*) etw (dringend) brauchen; **those most in ~ of help** diejenigen, die Hilfe am nötigsten brauchen; **to be in ~ of repair** reparaturbedürftig sein; **to be in ~ of an overhaul** (dringend) überholt werden müssen; **this window is in ~ of a coat of paint** dieses Fenster könnte ein wenig Farbe gut gebrauchen; **to have no ~ of sth** etw nicht brauchen; **to have no ~ to do sth** etw nicht zu tun brauchen **b** *no pl* (= *misfortune*) Not *f*; **in time(s) of ~** in schwierigen Zeiten, in Zeiten der Not; **do not fail me in my hour of ~** (*usu iro*) verlass mich nicht in der Stunde der Not **c** *no pl* (= *poverty*) Not *f*; **to be in great ~** große Not leiden; **those in ~** die Notleidenden *pl*, die Not Leidenden *pl*

d (= *requirement*) Bedürfnis *nt*; **the body's ~ for oxygen** das Sauerstoffbedürfnis des Körpers; **my ~s are few** ich stelle nur geringe Ansprüche; **a list of all your ~s** eine Aufstellung all dessen, was Sie brauchen; **your ~ is greater than mine** Sie haben es nötiger als ich; **there is a great ~ for ...** es besteht ein großer Bedarf an (+*dat*) ...; **investment is one of the firm's greatest ~s** die Firma braucht dringend Investitionen

VT **a** (= *require*) brauchen; **he ~ed no second invitation** man musste ihn nicht zweimal bitten; **to ~ no introduction** keine spezielle Einführung brauchen; **much ~ed** dringend notwendig; **what I ~ is a good drink** ich brauche etwas zu trinken; **just what I ~ed** genau das Richtige; **that's/you're all I ~ed** (*iro*) das hat/du hast mir gerade noch gefehlt; **this incident ~s some explanation** dieser Vorfall bedarf einer Erklärung (*gen*); **it ~s a service/a coat of paint/ careful consideration** es muss gewartet/gestrichen/gründlich überlegt werden; **is a visa ~ed to enter the USA?** braucht man für die Einreise in die USA ein Visum?; **it ~ed a revolution to change that** es bedurfte einer Revolution, um das zu ändern; **it ~ed an accident to make him drive carefully** er musste erst einen Unfall haben, bevor er vernünftig fuhr

b (*in verbal constructions*) **sth ~s doing** *or* **to be done** etw muss gemacht werden; **he ~s watching/cheering up** man muss ihn beobachten/ aufheitern, er muss beobachtet/aufgeheitert werden; **to ~ to do sth** (= *have to*) etw tun müssen; **not to ~ to do sth** etw nicht zu tun brauchen; **he doesn't ~ to be told** man braucht es ihm nicht zu sagen; **you shouldn't ~ to be told** das müsste man dir nicht erst sagen müssen; **it doesn't ~ me to tell you that** das brauche ich dir ja wohl nicht zu sagen; **she ~s to have everything explained to her** man muss ihr alles erklären

VB AUX **a** (*indicating obligation: in positive contexts*) müssen; **~ he go?** muss er gehen?; **~ I say more?** mehr brauche ich ja wohl nicht zu sagen; **I ~ hardly say that ...** ich brauche wohl kaum zu erwähnen, dass ...; **no-one ~ go** *or* **~s to go home yet** es braucht noch keiner nach Hause zu gehen; **you only ~ed (to) ask** du hättest nur (zu) fragen brauchen; **one ~ only look** ein Blick genügt

b (*indicating obligation: in negative contexts*) brauchen; **you ~n't wait** du brauchst nicht (zu) warten; **we ~n't have come/gone** wir hätten gar nicht kommen/gehen brauchen; **I/you ~n't have bothered** das war nicht nötig

c (*indicating logical necessity*) **~ that be true?** ist das notwendigerweise wahr?; **that ~n't be the case** das muss nicht unbedingt der Fall sein; **it ~ not follow that ...** daraus folgt nicht unbedingt, dass ...

needful ['niːdfʊl] **ADJ** (*old*) notwendig, nötig (*for, to* für, zu) **N** (*inf:* = *what is necessary*) **to do the ~** das Nötige tun

neediness ['niːdɪnɪs] **N** Armut *f*, Bedürftigkeit *f*

needle ['niːdl] **N** (*all senses*) Nadel *f*; **it's like looking for a ~ in a haystack** es ist, als ob man eine Stecknadel im Heuhaufen suchte; **to give sb the ~** (*inf*) jdn reizen **VT** **a** (*inf:* = *goad*) ärgern, piesacken (*inf*); **what's needling him?** was ist ihm über die Leber gelaufen? (*inf*) **b** (*US, inf*) **to ~ a drink** einen Schuss Alkohol in ein Getränk geben

needle: needle-book **N** Nadelheft *nt*; **needle-case** **N** Nadeletui *nt*; **needlecraft** **N** handarbeitliches Geschick; **needle exchange** **N** (= *centre*) ≈ Fixerstube *f*; (= *drugs treatment programme*) Spritzentausch *m*; **needle match** **N** spannendes Spiel; **needle-sharp** **ADJ** (*inf*) clever (*inf*), schwer auf Zack (*inf*)

needless ['niːdlɪs] **ADJ** unnötig; *remark etc also* überflüssig; *death, killing, pain, destruction* sinnlos; **~ to say, he didn't come** er kam natürlich nicht

needlessly ['niːdlɪslɪ] **ADV** unnötig(erweise), überflüssig(erweise); *destroy, kill* sinnlos; **he was quite ~ rude** er war ganz unnötig grob; **you are worrying quite ~** Ihre Sorgen sind vollkommen unbegründet

needlessness ['niːdlɪsnɪs] **N** Unnötigkeit *f*

needle: needlewoman **N** Näherin *f*; **needlework** **N** Handarbeit *f*; **a piece of ~** eine Handarbeit

needs [niːdz] **ADV** (*obs*) **I must ~ away/obey** ich muss fort/notwendigerweise gehorchen; **~ must if the devil drives** (*prov*) nolens volens

need-to-know [ˌniːdtəˈnəʊ] **N on a ~ basis** nur bei tatsächlichem Informationsbedarf, nach dem „need to know"-Prinzip

needy ['niːdɪ] **ADJ** (*+er*) ärmlich, bedürftig **N the ~** die Bedürftigen *pl*

ne'er [nɛə ͬ] **ADV** (*old, poet:* = *never*) nie, niemals

ne'er-do-well ['nɛəduːˌwel] (*dated*) **N** Tunichtgut *m*, Taugenichts *m* (*dated*) **ADJ** nichtsnutzig

ne'ertheless [ˌnɛərðəˈles] **ADV** (*old, poet*) nichtsdestoweniger

nefarious [nɪˈfɛərɪəs] **ADJ** (*form*) schändlich, ruchlos (*liter*); **~ deed** Freveltat *f* (*liter*), ruchlose Tat

negate [nɪˈgeɪt] **VT** (= *nullify*) zunichte machen; (= *deny*) verneinen (*also Gram*), negieren (*geh*)

negation [nɪˈgeɪʃən] **N** Verneinung *f*; (*of statement, negative form also*) Negation *f*

negative ['negətɪv] **ADJ** negativ; *answer* verneinend; (*Gram*) *form* verneint; **~ ion** Anion *nt*; **~ cash flow** (*Fin*) Überhang *m* der Zahlungsausgänge; **~ campaigning** (*Pol*) *negativer Wahlkampf* **I got a ~ reply to my request** ich habe auf meinen Antrag einen abschlägigen Bescheid bekommen

N **a** (*also Gram*) Verneinung *f*; **to answer in the ~** eine verneinende Antwort geben; (= *say no*) mit Nein antworten; (= *refuse*) einen abschlägigen Bescheid geben; **his answer was a curt ~** er antwortete mit einem knappen Nein; **put this sentence into the ~** verneinen Sie diesen Satz; **how do you express this statement in the ~?** wie drückt man diesen Satz verneint *or* in der Verneinungsform aus?

b (*Gram:* = *word*) Verneinungswort *nt*, Negation *f*; (*Math*) negative Zahl; **two ~s make a positive** (*Math*) zweimal minus gibt plus

c (*Phot*) Negativ *nt*

d (*Elec*) negativer Pol

INTERJ nein

VT *amendment, plan* ablehnen; *statement* negieren

negative equity **N** (*Fin*) *Differenz zwischen dem gefallenen Wert einer Immobilie und der auf ihr lastenden höheren Hypothekenschuld*

negative feedback **N** (*Elec*) negative Rückkopplung, Gegenkopplung *f*; (= *criticism*) negatives Feedback, negative Reaktion; **to give sb ~ (about sb/sth)** jdm eine negative Rückmeldung (zu jdm/etw) geben; **to get ~ (about sb/ sth)** eine negative Rückmeldung (zu jdm/etw) erhalten

negatively ['negətɪvlɪ] **ADV** negativ; (= *in the negative*) verneinend; **to respond ~** ablehnend *or* negativ reagieren

negative sign **N** (*Math*) Minuszeichen *nt*, negatives Vorzeichen

negativity [negəˈtɪvɪtɪ] **N** negative Einstellung

neglect [nɪˈglekt] **VT** vernachlässigen; *promise* nicht einhalten; *advice* nicht befolgen; *opportunity* versäumen; **to ~ to do sth** es versäumen *or* unterlassen, etw zu tun **N** Vernachlässigung *f*; (*of promise*) Nichteinhalten *nt*; (*of opportunity*) Versäumen *nt*; (*of advice*) Nichtbefolgung *f*; (= *negligence*) Nachlässigkeit *f*; **~ of one's duties** Pflichtvergessenheit *f*, Pflichtversäumnis *nt*; **to be in a state of ~** verwahrlost sein, völlig vernachlässigt sein; **the garden suffered through (our) ~** der Garten hat darunter gelitten, dass wir ihn vernachlässigt haben

neglected [nɪˈglektɪd] **ADJ** vernachlässigt; *area, garden etc also* verwahrlost; **to feel ~** sich vernachlässigt fühlen

neglectful [nɪˈglektfʊl] **ADJ** nachlässig; *father, government etc* pflichtvergessen; **to be ~ of sb/ sth** sich nicht um jdn/etw kümmern, jdn/etw vernachlässigen

neglectfully [nɪˈglektfəlɪ] **ADV** nachlässig

négligé(e) ['neglɪʒeɪ] **N** Negligee *nt*, Negligé *nt*

negligence ['neglɪdʒəns] **N** (= *carelessness*) Nachlässigkeit *f*; (*causing danger, Jur*) Fahrlässigkeit *f*

negligent ['neglɪdʒənt] **ADJ** **a** nachlässig; (*causing danger, damage*) fahrlässig; **to be ~ of sb/sth** jdn/etw vernachlässigen; **to be ~ of one's duties** pflichtvergessen sein; **both drivers were ~** beide Fahrer haben sich fahrlässig verhalten **b** (= *off-hand*) lässig

negligently ['neglɪdʒəntlɪ] **ADV** **a** nachlässig; (= *causing danger, damage*) fahrlässig; **he very ~ forgot** in seiner Nachlässigkeit *or* nachlässigerweise vergaß er es **b** (= *in an offhand manner*) lässig

negligible ['neglɪdʒəbl] **ADJ** unwesentlich, unbedeutend; *quantity, amount, sum also* geringfügig, unerheblich; **the opposition in this race is ~** in diesem Rennen gibt es keinen ernst zu nehmenden Gegner

negotiable [nɪˈgəʊʃɪəbl] **ADJ** **a** (*Comm*) (= *can be sold*) verkäuflich, veräußerlich; (= *can be transferred*) übertragbar; **not ~** nicht verkäuflich/übertragbar **b these terms are ~** über diese Bedingungen kann verhandelt werden **c** *road* befahrbar; *river, mountain, pass* passierbar; *obstacle, difficulty* überwindbar

negotiate [nɪˈgəʊʃɪeɪt] **VT** **a** (= *discuss*) verhandeln über (+*acc*); (= *bring about*) aushandeln **b** *bend in road* nehmen; (*horse*) *fence* nehmen; *river, mountain, rapids* passieren; *obstacle, difficulty* überwinden **c** (*Comm*) *shares* handeln mit; *sale* tätigen (*form*) **VI** verhandeln (*for* über +*acc*)

negotiating table [nɪˈgəʊʃɪeɪtɪŋˌteɪbl] **N** Verhandlungstisch *m*

negotiation [nɪˌgəʊʃɪˈeɪʃən] **N** **a** (= *discussion*) Verhandlung *f*; (= *bringing about*) Aushandlung *f*; **the matter is still under ~** über diese Sache wird noch verhandelt; **it's a matter for ~** darüber muss verhandelt werden; **the price is a matter for ~** über den Preis kann verhandelt werden; **by ~** auf dem Verhandlungsweg **b** *usu pl* (= *talks*) Verhandlung *f*; **to begin ~s with sb** mit jdm Verhandlungen *pl* mit jdm aufnehmen; **to be in ~(s) with sb** mit jdm in Verhandlungen stehen **c** (*of river, mountain, rapids*) Passage *f*, Passieren *nt*; (*of obstacle, difficulty*) Überwindung *f*

negotiator [nɪˈgəʊʃɪeɪtə ͬ] **N** Unterhändler(in) *m(f)*

Negress ['niːgres] **N** Negerin *f*

Negro ['niːgrəʊ] **ADJ** Neger-; **~ slave** Negersklave *m*/-sklavin *f* **N** Neger *m*

Negroid ['niːgrɔɪd] **ADJ** negroid

neigh [neɪ] **VI** wiehern **N** Wiehern *nt*

neighbour, (*US*) **neighbor** ['neɪbə ͬ] **N** **a** Nachbar(in) *m(f)*; (*at table*) Tischnachbar(in) *m(f)* → **next-door** **b** (*Bibl*) Nächste(r) *mf* **VT** (= *adjoin*) *country, river* angrenzen an (+*acc*) **VI a to ~ on** (= *adjoin*) (an)grenzen an (+*acc*); (= *approach*) grenzen an (+*acc*) **b** (*US inf*) **to neighbor with sb** gutnachbarliche Beziehungen *pl* zu jdm haben

neighbourhood, (*US*) **neighborhood** ['neɪbəhʊd] **N** (= *district*) Gegend *f*, Viertel *nt*; (= *people*) Nachbarschaft *f*; **get to know your ~** lernen Sie Ihre nähere Umgebung *or* (*people also*) Ihre Nachbarschaft kennen; **all the children from the ~** all die Kinder aus der Nachbarschaft *or* der Gegend; **she is very popular in this ~** sie ist allen Nachbarn *or* in der ganzen Nachbarschaft sehr beliebt; **your friendly ~ policeman** der freundliche Polizist in Ihrer Nachbarschaft; **in the ~ of sth** in der Nähe von etw; (*fig:* = *approximately*) um etw herum

neighbourhood watch N (*Brit*) Vereinigung von Bürgern, die durch Straßenwachen etc in ihrem Bezirk die Polizei bei der Verbrechensbekämpfung unterstützen

neighbouring, (*US*) **neighboring** ['neɪbərɪŋ] ADJ benachbart, angrenzend; ~ **village/house** Nachbardorf/-haus *nt*; ~ **country** Nachbarland *nt*; **in ~ Latvia** im benachbarten Lettland

neighbourly, (*US*) **neighborly** ['neɪbəlɪ] ADJ *person* nachbarlich; *action, relations* gutnachbarlich; **they are ~ people** sie sind gute Nachbarn

neighing ['neɪɪŋ] N Wiehern *nt*

neither ['naɪðə'] ADV **~ ... nor** weder ... noch; **he ~ knows nor cares** er weiß es nicht und will es auch nicht wissen

▶ CONJ auch nicht; **if you don't go, ~ shall I** wenn du nicht gehst, gehe ich auch nicht; **I'm not going – ~ am I** ich gehe nicht – ich auch nicht; **he didn't do it (and) ~ did his sister** weder er noch seine Schwester haben es getan; **I can't go, ~ do I want to** ich kann und will auch nicht gehen

▶ ADJ keine(r, s) (der beiden); **~ one of them** keiner von beiden; **in ~ case** in keinem Fall, weder in dem einen noch in dem anderen Fall

▶ PRON keine(r, s); **~ of them** keiner von beiden; **which will you take? – ~** welches nehmen Sie? – keines (von beiden)

nelly ['nelɪ] N **not on your ~** (*Brit, hum inf*) nie im Leben

nelson ['nelsən] N (*Wrestling*) Nelson *m*

nem con [ˌnem'kɒn] ADV ohne Gegenstimme

nemesis ['nemɪsɪs] N Nemesis *f* (*liter*), die gerechte Strafe

neo- ['niːəʊ-] PREF neo-, Neo-; **neoclassical** ADJ klassizistisch; **neoclassicism** N Klassizismus *m*; **neocolonial** ADJ neokolonialistisch; **neocolonialism** N Neokolonialismus *m*

neodymium [ˌniːəʊ'dɪmɪəm] N (*Chem*) Neodym *nt*

neo: neofascism N Neofaschismus *m*; **neofascist** ADJ neofaschistisch ▶ N Neofaschist(in) *m(f)*

neolithic [ˌniːəʊ'lɪθɪk] ADJ jungsteinzeitlich, neolithisch

neologism [nɪ'ɒlədʒɪzəm] N (*Ling*) (Wort)neubildung *f*, Neologismus *m*

neologize [nɪ'ɒlədʒaɪz] VI (*Ling*) neue Wörter bilden *or* benutzen

neon ['niːɒn] N (*Chem*) Neon *nt* ADJ attr Neon-; ~ **tube** Neonröhre *f*

neo-Nazi [ˌniːəʊ'nɑːtsɪ] N Neonazi *m* ADJ neonazistisch

neon light N Neonlicht *nt*

neon sign N (= *name*) Neon- *or* Leuchtschild *nt*; (= *advertisement*) Neon- *or* Leuchtreklame *f* *no pl*

neophyte ['niːəʊfaɪt] N Neubekehrte(r) *mf*, Neophyt(in) *m(f)* (*spec*); (*in RC church*) neu geweihter Priester

Neo: Neo-Platonic ADJ neuplatonisch; **Neo-Platonism** N Neuplatonismus *m*; **Neo-Platonist** N Neuplatoniker(in) *m(f)*

Nepal [nɪ'pɔːl] N Nepal *nt*

Nepalese [ˌnepɑː'liːz], **Nepali** [nɪ'pɔːlɪ] ADJ nepalesisch, nepalisch ▶ N Nepalese *m*, Nepalesin *f* ▶ (*Ling*) Nepalesisch *nt*

nephew ['nevjuː, 'nefjuː] N Neffe *m*

nephritis [ne'fraɪtɪs] N Nierenentzündung *f*, Nephritis *f* (*spec*)

nepotism ['nepətɪzəm] N Vetternwirtschaft *f*, Nepotismus *m*

Neptune ['neptjuːn] N (*Astron, Myth*) Neptun *m*

neptunium [nep'tjuːnɪəm] N (*Chem*) Neptunium *nt*

nerd [nɜːd] N (*inf*) Dumpfbacke *f* (*sl*); **computer ~** Computerfreak *m* (*inf*)

nerdy ['nɜːdɪ] ADJ (*inf*) ▶ *person* freakig (*inf*), intelligent aber nicht gesellschaftsfähig ▶ *thing* beknackt (*sl*); (= *cool*) geil (*sl*)

nereid ['nɪərɪɪd] N (*Myth*) Nereide *f*, Meerjungfrau *f*

nerve [nɜːv] ▶ N ▶ (*Anat*) Nerv *m*; **to suffer from ~s** nervös sein; **to have an attack of ~s** in Panik geraten, durchdrehen (*inf*); (*before exam also*) Prüfungsangst haben; **to be in a terrible state of ~s** mit den Nerven völlig fertig *or* herunter sein; **it's only ~s** du bist/er ist *etc* nur nervös; **to be all ~s** ein Nervenbündel sein; **his ~s are bad** er hat schlechte Nerven; **to get on sb's ~s** (*inf*) jdm auf die Nerven gehen *or* fallen; **he doesn't know what ~s are** er hat die Ruhe weg (*inf*); **to live on one's ~s** nervlich angespannt sein, völlig überreizt sein; **to have ~s of steel** Nerven wie Drahtseile haben; **his speech touched *or* struck a (raw) ~** seine Rede berührte einen wunden Punkt

▶ **b** *no pl* (= *courage*) Mut *m*; **to lose/hold *or* keep one's ~** die Nerven verlieren/nicht verlieren; **to regain one's ~,** to get one's ~ back seine Angst überwinden; **his ~ failed him** ihn verließ der Mut, er bekam Angst; **to have the ~ to do sth** sich trauen, etw zu tun; **a test of ~** eine Nervenprobe

▶ **c** *no pl* (*inf*: = *impudence*) Frechheit *f*, Unverschämtheit *f*; **to have the ~ to do sth** die Frechheit besitzen, etw zu tun; **he's got a ~!** der hat Nerven! (*inf*); **what a ~!, the ~ of it!** so eine Frechheit!

▶ **d** (*Bot*) Ader *f*, Nerv *m*

▶ VR **to ~ oneself for sth/to do sth** sich seelisch und moralisch auf etw (*acc*) vorbereiten/darauf vorbereiten, etw zu tun; **I can't ~ myself to do it** ich bringe einfach den Mut nicht auf, das zu tun

▶ VT **to ~ sb for sth** jdm den Mut geben, etw zu tun

nerve *in cpds* Nerven-; **nerve cell** N Nervenzelle *f*; **nerve centre**, (*US*) **nerve center** N (*Anat*) Nervenzentrum *nt*; (*fig also*) Schaltstelle *or* -zentrale *f*; **nerve ending** N Nervende *nt*; **nerve gas** N Nervengas *nt*

nerveless ['nɜːvlɪs] ADJ ▶ (= *without nerves*) ohne Nerven; *plant* ohne Adern *or* Nerven ▶ (= *confident*) *person* gelassen, seelenruhig

nerve-racking, **nerve-wracking** ['nɜːvrækɪŋ] ADJ nervenaufreibend

nervous ['nɜːvəs] ADJ ▶ (*Anat*) Nerven-; (= *related to the nerves*) *problem, disorder* nervös (bedingt); *exhaustion, reflex* nervös; ~ **tension** Nervenanspannung *f*

▶ **b** (= *apprehensive, timid*) ängstlich; (= *on edge*) nervös; **to be *or* feel ~** (= *be afraid*) Angst haben; (= *be worried*) sich (*dat*) Sorgen machen; (= *be on edge*) nervös sein; **you make me (feel) ~** du machst mich (ganz) nervös; **I am ~ about the exam/him** mir ist bange vor dem Examen/um ihn; **I was rather ~ about giving him the job** mir war nicht wohl bei dem Gedanken, ihm die Stelle zu geben; **I am rather ~ about diving** ich habe eine ziemliche Angst vor dem Tauchen; **to be in a ~ state** nervös sein

nervous *in cpds* Nerven-; **nervous breakdown** N Nervenzusammenbruch *m*; **nervous energy** N Vitalität *f*; **after the exam I still had a lot of ~** nach dem Examen war ich noch ganz aufgedreht

nervously ['nɜːvəslɪ] ADV (= *apprehensively*) ängstlich; (= *on edge*) nervös

nervous Nellie [-'nelɪ] N (*US inf*) Flattermann *m* (*inf*)

nervousness ['nɜːvəsnɪs] N Ängstlichkeit *f*; (= *edgy state*) Nervosität *f*; **his ~ about flying** seine Angst vor dem Fliegen

nervous: nervous system N Nervensystem *nt*; **nervous wreck** N (*inf*) to be/look a ~ mit den Nerven völlig am Ende *or* fertig sein

nervy ['nɜːvɪ] ADJ (+*er*) ▶ **a** (*Brit*: = *tense*) nervös ▶ **b** (*dated US inf*: = *cheeky*) frech, unverschämt

nescient ['nesɪənt] ADJ (*geh*) unwissend

nest [nest] ▶ N ▶ **a** (*of birds, bees, ants*) Nest *nt*; **to leave *or* fly the ~** (*lit, fig*) das Nest verlassen ▶ **b** (*of boxes etc*) Satz *m*; **a ~ of tables** ein Satz *m*

Tische *or* von Tischen ▶ **c** (*fig*: = *den*) Schlupfwinkel *m*; **a ~ of spies/criminals** ein Agenten-/ Verbrechernest *nt*; **a ~ of machine guns** eine Maschinengewehrstellung ▶ VI ▶ **a** (*bird*) nisten ▶ **b** **to go ~ing** Nester ausheben *or* ausnehmen

nest egg N (*lit*) Nestei *nt*; (*fig*) Notgroschen *m*; **to have a nice little ~** (*fig*) sich (*dat*) einen Notgroschen zurückgelegt haben

nesting ['nestɪŋ]

nesting box N Nistkasten *m*

nesting instinct N (*lit, fig*) Nistinstinkt *m or* -trieb *m*

nestle ['nesl] VI **to ~ down in bed** sich ins Bett kuscheln; **to ~ up to sb** sich an jdn schmiegen *or* kuscheln; **to ~ against sb** sich an jdn anschmiegen; **the village nestling in the hills** das Dorf, das zwischen den Bergen eingebettet liegt; **a house nestling *or* ~d among the trees** ein von Bäumen eingerahmtes Haus

nestling ['nestlɪŋ] N Nestling *m*

Net [net] N (*inf*) **the ~** (*Comput*) das Internet

net¹ [net] ▶ N ▶ **a** (*lit, fig*) Netz *nt*; **to make ~s** Netze knüpfen; **to be caught in the ~** (*fig*) in die Falle gehen; **to be caught in the police ~** (*fig*) der Polizei ins Netz *or* Garn gehen; **he felt the ~ closing round him** (*fig*) er fühlte, wie sich die Schlinge immer enger zog; **to cast one's ~ wider** die Auswahl erweitern; **to slip through the ~** (*criminal*) durch die Maschen schlüpfen ▶ **b** (*Sport*) Netz *nt*; **to come up to the ~** ans Netz gehen; **the ball's in the ~** der Ball ist im Tor *or* Netz; **the ~s** (*Cricket*) *von Netzen umspannter Übungsplatz* ▶ **c** (*Tex*) Netzgewebe *nt*; (*for curtains, clothes etc*) Tüll *m*

▶ VT ▶ **a** *fish, game, butterfly* mit dem Netz fangen; (*fig*) *criminal* fangen; **the police have ~ted the criminals** die Verbrecher sind der Polizei ins Netz gegangen ▶ **b** (*Sport*) *ball* ins Netz schlagen; **to ~ a goal** ein Tor schießen *or* erzielen

net² ADJ ▶ **a** *price, income, weight* netto, Netto-; ~ **disposable income** verfügbares Nettoeinkommen; **it costs £15** – es kostet £ 15 netto ▶ **b** (*fig*) End-, letztendlich; ~ **result** Endergebnis *nt*; ~ **effect** Endeffekt *m* ▶ VT netto einnehmen; (*in wages, salary*) netto verdienen; (*show, deal etc*) einbringen; **I ~ted a salary of £850 a month** ich bezog ein Gehalt von £ 850 netto im Monat, ich hatte ein monatliches Nettogehalt von £ 850

net: net assets PL Nettovermögen *nt*; **net bag** N (Einkaufs)netz *nt*; **net balance** N (*Econ*) Nettosaldo *m*, Reinüberschuss *m*; **netball** N (*Brit*) Korbball *m*; **net cord** N (*Tennis*) Netzkante *f*; **net curtain** N (*Brit*) Tüllgardine *f*, Store *m*

nether ['neðə'] ADJ (*liter*) untere(r, s); ~ **regions** Unterwelt *f*; (*hum inf*) untere Regionen *pl* (*hum inf*)

Netherlander ['neðəˌlændə'] N Niederländer(in) *m(f)*

Netherlands ['neðələndz] PL **the ~** die Niederlande *pl*

nethermost ['neðəməʊst] ADJ (*liter*) unterste(r, s)

netherworld ['neðəwɜːld] N (*liter*) Unterwelt *f*

netiquette ['netɪket] N (*Comput*) Netiquette *f*, Net(t)ikette *f*

net: net play N (*Tennis*) Spiel *nt* am Netz; **net profit** N Reingewinn *m*, Nettoertrag *m*; **netspeak** N (*Comput inf*) Internetjargon *m*; **net stocking** N Netzstrumpf *m*

nett ADJ = **net²**

netting ['netɪŋ] N Netz *nt*; (= *wire netting*) Maschendraht *m*; (= *fabric*) Netzgewebe *nt*; (*for curtains etc*) Tüll *m*

nettle ['netl] ▶ N (*Bot*) Nessel *f*; **to grasp the ~** (*fig*) in den sauren Apfel beißen ▶ VT (*fig inf*) *person* ärgern, wurmen (*inf*), fuchsen (*inf*)

nettle: nettle rash N Nesselausschlag *m*; **nettle sting** N Brennnesselstich *m*; **her legs**

were covered in ~s ihre Beine waren von den Brennnesseln völlig zerstochen

network ['netwɜːk] **N** **a** (lit, fig) Netz nt **b** (Rad, TV) Sendenetz nt; (Elec, Comput) Netzwerk nt; **~ card/driver/server** (Comput) Netzwerkkarte f/-treiber m/-server m **VT** (inf) programme im ganzen Netzbereich ausstrahlen **VI** (= make contacts) Kontakte knüpfen

networking ['netwɜːkɪŋ] **N** **a** (Comput) Networking nt **b** (= making contacts) Knüpfen nt von Kontakten

neural ['njʊərəl] ADJ Nerven-; **~ cell** Nervenzelle f

neuralgia [njʊəˈrældʒə] N Neuralgie f, Nervenschmerzen pl

neural network N (Anat) Nervennetzwerk nt; (Comput) neurales Netz

neurasthenia [ˌnjʊərəsˈθiːnɪə] N Neurasthenie f, Nervenschwäche f

neurasthenic [ˌnjʊərəsˈθenɪk] **N** Neurastheniker(in) m(f) **ADJ** neurasthenisch

neuritis [njʊəˈraɪtɪs] N Neuritis f, Nervenentzündung f

neuro- ['njʊərəʊ-] in cpds Neuro-, neuro-; **neurobiology** N Neurobiologie f; **neurochemistry** N Neurochemie f; **neurolinguistic programming** N neurolinguistisches Programmieren

neurological [ˌnjʊərəˈlɒdʒɪkəl] ADJ neurologisch

neurologist [njʊəˈrɒlədʒɪst] N Neurologe m, Neurologin f, Nervenarzt m/-ärztin f

neurology [njʊəˈrɒlədʒɪ] N Neurologie f

neuron ['njʊərɒn], **neurone** ['njʊərəʊn] N (Biol) Neuron nt

neuropath ['njʊərəpæθ] N Nervenkranke(r) mf

neuropathic [njʊərəˈpæθɪk] ADJ neuropathisch

neuropathology [ˌnjʊərəʊpəˈθɒlədʒɪ] N Neuropathologie f, Lehre f von den Nervenkrankheiten

neurosis [njʊəˈrəʊsɪs] N pl **neuroses** [njʊəˈrəʊsiːz] Neurose f

neurosurgeon ['njʊərəʊˌsɜːdʒən] N Neurochirurg(in) m(f)

neurosurgery ['njʊərəʊˌsɜːdʒərɪ] N Neurochirurgie f

neurosurgical [ˌnjʊərəʊˈsɜːdʒɪkəl] ADJ neurochirurgisch

neurotic [njʊəˈrɒtɪk] **ADJ** neurotisch; **to be ~ about sth** in Bezug auf etw (acc) neurotisch sein; **he's getting rather ~ about this problem** das Problem ist bei ihm schon zur Neurose geworden **N** Neurotiker(in) m(f)

neurotically [njʊəˈrɒtɪkəlɪ] ADV neurotisch

neurotoxin [ˌnjʊərəʊˈtɒksɪn] N (Pharm) Neurotoxin nt (spec), Nervengift nt

neuter ['njuːtə'] **ADJ** **a** (Gram) sächlich; **this word is ~** dieses Wort ist sächlich or ein Neutrum **b** animal, person geschlechtslos; (= castrated) kastriert; plant ungeschlechtlich **N** **a** (Gram) Neutrum nt; (= noun) Neutrum nt, sächliches Substantiv; **in the ~** in der sächlichen Form, im Neutrum **b** (= animal) geschlechtsloses Wesen; (castrated) kastriertes Tier; (= plant) ungeschlechtliche Pflanze **VT** cat, dog kastrieren; female, male sterilisieren; (esp Brit fig: = render ineffective) kastrieren

neutral ['njuːtrəl] **ADJ** neutral; (= colourless) shoe cream farblos; **you have a very ~ English accent** an Ihrem Akzent erkennt man nicht, woher in England Sie stammen **N** **a** (= person) Neutrale(r) mf; (= country) neutrales Land **b** (Aut) Leerlauf m; **to be in ~** im Leerlauf sein; **to put the car/gear in ~** den Gang herausnehmen

neutralism ['njuːtrəlɪzəm] N Neutralismus m

neutrality [njuːˈtrælɪtɪ] N Neutralität f

neutralization [ˌnjuːtrəlaɪˈzeɪʃən] N Neutralisation f; (fig) Aufhebung f

neutralize ['njuːtrəlaɪz] VT neutralisieren (also Chem); (fig) aufheben; the force of an argument

die Spitze nehmen (+dat); **neutralizing agent** neutralisierender Wirkstoff

neutrino [njuːˈtriːnəʊ] N Neutrino nt

neutron ['njuːtrɒn] N Neutron nt

neutron: neutron bomb N Neutronenbombe f; **neutron star** N Neutronenstern m

never ['nevə'] ⊘ 6.3, 18.3 ADV **a** (= not ever) nie, niemals (geh); **I ~ eat it** das esse ich nie; **I have ~ seen him** ich habe ihn (noch) nie gesehen; **~ again** nie wieder; **~ do that again** mach das bloß nie wieder or nicht noch einmal; **~ say** sag niemals nie; **I'll ~ try that again** das werde ich nie wieder or nicht noch einmal versuchen; **~ again will I see my own country** ich werde meine Heimat nie wiedersehen; **~ before** noch nie; **I had ~ seen him before today** ich hatte ihn (vor heute) noch nie gesehen; **~ before have men climbed this peak** nie zuvor haben Menschen diesen Gipfel erklommen; **~ before had there been such a disaster** eine solche Katastrophe hatte es noch nie (zuvor) gegeben; **~ even** nicht einmal; **~ ever** absolut or garantiert nie; **I have ~ ever been so insulted** ich bin noch nie so beleidigt worden; **I have ~ yet been able to find ...** ich habe ... bisher noch nicht finden können; **I ~ heard such a thing!** so etwas ist mir noch nie zu Ohren gekommen!

b (emph: = not) **that will ~ do!** das geht ganz und gar nicht!; **I ~ slept a wink** (inf) ich habe kein Auge zugetan; **he ~ so much as smiled** er hat nicht einmal gelächelt; **he said ~ a word** er hat kein einziges Wort gesagt; **you've ~ left it behind!** (inf) du hast es doch wohl nicht etwa liegen lassen! (inf); **you've ~ done that!** hast du das wirklich gemacht?; **would you do it a-gain? – ~!** würdest du das noch einmal machen? – bestimmt nicht; **Spurs were beaten – ~!** (inf) Spurs ist geschlagen worden – das ist doch nicht möglich! or nein! or nein wirklich? (iro); **well I ~ (did)!** (inf) nein, so was!; **~ fear** keine Angst

never: never-ending ADJ endlos, unaufhörlich; discussions, negotiations also nicht enden wollend attr; **it seemed ~** es schien kein Ende nehmen zu wollen; **a ~ job** eine Arbeit ohne Ende; **never-failing** ADJ method etc unfehlbar; source, spring etc unversieglich; **nevermore** ADV (liter) nimmermehr (liter), niemals wieder; **he departed ~ to return** er ging und kehrte niemals wieder (liter); **never-never** N (Brit, inf) **on the ~** auf Pump (inf); **never-never land** N Wunsch- or Traumwelt f

nevertheless [ˌnevəðəˈles] ⊘ 26.2 ADV trotzdem, dennoch, nichtsdestoweniger (geh)

never-to-be-forgotten [ˈnevətəbiːfəˈgɒtn] ADJ attr unvergesslich

new [njuː] **ADJ** (+er) **a** neu; **the ~ people at number five** die Neuen in Nummer fünf; **that's nothing ~** das ist nichts Neues; **that's something ~** das ist wirklich ganz was Neues!; **what's ~?** (inf) was gibts Neues? (inf); **to make sth (look) like ~** etw wie neu machen; **as ~** wie neu; **this system is ~ to me** dieses System ist mir neu; **he is a ~ man** (fig) er ist ein neuer Mensch; **that's a ~ one on me** (inf) das ist mir ja ganz neu; (joke) den kenne ich noch nicht; **a ~ kind of engine** ein neuartiger Motor

b (= fresh) potatoes neu; wine neu, jung; bread frisch

c (= modern, novel) modern; fashion, style neu; **the ~ woman** die moderne Frau; **the ~ diplomacy** die neue Diplomatie; **the New Look** (Fashion) der Newlook, der New Look

d (= lately arrived, inexperienced) person, pupil, recruit neu; **the ~ boys/girls** die Neuen pl, die neuen Schüler pl; **the ~ rich** die Neureichen pl; **I'm quite ~ to this job/to the company** ich bin neu in dieser Stelle/Firma; **to be ~ to business** ein Neuling m im Geschäftsleben sein; **are you ~ here?** sind Sie neu hier?; **I am ~ to this place** ich bin erst seit kurzem hier; **she's ~ to the game** (Sport) sie ist erst seit kurzem bei diesem Sport dabei; (fig) sie ist neu auf diesem Gebiet

New Ager N (inf) Newagejünger(in) m(f), New-Age-Jünger(in) m(f)

New Age Traveller N (Brit) Aussteiger(in) m(f)

newbie ['njuːbɪ] N (inf, = newcomer) Neuling m, Neue(r) mf (inf)

new: new blood N (fig) frisches Blut; **newborn** ADJ neugeboren; **the ~ babies** die Neugeborenen; **new broom** N (fig) neuer Besen; **newcomer** N (who has just arrived) Neuankömmling m; (in job, subject etc) Neuling m (to in +dat); **they are ~s to this town** sie sind neu in dieser Stadt, sie sind Zuzügler; **for the ~s I will recap** für diejenigen, die neu dazugekommen sind, fasse ich kurz zusammen; **New Delhi** [ˌnjuːˈdelɪ] N Neu-Delhi nt

newel ['njuːəl] N (of spiral staircase) Spindel f; (supporting banister) Pfosten m

new: New England N Neuengland nt; **New Englander** N Neuengländer(in) m(f); **new face** N neues Gesicht, Neuling m; **newfangled** ADJ neumodisch; **new-fashioned** ADJ modisch, modern; **new-found** ADJ friend, happiness neu(gefunden); confidence neugeschöpft

Newfoundland ['njuːfəndlənd] **N** Neufundland nt **ADJ** attr neufundländisch; **~ dog** Neufundländer m

Newfoundlander [ˌnjuːfəndˈləndə'] N Neufundländer(in) m(f)

New Guinea N Neuguinea nt

newish ['njuːɪʃ] ADJ ziemlich neu

new: New Lad N (Brit inf) Macho m neuen Stils; **new-laid** ADJ frisch; **new-look** ADJ (inf) neu

newly ['njuːlɪ] ADV frisch; **a ~ dug trench** ein frisch gezogener Graben; **a ~ dug grave** ein frisches Grab; **~ made** ganz neu; bread, cake etc frisch gebacken; road, gardens etc neu angelegt; **~ arrived** neu angekommen; **~ awakened** neu erwacht; **~ formed/found** neu geschaffen/gefunden; **~ married** frisch vermählt; **a ~ industrialized** or **industrializing country** ein industrielles Schwellenland

newlyweds ['njuːlɪwedz] PL (inf) Neu- or Frischvermählte pl

new: New Mexico N New Mexico nt; **new moon** N Neumond m; **there's a ~ tonight** heute Nacht ist Neumond; **new-mown** ADJ frisch gemäht

newness ['njuːnɪs] N Neuheit f; (of bread, cheese etc) Frische f; **his ~ to this job/the trade/this town** die Tatsache, dass er neu in dieser Arbeit ist/dass er Neuling ist/dass er erst seit kurzem in dieser Stadt ist

New Orleans [ˌnjuːɔːˈliːnz] N New Orleans nt

news [njuːz] **N** , no pl **a** (= report, information) Nachricht f; (= recent development) Neuigkeit(en) f(pl); **a piece of ~** eine Neuigkeit; **I have ~/no ~ of him** ich habe von ihm gehört/ nicht von ihm gehört, ich weiß Neues/nichts Neues von ihm; **there is no ~** es gibt nichts Neues zu berichten; **have you heard the ~?** haben Sie schon (das Neueste) gehört?; **have you heard the ~ about Fred?** haben Sie schon das Neueste über Fred gehört?; **tell us your ~** erzähl uns die Neuigkeiten or das Neueste; **let us have** or **send us some ~ of yourself** lassen Sie mal von sich hören; **what's your ~?** was gibts Neues?; **is there any ~?** gibt es etwas Neues?; **I have ~ for you** (iro) ich habe eine Überraschung für dich; **bad/sad/good ~** schlimme or schlechte/traurige/gute Nachricht(en); **that is good** ~ das ist erfreulich zu hören, das sind gute Nachrichten; **that's bad ~ for English football** das ist ein schwerer Schlag für den englischen Fußball; **the ~ of his death/the ~ broke** als sein Tod/es bekannt wurde; **who will break the ~ to him?** wer wird es ihm sagen or beibringen?; **that is ~ (to me)!** das ist (mir) ganz neu!; **that isn't exactly ~** das ist nichts Neues; **it will be ~ to him that ...** er wird staunen, dass ...; **~ travels fast** wie sich doch alles herumspricht; **bad ~ travels fast** schlechte Nachrichten verbreiten sich schnell; **as far as**

I'm concerned, he's bad ~ (*inf*) für mich bedeutet er (nichts als) Ärger; **no** ~ **is good** ~ keine Nachricht ist gute Nachricht

b (*Press, Film, Rad, TV*) Nachrichten *pl*; ~ **in brief** Kurznachrichten *pl*; **financial** ~ Wirtschaftsbericht *m*; **sports** ~ Sportnachrichten *pl*; **it was on the** ~ das kam in den Nachrichten; **to be in the** ~ von sich reden machen; **to make** ~ Schlagzeilen machen; **that's not** ~ damit kann man keine Schlagzeilen machen

news: news agency N Nachrichtenagentur *f*, Nachrichtendienst *m*; **newsagent** N (*Brit*) Zeitungshändler(in) *m(f)*; **newsboy** N (*US*) Zeitungsjunge *m*; **news bulletin** N Bulletin *nt*; **newscast** N Nachrichtensendung *f*; **newscaster** N Nachrichtensprecher(in) *m(f)*; **news cinema** N Aktualitätenkino *nt*; **newscopy** N (*Press, TV*) Bericht *m*; **newsdealer** N (*US*) Zeitungshändler(in) *m(f)*; **news desk** N Nachrichtenredaktion *f*; **news editor** N Nachrichtenredakteur(in) *m(f)*; **newsflash** N Kurzmeldung *f*; **news gathering** N , *no pl* Sammeln *nt* von Informationen; **newsgirl** N (*US*) Reporterin *f*; **newsgroup** N (*Internet*) Newsgroup *f*; **news hawk** N (*inf*) Zeitungsmann *m*/-frau *f* (*inf*), Reporter(in) *m(f)*; **news headlines** PL Kurznachrichten *pl*; (= *recap*) Nachrichten *pl* in Kürze; **news hound** N = **news hawk**; **news item** N Neuigkeit *f*, Nachricht *f*; **the three main** ~**s today** die drei Hauptpunkte der Nachrichten; **a short** ~ (*in paper*) eine Pressenotiz, eine Zeitungsnotiz; **newsletter** N Rundschreiben *nt*, Mitteilungsblatt *nt*; **newsmaker** N *jd, der/etw, das Schlagzeilen macht*; **newsmonger** N Klatschmaul *nt*; (*in paper*) Klatschspaltenschreiber(in) *m(f)*

New South Wales N Neusüdwales *nt*

newspaper ['njuːˌpeɪpə'] N Zeitung *f*; **daily/ weekly** ~ Tages-/Wochenzeitung *f*; **he works on a** ~ er ist bei einer Zeitung beschäftigt

newspaper: newspaper article N Zeitungsartikel *m*; **newspaper boy** N Zeitungsjunge *m*; **newspaper cutting** N Zeitungsausschnitt *m*; **newspaperman** N Zeitungsverkäufer *m*, Zeitungsmann *m* (*inf*); (= *journalist*) Journalist *m*; **newspaper office** N Redaktion *f*; **newspaper report** N Zeitungsbericht *m*; **newspaperwoman** N Zeitungsverkäuferin *f*, Zeitungsfrau *f* (*inf*); (= *journalist*) Journalistin *f*

news: newsprint N Zeitungspapier *nt*; **newsreader** N Nachrichtensprecher(in) *m(f)*; **newsreel** N Wochenschau *f*; **news release** N (*esp US*) = **press release**; **newsroom** N (*of newspaper*) Nachrichtenredaktion *f*; (*TV, Rad also*) Nachrichtenstudio *nt or* -zentrale *f*; **news satellite** N Nachrichtensatellit *m*; **news sheet** N Informationsblatt *nt*; **newsstand** N Zeitungsstand *m*; **news story** N Bericht *m*; **news theatre** N Aktualitätenkino *nt*

new-style ['njuːˈstaɪl] ADJ im neuen Stil; ~ **calendar** Kalender *m* nach neuer Zeitrechnung

news vendor N Zeitungsverkäufer(in) *m(f)*

newsworthy ['njuːzwɜːðɪ] ADJ **to be** ~ Neuigkeitswert haben

newsy ['njuːzɪ] ADJ (+*er*) (*inf*) voller Neuigkeiten

newt [njuːt] N Wassermolch *m*; **as pissed as a** ~ (*Brit inf*) voll wie eine Strandhaubitze (*inf*), stockbesoffen (*inf*)

new: New Testament N *attr* das Neue Testament (*ADJ attr*) neutestamentlich, des Neuen Testaments; **new town** N neue Stadt, ≈ Retortenstadt *f* (*pej*); **new wave** N (*in films*) neue Welle (*ADJ attr*) der neuen Welle; **New World** N the ~ die Neue Welt

New Year ✪ 23.2 N neues Jahr; (= *New Year's Day*) Neujahr *nt*; **to bring in** *or* **see in the** ~ das neue Jahr begrüßen; **Happy** ~**!** (ein) glückliches *or* gutes neues Jahr!; **over/at** ~ über/an Neujahr; **she's expecting a baby in the** ~ sie erwartet im neuen Jahr ihr Baby; ~ **resolution** (guter) Vorsatz für das neue Jahr

New Year's ['njuːˈjɪəz] N (*US inf*) = **New Year's Day, New Year's Eve**

New Year's Day N Neujahr *nt*, Neujahrstag *m*

New Year's Eve N Sylvester *nt*

New: New York N New York *nt* (*ADJ attr*) New Yorker; **New Yorker** N New Yorker(in) *m(f)*; **New Zealand** N Neuseeland *nt* (*ADJ attr*) Neuseeländer *attr*, neuseeländisch; **New Zealander** N Neuseeländer(in) *m(f)*

next [nekst] (*ADJ*) **a** (*in place*) nächste(r, s)

b (*in time*) nächste(r, s); **come back** ~ **week/ Tuesday** kommen Sie nächste Woche/nächsten Dienstag wieder; **he came back the** ~ **day/week** er kam am nächsten Tag/in der nächsten Woche wieder; **(the)** ~ **time I see him** wenn ich ihn das nächste Mal sehe; **(the)** ~ **moment he was gone** im nächsten Moment war er weg; **from one moment to the** ~ von einem Moment zum anderen; **this time** ~ **week** nächste Woche um diese Zeit; **the year after** ~ übernächstes Jahr; **the week after** ~ übernächste Woche; **the** ~ **day but one** der übernächste Tag

c (*order*) nächste(r, s); **who's** ~**?** wer ist der Nächste?; **you're** ~ Sie sind dran (*inf*) *or* an der Reihe; ~ **please!** der Nächste bitte!; **I come** ~ **after you** ich bin nach Ihnen an der Reihe *or* dran (*inf*); **I knew I was the** ~ **person to speak** ich wusste, dass ich als Nächster sprechen sollte; **I'll ask the very** ~ **person (I see)** ich frage den Nächsten(, den ich sehe); **my name is** ~ **on the list** mein Name kommt als Nächstes auf der Liste; **the** ~ **but one** der/die/das Übernächste; **the** ~ **thing to do is (to)** polish it als Nächstes poliert man (es); **the** ~ **thing I knew I** ... bevor ich wusste, wie mir geschah, ... ich ...; (*after fainting etc*) das Nächste, woran ich mich erinnern kann, war, dass ich ...; **the** ~ **size up/ down** die nächstkleinere/nächstgrößere Größe

(*ADV*) **a** (= *the next time*) das nächste Mal; (= *afterwards*) danach; **what shall we do** ~**?** und was sollen wir als Nächstes machen?; **when shall we meet** ~**?** wann treffen wir uns wieder *or* das nächste Mal?; **a new dress! what** ~**?** ein neues Kleid? sonst noch was?; **whatever** ~**?** (*in surprise*) Sachen gibts! (*inf*); (*despairingly*) wo soll das nur hinführen?

b ~ **to sb/sth** neben jdm/etw; (*with motion*) neben jdn/etw; **the** ~ **to last row** die vorletzte Reihe; **he was** ~ **to last** er war der Vorletzte; **the** ~ **to bottom shelf** das vorletzte Brett, das zweitunterste Brett; ~ **to the skin** (*direkt*) auf der Haut; ~ **to nothing/nobody** so gut wie nichts/niemand; ~ **to impossible** nahezu unmöglich; **I kept it** ~ **to my heart** (*most important thing*) es lag mir am meisten am Herzen; (*dearest thing*) es war mir das Liebste

c **the** ~ **best** der/die/das Nächstbeste; **this is the** ~ **best thing** das ist das Nächstbeste; **the** ~ **tallest/oldest boy** (= *second in order*) der zweitgrößte/zweitälteste Junge; **she is my** ~ **best friend** sie ist meine zweitbeste Freundin

(*N*) Nächste(r) *mf*; (= *child*) Nächste(s) *nt*

(*PREP*) (*old*) neben (+*dat*)

next door ['neksˈdɔː'] ADV nebenan; **let's go** ~ gehen wir nach nebenan; **they live** ~ **to us** sie wohnen (direkt) neben uns *or* (*gleich*) nebenan; **he has the room** ~ **to me** er hat das Zimmer neben mir; **we live** ~ **to each other** wir wohnen Tür an Tür; **the boy** ~ der Junge von nebenan; **it's** ~ **to madness** das grenzt an Wahnsinn

next-door ['neksˈdɔː'] ADJ **the** ~ **neighbour** (*Brit*) *or* **neighbor** (*US*) der direkte Nachbar; **we are** ~ **neighbours** (*Brit*) *or* **neighbors** (*US*) wir wohnen Tür an Tür; **the** ~ **house** das Nebenhaus; **the** ~ **room** das Zimmer nebenan, das Nebenzimmer

next friend N (*Jur*) Prozesspfleger(in) *m(f)* (*eines Minderjährigen*)

next of kin N *pl* - nächster Verwandter, nächste Verwandte, nächste Verwandte *pl*

nexus ['neksəs] N Verknüpfung *f*, Verkettung *f*

NF (*Brit*) abbr of **National Front**

NFL (*US*) abbr of **National Football League** amerikanische Fußball-Nationalliga

NFU (*Brit*) abbr of **National Farmers' Union** Bauerngewerkschaft

NG (*US*) abbr of **National Guard**

NGO abbr of **non-governmental organization**

NHS (*Brit*) abbr of **National Health Service**

NHS

Der **National Health Service** oder auch **NHS** ist das Gesundheitswesen, das seit 1948 allen Einwohnern Großbritanniens eine kostenlose medizinische Versorgung garantiert. Der **NHS** wird überwiegend aus Steuergeldern finanziert. Dazu kommen noch andere Quellen wie die Beiträge zur **National Insurance**, die von Arbeitgebern wie Arbeitnehmern gezahlt werden, oder die Gebühren für Rezepte oder Zahnbehandlung.

Verschiedene Regierungen haben einige umstrittene Änderungen am System des **NHS** durchgeführt, doch immer mehr Menschen äußern ihre Unzufriedenheit über den **NHS**, weil man zur Behandlung durch einen Spezialisten zunächst eine Überweisung vom Hausarzt, dem **GP** braucht, oder weil z. B. Patienten, die eine Operation benötigen, recht lange Wartezeiten in Kauf nehmen müssen → NATIONAL INSURANCE

---

niacin ['naɪəsɪn] N Nikotinsäure *f*, Niacin *nt* (*spec*)

Niagara [naɪˈægrə] N Niagara *m*; ~ **Falls** die Niagarafälle *pl*

nib [nɪb] N Feder *f*; (= *point of nib*) (Feder)spitze *f*

nibble ['nɪbl] (*VT*) knabbern; (= *pick at*) food nur anessen, herumnagen an (+*dat*) (*inf*) (*VI*) (*at an* +*dat*) knabbern; (= *pick at*) herumnagen; (*fig*) sich interessiert zeigen; **to** ~ **at the bait** (*fig*) sich interessiert zeigen (*N*) **I think I've got a** ~ ich glaube, bei mir beißt einer an; **I feel like a** ~ ich habe Appetit auf etwas, ich brauche etwas zwischen die Zähne (*hum inf*); ~**s** (*Brit*: = *snacks*) Knabbereien *pl*

niblick ['nɪblɪk] N (*Golf*) Niblick *m*

nibs [nɪbz] N (*hum inf*) **his** ~ der hohe Herr (*hum*), Seine Herrlichkeit (*hum inf*)

NIC (*N*) **a** (*Brit*) abbr of **national insurance contribution** Sozialversicherungsbeitrag *m* **b** abbr of **newly industrialized** *or* **industrializing country** industrielles Schwellenland

Nicaragua [ˌnɪkəˈrægjʊə] N Nicaragua *nt*

Nicaraguan [ˌnɪkəˈrægjʊən] (*ADJ*) nicaraguanisch (*N*) Nicaraguaner(in) *m(f)*

nice [naɪs] ADJ (+*er*) **a** nett; *person, ways, voice* nett, sympathisch; (= *nice-looking*) girl, dress, looks etc nett, hübsch; *weather* schön, gut; *taste, smell, meal, whisky* gut; *warmth, feeling, car* schön; *food* gut, lecker; (= *skilful*) workmanship, work gut, schön, fein; **be** ~ **to him** sei nett zu ihm; **that's not** ~**!** das ist aber nicht nett; **be a** ~ **girl and** ... sei lieb und ...; **he always tries to be Mr Nice Guy** er will sich immer bei allen beliebt machen; **no more Mr Nice Guy** jetzt werden andere Saiten aufgezogen; **have a** ~ **time** sich gut amüsieren; **have a** ~ **day!** (*esp US*) schönen Tag noch!; **that was the** ~ **thing about Venice** das war das Schöne an Venedig; **it's (so)** ~ **to meet you at last/to see you again** es freut mich (sehr), Sie endlich (persönlich) kennen zu lernen/Sie wieder zu treffen; **it's been** ~ **meeting you** ich habe mich gefreut, Sie kennen zu lernen; **I had a** ~ **rest** ich habe mich gut *or* schön ausgeruht; **it's** ~ **to be needed** es ist schön, gebraucht zu werden; **how** ~ **of you to** ... wie nett *or* lieb von Ihnen, zu ...; ~ **one!** toll! (*inf*), sauber! (*inf*); **he has a** ~ **taste in ties** er hat einen guten Geschmack, was Krawatten angeht

b (*intensifier*) schön; **a** ~ **long bath** ein schönes, langes Bad; ~ **and warm/near/quickly** schön warm/nahe/schnell; ~ **and easy** ganz leicht; **take it** ~ **and easy** überanstrengen Sie sich nicht; ~ **and easy does it** immer schön sachte

c (= *respectable*) nett; *district* fein; *words* schön; (= *refined*) manners gut, fein; **not a** ~ **word/district/book** gar kein schönes Wort/Viertel/Buch

d (*iro*) nett, schön, sauber (*all iro*); **here's a** ~

state of affairs! das sind ja schöne *or* nette Zustände!; **you're in a ~ mess** du sitzt schön im Schlamassel (*inf*); **that's a ~ way to talk to your mother** das ist ja eine schöne Art, mit deiner Mutter zu sprechen, wie sprichst du denn mit deiner Mutter?

c (= *subtle*) *distinction, shade of meaning* fein, genau; **overly ~ distinctions** überfeine *or* subtile Unterscheidungen; **that was a ~ point** das war eine gute Bemerkung; **one or two ~ points** ein paar brauchbare *or* gute Gedanken

f (= *hard to please*) *person* anspruchsvoll; **to be ~ about one's food** in Bezug aufs Essen wählerisch sein

nice-looking ['naɪs'lʊkɪŋ] ADJ schön; *woman also, man* gut aussehend; *face, dress etc* nett; *hotel, village* hübsch; **to be ~** gut aussehen

nicely ['naɪslɪ] ADV **a** (= *pleasantly*) nett; (= *well*) *go, speak, behave, placed* gut; **to go ~** wie geschmiert laufen (*inf*); **to be coming along ~** sich gut machen *or* entwickeln; **she thanked me ~** sie hat sich nett bei mir bedankt; **to ask ~** höflich fragen; **eat up/say thank you ~!** iss mal schön auf/sag mal schön danke!; **that will do ~** das reicht vollauf; **how's it going? – ~, thank you** wie geht es so? – danke, ganz gut; **he's doing very ~ for himself** er ist sehr gut gestellt; (= *making money*) er scheffelt Geld (*inf*); **a ~ situated home** ein hübsch gelegenes Haus; **to be ~ spoken** sich gepflegt ausdrücken; **he's such a ~ spoken young man** es ist eine Freude, diesem jungen Mann zuzuhören; **~ done** gut gemacht, prima (*inf*); **when the engine's ~ warmed up** wenn der Motor schön warm gelaufen ist

b (= *carefully*) *distinguish* genau, fein

niceness ['naɪsnɪs] N **a** (= *pleasantness: of person, behaviour*) Nettigkeit *f*; (= *nice appearance*) nettes *or* hübsches Aussehen; (= *skilfulness*) Qualität *f*, Feinheit *f* **b** (= *subtlety*) Feinheit *f*, Genauigkeit *f* **c** (= *fastidiousness*) anspruchsvolle Art, Pingeligkeit *f* (*inf*), Heikelkeit *f* (*dial*)

nicety ['naɪsɪtɪ] N **a** (= *subtlety*) Feinheit *f*; (*of judgement*) Schärfe *f*; (= *precision*) (peinliche) Genauigkeit *f*; **to a ~** äußerst *or* sehr genau **b niceties** PL Feinheiten *pl*, Details *pl*

niche [niːʃ] N (*Archit*) Nische *f*; (*fig*) Plätzchen *nt*; **to carve a ~ for oneself** eine Nische für sich finden; **~ market** (*Comm*) Nischenmarkt *m*

Nicholas ['nɪkələs] N Nikolaus *m*

nick[1] [nɪk] **N a** Kerbe *f*; **I got a little ~ on my chin** ich habe mich leicht am Kinn geschnitten **b in the ~ of time** gerade noch (rechtzeitig) **c** (*Brit inf:* = *condition*) **in good/bad ~** gut/nicht gut in Schuss (*inf*) **VT a** *wood, stick* einkerben; **to ~ oneself** sich schneiden; **to ~ one's chin** (*inf*) sich am Kinn schneiden **b** (*bullet*) *person, wall, arm* streifen

nick[2] (*Brit*) **VT** (*inf*) **a** (= *arrest*) einsperren (*inf*), einlochen (*inf*); (= *catch*) schnappen (*inf*); **he got ~ed** den haben sie sich (*dat*) gegriffen (*sl*) *or* geschnappt (*inf*); **you're ~ed!** Sie sind verhaftet! **b** (= *steal*) klauen (*inf*), mitgehen lassen (*inf*) **N** (*inf*) (= *prison*) Kittchen *nt* (*inf*), Knast *m* (*inf*); (= *police station*) Wache *f*, Revier *nt*

nick[3] VT (*US sl*) **to ~ sb for sth** jdm etw abknöpfen (*inf*)

Nick [nɪk] N *abbr of* **Nicholas Old ~** (*inf*) der Böse, der Leibhaftige (*old*)

nickel ['nɪkl] N **a** (= *metal*) Nickel *nt* **b** (*US*) Nickel *m*, Fünfcentstück *nt*

nickel-and-dime ['nɪklən'daɪm] (*US inf*) **ADJ** billig; *criminal etc* klein (*inf*) **VT to ~ sb** jdm sehr kleine (Geld)beträge abknöpfen (*inf*)

nickelodeon [ˌnɪkəl'əʊdɪən] N (*dated US*) **a** (Film)theater *nt* (*mit Eintrittspreisen von 5 Cent*) **b** (= *juke-box*) Musikbox *f*

nickel-plated ['nɪkl͵pleɪtɪd] ADJ vernickelt

nicker ['nɪkə'] N *pl* - (*Brit inf:* = *pound*) **50 ~** 50 Eier (*sl*)

nickel silver N Neusilber *nt*

nickname ['nɪkneɪm] **N** Spitzname *m* **VT** *person* betiteln, taufen (*inf*); **they ~d him Baldy** sie gaben ihm den Spitznamen Glatzköpfchen; **Chicago is ~d the Windy City** Chicago hat den Spitznamen Windy City

nicotine ['nɪkəti:n] N Nikotin *nt*

nicotine: nicotine patch N Nikotinpflaster *nt*; **nicotine poisoning** N Nikotinvergiftung *f*; **nicotine-stained** ADJ gelb von Nikotin; *fingers also* nikotingelb

niece [ni:s] N Nichte *f*

Nielsen rating ['ni:lsən͵reɪtɪŋ] N (*US*) Zuschauerquote *f*

niff [nɪf] N (*Brit inf*) Mief *m* (*inf*)

niffy ['nɪfɪ] ADJ (+*er*) (*inf*) muffig (*inf*)

nifty ['nɪftɪ] ADJ (+*er*) (*inf*) (= *smart*) flott (*inf*); *gadget, tool* schlau (*inf*); (= *quick*) *person* flott (*inf*), fix (*inf*); **~ footwork** (*fig*) flotte Fußarbeit; **a ~ piece of work** gute Arbeit; **he's pretty ~ with a gun** er hat ein lockeres Händchen mit dem Schießeisen (*inf*); **you'd better be ~ about it!** und ein bisschen dalli (*inf*); **a ~ little car** ein wendiger kleiner Flitzer (*inf*)

Niger ['naɪdʒə'] N Niger *m*

Nigeria [naɪ'dʒɪərɪə] N Nigeria *nt*

Nigerian [naɪ'dʒɪərɪən] **ADJ** nigerianisch **N** Nigerianer(in) *m(f)*

niggard ['nɪgəd] N (= *miser*) Geizhals *m* (*pej*)

niggardliness ['nɪgədlɪnɪs] N (*of person*) Knaus(e)rigkeit *f*; (*of amount, portion also*) Armseligkeit *f*, Kümmerlichkeit *f*

niggardly ['nɪgədlɪ] ADJ *person* knaus(e)rig; *amount, portion also* armselig, kümmerlich

nigger ['nɪgə'] N (*pej*) Nigger *m* (*pej*); **so you're the ~ in the woodpile** (*Brit inf*) Sie sind es also, der quer schießt; **there's a ~ in the woodpile** (*Brit inf*) irgendjemand schießt quer (*inf*); (= *snag*) da ist ein Haken dran (*inf*)

niggle ['nɪgl] **VI** (= *complain*) (herum)kritteln (*inf*), herumkritisieren (*about an* +*dat*) **VT** (= *worry*) plagen, quälen, zu schaffen machen (+*dat*)

niggling ['nɪglɪŋ] **ADJ** *person* kritt(e)lig (*inf*), überkritisch; *question, doubt, pain* bohrend, quälend; *injury* lästig; *detail* pingelig (*inf*); *feeling* ungut **N** Krittelei *nt*, Meckern *nt* (*inf*)

nigh [naɪ] **ADJ** (*old, liter*) nahe; **the end (of the world) is ~** das Ende der Welt ist nah **ADV a** (*old, liter*) **to draw ~** sich nahen (*old, geh*) (*to* +*dat*) **b** **~ on** nahezu (*geh*); **well ~ impossible** nahezu unmöglich **PREP** (*old, liter*) nahe (+*dat*)

night [naɪt] **ADJ a** (= *evening*) Abend *m*; **~ is falling** die Nacht bricht herein; **I saw him last ~** ich habe ihn gestern Abend gesehen; **I'll see him tomorrow ~** ich treffe ihn morgen Abend; **I stayed with them last ~** ich habe heute *or* letzte Nacht bei ihnen übernachtet; **to stay four ~s with sb** vier Nächte lang bei jdm bleiben; **I'll stay with them tomorrow ~** ich übernachte morgen Nacht bei ihnen; **on Friday ~** Freitag Abend/Nacht; **on the ~ of (Saturday) the 11th** am (Samstag dem) 11. nachts; **11 o'clock at ~** 11 Uhr nachts; **6 o'clock at ~** 6 Uhr abends; **she works at ~** sie arbeitet nachts; **to travel by ~** nachts reisen; **to see Paris by ~** Paris bei Nacht sehen; **far into the ~** bis spät in die Nacht, bis in die späte Nacht; **in/during the ~** in/während der Nacht; **the ~ before they were ...** am Abend/die Nacht zuvor waren sie ...; **the ~ before last they were ...** vorgestern Abend/vorletzte Nacht waren sie ...; **to spend the ~ at a hotel** in einem Hotel übernachten; **to have a good/bad ~ *or* ~'s sleep** gut/schlecht schlafen; (*patient also*) eine gute/schlechte Nacht haben; **I need a good ~'s sleep** ich muss mal wieder ordentlich schlafen; **~-night!** (*inf*) gut Nacht! (*inf*); **~ after ~** jede Nacht, Nacht um Nacht (*geh*); **all ~ (long)** die ganze Nacht; **~ and day** (*lit, fig*) Tag und Nacht; **to have a ~ out** (abends) ausgehen; **a ~ out with the lads** (*Brit*) *or* **boys** ein Abend mit den Kumpeln; **to make a ~ of it** durchmachen (*inf*); **to have a late/an early ~** spät/früh ins Bett kommen,

spät/früh schlafen gehen; **too many late ~s!** zu wenig Schlaf!; **after your early ~** nachdem du so früh schlafen gegangen bist; **to work ~s** Nachtdienst haben; **to be on ~s** Nachtdienst haben; (*shift worker*) Nachtschicht haben; **the dark ~ of the soul** (*fig*) die dunkle Nacht der Seele

b (*Theat*) Abend *m*; **the last three ~s of ...** die letzten drei Abende von ...; **a Mozart ~** ein Mozartabend *m* → **first night**

ADV ~s (*esp US*) nachts

night *in cpds* Nacht-; **night bird** N Nachtvogel *m*; (*fig*) Nachteule *f* (*inf*), Nachtschwärmer(in) *m(f)*; **night blindness** N Nachtblindheit *f*; **nightcap** N **a** (= *garment*) Nachtmütze *f*; (*for woman*) Nachthaube *f* **b** (= *drink*) Schlaftrunk *m* (*inf*); **nightclothes** PL Nachtzeug *nt*, Nachtwäsche *f* (*esp Comm*); **nightclub** N Nachtlokal *nt* *or* -klub *m*; **nightdress** N Nachthemd *nt*; **night editor** N Nachtredakteur(in) *m(f)*; **nightfall** N Einbruch der Dunkelheit; **at ~** bei Einbruch der Dunkelheit; **night fighter** N Nachtjäger *m*; **night flight** N Nachtflug *m*; **nightgown** N Nachthemd *nt*; **nighthawk** N (*US*) (*lit*) Amerikanischer Ziegenmelker; (*fig*) Nachtschwärmer(in) *m(f)*

nightie ['naɪtɪ] N (*inf*) Nachthemd *nt*

nightingale ['naɪtɪŋgeɪl] N Nachtigall *f*

night: nightjar N Ziegenmelker *m*, Nachtschwalbe *f*; **night leave** N (*Mil*) Urlaub *m* bis zum Wecken; **night letter** N (*US*) (*zu billigem Tarif gesandtes*) Nachttelegramm *nt*; **nightlife** N Nachtleben *nt*; **night-light** N **a** (*for child etc*) Nachtlicht *nt* **b** (*for teapot etc*) Teelicht *nt*; **nightlong** ADJ sich über die ganze Nacht hinziehend; (= *lasting several nights*) nächtelang; **after their ~ vigil** nachdem sie die ganze Nacht gewacht hatten

nightly ['naɪtlɪ] **ADJ** (= *every night*) (all)nächtlich; (= *every evening*) (all)abendlich; **~ performances** (*Theat*) allabendliche Vorstellung; **the ~ television news** die Abendnachrichten im Fernsehen **ADV** (= *every night*) jede Nacht; (= *every evening*) jeden Abend; **performances ~** jeden Abend Vorstellung; **three performances ~** jeden Abend drei Vorstellungen; **twice ~** zweimal pro Abend

nightmare ['naɪtmeə'] N (*lit, fig*) Albtraum *m*, Alptraum *m*; **that was a ~ of a journey** die Reise war ein Albtraum; **~ scenario** eine Albtraum- *or* Schreckensvision

nightmarish ['naɪtmeərɪʃ] ADJ grauenhaft, albtraumhaft, alptraumhaft

night: night nurse N Nachtschwester *f*; (= *man*) Nachtpfleger *m*; **night owl** N (*inf*) Nachteule *f* (*inf*); **night porter** N Nachtportier *m*; **night safe** N Nachtsafe *m*; **night school** N Abendschule *f*

nightshade ['naɪtʃeɪd] N Nachtschatten *m* → **deadly nightshade**

night: night shelter N Nachtquartier *nt*; **night shift** N Nachtschicht *f*; **to be** *or* **work on ~** Nachtschicht haben *or* arbeiten; **nightshirt** N (Herren)nachthemd *nt*; **night sky** N nächtlicher Himmel; **nightspot** N Nachtlokal *nt*; **night stand** N (*US*) Nachttisch *m*; **night stick** N (*US*) Schlagstock *m*; **night-storage heater** N Nachtspeicherofen *m*; **night table** N (*US*) Nachttisch *m*; **night-time** N Nacht *f*; **at ~** nachts; **in the ~** während der Nacht, nachts **ADJ** *attr* nächtlich; **~ temperature** Nachttemperatur *f*; **night vision** N Nachtsichtigkeit *f*; **night-vision** ADJ Nachtsicht-; **night vision aid, night vision scope** N Nachtsichtgerät *nt*; **night watch** N Nachtwache *f*; **night watchman** N Nachtwächter(in) *m(f)*; **nightwear** N Nachtzeug *nt*, Nachtwäsche *f* (*esp Comm*)

nihilism ['naɪɪlɪzəm] N Nihilismus *m*

nihilist ['naɪɪlɪst] N Nihilist(in) *m(f)*

nihilistic [ˌnaɪɪ'lɪstɪk] ADJ nihilistisch

Nikkei average [nɪˌkeɪ'ævərɪdʒ], **Nikkei index** [nɪˌkeɪ'ɪndeks] N Nikkei-(Durchschnitts)index *m*

nil [nɪl] N (= zero) null (also Sport); (= nothing) nichts; **the score was one-nil** es stand eins zu null; **the response** etc **was ~** die Reaktion etc war gleich null → also **zero**

Nile [naɪl] N Nil m

nimble [nɪmbl] ADJ (+er) (= quick) fingers, feet flink; person also behände (geh); (= agile) gelenkig, wendig, beweglich; car wendig; (= skilful) geschickt; mind beweglich; **to be very ~ at operating sth** sehr geschickt im Umgang mit etw sein; **as ~ as a goat** leichtfüßig (wie eine Gämse); **she is still ~** sie ist noch sehr rüstig

nimble: **nimble-fingered** ADJ fingerfertig; **nimble-footed** ADJ leichtfüßig

nimbleness [nɪmblnɪs] N (of fingers, feet) Flinkheit f; (of person) Flinkheit f, Behändigkeit f (geh); (= agility) Gelenkigkeit f, Wendigkeit f, Beweglichkeit f; (= skilfulness) Geschicklichkeit f, Geschick nt; (of mind) Beweglichkeit f

nimble-witted [nɪmbl'wɪtɪd] ADJ schlagfertig

nimbly [nɪmblɪ] ADV work, respond flink; dance leicht(füßig); jump, climb, step gelenkig, behände (geh); **her fingers moved ~** ihre Finger bewegten sich leicht und flink

nimbus [nɪmbəs] N **a** (Liter. = halo) Nimbus m (geh), Heiligenschein m **b** (Met) → **cumulonimbus**

nimby, Nimby [nɪmbɪ] abbr of **not in my back yard** jd, der Unangenehmes aber Notwendiges nicht in seiner Nachbarschaft haben will, sondern möglichst weit weg

nincompoop [nɪŋkəmpuːp] N (inf) Trottel m (inf), Simpel m (inf)

nine [naɪn] ADJ neun; **~ times out of ten** in neun Zehntel der Fälle, so gut wie immer; **to have ~ lives** ein zähes Leben haben; **a ~ days' wonder** eine Eintagsfliege (inf) N Neun f (inf); **dressed (up) to the ~s** in Schale (inf) → also **six**

ninepins [naɪnpɪnz] N (= game) Kegeln nt; **to go down like ~** (fig) wie die Fliegen umfallen (inf)

nineteen [naɪn'tiːn] ADJ neunzehn N Neunzehn f; **she talks ~ to the dozen** (Brit inf) sie redet wie ein Wasserfall (inf); **they were talking ~ to the dozen** (Brit inf) sie redeten, was das Zeug hielt (inf)

nineteenth [naɪn'tiːnθ] ADJ (in series) neunzehnte(r, s); (as fraction) neunzehntel; **the ~ (hole)** (Golf inf) das neunzehnte Loch (Bar im Klubhaus) N Neunzehnte(r, s); (= fraction) Neunzehntel nt → also **sixteenth**

ninetieth [naɪntɪθ] ADJ (in series) neunzigste(r, s); (as fraction) neunzigstel N Neunzigste(r, s); (= fraction) Neunzigstel nt

nine-to-five [naɪntə'faɪv] ADJ Büro-; **~ job/worker** Bürojob m/-angestellte(r) mf

nine-to-fiver [naɪntə'faɪvə] N (US, inf) Büroangestellte(r) mf, Bürohengst m (pej inf)

ninety [naɪntɪ] ADJ neunzig N Neunzig f → also **sixty**

ninny [nɪnɪ] N (inf) Dussel m (inf)

ninth [naɪnθ] ADJ (in series) neunte(r, s); (as fraction) neuntel N Neuntel nt; (Mus) None f → also **sixth**

niobium [naɪ'əʊbɪəm] N (Chem) Niob nt

Nip [nɪp] N (pej) Japs m (pej inf)

nip¹ [nɪp] N **a** (= pinch) Kniff m; (= bite: from animal etc) Biss m; **to give sb a ~ on the leg** jdn ins Bein zwicken or kneifen; (dog) jdn leicht ins Bein beißen; **the dog gave him a ~** der Hund hat kurz zugeschnappt → **nip and tuck**
b there's a **~ in the air today** es ist ganz schön frisch heute
VT **a** (= bite) zwicken; (= pinch) kneifen; **the dog nipped his ankle** der Hund hat ihn am Knöchel gezwickt
b (Hort) bud, shoot abknipsen; **to ~ sth in the bud** (fig) etw im Keim ersticken
c (cold, frost etc) plants angreifen; **the cold air ~ped our faces** die Kälte schnitt uns ins Gesicht; **the plants had been ~ped by the frost** die Pflanzen hatten Frost abbekommen
VI (Brit inf) sausen (inf), flitzen (inf); **to ~ up(stairs)/down(stairs)** hoch-/runtersausen (inf) or -flitzen (inf); **I'll just ~ down to the shops** ich gehe mal kurz einkaufen (inf); **I'll just ~ round to his place** ich gehe mal kurz bei ihm vorbei (inf); **I'll ~ on ahead** ich gehe schon mal voraus (inf)

▶ **nip along** VI (Brit inf) entlangsausen (inf) or -flitzen (inf); **nip along to Joan's house** lauf or saus mal schnell zu Joan rüber (inf)

▶ **nip in** VI (Brit inf) hereinsausen (inf); (= call in) auf einen Sprung vorbeikommen; **I've just nipped in for a chat** ich bin nur auf ein Schwätzchen vorbeigekommen (inf); **he just nipped into the pub for a drink** er ging auf einen Sprung or nur mal kurz in die Kneipe (inf); **to nip in and out of the traffic** sich durch den Verkehr schlängeln

▶ **nip off** VI (Brit inf) davonsausen (inf) VT sep twig abknicken; (with clippers etc) abzwicken; **he nipped off the end of his finger** er hat sich (dat) die Fingerspitze gekappt

▶ **nip out** VI (Brit inf) heraussausen (inf); (out of house etc) kurz weggehen (inf)

nip² N (inf: = drink) Schlückchen nt

nip and tuck [nɪpənd'tʌk] N (inf) **a** (= cosmetic surgery) Schönheitsoperation f **b** (esp US) **it was ~** das war eine knappe Sache; **to be ~** (in race etc) Kopf an Kopf liegen; **it was ~ as they came up to the finishing line** sie lagen vor dem Ziel praktisch auf gleicher Höhe

nip-and-tuck [nɪpənd'tʌk] ADJ attr (inf) **a ~ race** ein Kopf-an-Kopf-Rennen

nipper [nɪpə] N **a** (Zool) Schere f, Zange f **b** (Brit inf: = child) Steppke m (inf)

nipple [nɪpl] N **a** (Anat) Brustwarze f, Nippel m (inf); (US: on baby's bottle) Sauger m, Schnuller m (inf) **b** (Tech) Nippel m

nippy [nɪpɪ] ADJ (+er) **a** (Brit inf) flink, flott; car, motor spritzig **b** (= sharp, cold) weather frisch; wind frisch, beißend

Nirvana [nɪə'vɑːnə] N Nirwana nt

nisi [naɪsaɪ] CONJ → **decree**

Nissen hut [nɪsn̩hʌt] N (Brit) Nissenhütte f

nit [nɪt] N **a** (Zool) Nisse f **b** (Brit, inf) Dummkopf m, Schwachkopf m (inf)

niter N (US) = **nitre**

nit-pick [nɪtpɪk] VI (inf) kleinlich or pingelig (inf) sein

nit-picker [nɪtpɪkə] N (inf) Kleinigkeitskrämer(in) m(f) (inf)

nit-picking [nɪtpɪkɪŋ] ADJ (inf) kleinlich, pingelig (inf)

nitrate [naɪtreɪt] N Nitrat nt

nitration [naɪ'treɪʃən] N Nitrierung f

nitre, (US) niter [naɪtə] N Salpeter m or nt

nitric [naɪtrɪk] in cpds (= of nitrogen) Stickstoff-; (= of nitre) Salpeter-; **nitric acid** N Salpetersäure f; **nitric oxide** N Stick(stoffmon)oxid nt

nitro [naɪtrəʊ] (inf) abbr of **nitroglycerin(e)** Nitroglyzerin nt

nitro- PREF Nitro-; **~phosphates** Nitrophosphate pl

nitrogen [naɪtrədʒən] N Stickstoff m

nitrogen in cpds Stickstoff-; **~ compound** Stickstoffverbindung f

nitrogen dioxide N Stickstoffdioxid nt

nitroglycerin(e) [naɪtrəʊ'glɪsəriːn] N Nitroglyzerin nt

nitrous [naɪtrəs]: **nitrous acid** N salpetrige Säure f; **nitrous oxide** N Distickstoffmonoxid nt, Lachgas nt

nitty-gritty [nɪtɪ'grɪtɪ] N (inf) **to get down to the ~** zur Sache kommen; **the ~ of everyday life/of politics** die wahre Realität des alltäglichen Lebens/der Politik

nitwit [nɪtwɪt] N (inf) Dummkopf m, Schwachkopf m (inf)

nix [nɪks] N (inf) nix (inf) VI (US, inf) proposal über den Haufen werfen (inf)

NLP abbr of **neurolinguistic programming** NLP nt

NLQ abbr of **near letter-quality** NLQ; **in ~ mode** im NLQ-Druckmodus

NNE abbr of **north-northeast** NNO

NNW abbr of **north-northwest** NNW

No, no **a** abbr of **north** N **b** abbr of **number** Nr.

no [nəʊ] ADV **a** (negative) nein; **oh no!** o nein!; **to answer no** (to question) mit Nein antworten, verneinen; (to request) Nein or nein sagen; **she can't say no** sie kann nicht Nein or nein sagen; **the answer is no** da muss ich Nein or nein sagen; (as emphatic reply also) nein (und noch mal nein)
b (= not) nicht; **whether he comes or no** ob er kommt oder nicht; **hungry or no, you'll eat it** ob du Hunger hast oder nicht, das wird gegessen (inf)
c (with comp) nicht; **I can bear it no longer** ich kann es nicht länger ertragen; **I have no more money** ich habe kein Geld mehr; **he has no more than anyone else** er hat auch nicht mehr als jeder andere; **I'm no less tired than you are** ich bin auch nicht weniger müde als du; **he returned to England in an aircraft carrier no less** er kehrte auf nichts Geringerem als einem Flugzeugträger nach England zurück; **no later than Monday** spätestens Montag; **no longer ago than last week** erst letzte Woche
ADJ **a** (= not any: also with numerals and "other") kein; **a person of no intelligence** ein Mensch ohne jede Intelligenz; **he has no integrity** er ist ein unredlicher Mensch; **no one person could do it** keiner könnte das allein tun; **no two men could be less alike** zwei verschiedenere Menschen könnte es nicht geben; **no other man kein anderer**; **it's of no interest/importance** das ist belanglos/unwichtig; **it's no use** or **no good** das hat keinen Zweck
b (forbidding) **no parking/smoking** Parken/Rauchen verboten; **no surrender!** wir kapitulieren nicht!
c (with gerund) **there's no saying** or **telling what he'll do next** man kann nie wissen, was er als Nächstes tun wird; **there's no denying it** es lässt sich nicht leugnen; **there's no pleasing him** ihm kann man es auch nie recht machen
d (emph) **he's no genius** er ist nicht gerade ein Genie; **she's no beauty** sie ist nicht gerade eine Schönheit; **president or no president** Präsident oder nicht; **this is no place for children** das ist hier nichts für Kinder; **I'm no expert, but ...** ich bin ja kein Fachmann, aber ...; **in no time** im Nu; **it's no small matter** das ist keine Kleinigkeit; **at no little expense** zu großen Kosten; **theirs is no easy task** sie haben keine leichte Aufgabe; **there is no such thing** so etwas gibt es nicht; **it was/we did no such thing** bestimmt nicht, nichts dergleichen; **I'll do no such thing** ich werde mich hüten
N pl **-es** Nein nt; (= no vote) Neinstimme f; **I won't take no for an answer** ich bestehe darauf, ich lasse nicht locker; **he's the type who won't take no for an answer** er lässt sich nicht mit einem Nein abspeisen; **the noes have it** die Mehrheit ist dagegen

no-account [nəʊə'kaʊnt] (US inf) ADJ (= no use) nutzlos; (= up to no good) nichtsnutzig N (no use) Niete f (inf); (up to no good) Nichtsnutz m

Noah [nəʊə] N Noah m

Noah's ark [nəʊəz'ɑːk] N (Bibl) die Arche Noah

nob¹ [nɒb] N (inf) einer der besseren Leute (inf); **all the ~s** all die besseren Leute (inf), alles, was Rang und Namen hat

nob² N (inf, = head) Rübe f (inf)

no-ball [nəʊ'bɔːl] N (Cricket) wegen Übertreten ungültiger Ball

nobble [nɒbl] VT (Brit, inf) **a** horse, dog lahm legen (inf) **b** (= catch) sich (dat) schnappen (inf) **c** (= obtain dishonestly) votes etc sich (dat) kaufen; money einsacken (inf) **d** jury, witness bestechen **e** (= thwart) plan durchkreuzen

Nobel ['nəʊbel] N ~ **prize** Nobelpreis *m*; ~ **peace prize** Friedensnobelpreis *m*; ~ **prize winner** Nobelpreisträger(in) *m(f)*

nobelium [nəʊ'biːliəm] N Nobelium *nt*

nobility [nəʊ'bɪlɪtɪ] N , *no pl* **a** (= *people*) (Hoch)adel *m*; **she is one of the** ~ sie ist eine Adlige **b** (= *quality*) Adel *m*, Edle(s) *nt*; ~ **of mind/thought** geistiger Adel; ~ **of sentiment** edles Gefühl

noble ['nəʊbl] ADJ (+er) **a** (= *aristocratic*) *person, rank* adlig; **to be of ~ birth** adlig sein, von edler or adliger Geburt sein **b** (= *fine, distinguished*) *person, deed, thought etc* edel, nobel; *appearance* vornehm; *monument* stattlich, prächtig; *stag also* kapital; (= *brave*) *resistance* heldenhaft, wacker; **the ~ art of self-defence** die edle Kunst der Selbstverteidigung; **that was a ~ attempt** das war ein heldenhafter Versuch; **the ~ savage** (*Liter*) der edle Wilde **c** (*inf*: = *selfless*) edel, großmütig, edelmütig; **how ~ of you!** (*iro*) zu gütig **d** *metal* edel **N** Adlige(r) *mf*, Edelmann *m* (*Hist*); **the ~s** die Adligen or Edelleute (*Hist*)

noble: noble gas N Edelgas *nt*; **nobleman** N Adlige(r) *m*, Edelmann *m* (*Hist*); **noble--minded** ADJ edel gesinnt, vornehm

nobleness ['nəʊblnɪs] N **a** (*of person*) Adligkeit *f*; (*of birth, rank*) Vornehmheit *f* **b** (*of deed, thought etc*) Vornehmheit *f*; (*of person*) edle or noble Gesinnung; (= *braveness*) Heldenhaftigkeit *f* **c** (= *impressiveness*) Stattlichkeit *f* **d** (*inf*: = *selflessness*) Großmütigkeit *f*; (*of person*) Großmut *m*, Edelmut *m*

noblesse [nəʊ'bles] N Noblesse *f*; ~ **oblige** Adel verpflichtet, noblesse oblige

noblewoman ['nəʊblwʊmən] N *pl* -**women** [-wɪmɪn] Adlige *f*; (*married also*) Edelfrau *f* (*Hist*); (*unmarried also*) Edelfräulein *nt* (*Hist*)

nobly ['nəʊblɪ] ADV **a** (= *aristocratically*) vornehm; ~ **born** von edler Geburt **b** (= *finely*) edel, vornehm; (= *bravely*) wacker, heldenhaft; **you've done** ~ du hast dich wacker geschlagen (*inf*) **c** (= *impressively*) proportioned prächtig, prachtvoll **d** (*inf*: = *selflessly*) großmütig; **he ~ gave up his weekend** großmütigerweise opferte er sein Wochenende

nobody ['nəʊbədɪ] PRON niemand, keiner; **who saw him? – ~** wer hat ihn gesehen? – niemand; ~ **knows better than I** niemand or keiner weiß besser als ich; **there was ~ else** da war niemand anderes or sonst niemand; ~ **else could have done it** es kann niemand anders or kein anderer gewesen sein; ~ **else but you can do it** nur du kannst das, außer dir kann das niemand; ~ **else offered to give them money** sonst hat sich keiner or niemand angeboten, ihnen Geld zu geben; **like ~'s business** wie nichts; **he's ~'s fool** er ist nicht auf den Kopf gefallen **N** Niemand *m no pl*, Nichts *nt no pl*; **he's a mere ~** er ist überhaupt nichts, er ist doch ein Niemand or Nichts; **to marry a ~** ein heiraten, der nichts ist und nichts hat; **they are nobodies** sie sind doch niemand; **I worked with him when he was (a) ~** ich habe mit ihm gearbeitet, als er noch ein Niemand war

no-claim(s) bonus ['nəʊ,kleɪm(z)'bəʊnəs] N Schadenfreiheitsrabatt *m*

nocturnal [nɒk'tɜːnl] ADJ nächtlich; *sound also* der Nacht; ~ **animal/bird** Nachttier *nt*/-vogel *m*; ~ **flowers** Nachtblüher *pl*

nocturne [nɒk'tɜːn] N (*Mus*) Nocturne *f*

nod [nɒd] **N** Nicken *nt*; **he gave a quick ~** er nickte kurz; **to give sb a ~** jdm zunicken; **to give sb the ~** (*fig*) jdm grünes Licht geben; **to answer with a ~** (zustimmend) nicken; **to give sb a ~ and a wink** (*fig*) jdm im Stillen zustimmen; **a ~ is as good as a wink (to a blind man)** (*inf*) schon verstanden, das wird er schon verstehen; **to go through on the ~** (*inf*) ohne Einwände angenommen werden **b** (*inf*, = *sleep*) **the land of Nod** das Land der Träume **VI a** (*person, flowers*) nicken; (*plumes*) wippen;

---

to ~ to sb jdm zunicken; **to ~ toward(s) sth** mit dem Kopf auf etw zeigen; **to ~ in agreement** zustimmend nicken; **he ~ded to me to leave** er gab mir durch ein Nicken zu verstehen, dass ich gehen sollte **b** (= *doze*) ein Nickerchen machen (*inf*); **she was ~ding over a book** sie war über einem Buch eingenickt (*inf*) **c** **even Homer ~s** Irren or irren ist menschlich (*Prov*) **VT a** **to ~ one's head** mit dem Kopf nicken; **to ~ one's agreement/approval** zustimmend nicken; **to ~ a greeting/welcome to sb** jdm zum Gruß/zur Begrüßung zunicken **b** (*Sport*) *ball* köpfen

▶ **nod in** VT SEP *goal, ball* einköpfen
▶ **nod off** VI einnicken (*inf*)

nodal ['nəʊdl] ADJ knotenartig; ~ **point** (*fig*) Knotenpunkt *m*

nodding ['nɒdɪŋ] ADJ **to have a ~ acquaintance with sb** jdn flüchtig kennen

noddle ['nɒdl] N (*Brit, inf,* = *head*) Dez *m* (*inf*), Schädel *m* (*inf*)

node [nəʊd] N Knoten *m*

nodular ['nɒdjʊlə'] ADJ knötchenartig

nodule ['nɒdjuːl] N (*Med, Bot*) Knötchen *nt*; (*Geol*) Klümpchen *nt*

no-fault ['nəʊ,fɔːlt] (*US*) ADJ **a** *divorce* in gegenseitigem Einvernehmen **b** (*Insur*) *coverage* mit garantierter Entschädigungssumme **N** (*also* **no-fault insurance**) *Kraftfahrzeugversicherung mit garantierter Auszahlung einer Entschädigungssumme ohne vorherige Klärung der Unfallschuld*

no-fly zone ['nəʊ,flaɪ'zəʊn] N (*Mil*) Flugverbotszone *f*

no-frills ['nəʊ'frɪlz] ADJ *attr package, deal etc* ohne (alle) Extras; *style, decor etc* (schlicht und) einfach

noggin ['nɒɡɪn] N **a** (*inf,* = *head*) Birne *f* (*inf*) **b** (*Measure*) Becher *m* (*ca. 0,15 Liter*); **let's have a ~** (*inf*) wie wärs mit 'nem Gläschen? (*inf*)

no-go area ['nəʊ,ɡəʊ'eərɪə] N Sperrgebiet *nt*; **this street is a ~** diese Straße sollte man meiden

no: no-good ADJ *person* nichtsnutzig **N** (= *person*) Nichtsnutz *m*; **no-growth** ADJ *attr* nicht wachstumsorientiert; (= *preventing growth*) wachstumshemmend; **we have a ~ economy** unsere Wirtschaft zeigt kein Wachstum; **no--holds-barred** ADJ *contest, attack* kompromisslos; **no-hoper** N (*inf*) völlige Niete (*inf*), Nulpe *f* (*dial inf*); **nohow** ADV (*incorrect, hum*) **not never not ~** nie und nimmer

noise [nɔɪz] **N** Geräusch *nt*; (= *loud, irritating sound*) Lärm *m*, Krach *m*; (*Elec,* = *interference*) Rauschen *nt*; **what was that ~?** was war das für ein Geräusch?; **a hammering ~** ein hämmerndes Geräusch; **the ~ of (the) jet planes** der Düsenlärm; **the ~ of the traffic** der Straßenlärm; **the ~ of the bells** der Lärm der Glocken; **the ~ of horses coming up the street** Pferdegetrappel die Straße herauf; ~**s in the ears** (*Med*) Ohrensausen *nt*; **the rain made a ~ on the roof** der Regen prasselte aufs Dach; **it made a lot of ~** es war sehr laut, es hat viel Krach gemacht; **don't make a ~!** sei leise!; **stop making such a (lot of) ~** hör auf, solchen Lärm or Krach zu machen; **she made ~s about leaving early** sie ließ immer wieder fallen, dass sie früh gehen wollte (*inf*); **he's always making ~s about resigning** er redet dauernd davon, dass er zurücktreten will; **to make reassuring/placatory ~s** beruhigende/besänftigende Geräusche machen; **she made (all) the right ~s** sie reagierte richtig; **to make a lot of ~ about sth** (*inf*) viel Geschrei or etw machen; **to make a ~ in the world** Aufsehen erregen, von sich reden machen; **a big ~** (*fig inf*) ein großes Tier (*inf*); ~ **abatement/prevention** Lärmbekämpfung *f* **VT to ~ sth abroad** or **about** (*old, hum*) etw verbreiten; **it was ~d about that ...** es ging das Gerücht (um), dass ...

---

noise: noiseless ['nɔɪzlɪs] ADJ geräuschlos; *tread, step also* lautlos; **noiselessly** ['nɔɪzlɪslɪ] ADV geräuschlos; *move also* lautlos; **noise level** N Geräuschpegel *m*; **noise nuisance, noise pollution** N Lärmbelästigung *f*

noisily ['nɔɪzɪlɪ] ADV laut; *protest, welcome, debate* lautstark

noisiness ['nɔɪzɪnɪs] N Lärm *m*; (*of person*) laute Art; (*of children*) Krachmacherei *f* (*inf*); (*of protest, welcome, debate*) Lautstärke *f*; **the ~ of these pupils/this car** der Lärm or Krach, den diese Schüler machen/dieses Auto macht

noisome ['nɔɪsəm] ADJ **a** *smell* widerlich, eklig **b** (= *noxious*) giftig, (gesundheits)schädlich

noisy ['nɔɪzɪ] ADJ (+er) laut; *traffic, child also* lärmend; *machine, behaviour, work also* geräuschvoll; *protest, welcome, debate* lautstark; **don't be so ~** sei nicht so laut, mach nicht so viel Lärm; **this is a ~ house** in dem Haus ist es laut

no-jump ['nəʊdʒʌmp] N Fehlsprung *m*

nomad ['nəʊmæd] N Nomade *m*, Nomadin *f*

nomadic [nəʊ'mædɪk] ADJ nomadisch, Nomaden-; ~ **tribe** Nomadenstamm *m*; ~ **lifestyle** Nomadenleben *m*

no-man's-land ['nəʊmænzlænd] N (*lit, fig*) Niemandsland *nt*

nom de plume ['nɒmdə'pluːm] N Pseudonym *nt*

nomenclature [nəʊ'menklətʃə'] N Nomenklatur *f*

nomenklatura [,nəʊmenklə'tʊərə] N **the ~** (*Pol*) die Nomenklatura

nominal ['nɒmɪnl] ADJ **a** (= *in name*) nominell; ~ **shares** Stamm- or Gründungsaktien *pl* **b** (= *small*) *salary, fee, amount, rent* nominell, symbolisch **c** (*Gram*) Nominal-; ~ **clause** Nominalphrase *f*

nominal interest N (*Fin*) Nominalzins *m*, Nominalzinsfuß *m*

nominalism ['nɒmɪnəlɪzəm] N (*Philos*) Nominalismus *m*

nominalize ['nɒmɪnəlaɪz] VT (*Gram*) nominalisieren; *word also* substantivieren

nominally ['nɒmɪnəlɪ] ADV nominell; **it's worth £500** auf dem Papier ist es £ 500 wert

nominal value N (*of shares, voucher, banknote etc*) Nennwert *m*

nominate ['nɒmɪneɪt] VT **a** (= *appoint*) ernennen; **he was ~d chairman** er wurde zum Vorsitzenden ernannt **b** (= *propose*) nominieren, aufstellen; **he was ~d for the presidency** er wurde als Präsidentschaftskandidat aufgestellt; **to ~ sb/sth for an award** jdn/etw für eine Auszeichnung nominieren

nomination [,nɒmɪ'neɪʃən] N **a** (= *appointment*) Ernennung *f* **b** (= *proposal*) Nominierung *f*, Kandidatenvorschlag *m*

nominative ['nɒmɪnətɪv] (*Gram*) **N** Nominativ *m*, Werfall *m* ADJ **(the) ~ case** der Nominativ, der Werfall

nominee [,nɒmɪ'niː] N Kandidat(in) *m(f)*

non- [nɒn-] PREF nicht-; **non-absorbent** ADJ nicht absorbierend; **nonacceptance** N (*Comm, Fin*) Nichtannahme *f*, Annahmeverweigerung *f*; **non-achiever** N Leistungsschwache(r) *mf*; **non-adjustable** ADJ nicht verstellbar, unverstellbar; **non-affiliated** ADJ (*to an +acc*) *business, industry* nichtangeschlossen *attr*, nicht angeschlossen *pred*

nonagenarian [,nɒnədʒɪ'neərɪən] **N** Neunziger(in) *m(f)* ADJ in den Neunzigern

nonaggression [nɒnə'ɡreʃən] N Nichtangriff *m*; ~ **treaty** or **pact** Nichtangriffspakt *m*

nonagon ['nɒnəɡɒn] N Neuneck *nt*, Nonagon *nt*

non: nonalcoholic ADJ nichtalkoholisch, nicht alkoholisch, alkoholfrei; **nonaligned** ADJ (*Pol*) blockfrei, bündnisfrei; **nonalignment** N (*Pol*) Blockfreiheit *f*, Bündnisfreiheit *f*; ~ **policy** Neutralitätspolitik *f*; **nonappearance** N Nichterscheinen *nt*; **nonarrival** N Ausbleiben *nt*; (*of train, plane, letter also*) Nichteintreffen *nt*; **nonattendance** N Nichtteilnahme *f* (at an +*dat*); **nonavailability** N Unerhältlichkeit *f*; (*of person*) Unabkömmlichkeit *f*; **nonavailable** ADJ nicht erhältlich; *person* unabkömmlich; **nonbelligerent** N Kriegsunbeteiligte(r) *mf*; **to be a** ~ nicht am Krieg teilnehmen ADJ nicht Krieg führend, kriegsunbeteiligt; **non-breakable** ADJ unzerbrechlich, nicht zerbrechlich; **non-cash** ADJ (*Fin*) *payment* bargeldlos; ~ **assets** Sachwerte *pl*; ~ **benefits** geldwerte Vorteile *pl*

nonce word ['nɒnswɜːd] N Ad-hoc-Bildung *f*

nonchalance ['nɒnʃələns] N Lässigkeit *f*, Nonchalance *f*

nonchalant ADJ , **nonchalantly** ADV ['nɒnʃələnt, -lɪ] lässig, nonchalant

non: non-Christian N Nichtchrist(in) *m(f)* ADJ nichtchristlich, nicht christlich; **non-collegiate** ADJ *university* nicht aus Colleges bestehend; **non-com** N (*Mil inf*) Uffz *m* (*sl*); **noncombatant** N Nichtkämpfer(in) *m(f)*, Nonkombattant(in) *m(f)* (*spec*) ADJ nicht am Kampf beteiligt; **noncombustible** ADJ nicht brennbar N nicht brennbarer Stoff; **noncommissioned** ADJ (*Mil*) ~ **officer** Unteroffizier(in) *m(f)*; **noncommittal** ADJ zurückhaltend; *answer also* unverbindlich; **to be ~ about whether ...** sich nicht festlegen, ob ...; **he's so** ~ er legt sich nie fest; **noncommittally** ADV *answer, say* unverbindlich; **non-communicant** N (*Eccl*) Nichtkommunikant(in) *m(f)*; **non-completion** N Nichtbeendung *f*; (*of work also, contract*) Nichtabschluss *m*; **noncompliance** N (*with regulations etc*) Nichteinhaltung *f*, Nichterfüllung *f* (*with +gen*); (*with wishes, orders*) Zuwiderhandlung *f*, Zuwiderhandeln *nt* (*with gegen*)

non compos mentis ['nɒnˌkɒmpəs'mentɪs] ADJ nicht zurechnungsfähig, unzurechnungsfähig; **to be ~** (*inf*) nicht ganz da sein (*inf*)

non: nonconformism N Nonkonformismus *m*; **his social** ~ seine mangelnde Anpassung an die Gesellschaft; **the ~ of his views** seine nonkonformistischen Ansichten; **nonconformist** N Nonkonformist(in) *m(f)* ADJ nonkonformistisch; **nonconformity** N (*with rules*) Nichteinhaltung *f* (*with +gen*), Nichtkonformgehen *nt* (*form*) (*with mit*); **noncontributory** ADJ *benefits, insurance, pension scheme* ohne Eigenbeteiligung; *member* beitragsfrei; **noncontroversial** ADJ für alle annehmbar, nicht kontrovers; **to be ~** keinen Anlass zu Kontroversen bieten; **nonconvertible** ADJ (*Fin*) nicht konvertierbar; **noncooperation** N unkooperative Haltung; **noncooperative** ADJ unkooperativ; **non-deciduous** [ˌnɒndɪ'sɪdjʊəs] ADJ (*Bot*) *tree* immergrün; *leaves* nicht abfallend; **non-delivery** N Nichtlieferung *f*; **nondenominational** ADJ konfessionslos; **non-departure** N (*of train, flight*) Ausfall *m*

nondescript ['nɒndɪskrɪpt] ADJ *taste, colour* unbestimmt; *person, appearance* unauffällig, unscheinbar (*pej*)

non: nondetachable ADJ *handle, hood etc* nicht abnehmbar, fest angebracht; *lining* nicht ausknöpfbar; (*without zip*) nicht ausreißbar; **nondiscrimination** N Nichtdiskriminierung *f* (*against, towards +gen*); **nondiscriminatory** ADJ nicht diskriminierend; **nondrinker** N Nichttrinker(in) *m(f)*; **she is a** ~ sie trinkt keinen Alkohol; **nondriver** N Nichtfahrer(in) *m(f)*; ~**s are ...** wer selbst nicht (Auto) fährt, ist ...; **non-dutiable** ADJ unverzollbar

none [nʌn] PRON keine(r, s), keine; (*on form*) keine; ~ **of the boys/the chairs/them** keiner der Jungen/Stühle/von ihnen; ~ **of the girls** keines der Mädchen; ~ **of this/the cake** nichts davon/von dem Kuchen; ~ **of this is any good** das ist alles nicht gut; ~ **of this money is mine** von dem Geld gehört mir nichts; **do you have any bread/apples?** – ~ (**at all**) haben Sie Brot/Äpfel? – nein, gar keine/keins; **there is** ~ **left** es ist nichts übrig; **money have I** ~ (*liter*) Geld hab ich keines; ~ **but** he nur er; **their guest was** ~ **other than ...** ihr Gast war kein anderer als ...;

there is ~ **better than him at climbing** niemand kann besser klettern als er; **but** ~ **of your silly jokes** aber lass bitte deine dummen Witze; **I want** ~ **of your excuses** und ich will keine Entschuldigungen hören; (**we'll have**) ~ **of that!** jetzt reichts aber!; **I want** ~ **of this/this nonsense** ich will davon/von diesem Unsinn nichts hören; **I'll have** ~ **of your rudeness** (*inf*) ich dulde diese Unhöflichkeit nicht; **he would have** ~ **of it** er wollte davon nichts wissen ADV **to be** ~ **the wiser** um nichts schlauer sein; **she looks** ~ **the worse for her ordeal** trotz allem, was sie durchzustehen hatte, sieht sie gut aus; **it's** ~ **too warm** es ist nicht *or* keineswegs zu warm; **he was** ~ **too happy about it** er war darüber gar nicht erfreut; ~ **too sure/easy** durchaus nicht sicher/einfach

nonentity [nɒ'nentɪtɪ] N (= *person*) Nullität *f*, unbedeutende Figur

nonessential [nɒnɪ'senʃəl] ADJ unnötig; *workers* nicht unbedingt nötig; *services* nicht lebenswichtig N **nonessentials** PL nicht (lebens-)notwendige Dinge *pl*

nonetheless [ˌnʌnðə'les] ✪ 26.3 ADV nichtsdestoweniger, trotzdem

non: nonevent N (*inf*) Reinfall *m* (*inf*), Pleite *f* (*inf*), Schlag *m* ins Wasser (*inf*); **nonexecutive** ADJ **in a** ~ **capacity** ohne Entscheidungsbefugnis; ~ **director** ≈ Aufsichtsratsmitglied *nt* (*ohne Entscheidungsbefugnis*); **nonexistence** N Nichtvorhandensein *nt*; (*Philos*) Nichtexistenz *f*; **nonexistent** ADJ nicht vorhanden; (*Philos*) nicht existent; **discipline is practically** ~ **here** hier herrscht praktisch keine Disziplin; **non-fat** ADJ *diet* fettlos; *food* fettarm; **non-fat creamer** N milchfreier Kaffeeweißer; **non-fat milk** N Milchersatz *m* (*auf pflanzlicher Basis*); **nonfattening** ADJ nicht dick machend *attr*; *fruit is* ~ Obst macht nicht dick; **nonferrous** ADJ nicht eisenhaltig; **nonfiction** N Sachbücher *pl* ADJ ~ **book/publication** Sachbuch *nt*; ~ **department** Sachbuchabteilung *f*; **nonfinite** ADJ (*Gram*) infinit; **nonflammable** ADJ nichtentzündbar, nicht entzündbar; **nonflowering** ADJ nichtblühend, nicht blühend; **nonhereditary** ADJ nichtvererbbar, nicht vererbbar; *disease also* nichtvererblich, nicht vererblich; **non-impact printer** N Non-Impact-Drucker *m*, anschlagfreier Drucker; **non-infectious** ADJ nichtansteckend, nicht ansteckend, nicht infektiös (*form*); **non-inflammable** ADJ nicht feuergefährlich; **non-interest-bearing** ADJ zinslos, unverzinslich; **non-interference** N Nichteinmischung *f* (*in* in +*acc*); **nonintervention** N (*Pol etc*) Nichteinmischung *f*, Nichteingreifen *nt* (*in* in +*acc*); **noninterventionist** ADJ *policy* der Nichteinmischung; **noniron** ADJ bügelfrei; **non-league** ADJ (*Brit, Sport*) außerhalb der Spitzenligen, Amateur-; ~ **football** Amateurfußball *m*; **non-medical practitioner** N Heilpraktiker(in) *m(f)*; **nonmember** N Nichtmitglied *nt*; (*of society also*) Nichtangehörige(r) *mf*; **open to** ~**s** Gäste willkommen; **non-migratory** ADJ ~ **bird** Standvogel *m*, Nichtzieher *m* (*spec*); **non-milk** ADJ ~ **fat(s)** nichttierische *or* nicht tierische Fette *pl*; **non-negotiable** ADJ *ticket* nicht übertragbar; **the price is** ~ über den Preis lässt sich nicht verhandeln; **non-nuclear** ADJ *weapons, forces, energy* nicht nuklear; *world* atomwaffenfrei; ~ **state** Nichtnuklearstaat *m*

no-no ['nəʊnəʊ] N (*inf*) **that's/she's a** ~! das/sie kommt nicht infrage *or* in Frage! (*inf*); **that's a** ~! (= *you mustn't do it*) das gibts nicht!

non: non-obligatory ADJ freiwillig, nicht Pflicht, freigestellt *pred*; **non-observance** N Nicht(be)achtung *f*

no-nonsense ['nəʊˌnɒnsəns] ADJ (kühl und) sachlich, nüchtern

non: nonpareil [nɒnpə'reɪl] ADJ (*liter*) unerreicht N (*liter*) (= *thing*) Nonplusultra *nt*; (= *person*) unerreichter Meister; **nonpartisan** ADJ unparteiisch; **nonpayment** N Nichtzahlung *f*, Zahlungsverweigerung *f*; **nonperishable** ADJ dauerhaft, haltbar; **non-person** N Unperson *f*

nonplus ['nɒn'plʌs] VT verblüffen; **completely** ~**sed** völlig verdutzt *or* verblüfft

non: nonpoisonous ADJ nicht giftig, ungiftig; **nonpolitical** ADJ nichtpolitisch, nicht politisch; **nonpolluting** ADJ umweltschonend; **nonporous** ADJ nichtporös, nicht porös; **nonproductive** ADJ ~ **industries** Dienstleistungssektor *m*; ~ **worker** Angestellte(r) *mf* im Dienstleistungssektor; **non-profit-making**, (*US*) **nonprofit** ADJ keinen Gewinn anstrebend *attr*; *charity etc also* gemeinnützig; **on a** ~ **basis** auf gemeinnütziger Basis; **nonproliferation** N Nichtverbreitung *f* von Atomwaffen; ~ **treaty** Atomsperrvertrag *m*; **nonpublication** N Nichterscheinen *nt*; **nonradioactive** ADJ *substance* nicht radioaktiv, strahlenfrei; **nonreader** N Analphabet(in) *m(f)*; **there are still five** ~**s in this class** in dieser Klasse können fünf Schüler noch nicht lesen; **nonrecognition** N Nichtanerkennung *f*; **nonrefillable** ADJ Wegwerf-, Einweg-; ~ **bottle** Wegwerf- *or* Einwegflasche *f*; **nonresident** ADJ nicht ansässig; (*in hotel*) nicht im Hause wohnend N Nicht(orts)ansässige(r) *mf*; (*in hotel*) nicht im Haus wohnender Gast; **open to** ~**s** auch für Nichthotelgäste; **nonreturnable** ADJ ~ **bottle** Einwegflasche *f*; ~ **deposit** Anzahlung *f*; **non-run** ADJ (*esp US*) *stockings* maschenfest, laufmaschensicher; **non-scene** N (*inf*) *gay* der nicht zur Szene gehört; **nonscheduled** ADJ *flight, train* außerplanmäßig; **nonsectarian** ADJ nichtkonfessionell, nicht konfessionell; *assembly* nicht konfessionsgebunden

nonsense ['nɒnsəns] N , *no pl* (*also as interjection*) Unsinn *m*, Quatsch *m* (*inf*), Nonsens *m* (*geh*); (*verbal also*) dummes Zeug; (= *silly behaviour*) Dummheiten *pl*; **a piece of** ~ ein Quatsch *m* (*inf*) *or* Unsinn *m*; **that's a lot of** ~! das ist (ja) alles dummes Zeug!; **I've had enough of this** ~ jetzt reichts mir aber; **to make (a)** ~ **of sth** etw ad absurdum führen, etw sinnlos machen; **what's all this** ~ **about a cut in salary/about them not wanting to go?** was soll all das Gerede von einer Gehaltskürzung/all das Gerede, dass sie nicht mitgehen wollen?; **no more of your** ~! Schluss mit dem Unsinn!; **and no** ~ und keine Dummheiten; **I will stand** *or* **have no** ~ **from you** ich werde keinen Unsinn *or* keine Dummheiten dulden; **he will stand no** ~ **from anybody** er lässt nicht mit sich spaßen; **he won't stand any** ~ **over that** was das betrifft, verträgt er keinen Spaß; **a man with no** ~ **about him** ein nüchterner *or* kühler und sachlicher Mensch → **stuff** N a

nonsense verse N Nonsensvers *m*, Unsinnsvers *m*; (= *genre*) Nonsensverse *pl*, Unsinnsverse *pl*

nonsensical [nɒn'sensɪkəl] ADJ *idea, action* unsinnig

nonsensically [nɒn'sensɪkəlɪ] ADV *argue etc* unsinnigerweise

non sequitur [ˌnɒn'sekwɪtəʳ] N unlogische (Schluss)folgerung

non: nonshrink ADJ nicht einlaufend; **to be** ~ nicht einlaufen; **nonskid** ADJ rutschsicher; **nonslip** ADJ rutschfest; **nonsmoker** N (= *person*) Nichtraucher(in) *m(f)* b (*Rail*) Nichtraucherabteil *nt*; **nonsmoking** ADJ Nichtraucher-; ~ **area** *or* **section** Nichtraucherbereich *m*; **we have a** ~ **policy** bei uns herrscht Rauchverbot, bei uns darf nicht geraucht werden; **nonspecific** ADJ a (*Med*) unspezifisch b (= *imprecise*) allgemein; **nonstandard** ADJ nicht der Norm entsprechend; (= *not usually supplied*) *fittings* nicht üblich; ~ **size** Sondergröße *f*; **nonstarter** N a (*in race*) (= *person*) Nichtstartende(r) *mf*; (= *horse*) nicht startendes Pferd; **there were two** ~**s** zwei traten nicht an b (*fig*) (= *idea*) Blindgänger *m*; (= *person*) Blindgänger(in) *m(f)*; **nonstick** ADJ *pan, surface* kunststoffbeschichtet, Teflon-®; **nonstop** ADJ *train* durchgehend; *journey, performances* ohne Unterbrechung; *music* dauernd; ~ **flight** Nonstopflug *m*, Non-Stop-Flug *m* ADV *talk, work* ununterbrochen; *fly* nonstop; *travel* ohne Unterbrechung, nonstop; **non-survival** N Aussterben *nt*; **nonswimmer** N Nichtschwimmer(in) *m(f)*; **nontaxable** ADJ nicht steuerpflichtig; **nontechnical** ADJ *language etc* für den Laien verständlich; *subject* nichttechnisch, nicht technisch; ~ **people** technische Laien *pl*; **nontoxic** ADJ ungiftig; **non-U** ADJ *(Brit)* charakteristisch für die Gewohnheiten, Sprechweise etc des Kleinbürgertums, nicht vornehm; **nonunion** ADJ *worker, labour* nicht organisiert; **nonverbal** ADJ *communication* nichtverbal, nicht verbal, wortlos, ohne Worte; **nonviolence** N Gewaltlosigkeit *f*; **nonviolent** ADJ gewaltlos; *crime, offender* nicht gewalttätig; **nonvocational** ADJ *subject, course* nicht berufsorientiert; **nonvolatile** ADJ *(Chem, Comput)* nicht flüchtig; **nonvoter** N Nichtwähler(in) *m(f)*; **nonvoting** ADJ ~ **shares** stimmrechtslose Aktien *pl*; **non-White** Ⓝ Farbige(r) *mf* ADJ farbig

noodle ['nu:dl] N ⓐ *(Cook)* Nudel *f* ⓑ *(dated inf, = fool)* Dummerjan *m (dated inf)* ⓒ *(US, inf, = head)* Birne *f (inf)*; **use your** ~ streng deinen Grips an *(inf)*

nook [nʊk] N *(= corner)* Ecke *f*, Winkel *m*; *(= remote spot)* Winkel *m*; **a shady** ~ ein schattiges Fleckchen; **a cosy** ~ ein gemütliches Eckchen; **in every** ~ **and cranny** in jedem Winkel

nooky, nookie ['nʊkɪ] N *(inf)* **to have a bit of** ~ (ein bisschen) bumsen *(inf)*

noon [nu:n] Ⓝ Mittag *m*; **at** ~ um 12 Uhr mittags ADJ 12-Uhr-; *deadline* bis 12 Uhr; ~ **flight** 12-Uhr-Flug *m*

noonday ['nu:ndeɪ] ADJ *attr* Mittags-, mittäglich; ~ **sun** Mittagssonne *f*

no-one, **no one** ['nəʊwʌn] PRON = **nobody** PRON

noon: noontide N *(liter)* = **noontime; noontime** *(esp US)* Ⓝ Mittagszeit *f*, Mittagsstunde *f (geh)*; **at** ~ um die Mittagsstunde *(geh)* ADJ *meal, sun, light, class, service, crowd* zur Mittagszeit

noose [nu:s] N Schlinge *f*; **to put one's head in the** ~ *(prov)* den Kopf in die Schlinge stecken

no-passing zone N *(US: Mot)* Überholverbotszone *f*

nope [nəʊp] ADV *(inf)* ne(e) *(dial)*, nein

no place ADV *(esp US inf)* = **nowhere**

nor [nɔ:] CONJ ⓐ noch; **neither ...** ~ weder ... noch ⓑ *(= and not)* und ... auch nicht; **I shan't go,** ~ **will you** ich gehe nicht, und du auch nicht; ~ **do/have/am I** ich auch nicht; ~ **was this all** und das war noch nicht alles

Nordic ['nɔ:dɪk] ADJ nordisch

nor'east [nɔ:'ri:st] *(Naut)* = **northeast**

norm [nɔ:m] N Norm *f*; **our** ~ **is ...** unsere Norm liegt bei ...

normal ['nɔ:məl] Ⓝ ⓐ normal; *(= customary)* üblich; **it's a perfectly** *or* **quite a** ~ **thing** das ist völlig normal; **it's perfectly** ~ **for you to feel that way** es ist vollkommen normal, dass Sie so empfinden; **it's** ~ **practice** das ist so üblich; ~ **temperature/consumption/output** Normaltemperatur *f*/-verbrauch *m*/-leistung *f*; **he is not his** ~ **self today** er ist heute so anders; **a higher than** ~ **risk of infection** ein Infektionsrisiko, das über dem Normalen liegt ⓑ *(Math)* senkrecht ⓒ *(Chem)* ~ **solution** Normallösung *f* Ⓝ *no pl (of temperature)* Normalwert *m*, Durchschnitt *m*; *(Math)* Senkrechte *f*; *(to tangent)* Normale *f*; **temperatures below** ~ Temperaturen unter dem Durchschnitt; **her temperature is below/above** ~ sie hat Untertemperatur/erhöhte Temperatur; **when things/we are back to** *or* **return to** ~ wenn sich alles wieder normalisiert hat; **just carry on as** ~ machen Sie einfach normal weiter; **life went on as** ~ das Leben ging normal weiter

normalcy ['nɔ:məlsɪ] N = **normality**

normal hill N *(ski jumping)* Normalschanze *f*

normality [nɔ:'mælɪtɪ] N Normalität *f*; **the return to** ~ **after war** die Normalisierung (des Le-

bens) *or* die Wiederaufnahme eines normalen Lebens nach dem Krieg; **to return to** ~ sich wieder normalisieren; **despite his apparent** ~ obwohl er ganz normal zu sein scheint

normalization [nɔ:məlaɪˈzeɪʃən] N Normalisierung *f*

normalize ['nɔ:məlaɪz] VT normalisieren; *relations* wieder herstellen; **to be ~d** sich normalisiert haben

normally ['nɔ:məlɪ] ADV *(= usually)* normalerweise, gewöhnlich; *(= in normal way)* normal

normal school N *(US, old)* pädagogische Hochschule

Norman ['nɔ:mən] ADJ normannisch; **the** ~ **Conquest** der normannische Eroberungszug Ⓝ Normanne *m*, Normannin *f*

Normandy ['nɔ:məndɪ] N Normandie *f*

normative ['nɔ:mətɪv] ADJ normativ

nor'-nor'east [nɔ:nɔ:'ri:st] *(Naut)* = **north-north-east**

nor'-nor'west [nɔ:nɔ:'west] *(Naut)* = **north-northwest**

Norse [nɔ:s] ADJ *mythology* altnordisch Ⓝ *(Ling)* **Old** ~ Altnordisch *nt*

Norse: Norseman N *(Hist)* Normanne *m*, Wikinger *m*; **Norsewoman** N *(Hist)* Normannin *f*, Wikingerin *f*

north [nɔ:θ] Ⓝ ⓐ Norden *m*; **in/from the** ~ im/aus dem Norden; **to live in the** ~ im Norden leben; **to the** ~ **of** nördlich von, im Norden von; **to veer/go to the** ~ in nördliche Richtung *or* nach Norden drehen/gehen; **the wind is in the** ~ es ist Nordwind; **to face (the)** ~ nach Norden liegen; **the North (of Scotland/England)** Nordschottland/-england *nt* ⓑ *(US Hist)* **the North** der Norden, die Nordstaaten *pl* ADJ *attr* Nord-; **North German** norddeutsch ADV *(= towards North)* nach Norden, gen Norden *(liter)*, nordwärts *(liter, Naut)*; *(Met)* in nördliche Richtung; ~ **of** nördlich *or* im Norden von

north *in cpds* Nord-; **North Africa** N Nordafrika *nt*; **North African** ADJ nordafrikanisch Ⓝ Nordafrikaner(in) *m(f)*; **North America** N Nordamerika *nt*; **North American** ADJ nordamerikanisch Ⓝ Nordamerikaner(in) *m(f)*

Northants [nɔ:'θænts] *abbr of* **Northamptonshire**

north: North Atlantic N Nordatlantik *m*; **northbound** ADJ *carriageway* nach Norden (führend); *traffic* in Richtung Norden; **north country** N **the** ~ Nordengland *nt*; **north-country** ADJ nordenglisch; **North Dakota** ['nɔ:θdə'kəʊtə] N Norddakota *nt*; **northeast** Ⓝ Nordosten *m*, Nordost *m (esp Naut)*; **in the** ~ im Nordosten; **from the** ~ von Nordost ADJ Nordost-, nordöstlich; ~ **England** Nordostengland *nt* ADV nach Nordosten; ~ **of** nordöstlich von; **northeasterly** ADJ nordöstlich Ⓝ *(= wind)* Nordostwind *m*; **northeastern** ADJ *provinces* nordöstlich, im Nordosten; **northeastwards** ADV nordostwärts, nach Nordosten

northerly ['nɔ:ðəlɪ] ADJ *wind, direction, latitude* nördlich ADV nach Norden, nordwärts *(liter, Naut)* Ⓝ Nordwind *m*

northern ['nɔ:ðən] ADJ *hemisphere, counties* nördlich; ~ **Germany/Italy** Norddeutschland/-italien *nt*; **Northern Irish** nordirisch; **with a** ~ **outlook** mit Blick nach Norden

northerner ['nɔ:ðənə'] Ⓝ ⓐ Bewohner(in) *m(f)* des Nordens, Nordengländer(in) *m(f)*/-deutsche(r) *mf etc*; **he is a** ~ er kommt aus dem Norden (des Landes) ⓑ *(US)* Nordstaatler(in) *m(f)*

Northern Ireland N Nordirland *nt*

northern lights PL **the** ~ das Nordlicht

northernmost ['nɔ:ðənməʊst] ADJ *area* nördlichste(r, s)

northing ['nɔ:ðɪŋ] N ⓐ *(Astron)* nördliche Deklination *(eines Planeten)* ⓑ *(= Naut)* Weg *m* *or* Distanz *f* nach Norden

north: North Korea N Nordkorea *nt*; **North Korean** ADJ nordkoreanisch Ⓝ Nordkoreaner(in) *m(f)*; **north-northeast** Ⓝ Nordnord-

osten *m*, Nordnordost *m (esp Naut)* ADJ nordnordöstlich ADV nach Nordnordost(en); ~ **of** nordnordöstlich von; **north-northwest** Ⓝ Nordnordwesten *m*, Nordnordwest *m (esp Naut)* ADJ nordnordwestlich ADV nach Nordnordwest(en); ~ **of** nordnordwestlich von; **North Pole** N Nordpol *m*; **North Sea** Ⓝ Nordsee *f* ADJ Nordsee-; ~ **gas/oil** Nordseegas *nt*/-öl *nt*; **North-South divide** N Nord-Süd-Gefälle *nt*

North Star N Nordstern *m*

Northumb *(Brit) abbr of* **Northumberland**

north: North Vietnam N Nordvietnam *nt*; **North Vietnamese** ADJ nordvietnamesisch Ⓝ Nordvietnamese *m*/-vietnamesin *f*; **northward** ADJ nördlich; **in a** ~ **direction** nach Norden, (in) Richtung Norden ADV *(also* **northwards)** nach Norden, nordwärts; **northwardly** ADJ, ADV = **northward; northwest** Ⓝ Nordwesten *m*, Nordwest *m (esp Naut)* ADJ Nordwest-, nordwestlich; ~ **England** Nordwestengland *nt*; **the Northwest Passage** die Nordwestpassage ADV nach Nordwest(en); ~ **of** nordwestlich von; **northwesterly** ADJ nordwestlich Ⓝ Nordwestwind *m*

Norway ['nɔ:weɪ] N Norwegen *nt*

Norwegian [nɔ:'wi:dʒən] ADJ norwegisch Ⓝ ⓐ Norweger(in) *m(f)* ⓑ *(Ling)* Norwegisch *nt*

nor'west [nɔ:'west] *(Naut)* = **northwest**

Nos., **nos.** *abbr of* **numbers** Nrn.

nose [nəʊz] Ⓝ ⓐ Nase *f*; **to hold one's** ~ sich *(dat)* die Nase zuhalten; **to speak through one's** ~ durch die Nase sprechen; **the tip of one's** ~ die Nasenspitze; **my** ~ **is bleeding** ich habe Nasenbluten; **follow your** ~ immer der Nase nach; **she always has her** ~ **in a book** sie hat dauernd den Kopf in einem Buch (vergraben); **to do sth under sb's (very)** ~ etw vor jds Augen tun; **it was right under his** ~ **all the time** er hatte es die ganze Zeit direkt vor der Nase; **I just followed my** ~ ich bin immer der Nase nach gegangen; **she leads him by the** ~ er tanzt ganz nach ihrer Pfeife *(inf)*; **don't let him lead you by the** ~ lass dich von ihm nicht unterbuttern!; **he can't see beyond** *or* **further than the end of his** ~ er kann nicht weiter sehen, als sein eigener Schatten reicht; **to get up sb's** ~ *(fig inf)* jdm auf den Geist *or* auf die Nerven gehen *(inf)*; **to poke** *or* **stick one's** ~ **into sth** *(fig)* seine Nase in etw *(acc)* stecken; **you keep your** ~ **out of this** *(inf)* halt du dich da raus *(inf)*; **to cut off one's** ~ **to spite one's face** *(prov)* sich ins eigene Fleisch schneiden; **to look down one's** ~ **at sb/sth** auf jdn/etw herabblicken; **with one's** ~ **in the air** mit hoch erhobenem Kopf, hochnäsig; **to pay through the** ~ *(inf)* viel blechen *(inf)*, sich dumm und dämlich zahlen *(inf)*; **to win by a** ~ *(horse)* um eine Nasenlänge gewinnen; **to put sb's** ~ **out of joint** jdn vor den Kopf stoßen; **his** ~ **is out of joint over this** er fühlt sich dadurch vor den Kopf gestoßen; **to keep one's** ~ **clean** *(inf)* sauber bleiben *(inf)*, eine saubere Weste behalten *(inf)*; **to pay on the** ~ sofort bezahlen ⓑ *(= sense of smell)* Nase *f*; *(fig)* Riecher *m* (*inf*), Nase *f*; **to have a ~ for sth** (*fig*) eine Nase or einen Riecher (*inf*) für etw haben

c (*of wines*) Blume *f*

d (*of plane*) Nase *f*; (*of car*) Schnauze *f*; (*of boat*) Bug *m*; (*of torpedo*) Kopf *m*; **~ to tail** (*cars*) Stoßstange an Stoßstange

VT **the car/ship ~d its way through the fog** das Auto/Schiff tastete sich durch den Nebel; **the car ~d its way into the stream of traffic** das Auto schob sich in den fließenden Verkehr vor; **I ~d the car toward(s) the gate** ich manövrierte das Auto langsam zum Tor

VI **a boat ~d through the mist** ein Boot tastete sich durch den Nebel; **the car ~d forward** das Auto schob sich langsam vor; **to ~ into sb's affairs** (*fig*) seine Nase in jds Angelegenheiten (*acc*) stecken (*inf*)

▶**nose about** (*Brit*) or **around** VI herumschnüffeln (*inf*); (*person also*) herumspionieren (*inf*)

▶**nose out** **VT** *sep* (*Brit inf*) aufspüren; *secret, scandal* ausspionieren (*inf*), ausschnüffeln (*inf*) **VI** (*car*) sich vorschieben

nose: **nosebag** N Futtersack *m*; **noseband** N Nasenriemen *m*; **nosebleed** N Nasenbluten *nt*; **to have a ~** Nasenbluten haben; **nose cone** N (*Aviat*) Raketenspitze *f*; **nosedive** **N** (*Aviat*) Sturzflug *m*; **to go into a ~** zum Sturzflug ansetzen; **the car/he took a ~ into the sea** das Auto stürzte vornüber/er stürzte kopfüber ins Meer; **the company's profits took a ~** mit der Firma ging es rapide bergab; **his career took a ~** seine Karriere nahm einen scharfen Knick nach unten; **his reputation took a ~** sein Ruf nahm starken Schaden **VI** (*plane*) im Sturzflug herabgehen; (*fig: career, reputation*) den Bach runtergehen (*inf*); **to ~ off sth** vornüber von etw stürzen; (*person*) kopfüber von etw stürzen; **nosedrops** PL Nasentropfen *pl*; **nose flute** N Nasenflöte *f*; **nosegay** N (*Biedermeier*)sträußchen *nt*; **nose job** N (*inf*) Nasenkorrektur *f*; **to have a ~** sich einer Nasenkorrektur unterziehen; **nose-picking** N Nasenbohren *nt*; **nose ring** N Nasenring *m*; **nosewheel** N Bugrad *nt*

nosey ADJ = **nosy**

nosey parker [ˌnəʊzɪˈpɑːkə] N (*Brit inf*) Schnüffler(in) *m(f)* (*inf*); **I don't like ~s** ich mag Leute nicht, die ihre Nase in alles stecken (*inf*); **~!** sei doch nicht so neugierig!

nosh [nɒʃ] (*Brit sl*) **N** (= *food*) Futter *nt* (*inf*); (= *meal*) Schmaus *m*; **to have some ~** was essen or futtern (*inf*) **VI** futtern (*inf*)

no-show ['nəʊʃəʊ] N (*Aviat*) No-Show *m*, fehlender Flugpassagier

nosh-up ['nɒʃʌp] N (*Brit inf*) Schmaus *m*, Fressgelage *nt* (*inf*)

nostalgia [nɒsˈtældʒɪə] N Nostalgie *f* (*for nach*); **to feel ~ for sth** sich nach etw zurücksehnen

nostalgic [nɒsˈtældʒɪk] ADJ nostalgisch; (= *wistful*) wehmütig; **to feel/be ~ for** or **about sth** sich nach etw zurücksehnen

nostalgically [nɒsˈtældʒɪklɪ] ADV nostalgisch; (= *wistfully*) wehmütig; **they look back ~ to the war** sie blicken mit Nostalgie auf den Krieg zurück

no-strike ['nəʊstraɪk] ADJ *attr* **~ deal/agreement** Streikverzichtabkommen *nt*

nostril ['nɒstrəl] N Nasenloch *nt*; (*of horse, zebra etc*) Nüster *f*

nostrum ['nɒstrəm] N (*old lit, fig*) Patentrezept *nt*

nosy ['nəʊzɪ] ADJ (+*er*) (*inf*) neugierig

not [nɒt] ADV **a** nicht; **he told me ~ to come/to do that** er sagte, ich solle nicht kommen/ich solle nicht tun; **do ~** or **don't come** kommen Sie nicht; **that's how ~ to do it** so sollte man das nicht machen; **he was wrong in ~ making a protest** es war falsch von ihm, nicht zu protestieren; **~ wanting to be heard, he ~** da er nicht gehört werden wollte, ... er ...; **~ I!** ich nicht!; **fear ~!** (*old*) fürchte dich nicht!

b (*emphatic*) nicht; **~ a sound/word etc** kein Ton/Wort *etc*, nicht EIN Ton/Wort *etc*; **~ a bit**

kein bisschen; **~ a sign of ...** keine Spur von ...; **~ one of them** kein Einziger, nicht einer; **~ a thing** überhaupt nichts; **they were here ~ ten minutes ago** vor nicht einmal zehn Minuten waren sie noch hier; **~ any more** nicht mehr; **~ yet** noch nicht; **~ even** nicht einmal; **~ so** (*as reply*) nein; **say ~ so** (*old*) sag, dass es nicht wahr ist

c (*in tag or rhetorical questions*) **it's hot, isn't it?** or (*form*) **is it ~?** es ist heiß, nicht wahr or nicht? (*inf*) **isn't it hot?** (es ist) heiß, nicht wahr?, ist das vielleicht heiß!; **isn't he naughty!** ist er nicht frech?, (er ist) ganz schön frech, nicht! (*inf*) **you are coming, aren't you** or **are you ~?** Sie kommen doch, oder?; **you have got it, haven't you?** Sie haben es doch, oder?, Sie haben es, nicht wahr?; **you like it, don't you?** or (*form*) **do you ~?** das gefällt dir, nicht (wahr)?; **you are ~ angry, are you?** Sie sind nicht böse, oder?; **you are ~ angry - or are you?** Sie sind doch nicht etwa böse?

d (*as substitute for clause*) nicht; **is he coming? – I hope/I believe ~** kommt er? – ich hoffe/glaube nicht; **it would seem** or **appear ~** anscheinend nicht; **he's decided ~ to do it – I should think/hope ~** er hat sich entschlossen, es nicht zu tun – das möchte ich auch meinen/hoffen

e (*elliptically*) **are you cold? – ~ at all** ist dir kalt? – überhaupt or gar nicht; **thank you very much – ~ at all** vielen Dank – keine Ursache or gern geschehen; **~ in the least** überhaupt or gar nicht, nicht im Geringsten; **~ that I care** nicht, dass es mir etwas ausmacht(e); **~ that I know of** nicht, dass ich wüsste; **it's ~ that I don't believe him** ich glaube ihm ja, es ist ja nicht so, dass ich ihm nicht glaube

notability [ˌnəʊtəˈbɪlɪtɪ] N **a** (= *person*) bedeutende Persönlichkeit; **the notabilities of the town** die Honoratioren *pl* der Stadt **b** (= *eminence*) Berühmtheit *f*, Bedeutung *f*

notable ['nəʊtəbl] **ADJ** (= *eminent*) *person* bedeutend; (= *worthy of note*) *success, fact, event also* bemerkenswert, beachtenswert (*for wegen*); (= *big*) *difference, improvement* beträchtlich, beachtlich; (= *conspicuous*) auffallend; **with a few ~ exceptions** bis auf einige rühmliche Ausnahmen; **he was ~ by his absence** er glänzte durch Abwesenheit **N** = **notability a**

notably ['nəʊtəblɪ] ADV **a** (= *strikingly*) auffallend; *improved, different* beträchtlich; **to be ~ absent** durch Abwesenheit glänzen; **they were ~ unimpressed** sie zeigten sich bemerkenswert unbeeindruckt **b** (= *in particular*) hauptsächlich, insbesondere; **most ~** vor allem

notarial [nəʊˈtɛərɪəl] ADJ *seal, deed, style* notariell; *fees* Notar-

notarize ['nəʊtəraɪz] VT notariell beglaubigen

notary (public) ['nəʊtərɪ('pʌblɪk)] N Notar(in) *m(f)*

notate [nəʊˈteɪt] VT (*Mus*) in Notenschrift schreiben

notation [nəʊˈteɪʃən] N **a** (= *system*) Zeichensystem *nt*, Notation *f* (*spec*); (= *symbols*) Zeichen *pl*; (*Mus*) Notenschrift *f*, Notation *f* **b** (= *note*) Notiz *f*, Anmerkung *f*

notch [nɒtʃ] **N** Kerbe *f*; (*of handbrake, for adjustment etc*) Raste *f*; (*in belt*) Loch *nt*; (*on damaged blade etc*) Scharte *f*; (*US Geog*) Schlucht *f*; **to cut a ~ in sth** eine Kerbe in etw (*acc*) machen; **our team is a ~ above theirs** unsere Mannschaft ist eine Klasse besser als ihre → **top-notch** **VT** einkerben; einschneiden; (*esp Sport*) *win, success* verzeichnen können

▶**notch up** VT *sep score, points* erzielen, einheimsen (*inf*); *record* erringen, verzeichnen; *success* verzeichnen können

note [nəʊt] ✪ 20.7, 26.3 **N** **a** Notiz *f*, Anmerkung *f*; (= *footnote*) Anmerkung *f*, Fußnote *f*; (*official: in file etc*) Vermerk *m*; (= *diplomatic note*) Note *f*; (= *informal letter*) Briefchen *nt*, paar Zeilen *pl*; **~s** (= *summary*) Aufzeichnungen *pl*; (= *plan, draft*) Konzept *nt*; **a few rough ~s** ein paar Stichworte *pl*; **lecture ~s** (*professor's*) Manuskript *nt*; (*student's*) Aufzeichnungen *pl*; (=

handout) Vorlesungsskript *nt*; **to speak without ~s** frei sprechen, ohne Vorlage sprechen; **to speak from ~s** (von einer Vorlage) ablesen; **"Author's Note"** „Anmerkung des Verfassers"; **exchange of ~s** (*Pol*) Notenaustausch *m*; **to send/leave sb a ~** jdm ein paar Zeilen schicken; **to write a hasty ~** schnell ein paar Zeilen schreiben; **to take** or **make ~s** Notizen machen; (*in lecture also, in interrogation*) mitschreiben; **to make ~s on a case** (sich *dat*) Notizen zu einem Fall machen; **to take** or **make a ~ of sth** sich (*dat*) etw notieren

b *no pl* (= *notice*) **to take ~ of sth** von etw Notiz nehmen, etw zur Kenntnis nehmen; (= *heed*) einer Sache (*dat*) Beachtung schenken; **take no ~ of what he says** nehmen Sie keine Notiz von dem, was er sagt, achten Sie nicht darauf, was er sagt; **take ~ of what I tell you** hören Sie auf das, was ich zu sagen habe; **worthy of ~** beachtenswert, erwähnenswert

c *no pl* (= *importance*) **a man of ~** ein bedeutender Mann; **nothing of ~** nichts Beachtens- or Erwähnenswertes

d (*Mus*) (= *sign*) Note *f*; (= *sound: on piano etc*) Ton *m*; (= *song of bird etc*) Lied *nt*, Gesang *m*; **to give the ~** den Ton angeben; **to play/sing the right/wrong ~** richtig/falsch spielen/singen; **to strike the right ~** (*fig*) den richtigen Ton treffen; **it struck a wrong** or **false ~** (*fig*) da hat er *etc* sich im Ton vergriffen; (= *wasn't genuine*) es klang nicht echt

e (= *quality, tone*) Ton *m*, Klang *m*; **on a personal ~** persönlich gesprochen; **on a more optimistic/positive ~** aus optimistischer/positiver Sicht; **his voice took on a ~ of desperation** aus seiner Stimme klang Verzweiflung, seine Stimme hatte einen verzweifelten Klang; **a ~ of nostalgia** eine nostalgische Note; **to sound** or **strike a ~ of warning** warnen; **to sound a ~ of caution** zur Vorsicht mahnen; **there was a ~ of warning in his voice** seine Stimme hatte einen warnenden Unterton

f (*Brit Fin*) Note *f*, Schein *m*; **a £5 ~, a five-pound ~** eine Fünfpfundnote, ein Fünfpfundschein *m*

VT **a** (= *notice*) bemerken; (= *take note of*) zur Kenntnis nehmen; (= *pay attention to*) beachten **b** = **note down**

▶**note down** VT *sep* notieren, aufschreiben; (*as reminder*) sich (*dat*) notieren or aufschreiben

note: **notebook** N Notizbuch or -heft *nt*; (= *computer*) Notebook *nt*, Notebookcomputer *m*; **notecase** N Brieftasche *f*

noted ['nəʊtɪd] ADJ bekannt, berühmt (*for für, wegen*)

notelet ['nəʊtlɪt] N Briefkarte *f*

note: **notepad** N Notizblock *m*; **notepaper** N Briefpapier *nt*; **note row** ['nəʊtrəʊ] N (*twelve-tone music*) Reihe *f*

noteworthy ['nəʊtwɜːðɪ] ADJ beachtenswert, erwähnenswert

nothing ['nʌθɪŋ] **N, PRON, ADV** **a** nichts; **~ pleases him** nichts gefällt ihm, ihm gefällt nichts; **~ could be easier** nichts wäre einfacher; **it was reduced to ~** es blieb nichts davon übrig; **she is five foot ~** (*inf*) sie ist genau fünf Fuß; **it was all or ~** es ging um alles oder nichts

b (*with vb*) nichts; **she is** or **means ~ to him** sie bedeutet ihm nichts; **£500 is ~ to her** £ 500 sind für sie gar nichts; **she is ~ (compared) to her sister** sie ist nichts im Vergleich zu ihrer Schwester; **that's ~ to what is to come** das ist noch gar nichts im Vergleich zu dem, was noch kommen wird; **it came to ~** da ist nichts draus geworden; **I can make ~ of it** das sagt mir nichts, ich werde daraus nicht schlau; **he thinks ~ of doing that** er findet nichts dabei(, das zu tun); **think ~ of it** keine Ursache!; **will you come? – ~ doing!** (*inf*) kommst du? – ausgeschlossen! or kein Gedanke (*inf*); **there was ~ doing at the club** (*inf*) im Klub war nichts los; **I tried, but there's ~ doing** (*inf*) ich habs versucht, aber keine Chance (*inf*) or aber da ist nichts zu machen

c (with prep) **all his fame stood** or **counted for ~** (liter) sein Ruhm galt nichts; **for ~** (= free, in vain) umsonst; **it's not for ~ that he's called X** er heißt nicht umsonst or ohne Grund X; **there's ~ (else) for it but to leave** da bleibt einem nichts übrig als zu gehen; **there's ~ (else) for it, we'll have to ...** da hilft alles nichts, wir müssen ...; **there was ~ in it for me** das hat sich für mich nicht gelohnt, ich hatte nichts davon; (financially also) dabei sprang nichts für mich heraus (inf); **there's ~ in the rumour** (Brit) or **rumor** (US) das Gerücht ist völlig unfundiert or aus der Luft gegriffen, an dem Gerücht ist nichts (Wahres); **that is ~ to you** für dich ist das doch gar nichts; (= isn't important) das kümmert or berührt dich nicht, das ist dir egal; **there's ~ to it** (inf) das ist kinderleicht (inf)

d (with adj, adv) **~ but** nur; **he does ~ but eat** er isst nur or ständig, er tut nichts anderes als essen; **~ else** sonst nichts; **~ more** sonst nichts; **I'd like ~ more than that** ich möchte nichts lieber als das; **I'd like ~ more than to go to Canada** ich würde (nur) zu gern nach Kanada gehen; **~ much** nicht viel; **~ less than** nur; **~ if not polite** äußerst or überaus höflich; **~ new** nichts Neues; **it was ~ like as big as we thought** es war lange nicht so groß, wie wir dachten

e **in ~ flat** (US inf) in null Komma nichts (inf); **you don't know from ~** (US inf) du hast (überhaupt) keine Ahnung (inf); **he has ~ on her** (inf) er kann ihr nicht das Wasser reichen (inf) **N** **a** (Math) Null f

b (= thing, person of no value) Nichts nt; **it's a mere ~ compared to what he spent last year** im Vergleich zu dem, was er letztes Jahr ausgegeben hat, ist das gar nichts; **it was a mere ~** das war doch nicht der Rede wert, das war doch nur eine winzige Kleinigkeit; **thank you – it was ~** danke – das war doch selbstverständlich; **don't apologize, it's ~** entschuldige dich nicht, es ist nicht der Rede wert; **what's wrong with you? – (it's) ~** was ist mit dir los? – nichts; **to whisper sweet ~s to sb** jdm Zärtlichkeiten ins Ohr flüstern

nothingness ['nʌθɪŋnɪs] N Nichts nt

no through road N **it's a ~** es ist keine Durchfahrt

no-throw ['nəʊ'θrəʊ] N Fehlwurf m

notice ['nəʊtɪs] **N** **a** (= warning, communication) Bescheid m, Benachrichtigung f; (= written notification) Mitteilung f; (of forthcoming event, film etc) Ankündigung f; **~ to pay** (Comm) Zahlungsaufforderung f; **final ~** letzte Aufforderung; **we need three weeks' ~** wir müssen drei Wochen vorher Bescheid wissen; **to give ~ of sth** von etw Bescheid geben; (of film, change etc) etw ankündigen; (of arrival etc) etw melden; **to give sb one week's ~ of sth** jdn eine Woche vorher von etw benachrichtigen, jdm eine Woche vorher über etw (acc) Bescheid geben; **to give sb ~ of sth** jdn von etw benachrichtigen, jdm etw mitteilen; **to give ~ of appeal** (Jur) Berufung einlegen; **we must give advance ~ of the meeting** wir müssen das Treffen ankündigen; **to give official ~ that ...** öffentlich bekannt geben, dass ...; (referring to future event) öffentlich ankündigen, dass ...; **without ~** ohne Ankündigung; (of arrival also) unangemeldet; **~ is hereby given that ...** hiermit wird bekannt gegeben, dass ...; **he didn't give us much ~, he gave us rather short ~** er hat uns nicht viel Zeit gelassen or gegeben; **to have ~ of sth** von etw Kenntnis haben; **I must have ~** or **you must give me some ~ of what you intend to do** ich muss Bescheid wissen or Kenntnis davon haben (form), was Sie vorhaben; **to serve ~ on sb** (Jur, to appear in court) jdn vorladen; **at short ~** kurzfristig; **at a moment's ~** jederzeit, sofort; **at three days' ~** binnen drei Tagen, innerhalb von drei Tagen; **until further ~** bis auf weiteres

b (= public announcement) (on notice board etc) Bekanntmachung f, Anschlag m; (= poster) Plakat nt; (= sign) Schild nt; (in newspaper) Mitteilung f, Bekanntmachung f; (short) Notiz f; (of birth, wedding, vacancy etc) Anzeige f; **the ~ says**

... da steht ...; **to post a ~** einen Anschlag machen, ein Plakat nt aufhängen; **public ~** öffentliche Bekanntmachung; **birth/marriage/death ~** Geburts-/Heirats-/Todesanzeige f; **I saw a ~ in the paper about the concert** ich habe das Konzert in der Zeitung angekündigt gesehen

c (prior to end of employment, residence etc) Kündigung f; **~ to quit** (Brit) or **vacate** (US) Kündigung f; **to give sb ~** (employer, landlord) jdm kündigen; (lodger, employee also) bei jdm kündigen; **to give** or **hand** or **turn** (US) **in one's ~** kündigen; **I am under ~ of redundancy, I got my ~** mir ist gekündigt worden; **a month's ~** eine einmonatige Kündigungsfrist; **I have to give (my landlady) a week's ~** ich habe eine einwöchige Kündigungsfrist; **she gave me** or **I was given a month's ~** mir wurde zum nächsten Monat gekündigt

d (= review) Kritik f, Rezension f

e (= attention) **to take ~ of sth** von etw Notiz nehmen; (= heed) etw beachten, einer Sache (dat) Beachtung schenken; **I'm afraid I wasn't taking much ~ of what they were doing** ich muss gestehen, ich habe nicht aufgepasst, was sie machten; **to take no ~ of sb/sth** jdn/etw ignorieren, von jdm/etw keine Notiz nehmen, jdm/etw keine Beachtung schenken; **take no ~!** kümmern Sie sich nicht darum!; **a lot of ~ he takes of me!** als ob er mich beachten würde!; **to attract ~** Aufmerksamkeit erregen; **that has escaped his ~** das hat er nicht bemerkt; **it might not have escaped your ~ that ...** Sie haben vielleicht bemerkt, dass ...; **to bring sth to sb's ~** auf etw (acc) aufmerksam machen; (in letter etc) jdn von etw in Kenntnis setzen; **it came to his ~ that ...** er erfuhr, dass ..., es ist ihm zu Ohren gekommen, dass ...

VT bemerken; (= feel, hear, touch also) wahrnehmen; (= realize also) merken; (= recognize, acknowledge existence of) zur Kenntnis nehmen; difference feststellen; **~ the beautiful details** achten Sie auf die schönen Einzelheiten; **without my noticing it** ohne dass ich etwas gemerkt or bemerkt habe, von mir unbemerkt; **did anybody ~ him leave?** hat jemand sein Gehen bemerkt?; **I ~d her hesitating** ich bemerkte or merkte, dass sie zögerte; **did he wave? – I never ~d** hat er gewinkt? – ich habe es nicht bemerkt or gesehen; **I ~ you have a new dress** ich stelle fest, du hast ein neues Kleid, ich sehe, hast du ein neues Kleid; **to get oneself ~d** Aufmerksamkeit erregen, auf sich (acc) aufmerksam machen; (negatively) auffallen

noticeable ['nəʊtɪsəbl] ADJ erkennbar, wahrnehmbar; (= visible) sichtbar; (= obvious, considerable) deutlich; relief, pleasure, disgust etc sichtlich, merklich; **the stain is very ~** der Fleck fällt ziemlich auf; **his incompetence was very ~** seine Unfähigkeit trat klar zum Vorschein or zeigte sich deutlich; **the change was ~** man konnte eine Veränderung feststellen; **it is hardly ~, it isn't really ~** man merkt es kaum; (= visible also) man sieht es kaum; **it is ~ that ...** man merkt, dass ...; **she was ~ by her absence/because of her large hat** sie fiel durch ihre Abwesenheit/ihren großen Hut auf

noticeably ['nəʊtɪsəblɪ] ADV deutlich, merklich; relieved, pleased, annoyed etc sichtlich; **he was ~ lacking in confidence** es war deutlich, dass ihm das Selbstvertrauen fehlte

notice board ['nəʊtɪsbɔːd] N (esp Brit) Anschlagbrett nt; (in school etc also) schwarzes Brett nt; (= sign) Schild nt, Tafel f

notifiable ['nəʊtɪfaɪəbl] ADJ meldepflichtig

notification [ˌnəʊtɪfɪ'keɪʃən] N Benachrichtigung f, Benachrichtigung f; (of disease, crime, loss, damage etc) Meldung f; (= written notification: of birth etc) Anzeige f; **to send ~ of sth to sb** jdm etw schriftlich mitteilen

notify ['nəʊtɪfaɪ] VT person, candidate benachrichtigen, unterrichten (form); change of address, loss, disease etc melden; **to ~ sb of sth** jdn von etw benachrichtigen, jdm etw mitteilen; authorities, insurance company jdm etw melden; **to be notified of sth** über etw (acc) informiert

werden or etw benachrichtigt or unterrichtet (form) werden

notion ['nəʊʃən] N **a** (= idea, thought) Idee f; (= conception) Vorstellung f, Idee f; (= vague knowledge) Ahnung f; (= opinion) Meinung f, Ansicht f; **I haven't the foggiest** (inf) or **slightest ~ (of what he means)** ich habe keine Ahnung or nicht die leiseste Ahnung(, was er meint); **I have no ~ of time** ich habe überhaupt kein Zeitgefühl; **to give sb ~s** jdn auf Gedanken or Ideen bringen; **that gave me the ~ of inviting her** das brachte mich auf die Idee or den Gedanken, sie einzuladen; **where did you get the ~** or **what gave you the ~ that I ...?** wie kommst du denn auf die Idee, dass ich ...?; **he got the ~ (into his head) that she wouldn't help him** irgendwie hat er sich das eingebildet, sie würde ihm nicht helfen; **I have a ~ that ...** ich habe den Verdacht, dass ...

b (= whim) Idee f; **to have a ~ to do sth** Lust haben, etw zu tun; **if he gets a ~ to do something, nothing can stop him** wenn er sich (dat) etwas in den Kopf gesetzt hat, kann ihn keiner davon abhalten; **she has some strange ~s** sie kommt manchmal auf seltsame Ideen or Gedanken; **I hit (up)on** or **suddenly had the ~ of going to see her** mir kam plötzlich die Idee, sie zu besuchen

c notions PL (esp US inf) Kurzwaren pl

notional ['nəʊʃənl] ADJ **a** (= hypothetical) fiktiv, angenommen; (= nominal) payment nominell, symbolisch **b** (esp US) versponnen, verträumt **c** (Philos) spekulativ

notionally ['nəʊʃənəlɪ] ADV nominell

notoriety [ˌnəʊtə'raɪətɪ] N traurige Berühmtheit

notorious [nəʊ'tɔːrɪəs] ADJ person, fact berüchtigt; place also verrufen, verschrieen; (= well-known) gambler, criminal, liar notorisch; **a ~ woman** eine Frau von schlechtem Ruf; **to be ~ for/as sth** für/als etw berüchtigt sein; **it is a ~ fact that ...** es ist leider nur allzu bekannt, dass ...

notoriously [nəʊ'tɔːrɪəslɪ] ADV notorisch; (= as is well known) bekanntlich; **it is ~ difficult to treat** es lässt sich bekanntlich nur sehr schwer behandeln; **to be ~ unreliable/inefficient/violent** etc für seine Unzuverlässigkeit/Untüchtigkeit/Gewalttätigkeit etc berüchtigt or bekannt sein

no-trump ['nəʊtrʌmp] (Cards) ADJ Sans-Atout-; **~ contract** Sans-Atout-Kontrakt m **N** (also **no-trumps**) Sans-Atout m

Notts [nɒts] abbr of **Nottinghamshire**

notwithstanding [ˌnɒtwɪθ'stændɪŋ] (form) PREP ungeachtet (+gen) (form), trotz (+gen) ADV dennoch, trotzdem, nichtsdestotrotz (form) CONJ **~ that** obwohl or obgleich ...

nougat ['nuːgɑː] N Nougat m, Nugat m

nought [nɔːt] N **a** (= number) Null f; **~s and crosses** (Brit) Tic Tac Toe nt, Kinderspiel mit Nullen und Kreuzen → also **zero** **b** (liter, = nothing) Nichts nt; **to come to ~** sich zerschlagen; **to bring to ~** zunichte machen

noun [naʊn] N Substantiv(um) nt, Hauptwort nt; abstract ~ Abstraktum nt; collective ~ Sammelbegriff m; common ~ Gattungsname or -begriff m; proper ~ Name m; **~ group** or **phrase** Nominalphrase f

nourish ['nʌrɪʃ] VT **a** (lit) nähren; person ernähren; leather pflegen; **a good diet ~ed her back to health** gute Ernährung brachte sie wieder zu Kräften **b** (fig) hopes etc nähren, hegen; **literature to ~ their minds** Literatur als geistige Nahrung **VI** nahrhaft sein

nourishing ['nʌrɪʃɪŋ] ADJ food, diet, drink nahrhaft

nourishment ['nʌrɪʃmənt] N (= food) Nahrung f; **to take ~** Nahrung f zu sich (dat) nehmen; **you need some real ~** du brauchst gutes Essen

nous [naʊs] N (Brit inf) Grips m (inf)

nouveau riche [ˌnuːvəʊ'riːʃ] **N** pl **-x -s** [ˌnuːvəʊ'riːʃ] Neureiche(r) mf ADJ typisch neureich

nouvelle cuisine [ˌnuːvelkwɪ'ziːn] N Nouvelle cuisine f

Nov *abbr of* **November** Nov

nova ['nəʊvə] N *pl* **-s** *or* **-e** ['nəʊviː] Nova *f*

Nova Scotia ['nəʊvə'skəʊʃə] N Neuschottland *nt*

Nova Scotian ['nəʊvə'skəʊʃən] ADJ neuschottisch N Neuschotte *m*, Neuschottin *f*

novel¹ ['nɒvəl] N Roman *m*

novel² ADJ neu(artig)

novelette [ˌnɒvə'let] N *(pej)* Romänchen *nt*, Kitschroman *m*

novelettish [ˌnɒvə'letɪʃ] ADJ *(pej)* situation rührselig, kitschig

novelist ['nɒvəlɪst] N Romanschriftsteller(in) *m(f)*, Romancier *m*

novelistic [nɒvə'lɪstɪk] ADJ romanhaft

novella [nə'velə] N Novelle *f*

novelty ['nɒvəltɪ] N **a** (= *newness*) Neuheit *f*; **once the ~ has worn off** wenn der Reiz des Neuen or der Neuheit vorbei ist **b** (= *innovation*) Neuheit *f*, Novum *nt*; **it was quite a ~** das war etwas ganz Neues, das war ein Novum **c** (*Comm, = trinket*) Krimskrams *m*

November [nəʊ'vembə] N November *m* → *also* **September**

novena [nəʊ'viːnə] N Novene *f*

novice ['nɒvɪs] N (*Eccl*) Novize *m*, Novizin *f*; (= *racehorse*) Pferd, das noch nicht eine bestimmte Anzahl von Rennen gewonnen hat *(fig)* Neuling *m*, Anfänger(in) *m(f)* (*at* bei, *in* +*dat*)

noviciate, novitiate [nəʊ'vɪʃɪt] N (*Eccl*) **a** (= *state*) Noviziat *nt* **b** (= *place*) Novizenhaus *nt*

Novocaine® ['nəʊvəʊkeɪn] N Novokain *nt*, Novocain® *nt*

now [naʊ] ⊘ 26.1 ADV **a** jetzt, nun; (= *immediately*) jetzt, sofort, gleich; (= *at this very moment*) gerade, (so)eben; (= *nowadays*) heute, heutzutage; **she ~ realized why ...** nun or da erkannte sie, warum ...; **just ~** gerade; (= *immediately*) gleich, sofort; **~ is the time to do it** jetzt ist der richtige Moment dafür; **I'll do it just or right ~** ich mache es jetzt gleich or sofort; **do it (right) ~** mach es jetzt (sofort); **it's ~ or never** jetzt oder nie; **even ~ it's not right** es ist immer noch nicht richtig; **~ for it** los!; **~ for a look at the weather forecast** und nun zum Wetterbericht; **what is it ~?** was ist denn jetzt or nun schon wieder?; **by ~** (*present, past*) inzwischen, mittlerweile; **they have/had never met before ~** sie haben sich bis jetzt/sie hatten sich bis dahin noch nie getroffen; **before ~ it was thought ...** früher dachte man, dass ...; **we'd have heard before ~** das hätten wir (inzwischen) schon gehört; **I've been there before ~** ich war schon (früher) da; **for ~** (jetzt) erst einmal, im Moment, vorläufig; **even ~** auch or selbst jetzt noch; **any day/moment ~** jetzt jeden Tag/Moment; **from ~ on(wards)** von nun an; **between ~ and the end of the week** bis zum Ende der Woche; **in three days from ~** (heute) in drei Tagen; **from ~ until then** bis dahin; **up to ~, till ~, until ~** bis jetzt

b (*alternation*) **~ ... ...** bald ... bald ...; **(every) ~ and then, ~ and again** ab und zu, von Zeit zu Zeit, gelegentlich

CONJ **a** **~ (that) you've seen him** jetzt, wo Sie ihn gesehen haben, nun, da Sie ihn gesehen haben *(geh)*

b (*in explanation etc*) nun

INTERJ also; **~, ~!** na, na!; **well ~** also; **~ then** also (jetzt); **stop that ~!** Schluss jetzt!; **come ~, don't exaggerate** nun übertreib mal nicht; **~, why didn't I think of that?** warum habe ich bloß nicht daran gedacht?

nowadays ['naʊədeɪz] ⊘ 26.1 ADV heute, heutzutage

no way ['nəʊ'weɪ] ADV → **way 1 g**

nowhere ['nəʊweə] ADV nirgendwo, nirgends; (*with verbs of motion*) nirgendwohin; **~ special** irgendwo; (*with motion*) irgendwohin; **~ is or there is ~ more romantic than Paris** nirgends ist es romantischer als in Paris; **there's ~ I'd rather be** nirgends wäre ich lieber; **it's ~ you know** du

kennst den Ort nicht; **it's ~ you'll ever find it** es ist an einem Platz, wo du es bestimmt nicht findest; **he was ~ to be seen** er war nirgends zu sehen; **they have ~ (else) to go** sie können (sonst) nirgends unterkommen; *(fig: = have no escape)* es gibt für sie (sonst) keinen Ausweg; **there was ~ to hide** man konnte sich nirgends verstecken; **there was ~ to hide from the wind** es gab keinen Schutz vor dem Wind; **to appear from** *or* **out of ~** ganz plötzlich *or* aus heiterem Himmel auftauchen; **to come ~** (*Sport*) unter „ferner liefen" kommen *or* enden; **to come from ~ and win** (*Sport*) überraschend siegen; **we're getting ~ (fast)** wir machen keine Fortschritte, wir kommen nicht weiter; **rudeness will get you ~** Grobheit bringt dir gar nichts ein, mit Grobheit bringst du es auch nicht weiter; **a pound goes ~ these days** mit einem Pfund kommt man heute nicht mehr weit → **near 1 d**

no-win situation [ˌnəʊwɪnsɪtjʊ'eɪʃən] N verzwickte Situation (*in der man so oder so nicht gewinnen kann*); **it's a ~** wie mans macht ists falsch

nowt [naʊt] N, PRON, ADV (*Brit, dial*) nix (*inf*), nischt (*dial, inf*)

noxious ['nɒkʃəs] ADJ **a** (= *harmful*) schädlich; (= *toxic*) fumes, gas, substance giftig **b** (= *repugnant*) smell, habit übel; *attitude* widerlich

nozzle ['nɒzl] N Düse *f*; (*of syringe*) Kanüle *f*

nr *abbr of* **near** b., bei

NRA (*US*) *abbr of* **National Rifle Association** *amerikanische Organisation, die das Recht der Bürger auf freien Kauf und Besitz von Waffen verteidigt*

NS *abbr of* **Nova Scotia**

n/s N *abbr of* **nonsmoker** Nichtraucher(in) *m* ADJ *abbr of* **nonsmoking** Nichtraucher-

NSB (*Brit*) *abbr of* **National Savings Bank** ≈ Postsparkasse *f*

NSPCC (*Brit*) *abbr of* **National Society for the Prevention of Cruelty to Children** ≈ Kinderschutzbund *m*

NSU (*Med*) *abbr of* **nonspecific urethritis** unspezifische Urethritis, unspezifische Harnröhrenentzündung

NSW *abbr of* **New South Wales**

NT a *abbr of* **New Testament** N. T. *nt* **b** *abbr of* **Northern Territory**

nth [enθ] ADJ **the ~ power** *or* **degree** die n-te Potenz; **for the ~ time** zum x-ten Mal (*inf*)

nt. wt. *abbr of* **net weight**

nuance ['njuːɑ̃ːns] N Nuance *f*; (*of colour also*) Schattierung *f*

nub [nʌb] N **a** (= *piece*) Stückchen *nt*, Klümpchen *nt* **b** (*fig*) **the ~ of the matter** der springende Punkt, der Kernpunkt

Nubia ['njuːbɪə] N Nubien *nt*

Nubian ['njuːbɪən] ADJ nubisch N Nubier(in) *m(f)*

nubile ['njuːbaɪl] ADJ *girl* heiratsfähig; (= *attractive*) gut entwickelt

nuclear ['njuːklɪə] ADJ Atom-; *fuel* nuklear, atomar; *bomb* Atom-; (= *country, = develop nuclear weapons*) Atomwaffen entwickeln; (= *use nuclear energy*) zur Atomenergie übergehen

nuclear: nuclear attack N Atomangriff *m*; **nuclear deterrent** N nukleares Abschreckungsmittel; **nuclear disarmament** N nukleare *or* atomare Abrüstung; **nuclear energy** N = **nuclear power**; **nuclear family** N Klein- *or* Kernfamilie *f*; **nuclear fission** N Kernspaltung *f*; **nuclear-free** ADJ atomwaffenfrei; **nuclear fuel rod** N Kernbrennstab *m*; **nuclear holocaust** N Atominferno *nt*; **nuclear magnetic resonance** N kernmagnetische Resonanz; **nuclear medicine** N Nuklearmedizin *f*; **nuclear missile** N Atomrakete *f*; **Nuclear Non-Proliferation Treaty** N Atomwaffensperrvertrag *m*; **nuclear physicist** N Kernphysiker(in) *m(f)*; **nuclear physics** N Kernphysik *f*; **nuclear pile** N Atommeiler *m*; **nuclear plant** N Atomanlage *f*; **nuclear power**

N Atomkraft *f*, Kernenergie *f*; **nuclear-powered** ADJ atomgetrieben; **nuclear power station** N Kern- *or* Atomkraftwerk *nt*; **nuclear reaction** N Kernreaktion *f*; **nuclear reactor** N Kern- *or* Atomreaktor *m*; **nuclear reprocessing plant** N nukleare Wiederaufbereitungsanlage; **nuclear scientist** N Nuklearwissenschaftler(in) *m(f)*; **nuclear submarine** N Atom-U-Boot *nt*; **nuclear test** N Atom(-waffen)test *m*; **nuclear umbrella** N Atom- *or* Nuklearschirm *m*; **nuclear war** N Atomkrieg *m*; **nuclear warfare** N Atomkrieg *m*; **nuclear warhead** N Atomsprengkopf *m*; **nuclear waste** N Atommüll *m*; **nuclear weapon** N Atomwaffe *f*; **nuclear winter** N nuklearer Winter

nuclei ['njuːklɪaɪ] PL *of* **nucleus**

nucleic acid [njuː'kleɪk'æsɪd] N Nukleinsäure *f*

nucleus ['njuːklɪəs] N *pl* **nuclei** (*Phys, Astron, fig*) Kern *m*; (*Biol, of cell also*) Nukleus *m*; **atomic ~** Atomkern *m*

nude [njuːd] ADJ nackt; (*Art*) Akt-; **~ photograph** Aktfoto *nt*; **~ study** (*Art*) Akt *m*, Aktstudie *f*; **~ figure/portrait** Akt *m*; **~ scene** (*Film*) Nacktszene *f* N (= *person*) Nackte(r) *mf*; (*Art*) (= *painting, sculpture etc*) Akt *m*; (= *model*) Aktmodell *nt*; **to paint from the ~** einen Akt malen; **in the ~** nackt

nudge [nʌdʒ] VT stupsen, anstoßen; **she ~d him forward** sie schubste ihn vorwärts; **to ~ sb into doing sth** jdn den Anstoß dazu geben, etw zu tun; **to ~ sb's memory** (*fig*) jds Gedächtnis (*dat*) (ein wenig) nachhelfen; **the temperature was nudging 35°C** die Temperatur erreichte fast 35°C; **she's nudging 40** sie geht stramm auf die 40 zu N Stups *m*, kleiner Stoß; **to give sb a ~** jdm einen Stups geben, jdn stupsen; **a ~ and a wink** ein Augenzwinkern *nt*; **~-nudge, wink-wink** (*inf*) na, du weißt schon

nudie ['njuːdɪ] ADJ (*inf*) **~ picture** Nacktfoto *nt*; **~ magazine** Pornomagazin *nt*

nudism ['njuːdɪzəm] N Freikörperkultur *f*, Nudismus *m*

nudist ['njuːdɪst] N Anhänger(in) *m(f)* der Freikörperkultur, FKK-Anhänger(in) *m(f)*, Nudist(in) *m(f)*

nudist: nudist beach N FKK-Strand *m*, Nacktbadestrand *m*; **nudist camp** N FKK-Platz *m*, Nudistenplatz *m*; **nudist colony** N FKK-Kolonie *f*, Nudistenkolonie *f*

nudity ['njuːdɪtɪ] N Nacktheit *f*

nugatory ['njuːgətərɪ] ADJ (*liter*) belanglos, nichtig (*geh*)

nugget ['nʌgɪt] N (*of gold etc*) Klumpen *m*; (*fig: of information, knowledge*) Brocken *m*, Bröckchen *nt*

nuisance ['njuːsns] N **a** (= *person*) Plage *f*; (*esp pestering*) Nervensäge *f*; (*esp child*) Quälgeist *m*; **he can be a ~** er kann einen aufregen, er kann auf die Nerven *or* den Geist (*inf*) gehen; **sorry to be a ~** entschuldigen Sie, wenn ich störe; **to make a ~ of oneself** lästig werden; **to have ~ value** als Störfaktor wirken **b** (= *thing, event*) **to be a ~** lästig sein; (*annoying*) ärgerlich sein; **what a ~, having to do it again** wie ärgerlich *or* lästig, das noch einmal machen zu müssen; **to become a ~** lästig werden; **this wind is a ~** dieser Wind ist eine Plage **c** (*Jur*) **public ~** öffentliches Ärgernis; **to cause a (public) ~** (öffentliches) Ärgernis erregen

nuisance: nuisance call N (*Telec*) Schockanruf *m*; **~s** *pl* Telefonterror *m* (*inf*); **nuisance caller** N (*Telec*) Schockanrufer(in) *m(f)*

NUJ (*Brit*) *abbr of* **National Union of Journalists** *Journalistengewerkschaft*

nuke [njuːk] (*sl*) N **a** (*US: = power plant*) Kern- *or* Atomkraftwerk *nt* **b** (= *bomb*) Atombombe *f* VT (= *attack*) mit Atomwaffen angreifen; (= *destroy*) atomar vernichten

null [nʌl] ADJ (*Jur*) *act, decree* (null und) nichtig, ungültig; **to render sth ~ and void** etw null und nichtig machen

nullification [ˌnʌlɪfɪˈkeɪʃən] N **a** Annullierung f, Aufhebung f **b** (US) unterlassene Amts- or Rechtshilfe

nullify [ˈnʌlɪfaɪ] VT annullieren, für (null und) nichtig erklären

nullity [ˈnʌlɪtɪ] N (Jur) Ungültigkeit f, Nichtigkeit f

NUM (Brit) abbr of **National Union of Mineworkers** Bergarbeitergewerkschaft

numb [nʌm] ADJ (+er) taub, empfindungslos, gefühllos; feeling taub; (emotionally) benommen, wie betäubt; **hands ~ with cold** Hände, die vor Kälte taub or gefühllos sind; **~ with grief** starr or wie betäubt vor Schmerz; **~ with disbelief** starr vor Ungläubigkeit VT (cold) taub or gefühllos machen; (injection, fig) betäuben; **~ed with fear/grief** starr vor Furcht/Schmerz

number [ˈnʌmbə] ✪ 27.1, 27.3, 27.4, 27.7 N **a** (Math) Zahl f; (= numeral) Ziffer f; **the ~ of votes cast** die abgegebenen Stimmen **b** (= quantity, amount) Anzahl f; **a ~ of problems/applicants** eine (ganze) Anzahl von Problemen/Bewerbern; **large ~s of people/books** (sehr) viele Leute/Bücher; **on a ~ of occasions** des Öfteren; **boys and girls in equal ~s** ebenso viele Jungen wie Mädchen, Jungen und Mädchen zu gleicher Zahl (geh); **in a small ~ of cases** in wenigen Fällen; **ten in ~** zehn an der Zahl; **they were few in ~** es waren nur wenige; **to be found in large ~s** zahlreich vorhanden sein, häufig zu finden sein; **in small/large ~s** in kleinen/großen Mengen; **many in ~** zahlreich; **a fair ~ of times** ziemlich oft; **times without ~** unzählige Male pl; **any ~ can play** beliebig viele Spieler können teilnehmen; **any ~ of cards** etc (when choosing) beliebig viele Karten etc; (= many) sehr viele Karten etc; **I've told you any ~ of times** ich habe es dir zigmal or x-mal gesagt (inf); **to win by force of ~s** aufgrund or auf Grund zahlenmäßiger Überlegenheit gewinnen; **they have the advantage of ~s** sie sind zahlenmäßig überlegen; **they were defeated by superior ~s** sie wurden von einer zahlenmäßigen Übermacht geschlagen

c (of house, room, phone) Nummer f; (of page) Seitenzahl f; (of car) (Auto)nummer f; (Mil, of soldier etc) Kennnummer f; **at ~ 4** (in) Nummer 4; **Number Ten (Downing Street)** Nummer zehn (Downing Street); **the ~ 47 bus** die Buslinie 47, der 47er (inf); **I've got the wrong ~** ich habe mich verwählt; **it was a wrong ~** ich/er etc war falsch verbunden; **one pop star/tennis player** (inf) der Popstar/Tennisspieler Nummer eins (inf); **the single went straight to** or **straight in at ~ one** die Single stieg gleich auf Nummer eins ein; **he has never had a ~ one** (inf) er hat nie einen Nummer-Eins-Hit gehabt; **to take care of** or **look after ~ one** (inf) (vor allem) an sich (acc) selbst denken; **he's my ~ two** (inf) er ist mein Vize (inf) or Stellvertreter m; **I'm (the) ~ two in the department** ich bin die Nummer zwei in der Abteilung; **his ~'s up** (inf) er ist dran (inf); **to do a ~ one/two** (baby-talk) klein/groß machen (baby-talk); **to get sb's ~** (inf) jdn einschätzen or einordnen or durchschauen; **to do sth by (the** US**) ~s** etw nach Schema F (esp pej) or rein mechanisch erledigen

d (= song, act etc) Nummer f; (= issue of magazine etc) Ausgabe f, Nummer f, Heft nt; (= dress) Kreation f; **the June ~** das Juniheft, die Juniausgabe or -nummer

e (Gram) Numerus m

f (Eccl) **The Book of Numbers** das Vierte Buch Mose, Numeri pl

g (= company) **one of their/our ~** eine(r) aus ihren/unseren Reihen

h numbers PL (= arithmetic) Rechnen nt VT **a** (= give a number to) nummerieren; **~ed account** Nummernkonto nt

b (= include) zählen (among zu)

c (= amount to) zählen; **the group ~ed 50** es waren 50 (Leute in der Gruppe); **the library ~s 30,000 volumes** die Bibliothek hat 30.000 Bände

d (= count) zählen; **to be ~ed** (= limited) be-

grenzt sein; **his days are ~ed** seine Tage sind gezählt

VI (Brit Mil etc: also **number off**) abzählen

number cruncher [ˈnʌmbəˈkrʌntʃə] N (Comput) Numbercruncher m, Number Cruncher m, Supercomputer m; (= person) Zahlenzauberer m, Zahlenzauberin f

number crunching [ˈnʌmbəˈkrʌntʃɪŋ] N (Comput) Numbercrunching nt, Number Crunching nt

numbering [ˈnʌmbərɪŋ] N (of houses etc) Numerierung f; **~ system** Nummeriersystem nt

numbering machine N Nummernstempel m

number: numberless ADJ zahllos, unzählig; **numberplate** N (Brit) Nummernschild nt, Kennzeichen nt; **number pool** N (US) ≈ Zahlenlotto nt; **numbers game** N Zahlenspiel nt; **to play the ~** Zahlenspielerei betreiben; **numbers lock** N (Comput) Zahlenverriegelung f

numbly [ˈnʌmlɪ] ADV benommen, wie betäubt

numbness [ˈnʌmnɪs] N (of limbs etc) Taubheit f, Starre f; (fig: of mind, senses) Benommenheit f, Betäubung f

numbskull [ˈnʌmskʌl] N (inf) Holzkopf m (inf)

numeracy [ˈnjuːmərəsɪ] N Rechnen nt; **his ~** seine rechnerischen Fähigkeiten

numeral [ˈnjuːmərəl] N Ziffer f

numerate [ˈnjuːmərɪt] ADJ rechenkundig; **to be (very) ~** (gut) rechnen können

numeration [ˌnjuːməˈreɪʃən] N Nummerierung f

numerator [ˈnjuːməreɪtə] N (Math) Zähler m, Dividend m

numeric [njuːˈmerɪk] ADJ **~ keypad** Zehnertastatur f, numerisches Tastenfeld

numerical [njuːˈmerɪkəl] ADJ equation, order, data numerisch; superiority zahlenmäßig; **~ symbols** Zahlensymbole pl; **~ value** Zahlenwert m

numerically [njuːˈmerɪkəlɪ] ADV zahlenmäßig; **the reports are ~ incorrect** die Zahlenangaben in den Berichten stimmen nicht

numerous [ˈnjuːmərəs] ADJ zahlreich; family kinderreich; **on ~ occasions** bei vielen Gelegenheiten

numismatic [ˌnjuːmɪzˈmætɪk] ADJ numismatisch

numismatics [ˌnjuːmɪzˈmætɪks] N sing Münzkunde f, Numismatik f

numismatist [njuːˈmɪzmətɪst] N Numismatiker(in) m(f)

numskull [ˈnʌmskʌl] N (inf) Holzkopf m (inf)

nun [nʌn] N Nonne f

nunciature [ˈnʌnʃɪətjʊə] N Nuntiatur f

nuncio [ˈnʌnʃɪəʊ] N (= Papal nuncio) Nuntius m

nunnery [ˈnʌnərɪ] N (old) (Nonnen)kloster nt

NUPE [ˈnjuːpɪ] (Brit) abbr of **National Union of Public Employees** Gewerkschaft der Angestellten im öffentlichen Dienst

nuptial [ˈnʌpʃəl] ADJ bliss ehelich; **~ celebrations** Hochzeitsfeier f; **~ vows** Ehegelöbnis nt or -gelübde nt; **the ~ day** (hum) der Hochzeitstag N **nuptials** PL (hum, liter) **the ~s** die Hochzeit f

NUR (Brit old) abbr of **National Union of Railwaymen** Eisenbahnergewerkschaft

nurd N (US sl) = **nerd**

Nuremberg [ˈnjʊərəmˌbɜːg] N Nürnberg nt

nurse [nɜːs] N Schwester f; (as professional title) Krankenschwester f; (= nanny) Kindermädchen nt, Kinderfrau f; (= wet nurse) Amme f; **male ~** Krankenpfleger m

VT **a** sb pflegen; plant also hegen; (fig) plan hegen; hope, wrath etc hegen, nähren (geh); fire bewachen; (= treat carefully) schonen; business sorgsam verwalten; **to ~ sb back to health** jdn gesund pflegen; **to ~ sb through an illness** jdn während einer Krankheit pflegen; **to ~ a cold** an einer Erkältung herumlaborieren (inf); **he stood there nursing his bruised arm** er stand da und hielt seinen verletzten Arm; **to ~ a grudge (against sb)** (gegen jdn) einen Groll hegen; **to ~ the economy** die Wirtschaft hegen und pflegen

b (= suckle) child stillen; (= cradle) (in den Armen) wiegen

VI (baby) gestillt werden

nurseling [ˈnɜːslɪŋ] N = **nursling**

nursemaid [ˈnɜːsmeɪd] N (= nanny, hum, = servant) Kindermädchen nt

nursery [ˈnɜːsərɪ] N **a** (= room) Kinderzimmer nt; (in hospital) Säuglingssaal m **b** (= institution) Kindergarten m; (all-day) Kindertagesstätte f, Hort m **c** (Agr, Hort) (for plants) Gärtnerei f; (for trees) Baumschule f; (fig) Zuchtstätte f

nursery: nurseryman N Gärtner m; **nursery nurse** N Kindermädchen nt, Kinderfrau f; **nursery rhyme** N Kinderreim m; **nursery school** N Kindergarten m; **nursery school teacher** N Kindergärtner(in) m(f); **nursery slope** N (Ski) Idiotenhügel m (hum), Anfängerhügel m

nursing [ˈnɜːsɪŋ] N **a** (= care of invalids) Pflege f, Pflegen nt **b** (= profession) Krankenpflege f; **she's going in for ~** sie will in der Krankenpflege arbeiten **c** (= feeding) Stillen nt ADJ attr Pflege-; abilities pflegerisch; **~ staff** Pflegepersonal nt; **the ~ profession** die Krankenpflege; (= nurses collectively) die pflegerischen Berufe, die Pflegeberufe pl

nursing: nursing auxiliary N Schwesternhelferin f; **nursing bottle** N (US) Flasche f, Fläschchen nt; **nursing bra** N Still-BH m; **nursing care** N Pflege f; **nursing home** N Privatklinik f; (Brit: = maternity hospital) Entbindungsklinik f; (= convalescent home) Pflegeheim nt; **nursing mother** N stillende Mutter; **nursing officer** N (Brit) Oberpfleger m, Oberschwester f; **nursing sister** N Oberschwester f

nursling [ˈnɜːslɪŋ] N Pflegling m

nurture [ˈnɜːtʃə] N (= nourishing) Hegen nt; (= upbringing) Erziehung f, Bildung f VT **a** sb's talent entwickeln; idea, ambitions hegen; **to ~ sb on sth** (lit, fig) jdn mit etw aufziehen **b** (fig: = train) hegen und pflegen

NUS (Brit) **a** abbr of **National Union of Students** Studentengewerkschaft **b** abbr of **National Union of Seamen** Seeleutegewerkschaft

NUT (Brit) abbr of **National Union of Teachers**

nut [nʌt] N **a** (Bot) Nuss f; (of coal) kleines Stück; **a packet of ~s and raisins** eine Tüte Studentenfutter; **a hard** or **tough ~ to crack** (fig) eine harte Nuss

b (inf, = head) Nuss f (inf), Birne f (inf); **use your ~!** streng deinen Grips an! (inf); **to be off one's ~** nicht ganz bei Trost sein (inf), spinnen (inf); **to go off one's ~** durchdrehen (inf); **to do one's ~** (Brit inf) durchdrehen (inf) → also **nuts**

c (inf, = person) Spinner(in) m(f) (inf); **he's a tough ~** (inf) er ist ein harter or zäher Brocken (inf)

d (Mech) (Schrauben)mutter f; **the ~s and bolts of a theory** die Grundbestandteile einer Theorie

e nuts PL (sl: = testicles) Eier pl (sl)

nut: nutbrown ADJ nussbraun; **nutcase** N (inf) Spinner(in) m(f) (inf); **nutcracker** N , **nutcrackers** PL Nussknacker m; **nuthatch** N Kleiber m; **nuthouse** N (inf, lit, fig) Irrenhaus nt (inf); (lit also) Klapsmühle f (inf); **nutmeg** N (= spice) Muskat(nuss f) m; (also **nutmeg tree**) Muskatnussbaum m

Nutrasweet® [ˈnjuːtrəswiːt] N Süßstoff m

nutrient [ˈnjuːtrɪənt] ADJ substance nahrhaft; **~ solution** Nährlösung f N Nährstoff m

nutriment [ˈnjuːtrɪmənt] N (form) Nahrung f

nutrition [njuːˈtrɪʃən] N (= diet, science) Ernährung f

nutritional [njuːˈtrɪʃənl] ADJ Nähr-; **~ value** Nährkraft f, Nährwert m; **~ content** Nähr(stoff)gehalt m; **~ information** Nährwertangaben pl; **~ supplements** Nahrungsergänzungsmittel pl

nutritionist [njuːˈtrɪʃənɪst] N Ernährungswissenschaftler(in) m(f)

nutritious [njuːˈtrɪʃəs] ADJ nahrhaft

nutritiousness [njuː'trɪʃəsnɪs] N Nahrhaftigkeit f

nutritive ['njuːtrɪtɪv] ADJ nahrhaft

nuts [nʌts] ADJ *pred* (*inf*) **to be ~** spinnen (*inf*); **to go ~** durchdrehen (*inf*), anfangen zu spinnen (*inf*); **to be ~ about sb/sth** ganz verrückt nach jdm/auf etw (*acc*) sein (*inf*); **~!** (*dated US*) Quatsch! (*inf*); (*in annoyance*) Mist (*inf*)!; **~ to him!** (*dated US*) er kann mich mal (gern haben)! (*inf*)

nutshell ['nʌtʃel] N Nussschale f; **in a ~** (*fig*) kurz gesagt, mit einem Wort; **to put the matter in a ~** (*fig*) um es (ganz) kurz or kurz und bündig zu sagen

nutter ['nʌtə'] N (*Brit inf*) Spinner(in) *m(f)* (*inf*); (*dangerous*) Verrückte(r) *mf*; **he's a ~** er hat einen Stich (*inf*) or Vogel (*inf*)

nutty ['nʌtɪ] ADJ (+*er*) **a** (= *like nuts*) nussartig; (= *with nuts*) mit Nüssen; *aroma* nussig; **~ flavour** Nussgeschmack *m* **b** (*inf*, = *crazy*) bekloppt (*inf*); **to be ~ about sb/sth** ganz verrückt nach jdm/auf etw (*acc*) sein (*inf*)

nuzzle ['nʌzl] **VT** (*pig*) aufwühlen; (*dog*) beschnüffeln, beschnuppern **VI** **to ~ (up) against sb**, **to ~ up to sb** (*person, animal*) sich an jdn schmiegen or drücken

---

NVQ

National Vocational Qualifications oder NVQs sind berufsbezogene Qualifizierungen, die überwiegend für Menschen gedacht sind, die bereits im Berufsleben stehen, auch wenn einige Schulen diesen Abschluss zusätzlich zu oder anstelle der Hochschulzugangsqualifikationen wie GSCE oder A levels anbieten. Die Beurteilung erfolgt aufgrund der Leistungen im praktischen und theoretischen Unterricht sowie mündlichen und schriftlichen Prüfungen. Das System gilt in England, Wales und Nordirland, wobei es in Schottland ein ähnliches System, die **Scottish Vocational Qualifications** (oder auch „SVQs") gibt. → A LEVELS, GCSE

NW *abbr of* **north-west** NW

NY *abbr of* **New York**

Nyasaland [naɪ'æsəlænd] N Njassaland *nt*

NYC *abbr of* **New York City**

nylon ['naɪlɒn] **N** **a** (*Tex*) Nylon *nt* **b** **nylons** PL Nylonstrümpfe *pl* **ADJ** Nylon-; **~ shirt** Nylonhemd *nt*; **~ material** Nylon *nt*

nymph [nɪmf] N **a** (*Myth*) Nymphe f **b** (*Zool*) Nymphe f

nymphet [nɪm'fet] N Nymphchen *nt*

nympho ['nɪmfəʊ] N (*inf*) Nymphomanin f

nymphomania [ˌnɪmfəʊ'meɪnɪə] N Nymphomanie f

nymphomaniac [ˌnɪmfəʊ'meɪnɪæk] N Nymphomanin f

NYPD (*US*) *abbr of* **New York Police Department**

NYSE (*US*) *abbr of* **New York Stock Exchange**

NZ *abbr of* **New Zealand**

O

O INTERJ **a** (*Poet*) o; **O my people** o du mein Volk! **b** (*expressing feeling*) oh, ach; **O how wrong he was** wie hatte er sich da (doch) geirrt; **O for a bit of fresh air!** ach, wenn es doch nur ein bisschen frische Luft gäbe!; **O to be in France** (ach,) wäre ich nur in Frankreich! → *also* **oh**

O, o [əʊ] N **a** O *nt*, o *nt* **b** [(*Brit*) əʊ] [(*US*) 'zɪərəʊ] (*Telec*) Null *f*

O' [ə] PREP *abbr of* **of**

oaf [əʊf] N *pl* **-s** *or* **oaves** Flegel *m*, Lümmel *m*; **you clumsy ~!** du altes Trampel! (*inf*)

oafish ['əʊfɪʃ] ADJ flegelhaft, lümmelhaft; (= *clumsy*) tölpelhaft

oak [əʊk] N Eiche *f*; (= *wood also*) Eichenholz *nt*; **he has a heart of ~** er hat ein unerschütterliches Gemüt; **dark ~** (= *colour*) (in) dunkel Eiche; **great ~s from little acorns grow** (*prov*) aus kleinen Dingen entwickeln sich oft erstaunliche Sachen

oak *in cpds* Eichen-; **~ tree** Eichenbaum *m*

oak apple N Gallapfel *m*

oaken ['əʊkən] ADJ (*liter*) Eichen-, eichen; **~ door** Eichentür *f*

oakum ['əʊkəm] N Werg *nt*

OAP (*Brit*) *abbr of* **old-age pensioner**

OAPEC [əʊ'eɪpek] *abbr of* **Organization of Arab Petroleum Exporting Countries**

oar [ɔː'] N **a** Ruder *nt*, Riemen *m* (*spec*); **to pull at the ~s** sich in die Riemen legen; **he always has to put** *or* **stick his ~ in** (*fig inf*) er muss (aber auch) immer mitmischen (*inf*); **to rest on one's ~s** (*fig*) langsamer treten (*inf*) **b** (= *person*) Ruderer *m*, Ruderin *f*

-oared [-ɔːd] ADJ *suf* mit ... Rudern; **four-oared boat** Boot mit vier Rudern

oarlock ['ɔːlɒk] N (*US*) (Ruder)dolle *f*

oarsman ['ɔːzmən] N Ruderer *m*

oarsmanship ['ɔːzmənʃɪp] N Rudertechnik *or* -kunst *f*

OAS *abbr of* **Organization of American States** OAS *f*

oasis [əʊ'eɪsɪs] N *pl* **oases** [əʊ'eɪsiːz] (*lit*, *fig*) Oase *f*

oast [əʊst] N Darre *f*, Trockenboden *m*

oast house N Trockenschuppen *m or* -haus *nt*

oat [əʊt] N *usu pl* Hafer *m*; **~s** *pl* (*Cook*) Haferflocken *pl*; **to sow one's wild ~s** (*fig*) sich (*dat*) die Hörner abstoßen; **he's feeling his ~s** (*hum inf*) sticht der Hafer; **to be off one's ~s** (*hum inf*) keinen Appetit haben; **he hasn't had his ~s for some time** (*hum inf*) der hat schon lange keine mehr vernascht (*hum sl*)

oatcake ['əʊtkeɪk] N Haferkeks *m*

oaten ['əʊtn] ADJ *attr* **a** (*of oat straw*) aus Haferstroh **b** (*of oatmeal*) Hafer(mehl)-, aus Hafermehl

oath [əʊθ] N **a** Schwur *m*; (*Jur*) Eid *m*; **to take** *or* **make** *or* **swear an ~** schwören; (*Jur*) einen Eid ablegen *or* leisten; **he took an ~ of loyalty to the government** er schwor der Regierung Loyalität; **to declare under ~** *or* **on ~** (*Jur*) unter Eid aussagen; **to be under ~** (*Jur*) unter Eid stehen; **to break one's ~** seinen Schwur brechen; **to put sb on ~** (*Jur*) jdn vereidigen; **to take the ~**

(*Jur*) vereidigt werden; **he refused to take the ~** (*Jur*) er verweigerte den Eid; **on my ~!** (*obs*) bei meiner Seele! (*obs*) **b** (= *curse*, *profanity*) Fluch *m*

oatmeal ['əʊtmiːl] **N** , *no pl* Haferschrot *m*, Hafermehl *nt* ADJ **a** *biscuits*, *bread* aus Hafermehl **b** *colour*, *dress* hellbeige

OAU *abbr of* **Organization of African Unity** OAU *f*

oaves [əʊvz] PL *of* **oaf**

OB (*Brit*) *abbr of* **outside broadcast** Außenreportage *f*

ob *abbr of* **obiit** gest.

obbligato N, ADJ = **obligato**

obduracy ['ɒbdjʊrəsɪ] N (= *stubbornness*) Hartnäckigkeit *f*; (*of sinner*) Verstocktheit *f*, Halsstarrigkeit *f*; (= *hardheartedness*) Unnachgiebigkeit *f*

obdurate ['ɒbdjʊrɪt] ADJ (= *stubborn*) hartnäckig; *sinner* verstockt, halsstarrig; (= *hardhearted*) unnachgiebig, unerbittlich

obdurately ['ɒbdjʊrɪtlɪ] ADV (= *stubbornly*) hartnäckig; (= *hardheartedly*) unerbittlich; **she remained ~ silent** sie verharrte verbissen in Schweigen

OBE *abbr of* **Officer of the Order of the British Empire** britischer Verdienstorden

obedience [ə'biːdɪəns] N , *no pl* Gehorsam *m*; **in ~ to the law** dem Gesetz entsprechend; **in ~ to your wishes** (*form*) Ihren Wünschen gemäß; **to teach sb ~** jdn gehorchen lehren

obedient [ə'biːdɪənt] ADJ gehorsam; *child*, *dog also* folgsam; **to be ~** gehorchen (*to* +*dat*); (*child*, *dog also*) folgen (*to* +*dat*); (*steering*, *controls*, *car also*) reagieren, ansprechen (*to auf* +*acc*); **your ~ servant** (*old*, *in letters*) Ihr ergebenster Diener, Ihre ergebenste Dienerin (*old*)

obediently [ə'biːdɪəntlɪ] ADV gehorsam; **the car responded ~** das Auto reagierte prompt

obeisance [əʊ'beɪsəns] N **a** (*form*, = *homage*, = *respect*) Ehrerbietung *f*, Reverenz *f* (*geh*), Huldigung *f* (*liter*); **to make** *or* **pay ~ (to sb)** (jdm) seine Huldigung darbringen, (jdm) huldigen **b** (*obs*, = *deep bow*) Verbeugung *f*, Verneigung *f*

obelisk ['ɒbɪlɪsk] N **a** (*Archit*) Obelisk *m* **b** (*Typ*) Kreuz *nt*

obese [əʊ'biːs] ADJ fettleibig (*form*, *Med*), feist (*pej*)

obeseness [əʊ'biːsnɪs], **obesity** [əʊ'biːsɪtɪ] N Fettleibigkeit *f* (*form*, *Med*), Feistheit *f* (*pej*)

obey [ə'beɪ] VT gehorchen (+*dat*); *conscience also* folgen (+*dat*); (*child*, *dog also*) folgen (+*dat*); *law*, *rules* sich halten an (+*acc*), befolgen; *order* befolgen; (*Jur*) *summons* nachkommen (+*dat*), Folge leisten (+*dat*); (*machine*, *vehicle*) *controls* reagieren *or* ansprechen auf (+*acc*); *driver* gehorchen (+*dat*); **to ~ sb implicitly** jdm absoluten Gehorsam leisten; **I expect to be ~ed** ich erwarte, dass man meine Anordnungen befolgt VI gehorchen; (*child*, *dog also*) folgen; (*machine*, *vehicle also*) reagieren; **the troops refused to ~** die Truppen verweigerten den Gehorsam

obfuscate ['ɒbfʌskeɪt] VT (*liter*) *mind* verwirren, trüben; *issue* unklar *or* verworren machen, vernebeln

obituarist [ə'bɪtjʊərɪst] N Nachrufverfasser(in) *m(f)*

obituary [ə'bɪtjʊərɪ] N Nachruf *m*; **~ notice** Todesanzeige *f*; **I saw his ~ notice today** ich habe seinen Namen heute im Sterberegister gelesen; **~ column** Sterberegister *nt*

object¹ ['ɒbdʒɪkt] N **a** (= *thing*) Gegenstand *m*, Ding *nt*; (*Philos*, *abstract etc*) Objekt *nt*, Ding *nt*; **he treats her like an ~** er behandelt sie wie ein Ding *or* Objekt; **she became an ~ of pity** mit ihr musste man Mitleid haben; **he was an ~ of scorn** er war die Zielscheibe der Verachtung; **the cat is the sole ~ of her love** ihre ganze Liebe gilt ihrer Katze

b (= *aim*) Ziel *nt*, Absicht *f*, Zweck *m*; **with this ~ in view** *or* **in mind** mit diesem Ziel vor Augen; **with the sole ~ (of doing)** mit dem einzigen Ziel *or* nur in der Absicht(, zu ...); **he has no ~ in life** er hat kein Ziel im Leben *or* kein Lebensziel; **what's the ~ (of staying here)?** wozu *or* zu welchem Zweck (bleiben wir hier)?; **the ~ of the exercise** der Zweck *or* (*fig also*) Sinn der Übung; **that defeats the ~** das macht es sinnlos, das verfehlt seinen Sinn *or* Zweck; **he made it his ~ to ...** er setzte es sich (*dat*) zum Ziel, zu ...

c (= *obstacle*) Hinderungsgrund *m*; **money/distance is no ~** Geld/Entfernung spielt keine Rolle, Geld/Entfernung (ist) nebensächlich

d (*Gram*) Objekt *nt*; **direct/indirect ~** direktes/indirektes Objekt, Akkusativ-/Dativobjekt *nt*

e (*inf*, = *odd thing*) Ding *nt*, Dings *nt* (*inf*); (= *odd person*) Subjekt *nt*, Vogel *m* (*inf*)

object² [əb'dʒekt] ⊙ 9.2, 12.1, 26.3 VI dagegen sein; (= *make objection*, *protest*) protestieren; (= *be against: in discussion etc*) Einwände haben (*to* gegen); (= *raise objection*) Einwände erheben; (= *disapprove*) Anstoß nehmen (*to an* +*dat*), sich stören (*to an* +*dat*); **to ~ to sth** (= *disapprove*) etw ablehnen *or* missbilligen; **I don't ~ to that** ich habe nichts dagegen (einzuwenden); **if you don't ~** wenn es (Ihnen) recht ist, wenn Sie nichts dagegen haben; **do you ~ to my smoking?** stört es (Sie), wenn ich rauche?, haben Sie etwas dagegen, wenn ich rauche?; **he ~s to my drinking** er nimmt daran Anstoß *or* er hat etwas dagegen, dass ich trinke; **I ~ to your tone** ich verbitte mir diesen Ton; **I ~ to people smoking in my living room** ich verbitte mir, dass in meinem Wohnzimmer geraucht wird; **I ~ most strongly to his smoking** ich missbillige es aufs Äußerste, dass er raucht; **I ~ most strongly to his argument** ich lehne seine Argumentation energisch ab; **I ~ to him bossing me around** ich wehre mich dagegen, dass er mich (so) herumkommandiert; **I ~ to orange curtains with green wallpaper** Vorhänge in Orange mit grünen Tapeten, da protestiere ich!; **she ~s to all that noise** sie stört sich an dem vielen Lärm; **he doesn't ~ to the odd drink** er hat nichts gegen ein Gläschen ab und zu (einzuwenden); **I ~!** ich protestiere!, ich erhebe Einspruch (*form*); **to ~ to a witness** (*Jur*) einen Zeugen ablehnen

VT einwenden

object: object clause N Objektsatz *m*; **object deletion** N (*Gram*) Unterdrückung *f* des Objekts

objection [əbˈdʒekʃən] N **a** (= *reason against*) Einwand *m* (*to gegen*); **to make** or **raise an ~ (to sth)** einen Einwand (gegen etw) machen or erheben (*geh*); **I have no ~ to his going away** ich habe nichts dagegen (einzuwenden), dass er weggeht; **are there any ~s?** irgendwelche Einwände?; **I see no ~ to it** ich sehe nichts, was dagegen spricht; **what are your ~s to it/ him?** was haben Sie dagegen/gegen ihn (einzuwenden)?, welche Einwände haben Sie dagegen/gegen ihn?; **~!** (*Jur*) Einspruch!

b (= *dislike*) Abneigung *f*; (= *disapproval*) Einspruch *m*, Widerspruch *m*; **I have no ~ to him** (*as a person*) ich habe nichts gegen ihn

objectionable [əbˈdʒekʃənəbl] ADJ störend; *conduct* anstößig, nicht einwandfrei; *remark, language* anstößig, unanständig; *smell* unangenehm, übel; **he's a most ~ person** er ist unausstehlich or ekelhaft; **he became ~** er wurde unangenehm; **I find this (really) ~** ich habe starke Einwände dagegen; (= *offensive*) ich finde das anstößig; **this attitude was ~ to them** sie fanden diese Einstellung anstößig

objectionably [əbˈdʒekʃənəbli] ADV unangenehm

objective [əbˈdʒektɪv] **ADJ a** (= *impartial*) *person, article* objektiv, sachlich; **to take an ~ look at sth** etw objektiv betrachten **b** (= *real*) objektiv; **~ fact** Tatsache *f* **N a** (= *aim*) Ziel *nt*; (*esp Comm*) Zielvorstellung *f*; (*Mil*) Angriffsziel *nt*; **in establishing our ~s** bei unserer Zielsetzung **b** (*Opt, Phot*) Objektiv *nt*

objectively [əbˈdʒektɪvli] ADV **a** (= *unemotionally*) objektiv, sachlich **b** (= *in real life etc*) tatsächlich, wirklich

objectivism [əbˈdʒektɪvɪzəm] N Objektivismus *m*

objectivity [ˌɒbdʒekˈtɪvɪti] N Objektivität *f*

object lesson [ˈɒbdʒɪktˌlesn] N **a** (*fig*) Paradebeispiel *nt*, Musterbeispiel *nt* (*in, on* für, +*gen*) **b** (*Sch*) Anschauungsunterricht *m*

objector [əbˈdʒektə] N Gegner(in) *m(f)* (*to* +*gen*)

objet d'art [ˌɒbʒeɪˈdɑː] N Kunstgegenstand *m*

objurgate [ˈɒbdʒɜːɡeɪt] VT (*form*) rügen (*geh*), tadeln

objurgation [ˌɒbdʒɜːˈɡeɪʃən] N (*form*) Tadel *m*, Rüge *f*

oblate¹ [ˈɒbleɪt] ADJ (*Math*) abgeplattet

oblate² N (*Eccl*) Oblate *m*

oblation [əʊˈbleɪʃən] N (*Eccl*) Opfergabe *f*, Opfer *nt*

obligate [ˈɒblɪɡeɪt] VT (*form*) verpflichten (*sb to do sth* jdn, etw zu tun)

obligated [ˈɒblɪɡeɪtɪd] ADJ (*form*) verpflichtet; **to be ~ to sb** in jds Schuld sein or stehen; **to feel ~ to do sth** sich verpflichtet fühlen, etw zu tun

obligation [ˌɒblɪˈɡeɪʃən] N Verpflichtung *f*, Pflicht *f*; **to be under an ~ to do sth** verpflichtet sein or die Pflicht haben, etw zu tun; **to be under no ~ to do sth** nicht verpflichtet sein, etw zu tun; **to be under** or **have an ~ to sb** jdm verpflichtet sein; **you have placed us all under a great ~** wir sind Ihnen alle sehr verpflichtet; **without ~** (*Comm*) unverbindlich, ohne Obligo (*form*); **with no ~ to buy** ohne Kaufzwang

obligato [ˌɒblɪˈɡɑːtəʊ] **N** (= *part*) Obligato *nt* **ADJ** obligato

obligatory [əˈblɪɡətəri] ADJ obligatorisch; *rule* verbindlich; **~ subject** Pflichtfach *nt*; **biology is ~** Biologie ist Pflicht; **attendance is ~** Anwesenheit ist vorgeschrieben; **it's ~ to pay tax** jeder ist steuerpflichtig; **to make it ~ to do sth/ for sb to do sth** vorschreiben, dass etw getan wird/dass jd etw tut; **identity cards were made ~** Personalausweise wurden Vorschrift; **with the ~ piper** mit dem obligaten Dudelsackpfeifer

oblige [əˈblaɪdʒ] ◆ 4 **VT a** (= *compel*) zwingen; (*because of duty*) verpflichten (*sb to do sth* jdn, etw zu tun); (*Jur*) vorschreiben (*sb to do sth* jdm, etw zu tun); **to feel ~d to do sth** sich ver-

pflichtet fühlen, etw zu tun; **I was ~d to go** ich sah mich gezwungen zu gehen; **you are not ~d to do it** Sie sind nicht dazu verpflichtet; **you are not ~d to answer this question** Sie brauchen diese Frage nicht zu beantworten

b (= *do a favour to*) einen Gefallen tun (+*dat*), gefällig sein (+*dat*); **could you ~ me with a light?** wären Sie so gut, mir Feuer zu geben?; **please ~ me by opening a window** würden Sie mir bitte den Gefallen tun und ein Fenster öffnen?; **he ~d us with a song** er gab uns ein Lied zum Besten; **would you ~ me by not interrupting, I would be ~d if you wouldn't interrupt** hätten Sie die Güte, mich nicht zu unterbrechen; **anything to ~ a friend** was tut man nicht alles für einen Freund!

c much ~d! herzlichen Dank!; **I am much ~d to you for this!** ich bin Ihnen dafür sehr verbunden or dankbar

VI she is always ready to ~ sie ist immer sehr gefällig or hilfsbereit; (*hum*) sie ist niemals abgeneigt; **they called for a song, but no-one ~d** sie verlangten nach einem Lied, aber niemand kam der Aufforderung nach; **we asked him the way and he ~d with directions** wir fragten ihn nach dem Weg, und er gab bereitwillig Auskunft; **anything to ~** stets zu Diensten!; **a prompt reply would ~** (*Comm*) wir bitten um baldige Antwort

obliging [əˈblaɪdʒɪŋ] ADJ entgegenkommend, gefällig; *personality* zuvorkommend

obligingly [əˈblaɪdʒɪŋli] ADV entgegenkommenderweise, freundlicherweise, liebenswürdigerweise

obligingness [əˈblaɪdʒɪŋnɪs] N Gefälligkeit *f*, Zuvorkommenheit *f*

oblique [əˈbliːk] **ADJ a** *line* schief, schräg, geneigt; *angle* schief; (*Gram*) *case* abhängig; **~ stroke** Schrägstrich *m* **b** (*fig*) *look* schief, schräg; *course* schräg; *method, style, reply* indirekt; *hint, reference* indirekt, versteckt; *warning* versteckt; *criticism* verdeckt; **an ~ approach to the problem** eine indirekte Art, an das Problem heranzugehen; **he achieved his goal by rather ~ means** er erreichte sein Ziel auf Umwegen or (*dishonestly*) auf krummen Wegen **N** Schrägstrich *m*; **and ~ or** und Strich oder

obliquely [əˈbliːkli] ADV **a** schräg **b** (*fig*) indirekt

obliqueness [əˈbliːknɪs] N **a** Schiefe *f*, Schräge *f*, Neigung *f* **b** (*fig: of means*) Indirektheit *f*

obliterate [əˈblɪtəreɪt] VT (= *erase, abolish*) auslöschen; *past, memory also* tilgen (*geh*); *city also* vernichten; (*inf*) *opposite team etc* vernichten; (= *hide from sight*) *sun, view* verdecken; **the coffee stain has ~d most of the text** der Kaffeefleck hat den Text fast ganz unkenntlich gemacht; **by the 19th century this disease had been completely ~d** im 19. Jahrhundert war dann diese Krankheit völlig ausgerottet

obliteration [əˌblɪtəˈreɪʃən] N Auslöschen *nt*; (*inf: of opponent*) Vernichtung *f*; (= *hiding*) Verdecken *nt*

oblivion [əˈblɪvɪən] N **a** Vergessenheit *f*, Vergessen *nt*; **to sink** or **fall into ~** in Vergessenheit geraten, der Vergessenheit anheim fallen (*geh*); **to rescue sb/sth from ~** jdn/etw wieder ins Bewusstsein or ans Tageslicht bringen; **he drank himself into ~** er trank bis zur Bewusstlosigkeit; **to be bombed/blasted into ~** (*town etc*) dem Erdboden gleichgemacht werden **b** (= *unawareness*) = **obliviousness**

oblivious [əˈblɪvɪəs] ADJ **to be ~ of** or **to sth** sich (*dat*) etw nicht bewusst machen, sich (*dat*) einer Sache (*gen*) nicht bewusst sein; **he was quite ~ of his surroundings** er nahm seine Umgebung gar nicht wahr; **they are ~ to the beauty of their surroundings** sie haben für die Schönheit ihrer Umgebung keinen Sinn; **he was totally ~ of what was going on in his marriage** er (be)merkte gar nicht, was in seiner Ehe vor sich ging; **~ of the world** weltvergessen

obliviously [əˈblɪvɪəsli] ADV **to carry on ~** einfach (unbeirrt) weitermachen

obliviousness [əˈblɪvɪəsnɪs] N **because of his ~ to the danger he was in** weil er sich (*dat*) nicht der Gefahr bewusst war, in der er schwebte; **a state of blissful ~ to the world** ein Zustand *m* seliger Weltvergessenheit

oblong [ˈɒblɒŋ] **ADJ** rechteckig **N** Rechteck *nt*

obloquy [ˈɒbləkwɪ] N (*liter*) **a** (= *blame, abuse*) Schmähung *f* (*liter*), Beschimpfung *f* **b** (= *disgrace*) Schande *f*, Schmach *f*

obnoxious [əbˈnɒkʃəs] ADJ widerlich, widerwärtig; *person also, behaviour* unausstehlich; **an ~ person** ein Ekel *nt* (*inf*); **don't be so ~ to her** sei nicht so gemein or fies (*inf*) zu ihr

obnoxiously [əbˈnɒkʃəsli] ADV widerlich; *behave* unausstehlich

obnoxiousness [əbˈnɒkʃəsnɪs] N Widerlichkeit *f*, Widerwärtigkeit *f*; (*of person also, behaviour*) Unausstehlichkeit *f*

o.b.o. *abbr of* **or best offer** ≈ VB, Verhandlungsbasis *f* → **offer**

oboe [ˈəʊbəʊ] N Oboe *f*

oboist [ˈəʊbəʊɪst] N Oboist(in) *m(f)*

obscene [əbˈsiːn] ADJ obszön; *word, picture, book also* unzüchtig; *language, joke also* zotig; *gesture, posture, thought also* schamlos, unzüchtig; (*non-sexually*): = *repulsive*) Ekel erregend; *prices, demands* unverschämt; **~ publication** Veröffentlichung *f* mit pornografischem Inhalt; **Obscene Publications Act** (*Brit*) Gesetz *über die Veröffentlichung pornografischen Materials*; **this colour scheme is positively ~** diese Farbzusammenstellung widert einen an or ist widerlich

obscenely [əbˈsiːnli] ADV obszön; (= *repulsively*) Ekel erregend; **she earns ~ large amounts of money** sie verdient unverschämt viel Geld

obscenity [əbˈsenɪti] N Obszönität *f*; **he used an ~** er benutzte or gebrauchte einen ordinären Ausdruck

obscurantism [ˌɒbskjʊəˈræntɪzəm] N Obskurantismus *m*, Aufklärungsfeindlichkeit *f*

obscurantist [ˌɒbskjʊəˈræntɪst] N Gegner(in) *m(f)* der Aufklärung

obscuration [ˌɒbskjʊəˈreɪʃən] N Verdunkelung *f*

obscure [əbˈskjʊə] **ADJ** (+*er*) **a** (= *hard to understand*) dunkel; *style* unklar, undurchsichtig; *argument* verworren; *language, word, book, poet* schwer verständlich

b (= *indistinct*) *feeling, memory* dunkel, undeutlich, unklar; **for some ~ reason** aus einem unerfindlichen Grund

c (= *unknown, little known*) obskur; *poet, village* unbekannt; (= *humble*) *beginnings* unbedeutend; *life* wenig beachtenswert; **of ~ birth** von unbekannter Herkunft; **he holds some ~ post in the Civil Service** er hat so ein obskures Pöstchen im Staatsdienst

d (*rare*, = *dark*) düster, finster

VT a (= *hide*) *sun, view* verdecken; **the tree ~d the bay from our view** der Baum nahm uns (*dat*) die Sicht auf die Bucht

b (= *confuse*) verworren or unklar machen; *mind* verwirren; *truth, facts, issues* verschleiern

obscurely [əbˈskjʊəli] ADV **a** *written, presented, argued, remember* undeutlich, unklar **b** **a movement which began ~ in the depths of Russia** eine Bewegung mit obskuren Anfängen im tiefsten Russland **c** *lit* schwach

obscurity [əbˈskjʊərɪti] N **a** *no pl* (*of a wood, night*) Dunkelheit *f*, Finsternis *f*, Dunkel *nt* **b** (*of style, ideas, argument*) Unklarheit *f*, Unverständlichkeit *f*, Verworrenheit *f*; **to lapse into ~** verworren or unklar werden; **he threw some light on the obscurities of the text** er erhellte einige der unklaren Textstellen **c** *no pl* (*of birth, origins*) Dunkel *nt*; **to live in ~** zurückgezogen leben; **to rise from ~** aus dem Nichts auftauchen; **in spite of the ~ of his origins** trotz seiner unbekannten Herkunft; **to sink into ~** in Vergessenheit geraten

obsequies [ˈɒbsɪkwɪz] PL (*form*) Beerdigungsfeier *f*, Leichenbegängnis *nt* (*liter*)

obsequious [əbˈsiːkwɪəs] ADJ unterwürfig, servil (*geh*) (*to(wards)* gegen, gegenüber)

obsequiously [əb'si:kwɪəslɪ] ADV unterwürfig

obsequiousness [əb'si:kwɪəsnɪs] N Unterwürfigkeit f, Servilität f (geh)

observable [əb'zɜ:vəbl] ADJ sichtbar, erkennbar; universe sichtbar; **as is ~ in rabbits** wie bei Kaninchen zu beobachten ist or beobachtet wird; **a welcome improvement has recently become ~** in letzter Zeit zeichnet sich eine willkommene Verbesserung ab; **there has been no ~ change in his condition today** es wurde heute keine Veränderung seines Befindens beobachtet

observably [əb'zɜ:vəblɪ] ADV (= visibly) sichtlich

observance [əb'zɜ:vəns] N **a** (of law) Befolgung f, Beachtung f, Beachten nt **b** (Eccl) (= keeping: of rites etc) Einhalten nt, Einhaltung f, Beachten nt; (= celebration) Kirchenfest nt; (in a convent etc) (Ordens)regel f, Observanz f; **~ of the Sabbath** Einhaltung f des Sabbats or (non--Jewish) des Sonntagsgebots; **religious ~s** religiöse or (Christian also) kirchliche Feste

observant [əb'zɜ:vənt] ADJ **a** (= watchful) person aufmerksam, wach(sam), achtsam; **that's very ~ of you** das hast du aber gut bemerkt; **if you'd been a little more ~** wenn du etwas besser aufgepasst hättest **b** (= strict in obeying rules) **you should be a little more ~ of the law** Sie sollten sich etwas mehr an das Gesetz halten

observantly [əb'zɜ:vəntlɪ] ADV aufmerksam; **... which he very ~ spotted** ..., wie er sehr gut bemerkt hat

observation [ˌɒbzə'veɪʃən] N **a** Beobachtung f; **to keep sb/sth under ~** jdn/etw unter Beobachtung halten; (by police) jdn/etw überwachen or observieren (form); **~ of nature** Naturbeobachtung f; **to take an ~** (Naut) das Besteck nehmen; **powers of ~** Beobachtungsgabe f; **he's in hospital for ~** er ist zur Beobachtung im Krankenhaus; **to escape sb's ~** (von jdm) unbemerkt bleiben, jdm entgehen **b** (of rules, Sabbath) Einhalten nt **c** (= remark) Bemerkung f, Äußerung f; **~s on Kant** Betrachtungen über or zu Kant; **his ~s on the experiment** seine Versuchserläuterungen

observational [ˌɒbzə'veɪʃənəl] ADJ empirisch, aufgrund or auf Grund von Beobachtungen gewonnen; **~ skills** or **faculties** Beobachtungsgabe f; **~ study** Beobachtungsstudie f

observation: observation car N (Rail) Aussichtswagen m, Panoramawagen m; **observation deck** N Aussichtsdeck nt; **observation lounge** N Aussichtsrestaurant nt; **observation post** N Beobachtungsposten m; **observation tower** N Aussichtsturm m; **observation ward** N Beobachtungsstation f

observatory [əb'zɜ:vətrɪ] N Observatorium nt, Sternwarte f; (Met) Observatorium nt, Wetterwarte f

observe [əb'zɜ:v] **⊙** 26.2 **VT a** (= see, notice) beobachten, bemerken; difference, change beobachten, bemerken, wahrnehmen; **did you actually ~ him do it?** haben Sie ihn wirklich dabei beobachtet?; **the thief was ~d to ...** der Dieb wurde dabei beobachtet, wie er ... **b** (= watch carefully, study) beobachten; (by police) überwachen **c** (= remark) bemerken, feststellen, äußern **d** (= obey) achten auf (+acc); rule, custom, ceasefire, Sabbath einhalten; anniversary etc begehen, feiern; **to ~ a minute's silence** or **a moment's silence** (US) eine Schweigeminute einlegen; **failure to ~ the law** ein Verstoß m gegen das Gesetz **VI a** (= watch) zusehen; (= act as an observer) beobachten **b** (= remark) bemerken, feststellen (on zu, über +acc); **you were about to ~ ...?** Sie wollten gerade sagen ...?

observer [əb'zɜ:və'] N (= watcher) Zuschauer(in) m(f); (Mil, Aviat, Pol) Beobachter(in) m(f)

obsess [əb'ses] VT **to be ~ed by** or **with sb/sth** von jdm/etw besessen sein; **to be ~ed about sth** von etw besessen sein; **to be ~ed about doing sth** davon besessen sein, etw zu tun; **sth**

~es sb jd ist von etw besessen; **his one ~ing thought** der ihn ständig verfolgende Gedanke; **don't become ~ed by it** lass das nicht zum Zwang or zur Manie werden

obsession [əb'seʃən] N **a** (= fixed idea) fixe Idee, Manie f; (= fear etc) Zwangsvorstellung f, Obsession f (spec); **she has an ~ with her cat** die Katze ist ihre ganze Leidenschaft; **it's an ~ with him** das ist eine fixe Idee von ihm; (hobby etc) er ist davon besessen; **watching TV is an ~ with him** Fernsehen ist bei ihm zur Sucht geworden **b** (= state) Besessenheit f (with von), Monomanie f; **this ~ with order/quality** dieser Ordnungs-/Qualitätswahn m; **an unnatural ~ with detail** eine (ganz) unnatürliche Detailbesessenheit; **because of his ~ with her** weil er ihr gänzlich verfallen ist

obsessional [əb'seʃənl] ADJ (Psych) behaviour, personality zwanghaft; love, hatred, jealousy obsessiv

obsessionally [əb'seʃənlɪ] ADV (Psych) (+adj) zwanghaft, obsessiv; jealous zwanghaft; (+vb) wie besessen, fanatisch

obsessive [əb'sesɪv] ADJ zwanghaft, obsessiv (spec); **to be ~ about sth** von etw besessen sein; **to be ~ about tidiness** eine übertriebene Ordnungsliebe haben; **to be ~ about cleanliness** einen Sauberkeitsfimmel haben (inf); **she's ~ about organic food** Biokost ist bei ihr zur Manie geworden; **to have an ~ need to do sth** den Zwang verspüren, etw tun zu müssen; **to become ~** zum Zwang or zur Manie werden; **an ~ thought/memory** ein Gedanke, der/eine Erinnerung, die einen nicht loslässt; **an ~ desire for wealth** eine Sucht nach Reichtum; **he is an ~ reader** er liest wie besessen, er hat die Lesewut (inf) **N** Zwangsneurotiker(in) m(f)

obsessive-compulsive disorder [əb'sesɪvkəm'pʌlsɪvdɪs'ɔ:də'] N (Psych) zwanghafte Verhaltensstörung

obsessively [əb'sesɪvlɪ] ADV wie besessen; **to be ~ concerned about sb/sth** von der Sorge um jdn/etw besessen sein; **she is ~ preoccupied with cleanliness** sie huldigt einem Sauberkeitswahn; **he is ~ devoted to her** er ist ihr bedingungslos ergeben; (lover) er liebt sie wie besessen

obsessive neurosis N (Psych) Zwangsneurose f

obsolescence [ˌɒbsə'lesns] N Veralten nt ⟶ **planned obsolescence**

obsolescent [ˌɒbsə'lesnt] ADJ allmählich außer Gebrauch kommend; **to be ~** anfangen zu veralten; (machine, process etc) technisch (fast) überholt sein

obsolete ['ɒbsəli:t] ADJ veraltet, überholt, obsolet (geh); **to become ~** veralten

obstacle ['ɒbstəkl] N (lit, fig) Hindernis nt; **to be an ~ to sb/sth** jdm/einer Sache im Weg(e) stehen, jdn/etw (be)hindern; **if they put any ~ in the way of our plans** wenn man uns Steine in den Weg legt or unsere Pläne behindert; **that's no ~ to our doing it** das wird uns nicht daran hindern; **all the ~s to progress/peace** etc alles, was den Fortschritt/Frieden etc behindert

obstacle course N Hindernisstrecke f; **getting from the desk to the door is a real ~** der Weg vom Schreibtisch zur Tür ist mit Hindernissen übersät

obstacle race N (Sport, fig) Hindernisrennen nt

obstetric(al) [ɒb'stetrɪk(əl)] ADJ (Med) techniques etc bei der Geburtshilfe; **obstetric care** Geburtshilfe f; **obstetric problems** Probleme pl bei der Entbindung; **obstetric specialist** Geburtshelfer(in) m(f)

obstetric clinic N Entbindungsheim nt, Geburtsklinik f

obstetrician [ˌɒbstə'trɪʃən] N Geburtshelfer(in) m(f)

obstetrics [ɒb'stetrɪks] N sing Geburtshilfe f, Obstetrik f (spec); (= ward) Wöchnerinnenstation f

obstetric ward N Entbindungsstation f

obstinacy ['ɒbstɪnəsɪ] N **a** (of person) Hartnäckigkeit f, Starrsinn m; **his ~ in doing sth** die Hartnäckigkeit, mit der er etw tut **b** (of illness, resistance) Hartnäckigkeit f

obstinate ['ɒbstɪnɪt] ADJ **a** person hartnäckig, starrsinnig; stain, weeds hartnäckig; nail etc widerspenstig; **to remain ~** stur bleiben; **to have an ~ streak** zur Starheit neigen; **he was ~ in insisting that ...** er bestand stur or hartnäckig darauf, dass ... **b** resistance, illness hartnäckig

obstinately ['ɒbstɪnɪtlɪ] ADV hartnäckig, stur; **unemployment figures remain ~ high** die Arbeitslosenzahlen verharren auf unverändert hohem Niveau

obstreperous [əb'strepərəs] ADJ aufmüpfig (inf); child aufsässig; **the drunk became ~** der Betrunkene fing an zu randalieren; **it's not a real complaint, he's just being ~** es ist keine echte Beschwerde, er will nur Schwierigkeiten machen

obstreperously [əb'strepərəslɪ] ADV aufmüpfig (inf); (referring to child) aufsässig

obstreperousness [əb'strepərəsnɪs] N Aufmüpfigkeit f (inf); (of child) Aufsässigkeit f

obstruct [əb'strʌkt] **VT a** (= block) blockieren; passage, road versperren, blockieren; view versperren; (Med) artery, pipe blockieren, verstopfen; **you're ~ing my view** Sie nehmen or versperren mir die Sicht **b** (= hinder) (be)hindern; navigation behindern; traffic, progress behindern, aufhalten; (Sport) behindern; (in possession of ball) sperren; **to ~ a bill** (Parl) einen Gesetzentwurf blockieren; **to ~ (the course of) justice** die Rechtsfindung behindern; **to ~ the police** die Arbeit der Polizei behindern **VI** (= be obstructionist) obstruieren, Obstruktion treiben; (Sport) sperren

obstruction [əb'strʌkʃən] N **a** (= blocking) Blockierung f; (of view) Versperren nt; (of artery, pipe also) Verstopfung f; (of road) Sperrung f **b** (= hindering) Behinderung f; (Sport) Sperren nt; **to cause an ~** den Verkehr behindern **c** (= obstacle) Hindernis nt, Hemmnis nt (esp fig); **there is an ~ in the pipe** das Rohr ist blockiert or verstopft; **all ~s to progress** alles, was den Fortschritt aufhält or hemmt **d** (Pol) Obstruktion f, Behinderung f

obstructionism [əb'strʌkʃənɪzəm] N Obstruktionspolitik f

obstructionist [əb'strʌkʃənɪst] N Obstruktionspolitiker(in) m(f)

obstructive [əb'strʌktɪv] ADJ obstruktiv (esp Pol), behindernd; **to be ~** (person) Schwierigkeiten machen, sich quer stellen (inf); **to be ~ to progress** dem Fortschritt hinderlich sein

obtain [əb'teɪn] **VT** erhalten, bekommen; result, votes also erzielen; knowledge erwerben; **to ~ sth through hard work** etw durch harte Arbeit erreichen; possession sich (dat) etw mühsam erarbeiten; **to ~ a divorce** die Scheidung ausgesprochen bekommen; **to ~ an injunction** eine einstweilige Verfügung erteilt bekommen; **to ~ sth for sb** jdm etw beschaffen or verschaffen; **they ~ed the release of the hostages** sie erreichten die Freilassung der Geiseln **VI** (form) gelten; (rules also) in Kraft sein; (customs) bestehen, herrschen

obtainable [əb'teɪnəbl] ADJ erhältlich

obtrude [əb'tru:d] **VT a to ~ oneself** sich anderen aufdrängen **b** (= push out) hervorstrecken, hervorschieben **VI a** (= intrude) sich aufdrängen **b** (= protrude) (her)vorstehen; (fig) hervortreten

obtrusion [əb'tru:ʒən] N **a** Aufdrängen nt; **because of this ~ of himself/his ideas upon others** weil er sich/seine Ideen anderen aufdrängen will **b** (= pushing out) Hervorstrecken nt **c** (= sticking out) Herausragen nt

obtrusive [əb'truːsɪv] ADJ *person, music* aufdringlich; *smell also* penetrant; *building, furniture* zu auffällig

obtrusively [əb'truːsɪvlɪ] ADV (zu) auffällig; *smell* penetrant

obtrusiveness [əb'truːsɪvnɪs] N (*of person*) Aufdringlichkeit f; (*of smell also*) Penetranz f; (*of appearance, dress, building*) Auffälligkeit f

obtuse [əb'tjuːs] ADJ **a** (*Geometry*) stumpf **b** *person* begriffsstutzig, beschränkt; **are you just being ~?** tust du nur so beschränkt?

obtuseness [əb'tjuːsnɪs] N Begriffsstutzigkeit f, Beschränktheit f

OB van [ˌəʊbiː'væn] , **outside broadcast van** N (*Rad, TV*) Übertragungswagen m

obverse [ˈɒbvɜːs] ADJ ~ **side** Vorderseite f **a** (*of coin*) Vorderseite f, Avers m (*spec*) **b** (*of statement, truth*) andere Seite, Kehrseite f

obviate [ˈɒbvɪeɪt] VT vermeiden, umgehen; *need* vorbeugen (+*dat*)

obvious [ˈɒbvɪəs] ADJ offensichtlich, deutlich; (*visually also*) augenfällig; (= *not subtle*) plump; *proof* klar, eindeutig; *difference, fact* eindeutig, offensichtlich, offenkundig; *statement* nahe liegend, selbstverständlich; *reason* (leicht) ersichtlich; *dislike, reluctance, surprise* sichtlich; **an ~ truth** eine offenkundige Tatsache; **because of the ~ truth of what he maintains** da es so eindeutig *or* offensichtlich wahr ist, was er sagt; **that's the ~ translation/solution** das ist die am nächsten liegende *or* nächstliegende Übersetzung/Lösung; **for ~ reasons** aus nahe liegenden Gründen; **he was the ~ choice** es lag nahe, ihn zu wählen; **it was ~ he didn't want to come** er wollte offensichtlich nicht kommen; **it's quite ~ he doesn't understand** man merkt doch (sofort) *or* es ist doch klar, dass er nicht versteht; **to make sth a little more ~** etw etwas deutlicher *or* eindeutiger machen; **there's no need to make it so ~** man braucht das (doch) nicht so deutlich werden zu lassen; **do I have to make it even more ~?** muss ich denn noch deutlicher werden?; **we must not be too ~ about it** wir dürfen es nicht so auffällig machen; **I would have thought that was perfectly ~** das liegt doch auf der Hand; (= *noticeable*) das springt doch ins Auge; **that should be ~ to you** das sollte für Sie offensichtlich sein; **with the ~ exception of ...** natürlich mit Ausnahme von ...; **subtle? he's the most ~ person I know** raffiniert? ich kenne niemanden, der einfacher zu durchschauen wäre!; **even if I am stating the ~** selbst wenn ich hier etwas längst Bekanntes sage; **he has a gift for stating the ~** der merkt aber auch alles! (*inf*); **don't just state the ~, try to be original** sagen Sie nicht, was sich von selbst versteht, sondern bemühen Sie sich um Originalität; **what's the ~ thing to do?** was ist das Naheliegendste?, was bietet sich am ehesten an?

obviously [ˈɒbvɪəslɪ] ADV offensichtlich, offenbar; (= *noticeably*) (offen)sichtlich; **he's ~ French** er ist eindeutig ein Franzose; **she is not ~ drunk** es ist nicht offensichtlich, dass sie betrunken ist; **~!** natürlich!, selbstverständlich!; **is he there? – well, ~ not** ist er da? – offensichtlich nicht; **he's not going to like it** das wird ihm natürlich nicht gefallen; **he's ~ not going to get the job** er bekommt die Stelle nicht, das ist ja klar (*inf*)

obviousness [ˈɒbvɪəsnɪs] N Offensichtlichkeit f, Deutlichkeit f; **amused by the ~ of his reply** belustigt über die Eindeutigkeit *or* Plumpheit seiner Antwort

OC N abbr of **Officer Commanding** (*Mil*) Oberbefehlshaber(in) m(f); **who's OC paper supply in the office?** (*inf*) wer ist hier im Büro der Papierhengst? (*inf*)

ocarina [ˌɒkəˈriːnə] N Okarina f

Occam's razor [ˈɒkəmzˈreɪzə] N **to apply ~ to sth** etw komprimieren, etw auf das Wesentliche beschränken

occasion [əˈkeɪʒən] N **a** (= *point in time*) Gelegenheit f, Anlass m; **on that ~** damals, bei jener Gelegenheit *or* jenem Anlass (*geh*); **on another ~** ein anderes Mal, bei einer anderen Gelegenheit etc; **on several ~s** mehrmals, bei *or* zu mehreren Gelegenheiten etc; **(on) the first ~** beim ersten Mal, das erste Mal; **on ~** gelegentlich; (= *if need be*) wenn nötig; **it does not befit the ~** es ist unpassend für diesen *or* zu diesem Anlass; **to rise to the ~** sich der Lage gewachsen zeigen

b (= *special time*) Ereignis nt; **~s of state** Staatsanlässe pl; **on the ~ of his birthday** anlässlich *or* aus Anlass seines Geburtstages (*geh*); **one's 21st birthday should be something of an ~** ein 21. Geburtstag sollte schon ein besonderes Ereignis sein

c (= *opportunity*) Gelegenheit f, Möglichkeit f; **I never had the ~ to congratulate him** es bot sich mir keine Gelegenheit *or* ich hatte nicht die Möglichkeit, ihm zu gratulieren; **I would like to take this ~ to ...** (*form*) ich möchte diese Gelegenheit ergreifen, um ...

d (= *reason*) Grund m, Anlass m, Veranlassung f; **should the ~ arise** sollte es nötig sein *or* werden; **to give ~ to sth** (*form*) zu etw Anlass geben; **if you have ~ to ...** sollten Sie Veranlassung haben, zu ...; **not an ~ for merriment** kein Grund zur Freude

VT (*form*) verursachen, Anlass geben zu, zeitigen (*geh*); **to ~ sb to do sth** jdn dazu veranlassen, etw zu tun

occasional [əˈkeɪʒənl] ADJ **a** *visit, visitor, meeting, outburst, lapse* gelegentlich; **he likes an ~ or the ~ cigar** er raucht hin und wieder ganz gerne *or* gelegentlich ganz gern eine Zigarre; **she made ~ visits to England** sie fuhr ab und zu nach England **b** (= *designed for special event*) Gelegenheits-; **~ poem** Gelegenheitsgedicht nt

occasionally [əˈkeɪʒənlɪ] ADV gelegentlich, hin und wieder, zuweilen (*geh*); **very ~** sehr selten, sehr oft

occasional table N kleiner Wohnzimmertisch

occident [ˈɒksɪdənt] N (*liter*) Abendland nt, Okzident m (*geh*); **the Occident** (*Pol*) der Westen

occidental [ˌɒksɪˈdentəl] ADJ (*liter*) abendländisch N (*rare*) Abendländer(in) m(f)

occipital [ɒkˈsɪpɪtəl] ADJ (*spec*) des Hinterkopfs

occiput [ˈɒksɪpʌt] N (*spec*) Hinterkopf m

occlude [ɒˈkluːd] (*spec*) VT (*Anat, Med*) *pores, artery* verschließen, verstopfen, okkludieren (*spec*); (*Chem*) *gas* adsorbieren VI (*Dentistry*) eine normale Bissstellung haben

occluded front [ɒˈkluːdɪdˈfrʌnt] N (*Met*) Okklusion f

occlusion [ɒˈkluːʒən] N (*spec*) (*Med: of artery*) Verschluss m, Okklusion f (*spec*); (*Dentistry*) Biss m, normale Bissstellung; (*Phon*) Verschluss m; (*Chem*) Adsorption f; (*Met*) Okklusion f

occult [ɒˈkʌlt] ADJ okkult; (= *of occultism*) okkultistisch; (= *secret*) geheimnisvoll N Okkulte(s) nt

occultism [ˈɒkʌltɪzəm] N Okkultismus m

occultist [ɒˈkʌltɪst] N Okkultist(in) m(f)

occupancy [ˈɒkjʊpənsɪ] N Bewohnen nt; (= *period*) Wohndauer f; **a change of ~** ein Besitzerwechsel m; (*of rented property*) ein Mieterwechsel m; **multiple ~** Mehrfachbelegung f von Wohnraum; **levels of hotel ~** Übernachtungsziffern pl

occupant [ˈɒkjʊpənt] N (*of house*) Bewohner(in) m(f); (*of post*) Inhaber(in) m(f); (*of car*) Insasse m, Insassin f

occupation [ˌɒkjʊˈpeɪʃən] N **a** (= *employment*) Beruf m, Tätigkeit f; **what is his ~?** was ist er von Beruf?, welche Tätigkeit übt er aus?; **he is a teacher by ~** er ist Lehrer von Beruf

b (= *pastime*) Beschäftigung f, Betätigung f, Tätigkeit f

c (*Mil*) Okkupation f; (= *act*) Besetzung f (*of* von), Okkupation f; **army of ~** Besatzungsarmee f

d (*of house etc*) Besetzung f; **to be in ~ of a house** ein Haus bewohnen; **ready for ~** bezugsfertig, schlüsselfertig; **we found them already in ~** wir sahen, dass sie schon eingezogen waren ADJ Besatzungs-, Okkupations-; **~ troops** Besatzungs- *or* Okkupationstruppen pl

occupational [ˌɒkjʊˈpeɪʃənl] ADJ Berufs-, beruflich; **~ accident** Berufsunfall m; **~ disease** Berufskrankheit f; **~ group** Berufsgruppe f; **~ hazard** *or* **risk** Berufsrisiko nt

occupationally [ˌɒkjʊˈpeɪʃənlɪ] ADV beruflich; **equality for women politically and ~** die Gleichberechtigung der Frau in Politik und Beruf

occupational: occupational pension (scheme) N betriebliche Altersversorgung; **Occupational Safety and Health Administration** N (*US*) Arbeitsschutzbehörde f; **occupational therapist** N Beschäftigungstherapeut(in) m(f); **occupational therapy** N Beschäftigungstherapie f

occupied [ˈɒkjʊpaɪd] ADJ **a** *house, room* belegt; **a room ~ by four people** ein von vier Personen bewohntes Zimmer; **is this seat ~?** ist dieser Platz belegt? **b** (*Mil etc*) *country, territory* besetzt **c** (= *busy*) beschäftigt; **to be ~ with sth** mit etw beschäftigt sein; **to keep sb ~** jdn beschäftigen; **that'll keep him ~** dann hat er was zu tun, dann ist er beschäftigt; **he kept his mind ~** er beschäftigte sich geistig

occupier [ˈɒkjʊpaɪə] N (*of house, land*) Bewohner(in) m(f); (*of post*) Inhaber(in) m(f)

occupy [ˈɒkjʊpaɪ] VT **a** *house* bewohnen; *seat, room* belegen, besetzen; *hotel room* belegen; **you ~ a special place in my heart** du hast einen besonderen Platz in meinem Herzen (inne) **b** (*Mil etc*) besetzen; *country* okkupieren, besetzen **c** *post, position* innehaben, bekleiden (*geh*) **d** (= *take up*) beanspruchen; *space* einnehmen; *time* in Anspruch nehmen, beanspruchen; (= *help pass*) ausfüllen; **can't you find some better way of ~ing your time?** kannst du mit deiner Zeit nicht etwas Besseres anfangen? **e** (= *busy*) beschäftigen; **to ~ oneself** sich beschäftigen; **a thought which has been ~ing my mind** ein Gedanke, der mich beschäftigt

occur [əˈkɜː] VI **a** (= *take place*) (*event*) geschehen, sich ereignen, vorkommen; (*difficulty*) sich ergeben; (*change*) stattfinden; **that doesn't ~ very often** das kommt nicht oft vor, das gibt es nicht oft; **don't let it ~ again** lassen Sie das nicht wieder vorkommen, dass das nicht wieder passiert!; **should a fault ~** sollte ein Fehler auftreten; **if the opportunity ~s** sich die Gelegenheit bietet *or* ergibt **b** (= *be found: disease*) vorkommen **c** (= *come to mind*) einfallen, in den Sinn kommen (*geh*) (*to sb* jdm); **if it ~s to you that he is wrong** falls es Ihnen so vorkommt, als habe er sich geirrt; **it ~s to me that ...** ich habe den Eindruck, dass ...; **the idea just ~red to me** es ist mir gerade eingefallen; **it never ~red to me** darauf bin ich noch nie gekommen; **it didn't even ~ to him to ask** er kam erst gar nicht auf den Gedanken, zu fragen; **did it ever ~ to you to apologize?** hast du eigentlich je daran gedacht, dich zu entschuldigen?

occurrence [əˈkʌrəns] N **a** (= *event*) Ereignis nt, Begebenheit f **b** (= *presence, taking place*) Auftreten nt; (*of minerals*) Vorkommen nt; **further ~s of this nature must be avoided** weitere Vorkommnisse dieser Art müssen vermieden werden

ocean [ˈəʊʃən] N **a** Ozean m, Meer nt **b** **an ~ of flowers** ein Blumenmeer nt; **~s of** (*inf*) jede Menge (*inf*), massenhaft

ocean: ocean bed N Meeresboden m *or* -grund m; **ocean chart** N Seekarte f; **ocean climate** N Meeresklima nt, maritimes Klima; **ocean-going** ADJ hochseetauglich; **~ tug** Hochseeschlepper m

Oceania [ˌəʊʃɪˈeɪnɪə] N Ozeanien nt

Oceanian [ˌəʊʃɪˈeɪnɪən] ADJ ozeanisch N Ozeanier(in) m(f)

oceanic [ˌəʊʃɪˈænɪk] ADJ **a** Meeres-; ~ **plant** Meerespflanze f **b** (fig) riesenhaft

ocean liner N Ozeandampfer m

oceanographer [ˌəʊʃəˈnɒɡrəfəʳ] N Ozeanograf(in) m(f), Meereskundler(in) m(f)

oceanography [ˌəʊʃəˈnɒɡrəfɪ] N Ozeanografie f, Meereskunde f

ocean: Ocean State N the ~ (US) Rhode Island nt; **ocean voyage** N Schiffsreise f, Seereise f

ocelot [ˈɒsɪlɒt] N Ozelot m

och [ɒx] INTERJ (Scot) ach was, ach wo; ~ **aye** ach ja

ochre, (US) **ocher** [ˈəʊkəʳ] N Ocker m or nt; **red** ~ roter or rotes Ocker; **yellow** ~ (= substance) Ocker m or nt; (= colour) Ocker m or nt, Ockergelb nt ADJ ockerfarben

o'clock [əˈklɒk] ADV **a** at 5 ~ um 5 Uhr; **it is 5 ~ in the morning/evening** es ist 5 Uhr morgens/abends; **what** ~ **is it?** (obs) wie spät ist die Uhr?; **the 9 ~ news** die 9-Uhr-Nachrichten; **the 9 ~ train** der 9-Uhr-Zug **b** aircraft approaching at 5 ~ Flugzeug aus Südsüdost

OCR abbr of **optical character reader** of **optical character recognition** ~ **font** OCR-Schrift f

Oct abbr of **October** Okt.

octagon [ˈɒktəɡən] N Achteck nt, Oktogon nt, Oktagon nt

octagonal [ɒkˈtæɡənl] ADJ achteckig, oktogonal

octahedron [ˌɒktəˈhiːdrən] N Oktaeder m, Achtflächner m

octane [ˈɒkteɪn] N Oktan nt; **high-octane fuel** Benzin nt mit hoher Oktanzahl

octane number, octane rating N Oktanzahl f

octangle [ˈɒktæŋɡl] N (Math) Achteck nt

octave [ˈɒktɪv] N **a** (Mus) Oktave f **b** (of sonnet) Oktett nt

octavo [ɒkˈteɪvəʊ] N Oktav(format) nt; (also **octavo volume**) Oktavband m

octet [ɒkˈtet] N (Mus, Poet) Oktett nt

October [ɒkˈtəʊbəʳ] N Oktober m; **the ~ Revolution** die Oktoberrevolution → also **September**

octogenarian [ˌɒktəʊdʒɪˈneərɪən] N Achtziger(in) m(f), Achtzigjährige(r) mf ADJ achtzigjährig

octopus [ˈɒktəpəs] N Tintenfisch m, Krake f

ocular [ˈɒkjʊlə] ADJ (form) okular (spec)

oculist [ˈɒkjʊlɪst] N Augenspezialist(in) m(f)

OD (inf) ■ N Überdosis f ■ VI eine Überdosis nehmen; **to OD on heroin** sich (dat) den goldenen Schuss setzen (inf)

odalisque [ˈəʊdəlɪsk] N Odaliske f

odd [ɒd] ADJ (+er) **a** (= peculiar) merkwürdig, seltsam, sonderbar; person, thing, idea eigenartig, seltsam; **how** ~ **that we should meet him** (wie) eigenartig or seltsam, dass wir ihn trafen; **it is an** ~ **thing to do** es ist seltsam, so etwas zu tun; **the** ~ **thing about it is that** ... das Merkwürdige etc daran ist, dass ...; **there was something ~ about it** daran stimmte irgendetwas nicht; **it seemed** ~ **to me** es kam mir komisch vor; **he's got some ~ ways** er hat eine schrullige or verschrobene Art **b** number ungerade **c** (= one of a pair or a set) shoe, glove einzeln; **he/she is (the) ~ man** or **one out** er/sie ist übrig or überzählig or das fünfte Rad am Wagen; (in character) er/sie steht (immer) abseits, er/sie ist ein Außenseiter/eine Außenseiterin; **in each group underline the word/picture which is the ~ man** or **one out** unterstreichen Sie in jeder Gruppe das nicht dazugehörige Wort/Bild **d** (= slightly over) **600-odd euros** gut 600 Euro **e** (= surplus, extra) übrig, restlich, überzählig; **the ~ one left over** der/die/das Überzählige; **have you got an ~ piece of paper?** haben Sie ein Blatt Papier übrig? **f** (= not regular or specific) moments, times zeitweilig; (Comm) size ausgefallen; **any ~ piece of wood** irgendein Stück(chen) Holz; **at ~ mo-**

ments or times ab und zu; **at ~ moments during the day** zwischendurch; **he likes the ~ drink** er trinkt gerne mal einen; ~ **job** (gelegentlich) anfallende Arbeit; **he does all the ~ jobs** er macht alles, was an Arbeit anfällt

ADV (inf) **he was acting a bit** ~ er benahm sich etwas komisch

oddball [ˈɒdbɔːl] (inf) ■ N Spinner(in) m(f); (more harmless) komischer Kauz; (less harmless: = weirdo) Verrückte(r) mf ADJ ideas, friends komisch

odd bod [ˈɒdbɒd] N (Brit inf) komischer Kauz

oddity [ˈɒdɪtɪ] N **a** (= strangeness) (of person) Wunderlichkeit f, Absonderlichkeit f, Eigenartigkeit f; (of thing) Ausgefallenheit f **b** (= odd person) komischer Kauz or Vogel; (who doesn't fit) Kuriosität f; (= odd thing) Kuriosität f

odd-jobman [ˌɒdˈdʒɒbmæn] N Mädchen nt für alles

oddly [ˈɒdlɪ] ADV speak, behave eigenartig, sonderbar, merkwürdig; **an ~ shaped room** ein Raum, der eine seltsame Form hat; **I find her ~ attractive** ich finde sie auf (eine) seltsame Art anziehend; **they are ~ similar** sie sind sich seltsam or merkwürdig ähnlich; **the street was ~ familiar** die Straße kam mir merkwürdig bekannt vor; ~ **enough she was at home** merkwürdigerweise or seltsamerweise war sie zu Hause; ~ **enough you are right** Sie werden überrascht sein, aber das stimmt

oddment [ˈɒdmənt] N usu pl Restposten m; (of cloth also) Rest m; (= single piece also) Einzelstück nt

oddness [ˈɒdnɪs] N Merkwürdigkeit f, Seltsamkeit f

odds [ɒdz] PL **a** (Betting) Odds pl; (of bookmaker) Kurse pl, Odds pl; **the ~ are 6 to 1** die Chancen stehen 6 zu 1 (written: 6:1); **long/short ~** geringe/hohe Gewinnchancen pl; **he won at long ~** er hat mit einer hohen Gewinnquote gewonnen; **fixed ~** feste Kurse pl; **to lay** or **give ~ of 2 to 1 (against sb)** den Kurs mit 2 zu 1 (written: 2:1) (gegen jdn) angeben; **I'll lay ~ (of 3 to 1) that ...** (fig) ich wette (3 gegen 1), dass ...

b (= chances for or against) Chance(n) f(pl); **the ~ were against us** alles sprach gegen uns; **in spite of the tremendous ~ against him ...** obwohl alles so völlig gegen ihn sprach or war ...; **the ~ were in our favour** (Brit) or **favor** (US) alles sprach für uns; **against all the ~ he won** sie war wider Erwarten or entgegen allen Erwartungen gewann er; **what are the ~ on/against ...?** wie sind or stehen die Chancen, dass .../dass ... nicht?; **to fight against heavy/overwhelming ~** (Mil) gegen eine große/überwältigende gegnerische Übermacht ankämpfen; **to struggle against impossible ~** so gut wie keine Aussicht auf Erfolg haben; **the ~ are that he will come** es sieht ganz so aus, als ob er käme or kommen würde; **to lengthen/shorten the ~** die Chancen erhöhen/verringern

c (inf) **to pay over the ~** zu viel bezahlen; **foreign buyers who are prepared to pay over the ~** Ausländer, die gewillt sind, überhöhte Preise zu bezahlen

d (= difference) **what's the ~?** was macht das schon (aus)?; **it makes no ~** es spielt keine Rolle; **it makes no ~ to me** es ist mir (völlig) einerlei; **does it really make any ~ if I don't come?** macht es etwas aus, wenn ich nicht komme?

e (= variance) **to be at ~ with sb over sth** mit jdm in etw (dat) nicht übereinstimmen; **we are at ~ as to the best solution** wir gehen nicht darin einig, wie das am besten gelöst werden soll; **to be at ~ with oneself** mit sich selbst nicht klarkommen

odds and ends PL Krimskrams m, Kram m; (of food) Reste pl; (of cloth) Reste pl, Flicken pl; **bring all your ~** bringen Sie Ihren ganzen Kram or Ihre Siebensachen (inf)

odds and sods PL (Brit hum inf) Kleinkram m; **I've got a few ~ to tidy up** ich muss hier und da noch ein paar Sachen in Ordnung bringen; **a few ~** (= people) ein paar Leute

odds-on [ˈɒdzɒn] ADJ **the ~ favourite** (Brit) or **favorite** (US) der klare Favorit; **she's ~ favourite** (Brit) or **favorite** (US) **for the job** sie hat die größten Aussichten, die Stelle zu bekommen; **he has an ~ chance (of winning)** er hat die besten (Gewinn)chancen ADV **it's ~ that he'll come** es ist so gut wie sicher, dass er kommt

ode [əʊd] N Ode f (to, on an +acc)

odious [ˈəʊdɪəs] ADJ person abstoßend, ekelhaft; action abscheulich, verabscheuenswürdig; **an ~ person** ein Ekel nt; **what an ~ thing to say** wie abscheulich, so etwas zu sagen; **to make ~ comparisons** hässliche Vergleiche machen

odium [ˈəʊdɪəm] N (= being hated) Hass m; (= repugnance) Abscheu m

odometer [ɒˈdɒmɪtəʳ] N Kilometerzähler m

odontologist [ˌɒdɒnˈtɒlədʒɪst] N Odontologe m, Odontologin f, Facharzt m/-ärztin f für Zahnheilkunde

odontology [ˌɒdɒnˈtɒlədʒɪ] N Odontologie f, Zahnheilkunde f

odor etc (US) = **odour** etc

odoriferous [ˌəʊdəˈrɪfərəs] ADJ (form) wohlriechend, duftend

odorous [ˈəʊdərəs] ADJ (esp poet) duftend, wohlriechend

odour, (US) **odor** [ˈəʊdəʳ] N **a** (lit, fig) Geruch m; (= sweet smell) Duft m, Wohlgeruch m; (= bad smell) Gestank m **b** **to be in good/bad ~ with sb** gut/schlecht bei jdm angeschrieben sein

odour-free, (US) **odor-free** [ˈəʊdəfriː] ADJ geruchsfrei

odourless, (US) **odorless** [ˈəʊdəlɪs] ADJ geruchlos

Odyssey [ˈɒdɪsɪ] N (Myth, fig) Odyssee f

OE abbr of **Old English**

OECD abbr of **Organization for Economic Cooperation and Development** OECD f

oecumenical [ˌiːkjuːˈmenɪkəl] ADJ = **ecumenical**

oedema, (US) **edema** [ɪˈdiːmə] N Ödem nt

Oedipus [ˈiːdɪpəs] N Ödipus m

Oedipus complex N Ödipuskomplex m

OEIC [ɔɪk] N ABBR of **open-ended investment company** (Brit, Fin) Investmentgesellschaft f (mit eingeschränkten Befugnissen)

o'er [ˈəʊə] PREP, ADV (poet) contr of **over**

oesophagus, (US) **esophagus** [iːˈsɒfəɡəs] N Speiseröhre f

of [ɒv, əv] PREP **a** (indicating possession or relation) von (+dat), use of gen **the wife of the doctor** die Frau des Arztes, die Frau vom Arzt; **a friend of ours** ein Freund/eine Freundin von uns; **a painting of the Queen** ein Gemälde nt der or von der Königin; **a painting of the Queen's** (= belonging to her) ein Gemälde (im Besitz) der Königin; (= painted by her) ein Gemälde (von) der Königin; **of it** davon; **the first of May** der Erste Mai; **the first of the month** der Erste (des Monats), der Monatserste; **that damn dog of theirs** (inf) ihr verdammter Hund (inf); **it is very kind of you** es ist sehr freundlich von Ihnen; **it was nasty of him to say that** es war gemein von ihm, das zu sagen

b (indicating separation in space or time) **south of Paris** südlich von Paris; **within a month of his death** einen Monat nach seinem Tod; **a quarter of six** (US) Viertel vor sechs

c (indicating cause) **he died of poison/cancer** er starb an Gift/Krebs; **he died of hunger** er verhungerte, er starb hungers (geh); **it did not happen of itself** (liter) das ist nicht von selbst or von allein geschehen; **it tastes of garlic** es schmeckt nach Knoblauch; **she is proud of him** sie ist stolz auf ihn; **I am ashamed of it** ich schäme mich dafür

d (indicating deprivation, riddance) **he was cured of the illness** er wurde von der Krankheit geheilt; **trees bare of leaves** Bäume ohne Blätter; **free of charge** kostenlos

e (indicating material) aus; **dress made of wool** Wollkleid nt, Kleid nt aus Wolle

f (*indicating quality, identity etc*) **house of ten rooms** Haus *nt* mit zehn Zimmern; **man of courage** mutiger Mensch, Mensch *m* mit Mut; **girl of ten** zehnjähriges Mädchen, Mädchen *nt* von zehn Jahren; **a matter of no importance** eine Sache ohne Bedeutung; **the city of Paris** die Stadt Paris; **person of swarthy complexion** dunkelhäutige Person; **a town of narrow streets** eine Stadt mit engen Straßen; **where is that rascal of a boy?** wo ist dieser verflixte Bengel?; **that idiot of a waiter** dieser Idiot von Kellner

g (*objective genitive*) **fear of God** Gottesfurcht *f*; **his love of his father** die Liebe zu seinem Vater; **he is a leader of men** er hat die Fähigkeit, Menschen zu führen; **great eaters of fruit** große Obstesser *pl*; **writer of legal articles** Verfasser *m* von juristischen Artikeln; **love of money** Liebe zum Geld

h (*subjective genitive*) **love of God for man** Liebe Gottes zu den Menschen; **affection of a mother** Mutterliebe *f*

i (*partitive genitive*) **the whole of the house** das ganze Haus; **half of the house** das halbe Haus; **how many of them do you want?** wie viele möchten Sie (davon)?; **many of them came** viele (von ihnen) kamen; **there were six of us** wir waren zu sechst, wir waren sechs; **he is not one of us** er gehört nicht zu uns; **one of the best** einer der Besten; **he asked the six of us to lunch** er lud uns sechs zum Mittagessen ein; **of the ten only one was absent** von den zehn fehlte nur einer; **today of all days** ausgerechnet heute; **you of all people ought to know** gerade Sie sollten das wissen; **they are the best of friends** sie sind die besten Freunde; **the best of teachers** der (aller)beste Lehrer; **the bravest of the brave** der Mutigste der Mutigen; **he drank of the wine** (*liter*) er trank von dem Weine (*liter*)

j (= *concerning*) **what do you think of him?** was halten Sie von ihm?; **what has become of him?** was ist aus ihm geworden?; **he warned us of the danger** er warnte uns vor der Gefahr; **doctor of medicine** Doktor der Medizin; **what of it?** ja und?

k (*obs, liter,* = *by*) **forsaken of men** von allen verlassen; **beloved of all** von allen geliebt

l (*in temporal phrases*) **he's become very quiet of late** er ist letztlich *or* seit neuestem so ruhig geworden; **they go out of an evening** (*inf*) sie gehen abends (schon mal) aus (*inf*); **he died of a Saturday morning** (*dial*) er starb an einem Samstagmorgen

off [ɒf] **ADV a** (*distance*) **the house is 5 km ~** das Haus ist 5 km entfernt; **some way ~ (from here)** in einiger Entfernung (von hier); **it's a long way ~** das ist weit weg; (*time*) das liegt in weiter Ferne; **August isn't/the exams aren't very far ~** es ist nicht mehr lang bis August/bis zu den Prüfungen; **Christmas is only a week ~** es ist nur noch eine Woche bis Weihnachten; **noises ~** (*Theat*) Geräusche *pl* hinter den Kulissen

b (*departure*) **to be/go ~** gehen; **he's ~ to school** er ist zur Schule gegangen; **(be) ~ with you!** fort mit dir!, mach, dass du wegkommst!; **~ with him!** fort *or* weg mit ihm!; **I must be ~** ich muss (jetzt) gehen *or* weg (*inf*); **it's time I was ~** es wird *or* ist (höchste) Zeit, dass ich gehe; **where are you ~ to?** wohin gehen Sie denn?, wohin gehts denn? (*inf*); **~ we go!** los!, auf los gehts los!, na denn man los! (*inf*); **he's ~ playing tennis every evening** er geht jeden Abend Tennis spielen; **they're ~** (*Sport*) sie sind vom Start; **she's ~ again** (*inf, = complaining etc*) sie legt schon wieder los (*inf*)

c (*removal*) **he had his coat ~** er hatte den Mantel aus; **he helped me ~ with my coat** er half mir aus dem Mantel; **with his shirt ~** ohne Hemd; **~ with those wet clothes!** raus aus den nassen Kleidern!; **the handle has come ~** der Griff ist abgegangen; **there are two buttons ~** es fehlen zwei Knöpfe, da sind zwei Knöpfe ab (*inf*); **~ with his head!** herunter mit seinem Kopf!, Kopf ab!; **he had the back of the TV ~** er hatte die Rückwand des Fernsehers abge-

nommen; **the lid is ~** der Deckel ist nicht drauf

d (= *discount*) **3% ~** (*Comm*) 3% Nachlass *or* Abzug; **3% ~ for cash** (*Comm*) 3% Skonto, bei Barzahlung 3%; **to give sb £5/something ~** jdm £ 5 Ermäßigung/eine Ermäßigung geben; **he let me have £5 ~** er gab es mir (um) £ 5 billiger

e (= *not at work*) **to have time ~ to do sth** (Zeit) freibekommen haben, um etw zu tun; **I've got a day ~** ich habe einen Tag frei(bekommen); **she's nearly always ~ on Tuesdays** dienstags hat sie fast immer frei; **to be ~ sick** wegen Krankheit fehlen

f (*in phrases*) **~ and on, on and ~** ab und zu, ab und an; **it rained ~ and on** es regnete mit Unterbrechungen; **right** *or* **straight ~** gleich

ADJ a *attr* (= *substandard*) **year, day etc** schlecht; **I'm having an ~ day today** ich bin heute nicht in Form

b *pred* (*Brit: = not fresh*) verdorben, schlecht; *milk* schlecht, sauer; *butter* ranzig; **to go ~** schlecht werden

c *pred* (= *cancelled*) *match, party, talks* abgesagt; (= *not available: in restaurant*) *chops, fish* aus; **I'm afraid veal is ~ today** Kalbfleisch gibt es heute leider nicht; **the bet/agreement is ~** die Wette/Abmachung gilt nicht (mehr); **their engagement is ~** ihre Verlobung ist gelöst; **the play is ~** (= *cancelled*) das Stück wurde abgesagt; (= *no longer running*) das Stück wurde abgesetzt

d *TV, light, machine* aus(geschaltet); *tap* zu(gedreht); **the gas/electricity was ~** das Gas/der Strom war abgeschaltet; **the brake was ~** die Bremse war gelöst

e **they are badly/well** *or* **comfortably ~** sie sind nicht gut/(ganz) gut gestellt, sie stehen sich schlecht/(ganz) gut; **I am badly ~ for money/time** mit Geld/Zeit sieht es bei mir nicht gut aus; **how are we ~ for time?** wie sieht es mit der Zeit aus?, wie viel Zeit haben wir noch?; **he is better/worse ~ staying in England** er steht sich in England besser/schlechter

f *pred* (= *wide of the truth etc*) **you're ~ there** da irrst du gewaltig, da vertust du dich; **he was quite a bit ~ in his calculations** er hatte sich in seinen Berechnungen ziemlich *or* schwer (*inf*) vertan

g *pred* (*inf*) **that's a bit ~!** das ist ein dicker Hund! (*inf*); **it's a bit ~ not letting me know** das ist ja nicht die feine Art, mir nicht Bescheid zu sagen; **his behaviour** (*Brit*) *or* **behavior** (*US*) **was a bit ~** er hat sich ziemlich danebenbenommen; **she's been a bit ~ with me all week** sie hat sich die ganze Woche mir gegenüber etwas komisch verhalten; (= *has been angry*) sie war die ganze Woche über etwas sauer auf mich (*inf*)

PREP a (*indicating motion, removal etc*) von (+*dat*); **he jumped ~ the roof** er sprang vom Dach; **once you are ~ the premises** sobald Sie vom Gelände (herunter) sind; **I got it ~ my friend** (*inf*) ich habs von meinem Freund (gekriegt) (*inf*); **he borrowed money ~ his father** (*inf*) er lieh sich (*dat*) von seinem Vater Geld; **they dined ~ chicken** sie aßen Hühnchen; **we live ~ cheese on toast** wir leben von Käse und Toastbrot; **I'll take something ~ the price for you** ich lasse Ihnen vom *or* im Preis etwas nach; **he got £2 ~ the shirt** er bekam das Hemd £ 2 billiger; **the lid had been left ~ the tin** jemand hatte den Deckel nicht wieder auf die Büchse getan; **the coat has two buttons ~ it** am Mantel fehlen zwei Knöpfe; **which coat is that button ~?** von welchem Mantel ist dieser Knopf?

b (= *distant from*) ab(gelegen) von (+*dat*); (= *in a side street from*) in einer Nebenstraße von (+*dat*); (*Naut*) vor (+*dat*); **the house was just ~ the main road** das Haus lag in unmittelbarer Nähe der Hauptstraße; **one mile ~ the main road** eine Meile von der Hauptstraße weg *or* entfernt; **height ~ the ground** Höhe vom Boden (weg); **just ~ Piccadilly** in der Nähe von Piccadilly, gleich bei Piccadilly; **a road ~ Bank Street** eine Querstraße zur Bank Street

c **~ the map** nicht auf der Karte; **I just want it**

~ my hands ich möchte das nur loswerden → **duty, food** *etc*

d **I'm ~ sausages/beer/him** (= *don't like at the moment*) Wurst/Bier/er kann mich zur Zeit nicht reizen

off: off air ADV (*TV, Rad*) nicht auf Sendung; **to go ~** (*broadcast*) enden; (*for good: station*) den Sendebetrieb einstellen; **off-air** ADJ (*TV, Rad*) *argument, discussion* bei abgeschaltetem Mikrofon; **a special ~ advice line** ein besonderes Sorgentelefon, dessen Gespräche nicht gesendet werden

offal [ˈɒfəl] N , *no pl* Innereien *pl*; (*fig*) Abfall *m*, Ausschuss *m*

off: off-balance ADJ nicht im Gleichgewicht *pred*; **he was in an ~ position** er war aus dem Gleichgewicht gekommen → *also* **balance; off-beam** ADJ (*inf*) **to be ~** (*person, statement*) danebenliegen (*inf*); **offbeat** ADJ (= *unusual*) unkonventionell, ausgefallen, ungewöhnlich; **b** *jazz* synkopiert N unbetonte Taktzeit; **off-Broadway** ADJ *in New York außerhalb des Broadway* aufgeführt/gelegen, Off-Broadway-; **~ musical** Off-Broadway-Musical *nt* ADV *in New York außerhalb des Broadway*, off-Broadway

OFF-BROADWAY

Off-Broadway heißen in New York diejenigen Theaterproduktionen, die nicht in den berühmten Broadway-Häusern gespielt werden. Der Ausdruck wurde in den fünfziger Jahren geprägt, als Dramatiker wie Tennessee Williams und Edward Albee kreative Low-Budget-Produktionen zur Aufführung brachten. Off-Broadway-Theater sind normalerweise kleiner und die Eintrittskarten kosten weniger als bei den berühmteren Häusern, wobei neben professionellen Truppen auch Laiengruppen Aufführungen anbieten.
Heute werden insbesondere avantgardistische Theater als „off-off-Broadway" bezeichnet.

off: off-campus ADJ (*Univ*) *activities* außerhalb der Universität; *area* außerhalb des Universitätsgeländes; **several colleges hold classes at ~ sites** mehrere Institute halten außerhalb des Universitätsgeländes Lehrveranstaltungen ab ADV außerhalb des Universitätsgeländes; **off-centre**, (*US*) **off-center** ADJ (*lit*) nicht in der Mitte; *construction* asymmetrisch; **his translation/explanation was a bit ~** seine Übersetzung/Erklärung war schief *or* ging an der Sache vorbei ADV (= *askew*) schief; **the tablecloth was hanging ~** die Tischdecke hing an einer Seite zu weit herunter; **off chance** N **I just did it on the ~** ich habe es auf gut Glück getan; **to do sth on the ~ that ...** etw auf den Verdacht hin *or* in der unbestimmten Hoffnung tun, dass ...; **he bought it on the ~ that it would come in useful** er kaufte es, weil es vielleicht irgendwann mal nützlich sein könnte; **I came on the ~ of seeing her** ich kam in der Hoffnung, sie vielleicht zu sehen; **off-colour**, (*US*) **off-color** ADJ (*esp Brit*) **a** (= *unwell*) unwohl; **to feel/be ~** sich nicht wohl fühlen, sich daneben fühlen (*inf*) **b** (= *indecent*) schlüpfrig, gewagt; **off-duty** ADJ *attr soldier, nurse, policeman* außer Dienst; *hours* dienstfrei; **there was nothing to do in their ~ hours** wenn sie außer Dienst waren, gab es für sie nichts zu tun

offence, (*US*) **offense** [əˈfens] N **a** (*Jur*) (= *crime*) Straftat *f*, Delikt *nt*; (*minor*) Vergehen *nt*; **to commit an ~** sich strafbar machen; **it is an ~ to ...** ... ist bei Strafe verboten; **first ~** erste Straftat, erstes Vergehen; **second ~** Rückfall *m*; **an ~ against ...** ein Verstoß *m* gegen ...

b (*fig*) **an ~ against good taste** eine Beleidigung des guten Geschmacks; **an ~ against common decency** eine Erregung öffentlichen Ärgernisses

c *no pl* (*to sb's feelings*) Kränkung *f*, Beleidigung *f*; (*to sense of decency, morality etc*) Anstoß *m*; **to cause** *or* **give ~ to sb** jdn kränken *or* beleidigen; **without giving ~** ohne kränkend zu sein; **to take ~ at sth** wegen etw gekränkt or beleidigt sein; **she is quick to take ~** sie ist leicht gekränkt or beleidigt; **I meant no ~** ich habe es nicht böse gemeint; **no ~ to the Germans, of course!** damit will/wollte ich natürlich nichts gegen die Deutschen gesagt haben; **no ~ (meant)** nichts für ungut; **no ~ (taken)** ich nehme dir das nicht übel

d (*Eccl, = sin*) Sünde *f*

e [ɒˈfens] (*= attack, US: = attacking part of team*) Angriff *m*; **~ is the best defence** (*Brit*) **offense is the best defense** (*US*) Angriff ist die beste Verteidigung

offend [əˈfend] **VT** **a** (*= hurt feelings of*) kränken; (*= be disagreeable to*) Anstoß erregen bei; **this novel would ~ a lot of people** dieser Roman würde bei vielen Leuten Anstoß erregen **b** *ear, eye* beleidigen; *reason* verstoßen gegen; *sense of justice* gehen gegen, verletzen **VI** **a** (*= give offence*) beleidigend sein **b** (*= do wrong*) (ein) Unrecht tun, unrecht tun

▶ **offend against** VI +prep obj *taste, common sense* verstoßen gegen; *God* sündigen gegen

offended [əˈfendɪd] ADJ beleidigt, gekränkt; **don't be ~** seien Sie (doch) nicht beleidigt, nehmen Sie mir etc das nicht übel; **to be ~ by sth** sich von etw verletzt fühlen; **to look ~** eine beleidigte Miene machen

offender [əˈfendə^r] N (*= law-breaker*) (Straf)täter(in) *m(f)*; (*against traffic laws*) Verkehrssünder(in) *m(f)*; **sex ~** Sexualstraftäter(in) *m(f)*; **who left that here? – I'm afraid I was the ~** wer hat das da liegen lassen? – ich war der Übeltäter; **they are the worst ~s when it comes to ...** wenn es um ... geht, sind sie die schlimmsten → **first offender, young offender**

offending [əˈfendɪŋ] ADJ **a** (*= giving offence*) *remark* kränkend, beleidigend **b** (*= law-breaking*) *person* zuwiderhandelnd; *behaviour* kriminell; **the ~ party** (*Jur*) die schuldige Partei; (*fig*) der/ die Schuldige **c** (*= causing problem*) störend; (*= faulty*) *wire, part* defekt; **the ~ object** der Stein des Anstoßes

offense N (*US*) = **offence**

offensive [əˈfensɪv] ADJ **a** (*Jur*) Angriffs-; (*Mil*) Offensiv-; *action* offensiv; **~ play** (*Sport*) Offensivspiel *nt*; **~ player** Offensivspieler(in) *m(f)* **b** (*= unpleasant*) *smell, sight* übel, abstoßend, widerlich; *language, film, book* anstößig, Anstoß erregend (*= insulting, abusive*) *remark, gesture, behaviour* beleidigend, unverschämt; **his language was ~ to his parents** seine Ausdrucksweise erregte Anstoß bei seinen Eltern; **to find sb/sth ~** jdn/etw abstoßend finden; *behaviour, language* Anstoß an etw (*dat*) nehmen; **he was ~ to her** er beleidigte sie; **I don't mean to be ~** ich möchte nicht beleidigend wirken; **there's no need to get ~** kein Grund, ausfällig or ausfallend zu werden

N (*Mil, Sport*) Angriff *m*, Offensive *f*; **to take the ~** in die Offensive gehen; **to go over** or **on to the ~** zum Angriff übergehen; **on the ~** in der Offensive; **to mount an ~ (against sb/sth)** eine Offensive (gegen jdn/etw) starten

offensive capability N (*Mil*) Angriffsfähigkeit *f*

offensively [əˈfensɪvlɪ] ADV **a** (*= unpleasantly*) übel, widerlich; (*in moral sense*) anstößig; (*= abusively*) unverschämt; (*= obscenely*) unflätig **b** (*Mil, Sport*) offensiv

offensiveness [əˈfensɪvnɪs] N (*of smell, sight*) Widerlichkeit *f*; (*of language, film, book*) Anstößigkeit *f*; (*of remark, gesture, behaviour*) Unverschämtheit *f*

offensive operation N (*Mil*) Angriffsaktion *f*

offensive weapon N Angriffswaffe *f*, Offensivwaffe *f*

Offer [ˈɒfə] N (*Brit*) abbr of **Office of Electricity Regulation** *Regulierungsbehörde für die Stromindustrie*

offer [ˈɒfə^r] ❸ 3.1, 18.1, 19.5, 20.2, 26.1 **N** Angebot *nt*; (*also* **offer of marriage**) (Heirats-) antrag *m*; **the ~'s there** das Angebot gilt or

steht; **did you have many ~s of help?** haben Ihnen viele Leute ihre Hilfe angeboten?; **any ~s?** ist jemand interessiert?; **to make sb an ~ of sth** jdm etw anbieten; **he made me an ~ (of £50)** er machte mir ein Angebot (von £ 50); **an ~ I couldn't refuse** ein Angebot, zu dem ich nicht Nein or nein sagen konnte; **~s over £75,000** Angebote nicht unter £ 75.000; **on ~** (*Comm*) (*= on special offer*) im Angebot; (*= for sale*) verkäuflich → **near 3 b**

VT **a** *help, money, job, food, friendship etc* anbieten; *reward, prize* aussetzen; **to ~ to do sth** anbieten, etw zu tun; (*= offer one's services*) sich bereit erklären, etw zu tun; **he ~ed to give me £5 for it** er bot mir dafür £ 5 an; **he ~ed to help** er bot seine Hilfe an; **to ~ one's services** sich anbieten; **he was ~ed the job** ihm wurde die Stelle angeboten; **did he ~ to?** hat er sich angeboten?; **he's got nothing to ~** er hat nichts zu bieten

b *advice* anbieten; *plan, suggestion* unterbreiten; *remark* beisteuern; *excuse* vorbringen; *consolation* spenden; *condolences* aussprechen; **to ~ an opinion** sich (dazu) äußern; **to ~ one's resignation** seinen Rücktritt anbieten

c (*= present in worship or sacrifice*) *prayers, homage, sacrifice* darbringen; *one's life* opfern; **nuns ~ their lives to God** Nonnen stellen ihr Leben in den Dienst Gottes

d (*= put up, attempt to inflict*) *resistance* bieten; **to ~ violence** gewalttätig werden (*to gegen*) → **battle**

e (*= afford, make available*) *sleeping accommodation etc* bieten; **the bay ~ed a fine view** von der Bucht bot sich eine schöne Aussicht

f *subject* (*for exam*) machen

VI **whenever the opportunity ~s** wann immer sich die Gelegenheit bietet or ergibt; **did he ~?** hat er es angeboten?

▶ **offer up** VT *sep prayers, sacrifice* darbringen (*to sb* jdm); **to offer up one's life** sein Leben opfern; **to offer oneself up to a life of public service** sein Leben in den Dienst der Öffentlichkeit stellen

offering [ˈɒfərɪŋ] N Gabe *f*; (*Rel*) (*= collection*) Opfergabe *f*; (*= sacrifice*) Opfer *nt*; (*iro, = essay, play etc*) Vorstellung *f*

offer price N Angebotspreis *m*

offertory [ˈɒfətərɪ] N (*Eccl*) (*= part of service*) Opferung *f*, Offertorium *nt*; (*= collection*) Kollekte *f*, Geldsammlung *f*; **~ hymn** Lied *nt* während der Opferung

offertory box N (*Eccl*) Opferstock *m*

offhand [ˈɒfˈhænd] ADJ (*also* **off-handed**: *= casual*) *remark, manner* lässig; **to be ~ with sb** sich jdm gegenüber lässig benehmen; **to be ~ about sth** etw leichthin abtun ADV so ohne weiteres, aus dem Stand (*inf*); **I couldn't tell you ~** das könnte ich Ihnen auf Anhieb or so ohne weiteres nicht sagen

offhandedly [ˈɒfˈhændɪdlɪ] ADV lässig, leichthin

offhandedness [ˈɒfˈhændɪdnɪs] N Lässigkeit *f*

office [ˈɒfɪs] N **a** Büro *nt*; (*of lawyer*) Kanzlei *f*; (*= part of organization*) Abteilung *f*; (*= branch*) Geschäftsstelle *f*; **at the ~** im Büro; **local government ~s** Gemeindeverwaltung *f*

b (*= public position*) Amt *nt*; **to take ~** sein or das Amt antreten; (*political party*) die Regierung übernehmen, an die Regierung kommen; **to be in** or **hold ~** im Amt sein; (*party*) an der Regierung sein; **to be out of ~** nicht mehr an der Regierung sein; (*person*) nicht im Amt sein; **to be barred** or **disqualified from (holding) public ~** von allen öffentlichen Ämtern ausgeschlossen sein

c (*= duty*) Aufgabe *f*, Pflicht *f*

d *usu pl* (*= attention, help*) **through his good ~s** durch seine guten Dienste; **through the ~s of ...** durch Vermittlung von ...

e (*Eccl*) Gottesdienst *m*; **~ for the dead** Totenamt *nt*; (*RC*) Totenmesse *f*

f (*Brit*) **"usual ~s"** „übliche Nebenräume"

office: **office automation** N Büroautomation *f*; **office bearer** N Amtsträger(in) *m(f)*, Amts-

inhaber(in) *m(f)*; **office block** N Bürohaus or -gebäude *nt*; **office boy** N Laufjunge *m*; **office clerk** N Büroangestellte(r) *mf*; **office furniture** N Büromöbel *pl*; **office holder** N Amtsinhaber(in) *m(f)*; **office hours** PL Arbeitsstunden *pl*, Dienstzeit *f*; (*on sign*) Geschäfts- or Öffnungszeiten *pl*; **to work ~** normale Arbeitszeiten haben; **office hunter** N Postenjäger(in) *m(f)*; **office job** N Stelle *f* im Büro; **office junior** N Bürogehilfe *m*/-gehilfin *f*; **office manager(ess)** N Büroleiter(in) *m(f)*; **Office of Fair Trading** N (*Brit*) Behörde *f* gegen unlauteren Wettbewerb; **Office of Management and Budget** N (*US*) *US-Behörde für die Verwaltung der Ministerien und der Vorbereitung des Haushalts*; **office party** N Büroparty *f*

officer [ˈɒfɪsə^r] N **a** (*Mil, Naut, Aviat*) Offizier(in) *m(f)*; **~ of the day** Dienst habender Offizier, Offizier *m* vom Dienst; **Officers' Training Corps** (*Brit*) *Verband zur Offiziersausbildung* **b** (*= official*) Beamte(r) *m*, Beamtin *f*; (*= police officer*) Polizeibeamte(r) *m*/-beamtin *f*, Polizist(in) *m(f)*; (*of club, society*) Vorstandsmitglied *nt*, Funktionär(in) *m(f)*; **medical ~** Amtsarzt *m*/ -ärztin *f*; (*Mil*) Stabsarzt *m*/-ärztin *f*

officers' mess [ˈɒfɪsəz'mes] N Offizierskasino *nt*

office: **office seeker** N (*esp US*) **a** (*= job seeker*) Stellensuchende(r) *mf* **b** (*= office hunter*) Postenjäger(in) *m(f)*; **office supplies** PL Büroartikel *pl*, Bürobedarf *m*; **office worker** N Büroangestellte(r) *mf*

official [əˈfɪʃəl] ADJ offiziell; *report, duties, meeting, visit also* amtlich; (*= formal*) *ceremony, style* förmlich, formell; (*= authorized*) *biography* autorisiert; **~ language** Amtssprache *f*; **~ religion** Staatsreligion *f*; **~ statement** amtliche Verlautbarung; **is that ~?** ist das amtlich?; (*= publicly announced*) ist das offiziell?; **~ strike** offizieller Streik, gewerkschaftlich genehmigter Streik; **acting in one's ~ capacity** in Ausübung seiner Amtsgewalt; **~ uniform** Dienstuniform *f*

N (*= railway official, post office official etc*) Beamte(r) *m*, Beamtin *f*; (*of club, at race-meeting*) Funktionär(in) *m(f)*; **government ~** Regierungsbeamte(r) *m*/-beamtin *f*; **trade union ~** (*Brit*) Gewerkschaftsfunktionär(in) *m(f)*

officialdom [əˈfɪʃəldəm] N (*pej*) Bürokratie *f*, Beamtentum *nt*

officialese [ə,fɪʃə'liːz] N Behördensprache *f*, Beamtenchinesisch *nt* (*pej*)

officially [əˈfɪʃəlɪ] ADV offiziell; **~ approved** offiziell anerkannt

official: **Official Receiver** N Konkursverwalter(in) *m(f)*; **official seal** N Dienstsiegel *nt*, Amtssiegel *nt*; **official secret** N Dienstgeheimnis *nt*, Amtsgeheimnis *nt*; **Official Secrets Act** (*Brit*) *Gesetz nt zur amtlichen Schweigepflicht*

officiate [əˈfɪʃɪeɪt] VT amtieren, fungieren (*at* bei); **to ~ as president** als Präsident fungieren, das Amt des Präsidenten ausüben; **to ~ at a wedding** eine Trauung vornehmen

officious [əˈfɪʃəs] ADJ (*dienst*)beflissen, übereifrig; **to be ~** sich vor (Dienst)eifer überschlagen

officiousness [əˈfɪʃəsnɪs] N (Dienst)beflissenheit *f*, Übereifer *m*

offing [ˈɒfɪŋ] N **in the ~** in Sicht; **there's a pay rise** (*Brit*) or **raise** (*US*) **in the ~ for us** uns steht eine Gehaltserhöhung bevor, wir haben Aussicht auf eine Gehaltserhöhung

offish ADJ , **offishly** ADV [ˈɒfɪʃ, -lɪ] (*inf*) reserviert, unnahbar, kühl (*fig*), steif (*fig*)

off: **off-key** ADJ *attr*, **off key** ADJ *pred* (*Mus*) falsch; **off-licence** N (*Brit*) **a** (*= shop*) Weinund Spirituosenhandlung *f* **b** (*= permit*) Lizenz *f* zum Alkoholvertrieb or -verkauf, Alkohollizenz *f*; **off-limits** ADJ *attr*, **off limits** ADJ *pred* **a** (*= out of bounds*) *place* gesperrt; **this area is off limits** das Betreten dieses Gebiets ist verboten; **this room is off limits to** or **for the kids** die Kinder dürfen diesen Raum nicht betreten → *also* **limit N a** **b** (*fig: = forbidden*) *activity* verboten; **chocolates are off limits** Pralinen sind nicht erlaubt; **all drugs should be declared off limits for teenagers** alle Drogen sollten für Teenager verboten sein; **off line** (Comput) ADJ pred offline ADV off line; **to go ~** auf Offlinebetrieb schalten; **to put a printer ~** einen Drucker auf Offlinebetrieb schalten; **off-line** ADJ attr (Comput) Offline-; **off-load** VT goods ausladen, entladen; passengers aussteigen lassen; **off-peak** ADJ ~ central heating Nacht(strom)speicherheizung f; **~ electricity** Strom m außerhalb der Hauptabnahmezeit, Nachtstrom m; **~ charges** verbilligter Tarif; (Elec) ≈ Nachttarif m; **at ~ times, during ~ hours** außerhalb der Stoßzeiten; (Telec) außerhalb der Spitzenzeiten; **~ service** (Rail) Zugverkehr m außerhalb der Hauptverkehrszeit; **~ trains** Züge pl außerhalb der Hauptverkehrszeit; **~ ticket** verbilligte Fahrkarte/Flugkarte außerhalb der Stoßzeit; **off-piste** ADJ, ADV abseits der Piste; **offprint** N Sonderabdruck m; **off-putting** ADJ (esp Brit) smell, behaviour abstoßend; sight also, meal wenig einladend; thought, idea, story wenig ermutigend; (= daunting) entmutigend; interviewer wenig entgegenkommend; job unsympathisch; **it can be rather ~ to see how sausages are made** es kann einem den Appetit verderben or die Lust am Essen nehmen, wenn man sieht, wie Wurst gemacht wird; **off-road** ADJ driving, racing im Gelände; **~ vehicle** Geländefahrzeug nt; **off-roader** N Geländefahrzeug nt; **off--sales** (Brit) a pl Verkauf m aus dem Haus b sing = **off-licence** a; **off-screen** ADJ, ADV (Film, TV: = in real life) im wirklichen Leben; **off season** (in tourism) Nebensaison f; **in the ~** außerhalb der Saison; **off-season** ADJ travel, prices außerhalb der Saison

offset ['ɒfset] vb: pret, ptp **offset** VT a (financially, statistically etc) ausgleichen; (= make up for) wettmachen, aufwiegen b ['ɒfset] (= place non--centrally) versetzen N a (Typ) ~ (lithography/printing) Offsetdruck m b (Hort) Ableger m c (fig: = counterbalancing factor) Ausgleich m; **as an ~** zum Ausgleich, als Ausgleich (o für)

off: offshoot N a (of plant) Ausläufer m, Ableger m; (of tree) Schössling m, Spross m b (fig) (of family) Nebenlinie f; (of discussion, action etc) Randergebnis nt; **offshore** ADJ a island küstennah; wind ablandig; oilfield, installations etc im Meer; **drilling rig** Bohrinsel f; **the ~ industry/business** (= oil) die Offshoreindustrie f (Fin: = abroad) investment, funds im Ausland ADV a drill, explore im Meer; work, live auf einer Bohrinsel; **20 miles ~** 20 Meilen vor der Küste; **the wind blew ~** der Wind kam vom Land; **the ship anchored ~** das Schiff ankerte vor der Küste; **a gentle current carried him ~** eine leichte Strömung trug ihn aufs Meer hinaus; **50% of our oil comes from ~** 50% unseres Erdöls kommt or stammt aus dem Meer b (Fin: = abroad) im Ausland; **to move one's operation ~** sein Unternehmen ins Ausland verlegen

offshore: offshore banking N (Fin) Offshore-bankgeschäfte pl; **offshore company** N (Fin) Offshorefirma f; **offshore fishery** N Küstenfischerei f; **offshore well** N Offshorebohrloch nt; **offshore worker** N Offshorearbeiter(in) m(f)

offside [ɒf'saɪd] ADJ a (Sport) im Abseits; **to be ~** (player) im Abseits sein or stehen; (goal) ein Abseitstreffer m sein; **in an ~ position** in einer Abseitsposition, im Abseits; **~ rule** Abseitsregel f; **~ trap** Abseitsfalle f b (Aut) auf der Fahrerseite; (when driving on the left also) rechte(r, s); (when driving on the right also) linke(r, s) N (Aut) Fahrerseite f ADV (Sport) abseits, im Abseits

off site ADV außerhalb des Geländes

off-site [ɒf'saɪt] ADJ außerhalb des Geländes befindlich

offspring ['ɒfsprɪŋ] N a sing Sprössling m, Kind nt, Abkömmling m; (of animal) Junge(s) nt b pl (form, hum, of people) Nachwuchs m (hum), Nachkommen pl; (of animals) Junge pl;

how are your ~? (hum) wie gehts dem Nachwuchs? (hum)

offstage [ˌɒfˈsteɪdʒ] ADJ hinter den Kulissen; voice, music etc aus den Kulissen; **his ~ life** sein Leben abseits der Bühne ADV go, walk von der Bühne; stand hinter den Kulissen; **she was booed ~** sie wurde von der Bühne gebuht

off: off-street parking N (provided with flat/house, = single place) Stellplatz m; (= spaces) Stellplätze pl; **there isn't much ~ in this area** in dieser Gegend gibt es wenige Parkhäuser und Parkplätze; **off-the-cuff** ADJ remark, speech aus dem Stegreif; **off-the-job training** N außerbetriebliche Weiterbildung; **off-the-peg** ADJ attr, **off the peg** ADJ pred (Brit), **off-the--rack** ADJ attr, **off the rack** ADJ pred (US) dress, suit von der Stange; **~ clothes** Konfektionskleidung f; **off-the-record** ADJ attr, **off the record** ADJ pred remark, statement inoffiziell; (= confidential) vertraulich; **off-the-shelf** ADJ attr a (= take-away, cash-and-carry) goods, merchandise Mitnahme-, zum Mitnehmen b solution, computer, software etc Standard-; **off-the--shoulder** ADJ dress schulterfrei; **off-the-wall** ADJ attr, **off the wall** ADJ pred (inf, = zany) irre (inf), verrückt; **off-white** ADJ gebrochen weiß N gebrochenes Weiß

Ofgas ['ɒfgæs] N (Brit) abbr of **Office of Gas Supply** Regulierungsbehörde für die Gasindustrie

Ofgem ['ɒfdʒem] N (Brit) abbr of **Office of Gas and Electricity Markets** Regulierungsbehörde für die Stromindustrie

Oflot ['ɒflɒt] N (Brit) abbr of **Office of the National Lottery** Regulierungsbehörde für die britische Staatslotterie

OFT (Brit) abbr of **Office of Fair Trading**

oft [ɒft] ADV (liter) oft; **an ~-told story** eine gar oft erzählte Geschichte (liter)

Oftel ['ɒftel] N (Brit) abbr of **Office of Telecommunications** Regulierungsbehörde für die Telekommunikationsindustrie

often ['ɒfən] ✪ 26.1 ADV oft, häufig; **he went there ~, he ~ went there** er ging oft or häufig da hin; **you have been there as ~ as I have** Sie sind schon (eben)so oft wie ich dort gewesen; **do you go there as ~ as twice a week?** gehen Sie tatsächlich zweimal in der Woche dahin?; **not as ~ as twice a week** weniger als zweimal in der Woche; **as ~ as I ask you ...** jedes Mal wenn ich Sie frage ...; **more ~ than not, as ~ as not** meistens; **every so ~** öfters, von Zeit zu Zeit; **he did it once too ~** er hat es einmal zu oft or zu viel getan; **how ~?** wie oft?; **it is not ~ that ...** es kommt selten vor, dass ..., es geschieht nicht oft, dass ...; **oft(en) times** (obs) oftmals, gar viele Male (old)

Ofwat ['ɒfwɒt] N (Brit) abbr of **Office of Water Services** Regulierungsbehörde für die Wasserindustrie

ogle ['əʊgl] VT kein Auge lassen or wenden von, begaffen (pej); (flirtatiously) liebäugeln mit, schöne Augen machen (+dat); legs, girls schielen nach, beäuge(l)n (esp hum), beaugapfeln (hum)

O grade ['əʊgreɪd] N (Scot formerly) = **O level**

ogre ['əʊgə] N (Myth) Menschen fressender Riese; (fig) Ungeheuer nt, Unmensch m

ogress ['əʊgrɪs] N (Myth) Menschen fressende Riesin; (fig) Ungeheuer nt, Unmensch m

oh [əʊ] INTERJ ach; (admiring, surprised, disappointed) oh; (questioning, disinterested, in confirmation) tatsächlich, wahrhaftig; **oh good!** prima! (inf); **oh well** na ja! (inf); **oh bother!** (dated Brit) Mist! (inf); **oh damn!** (inf) verdammt! (inf); **oh dear!** o je!; **oh yes?** (interested) ach ja?; (disbelieving) so, so; **oh yes, that's right** ach ja, das stimmt; **oh yes, of course there'll be room** o ja, klar haben wir Platz!; **oh my God!** o Gott!, ach du lieber Gott!

ohm [əʊm] N Ohm nt

OHMS abbr of **On His/Her Majesty's Service** Aufdruck auf amtlichen Postsendungen

Ohm's law ['əʊmz'lɔː] N ohmsches Gesetz

OHP abbr of **overhead projector**

oi(c)k [ɔɪk] N (Brit, pej sl) Prolo m (sl)

oil [ɔɪl] N a Öl nt; **to pour ~ on troubled waters** die Wogen glätten, Öl auf die Wogen gießen b (= petroleum) (Erd)öl nt; **to strike ~** (lit) auf Öl stoßen b; (fig) einen Fund machen; (= get rich) das große Los ziehen c (Art, = painting) Ölgemälde nt; **to paint in ~s** in Öl malen; **a painting in ~s** ein Ölgemälde nt d (inf, = flattery) Schmeicheleien pl VT ölen, schmieren; table, furniture einölen; **to ~ sb's tongue** (fig) jdm die Zunge ölen or schmieren; **to ~ the wheels** (fig) die Dinge erleichtern

oil in cpds Öl-; **oil baron** N Ölmagnat m; **oil--based** ADJ auf Ölbasis; **~ paint** Ölfarbe f; **oil--bearing** ADJ a materials ölhaltig b (Geol) layer etc Öl führend; **oil-burning** ADJ Öl-; **~ lamp/stove** Öllampe f/-ofen m; **oilcake** N Ölkuchen m; **oilcan** N Ölkanne f; (for lubricating also) Ölkännchen nt; **oil change** N Ölwechsel m; **to do an ~** einen Ölwechsel machen or vornehmen; **I took the car in for an ~** ich habe den Wagen zum Ölwechsel(n) gebracht; **oilcloth** N Wachstuch nt; **oil colours**, (US) **oil colors** PL Ölfarben pl; **oil company** N Ölkonzern m; **oil drum** N Ölfass nt

oiled [ɔɪld] ADJ a ~ silk Ölhaut f b **he's well--oiled** (inf: = drunk) der ist ganz schön voll (inf), der hat ganz schön getankt (inf)

oil: oil-exporting ADJ öl exportierend; **oil-field** N Ölfeld nt; **oil-fired** ADJ Öl-, mit Öl befeuert; **~ power station** Ölkraftwerk nt; **oil gauge**, (US) **oil gage** N Ölstandsanzeiger m, Ölstandsmesser m; **oil industry** N Ölindustrie f

oiliness ['ɔɪlɪnɪs] N a ölige Beschaffenheit; (of food) Fettigkeit f b (fig: of person) aalglattes Wesen

oil: oil lamp N Öllampe f; **oil level** N Ölstand m; **oilman** N Ölindustrielle(r) mf; (= trader) Ölhändler(in) m(f); **oil paint** N Ölfarbe f; **oil painting** N (= picture) Ölgemälde nt; (= art) Ölmalerei f; **she's no ~** (inf) sie ist nicht gerade eine Schönheit; **oilpan** N Ölwanne f; **oil platform** N Bohrinsel f, Bohrplattform f; **oil pollution** N Ölverschmutzung f; **oil-producing** ADJ ölproduzierend; **oil refinery** N (Erd-)ölraffinerie f; **oil-rich** ADJ ölreich; **oil rig** N (Öl)bohrinsel f; **oil sheik** N Ölscheich m; **oil-skin** N a (= cloth) Öltuch nt b **oilskins** PL (= clothing) Ölzeug nt; **oil slick** N Ölteppich m; **oil spill** N Ölkatastrophe f; **oilstone** N geölter Wetzstein; **oil stove** N Ölofen m; **oil tanker** N (= ship) (Öl)tanker m, Tankschiff nt; (= lorry) Tankwagen m; **oil terminal** N Ölhafen m; **oil well** N Ölquelle f

oily ['ɔɪlɪ] ADJ (+er) a ölig; hair, skin, food fettig; clothes, fingers voller Öl; **~ fish** Fisch m mit hohem Ölgehalt b (fig) aalglatt, schleimig, ölig

oink [ɔɪŋk] INTERJ (pig) grunz

ointment ['ɔɪntmənt] N Salbe f

OK, okay ['əʊ'keɪ] (inf) INTERJ okay (inf); (= agreed also) einverstanden, in Ordnung; **OK, OK!** ist ja gut! (inf), okay, okay! (inf); **I'll come too, OK?** ich komme auch, okay or einverstanden?; **OK, that's enough of that** (call for attention) nun mal Schluss damit!; **OK, let's go!** also, gehen wir! ADJ in Ordnung, okay (inf); **that's OK with or by me** (= that's convenient) das ist mir recht, mir ists recht; (= I don't mind that) von mir aus, mir solls recht sein; **is it OK with or if ...?** macht es (dir) etwas aus, wenn ...?; **how's your mother? – she's OK** wie gehts deiner Mutter? – gut or (not too well) so einigermaßen (inf); **I feel OK** es geht mir einigermaßen (inf); **she looks OK** sie sieht einigermaßen aus (inf); **to be OK (for time/money** etc) (noch) genug (Zeit/Geld etc) haben; **is your car OK?** ist Ihr Auto in Ordnung; **is that OK?** geht das?, ist das okay? (inf); **what do you think of him? – he's OK** was halten Sie von ihm? – der ist in Ordnung (inf); **he's an OK guy** (esp US) er ist ein prima Kerl (inf)

ADV **a** (= *well*) gut; (= *not too badly*) einigermaßen (gut); (= *for sure*) schon; **to do OK** ganz gut zurechtkommen; (*Sch, in subject*) nicht schlecht sein; **they must be doing OK** (= *be affluent*) es muss ihnen ganz gut gehen; **can you mend it OK?** kannst du das reparieren?; **can you manage it OK?** kommst du damit klar?; **he'll come OK** der kommt schon

b (*inf, = admittedly*) **OK it's difficult but ...** zugeben, es ist schwer, aber ...; **OK, so he's not a real count** na gut, er ist also kein richtiger Graf

VT *order, plan, suggestion* gutheißen, billigen; *document, proposed expenses* genehmigen; **you have to get the boss to OK it, you have to OK it with the boss** das muss der Chef bewilligen

N Zustimmung *f*; **to give (sb/sth) the OK** (jdm/zu etw) seine Zustimmung geben; **if the boss gives his OK** wenn der Chef das bewilligt; **I can start work as soon as I get the OK** ich kann mit der Arbeit anfangen, sobald ich grünes Licht bekomme

okapi [əʊ'kɑːpɪ] **N** *pl* **-s** *or* - Okapi *nt*

okey-doke ['əʊkɪ'dəʊk], **okey-dokey** ['əʊkɪ'dəʊkɪ] **INTERJ** (*inf*) okay (*inf*)

Okla *abbr of* **Oklahoma**

okra ['ɒkrə] **N** Okra *f*

ol' [əʊl] **ADJ** (*esp US inf*) = **old**

old [əʊld] **ADJ** (*+er*) **a** alt; **~ people** *or* **folk(s)** alte Leute, die Alten *pl*; **if I live to be that ~** wenn ich (je) so alt werde; **~ Mr Smith, ~ man Smith** (*esp US*) der alte (Herr) Smith; **he/the building is 40 years ~** er/das Gebäude ist 40 Jahre alt; **at ten months ~** im Alter von zehn Monaten; **two-year-old** Zweijährige(r) *mf*; **the ~ part of Ulm** die Ulmer Altstadt; **the ~ (part of) town** die Altstadt; **in the ~ days** früher; **the good/bad ~ days** die gute/schlechte alte Zeit; **my ~ school** (= *former*) meine alte *or* ehemalige Schule

b (*inf, as intensifier*) **she dresses any ~ how** die ist vielleicht immer angezogen (*inf*); **any ~ thing** irgendwas, irgendein Dings (*inf*); **any ~ bottle/blouse** *etc* irgendeine Flasche/Bluse *etc* (*inf*); **~ Mike** der Michael (*inf*); **good ~ Tim** (*inf*) der gute alte Tim; **always the same ~ excuse** immer wieder dieselbe Ausrede; **we had a great ~ time** wir haben uns prächtig amüsiert; **funny ~ guy** komischer Typ (*inf*)

N **a** *pl* (= *old people*) **the ~** die Alten; **it caters for young and ~** es hat Angebote für Jung und Alt

b **in days of ~** (= *former times*) in alten *or* früheren Zeiten; **I know him of ~** ich kenne ihn von früher; **as of ~** wie in alten Zeiten

old: old age **N** das Alter; **to reach ~** ein hohes Alter erreichen; **in one's ~** im Alter, auf seine alten Tage (*also hum*); **old-age pension** **N** (Alters)rente *f*; **old-age pensioner** **N** Rentner(in) *m(f)*; **Old Bill** PL (*Brit, inf*) **the ~** die Bullen *pl* (*sl*); **old boy** **N** **a** (*Brit Sch*) ehemaliger Schüler, Ehemalige(r) *m*; **the old-boy network** Beziehungen *pl* (von der Schule her) **b** (*inf, old man*) **the ~ next door** der Alte von nebenan **c** (*dated inf, as address*) alter Junge (*inf*); **old country** **N** Mutterland *nt*, alte Heimat; **Old Dominion** **N** (*US: = Virginia*) Virginia *nt*

olde ['əʊldɪ] **ADJ** (*archaic*) alt, aus alter Zeit

olden ['əʊldən] **ADJ** (*liter*) alt; **in ~ times** *or* **days** früher, vordem (*liter*), in alten Zeiten; **city of ~ times** Stadt vergangener Zeiten

old: Old English **N** Altenglisch *nt* **ADJ** altenglisch; **Old English sheepdog** **N** Bobtail *m*; **old-established** **ADJ** *family, firm* alteingesessen; *custom* seit langem bestehend, alt

olde-worlde ['əʊldɪ'wɜːldɪ] **ADJ** altertümlich; (*pej*) auf alt getrimmt (*inf*) *or* gemacht

old: old-fashioned ['əʊld'fæʃnd] **ADJ** altmodisch; **a good ~ love story** eine Liebesgeschichte wie sie sonst nie sollte; **to give sb an ~ look** jdn missbilligend ansehen **N** (*US: = cocktail*) Cocktail aus Whiskey, Bitterlikör, Zucker und Früchten; **old flame** **N** alte Liebe; **old folk's home** **N** (*inf*) Altenheim *nt*; **Old**

French **N** (*Ling*) Altfranzösisch *nt*; **old girl** **N** **a** (*inf: = old woman*) Alte *f*, alte Dame; (= *animal*) altes Mädchen; **my ~** (*dated: = wife*) meine Alte **b** (*Brit Sch*) Ehemalige *f*, ehemalige Schülerin; **Old Glory** **N** (*US: = flag*) das Sternenbanner; **old gold** **N** Altgold *nt*; **old guard** **N** (*fig*) alte Garde; **old hand** **N** alter Hase (*at sth* in etw *dat*); **Old Harry** **N** (= *Devil*) der Leibhaftige; **to play ~ with sth** etw vollständig durcheinander bringen; **old hat** **N** (*fig*) alter Hut (*fig*); **that's ~** das ist ein alter Hut, das ist uninteressant; **Old High German** **N** (*Ling*) Althochdeutsch *nt*

oldie ['əʊldɪ] **N** (*inf*) (= *joke*) alter Witz; (= *song*) Oldie *m*; (= *record*) alte Platte, Oldie *m*; **the ~s** (= *people*) die Alten *pl*, die Oldies *pl* (*inf*); **that's a real ~** (= *joke*) der hat so einen Bart (*inf*)

oldish ['əʊldɪʃ] **ADJ** ältlich

old: old lady **N** (*inf*) **my ~** (= *wife*) meine Alte (*inf*); (= *mother also*) meine alte Dame (*inf*); **old lag** **N** (*sl*) Knastbruder *m* (*inf*); **old-line** **ADJ** (= *following tradition*) der alten Schule; (= *long-established*) alteingesessen; **old maid** **N** alte Jungfer; **old-maidish** **ADJ** altjüngferlich, altbacken; **old man** **N** (*inf*) **my ~** (= *husband*) mein Alter (*inf*); (= *father also*) mein alter Herr (*inf*); **the ~** (= *boss etc*) der Alte; **old master** **N** alter Meister; **Old Nick** **N** (*hum: = the devil*) der Leibhaftige; **old people's home** **N** Altenheim *nt*; **old rose** **ADJ** Altrosa *nt*; **old salt** **N** (alter) Seebär; **old school** **N** (*fig*) alte Schule; **old school tie** **N** (*lit*) Schulschlips *m*; (*fig*) Gehabe, das von Ehemaligen einer Public School erwartet wird; **old soldier** **N** alter Soldat; (*fig: = old hand*) alter Hase; **Old South** **N** Südstaaten der USA vor dem amerikanischen Bürgerkrieg; **old stager** **N** (*inf*) alter Hase (*inf*)

oldster ['əʊldstə'] **N** (*US, inf*) älterer Mann; **some of us ~s** einige von uns Alten

old: old-style **ADJ** im alten Stil; *furniture, car etc* altertümlich; **~ calendar** Kalender *m* alten Stils *or* nach alter Zeitrechnung; **Old Testament** (*Bibl*) **N** Altes Testament **ADJ** *prophet* alttestamentarisch; **old-timer** **N** Veteran(in) *m(f)*; **old wives' tale** **N** Ammenmärchen *nt*; **old woman** **N** **a** = **old lady b** **he's an ~** er ist wie ein altes Weib; **old-womanish** **ADJ** tuntig (*inf*); **Old World** **N** **the ~** die Alte Welt; **old-world** **ADJ** (= *quaint*) politeness, manners altväterlich; *cottage, atmosphere* altehrwürdig, heimelig **b** (*esp US: = European etc*) zur Alten Welt gehörend

OLE (*Comput*) *abbr of* **object linking and embedding** OLE *nt*

oleaginous [əʊlɪ'ædʒɪnəs] **ADJ** (*form*) *consistency* ölig; (= *containing oil*) ölhaltig; (*fig*) *person* ölig

oleander [əʊlɪ'ændə'] **N** Oleander *m*

oleomargarine ['əʊlɪəʊˌmɑː'dʒə'riːn] **N** (*esp US*) Margarine *f*

O level ['əʊlevl] **N** (*Brit formerly*) Abschluss *m* der Sekundarstufe 1, ≈ mittlere Reife; **to do one's ~s** ≈ die mittlere Reife machen; **to have an ~ in English** ≈ bis zur mittleren Reife Englisch gelernt haben; **he failed his English ~** er fiel durch die O-Level-Prüfung in Englisch; **3 ~s** ≈ die mittlere Reife in 3 Fächern

olfactory [ɒl'fæktərɪ] **ADJ** Geruchs-, olfaktorisch (*spec*)

olfactory nerve **N** Geruchsnerv *m*

oligarchic(al) [ˌɒlɪ'gɑːkɪk(əl)] **ADJ** oligarchisch

oligarchy ['ɒlɪgɑːkɪ] **N** Oligarchie *f*

olive ['ɒlɪv] **N** **a** Olive *f*; (*also* **olive tree**) Olivenbaum *m*; (*also* **olive wood**) Olive(nholz *nt*) *f* **b** (= *colour*) Olive *nt* **ADJ** (*also* **olive-coloured**) olivgrün; *complexion* dunkel

olive: olive branch **N** (*lit, fig*) Ölzweig *m*; **to hold out** *or* **offer the ~ to sb** (*fig*) jdm seinen Willen zum Frieden bekunden; **olive green** **N** Olivgrün *nt*; **olive-green** **ADJ** *cloth* olivgrün; **olive grove** **N** Olivenhain *m*; **olive oil** **N** Olivenöl *nt*

Olympiad [əʊ'lɪmpɪæd] **N** Olympiade *f*

Olympian [əʊ'lɪmpɪən] **ADJ** olympisch **N** **the ~s** die Olympier *pl*

Olympic [əʊ'lɪmpɪk] **ADJ** olympisch; **~ medallist** (*Brit*) *or* **medalist** (*US*) Olympiamedaillengewinner(in) *m(f)* **N** **Olympics** PL **the ~s** die Olympiade, die Olympischen Spiele

Olympic: Olympic champion **N** Olympiasieger(in) *m(f)*; **Olympic flame** **N** olympisches Feuer; **Olympic Games** PL **the ~** die Olympiade, die Olympischen Spiele; **Olympic stadium** **N** Olympiastadion *nt*; **Olympic torch** **N** olympisches Feuer

Olympus [əʊ'lɪmpəs] **N** (*also* **Mount Olympus**) der Olymp

OM *abbr of* **Order of Merit**

Oman [əʊ'mɑːn] **N** Oman *nt*

Omani [əʊ'mɑːnɪ] **ADJ** omanisch **N** Omaner(in) *m(f)*

omasum [əʊ'mɑːsəm] **N** Blättermagen *m*

OMB (*US*) *abbr of* **Office of Management and Budget**

ombudsman ['ɒmbʊdzmən] **N** *pl* **-men** [-mən] Ombudsmann *m*

ombudswoman [ˌɒmbʊdzwʊmən] **N** *pl* **-women** [-wɪmɪn] Ombudsfrau *f*

omega ['əʊmɪgə] **N** Omega *nt*

omelette, (*US*) **omelet** ['ɒmlɪt] **N** Omelett(e) *nt*; **you can't make an ~ without breaking eggs** (*Prov*) wo gehobelt wird, da fallen Späne (*Prov*)

omen ['əʊmen] **N** Omen *nt*, Zeichen *nt*; **it is an ~ of greatness** das bedeutet Erfolg; **a bird of ill ~** ein Unglücksvogel *m*

ominous ['ɒmɪnəs] **ADJ** bedrohlich, ominös; *event, appearance also* drohend; *look, voice also* Unheil verkündend, unheilschwanger; *sign also* verhängnisvoll; *sky* bedrohlich; **that's ~** das lässt nichts Gutes ahnen; **that sounds/looks ~** (*fig*) das verspricht nichts Gutes

ominously ['ɒmɪnəslɪ] **ADV** bedrohlich, ominös; *say* in einem Unheil verkündenden Ton; **it sounds ~ like a declaration of war** es klingt ominös nach einer Kriegserklärung; **more ~, the government is talking of reprisals** schlimmer noch, die Regierung spricht von Vergeltungsmaßnahmen

omission [əʊ'mɪʃən] **N** (= *omitting: of word, detail etc*) Auslassen *nt*; (= *word, thing etc left out*) Auslassung *f*; (= *failure to do sth*) Unterlassung *f*; **with the ~ of ...** unter Auslassung (*+gen*) ...; **sin of ~** (*Eccl, fig*) Unterlassungssünde *f*

omit [əʊ'mɪt] **VT** **a** (= *leave out*) auslassen; **please ~ any reference to me** bitte erwähnen Sie mich nicht, bitte unterlassen Sie jeden Hinweis auf mich **b** (= *fail*) (*to do sth* etw zu tun) unterlassen; (*accidentally*) versäumen

omnibus ['ɒmnɪbəs] **N** **a** (*form, = bus*) Omnibus *m*, Autobus *m* **b** (*also* **omnibus edition**: = *book*) Sammelausgabe *f*, Sammelband *m*; (*TV*) Fernseh- oder Radioprogramm, das zwei oder mehrere Folgen einer Serie als eine Sendung zeigt **ADJ** (*esp US*) allgemein, umfassend; **~ bill** (*Parl*) Sammelgesetz *nt*

omnibus edition **N** → **omnibus N b**

omnidirectional [ˌɒmnɪdɪ'rekʃənl] **ADJ** Rundstrahl-; **~ antenna** Rundstrahlantenne *f*

omnipotence [ɒm'nɪpətəns] **N** , *no pl* Allmacht *f*, Omnipotenz *f*

omnipotent [ɒm'nɪpətənt] **ADJ** allmächtig, omnipotent **N** **The Omnipotent** der Allmächtige

omnipresence ['ɒmnɪ'prezəns] **N** Allgegenwart *f*

omnipresent ['ɒmnɪ'prezənt] **ADJ** allgegenwärtig

omniscience [ɒm'nɪsɪəns] **N** Allwissenheit *f*

omniscient [ɒm'nɪsɪənt] **ADJ** allwissend

omnivore ['ɒmnɪˌvɔː'] **N** Allesfresser *m*, Omnivore *m* (*spec*)

omnivorous [ɒmˈnɪvərəs] ADJ (*lit*) alles fressend, omnivor (*spec*); **an ~ reader** ein Vielfraß *m*, was Bücher angeht

---

on [ɒn]

1 PREPOSITION	3 ADJECTIVE
2 ADVERB	

1 – PREPOSITION

> When **on** is the second element in a phrasal verb, eg **live on**, **lecture on**, look up the verb. When it is part of a set combination, eg **on the right**, **on request**, **on occasion**, look up the other word.

a indicating place, position auf (+*dat*); (*with vb of motion*) auf (+*acc*); (*on vertical surface, part of body*) an (+*dat*); (*with vb of motion*) an (+*acc*); **the book is on the table** das Buch ist auf dem Tisch; **he put the book on the table** er legte das Buch auf den Tisch; **it was on the blackboard** es stand an der Tafel; **he hung it on the wall/nail** er hängte es an die Wand/den Nagel; **a house on the coast/main road** ein Haus am Meer/an der Hauptstraße; **on the bank of the river** am Flussufer; **with a smile on her face** mit einem Lächeln auf den Lippen; **a ring on his finger** ein Ring am Finger; **her name is on the list** ihr Name ist auf der Liste; **he hit his head on the table/on the ground** er hat sich (*dat*) den Kopf am Tisch/auf dem *or* am Boden angeschlagen; **they came on(to) the stage** sie kamen auf die Bühne; **they advanced on the fort** sie rückten zum Fort vor; **on TV/the radio** im Fernsehen/Radio; **on video** auf Video; **held on computer** auf Computer (*dat*) gespeichert; **who's on his show tonight?** wer ist heute in seiner Show?; **I have no money on me** ich habe kein Geld bei mir; **we had something to eat on the train** wir haben im Zug etwas gegessen → *also* **onto**

b = by means of, using **we went on the train/bus** wir fuhren mit dem Zug/Bus; **on a bicycle** mit dem (Fahr)rad; **on foot/horseback** zu Fuß/Pferd; **the heating runs on oil** die Heizung wird mit Öl betrieben; **to count sth on one's fingers** etw an den Fingern abzählen

c = about, concerning über (+*acc*); **a book on German grammar** ein Buch über deutsche Grammatik; **we read Stalin on Marx** wir lasen Stalins Ausführungen zu Marx; **have you heard him on the subject?** haben Sie ihn zu diesem Thema gehört?; **he has nothing on me** (= *no damaging information etc*) er hat nichts gegen mich in der Hand, er kann mir nichts anhaben

d in expressions of time an (+*dat*); **on Sunday** (am) Sonntag; **on Sundays** sonntags; **on December the first** am ersten Dezember; **stars visible on clear nights** Sterne, die in klaren Nächten sichtbar sind; **on or about the twentieth** um den Zwanzigsten herum; **on and after the twentieth** am Zwanzigsten und danach

e = earning, getting **I'm on £18,000 a year** ich bekomme £ 18.000 im Jahr; **how much are you on?** wie viel verdienst *or* bekommst du?; **he retired on a good pension** er trat mit einer guten Rente in den Ruhestand

f = at the time of bei (+*dat*); **on my arrival** bei meiner Ankunft; **on examination** bei der Untersuchung; **on hearing this** he left als er das hörte, ging er

g = as a result of auf ... (*acc*) hin; **on receiving my letter** auf meinen Brief hin

h indicating membership in (+*dat*); **he is on the committee/the board** er gehört dem Ausschuss/Vorstand an, er sitzt im Ausschuss/Vorstand; **he is on the "Evening News"** er ist bei der „Evening News"; **he is on the teaching staff** er gehört zum Lehrpersonal

i = doing **to be on a course** (*Sch, Univ*) an einem Kurs teilnehmen; **I am working on a new project** ich arbeite gerade an einem neuen Projekt; **he was away on business** er war geschäftlich unterwegs; **I am on overtime** ich mache Überstunden; **we're on the past tense**

(*Sch*) wir sind bei der Vergangenheit; **we were on page 72** wir waren auf Seite 72

j = at the expense of **this round is on me** diese Runde geht auf meine Kosten; **have it on me** das spendiere ich (dir), ich gebe (dir) das aus → **house**

k = compared with im Vergleich zu; **prices are up on last year('s)** im Vergleich zum letzten Jahr sind die Preise gestiegen; **he has nothing on me** (= *not as good as*) er kann mir nicht das Wasser reichen

l = taking **to be on drugs/the pill** Drogen/die Pille nehmen; **what is he on?** (*inf*) er tickt wohl nicht ganz richtig! (*inf*)

m indicating repetition **he made mistake on mistake** er machte einen Fehler nach dem anderen

n musical instrument **he played (it) on the violin/trumpet** er spielte (es) auf der Geige/Trompete; **on drums/piano** am Schlagzeug/Klavier; **Roland Kirk on tenor sax** Roland Kirk, Tenorsaxophon

o = according to nach (+*dat*); **on your theory** Ihrer Theorie nach *or* zufolge, nach Ihrer Theorie

2 – ADVERB

a = in place, covering **he screwed the lid on** er schraubte den Deckel drauf; **she had nothing on** sie hatte nichts an; **what did he have on?** was hatte er an?; **he had his hat on crooked** er hatte den Hut schief auf; **he put his hat on** er setzte seinen Hut auf; **he put his coat on** er zog seinen Mantel an

b indicating position **put it this way on** stellen/legen Sie es so herum (darauf); **sideways on** längs

c indicating forward movement **move on!** gehen Sie weiter!, weitergehen!; **on! on!** weiter! weiter!; **to pass a message on** eine Nachricht weitergeben

d indicating time **from now on** von jetzt an; **from that day on** von diesem Tag an; **later on** später; **it was well on in the night** es war zu vorgerückter Stunde, es war spät in der Nacht; **it was well on into September** es war spät im September; **early on in her career** schon früh in ihrer Karriere

e indicating continuation **to keep on talking** immer weiterreden, in einem fort reden; **they walked on in silence** sie gingen schweigend weiter; **go on with your work** machen Sie Ihre Arbeit weiter

f set structures

♦ **on and on they talked on and on** sie redeten und redeten, sie redeten unentwegt; **the noise went on and on** der Lärm hörte überhaupt nicht auf; **she went on and on** sie hörte gar nicht mehr auf

♦ **to be on at sb** (*inf*) **he's always on at me** er hackt dauernd auf mir herum, er meckert dauernd an mir herum (*inf*); **he's always on at me to get my hair cut** er liegt mir dauernd in den Ohren, dass ich mir die Haare schneiden lassen soll; **he's been on at me about that several times** er ist mir ein paar Mal damit gekommen (*inf*)

♦ **to be on about sth** (*inf*) **she's always on about her experiences in Italy** sie kommt dauernd mit ihren Italienerfahrungen (*inf*); **what's he on about?** wovon redet er nun schon wieder?; **he knows what he's on about** er weiß, wovon er redet

3 – ADJECTIVE

a = switched on, functioning lights, TV, radio an; brake angezogen; electricity, gas an(gestellt); **to leave the engine on** den Motor laufen lassen; **the "on" switch** der Einschalter; **in the "on" position** auf „ein" gestellt; **it wasn't one of his on days** (*inf*) er war nicht gerade in Form

b = in place lid, cover drauf; **his hat/tie was on crookedly** sein Hut saß/sein Schlips hing schief; **his hat/coat was already on** er hatte den Hut schon auf/den Mantel schon an

c = taking place **there's a tennis match on at the moment** ein Tennismatch ist gerade im Gang; **there's a tennis match on tomorrow** morgen findet ein Tennismatch statt; **I have nothing on tonight** ich habe heute Abend nichts vor; **what's on in London?** was ist los in London?; **there's never anything on in this town** in dieser Stadt ist nie was los; **the search is on for a new managing director** jetzt wird nach einem neuen Geschäftsführer gesucht

d = being performed, performing **to be on** (*in theatre, cinema*) gegeben *or* gezeigt werden; (*on TV, radio*) gesendet *or* gezeigt werden; **is that programme** (*Brit*) *or* **program** (*US*) **still on?** läuft das Programm noch?; **the play is still on** (= *still running*) das Stück wird immer noch gegeben *or* gespielt; **what's on tonight?** was ist *or* steht heute Abend auf dem Programm?; **who's on tonight?** (*Theat, Film*) wer spielt heute Abend?, wer tritt heute Abend auf?; (*TV*) wer kommt heute Abend (im Fernsehen)?; **you're on now** (*Theat, Rad, TV*) Ihr Auftritt!, Sie sind (jetzt) dran (*inf*); **tell me when the English team is on** sagen Sie mir, wenn die englische Mannschaft dran ist *or* drankommt

e indicating agreement, acceptability **to be on** (*bet, agreement*) gelten; **you're on!** abgemacht!; **are you on?** (*inf*, = *are you with us*) bist du mit von der Partie? (*inf*), machst du mit?; **are you on for dinner tonight?** sehen wir uns zum Abendessen?; **you're/he's not on** (*Brit inf*) das ist nicht drin (*inf*); **it's just not on** (*Brit inf*, = *not acceptable*) das ist einfach nicht drin (*inf*), das gibt es einfach nicht; **his behaviour was really not on** (*Brit inf*) sein Benehmen war unmöglich

onanism [ˈəʊnənɪzm] N (*form*) Coitus interruptus *m*; (= *masturbation*) Onanie *f*, Masturbation *f*

on-camera ADJ, ADV (*Film, TV*) vor der Kamera

once [wʌns] ADV **a** (= *on one occasion*) einmal; **~ a week/month/year** einmal in der Woche/im Monat/im Jahr, einmal pro Woche/Monat/Jahr; **~ only** nur einmal; **this has happened only ~ before** das ist nur einmal zuvor passiert; **he tried this ~ before** er hat das schon einmal probiert; **~ again** *or* **more** noch einmal; **~ again we find that ...** wir stellen wiederum *or* erneut fest, dass ...; **~ or twice** (*lit*) ein- oder zweimal; (*fig*) nur ein paar Mal; **~ and for all** ein für alle Mal; **(every) ~ in a while**, **~ in a way** ab und zu mal; **you can come (just) this ~** dieses eine Mal können Sie kommen; **for ~** ausnahmsweise einmal; **I never ~ wondered where you were** ich habe mich kein einziges Mal gefragt, wo Sie wohl waren; **she walked away, without ~ looking back** sie ging davon, ohne auch nur ein einziges Mal zurückzublicken; **if ~ you begin to hesitate** wenn Sie erst einmal anfangen zu zögern; **~ a smoker, always a smoker** einmal Raucher, immer Raucher; **~ is enough** einmal reicht

b (= *in past*) einmal; **he was ~ famous** er war früher einmal berühmt; **~ upon a time there was ...** es war einmal ...

c **at ~** (= *immediately*) sofort, auf der Stelle; (= *at the same time*) auf einmal, gleichzeitig; **all at ~** auf einmal; (= *suddenly*) ganz plötzlich; **they came all at ~** sie kamen alle zur gleichen Zeit; **don't spend it all at ~** gib es nicht alles auf einmal aus

CONJ wenn; (*with past tense*) als; **~ you understand, it's easy** wenn Sie es einmal verstehen, ist es einfach; **~ the sun had set, it turned cold** als die Sonne erst einmal untergegangen war, wurde es kalt; **~ learned, it isn't easily forgotten** wenn man das erst einmal gelernt hat, vergisst man es nicht so leicht wieder

once-in-a-lifetime ADJ attr chance etc einmalig

once-over [ˈwʌnsəʊvə] N (*inf*, = *quick look*) flüchtige Überprüfung, kurze Untersuchung; **to give sb/sth the** *or* **a ~** (= *appraisal*) jdn/etw mal begucken (*inf*) *or* kurz überprüfen *or* inspizieren; (= *clean*) mal kurz über etw (*acc*) gehen (*inf*); **to give sb the** *or* **a ~** (= *beat up*) jdn in die Mache nehmen (*inf*)

oncologist [ɒŋˈkɒlədʒɪst] N Onkologe *m*, Onkologin *f*

oncology [ɒŋˈkɒlədʒɪ] N Onkologie *f*

oncoming [ˈɒnkʌmɪŋ] **ADJ** **a** (= *approaching*) *car, traffic* entgegenkommend; *troops, forces* heranrückend; *danger* nahend, drohend; **the ~ traffic** der Gegenverkehr **b** (= *imminent*) *winter, night* (her)einbrechend **N** (*of winter etc*) Nahen *nt*, Kommen *nt*

OND (*Brit*) *abbr of* **Ordinary National Diploma**

one [wʌn] **ADJ** **a** (= *number*) ein/eine/ein; (*counting*) eins; **~ man in a thousand** einer von tausend; **there was ~ person too many** da war einer zu viel; **~ girl was pretty, the other was ugly** das eine Mädchen war hübsch, das andere hässlich; **she was in ~ room, he was in the other** sie war im einen Zimmer, er im anderen; **the baby is ~ (year old)** das Kind ist ein Jahr (alt); **it is ~ (o'clock)** es ist eins, es ist ein Uhr; **~ hundred pounds** hundert Pfund; (*on cheque etc*) einhundert Pfund; **that's ~ way of doing it** so kann mans (natürlich) auch machen **b** (*indefinite*) **~ morning/day** *etc* **he realized ...** eines Morgens/Tages bemerkte er ...; **~ morning next week** nächste Woche einmal morgens; **~ day next week** nächste Woche einmal; **~ day soon** bald einmal; **~ sunny summer's day** an einem sonnigen Sommertag **c** (= *a certain*) **~ Mr Smith** ein gewisser Herr Smith **d** (= *sole, only*) **he is the ~ man to tell you** er ist der Einzige, der es Ihnen sagen kann; **no ~ man could do it** niemand konnte es allein tun; **my ~ (and only) hope** meine einzige Hoffnung; **the ~ and only Brigitte Bardot** die unvergleichliche Brigitte Bardot **e** (= *same*) **they all came in the ~ car** sie kamen alle in dem einen Auto; **they are ~ and the same person** das ist ein und dieselbe Person; **it is ~ and the same thing** das ist ein und dasselbe; **it's all ~ to me** das ist mir alles einerlei **f** (= *united*) **God is ~** Gott ist unteilbar; **are they ~ with us?** sind sie mit uns eins?; **we are ~ on the subject** wir sind uns über dieses Thema einig; **they were ~ in wanting that** sie waren sich darin einig, dass sie das wollten; **the crowd rose as ~** die Menge erhob sich geschlossen

PRON **a** eine(r, s); **the ~ who ...** der(jenige), der .../die(jenige), die .../das(jenige), das ...; **he/that was the ~** er/das wars; **do you have ~?** haben Sie einen/eine/ein(e)s?; **the red/big** *etc* **~** der/die/das Rote/Große *etc*; **he has some very fine ~s** er hat sehr Schöne; **my ~** (*inf*) meiner/meine/mein(e)s; **his ~** (*inf*) seiner/seine/sein(e)s; **not (a single) ~ of them, never ~ of them** nie eine(r, s) von ihnen, kein Einziger/keine Einzige/kein Einziges; **no ~ of these people** keiner dieser Leute; **any ~** irgendeine(r, s); **every ~** jede(r, s); **this ~** diese(r, s); **that ~** der/die/das, jene(r, s) (*geh*); **which ~?** welche(r, s)?; **the little ~s** (= *children*) die Kleinen *pl*; (= *animals*) die Jungen *pl*; **that's a good ~** (*inf*) der (Witz) ist gut; (*iro, excuse etc*) das ist ein guter Witz; **let's have a quick ~ after work** (*inf*) lasst uns nach der Arbeit noch kurz einen trinken gehen; **I'm not ~ to go out often** ich bin nicht der Typ, der oft ausgeht; **I'm not usually ~ to go out on a week night, but today ...** ich gehe sonst eigentlich nicht an Wochentagen aus, aber heute ...; **I am not much of a ~ for cakes** (*inf*) ich bin kein großer Freund von Kuchen (*inf*), Kuchen ist eigentlich nicht mein Fall (*inf*); **she was never ~ to cry** Weinen war noch nie ihre Art; (*but she did*) sonst weinte sie nie; **he's never ~ to say no** er sagt nie Nein or nein; **what a ~ he is for the girls!** der ist vielleicht ein Schwerenöter! (*inf*); **he's a great ~ for discipline/turning up late** der ist ganz groß, wenns um Disziplin/ums Zuspätkommen geht; **ooh, you are a ~!** (*inf*) oh, Sie sind mir vielleicht eine(r)! (*inf*); **she is a teacher, and he/her sister wants to be ~ too** sie ist Lehrerin, und er

möchte auch gern Lehrer werden/ihre Schwester möchte auch gern eine werden; **I, for ~, think otherwise** ich, zum Beispiel, denke anders; **they came ~ and all** sie kamen alle (ohne Ausnahme); **~ by ~** einzeln; **~ after the other** eine(r, s) nach dem/der/dem anderen; **take ~ or the other** nehmen Sie das eine oder das andere/den einen oder den anderen/die eine oder die andere; **you can't have ~ without the other** Sie können das eine nicht ohne das andere haben; **~ or other of them will do it** der/die eine oder andere wird es tun; **he's not ~ of our group** er gehört nicht zu unserer Gruppe; **he is ~ of us** er ist einer von uns; **~ who knows the country** jemand, der das Land kennt; **in the manner of ~ who ...** in der Art von jemandem, der ...; **like ~ demented/possessed** wie verrückt/besessen

b (*impers*) (*nom*) man; (*acc*) einen; (*dat*) einem; **~ must learn to keep quiet** man muss lernen, still zu sein; **to hurt ~'s foot** sich (*dat*) den Fuß verletzen; **to wash ~'s face/hair** sich (*dat*) das Gesicht/die Haare waschen; **~ likes to see ~'s** *or* **his** (*US*) **friends happy** man sieht seine Freunde gern glücklich

N (= *written figure*) Eins *f*; **Chapter ~** Kapitel eins; **in ~s and twos** in kleinen Gruppen; **they became ~** sie wurden eins; **they were made ~** sie wurden vereint; **to be at ~ (with sb)** sich (*dat*) (mit jdm) einig sein; **he was at ~ with the world** er war mit der Welt im Einklang; **he is not at ~ with himself** er ist mit sich selbst nicht im Reinen; **it was a bedroom and sitting room (all) in ~** es war Schlaf- und Wohnzimmer in einem; **T-shirt and shorts all in ~** T-shirt und Shorts in einem Stück; **I landed him ~** (*inf*) dem habe ich eine(n) or eins verpasst (*inf*); **to be ~ up on sb** (*inf*) (= *know more*) jdm eins voraus sein; (= *have more*) jdm etwas voraushaben; **Rangers were ~ up after the first half** Rangers hatten nach der ersten Halbzeit ein Tor Vorsprung

one-acter [ˈwʌnˌæktə], **one-act play** [ˈwʌnækt'pleɪ] N Einakter *m*

one another = **each other** → **each** PRON b

one: one-armed ADJ einarmig; **one-armed bandit** N (*inf*) einarmiger Bandit; **one-day** ADJ *seminar, course* eintägig; **one-dimensional** ADJ (*Math*) eindimensional; (*fig*) *character* eindimensional; *story* eindimensional, einfallslos; **one-eyed** ADJ einäugig; **one-handed** ADJ *person* einhändig ADV mit einer Hand; **one-horse** ADJ **a** *vehicle* einspännig; **to be a ~ race** (*fig*) einen sicheren Sieger haben **b** (*inf*, = *inferior*) **~ town** Kuhdorf *nt* (*inf*); **one-legged** ADJ *person* einbeinig; **one-line** ADJ *message etc* einzeilig; **one-liner** N (*inf*) witzige Bemerkung; **one-man** ADJ Einmann-; **~ canoe** Einerkanu *nt*; **~ job** Arbeit *f* für einen Einzelnen; **she's a ~ woman** ihr liegt nur an einem Mann etwas; **one-man band** N Einmannkapelle *f*; (*fig inf*) Einmannbetrieb *m*; **one-man show** N (*Art*) Ausstellung *f* eines (einzigen) Künstlers; (*Theat etc*) Einmannshow *f*

oneness [ˈwʌnnɪs] N Einheit *f*; (*of personality, thought*) Geschlossenheit *f*; (= *concord: with nature, fellow men*) Einklang *m*

one: one-night stand N (*Theat*) einmalige Vorstellung; (*fig*) einmalige Angelegenheit; **he's just after a ~** er sucht nur eine Nacht für eine Nacht; **one-off** (*Brit, inf*) **ADJ** einmalig **N a ~** etwas Einmaliges; **that mistake** *etc* **was just a ~** dieser Fehler *etc* war eine Ausnahme; **one-one, one-on-one** ADJ (*US*) = **one-to-one**; **one-parent family** N Einelternteilfamilie *f*; **one-party** ADJ (*Pol*) Einparteien-; **~ state/system** Einparteienstaat *m*/-system *nt*; **one-piece** **ADJ** einteilig **N** (= *bathing costume*) (einteiliger) Badeanzug, Einteiler *m*; **one-room** ATTR , **one-roomed** ADJ Einzimmer-; **~ flat** (*Brit*) *or* **apartment** Einzimmerwohnung *f*

onerous [ˈɒnərəs] ADJ *responsibility* schwer(wiegend); *task, duty* beschwerlich, schwer

oneself [wʌn'self] PRON **a** (*dir and indir, with prep*) sich; (= *oneself personally*) sich selbst *or* selber **b** (*emph*) (sich) selbst → *also* **myself**

one: one-shot ADJ, N (*US*) = **one-off**; **one-sided** ADJ einseitig; *judgement, account also* parteiisch; **one-time** ADJ ehemalig; **one-to-one** **ADJ a** (= *between two people*) *conversation, meeting* unter vier Augen; **~ teaching** *or* **tuition** Einzelunterricht *m*; **~ therapy** Einzeltherapie *f*; **~ relationship** Zweierbeziehung *f* **b** (= *corresponding exactly*) *correspondence, correlation* sich Punkt für Punkt entsprechend, eins zu eins; **a ~ exchange rate** ein Wechselkurs *m* im Verhältnis eins zu eins **ADV a** (= *person to person*) *talk, discuss* unter vier Augen; **they fought ~** sie kämpften einzeln gegeneinander **b** (= *in exact correspondence*) im Verhältnis eins-zu-eins **N** (= *conversation*) Gespräch *nt* unter vier Augen; **to have a ~ with sb** ein Gespräch *nt* unter vier Augen mit jdm führen; **one-track** ADJ **he's got a ~ mind** der hat immer nur das eine im Sinn *or* Kopf; **one-two** N **a** (*Boxing*) Rechts-links-Kombination *f*; **to give sb the old ~** jdm eine klassische Rechts-links-Kombination verpassen **b** (*Ftbl*) Doppelpass *m* **c** (*in race*) erster und zweiter Platz für Teamkollegen; **one-upmanship** [ˌwʌn'ʌpmənʃɪp] N **that's just a form of ~** damit will er *etc* anderen nur um eine Nasenlänge voraus sein; **the game of ~** (*hum*) die Kunst, allen anderen um einen Schritt *or* eine Nasenlänge voraus zu sein; **one-way** ADJ **a** (= *in one direction*) *traffic etc* in einer Richtung; **~ street** Einbahnstraße *f*; **~ system** System *nt* von Einbahnstraßen; **~ ticket** (*US Rail*) einfache Fahrkarte; **~ trip** einfache Fahrt **b** (= *one-sided*) *relationship, deal* einseitig; *process* einseitig, eingleisig **c** *mirror, glass* von einer Seite durchsichtig; **one-woman** ADJ Einfrau-; **~ show** eine Einfraushow *f*

ongoing [ˈɒngəʊɪŋ] ADJ (= *in progress*) *research, project* im Gang befindlich, laufend; (= *long-term, continuing*) *development, relationship* andauernd; **~ crisis** Dauerkrise *f*; **this is an ~ situation** diese Situation ist von Dauer

onion [ˈʌnjən] N Zwiebel *f*; **he knows his ~s** (*Brit, inf*) er kennt seinen Kram (*inf*)

onion: onion dome N Zwiebelturm *m*; **onion ring** N (*Cook*) Zwiebelring *m*; **onion-shaped** ADJ zwiebelförmig; **onionskin** N Zwiebelschale *f*; (= *paper*) Florpost *f*; **onion soup** N Zwiebelsuppe *f*

on line [ɒn'laɪn] (*Comput*) **ADJ** pred online **ADV** online, on line; **to go ~** auf Onlinebetrieb schalten; **to put a printer ~** einen Drucker auf Onlinebetrieb schalten; **to be ~ to sb/sth** mit jdm/etw verbunden sein

on-line [ˈɒnlaɪn] ADJ attr (*Comput*) Online-; **~ database** Onlinedatenbank *f*; **~ help** Online-Hilfe *f*

onlooker [ˈɒnlʊkə] N Zuschauer(in) *m(f)*

only [ˈəʊnlɪ] **ADJ** attr einzige(r, s); **he's an/my ~ child** er ist ein Einzelkind *nt*/mein einziges Kind; **the ~ one** *or* **person** der/die Einzige; **the ~ ones** *or* **people** die Einzigen; **he was the ~ one to leave** *or* **who left** er ist als Einziger gegangen; **the ~ thing** das Einzige; **the ~ thing I could suggest would be to invite him too** ich könnte höchstens vorschlagen, dass wir *etc* ihn auch einladen; **that's the ~ thing for it/the ~ thing to do** das ist die einzige Möglichkeit; **the ~ thing I have against it is that ...** ich habe nur eins dagegen einzuwenden, nämlich, dass ...; **the ~ thing** *or* **problem is ...** nur ...; **the ~ thing is (that) it's too late** es ist bloß *or* nur schon zu spät; **my ~ wish/regret** das einzige, was ich mir wünsche/was ich bedaure; **the ~ real problem** das einzig wirkliche Problem; **her ~ answer was a grin** *or* **to grin** ihre Antwort bestand nur aus einem Grinsen → **one** ADJ d **ADV a** nur; **it's ~ five o'clock** es ist erst fünf Uhr; **~ yesterday/last week** erst gestern/letzte Woche; **I ~ hope he gets here in time** ich hoffe nur, dass er es noch rechtzeitig hier eintrifft; **I ~ wanted to be with you** ich wollte nur mit dir zusammen sein; **you ~ have to ask** Sie brauchen nur zu fragen; **I wanted ~ to be with you** (*esp liter*) ich wollte weiter nichts, als mit dir zusammen zu sein; **"members ~"** „(Zutritt) nur für Mitglieder"; **~ think of it!** stellen Sie sich das nur (mal) vor!; **to think of it made him ill** der bloße Gedanke *or* schon der Gedanke daran machte ihn krank

b (*in constructions*) **~ too true/easy** *etc* nur (all)zu wahr/leicht *etc*; **I'd be ~ too pleased to help** ich würde nur zu gerne helfen; **if ~ that hadn't happened** wenn das bloß *or* nur nicht passiert wäre; **we ~ just caught the train** wir haben den Zug gerade noch gekriegt; **he has ~ just arrived** er ist gerade erst angekommen; **I've ~ just got enough** ich habe gerade genug; **not ~ ... but also ...** nicht nur ..., sondern auch ...

CONJ bloß, nur; **I would do it myself, ~ I haven't time** ich würde es selbst machen, ich habe bloß *or* nur keine Zeit; **she looks like me, ~ taller** sie sieht aus wie ich, nur dass sie etwas größer ist

ono, o.n.o. *abbr of* **or near(est) offer**

on-off switch [ˈɒnˈɒfswɪtʃ] N Ein- und Ausschalter *m*

onomatopoeia [ˌɒnəʊmætəʊˈpiːə] N Lautmalerei *f*, Onomatopöie *f* (*spec*)

onomatopoeic [ˌɒnəˌmætəʊˈpiːɪk], **onomatopoetic** [ˌɒnəˌmætəpəʊˈetɪk] ADJ lautmalend, onomatopoetisch (*spec*)

onrush [ˈɒnrʌʃ] N (*of people*) Ansturm *m*; (*of water*) Schwall *m*

onrushing [ˈɒnˌrʌʃɪŋ] ADJ *vehicle* heranbrausend; *tide, water* hereinbrechend

on-screen [ˈɒnskriːn] ADJ **a** (*Comput*) auf dem Bildschirm; **read the ~ text** lesen Sie den Text auf dem Bildschirm; **~ display** Bildschirmanzeige *f*; **b** *romance, kiss etc* (*TV*) Bildschirm-; (*Film*) Film-; **an ~ adventure** ein Bildschirm-/Filmabenteuer *nt* ADV [ˌɒnˈskriːn] (*Film*) auf der Leinwand; (*TV, Comput*) auf dem Bildschirm

onset [ˈɒnset] N Beginn *m*; (*of cold weather also*) Einbruch *m*; (*of illness*) Ausbruch *m*; **the sudden ~ of winter** der plötzliche Wintereinbruch; **the ~ of this illness is quite gradual** diese Krankheit kommt nur allmählich zum Ausbruch; **with the ~ of old age he ...** als er alt zu werden begann ...

onshore [ˈɒnʃɔː] ADJ *oilfield, job* auf dem Festland; **~ wind** Seewind *m* ADV [ɒnˈʃɔː] (*also* **on shore**) an Land; (*= on the mainland*) auf dem Festland; *blow* landwärts, küstenwärts

onside [ɒnˈsaɪd] ADV nicht im Abseits; **to stay ~** nicht ins Abseits laufen

on-site [ɒnˈsaɪt] ADJ *supervision, maintenance, personnel etc* vor Ort

onslaught [ˈɒnslɔːt] N (*Mil*) (heftiger) Angriff (*on auf +acc*); (*fig also*) Attacke *f* (*on auf +acc*); **to make an ~ on sb/sth** (*fig*) jdn/etw angreifen *or* attackieren; (*on work*) einer Sache (*dat*) zu Leibe rücken; **the constant ~ of advertisements on TV** das ständige Bombardement der Fernsehzuschauer mit Werbung

on-street parking [ˈɒnstriːtˈpɑːkɪŋ] N Parken *nt* auf der Straße

Ont *abbr of* **Ontario**

on-the-job training [ˈɒnðəˌdʒɒbˈtreɪnɪŋ] N Ausbildung *f* am Arbeitsplatz, innerbetriebliche Ausbildung

on-the-spot [ˌɒnðəˈspɒt] ADJ *fine* an Ort und Stelle verhängt; *decision, diagnosis, investigation, assessment* an Ort und Stelle; *reporting, coverage* vom Ort des Geschehens → *also* **spot**

onto [ˈɒntʊ] PREP **a** (*= upon, on top of*) auf (*+acc*); (*on sth vertical*) an (*+acc*); **to clip sth ~ sth** etw an etw (*acc*) anklemmen; **to get ~ the committee** in den Ausschuss kommen

b (*in verbal expressions, see also vb +on*) **to get/come ~ a subject** auf ein Thema zu sprechen kommen; **to come ~ the market** auf den Markt kommen; **are you ~ the next chapter already?** sind Sie schon beim nächsten Kapitel?; **when will you get ~ the next chapter?** wann kommen Sie zum nächsten Kapitel?; **the windows**

look ~ the lake die Fenster gehen zur Seeseite hinaus; **to be ~ or on to sb** (*= find sb out*) jdm auf die Schliche gekommen sein (*inf*); (*police*) jdm auf der Spur sein; **I think we're ~ something** ich glaube, hier sind wir auf etwas gestoßen

ontogeny [ɒnˈtɒdʒənɪ] N Ontogenese *f*

ontological [ˌɒntəˈlɒdʒɪkəl] ADJ ontologisch

ontology [ɒnˈtɒlədʒɪ] N Ontologie *f*

onus [ˈəʊnəs] N , *no pl* Pflicht *f*; (*= burden*) Last *f*, Bürde *f* (*geh*); **to shift the ~ for sth onto sb** jdm die Verantwortung für etw zuschieben; **the ~ to do it is on him** *or* **lies with him** es liegt an ihm, das zu tun; **the ~ of proof lies with the prosecution** die Anklage trägt die Beweislast

onward [ˈɒnwəd] ADJ **a** (*lit*) **~ flight** Anschlussflug *m*; **~ journey** Weiterreise *f*; **~ movement** Weiterbewegung *f*; (*on journey*) Weiterreise *f*; (*of goods*) Weitertransport *m* **b** (*fig*) **~ progress** weitere Fortschritte *pl*; **the ~ march of time/progress** das Fortschreiten der Zeit/der Vormarsch des Fortschritts ADV (*also* **onwards**) voran, vorwärts; *march* weiter; **from today/this time ~** von heute/der Zeit an INTERJ (*also* **onwards**) voran, vorwärts

onyx [ˈɒnɪks] N Onyx *m* ADJ Onyx-; **~ jewellery** (*Brit*) *or* **jewelry** (*US*) Onyxschmuck *m*

oodles [ˈuːdlz] PL (*inf*) jede Menge (*inf*); **~ and ~ Unmengen** *pl* (*inf*); **~ (and ~) of money** Geld wie Heu (*inf*); **~ (and ~) of time** massenhaft Zeit (*inf*)

ooh [uː] INTERJ oh **VI there was a lot of ~ing and ahing** es gab viele Ohs und Ahs

oomph [ʊmf] N (*inf*) **a** (*= energy*) Pep *m* (*inf*), Schwung *m* **b** (*= sex appeal*) Sex *m* (*inf*); **to have ~** sexy sein (*inf*)

oops [uːps, ʊps] INTERJ (*inf*) hoppla!

ooze [uːz] N **a** (*of mud, glue, resin*) Quellen *nt*; (*of water, blood*) Sickern *nt*, Triefen *nt* **b** (*= mud*) Schlamm *m* **VI a** (*lit*) triefen; (*water, blood*) sickern, triefen; (*wound*) nässen; (*resin, mud, glue*) (heraus)quellen **b** (*fig*) **to ~ with charm/kindness** Liebenswürdigkeit/Güte verströmen; **the house ~s with wealth** *or* **money/culture** das Haus verströmt eine Atmosphäre von Reichtum/Kultur; **he stood there, charm oozing out of** *or* **from every pore** er stand da, förmlich triefend vor Liebenswürdigkeit **VT a** (aus)schwitzen, absondern; *blood* triefen von; **my shoes were oozing water** das Wasser quoll mir aus den Schuhen **b** (*fig*) *charm* triefen von (*pej*), verströmen; *confidence, sex appeal* strotzen von; *insincerity* stinken vor (*+dat*) (*inf*)

▶ **ooze away** VI wegsickern; (*into ground*) versickern; (*fig: courage, pride, affection etc*) schwinden

▶ **ooze out** VI herausquellen; (*water, blood etc*) heraussickern

op¹ *abbr of* **opus** op

op² [ɒp] N (*inf*) = **operation**

opacity [əʊˈpæsɪtɪ] N **a** Undurchsichtigkeit *f*, Lichtundurchlässigkeit *f*; (*of paint*) Deckkraft *f* **b** (*fig: of essay, meaning etc*) Undurchsichtigkeit *f*

opal [ˈəʊpəl] N (*= stone*) Opal *m*; (*= colour*) beigegraue Farbe ADJ Opal-, opal-; (*colour*) opalen (*liter*), beigegrau schimmernd; **~ blue** opalblau; **~ ring** Opalring *m*

opalescence [ˌəʊpəˈlesns] N Schimmern *nt*, Opaleszenz *f*

opalescent [ˌəʊpəˈlesnt] ADJ schimmernd, opaleszierend

opal glass N Opalglas *nt*

opaline [ˈəʊpəlaɪn] ADJ opalen (*liter*)

opaque [əʊˈpeɪk] ADJ **a** opak; *liquid* trüb; *paper, glass, window* undurchsichtig; *tights, stockings* blickdicht **b** (*fig*) *essay, prose, text* undurchsichtig, unklar

op art [ˈɒpˈɑːt] N Op-Art *f*

op cit [ɒpˈsɪt] *abbr of* **opere citato** op. cit.

OPEC [ˈəʊpek] *abbr of* **Organization of Petroleum Exporting Countries** OPEC *f*

open [ˈəʊpən] ADJ **a** *door, bottle, book, eye, flower etc* offen, auf *pred*, geöffnet; *circuit* offen; *lines of communication* frei; *wound etc* offen; **to keep/hold the door ~** die Tür offen lassen *or* auflassen/offen halten *or* aufhalten; **to fling** *or* **throw the door ~** die Tür aufstoßen; **I can't keep my eyes ~** ich kann die Augen nicht offen halten *or* aufhalten; **the window flew ~** das Fenster flog auf; **the thugs split his head ~** die Schläger brachten ihm eine klaffende Wunde am Kopf bei; **his defeat blew the competition wide ~** durch seine Niederlage war der Ausgang des Wettbewerbs weit offen; **he threatened to blow the operation wide ~** (*= reveal sth secret*) er drohte damit, die Aktion offen zu legen; **a shirt ~ at the neck** ein am Hals offenes Hemd

b (*= open for business: shop, bank etc*) geöffnet; **the baker/baker's shop is ~** der Bäcker hat/der Bäckerladen ist *or* hat geöffnet *or* hat auf (*inf*)

c (*= not enclosed*) offen; *country, ground* offen, frei; *view* frei; *carriage, car* offen, ohne Verdeck; **in the ~ air** im Freien; **on ~ ground** auf offenem *or* freiem Gelände; (*= waste ground*) auf unbebautem Gelände

d (*= not blocked*) *Ling* offen; *road, canal, pores* offen, frei (*to für*), geöffnet; *rail track, river* frei (*to für*); (*Mus*) *string* leer; *pipe* offen; **~ note** Grundton *m*; **have you had your bowels ~ today?** (*Med form*) haben Sie heute Stuhlgang gehabt?; **~ to traffic/shipping** für den Verkehr/die Schifffahrt freigegeben; **"road ~ to traffic"** „Durchfahrt frei"

e (*= officially in use*) *building* eingeweiht; *road, bridge* (offiziell) freigegeben; *exhibition* eröffnet; **to declare sth ~** etw einweihen/freigeben/für eröffnet erklären

f (*= not restricted, accessible*) *letter, scholarship* offen; *market, competition* offen, frei; (*= public*) *meeting, trial* öffentlich; **to be ~ to sb** (*competition, membership, possibility*) jdm offen stehen; (*admission*) jdm freistehen; (*place*) für jdn geöffnet sein; (*park*) jdm zur Verfügung stehen; **my house is always ~ to you** mein Haus steht dir immer offen; **the director's door is always ~** die Tür des Direktors ist immer offen; **in ~ court** (*Jur*) in öffentlicher Verhandlung; **~ to the public** der Öffentlichkeit zugänglich; **park ~ to the public** öffentlicher Park; **~ forum** öffentliches Forum; **she gave us an ~ invitation to visit** sie lud uns ein, jederzeit bei ihr vorbeizukommen; **an unlocked window is an ~ invitation to a thief** ein unverschlossenes Fenster lädt geradezu zum Diebstahl ein

g **to be ~ to advice/suggestions/ideas** Ratschlägen/Vorschlägen/Ideen zugänglich sein *or* gegenüber offen sein; **I'm ~ to persuasion** ich lasse mich gern überreden; **I'm ~ to offers** ich lasse gern mit mir handeln *or* reden; **~ to bribes** Bestechungen zugänglich

h (*= not filled*) *evening, time* frei; *job, post* frei, offen

i (*= not concealed*) *campaign, secret, resistance* offen; *hostility* offen, unverhüllt

j (*= not decided or settled*) *question* offen, ungeklärt, ungelöst; **they left the matter ~** sie ließen die Angelegenheit offen *or* ungeklärt; **to keep one's options ~** es offen lassen; **to keep an ~ mind** alles offen lassen; (*judge, jury*) unvoreingenommen sein; **to have an ~ mind on sth** einer Sache (*dat*) aufgeschlossen gegenüberstehen; **keep your mind ~ to new suggestions** verschließen Sie sich nicht neuen Vorschlägen; **to be ~ to debate** zur Debatte stehen

k (*= exposed, not protected*) (*Mil*) *town* offen; *coast* ungeschützt; **a position ~ to attack** eine exponierte *or* leicht angreifbare Position; **~ to the elements** Wind und Wetter ausgesetzt; **to be ~ to criticism/attack** der Kritik/Angriffen ausgesetzt sein; **to lay oneself ~ to criticism/attack** sich der Kritik/Angriffen aussetzen; **he left himself wide ~ to criticism** er setzte sich breiter Kritik aus; **a theory ~ to criticism** eine anfechtbare Theorie; **to be ~ to abuse** sich leicht missbrauchen lassen; **to be ~ to doubt** anzweifelbar sein

l *weave* locker; *fabric, pattern* durchbrochen

m (= *frank*) *character, face, person* offen, aufrichtig; **he was ~ with us** er war ganz offen mit uns **N in the ~** (= *outside*) im Freien; (= *on open ground*) auf freiem Feld; **it's all out in the ~ now** nun ist alles heraus (*inf*), nun ist es alles zur Sprache gekommen; **to bring sth out into the ~** mit etw nicht länger hinterm Berg halten; **to come out into the ~** (*fig, person*) Farbe bekennen, sich erklären; (*affair*) herauskommen; **he eventually came out into the ~ about what he meant to do** er rückte endlich mit der Sprache heraus (*inf*), was er tun wollte; **to force sb out into the ~** jdn zwingen, sich zu stellen; (*fig*) jdn zwingen, Farbe zu bekennen; **to force sth out into the ~** (*fig*) etw zur Sprache bringen

VT a *door, mouth, bottle, letter etc* öffnen, aufmachen (*inf*); *book* aufschlagen, öffnen; *newspaper* aufschlagen; *throttle, circuit* öffnen; **he didn't ~ his mouth once** er hat kein einziges Mal den Mund aufgemacht (*inf*); **to ~ ranks** (*Mil*) weg- or abtreten

b (*officially*) *exhibition* eröffnen; *building* einweihen; *motorway* (für den Verkehr) freigeben

c *region* erschließen; **they ~ed a road through the mountains** durch die Berge wurde eine Straße gebaut

d (= *reveal, unfold*) öffnen; **to ~ one's heart to sb** sich jdm eröffnen (*geh*), jdm sein Herz aufschließen (*geh*); **to ~ sb's mind** jds Horizont erweitern; **~ your mind to new possibilities** öffnen Sie sich (*dat*) den Blick für neue Möglichkeiten; **it had ~ed new horizons for him** dadurch erschlossen sich ihm neue Horizonte

e (= *start*) *case, trial, account* eröffnen; *debate, conversation etc* beginnen

f (= *set up*) *shop* eröffnen, aufmachen (*inf*); *school* einrichten

g (*Med*) *pores* öffnen; **to ~ the bowels** (*person*) Stuhlgang haben; (*medicine*) abführen

h **to ~ fire** (*Mil*) das Feuer eröffnen (*on* auf +*acc*)

VI a aufgehen; (*eyes*) sich öffnen; (*door, flower, book, wound, pores, window*) sich öffnen, aufgehen; **I couldn't get the box/bottle to ~** ich habe die Schachtel/Flasche nicht aufbekommen; **it won't ~** es geht nicht auf

b (*shop, museum*) öffnen, aufmachen

c (= *afford access*: *door*) führen (*into* in +*acc*); **the two rooms ~ into one another** diese zwei Zimmer sind durch eine Tür verbunden → *also* **open on to**

d (= *start*) beginnen (*with* mit); (*Cards, Chess*) eröffnen; **the play ~s next week** das Stück wird ab nächster Woche gegeben; **when the play ~ed in Hull** bei der ersten Vorstellung in Hull

▶ **open on to** VI +*prep obj* (*window*) gehen auf (+*acc*); (*door* also) führen auf (+*acc*)

▶ **open out VI a** (= *become wider*) *river, street* sich verbreitern (*into* zu); (*view*) sich weiten, sich öffnen **b** (*flower*) sich öffnen, aufgehen **c** (*map*) sich ausfalten lassen **d** (*fig*) (*person*) aus sich herausgehen; (*business*) sich ausdehnen (*into* auf +*acc*); (*new horizons*) sich auftun **VT** *sep* **a** (= *unfold*) *map, newspaper etc* auseinander falten, aufmachen (*inf*) **b** (= *make wider*) *hole* erweitern, vergrößern **c** (*fig*) (= *make expansive*) *person* aus der Reserve locken; (= *develop*) *business* ausdehnen, erweitern

▶ **open up VI a** (*flower*) sich öffnen, aufgehen; (*fig*) (*prospects*) sich eröffnen, sich ergeben; (*field, new horizons*) sich auftun, sich erschließen

b (= *become expansive*) gesprächiger werden; (*fig*) **to get sb to open up** jdn zum Reden bringen; **to open up about sth** über etw (*acc*) sprechen or reden

c (*inf*: *accelerate*) aufdrehen (*inf*)

d (= *unlock doors*: *of house, shop etc*) aufschließen, aufmachen; **open up!** aufmachen!

e (= *start up*: *new shop*) aufmachen

f (= *start firing*: *guns, enemy*) das Feuer eröffnen

g (*Sport*: *game*) sich auflockern

VT *sep* **a** (= *make accessible*) *territory, mine, prospects* erschließen; *new horizons etc* auftun, erschließen; (= *unblock*) *disused tunnel etc* freimachen; **to open up a country to trade** ein Land für den Handel erschließen; **to open oneself up to sth** sich für etw öffnen

b (= *cut, make*) *passage* bauen; *gap* schaffen; *hole* machen; (= *make wider*) *hole* größer or weiter machen, vergrößern

c (= *unlock*) *house, shop, car etc* aufschließen, aufmachen

d (= *start*) *business* eröffnen; *shop* also aufmachen; *debate* eröffnen

e (*Sport*) *game* auflockern; **to open up a lead** eine Führung herausarbeiten

open: open-access library N (*Brit*) Freihandbibliothek *f*; **open-air** ADJ im Freien; **open-air concert** N Freilichtkonzert *nt*; **open-air performance** N Freilichtaufführung *f*, Openairaufführung *f*, Open-Air-Aufführung *f*; **open-air swimming pool** N Freibad *nt*; **open-air theatre**, (*US*) **open-air theater** N Freilichtbühne *f*, Freilichttheater *nt*; **open-and-shut** ADJ simpel; **it's an ~ case** es ist ein glasklarer Fall; **open-cast** ADJ *coal mine* über Tage *pred*; **~ mining** Tagebau *m*; **open cheque** N (*Brit*) Barscheck *m*; **open-cut** ADJ (*US*) = **open-cast**; **open day** N (*Brit*) Tag *m* der offenen Tür; **open-door** ADJ **~ policy** Politik *f* der Offenheit or der offenen Tür; **open-ended** ADJ (*lit*) *box, tube, barrel* (an einer Seite) offen **b** (*fig*) *contract* offen, zeitlich nicht begrenzt; *offer, commitment* unbegrenzt; *discussion* alles offen lassend *attr*; *subject, category* endlos, uferlos; **this question/subject is ~** über diese Frage/dieses Thema kann man endlos weiterdiskutieren; **open enrollment** N (*US Univ*) Einschreibung ohne Zulassungsvoraussetzungen

opener ['əʊpnə'] N **a** Öffner *m* **b** **for ~s** (*inf*) für den Anfang

open: open-eyed ADJ mit weit offenen Augen; **open-face sandwich** N (*US*) belegtes Brot; **open government** N transparente Politik; **open-handed** ADJ freigebig, großzügig; **open-handedness** N Freigebigkeit *f*, Großzügigkeit *f*; **open-hearted** ADJ offen, offenherzig; **open-hearth** ADJ (*Tech*) **~ furnace** Herdofen *m*; **~ process** Siemens-Martin-Verfahren *nt*; **open-heart surgery** N Eingriff *m* am offenen Herzen; **open house** N **it's ~ there** das ist ein gastfreundliches Haus, das ist ein Haus der offenen Tür; **to keep ~** ein offenes Haus führen; **open housing** N (*US*) Wohnraumvergabe ohne (Rassen)diskriminierung

opening ['əʊpnɪŋ] **N a** Öffnung *f*; (*in hedge, branches, clouds, wall etc* also) Loch *nt*; (= *cleft*) Spalt *m*; (*in traffic stream*) Lücke *f*; (= *forest clearing*) Lichtung *f*; (*fig*: *in conversation*) Anknüpfungspunkt *m*

b (= *beginning, initial stages*) Anfang *m*; (*Chess, Cards*) Eröffnung *f*

c (= *official opening*) (*of exhibition, stores*) Eröffnung *f*; (*of building*) Einweihung *f*, Eröffnung *f*; (*of motorway*) Freigabe *f* (für den Verkehr); **opening of Parliament** Parlamentseröffnung *f*

d (= *action*) (*of door, mouth, bottle, pub, shop etc*) Öffnen *nt*; (*of flower*) Aufgehen *nt*; (*of account*) Eröffnung *f*; (= *setting up*: *of shop, school etc*) Eröffnung *f*, Aufmachen *nt*; **hours of ~** Öffnungszeiten *pl*

e (= *opportunity*) Möglichkeit *f*, Chance *f*; (= *job vacancy*) (freie) Stelle *f*; **he gave his adversary an ~** er bot seinem Gegner eine Blöße; **leave an ~ for negotiations** lassen Sie die Möglichkeit für Verhandlungen offen

ATTR (= *initial, first*) erste(r, s); *remarks* einführend; **~ speech** Eröffnungsrede *f*; **~ move** erster Zug; (*Chess* also) Eröffnungszug *m*

opening: opening ceremony N Eröffnungsfeierlichkeiten *pl*; **opening hours** PL Öffnungszeiten *pl*; **opening night** N Eröffnungsvorstellung *f* (am Abend); **opening price** N (*St Ex*) Eröffnungs- or Anfangskurs *m*; **open-**

ing time N Öffnungszeit *f*; **what are the bank's ~s?** wann hat die Bank geöffnet?; **when is ~ on Sundays?** wann machen am Sonntag die Lokale auf?

openly ['əʊpənlɪ] ADV (= *without concealment*) offen; *speak* also freiheraus; (= *publicly*) öffentlich; **to be ~ critical of sb/sth** jdn/etw offen kritisieren; **he was ~ gay** er machte keinen Hehl aus seiner Homosexualität

open: open-minded ADJ aufgeschlossen; **open-mindedness** N Aufgeschlossenheit *f*; **open-mouthed** ['əʊpn'maʊðd] ADJ (*in surprise or stupidity*) mit offenem Mund, baff *pred* (*inf*); **she stood in ~ amazement** sie sperrte vor Staunen den Mund auf; **open-necked** ADJ *shirt* mit offenem Kragen

openness ['əʊpnnɪs] N **a** (= *frankness*) Offenheit *f*, Aufrichtigkeit *f*; (= *publicness*) Öffentlichkeit *f*, Offenheit *f* **b** (*fig*: *of mind*) Aufgeschlossenheit *f* (*to* für) **c** (*of countryside, coast*) Offenheit *f* **d** (= *looseness*: *of weave*) Lockerheit *f*

open: open-plan ADJ *flat etc* offen angelegt; **~ office** Großraumbüro *nt*; **open prison** N offenes Gefängnis; **open sandwich** N (*Brit*) belegtes Brot; **open season** N (*Hunt*) Jagdzeit *f*; **open-shelf library** N (*US*) Freihandbibliothek *f*; **open shop** N Open Shop *m*; **we have an ~** wir haben keinen Gewerkschaftszwang; **open-stack library** N (*US*) Freihandbibliothek *f*; **open-top(ped)** ADJ *bus* mit offenem Oberdeck; *car* mit offenem Verdeck; **Open University** N (*Brit*) Fernuniversität *f*; **to do an ~ course** ein Fernstudium machen or absolvieren

> ### OPEN UNIVERSITY
> Die **Open University** ist eine britische Fernuniversität, die 1969 gegründet wurde. Für die Kurse, die mit einem ersten akademischen Grad abschließen, werden keine formellen Aufnahmeanforderungen gestellt. Der Unterricht erfolgt über Radio- und Fernsehprogramme, die von der BBC ausgestrahlt werden. Schriftliche Arbeiten werden per Post verschickt. Zusätzlich müssen bestimmte Kurse, häufig im Sommer, in einer Art Internat besucht werden.

open verdict N **to record an ~** keine Erklärung zur Todesursache abgeben

openwork ['əʊpənwɜːk] **N** (*Sew*) Durchbrucharbeit *f*; (*Archit*) Durchbruchmauerwerk *nt* **ADJ** durchbrochen

opera ['ɒpərə] N Oper *f*; **to go to the ~** in die Oper gehen

operable ['ɒpərəbl] ADJ **a** (*Med*) operierbar, operabel **b** (= *practicable*) durchführbar, praktikabel

opera *in cpds* Opern-; **opera company** N Opernensemble *nt*; **opera glasses** PL Opernglas *nt*; **opera hat** N Chapeau claque *m*; **opera house** N Opernhaus *nt*

operand ['ɒpə‚rænd] N (*Math, Comput*) Operand *m*

opera singer N Opernsänger(in) *m(f)*

operate ['ɒpəreɪt] **VI a** (*machine, mechanism*) funktionieren; (= *be powered*) betrieben werden (*by, on* mit); (= *be in operation*) laufen, in Betrieb sein; (*fig*: *worker*) arbeiten; **how does it ~?** wie funktioniert es?; **to ~ at maximum capacity** (*lit, fig*) Höchstleistung bringen

b (*theory, plan, law*) sich auswirken; (*causes, factors*) hinwirken (*on, for* auf +*acc*); (*organization, system*) wirken; (*medicine*) wirken; **I don't understand how his mind ~s** ich verstehe seine Gedankengänge nicht; **to ~ against sb/sth** gegen jdn/etw wirken; **to ~ in favour of sb/sth** zugunsten or zu Gunsten von jdm/etw wirken

c (= *carry on one's business*) operieren; (*company*) operieren, Geschäfte tätigen; (*airport, station*) in Betrieb sein; (*buses, planes*) verkehren; **I don't like the way he ~s** ich mag seine Methoden nicht; **that firm ~s by defrauding its customers** es gehört zu den (Geschäfts)methoden der Firma, die Kunden zu betrügen

d (*Mil*) operieren
e (*Med*) operieren (*on sb/sth* jdn/etw); **to be ~d on** operiert werden; **he ~d on him for appendicitis/a cataract** er operierte ihn am Blinddarm/auf grauen Star
VT a (*person*) *machine, switchboard etc* bedienen; (= *set in operation*) in Betrieb setzen; *brakes etc* betätigen; (*lever, button etc*) betätigen; (*electricity, batteries etc*) betreiben
b (= *manage*) *business* betreiben, führen
c (= *put into practice*) *system, law* anwenden, arbeiten nach; *policy also* betreiben
d (*airline etc*) *route* betreiben; *bus etc* *service* unterhalten; *holiday, tours* veranstalten

operatic [ˌɒpəˈrætɪk] ADJ Opern-; **~ aria/singer** Opernarie *f*/-sänger(in) *m(f)*

operatics [ˌɒpəˈrætɪks] N *sing* (**amateur**) ~ Amateuropern *pl*

operating [ˈɒpəreɪtɪŋ] ADJ *attr* **a** (*Tech, Comm*) Betriebs-; **~ pressure** Betriebsdruck *m*; **~ profit** Betriebsgewinn *m*; **~ statement** (*US*) Gewinn- und Verlustrechnung *f* **b** (*Med*) Operations-

operating: operating manual N Betriebsanleitung *f*, Bedienungsanleitung *f*; **operating room** N (*US Med*) Operationssaal *m*, OP *m*; **operating system** N (*Comput*) Betriebssystem *nt*; **operating table** N (*Med*) Operationstisch *m*; **operating theatre** N (*Brit Med*) Operationssaal *m*, OP *m*

operation [ˌɒpəˈreɪʃən] N **a** (= *act of operating as in vi*) (*of machine, mechanism, system*) Funktionieren *nt*; (*of plan*) Durchführung *f*; (*of theory*) Anwendung *f*; (= *method of functioning*) (*of machine, organization*) Arbeitsweise *f*; (*of system, organ*) Funktionsweise *f*; (*of law*) Wirkungsweise *f*; **to be in ~** (*machine*) in Betrieb sein; (*law*) in Kraft sein; (*plan*) durchgeführt werden; **to be out of ~** außer Betrieb sein; (*fig: person*) nicht einsatzfähig sein; **to come into ~** (*machine*) in Gang kommen; (*law*) in Kraft treten; (*plan*) zur Anwendung gelangen; **to bring** *or* **put a law into ~** ein Gesetz in Kraft setzen
b (= *act of operating as in vt*) (*of machine etc*) Bedienung *f*, Handhabung *f*; (*of small mechanism*) Betätigung *f*; (*of business*) Betreiben *nt*, Führen *nt*; (*of system, policy*) Anwendung *f*; (*of plan, law*) Durchführung *f*; (*of route*) Bedienung *f*; (*of bus service etc*) Unterhaltung *f*; (*of tours*) Veranstaltung *f*
c (*Med*) Operation *f* (*on an* +*dat*); **to have an ~** operiert werden; **to have a serious/heart ~** sich einer schweren Operation/einer Herzoperation unterziehen; **to have an ~ for a hernia** wegen eines Bruchs operiert werden
d (= *enterprise*) Unternehmen *nt*, Unternehmung *f*, Operation *f*; (= *task, stage in undertaking*) Arbeitsgang *m*; (*Math*) Rechenvorgang *m*, Operation *f*; (**business**) **~s** Geschäfte *pl*; **to cease/resume ~s** den Geschäftsverkehr einstellen/wieder aufnehmen
e (*esp Mil*: = *campaign*) Operation *f*, Einsatz *m*, Unternehmen *nt*; (*in police force etc*) Einsatz *m*; **Operation Cynthia** Operation Cynthia

operational [ˌɒpəˈreɪʃənl] ADJ **a** (= *ready for use or action*) *machine, vehicle* betriebsbereit *or* -fähig; *army unit, aeroplane, tank etc* einsatzbereit *or* -fähig; (*fig*) *worker etc* einsatzbereit *or* -fähig; (= *in use or action*) *machine, vehicle etc* in Betrieb, in *or* im Gebrauch; *airport* in Betrieb; *army unit etc* im Einsatz
b (= *relating to operation, Tech, Comm*) Betriebs-; (*Mil*) Einsatz-; *problems, duties* operativ; **~ costs** Betriebskosten *pl*; **for ~ reasons** aus operativen Gründen; **~ staff** (*for machinery*) Bedienungspersonal *nt*; (*in military, police action*) Einsatzkräfte *pl*; **~ range** (*of radar etc*) Einflussbereich *m*; (*of aircraft*) Flugbereich *m*; **~ plan** (*Mil*) Einsatzplan *m*; **~ flight** (*Mil*) Einsatzflug *m*; **~ base** (*Mil*) Operationsbasis *f*; **these submarines have never seen ~ service** diese U-Boote sind nie eingesetzt worden *or* kamen nie zum Einsatz

operations room [ˌɒpəˈreɪʃənzˈruːm] N (*Mil, Police*) Hauptquartier *nt*

operative [ˈɒpərətɪv] ADJ **a** (= *producing an effect*) *measure, laws* wirksam; *clause* maßgeblich,

---

entscheidend; (= *in effect*) *law* rechtsgültig, geltend; *plan, system, service* operativ; **"if" being the ~ word** wobei „wenn" das entscheidende Wort ist; **to become ~** (*law*) in Kraft treten; (*system etc*) verbindlich eingeführt werden **b** (*Med*) *treatment* operativ; **~ report** Operationsbericht *m*; **~ risk** Operationsrisiko *nt* **N** (*of machinery*) Maschinenarbeiter(in) *m(f)*; (= *detective*) Detektiv(in) *m(f)*; (= *spy*) Agent(in) *m(f)*; (*US Pol*: = *campaign worker*) Parteiarbeiter(in) *m(f)*

operator [ˈɒpəreɪtə] N **a** (*Telec*) ≈ Vermittlung *f*; **a call through the ~** ein handvermitteltes Gespräch **b** (*of machinery*) (Maschinen)arbeiter(in) *m(f)*; (*of vehicle, lift*) Führer(in) *m(f)*; (*of electrical equipment*) Bediener(in) *m(f)*; (*of computer etc*) Operator(in) *m(f)*; *lathe etc* ~ Arbeiter(in) *m(f)* an der Drehbank etc **c** (= *private company*) Unternehmen *nt*; (= *company owner*) Unternehmer(in) *m(f)*; (*Fin*) (Börsen-) makler(in) *m(f)*; (= *tour operator*) Veranstalter(in) *m(f)* **d** (*inf*) raffinierter Typ *m* (*inf*); (= *criminal*) Gauner(in) *m(f)*; **to be a smooth/clever ~** raffiniert vorgehen

operetta [ˌɒpəˈretə] N Operette *f*

ophthalmic [ɒfˈθælmɪk] ADJ Augen-

ophthalmic optician N Optiker(in) *m(f)*; (*prescribing*) Augenarzt *m*, Augenärztin *f*; (*dispensing*) Optiker(in) *m(f)*

ophthalmic surgeon N Augenchirurg(in) *m(f)*

ophthalmologist [ˌɒfθælˈmɒlədʒɪst] N Ophthalmologe *m*, Ophthalmologin *f*

ophthalmology [ˌɒfθælˈmɒlədʒɪ] N Augenheilkunde *f*, Ophthalmologie *f* (*spec*)

ophthalmoscope [ɒfˈθælməskəʊp] N Augenspiegel *m*

opiate [ˈəʊpɪɪt] **N** Opiat *nt*; (*fig*) Beruhigungsmittel *nt* **ADJ** opiumhaltig

opine [əʊˈpaɪn] VT (*liter*) dafürhalten (*geh*), meinen

opinion [əˈpɪnjən] ✪ 1.1, 2.1, 6.1, 6.2, 6.3, 11.1, 13, 26.2 N **a** (= *belief, view*) Meinung *f* (*about, on* zu), Ansicht *f* (*about, on* zu); (*political, religious*) Anschauung *f*; **in my ~** meiner Meinung *or* Ansicht nach, meines Erachtens; **in the ~ of the experts** nach Ansicht der Experten; **to be of the ~ that ...** der Meinung *or* Ansicht sein, dass ...; **to express** *or* **put forward an ~** seine Meinung äußern *or* vorbringen; **to ask sb's ~** jdn nach seiner Meinung fragen; **it is a matter of ~** das ist Ansichtssache; **I have no ~ about it** *or* **on the matter** dazu habe ich keine Meinung
b *no pl* (= *estimation*) Meinung *f*; **to have a good ~ of** eine gute *or* hohe Meinung von jdm/etw haben; **to have a high/low** *or* **poor ~ of sb/sth** eine gute *or* hohe/keine gute *or* eine schlechte Meinung von jdm/etw haben; **to form an ~ of sb/sth** sich (*dat*) eine Meinung über jdn/etw bilden
c (= *professional advice*) Gutachten *nt*; (*esp Med*) Befund *m*; **it is the ~ of the court that ...** das Gericht ist zu der Auffassung *or* Ansicht gekommen, dass ...; **to seek** *or* **get a second ~** (*esp Med*) ein zweites Gutachten *or* einen zweiten Befund einholen

opinionated [əˈpɪnjəneɪtɪd] ADJ selbstherrlich, rechthaberisch

opinion poll N Meinungsumfrage *f*

opium [ˈəʊpɪəm] N (*lit, fig*) Opium *nt*; **the ~ of the masses** Opium *nt* für das Volk

opium *in cpds* Opium-; **opium den** N Opiumhöhle *f*; **opium fiend** N Opiumsüchtige(r) *mf*; **opium poppy** N Schlafmohn *m*

opossum [əˈpɒsəm] N Opossum *nt*

opp. *abbr of* **opposite a** (= *reverse*) Gegent. **b** (= *opposite from*) ggb.

opponent [əˈpəʊnənt] ✪ 14 N Gegner(in) *m(f)*; (*in debate, battle of wits etc also*) Opponent *m*

opportune [ˈɒpətjuːn] ADJ *time* gelegen, günstig; *remark* an passender Stelle; *action, event* rechtzeitig, opportun (*geh*); **at an ~ moment** zu einem günstigen Zeitpunkt

---

opportunely [ˈɒpətjuːnlɪ] ADV gelegen, günstig, opportun (*geh*); *remark* an passender Stelle

opportunism [ˌɒpəˈtjuːnɪzəm] N Opportunismus *m*

opportunist [ˌɒpəˈtjuːnɪst] **N** Opportunist(in) *m(f)* **ADJ** opportunistisch; **~ goal** Gelegenheitstor *nt*; **~ thief** Gelegenheitsdieb(in) *m(f)*

opportunity [ˌɒpəˈtjuːnɪtɪ] N **a** Gelegenheit *f*; **at the first** *or* **earliest ~** bei der erstbesten Gelegenheit; **I have little/no ~ for listening** *or* **to listen to music** ich habe wenig/nie Gelegenheit, Musik zu hören; **to take/seize the ~ to do sth** *or* **of doing sth** die Gelegenheit nutzen/ergreifen, etw zu tun; **as soon as the ~ arises** sobald sich die Gelegenheit ergibt; **~ makes the thief** (*Prov*) Gelegenheit macht Diebe (*Prov*) **b** (= *chance to better oneself*) Chance *f*, Möglichkeit *f*; **opportunities for promotion** Aufstiegsmöglichkeiten *or* -chancen *pl*; **equality of ~** Chancengleichheit *f*

oppose [əˈpəʊz] VT **a** (= *be against*) ablehnen; (= *fight against*) sich einsetzen *or* entgegensetzen (+*dat*), opponieren gegen (*form*); *leadership, orders, plans, decisions, sb's wishes* sich widersetzen (+*dat*); *government* sich stellen gegen; **if you think he is the best I won't ~ you** wenn Sie meinen, dass er der Beste ist, werde ich mich nicht dagegen stellen; **he ~s our coming** er ist absolut dagegen, dass wir kommen; **the President ~s sending the refugees back** der Präsident lehnt eine Rückführung der Flüchtlinge ab
b (= *stand in opposition: candidate*) kandidieren gegen
c (*form*) (*against, to* +*dat*) (= *set up in opposition*) entgegensetzen, entgegenstellen; (= *contrast*) gegenüberstellen

opposed [əˈpəʊzd] ✪ 12.1, 14 ADJ **a** *pred* (= *hostile*) dagegen; **to be ~ to sb/sth** gegen jdn/etw sein; **I am ~ to your going away** ich bin dagegen, dass Sie weggehen **b** (= *opposite, contrasted*) entgegengesetzt, gegensätzlich; *aims, views, attitudes* gegensätzlich; **~ to all reason** entgegen aller Vernunft **c** **as ~ to** im Gegensatz zu

opposing [əˈpəʊzɪŋ] ADJ *team* gegnerisch; *army* feindlich; *characters* entgegengesetzt, gegensätzlich; *views* gegensätzlich; *minority* opponierend; **to be on ~ sides** auf entgegengesetzten Seiten stehen

opposing counsel N (*Jur*) Anwalt *m*/Anwältin *f* der Gegenpartei

opposing party N (*Jur*) Gegenpartei *f*

opposite [ˈɒpəzɪt] **ADJ a** (*in place*) entgegengesetzt; (= *facing*) gegenüberliegend *attr*, gegenüber *pred*; **to be ~** gegenüberliegen/-stehen/-sitzen *etc*; **on the ~ page** auf der Seite gegenüber, auf der gegenüberliegenden *or* anderen Seite
b (= *contrary*) entgegengesetzt (*to, from* +*dat*, zu); **in the ~ direction** in entgegengesetzter Richtung; **the ~ sex** das andere Geschlecht; **~ poles** (*Geog*) entgegengesetzte Pole *pl*; (*Elec also*) Gegenpole *pl*; (*fig*) zwei Extreme; **they've got quite ~ characters** sie sind ganz gegensätzliche Charaktere; **it had the ~ effect** es bewirkte das genaue Gegenteil
N Gegenteil *nt*; (= *contrast: of pair*) Gegensatz *m*; **black and white are ~s** Schwarz und Weiß sind Gegensätze; **quite the ~!** ganz im Gegenteil!; **she's quite the ~ of her husband** sie ist genau das Gegenteil von ihrem Mann
ADV gegenüber, auf der anderen *or* gegenüberliegenden Seite; **they sat ~** sie saßen uns/ihnen/sich *etc* gegenüber
PREP gegenüber (+*dat*); **~ one another** sich gegenüber; **they live ~ us** sie wohnen uns gegenüber, sie wohnen gegenüber von uns; **to play ~ sb** (*Theat*) jds Gegenspieler(in) sein, die Gegenrolle zu jdm spielen

opposite number N Pendant *nt*

opposition [ˌɒpəˈzɪʃən] N **a** (= *resistance*) Widerstand *m*, Opposition *f*; (= *people resisting*) Opposition *f*; **to offer ~ to sb/sth** jdm/einer Sache Widerstand entgegensetzen; **to act in ~ to sth** einer Sache (*dat*) zuwiderhandeln; **to**

start up a business in ~ to sb ein Konkurrenzunternehmen zu jdm aufmachen; **without ~** widerstandslos

b (= *contrast*) Gegensatz *m*; **to be in ~ to sb** anderer Meinung als jd sein; **to be in ~ to sth** im Gegensatz zu etw stehen; **he found himself in ~ to the general opinion** er sah sich im Widerspruch zur allgemeinen Meinung

c (*Astron*) Opposition *f*, Gegenschein *m*; **planet in ~** Planet *m* in Opposition *or* im Gegenschein

d (*esp Brit Parl*) Opposition *f*; **the Opposition, Her Majesty's Opposition** die Opposition; **leader of the Opposition** Oppositionsführer(in) *m(f)*

e (*Sport*) Gegner *pl*

Opposition benches PL (*esp Brit Parl*) Oppositionsbank *f*

oppositionist [ˌɒpəˈzɪʃənɪst] N (*Pol*) Oppositionelle(r) *mf*

opposition parties PL (*Pol*) Oppositionsparteien *pl*

oppress [əˈpres] VT **a** (= *tyrannize*) unterdrücken **b** (= *weigh down*) bedrücken, lasten auf (+*dat*); (*heat*) lasten auf (+*dat*); **the climate ~es me** das Klima macht mir schwer zu schaffen; **I feel ~ed by the heat** die Hitze lastet schwer auf mir

oppression [əˈpreʃən] N **a** (= *tyranny*) Unterdrückung *f* **b** (*fig*: = *depression*) Bedrängnis *f*, Bedrücktheit *f*; (*due to heat, climate*) bedrückende Atmosphäre; **the ~ of his spirits** seine Bedrängtheit

oppressive [əˈpresɪv] ADJ **a** (= *tyrannical*) *regime, laws* repressiv; *taxes* (er)drückend **b** (*fig*) *thought, mood* bedrückend; *heat* drückend, schwül

oppressively [əˈpresɪvlɪ] ADV **a** *rule* repressiv; **to tax ~** drückende Steuern *pl* erheben **b** (*fig*) *hot* drückend; **~ drab and grey** bedrückend grau in grau

oppressiveness [əˈpresɪvnɪs] N **a** Unterdrückung *f* (*of durch*); (*of taxes*) (er)drückende Last **b** (*fig*) bedrückende Atmosphäre; (*of thought*) schwere Last; (*of heat, climate*) Schwüle *f*

oppressor [əˈpresə] N Unterdrücker(in) *m(f)*

opprobrious [əˈprəʊbrɪəs] ADJ *invective, remark* verächtlich, schmähend; *conduct* schändlich, schandhaft, schimpflich

opprobrium [əˈprəʊbrɪəm] N (= *disgrace*) Schande *f*, Schmach *f*; (= *scorn, reproach*) Schmähung *f*; **a term of ~** ein Schmähwort *nt*

opt [ɒpt] VI **to ~ for sth** sich für etw entscheiden; **to ~ to do sth** sich entscheiden, etw zu tun; **to ~ to join the single currency** seine Option wahrnehmen, der Währungsunion beizutreten

▶ **opt in** VI beitreten (+*dat*)

▶ **opt out** VI sich anders entscheiden; (*of awkward situation also*) abspringen (*of bei*); (*of responsibility, invitation*) ablehnen (*of* +*acc*); (= *give up membership*) (*also Rad, TV*) austreten (*of aus*); (*of insurance scheme*) kündigen (*of* +*acc*); (*Brit: school, hospital*) aus der Kontrolle der Kommunalverwaltung austreten; **he opted out of going to the party** er entschied sich, doch nicht zur Party zu gehen

optative [ˈɒptətɪv] N Optativ *m*, Wunschform *f* ADJ optativ

optic [ˈɒptɪk] ADJ optisch

optical [ˈɒptɪkəl] ADJ optisch

optical: optical character reader N (*Comput*) optischer Klarschriftleser; **optical character recognition** N (*Comput*) optische Zeichenerkennung; **optical disk** N optische Platte; **optical fibre**, (*US*) **optical fiber** N (= *material*) Glasfaser *f*; (= *cable*) Glasfaserkabel *nt*; **optical illusion** N optische Täuschung; **optical scanner** N optischer Scanner

optician [ɒpˈtɪʃən] N Augenarzt *m*, Augenärztin *f*, Optiker(in) *m(f)*

optic nerve N Sehnerv *m*

optics [ˈɒptɪks] N *sing* Optik *f*

optima [ˈɒptɪmə] *pl* of **optimum**

optimal [ˈɒptɪml] ADJ optimal

optimism [ˈɒptɪmɪzəm] N Optimismus *m*

optimist [ˈɒptɪmɪst] N Optimist(in) *m(f)*

optimistic [ˌɒptɪˈmɪstɪk] ADJ optimistisch; **to be ~ about sth** in Bezug auf etw (*acc*) optimistisch sein; **I'm not very ~ about it** da bin ich nicht sehr optimistisch; **the talks ended on an ~ note** die Gespräche endeten optimistisch

optimistically [ˌɒptɪˈmɪstɪkəlɪ] ADV optimistisch

optimize [ˈɒptɪmaɪz] VT optimieren

optimum [ˈɒptɪməm] ADJ optimal; *results, conditions also* bestmöglich; **for ~ health** für beste Gesundheit N *pl* **optima** *or* **-s** Optimum *nt*; **at an ~** optimal

option [ˈɒpʃən] N **a** (= *choice*) Wahl *f no pl*; (= *possible course of action*) Möglichkeit *f*; **you have the ~ of leaving or staying** Sie haben die Wahl, ob Sie gehen oder bleiben wollen; **to give sb the ~ of doing sth** jdm die Wahl lassen, etw zu tun; **I have little/no ~** mir bleibt kaum eine/keine andere Wahl; **he had no ~ but to come** ihm blieb nichts anderes übrig, als zu kommen; **you have only two ~s (open to you)** es stehen Ihnen nur zwei Möglichkeiten zur Wahl; **that leaves us no ~** das lässt uns keine andere Wahl; **to keep** *or* **leave one's ~s open** sich (*dat*) alle Möglichkeiten offen lassen; **imprisonment without the ~ of a fine** (*Jur*) Gefängnisstrafe *f* ohne Zulassung einer ersatzweisen Geldstrafe; **the military ~** die militärische Lösung

b (*Comm*) Option *f* (*on auf* +*acc*); (*on house, goods etc*) Vorkaufsrecht *nt* (*on an* +*dat*); (*on shares*) Bezugsrecht *nt* (*on für*); **with an ~ to buy** mit einer Kaufoption *or* (*on shares*) Bezugsoption; (= *on approval*) zur Ansicht; **to have a 20-day ~** eine Option mit einer Frist von 20 Tagen haben

c (*Univ, Sch*) Wahlfach *nt*

optional [ˈɒpʃənl] ADJ (= *not compulsory*) freiwillig; (= *not basic*) *trim, mirror etc* auf Wunsch erhältlich; **"evening dress ~"** „Abendkleidung nicht Vorschrift"; **"fancy dress ~"** „kein Kostümzwang"; **~ extras** Extras *pl*; **the cigar lighter is an ~ extra** der Zigarettenanzünder wird auf Wunsch eingebaut; **~ subject** (*Sch, Univ*) Wahlfach *nt*

optometrist [ɒpˈtɒmətrɪst] N (*US: = optician*) Optiker(in) *m(f)*

optometry [ɒpˈtɒmətrɪ] N Optometrie *f*

opt-out [ˈɒptaʊt] ADJ *attr* **a** (*Brit*) *school, hospital* aus der Kontrolle der Kommunalverwaltung ausgetreten **b** **~ clause** Rücktrittsklausel *f* N **a** (*Brit: by school, hospital*) Austritt *m* aus der Kontrolle der Kommunalverwaltung **b** (*from agreement, treaty*) Rücktritt *m*

opulence [ˈɒpjʊləns] N , *no pl* Reichtum *m*; (*of person's appearance also*) Wohlhabenheit *f*; (*of clothes, building, room*) Prunk *m*, Stattlichkeit *f*; (*of car, chairs, carpet*) Feudalität *f*; (*of décor, lifestyle, vegetation*) Üppigkeit *f*; (*of figure*) Üppigkeit *f*, Fülligkeit *f*; **to live in ~** im Überfluss leben

opulent [ˈɒpjʊlənt] ADJ reich; *appearance* (*of person*) *also* wohlhabend; *clothes, building, room* prunkvoll, stattlich; *car, chairs, carpets* feudal; *décor, lifestyle, vegetation* üppig; *figure* üppig, füllig; *feel, look, film, production* opulent

opus [ˈəʊpəs] N *pl* **opera** [ˈɒpərə] (*Mus*) Opus *nt*

OR (*Sport*) *abbr of* **Olympic record**

or¹ [ɔː] N (*Her*) Gold *nt*

or² ✪ 26.2 CONJ **a** oder; (*with neg*) noch; **he could not read** *or* **write** er konnte weder lesen noch schreiben; **without food** *or* **water** ohne Nahrung oder Wasser; **in a day/month or two** in ein bis *or* zwei Tagen/Monaten; **I'm coming, ready** *or* **not** ich komme!; **we're going outside, rain** *or* **no rain** wir gehen nach draußen, ob es nun regnet oder nicht

b (= *that is*) (oder) auch; **the Lacedaemonians,** *or* **Spartans** die Lazedämonier, (oder) auch Spartaner; **Rhodesia, or rather, Zimbabwe** Rhodesien, beziehungsweise Simbabwe

c (= *otherwise*) sonst; **you'd better go or (else) you'll be late** gehen Sie jetzt besser, sonst kommen Sie zu spät; **you'd better do it or else!** tu das lieber, sonst ...!

oracle [ˈɒrəkl] N **a** Orakel *nt*; (= *person*) Seher(in) *m(f)*; (*fig*) Alleswisser(in) *m(f)* **b** Oracle® britisches Videotext-System

oracular [ɒˈrækjʊlə] ADJ *inscriptions, utterances, tone* orakelhaft; *powers* seherisch; (*fig*) *weise*; **~ shrine** Orakelstätte *f*

oral [ˈɔːrəl] **a** ADJ *consonant, phase, contraceptive* oral; *vaccine* oral verabreicht; *medicine* zum Einnehmen **b** (= *verbal*) *communication, agreement, examination, tradition etc* mündlich; **to give ~ evidence to a committee** vor einer Kommission aussagen; **to improve one's ~ skills in a language** eine Sprache besser sprechen lernen N Mündliche(s) *nt*

oral: oral cavity N Mundhöhle *f*; **oral history** N Oral History *f*, mündliche Geschichtsdokumentation; **oral hygiene** N Mundhygiene *f*

orally [ˈɔːrəlɪ] ADV **a** oral; **to take a medicine ~** eine Medizin oral einnehmen **b** (= *verbally*) mündlich

oral sex N Mund- *or* Oralverkehr *m*

orange [ˈɒrɪndʒ] N **a** (= *fruit*) Orange *f*, Apfelsine *f*; (= *tree*) Orangen- *or* Apfelsinenbaum *m*; (= *drink*) Orangensaft *m* **b** (= *colour*) Orange *nt* ADJ **a** Orangen-; **~ flavour** (*Brit*) *or* **flavor** (*US*) Orangengeschmack *m* **b** (*colour*) orange *inv*, orange(n)farben *or* -farbig; **bright ~** grellorange

orangeade [ˈɒrɪndʒeɪd] N Orangeade *f*, Orangenlimonade *f*

orange: orange blossom N Orangenblüte *f* (*wird von Bräuten zur Hochzeit getragen*); **orange box** N Obst- *or* Apfelsinenkiste *f*; **orange-coloured**, (*US*) **orange-colored** ADJ orange(n)farben *or* -farbig; **Orange Day** N *Jahrestag der Schlacht an der Boyne (1690) am 12. Juli (Festtag der Protestanten in Nordirland)*; **orange flower water** N Orangenblütenwasser *nt*; **Orange Free State** N Oranjefreistaat *m*; **orange grove** N Orangenhain *m*; **orange juice** N Orangensaft *m*, O-Saft *m* (*inf*); **Orangeman** N Mitglied *nt* des Oranierordens; **Orangeman's Day** N = **Orange Day**; **Orange March** N Demonstration *f* des Oranierordens; **orange marmalade** N Orangenmarmelade *f*; **Orange Order** N Oranienorden *m* (*protestantische Vereinigung, die den Namen Wilhelms von Oranien trägt*); **orange peel** N Orangen- *or* Apfelsinenschale *f*

orangery [ˈɒrɪndʒərɪ] N Orangerie *f*

orange: orange squash N (*Brit*) Orangenkonzentrat *nt*; (*diluted*) Orangengetränk *nt*; **orange stick** N Manikürstäbchen *nt*; **orange zest** N geriebene Orangenschale

orang-outang, **orang-utan** [ɔːˌræŋuːˈtæŋ, -n] N Orang-Utan *m*

orate [ɒˈreɪt] VI Reden/eine Rede halten (*to vor* +*dat*)

oration [ɒˈreɪʃən] N Ansprache *f*; **funeral ~** Grabrede *f*

orator [ˈɒrətə] N Redner(in) *m(f)*, Orator *m* (*rare, Hist*)

oratorical [ˌɒrəˈtɒrɪkəl] ADJ oratorisch

oratorio [ˌɒrəˈtɔːrɪəʊ] N (*Mus*) Oratorium *nt*

oratory¹ [ˈɒrətərɪ] N (= *art of making speeches*) Redekunst *f*

oratory² N (*Eccl*) Oratorium *nt*

orb [ɔːb] N **a** (*poet*) Ball *m*; (= *star*) Gestirn *nt* (*geh*); (= *eye*) Auge *nt* **b** (*of sovereignty*) Reichsapfel *m*

orbit [ˈɔːbɪt] N **a** (*Astron, Space*) (= *path*) Umlaufbahn *f*, Kreisbahn *f*, Orbit *m*; (= *single circuit*) Umkreisung *f*, Umlauf *m*; **to be in ~ ((a)round the earth)** in der (Erd)umlaufbahn sein; **to go into ~ ((a)round the sun)** in die (Sonnen)umlaufbahn eintreten; **to put a satel-**

lite into ~ einen Satelliten in die Umlaufbahn schießen **b** (fig) Kreis m; (= sphere of influence) (Macht)bereich m, Einflusssphäre f **VT** umkreisen **VI** kreisen

orbital ['ɔːbɪtl] **ADJ** orbital; flight im Orbit; **~ motion** Kreisbewegung f **N** (also **orbital motorway**) Ringautobahn f

orbiter ['ɔːbɪtə'] **N** (Space) Orbiter m, Raumflugkörper m

orchard ['ɔːtʃəd] **N** Obstgarten m; (commercial) Obstplantage f; **apple/cherry ~** Obstgarten m mit Apfel-/Kirschbäumen; (commercial) Apfel-/Kirschplantage f

orchestra ['ɔːkɪstrə] **N** Orchester nt

orchestral [ɔː'kestrəl] **ADJ** Orchester-, orchestral; **~ music** Orchestermusik f; **~ musician** or **player** Orchestermusiker(in) m(f); **~ work** Orchesterwerk nt

orchestrally [ɔː'kestrəlɪ] **ADV** orchestral

orchestra: orchestra pit N Orchestergraben m; **orchestra stalls PL** Orchestersitze pl; **a seat in the ~** ein Orchestersitz m

orchestrate ['ɔːkɪstreɪt] **VT** orchestrieren

orchestrated ['ɔːkɪstreɪtɪd] **ADJ** (fig) attempt, campaign gezielt; **a carefully ~ protest** eine sorgfältig organisierte Protestaktion

orchestration [ɔːkɪs'treɪʃən] **N** Orchestrierung f, Orchesterbearbeitung f

orchid ['ɔːkɪd] **N** Orchidee f

ordain [ɔː'deɪn] **VT a** sb ordinieren; (Eccl) a priest weihen; **to be ~ed priest/to the ministry** ordiniert werden; (Catholic also) zum Priester geweiht werden **b** (= destine: God, fate) wollen, bestimmen; **God has ~ed that man should die** Gott hat es gewollt or hat bestimmt, dass der Mensch sterbe; **fate ~ed that he should die, it was ~ed that he should die** das Schicksal hat es so gefügt or es war ihm vom Schicksal bestimmt, dass er sterben sollte **c** (= decree) (law) bestimmen; (ruler) verfügen

ordeal [ɔː'diːl] **N a** Tortur f; (stronger, long-lasting) Martyrium nt; (= torment, emotional ordeal) Qual f **b** (Hist: = trial) Gottesurteil nt; **~ by fire/water** Feuer-/Wasserprobe f

order ['ɔːdə'] ✪ **20.3, 20.4 N a** (= sequence) (Reihen)folge f, (An)ordnung f; **word ~** Wortstellung f, Wortfolge f; **are they in ~/in the right ~?** sind sie geordnet/in der richtigen Reihenfolge?; **in ~ of preference/merit** in der bevorzugten/in der ihren Auszeichnungen entsprechenden Reihenfolge; **to put sth in (the right) ~** etw ordnen; **to be in the wrong ~** or out of ~ durcheinander sein; (one item) nicht am richtigen Platz sein; **to get out of ~** durcheinander geraten; (one item) an eine falsche Stelle kommen → **cast N d**
b (= system) Ordnung f; **there's no ~ in his work** seiner Arbeit fehlt die Systematik; **he has no sense of ~** er hat kein Gefühl für Systematik or Methode; **the ~ of the world** die Weltordnung; **it is in the ~ of things** es liegt in der Natur der Dinge; **a new social/political ~** eine neue soziale/politische Ordnung
c (= tidy or satisfactory state) Ordnung f; **his passport was in ~** sein Pass war in Ordnung; **to put** or **set one's life/affairs in ~** Ordnung in sein Leben/seine Angelegenheiten bringen
d (= discipline) (in society) Ordnung f; (in school, team) Disziplin f, Ordnung f; **to keep ~** die Ordnung wahren, die Disziplin aufrechterhalten; **to keep the children in ~** die Kinder unter Kontrolle halten; **~ in court** (Brit) or **the courtroom** (US)! Ruhe im Gerichtssaal!; **~, ~!** Ruhe!
e (= working condition) Zustand m; **to be in good ~** in gutem Zustand sein; (= work well) in Ordnung sein; **to be out of/in ~** (car, radio, telephone) nicht funktionieren/funktionieren; (machine, lift also) außer/in Betrieb sein; **"out of ~"** „außer Betrieb" → **working ADJ c**
f (= command) Befehl m, Order f (old, hum); **by ~ of the court** laut gerichtlicher Anweisung; **~s are ~s** Befehl ist Befehl; **"no parking/smoking by ~"** „Parken/Rauchen verboten!"; **"no parking - by ~ of the Town Council"** „Parken

verboten - die Stadtverwaltung"; **by ~ of the minister** auf Anordnung des Ministers; **I don't take ~s from anyone** ich lasse mir von niemandem befehlen; **to be under ~s to do sth** Instruktionen haben, etw zu tun; **until further ~s** bis auf weiteren Befehl
g (in restaurant etc, Comm) Bestellung f; (= contract to manufacture or supply) Auftrag m; **to place an ~ with sb** eine Bestellung bei jdm aufgeben or machen/jdm einen Auftrag geben; **to put sth on ~** etw in Bestellung/Auftrag geben; **to be on ~** bestellt sein; **two ~s of French fries** (esp US) zwei Portionen Pommes frites; **made to ~** auf Bestellung (gemacht or hergestellt)
h (Fin) cheque (Brit) or check (US) **to ~** Orderscheck m, Namensscheck m; **pay to the ~ of** zahlbar an (+acc); **pay X or Order** (zahlbar) an X oder dessen Order
i in ~ to do sth um etw zu tun; **in ~ that** damit
j (= correct procedure at meeting, Parl etc) **a point of ~** eine Verfahrensfrage; **to be out of ~** gegen die Verfahrensordnung verstoßen; (Jur: evidence) unzulässig sein; (fig) aus dem Rahmen fallen; **to call sb to ~** jdn ermahnen, sich an die Verfahrensordnung zu halten; **to call the meeting/delegates to ~** die Versammlung/die Delegierten zur Ordnung rufen; **an explanation/a drink would seem to be in ~** eine Erklärung/ein Drink wäre angebracht; **is it in ~ for me to go to Paris?** ist es in Ordnung, wenn ich nach Paris fahre?; **his demand is quite in ~** seine Forderung ist völlig berechtigt; **what's the ~ of the day?** was steht auf dem Programm (also fig) or auf der Tagesordnung?; (Mil) wie lautet der Tagesbefehl?
k (Archit) Säulenordnung f; (Biol) Ordnung f; (fig: = class, degree) Art f; **intelligence of a high** or **the first ~** hochgradige Intelligenz; **the present crisis is of a different ~** die gegenwärtige Krise ist anders geartet; **something in the ~ of ten per cent** in der Größenordnung von zehn Prozent; **something in the ~ of one in ten applicants** etwa einer von zehn Bewerbern
l (Mil: = formation) Ordnung f
m (social) Schicht f; **the higher/lower ~s** die oberen/unteren Schichten; **the ~ of baronets** der Freiherrnstand
n (Eccl: of monks etc) Orden m; **Benedictine ~** Benediktinerorden m
o orders PL (holy) **~s** (Eccl) Weihe(n) f(pl); (of priesthood) Priesterweihe f; **to take (holy) ~s** die Weihen empfangen; **he is in (holy) ~s** er gehört dem geistlichen Stand an
p (= honour, society of knights) Orden m; **Order of Merit** (Brit) Verdienstorden m → **garter**
VT a (= command, decree) sth befehlen, anordnen; (= prescribe: doctor) verordnen (for sb jdm); **to ~ sb to do sth** jdn etw tun heißen (geh), jdm befehlen or (doctor) verordnen, etw zu tun; (esp Mil) jdn dazu beordern, etw zu tun; **to ~ sb's arrest** jds Verhaftung anordnen; **he was ~ed to be quiet** man befahl ihm, still zu sein; (in public) er wurde zur Ruhe gerufen; **the army was ~ed to retreat** dem Heer wurde der Rückzug befohlen; **he ~ed his gun to be brought (to him)** er ließ sein Gewehr bringen; **to ~ sb out/home** jdn heraus-/heimbeordern (form, hum) or -rufen; (= send out etc) jdn hinaus-/heimbeordern (form, hum) or -schicken
b (= direct, arrange) one's affairs, life ordnen; **to ~ arms** (Mil) das Gewehr abnehmen
c (Comm etc) goods, dinner, taxi bestellen; (to be manufactured) ship, suit, machinery etc in Auftrag geben (from sb bei jdm)
VI bestellen

▶ **order about** (Brit) or **around VT sep** herumkommandieren

order: order book N (Comm) Auftragsbuch nt; **the ~s are full** die Auftragsbücher sind voll; **order cheque N** Orderscheck m, Namensscheck m; **order form N** Bestellformular nt, Bestellschein m

orderliness ['ɔːdəlɪnɪs] **N a** Ordentlichkeit f; **the ~ of his life** sein geregeltes Leben **b** (of

group, demonstration) Friedlichkeit f, Gesittetheit f

orderly ['ɔːdəlɪ] **ADJ a** (= tidy, methodical) ordentlich, geordnet; life geordnet, geregelt; person, mind ordentlich, methodisch; **in an ~ fashion** or **manner** geordnet **b** group, demonstration ruhig, friedlich, gesittet **N a** (Mil, attached to officer) Bursche m (dated) **b** (medical) **~** Pfleger(in) m(f); (Mil) Sanitäter(in) m(f)

orderly: orderly officer N Dienst habender Offizier, Dienst habende Offizierin, Offizier(in) m(f) vom Dienst; **orderly room N** Schreibstube f

order paper N (esp Parl) Tagesordnung f

ordinal ['ɔːdɪnl] (Math) **ADJ** Ordnungs-, Ordinal- **N** Ordnungs- or Ordinalzahl f, Ordinale f (spec)

ordinal number N (Math) Ordnungszahl f, Ordinalzahl f

ordinance ['ɔːdɪnəns] **N a** (= order) (of government) Verordnung f; (Jur) Anordnung f; (of fate) Fügung f (geh) **b** (Eccl) (= sacrament) Sakrament nt; (= rite) Ritus m

ordinand ['ɔːdɪnænd] **N** Priesteramtskandidat(in) m(f)

ordinarily ['ɔːdɪnrɪlɪ] **ADV** normalerweise, gewöhnlich; (+adj) normal, wie gewöhnlich; **more than ~ stupid/intelligent** außergewöhnlich dumm/intelligent

ordinary ['ɔːdnrɪ] **ADJ a** (= usual) gewöhnlich, normal; **to do sth in the ~ way** etw auf die normale or gewöhnliche Art und Weise tun; **in the ~ way I would ...** normalerweise or gewöhnlich würde ich ...; **~ use** normaler Gebrauch; **my doctor** der Arzt, zu dem ich normalerweise gehe
b (= average) normal, durchschnittlich; (= nothing special, commonplace) gewöhnlich, alltäglich; **the ~ Englishman** der normale Engländer; **a very ~ kind of person** ein ganz gewöhnlicher Mensch; **this is no ~ car** dies ist kein gewöhnliches Auto
N a out of the ~ außergewöhnlich, außerordentlich; **nothing/something out of the ~** nichts/etwas Außergewöhnliches or Ungewöhnliches; **to be a cut above the ~** besser als der Durchschnitt sein; **intelligence above the ~** überdurchschnittliche or außergewöhnliche Intelligenz
b (form) physician/painter **in ~ to the king** königlicher Leibarzt/Hofmaler
c (Eccl) **the ~ of the mass** Ordo m Missae

ordinary: Ordinary grade N (Brit) = **O grade**; **Ordinary level N** (Brit) = **O level**; **Ordinary National Certificate N** (Brit) Qualifikationsnachweis von einer Fachschule; **Ordinary National Diploma N** (Brit) Diplom einer technischen Fachschule; **ordinary seaman N** Maat m; **ordinary share N** (Fin) Stammaktie f

ordination [ɔːdɪ'neɪʃən] **N** Ordination f

ordnance ['ɔːdnəns] (Mil) **N a** (= artillery) (Wehr)material nt **b** (= supply) Material nt, Versorgung f (= troops) Technische Truppe; (in times of war) Nachschub m

ordnance: ordnance factory N Munitionsfabrik f; **ordnance map N a** (Brit) → **Ordnance Survey map b** (US Mil) Generalstabskarte f; **Ordnance Survey N** (Brit) ≈ Landesvermessungsamt nt; **Ordnance Survey map N** (Brit) amtliche topografische Karte (form), Messtischblatt nt

ordure ['ɔːdjʊə'] **N** (liter) (= excrement) Kot m; (= rubbish) Unrat m, Unflat m (geh); (fig) Schmutz m no pl

ore [ɔː'] **N** Erz nt

ore-bearing ADJ (Geol) layer etc Erz führend, erzhaltig

Ore(g) abbr of **Oregon**

oregano [ɒrɪ'gɑːnəʊ] **N** Origano m, Oregano m

organ ['ɔːgən] **N a** (Anat) Organ nt; (= penis) Geschlecht nt; **~ of speech** Sprechorgan nt **b** (Mus) Orgel f; **to be at the ~** die Orgel spielen

c (= *mouthpiece of opinion*) Sprachrohr *nt*; (= *newspaper*) Organ *nt* **d** (= *means of action*) Organ *nt*

organ bank N (*Med*) Organbank *f*

organdie, (*US*) **organdy** [ˈɔːgəndɪ] N Organdy *m*

organ: organ donor N Organspender(in) *m(f)*; **organ-grinder** N Drehorgelspieler(in) *m(f)*; (= *man also*) Leierkastenmann *m*; **I want to talk to the ~, not the monkey** (*inf*) ich will den sprechen, der das Sagen hat

organic [ɔːˈgænɪk] ADJ **a** (*Sci, Med*) organisch **b** *vegetables, farming* biodynamisch; **~ wine/flour** Wein *m*/Mehl *nt* aus biologisch kontrolliertem Anbau; **~ beer** *Bier aus Zutaten, die aus biologisch kontrolliertem Anbau stammen* **~ meat** Fleisch *nt* aus biologisch kontrollierter Zucht **c** (*fig*) *whole, unity* organisch; *part of whole* substanziell, substantiell; *fault* immanent

organically [ɔːˈgænɪkəlɪ] ADV **a** (*Sci, Med*) organisch **b** *farm, grow* biodynamisch **c** (*fig*) *integrated, connected etc* organisch

organic: organic chemistry N organische Chemie; **organic farm** N Bio-Landwirtschaftsbetrieb *m*; **organic farmer** N Bio-Bauer *m*, Bio-Bäuerin *f*

organism [ˈɔːgənɪzəm] N (*Biol, fig*) Organismus *m*

organist [ˈɔːgənɪst] N Organist(in) *m(f)*

organization [ˌɔːgənaɪˈzeɪʃən] N **a** (= *act*) Organisation *f* (*also Pol*); (*of time*) Einteilung *f* **b** (= *arrangement*) Ordnung *f*; (*of facts, work*) Organisation *f*; (*of time*) Einteilung *f*; (*of essay*) Aufbau *m*; (*of sb's life*) Planung *f* **c** (= *institution*) Organisation *f*; (*Comm*) Unternehmen *nt*

organizational [ˌɔːgənaɪˈzeɪʃənəl] ADJ organisatorisch; **at an ~ level** im strukturellem Bereich

organization: organization chart N Organisationsplan *m*; **Organization for Economic Cooperation and Development** N Organisation *f* für wirtschaftliche Zusammenarbeit und Entwicklung; **Organization of African Unity** N Organisation *f* für Afrikanische Einheit; **Organization of American States** N Organisation *f* Amerikanischer Staaten; **Organization of Arab Petroleum Exporting Countries** N Organisation *f* der arabischen Erdöl exportierenden Länder; **Organization of Petroleum Exporting Countries** N Organisation *f* der Erdöl exportierenden Länder

organize [ˈɔːgənaɪz] VT **a** (= *give structure to, systematize*) ordnen; *facts* organisieren, ordnen; *time* einteilen; *work* organisieren, einteilen; *essay* aufbauen; *one's/sb's life* planen; *one's thoughts* ordnen; **to get (oneself) ~d** (= *get ready*) alles vorbereiten; (*to go out*) sich fertig machen; (*for term, holiday etc*) sich vorbereiten; (= *sort things out*) seine Sachen in Ordnung bringen; (= *sort out one's life*) ein geregeltes Leben anfangen; **I'll have to get better ~d** ich muss das alles besser organisieren; **I'll come as soon as I've got (myself) ~d** ich komme, sobald ich so weit bin; **I've only just taken over the business, but as soon as I've got ~d I'll contact you** ich habe das Geschäft gerade erst übernommen, aber sobald alles (richtig) läuft, melde ich mich bei Ihnen; **it took us quite a while to get ~d in our new house** wir haben eine ganze Zeit gebraucht, uns in unserem neuen Haus (richtig) einzurichten

b (= *arrange*) *party, meeting etc* organisieren; *food, music for party etc* sorgen für; *sports event* organisieren, ausrichten; (*into teams, groups*) einteilen; **to ~ things so that ...** es so einrichten, dass ...; **they ~d (it) for me to go to London** sie haben meine Londonreise arrangiert; **organizing committee** Organisationskomitee *nt* **c** (*Pol: = unionize*) organisieren

VI (*Pol*) sich organisieren

organized [ˈɔːgənaɪzd] ADJ **a** (*Sci*) organisch **b** (= *structured, systematized*) organisiert; *life* geregelt; **he isn't very ~** bei ihm geht alles drunter und drüber (*inf*); **you have to be ~** du musst

planvoll *or* systematisch *or* mit System vorgehen; **as far as his work/social life is concerned, he's well ~** was seine Arbeit/sein gesellschaftliches Leben angeht, so läuft bei ihm alles sehr geregelt ab; **he's well ~** (*in new flat etc*) er ist bestens eingerichtet; (= *well-prepared*) er ist gut vorbereitet **c** (*Pol, = unionized*) organisiert

organized crime N organisiertes Verbrechen

organized labour, (*US*) **organized labor** N organisierte Arbeitnehmerschaft

organizer [ˈɔːgənaɪzə] N **a** Organisator(in) *m(f)*, Veranstalter(in) *m(f)*; (*of sports event*) Ausrichter(in) *m(f)* **b** = **personal organizer**

organ loft N Orgelempore *f*, Orgelbühne *f*

organophosphate [ɔːgənəʊˈfɒsfeɪt] N Organophosphat *nt*

organ: organ pipe N (*Mus*) Orgelpfeife *f*; **organ stop** N (*Mus*) Orgelregister *nt*, -zug *m*; **organ transplant** N **a** (= *operation*) Organtransplantation *f* **b** (= *organ*) Organtransplantat *nt*

organza [ɔːˈgænzə] N Organza *m*

orgasm [ˈɔːgæzəm] **N** (*lit, fig*) Orgasmus *m*; **to go into ~s** (*fig inf*) einen Orgasmus nach dem anderen kriegen (*inf*); **to be having ~s** (*fig inf*) ganz aus dem Häuschen sein (*inf*); **~** einen Orgasmus haben

orgasmic [ɔːˈgæzmɪk] ADJ orgasmisch

orgiastic [ɔːdʒɪˈæstɪk] ADJ orgiastisch

orgy [ˈɔːdʒɪ] N (*lit, fig*) Orgie *f*; **drunken ~** Saufgelage *f*; **an ~ of killing** eine Blutorgie; **~ of spending** Kauforgie *f*; **an ~ of colour** (*Brit*) *or* **color** (*US*) eine orgiastische Farbenpracht

oriel (window) [ˈɔːrɪəl(ˈwɪndəʊ)] N Erker(fenster *nt*) *m*

orient [ˈɔːrɪənt] N (*also* **Orient**) Orient *m*; (*poet also*) Morgenland *nt* ADJ (*poet*) *sun, moon* aufgehend **VT** = **orientate**

oriental [ɔːrɪˈentl] ADJ orientalisch; *languages also* östlich; (*Univ*) orientalistisch; **~ rug** Orientteppich *m*; **~ studies** *pl* Orientalistik *f* **N** (= *person*) **Oriental** Orientale *m*, Orientalin *f*

orientalist [ɔːrɪˈentəlɪst] N Orientalist(in) *m(f)*

orientate [ˈɔːrɪənteɪt] **VR** (*lit*) sich orientieren (*by an +dat, by the map nach der Karte*); (*fig also*) sich zurechtfinden **VT** ausrichten (*towards auf +acc*); *new employees etc* einführen; *thinking* orientieren (*towards an +dat*); **money-orientated** materiell ausgerichtet; **family-orientated** familienorientiert

orientation [ɔːrɪənˈteɪʃən] N **a** (= *getting one's bearing*) Orientierung *f*; (*fig*) Ausrichtung *f*, Orientierung *f* **b** (= *position, direction*) (*lit: of boat, spaceship etc*) Kurs *m*; (*fig*) Orientierung *f*; (= *attitude*) Einstellung *f* (*towards* zu); (= *leaning*) Ausrichtung *f* (*towards* auf *+acc*); **sexual ~** sexuelle Orientierung

-oriented [ˈɔːrɪəntɪd] ADJ *suf* -orientiert; **market--oriented** marktorientiert

orienteering [ɔːrɪənˈtɪərɪŋ] N Orientierungslauf *m*

orifice [ˈɒrɪfɪs] N Öffnung *f*

origami [ɒrɪˈgɑːmɪ] N Origami *nt*

origin [ˈɒrɪdʒɪn] N **a** Ursprung *m*, Herkunft *f*; (*of person, family*) Herkunft *f*, Abstammung *f*; (*of world*) Entstehung *f*; (*of river*) Ursprung *m* (*geh*); **to have its ~ in sth** auf etw (*acc*) zurückgehen; (*river*) in etw (*dat*) entspringen; **his family had its ~ in France** seine Familie ist französischer Herkunft; **country of ~** Herkunftsland *nt*; **nobody knew the ~ of that story** niemand wusste, wie die Geschichte entstanden war; **what are his ~s?** was für eine Herkunft hat er? **b** (*Math*) Ursprung *m*

original [əˈrɪdʒɪnl] ADJ **a** (= *first, earliest*) ursprünglich; **in its ~ form** in seiner ursprünglichen Form; **~ inhabitants of a country** Ureinwohner *pl* eines Landes; **~ text** Urtext *m*; **~ version** (*of book, play*) Urfassung *f*; (*of film, song*) Originalversion *or* -fassung *f*; **~ edition** Originalausgabe *f*; **in the ~ German** im deutschen Originaltext

b (= *not imitative*) *painting* original; *idea, writer, play* originell; (= *research*) eigene Forschung; **~ document** (*Jur*) Originaldokument *nt* **c** (= *unconventional, eccentric*) *character, person* originell **N a** Original *nt*; (*of model*) Vorlage *f* **b** (= *eccentric person*) Original *nt*

originality [əˌrɪdʒɪˈnælɪt] N Originalität *f*

originally [əˈrɪdʒənəlɪ] ADV **a** ursprünglich **b** (= *in an original way*) originell

original sin N die Erbsünde

originate [əˈrɪdʒɪneɪt] **VT** hervorbringen; *policy, company* ins Leben rufen; *product* erfinden; **who ~d the idea?** von wem stammt die Idee? **VI a** entstehen; **the legend ~d in ...** die Legende ist in (*+dat*) ... entstanden *or* hat ihren Ursprung in (*+dat*) ...; **to ~ from a country** aus einem Land stammen; **to ~ from** *or* **with sb** von jdm stammen; **the company ~d as a family concern** die Firma war ursprünglich *or* anfänglich ein Familienbetrieb **b** (*US: bus, train etc*) ausgehen (*in* von)

originator [əˈrɪdʒɪneɪtə] N (*of plan, idea*) Urheber(in) *m(f)*; (*of company*) Gründer(in) *m(f)*; (*of product*) Erfinder(in) *m(f)*

oriole [ˈɔːrɪəʊl] N Pirol *m*

Orkney Islands [ˈɔːknɪˈaɪləndz], **Orkneys** [ˈɔːknɪz] PL Orkneyinseln *pl*

Orlon® [ˈɔːlɒn] N Orlon® *nt*

ormolu [ˈɔːməʊluː] N **a** (= *alloy*) Messing *nt*; (= *decoration*) Messingverzierungen *pl*; (= *mountings*) Messingbeschläge *pl* **ADJ** aus Messing

ornament [ˈɔːnəmənt] **N a** (= *decorative object*) Schmuckgegenstand *m*, Verzierung *f*; (*on mantelpiece etc*) Ziergegenstand *m*; (*fig*) Zierde *f* (*to +gen*); **his secretary is just an ~** seine Sekretärin ist nur zur Verzierung *or* Dekoration da; **she has the house full of ~s** sie hat das Haus voller Nippes (*pej*) *or* Ziergegenstände; **altar ~s** (*Eccl*) Altarschmuck *m* **b** *no pl* (= *ornamentation*) Ornamente *pl*; (= *decorative articles, on clothes etc*) Verzierungen *pl*, Zierrat *m* (*geh*); **by way of ~, for ~** zur Verzierung **c** (*Mus*) Verzierung *f*, Ornament *nt* **VT** [ˈɔːnəmənt] verzieren; *room* ausschmücken

ornamental [ɔːnəˈmentl] ADJ dekorativ; *detail* schmückend, zierend; **for ~ purposes** zur Dekoration; **to be purely ~** zur Verzierung *or* Zierde (da) sein; **wives were only expected to look ~** Ehefrauen hatten nur zur Dekoration da zu sein; **~ object** *or* **piece** Zier- *or* Schmuckgegenstand *m*, Zierat *m* (*geh*); **~ garden/pond** Ziergarten *m*/-teich *m*; **~ plant** Zierpflanze *f*

ornamentation [ɔːnəmenˈteɪʃən] N **a** (= *ornamenting*) Verzieren *nt*, Verzierung *f*; (*of room*) Ausschmücken *nt*, Ausschmückung *f* **b** (= *ornamental detail*) Verzierungen *pl*, Zierrat *m* (*geh*); (*Art, Archit*) Ornamentik *f*; (= *ornaments: in room etc*) Schmuck *m*

ornate [ɔːˈneɪt] ADJ kunstvoll; (*of larger objects*) prunkvoll; *decoration* aufwändig, aufwendig; *music* ornamentreich; *description* reich ausgeschmückt, umständlich (*pej*); *language, style* umständlich (*pej*), überladen (*pej*), reich

ornately [ɔːˈneɪtlɪ] ADV kunstvoll; *describe* mit beredten Worten, umständlich (*pej*); *written in* reicher Sprache

ornateness [ɔːˈneɪtnɪs] N Verzierungsreichtum *m*; (*of baroque church, palace etc*) Prunk *m*, Prachtentfaltung *f*; (*of music*) ornamentaler Reichtum *m*; (*of style*) Reichtum *m*; (*of description*) Wortreichtum *m*, Umständlichkeit *f* (*pej*); (*of decoration*) Reichtum *m*, Aufwändigkeit *f*, Aufwendigkeit *f*

ornithological [ɔːnɪθəˈlɒdʒɪkəl] ADJ ornithologisch, vogelkundlich

ornithologist [ɔːnɪˈθɒlədʒɪst] N Ornithologe *m*, Ornithologin *f*, Vogelkundler(in) *m(f)*

ornithology [ɔːnɪˈθɒlədʒɪ] N Ornithologie *f*, Vogelkunde *f*

orphan [ˈɔːfən] **N** Waise *f*, Waisenkind *nt*; **the accident left him an ~** der Unfall machte ihn zur Waise or zum Waisenkind; **like ~ Annie** (*inf*) wie bestellt und nicht abgeholt **ADJ** Waisen-; **~ child** Waisenkind *nt* **VT** zur Waise machen; **to be ~ed** zur Waise werden; **he was ~ed by the war** er ist (eine) Kriegswaise; **he was ~ed at the age of three** er wurde Waise, als er drei Jahre alt war

orphanage ['ɔːfənɪdʒ] N Waisenhaus *nt*

Orpheus ['ɔːfjuːs] N (*Myth*) Orpheus *m*

orthodontic [ɔːθəʊ'dɒntɪk] ADJ kieferorthopädisch

orthodontics [ɔːθəʊ'dɒntɪks] N *sing* Kieferorthopädie *f*

orthodontist [ɔːθəʊ'dɒntɪst] N Kieferorthopäde *m*/-orthopädin *f*

orthodox ['ɔːθədɒks] ADJ **a** (*Rel*) orthodox; **the Orthodox (Eastern) Church** die orthodoxe (Ost)kirche **b** (*fig*) konventionell; *view, method, approach etc* orthodox

orthodoxy ['ɔːθədɒksɪ] N **a** Orthodoxie *f* **b** (*fig*) Konventionalität *f*; (*of view, method, approach etc*) Orthodoxie *f* **c** (= *orthodox belief, practice etc*) orthodoxe Konvention

orthographic(al) [ɔːθə'græfɪk(əl)] ADJ orthografisch

orthography [ɔː'θɒɡrəfɪ] N Rechtschreibung *f*, Orthografie *f*

orthopaedic, (*US*) **orthopedic** [ɔːθəʊ'piːdɪk] ADJ orthopädisch; **~ bed** orthopädisches Bett; **~ surgeon** orthopädischer Chirurg, orthopädische Chirurgin

orthopaedics, (*US*) **orthopedics** [ɔːθəʊ'piːdɪks] N *sing* Orthopädie *f*

orthopaedist, (*US*) **orthopedist** [ɔːθəʊ'piːdɪst] N Orthopäde *m*, Orthopädin *f*

orthoptic [ɔː'θɒptɪk] ADJ (*Med*) normalsichtig; **~ exercises** mechanische Sehübungen

OS a *abbr of* **ordinary seaman b** *abbr of* **Ordnance Survey c** *abbr of* **outsize**

Oscar ['ɒskə'] N (*Film*) Oscar *m*; **Dustin Hoffman in his ~-winning performance** Dustin Hoffman in der Rolle, für die er den Oscar bekam

oscillate ['ɒsɪleɪt] VI (*Phys*) oszillieren, schwingen; (*compass needle etc*) schwanken; (*rapidly*) zittern; (*fig*) schwanken; **the needle ~d violently** die Nadel schlug stark aus

oscillating ['ɒsɪleɪtɪŋ] ADJ **a** (*Phys*) schwingend; *needle* ausschlagend; (*rapidly*) zitternd **b** (*fig*) schwankend

oscillation [ɒsɪ'leɪʃən] N (*Phys*) Oszillation *f*, Schwingung *f*; (*of compass needle etc*) Schwanken *nt*; (*rapid*) Zittern *nt*; (= *individual movement etc*) Schwankung *f*

oscillator ['ɒsɪleɪtə'] N Oszillator *m*

oscillograph [ə'sɪləgræf] N Oszillograf *m*

oscilloscope [ə'sɪləskəʊp] N Oszilloskop *nt*

OSHA (*US*) *abbr of* **Occupational Safety and Health Administration** Arbeitsschutzbehörde *f*

osier ['əʊzɪə'] N Korbweide *f*; (= *twig*) Weidenrute or -gerte *f* ATTR Weiden-; **~ basket** Weidenkorb *m*; **~ chair** Korbstuhl *m*

osmium ['ɒzmɪəm] N Osmium *nt*

osmosis [ɒz'məʊsɪs] N Osmose *f*

osmotic [ɒz'mɒtɪk] ADJ osmotisch

osprey ['ɒspreɪ] N Fischadler *m*

osseous ['ɒsɪəs] ADJ knöchern

ossification [ɒsɪfɪ'keɪʃən] N Verknöcherung *f*, Ossifikation *f* (*spec*)

ossify ['ɒsɪfaɪ] VT (*lit*) verknöchern lassen; (*fig*) erstarren lassen; *mind* unbeweglich machen; **to be ossified** (*lit*) verknöchert sein; (*fig*) erstarrt sein; (*mind*) unbeweglich sein; **to become ossified** (*lit*) verknöchern; (*fig*) erstarren; (*mind*) unbeweglich werden VI (*lit*) verknöchern; (*fig*) erstarren; (*mind*) unbeweglich werden

ossuary ['ɒsjʊərɪ] N Ossarium *nt*; (= *building also*) Beinhaus *nt*

Ostend [ɒ'stend] N Ostende *nt*

ostensible ADJ , **ostensibly** ADV [ɒ'stensəbl, -ɪ] angeblich

ostentation [ɒsten'teɪʃən] N **a** (= *pretentious display*) (*of wealth etc*) Pomp *m*; (*of skills etc*) Großtuerei *f* **b** (= *obviousness*) aufdringliche or penetrante Deutlichkeit; **with ~** demonstrativ, ostentativ; **without ~** betont unauffällig

ostentatious [ɒsten'teɪʃəs] ADJ **a** (= *pretentious*) pompös, protzig (*inf*) **b** (= *conspicuous*) ostentativ, betont auffällig

ostentatiously [ɒsten'teɪʃəslɪ] ADV **a** (= *pretentiously*) pompös, protzig (*inf*); *live* pompös, in Pomp, auf großem Fuße **b** (= *conspicuously*) ostentativ, betont auffällig

ostentatiousness [ɒsten'teɪʃəsnɪs] N = **ostentation**

osteoarthritis ['ɒstɪəʊɑː'θraɪtɪs] N Arthrose *f*

osteopath ['ɒstɪəpæθ] N Osteopath(in) *m(f)*

osteopathy [ɒstɪ'ɒpəθɪ] N Osteopathie *f*

ostler ['ɒslə'] N (*Hist*) Stallknecht *m*

ostracism ['ɒstrəsɪzəm] N Ächtung *f*

ostracize ['ɒstrəsaɪz] VT ächten; (*Hist*) verbannen

ostrich ['ɒstrɪtʃ] N Strauß *m*; **~ policy** Vogel--Strauß-Politik *f*

OT *abbr of* **Old Testament** A. T. *nt*

OTC *abbr of* **Officers' Training Corps**

other ['ʌðə'] ADJ **a** andere(r, s); **~ people** andere (Leute); **some ~ people will come later** später kommen noch ein paar; **there were 6 ~ people there** es waren auch noch 6 andere (Leute) da; **do you have any ~ questions?** haben Sie sonst noch Fragen?; **he had no ~ questions** er hatte sonst keine Fragen; **he could be no ~ than strict** er konnte nicht anders als streng sein, er konnte nur streng sein; **the man was none ~ than my father** der Mann war niemand anders als mein Vater; **the ~ day** neulich; **the ~ world** das Jenseits, jene andere Welt (*liter*); **some ~ time** (*in future*) ein andermal; (*in past*) ein anderes Mal; **~ people's property** fremdes Eigentum; **to see how the ~ half lives** sehen, wie andere leben **b every ~ …** (= *alternate*) jede(r, s) zweite … **c ~ than** (= *except*) außer (+*dat*); (= *different to*) anders als **d** **some time or ~** irgendwann (einmal); **some writer/house etc or ~** irgend so ein or irgendein Schriftsteller/Haus *etc* PRON andere(r, s); **he doesn't like hurting ~s** er mag niemanden verletzen, er mag niemandem wehtun; **there are 6 ~s** da sind noch 6 (andere); **are there any ~s there?** sind noch welche da?; **there were no ~s there** es waren sonst keine da; **something/someone or ~** irgendetwas/-jemand; **one or ~ of them** will come either (von ihnen) wird kommen; **can you tell one from the ~?** kannst du sie auseinander halten?; **he fancied a bit of the ~** (*inf*) ihm war nach ein bisschen - na ja, du weißt schon (*inf*), er wollte ein bisschen bumsen (*inf*) → **each, one** ADV **he could do no ~ (than come)** er konnte nicht anders (als kommen), er konnte nichts anderes tun (als kommen); **I've never seen her ~ than with her husband** ich habe sie immer nur mit ihrem Mann gesehen; **somehow or ~** irgendwie, auf die eine oder andere Weise; **somewhere or ~** irgendwo

other-directed ['ʌðədaɪ'rektɪd] ADJ fremdbestimmt

otherness ['ʌðənɪs] N Anderssein *nt*, Andersartigkeit *f*

other ranks PL (*Brit Mil*) Angehörige der britischen Streitkräfte unterhalb des Offiziersrangs

otherwise ['ʌðəwaɪz] **2.3** ADV **a** (= *in a different way*) anders; **I am ~ engaged** (*form*) ich bin anderweitig beschäftigt; **except where ~ stated** (*form*) sofern nicht anders angegeben; **Richard I, ~ (known as) the Lionheart** Richard I., auch bekannt als Löwenherz, Richard I. oder auch Löwenherz; **you seem to think ~** Sie scheinen anderer Meinung zu sein **b** (= *in other respects*) sonst, ansonsten, im Übrigen CONJ

(= *or else*) sonst, andernfalls ADJ *pred* anders; **poems tragic and ~** tragische und andere Gedichte

otherworldliness [ʌðə'wɜːldlɪnɪs] N (*of person, attitude*) Weltferne *f*; (*of expression*) Entrücktheit *f*

otherworldly [ʌðə'wɜːldlɪ] ADJ *attitude, person* weltfern; *smile, expression* entrückt

otiose ['əʊʃɪəʊs] ADJ (*liter*) müßig (*geh*)

OTT (*inf*) *abbr of* **over the top**

otter ['ɒtə'] N Otter *m*

Ottoman ['ɒtəmən] ADJ osmanisch, ottomanisch (*rare*) N Osmane *m*, Osmanin *f*, Ottomane *m* (*rare*), Ottomanin *f* (*rare*)

ottoman ['ɒtəmən] N Polstertruhe *f*

ouch [aʊtʃ] INTERJ autsch

ought¹ [ɔːt] ✪ **1.1, 2.2** VB AUX **a** (*indicating moral obligation*) **I ~ to do it** ich sollte or müsste es tun; **he ~ to have come** er hätte kommen sollen or müssen; **this ~ to have been done** das hätte man tun sollen or müssen; **~ I to go too? - yes, you ~ (to)/no, you ~n't (to)** sollte or müsste ich auch (hin)gehen? - ja doch/nein, das sollen Sie nicht; **he thought he ~ to tell you/you ~ to know** er meinte, er sollte Ihnen das sagen/Sie sollten das wissen; **people have come who ~ not to have done** es sind Leute gekommen, die nicht hätten kommen sollen; **~n't you to have left?** hätten Sie nicht schon gehen müssen?; **cars are parked where they ~ not to be** Autos sind an Stellen geparkt, wo sie nicht hingehören; **he behaved just as he ~ (to have)** (= *was well-behaved*) er hat sich völlig korrekt benommen; (= *did the right thing*) er hat sich völlig richtig verhalten **b** (*indicating what is right, advisable, desirable*) **you ~ to see that film** den Film solltest du sehen; **you ~ to have seen his face** sein Gesicht hätten Sie sehen müssen; **she ~ to have been a teacher** sie hätte Lehrerin werden sollen **c** (*indicating probability*) **he ~ to win the race** er müsste (eigentlich) das Rennen gewinnen; **come at six, that ~ to be early enough** komm (mal) um sechs, das sollte or müsste früh genug sein; **that ~ to do** das dürfte wohl or müsste reichen; **he ~ to be here soon** er müsste bald hier sein; **he ~ to have left by now** er müsste inzwischen gegangen sein; **… and I ~ to know!** … und ich muss es doch wissen!

ought² N = **aught**

ouija (board) ['wiːdʒə('bɔːd)] N Buchstabenbrett für spiritistische Sitzungen

ounce [aʊns] N Unze *f*; **there's not an ~ of truth in it** daran ist kein Fünkchen Wahrheit; **if he had an ~ of sense** wenn er nur einen Funken or für fünf Pfennig (*inf*) Verstand hätte

our ['aʊə'] POSS ADJ unser; **these are ~ own make** die stellen wir selbst her; **Our Father** (*in prayer*) Vater unser; **the Our Father** das Vaterunser or Unservater (*Sw*) → *also* **my POSS ADJ**

ours ['aʊəz] POSS PRON unsere(r, s); **~ not to reason why(, ~ but to do or die)** (*prov*) das wissen die Götter (*inf*), es ist nicht an uns, nach dem Warum zu fragen → *also* **mine¹**

ourself [aʊə'self] PERS PRON (*form*) (wir) selbst

ourselves [aʊə'selvz] PERS PRON (*dir, indir obj +prep*) uns; (*emph*) selbst → *also* **myself**

oust [aʊst] VT (= *get, drive out*) herausbekommen; *government* absetzen; *politician, colleague etc* ausbooten (*inf*), absägen (*inf*); *heckler, anglicisms* entfernen; *rivals* ausschalten; (= *take place of*) verdrängen; **to ~ sb from office/his position** jdn aus seinem Amt/seiner Stellung entfernen or (*by intrigue*) hinausmanövrieren; **to ~ sb from power** jdn von der Macht verdrängen

out [aʊt] ADV **a** (= *not in container, car etc*) außen; (= *not in building, room*) draußen; (*indicating motion*) (*seen from inside*) hinaus, raus (*inf*); (*seen from outside*) heraus, raus (*inf*); **to be ~** weg sein; (*when visitors come*) nicht da sein; **they're ~ in the garden** sie sind draußen im Garten; **they're ~ playing** sie spielen draußen; **they are ~ fishing/shopping** sie sind zum Fischen/Einkaufen (gegangen), sie sind fischen/einkaufen; **he's ~ in his car** er ist mit dem Auto unterwegs; **she was ~ all night** sie war die ganze Nacht weg; **it's cold ~ here/there** es ist kalt hier/da *or* dort draußen; **~ you go!** hinaus *or* raus (*inf*) mit dir!; **~!** raus (hier)! (*inf*); **~ with him!** hinaus *or* raus (*inf*) mit ihm!; **~ it goes!** hinaus damit, raus damit (*inf*); **everybody ~!** alle Mann *or* alles raus! (*inf*); **he likes to be ~ and about** er ist gern unterwegs; **at weekends I like to be ~ and about** an den Wochenenden will ich (immer) raus; **we had a day ~ at the beach/ in London** wir haben einen Tag am Meer/in London verbracht; **we had a day ~ at the shops** wir haben einen Einkaufsbummel gemacht; **the journey ~** die Hinreise; (*seen from destination*) die Herfahrt; **the goods were damaged on the journey ~** die Waren sind auf dem Transport beschädigt worden; **the book is ~** (*from library*) das Buch ist ausgeliehen *or* unterwegs (*inf*); **the Socialists are ~** die Sozialisten sind nicht mehr an der Regierung; **the workers are ~** (= *on strike*) die Arbeiter streiken *or* sind im Ausstand; **school is ~** die Schule ist aus; **the tide is ~** es ist Ebbe; **the chicks should be ~ tomorrow** die Küken sollten bis morgen heraus sein

b (*indicating distance*) **when he was ~ in Persia** als er in Persien war; **to go ~ to China** nach China fahren; **~ in the Far East** im Fernen Osten; **~ here in Australia** hier in Australien; **Wilton Street? isn't that ~ your way?** Wilton Street? ist das nicht da (hinten) bei euch in der Gegend?; **the boat was ten miles ~** das Schiff war zehn Meilen weit draußen; **five days ~ from Liverpool** (*Naut*) fünf Tage nach dem Auslaufen aus Liverpool; **five miles ~ from shore** fünf Meilen von der Küste weg, fünf Meilen vor der Küste

c to be ~ (*sun*) (he)raus *or* draußen sein; (*stars, moon*) am Himmel stehen (*geh*), da sein; (*flowers*) blühen

d (= *in existence*) **the worst newspaper/best car ~** die schlechteste Zeitung, die/das beste Auto, das es zur Zeit gibt, die schlechteste Zeitung/ das beste Auto überhaupt; **to be ~** (= *be published*) herausgekommen sein; **when will it be ~?** wann kommt es heraus?; **there's a warrant ~ for him** *or* **for his arrest** es besteht Haftbefehl gegen ihn

e (= *not in prison*) **to be ~** draußen sein; (*seen from outside also*) (he)raus sein; **to come ~** (he)rauskommen

f (= *in the open, known*) **their secret was ~** ihr Geheimnis war bekannt geworden *or* herausgekommen; **it's ~ now** jetzt ist es heraus; **the results are ~** die Ergebnisse sind (he)raus; **the truth will ~** die Wahrheit wird heraus; **~ with it!** heraus damit!, heraus mit der Sprache!

g (= *to or at an end*) **before the day/month is/ was ~** vor Ende des Tages/Monats, noch am selben Tag/im selben Monat

h (*light, fire*) aus

i (= *not in fashion*) aus der Mode, passé, out (*inf*)

j (*Sport, ball*) aus; (*player*) aus(geschlagen), out (*inf*)

k (= *out of the question, not permissible*) ausgeschlossen, nicht drin (*inf*)

l (= *worn out*) **the jacket is ~ at the elbows** die Jacke ist an den Ellbogen durch

m (*indicating error*) **he was ~ in his calculations, his calculations were ~** er lag mit seinen Berechnungen daneben (*inf*) *or* falsch, er hatte sich in seinen Berechnungen geirrt; **not far ~!** beinah(e) (richtig)!; **you're not far ~** Sie haben es fast (getroffen); **you're far** *or* **way ~** weit gefehlt! (*geh*), da hast du dich völlig vertan (*inf*); **you're a little bit ~ there** das stimmt nicht ganz; **we were £5/20% ~** wir hatten uns um £ 5/20% verrechnet *or* vertan (*inf*); **that's £5/20% ~** das stimmt um £ 5/20% nicht; **the post isn't quite vertical yet, it's still a bit ~** der Pfahl ist noch nicht ganz senkrecht, er ist noch etwas schief; **my clock is 20 minutes ~** meine Uhr geht 20 Minuten falsch *or* verkehrt

n (*indicating loudness, clearness*) **speak ~ (loud)** sprechen Sie laut/lauter; **they shouted ~ (loud)**

sie riefen laut (und vernehmlich)

o (*indicating purpose*) **to be ~ for sth** auf etw (*acc*) aus sein; **to be ~ for a good time** sich amüsieren wollen; **she was ~ to pass the exam** sie war (fest) entschlossen, die Prüfung zu bestehen; **he's ~ for all he can get** er will haben, was er nur bekommen kann; **he's ~ to get her** er ist hinter ihr her; **he's just ~ to make money** er ist nur auf Geld aus, ihm geht es nur um Geld; **he was always ~ to make money** er wollte immer das große Geld machen; **she's ~ to find a husband** sie ist auf der Suche nach einem Mann

p (= *unconscious*) **to be ~** bewusstlos *or* weg (*inf*) sein; (= *drunk*) weg *or* hinüber sein (*inf*); (= *asleep*) weg (*inf*) *or* eingeschlafen sein; **she went straight ~** sie war sofort weg (*inf*)

q (*dirt, stain etc*) (he)raus

r ~ and away weitaus, mit Abstand

N a → in

b (*esp US inf: = way out*) Hintertür(chen *nt*) *f*

PREP aus (+*dat*); **to go ~ the door/window** zur Tür/zum Fenster hinausgehen; **from ~ the wood** (*poet*) aus dem Walde heraus → *also* **out of**

VT homosexual outen

out- PREF *with vbs* **to ~dance** *etc* **sb** jdn im Tanzen *etc* übertreffen, besser als jd tanzen *etc*

outact [aʊtˈækt] VT an die Wand spielen

out-and-out [ˈaʊtənˈaʊt] ADJ *liar, lie* ausgemacht; *fool* vollkommen, ausgemacht; *racist, fascist* eingefleischt; *winner, success* überragend; *defeat* völlig, total; **he is an ~ revolutionary/ conservative** er ist ein Revolutionär durch und durch/ein Erzkonservativer; **it's an ~ disgrace** das ist eine bodenlose Schande

outargue [aʊtˈɑːɡjuː] VT in der Diskussion überlegen sein (+*dat*), argumentativ überlegen sein (+*dat*) (*geh*)

outback [ˈaʊtbæk] (*in Australia*) **N the ~** das Hinterland **ATTR an ~ farm** eine Farm im Hinterland

out: outbalance [aʊtəˈbæləns] VT überwiegen, übertreffen; **outbid** *pret, ptp* **outbid** VT überbieten; **outboard** ADJ Außenbord-; **~ motor** Außenbordmotor *m* **N** Außenborder *m* (*inf*); **outbound** ADJ *ship* auslaufend, ausfahrend; *flight/journey* Hinflug *m*/-reise *f*; **outbox** VT *sb* besser boxen als; **for once he was completely ~ed** er ließ ihn seine Technik völlig im Stich; **he was ~ed by the younger man** der jüngere Boxer war ihm (technisch) überlegen

outbreak [ˈaʊtbreɪk] N (*of war, hostility, disease*) Ausbruch *m*; **a recent ~ of fire caused ...** ein Brand verursachte kürzlich ...; **if there should be an ~ of fire** wenn ein Brand *or* Feuer ausbricht; **at the ~ of war** bei Kriegsausbruch

outbuilding [ˈaʊtbɪldɪŋ] N Nebengebäude *nt*

outburst [ˈaʊtbɜːst] N (*of joy, anger*) Ausbruch *m*; **~ of temper** *or* **anger** Wutanfall *m*; **~ of feeling** Gefühlsausbruch *m*; **and to what do we owe that little ~?** und warum dieser kleine Gefühlsausbruch, wenn ich mal fragen darf?

outcast [ˈaʊtkɑːst] **N** Ausgestoßene(r) *mf*; **social ~** Außenseiter(in) *m(f)* der Gesellschaft; **he was treated as an ~** er wurde zum Außenseiter gestempelt; **one of the party's ~s** einer, den die Partei verstoßen hat **ADJ** ausgestoßen, verstoßen

outclass [aʊtˈklɑːs] VT voraus *or* überlegen sein (+*dat*), in den Schatten stellen

outcome [ˈaʊtkʌm] N Ergebnis *nt*, Resultat *nt*; **what was the ~ of your meeting?** was ist bei eurem Treffen herausgekommen?; **what was the ~?** was ist dabei herausgekommen?; **I don't know whether there'll be any immediate ~** ich weiß nicht, ob es unmittelbar zu einem Ergebnis führen wird

outcrop [ˈaʊtkrɒp] N **a** (*Geol*) **an ~ (of rock)** eine Felsnase **b** (*fig: of riots etc*) (plötzlicher) Ausbruch

outcry [ˈaʊtkraɪ] N Aufschrei *m* der Empörung (*against* über +*acc*); (= *public protest*) Protestwel-

le *f* (*against* gegen); **to cause an ~ against sb/ sth** zu lautstarkem Protest gegen jdn/etw führen; **to raise an ~ against sb/sth** gegen jdn/etw lautstarken Protest erheben; **there was a general ~ about the increase in taxes** eine Welle des Protests erhob sich wegen der Steuererhöhung

out: outdated ADJ *idea, theory* überholt; *technology, equipment, method, word, style, custom* veraltet; *image, concept, practice* überkommen; **outdid** *pret of* **outdo; outdistance** VT hinter sich (*dat*) lassen, abhängen (*inf*); **Y was ~d by X** Y fiel hinter X (*dat*) zurück, Y wurde von X abgehängt (*inf*)

outdo [aʊtˈduː] *pret* **outdid** [aʊtˈdɪd] *ptp* **outdone** [aʊtˈdʌn] VT übertreffen, überragen, überbieten (*sb in sth* jdn an etw *dat*); **he can ~ him in every sport** er ist ihm in jeder Sportart überlegen; **but Jimmy was not to be ~ne** aber Jimmy wollte da nicht zurückstehen

outdoor [ˈaʊtdɔː] ADJ *activities, recreation, work, use, tennis court* im Freien; **~ sports** im Freien ausgeübte Sportarten *pl*; **~ café** Café *nt* im Freien; (*in street*) Straßencafé *nt*; **~ clothes** Kleidung *f* für draußen; **~ shoes** Straßenschuhe *pl*; **~ market** Markt *m* im Freien; (*in street*) Straßenmarkt *m*; **~ games** Freiluftspiele *pl*, Spiele *pl* für draußen *or* im Freien; **~ living** Leben *nt* in freier Natur; **the ~ life** das Leben im Freien; **to lead an ~ life** viel im Freien sein; **~ swimming pool** Freibad *nt*

outdoors [ˈaʊtˈdɔːz] ADV *live, play, sleep* draußen, im Freien; **to go ~** nach draußen gehen, rausgehen (*inf*); **go ~ and play** geh draußen spielen **N the great ~** (*hum*) die freie Natur

outdoor: outdoor shot N (*Film*) Außenaufnahme *f*; **outdoor type** N sportlicher Typ

outer [ˈaʊtə] ADJ *attr* äußere(r, s); **~ harbour** Außen- *or* Vorhafen *m*; **~ office** (= *reception area*) Vorzimmer *nt*; **~ man** (= *appearance*) äußere Erscheinung, Äußere(s) *nt*; **the ~ world** die Außenwelt; **the ~ reaches of the solar system** die Weiten *pl* des Sonnensystems

outer: outer door N Außentür *f*; **outer garments** PL Oberbekleidung *f*, Überkleidung *f*; **Outer Hebrides** PL Äußere Hebriden *pl*; **Outer London** N die Peripherie Londons; **Outer Mongolia** N die Äußere Mongolei

outermost [ˈaʊtəməʊst] ADJ äußerste(r, s)

outer space N der Weltraum

out: outfall N (*of drain, sewer*) Ausfluss *m* **ATTR** Ausfluss-, Abfluss-; **~ pipe** Ausfluss- *or* Abflussrohr *nt*; **outfield** N (*Sport*) (= *place*) Außenfeld *nt*; (= *people*) Außenfeldspieler *pl*; **outfielder** N (*Baseball, Cricket*) Außenfeldspieler(in) *m(f)*; **outfight** *pret, ptp* **outfought** VT besser kämpfen als; (= *defeat*) bezwingen

outfit [ˈaʊtfɪt] N **a** (= *clothes*) Kleidung *f*, Kleider *pl*; (*Fashion*) Ensemble *nt*; (= *fancy dress*) Kostüm *nt*; (= *uniform*) Uniform *f*; (*of scout*) Kluft *f*; **is that a new ~ you're wearing?** hast du dich neu eingekleidet?; **she has so many ~s** sie hat so viel anzuziehen; **her ~s include ...** ihre Garderobe reicht von ... **b** (= *equipment*) Ausrüstung *f* **c** (*inf, = organization*) Laden *m* (*inf*), Verein *m* (*inf*); (*Mil*) Einheit *f*, Truppe *f*

outfitter [ˈaʊtfɪtə] N (*of ships*) Ausrüster *m*; **gentlemen's ~'s** Herrenausstatter *m*; **sports ~'s** Sport(artikel)geschäft *nt*

out: outflank VT **a** (*Mil*) *enemy* umfassen, von der Flanke/den Flanken angreifen; **~ing movement** Umfassungsangriff *m or* -bewegung *f* **b** (*fig: = outwit*) überlisten; **outflow** N (*of gutter*) Ausfluss *m*, Abfluss *m*; (*of water etc*) (= *act*) Abfließen *nt*, Ausfluss *m*; (= *amount*) Ausflussmenge *f*; (*of lava*) Ausfließen *nt*; (= *amount*) Ausfluss *m*, Auswurf *m*; (*of gas*) Ausströmen *nt*; (= *amount*) Ausströmungsmenge *f*; (*of money*) Abfließen *nt*; (= *amount*) Abfluss *m*; (*of refugees*) Strom *m*; **outfly** *pret* **outflew**, *ptp* **outflown** VT (fliegerisch) überlegen sein (*sb/sth* jdm/etw); **outfought** *pret, ptp of* **outfight; outfox** VT überlisten, austricksen (*inf*); **outgeneral** VT taktisch überlegen sein (+*dat*); **outgo** N (*US*) Ausgabe(n) *f(pl)*

outgoing [ˌaʊtˈɡəʊɪŋ] **ADJ** **a** *tenant* ausziehend; *office holder* scheidend; *train, boat* hinausfahrend; *flight* hinausgehend; (*Telec*) *cable* wegführend, hinausführend; *call* abgehend; ~ **tide** ablaufendes Wasser, Ebbe *f*; **the ~ flight for New York** der Flug nach New York **b** *personality* aus sich herausgehend, kontaktfreudig **PL** ~**s** Ausgaben *pl*

outgrow [ˌaʊtˈɡrəʊ] *pret* **outgrew** [ˌaʊtˈɡruː] *ptp* **outgrown** [ˌaʊtˈɡrəʊn] **VT** **a** *clothes* herauswachsen aus; **they outgrew their apartment** die Wohnung ist zu klein für sie geworden **b** *habit* entwachsen (+*dat*), hinauswachsen über (+*acc*); *interest* sich hinausentwickeln über (+*acc*); **he has ~n such childish pastimes** über solche Kindereien ist er hinaus **c** (= *grow taller than*) (*tree*) hinauswachsen über (+*acc*); (*person*) über den Kopf wachsen (+*dat*)

outgrowth [ˈaʊtɡrəʊθ] **N** (= *offshoot*) Auswuchs *m*; (*fig*) Folge *f*

out: out-Herod **VT** **to ~ Herod** dem Teufel Konkurrenz machen; **outhouse** **N** Seitengebäude *nt*

outing [ˈaʊtɪŋ] **N** **a** Ausflug *m*; **school/firm's ~** Schul-/Betriebsausflug *m*; **to go on an ~** einen Ausflug machen **b** (*of homosexual*) Outing *nt*, Outen *nt*

outlandish [aʊtˈlændɪʃ] **ADJ** absonderlich, sonderbar; *behaviour also* befremdend, befremdlich; *prose, style, description etc* eigenwillig; *name, clothes, appearance, colour combination etc* ausgefallen; *prices* haarsträubend; *theory* obskur

outlandishly [aʊtˈlændɪʃlɪ] **ADV** sonderbar, absonderlich; *decorated, portrayed* eigenwillig; *expensive* haarsträubend

outlandishness [aʊtˈlændɪʃnɪs] **N** Absonderlichkeit *f*, Sonderbarkeit *f*; (*of prose, style, description*) Eigenwilligkeit *f*; (*of name, colours, clothes, appearance etc*) Ausgefallenheit *f*; (*of theory*) Obskurität *f*

outlast [aʊtˈlɑːst] **VT** (*person*) (= *live longer*) überleben; (= *endure longer*) länger aus- or durchhalten als; (*thing*) länger halten als; (*idea etc*) überdauern, sich länger halten als

outlaw [ˈaʊtlɔː] **N** Geächtete(r) *mf*; (*in Western etc*) Bandit *m*; **to declare sb an ~** jdn ächten **VT** ächten; *newspaper, action etc* für ungesetzlich erklären, verbieten

outlawry [ˈaʊtlɔːrɪ] **N** Ächtung *f*; (= *defiance*) Gesetzlosigkeit *f*

outlay [ˈaʊtleɪ] **N** (Kosten)aufwand *m*; (*recurring, continuous*) Kosten *pl*; **the initial ~** die anfänglichen Aufwendungen; **capital ~** Kapitalaufwand *m*; **to recoup one's ~** seine Auslagen wieder hereinholen or -bekommen; (*business*) die Unkosten hereinwirtschaften

outlet [ˈaʊtlet] **N** **a** (*for water etc*) Abfluss *m*, Auslass *m*; (*for steam etc*) Abzug *m*; (*of river*) Ausfluss *m* **b** (*Comm*) Absatzmöglichkeit *f* or -markt *m*; (= *merchant*) Abnehmer(in) *m(f)*; (= *shop*) Verkaufsstelle *f* **c** (*fig*) (*for talents etc*) Betätigungsmöglichkeit *f*; (*for emotion*) Ventil *nt* **ATTR** (*Tech*) Ausfluss-, Abfluss-; ~ **pipe** Ausfluss- or Abflussrohr *nt*; ~ **valve** Auslassventil *nt*

outline [ˈaʊtlaɪn] **N** **a** (*of objects*) Umriss *m*; (= *line itself*) Umrisslinie *f*; (= *silhouette*) Silhouette *f*; (*of face*) Züge *pl*; **he drew the ~ of a head** er zeichnete einen Kopf im Umriss **b** (*fig*: = *summary*) Grundriss *m*, Abriss *m*; **in (broad) ~** in großen or groben Zügen; **just give (me) the broad ~s** umreißen or skizzieren Sie es (mir) grob; ~**s of botany** Abriss *m* or Grundriss *m* or Grundzüge *pl* der Botanik **c** (*Shorthand*) Kürzel *nt*, Sigel *nt*, Sigle *nt* **ATTR** ~ **drawing** Umrisszeichnung *f* **VT** **a** (= *draw outer edge of*) umreißen, den Umriss or die Silhouette zeichnen (+*gen*); **the mountain was ~d against the sky** die Umrisse des Berges zeichneten sich gegen den Himmel ab; **she stood there ~d against the sunset** ihre Silhouette zeichnete sich gegen die untergehende Sonne ab **b** (= *give summary of*) umreißen, skizzieren

outlive [aʊtˈlɪv] **VT** **a** (= *live longer than*) *person* überleben; *century* überdauern; **to have ~d one's day** nicht mehr der/die sein, der/die man einmal war; **to have ~d one's/its usefulness** ausgedient haben **b** (= *come safely through*) *storm etc* überstehen; (*method, system*) sich überlebt haben **b** (= *come safely through*) *storm etc* überstehen; *disgrace etc* sich reinigen (können) von (*geh*), frei werden von

outlook [ˈaʊtlʊk] **N** **a** (= *view*) (Aus)blick *m*, Aussicht *f* (*over* über +*acc*, *on to* auf +*acc*) **b** (= *prospects*) (Zukunfts)aussichten *pl*; (*Met*) Aussichten *pl*; **what's the ~ for the mining industry?** wie sind die (Zukunfts)aussichten im Bergbau? **c** (= *mental attitude*) Einstellung *f*; **his ~ (up)on life** seine Lebensauffassung, seine Einstellung zum Leben; **what's his ~ on the matter?** wie steht er zu der Sache?; **his broad ~** sein weiter Horizont; **narrow ~** beschränkter Horizont, (geistige) Beschränktheit; **if you adopt such a narrow ~** wenn Sie die Dinge so eng sehen

out: outlying **ADJ** (= *distant*) entlegen, abgelegen; (= *outside the town boundary*) umliegend; ~ **district** (*of town*) Außenbezirk *m*; ~ **suburbs** Außenbezirke *pl*, äußere Vororte *pl*; **outmanoeuvre**, (*US*) **outmaneuver** **VT** (*fig*) ausmanövrieren; (*in rivalry*) ausstechen; **outmatch** **VT** übertreffen, überlegen sein (+*dat*); **Y was ~ed by X** Y konnte gegen X nichts ausrichten; **outmoded** **ADJ** unzeitgemäß, altmodisch; *design etc also* antiquiert; *technology etc also* überholt, veraltet; **outmost** **ADJ** äußerste(r, s); *regions etc also* entlegenste(r, s) **N** **at the ~** äußerstenfalls, im äußersten Falle

outnumber [aʊtˈnʌmbəʳ] **VT** in der Mehrzahl sein gegenüber; (*in fight etc also*) zahlenmäßig überlegen sein (+*dat*); **we were ~ed (by them)** wir waren (ihnen gegenüber) in der Minderzahl or Minderheit, wir waren (ihnen) zahlenmäßig unterlegen; **we were ~ed five to one** sie waren fünfmal so viele wie wir, wir waren (ihnen) zahlenmäßig fünffach unterlegen

out of **PREP** **a** (= *outside, away from*) (*position*) nicht in (+*dat*), außerhalb (+*gen*); (*motion*) aus (+*dat*); (*fig*) außer (+*dat*); **I'll be ~ town all week** ich werde die ganze Woche (über) nicht in der Stadt sein; **to go/be ~ the country** außer Landes gehen/sein; **he was ~ the room at the time** er war zu dem Zeitpunkt nicht im Zimmer; **he walked ~ the room** er ging aus dem Zimmer (hinaus); **he went ~ the door** er ging zur Tür hinaus; **as soon as he was ~ the door** sobald er draußen war or zur Tür hinaus war; **to look ~ the window** aus dem Fenster sehen, zum Fenster hinaussehen; **I saw him ~ the window** ich sah ihn durchs Fenster; **to keep ~ the sun** nicht in die Sonne gehen; **~ danger/sight** außer Gefahr/Sicht; **get ~ my sight!** geh mir aus den Augen!; **he's ~ the tournament** er ist aus dem Turnier ausgeschieden; **he feels ~ it** (*inf*) er kommt sich (*dat*) ausgeschlossen vor, er fühlt sich ausgeschlossen; **they were 150 miles ~ Hamburg** (*Naut*) sie waren 150 Meilen von Hamburg weg or vor Hamburg; **three days ~ port** drei Tage nach dem Auslaufen aus dem Hafen/vor dem Einlaufen in den Hafen; **he lives 10 miles ~ London** er wohnt 10 Meilen außerhalb Londons; **you're well ~ it** (*inf*) so ist es besser für dich **b** (*cause, motive*) aus (+*dat*); ~ **curiosity** aus Neugier **c** (*indicating origins or source*) aus (+*dat*); **to drink ~ a glass** aus einem Glas trinken; **made ~ silver** aus Silber (gemacht); **a filly ~ the same mare** ein Fohlen *nt* von derselben Stute **d** (= *from among*) von (+*dat*); **in seven cases ~ ten** in sieben von zehn Fällen; **one ~ every four smokers** einer von vier Rauchern; **he picked one ~ the pile** er nahm einen aus dem Stapel (heraus) **e** (= *without*) ~ **breath** außer Atem; **we are ~ money/bread** wir haben kein Geld/Brot mehr, das Geld/Brot ist alle (*inf*)

out: out-of-bounds **ADJ** ~ **park** Park, dessen Betreten verboten ist (*to* für); ~ **area** Sperrgebiet *nt*; **out-of-court** **ADJ** *settlement* außerge-

richtlich; **out-of-date** **ADJ** *attr*, **out of date** **ADJ** *pred* **a** *methods, technology, ideas* überholt, veraltet; *clothes, records* altmodisch, veraltet; *customs* veraltet; **you're out of date** Sie sind nicht auf dem Laufenden **b** (= *expired*) *ticket* abgelaufen; *food, medicine* mit abgelaufenem Verfallsdatum; **out-of-doors** **ADV** = **outdoors** **ADV**; **out of office reply** **N** (*Comput*) Abwesenheitsnotiz *f*; **out of place** **ADJ** *pred*, **out-of-place** **ADJ** *attr* *remark etc* unangebracht, deplatziert; **out-of-pocket** **ADJ** *attr*, **out of pocket** **ADJ** *pred* (*Brit*) ~ **expenses** Barauslagen *pl*; **to be out of pocket** drauflegen, draufzahlen; **I was £5 out of pocket** ich habe £ 5 aus eigener Tasche bezahlt; **I'm still £2 out of pocket** ich habe immer noch £ 2 zu wenig; **out-of-the-way** **ADJ** *attr*, **out of the way** **ADJ** *pred* (= *remote*) *spot* abgelegen, aus der Welt; (= *unusual*) *theory* ungewöhnlich; (= *not commonly known*) *facts* wenig bekannt; **out-of--towner** **N** (*esp US*) Auswärtige(r) *mf*; **outpace** **VT** schneller sein als; **outpatient** **N** ambulanter Patient, ambulante Patientin; ~**s' (department)** Ambulanz *f*; ~**s' clinic** Poliklinik *f*; **outperform** **VT** ausstechen (*inf*); **outplacement** [ˈaʊtpleɪsmənt] **N** (*Econ*) Outplacement *nt*; **outplay** **VT** (*Sport*) besser spielen als, überlegen sein (+*dat*); **we were completely ~ed (by them)** wir konnten (gegen sie) absolut nichts ausrichten, sie waren uns haushoch überlegen; **outpoint** **VT** auspunkten; **outpost** **N** (*Mil, fig*) Vorposten *m*; **outpouring** **N** *often pl* Erguss *m* (*fig*)

output [ˈaʊtpʊt] **N** (*of machine, factory, person*) (= *act*) Produktion *f*; (= *quantity also*) Ausstoß *m*, Output *m* or *nt*; (= *rate of output also*) (Produktions)leistung *f*, Output *m* or *nt*; (= *quantity in agriculture also*) Ertrag *m*; (*Elec*) Leistung *f*; (= *output terminal*) Ausgang *m*; (= *capacity of amplifier*) (Ausgangs)leistung *f*; (*of mine*) Förderung *f*; (= *quantity*) Fördermenge *f*, Förderung *f*; (= *rate of output*) Förderleistung *f*, Förderung *f*; (= *of computer*) Ausgabe *f*, Output *m* or *nt*; **effective ~ of a machine** Nutzleistung *f* einer Maschine; **this factory has an ~ of 600 radios a day** diese Fabrik produziert täglich 600 Radios

output device **N** (*Comput*) Ausgabegerät *nt*

outrage [ˈaʊtreɪdʒ] **N** **a** (= *wicked, violent deed*) Untat *f*; (*cruel*) Gräueltat *f*; (*by police, demonstrators etc*) Ausschreitung *f*; **bomb ~** verbrecherischer Bombenanschlag; **an ~ against the State** ein schändliches or ruchloses (*liter*) Verbrechen gegen den Staat **b** (= *indecency, injustice*) Skandal *m*; **it's an ~ to waste food** es ist ein Skandal or Frevel, Essen verkommen zu lassen; **an ~ against humanity** ein Verbrechen *nt* gegen die Menschlichkeit; **an ~ to common decency** eine empörende Verletzung des allgemeinen Anstandsgefühls; **an ~ against public morality** ein empörender Verstoß gegen die guten Sitten or die öffentliche Moral **c** (= *sense of outrage*) Empörung *f* (*at* über +*acc*), Entrüstung *f* (*at* über +*acc*); **he reacted with (a sense of) ~** er war empört or entrüstet **VT** [ˈaʊtreɪdʒ] *morals, conventions* ins Gesicht schlagen (+*dat*), Hohn sprechen (+*dat*), hohnsprechen (+*dat*) (*geh*); *sense of decency* beleidigen; *ideals* mit Füßen treten; *person* empören, entrüsten; **public opinion was ~d by this cruelty/injustice** die öffentliche Meinung war über diese Grausamkeit/Ungerechtigkeit empört; **he deliberately set out to ~ his critics** er hatte es darauf angelegt, seine Kritiker zu schockieren

outraged [ˈaʊtreɪdʒd] **ADJ** empört (*at, about* über +*acc*)

outrageous [aʊtˈreɪdʒəs] **ADJ** **a** (= *cruel, violent*) gräulich, verabscheuenswürdig; **murder, rape, and other ~ deeds** Mord, Vergewaltigung und andere Untaten **b** *remark, story, price, claim, behaviour* unerhört; *demand, insolence, lie, arrogance etc* unerhört, unverschämt; *nonsense* haarsträubend; *language* entsetzlich, unflätig; *charge, defamation etc* ungeheuerlich; *clothes, make-up etc* ausgefallen, unmöglich (*inf*); (= *indecent*) geschmacklos; *complexity, selfishness* unglaublich, unerhört; **~ colour** Schockfarbe *f*; **he's ~!** er ist unmöglich!; **it's absolutely ~ that ...** es ist einfach unerhört, dass ...

outrageously [aʊtˈreɪdʒəslɪ] ADV *expensive* unerhört; *flirt* unverschämt; *behave* unerhört, unmöglich; *lie* schamlos; *exaggerate also* masslos; *made-up also, dressed* unmöglich (*inf*); **he suggested/demanded quite ~ that ...** er machte den unerhörten Vorschlag/er stellte die unerhörte Forderung, dass ...; **an ~ low neckline** ein schamlos tiefer Ausschnitt; **he's ~ over the top** er ist total ausgefallen; **~ funny** zum Schreien komisch

out: outran *pret of* **outrun**; **outrange** VT eine größere Reichweite haben als; **we were ~d** die anderen hatten/der Feind *etc* hatte eine größere Reichweite; **outrank** VT (*Mil*) rangmäßig stehen über (+*dat*); **he was ~ed** er war rangniedriger

outré [ˈuːtreɪ] ADJ überspannt, extravagant

out: outride *pret* **outrode** **outridden** VT besser reiten als; (*on bike*) besser fahren als; (= *outdistance*) davonreiten/-fahren (+*dat*); **he was completely outridden** er konnte absolut nicht mithalten; **he can't be outridden** mit ihm kann keiner mithalten; **outrider** N (*on motorcycle*) Kradbegleiter(in) *m(f)*; **outrigger** N (*Naut*) Ausleger *m*; (= *boat*) Auslegerboot *nt*

outright [aʊtˈraɪt] **ADV** **a** (= *entirely*) *reject* rundweg; *own* vollständig; **to buy sth ~** etw komplett kaufen; (= *not on HP*) den ganzen Preis für etw sofort bezahlen; **to win ~** einen klaren Sieg davontragen
   b (= *at once*) *kill* sofort, auf der Stelle, gleich; **he was killed ~** er war sofort tot; **he felled him ~** er streckte ihn mit einem einzigen Schlag zu Boden
   c (= *openly*) geradeheraus, unumwunden, ohne Umschweife
   ADJ [ˈaʊtraɪt] **a** (= *complete*) *deception, lie* rein, glatt (*inf*); *nonsense, ban, victory* total, absolut; *disaster, loss* völlig, vollkommen, total; *refusal, denial* total, absolut, glatt (*inf*); *majority* absolut; *hostility, condemnation* offen, unverhohlen; *support* uneingeschränkt; *opponent* eingefleischt; *winner* klar; *defeat, error* gründlich, ausgesprochen, absolut; *independence* vollkommen; **that's ~ arrogance/impertinence** das ist die reine Arroganz/Unverschämtheit; **that's ~ deception/selfishness** das ist reiner *or* glatter (*inf*) Betrug/reiner Egoismus
   b (*Comm*: = *full*) **~ sale/purchase** Verkauf *m*/Kauf *m* gegen sofortige Zahlung der Gesamtsumme; **~ owner** Volleigentümer(in) *m(f)*; **~ ownership** Volleigentum *nt*
   c (= *open*) *person* offen

out: outrode *pret of* **outride**; **outrun** *pret* **outran**, *ptp* **outrun** VT schneller laufen als; (= *outdistance*) davonlaufen (+*dat*); (*fig*) übersteigen; **the white horse outran the rest of the field** der Schimmel ließ das übrige Feld hinter sich (*dat*); **outset** N Beginn *m*, Anfang *m*; **at the ~** zu *or* am Anfang; **from the ~** von Anfang an, von Anbeginn (*geh*); **let me make it quite clear at the ~ that ...** lassen Sie mich von vornherein klarstellen, dass ...; **outshine** *pret, ptp* **outshone** VT überstrahlen (*geh*), heller sein als; (*fig*) in den Schatten stellen

outside [ˈaʊtsaɪd] **N** **a** (*of house, car, object*) Außenseite *f*; **the ~ of the car is green** das Auto ist (von) außen grün; **to open the door from the ~** die Tür von außen öffnen; **they were smuggled in from the ~** sie wurden von draußen eingeschmuggelt; **to stay on the ~ of a group** sich in einer Gruppe im Hintergrund halten; **people on the ~ (of society)** Menschen außerhalb der Gesellschaft; **to overtake on the ~** (*Brit*) außen überholen; **judging from the ~** (*fig*) wenn man es als Außenstehender beurteilt
   b (= *extreme limit*) **at the (very) ~** im äußersten Falle, äußerstenfalls
   ADJ **a** (= *external*) Außen-, äußere(r, s); *consultant, investor, examiner, opinion* extern; **an ~ broadcast** eine nicht im Studio produzierte

Sendung; **an ~ broadcast from Wimbledon** eine Sendung aus Wimbledon; **~ call** (*Telec*) externer Anruf; **to get some ~ help** Hilfe von außen holen; **~ influences** äußere Einflüsse, Einflüsse von außen; **~ seat** (*in a row*) Außensitz *m*, Platz *m* am Gang; **~ work** freie Mitarbeit; **I'm doing ~ work on the dictionary** ich arbeite freiberuflich am Wörterbuch mit
   b *price* äußerste(r, s); **at an ~ estimate** maximal
   c (= *very unlikely*) **an ~ chance** eine kleine Chance
   ADV (= *on the outer side*) außen; (*of house, room, vehicle*) draußen; **to be ~** draußen sein; **to go ~** nach draußen gehen; **seen from ~** von außen gesehen; **put the cat ~** bring die Katze raus (*inf*) or nach draußen; **I feel ~ it all** ich komme mir so ausgeschlossen vor
   PREP (*also* **outside of**) **a** (= *on the outer side of*) außerhalb (+*gen*); **~ California** außerhalb Kaliforniens; **~ London** außerhalb von London; **visitors from ~ the area** Besucher *pl* von außerhalb; **to be ~ sth** außerhalb einer Sache sein; **to go ~ sth** aus etw gehen; **he went ~ the house** er ging aus dem/vors/hinters Haus, er ging nach draußen; **the noise was coming from ~ the house** der Lärm kam von draußen; **he is waiting ~ the door** er wartet vor der Tür; **the car ~ the house** das Auto vorm Haus
   b (= *beyond limits of*) außerhalb (+*gen*); **it is ~ our agreement** es geht über unsere Vereinbarung hinaus; **~ the Festival** außerhalb des Festspiele; **this falls ~ the scope of ...** das geht über den Rahmen (+*gen*) ... hinaus; **to marry ~ one's religion** eine konfessionsverschiedene Ehe eingehen; **babies born ~ marriage** außerehelich geborene Kinder *pl*; **sex ~ marriage** Sex *m* außerhalb der Ehe; **you'll have to do it ~ office hours** Sie müssen das nach Büroschluss erledigen
   c (= *apart from*) außer (+*dat*), abgesehen von (+*dat*)

outside: outside aerial N (*Brit*) Außenantenne *f*; **outside half** N (*Rugby*) äußerer Halb (-spieler); **outside lane** N Überholspur *f*; **outside left** N (*Ftbl, Hockey*) Linksaußenspieler(in) *m(f)*; **outside line** N (*Tel*) Amtsanschluss *m*

outsider [aʊtˈsaɪdəʳ] N Außenseiter(in) *m(f)*, Outsider *m*

outside: outside right N (*Ftbl, Hockey*) Rechtsaußenspieler(in) *m(f)*; **outside temperature** N Außentemperatur *f*; **outside toilet** N Außentoilette *f*; **outside wall** N Außenwand *f*; **outside world** N Außenwelt *f*

out: outsize ADJ **a** übergroß; **~ clothes** Kleidung *f* in Übergröße, Übergrößen *pl*; **the ~ department** die Abteilung für Übergrößen **b** (*inf*: = *enormous*) riesig; **outskirts** PL (*of town*) Außen- or Randgebiete *pl*, Stadtrand *m*; (*of wood*) Rand *m*; **outslept** *pret, ptp* **outslept** VT verschlafen; **outsmart** VT (*inf*) überlisten, austricksen (*inf*)

outsource [ˈaʊtsɔːs] VT (*Econ*) *work* outsourcen, außer Haus geben, auslagern

outsourcing [ˈaʊtsɔːsɪŋ] N (*Econ*) Auslagerung *f*, Outsourcing *nt*

outspoken [ˌaʊtˈspəʊkən] ADJ *person, criticism, speech, book* freimütig; *attack, remark* direkt; *answer* freimütig, unverblümt; **he is ~** er nimmt kein Blatt vor den Mund; **there was no need for you to be so ~** so deutlich hättest du nicht zu sein brauchen

outspokenly [ˌaʊtˈspəʊkənlɪ] ADV geradeheraus, unverblümt; *answer, write also* freimütig; *remark also* direkt

outspokenness [ˌaʊtˈspəʊkənnɪs] N (*of person, criticism, speech, book*) Freimütigkeit *f*; (*of attack, remark*) Direktheit *f*; (*of answer*) Unverblümtheit *f*

outspread [ˈaʊtspred] *vb: pret, ptp* **outspread** **ADJ** ausgebreitet **VT** ausbreiten

outstanding [ˌaʊtˈstændɪŋ] ADJ **a** (= *exceptional*) hervorragend; *talent, beauty, brilliance* außerordentlich, überragend; **of ~ ability** hervorra-

gend or außerordentlich begabt; **work of ~ excellence** ganz ausgezeichnete Arbeit; **of ~ importance** von höchster Bedeutung; **area of ~ natural beauty** (*Brit*) Naturschutzgebiet *nt* (von besonderer Schönheit)
   b (= *prominent, conspicuous*) *event* bemerkenswert; *detail* auffallend; *feature* hervorstechend, auffallend
   c (*Comm, Fin*) *business* unerledigt; *amount, account, bill, interest* ausstehend; **a lot of work is still ~** viel Arbeit ist noch unerledigt; **are there any problems still ~?** gibt es noch irgendwelche ungeklärten Probleme?; **~ debts** Außenstände *pl*

outstandingly [ˌaʊtˈstændɪŋlɪ] ADV hervorragend; *good, beautiful, successful* außergewöhnlich; **the party did ~ well in the elections** die Partei hat in den Wahlen außergewöhnlich gut abgeschnitten

out: outstation N Vorposten *m*; **outstay** VT länger bleiben als; **I don't want to ~ my welcome** ich will eure Gastfreundschaft nicht überbeanspruchen *or* nicht zu lange in Anspruch nehmen; **outstretched** ADJ *body* ausgestreckt; *arms also* ausgebreitet; **outstrip** VT **a** (*Sport*) überholen; (*fig*) übertreffen (in +*dat*); **outswim** *pret* **outswam**, *ptp* **outswum** VT **to ~ sb** jdm davonschwimmen; **outtake** N *für die endgültige Fassung nicht verwendete, herausgeschnittene Filmsequenz*, Outtake *m* (*spec*); **out tray** N Ablage *f* für Ausgänge; **outvote** VT überstimmen

outward [ˈaʊtwəd] **ADJ** **a** (= *of or on the outside*) *appearance, form* äußere(r, s); *beauty* äußerlich; **he put on an ~ show of confidence** er gab sich den Anstrich von Selbstsicherheit **b** (= *going out*) *movement* nach außen führend *or* gehend; *freight* ausgehend; **~ flow of traffic** der Verkehr(sstrom) aus der Stadt heraus; **~ journey/voyage** Hinreise *f*; **~ flight** Hinflug *m*; **~ investment** Auslandsinvestitionen *pl* **ADV** nach außen; **the door opens ~** die Tür geht nach außen auf; **~ bound** (*ship*) auslaufend (*from* von, *for* mit Bestimmung, mit Kurs auf +*acc*); **Outward Bound course** Abenteuerkurs *m*

outward-looking [ˈaʊtwədˌlʊkɪŋ] ADJ *person, organization, country* aufgeschlossen; *attitude, approach* nach vorne gerichtet, aufgeschlossen; *policy* offen

outwardly [ˈaʊtwədlɪ] ADV nach außen hin

outwards [ˈaʊtwədz] ADV nach außen; **the journey ~** die Hinreise

out: outwear *pret* **outwore**, *ptp* **outworn** VT **a** (= *last longer than*) überdauern, länger halten als **b** (= *wear out*) *clothes* abtragen → *also* **outworn**; **outweigh** VT überwiegen, mehr Gewicht haben als; **outwit** VT überlisten; (*in card games etc*) austricksen (*inf*); **outwork** N (*Mil*) Außenwerk *nt*; **outworker** N **a** (*away from the office/factory*) Außenarbeiter(in) *m(f)* **b** (= *homeworker*) Heimarbeiter(in) *m(f)*; **outworn** ADJ *idea, subject, expression* abgedroschen, abgenutzt; *custom, doctrine* veraltet

ouzo [ˈuːzəʊ] N Ouzo *m*

ova [ˈəʊvə] *pl of* **ovum**

oval [ˈəʊvəl] **ADJ** oval; **~-shaped** oval **N** Oval *nt*

Oval Office N (*US*) Oval Office *nt*, Büro des US-Präsidenten

ovarian [əʊˈvɛərɪən] ADJ **a** (*Anat*) des Eierstocks/der Eierstöcke; **~ cyst** Zyste *f* im Eierstock **b** (*Bot*) des Fruchtknotens

ovary [ˈəʊvərɪ] N **a** (*Anat*) Eierstock *m* **b** (*Bot*) Fruchtknoten *m*

ovation [əʊˈveɪʃən] N Ovation *f*, stürmischer Beifall; **to give sb an ~** jdm eine Ovation darbringen, jdm stürmischen Beifall zollen; **to get an ~** stürmischen Beifall ernten → **standing**

oven [ˈʌvn] N (*Cook*) (Back)ofen *m*; (*Tech*) (for drying) (Trocken)ofen *m*; (for baking pottery etc) (Brenn)ofen *m*; **to put sth in the ~** etw in den Ofen tun *or* stecken; **put it in the ~ for two hours** backen Sie es zwei Stunden; *pottery* brennen Sie es zwei Stunden; **to cook in a hot or quick/moderate/slow ~** bei starker/mittlerer/

schwacher Hitze backen; **it's like an ~ in here** hier ist ja der reinste Backofen

oven: ovenable [ˈʌvnəbl] ADJ *dish* ofenfertig; **oven cleaner** N Ofenreiniger *m*; **oven cloth** N Topflappen *m*; **oven door** N Ofentür *f*, Ofenklappe *f*; **oven glove** N (*Brit*) Topfhandschuh *m*; **ovenproof** ADJ *dish* feuerfest, hitzebeständig; **oven-ready** ADJ bratfertig; **oven-to-table-ware** N feuerfestes Geschirr; **ovenware** N feuerfeste Formen *pl*

over [ˈəʊvəʳ] PREP **a** (*indicating motion*) über (+*acc*); **he spread the blanket ~ the bed** er breitete die Decke über das Bett; **he spilled coffee ~ it** er goss Kaffee darüber, er vergoss Kaffee darauf; **to hit sb ~ the head** jdm auf den Kopf schlagen **b** (*indicating position: = above, on top of*) über (+*dat*); **if you hang the picture ~ the desk** wenn du das Bild über dem Schreibtisch aufhängst *or* über den Schreibtisch hängst; **bent ~ one's books** über die Bücher gebeugt **c** (= *on the other side of*) über (+*dat*); (= *to the other side of*) über (+*acc*); **to look ~ the wall** über die Mauer schauen; **the noise came from ~ the wall** der Lärm kam von der anderen Seite der Mauer; **it's ~ the page** es ist auf der nächsten Seite; **I looked ~ my shoulder** ich sah mir über meine Schulter; **he looked ~ my shoulder** er sah über die Schulter; **she has to keep looking ~ her shoulder** (*fig*) sie ist verängstigt; **the house ~ the road** das Haus gegenüber; **the family from ~ the road** die Familie von gegenüber; **it's just ~ the road from us** das ist von uns (aus) nur über die Straße; **the bridge ~ the river** die Brücke über den Fluss; **we're ~ the main obstacles now** wir haben jetzt die größten Hindernisse hinter uns (*dat*); **when they were ~ the river** als sie über den Fluss hinüber waren; **they're all safely ~ the first fence** sie sind alle sicher über die erste Hürde gekommen **d** (= *in or across every part of*) in (+*dat*); **it was raining ~ London** es regnete in (ganz) London; **they came from all ~ England** sie kamen aus allen Teilen Englands *or* aus ganz England; **I'll show you ~ the house** ich zeige Ihnen das Haus; **you've got ink all ~ you/your hands** Sie/Ihre Hände sind ganz voller Tinte; **a smile spread ~ her face** ein Lächeln breitete sich auf ihrem Gesicht aus; **to be all ~ sb** (*inf*) ein Mordstheater um jdn machen (*inf*) **e** (= *superior to*) über (+*dat*); **to have authority ~ sb** Autorität über jdn haben; **he has no control ~ his urges/his staff** er hat seine Triebe/seine Angestellten nicht unter Kontrolle; **he was promoted ~ me** er wurde über mich befördert; **we were all ~ them** (*inf*) wir waren ihnen haushoch überlegen **f** (= *more than, longer than*) über (+*acc*); **~ and above that** darüber hinaus; **~ and above the expenses** über die Ausgaben hinaus; **that was well ~ a year ago** das ist gut ein Jahr her, das war vor gut einem Jahr; **she will not live ~ the winter** sie wird den Winter nicht überleben **g** (= *indicating time*) über (+*acc*); (= *during*) während (+*gen*), in (+*dat*); **can we stay ~ the weekend?** können wir übers Wochenende bleiben?; **~ Christmas** über Weihnachten; **~ the summer** den Sommer über; **~ the summer we have been trying ...** während des Sommers haben wir versucht ...; **~ the (past) years I've come to realize ...** im Laufe der (letzten) Jahre ist mir klar geworden ...; **he has mellowed ~ the years** er ist mit den Jahren milder geworden; **the visits were spread ~ several months** die Besuche verteilten sich über mehrere Monate **h** **they talked ~ a cup of coffee** sie unterhielten sich bei einer Tasse Kaffee; **the speeches were made ~ coffee** die Reden wurden beim Kaffee gehalten; **let's discuss that ~ dinner/a beer** wir besprechen das beim Essen/bei einem Bier; **they'll be a long time ~ it** sie werden dazu lange brauchen; **he nodded off ~ his work** er nickte über seiner Arbeit ein; **to get stuck ~ a difficulty** bei einer Schwierigkeit stecken bleiben

i **he told me ~ the phone** er hat es mir am Telefon gesagt; **I heard it ~ the radio** ich habe es im Radio gehört; **a voice came ~ the intercom** eine Stimme kam über die Sprechanlage **j** (= *about*) über (+*acc*); **it's not worth arguing ~** es lohnt (sich) nicht, darüber zu streiten; **that's nothing for you to get upset ~** darüber brauchst du dich nicht aufzuregen **k** **what is 7 ~ 3?** wie viel ist 7 durch 3?; **blood pressure of 150 ~ 120** Blutdruck *m* von 150 zu 120

ADV **a** (= *across*) (*away from speaker*) hinüber; (*towards speaker*) herüber; (= *on the other side*) drüben; **they swam ~ to us** sie schwammen zu uns herüber; **he took the fruit ~ to his mother** er brachte das Obst zu seiner Mutter hinüber; **when the first man is ~ the second starts to climb/swim** wenn der Erste drüben angekommen ist, klettert/schwimmt der Zweite los; **come ~ tonight** kommen Sie heute Abend vorbei; **I just thought I'd come ~** ich dachte, ich komme mal rüber (*inf*); **he is ~ here/there** er ist hier/dort drüben; **~ to you!** Sie sind daran; **and now ~ to our reporter in Belfast** und nun schalten wir zu unserem Reporter in Belfast um; **and now ~ to Paris where ...** und nun (schalten wir um) nach Paris, wo ...; **he has gone ~ to America** er ist nach Amerika gefahren; **~ in America** drüben in Amerika; **he drove us ~ to the other side of town** er fuhr uns ans andere Ende der Stadt; **he went ~ to the enemy** er lief zum Feind über **b** **famous the world ~** in der ganzen Welt berühmt; **I've been looking for it all ~** ich habe überall danach gesucht; **I am aching all ~** mir tut alles weh; **you've got dirt all ~** Sie sind voller Schmutz, Sie sind ganz schmutzig; **he was shaking all ~** er zitterte am ganzen Leib; **I'm wet all ~** ich bin völlig nass; **he was black all ~** er war von oben bis unten schwarz; **the dog licked him all ~** der Hund leckte ihn von oben bis unten ab; **that's Fred all ~** das ist typisch (für) Fred; **it happens all ~** das gibt es überall **c** (*indicating movement from one side to another, from upright position*) **to turn an object ~ (and ~)** einen Gegenstand (immer wieder) herumdrehen; **he hit her and ~ she went** er schlug sie, und sie fiel um **d** (= *ended*) *film, first act, operation, fight etc* zu Ende; *romance, summer* vorbei, zu Ende; **the rain is ~** der Regen hat aufgehört; **the pain will soon be ~** der Schmerz wird bald vorbei sein; **the danger was ~** die Gefahr war vorüber, es bestand keine Gefahr mehr; **when all this is ~** wenn das alles vorbei ist; **it's all ~ with him** es ist Schluss *or* aus mit ihm; **it's all ~ between us** es ist aus zwischen uns **e** (*indicating repetition*) **he counted them ~ again** (*Brit*) *or* **~** (*US*) er zählte sie noch einmal; **to start (all) ~ again** (*Brit*) *or* **~** (*US*) noch einmal (ganz) von vorn anfangen; **~ and ~ (again)** immer (und immer) wieder, wieder und wieder; **he did it five times ~** er hat es fünfmal wiederholt; **must I say everything twice ~!** muss ich denn immer alles zweimal sagen! **f** (= *excessively*) übermäßig, allzu; **he has not done it ~ well** er hat es nicht gerade übermäßig gut gemacht; **he is not ~ healthy** er ist nicht allzu gesund; **there's not ~ much left** es ist nicht allzu viel übrig **g** (= *remaining*) übrig; **there was no/a lot of meat (left) ~** es war kein Fleisch mehr übrig/viel Fleisch übrig; **7 into 22 goes 3 and 1 ~** 22 durch 7 ist 3, Rest 1; **6 feet and a little ~** 6 Fuß und ein bisschen **h** (= *more*) **children of 8 and ~** Kinder ab 8; **all results of 5.3 and ~** alle Ergebnisse ab 5,3 *or* von 5,3 und darüber; **if it takes three hours or ~** wenn es drei oder mehr Stunden dauert **i** (*Telec*) **come in, please,** **~** bitte kommen, over; **~ and out** Ende der Durchsage; (*Aviat*) over and out

N (*Cricket*) 6 aufeinanderfolgende Würfe

over- PREF über-, Über-; **overabundance** N Überfülle *f* (*of* von); **overabundant** ADJ überreichlich, sehr reichlich; **to have an ~ supply**

of sth überreichlich mit etw versorgt sein; **overachieve** VI leistungsorientiert sein; **a society which encourages people to ~** ein Gesellschaftssystem, das vom Menschen immer größere Leistungen fordert; **overachiever** N leistungsorientierter Mensch; **a chronic ~** ein typischer Erfolgsmensch; **overact** (*Theat*) VT *role* übertreiben, übertrieben gestalten VI übertreiben (*also fig*), chargieren; **overactive** ADJ überaktiv, zu aktiv; **~ thyroid** (*Med*) Schilddrüsenüberfunktion *f*

overage¹ [ˌəʊvərˈeɪdʒ] ADJ zu alt

overage² [ˈəʊvərɪdʒ] N (*US*) **a** (*Comm*) Überschuss *m* **b** (*mobile phone*) **~s** über die Freiminuten hinaus zu zahlende Telefonminuten

overall¹ [ˈəʊvərɔːl] ADJ **a** gesamt, Gesamt-; **~ width/length** Gesamtbreite *f*/-länge *f*; **~ dimensions** (*Aut*) Außenmaße *pl*; **~ majority** absolute Mehrheit; **~ winner** Gesamtsieger(in) *m(f)*; **he is the ~ leader** (*Sport*) er führt in der Gesamtwertung; **Labour gained ~ control** Labour erlangte die vollständige Kontrolle **b** (= *general*) allgemein; **there's been an ~ improvement recently in his work/health** sein Gesundheitszustand hat sich/seine Leistungen haben sich in letzter Zeit allgemein verbessert; **the ~ effect of this was to ...** dies hatte das Endergebnis, dass ... **ADV** **a** insgesamt; **what does it measure ~?** wie sind die Gesamtmaße?; **he came second ~** (*Sport*) er belegte in der Gesamtwertung den zweiten Platz **b** (= *in general, on the whole*) im Großen und Ganzen

overall² [ˈəʊvərɔːl] N (*Brit*) Kittel *m*; (*for women also*) Kittelschürze *f*; (*for children*) Kittelchen *nt*

overalls [ˈəʊvərɔːlz] PL Overall *m*, Arbeitsanzug *m*; (*US* = *dungarees*) Latzhose *f*

over: overambitious ADJ überehrgeizig, zu ehrgeizig; **overanxiety** N übersteigerte Angst; **overanxious** ADJ übertrieben besorgt; (*on particular occasion*) übermäßig aufgeregt, übermäßig nervös; **he's ~ to please** er überschlägt sich, um zu gefallen; **I'm not exactly ~ to go** ich bin nicht gerade scharf darauf, zu gehen

overarching [ˈəʊvərˈɑːtʃɪŋ] ADJ allumfassend

over: overarm ADJ, ADV (*Sport*) *throw* mit gestrecktem (erhobenem) Arm; *serve* über Kopf; **~ stroke** (*Swimming*) Kraulschlag *m*; **overate** *pret of* **overeat**; **overawe** VT (= *intimidate*) einschüchtern; (= *impress*) überwältigen, tief beeindrucken; **overbalance** VI (*person, object*) aus dem Gleichgewicht kommen, Übergewicht bekommen, das Gleichgewicht verlieren VT *object* umwerfen, umstoßen; *boat* kippen; *person* aus dem Gleichgewicht bringen

overbearing [ˈəʊvərˈbɛərɪŋ] ADJ herrisch; *arrogance* anmaßend

overbearingly [ˈəʊvərˈbɛərɪŋlɪ] ADV herrisch; **so ~ arrogant** von einer derartig anmaßenden Arroganz

over: overbid *pret, ptp* **overbid** VT **a** (*at auction*) überbieten **b** (*Cards*) überreizen; **to ~ one's hand** zu hoch reizen VI **a** (*at auction*) mehr bieten, ein höheres Gebot machen **b** (*Cards*) überreizen; **overblouse** N Überbluse *f*; **overblow** *pret* **overblew**, *ptp* **overblown** VT (*Mus*) überblasen; **overblown** ADJ **a** *flower* verblühend **b** *prose, rhetoric* geschwollen, schwülstig, hochtrabend **c** (*Mus*) *note* überblasen

overboard [ˈəʊvərbɔːd] ADV **a** (*Naut*) über Bord; **to fall ~** über Bord gehen *or* fallen; **man ~!** Mann über Bord!; **to throw sb/sth ~** jdn/etw über Bord werfen; **to throw sth ~** (*fig*) etw verwerfen **b** (*fig inf*) **to go ~** übers Ziel hinausschießen, zu weit gehen, es übertreiben; **to go ~ for** *or* **about sb** von jdm ganz hingerissen sein, Feuer und Flamme für jdn sein (*inf*); **there's no need to go ~ (about it)** übertreib es nicht, kein Grund zum Übertreiben

over: overbold ADJ *person, action* verwegen; **overbook** VI zu viele Buchungen vornehmen VT zu viele Buchungen vornehmen für; **o-**

verburden VT (*lit*) überladen; (*fig*) überlasten; **overbuy** *pret*, *ptp* **overbought** VI zu viel kaufen, über Bedarf einkaufen; **overcall** (*Cards*) VT überbieten N höheres Gebot; **overcame** *pret of* **overcome**; **overcapacity** N Überkapazität *f*; **overcapitalize** VT überkapitalisieren; **overcareful** ADJ übervorsichtig; **overcast** ADJ **a** *weather* bedeckt; *sky* bewölkt, bedeckt; **it's getting rather ~** es zieht sich zu **b** (*Sew*) *stitch* überwendlich; ~ **seam** überwendliche Naht; **overcautious** ADJ übervorsichtig, übertrieben vorsichtig; **overcautiousness** N übertriebene Vorsicht

overcharge [ˌəʊvəˈtʃɑːdʒ] VT **a** *person* zu viel berechnen (+*dat*) *or* abverlangen (+*dat*) (*for* für); **you've been ~d** man hat dir zu viel berechnet; **they ~d me by £2** sie haben mir £ 2 zu viel berechnet **b** *electric circuit* überlasten **c** (*with detail, emotion*) *painting, style* überladen N zu viel verlangen (*for* für); **to ~ on a bill** zu viel berechnen *or* anrechnen

overcoat [ˈəʊvəkəʊt] N Mantel *m*, Überzieher *m*

overcome [ˌəʊvəˈkʌm] *pret* **overcame** [ˌəʊvəˈkeɪm] *ptp* **overcome** VT *enemy* überwältigen, bezwingen; *bad habit* sich (*dat*) abgewöhnen; *shyness, nerves, difficulty, anger, obstacle etc* überwinden; *temptation* widerstehen (+*dat*), bezwingen; *disappointment* hinwegkommen über (+*acc*); **he was ~ by the fumes** die giftigen Gase machten ihn bewusstlos; **sleep overcame him** der Schlaf übermannte ihn; **he was ~ by grief/by emotion** Schmerz/Rührung übermannte ihn; **he was ~ by remorse/(a feeling of) despair** Reue *f*/(ein Gefühl *nt* der) Verzweiflung *f* überkam ihn; ~ **with fear** von Furcht ergriffen *or* übermannt; ~ **(with emotion)** ergriffen, gerührt VI siegen, siegreich sein; **we shall ~** wir werden siegen

over: overcompensate VI **to ~ for sth** etw überkompensieren; **overcompensation** N Überkompensation *f*; **overconfidence** N **a** (= *extreme self-assurance*) übersteigertes Selbstvertrauen *or* Selbstbewusstsein **b** (= *over-optimism*) zu großer Optimismus **c** (= *excessive trust*) blindes Vertrauen (*in* in +*acc*); **overconfident** ADJ **a** (= *extremely self-assured*) übertrieben selbstsicher *or* selbstbewusst **b** (= *too optimistic*) zu optimistisch; **he was ~ of success** er war sich (*dat*) seines Erfolges zu sicher **c** (= *excessively trustful*) blind vertrauend (*in* auf +*acc*); **you are ~ in him** Sie haben zu großes Vertrauen in ihn; **overconsumption** N zu starker Verbrauch (*of* an +*dat*); **overcook** VT verbraten, (= *boil too long*) verkochen; **overcorrect** VT überkorrigieren ADJ überkorrekt; **overcritical** ADJ zu kritisch; **overcrop** VT (*Agr*) *land* Raubbau treiben mit, zugrunde wirtschaften; **overcrowd** VT überladen; *bus etc also, room* (*with people*) überfüllen; **overcrowded** ADJ (*with things*) überfüllt; *town also* überbevölkert; (= *overpopulated*) überbevölkert; **overcrowding** N (*of bus, room, flat, classroom*) Überfüllung *f*; (*of town*) Überbevölkerung *f*; **overdependent** ADJ zu abhängig (*on* von); **overdeveloped** ADJ überentwickelt

overdo [ˌəʊvəˈduː] *pret* **overdid** [ˌəʊvəˈdɪd] *ptp* **overdone** [ˌəʊvəˈdʌn] VT **a** (= *exaggerate*) übertreiben; **you are ~ing it** *or* **things** (= *going too far*) Sie übertreiben, Sie gehen zu weit; (= *tiring yourself*) Sie übernehmen *or* überlasten sich; **don't ~ the drink/sympathy** übertreibe es nicht mit dem Trinken/Mitleid; **she rather overdid the loving wife (bit)** (*inf*) sie hat die liebevolle Ehefrau etwas zu dick aufgetragen; **gin? – please, but don't ~ the tonic** Gin? – ja bitte, aber nicht zu viel Tonic; **I'm afraid you've rather ~ne it with the garlic** ich fürchte, du hast es mit dem Knoblauch etwas zu gut gemeint **b** (= *cook too long*) verbraten; (= *boil too long*) verkochen

over: overdone ADJ **a** (= *exaggerated*) übertrieben **b** (= *cooked too long*) verbraten; (= *boiled too long*) verkocht; **overdose** N (*lit*)

Überdosis *f*; (*fig*) Zuviel *nt* (*of* an +*dat*); **he died of an ~ of sleeping pills/a drug ~** er starb an einer Überdosis Schlaftabletten/Drogen VI eine Überdosis nehmen; **to ~ on heroin** eine Überdosis Heroin nehmen; **to ~ on sun** zu viel Sonne bekommen; **to ~ on TV** zu viel fernsehen VT überdosieren; **overdraft** N Kontoüberziehung *f*; **my bank manager wouldn't let me have a bigger ~** der Direktor meiner Bank wollte mir ein weiteres Überziehen meines Kontos nicht gestatten; **to have an ~ of £100** (= *be in debt*) sein Konto um £ 100 überzogen haben; (= *have an overdraft facility*) einen Überziehungskredit *or* £ 100 haben; **I've still got an ~** mein Konto ist immer noch überzogen; **overdraft facility** N Überziehungs- *or* Dispositionskredit *m*; **overdramatize** VT (*fig*) überdramatisieren; **overdraw** *pret* **overdrew**, *ptp* **overdrawn** VT *one's account* überziehen; **overdrawn** [ˌəʊvəˈdrɔːn] ADJ (*Fin*: = *in the red*) *account* überzogen; **she is ~** sie hat ihr Bankkonto überzogen; **I'm always ~ at the end of the month** mein Konto ist am Ende des Monats immer überzogen; **to be £100 ~**, **to be ~ by £100** sein Konto um £ 100 überzogen haben → *also* **overdraw**; **overdress** [ˌəʊvəˈdres] VI (sich) übertrieben *or* zu fein kleiden VT **to be ~ed** zu vornehm *or* elegant angezogen sein; **do you think I'm ~ed?** was meinst du, bin ich zu elegant angezogen? N [ˈəʊvədres] Überkleid *nt*; **overdrive** N (*Aut*) Schnellgang *m*, Schongang *m*; **overdue** ADJ **a** (= *late*) *book, change, visit* überfällig; *sum of money, salary* fällig; **long ~** schon seit langem fällig; ~ **interest** Zinsrückstände *pl*; **he is ~** er müsste schon lange da sein; **the US market is ~ for changes** am US--Markt sind Veränderungen überfällig **b** (*inf*: = *late according to biological cycle*) *baby, period* überfällig; **overeager** ADJ übereifrig; **he was ~ to impress** er war (zu) sehr darauf aus, Eindruck zu machen; **he was ~ to start** er konnte den Start kaum abwarten; **they're not exactly ~ to learn** sie sind nicht gerade übermäßig lernbegierig; **overeagerness** N Übereifer *m*; **overeat** *pret* **overate**, *ptp* **overeaten** VI zu viel essen, sich überessen; **overeating** N Überessen *nt*; **over-egg** VT (*Brit inf fig*) **to ~ the pudding** übertreiben; **overelaborate** ADJ *design, style* manieriert, gekünstelt; *excuse, plan, scheme* (viel zu) umständlich, zu ausgeklügelt; *hairstyle, dress* überladen; **overemphasis** N Überbetonung *f*; **an ~ on money** eine Überbewertung des Geldes; **overemphasize** VT überbetonen; **one cannot ~ the importance of this** man kann nicht genug betonen, wie wichtig das ist; **overemployed** ADJ (*beruflich*) überfordert; **overenthusiastic** ADJ übertrieben begeistert; **not exactly ~** nicht gerade hingerissen; **overestimate** ⚙ 26.1 [ˌəʊvərˈestɪmeɪt] VT überschätzen N [ˌəʊvərˈestɪmɪt] (*of price*) Überbewertung *f*, zu hohe Schätzung *f*; **overexcite** VT zu sehr aufregen; **overexcited** ADJ *person* überreizt, zu aufgeregt; *children* aufgedreht, zu aufgeregt; **overexcitement** N Überreiztheit *f*, zu starke Aufregung *f*; (*of children*) Aufgedrehtheit *f*; **overexercise** VT übertrainieren VI übermäßig viel trainieren; **the dangers of overexercising** die Gefahren übermäßigen Trainings; **overexert** VT überanstrengen; **overexertion** N Überanstrengung *f*; **overexploit** VT *land etc* Raubbau treiben (*sth* an +*dat*/mit); **overexpose** VT (*Phot*) überbelichten; **overexposure** N (*Phot*) Überbelichtung *f*; (*in media etc*: *of topic*) Überbehandlung *f*; **the President's image is suffering from ~ (in the media)** das Image des Präsidenten leidet darunter, dass er zu oft in den Medien erscheint; **overextended** ADJ (= *over-stretched*) *person* überlastet; **the company was ~ and faced bankruptcy** die Firma hatte sich übernommen und stand vor dem Bankrott; **overfamiliar** ADJ **to be ~ with sb** etwas zu vertraulich *or* intim mit jdm sein; (= *too pally also*) plumpvertraulich mit jdm sein; **I'm not ~ with their methods** ich bin nicht allzu vertraut mit ihren Methoden; **overfeed** *pret*, *ptp* **overfed** VT überfüttern; **overfill** VT überfüllen, zu voll machen; **overfish** VT *the sea etc* überfi-

schen; **overfishing** N Überfischung *f*; **overflew** *pret of* **overfly**; **overflight** N Überflug *m*

overflow [ˈəʊvəfləʊ] N **a** (= *act*) Überlaufen *nt* **b** (= *amount*) Übergelaufene(s) *nt*, Übergeflossene(s) *nt* **c** (= *outlet*) Überlauf *m* **d** (= *excess*: *of people*) Überschuss *m* (*of* an +*dat*) VT [ˌəʊvəˈfləʊ] *area* überschwemmen; *container, tank* überlaufen lassen; **the river has ~ed its banks** der Fluss ist über die Ufer getreten VI [ˌəʊvəˈfləʊ] **a** (*liquid, river etc*) überlaufen, überfließen; (*container*) überlaufen; (*room, vehicle*) zum Platzen gefüllt sein, überfüllt sein (*with* mit); **full to ~ing** (*bowl, cup*) bis oben hin voll, zum Überlaufen voll; *room* überfüllt, zu voll; **the crowd at the meeting ~ed into the street** die Leute bei der Versammlung standen bis auf die Straße; **you'll have to open the doors and let the people ~ into the grounds** man wird die Türen öffnen müssen, damit die Leute in die Gartenanlagen ausweichen können **b** (*fig*: = *be full of*) überfließen (*with* von); **his heart was ~ing with love** sein Herz lief *or* floss über vor Liebe

over: overflow meeting N Parallelversammlung *f*; **overflow pipe** N Überlaufrohr *nt*; **o-verfly** *pret* **overflew**, *ptp* **overflown** VT **a** (= *fly over*) *town* überfliegen **b** (= *fly beyond*) *runway, airport* hinausfliegen über (+*acc*); **overfond** ADJ **to be ~ of sth/of doing sth** etw nur zu gern haben/tun; **I'm not exactly ~ of ...** ich bin nicht gerade begeistert von ...; **overfull** ADJ übervoll (*with* von, mit); **overgenerous** ADJ zu *or* übertrieben großzügig; **she was ~ in her praise** sie geizte nicht mit Lob, sie spendete überreichliches Lob; **he gave me an ~ helping** er überhäufte meinen Teller; **overground** (*Transport*) ADJ oberirdisch ADV oberirdisch; **overgrow** *pret* **overgrew**, *ptp* **overgrown** VT *path, garden, wall* überwachsen, überwuchern; **overgrown** ADJ **a** (= *overwuchert*) überwuchert (*with* von); (= *untrimmed*) *hedge, grass* ungeschnitten **b** *child* aufgeschossen, zu groß; **he's just an ~ schoolboy** er ist ein großes Kind; **you're just an ~ baby** du bist der reinste Säugling; **at forty-five, she still looked like an ~ schoolgirl** mit fünfundvierzig sah sie immer noch wie ein zu groß geratenes Schulmädchen aus; **overhand** ADJ, ADV (*Sport*) überarm; **overhand knot** N (*Naut*) einfacher Knoten; **overhang** [ˌəʊvəˈhæŋ] *vb*: *pret*, *ptp* **overhung** VT hängen über (+*acc*); (= *project over*: *rocks, balcony*) hinausragen über (+*acc*), vorstehen über (+*acc*) N [ˈəʊvəhæŋ] (*of rock, building*) Überhang *m*; (*Archit*) Überkragung *f*; **overhanging** ADJ *cliff, wall* überhängend; *vegetation* ADJ voreilig, übereilt; **am I being ~?** bin ich da zu voreilig?; **overhaul** [ˈəʊvəhɔːl] N Überholung *f*, Überholen *nt*; (*inf, of patient*) Generalüberholung *f* (*inf*); **the machine needs an ~** die Maschine muss überholt werden VT [ˌəʊvəˈhɔːl] **a** *engine* überholen; *plans* revidieren, überprüfen; (*inf*) *patient* gründlich untersuchen **b** (= *pass*) überholen; (= *catch up*) einholen

overhead[1] [ˌəʊvəˈhed] ADV oben; (= *in the sky*: *position*) am Himmel, in der Luft; **the people ~** (= *above us*) die Leute über uns; (= *above them*) die Leute darüber; **a plane flew ~** ein Flugzeug flog über uns *etc* (*acc*) (hinweg) ADJ [ˈəʊvəhed] ~ **compartment** Gepäckfach *nt*; ~ **railway** (*Brit*) Hochbahn *f*; ~ **kick** (*Ftbl*) Fallrückzieher *m*; ~ **lighting** Deckenbeleuchtung *f*; ~ **travelling crane** Laufkran *m*; ~ **volley** (*Sport*) Hochball *m*

overhead[2] [ˈəʊvəhed] (*Comm*) ADJ ~ **charges** *or* **costs** *or* **expenses** allgemeine Unkosten *pl* N (*US*) = **overheads**

overhead: overhead cable N Überlandleitung *f*; (*high voltage*) Hochspannungsleitung *f*; (*Rail*) Oberleitung *f*; **overhead cam(shaft)** N oben liegende Nockenwelle; **overhead projector** N Overheadprojektor *m*

overheads [ˈəʊvəhedz] PL (*Brit*) allgemeine Unkosten *pl*; **company** ~ allgemeine Geschäftskosten *or* Betriebs(un)kosten *pl*

overhead: overhead-valve engine N oben gesteuerter Motor; **overhead valves** PL oben gesteuerte Ventile pl

overhear [ˌəʊvəˈhɪə] pret, ptp **overheard** [ˌəʊvəˈhɜːd] VT zufällig mit anhören, zufällig mitbekommen; **we don't want him to ~ us** wir wollen nicht, dass er uns zuhören kann or dass er mitbekommt, was wir sagen; **I ~d them plotting** ich hörte zufällig, wie sie etwas aussheckten; **things you ~ in bars** Dinge, die man in Bars so mit anhört or mitbekommt; **the other day he was ~d to say that …** neulich hat ihn jemand sagen hören, dass …; **he was being ~d** jemand hörte mit

over: overheat 〈VT〉 engine überhitzen; room überheizen 〈VI〉 (engine) heißlaufen; (fig: economy) sich überhitzen; **overheated** ADJ **a** heißgelaufen; room überheizt; **to become** or **get ~** (person) einen Hitzschlag erleiden **b** discussion erhitzt; economy, market überhitzt **c** (= exaggerated) ~ **prose** überhitzte Prosa; **overhung** pret, ptp of **overhang; overimpressed** ADJ **I'm not ~ with him** er imponiert mir nicht besonders, von dem halte ich nicht besonders viel; **I'm not ~ with his work** ich bin nicht gerade von seiner Arbeit begeistert, seine Arbeit haut mich nicht vom Hocker (inf)

overindulge [ˈəʊvərɪnˈdʌldʒ] 〈VT〉 **a** person zu nachsichtig sein mit, zu viel durchgehen lassen (+dat) **b** fantasies, passion etc allzu freien Lauf lassen (+dat) 〈VI〉 zu viel genießen; (as regards eating also) Völlerei betreiben; **I ~d at the party** ich habe auf der Party ein bisschen zu viel des Guten gehabt; **to ~ in wine** zu viel Wein trinken

overindulgence [ˈəʊvərɪnˈdʌldʒəns] N **a** allzu große Nachsicht or Nachgiebigkeit (of sb jdm gegenüber) **b** (as regards eating) Völlerei f; **~ in wine** übermäßiger Weingenuss; **~ in cigarettes** zu starkes Rauchen; **the author's regrettable ~ in the use of metaphor** die bedauerlicherweise ungezügelte Vorliebe dieses Autors für Metaphern

overindulgent [ˈəʊvərɪnˈdʌldʒənt] ADJ parent zu nachsichtig, zu gutmütig (to(wards) sb jdm gegenüber, mit jdm); **should I have another or would that be ~?** soll ich mir noch einen nehmen oder wäre das des Guten zu viel?

overjoyed [ˌəʊvəˈdʒɔɪd] ADJ überglücklich, äußerst erfreut (at, by, with über +acc); **to be ~ to see sb** überglücklich sein, jdn zu sehen; **she was ~ with the present** sie war überglücklich über das Geschenk; **not exactly ~** nicht gerade erfreut

over: overkill N (Mil) Overkill m; (fig: = getting rid of too much etc) Rundumschlag m, Kahlschlag m; **repainting the whole room would definitely be ~** das ganze Zimmer neu zu streichen wäre des Guten zu viel or wäre übertrieben; **overladen** ADJ (lit, fig) überladen (with mit); lorry, circuit also überlastet; **overlaid** pret, ptp of **overlay; overland** ADJ journey auf dem Landweg; **~ route** Route f auf dem Landweg 〈ADV〉 travel etc über Land, auf dem Landweg

overlap [ˈəʊvəlæp] 〈N〉 Überschneidung f; (spatial) Überlappung f; (of concepts) teilweise Entsprechung or Deckung; **3 inches' ~** 3 Zoll Überlapp(ung); **there is an ~ of two days between our exams** unsere Prüfungen überschneiden sich um zwei Tage 〈VI〉 [ˌəʊvəˈlæp] **a** (tiles, boards) einander überdecken, überlappen; (teeth) übereinander stehen; **made of ~ping planks** aus (einander) überlappenden Brettern **b** (visits, dates, responsibilities) sich überschneiden; (ideas, concepts, plans, work areas) sich teilweise decken 〈VT〉 [ˌəʊvəˈlæp] **a** part gehen über (+acc), liegen über (+dat); (person) überlappen; **the tiles ~ each other** die Dachziegel überlappen sich or liegen übereinander **b** holiday, visit etc sich überschneiden mit; idea etc sich teilweise decken mit

over: overlay vb: pret, ptp **overlaid** [ˌəʊvəˈleɪ] 〈VT〉 überziehen; (with metal) belegen; wall verklei-

---

den 〈N〉 [ˈəʊvəleɪ] Überzug m; (metal) Auflage f; (on map) Auflegemaske f; (Typ) Zurichtung f, Zurichtbogen m; (for fridge etc) Verkleidung f; **overleaf** ADV umseitig; **the illustration ~** die umseitige Abbildung; **see ~** siehe umseitig; **o-verlie** VT bedecken; **overload** 〈N〉 Übergewicht nt, zu große Last, Überbelastung f; (Elec) Überlast f 〈VT〉 überladen; car, lorry, animal also überlasten; (Elec, Mech) überlasten; **overlong** ADJ überlang 〈ADV〉 zu lang

overlook [ˌəʊvəˈlʊk] VT **a** (= have view onto) überblicken; **we had a room ~ing the park** wir hatten ein Zimmer mit Blick auf den Park; **the castle ~s the whole town** vom Schloss aus hat man Aussicht auf die ganze Stadt; **the garden is not ~ed** niemand kann in den Garten hineinsehen **b** (= fail to notice) detail übersehen, nicht bemerken; **it is easy to ~** man übersieht es leicht **c** (= ignore) mistake hinwegsehen über (+acc), durchgehen lassen; **I am prepared to ~ it this time** diesmal will ich noch ein Auge zudrücken

over: overlord N (Hist) Oberherr m; **overlordship** N (Hist) Oberherrschaft f

overly [ˈəʊvəlɪ] ADV übermäßig, allzu

over: overmanned ADJ **to be ~** eine zu große Belegschaft haben; **overmanning** N zu große Belegschaft(en pl); **overmantel** N (Archit) Kaminaufsatz or -aufbau m; **overmuch** 〈ADV〉 zu viel, übermäßig; **they're not paid ~** sie bekommen nicht übermäßig viel bezahlt 〈ADJ〉 zu viel; **overnice** ADJ distinction spitzfindig, zu genau

overnight [ˈəʊvənaɪt] 〈ADV〉 **a** über Nacht; **we drove ~** wir sind die Nacht durchgefahren; **to stay ~ (with sb)** (bei jdm) übernachten, (bei jdm) über Nacht bleiben **b** (fig) von heute auf morgen, über Nacht; **the place had changed ~** der Ort hatte sich über Nacht verändert 〈ADJ〉 **a** Nacht-; **~ accommodation** Übernachtungsmöglichkeit f; **including ~ accommodation the cost is £50** der Kosten betragen £ 50 inklusive Übernachtung; **~ train** Nachtzug m **b** (fig: = sudden) ganz plötzlich; **an ~ success** ein Blitzerfolg m; **she became an ~ star** sie wurde über Nacht zum Star; **the play was an ~ success** das Stück wurde über Nacht ein Erfolg

overnight: overnight bag N Reisetasche f; **overnight case** N kleine Reisetasche (für eine einzelne Übernachtung); **overnight stay** N Übernachtung f

over: overpaid pret, ptp of **overpay; overparticular** ADJ zu genau, pingelig (inf); **he's not ~ about what he eats** er ist nicht wählerisch or pingelig (inf), was (das) Essen angeht; **he wasn't ~ about filling in his expenses form correctly** er nahm es mit dem Ausfüllen seines Spesenantrages nicht zu or so genau; **overpass** N Überführung f; **overpay** pret, ptp **overpaid** VT überbezahlen, zu viel bezahlen (+dat); **he was overpaid by about £5** man hat ihm etwa £ 5 zu viel bezahlt; **overpayment** N (= act) Überbezahlung f; (= amount) zu viel bezahlter Betrag; **overpeople** VT country übervölkern; **overphysical** ADJ (Sport) **to be ~** den körperlichen Einsatz übertreiben; **overplay** VT (= overact) übertrieben darstellen or spielen; **to ~ one's hand** (fig) es übertreiben, den Bogen überspannen; **overplus** N (esp US) Überschuss m, Mehr nt (of an +dat); **overpopulated** ADJ überbevölkert; **overpopulation** N Überbevölkerung f

overpower [ˌəʊvəˈpaʊə] VT **a** person, team, player überwältigen, bezwingen **b** (emotion, heat) überwältigen, übermannen **c** (Mech) **to be ~ed** übermotorisiert sein

overpowering [ˌəʊvəˈpaʊərɪŋ] ADJ überwältigend; smell penetrant; colour, decoration, perfume, person aufdringlich; heat glühend; **I felt an ~ desire …** ich fühlte den unwiderstehlichen Drang, …; **he's a bit ~ at times** seine Art kann einem manchmal zu viel werden

over: overpraise VT übertrieben or zu sehr loben; **overprice** VT einen zu hohen Preis ver-

---

langen für; **if the public will pay for it then it's not ~d** wenn es die Leute bezahlen, dann ist der Preis nicht zu hoch angesetzt; **at £50 it's ~d** £ 50 ist zu viel dafür; **overprint** 〈VT〉 **a** stamp, text überdrucken; (Phot) überkopieren **b** (= print too many copies of) in zu großer Auflage drucken 〈N〉 (on stamp) Überdruck m; **o-verproduce** VI überproduzieren, zu viel produzieren; **overproduction** N Überproduktion f; **overprotect** VT child überbehüten, zu sehr behüten; **overprotective** ADJ parent überängstlich; **overran** pret of **overrun; overrate** VT überschätzen; book, play, system etc also überbewerten; **to be ~d** überschätzt werden; **o-verreach** VI sich übernehmen; **overreact** VI übertrieben reagieren (to auf +acc); **overreaction** N übertriebene Reaktion (to auf +acc)

override [ˌəʊvəˈraɪd] pret **overrode** [ˌəʊvəˈrəʊd] ptp **overridden** [ˌəʊvəˈrɪdn] VT **a** (= disregard) sich hinwegsetzen über (+acc) **b** (= prevail over, cancel out) order, decision, ruling aufheben, außer Kraft setzen; objection ablehnen; **I'm a-fraid I'll have to ~ you there**, said the chairman da muss ich leider gegen Sie entscheiden, sagte der Vorsitzende **c** horse müde reiten **d** (teeth) gehen über (+acc)

overriding [ˌəʊvəˈraɪdɪŋ] ADJ principle vorrangig, wichtigste(r, s); priority vordringlich; desire dringendste(r, s); **matters of ~ importance** äußerst bedeutende Angelegenheiten; **my ~ ambition is to …** mein allergrößter Ehrgeiz ist es, zu …; **~ clause** (Jur) Aufhebungsklausel f

over: overripe ADJ überreif; **overrode** pret of **override**

overrule [ˌəʊvəˈruːl] VT ablehnen; claim also nicht anerkennen; objection also zurückweisen; verdict, decision aufheben; **his objection was ~d** sein Einspruch wurde abgewiesen; **we were ~d** unser Vorschlag/unsere Entscheidung etc wurde abgelehnt; **he was ~d by the majority** er wurde überstimmt

overrun [ˌəʊvəˈrʌn] pret **overran** [ˌəʊvəˈræn] ptp **o-verrun** 〈VT〉 **a** (weeds) überwuchern, überwachsen; **the town was ~ by tourists** die Stadt war von Touristen überlaufen; **the house was ~ by mice** das Haus war voller Mäuse **b** (troops etc: = invade) country, district einfallen in (+dat), herfallen über (+acc); enemy position überrennen **c** (= go past) mark hinauslaufen über (+acc); (Rail) signal überfahren; (train) platform hinausfahren über (+acc); (plane) runway hinausrollen über (+acc) **d** (= go beyond) time überziehen, überschreiten; **the TV documentary overran its time** die Fernsehdokumentation überzog **e** (= overflow) banks überfluten 〈VI〉 **a** (in time: speaker, concert etc) überziehen; **his speech overran by ten minutes** seine Rede dauerte zehn Minuten zu lang **b** (costs) überziehen

oversaw [ˌəʊvəˈsɔː] pret of **oversee**

overseas [ˈəʊvəˈsiːz] ADJ **a** (= beyond the sea) in Übersee pred; country, market überseeisch, in Übersee; telegram nach/aus Übersee; **our ~ office** unsere Zweigstelle in Übersee; **an ~ visitor** ein Besucher m aus Übersee **b** (= abroad) ausländisch, im Ausland; student, investment ausländisch; **in ~ countries** im Ausland; **an ~ visitor** ein Besucher m aus dem Ausland, ein ausländischer Besucher; **~ trip** Auslandsreise f; **he won his first ~ cap this year** er hat dieses Jahr zum ersten Mal bei einem Auswärtsspiel in der Nationalmannschaft gespielt 〈ADV〉 **to be/work ~** in Übersee/im Ausland sein/arbeiten; **to go ~** nach Übersee/ins Ausland gehen; **to be sent ~** nach Übersee/ins Ausland geschickt werden; **from ~** aus Übersee/dem Ausland

overseas: overseas aid N Entwicklungshilfe f; **Overseas Development** N (Brit Pol) ≈ Entwicklungshilfe f; **Minister for ~** ≈ Entwicklungshilfeminister(in) m(f); **~ Administration/A-**

gency ≈ Entwicklungshilfeministerium *nt*; **o-verseas trade** N Überseehandel *m*

over: oversee *pret* **oversaw**, *ptp* **overseen** VT (= *supervise*) *person, work* beaufsichtigen, überwachen; **overseer** N Aufseher(in) *m(f)*; (= *foreman*) Vorarbeiter(in) *m(f)*; (*in coal mine*) Steiger *m*; **oversell** *pret, ptp* **oversold** VT **a** (= *sell too many*) **to ~ sth** von etw mehr verkaufen, als geliefert werden kann; *concert, match etc* für etw zu viele Karten verkaufen **b** (= *promote too much*) zu viel Reklame machen für; **to ~ one-self** sich zu gut verkaufen VI (= *sell too many*) mehr verkaufen, als geliefert werden kann; (*for concert, match etc*) zu viele Karten verkaufen; **o-versensitive** ADJ überempfindlich; **oversew** *pret* **oversewed**, *ptp* **oversewed** *or* **oversewn** VT umnähen; **oversexed** ADJ **to be ~** einen übermäßig starken Sexualtrieb haben; **you're ~!** du bist unersättlich; **overshadow** VT (*lit, fig*) überschatten; **overshoe** N Überschuh *m*

overshoot [əʊvə'ʃuːt] *pret, ptp* **overshot** [əʊvə-'ʃɒt] VT *target, runway* hinausschießen über (+*acc*); *production target etc* übertreffen; **the golfer overshot the green** der Golfer schlug (den Ball) über das Grün hinaus; **to ~ the mark** (*lit, fig*) übers Ziel hinausschießen VI (*plane*) durchstarten

oversight ['əʊvəsaɪt] N **a** Versehen *nt*; **by** *or* **through an ~** aus Versehen **b** (= *supervision*) Aufsicht *f*, Beaufsichtigung *f*

over: oversimplification N (zu) grobe Vereinfachung; **oversimplify** VT zu sehr vereinfachen, zu einfach darstellen; **oversize(d)** ADJ übergroß; **~ classes** zu große Klassen *pl*; **o-versleep** *pret, ptp* **overslept** VI verschlafen; **oversold** *pret, ptp* of **oversell**; **overspend** [əʊvə'spend] *vb: pret, ptp* **overspent** VI zu viel ausgeben; **we've overspent by £10 wir haben £ 10 zu viel ausgegeben; ~ing city councils** Stadträte *pl* mit zu hoher Ausgabenpolitik VT überschreiten [əʊvəspend] zu hohe Ausgaben *pl*; **overspending** N zu hohe Ausgaben *pl*; **o-verspill** (*Brit*) ['əʊvəspɪl] N Bevölkerungsüberschuss *m*; **~ town** Trabantenstadt *f* VI [əʊvə-'spɪl] = **overflow** VI ban; **overstaffed** ADJ überbesetzt; **this office is ~** dieses Büro hat zu viel Personal; **overstaffing** N Personalüberschuss *m*; **~ problems** Probleme aufgrund *or* auf Grund von Personalüberschuss; **overstate** VT *facts, case* übertreiben, übertrieben darstellen; **overstatement** N Übertreibung *f*, übertriebene Darstellung; **overstay** VT = **outstay**; **o-versteer** N Übersteuern *nt* VI übersteuern; **overstep** VT überschreiten; **to ~ the mark** zu weit gehen

overstock [əʊvə'stɒk] VT *farm, pond* zu hoch bestücken; **the farm/pond is ~ed** der Hof/der Teich hat einen zu großen Vieh-/Fischbestand; **the shop is ~ed** der Laden hat zu große Bestände VI (*shop*) zu große (Lager)bestände haben, zu viel lagern; (*farm*) zu große (Vieh)bestände haben

overstrain [əʊvə'streɪn] VT *horse, person* überanstrengen, überfordern; *metal* überbelasten; *resources, strength, theory* überbeanspruchen; **to ~ oneself** sich übernehmen, sich überanstrengen; **don't ~ yourself** (*iro*) übernimm dich bloß nicht

overstretch [əʊvə'stretʃ] VT **a** (*lit*) *muscles, legs* überdehnen **b** (*fig*) *resources, budget, finances* zu sehr belasten; *abilities* überfordern; **to ~ oneself** sich übernehmen VI (*lit, person*) die Muskeln überdehnen; (*muscles, legs*) sich überdehnen

over: overstrung ADJ **a** *person* überspannt **b** *piano* kreuzsaitig; **oversubscribe** VT (*Fin*) überzeichnen; **the zoo outing was ~d** zu viele (Leute) hatten sich für den Ausflug in den Zoo angemeldet; **oversupply** VT überliefern N Überangebot *nt* (*of an* +*dat*), Überversorgung *f* (*of* mit)

overt [əʊ'vɜːt] ADJ *behaviour, campaign, operation, sexuality* offen; *hostility* unverhohlen

overtake [əʊvə'teɪk] *pret* **overtook** [əʊvə'tʊk] *ptp* **overtaken** [əʊvə'teɪkn] VT **a** *competitor, rival* einholen; (*esp Brit*: = *pass*) *runner, car etc* überho-

---

len **b** (= *take by surprise*) (*storm, night*) überraschen; (*fate*) ereilen (*geh*); **~n by fear** vor Furcht gelähmt; **we were ~n by events, events have ~n us** wir waren auf die Entwicklung der Dinge nicht gefasst VI (*esp Brit*) überholen

overtaking [əʊvə'teɪkɪŋ] N (*esp Brit*) Überholen *nt*

over: overtax VT **a** (*fig*) *person, heart* überlasten, überfordern; **to ~ one's strength** sich übernehmen **b** (*lit*, = *tax too heavily*) übermäßig besteuern; **overtechnical** ADJ zu fachspezifisch; (*regarding technology*) zu technisch; **over-the--counter** ADJ *drugs* nicht rezeptpflichtig; *sale* offen; (*St Ex*) *securities, transactions* außerbörslich; **~ market** (*St Ex*) Freiverkehr *m*, Freiverkehrsmarkt *m*; **overthrow** *vb: pret* **overthrew**, *ptp* **overthrown** ['əʊvəθrəʊ] N **a** Sieg *m* (*of* über +*acc*); (= *being overthrown*) Niederlage *f*; (*of dictator, government, empire*) Sturz *m*; (*of country*) Eroberung *f* **b** (*Cricket*) zu weiter Wurf VT [əʊvə'θrəʊ](= *defeat*) *enemy* besiegen; *government, dictator, general* stürzen, zu Fall bringen; *plans* umstoßen; *country* erobern

overtime ['əʊvətaɪm] N **a** Überstunden *pl*; **I am on ~** *or* **doing ~** ich mache Überstunden; **he did four hours' ~** er hat vier (Stunden) Überstunden gemacht **b** (*US Sport*) Verlängerung *f*; **we had to play ~** es gab eine Verlängerung ADV **to work ~** Überstunden machen; **my imagination was working ~** (*inf*) meine Fantasie *or* Phantasie lief auf Hochtouren (*inf*); **his liver's been working ~ to keep up with all this alcohol** (*inf*) seine Leber musste sich ganz schön anhalten (*inf*) *or* lief auf Hochtouren (*inf*), um all den Alkohol zu verkraften; **we shall have to work ~ to regain the advantage we have lost** (*fig*) wir müssen uns mächtig ranhalten, wenn wir den verlorenen Vorsprung wieder wettmachen wollen (*inf*) VT (*Phot*) überbelichten; **the programme planners ~d the symphony** die Programmgestalter hatten zu viel Zeit für die Sinfonie *or* Symphonie eingeplant

overtime: overtime ban N Überstundensperre *f*; **overtime pay** N Überstundenlohn *m*; **overtime rates** PL Überstundentarif *m*

overtired [əʊvə'taɪəd] ADJ übermüdet

overtly [əʊ'vɜːtlɪ] ADV offen

overtone ['əʊvətəʊn] N **a** (*Mus*) Oberton *m* **b** (*fig*) Unterton *m*; **political ~s** politische Untertöne *pl*; **what are the precise ~s of this word?** was klingt bei diesem Wort alles mit?

over: overtook *pret* of **overtake**; **overtop** VT überragen; **overtrain** VTI zu viel *or* zu hart trainieren; **~ed** übertrainiert; **overtrick** N (*Cards*) überzähliger Stich; **overtrump** VT übertrumpfen

overture ['əʊvətjʊə'] N **a** (*Mus*) Ouvertüre *f* **b** *usu pl* (= *approach*) Annäherungsversuch *m*; **to make ~s to sb** Annäherungsversuche bei jdm machen; **peace ~s** Friedensannäherungen *pl*

overturn [əʊvə'tɜːn] VT **a** (*lit*) umkippen, umwerfen; (= *capsize*) *boat* zum Kentern bringen, umkippen; **the ship rocked violently ~ing chairs and tables** das Schiff schwankte so heftig, dass Tische und Stühle umkippten **b** (*fig*) *regime* stürzen; *philosophy, world view* umstoßen; *law, ban, conviction* aufheben VI (*chair*) umkippen; (*boat also*) kentern N ['əʊvətɜːn](*of government*) Sturz *m*; (*of world view etc*) Umsturz *m*; (*of law, ban, conviction*) Aufhebung *f*

over: overtype VT (*Comput*) *text* überschreiben; **overuse** [əʊvə'juːs] N übermäßiger *or* zu häufiger Gebrauch VT [əʊvə'juːz] übermäßig oft *or* zu häufig gebrauchen; **overvalue** VT *goods* zu hoch schätzen; *idea, object, person* überbewerten; **overview** N Überblick *m* (*of* über +*acc*)

overweening [əʊvə'wiːnɪŋ] ADJ überheblich, anmaßend; *arrogance, pride, ambition* maßlos

overweight ['əʊvə'weɪt] ADJ *thing* zu schwer; *person also* übergewichtig; **to be five kilos ~** (*person, box etc*) fünf Kilo Übergewicht haben;

~ luggage Übergepäck *nt*; **you're ~** Sie haben Übergewicht N Übergewicht *nt*

overwhelm [əʊvə'welm] VT **a** (= *overpower: strong feelings*) überwältigen; **he was ~ed when they gave him the present** er war zutiefst gerührt, als sie ihm das Geschenk gaben; **Venice ~ed me** ich fand Venedig überwältigend; **to be ~ed with joy/grief** von Freude/Trauer überwältigt sein; **you ~ me!** (*iro*) da bin ich aber sprachlos! **b** (= *ruin, crush*) *enemy* überwältigen; *country* besiegen; (*Sport*) *defence* überrennen **c** (= *submerge*) (*water*) überschwemmen, überfluten; (*earth, lava*) verschütten, begraben **d** (*fig*) (*with favours, praise*) überschütten, überhäufen; (*with questions*) bestürmen; (*with work*) überhäufen

overwhelming [əʊvə'welmɪŋ] ADJ überwältigend; *desire, power* unwiderstehlich; *misfortune* erschütternd; **an ~ majority** eine überwältigende Mehrheit; **they won despite ~ odds** sie gewannen obwohl ihre Chancen sehr schlecht standen

overwhelmingly [əʊvə'welmɪŋlɪ] ADV **a** (= *extremely*) **he was quite ~ friendly** er war umwerfend freundlich; **he began to feel ~ anxious** er begann, sich unwahrscheinlich ängstlich zu fühlen **b** (= *predominantly*) *approve, reject, support* mit überwältigender Mehrheit; *white, positive* größtenteils; **they voted ~ for it** sie haben mit überwältigender Mehrheit dafür gestimmt

over: overwind *pret, ptp* **overwound** VT *watch* überdrehen; **overwinter** VTI überwintern; **o-verwork** N Überarbeitung *f*, Arbeitsüberlastung *f*; **he is ill from ~** er hat sich krank gearbeitet VT *horse etc* schinden; *person* überanstrengen; *image, idea, theme etc* überstrapazieren; **to ~ oneself** sich überarbeiten VI sich überarbeiten; **overwrite** *pret* **overwrote**, *ptp* **overwritten** VTI (*Comput*) überschreiben; **overwrite mode** N (*Comput*) Überschreibmodus *m*; **overwritten** ADJ (= *too flowery etc*) zu blumig (geschrieben); (= *too strong*) zu stark formuliert; (= *too rhetorical*) zu schwülstig

overwrought [əʊvə'rɔːt] ADJ **a** *person* überreizt **b** (= *too elaborate*) *style* überfeinert, verkünstelt

overzealous [əʊvə'zeləs] ADJ übereifrig

Ovid ['ɒvɪd] N Ovid *m*

oviduct ['əʊvɪdʌkt] N Eileiter *m*

oviform ['əʊvɪfɔːm] ADJ (*form*) eiförmig

oviparous [əʊ'vɪpərəs] ADJ Eier legend, ovipar (*spec*)

ovipositor [əʊvɪ'pɒzɪtə'] N Legebohrer *m*, Legestachel *m*

ovoid ['əʊvɔɪd] ADJ eiförmig, ovoid

ovulate ['ɒvjʊleɪt] VI ovulieren

ovulation [ˌɒvjʊ'leɪʃən] N Eisprung *m*, Ovulation *f*

ovule ['ɒvjuːl] N (*Zool*) Ovulum *nt*, Ei *nt*; (*Bot*) Samenanlage *f*

ovum ['əʊvəm] N *pl* **ova** Eizelle *f*, Ovum *nt*

owe [əʊ] VT **a** *money* schulden, schuldig sein (*sb sth, sth to sb* jdm etw); **can I ~ you the rest?** kann ich dir den Rest schuldig bleiben?; **I ~ him a meal** ich bin ihm noch ein Essen schuldig, ich schulde ihm noch ein Essen; **how much do I ~ you?** (*in shop etc*) was bin ich schuldig? **b** *reverence, obedience, loyalty* schulden, schuldig sein (*to sb* jdm); *allegiance* schulden (*to sb* jdm) **c** (= *be under an obligation for*) verdanken (*sth to sb* jdm etw); **I ~ my life to him** ich verdanke ihm mein Leben; **to what do I ~ the honour** (*Brit*) *or* **honor** (*US*) **of your visit?** (*iro*) und was verschafft mir die Ehre Ihres Besuches?; **we ~ it to them that we are alive today** wir haben es ihnen zu verdanken, dass wir heute noch leben; **you ~ it to yourself to keep fit** du bist es dir schuldig, fit zu bleiben; **we ~ nothing to him, we ~ him nothing** wir sind ihm (gar) nichts schuldig; **I think you ~ me an explana-**

tion ich glaube, du bist mir eine Erklärung schuldig

VI **to ~ sb for sth** jdm Geld für etw schulden; **can I ~ you for the rest?** kann ich Ihnen den Rest schuldig bleiben?; **I still ~ him for the meal** ich muss ihm das Essen noch bezahlen

owing ['əʊɪŋ] ❷ 17.1, 21.4 **ADJ** unbezahlt; **the amount ~ on the house** die Schulden, die auf dem Haus liegen; **how much is still ~?** wie viel steht noch aus?; **a lot of money is ~ to me** man schuldet mir viel Geld; **the money still ~ to us** (*Comm*) die Außenstände *pl*; **to pay what is ~** den ausstehenden Betrag bezahlen **PREP** **to** wegen (+*gen or* (*inf*) +*dat*), infolge (+*gen*); **~ to the circumstances** umständehalber; **~ to his being foreign** weil er Ausländer ist; **and it's all ~ to him that we succeeded** und unser Erfolg ist ihm allein zuzuschreiben

owl [aʊl] **N** Eule *f*; **wise old ~** weise Eule

owlet ['aʊlɪt] **N** junge Eule

owlish ['aʊlɪʃ] **ADJ** **the glasses gave him a somewhat ~ look** die Brille ließ ihn ein wenig eulenhaft erscheinen; **his ~ face** sein Eulengesicht *nt*

owlishly ['aʊlɪʃlɪ] **ADV** *look, stare* wie eine Eule

own¹ [əʊn] **VT** **a** (= *possess*) besitzen, haben; **who ~s that?** wem gehört das?; **we used to rent the house, now we ~ it** wir hatten das Haus vorher gemietet, jetzt gehört es uns; **he looks as if he ~s the place** er sieht so aus, als wäre er hier zu Hause; **the tourists behaved as if they ~ed the hotel** die Touristen benahmen sich, als gehöre das Hotel ihnen; **you don't ~ me, she said** ich bin nicht dein Privateigentum, sagte sie **b** (= *admit*) zugeben, zugestehen; (= *recognize*) anerkennen; **he ~ed that the claim was reasonable** er erkannte die Forderung als gerechtfertigt an, er gab zu, dass die Forderung gerechtfertigt war; **to ~ a child** (*Jur*) ein Kind (als seines) anerkennen

VI **to ~ to sth** etw eingestehen; **to debts** etw anerkennen; **he ~ed to having done it** er gestand, es getan zu haben; **he didn't ~ to having done it** er hat nicht zugegeben, dass er es getan hat

▶ **own up** **VI** es zugeben; **come on, own up** (*nun*) gib schon zu; **to own up to sth** etw zugeben; **he owned up to stealing the money** er gab zu or er gestand, das Geld gestohlen zu haben

own² **ADJ** *attr* eigen; **his ~ car** sein eigenes Auto; **one's ~ car** ein eigenes Auto; **he's his ~ man** er geht seinen eigenen Weg; **he likes beauty for its ~ sake** er liebt die Schönheit um ihrer selbst willen; **he does (all) his ~ cooking** er kocht für sich selbst; **thank you, I'm quite capable of finding my ~ way out** danke, ich finde sehr gut alleine hinaus; **my ~ one is smaller** meine(r, s) ist kleiner; **my ~ one** (*liter, hum*: = *beloved*) mein Einziger, meine Einzige

PRON **a** **that's my ~** das ist mein Eigenes; **those are my ~** die gehören mir; **my ~ is bigger** meine(r, s) ist größer; **to make sth one's ~** sich (*dat*) etw zu eigen machen; **my time is my ~** ich kann mit meiner Zeit machen, was ich will; **I can scarcely call my time my ~** ich kann kaum sagen, dass ich über meine Zeit frei verfügen kann; **his ideas were his ~** die Ideen stammten von ihm selbst; **I'd like a little house to call my ~** ich würde gern ein kleines Häuschen mein Eigen nennen; **a house of one's ~** ein eigenes Haus; **I have money of my ~** ich habe selbst Geld; **it has a**

beauty all its ~ *or* **of its ~** es hat eine ganz eigene *or* eigenartige Schönheit; **for reasons of his ~** aus irgendwelchen Gründen; **he gave me one of his ~** er gab mir eins von seinen (eigenen) **b** (*in phrases*) **can I have it for my (very) ~?** darf ich das ganz für mich allein behalten?; **to get one's ~ back on sb** (*esp Brit*) er jdm heimzahlen; **he was determined to get his ~ back** (*esp Brit*) er war entschlossen, sich zu revanchieren; **(all) on one's ~** (ganz) allein; (= *without help also*) selbst; **on its ~** von selbst, von allein; **if I can get him on his ~** wenn ich ihn allein erwische; **the goalkeeper came into his ~ with a series of brilliant saves** der Torwart zeigte sich von seiner besten Seite, als er eine Reihe von Bällen geradezu fantastisch abwehrte

own brand **N** Hausmarke *f*

own-brand ['əʊn‚brænd] **ADJ** **~ label** Hausmarke *f*

owner ['əʊnə'] **N** Besitzer(in) *m(f)*, Eigentümer(in) *m(f)*; (*of shop, factory, firm etc*) Inhaber(in) *m(f)*; (*of dogs, car, slaves*) Halter(in) *m(f)*; **who's the ~ of this umbrella?** wem gehört dieser Schirm?; **at ~'s risk** auf eigene Gefahr

owner: owner-driver **N** *Fahrzeughalter, der sein eigenes Auto fährt*; **owner-editor** **N** Redakteur(in) *m(f)* im eigenen Hause; **ownerless** **N** herrenlos; **owner-occupancy** **N** **there's a growing level of ~** immer mehr Häuser/Wohnungen werden eigengenutzt *or* befinden sich im Besitz der Bewohner; **owner-occupied** **ADJ** *house* vom Besitzer bewohnt; **owner-occupier** **N** Bewohner(in) *m(f)* im eigenen Haus, Eigennutzer(in) *m(f)* (*form*)

ownership ['əʊnəʃɪp] **N** Besitz *m*; **to establish the ~ of sth** den Besitzer einer Sache (*gen*) feststellen; **there are doubts as to the ~ of the property** es ist nicht klar, wer der Eigentümer dieses Grundstücks ist; **under his ~ the business flourished** das Geschäft blühte in der Zeit, als es sich in seinem Besitz befand; **under new ~** unter neuer Leitung; **since we've been under new ~** seit der Eigentümer gewechselt hat; **this certifies your ~ of ...** das weist Sie als Eigentümer von ... aus

own goal **N** (*lit, fig*) Eigentor *nt*; **to score an ~** (*lit, fig*) ein Eigentor schießen

ownsome ['əʊnsəm] **N** **on one's ~** (*inf*) mutterseelenallein

owt [aʊt] **PRON** (*N Engl*) = **anything PRON**

ox [ɒks] **N** *pl* **-en** Ochse *m*; **as strong as an ox** bärenstark

oxalic acid [ɒk'sælɪk'æsɪd] **N** Oxalsäure *f*

oxbow lake ['ɒksbəʊ'leɪk] **N** toter Flussarm

Oxbridge ['ɒksbrɪdʒ] **N** Oxford und/oder Cambridge *f*; **~ people** der Universität (*gen*) Oxford oder Cambridge

ox cart **N** Ochsenkarren *m*

oxen ['ɒksən] *pl* of **ox**

oxeye daisy ['ɒks‚aɪ'deɪzɪ] **N** Margerite *f*

Oxfam ['ɒksfæm] **N** *abbr of* **Oxford Committee for Famine Relief** **a** *britische karitative Vereinigung zur Hungerhilfe* **b** (*also* **Oxfam shop**) *Gebrauchtwarenladen, dessen Verkaufserlös der Hungerhilfe zugute kommt*, ≈ Dritte-Welt-Laden *m*

Oxford ['ɒksfəd] **N** Oxford *nt*; **my brother is at ~** mein Bruder studiert in Oxford

oxford ['ɒksfəd] **N** = **Oxford shoe**

Oxford: Oxford bags **PL** sehr weite Hosen *pl*; **Oxford blue** **N** *Mitglied eines Oxforder Studentensportklubs, das für die Universität angetreten ist*; **Oxford English** **N** Oxford-Englisch *nt*; **Oxford shoe** **N** geschnürter Halbschuh

oxidation [‚ɒksɪ'deɪʃən] **N** (*Chem*) Oxidation *f*

oxide ['ɒksaɪd] **N** (*Chem*) Oxid *nt*

oxidize ['ɒksɪdaɪz] **VTI** oxidieren

oxidizing agent ['ɒksɪdaɪzɪŋ‚eɪdʒənt] **N** (*Chem*) Oxidationsmittel *nt*, Oxidans *nt* (*spec*)

oxlip ['ɒkslɪp] **N** (*Bot*) hohe *or* weiße Schlüsselblume

Oxon ['ɒksən] **a** *abbr of* **Oxfordshire** **b** *abbr of* **Oxoniensis** der Universität Oxford

Oxonian [ɒk'səʊnɪən] **N** Oxfordstudent(in) *m(f)* **ADJ** der Oxforder Universität angehörend

ox: oxtail **N** Ochsenschwanz *m*; **oxtail soup** **N** Ochsenschwanzsuppe *f*

oxyacetylene ['ɒksɪə'setɪliːn] **ADJ** **~ burner** *or* **lamp** *or* **torch** Schweißbrenner *m*; **~ welding** Autogenschweißen *nt*

oxygen ['ɒksɪdʒən] **N** Sauerstoff *m*; **the ~ of publicity** (*fig*) öffentlichkeitswirksame Auftritte *pl*

oxygenate ['ɒksɪdʒəneɪt] **VT** oxygenieren, mit Sauerstoff behandeln *or* anreichern

oxygenation [‚ɒksɪdʒə'neɪʃən] **N** Oxygenierung *f*, Anreicherung *or* Behandlung *f* mit Sauerstoff

oxygen: oxygen bottle, oxygen cylinder **N** Sauerstoffflasche *f*; **oxygen mask** **N** Sauerstoff- *or* Atemmaske *f*; **oxygen tank** **N** Sauerstoffbehälter *m*; **oxygen tent** **N** Sauerstoffzelt *nt*

oxymoron [‚ɒksɪ'mɔːrɒn] **N** Oxymoron *nt*

oyez ['əʊjez] **INTERJ** (*old*) Achtung, Achtung

oyster ['ɔɪstə'] **N** Auster *f*; **the world's his ~** die Welt steht ihm offen; **to shut up** *or* **clam up like an ~** kein Wort mehr sagen

oyster: oyster bank, oyster bed **N** Austernbank *f*; **oyster-breeding** **N** Austernzucht *f*; **oystercatcher** **N** (*Orn*) Austernfischer *m*; **oyster cracker** **N** (*US*) Kräcker *m*; **oyster farm** **N** Austernpark *m*; **oyster mushroom** **N** Austernpilz *m*; **oyster shell** **N** Austernschale *f*

oz *abbr of* **ounce(s)**

ozalid ['ɒzəlɪd] **N** (*Typ*) Blaukopie *f*

ozone ['əʊzəʊn] **N** Ozon *nt*

ozone: ozone-friendly **ADJ** *spray etc* ohne Treibgas *pred*, FCKW-frei; **ozone hole** **N** Ozonloch *nt*; **ozone layer** **N** Ozonschicht *f*; **a hole in the ~** ein Ozonloch *nt*; **ozone-safe** **ADJ** = **ozone-friendly**

P

P, p [piː] N P *nt*, p *nt*; **to mind one's P's and Q's** (*inf*) sich anständig benehmen

p a *abbr of* **page** S. **b** *abbr of* **penny** *of* **pence**

P45

P45 nennt sich eine Bescheinigung, die Arbeitnehmern in Großbritannien am Ende ihres Beschäftigungsverhältnisses vom Arbeitgeber ausgehändigt wird. Darauf sind die Gesamtsumme des Einkommens sowie die Steuer- und Sozialversicherungsbeiträge des Arbeitnehmers im laufenden Steuerjahr aufgeführt. Bei Aufnahme eines neuen Beschäftigungsverhältnisses muss die Karte dem neuen Arbeitgeber übergeben werden.
„To get one's P45" wird oft als Umschreibung dafür genommen, dass jemand von seinem Arbeitgeber entlassen wird, auch wenn das genau genommen nicht ganz korrekt ist; ein Beispiel: „He is perilously close to getting his P45 if his players let him down again today" – „Er steht gefährlich knapp davor, seine Papiere zu bekommen, wenn ihn seine Spieler heute wieder im Stich lassen."

PA a *abbr of* **Press Association b** *abbr of* **personal assistant c** *abbr of* **public address (system)**

pa [pɑː] N (*inf*) Papa *m*, Papi *m*, Vati *m* (*all inf*)

p.a. *abbr of* **per annum**

PAC (*US*) *abbr of* **political action committee**

pace¹ ['peɪsɪ] PREP ohne ... (*dat*) nahe treten zu wollen

pace² [peɪs] **N** **a** (= *step*) Schritt *m*; (*of horse*) Gangart *f*; (*lifting both legs on same side*) Passgang *m*; **twelve ~s away** zwölf Schritt(e) entfernt; **at 20 ~s** auf 20 Schritte Entfernung; **to put a horse through its ~s** ein Pferd alle Gangarten machen lassen; **to put sb/a new car through his/its ~s** (*fig*) jdn/ein neues Auto auf Herz und Nieren prüfen; **to go through** *or* **show one's ~s** zeigen, was man drauf hat (*inf*) **b** (= *speed*) Tempo *nt*; **the more leisurely ~ of life in those days** das geruhsamere Leben damals; **at a good** *or* **smart ~** recht schnell; **at an incredible ~** unglaublich schnell, mit *or* in unglaublichem Tempo; **at a slow ~** langsam; **to learn at one's own ~** in seinem eigenen Tempo lernen; **to keep ~** Schritt halten; (*in discussing*) mitkommen; **I can't keep ~ with events** ich komme mit den Ereignissen nicht mehr mit; **to make** *or* **set the ~** das Tempo angeben; **to quicken one's ~** seinen Schritt beschleunigen; (*working*) sein Tempo beschleunigen; **to speed up the ~ of reforms** das Tempo der Reformen erhöhen; **I'm getting old, I can't stand the ~ any more** (*inf*) ich werde alt, ich kann nicht mehr mithalten; **the change of ~ in the narrative** der Tempowechsel in der Erzählung; **he has a good change of ~** (*runner*) er kann sein Tempo gut beschleunigen **VT a** (= *measure*) *floor, room* mit Schritten ausmessen **b** (*in anxiety etc*) auf und ab gehen *or* schreiten in (+*dat*) **c** *competitor* das Tempo angeben (+*dat*) **d** *horse* im Passgang gehen lassen **VI a** **to ~ around** hin und her laufen; **to ~ up**

and down auf und ab gehen *or* schreiten; **to ~ round the room** im Zimmer umhergehen **b** (*horse*) im Passgang gehen

▶ **pace off** *or* **out** VT *sep distance* ausschreiten, mit Schritten ausmessen *or* abmessen

pace bowler N (*Cricket*) Pace Bowler *m*, *Werfer, der die Bälle sehr schnell wirft*

-paced [peɪst] ADJ *suf* **fast-paced** flott, schwungvoll; **well-paced** schnell

pace lap N (*Motor sport*) Aufwärmrunde *f*

pacemaker ['peɪsmeɪkə'] N (*Med*) Schrittmacher *m* (*Sport*) = **pacesetter**

pacer ['peɪsə'], **pacesetter** ['peɪssetə'] N (*Sport*) Tempomacher(in) *m(f)*

pachyderm ['pækɪdɜːm] N Dickhäuter *m*

Pacific [pə'sɪfɪk] N **the ~ (Ocean)** der Pazifische *or* Stille Ozean, der Pazifik; **the ~ islands** die pazifischen Inseln; **a ~ island** eine Insel im Pazifik

pacific [pə'sɪfɪk] ADJ *people, nation* friedliebend, friedfertig

pacifically [pə'sɪfɪkəlɪ] ADV *live* in Frieden; *say* besänftigend

pacification [ˌpæsɪfɪ'keɪʃən] N Versöhnung *f*; (*of area*) Befriedung *f*; **attempts at ~** Friedensbemühungen *pl*

Pacific Standard Time N pazifische Zeit

pacifier ['pæsɪfaɪə'] N **a** (= *peacemaker*) Friedensstifter(in) *m(f)* **b** (*US: for baby*) Schnuller *m*

pacifism ['pæsɪfɪzəm] N Pazifismus *m*

pacifist ['pæsɪfɪst] **ADJ** pazifistisch **N** Pazifist(in) *m(f)*

pacifistic ['pæsɪfɪstɪk] ADJ pazifistisch

pacify ['pæsɪfaɪ] VT *baby* beruhigen; *warring countries* miteinander aussöhnen; *area* befrieden; *critics* besänftigen; **just to ~ the unions** nur damit die Gewerkschaften stillhalten

pack [pæk] **N** **a** (= *bundle*) Bündel *nt*; (*on animal*) Last *f*; (= *rucksack*) Rucksack *m*; (*Mil*) Gepäck *nt no pl*, Tornister *m* (*dated*) **b** (= *packet: for cereal, washing powder, frozen food*) Paket *nt*; (*esp US: of cigarettes*) Packung *f*, Schachtel *f*; **a ~ of six** ein Sechserpack *m* **c** (*Hunt*) Meute *f* **d** (*of wolves, cubs*) Rudel *nt*; (*of submarines*) Gruppe *f* **e** (*pej, = group*) Horde *f*, Meute *f*; **to stay ahead of the ~** (*fig*) der Konkurrenz (*dat*) immer um eine Nasenlänge voraus sein; **a ~ of thieves** eine Diebesbande; **he told us a ~ of lies** er tischte uns einen Sack voll Lügen auf; **it's all a ~ of lies** es ist alles erlogen **f** (*of cards*) (Karten)spiel *nt*; **52 cards make a ~** ein Blatt *nt* besteht aus 52 Karten **g** (*Rugby*) Stürmer *pl* **h** (*Med, Cosmetics*) Packung *f* **i** (*of ice*) Scholle *f* **VT a** *crate, container etc* voll packen; *fish, meat* in tin etc abpacken; **~ed in dozens** im Dutzend abgepackt **b** *case, trunk* packen; *things in case, clothes etc* einpacken **c** (= *wrap, put into parcel*) einpacken; **it comes ~ed in polythene** es ist in Cellophan *or* Zellophan verpackt

d (= *crowd, cram*) packen; *articles* stopfen, packen; **the box was ~ed full of explosives** die Kiste war voll mit Sprengstoff; **the crowds that ~ed the stadium** die Menschenmassen, die sich im Stadium drängten; **he ~ed the committee with his own supporters** er füllte das Komitee mit seinen eigenen Anhängern; **the comedy was playing to ~ed houses** die Komödie lief vor ausverkauften Häusern; **to be ~ed** (= *full*) gerammelt voll sein (*inf*); **the bus/square was ~ed solid** der Bus/der Platz war rappelvoll (*inf*); **all this information is ~ed into one chapter** all diese Informationen sind in einem Kapitel zusammengedrängt; **a weekend ~ed with excitement** ein Wochenende voller aufregender Erlebnisse; **a speech ~ed with jokes** eine mit Witzen gespickte Rede; **a thrill-packed film** ein packender Film; **the coast is ~ed with tourists** an der Küste wimmelt es von Touristen **e** (= *make firm*) *soil etc* festdrücken; **the snow on the path was ~ed hard** der Schnee auf dem Weg war festgetrampelt **f** *jury* mit den eigenen Leuten besetzen **g** (*US inf: = carry*) *gun* tragen, dabei haben; **to ~ one's lunch** sich (*dat*) sein Mittagessen mitnehmen **h** (*inf*) **to ~ a (heavy) punch** (*person*) kräftig zuschlagen; **he ~s a nasty left** er hat *or* schlägt eine ganz gemeine Linke (*inf*); **the film ~s a real punch** (*fig*) der Film ist total spannend **i** *leak, pipe* (zu)stopfen **VI a** (*items*) passen; **that won't all ~ into one suitcase** das passt *or* geht nicht alles in einen Koffer; **it ~s (in) nicely** es lässt sich gut verpacken; **the boxes are designed to ~ into this container** die Kästen sind so gemacht, dass sie in diesen Behälter hineinpassen **b** (*person*) packen; **I'm still ~ing** ich bin noch beim Packen **c** (= *crowd*) **the crowds ~ed into the stadium** die Menge drängte sich in das Stadion; **we can't all ~ into one car** wir können uns nicht alle in ein Auto zwängen; **they ~ed around the president** sie belagerten *or* umringten den Präsidenten **d** (= *become firm*) fest werden; **the snow had ~ed round the wheels** an den Rädern klebte eine feste Schneeschicht **e** (*inf*) **to send sb ~ing** jdn kurz abfertigen; **what should I do with my drunken husband? – I'd send him ~ing** was soll ich mit meinem Trunkenbold von Mann machen? – ich würde ihn vor die Tür setzen

▶ **pack away** **VT** *sep* **a** *clothes, boxes etc* wegpacken; **pack your toys away before you go out** räum deine Spielsachen weg, bevor du rausgehst; **I've packed all your books away in the attic** ich habe alle deine Bücher auf den Boden geräumt; **he packed the deck chairs away for the winter** er räumte die Liegestühle für den Winter weg **b** (*inf*) **he can really pack it away** (*food*) er kann ganz schön was verdrücken (*inf*) *or* verputzen (*inf*) **VI** **the bed packs away into a cupboard** man kann das Bett in einem Schrank verschwinden lassen

▶ **pack down** VI (*Rugby*) ein Gedränge *nt* bilden

▶ **pack in** **VT** *sep* **a** *clothes etc* einpacken **b** *people* hineinpferchen in (+*acc*); **we can't**

pack any more in here (*people*) hier geht *or* passt keiner mehr rein; (*things*) hier geht *or* passt nichts mehr rein

c (*inf: play, actor etc*) in Scharen anziehen; **this film is really packing them in** dieser Film zieht die Leute in Scharen an

d (*Brit, inf*) (= *give up*) *job* hinschmeißen (*inf*); *girlfriend* sausen lassen (*inf*); (= *stop*) *noise* aufhören mit; *work, activity* Schluss *or* Feierabend (*inf*) machen mit; **a footballer should know when it's time to pack it in** ein Fußballspieler sollte wissen, wann es Zeit ist, Schluss zu machen *or* aufzuhören; **to pack it all in** Schluss machen; **pack it in!** hör auf!, lass es gut sein!; (*job*) schmeiß die Sache hin!

VI a (= *crowd in*) sich hineindrängen; **we all packed into his car** wir zwängten uns alle in sein Auto

b (*Brit inf:* = *stop working*) (*engine*) seinen Geist aufgeben (*hum*); (*person*) zusammenpacken, Feierabend machen (*inf*)

▸ **pack off** VT *sep* **she packed them off to bed/school** sie schickte sie ins Bett/in die Schule

▸ **pack out** VT *sep usu pass* **to be packed out** (*hall, theatre etc*) gerammelt voll sein (*inf*), überfüllt sein

▸ **pack up** **VII** *sep clothes etc* zusammenpacken

VI a (= *prepare luggage*) packen; **he just packed up and left** er packte seine Sachen und ging **b** (*Brit inf:* = *stop working*) (*engine*) seinen Geist aufgeben (*hum*); (*person*) Feierabend machen (*inf*) **c the tent packs up easily** das Zelt lässt sich gut verpacken

package ['pækɪdʒ] **N a** (= *parcel, esp US:* = *packet*) Paket *nt*; (*of cardboard*) Schachtel *f* **b** (*esp Comm:* = *group, set*) Paket *nt*, Bündel *nt*; **software ~** Softwarepaket *nt* **VII a** *goods* verpacken **b** (*in order to enhance sales*) präsentieren

package: package deal N Pauschalangebot *nt*; **package holiday** N Pauschalreise *f*; **package insert** ['pækɪdʒ,ɪnsɜːt] N (*of medicine etc*) Packungsbeilage *f*

packager ['pækɪdʒə'] N Produktionsfirma *f*; (*for books*) Redaktionsbüro *nt*

package: package store N (*US*) Spirituosenhandlung *f*; **package tour** N Pauschalreise *f*

packaging ['pækɪdʒɪŋ] N **a** (= *material*) Verpackung *f*; **this is where they do the ~** hier werden die Sachen verpackt **b** (= *presentation of product*) Präsentation *f*; **the public don't buy the product, they buy the ~** die Leute kaufen nicht das Produkt, sondern die Verpackung **c** (= *act*) Verpacken *nt*

pack: pack animal N Packtier *nt*, Lasttier *nt*; **pack drill** N Strafexerzieren *nt* in gefechtsmäßiger Ausrüstung

packed lunch [pækt'lʌntʃ] N (*Brit*) Lunchpaket *nt*

packer ['pækə'] N Packer(in) *m(f)*; **he's a very untidy ~** er packt sehr unordentlich

packet ['pækɪt] N **a** (*esp Brit*) Paket *nt*; (*of cigarettes*) Päckchen *nt*, Schachtel *f*, Packung *f*; (= *small box*) Schachtel *f* **b** (*Naut*) Paketboot *nt* **c** (*Brit, inf:* = *lot of money*) **to make a ~** ein Schweinegeld verdienen (*inf*); **that must have cost a ~** das muss ein Heidengeld gekostet haben (*inf*)

packet: packet boat N Paketboot *nt*; **packet soup** N (*esp Brit*) Tütensuppe *f*; **packet switching** N (*Telec, Comput*) Paketvermittlung *f*

pack: packhorse N Packpferd *nt*; **I'm not your ~!** ich bin nicht dein Packesel!; **pack ice** N Packeis *nt*

packing ['pækɪŋ] N **a** (= *act*) (*in suitcases*) Packen *nt*; (*in factories etc*) Verpackung *f*; **to do one's ~** packen **b** (= *material*) Verpackung *f*; (*for leak*) Dichtung *f*

packing: packing case N Kiste *f*; **packing house** N (*US*) Abpackbetrieb *m*; **packing list** N (*Comm*) Packliste *f*; **packing plant** N (*US*) = **packing house**

pack: pack rat N Buschschwanzratte *f*; **packsack** N (*US*) Rucksack *m*; **packsaddle** N Packsattel *m*; **packthread** N Zwirn *m*; **pack train** N Tragtierkolonne *f*

pact [pækt] N Pakt *m*; **to make a ~ with sb** mit jdm einen Pakt schließen

pad¹ [pæd] VI **to ~ about** (*Brit*) *or* **around** umhertapsen; **to ~ along** entlangtrotten; **the panther ~ded up and down** der Pant(h)er trottete auf und ab; **the tiger ~ded off into the bushes** der Tiger trottete ins Gebüsch

pad² **N a** (= *stuffing*) (*for comfort etc*) Polster *nt*; (*for protection*) Schützer *m*; (*in bra*) Einlage *f*; (= *brake pad etc*) Belag *m* **b** (*of paper*) Block *m*; (*of blotting paper*) Schreibunterlage *f* **c** (*for inking*) Stempelkissen *nt* **d** (*of animal's foot*) Ballen *m* **e** (= *launch pad*) (Abschuss)rampe *f* **f** (*inf:* = *room, home*) Bude *f* (*inf*); **at your ~** in deiner Bude, bei dir **VII** *shoulders etc* polstern

▸ **pad out** VT *sep* **a** *shoulders* polstern **b** (*fig*) *article, essay etc* auffüllen; *speech* ausdehnen, strecken

padded ['pædɪd] ADJ **a** *shoulders, armour, bra* wattiert; *dashboard, seat* gepolstert; **~ envelope** gefütterter (Brief)umschlag **b** (*euph:* = *fat*) gut gepolstert

padded cell N Gummizelle *f*

padding ['pædɪŋ] N **a** (= *material*) Polsterung *f* **b** (*fig: in essay etc*) Füllwerk *nt*, Füllsel *pl*

paddle ['pædl] **N a** (= *oar*) Paddel *nt* **b** (= *blade of wheel*) Schaufel *f*; (= *wheel*) Schaufelrad *nt* (*for mixing*) Rührschaufel *f* **d Grandpa still enjoys a ~** Opa plan(t)scht noch gern durchs Wasser; **to go for a ~, to have a ~** durchs Wasser waten **e** (*in table tennis*) Schläger *m* **VII a** *boat* paddeln **b** (= *one's feet in the water*) mit den Füßen im Wasser plan(t)schen; **~ your feet and you'll stay afloat** du musst mit den Füßen paddeln, dann gehst du nicht unter **c** (*US:* = *spank*) verhauen, versohlen (*inf*) **VI a** (*in boat*) paddeln **b** (*with feet, swimming*) paddeln **c** (= *walk in shallow water*) waten

paddle: paddle boat N Raddampfer *m*; (*small, on pond*) Paddelboot *nt*; **paddle box** N Radkasten *m*; **paddle steamer** N Raddampfer *m*; **paddle wheel** N Schaufelrad *nt*

paddling pool ['pædlɪŋ,puːl] N (*Brit*) Plan(t)schbecken *nt*

paddock ['pædək] N (= *field*) Koppel *f*; (*of racecourse*) Sattelplatz *m*; (*Motor Racing*) Fahrerlager *nt*

Paddy ['pædɪ] N (*inf*) Paddy *m* (*Spitzname der Iren*)

paddy¹ ['pædɪ] N **a** (= *rice*) ungeschälter Reis **b** (*also* **paddy field**) Reisfeld *nt*

paddy² N (*Brit, inf*) Koller *m* (*inf*); **to get into a ~** einen Koller kriegen (*inf*); **to be in a ~** einen Koller haben (*inf*)

paddy wagon N (*US, inf*) grüne Minna (*inf*)

paddywhack ['pædɪwæk] N (*inf*) **a =** **paddy²** **b** (= *spank*) Klaps *m*

padlock ['pædlɒk] **N** Vorhängeschloss *nt* **VII** (*mit einem Vorhängeschloss*) verschließen

padre ['pɑːdrɪ] N (*Mil*) Feldkaplan *m*, Feldgeistliche(r) *m*; **yes, ~** ja, Herr Kaplan

paean ['piːən] N Lobrede *f*

paediatric, (*US*) **pediatric** [,piːdɪ'ætrɪk] ADJ Kinder-, pädiatrisch (*spec*)

paediatric clinic, (*US*) **pediatric clinic** N Kinderklinik *f*

paediatrician, (*US*) **pediatrician** [,piːdɪə'trɪʃən] N Kinderarzt *m*/-ärztin *f*, Pädiater *m* (*spec*)

paediatrics, (*US*) **pediatrics** [,piːdɪ'ætrɪks] N Kinderheilkunde *f*, Pädiatrie *f* (*spec*)

paedological, (*US*) **pedological** [,piːdə'lɒdʒɪkəl] ADJ pädologisch

paedology, (*US*) **pedology** [piː'dɒlədʒɪ] N Pädologie *f*

paedophile, (*US*) **pedophile** ['piːdəfaɪl] N Pädophile(r) *mf*; **~ ring** Pädophilenring *m*

paedophilia, (*US*) **pedophilia** [,piːdəʊ'fɪlɪə] N Pädophilie *f*

paedophiliac, (*US*) **pedophiliac** [,piːdə'fɪlɪæk] **N** Pädophile(r) *mf* **ADJ** pädophil

pagan ['peɪgən] **ADJ** heidnisch **N** Heide *m*, Heidin *f*

paganism ['peɪgənɪzəm] N Heidentum *nt*

page¹ [peɪdʒ] N (*also* **pageboy**) Page *m*; (*of knight*) Page *m*, Edelknabe *m* VT **to ~ sb** jdn ausrufen lassen; **paging Mr Cousin** Herr Cousin, bitte!

page² **N a** Seite *f*; **on ~ 14** auf Seite 14; **write on both sides of the ~** beschreiben Sie beide Seiten; **to be on the same ~** (*US:* = *in agreement*) auf der gleichen Wellenlänge liegen; **the sports ~s** die Sportseiten *pl* **a glorious ~ of English history** ein Ruhmesblatt *nt* in der Geschichte Englands; **to go down in the ~s of history** in die Geschichte *or* die Annalen der Geschichte eingehen **VII** (*Typ*) paginieren, mit Seitenzahlen versehen

pageant ['pædʒənt] N (= *show*) historische Aufführung, Historienspiel *nt*; (= *procession*) Festzug *m*; **Christmas ~** Weihnachtsspiel *nt*; **a ~ of Elizabethan times** (= *series of theatrical tableaux etc*) eine historische Darstellung des Elisabethanischen Zeitalters; (= *procession*) ein Festzug *m or* festlicher Umzug im Stil des Elisabethanischen Zeitalters; **the whole ~ of life** die breite Fülle des Lebens

pageantry ['pædʒəntrɪ] N Prunk *m*, Gepränge *nt*; **the ~ of history** die ganze Pracht der Geschichte; **the coronation was celebrated with great ~** die Krönung wurde sehr prunkvoll *or* mit großem Prunk gefeiert

page: pageboy N Page *m*; (*Brit:* = *attendant at wedding*) Junge, *der bei der Hochzeitszeremonie assistiert* **b** (= *hairstyle*) Pagenkopf *m*; **page break** N (*Comput*) Seitenwechsel *m*; **page make-up** N (*Typ*) Umbruch *m*; **page number** N Seitenzahl *f*; **page preview** N (*Comput*) Preview *m*; **page printer** N (*Comput*) Seitendrucker *m*; **page proof** N Korrekturfahne *f*

pager ['peɪdʒə'] N (*Telec*) Funkempfänger *m*, Pieper *m* (*inf*)

page-turner N **a** (*inf:* = *book*) spannendes Buch **b** (*person*) *jd, der Noten umblättert*

paginate ['pædʒɪneɪt] VT paginieren

pagination [,pædʒɪ'neɪʃən] N Paginierung *f*

pagoda [pə'gəʊdə] N Pagode *f*

paid [peɪd] *pret, ptp of* **pay** **ADJ** *official, work* bezahlt; **a highly ~ job** ein hoch bezahlter Posten; **a highly ~ manager** ein hoch bezahlter Manager, eine hoch bezahlte Managerin; **~ leave** bezahlter Urlaub *m* (*esp Brit*) **to put ~ to sth** etw zunichte machen; **that's put ~ to my weekend** damit ist mein Wochenende geplatzt *or* gestorben (*inf*); **that's put ~ to him** damit ist für ihn der Ofen aus (*inf*), das wars dann wohl für ihn (*inf*) **N the low/well ~** die Gering-/Gutverdienenden *pl*

paid-up ['peɪd'ʌp] ADJ *share* eingezahlt; **500 ~ members** 500 zahlende Mitglieder; **fully ~ member** Mitglied *nt* ohne Beitragsrückstände; **is he fully ~?** hat er alle Beiträge bezahlt?; **to make an insurance policy ~** eine Versicherung beitragsfrei stellen

pail [peɪl] N Eimer *m*; (*child's*) Eimerchen *nt*

pailful ['peɪlfʊl] N Eimer *m*

paillasse ['pælɪæs] N Strohsack *m*

pain [peɪn] N **a** Schmerz *m*; **is the ~ still there?** hast du noch Schmerzen?; **where is the ~ exactly?** wo tut es denn genau weh?; **this will help the ~** das ist gut gegen die Schmerzen; **to be in ~** Schmerzen haben; **you can't just leave him in ~** du kannst ihn nicht einfach leiden lassen; **he screamed in ~** er schrie vor Schmerzen; **do insects feel ~?** können Insekten Schmerz empfinden?; **a sharp ~** ein stechender Schmerz; **stomach/chest ~s** Magen-/Brustschmerzen *pl*; **my ankle has been giving** *or* **causing me a lot of ~** mein Knöchel tut mir sehr weh; **I felt a ~ in my leg** mein Bein tat mir weh, ich hatte Schmerzen im Bein; **to put sb out of his ~** jdn von seinen Schmerzen erlösen **b** (*mental*) Qualen *pl*; **the ~ of parting** der Abschiedsschmerz; **Werther: a soul in ~** Werther: eine gequälte Seele; **being so totally ignored like that was a source of great ~ to her** so vollkommen ignoriert zu werden, war für sie sehr schmerzlich; **he suffered great mental ~** er litt Seelenqualen; **the decision caused me a lot of ~** die Entscheidung war sehr schmerzlich für mich; **a look of ~ came over his face** sein Gesicht nahm einen schmerzlichen Ausdruck an; **no ~, no gain** ohne Fleiß kein Preis (*Prov*) **c pains** PL (= *efforts*) Mühe *f*; **to be at (great) ~s to do sth** sich (*dat*) (große) Mühe geben, etw zu tun; **to take ~s over sth** sich (*dat*) Mühe mit etw geben; **to take ~s to do sth** sich (*dat*) Mühe geben, etw zu tun; **great ~s have been taken to ...** besondere Mühe wurde darauf verwendet ...; **she takes great ~s with her appearance** sie verwendet sehr viel Sorgfalt auf ihr Äußeres; **all he got for his ~s was a curt refusal** zum Dank für seine Mühe wurde er schroff abgewiesen; **see what you get for your ~!** das hast du nun für deine Mühe! **d** (= *penalty*) **on** *or* **under ~ of death** bei Todesstrafe, bei Strafe des Todes (*old*), unter Androhung der Todesstrafe **e** (*inf: also* **pain in the neck** *or* **arse** *Brit sl*) **to be a (real) ~** einem auf den Wecker (*inf*) *or* Sack (*sl*) gehen; **this job is getting to be a ~** dieser Job geht mir langsam auf den Wecker (*inf*) *or* Sack (*sl*) ▶ VT (*mentally*) schmerzen; **it ~s me to see their ignorance** ihre Unwissenheit tut schon weh; **his laziness ~ed his parents** mit seiner Faulheit bereitete er seinen Eltern (*dat*) großen Kummer; **it ~s me to have to tell you this but ...** es schmerzt mich, Ihnen dies mitteilen zu müssen, aber ...

pain: pain barrier N Schmerzgrenze *f*; **to go through the ~** trotz Schmerzen weitermachen *or* durchhalten; **pain clinic** N Schmerzklinik *f*

pained [peɪnd] ADJ *expression, voice* schmerzerfüllt; **to look ~** schmerzerfüllt aussehen

painful ['peɪnfʊl] ADJ **a** (*physically*) *injury* schmerzhaft; **is it ~?** tut es weh?; **it's ~ to the touch** es tut weh, wenn man es berührt; **my arm was becoming ~** mein Arm fing an zu schmerzen; **my boots are still ~** meine Stiefel drücken immer noch **b** (= *unpleasant, distressing*) *task, decision, feeling, subject, fact* schmerzlich; *process, reminder, memory, experience* schmerzhaft; **it was ~ to admit that ...** es war schmerzlich zuzugeben, dass...; **it is my ~ duty to tell you that ...** ich habe die traurige Pflicht, Ihnen mitteilen zu müssen, dass ...; **~ to behold** ein qualvoller Anblick **c** (*inf*: = *terrible*) peinlich; **~, isn't it?** das tut weh, was?; **I went to the party but it was really ~** (= *boring*) ich war auf der Party, aber es war zum Sterben langweilig; (= *embarrassing*) ich war auf der Party, eine äußerst peinliche Angelegenheit; **she gave a ~ performance** ihre Vorführung war mehr als peinlich **d** (= *laborious*) schmerzlich; **it was a long and ~ process** es war ein langer und schmerzlicher Prozess

painfully ['peɪnfəlɪ] ADV **a** (*physically*) schmerzhaft; *move, walk* unter Schmerzen; **~ swollen** schmerzhaft angeschwollen; **he dragged himself ~ along** er quälte sich mühsam weiter **b** (*fig*) *learn, understand* schmerzlich; **Eleanor thought ~ of Eric** der Gedanke an Eric schmerzte Eleanor **c** (= *very*) schrecklich; *thin* furchtbar; *slow* schmerzlich; **it was ~ obvious** es war nicht zu übersehen; **he was being ~ overpolite** es war peinlich, wie betont höflich er sich benahm; **he became ~ aware that ...** ihm wurde schmerzlich bewusst, dass ... **d** (= *laboriously*) unter großen Anstrengungen; **the convict could scarcely write but had ~ scrawled out a statement** der Häftling konnte kaum schreiben, hatte aber unter großen Anstrengungen eine Erklärung hingekritzelt

pain: painkiller N schmerzstillendes Mittel; **painkilling** ADJ *drug* schmerzstillend

painless ['peɪnlɪs] ADJ schmerzlos; **I promise you the interview will be quite ~** (*inf*) ich versichere Ihnen, dass das Interview kurz und schmerzlos wird (*inf*); **a procedure which makes paying completely ~** (*inf*) ein Verfahren, bei dem Sie von der Bezahlung überhaupt nichts merken; **don't worry, it's quite ~** (*inf*) keine Angst, es tut gar nicht weh

painlessly ['peɪnlɪslɪ] ADV schmerzlos

painstaking ['peɪnz,teɪkɪŋ] ADJ *person, piece of work* sorgfältig; **with ~ accuracy** mit peinlicher Genauigkeit

painstakingly ['peɪnz,teɪkɪŋlɪ] ADV sorgfältig, gewissenhaft; **one has to be so ~ precise** man muss äußerst genau sein

paint [peɪnt] N **a** Farbe *f*; (*on car, furniture*) Lack *m*; (= *make-up*) Schminke *f*; **there's too much ~ on your face** (= *make-up*) du hast zu viel Farbe im Gesicht, du bist zu stark angemalt (*inf*) **b** **paints** PL Farben *pl*; **box of ~s** Farb- *or* Malkasten *m* **c** (*US*: = *piebald horse*) Schecke *m* ▶ VT **a** *wall, fence etc* streichen; *car* lackieren; *door* streichen, lackieren; **to ~ one's face** (*with make-up*) sich anmalen (*inf*); (*Theat*) sich schminken; **to ~ one's lips** sich (*dat*) die Lippen anmalen (*inf*); **to ~ the town red** (*inf*) die Stadt unsicher machen (*inf*); **to ~ oneself/sb into a corner** (*fig*) sich selbst/jdn in die Enge treiben **b** *picture, person* malen; **he ~ed a very convincing picture of life on the moon** er zeichnete ein sehr überzeugendes Bild vom Leben auf dem Mond → **black** ADJ **d** ▶ VI malen; (= *decorate*) (an)streichen

▶ **paint in** VT *sep* (= *add*) dazumalen; (= *fill in*) ausmalen

▶ **paint on** VT *sep* aufmalen

▶ **paint out** *or* **over** VT *sep* übermalen; (*on wall*) überstreichen

▶ **paint up** VT *sep building* neu *or* frisch anstreichen; *face* anmalen; **she gets all painted up on a Friday night** freitags abends legt sie immer ihre Kriegsbemalung an (*inf*)

paint: paintbox N Farb- *or* Malkasten *m*; **paintbrush** N Pinsel *m*

painted woman ['peɪntɪd'wʊmən] N Flittchen *nt* (*inf*)

painter[1] ['peɪntə'] N (*Art*) Maler(in) *m(f)*; (= *decorator also*) Anstreicher(in) *m(f)*

painter[2] N (*Naut*) Fangleine *f*

painterly ['peɪntəlɪ] ADJ malerisch; **his ~ talents** seine Begabung als Maler; **Magritte's prosaic ~ style** Magrittes prosaischer Malstil; **a ~ effect** ein gemalter Effekt

pain threshold N Schmerzschwelle *f*, -grenze *f*

painting ['peɪntɪŋ] N **a** (= *picture*) Bild *nt*, Gemälde *nt* **b** *no pl* (*Art*) Malerei *f* **c** *no pl* (*of flat etc*) Anstreichen *nt*

paint: paint pot N Farbtopf *m*; **paint remover** N Abbeizmittel *nt*; **paint roller** N Farbrolle *f*; **paint shop** N (*Ind*) Lackiererei *f*; **paint**

spray(er) N Spritzpistole *f*; **paint stripper** N Abbeizmittel *nt*; **paintwork** N (*on car etc*) Lack *m*; (*on wall, furniture*) Anstrich *m*

pair [peə'] N **a** (*of gloves, shoes, people*) Paar *nt*; (*of animals, cards*) Pärchen *nt*; (*hum sl*: = *breasts*) Vorbau *m* (*inf*), Dinger *pl* (*sl*); **these socks are not a ~** diese beiden Socken gehören nicht zusammen; **a ~ of scissors** eine Schere; **six ~s of scissors** sechs Scheren; **a new ~** (*of trousers*) eine neue (Hose); (*of shoes*) (ein Paar) neue; **I've lost my scissors, could I borrow your ~?** ich habe meine Schere verloren, kannst du mir deine leihen?; **I've only got one ~ of hands** ich habe auch nur zwei Hände; **he has a useful ~ of hands** (*boxer*) er ist ein guter Boxer; **to be** *or* **have a safe ~ of hands** zuverlässig sein; **a huge ~ of eyes** ein riesiges Augenpaar; **she has a great ~ of legs** sie hat tolle Beine (*inf*); **in ~s** paarweise; *hunt, arrive, go out* zu zweit; *be seated* in Zweiergruppen; **they're a ~ of rascals** das sind vielleicht zwei Lausejungen; **what a ~ of fools we are!** wir (beide) sind vielleicht dumm!; **you're a fine ~ you are!** (*iro*) ihr seid mir (vielleicht) ein sauberes Pärchen (*iro*) → **carriage** **b pairs** SING OR PL **the ~s** (*Skating*) Paarlauf *m*; (*Rowing*) Zweier *m*; **in the ~s** im Paarlauf/Zweier ▶ VT in Paaren *or* paarweise anordnen; **I was ~ed with Bob for the next round** in der nächsten Runde musste ich mit Bob ein Paar bilden; **to be ~ed against sb** gegen jdn spielen

▶ **pair off** VT *sep* in Zweiergruppen einteilen; **to pair sb off with sb** (= *find boyfriend etc for*) jdn mit jdm zusammenbringen *or* verkuppeln (*inf*); **she was paired off with Jean in the tournament** sie wurde beim Turnier mit Jean zusammengebracht; **pair off each word with its opposite** ordnen Sie jedem Wort den jeweiligen Gegensatz zu ▶ VI Paare bilden (*with* mit); **all the people at the party had paired off** bei der Party hatten alle Pärchen gebildet; **Marcel paired off with Emma** Marcel und Emma wurden ein Pärchen

pairing ['peərɪŋ] N **a** Paarung *f* **b** (*Parl*) Absprache zwischen Regierungs- und Oppositionsabgeordneten, an einer Abstimmung nicht teilzunehmen, um die Mehrheitsverhältnisse nicht zu verändern, Pairing *nt*

pair-skating ['peə,skeɪtɪŋ] N Paarlaufen *nt*

paisley ['peɪzlɪ] N türkisches Muster ADJ *pattern* türkisch; *shirt* türkisch gemustert

pajamas [pə'dʒɑːməz] PL (*US*) = **pyjamas**

Paki ['pækɪ] (*pej inf*) N (= *person*) Pakistani *mf* ADJ *shop etc* pakistanisch

Pakistan [,pɑːkɪs'tɑːn] N Pakistan *nt*

Pakistani [,pɑːkɪs'tɑːnɪ] ADJ pakistanisch N Pakistani *mf*, Pakistaner(in) *m(f)*

pal [pæl] N (*inf*) Kumpel *m* (*inf*); **OK, let's be ~s again** na gut, vertragen wir uns wieder!; **be a ~!** sei so nett!; **help me with this, there's a ~** sei doch so nett und hilf mir dabei

▶ **pal up** VI (*inf*) sich anfreunden (*with* mit)

palace ['pælɪs] N (*lit, fig*) Palast *m*; **bishop's ~** schöfliches Palais, bischöfliche Residenz; **royal ~** (Königs)schloss *nt*; **the PM was summoned to the ~** der Premierminister wurde zur Königin/zum König bestellt

palace: palace grounds PL Schlossgelände *nt*; **palace guard** N Schlosswache *f*; **palace revolution** N (*lit, fig*) Palastrevolution *f*; **palace wall** N Schlossmauer *f*

paladin ['pælədɪn] N Paladin *m*

palaeo- ['pælɪəʊ-] PREF = **paleo-**

palanquin [,pælən'kiːn] N Sänfte *f*

palatability [,pælətə'bɪlɪtɪ] N **a** Schmackhaftigkeit *f* **b** (*fig*) Attraktivität *f*

palatable ['pælətəbl] ADJ **a** genießbar; *food also* schmackhaft (*to* für); **to make sth ~** (*Cook*) etw geschmacklich verfeinern **b** (*fig*) *experience* attraktiv; **to some the truth is not always ~** manchen Leuten schmeckt die Wahrheit nicht immer; **to make sth ~ to sb** jdm etw schmackhaft machen

palatably ['pælətəblɪ] ADV schmackhaft; (*fig also*) attraktiv

palatal ['pælətl] ADJ Gaumen-; (*Phon*) palatal; ~ **muscle** Gaumenmuskel *m* N (*Phon*) Palatal (-laut) *m*

palatalize ['pælətəlaɪz] (*Phon*) VT palatalisieren; **the "t" is ~d** das „t" wird im vorderen Gaumen gebildet VI palatalisieren

palate ['pælɪt] N (*lit*) Gaumen *m*; **to have a sensitive ~** einen empfindlichen Gaumen haben; **to have no ~ for sth** (*fig*) keinen Sinn für etw haben

palatial [pə'leɪʃəl] ADJ (= *spacious*) palastartig; (= *luxurious*) luxuriös, prunkvoll, feudal (*hum inf*)

palatially [pə'leɪʃəlɪ] ADV luxuriös, prunkvoll, feudal (*hum inf*)

palatinate [pə'lætɪnɪt] N Pfalz *f*

palatine ['pælətaɪn] N (*also* **count palatine**) Pfalzgraf *m*

palaver [pə'lɑːvə'] N (*inf*) **a** (= *fuss and bother*) Umstand *m*, Theater *nt* (*inf*) **b** (= *conference*) Palaver *nt*

pale[1] [peɪl] ADJ (+*er*) **a** *colour, complexion, material* blass; *light* blass, fahl; (*implying unhealthy etc*) bleich, fahl; *light* blass, bleich, fahl; **she has ~ gold hair** sie hat rötlich blondes Haar; **~ green/ orange** *etc* blass- or zartgrün/-orange *etc*; **to go** or **turn ~ with fear** vor Schreck bleich or blass werden; **but a ~ imitation of the real thing** nur ein Abklatsch *m* des Originals **b** (= *faint*) *moon, sun* fahl VI (*person*) erbleichen, blass or bleich werden; (*paper etc*) verblassen; **to ~ with fear** vor Angst erblassen; **but X ~s beside Y** neben Y verblasst X direkt; **to sink into insignificance** or **to ~ (into insignificance) beside** or **alongside sth** neben etw (*dat*) bedeutungslos sein

pale[2] N (= *stake*) Pfahl *m*; **those last few remarks were quite beyond the ~** diese letzten Bemerkungen haben eindeutig die Grenzen überschritten; **he is now regarded as beyond the ~** man betrachtet ihn jetzt als indiskutabel

pale: pale ale N (*Brit*) helleres Dunkelbier; **paleface** N Bleichgesicht *nt*; **pale-faced** ADJ bleich, blass

palely ['peɪlɪ] ADV *shine, lit* schwach, matt

paleness ['peɪlnɪs] N Blässe *f*

paleo- ['pælɪəʊ-] PREF paläo-, Paläo-; **paleoanthropology** Paläoanthropologie *f*

paleography [,pælɪ'ɒɡrəfɪ] N Paläografie *f*

paleolithic [,pælɪəʊ'lɪθɪk] ADJ paläolithisch, altsteinzeitlich

paleontology [,pælɪɒn'tɒlədʒɪ] N Paläontologie *f*

Paleozoic [,pælɪəʊ'zəʊɪk] ADJ paläozoisch

Palestine ['pælɪstaɪn] N Palästina *nt*

Palestinian [,pælə'stɪnɪən] ADJ palästinensisch; **he is ~** er ist Palästinenser N Palästinenser(in) *m(f)*

palette ['pælɪt] N Palette *f*

palette knife N Palettenmesser *nt*

palfrey ['pɔːlfrɪ] N Zelter *m*

palimony ['pælɪmənɪ] N (*esp US inf*) Unterhaltszahlung *f* (*bei der Auflösung einer Ehe ohne Trauschein*)

palimpsest ['pælɪmpsest] N Palimpsest *m*

palindrome ['pælɪndrəʊm] N Palindrom *nt*

paling ['peɪlɪŋ] N (= *stake*) Zaunpfahl *m*; (= *fence*) Lattenzaun *m*; (*bigger*) Palisadenzaun *m*

palisade [,pælɪ'seɪd] N **a** Palisade *f* **b** **palisades** PL (*US*) Steilufer *nt* VT einpfählen

pall[1] [pɔːl] N **a** (*over coffin*) Bahrtuch *nt*, Sargtuch *nt*; **a ~ of smoke** (*fig*) (= *covering*) eine Dunstglocke; (*rising in air*) eine Rauchwolke; **her death cast a ~ over the celebrations** (*fig*) ihr Tod trübte die Stimmung auf der Feier **b** (*Eccl*) Pallium *nt*

pall[2] VI an Reiz verlieren (*on sb* für jdn)

palladium [pə'leɪdɪəm] N (*Chem*) Palladium *nt*

pallbearer ['pɔːl,beərə'] N Sargträger(in) *m(f)*

pallet ['pælɪt] N (= *bed*) Pritsche *f*; (*for storage*) Palette *f*

palletization [,pælɪtar'zeɪʃən] N Palettisierung *f*

palliasse ['pælɪæs] N Strohsack *m*

palliate ['pælɪeɪt] VT (*form*) **a** *disease* lindern **b** *offence, seriousness of situation* (= *make less serious*) mildern; (= *make seem less serious*) beschönigen

palliative ['pælɪətɪv] (*form*) ADJ *drug, remedy, effect* lindernd; *explanation* beschönigend N Linderungsmittel *nt*, Palliativ(um) *nt*

palliatory ['pælɪətərɪ] (*form*) ADJ = **palliative** ADJ

pallid ['pælɪd] ADJ blass, fahl; (= *unhealthy looking*) bleich, fahl

pallor ['pælə'] N Blässe *f*, Fahlheit *f*

pally ['pælɪ] ADJ (+*er*) (*Brit inf*) **they're very ~** sie sind dicke Freunde (*inf*); **to be ~ with sb** mit jdm gut Freund sein; **to get ~ with sb** sich mit jdm anfreunden; **he immediately tried to get ~ with the boss** er versuchte sofort, sich beim Chef anzubiedern

palm[1] [pɑːm] N (*Bot*) Palme *f*; (*as carried at Easter*) Palmzweig *m*; **to carry off** or **bear the ~** die Siegespalme erringen, gewinnen

palm[2] N (*Anat*) Handteller *m*, Handfläche *f*; (*of glove*) Innenfläche *f*; **the magician had concealed the ball in the ~ of his hand** der Zauberkünstler hielt den Ball in der hohlen Hand versteckt; **he had the audience in the ~ of his hand** er hielt das Publikum ganz in seinem Bann; **to grease sb's ~** (*fig*) jdn schmieren (*inf*); **to read sb's ~** jdm aus der Hand lesen → **itching** VT **a** *card* im Ärmel verstecken **b** **the goalie just managed to ~ the ball over the crossbar** der Torwart schaffte es gerade noch, den Ball mit der Handfläche über die Querlatte zu lenken

▶ **palm off** VT *sep* (*inf*) *rubbish, goods* andrehen (*on(to) sb* jdm) (*inf*); *person (with explanation)* abspeisen (*inf*); **they palmed him off on me** sie haben ihn mir aufgehalst (*inf*)

palmcorder ['pɑːmkɔːdə'] N Palmcorder *m*

palmetto [pæl'metəʊ] N Palmetto *f*

palmist ['pɑːmɪst] N Handliniendeuter(in) *m(f)*, Handleser(in) *m(f)*

palmistry ['pɑːmɪstrɪ] N Handliniendeutung *f*, Handlesekunst *f*

palm: palm leaf N Palmwedel *m*; **palm oil** N Palmöl *nt*; **Palm Sunday** N Palmsonntag *m*; **palmtop** ['pɑːmtɒp] N (*Comput*) Palmtop *m*; **palm tree** N Palme *f*; **palm wine** N Palmwein *m*

palmy ['pɑːmɪ] ADJ (+*er*) *days* glücklich, unbeschwert

palomino [,pælə'miːnəʊ] N Palomino *nt*

palpable ['pælpəbl] ADJ **a** greifbar; (*Med*) tastbar, palpabel (*spec*) **b** (= *clear*) *lie, error* offensichtlich; *nonsense* vollkommen; *injustice* grob

palpably ['pælpəblɪ] ADV (= *clearly*) eindeutig; (= *tangibly*) spürbar; **the scene was ~ intense to watch** man konnte die Spannung in dieser Szene regelrecht spüren

palpate [pæl'peɪt] VT (*Med*) palpieren

palpitate ['pælpɪteɪt] VI (*heart*) heftig klopfen; (= *tremble*) zittern

palpitation [,pælpɪ'teɪʃən] N (*of heart*) Herzklopfen *nt*; (= *trembling*) Zittern *nt*; **to have ~s** Herzklopfen haben

palsgrave ['pɔːlzɡreɪv] N (*Hist*) Pfalzgraf *m*

palsgravine ['pɔːlzɡrəviːn] N (*Hist*) Pfalzgräfin *f*

palsied ['pɔːlzɪd] ADJ gelähmt

palsy ['pɔːlzɪ] N Lähmung *f*; **sick of the ~** (*hum inf*) krank; (*Bibl*) gelähmt → **cerebral**

palsy-walsy ['pælzɪ'wælzɪ] ADJ (*hum inf*) **they are all ~** sie sind wieder ein Herz und eine Seele → *also* **pally**

paltriness ['pɔːltrɪnɪs] N Armseligkeit *f*, Schäbigkeit *f*; (*of reason*) Unbedeutendheit *f*, Geringfügigkeit *f*

paltry ['pɔːltrɪ] ADJ armselig, schäbig; **for a few ~ pounds** für ein paar lumpige or armselige Pfund; **he gave some ~ excuse** er brachte irgendeine armselige Entschuldigung hervor

pampas ['pæmpəs] PL Pampas *pl*

pampas grass N Pampasgras *nt*

pamper ['pæmpə'] VT verwöhnen; *child also* verhätscheln, verzärteln; *dog* verhätscheln; **why don't you ~ yourself and buy the de luxe edition?** warum gönnst du dir nicht mal etwas und kaufst die Luxusausgabe?

pamphlet ['pæmflɪt] N (= *informative brochure*) Broschüre *f*; (*literary*) Druckschrift *f*; (*political, handed out in street*) Flugblatt *nt*, Flugschrift *f*

pamphleteer [,pæmflɪ'tɪə'] N Verfasser(in) *m(f)* von Druckschriften/Flugblättern

pan[1] [pæn] N **a** (*Cook*) Pfanne *f*; (= *saucepan*) Topf *m* **b** (*of scales*) Waagschale *f*; (*for gold etc*) Goldpfanne *f*; (*of lavatory*) Becken *nt* **c** (*in ground*) Mulde *f* VT **a** *gold* waschen **c** (*US*) *fish* braten **c** (*inf: = slate*) *new play etc* verreißen VI **to ~ for gold** Gold waschen

▶ **pan out** VI (*inf*) sich entwickeln; **it didn't pan out** es hat nicht geklappt (*inf*); **if it pans out as we hope** wenns so wird, wie wir es uns erhoffen

pan[2] (*Film*) N (*Kamera*)schwenk *m* VI panoramieren; **a ~ning shot** ein Schwenk *m*; **the camera ~ned along the wall** die Kamera fuhr langsam die Mauer ab; **the camera ~ned in to the group in the centre** die Kamera schwenkte auf die Gruppe in der Mitte ein VI **they ~ned the camera across the whole scene** sie fuhren mit der Kamera die ganze Szene ab

pan- PREF pan-, Pan-

panacea [,pænə'sɪə] N Allheilmittel *nt*; **there's no universal ~ for ...** es gibt kein Allheilmittel für ...

panache [pə'næʃ] N Schwung *m*, Elan *m*; **she dresses with ~** sie kleidet sich sehr extravagant

Pan-African ['pæn'æfrɪkən] ADJ panafrikanisch

Pan-Africanism ['pæn'æfrɪkənɪzəm] N Panafrikanismus *m*

Panama [,pænə'mɑː] N Panama *nt*; **~ Canal** Panamakanal *m*

panama (hat) N Panamahut *m*

Panamanian [,pænə'meɪnɪən] ADJ panamaisch N Panamaer(in) *m(f)*, Panamese *m*, Panamesin *f*

Pan-American ['pænə'merɪkən] ADJ panamerikanisch

Pan-Americanism ['pænə'merɪkənɪzəm] N Pan-amerikanismus *m*

Pan-Arabic ['pæn'ærəbɪk] ADJ panarabisch

Pan-Arabism ['pæn'ærəbɪzəm] N Panarabismus *m*

panatella [,pænə'telə] N (*dünne, lange*) Zigarre *f*

pancake ['pænkeɪk] N Pfannkuchen *m*; **~ landing** Bauchlandung *f*; **~ roll** ≈ Frühlingsrolle *f* VI (*aeroplane*) eine Bauchlandung machen

Pancake Day N (*Brit*) Fastnachtsdienstag *m*

panchromatic ['pænkrəʊ'mætɪk] ADJ panchromatisch

pancreas ['pæŋkrɪəs] N Bauchspeicheldrüse *f*, Pankreas *nt*

pancreatic ['pæŋkrɪ'ætɪk] ADJ der Bauchspeicheldrüse; **~ cancer** Bauchspeicheldrüsenkrebs *m*

panda ['pændə] N Panda *m*, Katzenbär *m*

panda car N (*Brit*) (*Funk*)streifenwagen *m*

pandemic [pæn'demɪk] N Pandemie *f* (*geh*) ADJ pandemisch; ~ *disease* Seuche *f*

pandemonium [,pændɪ'məʊnɪəm] N Chaos *nt*; **at this there was ~** or **~ broke out** daraufhin brach ein Chaos aus or die Hölle los; **scenes of ~** chaotische Szenen *pl*; **judging by the ~ coming from the classroom** dem Höllenlärm in der Klasse nach zu urteilen

pander ['pændə'] N (*rare*) Kuppler(in) *m(f)* VI nachgeben (*to +dat*); **to ~ to sb's whims** jds

Launen (*acc*) befriedigen wollen; **to ~ to sb's ego** jdm um den Bart gehen; **this is ~ing to the public's basest instincts** damit wird an die niedrigsten Instinkte der Öffentlichkeit appelliert

Pandora's box [pæn'dɔːrəz'bɒks] N Büchse *f* der Pandora

p and p *abbr of* **post(age) and packing**

pane [peɪn] N Glasscheibe *f*

panegyric [ˌpænɪ'dʒɪrɪk] N Lobrede *f*, Panegyrikus *m* (*Liter*)

panel ['pænl] **N a** (= *piece of wood*) Platte *f*, Tafel *f*; (*in wainscoting, ceiling, door*) Feld *nt*; (*Sew*) Streifen *m*, Einsatz *m*; (*Art*) Tafel *f*; (= *painting*) Tafelbild *nt*; (= *part of a plane's wing, fuselage*) Verschalung(bau)teil *nt*; (= *part of bodywork of a car*) Karosserieteil *nt*; **door ~** (*on car*) Türblech *nt*; **wing ~** (*on plane*) Tragfläche *f* **b** (*of instruments, switches*) Schalttafel *f*; **instrument ~** Armaturenbrett *nt*; (*on machine*) Kontrolltafel *f* **c** (*Jur*, = *list of names*) Geschworenenliste *f*; (*Brit, Med*) ≈ Liste *f* der Kassenärzte **d** (*of interviewers etc*) Gremium *nt*; (*in discussion*) Diskussionsrunde *f*; (*in quiz*) Rateteam *nt*; **a ~ of experts** ein Sachverständigengremium *nt*; **on the ~ tonight we have ...** als Teilnehmer der Diskussionsrunde/des Rateteams begrüßen wir heute Abend ...; **a ~ of judges** eine Jury **VT** *wall, ceiling* täfeln, paneelieren

panel: panel beater N Autoschlosser(in) *m(f)*; **panel-beating** N (= *repair work*) Ausbeulen *nt*; **panel discussion** N Podiumsdiskussion *f*; **panel doctor** N Kassenarzt *m*, Kassenärztin *f*; **panel game** N Ratespiel *nt*

panelled, (*US*) **paneled** ['pænld] ADJ (*Archit*: = *decorated*) *room, wall, door* paneeliert; **to be ~ in** or **with sth** mit etw paneeliert sein

panel lighting N indirekte Beleuchtung

panelling, (*US*) **paneling** ['pænlɪŋ] N Täfelung *f*, Paneel *nt*; (*to conceal radiator etc, of plane*) Verschalung *f*

panellist, (*US*) **panelist** ['pænəlɪst] N Diskussionsteilnehmer(in) *m(f)*

panel: panel pin N Stift *m*; **panel saw** Laubsäge *f*; **panel truck** N (*US*) Lieferwagen *m*

Pan-European ADJ paneuropäisch

pang [pæŋ] N **~ of conscience** Gewissensbisse *pl*; **I felt a ~ of conscience** ich hatte Gewissensbisse; **a ~ of jealousy** ein Eifersuchtsanfall *m*; **a ~ of regret** ein Anfall *m* von Bedauern; **~s of hunger** quälender Hunger; **~s of childbirth** (*old*) Geburtswehen *pl*

pan: panhandle (*US*) **N** Pfannenstiel *m*; (= *shape of land*) Zipfel *m* (*US*, *inf*) die Leute anhauen (*inf*); **panhandler** N (*US, inf*) Bettler(in) *m(f)*, Schnorrer(in) *m(f)* (*inf*)

panic ['pænɪk] *vb*: *pret*, *ptp* **panicked N** Panik *f*; **~ on the stock exchange** Börsenpanik *f*; **in a (blind) ~** in (heller) Panik; **to flee in ~** panikartig die Flucht ergreifen; **a ~ reaction** eine Kurzschlussreaktion; **the country was thrown into a (state of)** ~ das Land wurde von Panik erfasst; **~ buying/selling** (*esp St Ex*) Panikkäufe *pl*/-verkäufe *pl*; (*of goods also*) Hamsterkäufe *pl*/Angstverkäufe *pl*; **to hit the ~ button** (*fig inf*, = *panic*) in Panik geraten, durchdrehen (*inf*) **VI** in Panik geraten; **don't ~** nur keine Panik! **VT** Panik auslösen unter (+*dat*); **to ~ sb into doing sth** jdn veranlassen, etw überstürzt zu tun

panic attack N (*Psych*) Panikanfall *m*; **to have a ~** einen Panikanfall bekommen

panicky ['pænɪkɪ] ADJ *person* überängstlich; *voice* panisch; *measure, behaviour* panikartig; **to feel ~** panische Angst haben; **I get this ~ feeling whenever ...** ich werde immer nervös or gerate immer in Panik, wenn ...; **to get ~** in Panik geraten; **don't get ~!** keine Panik!, dreh bloß nicht durch! (*inf*); **~ reaction** Kurzschlussreaktion *f*

panic: panic-mongering ['pænɪkˌmʌŋgərɪŋ] N (*pej*) Panikmache *f* (*pej*); **panic-stricken**

['pænɪkˌstrɪkən], **panic-struck** ['pænɪkstrʌk] ADJ von panischem Schrecken ergriffen; *look* panisch

panjandrum [pæn'dʒændrəm] N (*hum, pej*) Wichtigtuer(in) *m(f)* (*pej*)

pannier ['pænɪə'] N Korb *m*; (*on motor-cycle etc*) Satteltasche *f*; (*for mule etc*) Tragkorb *m*

panoplied ['pænəplɪd] ADJ *knight* in Rüstung

panoply ['pænəplɪ] N (= *armour*) Rüstung *f*; (= *covering*) Baldachin *m*; (*fig liter*) Dach *nt*; (= *array*) Palette *f*, Spektrum *nt*; **beneath the oak's ~ of leaves** unter dem Blätterdach der Eiche; **the ~ of the sky/of stars** das Himmels-/Sternenzelt (*liter*)

panorama [ˌpænə'rɑːmə] N (= *view, also fig: of life etc*) Panorama *nt* (*of* +*gen*); (= *survey*) Übersicht *f* (*of* über +*acc*)

panoramic [ˌpænə'ræmɪk] ADJ Panorama-; **~ shot** (*Phot*) Panoramaaufnahme *f*; **~ sight** (*Mil*) Rundblickzielfernrohr *nt*; **~ window** Panoramafenster *nt*

panoramic view N Panoramablick *m*; **a ~ of the hills** ein Blick *m* auf das Bergpanorama

panpipes ['pænpaɪps] PL Panflöte *f*

pansy ['pænzɪ] **N a** (*Bot*) Stiefmütterchen *nt* **b** (*Brit pej*: = *homosexual*) Schwuchtel *f* (*pej inf*)

pant [pænt] **N** Atemstoß *m* **VI a** (*person*) keuchen; (*dog*) hecheln; **to be ~ing for a drink** nach etwas zu trinken lechzen; **he was ~ing for breath** er schnappte nach Luft (*inf*), er rang nach Atem **b** (*inf*, = *desire*) lechzen (*for* nach); **to be ~ing to do sth** danach lechzen or darauf brennen, etw zu tun **VT** (*also* **pant out**) *message* hervorstoßen

pantaloon [ˌpæntə'luːn] N (*Theat*) Hanswurst *m*

pantaloons [ˌpæntə'luːnz] PL (*Hist*) Pantalons *pl*

pantechnicon [pæn'teknɪkən] N (*Brit*) Möbelwagen *m*

pantheism ['pænθiːɪzəm] N Pantheismus *m*

pantheist ['pænθiːɪst] N Pantheist(in) *m(f)*

pantheistic [ˌpænθiː'ɪstɪk] ADJ pantheistisch

pantheon ['pænθɪən] N Pantheon *nt*

panther ['pænθə'] N Pant(h)er *m*

panties ['pæntɪz] PL (*for children*) Höschen *nt*; (*for women also*) (Damen)slip *m*; **a pair of ~** ein Höschen *nt*/ein Slip *m*

pantile ['pæntaɪl] N Dachpfanne *f*

panto ['pæntəu] N (*Brit, inf*) = **pantomime a**

pantograph ['pæntəgrɑːf] N Pantograf *m*

pantomime ['pæntəmaɪm] N **a** (*in GB*) ≈ Weihnachtsmärchen *nt*; **what a ~!** (*inf*) was für ein Theater! (*inf*); **the government should abandon this ~ of secrecy** die Regierung sollte endlich diese Posse der Geheimhaltung beenden **b** (= *mime*) Pantomime *f*

PANTOMIME

Eine **pantomime**, oder kurz **panto**, hat mit der deutschen Form von Pantomime wenig gemein. Es handelt sich dabei vielmehr um ein normalerweise zur Weihnachtszeit aufgeführtes Märchenspiel für die ganze Familie. Die Handlung basiert auf einer bekannten Geschichte, wie z. B. Aschenputtel oder Aladin. Häufig ist die Mithilfe des Publikums, vor allem der Kinder, gefordert. Für die größeren Zuschauer werden Scherze zum aktuellen Zeitgeschehen eingebaut. Außerdem gehören dazu Musik, Slapstick sowie aufwändige Kostüme und Dekorationen. Die männlichen und weiblichen Hauptrollen werden gern Vertretern des jeweils anderen Geschlechts übertragen, wobei bei den bekannten Aufführungen Prominente die Rollen übernehmen.

---

pantomime: pantomime dame N (*Brit*) Figur einer grotesken, alten Dame im Weihnachtsstück, meist von einem Mann gespielt; **pantomime horse** N (*Brit*) von zwei Schau-

spielern in einem Kostüm gespieltes, komisches Pferd, meist im Weihnachtsstück

pantry ['pæntrɪ] N Speisekammer *f*

pants [pænts] PL (*esp US*: = *trousers*) Hose *f*; (*Brit*: = *underpants*) Unterhose *f*; **a pair of ~** eine Hose/Unterhose; **to beat the ~ off sb** (*inf*) es jdm ordentlich zeigen; **to charm the ~ off sb** (*inf*) jdm um den Bart gehen; **to wear the ~** (*US fig*) die Hosen anhaben (*inf*); **to be caught with one's ~ down** (*fig*) auf frischer Tat ertappt werden (*inf*); **to be ~** (*Brit sl*: = *awful*) beknackt or beschissen sein (*sl*)

pant: pantskirt ['pæntskɜːt] N (*esp US*) Hosenrock *m*

panty: pantsuit ['pæntsuːt] N (*US*) Hosenanzug *m*

panty ['pæntɪ]: **panty girdle** N Miederhöschen *nt*; **pantyhose** N (*US*) Strumpfhose *f*; **pantyliner** N Slipeinlage *f*; **pantywaist** N (*dated US, sl*) Schwächling *m*, Memme *f* (*inf*)

pap [pæp] N (= *food*) Brei *m*

papa [pə'pɑː] N (*dated inf*) Papa *m*

papacy ['peɪpəsɪ] N Papsttum *nt*; **during the ~ of ...** während der Amtszeit des Papstes ..., unter Papst ...

papadum, papadam ['pæpədəm] N = **poppadom**

papal ['peɪpəl] ADJ päpstlich

Papal States PL (*Hist*) Kirchenstaat *m*

Papanicolaou smear [ˌpæpə'nɪkəluː-], **Papanicolaou test** N (*esp US Med*: = *cervical smear*) Papanicolaou-Abstrich *m* or -Test *m*

paparazzo [ˌpæpə'rætsəu] *pl* **paparazzi** [ˌpæpə'rætsɪ] N Paparazzo *m*, Fotojäger *m*

papaya [pə'paɪə] N Papayabaum *m*; (= *fruit*) Papaya *f*

paper ['peɪpə'] **N a** (= *material*) Papier *nt*; **a piece of ~** ein Stück *nt* Papier; **a sheet of ~** ein Blatt *nt* Papier; **a writer who finds it hard to commit himself to ~** ein Schriftsteller, der nur zögernd etwas zu Papier bringt; **to get** or **put sth down on ~** etw schriftlich festhalten; **can we get your acceptance down on ~?** können wir Ihre Einwilligung schriftlich haben?; **on ~ they're the best firm** auf dem Papier ist das die beste Firma; **it's not worth the ~ it's written on** das ist schade ums Papier, auf dem es steht; **the walls are like ~** die Wände sind wie Pappe **b** (= *newspaper*) Zeitung *f*; **to write to the ~s about sth** Leserbriefe/einen Leserbrief über etw (*acc*) schreiben; **he's/his name is always in the ~s** er/sein Name steht ständig in der Zeitung **c papers** PL (= *identity papers*) Papiere *pl* **d papers** PL (= *writings, documents*) Papiere *pl*; **private ~s** private Unterlagen *pl* **e** (= *set of questions in exam*) Testbogen *m*; (= *exam*) (*Univ*) Klausur *f*; (*Sch*) Arbeit *f*; **to do a good ~ in maths** eine gute Mathematikklausur/-arbeit schreiben **f** (*academic*) Referat *nt*, Paper *nt* (*inf*); **he's going to give** or **read a ~ to the society** er wird vor der Gesellschaft ein Referat halten **g** (= *wallpaper*) Tapete *f* **h** (*Parl*) **a white ~** ein Weißbuch *nt* **i** (= *packet*) **a ~ of pins** ein Päckchen *nt* Stecknadeln **VT** *wall, room* tapezieren

▶ **paper over** VT *sep* überkleben; **to paper over the cracks** (*fig*) die Risse übertünchen; (= *cover up mistakes*) die Fehler übertünchen

paper *in cpds* Papier-; **paperback** N Taschenbuch *nt*, Paperback *nt*; **paperback** *in cpds* Taschenbuch-; **~ edition** Taschenbuchausgabe *f*; **~ book** Taschenbuch *nt*; **paper bag** N Papiertüte *f*; **they couldn't fight/play their way out of a (wet) ~** (*hum*) sie sind zu (überhaupt) nichts zu gebrauchen; **paper-bound** *book* broschiert; **paperboy** N Zeitungsjunge *m*; **paper chain** N Girlande *f*; **paper chase** N Schnitzeljagd *f*; **paperclip** N Büroklammer *f*; **paper cup** N Pappbecher *m*; **paper feed** N (*Comput*) Papiervorschub *m*; **paper girl** N Zeitungsmädchen *nt*; **paper handkerchief** N Tempo(taschen)tuch® *nt*, Papiertaschentuch *nt*; **paper handling** N (*Comput, of printer*) Papierführung *f*; **paperhanger** N Tapezierer(in) *m(f)*; **paperhanging** N Tapezieren *nt*; **paper jam** N (*of printer etc*) Papierstau *m*; **paperknife** N Brieföffner *m*; **paper lantern** N Lampion *m*; **paperless** ADJ papierlos; **paper mill** N Papierfabrik *f*, Papiermühle *f*; **paper money** N Papiergeld *nt*; **paper napkin** N Papierserviette *f*; **paper plate** N Pappteller *m*; **paper profit** N rechnerischer Gewinn; **paper round** N to have *or* do a ~ Zeitungen austragen; **paper shop** N (*Brit*) Zeitungsladen *m*; **paper tape** N Lochstreifen *m*; **paper-thin** ADJ *slice* hauchdünn; (*fig*) *wall* hauchdünn, hellhörig; **a ~ majority** eine hauchdünne Mehrheit; **paper tiger** N Papiertiger *m*; **paper tissue** N Papiertuch *nt*; **paper trail** N (*US*) belastende Unterlagen *pl*; **investigations found a ~ of documents** Nachforschungen brachten belastende Dokumente zutage; **paper tray** N (*Comput, for printer etc*) Papierschacht *m*; **paperweight** N Briefbeschwerer *m*; **paperwork** N Schreibarbeit *f*

papery ['peɪpərɪ] ADJ *plaster, pastry* bröckelig, krümelig; *skin* pergamenten

papier mâché ['pæpɪeɪ'mæʃeɪ] **N** Pappmaché *nt*, Pappmaschee *nt* ADJ aus Pappmaché

papism ['peɪpɪzəm] N (*pej*) Papismus *m*

papist ['peɪpɪst] N (*pej*) Papist(in) *m(f)*

papistry ['peɪpɪstrɪ] N (*pej*) Papismus *m*

papoose [pə'puːs] N Indianerbaby *nt*; (= *carrier for Indian baby*) Winkelbrettwiege *f*; (= *carrier for baby*) Tragegestell *nt*

pappadam, pappadum ['pæpədəm] N = **poppadom**

pappy ['pæpɪ] N (*US, inf*) Papi *m* (*inf*)

paprika ['pæprɪkə] N Paprika *m*

Pap smear ['pæpsmɪə'], **Pap test** ['pæptest] N (*esp US, Med*: = *cervical smear*) Pap-Test *m*

Papua ['pæpjʊə] N Papua *nt*

Papuan ['pæpjʊən] ADJ papuanisch **N a** Papua *mf* **b** (*Ling*) Papuasprache *f*

Papua New Guinea N Papua-Neuguinea *nt*

papyrus [pə'paɪərəs] N *pl* **papyri** [pə'paɪəraɪ] (= *plant*) Papyrusstaude *f*, Papyrus *m*; (= *paper*) Papyrus *m*; (= *scroll*) Papyrusrolle *f*, Papyrus *m*

par [pɑː'] N **a** (*Fin*) Nennwert *m*; **to be above/below ~** über/unter pari *or* dem Nennwert stehen; **at ~** zum Nennwert, al pari **b** to be on a ~ with sb/sth sich mit jdm/etw messen können; **this objection is on a ~ with Harry's** dieser Einwand liegt auf der gleichen Ebene wie Harrys; **he's nowhere near on a ~ with her** er kann ihr nicht das Wasser reichen; **culturally, the two countries are on a ~ or can be put on a ~** in kultureller Hinsicht sind die beiden Länder miteinander vergleichbar; **this puts him on a ~ with the champion** dadurch hat er mit dem Meister gleichgezogen; **an above-par performance** eine überdurchschnittliche Leistung **c** below ~ (*fig*) unter Niveau; **I'm feeling physically/mentally below** *or* **under ~** ich fühle mich körperlich/seelisch nicht auf der Höhe; **I'm not feeling quite up to ~ today** ich bin heute nicht ganz auf dem Damm (*inf*) *or* Posten (*inf*) **d** (*Golf*) Par *nt*; **~ three** Par 3; **a ~-five hole** ein Par-5-Loch *nt*; **to go round in under/over ~** sechs Schläge unter/über Par spielen; **that's ~ for the course for him** (*fig inf*) das kann man von ihm erwarten

par, para [pɑː'] *abbr of* **paragraph** Abschn.

parable ['pærəbl] N Parabel *f*, Gleichnis *nt*

parabola [pə'ræbələ] N (*Math*) Parabel *f*

parabolic [pærə'bɒlɪk] ADJ **a** Parabol-; *curve* parabelförmig; **~ mirror** Parabolspiegel *m* **b** (*Liter*) gleichnishaft

parabrake ['pærəbreɪk] N (*Aviat, Motor sport*) Bremsschirm *m*

paracetamol [pærə'siːtəmɒl] N Schmerztablette *f*

---

parachute ['pærəʃuːt] **N** Fallschirm *m*; **by ~** mit dem Fallschirm; **~ training** Übung *f* im Fallschirmspringen **VT** *troops* mit dem Fallschirm absetzen; *supplies* abwerfen; **to ~ food to sb** für jdn Lebensmittel abwerfen **VI** (*also* **parachute down**) (mit dem Fallschirm) abspringen; **they ~d into the wrong zone** sie sprangen über dem falschen Gebiet ab; **to ~ to safety** sich mit dem Fallschirm retten

▶ **parachute in** **VT** *sep* troops mit dem Fallschirm absetzen; *supplies* abwerfen **VI** (mit dem Fallschirm) abspringen

parachute: parachute brake N Bremsfallschirm *m*; **parachute drop** N (*by person*) (Fallschirm)absprung *m*; (*of supplies*) (Fallschirm)abwurf *m*; **there was a ~ of ten men** zehn Leute sprangen (mit dem Fallschirm) ab; **they got a ~ of medical supplies** medizinische Versorgungsmittel wurden (mit dem Fallschirm) für sie abgeworfen; **parachute jump** N Absprung *m* (mit dem Fallschirm); **parachute regiment** N Fallschirmjägertruppe *f*

parachutist ['pærəʃuːtɪst] N Fallschirmspringer(in) *m(f)*

parade [pə'reɪd] **N a** (= *procession*) Umzug *m*; (*Mil, of boy scouts, circus*) Parade *f*; (*political*) Demonstration *f*; (*fig*: = *long series*) (lange) Reihe; **church ~** Prozession *f*; **to be on ~** (*Mil*) eine Parade abhalten; **the regiment on ~** das Regiment bei der Parade; **in the school procession you'll be on ~ in front of the public** bei der Schulparade sieht dich alle Welt **b** (= *public walk*) Promenade *f* **c** (= *fashion parade*) Modenschau *f* **d** (= *display*) Parade *f*; (*of wealth etc*) Zurschaustellung *f* **e** (*US Mil*) (= *review*) Truppeninspektion *f*; (= *ground*) Truppenübungsplatz *m*, Exerzierplatz *m* **f** (= *shopping parade*) Reihe *f* Geschäfte *or* Läden **VT a** *troops* auf- *or* vorbeimarschieren lassen; *military might* demonstrieren; *placards* vor sich her tragen **b** (= *show off*) zur Schau stellen **VI** auf- *or* vorbeimarschieren; (*political party*) eine Demonstration veranstalten; **the strikers ~d through the town** die Streikenden zogen durch die Stadt; **she ~d up and down with the hat on** sie stolzierte mit ihrem Hut auf und ab

parade ground N Truppenübungsplatz *m*, Exerzierplatz *m*

paradigm ['pærədaɪm] N Musterbeispiel *nt*; (*Gram*) Paradigma *nt*

paradigmatic [pærədɪg'mætɪk] ADJ beispielhaft, paradigmatisch

paradise ['pærədaɪs] N (*lit, fig*) Paradies *nt*; **a shopper's ~** ein Einkaufsparadies *nt*; **an architect's ~** ein Paradies *nt* für Architekten; **living there must be ~ compared with this place** dort zu leben muss geradezu paradiesisch sein verglichen mit hier; **~, she sighed** himmlisch, seufzte sie; **I'm in ~** ich bin im Paradies; **~!** wie im Paradies!, paradiesisch!

paradisiac(al) [pærə'dɪzɪæk(əl)] ADJ paradiesisch

paradox ['pærədɒks] N Paradox *nt*, Paradoxon *nt* (*liter*); **life/he is full of ~es** das Leben/er steckt voller Widersprüche

paradoxical [pærə'dɒksɪkəl] ADJ paradox; *person* widersprüchlich

paradoxically [pærə'dɒksɪkəlɪ] ADV paradoxerweise; *worded* paradox

paraffin ['pærəfɪn] N (*Brit*: = *oil, US*: = *wax*) Paraffin *nt*

paraffin: paraffin lamp N Paraffinlampe *f*; **paraffin oil** N (*Brit*) Paraffinöl *nt*; **paraffin stove** N (*Brit*) Paraffinofen *m*; **paraffin wax** N Paraffin *nt*

paraglider ['pærəglaɪdə'] **N a** (= *person*) Paraglider(in) *m(f)* **b** (= *object*) Paraglider *m*

---

paragliding ['pærəglaɪdɪŋ] N Gleitschirmfliegen *nt*, Paragliding *nt*

paragon ['pærəgən] N Muster *nt*; **a ~ of virtue** ein Muster *nt* an Tugendhaftigkeit, ein Ausbund *m* an Tugend (*hum*)

paragraph ['pærəgrɑːf] **N a** Absatz *m*, Abschnitt *m*; **"new ~"** „(neuer) Absatz" **b** (= *brief article*) Notiz *f* **VT** (in Abschnitte) gliedern, aufgliedern

Paraguay ['pærəgwaɪ] N Paraguay *nt*

Paraguayan [pærə'gwaɪən] ADJ paraguayisch **N** Paraguayer(in) *m(f)*

parakeet ['pærəkiːt] N Sittich *m*

paraldehyde [pə'rældɪhaɪd] N Paraldehyd *nt*

paralegal [pærə'liːgəl] (*esp US*) **N** Rechtsassistent(in) *m(f)* ADJ **~ assistant** Rechtsassistent(in) *m(f)*; **~ secretary** Sekretär(in) und Rechtsassistent(in) *m(f)*

parallax ['pærəlæks] N Parallaxe *f*

parallel ['pærəlel] ADJ **a** *lines, streets* parallel; (*Comput*) parallel; **at this point the road and river are ~** an dieser Stelle verlaufen Straße und Fluss parallel (zueinander); **~ to** *or* **with** parallel zu *or* mit; **to lie ~ to** *or* **with sth** parallel zu etw liegen; **in a ~ direction** parallel; **~ connection** (*Elec*) Parallelschaltung *f*; **~ interface** (*Comput*) Parallelschnittstelle *f*; **~ market** (*Econ*) Parallelmarkt *m*; **~ printer** Paralleldrucker *m* **b** (*fig*) *career, development* vergleichbar, parallel verlaufend; *universe, talks, process* parallel; **a ~ case** ein Parallelfall *m*, ein vergleichbarer Fall; **the two systems developed along ~ lines** die Entwicklung der beiden Systeme verlief vergleichbar; **he argues along ~ lines to me** er argumentiert ähnlich wie ich **ADV to run ~** (*roads, careers*) parallel verlaufen (*to sth* zu etw); **to ski ~** Parallelslalom fahren **N a** (*Geometry*) Parallele *f* **b** (*Geog*) Breitenkreis *m*; **the 49th ~** der 49. Breitengrad **c** (*Elec*) **connected in ~** parallel geschaltet **d** (*fig*) Parallele *f*; **without ~** ohne Parallele; **it has no ~** es gibt dazu keine Parallele; **to draw a ~ between X and Y** eine Parallele zwischen X und Y ziehen; **in ~ with** parallel mit **VT** (*fig*) gleichen (+*dat*); **a case ~led only by ...** ein Fall, zu dem es nur eine einzige Parallele gibt, nämlich ...; **it is ~led by ...** es ist vergleichbar mit ...

parallel bars PL (*Sport*) Barren *m*

parallel import N (*Econ*) Parallelimport *m*

parallelism ['pærəlelɪzəm] N (*of lines*) Parallelität *f*; (*of cases also*) Ähnlichkeit *f*

parallelogram [pærə'leləʊgræm] N Parallelogramm *nt*

parallel processing N (*Comput*) Parallelverarbeitung *f*

parallel turn N (*Ski*) Parallelschwung *m*

Paralympic [pærə'lɪmpɪk] ADJ paralympisch; **~ Games** Paralympische Spiele *pl* **N** **Paralympics** PL Paralympics *pl* (*inf*), Paralympische Spiele *pl*, Behindertenolympiade *f*

paralysis [pə'ræləsɪs] N *pl* **paralyses** [pə'rælɪsiːz] Lähmung *f*, Paralyse *f*; (*of industry etc*) Lahmlegung *f*; **creeping ~** progressive Paralyse

paralytic [pærə'lɪtɪk] ADJ **a** paralytisch **b** (*Brit, inf*: = *very drunk*) voll dicht (*sl*), hacke(zu) (*inf*) **N** Paralytiker(in) *m(f)*, Gelähmte(r) *mf*

paralyze ['pærəlaɪz] VT **a** (*lit*) *person, legs* lähmen, paralysieren (*spec*) **b** (*fig*) *industry, economy* lahm legen; *traffic* zum Erliegen bringen, lahm legen

paralyzed ['pærəlaɪzd] ADJ **a** (*lit*) *person, legs* gelähmt; **he was left partially ~** er behielt teilweise Lähmungen zurück; **to be ~ in both legs** in beiden Beinen gelähmt sein; **~ from the neck/waist down** vom Hals/von der Hüfte abwärts gelähmt **b** (*fig*) **to be ~ with fear/shock/fright** vor Angst/Schock/Schreck (wie) gelähmt sein; **to be ~ by guilt** von Schuldgefühlen gepeinigt werden

paralyzing ['pærəlaɪzɪŋ] ADJ **a** (*lit*) **a ~ injury/ disease** eine Verletzung/Krankheit, die Lähmungen verursacht **b** (*fig*) *fear, jealousy, shyness* lähmend

paramedic [ˌpærə'medɪk] N Sanitäter(in) *m(f)*; (*in hospital*) medizinisch-technischer Assistent, medizinisch-technische Assistentin

parameter [pə'ræmɪtə'] N **a** (*Math*) Parameter *m* **b** **parameters** PL (= *framework, limits*) Rahmen *m*; **to define** *or* **establish** *or* **set the ~s of** *or* **for sth** die Parameter für etw festsetzen; **to fall within the ~s of sth** sich im Rahmen von etw bewegen *or* halten

paramilitary [ˌpærə'mɪlɪtərɪ] ADJ paramilitärisch

paramount ['pærəmaʊnt] ADJ Haupt-; **to be ~** Priorität haben; **our ~ aim** unser Hauptziel *nt*; **of ~ importance** von größter *or* höchster Wichtigkeit; **the interests of the child must be ~** den Interessen des Kindes muss Priorität eingeräumt werden

paramountcy ['pærəmaʊntsɪ] N größte Bedeutung

paramour ['pærəmʊə'] N (*old*) Liebhaber *m*, Buhle *mf* (*old*); (*hum*) (= *man*) Hausfreund *m* (*hum*); (= *woman*) Geliebte *f*

paranoia [ˌpærə'nɔɪə] N Paranoia *f*; (*inf*) Verfolgungswahn *m*; **this ~ which stops nations trusting each other** dieses krankhafte Misstrauen, das die Völker voneinander trennt

paranoiac [ˌpærə'nɔɪɪk] N Paranoiker(in) *m(f)* ADJ paranoisch

paranoid ['pærənɔɪd] ADJ paranoid; **or am I just being ~?** oder bilde ich mir das nur ein?; **aren't you being rather ~?** du scheinst unter Wahnvorstellungen zu leiden; **to be ~ about sth** von etw Wahnvorstellungen haben; **she's getting ~ about what other people think of her** die Angst vor dem, was andere von ihr denken, wird bei ihr langsam zur Manie; **~ schizophrenia** paranoide Schizophrenie

paranormal [ˌpærə'nɔːməl] ADJ paranormal N **the ~** das Paranormale

parapet ['pærəpɪt] N (*on rampart, of bridge*) Brüstung *f*; (*of well*) (Brunnen)wand *f*; **to put one's head above the ~** (*fig*) sich in die Schusslinie begeben; **to keep one's head below the ~** (*fig*) sich bedeckt halten

paraphernalia ['pærəfə'neɪlɪə] PL Brimborium *nt*, Drum und Dran *nt*

paraphrase ['pærəfreɪz] N Umschreibung *f*, Paraphrase *f* (*geh*) VT umschreiben, paraphrasieren (*geh*)

paraplegia [ˌpærə'pliːdʒə] N doppelseitige Lähmung

paraplegic [ˌpærə'pliːdʒɪk] ADJ doppelseitig gelähmt, paraplegisch (*spec*) N Paraplegiker(in) *m(f)* (*spec*)

parapsychology [ˌpærəsaɪ'kɒlədʒɪ] N Parapsychologie *f*

paras ['pærəz] PL (*Brit inf*) Fallschirmjäger *pl*

parasailing ['pærəˌseɪlɪŋ] N Gleitsegeln *nt*

parascending ['pærəˌsendɪŋ] N Paragliding *nt* (*bei dem der Start mit Hilfe eines Schnellboots erfolgt*)

parasite ['pærəsaɪt] N (*lit*) Parasit *m*, Schmarotzer *m*; (*fig*) Schmarotzer(in) *m(f)*

parasitic(al) [ˌpærə'sɪtɪk(əl)] ADJ parasitisch, parasitär (*also fig*); **to be ~ (up)on sth** von etw schmarotzen; **parasitic insect/plant** Parasit *m*, Schmarotzer *m*

parasitology [ˌpærəsɪ'tɒlədʒɪ] N Parasitologie *f*

parasol ['pærəsɒl] N Sonnenschirm *m*, Parasol *m* (*dated*)

paratactic [ˌpærə'tæktɪk] N (*Ling*) *clause, phrase* parataktisch, nebenordnend

paratrooper ['pærətruːpə'] N Fallschirmjäger(in) *m(f)*

paratroops ['pærətruːps] PL (= *soldiers*) Fallschirmjäger *pl*; (= *division also*) Fallschirmjägertruppe *f*

paratyphoid [ˌpærə'taɪfɔɪd] N Paratyphus *m*

---

parboil ['pɑːbɔɪl] VT vorkochen, halb gar kochen

parcel ['pɑːsl] N **a** (*esp Brit*) Paket *nt*; **to do sth up in a ~** etw als Paket packen; **~ post** Paketpost *f*; **to send sth (by) ~ post** etw als Paket schicken **b** **a ~ of land** ein Stück *nt* Land → **part N a**

▶ **parcel out** VT *sep land, inheritance* aufteilen; *business, tasks* delegieren

▶ **parcel up** VT *sep* als Paket verpacken

parcel bomb N (*Brit*) Paketbombe *f*

parcel delivery N Paketzustellung *f*

parcel(s) office N (*Brit Rail*) Paketstelle *f*

parch [pɑːtʃ] VT ausdörren, austrocknen

parched [pɑːtʃt] ADJ *lips, throat* ausgetrocknet; *land also* verdorrt; **I'm ~** ich habe furchtbaren Durst

parchment ['pɑːtʃmənt] N Pergament *nt*

pard [pɑːd] N (*obs* = *leopard*) Leopard *m*

pardner ['pɑːdnə'] N (*US inf hum*) Partner(in) *m(f)*, Kumpel *m* (*inf*)

pardon ['pɑːdn] N **a** (*Jur*) Begnadigung *f*; **there will be no ~ for deserters** für Fahnenflüchtige gibt es keinen Pardon; **to grant sb a ~** jdn begnadigen; **general ~** Amnestie *f* **b** **to beg sb's ~** jdn um Verzeihung bitten; **I beg your ~, but could you ...?** verzeihen *or* entschuldigen Sie bitte, könnten Sie ...?; **I beg your ~!** erlauben Sie mal!, ich muss doch sehr bitten!; (*beg*) **~?** (*Brit*) **I beg your ~?** (*Brit*) bitte?, wie bitte?; **I beg your ~, beg ~** (*apology*) verzeihen *or* entschuldigen Sie, Verzeihung, Entschuldigung; **a thousand ~s!** ich bitte tausendmal um Verzeihung *or* Entschuldigung!; **we beg the reader's ~ for ...** wir bitten den Leser für ... um Nachsicht

VT **a** (*Jur*) begnadigen **b** (= *forgive*) verzeihen, vergeben (*sb* jdm, *sth* etw); **to ~ sb sth** jdm etw verzeihen *or* vergeben; **~ me, but could you ...?** entschuldigen *or* verzeihen Sie bitte, könnten Sie ...?; **~ me!** Entschuldigung!, Verzeihung!; **~ me?** (*US*) bitte?, wie bitte?; **~ my mentioning it** entschuldigen *or* verzeihen Sie bitte, dass ich das erwähne; **~ me for asking!** (*iro*) entschuldige bitte, dass ich es gewagt habe zu fragen! (*iro*); **~ my French!** (*hum*) wenn ich den Ausdruck mal benutzen darf

pardonable ['pɑːdnəbl] ADJ *offence* entschuldbar; *weakness, mistake also* verzeihlich

pardonably ['pɑːdnəblɪ] ADV **he was ~ angry** sein Ärger war verständlich; **and ~ so** und das war verständlich

pare [pɛə'] VT **a** *nails* schneiden; *fruit, stick* schälen; **she ~d the skin off the apple** sie schälte den Apfel **b** (*fig*) *spending, budget* zurückschneiden; **~d to the bone** auf das Allernotwendigste zurückgeschnitten

▶ **pare back** VT *sep budget, costs, prices* zurückschneiden

▶ **pare down** VT *sep* (*fig*) *expenses* einschränken; *personnel* verringern; **to pare sth down to the minimum** etw auf ein Minimum beschränken

parent ['pɛərənt] N **a** Elternteil *m*; **~s** Eltern *pl*; **the duties of a ~** die elterlichen Pflichten; **his father was his favourite ~** von seinen Eltern hatte er seinen Vater am liebsten **b** (*fig*) Vorläufer *m*; **the Copernican theory is the ~ of modern astronomy** die moderne Astronomie geht auf die Lehren des Kopernikus zurück ATTR **~ birds** Vogeleltern *pl*; **~ plant** Mutterpflanze *f*; **~ ship** (*Space*) Mutterschiff *nt*

parentage ['pɛərəntɪdʒ] N Herkunft *f*; **of humble/uncertain ~** von einfacher/ungewisser Herkunft; **children of racially mixed ~** gemischtrassige Kinder *pl*

parental [pə'rentl] ADJ *care, guidance etc* elterlich *attr*; **~ choice** Wahlfreiheit *f* der Eltern, elterliche Wahl; **the ~ home** das Elternhaus *nt*; **~ leave** Elternzeit *f*

parent company N Muttergesellschaft *f*

---

parenthesis [pə'renθɪsɪs] N *pl* **parentheses** [pə'renθɪsiːz] Klammer(zeichen *nt*) *f*, Parenthese *f*; (= *words, statement*) Einschub *m*, Parenthese *f*; **in ~** in Klammern; **could I just say in ~ that ...** darf ich vielleicht einflechten, dass ...

parenthetical [ˌpærən'θetɪk(əl)] ADJ beiläufig; **could I make one ~ comment?** darf ich eine Bemerkung einflechten?

parenthetically [ˌpærən'θetɪkəlɪ] ADV nebenbei, beiläufig

parenthood ['pɛərənthʊd] N Elternschaft *f*; **the joys of ~** die Vater-/Mutterfreuden *pl*; **the idea of ~ frightened her** sie schrak zurück vor dem Gedanken, Mutter zu sein

parent power N Mitbestimmung *f* der Eltern

parent teacher association N (*Sch*) Lehrer- und Elternverband *m*

parer ['pɛərə'] N (= *apple-/fruit-parer*) Schälmesser *nt*

par excellence [ˌpɑːr'eksəlɑːns] ADV par excellence

parhelion [pɑː'hiːlɪən] N (*Astron*) Nebensonne *f*

pariah [pə'raɪə] N (*lit*) Paria *m*; (*fig also*) Ausgestoßene(r) *mf*

parietal [pə'raɪtl] ADJ (*Anat*) parietal; **~ bone** Scheitelbein *nt*

pari mutuel [ˌpærɪ'mjuːtʊəl] N Wettsystem, bei dem der gesamte Einsatz abzüglich der Verwaltungskosten prozentual an die Gewinner verteilt wird

paring: paring gouge ['pɛərɪŋˌgaʊdʒ] N (*Tech*) Hohlbeitel *m*; **paring knife** ['pɛərɪŋˌnaɪf] N Schälmesser *nt*

parings ['pɛərɪŋz] PL (*of nails*) abgeschnittene Fingernägel *pl*; (*of apple*) Schalen *pl*

pari passu ['pærɪ'pæsuː] ADV gleichlaufend, synchron

Paris ['pærɪs] N Paris *nt*

parish ['pærɪʃ] N Gemeinde *f*; (= *district also*) Pfarrbezirk *m*, Pfarre *f*, Pfarrei *f*

parish: parish church N Pfarrkirche *f*; **parish clerk** N Verwaltungsangestellte(r) des Gemeinderates; **parish council** N Gemeinderat *m*

parishioner [pə'rɪʃənə'] N Gemeinde(mit)glied *nt*

parish: parish priest N Pfarrer *m*; **parish pump politics** N Kirchturmpolitik *f*; **parish register** N Kirchenbuch *nt*, Kirchenregister *nt*

Parisian [pə'rɪzɪən] ADJ Pariser *inv*; **she is ~** sie ist Pariserin N Pariser(in) *m(f)*

parity ['pærɪtɪ] N **a** (= *equality*) Gleichstellung *f*; (*of opportunities*) Gleichheit *f*; **~ of treatment** Gleichstellung *f*; **~ of pay** Lohngleichheit *f* **b** (= *equivalence*) Übereinstimmung *f*; **by ~ of reasoning** mit den gleichen Argumenten **c** (*Fin, Sci*) Parität *f*; **the ~ of the dollar** die Dollarparität *f* (*US Agr*) Preisparität *f* **e** (*Comput*) Parität *f*; **odd/even ~** ungerade/gerade Parität *f*

park [pɑːk] N **a** Park *m*; **national ~** Nationalpark *m* **b** (*Brit Sport:* = *field*) (Sport)platz *m* **c** (*US:* = *car park*) Parkplatz *m* **d** (*Mil*) Arsenal *nt* **e** (*Aut*) **to put/leave a car in ~** das Getriebe in Parkstellung bringen/lassen

VT **a** *car* parken; *bicycle* abstellen; **a ~ed car** ein parkendes Auto; **there's been a car ~ed outside for days** draußen parkt schon seit Tagen ein Auto; **he was very badly ~ed** er hatte miserabel geparkt **b** (*inf:* = *put*) *luggage etc* abstellen; **he ~ed himself right in front of the fire** er pflanzte sich direkt vor den Kamin (*inf*); **we ~ed the children with the neighbours** wir haben die Kinder bei den Nachbarn abgegeben *or* gelassen; **find somewhere to ~ your backside** such dir was, wo du dich platzen kannst (*hum*) **c** (*Comput*) *hard disk* parken

VI parken; **there was nowhere to ~** es gab irgendwo einen Parkplatz; **to find a place to ~** einen Parkplatz finden; (*in line of cars*) eine Parklücke finden

parka [ˈpɑːkə] N Parka m

park-and-ride [ˌpɑːkənˈraɪd] N Park-and-Ride- -System nt

park bench N Parkbank f

parking [ˈpɑːkɪŋ] N Parken nt; **women are usually good at ~** Frauen sind gewöhnlich gut im Einparken; **there's no ~ on this street** in dieser Straße ist Parken verboten or ist Parkverbot; **there's plenty of ~** es gibt genug Parkplätze; **"no ~"** „Parken verboten"; **"good ~ facilities"** „gute Parkmöglichkeiten"; **"parking for 50 cars"** „50 (Park)plätze"

parking: parking attendant N Parkplatzwächter(in) m(f); **parking bay** N Parkbucht f; **parking brake** N (US Aut) Handbremse f; **parking disk** N Parkscheibe f; **parking fine** N Geldbuße f (für Parkvergehen); **parking garage** N (US) Parkhaus nt; **parking level** N (in multi-storey car park) Parkdeck nt; **parking lot** N (US) Parkplatz m; **parking meter** N Parkuhr f; **parking offender** N Parksünder(in) m(f); **parking orbit** N (Space) Parkbahn f; **parking place** N (for single vehicle) Parkplatz m; **parking space** N (for single vehicle) Parkplatz m, Abstellfläche f; **parking ticket** N Strafzettel m, Knöllchen nt (inf)

Parkinson's (disease) [ˈpɑːkɪnsənz(dɪˈziːz)] N parkinsonsche Krankheit

park: park keeper N Parkwächter(in) m(f); **parkland** N Grünland nt; **park ranger, park warden** N (in national park) Nationalparkwächter(in) m(f), Aufseher(in) m(f) in einem Nationalpark; (in forest) Förster(in) m(f); (in game reserve) Wildhüter(in) m(f); **parkway** N (US) Allee f

parky [ˈpɑːkɪ] ADJ (+er) (Brit, inf) kühl, frisch; **(it's a bit) ~ today** ganz schön kühl heute

parlance [ˈpɑːləns] N **in common/modern ~** im allgemeinen/modernen Sprachgebrauch; **in technical/legal ~** in der Fachsprache/Rechtssprache

parley [ˈpɑːlɪ] N Verhandlungen pl VI verhandeln

parliament [ˈpɑːləmənt] N Parlament nt; **to get into ~** ins Parlament kommen; **to open ~** das Parlament eröffnen; **~ reconvenes in the early autumn** das Parlament tritt Anfang Herbst wieder zusammen; **the German ~** der Bundestag; **the Swiss ~** die Bundesversammlung; **the Austrian ~** der Nationalrat

parliamentarian [ˌpɑːləmənˈtɛərɪən] N Parlamentarier(in) m(f)

parliamentarianism [ˌpɑːləmənˈtɛərɪənɪzəm] N Parlamentarismus m

parliamentary [ˌpɑːləˈmentərɪ] ADJ parlamentarisch; **the ~ Labour Party** die Parlamentsfraktion der Labour Party; **~ debates** Parlamentsdebatten pl; **~ seat** Parlamentssitz m

parliamentary: parliamentary agent N Parlamentsbeauftragte(r) mf; **parliamentary candidate** N Parlamentskandidat(in) m(f); **parliamentary election** N Parlamentswahlen pl; **parliamentary private secretary** N (Brit) Abgeordnete(r), der/die einem Minister zuarbeitet; **parliamentary privilege** N parlamentarische Sonderrechte pl; (= immunity) parlamentarische Immunität

parlor car N (US) Salonwagen m

parlour, (US) **parlor** [ˈpɑːlə] N **a** (in house) Salon m **b** (= beauty parlour, massage parlour etc) Salon m; **ice-cream ~** Eisdiele f

parlour: parlour game N Gesellschaftsspiel nt; **parlourmaid** N (Brit) Dienstmädchen nt

parlous [ˈpɑːləs] ADJ (old, liter) **to be in a ~ state** sich in einem prekären Zustand befinden

Parma ham [ˈpɑːməˈhæm] N Parmaschinken m

Parmesan [ˌpɑːmɪˈzæn] N Parmesan m

Parnassus [pɑːˈnæsəs] N **Mount ~** der Parnass

parochial [pəˈrəʊkɪəl] ADJ **a** (Eccl) Pfarr-; **~ ministry** Pfarramt nt; **the ~ duties of a priest** die Aufgaben eines Gemeindepfarrers; **the ~ boundaries** die Grenzen des Pfarrbezirks; **~ school** (US) Konfessionsschule f **b** (fig) attitude, person engstirnig; mind, ideas beschränkt; **he's so ~ in his outlook** er hat einen sehr beschränkten Gesichtskreis

parochialism [pəˈrəʊkɪəlɪzəm] N (fig) Engstirnigkeit f

parodist [ˈpærədɪst] N Parodist(in) m(f)

parody [ˈpærədɪ] **N a** Parodie f (of auf +acc) **b** (= travesty) Abklatsch m; **a ~ of justice** eine Parodie auf die Gerechtigkeit **VT** parodieren

parole [pəˈrəʊl] **N a** (Jur) Bewährung f; (= temporary release) Strafunterbrechung f, Kurzurlaub m; **to let sb out on ~** jdn auf Bewährung entlassen; (temporarily) jdm Strafunterbrechung or Kurzurlaub gewähren; **to be on ~** unter Bewährung stehen; (temporarily) auf Kurzurlaub sein; **he's on six months' ~** er hat sechs Monate Bewährung(sfrist); **to break one's ~** den Kurzurlaub zur Flucht benutzen **b** (Mil) Parole f **VT** prisoner auf Bewährung entlassen; (temporarily) Strafunterbrechung or Kurzurlaub gewähren (+dat)

paroxysm [ˈpærəksɪzəm] N Anfall m; **~ of grief** Verzweiflungsanfall m; **to be seized by a ~ of rage** einen Wutanfall bekommen; **~s of laughter** ein Lachkrampf m

parquet [ˈpɑːkeɪ] N **a** Parkett nt; **~ floor** Parkettboden m **b** (US Theat) Parkett nt; **~ circle** Parkett nt

parquetry [ˈpɑːkɪtrɪ] N Mosaikparkett nt

parricide [ˈpærɪsaɪd] N (= act) Vater-/Muttermord m; (= person) Vater-/Muttermörder(in) m(f)

parrot [ˈpærət] **N** Papagei m; **he felt as sick as a ~** (Brit inf) ihm war kotzübel (inf); **he was as sick as a ~** (Brit inf: = vomited) er kotzte wie ein Reiher (inf) **VT** (wie ein Papagei) nachplappern (sb jdm)

parrot: parrot cry N (fig) populäres Schlagwort; **parrot disease** N Papageienkrankheit f; **parrot-fashion** ADV **to repeat sth ~** etw wie ein Papagei nachplappern; **he learned the poem ~** er lernte das Gedicht stur auswendig; **parrot fever** N Papageienkrankheit f; **parrotfish** N Papageifisch m; **parrot-like** ADJ papageienhaft; **this ~ way of learning** dies sture Auswendiglernen; **parrot phrase** N = parrot cry

parry [ˈpærɪ] **N** (Fencing, fig) Parade f; (Boxing) Abwehr f **VT** (Fencing, fig) parieren; (Boxing) blow abwehren; ball, shot abwehren **VI** (Fencing) parieren; (Boxing, Ftbl) abwehren

parse [pɑːz] **VT** grammatisch analysieren **VI** analysieren; **this sentence doesn't ~ very easily** die Struktur dieses Satzes ist nicht leicht zu analysieren

parser [ˈpɑːsə] N (Comput) Parser m

parsimonious [ˌpɑːsɪˈməʊnɪəs] ADJ geizig

parsimoniously [ˌpɑːsɪˈməʊnɪəslɪ] ADV geizig; **he ~ refused to lend me any money at all** er war zu geizig, mir auch nur einen einzigen Cent zu leihen

parsimony [ˈpɑːsɪmənɪ] N Geiz m

parsing [ˈpɑːsɪŋ] N (Gram) Syntaxanalyse f; (Comput) Parsing nt

parsley [ˈpɑːslɪ] N Petersilie f

parsnip [ˈpɑːsnɪp] N Pastinak m, Pastinake f

parson [ˈpɑːsn] N Pfarrer m, Pastor m, Pfaffe m (pej); **~'s nose** Bürzel m, Sterz m

parsonage [ˈpɑːsənɪdʒ] N Pfarrhaus nt

Parsons table [ˈpɑːsnzˈteɪbl] N (US) Tisch m aus Plastik

part [pɑːt] **N a** (= portion, fragment) Teil m; **5 ~s of sand to 1 of cement** 5 Teile Sand auf ein (-en) Teil Zement; **it's 3 ~s gone** drei Viertel sind schon weg; **the stupid ~ of it that ...** das Dumme daran ist, dass ...; **you haven't heard the best ~ yet** ihr habt ja das Beste noch gar nicht gehört; **the book is good in ~s** teilweise or streckenweise ist das Buch gut; **in ~** teilweise, zum Teil; **the greater ~ of it/of the work is done** der größte Teil davon/der Arbeit ist fertig; **it is in large ~ finished/true** das ist zum großen Teil erledigt/wahr; **a ~ of the country/city I don't know** eine Gegend, die ich nicht kenne; **this is in great ~ due to ...** das liegt größtenteils or vor allem an (+dat) ...; **during the darkest ~ of the night** in tiefster Nacht; **I kept ~ of it for myself** ich habe einen Teil davon für mich behalten; **I lost ~ of the manuscript** ich habe einen Teil des Manuskripts verloren; **that's ~ of the truth** das ist ein Teil der Wahrheit; **for the most ~** zum größten Teil; **her performance was for the most ~ well executed** ihre Leistung war im Großen und Ganzen gelungen; **in the latter ~ of the year** gegen Ende des Jahres; **the remaining ~ of our holidays** der Rest unseres Urlaubs; **~ of him wanted to call her, ~ of him wanted to forget about her** ein Teil von ihm wollte sie anrufen, ein anderer sie vergessen; **she's become (a) ~ of me** sie ist ein Teil von mir geworden; **it's all ~ of growing up** das gehört alles zum Erwachsenwerden dazu; **to be ~ and parcel of sth** fester Bestandteil einer Sache (gen) sein; **it is ~ and parcel of the job** das gehört zu der Arbeit dazu; **are transport costs included? – yes, they're all ~ and parcel of the scheme** sind die Transportkosten enthalten? – ja, es ist alles inbegriffen

b (Mech, of kit etc) Teil nt; **spare ~** Ersatzteil nt; **moving ~s** bewegliche Teile pl

c (Gram) **~ of speech** Wortart f; **principal ~s of a verb** Stammformen pl

d (of series) Folge f; (of serial) Fortsetzung f; (of encyclopaedia etc) Lieferung f; **end of ~ one** (TV) Ende des ersten Teils

e (= share, role) (An)teil m, Rolle f; (Theat) Rolle f, Part m (geh); **to play one's ~** (fig) seinen Beitrag leisten; **to take ~ in sth** an etw (dat) teilnehmen, bei etw (dat) mitmachen, sich an etw (dat) beteiligen; **who is taking ~?** wer macht mit?, wer ist dabei?; **he's taking ~ in the play** er spielt in dem Stück mit; **in the ~ of Lear** in der Rolle des Lear; **he looks the ~** (Theat) die Rolle passt zu ihm; (fig) so sieht (d)er auch aus; **to play a ~** (Theat, fig) eine Rolle spielen; **to play no ~ in sth** (person) nicht an etw (dat) beteiligt sein; **we want no ~ of it** wir wollen damit nichts zu tun haben; **he's just playing a ~** (fig) der tut nur so

f (Mus) Stimme f, Part m; **the soprano ~** der Sopranpart, die Sopranstimme; **the piano ~** der Klavierpart, die Klavierstimme; **to sing in ~s** mehrstimmig singen

g **parts** PL (= region) Gegend f; **from all ~s** überallher, von überall her; **in** or **around these ~s** hier in der Gegend, in dieser Gegend; **in foreign ~s** in der Fremde, in fremden Ländern; **what ~s are you from?** aus welcher Gegend sind Sie?; **he's not from these ~s** er ist nicht aus dieser Gegend or nicht von hier

h (= side) Seite f; **to take sb's ~** sich auf jds Seite (acc) stellen, für jdn Partei ergreifen; **for my ~** was mich betrifft, meinerseits; **a miscalculation on my ~** eine Fehlkalkulation meinerseits; **on the ~ of** vonseiten (+gen), von Seiten (+gen), seitens (+gen)

i **to take sth in good ~** etw nicht übel nehmen

j **a man of ~s** ein vielseitiges Talent; **a man of many ~s** ein vielseitiger Mensch

k (US: in hair) Scheitel m

l **parts** PL (= male genitals) Geschlechtsteile pl

ADV teils, teilweise; **is it X or Y? – ~ one and ~ the other** ist es X oder Y? – teils (das eine), teils (das andere); **it is ~ iron and ~ copper** es ist teils aus Eisen, teils aus Kupfer; **it was ~ eaten** es war halb aufgegessen; **he's ~ French, ~ Scottish and ~ Latvian** er ist teils Franzose, teils Schotte und teils Lette

VT a (= divide) teilen; hair scheiteln; curtain zur Seite schieben; legs aufmachen; lips öffnen; **the police tried to ~ the crowd** (= make path through) die Polizei versuchte, eine Gasse durch die Menge zu bahnen

b (= separate) trennen; **to ~ sb from sb/sth** jdn von jdm/etw trennen; **till death us do ~** bis dass der Tod uns scheidet; **she's not easily ~ed from her money** sie trennt sich nicht gern von ihrem Geld; **to ~ company** sich trennen; **to ~ company with sb/sth** sich von jdm/etw trennen; (*in opinion*) mit jdm nicht gleicher Meinung sein; **on that issue, I must ~ company with you** in dem Punkt gehen unsere Meinungen auseinander

Ⅵ **a** (= *divide*) sich teilen; (*curtains*) sich öffnen; **her lips ~ed in a smile** ihre Lippen öffneten sich zu einem Lächeln

b (= *separate*) (*people*) sich trennen; (*things*) sich lösen, abgehen; **to ~ from** or **with sb** sich von jdm trennen; **we ~ed friends** wir gingen als Freunde auseinander, wir schieden als Freunde (*geh*); **to ~ with sth** sich von etw trennen; **to ~ with money** Geld ausgeben or lockermachen (*inf*); **to ~ from this life** (*liter*) aus diesem Leben scheiden (*geh*)

partake [pɑːˈteɪk] *pret* **partook**, *ptp* **partaken** [pɑːˈteɪkn] **Ⅵ** (*form*) **a** **to ~ of** (*food, drink*) zu sich (+*dat*) nehmen; **will you ~ of a glass of sherry?** darf ich Ihnen ein Glas Sherry anbieten?; **will** or **do you ~?** (*form, hum*) darf or kann ich Ihnen etwas anbieten? **b** (= *share in*) **to ~ of an experience** an einer Erfahrung (*dat*) teilhaben, jds Erfahrung (*acc*) teilen **c** **to ~ of a quality** eine Eigenschaft an sich (*dat*) haben; **to a certain extent he ~s of his father's arrogance** er hat etwas von der Arroganz seines Vaters **d** **to ~ in sth** (*in activity*) an etw (*dat*) teilnehmen

parterre [pɑːˈteə] N (*US*) Parterre *nt*

part exchange N **to offer/take sth in ~** etw in Zahlung geben/nehmen

parthenogenesis [ˌpɑːθɪnəʊˈdʒenɪsɪs] N Parthenogenese *f*, Jungfernzeugung *f*

Parthian shot [ˈpɑːθɪənˈʃɒt] N zum Abschied fallen gelassene spitze Bemerkung

partial [ˈpɑːʃəl] ADJ **a** (= *not complete*) Teil-, partiell (*geh*), teilweise; *paralysis, eclipse* teilweise, partiell; **a ~ success** ein Teilerfolg *m*, ein teilweiser Erfolg; **to make a ~ recovery** eine teilweise Erholung or Genesung durchmachen; **to give sth ~ support** eine Sache teilweise unterstützen; **to reach a ~ agreement** teilweise Übereinstimmung erzielen

b (= *biased*) voreingenommen; *judgement* parteiisch

c **to be ~ to sth** eine Vorliebe or Schwäche für etw haben; **after a while I became rather ~ to it** nach einiger Zeit hatte ich eine ziemliche Vorliebe dafür entwickelt; **to be ~ to doing sth** eine Vorliebe or Schwäche dafür haben, etw zu tun

partiality [ˌpɑːʃɪˈælɪtɪ] N **a** (= *bias*) Voreingenommenheit *f*; (*of judgement*) Parteilichkeit *f*; **without ~** unvoreingenommen, unparteiisch **b** (= *liking*) Vorliebe *f* (*for* für), Schwäche *f* (*for* für)

partially [ˈpɑːʃəlɪ] ADV **a** (= *not completely*) zum Teil, teilweise; **~ deaf** eingeschränkt hörfähig; **~ clothed** halb angezogen, teilweise bekleidet **b** (= *in part*) zum Teil, teils; **~ because ...** zum Teil deswegen, weil ... **c** (= *with bias*) parteiisch

partially sighted ADJ eingeschränkt sehfähig

participant [pɑːˈtɪsɪpənt] N Teilnehmer(in) *m(f)* (*in* +*gen*, an +*dat*); (*in scuffle etc*) Beteiligte(r) *mf* (*in* +*gen*, an +*dat*); **the bank will not be a ~ in this project** die Bank wird sich nicht an diesem Vorhaben beteiligen

participate [pɑːˈtɪsɪpeɪt] **Ⅵ** **a** (= *take part*) sich beteiligen, teilnehmen (*in* an +*dat*); **to ~ in sport** (*Sch*) am Schulsport teilnehmen; **the council was accused of participating in a housing swindle** man beschuldigte die Stadtverwaltung der Beteiligung an einem Bauschwindel; **it's no good complaining of being lonely if you don't ~** es hat keinen Sinn, über deine Einsamkeit zu klagen, wenn du nirgends mitmachst **b** (= *share*) beteiligt sein (*in* an +*dat*); **to ~ in sb's sorrow** an jds Kummer (*dat*) Anteil nehmen

participation [pɑːˌtɪsɪˈpeɪʃən] N Beteiligung *f*; (*in competition etc*) Teilnahme *f*; (= *worker partici-*

pation) Mitbestimmung *f*; **~ in the profits** Gewinnbeteiligung *f*

participative [pɑːˈtɪsɪpətɪv] ADJ mitbestimmend; **a genuinely ~ democracy** eine Demokratie, in der es echte Mitbestimmung gibt

participator [pɑːˈtɪsɪpeɪtə] N Teilnehmer(in) *m(f)*

participatory [ˌpɑːtɪsɪˈpeɪtərɪ] ADJ teilnehmend; (*Ind*) auf Mitbestimmung ausgerichtet; **~ democracy** Bürgerdemokratie *f*

participial [ˌpɑːtɪˈsɪpɪəl] ADJ Partizipial-, partizipial; **~ clause** Partizipialsatz *m*

participle [ˈpɑːtɪsɪpl] N Partizip *nt* → **present, past**

particle [ˈpɑːtɪkl] N **a** (*of sand etc*) Teilchen *nt*, Körnchen *nt*; (*Phys*) Teilchen *nt*; (*fig*) Körnchen *nt*; **~ of dust, dust ~** Stäubchen *nt*, Staubkörnchen *nt*, Staubpartikel *nt* (*spec*); **food ~s** Nahrungspartikel *pl*; **there's not a ~ of truth in it** darin steckt kein Körnchen Wahrheit **b** (*Gram*) Partikel *f*

particle: particle accelerator N Teilchenbeschleuniger *m*; **particle board** N (*US*) Spanplatte *f*

parti-coloured, (*US*) **parti-colored** [ˈpɑːtɪˌkʌləd] ADJ bunt, vielfarbig

particular [pɑːˈtɪkjʊlə] ❍ 6.3, 7.5, 26.2 **ADJ** **a** (= *as against others*) **this ~ house is very nice** dies (eine) Haus ist sehr hübsch; **it varies according to the ~ case** das ist von Fall zu Fall verschieden; **in this ~ instance** in diesem besonderen Fall; **in certain ~ cases** in einigen besonderen Fällen; **there's a ~ town in France where ...** in Frankreich gibt es eine Stadt, wo ...; **is there any one ~ city you prefer?** bevorzugen Sie eine bestimmte Stadt?

b (= *special*) besondere(r, s); *problem* besondere(r, s), bestimmt; **in ~** besonders, vor allem, insbesondere; **the wine in ~ was excellent** vor allem der Wein war hervorragend; **nothing in ~** nichts Besonderes or Bestimmtes; **is there anything in ~ you'd like?** haben Sie einen besonderen Wunsch?; **did you want to speak to anyone in ~?** wollten Sie mit jemand(em) Bestimmtem sprechen?; **I'm not waiting for anyone in ~** ich warte auf niemand Bestimmten; **he's a ~ friend of mine** er ist ein guter Freund von mir; **for no ~ reason** aus keinem besonderen or bestimmten Grund; **no ~ reason for sth/ for doing sth** kein besonderer Grund für etw/ dafür, etw zu tun; **at a ~ time** zu einer bestimmten Zeit; **at that ~ time** zu (genau) diesem Zeitpunkt; **in a ~ way** auf bestimmte Art und Weise; **to be of ~ interest** von besonderem Interesse sein; **to be of ~ concern to sb** jdm ein besonderes Anliegen sein; **with ~ reference to ...** mit besonderem Hinweis auf ... (*acc*); **to take ~ care to ...** besonders darauf achten, dass ...

c (= *fussy, fastidious*) eigen; (= *choosy*) wählerisch; **he is very ~ about cleanliness/his children's education** er nimmt es mit der Sauberkeit/der Erziehung seiner Kinder sehr genau; **he's ~ about his car** er ist sehr eigen or pingelig (*inf*) mit seinem Auto; **I'm ~ about my friends** ich suche mir meine Freunde genau aus; **you can't be too ~** man kann gar nicht wählerisch genug sein; **I'm not too ~ (about it)** es kommt mir nicht so darauf an, mir ist es gleich; **she was most ~ about it** (= *was definite*) sie bestand darauf

N **a** Besondere(s) *nt*; **the ~ and the general** das Besondere und das Allgemeine

b **particulars** PL Einzelheiten *pl*; (*about person*) Personalien *pl*; **in this ~** in diesem Punkt; **correct in every ~** in jedem Punkt richtig; **for further ~s apply to the personnel manager** weitere Auskünfte erteilt der Personalchef; **to go into ~s** ins Detail or in Einzelheiten gehen; **to give ~s** Angaben machen; **please give full ~s** bitte genaue Angaben machen

particularism [pɑːˈtɪkjʊlərɪzəm] N (*Pol*) Partikularismus *m*; (*adherence to one's own aims*) Sonderbestrebungen *pl*; (*of country*) Kleinstaaterei *f* **b** (*Rel*) Lehre *f* von der Gnadenwahl

particularity [pəˌtɪkjʊˈlærɪtɪ] N **a** (= *individuality*) Besonderheit *f* **b** (= *detailedness*) Ausführlichkeit *f* **c** (= *fastidiousness*) Eigenheit *f*

particularize [pəˈtɪkjʊləraɪz] **VT** spezifizieren, genau angeben **Ⅵ** ins Detail or Einzelne gehen; **he did not ~** er nannte keine Einzelheiten

particularly [pəˈtɪkjʊləlɪ] ADV besonders, vor allem; **everybody, but ~ Smith** alle, aber vor allem or ganz besonders Smith; **he said most ~ not to do it** er hat ausdrücklich gesagt, dass man das nicht tun soll; **do you want it ~ for tomorrow?** brauchen Sie es unbedingt morgen?; **we are ~ pleased to have with us today ...** wir freuen uns besonders, heute ... bei uns zu haben; **he was not ~ pleased** er war nicht besonders erfreut; **not ~** nicht besonders; **it's important, ~ since time is getting short** es ist wichtig, zumal die Zeit knapp wird

parting [ˈpɑːtɪŋ] **N** **a** Abschied *m*; **~ is such sweet sorrow** (*prov*) o süßer Abschiedsschmerz!; **after the ~ of the ways** nachdem sich ihre Wege getrennt hatten; **is this the ~ of the ways then?** das ist also das Ende (unserer Beziehung)?; **this meeting was the ~ of the ways for the Leninists and the Trotskyites** seit dieser Tagung sind die Leninisten und Trotzkisten getrennte Wege gegangen **b** (*Brit: in hair*) Scheitel *m*

ADJ Abschieds-, abschließend; **a ~ present/kiss** ein Abschiedsgeschenk *nt*/-kuss *m*; **Charles knows all about it already, was her ~ shot** Charles weiß schon alles, schleuderte sie ihm nach; **he made a ~ threat** zum Abschied stieß er eine Drohung aus; **his ~ words** seine Abschiedsworte *pl*

partisan [ˌpɑːtɪˈzæn] **ADJ** **a** parteiisch (*esp pej*), parteilich; *person* voreingenommen; *argument* parteiisch, voreingenommen; **~ politics** Parteipolitik *f*; **~ spirit** Partei- or Vereinsgeist *m* **b** (*Mil*) Partisanen-; **~ warfare** Partisanenkrieg *m* **N** Parteigänger(in) *m(f)* **b** (*Mil*) Partisan(in) *m(f)*, Freischärler(in) *m(f)*

partisanship [ˌpɑːtɪˈzænʃɪp] N Parteilichkeit *f*

partition [pɑːˈtɪʃən] **N** **a** Teilung *f* **b** (= *wall*) Trennwand *f* **c** (= *section*) Abteilung *f* **VT** *country* teilen, spalten; *room* aufteilen

▶ **partition off** VT *sep* abteilen, abtrennen

partitive [ˈpɑːtɪtɪv] ADJ (*Gram*) partitiv

part load N (*Comm*) Teilladung *f*

partly [ˈpɑːtlɪ] ADV zum Teil, teilweise, teils

partner [ˈpɑːtnə] **N** Partner(in) *m(f)*; (*in limited company also*) Gesellschafter(in) *m(f)*; (*in crime*) Komplize *m*, Komplizin *f*; **they were/became ~s in crime** sie waren/wurden Komplizen; **junior/senior ~** Junior-/Seniorpartner(in) *m(f)* **VT to ~ sb** jds Partner sein; **to be ~ed by sb** jdn zum Partner haben

partnership [ˈpɑːtnəʃɪp] N **a** Partnerschaft *f*, Gemeinschaft *f*; (*in sport, dancing etc*) Paar *nt*; **we're** or **we make a pretty good ~** wir sind ein ziemlich gutes Paar; **a relationship based on ~** eine partnerschaftliche Beziehung; **to do sth in ~ with sb** etw mit jdm gemeinsam or in Zusammenarbeit machen **b** (*Comm*) Personengesellschaft *f*; **to enter into a ~** eine Gesellschaft eintreten; **to go into ~ with sb** mit jdm eine Personengesellschaft gründen; **general ~** offene Handelsgesellschaft; **he left the ~** er ist aus der Gesellschaft ausgeschieden

partook [pɑːˈtʊk] *pret* of **partake**

part: part owner N Mitbesitzer(in) *m(f)*, Mitinhaber(in) *m(f)*; **part payment** N Teilzahlung *f*

partridge [ˈpɑːtrɪdʒ] N Rebhuhn *nt*

part: part song N (= *song*) mehrstimmiges Lied; (= *genre*) mehrstimmiger Gesang; **part-time** **ADJ** Teilzeit-; **~ job/worker** Teilzeitarbeit *f*/-arbeiter(in) *m(f)*; **I'm just ~** ich arbeite nur Teilzeit; **on a ~ basis** auf Teilzeitbasis **ADV can I do the job ~?** kann ich (auf) Teilzeit arbeiten?; **she only teaches ~** sie unterrichtet nur stundenweise; **she is studying ~** sie ist Teilzeitstudentin; **part-timer** N Teilzeitbeschäftigte(r) *mf*

parturition [ˌpɑːtjʊəˈrɪʃən] N (*form*) Entbindung *f*

partway [ˈpɑːtˈweɪ] ADV (*inf*, = *halfway*) halb; ~ **through the meal she became suspicious** mitten während des Essens schöpfte sie Verdacht

part work N (*printing*) Partwork *nt*, Lieferungswerk *nt*, Fortsetzungswerk *nt*

party [ˈpɑːtɪ] ✪ 25.2 **a** (*Pol*) Partei *f*; **to be a member of the ~** Parteimitglied sein, in der Partei sein (*inf*)
b (= *group*) Gruppe *f*, Gesellschaft *f*; (*Mil*) Kommando *nt*, Trupp *m*; **a ~ of tourists** eine Reisegesellschaft; **we were a ~ of five** wir waren zu fünft; **I was one of the ~** ich war dabei; **to join sb's ~** sich jdm anschließen
c (= *celebration*) Party *f*, Fete *f* (*inf*); (*more formal*) Gesellschaft *f*; **to have** *or* **give** *or* **throw** (*inf*) **a ~** eine Party geben *or* machen *or* schmeißen (*inf*); **at the ~** auf der Party; (*more formal*) bei der Gesellschaft; **what does he bring to the ~?** (*fig*) was steuert er bei?
d (*Jur, fig*) Partei *f*; **a third ~** ein Dritter *m*; **the third ~** der Dritte *m*; **the parties to a dispute** die streitenden Parteien; **to be a ~ to an agreement** einer Übereinkunft (*dat*) zustimmen, **to be a ~ to a crime** an einem Verbrechen beteiligt sein; **were you a ~ to this?** waren Sie daran beteiligt?
e (*inf, = person*) **a ~ by the name of Johnson** ein gewisser Johnson
VI (*inf*) feiern

party: **party dress** N Partykleid *nt*; **party-goer** N Partygänger(in) *m(f)*; **party hat** N Partyhut *m*; **party line** **a** (*Pol*) Parteilinie *f* **b** (*Telec*) Gemeinschaftsanschluss *m*; **party liner** N (*Pol*) linientreues Parteimitglied *nt*; **party man** N Gefolgsmann *m*; **party political** ADJ parteipolitisch; **party political broadcast** N parteipolitische Sendung; **party politics** PL Parteipolitik *f*; **party pooper** N (*inf*) Partymuffel *m* (*inf*); **party spirit** N **a** (*Pol*) Parteigeist *m or* -gesinnung *f* **b** (= *party mood*) Partylaune *f*; **to be in the ~** in Partylaune sein; **party spokesperson** N Parteisprecher(in) *m(f)*; **party ticket** N **a** (*Rail*) Gruppenfahrkarte *f* **b** (*US Pol*) (Kandidaten)liste *f* einer Partei

parvenu [ˈpɑːvənuː] N Emporkömmling *m*, Parvenü *m*

PASCAL [ˈpæskæl] N (*Comput*) PASCAL *nt*

paschal [ˈpæskəl] ADJ Passah-, Oster-; **~ feast** Passahfest *nt*

Paschal Lamb N Osterlamm *nt*

pas de deux [ˈpɑːdəˈdɜː] N Pas de deux *m*

pasha [ˈpæʃə] N Pascha *m*

paso doble [ˈpæsəʊˈdəʊbleɪ] N Paso doble *m*

pass [pɑːs] N **a** (= *permit*) Ausweis *m*; (*Mil etc*) Passierschein *m*; **a free ~** eine Freikarte; (*permanent*) ein Sonderausweis *m*
b (*Brit, Univ*) Bestehen *nt* einer Prüfung; **to get a ~ in German** seine Deutschprüfung bestehen; (*lowest level*) seine Deutschprüfung mit „ausreichend" bestehen; **I still need a ~ in physics** ich muss noch einen Abschluss in Physik machen
c (*Geog, Sport*) Pass *m*; (*Ftbl, for shot at goal*) Vorlage *f*
d (*Fencing*) Ausfall *m*
e (= *movement: by conjurer, hypnotist*) Bewegung *f*, Geste *f*; **the conjurer made a few quick ~es with his hand over the top of the hat** der Zauberer fuhr mit der Hand ein paar Mal schnell über dem Hut hin und her; **the text had a special hyphenation ~** der Text wurde eigens in Bezug auf Silbentrennung überprüft
f (*inf*) **things came to a ~ that ...** die Lage hatte sich so zugespitzt, dass ...; **things have come to a pretty ~ when ...** so weit ist es schon gekommen, dass ...; **this is a pretty ~!** das ist ja eine schöne Bescherung!
g **to make a ~ at sb** bei jdm Annäherungsversuche machen

h (*Aviat*) **the jet made three ~es over the ship** der Düsenjäger flog dreimal über das Schiff; **on its fourth ~ over the area the plane was almost hit** beim vierten Überfliegen des Gebietes wurde das Flugzeug fast getroffen; **the pilot made two ~es over the landing strip before deciding to come down** der Pilot passierte die Landebahn zweimal, ehe er sich zur Landung entschloss

VT **a** (= *move past*) vorbeigehen/-fahren/-fliegen an (+*dat*); **he ~ed me without even saying hello** er ging ohne zu grüßen an mir vorbei; **the ship ~ed the mouth of the estuary** das Schiff passierte die Flussmündung
b (= *overtake*) *athlete, car* überholen; **he's ~ed all the other candidates** er hat alle anderen Kandidaten überflügelt
c (= *cross*) *frontier etc* überschreiten, überqueren, passieren; *deadline* überschreiten; **not a word ~ed her lips** kein Wort kam über ihre Lippen
d (= *reach, hand*) reichen; **they ~ed the photograph around** sie reichten *or* gaben das Foto herum; **~ (me) the salt, please** reich mir doch bitte das Salz; **he ~ed the hammer up** er reichte den Hammer hinauf; **the characteristics which he ~ed to his son** die Eigenschaften, die er an seinen Sohn weitergab
e **it ~es belief** es ist kaum zu fassen; **it ~es my comprehension that ...** es geht über meinen Verstand *or* meine Fassungskraft, dass ...; **love which ~es all understanding** Liebe, die jenseits allen Verstehens liegt
f (*Univ etc*) *exam* bestehen; *candidate* bestehen lassen
g **this film will never ~ the censors** dieser Film kommt nie und nimmer durch die Zensur
h (= *approve*) *motion* annehmen; *plan* gutheißen, genehmigen; (*Parl*) verabschieden; **the censors will never ~ this film** die Zensur gibt diesen Film bestimmt nicht frei
i (*Sport*) **to ~ the ball to sb** jdm den Ball zuspielen; **you should learn to ~ the ball and not hang on to it** du solltest lernen abzuspielen, statt am Ball zu kleben
j *forged bank notes* weitergeben
k **he ~ed his hand across his forehead** er fuhr sich (*dat*) mit der Hand über die Stirn; **~ the thread through the hole** führen Sie den Faden durch die Öffnung; **he ~ed a chain around the front axle** er legte eine Kette um die Vorderachse
l (= *spend*) *time* verbringen; **he did it just to ~ time** er tat das nur, um sich (*dat*) die Zeit zu vertreiben
m *remark* von sich geben; *opinion* abgeben; (*Jur*) *sentence* verhängen; *judgement* fällen; **to ~ comment (on sth)** einen Kommentar (zu etw) abgeben
n (= *discharge*) *excrement, blood* absondern, ausscheiden; **to ~ water** Wasser *or* Harn lassen

VI **a** (= *move past*) vorbeigehen/-fahren; **the street was too narrow for the cars to ~** die Straße war so eng, dass die Wagen nicht aneinander vorbeikamen; **we ~ed in the corridor** wir gingen im Korridor aneinander vorbei; **there isn't room for him to ~** es ist so eng, dass er nicht vorbeikommt
b (= *overtake*) überholen
c (= *move, go*) **no letters ~ed between them** sie wechselten keine Briefe; **words ~ed between them** es gab einige Meinungsverschiedenheiten; **what has ~ed between us** was sich zwischen uns zugetragen hat; **a knowing look ~ed between them** sie tauschten wissende Blicke aus; **if you ~ by the grocer's ...** wenn du beim Kaufmann vorbeikommst ...; **we ~ed by a line of hotels** wir kamen an einer Reihe Hotels vorbei; **the procession ~ed down the street** die Prozession zog die Straße entlang; **the cars ~ down the assembly line** die Autos kommen das Fließband herunter; **as we ~ from feudalism to more open societies** beim Übergang vom Feudalismus zu offeneren Gesellschaftsformen; **as we ~ from youth to old age** mit zunehmendem Alter; **the virus ~es easily from one person to another** der Virus ist leicht von

einer Person auf die andere übertragbar; **people were ~ing in and out of the building** die Leute gingen in dem Gebäude ein und aus; **the land has now ~ed into private hands** das Land ist jetzt in Privatbesitz übergegangen; **to ~ into oblivion** in Vergessenheit geraten; **expressions which have ~ed into/out of the language** Redensarten, die in die Sprache eingegangen sind/aus der Sprache verschwunden sind; **to ~ into history/legend** in die Geschichte/Legende eingehen; **to ~ out of sight** außer Sichtweite geraten; **the firm has ~ed out of existence** die Firma hat aufgehört zu bestehen; **he ~ed out of our lives** er ist aus unserem Leben verschwunden; **everything he said just ~ed over my head** was er sagte, war mir alles zu hoch; **we're now ~ing over Paris** wir fliegen jetzt über Paris; **I'll just ~ quickly over the main points again** ich werde jetzt die Hauptpunkte noch einmal kurz durchgehen; **he's ~ing through a difficult period** er macht gerade eine schwere Zeit durch; **the manuscript has ~ed through a lot of hands** das Manuskript ist durch viele Hände gegangen; **the thread ~es through this hole** der Faden geht durch diese Öffnung; **you have to ~ through Berlin** Sie müssen über Berlin fahren; **shall we ~ to the second subject on the agenda?** wollen wir zum zweiten Punkt der Tagesordnung übergehen?; **the crown always ~es to the eldest son** die Krone geht immer auf den ältesten Sohn über; **the area then ~ed under Roman rule** das Gebiet geriet dann unter römische Herrschaft; **he ~ed under the archway** er ging/fuhr durch das Tor
d (*time: also* **pass by**) vergehen; (*deadline*) verfallen
e (= *disappear, end: anger, hope, era etc*) vorübergehen, vorbeigehen; (*storm*) (= *go over*) vorüberziehen; (= *abate*) sich legen; (*rain*) vorbeigehen; **to let an opportunity ~** eine Gelegenheit verstreichen lassen; **it'll ~** das geht vorüber!
f (= *be acceptable*) gehen; **to let sth ~** etw durchgehen lassen; **let it ~!** vergiss es!, vergessen wirs!; **it'll ~** das geht
g (= *be considered, be accepted*) angesehen werden (*for or as sth* als etw); **this little room has to ~ for an office** dieses kleine Zimmer dient als Büro; **in her day she ~ed for a great beauty** zu ihrer Zeit galt sie als große Schönheit; **she could easily ~ for 25** sie könnte leicht für 25 durchgehen; **or what ~es nowadays for a hat** oder was heute so als Hut betrachtet wird
h (*in exam*) bestehen; **I ~ed!** ich habe bestanden!; **did you ~ in chemistry?** hast du deine Chemieprüfung bestanden?
i (*Sport*) abspielen; **to ~ to sb** jdm zuspielen, an jdn abgeben
j (*Cards*) passen; **(I) ~!** (ich) passe!; **~** (*in quiz etc*) passe!; **I'll ~ on that** da passe ich
k (*old: = happen*) **to come to ~** sich begeben; **and it came to ~ in those days ...** und es begab sich zu jener Zeit ...; **to bring sth to ~** etw bewirken

▶ **pass away** **VI** **a** (= *end*) zu Ende gehen **b** (*euph: = die*) entschlafen, hinscheiden **VT** *sep hours* sich (*dat*) vertreiben

▶ **pass by** **VI** (= *go past*) vorbeigehen; (*car etc*) vorbeifahren; (*time, months etc*) vergehen; **there was no room for the lorry to pass by** der Lastwagen kam nicht vorbei; **I can't let that pass by without comment** ich kann das nicht kommentarlos durchgehen lassen; **to pass by on the other side** (*fig*) achtlos vorbeigehen **VT** *sep* (= *ignore*) *problems* übergehen; **life has passed her by** das Leben ist an ihr vorübergegangen

▶ **pass down** VT *sep* **a** *traditions* weitergeben (*to an +acc*), überliefern (*to +dat*); *characteristics* weitergeben (*to an +acc*); **passed down by word of mouth** mündlich überliefert **b** (= *transmit*) **the story was passed down through the ranks** die Sache sprach sich (bis) zu den Soldaten durch

▶ **pass off** **VI** **a** (= *take place*) ablaufen, vonstatten gehen **b** (= *end*) vorüber- *or* vorbeigehen **c** (= *be taken as*) durchgehen (*as* als); **she could pass off as an Italian** sie würde als Italienerin durchgehen **VT** *sep* **to pass oneself/ sb/sth off as sth** sich/jdn/etw als *or* für etw ausgeben

▶ **pass on VI** **a** (*euph:* = *die*) entschlafen, verscheiden **b** (= *proceed*) übergehen (*to* zu); **right gentlemen, shall we pass on?** gut, meine Herren, wollen wir nun zum nächsten Punkt übergehen? **VT** *sep* **a** *news, information* weitergeben; *disease* übertragen; **pass it on!** weitersagen!; **take a leaflet and pass them on** nehmen Sie ein Blatt und geben Sie die anderen weiter; **we passed the information on to the police** wir gaben die Informationen an die Polizei weiter **b** *cost, savings* weitergeben, weiterreichen

▶ **pass out VI** **a** (= *become unconscious*) in Ohnmacht fallen, umkippen (*inf*); **he drank till he passed out** er trank bis zum Umfallen **b** (*new officer*) ernannt werden, sein Patent bekommen (*dated*) **VT** *sep leaflets* austeilen, verteilen

▶ **pass over VT** *sep* übergehen; **he's been passed over again** er ist schon wieder übergangen worden; **to pass sth over in silence** etw stillschweigend übergehen **VI** (*euph:* = *die*) entschlafen

▶ **pass through VI I'm only passing through** ich bin nur auf der Durchreise

▶ **pass up VT** *sep chance* vorübergehen lassen

passable [ˈpɑːsəbl] **ADJ** **a** passierbar; *road etc* befahrbar, passierbar **b** (= *tolerable*) leidlich, passabel

passably [ˈpɑːsəblɪ] **ADV** (+*adj*) einigermaßen, leidlich; (+*vb*) ganz passabel; **she sings ~ well** sie singt ganz passabel

passage [ˈpæsɪdʒ] **N** **a** (= *transition: from youth to manhood etc*) Übergang *m*; **the ~ of time** der Verlauf *or* Strom (*geh*) der Zeit; **in** *or* **with the ~ of time** mit der Zeit **b** (*through country*) Durchfahrt *f*, Durchreise *f*; (= *right of passage*) Durchreise *f*, Transit *m*, Durchreise- *or* Transitgenehmigung *f*; **to grant sb ~ through an area** jdm die Durchreise durch ein Gebiet genehmigen **c** (= *voyage*) Überfahrt *f*, Schiffsreise *f*; (= *fare*) Überfahrt *f*, Passage *f* → **work** **d** (*Parl:* = *process*) parlamentarische Behandlung; (*final*) Annahme *f*, Verabschiedung *f* **e** (= *corridor*) Gang *m*; **the narrow ~ between Denmark and Sweden** die schmale Durchfahrt zwischen Dänemark und Schweden; **secret ~** Geheimgang *m*; **he forced a ~ through the crowd** er bahnte sich (*dat*) einen Weg durch die Menge **f** (*in book*) Passage *f*; (*Mus*) Stück *nt*, Passage *f*; **a ~ from Shakespeare/the Bible** eine Shakespeare-/Bibelstelle

passageway [ˈpæsɪdʒweɪ] **N** Durchgang *m*

pass: passbook N Sparbuch *nt*; **passcard N** (digitale) Ausweiskarte (*auf der persönliche Daten und Passwörter gespeichert sind*); (*Internet*) Passcard *f*; **pass degree N** niedrigster Grad an britischen Universitäten, „Bestanden"

passé [ˈpæseɪ] **ADJ** überholt, passé (*inf*)

passenger [ˈpæsɪndʒə] **N** **a** (*on bus, in taxi*) Fahrgast *m*; (*on train*) Reisende(r) *mf*; (*on ship*) Passagier(in) *m(f)*; (*on plane*) Fluggast *m*, Passagier(in) *m(f)*; (*in car*) Mitfahrer(in) *m(f)*, Beifahrer(in) *m(f)*; (*on motorcycle*) Beifahrer(in) *m(f)* **b** (*inf*) **we can't afford to carry any ~s** (= *incompetent people*) wir können es uns nicht leisten, Leute mit durchzuschleppen; (= *idle people*) wir können uns keine Drückeberger leisten; **he's just a ~ in the team** er wird von den anderen mit durchgeschleppt

passenger: passenger aircraft N Passagierflugzeug *nt*; **passenger door N** (*in car*) Beifahrertür *f*; **passenger ferry N** Personenfähre *f*; **passenger jet N** Passagierflugzeug *nt*; **passenger liner N** Passagierschiff *nt*; **passenger list N** Passagierliste *f*; **passenger mile N** (*Aviat*) Flugkilometer *m* je Fluggast; (*Rail*) Bahnkilometer *m* je Reisender; **passenger seat N** (*in car*) Beifahrersitz *m*; **passenger ship N**

Passagierschiff *nt*; **passenger train N** Zug *m* im Personenverkehr

passe-partout [ˈpæspɑːtuː] **N** Passepartout *nt*

passer-by [ˈpɑːsəˈbaɪ] **N** *pl* **passers-by** Passant(in) *m(f)*, Vorübergehende(r) *mf*

passim [ˈpæsɪm] **ADV** passim, verstreut

passing [ˈpɑːsɪŋ] **N** **a** (= *going by*) Vorübergehen *nt*; (*of procession*) Passieren *nt*, Vorüberziehen *nt*; **a swirling wind accompanies the ~ of each train** ein wirbelnder Wind begleitet jeden vorbeifahrenden Zug; **with the ~ of time/the years** im Lauf(e) der Zeit/der Jahre; **I would like to mention in ~ that ...** ich möchte beiläufig noch erwähnen, dass ... **b** (= *overtaking*) Überholen *nt* **c** (= *disappearance*) Niedergang *m*; (*of customs*) Aussterben *nt*; (*euph:* = *death*) Heimgang *m*; **the ~ of the old year** der Ausklang des alten Jahres **d** (*of deadline*) Überschreiten *nt* **e** (= *transmission: of information*) Weitergabe *f* **f** (*Ftbl*) Ballabgabe *f* **g** (*Parl, of bill*) = **passage d** **ADJ** **a** *car* vorbeifahrend; *clouds* vorüberziehend; *years* vergehend; **with every** *or* **each ~ day** mit jedem Tag, der vergeht **b** (= *casual*) *glance, thought, interest* flüchtig; *comments* beiläufig; *fancy* flüchtig, vorübergehend; *fashion, fad* vorübergehend; **to make (a) ~ reference to sth** auf etw (*acc*) beiläufig hinweisen; **to bear a ~ resemblance to sb/sth** mit jdn/ etw eine flüchtige Ähnlichkeit haben; **to have a ~ acquaintance with sb** jdn flüchtig kennen; **to have a ~ acquaintance with sth** flüchtige Kenntnis von etw haben **ADV** (*old:* = *very*) gar (*old*), überaus (*liter*)

passing: passing lane N (*Mot*) Überholspur *f*; **passing note N** Durchgangston *m*; **passing-out (ceremony) N** (*Mil*) Abschlussfeier *f*; **passing-out parade N** (*Mil*) Abschlussparade *f*; **passing place N** (*on narrow road*) Ausweichstelle *f*; **passing shot N** (*Tennis*) Passierball *m*

passion [ˈpæʃən] **N** **a** Leidenschaft *f*; (= *fervour*) Leidenschaftlichkeit *f*; (= *enthusiasm*) Begeisterung *f*, Leidenschaft *f*; **to have a ~ for sth** eine Passion *or* Leidenschaft für etw haben; **her ~ for oysters/all things Greek** ihre Passion *or* ausgeprägte Vorliebe für Austern/alles Griechische; **~s were running high** die Erregung schlug hohe Wellen; **his ~ for the cause** sein leidenschaftliches Engagement für die Sache; **music is a ~ with him** die Musik ist bei ihm eine Leidenschaft; **his ~ is Mozart** Mozart ist seine Passion; **to be in a ~** erregt sein; **to fly into a ~** in Erregung geraten, sich erregen **b** (*Rel, Art, Mus*) Passion *f*; **St Matthew Passion** Matthäuspassion *f*

passionate [ˈpæʃənɪt] **ADJ** leidenschaftlich; **to be ~ about sth** für etw eine Leidenschaft haben

passionately [ˈpæʃənɪtlɪ] **ADV** leidenschaftlich; **oh yes, she said ~** o ja, sagte sie voller Leidenschaft; **she wept ~** sie weinte heiße Tränen; **to be ~ fond of sth** etw unwahrscheinlich gern haben; **to be ~ in love with sb** leidenschaftlich in jdn verliebt sein; **a ~ held belief** eine felsenfeste Überzeugung

passion: passionflower N Passionsblume *f*; (*hum inf, as address*) Schatz *m*, Schätzchen *nt*; **passion fruit N** Passionsfrucht *f*; **passionless ADJ** leidenschaftslos; **Passion play N** Passionsspiel *nt*; **Passion Sunday N** (*erster*) Passionssonntag; (*in Protestant church*) Sonntag *m* Judika; **Passion Week N** Karwoche *f*

passive [ˈpæsɪv] **ADJ** **a** passiv; *acceptance* widerspruchslos, widerstandslos **b** (*Gram*) passivisch, passiv, Passiv-; **~ form** Passivform *f* **N** (*Gram*) Passiv *nt*, Leideform *f*; **in the ~** im Passiv

passively [ˈpæsɪvlɪ] **ADV** passiv; *accept* widerstandslos, widerspruchslos; *watch etc* tatenlos

passiveness [ˈpæsɪvnɪs], **passivity** [pæˈsɪvɪtɪ] **N** Passivität *f*

passive: passive resistance N passiver Widerstand; **passive smoker N** Passivraucher(in) *m(f)*, passiver Raucher, passive Raucherin; **passive smoking N** passives Rauchen, Passivrauchen *nt*; **passive vocabulary N** passiver Wortschatz

passkey [ˈpɑːskiː] **N** Hauptschlüssel *m*

Passover [ˈpɑːsəʊvə] **N** Passah *nt*

passport [ˈpɑːspɔːt] **N** (Reise)pass *m*; (*fig*) Schlüssel *m* (*to* für, zu)

passport: passport control N Passkontrolle *f*; **passport holder N** Passinhaber(in) *m(f)*; **are you a British ~?** haben Sie einen britischen Pass?; **passport office N** (= *building, organization*) Passamt *nt*

password [ˈpɑːswɜːd] **N** Losungs- *or* Kennwort *nt*, Parole *f*; (*Comput*) Passwort *nt*

past [pɑːst] **ADJ** **a** frühe(r, s) *attr*, vergangene(r, s) *attr*; **for some time ~** seit einiger Zeit; **in times ~** in früheren *or* vergangenen Zeiten; **it's ~ history now** das gehört jetzt der Vergangenheit an; **all that is now ~** das ist jetzt alles vorüber *or* vorbei; **what's ~ is ~** was vorbei ist, ist vorbei; **in the ~ week** letzte *or* vorige *or* vergangene Woche, in der letzten *or* vergangenen Woche; **~ president** früherer Präsident **b** (*Gram*) **~ tense** Vergangenheit *f*, Vergangenheitsform *f* **N** **a** Vergangenheit *f*; **to learn the lessons of the ~** die Lehren aus der Vergangenheit ziehen; **in the ~** in der Vergangenheit, früher; **events in the recent ~ have shown that ...** die jüngsten Ereignisse haben gezeigt, dass ...; **to live in the ~** in der Vergangenheit leben; **to be a thing of the ~** der Vergangenheit (*dat*) angehören; **that's all in the ~** das ist jetzt alles Vergangenheit; **a town/woman with a ~** eine Stadt/Frau mit Vergangenheit; **he was believed to have a "past"** man nahm an, dass er kein unbeschriebenes Blatt sei **b** (*Gram*) Vergangenheit *f*, Präteritum *nt*; **the verb is in the ~** das Verb steht in der Vergangenheit **PREP** **a** (*motion*) an (+*dat*) ... vorbei *or* vorüber; (*position:* = *beyond*) hinter (+*dat*), nach (+*dat*); **just ~ the library** kurz nach *or* hinter der Bücherei; **to run ~ sb** an jdm vorbeilaufen; **he stared straight ~ me** er starrte geradeaus an mir vorbei **b** (*time*) nach (+*dat*); **ten (minutes) ~ three** zehn (Minuten) nach drei; **half ~ four** halb fünf; **a quarter ~ nine** Viertel nach neun; **it's ~ 12** es ist schon nach 12 *or* 12 vorbei; **the trains run at a quarter ~ the hour** die Züge gehen jeweils um Viertel nach; **it's (well) ~ your bedtime** du solltest schon längst im Bett liegen **c** (= *beyond*) über (+*acc*); **~ forty** über vierzig; **the patient is ~ saving** der Patient ist nicht mehr zu retten; **we're ~ caring** es kümmert uns nicht mehr; **to be ~ sth** für etw zu alt sein; **my car is getting ~ it** (*inf*) mein Auto tuts allmählich nicht mehr, mein Auto bringts nicht mehr (*inf*); **he's ~ it** (*inf*) er ist zu alt, er ist ein bisschen alt (*dafür*), er bringts nicht mehr (*sl*); **she's getting a bit ~ it** (*inf*) sie wird allmählich alt; **I wouldn't put it ~ him** (*inf*) ich würde es ihm schon zutrauen **ADV** vorbei, vorüber; **to walk ~** vorüber- *or* vorbeigehen; **to run ~** vorbeirennen

pasta [ˈpæstə] **N** Teigwaren *pl*, Nudeln *pl*

past anterior N (*Gram*) Vorvergangenheit *f*

paste [peɪst] **N** **a** (*for sticking*) Kleister *m*; **wallpaper ~** Tapetenkleister *m* **b** **mix to a smooth/firm ~** (*glue etc*) zu einem lockeren/festen Brei anrühren; (*cake mixture etc*) zu einem glatten/festen Teig anrühren **c** (= *spread*) Brotaufstrich *m*; (= *tomato paste*) Mark *nt* **d** (*jewellery*) Similistein *m*, Strass *m* **VT** **a** (= *apply paste to*) *wallpaper etc* einkleistern, mit Kleister bestreichen; (= *affix*) kleben; (*Comput*) einfügen; **to ~ pictures into a book** Bilder in ein Buch (ein)kleben; **to ~ sth to sth** etw an etw (*acc*) kleben **b** (*inf*) *opponent* fertig machen (*inf*); *new play* *etc* verreißen; **to ~ sb (one)** *(lit)* jdm eins vor den Latz knallen *(sl)*; **to ~ sb** *(= defeat)* jdn in die Pfanne hauen *(inf)*; **to ~ sth** *(fig)* etw ver-hackstücken *(inf)*

▶ **paste up** VT *sep* aufkleben, ankleben; *(in publishing)* einen Klebeumbruch machen von

pasteboard ['peɪstbɔːd] N Karton *m*, Pappe *f*

pastedown ['peɪstdaʊn] N *(bookbinding)* Vorsatz *m or nt*, Vorsatzblatt *nt*

pastel ['pæstl] **N** *(= crayon)* Pastellstift *m*, Pastellkreide *f*; *(= drawing)* Pastellzeichnung *f*, Pastell *nt*; *(= colour)* Pastellton *m* **ADJ** *attr* Pastell-, pastellfarben; **~ colour** *(Brit)* or **color** *(US)* Pastellfarbe *f*, Pastellton *m*; **~ drawing** Pastellzeichnung *f*

paste-up ['peɪstʌp] N Klebeumbruch *m*

pasteurization [ˌpæstəraɪˈzeɪʃən] N Pasteurisierung *f*, Pasteurisation *f*

pasteurize ['pæstəraɪz] VT pasteurisieren, keimfrei machen

pastiche [pæˈstiːʃ] N Pastiche *m*; *(= satirical writing)* Persiflage *f*

pastille ['pæstɪl] N Pastille *f*

pastime ['pɑːstaɪm] N Zeitvertreib *m*

pastiness ['peɪstɪnɪs] N **the ~ of her complexion** ihr blasses or kränkliches Aussehen

pasting ['peɪstɪŋ] N *(inf)* **to take a ~ (from sb)** *(von jdm)* fertig gemacht werden *(inf)*; **to give sb a ~** jdn fertig machen *(inf)*

past master N erfahrener Könner, erfahrene Könnerin; *(Art, Sport also)* Altmeister(in) *m(f)*; **to be a ~ at doing sth** ein Experte *m*/eine Expertin darin sein, etw zu tun

pastor ['pɑːstəʳ] N Pfarrer(in) *m(f)*, Pastor(in) *m(f) (esp N Ger)*

pastoral ['pɑːstərəl] **ADJ a** *land, farming, life* ländlich; *(Art, Liter, Mus)* pastoral; **Beethoven's Pastoral Symphony** Beethovens Pastorale *f*; **~ poem** Schäfer- or Hirtengedicht *nt*; **~ picture** Pastorale *f or nt* **b** *(Eccl)* pastoral, pfarramtlich; *duties, responsibility* seelsorgerisch; **~ staff** Bischofsstab *m*; **~ letter** Hirtenbrief *m* **N a** *(Liter, Art, Mus)* Pastorale *f or nt* **b** *(Eccl)* Hirtenbrief *m*

pastoral care N *(Eccl)* Seelsorge *f*

pastorale [ˌpæstəˈrɑːl] N *(Mus)* Pastorale *f*

past: past participle N Partizip Perfekt *nt*, zweites Partizip; **past perfect** N Plusquamperfekt *nt*, Vorvergangenheit *f*

pastrami [pəˈstrɑːmɪ] N geräuchertes, stark gewürztes Rindfleisch

pastry ['peɪstrɪ] N Teig *m*; *(= cake etc)* Stückchen *nt*; **pastries** *pl* Gebäck *nt* → **Danish pastry**

pastry: pastry brush N Backpinsel *m*; **pastry case** N Törtchenform *f*; **pastry chef, pastry cook** N Konditor(in) *m(f)*; *(with higher qualification)* Konditormeister(in) *m(f)*

pasturage ['pɑːstjʊrɪdʒ] N **a** *(= grass)* Weide *f* **b** *(= right of pasture)* Weiderecht *nt*

pasture ['pɑːstʃəʳ] **N a** *(= field)* Weide *f*; **to put out to ~** auf die Weide treiben; *(fig inf, employee)* aufs Abstellgleis schieben; **greener ~s** *(fig)* bessere Weidegründe; **to move on to ~s new** *(fig)* sich *(dat)* etwas Neues suchen, nach neuen Weidegründen *(geh)* umsehen; **to seek ~s new** *(fig)* nach neuen Weidegründen suchen **b** *no pl (also* **pasture land***)* Weideland *nt* **c** *no pl (= food)* Futter *nt* **VT** *animals* weiden lassen **VI** grasen

pasty¹ ['peɪstɪ] ADJ **a** *consistency* zähflüssig **b** *colour* blässlich; *look* blass, kränklich

pasty² ['pæstɪ] N *(esp Brit)* Pastete *f*

pasty-faced ['peɪstɪ'feɪst] ADJ blass- or bleichgesichtig

Pat [pæt] N *(sl)* Ire *m*

pat¹ [pæt] N *(of butter)* Portion *f*; **cow ~** Kuhfladen *m*

pat² **ADV** **to know** or **have sth off ~** etw wie am Schnürchen *(inf)* or wie aus dem Effeff *(inf)* können; **he knows the rules off ~** er kennt die Regeln in- und auswendig or aus dem Effeff

(inf); **to learn sth off ~** etw in- und auswendig lernen; **he's always got an answer off ~** er hat immer eine Antwort parat; **to stand ~** keinen Zollbreit nachgeben **ADJ** *answer, explanation* glatt; **somehow his excuses seem a bit ~ to me** er ist mir immer ein bisschen zu schnell mit Ausreden bei der Hand

pat³ **N** Klaps *m*; **he gave his nephew a ~ on the head** er tätschelte seinem Neffen den Kopf; **excellent work, said the teacher, giving her a ~ on the shoulder** hervorragende Arbeit, sagte der Lehrer und klopfte ihr auf die Schulter; **he gave his knee an affectionate ~** er tätschelte ihr liebevoll das Knie; **to give one's horse/the dog a ~** sein Pferd/ seinen Hund tätscheln; *(once)* seinem Pferd/Hund einen Klaps geben; **to give sb/oneself a ~ on the back** *(fig)* jdm/ sich selbst auf die Schulter klopfen; **that's a ~ on the back for you** das ist ein Kompliment für dich **VT** *(= touch lightly)* tätscheln; *(= hit gently)* ball leicht schlagen; *sand* festklopfen; *face* abtupfen; **to ~ sb/the dog on the head** jdm/dem Hund den Kopf tätscheln; **to ~ sth/one's face dry** etw/sein Gesicht trockentupfen; **she ~ted a few loose curls into place** sie drückte ein paar Locken an, die sich gelöst hatten; **the sculptor ~ted the plaster into shape** der Bildhauer klopfte den Gips in die richtige Form; **he ~ted aftershave onto his face** er betupfte sein Gesicht mit Rasierwasser; **to ~ sb on the back** *(lit)* jdm auf den Rücken klopfen; **to ~ sb/oneself on the back** *(fig)* jdm/sich selbst auf die Schulter klopfen

▶ **pat down** VT *sep* festklopfen; *hair* festdrücken, andrücken

pat⁴ *abbr of* **patent**

Patagonia [ˌpætəˈgəʊnɪə] N Patagonien *nt*

Patagonian [ˌpætəˈgəʊnɪən] **ADJ** patagonisch **N** Patagonier(in) *m(f)*

patch [pætʃ] **N a** *(for mending)* Flicken *m*; *(on new garments)* Flecken *m*; *(= eye patch)* Augenklappe *f*

b **it's/he's not a ~ on ...** *(Brit inf)* das/er ist gar nichts gegen ...

c *(= small area, stain)* Fleck *m*; *(= piece of land)* Stück *nt*; *(= subdivision of garden)* Beet *nt*; *(= part, section)* Stelle *f*; *(of time)* Phase *f*; *(of policeman, prostitute)* Revier *nt*; **a ~ of blue sky** ein Stückchen *nt* blauer Himmel; **purple ~es on the skin** violette Flecke auf der Haut; **~es of colour** Farbtupfer *pl*; **a ~ of oil** ein Ölfleck *m*; **~es of sunlight dappled the floor of the forest** (die) Sonnenstrahlen tanzten auf dem Waldboden; **the cabbage ~** das Kohlbeet; **we drove through a few ~es of rain on our way here** wir hatten auf dem Weg stellenweise Regen; **there were sunny ~es during the day** hin und wieder schien die Sonne; **he's going through a bad ~ or rough ~ at the moment** ihm gehts im Augenblick nicht sonderlich gut

d *(= cosmetic beauty spot)* Schönheitspflästerchen *nt*

e *(Comput)* Korrekturroutine *f*

VT flicken; **this piece of cloth will just ~ that hole nicely** dieses Stück Stoff ist gerade richtig für das Loch; **a new government was hastily ~ed together** in aller Eile wurde eine neue Regierung zusammengeflickt or -gestückelt

▶ **patch up** VT *sep* zusammenflicken; *quarrel* beilegen; **to patch things up temporarily** die Dinge notdürftig zusammenflicken; **they managed to patch up their relationship** sie haben sich schließlich wieder ausgesöhnt; **I want to patch things up between us** ich möchte unsere Beziehung wieder ins Lot bringen

patchiness ['pætʃɪnɪs] N *(of work)* Unregelmäßigkeit *f*; *(of knowledge)* Lückenhaftigkeit *f*; *(of film, book, essay etc)* unterschiedliche Qualität

patch: patch pocket N Flickzeug *nt*; **patch pocket** N aufgesetzte Tasche; **patch-up** *(inf)* Flickwerk *nt no art*; **patchwork** N Patchwork *nt*; **~ quilt** Patchwork- or Flickendecke *f*; *(fig)* **a ~ of fields** ein Mosaik *nt* von Feldern

patchy ['pætʃɪ] ADJ *(+er)* **a** *work* ungleichmäßig, unterschiedlich; *knowledge, memory, evidence* lückenhaft; **what was the performance like? – ~ ~** wie war die Aufführung? – gemischt; **his second novel however was much patchier** sein zweiter Roman war wesentlicher unausgeglichener; **this is the patchiest production I've seen them do for a long time** eine derart ungleichmäßige Inszenierung habe ich von ihnen lange nicht mehr gesehen; **what's his work like? – ~ ~** wie ist seine Arbeit? – unterschiedlich

b *(lit)* *material* gefleckt; *beard, grass* licht; **~ fog on the coast** an der Küste stellenweise Nebel; **the ~ appearance of the half rebuilt city** der Eindruck von Flickwerk, den die zur Hälfte neu aufgebaute Stadt vermittelt

pate [peɪt] N Rübe *f (inf)*, Birne *f (inf)*; **bald ~** Platte *f (inf)*, Glatze *f*

pâté ['pæteɪ] N Pastete *f*

patella [pəˈtelə] N *(Anat)* Patella *f (spec)*, Kniescheibe *f*

paten ['pætən] N *(Eccl)* Patene *f*, Hostienteller *m*

patent ['peɪtənt] **N** Patent *nt*; **~ applied for** or **pending** Patent angemeldet; **to take out a ~ on sth** etw *(acc)* patentieren lassen → **letter** patentieren lassen; **is it ~ed?** ist das patentrechtlich geschützt? **ADJ** **a** *(= obvious)* offensichtlich **b** *(= patented)* *invention* patentiert; **he's got his own ~ method of doing it** *(fig)* dafür hat er seine Spezialmethode; **his ~ remedy for hangovers** *(fig)* sein Patent- or Spezialrezept gegen Kater

patentable ['peɪtəntəbl] ADJ patentierbar, patentfähig

patent: patent application N Patentanmeldung *f*; **patent attorney** N Patentanwalt *m*/-anwältin *f*

patentee [ˌpeɪtənˈtiː] N Patentinhaber(in) *m(f)*

patent: patent holder N Patentinhaber(in) *m(f)*; **patent leather** N Lackleder *nt*; **~ shoes** Lackschuhe *pl*

patently ['peɪtəntlɪ] ADV offenkundig, offensichtlich; **~ obvious/clear** ganz offensichtlich/ klar; **I would have thought that was ~ obvious** ich würde meinen, das liegt doch auf der Hand

patent: patent medicine N patentrechtlich geschütztes Arzneimittel; **Patent Office** N Patentamt *nt*

patentor [ˌpeɪtənˈtɔːʳ] N Patentgeber(in) *m(f)*

pater ['peɪtəʳ] N *(dated Brit inf)* Herr Vater *(dated)*

paterfamilias ['pɑːtəfəˈmiːlɪəs] N Familienvater *m*, Paterfamilias *m (geh)*

paternal [pəˈtɜːnl] ADJ väterlich; **my ~ uncle/ grandmother** *etc* mein Onkel *m*/meine Großmutter *etc* väterlicherseits

paternalism [pəˈtɜːnəlɪzəm] N Bevormundung *f*

paternalist [pəˈtɜːnəlɪst] N Patriarch *m*

paternalist(ic) [pəˈtɜːnəlɪst, pəˌtɜːnəˈlɪstɪk] ADJ , **paternalistically** [pəˌtɜːnəˈlɪstɪkəlɪ] ADV patriarchalisch

paternally [pəˈtɜːnəlɪ] ADV väterlich

paternity [pəˈtɜːnɪtɪ] N Vaterschaft *f*; **he denied ~ of the child** er bestritt die Vaterschaft an dem Kind

paternity leave N Vaterschaftsurlaub *m*

paternity suit N Vaterschaftsprozess *m*

paternoster ['pætəˈnɒstəʳ] N *(= prayer)* Vaterunser *nt*, Paternoster *nt*; *(= paternoster bead)* Vaterunserperle *f*; *(= lift)* Paternoster *m*

path [pɑːθ] **N a** *(lit)* *(trodden)* Weg *m*, Pfad *m*; *(surfaced)* Weg *m*; *(in field)* Feldweg *m*; **we took a ~ across the fields** wir nahmen den Weg über das Feld **b** *(= trajectory, route)* Bahn *f*; *(of hurricane)* Weg *m* **c** *(fig)* Weg *m*; **the Christian ~** der Weg des Christentums; **the ~ of** or **to salvation** der Weg des Heils; **the ~ of virtue** der Pfad der Tugend **d** *(Comput)* Pfad *m*

path-breaking ['pɑːˌbreɪkɪŋ] ADJ *(esp US)* bahnbrechend

pathetic [pəˈθetɪk] ADJ **a** (= *piteous*) Mitleid erregend; **the exhausted refugees made a ~ sight** die erschöpften Flüchtlinge boten ein Bild des Jammers; **it was ~ to see** es war ein Bild des Jammers **b** (= *poor*) erbärmlich, jämmerlich; **it's ~** es ist zum Weinen *or* Heulen (*inf*); **what a ~ bunch they are!** oh, was ist das für ein jämmerlicher Haufen!; **honestly you're ~, can't you even boil an egg?** ehrlich, dich kann man zu nichts brauchen, kannst du nicht einmal ein Ei kochen? **c the ~ fallacy** die Vermenschlichung der Natur

pathetically [pəˈθetɪkəlɪ] ADV **a** (= *piteously*) Mitleid erregend; **he limped along ~** es war ein Mitleid erregender Anblick, wie er einherhumpelte; **~ thin/weak** erschreckend dünn/schwach
　b *slow, stupid, inefficient* erbärmlich; **a ~ inadequate answer** eine äußerst dürftige Antwort; **a ~ weak attempt** ein kläglicher Versuch; **~ incapable** absolut unfähig; **the goalie dived ~ late** es war zum Weinen, wie spät sich der Torwart nach dem Ball warf; **the trains are ~ late** es ist zum Weinen *or* ein Jammer, wie unpünktlich die Züge sind; **it had become ~ obvious that she was ignoring him** es war schon peinlich zu sehen, wie sie ihn ignorierte

path: pathfinder N (*lit*) Führer(in) *m(f)*; (*fig: = innovator*) Wegbereiter(in) *m(f)*; **pathless** ADJ weglos; **path name** N (*Comput*) Pfad(name) *m*

pathogen [ˈpæθədʒɪn] N (*Med*) Krankheitserreger *m*

pathogenic [ˌpæθəˈdʒenɪk] ADJ pathogen, krankheitserregend

pathological [ˌpæθəˈlɒdʒɪkəl] ADJ (*lit, fig*) pathologisch, krankhaft; *studies etc* pathologisch

pathologically [ˌpæθəˈlɒdʒɪkəlɪ] ADV *jealous, violent* krankhaft

pathologist [pəˈθɒlədʒɪst] N Pathologe *m*, Pathologin *f*

pathology [pəˈθɒlədʒɪ] N (*science*) Pathologie *f*; **the ~ of a disease** das Krankheitsbild

pathos [ˈpeɪθɒs] N Pathos *nt*

pathway [ˈpɑːθweɪ] N = **path a**

patience [ˈpeɪʃəns] N **a** Geduld *f*; **to have ~/no ~ (with sb/sth)** Geduld/keine Geduld (mit jdm/etw) haben; **to have no ~ with sb/sth** (*fig inf: = dislike*) für jdn/etw nichts übrig haben; **to lose (one's) ~ (with sb/sth)** (mit jdm/etw) die Geduld verlieren; **to try** *or* **test sb's ~** jds Geduld auf die Probe stellen; **~ is a virtue** (*prov*) Geduld ist eine Tugend; **~, ~!** nur Geduld!, immer mit der Ruhe! → **patience b** (*Brit Cards*) Patience *f*; **to play ~** eine Patience legen

patient [ˈpeɪʃənt] ADJ geduldig; **to be ~ with sb/sth** mit jdm/etw geduldig sein; **you must be very ~ about it** du musst sehr viel Geduld haben *or* sehr geduldig sein; **we have been ~ long enough!** unsere Geduld ist erschöpft!; **his years of ~ work paid off** seine jahrelange geduldige Arbeit zahlte sich aus; **~ endurance** zähe Geduld **N** Patient(in) *m(f)*; **cancer/heart ~** Krebs-/Herzpatient(in) *m(f)*

patiently [ˈpeɪʃəntlɪ] ADV geduldig; **to wait ~** geduldig warten; **a very ~ reconstructed picture of Babylonian life** ein mit Akribie rekonstruiertes Bild babylonischer Lebensweise

patina [ˈpætɪnə] N (*lit, fig*) Patina *f*

patio [ˈpætɪəʊ] N Veranda *f*, Terrasse *f*; (= *inner court*) Innenhof *m*, Patio *m*; **~ door(s)** Terrassentür *f*

patisserie [pəˈtiːsərɪ] N **a** (= *pastry shop*) Konditorei *f* **b** (= *pastries*) Feingebäck *nt*

patois [ˈpætwɑː] N Mundart *f*

patriarch [ˈpeɪtrɪɑːk] N Patriarch *m*

patriarchal [ˌpeɪtrɪˈɑːkəl] ADJ patriarchalisch

patriarchy [ˈpeɪtrɪɑːkɪ] N Patriarchat *nt*

patrician [pəˈtrɪʃən] ADJ patrizisch; **the ~ classes** das Patriziertum; **the old ~ houses** die alten Patrizierhäuser **N** Patrizier(in) *m(f)*

patricide [ˈpætrɪsaɪd] N Vatermord *m*; (= *murderer*) Vatermörder(in) *m(f)*

patrimony [ˈpætrɪmənɪ] N Patrimonium *nt*

patriot [ˈpeɪtrɪət] N Patriot(in) *m(f)*

patriotic [ˌpætrɪˈɒtɪk] ADJ , **patriotically** ADV [ˌpætrɪˈɒtɪk, -əlɪ] patriotisch

patriotism [ˈpætrɪətɪzəm] N Patriotismus *m*, Vaterlandsliebe *f*

patrol [pəˈtrəʊl] **N a** (= *patrolling*) (*by police*) Streife *f*; (*by aircraft, ship*) Patrouille *f*; (*by watchman etc*) Runde *f*, Rundgang *m*; **the army/navy carry out** *or* **make weekly ~s of the area** das Heer/die Marine patrouilliert das Gebiet wöchentlich; **the army/navy maintain a constant ~** das Heer/die Marine führt ständige Patrouillen durch; **on ~** (*Mil*) auf Patrouille; (*police*) auf Streife; (*guard dogs, squad car, detectives*) im Einsatz
　b (= *patrol unit*) (*Mil*) Patrouille *f*; (= *police patrol*) (Polizei)streife *f*; (*of boy scouts*) Fähnlein *nt*; (*of girl guides*) Gilde *f*
　VT (*Mil*) *district, waters, sky, streets* patrouillieren, patrouillieren in (+*dat*); *frontier, coast* patrouillieren, patrouillieren vor (+*dat*); (*policeman, watchman*) seine Runden machen in (+*dat*); (*police car*) Streife fahren in (+*dat*); (*guard dogs, gamewarden*) einen Rund- *or* Streifengang *or* eine Runde machen in (+*dat*); **the frontier is not ~led** die Grenze wird nicht bewacht *or* ist unbewacht
　VI (*soldiers, ships, planes*) patrouillieren; (*planes also*) Patrouille fliegen; (*policeman*) seine Streife machen; (*watchman, store detective etc*) seine Runden machen; **to ~ up and down** auf und ab gehen

patrol: patrol boat N Patrouillenboot *nt*; **patrol car** N Streifenwagen *m*; **patrol leader** N (*of scouts*) Fähnleinführer *m*; (*of girl guides*) Gildenführerin *f*; **patrolman** N Wächter *m*; (*US: = policeman*) Polizist *m*; **patrol wagon** N (*US*) grüne Minna (*inf*), Gefangenenwagen *m*; **patrolwoman** N Wächterin *f*; (*US: = policewoman*) Polizistin *f*

patron [ˈpeɪtrən] N (= *customer of shop*) Kunde *m*, Kundin *f*; (= *customer of restaurant, hotel*) Gast *m*; (*of society*) Schirmherr(in) *m(f)*; (*of artist*) Förderer *m*, Förderin *f*, Gönner(in) *m(f)*; (= *patron saint*) Schutzpatron(in) *m(f)*; **~s only** nur für Kunden/Gäste; **~ of the arts** Kunstmäzen(in) *m(f)*; **our ~s** (*of shop*) unsere Kundschaft

patronage [ˈpætrənɪdʒ] N **a** (= *support*) Schirmherrschaft *f*; **under the ~ of ...** unter der Schirmherrschaft von ...; **his lifelong ~ of the arts** seine lebenslange Förderung der Künste
　b (*form, of a shop etc*) **we enjoy the ~ of ...** zu unseren Kunden zählen ...; **we thank you for your ~** wir danken Ihnen für Ihr Vertrauen; **the attitude of the new sales assistant caused her to withdraw her ~** das Benehmen des neuen Verkäufers veranlasste sie, dort nicht mehr einzukaufen
　c (= *right to appoint to government jobs*) Patronat *nt*; **under (the) ~ of** unter der Schirmherrschaft von
　d (*rare: = condescension*) **an air of ~** eine gönnerhafte Miene

patroness [ˈpeɪtrənɪs] N (= *sponsor*) Gönnerin *f*; **~ of the arts** Kunstmäzenin *f*

patronize [ˈpætrənaɪz] VT **a** *pub, cinema etc* besuchen; **I hope you will continue to ~ our store** ich hoffe, dass Sie uns weiterhin beehren; **it's not a shop I ~** in dem Geschäft kaufe ich nicht; **the shop is well ~d** das Geschäft hat viel Kundschaft **b** (= *treat condescendingly*) gönnerhaft *or* herablassend behandeln, von oben herab behandeln **c** (= *support*) *the arts etc* unterstützen, fördern

patronizing [ˈpætrənaɪzɪŋ] ADJ gönnerhaft, herablassend; **to be ~ to** *or* **toward(s) sb** jdn herablassend *or* von oben herab behandeln; **there's no need to be so ~** du brauchst gar nicht so herablassend *or* von oben herab zu tun

patronizingly [ˈpætrənaɪzɪŋlɪ] ADV gönnerhaft, herablassend; **a ~ tolerant attitude** herablassende Nachsicht

patron saint [ˌpeɪtrənˈseɪnt] N (*of church etc*) Schutzpatron(in) *m(f)*, Schutzheilige(r) *mf*

patronymic [ˌpætrəˈnɪmɪk] ADJ patronymisch **N** Patronymikon *nt*, Vatersname *m*

patsy [ˈpætsɪ] N (*US inf*) (= *scapegoat*) Sündenbock *m*; (= *easy victim*) Leichtgläubige(r) *mf*; (= *weak man*) Schlappschwanz *m* (*inf*), Schwächling *m*

patten [ˈpætən] N Stelzenschuh *m*

patter [ˈpætə] **N a** (*of feet*) Getrippel *nt*; (*of rain*) Platschen *nt*; **the ~ of tiny feet** (*fig*) Kindergetrappel *nt* **b** (*of salesman, comedian, conjurer, disc jockey*) Sprüche *pl* (*inf*); **to start one's ~** seine Sprüche loslassen; **you'll never pick up a girl unless you're good with the ~** (*inf*) du wirst nie eine Freundin aufreißen, wenn du nicht gut quatschen kannst (*inf*); **to have a good line in ~** (*of comedian, disc jockey etc*) gute Sprüche draufhaben *or* auf Lager haben (*inf*); **sales ~** Vertretersprüche *pl* **c** (*inf: = jargon*) Fachjargon *m* (*inf*) **VI** (*person, feet*) trippeln; (*rain: also* **patter down**) platschen

patter-merchant [ˈpætəmɜːtʃənt] N (*Brit inf*) Schönredner(in) *m(f)*, Sprücheklopfer(in) *m(f)* (*inf*)

pattern [ˈpætən] **N a** Muster *nt*; **to make a ~** ein Muster bilden
　b (*Sew*) Schnitt *m*, Schnittmuster *nt*; (*Knitting*) Strickanleitung *f*
　c (*fig: = model*) Vorbild *nt*; **according to a ~** nach einem (festen) Schema; **on the ~ of Albania, on the Albanian ~** nach albanischem Vorbild *or* Muster; **to set a** *or* **the ~ for sth** ein Muster *or* Vorbild für etw sein
　d (*fig: in events, behaviour etc*) Muster *nt*; (*set*) Schema *nt*; (*recurrent*) Regelmäßigkeit *f*; **there's a distinct ~/no ~ to these crimes** in diesen Verbrechen steckt ein bestimmtes Schema/kein Schema; **what ~ can we find in these events?** was verbindet diese Ereignisse?; **the ~ of events leading up to the war** der Ablauf der Ereignisse, die zum Krieg geführt haben; **a certain ~ emerged** es ließ sich ein gewisses Schema *or* Muster erkennen; **behaviour ~s** Verhaltensmuster *pl*; **eating/sleeping ~s** Ess-/Schlafverhalten *nt*; **the natural ~ of life in the wild** die natürlichen Lebensvorgänge in der Wildnis; **the daily ~ of his existence** die tägliche Routine seines Lebens; **to follow the usual/same ~** nach dem üblichen/gleichen Schema verlaufen; **the town's new buildings follow the usual ~ of concrete and glass** die Neubauten der Stadt entsprechen dem üblichen Baustil aus Beton und Glas; **it's the usual ~, the rich get richer and the poor get poorer** es läuft immer nach demselben Muster ab - die Reichen werden reicher und die Armen ärmer
　e (= *verb pattern, sentence pattern etc*) Struktur *f* **VT a** (*esp US: = model*) machen (*on* nach); **this design is ~ed on one I saw in a magazine** die Idee für dieses Muster habe ich aus einer Illustrierten; **many countries ~ their laws on the Roman system** viele Länder orientieren sich bei ihrer Gesetzgebung am römischen Vorbild; **to be ~ed on sth** einer Sache (*dat*) nachgebildet sein; (*music, poem, style etc*) einer Sache (*dat*) nachempfunden sein; **to ~ oneself on sb** sich (*dat*) jdn zum Vorbild nehmen; **he ~ed his lifestyle on that of a country squire** er ahmte den Lebensstil eines Landadligen nach
　b (= *put patterns on*) mit einem Muster versehen → *also* **patterned**

pattern book N Musterbuch *nt*

patterned [ˈpætənd] ADJ gemustert

patty [ˈpætɪ] N (*esp US*) Pastetchen *nt*

paucity [ˈpɔːsɪtɪ] N (*liter*) Mangel *m* (*of an* +*dat*)

Paul [pɔːl] N Paul *m*; (*Bibl*) Paulus *m*

Pauline [ˈpɔːlaɪn] ADJ paulinisch

paunch [pɔːntʃ] N Bauch *m*, Wanst *m*; (*of cow etc*) Pansen *m*

paunchy [ˈpɔːntʃɪ] ADJ (+er) dick

pauper [ˈpɔːpə] N Arme(r) *mf*; (*supported by charity*) Almosenempfänger(in) *m(f)*; **~'s grave** Armengrab *nt*

pauperism ['pɔ:pərɪzəm] N (*lit, fig*) Armut *f*

pauperization [ˌpɔ:pəraɪ'zeɪʃən] N Verarmung *f*; (*fig also*) Verkümmerung *f*

pauperize ['pɔ:pəraɪz] VT arm machen; (*fig*) verkümmern lassen

pause [pɔ:z] **N** Pause *f*; **a hesitant ~** ein kurzes Zögern; **an anxious/a pregnant ~** ein ängstliches/vielsagendes Schweigen; **there was a ~ while ...** es entstand eine Pause, während ...; **to have a ~** (eine) Pause machen; **without (a) ~** ohne Unterbrechung, pausenlos, ununterbrochen; **to give sb ~ (for thought)** (*esp liter*) jdm zu denken geben, jdn nachdenklich stimmen **VI** **a** (= *stop for a short while*) stehen bleiben, stoppen, (*inf*); (*speaker*) innehalten; **can't we ~ for a bit, I'm exhausted** können wir nicht eine kurze Pause machen, ich bin erschöpft; **he ~d dramatically** er legte eine Kunstpause ein; **~ before you act** überlege erst mal, bevor du etwas tust; **he ~d for breath/for a drink** er machte eine Pause, um Luft zu holen/etwas zu trinken; **to ~ for thought** (zum Nachdenken) innehalten; **he spoke for thirty minutes without once pausing** er sprach eine halbe Stunde ohne eine einzige Pause; **let's ~ here** machen wir hier Pause; **it made him ~** das machte ihn nachdenklich

b (= *dwell on*) **to ~ (up)on sth** auf etw (*acc*) näher eingehen **VT** *video, tape etc* anhalten

pave [peɪv] VT befestigen (*in, with* mit); *road, path* (*with stones also*) pflastern; *floor* (*with tiles*) fliesen, mit Fliesen auslegen; (*with slabs*) mit Platten auslegen; **to ~ the way for sb/sth** (*fig*) jdm/einer Sache (*dat*) den Weg ebnen; **where the streets are ~d with gold** wo die Straßen mit Gold gepflastert sind, wo das Geld auf der Straße liegt; **the path to hell is ~d with good intentions** (*prov*) der Weg zur Hölle ist mit guten Vorsätzen gepflastert (*prov*); **the paths are ~d in** *or* **with purest marble** die Wege sind mit feinstem Marmor ausgelegt

▶ **pave over** VT *sep* betonieren; (*with slabs*) mit Platten auslegen

pavement ['peɪvmənt] N (*Brit*) Gehsteig *m*, Bürgersteig *m*, Trottoir *nt*; (*US, PY, VY, = paved road*) Straße *f*; (= *material*) Bodenbelag *m*; **to leave the ~** (*US Aut*) von der Straße abkommen; **~ artist** Pflastermaler(in) *m(f)*

pavilion [pə'vɪlɪən] N Pavillon *m*; (*old: = tent*) Zelt *nt*; (*Brit Sport*) (= *changing pavilion*) Umkleideräume *pl*; (= *clubhouse*) Klubhaus *nt*

paving ['peɪvɪŋ] N Belag *m*; (*US: of road*) Decke *f*; (= *material*) Belag *m*; (= *action*) Pflastern *nt*; **~ stone** (Stein)platte *f*, Pflasterstein *m*; **~ tile** Fliese *f*

pavlova ['pævlə] N (*Cook*) Baiser *nt* Pawlowa

Pavlovian [pæv'ləʊvɪən] ADJ pawlowsch *attr*

paw[1] [pɔ:] **N** (*of animal*) Pfote *f*; (*of lion, bear*) Pranke *f*, Tatze *f*; (*pej inf:* = *hand*) Pfote *f* (*inf*); **keep your ~s off!** Pfoten weg! (*inf*) **VT** **a** (= *touch*) tätscheln; (*lion etc*) mit der Pfote *or* Tatze berühren; **to ~ the ground** (*lit*) scharren **b** (*pej inf:* = *handle*) betatschen (*inf*) **VI** **to ~ at sb/sth** jdn/etw betätscheln *or* betatschen (*inf*)

paw[2] N (*US, dial inf*) Pa *m* (*inf*)

pawl [pɔ:l] N Sperrklinke *f*

pawn[1] [pɔ:n] N (*Chess*) Bauer *m*; (*fig*) Schachfigur *f*

pawn[2] **N** (= *security*) Pfand *nt*; **in ~** verpfändet, versetzt; **to leave** *or* **put sth in ~** etw versetzen *or* auf die Pfandleihe *or* ins Leihhaus bringen; **the company is in ~ to foreigners** das Unternehmen ist an ausländische Kapitalgeber verpfändet **VT** verpfänden, versetzen

pawn: pawnbroker N Pfandleiher(in) *m(f)*; **pawnbroker's (shop)**, **pawnshop** N Pfandhaus *nt*, Leihhaus *nt*; **pawn ticket** N Pfandschein *m*, Leihschein *m*

pawpaw ['pɔ:pɔ:] N Papaya *f*

pax [pæks] INTERJ (*Brit*) Friede

pay [peɪ] *vb*: pret, ptp **paid** **N** Lohn *m*; (*of salaried employee*) Gehalt *nt*; (*Mil*) Sold *m*; (*of civil servant*) Gehalt *nt*, Bezüge *pl*, Besoldung *f*; **three months'** ~ drei Monatslöhne; (*of salaried employees*) drei Monatsgehälter; **what's the ~ like?** wie ist die Bezahlung?; **it comes out of my ~** es wird mir vom Gehalt/Lohn abgezogen; **to be suspended on half/full ~** bei halben/vollen Bezügen vom Dienst suspendiert sein; **a low-pay country** ein Land mit niedrigen Löhnen, ein Niedriglohnland; **the discussions were about ~** in den Diskussionen ging es um die Löhne/Gehälter; **to be in sb's ~** für jdn arbeiten

VT **a** zahlen; *person, bill, debt, account* bezahlen; *dividend* ausschütten, zahlen; **to ~ sb £10 (for sth)** jdm £ 10 (für etw) zahlen; **to ~ shareholders** Dividenden ausschütten *or* zahlen; **how much is their share still to ~?** wie viel steht noch aus?; **to be** *or* **get paid** (*in regular job*) seinen Lohn/sein Gehalt bekommen; **when do I get paid for doing that?** wann bekomme ich mein Geld dafür?, wann werde ich dafür bezahlt?; **savings accounts that ~ 5%** Sparkonten, die 5% Zinsen bringen; **I ~ you to prevent such mistakes** Sie werden schließlich dafür bezahlt, dass solche Fehler nicht vorkommen; **"paid"** (*on bill*) „bezahlt"; **to ~ the price/a high price for sth** den Preis/einen hohen Preis für etw zahlen → **paid**

b (*lit, fig:* = *be profitable to*) sich lohnen für; (*honesty*) sich auszahlen für; **it doesn't ~ them to work longer hours** es lohnt sich für sie nicht, mehr zu arbeiten; **in future it would ~ you to ask** in Zukunft solltest du besser vorher fragen; **but it paid him in the long run** aber auf die Dauer hat es sich doch ausgezahlt

c **to ~ (sb/a place) a visit** *or* **call, to ~ a visit to** *or* **a call on sb/a place** jdn/einen Ort besuchen; (*more formal*) jdm/einem Ort einen Besuch abstatten; **to ~ a visit to the doctor** den Arzt aufsuchen → **attention, compliment, respect**

VI **a** zahlen; **to ~ on account** auf Rechnung zahlen; **they ~ well for this sort of work** diese Arbeit wird gut bezahlt; **no, no, I'm ~ing** nein, nein, ich (be)zahle; **to ~ for sth** etw bezahlen; **it's already paid for** es ist schon bezahlt; **how much did you ~ for it?** wie viel hast du dafür bezahlt?; **I'd like to know what I'm ~ing for** ich wüsste gern, für was ich eigentlich mein Geld ausgebe; **to ~ for sb** für jdn zahlen; **I'll ~ for you this time** dieses Mal zahle ich; **they paid for her to go to America** sie zahlten ihr die Reise nach Amerika

b (= *be profitable*) sich lohnen; **it's a business that ~s** es ist ein rentables Geschäft; **it will ~ for itself within two years** innerhalb von zwei Jahren wird sich das rentiert haben; **crime doesn't ~** (*prov*) Verbrechen lohnt sich nicht

c (*fig:* = *suffer*) **to ~ for sth (with sth)** für etw (mit etw) büßen; **you'll ~ for that!** dafür wirst du (mir) büßen; **to make sb ~ (for sth)** jdn für etw büßen lassen; **I'll make you ~ for this!** das wirst du mir büßen, das werde ich dir heimzahlen!

▶ **pay back** VT *sep* **a** *money* zurückzahlen; **when do you want me to pay you back?** wann willst du das Geld wiederhaben?; **pay me back when you like** zahls *or* gibs mir zurück, wenn du willst **b** *compliment, visit* erwidern; *insult, trick* sich revanchieren für; **to pay sb back** es jdm heimzahlen

▶ **pay in** VT *sep* einzahlen; **to pay money into an account** Geld auf ein Konto einzahlen **VI** einzahlen

▶ **pay off** VT *sep* *workmen* auszahlen; *seamen* abmustern; *debt* abbezahlen, tilgen; *HP* ab(be)zahlen; *mortgage* abtragen; *creditor* befriedigen; **if this happens again we'll have to pay him off** wenn das noch einmal vorkommt, müssen wir ihn entlassen **VI** sich auszahlen

▶ **pay out** VT *sep* **a** *money* (= *spend*) ausgeben; (= *count out*) auszahlen **b** *rope* ablaufen lassen **VI** bezahlen

▶ **pay over** VT *sep* aushändigen

▶ **pay up** **VT** *sep* *what one owes* zurückzahlen; *subscription* bezahlen; **his account is paid up er** hat alles bezahlt → **paid-up** **VI** zahlen

payable ['peɪəbl] ADJ zahlbar; (= *due*) fällig; **~ to order** zahlbar an Order; **to make a cheque** (*Brit*) *or* **check** (*US*) **to sb** einen Scheck auf jdn ausstellen; **~ over three months** zahlbar über einen Zeitraum von drei Monaten

pay: pay-and-display ADJ (*Brit*) **~ parking space** Parkplatz, auf dem der Parkschein sichtbar im Wagen ausgelegt werden muss; **pay-as-you-earn** ATTR **~ tax system** Lohnsteuerabzugsverfahren *nt*, Steuersystem, bei dem die Lohnsteuer direkt einbehalten wird; **pay-as-you-go (mobile phone)** N Handy *nt* mit Guthabenkarte; **pay award** N Lohn-/Gehaltserhöhung *f*; **payback** N (*fig*) **a** (= *return*) Ertrag *m*; **to have a ~ sb** einen Scheck auf jdn ausstellen; **b** (= *revenge*) Rache *f*; **it's ~ time** die Zeit der Rache ist gekommen; **pay bargaining** N Tarifverhandlungen *pl*; **pay bed** (*Brit Med*) Privatbett *nt*; **pay bracket** N Lohn-/Gehaltsgruppe *f*; **pay cheque**, (*US*) **paycheck** N Lohn-/Gehaltsscheck *m*; **pay claim** N Lohn-/Gehaltsforderung *f*; **payday** N Zahltag *m*; **pay dirt** N abbauwürdiges Erzlager; **to hit** *or* **strike ~** (*fig inf*) auf eine Goldader treffen

PAYE (*Brit*) *abbr* of **pay-as-you-earn**

payee [peɪ'i:] N Zahlungsempfänger(in) *m(f)*

pay envelope N (*US*) Lohntüte *f*

payer ['peɪə] N Zahler(in) *m(f)*; **late/slow ~** säumiger Zahler, säumige Zahlerin; **to be a bad ~** eine schlechte Zahlungsmoral haben

pay: pay freeze N Lohnstopp *m*; **pay increase** N Lohn-/Gehaltserhöhung *f*

paying ['peɪɪŋ] ADJ **a** (= *profitable*) rentabel **b** **~ guest** zahlender Gast; **~ patient** Privatpatient(in) *m(f)*

paying-in slip [ˌpeɪɪŋ'ɪnˌslɪp] N (*Brit*) Einzahlungsschein *m*

pay: payload N Nutzlast *f*; (*of bomber*) Bombenlast *f*; **paymaster** N Zahlmeister(in) *m(f)*; **Paymaster General** (*Brit*) für Lohn- und Gehaltszahlungen im öffentlichen Dienst zuständiges Kabinettsmitglied

payment ['peɪmənt] N (= *paying*) (*of person*) Bezahlung *f*, Entlohnung *f*; (*of bill, instalment etc*) Bezahlung *f*, Begleichung *f*; (*of debt, mortgage*) Abtragung *f*, Rückzahlung *f*; (*of interest, bank charge etc*) Zahlung *f*; (= *sum paid*) Zahlung *f*; (*fig:* = *reward*) Belohnung *f*; **three monthly ~s** drei Monatsraten; **in ~ of a debt/bill** in Begleichung einer Schuld/Rechnung; **as** *or* **in ~ for goods/his services** als Bezahlung für *or* von Waren/für seine Dienste; **to accept sth as** *or* **in ~ (for ...)** etw in Begleichung (für ...) annehmen; **on ~ of** bei Begleichung/Bezahlung von; **without ~** (= *free*) umsonst; **to make a ~** eine Zahlung leisten; **to make a ~ on sth** eine Rate für etw zahlen; **to present sth for ~** etw zur Zahlung vorlegen; **to stop ~s** die Zahlungen *pl* einstellen; **to stop ~ of a cheque** (*Brit*) *or* **check** (*US*) einen Scheck sperren

payment card N (= *debit card*) Kreditkarte *f*; (*prepaid*) Guthabenkarte *f*

pay: pay negotiations PL = **pay talks**; **payoff** N (= *final payment*) Abschlusszahlung *f*; (*inf:* = *bribe*) Bestechungsgeld *nt*; (= *final outcome, climax*) Quittung *f*; (*inf*) Pointe *f*

payola [peɪ'əʊlə] N (*esp US*) (= *bribery*) Bestechung *f*; (= *bribe*) Schmiergeld *nt*

pay: payout N (*in competition*) Preis *m*; (*from insurance*) (Aus)zahlung *f*; **pay packet** N Lohntüte *f*; **pay-per-view** ATTR *television, service* Pay-per-View-; **~ channel** Pay-per-View-Kanal *m*; **payphone** N Münzfernsprecher *m*; **pay rise** N Lohn-/Gehaltserhöhung *f*; **payroll** N **they have 500 people on the ~** sie haben eine Belegschaft von 500, sie haben 500 Beschäftigte; **a monthly ~ of £75,000** eine monatliche Lohn- und Gehaltssumme von £ 75.000; **pay round** N Tarifrunde *f*; **payslip** N Lohn-/Gehaltsstreifen *m*; **pay station** N (*US*) öffentlicher Fernsprecher; **pay talks** PL Lohnverhandlungen *pl*; *(for profession, area of industry)* Tarifverhandlungen *pl*; **pay television** N = **pay TV**; **pay tone** N *bei öffentlichen Fernsprechern: Ton, der anzeigt, dass Münzen eingeworfen werden müssen*; **pay TV** N Pay-TV *nt*

PBX *abbr of* **private branch exchange** Nebenstellenanlage *f*

PC *(Brit)* **a** *abbr of* **Police Constable** PC Plod *(inf)* Streifenpolizist(in) *m(f)* **b** *abbr of* **Privy Council** **c** *abbr of* **Privy Councillor** **d** *abbr of* **personal computer** PC *m* **e** *abbr of* **politically correct**

pc **a** *abbr of* **post card** **b** *abbr of* **per cent** **c** *abbr of* **politically correct**

PCA *(Brit)* **a** *abbr of* **Police Complaints Authority** **b** *abbr of* **Professional Chess Association**

PCB *abbr of* **printed circuit board**

PCI *(Comput)* *abbr of* **Peripheral Component Interconnect** PCI

pcm *abbr of* **per calendar month** monatl.; "rent £230 =" „Miete £ 230 monatl."

PCP **a** *(Drugs)* *abbr of* **phencyclidine** PCP *nt* **b** *(Med)* *abbr of* **pneumocystis carinii pneumonia** PCP *f* **c** *(Chem)* *abbr of* **pentachlorophenol** PCP *nt*

pcs *abbr of* **pieces**

pd *abbr of* **paid** bez.

PDA *(Comput)* *abbr of* **personal digital assistant** PDA *m*

PDQ *(inf)* *abbr of* **pretty damned quick** verdammt schnell *(inf)*

PDSA *(Brit)* *abbr of* **People's Dispensary for Sick Animals** *kostenloses Behandlungszentrum für Haustiere*

PDT *(US)* *abbr of* **Pacific Daylight Time** pazifische Sommerzeit

PE *abbr of* **physical education**

pea [piː] N Erbse *f*; **they are as like as two ~s (in a pod)** sie gleichen sich *(dat)* wie ein Ei dem anderen

peace [piːs] N **a** (= *freedom from war*) Frieden *m*, Friede *m (geh)*; **the Versailles** *etc* **~** der Friede von Versailles *etc*; **a man of ~** ein friedfertiger *or* friedliebender Mensch; **to be at ~ with sb/sth** mit jdm/etw in Frieden leben; **the two countries are now at ~** zwischen den beiden Ländern herrscht jetzt Frieden; **to be at ~ with oneself/the world** mit sich *(dat)* selbst/mit der Welt in Frieden leben; **to make one's ~ with the world** seinen Frieden mit der Welt schließen; **he is at ~** (*euph*: = *dead*) er ruht in Frieden; **to hold** *or* **keep one's ~** (*geh*) schweigen; **to make (one's) ~ (with sb)** sich (mit jdm) versöhnen *or* aussöhnen; **to make (one's) ~ with oneself** mit sich *(dat)* selbst ins Reine kommen; **to make ~ between ...** Frieden stiften zwischen (+*dat*) ...

b *(Jur)* öffentliche (Ruhe und) Ordnung; **the (King's/Queen's) ~** *(Jur)* die öffentliche Ordnung; **to keep the ~** *(Jur)* (*demonstrator, citizen*) die öffentliche Ordnung wahren; (*policeman*) die öffentliche Ordnung aufrechterhalten; *(fig)* Frieden bewahren

c (= *tranquillity, quiet*) Ruhe *f*; **~ of mind** innere Ruhe, Seelenfrieden *m*; **the Peace of God** der Friede Gottes, Gottes Friede; **~ and quiet** Ruhe und Frieden; **to give sb some ~** jdn in Ruhe *or* Frieden lassen; **to give sb no ~** jdm keine Ruhe lassen; **to get some/no ~** zur Ruhe/nicht zur Ruhe kommen

peaceable [ˈpiːsəbl] ADJ *settlement, discussion* friedlich; *person, nature also* friedfertig, friedliebend

peaceably [ˈpiːsəblɪ] ADV *settle, discuss* friedlich

peace: peace campaign N Friedenskampagne *f*; **peace campaigner** N Friedenskämpfer(in) *m(f)*; **peace conference** N Friedenskonferenz *f*; **Peace Corps** N *(US)* Friedenskorps *nt*; **peace dividend** N Friedensdividende *f*

peaceful [ˈpiːsfʊl] ADJ friedlich; (= *peaceable*) *nation, person etc* friedfertig, friedliebend; (= *calm, undisturbed*) *holiday, sleep etc* ruhig; *death* sanft;

use of nuclear power für friedliche Zwecke; **a ~ transition to independence** die Erlangung der Unabhängigkeit auf friedlichem Wege; **he had a ~ reign** während seiner Regierungszeit herrschte Frieden; **I didn't get a ~ moment all day long** ich bin den ganzen Tag keine Sekunde zur Ruhe gekommen; **to achieve sth by** *or* **through ~ means** etw mit friedlichen Mitteln erlangen; **for ~ purposes** für friedliche Zwecke

peacefully [ˈpiːsfəlɪ] ADV friedlich; **to die ~ (in one's sleep)** sanft sterben *or* entschlafen (*liter*)

peacefulness [ˈpiːsfʊlnɪs] N Friedlichkeit *f*; (*of person, nation*) Friedfertigkeit *f*, Friedensliebe *f*; (*of place, holiday, sleep*) Ruhe *f*; (*of death*) Sanftheit *f*; **the ~ of the demonstration** der friedliche Charakter der Demonstration; **the ~ of a summer's evening** die friedliche Atmosphäre eines Sommerabends

peace: peace initiative N Friedensinitiative *f*; **peacekeeper** N Friedenswächter(in) *m(f)*; **peacekeeping** **N** Friedenssicherung *f* **ADJ** *role, force* zur Friedenssicherung; **~ troops** Friedenstruppen *pl*; **UN troops have a purely ~ role** die UN-Truppen sind eine reine Friedenstruppe; **a ~ operation** Maßnahmen *pl* zur Sicherung des Friedens; **peace-loving** ADJ friedliebend; **peacemaker** N Friedensstifter(in) *m(f)*; **peacemaking** **N** Friedensbemühungen *pl* **ADJ** *role* friedensstiftend; **~ efforts** Friedensbemühungen *pl*; **~ process** Friedensprozess *m*; **peace movement** N Friedensbewegung *f*

peacenik [ˈpiːsnɪk] N *(inf)* Pazifist(in) *m(f)*

peace: peace offensive N Friedensoffensive *f*; **peace offering** N Friedensangebot *nt*; *(fig)* Versöhnungsgeschenk *nt*; **peace pipe** N Friedenspfeife *f*; **peace process** N Friedensprozess *m*; **peace studies** PL Friedensforschung *f*; **peace talks** PL Friedensverhandlungen *pl*; **peacetime** **N** Friedenszeiten *pl* **ADJ** in Friedenszeiten

peach [piːtʃ] **N** **a** (= *fruit*) Pfirsich *m*; (= *tree*) Pfirsichbaum *m*; **her complexion is like ~es and cream, she has a ~es-and-cream complexion** sie hat eine Haut wie ein Pfirsich, sie hat eine Pfirsichhaut **b** *(inf)* **she's a ~** sie ist klasse *(inf)*; **it's a ~** das ist prima *or* klasse *or* Spitze *(all inf)*; **a ~ of a girl/dress/film** *etc* ein klasse Mädchen/Kleid/Film *etc* *(all inf)* **c** (= *colour*) Pfirsichton *m* **ADJ** pfirsichfarben

peachick [ˈpiːtʃɪk] N junger Pfau

peach Melba [ˌpiːtʃˈmelbə] N Pfirsich Melba *m*

peachy [ˈpiːtʃɪ] ADJ **a** (*in colour*) *complexion* pfirsichfarben, Pfirsich- **b** (*esp US inf*: = *excellent*) prima; **how's it going? – just ~!** wie gehts? – prima!

pea: peacock N Pfau *m*; *(fig*: = *man*) Geck *m*; **to strut up and down like a ~** wie ein Pfau einherstolzieren; **peacock-blue** ADJ pfauenblau; **peacock butterfly** N *(Zool)* Tagpfauenauge *nt*; **pea green** N Erbsengrün *nt*; **pea-green** ADJ erbsengrün; **peahen** N Pfauenhenne *f*; **pea jacket** N *(esp US)* Pijacke *f*

peak [piːk] N **a** (*of mountain*) Gipfel *m*; (*of roof*) First *m*; (= *sharp point*) Spitze *f* **b** (*of cap*) Schirm *m* **c** (= *maximum*) Höhepunkt *m*; (*on graph*) Scheitelpunkt *m*; **he is at the ~ of his fitness** er ist in Höchstform *or* Topform *(inf)*; **when his career was at its ~** als er auf dem Höhepunkt seiner Karriere war; **when demand is at its ~** wenn die Nachfrage ihren Höhepunkt erreicht hat *or* am stärksten ist

ADJ *attr power, position* höchste(r, s); **at ~ time** *(TV, Radio)* zur Hauptsendezeit; **~ pressure** Höchstdruck *m*; **~ value** Spitzenwert *m*; **~ voltage** Höchst- *or* Spitzenspannung *f*; **a ~ year for new car sales** ein Rekordjahr *nt* für den Neuwagenabsatz; **in ~ condition** (*athlete*) in Höchstform

VI den Höchststand erreichen; (*athlete*: = *reach one's best*) seine Spitzenform erreichen; **inflation ~ed at 9%** die Inflationsrate erreichte ihren Höchststand bei 9%; **to have ~ed** (= *be on the way down*) auf dem absteigenden Ast sein *(inf)*

▶**peak off** VI zurückgehen

▶**peak out** VI den Höhepunkt erreichen

peaked [piːkt] ADJ **a** *cap, helmet etc* spitz **b** *person* verhärmt, abgehärmt

peak: peak-hour ADJ **~ consumption** Verbrauch *m* in der Hauptbelastungszeit *or* zu Spitzenzeiten; **~ travel costs more** in der Hauptverkehrszeit *or* zu Spitzenzeiten sind die öffentlichen Verkehrsmittel teurer; **measures to reduce ~ traffic** Maßnahmen zur Reduzierung der Belastung in der Hauptverkehrszeit *or* zu Spitzenzeiten; **peak hours** PL (*of traffic*) Hauptverkehrszeit *f*, Stoßzeit *f*; *(Telec, Elec)* Hauptbelastungszeit *f*; **peak rate** N *(Telec)* Höchsttarif *m*; **peak season** N Hochsaison *f*; **peak-time** ADJ *(Brit)* zu Spitzenzeiten; **~ programme** *(TV, Radio)* Programm *nt* zur besten Sendezeit; **~ traffic** Stoßverkehr *m*; **~ train services** Zugverbindungen *pl* während der Hauptbelastungszeit; **peak times** PL Hauptbelastungszeit *f*

peaky [ˈpiːkɪ] ADJ (+*er*) *(Brit, inf)* *complexion* blass; *face* verhärmt, abgehärmt; *look, child* kränklich; **to look ~** nicht gut aussehen, angeschlagen aussehen *(inf)*

peal [piːl] **N** **~ of bells** (= *sound*) Glockengeläut(e) *nt*, Glockenläuten *nt*; (= *set*) Glockenspiel *nt*; **~s of laughter** schallendes Gelächter; **~ of thunder** Donnerrollen *nt*, Donnerschlag *m* **VT** läuten **VI** (*bell*) läuten; (*thunder*) dröhnen

▶**peal out** VI verhallen; **the bells pealed out over the fields** das Geläut der Glocken verhallte über den Feldern

peanut [ˈpiːnʌt] N Erdnuss *f*; **~s** (*inf*: = *not much money*) Kleingeld *nt*, Peanuts *pl (inf)*; **the pay is ~s** die Bezahlung ist miserabel *or* lächerlich *(inf)*; **£2,000? that's ~s these days** £ 2.000? das ist doch ein Klacks *or* das sind doch Peanuts heutzutage *(inf)*; **if you pay ~s, you get monkeys** *(prov)* wer nichts zahlt, kann nichts erwarten

peanut: peanut butter N Erdnussbutter *f*; **peanut gallery** N *(US inf)* Olymp *m (inf)*; **peanut oil** N Erdnussöl *nt*

peapod [ˈpiːpɒd] N Erbsenschote *f*

pear [peəʳ] N Birne *f*; (= *tree*) Birnbaum *m*

pear: peardrop N (= *pendant*) tropfenförmiger Anhänger *m*; (= *sweet*) hartes Bonbon in Birnenform; **pear-drop** ADJ *earring etc* tropfenförmig

pearl¹ [pɜːl] N, VT, VI = **purl**

pearl² **N** (*lit, fig*) Perle *f*; (= *mother-of-pearl*) Perlmutt *nt*; (*of sweat etc*) Perle *f*, Tropfen *m*; (= *colour*) Grauweiß *nt*; **~ of wisdom** weiser Spruch; **to cast ~s before swine** *(prov)* Perlen *pl* vor die Säue werfen *(prov)* **ADJ** Perlen-; (= *pearl-coloured*) grauweiß; **~ necklace** Perlenkette *f*

pearl: pearl barley N Perlgraupen *pl*; **pearl-barley** ADJ silberblau; **pearl fisher** N Perlenfischer(in) *m(f)*; **pearl fishing** N Perlenfischerei *f*; **pearl-grey** ADJ silbergrau; **pearl-handled** ADJ perlmuttbesetzt; **pearl oyster** N Perlenauster *f*

pearly [ˈpɜːlɪ] ADJ (+*er*) (*in colour*) perlmuttarben; **~ buttons** Perlmuttknöpfe *pl*; **a ~ costume** ein Kostüm *nt* mit Perlmuttknöpfen

pearly: Pearly Gates PL Himmelstür *f*; **pearly king/queen** N *Straßenverkäufer(in) in London, der/die ein mit Perlmuttknöpfen und bunten Perlen besticktes Kostüm trägt*; **pearly-white** ADJ strahlend weiß; *teeth* perlweiß; *skin, fabric* blütenweiß

pear-shaped [ˈpeəʃeɪpt] ADJ birnenförmig; **to be ~** (*woman*) eine birnenförmige Körperform haben; **to go ~** *(Brit fig inf)* völlig danebengehen *(inf)*

peasant [ˈpezənt] **N** (*lit*) (armer) Bauer, (arme) Bäuerin *f*; (*pej inf*: = *ignoramus*) Banause *m*, Banausin *f*; (= *lout*) Bauer *m*; (= *pleb*) Prolet(in) *m(f)* **ADJ** *attr* bäuerlich; **~ boy/girl** Bauernjunge *m*/-mädchen *nt*; **~ farmer** (armer) Bauer; **~ labour** Landarbeiterschaft *f*, landwirtschaftliche Arbeitskräfte *pl*; **~ leader** Bauernführer(in) *m(f)*; **~ unrest** Bauernunruhen *pl*; **~ woman** (arme) Bäuerin; **to be from ~ stock** von bäuerlicher Herkunft sein

peasantry ['pezntrɪ] N Bauernschaft *f*; (= *class, status*) Bauerntum *nt*

pease pudding ['pi:z'pʊdɪŋ] N Erbspüree *nt*

pea: peashooter N Pusterohr *nt*; **pea soup** N Erbsensuppe *f*; **peasouper** [pi:'su:pə'] N Waschküche (*inf*), Suppe (*inf*) *f*

peat [pi:t] N Torf *m*; (= *piece*) Stück *nt* Torf

peat bog N Torfmoor *nt*

peaty ['pi:tɪ] ADJ (+*er*) torfig; *taste* nach Torf

pebble ['pebl] N Kiesel *m*, Kieselstein *m*; (= *rock crystal*) Bergkristall *m*; (*after polishing*) Kieselglas *nt*; **he/she is not the only ~ on the beach** (*inf*) es gibt noch andere

pebble: pebble dash N (*Brit*) (Kiesel)rauputz *m*; **pebble glasses** PL Brille *f* mit sehr dicken Gläsern

pebbly ['peblɪ] ADJ steinig

pecan [prˈkæn] N (= *nut*) Pecannuss *f*; (= *tree*) Hickory *m*

peccadillo [pekəˈdɪləʊ] N *pl* **-(e)s** kleine Sünde; (*of youth*) Jugendsünde *f*

peccary ['pekərɪ] N Pekari *nt*, Nabelschwein *nt*

peck¹ [pek] N (= *dry measure*) Viertelscheffel *m*

peck² N **a** (*inf*: = *kiss*) flüchtiger Kuss *m*, Küsschen *nt* **b the hen gave him a ~** die Henne hackte nach ihm **VT a** (*bird*) picken **b** (*inf*: = *kiss*) ein Küsschen *nt* geben (+*dat*) **VI** picken (*at* nach)

▶ **peck out** VT *sep* aushacken

pecker ['pekə'] N **a** (*Brit inf*) **keep your ~ up!** halt die Ohren steif! (*inf*) **b** (*US sl*: = *penis*) Schwanz *m* (*vulg*)

pecking order ['pekɪŋˌɔ:də'] N (*lit, fig*) Hackordnung *f*

peckish ['pekɪʃ] ADJ (*Brit inf*: = *hungry*) **I'm (feeling) a bit ~** ich könnte was zwischen die Zähne gebrauchen (*inf*)

Pecksniffian [pekˈsnɪfɪən] ADJ scheinheilig, heuchlerisch

pecs [peks] PL (*inf*) *abbr of* **pectorals** Muskeln *pl*

pectic ['pektɪk] ADJ pektisch

pectin ['pektɪn] N Pektin *nt*

pectoral ['pektərəl] ADJ Brust-, pektoral (*spec*)

pectoral fin N Brustflosse *f*

pectoral muscle N Brustmuskel *m*

peculate ['pekjʊleɪt] (*geh*) **VI** öffentliche Gelder *etc* unterschlagen, Unterschlagung begehen **VT** *money, funds etc* veruntreuen, unterschlagen

peculiar [prˈkju:lɪə'] ADJ **a** (= *strange*) seltsam, eigenartig; **funny** ~ merkwürdig-komisch; **to feel ~** sich komisch *or* seltsam fühlen **b** (= *exclusive, special*) eigentümlich; **to be ~ to sth** (*to period, religion, group*) für etw eigentümlich sein; **a method ~ to her** eine Methode, die nur sie benutzt; **an animal ~ to Africa** ein Tier, das nur in Afrika vorkommt; **his own ~ style** der ihm eigene Stil; **in his own ~ way** auf die ihm eigene Art und Weise

peculiarity [pɪˌkju:lɪˈærɪtɪ] N **a** (= *strangeness*) Seltsamkeit *f*, Eigenartigkeit *f* **b** (= *unusual feature*) Eigentümlichkeit *f*, Eigenheit *f*, Besonderheit *f*; **it has the ~ that it is** *or* **of being ... es** hat die Besonderheit, ... zu sein

peculiarly [prˈkju:lɪəlɪ] ADV **a** (= *strangely*) seltsam, eigenartig **b** (= *exceptionally*) besonders; **a ~ British characteristic** eine typisch britische Eigenart

pecuniary [prˈkju:nɪərɪ] ADJ (*form*) *gain, advantage, problem, difficulties* finanziell; **~ affairs** Geldangelegenheiten, Geldsachen *pl*; **~ resources** Geldmittel *pl*

ped [ped] N (*inf*: = *pedestrian*) Fußgänger(in) *m(f)*

pedagogic(al) [pedəˈɡɒdʒɪk(əl)] ADJ (*form*) pädagogisch

pedagogically [pedəˈɡɒdʒɪkəlɪ] ADV (*form*) pädagogisch

pedagogue ['pedəɡɒɡ] N (= *pedant*) Schulmeister(in) *m(f)*; (*form*: = *teacher*) Pädagoge *m*, Pädagogin *f*

pedagogy ['pedəɡɒɡɪ] N (*form*) Pädagogik *f*

pedal ['pedl] **N** Pedal *nt*; (*on waste bin etc*) Trethebel *m*; **to put the ~ to the metal** (*inf*) Vollgas geben **VT** **he ~led the bicycle up the hill** er strampelte mit dem Fahrrad den Berg hinauf (*inf*); **he ~led the three miles to the restaurant** er radelte die drei Meilen zur Gaststätte; **he ~led the organ** er trat das Pedal der Orgel **VI** (*on bicycle*) treten; (*on organ*) das Pedal treten; **he ~led for all he was worth** er trat in die Pedale, er strampelte (*inf*) so sehr er konnte; **to ~ off** (mit dem Rad) wegfahren

pedal: pedal bin N (*Brit*) Treteimer *m*; **pedal boat** N Tretboot *nt*; **pedal car** N Tretauto *nt*

pedal(l)o ['pedələʊ] N Tretboot *nt*

pedal pushers ['pedlˌpʊʃəz] PL *dreiviertellange Damen-/Mädchenhose*

pedant ['pedənt] N Pedant(in) *m(f)*, Kleinigkeitskrämer(in) *m(f)*

pedantic [prˈdæntɪk] ADJ pedantisch; **to be ~ about sth** in Bezug auf etw (*acc*) pedantisch sein

pedantically [prˈdæntɪkəlɪ] ADV pedantisch

pedantry ['pedəntrɪ] N Pedanterie *f*

peddle ['pedl] VT feilbieten, verkaufen; (*fig*) *gossip etc* verbreiten; **to ~ drugs** mit Drogen handeln

peddler ['pedlə'] N (*esp US*) = **pedlar**

pederast ['pedəræst] N Päderast *m*

pederasty ['pedəræstɪ] N Päderastie *f*

pedestal ['pedɪstl] N Sockel *m*; **to put** *or* **set sb (up) on a ~** (*fig*) jdn in den Himmel heben; **to knock sb off his ~** (*fig*) jdn von seinem Sockel stoßen

pedestrian [prˈdestrɪən] **N** Fußgänger(in) *m(f)* **ADJ** **a** *attr* (= *of pedestrians*) Fußgänger-; **~ lights** Fußgängerampel *f*; **~ precinct** *or* (*US*) **zone** Fußgängerzone *f*; **at a ~ pace** im Schritttempo **b** (= *prosaic*) *style etc* schwunglos; *method etc* umständlich

pedestrian crossing N Fußgängerüberweg *m* *or* -übergang *m*

pedestrianize [prˈdestrɪənaɪz] VT *street* in eine Fußgängerzone umwandeln

pediatric *etc* [ˌpi:dɪˈætrɪk] (*US*) = **paediatric** *etc*

pedicure ['pedɪkjʊə'] N Pediküre *f*

pedigree ['pedɪɡri:] **N** (*lit, fig*) Stammbaum *m*; (= *document*) Ahnentafel *f*; (*fig*) Geschichte *f* **ATTR** reinrassig

pedigreed ['pedɪɡri:d] ADJ reinrassig

pediment ['pedɪmənt] N Giebeldreieck *nt*

pedlar ['pedlə'] N Hausierer(in) *m(f)*; (*of drugs*) Dealer(in) *m(f)* (*inf*)

pedology *etc* (*US*) = **paedology** *etc*

pedometer [prˈdɒmɪtə'] N Pedometer *nt*, Schrittzähler *m*

pedophile *etc* (*US*) = **paedophile** *etc*

pee [pi:] (*inf*) **N** (= *urine*) Urin *m*, Pipi *nt* (*babytalk*); **to need a ~** pinkeln müssen (*inf*); **to have a ~** pinkeln (*inf*); **I'm just going for a ~** ich geh mal eben pinkeln (*inf*) **VI a** (*person, animal*) pinkeln (*inf*) **b** (*hum*, = *rain*, *also* **pee down**) pinkeln (*inf*)

peek [pi:k] N kurzer Blick; (*furtive, from under blindfold etc*) verstohlener Blick; **to take** *or* **have a ~** kurz/verstohlen gucken (*at* nach); **may I just have a ~?** darf ich mal kurz sehen *or* gucken?; **to get a ~ at sb/sth** jdn/etw kurz zu sehen bekommen **VI** gucken (*at* nach)

peekaboo ['pi:kəbu:] **N** Kuckuckspiel *nt*; **to play ~** kuckuck spielen **INTERJ** kuckuck

peel [pi:l] **N** Schale *f* **VI** schälen → **eye** **VI** (*wallpaper*) sich lösen; (*paint*) abblättern; (*skin, person*) sich schälen *or* pellen (*inf*); **the paper was ~ing off the wall** die Tapete löste sich von der Wand

▶ **peel away** **VT** *sep wallpaper, paint* abziehen, ablösen (*from* von); *wrapper* abstreifen (*from* von); *bark* abschälen (*from* von) **VI** (*lit, fig*) sich lösen (*from* von)

▶ **peel back** VT *sep cover, wrapping* abziehen

▶ **peel off** **VT** *sep* (+*prep obj* von) *sticky tape, wallpaper, paint* abziehen, ablösen; *tree bark* abschälen; *wrapper, dress, glove etc* abstreifen **VI** **a** = **peel away VI b** (= *leave formation*) ausscheren (*Aviat*) ausscheren, abdrehen

peeler¹ ['pi:lə'] N (*old Brit inf*) Gendarm *m* (*old*)

peeler² N **a** (= *potato peeler*) Schälmesser *nt*, Schäler *m* **b** (*dated US sl*: = *stripper*) Stripper(in) *m(f)* (*inf*)

peeling ['pi:lɪŋ] N **a** Abschälen *nt* **b peelings** PL Schalen *pl*

peep¹ [pi:p] N (= *sound*) (*of bird etc*) Piep *m*; (*of horn, whistle, inf, of person*) Ton *m*; **to give a ~** (*bird*) einen Piep von sich geben; (*horn, whistle*) einen Ton von sich geben; **not to give a ~** keinen Pieps von sich geben (*inf*); **we haven't heard a ~ out of him** wir haben keinen Pieps von ihm gehört (*inf*); **one ~ out of you and ...** (*inf*) noch einen Mucks (*inf*) *or* Pieps (*inf*) und ...; **~! ~!** (*of horn*) tut! tut!; (*of whistle*) tüt! tüt! **VI** (*bird etc*) piepen; (*horn, car*) tuten; (*whistle*) pfeifen; (*person: on horn*) tuten; (*on whistle*) pfeifen **VT** **I ~ed my horn at him, I ~ed him** (*inf*) ich habe ihn angehupt (*inf*)

peep² **N** (= *look*) kurzer Blick; (*furtive, when forbidden*) verstohlener Blick; **to get a ~ at sth** etw kurz zu sehen bekommen; **to take** *or* **have a ~ (at sth)** kurz/verstohlen (nach etw) gucken **VI** **she ~ed her head out** sie streckte ihren Kopf hervor **VI** gucken (*at* nach); **to ~ from behind sth** hinter etw (*dat*) hervorschauen; **to ~ over sth** über etw (*acc*) gucken; **to ~ through sth** durch etw gucken *or* lugen; **no ~ing!, don't ~!** (aber) nicht gucken!

▶ **peep out** VI herausgucken; **the sun peeped out from behind the clouds** die Sonne sah *or* kam hinter den Wolken hervor

peepers ['pi:pəz] PL (*inf*) Gucker *pl* (*inf*)

peephole ['pi:phəʊl] N Guckloch *nt*; (*in door also*) Spion *m*

Peeping Tom ['pi:pɪŋˈtɒm] N Spanner *m* (*inf*), Voyeur *m*

peep: peepshow N Peepshow *f*; **peep-toe** **ADJ** offen **N** (= *shoe*) offener Schuh

peer¹ [pɪə'] N **a** (= *noble*) Peer *m*; **~ of the realm** Peer *m* **b** (= *equal*) Gleichrangige(r) *mf*, Peer *m* (*spec*); **he was well-liked by his ~s** er war bei seinesgleichen beliebt; **to be tried by one's ~s** von seinesgleichen gerichtet werden; **as a musician he has no ~** *or* **is without ~** als Musiker sucht er seinesgleichen

peer² VI starren; (*short-sightedly, inquiringly*) schielen; **to ~ (hard) at sb** jdn anstarren/anschielen; **to ~ (hard) at sth** etw anstarren; **the driver ~ed through the fog** der Fahrer versuchte angestrengt, im Nebel etwas zu erkennen; **if you ~ through the mist you can just see ...** wenn es dir gelingt, im Nebel etwas zu erkennen, kannst du gerade noch ... sehen

peerage ['pɪərɪdʒ] N **a** (= *peers*) Adelsstand *m*; (*in GB*) Peers *pl* **b** (= *rank*) Adelsstand *m*, Adelswürde *f*; (*in GB*) Peerage *f*, Peerswürde *f*; **to raise** *or* **elevate sb to the ~** jdn in den Adelsstand erheben; **to give sb a ~** jdm einen Adelstitel verleihen, jdn adeln; **to get a ~** geadelt werden, einen Adelstitel verliehen bekommen **c** (= *book*) *das britische Adelsverzeichnis*

peeress ['pɪərɪs] N Peeress *f*

peer group N Peergroup *f*, Alterskohorte *f*

peerless ADJ , **peerlessly** ADV ['pɪəlɪs, -lɪ] einzigartig, unvergleichlich

peer pressure N Gruppen- *or* Erwartungsdruck *m* (*von seiten Gleichaltriger*)

peeve [pi:v] VT (*inf*) ärgern, reizen, fuchsen (*inf*)

peeved [pi:vd] ADJ (*inf*) eingeschnappt, ärgerlich, verärgert; *look* ärgerlich, verärgert

peevish ['pi:vɪʃ] ADJ (= irritated) gereizt, mürrisch, brummig; (= irritable) reizbar

peevishly ['pi:vɪʃlɪ] ADV gereizt

peevishness ['pi:vɪʃnɪs] N (= irritation) Gereiztheit f, Brummigkeit f; (= irritability) Reizbarkeit f

peewit ['pi:wɪt] N Kiebitz m

peg [peg] **N** (= stake) Pflock m; (= tent peg also) Hering m; (for pegboard, wood joints, in games) Stift m; (of musical instrument) Wirbel m; (Brit: = clothes peg) (Wäsche)klammer f; (= hook, for mountaineering) Haken m; (in barrel) Zapfen m, Spund m; **off the ~** von der Stange; **a ~ of rum** etc ein Gläschen nt Rum etc; **to take** or **bring sb down a ~** or **two** (inf) jdm einen Dämpfer geben; **a (convenient) ~ on which to hang one's prejudices** etc ein guter Aufhänger für seine Vorurteile etc
▪ **VT a** (= fasten) (with stake) anpflocken; (with clothes peg) anklammern; (to pegboard) anheften; (with tent peg) festpflocken
b (= mark out) area abstecken
c (fig) prices, wages festsetzen; **to have sb ~ged (as sth)** (inf) jdn (als etw) abstempeln

▸ **peg away** VI (inf) nicht locker lassen (at mit)

▸ **peg down** VT sep tent etc festpflocken

▸ **peg out VT** sep **a** washing aufhängen; skins ausspannen **b** (= mark out) area abstecken **VI** (Brit sl, = die) abkratzen (inf), den Löffel abgeben (inf); (with exhaustion) umkippen (inf); (= stop: machine) verrecken (inf)

▸ **peg up** VT sep washing aufhängen; notice heften (on an +acc)

Pegasus ['pegəsəs] N Pegasus m

pegboard ['pegbɔːd] N Lochbrett nt

peg leg N (inf) (= person) Stelzfuß m; (= leg also) Holzbein nt

peignoir ['peɪnwɑː] N Negligée nt, Negligee nt

pejorative ADJ , **pejoratively** ADV [prˈdʒɒrɪtɪv, -lɪ] pejorativ, abwertend, abschätzig

peke [pi:k] N (inf) = **pekin(g)ese**

Pekin(g) [pi:ˈkɪŋ] N Peking nt; **~ man** Pekingmensch m

pekin(g)ese [ˌpi:kɪˈni:z] N pl - = (dog) Pekinese m

pelerine ['pelərɪn] N (old) Pelerine f, Umhang m

pelican ['pelɪkən] N Pelikan m

pelican crossing N (Brit) Fußgängerüberweg m (mit Ampel)

pelisse [pəˈliːs] N (old) pelzbesetztes Kleid

pellet ['pelɪt] N Kügelchen nt; (for gun) Schrotkugel m; (Biol: = regurgitated pellet) Gewölle nt

pellicle ['pelɪkəl] N Film m; (Zool: = membrane) Pellicula f

pell-mell ['pel'mel] ADV durcheinander, wie Kraut und Rüben (inf); (with vbs of motion) in heillosem Durcheinander

pellucid [pe'lu:sɪd] ADJ liquid, meaning klar; argument also einleuchtend

pelmet ['pelmɪt] N (Brit) Blende f; (of fabric) Falbel f, Querbehang m

Peloponnese [ˌpeləpə'ni:z] N Peloponnes m

Peloponnesian [ˌpeləpə'ni:zɪən] ADJ peloponnesisch

pelt1 [pelt] N Pelz m, Fell nt

pelt2 VT a (= throw) schleudern (at nach); **to ~ sb/sth (with sth)** jdn/etw (mit etw) bewerfen **b** (= beat hard) verprügeln **VI** (inf) **a** (= go fast) pesen (inf) **b** **it ~ed (with rain)** es hat nur so geschüttet (inf); **the rain/hail ~ed against the windows** der Regen/Hagel prasselte an or schlug gegen die Fensterscheiben **N** (inf) **a** (= speed) **at full ~** volle Pulle (inf) **b** (= blow) Schlag m; **she gave him a good ~ round the ear** sie gab ihr eine kräftige Ohrfeige

▸ **pelt along** VI (inf) entlangrasen

▸ **pelt down** VI it or **the rain really pelted down** der Regen prasselte nur so herunter; **it's pelting down** es regnet in Strömen

peltry ['peltrɪ] N **a** (furs collectively) Rauchwaren pl, Pelzwaren pl **b** (= single furs) Felle pl, Häute pl

pelvic ['pelvɪk] ADJ Becken-; complaint, pains in der Beckengegend; **~ floor muscles** Beckenboden m, Beckenbodenmuskulatur f; **~ thrust** Hüftschwung m

pelvic: pelvic bone N Beckenknochen m; **pelvic girdle** N Beckengürtel m; **pelvic fin** Bauchflosse f

pelvis ['pelvɪs] N Becken nt

pen1 [pen] **N a** (= dip pen) Feder f; (= fountain pen) Füllfederhalter m, Füller m; (= ball-point pen) Kugelschreiber m, Kuli m (inf); **to put ~ to paper** zur Feder greifen; **the ~ is mightier than the sword** (prov) die Feder ist mächtiger als das Schwert **VT** niederschreiben; poem etc also verfassen

pen2 N a (for cattle etc) Pferch m; (for sheep) Hürde f; (for pigs) Koben m; (= play pen) Laufstall m, Ställchen nt, Laufgitter nt **b** (US inf: = prison) Bau m (inf), Knast m (inf) **c** (for submarines) Bunker m **VT** einsperren

▸ **pen in** VT sep einsperren; (fig) car etc einklemmen, einkeilen

▸ **pen up** VT sep einsperren

pen3 N (= swan) weiblicher Schwan

penal ['pi:nl] ADJ **a** Straf-; **~ institution** Strafanstalt f; **~ law** Strafrecht nt; **~ offence** Straftat f; **~ policy** Strafrechtspolitik f; **~ reform** Strafrechtsreform f **b** (= harsh) rates, taxation überzogen

penal code N Strafgesetzbuch nt

penal colony N Strafkolonie f

penalization [ˌpi:nəlaɪ'zeɪʃən] N **a** (= punishment) Bestrafung f; (fig) Benachteiligung f **b** (= making punishable) Unter-Strafe-Stellen nt

penalize ['pi:nəlaɪz] VT **a** (= punish, also Sport) bestrafen **b** (fig) benachteiligen; **we are ~d as we don't have a car** wir sind benachteiligt or im Nachteil, weil wir kein Auto haben **c** (= make punishable) unter Strafe stellen

penal servitude N Zwangsarbeit f

penal system N Strafrecht nt

penalty ['penəltɪ] N **a** (= punishment) Strafe f; (fig: = disadvantage) Nachteil m; **the ~ (for this) is death** darauf steht die Todesstrafe; **you know the ~** Sie wissen, welche Strafe darauf steht; **"penalty £50"** „bei Zuwiderhandlung wird eine Geldstrafe von £ 50 erhoben"; **to carry the death ~/the ~ of imprisonment** mit dem Tod/mit Gefängnis bestraft werden; **on ~ of £200** bei einer Geldstrafe von £ 200; **to pay the ~** dafür büßen; **that's the ~ you pay for ...** das ist die Strafe dafür, dass ...
b (Sport) Strafstoß m; (Ftbl) Elfmeter m; (Golf, Bridge) Strafpunkt m; **the match was decided on penalties** (Ftbl) die Partie wurde durch Elfmeterschießen entschieden

penalty: penalty area N Strafraum m; **penalty box** N (Ftbl) Strafraum m; (Ice Hockey) Strafbank f; **penalty clause** N Strafklausel f; **penalty goal** N (Rugby) Straftor nt; **penalty kick** N Strafstoß m; **penalty killer** N (Ice hockey) Penalty-Killer(in) m(f), Unterzahlspezialist(in) m(f); **penalty line** N Strafraumgrenze f; **penalty point** N (Aut, Jur, Sport) Strafpunkt m; **penalty shoot-out** N (Ftbl) Elfmeterschießen nt; **penalty shot** N (Ice hockey) Strafschuss m; (Golf) Strafschlag m; (Basketball US) Freiwurf m; **penalty spot** N (Ftbl) Elfmeterpunkt m; **penalty taker** N (Ftbl) Elfmeterschütze m/-schützin f

penance ['penəns] N (Rel) Buße f; (fig) Strafe f; **to do ~** Buße tun; (fig) büßen; **as a ~** (Rel) als Buße; (fig) zur or als Strafe; **to give sb ~** jdm Buße auferlegen

pen-and-ink ['penəndɪŋk] ADJ Feder-; **~ drawing** Federzeichnung f

pence [pens] N pl of **penny** Pence pl

penchant ['pɑ̃:ʃɑ̃:ŋ] N Schwäche f (for für), Vorliebe f (for für)

pencil ['pensl] **N** Bleistift m; (= eyebrow pencil) Augenbrauenstift m; (Math, Phys: of lines, rays etc) Büschel nt **VT** mit Bleistift schreiben/zeichnen etc; **~led eyebrows** nachgezogene Augenbrauen pl **ATTR** Bleistift-; line mit Bleistift gezogen; **~ sketch** Bleistiftskizze f

▸ **pencil in** VT sep **a** eyebrows aufzeichnen **b** (= make provisional arrangement with/for) vorläufig vormerken; **can I pencil you in for Tuesday?** kann ich Sie erst mal für Dienstag vormerken?

pencil: pencil box N Federkasten m; **pencil case** N Federmäppchen nt; **pencil sharpener** N (Bleistift)spitzer m; **pencil skirt** N enger Rock

pendant ['pendənt] N Anhänger m

pendent ['pendənt] ADJ herabhängend; **~ lamp** Hängelampe f

pending ['pendɪŋ] **ADJ** anstehend; lawsuit anhängig; **"pending"** „unerledigt"; **to be ~** (decision etc) noch anstehen; (trial) noch anhängig sein; **he knew my examination was ~** er wusste, dass meine Prüfung bevorstand; **four more charges are ~ against her** gegen sie sind noch vier weitere Klagen anhängig; **to leave sth ~** etw noch weiterverfolgen; **the offer is left ~ until the examination results are known** über das Angebot wird erst entschieden, wenn die Prüfungsergebnisse bekannt sind **PREP ~ his arrival/return** bis zu seiner Ankunft/Rückkehr; **~ a decision** bis eine Entscheidung getroffen worden ist

pendulous ['pendjʊləs] ADJ herabhängend; **~ breasts** or **bosom** Hängebrüste pl, Hängebusen m; **~ cheeks** Hängebacken pl

pendulum ['pendjʊləm] N Pendel nt; **the ~ has swung back in the opposite direction** (lit, fig) das Pendel ist in die entgegengesetzte Richtung ausgeschlagen; **the ~ has swung back in favour** (Brit) or **favor** (US) of or **toward(s) ...** (fig) die Tendenz geht wieder in Richtung (+gen) ...; **the swing of the ~** (fig) die Tendenzwende

penetrable ['penɪtrəbl] ADJ zu durchdringen; **the barely ~ jungle** der fast undurchdringliche Dschungel

penetrate ['penɪtreɪt] **VT** eindringen in (+acc); (= go right through) walls etc durchdringen; (Mil) enemy lines durchbrechen; (Med) vein durchstechen; (= infiltrate) party infiltrieren; market eindringen in; **is there anything that will ~ that thick skull of yours?** geht denn auch überhaupt nichts in deinen Schädel rein?; **to ~ sb's disguise** hinter jds Maske (acc) schauen **VI** eindringen; (= go right through) durchdringen; **I just didn't ~** (fig) das ist mir/ihm etc nicht klar geworden; **has that ~d?** hast du/habt ihr das endlich kapiert?

penetrating ['penɪtreɪtɪŋ] ADJ **a** (= perceptive) gaze durchdringend; insight, person scharfsinnig; question, analysis treffend; interview tief gehend; **a ~ mind** ein scharfer Verstand **b** (= piercing) cold durchdringend; light grell; pain stechend

penetratingly ['penɪtreɪtɪŋlɪ] ADV gaze durchdringend; comment, analyze scharfsinnig; shine grell; **a ~ accurate analysis** eine messerscharfe Analyse; **a ~ bright light** ein grelles Licht

penetration [ˌpenɪ'treɪʃən] N (by bullet etc) (= entering) Eindringen nt (into in +acc); (= going right through) Durchdringen nt (of +gen); (Mil) Durchbrechen nt, Durchbrechung f; (= infiltration: of party, group) Infiltration f; (during sex) Eindringen nt, Penetration f; **the ~ of his gaze** sein durchdringender Blick; **his powers of ~** sein Scharfsinn m

penetrative ['penɪtrətɪv] ADJ **a** **~ sex** penetrativer Sex **b** = **penetrating a**

pen friend N Brieffreund(in) m(f)

penguin ['peŋgwɪn] N Pinguin m; **~ suit** (hum) Frack m, Schwalbenschwanz m (hum)

penholder ['penˌhəʊldə] N Federhalter m

penicillin [ˌpenɪ'sɪlɪn] N Penizillin nt

peninsula [pr'nɪnsjʊlə] N Halbinsel f

peninsular [pr'nɪnsjʊlə] ADJ **the Peninsular War** der Krieg auf der Pyrenäenhalbinsel

penis ['pi:nɪs] N Penis *m*

penis envy N Penisneid *m*

penitence ['penɪtəns] N Reue *f* (*also Eccl*), Zerknirschtheit *f*

penitent ['penɪtənt] **ADJ** reuig (*also Eccl*), zerknirscht **N** Büßer(in) *m(f)*; (*Eccl*) reuiger Sünder, reuige Sünderin

penitential [,penɪ'tenʃəl] ADJ reuevoll, reumütig, reuig; (*Eccl*) eine Bußtat

penitentiary [,penɪ'tenʃərɪ] N (*esp US*: = *prison*) Strafanstalt *f*, Gefängnis *nt*

penknife ['pennaɪf] N Taschenmesser *nt*

Penn(a) (*dated US*) abbr of **Pennsylvania**

pen name N Pseudonym *nt*, Schriftstellername *m*

pennant ['penənt] N Wimpel *m*

pen nib N Feder *f*

penniless ['penɪlɪs] ADJ mittellos; **to be ~** keinen Cent haben; **her husband died, leaving her ~** ihr Mann starb, und sie stand völlig mittellos *or* ohne einen einzigen Cent da

Pennines ['penaɪnz] PL Pennines *pl*, Gebirgszug in Nordengland

pennon ['penən] N = **pennant**

penn'orth ['penəθ] N = **pennyworth**

Pennsylvania [,pensɪl'veɪnɪə] N Pennsylvania *nt*

Pennsylvania Dutch **N** **a** (*Ling*) Pennsylvania-Deutsch *nt* **b** *pl* (= *people*) Pennsylvania-Deutsche *pl* **ADJ** pennsylvania-deutsch

Pennsylvanian [,pensɪl'veɪnɪən] ADJ pennsylvanisch

penny ['penɪ] N *pl* (*coins*) **pennies** *or* (*sum*) **pence** Penny *m*; (*US*) Centstück *nt*; **it costs 50 pence** es kostet 50 Pence; **he hasn't got a ~** (**to his name**) er hat keinen Cent (Geld); **in for a ~, in for a pound** (*esp Brit prov*) wennschon, dennschon (*inf*); (*morally*) wer A sagt muss auch B sagen (*prov*); **I'm not a ~ the wiser** ich bin genauso klug wie zuvor; **take care of the pennies and the pounds** (*Brit*) *or* **dollars** (*US*) **will take care of themselves** (*Prov*) spare im Kleinen, dann hast du im Großen; **to count** *or* **watch the pennies** auf den Pfennig sehen; **a ~ for your thoughts** ich möchte deine Gedanken lesen können; **magpies are two** *or* **ten a ~ in this area** Elstern gibt es in dieser Gegend jede Menge; **he keeps turning up like a bad ~** (*inf*) der taucht immer wieder auf (*inf*); **to spend a ~** (*Brit inf*) austreten, mal eben verschwinden (*inf*); **the ~ dropped** (*inf*) der Groschen ist gefallen (*inf*) → **pretty, honest**

penny: penny arcade N Spielhalle *f*; **Penny Black** N (= *stamp*) Penny Black *f*; **penny-dreadful** N (*dated Brit*) Groschenroman *m*; **penny-farthing** N (*Brit*) Hochrad *nt*; **penny loafer** N (*US*) Slipper *m*, Mokassin *m*; **penny-pinch** VI jeden Cent *or* Pfennig umdrehen; **penny-pincher** ['penɪ,pɪntʃə] N (*pej*) Pfennigfuchser(in) *m(f)* (*pej*); **penny-pinching** ADJ knauserig (*inf*); **pennyweight** N Pennygewicht *nt*; **penny whistle** N Kinderflöte *f*; **penny-wise** ADJ **to be ~ and pound foolish** immer am falschen Ende sparen; **pennyworth** N (*dated*) **a ~ of liquorice** für einen Penny Lakritz; **a ~ of common sense** für fünf Cent gesunden Menschenverstand

penologist [pi:'nɒlədʒɪst] N Kriminalpädagoge *m*, Kriminalpädagogin *f*

penology [pi:'nɒlədʒɪ] N Kriminalpädagogik *f*

pen: pen pal N (*inf*) Brieffreund(in) *m(f)*; **penpusher** N Schreiberling *m*; **penpushing** **N** Schreiberei *f*, Schreibkram *m* **ADJ** Schreib-; **~ work** Schreibarbeit *f*; **~ clerk** Bürohengst *m* (*inf*)

pension ['penʃən] N Rente *f*; (*for civil servants also*) Pension *f*, Ruhegehalt *nt* (*form*); **company ~** betriebliche Altersversorgung; **to be entitled to a ~** Anspruch auf eine Rente *etc* haben, rentenberechtigt/pensionsberechtigt sein; **to be living on a ~** von der Rente *etc* leben; **to get a ~** eine Rente *etc* beziehen

▶**pension off** VT *sep* (*Brit inf*) vorzeitig pensionieren

pensionable ['penʃənəbl] ADJ *job* mit Pensionsberechtigung; **this position is ~** diese Stellung berechtigt zu einer Pension/einem Ruhegehalt; **of ~ age** im Renten-/Pensionsalter; **~ salary** Gehaltsanteil, der zur Berechnung des Rentenversicherungsbeitrages herangezogen wird

pension book N Rentenausweis *m*

pensioner ['penʃənə'] N Rentner(in) *m(f)*; (= *former civil servant also*) Pensionär(in) *m(f)*, Ruhegehaltsempfänger(in) *m(f)* (*form*)

pension: pension fund N Rentenfonds *m*; **pension rights** PL Rentenanspruch *m*; **pension scheme** N Rentenversicherung *f*

pensive ADJ , **pensively** ADV ['pensɪv, -lɪ] nachdenklich; (= *sadly serious*) schwermütig

pensiveness ['pensɪvnɪs] N Nachdenklichkeit *f*; (*sad*) Schwermütigkeit *f*

pentagon ['pentəgən] N Fünfeck *nt*, Pentagon *nt*; **the Pentagon** das Pentagon

pentagonal [pen'tægənl] ADJ fünfeckig

pentagram ['pentəgræm] N Drudenfuß *m*, Pentagramm *nt*

pentahedron [,pentə'hi:drən] N Fünfflächner *m*, Pentaeder *nt*

pentameter [pen'tæmɪtə'] N Pentameter *m* → **iambic**

Pentateuch ['pentətju:k] N die fünf Bücher *pl* Mose, Pentateuch *m*

pentathlete [pen'tæθli:t] N Fünfkämpfer(in) *m(f)*

pentathlon [pen'tæθlən] N Fünfkampf *m*

pentatonic [,pentə'tɒnɪk] ADJ pentatonisch; **~ scale** fünfstufige Tonleiter

Pentecost ['pentɪkɒst] N (*Jewish*) Erntefest *nt*; (*Christian*) Pfingsten *nt*

Pentecostal [,pentɪ'kɒstl] ADJ Pfingst-; *sect, service, revival* der Pfingstbewegung; **pentecostal church** Pfingstkirche *f*; **pentecostal minister** Pfarrer(in) *m(f)* einer Pfingstkirche

penthouse ['penthaus] N (= *apartment*) Penthouse *nt*, Dachterrassenwohnung *f*; (= *roof*) Überdachung *f*

Pentium processor® [,pentɪəm'prəusesə'] N Pentium-Prozessor® *m*

pent up ADJ *pred*, **pent-up** ['pent'ʌp] ADJ *attr person* (*with frustration, anger*) geladen *pred*; (*after traumatic experience*) aufgewühlt; (= *nervous, excited*) innerlich angespannt; *emotions, passion, excitement* aufgestaut; (*Econ*) *demand* rege, lebhaft; **she had been very ~** es hatte sich alles in ihr gestaut; **pent-up feelings** ein Emotionsstau *m*, angestaute Gefühle *pl*

penultimate [pe'nʌltɪmɪt] ADJ vorletzte(r, s)

penumbra [pɪ'nʌmbrə] N *pl* **-s** *or* **-e** [-bri:] Halbschatten *m*

penurious [pɪ'njʊərɪəs] ADJ (*liter*) (= *poor*) arm, armselig; *existence also* karg, dürftig; (= *mean*) geizig, knauserig

penuriously [pɪ'njʊərɪəslɪ] ADV (*liter*) *live* arm, armselig

penury ['penjʊrɪ] N Armut *f*, Not *f*; **in a state of ~** in Armut

peony ['pi:ənɪ] N Pfingstrose *f*, Päonie *f* (*spec*)

people ['pi:pl] **PL** **a** Menschen *pl*; (*not in formal context*) Leute *pl*; **we're concerned with ~** uns geht es um die Menschen; **French ~ are very fond of their food** die Franzosen lieben ihre gute Küche; **that's typical of Edinburgh ~** das ist typisch für (die) Leute aus Edinburgh; **a job where you meet ~** eine Arbeit, wo man mit Menschen *or* Leuten zusammenkommt; **~ who need ~** Menschen, die andere Menschen brauchen; **all the ~ in the world** alle Menschen auf der Welt; **all ~ with red hair** alle Rothaarigen; **some ~ don't like it** manche Leute mögen es nicht; **most ~ in show business** die meisten Leute im Showgeschäft; **aren't ~ funny?** was gibt es doch für seltsame Menschen *or* Leute?; **the ~ you meet!** Menschen *or* Leute gibts!; **why**

me of all ~? warum ausgerechnet ich/mich?; **I met Harry of all ~!** ausgerechnet Harry habe ich getroffen!; **of all ~ who do you think I should meet?** stell dir mal vor, wen ich getroffen habe?; **what do you ~ think?** was haltet ihr denn davon?; *poor* ~ arme Leute *pl*, Arme *pl*; *blind* ~ Blinde *pl*; *disabled* ~ Behinderte *pl*; *middle-aged* ~ Menschen *pl* mittleren Alters; *old* ~ Senioren *pl*; *city* ~ Stadtmenschen *pl*; *country* ~ Menschen *pl* vom Land, Landleute *pl* (*dated*); **some ~!** Leute gibts!; **some ~ have all the luck** manche Leute haben einfach Glück

b (= *inhabitants*) Bevölkerung *f*; **the ~ of Rome/Egypt** *etc* die Bevölkerung von Rom/Ägypten *etc*; **Madrid has over 5 million ~** Madrid hat über 5 Millionen Einwohner

c (= *one, they*) man; (= *people in general, the neighbours*) die Leute; **~ say that ...** man sagt, dass ...; **what will ~ think!** was sollen die Leute denken!; **~ in general tend to say ... in** Allgemeinen neigt man zu der Behauptung ...

d (= *nation, masses, subjects*) Volk *nt*; **the common ~** das einfache Volk, die breite Masse; **a man of the ~** ein Mann *m* des Volkes; **government by the ~ (of the ~)** eine Regierung des Volkes; **the Belgian ~** die Belgier *pl*, das belgische Volk; **People's police/Republic** *etc* Volkspolizei *f*/-republik *f etc*

VT besiedeln; **to be ~d by** bevölkert sein von; **the world seems to be ~d with idiots** die Welt scheint von Idioten bevölkert zu sein

people: people carrier N (*Aut*) Großraumlimousine *f*, Van *m*; **people mover** N **a** (= *moving pavement*) Rollband *nt* **b** (*Aut*) = **people carrier**; **people power** N Basisdemokratie *f*; **People's Dispensary for Sick Animals** N (*Brit*) *kostenloses Behandlungszentrum für Haustiere*

pep [pep] N (*inf*) Schwung *m*, Elan *m*, Pep *m* (*inf*)

▶**pep up** VT *sep* (*inf*) Schwung bringen in (+*acc*); *food, drink* pikanter machen; *person* munter machen; **pills to pep you up** Aufputschmittel *pl*

pepper ['pepə'] **N** Pfeffer *m*; (= *green, red pepper*) Paprika *m*; (= *plant*) Pfefferstrauch *m*; **two ~s** zwei Paprikaschoten **VT** **a** (*lit*) pfeffern **b** (*fig*) **to ~ sth with quotations** etw mit Zitaten spicken; **to ~ sb with shot** jdn mit Kugeln durchlöchern

pepper: pepper-and-salt ADJ Pfeffer-und-Salz-; *hair* meliert; **~ pattern** Pfeffer-und-Salz-Muster *nt*; **pepperbox** N (*US*) Pfefferstreuer *m*; **peppercorn** N Pfefferkorn *nt*; **peppercorn rent** N (= *nominal rent*) nominelle *or* symbolische Miete

peppered ['pepəd] ADJ **a** (*Cook*) gepfeffert; **~ mackerel fillets** gepfefferte Makrelenfilets **b** (*fig*) **to be ~ with sth** mit etw übersät sein; *with quotations etc* mit etw gespickt sein; **his hair is ~ with grey** sein Haar ist von grauen Strähnen durchzogen

pepper: pepper mill N Pfeffermühle *f*; **peppermint** N Pfefferminz *nt*; (*Bot*) Pfefferminze *f*; **pepper pot** N Pfefferstreuer *m*; **pepper steak** N Pfeffersteak *m*

peppery ['pepərɪ] ADJ gepfeffert; (*fig*) *old man etc* hitzig, hitzköpfig; **it tastes rather ~** es schmeckt stark nach Pfeffer

pep pill N Aufputschpille *f*, Peppille *f* (*inf*)

peppy ['pepɪ] ADJ (+*er*) (*inf*) peppig (*inf*)

PEP RALLY

Eine **pep rally** ist ein amerikanischer Begriff für ein Treffen von Schülern und Studenten von **high schools**, Colleges oder Universitäten vor einem sportlichen Ereignis, meist einem Football- oder Basketballspiel, auf dem die Stimmung für ihr Team aufgeheizt werden soll. Bei der Kundgebung, die einen Tag oder noch früher vor dem Spiel abgehalten wird, treten Cheerleader auf, die Blaskapelle der Schule spielt, und die Spieler und Trainer halten kurze Ansprachen. Manchmal wird der Begriff auch für politische Kundgebungen oder Firmenversammlungen verwendet, auf denen die Anhänger oder Arbeitnehmer durch öffentliche Belobigung und die Ankündigung neuer Pläne und zukünftiger Erfolge motiviert werden sollen.

pepsin ['pepsɪn] N Pepsin nt

pep talk N (inf) aufmunternde Worte pl; **to give sb a ~** jdm ein paar aufmunternde Worte sagen

peptic ['peptɪk] ADJ peptisch

peptic ulcer N Magengeschwür nt

per [pɜː'] PREP pro; **£500 ~ annum** £ 500 im or pro Jahr; **60 km ~ hour** 60 Stundenkilometer, 60 km pro Stunde or in der Stunde; **£2 ~ dozen** das Dutzend für £ 2, £ 2 das Dutzend; **£5 ~ copy** £ 5 pro or je Exemplar, £ 5 für jedes Exemplar; **as ~** gemäß (+dat); **~ se** an sich, per se (geh) → **usual**

peradventure [ˌperəd'ventʃə'] ADV (old: = perhaps) vielleicht; **if/lest ~** falls

perambulate [pə'ræmbjʊleɪt] (form) VT sich ergehen in (+dat) (geh) VI sich ergehen (liter)

perambulation [pəˌræmbjʊ'leɪʃən] N (form) Spaziergang m

perambulator ['præmbjʊleɪtə'] N (Brit, form) Kinderwagen m

per capita [pə'kæpɪtə] ADJ Pro-Kopf-; **~ income** Pro-Kopf-Einkommen nt ADV pro Kopf; **what is the average wage ~?** wie hoch ist der Durchschnittslohn pro Kopf?

perceivable [pə'siːvəbl] ADJ erkennbar; **barely ~** kaum auszumachen or zu erkennen

perceive [pə'siːv] VT wahrnehmen; (= understand, realize, recognize) erkennen; **do you ~ anything strange?** fällt Ihnen irgendetwas Ungewöhnliches auf?; **..., which we ~ to be the case** (form) ..., was wir als zutreffend erkennen; **to ~ oneself as ...** sich als ... empfinden

perceived [pə'siːvd] ADJ danger empfunden; need erkannt; failure, success wahrnehmbar

per cent, (US) **percent** [pə'sent] N Prozent nt; **what ~?** wie viel Prozent?; **20 ~** 20 Prozent; **a 10 ~ discount** 10 Prozent Rabatt; **a ten ~ increase** eine zehnprozentige Steigerung; **45 ~ of Americans** 45 Prozent der Amerikaner; **to increase sth by 10 ~** etw um 10 Prozent erhöhen; **to give 100 ~** 100 Prozent geben; **I'm 99 ~ certain that ...** ich bin (zu) 99 Prozent sicher, dass ...

percentage [pə'sentɪdʒ] N a Prozentsatz m; (= commission, payment) Anteil m; (= proportion) Teil m; **a small ~ of the population** ein geringer Teil der Bevölkerung; **expressed as a ~** prozentual or in Prozenten ausgedrückt; **what ~?** wie viel Prozent?; **to get a ~ of all sales** prozentual am Umsatz beteiligt sein (inf: = advantage) **there's no ~ in it** das bringt nichts (inf) ATTR prozentual; **on a ~ basis** prozentual, auf Prozentbasis; **~ sign** Prozentzeichen nt

percentile [pə'sentaɪl] N Prozent nt; **he's in the ninetieth ~ for reading and maths** in Lesen und Rechnen gehört er zu den besten zehn Prozent

perceptible [pə'septəbl] ADJ wahrnehmbar; improvement, trend, increase etc spürbar, deutlich; **there was a ~ pause** es trat eine deutliche Pause ein; **his unhappiness was ~ only to his close friends** nur seine engsten Freunde spürten or merkten, dass er unglücklich war

perceptibly [pə'septəblɪ] ADV merklich, spürbar; (to the eye) wahrnehmbar, sichtbar; **he paled ~** er wurde sichtbar blass

perception [pə'sepʃən] N a no pl Wahrnehmung f; **his colour ~ is impaired** seine Farbwahrnehmung ist beeinträchtigt; **his powers of ~** sein Wahrnehmungsvermögen nt
b (= mental image, conception) Auffassung f (of von); **he seems to have a clear ~ of the dilemma I face** er scheint meine schwierige Lage vollauf zu erkennen; **one's ~ of the situation**

die eigene Einschätzung der Lage
c no pl (= perceptiveness) Einsicht f; (= perceptive remark, observation) Beobachtung f
d no pl (= act of perceiving) (of object, visible difference) Wahrnehmung f; (of difficulties, meaning, illogicality etc) Erkennen nt; **his quick ~ of the danger saved us all from death** weil er die Gefahr blitzschnell erkannte, rettete er uns allen das Leben

perceptive [pə'septɪv] ADJ a Wahrnehmungs-; **~ ability** Wahrnehmungsvermögen nt b person (= quick to smell/see/hear) aufmerksam; (= quick to understand) scharfsinnig; (= penetrating) analysis, speech, study aufschlussreich, scharfsinnig; book, remark aufschlussreich; **he has the ~ mind of a true artist** er hat das Einfühlungsvermögen eines wahren Künstlers; **very ~ of you!** (iro) du merkst auch alles! (iro)

perceptively [pə'septɪvlɪ] ADV say, remark, write scharfsinnig

perceptiveness [pə'septɪvnɪs] N (of person) (= quickness to see/hear/smell) Aufmerksamkeit f; (= quick realization) Scharfsinnigkeit f; (of analysis, speech, study) Erkenntnisreichtum m, Scharfsinnigkeit f; (of argument) Einsichtigkeit f

perceptual [pə'septjʊəl] ADJ ATTR Wahrnehmungs-; **~ skills** Wahrnehmungsfähigkeit f; **~ problems** Wahrnehmungsprobleme pl

perch¹ [pɜːtʃ] N (= fish) Flussbarsch m

perch² N a (of bird) Stange f; (in tree) Ast m; (= hen-roost) Hühnerstange f; (fig: for person etc) Hochsitz m; **to fall** or **drop** or **topple off the** or **one's ~** (Brit fig inf) den Löffel abgeben (inf); **to knock sb off his ~** (Brit fig) jdn von seinem hohen Ross herunterholen b (Measure) Längenmaß (5.029 m) VT **to ~ sth on sth** etw auf etw (acc) setzen or (upright) stellen VI (bird, fig: person) hocken; (= alight) sich niederlassen; **the tower ~es on the edge of the cliff** der Turm thront über dem Rand der Klippe

perchance [pə'tʃɑːns] ADV (old) vielleicht

perched [pɜːtʃt] ADJ a (= situated) **~ on** thronend auf +dat; **a village ~ on a hillside/above the lake** ein Dorf, das auf dem Hang/über dem See thront b (= seated) **to be ~ on sth** auf etw (dat) hocken c (= resting) **with his glasses ~ on the end of his nose** mit der Brille auf der Nasenspitze

percipient [pə'sɪpɪənt] ADJ (form) = **perceptive**

percolate ['pɜːkəleɪt] VT filtrieren; coffee (in einer Kaffeemaschine) zubereiten; **~d coffee** mit der Kaffeemaschine gebrühter Kaffee VI (lit, fig) durchsickern; **the coffee is just percolating** der Kaffee läuft gerade durch; **the information was starting to ~ through** die Informationen begannen durchzusickern

percolator ['pɜːkəleɪtə'] N Kaffeemaschine f

percuss [pə'kʌs] VT (Med) perkutieren (spec), abklopfen

percussion [pə'kʌʃən] N a Perkussion f (also Med) b (Mus) Schlagzeug nt

percussion: percussion cap N Zündhütchen nt; **percussion drill** N Schlagbohrmaschine f; **percussion instrument** N (Mus) Schlaginstrument nt

percussionist [pə'kʌʃənɪst] N Schlagzeuger(in) m(f)

percussion section N (Mus) Schlagzeug nt

percussive [pə'kʌsɪv] ADJ perkussorisch (spec)

per diem [pɜː'diːem] ADV pro Tag ADJ pro Tag; **the ~ rate** der Tagessatz N (esp US) Tagessatz m

perdition [pə'dɪʃən] N ewige Verdammnis

peregrination [ˌperɪgrɪ'neɪʃən] N (liter) Fahrt f

peregrine (falcon) ['perɪgrɪn('fɔːlkən)] N Wanderfalke m

peremptorily [pə'remptərɪlɪ] ADV command, instruct kategorisch

peremptory [pə'remptərɪ] ADJ command, instruction kategorisch; gesture, voice gebieterisch; person herrisch; **~ challenge** (US Jur) Ablehnung

eines Geschworenen ohne Angabe von Gründen

perennial [pə'renɪəl] ADJ plant mehrjährig, perennierend; (= perpetual, constant) immer während, ewig; (= regularly recurring) immer wiederkehrend; **buying Christmas presents is a ~ problem** der Kauf von Weihnachtsgeschenken ist ein alljährlich wiederkehrendes Problem N (Bot) perennierende or mehrjährige Pflanze

perennially [pə'renɪəlɪ] ADV (= perpetually, constantly) ständig; (= recurrently) immer wieder

perestroika [pere'strɔɪkə] N Perestroika f

perfect ['pɜːfɪkt] ADJ a perfekt; wife, husband, teacher, host, relationship perfekt, vorbildlich; weather, day, holiday ideal, perfekt; (Comm: = not damaged) einwandfrei; **to be ~ for doing sth** bestens geeignet sein, um etw zu tun; **it was the ~ moment** es war genau der richtige Augenblick; **that's the ~ hairstyle/woman for you** das ist genau die richtige Frisur/Frau für dich; **his Spanish is far from ~** sein Spanisch ist bei weitem nicht perfekt; **with ~ self-confidence** mit absolutem Selbstvertrauen; **nobody is ~** niemand ist perfekt or vollkommen; **they make a ~ couple** sie sind das perfekte Paar; **in a ~ world** in einer idealen Welt; **he's the ~ gentleman** er ist der perfekte Gentleman; **~ number** (Math) vollkommene Zahl
b (= absolute, utter) völlig; fool, nonsense völlig, ausgemacht; **she's a ~ terror** sie ist einfach schrecklich; **he's a ~ bore** er ist ausgesprochen langweilig; **~ strangers** wildfremde Leute pl; **a ~ stranger** ein wildfremder Mensch; **he's a ~ stranger to me** er ist mir völlig fremd; **it's a ~ disgrace** es ist wirklich eine Schande
c (Gram) **~ tense** Perfekt nt; **~ ending** Endung f im Perfekt; **~ form** Vergangenheitsform f
d (Mus) fourth rein; cadence authentisch → **pitch²**
N (Gram) Perfekt nt; **in the ~** im Perfekt
VT [pə'fekt] vervollkommnen; technique, technology, process also perfektionieren; **to ~ the art of doing sth** die Kunst perfektionieren, etw zu tun

perfectibility [pəˌfektɪ'bɪlɪtɪ] N Vervollkommnungsfähigkeit f; (of technique, technology, process) Perfektionierbarkeit f

perfectible [pə'fektɪbl] ADJ vervollkommnungsfähig; technique, technology, process perfektionierbar

perfection [pə'fekʃən] N a Vollkommenheit f, Perfektion f; **to do sth to ~** etw perfekt tun b (= perfecting) Vervollkommnung f, Perfektionierung f; **the ~ of production methods** die Perfektionierung der Produktionsmethoden

perfectionism [pə'fekʃənɪzəm] N Perfektionismus m

perfectionist [pə'fekʃənɪst] N Perfektionist(in) m(f) ADJ perfektionistisch

perfective [pə'fektɪv] ADJ (also Gram) perfektiv

perfectly ['pɜːfɪktlɪ] ADV a (= flawlessly, completely) perfekt; **he timed his entry ~** er hat seinen Eintritt genau abgepasst; **a ~ finished piece of work** eine wirklich vollendete Arbeit; **the climate suited us ~** das Klima war ideal für uns; **I understand you ~** ich weiß genau, was Sie meinen
b (= absolutely, utterly) absolut, vollkommen; **we're ~ happy about it** wir sind damit völlig zufrieden; **a ~ lovely day** ein wirklich herrlicher Tag; **you know ~ well that ...** du weißt ganz genau, dass ...; **to be ~ honest, ...** um ganz ehrlich zu sein, ...; **a Lada is a ~ good car** ein Lada ist durchaus ein gutes Auto

perfect rhyme N rührender Reim

perfidious ADJ , **perfidiously** ADV [pɜː'fɪdɪəs, -lɪ] (liter) perfid(e) (liter)

perfidiousness [pɜː'fɪdɪəsnɪs], **perfidy** ['pɜːfɪdɪ] N (liter) Perfidie f (liter)

perforate ['pɜːfəreɪt] VT (with row of holes) perforieren; (= pierce once) durchstechen, lochen; (Med) perforieren VI (ulcer) durchbrechen

perforation [ˌpɜːfə'reɪʃən] N (= act) Perforieren nt; (= row of holes, Med) Perforation f

perforce [pəˈfɔːs] ADV (old, liter) notgedrungen

perform [pəˈfɔːm] VT play, concerto aufführen; solo, duet vortragen; part spielen; trick vorführen; miracle vollbringen; task verrichten, erfüllen; duty, function erfüllen; operation durchführen; ritual, ceremony vollziehen VI **a** (= appear: orchestra, circus act etc) auftreten; **to ~ on the violin** Geige spielen

b (car, machine, football team etc) leisten; (examination candidate etc) abschneiden; **the 2 litre version ~s better** die Zweiliterversion leistet mehr; **the car ~ed excellently in the speed trials** in den Geschwindigkeitsversuchen brachte der Wagen ausgezeichnete Ergebnisse; **the choir ~ed very well** der Chor war sehr gut or hat sehr gut gesungen; **this car ~s best between 50 and 60 kmph** dieser Wagen bringt seine optimale Leistung zwischen 50 und 60 Stundenkilometern; **how did he ~?** (actor, musician) wie war er?; **how did the car ~?** wie ist der Wagen gelaufen?; **he ~ed brilliantly as Hamlet** er spielte die Rolle des Hamlet brillant; **how does the metal ~ under pressure?** wie verhält sich das Metall unter Druck?; **the shares are ~ing strongly** die Aktien steigen stark; **he couldn't ~** (euph, sexually) er konnte nicht

c (euph: = excrete) sein Geschäft verrichten

performance [pəˈfɔːməns] N **a** (esp Theat, of play, opera etc) Aufführung f; (cinema) Vorstellung f; (by actor) Leistung f; (of a part) Darstellung f; **the late ~** die Spätvorstellung; **her ~ as Mother Courage was outstanding** ihre Darstellung der Mutter Courage war hervorragend; **he gave a splendid ~** er hat eine ausgezeichnete Leistung geboten, er hat ausgezeichnet gespielt/gesungen etc; **we are going to hear a ~ of Beethoven's 5th** wir werden Beethovens 5. Sinfonie hören

b (= carrying out) (of function, duty, task) Erfüllung f; (of operation) Durchführung f; (of ritual, ceremony) Vollzug m; (of trick) Vorführung f; (of miracle) Vollbringung f; (of play, concerto) Aufführung f; (of solo, duet) Vortrag m; (of part) Darstellung f; **in the ~ of his duties** in Ausübung seiner Pflicht; **he died in the ~ of duty** er starb in Erfüllung seiner Pflicht

c (= effectiveness) (of machine, vehicle, sportsman etc) Leistung f; (of examination candidate etc) Abschneiden nt; (of shares) Kursentwicklung f; **he put up a good ~** er hat sich gut geschlagen (inf); **what was his ~ like in the test?** wie hat er in der Prüfung abgeschnitten?; **the team gave a poor ~** die Mannschaft hat eine schlechte Leistung gezeigt

d (inf: = to-do, palaver) Umstand m; (= bad behaviour) Benehmen nt; **what a ~!** was für ein Umstand!, welch ein Benehmen!; **what a ~ to put on in front of all the guests** sich so vor den Gästen zu benehmen!

performance: performance art N Performance Art f; **performance artist** N Performancekünstler(in) m(f); **performance car** N leistungsstarker Wagen

performative [pəˈfɔːmətɪv] (Ling) N performativer Ausdruck ADJ performativ

performer [pəˈfɔːmə] N Künstler(in) m(f)

performing [pəˈfɔːmɪŋ] ADJ animal dressiert; artist darstellend; **the ~ arts** die darstellenden Künste; **~ rights** Aufführungsrechte pl

perfume [ˈpɜːfjuːm] N **a** (= substance) Parfüm nt; (= smell) Duft m VT [pəˈfjuːm] parfümieren; **the flowers ~d the air** der Duft der Blumen erfüllte die Luft

perfumed [ˈpɜːfjuːmd] ADJ **a** (= scented) substance parfümiert (with mit); handkerchief, envelope parfümiert **b** (naturally) flowers, air duftend; **a sweetly ~ oil** ein süßlich duftendes Öl

perfumer [pɜːˈfjuːmə] N (= maker) Parfümeur(in) m(f); (= seller) Parfümhändler(in) m(f); (= device) Parfümzerstäuber m

perfumery [pɜːˈfjuːməri] N (= making perfume) Parfümherstellung f; (= perfume factory) Parfümerie f; (= perfumes) Parfüm pl

perfunctorily [pəˈfʌŋktərili] ADV flüchtig

perfunctory [pəˈfʌŋktəri] ADJ flüchtig, der Form halber; **he said some ~ words of congratulation** er gratulierte mit ein paar flüchtig hingeworfenen Worten

pergola [ˈpɜːɡələ] N Pergola f, Laube f

perhaps [pəˈhæps, præps] ✪ 1.1, 15.3, 26.3 ADV vielleicht; **~ the greatest exponent of the art** der möglicherweise bedeutendste Vertreter dieser Kunst; **~ so** das kann or mag sein; **~ not** vielleicht (auch) nicht; **will he make a complete recovery? – ~ not, but we are doing our best** wird er sich ganz erholen? – das vielleicht nicht, aber wir tun unser Bestes; **~ I might keep it for a day or two?** könnte ich es vielleicht or eventuell für ein oder zwei Tage behalten?

pericarp [ˈperɪkɑːp] N Perikarp nt

perigee [ˈperɪdʒiː] N (Astron) Perigäum nt, Erdnähe f

peril [ˈperɪl] N Gefahr f; **he is in great ~** er schwebt in großer Gefahr; **to be in ~ of one's life** in Lebensgefahr sein; **the cliff is in ~ of collapsing** es besteht die Gefahr, dass die Klippen einstürzen; **do it at your (own) ~** auf Ihre eigene Gefahr

perilous [ˈperɪləs] ADJ gefährlich; situation also bedrohlich

perilously [ˈperɪləslɪ] ADV gefährlich; **he was clinging ~ to an outcrop of rock** er hing lebensgefährlich an einem Felsvorsprung; **we came ~ close to bankruptcy/the precipice** wir waren dem Bankrott/Abgrund gefährlich nahe; **she came ~ close to falling** sie wäre um ein Haar heruntergefallen

perimeter [pəˈrɪmɪtə] N (Math) Umfang m, Perimeter m; (Med) Perimeter m; (of grounds) Grenze f; **~ fence** Umzäunung f; **to walk round the ~** um das Gelände herumgehen

perinatal [perɪˈneɪtəl] ADJ (Med) perinatal

perineum [perɪˈniːəm] N (Anat) Damm m, Perineum nt (spec)

period [ˈpɪəriəd] N **a** (= length of time) Zeit f; (= age, epoch) Zeitalter nt, Epoche f; (Geol) Periode f; **Picasso's blue ~** Picassos blaue Periode; **for a ~ of eight weeks/two hours** für eine (Zeit)dauer or einen Zeitraum von acht Wochen/zwei Stunden; **within a three-month ~** innerhalb von drei Monaten; **for a three-month ~** drei Monate lang; **at that ~ (of my life)** zu diesem Zeitpunkt (in meinem Leben); **a ~ of cold weather** eine Kaltwetterperiode; **the costume etc of the ~** die Kleidung etc der damaligen Zeit; **a writer of the ~** ein zeitgenössischer Schriftsteller

b (Sch) (Schul)stunde f; **double ~** Doppelstunde f

c (form: of sentence) Periode f; (esp US: = full stop) Punkt m; **I don't know anything about American literature ~** (esp US) ich habe überhaupt keine Ahnung von amerikanischer Literatur; **I'm not going ~!** (esp US) ich gehe nicht, Schluss or und damit basta (inf)!

d (= menstruation) Periode f, Monatsblutung f, Tage pl (inf); **she missed a ~** sie bekam ihre Periode etc nicht

e (Chem) Periode f

period: period costume, period dress N zeitgenössische Kostüme pl; **period furniture** N antike Möbel pl

periodic [pɪəriˈɒdɪk] ADJ (= intermittent) periodisch; (= regular also) regelmäßig

periodical [pɪəriˈɒdɪkəl] ADJ = **periodic** N Zeitschrift f; (= academic also) Periodikum nt

periodically [pɪəriˈɒdɪkəli] ADV periodisch; (= regularly also) regelmäßig

periodicity [pɪəriəˈdɪsɪti] N (Chem) Periodizität f

periodic system, periodic table N (Chem) Periodensystem nt

periodontitis [perɪəʊdɒnˈtaɪtɪs] N Wurzelhautentzündung f

period: period pains PL Menstruationsbeschwerden pl; **period piece** N **a** antikes

Stück; (= painting, music etc) Zeitdokument nt **b** (also **period play**) Zeitstück nt

peripatetic [perɪpəˈtetɪk] ADJ umherreisend; existence rastlos; teacher an mehreren Schulen unterrichtend attr

peripheral [pəˈrɪfərəl] ADJ Rand-; (Anat) peripher; (fig) nebensächlich, peripher; (Comput) Peripherie-; **to be ~ to sth** (situation, person) für etw nebensächlich sein; **~ figure** (= person) Randfigur f; **~ role** Nebenrolle f; **~ device** (Comput) Peripheriegerät nt; **~ vision** peripheres Sehvermögen N (Comput) Peripheriegerät nt

periphery [pəˈrɪfəri] N Peripherie f; **young people on the ~ of society** junge Menschen am Rande der Gesellschaft

periphrastic [perɪˈfræstɪk] ADJ periphrastisch

periscope [ˈperɪskəʊp] N Periskop nt

perish [ˈperɪʃ] VI **a** (liter) (= die) umkommen, sterben; (= be destroyed: cities, civilization) untergehen; **we shall do it or ~ in the attempt** wir werden es machen, koste es, was es wolle; **he ~ed at sea** er fand den Tod auf See; **~ the thought!** (inf) Gott behüte or bewahre! **b** (rubber, leather etc) verschleißen, brüchig werden; (food) verderben, schlecht werden VT rubber, leather zerstören, brüchig werden lassen

perishable [ˈperɪʃəbl] ADJ food verderblich; **"perishable"** „leicht verderblich" PL **~s** leicht verderbliche Ware(n)

perished [ˈperɪʃt] ADJ (inf, with cold) durchgefroren

perisher [ˈperɪʃə] N (Brit, inf) Teufelsbraten m (inf)

perishing [ˈperɪʃɪŋ] ADJ (Brit inf) **a** (= very cold) room, weather eisig kalt; **I'm ~** ich geh fast ein vor Kälte (inf) **b** (= objectionable) verdammt (inf)

peristalsis [perɪˈstælsɪs] N Peristaltik f

peristyle [ˈperɪstaɪl] N Peristyl nt

peritoneum [perɪtəʊˈniːəm] N (Anat) Bauchfell nt, Peritoneum nt (spec)

peritonitis [perɪtəʊˈnaɪtɪs] N Bauchfellentzündung f

periwig [ˈperɪwɪɡ] N (Hist) Perücke f

periwinkle [ˈperɪwɪŋkl] N (Bot) Immergrün nt; (Zool) Strandschnecke f

perjure [ˈpɜːdʒə] VR einen Meineid leisten

perjured [ˈpɜːdʒəd] ADJ evidence, witness meineidig

perjury [ˈpɜːdʒəri] N Meineid m; **to commit ~** einen Meineid leisten

perk [pɜːk] N (= benefit) Vergünstigung f

▶ **perk up** VT sep **a** (= lift) head heben; **he perked up his ears** (dog, person) er spitzte die Ohren **b** **to perk sb up** (= make lively: coffee etc) jdn aufmöbeln (inf) or munter machen; (= make cheerful: visit, idea etc) jdn aufheitern; **she perked up her outfit with a bright scarf** sie peppte ihre Kleidung mit einem hellen Schal auf (inf) VI (= liven up: person, party) munter werden; (= cheer up) aufleben; (= become interested) hellhörig werden; **his ears perked up** er spitzte seine Ohren

perkily [ˈpɜːkɪli] ADV (= cheerfully) munter; (= cheekily) kess, keck

perkiness [ˈpɜːkɪnɪs] N (= cheerfulness) Lebhaftigkeit f; (= cheekiness) Keckheit f, forsche Art

perky [ˈpɜːki] ADJ (+er) (= cheerful, bright) munter; (= cheeky, pert) kess, keck

perm[1] [pɜːm] abbr of **permanent wave** N Dauerwelle f; **to give sb a ~** jdm eine Dauerwelle machen VT **to ~ sb's hair** jdm eine Dauerwelle machen; **she only had the ends ~ed** sie ließ sich (dat) nur an den Enden eine Dauerwelle machen VI **my hair doesn't ~ very easily** Dauerwelle hält bei mir sehr schlecht

perm[2] N (for football pools) abbr of **permutation**

permafrost [ˈpɜːməfrɒst] N Dauerfrostboden m

permanence [ˈpɜːmənəns], **permanency** [ˈpɜːmənsi] N Dauerhaftigkeit f, Permanenz f; (of relationship, marriage, arrangement also, of *job*) Beständigkeit *f*; **having bought a flat, she began to feel some degree of ~** nachdem sie sich (*dat*) eine Wohnung gekauft hatte, entwickelte sie ein gewisses Gefühl der Bodenständigkeit

permanent ['pɜːmənənt] **ADJ** **a** (= *lasting*) ständig, permanent; *arrangement, position, building* fest; *job, relationship, dye, effect, solution* dauerhaft; *damage* bleibend; *agreement* unbefristet; **on a ~ basis** dauerhaft; **to earn oneself a ~ place in history** sich (*dat*) einen bleibenden Platz in der Geschichte verdienen; **the ~ revolution** die permanente Revolution; **I hope this is not going to become ~** ich hoffe, das wird kein Dauerzustand; **~ assets** Anlagevermögen *nt*; **~ capital** Anlagekapital *nt*; **~ feature** fester Bestandteil; **~ fixture** (*lit*) fest installierte Einrichtung; **he is a ~ fixture here** er gehört schon mit zum Inventar; **~ magnet** Permanentmagnet *m*; **~ memory** (*Comput*) Festspeicher *m*; **~ pleats** Dauerfalten *pl*; **~ residence/address** ständiger *or* fester Wohnsitz; **one's ~ teeth** die zweiten Zähne **b** (= *constant*) *supply* permanent; *staff* fest angestellt; *member* ständig; **~ employees** Festangestellte *pl*; **to make sb ~** jdn fest anstellen; **I'm not ~ here** ich bin hier nicht fest angestellt **N** (*US*) = perm ¹ N

permanently ['pɜːmənəntlɪ] **ADV** **a** permanent, ständig; *fixed* fest; *damage* bleibend; *change* ständig; **a ~ depressing effect** eine anhaltend deprimierende Wirkung; **~ employed** fest angestellt; **~ glued together** dauerhaft verbunden; **~ pleated skirt** Rock mit Dauerfalten; **are you living ~ in Frankfurt?** ist Frankfurt Ihr fester *or* ständiger Wohnsitz? **b** (= *constantly*) *closed* dauernd; *tired* dauernd, ständig; *angry* ständig

permanent: Permanent Secretary N (*Brit Admin*) beamteter Staatssekretär, beamtete Staatssekretärin; **permanent wave** N → perm ¹ N; **permanent way** N (*Brit*) Bahnkörper *m*

permanganate [pɜːˈmæŋgənɪt] N Permanganat *nt*

permeability [ˌpɜːmɪəˈbɪlɪtɪ] N Durchlässigkeit *f*, Permeabilität *f* (*geh, Sci*)

permeable ['pɜːmɪəbl] **ADJ** durchlässig, permeabel (*geh, Sci*)

permeate ['pɜːmɪeɪt] **VT** (*lit, fig*) durchdringen **VI** dringen (*into* in +*acc*, *through* durch)

permissible [pəˈmɪsɪbl] **ADJ** **a** erlaubt (*for sb* jdm); **legally ~** gesetzlich erlaubt; **the maximum ~ levels of radiation** die maximal zulässige Strahlenbelastung **b** (= *acceptable*) annehmbar

permission [pəˈmɪʃən] **✪** 9.1, 9.2 N Erlaubnis *f*; **with your ~** mit Ihrer Erlaubnis, wenn Sie gestatten; **without ~ from sb** ohne jds Erlaubnis; **to do sth with/by sb's ~** etw mit jds Erlaubnis tun; **to get ~** eine Erlaubnis erhalten; **to get sb's ~** jds Erlaubnis erhalten; **to give ~ (for sth)** etw erlauben, die Erlaubnis (für etw) erteilen; **to give sb ~ (to do sth)** jdm die Erlaubnis geben *or* jdm erlauben(, etw zu tun); **you have my ~ to leave** Sie haben meine Erlaubnis zu gehen; **no ~ is needed** eine Erlaubnis ist nicht erforderlich; **to ask sb's ~, to ask ~ of sb** jdn um Erlaubnis bitten; **to ask ~ for sb to do sth** um Erlaubnis bitten, dass jd etw tun darf; **"by (kind) ~ of ..."** „mit (freundlicher) Genehmigung (+*gen*) ..."

permissive [pəˈmɪsɪv] **ADJ** nachgiebig, permissiv (*geh*); (= *tolerant*) *age, attitude, law, parents, school* freizügig; (*sexually*) freizügig; **it encourages youngsters to be ~** es führt zu allzu großer Freizügigkeit unter Jugendlichen; **the ~ society** die permissive Gesellschaft

permissiveness [pəˈmɪsɪvnɪs] N Nachgiebigkeit *f*, Permissivität *f* (*geh*); (*of age, attitude, law, parents, school*) Freizügigkeit *f*; (*sexually*) Freizügigkeit *f*

permit [pəˈmɪt] **✪** 9.1, 9.2, 9.4 **VT** *sth* erlauben, gestatten; **to ~ sb/oneself to do sth** jdm/sich (*dat*) erlauben, etw zu tun; **is it/am I ~ted to smoke?** darf man/ich rauchen?; **visitors are**

not **~ted after 10** nach 10 Uhr sind keine Besucher mehr erlaubt; **to ~ oneself sth** sich (*dat*) etw erlauben; **~ me!** gestatten Sie bitte! **VI** **a** **if you (will) ~** wenn Sie gestatten *or* erlauben; **if the weather ~s, weather ~ting** wenn es das Wetter erlaubt *or* zulässt; **if time ~s** wenn es die Zeit zulässt, wenn die Zeit reicht **b** (*form*) **to ~ of sth** etw zulassen **N** ['pɜːmɪt] Genehmigung *f*; **~ holder** Inhaber(in) *m(f)* eines Berechtigungsscheins *or* (*for parking*) Parkausweises; **"permit holders only"** (*for parking*) „Parken nur mit Parkausweis"

permutation [ˌpɜːmjʊˈteɪʃən] N Permutation *f*

permute [pəˈmjuːt] **VT** permutieren

pernicious [pɜːˈnɪʃəs] **ADJ** schädlich; (*Med*) perniziös, bösartig

pernicious anaemia N (*Med*) perniziöse Anämie

pernickety [pəˈnɪkɪtɪ] **ADJ** (*inf*) pingelig (*inf*); (= *tricky, delicate*) *work, point* heikel

perorate ['perəreɪt] **VI** (*liter*) (*conclude a speech*) eine Rede zusammenfassend abschließen; (*speak at length*) endlose Reden halten, sich auslassen (*inf*) (*against* über +*acc*)

peroration [ˌperəˈreɪʃən] N (*liter*) (= *concluding part*) Resümee *nt*, Zusammenfassung *f*; (= *lengthy speech*) endlose Rede

peroxide [pəˈrɒksaɪd] N Peroxid *nt*; **a ~ blonde** (*pej*) eine Wasserstoffblondine; **~ blonde hair** wasserstoffblonde Haare

perp [pɜːp] N (*inf*) = perpetrator

perpendicular [ˌpɜːpənˈdɪkjʊlə'] **ADJ** **a** senkrecht (*to* zu); **the wall is not quite ~ to the ceiling** die Mauer steht nicht ganz lotrecht zur Decke; **a ~ cliff** eine senkrecht abfallende Klippe **b** (*Archit*) perpendikular **N** Senkrechte *f*; **to drop a ~** ein Lot fällen; **to be out of ~** nicht im Lot sein

perpendicularly [ˌpɜːpənˈdɪkjʊləlɪ] **ADV** senkrecht

perpetrate ['pɜːpɪtreɪt] **VT** begehen; *crime also* verüben

perpetration [ˌpɜːpɪˈtreɪʃən] N Begehen *nt*, Begehung *f*; (*of crime also*) Verübung *f*

perpetrator ['pɜːpɪtreɪtə'] N Täter(in) *m(f)*; **the ~ of this crime** derjenige, der dieses Verbrechen begangen hat

perpetual [pəˈpetjʊəl] **ADJ** ständig, fortwährend, immer während; *joy* stet; *ice, snow* ewig; **you're a ~ source of amazement to me** ich muss mich immer wieder über dich wundern; **~ motion/motion machine** Perpetuum mobile *nt*

perpetually [pəˈpetjʊəlɪ] **ADV** ständig

perpetuate [pəˈpetjʊeɪt] **VT** aufrechterhalten; *memory* bewahren

perpetuation [pəˌpetjʊˈeɪʃən] N Aufrechterhaltung *f*; (*of memory*) Bewahrung *f*; (*of old names etc*) Beibehaltung *f*

perpetuity [ˌpɜːpɪˈtjuːɪtɪ] N (*form*) Ewigkeit *f*; **in ~** auf ewig; (*Jur*) lebenslänglich

perplex [pəˈpleks] **VT** verblüffen, verdutzen

perplexed **ADJ**, **perplexedly** **ADV** [pəˈplekst, -sɪdlɪ] verblüfft, verdutzt, perplex

perplexing [pəˈpleksɪŋ] **ADJ** verblüffend

perplexingly [pəˈpleksɪŋlɪ] **ADV** verwirrend; **a ~ difficult problem** ein schwieriges und verwirrendes Problem

perplexity [pəˈpleksɪtɪ] N **a** Verblüffung *f*; **in some ~** verblüfft, verdutzt, perplex **b** (= *complexity*) Komplexität *f*; **the perplexities of sth** die Komplexität einer Sache (*gen*)

perquisite ['pɜːkwɪzɪt] N (*form*) Vergünstigung *f*

perry ['perɪ] N Birnenmost *m*

per se ['pɜːˈseɪ] **ADV** an sich, per se (*geh*)

persecute ['pɜːsɪkjuːt] **VT** verfolgen

persecution [ˌpɜːsɪˈkjuːʃən] N Verfolgung *f* (*of* von); **his ~ by the press** seine Verfolgung durch die Presse; **to have a ~ complex** an Verfolgungswahn leiden

persecutional mania [ˌpɜːsɪˈkjuːʃənlˈmeɪnɪə] N (*Psych*) Verfolgungswahn *m*

persecutor ['pɜːsɪkjuːtə'] N Verfolger(in) *m(f)*

perseverance [ˌpɜːsɪˈvɪərəns] N Ausdauer *f* (*with* mit), Beharrlichkeit *f* (*with* bei)

perseverant **ADJ**, **perseverantly** **ADV** [ˌpɜːsɪˈvɪərənt, -lɪ] ausdauernd, beharrlich

persevere [ˌpɜːsɪˈvɪə'] **VI** durchhalten; **to ~ in one's studies** mit seinem Studium weitermachen; **he ~d with German** er machte mit Deutsch weiter; **to ~ in** *or* **with one's attempts/efforts to do sth** unermüdlich weiter versuchen, etw zu tun

persevering **ADJ**, **perseveringly** **ADV** [ˌpɜːsɪˈvɪərɪŋ, -lɪ] ausdauernd, beharrlich

Persia ['pɜːʃə] N Persien *nt*

Persian ['pɜːʃən] **ADJ** persisch; **the ~ Gulf** der Persische Golf; **~ lamb** (= *animal*) Karakulschaf *nt*; (= *skin, coat*) Persianer *m* **N** **a** Perser(in) *m(f)* **b** (*Ling*) Persisch *nt*

Persian carpet N Perser(teppich) *m*

Persian cat N Perserkatze *f*

persiflage [ˌpɜːsɪˈflɑːʒ] N Persiflage *f*

persimmon [pɜːˈsɪmən] N Persimone *f*; (= *wood*) Persimmon *nt*

persist [pəˈsɪst] **VI** (= *persevere*) nicht lockerlassen, unbeirrt fortfahren (*with* mit); (= *be tenacious*: *in belief, demand etc*) beharren, bestehen (*in* auf +*dat*); (= *last, continue*: *fog, pain etc*) anhalten, fortdauern; **if you ~ in misbehaving** wenn du dich weiterhin so schlecht benimmst; **if you ~ in coming late** wenn du weiterhin zu spät kommst; **if the rumours still ~** falls sich die Gerüchte halten sollten; **we shall ~ in** *or* **with our efforts** wir werden in unseren Bemühungen nicht nachlassen

persistence [pəˈsɪstəns], **persistency** [pəˈsɪstənsɪ] N (= *tenacity*) Beharrlichkeit *f*, Hartnäckigkeit *f*; (= *perseverance*) Ausdauer *f*; (*of disease*) Hartnäckigkeit *f*; (*of fog, pain etc*) Anhalten *nt*, Fortdauern *nt*; **the ~ of his questioning brought results** sein beharrliches Fragen hat schließlich doch zu etwas geführt; **the ~ of a high temperature** anhaltend hohes Fieber

persistent [pəˈsɪstənt] **ADJ** (= *tenacious*) *demands, questions* beharrlich; *person, smell* hartnäckig; *attempts, efforts* ausdauernd; (= *repeated, constant*) *drinking, drinker* gewohnheitsmäßig; *nagging, lateness, threats* ständig; *report* wiederholt; *rumour, problems* anhaltend; *cheerfulness* gleich bleibend; (= *continuing*) *rain, illness, pain, noise* anhaltend; *worry* nicht nachlassend; **~ offender** Wiederholungstäter(in) *m(f)*; **despite our ~ warnings ...** obwohl wir sie/ihn *etc* immer wieder gewarnt haben ...; **~ vegetative state** (*Med*) waches Koma, Wachkoma *nt*

persistently [pəˈsɪstəntlɪ] **ADV** *deny, ask* beharrlich; *claim, argue* hartnäckig; *fail, criticize* ständig; **to ~ break the law** wiederholt das Gesetz brechen; **~ high inflation** anhaltend hohe Inflation; **to be ~ late** ständig spät kommen

persnickety [pəˈsnɪkɪtɪ] **ADJ** (*US inf*) pingelig (*inf*); (= *tricky, delicate*) *work, point* heikel

person ['pɜːsn] N **a** *pl* **people** *or* (*form*) **-s** (= *human being*) Mensch *m*; (*in official contexts*) Person *f*; **I like him as a ~, but not as a teacher** ich mag ihn als Mensch, aber nicht als Lehrer; **no ~** kein Mensch, niemand; **I know no such ~** so jemanden kenne ich nicht; **any ~** jeder; **a certain ~** ein gewisser Jemand; **to ~ call** Gespräch mit Voranmeldung; **30 p per ~** 30 Pence pro Person; **the murder was committed by ~ or ~s unknown** der Mord wurde von einem oder mehreren unbekannten Tätern verübt; **I'm more of an outdoor/cat ~** ich bin mehr ein Typ *m* für draußen/ein Katzentyp *m* **b** *pl* **-s** (*Gram, Jur*: = *legal person*) Person *f*; **first ~ singular/plural** erste Person Singular/Plural **c** *pl* **-s** (= *body, physical presence*) Körper *m*; (= *appearance*) Äußere(s) *nt*; **in ~** persönlich; **in the ~ of** in Gestalt (+*gen*); **crime against the ~**

Vergehen *nt* gegen die Person; **on** *or* **about one's ~** bei sich

-person SUF *in Berufsbezeichnungen etc als neutralere Form anstelle von „-man"* **chairperson** Vorsitzende(r) *mf*; **salesperson** Verkäufer(in) *m(f)*

persona [pɜːˈsəʊnə] N *pl* **-e** *(Psych)* Persona *f*; **~ grata** *(Jur)* Persona grata *f*; **~ non grata** *(Jur, fig)* Persona non grata *f*

personable [ˈpɜːsnəbl] ADJ von angenehmer Erscheinung

personae [pɜːˈsəʊniː] *pl of* persona

personage [ˈpɜːsənɪdʒ] N Persönlichkeit *f*

personal [ˈpɜːsnl] ADJ **a** persönlich; **he gave several ~ performances to promote his new record** er trat mehrmals persönlich auf, um für seine neue Platte zu werben; **to make a ~ appearance** persönlich erscheinen; **the ~ touch** der persönliche Touch; **~ freshness** *or* **cleanliness/hygiene** Körperfrische *f*/-pflege *f*; **it's nothing ~, I just don't think you're the right person** nicht, dass ich etwas gegen Sie persönlich hätte, Sie sind nur nicht der/die Richtige; **I have no ~ knowledge of it** mir (persönlich) ist nichts davon bekannt; **~ call** Privatgespräch *nt*; **~ effects** persönliches Eigentum; **~ friend** persönlicher Freund, persönliche Freundin; **~ identification number** persönliche Identifikationsnummer, Geheimzahl *f (inf)*; **~ stationery** Briefpapier *nt* mit persönlichem Briefkopf **b** (= *private*) *problems* persönlich; **her ~ life** ihr Privatleben *nt*; **"personal"** (*on letter*) „privat" **c** (= *rude*) *insult, remark* persönlich; **don't get ~** nun werden Sie mal nicht persönlich **N** (*US Press:* = *advert*) Privatanzeige *f*

personal: personal ad N (*inf*) private Kleinanzeige *f*; **personal allowance** N (*for tax purposes*) persönlicher Freibetrag; **personal assistant** N persönlicher Assistent, persönliche Assistentin; (= *secretary*) Chefsekretär(in) *m(f)*; **personal best** N (*Sport*) persönliche Bestleistung; **to set a new ~** (*Sport*) eine neue persönliche Bestleistung aufstellen; **personal chair** N (*Brit Univ*) *Lehrstelle, die auf Grund außergewöhnlicher Leistungen des Inhabers eingerichtet wurde*; **personal column** N Familienanzeigen *pl*; **personal computer** N Personalcomputer *m*, PC *m*; **personal hygiene** N Körperpflege *f*; **personal insurance** N Privatversicherung *f*

personality [ˌpɜːsəˈnælɪtɪ] N **a** (= *character, person*) Persönlichkeit *f*; **~ development** Persönlichkeitsentfaltung *f* **b** (= *personal remark*) **let's keep personalities out of this** lassen wir persönliche Dinge aus dem Spiel

personality cult N Personenkult *m*

personality disorder N Persönlichkeitsstörung *f*

personalize [ˈpɜːsənəlaɪz] VT **a** (= *make more personal*) persönlicher gestalten; (= *put initials etc on*) *diary, calculator, shirt* eine persönliche *or* individuelle Note geben (+*dat*); **~d letterhead** persönliches *or* individuelles Briefpapier; **~d number plates** = **vanity plates** **b** (= *treat as personal issue*) personalisieren

personal loan N Personaldarlehen *nt*, Privatdarlehen *nt*

personally [ˈpɜːsənəlɪ] ✪ 6.1 ADV persönlich; **~, I think that ...** ich persönlich bin der Meinung, dass ...; **I like him ~, but not as an employer** ich mag ihn als Mensch, aber nicht als Arbeitgeber; **to be ~ responsible (for sth)** persönlich (für etw) verantwortlich sein; **to hold sb ~ responsible** jdn persönlich verantwortlich machen; **to be ~ involved** persönlich *or* selbst beteiligt sein; **to take sth ~** etw persönlich nehmen

personal: personal organizer N Terminplaner *m*, Zeitplaner *m*; (*electronic*) elektronisches Notizbuch, Datencenter *nt*; **personal pronoun** N (*Gram*) Personalpronomen *nt*, persönliches Fürwort; **personal property** N persönliches Eigentum, Privateigentum *nt*; **personal space** N persönlicher Freiraum; **to in-**

vade sb's **~** jdm zu nahe kommen; **personal stereo** N Walkman® *m*; **personal trainer** N privater Fitnesstrainer, private Fitnesstrainerin

personalty [ˈpɜːsnltɪ] N (*Jur*) bewegliches Vermögen

personification [pɜːˌsɒnɪfɪˈkeɪʃən] N Verkörperung *f*, Personifizierung *f*; **he is the ~ of good taste** er ist der personifizierte gute Geschmack

personify [pɜːˈsɒnɪfaɪ] VT personifizieren; (= *be the personification of also*) verkörpern; **he is evil personified** er ist das personifizierte Böse *or* das Böse in Person

personnel [ˌpɜːsəˈnel] **N** *sing or pl* **a** Personal *nt*; (*on plane*) Besatzung *f*; (*on ship*) Besatzung *f*, Mannschaft *f*; (*Mil*) Leute *pl*; **this firm employs 800 ~** diese Firma beschäftigt 800 Leute; **with a larger ~** mit mehr Personal **b** (= *personnel department*) die Personalabteilung; (= *personnel work*) Personalarbeit *f* ATTR Personal-; **~ agency** Personalagentur *f*; **~ carrier** (*Mil*) Mannschaftstransportwagen *m*/-transportflugzeug *nt*

personnel: personnel management N Personalführung *f*; **personnel manager** N Personalchef(in) *m(f)*; **personnel officer** N Personalleiter(in) *m(f)*

perspective [pəˈspektɪv] N (*lit*) Perspektive *f*; (*fig also*) Blickwinkel *m*; **to get a different ~ on a problem** ein Problem aus einer anderen Perspektive *or* aus einem anderen Blickwinkel sehen; **in ~** (*Art*) perspektivisch; **the foreground isn't in ~** der Vordergrund ist perspektivisch nicht richtig; **try to keep/get things in ~** versuchen Sie, nüchtern und sachlich zu bleiben/ das nüchtern und sachlich zu sehen; **to get sth out of ~** (*lit: artist etc*) etw perspektivisch verzerren; (*fig*) etw verzerrt sehen; **in historical ~** aus historischer Sicht; **to see things in their proper** *or* **true ~** die Dinge so sehen, wie sie sind; **to see things from a different ~** die Dinge aus einem anderen Blickwinkel betrachten

Perspex® [ˈpɜːspeks] N Acrylglas *nt*, Akrylglas *nt*

perspicacious [ˌpɜːspɪˈkeɪʃəs] ADJ *person, remark etc* scharfsinnig; *decision* weitsichtig

perspicacity [ˌpɜːspɪˈkæsɪtɪ] N Scharfsinn *m*, Scharfblick *m*; (*of decision*) Weitsicht *f*

perspicuity [ˌpɜːspɪˈkjuːɪtɪ] N Klarheit *f*; (= *clearness: of expression, statement also*) Verständlichkeit *f*

perspicuous [pəˈspɪkjʊəs] ADJ einleuchtend; (= *clear*) *expression, statement* klar, verständlich

perspiration [ˌpɜːspəˈreɪʃən] N (= *perspiring*) Schwitzen *nt*, Transpiration *f* (*geh*); (= *sweat*) Schweiß *m*; **he ~ was dripping off him, he was dripping with ~** ihm lief der Schweiß in Strömen herunter; **beads of ~** Schweißperlen *pl*

perspire [pəˈspaɪə] VI schwitzen, transpirieren (*geh*)

persuadable [pəˈsweɪdəbl] ADJ **he may be ~** (= *amenable*) vielleicht lässt er sich überreden, vielleicht ist er zu überreden; (= *convincible*) vielleicht lässt er sich überzeugen, vielleicht ist er zu überzeugen

persuade [pəˈsweɪd] VT überreden; (= *convince*) überzeugen; **to ~ sb to do sth** jdn überreden, etw zu tun; **to ~ sb into doing sth** jdn dazu überreden, etw zu tun; **to ~ sb out of sth** jdm etw ausreden; **to ~ sb out of doing sth** jdn dazu überreden, etw nicht zu tun; **to ~ oneself/ sb of sth** sich selbst/jdn von etw überzeugen; **to ~ sb of the need for sth** jdn von der Notwendigkeit einer Sache überzeugen; **to ~ sb of the need to do sth** jdn von der Notwendigkeit überzeugen, etw zu tun; **to ~ sb of/ ~ sb that ...** jdn von etw überzeugen/jdn davon überzeugen, dass ...; **I am ~d that ...** ich bin überzeugt, dass ...; **she is easily ~d** sie ist leicht zu überreden/überzeugen; **he doesn't take much persuading** ihn braucht man nicht lange zu überreden

persuader [pəˈsweɪdə] N Überredungskünstler(in) *m(f)*; **the hidden ~s** die geheimen Verführer

persuasible [pəˈsweɪzəbl] ADJ = **persuadable**

persuasion [pəˈsweɪʒən] N **a** (= *persuading*) Überredung *f*; **advertising uses many subtle means of ~** die Werbung arbeitet mit vielen subtilen Überzeugungsmechanismen; **her powers of ~** ihre Überredungskünste; **she tried every possible means of ~ to get him to agree** sie setzte ihre ganze Überredungskunst ein, um seine Zustimmung zu erlangen; **I don't need much ~ to stop working** man braucht mich nicht lange zu überreden, damit ich aufhöre zu arbeiten **b** (= *persuasiveness*) Überzeugungskraft *f* **c** (= *belief*) Überzeugung *f*; (= *sect, denomination*) Glaube *m*, Glaubensrichtung *f*; **I am not of that ~** (= *don't believe that*) davon bin ich nicht überzeugt; (= *don't belong to that sect*) ich gehöre nicht diesem Glauben an; **and others of that ~** und andere, die dieser Überzeugung anhängen; **to be of left-wing ~, to have left-wing ~s** linke Ansichten haben

persuasive [pəˈsweɪsɪv] ADJ *salesman, voice* beredsam; *arguments etc* überzeugend; **he can be very ~** er kann einen gut überreden; (= *convincing*) er kann einen leicht überzeugen; **I had to be very ~** ich musste meine ganze Überredungskunst aufwenden; **her ~ powers** ihre Überredungskünste *pl*

persuasively [pəˈsweɪsɪvlɪ] ADV *argue etc* überzeugend; **..., he said ...** ..., versuchte er sie/ihn *etc* zu überreden

persuasiveness [pəˈsweɪsɪvnɪs] N (*of person, salesman etc*) Überredungskunst *f*, Beredsamkeit *f*; (*of argument*) Überzeugungskraft *f*

pert [pɜːt] ADJ (+*er*) keck, kess; (= *impudent*) keck; **a ~ little smile** ein kesses *or* freches Lächeln

pertain [pɜːˈteɪn] VI **to ~ to sth** etw betreffen; (= *belong to: land etc*) zu etw gehören; **all documents ~ing to the case** alle den Fall betreffenden Dokumente; **and other matters ~ing to it** und andere damit verbundene Fragen; **of** *or* **~ing to sth** etw betreffend

pertinacious [ˌpɜːtɪˈneɪʃəs] ADJ (= *persevering*) beharrlich, ausdauernd; (= *tenacious, stubborn*) hartnäckig

pertinacity [ˌpɜːtɪˈnæsɪtɪ] N (= *perseverance*) Beharrlichkeit *f*, Ausdauer *f*; (= *stubbornness*) Hartnäckigkeit *f*

pertinence [ˈpɜːtɪnəns] N Relevanz *f* (*to* für); (*of information*) Sachdienlichkeit *f*

pertinent [ˈpɜːtɪnənt] ADJ relevant (*to* für); *information* sachdienlich

pertinently [ˈpɜːtɪnəntlɪ] ADV passend, völlig richtig; **he asked very ~ whether ...** er stellte zu Recht die Frage, ob ...

pertly [ˈpɜːtlɪ] ADV keck, kess; (= *impudently*) keck

pertness [ˈpɜːtnɪs] N Keckheit *f*, Kessheit *f*; (= *impudence*) Keckheit *f*

perturb [pəˈtɜːb] VT beunruhigen

perturbation [ˌpɜːtɜːˈbeɪʃən] N (= *state*) Unruhe *f*; (= *act*) Beunruhigung *f*; **to be in (a state of) ~** ziemlich in Unruhe sein

perturbed [pəˈtɜːbd] ADJ beunruhigt

perturbing ADJ , **perturbingly** ADV [pəˈtɜːbɪŋ, -lɪ] beunruhigend

Peru [pəˈruː] N Peru *nt*

perusal [pəˈruːzəl] N Lektüre *f*; (*careful*) sorgfältige Durchsicht, Prüfung *f*; **after a brief ~ of the newspaper he ...** nachdem er kurz einen Blick in die Zeitung geworfen hatte ...

peruse [pəˈruːz] VT (*durch*)lesen; (*carefully*) sorgfältig durchsehen, prüfen

Peruvian [pəˈruːvɪən] ADJ peruanisch **N** Peruaner(in) *m(f)*

pervade [pɜːˈveɪd] VT erfüllen; (*smell also*) durchziehen; (*light*) durchfluten; **his writing is ~d with dialect expressions** seine Bücher sind voller Dialektausdrücke; **the universities are ~d with subversive elements** die Universitäten sind mit subversiven Elementen durchsetzt

pervading [pɜːˈveɪdɪŋ] ADJ durchdringend

pervasive [pɜ:'veɪsɪv] ADJ *smell etc* durchdringend; *influence, feeling, ideas* um sich greifend

pervasively [pɜ:'veɪsɪvlɪ] ADV durchdringend; **to spread ~** (*smell etc*) sich überall ausbreiten (*through* in +*dat*); (*ideas, mood etc also*) um sich greifen (*through* in +*dat*)

pervasiveness [pɜ:'veɪsɪvnɪs] N (*of smell etc*) durchdringender Charakter; (*of influence, feeling, ideas*) um sich greifender Charakter

perverse [pə'vɜ:s] ADJ (= *contrary*) *idea* abwegig; (= *perverted*) pervers, widernatürlich; **it would be ~ to refuse** es wäre unsinnig abzulehnen

perversely [pə'vɜ:slɪ] ADV (= *paradoxically*) paradoxerweise; *think, believe, decide* abwegigerweise; **~, when the day of her departure came, she wanted to stay** als der Abreisetag gekommen war, wollte sie paradoxerweise noch bleiben; **~ enjoyable** auf perverse Art und Weise unterhaltsam; **do you have to be so ~ different?** musst du denn immer um jeden Preis anders sein?; **he is really ~ old-fashioned** er ist wirklich hoffnungslos altmodisch; **the translation still sounds ~ French** die Übersetzung klingt noch immer penetrant französisch

perverseness [pə'vɜ:snɪs] N (*of idea*) Abwegigkeit *f*; (= *perverted nature*) Perversität *f*, Widernatürlichkeit *f*

perversion [pə'vɜ:ʃən] N **a** (*esp sexual, Psych*) Perversion *f*; (*no pl*: = *act of perverting*) Pervertierung *f* **b** (*Rel*) Fehlglaube *m*; (*no pl*: = *act*) Irreleitung *f* **c** (= *distortion: of truth etc*) Verzerrung *f*

perversity [pə'vɜ:sɪtɪ] N (= *perverted nature*) Perversität *f*, Widernatürlichkeit *f*

pervert [pə'vɜ:t] VT (= *deprave*) *person, mind* verderben, pervertieren; (*Rel*) *believer* irreleiten; (= *change, distort*) *truth, sb's words* verzerren; **to ~ the course of justice** (*Jur*) die Rechtsfindung behindern; (*by official*) das Recht beugen N ['pɜ:vɜ:t] Perverse(r) *mf*

perverted [pə'vɜ:tɪd] ADJ *mind, person* verdorben, pervertiert; *phone call* pervers

pervious ['pɜ:vɪəs] ADJ (*lit*) durchlässig; (*fig*) zugänglich (*to* für); **chalk is ~ (to water)** Kalk ist wasserdurchlässig

perviousness ['pɜ:vɪəsnɪs] N (*lit*) Durchlässigkeit *f*; (*fig*) Zugänglichkeit *f* (*to* für)

peseta [pə'seɪtə] N Peseta *f*

pesky ['peskɪ] ADJ (+*er*) (*esp US, inf*) nervtötend (*inf*)

pessary ['pesərɪ] N (= *contraceptive*) Pessar *nt*; (= *suppository*) Zäpfchen *nt*, Suppositorium *nt* (*spec*)

pessimism ['pesɪmɪzəm] N Pessimismus *m*, Schwarzseherei *f*

pessimist ['pesɪmɪst] N Pessimist(in) *m(f)*, Schwarzseher(in) *m(f)*

pessimistic [pesɪ'mɪstɪk] ADJ pessimistisch; **I'm rather ~ about it** da bin ich ziemlich pessimistisch, da sehe ich ziemlich schwarz (*inf*); **I'm ~ about our chances of success** ich bin pessimistisch, was unsere Erfolgschancen angeht, ich sehe schwarz für unsere Erfolgschancen (*inf*)

pessimistically [pesɪ'mɪstɪkəlɪ] ADV pessimistisch

pest [pest] N **a** (*Zool*) Schädling *m*; **~ control** Schädlingsbekämpfung *f* **b** (*fig*) (= *person*) Nervensäge *f*; (= *thing*) Plage *f*; **sex ~** (lästige) Sexbestie **c** (*obs*: = *plague*) Pest *f*, Pestilenz *f* (*old*)

pester ['pestə'] VT belästigen; (= *keep on at: with requests etc*) plagen; **to ~ the life out of sb** jdm keine Ruhe lassen; **she ~ed me for the book** sie ließ mir keine Ruhe wegen des Buches; **to ~ sb to do sth** jdn bedrängen, etw zu tun

pesticide ['pestɪsaɪd] N Schädlingsbekämpfungsmittel *nt*, Pestizid *nt* (*spec*)

pestiferous [pe'stɪfərəs] ADJ verpestet; (*inf*: = *annoying*) lästig

pestilence ['pestɪləns] N (*old, liter*) Pest *f*, Pestilenz *f* (*old*)

pestilent ['pestɪlənt], **pestilential** [pestɪ'lenʃəl] ADJ pesterfüllt; (*fig*: = *pernicious*) schädlich, verderblich; (*inf*: = *loathsome*) ekelhaft; **a ~ disease** eine Seuche

pestle ['pesl] N Stößel *m*

pet¹ [pet] ADJ *attr* **a** (= *animal*) Haustier *nt*; **a ~ lion** ein zahmer Löwe; **her two ~ dogs** ihre beiden Hunde **b** (= *favourite*) Lieblings-; **~ idea/ theory** Lieblingsidee/-theorie *f*; **~ pupil** Lieblingsschüler(in) *m(f)*; **a ~ name** ein Kosename *m* → **hate** N **b** N **a** (= *animal*) Haustier *nt* **b** (= *favourite*) Liebling *m*; **teacher's ~** Lehrers Liebling *m or* Schätzchen *nt* (*inf*); (*as derogatory name*) Streber(in) *m(f)* **c** (*inf*, = *dear*) Schatz *m*; **yes, (my) ~** ja, (mein) Schatz; **he's rather a ~** er ist wirklich lieb *or* ein Schatz VT *animal* streicheln; *child also* liebkosen; (*fig*: = *spoil*) (ver)hätscheln VI (*sexually*) Petting machen

pet² N (*dated inf*, = *huff*) Verstimmung *f*; **to be in/fly into a ~** verstimmt *or* gekränkt sein/werden

petal ['petl] N Blütenblatt *nt*

petard [pe'tɑ:d] N Petarde *f* → **hoist**

pet dander allergy N Haustierallergie *f*

Pete [pi:t] N **for ~'s** *or* **pete's sake** (*inf*) um Himmels willen

Peter ['pi:tə'] N Peter *m*; (= *apostle*) Petrus *m*; **Saint ~** Sankt Peter, der Heilige Petrus; **to rob ~ to pay Paul** ein Loch mit dem anderen zustopfen; **he is a real ~ Pan** er will einfach nicht erwachsen werden; **~ Pan collar** Bubikragen *m*; **~ Pan figure** Peter Pan *m*

▶ **peter out** VI langsam zu Ende gehen; (*mineral vein*) versiegen; (*river*) versickern; (*song, noise*) verhallen; (*interest*) sich verlieren, sich totlaufen; (*excitement*) sich legen; (*plan*) im Sande verlaufen

peterman ['pi:təmən] N *pl* **-men** [-mən] (*sl*) Schränker *m* (*sl*), Panzerknacker *m* (*inf*)

petersham ['pi:təʃəm] N (= *ribbon*) Seidenripsband *nt*

pet food N Tierfutter *nt*

petiole ['petɪəʊl] N Stängel *m*

petit bourgeois ['petɪ'bʊəʒwɑ:] N Kleinbürger(in) *m(f)* ADJ kleinbürgerlich

petite [pə'ti:t] ADJ *woman, girl* zierlich

petite bourgeoisie [petɪ,bʊəʒwɑ:'zi:] N Kleinbürgertum *nt*

petit four ['petɪ'fɔ:r] N *pl* **-s -s** Petit Four *nt*

petition [pə'tɪʃən] N **a** (= *list of signatures*) Unterschriftenliste *f*; **to get up a ~** (for/against sth) Unterschriften (für/gegen etw) sammeln **b** (= *request*) Gesuch *nt*, Bittschrift *f*, Petition *f*; **~ for clemency** Gnadengesuch *nt* **c** (*Jur*) **~ for divorce** Scheidungsantrag *m*; **a ~ for** *or* **in bankruptcy** ein Konkursantrag *m* VT *person, authorities* (= *request, entreat*) ersuchen (*for* um); (= *hand petition to*) eine Unterschriftenliste vorlegen (+*dat*); **to ~ the court** das Gericht anrufen VI **a** (= *hand in petition*) eine Unterschriftenliste einreichen **b** (*Jur*) **to ~ for divorce** die Scheidung einreichen; **to ~ for bankruptcy** das Konkursverfahren eröffnen

petitioner [pə'tɪʃənə'] N Bittsteller(in) *m(f)*; (*Jur*) Kläger(in) *m(f)*

petit jury [petɪ'dʒʊərɪ] N ≈ Geschworene *pl*

petit larceny [petɪ'lɑ:sənɪ] N einfacher Diebstahl

petit mal [petɪ'mæl] N (*Med*) Petit Mal *nt*

petit point [petɪ'pwɛ] N Petit point *nt*

petits pois [petɪ'pwɑ:] PL (*form*) Petits Pois *pl*

pet passport N (*Brit*) Tierpass *m*

Petrarch ['petrɑ:k] N Petrarca *f*

petrel ['petrəl] N Sturmvogel *m*

Petri dish ['petrɪdɪʃ] N Petrischale *f*

petrifaction [petrɪ'fækʃən], **petrification** [petrɪfɪ'keɪʃən] N Versteinerung *f*, Petrifikation *f*

petrified ['petrɪfaɪd] ADJ **a** (*lit*) versteinert; **as though ~** wie erstarrt **b** (*fig*) **I was ~ (with fear)** ich war starr vor Schrecken; **she is ~ of spiders** sie hat panische Angst vor Spinnen; **to be ~ of doing sth** panische Angst davor haben, etw zu tun

petrify ['petrɪfaɪ] VT **a** (*lit*) versteinern **b** (= *frighten*) **he really petrifies me** er jagt mir schreckliche Angst ein; **a ~ing experience** ein schreckliches Erlebnis; **to be petrified by sth** sich panisch vor etw fürchten VI versteinern

petrochemical ['petrəʊ'kemɪkəl] N petrochemisches Erzeugnis ADJ petrochemisch

petrochemistry [petrəʊ'kemɪstrɪ] N Petrochemie *f*

petrodollar ['petrəʊdɒlə'] N Petrodollar *m*

petrol ['petrəl] N (*Brit*) Benzin *nt*

petrol *in cpds* Benzin-; **petrol bomb** N Benzinbombe *f*, Molotowcocktail *m*; **petrol can** N Reservekanister *m*; **petrol cap** N Tankdeckel *m*

petroleum [pɪ'trəʊlɪəm] N Petroleum *nt*

petroleum: petroleum ether N Petroläther *m*; **petroleum jelly** N Vaselin *nt*, Vaseline *f*; **petroleum refinery** N Erdölraffinerie *f*

petrol gauge N Benzinuhr *f*

petrology [pɪ'trɒlɪdʒɪ] N Gesteinskunde *f*, Petrologie *f*

petrol: petrol pump N (*in engine*) Benzinpumpe *f*; (*at garage*) Zapfsäule *f*; **petrol station** N Tankstelle *f*; **petrol tank** N Benzintank *m*; **petrol tanker** N (Benzin)tankwagen *m*

petticoat ['petɪkəʊt] N Unterrock *m*; (*stiffened*) Petticoat *m*; **~ government** Weiberherrschaft *f*, Weiberregiment *nt*

pettifogging ['petɪfɒgɪŋ] ADJ *objections* kleinlich; *details* belanglos; *person* pedantisch

pettiness ['petɪnɪs] N **a** (= *trivial nature*) Unbedeutendheit *f*, Belanglosigkeit *f*, Unwichtigkeit *f*; (*of excuse*) Billigkeit *f*; (*of crime*) Geringfügigkeit *f* **b** (= *small-mindedness*) Kleinlichkeit *f*; (*of remark*) spitzer Charakter

petting ['petɪŋ] N Petting *nt*; **heavy ~** Heavy Petting *nt*

petting zoo N (*US*) Streichelzoo *m*

pettish ADJ , **pettishly** ADV ['petɪʃ, -lɪ] bockig (*inf*)

pettishness ['petɪʃnɪs] N bockige Art (*inf*)

petty ['petɪ] ADJ (+*er*) **a** (= *trivial*) unbedeutend, belanglos, unwichtig; *excuse* billig; *crime* geringfügig **b** (= *small-minded*) kleinlich; (= *spiteful*) *remark* spitz; **you're being very ~ about it** du bist sehr kleinlich **c** (= *minor*) *chieftain etc* untergeordnet; (*pej*) *official* unbedeutend, untergeordnet; **the ~ wars of the time** die Kleinkriege jener Zeit

petty: petty average N (*Naut Jur*) Teilschaden *m*, kleine Havarie; **petty bourgeois** N, ADJ = **petit bourgeois**; **petty bourgeoisie** N = **petite bourgeoisie**; **petty cash** N Portokasse *f*; **petty crime** N *a no pl* (= *illegal activities*) Kleinkriminalität *f* **b** (= *illegal act*) Vergehen *nt*, Bagatelldelikt *nt*; **petty jury** N ≈ Geschworene *pl*; **petty larceny** N einfacher Diebstahl; **petty-minded** ADJ kleinlich; **petty officer** N Fähnrich *m* zur See; **petty theft** N einfacher Diebstahl

petulance ['petjʊləns], **petulancy** ['petjʊlənsɪ] N verdrießliche Art; (*of child*) bockige Art (*inf*)

petulant ['petjʊlənt] ADJ verdrießlich; *child* bockig (*inf*)

petulantly ['petjʊləntlɪ] ADV verdrießlich; (*used of child*) bockig (*inf*)

petunia [pɪ'tju:nɪə] N Petunie *f*

pew [pju:] N (*Eccl*) (Kirchen)bank *f*; (*hum, = chair*) Platz *m*; **take a ~!** (*hum*) lass dich nieder! (*hum*)

pewit ['pi:wɪt] N = **peewit**

pewter ['pju:tə'] N (= *alloy*) Zinn *nt*; (= *vessel*) Zinnbecher *m*; (= *articles*) Zinn(geschirr) *nt*

peyote [peɪˈəʊtɪ] N Peyotl *m*

PFI (*Brit, Pol*) abbr of **Private Finance Initiative**

PG (*Brit*) abbr of **parental guidance** *Klassifikation für Kinofilme, welche Kinder nur in Begleitung Erwachsener sehen dürfen*

PGA abbr of **Professional Golfers' Association** PGA *f*

PGCE (*Brit*) abbr of **Postgraduate Certificate of Education**

phalanx [ˈfælæŋks] N *pl* **-es** or **phalanges** [fæˈlændʒiːz] **a** (*Anat*) Finger-/Zehenglied *nt*, Phalanx *f* (*spec*) **b** (= *body of people, troops*) Phalanx *f*

phalli [ˈfælaɪ] *pl of* **phallus**

phallic [ˈfælɪk] ADJ phallisch; **~ symbol** Phallussymbol *nt*

phallus [ˈfæləs] N *pl* **-es** or **phalli** Phallus *m*

phantasm [ˈfæntæzəm], **phantasma** [fænˈtæzmə] N *pl* **phantasmata** Phantasma *nt*

phantasmagoria [ˌfæntæzməˈɡɔːrɪə] N Phantasmagorie *f*

phantasmagoric(al) [ˌfæntæzməˈɡɒrɪk(əl)] ADJ phantasmagorisch

phantasmal [fænˈtæzməl] ADJ imaginär

phantasmata [fænˈtæzmətə] *pl of* **phantasm** of **phantasma**

phantasy N = **fantasy**

phantom [ˈfæntəm] N Phantom *nt*; (= *ghost: esp of particular person*) Geist *m*; **~s of the imagination** Fantasiegebilde *pl*, Phantasiegebilde *pl* ADJ *attr* (= *imagined*) eingebildet; (= *mysterious*) Phantom-; **a ~ child/knight** *etc* der Geist eines Kindes/Ritters *etc*; **~ limb pains** Phantomschmerzen *pl*; **~ company** Briefkastenfirma *f*; **~ withdrawal** (*from cash dispenser*) falsche or irrtümliche Abbuchung, Falschbelastung *f*

phantom pregnancy N eingebildete Schwangerschaft

Pharaoh [ˈfɛərəʊ] N Pharao *m*; **the tombs of the ~s** die Pharaonengräber *pl*

Pharaonic [fɛəˈreɪɒnɪk] ADJ pharaonisch

Pharisaic(al) [ˌfærɪˈseɪk(əl)] ADJ **a** pharisäisch **b** **pharisaic(al)** (*fig*) pharisäerhaft

Pharisee [ˈfærɪsiː] N (*fig: also* **pharisee**) Pharisäer(in) *m(f)*

pharmaceutical [ˌfɑːməˈsjuːtɪkəl] ADJ pharmazeutisch N *usu pl* Arzneimittel *nt*; **~(s) company** Pharmaunternehmen *nt*

pharmaceutics [ˌfɑːməˈsjuːtɪks] N *sing* = **pharmacy a**

pharmacist [ˈfɑːməsɪst] N Apotheker(in) *m(f)*; (*in research*) Pharmazeut(in) *m(f)*

pharmacological [ˌfɑːməkəˈlɒdʒɪkəl] ADJ pharmakologisch

pharmacologist [ˌfɑːməˈkɒlədʒɪst] N Pharmakologe *m*, Pharmakologin *f*

pharmacology [ˌfɑːməˈkɒlədʒɪ] N Pharmakologie *f*

pharmacopoeia [ˌfɑːməkəˈpiːə] N Pharmakopöe *f* (*spec*), amtliches Arzneibuch

pharmacy [ˈfɑːməsɪ] N **a** (= *science*) Pharmazie *f* **b** (*esp US*: = *shop*) Apotheke *f*

pharyngeal [fəˈrɪndʒɪəl], **pharyngal** [fəˈrɪŋɡəl] ADJ Rachen-; **~ cancer** Rachenkrebs *m*

pharyngitis [ˌfærɪnˈdʒaɪtɪs] N Rachenkatarr(h) *m*, Pharyngitis *f* (*spec*)

pharynx [ˈfærɪŋks] N Rachen *m*, Pharynx *f* (*spec*)

phase [feɪz] N Phase *f*; (*of construction, project, history also*) Abschnitt *m*; (*of illness*) Stadium *nt*; **in ~** (*Tech, Elec*) phasengleich, in Phase; (*fig*) koordiniert; **out of ~** (*Tech, Elec*) phasenverschoben; (*fig*) unkoordiniert; **a passing ~** ein vorübergehender Zustand; **he's just going through a ~** das ist nur so eine Phase bei ihm; **he's out of ~ with the times** er ist nicht im Gleichklang mit seiner Zeit
VT **a** (= *introduce gradually*) *plan, change-over, withdrawal* schrittweise durchführen
b (= *coordinate, fit to one another*) *starting times, production stages, traffic lights* aufeinander ab-

stimmen; *machines etc* gleichschalten, synchronisieren; **the traffic lights are not ~d here** hier gibt es keine grüne Welle; **a ~d withdrawal of troops** ein schrittweiser Truppenabzug

▶ **phase in** VT *sep* allmählich einführen

▶ **phase out** VT *sep* auslaufen lassen

phase: phase-down N stufenweise Verringerung, stufenweiser Abbau; **phase modulation** N (*Elec*) Phasenmodulation *f*; **phase-out** N stufenweiser Abbau, stufenweise Außerkraftsetzung

phasing [ˈfeɪzɪŋ] N Synchronisierung *f*, Gleichschaltung *f*

phatic [ˈfætɪk] ADJ (*liter*) phatisch

pH-balanced [piːˈeɪtʃˌbælənst] ADJ (*Chem*) pH-neutral

PhD N Doktor *m*, Dr.; **~ thesis** Doktorarbeit *f*; **to do one's ~** seinen Doktor machen, promovieren; **to get one's ~** den Doktor bekommen; **he has a ~ in English** er hat in Anglistik promoviert; **John Smith ~** Dr. John Smith

pheasant [ˈfeznt] N Fasan *m*

phencyclidine [fenˈsɪklɪˌdiːn] N Phencyclidin *nt*

phenix [ˈfiːnɪks] N (*US*) = **phoenix**

phenobarbitone [ˌfiːnəʊˈbɑːbɪtəʊn], **phenobarbital** [ˌfiːnəʊˈbɑːbɪtəl] N Phenobarbital *nt*

phenol [ˈfiːnɒl] N Phenol *nt*

phenomena [frˈnɒmɪnə] *pl of* **phenomenon**

phenomenal [frˈnɒmɪnl] ADJ **a** phänomenal, sagenhaft (*inf*); *person, beauty, figure* fabelhaft; *boredom, heat* unglaublich; **at a ~ rate** in phänomenalem Tempo **b** (*Philos*) **the ~ world** die Erscheinungswelt

phenomenalism [frˈnɒmɪnəlɪzəm] N Phänomenalismus *m*

phenomenally [frˈnɒmɪnəlɪ] ADV außerordentlich; *bad, boring etc* unglaublich

phenomenology [frˌnɒmɪˈnɒlədʒɪ] N Phänomenologie *f*

phenomenon [frˈnɒmɪnən] N *pl* **phenomena** Phänomen *nt*

phenotype [ˈfiːnəʊtaɪp] N Phänotyp(us) *m*

phew [fjuː] INTERJ Mensch, puh

phial [ˈfaɪəl] N Fläschchen *nt*; (*for serum*) Ampulle *f*

PHI BETA KAPPA

Phi Beta Kappa ist die älteste und renommierteste landesweite Studentenverbindung der USA, die 1776 für College- und Universitätsstudenten mit herausragenden Leistungen gegründet wurde. Der Name besteht aus den griechischen Anfangsbuchstaben des Mottos der Verbindung: „philosophia biou kybernetes" - „Philosophie, der Führer des Lebens". Die Mitglieder werden in ihrem dritten oder vierten Studienjahr aufgenommen und werden dann auch **Phi Beta Kappa** oder „Phi Beta Kappa student" genannt.

Phil (*US*) abbr of **Philadelphia**

Philadelphia lawyer [ˌfɪləˈdelfɪəˈlɔːjəʳ] N (*esp US inf*) gerissener Anwalt/Jurist, gerissene Anwältin/Juristin

philander [frˈlændəʳ] VI tändeln (*liter*)

philanderer [frˈlændərəʳ] N Schwerenöter *m*

philandering [frˈlændərɪŋ] N Liebeleien *pl* ADJ **her ~ husband** ihr zu Seitensprüngen neigender Mann

philanthropic(al) [ˌfɪlənˈθrɒpɪk(əl)] ADJ menschenfreundlich; *person also, organization* philanthropisch (*geh*)

philanthropically [ˌfɪlənˈθrɒpɪkəlɪ] ADV menschenfreundlich

philanthropist [frˈlænθrəpɪst] N Menschenfreund(in) *m(f)*, Philanthrop(in) *m(f)* (*geh*)

philanthropy [frˈlænθrəpɪ] N Menschenfreundlichkeit *f*, Philanthropie *f* (*geh*)

philatelic [ˌfɪləˈtelɪk] ADJ philatelistisch

philatelist [frˈlætəlɪst] N Philatelist(in) *m(f)*, Briefmarkensammler(in) *m(f)*

philately [frˈlætəlɪ] N Philatelie *f*, Briefmarkenkunde *f*

-phile [-faɪl] SUF N -phile(r) *mf*, -freund(in) *m(f)*; **Anglophile** Anglophile(r) *mf*, Englandfreund(in) *m(f)* ADJ -phil, -freundlich; **Francophile** frankophil, frankreich- or franzosenfreundlich

philharmonic [ˌfɪlɑːˈmɒnɪk] ADJ philharmonisch; **~ hall/society** Philharmonie *f* N **Philharmonic** Philharmonie *f*

Philip [ˈfɪlɪp] N Philipp *m*; (*Bibl*) Philippus *m*

Philippians [frˈlɪpɪənz] N *sing* (*Bibl*) Philipper *pl*

philippic [frˈlɪpɪk] N (*lit, fig*) Philippika *f*

Philippine [ˈfɪlɪpiːn] ADJ philippinisch

Philippines [ˈfɪlɪpiːnz] PL Philippinen *pl*

philistine [ˈfɪlɪstaɪn] ADJ (*fig*) kulturlos, philisterhaft (*geh*); **tell that ~ friend of yours ...** sag deinem Freund, diesem Banausen ... N **a** (*lit*) **Philistine** Philister(in) *m(f)* **b** (*fig*) Banause *m*, Banausin *f*, Philister(in) *m(f)* (*geh*)

philistinism [ˈfɪlɪstɪnɪzəm] N Banausentum *nt*

Phillips® [ˈfɪlɪps]: **Phillips screw** N Kreuzschraube *f*; **Phillips screwdriver** N Kreuzschlitzschraubenzieher *m*

philological [ˌfɪləˈlɒdʒɪkəl] ADJ philologisch

philologist [frˈlɒlədʒɪst] N Philologe *m*, Philologin *f*

philology [frˈlɒlədʒɪ] N Philologie *f*

philosopher [frˈlɒsəfəʳ] N Philosoph(in) *m(f)*

philosopher's stone N [frˌlɒsəfəzˈstəʊn] N Stein *m* der Weisen

philosophic(al) [ˌfɪləˈsɒfɪk(əl)] ADJ philosophisch; (*fig also*) gelassen; **to be philosophical about sth** etw philosophisch betrachten

philosophically [ˌfɪləˈsɒfɪkəlɪ] ADV philosophisch; (*fig also*) gelassen; **his ideas are ~ naïve** philosophisch betrachtet sind seine Gedanken naiv; **~ speaking, ...** (rein) theoretisch gesehen, ...

philosophize [frˈlɒsəfaɪz] VI philosophieren (*about, on* über +*acc*)

philosophy [frˈlɒsəfɪ] N Philosophie *f*; **~ of life** Lebensphilosophie *f*; **that's my ~** das ist meine Philosophie or Einstellung; **~ of education** Erziehungsphilosophie *f*

philtre, (*US*) **philter** [ˈfɪltəʳ] N Zaubertrank *m*; (= *love philtre*) Liebestrank *m*

phiz [fɪz] N (*dated Brit sl*) Visage *f* (*inf*)

phlebitis [flrˈbaɪtɪs] N Venenentzündung *f*, Phlebitis *f* (*spec*)

phlegm [flem] N (= *mucus*) Schleim *m*; (*obs: humour*) Phlegma *nt*; (*fig*) (= *coolness*) Gemütsruhe *f*, stoische Ruhe; (= *stolidness*) Trägheit *f*, Schwerfälligkeit *f*, Phlegma *nt*

phlegmatic [flegˈmætɪk] ADJ (= *cool*) seelenruhig, stoisch; (= *stolid*) träge, schwerfällig, phlegmatisch

phlox [flɒks] N Phlox *m*

-phobe [-fəʊb] N *suf* -phobe(r) *mf*, -feind(in) *m(f)*; **Anglophobe** Anglophobe(r) *mf*, Englandfeind(in) *m(f)*

phobia [ˈfəʊbɪə] N Phobie *f*; **she has a ~ about it** sie hat krankhafte Angst davor

-phobic [-ˈfəʊbɪk] ADJ *suf* -phob, -feindlich; **Anglophobic** anglophob, englandfeindlich

Phoenicia [fəˈniːʃə] N Phönizien *nt*

Phoenician [fəˈniːʃən] ADJ phönizisch N Phönizier(in) *m(f)*

phoenix, (*US*) **phenix** [ˈfiːnɪks] N (*Myth*) Phönix *m*; **like a ~ from the ashes** wie ein Phönix aus der Asche

phoenix-like, (*US*) **phenix-like** [ˈfiːnɪkslaɪk] ADJ wie ein Phönix, dem Phönix gleich ADV wie ein Phönix; **to rise ~ from the ashes** wie ein Phönix aus der Asche (auf)steigen

phone[1] [fəʊn] ✆ 27.4 N Telefon *nt*; **to be on the ~** (= *be a subscriber*) Telefon haben; (= *be speaking*) am Telefon sein; **I'll give you a ~** (*inf*) ich ruf dich an **VT** *person* anrufen; *message* telefonisch übermitteln **VI** anrufen, telefonieren → *also* **telephone**

▶ **phone back VT** *sep* zurückrufen **VI** zurückrufen

▶ **phone in VI** anrufen **VT** *sep* telefonisch übermitteln

▶ **phone up VI** anrufen, telefonieren **VT** *sep* anrufen

phone² N (*Ling*) Phon *nt*

phone: phone bill N Telefonrechnung *f*; **phone booth** N **a** (*in station, hotel etc*) Fernsprechhaube *f* **b** (*US: = call box*) Telefonzelle *f*; **phonecard** N Telefonkarte *f*; **phone-in** N *Rundfunkprogramm, an dem sich Hörer per Telefon beteiligen können*, Phone-in *nt*

phoneme ['fəʊniːm] N Phonem *nt*

phonemic [fəʊ'niːmɪk] ADJ phonemisch

phone tapping ['fəʊnˌtæpɪŋ] N Abhören *nt* von Telefonen; **new measures to stop ~** neue Maßnahmen zum Abhörschutz

phonetic ADJ , **phonetically** ADV [fəʊ'netɪk, -əlɪ] phonetisch

phonetician [ˌfɒnɪ'tɪʃən] N Phonetiker(in) *m(f)*

phonetics [fəʊ'netɪks] N **a** *sing* (*= subject*) Phonetik *f* **b** *pl* (*= phonetic script*) Lautschrift *f*, phonetische Umschrift

phoney ['fəʊnɪ] (*inf*) **ADJ** **a** (*= fake, pretentious*) unecht; *excuse, deal, peace* faul (*inf*); *name, accent* falsch; *passport, money* gefälscht; *story, report* erfunden; **a ~ doctor** ein Scharlatan *m*; **a ~ policeman** ein zwielichtiger Polizist; **a ~ company** eine Schwindelfirma; **a ~ war** kein echter Krieg; **he's so ~** der ist doch nicht echt (*inf*); **there's something ~ about it** da ist was faul dran (*inf*) **b** (*= insincere*) *person* falsch; *emotion* unecht, vorgetäuscht **N** (*= thing*) Fälschung *f*; (*= banknote also*) Blüte *f* (*inf*); (*= bogus policeman etc*) Schwindler(in) *m(f)*; (*= doctor*) Scharlatan *m*; (*= pretentious person*) Angeber(in) *m(f)*

phonic ['fɒnɪk] ADJ phonisch

phonograph ['fəʊnəɡrɑːf] N (*old, US*) Phonograph *m*

phonological [ˌfəʊnə'lɒdʒɪkəl] ADJ phonologisch

phonology [fəʊ'nɒlədʒɪ] N (*= science*) Phonologie *f*; (*= system*) Lautsystem *nt*

phonometry [fəʊ'nɒmɪtrɪ] N (*acoustics*) Phonometrie *f*

phony ADJ, N (*US inf*) = **phoney**

phooey ['fuːɪ] INTERJ (*scorn*) pah, bah; (*disgust*) pfui

phosphate ['fɒsfeɪt] N (*Chem*) Phosphat *nt*; (*Agr, = fertilizer*) Phosphatdünger *m*

phosphide ['fɒsfaɪd] N Phosphid *nt*

phosphor ['fɒsfə'] N Phosphor *m*

phosphoresce [ˌfɒsfə'res] VI phosphoreszieren

phosphorescence [ˌfɒsfə'resns] N Phosphoreszenz *f*

phosphorescent [ˌfɒsfə'resnt] ADJ phosphoreszierend

phosphoric [fɒs'fɒrɪk] ADJ phosphorig

phosphorous ['fɒsfərəs] ADJ phosphorsauer

phosphorus ['fɒsfərəs] N Phosphor *m*

photo ['fəʊtəʊ] N Foto *nt*, Photo *nt*, Aufnahme *f* → *also* **photograph**

photo: photo booth N Passfotoautomat® *m*; **photo call** N Fototermin *m*; **photocell** N Photozelle *f*; **photocompose** VT (*esp US Typ*) lichtsetzen, fotosetzen; **photocomposition** N (*Typ*) Lichtsatz *m*, Filmsatz *m*; **photocopier** N (Foto)kopierer *m*, (Foto)kopiergerät *nt*; **photocopy N** Fotokopie *f* **VT** fotokopieren **VI** **this won't ~** das lässt sich nicht fotokopieren; **photoelectric** ADJ photoelektrisch; **photoelectric cell** N Photozelle *f*; **photoelectron** N Photoelektron *nt*; **photoengraving** N (*= process*) Klischieren *nt*; (*= plate*) Klischee *nt*; **photo finish** N Fotofinish *nt*; **Pho-**

tofit® N (*also* **Photofit picture**) Phantombild *nt*; **photoflash** N Blitzlicht *nt*; **~ lamp** Blitzgerät *nt*; **photoflood (lamp)** N Jupiterlampe *f*

photogenic [ˌfəʊtəʊ'dʒenɪk] ADJ fotogen

photograph ['fəʊtəɡrɑːf] N Fotografie *f*, Aufnahme *f*; **to take a ~ (of sb/sth)** (jdn/etw) fotografieren, eine Aufnahme *or* ein Bild (von jdm/etw) machen; **she takes a good ~** (= *is photogenic*) sie ist fotogen; **this camera takes good ~s** diese Kamera macht gute Aufnahmen *or* Bilder *or* Fotos; **~ album** Fotoalbum *nt* **VT** fotografieren, knipsen (*inf*); **"photographed by John Mayne"** „Foto/Fotos: John Mayne" **VI to ~ well** sich gut fotografieren lassen; **she doesn't ~ well** sie ist nicht sehr fotogen

photographer [fə'tɒɡrəfə'] N Fotograf(in) *m(f)*

photographic [ˌfəʊtə'ɡræfɪk] ADJ *film* für Fotos; *plate, library, studio, evidence, record* fotografisch; *style of painting, art* naturgetreu; **~ agency** Fotoagentur *f*; **~ magazine** Fotomagazin *nt*

photographically [ˌfəʊtə'ɡræfɪkəlɪ] ADV fotografisch; **to record sth ~** etw im Bild festhalten

photographic memory N fotografisches Gedächtnis

photography [fə'tɒɡrəfɪ] N Fotografie *f*; (*in film, book etc*) Fotografien *pl*, Aufnahmen *pl*, Bilder *pl*; **his ~ is marvellous** seine Fotografien *etc* sind hervorragend

photogravure [ˌfəʊtəʊɡrə'vjʊə'] N Photogravüre *f*, Heliogravüre *f*

photo: photojournalism N Fotojournalismus *m*; **photojournalist** N Fotojournalist(in) *m(f)*, Bildjournalist(in) *m(f)*

photomechanical ADJ fotomechanisch

photometer [fəʊ'tɒmɪtə'] N Photometer *nt*

photomontage ['fəʊtəʊmɒn'tɑːʒ] N Fotomontage *f*

photon ['fəʊtɒn] N Photon *nt*

photo: photo opportunity N Fototermin *m*; **photosensitive** ADJ lichtempfindlich; **photosensitize** VT lichtempfindlich machen; **photo session** N Fotosession *f*; **photoset** VT (*Typ*) im Lichtsatz herstellen; **photosetting** N Lichtsatz *m*; **Photostat®** N, VTI = **photocopy**; **photosynthesis** N Photosynthese *f*; **phototelegraphy** N Bildtelegrafie *f*; **phototropic** ADJ phototrop(isch); **phototropism** N Phototropismus *m*; **phototypesetting** N (*esp US Typ*) Lichtsatz *m*, Fotosatz *m*

phrasal ['freɪzəl] ADJ im Satz

phrasal verb N Verb *nt* mit Präposition

phrase [freɪz] **N** **a** (*Gram*) Phrase *f*, Satzglied *nt* *or* -teil *m*; (*in spoken language*) Phrase *f*; **noun/verb ~** Nominal-/Verbalphrase *f* **b** (= *mode of expression*) Ausdruck *m*; (*= set expression*) Redewendung *f*; **in a ~** kurz gesagt → **set 2 d**, **turn 1 b** **c** (*Mus*) Phrase *f* **VT** **a** (= *express*) formulieren; *criticism, suggestion* ausdrücken, formulieren **b** (*Mus*) phrasieren

phrase: phrase book N Sprachführer *m*; **phrase marker** N (*Ling*) P-Marker *m*, Formationsmarker *m*; **phrasemonger** N (*pej*) Phrasendrescher(in) *m(f)*

phraseology [ˌfreɪzɪ'ɒlədʒɪ] N Ausdrucksweise *f*; (*of letter etc*) Diktion *f*; (*= jargon*) Jargon *m*

phrase structure grammar N (*Ling*) Phrasenstrukturgrammatik *f*

phrasing ['freɪzɪŋ] N (= *act*) Formulierung *f*; (= *style*) Ausdrucksweise *f*, Stil *m*; (*Mus*) Phrasierung *f*

phrenetic ADJ = **frenetic**

phrenologist [frɪ'nɒlədʒɪst] N Phrenologe *m*, Phrenologin *f*

phrenology [frɪ'nɒlədʒɪ] N Phrenologie *f*

phthisis ['θaɪsɪs] N Schwindsucht *f*, (Lungen-)tuberkulose *f*

phut [fʌt] (*inf*) **N** Puff *m* **ADV to go ~** (= *make noise*) puff machen; (= *break down*) kaputtgehen (*inf*); (*plans etc*) platzen (*inf*)

pH-value [piː'eɪtʃvæljuː] N pH-Wert *m*

phylum ['faɪləm] N *pl* **phyla** ['faɪlə] (*Biol*) Stamm *m*

physic ['fɪzɪk] N (*obs*) Arznei *f*; (*cathartic*) Purgativ *nt*

physical ['fɪzɪkəl] **ADJ** **a** (= *of the body*) körperlich; *abuse, violence, punishment, discomfort* physisch, körperlich; *check-up* ärztlich; (= *not psychological*) physisch; **you don't take/get enough ~ exercise** Sie bewegen sich nicht genug; **he's very ~** (*inf*) er ist sehr sinnlich; **play got too ~** (*Sport inf*) das Spiel wurde so ruppig *or* rabiat (*inf*); **the ~ force of the impact** die Wucht des Aufpralls; **we don't actually need your ~ presence** Ihre persönliche Anwesenheit ist nicht unbedingt nötig **b** (= *sexual*) *love, relationship* körperlich **c** (= *material*) physisch, körperlich; *size* physisch; *world* fassbar **d** (*of physics*) *laws, properties* physikalisch; **it's a ~ impossibility** es ist ein Ding der Unmöglichkeit **e** (= *natural*) *environment* physisch, real; *conditions* physisch **f** (= *actual*) *possession* physisch, leibhaftig **N** ärztliche Untersuchung; (*Mil*) Musterung *f*

physical: physical chemistry N physikalische Chemie; **physical education** N (*abbr* **PE**) Sport *m*, Leibesübungen *pl* (*form*); **physical education college** N Sporthochschule *f*, Sportakademie *f*; **physical education teacher** N Sportlehrer(in) *m(f)*; **physical fitness** N körperliche Fitness *f*, physische Fitness *f*; **physical geography** N physische *or* physikalische Geografie, Physiogeografie *f*; **physical jerks** PL (*inf*) Gymnastik *f*

physically ['fɪzɪkəlɪ] ADV **a** körperlich, physisch; *restrain, separate* körperlich; (*Sci*) physikalisch; **to be ~ sick** sich übergeben; **to be ~ capable/incapable of (doing) sth** körperlich *or* physisch imstande *or* im Stande/außerstand *or* außer Stande sein, etw zu tun; **~ impossible** praktisch unmöglich; **the substance changed ~** die Substanz ging in einen anderen Zustand über; **the journey is ~ dangerous** die Reise ist gefährlich für Leib und Leben; **you don't have to be there ~** Ihre persönliche Anwesenheit ist nicht erforderlich; **they removed him ~ from the meeting** sie haben ihn mit Gewalt aus der Versammlung entfernt **b** (*emph, = actually*) **as long as is ~ possible** so lange wie nur irgend möglich

physical: physical science N Naturwissenschaft *f*; **physical therapist** N (*US Med*) Physiotherapeut(in) *m(f)*; **physical therapy** N (*US Med*) Physiotherapie *f*; **physical training** N (*abbr* **PT**) = **physical education**

physician [fɪ'zɪʃən] N Arzt *m*, Ärztin *f*

physicist ['fɪzɪsɪst] N Physiker(in) *m(f)*

physics ['fɪzɪks] N (*sing: = subject*) Physik *f*; **the ~ of this are quite complex** die physikalischen Zusammenhänge sind hierbei ziemlich komplex

physio ['fɪzɪəʊ] N (*esp Brit inf*) Physiotherapeut(in) *m(f)*

physiognomy [ˌfɪzɪ'ɒnəmɪ] N (= *face*) Physiognomie *f*; (= *study*) Physiognomik *f*; (*fig*) äußere Erscheinung, Aussehen *nt*; **the ~ of the Labour Party** das Gesicht der Labour Party

physiological [ˌfɪzɪə'lɒdʒɪkəl] ADJ physiologisch

physiologist [ˌfɪzɪ'ɒlədʒɪst] N Physiologe *m*, Physiologin *f*

physiology [ˌfɪzɪ'ɒlədʒɪ] N Physiologie *f*

physiotherapeutic ['fɪzɪəˌθerə'pjuːtɪk] ADJ physiotherapeutisch

physiotherapist [ˌfɪzɪə'θerəpɪst] N Physiotherapeut(in) *m(f)*

physiotherapy [ˌfɪzɪə'θerəpɪ] N Physiotherapie *f*, physikalische Therapie

physique [fɪ'ziːk] N Körperbau *m*, Statur *f*; **to be small in ~** von kleiner Statur sein

PI *abbr of* **private investigator** Privatdetektiv(in) *m(f)*

pi [paɪ] N (Math) Pi nt

pianissimo [pɪə'nɪsɪ,məʊ] (Mus) **ADV** pianissimo, sehr leise; **to play ~** pianissimo spielen **ADJ** pianissimo *inv*, sehr leise; **the ~ section** das Pianissimo

pianist ['pɪənɪst] N Klavierspieler(in) m(f); (= *concert pianist*) Pianist(in) m(f)

piano ['pjænəʊ] **N** (*upright*) Klavier nt, Piano nt (*geh, old*); (= *grand piano*) Flügel m; **who was at or on the ~?** wer war am Klavier? **ADV** ['pjɑːnəʊ] (Mus) piano, leise **ADJ** ['pjɑːnəʊ] piano, leise; **the ~ section** das Piano

piano: piano accordion N Pianoakkordeon nt; **piano concerto** N Klavierkonzert nt; **pianoforte** ['pjænəʊ'fɔːtɪ] (*form*) Pianoforte nt; **piano keys** PL Klaviertasten pl

Pianola® [pɪə'nəʊlə] N Pianola nt

piano: piano lesson N Klavierstunde f; **piano music** N Klaviermusik f; **piano player** N Klavierspieler(in) m(f); **piano recital** N Klavierkonzert nt; **piano stool** N Klavierhocker m; **piano teacher** N Klavierlehrer(in) m(f); **piano tuner** N Klavierstimmer(in) m(f); **piano wire** N Klaviersaitendraht m

piazza ['pjætsə] N Piazza f, (Markt)platz m; (US: = *veranda*) (überdachte) Veranda

pic [pɪk] N (*inf*, = *photo*) Foto nt

picaresque [,pɪkə'resk] ADJ pikaresk; **~ novel** Schelmenroman m, pikaresker Roman

picayune [,pɪkə'juːn], **picayunish** [-ɪʃ] ADJ (*US inf*: = *paltry*) gering, minimal; (= *petty*) kleinlich

piccalilli ['pɪkə,lɪlɪ] N Piccalilli pl

piccaninny [,pɪkə'nɪnɪ] N (*pej*) Negerkind nt

piccolo ['pɪkələʊ] N Pikkoloflöte f

pick [pɪk] **N a** (= *pickaxe*) Spitzhacke f, Picke f, Pickel m; (Mountaineering) Eispickel m; (= *toothpick*) Zahnstocher m
  b (*esp US*: = *plectrum*) Plektron nt, Plektrum nt
  c (= *choice*) **she could have her ~ of any man in the room** sie könnte jeden Mann im Raum haben; **to have first ~** die erste Wahl haben; **take your ~!** such dir etwas/einen *etc* aus!
  d (= *best*) Beste(s) nt → **bunch**
VT a (= *choose*) (aus)wählen; **to ~ a team** eine Mannschaft aufstellen; **to ~ sb to do sth** jdn auswählen, etw zu tun; **he has been ~ed for England** er ist für England aufgestellt worden; **to ~ sides** wählen; **to ~ a winner** (*lit*) den Sieger erraten; (*fig*) das große Los ziehen; **a handful of ~ed men** (Mil) ein paar ausgewählte Soldaten; **to ~ one's words** seine Worte mit Bedacht wählen; **to ~ one's time** den richtigen Zeitpunkt wählen; **you really ~ your times, don't you?** (*iro*) du suchst dir aber auch immer den günstigsten Augenblick aus! (*iro*) **to ~ one's way** seinen Weg suchen; **to ~ one's way through sth** seinen Weg durch etw finden; **he knows how to ~ 'em** (*inf*) er hat den richtigen Riecher (*inf*); **you do ~ 'em** (*iro*) du gerätst auch immer an die Falschen
  b (= *pull bits off, make holes in*) jumper, blanket *etc* zupfen an (+*dat*); spot, scab kratzen an (+*dat*); hole (*with fingers, instrument*) bohren; (*with beak*) picken, hacken; **to ~ one's nose** sich (+*dat*) in der Nase bohren; **to ~ one's teeth** sich (*dat*) in den Zähnen herumstochern; **to ~ a lock** ein Schloss knacken; **to ~ a bone** (*with fingers*) einen Knochen abzupfen; (*with teeth, beak*) einen Knochen abnagen; **to ~ sth to pieces** (*lit*) etw zerpflücken; (*fig*) kein gutes Haar an etw (*dat*) lassen, etw verreißen; **to ~ holes in sth** (*fig*) etw bemäkeln; *in argument, theory* etw in ein Punkten widerlegen; **to ~ a fight** or **quarrel (with sb)** (mit jdm) einen Streit vom Zaun brechen; **to ~ pockets** sich als Taschendieb betätigen; **he's very good at ~ing pockets** er ist ein sehr geschickter Taschendieb; **to ~ sb's pocket** jdn bestehlen; **to ~ sb's brains (about sth)** jdn (nach etw) ausfragen → **bone** N **a**
  c (= *pluck*) flowers, fruit pflücken; (= *pick out and remove*) fleas, splinter *etc* entfernen (*from* von)

  d (*US*, = *pluck*) chicken *etc* rupfen
  e (*esp US*) strings zupfen, anreißen; banjo zupfen
  f (= *peck up*) corn *etc* picken
VI a (= *choose*) wählen, aussuchen; **to ~ and choose** wählerisch sein
  b (*esp US*: *on guitar etc*) zupfen

▶ **pick at** VI +prep obj **a** **to pick at one's food** im Essen herumstochern, am Essen herumpicken **b** (*inf*, = *criticize*) **to pick at sb/sth** auf jdm/etw herumhacken

▶ **pick off** VT sep **a** (= *remove*) fluff *etc* wegzupfen; (= *pluck*) fruit pflücken; nail polish abschälen; **the crew were picked off by helicopter** die Mannschaft wurde von einem Hubschrauber aufgenommen *or* aufgelesen (*inf*) **b** (= *shoot*) abschießen, abknallen (*inf*)

▶ **pick on** VI +prep obj (*esp Brit*) (= *choose*) aussuchen; (= *victimize*) herumhacken auf (+*dat*); **why pick on me?** (*inf*) warum gerade ich?; **pick on somebody your own size!** (*inf*) leg dich doch mit einem Gleichstarken an! (*inf*); **stop picking on me!** hack nicht ständig auf mir herum!

▶ **pick out** VT sep **a** (= *choose*) aussuchen, auswählen; **to pick out a few examples** um ein paar Beispiele herauszugreifen **b** (= *remove*) bad apples *etc* heraussuchen, auslesen **c** (= *see, distinguish*) person, familiar face ausmachen, entdecken; **the spotlight picked out the leading dancer** der Scheinwerfer wurde auf den Haupttänzer gerichtet **d** (= *highlight*) hervorheben (*in, with durch*) **e** (*Mus*) **to pick out a tune (on the piano)** eine Melodie (auf dem Klavier) improvisieren; **he picked out a few notes** er spielte ein paar Takte

▶ **pick over** *or* **through** VI +prep obj durchsehen, untersuchen; **it's no good picking over the past** es hat keinen Sinn, über die Vergangenheit zu brüten

▶ **pick up** **VT** sep **a** (= *take up*) aufheben; (= *lift momentarily*) hochheben; stitch aufnehmen; **to pick up a child in one's arms** ein Kind auf den Arm nehmen; **pick up your feet when you walk!** heb deine Füße (beim Gehen)!; **to pick oneself up** aufstehen; **as soon as he picks up a book** sobald er ein Buch in die Hand nimmt; **it's the sort of book you can pick up when you have a free minute** das ist so ein Buch, das man mal zwischendurch lesen kann; **to pick up the phone** (den Hörer) abnehmen; **you just have to pick up the phone** du brauchst nur anzurufen; **to pick up the bill** (= *pay*) die Rechnung bezahlen; **to pick up a story** mit einer Geschichte fortfahren; **to pick up the pieces** (*lit, fig*) die Scherben aufsammeln *or* zusammenmensuchen; **to pick up the thread of a lecture** den Faden (eines Vortrags) wieder finden; **to pick up the threads of one's life** die Scherben seines Lebens wieder zusammenkitten; **the interviewer picked up this reference and ...** der Interviewer nahm diese Bemerkung auf *or* knüpfte an diese Bemerkung an und ...
  b (= *get*) holen; (= *buy*) bekommen; habit (*dat*) angewöhnen; news, gossip aufschnappen; illness sich (*dat*) holen *or* zuziehen; (= *earn*) verdienen; medal bekommen, erhalten; **to pick sth up at a sale** etw im Ausverkauf erwischen; **to pick up speed** schneller werden; **you never know what you'll pick up** (= *what illness etc*) man weiß nie, was man sich (*dat*) da holen *or* zuziehen kann; **he picked up a few extra points** er hat ein paar Extrapunkte gemacht; **he picked up a reputation as a womanizer** er geriet in den Ruf eines Frauenhelden
  c (= *learn*) skill *etc* sich (*dat*) aneignen; language lernen; accent, word aufschnappen; information, tips *etc* herausbekommen; idea aufgreifen; **you'll soon pick it up** du wirst das schnell lernen; **where did you pick up that idea?** wo hast du denn die Idee her?
  d (= *collect*) person, goods abholen; **I'll come and pick you up** ich hole dich ab, ich komme dich abholen
  e (bus *etc*) passengers aufnehmen; (*in car*) mitnehmen

  f (= *rescue: helicopter, lifeboat*) bergen
  g (= *arrest, catch*) wanted man, criminal schnappen (*inf*); **they picked him up for questioning** sie haben ihn geholt, um ihn zu vernehmen
  h (*inf*) girl aufgabeln (*inf*); **she got picked up at a party** die ist auf einer Party (von einem) abgeschleppt *or* aufgegabelt worden (*inf*)
  i (= *find*) road finden; **to pick up the trail** (Hunt, *fig*) die Fährte *or* Spur aufnehmen
  j (Rad) station hereinbekommen, (rein)kriegen (*inf*); message empfangen, auffangen; (= *see*) beacon *etc* ausmachen, sichten; (*on radar*) ausmachen; (*record stylus*) sound aufnehmen; **the surface was clearly picked up by the satellite's cameras** das Bild der Oberfläche wurde von den Satellitenkameras deutlich übermittelt; **we picked up a rabbit in the car headlights** wir sahen ein Kaninchen im Scheinwerferlicht
  k (*Brit*: = *correct, put right*) korrigieren; **he picked me up on my bad grammar** er wies auf meine schlechte Grammatik hin; **he picked me up for mispronouncing it** er hat meine falsche Aussprache korrigiert
  l (= *restore to health*) wieder auf die Beine stellen
  m (= *spot, identify*) mistakes finden
  n (*US, inf*, = *tidy*) room auf Vordermann bringen (*inf*)
VI a (= *improve*) besser werden; (*appetite*) zunehmen; (*currency*) sich erholen; (*business: after slump*) sich erholen; (*engine*) rund laufen; (= *accelerate*) schneller werden
  b (= *continue*) weitermachen; **to pick up where one left off** da weitermachen, wo man aufgehört hat
  c (*inf*) **to pick up with sb** (= *get to know*) jds Bekanntschaft machen; **he has picked up with a rather strange crowd** er hat sich mit merkwürdigen Leuten umgang; **to pick up on a point** einen Punkt aufgreifen

pickaback ['pɪkəbæk] N, ADV = **piggyback**

pick-and-mix N, ADJ = **pick 'n' mix**

pickaninny N (*US*) = **piccaninny**

pickaxe, (*US*) **pickax** ['pɪkæks] N Spitzhacke f, Picke f

picker ['pɪkə'] N (*of fruit etc*) Pflücker(in) m(f)

picket ['pɪkɪt] **N a** (*of strikers*) Streikposten m; **to mount a ~ (at** *or* **on a gate)** (an *or* bei einem Tor) Streikposten aufstellen **b** (Mil) Feldposten m, Vorposten m **c** (= *stake*) Pfahl m; **~ fence** Palisade f, Palisadenzaun m **VT** factory Streikposten aufstellen vor (+*dat*); (*demonstrators etc*) demonstrieren vor (+*dat*) **VI** Streikposten aufstellen; **he is ~ing at the front entrance** er ist Streikposten am Vordereingang

picket: picket boat N (*of port police*) Patrouillenboot nt; **picket duty** N Streikpostendienst m; **to be on ~** Streikposten sein

picketer ['pɪkɪtə'] N Streikposten m

picketing ['pɪkɪtɪŋ] N Aufstellen nt von Streikposten; **there was no ~** es wurden keine Streikposten aufgestellt; **the ~ of the factory went on for six months** es standen sechs Monate lang Streikposten vor dem Betrieb

picket line N Streikpostenkette f; **to cross a ~** eine Streikpostenkette durchbrechen

picking ['pɪkɪŋ] N **a** (= *amount of fruit picked*) Ernte f **b** **pickings** PL Ausbeute f; (= *stolen goods*) Beute f; **most office workers regard pens as legitimate ~s** die meisten Büroangestellten sehen es als ihr Recht an, Kulis mitgehen zu lassen (*inf*) *or* einzustecken; **she went along to see if there were any ~s** sie ging hin, um zu sehen, ob es für sie was zu holen gab; **there are rich ~s to be had** da gibt es reiche Beute; **easy ~s for thieves** leichte Beute für Diebe

pickle ['pɪkl] **N a** (= *food*) Pickles pl **b** (= *solution*) (= *brine*) Salzlake f, Pökel m; (= *vinegar*) Essigsoße f; (*for leather, wood*) Beize f; (Med, Sci) Nasspräparat nt **c** (*inf*: = *predicament*) Klemme f (*inf*); **he was in a bit of a ~** er steckte in einer Klemme (*inf*), er saß in der Tinte (*inf*); **to get (oneself) into a ~** in ein Kuddelmuddel geraten (*inf*); **what a ~!** so eine verzwickte Lage! **VT** einlegen; (*Med, Sci*) konservieren

pickled ['pɪkld] ADJ **a** eingelegt **b** pred (*inf, = drunk*) besoffen (*inf*), alkoholisiert (*inf*)

pick: picklock N (= *tool*) Dietrich *m*; (= *thief*) Einbrecher(in) *m(f)*; **pick-me-up** N (= *drink*) Muntermacher *m*, Stärkung *f*; (= *holiday etc*) Erholung *f*; **we stopped off at the pub for a ~** wir sind auf ein Gläschen *or* einen Schluck in die Kneipe gegangen; **hearing that was a real ~** das hat mir richtig Auftrieb gegeben

pick 'n' mix [ˌpɪkn'mɪks] N (= *sweets etc, fig*) bunte Mischung ADJ approach, selection, collection bunt gemischt, bunt zusammengewürfelt; morality, politics verschiedenste Elemente vereinend

pickpocket ['pɪkˌpɒkɪt] N Taschendieb(in) *m(f)*

pick-up ['pɪkʌp] N **a** Tonabnehmer *m*; **~ arm** Tonarm *m*
b (*also* **pick-up truck**) Kleinlieferwagen *m*, Kleintransporter *m*
c (*inf, = acquaintance*) Bekanntschaft *f*; **with his latest ~** mit seiner neusten Errungenschaft; **he's just looking for a ~** er will nur eine aufreißen (*inf*)
d (= *collection*) Abholen *nt*; **he was late for the ~** er kam zu spät zum Treffpunkt; **the mail van makes 3 ~s a day** der Postwagen kommt dreimal täglich(, um die Post abzuholen); **the bus makes four ~s** der Bus hält viermal(, um Leute aufzunehmen); **~ point** (*for excursion*) Sammelstelle *f*, Treffpunkt *m*; (*on regular basis*) Haltestelle *f*
e (= *improvement*) Verbesserung *f*; (= *increase*) Ansteigen *nt*
f (= *acceleration*) Beschleunigung *f*

picky ['pɪkɪ] ADJ (+er) (*inf*) pingelig (*inf*); eater wählerisch

picnic ['pɪknɪk] vb: pret, ptp **picnicked** N Picknick *nt*; **to have a ~** picknicken; **to go for** *or* **on a ~** ein Picknick veranstalten *or* machen; **a ~ lunch** ein Picknick *nt*; **it was no ~** (*fig inf*) es war kein Honiglecken **VI** picknicken, ein Picknick machen; **we went ~king every Sunday** wir machten jeden Sonntag ein Picknick

picnic basket, **picnic hamper** N Picknickkorb *m*

picnicker ['pɪknɪkə'] N jd, der picknickt *or* ein Picknick macht; **the ~s left all their rubbish behind them** die Ausflügler ließen ihre Abfälle liegen

picnic: picnic site N Rastplatz *m*; **picnic table** N Campingtisch *m*

pics [pɪks] PL abbr of **pictures** (*Brit, inf*) = **picture** N c

Pict [pɪkt] N Pikte *m*, Piktin *f*

Pictish ['pɪktɪʃ] ADJ piktisch N (*Ling*) Piktisch *nt*

pictogram ['pɪktəɡræm], **pictograph** ['pɪktəɡrɑːf] N Piktogramm *nt*

pictorial [pɪk'tɔːrɪəl] ADJ calendar bebildert; magazine also illustriert; impact bildlich; language, description bildhaft; **~ dictionary** Bildwörterbuch *nt*; **to keep a ~ record of** etw im Bild festhalten N (= *magazine*) Illustrierte *f*; (= *stamp*) Sondermarke *f*

pictorially [pɪk'tɔːrɪəlɪ] ADV (= *in pictures*) in Bildern, bildlich; describe bildhaft

picture ['pɪktʃə'] N **a** Bild *nt*; (*Art*) (= *painting*) Gemälde *nt*, Bild *nt*; (= *drawing*) Zeichnung *f*; **(as) pretty as a ~** bildschön
b (*TV*) Bild *nt*
c (*Film*) Film *m*; **the ~s** (*Brit*) das Kino; **to go to the ~s** (*Brit*) ins Kino gehen; **what's on at the ~s?** (*Brit*) was gibts im Kino?
d (= *mental image*) Vorstellung *f*, Bild *nt*; **these figures give the general ~** diese Zahlen geben ein allgemeines Bild; **have you got the general ~?** wissen Sie jetzt ungefähr Bescheid?; **to give you a ~ of what life is like here** damit Sie sich (*dat*) ein Bild vom Leben hier machen können; **to form a ~ of sth** sich (*dat*) ein Bild von etw machen; **the other side of the ~** die Kehr-

seite der Medaille; **to be in the ~** im Bilde sein; **to put sb in the ~** jdn ins Bild setzen; **to be left out of the ~** (= *be kept in the dark*) nicht informiert werden; **I get the ~** (*inf*) ich habs begriffen *or* kapiert (*inf*); **I'm beginning to get the ~** (*inf*) ich fange an zu begreifen *or* kapieren (*inf*); **he/that no longer comes into the ~** er/das spielt keine Rolle mehr
e (= *sight*) Bild *nt*; (*beautiful*) Traum *m*, Bild *nt*; **his face was a ~** sein Gesicht war ein Bild für die Götter (*inf*); **she looked a ~** sie war bildschön *or* traumhaft schön; **the garden is a ~** der Garten ist eine Pracht
f (= *embodiment*) Bild *nt*, Verkörperung *f*; (= *spitting image*) Abbild *nt*, Ebenbild *nt*; **she looked** *or* **was the ~ of happiness/health** sie sah wie das Glück/die Gesundheit in Person aus; **she looked** *or* **was the ~ of misery** sie war ein Bild des Elends
VT **a** (= *imagine*) sich (*dat*) vorstellen; **to ~ sth to oneself** sich (*dat*) etw vorstellen
b (= *describe*) beschreiben, darstellen
c (*by drawing, painting*) darstellen; (*in book*) abbilden

picture: picture book N Bildband *m*; (*for children*) Bilderbuch *nt*; **picture card** N Bild(-karte *f*) *nt*; **picture composition** N (*Art*) Bildkomposition *f*; **picture desk** N (*Press*) Bildredaktion *f*; **picture editor** N (*Press*) Bildredakteur(in) *m(f)*; **picture frame** N Bilderrahmen *m*; **picture gallery** N Gemäldegalerie *f*; **picturegoer** N (*Brit*) Kinogänger(in) *m(f)*, Kinobesucher(in) *m(f)*; **picture hat** N Florentiner(hut) *m*; **picture house** N (*dated Brit*) = **picture palace**; **picture-in-picture** N (*TV, Comput*) Bild-in-Bild *nt*; **picture library** N Bildarchiv *nt*; **picture messaging** N (*Telec*) Picture Messaging *nt*; **picture palace** N (*dated Brit*) Lichtspielhaus *nt* (*old*), Lichtspieltheater *nt* (*old*); **picture paper** N (*Brit*) Illustrierte *f*; **picture postcard** N Ansichts(post)karte *f*; **picture puzzle** N **a** Vexierbild *nt* **b** Bilderrätsel *nt*; **picture quality** N (*TV etc*) Bildqualität *f*; **picture rail** N Bilderleiste *f*; **picture researcher** N Bildbeschaffer(in) *m(f)*, Pictureresearcher(in) *m(f)*; **picture search** N (*on video*) Bildsuchlauf *m*

picturesque [ˌpɪktʃə'resk] ADJ malerisch, pittoresk (*geh*); (*fig*) description anschaulich, bildhaft

picturesquely [ˌpɪktʃə'resklɪ] ADV malerisch, pittoresk (*geh*); (*fig*) describe anschaulich, bildhaft; **a place ~ known as Devil's Dyke** ein Ort mit dem malerischen Namen Devils Dyke

picturesqueness [ˌpɪktʃə'resknɪs] N Malerische(s) *nt*; (*fig: of account, language*) Bildhaftigkeit *f*, Anschaulichkeit *f*

picture: picture tube N Bildröhre *f*; **picture window** N Aussichtsfenster *nt*; **picture writing** N Bilderschrift *f*

piddle ['pɪdl] (*inf*) N Pipi *nt* (*inf*); **to do a ~** pinkeln (*inf*) **VI** **a** (*person, animal*) pinkeln (*inf*); (*esp child*) Pipi machen (*inf*) **b** **to ~ around** herumpatchen

piddling ['pɪdlɪŋ] ADJ (*inf*) lächerlich

pidgin ['pɪdʒɪn] N Mischsprache *f*

pidgin English N Pidgin-English *nt*

pie [paɪ] N Pastete *f*; (*sweet*) Obstkuchen *m*; (*individual*) Törtelett *nt*; **that's all ~ in the sky** (*inf*) das sind nur verrückte Ideen; **as nice/sweet as ~** (*inf*) superfreundlich (*inf*); **as easy as ~** (*inf*) kinderleicht; **she's got a finger in every ~** (*fig inf*) sie hat überall ihre Finger drin (*inf*)

piebald ['paɪbɔːld] ADJ scheckig N Schecke *mf*

piece [piːs] N **a** Stück *nt*; (= *part, member of a set*) Teil *nt*; (= *component part*) Einzelteil *nt*; (= *fragment: of glass, pottery etc*) Scherbe *f*; (*in draughts etc*) Stein *m*; (*in chess*) Figur *f*; (*Press*: = *article*) Artikel *m*; (*Mil*) Geschütz *nt*; (= *firearm*) Waffe *f*; (= *coin*) Münze *f*; **a 50p ~** ein 50-Pence-Stück, eine 50-Pence-Münze; **a ~ of cake/land/paper** ein Stück *nt* Kuchen/Land/Papier; **a ~ of furniture/luggage/clothing** ein Möbel-/Gepäck-/Kleidungsstück *nt*; **a seven--piece band** eine siebenköpfige Band; **a 30-**

-piece dinner service ein dreißigteiliges Speiseservice; **a ~ of news** eine Nachricht; **a ~ of information** eine Information; **a ~ of advice** ein Rat *m*; **a ~ of luck** ein Glücksfall *m*; **by a ~ of good luck** glücklicherweise; **a ~ of nonsense** Unsinn *m*; **a ~ of work** eine Arbeit; **~ by ~** Stück für Stück; **to be sold by the ~** stückweise verkauft werden; **to take sth to ~s** etw in seine Einzelteile zerlegen; **to come to ~s** (*collapsible furniture etc*) sich auseinander nehmen *or* zerlegen lassen; **to come** *or* **fall to ~s** (*broken chair, old book etc*) auseinander fallen; (*glass, pottery*) zerbrechen; **to be in ~s** (= *taken apart*) in Einzelteile zerlegt sein; (= *broken: vase etc*) in Scherben sein, zerbrochen sein; **to smash sth to ~s** etw kaputtschlagen; **he tore the letter (in)to ~s** er zerriss den Brief (in Stücke *or* Fetzen); **he tore me to ~s during the debate** er zerriss mich förmlich während der Debatte; **to put together the ~s of a mystery** die einzelnen Teile eines Rätsels zusammenfügen; **he said his ~ very nicely** (*poem etc*) er hat das sehr nett vorgetragen; **to recite a ~** etwas aufsagen; **a piano ~** ein Klavierstück *nt*; **down the road a ~** (*US, inf*) in Stückchen die Straße runter (*inf*) → **bit²** N a
b (*phrases*) **to go to ~s** (= *crack up*) durchdrehen (*inf*); (= *lose grip*) die Kontrolle verlieren; (*sportsman, team*) abbauen (*inf*); **he's going to ~s** mit ihm gehts bergab; **his confidence is shot to ~s** (*inf*) sein Selbstvertrauen ist am Boden *or* völlig zerstört; **all in one ~** (= *intact*) heil, unversehrt; **are you still in one ~ after your trip?** hast du deine Reise heil überstanden?; **it's all of a ~ with his usual behaviour** so benimmt er sich immer; **his behaviour is all of a ~** sein Verhalten ist konsequent; **to give sb a ~ of one's mind** jdm gehörig *or* ordentlich die Meinung sagen; **he got a ~ of my mind** ich habe ihm meine Meinung gesagt, ich habe ihm Bescheid gestoßen (*inf*); **to say one's ~** seine Meinung sagen
c (*inf, = woman*) Tussi *f* (*sl*)

▶ **piece together** VT sep (*lit*) zusammenstückeln; (*fig*) sich (*dat*) zusammenreimen; evidence zusammenfügen; **to piece together a mystery** die einzelnen Teile eines Rätsels zusammenfügen; **police are trying to piece together his last hours** die Polizei versucht, seine letzten Stunden zu rekonstruieren

pièce de résistance ['pjɛːsdə'reɪziːstɑ̃ŋs] N Krönung *f*; **and now the** *or* **my ~** und nun die Krönung!

piece: piece goods PL (*Sew*) Meterware *f*, Schnittware *f*; **piecemeal** ADV Stück für Stück, stückweise; (= *haphazardly*) kunterbunt durcheinander ADJ stückweise; (= *haphazard*) wenig systematisch; **in ~ fashion** auf unsystematische Weise; **piece rate** N Akkordlohnsatz *m*; **piece to camera** N (*TV*) Szene *f* direkt in die Kamera; **to do a ~** in die Kamera sprechen; **piece wages** PL Akkordlohn *m*, Stücklohn *m*; **piecework** N Akkordarbeit *f*; **to be on ~** im Akkord arbeiten; **pieceworker** N Akkordarbeiter(in) *m(f)*

pie: pie chart N Kreisdiagramm *nt*; **piecrust** N Teigdecke *f*

pied [paɪd] ADJ gescheckt, gefleckt; **the Pied Piper of Hamelin** der Rattenfänger von Hameln

pied-à-terre [ˌpjeɪdɑː'teə'] N Zweitwohnung *f*

pie dish N Pastetenform *f*

piedmont ['piːdmɒnt] N **a** (*Geol*) Piedmontfläche *f* **b** (*Geog, Region of Italy*) Piemont *nt*

pie-dog ['paɪdɒɡ] N (*Brit*) streunender Hundebastard

pied wagtail N Trauerbachstelze *f*

pie: pie-eater N (*Austral inf*: = *nonentity*) Null *f* (*inf*); **pie-eyed** ['paɪaɪd] ADJ (*inf*) blau (wie ein Veilchen) (*inf*); **pie-flinging** ['paɪˌflɪŋɪŋ] N (*inf*: *in films*) Tortenschlacht *f* (*inf*)

pier [pɪə'] N **a** Pier *m or f*; (= *landing place*) Anlegestelle *f*, Pier *m or f* **b** (*of bridge etc*) Pfeiler *m*

pierce [pɪəs] VT durchstechen; (*knife, spear*) durchstoßen, durchbohren; (*bullet*) durchbohren; (*fig: sound, coldness etc*) durchdringen; **to ~ a hole in sth** etw durchstechen; **to have** or **get one's ears/nose ~d** sich (*dat*) die Ohren/Nase durchstechen lassen; **to ~ sth through (and through)** (*lit, fig*) etw durchbohren; **the news ~d him to the heart** die Nachricht traf ihn bis ins Herz

pierced [pɪəst] ADJ *object* durchstochen; *nose, nipple* gepierct; **to have ~ ears** Löcher in den Ohrläppchen haben

piercing [ˈpɪəsɪŋ] ADJ **a** durchdringend; *cold, wind also* schneidend; *stare* stechend, durchdringend; *sarcasm* beißend; *wit* scharf; **~ blue eyes** durchdringende blaue Augen **b** (*liter, = painful*) durchdringend

piercingly [ˈpɪəsɪŋlɪ] ADV **a** *scream, look at* durchdringend **b** (*liter: = painfully*) scharf, schneidend

pierrot [ˈpɪərəʊ] N Pierrot *m*

pietà [pɪeˈtɑː] N Pieta *f*, Pietà *f*

pietism [ˈpaɪətɪzəm] N **a Pietism** der Pietismus **b** (*= piety*) Pietät *f*, Frömmigkeit *f*; (*pej*) Frömmelei *f*

pietist [ˈpaɪətɪst] N Pietist(in) *m(f)*; (*= pious person*) frommer Mensch; (*pej*) Frömmler(in) *m(f)*

pietistic [paɪəˈtɪstɪk] ADJ (*pej*) frömmelnd

piety [ˈpaɪətɪ] N **a** Pietät *f*, Frömmigkeit *f*; **filial ~** Respekt *m* gegenüber den Eltern **b pieties** PL (*pej*) Frömmeleien *pl* (*pej*)

piffle [ˈpɪfl] N (*inf*) Quatsch *m* (*inf*), Schnickschnack *m* (*inf*)

piffling [ˈpɪflɪŋ] ADJ (*inf*) lächerlich

pig [pɪg] **N a** Schwein *nt*; **to buy a ~ in a poke** (*prov*) die Katze im Sack kaufen; **~s might fly** (*Brit prov*) wers glaubt, wird selig; **they were living like ~s** sie haben wie die Schweine gehaust; **as happy as a ~ in muck** (*inf*) or **shit** (*sl*) voll gut drauf (*inf*); **in a ~'s eye** (*US, inf*) du spinnst wohl! (*inf*) **b** (*inf: person: dirty, nasty*) Schwein *nt*, Sau *f* (*inf*); (*greedy*) Vielfraß *m* (*inf*); **to make a ~ of oneself** sich (*dat*) den Bauch voll schlagen (*inf*), kräftig zulangen **c** (*inf, = awkward thing*) fieses Ding (*inf*) **d** (*sl, = policeman*) Bulle *m* (*sl*) **e** (*Metal*) (*= ingot*) Massel *f*; (*= mould*) Kokille *f* **VT to ~ it** (*inf*) hausen **VR to ~ oneself** (*inf*) sich voll stopfen (*inf*)

▶ **pig out** VI (*inf*) sich voll stopfen (*inf*)

pigeon [ˈpɪdʒən] N **a** Taube *f* **b** (*inf*) **that's not my ~** das ist nicht mein Bier (*inf*)

pigeon: pigeon breast N (*Brit Med*) Hühnerbrust *f*; **pigeon-breasted** ADJ (*Brit Med*) hühnerbrüstig; **pigeon fancier** N Taubenzüchter(in) *m(f)*; **pigeon-hearted** [ˈpɪdʒənˈhɑːtɪd] ADJ feige, ängstlich; **pigeonhole N** (*in desk etc*) Fach *nt*; **to put people in ~s** (*fig*) Menschen (in Kategorien) einordnen, Leute abstempeln **VT** (*lit*) (in Fächer) einordnen; (*fig: = categorize*) einordnen, ein- or aufteilen; **pigeon house, pigeon loft** N Taubenschlag *m*; **pigeon-livered** [ˈpɪdʒənˈlɪvəd] ADJ ängstlich, feige; **pigeon post** N Brieftaubenpost *f*; **pigeon-toed** ADJ, ADV mit einwärts gerichteten Fußspitzen; **he is/walks ~** er geht über die großen Onkel (*inf*)

pig farmer N Schweinezüchter(in) *m(f)*

piggery [ˈpɪgərɪ] N **a** Schweinefarm *f*, Schweinemästerei *f* **b** (*inf, = gluttony*) Völlerei *f*

piggish [ˈpɪgɪʃ] ADJ **a** *eyes, face* Schweins- **b** (*= greedy*) gefräßig; *person* verfressen (*inf*), gefräßig; *appetite* unmäßig, kannibalisch; (*= dirty*) saumäßig (*inf*; *= nasty*) fies (*inf*), schweinisch (*inf*); (*= stubborn*) fies (*inf*)

piggy [ˈpɪgɪ] **N** (*baby-talk*) Schweinchen *nt* **ADJ** (+*er*) **a** *attr* Schweins-; **~ eyes** Schweinsaugen *pl* **b** (*inf, = greedy*) verfressen (*inf*)

piggyback [ˈpɪgɪbæk] **N to give sb a ~** jdn huckepack nehmen; **the little girl wanted a ~** das kleine Mädchen wollte huckepack getragen werden **ADV** (*US Rail, also Comput*) huckepack

inv **VI to ~ on sth** (*fig*) etw (zu seinem Vorteil) ausnutzen

piggy bank N Sparschwein *nt*

pig-headed [ˈpɪgˈhedɪd] ADJ stur; **that was a ~ thing to do** so was von stur (*inf*)

pig-headedly [ˈpɪgˈhedɪdlɪ] ADV stur

pig-headedness [ˈpɪgˈhedɪdnɪs] N Sturheit *f*

pig: pig in the middle N (*Brit*) Spiel, *bei dem ein zwischen zwei anderen stehender Spieler einen Ball, den diese sich zuwerfen, zu fangen versucht* **I'm just ~ on this project** (*inf*) ich stehe bei diesem Projekt nur hilflos dazwischen or in der Mitte; **pig iron** N Roheisen *nt*; **pig Latin** N *kindliche Geheimsprache durch Anfügen von Silben*

piglet [ˈpɪglɪt], **pigling** [ˈpɪglɪŋ] N Ferkel *nt*

pigman [ˈpɪgmən] N *pl* **-men** [-mən] Schweinehirt(e) *m*

pigment [ˈpɪgmənt] N Pigment *nt*

pigmentation [pɪgmənˈteɪʃən] N Pigmentierung *f*

pigmy N = pygmy

pig: pigpen N (*US*) = pigsty; **pig's ear N to make a ~ of sth** (*Brit, inf*) etw vermasseln (*inf*); **pigskin N a** Schweinsleder *nt* **b** (*US, inf, = football*) Pille *f* (*inf*), Leder *nt* (*inf*); **pigsty** N Schweinestall *m*; (*fig also*) Saustall *m* (*inf*); **pigswill** N Schweinefutter *nt*; (*fig*) (*= coffee, soup etc*) Spülwasser *nt* (*inf*); (*= porridge etc*) Schweinefraß *m* (*inf*); **pigtail** N Zopf *m*; **pigwoman** N Schweinehirtin *f*

pike¹ [paɪk] N (*= weapon*) Pike *f*, Spieß *m*

pike² N (*fish*) Hecht *m*

pike³ N (*US inf, = toll-road*) Mautstraße *f*; (*= barrier*) Mautschranke *f*

piker [ˈpaɪkə] N (*pej*) **a** (*US sl: = cautious gambler*) vorsichtige(r) Spieler(in) **b** (*US sl: = miser*) Geizhals *m* **c** (*Austral sl: = shirker*) Drückeberger(in) *m(f)* (*pej*), Memme *f* (*pej*), Faulenzer(in) *m(f)* (*pej*)

pikestaff [ˈpaɪkstɑːf] N **as plain as a ~** sonnenklar

pilaf [ˈpiːlæf] N = pilau

pilaster [pɪˈlæstə] N Pilaster *m*, Halbpfeiler *m*

pilau [pɪˈlaʊ] N (*also* **pilau rice**) Pilaw *nt*

pilchard [ˈpɪltʃəd] N Sardine *f*

pile¹ [paɪl] **N a** (*= heap*) Stapel *m*, Stoß *m*; **to put things in a ~** etw (auf)stapeln; **her things lay** or **were in a ~** ihre Sachen lagen auf einem Haufen; **he made a ~ of the books** er stapelte die Bücher aufeinander; **at the bottom/top of the ~** (*fig*) untenan/obenauf **b** (*inf, = large amount*) Haufen *m*, Menge *f*, Masse *f* (*inf*); **~s of work** eine Menge or Masse (*inf*) Arbeit; **~s of money/trouble/food** eine or jede Menge (*inf*) Geld/Ärger/Essen; **a ~ of things to do** massenhaft zu tun (*inf*) **c** (*inf, = fortune*) Vermögen *nt*; **to make a ~** einen Haufen Geld verdienen; **to make one's ~** sein Vermögen machen **d** (*= funeral pile*) Scheiterhaufen *m* **e** (*liter, hum, = building*) ehrwürdiges Gebäude **f** (*= atomic pile*) Atommeiler *m* **VT** stapeln; **a table ~d high with books** ein Tisch mit Stapeln von Büchern; **the sideboard was ~d high with presents** auf der Anrichte stapelten sich die Geschenke

▶ **pile in** VI (*inf*) (*-to in +acc*) hineindrängen; (*= get in*) einsteigen; **pile in!** immer herein! **VT** *sep* einladen (*-to in +acc*)

▶ **pile off** VI (*inf*) hinausdrängen (*prep obj aus*)

▶ **pile on** VI (*inf*) hineindrängen (*-to in +acc*) **VT** *sep* (*lit*) aufhäufen (*-to auf +acc*); **she piled rice on(to) my plate** sie häufte Reis auf meinen Teller; **he's piling work on(to) his staff** er überhäuft seine Leute mit Arbeit; **they are really piling on the pressure** sie setzen uns/euch etc ganz gehörig unter Druck; **to pile on weight** or **the pounds** Gewicht *nt*/Pfunde *pl* ansetzen; **to pile on the agony** (*inf*) dick auftragen (*inf*); **to pile it on** (*inf*) dick auftragen (*inf*)

▶ **pile out** VI (*inf*) hinausdrängen (*of aus*)

▶ **pile up** **VI a** (*lit, fig*) sich (an)sammeln or anhäufen; (*traffic*) sich stauen; (*snow, work*) sich (auf)türmen or anhäufen; (*reasons*) sich häufen; (*evidence*) sich verdichten; (*points*) sich ansammeln; **he let the work pile up** die Arbeit türmte sich auf **b** (*= crash*) aufeinander auffahren **VT** *sep* **a** (*= stack up*) (auf)stapeln; *money* horten; (*fig*) *debts* anhäufen; *evidence* sammeln; **her hair was piled up on top of her head** sie trug ihre Haare hoch aufgetürmt; **to pile the fire up (with logs/coal)** (Holz/Kohle) nachlegen; **he's piling up trouble for himself** er handelt sich (*dat*) Ärger ein **b** (*inf, = crash*) *car* kaputtfahren

pile² N (*= post*) Pfahl *m*

pile³ N (*of carpet, cloth*) Flor *m*

pile: pile bridge N (Pfahl)jochbrücke *f*; **pile-driver** N Ramme *f*; **pile dwelling** N Pfahlbau *m*

piles [paɪlz] PL Hämorr(ho)iden *pl*

pile-up [ˈpaɪlʌp] N (*= car crash*) (Massen)karambolage *f*, Massenzusammenstoß *m*

pilfer [ˈpɪlfə] **VT** stehlen, klauen (*inf*); **a lot of ~ing goes on in the office** im Büro wird viel geklaut (*inf*) **VI** stehlen, klauen (*inf*)

pilferage [ˈpɪlfərɪdʒ] N Diebstähle *pl* (*in kleinem Rahmen*), Beraubung *f* (*Insur*)

pilferer [ˈpɪlfərə] N Dieb(in) *m(f)*, Langfinger *m* (*inf*)

pilgrim [ˈpɪlgrɪm] N Pilger(in) *m(f)*; **the Pilgrim Fathers** die Pilgerväter *pl*

PILGRIM FATHERS

Die **Pilgrim Fathers**, die Pilgerväter, waren eine Gruppe von Puritanern, die 1620 England verließen, um der religiösen Verfolgung zu entgehen. Sie segelten in einem Schiff namens „Mayflower" über den Atlantik und gründeten New Plymouth in Neuengland, das im heutigen Bundesstaat Massachusetts liegt, wo sie sich ansiedelten. Damit begann die britische Kolonisierung Amerikas. Die **Pilgrim Fathers** gelten als die Gründerväter der Vereinigten Staaten, und jedes Jahr wird am Thanksgiving Day wieder ihre erste Ernte gefeiert. → THANKSGIVING

pilgrimage [ˈpɪlgrɪmɪdʒ] N Wallfahrt *f*, Pilgerfahrt *f*; **to go on** or **make a ~** pilgern, wallfahren, eine Pilger- or Wallfahrt machen; **in our ~ through this life** (*liter*) auf unserem langen Weg or unserer langen Reise durch dieses Leben

piling [ˈpaɪlɪŋ] N (*= posts*) Pfähle *pl*

pill [pɪl] **N a** Tablette *f*; **the ~** die Pille; **to be/ go on the ~** die Pille nehmen → **bitter** ADJ a **b** (*sl, = ball*) Pille *f* (*sl*)

pillage [ˈpɪlɪdʒ] **N** (*= act*) Plünderung *f*; (*= booty*) Beute *f* **VT VI** plündern

pillar [ˈpɪlə] N Säule *f*; **~ of salt** Salzsäule *f*; **~ of smoke** Rauchsäule *f*; **the Pillars of Hercules** die Säulen *pl* des Herkules; **a ~ of society/the community** eine Säule or Stütze der Gesellschaft/der Gemeinschaft; **from ~ to post** (*Brit*) von Pontius zu Pilatus

pillar box [ˈpɪləbɒks] N (*Brit*) Briefkasten *m*; **pillar-box red** knallrot

pillbox [ˈpɪlbɒks] N **a** (*Med*) Pillenschachtel *f* **b** (*Mil*) Bunker *m* **c** (*also* **pillbox hat**) Pagenkäppi *nt*; (*for women*) Pillbox *f*

pillion [ˈpɪljən] **N a** (*on motorbike*) Soziussitz *m*; **~ passenger** Sozius *m*, Beifahrer(in) *m(f)* **b** (*Hist*) Damensattel *m* **ADV to ride ~** auf dem Sozius- or Beifahrersitz mitfahren; (*on horse*) hinter dem Sattel sitzen

pillock [ˈpɪlək] N (*Brit inf pej*) Blödmann *m* (*pej*), Schwachkopf *m* (*pej*)

pillory [ˈpɪlərɪ] **N** (*Hist*) Pranger *m*; **to be in the ~** am Pranger stehen **VT** (*fig*) anprangern

pillow [ˈpɪləʊ] **N** (Kopf)kissen *nt* **VT** betten

pillow: pillowcase N (Kopf)kissenbezug *m*; **pillow fight** N Kissenschlacht *f*; **pillow lace**

N Klöppel-/Kissenspitzen *pl*; **pillow lava** N (*Geol*) Kissenlava *f*; **pillowslip** N = **pillowcase**; **pillow talk** N Bettgeflüster *nt*

pill popper N (*inf*) Tablettensüchtige(r) *mf*

pilot ['paɪlət] **N** **a** (*Aviat*) Pilot(in) *m(f)*, Flugzeugführer(in) *m(f)*; ~'s **licence** Flugschein *m*, Flugzeugführerlaubnis *f* (*form*) **b** (*Naut*) Lotse *m*, Lotsin *f* **c** (= *pilot light*) Zündflamme *f* **d** (*US: on train*) Schienenräumer *m* **e** (*TV*) **(episode)** Pilotfilm *m* **VT** *plane* führen, fliegen; *ship* lotsen; (*fig*) führen, leiten

pilot: pilot beam N (*Tech*) Leitstrahl *f*; **pilot boat** N Lotsenboot *nt*; **pilot fish** N Lotsenor Pilotfisch *m*; **pilot flag** N Lotsenrufflagge *f*; **pilot house** N Ruderhaus *nt*, Steuerhaus *nt*; **pilot lamp** N Kontrolllampe *f*; **pilotless** ADJ führerlos; **pilot light** N Zündflamme *f*; **pilot officer** N (*Brit Aviat*) Leutnant *m*; **pilot plant** N (= *experimental plant*) Pilot-/Versuchsanlage *f* **b** (= *model company*) Musterbetrieb *m*; **pilot scheme** N Pilotprojekt *nt*; **pilot study** N Pilotstudie *f*, Musterstudie *f*

pimento [pɪˈmɛntəʊ] N **a** Paprikaschote *f* **b** (= *allspice*) Piment *m or nt*, Nelkenpfeffer *m*; (= *tree*) Pimentbaum *m*

pimp[1] [pɪmp] **N** Zuhälter *m* **VI** Zuhälter sein; **to ~ for sb** für jdn den Zuhälter machen

pimp[2] N (*Austral sl pej*) Spitzel *m* (*pej*), Informant(in) *m(f)*

pimpernel ['pɪmpənɛl] N (*Bot: also* **scarlet pimpernel**) (Acker)gauchheil *m*

pimple ['pɪmpl] N Pickel *m*, Pustel *f*; **to get ~s** Pickel bekommen; **her face breaks out in ~s** sie bekommt Pickel im Gesicht

pimply ['pɪmplɪ] ADJ (+er) pickelig

PIN [pɪn] N *abbr of* **personal identification number ~ number** (*for cash card*) Geheimnummer *f*

pin [pɪn] **N** **a** (*Sew*) Stecknadel *f*; (= *tie pin, hatpin, on brooch, hair pin*) Nadel *f*; (*Mech*) Bolzen *m*, Stift *m*; (= *small nail*) Stift *m*; (*in grenade*) Sicherungsstift *m*; (*on guitar*) Wirbel *m*; (*Med*) Stift *m*, Nagel *m*; (*Elec, of plug*) Pol *m*; (*Comput on connector*) Pin *m*; (*on printhead*) Nadel *f*; **a two-pin plug** ein zweipoliger Stecker; **~s and needles** *sing or pl* ein Kribbeln *nt*; **I've got ~s and needles in my foot** mir ist der Fuß eingeschlafen; **to be on ~s and needles** wie auf (glühenden) Kohlen sitzen; **like a new ~** blitzsauber, funkelnagelneu; **neat as a (new) ~** wie aus dem Ei gepellt; **for two ~s I'd pack up and go** (*inf*) es fehlt nicht mehr viel, dann gehe ich; **I don't care a ~** (*dated inf*) es ist mir völlig egal or schnuppe (*inf*); **you could have heard a ~ drop** man hätte eine Stecknadel fallen hören können **b** (*esp US*) (= *brooch*) Brosche *f*, Schmucknadel *f*; (= *badge: also* **lapel pin, fraternity pin**) Anstecknadel *f*, Abzeichen *nt* **c** (*Golf*) Flaggenstock *m*; (*Bowling*) Kegel *m* **d pins** PL (*esp Brit inf*: = *legs*) Gestell *nt* (*inf*); **he wasn't very steady on his ~s** er war etwas wackelig auf den Beinen; **to be quick on one's ~s** gut zu Fuß sein **VT** **a** *dress* stecken; **to ~ sth to sth** etw an etw (*acc*) heften; **to ~ papers together** Blätter zusammenheften; **the bone had to be ~ned in place** der Knochen musste genagelt werden; **she ~ned her hair back** sie hatte ihr Haar hinten zusammengesteckt **b** (*fig*) **to ~ sb to the ground/against a wall** jdn an den Boden/an eine Wand pressen; **to ~ sb's arms to his side** jdm die Arme an den Körper pressen; **to ~ sb's arm behind his back** jdm den Arm auf den Rücken drehen; **to ~ one's hopes/faith on sb/sth** seine Hoffnungen/sein Vertrauen auf jdn/etw setzen; **you shouldn't ~ everything on one chance** Sie sollten nicht alles auf eine Karte setzen; **to ~ back one's ears** die Ohren spitzen (*inf*) **c** (*inf*, = *accuse of*) **to ~ sth on sb** jdm etw anhängen; **to ~ the blame (for sth) on sb** jdm die Schuld (an etw *dat*) anhängen **d** (*US, inf*) **to be ~ned** verlobt sein; **to get ~ned** sich verloben

▶ **pin down** VT *sep* **a** (= *fix down: with pins*) anor festheften; (= *hold, weight down*) beschweren, niederhalten; (= *trap: rockfall etc*) einklemmen; **he pinned him down on the canvas** er drückte ihn auf die Matte; **two of the gang pinned him down** zwei aus der Bande drückten ihn zu Boden; **our troops were pinned down by heavy artillery fire** unsere Truppen wurden durch heftiges Artilleriefeuer festgehalten **b** (*fig*) **to pin sb down** jdn festnageln or festlegen; **he wouldn't be pinned down to any particular date** er ließ sich nicht auf ein bestimmtes Datum festnageln or festlegen; **he's a difficult man to pin down** man kann ihn nur schwer dazu bringen, sich festzulegen; **I've seen him/it somewhere before but I can't pin him/it down** ich habe ihn/es schon mal irgendwo gesehen, kann ihn/es aber nicht einordnen; **we can't pin down the source of the rumours** wir können die Quelle der Gerüchte nicht lokalisieren; **it's not easy to pin down the precise cause of this** es ist nicht leicht, die genaue Ursache dafür festzustellen; **there's something odd here, but I can't pin it down** irgendetwas ist hier merkwürdig, aber ich kann nicht genau sagen, was

▶ **pin up** VT *sep notice* anheften; *hair* aufstecken, hochstecken; *hem, dress, sleeves* stecken

pina colada [ˌpiːnəkəˈlɑːdə] N Pina Colada *m*

pinafore ['pɪnəfɔː'] N (= *overall: for children*) Kinderkittel *m*; (= *apron*) Schürze *f*, Kittel *m*; ~ **dress** (*Brit*) Trägerkleid *nt*

pinball ['pɪnbɔːl] N Flipper *m*; **to have a game of** ~ Flipper spielen, flippern; ~ **machine** Flipper *m*

pince-nez ['pɪnsneɪ] N Kneifer *m*, Pincenez *nt* (*old*)

pincer movement ['pɪnsə-] N (*Mil, fig*) Zangenbewegung *f*

pincers ['pɪnsəz] PL **a** Kneifzange *f*, Beißzange *f*; **a pair of** ~ eine Kneifzange, eine Beißzange **b** (*Zool*) Schere *f*, Zange *f*

pinch [pɪntʃ] **N** **a** (*with fingers*) Kneifen *nt no pl*, Zwicken *nt no pl*; **to give sb a ~ on the arm** jdn in den Arm kneifen or zwicken **b** (= *small quantity*) Quäntchen *nt*; (*Cook*) Prise *f*; **a ~ of snuff** eine Prise Schnupftabak **c** (= *pressure*) **to feel the ~** die schlechte Lage zu spüren bekommen; **I'm feeling the ~ a bit at the moment** ich bin im Augenblick ziemlich knapp bei Kasse (*inf*); **if it comes to the ~** wenn es zum Schlimmsten or Äußersten kommt; **at** (*Brit*) **or in** (*US*) **a ~** zur Not **VT** **a** (*with fingers*) kneifen, zwicken; (*with implement*: = *squeeze*) *end of wire etc* zusammendrücken, zusammenklemmen; (*shoe*) drücken; **to ~ sb's bottom** jdn in den Hintern kneifen; **to ~ oneself** sich kneifen; **to ~ one's finger in the door** sich (*dat*) den Finger in der Tür (ein-)klemmen **b** (*Brit inf, = steal*) klauen, stibitzen, mopsen (*all inf*); **don't let anyone ~ my seat** pass auf, dass mir niemand den Platz wegnimmt; **he ~ed Johnny's girlfriend** er hat Johnny (*dat*) die Freundin ausgespannt (*inf*); **he ~ed that idea from Shaw** die Idee hat er bei Shaw geklaut (*inf*); **I had my car ~ed** mein Auto ist geklaut worden (*inf*) **c** (*inf*, = *arrest*) schnappen (*inf*), erwischen **VI** **a** (*shoe, also fig*) drücken **b** **to ~ and scrape** sich einschränken

▶ **pinch back** or **off** VT *sep bud* abknipsen

pinchbeck ['pɪntʃbɛk] **N** (*lit, fig*) Talmi *nt* **ADJ** *jewels* aus Talmi

pinched [pɪntʃt] ADJ **a** verhärmt; (*from cold*) verfroren; (*from fatigue*) erschöpft **b** (*inf*, = *short*) **to be ~ for money** knapp bei Kasse sein (*inf*); **to be ~ for time** keine Zeit haben

pin cherry N (*Bot*) Amerikanische Weichselkirsche

pinch-hit ['pɪntʃhɪt] VI (*US*) Ersatzspieler sein; (*fig*) einspringen

pinch hitter ['pɪntʃhɪtə'] N (*US*) Ersatzspieler(in) *m(f)*; (*fig*) Ersatz *m*

pinchpenny ['pɪntʃpɛnɪ] ADJ knauserig, pfennigfuchserisch

pin: pin curl N Löckchen *nt*; **pincushion** N Nadelkissen *nt*

pine[1] [paɪn] N Kiefer *f*

pine[2] VI **a** **to ~ for sb/sth** sich nach jdm/etw sehnen or verzehren **b** (= *pine away, be sad*) sich vor Kummer verzehren

▶ **pine away** VI (*from grief*) sich (vor Kummer) verzehren, vor Gram vergehen; (*from disease*) (dahin)siechen; (*of animal, plant*) eingehen; **she pined away and died** sie starb an gebrochenem Herzen; **the dog just pined away and died** der Hund ging langsam ein

pineal gland ['paɪnɪəl-] N Zirbeldrüse *f*, Epiphyse *f* (*spec*)

pineapple ['paɪnæpl] N Ananas *f*; ~ **chunks** Ananasstücke *pl*; ~ **juice** Ananassaft *m*

pine: pine cone N Kiefernzapfen *m*; **pine forest** N Kiefernwald *m*; **pine marten** N Baummarder *m*; **pine needle** N Kiefernnadel *f*; **pine tree** N Kiefer *f*; **pine wood** N Kiefernwald *m*; (= *material*) Kiefernholz *nt*

▶ **ping** [pɪŋ] **N** (*of bell*) Klingeln *nt*; (*of bullet*) Peng *nt*; **to make a ~** (*sonar, tilt bell etc*) klingeln; **the stone made a ~ as it hit the glass** der Stein machte klick, als er auf das Glas traf **VI** (*bell*) klingeln; (*bullet*) peng machen

ping pong ['pɪŋpɒŋ] N Pingpong *nt*; ~ **ball** Pingpongball *m*

pin: pinhead N (Steck)nadelkopf *m*; (*inf*, = *stupid person*) Holzkopf *m* (*inf*), Strohkopf *m* (*inf*); **pinheaded** ADJ (*inf*) schwachköpfig (*inf*), blöd(e) (*inf*); **pin holder** N Blumenigel *m*; **pinhole** N Loch *nt*; **pinhole camera** N Lochkamera *f*, Camera obscura *f*

pinion ['pɪnjən] **N** **a** (*Mech*) Ritzel *nt*, Treibrad *nt* **b** (*poet*, = *wing*) Fittich *m* (*poet*), Schwinge *f* (*poet*) **c** (*Orn*) Flügelspitze *f* **VT** **to ~ sb to the ground/against the wall** jdn zu Boden/gegen eine Wand drücken

pink[1] [pɪŋk] **N** **a** (= *colour*) Rosa *nt*; (= *hunting pink*) Rot *nt* **b** (= *plant*) Gartennelke *f* **c** (*Brit*) **to be in the ~ (of health)** vor Gesundheit strotzen; **I'm in the ~** mir gehts prächtig; **to feel in the ~** sich bestens fühlen; **in the ~ of condition** in Top- or Hochform **ADJ** **a** (= *colour*) rosa *inv*, rosarot, rosafarben; *cheeks, face* rosig; **to go or turn ~** sich röten; **to see ~ elephants or mice** (*inf*) weiße Mäuse sehen (*inf*); **the ~ pound** (*inf*) die Kaufkraft der Homosexuellen **b** (*Pol inf*) rot angehaucht

pink[2] VT **a** (*Sew*) mit der Zickzackschere schneiden **b** (= *nick*) streifen

pink[3] VI (*Aut*) klopfen

pink-collar ADJ *attr* Frauen-; ~ **jobs** typische Frauenberufe *pl*

pinkeye ['pɪŋkaɪ] N (*inf*) Bindehautentzündung *f*

pink gin N Pink Gin *m*

pinkie ['pɪŋkɪ] N (*Scot, US: inf*) kleiner Finger

pinking shears ['pɪŋkɪŋʃɪəz] PL Zickzackschere *f*

pinkish ['pɪŋkɪʃ] ADJ rötlich; ~ **white** blassrosa

pinko ['pɪŋkəʊ] N (*Pol pej inf*) roter Bruder (*inf*), rote Schwester (*inf*)

pink slip N (*US inf*) Entlassungspapiere *pl*

PINK SLIP

In den USA ist **pink slip** der umgangssprachliche Ausdruck für das Schreiben, mit dem ein Arbeitgeber seinem Angestellten die Kündigung mitteilt. Der Begriff stammt aus den zwanziger Jahren, als ein rosafarbener Durchschlag mit der Kündigung in die Lohntüte gesteckt wurde. Es gibt davon auch eine verbale („they pink-slipped him") und eine adjektivische („a pink-slipped worker") Form.

---

pink-slip VT (*US inf*) entlassen; **to ~ sb** jdm den blauen Brief schicken (*inf*); **to be ~ped** den blauen Brief bekommen

pin money N Taschengeld nt, Nadelgeld nt (old)

pinnace ['pɪnɪs] N Pinasse f

pinnacle ['pɪnəkl] N (Archit) Fiale f; (of rock, mountain) Gipfel m, Spitze f; (fig) Gipfel m, Höhepunkt m

pinnate ['pɪneɪt] ADJ (Bot) gefiedert

pinny ['pɪnɪ] N (Brit inf) Schürze f

pinoc(h)le ['piːnʌkəl] N (Cards) Binokel nt

pin: pinpoint N Punkt m; **the buildings were mere ~s on the horizon** die Gebäude zeichneten sich wie Stecknadelköpfe am Horizont ab; **a ~ of light** ein Lichtpunkt m; **~ bombing** Punktzielbombardement nt VT (= locate) genau an- or aufzeigen; (= define, identify) genau feststellen or -legen; **pinprick** N Nadelstich m; (fig) Kleinigkeit f; **pinstripe** N (= stripe) Nadelstreifen m; (= cloth) Tuch nt mit Nadelstreifen; (= pinstripe suit) Nadelstreifenanzug m; **pinstriped** ADJ Nadelstreifen-; **~ suit** Nadelstreifenanzug m

pint [paɪnt] N a (= measure) Pint nt b (esp Brit: = quantity) (of milk) Tüte f; (= bottle) Flasche f; (of beer) Halbe f, Glas nt Bier; **to have a ~** ein Bier trinken; **to go (out) for a ~** auf ein Bier ausgehen; **he likes a ~** er hebt ganz gern mal einen (inf); **she's had a few ~s** (inf) sie hat ein paar intus (inf); **a good ~** ein gutes Bier

pinta ['paɪntə] N (Brit, inf) halber Liter Milch

pin table N Flipper m

pint mug ['paɪnt'mʌg] N Humpen m (der ein Pint fasst)

pinto ['pɪntəʊ] (US) ADJ horse scheckig N Schecke mf

pinto bean N Pintobohne f

pint-size(d) ['paɪntsaɪz(d)] ADJ (inf) stöpselig (inf), knirpsig (inf); **a ~ boxer** ein Knirps m von einem Boxer

pin: pin tuck N Biese f; **pin-up** N (= picture) Pin-up-Foto nt; (= woman) Pin-up-Girl nt; (= man) Idol nt; **pin-up girl** N Pin-up-Girl nt; **pinwheel** N (= firework) Feuerrad nt; (US: = toy) Windrädchen nt

Pinyin ['pɪnˈjɪn] N Pinyin(umschrift f) nt

piolet ['piːəleɪ] N (Mountaineering) Eispickel m

pioneer [ˌpaɪə'nɪəʳ] N (Mil) Pionier m; (fig) Pionier(in) m(f), Wegbereiter(in) m(f) ADJ attr → **pioneering** VT way vorbereiten, bahnen; (fig) Pionierarbeit f leisten für; **the use of sth** (= use for the first time) etw zum ersten Mal anwenden; **the firm which ~ed its technical development** die Firma, die die technische Pionierarbeit dafür geleistet hat VT Pionierarbeit or Vorarbeit leisten, den Weg bahnen

pioneering [ˌpaɪə'nɪərɪŋ] ADJ attr method, research wegbereitend; **~ spirit** Pioniergeist m; **~ work** Pionierarbeit f; **the pride they take in their ~ ancestors** der Stolz auf ihre Vorfahren, die Pioniere; **in the ~ days of radio** in den Kindertagen des Radios

pious ['paɪəs] ADJ a (= devout) fromm; (pej also) frömmlerisch b (pej: = hypocritical) person, words unaufrichtig, falsch; **a ~ hope** ein frommer Wunsch

piously ['paɪəslɪ] ADV fromm

piousness ['paɪəsnɪs] N Frömmigkeit f; (pej also) Frömmelei f

pip[1] [pɪp] N a (Bot) Kern m b (on card, dice) Auge nt; (Brit Mil inf) Stern m; (on radar screen) Pip m, Echozeichen nt c (Rad, Telec) **the ~s** das Zeitzeichen; (in public telephone) das Tut-Tut-Tut; **at the third ~ it will be …** beim dritten Ton des Zeitzeichens ist es …; **put more money in when you hear the ~s** bitte Geld nachwerfen, sobald die Zeichen ertönt

pip[2] N (Vet) Pips m; **to give sb the ~** (Brit, inf) jdn aufregen (inf)

pip[3] VT (Brit, inf) knapp besiegen or schlagen; **to ~ sb at or to the post** (in race) jdn um Haaresbreite schlagen; (fig) jdm um Haaresbreite zuvorkommen; (in getting orders etc) jdm etw vor der Nase wegschnappen; **I was ~ped at or to**

---

the post again (fig) da war mir wieder jemand zuvorgekommen; **he was ~ped for second place by Moore** er wurde von Moore nur knapp vom zweiten Platz verdrängt

pipe [paɪp] N a (= tube: for water, gas, sewage) Rohr nt, Leitung f; (= fuel pipe, for steam) Leitung f; (in body) Röhre f
b (Mus) Flöte f; **~s** (= bagpipes) Dudelsack m; **~s of Pan** Panflöte f
c (for smoking) Pfeife f; **~ of peace** Friedenspfeife; **to smoke a ~** Pfeife rauchen; **put that in your ~ and smoke it!** (inf) steck dir das hinter den Spiegel! (inf)
VT a water, oil etc in Rohren leiten; music, broadcast ausstrahlen; **water has to be ~d in from the next state** Wasser muss in Rohrleitungen aus dem Nachbarstaat herangeschafft werden; **~d music** (pej) Musikberieselung f (inf)
b (Mus) tune flöten, pfeifen; (= sing in high voice) krähen; (= speak in high voice) piepsen; (Naut) pfeifen; **to ~ sb aboard** jdn mit Pfeifensignal an Bord begrüßen or empfangen; **he was even ~d to the gallows** selbst zum Galgen wurde er mit Dudelsackmusik geleitet
c (Cook) spritzen; cake mit Spritzguss verzieren; (Sew) paspelieren, paspeln
VI (Mus) flöten, (die) Flöte spielen; (bird) pfeifen; (young bird: anxiously) piep(s)en

▶ **pipe down** VI (= be less noisy) die Luft anhalten (inf), ruhig sein; (= become less confident) (ganz) klein werden (inf)

▶ **pipe up** VI (inf) (person) den Mund aufmachen, sich melden; **suddenly a little voice piped up** plötzlich machte sich ein Stimmchen bemerkbar; **then he piped up with another objection** dann kam er mit noch einem Einwand

pipe: pipe band N Dudelsackkapelle f; **pipe bomb** N Rohrbombe f; **pipe burst** N Rohrbruch m; **pipe clamp** N (Tech) Rohrschelle f; **pipeclay** N (for making pipes) Pfeifenton m; **pipe cleaner** N Pfeifenreiniger m; **pipe clip** N (Tech) Rohrschelle f; **pipe dream** N Hirngespinst nt; **that's just a ~** das ist ja wohl nur ein frommer Wunsch; **pipe-layer** N Rohrleitungs(ver)leger(in) m(f), Rohrleitungsmonteur(in) m(f); **pipe-laying** N Verlegen nt von Rohrleitungen; **pipeline** N (Rohr)leitung f; (for oil, gas also) Pipeline f; **to be in the ~** (fig) in Vorbereitung sein; **the pay rise hasn't come through yet but it's in the ~** die Lohnerhöhung ist noch nicht durch, steht aber kurz bevor; **we've got a few changes in the ~** wir müssen auf einige Änderungen gefasst sein

piper ['paɪpəʳ] N Flötenspieler(in) m(f); (on fife) Pfeifer(in) m(f); (on bagpipes) Dudelsackpfeifer(in) m(f); **to pay the ~** (fig) die Kosten tragen, für die Kosten aufkommen; **he who pays the ~ calls the tune** (Prov) wer bezahlt, darf auch bestimmen

pipe: pipe rack N Pfeifenständer m; **pipe smoker** N Pfeifenraucher(in) m(f); **pipe tobacco** N Pfeifentabak m; **pipe tool** N (for pipe-smokers) Pfeifenbesteck nt

pipette [pɪ'pet] N Pipette f, Saugröhrchen nt

pipe: pipework ['paɪpwɜːk] N Rohre pl; **pipe wrench** N (Tech) Rohrzange f

piping ['paɪpɪŋ] N a (= pipework) Rohrleitungssystem nt; (= pipe) Rohrleitung f b (Sew) Paspelierung f; (on furniture) Kordel f; (Cook) Spritzgussverzierung f; (Mus) Flötenspiel nt; (on bagpipes) Dudelsackpfeifen nt ADJ voice piepsend ADV **~ hot** kochend heiß

piping bag N Spritzbeutel m

pipistrelle [ˌpɪpɪ'strel] N Zwergfledermaus f

pipit ['pɪpɪt] N Pieper m

pippin ['pɪpɪn] N Cox m

pipsqueak ['pɪpskwiːk] N (inf) Winzling m (inf)

piquancy ['piːkənsɪ] N Pikantheit f, Würze f; (fig) Pikanterie f

piquant ['piːkənt] ADJ (lit, fig) pikant

pique [piːk] N Groll m, Vergrämtheit f; **he resigned in a fit of ~** er kündigte, weil er ver-

---

grämt war; **you needn't have a fit of ~ just because …** du brauchst nicht gleich pikiert or beleidigt zu sein, nur weil …; **to do sth out of ~** etw aus Groll (dat) tun; **to be in a ~ with sb** (old) gegen jdn einen Groll hegen VT (= offend, wound) kränken, verletzen; **to be ~d at or by sth** über jdn/etw (acc) ungehalten or pikiert sein VR **to ~ oneself on sth** sich (dat) viel auf etw (acc) einbilden

piqué ['piːkeɪ] N Pikee m, Piqué m

piracy ['paɪərəsɪ] N Seeräuberei f, Piraterie f; (of book etc) Raubdruck m; (of record) Raubpressung f; **an act of ~** Seeräuberei f, Piraterie f

piranha (fish) [pɪ'rɑːnjə(ˌfɪʃ)] N Piranha m

pirate ['paɪərɪt] N Seeräuber(in) m(f), Pirat(in) m(f); (= pirate ship) Seeräuberschiff nt, Piratenschiff nt; (also **pirate cab**) nicht konzessioniertes Taxi VT book einen Raubdruck herstellen von; invention, idea stehlen; **a ~d copy of the record** eine Raubpressung; **~d edition** Raubdruck m

pirate radio N (Brit) Piratensender m

piratical [paɪ'rætɪkəl] ADJ seeräuberisch, piratenhaft

pirogue [pɪ'rəʊg] N (= dug-out canoe) Einbaum m, Piragua f

pirouette [ˌpɪruː'et] N Pirouette f VI Pirouetten drehen, pirouettieren

Pisces ['paɪsiːz] PL Fische pl; **I'm (a) ~** ich bin Fisch

pisciculture ['pɪsɪkʌltʃəʳ] N (spec) Fischzucht f

pishogue [pɪ'ʃəʊg] N (Irish) Hexerei f

piss [pɪs] (sl) N (= urine) Pisse f (vulg); **to have a ~** pissen (vulg); **to go for a ~** pissen gehen (vulg); **to take the ~ out of sb/sth** (Brit sl) jdn/etw verarschen (inf) VI pissen (inf); **it's ~ing with rain** (inf) es pisst (sl) VT pissen (sl) VR sich bepissen (vulg); **we ~ed ourselves (laughing)** wir haben uns bepisst (sl)

▶ **piss about** or **around** VI (Brit inf) herummachen (inf)

▶ **piss down** VI (Brit inf) **it's pissing down** es pisst (sl)

▶ **piss off** VI (esp Brit sl) sich verpissen (sl); **piss off!** (= go away) verpiss dich! (sl); (= don't be stupid) du kannst mich mal (inf) VT (esp Brit, inf) ankotzen (sl); **to be pissed off with sb/sth** von jdm/etw die Schnauze voll haben (inf)

piss artist N (inf) (= drunk) Säufer(in) m(f); (= boaster) Großmaul nt (inf); (= incompetent) Niete f (inf); (= silly bastard) Arschloch nt (vulg)

pissed [pɪst] ADJ (inf) (Brit: = drunk) stockbesoffen (inf), dicht (sl); (US: = angry) stocksauer (inf)

piss: pisshead N (Brit inf) Saufkopf m (sl); **piss-poor** ADJ job, performance hundsmiserabel (inf); **piss-take** N (Brit sl) Verarschung f (inf); **piss-up** N (Brit sl) Saufgelage nt (inf); **he couldn't organize a ~ in a brewery** er ist dümmer als die Polizei erlaubt (inf)

pistachio [pɪ'stɑːʃɪəʊ] N Pistazie f ADJ (colour) pistazienfarben

piste [piːst] N (Ski) Piste f

pistil ['pɪstɪl] N Stempel m, Pistill nt (spec)

pistol ['pɪstl] N Pistole f; **~ shot** Pistolenschuss m; (= person) Pistolenschütze m/-schützin f; **to hold a ~ to sb's head** (fig) jdm die Pistole auf die Brust setzen; **~-grip camera** Kamera f mit Handgriff

pistol-whip ['pɪstəlwɪp] VT (US) mit einer Pistole ein paar überziehen (+dat) (inf)

piston ['pɪstən] N Kolben m; **~ stroke** Kolbenhub m

piston: piston engine N Kolbenmotor m; **piston ring** N Kolbenring m; **piston rod** N Pleuel- or Kolbenstange f

pit[1] [pɪt] N a (= hole) Grube f; (Brit: = coal mine) Zeche f, Grube f; (= quarry) Steinbruch m; (= trap) Fallgrube f; (in zoo etc) Grube f; (for cockfighting) (Kampf)arena f; (= stomach) Magengrube f; **to have a sinking feeling in the ~ of one's stomach** ein ungutes Gefühl in der Magengegend haben; **it makes me feel sick to the ~ of my stomach** da kommt mir die Galle hoch; **to go down the ~** Bergmann or Bergarbeiter werden; **he works down the ~(s)** er arbeitet unter Tage; **the ~** (= *hell*) die Hölle → **bottomless**

b (*Aut, in garage*) Grube *f*; (*Sport*) (*for long jump*) Sprunggrube *f*; (*for high jump*) Sprunghügel *m*; **the ~s** (*Motor Racing*) die Box; **to make a ~ stop** einen Boxenstopp machen

c (*Theat*) (*Brit: usu pl: for audience*) Parkett *nt*; (= *orchestra pit*) Orchestergraben *m* or -versenkung *f* or -raum *m*

d (*US St Ex*) Börsensaal *m*

e (= *scar*) (*on ceramics*) Vertiefung *f*; (*on skin*) Narbe *f*

f the ~s (*inf, = very bad*) das Allerletzte

g (*inf, = bed*) Falle *f* (*inf*)

VT a the surface of the moon is ~ted with small craters die Mondoberfläche ist mit kleinen Kratern übersät; **where the meteorites have ~ted the surface** wo die Meteoriten Einschläge hinterlassen haben; **his face was ~ted with smallpox scars** sein Gesicht war voller Pockennarben; **the underside of the car was ~ted with rust holes** die Unterseite des Wagens war mit Rostlöchern übersät; **a ~ted road surface** eine mit Schlaglöchern übersäte Fahrbahn

b to ~ one's strength/wits against sb/sth seine Kraft/seinen Verstand an jdm/etw messen; **to ~ oneself against** sb den Kampf gegen jdn aufnehmen; **in the next round A is ~ted against B** in der nächsten Runde stehen sich A und B gegenüber; **they are clearly ~ting their new model against ours** mit ihrem neuen Modell nehmen sie offensichtlich den Kampf gegen uns auf

pit² (*US*) **N** Stein *m* **VT** entsteinen

pita (bread) ['pɪtə] **N** (*US*) = **pitta (bread)**

pitapat ['pɪtəˈpæt] **ADV** (*of heart*) poch poch, klopf klopf; (*of feet*) tapp tapp; **to go ~** (*heart*) pochen, klopfen (*of rain, heart*) Klopfen *nt*; (*of feet*) Getrappel *nt*, Getrippel *nt*

pit bull terrier **N** Pitbullterrier *m*

pitch¹ [pɪtʃ] **N** Pech *nt*; **as black as ~** pechschwarz

pitch² **N a** (= *throw*) Wurf *m*; **he threw a good ~** (*Baseball*) ihm gelang ein guter Wurf

b (*Naut*) Stampfen *nt*

c (*esp Brit Sport*) Platz *m*, Feld *nt*

d (*Brit: for doing one's business, in market, outside theatre etc*) Stand *m*; (*fig, = usual place: on beach etc*) Platz *m*; **keep off my ~!** (*fig*) komm mir nicht ins Gehege! → **queer**

e (*inf. = sales pitch*) (= *long talk*) Sermon *m* (*inf*); (= *technique*) Verkaufstaktik *f*, Masche *f* (*inf*); **to make a ~ for sth** etw anpreisen; **he gave us his ~ about the need to change our policy** er hielt uns (wieder einmal) einen Vortrag über die Notwendigkeit, unsere Politik zu ändern

f (*Phon, also of note*) Tonhöhe *f*; (*of instrument*) Tonlage *f*; (*of voice*) Stimmlage *f*; **to have perfect ~** das absolute Gehör haben; **their speaking voices are similar in ~** ihre Stimmlagen sind ähnlich

g (= *angle, slope: of roof*) Schräge *f*, Neigung *f*; (*of propeller*) Steigung *f*; **the roofs have a steep ~** die Dächer sind sehr steil; **the floor was sloping at a precarious ~** der Boden neigte sich gefährlich

h (*fig: = degree*) **he roused the mob to such a ~ that ...** er brachte die Massen so sehr auf, dass ...; **the tension/their frustration had reached such a ~ that ...** die Spannung/ihre Frustration hatte einen derartigen Grad erreicht, dass ...; **matters had reached such a ~ that ...** die Sache hatte sich derart zugespitzt, dass ...; **at its highest ~** auf dem Höhepunkt or Gipfel; **we can't keep on working at this ~ much longer** wir können dieses Arbeitstempo nicht mehr lange durchhalten → **fever b**

i (*US, inf*) **what's the ~?** wie siehts aus?, was liegt an? (*inf*), was geht? (*sl*)

VT a (= *throw*) hay gabeln; *ball* werfen; **he was ~ed from** or **off his horse** er wurde vom Pferd geworfen; **he was ~ed through the windscreen** er wurde durch die Windschutzscheibe geschleudert; **as soon as he got the job he was ~ed into a departmental battle** kaum hatte er die Stelle, wurde er schon in einen Abteilungskrieg verwickelt

b (*Mus*) *song* anstimmen; *note* (= *give*) angeben; (= *hit*) treffen; *instrument* stimmen; **she ~ed her voice higher** sie sprach mit einer höheren Stimme

c (*fig*) **to ~ one's aspirations too high** seine Erwartungen or Hoffnungen zu hoch stecken; **the prices of these cars are ~ed extremely competitively** diese Autos haben sehr attraktive Preise; **the production must be ~ed at the right level for London audiences** das Stück muss auf das Niveau des Londoner Publikums abgestimmt werden; **she ~ed the plan to business leaders** sie machte ihren Plan führenden Geschäftsleuten schmackhaft; **that's ~ing it rather strong** das ist ein bisschen übertrieben; **to ~ sb a story** (*inf*) jdm eine Geschichte or ein Märchen auftischen (*inf*)

d (= *put up*) *camp, tent* aufschlagen; *stand* aufstellen

e (*Baseball*) *ball* werfen; **he ~ed the first two innings** er spielte or machte in den ersten beiden Runden den Werfer

VI a (= *fall*) fallen, stürzen; **to ~ forward** vornüberfallen; **he ~ed off his horse** er fiel kopfüber vom Pferd; **he ~ed forward as the bus braked** er fiel nach vorn, als der Bus bremste

b (*Naut*) stampfen; (*Aviat*) absacken; **the ship ~ed and rolled** das Schiff stampfte und rollte

c (*Baseball*) werfen; **he's in there ~ing** (*US fig inf*) er schuftete wie ein Ochse (*inf*)

▶ **pitch for** VI +*prep obj* anpreisen

▶ **pitch in** **VT** *sep* hineinwerfen or -schleudern **VI** (*inf*) einspringen; **if we all pitch in and help** wenn wir alle einspringen; **so we all pitched in together** also packten wir alle mit an

▶ **pitch into** **VI** +*prep obj* (= *attack*) herfallen über (+*acc*); *food also, work* sich hermachen über (+*acc*); (= *criticize*) heruntermachen (*inf*) **VT** *sep* **to pitch sb into fame/gloom** jdn berühmt/traurig machen

▶ **pitch on** VI +*prep obj* (*inf, = choose*) herauspicken (*inf*)

▶ **pitch out** VT *sep* (*lit, fig*) hinauswerfen; (= *get rid of*) wegwerfen; **he was pitched out when the car crashed** beim Unfall wurde er aus dem Wagen geschleudert

pitch: pitch accent N (*Phon*) musikalischer (Ton)akzent; **pitch angle** N Steigungswinkel *m*; **pitch-black** ADJ pechschwarz; **pitchblende** N Pechblende *f*; **pitch-dark** ADJ pechschwarz **N** (tiefe) Finsternis

pitched [pɪtʃt] ADJ **a ~ roof** Sattel- or Giebeldach *nt* **b** *battle* offen

pitcher¹ ['pɪtʃə'] N (*esp US*) Krug *m*; (*two-handled*) Henkelkrug *m*

pitcher² N (*Baseball*) Werfer(in) *m(f)*

pitch: pitchfork **N** Heugabel *f*; (*for manure*) Mistgabel *f* **VT** gabeln; (*fig*) hineinwerfen; **pitch invasion** N Sturm *m* auf das Spielfeld; **pitch pine** N Pechkiefer *f*; **pitch pipe** N (*Mus*) Stimmpfeife *f*

pit disaster N (*Min*) Grubenunglück *nt*

piteous ['pɪtɪəs] ADJ Mitleid erregend; *sounds* kläglich

piteously ['pɪtɪəslɪ] ADV Mitleid erregend; *cry etc also* kläglich

pitfall ['pɪtfɔːl] N (*fig*) Falle *f*, Fallstrick *m*; "**Pitfalls of English**" „Hauptschwierigkeiten der englischen Sprache"

pith [pɪθ] N (*Bot*) Mark *nt*; (*of orange, lemon etc*) weiße Haut; (*fig: = core*) Kern *m*, Wesentliche(s) *nt*; **remarks of ~ (and moment)** bedeutungsschwere Äußerungen

pithead ['pɪthed] N Übertageanlagen *pl*; **at the ~** über Tage; **~ ballot** Abstimmung *f* der Bergarbeiter

pith hat, **pith helmet** N Tropenhelm *m*

pithily ['pɪθɪlɪ] ADV prägnant, kernig, markig

pithiness ['pɪθɪnɪs] N (*fig*) Prägnanz *f*, Markigkeit *f*

pithy ['pɪθɪ] ADJ (+*er*) (*Bot*) reich an Mark; *oranges etc* dickschalig; (*fig*) prägnant, markig; **~ remarks** Kraftsprüche *pl*

pitiable ['pɪtɪəbl] ADJ Mitleid erregend, bemitleidenswert

pitiably ['pɪtɪəblɪ] ADV (= *pitifully*) erbärmlich, jämmerlich; **her dowry is ~ small** ihre Mitgift ist jämmerlich, sie hat nur eine klägliche Mitgift; **he found her lying on the bed, crying ~** er fand sie auf dem Bett, jämmerlich weinend

pitiful ['pɪtɪfʊl] ADJ **a** (= *moving to pity*) *sight, story* Mitleid erregend; *person* bemitleidenswert, bedauernswert; *cry, whimper* jämmerlich; **to be in a ~ state** in einem erbärmlichen Zustand sein **b** (= *poor, wretched*) erbärmlich, jämmerlich, kläglich; **what a ~ little wretch you are** was bist du doch für ein erbärmlicher kleiner Schuft

pitifully ['pɪtɪfəlɪ] ADV **a** jämmerlich, erbärmlich; *look, say, complain* Mitleid erregend; **it was ~ obvious that ...** es war schon qualvoll offensichtlich, dass ... **b** (= *woefully*) *inadequate* erbärmlich, schmerzlich

pitiless ['pɪtɪlɪs] ADJ mitleidlos; *person also, sun, glare* unbarmherzig; *cruelty also* gnadenlos, erbarmungslos

pitilessly ['pɪtɪlɪslɪ] ADV mitleidlos; *cruel* gnadenlos, erbarmungslos

pitman ['pɪtmən] N *pl* **-men** [-mən] (*Brit*) Bergmann *m*, Kumpel *m* (*inf*)

piton ['piːtɒn] N (*Mountaineering*) Felshaken *m*

pit: pit pony N Grubenpony *nt*; **pit prop** N Grubenstempel *m*

pits [pɪts] PL → **pit¹ N f**

pitta (bread) ['piːtə] N ≈ Fladenbrot *nt*

pittance ['pɪtəns] N Hungerlohn *m*

pitter-patter ['pɪtəˈpætə'] N (*of rain*) Klatschen *nt*; (*of feet*) Getrappel *nt*, Getrippel *nt* **ADV** **her heart went ~** ihr Herz klopfte or pochte **VI** (*rain*) platschen, klatschen; (= *run*) trappeln, trippeln

pituitary (gland) [pɪ'tjʊətrɪ(ˌglænd)] N Hirnhangdrüse *f*

pit worker N (*Brit*) Grubenarbeiter(in) *m(f)*

pity ['pɪtɪ] **☉ 26.3** **N a** Mitleid *nt*, Mitgefühl *nt*, Erbarmen *nt*; **for ~'s sake!** Erbarmen!; (*less seriously*) um Himmels willen!; **to have** or **take ~ on sb, to feel ~ for sb** mit jdm Mitleid haben; **but the king took ~ on him and spared his life** aber der König hatte Erbarmen mit ihm und schonte sein Leben; **have you no ~?** hast du kein Mitleid?; **to do sth out of ~ (for sb)** etw aus Mitleid (mit jdm) tun; **to feel no ~** kein Mitgefühl *etc* haben, kein Mitleid fühlen; **to move sb to ~** jds Mitleid (*acc*) erregen

b (= *cause of regret*) **(what a) ~!** (wie) schade!; **what a ~ he can't come** (wie) schade, dass er nicht kommen kann; **it's a ~ about the lack of tickets** es ist schade, dass es nicht genug Eintrittskarten gibt; **more's the ~!** leider; **and I won't be able to attend, more's the ~** und ich kann leider nicht teilnehmen; **it is a ~ that ...** es ist schade, dass ...; **the ~ of it was that ...** das Traurige daran war, dass ...; **it's a great ~** es ist sehr schade, es ist jammerschade; (*more formally*) es ist sehr bedauerlich; **it would be a ~ if he lost** or **were to lose this job** es wäre bedauerlich, wenn er seine Arbeit verlieren sollte; **it would be a ~ to waste this opportunity** es wäre bedauerlich, diese Gelegenheit ungenutzt verstreichen zu lassen

VT bemitleiden, bedauern; (*contemptuously*) bedauern; **all I can say is that I ~ you** ich kann nur sagen, du tust mir Leid

pitying ADJ , **pityingly** ADV ['pɪtɪŋ, -lɪ] mitleidig; *glance also* bedauernd; (*with contempt*) verächtlich

pivot ['pɪvət] *vb: pret, ptp* pivoted **N** Lagerzapfen *m*, Drehzapfen *m*; (*Mil*) Flügelmann *m*; (*fig*)

Dreh- und Angelpunkt *m*; ~ **bearing** Zapfenlager *nt*; drehbar lagern; **he ~ed it on his hand** er ließ es auf seiner Hand kreiseln **VI** sich drehen; **to ~ on sth** (*fig*) sich um etw drehen

pivotal ['pɪvətl] ADJ (*fig*) zentral

pivot: pivot bridge N (*Tech*) Drehbrücke *f*; **pivot tooth** N (*Med*) Stiftzahn *m*

pixel ['pɪksl] N (*Comput*) Pixel *nt*

pixelate ['pɪksəleɪt] VT (*TV etc*) unkenntlich machen (*durch Vergrößern der Bildpunkte*)

pixie, pixy ['pɪksɪ] N Elf *m*, Elfin *f*; ~ **hat** *or* **hood** Rotkäppchenmütze *f*

pixilated ['pɪksɪleɪtɪd] ADJ (*hum inf*) (= *crazy, eccentric*) überspannt, überkandidelt (*inf*); (= *drunk*) angeheitert (*inf*)

pizazz [pɪ'zæz] N = **pzazz**

pizza ['pi:tsə] N Pizza *f*

pizzazz [pɪ'zæz] N = **pzazz**

pizzeria [,pi:tsə'ri:ə] N Pizzeria *f*

pizzicato [,pɪtsɪ'kɑ:təʊ] (*Mus*) ADV pizzicato ADJ pizzicato; **the ~ section** das Pizzicato **N** Pizzicato *nt*

pizzle ['pɪzl] N Ochsenziemer *m*

pkt *abbr of* **packet** Pckg.

pl *abbr of* **plural** Pl.

Pl *abbr of* **Place** Pl., **placable** ADJ

placably ADV ['plækəbl, -ɪ] versöhnlich, nachgiebig

placard ['plækɑːd] **N** Plakat *nt*; (*at demonstrations also*) Transparent *nt* **VT** plakatieren; **to ~ a wall with posters** eine Wand mit Plakaten bekleben

placate [plə'keɪt] VT besänftigen, beschwichtigen

placatory [plə'keɪtərɪ] ADJ beschwichtigend, besänftigend; *gesture also* versöhnlich; **he held out a ~ hand** er streckte seine Hand zur Versöhnung aus

place [pleɪs]

1 NOUN	2 TRANSITIVE VERB

1 – NOUN

a general Platz *m*, Stelle *f*; **this is the place where he was born** hier *or* an dieser Stelle wurde er geboren; **do the spoons have a special place?** haben die Löffel einen bestimmten Platz?; **water is coming through in several places** an mehreren Stellen kommt Wasser durch; **from place to place** von einem Ort zum anderen; **in another place** woanders; **bed is the best place for him** im Bett ist er am besten aufgehoben; **we found a good place to watch the procession from** wir fanden einen Platz, von dem wir den Umzug gut sehen konnten; **in the right/wrong place** an der richtigen/falschen Stelle; **some/any place** irgendwo; **a poor man with no place to go** ein armer Mann, der nicht weiß, wohin; **this is no place for you/children** das ist nichts *or* kein Platz für dich/für Kinder; **there is no place for the unsuccessful in our society** für Erfolglose ist in unserer Gesellschaft kein Platz; **your place is by his side** dein Platz ist an seiner Seite; **it was the last place I expected to find him** da hätte ich ihn zuletzt *or* am wenigsten vermutet; **this isn't the place to discuss politics** dies ist nicht der Ort, um über Politik zu sprechen; **to laugh in the right places** an den richtigen Stellen lachen; **I can't be in two places at once!** ich kann doch nicht an zwei Stellen gleichzeitig sein; **she likes to have a place for everything and everything in its place** sie hält sehr auf Ordnung und achtet darauf, dass alles an seinem Platz liegt

b = geographical location (= *district*) Gegend *f*; (= *country*) Land *nt*; (= *building*) Gebäude *nt*; (= *town*) Ort *m*; **there's nothing to do in the evenings in this place** hier kann man abends nichts unternehmen; **Sweden's a great place** Schweden ist ein tolles Land; **they're building**

a new place out in the suburbs sie bauen ein neues Gebäude am Stadtrand; **a little place at the seaside** (= *village*) ein kleiner Ort am Meer; (= *house*) ein Häuschen *nt* am Meer

c = home Haus *nt*, Wohnung *f*; **come round to my place some time** besuch mich mal, komm doch mal vorbei; **let's go back to my place** lass uns zu mir gehen; **I've never been to his place** ich bin noch nie bei ihm gewesen; **where's your place?** wo wohnst du?; **at Peter's place** bei Peter; **your place or mine?** (*hum inf*) gehen wir zu dir oder zu mir?

d in book etc Stelle *f*; **to find one's place** die richtige Stelle finden; **to keep one's place** sich (*dat*) die richtige Stelle markieren; **to lose one's place** die Seite verblättern; (*on page*) die Zeile verlieren

e = seat, position (*at table, in team, school, hospital*) Platz *m*; (*at university*) Studienplatz *m*; (*job*) Stelle *f*; **to lay an extra place for sb** ein zusätzliches Gedeck für jdn auflegen; **to take one's place (at table)** Platz nehmen; **take your places for a square dance!** Aufstellung zur Quadrille, bitte!; **places for 500 students** 500 Studienplätze; **to give up one's place** (*in a queue*) jdm den Vortritt lassen; **to lose one's place** (*in a queue*) sich wieder hinten anstellen müssen; **if I were in your place** an Ihrer Stelle, wenn ich an Ihrer Stelle wäre; **put yourself in my place** versetzen Sie sich in meine Lage; **to take the place of sb/sth** jdn/etw ersetzen, jds Platz *or* den Platz von jdm/etw einnehmen

f in hierarchy Rang *m*, Stellung *f*; **people in high places** Leute in hohen Positionen; **to know one's place** wissen, was sich (für einen) gehört; **of course I'm not criticizing you, I know my place!** (*hum*) ich kritisiere dich selbstverständlich nicht, das steht mir gar nicht zu; **it's not my place to comment/tell him what to do** es steht mir nicht zu, einen Kommentar abzugeben/ihm zu sagen, was er tun soll; **to keep** *or* **put sb in his place** jdn in seine Schranken weisen; **that put him in his place!** das hat ihn erst mal zum Schweigen gebracht, da hab ichs/hat ers *etc* ihm gezeigt (*inf*)

g in exam, competition Platz *m*, Stelle *f*; **Lunt won, with Moore in second place** Lunt hat gewonnen, auf zweiter Stelle *or* auf dem zweiten Platz lag Moore; **to win first place** Erste(r, s) sein; **to take second place to sth** einer Sache (*dat*) gegenüber zweitrangig sein

h Sport Platzierung *f*; **to get a place** eine Platzierung erreichen, einen der ersten drei Plätze belegen; **to back a horse for a place** auf Platz wetten, eine Platzwette abschließen

i in street names Platz *m*

j Math Stelle *f*; **to work sth out to three decimal places** etw auf drei Stellen nach dem Komma berechnen

k set structures

♦ **place of** + *noun* **place of amusement** Vergnügungsstätte *f*; **place of birth** Geburtsort *m*; **place of residence** Wohnort *m*; **place of business** *or* **work** Arbeitsstelle *f*

♦ **in places** stellenweise; **the snow was up to a metre deep in places** der Schnee lag stellenweise bis zu einem Meter hoch

♦ **in place** everything was in place alles war an seiner Stelle; **make sure the wire/screw is properly in place** achten Sie darauf, dass der Draht/die Schraube richtig sitzt; **the legislation is already in place** die gesetzlichen Regelungen gelten schon

♦ **out of place** (= *in the wrong place*) nicht an der richtigen Stelle sein; (= *untidy*) in Unordnung sein; (*fig, remark*) unangebracht *or* deplatziert sein; (*person*) fehl am Platz *or* deplatziert sein; **to look out of place** fehl am Platz *or* deplatziert wirken; **to feel out of place** sich fehl am Platz *or* deplatziert fühlen; **not a hair out of place** tipptopp frisiert (*inf*)

♦ **all over the place** (= *everywhere*) überall; **she's all over the place** (*inf*, = *disorganized*) sie ist total chaotisch (*inf*)

♦ **in place of** statt (+*gen*); **McCormack played in goal in place of Miller** McCormack stand anstelle von Miller im Tor

♦ **to fall into place** Gestalt annehmen

♦ **in the first place** (= *firstly*) erstens; **in the first place ..., in the second place ...** erstens ..., zweitens ...; **she shouldn't have been there in the first place** (= *anyway*) sie hätte überhaupt nicht *or* erst gar nicht dort sein sollen

♦ **to take place** stattfinden; **the meeting will take place on Monday** das Treffen findet am Montag statt

♦ **to go places** (= *travel*) Ausflüge machen, herumreisen; **he's going places** (*fig inf*) er bringts zu was (*inf*)

♦ **to give place to sth** einer Sache (*dat*) Platz machen

2 – TRANSITIVE VERB

a = put setzen, stellen; (= *lay down*) legen; *person at table etc* setzen; *guards* aufstellen; *shot* (*with gun*) anbringen; (*Ftbl, Tennis*) platzieren; *troops* in Stellung bringen; *announcement* (*in paper*) inserieren (*in* in +*dat*); *advertisement* setzen (*in* in +*acc*); **the magician placed one hand over the other** der Zauberer legte eine Hand über die andere; **she slowly placed one foot in front of the other** sie setzte langsam einen Fuß vor den anderen; **he placed the cue ball right behind the black** er setzte die Spielkugel direkt hinter die schwarze Kugel; **he placed a gun to my head** er setzte mir eine Pistole an den Kopf; **she placed a finger on her lips** sie legte den Finger auf die Lippen; **the vase was precariously placed** die Vase stand an einer gefährlichen Stelle; **to place a matter before sb** jdm eine Angelegenheit vorlegen; **I shall place the matter in the hands of a lawyer** ich werde die Angelegenheit einem Rechtsanwalt übergeben; **to place a strain on sth** etw belasten; **this placed him under a lot of pressure** dadurch geriet er stark unter Druck; **to place confidence/trust in sb/sth** Vertrauen in jdn/etw setzen; **to be placed** (*shop, town, house etc*) liegen; **how are you placed for time/money?** wie sieht es mit deiner Zeit/deinem Geld aus?

♦ **well/better placed** we are well placed for the shops was Einkaufsmöglichkeiten angeht, wohnen wir günstig; **Liverpool are well placed in the league** Liverpool liegt gut in der Tabelle; **they were well placed to observe the whole battle** sie hatten einen günstigen Platz, von dem sie die ganze Schlacht verfolgen konnten; **we are well placed now to finish the job by next year** wir stehen jetzt so gut da, dass wir die Arbeit im nächsten Jahr fertig stellen können; **with the extra staff we are better placed now than we were last month** mit dem zusätzlichen Personal stehen wir jetzt besser da als vor einem Monat; **he is well placed** (*to get hold of things*) er sitzt an der Quelle; **he is well placed to get information** er kommt leicht an Informationen

b = rank stellen; **to place local interests above** *or* **before** *or* **over those of central government** kommunale Interessen über die der Zentralregierung stellen; **that should be placed first** das sollte an erster Stelle stehen; **where do you place love on your list of priorities?** an welcher Stelle steht die Liebe für dich?; **the German runner was placed third** der deutsche Läufer belegte den dritten Platz *or* wurde Dritter; **to be placed** (*Sport*) sich platzieren

c = identify context of einordnen; **in which school would you place this painting?** welcher Schule würden Sie dieses Gemälde zuordnen?; **I don't know, it's very difficult to place** ich weiß es nicht, es ist sehr schwer einzuordnen; **I can't quite place him/his accent** ich kann ihn/seinen Akzent nicht einordnen; **historians place the book in the 5th century AD** Historiker datieren das Buch auf das 5. Jahrhundert

d Comm *goods* absetzen; *order* erteilen (*with sb* jdm); *contract* abschließen (*with sb* mit jdm); **who did you place the computer typesetting job with?** wem haben Sie den Auftrag für den

Computersatz erteilt?; **this is the last time we place any work with you** das ist das letzte Mal, dass wir Ihnen einen Auftrag erteilt haben **e** money (= *deposit*) deponieren; (= *invest*) investieren; **to place money at sb's credit** jdm eine Geldsumme gutschreiben **f** phone call anmelden **g** = find job for unterbringen (*with* bei); **the agency is trying to place him with a building firm** die Agentur versucht, ihn bei einer Baufirma unterzubringen

placebo [pləˈsiːbəʊ] N (*Med*) Placebo *nt*
placebo effect N Placeboeffekt *m*
place: place card N Tischkarte *f*; **place kick** N Platztritt *m*; **placeman** N (*pej*) Strohmann *m*; **place mat** N Set *nt*
placement [ˈpleɪsmənt] N **a** (= *act: of social worker, teacher etc*) Platzierung *f*; (= *finding job for*) Vermittlung *f* **b** (*Brit*) (= *period: of trainee*) Praktikum *nt*; **I'm here on a six-month ~** (*for in-service training etc*) ich bin hier für sechs Monate zur Weiterbildung; (*on secondment*) ich bin für sechs Monate hierhin überwiesen worden
place name N Ortsname *m*
placenta [pləˈsentə] N Plazenta *f*
placer mining N (*in rivers*) Goldwaschen *nt*
place setting N Gedeck *nt*
placid [ˈplæsɪd] ADJ ruhig; *person also* gelassen; *disposition* friedfertig; *smile* still; *scene* beschaulich, friedvoll
placidity [pləˈsɪdɪtɪ] N Ruhe *f*; (*of person also*) Gelassenheit *f*; (*of disposition*) Friedfertigkeit *f*; (*of smile*) Stille *f*
placidly [ˈplæsɪdlɪ] ADV ruhig, friedlich; *speak* bedächtig
placings [ˈpleɪsɪŋz] PL Platzierungen *pl*
placket [ˈplækɪt] N Schlitz *m*
plagiarism [ˈpleɪdʒərɪzəm] N Plagiat *nt*
plagiarist [ˈpleɪdʒərɪst] N Plagiator(in) *m(f)*
plagiarize [ˈpleɪdʒəraɪz] VT *book, idea* plagiieren
plague [pleɪg] **N** (*Med*) Seuche *f*; (*Bibl, fig*) Plage *f*; **the ~** die Pest; **to avoid sb/sth like the ~** jdn/etw wie die Pest meiden; **we're suffering from a ~ of crime** wir leiden unter einer wahren Flut an Verbrechen; **a ~ of reporters descended on the town** eine Horde von Reportern suchte die Stadt heim; **a ~ on him!** (*old*) die Pest möge über ihn kommen! (*old*) **VT** plagen; **to ~ the life out of sb** jdn (bis aufs Blut) quälen, jdm das Leben schwer machen; **to be ~d by doubts/injury** von Zweifeln/Verletzungen geplagt werden; **to be ~d by bad luck** vom Pech verfolgt werden; **to ~ sb with questions** jdn ständig mit Fragen belästigen
plaice [pleɪs] N , *no pl* Scholle *f*
plaid [plæd] N Plaid *nt*; **~ skirt** karierter Rock
plain [pleɪn] **ADJ** (+*er*) **a** klar; (= *obvious*) offensichtlich, klar; *tracks, differences* deutlich; **it is ~ to see that ...** es ist offensichtlich, dass ...; **it's as ~ as the nose on your face** (*inf*) das sieht doch ein Blinder (mit Krückstock) (*inf*); **(as) ~ as day** sonnenklar; **to make sth ~ to sb** jdm etw klarmachen *or* klar zu verstehen geben; **the reason is ~ to see** der Grund ist leicht einzusehen; **I'd like to make it quite ~ that ...** ich möchte gern klarstellen, dass ...; **did I make myself** *or* **my meaning ~?** habe ich mich klar ausgedrückt?; **to make sb's point of view ~** seine Meinung klar zum Ausdruck bringen **b** (= *frank, straightforward*) *question, answer* klar; *truth* schlicht; *statement* klar, deutlich; **~ dealing** Redlichkeit *f*; **to be ~ with sb** jdm gegenüber offen *or* direkt sein; **in ~ language** *or* **English** unmissverständlich, auf gut Deutsch; **in ~ language** *or* **English, the answer is no** um es klar *or* auf gut Deutsch zu sagen: die Antwort ist nein; **it was ~ sailing** es ging glatt (über die Bühne) (*inf*); **it won't all be ~ sailing** es wird gar nicht so einfach sein; **from now on it'll be ~ sailing** von jetzt an geht es ganz einfach **c** (= *simple, with nothing added*) einfach; *dress, design, living* schlicht; *cooking, food*

(*gut*)bürgerlich; *cook* einfach, gutbürgerlich; *water* klar; *paper* unliniert; *envelope* neutral; *colour* einheitlich; *cigarette* filterlos, ohne Filter; **in a ~ colour** (*Brit*) *or* **color** (*US*) einfarbig, uni *pred*; **under ~ cover** in neutraler Verpackung; (= *in envelope*) in neutralem Umschlag; **he's a ~ Mr** er ist einfach Herr Sowieso; **he used to be ~ Mr X** früher war er einfach *or* schlicht Herr X **d** (= *sheer*) rein; *nonsense etc* rein, völlig, blank (*inf*); **it's just ~ common sense** das ist einfach gesunder Menschenverstand **e** (= *not beautiful*) *person, appearance, face* unattraktiv; **she really is so ~** sie ist nicht unansehnlich; **~ Jane** unattraktives *or* unansehnliches Mädchen; **she's a real ~ Jane** sie ist nicht gerade hübsch *or* eine Schönheit **ADV a** (*inf*: = *simply, completely*) (ganz) einfach; **~ stupid/wrong** einfach dumm/falsch **b** **I can't put it ~er than that** deutlicher kann ich es nicht sagen **N a** (*Geog*) Ebene *f*, Flachland *nt*; **the ~s** das Flachland, die Ebene; (*in North America*) die Prärie **b** (*Knitting*) rechte Masche
plain: plain chocolate N (*Brit*) (Zart)bitterschokolade *f*; **plain clothes** **PL** **in ~** in Zivil **ADJ** **plain-clothes** in Zivil; **a plain-clothes policeman** ein Polizist in Zivil; **plainclothesman** N *pl* -men Polizist *m* in Zivil, Zivile(r) *m* (*inf*); **plain flour** N Mehl *nt* (*ohne beigemischtes Backpulver*)
plainly [ˈpleɪnlɪ] ADV **a** (= *clearly*) eindeutig; *explain, remember, state* klar, deutlich; **~, these new techniques are impractical** es ist ganz klar, dass diese neuen Verfahren unpraktisch sind **b** (= *frankly*) offen, direkt **c** (= *simply, unsophisticatedly*) einfach
plainness [ˈpleɪnnɪs] N **a** (= *frankness, straightforwardness*) Direktheit *f*, Offenheit *f* **b** (= *simplicity*) Einfachheit *f* **c** (= *lack of beauty*) Unansehnlichkeit *f*
Plain People PL (*US*) *Sammelbegriff for Mitglieder christlicher Glaubensgruppen wie den Amish, die bewusst einfach leben*
plainsman [ˈpleɪnzmən] N *pl* -men [-mən] Flachländer *m*
plain: plainsong N Cantus planus *m*, gregorianischer Gesang; **plain speaking** N Offenheit *f*; **some/a bit of ~** ein paar offene Worte; **plain-spoken** ADJ offen, direkt; *criticism also* unverhohlen; **to be ~** sagen, was man denkt
plaint [pleɪnt] N (*liter*) **a** (= *complaint*) Wehklage *f* (*geh*) **b** (= *cry*) Gejammer *nt*; **the moans and ~s of their children** das Gequäke und Gejammer ihrer Kinder
plaintiff [ˈpleɪntɪf] N Kläger(in) *m(f)*
plaintive [ˈpleɪntɪv] ADJ klagend; *voice etc also* wehleidig (*pej*); *song etc also* schwermütig, elegisch (*geh*); *look etc* leidend; **the letter ended on a ~ note** der Brief schloss mit einer Klage
plaintively [ˈpleɪntɪvlɪ] ADV *say, ask* klagend
plait [plæt] **N** (*esp Brit*) Zopf *m*; **she wears her hair in ~s** sie trägt Zöpfe **VT** flechten
plan [plæn] **○** 8.1, 8.2, 25.2 **N a** (= *scheme*) Plan *m*; (*Pol, Econ*) Programm *nt*, Plan *m*; **~ of action** (*Mil*) Aktionsprogramm *nt*; (*of campaign*) Strategie *f*; **the ~ is to meet at six** es ist geplant, sich um sechs zu treffen; **so, what's the ~?** was ist also geplant?; **the best ~ is to tell him first** am besten sagt man es ihm zuerst; **to make ~s (for sth)** Pläne (für etw) machen, (etw) planen; **to have great ~s for sb** mit jdm Großes vorhaben, große Pläne mit jdm haben; **what ~s do you have for the holidays/ your son?** welche Pläne haben Sie für den Urlaub/Ihren Sohn?; **have you any ~s for tonight?** hast du (für) heute Abend (schon) etwas vor?; **according to ~** planmäßig, wie vorgesehen, programmgemäß **b** (= *diagram*) Plan *m*; (*for novel etc also*) Entwurf *m*; (*for essay, speech*) Konzept *nt*; (= *town plan*) Stadtplan *m* **VT a** (= *arrange*) planen; *programme etc* erstellen

b (= *intend*) vorhaben; **we weren't ~ning to** wir hatten es nicht vorgehabt; **she's ~ning a career in law** sie will ins Justizwesen gehen; **this development was not ~ned** diese Entwicklung war nicht eingeplant **c** (= *design*) planen; *buildings etc* planen, entwerfen **VI** planen; **to ~ for sth** sich einstellen auf (+*acc*), rechnen mit; **to ~ months ahead** (auf) Monate vorausplanen
▶ **plan on** VI +*prep obj* **a** (= *intend*) **to plan on a trip to London** vorhaben, eine Reise nach London zu machen; **I'm planning on a hot bath and an early night** ich beabsichtige, ein heißes Bad zu nehmen und früh ins Bett zu gehen; **to plan on doing sth** vorhaben, etw zu tun; **she plans on staying in London** sie hat vor, in London zu bleiben **b** (= *foresee*) **to plan on sth** mit etwas rechnen; **he hadn't planned on the bad weather** er hatte nicht mit dem schlechten Wetter gerechnet; **I hadn't planned on being paid for my help** ich hatte nicht damit gerechnet, für meine Hilfe bezahlt zu werden
▶ **plan out** VT *sep* in Einzelheiten planen
plane¹ [pleɪn] N (*also* **plane tree**) Platane *f*
plane² [pleɪn] N **a** eben (*also Math*); *surface also* plan **a** (*Math*) Ebene *f* **b** (= *aeroplane*) Flugzeug *nt*; **to go by ~**, **to take a ~** fliegen **c** (= *tool*) Hobel *m* **d** (*fig*) Ebene *f*; (*intellectual*) Niveau *nt*; (= *social plane*) Schicht *f*; **he lives on a different ~** er lebt in anderen Sphären; **a higher ~ of consciousness** eine höhere Bewusstseinsebene **VT** hobeln; **to ~ sth down** etw abhobeln, etw glatt hobeln **VI** (*bird, glider, speedboat*) gleiten
plane chart N (*Naut*) Plankarte *f*
planeload [ˈpleɪnləʊd] N Flugzeugladung *f*
plane geometry N (*Math*) Planimetrie *f*
planet [ˈplænɪt] N Planet *m*
planetarium [ˌplænɪˈtɛərɪəm] N Planetarium *nt*
planetary [ˈplænɪtərɪ] ADJ planetarisch, Planeten-; *travel* zu anderen Planeten; **~ system** Planetensystem *nt*; **the laws of ~ motion** die Gesetze *pl* der Planetenbewegung
planetoid [ˈplænɪtɔɪd] N (*Astron*) Planetoid *m*
plangent [ˈplændʒənt] ADJ (*liter*) getragen, klagend
planify [ˈplænɪfaɪ] VTI (*esp US inf*) systematisch planen
planimetry [plæˈnɪmɪtrɪ] N (*Math*) Planimetrie *f*
plank [plæŋk] **N a** Brett *nt*; (*Naut*) Planke *f* → **walk b** (*Pol*) Schwerpunkt *m*; **the main ~ of their argument is that ...** ihr Argument stützt sich vor allem darauf, dass ... **VT** (*inf*) = **plonk¹**
planking [ˈplæŋkɪŋ] N Beplankung *f*, Planken *pl*
plankton [ˈplæŋktən] N Plankton *nt*
planless ADJ , **planlessly** ADV [ˈplænlɪs, -lɪ] planlos
planned [plænd] ADJ geplant
planned economy N Planwirtschaft *f*
planned obsolescence N geplanter Verschleiß
planner [ˈplænə] N Planer(in) *m(f)*
planning [ˈplænɪŋ] N Planung *f*
planning *in cpds* Planungs-; **~ commission** Planungsausschuss *m*; **~ permission** Baugenehmigung *f*
plant [plɑːnt] **N a** (*Bot*) Pflanze *f*; **rare/tropical ~s** seltene/tropische Gewächse *pl* **b** *no pl* (= *equipment*) Anlagen *pl*; (= *equipment and buildings*) Produktionsanlage *f*; (*US: of school, bank*) Einrichtungen *pl*; (= *factory*) Werk *nt*; **~-hire** Baumaschinenvermietung *f*; **"heavy crossing"** „Baustellenverkehr" **c** (*inf*: = *frame-up*) eingeschmuggelter Gegenstand *etc, der jdn kompromittieren soll*, Komplott *nt* **ATTR** Pflanzen-; **~ life** Pflanzenwelt *f* **VT a** *plants, trees* pflanzen, ein- *or* anpflanzen; *field* bepflanzen; **to ~ a field with turnips/wheat** auf einem Feld Rüben anbauen *or* anpflanzen/ Weizen anbauen *or* säen

b (= *place in position*) setzen; *bomb* legen; *kiss* drücken; *fist* pflanzen (*inf*); (*in the ground*) stick stecken; *flag* pflanzen; **to ~ sth in sb's mind** jdm etw in den Kopf setzen, jdn auf etw (*acc*) bringen; **a policeman was ~ed at each entrance** an jedem Eingang wurde ein Polizist aufgestellt *or* postiert; **he ~ed himself right in front of the fire** (*inf*) er pflanzte sich genau vor dem Kamin auf (*inf*); **she ~ed the children in the hall** sie stellte die Kinder im Flur ab (*inf*); **to ~ one on sb's chin** (*inf*) jdm einen Kinnhaken geben; **to ~ one's feet** (*lit*) die Füße aufsetzen

c (*inf*) *incriminating evidence, stolen goods etc* manipulieren, praktizieren; (*in sb's car, home*) schmuggeln; *informer, spy etc* (ein)schleusen; **to ~ sth on sb** (*inf*) jdm etw unterjubeln (*inf*), jdm etw in die Tasche praktizieren

▶ **plant out** VT *sep* auspflanzen

plantain ['plæntɪn] N (*Bot*) **a** Plantainbanane *f* **b** (= *weed*) Wegerich *m*

plantation [plæn'teɪʃən] N Plantage *f*, Pflanzung *f*; (*of trees*) Schonung *f*, Anpflanzung *f*

planter ['plɑːntə'] N Pflanzer(in) *m(f)*; (= *plantation owner also*) Plantagenbesitzer(in) *m(f)*; (= *machine*) Pflanzmaschine *f*; (= *seed planter*) Sämaschine *f*; (= *plant pot*) Übertopf *m*

plant kingdom N Pflanzenreich *nt*

plantlet ['plɑːntlɪt] N Pflänzchen *nt*

plant pot N (*esp Brit*) Blumentopf *m*

plaque [plæk] N **a** Plakette *f*, (*on building etc*) Tafel *f* **b** (*Med*) Belag *m*; (*on teeth*) (Zahn)belag *m*

plash [plæʃ] (*liter*) **N** (*of water, rain*) Plätschern *nt*; (*of oars*) Platschen *nt* **VI** (*water, rain*) plätschern; (*oars*) platschen

plasm ['plæzəm], **plasma** ['plæzmə] N Plasma *nt*

plaster ['plɑːstə'] **N** **a** (*Build*) (Ver)putz *m* **b** (*Art, Med: also* **plaster of Paris**) Gips *m*; (*Brit Med*: = *plaster cast*) Gipsverband *m*; **to have one's leg in ~** das Bein in Gips haben **c** (*Brit*: = *sticking plaster*) Pflaster *nt* **VT** **a** (*Build*) *wall* verputzen; **to ~ over a hole** ein Loch zugipsen **b** (*inf*: = *cover*) voll kleistern; **to ~ a wall with posters** eine Wand mit Plakaten voll kleistern *or* bepflastern (*inf*); **his picture was ~ed all over the newspapers** sein Bild war in allen Zeitungen; **to ~ one's face with make-up** sein Gesicht mit Make-up voll kleistern (*inf*); **~ed with mud** schlammbedeckt; **he ~ed down his wet hair with his hands** er klatschte sich das nasse Haar mit den Händen an

plaster: plaster bandage N (*Med*) Gipsbinde *f*; **plasterboard** N Gipskarton(platten *pl*) *m*; **a sheet of ~** eine Gipskartonplatte; **plaster cast** N (= *model, statue*) Gipsform *f*; (*of footprint etc*) Gipsabdruck *m*; (*Med*) Gipsverband *m*

plastered ['plɑːstəd] ADJ *pred* (*inf*) voll (*inf*); **to get ~** sich voll laufen lassen (*inf*)

plasterer ['plɑːstərə'] N Gipser(in) *m(f)*, Stuckateur(in) *m(f)*

plastering ['plɑːstərɪŋ] N **a** (= *plasterwork*) Verputz *m*, Bewurf *m*; (*action*) Verputzen *nt* **b** (= *stucco*) Stuck *m*, Stuckarbeit *f*, Stuckatur *f* **c** (= *application of plaster*) Gipsen *nt*; (*Med*) Eingipsen *nt*

plastic ['plæstɪk] **N** **a** Plastik *nt*; **~s** Kunststoffe *pl* **b** (*inf*: = *credit cards*) Kreditkarten *pl*, Plastikkarten *pl* (*inf*) **ADJ** **a** (= *made of plastic*) Plastik-, aus Plastik; (*pej inf*) *person* synthetisch; *smile* aufgesetzt, gekünstelt; *pub* steril; **~ bottle** Plastikflasche *f*; **~ food** (*pej inf*) Plastikessen *nt* (*inf*) **b** (= *flexible*) formbar *also fig*, modellierbar (*also fig*), plastisch; **the ~ arts** die gestaltenden Künste **c** (*Med*) plastisch

plastic: plastic bag N Plastiktüte *f*; **plastic bomb** N Plastikbombe *f*; **plastic bullet** N Plastikgeschoss *nt*; **plastic explosive** N Plastiksprengstoff *m*

Plasticine® ['plæstɪsiːn] N (*Brit*) Plastilin *nt*

plasticity [plæ'stɪsɪtɪ] N Formbarkeit *f*, Modellierbarkeit *f*

plastic: plastic money N (*inf*) Plastikgeld *nt*; **plastics industry** N Kunststoffindustrie *f*; **plastic surgeon** N plastischer Chirurg; **plastic surgery** N plastische Chirurgie; **he had to have ~** er musste sich einer Gesichtsoperation unterziehen; **she decided to have ~ on her nose** sie entschloss sich zu einer Schönheitsoperation an ihrer Nase

plate [pleɪt] **N** **a** (= *flat dish, plateful, collection plate*) Teller *m*; (= *warming plate*) Platte *f*; **~ supper** (*US*) Tellergericht *nt*; **a dinner at 45 dollars a ~** (*US*) ein Essen für *or* zu 45 Dollar pro Person; **cold ~** kalte Platte; **to have sth handed to one on a ~** (*Brit fig inf*) etw auf einem Tablett serviert bekommen (*inf*); **to have enough/a lot on one's ~** (*fig inf*) genug/viel am Hals haben (*inf*) **b** (= *gold, silver*) Silber und Gold *nt*; (= *tableware*) Tafelsilber/-gold *nt*; (= *plated metal*) vergoldetes/versilbertes Metall; (= *plated articles, jewellery*) Doublé *nt*, plattierte Ware, Doublee *nt*; **a piece of ~** ein Stück *or* Gegenstand aus Gold/Silber *etc*; (= *plated article*) ein vergoldeter/versilberter *etc* Gegenstand; **it's only ~** es ist bloß *or* nur vergoldet/versilbert *etc* **c** (*Tech, Phot, Typ*) Platte *f*; (= *name plate, number plate*) Schild *nt* **d** (= *illustration*) Tafel *f* **e** (= *dental plate*) (Gaumen)platte *f* **f** (*Racing*) Cup *m*, Pokal *m*; (= *race*) Cup- *or* Pokalrennen *nt* **g** (*Baseball*: = *home plate*) Gummiplatte *f* **VT** *ship* beplanken; (*with armour-plating*) panzern; **to ~ sth with gold/silver/nickel** etw vergolden/versilbern/vernickeln

plateau ['plætəʊ] N *pl* **-s** *or* **-x** (*Geog*) Plateau *nt*, Hochebene *f*; **the rising prices have reached a ~** die Preise steigen nicht mehr und haben sich eingependelt

plateful ['pleɪtfʊl] N Teller *m*; **two ~s of salad** zwei Teller (voll) Salat

plate: plate glass N Tafelglas *nt*; **plateholder** N (*Phot*) Plattenkassette *f*; **plate iron** N (*Tech*) Eisenblech *nt*, Walzeisen *nt*; **platelayer** N (*Brit Rail*) Streckenarbeiter(in) *m(f)*

platelet ['pleɪtlɪt] N (*Physiol*) Plättchen *nt*

platen ['plætən] N (*of typewriter, printer*) Walze *f*

plate: plate rack N (*Brit*) Geschirrständer *m*; **plate tectonics** N *sing* (*Geol*) Plattentektonik *f*; **plate warmer** N Warmhalteplatte *f*

platform ['plætfɔːm] **N** **a** Plattform *f*; (= *stage*) Podium *nt*, Bühne *f* **b** (*Rail*) Bahnsteig *m* **c** (*Pol*) Plattform *f*

platform: platform crane N (*Tech*) Laufkran *m*; **platform party** N Podiumsgäste *pl*; **platform shoe** N Plateauschuh *m*; **platform sole** N Plateausohle *f*; **platform ticket** N Bahnsteigkarte *f*

plating ['pleɪtɪŋ] N (= *act*) (*with gold*) Vergolden *nt*, Vergoldung *f*; (*with silver*) Versilbern *nt*, Versilberung *f*; (*with nickel*) Vernickeln *nt*, Vernickelung *f*; (= *material*) Auflage *f*; (*on ship*) Beplankung *f*, Außenhaut *f*; (= *armour-plating*) Panzerung *f*

platinum ['plætɪnəm] N Platin *nt*; **a ~ blonde** eine Platinblonde

platinum disc N Platinplatte *f*

platitude ['plætɪtjuːd] N (*pej*) Platitüde *f*, Plattheit *f*

platitudinize [,plætɪ'tjuːdɪnaɪz] VI (*pej*) sich in Gemeinplätzen ergehen (*geh*)

platitudinous [,plætɪ'tjuːdɪnəs] ADJ (*pej*) banal; *speech also* platt

Plato ['pleɪtəʊ] N Plato(n) *m*

Platonic [plə'tɒnɪk] ADJ *philosophy* Platonisch; **platonic** (*love, friendship*) platonisch

platoon [plə'tuːn] N (*Mil*) Zug *m*

platter ['plætə'] N Teller *m*; (= *wooden platter also*) Brett *nt*; (= *serving dish*) Platte *f*; (*inf*: = *record*) Platte *f*; **to have sth handed to one on a (silver) ~** (*fig*) etw auf einem (silbernen) Tablett serviert bekommen; **to demand sb's head on a ~** (*fig*) jds Kopf verlangen

platypus ['plætɪpəs] N Schnabeltier *nt*

plaudit ['plɔːdɪt] N *usu pl* (*liter*) Ovation *f* (*usu pl*), Huldigung *f* (*geh*); **the headmaster's ~s made him blush** die Lobeshymnen des Direktors ließen ihn erröten

plausibility [,plɔːzə'bɪlɪtɪ] N Plausibilität *f*; (*of story, excuse also*) Glaubwürdigkeit *f*; (*of liar*) Geschicktheit *f*; (*of manner, person*) überzeugende Art

plausible ['plɔːzəbl] ADJ plausibel; *argument also* einleuchtend; *story, excuse also* glaubwürdig, glaubhaft; *liar* gut, geschickt; *manner, person* überzeugend

plausibly ['plɔːzəblɪ] ADV plausibel; *argue also* einleuchtend; *lie, present one's excuses* geschickt; *tell a story, act a part* auf überzeugende Art, überzeugend

play [pleɪ] **N** **a** (= *amusement, gambling*) Spiel *nt*; **to be at ~** beim Spielen sein; **to do/say sth in ~** etw aus Spaß tun/sagen; **~ on words** Wortspiel *nt*; **children at ~** spielende Kinder; **children learn through ~** Kinder lernen beim Spiel; **he lost £800 in a few hours'** ~ er hat beim Spiel innerhalb von ein paar Stunden £ 800 verloren **b** (*Sport*) Spiel *nt*; **to abandon ~** das Spiel abbrechen; **because of bad weather ~ was impossible** es konnte wegen schlechten Wetters nicht gespielt werden; **in a clever piece of ~, in a clever ~** (*US*) in einem klugen Schachzug; **there was some exciting ~ toward(s) the end** gegen Ende gab es einige spannende (Spiel)szenen; **to be in ~/out of ~** (*ball*) im Spiel/im Aus sein; **to kick the ball out of ~** den Ball aus *or* ins Aus schießen **c** (*Tech, Mech*) Spiel *nt*; **1 mm (of) ~** 1 mm Spiel **d** (*Theat*) (Theater)stück *nt*; (*Rad*) Hörspiel *nt*; (*TV*) Fernsehspiel *nt*; **the ~s of Shakespeare** Shakespeares Dramen **e** (*fig*: = *moving patterns*) Spiel *nt* **f** (*fig phrases*) **to come into ~** ins Spiel kommen; **to give full ~ to one's imagination** seiner Fantasie *or* Phantasie (*dat*) freien Lauf lassen; **the game allows the child's imagination (to be given) full ~** das Spiel gestattet die freie Entfaltung der kindlichen Fantasie; **to bring** *or* **call sth into ~** etw aufbieten *or* einsetzen; **the ~ of opposing forces** das Widerspiel der Kräfte; **the free ~ of market forces** das freie Spiel der Marktkräfte; **to make great ~ of sth** (*Brit*) viel Aufhebens von etw machen; **to make great ~ of doing sth** (*Brit*) viel Wind darum machen, etw zu tun; **to make a ~ for sb** sich um jdn bemühen; **to make a ~ for sth** es auf etw (*acc*) abgesehen haben **VT** **a** *game, card, ball, position* spielen; *player* aufstellen, einsetzen; **to ~ sb (at a game)** gegen jdn (ein Spiel) spielen; **to ~ ball (with sb)** (mit jdm) mitspielen; **to ~ shop** (Kaufmanns)laden spielen, Kaufmann spielen; **to ~ a joke on sb** jdm einen Streich spielen; **to ~ a mean/dirty trick on sb** jdn auf gemeine/schmutzige Art hereinlegen; **to ~ the company game** sich in der Firma profilieren wollen; **they're all ~ing the game** die machen doch alle mit → **card** [1], **game** [1], **market**, **hell** *etc* **b** (*Theat, fig*) *part* spielen; (= *perform in*) *town* spielen in (+*dat*); **to ~ it safe** auf Nummer sicher gehen (*inf*); **to ~ it cautious/clever** vorsichtig/klug vorgehen; **to ~ the fool** den Clown spielen, herumblödeln (*inf*); **he was ~ing the jealous lover** er spielte den eifersüchtigen Liebhaber → **cool** ADJ d **c** *instrument, record, tune* spielen; **to ~ the piano** Klavier spielen; **to ~ sth through/over** etw durchspielen **d** (= *direct*) *lights, jet of water* richten **e** (*Fishing*) drillen **VI** **a** (*esp child*) spielen; **to go out to ~** rausgehen und spielen; **run away and ~!** geh spielen!; **can Johnny come out to ~?** darf Johnny zum Spielen rauskommen?; **he wouldn't ~** (*fig inf*) er wollte nicht mitspielen (*inf*) **b** (*Sport, at game*, = *gamble*) spielen; **England ~s against Scotland next week** England spielt nächste Woche gegen Schottland; **he ~s for Celtic** er spielt für Celtic; **to ~ at mothers and fathers/cowboys and Indians** Vater und Mutter/Cowboy und Indianer spielen; **to ~ at being a fireman** Feuerwehrmann spielen; **he was ~ing at being angry** seine Wut war gespielt; **~!** Anspiel!; **to ~ in defence** in der Abwehr spielen; **to ~ in goal** im Tor stehen; **he's just ~ing at it** er tut nur so; **what are you ~ing at?** (*inf*) was soll (denn) das? (*inf*); **to ~ for money** um Geld spielen; **to ~ for time** (*fig*) Zeit gewinnen wollen; **to ~ into sb's hands** (*fig*) jdm in die Hände spielen; **to ~ to one's strengths** seine Stärken ausspielen

c (*Mus*) spielen; **to ~ to sb** jdm vorspielen

d (= *move about, form patterns*) (*sun, light, water*) spielen; (*fountain*) tanzen; **a smile ~ed on his lips** ein Lächeln spielte um seine Lippen; **the firemen's hoses ~ed on the flames** die Schläuche der Feuerwehrmänner waren auf die Flammen gerichtet; **the searchlights ~ed over the roofs** die Suchscheinwerfer strichen über die Dächer

e (*Theat*) (= *act*) spielen; (= *be performed*) gespielt werden

f (*Sport: ground, pitch*) sich bespielen lassen; **the pitch ~s well/badly** auf dem Platz spielt es sich gut/schlecht

▸ **play about** (*Brit*) *or* **around** VI spielen; **I wish he'd stop playing around and settle down to a steady job** ich wollte, er würde mit dem ständigen Hin und Her aufhören und sich eine feste Arbeit suchen; **to play around with sth** mit etw (herum)spielen; **to play about** *or* **around with an idea** mit einer Idee spielen; **to play around with sb's/sb's feelings** mit jdm/mit jds Gefühlen spielen; **he's been playing around (with another woman)** er hat mit einer anderen Frau herumgemacht (*inf*)

▸ **play along** VI mitspielen; **he played along with the system** er arrangierte sich mit dem System; **to play along with a suggestion** auf einen Vorschlag eingehen; (= *pretend*) auf einen Vorschlag scheinbar eingehen; **to play along with sb** jdm zustimmen VT always separate hinters Licht führen, ein falsches Spiel spielen mit; (*in order to gain time*) hinhalten

▸ **play back** VT sep tape recording abspielen; **the conversation was played back to us** man spielte uns (*dat*) das Gespräch vor

▸ **play down** VT sep herunterspielen

▸ **play in** VT sep (= *with music*) musikalisch begrüßen

▸ **play off** VT sep **to play X off against Y** X gegen Y ausspielen; **he was playing them off against each other** er spielte sie gegeneinander aus VI (*Sport*) um die Entscheidung spielen

▸ **play on** VI weiterspielen VI +prep obj (*also* **play upon**) (= *exploit*) *sb's fears, feelings, good nature* geschickt ausnutzen; (= *emphasize*) *difficulties, similarities* herausstreichen; **the hours of waiting played on my nerves** das stundenlange Warten zermürbte mich; **the author is playing on words** der Autor macht Wortspiele/ein Wortspiel

▸ **play out** VT sep **a** (*Theat*) *scene* (= *enact*) darstellen; (= *finish acting*) zu Ende spielen (*also fig*); **their romance was played out against a background of civil war** ihre Romanze spielte sich vor dem Hintergrund des Bürgerkrieges ab

b (*esp pass*: = *use up*) *mine* ausbeuten; **to play out (the) time** die Zeit herumbringen; (*Sport also*) auf Zeit spielen, Zeit schinden (*pej*); **a played-out joke** (*inf*) ein abgedroschener Witz; **a played-out theory** (*inf*) eine überstrapazierte Theorie; **I was completely played out after the game** (*inf*) nach dem Spiel war ich völlig geschafft (*inf*)

c (*Mus*) mit Musik hinausgeleiten; **the organ played them out** das Spiel der Orgel geleitete sie hinaus

▸ **play through** VI +prep obj *a few bars etc* durchspielen

▸ **play up** VI **a** (= *play louder*) lauter spielen

b (*Sport inf*: = *play better*) aufdrehen (*inf*), (*richtig*) loslegen (*inf*); **play up!** vor!, ran! **c** (*Brit inf*: = *cause trouble: car, injury, child*) Schwierigkeiten machen, verrückt spielen (*inf*) **d** (*inf*, *flatter*) **to play up to sb** jdn umschmeicheln VT sep (*inf*) **a** (= *cause trouble to*) **to play sb up** jdm Schwierigkeiten machen; (*child, injury also*) jdn piesacken (*inf*) **b** (= *exaggerate*) hochspielen

▸ **play upon** VI +prep obj = **play on** VI +prep obj

▸ **play with** VI +prep obj **to play with the idea of doing sth** mit dem Gedanken spielen, etw zu tun; **we don't have much time/money to play with** wir haben zeitlich/finanziell nicht viel Spielraum; **we don't have that many alternatives to play with** so viele Alternativen haben wir nicht zur Verfügung; **to play with oneself** an sich (*dat*) herumfummeln

playa ['plaɪə] N (*Geol*) Playa *f*, Salztonebene *f*

playable ['pleɪəbl] ADJ *pitch* bespielbar; *ball* zu spielen *pred*

play: play-act VI (*dated Theat*) schauspielern; (*fig also*) Theater spielen; **play-acting** N (*dated Theat*) Schauspielerei *f*; (*fig also*) Theater(spiel) *nt*; **play-actor** N (*dated Theat*) Mime *m* (*old, geh*), Mimin *f* (*old, geh*), Schauspieler(in) *m(f)* (*also fig*); **playback** N (= *switch, recording*) Wiedergabe *f*; (= *playing-back also*) Abspielen *nt*; **the producer asked for a ~** der Produzent bat um eine Wiedergabe *or* ein Playback; **they listened to the ~ of their conversation** sie hörten sich (*dat*) die Aufnahme ihres Gespräches an; **playbill** N (= *poster*) Theaterplakat *nt*; (*US*: = *programme*) Theaterprogramm *nt*

play: playboy N Playboy *m*; **playclothes** PL (*US*) Sport-/Freizeitkleidung *f*

player ['pleɪə'] N (*Sport, Mus*) Spieler(in) *m(f)*; (*Theat*) Schauspieler(in) *m(f)*; **one of the main** *or* **major ~s in ...** (*fig*) einer der Hauptakteure in ... (+*dat*)

player piano N automatisches Klavier

playfellow ['pleɪfɛləʊ] N (*Brit*) Spielkamerad(in) *m(f)*

playful ['pleɪfʊl] ADJ neckisch; *remark, smile, look also* schelmisch; *child, animal* verspielt, munter; **the dog is in a ~ mood/just being ~** der Hund will spielen/spielt nur; **the boss is in a ~ mood today** der Chef ist heute zu Späßen aufgelegt; **to do sth in a ~ way** etw zum Scherz *or* aus Spaß tun; **she gave Philip's hand a ~ squeeze** sie drückte spielerisch Philips Hand; **in a ~ tone** in einem spielerischen Ton

playfully ['pleɪfəlɪ] ADV neckisch; *remark, smile, look also* schelmisch; **to do/say sth ~** etw zum Scherz tun/sagen; **he grasped her wrist ~** er ergriff spielerisch ihr Handgelenk

playfulness ['pleɪfʊlnɪs] N (*of child, animal*) Verspieltheit *f*; (*of adult*) Ausgelassenheit *f*, Lustigkeit *f*; **there was a touch of ~ in his manner as he replied** in der Art, wie er antwortete, lag etwas leicht Neckisches *or* Schelmisches

play: playgoer N Theaterbesucher(in) *m(f)*; **playground** N Spielplatz *m*; (*Sch*) (Schul)hof *m*; (*fig*) Tummelplatz *m*, Spielwiese *f*; **playgroup** N Spielgruppe *f*; **playhouse** N **a** (= *children's house*) Spielhaus *nt*; (*US*: = *doll's house*) Puppenstube *f* **b** (*Theat*) Schaubühne *f* (*dated*), Schauspielhaus *nt*

playing ['pleɪɪŋ]: **playing card** N Spielkarte *f*; **playing field** N Sportplatz *m*; **the school ~s** der Schulsportplatz; **playing method** N (*Sport*) Spielweise *f*; **playing time** N (*Sport*) Spielzeit *f*

playlet ['pleɪlɪt] N Spiel *nt*, Stück *nt*

play: playlist N (*Rad*) CDs, Platten etc, die von einem Radiosender gespielt werden **artists who don't often make it on to the ~s of radio stations** Künstler, die nicht oft im Radio gespielt werden; **playmaker** N (*Sport*) Spielmacher(in) *m(f)*; **playmate** N Spielkamerad(in) *m(f)*; **play-off** N Entscheidungsspiel *nt*; (= *extra time*) Verlängerung *f*; **play park** N Spielplatz *m*; **playpen** N Laufstall *m*, Laufgit-

ter *nt*; **playroom** N Spielzimmer *nt*; **playschool** N (*esp Brit*) Kindergarten *m*; **playsuit** N Kombination *f* mit kurzer Hose, Spielanzug *m*; **plaything** N (*lit, fig*) Spielzeug *nt*; **playtime** N Zeit *f* zum Spielen; (*Sch*) große Pause; **playwear** N (*US*) Sport-/Freizeitkleidung *f*

playwright ['pleɪraɪt] N Dramatiker(in) *m(f)*; (*contemporary also*) Stückeschreiber(in) *m(f)*

plaza ['plɑːzə] N Piazza *f*; (*US*: = *shopping complex*) Einkaufszentrum *or* -center *nt*

plc (*Brit*) abbr of **public limited company** ≈ AG *f*

plea [pli:] N **a** Bitte *f*; (= *general appeal*) Appell *m*; **to make a ~ for sth** zu etw aufrufen; **to make a ~ for mercy/leniency** um Gnade/ Milde bitten **b** (= *excuse*) Begründung *f*; **on the ~ of illness/ill health** aus Krankheitsgründen/gesundheitlichen Gründen **c** (*Jur*) Plädoyer *nt*; **to enter a ~ of guilty** sich schuldig bekennen; **to enter a ~ of not guilty** seine Unschuld erklären; **to enter a ~ of insanity** auf Zurechnungsunfähigkeit plädieren; **he put forward** *or* **he made a ~ of self-defence** er machte Notwehr geltend, er berief sich auf Notwehr

plea: plea bargain, plea agreement N *Verhandlung zwischen der Anklagevertretung und dem Verteidiger, um eine mildere Strafe zu erwirken, indem sich der Angeklagte für schuldig erklärt*; **plea-bargain** VI *verhandeln zwischen der Anklagevertretung und dem Verteidiger, um eine mildere Strafe zu erwirken, indem sich der Angeklagte für schuldig erklärt*; **plea bargaining** N = **plea bargain**

plead [pli:d] pret, ptp **pleaded** *or* (*Scot, US*) **pled** VT **a** (= *argue*) vertreten; **to ~ sb's case** (*Jur*) **to ~ the case for sb** (*Jur*) jdn vertreten; **to ~ the case for the defence** (*Jur*) die Verteidigung vertreten; **to ~ the case for sth** (*fig*) sich für etw einsetzen; **to ~ sb's cause** (*fig*) jds Sache vertreten, für jds Sache eintreten

b (*as excuse*) *ignorance, insanity* sich berufen auf (+*acc*)

VI **a** (= *beg*) bitten, nachsuchen (*for* um); **to ~ with sb to do sth** jdn bitten *or* ersuchen (*geh*), etw zu tun; **to ~ with sb for sth** (= *beg*) jdn um etw bitten *or* ersuchen (*geh*)

b (*Jur, counsel*) das Plädoyer halten; **to ~ guilty/not guilty** sich schuldig/nicht schuldig bekennen; **how do you ~?** bekennen Sie sich schuldig?; **to ~ for sth** (*fig*) für etw plädieren

pleading ['pli:dɪŋ] N Bitten *nt*; (*Jur*) Plädoyer *nt* ADJ *look, voice* flehend

pleadingly ['pli:dɪŋlɪ] ADV flehend

pleasant ['plɛznt] ADJ *aroma, taste* angenehm; *surprise also, news* erfreulich; *person also, face* nett; *manner also, smile* freundlich; *building* gefällig; **to make oneself ~ to sb** jdn ein wenig unterhalten

pleasantly ['plɛzntlɪ] ADV angenehm; *smile, greet, speak etc* freundlich; **~ decorated** nett *or* hübsch eingerichtet; **the room is ~ light and airy** das Zimmer ist angenehm hell und luftig; **to be ~ surprised** angenehm überrascht sein

pleasantness ['plɛzntnɪs] N Freundlichkeit *f*; (*of news, surprise*) Erfreulichkeit *f*; **the ~ of her manner** ihre freundliche Art; **the ~ of her face** ihr nettes Gesicht

pleasantry ['plɛzntrɪ] N (*joking remark*) Scherz *m*; (*polite remark*) Höflichkeit *f*, Nettigkeit *f*

pleasa(u)nce ['plɛzəns] N (*old*) Lustgarten *m* (*old*)

please [pli:z] ✪ 4 INTERJ bitte; (*yes,*) **~** (*acceptance*) (ja,) bitte; (*enthusiastic*) oh ja, gerne; **~ pass the salt, pass the salt, ~** würden Sie mir bitte das Salz reichen?; **may I? – ~ do!** darf ich? – bitte sehr!

VI **a** if you **~** (*form, in request*) wenn ich darum bitten darf; **do it now, if you ~** (*angrily*) aber sofort, wenn es recht ist *or* wenn ich bitten darf!; **and then, if you ~, he tried ...** und dann, stell dir vor, versuchte er ...; (*just*) **as you ~** ganz wie du willst, wie es Ihnen beliebt (*form*); **bold as you ~, he entered the room** frech wie Oskar kam er ins Zimmer (*inf*); **to do as one ~s** machen *or* tun, was man will, machen *or* tun, was einem gefällt

b (= *cause satisfaction*) gefallen; **eager to ~** darum bemüht, alles richtig zu machen; (*servant*) darum bemüht, jeden Wunsch zu erfüllen; **a gift that is sure to ~** ein Geschenk, das sicher gefällt; **we aim to ~** wir wollen, dass Sie zufrieden sind

VT **a** (= *give pleasure to*) eine Freude machen (+*dat*); (= *satisfy*) zufrieden stellen; (= *do as sb wants*) gefallen (+*dat*), gefällig sein (+*dat*); **the gift/idea ~d him** das Geschenk/die Idee hat ihm gefallen; **just to ~** you nur dir zuliebe; **it ~s me to see him so happy** es freut mich, dass er so glücklich ist; **well do it then if it ~s you** tus doch, wenn es dir Spaß macht; **you can't ~ everybody** man kann es nicht allen recht machen; **there's no pleasing him** er ist nie zufrieden; **he is easily ~d** *or* **easy to ~** er ist leicht zufrieden zu stellen; (*iro*) er ist eben ein bescheidener Mensch; **to be hard to ~** schwer zufrieden zu stellen sein → **pleased**

b (*iro, form*: = *be the will of*) belieben (+*dat*) (*iro, form*); **it ~d him to order that ...** er beliebte anzuordnen, dass ... (*form*); **may it ~ Your Honour** (*Jur*) mit Erlaubnis des Herrn Vorsitzenden; **if it ~s God** wenn es Gott gefällt; **~ God he will recover** gebe Gott, dass er wieder gesund wird; **he will return safely, ~ God!** er wird wohlbehalten zurückkehren, das gebe Gott!

VR **to ~ oneself** tun, was einem gefällt; **~ yourself!** wie Sie wollen!; **you can ~ yourself about where you sit** es ist Ihnen überlassen, wo Sie sitzen; **he has only himself to ~** er braucht auf keinen Menschen irgendwelche Rücksichten zu nehmen

N Bitte *nt*; **without so much as a ~** ohne auch nur, bitte zu sagen

pleased [pliːzd] ✪ 9.2, 19.3, 20.2, 25.2 ADJ (= *happy*) *expression* freudig; (= *satisfied*) zufrieden; **to be ~ (about sth)** sich (über etw *acc*) freuen; **I'm ~ to hear that ...** es freut mich zu hören, dass ...; **~ to meet you or make your acquaintance** angenehm (*form*), freut mich; **I'm ~ to be able to announce that ...** ich freue mich, mitteilen zu können, dass ...; **we are ~ to inform you that ...** wir freuen uns, Ihnen mitteilen zu können, dass ...; **to be ~ at sth** über etw (*acc*) erfreut sein; **to be ~ with sb/sth** mit jdm/etw zufrieden sein; **~ with oneself** mit sich selbst zufrieden, selbstgefällig (*pej*); **that's nothing to be ~ about** das ist aber gar nicht gut; **I was only too ~ to help** es war mir wirklich eine Freude zu helfen; **they will be only too ~ to let someone else take the risk** es wird ihnen nur zu recht sein, jemand anders das Risiko tragen zu lassen

pleasing [ˈpliːzɪŋ] ADJ angenehm; *sight* erfreulich; **to be ~ to the eye** ein netter Anblick sein; **to be ~ to the ear** sich angenehm anhören

pleasingly [ˈpliːzɪŋlɪ] ADV angenehm; **a ~ laid-out garden** ein hübsch angelegter Garten

pleasurable [ˈplɛʒərəbl] ADJ angenehm; *anticipation* freudig

pleasurably [ˈplɛʒərəblɪ] ADV freudig, angenehm; **he had often ~ anticipated this moment** er hatte oft voller Vorfreude diesem Augenblick entgegengesehen

pleasure [ˈplɛʒə] ✪ 3.2 N **a** (= *satisfaction, happiness*) Freude *f*; **it's a ~, (my) ~** gern (geschehen)!; **with ~** sehr gerne, mit Vergnügen (*form*); **the ~ is all mine** (*form*) das Vergnügen ist ganz meinerseits (*form*); **it's my very great ~ ...** es ist mir ein großes Vergnügen, ...; **it gives me great ~ to be here** (*form*) es ist mir eine große Freude, hier zu sein; **it would give me great ~ to ...** es wäre mir ein Vergnügen, zu ...; **if it gives you ~** wenn es dir Vergnügen bereitet; **I have much ~ in informing you that ...** ich freue mich (sehr), Ihnen mitteilen zu können, dass ...; **to have the ~ of doing sth** das Vergnügen haben, etw zu tun; **to do sth for ~** etw zum Vergnügen tun; **he finds ~ in books** er hat

Freude an Büchern; **he gets a lot of ~ out of his hobby** er hat viel Freude *or* Spaß an seinem Hobby; **to get ~ from** *or* **out of doing sth** Spaß daran haben, etw zu tun; **he seems to take ~ in annoying me** es scheint ihm Vergnügen zu bereiten, mich zu ärgern; **but don't think I'll take ~ in it** aber glaub nicht, dass mir das Spaß macht; **may I have the ~?** (*form*) darf ich (um den nächsten Tanz) bitten? (*form*); **will you do me the ~ of dining with me?** (*form*) machen Sie mir das Vergnügen, mit mir zu speisen? (*form*); **Mrs X requests the ~ of Mr Y's company** (*form*) Frau X gibt sich die Ehre, Herrn Y einzuladen (*form*); **Mr Y has great ~ in accepting ...** (*form*) Herr Y nimmt ... mit dem größten Vergnügen an (*form*)

b (= *amusement*) Vergnügen *nt*; **is it business or ~?** (ist es) geschäftlich oder zum Vergnügen?

c (= *source of pleasure*) Vergnügen *nt*; **it's a ~ to meet you** es freut mich, Sie kennenzulernen; **it's a ~ to work with him** es ist ein Vergnügen, mit ihm zusammenzuarbeiten; **he's a ~ to teach** es ist ein Vergnügen, ihn zu unterrichten; **the ~s of country life** die Freuden des Landlebens; **all the ~s of London** alle Vergnügungen Londons; **she has very few ~s in life** sie hat viel Freuden im Leben

d (*iro, form*: = *will*) Wunsch *m*; **at (one's) ~** nach Belieben, nach Gutdünken; **to await sb's ~** abwarten, was jd zu tun geruht; **during Her Majesty's ~** (*Jur*) auf unbestimmte Zeit

pleasure *in cpds* Vergnügungs-; **pleasure boat** N **a** Vergnügungsdampfer *m or* -schiff *nt*, Ausflugsdampfer *m or* -schiff *nt* **b** (= *yacht etc*) Hobbyboot *nt*; **pleasure craft** N Hobbyboot *nt*; **pleasure cruise** N Vergnügungsfahrt *f*, Kreuzfahrt *f*; **pleasure ground** N Parkanlage *f*; (= *fairground*) Vergnügungspark *m*; **pleasure-loving** ADJ lebenslustig, leichtlebig (*pej*); **pleasure principle** N (*Psych*) Lustprinzip *nt*; **pleasure-seeker** N Vergnügungshungrige(r) *mf*; **pleasure-seeking** ADJ vergnügungshungrig; **pleasure trip** N Vergnügungsausflug *m or* -reise *f*

pleat [pliːt] N Falte *f* **VT** fälteln

pleated [ˈpliːtɪd] ADJ gefältelt, Falten-; **~ skirt** Faltenrock *m*

pleb [plɛb] N (*Brit pej inf*) Plebejer(in) *m(f)* (*pej*), Prolet(in) *m(f)* (*pej inf*); **the ~s** die Proleten *pl* (*pej inf*), der Plebs (*pej*)

plebby [ˈplɛbɪ] ADJ (*pej inf*) primitiv

plebeian [plɪˈbiːən] ADJ plebejisch N Plebejer(in) *m(f)*

plebiscite [ˈplɛbɪsɪt] N Plebiszit *nt*, Volksentscheid *m*

plectrum [ˈplɛktrəm] N Plektron *nt*, Plektrum *nt*

pled [plɛd] (*US, Scot*) *pret, ptp of* **plead**

pledge [plɛdʒ] N **a** (*in pawnshop, of love*) Pfand *nt*; (= *promise*) Versprechen *nt*, Zusicherung *f*; **I give you my ~** ich gebe dir mein Wort; **we have given them a ~ of aid** wir haben versprochen, ihnen zu helfen; **as a ~ of** als Zeichen (+*gen*); **under (the) ~ of secrecy** unter dem Siegel der Verschwiegenheit; **election ~s** Wahlversprechen *pl*; **to sign or take the ~** (= *lit*) schriftlich zur Abstinenz verpflichten; (*hum inf*) dem Alkohol abschwören (*usu hum*)

b (*form*: = *toast*) Toast *m*, Trinkspruch *m*; **to drink a ~ to sb/sth** einen Toast *etc* auf jdn/etw ausbringen

VT **a** (= *give as security, pawn*) verpfänden

b (= *promise*) versprechen, zusichern; **to ~ one's word** sein Wort geben *or* verpfänden; **to ~ support for sb/sth** jdm/einer Sache seine Unterstützung zusichern; **I am ~d to secrecy** ich bin zum Schweigen verpflichtet; **~ me to secrecy** verpflichtete mich zum Schweigen; **to ~ (one's) allegiance to sb/sth** jdm/einer Sache Treue schwören *or* geloben

c (*form*: = *toast*) einen Trinkspruch ausbringen auf (+*acc*)

VR **to ~ oneself to do sth** geloben *or* sich verpflichten, etw zu tun

---

PLEDGE OF ALLEGIANCE

Die **Pledge of Allegiance**, ursprünglich 1892 geschrieben, wird jeden Tag von amerikanischen Schulkindern, besonders in der Grundschule, aufgesagt. Sie stellen sich dazu vor der amerikanischen Flagge auf, legen die rechte Hand aufs Herz und sprechen die folgenden Worte: „I pledge allegiance to the flag of the United States of America and to the Republic for which it stands, one nation under God, indivisible, with liberty and justice for all." Besonders die Traditionalisten halten an diesem Brauch fest, den sie als einen Kernpunkt des amerikanischen Patriotismus ansehen.

Pleiades [ˈplaɪədiːz] PL Plejaden *pl*

Pleistocene [ˈplaɪstəsiːn] N Pleistozän *nt* ADJ pleistozän, Pleistozän-; **~ period** Pleistozänzeit *f*

plenary [ˈpliːnərɪ] ADJ Plenar-, Voll-; **~ session** Plenarsitzung *f*, Vollversammlung *f*; **~ powers** unbeschränkte Vollmachten *pl*

plenipotentiary [ˌplenɪpəˈtenʃərɪ] N (General)bevollmächtigte(r) *mf* ADJ *ambassador* (general)bevollmächtigt; **~ powers** Generalvollmachten *pl*

plenitude [ˈplenɪtjuːd] N (*liter*) Fülle *f*

plenteous [ˈplentɪəs] ADJ (*liter*) = **plentiful**

plentiful [ˈplentɪfʊl] ADJ reichlich; *commodities, gold, minerals etc* reichlich *or* im Überfluss vorhanden; *hair* voll; **to be in ~ supply** reichlich *or* im Überfluss vorhanden sein

plentifully [ˈplentɪfəlɪ] ADV reichlich

plenty [ˈplentɪ] N **a** eine Menge; **land of ~** Land des Überflusses; **times of ~** Zeiten *pl* des Überflusses, fette Jahre *pl* (*Bibl*); **in ~** im Überfluss; **three kilos will be ~** drei Kilo sind reichlich; **there's ~ here for six** es gibt mehr als genug für sechs; **that's ~, thanks!** danke, das ist reichlich; **you've already had ~** du hast schon reichlich gehabt; **I met him once, and that was ~!** ich habe ihn nur einmal getroffen und das hat mir gereicht!; **to see ~ of sb** jdn oft sehen; **there had been ~ going on** es war einiges los gewesen; **there's ~ to do** es gibt viel zu tun; **I've got ~ to do** ich habe viel zu tun; **have I got problems? I've got ~** ob ich Probleme habe? mehr als genug!; **there's ~ more where that came from** davon gibt es genug; **take ~** nimm dir *or* bedien dich reichlich; **there are still ~ left** es sind immer noch eine ganze Menge da

b **~ of** viel, eine Menge; **~ of time/milk** Zeit/Milch, eine Menge Zeit/Milch; **~ of eggs/reasons** viele Eier/Gründe, eine Menge Eier/Gründe; **there is no longer ~ of oil** Öl ist nicht mehr im Überfluss vorhanden; **he's certainly got ~ of nerve** der hat vielleicht Nerven! (*inf*); **a country with ~ of natural resources** ein Land mit umfangreichen Bodenschätzen; **has everyone got ~ of potatoes?** hat jeder reichlich Kartoffeln?; **there will be ~ of things to drink** es gibt dort ausreichend zu trinken; **he had been given ~ of warning** er ist genügend oft gewarnt worden; **we arrived in ~ of time to get a good seat** wir kamen so rechtzeitig, dass wir einen guten Platz kriegten; **don't worry, there's ~ of time** keine Angst, es ist noch genug *or* viel Zeit; **take ~ of exercise** Sie müssen viel Sport treiben

ADJ (*US, inf*) reichlich; **~ bananas** reichlich Bananen

ADV (*esp US, inf*) **~ big (enough)** groß genug; **he's ~ mean** er ist ziemlich brutal; **he was ~ rude to her** er war zu ihr ziemlich grob zu ihr; **it rained ~** es hat viel geregnet; **sure, I like it ~** sicher, ich mag das sehr

plenum [ˈpliːnəm] N Plenum *nt*, Vollversammlung *f*

pleonasm [ˈpliːənæzəm] N Pleonasmus *m*

pleonastic [ˌpliːəˈnæstɪk] ADJ pleonastisch

plethora [ˈpleθərə] N (*form*) Fülle *f*

pleurisy ['plʊərɪsɪ] N Brustfellentzündung *f*, Pleuritis *f* (*spec*)

plexus ['pleksəs] N Plexus *m*; (*of nerves also*) Nervengeflecht *nt*; (*of blood vessels also*) Gefäßgeflecht *nt*

pliability [ˌplaɪə'bɪlɪtɪ] N Biegsamkeit *f*; (*of leather*) Geschmeidigkeit *f*; (*of character, mind, person*) Formbarkeit *f*; (= *docility*) Fügsamkeit *f*

pliable ['plaɪəbl], **pliant** ['plaɪənt] ADJ biegsam; *leather* geschmeidig; *character, mind, person* formbar; (= *docile*) fügsam

plied [plaɪd] *pret, ptp of* **ply**²

pliers ['plaɪəz] PL (*also* **pair of pliers**) (Kombi)zange *f*

plight¹ [plaɪt] VT (*liter*) **to ~ one's word** sein (Ehren)wort geben; **to ~ one's troth (to sb)** (*old, hum*) (jdm) die Ehe versprechen

plight² N Not *f*, Elend *nt*; (*of currency, economy etc*) Verfall *m*; **to be in a sorry ~** in einem traurigen Zustand sein; **the country's economic ~** die wirtschaftliche Misere des Landes

plimsole ['plɪmsəl], **plimsoll** ['plɪmsəl] N (*Brit*) Turnschuh *m*

Plimsoll line, Plimsoll mark N Höchstlademarke *f*

plinth [plɪnθ] N Sockel *m*, Fußplatte *f*, Plinthe *f* (*spec*)

Pliocene ['plaɪəʊsiːn] N Pliozän *nt* ADJ pliozän

PLO *abbr of* **Palestine Liberation Organization** PLO *f*

plod [plɒd] N Trott *m*, Zockeltrab *m* (*inf*); **a steady ~** ein gleichmäßiger Trott VI **a** (= *trudge*) trotten, zockeln (*inf*); **to ~ up a hill** einen Hügel hinaufstapfen; **to ~ along** *or* **on** weiterstapfen; **to ~ in/out** herein-/hinausstapfen **b** (*fig: in work etc*) sich abmühen *or* abplagen *or* herumquälen; **to ~ away at sth** sich mit etw abmühen *etc*; **to ~ on** sich weiterkämpfen, sich durchkämpfen; **I've already ~ded through 200 pages of this document** ich habe mich schon durch 200 Seiten dieses Dokuments gekämpft

plodder ['plɒdə] N zäher Arbeiter, zähe Arbeiterin

plodding ['plɒdɪŋ] ADJ *walk* schwerfällig, mühsam; *student, worker* hart arbeitend *attr*; *research* langwierig, mühsam

plonk¹ [plɒŋk] N (= *noise*) Bums *m* ADV *fall, land* bums, peng; **~ in the middle** genau in die/in der Mitte VT (*inf: also* **plonk down**) (= *drop, put down*) hinwerfen, hinschmeißen (*inf*); (= *bang down*) hinknallen (*inf*), hinhauen (*inf*); **to ~ oneself (down)** sich hinwerfen, sich hinpflanzen (*inf*); **he ~ed himself down in a chair** er warf sich in einen Sessel, er ließ sich in einen Sessel fallen; **just ~ yourself down somewhere** hau dich einfach irgendwo hin (*inf*)

plonk² N (*Brit inf:* = *wine*) (billiger) Wein, Gesöff *nt* (*hum, pej*)

plonker ['plɒŋkə] N (*Brit inf*) **a** (= *stupid person*) Niete *f* **b** (= *penis*) Pimmel *m* (*inf*)

plook [pluːk] N (*Scot inf:* = *pimple, zit*) Pickel *m*

plop [plɒp] N Plumps *m*; (*in water*) Platsch *m* ADV **it fell** *or* **went ~ into the water** es fiel mit einem Platsch ins Wasser VI **a** (= *make a plopping sound*) platschen **b** (*inf:* = *fall*) plumpsen (*inf*) VT (*inf:* = *put down*) hinlegen

plosive ['pləʊsɪv] ADJ Verschluss-, explosiv; **~ sound** Verschlusslaut *m*, Verschlusslaut *m*, Explosivlaut *m*, Explosivum *nt* (*spec*)

plot [plɒt] N **a** (*Agr*) Stück *nt* Land; (= *bed: in garden*) Beet *nt*; (= *building plot*) Grundstück *nt*; (= *allotment*) Parzelle *f*; (*in graveyard*) Grabstelle *f*; **a ~ of land** ein Stück Land; **a ~ of lettuces** ein Salatbeet *nt*; (*larger*) ein Salatfeld *nt* **b** (*US:* = *diagram, chart, of estate*) Plan *m*; (*of building*) Grundriss *m* **c** (= *conspiracy*) Verschwörung *f*, Komplott *nt* → **thicken VI b** **d** (*Liter, Theat*) Handlung *f*, Plot *m* (*spec*); **to lose the ~** (*fig inf*) den Faden verlieren VT **a** (= *plan*) planen, aushecken (*inf*); **what are you ~ting now?** was heckst du nun schon

wieder aus? (*inf*); **they ~ted to kill him** sie planten gemeinsam, ihn zu töten **b** *position, course* feststellen; (= *draw on map*) einzeichnen; (*Math, Med*) *curve* aufzeichnen VI sich verschwören; **to ~ against sb** sich gegen jdn verschwören, gegen jdn ein Komplott schmieden

plotless ['plɒtlɪs] ADJ handlungslos, ohne Handlung; **the film is riveting but almost ~** der Film ist faszinierend, hat aber fast keine Handlung

plotter¹ ['plɒtə] N Verschwörer(in) *m(f)*

plotter² N (*Comput*) Plotter *m*

plotting ['plɒtɪŋ] N Verschwörertum *nt*

plotting board, plotting table N Zeichentisch *m*

plough, (*US*) **plow** [plaʊ] N Pflug *m*; **the Plough** (*Astron*) der Wagen; **under the ~** unter dem Pflug; **to put one's hand to the ~** (*fig*) sich in die Riemen legen VT **a** (*Agr*) pflügen, umpflügen; *furrow* ziehen; **to ~ a lonely furrow** (*fig*) allein auf weiter Flur stehen **b** (*Brit Univ dated sl*) reinreißen (*inf*), durchfallen lassen VI **a** pflügen **b** (*Brit Univ dated sl*) durchrasseln (*inf*)

▶ **plough back** VT *sep* (*Agr*) unterpflügen; (*Comm*) *profits* wieder (hinein)stecken, reinvestieren (*into* in +*acc*)

▶ **plough in** VT *sep manure, crop etc* unterpflügen

▶ **plough into** VI +*prep obj car etc* hineinrasen in (+*acc*) VT SEP *money* reinstecken in (+*acc*) (*inf*)

▶ **plough through** VI +*prep obj* **a** **the ship ploughed through the heavy seas** das Schiff pflügte sich durch die schwere See; **we had to plough through the snow** wir mussten uns durch den Schnee kämpfen; **the car ploughed straight through our garden fence** der Wagen brach geradewegs durch unseren Gartenzaun **b** (*inf*) **to plough through a novel** *etc* sich durch einen Roman *etc* durchackern (*inf*) *or* hindurchquälen VT *sep* **a** **the ship ploughed its way through the waves** das Schiff pflügte sich durch die Wellen; **we ploughed our way through the long grass** wir bahnten uns unseren Weg durch das hohe Gras **b** (*inf*) **to plough one's way through a novel** *etc* sich durch einen Roman *etc* durchackern (*inf*)

▶ **plough up** VT *sep field* umpflügen; (= *uncover*) beim Pflügen zutage *or* zu Tage bringen; (= *uproot*) *tree* roden; **the lorries had completely ploughed up the village green** die Lastwagen hatten den Dorfanger vollkommen zerpflügt; **the train ploughed up the track for 40 metres** der Zug riss 40 Meter Schienen aus ihrer Verankerung

plough, (*US*) **plow: ploughboy** N Pflüger *m*; **ploughhorse** N Ackergaul *m*

ploughing, (*US*) **plowing** ['plaʊɪŋ] N Pflügen *nt*; **the ~ back of profits into the company** die Reinvestierung von Gewinnen in die Firma

plough, (*US*) **plow: ploughland** N Ackerland *nt*; **ploughman** N Pflüger *m*; **ploughman's lunch** N (*Brit*) Käse und Brot als Imbiss; **ploughshare** N Pflugschar *f*; **to turn** *or* **beat swords into ~s** (*fig*) Schwerter zu Pflugscharen machen

plover ['plʌvə] N Regenpfeifer *m*; (= *lapwing*) Kiebitz *m*

plow *etc* (*US*) = **plough** *etc*

ploy [plɔɪ] N (= *stratagem*) Trick *m*

PLP (*Brit*) *abbr of* **Parliamentary Labour Party** Parlamentsfraktion *f* der Labour Partei

pls *abbr of* **please** b.

pluck [plʌk] N **a** (= *courage*) Schneid *m* (*inf*), Mut *m* **b** (*of animal*) Innereien *pl* VT **a** *fruit, flower* pflücken; *chicken* rupfen; *guitar, eyebrows* zupfen; **to ~ (at) sb's sleeve** jdn am Ärmel zupfen; **he ~ed a stray hair off his coat** er zupfte sich (*dat*) ein Haar vom Mantel; **she was ~ed from obscurity to become a film**

star sie wurde von einer Unbekannten zum Filmstar gemacht; **his rescuers had ~ed him from the jaws of death** seine Retter hatten ihn den Klauen des Todes entrissen; **he was ~ed to safety** er wurde in Sicherheit gebracht; **to ~ sth out of the air** etw aus der Luft greifen; **to ~ up (one's) courage** all seinen Mut zusammennehmen **b** (*also* **pluck out**) *hair, feather* auszupfen; **if thy right eye offend thee ~ it out** (*Bibl*) wenn dir dein rechtes Auge zum Ärgernis wird, so reiß es aus VI **to ~ at sth** an etw (*dat*) (herum-)zupfen

plucked instrument ['plʌkt'ɪnstrʊmənt] N (*Mus*) Zupfinstrument *nt*

pluckily ['plʌkɪlɪ] ADV tapfer, mutig

pluckiness ['plʌkɪnɪs] N Unerschrockenheit *f*, Schneid *m* (*inf*)

plucky ['plʌkɪ] ADJ (+*er*) *person* tapfer, mutig; *smile* tapfer; *little pony, action* mutig

plug [plʌg] N **a** (= *stopper*) Stöpsel *m*; (*for stopping a leak*) Propfen *m*; (*in barrel*) Spund *m*; **a ~ of cotton wool** ein Wattebausch *m*; **to pull the ~** (*in lavatory*) die Spülung ziehen; **to pull the ~ on sb/sth** (*fig inf*) jdm/einer Sache den Boden unter den Füßen wegziehen **b** (*Elec*) Stecker *m*; (*incorrect:* = *socket*) Steckdose *f*; (*Aut:* = *spark plug*) (Zünd)kerze *f* **c** (*inf: piece of publicity*) Schleichwerbung *f no pl*; **to give sb/sth a ~** für jdn/etw Werbung machen **d** (*of tobacco*) Scheibe *f*; (*for chewing*) Priem *m* **e** (*Geol*) Vulkanstotzen *m* **f** (*US:* = *fireplug*) Hydrant *m* **g** (*inf:* = *punch*) **to take a ~ at sb** jdm eine verpassen *or* runterhauen (*inf*) VT **a** (= *stop*) *hole, gap, crevice, leak* verstopfen, zustopfen; *barrel* (ver)spunden; *tooth* plombieren; **the doctor ~ged the wound with cotton wool** der Arzt stillte die Blutung mit Watte; **to ~ one's ears** sich (*dat*) die Ohren zuhalten; (*with cotton wool etc*) sich (*dat*) etwas in die Ohren stopfen; **to ~ the gaps in the tax laws** die Lücken im Steuergesetz schließen **b** (= *insert*) stecken; **~ the TV into the socket, please** steck bitte den Stecker vom Fernseher in die Steckdose; **an old rag had been ~ged into the hole** man hatte einen alten Lappen in das Loch gestopft **c** (*inf:* = *publicize*) Schleichwerbung machen für **d** (*inf:* = *push, put forward*) *idea* hausieren gehen mit **e** (*inf:* = *shoot*) **to ~ sb in the head/stomach** *etc* jdm ein Loch in den Kopf/Bauch *etc* schießen; **they ~ged him full of lead** sie pumpten ihn mit Blei voll (*inf*) **f** (*inf:* = *punch*) eine verpassen (+*dat*) (*inf*)

▶ **plug away** VI (*inf*) ackern (*inf*); **to plug away at sth** sich mit etw abrackern *or* herumschlagen (*inf*); **keep plugging away** (nur) nicht lockerlassen

▶ **plug in** VT *sep TV, heater etc* hineinstecken, einstöpseln, anschließen; **to be plugged in** angeschlossen sein VI sich anschließen lassen; **where does the TV plug in?** wo wird der Fernseher angeschlossen?; **plug in, then switch on** schließen Sie das Gerät an und schalten Sie es dann ein

▶ **plug into** VI +*prep obj ideas* aufnehmen

▶ **plug up** VT *sep gap, hole, leak etc* verstopfen, zustopfen; *crack* zuspachteln, verspachteln

plug: plug-and-play ATTR (*Comput*) *technology* Plug-and-Play; **plug hat** N (*old US sl*) Angströhre *f* (*dated hum*); **plughole** N (*Brit*) Abflussloch *nt*, Abfluss *m*; **to go down the ~** (*fig inf*) kaputtgehen (*inf*); **plug tobacco** N Kautabak *m*; **plug-ugly** (*inf*) N Schlägertyp *m* (*inf*), Rabauke *m* (*inf*) ADJ potthässlich (*inf*)

plum [plʌm] N **a** (= *fruit, tree*) Pflaume *f*; (= *Victoria plum, dark blue*) Zwetsch(g)e *f*; **to speak with a ~ in one's mouth** (*Brit*) sprechen, als hätte man eine heiße Kartoffel im Mund **b** (= *colour*) Pflaumenblau *nt* (*fig inf:* = *good job*) **a real ~ (of a job)** ein Bombenjob *m* (*inf*)

ADJ *attr* **a** (*inf*) *job, position* Bomben-(*inf*), Mords-(*inf*) **b** (*colour*) pflaumenblau

plumage ['pluːmɪdʒ] N Gefieder *nt*, Federkleid *nt* (*liter*)

plumb [plʌm] **N** (= *plumbline*) Lot *nt*, Senkblei *nt*; **out of ~** nicht im Lot; **true to ~** (*Tech*) lotrecht

ADV **a** lotrecht, senkrecht

b (*inf*) (= *completely*) total (*inf*), komplett (*inf*); (= *exactly*) genau; **~ in the middle** (haar)genau in der Mitte; **it hit him ~ on the nose** es traf ihn genau *or* mitten auf die Nase

VT **a** *ocean, depth* (aus)loten

b (*fig*) *mystery etc* ergründen; **to ~ the depths of despair** die tiefste Verzweiflung erleben; **this song ~s the depths of bad taste** dieses Lied übertrifft alles bisher da Gewesene *or* Dagewesene an schlechtem Geschmack; **to ~ new depths** einen neuen Tiefstand erreichen; **a look that ~ed his very soul** ein Blick, der in die Tiefen seiner Seele drang

c (= *connect plumbing in*) *building* Klempnerarbeiten ausführen an (+*dat*)

▶ **plumb in** VT *sep* (*Brit*) *washing machine etc* anschließen

plumbago [plʌm'beɪgəʊ] N Graphit *m*, Grafit *m*

plumb bob N Lot *nt*, Senkblei *nt*

plumber ['plʌmə'] N Installateur(in) *m(f)*, Klempner(in) *m(f)*

plumbiferous [plʌm'bɪfərəs] ADJ bleihaltig, Blei führend

plumbing ['plʌmɪŋ] N **a** (= *work*) Installieren *nt*; **he decided to learn ~** er beschloss, Installateur *or* Klempner zu werden; **he does all his own ~** er macht alle Installations- *or* Klempnerarbeiten selbst **b** (= *fittings*) Rohre *pl*, Leitungen *pl*, Installationen *pl*; (= *bathroom fittings*) sanitäre Anlagen *pl*; **to inspect the ~** (*hum*) die Lokalitäten aufsuchen (*hum*)

plumb: plumb line N Lot *nt*, Senkblei *nt*; (*Naut also*) Bleilot *nt*; **plumb rule** N Lotwaage *f*

plum duff [plʌm'dʌf] N Plumpudding *m*

plume [pluːm] N Feder *f*; (*on helmet*) Federbusch *m*; **~ of smoke** Rauchwolke *f*, Rauchfahne *f*; **a ~ of water** eine Wasserfontäne; **in borrowed ~s** mit fremden Federn geschmückt **VR** **a** (*bird*) sich putzen **b** **to ~ oneself on sth** auf etw (*acc*) stolz sein wie ein Pfau

plumed [pluːmd] ADJ *helmet etc* federgeschmückt, mit Federschmuck; **the peacock with its magnificently ~ tail** der Pfau mit seinem prächtigen Schwanzgefieder

plummet ['plʌmɪt] **N** **a** (= *weight*) Senkblei *nt*; (*Fishing*) Grundsenker *m* **b** (= *falling*) (*plane*) Sturz *m*; (*of bird, plane*) Sturzflug *m* **VI** (*bird, plane etc*) hinunterstürzen; (*Econ*) (*sales figures etc*) stark zurückgehen; (*currency, shares etc*) fallen, absacken; **the pound has ~ted to EUR 1.40** das Pfund ist auf EUR 1,40 gefallen *or* abgesackt; **he has ~ted again to the depths of despair** er ist wieder in tiefster Verzweiflung

plummeting ['plʌmɪtɪŋ] ADJ *prices, profits, sales* fallend; *popularity also* schwindend; *temperatures also* abnehmend

plummy ['plʌmɪ] ADJ (+*er*) (*Brit*) **a** (*inf*) *job* Bomben-(*inf*), Mords-(*inf*) **b** *voice* vornehm-sonor

plump [plʌmp] **ADJ** (+*er*) **a** rundlich, mollig, pummelig; *legs etc* stämmig; *face* rundlich, pausbäckig, voll; *chicken etc* gut genährt, fleischig; *fish* fett; *fruit* prall; **~ cheeks** Pausbacken *pl*

b *phrasing, reply* direkt, unverblümt

ADV **to fall ~ onto sth** mit einem Plumps auf etw (*acc*) fallen

VT **a** (= *drop*) fallen lassen; (= *throw*) werfen; (*angrily, noisily*) knallen (*inf*); **to ~ sth down** etw hinfallen lassen/hinwerfen/hinknallen (*inf*); **she ~ed herself down in the armchair** sie ließ sich in den Sessel fallen; **he had ~ed himself in the best chair** er hatte sich im besten Sessel breit gemacht (*inf*)

b (*also* **plump up**) *cushion, pillow* aufschütteln **VI** (= *fall*) fallen; **to ~ down onto a chair** auf einen Stuhl fallen *or* plumpsen (*inf*)

▶ **plump for** VI +*prep obj* sich entscheiden für

▶ **plump out** VI (*person*) (Gewicht) ansetzen

▶ **plump up** VT *sep cushion, pillow* aufschütteln; *chicken* mästen

plumply ['plʌmplɪ] ADV plump

plumpness ['plʌmpnɪs] N Rundlichkeit *f*, Molligkeit *f*, Pummeligkeit *f*; (*of legs etc*) Stämmigkeit *f*; (*of face*) Pausbäckigkeit *f*; (*of chicken*) Wohlgenährtheit *f*; **the ~ of her cheeks** ihre Pausbäckigkeit

plum: plum pudding N Plumpudding *m*; **plum tomato** N italienische Tomate; **plum tree** N Pflaumenbaum *m*; (= *Victoria plum tree*) Zwetsch(g)enbaum *m*

plunder ['plʌndə'] **N** **a** (= *act*) (*of place*) Plünderung *f*; (*of things*) Raub *m* **b** (= *loot*) Beute *f* **VT** *place* plündern; (*also hum*); (*completely*) ausplündern; *people* ausplündern; *thing* rauben **VI** plündern

plunderer ['plʌndərə'] N Plünderer *m*, Plünderin *f*

plundering ['plʌndərɪŋ] N (*of place*) Plünderung *f*, Plündern *nt*; (*of things*) Raub *m*

plunge [plʌndʒ] **VT** **a** (= *thrust*) stecken; (*into water etc*) tauchen; **he ~d the knife into his victim's back** er jagte seinem Opfer das Messer in den Rücken; **to ~ one's hand into sth** seine Hand tief in etw (*acc*) (hinein)stecken; **he ~d his hands into his pockets** er vergrub seine Hände in den Taschen

b (*fig*) **to ~ the country into war/debt** das Land in einen Krieg/in Schulden stürzen; **the room was ~d into darkness** das Zimmer war in Dunkelheit getaucht; **we were ~d into darkness** tiefe Dunkelheit umfing uns; **he was ~d into despair by the news** die Nachricht stürzte ihn in tiefe Verzweiflung

VI **a** (= *dive*) tauchen; (*goalkeeper*) sich werfen, hechten

b (= *rush: esp downward*) stürzen; **to ~ down the stairs** die Treppe hinunterstürzen; **to ~ to one's death** zu Tode stürzen; **he ~d into/through the crowd** er stürzte sich in/wühlte sich durch die Massen; **the road ~d down the hill** die Straße fiel steil ab

c (*share prices, currency etc*) stürzen, stark fallen; **sales have ~d by 24%** die Verkaufszahlen sind um 24% gefallen

d (*fig*) (*into debate, studies, preparations, debt*) sich stürzen (*into* in +*acc*); (*into recession*) stürzen (*into* in +*acc*)

e (= *dip*) (*horse*) bocken; (*ship*) stampfen

f (*neckline*) fallen; **the dress ~s at the back** das Kleid ist hinten tief ausgeschnitten

g (= *speculate rashly*) sich verspekulieren

VR (*into studies, job etc*) sich stürzen (*into* in +*acc*)

N **a** (= *dive*) (Kopf)sprung *m*, Köpper *m* (*inf*); (*of goalkeeper*) Hechtsprung *m*; **he enjoys a quick ~ before breakfast** vor dem Frühstück schwimmt er gern eine Runde; **to take the ~** (*fig inf*) den Sprung wagen

b (= *downward movement*) Sturz *m*

c (*fig: into debt, despair etc, of shares, currency etc*) Sturz *m*; **a downward ~** ein Absturz *m*; **his ~ into debt began when his business collapsed** nach dem Bankrott seines Geschäftes stürzte er in Schulden; **shares took a ~ after the government's announcement** nach der Ankündigung der Regierung kam es zu einem Kurssturz; **a ~ in the value of the pound** ein Kurssturz *m* des Pfunds

d (= *rash investment*) Fehlspekulation *f*

▶ **plunge in** VT *sep knife* hineinjagen; *hand* hineinstecken; (*into water*) hineintauchen; **he was plunged straight in (at the deep end)** (*fig*) er musste gleich richtig ran (*inf*), er musste gleich voll einsteigen (*inf*) **VI** (= *dive*) hineinspringen

plunge pool N Tauchbecken *nt*

plunger ['plʌndʒə'] N **a** (= *piston*) Tauchkolben *m* **b** (*for clearing pipes*) Sauger *m* **c** (= *speculator*) Spekulant(in) *m(f)*

plunging ['plʌndʒɪŋ] ADJ **a** *neckline, back* tief ausgeschnitten; **her deeply ~ neckline** der tiefe Ausschnitt ihres Kleides **b** (= *decreasing*) *cost, currency, prices* stark fallend

plunk¹ [plʌŋk] VT *banjo* zupfen

plunk² N, ADV, VT = **plonk¹**

pluperfect ['pluː'pɜːfɪkt] **N** Vorvergangenheit *f*, Plusquamperfekt *nt* **ADJ** in der Vorvergangenheit, im Plusquamperfekt; **~ tense** Vorvergangenheit *f*, Plusquamperfekt *nt*

plural ['plʊərəl] **ADJ** **a** (*Gram*) Plural-, Mehrzahl-; **~ ending** Plural- *or* Mehrzahlendung *f* **b** (= *diverse, pluralistic*) *society, system* pluralistisch **N** Plural *m*, Mehrzahl *f*; **in the ~** im Plural, in der Mehrzahl

pluralism ['plʊərəlɪzəm] N Pluralismus *m*

pluralist ['plʊərəlɪst] **ADJ** (= *mixed*) *society, system, values* pluralistisch **N** Pluralist(in) *m(f)*

pluralistic [,plʊərə'lɪstɪk] ADJ pluralistisch

plurality [,plʊə'rælɪtɪ] N **a** Vielfalt *f*, Mannigfaltigkeit *f* (*Sociol*) Pluralität *f* **b** (*US, Pol*) (Stimmen)vorsprung *m*

plural voting N Pluralwahlrecht *nt*, Mehrstimmenwahlrecht *nt*

plus [plʌs] **PREP** (= *added to, increased by*) plus (+*dat*); (= *together with*) und (außerdem); **the day's takings were ~ £100** die Tageseinnahmen lagen um £ 100 höher; **~ or minus 10%** plus minus 10%

ADJ **a** (*Math, Elec, fig*) **a ~ figure** eine positive Zahl; **the ~ terminal** der Pluspol; **a ~ factor** ein Pluspunkt *m*; **on the ~ side** auf der Habenseite; **~ 10 degrees** 10 Grad plus *or* über Null

b (= *more than*) **he got B ~ in the exam** ≈ er hat in der Prüfung eine Zwei plus bekommen; **50 pages/hours ~ a week** mehr als *or* über 50 Seiten/Stunden pro Woche; **she has personality ~** sie hat ein gewinnendes Wesen

N (= *sign*) Pluszeichen *nt*; (= *positive factor*) Pluspunkt *m*; (= *extra*) Plus *nt*; **if after all the deductions you still finish up with a ~** wenn dir nach allen Abzügen noch etwas übrig bleibt

plus fours ['plʌs'fɔːz] PL Knickerbocker *pl*

plush [plʌʃ] **N** Plüsch *m* **ADJ** (+*er*) **a** Plüsch-; **~ curtains** Plüschvorhänge *pl* **b** (*inf*: = *luxurious*) feudal (*inf*), elegant, vornehm; **a ~ hotel/restaurant** ein Nobelhotel/-restaurant *nt* (*inf*)

plushly ['plʌʃlɪ] ADV nobel, elegant; **a ~ appointed room in an exclusive club** ein elegant ausgestatteter Raum in einem exklusiven Klub

plushy ['plʌʃɪ] ADJ (+*er*) (*inf*) = **plush** ADJ **b**

plus sign N (*Math, Elec*) Pluszeichen *nt*

Plutarch ['pluːtɑːk] N Plutarch *m*

Pluto ['pluːtəʊ] N (*Myth*) Pluto *m*, Pluton *m*; (*Astron*) Pluto *m*

plutocracy [pluː'tɒkrəsɪ] N Plutokratie *f*

plutocrat ['pluːtəʊkræt] N Plutokrat(in) *m(f)*

plutocratic [,pluːtəʊ'krætɪk] ADJ plutokratisch

plutonium [pluː'təʊnɪəm] N Plutonium *nt*

pluvial ['pluːvɪəl] ADJ (*form*) Regen-; **~ erosion** Erosion *f* durch Regen, Regenerosion *f*

pluviometer [,pluːvɪ'ɒmɪtə'] N Regen- *or* Niederschlagsmesser *m*, Pluviometer *nt*

ply¹ [plaɪ] N **three-ply** (*wood*) dreischichtig; *tissues* dreilagig; **three-ply wool** Dreifachwolle *f*, dreifädige Wolle; **what ~ is this wool?** wievielfach ist diese Wolle?, wie viele Fäden hat diese Wolle?

ply² **VT** **a** (= *work with, use*) *tool, brush etc* gebrauchen, umgehen mit, führen; *needle* einsetzen; (= *work busily with*) *tool, brush etc* fleißig führen *or* umgehen mit; *needle* tanzen lassen (*geh*); *oars* kräftig einsetzen

b (= *work at*) *trade* ausüben, betreiben, nachgehen (+*dat*)

c (*ships*) *sea, river, route* befahren

d **to ~ sb with questions** jdn mit Fragen überhäufen; **to ~ sb with drink(s)** jdn immer wieder zum Trinken auffordern; **she kept her guests well plied with drinks** sie sorgte dafür, dass ihren Gästen die Getränke nicht ausgingen **VI** (*ship*) **to ~ between** verkehren zwischen; **to ~ for hire** seine Dienste anbieten

plywood ['plaɪwʊd] N Sperrholz *nt*

PM (*Brit inf*) *abbr of* **Prime Minister**

pm *abbr of* **post meridiem** p.m.

PMS [piːemˈes] N *abbr of* **pre-menstrual syndrome** PMS *nt*

PMT [piːemˈtiː] N (*Brit*) **a** *abbr of* **pre-menstrual tension** **b** *abbr of* **photomechanical transfer**

pneumatic [njuːˈmætɪk] ADJ **a** Druckluft-; ~ **valve** Druckluftventil *nt* **b** (*inf*) *young lady* vollbusig (*inf*); *breasts* prall

pneumatically [njuːˈmætɪkəlɪ] ADV mit *or* durch Druck- *or* Pressluft; **a ~ operated drill** ein pressluftbetriebener Bohrer

pneumatic: pneumatic brake N Druckluftbremse *f*; **pneumatic drill** N Pressluftbohrer *m*; **pneumatic hammer** N Presslu/thammer *m*; **pneumatic tyre** N Luftreifen *m*

pneumonia [njuːˈməʊnɪə] N Lungenentzündung *f*

PO **a** *abbr of* **post office** PA **b** *abbr of* **postal order**

po [pəʊ] N (*inf*) (Nacht)topf *m*, Pott *m* (*inf*)

POA (*Brit*) *abbr of* **Prison Officers' Association** Verband *m* der Justizvollzugsbeamten

poach[1] [pəʊtʃ] VT *egg* pochieren; *fish* (blau) dünsten; **~ed egg** pochiertes *or* verlorenes Ei; (*in poacher*) ≈ Ei *nt* im Glas

poach[2] **VT** unerlaubt fangen, schwarzfangen (*inf*); (*fig*) *idea* stehlen; *members, customers* abwerben **VI** **a** (*lit*) wildern (*for auf +acc*); **to ~ for salmon** Lachs ohne Berechtigung *or* schwarz (*inf*) fangen **b** (*fig*) **to ~ (on sb's territory)** (*in sport*) jdm ins Gehege *or* in die Quere kommen; (*in work also*) jdm ins Handwerk pfuschen

poacher[1] ['pəʊtʃə'] N Wilderer *m*, Wilderin *f*; (*of game also*) Wilddieb(in) *m(f)*; **it's a case of ~ turned gamekeeper** the new Arsenal manager (*Brit*) der neue Manager von Arsenal ist ein zum Paulus gewordener Saulus

poacher[2] N (*for eggs*) Pochierpfanne *f*

poaching ['pəʊtʃɪŋ] N Wildern *nt*, Wilderei *f*

pock [pɒk] N (= *pustule*) Pocke *f*, Blatter *f*; (= *mark*) Pocken- *or* Blatternarbe *f*

pocket ['pɒkɪt] **N** **a** (*in garment*) Tasche *f*; **take your hands out of your ~s!** nimm die Hände aus der Tasche!; **to have sb/sth in one's ~** (*fig*) jdn/etw in der Tasche haben (*inf*); **to be in sb's ~** (*fig*) jdm hörig sein; **money burns a hole in his ~** er gibt sein Geld immer schnell aus; **to live in each other's** *or* **one another's ~s** (*fig*) unzertrennlich sein **b** (= *receptacle*) (*in suitcase, file etc*) Fach *nt*; (*in book cover, for map etc*) Tasche *f*; (*Baseball*) Tasche *f*; (*Billiards*) Loch *nt* **c** (= *resources*) Geldbeutel *m*; **to be a drain on one's ~** jds Geldbeutel strapazieren (*inf*); **that hit his ~** das hat seinen Geldbeutel ganz schön strapaziert (*inf*); **I was £100 in ~ after the sale** nach dem Verkauf war ich um £ 100 reicher; **to pay for sth out of one's own ~** etw aus der eigenen Tasche bezahlen; **to put one's hand in one's ~** tief in die Tasche greifen; **to have deep ~s** (*fig*) großzügig sein; **investors with deep ~s** (*fig*) großzügige Investoren *pl* → **out-of-pocket** **d** (= *restricted area, space*) Gebiet *nt*; (*smaller*) Einsprengsel *nt*; ~ **of resistance** Widerstandsnest *nt*; ~ **of unemployment** Gebiet *nt* mit hoher Arbeitslosigkeit; **a ~ of infection** Ansteckungsgebiet *nt*; **a ~ of ore** ein Einschluss *m* von Erz **e** (*Aviat*: = *air pocket*) Luftloch *nt* **ADJ** (= *for the pocket*) Taschen-; ~ **diary** Taschenkalender *m*; ~ **dictionary** Taschenwörterbuch *nt* **VT** **a** (= *put in one's pocket*) einstecken; **to ~ one's pride** seinen Stolz überwinden

b (= *gain*) *money, prize, award* kassieren; (= *misappropriate*) einstecken (*inf*), einsacken (*inf*); **the treasurer ~ed the club funds** der Schatzmeister hat die Vereinsgelder in die eigene Tasche gesteckt **c** (*Billiards*) ins Loch bringen, einlochen **d** (*US Pol*) durch Veto aufschieben

pocket: pocket battleship N Westentaschenkreuzer *m*; **pocket billiards** N *sing* **a** (*US*) Poolbillard *nt* **b** (*hum sl*) Taschenbillard (*sl*) *nt*; **pocketbook** N **a** (= *notebook*) Notizbuch *nt* **b** (*esp US*: = *wallet*) Brieftasche *f* **c** (*US*: = *handbag*) Handtasche *f*; **pocket borough** N (*Brit, Hist*) vor 1832 ein Wahlbezirk, der sich praktisch in den Händen einer Person oder Familie befand; **pocket calculator** N Taschenrechner *m*; **pocket camera** N (*Phot*) Pocketkamera *f*

pocketful ['pɒkɪtfʊl] N **a** ~ eine Tasche voll

pocket: pocket handkerchief N Taschentuch *nt*; **a ~(-sized) garden** ein Garten *m* im Westentaschenformat; **pocketknife** N Taschenmesser *nt*; **pocket money** N (*esp Brit*) Taschengeld *nt*; **pocket-size(d)** ADJ *book* im Taschenformat; *person* winzig; *garden* im Westentaschenformat; ~ **camera/TV** Miniaturkamera *f*/-fernseher *m*; **pocket veto** N (*US Pol*) Verzögerung der Gesetzesverabschiedung durch aufschiebendes Veto des Präsidenten

pock: pockmark N Pocken- *or* Blatternarbe *f*; **pockmarked** ADJ *face* pockennarbig; *surface* narbig; **the ~ surface of the moon** die mit Kratern übersäte Oberfläche des Mondes; ~ **with bullet holes** mit Einschüssen übersät

pod [pɒd] **N** (*Bot*) Hülse *f*; (*of peas also*) Schote *f*; (*Aviat*) (*for missiles etc*) Magazin *nt*; (*for jet engine*) Gehäuse *nt* **VT** *peas* enthülsen, auslösen

podgy ['pɒdʒɪ] ADJ (*+er*) (*Brit inf*) rundlich, pummelig; *face* schwammig; ~ **fingers** Wurstfinger *pl*

podiatrist [pɒˈdiːətrɪst] N (*esp US*) Fußspezialist(in) *m(f)*

podiatry [pɒˈdiːətrɪ] N (*esp US*) Lehre *f* von den Fußkrankheiten; (= *treatment*) Fußpflege *f*

podium ['pəʊdɪəm] N Podest *nt*

Podunk ['pəʊdʌŋk] N (*US pej*: = *backwater, boring provincial town*) Krähwinkel *nt* (*pej*)

poem ['pəʊɪm] N Gedicht *nt*; **epic ~** Epos *nt*

poesy ['pəʊɪzɪ] N (*form*: = *poetry*) Lyrik *f*, Poesie *f* (*old*)

poet ['pəʊɪt] N Dichter *m*, Poet *m* (*old*) → **poet laureate**

poetaster [ˌpəʊɪˈtæstə'] N (*pej*) Poetaster *m*, Dichterling *m*

poetess ['pəʊɪtes] N Dichterin *f*, Poetin *f* (*old*)

poetic [pəʊˈetɪk] ADJ poetisch; *talent, ability also* dichterisch; *place, charm* stimmungsvoll, malerisch; ~ **beauty** (*visual*) malerische Schönheit; (*of thought, scene in play etc*) poetische Schönheit; **he's not at all ~** er hat überhaupt keinen Sinn für Poesie; **he became ~** er wurde poetisch *or* lyrisch

poetical [pəʊˈetɪkəl] ADJ = **poetic**

poetically [pəʊˈetɪkəlɪ] ADV *describe, write, named* poetisch; **very ~ put** sehr poetisch ausgedrückt; ~ **gifted** dichterisch begabt

poetic justice N poetische Gerechtigkeit

poetic licence N dichterische Freiheit

poetics [pəʊˈetɪks] N *sing* Poetik *f*

poet laureate ['pəʊɪt'lɔːrɪt] N Hofdichter(in) *m(f)*, Poeta laureatus *m*

poetry ['pəʊɪtrɪ] **N** **a** Dichtung *f*; (*not epic also*) Lyrik *f*; **to write ~** Gedichte schreiben, dichten; **the rules of ~** die Regeln der Versdichtung; ~ **reading** Dichterlesung *f* **b** (*fig*) Poesie *f*; **the dancing was ~ in motion** der Tanz war in Bewegung umgesetzte Poesie; **the sunset was sheer ~** der Sonnenuntergang war reinste Poesie

po-faced ['pəʊfeɪst] ADJ (*inf*, = *disapproving*) grimmig, mürrisch; **a ~ woman** (= *ugly*) eine Schrulle (*inf*)

pogo ['pəʊgəʊ] VI (= *dance*) Pogo tanzen

pogo stick N Springstock *m*

pogrom ['pɒgrəm] N Pogrom *m*

poignancy ['pɔɪnjənsɪ] N Ergreifende(s) *nt*; (*of look, memories*) Wehmut *f*; (*of distress, regret*) Schmerzlichkeit *f*; **the ~ of his message** die Wehmut, die in seinen Worten lag; **he writes with great ~** er schreibt sehr ergreifend

poignant ['pɔɪnjənt] ADJ ergreifend; *memories, look* wehmütig; *distress, regret* schmerzlich

poignantly ['pɔɪnjəntlɪ] ADV *describe, illustrate* ergreifend; **old memories stirred ~ within her** alte Erinnerungen rührten sich wehmütig in ihr; ~ **beautiful** auf wehmütige Art schön

poinsettia [pɔɪnˈsetɪə] N Weihnachtsstern *m*, Poinsettia *f* (*spec*)

---

point [pɔɪnt]
✪ 15.2, 20.7, 26

1 NOUN	4 INTRANSITIVE VERB
2 PLURAL NOUN	5 PHRASAL VERBS
3 TRANSITIVE VERB	

1 – NOUN

a = sharp end (*of chin, needle*) Spitze *f*; (*of a star*) Zacke *f*; (*of antler*) (Geweih)ende *nt*, (Geweih)spitze *f*; **at the point of a gun/sword** mit vorgehaltener Pistole/vorgehaltenem Schwert; **things look different at the point of a gun** alles sieht ein bisschen anders aus, wenn einem jemand die Pistole auf die Brust setzt → **fine**

b = marker (*on scale, compass*) Punkt *m*; (*on thermometer*) Grad *m*; **from all points (of the compass)** aus allen (Himmels)richtungen

♦ **up to a point** bis zu einem gewissen Grad *or* Punkt

c = unit, score (*in test, competition, St Ex etc*) Punkt *m*; **points for/against** Plus-/Minuspunkte *pl*; **points decision** Entscheidung *f* nach Punkten; **points win** Punktsieg *m*, Sieg *m* nach Punkten; **to win on points** nach Punkten gewinnen; **points system** Punktesystem *nt*

d = dot, punctuation mark (*Typ, Geometry*) Punkt *m*; (*in Hebrew texts*) Vokalzeichen *nt*; **(nought) point seven (0.7)** null Komma sieben (0,7)

e = place, time Punkt *m*, Stelle *f*; **the northernmost point of Scotland** der nördlichste Punkt Schottlands; **the train stops at Slough and all points east** der Zug hält in Slough und allen Orten östlich davon; **at this point** (*spatially*) an dieser Stelle, an diesem Punkt; (*in time*) (= *then*) in diesem Augenblick; (= *now*) jetzt; **from that point on they were friends** von da an waren sie Freunde; **at what point ...?** an welcher Stelle ...?; **at no point** nie; **at no point in the book** nirgends in dem Buch, an keiner Stelle des Buches; **they provoked him to the point where he lost his temper** sie reizten ihn so lange, bis er die Geduld verlor

♦ **point of + NOUN point of entry** (*over border*) Ort *m* der Einreise; (*of space capsule*) Ort *m* des Wiedereintritts; **point of departure** (*lit, fig*) Ausgangspunkt *m*; **to be at the point of death** am Rande *or* an der Schwelle des Todes stehen; **severe to the point of cruelty** streng bis an die Grenze der Grausamkeit; **to reach the point of no return** (*fig*) den Punkt erreichen, von dem es kein Zurück gibt; **point of view** Standpunkt *m*, Gesichtspunkt *m*; **from my point of view** von meinem Standpunkt aus, aus meiner Perspektive *or* Sicht; **from the point of view of productivity** von der Produktivität her gesehen

♦ **point of + -ing to be on the point of doing sth** im Begriff sein, etw zu tun; **he was on the point of telling me the story when ...** er wollte mir gerade die Geschichte erzählen, als ...; **he had reached the point of resigning** er war nahe daran, zu resignieren; **she was indulgent to the point of spoiling the child** sie war nachgiebig in einem Maße, das schon in Verwöhnung des Kindes umschlug

f = matter, question Punkt *m*; **on this point we are agreed** in diesem Punkt stimmen wir überein; **the point at issue** der strittige Punkt; **a**

12-point plan ein Zwölfpunkteplan *m*; **a useful point** ein nützlicher Hinweis; **point by point** Punkt für Punkt; **a point by point comparison** ein Vergleich Punkt für Punkt; **my point was ...** was ich sagen wollte, war ...; **you have a point there** darin mögen Sie Recht haben, da ist etwas dran (*inf*); **he may have a point, you know** da kann er Recht haben, weißt du; **can I put that same point another way?** können Sie das noch einmal anders formulieren?; **would you put that point more succinctly?** können Sie das etwas knapper fassen?; **to gain** *or* **carry one's point** sich durchsetzen

◆ **to make a/one's point** ein/sein Argument *nt* anbringen *or* vorbringen; **he made the point that ...** er betonte, dass ...; **you've made your point!** wissen wir ja schon!, das hast du ja schon gesagt!; **the chairman gave him just 30 seconds to make his point** der Vorsitzende gab ihm nur 30 Sekunden, um sein Argument zu erläutern; **he makes his points very clearly** er bringt seine Argumente sehr klar vor; **what point are you trying to make?** worauf wollen Sie hinaus?; **if I may make another point** wenn ich noch auf einen weiteren Punkt aufmerksam machen darf

◆ **to take the/sb's point I take your point, point taken** ich akzeptiere, was Sie sagen; (*in exasperation*) ich habe schon begriffen; **do you take my point?** verstehst du mich?

◆ **point of** + *NOUN* **a point of detail** eine Einzelfrage; **a point of interest** ein interessanter Punkt; **a point of law** eine Rechtsfrage; **a point of principle** eine grundsätzliche Frage → **honour, order**

g = *crux, main issue* **the point is that ...** es ist nämlich so ..., die Sache ist die, dass ...; **that's the whole point** das ist es ja gerade; **that's the whole point of doing it this way** gerade darum machen wir das so; **but the pound has been devalued – that's the whole point, your mark is worth more!** aber das Pfund wurde doch abgewertet – genau! deshalb ist die Mark jetzt mehr wert; **the point of the joke/story** die Pointe; **that's not the point** darum geht es nicht; **his remarks are very much to the point** seine Bemerkungen sind sehr sachbezogen

◆ **to get** *or* **see the point** verstehen, worum es geht; **do you see the point of what I'm saying?** weißt du, worauf ich hinauswill?

◆ **to miss the point** nicht verstehen, worum es geht; **he missed the point of what I was saying** er hat nicht begriffen, worauf ich hinauswollte

◆ **to come to the point** zur Sache kommen; **when it comes to the point** wenn es darauf ankommt

◆ **to keep** *or* **stick to the point** beim Thema bleiben

◆ **beside the point** unerheblich, irrelevant; **I'm afraid that's beside the point** das ist nicht relevant, das gehört nicht hierher

◆ **a case in point** ein einschlägiger Fall; **the case in point** der zur Debatte stehende Punkt

◆ **to make a point of doing sth** Wert darauf legen, etw zu tun; **he made a special point of being early** er legte besonderen Wert darauf, früh da zu sein; **we make a point of stressing colloquial usage** wir legen besonderen Nachdruck auf die Umgangssprache

h = *purpose, use* Zweck *m*, Sinn *m*; **there's no point in staying** es hat keinen Zweck *or* Sinn zu bleiben; **I don't see the point of carrying on/changing our system now** ich sehe keinen Sinn darin, weiterzumachen/unser System jetzt zu ändern; **what's the point?** was solls?; **I just don't see the point of it** *or* **any point in it** das sehe ich überhaupt nicht ein, ich sehe überhaupt keinen Sinn darin; **the point of this is ...** Sinn und Zweck ist davon ...; **what's the point of trying?** wozu (es) versuchen?; **he doesn't understand the point of doing this** er versteht nicht, weswegen wir/sie *etc* das machen; **the news gave point to his arguments** die Nachrichten verliehen seinen Argumenten Nachdruck *or* Gewicht; **life has lost its point**

das Leben hat jeden Sinn *or* all seinen Sinn verloren

i = *characteristic* **good/bad points** gute/schlechte Seiten *pl*; **he has his good points** er hat auch gute Seiten *or* seine guten Seiten; **the points to look for when buying a new car** die Punkte *or* Dinge, auf die man beim Kauf eines neuen Wagens achten muss

j Elec (*Brit*) Steckdose *f*

2 – points PLURAL NOUN

a Aut Unterbrecherkontakte *pl*

b Ballet Spitzen *pl*; **to dance on points** Spitzentanz *m* machen, auf den Spitzen tanzen

c Rail (*Brit*) Weichen *pl*

3 – TRANSITIVE VERB

a = *aim, direct* *gun, telescope etc* richten (*at* auf +*acc*); **he pointed his stick in the direction of the house** er zeigte *or* wies mit dem Stock auf das Haus; **he pointed his boat upstream** er drehte sein Boot stromaufwärts; **they pointed the drunk off in the right direction** sie schickten den Betrunkenen in die richtige Richtung → **finger**

b = *mark, show* zeigen; **to point the way** (*lit, fig*) den Weg weisen; **that really pointed the moral** das bewies, wie Recht wir/sie *etc* hatten; **he used the decline in the company's profits to point the moral that ...** er nahm das Absinken der Firmengewinne zum Anlass zu betonen, dass ...

c *toes* strecken

d Build *wall, brickwork* verfugen, ausfugen

e = *punctuate* *text* interpunktieren; *Hebrew* vokalisieren; *psalm* mit Deklarationszeichen versehen

f Hunt *game* anzeigen

4 – INTRANSITIVE VERB

a *with finger etc* zeigen, deuten (*at, to* auf +*acc*); **it's rude to point (at strangers)** es ist unhöflich, mit dem Finger (auf Fremde) zu zeigen; **don't point!** zeig nicht mit dem Finger!; **he pointed toward(s) the house/back towards the house** er zeigte *or* deutete zum Haus/zurück zum Haus; **the compass needle points (to the) north** die Kompassnadel zeigt *or* weist nach Norden

b = *indicate* (*facts, events*) hinweisen, hindeuten (*to* auf +*acc*); (*person*: = *point out*) hinweisen; **everything points that way** alles weist in diese Richtung; **the problems which you have pointed to in your paper** die Probleme, auf die du in deinem Aufsatz hingewiesen hast *or* die du in deinem Aufsatz aufgezeigt hast; **the poet doesn't state, he points in certain directions** der Dichter trifft keine Feststellungen, er deutet bestimmte Richtungen an; **all the signs point to success** alle Zeichen stehen auf Erfolg; **all the signs point to economic recovery** alles deutet *or* weist auf eine Erholung der Wirtschaft hin

c = *be aimed* (*gun, vehicle etc*) gerichtet sein; (= *face, be situated*: *building, valley*) liegen; **with his gun pointed** *or* **pointing right at me, he said ...** die Pistole direkt auf mich gerichtet, sagte er ...; **the wheels aren't pointing in the same direction** die Räder zeigen nicht in dieselbe Richtung; **in which direction is it pointing?** in welche Richtung zeigt es?

d Hunt (vor)stehen

5 – PHRASAL VERBS

▶ **point out** VT *sep* **a** (= *show*) zeigen auf (+*acc*); **to point sth out to sb** jdn auf etw hinweisen, jdn auf etw aufmerksam machen; **could you point him out to me?** kannst du mir zeigen, wer er ist?; **I'll point him out** ich zeige ihn dir; **the guide pointed out the most interesting paintings** der Führer machte auf die interessantesten Gemälde aufmerksam

b (= *mention*) **to point sth out (to sb)** (jdn) auf etw (*acc*) aufmerksam machen, (jdn) auf etw (*acc*) hinweisen; **may I point out that ...?** darf ich darauf aufmerksam machen *or* darauf

hinweisen, dass ...?; **thank you for pointing that out to me** vielen Dank, dass Sie mich darauf aufmerksam gemacht haben

▶ **point up** VT *sep* (= *emphasize*) unterstreichen, betonen; (= *make clear*) veranschaulichen, verdeutlichen

point-blank ['pɔɪnt'blæŋk] ADJ direkt; *refusal* glatt; **at** *or* **from ~ range** aus kürzester Entfernung *or* Distanz; **a ~ shot** (*from gun, Ftbl*) ein Schuss *m* aus kürzester Distanz *or* Entfernung ADV *fire* aus kürzester Distanz *or* Entfernung; *ask* rundheraus; **to ask sb ~** jdn geradeheraus fragen; **he refused ~ to help** er weigerte sich rundweg *or* lehnte es rundheraus ab zu helfen

pointed ['pɔɪntɪd] ADJ **a** (= *sharp*) *stick, roof, chin, nose, shoes* spitz; *window, arch* spitzbogig; **a stick with a sharply ~ end** ein Stock mit sehr spitzem Ende; **the ~ windows in the old church** die Spitzbogenfenster in der alten Kirche **b** (= *incisive*) *wit, criticism* scharf **c** (= *obvious in intention*) *remark, comment* scharf, spitz; *reference* unverblümt; *question* gezielt; *look* spitz; *absence, gesture, departure* ostentativ; **her ~ lack of interest in my problems** ihr ostentatives *or* betontes Desinteresse an meinen Problemen; **that was rather ~** das war ziemlich deutlich

pointedly ['pɔɪntɪdlɪ] ADV *speak, comment, look* spitz; *refer* unverblümt; *leave, stay away etc* ostentativ

pointer ['pɔɪntə] N **a** (= *indicator*) Zeiger *m* **b** (= *stick*) Zeigestock *m* **c** (= *dog*) Pointer *m*, Vorstehhund *m* **d** (*fig*: = *hint*) Hinweis *m*, Fingerzeig *m*, Tip *m*; **he gave me some ~s on how to behave** er gab mir ein paar Hinweise, wie ich mich benehmen sollte **e** (*esp Brit fig*: = *indication*) Anzeichen *nt*, Hinweis *m*; **a ~ to a possible solution** ein Hinweis auf eine mögliche Lösung

pointillism ['pwæntɪlɪzəm] N Pointillismus *m*

pointillist ['pwæntɪlɪst] N Pointillist(in) *m(f)* ADJ pointillistisch

pointing ['pɔɪntɪŋ] N (*Build*) (= *act*) Ausfugung *f*; (= *material*) Fugenmörtel *m*; **the ~ on these old buildings needs to be restored** das Mauerwerk dieser alten Gebäude muss neu verfugt *or* ausgefugt werden

pointless ['pɔɪntlɪs] ADJ sinnlos; **it is ~ to go** es ist sinnlos zu gehen; **it is ~ her going** *or* **for her to go** es ist sinnlos, dass sie geht; **a ~ exercise** eine sinnlose Angelegenheit

pointlessly ['pɔɪntlɪslɪ] ADV sinnlos

pointlessness ['pɔɪntlɪsnɪs] N Sinnlosigkeit *f*

point of sale N (*Comm*) Verkaufsstelle *f*

point-of-sale [ˌpɔɪntəv'seɪl] ADJ *attr advertising* an der Verkaufsstelle

point(s) duty N Verkehrsdienst *m*

pointsman ['pɔɪntsmən] N *pl* **-men** [-mən] (*Brit Rail*) Weichensteller *m*

point source N (*Phys*) Punktquelle *f*, punktförmige Lichtquelle

point-to-point [ˌpɔɪnttə'pɔɪnt] N (*also* **point-to-point race**) Geländejagdrennen *nt*

pointy ['pɔɪntɪ] ADJ *attr* (+*er*) spitz

pointy-headed [ˌpɔɪntɪ'hedɪd] ADJ (*US pej sl*) abgehoben (*pej inf*)

poise [pɔɪz] N **a** (= *carriage*: *of head, body*) Haltung *f*; (= *grace*) Grazie *f*; **the ~ of her head** ihre Kopfhaltung; **the graceful ~ of the dancer's body** die Grazie *or* graziöse Haltung der Tänzerin/des Tänzers

b (= *composure*) Gelassenheit *f*; (= *self-possession*) Selbstsicherheit *f*; **a woman of great ~ and charm** eine Frau voller Selbstsicherheit und Charme; **her ~ as a hostess** ihre Sicherheit als Gastgeberin; **to recover** *or* **regain one's ~** seine Selbstbeherrschung wiedererlangen; **he lacks ~** ihm fehlt die Gelassenheit

VT **a** (= *balance, hold balanced*) balancieren; **he ~d the knife ready to strike** er hielt das Messer so, dass er jederzeit zustechen konnte; **she ~d her pen over her notebook** sie hielt den Kugelschreiber schreibbereit über ihrem Notizblock; **the tiger ~d itself to spring** der Tiger machte sich sprungbereit **b** (*in passive*) **to be/hang ~d** (*bird, rock, sword*) schweben; **the diver was ~d on the edge of the pool** der Taucher stand sprungbereit auf dem Beckenrand; **the tiger was ~d ready to spring** der Tiger lauerte sprungbereit; **we sat ~d on the edge of our chairs** wir balancierten auf den Stuhlkanten → *also* **poised a, b** **VI** (für einen Moment) unbeweglich bleiben; (*bird, helicopter*) schweben; **he ~d for a second on the edge of the pool** er verharrte einen Augenblick am Beckenrand

poised ['pɔɪzd] ADJ **a** (= *suspended*) *hand* erhoben; *object* bereit; **a waitress approached us, pencil and pad ~** die Bedienung näherte sich uns, Stift und Block bereithaltend **b** (= *ready*) bereit; **to be ~ to do sth** bereit sein, etw zu tun; **to be ~ for sth** für etw bereit sein; **the enemy are ~ to attack** der Feind steht angriffsbereit; **he was ~ to become champion** er war auf dem besten Weg, die Meisterschaft zu gewinnen; **they sat in the hall, ~ for departure** sie saßen abfahrtbereit in der Halle; **to be ~ between peace and war** am Rande des Krieges stehen; **to be ~ on the brink of sth** dicht vor etw (*dat*) *or* am Rande von etw stehen; **a bright young man ~ on the brink of success** ein intelligenter junger Mann an der Schwelle zum Erfolg **c** (= *self-possessed*) gelassen, selbstsicher; **she was ~ and diplomatic on the telephone** am Telefon war sie selbstsicher und diplomatisch

poison ['pɔɪzn] **N** (*lit, fig*) Gift *nt*; **what's your ~?** (*inf*) **name your ~** (*inf*) was willst du trinken?; **to hate sb like ~** jdn glühend *or* wie die Pest (*inf*) hassen → **meat b** **VT** **a** (*lit*) vergiften; *atmosphere, rivers* verpesten; **it won't ~ you** (*inf*) das wird dich nicht umbringen (*inf*) **b** (*fig*) vergiften; *marriage* zerrütten; **to ~ sb's mind against sb** jdn gegen jdn aufstacheln

poisoned ['pɔɪznd] ADJ **a** *food, arrow* vergiftet; **a ~ chalice** (*esp Brit fig*) ein bitterer Kelch **b** (= *contaminated*) *air, water, soil* vergiftet **c** (*Med*: = *infected*) infiziert

poisoner ['pɔɪznə'] N Giftmörder(in) *m(f)*

poison: poison fang N (*of snake*) Giftzahn *m*; **poison gas** N Giftgas *nt*; **poison gland** N (*Zool*) Giftdrüse *f*

poisoning ['pɔɪznɪŋ] N (*lit, fig*) Vergiftung *f*; **the gradual ~ of the atmosphere by ...** die zunehmende Luftverpestung durch ...; **to die of ~** an einer Vergiftung sterben

poison: poison ivy N kletternder Giftsumach, Giftefeu *m*; **poison oak** N (*Bot*) Giftsumach *m*

poisonous ['pɔɪznəs] ADJ **a** giftig; **~ mushroom** Giftpilz *m*; **~ snake** Giftschlange *f*; **whisky on top of beer, that's absolutely ~** (*inf*) Whisky auf Bier, das ist tödlich (*inf*) **b** (*fig*) *literature, doctrine* zersetzend; *remark etc* giftig; **~ propaganda** Hetzpropaganda *f*; **she has a ~ tongue** sie hat eine giftige Zunge; **he's a ~ individual** er ist ein richtiger Giftzwerg; **a long-standing and ~ dispute** ein lang währender und zerrüttender Streit **c** **~ stuff** (*inf: usu hum*) Teufelszeug *nt*

poison: poison-pen letter N anonymer Brief; **poison pill** N (*Fin*) *zum Schutz gegen ein unerwünschtes Übernahmeangebot eingesetzte Maßnahme, die im Falle der Übernahme zu einem Wertverlust der Firma führen*; **poison sumach** N (*Bot*) Giftsumach *m*

poke¹ [pəʊk] N (*dial, Scot*) Beutel *m*, Sack *m* (*dial*); (*plastic, paper*) Tüte *f* → **pig**

poke² **N** **a** (= *jab*) Stoß *m*, Schubs *m* (*inf*); **to give sb/sth a ~** (*with stick*) jdn/etw stoßen; (*with finger*) stupsen; **I got a ~ in the eye from his umbrella** er stieß mir den Regenschirm ins Auge; **it's better than a ~ in the eye (with a sharp stick)** (*inf*) es ist besser als gar nichts **b** (*US inf*: = *punch*) Schlag *m*; **~ on the nose** Nasenstüber *m* **c** (*vulg*: = *act of intercourse*) Vögeln *nt* (*inf*); **to have a ~** vögeln (*inf*), ficken (*vulg*)

VT **a** (= *jab*) (*with stick*) stoßen; (*with finger*) stupsen; **to ~ the fire** das Feuer schüren, im Feuer stochern; **he ~d the ground with his stick** er stieß mit seinem Stock auf den Boden; **he accidentally ~d me in the eye** er hat mir aus Versehen ins Auge gestoßen **b** (*US inf*: = *punch*) hauen (*inf*); **to ~ sb on the nose** jdn auf die Nase hauen *or* schlagen **c** (= *thrust*) **to ~ one's head/finger/a stick** *etc* **into sth** seinen Kopf/Finger/einen Stock *etc* in etw (*acc*) stecken; **he ~d his head round the door/out of the window** er streckte seinen Kopf aus der Tür/aus dem Fenster **d** (*vulg*: = *have sex with*) vögeln (*inf*), ficken (*vulg*) **e** (= *make by poking*) *hole* bohren; **to ~ holes in sb's story** jds Geschichte zerpflücken **VI** his elbows were poking through his sleeves an seinen Ärmeln kamen schon die Ellenbogen durch; **to ~ at sth** (*testing*) etw prüfen; (*searching*) in etw (*dat*) stochern; **he ~d at me with his finger** (*touching*) er stupste mich; (*not touching*) er stieß mit dem Finger nach mir; **the doctor ~d at his ribs** der Arzt tastete seine Rippen ab; **she ~d at her food with a fork** sie stocherte mit einer Gabel in ihrem Essen herum; **well, if you will go poking into things that don't concern you ...** na ja, wenn du deine Nase ständig in Dinge steckst, die dich nichts angehen ...

▶ **poke about** (*Brit*) *or* **around** VI **a** (= *prod*) herumstochern **b** (*inf*: = *nose about*) stöbern, schnüffeln (*inf*) **c** +*prep obj* (*inf*: = *wander about*) (herum)bummeln; **we spent a pleasant day poking around the shops** wir haben einen netten Tag mit Geschäftsbummeln verbracht

▶ **poke in** VT *sep* hineinstecken *or* -strecken; **he poked his head in through the window** er steckte *or* streckte seinen Kopf zum Fenster herein; **I'll just poke my head in and say hello** (*inf*) ich will nur schnell vorbeischauen und Guten *or* guten Tag sagen

▶ **poke out** **VI** vorstehen; **the tortoise had its head poking out of its shell** die Schildkröte hatte ihren Kopf aus dem Panzer gestreckt; **a handkerchief was poking out of his top pocket** ein Taschentuch schaute *or* guckte aus seiner Brusttasche hervor **VT** *sep* **a** (= *extend*) hinausstrecken **b** (= *remove by poking*) **he poked the dirt out with his fingers** er pulte (*inf*) *or* kratzte den Schmutz mit den Fingern heraus; **to poke sb's eye out** jdm ein Auge ausstechen

▶ **poke up** VT *sep fire* schüren; **he poked his finger up his nose** er bohrte mit dem Finger in der Nase

poke bonnet N Kiepenhut *m*, Schute *f*

poker¹ ['pəʊkə'] N (*for fire*) Schürhaken *m*, Feuerhaken *m*

poker² N (*Cards*) Poker *nt*

poker: poker dice N **a** (= *single dice*) Pokerwürfel *m* **b** (= *set of five*) Pokerwürfel *pl* **c** *no pl* (= *game*) Würfelpoker *m*; **poker face** N Pokergesicht *nt*, Pokerface *nt*; **poker-faced** ADJ mit einem Pokergesicht *or* Pokerface; (= *bored*) mit unbewegter Miene; **pokerwork** N (*Brit*) Brandmalerei *f*

pokeweed ['pəʊkwi:d] N (*US*) Kermesbeere *f*

poky ['pəʊkɪ] ADJ (+*er*) (*pej*) *room, house* winzig; **it's so ~ in here** es ist so eng hier

Polack ['pəʊlæk] N (*pej*) Polack(e) *m* (*pej*), Polackin *f* (*pej*)

Poland ['pəʊlənd] N Polen *nt*

polar ['pəʊlə'] ADJ **a** Polar-, polar; **~ expedition** Polarexpedition *f* **b** (= *opposite*) polar

polar bear N Polarbär *m*, Eisbär *m*

polar circle N Polarkreis *m*

polarity [pəʊˈlærɪtɪ] N (*Phys, fig*) Polarität *f*

polarization [ˌpəʊləraɪˈzeɪʃən] N (*Phys*) Polarisation *f*; (*fig*) Polarisierung *f*

polarize ['pəʊləraɪz] **VT** polarisieren **VI** sich polarisieren

Polaroid® ['pəʊlərɔɪd] N (= *camera*) Polaroidkamera® *f*, Sofortbildkamera *f*; (= *photograph*) Sofortbild *nt*

polder ['pəʊldə'] N Polder *m*

Pole [pəʊl] N Pole *m*, Polin *f*

pole¹ [pəʊl] **N** **a** Stange *f*; (= *flagpole, telegraph pole*) Mast *m*, Stange *f*; (*of cart*) Deichsel *f*; (= *ski-pole*) Stock *m*; (*for vaulting*) Stab *m*; (*for punting*) Stange *f*, Stake *f* (*spec*); **to be up the ~** (*Brit, inf*) eine Schraube locker haben (*inf*); **to drive sb up the ~** (*inf*) jdn die Wände hoch treiben (*inf*); **I wouldn't touch it/him with a ten-foot ~** (*US inf*) von so etwas/so jemandem lasse ich die Finger (*inf*); (*because disgusting, unpleasant*) das/den würde ich noch nicht mal mit der Kneifzange anfassen (*inf*) **b** (*Measure: old*) Rute *f* (*old*) **VT** punt staken

pole² N (*Geog, Astron, Elec*) Pol *m*; **they are ~s apart** sie (*acc*) trennen Welten, Welten liegen zwischen ihnen; **at opposite ~s of sth** (*fig*) an entgegengesetzten Enden einer Sache (*gen*)

pole: poleaxe, (US) poleax **N** **a** (*Mil*) Streitaxt *f* **b** (*for slaughtering*) Schlachtbeil *nt* **VT** **a** (*Mil*) (mit der Streitaxt) niederschlagen *or* umhauen; (*fig*) verblüffen **b** *animal* (mit dem Schlachtbeil) töten; **polecat** N Iltis *m*; (*US*) Skunk *m*, Stinktier *nt*; **pole jump** N (*US*) = **pole vault**

polemic [pɒˈlemɪk] ADJ polemisch **N** Polemik *f*

polemical [pɒˈlemɪkəl] ADJ polemisch

polemicist [pɒˈlemɪsɪst] N Polemiker(in) *m(f)*

polemicize [pɒˈlemɪsaɪz] VI polemisieren (*against gegen*)

polemics [pɒˈlemɪks] N *sing* Polemik *f*

pole: pole position N **a** (*Motor Racing*) Poleposition *f*; **to be or start in ~** aus der Poleposition starten **b** (*fig*) günstige Ausgangsposition; **to be in ~** in einer günstigen Ausgangsposition sein; **pole star** N Polarstern *m*; **pole vault** **N** (= *event*) Stabhochsprung *m*; (= *one jump*) Sprung *m* mit dem Stab **VI** stabhochspringen; **pole-vaulter** N Stabhochspringer(in) *m(f)*; **pole-vaulting** N Stabhochspringen *nt*, Stabhochsprung *m*

police [pəˈliːs] N (+*sing vb*, = *institution*, +*pl vb*, = *policemen*) Polizei *f*; **to join the ~** zur Polizei gehen; **he is in** *or* **a member of the ~** er ist bei der Polizei; **all ~ leave was cancelled** allen Polizisten wurde der Urlaub gesperrt; **hundreds of ~** hunderte *or* Hunderte von Polizisten; **extra ~ were called in** es wurden zusätzliche Polizeikräfte angefordert; **three ~ were injured** drei Polizeibeamte *or* Polizisten wurden verletzt **VT** *road, frontier, territory* kontrollieren; *agreement, pop concert* überwachen, kontrollieren; **to ~ the peace** den Frieden überwachen; **a heavily ~d area** ein Gebiet *nt* mit hoher Polizeidichte

police: police car N Polizeiwagen *m*; **police constable** N (*Brit*) Polizist(in) *m(f)*, Wachtmeister(in) *m(f)* (*form*); **police court** N ≈ Polizeigericht *nt*; **police dog** N Polizeihund *m*; **police escort** N Polizeieskorte *f*; **police force** N Polizei *f*; **one of the best-equipped ~s in the world** eine der bestausgestatteten Polizeitruppen der Welt; **police headquarters** N *sing or pl* Polizeipräsidium *nt*; **policeman** N Polizist *m*; **police officer** N Polizeibeamte(r) *mf*; **police presence** N Polizeiaufgebot *nt*; **police protection** N Polizeischutz *m*; **police record** N Vorstrafen *pl*; **to have a ~** vorbestraft sein; **police state** N Polizeistaat *m*; **police station** N (Polizei)wache *f or* -revier *nt*; **police supervision** N Polizeiaufsicht *f*; **policewoman** N Polizistin *f*; **police work** N Polizeiarbeit *f*; (= *investigation*) polizeiliche Nachforschungen *pl*

policing [pəˈliːsɪŋ] N (*of road, frontier, territory*) Kontrolle *f*; (*of agreement, pop concert also*) Überwachung *f*; **new ~ policies for sports events** neue polizeiliche Richtlinien bei Sportveranstaltungen

policy[1] ['pɒlɪsɪ] N **a** Politik *f no pl*; *(of business)* Geschäfts- *or* Firmenpolitik *f* (*on* bei), Praktiken *pl* (*pej*) (*on* in Bezug auf +*acc*); *(of team, football manager: = tactics)* Taktik *f*; *(= principle)* Grundsatz *m*; **social and economic ~** Wirtschafts- und Sozialpolitik *f*; **our ~ on immigration/recruitment** unsere Einwanderungs-/Einstellungspolitik; **what is company ~ on this matter?** wie steht die Geschäfts- *or* Firmenpolitik in diesem Falle aus?; **the newspaper followed a ~ of attacking the church** die Zeitung verfolgte eine kirchenfeindliche Linie *or* Politik; **a ~ of restricting immigration** eine Politik zur Einschränkung der Einwanderung; **a matter of ~** eine Grundsatzfrage; **~ decision** Grundsatzentscheidung *f*; **~ statement** Grundsatzerklärung *f*; **your ~ should always be to give people a second chance** du solltest es dir zum Grundsatz machen, Menschen eine zweite Chance zu geben; **my ~ is to wait and see** meine Devise heißt abwarten; **it's our ~ to cater for the mid-twenties** wir wenden uns mit unserer Firmenpolitik an die Mittzwanziger; **our ~ is one of expansion** wir verfolgen eine expansionsorientierte Geschäftspolitik

b *(= prudence, a prudent procedure)* Taktik *f*; **~ demands that the government compromise** die Regierung muss aus taktischen Gründen Kompromisse eingehen; **it was good/bad ~** das war (taktisch) klug/unklug

policy[2] N *(also* **insurance policy***)* (Versicherungs)police *f*, Versicherungsschein *m*; **to take out a ~** eine Versicherung abschließen

policy: policy document N Grundsatzpapier *nt*, Grundsatzprogramm *nt*; **policyholder** N Versicherungsnehmer(in) *m(f)*; **policy-maker** N Parteiideologe *m/*-ideologin *f*; **policy-making** N Treffen *nt* von Grundsatzentscheidungen ADJ *body, process, role* grundsatzpolitisch; **policy paper** N = **policy document**; **policy unit** N (*Brit Pol*) Richtlinienkommission *f*

polio ['pəʊlɪəʊ] N Polio *f*, Kinderlähmung *f*; **~ vaccine** Impfstoff *m* gegen Kinderlähmung; **~ victim** Opfer *nt* der Kinderlähmung, Polioopfer *nt*

poliomyelitis ['pəʊlɪəʊmaɪə'laɪtɪs] N *(form)* Poliomyelitis *f* (*spec*), Kinderlähmung *f*

Polish ['pəʊlɪʃ] ADJ polnisch; **~ Corridor** Polnischer Korridor N (*Ling*) Polnisch *nt*

polish ['pɒlɪʃ] N **a** *(= material) (= shoe polish)* Creme *f*; *(= floor polish)* Bohnerwachs *nt*; *(= furniture polish)* Politur *f*; *(= metal polish)* Poliermittel *nt*; *(= nail polish)* Lack *m*

b *(= act)* **to give sth a ~** etw polieren; *shoes, silver* etw putzen; *floor* etw bohnern; **my shoes need a ~** meine Schuhe müssen geputzt werden

c *(= polished state, shine)* Glanz *m*; *(of furniture)* Politur *f*; **high ~** Hochglanz *m*, starker Glanz; **there was a high ~ on the floor** der Fußboden war stark gebohnert; **to put a ~ on sth** etw zum Glänzen bringen, Glanz auf etw (*acc*) bringen; **water will take the ~ off** Wasser nimmt den Glanz/greift die Politur an

d *(fig: = refinement) (of person, style, manners)* Schliff *m*; *(of performance)* Brillanz *f*; **he lacks ~** ihm fehlt der Schliff/die Brillanz; **his style lacks ~** an seinem Stil muss noch gearbeitet werden

VT **a** *(lit)* polieren; *silver, shoes* putzen, polieren; *floor* bohnern

b *(fig) person, performance* den letzten Schliff geben (+*dat*); *manner, style* polieren (*inf*), verfeinern

▶ **polish off** VT *sep (inf) food* verdrücken (*inf*), verputzen (*inf*); *drink* wegputzen (*inf*); *work* wegschaffen (*inf*), erledigen; *opponent, competitor* abfertigen, abservieren (*inf*)

▶ **polish up** VT *sep* **a** *shoes, floor, silver etc* polieren, auf Hochglanz bringen **b** *(fig: = improve) style* aufpolieren, verfeinern; *work* überarbeiten; *one's French etc* aufpolieren (*inf*); **you'd better polish up your ideas** (*inf*) du solltest dich besser auf den Hosenboden setzen (*inf*) VI sich polieren lassen

polished ['pɒlɪʃt] ADJ **a** *surface, furniture* poliert, glänzend; *ornaments* poliert; *floor* gebohnert; *stone, glass* geschliffen; **his highly ~ shoes** seine blank geputzten Schuhe **b** *style etc* verfeinert; *performance, performer* brillant; *language* geschliffen; *image* makellos, sauber **c** *manners* geschliffen; *(= refined, suave) person* gewandt

polisher ['pɒlɪʃə'] N *(= person)* Schleifer(in) *m(f)*; *(= machine)* Schleif-/Polier-/Bohnermaschine *f*

polite [pə'laɪt] ADJ (+*er*) **a** höflich; **it wouldn't be ~** es wäre unhöflich; **to be ~ to sb** höflich zu jdm sein; **be ~ about her cooking** mach ein paar höfliche Bemerkungen über ihre Kochkunst; **when I said it was good I was just being ~** als ich sagte, es sei gut, wollte ich nur höflich sein; **there's no need to be ~ about it if you don't like it** du kannst es ruhig sagen, wenn es dir nicht gefällt; **~ conversation** höfliche Konversation; **we sat around making ~ conversation** wir saßen zusammen und machten Konversation **b** *society* fein

politely [pə'laɪtlɪ] ADV höflich

politeness [pə'laɪtnɪs] N Höflichkeit *f*

politic ['pɒlɪtɪk] ADJ **a** klug; **it would be ~ to apologize** es wäre (taktisch) klug, sich zu entschuldigen; **he tended to do what was ~ rather than that which was proper** er machte eher (das), was klug *or* günstig war, als das, was recht gewesen wäre **b** **the body ~** das Staatswesen, das staatliche Gemeinwesen

political [pə'lɪtɪkəl] ADJ politisch; **~ action committee** (*US*) politische Aktionsgruppe

political: political analyst N politischer Analyst, politische Analystin; **political asylum** N politisches Asyl; **to ask for** *or* **seek ~** um politisches Asyl bitten *or* ersuchen, politisches Asyl beantragen; **he was granted/refused ~** ihm wurde politisches Asyl gewährt/nicht gewährt; **political commentator** N politischer Analytiker, politische Analytikerin; **political correctness** N politische Korrektheit; **our society's obsession with ~** die Besessenheit unserer Gesellschaft, politisch korrekt zu sein; **political economy** N Volkswirtschaft *f*; **political geography** N politische Geographie

politically [pə'lɪtɪkəlɪ] ADV *aware, expedient* politisch; **~ speaking** im politischen Sinne

politically correct ADJ politisch korrekt

POLITICALLY CORRECT

Die Woge der politischen Korrektheit entstand wie so vieles andere in den Vereinigten Staaten und hat sich mittlerweile auf der ganzen Welt ausgebreitet. Ursprünglich wollte man vermeiden, dass über ethnische Minderheiten, Frauen, Behinderte, Homosexuelle und benachteiligte Bevölkerungsgruppen in Worten gesprochen wird, die sie herabsetzen oder beleidigen. Wer überzeugt **politically correct**, oder auch kurz **PC**, ist, hält sich für den Verfechter einer Weltanschauung, in der all die Werte infrage gestellt werden, die die westliche Gesellschaft im Laufe der Jahrhunderte dem Rest der Welt aufgezwungen hat. Heute wird der Ausdruck **politically correct** überwiegend als Schimpfwort von den Gegnern dieser „liberalen" Ansichten gebraucht. Hier einige Beispiele für politisch korrekte Ausdrucksweise: **Native American** statt **Red Indian**, **visually impaired** statt **blind** und **vertically challenged** statt **short**.

---

politically incorrect ADJ politisch inkorrekt *or* nicht korrekt

political: political party N politische Partei; **political prisoner** N politischer Gefangener, politische Gefangene; **political science** N Politologie *f*; **political scientist** N Politologe *m*, Politologin *f*, Politikwissenschaftler(in) *m(f)*

politician [ˌpɒlɪ'tɪʃən] N Politiker(in) *m(f)*

politicization [pəˌlɪtɪsaɪ'zeɪʃən] N Politisierung *f*

politicize [pə'lɪtɪsaɪz] VT politisieren

politick ['pɒlɪtɪk] *(usu pej)* VI politisieren, sich politisch betätigen VT **to ~ a bill through parliament** durch seinen politischen Einsatz erreichen, dass ein Gesetz im Parlament verabschiedet wird

politicking [pə'lɪtɪkɪŋ] N *(pej)* politische Aktivitäten *pl*

politico [pə'lɪtɪkəʊ] N *(esp US, pej)* Politiker(in) *m(f)*

politico- PREF politisch-; **~military** politisch-militärisch

politics ['pɒlɪtɪks] N **a** *(+pl vb)* (*Pol*) Politik *f*; *(= views)* politische Ansichten *pl*; **what are his ~?** welche politischen Ansichten hat er? **b** *(+sing or pl vb) (= political affairs, idea)* Politik *f*; **to be in ~** in der Politik sein; **to go into ~** in die Politik gehen; **to talk ~** über Politik (*acc*) reden; **to study ~** Politik studieren; **interested in ~** politisch interessiert; **to play ~** (*pej*) große Politik spielen (*pej*); **office ~** Bürorangeleien *pl*; **sexual ~** Rangeleien *pl* zwischen den Geschlechtern

polity ['pɒlɪtɪ] N *(= form of government)* politische Ordnung, Staats- *or* Regierungsform *f*; *(= politically organized society)* Staat(swesen *nt*) *m*, Gemeinwesen *nt*; *(= management of public affairs)* Staatsverwaltung *f*

polka ['pɒlkə] N Polka *f*

polka dot N Tupfen *m* ADJ getupft, gepunktet

poll [pəʊl] N **a** (*Pol*) *(= voting)* Abstimmung *f*; *(= election)* Wahl *f*; **a ~ was taken among the villagers** unter den Dorfbewohnern wurde abgestimmt; **to head the ~** bei der Wahl führen; **~ of ~s** Politbarometer *nt*

b *(= total of votes cast)* Wahlbeteiligung *f*; *(for individual candidate)* Stimmenanteil *m*; **there was an 84% ~** die Wahlbeteiligung betrug 84%; **they got 34% of the ~** sie bekamen 34% der Stimmen

c **~s** *(= voting place)* Wahllokale *pl*; *(= election)* Wahl *f*; **to go to the ~s** wählen gehen, zur Wahl gehen; **a crushing defeat at the ~s** eine vernichtende Niederlage bei den Wahlen, eine vernichtende Wahlniederlage; **a photograph of Schröder at the ~s** ein Foto von Schröder bei der Stimmabgabe

d *(= opinion poll)* Umfrage *f*; **a telephone ~** eine telefonische Abstimmung; **to take a ~ (of 3,000 people)** (3000 Personen) abstimmen lassen

e *(old: = head, esp back of head)* Schädel *m* VT **a** *votes* erhalten, auf sich (*acc*) vereinigen **b** *(in opinion poll)* befragen; **40% of those ~ed supported the Government** 40% der Befragten waren für die Regierung **c** *horns, trees* stutzen; **~ed cattle** Rinder mit gestutzten Hörnern

VI **he ~ed badly (in the election)** er erhielt bei der Wahl wenige Stimmen, er schnitt bei der Wahl schlecht ab; **the nationalists ~ed well** die Nationalisten erhielten bei der Wahl viele Stimmen, die Nationalisten schnitten bei der Wahl gut ab

pollard ['pɒləd] N *(= tree)* gekappter Baum VT kappen

pollee [pəʊ'liː] N *(esp US, at opinion poll)* Befragte(r) *mf*

pollen ['pɒlən] N Blütenstaub *m*, Pollen *m*

pollen basket N Höschen *nt*, Hose *f*

pollen count N Pollenzahl *f*

pollinate ['pɒlɪneɪt] VT bestäuben

pollination [ˌpɒlɪ'neɪʃən] N Bestäubung *f*

pollinator ['pɒlɪneɪtə'] N *(Zool)* Bestäuber *m*

polling ['pəʊlɪŋ] N **a** Stimmabgabe *f*, Wahl *f*; **~ will be on Thursday** die Wahl ist am Donnerstag; **~ has been heavy** die Wahlbeteiligung war (sehr) hoch *or* stark; **the ~ was extremely low** die Wahlbeteiligung war äußerst gering **b** *(Comput)* Sendeaufruf *m*

polling: polling booth N Wahlkabine *f*, Wahlzelle *f*; **polling card** N Wahlausweis *m*; **polling day** N (*esp Brit*) Wahltag *m*; **polling station** N (*Brit*) Wahllokal *nt*

polliwog ['pɒlɪwɒg] N (*US*) Kaulquappe *f*

pollster ['pəʊlstə'] N Meinungsforscher(in) *m(f)*

poll tax N Kopfsteuer *f*

pollutant [pə'luːtənt] N Schadstoff *m*

pollute [pə'luːt] VT *environment* verschmutzen; *river, atmosphere etc also* verunreinigen; *atmosphere also* verpesten (*pej*); (*fig*) *mind, morals* verderben, korrumpieren

polluter [pə'luːtə'] N Umweltverschmutzer(in) *m(f)*

pollution [pə'luːʃən] N (*of environment*) Umweltverschmutzung *f*, Verschmutzung *f*; (*of atmosphere*) Verunreinigung *f*; (*of rivers*) Verunreinigung *f*, Verpestung *f* (*pej*); (*fig*) Korrumpierung *f*; **the fight against ~** der Kampf gegen die Umweltverschmutzung

poll watcher N Wahlbeobachter(in) *m(f)*

pollywog N = polliwog

polo ['pəʊləʊ] N Polo *nt*

polonaise [ˌpɒlə'neɪz] N Polonaise *f*, Polonäse *f*

polo neck (*Brit*) N Rollkragen *m*; (= *sweater*) Rollkragenpullover *m* ADJ Rollkragen-; **~ sweater** Rollkragenpullover *m*

polonium [pə'ləʊnɪəm] N (*Chem*) Polonium *nt*

poltergeist ['pɒltəgaɪst] N Poltergeist *m*, Klopfgeist *m*

poltroon [pɒl'truːn] N (*liter*) feiger Wicht, Memme *f*

poly ['pɒlɪ] a (*Brit*) abbr of **polytechnic** b abbr of **polythene** **~ bag** Plastetüte *f*, Plastiktüte *f*

polyandrous [ˌpɒlɪ'ændrəs] ADJ Vielmännerei betreibend, polyandrisch (*spec*); (*Bot*) polyadelphisch

polyandry ['pɒlɪændrɪ] N Vielmännerei *f*, Polyandrie *f* (*form*)

polyanthus [ˌpɒlɪ'ænθəs] N (= *primrose*) Gartenprimel *f*; (= *narcissus*) Tazette *f*

polychromatic [ˌpɒlɪkrəʊ'mætɪk] ADJ polychrom

polyclinic ['pɒlɪklɪnɪk] N Poliklinik *f*

polyester [ˌpɒlɪ'estə'] N Polyester *m*

polyethylene [ˌpɒlɪ'eθəliːn] N Polyäthylen *nt*

polygamist [pə'lɪɡəmɪst] N Polygamist(in) *m(f)*

polygamous [pə'lɪɡəməs] ADJ polygam

polygamy [pə'lɪɡəmɪ] N Polygamie *f*, Vielehe *f*, Vielweiberei *f*

polyglot ['pɒlɪɡlɒt] ADJ polyglott, vielsprachig N (= *person*) Polyglotte(r) *mf*

polygon ['pɒlɪɡən] N Polygon *nt*, Vieleck *nt*

polygonal [pɒ'lɪɡənl] ADJ polygonal, vieleckig

polygraph ['pɒlɪɡrɑːf] N (*US*: = *lie detector*) Lügendetektor *m*

polyhedron [ˌpɒlɪ'hiːdrən] N Polyeder *nt*, Vielflächner *m*

polymath ['pɒlɪmæθ] N Mensch *m* mit vielseitigem Wissen

polymer ['pɒlɪmə'] N Polymer *nt*

polymeric [ˌpɒlɪ'merɪk] ADJ polymer

polymerization [ˌpɒlɪmərɪ'zeɪʃən] N Polymerisation *f*

polymorphic [ˌpɒlɪ'mɔːfɪk] ADJ polymorph, vielgestaltig

polymorphism [ˌpɒlɪ'mɔːfɪzəm] N Polymorphismus *m*

Polynesia [ˌpɒlɪ'niːzɪə] N Polynesien *nt*

Polynesian [ˌpɒlɪ'niːzɪən] ADJ polynesisch N a Polynesier(in) *m(f)* b (*Ling*) Polynesisch *nt*

polynomial [ˌpɒlɪ'nəʊmɪəl] ADJ polynomisch N Polynom *nt*

polyp ['pɒlɪp] N Polyp *m*

polyphonic [ˌpɒlɪ'fɒnɪk] ADJ (*Mus*) polyphon

polyphonist [pə'lɪfənɪst] N (*Mus*) Polyphoniker(in) *m(f)*, Kontrapunktiker(in) *m(f)*

polyphony [pə'lɪfənɪ] N (*Mus*) Polyphonie *f*

polypropylene [ˌpɒlɪ'prəʊpɪliːn] N Polypropylen *nt*

polypus ['pɒlɪpəs] N Polyp *m*

polysemous [pɒ'lɪsəməs] ADJ polysem

polystyrene [ˌpɒlɪ'staɪriːn] N Polystyrol *nt*; (*extended also*) Styropor® *nt* ADJ Polystyrol-/Styropor-; **~ cup** Styroporbecher *m*

polysyllabic [ˌpɒlɪsɪ'læbɪk] ADJ viel- *or* mehrsilbig

polysyllable ['pɒlɪsɪləbl] N Polysyllabum *nt* (*spec*), vielsilbiges Wort

polytechnic [ˌpɒlɪ'teknɪk] N (*Brit*) ≈ Polytechnikum *nt*; (*degree-awarding*) technische Hochschule, TH *f*

polytheism ['pɒlɪθiːɪzəm] N Polytheismus *m*

polytheistic [ˌpɒlɪθiː'ɪstɪk] ADJ polytheistisch

polythene ['pɒlɪθiːn] N (*Brit*) Polyäthylen *nt*; (*in everyday language*) Plastik *nt*; **~ bag** Plastiktüte *f*

polyunsaturated fats [ˌpɒlɪʌn'sætjəreɪtɪd'fæts], **polyunsaturates** [ˌpɒlɪʌn'sætjʊrɪts] PL mehrfach ungesättigte Fettsäuren *pl*

polyurethane [ˌpɒlɪ'jʊərəθeɪn] N Polyurethan *nt*

polyvalent [pə'lɪvələnt] ADJ mehrwertig, polyvalent

pom¹ [pɒm] N (*Austral, inf*) Engländer(in) *m(f)*, Tommy *m* (*dated inf*)

pom² N (*inf*) = **Pomeranian N b**

pomade [pə'mɑːd] N Pomade *f* VT mit Pomade einreiben

pomander [pəʊ'mændə'] N Duftkugel *f*

pomegranate ['pɒməˌɡrænɪt] N Granatapfel *m*; (= *tree*) Granatapfelbaum *m*, Granatbaum *m*

pomelo ['pɒmɪləʊ] N (*esp US*) Grapefruit *f*, Pampelmuse *f*

Pomerania [ˌpɒmə'reɪnɪə] N Pommern *nt*

Pomeranian [ˌpɒmə'reɪnɪən] ADJ pommer(i)sch N a Pommer(in) *m(f)* b (= *dog*) Spitz *m*

pommel ['pʌml] N (*on sword*) Knauf *m*; (*on saddle*) Knopf *m* VT = **pummel**

pommy ['pɒmɪ] N (*Austral, inf*) Engländer(in) *m(f)*, Tommy *m* (*dated inf*); **~ bastard** Scheißengländer *m* (*inf*)

pomp [pɒmp] N Pomp *m*, Prunk *m*, Gepränge *nt*; **~ and circumstance** Pomp und Prunk *m*

pompadour ['pɒmpədʊə'] N (*Hist*) Pompadourfrisur *f*

Pompeian [pɒm'peɪən] ADJ pompej(an)isch N Pompej(an)er(in) *m(f)*

Pompeii [pɒm'peɪiː] N Pompej(i) *nt*

Pompey ['pɒmpɪ] N Pompejus *m*

pompom ['pɒmpɒm] N a (= *gun*) automatische Flugzeugabwehrkanone b (*on hat etc*) Troddel *f*, Bommel *f* (*dial*)

pomposity [pɒm'pɒsɪtɪ] N (*of person*) Aufgeblasenheit *f*, Wichtigtuerei *f*; (*of attitude, behaviour also, phrase*) Gespreiztheit *f*; (*of language, letter, remark*) Schwülstigkeit *f*, Bombast *m*

pompous ['pɒmpəs] ADJ a *person* aufgeblasen, wichtigtuerisch; *attitude, behaviour also, phrase* gespreizt; *language, letter, remark* schwülstig, bombastisch; **don't be so ~** tu nicht so aufgeblasen, sei nicht so wichtigtuerisch b (= *magnificent*) *building* grandios, bombastisch; *occasion* grandios

pompously ['pɒmpəslɪ] ADV *write, speak* schwülstig, bombastisch; *behave* aufgeblasen, wichtigtuerisch

'pon [pɒn] PREP (*old, poet*) contr of **upon**

ponce [pɒns] N (*Brit, inf*) N (= *pimp*) Loddel *m* (*inf*), Lude *m* (*sl*); (*pej*: = *homosexual*) Tunte *f* (*inf*) VI **to ~ for sb** jds Zuhälter sein

▶ **ponce about** *or* **around** VI (*Brit, inf*) herumtänzeln

poncho ['pɒntʃəʊ] N Poncho *m*

poncy ['pɒnsɪ] ADJ (+er) (*Brit inf*) a (= *flashy*) eingebildet b (*pej*: = *homosexual*) schwul (*inf*); (= *affected*) *walk, actor* tuntig (*inf*)

pond [pɒnd] N Teich *m*; **the ~** (*inf*: = *Atlantic*) der große Teich (*hum*); **~ life** Pflanzen- und Tierleben in Teichen

ponder ['pɒndə'] VT nachdenken über (+*acc*); *possibilities, consequences etc* erwägen, bedenken VI nachdenken (*on, over* über +*acc*)

pondering ADJ , **ponderingly** ADV ['pɒndərɪŋ, -lɪ] nachdenklich, grüblerisch

ponderous ['pɒndərəs] ADJ a (= *laboured, clumsy*) *person, movement, steps* schwerfällig; (= *heavy*) massiv b (= *too serious*) *book* gewichtig; *joke* schwerfällig

ponderously ['pɒndərəslɪ] ADV schwerfällig; (= *seriously*) *formal* gewichtig, gravitätisch

ponderousness ['pɒndərəsnɪs] N Schwerfälligkeit *f*; (= *heaviness*) Schwere *f*, Gewichtigkeit *f*

pondweed ['pɒndwiːd] N Laichkrautgewächs *nt*

pone [pəʊn] N (*US*) Maisbrot *nt*

pong [pɒŋ] (*Brit, inf*) N Gestank *m*, Mief *m* (*inf*); **there's a bit of a ~ in here** hier stinkts *or* mieft (*inf*) VI stinken, miefen (*inf*)

poniard ['pɒnjəd] N (*liter, old*) Dolch *m*

pontiff ['pɒntɪf] N Pontifex *m*; (= *pope also*) Papst *m*

pontifical [pɒn'tɪfɪkəl] ADJ a (*lit*) pontifikal; (= *papal*) **~ robes** Pontifikalien *pl*; (*of pope*) päpstliche Gewänder *pl*; **~ duties** Pontifikalien *pl*; (*of pope*) päpstliche Pflichten *pl*; **~ office** Pontifikat *nt* b (*fig*) päpstlich

pontifically [pɒn'tɪfɪkəlɪ] ADV (*fig*) päpstlich

Pontifical Mass N Pontifikalamt *nt*

pontificate [pɒn'tɪfɪkɪt] N Pontifikat *nt* [pɒn'tɪfɪkeɪt] VI (*fig*) dozieren; **I wish you wouldn't ~ to me** ich wünschte, du würdest nicht in diesem belehrenden Ton mit mir reden

Pontius Pilate ['pɒnʃəs'paɪlət] N Pontius Pilatus *m*

pontoon¹ [pɒn'tuːn] N Ponton *m*; (*on flying boat*) Schwimmer *m*; **~ bridge** Pontonbrücke *f*

pontoon² N (*Brit, Cards*) 17 und 4 *nt*

pony ['pəʊnɪ] N a Pony *nt* b (*Brit, sl*) 25 Pfund c (*US, sl*; = *crib*) Spickzettel *m* d (*US, inf*, = *small glass*) Gläschen *nt*

pony: pony express N Ponyexpress *m*; **ponytail** N Pferdeschwanz *m*; **she was wearing her hair in a ~** sie trug einen Pferdeschwanz; **pony trekking** N Ponyreiten *nt*; **a ~ holiday** ein Ponyreiturlaub *m*

poo [puː], N, VI (*baby-talk*) = **pooh N VI**

pooch [puːtʃ] N (*inf*) Hündchen *nt*

poodle ['puːdl] N Pudel *m*

poof(ter) ['pʊf(tə')] N (*dated Brit pej inf*) Warme(r) *m* (*dated inf*), Schwule(r) *m* (*inf*)

poofy ['pʊfɪ] ADJ (+er) (*Brit pej inf*) schwul (*inf*); *clothes, colour, actor* tuntig (*inf*), tuntenhaft (*inf*)

pooh [puː] INTERJ (*bad smell*) puh, pfui; (*disdain*) pah, bah N (*baby-talk*) Aa *nt* (*baby-talk*); **to do a ~** Aa machen (*baby-talk*) VI (*baby-talk*) Aa machen (*baby-talk*)

pooh-pooh ['puː'puː] VT verächtlich abtun

pool¹ [puːl] N a Teich *m*, Tümpel *m*; (*underground*) See *m*
b (*of rain*) Pfütze *f*; (*of spilled liquid*) Lache *f*; **a ~ of blood** eine Blutlache *f*; **~s of sunlight/shade** sonnige/schattige Stellen
c (*in river*) Loch *nt*
d (*artificial*) Teich *m*; (= *swimming pool*) (Schwimm)becken *nt*; (*in private garden, hotel*) Swimmingpool *m*, Schwimmbecken *nt*; (= *swimming baths*) Schwimmbad *nt*; **to go to the (swimming) ~** ins Schwimmbad gehen; **an Olympic ~ should measure ...** ein olympisches Wettkampfbecken muss ... groß sein; **in the kiddies' ~** im Kinderbecken; **we spent every afternoon down at the ~** wir verbrachten jeden Nachmittag im Schwimmbad; **she was sitting at the edge of the ~** sie saß am Beckenrand

pool² N a (= *common fund*) (gemeinsame) Kasse; **each player put £10 in the ~** jeder Spieler gab £10 in die Kasse; **the ~ stood at £40** es waren £ 40 in der Kasse

b (= supply, source) (= typing pool) Schreibzentrale f; (= car pool) Fahrbereitschaft f; (= carsharing) Fahrgemeinschaft f; **a ~ of labour** (Brit) or **labor** (US) ein Bestand m an Arbeitskräften, eine Arbeitskraftreserve; **the Prime Minister's ~ of advisers** der Beraterstab des Premierministers; **among them they have a great ~ of experience/ideas** zusammen verfügen sie über eine Menge Erfahrung/Ideen

c pools PL (Brit) **the ~s** (= football pools) Toto m or nt; **to do the ~s** Toto spielen; **to win the ~s** im Toto gewinnen; **he won £1000 on the ~s** er hat £ 1000 im Toto gewonnen

d (= form of snooker) Poolbillard nt

e (Comm) Interessengemeinschaft f; (US: = monopoly, trust) Pool m, Kartell nt

VT resources, savings zusammenlegen; efforts vereinen (geh); **if we ~ our efforts we'll get the work done sooner** mit vereinten Kräften werden wir schneller mit der Arbeit fertig (werden)

pool: **pool attendant** N Bademeister(in) m(f); **pool hall** N Billardzimmer nt; **pool room** N **a** (= pool hall) Billardzimmer nt **b** (= betting shop) Wettannahmestelle f; **pool table** N Billardtisch m

poop[1] [puːp] N Hütte f, Poop f

poop[2] N (inf: = exhaust) schlauchen (inf); **to be ~ed (out)** geschlaucht or fertig sein (inf)

poop[3] N (US inf, pej) Trottel m (pej), Einfaltspinsel f (pej)

poop deck N Hütten- or Poopdeck nt

poo-poo ['puːˈpuː] N (baby-talk: = excreta) Aa nt (baby-talk)

poor [pʊə] **ADJ** (+er) **a** arm; **to get** or **become ~er** ärmer werden, verarmen; **he was now one thousand pounds (the) ~er** er war nun um eintausend Pfund ärmer; **a ~ little rich girl** ein armes reiches Mädchen; **~ whites** arme weiße Bevölkerung im Süden der USA **a country ~ in natural resources** ein an Bodenschätzen armes Land; **to be ~ in nutrients** arm an Nährstoffen sein; **it's the ~ man's Mercedes/Monte Carlo** (inf) das ist der Mercedes/das Monte Carlo des kleinen Mannes (inf); **~ relation** (fig) Sorgenkind nt

b (= not good) schlecht; (= meagre) mangelhaft; health, effort, performance, excuse schlecht, schwach; sense of responsibility, leadership schwach; soil mager, schlecht; quality schlecht, minderwertig; **a ~ joke** (= weak) ein schwacher Witz; (= in bad taste) ein geschmackloser Witz; **to show sb/sth in a ~ light** jdn/etw in einem schlechten Licht darstellen; **to get** or **become ~er** eyesight, hearing, weather) schlechter werden, sich verschlechtern; **she was a very ~ swimmer** sie war ein sehr schlechter Schwimmer; **he is a ~ traveller/flier** er verträgt Reisen/Flugreisen nicht gut; **a ~ friend you are!** du bist mir ein schöner Freund!; **fruit wines are a ~ substitute for grape wine** Obstwein ist nur ein armseliger Ersatz für Wein aus Trauben; **a ~ imitation of sth** eine schlechte or minderwertige Nachahmung von etw; **a ~ chance of success** schlechte Erfolgsaussichten pl; **we had a ~ time of it last night** gestern Abend lief auch alles schief (inf); **only £55? that's pretty ~, isn't it?** nur £ 55? das ist aber ziemlich wenig!; **that's ~ consolation** das ist ein schwacher Trost; **it's a ~ thing for Britain if ...** es ist schlecht für Großbritannien, wenn ...; **it will be a ~ day for the world when ...** es wird ein schwarzer Tag für die Welt sein, wenn ...; **this is a pretty ~ state of affairs** das sieht aber gar nicht gut aus; **it's very ~ of them not to have replied** es ist sehr unhöflich, dass sie uns etc (dat) nicht geantwortet haben; **he has a very ~ grasp of the subject** er beherrscht das Fach sehr schlecht; **he showed a ~ grasp of the facts** er zeigte wenig Verständnis für die Fakten; **he is a ~ hand at public speaking** in der Öffentlichkeit zu sprechen liegt ihm nicht; **she was always ~ at languages** sie war immer schlecht

or schwach in Sprachen; **hospitals are ~ at collecting information** Krankenhäuser sind schlecht im Sammeln von Informationen

c (= pitiful, pitiable) arm; **you ~ (old) chap** (inf) du armer Kerl (inf); **~ you!** du Ärmste(r)!; **she's all alone, ~ woman** sie ist ganz allein, die arme Frau; **~ things, they look cold** die Ärmsten, ihnen scheint kalt zu sein; **~ miserable creature that he is ...** armseliger Kerl or Tropf (inf), der er ist ...; **in my ~ opinion** (iro) meiner bescheidenen or unmaßgeblichen Meinung nach (iro); **it fell to my ~ self to ...** es blieb meiner Wenigkeit (dat) überlassen, zu ... (iro)

PL the ~ die Armen pl

poor: **poor box** N Armen- or Almosenbüchse f; **poorhouse** N (old) Armenhaus nt (old); **poor laws** PL Armengesetze pl

poorly ['pʊəlɪ] **ADV** **a** arm; dressed, furnished ärmlich; **~ off** schlecht gestellt; **her husband left her very ~ off** ihr Mann ließ sie in sehr ärmlichen Verhältnissen zurück

b (= badly) schlecht; (= inadequately) supported, understood schlecht, unzureichend; **~-attended** schlecht besucht; **~-designed** schlecht konstruiert, nicht genügend durchdacht; **~-educated** ohne (ausreichende) Schulbildung; **~-equipped** schlecht ausgerüstet; **~-lit** schlecht or schwach beleuchtet; **~-paid** schlecht bezahlt; **~-trained** schlecht ausgebildet, ungeschult; **~-ventilated** schlecht gelüftet; **to do ~ (at sth)** (in etw dat) schwach or schlecht abschneiden; **we're rather ~ off for staff/new ideas** wir haben einen ziemlichen Mangel an Personal/neuen Ideen

ADJ pred (Brit: = ill) schlecht, krank, elend; **to be** or **feel ~** sich schlecht etc fühlen

poorness ['pʊənɪs] N **a** (= lack of money) Armut f **b** (= lack of quality) Dürftigkeit f, Mangelhaftigkeit f; (of soil) Magerkeit f, Unergiebigkeit f; (of effort, excuse, harvest, performance) Dürftigkeit f; (of quality) Minderwertigkeit f; (of weather, memory, health, eyesight) Unzulänglichkeit f; (of leadership) Schwäche f

poor-spirited ['pʊəˈspɪrɪtɪd] **ADJ** person ängstlich

poor white trash N (US inf, pej) weißer Pöbel

poove [puːv] N = **poof(ter)**

pop[1] abbr of **population**

pop[2] [pɒp] N (esp US inf) (= father) Papa m (inf); (= elderly man) Opa m (hum inf)

pop[3] N (= pop music) Popmusik f, Pop m

pop[4] N **a** (inf: = sound) Knall m; **the toy gun went off with a ~** peng, ging die Spielzeugpistole los; **the faint ~ of a stud unfastening** das leise „Popp" eines aufspringenden Druckknopfs

b (inf: = shot) Schuss m; **to have** or **take a ~ at sb/sth** auf jdn/etw (acc) ballern (inf); (= criticize) einen Seitenhieb gegen jdn/etw führen, auf jdn/etw losgehen; **to have** or **take a ~ at sth** (fig: = try) einen Versuch wagen mit etw, sich an etw versuchen

c (= fizzy drink) Brause f, Limo f (inf)

d (dated inf: = pawn) in ~ verpfändet, versetzt

e (inf: = each) **the drinks go for £3.50 a ~** jedes Getränk kostet £ 3,50

ADV **to go ~** (cork) knallen, hochgehen (inf); (balloon) platzen; (ears) mit einem Knacken aufgehen or (when going down) zugehen; (bulb) mit einem „Ping" durchbrennen; (press stud) Popp machen; **~!** peng!

VT **a** balloon, corn zum Platzen bringen; **to ~ corn** Popcorn machen

b (inf: = put) stecken; **to ~ a letter into the postbox** (Brit) or **mailbox** (US) einen Brief einwerfen or einschmeißen (inf); **he ~ped his head round the door** er streckte den Kopf durch die Tür; **to ~ a jacket/hat on** sich (dat) ein Jackett überziehen/einen Hut aufsetzen; **to ~ the question** einen (Heirats)antrag machen; **to ~ one's cork** (inf) sich begeistern

c (dated inf: = pawn) versetzen

d (inf) pills schlucken (inf)

VI (inf) **a** (= go pop, burst) (cork) knallen; (balloon) platzen; (seed pods, buttons, popcorn) auf-

platzen; (ears) knacken; **his eyes were ~ping out of his head** ihm gingen die Augen über, ihm fielen fast die Augen aus dem Kopf (inf); **suddenly her blouse ~ped open** plötzlich platzte or sprang ihre Bluse auf

b (= go quickly or suddenly) **to ~ along/down to the baker's** schnell zum Bäcker laufen; **I'll just ~ upstairs** ich laufe mal eben nach oben; **~ across/round and see me sometime** komm doch mal auf einen Sprung bei mir vorbei (inf); **I thought I'd just ~ down to London for the weekend** ich dachte, ich fahr mal eben übers Wochenende nach London

▶ **pop at** VI +prep obj (inf: = shoot at) ballern auf (+acc) (inf)

▶ **pop back** (inf) **VT** sep (schnell) zurücktun (inf); **pop the lid back on the box** klapp den Deckel wieder auf die Schachtel; **pop it back in(to) the box** tu es wieder in die Schachtel **VI** schnell zurücklaufen; **she popped back for her book** sie lief kurz zurück, um ihr Buch zu holen

▶ **pop in** (inf) **VT** sep hineintun; **to pop sth in(-to) sth** etw in etw (acc) stecken or werfen (inf) **VI** (= visit) auf einen Sprung vorbeikommen (inf); **to pop in for a short chat** auf einen kleinen Schwatz hereinschauen (inf); **she kept popping in and out** sie lief dauernd rein und raus; **we just popped into the pub for a quickie** wir gingen kurz in die Kneipe, um einen zu heben (inf); **just pop in any time you're passing** komm doch mal vorbei, wenn du in der Gegend bist (inf)

▶ **pop off** VI (Brit inf) **a** (= die suddenly) den Löffel abgeben (sl) **b** (= go off) verschwinden (inf) (to nach); **do you fancy popping off to Spain for a week?** wie wärs, wollen wir für eine Woche nach Spanien verschwinden?

▶ **pop out** VI (inf) **a** (= go out) (schnell) rausgehen (inf); (spring, rabbit) herausspringen (of aus); **he has just popped out for a beer** er ist schnell auf ein Bierchen gegangen (inf); **he has just popped out to buy a paper/to the shops** er ist schnell eine Zeitung kaufen gegangen/zum Einkaufen gegangen **b** (eyes) vorquellen; **his eyes were popping out (with amazement)** vor Staunen fielen ihm fast die Augen aus dem Kopf (inf)

▶ **pop up** (inf) **VT** sep **a** (= put up) head hochstrecken **b** (= bring up) schnell raufbringen (inf) **VI** **a** (= appear suddenly) auftauchen (inf); (head, toast) hochschießen (inf); (figures in illustrations) sich aufstellen **b** (= come up) (mal eben) raufkommen (inf); (head, toast) (mal eben) raufgehen (inf); **do you feel like popping up to my place?** hast du Lust, mal eben zu mir raufzukommen? (inf)

pop: **pop art** N Pop-Art f; **pop concert** N Popkonzert nt; **popcorn** N Popcorn nt

Pope [pəʊp] N Papst m

Popemobile ['pəʊpməʊˌbiːl] N (inf) Papamobil nt (inf)

popery ['pəʊpərɪ] N (pej) Pfaffentum nt; **no ~!** Pfaffen raus!

pop: **popeyed** ADJ person glotzäugig; (fig) mit Glotzaugen; **pop festival** N Popfestival nt; **pop group** N Popgruppe f; **popgun** N Spielzeugpistole f

popinjay ['pɒpɪndʒeɪ] N (old) Geck m, Laffe m

popish ['pəʊpɪʃ] ADJ (pej) papistisch

poplar ['pɒplə] N Pappel f

poplin ['pɒplɪn] N Popeline f; **~ dress** Popelinekleid nt

pop: **pop music** N Popmusik f; **popover** N (US) stark aufgehender hefiger Eierkuchen

poppa ['pɒpə] N (US inf) Papa m (inf)

poppadom, poppadum ['pɒpədəm] N großes, dünnes, rundes, knusprig gebratenes Teigstück als Beilage zu indischen Gerichten

popper ['pɒpə] N (Brit inf: = press-stud) Druckknopf m

poppet ['pɒpɪt] N (inf) Schatz m; (= term of address also) Schätzchen nt

poppy ['pɒpɪ] N Mohn m

poppycock ['pɒpɪkɒk] N *(dated inf)* Unsinn *m*, Blödsinn *m (inf)*

Poppy Day N *(Brit)* ≈ Volkstrauertag *m (in Germany)*

> ## POPPY DAY
> Poppy Day ist der volkstümliche Name für den **Remembrance Day**, den zweiten Sonntag im November, an dem in Großbritannien der Toten beider Weltkriege gedacht wird. Der Name geht auf den Brauch zurück, in der Zeit vor diesem Tag Papiermohnblumen zu verkaufen, um Spendengelder für die Unterstützung von Kriegsveteranen und ihren Familien zu sammeln.

poppy seed N Mohn *m*; **poppy-seed cake** Mohnkuchen *m*

pops ['pɒps] N *(esp US, inf)* Paps *m (inf)*

pop shop N *(dated inf)* Pfandhaus *nt*

Popsicle® ['pɒpsɪkl] N *(US)* Eis *nt* am Stiel

pop: pop singer N Popsänger(in) *m(f)*; **pop socks** PL Kniestrümpfe *pl*; **pop song** N Popsong *m*; **pop star** N Popstar *m*

popsy ['pɒpsɪ] N *(dated sl)* Biene *f (dated inf)*, Puppe *f (dated inf)*

populace ['pɒpjʊlɪs] N Bevölkerung *f*; (= *masses*) breite Öffentlichkeit; **the ~ of Rome** das Volk von Rom, die Bürger von Rom

popular ['pɒpjʊlə'] ADJ **a** (= *well-liked*) beliebt *(with* bei); *(with the public)* populär, beliebt *(with* bei); *decision, measure* populär; **I know I won't be ~ if I decide that, but ...** ich weiß, dass ich mich nicht gerade beliebt mache, wenn ich so entscheide, aber ...; **he's not the most ~ of men at the moment** er ist im Augenblick nicht gerade einer der Beliebtesten *or (with the public also)* Populärsten; **he was a very ~ choice** seine Wahl fand großen Anklang

b (= *suitable for the general public*) populär; *music* leicht; *prices* erschwinglich; *lectures, journal* populärwissenschaftlich; *television, entertainer* populär, beliebt; *newspaper* weit verbreitet; **~ appeal** Massenappeal *m*; **~ edition** Volksausgabe *f*; **~ science** Populärwissenschaft *f*; **~ theatre** Volkstheater *nt*, Boulevardtheater *nt*; **a series of ~ concerts** eine Reihe volkstümlicher Konzerte

c (= *widespread*) *belief, fallacy, conviction, discontent, myth* weitverbreitet, weit verbreitet; **~ remedy** Hausmittel *nt*; **contrary to ~ belief** *or* **opinion** entgegen der landläufigen Annahme *or* Meinung; **fruit teas are becoming increasingly ~** Früchtetees erfreuen sich zunehmender Beliebtheit; **it's ~ to despise politicians these days** es gehört heutzutage zum guten Ton, sich über Politiker abfällig zu äußern

d *(Pol)* (= *of or for the people*) *government, approval, consent, support* des Volkes; (= *democratic, public*) *vote* öffentlich, allgemein; *referendum* öffentlich, offen, allgemein; *demand* groß, allgemein; *democracy* allgemein; **~ uprising** Volksaufstand *m*; **~ movement** Volksbewegung *f*; **~ mandate** Mandat *nt*; **he isn't the ~ idea of a great leader** er entspricht nicht gerade der gängigen Vorstellung von einem großen Führer; **to rule by ~ consent** mit Zustimmung der Allgemeinheit regieren; **by ~ request** auf allgemeinen Wunsch

popular culture N Popkultur *f*

popular front N Volksfront *f*

popularity [ˌpɒpjʊˈlærɪtɪ] N Beliebtheit *f*; *(with the public also)* Popularität *f (with* bei); **he'd do anything to win ~** er würde alles tun, um sich beliebt zu machen; **he'd never win a ~ contest!** er ist nicht gerade beliebt; **the sport is growing/declining in ~** dieser Sport wird immer populärer/verliert immer mehr an Popularität

popularity rating N Beliebtheitsquote *f*; **to do well in the ~s** bei Meinungsumfragen eine hohe Beliebtheitsquote erzielen

popularization [ˌpɒpjʊləraɪˈzeɪʃən] N Popularisierung *f*; (= *act also*) allgemeine Verbreitung; **a ~ of Hamlet** eine Volksfassung des Hamlet

popularize ['pɒpjʊləraɪz] VT **a** (= *make well-liked*) populär machen, zum Durchbruch verhelfen (+*dat*) **b** (= *make understandable*) *science* popularisieren, unter das Volk bringen *(inf)*; *ideas* zum Durchbruch verhelfen (+*dat*), popularisieren

popularizer ['pɒpjʊləraɪzə'] N **he is a great ~ of political/scientific ideas** er macht politische/wissenschaftliche Ideen auch der breiten Masse zugänglich

popularly ['pɒpjʊləlɪ] ADV **a** allgemein; **he is ~ believed** *or* **held** *or* **thought to be a rich man** nach allgemeiner Ansicht ist er ein reicher Mann; **to be ~ known as sb/sth** allgemein als jd/etw bekannt sein; **~ supposed to be sb/sth** allgemein als jd/etw gelten; **to be ~ considered (as** *or* **to be) sb/sth** allgemein *or* weithin als jd/etw betrachtet werden, allgemein *or* weithin für jdn/etw gehalten werden **b** (= *democratically, publicly*) *elected, supported* vom Volk, öffentlich

popular press N Boulevardpresse *f*, Regenbogenpresse *f*

populate ['pɒpjʊleɪt] VT (= *inhabit*) bevölkern; (= *colonize*) besiedeln; **~d by** bevölkert von; **this area is ~d mainly by immigrants** in diesem Stadtteil leben *or* wohnen hauptsächlich Einwanderer; **densely ~d areas** dicht besiedelte Gebiete *pl*; **densely ~d cities** dicht bevölkerte Städte *pl*

population [ˌpɒpjʊˈleɪʃən] N *(of region, country)* Bevölkerung *f*; *(of village, town)* Bewohner *pl*, Einwohner *pl*; (= *colonization*) Besiedlung *f*; (= *number of inhabitants*) Bevölkerungszahl *f*; **the ~ explosion** die Bevölkerungsexplosion; **the growing black ~ of London** die wachsende Zahl von Schwarzen in London

population: population density N Bevölkerungsdichte *f*; **population statistics** PL Bevölkerungsstatistik *f*

populism ['pɒpjʊlɪzəm] N Populismus *m*

populist ['pɒpjʊlɪst] **N** Populist(in) *m(f)* **ADJ** populistisch

populous ['pɒpjʊləs] ADJ *country* dicht besiedelt; *town, area also* mit vielen Einwohnern, einwohnerstark

pop-up ['pɒpʌp] ADJ *toaster* automatisch; *book, picture* Hochklapp- *(inf)*; **~ menu** *(Comput)* Pop-up-Menü *nt*

pop valve N *(Tech)* Sicherheitsventil *nt*

porage ['pɒrɪdʒ] N = **porridge**

porcelain ['pɔːsəlɪn] **N** Porzellan *nt* **ADJ** Porzellan-; **~ doll** Porzellanpuppe *f*

porch [pɔːtʃ] N *(of house)* Vorbau *m*, Vordach *nt*; *(US)* Veranda *f*; *(of church)* Vorhalle *f*, Portal *nt*

porcine ['pɔːsaɪn] ADJ (= *pig-like*) schweineartig; (= *of pigs*) Schweine-; **... are members of the ~ family** ... gehören zur Familie der Schweine *or* zu den Schweineartigen

porcupine ['pɔːkjʊpaɪn] N Stachelschwein *nt*

porcupine fish N Igelfisch *m*

pore [pɔː'] N Pore *f*; **in/from every ~** *(fig)* aus allen Poren

▶ **pore over** VI +*prep obj* (= *scrutinize*) genau studieren; (= *meditate*) nachdenken *or* nachgrübeln über (+*acc*); **to pore over one's books** über seinen Büchern hocken

pork [pɔːk] N **a** Schweinefleisch *nt* **b** (*US, sl*) *von der Regierung aus politischen Gründen gewährte finanzielle Vergünstigungen oder Stellen*

pork: pork barrel N *(US, inf) Geldzuwendungen der Regierung an örtliche Verwaltungsstellen, um deren Unterstützung zu gewinnen*; **pork belly** N *(Cook)* Schweinebauch *m*; **pork butcher** N Schweinemetzger *m*; **pork chop** N Schweine- *or* Schweinskotelett *nt*

porker ['pɔːkə'] N Mastschwein *nt*

pork: pork pie N Schweinefleischpastete *f*; **pork pie hat** N *runder, niedriger Filzhut*; **pork sausage** N Schweinswurst *f*

porky¹ ['pɔːkɪ] *(inf)* **ADJ** (+*er*) (= *fat*) fett **N** Schwindelei *f*

porky² N *(US inf)* Stachelschwein *nt*

porn [pɔːn] *(inf)* **N** Pornografie *f*; **soft ~** weicher Porno, Soft-Porno *m*; **hard ~** harter Porno; **hardcore ~** Hardcorepornografie *f*; **child ~** Kinderpornografie *f* **ADJ** *magazine, film, video* pornografisch; **~ actor** Pornodarsteller *m*; **~ shop** Pornoladen *m (inf)*

pornographic ADJ , **pornographically** ADV [ˌpɔːnəˈgræfɪk, -əlɪ] pornografisch

pornography [pɔːˈnɒgrəfɪ] N Pornografie *f*

porosity [pɔːˈrɒsɪtɪ] N *(of rocks, substance)* Porosität *f*; *(of skin)* Porigkeit *f*

porous ['pɔːrəs] ADJ **a** *rock, substance* porös; *skin* porig **b** *border, defence* durchlässig

porousness ['pɔːrəsnɪs] N = **porosity**

porphyry ['pɔːfɪrɪ] N Porphyr *m*

porpoise ['pɔːpəs] N Tümmler *m*

porridge ['pɒrɪdʒ] N *(esp Brit)* Porridge *m*, Haferbrei *m*; **~ oats** Haferflocken *pl*

port¹ [pɔːt] N **a** (= *harbour*) Hafen *m*; **naval ~** Kriegshafen *m*; **to come/put into ~** in den Hafen einlaufen; **~ of call** Hafen *m*, Halt *m*; **to make ~** den/einen Hafen anlaufen; **~ authority** Hafenamt *nt*, Hafenbehörde *f*; **~ dues** Hafengelder *pl*; **any ~ in a storm** *(prov)* in der Not frisst der Teufel Fliegen *(Prov)*; **the yen is the safest ~ in the current economic storm** der Yen ist in der gegenwärtigen Wirtschaftskrise der sicherste Hafen **b** (= *city or town with a port*) Hafen *m*, Hafenstadt *f*

port² N **a** *(Naut, Aviat: = porthole)* Bullauge *nt* **b** *(Naut, for cargo)* (Lade)luke *f* **c** *(Tech)* Durchlass *m* **d** *(Comput)* Anschluss *m*, Port *m*

port³ **N** *(Naut, Aviat, = left side)* Backbord *m*; **land to ~!** Land an Backbord! **ADJ** *cabin, deck* auf der Backbordseite; **~ side** Backbordseite *f*; **on the ~ bow** Backbord voraus **VT** *(Naut)* **to ~ the helm** nach Backbord drehen

port⁴ N *(also* **port wine***)* Portwein *m*

port⁵ *(Mil)* **N** **to hold the rifle at ~** das Gewehr (schräg nach links) vor dem Körper halten **VT** *arms* vorlegen, schräg nach links vor dem Körper halten; **~ arms!** ≈ präsentiert das Gewehr!

portability [ˌpɔːtəˈbɪlɪtɪ] N Tragbarkeit *f*

portable ['pɔːtəbl] **ADJ** **a** *computer, sound system* tragbar; *generator, toilets* tragbar, mobil; *medical equipment* tragbar, transportierbar, mobil; **easily ~** leicht zu tragen; **~ radio** Kofferradio *nt*; **~ television** Portable *nt*, tragbarer Fernseher; **~ (tele)phone** Mobiltelefon *nt* **b** *pension* übertragbar; *(Comput) software* übertragbar, beweglich; *language* übertragbar **N** *(computer, TV)* Portable *nt*

portage ['pɔːtɪdʒ] **N** *(Comm)* (= *act*) Transport *m*, Beförderung *f*; (= *cost*) Rollgeld *nt*, Transportkosten *pl*, Beförderungsentgelt *nt*

Portakabin® ['pɔːtəˌkæbɪn] N Container *m*; *(used as accommodation also)* Wohncontainer *m*; *(used as office also)* Bürocontainer *m*

portal ['pɔːtl] N *(liter)* Portal *nt*, Pforte *f (geh)*, Tor *nt*; *(Comput)* Portal *nt*

Portaloo® ['pɔːtəluː] N *(Brit)* mobiles Toilettenhäuschen

portal vein N Pfortader *f*

portcullis [pɔːtˈkʌlɪs] N Fallgitter *nt*, Fallgatter *nt*

porte-cochère [ˌpɔːtkɒˈʃɛə'] N Wagenauffahrt *f*

portend [pɔːˈtend] VT *(form)* bedeuten, hindeuten auf (+*acc*); **what does this ~?** was hat das zu bedeuten?

portent [pɔːˈtent] N Zeichen *nt*, Omen *nt (geh)* *(of* für); **a matter of great ~ for us all** eine Angelegenheit (von) großer Tragweite für uns alle; **a ~ of things to come** ein Vorgeschmack *m* auf das, was noch bevorsteht; **to be a ~ of sth** etw ahnen lassen

portentous [pɔːˈtentəs] ADJ **a** (= *ominous*) unheilschwanger **b** (= *grave*) gewichtig; **c** (= *pompous*) bombastisch **c** (= *marvellous*) gewaltig

portentously [pɔː'tentəslɪ] ADV **a** (= ominously) unheilschwanger **b** (= pompously) say gewichtig; **he cleared his throat ~** er räusperte sich gewichtig

porter¹ ['pɔːtə'] N (of office etc) Pförtner(in) m(f), Portier m, Portiersfrau f; (= hospital porter) Assistent(in) m(f); (at hotel) Portier m, Portiersfrau f; (Rail, at airport) Gepäckträger(in) m(f); (= Sherpa etc) (Lasten)träger(in) m(f); (US Rail) Schlafwagenschaffner(in) m(f); **~'s lodge** Pförtnerloge f

porter² N (= beer) Porter m or nt

porterage ['pɔːtərɪdʒ] N (= charge) Trägerlohn m

porterhouse steak ['pɔːtəhaʊs'steɪk] N Porterhouse Steak nt

portfolio [pɔːt'fəʊlɪəʊ] N **a** (Akten)mappe f **b** (Pol: = office) Portefeuille nt (form), Geschäftsbereich m; **minister without ~** Minister ohne Portefeuille (form) or Geschäftsbereich **c** (Fin) Portefeuille nt **d** (of artist, designer) Kollektion f; (Comm: = range of products) Kollektion f

porthole ['pɔːthəʊl] N Bullauge nt

portico ['pɔːtɪkəʊ] N Portikus m

portion ['pɔːʃən] N **a** (= piece, part) Teil m; (of ticket) Abschnitt m; **your/my ~** dein/mein Anteil m **b** (of food) Portion f **c** (old, form, = marriage portion) Mitgift f, Heiratsgut nt (old) **d** (liter: = fate) Los nt, Schicksal f

▶ **portion out** VT sep aufteilen, verteilen (among unter +acc)

portliness ['pɔːtlɪnɪs] N Beleibtheit f, Korpulenz f

portly ['pɔːtlɪ] ADJ (+er) beleibt, korpulent

portmanteau [pɔːt'mæntəʊ] N pl **-s** or **-x** Handkoffer m

portmanteau word N Kombinationsform f

Porto Rico ['pɔːtəʊ'riːkəʊ] = **Puerto Rico**

portrait ['pɔːtrɪt] N (also in words) Porträt nt; **to have one's ~ painted** sich malen lassen; **to sit for one's ~** für sein Porträt sitzen; **to paint a ~ of sb** jdn porträtieren

portraitist ['pɔːtrɪtɪst] N Porträtist(in) m(f)

portrait: portrait painter N Porträtmaler(in) m(f); **portrait photographer** N Porträtfotograf(in) m(f); **portrait photography** N Porträtfotografie f

portraiture ['pɔːtrɪtʃə'] N (= portrait) Porträt nt; (= portraits collectively) Porträts pl; (= art of portraiture) (painting) Porträtmalerei f; (Phot) Porträtfotografie f

portray [pɔː'treɪ] VT darstellen; (= paint also) malen

portrayal [pɔː'treɪəl] N Darstellung f; (= description also) Schilderung f

Portugal ['pɔːtjʊgəl] N Portugal nt

Portuguese [pɔːtjʊ'giːz] ADJ portugiesisch; **he is ~** er ist Portugiese N Portugiese m, Portugiesin f; (Ling) Portugiesisch nt

Portuguese man-of-war N Staats- or Röhrenqualle f, Portugiesische Galeere f

pose [pəʊz] N **a** (= position, attitude) Haltung f; (of model, also pej) Pose f, Haltung f; **to take up a ~** (model) eine Pose or Haltung einnehmen; **to hold a ~** eine Pose or Haltung beibehalten; **to strike a (dramatic) ~** sich (dramatisch) in Positur werfen; **she's always striking ~s** sie benimmt sich immer so theatralisch **b** (= affectation) Pose f VT **a** (= position) model aufstellen **b** (= put forward) question, problem vortragen; **the question ~d by his speech** die in seiner Rede aufgeworfene Frage **c** (= formulate) question, problem formulieren **d** (= constitute, present) difficulties, problem aufwerfen; threat darstellen; **this could ~ a health risk** das könnte eine Gesundheitsgefährdung darstellen VI **a** (= model) posieren, Modell sitzen/stehen; **to ~ (in the) nude** für einen Akt posieren or Modell sitzen/stehen; **to ~ for photographs** für Fotografien posieren

b (= attitudinize) posieren, sich in Pose werfen **c** (= present oneself as) **to ~ as** sich ausgeben als

Poseidon [pə'saɪdən] N Poseidon m

poser ['pəʊzə'] N **a** (= person) Angeber(in) m(f) **b** (inf: = difficult problem or question) harte Nuss (inf)

posh [pɒʃ] (inf) ADJ (+er) piekfein (inf), vornehm; neighbourhood, hotel, wedding also nobel; friends vornehm, fein; occasion vornehm, elegant ADV (+er) **to talk ~** mit vornehmem Akzent sprechen VT **to ~ sth up** (inf) etw verschönern (inf)

poshly ['pɒʃlɪ] ADJ piekfein (inf), vornehm; talk vornehm

poshness ['pɒʃnɪs] N Feinheit f, Vornehmheit f; (of accent) Vornehmheit f, Distinguierte(s) nt

posing pouch N knappe Herrenbadehose

posit ['pɒzɪt] N (= claim) Postulat nt, Grundannahme f VT **a** (rare: = put down) absetzen **b** (= claim) postulieren; hypothesis aufstellen

position [pə'zɪʃən] ⚙ 12.3, 19.1 N **a** (= location, place where sb/sth is, of person) Platz m; (of object) Stelle f, Platz m; (of microphone, statue, wardrobe, plant etc) Standort m; (of spotlight, table, in picture, painting) Anordnung f; (of town, house etc) Lage f; (of plane, ship, Sport: = starting position, Ftbl etc) Position f; (Mil: = strategic site) Stellung f; **to be in/out of ~** an der richtigen/falschen Stelle sein; **the actors were in ~ on the stage** die Schauspieler hatten ihre Plätze auf der Bühne eingenommen; **to jockey or jostle for ~** (lit) um eine gute Ausgangsposition kämpfen; (fig) um eine gute Position rangeln; **the ~ of the fireplace isn't very good** der Kamin hat keinen sehr günstigen Platz; **what ~ do you play?** auf or in welcher Position spielst du?; **his ~ is full-back/goalkeeper** er spielt Außenverteidiger/Torwart **b** (= posture, way of standing, sitting etc) Haltung f; (in love-making, Art: of model) Stellung f; (Ballet) Position f; **in a sitting ~** sitzend; **in a reclining ~** zurückgelehnt **c** (in class, league etc) Platz m; **after the third lap he was in fourth ~** nach der dritten Runde lag er auf dem vierten Platz or war er Vierter; **to finish in third ~** Dritter werden, auf dem dritten Platz landen (inf) **d** (= social, professional standing) Stellung f, Position f; **a man of ~** eine hoch gestellte Persönlichkeit **e** (= job) Stelle f; **he has a high ~ in the Ministry of Defence** er bekleidet eine hohe Stellung or Position im Verteidigungsministerium; **a ~ of trust** eine Vertrauensstellung; **to be in a ~ of power** eine Machtposition innehaben **f** (fig: = situation, circumstance) Lage f; **to be in a ~ to do sth** in der Lage sein, etw zu tun; **what is the ~ regarding ...?** wie sieht es mit ... aus?; **I'm not in a ~ to say anything about that** ich kann dazu nichts sagen; **my ~ is that I don't have the qualifications/money** mir geht es so, dass mir die Qualifikation/das Geld fehlt **g** (fig: = point of view, attitude) Standpunkt m, Haltung f, Einstellung f; **what is the government's ~ on ...?** welchen Standpunkt vertritt die Regierung zu ...?; **to take (up) a ~ on sth** eine Haltung zu einer Sache einnehmen VT **a** (= place in position) microphone, ladder, guards aufstellen; soldiers, policemen positionieren; (artist, photographer etc) platzieren; (Comput) cursor positionieren, platzieren; **he ~ed himself where he could see her** er stellte or (seated) setzte sich so, dass er sie sehen konnte; **he has ~ed himself as a moderate** er hat sich als (ein) Gemäßigter etabliert **b** (in marketing) product positionieren

position: position finder N (Aviat, Naut, Tech) Ortungsgerät nt; **position paper** N (Pol) Positionspapier nt

positive ['pɒzɪtɪv] ADJ **a** (Math, Phot, Elec, Gram) positiv; **~ pole** Pluspol m; **the ~ degree** (Gram) der Positiv **b** (= affirmative, constructive) result, answer, attitude positiv; criticism, suggestion konstruktiv; **he is a very ~ person** er hat eine sehr positive Einstellung zum Leben; **on the ~ side** auf der positiven Seite; **to take ~ action** positive Schritte unternehmen; **~ thinking** positive Haltung, positives Denken **c** (= definite) person, tone of voice bestimmt; instructions streng; evidence, answer definitiv, eindeutig; rule fest; **that is ~ proof of** proof **~** das ist der sichere or eindeutige Beweis; **to be ~ that ...** sicher sein, dass ..., definitiv wissen, dass ...; **to be ~ about or of sth** sich (dat) einer Sache (gen) absolut sicher sein; **to make a ~ identification** or **ID** (Police) eindeutig identifizieren, die Identität eindeutig feststellen; **this may even do some ~ good** damit tut man vielleicht sogar etwas wirklich or richtig Gutes; **are you sure you don't want her address? – –** bist du sicher, dass du nicht ihre Adresse willst? – absolut or ganz bestimmt **d** (= real, downright) **this is a ~ miracle/crime/disgrace** das ist wirklich ein Wunder/Verbrechen/eine Schande; **he's a ~ genius/menace** er ist wirklich ein Genie/Ärgernis, er ist ein wahres Genie/wirkliches Ärgernis N **a** (Phot) Positiv nt; (Gram) Positiv m; (Elec) Pluspol m; (Math) positive Zahl **b** (= advantage) Positive(s) nt; **the ~s far outweigh the negatives** das Positive wiegt viel schwerer als das Negative, das Positive gleicht das Negative mehr als aus ADV **a** (Med) **to test ~** einen positiven Befund haben; **to show ~ (for sth)** einen positiven Befund (auf etw) zeigen **b** **to think ~** positiv denken

positive discrimination N (Brit) positive Diskriminierung

positive feedback N positives Feedback, positive Reaktion; (Elec) Rückkopplung f; **to give sb ~ (about sb/sth)** jdm eine positive Rückmeldung (zu jdm/etw) geben; **to get ~ (about sb/sth)** eine positive Rückmeldung (zu jdm/etw) erhalten

positively ['pɒzɪtɪvlɪ] ADV **a** (= affirmatively, constructively, also Sci) positiv **b** (= decisively) bestimmt; (= definitely, indisputably) prove definitiv, eindeutig; (= conclusively) identify eindeutig, bestimmt, definitiv; **to test ~ for drugs** positiv auf Drogen getestet werden; **I ~ forbid it** ich verbiete es absolut or definitiv **c** (= really, absolutely) wirklich, echt (inf); (emph: = actively) eindeutig, bestimmt; **she glowed with pride** sie strahlte regelrecht vor Stolz; **Jane doesn't mind being photographed, she ~ loves it** Jane hat nichts dagegen, fotografiert zu werden, im Gegenteil, sie hat es sehr gern or sie hat es eindeutig sehr gern **d** (Elec, Phys) charged positiv; **~ charged terminal** Plus-Klemme f

positiveness ['pɒzɪtɪvnɪs] N **a** (= constructiveness) Positive(s) nt; **I was reassured by the ~ of his attitude** ich wurde durch seine positive Haltung bestärkt **b** (= certainty) Überzeugung f; (of voice) Bestimmtheit f; (of evidence) Überzeugungskraft f; **her ~ that he was innocent** die Überzeugung, mit der sie an seine Unschuld glaubte

positive vetting N Sicherheitsüberprüfung f

positivism ['pɒzɪtɪvɪzəm] N Positivismus m

positivist ['pɒzɪtɪvɪst] ADJ positivistisch N Positivist(in) m(f)

positivistic ADJ , **positivistically** ADV [pɒzɪtɪ'vɪstɪk, -əlɪ] positivistisch

positron ['pɒzɪtrɒn] N Positron nt

poss [pɒs] abbr of **possible** of **possibly** mögl.

posse ['pɒsɪ] N (US: = sheriff's posse) Aufgebot nt; (fig) Gruppe f, Schar f; **~ of searchers** Suchtrupp m

possess [pə'zes] VT besitzen; (form) foreign language, facts verfügen über (+acc); **to be ~ed of sth** (form) über etw (acc) verfügen; **it ~s many advantages** es hat viele Vorteile; **to be ~ed by demons** von Dämonen besessen sein; **to be ~ed by the urge to do sth** von dem Drang besessen sein, etw tun zu müssen; **like a man/ woman ~ed** wie ein Besessener/eine Besessene; **to fight like one ~ed** wie ein Besessener kämpfen; **whatever ~ed you to do that?** was ist bloß in Sie gefahren, so etwas zu tun?; **to ~ one's soul in patience** (form) sich in Geduld fassen

possession [pəˈzeʃən] N **a** (= ownership) Besitz m; (Sport: of ball) Ballbesitz m; (fig = control) (of feelings, oneself) Kontrolle f; **to have sth in one's ~** etw in seinem Besitz haben; **to have/take ~ of sth** etw in Besitz haben/nehmen; **to come into/get ~ of sth** in den Besitz von etw gelangen/kommen; **to get/have ~ of the ball** in Ballbesitz gelangen/sein; **to be in ~ of sth** im Besitz von etw sein; **I'm in full ~ of the facts** ich verfüge über alle Tatsachen; **he put me in ~ of the information I required** er lieferte or verschaffte mir die Informationen, die ich benötigte; **according to the information in my ~** nach der mir zur Verfügung stehenden Informationen; **to be in ~ of a house** ein Haus in Besitz haben; **to take ~ of a house** ein Haus in Besitz nehmen; **~ is nine points of the law** (prov) das Recht steht auf der Seite der Besitzenden
 b (by demons) Besessenheit f
 c (= thing possessed) Besitz m no pl; (= territory) Besitzung f; **all his ~s** sein gesamter Besitz, seine gesamten Besitztümer

possession order N (Brit Jur) Räumungsbefehl m

possessive [pəˈzesɪv] ADJ (towards belongings) eigen; mother, boyfriend, love, manner etc besitzergreifend; streak besitzergreifend, habgierig; **to be ~ about sth** seine Besitzansprüche auf etw (acc) betonen; **to be ~ toward(s) sb** an jdn Besitzansprüche stellen **N** (Gram: = pronoun, adjective) Possessiv(um) nt

possessive case N (Gram) Genitiv m, zweiter Fall

possessively [pəˈzesɪvlɪ] ADV (about things) eigen; (towards people) besitzergreifend

possessiveness [pəˈzesɪvnɪs] N eigene Art (about mit); (towards people) besitzergreifende Art (towards gegenüber)

possessive pronoun N (Gram) besitzanzeigendes Fürwort, Possessivpronomen nt

possessor [pəˈzesə'] N Besitzer(in) m(f); **to be the proud ~ of sth** der stolze Besitzer von etw sein

posset [ˈpɒsɪt] N **a** heiße Milch mit Bier oder Wein und Gewürzen **b** (of baby) erbrochene Milch

possibility [ˌpɒsəˈbɪlɪtɪ] ✪ 15.2, 26.3 N Möglichkeit f; **there's not much ~ of success/of his** or **him being successful** die Aussichten auf Erfolg/darauf, dass er Erfolg hat, sind nicht sehr groß; **within the realms** or **bounds of ~** im Bereich des Möglichen; **it's not beyond the realms** or **bounds of ~** es ist durchaus im Bereich des Möglichen; **do you by any ~ happen to know ...?** wissen Sie zufällig ...?; **the ~ of doing sth** die Möglichkeit or Chance, etw zu tun; **it's a distinct ~ that ...** es besteht eindeutig die Möglichkeit, dass ...; **he is a ~ for the job** er kommt für die Stelle infrage or in Frage or in Betracht; **there is some** or **a ~ that ...** es besteht die Möglichkeit, dass ...; **a job with real possibilities** eine Stelle mit echten Möglichkeiten or Chancen; **he/that has possibilities** in ihm/darin stecken Möglichkeiten

possible [ˈpɒsəbl] ✪ 9.1, 15.3, 19.4, 26.3 **ADJ** möglich; **anything is ~** möglich ist alles; **as soon/often/far as ~** so bald/oft/weit wie möglich; **as quickly as ~** so rasch or schnell wie möglich; **the best/worst/quickest ~ ...** der/die/ das bestmögliche/schlechtestmögliche/ schnellstmögliche ...; **if (at all) ~** falls (irgend) möglich; **it's just ~ that I'll see you before then** eventuell sehe ich dich vorher noch; **it's just ~, I suppose** es ist unwahrscheinlich, aber möglich; **there is no ~ excuse for his behaviour** für sein Verhalten gibt es absolut keine Entschuldigung; **the only ~ choice, the only choice**

die einzig mögliche Wahl; **it will be ~ for you to return the same day** es besteht or Sie haben die Möglichkeit, am selben Tag zurückzukommen; **to make sth ~** etw ermöglichen, etw möglich machen; **to make it ~ for sb to do sth** es jdm ermöglichen, etw zu tun; **where ~** wo möglich; **wherever ~** wo immer möglich, wo immer es möglich ist
 N Möglichkeit f; **a long list of ~s for the job** eine lange Liste möglicher Kandidaten für die Stelle; **the ~s played the probables** (Sport) die möglichen Kandidaten spielten gegen die wahrscheinlichen (Kandidaten); **he is a ~ for the English team** er kommt für die englische Mannschaft infrage or in Frage; **the first three houses were all ~s** die ersten drei Häuser kamen alle infrage or in Frage

possibly [ˈpɒsəblɪ] ✪ 12.3, 16.3, 26.3 ADV **not ~** unmöglich; **I can't ~ stay indoors all weekend** ich kann unmöglich das ganze Wochenende in der Wohnung sitzen; **nobody could ~ tell the difference** es war unmöglich, einen Unterschied zu erkennen; **that can't ~ be true** das kann unmöglich wahr sein; **can that ~ be true?** kann das (vielleicht doch) stimmen?; **very** or **quite ~** absolut or durchaus möglich; **how could I ~ have come?** wie hätte ich denn kommen können?; **how could he ~ have known that?** wie konnte er das nur wissen?; **he did all he ~ could** er tat, was er nur konnte; **I have made myself as comfortable as I ~ can** ich habe es mir so bequem wie möglich gemacht; **if I ~ can** wenn ich irgend kann; **I couldn't ~ ...** (polite formula) ich kann unmöglich ...
 b (= perhaps) vielleicht, möglicherweise; **~ not** vielleicht nicht, möglicherweise nicht

possum [ˈpɒsəm] N Opossum nt, Beutelratte f; **to play ~** (sleeping) sich schlafend stellen; (dead) sich tot stellen

post¹ [pəʊst] **N a** (= pole, doorpost etc) Pfosten m; (= lamp post) Pfahl m; (= telegraph post) Mast m; **a wooden ~** ein Holzpfosten or -pfahl m; **a metal ~** ein Metallpfosten m; **starting/winning** or **finishing ~** Start-/Zielpfosten m; **the horses were at the ~** die Pferde standen am Start; **he was left at the ~** sie ließen ihn stehen → **deaf**
 VT a (= display: also **post up**) anschlagen; **"post no bills"** „Plakate ankleben verboten"; **to ~ a wall with advertisements** eine Wand plakatieren or mit Werbeplakaten bekleben
 b (= announce) concert etc durch Anschlag bekannt machen; gains, profits veröffentlichen; **to ~ a reward** eine Belohnung ausschreiben; **to be ~ed (as) missing** als vermisst gemeldet sein

post² ✪ 19.1, 19.4 **N a** (Brit: = job) Stelle f, Posten m; **to look for/take up a ~** eine Stelle suchen/antreten; **to hold a ~** eine Stelle innehaben
 b (esp Mil: = place of duty) Posten m; **at one's ~** auf seinem Posten; **to die at one's ~** im Dienst sterben
 c (Mil: = camp, station) Posten m; **a frontier** or **border ~** ein Grenzposten m; **a chain of ~s along the border** eine Postenkette entlang der Grenze; **~ exchange** (abbr **PX**) (US) von der Regierung betriebener Vorzugsladen für Truppenangehörige; **to return to the ~** zur Garnison zurückkehren; **to leave the ~** die Garnison verlassen; **most of the officers live on the ~** die meisten Offiziere leben in der Garnison; **the whole ~ fell sick** die ganze Garnison wurde krank
 d (Brit Mil: = bugle call) **first ~** Wecksignal nt; **last ~** Zapfenstreich m
 e (= trading post) Handelsniederlassung f
 VT a (= position) postieren; sentry, guard postieren, aufstellen
 b (= send, assign) versetzen; (Mil) abkommandieren; **to be ~ed to a battalion/an embassy/a ship** zu einem Bataillon/an eine Botschaft/auf ein Schiff versetzt or (Mil) abkommandiert werden; **he has been ~ed away** er ist versetzt or (Mil) abkommandiert worden

post³ N a (Brit: = mail) Post f; **by ~** mit der Post, auf dem Postweg (form); **it's in the ~** es

ist unterwegs or in der Post; **to drop sth in the ~** (in den Briefkasten) einwerfen; (= in post office) etw zur Post bringen; **to catch the ~** (letter) noch mit der Post mitkommen; (person) rechtzeitig zur Leerung kommen; **to miss the ~** (letter) nicht mehr mit der Post mitkommen; (person) die Leerung verpassen; **there is no ~ today** (= no delivery) heute kommt keine Post, heute wird keine Post ausgetragen; (= no letters) heute ist keine Post (für uns) gekommen; **has the ~ been?** war die Post schon da?
 b (Hist) Post f; **to travel ~** mit der Post(kutsche) reisen
 VT a (Brit, = put in the post) aufgeben; (in letterbox) einwerfen, einstecken; (= send by post) mit der Post schicken; (Comput) abschicken; **I ~ed it to you on Monday** ich habe es am Montag an Sie abgeschickt
 b (= inform) **to keep sb ~ed** jdn auf dem Laufenden halten
 c (= enter in ledger: also **post up**) eintragen (to in +acc); **all transactions must be ~ed (up) weekly** alle Geschäftsvorgänge müssen wöchentlich verbucht werden VI (old: = travel by post) mit der Post(kutsche) reisen

▸ **post off** VT sep abschicken

post- [pəʊst-] PREF nach-; (esp with words derived from Latin or Greek) post-; **postcommunist** post- or nachkommunistisch; **~traumatic** posttraumatisch

postage [ˈpəʊstɪdʒ] N Porto nt, Postgebühr f (form); **~ and packing** (abbr **p&p**) Porto und Verpackung; **what is the ~ to Germany?** wie hoch ist das Porto nach Deutschland?

postage: postage meter N (US) Frankiermaschine f; **postage paid** ADJ portofrei; envelope frankiert, freigemacht **ADV** portofrei; **postage rate** N Porto nt, Postgebühr f (form); **postage stamp** N Briefmarke f, Postwertzeichen nt (form); **what she knows about children would fit on the back of a ~** ihre Kenntnisse über Kinder sind verschwindend gering

postal [ˈpəʊstl] ADJ Post-, postalisch (form); **~ charges** Postgebühren pl **N** (US, inf) = **postal card**

postal: postal area N Zustellbereich m (form), Postbezirk m; **postal ballot** N Briefwahl f; **postal card** N (US) (= letter card) Postkarte mit aufgedruckter Briefmarke für offizielle Zwecke (= postcard) Briefkarte f; (with picture) Ansichtskarte f; **postal code** N (Brit) Postleitzahl f; **postal district** N (of main sorting office) ≈ Postort m (form), (of local sorting office) ≈ Postzustellbereich m (form); **postal order** N (Brit) ≈ Postanweisung f, Geldgutschein, der bei der Post gekauft und eingelöst wird; **postal service** N Postdienst m; **postal tuition** N Fernunterricht m; **postal vote** N **to have a ~** per Briefwahl wählen; **postal worker** N Postbeamte(r) m, Postbeamtin f, Postbedienstete(r) mf, Postler(in) m(f) (inf)

post: postbag N (Brit) Postsack m; **postbox** N (Brit) Briefkasten m; **postcard** N Postkarte f; **(picture) ~** Ansichtskarte f; **post chaise** N (Hist) Postkutsche f; **postclassical** ADJ nachklassisch; **post code** N (Brit) Postleitzahl f

---

POST CODE

Der britische **post code** setzt sich aus zwei Gruppen mit jeweils drei Elementen zusammen, normalerweise ein oder zwei Buchstaben plus eine Zahl, danach eine Zahl und zwei Buchstaben: z.B. EH9 2HZ. Die erste Gruppe bezieht sich auf die Gegend, wobei in diesem Fall „EH" für die Gegend um Edinburgh und „9" für einen bestimmten Bezirk darin steht. Die zweite Gruppe bezeichnet einen bestimmten Straßenabschnitt in dieser Gegend.

---

post: postdate VT **a** cheque etc vordatieren
 b (= be later than) später datieren als (+nom); **postdoctoral** ADJ nach der or im Anschluss an die Promotion; **postedit** VTI (Comput, in

machine translations) redaktionell nachbearbeiten

poster ['pəʊstə'] N (*advertising*) Plakat *nt*; (*for decoration also*) Poster *nt*; ~ **colour** or **paint** Plakatfarbe *f*, Plakafarbe® *f*

poste restante ['pəʊst'resta:nt] (*Brit*) **N** Aufbewahrungsstelle *f* für postlagernde Sendungen **ADJ** *address, facility* für postlagernde Sendungen **ADV** postlagernd

posterior [pɒ'stɪərɪə'] **ADJ** (*form*) hintere(r, s); (*in time*) spätere(r, s); **to be** ~ **to sth** hinter etw (*dat*) liegen; (*in time*) nach etw (*dat*) kommen, auf etw (*acc*) folgen **N** (*hum*) Allerwerteste(r) *m* (*hum*)

posterity [pɒ'sterɪtɪ] N die Nachwelt; **they videoed it for** ~ sie haben es für die Nachwelt auf Video aufgenommen

postern ['pɒstɜ:n] N (*old*) Seitenpforte *f*, Nebenpforte *f*

post: post-free ADJ, ADV portofrei, gebührenfrei; **postglacial** ADJ postglazial, nacheiszeitlich; **postgrad** ['pəʊst'græd] N, ADJ (*Brit inf*) = **postgraduate; postgraduate N** *jd, der seine Studien an den ersten akademischen Grad weiterführt*, Postgraduierte(r) *mf* **ADJ** *work, studies, research* weiterführend, postgradual; ~ **course** Anschlusskurs *m*; ~ **degree** zweiter akademischer Abschluss or Grad; ~ **diploma/scholarship** Postgraduiertendiplom *nt*/-stipendium *nt*; ~ **student** Postgraduierte(r) *mf*; **posthaste** ADV schnellstens, auf dem schnellsten Wege; **post horn** N Posthorn *nt*; **post house** N (*Hist*) Posthalterei *f*

posthumous ['pɒstjʊməs] ADJ post(h)um; *child* nachgeboren

posthumously ['pɒstjʊməslɪ] ADV post(h)um

postie ['pəʊstɪ] N (*Scot, Austral: inf*) Briefträger(in) *m(f)*

postil(l)ion [pə'stɪlɪən] N Reiter(in) *m(f)* des Sattelpferdes

postimpressionism ['pəʊstɪm'preʃənɪzəm] N Nachimpressionismus *m*

postimpressionist ['pəʊstɪm'preʃənɪst] **ADJ** nachimpressionistisch **N** Nachimpressionist(in) *m(f)*

postindustrial [ˌpəʊstɪn'dʌstrɪəl] ADJ post- or nachindustriell

posting ['pəʊstɪŋ] N (= *transfer, assignment*) Versetzung *f*; (*Mil also*) Abkommandierung *f*; **he's got a new** ~ er ist wieder versetzt/abkommandiert worden; **I've been given an overseas** ~ **to Japan** ich bin auf einen Auslandsposten nach Japan versetzt worden

Post-it® ['pəʊstɪt], **Post-it note**® N Haftnotiz *f*

postlude ['pəʊstlu:d] N Nachspiel *nt*

post: postman N (*Brit*) Briefträger *m*, Postbote *m*; **postman's knock** N *Kinderspiel, bei dem für einen Brief mit einem Kuss bezahlt wird*; **postmark N** Poststempel *m*; **date as** ~ Datum *nt* des Poststempels **VT** (ab)stempeln; **the letter is ~ed "Birmingham"** der Brief ist in Birmingham abgestempelt; **postmaster** N (*Brit*) Postmeister *m*; **postmaster general** *pl* ~**masters general** = Postminister(in) *m(f)*; **postmeridian** ADJ (*form*) nachmittäglich; **post meridiem** ['pəʊstmə'rɪdɪəm] ADV (*form*) nachmittags; **postmistress** N (*Brit*) Postmeisterin *f*; **postmodern** ADJ postmodern; **postmodernism** N Postmodernismus *m*; **postmodernist N** Postmodernist(in) *m(f)* **ADJ** postmodernistisch; **postmortem** [ˌpəʊst'mɔ:təm] **N a** (*also* **postmortem examination**) Obduktion *f*, Autopsie *f*, Leichenöffnung *f* **b** (*fig*) nachträgliche Erörterung; **to hold** or **have a** ~ **on sth** etw hinterher erörtern; **postnatal** ADJ nach der Geburt, postnatal (*spec*); **post office** N Postamt *nt*; **the Post Office** (= *institution*) die Post; ~ **box** (*abbr* **PO Box**) Postfach *nt*; **~ worker** Postarbeiter(in) *m(f)*; **he has £2000 in ~ savings** or **in the Post Office Savings Bank** (*Brit*) er hat £ 2000 auf dem Postsparbuch; **postoperative** ADJ post-

operativ; **post-paid ADJ** portofrei; *envelope* frankiert, freigemacht **ADV** **to reply** ~ mit freigemachter Postkarte/freigemachtem Briefumschlag antworten; **postpartum** [ˌpəʊst'pɑ:təm] **ADJ** post partum, postpartal; ~ **depression** post-Partum-Depression *f*

postpone [pəʊst'pəʊn] VT **a** aufschieben, hinausschieben; (*for specified period*) verschieben; **it has been ~d till Tuesday** es ist auf Dienstag verschoben worden; **you mustn't** ~ **answering a day longer** Sie dürfen die Antwort keinen Tag länger hinausschieben **b** (*Gram form*) nachstellen

postponement [pəʊst'pəʊnmənt] N (= *act*) Verschiebung *f*; (= *result*) Aufschub *m*

post: postposition N (*Gram*) Nachstellung *f*; (= *part of speech*) Postposition *f*; **postpositive** ADJ (*Gram*) nachgestellt; **postprandial** [ˌpəʊst'prændɪəl] **ADJ** (*hum*) nach dem Essen; ~ **walk** Verdauungsspaziergang *m*; **post road** N (*Hist*) Poststraße *f*; **postscript(um)** N (*abbr* **PS**) (*to letter*) Postskriptum *nt*; (*to book, article etc*) Nachwort *nt*; (*fig: to affair*) Nachspiel *nt*; **he added a postscript** (*fig: in speech*) er fügte noch eine Bemerkung hinzu

postulant ['pɒstjʊlənt] N (*Rel*) Postulant(in) *m(f)*

postulate ['pɒstjʊlɪt] **N** Postulat *nt* **VT** ['pɒstjʊleɪt] postulieren; *theory* aufstellen

postulation [ˌpɒstjʊ'leɪʃən] N (= *act*) Postulieren *nt*; (*theory*) Postulat *nt*

postural ['pɒstjərəl] ADJ Haltungs-; ~ **exercises** Haltungsübungen *pl*; **children can develop bad** ~ **habits** Kinder können sich eine schlechte Haltung angewöhnen

posture ['pɒstʃə'] **N** (*lit, fig*) Haltung *f*; (*pej*) Pose *f*; **she has very poor** ~ sie hat eine sehr schlechte Haltung; **in the** ~ **of** in der Pose (+*gen*) **VI** sich in Positur or Pose werfen; **is he merely posturing (because of the election)?** ist das nur eine (Wahl)pose seinerseits?

post-war ADJ Nachkriegs-; *event also* in der Nachkriegszeit; ~ **era** Nachkriegszeit *f*; **of the** ~ **era** aus der Nachkriegszeit; ~ **London** das London der Nachkriegszeit

postwoman N (*esp Brit*) Briefträgerin *f*, Postbotin *f*

posy ['pəʊzɪ] N Sträußchen *nt*

pot [pɒt] **N a** Topf *m*; (= *teapot, coffee pot*) Kanne *f*; (*dated:* = *tankard*) Krug *m*; (= *lobster pot*) Korb *m*; (= *chimneypot*) Kaminaufsatz *m*; ~**s and pans** Töpfe und Pfannen; **a pint** ~ = ein Humpen *m*; **to keep the** ~ **boiling** (= *earn living*) dafür sorgen, dass der Schornstein raucht (*inf*); (= *keep sth going*) den Betrieb aufrechterhalten; **that's (a case of) the** ~ **calling the kettle black** (*prov*) ein Esel schimpft den anderen Langohr (*prov*); **to go to** ~ (*inf*) (*person, business*) auf den Hund kommen (*inf*); (*plan, arrangement*) ins Wasser fallen (*inf*) **b** (*inf:* = *large amount*) **to have ~s of money/time** massenhaft (*inf*) or jede Menge (*inf*) Geld/Zeit haben **c** (*inf:* = *important person*) **a big** ~ ein hohes Tier (*inf*) **d** (*inf:* = *marijuana*) Pot *nt* (*sl*) **e** (*Cards:* = *pool*) Topf *m*, Pott *m* **f** (*inf:* = *prize, cup*) Topf *m* (*inf*) **g** (= *potshot*) Schuss *m* aufs Geratewohl **h** (*inf:* = *potbelly*) Spitzbauch *m* **VT a** *meat* einmachen, einkochen; *jam* einfüllen **b** *plant* eintopfen **c** (= *shoot*) *game* schießen **d** (*Billiards*) *ball* einlochen **e** (*inf*) *baby* auf den Topf setzen **VI a** **to** ~ **at** schießen auf (+*acc*) **b** (*inf:* = *make pottery*) töpfern (*inf*)

potable ['pəʊtəbl] ADJ (*esp US form*) trinkbar

potage ['pəʊtɪdʒ] N (*Cook*) dicke Suppe (*mit Rahm*)

potash ['pɒtæʃ] N Pottasche *f*, Kaliumkarbonat *nt*

potassic [pə'tæsɪk] ADJ (*Chem*) Kalium-, Kali-

potassium [pə'tæsɪəm] N Kalium *nt*

potassium cyanide N Kaliumzyanid *nt*, Zyankali *nt*

potassium nitrate N Kaliumnitrat *nt*, Kalisalpeter *m*

potations [pə'teɪʃənz] PL (*liter*) Zecherei *f*

potato [pə'teɪtəʊ] N *pl* **-es** Kartoffel *f* → **hot potato**

potato: potato beetle, (*esp US*) **potato bug** N Kartoffelkäfer *m*; **potato blight** N Kartoffelfäule *f*/-krankheit *f*; **potato chip a** (*esp US*) = **potato crisp b** (*Brit:* = *chip*) Pomme frite *f*; **potato crisp** (*Brit*) Kartoffelchip *m*; **potato masher** N Kartoffelstampfer *m*; **potato peeler** N Kartoffelschäler *m*; **potato rot** N Kartoffelfäule *f*/-krankheit *f*; **potato salad** N Kartoffelsalat *m*; **potato soup** N Kartoffelsuppe *f*

pot: potbellied ['pɒt'belɪd] ADJ *person* spitzbäuchig; (*through hunger*) blähbäuchig; ~ **pig** Hängebauchschwein *nt*; ~ **stove** Kanonenofen *m*; **potbelly** N (= *stomach*) (*from overeating*) Spitzbauch *m*; (*from malnutrition*) Blähbauch *m*; (= *stove*) Kanonenofen *m*; **potboiler** N rein kommerzielles Werk; **pot-bound** ADJ *plant* eingewachsen; **pot cheese** ADJ (*US*) = **cottage cheese**

poteen [pɒ'ti:n, pɒ'tʃi:n] N *illegal destillierter irischer Whisky*

potency ['pəʊtənsɪ] N (*of drink, drug, charm etc*) Stärke *f*; (*of argument, reason etc*) Durchschlagskraft *f*; (*of weapon, combination, image*) Schlagkraft *f*; (*of man*) Potenz *f*

potent ['pəʊtənt] ADJ *drink, drug, charm, motive etc* stark; *argument, reason etc* durchschlagend; *weapon, combination, image* stark, mächtig, durchschlagend; *reminder* stark, beeindruckend; *man* potent; *ruler* mächtig

potentate ['pəʊtənteɪt] N Potentat *m*

potential [pəʊ'tenʃəl] **ADJ** (*also Phys*) potenziell, potentiell **N** Potenzial *nt*, Potential *nt* (*also Elec, Math, Phys*); **the** ~ **for growth** Wachstumspotenzial *nt*, Wachstumspotential *nt*; **to have** ~ ausbaufähig sein (*inf*); **he shows quite a bit of** ~ es steckt einiges in ihm; **to achieve** or **fulfil** or **realize one's** ~ die Grenze seiner Möglichkeiten erreichen or erfüllen or verwirklichen; **to do sth to one's full** ~ etw bis an die Grenzen seiner Möglichkeiten tun; **to have great** ~ **(as/for)** große Möglichkeiten bergen (als/für); **to have the** ~ **for sth** das Potenzial or Potential für etw haben; **to have the** ~ **to do sth** das Potenzial or Potential haben, um etw zu tun; **to have no/ little** ~ kein/kaum Potenzial or Potential haben; **creative** ~ kreatives Potenzial or Potential, kreative Möglichkeiten *pl*; **military** ~ militärisches Potenzial or Potential; **employment** ~ Arbeitsmöglichkeiten *pl*; **management** ~ Möglichkeiten *pl* im Management; **she has management** ~ sie hat das Zeug zur Managerin; **commercial** ~ kommerzielle Möglichkeiten *pl*

potential difference N (*Phys, Elec*) potenzieller or potentieller Unterschied

potential energy N (*Phys*) potenzielle or potentielle Energie

potentiality [pəʊ̩tenʃɪ'ælɪtɪ] N Möglichkeit *f*

potentially ['pəʊ'tenʃəlɪ] ❂ 15.3 ADV potenziell, potentiell; ~, **these problems are very serious** diese Probleme könnten sich als gravierend herausstellen

potentiometer [pəʊ̩tenʃɪ'ɒmɪtə'] N (*Tech*) Potenziometer *nt*, Potentiometer *nt*

potful ['pɒtfʊl] N Topf *m*; (*of coffee, tea*) Kanne *f*

pothead ['pɒthed] N (*inf*) Kiffer(in) *m(f)* (*inf*)

pother ['pɒðə'] N (*old*) Aufruhr *m*, Wirbel *m*; **to make a** ~ **about sth** wegen etw (ein) Theater machen

pot: potherb N Küchenkraut *nt*; **potholder** N (*US*) Topflappen *m*; **pothole N a** (*in road*) Schlagloch *nt* **b** (*Geol*) Höhle *f*; **potholed** ADJ voller Schlaglöcher; **workmen are already beginning to mend the** ~ **roads** Arbeiter haben schon damit begonnen, die Schlaglöcher in den Straßen auszubessern; **potholer** N Höhlenforscher(in) *m(f)*; **potholing** N Höhlenforschung *f*; **pothook** N **a** (*for pot*) Kesselhaken *m* **b** (*in writing*) Krakel *m*; **pothunter** N **a** (*Sport*) unwaidmännischer Jäger **b** (*for prizes*) Pokalsammler(in) *m(f)*

potion ['pəʊʃən] N Trank *m*

pot: pot luck N **to take ~** nehmen, was es gerade gibt; **we took ~ and went to the nearest pub** wir gingen aufs Geratewohl in die nächste Kneipe; **potluck dinner** N (*esp US*) *großes Abendessen, bei dem sich alle Anwesenden selbst mitgebrachte Speisen teilen*; **potpie** N (*US*) in einer Auflaufform gebackene Pastete; **pot plant** N Topfpflanze *f*

potpourri [pəʊ'pʊərɪ] N **a** (*lit*) Duftsträußchen *nt* **b** (*fig: = mixture, medley*) (kunter)bunte Mischung; (*of music*) Potpourri *nt*

pot: pot roast N Schmorbraten *m* VT schmoren; **potsherd** N (*Archeol*) Scherbe *f*; **pot shot** N Schuss *m* aufs Geratewohl; **to take a ~ at sb/sth** aufs Geratewohl auf jdn/etw schießen; (*fig inf: = criticize*) jdn/etw herunterputzen (*inf*)

potted ['pɒtɪd] ADJ **a** *meat* eingemacht; *fish* eingelegt; **~ flower/plant/palm** Topfblume *f*/-pflanze *f*/-palme *f* **b** (*= shortened*) *history, biography* gekürzt, zusammengefasst; **he gave me a ~ version of the film** er erzählte mir in kurzen Worten, wovon der Film handelte

potter[1] ['pɒtə'] N Töpfer(in) *m(f)*; **~'s clay** Töpferton *m*; **~'s wheel** Töpferscheibe *f*

potter[2], (*US also*) **putter** ['pʌtə'] VI (*= do little jobs*) herumwerkeln; (*= wander aimlessly*) herumschlendern; **she ~s away in the kitchen for hours** sie hantiert stundenlang in der Küche herum; **to ~ round the house** im Haus herumwerkeln; **to ~ round the shops** einen Geschäftebummel machen; **to ~ along the road** (*car, driver*) dahinzuckeln; **we ~ along quite happily** wir leben recht zufrieden vor uns hin

potterer ['pɒtərə'] N Trödelheini *m*, Trödelsuse *f*

pottery ['pɒtərɪ] N (*= workshop, craft*) Töpferei *f*; (*= pots*) Töpferwaren *pl*, Tonwaren *pl*; (*glazed*) Keramik *f*; (*= archaeological remains*) Tonscherben *pl*

potting ['pɒtɪŋ]: **potting compost** N Pflanzerde *f*; **potting shed** N Schuppen *m*

potty[1] ['pɒtɪ] N Töpfchen *nt*; **~-trained** (*Brit*) sauber

potty[2] ADJ (*+er*) (*Brit, inf: = mad*) verrückt; **to go ~** verrückt werden, durchdrehen; **to drive sb ~** jdn zum Wahnsinn treiben; **to be ~ about sth** (*about hobby etc*) ganz verrückt nach etw sein; **he's ~ about her** er ist verrückt nach ihr

pouch [paʊtʃ] N Beutel *m*; (*under eyes*) (Tränen-)sack *m*; (*of pelican, hamster*) Tasche *f*; (*Mil*) (Patronen)tasche *f*; (*Hist: for gunpowder*) (Pulver-)beutel *m*; (*esp US: = mail pouch*) Postsack *m*

pouf(fe) [puːf] N **a** (*= seat*) Puff *m* **b** (*Brit inf*) = poof(ter)

poult [pəʊlt] N (*Farming*) **a** (*= chicken*) junges Huhn **b** (*= turkey*) junger Truthahn **c** (*= pheasant*) junger Fasan

poulterer ['pəʊltərə'] N (*Brit*) Geflügelhändler(in) *m(f)*; **~'s (shop)** Geflügelhandlung *f*

poultice ['pəʊltɪs] N Umschlag *m*, Wickel *m*; (*for boil*) Zugpflaster *nt* VT einen Umschlag *or* Wickel machen um; *boil* ein Zugpflaster kleben auf (+*acc*)

poultry ['pəʊltrɪ] N Geflügel *nt*

poultry: poultry farm N Geflügelfarm *f*; **poultry farmer** N Geflügelzüchter(in) *m(f)*; **poultry farming** N Geflügelzucht *f*; **poultry house** N Hühnerhaus *nt*; **poultryman** N (*esp US*) (*= farmer*) Geflügelzüchter(in) *m(f)*; (*= dealer*) Geflügelhändler(in) *m(f)*

pounce [paʊns] N Sprung *m*, Satz *m*; (*= swoop*) (*by bird*) Angriff *m*; (*by police*) Zugriff *m* VI (*cat, lion etc*) einen Satz machen; (*bird*) niederstoßen; (*fig*) zuschlagen; **to ~ on sb/sth** (*lit, fig*)

sich auf jdn/etw stürzen; **the tiger ~d on its prey** der Tiger stürzte sich auf seine Beute; **the police ~d on him** die Polizei griff sich (*dat*) ihn

pound[1] [paʊnd] N **a** (*= weight*) ≈ Pfund *nt*; **two ~s of apples** zwei Pfund Äpfel; **by the ~** pfundweise; **he is making sure he gets his ~ of flesh** er sorgt dafür, dass er bekommt, was ihm zusteht **b** (*= money*) Pfund *nt*; **one ~ sterling** ein Pfund *nt* Sterling; **five ~s** fünf Pfund; **a five-pound note** eine Fünfpfundnote, ein Fünfpfundschein *m* → **penny**

pound[2] VT **a** (*= hammer, strike*) hämmern; *earth, paving slabs* feststampfen; *meat* klopfen; *dough* kneten, schlagen; *piano, typewriter* hämmern auf (+*dat*); *table* hämmern auf (+*acc*); *door, wall* hämmern gegen; (*waves, sea*) *ship* schlagen gegen; (*guns, shells, bombs*) ununterbrochen beschießen; (*troops, artillery*) unter Beschuss haben; **to ~ the streets** (*= jog*) durch die Straßen joggen; **the boxer ~ed his opponent with his fists** der Boxer hämmerte mit den Fäusten auf seinen Gegner ein; **the ship was ~ed by the waves** die Wellen schlugen gegen das Schiff; **the old-style policeman ~ing his beat** der Polizist alten Stils, der seine Runde abmarschierte

b (*= pulverize*) *corn etc* (zer)stampfen; *drugs, spices* zerstoßen; **to ~ sth to pieces** etw klein stampfen; **the guns ~ed the walls to pieces** die Kanonen zertrümmerten die Mauern; **the waves ~ed the boat to pieces** die Wellen zertrümmerten das Boot

VI **a** (*= beat*) hämmern; (*heart*) (wild) pochen; (*waves, sea*) schlagen (*on, against* gegen); (*drums*) dröhnen; (*engine, steamer, hooves*) stampfen; **he ~ed at** *or* **on the door/on the table** er hämmerte an *or* gegen die Tür/auf den Tisch

b (*= run heavily*) stampfen; (*= walk heavily, stamp*) stapfen; **the sound of ~ing feet** das Geräusch stampfender Füße; **the messenger ~ed up to me and handed me a telegram** der Bote stampfte auf mich zu und übergab mir ein Telegramm

▶ **pound away** VI hämmern; (*music, drums, guns*) dröhnen; **our guns were pounding away at the enemy position** wir hatten die feindliche Stellung unter anhaltendem Beschuss; **he was pounding away at the typewriter** er hämmerte auf die Schreibmaschine herum

▶ **pound down** VT *sep earth, rocks* feststampfen; **to pound sth down to a powder** etw pulverisieren

▶ **pound out** VT *sep* **to pound out a tune** eine Melodie herunterhämmern

pound[3] N (*for stray dogs*) städtischer Hundezwinger; (*esp Brit: for cars*) Abstellplatz *m* (*für amtlich abgeschleppte Fahrzeuge*)

poundage ['paʊndɪdʒ] N **a** *auf Pfundbasis berechnete Gebühr oder Abgabe* **b** (*= weight*) Gewicht *nt* (*in Pfund*)

pound cake N (*esp US*) reichhaltiger Früchtekuchen

-pounder [-'paʊndə'] N *suf* -pfünder *m*; **quarterpounder** Viertelpfünder *m*

pound foolish ADJ → **penny wise**

pounding ['paʊndɪŋ] N **a** Hämmern *nt*; (*of heart*) Pochen *nt*; (*of music, drums*) Dröhnen *nt*; (*of waves, sea*) Schlagen *nt*; (*of engine, steamer, pile-driver, hooves, feet etc*) Stampfen *nt*; (*of guns, shells, bombs*) Bombardement *nt*; **the ship took a ~ from the waves** das Schiff wurde von den Wellen stark mitgenommen; **the city took a ~ last night** gestern Nacht wurde die Stadt schwer bombardiert; **his theory took a ~ from the critics** seine Theorie wurde von den Kritikern scharf angegriffen; **our team took quite a ~ on Saturday** unsere Mannschaft hat am Samstag eine ziemliche Schlappe einstecken müssen (*inf*); **he took a ~ in the fight** er musste in dem Kampf einige Schläge einstecken

b (*of corn etc*) Zerstampfen *nt*; (*of drugs*) Zerstoßen *nt*

ADJ *heart* trommelnd, klopfend; *feet* trommelnd; *hooves, drums* donnernd, trommelnd;

headache pochend; *waves* donnernd, aufschlagend

pour [pɔː'] VT *liquid* gießen; *large amount also, sugar, rice etc* schütten; *drink* eingießen, einschenken; **to ~ sth for sb** jdm etw eingießen *or* einschenken; **she looks as if she's been ~ed into that dress!** (*inf*) das Kleid sitzt wie angegossen (*inf*); **to ~ money into a project/men into a war** Geld in ein Projekt/Männer in einen Krieg pumpen (*inf*); **he ~ed all his ideas into a book** alle seine Gedanken flossen in ein Buch VI **a** (*lit, fig*) strömen; **the sweat ~ed off him** der Schweiß floss in Strömen an ihm herunter; **books are ~ing off the presses** Bücher werden in Massen ausgestoßen; **cars ~ed off the ferry** Autokolonnen rollten von der Fähre

b (*= rain*) **it's ~ing (with rain)** es gießt (in Strömen), es schüttet (*inf*); **the rain ~ed down** es regnete *or* goss in Strömen → **rain**

c (*= pour out tea, coffee etc*) eingießen, einschenken; (*US: = act as hostess*) als Gastgeberin fungieren

d **this jug doesn't ~ well** dieser Krug gießt nicht gut

▶ **pour away** VT *sep* weggießen

▶ **pour forth** VI, VT *sep* = **pour out** VI VT b, c

▶ **pour in** VI hereinströmen; (*donations, protests*) in Strömen eintreffen VT *sep money, men* hineinpumpen (*inf*)

▶ **pour out** VI herausströmen (*of aus*); (*smoke also*) hervorquellen (*of aus*); (*words*) heraussprudeln (*of aus*) VT *sep* **a** *liquid* ausgießen; *in large quantities* sugar, rice etc ausschütten; *drink* eingießen, einschenken; **he poured out two glasses of wine** er goss zwei Gläser Wein aus **b** (*factories, schools*) *cars, students* ausstoßen **c** (*fig*) *feelings, troubles, story* sich (*dat*) von der Seele reden; **to pour out one's thanks** sich überströmend bedanken; **to pour out one's heart (to sb)** (jdm) sein Herz ausschütten

pouring ['pɔːrɪŋ] ADJ **~ rain** strömender Regen; **a ~ wet day** ein völlig verregneter Tag; **~ cream** Sahne *f*

pout[1] [paʊt] N **a** (*= facial expression*) Schmollmund *m* **b** (*= sulking fit*) Schmollen *nt*; **to have a ~** schmollen VI **a** (*with lips*) einen Schmollmund machen, einen Flunsch *or* eine Schnute ziehen (*inf*) **b** (*= sulk*) schmollen VT *lips* schürzen; (*sulkingly*) zu einem Schmollmund *or* Schmollen verziehen

pout[2] N (*= kind of cod*) Schellfisch *m*

poverty ['pɒvətɪ] N Armut *f*; **~ of ideas/information** Ideen-/Informationsarmut *f*; **to be above/below/on the ~ line** oberhalb/unterhalb/an der Armutsgrenze leben

poverty: poverty level N Ausmaß *nt* an Armut; **poverty-stricken** ['pɒvətɪstrɪkən] ADJ Not leidend; *conditions* kümmerlich; **to be ~** Armut leiden; (*hum inf*) am Hungertuch nagen (*hum*); **poverty trap** N *Situation, wobei (vermehrte) Einkünfte zu einer Verringerung/zum Wegfall von Sozialleistungen führen*, Armutsfalle *f*

POW *abbr of* **prisoner of war**

powder ['paʊdə'] N Pulver *nt*; (*= face, talcum powder etc*) Puder *m*; (*= dust*) Staub *m*; **to grind sth to (a) ~** etw pulverig *or* zu Pulver mahlen; **to reduce sth to (a) ~** etw zu Pulver machen VT **a** *milk* pulverisieren; *sugar* stoßen; *chalk* zermahlen **b** (*= apply powder to*) *face, body, oneself* pudern; **to ~ one's nose** (*lit*) sich (*dat*) die Nase pudern; (*euph*) kurz verschwinden (*euph*); **the trees were ~ed with snow** die Bäume waren mit Schnee überzuckert VI (*= crumble*) (zu Staub) zerfallen; **the cement had ~ed away** der Mörtel war zu Staub zerfallen

powder: powder blue ADJ taubenblau N Taubenblau *nt*; **powder compact** N Puderdose *f*

powdered ['paʊdəd] ADJ **a** (*= covered with powder*) *face, wig* gepudert **b** (*= in powder form*) *coffee* löslich; *egg* pulverisiert; **~ chalk** Kreidepulver *nt*; **~ sugar** (*US*) Puderzucker *m*, Staubzucker *m* (*Aus*)

powdered milk N Milchpulver nt

powder horn N Pulverhorn nt

powdering ['paʊdərɪŋ] N (liter) **there was a thin ~ of snow on the grass** auf dem Gras lag eine dünne Schneeschicht wie Puderzucker

powder: powder keg N (lit, fig) Pulverfass nt; **powder magazine** N Pulvermagazin nt, Pulverkammer f; **powder monkey** N (Mil Hist) Pulverjunge m; (= explosives man) Sprengmeister m; **powder puff** N Puderquaste f; **powder room** N Damentoilette f; **powder snow** N Pulverschnee m

powdery ['paʊdərɪ] ADJ **a** (= like powder) pulvrig **b** (= crumbly) bröckelig; bones morsch **c** (= covered with powder) gepudert

power ['paʊə'] **N a** no pl (= physical strength) Kraft f; (= force: of blow, explosion etc) Stärke f, Gewalt f, Wucht f; (fig: of argument etc) Überzeugungskraft f; **the ~ of love/logic/tradition** die Macht der Liebe/Logik/Tradition; **earning ~** mögliche Verdiensthöhe; **purchasing** or **spending ~** Kaufkraft f
b (= faculty, ability: of hearing, imagination) Vermögen nt no pl; **his ~s of hearing** sein Hörvermögen nt; **mental/hypnotic ~s** geistige/hypnotische Kräfte pl; **to weaken their ~(s) of resistance** ihre Widerstandskraft zu schwächen
c (= capacity, ability to help etc) Macht f; **he did all in his ~ to help them** er tat (alles), was in seiner Macht or in seinen Kräften stand, um ihnen zu helfen; **it's beyond my ~ or not within my ~ to ...** es steht nicht in meiner Macht, zu ...
d (no pl: = sphere or strength of influence, authority) Macht f; (Jur, parental) Gewalt f; (usu pl: = thing one has authority to do) Befugnis f; **he has the ~ to act** er ist handlungsberechtigt; **the ~ of the police/of the law** die Macht der Polizei/des Gesetzes; **to be in sb's ~** in jds Gewalt (dat) sein; **that does not fall within my ~(s)** das fällt nicht in meinen Machtbereich; **that is beyond** or **outside my ~(s)** das überschreitet meine Befugnisse; **~ of attorney** (Jur) (Handlungs)vollmacht f; **the party now in ~** die Partei, die im Augenblick an der Macht ist; **to fall from ~** abgesetzt werden; **to come into ~** an die Macht kommen; **they have no ~ over economic matters** in Wirtschaftsfragen haben sie keine Befugnisse; **I have no ~ over her** ich habe keine Gewalt über sie; **he has been given full ~(s) to make all decisions** man hat ihm volle Entscheidungsgewalt übertragen; **that man has no ~ over his destiny** dass der Mensch keine Gewalt über sein Schicksal hat; **"student/worker ~"** „Macht den Studenten/Arbeitern"
c (= person or institution having authority) Autorität f, Machtfaktor m; **to be the ~ behind the scenes/throne** die graue Eminenz sein; **the ~s that be** (inf) die da oben (inf); **the ~s of darkness/evil** die Mächte der Finsternis/des Bösen
f (= nation) Macht f; **a four-power conference** eine Viermächtekonferenz; **a naval ~** eine Seemacht
g (= source of energy: nuclear, electric power etc) Energie f; (of water, steam) Energie f, Kraft f; **the ship made port under her own ~** das Schiff lief mit eigener Kraft in den Hafen ein; **they cut off the ~** (= electricity) sie haben den Strom abgestellt
h (of engine, machine, loudspeakers, transmitter) Leistung f; (of microscope, lens, sun's rays, drug, chemical) Stärke f; **the ~ of suggestion** die Wirkung or Wirkkraft des Unterschwelligen; **a low--power microscope** ein schwaches Mikroskop; **a 10-power magnification** eine 10fache Vergrößerung; **microwave on full ~ for one minute** eine Minute bei voller Leistung in der Mikrowelle erhitzen
i (Math) Potenz f; **to the ~ (of) 2** hoch 2, in der 2. Potenz
j (inf: = a lot of) **a ~ of help** eine wertvolle or große Hilfe; **that did me a ~ of good** das hat mir unheimlich gut getan (inf)
VT (engine) antreiben; (fuel) betreiben; **~ed by electricity/by jet engines** mit Elektro-/Düsenantrieb; **as he ~s his way down the straight** wie er die Gerade entlangbraust; **he ~ed the ball into the net** er schoss den Ball mit Wucht ins Netz
VI (runner, racing car) rasen; **he ~ed away from the rest of the field** er raste dem übrigen Feld davon; **the swimmer ~ed through the water** der Schwimmer wuchtete sich durch das Wasser; **we're ~ing through the work now** unsere Arbeit geht jetzt mit Riesenschritten voran

▸**power down** VI (engine, turbine) zum Stillstand kommen

▸**power up** **VT** sep starten **VI** starten

power: power amplifier N (Tech) Endverstärker m; **power-assisted** ADJ (Aut, Tech) Servo-; **~ steering** Servolenkung f; **power base** N Machtbasis f; **powerboat** N Rennboot nt; **power brakes** PL Servobremsen pl; **power broker** N (esp US Pol) Drahtzieher(in) m(f) (inf); **power cable** N Stromkabel nt; **power consumption** N Strom- or Energieverbrauch m; **power cut** N Stromsperre f; (accidental) Stromausfall m; **power demand** N Strom- or Energiebedarf m; **power dive** N (Aviat) (Voll)gas)sturzflug m; **power-dive** VI (Aviat) einen Sturzflug machen; **power dressing** N Karriererelook m; **power drill** N Bohrmaschine f; **power-driven** ADJ mit Motorantrieb; **power failure** N Stromausfall m

powerful ['paʊəfʊl] ADJ **a** (= influential) government, person mächtig, einflussreich
b (= strong) boxer, engine, drug, emotions, computer, evidence, influence, message stark; swimmer kraftvoll, stark; build, arm, kick, light kräftig; stroke, punch, detergent kraftvoll; bomb stark, zerstörisch, von großer Durchschlagskraft; earthquake, storm stark, massiv; smell massiv, überwältigend; voice kräftig, kraftvoll
c (fig) speaker, actor mitreißend; music, film, performance ausdrucksvoll, mitreißend; argument durchschlagend, massiv (inf); salesman überzeugend
d **a ~ lot of** (dial) ganz schön viel (inf), gehörig viel (inf)

powerfully ['paʊəfʊlɪ] ADV **a** (= strongly) influence mächtig, gewaltig, stark; reinforce massiv, gewaltig; moving mächtig, stark; erotic stark; **a ~ addictive drug** eine stark Sucht erregende Droge; **~ built** kräftig gebaut; **the room smelled ~ of cats** der Katzengeruch in dem Raum war überwältigend **b** (fig) speak kraftvoll; describe, act mitreißend, kraftvoll; argue massiv (inf); ~ written mitreißend geschrieben; **I was ~ affected by the book** das Buch hat mich mächtig (inf) or stark beeindruckt

power glider N (Aviat) Motorsegler m

powerhouse ['paʊəhaʊs] N **a** (lit) = **power station b** (fig) treibende Kraft (behind hinter +dat); **he's a real ~** er ist ein äußerst dynamischer Mensch; **she's an intellectual ~** sie hat eine erstaunliche intellektuelle Kapazität; **he's a ~ of new ideas** er hat einen unerschöpflichen Vorrat an neuen Ideen

power: powerless ADJ (physically) punch, body kraftlos; (as regards ability to act) committee, person machtlos; **to be ~ to resist** nicht die Kraft haben, zu widerstehen; **the government is ~ to deal with inflation** die Regierung steht der Inflation machtlos gegenüber; **we are ~ to help you** es steht nicht in unserer Macht, Ihnen zu helfen, wir sind machtlos(, Ihnen zu helfen); **power-lifting** N Powerlifting nt, Kraftdreikampf m; **power line** N (Elec) **a** (for heavy current) Starkstromleitung f **b** (on pylons or poles) Überlandleitung f; **power loom** N Webmaschine f; **power lunch** N Geschäftsessen nt unter Führungskräften; **power mower** N Motorrasenmäher m; (electric) Elektrorasenmäher m; **power outage** ['paʊər,aʊtɪdʒ] N Stromsperre f; (accidental) Stromausfall m; **power pack** N (Elec) Netzteil nt; (inf: = engine) Motor m, Kraftpaket nt (inf); **power plant** N **a** = **power station b** (= engine) Motor m; **power play** N **a** (Ice Hockey) Powerplay nt, Übermachtspiel nt **b** (fig = attack) Powerplay nt; (= struggle) Kraftprobe f; **power point** N (Elec)

Steckdose f; **power politics** PL Machtpolitik f; **power saw** N Motorsäge f; (electric) Elektrosäge f; **power sharing** N (Pol) Machtteilung f; **power-sharing** ADJ (Pol) executive mit Machtteilung pred; **~ agreement** Machtteilungsabkommen nt; **power station** N Kraftwerk nt, Elektrizitätswerk nt; **power steering** N (Aut) Servolenkung f; **power structure** N Machtstruktur f; **power struggle** N Machtkampf m; **power supply** N (Elec) Stromversorgung f; **power surge** N (Elec) Überspannung f; **power tool** N Elektrowerkzeug nt; **power-up** N Start m; **power walking** N Walking nt, Walken nt; **power worker** N Elektrizitätsarbeiter(in) m(f)

powwow ['paʊwaʊ] N (of Native Americans) Versammlung f; (with Native Americans) indianische Verhandlungen pl; (inf) Besprechung f; (to solve problem) Kriegsrat m (hum); **a family ~** ein Familienrat m

pox [pɒks] N (old) (= smallpox) Pocken pl, Blattern pl; (= syphilis) Syphilis f; **a ~ on ...!** (old) zur Hölle mit ...!

pp a abbr of **pages** S. **b** abbr of **per procurationem** (= on behalf of) pp., ppa.

PPE abbr of **Philosophy, Politics and Economics**

ppm abbr of **parts per million**

PPS a (Brit) abbr of **parliamentary private secretary b** abbr of **post postscriptum** PPS nt

PPV abbr of **pay-per-view**

PR [piː'ɑː'] N **a** abbr of **proportional representation b** abbr of **public relations** PR f; **PR agency** PR-Agentur f; **PR man** PR-Mann m; **PR woman** PR-Frau f; **PR work** PR-Arbeit f, Öffentlichkeitsarbeit f

pr abbr of **pair**

practicability [ˌpræktɪkə'bɪlɪtɪ] N Durchführbarkeit f, Praktikabilität f (rare); (of road) Befahrbarkeit f

practicable ['præktɪkəbl] ADJ durchführbar, praktikabel; road befahrbar

practicably ['præktɪkəblɪ] ADV **if it can ~ be done** falls (es) durchführbar (ist)

practical ['præktɪkəl] ADJ **a** praktisch; person praktisch (veranlagt); **to have a ~ mind** praktisch denken; **his ideas have no ~ application** seine Ideen sind nicht praxisnah or sind praktisch nicht anwendbar; **for (all) ~ purposes** in der Praxis; **to be of no ~ use** ohne (jeden) praktischen Nutzen sein **b** (= handy) praktisch; **they are both very ~ about the house** sie sind beide sehr geschickt or praktisch in allem, was in einem Haus anfällt **c** (= virtual) **it was a ~ certainty** es war praktisch eine Gewissheit

practicality [ˌpræktɪ'kælɪtɪ] N **a** no pl (of person) praktische Veranlagung f **b** no pl (of scheme etc) Durchführbarkeit f; **your solution shows/lacks ~** Ihre Lösung ist praxisnah/praxisfremd **c** (= practical detail) praktisches Detail

practical: practical joke N Streich m; **practical joker** N Witzbold m (inf)

practically ['præktɪkəlɪ] ADV (all senses) praktisch; **~ speaking** konkret gesagt; **~ minded** praktisch veranlagt

practical nurse N (US) ≈ Hilfsschwester f

practice ['præktɪs] **N a** (= habit, custom) (of individual) Gewohnheit f, Angewohnheit f; (of group, in country) Brauch m, Sitte f; (= bad habit) Unsitte f; (in business) Verfahrensweise, Praktik f; **he opposes the ~ of pubs being open on Sundays** er ist dagegen, dass Lokale am Sonntag geöffnet sind; **this is normal business ~** das ist im Geschäftsleben so üblich; **as is my (usual) ~** wie es meine Gewohnheit ist; **to make a ~ of doing sth, to make it a ~ to do sth** es sich (dat) zur Gewohnheit machen, etw zu tun; **Christian ~ dictates ...** das christliche Brauchtum verlangt ...; **it is the ~ of this Court to ...** es ist an diesem Gericht üblich, zu ...; **that's common ~** das ist allgemeine Praxis, das ist allgemein üblich
b (= exercise, training) Übung f; (= rehearsal, trial run) Probe f; (Sport) Training nt; (= practice

game) Trainingsspiel *nt*; **~ makes perfect** (*Prov*) Übung macht den Meister (*Prov*); **Michael Schuhmacher had the fastest time in** ~ Michael Schuhmacher fuhr im Training die schnellste Zeit; **this piece of music needs a lot of** ~ für dieses (Musik)stück muss man viel üben; **you should do 10 minutes'** ~ **each day** du solltest täglich 10 Minuten (lang) üben; **to be out of** ~ aus der Übung sein; **that was just a** ~ **run** das war nur mal zur Probe; **to have a** ~ **session** üben; (= *rehearse*) Probe haben; (*Sport*) trainieren; **the first** ~ **session** die erste Übung/Probe/ das erste Training

c (= *doing, as opposed to theory*) Praxis *f*; **in** ~ in der Praxis; **that won't work in** ~ das lässt sich praktisch nicht durchführen; **to put one's ideas into** ~ seine Ideen in die Praxis umsetzen

d (*of doctor, lawyer etc*) Praxis *f*; **he returned to the** ~ **of law/medicine** er praktizierte wieder als Rechtsanwalt/Arzt; **to go into** *or* **set up in** ~ eine Praxis aufmachen *or* eröffnen, sich als Arzt/ Rechtsanwalt *etc* niederlassen; **he's not in** ~ **any more** er praktiziert nicht mehr; **to retire from** ~ sich aus der Praxis zurückziehen; **a large legal** ~ eine große Rechtsanwaltspraxis

VTI (*US*) = **practise**

practice teacher N (*US Sch*) Referendar(in) *m(f)*

practise, (*US*) **practice** ['præktɪs] **VT** **a** *thrift, patience etc* üben; *self-denial, Christian charity, torture* praktizieren; **to** ~ **what one preaches** (*prov*) seine Lehren in die Tat umsetzen

b (*in order to acquire skill*) üben; *song, chorus* proben; **to** ~ **the violin** Geige üben; **to** ~ **the high jump/one's golf swing** Hochsprung/seinen Schlag im Golf üben *or* trainieren; **to** ~ **doing sth** etw üben; **I'm practising my German on him** ich probiere mein Deutsch an ihm aus

c (= *follow, exercise*) *profession, religion* ausüben, praktizieren; **to** ~ **law/medicine** als Anwalt/ Arzt praktizieren; **all a writer wants is peace to** ~ **his art** alles, was ein Schriftsteller braucht, ist Ruhe, um sich seiner Kunst widmen zu können

VI **a** (*in order to acquire skill*) üben

b (*lawyer, doctor etc*) praktizieren; **to** ~ **at the Bar** als Anwalt bei Gericht praktizieren

practised, (*US*) **practiced** ['præktɪst] ADJ geübt; *politician, marksman, liar also* erfahren; *performance also* professionell; **with a** ~ **eye/hand** mit geübtem Auge/geübter Hand; **he's** ~ **in getting his own way** er hat Übung darin, seinen Willen durchzusetzen; **with** ~ **skill** gekonnt

practising, (*US*) **practicing** ['præktɪsɪŋ] ADJ *lawyer, doctor, homosexual* praktizierend; *Christian also, socialist* aktiv; *teacher* im Beruf stehend, seinen Beruf ausübend

practitioner [præk'tɪʃənə'] N (*of method*) Benutzer(in) *m(f)*, Anwender(in) *m(f)*; (= *medical practitioner*) praktischer Arzt, praktische Ärztin; (= *dental practitioner*) Zahnarzt *m*/-ärztin *f*; (= *legal practitioner*) Rechtsanwalt *m*/-anwältin *f*; **~s of this profession** diejenigen, die diesen Beruf ausüben; **he is a** ~ **of Zen Buddhism** er ist ein Anhänger des Zen-Buddhismus → **general practitioner**

praesidium [prɪ'sɪdɪəm] N = **presidium**

praetor ['pri:tə'] N Prätor *m*

praetorian guard [prɪ'tɔːrɪən'gɑːd] N **a** (*Hist*) **the Praetorian Guard** (= *body*) die Prätorianergarde **b** (*fig*: = *loyal group*) Prätorianergarde *f*, Prätorianer *pl*; **that** ~ **of foreigners around the President** die ausländischen Prätorianer in der Umgebung des Präsidenten

pragmatic ADJ , **pragmatically** ADV ['præg'mætɪk, -əlɪ] pragmatisch

pragmatism ['prægmətɪzəm] N Pragmatismus *m*

pragmatist ['prægmətɪst] N Pragmatiker(in) *m(f)*

Prague [prɑːg] N Prag *nt*

prairie ['preərɪ] N Grassteppe *f*; (*in North America*) Prärie *f*

prairie: prairie chicken N (*US*) Präriehuhn *nt*; **prairie dog** N Präriehund *m*; **prairie oyster** N Prärieauster *f*; **prairie schooner** N Planwagen *m*; **prairie wolf** N Präriewolf *m*

praise [preɪz] **VT** loben; (*to others, in worship also*) preisen (*geh*), rühmen (*geh*); **to** ~ **sb for having done sth** jdn dafür loben, etw getan zu haben; **to** ~ **the virtues of sth** die Vorzüge einer Sache (*gen*) loben *or* preisen (*geh*); ~ **God!** gelobt sei Gott!

N Lob *nt no pl*; **a hymn of** ~ eine Lobeshymne; **a poem in** ~ **of beer** ein Loblied *nt* auf das Bier; **he spoke/made a speech in** ~ **of their efforts** er sprach lobend von ihren Bemühungen/hielt eine Lobrede auf ihre Bemühungen; **to win** ~ (*person*) Lob ernten; (*efforts*) Lob einbringen; **to give** ~ (**to sb**) (jdn) loben; **to be loud** *or* **warm in one's** ~ (**of sth**) voll des Lobes (für etw) sein; **I have nothing but** ~ **for him** ich kann ihn nur loben; **he's beyond** ~ er ist über jedes *or* alles Lob erhaben; **all** ~ **to him** alle Achtung!; ~ **indeed!** (*also iro*) ein hohes Lob; ~ **from him is** ~ **indeed** Lob aus seinem Mund will etwas heißen; ~ **be to God!** (*in church*) gelobt sei der Herr!; ~(**s**) **be!** Gott sei Dank! → **sing**

praiseworthiness ['preɪz,wɜːðɪnɪs] N (*of attempt, effort*) Löblichkeit *f*; **I don't doubt his** ~**/the** ~ **of his motives** ich zweifle nicht an seinen lobenswerten Absichten/daran, dass seine Motive lobenswert sind

praiseworthy ['preɪz,wɜːðɪ] ADJ lobenswert

praline ['prɑːliːn] N Praline *f* mit Nuss-Karamellfüllung

pram [præm] N (*Brit*) Kinderwagen *m*; (*dolls'*) Puppenwagen *m*

prance [prɑːns] VI (*horse*) tänzeln; (*person*) (= *jump around*) herumhüpfen *or* -tanzen; (= *walk gaily, mince*) tänzeln; **she was prancing about with nothing on** sie lief nackt durch die Gegend; **to** ~ **in/out** (*person*) herein-/hinausspazieren

prandial ['prændɪəl] ADJ (*form, often hum*) Essens-, Tisch-

prang [præŋ] (*esp Brit, inf*) **N** (= *crash*) Bums *m* (*inf*); (*of plane*) Bruchlandung *f* **INTERJ** krach **VT** **a** (= *crash*) *car* ramponieren (*inf*), lädieren; *plane* eine Bruchlandung machen **b** (= *bomb*) zerbomben, zusammenbomben (*inf*)

prank [præŋk] N Streich *m*; (*harmless also*) Ulk *m*; **to play a** ~ **on sb** jdm einen Streich spielen; (*harmless also*) einen Ulk mit jdm machen

prankish ['præŋkɪʃ] ADJ *person* zu Streichen aufgelegt *or* bereit; *behaviour, act* schelmisch

prankster ['præŋkstə'] N Schelm(in) *m(f)*

praseodymium [,preɪzɪəʊ'dɪmɪəm] N (*Chem*) Praseodym *nt*

prat [præt] N (*Brit inf*: = *idiot*) Trottel *m* (*inf*)

prate [preɪt] VI faseln, schwafeln

pratfall ['prætfɔːl] N (*esp US inf*) Sturz auf den Hintern (*inf*); (*fig*) Bauchlandung *f* (*fig*); **to take a** ~ (*also fig*) auf den Hintern fallen

prating ['preɪtɪŋ] **N** Gefasel *nt*, Geschwafel *nt* **ADJ** faselnd, schwafelnd

prattle ['prætl] **N** Geplapper *nt* **VI** plappern

prattler ['prætlə'] N (*pej*: = *chatterbox*) Plappermaul *nt*

prawn [prɔːn] N Garnele *f*

prawn cocktail N Krabbencocktail *m*

prawn crackers PL Krabbenchips *pl*

pray [preɪ] **VI** **a** (= *say prayers*) beten; **let us** ~ lasset uns beten; **to** ~ **for sb/sth** für jdn/um etw beten; **to** ~ **for sth** (= *want it badly*) stark auf etw (*acc*) hoffen

b (*old, liter*) ~ **take a seat** bitte, nehmen Sie doch Platz, wollen Sie bitte Platz nehmen?; **what good is that,** ~ (**tell**)? was hilft das, wenn ich mir die Frage gestatten darf?

VT (*old, liter*) inständig bitten, ersuchen (*geh*); **I** ~ **you tell me** (*old*) bitte, erzählen Sie mir doch; (*stronger*) ich bitte Sie inständig, erzählen Sie mir doch; **and what is that, I** ~ **you?** und was ist das, wenn ich mir die Frage gestatten darf?;

they ~**ed the king for mercy** sie flehten den König um Gnade an (*geh*)

prayer [preə'] N Gebet *nt*; (= *service, prayer meeting*) Andacht *f*; **to say one's** ~**s** beten, seine Gebete verrichten (*geh*); **to be at** ~ beim Gebet sein; **he will lead our** ~**s** er wird uns im Gebet führen; **a** ~ **for peace** ein Gebet für den Frieden; **a life of** ~ ein Leben im Gebet; **Evening Prayer** Abendandacht *f*; **we attended Morning Prayer** wir besuchten die Morgenandacht; **we have** ~**s every morning** wir haben jeden Morgen eine Andacht; **family** ~**s** Hausandacht *f*; **the Book of Common Prayer** *das Gebetbuch der anglikanischen Kirche* **my one** ~ **is that ...** ich bete nur, dass ...

prayer: prayer beads PL Gebetsperlen *pl*; **prayer book** N Gebetbuch *nt*; **prayer mat** N Gebetsteppich *m*; **prayer meeting** N Gebetsstunde *f*; **prayer rug** N = **prayer mat**; **prayer shawl** N Gebetsmantel *m*; **prayer wheel** N Gebetsmühle *f*

praying mantis ['preɪŋ'mæntɪs] N Gottesanbeterin *f*

pre- [priː-] PREF vor-; (*esp with words derived from Latin or Greek*) prä-; **preschool** vorschulisch; **prefascist** präfaschistisch; **at** ~**1980 prices** zu Preisen von vor 1980

preach [priːtʃ] **VT** predigen; (*fig*) *advantages etc* propagieren; **to** ~ **a sermon** (*lit, fig*) eine Predigt halten; **to** ~ **the gospel** das Evangelium verkünden **VI** (= *give a sermon, be moralistic*) predigen; **who's** ~**ing today?** wer predigt heute?, wer hält heute die Predigt?; **to** ~ **to/at sb** jdm eine Predigt halten; **to** ~ **to the converted** (*prov*) offene Türen einrennen

preacher ['priːtʃə'] N Prediger(in) *m(f)*; (*fig*: = *moralizer*) Moralprediger(in) *m(f)*; **all these** ~**s of détente** alle diese Entspannungsprediger

preachify ['priːtʃɪfaɪ] VI (*pej inf*) predigen, moralisieren

preaching ['priːtʃɪŋ] N (*lit, fig*) (= *act*) Predigen *nt*; (= *sermon*) Predigt *f*

preachy ['priːtʃɪ] ADJ (*inf*) moralisierend

preadolescent [,priːædə'lesənt] ADJ vorpubertär

preamble [priː'æmbl] N Einleitung *f*; (*of book*) Vorwort *nt*; (*Jur*) Präambel *f*

preamplifier [priː'æmplɪˌfaɪə'], **preamp** (*inf*) [priː'æmp] N Vorverstärker *m*

prearrange ['priːə'reɪndʒ] VT im voraus vereinbaren

prearranged ['priːə'reɪndʒd], **pre-arranged** ADJ (= *predetermined*) *meeting, sign* im Voraus verabredet; *route, location* im Voraus bestimmt *or* festgelegt

prebend ['prebənd] N (*form*) (= *stipend*) Pfründe *f*, Präbende *f*; (= *person*) Pfründner *m*, Pfründeninhaber *m*, Präbendar(ius) *m*

prebendary ['prebəndərɪ] N Pfründner *m*, Pfründeninhaber *m*, Präbendar(ius) *m*

Pre-Cambrian [priː'kæmbrɪən] ADJ präkambrisch

precarious [prɪ'keərɪəs] ADJ unsicher; *situation also, relationship* prekär; *theory, assertion* anfechtbar; *position* unsicher, schwankend; *balance* unsicher, schwankend, instabil; *peace* gefährdet, instabil, unsicher; **at a** ~ **angle** in einem gefährlich aussehenden Winkel; **that cup/that shelf looks somewhat** ~ die Tasse/das Regal sieht ziemlich gefährlich aus

precariously [prɪ'keərɪəslɪ] ADV *cling, dangle* unsicher; **to be** ~ **balanced** (*lit, fig*) auf der Kippe stehen; **with a cup** ~ **balanced on the end of his nose** eine Tasse auf der Nase balancierend; ~ **perched on the edge of the table** gefährlich nahe am Tischrand; **he lived rather** ~ **from his work as a photographer** er verdiente einen ziemlich unsicheren Lebensunterhalt als Fotograf

precast [priː'kɑːst] *vb*: pret, ptp **precast** **VT** vorfertigen **ADJ** vorgefertigt; ~ **concrete** Fertig(teil)beton *m*

precaution [prɪˈkɔːʃən] N Sicherheitsmaßnahme f, (Sicherheits)vorkehrung f, Vorsichtsmaßnahme f; **security ~s** Sicherheitsmaßnahmen or -vorkehrungen pl; **fire ~s** Brandschutzmaßnahmen pl; **to take ~s against sth** Vorsichtsmaßnahmen pl gegen etw treffen; **do you take ~s?** (euph: = use contraception) nimmst or machst du (irgend)etwas?; **to take the ~ of doing sth** vorsichtshalber or sicherheitshalber etw tun

precautionary [prɪˈkɔːʃənərɪ] ADJ Vorsichts-, Sicherheits-, vorbeugend; **~ measure** Vorsichts- or Sicherheitsmaßnahme f; **it's purely ~** es ist eine reine or nur eine Vorsichtsmaßnahme

precede [prɪˈsiːd] VT (in order, time) vorangehen (+dat); (in importance) gehen vor (+dat); (in rank) stehen über (+dat); **for the month preceding this** den (ganzen) Monat davor; **to ~ a lecture with a joke** einem Vortrag einen Witz vorausschicken

precedence [ˈpresɪdəns] N (of person) vorrangige Stellung (over gegenüber); (of problem etc) Vorrang m (over vor +dat); **to take or have ~ over sb/sth** vor jdm/etw Vorrang haben; **to give ~ to sb/sth** jdm/einer Sache Vorrang geben; **the guests entered the hall in order of ~** die Gäste betraten die Halle in der Reihenfolge ihres (gesellschaftlichen) Rangs; **dukes have ~ over barons** Herzöge stehen im Rang höher als Barone

precedent [ˈpresɪdənt] N Präzedenzfall m; (Jur also) Präjudiz nt; **according to ~** nach den bisherigen Fällen; **against all the ~s** entgegen allen früheren Fällen; **without ~** noch nie da gewesen; **to establish** or **create** or **set a ~** einen Präzedenzfall schaffen; **to break with ~** dem Präzedenzfall nicht mehr folgen; **is there any ~ for this?** ist der Fall schon einmal da gewesen?; **there is no ~ for this decision** diese Entscheidung kann sich nicht an einem vergleichbaren Fall ausrichten

preceding [prɪˈsiːdɪŋ] ADJ time, month etc vorangegangen; page, example also vorhergehend

precensor [ˌpriːˈsensəʳ] VT newspaper article etc vorzensieren, einer Vorzensur unterwerfen (geh)

precentor [prɪˈsentəʳ] N Vorsänger(in) m(f), Präzentor(in) m(f) (spec)

precept [ˈpriːsept] N Grundsatz m, Prinzip nt

preceptor [prɪˈseptəʳ] N (old, form) Lehrer m, Präzeptor m (old)

precession [prɪˈseʃən] N Präzession f; **~ of the equinoxes** (Astron) Präzession f der Äquinoktien

pre-Christian [priːˈkrɪstɪən] ADJ vorchristlich

precinct [ˈpriːsɪŋkt] N **a** (Brit) (= pedestrian precinct) Fußgängerzone f; (= shopping precinct) Geschäfts- or Einkaufsviertel nt; (US) (= police precinct) Revier nt; (= voting precinct) Bezirk m **b** **precincts** PL (= grounds, premises) Gelände nt, Areal nt; (= environs) Umgebung f; (of cathedral) Domfreiheit f

preciosity [ˌpresɪˈɒsɪtɪ] N Pretiosität f, Preziosität f

precious [ˈpreʃəs] ADJ **a** (= costly) wertvoll, kostbar, **b** (= rare) commodity kostbar, wertvoll **c** (= treasured) wertvoll, (iro) hochverehrt, heiß geliebt; **my ~ (one)!** mein Schatz!; **I have very ~ memories of that time/of him** ich habe Erinnerungen an diese Zeit/an ihn, die mir sehr wertvoll or teuer (geh) sind; **the loss of our ~ daughter** der Verlust unserer heißgeliebten Tochter **d** (pej: = mannered, affected) language, humour etc pretiös, preziös; person geziert, geschraubt; style geziert, gekünstelt

ADV (inf) **little/few** herzlich wenig/wenige (inf), **little else** herzlich wenig sonst; **I had ~ little choice** ich hatte keine große Wahl

precious metal N Edelmetall nt

precious stone N Edelstein m

precipice [ˈpresɪpɪs] N (lit, fig) Abgrund m

---

precipitance [prɪˈsɪpɪtəns], **precipitancy** [prɪˈsɪpɪtənsɪ] N (= hastiness) Hast f, Eile f; (= overhastiness) Voreiligkeit f, Überstürztheit f, Überstürzung f

precipitant [prɪˈsɪpɪtənt] N (Aus)fällungsmittel nt ADJ = precipitate ADJ

precipitate [prɪˈsɪpɪtɪt] N (Met) Niederschlag m; (Chem also) Präzipitat nt (spec) ADJ [prɪˈsɪpɪtɪt] (= hasty) hastig, eilig; (= over-hasty) übereilt, voreilig, überstürzt VT **a** (= hurl) schleudern; (downwards) hinunter- or hinabschleudern; (fig) stürzen **b** (= hasten) beschleunigen **c** (Chem) (aus)fällen; (Met) niederschlagen VI (Chem) ausfallen; (Met) sich niederschlagen

precipitately [prɪˈsɪpɪtɪtlɪ] ADV (= hastily) hastig, eilig; (= over-hastily) übereilt, voreilig, überstürzt

precipitation [prɪˌsɪpɪˈteɪʃən] N **a** (Met) Niederschlag m **b** (= haste) Hast f, Eile f; (= overhastiness) Übereile f, Übereiltheit f, Überstürztheit f

precipitous [prɪˈsɪpɪtəs] ADJ **a** (= steep) steil **b** (= hasty) überstürzt

precipitously [prɪˈsɪpɪtəslɪ] ADV **a** (= steeply) steil; **to fall away ~** (ground etc) senkrecht or jäh abfallen **b** (= hastily) überstürzt

précis [ˈpreɪsiː] N Zusammenfassung f; (Sch) Inhaltsangabe f

precise [prɪˈsaɪs] ADJ **a** genau; answer, description also präzise; **at that ~ moment** genau in dem Augenblick; **this was the ~ amount I needed** das war genau or exakt der Betrag, den ich brauchte; **please be more ~** drücken Sie sich bitte etwas genauer or deutlicher aus; **but was it this ~ colour?** aber war es genau diese Farbe?; **18, to be ~** 18, um genau zu sein; **or, to be more ~, ...** oder, um es genauer zu sagen, ...; **in that ~ voice of hers** präzise or exakt, wie sie nun einmal spricht; **these ~ British accents** die akzentuierte Aussprache der Briten **b** (= meticulous) worker exakt, genau, präzise

precisely [prɪˈsaɪslɪ] ADV genau; answer, describe, work also präzise; use instrument exakt; **at ~ 7 o'clock, at 7 o'clock ~** Punkt 7 Uhr, genau um 7 Uhr; **what ~ do you mean/want?** was meinen/wollen Sie eigentlich genau?; **but it is ~ because the money supply is ...** aber gerade deshalb, weil das Kapital ... ist; **that is ~ why I don't want it** genau deshalb will ich es nicht; **~ nothing** gar nichts; **or more ~ ...** oder genauer ...

preciseness [prɪˈsaɪsnɪs] N Genauigkeit f, Exaktheit f

precision [prɪˈsɪʒən] N Genauigkeit f; (of work, movement also) Präzision f

precision: precision bombing N gezielter Bombenabwurf; **precision-engineered** ADJ präzisionsgefertigt; **precision engineering** N Präzisionstechnik f; **precision instrument** N Präzisionsinstrument nt; **precision-made** ADJ präzisionsgefertigt; **precision tool** N Präzisionswerkzeug nt; **precision work** N Präzisionsarbeit f

preclassical [priːˈklæsɪkəl] ADJ vorklassisch

preclinical [priːˈklɪnɪkəl] ADJ (Med) Studium vorklinisch

preclude [prɪˈkluːd] VT possibility ausschließen; **to ~ sb from doing sth** jdn daran hindern, etw zu tun; **to ~ sth happening** die Möglichkeit ausschließen, dass etw geschieht

preclusion [prɪˈkluːʒən] N **a** (of possibility) Ausschließung f, Ausschluss m **b** (= prevention) Verhinderung f

precocious [prɪˈkəʊʃəs] ADJ interest, teenager, behaviour frühreif; way of speaking altklug; talent, development frühreif, früh entwickelt; **at a ~ age** im frühen Alter

precociously [prɪˈkəʊʃəslɪ] ADV frühreif; talk altklug; **a ~ articulate child** ein erstaunlich beredsames or wortgewandtes Kind, ein Kind von altkluger Beredsamkeit; **~ talented** früh begabt; **~ dressed** auf alt angezogen (inf)

---

precociousness [prɪˈkəʊʃəsnɪs], **precocity** [prɪˈkɒsɪtɪ] N (of child, behaviour) Frühreife f; (of way of speaking) Altklugheit f

precognition [ˌpriːkɒgˈnɪʃən] N (Psych) Präkognition f; (= knowledge) vorherige Kenntnis, vorheriges Wissen

preconceived [ˌpriːkənˈsiːvd] ADJ opinion, idea vorgefasst; **to have ~ ideas about sth** eine vorgefasste Meinung zu etw haben

preconception [ˌpriːkənˈsepʃən] N vorgefasste Meinung

precondemn [ˌpriːkənˈdem] VT vorverurteilen

precondition [ˌpriːkənˈdɪʃən] N (Vor)bedingung f, Voraussetzung f; **to make sth a ~** etw zur Voraussetzung or Bedingung machen

precook [priːˈkʊk] VT vorkochen

precursor [prɪˈkɜːsəʳ] N **a** Vorläufer(in) m(f); (= herald: of event etc) Vorbote m, Vorbotin f; (in office) (Amts)vorgänger(in) m(f)

precursory [prɪˈkɜːsərɪ] ADJ einleitend

predate [ˌpriːˈdeɪt] VT (= precede) zeitlich vorangehen (+dat); cheque, letter zurückdatieren

predator [ˈpredətəʳ] N (= animal) Raubtier nt; (= person) Plünderer m, Plünderin f; **the main ~s of the gazelle** die Hauptfeinde der Gazelle

predatory [ˈpredətərɪ] ADJ **a** (= involving killing) attack, tribe, behaviour räuberisch; **~ animal** Raubtier nt; **~ instinct** Raubtierinstinkt m **b** (financially etc) person, behaviour raubtierhaft **c** (sexually) person raubtierhaft; **he has a ~ attitude toward(s) all the girls in the office** er betrachtet alle Mädchen im Büro als Freiwild

predecease [ˌpriːdɪˈsiːs] VT **to ~ sb** vor jdm sterben

predecessor [ˈpriːdɪsesəʳ] N (= person) Vorgänger(in) m(f); (= thing) Vorläufer(in) m(f); **our ~s** (= ancestors) unsere Ahnen or Vorfahren pl; **his latest book is certainly better than its ~s** sein neuestes Buch ist zweifellos besser als seine vorherigen

predefine [ˌpriːdɪˈfaɪn] VT vorher abgrenzen or bestimmen

predestination [priːˌdestɪˈneɪʃən] N Vorherbestimmung f, Prädestination f

predestine [priːˈdestɪn] VT vorherbestimmen, prädestinieren; person prädestinieren

predetermination [ˈpriːdɪˌtɜːmɪˈneɪʃən] N (Philos) Prädetermination f; (of course of events, sb's future etc) Vorherbestimmung f

predetermine [ˌpriːdɪˈtɜːmɪn] VT course of events, sb's future etc vorherbestimmen; (Philos) prädeterminieren; (= fix in advance) price, date etc vorher or im Voraus festlegen or festsetzen; (= ascertain in advance) costs vorher ermitteln

predetermined [ˌpriːdɪˈtɜːmɪnd] ADJ (= prearranged) outcome verabredet, im Voraus festgelegt; size vorgegeben; position vorherbestimmt; **for a ~ period** für einen vorherbestimmten Zeitabschnitt; **at ~ times** zu (vorher) festgesetzten Zeiten

predicable [ˈpredɪkəbl] ADJ **to be ~ of sth** von etw ausgesagt or behauptet werden können

predicament [prɪˈdɪkəmənt] N Zwangslage f, Dilemma nt; **to be in a ~** in einem Dilemma or in einer Zwangslage sein

predicate [ˈpredɪkɪt] N (Gram) Prädikat nt, Satzaussage f; (Logic) Aussage f; **~ noun** prädikatives Substantiv, Prädikativ(um) nt VT [ˈpredɪkeɪt] (= imply, connote) aussagen; (= assert, state) behaupten; **to ~ sth on sth** (= base) etw auf etw (dat) gründen; **to ~ sth of sth** (= assert as quality of) etw von etw behaupten

predicative ADJ , **predicatively** ADV [prɪˈdɪkətɪv, -lɪ] prädikativ

predict [prɪˈdɪkt] VT vorher- or voraussagen, prophezeien

predictability [prədɪktəˈbɪlɪtɪ] N Vorhersagbarkeit f

predictable [prɪˈdɪktəbl] ADJ event, reaction vorher- or voraussagbar; person durchschaubar; **to be ~** vorher- or voraussagbar sein, vorher- or vorauszusagen sein; **that was ~!** das war vorherzusehen!; **you're so ~** man weiß doch genau, wie Sie reagieren; **with ~ consequences** mit vorhersehbaren *or* voraussagbaren Folgen; **to follow a ~ pattern** einem vorhersehbaren *or* voraussagbaren Muster folgen

predictably [prɪˈdɪktəblɪ] ADV react vorher- *or* voraussagbar; **~ (enough), he was late** wie vorauszusehen, kam er zu spät

prediction [prɪˈdɪkʃən] N Prophezeiung f, Voraussage f

predictive [prɪˈdɪktɪv] ADJ (form: = prophetic) power, value, test vorausdeutend, vorhersagend; **to be ~ of sth** ein Vorzeichen für etw sein, etw anzeigen

predictor [prɪˈdɪktə'] N (= indication) Anzeichen nt (of für); **opinion polls are an unreliable ~ of election outcomes** Umfragen können Wahlergebnisse nicht zuverlässig voraussagen

predigest [ˌpriːdaɪˈdʒest] VT vorverdauen; (artificially, chemically) aufschließen; (fig) vorkauen

predilection [ˌpriːdɪˈlekʃən] N Vorliebe f, Faible nt (for für)

predispose [ˌpriːdɪˈspəʊz] VT geneigt machen; (Med) prädisponieren, anfällig machen (to für); **to ~ sb toward(s) sb/sth** jdn für jdn/etw einnehmen; **it ~s me to believe that ...** das führt mich zu der Annahme, dass ...; **people are ~d to behave in certain ways** die Menschen sind so veranlagt, sich in einer bestimmten Weise zu verhalten; **I'm not ~d to help him** ich bin nicht geneigt, ihm zu helfen

predisposition [ˌpriːdɪspəˈzɪʃən] N (= tendency, inclination) Neigung f (to zu); (Med) Prädisposition f (to für), Anfälligkeit f (to für); **he has a natural ~ to violence** er hat eine natürliche Veranlagung zur Gewalttätigkeit

predominance [prɪˈdɒmɪnəns] N (= control) Vorherrschaft f, Vormachtstellung f; (= prevalence) Überwiegen nt; **the ~ of women in the office** die weibliche Überzahl im Büro

predominant [prɪˈdɒmɪnənt] ADJ (= most prevalent) idea, theory vorherrschend; (= dominating) person, animal beherrschend; **to be ~ in sth** überwiegend in etw sein; **those things which are ~ in your life** die Dinge, die in Ihrem Leben von größter Bedeutung sind; **he was the ~ member of the group** er war in der Gruppe tonangebend

predominantly [prɪˈdɒmɪnəntlɪ] ADV überwiegend

predominate [prɪˈdɒmɪneɪt] VI a (in numbers) vorherrschen b (in influence etc) überwiegen; **Good will always ~ over Evil** das Gute wird immer über das Böse siegen; **if you allow any one individual to ~ (over the others)** wenn man einem einzigen gestattet, die anderen zu beherrschen

predominately [prɪˈdɒmɪnɪtlɪ] ADV (= largely, mainly) überwiegend

pre-eclampsia [ˌpriːɪˈklæmpsɪə] N (Med) Präeklampsie f (spec)

pre-election [ˌpriːɪˈlekʃən] ADJ poll, campaign, rally vor der Wahl (durchgeführt); **~ atmosphere** Wahlkampfatmosphäre f; **~ promise** Wahlversprechen nt

pre-eminence [priːˈemɪnəns] N überragende Bedeutung

pre-eminent [priːˈemɪnənt] ADJ herausragend, überragend

pre-eminently [priːˈemɪnəntlɪ] ADV hauptsächlich, vor allem, in erster Linie; (= excellently) hervorragend

pre-empt [priːˈempt] VT zuvorkommen (+dat); (Bridge) seinen Gegenspielern durch eine schwer zu überbietende Ansage zuvorkommen **his decision to leave was ~ed by his dismissal** die Entlassung kam seinem Entschluss wegzugehen zuvor

pre-emption [priːˈempʃən] N Zuvorkommen nt

pre-emptive [priːˈemptɪv] ADJ präventiv, Präventiv-; **~ attack** Präventivschlag m; **~ bid**

(Bridge) Ansage, die durch ihre Höhe weitere Ansagen erschwert

preen [priːn] VT feathers putzen VI (bird) sich putzen VR **to ~ oneself** (bird) sich putzen; (person) (= be smug) sich brüsten (on mit); (= dress up) sich herausputzen, sich aufputzen

pre-exist [ˌpriːɪgˈzɪst] VI (= exist beforehand) vorher existieren, vorher vorhanden sein; (= exist in previous life) präexistieren

pre-existence [ˌpriːɪgˈzɪstəns] N (no pl: = existing before) vorherige Existenz, vorheriges Vorhandensein; (= previous life) früheres Leben or Dasein, Präexistenz f

pre-existent [ˌpriːɪgˈzɪstənt] ADJ (= existing before) vorher vorhanden or existent; (= of an earlier life) präexistent

prefab [ˈpriːfæb] N Fertighaus nt

prefabricate [ˌpriːˈfæbrɪkeɪt] VT vorfertigen

prefabricated [ˌpriːˈfæbrɪkeɪtɪd] ADJ vorgefertigt, Fertig-; **~ building** Fertighaus nt

prefabrication [priːˌfæbrɪˈkeɪʃən] N Vorfertigung f

preface [ˈprefɪs] N Vorwort nt; (of speech) Vorrede f VT einleiten; book mit einem Vorwort versehen

prefaded [ˈpriːfeɪdɪd] ADJ denims gebleicht, bleached pred

prefatory [ˈprefətərɪ] ADJ einleitend

prefect [ˈpriːfekt] N Präfekt(in) m(f); (Brit Sch) Aufsichtsschüler(in) m(f); form ~ (Sch) ≈ Klassensprecher(in) m(f)

prefecture [ˈpriːfektjʊə'] N Präfektur f

prefer [prɪˈfɜː'] ○ 5.2, 7.1, 7.4, 26.3 VT a (= like better) vorziehen (to dat), lieber mögen (to als); applicant, solution vorziehen, bevorzugen; (= be more fond of) person lieber haben (to als); **he ~s coffee to tea** er trinkt lieber Kaffee als Tee; **he ~s blondes/hot countries** er bevorzugt Blondinen/warme Länder; **I ~ it that way** es ist mir lieber so; **which (of them) do you ~?** (of people) wen ziehen Sie vor?; (emotionally) wen mögen or haben Sie lieber?; (of things) welche(n, s) ziehen Sie vor or finden Sie besser?; (= find more pleasing) welche(r, s) gefällt Ihnen besser?; **I'd ~ something less ornate** ich hätte lieber etwas Schlichteres; **to ~ to do sth** etw lieber tun, es vorziehen, etw zu tun; **I ~ to resign rather than ...** eher kündige ich, als dass ...; **I ~ walking to cycling)** ich gehe lieber zu Fuß(, als mit dem Fahrrad zu fahren); **I ~ flying** ich fliege lieber; **I ~ not to say** ich sage es lieber nicht; **would you ~ me to drive?** soll ich lieber fahren?; **I would ~ you to do it today** or that **you did it today** mir wäre es lieber, wenn Sie es heute täten

b (Jur) **to ~ charges (against sb)** (gegen jdn) klagen, Klage (gegen jdn) einreichen or erheben

c (esp Eccl: = promote) befördern; **the bishop was ~red to the archbishopric of York** dem Bischof wurde die Würde eines Erzbischofs von York verliehen

preferable [ˈprefərəbl] ADJ **X is ~ to Y** X ist Y (dat) vorzuziehen; **anything would be ~ to sharing a flat with Sophie** alles wäre besser, als mit Sophie zusammen wohnen zu müssen; **death is ~ to dishonour** lieber tot als ehrlos; **it is ~ to use vegetable oil for cooking** zum Kochen eignet sich pflanzliches Öl besser or am besten, zum Kochen ist pflanzliches Öl vorzuziehen; **it would be ~ to do it that way** es wäre besser, es so zu machen; **to find sth ~** etw vorziehen, einer Sache (dat) den Vorzug geben; **infinitely ~** hundertmal besser or lieber

preferably [ˈprefərəblɪ] ADV am liebsten; **tea or coffee? – coffee, ~** Tee oder Kaffee? – lieber Kaffee; **but ~ not Tuesday** aber, wenn möglich, nicht Dienstag

preference [ˈprefərəns] ○ 7.4, 7.5 N a (= greater liking) Vorliebe f; **for ~** lieber; **to have a ~ for sth** eine Vorliebe für etw haben or bevorzugen; **my ~ is for country life** ich ziehe das Leben auf dem Land vor; **I drink coffee in ~ to tea** ich trinke lieber Kaffee als Tee

b (= thing preferred) **what is your ~?** was wäre Ihnen am liebsten?; **just state your ~** nennen Sie einfach Ihre Wünsche; **I have no ~** mir ist das eigentlich gleich; **what are your ~s as regards food?** was essen Sie am liebsten?

c (= greater favour) Vorzug m; **to show ~ for sb** jdn bevorzugen; **to give ~ to sb/sth** jdn/etw bevorzugen, jdm/etw den Vorzug geben (over gegenüber); **to give certain imports ~** Vorzugs- or Präferenzzölle auf bestimmte Einfuhrartikel gewähren

preference shares [ˈprefərənsˌʃeəz] PL (Brit Fin) Vorzugsaktien pl

preferential [ˌprefəˈrenʃəl] ADJ bevorzugt, Sonder-; **~ rate** Sonderpreis m; **to give sb ~ treatment** jdn bevorzugt behandeln; **to get** or **receive ~ treatment** eine Vorzugsbehandlung genießen or bekommen; **~ trade** (Comm) Präferenz- or Vorzugshandel m; **~ trade agreement** Vereinbarung f über Präferenzhandel or Vorzugshandel; **~ trade area** präferenzielle or präferentielle or vorzugsweise Handelszone; **~ trading status** präferenzieller or präferentieller or bevorzugter Handelsstatus; **~ tariff** (Comm) Präferenz- or Vorzugszoll m; **~ ballot** (Pol) Präferenzwahl f; **~ voting** (Pol) Präferenzwahlsystem nt

preferentially [ˌprefəˈrenʃəlɪ] ADV treat etc bevorzugt

preferment [prɪˈfɜːmənt] N a (esp Eccl: = promotion) Beförderung f b (Jur) **~ of charges** Klageerhebung f

preferred [prɪˈfɜːd] ADJ creditor bevorrechtigt

preferred stock N (US Fin) Vorzugsaktien pl

prefigure [priːˈfɪgə'] VT (= indicate) anzeigen, ankündigen; (= imagine beforehand) sich (dat) ausmalen

prefix [ˈpriːfɪks] N (Gram) Vorsilbe f, Präfix nt; (= title) Namensvorsatz m; (in code) Vorsatz m; (Telec) Vorwahl f VT [priːˈfɪks] (Gram) präfigieren, mit einer Vorsilbe or einem Präfix versehen; name mit einem Namensvorsatz versehen; number (with code) voranstellen (+dat), voransetzen (+dat); **words ~ed by "un"** Wörter mit der Vorsilbe or dem Präfix „un"

preflight [ˈpriːflaɪt] ADJ attr **~ checks/instructions** Kontrollen pl/Anweisungen pl vor dem Flug

preform [priːˈfɔːm] VT vorformen

prefrontal [ˌpriːˈfrʌntl] ADJ des Stirnbeins

preggers [ˈpregəz] ADJ pred (esp Brit, inf) schwanger

pregnancy [ˈpregnənsɪ] N Schwangerschaft f; (of animal) Trächtigkeit f; (fig) (of remarks etc) Bedeutungsgehalt m; (of silence, pause) Bedeutungsschwere f, Bedeutungsgeladenheit f

pregnancy test N Schwangerschaftsuntersuchung f, Schwangerschaftstest m

pregnant [ˈpregnənt] ADJ a woman schwanger; animal trächtig, tragend; **3 months ~** im vierten Monat schwanger; **she is ~ with her first child** sie ist zum ersten Mal schwanger; **Gill was ~ by her new boyfriend** Gill war von ihrem neuen Freund schwanger; **to become** or **get ~** (woman) schwanger werden b (fig) remark, silence, pause bedeutungsvoll or -schwer or -geladen; **~ with meaning** bedeutungsvoll or -geladen or -schwanger (iro); **~ with consequences** folgenschwer

preheat [priːˈhiːt] VT vorheizen

prehensile [prɪˈhensaɪl] ADJ Greif-; **~ tail** Greifschwanz m

prehistoric [ˌpriːhɪˈstɒrɪk] ADJ a prähistorisch, vorgeschichtlich b (fig) mittelalterlich, uralt; **it is based on almost ~ technology** es basiert auf geradezu mittelalterlicher Technologie

prehistory [ˌpriːˈhɪstərɪ] N Vorgeschichte f

pre-ignition [ˌpriːɪgˈnɪʃən] N Frühzündung f

pre-industrial [ˌpriːɪnˈdʌstrɪəl] ADJ vorindustriell

prejudge [priːˈdʒʌdʒ] VT case, issue, person im voraus beurteilen; (negatively) person im Voraus verurteilen

prejudice ['predʒʊdɪs] **N** **a** (= biased opinion) Vorurteil nt; **his ~ against** ... seine Voreingenommenheit gegen ...; **that's pure** ~ das ist reine Voreingenommenheit; **the newspaper report was full of ~ against** ... der Zeitungsbericht steckte voller Vorurteile gegen ...; **to have a ~ against sb/sth** ein Vorurteil nt gegen jdn/etw haben, gegen jdn/etw voreingenommen sein; **racial** ~ Rassenvorurteile pl; **colour** ~ Vorurteile pl gegen Andersfarbige or aufgrund or auf Grund der Hautfarbe

b (esp Jur: = detriment, injury) Schaden m; **to the ~ of sb** (form) zu jds Schaden; **to the ~ of sth** (form) unter Beeinträchtigung einer Sache (gen); **without** ~ (Jur) ohne Verbindlichkeit or Obligo; **without ~ to one's rights** ohne sich (dat) selbst zu schaden; **without ~ to any claim** (Jur) ohne Beeinträchtigung or unbeschadet irgendwelcher Ansprüche

VT **a** (= bias) einnehmen, beeinflussen → also **prejudiced**

b (= injure) gefährden; chances beeinträchtigen, gefährden

prejudiced ['predʒʊdɪst] **ADJ** person voreingenommen (against gegen); opinion vorgefasst; judge befangen; **to be ~ in favour of sb/sth** für jdn/etw voreingenommen sein; **to be racially ~** Rassenvorurteile haben

prejudicial [predʒʊ'dɪʃəl] **ADJ** abträglich (to sth einer Sache dat); **to be ~ to a cause** einer Sache (dat) schaden; **to be ~ to sb's interests** jds Chancen gefährden

prelacy ['prelǝsɪ] **N** (= office) Prälatur f; (= bishops etc) geistliche Würdenträger pl; (= system) Kirchenhierarchie f

prelate ['prelɪt] **N** Prälat m

preliminary [prɪ'lɪmɪnǝrɪ] **ADJ** remarks, chapter einleitend; steps, measures vorbereitend; report, results, tests vorläufig; stage früh; ~ **negotiations** Vorverhandlungen pl; ~ **investigation** Voruntersuchung f; ~ **contacts** erste Kontakte; ~ **round** Vorrunde f

N Einleitung f (to zu); (= preparatory measure) Vorbereitung f, vorbereitende Maßnahme; (Sport) Vorspiel nt; **preliminaries** Präliminarien pl (geh, Jur); (for speech) einführende or einleitende Worte; (Sport) Vorrunde f; **the preliminaries are complete, now the actual work can begin** die Vorarbeit ist getan, jetzt kann die eigentliche Arbeit anfangen; **all the preliminaries to sth** alles, was einer Sache (dat) vorausgeht; **let's dispense with the preliminaries** kommen wir gleich zur Sache; **as a** ~ als Vorarbeit, als Vorbereitung

preliminary hearing **N** (Jur) Voruntersuchung f

Preliminary Scholastic Aptitude Test **N** (US Sch, Univ) Eignungstest vor Aufnahme in eine Universität

prelims ['pri:lɪmz] **PL** **a** (Sch, Univ) Vorprüfung f **b** (in book) Vorbemerkungen pl

prelude ['prelju:d] **N** Vorspiel nt; (Mus: = introduction to fugue) Präludium nt; (fig) Auftakt m **VT** einleiten, den Auftakt (+gen) bilden

prem [prem] **N** (inf: = premature baby) Frühchen nt (inf)

premarital [pri:'mærɪtl] **ADJ** vorehelich

premature ['premǝtʃʊǝ] **ADJ** baldness, birth, arrival vorzeitig; labour, death, retirement frühzeitig, vorzeitig; decision, action verfrüht; **you were a little** ~ da waren Sie ein wenig voreilig; **the baby was three weeks** ~ das Baby wurde drei Wochen zu früh geboren; **it is ~ to talk of sanctions** es ist voreilig or verfrüht, von Sanktionen zu sprechen; ~ **baby** Frühgeburt f; ~ **ejaculation** vorzeitiger Samenerguss

prematurely ['premǝtʃʊǝlɪ] **ADV** bald vorzeitig; aged, middle-aged, menopausal frühzeitig, vorzeitig; decide verfrüht; act voreilig; **he was born** ~ er war eine Frühgeburt

premed [pri:'med] **N** (inf) **a** = **premedication** **b** (US) (person) Medizinstudent, der auf das Medizinstudium vorbereitende Einführungs-

kurse besucht (class) vorbereitender medizinischer Einführungskurs

premedic [pri:'medɪk] **ADJ** (inf: = premedical student) Student im vorklinischen Studium

premedical [pri:'medɪkl] **ADJ** (US) course auf das (eigentliche) Medizinstudium vorbereitend attr

premedication [pri:medɪ'keɪʃǝn] **N** Beruhigungsspritze f (vor Anästhesie)

premeditate [pri:'medɪteɪt] **VT** vorsätzlich planen

premeditated [pri:'medɪteɪtɪd] **ADJ** vorsätzlich

premeditation [pri:medɪ'teɪʃǝn] **N** Vorsatz m

premenstrual [pri:'menstrʊǝl] **ADJ** prämenstruell, vor der Menstruation auftretend

premenstrual syndrome, **premenstrual tension** **N** (esp Brit) prämenstruelles Syndrom, prämenstruelle Phase

premier ['premɪǝ] **ADJ** führend **N** Premier m, Premierminister(in) m(f)

Premier Division **N** (Ftbl, in Scotland) = **Premier League**

première ['premɪɛǝ] **N** Premiere f; (first ever also) Uraufführung f; (in particular place also) Erstaufführung f **VT** uraufführen, erstaufführen

Premier League **N** (Ftbl) erste Liga

Premiership ['premɪǝʃɪp] **N** (Ftbl) erste Liga

premiership **N** (= period) Amtsperiode or -zeit f als Premierminister(in); (= office) Amt nt des Premierministers/der Premierministerin

premise ['premɪs] **N** **a** (esp Logic) Prämisse f (spec), Voraussetzung f

b **premises** PL (of school, factory) Gelände nt; (= building) Gebäude nt; (= shop) Räumlichkeiten pl; (form, = house) Besitz m, Anwesen nt; **licensed ~s** Schankort m; **business ~s** Geschäftsräume pl; **to use as business ~s** geschäftlich nutzen; **drinking is not allowed in or on these ~s** es ist nicht erlaubt, hier Alkohol zu trinken; **will you escort him off the ~s?** würden Sie ihn bitte hinausbegleiten?; **he was asked to leave the ~s** man forderte ihn auf, das Gelände etc zu verlassen; **get off my ~s** verlassen Sie sofort mein Land or Grundstück! **VT** **to be ~d on sth** (form) auf etw (dat) basieren

premiss **N** = **premise a**

premium ['pri:mɪǝm] **N** (= bonus, additional sum) Bonus m, Prämie f; (= surcharge) Zuschlag m; (= insurance premium) Prämie f; (St Ex) Aufgeld nt, Agio nt; ~ **bond** (Brit) Los- or Lotterieanleihe f; **to sell sth at a** ~ etw über seinem Wert verkaufen; **to be at a** ~ (St Ex) über pari stehen; (fig) hoch im Kurs stehen; **to place** or **put a (high)** ~ **on sth** (fig) etw hoch einschätzen or bewerten

ADJ **a** (= top-quality) goods, brand erstklassig; ~ **petrol** (Brit) or **gas** (US) Super nt, Superbenzin nt

b (= inflated) ~ **price** Höchstpreis m; **callers are charged a ~ rate of 48p a minute** Anrufern wird der Höchsttarif von 48 Pence pro Minute berechnet

premium-rate ['pri:mɪǝmreɪt] **ADJ** (Telec) call zum Höchsttarif; ~ **telephone numbers** Telefonnummern pl, die man zum Höchsttarif anrufen kann; ~ **services** Leistungen pl, für die man den Höchsttarif bezahlen muss

premolar [pri:'mǝʊlǝ] **N** vorderer Backenzahn

premonition [premǝ'nɪʃǝn] **N** (= presentiment) (böse or schlechte) Vorahnung, (böses or schlechtes) Vorgefühl; (= forewarning) Vorwarnung f

premonitory [prɪ'mɒnɪtǝ rɪ] **ADJ** warnend

prenatal [pri:'neɪtl] **ADJ** pränatal, vor der Geburt

prenuptial [pri:'nʌpʃǝl] **ADJ** vor der Hochzeit

prenuptial agreement **N** vorehelicher Vertrag

preoccupation [pri:ɒkjʊ'peɪʃǝn] **N** **his face had a look of** ~ seinem Gesicht sah man an, dass ihn etwas beschäftigte; **her ~ with her ap-**

pearance ihre ständige Sorge um ihr Äußeres; **her ~ with making money was such that** ... sie war so sehr mit dem Geldverdienen beschäftigt, dass ...; **that was his main** ~ das war sein Hauptanliegen

preoccupied [pri:'ɒkjʊpaɪd] **ADJ** look, tone of voice, smile gedankenverloren; **to be ~ with sth** nur an etw (acc) denken, sich ganz auf etw (acc) konzentrieren; **he has been (looking) rather ~ recently** er sieht in letzter Zeit so aus, als beschäftige ihn etwas; **he was too ~ to notice her** er war zu sehr mit anderen Dingen beschäftigt, um sie zu bemerken

preoccupy [pri:'ɒkjʊpaɪ] **VT** (stark) beschäftigen

pre-op ['pri:ɒp] **ADJ** (inf) vor der Operation, präoperativ; ~ **medication** vor der Operation verabreichte Medikamente pl

preordain ['pri:ɔ:'deɪn] **VT** vorherbestimmen

prep [prep] (inf) **N** (Brit Sch) (= homework) Hausaufgaben pl, Hausarbeit f; (= homework period) Lernstunde f

prepackaged [pri:'pækɪdʒd], **prepacked** [pri:'pækt] **ADJ** abgepackt

prepaid [pri:'peɪd] **ptp** of **prepay ADJ** postage, goods vorausbezahlt; envelope vorfrankiert, freigemacht; **reply ~ envelope** (Comm) frankierter Rückumschlag; ~ **mobile phone** Handy nt (mit im Voraus entrichteter Grundgebühr)

preparation [prepǝ'reɪʃǝn] **N** **a** (= preparing) Vorbereitung f; (of meal, medicine etc) Zubereitung f; **in ~ for sth** als Vorbereitung für etw; **to be in** ~ in Vorbereitung sein **b** (= preparatory measure) Vorbereitung f; ~**s for war/a journey** Kriegs-/Reisevorbereitungen pl; **to make ~s** Vorbereitungen treffen **c** (Med, Sci) Präparat nt; **beauty ~s** Schönheitspräparate pl; **a ~ of herbs** (Med) ein Kräuterpräparat nt; (Cook) eine Kräutermischung **d** = **prep**

preparatory [prɪ'pærǝtǝrɪ] **ADJ** **a** step, measure, talks, plan vorbereitend; ~ **work** Vorbereitungsarbeit f; **the ~ arrangements** die Vorbereitungen pl **b** (Sch) ~ **education** Erziehung f or Ausbildung f in Vorbereitungsschulen; ~ **student** (US) Schüler(in) einer privaten Vorbereitungsschule für die Hochschule; ~ **talks were held** ~ **to the summit conference** es wurden Gespräche geführt, um die Gipfelkonferenz vorzubereiten; **he cleared his throat** ~ **to speaking** er räusperte sich vorbereitend or er räusperte sich, bevor er zum Sprechen ansetzte

prepare [prɪ'pɛǝ] **VT** vorbereiten (sb for sth jdn auf etw acc, sth for sth etw für etw); meal, medicine zubereiten; guest room zurechtmachen, fertig machen; (Sci) präparieren; data aufbereiten;

~ yourself for a shock! mach dich auf einen Schock gefasst!; **we ~d ourselves for a long wait** wir machten uns auf eine lange Wartezeit gefasst; **to ~ the ground for sth** den Boden für etw bereiten **VI** **to ~ for sth** sich auf etw (*acc*) vorbereiten; **the country is preparing for war** das Land trifft Kriegsvorbereitungen; **to ~ to do sth** Anstalten machen, etw zu tun

prepared [prɪˈpɛəd] ADJ **a** (*also* **ready prepared**) vorbereitet; **~ meal** Fertiggericht *nt* **b** (= *in a state of readiness*) vorbereitet (*for* auf +*acc*); **I wasn't ~ for that!** darauf war ich nicht vorbereitet *or* gefasst; **to be ~ for the worst** auf das Schlimmste vorbereitet sein; **I wasn't ~ for him** to do that ich war nicht darauf vorbereitet, dass er das tut; **the country is ~ for war** das Land ist kriegsbereit *or* bereit zum Krieg; **are you ~ for your journey?** sind Sie reisefertig?; "**be ~**" „allzeit bereit" **c** (= *willing*) **to be ~ to do sth** bereit sein, etw zu tun

preparedness [prɪˈpɛədnɪs] N (= *readiness*) Vorbereitetsein *nt* (*for* auf +*acc*); (*for untoward events*) Gefasstsein *nt* (*for* auf +*acc*); (= *willingness*) Bereitschaft *f*; **lack of ~** mangelnde Vorbereitung (*for* auf +*acc*); **~ for war** Kriegsbereitschaft *f*; (*of army*) Einsatzbereitschaft *f*

prepay [priːˈpeɪ] *pret, ptp* **prepaid** VT im Voraus bezahlen

prepayment [priːˈpeɪmənt] N Vorauszahlung *f*

preponderance [prɪˈpɒndərəns] N Übergewicht *nt*; (*in number also*) Überwiegen *nt*

preponderant [prɪˈpɒndərənt] ADJ überwiegend

preponderantly [prɪˈpɒndərəntlɪ] ADV überwiegend, mehrheitlich

preponderate [prɪˈpɒndəreɪt] VI überwiegen

preposition [ˌprɛpəˈzɪʃən] N Präposition *f*, Verhältniswort *nt*

prepositional [ˌprɛpəˈzɪʃənl] ADJ präpositional; **~ phrase** Präpositionalphrase *f*

prepossess [ˌpriːpəˈzɛs] VT einnehmen (*in sb's favour* für jdn)

prepossessing [ˌpriːpəˈzɛsɪŋ] ADJ einnehmend, anziehend

preposterous [prɪˈpɒstərəs] ADJ grotesk, absurd; **you're being ~** das ist ja grotesk; **it is ~ to suggest that ...** es ist absurd vorzuschlagen, dass ...

preposterously [prɪˈpɒstərəslɪ] ADV grotesk; **he suggested, quite ~ ...** er machte den grotesken *or* absurden Vorschlag ...; **it took a ~ long time** es dauerte absurd lange

preposterousness [prɪˈpɒstərəsnɪs] N Absurdität *f*

preppie, preppy [ˈprɛpɪ] ADJ adrett, popperhaft (*esp pej*)

preprinted [ˈpriːˈprɪntɪd] ADJ vorgedruckt

preprogram [ˈpriːˈprəʊgræm] VT (*lit, fig*) vorprogrammieren; **~med** vorprogrammiert

prep school N = **preparatory school**

prepublication [ˌpriːpʌblɪˈkeɪʃən] ADJ *attr* vor der Veröffentlichung

prepuce [ˈpriːpjuːs] N Vorhaut *f*, Präputium *nt* (*spec*)

prequel [ˈpriːkwəl] N (*Film*) Film, der die Vorgeschichte eines bereits erfolgreich gelaufenen Films erzählt

pre-Raphaelite [priːˈræfəlaɪt] ADJ präraffaelitisch **N** Präraffaelit *m*

prerecord [ˌpriːrɪˈkɔːd] VT vorher aufzeichnen; **~ed cassette** bespielte Kassette

prerequisite [ˌpriːˈrɛkwɪzɪt] N (Grund)voraussetzung *f*, Vorbedingung *f* ADJ erforderlich, notwendig

prerogative [prɪˈrɒgətɪv] N Vorrecht *nt*, Prärogativ *nt* (*geh*); **that's a woman's ~** das ist das Vorrecht einer Frau

Pres *abbr* = **president** Präs.

presage [ˈprɛsɪdʒ] **N** (= *omen*) Vorzeichen *nt*, Anzeichen *nt*, Vorbote *m*; (= *feeling*) Vorahnung *f* VT ankünd(ig)en, andeuten

---

Presbyterian [ˌprɛzbɪˈtɪərɪən] ADJ presbyterianisch **N** Presbyterianer(in) *m(f)*

presbytery [ˈprɛzbɪtərɪ] N (= *priest's house*) (katholisches) Pfarrhaus; (*part of church*) Presbyterium *nt*

preschool [ˈpriːˈskuːl] ADJ *attr* vorschulisch; **a child of ~ age** ein Kind *nt* im Vorschulalter; **~ children** Kinder *pl* im Vorschulalter; **~ education** Vorschulerziehung *f*; **~ years** Vorschuljahre *pl*

preschooler [ˈpriːˈskuːlə'] N Vorschulkind *nt*

preschooling [ˈpriːˈskuːlɪŋ] N Vorschulerziehung *f*

prescience [ˈprɛsɪəns] N vorheriges Wissen, vorherige Kenntnis, Vorherwissen *nt*

prescore [ˌpriːˈskɔː'] VT (*Film, TV*) vorsynchronisieren

prescribe [prɪˈskraɪb] **VT** **a** (= *order, lay down*) vorschreiben; **~d reading** Pflichtlektüre *f* **b** (*Med, fig*) verschreiben, verordnen (*sth for sb* jdm etw); **the ~d dose/punishment** die verordnete Dosis/Strafe **VI** (= *lay down rules*) Vorschriften machen

prescription [prɪˈskrɪpʃən] N **a** (*Med*) Rezept *nt*; (*act of prescribing*) Verschreiben *nt*, Verordnen *nt*; **to make up** *or* **fill** (*US*) **a ~** eine Medizin zubereiten; **on ~** auf Rezept; **only available on ~** rezeptpflichtig, nur auf Rezept erhältlich **b** (= *regulation*) Vorschrift *f*

prescription charge N Rezeptgebühr *f*

prescription drugs PL verschreibungspflichtige Medikamente *pl*

prescriptive [prɪˈskrɪptɪv] ADJ normativ; **to be ~** Vorschriften machen

prescriptivism [prɪˈskrɪptɪvɪzəm] N Präskriptivismus *m*

presealed [ˈpriːˈsiːld] ADJ versiegelt; *containers etc* plombiert

preseason [ˈpriːˈsiːzn] ADJ (*Sport*) *match, training* vor der Saison; (*in tourism*) Vorsaison-; **~ rates** Vorsaisonpreise *pl*

preselect [ˌpriːsɪˈlɛkt] VT vorher auswählen; *gear* vorwählen

presence [ˈprɛzns] N **a** Gegenwart *f*, Anwesenheit *f*; **in sb's ~, in the ~ of sb** in jds (*dat*) Gegenwart *or* Anwesenheit, in Gegenwart *or* im Beisein von jdm; **he was admitted to the king's ~** er wurde zum König vorgelassen; **your ~ is requested** Ihre Anwesenheit ist erforderlich; **to make one's ~ felt** sich bemerkbar machen; **in the ~ of danger** im Angesicht der Gefahr; **there is a strong German ~ in the 1500 metres** die Deutschen sind beim 1500-Meter-Lauf stark vertreten

b *military/police ~* Militär-/Polizeipräsenz *f*

c (= *bearing, dignity*) Auftreten *nt*, Haltung *f*; (*of actor: also* **stage presence**) Ausstrahlung *f*

d **they felt a ghostly/an invisible ~** sie spürten, dass etwas Geisterhaftes/Unsichtbares anwesend war

presence of mind N Geistesgegenwart *f*

present¹ [ˈprɛznt] ADJ **a** (= *in attendance*) anwesend; **to be ~** anwesend sein; **he was ever ~ in her thoughts** er war in ihren Gedanken immer gegenwärtig; **to be ~ at sth** bei etw (anwesend) sein; **~ company excepted** Anwesende ausgenommen; **all those ~** alle Anwesenden; **all ~ and correct** alle da und vollständig

b (= *existing in sth*) vorhanden; **gases ~ in the atmosphere** in der Atmosphäre vorhandene Gase; **carbon is ~ in organic matter** Kohlenstoff ist in organischen Stoffen enthalten; **a quality ~ in all great men** eine Eigenschaft, die man bei allen großen Männern findet

c (= *time*) gegenwärtig, derzeitig, augenblicklich; *year, season etc* laufend; *century* gegenwärtig, jetzig; (= *at the present moment or time*) zum gegenwärtigen *or* jetzigen Zeitpunkt; **the ~ day** (= *nowadays*) heutzutage; **of the ~ day** heutig, modern; **till** *or* **to** *or* **until the ~ day** bis zum heutigen Tag, bis auf den heutigen Tag; **in the ~ circumstances** unter den gegenwärtigen

---

or gegebenen Umständen; **in the ~ case** im vorliegenden Fall; **the ~ writer** (*form*) der Autor des hier vorliegenden Werkes

d (*Gram*) **in the ~ tense** in der Gegenwart, im Präsens; **~ participle** Partizip *nt* Präsens, Mittelwort *nt* der Gegenwart; **~ perfect (tense)** zweite Vergangenheit, Perfekt *nt*

N **a** Gegenwart *f*; **at ~** zur Zeit, im Moment *or* Augenblick, derzeit; **up to the ~** bislang, bis jetzt; **there's no time like the ~** (*prov*) was du heute kannst besorgen, das verschiebe nicht auf morgen (*Prov*); **to live for the ~** ganz in der Gegenwart *or* im Hier und Heute leben; **that will be all for the ~** das ist vorläufig *or* einstweilen alles

b (*Gram*) Gegenwart *f*, Präsens *nt*; **~ continuous/simple** erweitertes/einfaches Präsens, aktuelles/generelles Präsens

present² **N** (= *gift*) Geschenk *nt*; **to make sb a ~ of sth** jdm etw schenken (*also fig*), jdm etw zum Geschenk machen (*form*); **I got it** *or* **was given it as a ~** das habe ich geschenkt bekommen

VT [prɪˈzɛnt] **a** (= *hand over formally*) *medal, prize etc* überreichen; (= *give as a gift*) *art collection, book etc* schenken, zum Geschenk machen (*form*); **to ~ sb with sth, to ~ sth to sb** jdm etw übergeben *or* überreichen; (*as a gift*) jdm etw schenken *or* zum Geschenk machen (*form*); **they ~ed us with a hefty bill** sie präsentierten *or* überreichten uns (*dat*) eine gesalzene Rechnung; **she ~ed him with a son** sie schenkte ihm einen Sohn

b (= *put forward*) vorlegen; *cheque* (*for payment*) präsentieren; *proof* vorlegen, erbringen (*of sth* für etw); *proposal* vorlegen, unterbreiten; **she asked me to ~ her apologies/compliments** (*form*) sie bat mich, ihre Entschuldigung/Komplimente weiterzuleiten; **please ~ my apologies to your mother** (*form*) bitte entschuldigen Sie mich bei Ihrer Mutter; **his report ~s the matter in another light** sein Bericht zeigt die Angelegenheit in anderem Licht *or* stellt die Angelegenheit in anderem Licht dar

c (= *offer, provide*) *target, view, opportunity* bieten; **to ~ a brave face to the world** sich (*dat*) nichts anmerken lassen; **his action ~ed us with a problem** seine Tat stellte uns vor ein Problem; **he ~ed the appearance of normality** nach außen hin wirkte er ganz normal

d (*Rad, TV*) präsentieren; (*Theat*) zeigen, aufführen; (*commentator*) moderieren; **~s, in the blue corner ...** in der blauen Ecke des Rings ...

e (= *introduce*) vorstellen; **to ~ Mr X to Miss Y** Herrn X Fräulein Y (*dat*) vorstellen; **may I ~ Mr X?** (*form*) erlauben Sie mir, Herrn X vorzustellen (*form*); **to be ~ed at Court** bei Hof eingeführt werden

f (= *point*) *gun etc* richten, zielen (*at* auf +*acc*); **~ arms!** (*Mil*) präsentiert das Gewehr!

VR [prɪˈzɛnt] (*opportunity, problem etc*) sich ergeben; **how you ~ yourself is very important** es ist sehr wichtig, wie man sich präsentiert; **to ~ oneself as a candidate** sich aufstellen lassen; **to ~ oneself for an exam** sich zu einer Prüfung anmelden; **he was asked to ~ himself for interview** er wurde gebeten, zu einem Vorstellungsgespräch zu erscheinen; **to ~ oneself at an ideal moment** im idealen Augenblick erscheinen

presentable [prɪˈzɛntəbl] ADJ *clothes, room* präsentabel, vorzeigbar; *food* akzeptabel, in Ordnung; **to be ~** (*person*) sich sehen lassen können; **to look ~** (*person*) akzeptabel aussehen, präsentabel aussehen; **it's not very ~** damit kann man sich nicht gut sehen lassen; **to make sth ~** etw so herrichten, dass man es zeigen kann; **to make oneself ~** sich zurechtmachen; **you're not ~ enough to go** du siehst nicht akzeptabel genug aus, um dorthin zu gehen

presentably [prɪˈzɛntəblɪ] ADV annehmbar, akzeptabel; **you have to be ~ dressed to get into that bar** man muss angemessen angezogen sein, wenn man in diese Bar will

presentation [ˌprɛzənˈteɪʃən] N **a** (*of gift etc*) Überreichung *f*; (*of prize, medal*) Verleihung *f*; (= *ceremony*) Verleihung(szeremonie) *f*; (= *gift*)

Geschenk nt; **to make the ~** die Preise/Auszeichnungen etc verleihen; **to make sb a ~** jdm ein Geschenk überreichen **b** (= act of presenting) (of report, voucher, cheque etc) Vorlage, Präsentation f; (of petition) Überreichung f; (Jur, of case, evidence) Darlegung f; **on ~ of a certificate** gegen Vorlage einer Bescheinigung (gen) **c** (= manner of presenting) Darbietung f, Präsentation f **d** (Theat) Inszenierung f; (TV, Rad) Produktion f; (= announcing, commentary) Moderation f **e** (Med, at birth) Lage f

presentation copy N Dedikationsexemplar nt

present-day ['preznt'deɪ] ADJ attr morality, problems, fashions heutig; **~ Britain** das heutige Großbritannien

presenter [prɪ'zentə'] N **a** (of cheque) Überbringer(in) m(f); **the ~ of the prize was a child** der Preis wurde von einem Kind überreicht **b** (esp Brit: TV, Rad) Moderator(in) m(f)

presentiment [prɪ'zentɪmənt] N (Vor)ahnung f, Vorgefühl nt; **to have a ~ of sth** eine Vorahnung von etw haben; **to have a ~ that ...** das Gefühl haben, dass ...

presently ['prezntlɪ] ADV **a** (= soon) bald; (= shortly afterwards) bald, bald darauf **b** (= at present) zurzeit, derzeit, gegenwärtig

preservation [prezə'veɪʃən] N **a** (= maintaining) (of custom, building, manuscript) Erhaltung f; (of peace) Wahrung f, Erhaltung f; (of dignity) Wahrung f; (of memory, reputation) Aufrechterhaltung f, Wahrung f **b** (to prevent decay) Konservierung f; (of specimens) Präservierung f; **to be in a good state of ~** gut erhalten sein

preservation order N (Brit) **to put a ~ on sth** etw unter Denkmalschutz stellen

preservation society N (for buildings) Denkmalschutzverband m; (for nature) Landschaftsschutzverband m

preservative [prɪ'zɜːvətɪv] ADJ Konservierungs-; **~ chemical** Konservierungsmittel nt N Konservierungsmittel nt

preserve [prɪ'zɜːv] VT **a** (= keep intact, maintain) customs, building, position, eyesight, manuscript erhalten; peace wahren, erhalten; dignity, appearances wahren; memory, reputation aufrechterhalten, wahren; sense of humour, silence bewahren **b** (= keep from decay) konservieren; specimens etc präservieren; leather, wood schützen **c** (Cook) einmachen, einkochen; (= pickle) einlegen; **preserving jar** Weck- or Einmachglas nt **d** (= keep from harm, save) bewahren; **may God ~ you!** Gott behüte dich!; **to ~ sb from sth** jdn vor etw (dat) schützen or bewahren; **heaven or the saints ~ me from that!** (iro) der Himmel möge mich damit verschonen or möge mir das ersparen! **e** (Hunt) game, fish schützen, hegen; **~d fishing/river/wood** unter Schutz stehende Fische/stehender Fluss/Wald N **preserves** PL (Cook) Eingemachtes nt; **peach ~(s)** eingemachte Pfirsiche pl; (= jam) Pfirsichmarmelade f **b** (= special domain) Ressort nt; **this was once the ~ of the wealthy** dies war einst eine Domäne der Reichen; **to poach on sb's ~(s)** jdm ins Handwerk pfuschen **c** game ~ (Hunt) Jagd f, Jagdrevier nt

preserved [prɪ'zɜːvd] ADJ **a** food konserviert; (in jars) eingekocht, eingeweckt, eingemacht; (= pickled) eingelegt **b** (= conserved) präserviert, erhalten; **well-preserved** (building, village, fossil) gut präserviert, gut erhalten; **he is well-preserved** (hum) er hat sich gut gehalten (hum)

preserver [prɪ'zɜːvə'] N Retter(in) m(f)

preset [priː'set] pret, ptp **preset** VT vorher einstellen

preshrink [priː'ʃrɪŋk] pret **preshrank** [priː'ʃræŋk] ptp **preshrunk** [priː'ʃrʌŋk] VT vorwaschen

preside [prɪ'zaɪd] VI (at meeting etc) den Vorsitz haben or führen (at bei); (at meal) den Vorsitz haben (at bei); **to ~ over an organization** etc eine Organisation etc leiten

presidency ['prezɪdənsɪ] N Präsidentschaft f; (esp US: of company) Aufsichtsratsvorsitz m; (US Univ) Rektorat nt

president ['prezɪdənt] N Präsident(in) m(f); (esp US: of company) Aufsichtsratsvorsitzende(r) mf; (US Univ) Rektor(in) m(f)

president elect [prezɪdntɪ'lekt] N gewählter Präsident/gewählte Präsidentin (vor Amtsantritt)

presidential [prezɪ'denʃəl] ADJ (Pol) decree, decision, spokesman des Präsidenten; **~ debate** Präsidentschaftsdebatte f; **~ guard** Wache f des Präsidenten; **~ palace** Präsidentenpalast m; **his ~ duties** seine Pflichten als Präsident

presidential (Pol): **presidential adviser** N Berater(in) m(f) des Präsidenten; **presidential campaign** N Präsidentschaftskampagne f; **presidential candidate** N Präsidentschaftskandidat(in) m(f); **presidential election** N Präsidentenwahl f; **presidential primary** N Vorwahl f für die Präsidentschaft; **presidential year** N Jahr nt der Präsidentschaft, Jahr nt als Präsident

President's Day ['prezɪdənts,deɪ] N (US) Feiertag am dritten Montag im Februar zum Gedenken an die Geburtstage der Präsidenten Lincoln und Washington

presidium [prɪ'sɪdɪəm] N (Partei)präsidium nt

press [pres] N **a** (= machine: trouser press, flower press) Presse f; (= racket press) Spanner m **b** (Typ) (Drucker)presse f; (= publishing firm) Verlag m; **to go to ~** in Druck gehen; **to be in the ~** im Druck sein **c** (= newspapers, journalists) Presse f; **the daily/sporting ~** die Tages-/Sportpresse; **the weekly ~** die Wochenzeitungen pl; **to get a good/bad ~** eine gute/schlechte Presse bekommen **d** (= squeeze, push) Druck m; **to give sth a ~** etw drücken; (= iron) dress etc etw bügeln **e** (dial, US: = cupboard) Wandschrank m **f** (= crush) Gedränge nt; **a ~ of people** eine Menschenmenge **g** (Weightlifting) Drücken nt VT **a** (= push, squeeze) drücken (to an +acc); button, doorbell, knob, brake pedal drücken auf (+acc); clutch, piano pedal treten; grapes, fruit (aus)pressen; flowers pressen; **to ~ the accelerator** Gas geben; **to ~ the trigger (of a gun)** abdrücken, den Abzug betätigen; **the shoe ~es my foot here** der Schuh drückt (mich) hier **b** (= iron) clothes bügeln **c** (= urge, persuade) drängen; (= harass, importune) bedrängen, unter Druck setzen; (= insist on) claim, argument bestehen auf (+dat); **to ~ sb hard** jdm (hart) zusetzen; **he didn't need much ~ing** man brauchte ihn nicht lange zu drängen; **to ~ sb for an answer** auf jds Antwort (acc) drängen; **to ~ the point** darauf beharren or herumreiten (inf); **to ~ home an advantage** einen Vorteil ausnutzen, sich (dat) einen Vorteil zunutze or zu Nutze machen; **to ~ home an attack** einen Angriff energisch vortragen; **to ~ money/one's views on sb** jdm Geld/seine Ansichten aufdrängen; **to be ~ed for money** in Geldnot sein; **to be ~ed for time** unter Zeitdruck stehen, in Zeitnot sein; **to ~ sb/sth into service** jdn/etw einspannen **d** machine part, record etc pressen; **~ed steel** gepresster Stahl, Pressstahl m VI **a** (lit, fig: = bear down, exert pressure) drücken; **to ~ (down) on sb** (debts, troubles) schwer auf jdm lasten **b** (= urge, agitate) drängen; **to ~ for sth** auf etw (acc) drängen; **time ~es** die Zeit drängt **c** (= move, push) sich drängen; **crowds ~ed round him** Massen drängten sich um ihn; **to ~ ahead or forward (with sth)** (fig) (mit etw) weitermachen; (with plans) etw weiterführen

▶ **press on** VI weitermachen; (with journey) weiterfahren

▶ **press out** VT sep juice auspressen; pop-out models etc herausdrücken

press: **press agency** N Presseagentur f; **press agent** N Presseagent(in) m(f); **Press Association** N (Brit) Presseagentur f; **press attaché**

N Presseattaché m; **press baron** N Pressezar m; **press box** N Pressetribüne f; **press-button** N = push-button; **press campaign** N Pressekampagne f or -feldzug m; **press card** N Presseausweis m; **press centre**, (US) **press center** N Pressezentrum nt; **press clipping** N Presseausschnitt m; (from newspaper) Zeitungsausschnitt m; **Press Complaints Commission** N (Brit) Presseaufsichtsrat m; **press conference** N Pressekonferenz f; **press coverage** N Berichterstattung f in der Presse (über ein bestimmtes Thema); **press cutting** N (esp Brit) Presseausschnitt m; (from newspaper) Zeitungsausschnitt m; **press gallery** N (esp Jur, Parl) Pressetribüne f; **press gang** N (Hist) (for navy) Presspatrouille f; (for army) Werber pl VT (esp Brit inf) dazu drängen; **to press-gang sb into (doing) sth** jdn drängen, etw zu tun

pressing ['presɪŋ] ADJ **a** (= urgent) issue brennend, dringend; task dringend **b** (= insistent) requests nachdrücklich; **he was very ~ in his invitation** er drängte mir etc seine Einladung richtig auf N (= records issued at one time) Auflage f; (= copy of record) Pressung f

press: **press kit** N Pressemappe f; **press lord** N = press baron; **pressman** N (esp Brit: = reporter) Zeitungsmann m, Pressemann m **b** (Typ) Drucker m; **pressmark** N Signatur f; **press office** N Pressestelle f; **press officer** N Pressesprecher(in) m(f)

pressor ['presə'] ADJ attr (Med) blutdruckerhöhend

press: **press photographer** N Pressefotograf(in) m(f); **press release** N Pressemitteilung f or -verlautbarung f; **press report** N Pressebericht m; **pressroom** N Druckerei f, (Druck)maschinensaal m; **press spokesman** N Pressesprecher m; **press spokeswoman** N Pressesprecherin f; **press stud** N (Brit) Druckknopf m; **press-up** N (Brit) Liegestütz m

pressure ['preʃə'] N **a** Druck m (also Phys, Met); **at high/full ~** unter Hochdruck; **oil ~** Öldruck m **b** (= compulsion, influence) Druck m, Zwang m; **parental ~** Druck von seiten or von Seiten der Eltern; **social ~s** gesellschaftliche Zwänge pl; **to do sth under ~** etw unter Druck or Zwang tun; **to be/come under ~ to do sth** unter Druck (dat) stehen/geraten, etw zu tun; **to be under ~ from sb** (to do sth) von jdm gedrängt werden(, etw zu tun); **to put ~ on sb** jdn unter Druck (dat) setzen; **to put the ~ on** (inf) Druck dahinter machen (inf), Dampf machen (inf) **c** (= urgent demands, stress) Druck m no pl, Stress m no pl; **~ of work prevents me** Arbeitsüberlastung hindert mich daran; **the ~ of events** der Druck der Ereignisse; **business ~s** geschäftliche Belastungen pl; **the ~s of modern life** die Belastungen pl or der Stress des modernen Lebens; **the ~s of meeting deadlines** der Stress, Termine einzuhalten; **he works better under ~** er arbeitet besser unter Druck; **to be subjected to ~, to be under ~** unter Druck (dat) stehen or sein VT = pressurize b

pressure: **pressure cabin** N (Aviat) Überdruckkabine f; **pressure-cook** VT mit Dampf kochen; **pressure cooker** N Druckkochtopf m, Schnellkochtopf m; **pressure gauge** N Manometer nt, Druckmesser m; **pressure group** N Pressuregroup f; **pressure point** N (Anat) Druckpunkt m; **pressure suit** N (Aviat) Druckanzug m

pressurization [preʃəraɪ'zeɪʃən] N (Aviat etc) Druckausgleich m

pressurize ['preʃəraɪz] VT **a** cabin, spacesuit auf Normaldruck halten; **the cabin is only ~d when ...** der Druckausgleich in der Kabine wird erst hergestellt, wenn ... **b** (= pressure) sb unter Druck setzen; **to ~ sb into doing sth** jdn so unter Druck setzen, dass er schließlich etw tut; **I refuse to be ~d into agreeing** ich lasse mir meine Zustimmung nicht abpressen; **she refused to be ~d into going** sie ließ sich nicht zwingen zu gehen

pressurized ['preʃəraɪzd] ADJ **a** *aircraft, container* mit Druckausgleich; **~ chamber** Druckkammer *f* **b** (= *compressed*) *water, gas* komprimiert, verdichtet, gepresst **c** (*fig*) unter Druck; **to feel ~** sich unter Druck (gesetzt) fühlen; **to feel ~ into sth** sich zu etw gedrängt fühlen; **to feel ~ into doing sth** sich dazu gedrängt fühlen, etw zu tun

pressurized cabin N Druckkabine *f*

pressurized-water reactor ['preʃəraɪzd'wɔ:-tərɪ'æktə'] N Druckwasserreaktor *m*

presswoman ['pres,wʊmən] N **a** (*esp Brit*: = *reporter*) Zeitungsfrau *f*, Pressefrau *f* **b** (*Typ*) Druckerin *f*

Prestel® ['prestel] N (*Brit Telec*) ≈ Bildschirmtext *m*

prestidigitation ['presti,dɪdʒi'teɪʃən] N (*form*) Fingerfertigkeit *f*, Geschicklichkeit *f*

prestidigitator [,presti'dɪdʒiteɪtə'] N (*form*) Taschenspieler(in) *m(f)*

prestige [pre'sti:ʒ] N Prestige *nt*; **~ value** Prestigewert *m*

prestigious [pre'stɪdʒəs] ADJ Prestige-; **a ~ job** ein Prestigeberuf *m*; **to be (very) ~** (einen hohen) Prestigewert haben

presto ['prestəʊ] ADV → **hey**

prestressed ['pri:strest] ADJ vorgespannt; **~ concrete** Spannbeton *m*

presumable [prɪ'zju:məbl] ADJ vermutlich

presumably [prɪ'zju:məblɪ] ADV vermutlich; **he is ~ very rich, is he?** ich nehme an, er ist sehr reich, oder?; vermutlich ist er sehr reich, nicht wahr?; **~ he'll come later** er wird voraussichtlich später kommen, vermutlich wird er später kommen

presume [prɪ'zju:m] **VT a** (= *suppose*) annehmen, vermuten; *sb's death* unterstellen (*form*); **~d dead** mutmaßlich verstorben; **to be ~d innocent** als unschuldig gelten; **he is ~d to be living in Spain** es wird vermutet, dass er in Spanien lebt

b (= *venture*) **to ~ to do sth** sich (*dat*) erlauben or sich (*dat*) herausnehmen or sich erdreisten, etw zu tun

VI a (= *suppose*) annehmen, vermuten; **Dr Livingstone, I ~** Dr. Livingstone, wie ich annehme; **it was his decision, I ~** ich nehme an or vermute, das war seine Entscheidung; **I ~ not** ich glaube nein

b (= *take liberties, be presumptuous*) **I didn't want to ~** ich wollte nicht aufdringlich sein; **you ~ too much** Sie sind wirklich vermessen; **to ~ on** or **upon sth** etw überbeanspruchen

presumedly [prɪ'zju:mɪdlɪ] ADV vermutlich, mutmaßlich

presumption [prɪ'zʌmpʃən] N **a** (= *assumption*) Annahme *f*, Vermutung *f*; **the ~ is that ...** es wird angenommen or man vermutet, dass ...; **~ of death/innocence** Todes-/Unschuldsvermutung *f* **b** (= *boldness, arrogance*) Unverschämtheit *f*, Dreistigkeit *f*; (*in connection with one's abilities*) Überheblichkeit *f*, Anmaßung *f*, Vermessenheit *f* (*geh*)

presumptive [prɪ'zʌmptɪv] ADJ **a** (*Jur*) **~ evidence** Indizien(beweis *m*) *pl*; **~ case** Indizienprozess *m* **b** (= *likely*) **heir ~** mutmaßlicher Erbe

presumptuous [prɪ'zʌmptjʊəs] ADJ *person, remark* anmaßend, unverschämt, dreist; (*in connection with one's abilities*) überheblich, anmaßend, vermessen (*geh*); *behaviour* anmaßend, unverschämt; *idea* anmaßend, vermessen, großspurig; **it would be ~ of me to ...** es wäre eine Anmaßung von mir, zu ...

presumptuously [prɪ'zʌmptjʊəslɪ] ADV **I had assumed, somewhat ~, that ...** es war vielleicht vermessen, aber ich hatte angenommen, dass ...

presumptuousness [prɪ'zʌmptjʊəsnɪs] N (*of person, remark*) Unverschämtheit *f*, Dreistigkeit *f*; (*in connection with one's abilities*) Überheblichkeit *f*, Anmaßung *f*, Vermessenheit *f* (*geh*); (*of behaviour*) Unverschämtheit *f*

presuppose [,pri:sə'pəʊz] VT voraussetzen; (= *require also*) zur Voraussetzung haben

presupposition [,pri:sʌpə'zɪʃən] N Voraussetzung *f*

pre-tax [pri:'tæks] ADJ unversteuert, vor Besteuerung

pre-teen ['pri:'ti:n] ADJ im Kindesalter

pretence, (*US*) **pretense** [prɪ'tens] N **a** (= *make-believe story*) erfundene Geschichte; (= *make-believe person*) erfundene Gestalt; **he didn't really shoot me, it was just ~** er hat nicht auf mich geschossen, er hat nur so getan; **we soon saw through his ~ of being a foreigner** wir durchschauten bald, dass er nur vorspiegelte or vorgab, Ausländer zu sein; **to make a ~ of doing sth** so tun, als ob man etw tut; **he made not even the slightest ~ of being interested** er gab sich (*dat*) nicht einmal den Anschein des Interesses; **this constant ~ that all is well** die ständige Vorspiegelung, dass alles in Ordnung ist; **to maintain a ~ of democracy** den (An)schein einer Demokratie wahren; **it's all a ~** das ist alles nur gespielt or Mache (*inf*)

b (= *feigning, insincerity*) Heuchelei *f*, Verstellung *f*; **his coolness is just (a) ~** seine Kühle ist nur gespielt; **his ~ of normality** seine vorgespiegelte Normalität; **he made a ~ of friendship** er heuchelte Freundschaft, er gab Freundschaft vor; **let's stop all this ~** hören wir mit der Heuchelei auf, hören wir auf, uns (*dat*) etwas vorzumachen; **he is incapable of ~** er kann sich nicht verstellen

c (= *affectation*) Unnatürlichkeit *f*, Geziertheit *f*

d **to make no ~ to sth** keinen Anspruch auf etw (*acc*) erheben

e (= *pretext, excuse*) Vorwand *m*; **on** or **under the ~ of doing sth** unter dem Vorwand, etw zu tun → **false** ADJ **a**

pretend [prɪ'tend] **VT a** (= *make believe*) so tun, als ob; (= *feign*) vortäuschen, vorgeben; **to ~ to be interested** so tun, als ob man interessiert wäre; **to ~ to be sick/to have a cold** eine Krankheit/Erkältung vortäuschen or vorschützen; **to ~ to be asleep** sich schlafend stellen

b (= *claim*) **I don't ~ to ...** ich behaupte nicht, dass ich ...

VI a (= *make believe*) so tun, als ob; (= *keep up facade*) sich verstellen; **he is only ~ing** er tut nur so (als ob); **let's stop ~ing** hören wir auf, uns (*dat*) etwas vorzumachen

b (= *lay claim*) **to ~ to sth** auf etw (*acc*) Anspruch erheben

ADJ (*inf, child language*) Spiel-; **~ money** Spielgeld *nt*; **~ gun** Spielzeuggewehr *nt*; **it's just ~** (*story etc*) das ist nur Spaß (*inf*)

pretended [prɪ'tendɪd] ADJ vorgetäuscht, angeblich, vorgeblich

pretender [prɪ'tendə'] N (*to throne*) Prätendent(in) *m(f)* (*to* auf +*acc*)

pretense N (*US*) = **pretence**

pretension [prɪ'tenʃən] N **a** (= *claim*) Anspruch *m*; (*social, cultural*) Ambition *f*; **he makes no ~(s) to originality** er beansprucht keineswegs, originell zu sein **b** (= *ostentation*) Prahlerei *f*, Protzerei *f* (*pej inf*); (= *affectation*) Anmaßung *f*

pretentious [prɪ'tenʃəs] ADJ (= *pretending to be important*) anmaßend; *speech, style, book* hochtrabend, hochgestochen; (= *ostentatious*) angeberisch, protzig (*inf*), großkotzig (*inf*); *house, restaurant, décor* pompös, bombastisch

pretentiously [prɪ'tenʃəslɪ] ADV *say, describe* hochtrabend; *decorated* pompös, protzig (*inf*)

pretentiousness [prɪ'tenʃəsnɪs] N (= *self-importance*) Anmaßung *f*; (*of speech, style, book*) Hochgestochenheit *f*; (= *ostentatiousness*) Angeberei *f*, Protzigkeit *f* (*inf*), Großkotzigkeit *f* (*inf*); (*of house, restaurant, décor*) Pomp *m*, Bombast *m*

preter- ['pri:tə'-] PREF über-; **preterhuman** übernatürlich

preterite, (*esp US*) **preterit** ['pretərɪt] **ADJ** *verb* im Imperfekt; (*in English*) im Präteritum; **~ form** Imperfekt-/Präteritumsform *f*; **the ~ tense** das Imperfekt, das Präteritum **N** Imperfekt *nt*, Präteritum *nt*; **in the ~** im Imperfekt/Präteritum

preternatural [,pri:tə'nætʃrəl] ADJ **a** (= *supernatural*) übernatürlich **b** (= *abnormal, exceptional*) außergewöhnlich

preternaturally [,pri:tə'nætʃrəlɪ] ADV übernatürlich, außergewöhnlich, unheimlich; **it was suddenly ~ quiet** plötzlich war es unheimlich still

pretext ['pri:tekst] N Vorwand *m*; **on** or **under the ~ of doing sth** unter dem Vorwand, etw zu tun

pretorian [prɪ'tɔ:rɪən] ADJ (*US*) = **praetorian**

pretrial [,pri:'traɪəl] ADJ (*Jur*) vor der Hauptverhandlung

prettify ['prɪtɪfaɪ] VT verschönern

prettily ['prɪtɪlɪ] ADV nett; *dress also* hübsch; (= *charmingly*) reizend, hübsch

prettiness ['prɪtɪnɪs] N (= *pretty appearance*) hübsches Aussehen; (*of place*) Schönheit *f*; (= *charm*) (*of woman*) Anmut *f*, Schönheit *f*; (*of manners, compliment etc*) Artigkeit *f*; **the ~ of her hair/face** ihr hübsches Haar/Gesicht

pretty ['prɪtɪ] **ADJ** (*+er*) **a** hübsch, nett; *manners, compliment, speech* artig; **to be ~** (*also pej*: *man*) hübsch sein; **a ~ man** (*pej*) ein Schönling *m*; **to make oneself ~** sich hübsch machen; **I'm not just a ~ face!** (*inf*) ich bin gar nicht so dumm (wie ich aussehe) (*inf*); **she's not just a ~ face!** (*inf*) sie hat auch Köpfchen!; **~ Polly!** (*to parrot*) Lora, Lora!; **it wasn't ~** das war alles andere als schön; **it wasn't a ~ sight** das war kein schöner Anblick; **~-pretty** (*inf*) niedlich

b (*inf*) hübsch (*inf*); *price, sum* hübsch, stolz; **it'll cost a ~ penny** das wird eine schöne Stange Geld kosten (*inf*); **a ~ state of affairs** eine schöne Geschichte; **a ~ mess we're in!** da sitzen wir ganz schön in der Tinte! (*inf*); **say ~ please** sag mal schön bitte

ADV (= *rather*) ziemlich; *good also* ganz; (= *very also*) ganz hübsch (*inf*), ganz hübsch (*inf*); **~ damn** or **damned good/quick** verdammt gut/ schnell (*inf*), ganz schön gut/schnell; **~ nearly** or **well finished** so gut wie or so ziemlich fertig (*inf*); **how's your job/the patient? – ~ much the same** was macht die Arbeit/der Patient? – so ziemlich wie immer/immer noch so ziemlich gleich

N my **~** mein Sternchen

VT (*inf*) **to ~ up** schönmachen, verschönern

pretzel ['pretsl] N Brezel *f*

prevail [prɪ'veɪl] **VI a** (= *gain mastery*) sich durchsetzen (*over, against* gegenüber) **b** (*conditions, wind etc*) vorherrschen; (= *be widespread*: *customs*) weit verbreitet sein **c** (= *persuade*) **to ~ (up)on sb to do sth** jdn dazu bewegen or bringen, etw zu tun

prevailing [prɪ'veɪlɪŋ] ADJ **a** (= *current*) *fashion, conditions* derzeitig, derzeit herrschend; *opinion* aktuell, (vor)herrschend; **the ~ wisdom** die vorherrschende or derzeitige Überzeugung **b** *wind* vorherrschend

prevalence ['prevələns] N (= *widespread occurrence*) Vorherrschen *nt*, weite Verbreitung; (*of crime, disease*) Häufigkeit *f*; (*of fashion, style*) Beliebtheit *f*

prevalent ['prevələnt] ADJ (= *widespread*) vorherrschend, weit verbreitet, weitverbreitet; *opinion, attitude* geläufig, weit verbreitet, weitverbreitet; *custom, disease* weit verbreitet, weitverbreitet; *conditions, situation* herrschend; *fashions, style* beliebt; **that is very ~ these days** das ist heutzutage häufig anzutreffen

prevaricate [prɪ'værɪkeɪt] VI Ausflüchte machen

prevarication [prɪ,værɪ'keɪʃən] N Ausflucht *f*; (= *prevaricating*) Ausflüchte *pl*, Ausweichmanöver *pl*

prevaricator [prɪ'værɪkeɪtə'] N Ausweichtaktiker(in) *m(f)*

prevent [prɪˈvent] ❂ 26.3 VT *sth* verhindern, verhüten; (*through preventive measures*) vorbeugen (+*dat*); **to ~ sb (from) doing sth** jdn daran hindern *or* davon abhalten, etw zu tun; **the gate is there to ~ them from falling down the stairs** das Gitter ist dazu da, dass sie nicht die Treppe hinunterfallen; **to ~ sb from coming** jdn am Kommen hindern; **there is nothing to ~ me** nichts kann mich daran hindern *or* davon abhalten; **to ~ sth (from) happening** verhindern, dass etw geschieht

preventable [prɪˈventəbl] ADJ vermeidbar, verhütbar

prevention [prɪˈvenʃən] N Verhinderung *f*, Verhütung *f*; (*through preventive measures*) Vorbeugung *f* (*of gegen*); **~ is better than cure** vorbeugen ist besser als heilen; **society for the ~ of cruelty to animals** ≈ Tierschutzverein *m*; **society for the ~ of cruelty to children** Kinderschutzbund *m*; **fire ~** Feuerschutz *m*

preventive [prɪˈventɪv] ADJ *action, measure* vorbeugend, präventiv; **to be ~** zur Vorbeugung dienen; **~ detention** (*Brit Jur*) Vorbeugehaft *f*; (*of habitual criminal*) Sicherungsverwahrung *f*; **~ war** Präventivkrieg *m* N (= *preventive measure*) Präventivmaßnahme *f*; (*Med*) vorbeugendes Mittel, Präventiv *nt*; **as a ~** als Vorbeugung

preventive medicine N vorbeugende Medizin, Präventivmedizin *f*

preview [ˈpriːvjuː] N a (*of play, film*) Vorpremiere *f*; (*of exhibition*) Vorbesichtigung *f*; **to give sb a ~ of sth** (*fig*) jdm eine Vorschau auf etw (*acc*) geben b (*Film, TV:* = *trailer*) Vorschau *f* (*of auf* +*acc*) VT a (= *view beforehand*) vorher ansehen; (= *show beforehand*) film vorher aufführen; *paintings, fashions* vorher zeigen

previous [ˈpriːvɪəs] ADJ a (= *immediately preceding*) vorherig; *page, day* vorhergehend; *year* vorangegangen; (*with indef art*) früher; **the ~ page/day/year** die Seite/der Tag/das Jahr davor; **the/a ~ holder of the title** der vorherige/ein früherer Titelträger; **in ~ years** in früheren Jahren, früher; **he's already been the target of two ~ attacks** er war schon das Opfer von zwei früheren Angriffen; **in a ~ incarnation** *or* **life** (*lit*) in einem früheren Leben; (*fig*) früher im Leben; **from a ~ relationship** aus einer früheren Beziehung; **he beat his ~ best** (*Sport*) er hat seine bisherige Höchstleistung überboten; **have you made any ~ applications?** haben Sie sich davor *or* früher schon einmal beworben?; **on a ~ occasion** zuvor, bei einer früheren Gelegenheit; **I have a ~ engagement** ich habe schon einen Termin; **no ~ experience necessary** Vorkenntnisse (sind) nicht erforderlich; **~ conviction** (*Jur*) Vorstrafe *f*; **to have a ~ conviction** vorbestraft sein; **~ owner** Vorbesitzer(in) *m(f)* b (*dated inf:* = *premature*) vorschnell, voreilig; **this seems somewhat ~** das scheint etwas voreilig *or* verfrüht c **~ to** vor (+*dat*); **~ to going out** bevor ich/er *etc* ausging

previously [ˈpriːvɪəslɪ] ADV vorher, früher; **~ I had very little time to cook** früher hatte ich nur sehr wenig Zeit zum Kochen; **he'd arrived three hours ~** er war drei Stunden zuvor angekommen; **~ unreleased/unpublished** bislang *or* bisher unveröffentlicht; **~ unknown** bislang *or* bisher unbekannt

pre-vocational [ˌpriːvəˈkeɪʃənl] ADJ vorberuflich; **~ training** Berufsschulausbildung *f*

pre-war [ˈpriːˈwɔː] ADJ Vorkriegs-; **the ~ years** die Vorkriegsjahre *pl*

prewash [ˈpriːwɒʃ] N (*on washing machine*) Vorwaschgang *m*

prey [preɪ] N (*lit, fig*) Beute *f*; (= *animal also*) Beutetier *nt*; **beast of ~** Raubtier *nt*; **bird of ~** Raubvogel *m*; **to be/fall ~ to sth** (*lit*) eine Beute von jdm/etw werden; (*fig*) ein Opfer von jdm/etw werden; **she was (a) ~ to anxiety** sie war leicht in Angst zu versetzen; **she was (a) ~ to illness** sie wurde leicht krank VI **to ~ (up-) on** (*animals*) Beute machen auf (+*acc*); (*pirates, thieves*) (aus)plündern; (*swindler etc*) als Opfer aussuchen; (*doubts*) nagen an (+*dat*); (*anxiety*)

quälen; **it ~ed (up)on his mind** es ließ ihn nicht los, der Gedanke daran quälte ihn

prezzie [ˈprezɪ] N (*Brit inf:* = *present*) Geschenk *nt*

price [praɪs] N a Preis *m*; **the ~ of coffee/cars** die Kaffee-/Autopreise *pl*; **~s and incomes policy** Lohn-Preis-Politik *f*; **to go up** *or* **rise/to go down** *or* **fall in ~** teurer/billiger werden, im Preis steigen/fallen; **they range in ~ from £10 to £30** die Preise dafür bewegen sich zwischen £ 10 und £ 30; **what is the ~ of that?** was kostet das?; **at a ~ of ...** zum Preis(e) von ...; **at a ~** zum entsprechenden Preis, wenn man genug dafür hinlegt (*inf*); **at a reduced ~** verbilligt, zu herabgesetztem *or* reduziertem Preis (*form*); **if the ~ is right** wenn der Preis stimmt; **ask him for a ~ for the job** frag ihn (mal), was das kostet

b (*fig*) Preis *m*; **everybody has his ~** jeder hat seinen Preis; **the ~ of victory/freedom/fame** der Preis des Sieges/der Freiheit/des Ruhms *or* für den Sieg/die Freiheit/den Ruhm; **but at what ~!** aber zu welchem Preis!; **at any ~** um jeden Preis; **not at any ~** um keinen Preis; **at the ~ of losing his health and his family** auf Kosten seiner Gesundheit und seiner Familie; **that's too big a ~ to pay** das ist ein zu hoher Preis; **but what ~ honour?** wie kann man Ehre bezahlen?

c (= *value, valuation*) **a diamond of great ~** ein sehr wertvoller Diamant; **to put a ~ on sth** einen Preis für etw nennen; **but what ~ do you put on freedom?** aber wie ließe sich die Freiheit mit Gold aufwiegen?; **to be beyond/without ~** nicht mit Geld zu bezahlen *or* mit Gold aufzuwiegen sein

d (= *reward*) Preis *m*; **to put a ~ on sb's head** eine Belohnung auf jds Kopf (*acc*) aussetzen; **to have a ~ on one's head** steckbrieflich gesucht werden

e (*Betting:* = *odds*) Quote *f*; **what ~ are they giving on that horse?** wie stehen die Wetten für das Pferd?; **the horse had a starting ~ of 3 to 1** das Pferd wurde vor dem Start mit 3:1 gewettet; **what ~ our being able to ...?** (*inf*) wetten, dass wir ... können?; **what ~ freedom/workers' solidarity now?** (*inf*) wie steht es jetzt mit der Freiheit/der Solidarität der Arbeiter?

VT **a** (= *fix price of*) den Preis festsetzen von; (= *put price label on*) auszeichnen (*at* mit); (= *ask price of*) nach dem Preis fragen von; (*fig:* = *estimate value of*) schätzen; **it was ~d at £5** (= *marked £5*) es wurde mit £ 5 ausgezeichnet; (= *cost £5*) es kostete £ 5; **tickets ~d at £20** Karten zum Preis von £ 20; **reasonably ~d** angemessen im Preis; **~d too high/low** zu teuer/billig; **to ~ one's goods/oneself out of the market** seine Waren/sich selbst durch zu hohe Preise konkurrenzunfähig machen; **to ~ sb out of the market** jdn durch niedrigere Preise vom Markt verdrängen

▶ **price down** VT *sep* heruntersetzen, herabsetzen

▶ **price up** VT *sep* heraufsetzen, teurer machen

price: price agreement N Preisvereinbarung *f*, Preisabsprache *f*; **price bracket** N = **price range**; **price ceiling** N Preis(ober)grenze *f*; **price control** N Preiskontrolle *f*; **price-controlled** ADJ preisgebunden; **price cut** N Preissenkung *f*; **price cutter** N Preisbrecher(in) *m(f)*; **price cutting** N (starke) Preissenkungen *pl*; **price-earnings ratio** N (*of shares*) Kurs-Gewinn-Verhältnis *nt*; **price fixing** N Preisfestlegung *f*; **price freeze** N Preisstopp *m*; **price increase** N Preisanstieg *m*, Preiserhöhung *f*; **price index** N Preisindex *m*

priceless [ˈpraɪslɪs] ADJ unschätzbar, von unschätzbarem Wert; (*inf:* = *amusing*) joke, film köstlich; *person* unbezahlbar; **Amy, you are ~!** (*inf:* = *amusing*) Amy, du bist wirklich zum Totlachen

price: price level N Preisniveau *nt*; **price limit** N Preisgrenze *f*; **price list** N Preisliste *f*; **price-maintained** ADJ preisgebunden; **price range** N Preisklasse *f*; **price rigging** N Preisabsprachen *pl*; **price ring** N Preiskartell *nt*;

price rise N Preiserhöhung *f*; **price support** N (*US*) Subvention *f*, Preisstützung *f*; **price tag, price ticket** N Preisschild *nt*; **price war** N Preiskrieg *m*

pricey [ˈpraɪsɪ] ADJ (*inf*) kostspielig; **that's a bit ~!** das ist ein bisschen happig (*inf*)

pricing policy [ˈpraɪsɪŋˌpɒlɪsɪ] N Preispolitik *f*

prick [prɪk] N a (= *puncture, pricking sensation*) Stich *m*; **to give sb/oneself a ~** jdn/sich stechen; **~ of conscience** Gewissensbisse *pl* b (*sl:* = *penis*) Schwanz *m* (*sl*) c (*sl:* = *person*) Arsch *m* (*vulg*), Arschloch *nt* (*vulg*)

VT a (= *puncture*) oneself, sb stechen; *balloon* durchstechen; *blister* outline (durch Löcher) markieren; **to ~ holes in sth** Löcher in etw stechen; **to ~ one's finger (with sth)** sich (*dat*) (mit etw) in den Finger stechen; **to ~ one's finger (on sth)** sich (*dat*) (an etw *dat*) den Finger stechen; **to ~ the bubble of sth** (*fig*) etw in sich zusammenfallen lassen; **his conscience ~ed him** er bekam *or* hatte Gewissensbisse; **it/she ~ed his conscience** es/sie bereitete ihm Gewissensbisse; **tears ~ed his eyes** (*liter*) er fühlte die Tränen kommen b **to ~ one's ears** die Ohren spitzen → *also* **prick up** VT

VI (*thorn, injection etc*) stechen; (*eyes*) brennen

▶ **prick out** VT *sep* a *seedlings* pflanzen, setzen, pikieren (*spec*) b (= *mark*) pattern, shape, design punktieren; (*with marking wheel*) ausrädeln

▶ **prick up** VI **her/its ears pricked up** sie/es spitzte die Ohren VT *sep* **to prick up its/one's ears** (*lit, fig*) die Ohren spitzen

pricking [ˈprɪkɪŋ] N (= *sensation*) Stechen *nt*

prickle [ˈprɪkl] N a (= *sharp point*) Stachel *m*; (*on plants*) Dorn *m*, Stachel *m* b (= *sensation*) Stechen *nt*; (*caused by wool, beard etc*) Kratzen *nt*; (= *tingle, also fig*) Prickeln *nt* VI stechen; (*wool, beard*) kratzen; (= *tingle, also fig*) prickeln

prickleback N (*fish*) Stichling *m*

prickly [ˈprɪklɪ] ADJ (+*er*) a *plant, fish, animal* stach(e)lig; *beard, material* kratzig; *sensation* stechend; (= *tingling*) prickelnd (*also fig*) b (*fig*) *person* bissig; *woman also* kratzbürstig (*inf*); **as ~ as a hedgehog** stachelig wie ein Igel c (= *sore*) *eyes* schmerzend, gereizt

prickly: prickly ash N (*Bot*) Stachelesche *f*; **prickly heat** N Hitzepocken *pl*; **prickly pear** N (= *plant*) Feigenkaktus *m*; (= *fruit*) Kaktusfeige *f*

prick: prick-tease [ˈprɪktiːz] (*sl*) VI **she's always prick-teasing** sie geilt die Männer auf und lässt sie dann abblitzen (*sl*) VT aufgeilen und dann abblitzen lassen (*sl*); **prick-teaser, prick-tease** N (*sl*) **she's just a ~** sie geilt die Männer nur auf (*sl*)

pricy [ˈpraɪsɪ] ADJ = **pricey**

pride [praɪd] N a Stolz *m*; (= *arrogance*) Hochmut *m*; **to have too much ~ to do sth** zu stolz sein, um etw zu tun; **to take (a) ~ in sth** auf etw (*acc*) stolz sein; **to take (a) ~ in one's appearance** Wert auf sein Äußeres legen; **to be a (great) source of ~ to sb** jdn mit (großem) Stolz erfüllen; **her ~ and joy** ihr ganzer Stolz; **the ~ of the army** der Stolz der Armee; **to have** *or* **take ~ of place** den Ehrenplatz einnehmen; **~ comes before a fall** (*prov*) Hochmut kommt vor dem Fall (*Prov*) b (*of lions*) Rudel *nt*

VR **to ~ oneself on sth** sich einer Sache (*gen*) rühmen; **I ~ myself on being an expert in this field** ich darf wohl behaupten, mich auf diesem Gebiet auszukennen; **he ~s himself on the succinctness of his prose** er rühmt sich des knappen Stils seiner Prosa

prie-dieu [ˈpriːdjɜː] N Betpult *nt*

priest [priːst] N Priester(in) *m(f)*, Geistliche(r) *mf*

priestess [ˈpriːstɪs] N Priesterin *f*

priest: priest-hole N verborgener Winkel (*in dem verfolgte Priester versteckt wurden*);

priesthood N Priestertum *nt*; (= *priests collectively*) Priesterschaft *f*; **to enter the ~** Priester werden

priestly ['priːstlɪ] ADJ priesterlich; **~ robes** Priestergewand *nt*

priest-ridden ['priːstˌrɪdn] ADJ klerikalistisch

prig [prɪg] N (= *goody-goody*) Tugendlamm *nt* (*inf*); (= *boy also*) Musterknabe *m*; (= *snob*) Schnösel *m* (*inf*); **don't be such a ~** tu doch nicht so

priggish ['prɪgɪʃ] ADJ tugendhaft; (= *snobbish*) hochnäsig

priggishness ['prɪgɪʃnɪs] N tugendhaftes Getue, Tugendhaftigkeit *f*; (= *snobbishness*) Hochnäsigkeit *f*

prim [prɪm] ADJ (+er) **a** (*also* **prim and proper**) etepetete *pred* (*inf*); *woman, manner* steif, prüde; *mouth, expression* verkniffen; (= *prudish*) prüde **b** (= *neat*) *clothes* sittsam, züchtig; *house* untadelig, mustergültig; *furnishings* steif; (= *demure*) *person* sittsam, züchtig

prima ballerina ['priːməˌbæləˈriːnə] N Primaballerina *f*

primacy ['praɪməsɪ] N **a** (= *supremacy*) Vorrang *m*; (= *position*) Vorrangstellung *f* **b** (*Eccl*) Primat *nt or m*

prima donna ['priːməˈdɒnə] N (*lit, fig*) Primadonna *f*

primaeval ADJ = **primeval**

prima facie ['praɪməˈfeɪʃɪ] ADV allem Anschein nach ◆ ADJ **~ evidence** glaubhafter Beweis; **the police have a ~ case** die Polizei hat genügend Beweise; **a ~ case of …** auf den ersten Blick ein Fall von …

primal ['praɪməl] ADJ ursprünglich, Ur-; **~ scream** Urschrei *m*

primarily ['praɪmərɪlɪ] ADV hauptsächlich, in erster Linie

primary ['praɪmərɪ] ADJ (= *chief, main*) Haupt-, wesentlich, primär (*form*); **that is our ~ concern** das ist unser Hauptanliegen *or* unsere Hauptsorge; **of ~ importance** von größter Bedeutung, von äußerster Wichtigkeit; **the ~ meaning of a word** die Grundbedeutung eines Wortes; **~ source of income** Haupteinnahmequelle *f*; **at ~ level** (*Brit Sch*) in der Grundschule, auf Grundschulniveau ◆ N **a** (= *colour*) Grundfarbe *f* **b** (*esp Brit*: = *primary school*) Grundschule *f* **c** (*US*: = *election*) (innerparteiliche) Vorwahl

primary: primary care N (*Med*) Gesundheitsfürsorge *f* auf kommunaler Ebene; **primary cell** N Primärzelle *f*; **primary colour**, (*US*) **primary color** N Grundfarbe *f*; **primary education** N Grundschul(aus)bildung *f*; **primary election** N (*US*) (innerparteiliche) Vorwahl; **primary feather** N Handschwinge *f*; **primary industry** N Grund(stoff)industrie *f*; (*agriculture etc*) Urindustrie *f*, primäre Industrie (*form*); (= *main industry*) Hauptindustrie *f*; **primary institution** N Ureinrichtung *f*; **primary producer** N Lieferant(in) *m(f)* von Rohmaterial; **primary product** N Primärprodukt *nt*; (= *main product*) Hauptprodukt *nt*; **primary school** N (*esp Brit*) Grundschule *f*; **primary school teacher** N (*esp Brit*) Grundschullehrer(in) *m(f)*; **primary stress** N Haupton *m*; **primary teacher** N (*esp Brit*) Grundschullehrer(in) *m(f)*; **primary winding** N Primärwindung *f*

primate ['praɪmɪt] N **a** (*Zool*) Primat *m* **b** (*Eccl*) Primas *m*; **Primate of England/all England** Erzbischof von York/Canterbury

prime [praɪm] ADJ **a** (= *major, chief*) Haupt-, wesentlich; *target, objective* hauptsächlich, oberste(r, s), höchste(r, s); *candidate* erste(r, s); *cause* hauptsächlich, häufigste(r, s); *requirement* erste(r, s), oberste(r, s); **~ suspect** Hauptverdächtige(r) *mf*; **of ~ importance** von größter Bedeutung, von äußerster Wichtigkeit; **my ~ concern** mein Hauptanliegen *nt*; **she was a ~ favourite** sie war eine hohe Favoritin **b** (= *excellent*) erstklassig, beste(r, s); *example*

erstklassig; **in ~ condition** (*meat, fruit etc*) von hervorragender Qualität; *athlete, car etc* in erstklassiger *or* hervorragender Verfassung; **~ cut** Stück *nt* bester Qualität ◆ N **a** (= *full vigour*) **in the ~ of life** in der Blüte seiner Jahre; **he is in his ~** er ist im besten Alter *or* in den besten Jahren; (*singer, artist*) er ist an seinem Höhepunkt angelangt; **he was cut down in his ~** er wurde in der Blüte seiner Jahre dahingerafft; **he is past his ~** er ist über sein bestes Alter *or* seine besten Jahre hinaus; (*singer, artist*) er hat seine beste Zeit hinter sich; **this city is past its ~** diese Stadt hat auch schon bessere Zeiten gesehen **b** (*Math*) Primzahl *f* **c** (*Eccl: also* **Prime**) Prim *f* ◆ VT **a** *gun* schussfertig machen; *bomb* scharf machen; *pump* vorpumpen; *carburettor* Anlasskraftstoff einspritzen in (+acc) **b** *surface* (*for painting*) grundieren **c** (*with advice, information*) instruieren **d** *person* (*with drink*) alkoholisieren, unter Alkohol setzen

prime costs PL (*Comm*) Selbstkosten *pl*, Gestehungskosten *pl*

primed [praɪmd] ADJ **a** *person* präpariert, vorbereitet, instruiert, gerüstet; **to be ~ for the interview/game** für das Interview/Spiel gut gerüstet sein; **to do sth** gut vorbereitet *or* gerüstet, etw zu tun **b** (= *drunk*) *person* angetrunken, alkoholisiert, unter Alkohol; **~ with drink** unter Alkohol gesetzt; **well ~** gut geölt (*inf*) **c** (= *prepared*) *surface* grundiert, präpariert, vorbereitet **d** *bomb, gun* präpariert

prime: prime factor N (*Math*) Primfaktor *m*; **prime meridian** N Nullmeridian *m*; **prime minister** N Ministerpräsident(in) *m(f)*, Premierminister(in) *m(f)*; **prime ministerial** ADJ des Premierministers, der Premierministerin; **prime ministership** N Amt *nt* des Premierministers; **during her ~** während ihrer Amtszeit als Premierministerin; **prime mover** N (*Phys, Tech*) Zugmaschine *f*; (*Philos*) bewegende Kraft, Triebfeder *f*; (*fig*: = *person*) treibende Kraft; **prime number** N (*Math*) Primzahl *f*

primer ['praɪmə] N **a** (= *paint*) Grundierfarbe *f*, Grundierung *f*; (= *coat*) Grundierung *f*, Grundieranstrich *m* **b** (*esp Sch*: = *book*) Elementarbuch *nt*, Anfangslehrbuch *nt*, Fibel *f* **c** (= *explosive*) Zündhütchen *nt*, Treibladungszünder *m*

prime: prime rate N (*Econ, Fin*) Prime Rate *f*, Vorzugszins *nt*; **prime ribs** PL Hochrippen *pl*; **prime time** N Hauptsendezeit *f*

primeval [praɪˈmiːvəl] ADJ urzeitlich, Ur-; **~ soup** Ursuppe *f*; **~ slime** Urschleim *m*; **~ forest** Urwald *m*; **~ instinct** Urinstinkt *m*

primitive ['prɪmɪtɪv] ADJ primitiv; (*Art*) naiv ◆ N (*Art*) (= *artist*) Naive(r) *mf*; (= *work*) naives Werk

primitivism ['prɪmɪtɪvɪzəm] N (*Art*) naive Kunst

primly ['prɪmlɪ] ADV (= *demurely*) sittsam, züchtig, überkorrekt; (= *prudishly*) prüde; **she was sitting ~ sipping tea** sie saß steif und vornehm da und nippte an ihrem Tee

primness ['prɪmnɪs] N (= *demureness*) Sittsamkeit *f*, Züchtigkeit *f*; (= *prudishness*) Prüderie *f*

primogenitor [ˌpraɪməʊˈdʒenɪtə] N (= *ancestor*) Ahn(e) *m*, Vorfahr *m*; (= *first ancestor*) Urahn(e) *m*, Stammvater *m*

primogeniture [ˌpraɪməʊˈdʒenɪtʃə] N Erstgeburt *f*; **law of ~** Erstgeburtsrecht *nt*

primordial [praɪˈmɔːdɪəl] ADJ primordial (*spec*), ursprünglich; **~ slime** Urschleim *m*

primp [prɪmp] VT zurechtmachen; *hair also* richten; **to ~ oneself (up)** sich fein machen, sich schniegeln ◆ VI sich zurechtmachen

primrose ['prɪmrəʊz] N (*Bot*) Erdschlüsselblume *f*; (= *colour*) Blassgelb *nt* ◆ ADJ blassgelb; **the ~ path** (*fig*) der Rosenpfad

primula ['prɪmjʊlə] N Primel *f*

Primus (stove)® ['praɪməsˌstəʊv)] N Primuskocher *m*

prince [prɪns] N (= *king's son*) Prinz *m*; (= *ruler*) Fürst *m*; **Prince Charming** (*in fairy story*) der Königssohn; (*fig*) der Märchenprinz; **the Prince of Darkness** der Fürst der Finsternis; **the Prince of Peace** der Friedensfürst; **a ~ among men** eine herausragende Erscheinung; **he is ~ of architects/architecture** (*liter*) er ist einer der herausragendsten Architekten

prince consort N Prinzgemahl *m*

princedom ['prɪnsdəm] N (*old*) Fürstentum *nt*

princeling ['prɪnslɪŋ] N (*old, liter*) Prinzchen *nt*

princely ['prɪnslɪ] ADJ (*lit, fig*) fürstlich

prince regent N Prinzregent *m*

princess [prɪnˈses] N Prinzessin *f*; (= *wife of ruler*) Fürstin *f*

Princess Royal N (*Brit*) *Titel einer der Töchter des regierenden Monarchen*

principal ['prɪnsɪpəl] ADJ Haupt-, hauptsächlich; **the ~ cities of China** die wichtigsten Städte Chinas; **my ~ concern** mein Hauptanliegen *nt*; **~ person** Hauptperson *f*; **~ teacher** Rektor(in) *m(f)*; **~ horn in the Philharmonic Orchestra** erster Hornist/erste Hornistin der Philharmoniker ◆ N **a** (*of school, college*) Rektor(in) *m(f)*; (*in play*) Hauptperson *f*; (*in duel*) Duellant *m* **b** (*Fin, of investment*) Kapitalsumme *f*; (*of debt*) Kreditsumme *f* **c** (*esp Jur*: = *client*) Klient(in) *m(f)*, Mandant(in) *m(f)*

principal boy N (*Theat*) *jugendliche Hauptrolle in britischen Weihnachtsrevuen, die traditionsgemäß von einem Mädchen gespielt wird*

principality [ˌprɪnsɪˈpælɪtɪ] N Fürstentum *nt*

principally ['prɪnsɪpəlɪ] ADV vornehmlich, in erster Linie

principal parts PL (*Gram*: *of verb*) Stammformen *pl*

principle ['prɪnsɪpl] N **a** Prinzip *nt*; **to go back to first ~s** zu den Grundlagen zurückgehen **b** (= *moral precept*) Prinzip *nt*, Grundsatz *m*; (*no pl*: = *integrity*) Prinzipien *pl*, Grundsätze *pl*; **in/on ~** im/aus Prinzip, prinzipiell; **a man of ~(s)** ein Mensch mit *or* von Prinzipien *or* Grundsätzen; **it's against my ~s** es geht gegen meine Prinzipien; **it's a matter of ~**, **it's the ~ of the thing** es geht dabei ums Prinzip; **I'm doing it for reasons of ~** ich tue das aus Prinzip **c** (= *basic element*) Element *nt*

principled ['prɪnsɪpld] ADJ *man, statesman* mit Prinzipien *or* Grundsätzen, prinzipientreu; **high-principled** mit hohen Prinzipien *or* Grundsätzen; **to take a ~ stand** seinen Prinzipien treu bleiben; **on ~ grounds** aus prinzipiellen Gründen

prink [prɪŋk] VTI = **primp**

print [prɪnt] N **a** (= *typeface, characters*) Schrift *f*; (= *printed matter*) Gedruckte(s) *nt*; **out of ~** vergriffen; **in ~** gedruckt; **to be in ~ again** wieder erhältlich sein; **to see sth in cold ~** etw schwarz auf weiß sehen; **he'll never get into ~** er wird nie etwas veröffentlichen; **don't let that get into ~** das darf nicht erscheinen; **in large** *or* **big ~** in Großbuchstaben → *also* **small print** **b** (= *picture*) Druck *m* **c** (*Phot*) Abzug *m*, Kopie *f*; (*of cinema film*) Kopie *f* **d** (= *fabric*) bedruckter Stoff; (= *cotton print*) Kattun *m*; (= *dress*) bedrucktes Kleid; (*of cotton*) Kattunkleid *nt* **e** (= *impression*: *of foot, hand etc*) Abdruck *m*; **a thumb/paw ~** ein Daumen-/Pfotenabdruck *m*; **to take sb's ~s** (*police*) von jdm Fingerabdrücke machen *or* nehmen ◆ VT **a** *book, design, money* drucken; (*Comput*) (aus)drucken; *fabric* bedrucken **b** (= *publish*) *story, picture* veröffentlichen **c** (= *write in block letters*) in Druckschrift schreiben; **to ~ sth in large letters** etw in Großbuchstaben schreiben **d** (*Phot*) abziehen **e** **hoof marks ~ed in the sand** Hufabdrücke *pl* im Sand ◆ VI **a** (*printer, printing machine*) drucken; **ready to ~** (*book*) druckfertig; *machine* druckbereit;

the book is ~ing now das Buch ist gerade im Druck
b (= *write in block letters*) in Druckschrift schreiben

▶ **print off** VT *sep* (*Typ*) drucken; (*Phot*) abziehen

▶ **print out** VT *sep* (*Comput*) ausdrucken; **print out the results, please** würden Sie bitte die Ergebnisse ausdrucken lassen

printable ['prɪntəbl] ADJ druckfähig; *photograph* abzugsfähig, reproduzierbar

print drum N (*Comput*) Drucktrommel *f*

printed ['prɪntɪd] ADJ Druck-, gedruckt; (= *written in capitals*) in Großbuchstaben; *fabric* bedruckt; **~ matter/papers** Büchersendung *f*; **the ~ word** das ~ **book** das gedruckte *or* veröffentlichte Buch; **the ~ page** die gedruckte Seite; **in ~ form** in gedruckter Form; **~ circuit** gedruckte Schaltung; **~ circuit board** Leiterplatte *f*

printer ['prɪntə] N Drucker *m*; **the text has gone to the ~** der Text ist in Druck gegangen

printer driver N (*Comput*) Druckertreiber *m*

printer's ['prɪntəz]: **printer's devil** N Setzerjunge *m*; **printer's error** N Druckfehler *m*; **printer's ink** N Druckerschwärze *f*

printery ['prɪntərɪ] N Druckerei *f*

print head N (*Comput*) Druckkopf *m*

printing ['prɪntɪŋ] N **a** (= *process*) Drucken *nt* **b** (= *unjoined writing*) Druckschrift *f*; (= *characters, print*) Schrift *f* **c** (= *quantity printed*) Auflage *f*

printing: printing block N (*Typ*) Druckform *f*, Klischee *nt*; **printing frame** N Kopierrahmen *m*; **printing ink** N Druckerschwärze *f*; **printing office** N (*Buch*)druckerei *f*; **printing paper** N Druckerpapier *nt*, Kopierpapier *nt*; **printing press** N Druckerpresse *f*; **printing works** N *sing or pl* Druckerei *f*

print: print journalist N Journalist(in) *m(f)* in den Printmedien; **print list** N (*Comput*) Druckliste *f*; **printmaker** ['prɪntˌmeɪkə] N (= *artist*) Grafiker(in) *m(f)*; (= *manufacturer*) Druckhersteller(in) *m(f)*; **printmaking** N Grafik *f*; **print media** PL Print- *or* Druckmedien *pl*; **print menu** N (*Comput*) Druckmenü *nt*; **print-out** N (*Comput*) Ausdruck *m*; **print queue** N (*Comput*) Druckerwarteschlange *f*; **print run** N Auflage *f*; **print seller** N Grafikhändler(in) *m(f)*; **print shop** N (*in printing works*) Druckmaschinensaal *m*; **print speed** N (*Comput*) Druckgeschwindigkeit *f*; **print-through paper** N (*Comput*) Durchschlagpapier *nt*; **printwheel** ['prɪntˌwiːl] N (*Comput*) Typenrad *nt*

prion ['praɪɒn] N Prion *nt*; **~ protein** Prion-Protein *nt*

prior¹ ['praɪə] ADJ **a** *knowledge, agreement* vorherig; (= *earlier*) früher; **without ~ warning** ohne vorherige Warnung, ohne Vorwarnung; **~ claim** Vorrecht *nt* (*to* auf +*acc*); **a ~ engagement** eine vorher getroffene Verabredung **b** (= *stronger*) *obligation* vorrangig **c** **~ to sth** vor etw (*dat*); **~ to this/that** zuvor; **~ to going out** bevor ich/er *etc* ausging

prior² N (*Eccl*) Prior *m*

prioress ['praɪərɪs] N Priorin *f*

prioritization [praɪˌɒrɪtaˈzeɪʃən] N **a** (= *arranging in order of priority*) Ordnung *f* nach Priorität **b** (= *making a priority*) **~ of these issues was a mistake** es war falsch, diesen Dingen Priorität einzuräumen

prioritize [praɪˈɒrɪtaɪz] VT **a** (= *arrange in order of priority*) der Priorität nach ordnen **b** (= *make a priority*) Priorität einräumen (+*dat*)

priority [praɪˈɒrɪtɪ] N Vorrang *m*, Priorität *f*; (= *thing having precedence*) vorrangige Sache *or* Angelegenheit; **a top ~** eine Sache *or* Angelegenheit (von) äußerster Dringlichkeit *or* höchster Priorität; **what is your top ~?** was steht bei Ihnen an erster Stelle?; **it must be given top ~** das muss vorrangig behandelt werden; **to have ~ Vorrang *or* Priorität haben; **to give ~ to sth**

etw vorrangig behandeln, einer Sache (*dat*) Priorität geben; **in strict order of ~** ganz nach Dringlichkeit; **we must get our priorities right** wir müssen unsere Prioritäten richtig setzen; **you've got your priorities all wrong** du weißt ja nicht, was wirklich wichtig ist; **you should get your priorities right** du solltest deine Prioritäten finden; **high/low on the list of priorities** *or* **the ~ list** oben/unten auf der Prioritätenliste

priority: priority share N (*Fin*) Vorzugsaktie *f*; **priority treatment** N Vorzugsbehandlung *f*; **to get ~** bevorzugt behandelt werden

priory ['praɪərɪ] N Priorat *nt*; (*in church names*) ≈ Münster *nt*

prise, (*US*) **prize** [praɪz] VT **to ~ sth open** etw aufbrechen; **to ~ the lid up/off** den Deckel auf-/abbekommen; **to ~ sth out (of sth)** etw aus etw herausbekommen; **to ~ a secret out of sb** jdm ein Geheimnis entlocken

prism ['prɪzəm] N Prisma *nt*

prismatic [prɪzˈmætɪk] ADJ prismatisch; (= *multi-coloured*) in den Farben des Spektrums; **~ colour** Spektralfarbe *f*

prison ['prɪzn] N **a** (*lit, fig*) Gefängnis *nt*; **to be in ~** im Gefängnis sein *or* sitzen; **to go to ~ for 5 years** für *or* auf 5 Jahre ins Gefängnis gehen *or* wandern (*inf*); **to send sb to ~** jdn ins Gefängnis schicken, jdn zu einer Freiheitsstrafe verurteilen ATTR Gefängnis-

prison: prison breach, prison breaking N Gefängnisausbruch *m*, Ausbruch *m* aus dem Gefängnis; **prison camp** N Gefangenenlager *nt*; **prisoner** ['prɪznə] N **a** (*lit, fig*) Gefangene(r) *mf*; **to hold** *or* **keep sb ~** jdn gefangen halten; **to take sb ~** jdn gefangen nehmen; **to take no ~s** (*fig*) keine Gefangenen machen; **~ of war** Kriegsgefangene(r) *mf*; **~ of war camp** (Kriegs)gefangenenlager *nt* **b** (*Jur*) (*under arrest*) Festgenommene(r) *mf*; (*facing charge, at the bar*) Angeklagte(r) *mf*

prison: prison guard N (*US*) = **prison officer**; **prison life** N das Leben im Gefängnis; **prison officer** N (*Brit*) Gefängniswärter(in) *or* -aufseher(in) *m(f)*; **prison system** N Strafvollzugssystem *nt*; **prison visitor** N Gefangenenbetreuer(in) *m(f)*

prissy ['prɪsɪ] ADJ (*pej*) zimperlich; *dress, hairstyle* brav

pristine ['prɪstaɪn] ADJ (= *in unspoilt state*) *beauty* unberührt, ursprünglich; *condition* tadellos, makellos; (= *original*) urtümlich, ursprünglich

prithee ['prɪðiː] INTERJ (*obs*) bitte

privacy ['prɪvəsɪ, 'praɪvəsɪ] N Privatleben *nt*; **there is no ~ in these flats** in diesen Wohnungen kann man kein Privatleben führen; **in an open-plan office one has no ~** in einem Großraumbüro hat man keinen privaten Bereich; **in the ~ of one's own home** im eigenen Heim; **in the strictest ~** (*meeting, preparations*) unter strengster Geheimhaltung

private ['praɪvɪt] ADJ **a** privat; (= *personal*) *letter, reasons* persönlich, privat; (= *confidential*) *matter, affair* vertraulich; *conversation, meeting, interview* privat, vertraulich; (= *secluded*) *place* abgelegen; *dining room* separat; (= *not public*) *funeral, wedding* im engsten Kreis; *hearing, sitting* nicht öffentlich, nichtöffentlich; **they were sharing a ~ joke** sie fanden irgend etwas lustig; **it's just a ~ joke between us** das ist ein Privatwitz von uns; **no ~ jokes!** lass uns auch mitlachen!; **~ and confidential** streng vertraulich; **he acted in a ~ capacity** er handelte als Privatperson; **they wanted to be ~** sie wollten allein *or* für sich sein; **to keep sth ~** etw für sich behalten; **his ~ life** sein Privatleben *nt*; **in his ~ thoughts** in seinen ganz persönlichen Gedanken

b **~ branch exchange** (*Brit Telec*) Nebenstellenanlage *f*; **~ car** Privatwagen *m*; **~ citizen** Privatperson *f*; **~ education** Ausbildung *f* in Privatschulen; **~ health insurance** private Krankenversicherung *f*; **~ individual** Einzelne(r) *mf*; **~ law** Privatrecht *nt*; **~ limited company** = Aktiengesellschaft *f* (*die nicht an der Börse notiert ist*); **~ means** Privatvermögen *nt*; **~ pupil** Pri-

vatschüler(in) *m(f)*; **~ soldier** (*Mil*) gemeiner *or* einfacher Soldat; **~ treatment** Privatbehandlung *f*; **~ tutor** Privatlehrer(in) *m(f)*; **~ ward** Privatabteilung *or* -station *f*

c (= *withdrawn, reserved*) *person* reserviert, zurückhaltend

N a (*Mil*) Gefreite(r) *mf*; **Private X** der Gefreite X; (*in address*) Gefreiter X; **~ first class** (*US*) Obergefreite(r) *mf*

b **privates** PL (= *genitals*) Geschlechtsteile *pl*
c **in ~** privat; (*Jur*) unter Ausschluss der Öffentlichkeit; **we must talk in ~** wir müssen das unter uns besprechen

private: private company N Privatgesellschaft *f*; **private detective** N Privatdetektiv(in) *m(f)*; **private enterprise** N Privatunternehmen *nt*; (= *free enterprise*) freies Unternehmertum

privateer [ˌpraɪvəˈtɪə] N (= *ship*) Freibeuter *m*, Kaperschiff *nt*; (= *crew member*) Freibeuter *m*, Kaperer *m*

private: private eye N (*inf*) Privatdetektiv(in) *m(f)*, Schnüffler(in) *m(f)* (*pej inf*); **Private Finance Initiative** N (*Brit, Pol*) *Regierungsprogramm zur Privatfinanzierung öffentlicher Projekte*; **private hotel** N Privathotel *nt*; **private investigator** N Privatdetektiv(in) *m(f)*

privately ['praɪvɪtlɪ] ADV **a** (= *not publicly*) privat; **may I speak to you ~?** kann ich Sie privat sprechen *or* unter vier Augen sprechen?; **the meeting was held ~** das Treffen wurde in kleinem Kreis *or* Rahmen abgehalten; **a ~ owned company** ein Unternehmen in Privatbesitz; **he is being ~ educated** er wird privat erzogen; **she is having the operation ~** sie lässt sich auf eigene Kosten operieren; **I sold/bought my car ~** ich habe meinen Wagen privat verkauft/privat *or* von Privat gekauft

b (= *secretly, personally, unofficially*) persönlich; **I have been told ~ that ...** mir wurde vertraulich mitgeteilt, dass ...; **~ I think that ...** ich persönlich glaube, dass ...; **but ~ he was very upset** doch innerlich war er sehr aufgebracht

private: private member N (*Brit Parl*) Abgeordnete(r) *mf* (*der/die nicht der Regierung angehört*); **~'s bill** Gesetzesinitiative *f* eines Abgeordneten; **private parts** PL (= *genitals*) Geschlechtsteile *pl* → *also* **private N b**; **private patient** N Privatpatient(in) *m(f)*; **private practice** N (*Brit*) Privatpraxis *f*; **he is in ~** er hat Privatpatienten; **private property** N Privateigentum *nt*; **private prosecution** N (*Jur*) Zivilklage *f*; **private school** N Privatschule *f*; **private secretary** N Privatsekretär(in) *m(f)*; **private sector** N privater Sektor; **private-sector company** N Unternehmen *nt* des privaten Sektors, privatwirtschaftliches Unternehmen; **private tuition** N Privatunterricht *m*; **private view** N Vorabbesichtigung *f*

privation [praɪˈveɪʃən] N **a** (= *state*) Armut *f*, Not *f*; **a life of ~** ein Leben in Armut *or* Not **b** (= *hardship*) Entbehrung *f*, Einschränkung *f*; **to suffer many ~s** viele Entbehrungen erleiden; **wartime ~s** die Entbehrungen *pl* der Kriegszeit

privatization [ˌpraɪvətaɪˈzeɪʃən] N Privatisierung *f*

privatize ['praɪvətaɪz] VT privatisieren

privet ['prɪvɪt] N (*gemeiner*) Liguster; **~ hedge** Ligusterhecke *f*

privilege ['prɪvɪlɪdʒ] N (= *prerogative*) Privileg *nt*, Sonderrecht *nt*; (= *honour*) Ehre *f*; (*Parl*) Immunität *f*; **it's a lady's ~** es ist das Vorrecht einer Dame VT privilegieren, bevorrechtigen

privileged ['prɪvɪlɪdʒd] ADJ *a person, classes* privilegiert; (*Parl*) *speech* der Immunität unterliegend *attr*; *claim, debt* bevorrechtigt; **for a ~ few** für wenige Privilegierte, für eine kleine Gruppe von Privilegierten; **to be ~ to do sth** das Privileg genießen, etw zu tun; **I was ~ to meet him** ich hatte das Privileg *or* die Ehre, ihm vorgestellt zu werden; **in a ~ position** in einer privilegierten Position; **~ stock** Vorzugsaktien *pl* **b** (= *secret*) *information* vertraulich **c** (*Jur*) *document* vertraulich; **~ communication**

vertrauliche Mitteilung **N** **the ~** *pl* (= *elite*) die Privilegierten

privily ['prɪvɪlɪ] ADV (*old*) insgeheim, im Geheimen

privy ['prɪvɪ] **ADJ** **to be ~ to sth** in etw (*acc*) eingeweiht sein **N** Abort *m*, Abtritt *m*

Privy: Privy Council N Geheimer Rat; **Privy Councillor** ['praɪzfaɪt], (*US*) **Privy Councilor** N Geheimrat *m*, Geheimrätin *f*; **Privy Purse** N Privatschatulle *f*

prize¹ [praɪz] **N** **a** Preis *m*; (*in lottery*) Gewinn *m*, Preis *m*; **the glittering ~s of the pop world** der Flimmerglanz der Popwelt; **(there are) no ~s for guessing** (*inf*) dreimal darfst du raten **b** (*Naut: = captured ship*) Prise *f* (*old*)
ADJ **a** (= *awarded a prize*) *entry, essay, sheep* preisgekrönt; **~ idiot** (*inf*) Vollidiot(in) *m(f)* (*inf*) **b** (= *awarded as a prize*) **~ trophy** Siegestrophäe *f*; **~ cup** (Sieger)pokal *m*; **~ medal** (Sieger)medaille *f* **c** (= *offering a prize*) **~ competition** Preisausschreiben *nt* **VT** (hoch)schätzen; **to ~ sth highly** etw sehr *or* hoch schätzen; **to ~ sth above sth** etw über *or* vor etw (*acc*) stellen; **~d possession** wertvollster Besitz, wertvollstes Stück; (*of museum etc*) Glanzstück *nt*, Paradestück *nt*

prize² VT (*US*) = **prise**

prize: prize day N (*Sch*) (Tag *m* der) Preisverleihung *f*; **prize draw** N Lotterie *f*, Tombola *f*; **prizefight** ['praɪzfaɪt] N Profiboxkampf *m*; **prizefighter** ['praɪzfaɪtə'] N Profi- *or* Berufsboxer(in) *m(f)*; **prizefighting** ['praɪzfaɪtɪŋ] N Profi- *or* Berufsboxkampf *m*; **prize-giving** N (*Sch*) Preisverleihung *or* -verteilung *f*; **prize list** N (*in lottery, competition*) Gewinnerliste *f*; **prize money** N **a** (= *cash prize*) Geld- *or* Barpreis *m*; (*Boxing*) (Sieges)prämie *f*; (*in competition*) Gewinn *m* **b** (*old Naut*) Prisengeld *nt*; **prize ring** N (*Boxing*) Ring *m*; **prizewinner** N (Preis)gewinner(in) *m(f)*; **prizewinning** ADJ *entry, novel* preisgekrönt; **~ ticket** Gewinnlos *nt*

PRO *abbr of* **public relations officer**

pro¹ [prəʊ] N (*inf*) Profi *m*

pro² N (*inf: = prostitute*) Nutte *f* (*inf*)

pro³ **PREP** (= *in favour of*) für **N** **the ~s and cons** das Für und Wider, das Pro und Kontra

pro- PREF pro-, Pro-; **~European** proeuropäisch

proactive [prəʊˈæktɪv] ADJ proaktiv

pro-am ['prəʊˈæm] ADJ **~ golf tournament** *Golftournier, bei dem Profis gegen (prominente) Amateure spielen*

probabilistic [ˌprɒbəbəˈlɪstɪk] ADJ (*esp Philos*) probabilistisch; **these are all ~ models** dies sind alles wahrscheinliche Modelle

probability [ˌprɒbəˈbɪlɪtɪ] ✪ 15.2 N Wahrscheinlichkeit *f*; **in all ~** aller Wahrscheinlichkeit nach, höchstwahrscheinlich; **the ~ of sth** die Wahrscheinlichkeit einer Sache (*gen*); **what's the ~ of that happening?** wie groß ist die Wahrscheinlichkeit, dass das geschieht?; **the ~ is that he will leave** wahrscheinlich wird er weggehen

probable ['prɒbəbl] ✪ 15.2 ADJ wahrscheinlich

probably ['prɒbəblɪ] ✪ 15.2, 16.2 ADV wahrscheinlich; **very ~, but ...** sehr wahrscheinlich, aber ...; **most ~, more ~ than not** höchstwahrscheinlich; **~ not** wahrscheinlich nicht

probate ['prəʊbɪt] N (= *examination*) gerichtliche Testamentsbestätigung; (= *will*) beglaubigte Testamentsabschrift *f*; **grant of ~** Erbscheinerteilung *f*

probate court N Nachlassgericht *nt*

probation [prəˈbeɪʃən] N **a** (*Jur*) Bewährung *f*; **to put sb on ~ (for a year)** jdm (ein Jahr) Bewährung geben; **to be on ~** auf Bewährung sein, Bewährung haben **b** (*of employee*) Probe *f*; (= *probation period*) Probezeit *f*; (*Rel*) Noviziat *nt*

probational [prəˈbeɪʃənl] ADJ Probe-; **~ period** Probezeit *f*

probationary [prəˈbeɪʃənrɪ] ADJ Probe-; **~ period** Probezeit *f*; (*Jur*) Bewährungsfrist *f*

probationer [prəˈbeɪʃnə'] N (*Jur*) auf Bewährung Freigelassene(r) *mf*; (*Med*) Lernschwester *f*; (*Rel*) Novize *m*, Novizin *f*

probation officer N Bewährungshelfer(in) *m(f)*

probe [prəʊb] **N** **a** (= *device*) Sonde *f* **b** (= *investigation*) Untersuchung *f* (*into +gen*); **a police ~ revealed ...** Nachforschungen der Polizei ergaben ... **VT** untersuchen; (*esp with device*) sondieren; *space, sb's past, subconscious, private life* erforschen; *mystery* ergründen, erforschen **VI** suchen, forschen (*for* nach); (*Med*) untersuchen (*for* auf +*acc*); (= *inquire*) forschen, bohren (*for* nach); **to ~ into a wound** eine Wunde mit der Sonde untersuchen; **to ~ into sb's private life/sb's past** in jds Privatleben/Vergangenheit (*dat*) herumschnüffeln

probing ['prəʊbɪŋ] **N** Untersuchung *f*; (*esp with device*) Sondierung *f*, Sondieren *nt*; **all this ~ into people's private affairs** dieses Herumschnüffeln in den privaten Angelegenheiten der Leute **ADJ** *question, study, fingers* prüfend

probity ['prəʊbɪtɪ] N (*form*) Redlichkeit *f*, Integrität *f* (*also*)

problem ['prɒbləm] ✪ 26.1 N Problem *nt*; (*Math: as school exercise*) Aufgabe *f*; (= *problematic area*) Problematik *f*; **what's the ~?** wo fehlt's?; **he's got a drink(ing) ~** er trinkt (zu viel); **to have no ~ with sth** kein Problem *or* keine Schwierigkeiten mit etw haben, etw nicht problematisch finden; **I had no ~ in getting the money** ich habe das Geld ohne Schwierigkeiten bekommen; **no ~!** (*inf*) kein Problem!; **the whole ~ of modernization** die ganze Modernisierungsproblematik; **~ area** Problembereich *m*

problematic(al) [ˌprɒbləˈmætɪk(əl)] ADJ problematisch

problem: problem child N Problemkind *nt*; **problem family** N Problemfamilie *f*; **problem-oriented** ADJ (*Comput*) problemorientiert; **problem page** N Problemseite *f*; **problem play** N Problemstück *nt*; **problem-solving** N Problemlösung *f*; **~ skills** Problemlösungsfähigkeit *f*

proboscis [prəʊˈbɒsɪs] N (*Zool, hum inf*) Rüssel *m*

procedural [prəˈsiːdjʊrəl] **ADJ** verfahrenstechnisch; (*Jur*) verfahrensrechtlich **N (police) ~** (= *novel*) Kriminalroman *m*; (= *film*) Kriminalfilm *m*

procedure [prəˈsiːdʒə'] N Verfahren *nt*; **parliamentary/legal ~** parlamentarisches/gerichtliches Verfahren; **what would be the correct ~ in such a case?** wie geht man in einem solchen Falle vor?, wie verfährt man in einem solchen Falle?; **business ~** geschäftliche Verfahrensweise; **rules of ~** Vorschriften *pl*; **questions of ~** verfahrenstechnische *or* (*Jur*) verfahrensrechtliche Fragen *pl*; **~-oriented** (*Comput*) prozedurorientiert

proceed [prəˈsiːd] **VI** **a** (*form: = go*) **vehicles must ~ with caution** vorsichtig fahren!; **I was ~ing along the High Street** ich ging die High Street entlang; **please ~ to gate 3** begeben Sie sich zum Flugsteig 3 **b** (*form: = go on*) (*person*) weitergehen; (*vehicle, by vehicle*) weiterfahren; **we then ~ed to London** wir fuhren dann nach London weiter, wir begaben uns dann nach London (*geh*); **to ~ on one's way** seinen Weg fortsetzen **c** (= *carry on, continue*) fortfahren; **can we now ~ to the next item on the agenda?** können wir jetzt zum nächsten Punkt der Tagesordnung übergehen?; **they ~ed with their plan** sie führten ihren Plan weiter; (= *start*) sie gingen nach ihrem Plan vor; **to ~ about one's business** (*form*) seinen Geschäften (*dat*) nachgehen (*geh*); **~ with your work** fahren Sie mit Ihrer Arbeit fort; **the text ~s as follows** der Text lautet

dann wie folgt; **everything is ~ing smoothly** alles läuft bestens; **negotiations are ~ing well** die Verhandlungen kommen gut voran; **you may ~** (= *speak*) Sie haben das Wort; **I would like to make a statement – ~** ich möchte eine Aussage machen – bitte!
d (= *set about sth*) vorgehen; **how does one ~ in such cases?** wie verfährt man in solchen Fällen?, wie geht man in solchen Fällen vor?; **to ~ on the assumption that ...** von der Voraussetzung ausgehen, dass ... **e** (= *originate*) **to ~ from** kommen von; (*fig*) herrühren von; **all life ~s from the sea** alles Leben kommt aus dem Meer **f** (*Jur*) **to ~ against sb** gegen jdn gerichtlich vorgehen; **to ~ with a case** einen Prozess anstrengen **VT** now, he ~ed nun, fuhr er fort; **to ~ to do sth** (dann) etw tun

proceeding [prəˈsiːdɪŋ] N **a** (= *action, course of action*) Vorgehen *nt*; **the best/safest way of ~ would be to ask him** am besten/sichersten wäre es, wenn wir ihn fragten **b** **proceedings** PL (= *function*) Veranstaltung *f* **c** **proceedings** PL (*esp Jur*) Verfahren *nt*; (*Jur*) court ~ Gerichtsverhandlung *f*; **to take/start ~s against sb** gegen jdn gerichtlich vorgehen; **to take legal ~s** ein Gerichtsverfahren *or* einen Prozess anstrengen; **to start divorce ~s** die Scheidung einreichen **d** **proceedings** PL (= *record, written minutes etc*) Protokoll *nt*; (= *published report*) Tätigkeitsbericht *m*

proceeds ['prəʊsiːdz] PL (= *yield*) Ertrag *m*; (*from sale, bazaar, raffle*) Erlös *m*; (= *takings*) Einnahmen *pl*

process¹ ['prəʊses] **N** **a** Prozess *m*; **the ~es of the law** der Gesetzesweg; **the ~ of time will ...** die Zeit wird ...; **in the ~ of time** im Laufe der Zeit, mit der Zeit; **in the ~** dabei; **in the ~ of learning** beim Lernen; **in the ~ of construction** im Bau; **to be in the ~ of doing sth** dabei sein, etw zu tun
b (= *specific method, technique*) Verfahren *nt*; (*Ind*) Prozess *m*, Verfahren *nt* **c** (*Jur*) Prozess *m*; **to serve a ~ on sb** jdn vorladen **d** (*Biol*) vorstehender Teil; **a ~ of a bone/of the jaw** ein Knochen-/Kiefervorsprung *m* **VT** (= *treat*) *raw materials, data, information, waste* verarbeiten; *food* konservieren; *milk* sterilisieren; *application, loan, wood* bearbeiten; *film* entwickeln; (= *deal with*) *applicants, people* abfertigen

process² [prəˈses] VI (*Brit: = go in procession*) ziehen, schreiten

processed cheese ['prəʊsestˈtʃiːz], (*US*) **process cheese** N Schmelzkäse *m*

processed peas ['prəʊsestˈpiːz] PL Dosenerbsen *pl*

process engineering N Prozess- *or* Verfahrenstechnik *f*

processing ['prəʊsesɪŋ] N (*of raw materials, data, information, waste*) Verarbeitung *f*; (*of food*) Konservierung *f*; (*of milk*) Sterilisierung *f*; (*of application, loan, wood*) Bearbeitung *f*; (*of film*) Entwicklung *f*; (*of applicants, people*) Abfertigung *f*

processing: processing language N (*Comput*) Prozesssprache *f*; **processing plant** N Aufbereitungsanlage *f*; **processing speed** N (*Comput*) Verarbeitungsgeschwindigkeit *f*; **processing unit** N (*Comput*) Prozessor *m*

procession [prəˈseʃən] N (*organized*) Umzug *m*; (*solemn*) Prozession *f*; (= *line of people, cars etc*) Reihe *f*, Schlange *f*; **funeral/carnival ~** Trauer-/Karnevalszug *m*; **to go** *or* **walk in ~** einen Umzug/eine Prozession machen

processional [prəˈseʃənl] (*Eccl*) **N** (= *hymn*) Prozessionshymne *f*, Prozessionslied *nt*; (= *book*) Prozessionsbuch *nt* **ADJ** Prozessions-; *pace* gemessen

processor ['prəʊsesə'] N (*Comput*) Prozessor *m*; (= *food processor*) Küchenmaschine *f*

process printing N (*Typ*) Vierfarbendruck *m*

process-server N (*Jur*) Zustellungsbeamte(r) *m*/-beamtin *f*

pro-choice [prəʊ'tʃɔɪs] ADJ *group, organization* für Abtreibung *pred*; ~ **movement** Bewegung *f* der Abtreibungsbefürworter

pro-choicer [ˌprəʊ'tʃɔɪsə'] N (*inf*) Abtreibungsbefürworter(in) *m(f)*

proclaim [prə'kleɪm] VT **a** (= *announce*) erklären; *revolution* ausrufen; **to ~ sb king** jdn zum König erklären *or* ausrufen *or* proklamieren; **the day had been ~ed a holiday** der Tag war zum Feiertag erklärt worden; **it was ~ed a success** es wurde zu einem Erfolg erklärt **b** (= *reveal*) verraten, beweisen **VR to ~ oneself king** sich zum König erklären

proclamation [ˌprɒklə'meɪʃən] N **a** (= *act*) (*of war*) Erklärung *f*; (*of laws, measures*) Verkündung *f*; (*of state of emergency*) Ausrufung *f*; **after his ~ as Emperor** nach seiner Proklamation zum Kaiser **b** (= *thing proclaimed*) Erklärung *f*, Proklamation *f*

proclivity [prə'klɪvɪtɪ] N Schwäche *f* (*for* für), Vorliebe *f* (*for* für)

proconsul [prəʊ'kɒnsəl] N Prokonsul(in) *m(f)*

procrastinate [prəʊ'kræstɪneɪt] VI zögern, zaudern; **he always ~s** er schiebt die Dinge immer vor sich (*dat*) her

procrastination [prəʊˌkræstɪ'neɪʃən] N Zögern *nt*, Zaudern *nt*; **~ won't solve your problems** durch Aufschieben lösen sich Ihre Probleme nicht

procrastinator [prəʊ'kræstɪneɪtə'] N Zögerer *m*, Zögerin *f*, Zauderer *m*, Zauderin *f*

procreate ['prəʊkrɪeɪt] VI zeugen, sich fortpflanzen VT zeugen, hervorbringen

procreation [ˌprəʊkrɪ'eɪʃən] N Zeugung *f*, Fortpflanzung *f*; (*of species*) Fortpflanzung *f*

Procrustean [prəʊ'krʌstɪən] ADJ unnachgiebig, starr; ~ **bed** Prokrustesbett *nt*

proctor ['prɒktə'] N (*Jur*) Prokurator(in) *m(f)*; (*Univ*) Proktor(in) *m(f)*; (*US: = supervisor*) (Prüfungs)aufsicht *f*

proctoscope ['prɒktəskəʊp] N (*Med*) Proktoskop *nt*

procurable [prə'kjʊərəbl] ADJ erhältlich, zu beschaffen *pred*

procurator ['prɒkjʊəreɪtə'] N (*Hist*) Prokurator *m*; (*Jur*: = *agent also*) Bevollmächtigte(r) *mf*

procurator fiscal N (*Scot Jur*) ≈ Staatsanwalt *m*, ≈ Staatsanwältin *f*

procure [prə'kjʊə'] VT **a** (= *obtain*) beschaffen, sich (*dat*) verschaffen *or* beschaffen, besorgen; (= *bring about*) bewirken, herbeiführen; **to ~ sth for sb/oneself** jdm/sich etw beschaffen *or* besorgen, etw für jdn/sich beschaffen *or* besorgen; **to ~ sb's release** jds Freilassung bewirken *or* erreichen **b** (*for prostitution*) beschaffen (*for sb* jdm) VI Kuppelei betreiben

procurement [prə'kjʊəmənt] N Beschaffung *f*; (*of release*) Bewirkung *f*; (*of prostitutes*) Beschaffung *f*

procurer [prə'kjʊərə'] N (= *pimp*) Zuhälter *m*, Kuppler *m*

procuress [prə'kjʊərɪs] N Kupplerin *f*

procuring [prə'kjʊərɪŋ] N (*for prostitution*) Zuhälterei *f*

Prod [prɒd] N (*Ir, Scot: pej sl*) Protestant(in) *m(f)*

prod [prɒd] N **a** (*lit*) Stoß *m*, Knuff *m* (*inf*), Puff *m* (*inf*); **to give sb a ~** jdm einen Stoß *etc* versetzen; **a ~ in the ribs** ein Rippenstoß *m* **b** (*fig*) Ansporn *m*, Anstoß *m*, Schubs *m* (*inf*); **to give sb a ~** jdn anstoßen VT **a** (*lit*) stoßen, knuffen (*inf*), puffen (*inf*); **he ~ded the donkey (on) with his stick** er trieb den Esel mit seinem Stock vorwärts; **he ~ded the hay with his stick** er stach mit seinem Stock ins Heu; **..., he said, ~ding the map with his finger** ..., sagte er und stieß mit dem Finger auf die Karte **b** (*fig*) anspornen, anstacheln (*into sth zu etw*); **to ~ sb into action** jdm einen Stoß geben VI stoßen; **he ~ded at the picture with his fin-**ger er stieß mit dem Finger auf das Bild; **he ~ded at the cows with his stick** er trieb die Kühe mit seinem Stock an; **he doesn't need any ~ding** man braucht ihn nicht anzuspornen

Proddie ['prɒdɪ] N = **Prod**

prodigal ['prɒdɪgl] ADJ verschwenderisch; **to be ~ of sth** verschwenderisch mit etw umgehen; **the ~ son** (*Bibl, fig*) der verlorene Sohn **N** Verschwender(in) *m(f)*

prodigality [ˌprɒdɪ'gælɪtɪ] N (*liter*) Verschwendungssucht *f*; (= *lavishness*) Fülle *f*, Üppigkeit *f*

prodigious [prə'dɪdʒəs] ADJ (= *vast*) ungeheuer, außerordentlich; (= *marvellous*) erstaunlich, wunderbar

prodigiously [prə'dɪdʒəslɪ] ADV *drink* ungeheuer viel; *eat* üppig, ungeheuer viel; *talented, gifted, successful* außerordentlich

prodigy ['prɒdɪdʒɪ] N Wunder *nt*; **child** *or* **infant ~** Wunderkind *nt*

produce ['prɒdjuːs] **N** *no pl* (*Agr*) Produkt(e *pl*), Erzeugnis(se) *nt(pl)*; **Italian ~, ~ of Italy** italienisches Erzeugnis; **the ~ of the soil** die Bodenprodukte *or* -erzeugnisse *pl*

VT [prə'djuːs] **a** (= *yield*) produzieren; (*Ind*) produzieren, herstellen; *electricity, energy, heat* erzeugen; *crop* abwerfen; *coal* fördern, produzieren; (= *create*) *book, article, essay* schreiben; *painting, sculpture* anfertigen; *ideas, novel etc, masterpiece* hervorbringen; *interest, return on capital* bringen, abwerfen; *meal* machen, herstellen; **the sort of environment that ~s criminal types** das Milieu, das Kriminelle hervorbringt; **to ~ offspring** Junge bekommen; (*hum: people*) Nachwuchs bekommen; **to be well ~d** gut aussehen; (*goods also*) gut gearbeitet sein; **hopefully he can ~ the goods** (*fig inf*) hoffentlich bringt er es auch (*inf*) **b** (= *bring forward, show*) *gift, wallet etc* hervorholen (*from, out of aus*); *pistol* ziehen (*from, out of aus*); *proof, evidence* liefern, beibringen; *results* liefern; *effect* erzielen; *witness* beibringen; *ticket, documents* vorzeigen; **she managed to ~ something special for dinner** es gelang ihr, zum Abendessen etwas Besonderes auf den Tisch zu bringen; **I can't ~ it out of thin air** ich kann es doch nicht aus dem Nichts hervorzaubern *or* aus dem Ärmel schütteln (*inf*); **if we don't ~ results soon** wenn wir nicht bald Ergebnisse vorweisen können; **he ~d an incredible backhand** ihm gelang ein unglaublicher Rückhandschlag; **he ~d a sudden burst of speed** er rannte plötzlich kurz los **c** *play* inszenieren; *film* produzieren; **who's producing you?** wer ist Ihr Regisseur? **d** (= *cause*) *famine, bitterness, impression, interest etc* hervorrufen; *spark* erzeugen **e** (*Math*) *line* verlängern VI [prə'djuːs] **a** (*Theat*) das/ein Stück inszenieren; (*Film*) den/einen Film produzieren **b** (*factory, mine*) produzieren; (*land*) Ertrag bringen; (*tree*) tragen; **this cow hasn't ~d for years** (*produced calf*) diese Kuh hat jahrelang nicht mehr gekalbt; (*produced milk*) diese Kuh hat jahrelang keine Milch mehr gegeben; **when is she going to ~?** (*hum*) wann ist es denn so weit?; **it's about time that you ~d** (*hum*) es wird bald Zeit, dass ihr mal an Nachwuchs denkt

producer [prə'djuːsə'] N Produzent(in) *m(f)*; (*Ind also*) Hersteller(in) *m(f)*; (*Theat*) Regisseur(in) *m(f)*; (*Film, TV, Rad*) Produzent(in) *m(f)*; ~ **goods** Produktionsgüter *pl*

-producing [-prə'djuːsɪŋ] ADJ *suf* erzeugend, produzierend; **oil-producing country** Öl erzeugendes *or* produzierendes Land, Ölland *nt*; **coal-producing countries** Kohleförderländer *pl*; **wine-producing area** Weinregion *f*

product ['prɒdʌkt] N Produkt *nt*, Erzeugnis *nt*; (*fig*: = *result, also Math, Chem*) Produkt *nt*; **food ~s** Nahrungsmittel *pl*; ~ **placement** Produktplacement *nt*

production [prə'dʌkʃən] N **a** Produktion *f*; (*Ind*) Produktion *f*, Herstellung *f*; (*of electricity, energy, heat*) Erzeugung *f*; (*of crop*) Anbau *m*; (*of coal*) Förderung *f*, Produktion *f*; (*of book, article,* *essay*) Schreiben *nt*; (*of painting, sculpture*) Anfertigung *f*; (*of ideas, novel etc, masterpiece*) Hervorbringung *f*; **to put sth into ~** die Herstellung *or* Produktion von etw aufnehmen; **when the new car goes into ~** wenn der neue Wagen in die Produktion *or* Herstellung geht; **when we go into ~ (with this new model)** wenn wir (mit diesem neuen Modell) in die Produktion *or* Herstellung gehen; **is it still in ~?** wird das noch hergestellt?; **to take sth out of ~** etw aus der Produktion nehmen **b** (= *output*) Produktion *f* **c** (= *bringing forward, showing*) (*of ticket, documents*) Vorzeigen *nt*; (*of proof, evidence*) Lieferung *f*, Beibringung *f*; (*of witness*) Beibringung *f*; **on ~ of this ticket** gegen Vorlage dieser Eintrittskarte **d** (*of play*) Inszenierung *f*; (*of film*) Produktion *f*; **there's no need to make a ~ (number) (out) of it** (*inf*) es ist nicht notwendig, daraus eine Staatsaffäre zu machen (*inf*)

production: production capacity N Produktionskapazität *f*; **production car** N (*Aut*) Serienwagen *m*; **production company** N (*TV, Video, also Theat*) Produktionsgesellschaft *f*; **production control** N Fertigungskontrolle *f*; **production costs** PL Produktions- *or* Herstellungskosten *pl*; **production department** N (*of publishing company etc*) Herstellungsabteilung *f*; **production director** N (*Radio, TV*) Sendeleiter(in) *m(f)*; **production engineer** N Betriebsingenieur(in) *m(f)*; **production line** N Fließband *nt*, Fertigungsstraße *f*; **production manager** N Produktionsleiter(in) *m(f)*; **production method** N Produktions- *or* Herstellungsverfahren *nt*; **production model** N (*of car*) Serienmodell *nt*; **production planning** N Produktions-/Fertigungsplanung *f*; **production platform** N (*for oil*) Förderplattform *f*; **production site** N Produktionsstätte *f*

productive [prə'dʌktɪv] ADJ produktiv; *mind also* schöpferisch; *land* ertragreich, fruchtbar; *well, mine* ergiebig, ertragreich; *business, shop* rentabel; **to be ~ of sth** etw einbringen; **to lead a ~ life** ein reiches *or* aktives Leben führen; **I don't think it would be very ~ to argue with him** ich halte es nicht für sehr lohnenswert, mit ihm zu streiten (*inf*)

productively [prə'dʌktɪvlɪ] ADV produktiv

productivity [ˌprɒdʌk'tɪvɪtɪ] N Produktivität *f*; (*of land*) Fruchtbarkeit *f*, Ergiebigkeit *f*; (*of well, mine*) Ergiebigkeit *f*; (*of business, shop*) Rentabilität *f*

productivity: productivity agreement N Produktivitätsvereinbarung *f*; **productivity bonus** N Leistungszulage *f*; **productivity incentive** N Leistungsanreiz *m*

proem ['prəʊem] N Einleitung *f*

prof [prɒf] N (*inf*) Prof *m* (*inf*)

profanation [ˌprɒfə'neɪʃən] N Entweihung *f*, Profanierung *f*

profane [prə'feɪn] ADJ **a** (= *irreverent, sacrilegious*) (gottes)lästerlich; **don't be ~** lästere nicht; **to use ~ language** gotteslästerlich fluchen, lästern; **~ expression** eine Gotteslästerung **b** (= *secular*) weltlich, profan VT entweihen, profanieren

profanity [prə'fænɪtɪ] N **a** (= *sacrilegious nature*) Gotteslästerlichkeit *f* **b** (= *act, utterance*) (Gottes)lästerung *f* **c** (= *secular nature*) Weltlichkeit *f*, Profanität *f*

profess [prə'fes] VT **a** *faith, belief etc* sich bekennen zu **b** (= *claim to have*) *interest, enthusiasm, distaste* bekunden; *belief, disbelief* kundtun; *weakness, ignorance* zugeben; **to ~ to love sb/sth** seine Liebe zu jdm/etw bekennen; **to ~ to hate sb/sth** sich dazu bekennen, jdn/etw zu hassen; **she ~es to be 25/a good driver** sie behauptet, 25/ eine gute Fahrerin zu sein; **I don't ~ to ...** ich behauptet nicht, zu ... VR **to ~ oneself satisfied** seine Zufriedenheit bekunden (*with über +acc*); **the judge ~ed himself satisfied that this was so** der Richter fand den Sachverhalt als hinlänglich erwiesen; **to ~ oneself unable/willing to do sth** sich außerstande *or* außer Stande sehen/sich bereit erklären, etw zu tun

professed [prəˈfest] ADJ erklärt; (*pej: = purported*) angeblich; **a ~ nun/monk** (*Eccl*) eine Nonne, die/ein Mönch, der die Gelübde abgelegt hat; **to be a ~ Christian** sich zum christlichen Glauben bekennen; **he is a ~ coward** er gibt zu, ein Feigling zu sein; **a ~ love of sth** eine erklärte Liebe zu etw

professedly [prəˈfesɪdlɪ] ADV zugegebenermaßen; (*pej: = purportedly*) angeblich

profession [prəˈfeʃən] N **a** (*= occupation*) Beruf *m*; **the medical/teaching ~** der Arzt-/Lehrberuf; **by ~** von Beruf; **the ~s** die gehobenen Berufe; **the oldest ~ in the world** (*hum*) das älteste Gewerbe der Welt
b (*= members of the profession*) **the medical ~** die Ärzteschaft; **the architectural ~** die Architekten *pl*; **the whole ~ was outraged** der gesamte Berufsstand war empört
c (*= declaration, also Eccl*) Gelübde *nt*; **~ of faith** Glaubensbekenntnis *nt*; **a ~ of love** eine Liebeserklärung; **a ~ of contempt** eine Missfallensäußerung; **a ~ of loyalty** ein Treuegelöbnis *nt*; **the ~ of Christianity** das Bekenntnis zum Christentum; **he is, by his own ~, …** nach eigenem Bekunden ist er …

professional [prəˈfeʃənl] **ADJ a** Berufs-, beruflich; *opinion* fachmännisch, fachlich; *football, tennis* professionell; **their ~ ability** ihre beruflichen Fähigkeiten; **~ army/soldier** Berufsarmee *m/*-soldat(in) *m(f)*; **his ~ life** sein Berufsleben; **our relationship is purely ~** unsere Beziehung ist rein geschäftlich(er Natur); **a ~ thief** ein professioneller Dieb; **~ criminal** Berufsverbrecher(in) *m(f)*; **we need your ~ help here** hier brauchen wir Ihre fachmännische Hilfe; **he's now doing it on a ~ basis** er macht das jetzt hauptberuflich; **in his ~ capacity as a doctor** in seiner Eigenschaft als Arzt; **to be a ~ singer/ author** *etc* von Beruf Sänger/Schriftsteller *etc* sein; **"flat to let to quiet ~ gentleman"** „Wohnung zu vermieten an ruhigen gut situierten Herrn"; **the pub is used mainly by ~ men** das Lokal wird hauptsächlich von Angehörigen der gehobenen Berufe besucht; **the ~ classes** die gehobenen Berufe, die höheren Berufsstände (*dated*); **to seek/take ~ advice** fachmännischen Rat suchen/einholen; **it's not our ~ practice** es gehört nicht zu unseren geschäftlichen Gepflogenheiten; **to turn** *or* **go ~** Profi werden
b (*= skilled, competent*) *piece of work etc* fachmännisch, fachgemäß, fachgerecht; *worker, person* gewissenhaft; *company, approach* professionell; (*= expert*) *performance* kompetent, sachkundig, professionell; **he didn't make a very ~ job of that** er hat das nicht sehr fachmännisch erledigt; **he handled the matter in a very ~ manner** er hat die Angelegenheit in sehr kompetenter Weise gehandhabt; **that's not a very ~ attitude to your work** das ist doch nicht die richtige Einstellung (zu Ihrem Beruf); **it's not up to ~ standards** es entspricht nicht fachlichen Normen; **a typed letter looks more ~** ein maschine(n)geschriebener Brief sieht professioneller aus
c (*inf*) *worrier, moaner* notorisch, gewohnheitsmäßig
N Profi *m*

professional: professional footballer N Berufsfußballer(in) *m(f)*; **professional foul** N absichtliches Foul; **Professional Golfers' Association** N Professional Golfers' Association *f*, Verband professioneller Golfspieler

professionalism [prəˈfeʃnəlɪzm] N Professionalismus *m*; (*of job, piece of work*) Perfektion *f*; (*Sport*) Profitum *nt*

professionally [prəˈfeʃnəlɪ] ADV beruflich; (*= in accomplished manner*) fachmännisch; **he sings/ dances ~** er singt/tanzt von Berufs wegen *or* beruflich, er ist ein professioneller Sänger/Tänzer; **now he plays ~** jetzt ist er Berufsspieler *or* Profi; **he is ~ recognized as the best …** er ist in

Fachkreisen als der beste … bekannt; **X, ~ known as Y** (*of artist, musician etc*) X, unter dem Künstlernamen Y bekannt; (*of writer*) X, unter dem Pseudonym Y bekannt; **to know sb ~** jdn beruflich kennen; **they acted most ~ in refusing to …** dass sie … ablehnten, zeugte von hohem Berufsethos

professor [prəˈfesə] N **a** Professor(in) *m(f)*; (*US: = lecturer of highest rank*) Dozent(in) *m(f)*; **the ~s** die Professorenschaft **b** (*of a faith*) Bekenner(in) *m(f)*

professorial [ˌprɒfəˈsɔːrɪəl] ADJ (*of a professor*) eines Professors; (*= professorlike*) wie ein Professor, professoral (*pej*)

professorship [prəˈfesəʃɪp] N Professur *f*, Lehrstuhl *m*

proffer [ˈprɒfə] VT *arm, gift, drink* anbieten; *apologies, thanks etc* aussprechen; *remark* machen; *suggestion* vorbringen

proficiency [prəˈfɪʃənsɪ] N **her ~ at teaching/as a secretary** ihre Tüchtigkeit als Lehrerin/Sekretärin; **his ~ in English** seine Englischkenntnisse; **her ~ in translating/accountancy** ihr Können als Übersetzerin/Buchhalterin; **his ~ with figures** sein Können im Umgang mit Zahlen; **level of ~** Leistungsstand *m*; **~ test** Leistungstest *m*

proficient [prəˈfɪʃənt] ADJ tüchtig, fähig; **he is just about ~ in German** seine Deutschkenntnisse reichen gerade aus; **how long would it take to become ~ in Japanese?** wie lange würde es dauern, bis man Japanisch beherrscht?

profile [ˈprəʊfaɪl] **N a** Profil *nt*; (*= picture, photograph*) Profilbild *nt*, Seitenansicht *f*; (*= biographical profile*) Porträt *nt*; (*Tech: = section*) (*vertical*) Längsschnitt *m*; (*horizontal*) Querschnitt *m*; **in ~** (*person, head*) im Profil; **to keep a low ~** sich zurückhalten **VT** (*= draw a profile of*) (*pictorially*) im Profil darstellen; (*biographically*) porträtieren; (*Tech*) im Längs- *or* Querschnitt zeichnen *or* darstellen

profiler [ˈprəʊfaɪlə] N **a** (*Police, Psych*) Profilfahnder(in) *m(f)*, Profiler(in) *m(f)* **b** (*Tech: = profiling machine*) Profilfräsmaschine *f*

profit [ˈprɒfɪt] **N a** (*Comm*) Gewinn *m*, Profit *m* (*also pej*); **there's not much (of a) ~ in this business** dieses Geschäft wirft kaum Gewinn *or* Profit ab; **~ and loss account** Gewinn-und--Verlustrechnung *f*; **to make a ~ (out of** *or* **on sth)** (mit etw) einen Profit *or* Gewinn machen, (mit etw) ein Geschäft machen; **to show** *or* **yield a ~** einen Gewinn *or* Profit verzeichnen; **to sell sth at a ~** etw mit Gewinn verkaufen; **the business is now running at a ~** das Geschäft wirft jetzt Gewinn *or* Profit ab, das Geschäft rentiert sich jetzt; **I'm not doing it for ~** ich tue das nicht, um damit Geld zu verdienen; **a with-profits policy** (*Insur*) eine Police mit Gewinnbeteiligung
b (*fig*) Nutzen *m*, Vorteil *m*; **to turn sth to ~** Nutzen aus etw ziehen; **you might well learn something to your ~** Sie können etwas lernen, was Ihnen von Nutzen *or* Vorteil ist
VT (*liter*) nutzen, nützen (*sb* jdm), von Nutzen sein (*sb* für jdn); **what does it ~ a man if …** was nützt es dem Menschen, wenn …
VI (*= gain*) profitieren (*by, from* von), Nutzen *or* Gewinn ziehen (*by, from* aus)

profitability [ˌprɒfɪtəˈbɪlɪtɪ] N Rentabilität *f*, Einträglichkeit *f*

profitability study N Rentabilitäts- *or* Wirtschaftlichkeitsstudie *f*

profitable [ˈprɒfɪtəbl] ADJ (*Comm*) Gewinn *or* Profit bringend, gewinn- *or* profitbringend, rentabel, profitabel; (*fig: = beneficial*) nützlich, vorteilhaft; **could you not find a more ~ way of spending your time?** kannst du nichts Besseres mit deiner Zeit anfangen?

profitably [ˈprɒfɪtəblɪ] ADV (*Comm*) *sell, trade* Gewinn *or* Profit bringend, gewinn- *or* profitbringend, rentabel, profitabel; (*fig: = beneficially*) nützlich, vorteilhaft; **you could ~ spend a couple of hours reading a book** es käme dir sehr zugute, wenn du ein paar Stunden mit Lesen

verbringen würdest; **there was little I could ~ do sitting at my desk** von meinem Schreibtisch aus konnte ich nur wenig Sinnvolles *or* Nützliches tun

profit centre, (*US*) **profit center** N Profitcenter *nt*

profiteer [ˌprɒfɪˈtɪə] **N** Profitmacher(in), Profitjäger(in) *m(f)*, Profitgeier *m*; **war ~** Kriegsgewinnler(in) *m(f)* **VI** sich bereichern

profiteering [ˌprɒfɪˈtɪərɪŋ] N Wucherei *f*, Wucher *m*

profiterole [prəˈfɪtərəʊl] N Profiterol(e) *nt*, kleiner Windbeutel mit süßer oder pikanter Füllung

profitless [ˈprɒfɪtlɪs] ADJ **a** (*Comm*) unrentabel **b** *discussion, exercise* zwecklos

profitlessly [ˈprɒfɪtlɪslɪ] ADV **a** (*Comm*) ohne Gewinn **b** *argue* zwecklos

profit: profit-making ADJ *organization* rentabel; (*= profit-orientated*) auf Gewinn gerichtet; **profit margin** N Gewinnspanne *f*; **profit motive** N Gewinnstreben *nt*; **profit-seeking** ADJ gewinnorientiert; **profit-sharing** N Gewinnbeteiligung *f*; **~ scheme** Gewinnbeteiligungsplan *m*

profligacy [ˈprɒflɪɡəsɪ] N (*= dissoluteness*) Lasterhaftigkeit *f*, Verworfenheit *f*; (*= extravagance*) Verschwendungssucht *f*; (*= an extravagance*) Verschwendung *f*

profligate [ˈprɒflɪɡɪt] **ADJ** (*= dissolute*) lasterhaft, verworfen; (*= extravagant*) verschwenderisch **N** (*= roué*) Leichtfuß *m*, Liederjan *m* (*inf*); (*= prodigal*) Verschwender(in) *m(f)*

pro forma (invoice) [ˌprəʊˈfɔːmə(ɪnvɔɪs)] N Pro-forma-Rechnung *f*

profound [prəˈfaʊnd] ADJ **a** *sleep, sigh, sorrow, love, concern, depression* tief; *thought, idea, art* tiefsinnig, tief schürfend, tiefgründig; *experience* tief gehend, im Innersten ergreifend; *book* gehaltvoll, profund (*geh*); *thinker, knowledge* profund (*geh*), tief gehend; *regret* tief gehend; *hatred, mistrust, difference, belief, respect, ignorance* tief sitzend; *effect, influence, implications* tief greifend, weittragend, weit tragend; *problem* tief sitzend, tief gehend; *indifference* vollkommen, völlig; *interest* stark; *changes* tief greifend; **you're very ~ today** (*also iro*) du bist heute sehr tiefsinnig; **that's very ~** (*also iro*) das ist sehr tiefsinnig
b *deafness* vollkommen; *clinical shock, unconsciousness* tief

profoundly [prəˈfaʊndlɪ] ADV *different* zutiefst; **~ sad** tieftraurig; **~ deaf** vollkommen taub; **~ significant** äußerst bedeutsam; **~ indifferent** völlig *or* vollkommen gleichgültig; **…, he said ~** …, sagte er tiefsinnig; **to be ~ ignorant of sth** überhaupt keine Ahnung von etw haben

profundity [prəˈfʌndɪtɪ] N **a** *no pl* Tiefe *f*; (*of thought, thinker, book etc*) Tiefgründigkeit *f*, Tiefsinnigkeit *f*; (*of knowledge*) Gründlichkeit *f* **b** (*= profound remark*) Tiefsinnigkeit *f*

profuse [prəˈfjuːs] ADJ *vegetation* üppig; *bleeding* stark; *thanks, praise* überschwänglich; *apologies* überreichlich; *vomiting* heftig, stark; **to be ~ in one's thanks** sich überschwänglich bedanken; **to be ~ in one's apologies** sich vielmals entschuldigen; **he was ~ in his praise** er geizte nicht mit seinem Lob; **where flowers grow in ~ abundance** wo Blumen in üppiger *or* verschwenderischer Fülle wachsen

profusely [prəˈfjuːslɪ] ADV *grow* üppig; *bleed* stark; *thank, praise* überschwänglich; *sweat* heftig, stark; **he apologized ~** er entschuldigte sich vielmals, er bat vielmals um Entschuldigung; **~ illustrated** reich illustriert

profusion [prəˈfjuːʒən] N Überfülle *f*, verschwenderische Fülle; **trees in ~** Bäume in Hülle und Fülle; **his painting was a wild ~ of reds and blues** sein Gemälde war eine Orgie in Rot und Blau

progenitor [prəʊˈdʒenɪtə] N (*form*) Vorfahr(in) *m(f)*, Ahn *m*, Ahne *f*; (*fig*) Vorläufer *m*

progenitrix [prəʊˈdʒenɪtrɪks] N (*form*) Vorfahrin *f*, Ahne *f*

progeny ['prɒdʒɪnɪ] N Nachkommen *pl*, Nachkommenschaft *f*

progesterone [prəʊ'dʒestərəʊn] N Progesteron *nt*, Gelbkörperhormon *nt*

prognosis [prɒg'nəʊsɪs] N *pl* **prognoses** [prɒg'nəʊsiːz] Prognose *f*, Vorhersage *f*, Voraussage *f*

prognostic [prɒg'nɒstɪk] ADJ (*form*) prognostisch

prognosticate [prɒg'nɒstɪkeɪt] **VI** (*often hum*) Prognosen stellen, Vorsagen machen **VT** prognostizieren

prognostication [prɒg,nɒstɪ'keɪʃən] N Prognose *f*, Vorhersage *f*, Voraussage *f*

program ['prəʊgræm] **N a** (*Comput*) Programm *nt* **b** (*US*) = **programme** N **VT a** computer programmieren **b** (*fig*) *person* vorprogrammieren

programmable ['prəʊgræməbl] ADJ *computer, device, oven etc* programmierbar

programme, (*US*) **program** ['prəʊgræm] **N** Programm *nt*; (*Rad, TV also*) Sendung *f*; **we've got a very heavy ~ of meetings** wir haben sehr viele Besprechungen auf unserem Programm; **what's the ~ for tomorrow?** was steht für morgen auf dem Programm?; **what's on the other ~?** was gibt es *or* läuft im anderen Programm?; **our ~s for this evening** das Programm des heutigen Abends **VT** programmieren; **~d course** programmierter Unterricht; **~d learning** programmiertes Lernen

programme, (*US*) **program**: **programme--maker**, (*US*) **program-maker** N (*TV, Rad*) Programmmacher(in) *m(f)*; **programme music** N Programmmusik *f*; **programme notes** PL Programmhinweise *pl*; **programme planner** N (*TV*) Programmplaner(in) *m(f)*

programmer ['prəʊgræmə'] N Programmierer(in) *m(f)*

programme seller N (*in theatre etc*) Programmverkäufer(in) *m(f)*

programming ['prəʊgræmɪŋ] N Programmieren *nt*; **~ language** Programmiersprache *f*

progress ['prəʊgres] **N a** *no pl* (= *movement forwards*) Fortschreiten *nt*, Vorwärtskommen *nt*; (*Mil*) Vorrücken *nt*, Vordringen *nt*; **we made slow ~ through the mud** wir kamen im Schlamm nur langsam vorwärts; **they made good ~ across the open country** sie kamen im offenen Gelände gut vorwärts

b *no pl* (= *advance*) Fortschritt *m*; **the ~ of events** der Gang der Ereignisse; **to make (good/slow) ~** (gute/langsame) Fortschritte machen; **I want to see some ~!** ich möchte Fortschritte sehen!

c **in ~** im Gange; **in full ~** in vollem Gange; **"silence please, meeting in ~"** „Sitzung! Ruhe bitte"; **the work still in ~** die noch zu erledigende Arbeit

d (*obs*: = *journey*) Reise *f*

VI [prə'gres] **a** (= *move, go forward*) sich vorwärts bewegen, vorwärts schreiten; **we ~ed slowly across the ice** wir bewegten uns langsam über das Eis vorwärts; **by the third day the enemy/expedition had ~ed as far as ...** am dritten Tag war der Feind bis ... vorgerückt *or* vorgedrungen/die Expedition bis ... vorgedrungen *or* gekommen

b (*in time*) **as the work ~es** mit dem Fortschreiten der Arbeit; **as the game ~ed** im Laufe des Spiels; **while negotiations were actually ~ing** während die Verhandlungen im Gange waren

c (= *improve, make progress*: *student, patient*) Fortschritte machen; **how far have you ~ed since our last meeting?** wie weit sind Sie seit unserer letzten Sitzung gekommen?; **investigations are ~ing well** die Untersuchungen kommen gut voran *or* machen gute Fortschritte; **we are, in fact, ~ing toward(s) a solution** wir nähern uns in der Tat einer Lösung; **that civilization is constantly ~ing toward(s) a state of perfection** dass sich die Zivilisation ständig (auf einen Zustand der Perfektion hin) weiterentwickelt; **that mankind is ~ing toward(s) some goal**

dass sich die Menschheit auf ein Ziel zubewegt **d** (*through hierarchy etc*) **as you ~ through the ranks** bei Ihrem Aufstieg durch die Ränge; **the employee ~es upwards through the company hierarchy** der Angestellte macht seinen Weg durch die Firmenhierarchie

VT [prə'gres] (*esp Comm*) *matters etc* weiterverfolgen

progression [prə'greʃən] N Folge *f*; (*Math*) Reihe *f*, Progression *f*; (*Mus*) Sequenz *f*; (= *development*) Entwicklung *f*; (*in taxation*) Progression *f*; (*of discount rates etc*) Staffelung *f*; **sales have shown a continuous ~** im Absatz wurde eine stete Aufwärtsentwicklung verzeichnet; **his ~ from a junior clerk to managing director** sein Aufstieg vom kleinen Angestellten zum Direktor; **is there a natural ~ from marijuana to heroin?** ist das Umsteigen von Marihuana auf Heroin zwangsläufig?; **a ~ of ...** eine Folge *or* Reihe von ...

progressional ADJ [prə'greʃənl] *development* fortschreitend; *examinations* aufeinander folgend, im Schwierigkeitsgrad ansteigend; *training, development* kontinuierlich (verlaufend *or* weitergehend)

progressive [prə'gresɪv] **ADJ a** (= *increasing*) zunehmend; *disease etc* fortschreitend; *action* allmählich steigernd, fortschreitend; *paralysis, taxation* progressiv; **~ form/tense** (*Gram*) Verlaufsform *f* **b** (= *favouring progress*) progressiv, fortschrittlich; (*Mus*) progressiv **N** (= *person*) Progressive(r) *mf*

progressive jazz N progressiver Jazz

progressively [prə'gresɪvlɪ] ADV zunehmend; **he is becoming ~ more addicted** er wird zunehmend *or* immer abhängiger

progressiveness [prə'gresɪvnɪs] N Fortschrittlichkeit *f*, Progressivität *f*

progressive party N (*Pol*) fortschrittliche Partei, Fortschrittspartei *f*

progress report N Fortschrittsbericht *m*

prohibit [prə'hɪbɪt] VT **a** (= *forbid*) verbieten, untersagen; **to ~ sb from doing sth** jdm verbieten *or* untersagen, etw zu tun; **his health ~s him from swimming** sein Gesundheitszustand verbietet (es) ihm zu schwimmen; **"smoking ~ed"** „Rauchen verboten" **b** (= *prevent*) verhindern; **to ~ sth being done** verhindern, dass etw geschieht; **to ~ sb from doing sth** jdn daran hindern, etw zu tun

prohibited substance [prə'hɪbɪtɪd'sʌbstəns] N verbotene Substanz

prohibition [ˌprəʊɪ'bɪʃən] N **a** Verbot *nt*; **the ~ of alcohol** das Alkoholverbot **b** (**the**) **Prohibition** (*US Hist*) die Prohibition; **the Prohibition era** (*US Hist*) die Prohibitionszeit

prohibitionism [ˌprəʊɪ'bɪʃənɪzəm] N Prohibition *f*

prohibitionist [ˌprəʊɪ'bɪʃənɪst] N Prohibitionist(in) *m(f)*

prohibitive [prə'hɪbɪtɪv] ADJ **a** *tax* prohibitiv; **~ duty** Sperrzoll *m*; **~ laws** Verbotsgesetze *pl*; **~ signs** Verbotsschilder *pl*; **~ rules** Verbote *pl* **b** *price, cost* unerschwinglich; **the costs of producing this model have become ~** die Kosten für die Herstellung dieses Modells sind untragbar geworden

prohibitively [prə'hɪbɪtɪvlɪ] ADV (= *extremely*) ungeheuerlich; **~ expensive** unerschwinglich (teuer)

prohibitory [prə'hɪbɪtərɪ] ADJ = **prohibitive** a

project¹ ['prɒdʒekt] N Projekt *nt*; (= *scheme*) Unternehmen *nt*, Vorhaben *nt*; (*Sch, Univ*) Referat *nt*; (*in primary school*) Arbeit *f*; **~ engineer** Projektingenieur(in) *m*

project² [prə'dʒekt] **VT a** *film, map* projizieren; **to ~ oneself/one's personality** sich selbst/seine eigene Person zur Geltung bringen; **to ~ one's emotions onto somebody else** seine Emotionen auf einen anderen projizieren; **to ~ one's voice** seine Stimme zum Tragen bringen; **to ~ one's voice to the back of the hall** seine Stimme so erheben, dass sie auch im hinteren Teil

des Saals zu hören ist; **in order to ~ an adequate picture of our country** um ein angemessenes Bild unseres Landes zu vermitteln

b *plan* (voraus)planen; *costs* überschlagen; *figures* projizieren; (*esp in elections*) hochrechnen **c** (*Math*) *line* verlängern; *solid* projizieren **d** (= *propel*) abschießen; **to ~ a missile into space** eine Rakete in den Weltraum schießen **e** (= *cause to jut*) *part of building etc* vorspringen lassen

VI a (= *jut out*) hervorragen (*from* aus); **the upper storey ~s over the road** das obere Stockwerk ragt über die Straße **b** (*Psych*) projizieren, von sich auf andere schließen **c** (*with one's voice: actor/singer*) **you'll have to ~ more than that, we can't hear you at the back** Sie müssen lauter singen/sprechen, wir können Sie hier hinten nicht hören

projectile [prə'dʒektaɪl] N (Wurf)geschoss *nt*, (Wurf)geschoß *nt* (*Aus*); (*Mil*) Geschoss *nt*, Geschoß *nt* (*Aus*), Projektil *nt* (*spec*)

projection [prə'dʒekʃən] N **a** (*of films, guilt feelings, map*) Projektion *f* **b** (= *protrusion, overhang, ledge etc*) Vorsprung *m*, Überhang *m* **c** (= *extension: of line*) Verlängerung *f* **d** (= *prediction, estimate*) (Voraus)planung *f*; (*of cost*) Überschlagung *f*; (*of figures, esp in elections*) Hochrechnung *f*

projection booth N Vorführraum *m*

projectionist [prə'dʒekʃnɪst] N Filmvorführer(in) *m(f)*

projection room N Vorführraum *m*

projective [prə'dʒektɪv] ADJ **a** **~ geometry** Projektionsgeometrie *f* **b** (*Psych*) projizierend

projector [prə'dʒektə'] N (*Film*) Projektor *m*, Vorführgerät *nt*

prolapse ['prəʊlæps] N (*Med*) Vorfall *m*, Prolaps *m* (*spec*)

prole [prəʊl] N (*esp Brit, pej inf*) Prolet(in) *m(f)* (*inf*)

proletarian [ˌprəʊlə'teərɪən] ADJ proletarisch **N** Proletarier(in) *m(f)*

proletariat [ˌprəʊlə'teərɪət] N Proletariat *nt*

pro-life ['prəʊ'laɪf] ADJ *group, organization* gegen Abtreibung *pred*; **~ movement** Antiabtreibungsbewegung *f*

pro-lifer [ˌprəʊ'laɪfə'] N (*inf*) Abtreibungsgegner(in) *m(f)*

proliferate [prə'lɪfəreɪt] VI (*number*) sich stark erhöhen; (*ideas*) um sich greifen; (*insects, animals*) sich stark vermehren; (*weeds, cells*) wuchern, sich rasch ausbreiten

proliferation [prəˌlɪfə'reɪʃən] N (*in numbers*) starke Erhöhung; (*of animals*) zahlreiche Vermehrung; (*of nuclear weapons*) Weitergabe *f*; (*of ideas*) Ausbreitung *f*, Umsichgreifen *nt*; (*of sects*) Umsichgreifen *nt*, Wuchern *nt*; (*of weeds*) Wuchern *nt*

prolific [prə'lɪfɪk] ADJ **a** (= *productive*) fruchtbar; *writer also* sehr produktiv; *scorer* erfolgreich **b** (= *producing young*) *person* fruchtbar **c** (= *abundant*) zahlreich, üppig

prolix ['prəʊlɪks] ADJ weitschweifig

prolixity [prəʊ'lɪksɪtɪ] N Weitschweifigkeit *f*

prolly ['prɒlɪ] ADV (*sl*) wahrscheinlich

prologue, (*US*) **prolog** ['prəʊlɒg] N Prolog *m*; (*of book*) Vorwort *nt*; (*fig*) Vorspiel *nt*

prolong [prə'lɒŋ] VT verlängern; (*unpleasantly*) *process, pain* hinauszögern; (*Fin*) *draft* prolongieren; **to ~ the agony** (*fig*) das Leiden verlängern

prolongation [ˌprəʊlɒŋ'geɪʃən] N Verlängerung *f*; (*unpleasant: of process, pain*) Hinauszögern *nt*; (*Fin, of draft*) Prolongation *f*, Prolongierung *f*

prolonged-action [prəˈlɒŋdækʃən] ADJ (*Pharm*) *medicine* mit Langzeitwirkung *pred*

PROM [prɒm] N (*Comput*) *abbr of* **Programmable Read Only Memory** PROM *m*

prom [prɒm] N (*inf*) (*Brit*: = *promenade*) (Strand)promenade *f*; (*Brit*: = *concert*) Konzert *nt* (*in gelockertem Rahmen*); (*US*: = *ball*) Studenten-/Schülerball *m*

PROM

In Großbritannien versteht man unter einem **prom** (Kurzform von **promenade concert**) ein klassisches Musikkonzert, bei dem ein Großteil des Publikums im Parkett Stehplätze hat. Die bekanntesten **proms** sind die Konzerte, die jeden Sommer in der Londoner Royal Albert Hall abgehalten werden. Der Abschlussabend, „Last Night of the Proms", ist ein ganz besonderes Ereignis, das ganz im Zeichen des Patriotismus steht und im Singen von „Land of Hope and Glory" gipfelt.

In den USA und Kanada dagegen ist ein **prom** ein Ball für die Schüler und Studenten von Highschools oder Colleges. Ein ganz besonders wichtiges gesellschaftliches Ereignis ist der **senior prom** zum Abschluss der Highschool-Zeit. Zu diesen Bällen geht man normalerweise in Begleitung und in formeller Kleidung.

---

promenade [ˌprɒmɪ'nɑːd] **N** (= stroll: also in dancing) Promenade f; (esp Brit: = esplanade) (Strand)promenade f; (US: = ball) Studenten-/Schülerball m; ~ **concert** (Brit) Konzert nt (in gelockertem Rahmen); ~ **deck** (Brit) Promenadendeck nt **VT** (= stroll through) promenieren in (+dat); avenue entlangpromenieren; (= stroll with) spazieren führen; (in dance) eine Promenade machen mit **VI** (= stroll) promenieren; (in dance) eine Promenade machen

promenader [ˌprɒmɪ'nɑːdə'] N **a** (= walker) Spaziergänger(in) m(f) **b** (Brit: in concert) Stehplatzbesucher(in) m(f); **Promenader** Besucher(in) m(f) der Londoner Prom-Konzerte

Promethean [prə'miːθɪən] ADJ (liter) prometheisch (liter)

Prometheus [prə'miːθjuːs] N Prometheus m

promethium [prəʊ'miːθɪəm] N (Chem) Promethium nt

prominence ['prɒmɪnəns] N **a** no pl **the ~ of his cheekbones/eyes** seine ausgeprägten Wangenknochen/Augen; **because of the ~ of the castle in the middle of the city** wegen der exponierten Lage des Schlosses inmitten der Stadt
b (of ideas, beliefs) Beliebtheit f; (of writer, politician etc) Bekanntheit f; **the undisputed ~ of his position as ...** seine unbestritten führende Position als ...; **if you give too much ~ to any one particular aspect** wenn Sie einen bestimmten Aspekt zu sehr in den Vordergrund stellen; **to bring sb/sth (in)to ~** (= attract attention to) jdn/etw herausstellen or in den Vordergrund rücken; (= make famous) jdn/etw berühmt machen; **he came or rose to ~ in the Cuba affair** er wurde durch die Kuba-Affäre bekannt
c (= prominent part) Vorsprung m

prominent ['prɒmɪnənt] ADJ **a** (= jutting out) cheekbones, teeth vorstehend attr; crag vorspringend attr; **to be ~** vorstehen, vorspringen
b (= conspicuous) markings auffällig; feature, characteristic hervorstechend, auffallend; position hervorragend, herausragend, prominent; **put it in a ~ position** stellen Sie es deutlich sichtbar hin; **the castle occupies a ~ position on the hill** das Schloss hat eine exponierte Lage auf dem Hügel
c (= leading) role führend; (= large, significant) wichtig
d (= well-known) personality, publisher prominent; **she is ~ in London society** sie ist ein bekanntes Mitglied der Londoner Gesellschaft

prominently ['prɒmɪnəntlɪ] ADV display, place deutlich sichtbar; **he figured ~ in the case** er spielte in dem Fall eine bedeutende Rolle; **the murder was ~ reported in the press** in der Presse wurde ausführlich über den Mordfall berichtet; der Mordfall füllte die Schlagzeilen

promiscuity [ˌprɒmɪ'skjuːɪtɪ] N **a** Promiskuität f, häufiger Partnerwechsel m **b** (liter: = confusion) Wirrwarr m

promiscuous [prə'mɪskjʊəs] ADJ **a** (sexually) promisk, promiskuitiv (spec); **to be ~** häufig

den Partner wechseln; **~ behaviour** häufiger Partnerwechsel **b** (liter) wirr

promiscuously [prə'mɪskjʊəslɪ] ADV (sexually) promisk, promiskuitiv (spec)

promise ['prɒmɪs] **N** **a** (= pledge) Versprechen nt; **their ~ of help** ihr Versprechen zu helfen; **~ of marriage** Eheversprechen nt; **under ~ of** (form) mit dem Versprechen (+gen); **is that a ~?** ganz bestimmt?; **to make sb a ~** jdm ein Versprechen geben or machen; **make me one ~** versprich mir eins; **I'm not making any ~s** versprechen kann ich nichts; **to hold** or **keep sb to his ~** jdn an sein Versprechen binden; **~s, ~s!** Versprechen, nichts als Versprechen!
b (= hope, prospect) Hoffnung f, Aussicht f; **a young woman of ~** eine viel versprechende junge Frau; **to hold out a** or **the ~ of sth to sb** jdm Hoffnungen auf etw (acc) machen; **to show ~** zu den besten Hoffnungen berechtigen; **she had a ~ of passion in her eyes** ihre Augen verrieten Leidenschaft
VT (= pledge) versprechen; (= forecast, augur) hindeuten auf (+acc); **to ~ (sb) to do sth** (jdm) versprechen, etw zu tun; **to ~ sb sth, to ~ sth to sb** jdm etw versprechen; **to ~ sb the earth** jdm das Blaue vom Himmel herunter versprechen; **~ me one thing** versprich mir eins; **to be ~d to sb** (dated) jdm versprochen sein (old); **I'm not promising anything but ...** ich will nichts versprechen, aber ...; **I won't do it again, I ~ you** ich werde es nie wieder tun, das verspreche ich Ihnen; **you'll regret this, I ~ you** ich verspreche dir, das wirst du bereuen; **this ~s trouble** das sieht nach Ärger aus; **this ~s better things to come** das lässt auf Besseres hoffen; **it ~d to be another scorching day** der Tag versprach wieder heiß zu werden; **the Promised Land** (Bibl, fig) das Gelobte Land
VI **a** (= pledge) versprechen; **(do you) ~?** versprichst du es?; **~!** (= will you promise) versprichs mir, ehrlich?; (= I promise) ehrlich!; **I'll try, but I'm not promising** ich werde es versuchen, aber ich kann nichts versprechen; **but you ~d!** aber du hast es doch versprochen!
b **to ~ well** viel versprechend sein
VR **to ~ oneself sth** sich (dat) etw versprechen; **I've ~d myself never to do it again** ich habe mir geschworen, dass ich das nicht noch einmal mache

promising ['prɒmɪsɪŋ] ADJ viel versprechend; **that sounds ~** das klingt viel versprechend; **so far the signs are not ~** bislang sind die Anzeichen nicht viel versprechend

promisingly ['prɒmɪsɪŋlɪ] ADV viel versprechend

promissory note ['prɒmɪsərɪ'nəʊt] N Schuldschein m

prommer, Prommer ['prɒmə'] N (inf) Besucher(in) m(f) der Londoner Prom-Konzerte

promo ['prəʊməʊ] N (inf: = promotional video) Werbevideo nt

promontory ['prɒməntrɪ] N Vorgebirge nt, Kap nt

promote [prə'məʊt] VT **a** (in rank) befördern; **he has been ~d (to) colonel** or **to the rank of colonel** er ist zum Obersten befördert worden; **our team was ~d** (Ftbl) unsere Mannschaft ist aufgestiegen **b** (= foster) fördern; (Parl) bill sich einsetzen für **c** (= organize, put on) conference, race meeting, boxing match etc veranstalten **d** (= advertise) werben für; (= put on the market) auf den Markt bringen; **the new model has been widely ~d in the media** für das neue Modell ist in den Medien intensiv geworben worden or Werbung gemacht worden

promoter [prə'məʊtə'] N (Sport, of beauty contest etc) Promoter m, Veranstalter m; (of company) Promoter m; **sales ~** Verkaufsleiter(in) m(f), Salespromoter(in) m(f) (Comm)

promotion [prə'məʊʃən] N **a** (in rank) Beförderung f; (of football team) Aufstieg m; **to get** or **win ~** befördert werden; (football team) aufsteigen **b** (= fostering) Förderung f; (Parl: of bill) Einsatz m (of für) **c** (= organization: of conference etc) Veranstaltung f **d** (= advertising) Wer-

bung f (of für); (= advertising campaign) Werbekampagne f; (= marketing) Einführung f auf dem Markt; **Rochas are doing a special ~ in the store this week** wir haben diese Woche eine Rochas-Werbekampagne im Warenhaus

prompt [prɒmpt] **ADJ** (+er) prompt; action unverzüglich, sofortig; **he is always very ~ with such things** solche Dinge erledigt er immer prompt or sofort; **he is always very ~** (= on time) er ist immer sehr pünktlich; **to ~ to do sth** (= quick) prompt or rasch or schnell dabei, etw zu tun; **the company was ~ in its response to these accusations** die Firma hat prompt auf diese Vorwürfe reagiert
ADV **at 6 o'clock ~** pünktlich um 6 Uhr, Punkt 6 Uhr
VT **a** (= motivate) veranlassen (to zu); **to ~ sb to do sth** jdn (dazu) veranlassen, etw zu tun; **what ~ed you to do it?** was hat Sie dazu veranlasst?; **he was ~ed purely by a desire to help** sein Beweggrund war einzig und allein der Wunsch zu helfen; **in the hope that this might ~ a discussion** in der Hoffnung, dass das eine Diskussion in Gang setzen wird; **he didn't need any ~ing to ask her** man brauchte ihn nicht darum zu bitten, sie zu fragen; **he's a bit lazy, he needs a little ~ing** er ist ein bisschen faul, man muss ihn manchmal auf die Sprünge helfen; **I'll do it myself, I don't need you to ~ me** ich mache das schon selbst, du brauchst mich nicht erst zu ermahnen; **he doesn't need any ~ing, he's cheeky enough as it is** er braucht keine Ermunterung, er ist auch so schon frech genug
b (= evoke) memories, feelings wecken; conclusion nahe legen; **it ~d the thought that ...** es drängt einem den Gedanken auf, dass ...
c (= help with speech) vorsagen (sb jdm); (Theat) soufflieren (sb jdm); **he recited the whole poem without any ~ing** er sagte das ganze Gedicht auf, ohne dass ihm jemand (etwas) vorsagen musste; **the teacher had to keep ~ing him** der Lehrer musste ihm immer wieder Hilfestellung geben; **he forgot his speech and had to be ~ed** er hatte seine Rede vergessen, so dass or sodass man ihm mit Stichworten auf die Sprünge helfen musste
VI (Theat) soufflieren
N **a** (Theat) **he needed a ~** ihm musste souffliert werden; **he couldn't hear the ~** er hörte die Souffleuse nicht; **to give sb a ~** jdm weiterhelfen; (Theat) jdm soufflieren
b (= reminder, encouragement) **to give sb a ~** jdm einen Schubs geben (inf), jdn anstoßen; **we have to give our debtors the occasional ~** wir müssen uns bei unseren Schuldnern hin und wieder in Erinnerung bringen
c (Comput) Prompt m, Aufforderungsmeldung f

prompt: prompt book N (Theat) Soufflierbuch nt; **prompt box** N (Theat) Souffleurkasten m; **prompt copy** N (Theat) Rollenheft nt

prompter ['prɒmptə'] N Souffleur m, Souffleuse f; (= tele-prompter) Teleprompter m

prompting ['prɒmptɪŋ] N **a** (Theat) Soufflieren nt **b** **the ~s of conscience/the heart** die Stimme des Gewissens/Herzens

promptitude ['prɒmptɪtjuːd] N = promptness

promptly ['prɒmptlɪ] ADV **a** prompt; **of course he ~ forgot it all** er hat natürlich prompt alles vergessen; **they left ~ at 6** sie gingen pünktlich um 6 Uhr or Punkt 6 Uhr; **when you receive orders you must obey them ~** wenn Sie Anweisungen erhalten, müssen Sie sie auf der Stelle befolgen; **she sat down and ~ fell asleep** sie setzte sich hin und schlief auf der Stelle or prompt ein **b** (= without further ado) **she ~ gave him a left hook** sie versetzte ihm unverzüglich einen linken Haken

promptness ['prɒmptnɪs] N Promptheit f; **the fire brigade's ~** der prompte Einsatz der Feuerwehr

prompt note N (Comm) Ermahnung f

promulgate ['prɒməlgeɪt] VT verbreiten; law verkünden

promulgation [ˌprɒməlˈɡeɪʃən] N Verbreitung *f*; (*of law*) Verkündung *f*

prone [prəʊn] ADJ **a** (= *lying*) **to be** *or* **lie ~** auf dem Bauch liegen; **in a ~ position** in Bauchlage **b** (= *liable*) **to be ~ to sth** zu etw neigen; **to be ~ to do sth** dazu neigen, etw zu tun

proneness [ˈprəʊnnɪs] N Neigung *f* (*to* zu)

prong [prɒŋ] N **a** (*of fork*) Zacke *f*, Zinke *f*; (*of antler*) Sprosse *f*, Ende *nt* **b** (*fig*) (*of argument*) Punkt *m*; (*of policy, strategy*) Element *nt*; (*of attack*) (Angriffs)spitze *f* VT aufspießen

pronged [prɒŋd] ADJ zackig, gezinkt

-pronged [-prɒŋd] ADJ *suf fork* -zackig, -zinkig; **three-pronged** dreizackig, dreizinkig; **a three--pronged attack** ein Angriff mit drei Spitzen; **a two-pronged approach** eine zweigleisige Vorgehensweise

pronominal [prəʊˈnɒmɪnl] ADJ pronominal

pronoun [ˈprəʊnaʊn] N Fürwort *nt*, Pronomen *nt*

pronounce [prəˈnaʊns] VT **a** *word etc* aussprechen; **I find Russian hard to ~** ich finde die russische Aussprache schwierig; **the "p" isn't ~d** das „p" wird nicht ausgesprochen **b** (= *declare*) erklären für; **the doctors ~d him unfit for work** die Ärzte erklärten ihn für arbeitsunfähig; **to ~ oneself in favour of/against sth** sich für/gegen etw aussprechen; **to ~ sentence** das Urteil verkünden VI **to ~ in favour of/against sth** sich für/gegen etw aussprechen; **to ~ on sth** zu etw Stellung nehmen

pronounceable [prəˈnaʊnsəbl] ADJ aussprechbar

pronounced [prəˈnaʊnst] ADJ (= *marked*) ausgesprochen; *accent* ausgeprägt, stark, schwer; *flavour* ausgeprägt, stark; *hipbones* ausgeprägt; *improvement, deterioration* deutlich; *views* pronounciert; **he has a ~ limp** er hinkt sehr stark

pronouncedly [prəˈnaʊnsɪdlɪ, -stlɪ] ADV (= *really*) ausgesprochen; **~ good** ausgesprochen gut

pronouncement [prəˈnaʊnsmənt] N Erklärung *f*; (*Jur, of sentence*) Verkündung *f*; **to make a ~** eine Erklärung abgeben

pronto [ˈprɒntəʊ] ADV (*inf*) fix (*inf*); **do it ~** aber dalli! (*inf*)

pronunciation [prəˌnʌnsɪˈeɪʃən] N Aussprache *f*

proof [pruːf] N **a** Beweis *m* (*of* für); **you'll need more ~ than that** die Beweise reichen nicht aus; **as ~ of** als *or* zum Beweis für; **to put sth to the ~** etw auf die Probe stellen; (*Tech*) etw erproben; **that is ~ that ...** das ist der Beweis dafür, dass ...; **to give** *or* **show ~ of sth** etw nachweisen, den Nachweis für etw liefern; **can you give us any ~ of that?** können Sie (uns) dafür Beweise liefern?; **show me your ~** beweisen Sie (mir) das; **what ~ is there that he meant it?** und was beweist, dass er es ernst gemeint hat?; **~ of purchase** (= *receipt*) Kaufbeleg *m*

b (= *test, trial*) Probe *f*; **withstanding these conditions is the ~ of a good paint** es ist der Beweis für die Qualität einer Farbe, wenn sie solchen Bedingungen standhält; **the ~ of the pudding is in the eating** (*Prov*) Probieren *or* probieren geht über Studieren *or* studieren (*Prov*)

c (*Typ*) (Korrektur)fahne *f*; (*Phot*) Probeabzug *m*

d (*of alcohol*) Alkoholgehalt *m*; **70% ~** ≈ 40 Vol-%

ADJ (= *resistant*) **to be ~ against fire/bullets** feuersicher/kugelsicher sein; **to be ~ against water** wasserdicht sein; **~ against inflation** inflationssicher

VT **a** (*against water*) imprägnieren

b (*Typ*) (= *make proof*) einen Korrekturabzug herstellen; (= *read proof*) Korrektur lesen

proof: **proofread** [ˈpruːfriːd] VI Korrektur lesen VT Korrektur lesen; **proofreader** [ˈpruːfˌriːdə] N Korrektor(in) *m(f)*; **proofreading** [ˈpruːfˌriːdɪŋ] N Korrekturlesen *nt*; **at the ~ stage** im Korrekturstadium; **proof sheet** N

(*Typ*) Korrekturfahne *f*/-bogen *m*; (= *trial print*) Probedruck *m*/-abzug *m*

prop¹ [prɒp] N (*lit*) Stütze *f*; (*fig also*) Halt *m* VT **to ~ the door open** die Tür offen halten; **to ~ oneself/sth against sth** sich/etw gegen etw lehnen → **prop up**

▶ **prop up** VT *sep* **a** (= *rest, lean*) **to prop oneself/sth up against sth** sich/etw gegen etw lehnen **b** (= *support*) stützen; *tunnel, wall* abstützen; *engine* aufbocken; (*fig*) *régime, company, the pound* stützen; *organization* unterstützen; **to prop oneself up on sth** sich auf etw (*acc*) stützen; **he spends most of his time propping up the bar** (*inf*) er hängt die meiste Zeit an der Bar

prop² N (*inf:* = *propeller*) Propeller *m*; **~ shaft** = **propeller shaft**

prop³ N (*Theat inf*) = **property d**

prop⁴ *abbr of* **proprietor**

propaedeutic [ˌprəʊpiːˈdjuːtɪk] N (*form*) Propädeutik *f*

propaganda [ˌprɒpəˈɡændə] N Propaganda *f*; **~ machine** Propagandamaschinerie *f*

propagandist [ˌprɒpəˈɡændɪst] N Propagandist(in) *m(f)*; **a tireless ~ for penal reform** ein unermüdlicher Verfechter der Strafrechtsreform ADJ propagandistisch

propagate [ˈprɒpəɡeɪt] VT **a** (= *reproduce*) fortpflanzen **b** (= *disseminate*) verbreiten; *views* verbreiten, propagieren **c** (*Phys*) *sound, waves* fortpflanzen **d** (*Hort*) *plant* vermehren VI **a** sich fortpflanzen *or* vermehren; (*views*) sich aus- *or* verbreiten

propagation [ˌprɒpəˈɡeɪʃən] N (= *reproduction*) Fortpflanzung *f*; (*Hort: of plants*) Vermehrung *f*; (= *dissemination*) Verbreitung *f*; (*of views*) Verbreitung *f*, Propagierung *f*

propane [ˈprəʊpeɪn] N Propan *nt*

propel [prəˈpel] VT antreiben; *fuel* betreiben; **~led along by the wind** vom Wind getrieben; **~led by greed** von Habgier getrieben; **he was ~led through the window** er wurde aus dem Fenster geworfen

propellant, propellent [prəˈpelənt] N Treibstoff *m*; (*in spray can*) Treibgas *nt* ADJ treibend

propeller [prəˈpelə] N Propeller *m*; **~ blade** (*Aviat*) Luftschrauben-/Propellerblatt *nt*; (*Naut*) Schraubenflügel *m*; **~ shaft** Antriebswelle *f*; (*Aut*) Kardanwelle *f*; (*Naut*) Schraubenwelle *f*

propelling: **propelling force** N (*lit, fig*) Triebkraft *f*; **propelling pencil** N Drehbleistift *m*

propensity [prəˈpensɪtɪ] N Hang *m*, Neigung *f* (*to* zu); **to have a ~ for sth** einen Hang zu etw haben; **to have a ~ to do sth** *or* **for doing sth** dazu neigen, etw zu tun, die Neigung *or* den Hang haben, etw zu tun

proper [ˈprɒpə] ADJ **a** (= *actual*) eigentlich; **physics ~** die eigentliche Physik; **in the ~ sense of the word** in der eigentlichen Bedeutung des Wortes; **is that a ~ policeman's helmet?** ist das ein richtiger Polizeihelm?; **he's never had a ~ job** er hat noch nie einen richtigen Job gehabt; **he's not a ~ electrician** er ist kein richtiger Elektriker; **not in Berlin ~** nicht in Berlin selbst **b** (*inf*) (= *real*) *fool etc* richtig; (= *thorough*) *beating* gehörig, anständig (*inf*), tüchtig (*inf*); **we got a ~ beating** (*team etc*) wir sind ganz schön geschlagen worden (*inf*) **c** (= *fitting, suitable*) richtig; **in ~ condition** in ordnungsgemäßem Zustand; **in the ~ way** richtig; **as you think ~** wie Sie es für richtig halten; **it's only right and ~** es ist nur recht und billig; **to do the ~ thing** das tun, was sich gehört; **the ~ thing to do would be to apologize** es gehört sich eigentlich, dass man sich entschuldigt; **don't touch the injured man unless you know the ~ thing to do** lassen Sie den Verletzten liegen, solange Sie nicht genau wissen, was man machen muss; **it wasn't really the ~ thing to say** es war ziemlich unpassend, das zu sagen; **we considered** *or* **thought it only ~ to ...** wir dachten, es gehört sich einfach zu ...

d (= *seemly*) anständig; **what is ~** was sich gehört; **it is not ~ for you to ...** es gehört sich nicht, dass Sie ...

e (= *prim and proper*) korrekt

f (= *peculiar, characteristic*) **~ to** angestammt (+*dat*), angehörig (+*dat*); **a species ~ to the Galapagos** eine Gattung, die den Galapagosinseln angestammt ist; **~ to the species** der Art eigen, arteigen

ADV **a** (*dial*) *cruel, poorly* richtig (*inf*)

b (*incorrect usage*) *behave* anständig; *talk* richtig

proper fraction N echter Bruch

properly [ˈprɒpəlɪ] ADV **a** (= *correctly*) richtig; **~ speaking** genau genommen, streng genommen; **Holland, more ~ called the Netherlands** Holland, eigentlich *or* richtiger die Niederlande; **Irish is ~ called Gaelic** Irisch heißt korrekt Gälisch **b** (= *in seemly fashion*) anständig; **to conduct oneself ~** sich korrekt verhalten; **she very ~ refused** sie hat sich zu Recht geweigert **c** (= *justifiably*) zu Recht **d** (*inf:* = *really, thoroughly*) ganz schön (*inf*)

proper name, proper noun N Eigenname *m*

propertied [ˈprɒpətɪd] ADJ besitzend; *person* begütert; **the ~ classes** die besitzenden Schichten, das Besitzbürgertum

property [ˈprɒpətɪ] N **a** (= *characteristic, Philos*) Eigenschaft *f*; **it has healing properties** es besitzt heilende Kräfte

b (= *thing owned*) Eigentum *nt*; **government/company ~** Eigentum *nt* der Regierung/Firma, Regierungs-/Firmeneigentum *nt*; **that's my ~** das gehört mir; **common ~** (*lit*) gemeinsames Eigentum; (*fig*) Gemeingut *nt*; **~ is theft** Eigentum ist Diebstahl; **to become the ~ of sb** in jds Eigentum (*acc*) übergehen; **a man of ~** ein begüterter Mann

c (= *building*) Haus *nt*, Wohnung *f*; (= *office*) Gebäude *nt*; (= *land*) Besitztum *nt*; (= *estate*) Besitz *m*; **this house is a very valuable ~** dieses Haus ist ein sehr wertvoller Besitz; **invest your money in ~** legen Sie Ihr Geld in Immobilien an; **~ in London is dearer** die Preise auf dem Londoner Immobilienmarkt sind höher

d (*Theat*) Requisit *nt*

property: property assets PL Vermögenswerte *pl*; **property consultant** N Vermögensberater(in) *m(f)*; **property developer** N Häusermakler(in) *m(f)*; **property giant** N Baulöwe *m*/-löwin *f* (*inf*); **property man** N (*Theat*) Requisiteur *m*; **property manager** N (*Theat*) Requisiteur(in) *m(f)*; **property master** N (*Theat*) Requisiteur(in) *m(f)*; **property market** N Immobilienmarkt *m*; **property mistress** N (*Theat*) Requisiteurin *f*; **property owner** N Haus- und Grundbesitzer(in) *m(f)*; **property speculation** N Immobilienspekulation *f*; **property speculator** N Immobilienspekulant(in) *m(f)*; **property tax** N Vermögenssteuer *f*

prophecy [ˈprɒfɪsɪ] N Prophezeiung *f*; **one skilled in the ~ of the future** jemand, der zukünftige Ereignisse vorhersagen kann *or* der die Gabe der Prophetie hat

prophesy [ˈprɒfɪsaɪ] VT prophezeien VI Prophezeiungen machen

prophet [ˈprɒfɪt] N Prophet(in) *m(f)*; **~ of doom** Unheilsverkünder(in) *m(f)*, Unheilsprophet(in) *m(f)*

prophetess [ˈprɒfɪtɪs] N Prophetin *f*

prophetic ADJ , **prophetically** ADV [prəˈfetɪk, -əlɪ] prophetisch

prophylactic [ˌprɒfɪˈlæktɪk] ADJ prophylaktisch, vorbeugend N Prophylaktikum *nt*; (= *contraceptive*) Präservativ *nt*

prophylaxis [ˌprɒfɪˈlæksɪs] N Prophylaxe *f*

propinquity [prəˈpɪŋkwɪtɪ] N (*form*) Nähe *f* (*to* zu); (*in time*) zeitliche Nähe (*to* zu); (*of relationship*) nahe Verwandtschaft (*to* mit)

propitiate [prəˈpɪʃɪeɪt] VT (*liter*) versöhnlich stimmen, besänftigen

propitiation [prəˌpɪʃɪˈeɪʃən] N (*liter*) Versöhnung *f*, Besänftigung *f*; **as ~ for, in ~ of** als Sühne für

propitiatory [prə'pɪʃɪətərɪ] ADJ versöhnend, besänftigend; *mood* versöhnlich

propitious ADJ , **propitiously** ADV [prə'pɪʃəs, -lɪ] günstig (*to, for* für)

propjet ['prɒpdʒet] N = **turboprop**

propman ['prɒpmæn, -mən] N (*Theat*) Requisiteur(in) *m(f)*

proponent [prə'pəʊnənt] N Befürworter(in) *m(f)*

proportion [prə'pɔːʃən] **N** **a** (= *ratio, relationship in number*) Verhältnis *nt* (*of x to y* zwischen x und y); (= *relationship in size, Art*) Proportionen *pl*; **~s** (= *size*) Ausmaß *nt*; (*of building*) Ausmaße *pl*; (*relative to one another, Art: of building etc*) Proportionen *pl*; **to be in/out of ~ (to one another)** (*in number*) (im richtigen/nicht im richtigen Verhältnis zueinander stehen; (*in size, Art*) in den Proportionen stimmen/nicht stimmen; (*in time, effort etc*) im richtigen/in keinem Verhältnis zueinander stehen; **to be in/out of ~ to** *or* **with sth** im Verhältnis/in keinem Verhältnis zu etw stehen; (*in size, Art*) in den Proportionen zu etw passen/nicht zu etw passen; **in ~ to what she earns her contributions are very small** im Verhältnis zu dem, was sie verdient, ist ihr Beitrag äußerst bescheiden; **in direct/inverse ~ to sth** in direktem/umgekehrtem Verhältnis zu etw; (*Math*) direkt/indirekt proportional zu etw; **to get sth in ~** (*Art*) etw proportional richtig darstellen; (*fig*) etw objektiv betrachten; **he has got the arms out of ~** er hat die Arme proportional falsch dargestellt; **he has let it all get out of ~** (*fig*) er hat den Blick für die Proportionen verloren; **it's out of all ~!** das geht über jedes Maß hinaus!; **sense of ~** (*lit, fig*) Sinn *m* für Proportionen; **in due ~** in angemessenem Verhältnis; **in ~ as** in dem Maße wie; **a man of huge ~s** ein Koloss von einem Mann; **he admired her ample ~s** er bewunderte ihre üppigen Formen; **a room of good ~s** ein Zimmer mit guter Raumaufteilung

b (= *part, amount*) Teil *m*; **a certain ~ of the population** ein bestimmter Teil der Bevölkerung; **the ~ of drinkers in our society is rising constantly** der Anteil der Trinker in unserer Gesellschaft nimmt ständig zu; **what ~ of the industry is in private hands?** wie groß ist der Anteil der Industrie, der sich in Privathand befindet?; **a ~ of the industry is in private hands** ein Teil der Industrie befindet sich in Privathand

VT **you haven't ~ed the head properly** Sie haben den Kopf proportional falsch dargestellt; **he ~ed the building beautifully** er hat das Gebäude wunderbar ausgewogen gestaltet; **a realistically ~ed model** ein maßstabgetreues Modell; **a nicely ~ed woman** eine wohlproportionierte Frau

proportional [prə'pɔːʃənl] ADJ proportional (*to* zu); *share, distribution also* anteilmäßig (*to* zu)

proportionality [prə,pɔːʃə'nælɪtɪ] N Proportionalität *f*; (*of means*) Verhältnismäßigkeit *f*

proportionally [prə'pɔːʃnlɪ] ADV proportional; *share, distribute also* anteilmäßig; *more, less* entsprechend; *elect* durch Verhältnis- *or* Proportionalwahl

proportional: proportional printing N (*Typ, Printing*) Proportionaldruck *m*; **proportional representation** N (*Pol*) Verhältniswahlrecht *nt*; **proportional spacing** N (*Typ, Printing*) Proportionalschrift *f*; **proportional voting** N (*Pol*) Verhältniswahlrecht *nt*

proportionate [prə'pɔːʃnɪt] ADJ proportional; *share also* anteil(s)mäßig; **to be/not to be ~ to sth** im Verhältnis/in keinem Verhältnis zu etw stehen

proportionately [prə'pɔːʃnɪtlɪ] ADV proportional; *share, distribute also* anteil(s)mäßig; *more, less* entsprechend

proposal [prə'pəʊzl] N **a** Vorschlag *m* (*on, about* zu); (= *proposal of marriage*) (Heirats)antrag *m*; **to make sb a ~** jdm einen Vorschlag/(Heirats)antrag machen **b** (= *act of proposing*) (*of toast*) Ausbringen *nt*; (*of motion*) Einbringen *nt*;

his ~ of this plan surprised his colleagues dass er den Vorschlag zu diesem Plan machte, überraschte seine Kollegen; **his ~ of John as chairman was expected** dass er John zum Vorsitzenden vorschlägt, war erwartet worden

propose [prə'pəʊz] ⊘ 8.1, 8.3 **VT** **a** (= *suggest*) vorschlagen; *motion* stellen, einbringen; **to ~ marriage to sb** jdm einen (Heirats)antrag machen; **I ~ leaving now** *or* **that we leave now** ich schlage vor, wir gehen jetzt *or* dass wir jetzt gehen; **to ~ sb's health** einen Toast auf jdn ausbringen → **toast** ²

b (= *have in mind*) beabsichtigen, vorhaben; **I don't ~ having any more to do with it/him** ich will nichts mehr damit/mit ihm zu tun haben; **but I don't ~ to** ich habe aber nicht die Absicht; **how do you ~ to pay for it?** wie wollen Sie das bezahlen?; **and just how do you ~ we pay for all that?** können Sie uns denn auch verraten, wie wir das alles bezahlen sollen?

VI (= *offer marriage*) einen (Heirats)antrag machen (*to* +*dat*)

b **man ~s, God disposes** (*Prov*) der Mensch denkt, Gott lenkt (*Prov*)

proposer [prə'pəʊzə'] N (*in debate*) Antragsteller(in) *m(f)*; **if you want to stand for the committee you'll have to find a ~** wenn Sie sich in den Ausschuss wählen lassen wollen, müssen Sie jemanden finden, der Sie vorschlägt

proposition [,prɒpə'zɪʃən] **N** **a** (= *statement*) Aussage *f*; (*Philos, Logic*) Satz *m*; (*Math*) (Lehr)satz *m* **b** (= *proposal*) Vorschlag *m*; (= *argument*) These *f*; **a paying ~** ein lohnendes Geschäft **c** (= *person or thing to be dealt with*) (= *objective*) Unternehmen *nt*; (= *opponent*) Fall *m*; (= *prospect*) Aussicht *f* **d** (*pej: = improper proposition*) unsittlicher Antrag **VT** **he ~ed me** er hat mich gefragt, ob ich mit ihm schlafen würde

propound [prə'paʊnd] VT darlegen

proprietary [prə'praɪətərɪ] ADJ *class* besitzend; *attitude, manner* besitzergreifend; **~ rights** Besitzrecht *nt*; **~ article/name** Markenartikel/-name *m*; **~ drug** Markenpräparat *nt*; **the author has rather strong ~ feelings about his work** der Autor sieht sein Werk als persönlichen Besitz an

proprietary article N Markenartikel *m*
proprietary name N Markenname *m*

proprietor [prə'praɪətə'] N (*of pub, hotel, patent*) Inhaber(in) *m(f)*; (*of house, newspaper*) Besitzer(in) *m(f)*

proprietorship [prə'praɪətəʃɪp] N → **proprietor**; **under his ~** während er der Inhaber/Besitzer war

proprietress [prə'praɪətrɪs] N (*of pub, hotel*) Inhaberin *f*; (*of newspaper*) Besitzerin *f*

propriety [prə'praɪətɪ] N (= *correctness*) Korrektheit *f*, Richtigkeit *f*; (= *decency*) Anstand *m*; (*of clothing*) Gesellschaftsfähigkeit *f*, Züchtigkeit *f* (*liter*); **some countries still have doubts about the ~ of bikinis** in manchen Ländern werden Bikinis noch als anstößig betrachtet; **~ of conduct** korrektes Verhalten; **breach of ~** Verstoß *m* gegen die guten Sitten; **the proprieties** die Regeln *pl* des Anstands

props [prɒps] PL (*Theat*) Requisiten *pl*

propulsion [prə'pʌlʃən] N Antrieb *m*

pro rata ['prəʊ'rɑːtə] ADJ, ADV anteil(s)mäßig; **on a ~ basis** auf einer proportionalen Basis

prorate ['prəʊreɪt] VT (*US*) anteil(s)mäßig aufteilen *or* verteilen

prorogation [,prəʊrə'geɪʃən] N Vertagung *f*

prorogue [prə'rəʊg] **VT** vertagen **VI** sich vertagen

prosaic [prəʊ'zeɪɪk] ADJ *task, explanation, job, name* prosaisch; *approach, message* nüchtern; *life, joke* alltäglich

prosaically [prəʊ'zeɪɪkəlɪ] ADV *say, explain* prosaisch; *approach* nüchtern

proscenium [prəʊ'siːnɪəm] N *pl* **proscenia** [prəʊ'siːnɪə] (*also* **proscenium arch**) Proszenium *nt*; **~ stage** Bühne *f* mit Vorbühne

proscribe [prəʊ'skraɪb] VT (= *forbid*) verbieten; (= *outlaw*) ächten; (= *banish, exile*) verbannen

proscription [prəʊ'skrɪpʃən] N Verbot *nt*; (= *ostracism*) Ächtung *f*; (= *banishment*) Verbannung *f*

prose [prəʊz] N Prosa *f*; (= *writing, style*) Stil *m*; (*Sch, Univ: = translation text*) Übersetzung *f* in die Fremdsprache, Hinübersetzung *f*

prose composition N Prosa *f*

prosecutable ['prɒsɪkjuːtəbl] ADJ strafbar

prosecute ['prɒsɪkjuːt] **VT** **a** *person* strafrechtlich verfolgen *or* belangen (*for wegen*); **prosecuting counsel** *or* **attorney** (*US*) Staatsanwalt *m*/-anwältin *f*; **"trespassers will be ~d"** „widerrechtliches Betreten wird strafrechtlich verfolgt" **b** (*form: = carry on*) *inquiry, campaign etc* durchführen; *claim* weiterverfolgen **VI** Anzeige erstatten, gerichtlich vorgehen; **"shoplifting – we always ~"** „jeder Ladendiebstahl wird angezeigt *or* strafrechtlich verfolgt"; **Mr Jones, prosecuting, said …** Herr Jones, der Vertreter der Anklage, sagte …

prosecution [,prɒsɪ'kjuːʃən] N **a** (*Jur, = act of prosecuting*) strafrechtliche Verfolgung; (*in court: = case, side*) Anklage *f* (*for wegen*); **(the) counsel for the ~** die Anklage(vertretung), der Vertreter/die Vertreterin der Anklage; **witness for the ~** Zeuge *m*/Zeugin *f* der Anklage, Belastungszeuge *m*/-zeugin *f* **b** (*form: = carrying on*) (*of inquiry, campaign etc*) Durchführung *f*; (*of claim*) Weiterverfolgung *f*

prosecutor ['prɒsɪkjuːtə'] N Ankläger(in) *m(f)*

proselyte ['prɒsɪlaɪt] N Neubekehrte(r) *mf*, Proselyt(in) *m(f)*

proselytize ['prɒsɪlɪtaɪz] **VT** bekehren **VI** Leute bekehren

prose: prose poem N Prosagedicht *nt*; **prose style** N Stil *m*; **prose writer** N Prosaschriftsteller(in) *m(f)*; **prose writing** N Prosadichtung *f*

prosodic [prə'sɒdɪk] ADJ prosodisch

prosody ['prɒsədɪ] N Verslehre *f*

prospect ['prɒspekt] **N** **a** (= *outlook, chance*) Aussicht *f* (*of auf* +*acc*); **what a ~!** (*iro*) das sind ja schöne Aussichten!; **he has no ~s** er hat keine Zukunft; **a job with no ~s** eine Stelle ohne Zukunft; **to face the ~ of sth** mit etw rechnen müssen; **to hold out the ~ of sth** etw in Aussicht stellen; **to have sth in ~** etw in Aussicht haben

b (= *person, thing*) **he's not much of a ~ for her** er hat ihr nicht viel zu bieten; **I think this product would be a good ~** ich glaube, dieses Produkt ist sehr aussichtsreich; **Manchester is a good ~ for the cup** Manchester ist ein aussichtsreicher Kandidat für den Pokal; **a likely ~ as a customer/candidate** ein aussichtsreicher Kunde/Kandidat; **a likely ~ as a husband** ein Mann, der als Ehemann infrage *or* in Frage kommt; **he's a good ~ for the team** (*could benefit it*) mit ihm hat die Mannschaft gute Aussichten

c (*old, form: = view*) Aussicht *f* (*of auf* +*acc*); (= *painting*) Ansicht *f* (*of von*)

d (*Min*) Schürfstelle *f*

VT [prə'spekt] (*Min*) nach Bodenschätzen suchen in (+*dat*)

VI [prə'spekt] (*Min*) nach Bodenschätzen suchen; **to ~ for gold** nach Gold suchen

prospecting [prə'spektɪŋ] N (*Min*) Suche *f* nach Bodenschätzen

prospective [prə'spektɪv] ADJ *attr* (= *likely to happen*) *journey, return* voraussichtlich; (= *future*) *son-in-law, change* zukünftig; *buyer* interessiert; **~ candidate** Kandidat(in) *m(f)*; **all the ~ cases** alle infrage *or* in Frage kommenden Fälle; **~ earnings** voraussichtliche Einkünfte *pl*

prospector [prə'spektə'] N Prospektor *m* (*spec*), Gold-/Erz-/Ölsucher(in) *m(f)*

prospectus [prə'spektəs] N Prospekt *m*; (*Sch, Univ*) Lehrprogramm *nt*

prosper ['prɒspə'] VI (*town, country, crime*) gedeihen, blühen; (*financially*) florieren, blühen;

(plan) erfolgreich sein; **how's he ~ing these days?** wie geht es ihm?

prosperity [prɒsˈperɪtɪ] N Wohlstand m, Reichtum m; (of business) Prosperität f

prosperous [ˈprɒspərəs] ADJ person wohlhabend, reich; business gut gehend, florierend; economy florierend, blühend; (liter) wind gut; **those were ~ times/years** das waren Zeiten/ Jahre des Wohlstands; **he had a ~ look about him** er sah wohlhabend aus

prosperously [ˈprɒspərəslɪ] ADV live im Wohlstand

prostaglandin [ˌprɒstəˈɡlændɪn] N Prostaglandin nt

prostate (gland) [ˈprɒsteɪt(ˌɡlænd)] N Prostata f, Vorsteherdrüse f

prosthesis [prɒsˈθiːsɪs] N (spec) Prothese f

prostitute [ˈprɒstɪtjuːt] **N** Prostituierte(r) mf **VT** (lit) prostituieren; one's talents, honour, ideals verkaufen **VR** sich prostituieren; (fig also) sich verkaufen

prostitution [ˌprɒstɪˈtjuːʃən] N (lit, fig) Prostitution f; (of one's talents, honour, ideals) Verkaufen nt

prostrate [ˈprɒstreɪt] ADJ ausgestreckt; **he was found ~ on the floor** man fand ihn ausgestreckt am Boden liegend; **the servants lay ~ at their master's feet** die Diener lagen demütig or unterwürfig zu Füßen ihres Herrn; **~ with grief** vor Gram gebrochen; **she was ~ with exhaustion** sie brach fast zusammen vor Erschöpfung **VT** [prɒˈstreɪt] usu pass (lit) zu Boden werfen; (fig) (with fatigue) erschöpfen, mitnehmen; (with shock) zusammenbrechen lassen, niederschmettern; **to be ~d by an illness** einer Krankheit (dat) zum Opfer gefallen sein; **to be ~d with grief** vor Gram gebrochen sein **VR** [prɒˈstreɪt] sich niederwerfen (before vor +dat)

prostration [prɒˈstreɪʃən] N (lit) Fußfall m; (fig: = exhaustion) Erschöpfung f

prosy [ˈprəʊzɪ] ADJ (+er) (= boring) redselig; (= over-literary) schwülstig

Prot abbr of **Protestant** ≈ ev.

protactinium [ˌprəʊtækˈtɪnɪəm] N (Chem) Protaktinium nt

protagonist [prəʊˈtæɡənɪst] N (esp Liter) Protagonist(in) m(f); (= champion, supporter) Verfechter(in) m(f)

protean [ˈprəʊtɪən] ADJ (liter) proteisch (liter)

protect [prəˈtekt] **VT** schützen (against gegen, from vor +dat); (person, animal) sth, young beschützen (against gegen, from vor +dat); one's interests, rights schützen, wahren; (Comput) cell etc sichern; **don't try to ~ the culprit** versuchen Sie nicht, den Schuldigen zu decken **VI** schützen (against vor +dat)

protected species [prəˌtektɪdˈspiːʃiːz] N geschützte Art

protection [prəˈtekʃən] N **a** Schutz m (against gegen, from vor +dat); (of interests, rights) Wahrung f; **to be under sb's ~** unter jds Schutz (dat) stehen **b** (also **protection money**) Schutzgeld nt

protection factor N (of sun lotion) Lichtschutzfaktor m

protectionism [prəˈtekʃənɪzəm] N Protektionismus m

protectionist [prəˈtekʃənɪst] ADJ protektionistisch **N** Protektionist(in) m(f)

protection racket N organisiertes Erpresserunwesen

protective [prəˈtektɪv] ADJ **a** Schutz-; attitude, gesture beschützend; equipment, layer, covering schützend; **~ instinct** Beschützerinstinkt m; **the mother is very ~ toward(s) her children** die Mutter ist sehr fürsorglich ihren Kindern gegenüber; **some parents can be too ~** manche Eltern sind übermäßig besorgt **b** (Econ) system protektionistisch; **~ duty** Schutzzoll m

protective: protective clothing N Schutzkleidung f, Schutzbekleidung f; **protective**

colouring, (US) **protective coloring** N Tarnfarbe f, Schutzfarbe f; **protective custody** N Schutzhaft f

protectively [prəˈtektɪvlɪ] ADV schützend; (with regard to people) beschützend; **don't be frightened, he said ~** hab keine Angst, sagte er in beschützendem Ton

protective tariff N (Econ) Schutzzoll m, Schutzgebühr f

protector [prəˈtektər] N **a** (= defender) Beschützer(in) m(f) **b** (= protective wear) Schutz m

protectorate [prəˈtektərɪt] N Protektorat nt

protectory [prəˈtektərɪ] N (Kinder)fürsorgeheim nt

protectress [prəˈtektrɪs] N Beschützerin f

protégé, protégée [ˈprɒtəʒeɪ] N Protegé m, Schützling m

protein [ˈprəʊtiːn] N Eiweiß nt, Protein nt; **a high-protein diet** eine eiweißreiche or stark proteinhaltige Kost

pro tem [ˈprəʊtem] abbr of **pro tempore** zurzeit, zzt.; **on a ~ basis** auf vorübergehender Basis

protest [ˈprəʊtest] **○** 12.2, 14 **N** Protest m; (= demonstration) Protestkundgebung f; **under ~** unter Protest; **in ~** aus Protest; **to make a/one's ~ Protest** or Widerspruch erheben; **letter of ~, ~ letter** Protestschreiben nt **VI** [prəʊˈtest] (against, about gegen) protestieren; (= demonstrate) demonstrieren; **the ~ing scream of the brakes** das gequälte Aufkreischen der Bremsen **VT** [prəʊˈtest] **a** innocence beteuern **b** (= dispute) decision protestieren gegen, Protest or Einspruch erheben gegen; **it's mine, he ~ed** das gehört mir, protestierte er

Protestant [ˈprɒtɪstənt] ADJ protestantisch; (esp in Germany) evangelisch **N** Protestant(in) m(f), Evangelische(r) mf

Protestantism [ˈprɒtɪstəntɪzəm] N Protestantismus m

protestation [ˌprɒteˈsteɪʃən] N **a** (of love, loyalty etc) Beteuerung f **b** (= protest) Protest m

protester [prəˈtestər] N Protestierende(r) mf; (in demonstration) Demonstrant(in) m(f)

protest march N Protestmarsch m

protest vote N Proteststimme f

proto- [ˈprəʊtəʊ-] PREF **a** (Chem, Biol) proto-, Proto-; **protolysis** Protolyse f **b** (Ling) ur-, Ur-; **protolanguage** Ursprache f

protocol [ˈprəʊtəkɒl] N Protokoll nt

protohistory [ˌprəʊtəʊˈhɪstərɪ] N (Hist) Urgeschichte f

proton [ˈprəʊtɒn] N Proton nt

protoplasm [ˈprəʊtəʊplæzəm] N Protoplasma nt

protoplast [ˈprəʊtəʊplæst] N (Bot) Protoplast m

prototype [ˈprəʊtəʊtaɪp] N Prototyp m

prototypical [ˌprəʊtəʊˈtɪpɪkəl] ADJ (= typical) typisch

protozoan [ˌprəʊtəʊˈzəʊən] ADJ einzellig **N** Protozoon nt (spec), Urtierchen nt

protozoic [ˌprəʊtəʊˈzəʊɪk] ADJ einzellig

protract [prəˈtrækt] VT hinausziehen, in die Länge ziehen; illness verlängern; decision hinauszögern

protracted [prəˈtræktɪd] ADJ illness langwierig; discussion, debate, negotiations also sich hinziehend attr; description lang gezogen; absence, dispute längere(r, s)

protraction [prəˈtrækʃən] N **that can only lead to the ~ of the discussion/illness** das kann nur dazu führen, dass sich die Diskussion/Krankheit hinzieht

protractor [prəˈtræktər] N (Math) Winkelmesser m

protrude [prəˈtruːd] **VI** (out of, from aus) vorstehen; (ears) abstehen; (eyes) vortreten **VT** hervorstrecken, herausstrecken

protruding [prəˈtruːdɪŋ] ADJ vorstehend; rock, ledge vorstehend, herausragend; ears abstehend; eyes vortretend; forehead, chin vorsprin-

gend; stomach vorstehend, vorspringend; teeth vorstehend; ribs hervorstehend, hervortretend

protrusion [prəˈtruːʒən] N **a** (= protruding object) Vorsprung m **b** (= protruding) (of rock, buttress, teeth etc) Vorstehen nt; (of forehead, chin) Vorspringen nt; (of eyes) Vortreten nt

protrusive [prəˈtruːsɪv] ADJ = protruding

protuberance [prəˈtjuːbərəns] N (= bulge) Beule f; (of stomach) Vorstehen nt; (of eyes) Vortreten nt

protuberant [prəˈtjuːbərənt] ADJ vorstehend; eyes vortretend

proud [praʊd] **ADJ** **a** person, expression stolz (of auf +acc); **it made his parents feel very ~** das erfüllte seine Eltern mit Stolz; **to be the ~ owner** or **possessor of sth** der stolze Eigentümer or Besitzer von etw sein; **as ~ as a peacock** eitel wie ein Pfau, stolz wie ein Hahn; **~ boast** stolze Behauptung; **a ~ day for ...** ein stolzer Tag für ...; **~ history** stolze Geschichte; **a ~ moment** ein stolzer Moment; **to be ~ that ...** stolz (darauf) sein, dass ...; **to be ~ to do sth** stolz darauf sein, etw zu tun; **I hope you're ~ of yourself** (iro) ich hoffe, du bist stolz auf dich; **that's nothing to be ~ of** das ist nichts, worauf man stolz sein kann

b (dated Brit: = projecting) **to be** or **stand ~** (nail etc) herausragen, hervorragen; (Typ: character) erhaben sein; **~ flesh** wildes Fleisch

c (liter: = high, noble) stolz

ADV to do sb/oneself ~ jdn/sich verwöhnen

proudly [ˈpraʊdlɪ] ADV stolz

provable [ˈpruːvəbl] ADJ hypothesis, story, law beweisbar; guilt, innocence also nachweisbar

prove [pruːv] **V** **○** 26.1 pret **proved**, ptp **proved** or **proven** **a** (= verify) beweisen; will beglaubigen; **he ~d that she did it** er bewies or er wies nach, dass sie das getan hat; **to ~ sb innocent** or **sb's innocence** jds Unschuld beweisen or nachweisen; **to ~ something against sb** jdm etwas nachweisen; **whether his judgement was right remains to be ~d** or **~n** es muss sich erst noch erweisen, ob seine Beurteilung zutrifft; **it all goes to ~ that ...** das beweist mal wieder, dass ...; **he was ~d right in the end** er hat schließlich doch Recht behalten

b (= test out, put to the proof) rifle, aircraft etc erproben; one's worth, courage unter Beweis stellen, beweisen; **he did it just to ~ a point** er tat es nur der Sache wegen

c (Cook) dough gehen lassen **VI** (Cook: dough) gehen

b (= turn out) **to ~ (to be) hot/useful etc** sich als heiß/nützlich etc erweisen; **if it ~s otherwise** wenn sich das Gegenteil herausstellt **VR** **a** (= show one's value, courage etc) sich bewähren

b **to ~ oneself innocent/indispensable etc** sich als unschuldig/unentbehrlich etc erweisen

proven [ˈpruːvən] ptp of **prove** ADJ [ˈprəʊvən] bewährt; **not ~** (Scot Jur) unbewiesen

provenance [ˈprɒvɪnəns] N Herkunft f, Ursprung m; **country of ~** Herkunfts- or Ursprungsland nt

provender [ˈprɒvɪndər] N Futter nt

proverb [ˈprɒvɜːb] N Sprichwort nt; **(the Book of) Proverbs** die Sprüche pl

proverbial [prəˈvɜːbɪəl] ADJ (lit, fig) sprichwörtlich

proverbially [prəˈvɜːbɪəlɪ] ADV (lit) express in Form eines Sprichworts; (fig) sprichwörtlich; **the weather there is ~ unreliable** das Wetter dort ist sprichwörtlich wechselhaft; **prevention is ~ better than cure** wie das Sprichwort sagt, Vorsicht ist besser als Nachsicht

provide [prəˈvaɪd] **VT** **a** (= make available) zur Verfügung stellen; (agency) personnel vermitteln; money bereitstellen; (= lay on, as part of service) chairs, materials, food etc (zur Verfügung) stellen; (= see to, bring along) food, records etc sorgen für; (= produce, give) ideas, specialist knowledge, electricity liefern; light, shade spenden, geben; privacy sorgen für, schaffen; topic of conversation sorgen für, liefern; **X ~d the money and Y (~d) the ex-**

pertise X stellte das Geld bereit und Y lieferte das Fachwissen; **a local band ~d the music** eine örtliche Kapelle sorgte für die Musik; **candidates must ~ their own pens** die Kandidaten müssen ihr Schreibgerät selbst stellen

b **to ~ sth for sb** etw für jdn stellen; (= *make available*) jdm etw zur Verfügung stellen; (= *find, supply: agency etc*) jdm etw besorgen; **to ~ food and clothes for one's family** für Nahrung und Kleidung seiner Familie sorgen; **I can't ~ enough food for everyone** ich kann nicht genug Essen für alle stellen; **it ~s a certain amount of privacy/shade for the inhabitants** es gibt den Bewohnern eine gewisse Abgeschlossenheit/etwas Schatten; **they ~ a restroom/bus for their workers** sie stellen einen Ruheraum/Bus für ihre Arbeiter

c **to ~ sb with sth** (*with food, clothing etc*) jdn mit etw versorgen; (= *equip*) jdn mit etw versehen or ausstatten; *with excuse, idea, answer* jdm etw geben or liefern; *with opportunity, information* jdm etw verschaffen or geben or liefern; **the job ~d him with a good salary/with the necessary experience** die Stelle verschaffte ihm genug Geld/die nötige Erfahrung; **this ~d the school with enough money to build a gymnasium** dadurch hatte die Schule genügend Geld zur Verfügung, um eine Turnhalle zu bauen

d (= *stipulate: clause, agreement*) vorsehen; **unless otherwise ~d** sofern nichts Gegenteiliges bestimmt ist → **provided (that), providing (that)**

VI **the Lord will ~** (*prov*) der Herr wirds schon geben; **a husband who ~s well** ein Ehemann, der gut für seine Familie/Frau sorgt

VR **to ~ oneself with sth** sich mit etw ausstatten; **to ~ oneself with a good excuse** sich (*dat*) eine gute Entschuldigung zurechtlegen

▶ **provide against** VI +*prep obj* vorsorgen für, Vorsorge or Vorkehrungen treffen für; **the law provides against such abuses** das Gesetz schützt vor solchem Missbrauch

▶ **provide for** VI +*prep obj* **a** *family etc* versorgen, sorgen für, Sorge tragen für; **he made sure that his family would be well provided for** er stellte sicher, dass seine Familie gut versorgt war or dass für seine Familie gut gesorgt war

b *the law/treaty provides for penalties against abuses* bei Missbrauch sieht das Gesetz/der Vertrag Strafe vor; **as provided for in the 1970 contract** wie in dem Vertrag von 1970 vorgesehen; **we provided for all emergencies** wir haben für alle Notfälle vorgesorgt; **we have provided for an increase in costs of 25%** wir haben eine Kostensteigerung von 25% einkalkuliert

provided (that) [prəˈvaɪdɪd(ˈðæt)] CONJ vorausgesetzt(, dass), gesetzt den Fall(, dass)

providence [ˈprɒvɪdəns] N **a** (= *fate*) die Vorsehung **b** (*dated*: = *prudent thriftiness*) Vorsorge *f*

provident [ˈprɒvɪdənt] ADJ vorsorglich, vorsorgend, vorausschauend; **~ fund** Unterstützungskasse *f*; **~ society** *private Altersversicherung*

providential [ˌprɒvɪˈdɛnʃəl] ADJ **a** **God's ~ care** die göttliche Vorsehung **b** (= *lucky*) glücklich; **to be ~** (ein) Glück sein

providentially [ˌprɒvɪˈdɛnʃəlɪ] ADV (= *luckily*) glücklicherweise; **it happened almost ~** das war gleichsam eine Fügung (des Schicksals)

providently [ˈprɒvɪdəntlɪ] ADV vorsorglich, vorsorgend, vorausschauend

provider [prəˈvaɪdə] N (*for family*) Ernährer(in) *m(f)*

providing (that) [prəˈvaɪdɪŋ(ˈðæt)] CONJ vorausgesetzt(, dass), gesetzt den Fall(, dass)

province [ˈprɒvɪns] N **a** Provinz *f* **b** **provinces** PL **the ~s** die Provinz **c** (*fig*: = *area of knowledge, activity etc*) Gebiet *nt*, Bereich *m*; **it's not (within) my ~** das fällt nicht in meinen Bereich or mein Gebiet; **it's outside the ~ of science** es liegt außerhalb des wissenschaftlichen Gebiets or Bereichs **d** (= *area of authority*) Kompetenzbereich *m*; **that's not my ~** dafür bin ich nicht zuständig

provincial [prəˈvɪnʃəl] ADJ Provinz-; *custom, accent* ländlich; (*pej*) provinzlerisch; **~ capital**

Provinzhauptstadt *f*; **~ narrowness** Engstirnigkeit *f*; **the World War did not affect daily life in ~ France** der Weltkrieg hatte keinen Einfluss auf den Alltag in den ländlichen Teilen Frankreichs **N** Provinzbewohner(in) *m(f)*; (*pej*) Provinzler(in) *m(f)*

provincialism [prəˈvɪnʃəlɪzəm] N Provinzialismus *m*

provincialize [prəˈvɪnʃəlaɪz] VT **to ~ sth** etw provinziell machen, etw *dat* einen provinzlerischen Charakter geben

proving ground [ˈpruːvɪŋˌɡraʊnd] N (*for theory*) Versuchsfeld *nt*; (= *situation: for sb, sb's abilities*) Bewährungsprobe *f*; **Belfast was his ~** Belfast war für ihn die Bewährungsprobe

provision [prəˈvɪʒən] **N** **a** (= *act of supplying*) (*for others*) Bereitstellung *f*; (*for one's own team, expedition etc*) Beschaffung *f*; (*of food, gas, water etc*) Versorgung *f* (*of mit, to sb jds*) **b** (= *supply*) Vorrat *m* (*of an +dat*); **we had an ample ~ of reference books/houses** *etc* uns (*dat*) standen genügend Nachschlagewerke/Häuser *etc* zur Verfügung **c** **~s** *pl* (= *food*) Lebensmittel *pl*; (*Mil: for journey, expedition*) Verpflegung *f*, Proviant *m*; **~s ship** Versorgungsschiff *nt* **d** (= *allowance*) Berücksichtigung *f*; (= *arrangement*) Vorkehrung *f*; (= *stipulation*) Bestimmung *f*; **with the ~ that ...** mit dem Vorbehalt or der Bedingung, dass ...; **is there no ~ for such cases in the legislation?** sind solche Fälle im Gesetz nicht berücksichtigt or vorgesehen?; **there's no ~ for later additions** spätere Erweiterungen sind nicht vorgesehen; **to make ~ for sb/one's family/the future** für jdn/für seine Familie/für die Zukunft Vorsorge or Vorkehrungen treffen; **to make ~ for sth** etw vorsehen; (*in legislation, rules also*) etw berücksichtigen; (*in margin of error etc*) etw einkalkulieren; **the council made ~ for recreation** die Stadt hat Freizeiteinrichtungen geschaffen; **to make (a) ~ against sth** gegen etw Vorkehrungen treffen **VT** die Verpflegung liefern für; *expedition* verproviantieren; *troops* (mit Proviant) beliefern or versorgen

provisional [prəˈvɪʒənl] ADJ provisorisch; *measures, solution also, offer, acceptance, decision, legislation* vorläufig; **~ driving licence** (*Brit*) vorläufige Fahrerlaubnis für Fahrschüler; **the ~ IRA** die provisorische irisch-republikanische Armee **N** (*Ir Pol*) **the Provisionals** Mitglieder der provisorischen irisch-republikanischen Armee

provisionally [prəˈvɪʒnəlɪ] ADV vorläufig; *appoint also* provisorisch; **~ titled ...** mit dem vorläufigen Titel or Arbeitstitel ..., vorläufig ... benannt

proviso [prəˈvaɪzəʊ] N (= *condition*) Vorbehalt *m*, Bedingung *f*; (= *clause*) Vorbehaltsklausel *f*; **with the ~ that ...** unter der Bedingung, dass ...

provisorily [prəˈvaɪzərɪlɪ] ADV **a** (= *with a proviso*) mit Vorbehalt, bedingt **b** (= *tentatively*) provisorisch, vorläufig

provisory [prəˈvaɪzərɪ] ADJ **a** (= *with a proviso*) vorbehaltlich; **a ~ clause** eine Vorbehaltsklausel **b** = **provisional** ADJ

Provo [ˈprəʊvəʊ] N (*Ir, Pol*) = **provisional** N

provocation [ˌprɒvəˈkeɪʃən] N Provokation *f*, Herausforderung *f*; **what ~ was there for you to hit him?** was hat dich dazu provoziert, ihn zu schlagen?; **he acted under ~** er wurde dazu provoziert or herausgefordert; **his deliberate ~ of a quarrel** seine bewusste Herbeiführung eines Streits; **to suffer great ~** sehr stark provoziert werden; **at the slightest ~** bei der geringsten Provokation or Herausforderung; **he hit me without any ~** er hat mich geschlagen, ohne dass ich ihn dazu provoziert hätte

provocative [prəˈvɒkətɪv] ADJ **a** (= *thought-provoking*) provozierend, provokatorisch; *film, discussion* anregend, kontrovers; **he's just trying to be ~** er versucht nur zu provozieren **b** (= *erotic, seductive*) *dress* provozierend; *remark* herausfordernd; *pose, manner, behaviour* aufreizend, herausfordernd, provozierend

provocatively [prəˈvɒkətɪvlɪ] ADV **a** provozierend, provokatorisch; **~ entitled ...** mit dem provokativen Titel ... **b** (= *erotically, seductively*) *say, behave* herausfordernd; *dress* provozierend; **~ dressed** aufreizend gekleidet; **she smiled ~** sie lächelte aufreizend

provoke [prəˈvəʊk] VT *sb* provozieren, reizen, herausfordern; *animal* reizen; *reaction, anger, criticism, dismay, smile* hervorrufen; *lust, pity* erwecken, erregen; *reply, dispute* provozieren; *discussion, revolt, showdown* herbeiführen, auslösen; **to ~ a quarrel** or **an argument** (*person*) Streit suchen; (*action*) zu einem Streit führen; **to ~ sb into doing sth** or **to do sth** jdn dazu bringen, dass er etw tut; (= *taunt*) jdn dazu treiben or so provozieren, dass er etw tut

provoking [prəˈvəʊkɪŋ] ADJ provozierend; (= *annoying*) *fact, circumstance* ärgerlich; **how very ~!** wie ärgerlich!

provokingly [prəˈvəʊkɪŋlɪ] ADV provozierend

provost [ˈprɒvəst] N **a** (*Scot*) Bürgermeister(in) *m(f)* **b** (*Univ*) ≈ Dekan(in) *m(f)* **c** (*Eccl*) Propst *m*

provost marshal [prəˈvəʊstˈmɑːʃəl] N Kommandeur(in) *m(f)* der Militärpolizei

prow [praʊ] N Bug *m*

prowess [ˈpraʊɪs] N (= *skill*) Fähigkeiten *pl*, Können *nt*; (= *courage*) Tapferkeit *f*; **his (sexual) ~** seine Potenz, seine Manneskraft

prowl [praʊl] **N** Streifzug *m*; **to be on the ~** (*cat, lion, burglar*) auf Streifzug sein; (*headmaster, boss*) herumschleichen; (*police car*) auf Streife sein; (*inf: for pick-up*) auf Frauen-/Männerjagd sein **VT** durchstreifen **VI** (*also* **prowl about** or **around**) herumstreichen; (*boss, headmaster*) herumschleichen; **he ~ed round the house** er schlich im Haus

prowl car N (*US*) Streifenwagen *m*

prowler [ˈpraʊlə] N Herumtreiber(in) *m(f)*; (= *peeping Tom*) Spanner *m* (*inf*); **he heard a ~ outside** er hörte, wie draußen jemand herumschlich

prox [prɒks] *abbr of* **proximo**

proximate [ˈprɒksɪmɪt] ADJ **a** (= *next*) nächste(r, s), folgende(r, s), sich unmittelbar anschließend, unmittelbar; **~ cause** unmittelbare Ursache **b** (= *close, very near*) nahe liegend **c** (= *forthcoming, imminent*) kurz bevorstehend **d** (= *approximate*) annähernd, ungefähr; **~ estimate** ungefähre Schätzung; **~ analysis** (*Chem*) quantitative Analyse

proximity [prɒkˈsɪmɪtɪ] N Nähe *f*; **in ~ to** in der Nähe (+*gen*); **in close ~ to** in unmittelbarer Nähe (+*gen*); **~ in time** zeitliche Nähe

proximo [ˈprɒksɪməʊ] ADV (*Comm*) (des) nächsten Monats

proxy [ˈprɒksɪ] N (= *power, document*) (Handlungs)vollmacht *f*; (= *person*) Stellvertreter(in) *m(f)*; **by ~** durch einen Stellvertreter; **to be married by ~** ferngetraut werden

proxy vote N stellvertretend abgegebene Stimme

Prozac® [ˈprəʊzæk] N Prozac® *nt*

prude [pruːd] N **to be a ~** prüde sein; **only ~s would object to that** nur prüde Leute würden sich daran stoßen

prudence [ˈpruːdəns] N (*of person*) Umsicht *f*; (*of measure, action, decision*) Klugheit *f*; (*of answer*) Überlegtheit *f*; **simple ~ should have made you stop** der gesunde Menschenverstand hätte Sie davon abbringen müssen

prudent [ˈpruːdənt] ADJ *person* umsichtig; *measure, action, decision* klug; *answer* wohl überlegt; **I thought it ~ to change the subject** ich hielt es für klüger, das Thema zu wechseln; **how ~!** sehr klug or weise!; **that was the ~ thing to do** es war klug, das zu tun

prudential [pruːˈdɛnʃəl] ADJ (*geh*) **a** → **prudent** **b** (= *sensible*) verständig **c** (= *expert, competent*) sachverständig; **~ committee** (*US*) beratender Ausschuss

prudently [ˈpruːdəntlɪ] ADV wohlweislich; *act* umsichtig; *answer* überlegt

prudery ['pruːdərɪ] N Prüderie f

prudish ['pruːdɪʃ] ADJ prüde; *clothes* sittsam, züchtig

prudishly ['pruːdɪʃlɪ] ADV *say, behave* prüde; *dress* sittsam, züchtig; **they ~ cut out all the swearwords** prüde wie sie sind, haben sie alle Kraftausdrücke gestrichen

prudishness ['pruːdɪʃnɪs] N (= *prudish behaviour*) Prüderie f; (= *prudish nature*) prüde Art; (*of clothes*) Sittsamkeit f

prune[1] [pruːn] N Backpflaume f; (*inf*, = *person*) Muffel m (*inf*)

prune[2] VT (*also* **prune down**) beschneiden, stutzen; *hedge* schneiden, zurechtstutzen; (*fig*) *expenditure* kürzen; *workforce* reduzieren; *firm* schrumpfen lassen; *book, essay* zusammenstreichen, kürzen; **to ~ away** ab- *or* wegschneiden; *unnecessary details etc* wegstreichen; **to ~ superfluous matter from an essay** einen Aufsatz straffen

pruners ['pruːnəz] PL Gartenschere f, Rebschere f

pruning ['pruːnɪŋ] N Beschneiden nt, Stutzen nt; (*of hedge*) Schneiden nt, Zurechtstutzen nt; (*fig*) (*of expenditure*) Kürzung f; (*of workforce*) Reduzierung f; (*of firm*) Schrumpfung f; (*of book, essay*) Zusammenstreichen nt, Kürzung f; **the tree needs ~** der Baum muss beschnitten *or* gestutzt werden

pruning: pruning hook N Rebmesser nt; **pruning knife** N Gartenmesser nt, Hippe f; **pruning shears** PL Gartenschere f, Rebschere f

prurience ['proərɪəns] N Anzüglichkeit f; (*of person*) Lüsternheit f

prurient ['proərɪənt] ADJ anzüglich; *person* lüstern

Prussia ['prʌʃə] N Preußen nt

Prussian ['prʌʃən] ADJ preußisch; ~ **blue** preußischblau N a Preuße m, Preußin f b (*Ling*) Preußisch nt; **Old** ~ Altpreußisch nt

prussic acid ['prʌsɪkˈæsɪd] N Blausäure f

pry[1] [praɪ] VI neugierig sein; (*in drawers etc*) (herum)schnüffeln (in in +*dat*); **I don't mean to ~, but ...** es geht mich ja nichts an, aber ...; **to ~ into sb's affairs** seine Nase in jds Angelegenheiten (*acc*) stecken; **to ~ into sb's secrets** jds Geheimnisse ausspionieren wollen; **to ~ around** herumschnüffeln

pry[2] VT (*US*) = **prise**

prying ['praɪɪŋ] ADJ neugierig

PS abbr of **postscript** PS

psalm [sɑːm] N Psalm m; (**the Book of**) **Psalms** der Psalter; ~ **book** Psalmenbuch nt

psalmist ['sɑːmɪst] N Psalmist m

psalmody ['sælmədɪ] N Psalmodie f

psalter ['sɔːltə] N Psalter m

psaltery ['sɔːltərɪ] N Psalterium nt

PSAT N (*US: Sch, Univ*) abbr of **Preliminary Scholastic Aptitude Test** Eignungstest *vor Aufnahme in eine Universität* → also **SAT**

PSBR (*Brit*) abbr of **public sector borrowing requirement**

psephological [sefə'lɒdʒɪkəl] ADJ Wahlforschungs-; ~ **study** Wahlforschungsstudie f

psephologist [se'fɒlədʒɪst] N Wahlforscher(in) m(f), Psephologe m, Psephologin f

psephology [se'fɒlədʒɪ] N Wahlforschung f

pseud [sjuːd] (*Brit inf*) N Möchtegern m (*inf*); **you ~!** du Angeber(in)! ADJ *book, film* auf intellektuell gemacht (*inf*), gewollt; *views, ideas* hochgestochen; *décor, pub etc* auf schick gemacht (*inf*); *person* affektiert, pseudointellektuell

pseudo ['sjuːdəʊ] (*inf*) ADJ a = **pseud** ADJ b (= *pretended*) unecht; *affection, simplicity* aufgesetzt; ~ **revolutionary/intellectual** Pseudorevolutionär(in) m(f)/-intellektuelle(r) mf N = **pseud** N

pseudo- PREF Pseudo-, pseudo; ~**scientific** pseudowissenschaftlich

pseudonym ['sjuːdənɪm] N Pseudonym nt

pseudopregnancy [ˌsjuːdəʊˈpregnənsɪ] N (*Med*) Scheinschwangerschaft f

pseudy ['sjuːdɪ] ADJ (+*er*) (*inf*) = **pseud** ADJ

pshaw [pʃɔː] INTERJ (*dated*) pah

psi [psaɪ] N , *no pl* a (= *letter*) Psi nt b (= *psychic phenomena*) Psi nt

psittacosis [ˌpsɪtə'kəʊsɪs] N Papageienkrankheit f, Psittakose f (*spec*)

psoriasis [sɒ'raɪəsɪs] N Schuppenflechte f, Psoriasis f (*spec*)

PST (*US*) abbr of **Pacific Standard Time** pazifische Zeit

Psyche ['saɪkɪ] N (*Myth*) Psyche f

psych [saɪk] VT (*inf*) a (*psychoanalyst*) analysieren b (= *understand, get taped*) **to ~ sb (out)**, **to get sb ~ed (out)** jdn durchschauen

▸**psych out** VT sep (*inf*) psychologisch fertig machen VI (= *freak out*) ausflippen (*inf*)

▸**psych up** VT sep (*inf*) hochputschen (*inf*); **to psych oneself up, to get oneself psyched up** sich hochputschen (*inf*); **he was all psyched up for the match** er hatte sich für das Spiel so richtig hochgeputscht (*inf*)

psyche ['saɪkɪ] N Psyche f

psychedelic [ˌsaɪkɪ'delɪk] ADJ psychedelisch; *drugs also* bewusstseinserweiternd

psychiatric [ˌsaɪkɪ'ætrɪk] ADJ psychiatrisch; *illness, problem* psychisch; ~ **hospital** psychiatrische Klinik; ~ **nurse** Psychiatrieschwester f, psychiatrisch ausgebildete Krankenschwester; ~ **unit** psychiatrische Abteilung; ~ **ward** Psychiatrie f

psychiatrist [saɪ'kaɪətrɪst] N Psychiater(in) m(f)

psychiatry [saɪ'kaɪətrɪ] N Psychiatrie f

psychic ['saɪkɪk] ADJ a übersinnlich; *powers* übernatürlich; ~ **research** Parapsychologie f; **she is ~** sie besitzt übernatürliche Kräfte *or* übersinnliche Wahrnehmung; **you must be ~!** Sie müssen hellsehen können! b (*Psych:* = *mental*) psychisch N Mensch m mit übernatürlichen Kräften *or* übersinnlicher Wahrnehmung

psychical ['saɪkɪkəl] ADJ → **psychic** ADJ

psycho ['saɪkəʊ] N (*inf*) Verrückte(r) mf

psychoanalyse, (*US*) **psychoanalyze** [ˌsaɪkəʊ'ænəlaɪz] VT psychoanalytisch behandeln, psychoanalysieren

psychoanalysis [ˌsaɪkəʊə'nælɪsɪs] N Psychoanalyse f

psychoanalyst [ˌsaɪkəʊ'ænəlɪst] N Psychoanalytiker(in) m(f)

psychoanalytic [ˌsaɪkəʊænə'lɪtɪk] ADJ psychoanalytisch

psychobabble ['saɪkəʊˌbæbl] N (*inf*) Psychogeschwätz nt

psychodynamic [ˌsaɪkəʊdaɪ'næmɪk] ADJ psychodynamisch N **psychodynamics** sing Psychodynamik f

psychogenic [ˌsaɪkəʊ'dʒenɪk] ADJ *disease, complaint* psychogen, seelisch bedingt

psychokinesis [ˌsaɪkəʊkaɪ'niːsɪs] N , *no pl* (*Parapsychology*) Psychokinese f

psycholinguistic [ˌsaɪkəʊlɪŋ'gwɪstɪk] ADJ psycholinguistisch

psycholinguistics [ˌsaɪkəʊlɪŋ'gwɪstɪks] N sing Psycholinguistik f

psychological [ˌsaɪkə'lɒdʒɪkəl] ADJ (= *mental*) psychisch; (= *concerning psychology*) psychologisch; **the ~ moment** der psychologisch günstige Augenblick; ~ **terror** Psychoterror m; **he's not really ill, it's all ~** er ist nicht wirklich krank, das ist alles psychisch bedingt

psychologically [ˌsaɪkə'lɒdʒɪklɪ] ADV (= *mentally*) psychisch; (= *concerning psychology*) psychologisch; **he is ~ very unstable** er ist psychisch sehr unausgeglichen; ~ **speaking** psychologisch ausgedrückt; **to be ~ prepared for sth** psychisch auf etw vorbereitet sein

psychological: psychological make-up N Psyche f; **psychological profile** N psychologisches Profil; **psychological profiling** N Ausfertigung f eines psychologischen Profils; **psychological thriller** N (*Film, Liter*) psychologischer Thriller, Psychothriller m; **psychological warfare** N psychologische Kriegführung

psychologist [saɪ'kɒlədʒɪst] N Psychologe m, Psychologin f

psychology [saɪ'kɒlədʒɪ] N (= *science*) Psychologie f; (= *make-up*) Psyche f; **it's all a matter of ~** (*inf*) das ist alles eine Frage der Psychologie

psychometrics [ˌsaɪkəʊ'metrɪks] N sing, **psychometry** [saɪ'kɒmɪtrɪ] N Psychometrie f

psychopath ['saɪkəʊpæθ] N Psychopath(in) m(f)

psychopathic [ˌsaɪkəʊ'pæθɪk] ADJ psychopathisch

psychopathy [saɪ'kɒpəθɪ] N (= *Med*) Psychopathie f, Geisteskrankheit f/-störung f

psychosexual [ˌsaɪkəʊ'seksjʊəl] ADJ psychosexuell

psychosis [saɪ'kəʊsɪs] N pl **psychoses** [saɪ'kəʊsiːz] Psychose f

psychosocial [ˌsaɪkəʊ'səʊʃəl] ADJ psychosozial

psychosociological [ˌsaɪkəʊˌsəʊsɪə'lɒdʒɪkəl] ADJ psychosoziologisch

psychosomatic [ˌsaɪkəʊsə'mætɪk] ADJ psychosomatisch; ~ **medicine** Psychosomatik f, psychosomatische Medizin

psychotherapeutic ADJ , **psychotherapeutically** ADV ['saɪkəʊˌθerə'pjuːtɪk, -klɪ] psychotherapeutisch

psychotherapist [ˌsaɪkəʊ'θerəpɪst] N Psychotherapeut(in) m(f)

psychotherapy [ˌsaɪkəʊ'θerəpɪ] N Psychotherapie f

psychotic [saɪ'kɒtɪk] ADJ psychotisch; ~ **illness** Psychose f N Psychotiker(in) m(f)

psychotropic [ˌsaɪkəʊ'trɒpɪk] ADJ *drug* psychotrop

PT (*old*) abbr of **physical training**

pt abbr of **part** of **pint** of **payment** of **point**

PTA abbr of **parent-teacher association** Lehrer-Eltern-Ausschuss m

ptarmigan ['tɑːmɪgən] N Schneehuhn nt

Pte (*Mil*) abbr of **Private**

pterodactyl [ˌterəʊ'dæktɪl] N Pterodaktylus m

pto abbr of **please turn over** bitte wenden, b.w.

Ptolemaic [ˌtɒlə'meɪɪk] ADJ ptolemäisch; ~ **system** ptolemäisches Weltbild *or* (Welt)system

Ptolemy ['tɒləmɪ] N (*astronomer*) Ptolemäus m; (*king*) Ptolemaios m; (*dynasty*) Ptolemäer pl

ptomaine ['təʊmeɪn] N Leichengift nt, Ptomain nt (*spec*)

ptomaine poisoning N Leichenvergiftung f

pub [pʌb] N (*esp Brit*) Kneipe f (*inf*), Wirtschaft f, Lokal nt; (*in the country*) Gasthaus nt, Wirtshaus nt; **let's go to the ~** komm, wir gehen einen trinken *or* wir gehen in die Kneipe (*inf*); ~ **grub/lunch** in Trinkgaststätten servierter Imbiss

---

PUB

Ein **pub** (Kurzform von **public house**) ist ein Lokal, in dem Wein, Bier, Spirituosen und alkoholfreie Getränke an alle Personen über 18 ausgeschenkt werden. In den Pubs kann man aber nicht nur trinken, sondern sie spielen auch eine bedeutsame Rolle im britischen Gesellschaftsleben. Spiele wie Poolbillard, Darts oder Domino stehen oft zur freien Verfügung. In vielen Pubs werden - allerdings meist nur mittags - Mahlzeiten angeboten, und einige verfügen über eigene Räumlichkeiten oder Biergärten für Familien mit Kindern. Normalerweise sind Pubs von 11 bis 23 Uhr geöffnet, in Schottland können die Zeiten flexibler gehandhabt werden.

Einige Pubs sind im Besitz großer Brauereigesellschaften und verkaufen nur eigene Produkte; andere, die sogenannten **free houses**, sind in Privatbesitz und bieten eine große Palette verschiedener Biere an → **BEER**

pub. *abbr of* **published** herausgegeben, erschienen

pub-crawl ['pʌbkrɔːl] N (*esp Brit, inf*) Kneipenbummel *m* (*inf*); **to go on a ~** einen Kneipenbummel machen (*inf*), einen Zug durch die Gemeinde machen (*hum inf*)

puberty ['pjuːbətɪ] N die Pubertät; **to reach the age of ~** ins Pubertätsalter *or* in die Pubertät kommen

pubes ['pjuːbiːz] *pl of* **pubis**

pubescence [pjuː'besəns] N die Pubertät

pubescent [pjuː'besənt] ADJ pubertierend

pubic ['pjuːbɪk] ADJ Scham–; **~ hair** Schamhaar *nt*

pubis ['pjuːbɪs] *n pl* **pubes** Schambein *nt*

public ['pʌblɪk] **ADJ** *support, pressure, subsidy* öffentlich; *official* öffentlich, staatlich; **to be ~ knowledge** allgemein bekannt sein; **to become ~** publik werden; **at ~ expense** aus öffentlichen Mitteln; **~ pressure** Druck *m* der Öffentlichkeit; **it's rather ~ here** es ist nicht gerade privat hier; **he is a ~ figure** *or* **person** er ist eine Persönlichkeit des öffentlichen Lebens; **in the ~ eye** im Blickpunkt der Öffentlichkeit; **to make sth ~** etw bekannt geben, etw publik machen; (*officially*) etw öffentlich bekannt machen; **in the ~ interest** im öffentlichen Interesse; **to create ~ awareness** öffentliches Interesse wecken; **to go ~** (*Comm*) in eine Aktiengesellschaft umgewandelt werden

N *sing or pl* Öffentlichkeit *f*; **in ~** in der Öffentlichkeit; *speak also, agree, admit* öffentlich; **our/ their** *etc* ~ unser/ihr *etc* Publikum; **the (general) ~** die (breite) Öffentlichkeit; **a member of the ~** ein Vertreter/eine Vertreterin der Öffentlichkeit; **the viewing ~** das Fernsehpublikum, die Zuschauer *pl*; **the reading/sporting ~** die lesende/sportinteressierte Öffentlichkeit; **the racing ~** die Freunde *pl* des Rennsports; **the great American/British ~** (*iro*) die breite amerikanische/britische Öffentlichkeit

public access channel N öffentlicher Fernsehkanal

PUBLIC ACCESS TELEVISION

Public access television in den USA besteht aus einer Reihe nichtkommerzieller Kabelkanäle, die Programmen von Wohlfahrtsverbänden und anderen gemeinnützigen Vereinen der ortsansässigen Bevölkerung vorbehalten sind. Dazu gehören auch Sendungen von Schulen, Freizeit-Entertainern oder sogar rassistischen Gruppierungen. **Public access television** wurde geschaffen, um lokalen Interessen ein Forum zu bieten und um die Vorherrschaft einiger weniger Lizenzinhaber zu vermeiden. Durch den **Cable Act** von 1984 können die Besitzer von Kabelkanälen durch die Kommunen verpflichtet werden, einen öffentlichen Kabelkanal mit Studio, technischer Ausrüstung und dazugehörigem Personal einzurichten.

---

public: Public Accounts Committee N (*Brit*) Haushaltsausschuss *m*; **public address system** N Lautsprecheranlage *f*

publican ['pʌblɪkən] N **a** (*Brit*) Gastwirt(in) *m(f)* **b** (*Hist: = tax collector*) Zöllner *m*

public: public analyst N Analytiker(in) *m(f)* in der Öffentlichkeitsarbeit; **public assistance** N (*US*) staatliche Fürsorge

publication [ˌpʌblɪ'keɪʃən] N Veröffentlichung *f*, Publikation *f* (*geh*); **when's ~?** wann erscheint das Buch?

publication date N Erscheinungsdatum *nt*, Datum *nt* der Veröffentlichung

public: public bar N (*Brit*) ≈ Ausschank *m*, Schänke *f*, Schenke *f*; **public building** N öffentliches Gebäude; **public company** N Aktiengesellschaft *f*; **public convenience** N (*Brit*) öffentliche Toilette; **public debt** N (*esp US*) Verschuldung *f* der öffentlichen Hand; (= *national debt*) Staatsverschuldung *f*; **public**

---

defender N (*US*) Pflichtverteidiger(in) *m(f)*;

public domain N **a** (= *land*) Domäne *f* **b** (= *unpatented status*) **this book/invention will soon become ~** das Copyright für dieses Buch/das Patent für diese Erfindung läuft bald ab; **to be in the ~** (= *not private property*) allgemein zugänglich sein; (= *generally known*) allgemein bekannt sein; **public enemy** N Staatsfeind(in) *m(f)*; **he is ~ number one** er ist Staatsfeind Nr. 1; **public enterprise** N öffentliches Unternehmentum; **public examination** N öffentliche Prüfung, der Öffentlichkeit zugängliche Prüfung; **public gallery** N (*in parliament, courtroom*) Besuchertribüne *f*, Besucherplätze *pl*; **public health** N (= *health of the public*) die allgemeine *or* öffentliche Gesundheit, die Volksgesundheit; (= *health care*) das (öffentliche) Gesundheitswesen; **a danger to ~** eine Gefahr für die Volksgesundheit; **public health service** N staatliche Gesundheitsfürsorge; **public holiday** N gesetzlicher Feiertag; **public house** N (*Brit, form*) Gaststätte *f*; **public housing** N (*US*) Sozialwohnungen *pl*; **public housing project** N (*US*) sozialer Wohnungsbau; **public inquiry** N öffentliche Untersuchung

publicist ['pʌblɪsɪst] N Publizist(in) *m(f)*

publicity [pʌb'lɪsɪtɪ] N **a** Publicity *f* **b** (*Comm, = advertising, advertisements*) Werbung *f*, Reklame *f*; **we must generate more ~ for this product** wir müssen mehr Werbung für dieses Produkt treiben

publicity: publicity agency N Publicity-Agentur *f*; (*Comm*) Werbeagentur *f*; **publicity agent** N Publicitymanager(in) *m(f)*; **publicity campaign** N Publicitykampagne *f*; (*Comm*) Werbekampagne *f*; **publicity department** N Publicity-Abteilung *f*; (*Comm*) Werbeabteilung *f*; **publicity film** N Publicity-Film *m*; (*Comm*) Werbefilm *m*; **publicity gimmick** N Publicity-Gag *m* (*inf*); (*Comm*) Werbegag *m* (*inf*); **publicity material** N Publicitymaterial *nt*; (*Comm*) Werbematerial *nt*; **publicity-shy** ADJ öffentlichkeitsscheu; **publicity stunt** N Werbegag *m*

publicize ['pʌblɪsaɪz] VT **a** (= *make public*) bekannt machen, an die Öffentlichkeit bringen; **I don't want this ~d** ich möchte nicht, dass das publik wird; **I don't ~ the fact** ich will das nicht an die große Glocke hängen (*inf*) **b** (= *get publicity for*) *film, author, product* Werbung *or* Reklame *or* Publicity machen für; **it has been well ~d** es hat viel Publicity bekommen, dafür ist viel Werbung *or* Reklame gemacht worden

public: public law N öffentliches Recht; **Public Lending Right** N Verleihrecht *nt*, Anspruch *m* auf Leihbücherei-Tantiemen; **public life** N öffentliches Leben

publicly ['pʌblɪklɪ] ADV öffentlich; **~ funded** durch öffentliche Mittel finanziert; **~ accountable** der Öffentlichkeit verantwortlich; **this factory is ~ owned** diese Fabrik ist gesellschaftliches Eigentum; **~ quoted company** ≈ Aktiengesellschaft *f*

public: public money N öffentliche Gelder *pl*; **public nuisance** N öffentliches Ärgernis; **to cause a ~** öffentliches Ärgernis erregen; **public opinion** N die öffentliche Meinung; **public opinion poll** N Meinungsumfrage *f*; **public ownership** N staatlicher Besitz; **under** *or* **in ~** in staatlichem Besitz; **to take sth (back) into ~** etw (wieder) verstaatlichen, etw (wieder) in Staatsbesitz überführen; **public property** N **a** (= *land etc*) öffentliches Eigentum, Gemeineigentum *nt* **b** (*fig*) **to be ~** (= *person*) im Rampenlicht der Öffentlichkeit stehen; (*private life*) Allgemeingut sein; **intimate aspects of her personal life had been made ~** intime Aspekte ihres Privatlebens waren allgemein bekannt geworden; **public prosecutor** N Staatsanwalt *m*/-anwältin *f*; **public prosecutor's office** N Staatsanwaltschaft *f*; **public purse** N Staatskasse *f*, Staatssäckel *m* (*inf*); **Public Record(s) Office** N (*Brit*) Nationalarchiv *nt*, ≈ Bundeszentralarchiv *nt* (*Ger*); **public relations** N *pl or sing* Publicrelations *pl*, Public Re-

---

lations *pl*, Öffentlichkeitsarbeit *f*; **public relations officer** N Öffentlichkeitsarbeiter(in) *m(f)*; **public room** N Gemeinschaftsraum *m*, öffentlich *or* allgemein zugänglicher Raum; **public school** N (*Brit*) Privatschule *f*, Public School *f*; (*US*) staatliche Schule; **public schoolboy** N (*Brit*) Schüler *m* einer Privatschule; **public schoolgirl** N (*Brit*) Schülerin *f* einer Privatschule; **public sector** N öffentlicher Sektor **ADJ** *attr* des öffentlichen Sektors; **~ borrowing** Anleihe *f* des öffentlichen Sektors, staatliche Kreditaufnahme; **~ borrowing requirement** Kreditbedarf *m* der öffentlichen Hand; **public servant** N Arbeitnehmer(in) *m(f)* im öffentlichen Dienst; **public service** N (*Civil Service*) öffentlicher Dienst; (*facility: = water, transport etc*) öffentlicher Dienstleistungsbetrieb; (= *benefit*) Dienst *m* an der Allgemeinheit; **public service broadcasting** N (*Rad*) ≈ öffentlich-rechtlicher Rundfunk; (*TV*) ≈ öffentlich-rechtliches Fernsehen; **public-service television** N ≈ öffentlich-rechtliches Fernsehen; **public service vehicle** N Redner(in) *m(f)*; **public speaker** N Redner(in) *m(f)*; **public speaking** N Redenhalten *nt*; **a course in ~** ein Rednerlehrgang *m*; **I'm no good at ~** ich kann nicht in der Öffentlichkeit reden; **public spending** N Ausgaben *pl* der öffentlichen Hand; **public spirit** N Gemeinsinn *m*; **public-spirited** ADJ *act, attitude* gemeinsinnig (*geh*), von Gemeinschaftssinn zeugend *attr*; **it's not very ~ of them to …** es spricht nicht gerade für ihren Gemeinschaftssinn, dass sie …; **public television** N (*US*) öffentliches Fernsehen; **public transport** N öffentlicher Nahverkehr, öffentliche Verkehrsmittel *pl*; **by ~** mit öffentlichen Verkehrsmitteln; **public utility** N öffentlicher Versorgungsbetrieb; **public works** PL staatliche Bauvorhaben *pl*

publish ['pʌblɪʃ] **VT** **a** (= *issue*) veröffentlichen; *book, magazine etc* veröffentlichen, herausbringen; **~ed by Collins** bei Collins erschienen; **"published monthly"** „erscheint monatlich"; **"just ~ed"** „neu erschienen"; **"to be ~ed shortly"** „erscheint in Kürze"; **who ~es that book?** in welchem Verlag ist das Buch erschienen?; **they ~ novels** sie verlegen Romane **b** (= *make public*) *news, banns* veröffentlichen, bekannt geben; *decree* herausgeben; *will* eröffnen; **to ~ sth abroad** (*fig*) etw überall herumerzählen

VI **when are we going to ~?** (*book*) wann bringen wir das Buch heraus?; (*research*) wann veröffentlichen *or* publizieren wir die Arbeit?; **he used to ~ with Collins** er hat seine Bücher früher bei Collins herausgebracht *or* veröffentlicht

publisher ['pʌblɪʃə] N (= *person*) Verleger(in) *m(f)*; (= *firm: also* **publishers**) Verlag *m*; **who are your ~s?** wer ist Ihr Verleger?

publishing ['pʌblɪʃɪŋ] N (= *trade*) das Verlagswesen; **~ company** *or* **house** Verlagshaus *nt*; **the decline of children's book ~** der Rückgang bei den Kinderbüchern

publishing business N (= *trade*) Verlagsgeschäft *nt*, Verlagsbuchhandel *m*; (= *company*) Verlagshaus *nt*, Verlag *m*

puce [pjuːs] **N** Braunrot *nt* **ADJ** braunrot; (*fig: with rage, shame*) rot

puck¹ [pʌk] N (= *goblin*) Kobold *m*, Puck *m*

puck² N (*Sport*) Puck *m*

pucker ['pʌkə] **N** (*in cloth*) Fältchen *nt* **VT** (*also* **pucker up**) *one's lips, mouth* verziehen; (*for kissing*) spitzen; *one's brow* runzeln; *material* Falten machen in (+*acc*) **VI** (*also* **pucker up**) (*lips*) sich verziehen; (*to be kissed*) sich spitzen; (*brow*) sich runzeln; (*material*) Falten werfen

puckered ['pʌkəd] ADJ *lips* gespitzt, geschürzt; *brow* gefurcht; *skin* zusammengezogen, höckerig; *scar* hervortretend; *seam* wellig, gewellt

puckish ADJ , **puckishly** ADV ['pʌkɪʃ, -lɪ] schelmisch, koboldhaft

pud [pʊd] N (*Brit inf*) = **pudding**

pudding ['pʊdɪŋ] N (*Brit*) **a** (= *dessert*) Nachspeise *f*; (= *crème caramel, instant whip etc*) Pudding *m*; **what's for ~?** was gibt es als Nachspeise *or* Nachtisch? **b** (*savoury*: = *meat in suet*) ≈ (Fleisch)pastete *f*; **black ~** ≈ Blutwurst *f*; **white ~** ≈ Presssack *m* **c** (*inf*) (= *idiot*) Knallkopp *m* (*inf*); (= *fatty*) Dickerchen *nt*

pudding: pudding basin N Puddingform *f*; **pudding-basin haircut** N Topfschnitt *m* (*inf*); **pudding club** N **to be in the ~** (*inf*) einen dicken Bauch haben (*inf*); **pudding-face** N (*inf*) Vollmondgesicht *nt* (*inf*); **pudding--head** N (*inf*) Knallkopp *m* (*inf*); **pudding stone** N Puddingstein *m*

puddle ['pʌdl] N Pfütze *f* (*also euph*)

pudendum [pjuː'dendəm] N *pl* **pudenda** [pjuː-'dendə] **a** (*of woman*) Vulva *f* **b** **pudenda** PL (*of either sex*) primäre Geschlechtsmerkmale *pl*, Scham *f* (*geh*)

pudgy ['pʌdʒɪ] ADJ (+*er*) = **podgy**

pueblo ['pwebləʊ] N **a** (= *Indian settlement*) Pueblo *m* **b** (= *town in Spanish-speaking America*) (Klein)stadt *f*

puerile ['pjʊəraɪl] ADJ infantil

puerility [pjʊə'rɪlɪtɪ] N Infantilität *f*

puerperal fever [pjuː'ɜːpərəl'fiːvə'] N Kindbettfieber *nt*, Puerperalfieber *nt* (*spec*)

Puerto Rican ['pwɜːtəʊ'riːkən] ADJ puertoricanisch N (= *person*) Puertoricaner(in) *m(f)*

Puerto Rico ['pwɜːtəʊ'riːkəʊ] N Puerto Rico *nt*

puff [pʌf] N **a** (*of breathing, of engine*) Schnaufen *nt no pl*; (*of horse*) Schnauben *nt no pl*; (*inf*: = *breath*) Puste *f* (*inf*); (*on cigarette etc*) Zug *m* (*at*, of an +*dat*); **a ~ of air/wind** ein Luft-/Windstoß *m*; **a ~ of smoke** eine Rauchwolke; **our hopes vanished in a ~ of smoke** unsere Hoffnungen lösten sich in nichts auf; **he blew out the candles with** *or* **in one ~** er blies die Kerzen auf einmal aus; **to be out of ~** (*Brit inf*) außer Puste sein (*inf*) **b** (= *powder puff*) Quaste *f* **c** (*Cook*) **cream ~** Windbeutel *m*; **jam ~** Blätterteigteilchen *nt* mit Marmelade **VT** **a** *smoke* ausstoßen; *cigarette, cigar* paffen (*inf*); **to ~ sth away** etw wegblasen; **stop ~ing smoke in my face** blas mir nicht dauernd den Rauch ins Gesicht **b** (*Sew*) bauschen; **~ed sleeves** Puffärmel *pl* **c** (*Cook*) **to ~ rice** Puffreis *m* herstellen **VI** (*person, train*) schnaufen; (*horse*) schnauben; (*wind*) blasen; (*chimney, smoke*) qualmen; **he was ~ing and panting** er pustete und schnaufte; **the train ~ed into the station** der Zug fuhr schnaufend in den Bahnhof ein; **to ~ (away) at** *or* **on a cigar** an einer Zigarre paffen

▶ **puff out** VT *sep* **a** (= *expand*) *chest* herausstrecken, herausdrücken; *cheeks* aufblasen; *feathers* (auf)plustern; *sail* blähen **b** (= *emit*) *air, smoke* ausstoßen; *words* hervorstoßen **c** (= *blow out*) auspusten **d** (*inf*) *always separate* (= *make out of breath*) außer Puste bringen (*inf*)

▶ **puff up** VT *sep* **a** *feathers* (auf)plustern; (= *blow up*) aufblasen **b** (*fig*) **to be puffed up** aufgeblasen sein; **to be puffed up with pride** ganz aufgeblasen sein; **to puff oneself up** sich aufblasen **VI** **a** (= *swell: eyes, face etc*) anschwellen **b** **he came puffing up (to me)** er kam angeschnauft

puff: puff adder N Puffotter *f*; **puffball** ['pʌfbɔːl] N (*Bot*) Bovist *m*

puffed [pʌft] ADJ (*inf*) außer Puste (*inf*)

puffed-up ['pʌft'ʌp] ADJ *face* aufgedunsen

puffer ['pʌfə'] N (*baby-talk*: = *train*) Puffpuff *f* (*baby-talk*)

puffin ['pʌfɪn] N Papageientaucher *m*, Lund *m*

puffin crossing N (*Brit*: *for pedestrians*) sensorgesteuerter Ampelübergang

puffiness ['pʌfɪnɪs] N Verschwollenheit *f*

puff: puff pastry, (*US*) **puff paste** N Blätterteig *m*; **puff-puff** N (*baby-talk*: = *train*) Puffpuff *f* (*baby-talk*); (= *sound*) Puffpuff *nt*; **puff sleeve** N Puffärmel *m*

puffy ['pʌfɪ] ADJ (+*er*) **a** (= *swollen*) geschwollen; *face, eyes also* verschwollen; (*from crying*) ver-

---

quollen **b** (= *voluminous*) *cloud* bauschig; **~ sleeve** Puffärmel *m*

pug [pʌg] N (*also* **pug dog**) Mops *m*

pugilism ['pjuːdʒɪlɪzəm] N (*form*) Faustkampf *m*

pugilist ['pjuːdʒɪlɪst] N (*form*) Faustkämpfer(in) *m(f)*

pugnacious [pʌg'neɪʃəs] ADJ kampfeslustig; (*verbally*) streitsüchtig; *expression, remark* herausfordernd; *support, defence* hartnäckig; *campaign* aggressiv

pugnaciously [pʌg'neɪʃəslɪ] ADV *behave* kampf(es)lustig; (*verbally*) streitsüchtig; *say, remark* herausfordernd; *support, defend* hartnäckig

pugnacity [pʌg'næsɪtɪ] N Kampfeslust *f*; (*verbal*) Streitsüchtigkeit *f*; (*of expression, remark*) Herausforderung *f* (*of in* +*dat*); (*of support, defence*) Hartnäckigkeit *f*; (*of campaign*) Aggressivität *f*; **the ~ of his approach** die Aggressivität seiner Vorgehensweise

pug: pug nose N Knollennase *f*; **pug-nosed** ADJ knollennasig

puke [pjuːk] (*sl*) **VI** kotzen (*inf*), spucken (*inf*); **to ~ all over sth** (*inf*) etw voll kotzen (*sl*); **he makes me ~** er kotzt mich an (*sl*) **VT** kotzen (*inf*), spucken (*inf*) N Kotze *f* (*vulg*)

▶ **puke up** VI (*inf*) kotzen (*sl*), spucken (*inf*)

pukey ['pjuːkɪ] ADJ (*inf*) *colour* kackig (*sl*), eklig (*inf*)

pukka, pucka ['pʌkə] ADJ (*inf*) (= *genuine*) echt; (= *proper*) anständig (*inf*); (= *excellent*) eins a (*inf*), erstklassig (*inf*); (= *posh, upper-class*) vornehm; **~ sahib** Gentleman *m*

pulchritude ['pʌlkrɪtjuːd] N (*liter*) Schönheit *f*

PULITZER PRIZES

Die Pulitzer-Preise sind die renommiertesten Auszeichnungen, die seit 1917 jedes Jahr in den USA für herausragende Leistungen in Journalismus, Literatur, Drama und Musikkomposition vergeben werden. In den vierzehn Kategorien im Bereich Journalismus werden Preise z. B. für Reportagen oder Kritiken vergeben. Im Bereich Literatur gibt es sechs Kategorien, darunter Belletristik, Lyrik und Drama. Die Auszeichnungen sind nach dem amerikanischen Pressemagnaten Joseph Pulitzer (1847 - 1911) benannt, der das Preisgeld in seinem Testament stiftete.

---

pull [pʊl] N **a** (= *tug*) Ziehen *nt*; (*short*) Ruck *m*; (*lit, fig*: = *attraction*) Anziehungskraft *f*; (*of current*) Sog *m*; **he gave her/the rope a ~** er zog sie/am Seil; **I felt a ~ at my sleeve** ich spürte, wie mich jemand am Ärmel zog; **the ~ of family ties brought him home again** familiäre Bande zogen ihn wieder nach Hause; **to be on the ~** (*Brit inf*) auf Mädchen/Männer aus sein **b** (= *uphill journey*) Anstieg *m* **c** (*inf*: = *influence*) Beziehungen *pl* (*with zu*); **she has some ~ with the manager** sie kann beim Chef was erreichen (*inf*); **he has ~ in the right places** er hat an den richtigen Stellen seine Leute sitzen **d** (*at pipe, beer*) Zug *m*; **he took a ~ at his cigar** er zog an seiner Zigarre; **he took a ~ at his glass** er nahm einen Schluck aus seinem Glas **e** (*Typ*: = *proof*) Abzug *m* **VT** **a** (= *draw, drag*) ziehen; **he ~ed the dog behind him** er zog den Hund hinter sich (*dat*) her; **to ~ a door shut** eine Tür zuziehen; **he ~ed her toward(s) him** er zog sie an sich (*acc*) **b** (= *tug*) *handle, rope, bell* ziehen an (+*dat*); *boat* rudern; **he ~ed her hair** er zog sie an den Haaren; **to ~ sth to pieces** (*lit*) etw zerreißen, etw in Stücke reißen; (*fig*: = *criticize*) etw verreißen; **to ~ sb's leg** (*fig inf*) jdn auf den Arm nehmen (*inf*); **the other one(, it's got bells on)** (*Brit inf*) das glaubst du ja selber nicht!, das kannst du deiner Großmutter erzählen! (*inf*); **she was the one ~ing the strings** sie war es, die alle Fäden in der Hand hielt; **to ~ rank (on sb)** (*jdm gegenüber*) den Vorgesetzten herauskehren; **to ~ one's punches** (*Boxing*) verhalten schlagen; (*fig*) sich zurückhalten; **when it came**

---

to criticizing other people he didn't ~ his *or* **any punches** wenn es darum ging, andere zu kritisieren, zog er ganz schön vom Leder (*inf*) **c** (= *extract, draw out*) *tooth, cork* (heraus)ziehen; *gun, knife* ziehen; *weeds, lettuce* ausreißen; *beer* zapfen; (*Cook*) *chicken* ausnehmen; **to ~ a gun on sb** jdn mit der Pistole bedrohen **d** (= *strain*) *muscle* sich (*dat*) zerren; (= *tear*) *thread, ziehen* **e** (= *attract*) *crowd* anziehen; (*Brit inf: sexually*) rumkriegen (*inf*); **a sports car always ~s the girls** (*inf*) mit einem Sportwagen kommt man leichter an die Mädchen ran (*inf*) **f** (*inf*: = *carry out, do*) *deal* durchziehen (*inf*); (*criminal*) *job* drehen (*inf*); **what are you trying to ~?** (*inf*) was heckst du wieder aus? (*inf*); **to ~ a stunt** Geschichten machen **g** (= *cancel*) *TV programme, concert etc* absagen **h** (*Typ*) **to ~ a proof** einen Abzug machen **i** (*Golf, Cricket, Baseball*) verziehen, *auf die der Schlaghand entgegengesetzte Seite schlagen* **VI** **a** (= *draw*) ziehen (*on, at* an +*dat*); **to ~ to the left/right** (*car, brakes*) nach links/rechts ziehen; **the car/engine isn't ~ing very well** der Wagen/Motor zieht nicht richtig; **to ~ on one's cigarette** an seiner Zigarette ziehen; **to ~ for sb/sth** (*US, inf*) jdn/etw unterstützen **b** (= *move*: *train, car etc*) fahren; **the car ~ed into the driveway** der Wagen fuhr in die Einfahrt; **he ~ed across to the left-hand lane** er wechselte auf die linke Spur über; **he ~ed into the next lay-by** er fuhr auf den nächsten Halteplatz; **he ~ed into the kerb/the side of the road** er fuhr an den Bordstein heran/an den Straßenrand; **to ~ alongside** seitlich heranfahren; (*Naut*) längsseits kommen; **to ~ off the road** am Straßenrand anhalten; **the oarsmen ~ed for** *or* **toward(s) the shore** die Ruderer hielten auf das Ufer zu **c** (*Brit inf: sexually*) jemanden rumkriegen (*inf*)

▶ **pull about** (*Brit*) *or* **around** VT *sep* (= *handle roughly*) *toy etc* herumzerren; *person* herumzerren an (+*dat*)

▶ **pull ahead** VI (*in race, poll, contest*) Vorsprung gewinnen; **to pull ahead of sb/sth** (*in race etc*) einen Vorsprung vor jdm/etw gewinnen; (*in poll, contest*) jdm/einer Sache (*dat*) davonziehen

▶ **pull apart** VT *sep* **a** (= *separate*) auseinander ziehen; *sheets of paper, fighting people* trennen; *radio etc* auseinander nehmen **b** (*fig inf*) (= *search thoroughly*) auseinander nehmen (*inf*); (= *criticize*) verreißen **VI** (*through design*) sich auseinander nehmen lassen; (= *break*) auseinander gehen

▶ **pull away** VT *sep* wegziehen; **she pulled it away from him** sie zog es von ihm weg; (*from his hands*) sie zog es ihm aus den Händen **VI** (= *move off*) wegfahren; (*ship*) ablegen; **the car/runner pulled away from the others** der Wagen/ Läufer setzte sich (von den anderen) ab

▶ **pull back** VT *sep* zurückziehen **VI** (*lit*) sich zurückziehen; **to pull back (from doing sth)** (*fig*) einen Rückzieher machen (und etw nicht tun) (*inf*); **he pulled back from confrontation** er zog sich aus der Konfrontation zurück

▶ **pull down** VT *sep* **a** (= *move down*) herunterziehen; **he pulled his hat down over his eyes** er zog sich (*dat*) den Hut über die Augen **b** (= *demolish*) *buildings* abreißen **c** (= *weaken, make worse*) (*illness*) *person* mitnehmen; (*exam, question*) *marks* herunterdrücken; (*failure, adverse conditions*) *company etc* mitnehmen; *profits, results* herunterdrücken; **this bad mark pulled you down** diese schlechte Zensur hat deinen Notenschnitt (herunter)gedrückt **d** (*US inf*: = *earn*) reinholen (*inf*), machen (*inf*) **VI** (*blind etc*) sich herunterziehen lassen

▶ **pull in** VT *sep* **a** *claws, rope, stomach etc* einziehen; (*into room, swimming pool etc*) hineinziehen; **to pull sb/sth in(to) sth** jdn/etw in etw (*acc*) ziehen **b** (= *rein in*) *horse* zügeln **c** (= *attract*) *crowds* anziehen **d** (*inf*: = *earn*) kassieren (*inf*) **e** (*inf*: = *take into custody*) einkassieren (*inf*) **VI** **a** (*claws*) sich einziehen lassen **b** (*in-*

to station, harbour, pier) einfahren, einlaufen (_into_ in +_acc_); (_into garage, driveway_) hineinfahren (_into_ in +_acc_); (= _stop, park_) anhalten

▶**pull off** VT _sep_ **a** _wrapping paper_ abziehen; _cover_ abnehmen; (_violently_) abreißen; _clothes, pullover, shoes_ ausziehen; _gloves, tights_ ausziehen, abstreifen; **he pulled his clothes off and jumped into the water** er riss sich (_dat_) die Kleider vom Leib und sprang ins Wasser; **he quickly pulled his/her coat off** er zog sich/ihr schnell den Mantel aus **b** (_inf:_ = _succeed in_) schaffen (_inf_); _deal, coup_ zuwege bringen (_inf_); _order_ an Land ziehen (_inf_); _bank job, burglary_ drehen (_inf_)

▶**pull on** VT _sep coat etc_ sich (_dat_) überziehen; _hat_ aufsetzen

▶**pull out** VT **a** (= _extract_) (_of_ aus) herausziehen; _tooth_ ziehen; _page_ herausziehen; **to be pulling one's hair out** (_fig_) sich (_dat_) die Haare ausreißen; **to pull the rug out from under sb** (_fig_) jdm den Boden unter den Füßen wegziehen; **to pull a rabbit out of the hat** (_fig_) etwas aus dem Hut ziehen **b** (= _elongate_) _table, dough_ ausziehen **c** (= _withdraw_) _troops_ abziehen **VI a** (= _come out, become detached_) sich herausziehen lassen; (_pages_) sich heraustrennen lassen **b** (= _elongate_) sich ausziehen lassen **c** (= _withdraw_) aussteigen (_of_ aus) (_inf_); (_troops_) abziehen **d** (= _leave: train etc_) herausfahren (_of_ aus); **to pull out of recession** (_economy_) aus der Rezession kommen **e** (= _move on_) herausfahren; **the car/driver pulled out from behind the lorry** der Wagen/Fahrer scherte hinter dem Lastwagen aus; **the boat pulled out into midstream** das Boot fuhr in die Flussmitte hinaus

▶**pull over** VI _sep_ **a** (= _move over_) herüberziehen (_prep obj_ über +_acc_) **b** (= _topple_) umreißen; **he pulled the whole bookcase over on top of him** er hat das ganze Bücherregal mit sich gerissen **c** (= _move over_) **the police pulled him over** die Polizei stoppte ihn am Straßenrand **VI** (_car, driver_) zur Seite fahren

▶**pull round** (_esp Brit_) **VI** _sep_ **a** (= _turn round_) herumdrehen **b** (= _bring back to consciousness_) wieder zu sich bringen; (= _help recover_) durchbringen **VI** (= _regain consciousness_) wieder zu sich kommen; (= _recover_) durchkommen

▶**pull through** VI _sep_ (_lit_) durchziehen; (_fig:_ = _help recover, help succeed_) durchbringen; **to pull sb/sth through sth** (_lit_) jdn/etw durch etw ziehen; **to pull sb through a difficult period** jdm helfen, eine schwierige Zeit zu überstehen **VI** (_fig:_ = _recover_) durchkommen; **to pull through sth** (_fig_) etw überstehen

▶**pull together** VI (_lit_) gemeinsam ziehen; (= _row jointly_) im gleichen Takt rudern; (_fig:_ = _cooperate_) an einem or am gleichen Strang ziehen **VI** _sep_ (_fig_) _political party, members of family etc_ zusammenschweißen; _novel etc_ in einen Zusammenhang bringen; **let me now pull together the threads of my argument** lassen Sie mich nunmehr meine Argumentation zusammenfassen **VR** sich zusammenreißen

▶**pull under** VT _sep swimmer_ nach unten ziehen

▶**pull up** VI _sep_ **a** (= _raise by pulling_) hochziehen → **sock**[1] **b** (= _uproot_) herausreißen; **to pull up one's roots, to pull up stakes** (_esp US_) alles aufgeben **c** (= _move closer_) _chair_ heranrücken **d** (= _stop_) anhalten **e** (_Brit:_ = _reprimand_) (_for behaviour_) zurechtweisen; (_for pronunciation, grammar_) korrigieren; **he pulled me up about that** er hat mich deswegen zurechtgewiesen/korrigiert **f** (= _improve_) _marks_ verbessern; **that good mark pulled you up a bit** durch diese gute Note hast du ein wenig aufgeholt **VI a** (= _stop_) anhalten **b** (= _improve one's position_) aufholen; **to pull up**

with sb/sth jdn/etw einholen, mit jdm/etw gleichziehen (_inf_)

pull: pullback N (_Mil_) Abzug _m_; **pull cord** N Zugleine _f_/-schnur _f_; **pull date** N (_US:_ = _eat-by date_) (Mindest)haltbarkeitsdatum _nt_; **pull-down** ADJ _bed_ Klapp-; **~ seat** Klappsitz _m_; **~ menu** (_Comput_) Pull-down-Menü _nt_

pullet ['pʊlɪt] N junges Huhn, Hühnchen _nt_

pulley ['pʊlɪ] N (= _wheel_) Rolle _f_; (= _block_) Flaschenzug _m_; (= _hospital apparatus_) Streckapparat _m_

pull-in ['pʊlɪn] N (_Brit_) (= _lay-by_) Halteplatz _m_; (= _café_) Raststätte _f_

Pullman® ['pʊlmən] N (= _Pullman car_) Pullmanwagen _m_; (= _Pullman train_) Pullman® _m_

pull: pull-out N **a** (= _withdrawal_) Abzug _m_ **b** (= _supplement_) heraustrennbarer Teil **ATTR** _supplement_ heraustrennbar; _table leaf, seat_ ausziehbar; **pullover** N Pullover _m_; **pull switch** N (_Elec_) Zugschalter _m_; **pull-up** N (_Sport_) Klimmzug _m_

pulmonary ['pʌlmənərɪ] ADJ Lungen-; **~ disease** Lungenkrankheit _f_; **~ hospital** Lungenklinik _f_

pulmonary artery N Lungenarterie _f_

pulp [pʌlp] N **a** (= _soft mass, paper pulp, wood pulp_) Brei _m_; **to reduce sth to ~** etw in Brei auflösen; _wood etc_ (_for paper_) etw zu einem Brei verarbeiten; **to beat sb to a ~** (_inf_) jdn zu Brei schlagen (_inf_), Matsch aus jdm machen (_sl_); **crushed to (a) ~** zu Brei zerquetscht **b** (_of plant stem_) Mark _nt_; (_of fruit, vegetable_) Fruchtfleisch _nt_; (_of tooth_) Zahnmark _nt_, Pulpa _f_ (_spec_) **c** (_pej: also_ **pulp magazine**) Schundmagazin _nt_ VT _fruit, vegetables_ zerdrücken; _paper, book_ einstampfen; _wood_ zu Brei verarbeiten

pulpboard ['pʌlpbɔːd] N Zellstoffpappe _f_

pulpit ['pʊlpɪt] N Kanzel _f_

pulpy ['pʌlpɪ] ADJ (+_er_) **a** breiig **b** (_inf:_ = _trashy_) _book_ trivial, billig; _newspaper_ billig, minderwertig; **~ magazine** Schundmagazin _nt_, Schundblatt _nt_

pulsar ['pʌlsɑː] N Pulsar _m_

pulsate ['pʌlseɪt] VI (_lit, fig_) pulsieren; (_head, heart_) klopfen, pochen; (_voice, building_) beben; (_music_) rhythmisch klingen; **the whole school ~d with excitement** die ganze Schule fieberte vor Aufregung; **the whole town was pulsating with life** die ganze Stadt war von pulsierendem Leben erfüllt

pulsation [pʌlˈseɪʃən] N (= _pulsating_) Pulsieren _nt_; (_of head, heart_) Klopfen _nt_, Pochen _nt_; (_one beat_) Schwingung _f_; (_of pulse, in artery_) Schlag _m_

pulse[1] [pʌls] N (_Anat_) Puls _m_; (_Phys_) Impuls _m_; (_fig: of drums, music_) Rhythmus _m_; **~ beat** Pulsschlag _m_; **to feel** or **take sb's ~** jdm den Puls fühlen; **he felt the ~ of life in his veins** er spürte, wie das Leben in seinen Adern pulsierte; **he still has** or **keeps his finger on the ~ of economic affairs** er hat in Wirtschaftsfragen immer noch den Finger am Puls der Zeit **VI** pulsieren; (_machines_) stampfen

pulse[2] N (_Bot, Cook_) Hülsenfrucht _f_

pulse rate N (_Anat_) Pulszahl _f_, Puls _m_

pulverization [ˌpʌlvəraɪˈzeɪʃən] N Pulverisierung _f_

pulverize ['pʌlvəraɪz] VT pulverisieren; (_fig inf_) (= _beat up_) Kleinholz machen aus (_inf_); (= _defeat_) fertig machen (_inf_)

puma ['pjuːmə] N Puma _m_

pumice (stone) ['pʌmɪs(ˌstəʊn)] N Bimsstein _m_

pummel ['pʌml] VT eintrommeln auf (+_acc_)

pump[1] [pʌmp] N Pumpe _f_

VT pumpen; _stomach_ auspumpen; _pedal_ mehrmals treten; **to ~ oil/water out of sth** Öl/Wasser aus etw (heraus)pumpen; **to ~ sth dry** etw leer pumpen; **to ~ bullets into sb** jdn mit Blei voll pumpen (_inf_); **to ~ sb full of drugs** jdn mit Drogen voll pumpen; **he ~ed my arm up and down** er riss meinen Arm wie einen Pumpen-

schwengel auf und ab; **to ~ money into sth** Geld in etw (_acc_) hineinpumpen; **to ~ sb (for information)** jdn aushorchen or löchern (_inf_); **to ~ information out of sb** Informationen aus jdm herausholen; **to ~ iron** (_inf_) Gewichte stemmen

VI a pumpen; (_water, blood_) herausschießen; **the piston ~ed up and down** der Kolben ging auf und ab

b (_Brit sl:_ = _have sex_) poppen (_sl_)

▶**pump in** VT _sep_ (_lit, fig_) hineinpumpen

▶**pump out** VT _sep liquid, air_ herauspumpen; _boat, cellar_ auspumpen, leer pumpen; _stomach_ auspumpen

▶**pump up** VT _sep_ **a** (= _inflate_) _tyre etc_ aufpumpen; _prices, profits_ hochtreiben **b** _liquid_ hochpumpen

pump[2] N (= _dancing shoe_) Lackschuh _m_; (= _ballet shoe_) Ballettschuh _m_; (_esp Brit:_ = _gym shoe_) Turnschuh _m_; (_US:_ = _court shoe_) Pumps _m_

pump-action shotgun N Pump-Gun _f_

pump attendant N Tankwart(in) _m(f)_

pumpernickel ['pʌmpənɪkl] N Pumpernickel _m_

pumping station ['pʌmpɪŋˌsteɪʃən] N Pumpwerk _nt_, Pumpstation _f_; (_on a pipeline_) Förderpumpe _f_

pumpkin ['pʌmpkɪn] N Kürbis _m_

pump: pump priming ['pʌmpˌpraɪmɪŋ] N (_fig_) Ankurbelung _f_ der Wirtschaft; **pump room** ['pʌmpruːm] N Trinkhalle _f_, Brunnenhaus _f_

pun [pʌn] **N** Wortspiel _nt_ **VI** Wortspiele machen

Punch [pʌntʃ] N (_Brit_) Kasper _m_, Kasperle _nt_; **~ and Judy show** Kasper(le)theater _nt_; **to be (as) pleased as ~** (_inf_) sich wie ein Schneekönig freuen (_inf_)

punch[1] [pʌntʃ] **N a** (= _blow_) Schlag _m_ **b** _no pl_ (_fig:_ = _vigour_) Schwung _m_ → **pack, pull** **VT** boxen; **I wanted to ~ him in the face when he said that** als er das sagte, hätte ich ihn or ihm am liebsten ins Gesicht geschlagen; **to ~ the air** die geballte Faust nach oben strecken **VI** boxen

punch[2] **N** (_for punching holes_) Locher _m_; (_in tickets_) Lochzange _f_; (_in leather_) Lochstanzer _m_; (_for stamping metal, leather etc_) Prägestempel _m_; (_for knocking out rivets etc_) Punze _f_ VT _ticket etc_ lochen; _leather, metal_ stanzen; _holes_ stechen, stanzen; (= _stamp_) _metal, pattern_ prägen; (_US_) _cattle_ hüten; **to ~ the card** (_of time clock_) die Stechkarte stempeln

▶**punch in** VT _sep_ **a** **I'll punch your face in** (_inf_) ich hau dir eine in die Fresse (_vulg_) or aufs Maul (_inf_) **b** (_Comput_) _data_ tasten, tippen (_inf_)

▶**punch out** VT _sep_ ausstechen, ausstanzen; _pattern etc_ prägen

punch[3] N (= _drink_) Bowle _f_; (_hot_) Punsch _m_

punch: punchbag N Sandsack _m_; **punchball** N Punchingball _m_; (_round_) Lederball _m_; **punchbowl** N Bowle _f_; **punch card** N Lochkarte _f_; **punch-drunk** ADJ (_Boxing_) benommen; (_fig_) durcheinander

Punchinello [pʌntʃɪˈneləʊ] N Pulcinella _f_; (= _clown_) Hanswurst _m_

punching: punching bag ['pʌntʃɪŋˌbæg] N (_US_) = **punch bag**; **punching power** ['pʌntʃɪŋˌpaʊə] N (_Boxing_) Schlagkraft _f_

punch': punch line N Pointe _f_; **punch operator** N Locher(in) _m(f)_; **punch power** N (_Boxing_) Schlagkraft _f_; **punch tape** N Lochstreifen _m_; **punch-up** N (_Brit, inf_) Schlägerei _f_

punchy ['pʌntʃɪ] ADJ (+_er_) (_inf_) **a** _sentence, speech etc_ schwungvoll (_inf_) **b** (_Boxing_) benommen; (_fig:_ = _confused_) benommen, durcheinander _pred_

punctilious [pʌŋkˈtɪlɪəs] ADJ (_regarding etiquette_) korrekt; (= _scrupulous, fastidious_) sehr or peinlich genau; **she is always ~ about arriving in time** sie nimmt es mit der Pünktlichkeit sehr genau; **he is always ~ about writing to thank his host**

er achtet immer darauf, dass er sich bei seinem Gastgeber schriftlich bedankt

punctiliously [pʌŋkˈtɪlɪəslɪ] ADV korrekt; (= *scrupulously, fastidiously*) (+*vb*) peinlich genau; (+*adj*) peinlich; *correct* höchst; **he was ~ polite to his mother-in-law** er war äußerst korrekt gegenüber seiner Schwiegermutter

punctiliousness [pʌŋkˈtɪlɪəsnɪs] N peinliche Genauigkeit *or* Korrektheit

punctual [ˈpʌŋktjʊəl] ADJ pünktlich; **to be ~** pünktlich kommen

punctuality [ˌpʌŋktjʊˈælɪtɪ] N Pünktlichkeit *f*

punctually [ˈpʌŋktjʊəlɪ] ADV pünktlich

punctuate [ˈpʌŋktjʊeɪt] VT **a** (*Gram*) mit Satzzeichen versehen, interpunktieren **b** (= *intersperse*) unterbrechen; **he ~d his talk with jokes** er spickte seine Rede mit Witzen; **a long happy life, ~d with** *or* **by short spells of sadness** ein langes glückliches Leben, das zeitweise von traurigen Augenblicken überschattet war **c** (= *emphasize*) betonen VI Satzzeichen setzen

punctuation [ˌpʌŋktjʊˈeɪʃən] N Zeichensetzung *f*, Interpunktion *f*; **~ mark** Satzzeichen *nt*, Interpunktionszeichen *nt*

puncture [ˈpʌŋktʃəʳ] N **a** (*in tyre, balloon etc*) Loch *nt*; (*in skin*) (Ein)stich *m*; (= *flat tyre*) Reifenpanne *f*, Platte(r) *m* (*inf*) VT stechen in (+*acc*); *membrane* durchstechen; *blister* aufstechen; *tyre, balloon* Löcher/ein Loch machen in (+*acc*); *pride* einen Stich versetzen (+*dat*); **a ~d lung** eine perforierte Lunge VI (*tyre*) einen Platten haben (*inf*); (*balloon*) platzen; **my front tyre ~d** ich hatte einen Platten am Vorderrad

puncture: puncture needle N (*Med*) Punktionsnadel *f*; **punctureproof** [ˈpʌŋktʃəˌpruːf] ADJ *tyre* nagel-/pannensicher; (*Elec*) durchschlagsicher

pundit [ˈpʌndɪt] N (*lit*) Pandit *m*; (*fig*) Experte *m*, Expertin *f*

pungency [ˈpʌndʒənsɪ] N (*lit, fig*) Schärfe *f*

pungent [ˈpʌndʒənt] ADJ (*lit, fig*) scharf; *smell* also stechend, durchdringend; **to have a ~ style of writing** eine spitze *or* scharfe Feder führen

pungently [ˈpʌndʒəntlɪ] ADV (*lit, fig*) scharf; *smell* also stechend, durchdringend

Punic [ˈpjuːnɪk] ADJ punisch; **the ~ Wars** die Punischen Kriege

puniness [ˈpjuːnɪnɪs] N Schwächlichkeit *f*, Mickerigkeit *f* (*pej*)

punish [ˈpʌnɪʃ] VT **a** *person* bestrafen, strafen (*geh*); *offence* bestrafen; **he was ~ed by a fine** er wurde mit einer Geldstrafe belegt; **he has been ~ed enough** er ist genug bestraft worden; (= *has suffered enough*) er ist gestraft genug; **our team was ~ed for making that mistake** unsere Mannschaft musste für diesen Fehler büßen; **the other team ~ed us for that mistake** die andere Mannschaft ließ uns für diesen Fehler büßen **b** (*fig inf*: = *drive hard, treat roughly*) strapazieren; *horses, oneself* schinden; *opponent* vorführen (*inf*), zusetzen (+*dat*)

punishable [ˈpʌnɪʃəbl] ADJ strafbar; **this offence** (*Brit*) *or* **offense** (*US*) **is ~ by 2 years' imprisonment** dieses Verbrechen wird mit 2 Jahren Gefängnis bestraft; **it is a ~ offence** (*Brit*) *or* **offense** (*US*) es ist strafbar

punishing [ˈpʌnɪʃɪŋ] ADJ *blow* hart; *routine, pace* strapaziös, tödlich; *workload* strapaziös, erdrückend; **to get** *or* **take some ~ treatment** (*cars, furniture*) strapaziert werden; (*Sport*) vorgeführt werden (*inf*), eins aufs Dach bekommen (*inf*) N **to take a ~** (*inf*: *team, boxer etc*) vorgeführt werden (*inf*); **he got a real ~ from his opponent** (*inf*) er wurde von seinem Gegner regelrecht vorgeführt (*inf*); **his self-confidence took a ~** sein Selbstbewusstsein litt darunter *or* bekam einen Knacks (*inf*)

punishment [ˈpʌnɪʃmənt] N **a** (= *penalty*) Strafe *f*; (= *punishing*) Bestrafung *f*; **you know the ~ for such offences** Sie wissen, was darauf steht; **to take one's ~** seine Strafe akzeptieren; **~ beating** Bestrafungsaktion *f* **b** (*fig inf*) **to take a lot of ~** (*car, furniture etc*) stark

strapaziert werden; (*Sport*) vorgeführt werden

punitive [ˈpjuːnɪtɪv] ADJ Straf-; *sanctions* strafend; *strike* vergeltend; (*fig*) *taxation, fines etc* extrem (hoch); **~ expedition** Strafexpedition *f*; **~ measures** Strafmaßnahmen *pl*; **~ sentence** Strafurteil *nt*; **to take ~ action against sb** eine Strafaktion gegen jdn führen

punitive damages PL (*Jur*) Schadensersatz *m*

Punjab [pʌnˈdʒɑːb] N **the ~** das Pandschab

Punjabi [pʌnˈdʒɑːbɪ] N **a** *state, capital* des Pandschab, pandschabisch **b** (*Ling*) Pandschabi *nt* ADJ **a** Pandschabi *mf* **b** (*Ling*) Pandschabi *nt*

punk [pʌŋk] N **a** (= *person: also* **punk rocker**) Punker(in), Punkrocker(in) *m(f)*; (= *music: also* **punk rock**) → **punk rock** (= *culture*) Punk *m* **b** (*US inf*: = *hoodlum*) Ganove *m* (*inf*) **c** (*dated inf*: = *nonsense*) Stuss *m* (*inf*) ADJ Punk-

punk rock N Punkrock *m*

punnet [ˈpʌnɪt] N (*Brit*) Körbchen *nt*

punster [ˈpʌnstəʳ] N **he is a brilliant ~** er versteht es hervorragend, Wortspiele zu machen

punt¹ [pʌnt] (*esp Brit*) N **a** (= *boat*) Stechkahn *m*, Stocherkahn *m* VI staken, stochern; (= *go by punt*) im Stechkahn fahren; **to go ~ing** Stechkahn fahren VT staken; (= *take by punt*) im Stechkahn fahren

punt² N **a** Schuss *m* (aus der Hand); **he gave the ball a ~** er schoss den Ball aus der Hand VT **to ~ the ball** den Ball aus der Hand schießen; **he ~ed the ball back** er schoss den Ball zurück VI (*Rugby*) den Ball aus der Hand schießen

punt³ N (= *bet*) Wette *f*; (= *gamble*) Spiel *nt* VI wetten, spielen

punt⁴ [pʊnt] N (= *Irish currency*) Punt *nt*, irisches Pfund

punter¹ [ˈpʌntəʳ] N (= *boater*) Stechkahnfahrer(in) *m(f)*

punter² [ˈpʌntəʳ] N **a** (*Brit inf*) (= *better*) Wetter(in) *m(f)*; (= *gambler*) Spieler(in) *m(f)* **b** (*esp Brit inf*: = *customer etc*) Kunde *m*, Kundin *f*; (*of prostitute*) Freier *m* (*inf*); **the average ~** Otto Normalverbraucher

puny [ˈpjuːnɪ] ADJ (+*er*) (= *weak*) *person* schwächlich, mick(e)rig (*pej*); *effort* kläglich; *resources* kläglich, winzig

PUP N (*Brit*) abbr of **Progressive Unionist Party**

pup [pʌp] N **a** Junge(s) *nt*; **in ~** (*bitch*) trächtig; **she's still a ~** sie ist noch jung *or* klein; **to be sold a ~** (*fig inf*) übers Ohr gehauen werden (*inf*) **b** (*pej*, = *youth*) = **puppy b** VI werfen

pupa [ˈpjuːpə] N *pl* **-e** [ˈpjuːpiː] Puppe *f*

pupate [ˈpjuːpeɪt] VI sich verpuppen

pupil¹ [ˈpjuːpl] N (*Sch, fig*) Schüler(in) *m(f)*

pupil² N (*Anat*) Pupille *f*

puppet [ˈpʌpɪt] N Puppe *f*; (= *glove puppet*) Handpuppe *f*; (= *string puppet, also fig*) Marionette *f*

puppeteer [ˌpʌpɪˈtɪəʳ] N Puppenspieler(in) *m(f)*

puppet: puppet government N Marionettenregierung *f*; **puppet régime** N Marionettenregime *nt*

puppetry [ˈpʌpɪtrɪ] N das Puppenspiel

puppet: puppet show N Puppenspiel *nt*; (*with string puppets also*) Marionettentheater *nt*; **puppet state** N Marionettenstaat *m*

puppy [ˈpʌpɪ] N **a** (= *young dog*) junger *or* kleiner Hund, Hündchen *nt*, Welpe *m*; **when he was still a ~** als er noch jung *or* klein war **b** (*pej dated*: = *youth*) Schnösel *m* (*inf*)

puppy: puppy dog N Hundchen *nt*; **puppy farm** N Hundezucht *f* (*wo junge Rassehunde zum Weiterverkauf an Tierhandlungen gezüchtet werden*); **puppy fat** N (*Brit*) Babyspeck *m*; **puppy love** N Schwärmerei *f*

pup tent N (*US Mil*) Zweimannzelt *nt*

purblind [ˈpɜːblaɪnd] ADJ (*liter*) (*lit*) halb blind; (*fig*) blind, borniert, dumm

purblindness [ˈpɜːblaɪndnɪs] ADJ (*liter*) (*lit*) Halbblindheit; (*fig*) Blindheit *f*, Borniertheit *f*, Dummheit *f*

purchasable [ˈpɜːtʃəsəbl] ADJ käuflich (zu erwerben *geh*)

purchase [ˈpɜːtʃɪs] N **a** Kauf *m*; (*of furniture, machine, flat, car*) Kauf *m*, Anschaffung *f*; **to make a ~** einen Kauf tätigen, eine Anschaffung machen **b** (= *grip*) Halt *m*; **he couldn't get a ~ on the wet rope** er konnte an dem nassen Seil keinen Halt finden VT (= *buy*) kaufen, erwerben (*geh*), erstehen (*geh*); (*fig*) *success, victory* erkaufen

purchase: purchase account N (*Comm*) Wareneingangskonto *nt*; **purchase money** N Kaufgeld *nt*; **purchase order** N Auftragsbestätigung *f*; **purchase price** N Kaufpreis *m*

purchaser [ˈpɜːtʃɪsəʳ] N Käufer(in) *m(f)*

purchase tax N (*Brit*) *nach dem Großhandelspreis berechnete Kaufsteuer*

purchasing [ˈpɜːtʃɪsɪŋ]: **purchasing agent** N (*Comm*) Einkäufer(in) *m(f)*; **purchasing association** N (*Comm*) Einkaufsgenossenschaft *f*; **purchasing power** N Kaufkraft *f*

purdah [ˈpɜːdə] N *Vorhang vor den Frauengemächern im Islam und Hinduismus*, Purdah *f*; **a woman in ~** (*lit*) eine Frau, die von (fremden) Männern fern gehalten wird; **he keeps his wife (like a woman) in ~** er hält seine Frau von allem fern

pure [pjʊəʳ] ADJ (+*er*) **a** rein; *motive* ehrlich, lauter (*geh*); (= *utter*) *madness, nonsense etc* also reinste(r, s); **she stared at him in ~ disbelief** sie starrte ihn ganz ungläubig an; **by ~ chance** durch puren Zufall, rein zufällig; *malice* **~ and simple** reine Bosheit; **a ~ wool dress** ein Kleid aus reiner Wolle, ein rein wollenes *or* reinwollenes Kleid; **blessed are the ~ in heart** (*Bibl*) selig, die reinen Herzens sind **b** (= *theoretical*) *chemistry* rein, theoretisch; *maths, research, science* rein

pureblood [ˈpjʊəblʌd], **purebred** [ˈpjʊəbred] ADJ reinrassig N reinrassiges Pferd *etc*

purée [ˈpjʊəreɪ] N Püree *nt*, Brei *m*; **tomato ~** Tomatenmark *nt* VT pürieren

purely [ˈpjʊəlɪ] ADV rein; **~ and simply** schlicht und einfach

pure-minded [ˈpjʊəˈmaɪndɪd] ADJ unverdorben

pureness [ˈpjʊənɪs] N = **purity**

purgation [pɜːˈgeɪʃən] N (*liter*) Reinigung *f*; (*of sin, guilt*) Buße *f*; (*form, of bowels*) Entleerung *f*

purgative [ˈpɜːgətɪv] ADJ (*Med*) abführend, purgativ (*spec*); (*fig liter*) läuternd (*geh*) N Abführmittel *nt*, Purgativ *nt* (*spec*)

purgatorial [ˌpɜːgəˈtɔːrɪəl] ADJ **a** (*Rel*) *concept* des Fegefeuers; *time* im Fegefeuer; **~ fire** Fegefeuer *nt* **b** (*fig*) höllisch

purgatory [ˈpɜːgətərɪ] N **a** (*Rel*) das Fegefeuer **b** (*fig*: = *state*) die Hölle

purge [pɜːdʒ] N **a** (*Med*) (starkes) Abführmittel *nt* **b** (*Pol etc*) Säuberung(saktion) *f*; **a ~ of all radical elements in the party** eine Säuberung der Partei von allen radikalen Elementen VT reinigen; *body* entschlacken; *guilt, offence, sin* büßen; (*Pol etc*) *party, organization* säubern (*of* von); *traitor, member* eliminieren (*from* aus); **to ~ the bowels** den Darm entleeren

purification [ˌpjʊərɪfɪˈkeɪʃən] N Reinigung *f*

purification plant N (*of factory*) Kläranlage *f*

purifier [ˈpjʊərɪfaɪəʳ] N Reinigungsanlage *f*; (= *air-freshener*) Luftreiniger *m*

purify [ˈpjʊərɪfaɪ] VT reinigen

purism [ˈpjʊərɪzəm] N Purismus *m*

purist [ˈpjʊərɪst] N Purist(in) *m(f)*

puristic ADJ , **puristically** ADV [pjʊəˈrɪstɪk, -lɪ] puristisch

puritan [ˈpjʊərɪtə] (*Rel: also* **Puritan**) ADJ puritanisch N Puritaner(in) *m(f)*

puritanical [ˌpjʊərɪˈtænɪkəl] ADJ puritanisch

puritanism [ˈpjʊərɪtənɪzəm] N (*Rel: also* **Puritanism**) Puritanismus *m*

purity [ˈpjʊərɪtɪ] N Reinheit *f*; (*of motives*) Lauterkeit *f* (*geh*), Ehrlichkeit *f*

purl [pɜːl] N linke Masche; **is the next row (in)
~?** ist die nächste Reihe links? VT links stricken; **~ two** zwei links VI links stricken

purlieus [ˈpɜːljuːz] PL (liter) Umgebung f

purloin [pɜːˈlɔɪn] VT (form, hum) entwenden
(form, hum)

purloiner [pɜːˈlɔɪnə] N (form, hum) Dieb(in)
m(f)

purple [ˈpɜːpl] ADJ violett, lila; face dunkelrot,
hochrot; (pej) prose, passage hochgestochen,
hochtrabend; **to go ~ (in the face)** hochrot
werden or anlaufen (inf) N a (= colour) Violett
nt, Lila nt b (fig) **the ~** (= nobility) der Adel; (=
bishops) der Kardinalsstand; **to be born to the
~** von königlichem Geblüt sein; **to be raised
to the ~** den Kardinalspurpur anlegen

purple heart N a (esp Brit inf) Amphetamin-
tablette f b (US) **Purple Heart** Purpurherz nt,
Verwundetenabzeichen nt

purplish [ˈpɜːplɪʃ] ADJ leicht violett or lila

purport [ˈpɜːpət] N Tenor m [pɜːˈpɔːt] VT a (=
convey, mean) hindeuten auf (+acc) b (= profess, claim) **to ~ to be/do sth** (person) vorgeben,
etw zu sein/tun; (object) etw sein/tun sollen;
he is ~ed to be a spy es wird behauptet, er sei
ein Spion; **the law is ~ed to be in the public
interest** das Gesetz soll dem Interesse der Öffentlichkeit dienen

purpose [ˈpɜːpəs] N a (= intention) Absicht f;
(= result aimed at, set goal) Zweck m; **on ~** mit
Absicht, absichtlich; **what was your ~ in doing
this?** was haben Sie damit beabsichtigt?, was
war Ihre Absicht dabei?; **he did it for or with
the ~ of improving his image** er tat es in der
Absicht or mit dem Ziel, sein Image zu verbessern; **he's a man with a ~ in life** er ist ein
Mensch mit einem Lebensziel; **a novel with a ~**
ein Roman, der einen Zweck erfüllen soll; **to
answer or serve sb's ~(s)** jds Zweck(en) entsprechen or dienen; **his activities seem to lack
~** seine Aktivitäten scheinen nicht zweckge-
richtet zu sein; **for our ~s** für unsere Zwecke;
for the ~s of this meeting zum Zweck dieser
Konferenz; **for all practical ~s** in der Praxis; **to
the ~** relevant; **to some/good/little ~** mit eini-
gem/gutem/wenig Erfolg; **to no ~** ohne Erfolg
b (= resolution, determination) Entschlossenheit f; **strength of ~** Entschlusskraft f, Entschlossenheit f; **sense of ~** Zielbewusstsein nt;
(of nation) Ziel nt, Zielvorstellungen pl; **to have
a sense of ~** zielbewusst sein; **to have no sense
of ~** kein Zielbewusstsein or kein Ziel haben
VT (liter) beabsichtigen; **to ~ to do sth** etw zu
tun gedenken

purpose-built [ˈpɜːpəsbɪlt] ADJ (esp Brit) speziell angefertigt, Spezial-; construction speziell gebaut; **~ vehicle** Spezialfahrzeug nt

purposeful ADJ , **purposefully** ADV [ˈpɜːpəs-
fʊl, -fəlɪ] entschlossen; activity, life sinnvoll

purposefulness [ˈpɜːpəsfʊlnɪs] N Entschlossenheit f

purposeless [ˈpɜːpəslɪs] ADJ sinnlos; person
ziellos

purposely [ˈpɜːpəslɪ] ADV bewusst, absichtlich

purpose-trained [ˈpɜːpəstreɪnd] ADJ (esp Brit)
troops etc mit Spezialausbildung pred, Spezial-

purposive [ˈpɜːpəsɪv] ADJ remark, statement, action, behaviour gezielt; **the ~ use of scientific
progress** der gezielte Einsatz des wissenschaftlichen Fortschritts; **to be ~** einen Zweck verfolgen

purr [pɜː] VI (cat, fig: person) schnurren; (engine)
surren VT (= say) säuseln N Schnurren nt no
pl, Surren nt no pl

purse [pɜːs] N a (dial) Portemonnaie nt,
Geldbeutel m, Geldbörse f (form); **to
hold the ~ strings** (Brit fig) über die Finanzen
bestimmen, die Finanzen in der Hand haben;
**the government decided to loosen the ~
strings for defence** die Regierung beschloss,
mehr Geld für die Verteidigung auszugeben;
**her husband spent too much, so she decided
to tighten the ~ strings** ihr Mann gab zu viel

Geld aus, also beschloss sie, ihn kurz zu halten
b (US: = handbag) Handtasche f
c (= funds) Gelder pl; **that's beyond my ~** das
übersteigt meine Finanzen (inf) → **public purse**
d (= sum of money) (as prize) Preisgeld nt; (as
gift) (to widow, refugee etc) (Geld)spende f; (on
retirement) Geldgeschenk nt
VT **to ~ one's lips/mouth (up)** einen Schmollmund machen

purser [ˈpɜːsə] N Zahlmeister(in) m(f)

purse snatcher N (US inf) Handtaschen-
dieb(in) m(f)

pursuance [pəˈsjuːəns] N (form) (of plan) Verfolgung f; (of instruction) Ausführung f; (of duties)
Erfüllung f

pursuant [pəˈsjuːənt] ADJ (form) **~ to** gemäß
(+dat), entsprechend (+dat); **~ to our agreement** unserem Abkommen gemäß or entsprechend

pursue [pəˈsjuː] VT a (= follow) verfolgen; girl,
film star etc nachlaufen (+dat), verfolgen; (=
strive for) pleasure, success nachjagen (+dat), aus
sein auf (+acc); happiness streben nach; **bad
luck seems to ~ him** er scheint vom Pech verfolgt zu sein b (= carry on) train of thought,
course of action, idea verfolgen; inquiry durchführen; profession, studies nachgehen (+dat); subject
weiterführen

pursuer [pəˈsjuːə] N Verfolger(in) m(f)

pursuit [pəˈsjuːt] N a (= act of pursuing) (of person) Verfolgung f (of +gen), Jagd f (of auf
+acc); (of knowledge) Streben nt (of nach),
Trachten nt (of nach); (of pleasure) Jagd f (of
nach); (of happiness) Streben nt (of nach); **he
set off in ~ (of her)** er rannte/fuhr (ihr) hinterher; **to go in ~ of sb/sth** sich auf die Jagd nach
jdm/etw machen; **hot ~** (Mil) Nacheile f; **in
hot ~ of sb** hart auf jds Fersen (dat); **to set off/be
in hot ~ of sb/sth** jdm/einer Sache nachjagen;
in hot ~ of the thief in wilder Jagd auf den
Dieb; **in (the) ~ of his goal** in Verfolgung seines Ziels; **Kissinger's ~ of peace** Kissingers
Friedensbemühungen pl
b (= occupation) Beschäftigung f; (= hobby, pastime) Freizeitbeschäftigung f, Zeitvertreib m;
his literary ~s seine Beschäftigung mit der Literatur
c (Sport: also **pursuit race**) Verfolgungsren-
nen nt

pursuit plane N Jagdflugzeug nt

purulence [ˈpjʊərʊləns], **purulency** [ˈpjʊərʊlən-
sɪ] N Eitern nt; (= pus) Eiter m

purulent [ˈpjʊərʊlənt] ADJ eitrig; **to become ~**
eitern

purvey [pɜːˈveɪ] VT (form) (= sell) verkaufen; **to ~
sth to sb** (= supply) jdm etw liefern; food also
jdn mit etw beliefern; information also jdn mit
etw versorgen

purveyance [pɜːˈveɪəns] N (form: = sale) Verkauf
m; **the ~ of food to the Navy** die Lieferung
von Lebensmitteln an die Marine

purveyor [pɜːˈveɪə] N (form) (= seller) Händ-
ler(in) m(f); (= supplier) Lieferant m

purview [ˈpɜːvjuː] N (form) Rahmen m; (of department) Aufgabenbereich m, Ressort nt; **to
come within/lie outside the ~ of an inquiry**
noch/nicht mehr im Rahmen einer Untersuchung liegen

pus [pʌs] N Eiter m

push [pʊʃ] N a Schubs m (inf); (short) Stoß m;
(in childbirth) Drücken nt no pl; **to give sb/sth a
~** jdn schieben, jdm/einer Sache einen
Stoß versetzen; **to give a car a ~** einen Wagen
anschieben; **he needs a little ~ now and then**
(fig) dem muss man mal ab und zu in die Rippen stoßen (inf); **to get the ~** (Brit inf) (employee) (raus)fliegen (inf) (from aus); (boyfriend)
Laufpass kriegen (inf); **to give sb the ~** (Brit inf,
employee) jdn rausschmeißen (inf); boyfriend
jdm den Laufpass geben (inf)
b (= effort) Anstrengung f; (= sales push) Kampagne f, Aktion f; (Mil: = offensive) Offensive f;
to make a ~ sich ranhalten (inf), Dampf ma-

chen (inf); (Mil) eine Offensive starten; **let's
make a ~ to get it finished** halten wir uns ran,
damit wir fertig werden (inf); **to have a ~ on
sales** eine Verkaufskampagne führen
c (= drive, aggression) Durchsetzungsvermögen
nt
d (inf) **at a ~** notfalls, im Notfall; **if/when it
comes to the ~** wenn es darauf ankommt; **if/
when ~ comes to shove** wenn der schlimmste
Fall eintritt
VT a (= shove, move by pushing) schieben;
(quickly, violently) stoßen, schubsen (inf); (=
press) button, controls drücken; **to ~ a door o-
pen/shut** eine Tür auf-/zuschieben; (quickly, violently) eine Tür auf-/zustoßen; **he ~ed the book
into my hand** er drückte mir das Buch in die
Hand; **to ~ a car to get it started** einen Wagen
anschieben; **he ~ed his way through the crowd**
er drängte sich durch die Menge; **he ~ed the
thought to the back of his mind** er schob den
Gedanken beiseite; **he ~ed the ball over the
bar** (Sport) er hat den Ball über die Latte gestoßen
b (fig) views, claims, interests durchzusetzen versuchen; candidate die Werbetrommel rühren
für; export side intensiv fördern; product propagieren, massiv Werbung machen für, puschen
(inf), puschen (inf); drugs schieben, pushen
(inf); **to ~ home one's advantage** seinen Vorteil
ausnützen; **the speaker ~ed home his points**
der Sprecher machte nachdrücklich seinen
Standpunkt klar; **don't ~ your luck** treibs nicht
zu weit!; **he's ~ing his luck trying to do that** er
legt es wirklich darauf an, wenn er das versucht; **he must be ~ing 70** (inf) er muss auf die
70 zugehen
c (fig: = put pressure on) drängen, drängeln
(inf); athlete, pupil, employee antreiben; **to ~ sb
into doing sth** jdn dazu treiben, etw zu tun; **to
~ sb to do sth** jdn dazu drängen, etw zu tun;
to ~ sb for payment jdn zum Zahlen drängen;
don't ~ him so hard to make a decision drängen or drängeln (inf) Sie ihn nicht zu sehr zu
einer Entscheidung; **they ~ed him to the limits**
sie trieben ihn bis an seine Grenzen; **that's
~ing it a bit** (inf) das ist ein bisschen übertrieben; **to be ~ed (for time)** (inf) mit der Zeit
knapp dran sein, unter Zeitdruck stehen; **to
be ~ed (for money)** (inf) knapp bei Kasse sein
(inf); **to ~ oneself hard** sich schinden
VI a (= shove) schieben; (quickly, violently) stoßen; (= press, also in childbirth) drücken; (in a
crowd) drängen, drängeln (inf); (= press onward)
sich (vorwärts) kämpfen; (fig: = be ambitious, assert oneself) kämpfen; (= apply pressure) drängen,
drängeln (inf); **"push"** (on door) „drücken"; (on
bell) „klingeln"; **~ harder!** fester schieben/sto-
ßen/drücken!; **he ~es too much** (fig) er ist zu
aggressiv
b **this door ~es (open)** bei dieser Tür muss
man drücken

▶ **push about** VT sep (Brit) = **push around**

▶ **push across** VT sep = **push over a**

▶ **push ahead** VI sich ranhalten (inf), voran-
machen (inf); **to push ahead with one's plans**
seine Pläne vorantreiben

▶ **push along** VT sep wheelbarrow etc vor sich
(dat) her schieben; (fig: = speed up) work etc voranbringen, vorantreiben; **to push things along**
(fig) die Dinge vorantreiben VI (inf) sich auf
den Weg or auf die Socken machen (inf)

▶ **push around** VT sep a (lit) herumschieben;
(quickly, violently) herumstoßen b (fig inf: = bully) child herumschubsen; adult herumkommandieren

▶ **push aside** VT sep zur Seite or beiseite schieben; (quickly, violently) zur Seite or beiseite stoßen; (fig) problems, suggestions einfach abtun; rival zur Seite drängen

▶ **push away** VT sep wegschieben; (quickly) wegstoßen

▶ **push back** VT sep people zurückdrängen;
(with one push) zurückstoßen; curtains, cover, lock
of hair zurückschieben; **to push back the**

boundaries (of sth) die Grenzen (einer Sache) zurückdrängen

▶ **push by** = push past

▶ **push down** VT *sep* **a** (= press down) nach unten drücken **b** (= knock over) umstoßen; *fence* niederreißen VI (= press down) hinunterdrücken, nach unten drücken; (in childbirth) drücken

▶ **push for** VI +*prep obj* drängen auf (+*acc*)

▶ **push forward** VI **a** (Mil) vorwärts drängen **b** = push ahead VT *sep* (lit) nach vorn schieben; (fig) claim geltend machen; ideas hervorheben, herausstellen; sb, oneself in den Vordergrund schieben

▶ **push in** VT *sep* **a** hineinschieben; (quickly, violently) hineinstoßen; **to push sb/sth in(to) sth** jdn/etw in etw (acc) schieben/stoßen; **to push one's way in** sich hineindrängen **b** (= break) window, sides of box eindrücken VI (lit: in queue, into room etc) sich hineindrängen or -drängeln (inf); (fig: = interfere) sich dazwischendrängen, sich reindrängen (inf); **he pushed into the queue** er drängelte sich (in der Schlange) vor

▶ **push off** VT *sep* **a** hinunterschieben; (quickly, violently) hinunterstoßen; lid, cap wegdrücken; **to push sb off sth** jdn von etw schieben/stoßen; **to push sth off sth** etw von etw schieben/stoßen/drücken; **I was pushed off the pavement** ich wurde vom Bürgersteig gedrängt **b** boat abstoßen VI **a** (in boat) abstoßen **b** (Brit inf, = leave) abhauen (inf); **push off!** mach 'ne Fliege! (sl), hau or zieh ab! (inf) **c** the top just pushes off der Deckel lässt sich einfach wegdrücken

▶ **push on** VI (with journey) weiterfahren; (walking) weitergehen; (with job) weitermachen VT *sep* **a** top, lid festdrücken; **he pushed the lid on(to) the jar** er drückte den Deckel auf das Glas **b** (fig: = urge on) antreiben; (= incite) anstacheln

▶ **push out** VT *sep* **a** (lit) hinausschieben; (quickly, violently) hinausstoßen; **to push sb/sth out of sth** jdn/etw aus etw schieben/stoßen; **to push one's way out (of sth)** sich (aus etw) hinausdrängen → boat N **a b** (fig) employee, government, member of group hinausdrängen; **to push sb out of sth** jdn aus etw drängen **c** (Bot) root, shoots treiben VI (Bot: roots, shoots) treiben

▶ **push over** VT *sep* **a** (= pass over, move over) hinüberschieben; (quickly, violently) hinüberstoßen; **to push sb/sth over sth** jdn/etw über etw (acc) schieben/stoßen **b** (= knock over) umwerfen

▶ **push past** VI sich vorbeischieben (prep obj an +dat); (= move violently) sich vorbeidrängen (prep obj an +dat)

▶ **push through** VT *sep* **a** (= shove through) durchschieben; (quickly, violently) durchstoßen; **to push sb/sth through sth** jdn/etw durch etw schieben/stoßen; **to push one's way through** sich durchdrängen; **she pushed her way through the crowd** sie drängte sich durch die Menge **b** (= get done quickly) bill, decision durchpeitschen (inf); business durchziehen (inf) VI (through crowd) sich durchschieben; (more violently) sich durchdrängen; (new shoots) sich herausschieben; **he pushed through the crowd** er schob/drängte sich durch die Menge

▶ **push to** VT *always separate* door anlehnen

▶ **push up** VT *sep* **a** (lit) hinaufschieben; (quickly, violently) hinaufstoßen; window hochschieben/-stoßen → daisy **b** (fig: = raise, increase) hoch treiben, hoch drücken

push: pushback N (Aviat) Zurückstoßen nt, Zurückschieben nt; **to be ready for ~** startklar sein; **pushball** N (esp US) Pushball m; **pushbar** N Riegel m; **push-bike** N (dated Brit) Fahrrad nt; **push-button** N Drucktaste f, Druckknopf m; **~ controls** Druckknopfsteuerung f; **~ radio** Radio nt mit Drucktasten; **~ telephone** Tastentelefon nt; **~ warfare** Krieg m auf Knopfdruck; **pushcart** ['pʊʃkɑːt] N

(Hand)karren m; **pushchair** N (Brit) Sportwagen m

pusher ['pʊʃə'] N (inf) **a** (of drugs) Pusher(in) m(f) (inf); (small-time) Dealer(in) m(f) (inf) **b** (= ambitious person) **he's a ~** er setzt sich durch

pusher barge, **pusher tug** N (inland navigation) Schubschiff nt

pushiness ['pʊʃɪnɪs] N (inf) penetrante Art (pej)

pushing ['pʊʃɪŋ] (inf) ADJ penetrant (pej)

push: push-off N (inf) Anfang m, Start m; **pushover** ['pʊʃəʊvə'] N (inf) (= job etc) Kinderspiel nt; (= match also) Geschenk nt (inf); (= person) leichtes Opfer; **a pretty face and she's a ~ for a pretty face** bei einem hübschen Gesicht wird er schwach; **pushpin** ['pʊʃpɪn] N (esp US) Pin-Nagel m; **push-pull** ADJ (Elec) Gegentakt-; **~ circuit** Gegentaktschaltung f; **pushrod** N (Mech) Stößelstange f; **push-start** VT car anschieben N **to give a car a ~** ein Auto anschieben; **push-up** N (US) Liegestütz m

pushy ['pʊʃɪ] ADJ (+er) (inf) penetrant (pej)

pusillanimity [ˌpjuːsɪlə'nɪmɪtɪ] N (liter) Unbeherztheit f, Feigheit f

pusillanimous [ˌpjuːsɪ'lænɪməs] ADJ (liter) unbeherzt, feige

puss [pʊs] N (inf) Mieze f (inf), Muschi f (inf); **~, ~!** Miez, Miez!; **Puss in Boots** der Gestiefelte Kater; **she's a sly ~** (inf) sie ist ein schlaues Ding (inf)

pussy ['pʊsɪ] N **a** (= cat) Mieze f (inf), Muschi f (inf) **b** (sl, = female genitals) Muschi f (inf)

pussy: pussycat ['pʊsɪkæt] N (baby-talk) Miezekatze f (baby-talk); **pussyfoot** VI (inf) **a** (= move cautiously) auf Zehenspitzen tappen, auf Samtpfoten schleichen **b** (= act cautiously) **to ~ (about** or **around) sth** (um etw) wie die Katze um den heißen Brei schleichen (inf); **pussyfooting** (inf) ADJ überängstlich N **I'm fed up with his ~** ich habe es satt, wie er immer wie die Katze um den heißen Brei schleicht; **pussy willow** N Salweide f

pustule ['pʌstjuːl] N Pustel f, Eiterpickel m

put[1] [pʊt] vb: pret, ptp **put** N (Sport) Stoß m VT **to ~ the shot** kugelstoßen; **~ting the shot** Kugelstoßen nt

---

put[2] [pʊt]
pret, ptp **put** [pʊt]

1 TRANSITIVE VERB	3 PHRASAL VERBS
2 INTRANSITIVE VERB	

For combinations of **put** with adverbs and prepositions, e.g. **put in**, **put on**, **put up** etc., see also the phrasal verbs section.

1 – TRANSITIVE VERB

a = place stellen, setzen; (= lay down) legen; (= push in) stecken; **you've put the picture too high up** du hast das Bild zu hoch (auf)gehängt; **put it there!** (concluding deal) abgemacht!; (congratulatory) gratuliere!; **I didn't know where to put myself** ich wusste gar nicht, wo ich hingucken sollte

◆ **to put + across** they put a plank across the stream sie legten ein Brett über den Bach

◆ **to put + down** he put the corpse down the well er warf die Leiche in den Brunnen

◆ **to put + in** to put sth in a drawer etw in eine Schublade tun or legen; **he put his hand in his pocket** er steckte die Hand in die Tasche; **he put his toe in the water** er steckte seinen Zeh ins Wasser; **put the dog in the kitchen** tu or steck den Hund in die Küche; **to put milk/sugar in one's coffee** Milch/Zucker in den Kaffee tun or geben; **to put the ball in the net** (Ftbl) den Ball ins Netz setzen; (Tennis) den Ball ins Netz schlagen; **to put a child in a home** ein Kind in ein Heim stecken; **I would put complete confidence in him** ich würde mein volles Vertrauen auf ihn or in ihn setzen; **to put sb in possession of the facts** jdn über den Stand der Dinge unterrichten; **to put sb in a good/bad mood** jdn fröhlich/missmutig stimmen;

that puts him in another category das stuft ihn in eine andere Klasse ein

◆ **to put + into** to put a lot of time into sth viel Zeit auf etw (acc) verwenden or in etw (acc) stecken; **to put a lot of effort into one's work** viel Mühe in seine Arbeit stecken; **she has put a lot into her marriage** sie hat eine Menge in ihre Ehe gesteckt or investiert; **to put money into sth** (sein) Geld in etw (acc) stecken; **to put a text into Greek** einen Text ins Griechische übersetzen; **to put a verb into the past tense** ein Verb in die Vergangenheit setzen

◆ **to put + on** put the lid on the box tu or mach den Deckel auf die Schachtel; **he put some more coal on the fire** er legte Kohle nach; **he put his hat on his head** er setzte sich (dat) den Hut auf; **he put his hand/head on my shoulder** er legte seine Hand/seinen Kopf auf meine Schulter; **his aunt put her on the train** ihre Tante setzte sie in den Zug; **to put men on the moon** Menschen auf den Mond bringen; **he put four men on the job** er setzte (für diese Arbeit) vier Leute ein; **to put a patch on sth** einen Flicken auf etw (acc) setzen; **to put money on a horse** auf ein Pferd setzen; **he put £10 on the favourite** er setzte £ 10 auf den Favoriten; **I'm putting my money on him** ich setzte auf ihn; **I'm putting my money on him to get the job** ich gehe jede Wette ein, dass er die Stelle bekommt; **to put a value of £100 on sth** den Wert einer Sache (gen) auf £ 100 schätzen; **I put the children on their best behaviour** ich habe den Kindern eingeschärft, sich ja gut zu benehmen

◆ **to put + over/under** he put his rucksack over the fence er setzte seinen Rucksack über den Zaun; **he put the ball over the wall** er schoss den Ball über die Mauer; **to put one's hand over one's/sb's mouth** sich/jdm die Hand vor den Mund halten; **they put someone over/under him in the office** im Büro haben sie jemanden über ihn gesetzt/ihm jemanden unterstellt; **he was put under the care of a nurse** er wurde in die Obhut einer Krankenschwester gegeben

◆ **to put + (a)round** he put his head (a)round the door er steckte den Kopf zur Tür herein

◆ **to put + through** to put one's fist through a window mit der Faust ein Fenster einschlagen; **to put a bullet through sb's head** jdm eine Kugel durch den Kopf schießen

◆ **to put + to** he put his lips to my ear and whispered ... er kam ganz dicht und flüsterte mir ins Ohr ...; **to put a glass to one's lips** ein Glas zum Mund(e) führen; **she put the shell to her ear** sie hielt (sich) (dat) die Muschel ans Ohr; **to put the children to bed** die Kinder ins Bett bringen; **to put a poem to music** ein Gedicht vertonen; **to put sb to great expense** jdm große Ausgaben verursachen; **I don't want to be put to a lot of expense** ich möchte nicht, dass mir damit große Ausgaben entstehen; **to be put to a lot of inconvenience over sth** mit etw viele Unannehmlichkeiten haben; **to put a horse to a fence** mit einem Pferd ein Hindernis angehen or anreiten; **to put a heifer to a bull** die Kuh mit dem Bullen zusammenbringen or -führen

◆ **to put + toward(s)** we'll each put £5 toward(s) the cost of it jeder von uns gibt £ 5 (zum Betrag) dazu

◆ **to put sb to do** or **doing sth** jdn abordnen, etw zu tun; **they put her to work on the new project** ihr wurde das neue Projekt als Arbeitsbereich zugewiesen

◆ **to stay put** liegen/stehen/hängen etc bleiben; (hair) halten; (person, = not move) sich nicht von der Stelle rühren; (= not stand up) sitzen bleiben; **just stay put!** bleib, wo du bist!

b = write schreiben; comma, line machen; (= draw) zeichnen, malen; **to put one's signature to a document** seine Unterschrift unter ein Schriftstück setzen; **put your name here** schreiben or setzen Sie Ihren Namen hierhin; **to put a cross/tick against sb's name** jds Namen ankreuzen/abhaken; **he put it in his next**

novel er brachte das in seinem nächsten Roman

c = put forward case, question, proposal vorbringen; **to put a matter before a committee** eine Angelegenheit vor einen Ausschuss bringen; **to put the arguments for and against sth** das Für und Wider von etw (dat) aufzählen; **to put sth on the agenda** etw auf die Tagesordnung setzen; **to put a question/suggestion to sb** jdm eine Frage stellen/einen Vorschlag unterbreiten

♦ **to put it to sb (that ...)** (= suggest) **I put it to you that ...** ich behaupte, dass ...; **it was put to me that ...** es wurde mir nahe gelegt, dass ...; **I put it to him that this might not fit in with his theory** ich gab ihm zu bedenken, dass dies vielleicht nicht in seine Theorie passen würde; **you might put it to him that a contribution would be welcome** du könntest ihm nahe legen, dass ein Beitrag erwünscht wäre; **how will you put it to him?** wie wirst du es ihm beibringen?

d = express ausdrücken, sagen; **the compliment was eloquently put** das Kompliment war gewandt formuliert

♦ **to put it... that's one way of putting it** so kann mans auch sagen; **as he would put it** wie er sich ausdrücken würde; **as Shakespeare puts it** wie Shakespeare es ausdrückt; **put it so as not to offend her** formulieren Sie es so, dass Sie sie nicht beleidigen; **how shall I put it?** wie soll ich (es) sagen?; **if I may put it so** wenn ich das so sagen darf, wenn ich mich (mal) so ausdrücken darf; **to put it bluntly** um es klipp und klar zu sagen

e = rate schätzen (at auf +acc)

♦ **to put sth above/amongst/before sth I put him above Tennyson** ich schätze ihn höher ein als Tennyson; **I wouldn't put him amongst the greatest poets** ich würde ihn nicht zu den größten Dichtern zählen; **he puts money before his family's happiness** er stellt Geld über das Glück seiner Familie

2 – INTRANSITIVE VERB

♦ **to put to sea** (Naut) in See stechen

3 – PHRASAL VERBS

▶ **put about** (esp Brit) **VT** sep **a** (= circulate) news, rumour verbreiten, in Umlauf bringen; **he put it about that ...** er verbreitete (das Gerücht), dass ...; **he's been putting himself about a lot lately** (inf) er hat sich in letzter Zeit ganz schön in Szene gesetzt **b** (Naut) **to put a ship about** den Kurs (eines Schiffes) ändern **VI** (Naut) den Kurs ändern

▶ **put across VT** sep **a** (= communicate) ideas verständlich machen (to sb jdm), klar zum Ausdruck bringen; knowledge vermitteln (to sb jdm); (= promote) an den Mann bringen (inf); **to put a product across to the public** ein Produkt an den Mann bringen (inf); **to put oneself across** den richtigen Eindruck von sich geben

b (inf, = play a trick) **to put one across sb** jdn anführen; **he's just trying to put one across (you)** er will dich nur anführen

▶ **put aside VT** sep **a** book, knitting etc beiseite legen **b** (= save for later use) beiseite or auf die Seite legen, zurücklegen; (in shop) zurücklegen **c** (fig: = forget, abandon) ablegen, über Bord werfen (inf); anger, grief, animosity begraben; thought aufgeben; differences vergessen

▶ **put away VT** sep **a** (in usual place) einräumen; toys aufräumen; (= tidy away) wegräumen; **put that money away in your bag** steck das Geld in deine Tasche; **put that money away!** steck das Geld weg!; **to put the car away** das Auto wegstellen

b (= save) zurücklegen

c (inf, = consume) schaffen (inf); **he can certainly put it away!** (food) der kann was verdrücken! (inf); (drink) der kann was schlucken! (inf)

d (= lock up: in prison, mental home) einsperren

e (= put to sleep) pet einschläfern

▶ **put back VT** sep **a** (= replace) → **put 1 a** zurückstellen or -setzen/-legen/-stecken **b** (esp Brit: postpone) meeting, date verschieben; (= set back) plans, production zurückwerfen; (= readjust) watch etc zurückstellen; **to be put back a class** (pupil) eine Klasse zurückgestuft werden → **clock VI** (Naut = go back) zurückkehren (to nach)

▶ **put by VT** sep (Brit) zurücklegen, auf die hohe Kante legen; **I've got a few pounds put by** ich habe ein paar Pfund auf der hohen Kante

▶ **put down** ✪ 17.2 **VT** sep **a** (= set down) object → **put 1 a** wegstellen or -setzen/-legen; surface verlegen; **to put it down on the floor** stellen or setzen Sie es auf den Boden; **I simply couldn't put that book down** ich konnte das Buch einfach nicht aus der Hand legen; **to put down the phone** (den Hörer) auflegen → **foot N b**

b (= lower) umbrella zumachen, zuklappen; aerial einschieben; car roof zurückklappen; lid zuklappen

c passenger absetzen

d (= land) landen

e (= crush) rebellion niederschlagen; rebels niederwerfen; crime besiegen; prostitution, gambling, drinking unterdrücken; rumour zum Verstummen bringen; critic, heckler zum Schweigen bringen; (= reject, humiliate) demütigen

f (= pay) anzahlen; deposit machen

g (= store) einlagern

h (esp Brit: = destroy) pet einschläfern; injured horse etc den Gnadenschuss geben (+dat); rats, vermin vernichten

i (= write down) niederschreiben, aufschreiben; (on form, in register) angeben; (Parl) motion, resolution vorlegen, einbringen; **to put one's name down for sth** sich or seinen Namen (in eine Liste) für etw eintragen; **to put one's son down for Eton** seinen Sohn für Eton anmelden; **you can put me down for £10** für mich können Sie £ 10 eintragen; **put it down to my account/my husband's account** schreiben Sie es mir/meinem Mann an; **put it down under sundries/on expenses** schreiben Sie es unter Verschiedenes an/als Spesen an → **paper N a, name**

j (= classify) halten (as für); **I'd put her down as about 30** ich würde sie auf etwa 30 schätzen

k (= attribute) zurückführen (to auf +acc), zuschreiben (to dat)

VI (Aviat) landen, niedergehen

▶ **put forth VI** +prep obj buds, shoots hervorbringen; plan, claim vorbringen; effort unternehmen

▶ **put forward VT** sep **a** (= propose) idea, suggestion, plan vorbringen; person (for job etc) vorschlagen; (as candidate) aufstellen; (= nominate) vorschlagen; **he put himself/his name forward for the job** er hat sich für den Posten angeboten **b** (esp Brit: = advance) date, meeting vorverlegen (to auf +acc); schedule voranbringen, weiterbringen (by um); watch etc vorstellen → **clock**

▶ **put in VT** sep **a** (= place in) → **put 1 a** hineinstellen or -setzen/-legen/-stecken; (= pack) einpacken; **he opened the drawer and put his hand in** er öffnete die Schublade und fuhr or griff mit der Hand hinein; **I'll just put the car in** ich stelle eben den Wagen weg

b (= insert in book, speech etc) einsetzen, einfügen; (= add) hinzufügen, dazusagen

c (= interpose) remark einfügen

d (= enter) application, protest, claim einreichen; **to put in a plea of not guilty** auf „nicht schuldig" plädieren; **to put one's name in for sth** sich um etw bewerben; for evening classes, exam sich für etw anmelden; **to put sb in for an exam/a race** jdn für eine Prüfung/für ein Rennen anmelden; **to put sb in for an award** jdn für eine Ehrung vorschlagen; **to put the car in for a service** das Auto zur Wartung (in die Werkstatt) bringen

e (= install) central heating, car radio einbauen

f (= employ) night watchman einsetzen; (= elect) political party an die Regierung bringen, ranbringen (inf)

g (Sport, = send in) player hereinnehmen; team to bat (als Innenmannschaft) hereinschicken

h (= devote, expend) time zubringen, verbringen (with mit), verwenden (with auf); **we have a couple of hours to put in at Heathrow** wir müssen uns in Heathrow ein paar Stunden die Zeit vertreiben; **to put in an hour at the piano** eine Stunde Klavier spielen; **to put in an hour's painting** eine Stunde lang malen; **could you put in a few hours' work at the weekend?** könnten Sie am Wochenende ein paar Stunden Arbeit einschieben?; **he put in a lot of hard work on the project** er hat eine Menge harter Arbeit in das Projekt gesteckt; **he always puts in a good day's work** er schafft jeden Tag ein ordentliches Arbeitspensum

VI a to put in for sth (for job) sich um etw bewerben; for leave, rise, house also etw beantragen

b (Naut, = enter port) **to put in at a port** in einen Hafen einlaufen; (= call at) einen Hafen anlaufen; **to put in to Bremen/harbour** in Bremen/in den Hafen einlaufen; **to put in for supplies** einen Hafen anlaufen, um die Vorräte aufzufüllen

▶ **put inside VT** sep (inf, in prison) einsperren (inf)

▶ **put off** ✪ 7.3 **VT** sep **a** (= set down) passengers aussteigen lassen (prep obj aus); (= forcibly) hinauswerfen (prep obj aus); **the conductor put us off at the theatre** der Schaffner sagte uns (dat) am Theater Bescheid, dass wir aussteigen müssten; **we asked to be put off at the theatre** wir baten darum, uns (dat) am Theater Bescheid zu sagen

b (= lay aside) uniform ablegen, ausziehen; responsibilities, worries ablegen

c (= postpone, delay) match, appointment etc verschieben; decision aufschieben; sth unpleasant hinauszögern; **it's too late to put our visitors off** es ist zu spät, die Besucher (wieder) auszuladen; **to put sth off till later** etw auf später verschieben; **to put sth off for 10 days/until January** etw um 10 Tage aufschieben/auf Januar verschieben

d (= make excuses to, be evasive with) questioner, boyfriend, creditor hinhalten; **he's not easily put off** er lässt sich nicht so leicht beirren; **I won't be put off any longer** ich lasse mich nicht länger hinhalten

e (= discourage) die Lust nehmen or verderben (+dat); **to put sb off sth** jdm etw verleiden, jdm die Lust an etw (dat) nehmen; **don't let his rudeness put you off** störe dich nicht an seiner Flegelhaftigkeit; **are you trying to put me off?** versuchst du, mir das mies zu machen (inf) or mir das zu verleiden?; **I've been put off the idea** diese Idee ist mir verleidet worden; **to put sb off doing sth** jdn davon abbringen or (person also) es jdm ausreden, etw zu tun

f (= distract) ablenken (prep obj von); **to put sb off the track** jdn von der Fährte abbringen; **he is easily put off his game** er lässt sich leicht vom Spiel ablenken; **I'd like to watch you if it won't put you off** ich würde dir gern zusehen, wenn es dich nicht stört

g (= switch off) light, TV, heater ausmachen, ausschalten; power, motor abstellen

▶ **put on VT** sep **a** coat, shoes etc anziehen; hat (sich dat) aufsetzen; make-up auftragen, auflegen; (fig: = assume) accent, manners annehmen; facade, front aufsetzen, vortäuschen; **to put on one's make-up** sich schminken; **to put on an air of innocence** eine unschuldige Miene aufsetzen; **his sorrow is put on** sein Kummer ist bloß Schau (inf); **to put it on** (inf) so tun(, als ob); **to put sb on** (inf) jdn verkohlen (inf) → **front**

b (= increase, add) **to put on weight** zunehmen; **to put on a few pounds** ein paar Pfund zunehmen; **to put on speed** schneller fahren, beschleunigen; **he put on fifty runs** (Cricket) erhöhte (das Gesamtergebnis) um fünfzig

Punkte; **ten pence was put on the price of petrol** (*Brit*) *or* **gas** (*US*) der Benzinpreis wurde um zehn Pence erhöht; **he saw I wanted it and promptly put another £10 on (the price)** er sah, dass ich es haben wollte, und hat gleich noch einmal £ 10 aufgeschlagen; **he's been putting it on a bit** (= *gaining weight*) er hat ganz schön zugenommen

c *play* aufführen; *party* geben; *exhibition* veranstalten; *film* vorführen; *train, bus* einsetzen; *food* (*on menu*) auf die Speisekarte setzen; (*fig*) *act, show* abziehen (*inf*); **Sobers was put on to bowl** Sobers wurde als Werfer eingesetzt; **he put on quite a show of being angry** er tat so, als wäre er wütend; **she put on a display of temper** sie inszenierte einen Wutanfall

d (*on telephone*) **to put sb on to sb** jdn mit jdm verbinden; **would you put him on?** könnten Sie ihn mir geben?

e (= *switch on*) *light, TV* anmachen, einschalten; **to put the kettle/dinner on** das Wasser/das Essen aufsetzen *or* aufstellen

f *watch etc* vorstellen → **clock**

g **to put sb on to sth** (= *inform about*) jdm etw vermitteln; **to put sb on to a plumber/garage etc** jdm einen Installateur/eine Reparaturwerkstatt *etc* empfehlen; **he put me on to a first--rate dentist** durch ihn bin ich an einen erstklassigen Zahnarzt gekommen; **what put you on to it?** was hat dich darauf gebracht?; **to put the police on to sb** die Polizei auf jds Spur bringen; **to put sb on to a winner/good thing** *etc* jdm einen heißen (*inf*) *or* todsicheren Tipp geben

▸ **put out** 🆅🆃 *sep* **a** (= *place outside*) *rubbish etc* hinausbringen; *cat, drunk* vor die Tür setzen; **to put the washing out (to dry)** die Wäsche (zum Trocknen) raushängen; **to be put out** (= *asked to leave*) vor die Tür gesetzt werden; **to be put out of a restaurant** aus einem Restaurant herausgeworfen werden; **to put sb out of business** jdn aus dem Markt drängen; **that goal put them out of the competition** mit diesem Tor waren sie aus dem Wettbewerb ausgeschieden; **she could not put him out of her mind** er ging ihr nicht aus dem Sinn; **to put sb's eyes out** jdm die Augen ausstechen → **grass**

b (= *stretch out, push out*) *hand, foot* ausstrecken; *tongue, head* herausstrecken; **to put one's head out of the window** den Kopf zum Fenster hinausstrecken → **feeler**

c (= *sprout*) *leaves, roots* hervorbringen, treiben

d *cards, dishes, cutlery* auflegen; *chessmen etc* aufstellen

e (= *farm out*) *work* weggeben, vergeben (*to an* +*acc*)

f (= *bring out, circulate*) *pamphlet, book* herausbringen; *propaganda* machen; *statement* abgeben; *message, appeal* durchgeben; *description* bekannt geben; (*on TV, radio*) *programme* bringen, senden

g (= *generate*) *kilowatts etc* abgeben; *horsepower* leisten

h (= *extinguish*) *fire, light, candle* ausmachen, löschen

i (= *make unconscious*) bewusstlos machen, betäuben; (*boxer*) k. o. schlagen

j (= *discontent, vex*) **to be put out (by sth)** (über etw *acc*) verärgert *or* ungehalten sein; **nothing seems to put her out** sie scheint sich über nichts zu ärgern

k (= *inconvenience*) **to put sb out** jdm Umstände bereiten *or* machen; **to put oneself out (for sb)** sich (*dat*) (wegen jdm) Umstände machen

l (= *dislocate*) *knee, shoulder* ausrenken; (*more severely*) auskugeln; *back* verrenken → **nose**

m (= *make inaccurate*) *instruments* ungenau machen; (*fig*) *calculations, figures* verfälschen

n **to put money out at interest/at 12%** Geld für Zinsen/zu 12% (Zinsen) verleihen

🆅🅸 **a** (*Naut*, = *set sail*) auslaufen; **to put out to sea** in See stechen; **to put out of port/from Bremen** aus dem Hafen/von Bremen auslaufen

▸ **put over** 🆅🆃 *sep* **a** = **put across** **b** (*esp US*: = *postpone*) verschieben (*to, until* auf +*acc*)

▸ **put through** 🆅🆃 *sep* **a** *plan, reform, proposal, bill* durchbringen; (+*prep obj*) bringen durch; *claim* weiterleiten; *job* durchführen, durchziehen (*inf*); *deal* tätigen

b +*prep obj* (= *cause to undergo*) durchmachen lassen; **to put sb through a test/an exam** jdn einem Test/einer Prüfung unterziehen; **he has put his family through a lot (of suffering)** seine Familie hat seinetwegen viel durchgemacht; **his guilty conscience put him through hell** sein schlechtes Gewissen machte ihm das Leben zur Hölle; **to put sb through university** jdn durch die Universität bringen; **they really put him through it!** (*inf*) den haben sie vielleicht durch die Mangel gedreht! (*inf*) → **mill, pace** [2] **N a**

c (= *connect by telephone*) *person* verbinden (*to* mit); *call* durchstellen (*to* zu); **to put a call through to Beirut** ein Gespräch nach Beirut vermitteln *or* (*caller*) anmelden

▸ **put together** 🆅🆃 *sep* **a** (= *put in same room, cage etc*) zusammentun; (= *seat together*) zusammensetzen; **he's better than all the others put together** er ist besser als alle anderen zusammen → **head 1 c** **b** (= *assemble*) zusammensetzen; *furniture, machine* zusammenbauen *or* -setzen; *book, essay, menu* zusammenstellen; *meal* auf die Beine stellen (*inf*); (*Jur*) *case* zusammenstellen; *collection, evidence, facts* zusammentragen → **two**

▸ **put under** 🆅🆃 *sep* (*doctor*) betäuben

▸ **put up** 🆅🆃 *sep* **a** (= *raise, lift up*) *hand* hochheben; *car window* zumachen; *sash window* hochschieben; *umbrella* aufklappen; *hair* hochstecken; *collar* hochschlagen, hochklappen; **put 'em up!** (*inf*) (*hands in surrender*) Hände hoch!; (*fists to fight*) na, mach schon! → **back N a, foot N a, wind** [1] **N a**

b (= *hoist*) *flag, sail* hissen, aufziehen

c (= *fasten up*) *picture, decorations, poster, curtains* aufhängen; *notice* anbringen

d (= *erect*) *building, fence, barrier* errichten; *ladder, scaffolding* aufstellen; *tent* aufschlagen

e (= *send up*) *missile, space probe* hochschießen

f (= *increase*) *numbers, sales, prices, demands* erhöhen; *rent* erhöhen, heraufsetzen; *sb's temperature, blood pressure* hoch treiben

g (= *propose*) *person* (*for job etc*) vorschlagen; (*as candidate*) aufstellen; (= *nominate*) vorschlagen; **he put himself up for the job** er hat sich für den Posten beworben

h (= *offer*) **to put sth up for sale/auction** etw zum Verkauf anbieten/zur Versteigerung geben; **to put one's child up for adoption** sein Kind zur Adoption freigeben; **to put up resistance (to sb)** (jdm) Widerstand leisten, sich (gegen jdn) wehren → **fight N a, struggle, performance**

i (= *feign*) *facade* vortäuschen

j (= *give accommodation to*) unterbringen

k (= *provide*) *capital* bereitstellen; *reward* aussetzen

l **to put sb up to sth** jdn zu etw anstiften

🆅🅸 **a** (= *stay*) wohnen; (*for one night*) übernachten

b **to put up for election** sich zur Wahl stellen

c **put up or shut up!** (*lit*) Geld her oder Maul halten! (*inf*); (*fig*) Butter bei die Fische! (*inf*)

▸ **put upon** 🆅🅸 +*prep obj* (= *impose on*) ausnutzen; **I won't be put upon any longer** ich lasse mich nicht länger ausnutzen

▸ **put up with** 🆅🅸 +*prep obj* sich abfinden mit; **I won't put up with that** das lasse ich mir nicht gefallen

put and call (option) N (*St Ex*) Stellagegeschäft *nt*

putative ['pjuːtətɪv] ADJ (*form*) vermutlich; *father, culprit* mutmaßlich

put: put-down N (= *snub*) Abfuhr *f*; **putoff** ['pʊtɒf] N (*inf*) faule Ausrede (*inf*); **put-on** (*inf*) 🅰🅳🅹 unecht, vorgetäuscht, aufgesetzt; *smile also* falsch → **put, Schau** *f* (*inf*); **it's just a ~** das ist nur Schau *or* (ein) Bluff; **put option** N (*St Ex*) Verkaufsoption *f*, Rückprämiengeschäft *nt*

put-put ['pʌtpʌt] N (= *sound*) Tuckern *nt* 🆅🅸 tuckern

putrefaction [ˌpjuːtrɪˈfækʃən] N Verwesung *f*

putrefy ['pjuːtrɪfaɪ] 🆅🅸 verwesen

putrescent [pjuːˈtresnt] ADJ (*form*) verwesend

putrid ['pjuːtrɪd] ADJ verfault; *smell* faulig; (*fig*: = *corrupt*) zersetzt; (*inf*: = *horrible*) grässlich, ekelhaft; **the rubbish had become ~** der Abfall war verfault

putsch [pʊtʃ] N Putsch *m*

putt [pʌt] 🅽 Schlag *m* (*mit dem man einlocht*); **he needed a long ~ at the 5th hole** am 5. Loch musste er aus großem Abstand einlochen 🆅🆃 putten, einlochen

puttee, putty ['pʌtɪ] N (Wickel)gamasche *f*

putter[1] ['pʌtə'] N (= *golf club*) Putter *m*; **he's a good ~** er kann gut einlochen

putter[2] (*US*) 🆅🅸 = **potter**

putting ['pʌtɪŋ] N Putten *nt*, Einlochen *nt*; (*as game*) Putten *nt*

putting green N (*Golf*) kleiner Rasenplatz zum Putten; (= *green*) Grün *nt*

putty[1] ['pʌtɪ] 🅽 Kitt *m*; **he was ~ in her hands** er war Wachs in ihren Händen 🆅🆃 kitten

putty[2] N = **puttee**

putty knife N Spachtel *m*

put: put-up ADJ (*inf*) **a ~ job** (*Brit inf*) ein abgekartetes Spiel; **put-upon** ADJ (*inf*) ausgenutzt; **she had a rather ~ air** sie guckte so, als fiele ihr ein Zacken aus der Krone; **put-you-up** N (*Brit, inf*) Schlafcouch *f*

putz [pʌts] N (*US*) **a** (*inf*: = *person*) Dussel *m* (*inf*) **b** (*vulg*: = *penis*) Schwanz *m* (*sl*)

puzzle ['pʌzl] 🅽 🅰 (= *wordgame etc*) Rätsel *nt*; (= *toy*) Geduldsspiel *nt*; (= *jigsaw*) Puzzle(spiel) *nt*; **books of ~s** *or* **~ books for children** Rätselbücher *pl* für Kinder 🅱 (= *mystery*) Rätsel *nt*; **it's a ~ to me** es ist mir ein Rätsel 🆅🆃 **a** (= *baffle*) verblüffen; **to be ~d about sth** sich über etw (*acc*) im Unklaren sein; **the authorities are ~d** die Behörden stehen vor einem Rätsel 🅱 **to ~ sth out** etw (her)austüfteln 🆅🅸 **to ~ about** *or* **over sth** sich (*dat*) über etw (*acc*) den Kopf zerbrechen

puzzled ['pʌzld] ADJ *look, frown* verdutzt, verblüfft; *person* verwirrt, verblüfft; **to be ~ why ...** verwundert *or* verdutzt sein, dass ...; **she was ~ why he didn't phone** sie wunderte sich, dass er nicht anrief

puzzle-headed ['pʌzl'hedɪd] ADJ *person* wirr, konfus

puzzlement ['pʌzlmənt] N Verblüffung *f*, Verwirrung *f*; **the look of ~ on her face** die Verwirrung in ihrem Gesicht

puzzler ['pʌzlə'] N (= *problem*) harter Brocken (*inf*)

puzzling ['pʌzlɪŋ] ADJ rätselhaft; *story, mechanism, attitude, question* verwirrend; **to be ~ to sb** jdm rätselhaft sein; **the ~ thing is that ...** das Verblüffende an der Sache ist, dass ...

PVC abbr of **polyvinyl chloride** PVC *nt*

PVS **a** abbr of **persistent vegetative state** **b** abbr of **postviral syndrome**

Pvt (*US Mil*) abbr of **Private**

PX (*US*) abbr of **Post Exchange**

pye-dog ['paɪdɒg] N (*Brit*) streunender Hundebastard

pygmy, pigmy ['pɪgmɪ] 🅽 🅰 **Pygmy** Pygmäe *m* 🅱 (= *small person, also fig*) Zwerg *m* 🅰🅳🅹 🅰 **Pygmy** Pygmäen-; **Pygmy tribe** Pygmäenvolk *nt* 🅱 Zwerg-; **~ goat** Zwergziege *f*

pyjama, (*US*) **pajama** [pə'dʒɑːmə] ADJ *attr* Schlafanzug-, Pyjama-; **~ jacket** Schlafanzug- *or* Pyjamajacke *f*; **~ party** Pyjamaparty *f*

pyjamas, (*US*) **pajamas** [pə'dʒɑːməz] PL Schlafanzug *m*, Pyjama *m*

pylon ['paɪlən] N Mast *m*

pyramid ['pɪrəmɪd] N Pyramide *f*

pyramidal [pɪ'ræmɪdl] ADJ pyramidenförmig *or* -artig

pyramid selling N ≈ Schneeballsystem *nt*

pyre ['paɪə'] N Scheiterhaufen *m* (*zum Verbrennen von Leichen*)

Pyrenean [pɪrə'niːən] ADJ pyrenäisch; ~ **mountain dog** Pyrenäenhund *m*

Pyrenees [pɪrə'niːz] PL Pyrenäen *pl*

pyretotherapy [paɪˌretəʊ'θerəpɪ] N (*Med*) Fiebertherapie *f*

Pyrex® ['paɪreks] N Hartglas *nt*, Jenaer Glas® *nt*

pyrite(s) ['paɪraɪt(s)] N Eisen- *or* Schwefelkies *m*, Pyrit *m*

pyroclastic [ˌpaɪərəʊ'klæstɪk] ADJ (*Geol*) *rocks* pyroklastisch; ~ **flow** pyroklastischer Strom

pyrolysis [paɪ'rɒlɪsɪs] N (*Chem*) Pyrolyse *f*

pyromania [ˌpaɪrəʊ'meɪnɪə] N Pyromanie *f*

pyromaniac [ˌpaɪrəʊ'meɪnɪæk] N Pyromane *m*, Pyromanin *f*

pyrotechnic [ˌpaɪərəʊ'teknɪk] ADJ (*lit*) pyrotechnisch; (*fig*) brillant

pyrotechnics [ˌpaɪrəʊ'teknɪks] N *sing* Pyrotechnik *f*; (*pl*: = *display*) Feuerwerk *nt*; **a display of** ~ (*lit, fig*) ein Feuerwerk *nt*

Pyrrhic ['pɪrɪk] ADJ ~ **victory** Pyrrhussieg *m*

Pythagoras [paɪ'θægərəs] N Pythagoras *m*

Pythagoras' theorem N der Satz des Pythagoras

Pythagorean [paɪˌθægə'rɪən] ADJ pythagoräisch

python ['paɪθən] N Python *m*, Pythonschlange *f*

pyx [pɪks] N Hostienkelch *m*; (*for sick communion*) Bursa *f*

pzazz [pzæz] N Flair *nt*, Pfiff *m* (*inf*)

Q

Q, **q** [kjuː] N Q *nt*, q *nt* → **P**

Q *abbr of* **Queen**

Qatar [kæˈtɑːˈ] N Katar *nt*

QC (*Brit*) *abbr of* **Queen's Counsel**

QED *abbr of* **quod erat demonstrandum** q.e.d.

qt *abbr of* **quart**

q.t. [kjuːˈtiː] N **on the ~** (*Brit inf*) heimlich

Q-tip® [ˈkjuːtɪp] N (*US*) Q-tip® *m*

qtr *abbr of* **quarter**

qua [kwɑː] ADV als

quack¹ [kwæk] N Schnattern *nt no pl*, Quaken *nt no pl*; **~~quack** (*baby-talk*) Entchen *nt* VI (*duck*) schnattern, quaken, quak machen (*inf*); **what? she ~ed** was?, quakte sie

quack² N (*also* **quack doctor**) Quacksalber *m*, Kurpfuscher *m*; (*hum*, = *doctor*) Doktor *m*, Medizinmann *m* (*hum*) ADJ *attr* Kurpfuscher-; **~ methods** Kurpfuschermethoden *pl*; **~ remedy** Mittelchen *nt*

quackery [ˈkwækərɪ] N Quacksalberei *f*, Kurpfuscherei *f*

quad [kwɒd] N **a** *abbr of* **quadrangle** Hof *m* **b** *abbr of* **quadruplet** Vierling *m* **c** (*Typ*) *abbr of* **quadrat** Quadrat *nt*, Blockade *f*; **em ~** Geviert *nt*; **en ~** Halbgeviert *nt* **d** (*Comput*) *abbr of* **quadruple ~ density** Vierfachdichte *f*

quad bike N Quad *nt*

Quadragesima [ˌkwɒdrəˈdʒesɪmə] N Quadragesima *f*

quadrangle [ˈkwɒdræŋgl] N **a** (*Math*) Viereck *nt* **b** (*Archit*) (viereckiger) (Innen)hof

quadrangular [kwɒˈdræŋgjʊlə] ADJ viereckig

quadrant [ˈkwɒdrənt] N Quadrant *m*

quadraphonic [ˌkwɒdrəˈfɒnɪk] ADJ quadrophonisch, quadrofonisch

quadrat [ˈkwɒdrət] N (*Typ*) = **quad c**

quadratic [kwɒˈdrætɪk] ADJ (*Math*) quadratisch

quadrature [ˈkwɒdrətʃə] N (*Math, Astron*) Quadratur *f*

quadrilateral [ˌkwɒdrɪˈlætərəl] ADJ (*Math*) vierseitig N Viereck *nt*

quadrille [kwəˈdrɪl] N Quadrille *f*

quadrillion [kwəˈdrɪljən] N (*Brit*) Quadrillion *f*; (*US*) Billiarde *f*

quadrinomial [ˌkwɒdrɪˈnəʊmɪəl] ADJ viergliedrig, vierteilig

quadripartite [ˌkwɒdrɪˈpɑːtaɪt] ADJ (*Pol, form*) Vierer-; **~ talks** Vierergespräche *pl*; **~ agreement** Viermächteabkommen *nt*; **the ~ division of Berlin** die Teilung Berlins in vier Sektoren

quadriplegia [ˌkwɒdrɪˈpliːdʒə] N Tetraplegie *f*

quadriplegic [ˌkwɒdrɪˈpliːdʒɪk] ADJ tetraplegisch N Tetraplegiker(in) *m(f)*

quadroon [kwɒˈdruːn] N Viertelneger(in) *m(f)*, Terzerone *m* (*spec*), Terzeronin *f* (*spec*)

quadrophonic [ˌkwɒdrəˈfɒnɪk] ADJ quadrophonisch, quadrofonisch

quadruped [ˈkwɒdrʊped] N Vierfüß(l)er *m* ADJ vierfüßig

quadruple [ˈkwɒdrʊpl] ADJ vierfach; (*Mus*) Vierer-; **~ time** (*Mus*) Viertakt *m* N Vierfache(s) *nt* VT vervierfachen VI sich vervierfachen

quadruplet [kwɒˈdruːplɪt] N (= *child*) Vierling *m*

quadruplicate [kwɒˈdruːplɪkɪt] ADJ vierfach N **in ~** in vierfacher Ausfertigung

quaff [kwɒf] (*old, hum*) VT trinken, schlürfen (*hum*) VI zechen (*old, hum*); (= *take a swig*) schlucken

quaffable [ˈkwɒfəbl] ADJ *wine* süffig

quagmire [ˈkwægmaɪə] N Sumpf *m*, Morast *m*; (*fig*) (*of vice etc*) Morast *m*; (= *difficult situation*) Schlamassel *m* (*inf*); **the paths were reduced to a ~** die Wege waren völlig aufgeweicht *or* matschig; **he was bogged down in a ~ of tiny details** er hatte sich in einem Wust von kleinen Einzelheiten festgebissen

quail¹ [kweɪl] VI (vor Angst) zittern *or* beben (*before* vor +*dat*)

quail² N (*Orn*) Wachtel *f*; **~s' eggs** Wachteleier *pl*

quaint [kweɪnt] ADJ (+*er*) (= *picturesque*) *cottage, village, scene* malerisch, idyllisch; (= *charmingly old-fashioned*) *pub, custom, expression* urig, reizend; (= *pleasantly odd*) *idea* kurios, schnurrig, putzig; *nickname* originell; *person, way of speaking* drollig; **how ~ to live in such an old house** das ist ja urig, in so einem alten Haus zu wohnen; **what a thought, my dear, how ~!** nein so was, meine Liebe, wie originell!

quaintly [ˈkweɪntlɪ] ADV **a** (= *picturesquely*) malerisch, idyllisch; *decorated, finished* malerisch, urig **b** *written* schnurrig; *dressed* putzig; *nicknamed* originell; *old-fashioned* schnurrig, kurios, skurril; **their little daughter got up and danced so ~ that ...** ihr Töchterchen ist aufgestanden und hat so drollig getanzt, dass ...

quaintness [ˈkweɪntnɪs] N **a** (= *picturesque nature*) malerischer *or* idyllischer Anblick; (= *old-fashioned charm*: *of pub, custom, expression*) Urigkeit *f* **b** (= *oddness*) (*of idea*) Kuriosität *f*, Schnurrigkeit *f*, Putzigkeit *f*; (*of nickname*) Originalität *f*; (*of person, way of speaking*) Drolligkeit *f*

quake [kweɪk] VI zittern, beben (*with* vor +*dat*); (*earth, rafters etc*) beben, erzittern N **a** (*inf*: = *earthquake*) (Erd)beben *nt* **b** (*of rafters etc*) Beben *nt*

quakeproof [ˈkweɪkpruːf] (*inf*) ADJ *building etc* erdbebensicher VT erdbebensicher machen

Quaker [ˈkweɪkə] N Quäker(in) *m(f)*; **~ school** Quäkerschule *f*, von Quäkern geleitete Schule; **~ meeting** Treffen *nt* der Quäker; **~ family** Quäkerfamilie *f*

Quakerism [ˈkweɪkərɪzəm] N Quäkertum *nt*

quaking grass [ˈkweɪkɪŋˌɡrɑːs] N Zittergras *nt*

quaky ADJ , **quakily** ADV [ˈkweɪkɪ, -lɪ] zitternd, zitt(e)rig

qualification [ˌkwɒlɪfɪˈkeɪʃən] N **a** (*on paper*) Qualifikation *f*; (= *document itself*) Zeugnis *nt*; (= *skill, ability, suitable quality*) Voraussetzung *f*; **what ~s do you have for this job?** welche Qualifikationen haben Sie für diese Stelle?; **English ~s are not recognized by Scottish schools** englische Zeugnisse werden von schottischen Schulen nicht anerkannt; **the only ~ needed is patience/is a knowledge of French** die einzige Voraussetzung ist Geduld/sind Französischkenntnisse

b (= *act of qualifying*) Abschluss *m* von jds Ausbildung; **after his ~ as a doctor/an insurance broker** nachdem er seine Ausbildung als Arzt/Versicherungsagent abgeschlossen hatte; **prior to his ~** vor Abschluss seines Studiums **c** (*Sport*) Qualifikation *f* **d** (= *prerequisite*) Voraussetzung *f* **e** (= *limitation*) Einschränkung *f*, Vorbehalt *m*; (= *modification*) Modifikation *f*; **to accept a plan with/without ~(s)** einen Plan unter Vorbehalt/ vorbehaltlos billigen **f** (*Gram*) nähere Bestimmung

qualified [ˈkwɒlɪfaɪd] ADJ **a** (= *having training*) ausgebildet; (= *with degree*) Diplom-; **~ engineer/interpreter** Diplomingenieur(in)/-dolmetscher(in) *m(f)*; **highly ~** hoch qualifiziert; **to be ~ to do sth** qualifiziert sein, etw zu tun; **~ to practise** (*doctor, lawyer*) zugelassen; **he is/is not ~ to teach** er besitzt die/keine Lehrbefähigung; **he was not ~ for the job** ihm fehlte die Qualifikation für die Stelle; **to be well ~ for sth** für etw hoch qualifiziert *or* gut geeignet sein; **he is fully ~** er ist voll ausgebildet; **now that you are ~** nachdem Sie nun Ihre Ausbildung abgeschlossen haben; **she's better ~ than any other candidate** sie ist besser qualifiziert als die anderen Kandidaten *or* als jeder andere Kandidat **b** (= *able, entitled*) berechtigt; *voter* berechtigt, zugelassen; **to be ~ to vote** wahlberechtigt sein; **I'm not ~ to speak for her** ich bin nicht kompetent, in ihrem Namen zu sprechen; **what makes you think you're ~ to judge her?** mit welchem Recht meinen Sie, sie beurteilen zu können?

c (= *limited*) *praise, approval* bedingt, nicht uneingeschränkt; **we're only prepared to make a ~ statement** wir können uns nur bedingt *or* mit Einschränkungen zu ... äußern; **his theory is so ~ as to be ...** seine Theorie hat so viele Einschränkungen, dass sie ...; **in a ~ sense** mit Einschränkung; **a ~ success** kein voller Erfolg; **a ~ yes** ein Ja *nt* mit Einschränkungen, ein bedingtes Ja; **~ acceptance** (*Comm*) bedingte Annahme

qualifier [ˈkwɒlɪfaɪə] N (*Gram*) Ausdruck *m* des Grades

qualify [ˈkwɒlɪfaɪ] VT **a** (= *make competent*) qualifizieren; (= *make legally entitled*) berechtigen, das Recht geben (+*dat*); **to ~ sb to do sth** (= *entitle*) jdn berechtigen, etw zu tun; **his experience qualifies him to make these decisions** aufgrund *or* auf Grund seiner Erfahrung ist er qualifiziert *or* kompetent, diese Entscheidungen zu treffen; **this qualifies him for promotion** dadurch kommt er für eine Beförderung in Betracht

b (= *limit*) *statement, criticism* einschränken; (= *change slightly*) *opinion, remark* modifizieren, relativieren

c (*Gram*) charakterisieren, näher bestimmen; **the adjective qualifies the noun** das Adjektiv bestimmt das Substantiv näher

d (= *describe*) bezeichnen, klassifizieren

VI **a** (= *acquire degree etc*) seine Ausbildung abschließen, sich qualifizieren; **to ~ as a lawyer/doctor** sein juristisches/medizinisches Staatsexamen machen; **to ~ as a teacher** die Lehrbefähigung erhalten; **to ~ as an officer** das Offizierspatent erwerben; **your salary increases**

when you ~ Sie bekommen nach bestandener Prüfung ein höheres Gehalt **b** (*Sport, in competition*) sich qualifizieren (*for* für); **those who pass the first round of tests ~ for the final interviews** diejenigen, die die erste Testreihe erfolgreich bearbeiten, kommen in die engere und letzte Auswahl **c** (= *fulfil required conditions*) infrage or in Frage kommen (*for* für); **does he ~ for admission to the club?** erfüllt er die Bedingungen für die Aufnahme in den Klub?; **he hardly qualifies as a poet** er kann kaum als Dichter angesehen werden

qualifying ['kwɒlɪfaɪɪŋ] ADJ *adjective* erläuternd; (*Sport*) Qualifikations-; **~ match** Qualifikationsspiel *nt*; **~ examination** Auswahlprüfung *f*

qualitative ADJ , **qualitatively** ADV ['kwɒlɪtətɪv, -lɪ] qualitativ

quality ['kwɒlɪtɪ] N **a** (= *degree of goodness*) Qualität *f*; (*Comm, categorized*) Güteklasse *f*, Qualität *f*; (*of justice, education etc*) (hoher) Stand; **of the best ~** von bester Qualität; **of good/poor ~** von guter/schlechter Qualität, qualitativ gut/schlecht; **~ matters more than quantity** Qualität geht vor Quantität; **they vary in ~** sie sind qualitativ verschieden; **the excellent ~ of her mind** ihr hervorragender Verstand; **~ of life** Lebensqualität *f* **b** (= *characteristics of person, thing*) Eigenschaft *f*; **he has the ~ of great patience** er hat viel or große Geduld, er ist sehr geduldig **c** (= *nature*) Art *f*; **because of the unique ~ of the relationship** da es eine einzigartige Beziehung war **d** (*of voice, sound*) Klangfarbe *f*; (*Ling*) Qualität *f*; (*of colour*) Farbqualität *f* **e** (*old, hum, = high rank*) vornehmer Stand; **the ~** die Oberschicht, die vornehme Welt; **people of ~** Leute *pl* von Rang und Namen; **a lady of ~** eine vornehme Dame **f the qualities** (*Brit*: = *newspapers*) die seriösen Zeitungen *pl* ◾ATTR **a** Qualitäts-; **~ goods** Qualitätsware *f*; **~ mark** Gütezeichen *nt* **b** (*inf*: = *good*) erstklassig (*inf*); *newspaper* angesehen, seriös; **the ~ press** (*Brit*) die seriöse Presse

quality: quality control N Qualitätskontrolle *f*; **quality controller** N (*Ind*) Qualitätskontrolleur(in) *m(f)*; **quality time** N intensiv genutzte Zeit; **today I spent some ~ with my children** heute habe ich mich einige Zeit den Kindern gewidmet

qualm [kwɑːm] N **a** (= *doubt, scruple*) Skrupel *m*, Bedenken *nt*; **I would feel** or **have no ~s about killing that dog** ich würde keine Bedenken or Skrupel haben, den Hund zu töten; **without the slightest ~** ohne die geringsten Skrupel or Bedenken; **without a ~** ohne jeden Skrupel; **~s of conscience** Gewissensbisse *pl*; **he suddenly had ~s about it** ihn überkamen plötzlich Skrupel or Bedenken **b** (= *misgiving*) Bedenken *nt*; **I had some ~s about his future** ich hatte mancherlei Bedenken hinsichtlich seiner Zukunft **c** (*old:* = *nausea*) Übelkeit *f*

qualmish ADJ , **qualmishly** ADV ['kwɑːmɪʃ, -lɪ] voller Skrupel; *person* immer wieder von Skrupeln geplagt

quandary ['kwɒndərɪ] N Verlegenheit *f*, Dilemma *nt*; **what a ~ he was in!** was für ein Dilemma!; **he was in a ~ as to** or **about what to do** er wusste nicht, was er tun sollte; **to put sb in a ~** jdn in Verlegenheit or in eine missliche Lage bringen

quango ['kwæŋgəʊ] N (*Brit*) *abbr of* **quasi-autonomous nongovernmental organization** *regierungsunabhängige Kommission*

QUANGO

Der Begriff **quango** (ein Akronym aus **quasi-autonomous nongovernmental organization**) kam in den siebziger Jahren in Großbritannien auf, als man eine Bezeichnung für Organisationen wie **Equal Opportunities Commission** oder **Race Relations Board** fin-

---

den musste, die von der Regierung eingerichtet werden, aber keiner Regierungsbehörde unterstellt waren. Einige **quangos** üben Regierungsfunktionen aus, andere dagegen haben nur beratende Funktion. Kritisiert wird mittlerweile die Praxis, zahlreiche Bereiche aus der Verantwortlichkeit der Regierung in **quangos** auszulagern, die der Öffentlichkeit gegenüber nicht rechenschaftspflichtig sind.

quanta ['kwɒntə] *pl of* **quantum**

quantification [ˌkwɒntɪfɪ'keɪʃən] N Quantifizierung *f*

quantifier ['kwɒntɪfaɪə'] N (*Logic*) Quantor *m*

quantify ['kwɒntɪfaɪ] VT quantifizieren (*form*), in Zahlen ausdrücken

quantitative ADJ , **quantitatively** ADV ['kwɒntɪtətɪv, -lɪ] quantitativ; *restrictions, controls* quantitativ, mengenmäßig; **in ~ terms** rein quantitativ or mengenmäßig betrachtet

quantity ['kwɒntɪtɪ] N **a** Quantität *f*; (= *amount*) Menge *f*; (= *proportion*) Anteil *m* (*of an* +*dat*), Quantum *nt*; **to prefer ~ to quality** Quantität der Qualität vorziehen; **in ~**, **in large quantities** in großen Mengen; **what ~ did you order?** welche Menge haben Sie bestellt?; **a tiny ~ of poison** eine kleine Menge Gift; **what ~ of yeast was used?** wie viel Hefe wurde benutzt?; **the ~ of meat in these sausages is very small** der Fleischanteil in diesen Würsten ist sehr klein; **in equal quantities** zu gleichen Mengen or Teilen **b** *often pl* (= *large amount or number*) Unmenge *f*; **quantities of books/beer** Unmengen von Büchern/Bier **c** (*Math, Phys, fig*) Größe *f* **d** (*Poet, Phon*) Quantität *f*

quantity: quantity mark N Quantitätszeichen *nt*; **quantity surveyor** N Baukostenkalkulator(in) *m(f)*

quantum ['kwɒntəm] N *pl* **quanta** (*Phys*) Quant *nt*; **the quality of life cannot be measured as a ~** Lebensqualität kann nicht in Zahlen ausgedrückt werden; **the ~ of satisfaction** das (Aus)Maß an Zufriedenheit

quantum: quantum jump, **quantum leap** N (*Phys*) Quantensprung *m*; (*fig*) Riesenschritt *m*; **quantum mechanics** N *sing* Quantenmechanik *f*; **quantum number** N Quantenzahl *f*; **quantum physics** N *sing* Quantenphysik *f*; **quantum theory** N Quantentheorie *f*

quarantine ['kwɒrəntiːn] N Quarantäne *f*; **to be in ~** in Quarantäne sein; (*ship*) unter Quarantäne liegen; **to put sb in ~** jdn unter Quarantäne stellen ◾ATTR Quarantäne-; **~ period** Quarantänezeit *f* ◾VT *person, animal, ship, area* unter Quarantäne stellen

quark¹ [kwɑːk] N (*Phys*) Quark *nt*

quark² N (= *cheese*) Quark *m*

quarrel¹ ['kwɒrəl] N (*in window*) rautenförmiges Fensterglas

quarrel² N **a** Streit *m*; (= *dispute*) Auseinandersetzung *f*; **they have had a ~** sie haben Streit gehabt, sie haben sich gestritten; **let's not have a ~ about it** wir wollen uns nicht darüber streiten; **to start** or **pick a ~** einen Streit anfangen (*with mit*) **b** (*cause for complaint*) Einwand *m* (*with gegen*); **I have no ~ with him** ich habe nichts gegen ihn ◾VI **a** (= *have a dispute*) sich streiten (*with mit, about, over über* +*acc*); (*more trivially*) sich zanken; **to ~ over sth** sich über etw (*acc*) streiten; (*over inheritance*) sich wegen or um etw streiten; **to ~ over a girl** sich wegen eines Mädchens or um ein Mädchen streiten **b** (= *find fault*) etwas auszusetzen haben (*with an* +*dat*); **you can't ~ with that** daran kann man doch nichts aussetzen

quarrelling, (*US*) **quarreling** ['kwɒrəlɪŋ] N Streiterei *f*

quarrelsome ['kwɒrəlsəm] ADJ streitsüchtig; *woman also* zänkisch

quarrelsomeness ['kwɒrəlsəmnɪs] N Streitsucht *f*

quarrier ['kwɒrɪə'] N = **quarryman**

quarry¹ ['kwɒrɪ] N **a** Steinbruch *m*; **sandstone/ slate etc ~** Sandstein-/Schieferbruch *etc* **b** (*fig*) Fundgrube *f* ◾VT brechen, hauen ◾VI Steine brechen or hauen; **to ~ for sth** etw hauen or brechen; (*fig*) nach etw suchen

▶ **quarry out** VT *sep block* heraushauen or -brechen

quarry² N **a** Beute *f* **b** (*fig*, = *thing*) Ziel *nt*; (= *person*) Opfer *nt*

quarryman ['kwɒrɪmən] N *pl* **-men** [-mən] Steinbrucharbeiter *m*, Steinhauer *m*

quart¹ [kwɔːt] N (*Measure*) Quart *nt*; **to try to put a ~ into a pint pot** (*fig*) Unmögliches versuchen

quart² N **a** (*Fencing*) Quart *f* **b** (*Cards*) Vierersequenz *f*, Quart *f*; **~ major** Quartmajor *f*

quarter ['kwɔːtə'] N **a** (= *fourth part*) Viertel *nt*; **to divide sth into ~s** etw in vier Teile teilen; **the bottle was a ~/three-quarters full** die Flasche war zu einem Viertel/zu drei Vierteln gefüllt, die Flasche war viertel/drei viertel voll; **a ~ (of a pound) of tea** ein Viertel(pfund) Tee; **a mile and a ~** eineinviertel Meilen; **a ~ of a mile** eine Viertelmeile; **it was a ~ as big as the other one** es war ein Viertel so groß wie das andere; **for a ~ (of) the price, for ~ the price** zu einem Viertel des Preises **b** (*in expressions of time*) Viertel *nt*; **a ~ of an hour** eine Viertelstunde; **a ~ to seven, a ~ of seven** (*US*) (ein) Viertel vor sieben, drei viertel sieben (*dial*); **a ~ past six, a ~ after six** (*US*) (ein) Viertel nach sechs, viertel sieben (*dial*); **it's just on the ~** es ist gerade Viertel; **the clock strikes the ~s** die Uhr schlägt alle Viertelstunde; **the clock has just struck the ~** die Uhr hat eben Viertel or die Viertelstunde geschlagen; **an hour and a ~** eineinviertel Stunden, fünf viertel Stunden **c** (= *fourth year*) Vierteljahr *nt*, Quartal *nt*; **paid by the ~** vierteljährlich bezahlt; **a ~'s rent** die Miete für ein Quartal **d** (*US*) Vierteldollar *m*, 25-Cent-Stück *nt* **e** (= *district in town*) Viertel *nt* **f** (= *area*) **he has travelled in every ~ of the globe** er hat schon alle Ecken der Welt bereist; **they came from all ~s of the earth** sie kamen aus allen Teilen der Welt; **in these ~s** in dieser Gegend **g** (= *direction*) (Himmels)richtung *f*; **they came from all ~s** sie kamen aus allen Himmelsrichtungen **h** (*Naut*: = *direction of wind*) Richtung *f*; **what ~ is the wind in?** aus welcher Richtung kommt der Wind? **i** (= *side*) Seite *f*; (= *place*) Stelle *f*; **he won't get help from that ~** von dieser Seite wird er keine Hilfe bekommen; **in high ~s** höheren Orts; **in various ~s** an verschiedenen Stellen; **at close ~s** in der Nähe; (= *from nearby*) aus der Nähe; **they were unaccustomed to fighting at close ~s** sie waren nicht an den Nahkampf gewöhnt **j quarters** PL (= *lodgings*) Quartier *nt* (*also Mil*), Unterkunft *f*; **to take up one's ~s** (*Mil*) sein Quartier beziehen; **to be confined to ~s** (*Mil*) Stubenarrest haben **k** (*Naut, for battle*) Posten *m*; **to take up one's ~s** Posten beziehen **l** (*Naut, = part of ship*) Achterschiff *nt*; **on the port ~** backbord; **on the starboard ~** steuerbord **m** (= *mercy in battle*) Schonung *f*, Pardon *m*; **to give ~** Schonung or Pardon gewähren; **he gave no ~** er kannte kein Pardon; **no ~ was asked for and none given** es wurde auf beiden Seiten schonungslos gekämpft **n** (*Her*) Wappenfeld *nt* **o** (*of moon*) Viertel *nt* **p** (*Sport, of match*) (Spiel)viertel *nt* **q** (*Measure*) ≈ Viertelzentner *m* ◾ADJ Viertel-; **~ pound/mile** Viertelpfund *nt*/-meile *f*; **the/a ~ part** das/ein Viertel ◾VT **a** (= *cut into four*) vierteln; *beef, horse* (in vier Teile) zerlegen; *traitor's body* vierteilen **b** (= *lodge*) unterbringen, einquartieren (*also Mil*) (*on* bei)

quarter: quarterback ['kwɔːtəbæk] N (*US Ftbl*) Quarterback *m*; **quarter day** N Quartalstag *m*; **quarterdeck** N (*Naut*) Achterdeck *nt*, Quarterdeck *nt*; **quarterfinal** [ˌkwɔːtə'faɪnl] N Viertelfinalspiel *nt*; **quarterfinalist** [ˌkwɔːtə-'faɪnlɪst] N Teilnehmer(in) *m(f)* am Viertelfinale; **quarter horse** N (*breed of horse*) Quarter Horse *nt*; **quarter-hour** **N** Viertelstunde *f* **ADJ** **a** (*lasting 15 minutes*) viertelstündig **b** (*every 15 minutes*) viertelstündlich

quartering ['kwɔːtərɪŋ] N **a** Vierteln *nt*; (= *division into four also*) Teilung *f* in vier Teile; (*of beef, horse*) Zerlegen *nt*; (*of traitor's body*) Vierteilen *nt* **b** (*Mil*) Einquartierung *f* **c** (*Her*) Einteilung *f* in vier Felder

quarterlight ['kwɔːtəlaɪt] N (*Brit*) Dreieckfenster *nt*; (*openable*) Ausstellfenster *nt*

quarterly ['kwɔːtəlɪ] **ADJ** vierteljährlich **N** Vierteljahresschrift *f* **ADV** vierteljährlich, alle Vierteljahre

quartermaster ['kwɔːtəˌmɑːstə'] N **a** (*Mil*) Quartiermeister *m* **b** (*Navy*) Steuermannsmaat *m*; **~'s store** Versorgungslager *nt*

Quartermaster General N Generalquartiermeister *m*

quarter: quarter note N (*US Mus*) Viertel(note *f*) *nt*; **quarter-note** **ADJ** **~ rest** Viertelpause *f*; **quarter-pounder** N (*Cook*) Viertelpfünder *m*; **quarter sessions** PL vierteljährliche Gerichtssitzungen *pl*; **quarterstaff** N (*Hist*) Schlagstock *m*; **quarter tone** N Viertelstonintervall *nt*

quartet(te) [kwɔː'tet] N (*Mus*, = *foursome*) Quartett *nt*

quarto ['kwɔːtəʊ] **N** (*Typ*) Quart(format) *nt* **ATTR** *paper, volume* in Quart

quartz ['kwɔːts] N Quarz *m*; **~ (iodine) lamp** Quarzlampe *f*

quartz: quartz clock N Quarzuhr *f*; **quartz crystal** N Quarzkristall *m*

quartzite ['kwɔːtsaɪt] N Quarzfels *m*

quartz watch N Quarzuhr *f*

quasar ['kweɪzɑː'] N Quasar *m*

quash [kwɒʃ] VT **a** (*Jur*) *verdict* aufheben, annullieren **b** *rebellion* unterdrücken; *suggestion, objection* ablehnen

quasi- ['kwɑːzɪ–] PREF quasi-, quasi; **~religious** quasireligiös; **acting in a ~managerial role** quasi als Manager handelnd

quatercentenary [ˌkwætəsen'tiːnərɪ] N (*also* **quatercentenary celebrations**) Vierhundertjahrfeier *f*; (= *anniversary*) vierhundertster Jahrestag

quaternary [kwə'tɜːnərɪ] **ADJ** (*Geol*) quartär; (*Chem*) quaternär, aus vier Teilen bestehend **N** (*Geol*) Quartär *nt*

quatrain ['kwɒtreɪn] N Vierzeiler *m*

quaver ['kweɪvə'] **N** **a** (*esp Brit Mus*) Achtel(note *f*) *nt*; **~ rest** Achtelpause *f* **b** (*in voice*) Beben *nt*, Zittern *nt*; **with a ~ in her voice** mit bebender *or* zitternder Stimme **VI** (*voice*) beben, zittern; (*Mus*) tremolieren **VT** mit bebender *or* zitternder Stimme sagen

quavering ['kweɪvərɪŋ], **quavery** ['kweɪvərɪ] ADJ *voice* bebend, zitternd; *notes* tremolierend

quay [kiː] N Kai *m*; **alongside the ~** am Kai

quayside ['kiːsaɪd] N Kai *m*; **the ~ bars** die Hafenkneipen *pl*

queasiness ['kwiːzɪnɪs] N Übelkeit *f*

queasy ['kwiːzɪ] ADJ (+*er*) *stomach* gereizt; **I feel ~** mir ist (leicht) übel; **it makes me ~** da wird mir übel; **don't do it if you feel ~ about it** wenn dir nicht wohl dabei ist, dann tus doch nicht; **a ~ feeling** (*unwell*) ein Gefühl *nt* der Übelkeit, ein Übelkeitsgefühl *nt*; **I had a ~ feeling about the whole thing** ich hatte ein ungutes Gefühl bei der ganzen Sache

queen [kwiːn] **N** **a** (*also fig*) Königin *f*; **she was ~ to George V** sie war die Gemahlin von Ge-

org V.; **~ of the May** Maikönigin *f* **b** (= *bee, ant etc*) Königin *f* **c** (*Cards*) Dame *f*; **~ of spades** Pikdame **d** (*Chess*) Dame *f*; **~'s bishop/ pawn** Damenläufer/-bauer *m* **e** (*inf*: = *homosexual*) Tunte *f* (*inf*) **VT** **a** (*Chess*) in eine Dame verwandeln *or* umwandeln **b** (*inf*) **to ~ it** die große Dame spielen; **to ~ it over sb** jdn herumkommandieren (*inf*) **VI** (*Chess*) sich in eine Dame verwandeln

queen: Queen-Anne ADJ *style, furniture, building* Queen-Anne-; **~ style furniture** Möbel *pl* im Queen-Anne-Stil; **queen bee** N Bienenkönigin *f*; **she's the ~ round here** (*fig inf*) sie ist hier die Nummer eins (*inf*); **queen cake** N kleiner Rosinenkuchen; **queen consort** N Königin *f*, Gemahlin *f* des Königs; **queen dowager** N Königinwitwe *f*

queenhood ['kwiːnhʊd] N Rang *m* einer Königin

queenly ['kwiːnlɪ] ADJ königlich; *rule also* der Königin

queen: queen mother N Königinmutter *f*; **Queen's Bench** N Oberster Gerichtshof

Queensberry rules ['kwiːnzbərɪ'ruːlz] PL Queensberry-Regeln *pl*

queen's: Queen's Counsel N (*Brit*) Kronanwalt *m*/-anwältin *f*, Anwalt *m*/Anwältin *f* der Krone, ≈ Staatsanwalt *m*/-anwältin *f*; (*as title*) Justizrat *m*/-rätin *f*; **queen's English** N englische Hochsprache; **don't you understand the ~?** verstehst du denn kein Englisch?; **queen's evidence** N **to turn ~** (*Brit*) als Kronzeuge auftreten; **Queen's Guide** N Pfadfinderin *f* mit den höchsten Auszeichnungen

queen-size bed ['kwiːnsaɪz'bed] N *ca.* 1,50 *m* breites Doppelbett

queen's: queen's peace N **to keep the ~** sich ordnungsgemäß verhalten; **a breach of the ~** öffentliche Ruhestörung; **Queen's Scout** N Pfadfinder *m* mit den höchsten Auszeichnungen; **queen's shilling** N **to take the ~** (*old*) des Königs Rock anziehen (*obs*); **Queen's Speech** N Thronrede *f*

QUEEN'S SPEECH, KING'S SPEECH

Die **Queen's Speech** (bzw. die **King's Speech**) ist die Rede, die der britische Monarch jedes Jahr zur feierlichen Parlamentseröffnung im Oberhaus vor den versammelten Parlamentsmitgliedern beider Häuser verliest. Sie wird vom Premierminister in Zusammenarbeit mit seinem Kabinett erstellt und enthält die Regierungserklärung für das kommende Jahr sowie Einzelheiten über geplante Gesetzesabkommen. In der Rede, die sowohl im Radio wie auch im Fernsehen direkt übertragen wird, bezieht sich der Monarch aus Tradition immer noch auf „My government".

---

queer [kwɪə'] **ADJ** (+*er*) **a** (= *strange*) eigenartig, seltsam, komisch; (= *eccentric*) komisch, kauzig; (*inf*: = *mentally unbalanced*) nicht ganz richtig (im Kopf) (*inf*); **a ~-sounding name** ein komischer Name; **he's a bit ~ in the head** (*inf*) er ist nicht ganz richtig im Kopf (*inf*); **doesn't it feel ~ being the only woman?** kommst du dir nicht komisch vor als einzige Frau? **b** (= *causing suspicion*) verdächtig, nicht ganz hasenrein (*inf*); **there's something ~ about it** da ist etwas faul dran (*inf*) **c** (*inf*) (= *unwell*) unwohl; (= *peculiar*) *feeling* komisch; **I feel ~** (= *unwell*) mir ist nicht gut; (= *peculiar*) mir ist ganz komisch (*inf*); **I came over all ~** mir wurde ganz anders (*inf*) *or* komisch (*inf*) **d** (*pej inf*: = *homosexual*) schwul (*inf*) **N** (*pej inf*: = *homosexual*) Schwule(r) *mf* (*inf*) **VT** (*inf*: = *spoil*) versauen (*inf*), vermasseln (*inf*); **to ~ sb's pitch** (*inf*) jdm einen Strich durch die Rechnung machen

queer-bashing ['kwɪəˌbæʃɪŋ] N (*Brit pej inf*) Überfälle *pl* auf Schwule

queerly ['kwɪəlɪ] ADV eigenartig, seltsam, komisch

queerness ['kwɪənɪs] N **a** Eigenartigkeit *f*, Merkwürdigkeit *f*, Seltsamkeit *f* **b** (*pej inf*: = *homosexuality*) Schwulheit *f* (*inf*)

Queer Street N (*Brit, inf*) **to be in ~** pleite *or* blank sein (*inf*); **we'll really be in ~ if that happens** wenn das passiert, sind wir wirklich in Schwulitäten (*inf*)

quell [kwel] VT *fear* bezwingen; *passion* bändigen, zügeln; *riot* unterdrücken, niederschlagen; *anxieties* überwinden

quench [kwentʃ] VT *flames, fire, thirst* löschen; (*liter*) *desire* stillen; *enthusiasm* dämpfen

quenchless ['kwentʃlɪs] ADJ (*liter*) *flames* unlöschbar; *curiosity* unstillbar

quenelle [kə'nel] N (*Cook*) (*of meat*) Fleischklößchen *nt*; (*of fish*) Fischklößchen *nt*

quern [kwɜːn] N Hand- *or* Drehmühle *f*; (*Archeol*) Mahlstein *m*

querulous ['kwerʊləs] ADJ nörglerisch, missmutig; **a ~ person** ein Querulant *m*, eine Querulantin

querulously ['kwerʊləslɪ] ADV nörglerisch, missmutig

query ['kwɪərɪ] **N** **a** (= *question*) Frage *f*; **there was a note of ~ in his voice** seine Stimme hatte einen fragenden Unterton; **that raises a ~ as to whether ...** das wirft die Frage auf, ob ...; **that raises a ~ about ...** das wirft die Frage (+*gen*) ... auf **b** (*Typ*) Fragezeichen *nt* **c** (*Comput*) Abfrage *f*; **~ language** Abfragesprache *f* **VT** **a** (= *express doubt about*) bezweifeln; *statement, motives* infrage *or* in Frage stellen; *bill, item, invoice* reklamieren; **I'm not ~ing your right to do that but ...** ich bezweifle ja nicht, dass Sie dazu berechtigt sind, aber ...; **£500! I'd ~ that if I were you** £ 500! da würde ich an Ihrer Stelle reklamieren; **I ~ whether ...** ich bezweifle, ob ... **b** (= *check*) **to ~ sth with sb** etw mit jdm abklären **c** (*with a question mark*) mit einem Fragezeichen versehen **d** (*Comput*) *database* abfragen

quest [kwest] **N** (= *search*) Suche *f* (*for* nach); (*for knowledge, happiness etc*) Streben *nt* (*for* nach); **to go in ~ of sth** (*old, liter*) sich auf die Suche nach etw machen **VI** **a** (*old, liter*: = *seek*) suchen (*for* nach); **to ~ for riches/truth** nach Reichtümern *or* Wahrheit streben **b** (*Hunt*) die Beute aufspüren

question ['kwestʃən] ❂ 8.3, 12.3, 16.3, 26.1, 26.3 **N** **a** (*Gram etc*) Frage *f* (*to an* +*acc*); (*Parl*) (An)frage *f* (*to an* +*acc*); **to ask sb a ~** jdm eine Frage stellen; **don't ask so many ~s** frag nicht so viel; **they'll buy anything, no ~s asked** sie kaufen alles und stellen keine dummen Fragen; **what a ~ (to ask)!** was für eine Frage!; **(that's a) good ~!** (das ist eine) gute Frage!; **let me put the ~ another way** ich werde die Frage anders formulieren **b** *no pl* (= *doubt*) Zweifel *m*, Frage *f*; **beyond (all) ~, without ~** ohne Frage, ohne (jeden) Zweifel; **his honesty is beyond ~** seine Ehrlichkeit steht außer Zweifel *or* Frage; **there is no ~ but that he has gone** (*form*) es besteht kein Zweifel darüber, er ist fort; **your sincerity is not in ~** niemand zweifelt an Ihrer Aufrichtigkeit; **to call sth into ~** etw infrage *or* in Frage stellen **c** (= *matter*) Frage *f*; **that's another ~ altogether** das ist etwas völlig anderes; **that's not the ~** darum geht es nicht; **the German ~** die deutsche Frage; **it's simply a ~ of time** das ist einfach eine Frage der Zeit; **it's not just a ~ of money** es ist nicht nur eine Geldfrage *or* eine Frage des Geldes; **if it's only a ~ of whether ...** wenn es nur darum geht (*inf*) *or* sich darum handelt, ob ... **d** *no pl* (= *possibility, likelihood*) **there is some ~ of whether ...** es ist ziemlich fraglich, ob ...;

there's no ~ of that happening es steht außer Diskussion *or* es kann keine Rede davon sein, dass das passiert; **there's no ~ of a strike** von einem Streik kann keine Rede sein; **that's out of the ~** das kommt nicht infrage *or* in Frage; **the person/matter in ~** die fragliche *or* infrage *or* in Frage stehende Person/Angelegenheit

VT **a** (= *ask questions of*) fragen (*about* nach); (*police etc*) befragen, vernehmen, verhören (*about* zu); (*examiner*) prüfen (*on* über +*acc*); **my father started ~ing me about where I'd been** mein Vater fing an, mich auszufragen, wo ich gewesen war; **they were ~ed by the immigration authorities** ihnen wurden von der Einwanderungsbehörde viele Fragen gestellt; **I don't like being ~ed, she said** ich mag diese Verhöre nicht, sagte sie

b (= *express doubt about*) bezweifeln, zweifeln an (+*dat*); (= *dispute, challenge*) infrage *or* in Frage stellen; **they ~ whether it's worth it** sie bezweifeln, dass es der Mühe wert ist; **but I'm not ~ing that!** das bezweifle *or* bestreite ich ja nicht; **he ~ed her inclusion on the committee** er äußerte Bedenken gegen ihre Aufnahme in den Ausschuss

questionable ['kwestʃənəbl] ✪ 26.3 ADJ **a** (= *suspect*) fragwürdig; **of ~ morals** von zweifelhaftem moralischem Standard; **in ~ taste** geschmacklos **b** (= *open to doubt*) *statement, figures* fraglich; *advantage* zweifelhaft; **of ~ value** von fragwürdigem Wert

questionary ['kwestʃənəri] N (*esp Med*) Fragebogen *m*

questioner ['kwestʃənə'] N Fragesteller(in) *m(f)*, Frager(in) *m(f)*

questioning ['kwestʃənɪŋ] ADJ **a** *nature* neugierig, interrogativ, kritisch, in Zweifel ziehend; **to have a ~ mind** eine kritische Haltung haben, seiner Natur nach den Dingen auf den Grund gehen **b** (= *doubting*) *look* fragend **N** (*by parents, husband*) Verhör *nt*; (*by police also*) Vernehmung *f*; (*of candidate*) Befragung *f*; **after hours of ~ by the immigration authorities** nach stundenlanger Befragung durch die Einwanderungsbehörde; **they brought him in for ~** sie holten ihn, um ihn zu vernehmen

questioningly ['kwestʃənɪŋlɪ] ADV fragend

question: question mark N Fragezeichen *nt*; **to put a ~ over sth** etw infrage *or* in Frage stellen; **question master** N Quizmaster *m*

questionnaire [ˌkwestʃə'neə'] N Fragebogen *m*

question: question tag N (*Ling*) Frageanhängsel *nt*; **question time** N Zeit *f* für Fragen; (*Brit Parl*) Fragestunde *f* **queue** [kju:] **N** **a** (*Brit: of people, cars*) Schlange *f*; **to form a ~** eine Schlange bilden; **to stand in a ~** Schlange stehen, anstehen; **to join the ~** sich (hinten) anstellen; **a ~ of cars** eine Autoschlange; **a long ~ of people** eine lange Schlange **b** (*old: = pigtail*) Zopf *m* **VI** (*Brit: also* **queue up**) Schlange stehen; (*people also*) anstehen; (= *form a queue*) eine Schlange bilden; (*people*) sich anstellen; **they were queuing outside the cinema** sie standen vor dem Kino Schlange; **we ~d for an hour** wir haben eine Stunde angestanden; **they were queuing for the bus** sie standen an der Bushaltestelle Schlange; **they were queuing for bread** sie standen nach Brot an; **people are queuing up to ...** (*fig*) die Leute schlagen sich darum, zu ...

queue: queue-jump VI (*Brit*) sich vordränge(l)n; (*Mot*) aus einer Kolonne ausscheren und überholen; **queue-jumper** N (*Brit*) jd, der sich vordräng(el)t (*Mot*) Kolonnenspringer(in) *m(f)*; **the ~s were booed** die, die sich vordräng(el)ten, wurden ausgebuht; **queue-jumping** N (*Brit*) Vordränge(l)n *nt*; (*Mot*) Kolonnenspringen *nt*; **hey you, no ~!** he, Vordränge(l)n gibts nicht! (*inf*)

quibble ['kwɪbl] **VI** (= *be petty-minded*) kleinlich sein (*over, about* wegen); (= *argue with sb*) sich herumstreiten (*over, about* wegen); **to ~ over details** auf Einzelheiten herumreiten; **he ~d about the design** er krittelte am Design herum; **they weren't arguing, just quibbling** sie disku-

---

tierten nicht, sondern stritten sich nur über Spitzfindigkeiten **N** **these aren't really serious criticisms at all, just ~s** das ist doch keine ernsthafte Kritik, das sind doch nur Spitzfindigkeiten *or* Haarspaltereien; **I've got a few ~s about her work/ the design** ich habe ein paar Kleinigkeiten an ihrer Arbeit/am Design auszusetzen; **I hope you don't think this is a ~, but ...** ich hoffe, Sie halten mich nicht für kleinlich, aber ...

quibbler ['kwɪblə'] N (= *petty critic*) Krittler(in) *m(f)*, Kritikaster *m* (*pej*); (= *hair-splitter*) Wortklauber(in) *m(f)*, Haarspalter(in) *m(f)*

quibbling ['kwɪblɪŋ] ADJ (= *petty*) *person* kleinlich; (= *hair-splitting*) *person, details, argument* spitzfindig **N** kleinliches Getue (*inf*); (= *petty criticism*) Krittelei *f*; (= *hair-splitting*) Haarspalterei *f*, Wortklauberei *f*; **all this ~ about details** dieses Herumreiten auf Einzelheiten

quiche [ki:ʃ] N Quiche *f*

quick [kwɪk] ADJ (+*er*) **a** (= *rapid*) schnell; *answer, temper, prompt*; **be ~!** mach schnell!; (*on telephone etc*) fass dich kurz!; **come on, ~, ~!** komm, schnell, schnell *or* zack, zack (*inf*); **and be ~ about it** aber ein bisschen dalli (*inf*); **you were ~** das ist ja schnell gegangen, das war ja schnell; **he's a ~ worker** er ist von der schnellen Truppe, er arbeitet schnell; **he was the ~est to be promoted** er wurde am schnellsten befördert; **he was too ~ for me** (*in speech*) das ging mir zu schnell; (*in escaping*) er war zu schnell für mich; **~ march!** (*Mil*) im Eilschritt, marsch!; **it's ~er by train** mit dem Zug geht es schneller; **to be ~ to do sth** etw ganz schnell tun; **he is ~ to criticize other people** er ist mit seiner Kritik schnell bei der Hand; **he is ~ to anger** er wird leicht zornig; **the ~est way to the station** der schnellste Weg zum Bahnhof; **what's the ~est way to the station?** wie komme ich am schnellsten zum Bahnhof?; **what's the ~est way to finish it?** wie werde ich am schnellsten damit fertig?

b (= *short, quickly done*) *kiss* flüchtig; *speech, synopsis* kurz; *rest* klein, kurz; **let me have a ~ look** lass mich mal schnell *or* kurz sehen; **we had a ~ meal** wir haben schnell etwas gegessen; **let's go for a ~ drive** komm, wir machen eine kleine Spritztour; **he took a ~ swig of whisky** er trank schnell einen Schluck Whisky; **to have a ~ chat (with sb)** (mit jdm) ein paar Worte wechseln; **could I have a ~ word?** könnte ich Sie mal kurz sprechen?; **could I have a ~ try?** darf ich mal schnell *or* kurz versuchen?; **I'll just write him a ~ note** ich schreibe ihm schnell mal *or* kurz; **I grabbed a ~ sleep** ich legte mich kurz hin; **time for a ~ beer** genügend Zeit, um schnell ein Bierchen zu trinken; **a ~ one** eine(r, s) auf die Schnelle (*inf*); (*question*) eine kurze Frage

c (= *lively, quick to understand*) *mind* wach; *person* schnell von Begriff (*inf*); *child* aufgeweckt; *temper* hitzig, heftig; *eye, ear* scharf; **the ~er children soon get bored** die Kinder, die schneller begreifen *or* die eine schnellere Auffassungsgabe haben, langweilen sich bald; **he is ~ at figures** er kann schnell rechnen; **to be ~ at doing sth** fix dabei sein, etw zu tun; **he's very ~** er begreift *or* kapiert (*inf*) schnell; **he's too ~ for me** mit ihm komme ich nicht mit; **~, isn't he?** ist das aber schlagfertig **N** (*Anat*) empfindliches Fleisch (*besonders unter den Fingernägeln*); **to bite one's nails to the ~** die Nägel bis zum Fleisch abkauen; **to be cut to the ~** (*Brit*) tief getroffen sein; **to cut sb to the ~** (*Brit*) jdn zutiefst verletzen

b *pl* (*liter*) **the ~ and the dead** die Lebenden und die Toten **ADV** (+*er*) schnell

quick: quick-acting ADJ *medicine* schnell wirkend *attr*; *person* schnell handelnd; **quickbeam** ['kwɪkbi:m] N (*Bot*) Vogelbeerbaum *m*, Eberesche *f*; **quick-change artist** N (*Theat*) Verwandlungskünstler(in) *m(f)*; **quick-drying** ADJ *paint, concrete* schnell trocknend

---

quicken ['kwɪkən] **VT** **a** (*also* **quicken up**) beschleunigen **b** (*liter.* = *make more lively*) *feelings* erhöhen; *imagination* beflügeln (*geh*), anregen **VI** **a** (*also* **quicken up**) schneller werden; **~, sich beschleunigen; **the pace ~ed** das Tempo nahm zu **b** (*liter, hope, interest*) wachsen; (*foetus*) sich bewegen

quick: quick-fire questions PL Fragen *pl* wie aus der Maschinenpistole; **quick-firing** ADJ (*Mil*) schnell feuernd; **quick fix** N Schnelllösung *f*; **quick-freeze** VT *food* einfrieren, einfrosten; **quick-frozen** ADJ Gefrier-, tiefgekühlt; **~ vegetables** Gefriergemüse *nt*

quickie ['kwɪkɪ] N (*inf* = *drink*) eine(r, s) auf die Schnelle (*inf*); (= *question*) kurze Frage; (= *sex*) Quickie *m* (*inf*); **the meeting has to be a ~** mit der Besprechung müssen wirs kurz machen (*inf*)

quicklime ['kwɪklaɪm] N ungelöschter Kalk

quickly ['kwɪklɪ] ADV schnell; **as ~ as I can** so schnell (wie) ich kann

quick motion N Schnellgang *m*; **in ~** (*Film*) im Zeitraffer

quickness ['kwɪknɪs] N **a** (= *speed*) Schnelligkeit *f*; **his ~ to appreciate the problem** die Schnelligkeit, mit der er das Problem erfasst hat **b** (= *intelligence*) schnelle Auffassungsgabe; **~ of mind** Fähigkeit *f*, schnell zu denken; **~ of eye** schnelle Auffassungsgabe; **~ of temper** heftiges *or* aufbrausendes Temperament

quick: quicksand N Treibsand *m*; **quickset hedge** N Hecke *f*; (= *hawthorn*) Weißdornhecke *f*; **quick-setting** ADJ *glue etc* schnell trocknend *attr*; *cement* schnell bindend *attr*; **quicksilver** N Quecksilber *nt* **ADJ** *attr* (*fig liter*) quecksilbrig, lebhaft; **quickstep** N Quickstepp *m*; **quick-tempered** ADJ hitzig, leicht erregbar; **to be ~** leicht aufbrausen; **quickthorn** N Rotdorn *m*; **quick time** N (*US Mil*) Marsch im Normaltempo; **quick-witted** ADJ geistesgegenwärtig; *answer* schlagfertig; **the more ~ candidates** die Kandidaten mit einer schnelleren Auffassungsgabe; **quick-wittedness** N Geistesgegenwart *f*, Schlagfertigkeit *f*, schnelle Auffassungsgabe

quid[1] [kwɪd] N *pl* - (*Brit inf*) Pfund *nt*; **20 ~** 20 Eier (*sl*); **to be ~s in** auf sein Geld kommen (*inf*)

quid[2] N (= *tobacco*) Priem *m*

quiddity ['kwɪdɪtɪ] N **a** (*Philos*) Quiddität *f* (*spec*), Wesen *nt* **b** (*liter.* = *quibble*) Spitzfindigkeit *f*

quid pro quo ['kwɪdprəʊ'kwəʊ] N Gegenleistung *f*

quiescence [kwɪ'esns] N Ruhe *f*, Stille *f*

quiescent [kwɪ'esnt] ADJ ruhig, still

quiet ['kwaɪət] ADJ (+*er*) **a** (= *silent*) still; *neighbours, person* ruhig, still; *engine* ruhig; *footsteps, music, car, voice* leise; **at night when the office is ~** nachts, wenn im Büro alles still ist; **double-glazing makes the house ~er** durch Doppelfenster wird das Haus ruhiger; **she was as ~ as a mouse** sie war mucksmäuschenstill (*inf*); **(be) ~!** Ruhe!; **to keep ~** (= *not speak*) still sein; (= *not make noise*) leise sein; **keep ~!** sei still!; **can't you keep your dog ~?** können Sie nicht zusehen, dass ihr Hund still ist?; **that book should keep him ~ for a while** das Buch sollte ihn eine Weile beschäftigt halten, mit dem Buch sollte er eine Weile zu tun haben; **to keep ~ about sth** über etw (*acc*) nichts sagen; **you've kept very ~ about it** du hast ja nicht viel darüber verlauten lassen; **to go ~** still werden; (*music etc*) leise werden; **could you make the class ~ for a minute?** könnten Sie die Klasse für eine Minute zur Ruhe bringen?; **turn the volume down** ~ dreh die Lautstärke zurück; **I can't make the radio any ~er** ich kann das Radio nicht (noch) leiser stellen

b (= *peaceful*) ruhig; *evening* geruhsam, ruhig; *conscience* gut, ruhig; *smile* leise; **this town is too ~ for me** die Stadt ist mir zu ruhig; **things are very ~ at the moment** im Augenblick ist nicht viel los; **business is ~** das Geschäft ist ruhig; **to have a ~ mind** beruhigt sein; **he had a ~**

sleep er hat ruhig geschlafen; **the patient had a ~ night** der Patient verbrachte eine ruhige or ungestörte Nacht; **to lead a ~ life** ein ruhiges Leben führen; **all ~ on the western front** im Westen nichts Neues; **yesterday everything was ~ on the Syrian border** gestern herrschte Ruhe or war alles ruhig an der syrischen Grenze; **I was just sitting there having a ~ drink** ich saß da und habe in aller Ruhe mein Bier etc getrunken

c (= gentle) face, character sanft; child ruhig; horse brav, gutwillig; irony leise

d (= unpretentious, simple) dress, tie, colour dezent; style einfach, schlicht; elegance schlicht; wedding, dinner, funeral im kleinen Rahmen

e (= not overt) hatred, envy, despair still; resentment heimlich; **I'll have a ~ word with him** ich werde mal ein Wörtchen (im Vertrauen) mit ihm reden; **could we have a ~ word together some time** könnten wir uns mal unter vier Augen unterhalten?; **I caught him having a ~ drink** ich habe ihn dabei erwischt, wie er heimlich getrunken hat; **they had a ~ laugh over it** sie haben im Stillen darüber gelacht; **he kept the matter ~** er behielt die Sache für sich; **keep it ~** behalte es für dich

f (= unobtrusive, confidential) dinner ruhig, im kleinen Kreis; negotiation besonnen, vertraulich; diplomacy besonnen; **there are grounds for ~ optimism** zurückhaltender Optimismus scheint angebracht or am Platz

N Ruhe f; **a period of ~** eine Zeit der Stille; **in the ~ of the night** in der Stille der Nacht; **on the ~** heimlich; **he left on the ~** er ist still und heimlich weggegangen → **peace**

VT = **quieten**

VI (US: = become quiet) nachlassen, erlahmen, erlöschen; **his sobs ~ed** sein Schluchzen ließ nach

quieten ['kwaɪətn] **VT** (Brit) **a** sb zum Schweigen bringen; noisy class, dog zur Ruhe bringen; crying baby beruhigen; engine ruhiger machen; **b** (= make calm) person, conscience beruhigen; suspicion, fear zerstreuen

▸**quieten down** (Brit) **VI** (= become silent) leiser werden; (= become calm) sich beruhigen; (after wild youth) ruhiger werden; **quieten down, boys!** ein bisschen ruhiger, Jungens!; **things have quietened down a lot** es ist viel ruhiger geworden **VT** sep person beruhigen; engine ruhiger machen; **to quieten things down** (situation) die Lage beruhigen

quietism ['kwaɪɪtɪzəm] **N** Quietismus m

quietist ['kwaɪɪtɪst] **N** Quietist(in) m(f) **ADJ** quietistisch

quietly ['kwaɪətlɪ] **ADV** (= making little noise) leise; (= peacefully, making little fuss) ruhig; (= secretly) still und heimlich; dressed dezent; (= placidly) still; **to live ~** ruhig or zurückgezogen leben; **he's very ~ spoken** er spricht sehr leise; **a very ~ spoken young man** ein sehr ruhiger junger Mann; **to be ~ confident** insgeheim sehr sicher sein; **I can only think how happy I am, how ~ content** ich kann mich nur glücklich und zutiefst zufrieden schätzen; **I was sitting here ~ sipping my wine** ich saß da und trank in aller Ruhe meinen Wein; **he sat down and ~ died** er setzte sich hin und starb in aller Stille; **he refused to go ~** er weigerte sich, unauffällig zu gehen; **are you going to come ~?** (said by policeman) kommen Sie widerstandslos mit?, kommen Sie ohne Widerstand zu leisten mit?; **he slipped off ~** er machte sich in aller Stille davon (inf); **they got married very ~** sie haben im kleinen Rahmen geheiratet; **and all the time he was ~ writing a novel about us** und die ganze Zeit hat er still und heimlich einen Roman über uns geschrieben

quietness ['kwaɪətnɪs] **N** **a** (= lack of noise) Stille f; (of engine, car) Geräuscharmut f; (of footsteps etc) Geräuschlosigkeit f, Lautlosigkeit f; (of person) stille Art; **the ~ of her voice** ihre leise Stimme; **then with the sudden ~ of the music ...** und dann, als die Musik plötzlich leise

wurde ... **b** (= peacefulness) Ruhe f **c** (of tie, colour) Dezentheit f; (of style) Schlichtheit f

quietude ['kwaɪətjuːd] **N** (liter) Ruhe f, Friede(n) m

quietus [kwaɪˈiːtəs] **N** (old, liter) Todesstoß m; **to give sb his/sth its ~** jdm/einer Sache den Todesstoß versetzen; **he found his ~** er schied von hinnen (liter)

quiff [kwɪf] **N** (esp Brit) Stirnlocke f, Tolle f

quill [kwɪl] **N** **a** (= feather) Feder f; (= feather stem) Federkiel m **b** (also **quill-pen**) Federkiel m, Feder f **c** (of porcupine) Stachel m

quilt [kwɪlt] **N** (= continental quilt) Steppdecke f; (unstitched) Federbett nt; (= bedspread) Bettdecke f **VT** absteppen; (with padding) wattieren; **~ed jacket** Steppjacke f

quilting ['kwɪltɪŋ] **N** **a** (= process) (Ab)steppen nt, Wattieren nt **b** (= material) Steppstoff m

quim [kwɪm] **N** (Brit sl) Möse f (vulg)

quin [kwɪn] **N** (Brit) abbr of **quintuplet** Fünfling m

quince [kwɪns] **N** (= fruit, tree) Quitte f; **~ jelly** Quittengelee nt

quincentenary [ˌkwɪnsenˈtiːnərɪ] **N** fünfhundertster Jahrestag; (also **quincentenary celebrations**) Fünfhundertjahrfeier f

quinine [kwɪˈniːn] **N** Chinin nt

Quinquagesima [ˌkwɪŋkwəˈdʒesɪmə] **N** Quinquagesima f

quinquennia [kwɪŋˈkwenɪə] pl of **quinquennium**

quinquennial [kwɪŋˈkwenɪəl] **ADJ** alle fünf Jahre (stattfindend); (= lasting five years) fünfjährig

quinquennium [kwɪŋˈkwenɪəm] **N** pl **quinquennia** (form) Jahrfünft nt

quinsy ['kwɪnzɪ] **N** (old) Mandelentzündung f

quint¹ [kwɪnt] **N** (US) abbr of **quintuplet** Fünfling m

quint² **N** (Mus) Quint(e) f

quintessence [kwɪnˈtesns] **N** (Philos, fig) Quintessenz f; (= embodiment) Inbegriff m

quintessential [ˌkwɪntɪˈsenʃəl] **ADJ** (liter) fundamental (geh); **the ~ English gentleman** der Inbegriff des englischen Gentleman; **an instance of his ~ bad taste** ein Beispiel für seinen von Grund auf schlechten Geschmack; **the ~ Catholicism of his whole attitude** seine fundamental (geh) or durch und durch katholische Haltung

quintessentially [ˌkwɪntɪˈsenʃəlɪ] **ADV** (liter) durch und durch; **they are ~ different** sie sind fundamental (geh) or von Grund auf verschieden; **this is ~ Bach** das ist Bach reinsten Wassers

quintet(te) [kwɪnˈtet] **N** (Mus: = group of five) Quintett nt

quintillion [kwɪnˈtɪljən] **N** (Brit) Quintillion f; (US) Trillion f

quintuple ['kwɪntjʊpl] **ADJ** fünffach **N** Fünffache(s) nt **VT** verfünffachen **VI** sich verfünffachen

quintuplet [kwɪnˈtjuːplɪt] **N** Fünfling m

quip [kwɪp] **N** witzige or geistreiche Bemerkung **VTI** witzeln

quipster ['kwɪpstə'] **N** Spaßvogel m

quire¹ ['kwaɪə'] **N** **a** (= 24 sheets) 24 Bogen Papier **b** (= folded, unbound sheets) Bogen m

quire² **N** (obs) = **choir**

quirk [kwɜːk] **N** Schrulle f, Marotte f; (of nature, fate) Laune f; **by a strange ~ of fate** durch eine Laune des Schicksals

quirkiness ['kwɜːkɪnɪs] **N** Schrulligkeit f

quirky ['kwɜːkɪ] **ADJ** (+er) person, character schrullig

quirt [kwɜːt] **N** (US) geflochtene Reitpeitsche

quisling ['kwɪzlɪŋ] **N** Quisling m

quit [kwɪt] vb: pret, ptp **quitted** or **quit** **VT** **a** (= leave) town, army verlassen; this life scheiden aus; (= give up) job aufgeben, kündigen; **I've given her notice to ~ the flat** (form) ich habe ihr die Wohnung gekündigt; **I've had notice to ~**

the flat (form) mir ist (die Wohnung) gekündigt worden; **the dog would not ~ his prey** (liter) der Hund wollte nicht von seiner Beute ablassen (liter)

b (inf: = stop) aufhören mit; **to ~ doing sth** aufhören, etw zu tun; **~ it!** hör (damit) auf!; **to ~ work** mit der Arbeit aufhören

c (Comput) job, program verlassen, aussteigen aus (inf)

VI **a** (= leave one's job) kündigen

b (= go away) weg- or fortgehen; **notice to ~** Kündigung f; **they gave me notice to ~** sie haben mir gekündigt

c (= accept defeat) aufgeben

d (Comput) das Programm/die Datei etc verlassen, aussteigen (inf)

ADJ **~ of** los or frei von, ledig (+gen) (geh); **we are ~ of him** wir sind ihn los

quite [kwaɪt] **ADV** **a** (= entirely) ganz; (emph) völlig; **I am ~ happy where I am** ich fühle mich hier ganz wohl; **it's ~ impossible to do that** das ist völlig or gänzlich unmöglich; **you're being ~ impossible** du bist einfach unmöglich; **are you ~ finished?** bist du dann fertig?; **when you're ~ ready ...** (iro) wenn du dann fertig bist ...; **he's ~ grown up now** er ist jetzt schon richtig erwachsen; **I ~ agree with you** ich stimme völlig mit Ihnen überein; **he ~ understands that he must go** er sieht es durchaus or völlig ein, dass er gehen muss; **he has ~ recovered** er ist völlig or ganz wiederhergestellt; **that's ~ another matter** das ist doch etwas ganz anderes; **he said it in ~ another tone** er sagte es in einem ganz anderen Ton; **that's ~ enough for me** das reicht wirklich; **that's ~ enough of that** das reicht jetzt aber; **it was ~ some time ago** es war vor einiger Zeit; **not ~** nicht ganz; **you weren't ~ early/tall enough** Sie waren ein bisschen zu spät dran/zu klein; **I don't ~ see what he means** ich verstehe nicht ganz, was er meint; **you don't ~ understand** Sie verstehen mich anscheinend nicht richtig; **that's not ~ your colour** das ist nicht ganz die richtige Farbe für Sie; **he's not ~ the James Bond type** er ist nicht gerade der James-Bond-Typ; **it was not ~ midnight** es war noch nicht ganz Mitternacht; **sorry! – that's ~ all right** entschuldige! – das macht nichts; **I'm ~ all right, thanks** danke, mir gehts gut; **thank you – that's ~ all right** danke – bitte schön; **it's ~ all right, thank you, I can manage alone** das geht schon, danke, ich komme alleine zurecht; **~ (so)!** genau!, sehr richtig!, ganz recht!; **~ the thing** (inf) ganz große Mode

b (= to some degree) ziemlich; **~ likely/unlikely** sehr wahrscheinlich/unwahrscheinlich; **he's had ~ a lot to drink** er hat ziemlich viel or ganz schön viel (inf) getrunken; **~ a few people** ziemlich viele Leute; **he is ~ a good singer** er ist ein ziemlich guter Sänger; **I ~ like this painting** dieses Bild gefällt mir ganz gut; **yes, I'd ~ like to** ja, eigentlich ganz gern

c (= really, truly) wirklich; **she was a ~ beautiful girl** sie war wirklich eine Schönheit; **she's ~ a girl/friend** etc sie ist ein tolles Mädchen/eine tolle Freundin etc; **it's ~ delightful** es ist entzückend, es ist einfach wunderbar; **it was ~ a shock** es war ein ziemlicher or ganz schöner (inf) Schock; **it was ~ a disappointment/change** es war eine ziemliche or ganz schöne (inf) Enttäuschung/Veränderung; **that's ~ some bruise/car** (inf) das ist vielleicht ein blauer Fleck/ein Auto (inf); **it was ~ a party** das war vielleicht eine Party! (inf); **it was ~ an experience** das war schon ein Erlebnis; **he's ~ the gentleman now** er ist jetzt ganz der feine Herr; **he's ~ a hero now** jetzt ist er ein richtiger Held; **~ the little party-goer, aren't we?** (inf) du bist wohl so eine richtige kleine Partynudel, wie? (inf); **he's ~ a comedian, isn't he?** er ist ja sehr komisch

quits [kwɪts] **ADJ** quitt; **to be ~ with sb** mit jdm quitt sein; **shall we call it ~?** (= agree to stop) lassen wirs (dabei bewenden)?; (when owing money) sind wir quitt? → **double**

quittance ['kwɪtəns] **N** Schuldenerlass m

quitter ['kwɪtə'] N (*inf*) **he's not a ~** er gibt nicht so leicht auf

quiver¹ ['kwɪvə'] **VI** zittern; (*person also*) beben (*with* vor +*dat*); (*wings*) flattern; (*lips, eyelids, heart*) zucken; (*flesh*) wabbeln **N** Zittern *nt*; Beben *nt*; Flattern *nt*; Zucken *nt*; Wabbeln *nt*

quiver² N Köcher *m*

quiverful ['kwɪvəfʊl] N (*of arrows*) Köchervoll *m*

qui vive [‚kiː'viːv] N **on the ~** auf dem Quivive (*dated*), auf der Hut

quixotic [kwɪk'sɒtɪk] ADJ *behaviour, gesture etc* edelmütig, ritterlich; *ideals* schwärmerisch, idealistisch; **a foolish ~ act** eine Donquichotterie; **don't you find that a little ~?** finden Sie das nicht etwas versponnen?

quixotically [kwɪk'sɒtɪkəlɪ] ADV *behave* edelmütig, ritterlich

quiz [kwɪz] **N** **a** Quiz *nt* **b** (*US Sch inf*) Prüfung *f* **VT** **a** (*= question closely*) ausfragen (*about* über +*acc*) **b** (*US Sch inf*) abfragen, prüfen **c** (*obs: = stare at impudently*) mustern, beäugen **d** (*obs: = mock*) necken (*geh*)

quiz: quizmaster N Quizmaster *m*; **quiz programme**, (*US*) **quiz program** N Quizsendung *f*; **quiz show** N Quiz *nt*

quizzical ['kwɪzɪkəl] ADJ **a** (*= knowing, shrewd*) *air, look* fragend; *smile* wissend, gewitzt **b** (*= odd*) eigenartig, drollig

quizzically ['kwɪzɪkəlɪ] ADV *look* fragend; *smile* zweifelnd

quodlibet ['kwɒdlɪbet] N (*Mus*) Quodlibet *nt*, (Lieder)potpourri *nt*

quoin [kwɔɪn] N **a** (*= outer corner of wall*) Ecke *f*; (*= cornerstone*) Eckstein *m* **b** (*Typ*) Schließzeug *nt*

quoit [kwɔɪt] N Wurfring *m*

quoits [kwɔɪts] N *sing* Wurfringspiel *nt*; **to play ~** Wurfring spielen

quondam ['kwɒndæm] ADJ (*liter*) ehemalig, früher; **his ~ wife** weiland seine Gattin (*obs*)

Quonset (hut)® ['kwɒnsɪt('hʌt)] N (*US*) Nissenhütte *f*

quorate ['kwɔːreɪt] ADJ (*form*) **to be ~** ein Quorum haben

quorum ['kwɔːrəm] N Quorum *nt*; **to make a ~** ein Quorum haben, beschlussfähig sein

quota ['kwəʊtə] N **a** (*of work*) Pensum *nt* **b** (*= permitted amount*) Quantum *nt*; (*= share allotted*) Anteil *m*; (*of goods*) Kontingent *nt*; **the ~ of immigrants allowed into the country** die zugelassene Einwanderungsquote; **import ~** Einfuhrkontingent *nt*

quotability [‚kwəʊtə'bɪlɪtɪ] N Zitierbarkeit *f*; **something with a little more ~ for the headlines** ein Zitat, das sich besser als Schlagzeile eignet

quotable ['kwəʊtəbl] ADJ zitierbar, zitierfähig; **a highly ~ author** ein gern zitierter Autor; **~ quips from his speech** geistreiche Bemerkungen aus seiner Rede, die sich als Zitate eignen

quotation [kwəʊ'teɪʃən] N **a** (*= passage cited*) Zitat *nt*; (*act*) Zitieren *nt*; **dictionary of ~s** Zitatenlexikon *nt*; **a ~ from Shakespeare** ein Shakespearezitat *nt*; **a ~ from the Bible** ein Bibelzitat *nt*; **a two-bar ~ from Bach** zwei Takte, die von Bach übernommen sind **b** (*Fin: = statement of price*) (Börsen- *or* Kurs)notierung *f* **c** (*Comm: = estimate*) (Preis)angebot *nt*; (*for building work etc*) Kostenvoranschlag *m*

quotation marks PL Anführungszeichen *pl*, Anführungsstriche *pl*; **open/close ~** Anführungsstriche unten/oben; **to put a word in ~** ein Wort in Anführungszeichen *or* -striche setzen

quote [kwəʊt] ⊙ 26.2 **VT** **a** *author, text* zitieren; **you can ~ me (on that)** Sie können das ruhig wörtlich wiedergeben; **please don't ~ me**

on this, but ... (*= this isn't authoritative*) ich kann mich nicht hundertprozentig dafür verbürgen, aber ...; (*= don't repeat it*) bitte wiederholen Sie nicht, was ich jetzt sage, aber ...; **he was ~d as saying that ...** er soll gesagt haben, dass ...; **~ ... end ~** *or* **unquote** Zitat Anfang ... Zitat Ende; **and the ~(, unquote) liberals** und die Liberalen in Anführungszeichen

b (*= cite*) anführen; **to ~ sb/sth as an example** jdn/etw als Beispiel anführen

c (*Comm*) *price* nennen; *reference number* angeben; **how much did they ~ you for that?** wie viel haben sie dafür verlangt?, wie viel wollten sie dafür haben?

d (*St Ex*) notieren; **the shares are ~d at £2** die Aktien werden mit £ 2 notiert

VI **a** (*from person, text*) zitieren; **to ~ from an author** einen Schriftsteller zitieren, aus dem Werk eines Schriftstellers zitieren; **... and I ~** ... und ich zitiere

b (*Comm*) ein (Preis)angebot machen; (*building firm etc*) einen Kostenvoranschlag machen; **we asked six companies to ~** wir baten sechs Firmen um Preisangaben

N (*from author, politician*) Zitat *nt*; **a two-bar ~ from Bach** zwei von Bach übernommene Takte

b **quotes** PL Anführungszeichen *pl*, Gänsefüßchen *pl* (*inf*); **in ~s** in Anführungszeichen

c (*Comm*) Preis *m*; (*= estimate*) Kostenvoranschlag *m*

quoth [kwəʊθ] DEFECTIVE VB (*obs, hum*) sagte, sprach (*liter*)

quotidian [kwəʊ'tɪdɪən] ADJ (*form: = daily*) täglich; **the ~ lives of the people** der Alltag der Menschen

quotient ['kwəʊʃənt] N (*Math*) Quotient *m*

qv *abbr of* **quod vide** s.d.

qwerty keyboard ['kwɜːtɪ'kiːbɔːd] N Qwertystatur *f*

R

R, **r** [ɑːʳ] N R nt, r nt → also **three Rs**

R **a** abbr of **Rex** of **Regina** **b** abbr of **river** **c** (US Film) abbr of **restricted** für Jugendliche nicht geeignet

r abbr of **right** r.

RA abbr of **Royal Academy**

rabbet ['ræbɪt] N (= notch) Nut f; (= joint) Nutnaht f

rabbi ['ræbaɪ] N Rabbiner m; (as title) Rabbi m

rabbinical [rə'bɪnɪkəl] ADJ rabbinisch

rabbit ['ræbɪt] **N** Kaninchen nt; (= fur also) Kanin nt (spec); **to behave like a ~ caught in the headlights** ängstlich und überrascht handeln **VI** **a** **to go ~ing** Kaninchen jagen, auf Kaninchenjagd gehen **b** (Brit inf: also **rabbit on**) quasseln, schwafeln, sülzen (all inf)

rabbit in cpds Kaninchen-; **rabbit burrow**, **rabbit hole** N Kaninchenbau m; **rabbit hutch** N Kaninchenstall m; **rabbit punch** N Nacken- or Genickschlag m; **rabbit warren** N **a** Gänge pl des Kaninchenbaus **b** (fig: = maze) Labyrinth nt

rabble ['ræbl] N (= disorderly crowd) lärmende Menge, lärmender Haufen (inf); (pej: = lower classes) Pöbel m

rabble: rabble-rouser N Hetzer(in), Volksverhetzer(in) m(f); **rabble-rousing** **N** Hetze f, Volksverhetzung f **ADJ** (auf)hetzerisch

Rabelaisian [ræbə'leɪzɪən] ADJ **a** (of Rabelais) des Rabelais **b** (= like Rabelais) im Stile Rabelais'

rabid ['ræbɪd] ADJ **a** (Vet) tollwütig **b** (= fanatical) fanatisch; reformer, hatred fanatisch, wild

rabidness ['ræbɪdnɪs] N (= fanaticism) Fanatismus m; (of reformer, hatred) Wildheit f

rabies ['reɪbiːz] N Tollwut f

RAC abbr of **Royal Automobile Club**

raccoon N = **racoon**

race[1] [reɪs] **N** **a** Rennen nt; (on foot) Rennen nt, (Wett)lauf m; (swimming) Wettschwimmen nt; **100 metres ~** 100-Meter-Lauf m; **to run a ~ (against sb)** um die Wette laufen; **to go to the ~s** zum Pferderennen gehen; **a day at the ~s** ein Tag auf der Pferderennbahn; **we were at the ~s yesterday** wir waren gestern beim Pferderennen; **the ~ for the Democratic nomination/the White House** das Rennen um die Nominierung des demokratischen Kandidaten/die amerikanische Präsidentschaft; **it was a ~ to get the work finished** es war eine Hetze, die Arbeit fertig zu machen; **a ~ against time** or **the clock** ein Wettlauf m mit der Zeit or gegen die Uhr; **his ~ is run** (fig) er ist erledigt (inf)
   b (= swift current) Strömung f; (= mill race) Gerinne nt
   c (liter: of sun, moon) Lauf m
   VT **a** (= compete with) um die Wette laufen/reiten/fahren/schwimmen etc mit; (Sport) laufen/reiten/fahren/schwimmen etc gegen; **I'll ~ you to school** ich mache mit dir ein Wettrennen bis zur Schule; **the car was racing the train** das Auto fuhr mit dem Zug um die Wette
   b engine hochjagen
   c (Sport) car ins Rennen schicken; horse laufen or rennen lassen
   VI **a** (= compete) laufen/reiten/fahren/ schwimmen etc; **to ~ with** or **against sb** gegen jdn laufen etc, mit jdm um die Wette laufen etc; **we're racing against time (to get this finished)** wir arbeiten gegen die Uhr(, um fertig zu werden); **he ~s at Newmarket** er lässt seine Pferde in Newmarket laufen
   b (= rush) rasen, jagen; (on foot) rennen, rasen; (with work) hetzen; **to ~ about** herumrasen/-rennen etc; **to ~ after sb/sth** hinter jdm/etw herhetzen or herjagen; **to ~ to get sth finished** Dampf machen, um etw fertig zu bekommen (inf); **he ~d through his work** er jagte durch sein Arbeitspensum; **to ~ ahead with one's plans/work** etc seine Pläne/Arbeit etc vorantreiben; **the project is racing ahead** die Arbeit am Projekt geht mit Riesenschritten voran; **clouds ~d across the sky** Wolken jagten über den Himmel; **memories of the past ~d through her mind** Erinnerungen an die Vergangenheit jagten ihr durch den Kopf
   c (engine) durchdrehen; (pulse) jagen, fliegen; (heart) rasen; (thoughts, mind) jagen

race[2] N **a** (= ethnic group, species) Rasse f; **of mixed ~** gemischtrassig; **of noble ~** (person) edler Herkunft or Abstammung; (horse) (von) edler Rasse; **~ is causing a problem in this town** es gibt Rassenprobleme in dieser Stadt **b** (fig: of authors, poets etc) Kaste f

race: raceboat N (Sport) Rennboot nt; **racecard** N Rennprogramm nt; **race conflict** N Rassenkonflikt m; **racecourse** N (Brit) Rennbahn f; **racegoer** N (esp Brit) Rennbesucher(in) m(f); **race hatred** N Rassenhass m; **racehorse** N Rennpferd nt; **race meeting** N (esp Brit) Rennveranstaltung f

racer ['reɪsə] N Rennfahrer(in) m(f); (= car) Rennwagen m; (= bicycle) Rennrad nt; (= yacht) Rennjacht f; (= horse) Rennpferd nt

race: race relations **a** pl Beziehungen pl zwischen den Rassen **b** sing (= subject) Rassenintegration f; **Race Relations Board** N (Brit) Amt nt für Rassenfragen; **race riot** N Rassenkrawall m usu pl; **racetrack** N Rennbahn f; **race walker** N (Sport) Geher(in) m(f); **race walking** N (Sport) Gehen nt

rachitic [rə'kɪtɪk] ADJ (Med) rachitisch

rachitis [rə'kaɪtɪs] N (Med) Rachitis f

Rachmanism ['rækmænɪzəm] N (Brit) Mietwucher m

racial ['reɪʃəl] ADJ rassisch, Rassen-; pride auf die Rasse; **~ discrimination** Rassendiskriminierung f; **~ equality** Rassengleichheit f; **~ minority** rassische Minderheit; **~ prejudice** Rassenvorurteil nt; **~ violence** rassistische Gewalt; **to promote ~ harmony** das harmonische Zusammenleben der verschiedenen Rassen fördern; **to do sth on ~ grounds** etw aus rassistischen Gründen tun; **to vote along ~ lines** entsprechend der Rassenzugehörigkeit wählen

racial harassment N rassistisch motivierte Schikanierung

racialism ['reɪʃəlɪzəm] N (esp Brit) Rassismus m

racialist ['reɪʃəlɪst] **N** Rassist(in) m(f) **ADJ** rassistisch

racially ['reɪʃəlɪ] ADV offensive, sensitive in Bezug auf die Rasse; abused aufgrund or auf Grund seiner Rasse, in Bezug auf die Rasse; diverse multikulturell; pure rassisch; **he is ~ bias(s)ed** er hat Rassenvorurteile; **to be of ~ mixed parentage** gemischtrassige Eltern haben; **~ mixed marriage** gemischtrassige Ehe; **the schools were ~ integrated** die Schulen waren multikulturell; **~ superior** rassenmäßig überlegen; **to be ~ motivated** (riots etc) rassistisch motiviert sein; **a ~ motivated attack** ein ausländerfeindlicher Überfall or Angriff

racily ['reɪsɪlɪ] ADV write schwungvoll, feurig

raciness ['reɪsɪnɪs] N (of speech, style, play) Schwung m, Feuer nt; (= risqué nature) Gewagtheit f

racing ['reɪsɪŋ] N (= horse-racing) Pferderennsport m, Pferderennen nt; (= motor racing) Motorrennen nt; **he often goes ~** er geht oft zu Pferderennen/Motorrennen; (= participates) er nimmt oft an Pferderennen/Motorrennen teil

racing in cpds Renn-; **racing bicycle** N Rennrad nt; **racing car** N Rennwagen m; **racing certainty** N (Brit, fig) absolute Sicherheit; **it's a ~ that ...** es ist absolut sicher, dass ...; **racing colours** PL Rennfarben pl; **racing cyclist** N Radrennfahrer(in) m(f); **racing driver** N Rennfahrer(in) m(f); **racing man** N Anhänger m des Pferderennsports; **racing pigeon** N Brieftaube f; **racing stable** N Rennstall m; **racing tyres** PL Rennreifen pl; **racing world** N Welt f des Rennsports; **racing yacht** N Rennjacht f

racism ['reɪsɪzəm] N Rassismus nt

racist ['reɪsɪst] **N** Rassist(in) m(f) **ADJ** rassistisch

rack[1] [ræk] **N** **a** (for hats, toast, pipes etc) Ständer m; (for bottles, plates) Gestell nt, Ständer m; (= shelves) Regal nt; (= luggage rack) Gepäcknetz nt; (on car, bicycle) Gepäckträger m; (for bombs) Bombenträger m; (for fodder) Raufe f; (Tech) Zahnstange f
   b (US Billiards) Rahmen m
   c (Hist) Folter(bank) f; **to put sb on the ~** (lit, fig) jdn auf die Folter spannen; **to be on the ~** (lit) auf der Folterbank sein; (fig) Folterqualen leiden
   VT **a** (to cause pain, also fig) quälen, plagen; **~ed with pain/by remorse** von Schmerz/Gewissensbissen gequält or geplagt
   b **to ~ one's brains** sich (dat) den Kopf zerbrechen, sich (dat) den Kopf or das Hirn zermartern (inf)
   c (Hist) auf die Folter spannen, auf die Folter strecken

▶ **rack up** VT sep einbringen, hereinholen; **to rack up £200,000 in sales** £ 200 000 aus Verkäufen hereinholen; **to rack up 61% of the vote** 61% der Stimmen auf sich (dat) vereinen

rack[2] N **to go to ~ and ruin** (person) verkommen, vor die Hunde gehen (inf); (country, economy) herunterkommen, vor die Hunde gehen (inf); (building) verfallen, in Schutt und Asche zerfallen

rack[3] VT wine, beer abfüllen

rack-and-pinion steering ['rækən'pɪnjən-ˌstɪrɪŋ] N (Aut) Zahnstangenlenkung f

rack car N (US Rail) Doppelstockwagen m (für Autotransport)

racket[1] ['rækɪt] N (Sport: for tennis etc) Schläger m

racket[2] N a (= uproar) Krach m, Lärm m, Krawall m (inf); **to make a ~** Krach etc machen b (inf: = dishonest business) Schwindelgeschäft nt (inf), Gaunerei f (inf); (making excessive profit) Wucher m; **the drugs ~** das Drogengeschäft; **to be in on a ~** bei einer Gaunerei mitmischen (inf) c (inf: = business, job) Job m (inf); **what's his ~?** was macht er? (inf); **what ~ are you in?** was ist Ihr Job? (inf)

racketeer [ˌrækɪ'tɪə'] N Gauner(in) m(f) (inf); (in serious crime) Gangster(in) m(f); (making excessive profit) Halsabschneider(in) m(f) (inf)

racketeering [ˌrækɪ'tɪərɪŋ] N Gaunereien pl (inf); (= organized crime) organisiertes Verbrechen; (= excessive profit-making) Beutelschneiderei f (inf); **drugs ~** Drogenhandel m, Drogenschieberei f (inf)

racket press N Spanner m

racking ['rækɪŋ] ADJ attr pain rasend, entsetzlich; cough fürchterlich, quälend; sob entsetzlich, fürchterlich

rack: **rack railway** N Zahnradbahn f; **rack-rent** N Wuchermiete f; **rack wheel** N (Tech) Zahnrad nt

raclette [rə'klɛt] N (Cook) Raclette f or nt

raconteur [ˌrækɒn'tɜː'] N Erzähler(in) m(f) von Anekdoten

racoon, raccoon [rə'kuːn] N Waschbär m

racquet ['rækɪt] N (Brit) = racket[1]

racquetball ['rækɪtbɔːl] N , no pl Racquetball m

racy ['reɪsɪ] ADJ (+er) a speech, style, play schwungvoll, feurig; (= risqué) gewagt b wine feurig c (inf) car rasant

RADA ['rɑːdə] abbr of **Royal Academy of Dramatic Art**

radar ['reɪdɑː'] N Radar nt or m

radar in cpds Radar-; **radar beacon** N Radarbake f, Radarfunkfeuer nt; **radar operator** N Bediener(in) m(f) eines/des Radargerätes; **radar scanner** N Rundsuchradargerät nt; **radar station** N Radarstation f; **radar trap** N Radarfalle f

raddle ['rædl] N Rötel m, Roteisenstein m VT sheep (mit Rötel) zeichnen

radial ['reɪdɪəl] ADJ (Tech) radial; beams, bars, lines also strahlenförmig; (Anat) Speichen- N Gürtelreifen m

radial: **radial artery** N Speichenschlagader f; **radial engine** N Sternmotor m; **radial(-ply) tyre** N Gürtelreifen m; **radial velocity** N Radialgeschwindigkeit f

radiance ['reɪdɪəns] N (of sun, smile) Strahlen nt; (of colours also) Leuchten nt

radian measure ['reɪdɪən‚meʒə'] N (Math) Bogenmaß nt

radiant ['reɪdɪənt] ADJ a sun strahlend; colours leuchtend; (fig) person, beauty, smile strahlend (with vor +dat); face leuchtend, strahlend; **to be ~ with health** vor Gesundheit strotzen; **to be ~ with joy** vor Freude strahlen; **~ optimism** blendender or strahlender Optimismus b (Phys) Strahlungs-; energy strahlend, ausstrahlend; heater strahlend, ausstrahlend, wärmend N (Phys, Math, Astron) Strahl m

radiant heat N Strahlungswärme f

radiantly ['reɪdɪəntlɪ] ADV a happy strahlend b (liter) shine blendend, hell

radiate ['reɪdɪeɪt] VI a Strahlen aussenden; (= emit heat) Wärme ausstrahlen; (heat, light, energy) ausgestrahlt werden b (lines, roads) strahlenförmig ausgehen (from von) VT heat, light ausstrahlen; electric waves, energy also abstrahlen; (fig) happiness, health, love (förmlich) ausstrahlen

radiation [ˌreɪdɪ'eɪʃən] N (of heat etc) (Aus)strahlung f; (= rays) radioaktive Strahlung; **contaminated by or with ~** verstrahlt, strahlenverseucht; **exposure to ~** Strahlenbelastung f; **~**

~ therapy or treatment Strahlenbehandlung f; **~ damage/injuries** Strahlenschäden pl

radiation sickness N Strahlenkrankheit f

radiator ['reɪdɪeɪtə'] N (for heating) Heizkörper m, Radiator m; (Aut) Kühler m; **~ cap** Kühlerverschlussdeckel m; **~ grill** Kühlergrill m; **~ mascot** Kühlerfigur f

radiator coil N (Tech) Kühlschlange f

radical ['rædɪkəl] ADJ a (= basic) fundamental, Grund-; difference, error fundamental; (= extreme) change, reform radikal, grundlegend; rethinking, re-examination total; measures einschneidend, radikal; reduction radikal, fundamental, rigoros b (Pol) person, organization, idea radikal; attitude radikal, rigoros; **to effect a ~ cure** eine Radikalkur machen; **~ surgery** Radikalchirurgie f c (Math) Wurzel-; **a ~ expression** eine Wurzel d (Bot) leaves bodenständig N (Pol) Radikale(r) mf; (Math, Gram) Wurzel f; (in Chinese) Radikal m; (Chem) Radikal nt

radicalism ['rædɪkəlɪzəm] N (Pol) Radikalismus m

radically ['rædɪkəlɪ] ADV change, differ, improve radikal, grundlegend; **there's something ~ wrong with this** hier stimmt etwas ganz und gar nicht

radical sign N (Math) Wurzelzeichen nt

radicchio [rə'dɪkɪəʊ] N (variety of chicory) Radicchio m

radices ['reɪdɪsiːz] pl of radix

radicle ['rædɪkl] N (Bot) Keimwurzel f; (= small root) Würzelchen nt; (Chem) Radikal nt

radii ['reɪdɪaɪ] pl of radius

radio ['reɪdɪəʊ] N a Rundfunk m; (also radio set) Radio nt; **to listen to the ~** Radio hören; **to hear sth on the ~** etw im Radio hören; **the programmes on the ~** die Radioprogramme pl; **he was on the ~ yesterday** er kam gestern im Radio b (in taxi etc) Funkgerät nt; **over the/by ~** über or per Funk; **to talk over the ~** über Funk sprechen; **they don't have (a) ~** sie haben kein Funkgerät VT person per or über Funk verständigen; message, one's position funken, durchgeben; **to ~ that all is well** funken or über Funk durchgeben, dass alles in Ordnung ist VI **to ~ for help** per Funk einen Hilferuf durchgeben

radio: **radioactive** ADJ radioaktiv; **radioactive waste** N radioaktiver Müll; **radioactivity** N Radioaktivität f; **radio alarm (clock)** N Radiowecker m; **radio amateur** N Funkamateur(in) m(f); **radio announcer** N Rundfunkansager(in) m(f), Rundfunksprecher(in) m(f); **radio astronomy** N Radioastronomie f; **radio beacon** N (Aviat, Naut) Funkfeuer nt, Funkbake f; **radio beam** N Funkleitstrahl m; **radio broadcast** N Radiosendung f; **radiocarbon dating** N Radiokarbonmethode f, Kohlenstoffdatierung f; **radio cassette recorder** N (Brit) Radiorekorder m; **radio communication** N Funkverbindung f; **radio compass** N Radiokompass m; **radio contact** N Funkkontakt m; **radio control** N Funksteuerung f; **radio-controlled** ADJ ferngesteuert, ferngelenkt; **radio direction finding** N Funkpeilung f; **radio engineer** N Rundfunktechniker(in) m(f); **radio frequency** N Radiofrequenz f

radiogram ['reɪdɪəʊgræm] N a (= apparatus) Musiktruhe f b (= message) Funkspruch m c = radiograph

radiograph ['reɪdɪəʊgrɑːf] N Radiogramm nt; (= X-ray) Röntgenogramm nt, Röntgenbild nt

radiographer [ˌreɪdɪ'ɒgrɑːfə'] N Röntgenassistent(in) m(f)

radiography [ˌreɪdɪ'ɒgrəfɪ] N Röntgenografie f

radio: **radio ham** N Funkamateur(in) m(f); **radioisotope** N Radioisotop nt

radiolarian [ˌreɪdɪəʊ'lɛərɪən] N (Zool) Strahlentierchen nt, Radiolarie f (spec)

radio link N Funkverbindung f

radiological [ˌreɪdɪəʊ'lɒdʒɪkəl] ADJ radiologisch

radiologist [ˌreɪdɪ'ɒlədʒɪst] N Röntgenologe m, Röntgenologin f

radiology [ˌreɪdɪ'ɒlədʒɪ] N Radiologie f; (X-ray also) Röntgenologie f

radio: **radio marker** N (Aviat) Markierungs-/Funk-/Anflugbake f; **radio mast** N Funkmast m; **radio message** N Funkmeldung f/-spruch m; **radio operator** N (Bord)funker(in) m(f); **radiopager** ['reɪdɪəʊ'peɪdʒə'] N Funkrufempfänger m, Piepser m (inf); **radiopaging** ['reɪdɪəʊ'peɪdʒɪŋ] N Funkruf m; **radio play** N Hörspiel nt; **radio programme** N Radio- or Rundfunkprogramm nt

radioscopy [ˌreɪdɪ'ɒskəpɪ] N Radioskopie f; (Med) Röntgenuntersuchung f

radio: **radio set** N Radioapparat m, Rundfunkgerät nt; **radio silence** N (Mil) Funkstille f; **radio station** N Rundfunkstation f; **radio taxi** N Funktaxi nt; **radiotelephone** N Funksprechgerät nt; **radiotelephony** N Sprechfunk m; **radio telescope** N Radioteleskop nt; **radiotherapy** N Strahlen- or Röntgentherapie f; **radio truck** (US), **radio van** (Brit) N Funk- or Übertragungswagen m; **radio wave** N Radiowelle f

radish ['rædɪʃ] N (small red variety) Radieschen nt; (all other varieties) Rettich m

radium ['reɪdɪəm] N Radium nt; **~ therapy or treatment** (Med) Radiumtherapie f

radius ['reɪdɪəs] N pl radii a (Math) Radius m, Halbmesser m; (of ship, aircraft) Aktionsradius m, Wirkungsbereich m; **within a 6 km ~ (of Hamburg)** in einem Umkreis von 6 km (von Hamburg) b (Anat) Speiche f

radix ['reɪdɪks] N pl radices (Math) Grundzahl f

radome ['reɪdəʊm] N (Tech) Radom nt, Radarkuppel f; (at tip of aircraft) Radarbug m/-nase f

radon ['reɪdɒn] N (Chem) Radon nt

RAF abbr of **Royal Air Force** königliche (britische) Luftwaffe

raffia ['ræfɪə] N (= plant) Raphia(palme) f; (= fibre) Raphiabast m; (for handicraft, garden) Bast m; **~ work** Bastarbeit f; **~ table mat** Bastuntersetzer m

raffish ['ræfɪʃ] ADJ appearance flott, verwegen; person flott, verwegen, schnittig; place, behaviour verwegen, zwielichtig

raffle ['ræfl] N Tombola f, Verlosung f VT (also **raffle off**) verlosen

raffle ticket N Los nt

raft [rɑːft] N Floß nt

rafter ['rɑːftə'] N (Dach)sparren m

rafting ['rɑːftɪŋ] N (Sport) Rafting nt; **to go ~** Raften gehen

rag[1] [ræg] N a Lumpen m, Fetzen m; (for cleaning) Lappen m, Lumpen m; (for paper) Lumpen pl, Hadern pl; (inf: = shirt, dress) Fetzen m (inf); **~s** Lumpen pl; (inf: = clothes) Klamotten pl (inf); **in ~s** zerlumpt, abgerissen; **~s and tatters** abgerissene Lumpen pl; **to go from ~s to riches** (by luck) vom armen Schlucker zum reichen Mann/zur reichen Frau werden; (by work) vom Tellerwäscher zum Millionär werden; **to feel like a wet ~** (inf) total ausgelaugt sein (inf); **to lose one's ~** (inf) in die Luft gehen (inf) → red rag b (pej inf: = newspaper) Käseblatt nt

rag[2] N (Brit, inf) a (= joke) Jux m (inf); (Univ) karnevalistische Veranstaltung der Studenten zu Wohltätigkeitszwecken **for a ~** aus Jux (inf); **~ week** (Univ) Woche, in der Studenten durch Aufführungen Geld für Wohltätigkeitszwecke sammeln VT (= tease) aufziehen, foppen b (Brit: = play a trick on) **to ~ sb** jdm einen Streich spielen, einen Jux mit jdm machen (inf)

raga ['rɑːgə] N (Mus) Raga m

ragamuffin ['rægə‚mʌfɪn] N Vogelscheuche f (inf); (boy) Bengel m; (girl) Göre f; **you little ~** du kleiner Fratz

rag: **rag-and-bone man** N (Brit) Lumpenhändler m, Lumpensammler m; **ragbag** N Lumpensack m; (woman) Schlampe f; (fig) Sammelsurium nt (inf); **rag doll** N Flickenpuppe f

rage [reɪdʒ] **N** Wut *f*, Zorn *m*; (*liter*) (*of sea*) Toben *nt*; (*of storm*) Toben *nt*, Rasen *nt*; **to be in a ~** wütend sein, toben; **to fly into a ~** einen Wutanfall bekommen; **fit of ~** Wutanfall *m*; **to send sb into a ~** jdn wütend *or* (*stronger*) rasend machen; **to be (all) the ~** (*inf*) der letzte Schrei sein (*inf*) **VI** toben, rasen; (*sea, war, debate*) toben; **to ~ against sb/sth** gegen jdn/etw wettern

ragged ['rægɪd] **ADJ** *person, clothes* zerlumpt, abgerissen; *beard, hair* zottig, strähnig; *animal's coat* zottig; *coastline, rocks, hole* zerklüftet; *wound* schartig, zerfetzt; *edge, cuff* ausgefranst; (*fig*) *performance, singing* stümperhaft; **to run sb ~** (*inf*: = *exhaust*) jdn fertig machen (*inf*); **to run oneself ~** (*inf*) sich selbst ganz fertig *or* fix und fertig *or* kaputt machen (*inf*); **on the ~ edge** (*US fig*) gefährlich nah am Rande (des Abgrunds); **~ right** (*Typ*) Flattersatz *m*; **to set sth ~ left/right** (*Typ*) etw rechts-/linksbündig setzen

raggedly ['rægɪdlɪ] **ADV a** (= *in torn clothes*) *dress* abgerissen, zerlumpt **b** (= *unevenly*) stotternd, unregelmäßig

ragged robin **N** Kuckucklichtnelke *f*, Kuckucksnelke *f*

raggle-taggle [,rægl'tægl] **ADJ** *gipsy* zerlumpt; *army, group* zusammengewürfelt

raging ['reɪdʒɪn] **ADJ** *person* wütend; *fever* heftig, sehr hoch; *temperature* sehr hoch; *thirst* brennend; *pain, toothache* rasend; *storm, sea, wind* tobend; *inflation* galoppierend; *debate* hitzig, wütend, heftig; *nationalist, feminist* radikal, extrem, heftig; *nationalism, feminism* radikal, extrem; **he was ~** er tobte; **to be in a ~ temper** eine fürchterliche Laune haben; **to be ~ mad** (*inf*) eine Stinkwut haben (*inf*); **a ~ success** ein überwältigender Erfolg **N** (*of person, storm*) Toben *nt*, Rasen *nt*; (*of sea*) Toben *nt*

raglan ['ræglən] **ADJ** Raglan-; **~ sleeve** Raglanärmel *m* **N** (= *raglan coat*) Raglan(mantel) *m*

ragman **N** = **rag-and-bone man**

ragout ['ræguː] **N** (*Cook*) Ragout *nt*

rag: rag rug **N** Flickenteppich *m*; **ragtag and bobtail** **N** Hinz und Kunz (+*pl or sing vb*); **the ~ of society** Krethi und Plethi (+*pl or sing vb*); **ragtime** **N** Ragtime *m*; **rag trade** **N** (*inf*) Kleiderbranche *f*; **ragweed** **N** (*Bot*) beifußblättrige Ambrosia; **ragwort** **N** (*Bot*) Jakobskraut *nt*

raid [reɪd] **N** Überfall *m*; (*Mil also*) Angriff *m*; (= *air raid*) Luftangriff *m*; (= *police raid*) Razzia *f*; (*by thieves*) Einbruch *m* **VT a** (*lit*) überfallen; (*police*) eine Razzia durchführen in (+*dat*); (*thieves*) einbrechen in (+*acc*) **b** (*fig hum*) plündern

raider ['reɪdə'] **N** (= *bandit*) Gangster(in) *m(f)*; (= *thief*) Einbrecher(in) *m(f)*; (*in bank*) Bankräuber(in) *m(f)*; (= *ship*) Kaperschiff *nt*; (= *plane*) Überfallflugzeug *nt*

rail¹ [reɪl] **N a** (*on bridge, stairs etc*) Geländer *nt*; (*Naut*) Reling *f*; (= *curtain rail*) Schiene *f*; (= *towel rail*) Handtuchhalter *m*; (= *altar rail*) Kommunionbank *f* **b** **~s** (= *fence*) Umzäunung *f*; (*for train, tram*) Schiene *f*, Gleis *nt*; **to go off the ~s** (*lit*) entgleisen; (*Brit fig*) (*morally*) auf die schiefe Bahn geraten; (*mentally*) zu spinnen anfangen (*inf*); **the project is back on the ~s** (*fig*) das Projekt verläuft wieder nach Plan **c** (= *rail travel, railway*) die (Eisen)bahn; **to travel by ~** mit der Bahn fahren **VT** *goods* per *or* mit der Bahn verschicken *or* senden

▶ **rail in** **VT** *sep* einzäunen

▶ **rail off** **VT** *sep* abzäunen; **railed off from the road** gegen die Straße abgezäunt

rail² **VI** **to ~ at sb/sth** jdn/etw beschimpfen; **to ~ against sb/sth** über jdn/etw schimpfen

rail *in cpds* Bahn-; **railcar** **N** Triebwagen *m*; **railcard** **N** (*Brit Rail*) ≈ Bahncard® *f*; (*for young people also*) ≈ Juniorenpass *m*, ≈ Bahncard® *f* (*für Junioren*); (*for families also*) ≈ Familienpass *m*, ≈ Bahncard® *f* (*für Familien*); (*for senior citizens also*) ≈ Seniorenpass *m*, ≈ Bahncard® *f* (*für Senioren*); **rail company** **N** Bahngesell-

schaft *f*; **railhead** **N** Endbahnhof *m*; (= *end of track*) Gleisende *nt*

railing ['reɪlɪŋ] **N** (= *rail*) Geländer *nt*; (*Naut*) Reling *f*; (= *fence*: also **railings**) Zaun *m*

raillery ['reɪlərɪ] **N** Neckerei *f*, Stichelei *f*, gutmütiger Spott

railroad ['reɪlrəʊd] **N** (*US*) (Eisen)bahn *f* **VT a** (*US*) *goods* per *or* mit der Bahn befördern **b** (*inf*) **to ~ a bill** eine Gesetzesvorlage durchpeitschen; **to ~ sb into doing sth** jdn dazu hetzen, etw zu tun

railroad car **N** (*US*) Eisenbahnwaggon *m*/-wagen *m*

railroader ['reɪlrəʊdə'] **N** (*US*) Eisenbahner(in) *m(f)*

rail: rail strike **N** Bahnstreik *m*; **rail traffic** **N** Bahnverkehr *m*

railway ['reɪlweɪ] **N** (*Brit*) (Eisen)bahn *f*; (= *track*) Gleis *nt*

railway (*Brit*): **railway carriage** **N** Eisenbahnwagen *m*; **railway crossing** **N** Bahnübergang *m*; **railway engine** **N** Lokomotive *f*; **railway engineering** **N** Bahntechnik *f*, Bahnbautechnik *f*; **railway guide** **N** Kursbuch *nt*; **railway line** **N** (Eisen)bahnlinie *f*; (= *track*) Gleis *nt*; **railwayman** **N** Eisenbahner *m*; **railway network** **N** Bahnnetz *nt*; **railway porter** **N** Gepäckträger(in) *m(f)*; **railway station** **N** Bahnhof *m*; **railwaywoman** **N** Eisenbahnerin *f*

railworker ['reɪlwɜːkə'] **N** Bahnarbeiter(in) *m(f)*

raiment ['reɪmənt] **N** (*liter*) Gewand *nt* (*liter*)

rain [reɪn] **N a** Regen *m*; **in the ~** im Regen; **(come) ~ or shine** (*lit*) ob es regnet oder schneit; (*fig*) was auch geschieht; **the ~s** die Regenzeit → **right b** (*fig: of arrows, bullets, blows*) Hagel *m* **VI** *impers* (*lit, fig*) regnen; **it is ~ing** es regnet; **it never ~s but it pours** (*prov*) **when it ~s, it pours** (*US prov*) ein Unglück kommt selten allein (*prov*); **to ~ on sb's parade** (*US fig*) jdm in die Suppe spucken (*inf*) **VT to ~ blows on sb** einen Hagel von Schlägen auf jdn niedergehen lassen **VT** *impers* **it's ~ing cats and dogs** (*inf*) es gießt wie aus Kübeln, es schüttet nur so (*inf*)

▶ **rain down** **VI** (*blows etc*) niederprasseln (*upon* auf +*acc*)

▶ **rain off**, (*US*) **rain out** **VT** *sep* **to be rained off** wegen Regen nicht stattfinden; (= *abandoned*) wegen Regen abgebrochen werden

rain *in cpds* Regen-; **rain belt** **N** Regenzone *f*

rainbow ['reɪnbəʊ] **N** Regenbogen *m*; **a dress (in) all the colours of the ~** ein Kleid in allen Regenbogenfarben; **a pot of gold at the end of the ~** ein Wunschtraum *m*

rainbow: rainbow coalition **N** Regenbogenkoalition *f*; **rainbow trout** **N** Regenbogenforelle *f*

rain: rain check **N** (*esp US*) **I'll take a ~ on that** (*fig inf*) das verschiebe ich auf ein andermal; **rain cloud** **N** Regenwolke *f*; **raincoat** **N** Regenmantel *m*; **rain dance** **N** Regentanz *m*; **raindrop** **N** Regentropfen *m*; **rainfall** **N** Niederschlag *m*; **rain forest** **N** Regenwald *m*; **rain gauge** **N** Regenmesser *m*; **rain hood** **N** Regenhaube *f*; (*of anorak etc*) Kapuze *f*

raininess ['reɪnɪnɪs] **N** regnerisches Wetter, Regenwetter *nt*; (*of season, area*) Neigung *f* zu regnerischem Wetter

rain: rainless **ADJ** niederschlagsfrei (*Met*), ohne Regen, regenfrei; **rainout** **N** (*US Sport*) wegen Regens abgesagtes Spiel *nt*; **rainproof** **ADJ** wasserdicht, regensicher **VT** imprägnieren; **rain-sodden** ['reɪnˌsɒdn] **ADJ** *soil* aufgeweicht; **rainstorm** **N** schwere Regenfälle *pl*; **rainswept** ['reɪnswept] **ADJ** *attr* regengepeitscht; *evening* regnerisch; **raintight** ['reɪntaɪt] **ADJ** wasserfest, wasserdicht; **rainwater** **N** Regenwasser *nt*; **rainwear** **N** Regenkleidung *f*

rainy ['reɪnɪ] **ADJ** (+*er*) regnerisch, Regen-; *day also* verregnet; *area also* regenreich; **~ season** Regenzeit *f*; **a ~ spell** ein regnerischer Abschnitt; **to keep** *or* **save sth for a ~ day** (*fig*) etw für schlechte Zeiten zurücklegen *or* aufheben

raise [reɪz] ✪ 26.1, 26.3 **VT a** (= *lift*) *object, arm, head* heben; *blinds, eyebrow* hochziehen; (*Theat*) *curtain* hochziehen; (*Naut*) *anchor* lichten; *sunken ship* heben; (*Med*) *blister* bilden; **to ~ one's hat to sb** (*lit, fig*) den Hut vor jdm ziehen *or* lüften; **to ~ one's glass to sb** jdm zutrinken; **to ~ one's fist to sb** jdm mit der Faust drohen; **to ~ one's hand against sb** die Hand gegen jdn erheben; **to ~ one's eyes to heaven** die Augen zum Himmel erheben; **to ~ the pitch** (*Mus*) eine höhere Tonlage wählen; **to ~ the dead** die Toten wieder zum Leben erwecken *or* auferstehen lassen; **to ~ sb from the dead** jdn von den Toten erwecken; **to ~ one's voice** lauter sprechen; (= *get angry*) laut werden; **not a voice was ~d in protest** nicht eine Stimme des Protests wurde laut; **to ~ sb's/one's hopes** jdm/sich Hoffnung machen; **to ~ the people to revolt** das Volk zur Revolution aufhetzen; **to ~ the roof** (*fig*) (*with noise*) das Haus zum Beben bringen; (*with approval*) in Begeisterungsstürme ausbrechen; (*with anger*) fürchterlich toben; **the Opposition ~d the roof at the Government's proposals** die Opposition buhte gewaltig, als sie die Vorschläge der Regierung hörte → **eyebrow** **b** (*in height*) (*by* um) *wall, ceiling* erhöhen; *level* anheben **c** (= *increase*) (*to* auf +*acc*) erhöhen; *price* erhöhen, anheben; *limit, standard* anheben, heraufsetzen; **to ~ the stakes** den Einsatz erhöhen; **to ~ the tone** das Niveau heben; **England has to ~ its game** das Spielniveau der englischen Mannschaft muss sich verbessern **d** (= *promote*) (er)heben (*to* in +*acc*) → **peerage** **e** (= *build, erect*) *statue, building* errichten **f** (= *create, evoke*) *problem, difficulty* schaffen, aufwerfen; *question* aufwerfen, vorbringen; *objection* erheben; *suspicion, hope* (er)wecken; *spirits, ghosts* (herauf)beschwören; *mutiny* anzetteln; **to ~ a cheer** (*in others*) Beifall ernten; (*oneself*) Beifall spenden; **to ~ a smile** (*in others*) ein Lächeln hervorrufen; (*oneself*) lächeln; **to ~ a protest** protestieren; **to ~ hell** (*inf*) einen Höllenspektakel machen (*inf*) **g** (= *grow, breed*) *children* aufziehen, großziehen; *animals* aufziehen; *crops* anbauen; **to ~ a family** Kinder großziehen **h** (= *get together*) *army* auf die Beine stellen, aufstellen; *taxes* erheben; *funds, money* aufbringen, auftreiben; *loan, mortgage* aufnehmen **i** (= *end*) *siege, embargo* aufheben, beenden **j** (*cards*) erhöhen; **I'll ~ you 6** (*Poker*) ich erhöhe um 6 **k** (*Telec*: = *contact*) Funkkontakt *m* aufnehmen mit **l** (*Math*) **to ~ a number to the power of 2/3** *etc* eine Zahl in die zweite/dritte *etc* Potenz erheben **N a** (*esp US*) (*in salary*) Gehaltserhöhung *f*; (*in wages*) Lohnerhöhung *f* **b** (*Cards*) Erhöhung *f*

▶ **raise up** **VT** *sep* heben; **he raised himself up on his elbow** er stützte sich auf den Ellbogen

raised [reɪzd] **ADJ** *arm* angehoben; *voice* erhoben, laut; **~ type** (*Typ*) erhabener Druck → **eyebrow**

raisin ['reɪzən] **N** Rosine *f*

raj [rɑːdʒ] **N** Herrschaft *f* eines Radscha; **the British Raj** die britische Oberherrschaft in Indien

rajah ['rɑːdʒə] **N** Radscha *m*

rake¹ [reɪk] **N** (= *garden rake, croupier's rake*) Harke *f*, Rechen *m* (*dial*); (*for grate*) Kaminrechen *m*; (*for furnace*) Ofenkrücke *f* **VT a** *garden, hay, leaves* harken, rechen (*dial*); *grate* säubern; *fire* ausräumen; **to ~ sb/sth over the coals** (*US fig*) jdn/etw ordentlich runterputzen (*inf*) **b** (*machine gun, searchlight*) bestreichen **c** (*liter, nails, branches*) kratzen **VI** (= *search*) **to ~ around** *or* **about** (*herum*)wühlen, (*herum*)stöbern; **to ~ through old papers** in alten Papieren wühlen *or* stöbern

▶ **rake in** VT sep (inf) money kassieren (inf); **he's raking it in** er scheffelt das Geld nur so

▶ **rake out** VT sep fire ausräumen; (inf) information auskundschaften, herausfinden

▶ **rake over** VT sep earth, plot harken; (fig) past durchwühlen; **to rake over the coals** or **ashes** (esp Brit fig) alte Wunden wieder öffnen

▶ **rake up** VT sep **a** leaves zusammenharken **b** (fig) people, things, money auftreiben (inf) **c** fire schüren; (fig) quarrel schüren; memories, grievance aufwärmen; **to rake up the past** in der Vergangenheit wühlen

rake² N (= person) Lebemann m, Schwerenöter m

rake³ N (Naut, of mast) schiefe Stellung, Neigung f; (of stage, seating) Neigung f; (Aviat, of wing) Anstellwinkel m; (Aut, of seat) verstellbare Rückenlehne VI (Naut) sich neigen; (Theat) ansteigen

rake-off ['reɪkɒf] N (inf) (Gewinn)anteil m, Prozente pl (inf)

rakish¹ ['reɪkɪʃ] ADJ person, appearance flott, verwegen; life verwegen, flott, ausschweifend; **to wear one's hat at a ~ angle** den Hut verwegen aufgesetzt haben

rakish² ADJ (Naut) schnittig

rakishly ['reɪkɪʃlɪ] ADV flott, verwegen; behave verwegen; **…, he said ~** …, sagte er verwegen

rally¹ ['rælɪ] N **a** (= gathering) (Massen)versammlung f; (with speaker) Kundgebung f; (of troops) (Ver)sammlung f; (Aut) Rallye f; **electoral ~** Wahlversammlung f; **peace ~** Friedenskundgebung f; **youth ~** Jugendtreffen nt **b** (in health, spirits) Erholung f **c** (Tennis etc) Ballwechsel m **d** (St Ex) Erholung f VT troops, supporters (ver)sammeln, zusammenrufen; **to ~ one's strength** all seine Kräfte sammeln or zusammennehmen; **~ing call** or **cry** Slogan m VI **a** (sick person) Fortschritte machen; (St Ex) sich erholen **b** (troops, people) sich sammeln, sich versammeln; **~ing point** Sammelplatz m; **to ~ to the support of sb** (fig) jdm in Scharen zu Hilfe eilen **c** (Aut) **to go ~ing** Rallyes/eine Rallye fahren or machen; **to enjoy ~ing** gern Rallyes fahren

▶ **rally (a)round** VI +prep obj leader sich scharen um; person in distress sich annehmen (+gen) VI sich seiner/ihrer etc annehmen

rally² VT (obs: = tease) necken, hänseln

rallycross ['rælɪkrɒs] N, no pl Rallyecross nt, Rallye-Cross nt

rally driver N Rallyefahrer(in) m(f)

rallying point ['rælɪŋpɔɪnt] N Sammelpunkt m/-platz m

RAM [ræm] N (Comput) abbr of **random access memory** RAM m or nt; **1 megabyte of ~** 1 Megabyte RAM

ram [ræm] N **a** (= animal) Widder m, Schafbock m; **the Ram** (Astrol) der Widder **b** (Tech) Ramme f, Rammbär m, Rammbock m; (of hydraulic press) Stoßheber m, hydraulischer Widder **c** (Mil) = **battering ram** **d** (inf: = man) Rammler m (inf) VT **a** (= push) stick, post, umbrella stoßen; (with great force) rammen; (= pack) zwängen; (Tech) pile rammen; **to ~ cotton wool in(to) one's ears** sich (dat) Watte in die Ohren stopfen; **to ~ a charge home** (Mil) laden; (Min) eine Sprengladung anbringen; **to ~ home a message** eine Botschaft an den Mann bringen; **to ~ sth down sb's throat** (inf) jdm etw eintrichtern (inf) **b** (= crash into) ship, car rammen; **the car ~med a lamppost** das Auto prallte gegen einen Laternenpfahl

▶ **ram down** VT sep earth feststampfen; (Tech) pile einrammen; **his hat was rammed down over his ears** sein Hut war fest über beide Ohren gezogen

▶ **ram in** VT sep hineinstoßen; (with great force) hineinrammen

Ramadan [ˌræməˈdæn] N der Ramadan

ramble ['ræmbl] N Streifzug m; (esp Brit = hike) Wanderung f; **to go for** or **on a ~** einen Streifzug/eine Wanderung machen VI **a** (= wander about) Streifzüge/einen Streifzug machen; (esp Brit: = go on hike) wandern **b** (in speech: old person) unzusammenhängendes Zeug reden, faseln (inf); (pej: also **ramble on**) schwafeln (inf), vom Hundertsten ins Tausendste kommen **c** (Hort) ranken, klettern

rambler ['ræmblə'] N **a** (esp Brit) (= person) Spaziergänger(in) m(f); (= member of club) Wanderer m, Wanderin f, Wanderfreund(in) m(f) **b** (also **rambler rose**) Kletterrose f

rambling ['ræmblɪŋ] ADJ **a** speech, writing weitschweifig, umständlich; old person faselnd (inf), schwafelnd (inf); building, town, garden weitläufig **b** plant rankend, kletternd; **~ rose** Kletterrose f **c** **~ club/society** (esp Brit) Wanderklub m/-verein m N **a** (= wandering about) Streifzüge pl; (esp Brit: = hiking) Wandern nt; **to go ~** wandern gehen, wandern **b** (in speech: also **ramblings**) Gefasel nt (inf), Geschwafel nt (inf)

Rambo ['ræmbəʊ] N (inf) Rambo m (inf)

rambunctious ADJ, **rambunctiously** ADV [ræm'bʌŋkʃəs, -lɪ] (esp US inf) (= exuberant and noisy) laut, lärmend; (= boisterous) übermütig, ausgelassen, wild

RAM chip N (Comput) RAM-Chip m

ramekin ['ræmɪkɪn] N (Cook) **a** kleiner Käseauflauf **b** (also **ramekin dish**) Auflaufförmchen nt

ramification [ˌræmɪfɪˈkeɪʃən] N (lit) Verzweigung f; (smaller) Verästelung f; (of arteries) Verästelung f, Geäst nt; **the ~s of this matter are several** (form) dies ist eine sehr verzweigte Angelegenheit; **the race question and its many ~s** die Rassenfrage und die damit verbundenen Probleme

ramified ['ræmɪfaɪd] ADJ (lit, fig) verzweigt; (more intricate) verästelt

ramify ['ræmɪfaɪ] VI (lit, fig) sich verzweigen; **the problem ramifies into several areas** das Problem greift in verschiedene Bereiche über

ramjet (engine) ['ræmdʒet('endʒɪn)] N Staustrahltriebwerk nt, Ramjet m

rammer ['ræmə'] N Ramme f

ramp [ræmp] N Rampe f; (= hydraulic ramp) Hebebühne f; (Aviat: also **approach** or **boarding ramp**) Gangway f; **"(beware** or **caution) ~"** (on road sign) „Vorsicht Rampe or unebene Fahrbahn"

rampage [ræm'peɪdʒ] N **to be/go on the ~** randalieren; (= be angry) (herum)toben/einen Wutanfall bekommen; (= looting) auf Raubzug sein/gehen VI (also **rampage about** or **around**) herumwüten; (angrily) herumtoben

rampancy ['ræmpənsɪ] N (of plants, growth) Üppigkeit f, Wuchern nt; (of evil, corruption) wilde(s) Wuchern

rampant ['ræmpənt] ADJ **a** (= unrestrained) plants, growth üppig, wuchernd attr; heresy, evil, social injustice etc wild wuchernd attr; inflation wuchernd, galloppierend; corruption wuchernd, überhand nehmend, zügellos, ungezügelt; crime um sich greifend, blühend; **the ~ growth of** das Wuchern (+gen); **to be ~** (wild) wuchern; heart disease **is ~ in my family** Herzkrankheiten liegen bei uns in der Familie; **to run ~** (condition) um sich greifen; (person) unbeaufsichtigt herumlaufen **b** (Her) (drohend) aufgerichtet; **lion ~** aufgerichteter Löwe

rampart ['ræmpɑːt] N Wall m; (fig: = defence) Schutzwall m

ram raid N (Brit) Raub, bei dem ein Geschäft etc mit dem Auto aufgebrochen wird

ram-raid ['ræmreɪd] VT (Brit) mit dem Auto einbrechen in (+acc)

ramrod ['ræmrɒd] N Ladestock m; **he's sitting there as stiff** or **straight as a ~** er sitzt da, als

hätte er einen Besenstiel verschluckt ADJ stocksteif; **he is tall and thin, with a ~ posture** er ist groß und dünn, mit einer Haltung wie ein Ladestock ADV stocksteif; **~ straight** stocksteif, gerade or aufrecht wie ein Ladestock

ramshackle ['ræmˌʃækl] ADJ building morsch, baufällig; car klapprig, altersschwach; group, movement schlecht organisiert

ran [ræn] pret of **run**

ranch [rɑːntʃ] N Ranch f, Viehfarm f; **~ hand** Farmhelfer(in) m(f); **~ house** (on ranch) Farmhaus nt; **~(-style) house** (US) Bungalow m VI Viehwirtschaft treiben

rancher ['rɑːntʃə'] N Rancher(in) m(f), Viehzüchter(in) m(f)

rancid ['rænsɪd] ADJ ranzig

rancidity [ræn'sɪdɪtɪ], **rancidness** ['rænsɪdnɪs] N Ranzigkeit f

rancor N (US) = **rancour**

rancorous ['ræŋkərəs] ADJ tone bitter; attack bösartig

rancour, (US) **rancor** ['ræŋkə'] N (of tone) Bitterkeit f, Verbitterung f; (of attack) Boshaftigkeit f

rand [rænd] N (= monetary unit) Rand m

randan ['ræn,dæn] N (Brit inf) **to be out on the ~** eine Sause machen (inf); (= rowdy behaviour) auf den Putz hauen (inf), Remmidemmi machen (inf)

R & B [ɑːrˈbiː] N (Mus) abbr of **Rhythm and Blues** R & B m

R & D [ɑːrənˈdiː] N abbr of **research and development** Forschung und Entwicklung f

randiness ['rændɪnɪs] N (Brit) Geilheit f

random ['rændəm] N **at ~** (speak, walk, drive) aufs Geratewohl; shoot, drop bombs ziellos; take wahllos; **to hit out at ~** ziellos um sich schlagen; **to talk at ~** ins Blaue hineinreden; **a few examples chosen** or **taken at ~** ein paar willkürlich gewählte Beispiele; **he just said anything at ~** er hat einfach irgendetwas gesagt, er hat einfach drauflosgeredet; **I (just) chose one at ~** ich wählte einfach irgendeine (Beliebige) ADJ selection willkürlich; sequence zufällig; **killed by a ~ bullet** von einer verirrten Kugel getötet; **~ breath/drug test** Stichprobe f auf Alkohol im Atem/auf Drogen

random access N (Comput) wahlfreier Zugriff

random access memory N (Comput) Direktzugriffsspeicher m

randomize ['rændəmaɪz] VTI (Statistics) randomisieren, eine zufällige Auswahl treffen (statt aus)

randomly ['rændəmlɪ] ADV (= haphazardly) wahllos, willkürlich

random: random number N Zufallszahl f; **random sample** N Stichprobe f; **random sampling** N Stichproben pl

R & R [ɑːrənˈɑː'] N (US, Mil) abbr of **rest and recreation**

randy ['rændɪ] ADJ (+er) (Brit) scharf (inf), geil; **you ~ old devil** du alter Lustmolch (inf)

rang [ræŋ] pret of **ring²**

range [reɪndʒ] N **a** (= scope, distance covered) (of missile, telescope) Reichweite f; (of gun) Reichweite f, Schussweite f; (of vehicle) Fahrbereich m; (of plane) Flugbereich m; **at a ~ of** auf eine Entfernung von; **at close** or **short/long ~** auf kurze/große Entfernung; **to find the ~** (Mil) das Visier einstellen; **to be out of ~** außer Reichweite sein; (of telescope) außer Sichtweite sein; (of gun) außer Schussweite sein; **within shouting ~** in Hörweite; **within (firing) ~** in Schussweite; **~ of vision** Gesichtsfeld nt **b** (= spread, selection) Reihe f; (of goods) Sortiment nt, Reihe f; (of colours) Skala f; (of patterns, sizes, models) Angebot nt, Auswahl f (of an +dat); (of interest, abilities) Palette f; **a wide ~** eine große Auswahl; **in this price ~** in dieser Preisklasse or Preislage; **in this temperature ~** in diesem Temperaturbereich; **out of/within my price ~** außerhalb/innerhalb meiner (finanziellen) Möglichkeiten or meiner Preisklasse; **what**

sort of price ~ were you thinking of? an welche Preislage haben Sie gedacht?; **a ~ of prices/temperatures/clients** unterschiedliche Preise pl/Temperaturen pl/Klienten pl; **models available in a whole ~ of prices** Modelle in unterschiedlichen Preislagen erhältlich; **we have the whole ~ of models/prices** wir führen sämtliche Modelle/Waren in allen Preislagen; **we cater for the whole ~ of customers** wir sind auf alle Kundenkreise eingestellt; **his ~ of knowledge is very limited** sein Wissen ist sehr beschränkt

c (Mus) (of instruments) (Ton)umfang m; (of voice) (Stimm)umfang m

d (= domain, sphere) Kompetenz f; (of influence) (Einfluss)bereich m; **this is outside the ~ of the department/the committee** dies liegt außerhalb der Kompetenz dieser Abteilung/dieses Komitees; **this is outside the ~ of his experience** dies liegt außerhalb seiner Erfahrung

e (also **shooting range**) (Mil) Schießplatz m; (= rifle range) Schießstand m; (at fair) Schießbude f

f (= cooking stove) Koch- or Küchenherd m

g (= row) Reihe f; (= mountain range) Kette f

h (US: = grazing land) Freiland nt, Weideland nt; **~ cattle** Freilandvieh nt

VT a (= place in a row) aufstellen; objects aufstellen, anordnen; **they ~d themselves along the pavement** sie stellten sich am Bürgersteig entlang auf; **to ~ oneself with sb** (fig) sich auf jds Seite (acc) stellen

b (= classify) person zählen (among, with zu)

c (= roam over) durchstreifen, durchziehen; **to ~ the seas** die Meere befahren

d (= direct) gun, telescope ausrichten (on auf +acc)

e (US) cattle grasen lassen

f (Comput) **~d left/right** links-/rechtsbündig

VI a (= extend) **to ~ (from ... to)** gehen (von ... bis); (temperature, value) liegen (zwischen ... und); **the discussion ~d from the president to the hot-water system** die Diskussion umfasste alles, vom Präsidenten bis zum Heißwassersystem; **his interests ~ from skiing to chess** seine Interessen reichen vom Skifahren bis zum Schachspielen; **the conversation ~d over a number of subjects** die Unterhaltung kreiste um eine ganze Reihe von Themen; **his knowledge ~s over a wide field** er hat ein sehr umfangreiches Wissen; **the search ~d over the whole country** die Suche erstreckte sich auf das ganze Land

b (= roam) streifen; **to ~ over the area** im Gebiet umherstreifen

rangefinder [ˈreɪndʒˌfaɪndə'] N Entfernungsmesser m

rangeland [ˈreɪndʒlænd] N (US) offenes Weideland

ranger [ˈreɪndʒə'] N **a** (of forest etc) Förster(in), Aufseher(in) m(f) **b** (US) (= mounted patrolman) Ranger m; (= commando) Überfallkommando nt **c** (Brit) **~ (scout)/(guide)** Ranger m

Rangoon [ræŋˈguːn] N Rangun nt

rangy [ˈreɪndʒɪ] ADJ (+er) langglied(e)rig

rani [ˈrɑːnɪ] N Rani f

rank¹ [ræŋk] **N a** (Mil: = grade) Rang m; **officer of high ~** hoher Offizier; **to reach the ~ of general** den Rang eines Generals erlangen → **pull**

b (= class, status) Stand m, Schicht f; **people of all ~s** Leute pl aller Stände; **a person of ~** eine hoch gestellte Persönlichkeit; **a singer of the first ~** ein erstklassiger Sänger

c (= row) Reihe f; (Brit: = taxi rank) Taxistand m; **the taxi at the head of the ~** das erste Taxi in der Reihe

d (Mil: = formation) Glied nt; **to break ~(s)** aus dem Glied treten; **to keep ~(s)** im Reih und Glied stehen; **to serve in the ~s** gemeiner Soldat sein; **the ~s, other ~s** (Brit) die Mannschaften und die Unteroffiziere; **the ~ and file** (Mil) die Mannschaft; **the ~ and file of the party/union** die Basis der Partei/Gewerkschaft, die einfachen Partei-/Gewerkschaftsmitglieder; **the ~ and file workers** die einfachen Arbeiter; **to rise**

from the ~s aus dem Mannschaftsstand zum Offizier aufsteigen; (fig) sich hocharbeiten; **to reduce sb to the ~s** jdn degradieren → **close²**

e (Mus) Register nt

VT (= class, consider) **to ~ sb among the best** jdn zu den Besten zählen; **where would you ~ Napoleon among the world's statesmen?** wie würden Sie Napoleon als Staatsmann einordnen or einstufen?

VI to ~ among zählen zu; **to ~ above/below sb** bedeutender/weniger bedeutend als jd sein; (athlete) leistungsmäßig über/unter jdm liegen; (officer) rangmäßig über/unter jdm stehen; **to ~ high among the world's statesmen** einer der großen Staatsmänner sein; **he ~s high among her friends** er hat eine Sonderstellung unter ihren Freunden; **it ~s with the best films of the decade** es zählt zu den besten Filmen des Jahrzehnts; **he ~s as a great composer** er gilt als großer Komponist; **to ~ 6th** den 6. Rang or Platz belegen

rank² ADJ (+er) **a** plants üppig; grass verwildert; soil überwuchert; **~ with weeds** von Unkraut überwuchert; **to grow ~** wuchern **b** (= offensive) smell übel; dustbin, drain stinkend attr; fat ranzig; person derb, vulgär; **to be ~** (dustbin, drains) stinken; (breath) stinken, übel riechend sein **c** attr (= utter) disgrace wahr; injustice schreiend; nonsense, insolence rein; outsider, amateur richtig, absolut, ausgesprochen; stupidity ausgesprochen

ranker [ˈræŋkə'] N (Mil) (= soldier) einfacher or gemeiner Soldat; (= officer) aus dem Mannschaftsstand aufgestiegener Offizier

ranking officer [ˈræŋkɪŋˈbfɪsə'] N ranghöchster/ranghöherer Offizier

rankings [ˈræŋkɪŋz] PL (Sport) **the ~** die Platzierungen pl

rankle [ˈræŋkl] VI **to ~ (with sb)** jdn wurmen

rankness [ˈræŋknɪs] N **a** (of plants) Üppigkeit f; (of grass) Verwildertheit f; (of soil) Überwucherung f **b** (of smell) Übelkeit f; (of dustbin, drain) Gestank m, Stinken nt; (of person) Derbheit f, Vulgarität f

ransack [ˈrænsæk] VT (= search) room, cupboards durchwühlen; (= pillage) house plündern; town, region herfallen über (+acc)

ransom [ˈrænsəm] **N a** (= rescue) Lösegeld nt; (= release) Freilassung f; (Rel) Erlösung f; **to hold sb to** (Brit) or **for** (US) **~** (lit) jdn als Geisel halten; (fig) jdn erpressen → **king** **VT** (= buy free) auslösen, Lösegeld bezahlen für; (= set free) gegen Lösegeld freilassen; (Rel) erlösen

rant [rænt] **VI** (emotionally, angrily) eine Schimpfkanonade loslassen (inf); (talk nonsense) irres Zeug reden (inf); **to ~ (and rave)** (= be angry) herumschimpfen; **to ~ (and rave) at sb** mit jdm schimpfen; **what's he ~ing (on) about?** worüber lässt er sich denn da aus? (inf) **N** Schimpfkanonade f (inf)

ranting [ˈræntɪŋ] **N a** (= outburst) Geschimpfe nt; (= incoherent talk) irres Zeug **ADJ** pathetisch

ranunculus [rəˈnʌŋkjʊləs] N (= garden flower) Ranunkel f

rap¹ [ræp] **N a** (= noise, blow) Klopfen nt no pl; **there was a ~ at** or **on the door** es hat geklopft; **to give sb a ~ on the knuckles** (lit, fig) jdm auf die Finger klopfen; **he got a ~ on the knuckles for that** (lit, fig) dafür hat er eins auf die Finger bekommen (inf); **to take the ~** (inf) die Schuld zugeschoben kriegen (inf); **to take the ~ for sb** (inf) für jdn den Kopf hinhalten (inf); **I don't care a ~** (inf) das ist mir piepe (inf); **to beat the ~** (US inf) (von der Anklage) freigesprochen werden

VT a table klopfen auf (+acc); window klopfen an (+acc); **to ~ sb's knuckles, to ~ sb over the knuckles** (lit, fig) jdm auf die Finger klopfen **b** (= criticize) kritisieren

VI klopfen; **to ~ at** or **on the door/window** an die Tür/ans Fenster klopfen

▶ **rap out** VT sep **a** (= say curtly) oath, order ausstoßen **b** (Spiritualism) message klopfen

rap² (Mus) **N** Rap m **VI** rappen

rapacious ADJ , **rapaciously** ADV [rəˈpeɪʃəs, -lɪ] habgierig

rapacity [rəˈpæsɪtɪ] N Habgier f

rape¹ [reɪp] **N** Vergewaltigung f, Notzucht f (Jur); (obs: = abduction) Raub m; **~ crisis centre** Beratungszentrum nt (für Frauen, die Opfer einer Vergewaltigung geworden sind) **VT** vergewaltigen, notzüchtigen (Jur)

rape² N (= plant) Raps m

rape³ N (= grape pulp) Trester pl

rape oil N Rapsöl nt

rapeseed [ˈreɪpsiːd] N Rapssamen m

rap group N (US inf) Diskussionsgruppe f

rapid [ˈræpɪd] **ADJ** schnell; action, movement also rasch; improvement, change, spread also rapide; decline, rise rapide, steil; smile kurz; loss of heat plötzlich; river, waterfall reißend; slope, descent steil **N rapids** PL (Geog) Stromschnellen pl; **to ride** or **run the ~s** die Stromschnellen hinunterfahren

rapid: rapid deployment force, rapid reaction force N (Mil) schnelle Eingreiftruppe; **rapid eye movement sleep** N REM-Phase f; **rapid fire** N (Mil) Schnellfeuer nt; **~ of questions** (fig) Feuerwerk nt von Fragen; **rapid-fire** ADJ attr (esp US) **~ gun** Schnellfeuergewehr nt; **~ questions** Fragen wie aus dem Schnellfeuergewehr

rapidity [rəˈpɪdɪtɪ] N Schnelligkeit f; (of action, movement also) Raschheit f; (of improvement, change, spread also) Rapidheit f; (of decline, rise) Steilheit f

rapidly [ˈræpɪdlɪ] ADV schnell; act, move also rasch; improve, change, spread also rapide; decline, rise rapide, steil

rapid transit system N Schnellbahnsystem nt

rapier [ˈreɪpɪə'] N Rapier nt; **~ thrust** (lit) Stoß m mit dem Rapier; (fig) (= remark) Hieb m; (= retort) Parade f; **~ wit** Schlagfertigkeit f

rapine [ˈræpaɪn] N (liter) Plünderung f

rapist [ˈreɪpɪst] N Vergewaltiger m

rappel [ræˈpel] VI, N (US) = **abseil**

rapper [ˈræpə'] N (Mus) Rapper(in) m(f)

rapping [ˈræpɪŋ] N **a** Klopfen nt **b** (Mus) Rappen nt

rapport [ræˈpɔː'] N **the ~ I have with my father** das enge Verhältnis zwischen mir und meinem Vater; **I envied them the obvious ~ that they had** ich beneidete sie um ihr offensichtlich enges Verhältnis zueinander; **in ~ with sb/oneself** in Harmonie mit jdm/sich (dat) selbst; **they are in ~ with each other** sie harmonieren gut (miteinander)

rapprochement [ræˈprɒʃmãːŋ] N Annäherung f

rapscallion [ræpˈskælɪən] N (old, hum) Halunke m, Gauner m

rap sheet N (US sl) Strafregister nt; **to have a ~** vorbestraft sein

rapt [ræpt] ADJ interest gespannt; attention atemlos, höchste(r, s); person gebannt, gespannt, hingerissen; audience hingerissen, gespannt, in Bann geschlagen; look, smile verzückt; **~ with concentration** atemlos vor Konzentration; **~ in contemplation/in thought** in Betrachtungen/Gedanken versunken

raptor [ˈræptə'] N (Zool) Raubvogel m

rapture [ˈræptʃə'] N (= delight) Entzücken nt; (= ecstasy) Verzückung f; **to be in ~s** entzückt sein (over über +acc, about von); **she was in ~s when she heard he was returning** sie war außer sich vor Freude, als sie hörte, dass er zurückkommt; **to go into ~s (about sb/sth)** (über jdn/etw) ins Schwärmen geraten; **to send sb into ~s** jdn in Entzücken versetzen

rapturous [ˈræptʃərəs] ADJ applause, reception stürmisch, begeistert; exclamation entzückt; look verzückt, hingerissen

rapturously [ˈræptʃərəslɪ] ADV applaud, receive stürmisch, begeistert; exclaim entzückt; look verzückt, hingerissen

rare [rɛəʳ] ADJ (+er) **a** (= *uncommon*) selten, rar; *occurrence* selten; **with very ~ exceptions** mit sehr wenigen Ausnahmen; **it's ~ for her to come** sie kommt nur selten; **that ~ bird, the man who remembers birthdays** dieser weiße Rabe *or* Ausnahmefall, ein Mann der sich Geburtstage merkt; **on the ~ occasions when he spoke** bei den seltenen Gelegenheiten, bei denen er sprach **b** *atmosphere* dünn; *earths* selten **c** *meat* roh; *steak* blutig, englisch **d** (*inf:* = *great*) irrsinnig (*inf*); **a person of ~ kindness** ein selten freundlicher Mensch (*inf*); **kind to a ~ degree** selten freundlich; **to have a ~ old time** sich selten gut amüsieren

rarebit [ˈrɛəbɪt] N → **Welsh rarebit**

rarefaction [ˌrɛərɪˈfækʃən] N Dünne *f*; (*fig*) Exklusivität *f*

rarefied [ˈrɛərɪfaɪd] ADJ *atmosphere, air* dünn; (*fig*) exklusiv

rarefy [ˈrɛərɪfaɪ] VT *air, atmosphere* verdünnen, dünn werden lassen; (*fig*) exklusiv machen VI (*air*) dünn werden

rare gas N Edelgas *nt*

rarely [ˈrɛəlɪ] ADV selten

rareness [ˈrɛənɪs] N **a** (= *scarcity*) Seltenheit *f*, Rarheit *f*; (*of occurrence*) Seltenheit *f* **b** (*of steak*) Rohheit *f*

raring [ˈrɛərɪŋ] ADJ **to be ~ to go** (*inf*) in den Startlöchern sein

rarity [ˈrɛərɪtɪ] N Seltenheit *f*; (= *rare occurrence also*) Rarität *f*

rascal [ˈrɑːskəl] N Gauner *m*; (= *child*) Schlingel *m*, Frechdachs *m*; (*old:* = *scoundrel*) Schurke *m*

rascally [ˈrɑːskəlɪ] ADJ (*old, liter*) *trick* schändlich, schimpflich (*old, liter*); *person* schurkisch; **a ~ fellow** ein Schurke *m*

rash¹ [ræʃ] N (*Med*) Ausschlag *m*; **to come out** *or* **break out in a ~** einen Ausschlag bekommen

rash² ADJ (+er) *person* unbesonnen; *act also* voreilig, überstürzt; *thoughts* voreilig; *promise, words, decision* voreilig, vorschnell; **it was ~ of him to promise that** es war etwas voreilig von ihm, das zu versprechen; **don't do anything ~** tu ja nichts Übereiltes *or* Überstürztes, nur nichts übereilen *or* überstürzen; **in a ~ moment** in einem unbedachten *or* unbesonnen Moment

rasher [ˈræʃəʳ] N Streifen *m*; **~ of bacon** Speckstreifen *m*

rashly [ˈræʃlɪ] ADV *act* voreilig, überstürzt; *promise, decide* voreilig, vorschnell

rashness [ˈræʃnɪs] N (*of person*) Unbesonnenheit *f*; (*of action*) Voreiligkeit *f*, Überstürztheit *f*; (*of promise, decision*) Voreiligkeit *f*

rasp [rɑːsp] N (= *tool*) Raspel *f*; (= *noise*) Kratzen *nt no pl*; (*of cough, when breathing*) Keuchen *nt no pl* VT **a** (*Tech*) raspeln, feilen; **to ~ sth away** etw wegraspeln *or* abfeilen VI **b** (= *say: also* **rasp out**) *insults* krächzen; *orders* schnarren VI kratzen; (*breath*) rasseln → *also* **rasping**

raspberry [ˈrɑːzbərɪ] N Himbeere *f*; (= *plant: also* **raspberry bush** *or* **cane**) Himbeerstrauch *m*; **to blow a ~ (at sb)** (*inf*) (über etw) verächtlich schnauben; **to get a ~ (from sb)** (*inf*) (von jdm) nur ein verächtliches Schnauben ernten; **"new proposals get ~ from electorate"** (*inf*) „Wähler erteilen neuen Vorschlägen eine Abfuhr" ADJ Himbeer-; (*colour*) himbeerrot; **~ jam** Himbeermarmelade *f*

rasper [ˈrɑːspəʳ] N (*Tech*) Raspel *f*, Grobfeile *f*; (*Cook*) Raspel *f*, Reibeisen *nt*

rasping [ˈrɑːspɪŋ] ADJ (= *sound*) kratzend; *voice* kratzig (*inf*), krächzend; *cough* keuchend; *breath* rasselnd, keuchend N (= *sound*) Kratzen *nt*; (*of voice*) Krächzen *nt*, Gekrächze *nt*

raspy [ˈrɑːspɪ] ADJ (= *hoarse*) *tone* krächzend; *voice* heiser

Rasta [ˈræstə] N Rasta *m*

Rastafarian [ˌræstəˈfɛərɪən] N Rastafari *m*, Rastafarier(in) *m(f)* ADJ der Rastafaris

raster [ˈræstəʳ] N Raster *m or nt*

---

rat [ræt] N (*Zool*) Ratte *f*; (*pej inf:* = *person*) elender Verräter (*inf*); **he's a dirty ~** (*inf*) er ist ein dreckiges *or* gemeines Schwein (*inf*); **you ~!** du Hund! (*inf*); **~s!** (*inf*) (*annoyance*) Mist! (*inf*); (*rejection*) Quatsch! (*inf*) → **smell** VI **a** **to ~ on sb** (*inf*) jdn sitzen lassen (*inf*); (= *inform on*) jdn verpfeifen (*inf*); **to ~ on sth** (*inf:* = *renege on*) etw nicht einhalten **b** **to go ~ting** auf Rattenfang gehen

ratable ADJ = **rateable**

rat *in cpds* Ratten-

rat-arsed ADJ (*Brit sl:* = *drunk*) stockbesoffen (*inf*); **to get ~** sich zuschütten (*inf*)

rat-a-tat [ˌrætəˈtæt], **rat-a-tat-tat** N Rattern; **the continual ~ of machine-gun fire** das kontinuierliche Rattern von Maschinengewehren ADV ratternd

ratatouille [ˌrætəˈtwiː] N Ratatouille *f*

ratbag N (*Brit pej inf*) Schrulle *f* (*inf*)

rat-catcher N Rattenfänger(in) *m(f)*

rat-catching N Rattenfang *m*

ratchet [ˈrætʃɪt] N Ratsche *f*; **~ wheel** Sperrrad *nt*; **it is one more ~ in the cycle of violence that exists here** das ist eine weitere Drehung der Spirale der Gewalt, die hier existiert

▶ **ratchet up** (*esp US*) VI zunehmen VT SEP anheizen (*inf*); *pressure* verschärfen; *interest rates, rent* anheben

rate¹ [reɪt] N **a** (= *ratio, proportion, frequency*) Rate *f*; (= *speed*) Tempo *nt*; **the failure ~ on this course** die Durchfallrate *or* -quote bei diesem Kurs; **the failure ~ for small businesses** die Zahl der Konkurse bei Kleinunternehmen; **at the ~ of 100 litres** (*Brit*) *or* **liters** (*US*) **an hour/14 feet per minute** (in einem Tempo von) 100 Liter pro Stunde/14 Fuß pro Minute; **~ of climb** (*Aviat*) Steigleistung *f*; **~ of consumption** Verbrauch *m*; **~ of flow** (*of water, electricity*) Fluss *m*; **pulse ~** Puls *m*; **at a great** *or* **terrific** (*inf*) **~, at a ~ of knots** (*inf*) in irrsinnigem Tempo (*inf*); (*move also*) mit hundert Sachen (*inf*); **if you continue at this ~** (*lit, fig*) wenn du so weitermachst, wenn du in diesem Tempo weitermachst; **at his ~ of working** bei seinem Arbeitstempo; **at the ~ you're going you'll be dead before long** wenn du so weitermachst, bist du bald unter der Erde; **at any ~** auf jeden Fall; **at that ~, I suppose I'll have to agree** wenn das so ist, muss ich wohl zustimmen **b** (*Comm, Fin*) Satz *m*; (*St Ex*) Kurs *m*; **~ of exchange** Wechselkurs *m*; **what's the ~ at the moment?** wie steht der Kurs momentan?; **what's the ~ of pay?** wie hoch ist der Satz (für die Bezahlung)?; **~ of interest** Zinssatz *m*; **~ of taxation** Steuersatz *m*; **~ of pay for overtime** Satz *m* für Überstunden; **postage/advertising/insurance ~s** Post-/Werbe-/Versicherungsgebühren *pl*; **there is a reduced ~ for children** Kinderermäßigung wird gewährt; **basic salary ~** Grundgehaltssatz *m*; **to pay sb at the ~ of £10 per hour** jdm einen Stundenlohn von £ 10 bezahlen **c** **rates** PL (*dated Brit:* = *municipal tax*) Gemeindesteuern *pl*, Kommunalsteuern *pl*; **~s and taxes** Kommunal- und Staatssteuern *pl*; **~(s) office** Gemeindesteueramt *nt* → **water-rate** VT **a** (= *estimate value or worth of*) (ein)schätzen; **to ~ sb/sth among ...** jdn/etw zu ... zählen *or* rechnen; **how does he ~ that film?** was hält er von dem Film?; **to ~ sb/sth as sth** jdn/etw für etw halten; **he is generally ~d as a great statesman** er gilt allgemein als großer Staatsmann; **to ~ sb/sth highly** jdn/etw hoch einschätzen; **Shearer was ~d at £1,000,000** Shearers Preis wurde auf £ 1.000.000 geschätzt **b** (*Brit Local Government*) veranlagen; **a shop ~d at £1,000 per annum** ein Laden, dessen steuerbarer Wert £ 1.000 pro Jahr ist **c** (= *deserve*) verdienen; **does this hotel ~ 3 stars?** verdient dieses Hotel 3 Sterne?; **I think he ~s a pass (mark)** ich finde, seine Leistung kann man mit „ausreichend" oder besser bewerten **d** (*inf:* = *think highly of*) gut finden (*inf*); **I really/don't really ~ him** ich finde ihn wirklich gut/mag ihn nicht besonders

---

VI (= *be classed*) **to ~ as ...** gelten als ...; **to ~ among ...** zählen zu ...; **reading does not ~ highly among young people** vom Lesen halten die jungen Leute nicht viel

rate² VT (*liter*) = **berate**

rateable, ratable [ˈreɪtəbl] ADJ (*Brit*) *property* steuerpflichtig, steuerbar

rateable value N (*Brit*) steuerbarer Wert

rate-cap [ˈreɪtkæp] VT (*Brit dated*) **the council was ~ped** dem Stadtrat wurde eine Höchstsatz für die Kommunalsteuer auferlegt

rate-capping [ˈreɪtkæpɪŋ] N (*Brit dated*) Festlegung eines Kommunalsteuer-Höchstsatzes durch die Zentralregierung

rated [ˈreɪtɪd] ADJ **a** (*Brit*) *property* kommunalsteuerpflichtig **b** (*Tech*) Nenn-; **~ output/power** Nennleistung *f*

ratepayer [ˈreɪtpeɪəʳ] N (*Brit dated*) Steuerzahler(in) *m(f)* (*von Kommunalsteuern*)

rate rebate N (*Brit dated*) Kommunalsteuer-Rückerstattung *f*

ratfink [ˈrætfɪŋk] N (*dated US, sl*) Arschloch *nt* (*sl*); (= *informer*) Spitzel *m*

rather [ˈrɑːðəʳ] 6.3, 7.4, 8.3, 26.1, 26.3 ADV **a** (= *for preference*) lieber; **~ than wait, he went away** er ging lieber, als dass er wartete; **I would ~ have the blue dress** ich hätte lieber das blaue Kleid; **I would ~ be happy than rich** ich wäre lieber glücklich als reich; **I would ~ you came yourself** mir wäre es lieber, Sie kämen selbst; **I'd ~ not** lieber nicht; **I'd ~ not go** ich würde lieber nicht gehen; **I'd ~ die!** eher sterbe ich!; **he expected me to phone ~ than (to) write** er erwartete eher einen Anruf als einen Brief von mir; **it would be better to phone ~ than (to) write** es wäre besser zu telefonieren als zu schreiben **b** (= *more accurately*) vielmehr; **he is, or ~ was, a soldier** er ist, beziehungsweise *or* vielmehr war, Soldat; **a car, or ~ an old banger** ein Auto, genauer gesagt eine alte Kiste **c** (= *to a considerable degree*) ziemlich; (= *somewhat, slightly*) etwas; **~ a clever person** *or* **a clever person** er ist ziemlich klug; **he felt ~ better** er fühlte sich bedeutend wohler; **it's ~ more difficult than you think** es ist um einiges schwieriger, als du denkst; **it's ~ too difficult for me** es ist etwas zu schwierig für mich; **she's ~ an idiot/a killjoy** sie ist reichlich doof/ein richtiger Spielverderber; **I ~ think he's wrong** ich glaube fast, er hat Unrecht; **I've ~ got the impression ...** ich habe ganz den Eindruck, ...; **~!** (*inf*) und ob! (*inf*), klar! (*inf*)

raticide [ˈrætɪsaɪd] N (*spec*) Rattengift *nt*

ratification [ˌrætɪfɪˈkeɪʃən] N Ratifizierung *f*

ratify [ˈrætɪfaɪ] VT ratifizieren

rating¹ [ˈreɪtɪŋ] N **a** (= *assessment*) (Ein)schätzung *f*; (*Brit, of house*) Veranlagung *f*; **what's your ~ of his abilities?** wie schätzen Sie seine Fähigkeiten ein? **b** (= *class, category, Sport: of yacht, car*) Klasse *f*; (*Fin: also* **credit rating**) Kreditfähigkeit *f*; (*Elec*) Leistung *f*; (*of petrol: also* **octane rating**) Oktanzahl *f*; **what's his ~?** wie wird er eingestuft?; **he has attained world-class ~** er hat Weltklasse(format) erreicht; **the popularity ~ of a TV programme** die Zuschauerzahlen eines Fernsehprogramms; **the government's low ~ in the opinion polls** die niedrigen Werte der Regierung in den Meinungsumfragen; **security ~** Sicherheitseinstufung *f*; **voltage ~** Grenzspannung *f*; **high/low ~s** (*TV*) hohe/niedrige Werte *pl*; **to boost ~s** (*TV*) die Werte stark verbessern; **the ~s war** (*TV*) der Krieg um hohe Einschaltquoten **c** (*Naut*) (= *rank*) Rang *m*; (= *sailor*) Matrose *m*

rating² N (= *scolding*) Schelte *f*

ratio [ˈreɪʃɪəʊ] N Verhältnis *nt*; **the ~ of men to women** das Verhältnis von Männern zu Frauen; **in the ~ of ~ of 100 to 1** im Verhältnis 100 zu 1 (*written: 100:1*); **inverse ~** umgekehrtes Verhältnis; **in inverse ~ to** (*Math*) umgekehrt proportional zu

ratiocinate [ˌrætɪˈɒsɪneɪt] VI (form) reflektieren

ration [ˈræʃən, (US) ˈræʃən] N Ration f; (fig) Quantum nt; **~s** (= food) Rationen pl; **to put sb on short ~s** jdn auf halbe Ration setzen; **~ book/card** Bezug(s)scheinbuch nt/Bezug(s)schein m; (for food) ≈ Lebensmittelkarte f/-marke f

VT goods, food rationieren; (state, government also) bewirtschaften; **there is a sugar shortage, so it's being ~ed** Zucker ist knapp und wird daher rationiert; **he was ~ed to 1 kg** ihm wurde nur 1 kg erlaubt; **I'm going to ~ you to one biscuit a day** ich werde dich kurz halten, du bekommst nur einen Keks pro Tag; **he ~ed himself to five cigarettes a day** er erlaubte sich (dat) nur fünf Zigaretten pro Tag

▶ **ration out** VT sep zuteilen

rational [ˈræʃənl] ADJ **a** (= having reason) creature, person vernunftbegabt, rational **b** (= sensible, reasonable) person, action, thinking vernünftig, rational; activity, solution vernünftig, sinnvoll; (Med: = lucid, sane) person bei klarem Verstand; **it was the only ~ thing to do** es war das einzig Vernünftige **c** (Math) rational

rationale [ˌræʃəˈnɑːl] N Gründe pl; **it lacks any ~** das entbehrt jeglicher Begründung

rationalism [ˈræʃnəlɪzəm] N Rationalismus m

rationalist [ˈræʃnəlɪst] N Rationalist(in) m(f)

rationalistic [ˌræʃnəˈlɪstɪk] ADJ rationalistisch

rationality [ˌræʃəˈnælɪtɪ] N (of person, action, thinking) Vernünftigkeit f, Rationalität f; (of activity, solution) Vernünftigkeit f; (Med) klarer Verstand

rationalization [ˌræʃnəlaɪˈzeɪʃən] N Rationalisierung f; (of problem) vernünftige Betrachtung

rationalize [ˈræʃnəlaɪz] VT **a** event, conduct etc rationalisieren; problem vernünftig sehen or betrachten **b** (= organize efficiently) industry, production, work rationalisieren **c** (Math) in eine rationale Gleichung umändern VI rationalisieren

rationally [ˈræʃnəlɪ] ADV act, behave, think vernünftig, rational; (Med) bei klarem Verstand; **~ (speaking), it should be possible to do it** rational gesehen sollte es möglich sein

rationing [ˈræʃənɪŋ] N (of goods, food) Rationierung f; (by state, government also) Bewirtschaftung f

ratline, ratlin [ˈrætlɪn] N (Naut) Webeleine f

rat: ratpack N (Brit, pej inf) Journalistenmeute f (pej inf); **rat poison** N Rattengift nt; **rat race** N ständiger Konkurrenzkampf; **rat run** N (Brit, inf) Schleichweg m (inf); **drivers were using the area as a ~** die Gegend wurde von Autofahrern als Schleichweg (inf) genutzt; **rats' tails** PL (pej) Zotteln pl (pej); (inf, = bunches) Rattenschwänze pl (inf); **her hair was** or **hung in ~** (pej) ihr Haar war zottelig or hing zottelig herunter

rattan [ræˈtæn] N (= plant) Rotangpalme f; (= cane) Rattan nt, Peddigrohr nt

ratted [ˈrætɪd] ADJ (Brit inf) stockbesoffen (inf)

ratter [ˈrætə] N (= dog or cat) Rattenfänger m

rattle [ˈrætl] VI klappern; (chains) rasseln, klirren; (bottles) klirren; (gunfire) knattern; (drums) schlagen; (hailstones) prasseln; (rattlesnake) klappern; **to ~ at the door** an der Tür rütteln; **there's something rattling** da klappert etwas; **to ~ along/away** (vehicle) entlang-/davonrattern; **they ~d through the village** sie ratterten durch das Dorf

VT box, dice, keys schütteln; bottles, cans zusammenschlagen; chains rasseln mit; windows rütteln an (+dat); **to ~ sb's cage** (inf) jdn verärgern

b (inf: = alarm) person durcheinander bringen; **don't get ~d!** reg dich nicht auf!; **she was ~d by the news, the news ~d her** die Nachricht hat ihr einen Schock versetzt

N **a** (= sound) Klappern nt no pl; (of chains) Rasseln nt no pl, Klirren nt no pl; (of bottles) Klirren nt no pl; (of gunfire) Knattern nt no pl; (of drums) Schlagen nt no pl; (of hailstones)

Prasseln nt no pl; (of rattlesnake) Klappern nt no pl; (Med: also **death rattle**) Todesröcheln nt

b (child's) Rassel f; (sports fan's) Schnarre f

▶ **rattle around** VI (fig: in house etc) herumgeistern (inf)

▶ **rattle down** VI herunterprasseln, herunterhageln

▶ **rattle off** VT sep poem, joke, list herunterrasseln (inf); win hinlegen (inf)

▶ **rattle on** VI (inf) (unentwegt) quasseln (inf) (about über +acc)

▶ **rattle through** VI +prep obj speech etc herunterrasseln; work, music rasen durch

rattlebrain [ˈrætlbreɪn] N (inf) Spatzenhirn nt (inf)

rattler [ˈrætlə] N (US, inf) Klapperschlange f

rattle: rattlesnake N Klapperschlange f; **rattletrap** N (hum inf) Klapperkiste f (hum inf)

rattling [ˈrætlɪŋ] N (= sound) Klappern nt; (of chains) Rasseln nt, Klirren nt; (of bottles) Klirren nt; (of gunfire) Knattern nt; (of drums) Schlagen nt; (of hailstones) Prasseln nt ADJ klappernd; chains rasselnd, klirrend; bottles klirrend; gunfire knatternd; drums schlagend; hailstones prasselnd; **a ~ noise** ein Klappern nt/Rasseln nt etc

rattrap, rat trap [ˈrættræp] N Rattenfalle f

ratty [ˈrætɪ] ADJ (+er) (inf) **a** (Brit: = irritable) gereizt **b** (US: = run-down) verlottert (inf)

raucous [ˈrɔːkəs] ADJ voice, laughter, shouts rau, heiser; crowd lärmend; party, music laut, lärmend; bird cry heiser, rau

raucously [ˈrɔːkəslɪ] ADV laugh, shout rau, heiser; sing mit rauer or heiserer Stimme

raucousness [ˈrɔːkəsnɪs] N (of voice, laughter) Rauheit f, Heiserkeit f; (of crowd) Rauheit f, Barschheit f; (of party, music) Rauheit f

raunchy [ˈrɔːntʃɪ] ADJ (+er) (inf) person sexy; film, scene erotisch, aufreizend; novel erotisch; clothing aufreizend, sexy

ravage [ˈrævɪdʒ] N (of war) verheerendes Wüten nt no pl; (of disease) Wüten nt no pl, Zerstörung f (of durch); **~s** (of war) Verheerung f (of durch); (of disease) Zerstörung f (of durch); **the ~s of time** die Spuren pl der Zeit; **a face marked by the ~s of time** ein von der Zeit schwer gezeichnetes Gesicht VT (= ruin) verwüsten, verheeren; (= plunder) plündern; **~d by disease** von Krankheit schwer gezeichnet

rave [reɪv] VI **a** (= be delirious) fantasieren, phantasieren, delirieren (spec); (= talk wildly) fantasieren, phantasieren, spinnen (inf); (= speak furiously) toben (inf, = speak, write enthusiastically) schwärmen (about, over von); (liter) storm) toben; (wind) brausen; (sea) toben; **to ~ against sb/sth** gegen jdn/etw wettern; **he ~d at the children for breaking the window** er donnerte die Kinder wegen der eingeworfenen Fensterscheibe an → rant

N **a** (Brit inf) Rave m (sl)

b (inf, = praise) Schwärmerei f; **to have a ~ about sth** von etw schwärmen, von etw ganz weg sein (inf); **the play got a ~ review** (inf) das Stück bekam eine glänzende or begeisterte Kritik

c (inf, = fashion) it's all the **~** das ist große Mode

rave culture N (Mus) Ravekultur f

ravel [ˈrævl] VT **a** (= disentangle) VI **ravel out** VT **b** (old: = entangle) verwirren VI (= become tangled) sich verwirren; (= fray) ausfransen

▶ **ravel out** VI ausfransen; (rope) faserig werden VT sep material ausfransen; threads entwirren; knitting auftrennen, aufziehen; (fig) difficulty klären

raven [ˈreɪvn] N Rabe m; **~-black** rabenschwarz

raven-haired [ˈreɪvnˈhɛəd] ADJ mit rabenschwarzem Haar

ravening [ˈrævnɪŋ] ADJ beutehungrig, räuberisch

ravenous [ˈrævənəs] ADJ animal ausgehungert; person also heißhungrig; appetite, hunger gewaltig; **I'm ~** ich habe einen Bärenhunger (inf)

ravenously [ˈrævənəslɪ] ADV eat wie ein Wolf; look ausgehungert; **to be ~ hungry** (animal) ausgehungert sein; (person also) einen Bärenhunger haben (inf)

raver [ˈreɪvə] N **a** (Brit inf) Raver(in) m(f) **b** (dated Brit sl) flotte Biene (dated inf); **she's a real little ~** sie führt ein flottes Leben

rave-up [ˈreɪvʌp] N (dated Brit, sl: = party) Fete f (inf), tolle Party f

ravine [rəˈviːn] N Schlucht f, Klamm f

raving [ˈreɪvɪŋ] ADJ **a** (= frenzied) wahnsinnig, verrückt; (= delirious) im Delirium, fantasierend attr, phantasierend attr; **his ~ fantasies** seine verrückten Fantastereien or Phantastereien; **a ~ lunatic** (inf) ein kompletter Idiot (inf) **b** (inf, = remarkable) success toll (inf); beauty hinreißend ADV **~ mad** (inf) total verrückt (inf); **to go ~ mad** (inf) total verrückt werden (inf) N **~(s)** Fantasien pl, Phantasien pl

ravioli [ˌrævɪˈəʊlɪ] N Ravioli pl

ravish [ˈrævɪʃ] VT **a** (= delight) hinreißen **b** (old, liter: = rape) schänden (geh); (obs: = abduct) rauben

ravisher [ˈrævɪʃə] N (old, liter) Schänder m (geh)

ravishing [ˈrævɪʃɪŋ] ADJ woman, sight atemberaubend; beauty also, meal hinreißend

ravishingly [ˈrævɪʃɪŋlɪ] ADV beautiful hinreißend, atemberaubend; dressed, decorated atemberaubend schön

ravishment [ˈrævɪʃmənt] N **a** (= delight) atemloses Staunen, Hingerissenheit f **b** (old, liter: = rape) Schändung f (geh); (obs: = abduction) Raub m

raw [rɔː] ADJ (+er) **a** (= uncooked) meat, food roh; (= unprocessed) roh, Roh-; alcohol rein, unvermischt; cloth ungewalkt; leather ungegerbt; cotton roh, naturbelassen, unbehandelt; rubber roh; sewage ungeklärt; **~ sugar** Rohzucker m; **~ brick** Rohziegel m; **~ edge** (of cloth etc) ungesäumte Kante; **~ spirits** reiner Alkohol; **it's a ~ deal** (inf) das ist eine Gemeinheit (inf); **to give sb a ~ deal** jdn benachteiligen, jdn unfair behandeln; **to get a ~ deal** schlecht wegkommen (inf); **the old get a ~ deal from the state** (inf) alte Leute werden vom Staat stiefmütterlich behandelt

b (= naked, pure, basic) emotion nackt, unverfälscht; energy ursprünglich, impulsiv, nackt; talent ungeschliffen, elementar; ambition, statistics nackt; courage elementar, unverfälscht; facts nackt, unverfälscht, ungeschönt; **~ data** (Comput) unaufbereitete Daten pl; **~ score** (US, Sch) bloße Punktergebnisse or Punkte pl

c (= inexperienced) troops, recruit neu, unerfahren

d (= sore) wound offen; skin wund; nerves empfindlich; **red and ~** gerötet und wund; **to touch a ~ nerve** (fig) einen wunden Punkt berühren, einen rohen or offen liegenden Nerv berühren

e (= frank) account ungeschönt, ungeschliffen; ungemildert

f (Met) climate, wind, air rau; night rau, stürmisch

g (esp US: = coarse) humour, story, person derb; colour grell

N **a** **to touch** or **get sb on the ~** (Brit) bei jdm einen wunden Punkt berühren

b **in the ~** (inf, = naked) im Naturzustand; **life/nature in the ~** die raue Seite des Lebens/der Natur

raw: rawboned ADJ mager, knochig; **rawhide** N (= leather) ungegerbtes Leder; (= whip) Lederpeitsche f

Rawlplug® [ˈrɔːlplʌɡ] N Dübel m

raw material N Rohmaterial nt

rawness [ˈrɔːnɪs] N **a** (of meat, food) Rohheit f **b** (= lack of experience) Unerfahrenheit f **c** (= soreness) Wundheit f **d** (of weather) Rauheit f **e** (esp US: = coarseness) Derbheit f

raw recruit N (fig) blutiger Anfänger (inf), blutige Anfängerin (inf)

raw silk N Rohseide f

ray[1] [reɪ] N **a** Strahl m; **a ~ of hope** ein Hoffnungsschimmer or -strahl m; **a ~ of sunshine** (fig) ein kleiner Trost **b** (of fish) Flossenstrahl m; (of starfish) Arm m

ray[2] N (= fish) Rochen m

ray gun N Strahlenpistole f

rayon ['reɪɒn] **N** Viskose f, Reyon nt **ADJ** aus Viskose or Reyon; **~ fibre** Viskose- or Reyonfaser f

raze [reɪz] VT zerstören; (Mil) schleifen; **to ~ sth to the ground** etw dem Erdboden gleichmachen

razor ['reɪzə'] N Rasierapparat m; (cutthroat) Rasiermesser nt; **electric ~** Elektrorasierer m; **~'s edge** (fig) = **razor-edge b**

razor: razorback N (Zool) Finnwal m; **razorbill** N (Zool) Tordalk m; **razor blade** N Rasierklinge f; **razor cut** N Messerschnitt m; **razor-cut** VT mit dem Messer schneiden; **razor edge** N **a** (= mountain ridge) Grat m **b** (fig) **we are living on a ~** wir stehen vor einem Abgrund; **razor-sharp** ADJ knife scharf (wie ein Rasiermesser); teeth rasiermesserscharf; (fig) person sehr scharfsinnig; mind, wit messerscharf; **razor wire** N Bandstacheldraht m, Natodraht m (inf)

razz [ræz] VT (US, inf) aufziehen (inf), verhohnepiepeln (inf)

razzle ['ræzl] N (inf) **to go on/be out on the ~** eine Sause machen (dated inf)

razzle-dazzle ['ræzl'dæzl], **razzmatazz** ['ræzmə'tæz] N (esp Brit inf) Rummel m, Trubel m

RC abbr of **Roman Catholic** r.-k.

RCP (Brit) abbr of **Royal College of Physicians** königlicher Ärzteverband

r-coloured, (US) **r-colored** ['ɑ:ˌkʌləd] ADJ (Ling) vowels mit R-Färbung

RCS (Brit) abbr of **Royal College of Surgeons** königlicher Chirurgenverband

Rd abbr of **Road** Str.

RDA abbr of **recommended daily allowance**

RE (Brit) abbr of **Religious Education**

re[1] [reɪ] N (Mus) re nt

re[2] [ri:] PREP (Admin, Comm etc, = referring to) betreffs (+gen), bezüglich (+gen); (Jur: also **in re**) in Sachen gegen; **re your letter of 16th June** Betr(eff): Ihr Brief vom 16. Juni

reach [ri:tʃ] **N a** (= act of reaching) **to make a ~ for sth** nach etw greifen **b** (denoting accessibility) **within/out of sb's ~** in/außer jds Reichweite (dat), in/außer Reichweite für jdn; **within arm's ~** in greifbarer Nähe; **put it out of the children's ~** or **out of the ~ of the children** stellen Sie es so, dass Kinder es nicht erreichen können; **keep out of ~ of children** von Kindern fern halten; **cars are within everyone's ~ nowadays** Autos sind heute für jeden erschwinglich; **mountains within easy ~** Berge, die leicht erreichbar sind; **within easy ~ of the sea** in unmittelbarer Nähe des Meers; **this town is within easy ~ of London for a day trip** man kann von dieser Stadt aus gut Tagesflüge nach London machen; **I keep it within easy ~** ich habe es in greifbarer Nähe; **she was beyond (the) ~ of help** für sie kam jede Hilfe zu spät; **this subject is beyond his ~** dieses Thema geht über seinen Horizont (inf) **c** (= distance one can reach) Reichweite f; (Boxing) Aktionsradius m; **a long ~** lange Arme pl, ein großer Aktionsradius **d** (= sphere of action, influence) Einflussbereich m; **beyond the ~ of the law** außerhalb des Gesetzes **e** (= stretch) **~es** (of beach, river) Strecke f; (of canal) Wasserhaltung f; (of woodland) Gebiet nt; **the upper ~es of the Rhine** der Oberfluss des Rheins

VT a (= arrive at) erreichen; point ankommen an (+dat); town, country ankommen in (+dat); perfection erlangen; agreement, understanding erzielen, kommen zu; conclusion kommen or gelangen zu; **we ~ed London at 3pm** wir kamen um 15 Uhr in London an; **when we ~ed him he was dead** als wir zu ihm kamen, war er tot; **to ~ the terrace you have to cross the garden** um auf die Terrasse zu kommen, muss man durch den Garten gehen; **to ~ page 50** bis Seite 50 kommen; **to ~ school age/the age of 50** das Schulalter/die 50 erreichen; **this advertisement is geared to ~ a younger audience** diese Werbung soll junge Leute ansprechen; **you can ~ me at my hotel** Sie erreichen mich in meinem Hotel; **to ~ the final of the Davis Cup** das Finale des Davis-Cups erreichen **b** (= stretch to get or touch) **to be able to ~ sth** an etw (acc) (heran)reichen können, bis zu etw langen können (inf); **can you ~ it?** kommen Sie dran?; **can you ~ the ceiling?** kannst du bis an die Decke reichen or langen? (inf) **c** (= come up to, go down to) reichen or gehen bis zu; **he ~es her shoulder** er reicht or geht ihr bis zur Schulter **d** (inf, = get and give) langen (inf), reichen; **~ me (over) that book** reiche or lang (inf) mir das Buch (herüber) **e** (US Jur) witness bestechen

VI a (to, as far as bis) (territory etc) sich erstrecken, gehen, reichen; (voice, sound) tragen **b** (= stretch out hand or arm) greifen; **to ~ for sth** nach etw greifen or langen (inf); **~ for the sky!** (US) Hände hoch!; **to ~ for the moon or stars** (fig) nach den Sternen greifen **c** **can you ~?** kommen Sie dran?

▶**reach across** VI hinübergreifen or -langen (inf)

▶**reach back** VI (in time) zurückreichen, zurückgehen (to bis)

▶**reach down** **VI** (clothes, curtains, hair etc) herunterreichen (to bis); (person) hinuntergreifen or -langen (inf) (for nach) **VT** sep herunterreichen

▶**reach out** **VT** sep **he reached out his hand to take the book** er streckte die Hand aus, um das Buch zu nehmen; **he reached out his hand for the cup** er griff nach der Tasse **VI** die Hand/Hände ausstrecken; **to reach out for sth** nach etw greifen or langen (inf); **he reached out to grasp the door handle** er griff or langte (inf) nach dem Türgriff; **she reached out and slapped him** sie holte aus und haute ihm eine runter (inf)

▶**reach over** VI = reach across

▶**reach up** **VI a** (water, level etc) (herauf)reichen or -gehen (to bis) **b** (person) hinaufgreifen (for nach) **VT** sep (inf) heraufreichen

reachable ['ri:tʃəbl] ADJ erreichbar

reach-me-down ['ri:tʃmɪˌdaʊn] N (inf) = **hand-me-down**

react [ri:'ækt] VI **a** (= respond, Chem, Phys) reagieren (to auf +acc); **slow to ~** (Chem) reaktionsträge; **she was slow to ~ to my offer** sie reagierte nur langsam auf mein Angebot; **to ~ against** negativ reagieren auf (+acc) **b** (= have an effect) wirken (on, upon auf +acc)

reaction [ri:'ækʃən] N **a** (= response, Chem, Phys) Reaktion f (to auf +acc, against gegen); **what was his ~ to your suggestion?** wie hat er auf Ihren Vorschlag reagiert?, wie war seine Reaktion auf Ihren Vorschlag?; **a ~ against feminism** eine Absage an den Feminismus; **action and ~** Wirkung und Gegenwirkung **b** (Pol) Reaktion f; **forces of ~** reaktionäre Kräfte pl **c** (Mil) Gegenschlag m **d** (St Ex) Umschwung m, Rückgang m

reactionary [ri:'ækʃənrɪ], **reactionist** [ri:'ækʃənɪst] **ADJ** reaktionär **N** Reaktionär(in) m(f)

reaction time N Reaktionszeit f

reactivate [ri:'æktɪveɪt] VT reaktivieren

reactive [ri:'æktɪv] ADJ (Chem, Phys) reaktiv

reactor [ri:'æktə'] N (Phys) Reaktor m; (Chem also) Reaktionsapparat m; (Elec) Blindwiderstand m

read[1] [ri:d] vb: pret, ptp **read** [red] **VT a** (also Comput) lesen; (to sb) vorlesen (to +dat); **do you ~ music?** können Sie Noten lesen?; **I ~ him to sleep** ich las ihm vor, bis er einschlief; **~ my lips!** höre meine Worte!; **to take sth as ~** (fig) (= as self-evident) etw als selbstverständlich voraussetzen; (= as agreed) etw für abgemacht halten; **they took the minutes as ~** (in meeting) sie setzten das Protokoll als bekannt voraus; **for "meet" ~ "met"** anstelle or an Stelle von „meet" soll „met" stehen **b** (= interpret) thoughts, feelings lesen; dream deuten; words einschätzen; person einschätzen können; **to ~ sb's thoughts/mind** jds Gedanken lesen; **to ~ sb's palm** jdm aus der Hand lesen; **to ~ the tea leaves** = aus dem Kaffeesatz lesen; **these words can be ~ in several ways** diese Wörter können unterschiedlich verstanden werden; **to ~ something into a text** etwas in einen Text (hinein)lesen; **don't ~ too much into his words** interpretieren Sie nicht zu viel in seine Worte hinein **c** (Brit Univ form: = study) studieren **d** thermometer, barometer etc sehen auf (+acc), ablesen; **to ~ a meter** einen Zähler(stand) ablesen **e** (meter) (an)zeigen, stehen auf (+dat); (flight etc instruments) anzeigen; **the thermometer ~s 37°** das Thermometer steht or zeigt 37° **f** (Telec) verstehen; **do you ~ me?** (Telec) können Sie mich verstehen?; (fig) haben Sie mich verstanden?

VI a (= read books etc) lesen; (to sb) vorlesen (to +dat); **she ~s well** sie liest gut; (learner, beginner) sie kann schon gut lesen; **to ~ aloud** or **out loud** laut lesen; **to ~ to oneself** für sich lesen; **he likes being ~ to** er lässt sich (dat) gern vorlesen; **will you ~ to me, Mummy?** Mutti, liest du mir etwas vor? **b** (= convey impression when read) **this paragraph ~s/doesn't ~ well** dieser Abschnitt liest sich gut/nicht gut; **this ~s like an official report/a translation** das klingt wie ein offizieller Bericht/eine Übersetzung; **that's how it ~s to me** so verstehe ich das **c** (= have wording) lauten; **the letter ~s as follows** der Brief geht so or lautet folgendermaßen **d** (Brit Univ form: = study) **to ~ for an examination** sich auf eine Prüfung vorbereiten → **bar**[1] **N** **she enjoys a good ~** sie liest gern; **this book is quite a good ~** das Buch liest sich gut

▶**read back** VT sep shorthand lesen; one's notes etc noch einmal lesen; (to sb) noch einmal vorlesen

▶**read in** VT sep (Comput) text, data einlesen

▶**read off** VT sep ablesen; (without pause) herunterlesen

▶**read on** VI weiterlesen

▶**read out** VT sep vorlesen; instrument readings ablesen

▶**read over** or **through** VT sep durchlesen

▶**read up** **VT** sep nachlesen über (+acc), sich informieren über (+acc) **VI** nachlesen, sich informieren (on über +acc)

read[2] [red] pret, ptp of **read**[1] ADJ **he is well/not very well ~** er ist sehr/wenig belesen

readability [ˌri:də'bɪlɪtɪ] N (= legibility, of handwriting etc) Leserlichkeit f, Lesbarkeit f; (= reading enjoyment) Lesevergnügen nt; (= comprehensibility, of book etc) Lesbarkeit f

readable ['ri:dəbl] ADJ (= legible) handwriting lesbar; (= worth reading) book etc lesenswert; **not very ~** (= illegible) schlecht lesbar; (= not worth reading) nicht besonders lesenswert

readdress [ˌri:ə'dres] VT **a** letter, parcel umadressieren **b** problem erneut ansprechen

reader ['ri:də'] N **a** Leser(in) m(f); **publisher's ~** Lektor(in) m(f) **b** (Brit Univ) ≈ Dozent(in) m(f) **c** (= schoolbook) Lesebuch nt; (to teach reading) Fibel f; (= foreign language text) Text m, Lektüre f; (= anthology) Sammelband m; **a ~ in the Classics** eine Klassikersammlung; **"first**

French ~" „Französisches Lesebuch für Anfänger"

readership ['riːdəʃɪp] N **a** (of newspaper, magazine) Leserschaft f, Leser pl; **a big** or **wide ~** eine große Leserschaft; **a ~ of millions** Millionen Leser **b** (Brit Univ) ≈ Dozentur f

read head N (Comput) Lesekopf m

readies ['rediz] PL (Brit inf, = ready cash) Bare(s) nt (inf); **the ~** das Bare (inf); **that'll cost you 100 in ~** das kostet dich 100 Bar auf die Hand (inf) or Kralle (sl); **I don't have the ~** ich hab nicht die Kohle (inf)

readily ['redɪlɪ] ADV bereitwillig; (= easily) leicht; **~ to hand** griffbereit; **~ available** leicht erhältlich; **~ accessible** leicht zugänglich; **~ apparent** offensichtlich, leicht ersichtlich

readiness ['redɪnɪs] N **a** Bereitschaft f; **~ for war** Kriegsbereitschaft f; **to be (kept) in ~ (for sth)** (für etw) bereitgehalten werden; **his ~ to help** seine Hilfsbereitschaft **b** (= ease) Leichtigkeit f

reading ['riːdɪŋ] N **a** (= action) Lesen nt **b** (= reading matter) Lektüre f; **this book makes (for) very interesting ~** dieses Buch ist sehr interessant zu lesen; **have you any light ~?** haben Sie eine leichte Lektüre? **c** (= recital, excerpt) Lesung f; **play ~** Lesen nt mit verteilten Rollen **d** (= interpretation) Interpretation f, Verständnis nt **e** (= variant) Version f **f** (from meter) Thermometer-/Barometer-/Zählerstand etc m; (on flight etc instruments) Anzeige f; (in scientific experiment) Messwert m; **to take a ~** den Thermometerstand etc/die Anzeige/den Messwert ablesen; **the ~ is …** das Thermometer etc steht auf …; die Anzeige/der Messwert ist … **g** (Parl, of bill) Lesung f; **the Senate gave the bill its first/a second ~** der Senat beriet das Gesetz in erster/zweiter Lesung **h** (= knowledge) Belesenheit f; **a man of wide ~** ein sehr belesener Mann

reading: reading age N a low/high **~** ein hohes/junges Lesalter; **a ~ of 7** die Lesefähigkeit eines 7-Jährigen; **reading book** N Lesebuch nt; **reading desk** N (Lese)tisch m; **reading glass** N Lupe f; **reading glasses** PL Lesebrille f; **reading head** N (Comput) Lesekopf m; **reading knowledge** N **to have a ~ of Spanish** Spanisch lesen können; **reading lamp** N Leselampe f; **reading list** N Leseliste f; **reading matter** N Lesestoff m; **reading public** N Leserschaft f, Leser pl; **reading room** N Lesesaal m; **reading speed** N (of child, Comput) Lesegeschwindigkeit f

readjust [ˌriːə'dʒʌst] **VT** instrument, mechanism neu einstellen; (= correct) nachstellen; prices, salary anpassen, neu regeln; opinion korrigieren **VI** sich neu or wieder anpassen (to an +acc), sich neu or wieder einstellen (to auf +acc)

readjustment [ˌriːə'dʒʌstmənt] N (of instrument, mechanism) Neueinstellung f; (= correction) Nachstellung f; (of prices, salary) Anpassung f, Neuregelung f; (of opinion) Korrektur f; (of person) Wiederanpassung f

read: read only memory N (Comput) (Nur)lesespeicher m, Festwertspeicher m; **readout** N (Comput etc) Anzeige f; **read-through** N (Theat etc) Leseprobe f; **read-write head** N (Comput) Schreib-/Lesekopf m; **read-write memory** N (Comput) Schreib-/Lesespeicher m

ready ['redɪ] **ADJ** **a** (= prepared) person, thing bereit, fertig; answer, excuse parat, vorformuliert; (= finished, cooked etc) fertig; **~ to leave** abmarschbereit; (for journey) abfahrtbereit, reisefertig; **~ to use** or **for use** gebrauchsfertig; **~ to serve** tischfertig; **~ for battle** kampfbereit; **~ for action** bereit zum Angriff, klar zum Angriff or Gefecht; **~ for anything** zu allem bereit; **dinner is ~** das Essen ist fertig; **"dinner's ~"** „essen kommen", „zum Essen"; **are you ~ to go?** sind Sie so weit?, kann es losgehen? (inf); **are you ~ to push?** alles fertig zum Schieben?; **are you ~ to take the weight?** können Sie das Gewicht

jetzt übernehmen?; **are you ~ to order?** sind Sie so weit?, möchten Sie jetzt bestellen?; **well, I think we're ~** ich glaube, wir sind so weit; **I'm not quite ~ yet** ich bin noch nicht ganz fertig; **everything is ~ for his visit** alles ist auf or für seinen Besuch vorbereitet; **the final treaty will be ~ for signing tomorrow** der endgültige Vertrag wird morgen zum Unterzeichnen fertig sein or bereitliegen; **flight 211 is now ~ for boarding** Flug 211 ist jetzt zum Einsteigen bereit; **the doctor's ~ for you now** der Doktor kann Sie jetzt sehen; **I'm ~ for him!** ich warte nur auf ihn, er soll nur kommen; **to be ~ with an excuse** eine Entschuldigung bereit haben or bereithalten; **to get (oneself) ~** sich fertig machen; **to get ready to go out/play tennis** sich zum Ausgehen/Tennisspielen fertig machen; **to get ~ for sth** sich auf etw (acc) vorbereiten; **get ~ for it!** (before blow etc) Achtung!, pass auf!; (before momentous news) mach dich auf was gefasst (inf); **to get** or **make sth ~** etw fertig machen, etw bereitmachen; room, bed, breakfast etc **to get sth/sb ~ (for sth/to do sth)** etw/jdn vorbereiten or fertig machen (für etw/zum Tun von etw); **to make ~ (for sth/to do sth)** sich fertig machen (für etw/zum Tun von etw); **we were all ~ to sleep** (expressing need) wir brauchten alle Schlaf, wir waren alle kurz davor, einzuschlafen; **~ and waiting** startbereit; **~ when you are** ich bin bereit or startbereit; **~ about!** (Naut) klar zum Wenden!; **~, steady, go!** (Brit) Achtung or auf die Plätze, fertig, los!

b (= quick) explanation fertig, zur Hand pred; smile rasch, schnell; supply griffbereit, zur Hand pred; market schnell; availability schnell, griffbereit, zur Hand; **~ to do sth** (= willing) bereit, etw zu tun; (= quick) schnell dabei, etw zu tun; **he's always ~ to find fault** er ist immer schnell dabei, wenn es gilt, Fehler zu finden; **they are only too ~ to let us do all the work** sie sind nur allzu bereit or immer gern bereit, die ganze Arbeit uns zu überlassen; **don't be so ~ to criticize** kritisieren Sie doch nicht so schnell; **I'm ~ to believe it** ich möchte das fast glauben; **he was ~ to cry** er war den Tränen nahe; **he's always ~ with an answer** er ist mit einer Antwort immer schnell bei der Hand; **~, willing and able (to do sth)** bereit, fertig und willens(, etw zu tun)

c (= prompt) reply prompt; wit schlagfertig; **to have a ~ tongue** schlagfertig sein **d** (= available) money jederzeit verfügbares Geld; **~ cash** Bargeld nt; **~ to pay in ~ cash** auf die Hand bezahlen; **~ to hand** zur Hand; **"now ~"** „jetzt zu haben" **e** (= practical) solution sauber; (= competent) speaker gewandt; **to have a ~ sale** (Comm) guten Absatz finden

N **a** (Mil) **to come to the ~** das Gewehr in Anschlag nehmen; **at the ~** (Mil) mit dem Gewehr im Anschlag; (fig) marsch-/fahrbereit etc; **with his pen at the ~** mit gezücktem Federhalter **b** (= money) **the ~** (inf) das nötige Kleingeld (inf) → also **readies**

VT (form, = prepare) object vorbereiten, fertig machen; **to oneself to do sth** sich vorbereiten, etw zu tun or sich vorbereiten für etw

VI (form) **to ~ for sth** auf dem Weg or unterwegs sein zu etw; **to ~ to do sth** im Begriff sein or stehen, etw zu tun, drauf und dran sein, etw zu tun

ready: ready-cooked ADJ vorgekocht; **ready-cut** ADJ zugeschnitten; **ready-furnished** ADJ fertig eingerichtet; **ready-made** **ADJ** **a** curtains fertig; meal vorgekocht; answer, ideas vorgefertigt; **~ clothes** Konfektionskleidung f **b** (= convenient) replacement nahtlos, übergangslos; topic jederzeit verfügbar, immer zur Hand; family komplett; **~ solution** Patentlösung f **ADV** komplett; **you can buy your greenhouse ~** Sie können Ihr Glashaus schon fertig zusammengesetzt or zusammengebaut kaufen, Sie können ein komplett fertiges Glashaus kaufen; **ready meal** N Fertiggericht nt; **ready-**

y-mix ADJ attr (Cook) aus einer Packung, aus der Packung; **ready-mixed** ADJ vorgemischt; **~ concrete** Fertigzement m; **ready-prepared** ADJ vorbereitet, im Voraus zubereitet; **ready reckoner** N Rechentabelle f; **ready-to-eat** ADJ tafelfertig, essfertig; **~ frozen meals** tiefgefrorene Fertiggerichte; **ready-to-serve** ADJ tischfertig; **ready-to-wear** ADJ attr, **ready to wear** ADJ pred Konfektions-, von der Stange (inf); **~ dress** Konfektionskleid nt; **ready-witted** ADJ person aufgeweckt, schlagfertig

reaffirm [ˌriːə'fɜːm] VT **a** (= assert again) wieder or erneut versichern, beteuern **b** (= strengthen, reconfirm) suspicion, doubts bestätigen; principles, wish bestärken

reaffirmation [ˌriːæfə'meɪʃən] N **a** (= assertion) erneute Versicherung f **b** (= confirmation) Bestätigung f, Bestärkung f

reafforest [ˌriːə'fɒrɪst] VT wieder aufforsten

reafforestation ['riːəˌfɒrɪs'teɪʃən] N (esp Brit) Wiederaufforstung f

reagent [riː'eɪdʒənt] N (Chem) Reagens nt

real [rɪəl] **ADJ** **a** (= genuine) gold, flowers, silk etc, sympathy, joy, desire echt; need, improvement echt, wirklich; (= as opposed to substitute) richtig; name richtig; (= true, as opposed to apparent) owner, boss, reason, purpose, state of affairs wirklich, tatsächlich, eigentlich; (= not imaginary) creature, object, life, world wirklich, real (esp Philos); (Phys, Math) reell; (Econ) real; **you can touch it, it's ~** das können Sie anfassen, es ist wirklich da; **was the unicorn ever a ~ creature?** gab es das Einhorn je wirklich or tatsächlich?; **in ~ life** im wirklichen Leben; **he has no ~ power** er hat keine wirkliche Macht; **his grief was very ~** sein Schmerz war echt, er empfand seinen Schmerz zutiefst; **the danger was very ~** das war eine ganz reale Gefahr; **it's the ~ thing** or **McCoy, this whisky!** dieser Whisky ist der echte; **it's not the ~ thing** das ist nicht das Wahre; (= not genuine) das ist nicht echt; **climbing this hill isn't much when you've done the ~ thing** dieser Hügel ist gar nichts, wenn man schon einmal richtig geklettert hat; **she wanted to see the ~ Africa** sie wollte das wirkliche Afrika or das tiefe Afrika erleben; **the ~ question is…** die wirkliche Frage ist …, der Kern der Frage ist …; **to keep in touch with the ~ world** auf dem Boden der Tatsachen bleiben, nicht die Berührung mit der wirklichen Leben verlieren; **Real Presence** (Rel) Realpräsenz f; **get ~!** (inf) wach auf!

b (= proper, complete) richtig; sportsman, gentleman, coward richtig, echt; champion, friend, friendship wahr, echt; threat echt, wirklich; idiot, disaster komplett; **it's a ~ miracle** das ist wirklich or echt (inf) ein Wunder, das ist ein wahres Wunder; **it's a ~ shame** es ist wirklich schade, es ist jammerschade; **he doesn't know what ~ contentment/family life is** er weiß ja nicht, was Zufriedenheit/Familienleben wirklich ist; **that's what I call a ~ car** das nenne ich ein Auto; **that's a ~ racket** das ist wirklich ein Schwindel; **I'm in ~ trouble** ich bin in großen Schwierigkeiten; **to make ~ money** wirklich viel Geld verdienen, das große Geld verdienen or machen (inf)

c (Fin, = net, overall) income, cost wirklich, tatsächlich; interest rate effektiv; **in ~ terms** effektiv; **this increase is equivalent in ~ terms to …** dieser Anstieg entspricht effektiv …

ADV (esp US, inf) echt (inf), wirklich; **~ soon** wirklich bald; **we had a ~ good laugh** wir haben so gelacht

N **a** **for ~** wirklich, echt (inf); **is that invitation for ~?** ist die Einladung ernst gemeint?; **he's not for ~** (= not sincere) er meint es nicht wirklich; (= not genuine) er ist nicht echt; **is this for ~ or is it another practice?** ist das echt (inf) or Ernst oder steckt wieder eine Übung? **b** (Philos) **the ~** das Reale, die Wirklichkeit

real: real ale N Real Ale nt; **real coffee** N Bohnenkaffee m; **real estate** N Immobilien pl; **~ developer** (US) Immobilienhändler(in) m(f); **~ agent** (US) Grundstücks- or Immobilienmakler(in) *m(f)*; **~ office** (*US*) Immobilienbüro *nt*; **~ register** (*US*) Grundbuch *nt*

realism [ˈrɪəlɪzəm] N Realismus *m*

realist [ˈrɪəlɪst] N Realist(in) *m(f)*

realistic [rɪəˈlɪstɪk] ADJ realistisch; *painting also* naturgetreu

realistically [rɪəˈlɪstɪkəlɪ] ADV *hope for* realistisch, realistischerweise; **it just isn't ~ possible** es ist realistisch gesehen nicht möglich, es ist einfach unrealistisch; **~, he had little chance of winning** realistisch gesehen hatte er kaum eine Chance zu gewinnen; **~ speaking** realistisch gesehen *or* gesagt

reality [riːˈælɪtɪ] ✪ 26.3 N **a** Wirklichkeit *f*, Realität *f*; **to become ~** sich verwirklichen; **(the) ~ is somewhat different** die Wirklichkeit *or* Realität sieht etwas anders aus; **in ~** (= *in fact*) in Wirklichkeit; (= *actually*) eigentlich; **to bring sb back to ~** jdn auf den Boden der Tatsachen zurückbringen; **the realities of the situation** der wirkliche Sachverhalt **b** (= *trueness to life*) Naturtreue *f*

reality TV N Reality TV *nt*

realizable [ˈrɪəlaɪzəbl] ADJ *assets* realisierbar, zu verflüssigen *pred*; *hope, plan* realisierbar, zu verwirklichen *pred*; *wealth* realisierbar

realization [ˌrɪəlaɪˈzeɪʃən] N **a** (*of assets*) Realisation *f*, Verflüssigung *f*; (*of hope, plan*) Realisierung *f*, Verwirklichung *f*; (*of potential*) Verwirklichung *f* **b** (= *awareness*) Erkenntnis *f*

realize [ˈrɪəlaɪz] VT **a** (= *become aware of*) erkennen, sich (*dat*) klar werden (+*gen*), (*dat*) bewusst werden (+*gen*); (= *be aware of*) sich (*dat*) klar sein über (+*acc*), sich (*dat*) bewusst sein (+*gen*); (= *appreciate, understand*) begreifen; (= *notice*) (be)merken; (= *discover*) feststellen; **does he ~ the problems?** sind ihm die Probleme bewusst *or* klar?; **he had not fully ~d that she was dead** es war ihm nicht voll bewusst, dass sie tot war; **I ~d what he meant** mir wurde klar *or* ich begriff, was er meinte; **I ~d how he had done it** ich erkannte *or* mir wurde klar, wie er es gemacht hatte; **I hadn't ~d you were going away** mir war nicht klar, dass Sie weggehen; **I've just ~d I won't be here** mir ist eben aufgegangen *or* klar geworden, dass ich dann nicht hier sein werde; **when will you ~ you can't ...?** wann werden Sie endlich begreifen, dass Sie nicht ... können?; **I hadn't ~d how late it was** ich habe gar nicht gemerkt, wie spät es war; **he didn't ~ she was cheating him** er merkte nicht, dass sie ihn betrog; **when the parents ~d their child was deaf** als die Eltern (be)merkten *or* feststellten, dass ihr Kind taub war; **I ~d I didn't have any money on me** ich stellte fest, dass ich kein Geld dabei hatte; **I made her ~ that I was right** ich machte ihr klar, dass ich Recht hatte; **you couldn't be expected to ~ that** das konnten Sie nicht wissen; **yes, I ~ that** ja, das ist mir klar *or* bewusst; **yes, I ~ that I was wrong** ja, ich sehe ein, dass ich Unrecht hatte

b *hope, plan* verwirklichen, realisieren; *potential* verwirklichen

c (*Fin*) *assets* realisieren, verflüssigen; *price* bringen, erzielen; *interest* abwerfen, erbringen; (*goods*) einbringen; **how much did you ~ on your Rembrandt?** wie viel hat Ihr Rembrandt (ein)gebracht?

VI **didn't you ~?** war Ihnen das nicht klar?; (= *notice*) haben Sie das nicht gemerkt?; **I've just ~d** das ist mir eben klar geworden; (= *noticed*) das habe ich eben gemerkt; **I thought you'd never ~** ich dachte, Sie merken es nie; **he'll never ~** (= *notice*) das wird er nie merken

real-life ADJ *situation* alltäglich, lebensecht, tatsächlich; *event* real, tatsächlich, wirklich; *person* wirklich, real; *story* wirklich, wahr

reallocate [riˈæləʊkeɪt] VT umverteilen, neu verteilen *or* zuteilen

reallocation [ˌriːæləʊˈkeɪʃən] N Umverteilung *f*, Neuverteilung *f*

---

really [ˈrɪəlɪ] ADV **a** (= *in reality*) wirklich, tatsächlich; **I ~ don't know what to think** ich weiß wirklich *or* tatsächlich nicht, was ich davon halten soll; **I don't ~ know what I'm going to do** ich weiß eigentlich nicht, was ich machen werde; **I don't ~ think so** das glaube ich eigentlich nicht; **well yes, I ~ think we should** ich finde eigentlich schon, dass wir das tun sollten; **before he ~ knew/understood** bevor er richtig *or* wirklich wusste/verstand; **~ and truly** wirklich

b (*intensifier*) wirklich, echt (*inf*); *glad, disappointed* wirklich, richtig, echt (*inf*); **he ~ is an idiot** er ist wirklich *or* echt (*inf*) ein Idiot; **you ~ must visit Paris** Sie müssen wirklich Paris besuchen; **I ~ must say ...** ich muss schon sagen ...

INTERJ (*in doubt, disbelief, surprise*) wirklich, tatsächlich; (*in protest, indignation*) also wirklich!; **not ~!** ach wirklich?

realm [relm] N (*liter, = kingdom*) Königreich *nt*; (*fig*) Reich *nt*; **within the ~s of possibility** im Bereich des Möglichen

real: real number N reelle Zahl; **real property** N (*US*) Grundbesitz *m*; **real tennis** N Ballhaustennis *nt*; **real time** N (*Comput*) Echtzeit *f*; **real-time clock** N (*Comput*) Echtzeituhr *f*; **real-time processing** N (*Comput*) Echtzeitverarbeitung *f*

realtor [ˈrɪəltɔː] N (*US*) Grundstücksmakler(in) *m(f)*

realty [ˈrɪəltɪ] N , *no pl* (*Jur*) Immobilien *pl*

ream [riːm] N (*of paper*) (altes) Ries; **he always writes ~s** (*inf*) er schreibt immer ganze Bände (*inf*)

reanimate [riːˈænɪmeɪt] VT (*Med, form*) *patient, person* wieder beleben; (*fig*) *party, conversation* also neu beleben

reanimation [ˌriːænɪˈmeɪʃən] N (*Med*) Wiederbelebung *f*; (*fig: of party, conversation also*) Neubelebung *f*

reap [riːp] VT **a** *corn* (= *cut*) schneiden, mähen; (= *harvest*) ernten; *field* abernten **b** (*fig*) *profit* ernten; *reward* bekommen; **to ~ the fruit of one's labours** die Früchte seiner Arbeit ernten; **to ~ a rich harvest** eine reiche Ernte einbringen; **to ~ what one has sown** ernten, was man gesät hat → **sow¹** VI schneiden, mähen; (*person*) ernten

reaper [ˈriːpə] N (= *person*) Schnitter(in) *m(f)*; (= *machine*) Mähbinder *m*; **the Reaper** (*fig: = death*) der Schnitter

reaping [ˈriːpɪŋ] N (*of corn*) (= *cutting*) Schneiden *nt*, Mähen *nt*; (= *harvesting*) Ernten *nt*; (*of field*) Abernten *nt*

reaping: reaping hook N Sichel *f*; **reaping machine** N Mähbinder *m*

reappear [ˌriːəˈpɪə] VI wieder erscheinen; (*person, sun also*) sich wieder zeigen; (*character in novel*) wieder auftauchen

reappearance [ˌriːəˈpɪərəns] N Wiedererscheinen *nt*; (*of character in novel*) Wiederauftauchen *nt*

reappoint [ˌriːəˈpɔɪnt] VT (*to a job*) wieder einstellen (*to* als); (*to a post*) wieder ernennen (*to* zu)

reappointment [ˌriːəˈpɔɪntmənt] N (*to a job*) Wiedereinstellung *f*; (*to a post*) Wiederernennung *f*

reapportion [ˌriːəˈpɔːʃən] VT *money, food, land* neu aufteilen; *duties* neu zuteilen

reappraisal [ˌriːəˈpreɪzəl] N (*of situation, problem*) Neubeurteilung *f*; (*of author, film etc also*) Neubewertung *f*

reappraise [ˌriːəˈpreɪz] VT *situation, problem* von neuem beurteilen; *author, film etc also* neu bewerten

rear¹ [rɪə] N **a** (= *back part*) hinterer Teil; (*inf, = buttocks*) Hintern *m* (*inf*); **in** *or* **at the ~** hinten (*of* in +*dat*); **to be situated at/to(wards) the ~ of the plane** hinten im Flugzeug/am hinteren Ende des Flugzeugs sein; **at** *or* **to the ~ of the building** (*outside*) hinter dem Haus; (*inside*) hin-

---

ten im Haus; **go to the ~ of the house** (*behind the house*) geh hinter das Haus; (*inside the house*) geh nach hinten; **from the ~** von hinten

b (*Mil*) Schwanz *m* (der Truppe); **to attack an army in the ~** eine Armee im Rücken angreifen; **to bring up the ~** (*lit, fig*) die Nachhut bilden

ADJ **a** Hinter-, hintere(r, s)

b (*Aut*) Heck-; **~ door** hintere Tür; **~ engine** Heckmotor *m*; **~ lights** Rücklichter *pl*; **~ wheel** Hinterrad *nt*; **~ window** Heckfenster *nt*; **~ windscreen** Heckscheibe *f*

rear² VT **a** (*esp Brit*) *animals, family* großziehen, aufziehen **b** *animal* ~**s its head** den Kopf zurückwerfen; (*snake*) sich aufstellen; *violence/racism* ~**ed its ugly head (again)** die Gewalt/der Rassismus kam (wieder) zum Vorschein; **sex** ~**s its ugly head** der Trieb meldet sich VI (*horse: also* **rear up**) sich aufbäumen

rear: rear admiral N Konteradmiral *m*; **rear end** N hinteres Ende; (*Aut*) Heck *nt*; (*fig; hum: = buttocks*) Hintern *m* (*inf*), Hinterteil *nt* (*inf*); **rear-end** VT (*esp US Inf*) *sb/sth* auffahren (*sb/sth* +*acc*); **rear-end collision** N (*Mot*), **rear-ender** [ˈrɪərˈendə] N (*esp US Inf Mot*) Auffahrunfall *m*; **rear-engined** ADJ (*Aut*) mit Heckmotor, heckmotorig; **rearguard** N (*Mil*) Nachhut *f*; **rearguard action** N Nachhutgefecht *nt*; **rear gunner** N (*Mil*) Heckschütze *m*/-schützin *f*

rearm [ˌriːˈɑːm] VT *country* wieder bewaffnen; *forces, troops* neu ausrüsten *or* ausstatten VI wieder aufrüsten, neue Ausrüstung anschaffen, sich neu ausrüsten

rearmament [ˌriːˈɑːməmənt] N (*of country*) Wiederbewaffnung *f*, Wiederaufrüstung *f*; (*of forces, troops*) Neuausrüstung *f*, Neuausstattung *f*

rearmost [ˈrɪəməʊst] ADJ hinterste(r, s)

rear: rear-mounted engine N (*Aut*) Heckmotor *m*; **rear projection** N (*Film, Theat*) Rückprojektion *f*

rearrange [ˌriːəˈreɪndʒ] VT *furniture, system* umstellen; *plans also, layout, formation, order, ideas* ändern; *appointment, meeting* neu abmachen

rearrangement [ˌriːəˈreɪndʒmənt] N (*of furniture, system*) Umstellung *f*; (*of plans, layout, formation, order, ideas*) Änderung *f*; (*of appointment, meeting*) Neuabmachung *f*

rear-view mirror [ˈrɪəˌvjuːˈmɪrə] N Rückspiegel *m*

rearward [ˈrɪəwəd] ADJ *part* hintere(r, s); *position* am Ende; *movement* nach hinten, rückwärtig ADV (*also* **rearwards**) rückwärts

rear-wheel drive [ˈrɪəˌwiːlˈdraɪv] N Heckantrieb *m*

reason [ˈriːzn] ✪ 16.1, 17.1, 17.2, 26.3 N **a** (= *cause, justification*) Grund *m* (*for* für); **~ for living** *or* **being** Grund *m* zum Leben; **my ~ for going, the ~ for my going** (der Grund,) weshalb ich gehe/gegangen bin; **to give sb ~ for complaint** jdm Anlass *or* Grund zu Klagen geben; **the police had no ~ to interfere** die Polizei hatte keinen Grund einzugreifen; (*but did*) die Polizei hat ohne Grund eingegriffen; **what's the ~ for this celebration?** aus welchem Anlass wird hier gefeiert?; **I want to know the ~ why** ich möchte wissen, weshalb; **and that's the ~ why ... and deshalb ...**; das ist der Grund dafür!; **I have (good) ~/every ~ to believe that ...** ich habe (guten) Grund/allen Grund anzunehmen, dass ...; **there is ~ to believe that ...** es gibt Gründe zu glauben, dass ...; **there is every ~ to believe ...** es spricht alles dafür ...; **for that very ~** eben deswegen; **with (good) ~** mit gutem Grund, mit Recht; **without any ~** ohne jeden Grund *or* Anlass, grundlos; **for no ~ at all** ohne ersichtlichen Grund; **for no particular/apparent ~** ohne einen bestimmten/ersichtlichen Grund; **why did you do that? – no particular ~** warum haben Sie das gemacht? – einfach nur so; **for no other ~ than that ...** aus keinem anderen Grund, als dass ...; **for some ~ (or (an)other)** aus irgendeinem Grund; **for ~s best known to himself/myself** aus unerfindlichen/bestimmten Gründen; **all the more ~ for doing it** *or* **to do it** umso mehr

Grund, das zu tun; **by ~ of** wegen (+*gen*); **for ~s of State this was never disclosed** die Staatsräson machte die Geheimhaltung erforderlich **b** *no pl* (= *mental faculty*) Verstand *m*; **to lose one's ~** den Verstand verlieren; **to reach the age of ~** verständig werden; **the Age of Reason** (*Hist*) das Zeitalter der Vernunft **c** *no pl* (= *common sense*) Vernunft *f*; **the voice of ~** die Stimme der Vernunft; **to listen to ~** auf die Stimme der Vernunft hören; **he won't listen to ~** er lässt sich (*dat*) nichts sagen; **he's beyond ~** ihm ist mit Vernunft nicht beizukommen; **that stands to ~** das ist logisch; **we'll do anything within ~ to ...** wir tun alles, was in unserer Macht steht, um zu ...; **you can have anything within ~** Sie können alles haben, solange es sich in Grenzen hält **VI** **a** (= *think logically*) vernünftig *or* logisch denken; **the ability to ~** logisches Denkvermögen **b** (= *argue*) **to ~ (with sb)** vernünftig mit jdm reden; **there's no ~ing with him** mit ihm kann man nicht vernünftig reden **VT** **a** **to ~ sb out of sth** jdm etw ausreden; **to ~ sb into sth** jdn zu etw überreden; **to ~ why/ what ...** sich (*dat*) klarmachen, warum/was ...; **ours is not to ~ why** es steht uns nicht an zu fragen, warum; **he ~ed that if we hurried we could get there by 6 o'clock** er argumentierte, dass wir um 6.00 Uhr dort ankommen könnten, wenn wir uns beeilen würden, er rechnete vor, dass wir bis 6.00 Uhr dort sein könnten **b** (*also* **reason out**) (= *deduce*) schließen, folgern; (*verbally*) argumentieren; (= *work out*) problem durchdenken

▶ **reason out** VT SEP = **reason** VT b

reasonable ['riːznəbl] ADJ **a** vernünftig; *chance* reell; *claim* berechtigt; *amount* angemessen; (= *acceptable*) *excuse, offer* akzeptabel, angemessen; **be ~!** sei vernünftig; **vegetables are ~ (in price) just now** Gemüse ist momentan preiswert; **to be ~ about sth** angemessen reagieren auf etw, vernünftig sein in einer Sache (*dat*); **to use ~ force** (*Jur*) angemessene Gewalt anwenden; **~ grounds** (*Jur*) zureichende Gründe *pl*; **~ doubt** berechtigter Zweifel; **beyond (all) ~ doubt** ohne (jeden) Zweifel; **guilty beyond (all) ~ doubt** (*Jur*) hinreichend schuldig; **within a ~ time** innerhalb eines angemessenen Zeitraums; **it would be ~ to assume that ...** man könnte durchaus annehmen, dass ... **b** (= *quite good*) ordentlich, ganz gut; **his work was only ~** seine Arbeit war nur einigermaßen (gut); **with a ~ amount of luck** mit einigem Glück

reasonableness ['riːznəblnɪs] N Vernünftigkeit *f*; (*of claim*) Berechtigung *f*; (*of amount*) Angemessenheit *f*

reasonably ['riːznəblɪ] ADV **a** *behave, act, think* vernünftig; **one could ~ think/argue that ...** man könnte durchaus annehmen/anführen, dass ...; **~ priced** preiswert **b** (= *quite, fairly*) ziemlich, ganz

reasoned ['riːznd] ADJ *argument, approach* durchdacht; *discussion* vernunftgeleitet, vernünftig; *explanation* wohl begründet, durchdacht; **~ thought** Vernunftdenken *nt*

reasoning ['riːznɪŋ] N logisches Denken; (= *arguing*) Argumentation *f*; **I don't follow your ~** ich kann Ihrem Gedankengang *or* Ihrer Argumentation nicht folgen; **this (piece of) ~ is faulty** das Argument ist falsch; **his ~ is all wrong** er argumentiert ganz falsch, seine Argumente sind total falsch

reassemble [ˌriːəˈsembl] **VT** **a** *people, troops* wieder versammeln **b** *tool, car, machine* wieder zusammenbauen **VI** sich wieder versammeln; (*troops*) sich wieder sammeln

reassert [ˌriːəˈsɜːt] VT mit Nachdruck behaupten; **to ~ oneself** seine Autorität wieder geltend machen; **his old habits ~ed themselves** seine alten Gewohnheiten kamen wieder durch

reassess [ˌriːəˈses] VT neu überdenken; *proposals, advantages* neu abwägen; (*for taxation*) neu veranlagen; *damages* neu schätzen

reassume [ˌriːəˈsjuːm] VT *work* wieder aufnehmen; *office* wieder übernehmen

reassurance [ˌriːəˈʃʊərəns] N **a** (= *feeling of security*) Beruhigung *f*; **to give sb ~** jdn beruhigen; **a mother's presence gives a child the ~ it needs** die Gegenwart der Mutter gibt dem Kind das nötige Gefühl der Sicherheit **b** (= *renewed confirmation*) Bestätigung *f*; **despite his ~(s)** trotz seiner Versicherungen; (*of lover etc*) trotz seiner Beteuerungen **c** = **reinsurance**

reassure [ˌriːəˈʃʊə] VT **a** (= *relieve sb's mind*) beruhigen; (= *give feeling of security to*) das Gefühl der Sicherheit geben (+*dat*) **b** (*verbally*) versichern (+*dat*); (*lover*) beteuern (+*dat*); **to ~ sb of sth** jdm etw versichern/beteuern; **she needs to be constantly ~d that her work is adequate** man muss ihr ständig versichern *or* bestätigen, dass ihre Arbeit gut genug ist **c** = **reinsure**

reassuring [ˌriːəˈʃʊərɪŋ] ADJ beruhigend; **they had been ~ about the technical problems** sie waren hinsichtlich der technischen Schwierigkeiten zuversichtlich gewesen, sie hatten sich beruhigend über die technischen Schwierigkeiten geäußert; **it is ~ to know that ...** es ist beruhigend zu wissen, dass ...

reassuringly [ˌriːəˈʃʊərɪŋlɪ] ADV *say, simple* beruhigend; *familiar* beruhigend, tröstlich

reawaken [ˌriːəˈweɪkən] **VT** *person* wieder erwecken; *love, passion, interest* neu erwecken **VI** *(interest, love, passion)* wieder aufleben, wieder erwachen

reawakening [ˌriːəˈweɪk/ɪŋ] N (*of person*) Wiedererwachen *nt*; (*of ideas, interest also*) Wiederaufleben *nt*

rebarbative [rɪˈbɑːbətɪv] ADJ (*form*) abstoßend

rebate ['riːbeɪt] N (= *discount*) Rabatt *m*, (Preis-)nachlass *m*; (= *money back*) Rückvergütung *f*, Rückzahlung *f*

rebel ['rebl] **N** Rebell(in) *m(f)*, Aufrührer(in) *m(f)*; (*by nature*) Rebell(in) *m(f)* **ADJ** *attr* rebellisch; *forces, troops also* aufständisch **VI** [rɪˈbel] rebellieren; (*troops, forces also*) sich erheben

rebellion [rɪˈbeljən] N Rebellion *f*, Aufstand *m*; **to rise (up) in ~** einen Aufstand machen, sich erheben

rebellious [rɪˈbeljəs] ADJ *soldiers, peasants etc* rebellisch, aufrührerisch; *child, nature* rebellisch, widerspenstig

rebelliously [rɪˈbeljəslɪ] ADV *say* rebellisch, aufmüpfig; *act* rebellisch

rebelliousness [rɪˈbeljəsnɪs] N (*of troops, subordinates etc*) Rebellion *f*; (= *nature: of child etc*) Widerspenstigkeit *f*

rebirth [ˌriːˈbɜːθ] N Wiedergeburt *f*; (*of desire*) Wiederaufflackern *nt*

rebirthing [ˌriːˈbɜːθɪŋ] N Rebirthing *nt*

reboot [ˌriːˈbuːt] VTI (*Comput*) neu laden, rebooten

rebore [ˌriːˈbɔː] **VT** wieder bohren; *hole* noch einmal bohren; (*Aut*) *engine* ausbohren **N** ['riː-ˌbɔː](*Aut*) **this engine needs a ~** der Motor muss ausgebohrt werden

reborn [ˌriːˈbɔːn] ADJ **to be ~** wieder geboren werden; **to be ~ in** (*fig*) weiterleben in (+*dat*); **to feel ~** sich wie neugeboren fühlen

rebound [rɪˈbaʊnd] **VI** (*ball, bullet*) zurückprallen, abprallen (*against, off* von); **your methods will ~ on you** Ihre Methoden werden auf Sie zurückfallen **N** ['riːbaʊnd] (*of ball, bullet*) Rückprall *m*; (*Baseball*) Rebound *m*; **to hit a ball on the ~** den zurück- *or* abgeprallten Ball schlagen; **she married him on the ~** sie heiratete ihn, um sich über einen anderen hinwegzutrösten

rebrand [rɪˈbrænd] VT *product* ein neues Markenimage geben (+*dat*)

rebranding [rɪˈbrændɪŋ] N **the ~ of a company** der Versuch, einer Firma ein neues Image zu geben

rebroadcast [ˌriːˈbrɔːdkɑːst] **N** Wiederholung(ssendung) *f* **VT** wiederholen, noch einmal senden

rebuff [rɪˈbʌf] **N** Abfuhr *f*, kurze Zurückweisung; **to suffer a ~** zurück- *or* abgewiesen werden, eine Abfuhr bekommen; (*from opposite sex*) einen Korb bekommen (*inf*) **VT** zurückweisen *or* abweisen, einen Korb geben (+*dat*) (*inf*)

rebuild [ˌriːˈbɪld] VT **a** (= *restore*) *house, wall* wieder aufbauen; (*fig*) *society, relationship* wieder herstellen; *country* wieder aufbauen; **to ~ one's life** sein Leben wieder aufbauen; **doctors worked to ~ his face** die Ärzte versuchten, sein Gesicht wiederherzustellen **b** (= *convert*) *house* umbauen; *society* umorganisieren

rebuilding [ˌriːˈbɪldɪŋ] N (= *restoration*: *of house, wall*) Wiederaufbau *m*; (*fig*: *of society, relationship*) Wiederherstellung *f*

rebuke [rɪˈbjuːk] **N** Verweis *m*, Tadel *m* **VT** zurechtweisen (*for* wegen), tadeln (*for* für); **to ~ sb for having spoken unkindly** jdn dafür tadeln, dass er so unfreundlich gesprochen hat

rebukingly [rɪˈbjuːkɪŋlɪ] ADV tadelnd

rebus ['riːbəs] N Bilderrätsel *nt*, Rebus *m or nt*

rebut [rɪˈbʌt] VT *argument, contention* widerlegen; *charges, allegations* entkräften

rebuttal [rɪˈbʌtl] N (*of argument, contention*) Widerlegung *f*; (*of charges, allegations*) Entkräftung *f*

rec *abbr of* **recommended** empf.

recalcitrance [rɪˈkælsɪtrəns] N Aufsässigkeit *f*

recalcitrant [rɪˈkælsɪtrənt] ADJ aufsässig

recall [rɪˈkɔːl] **VT** **a** (= *summon back*) zurückrufen; *ambassador* abberufen; *library book* zurückfordern; (*Fin*) *capital* zurückfordern, einziehen; **Ferguson was ~ed to the Scotland squad** Ferguson wurde in die schottische Mannschaft zurückberufen; **this music ~s the past** diese Musik ruft die Vergangenheit zurück; **to ~ sb to life** jdn ins Leben zurückrufen; **her voice ~ed him to the present** ihre Stimme brachte ihn in die Wirklichkeit zurück **b** (= *remember*) sich erinnern an (+*acc*), sich entsinnen (+*gen*); **I cannot ~ meeting him** *or* **having met him** ich kann mich nicht daran erinnern, dass ich ihn kennen gelernt habe; **as I ~ ...** soweit ich mich erinnere ... **c** (*Comput*) *file* wieder aufrufen **N** **a** (= *summoning back*) Rückruf *m*; (*of ambassador*) Abberufung *f*; (*of library book*) Rückforderung *f*, Einmahnung *f*; (*Fin*, *of capital*) Einzug *m*; **to sound the ~** (*Mil*) zum Rückzug blasen; **this book is on ~** das Buch wird zurückgefordert; **~ slip** Aufforderung *f* zur Rückgabe eines/des Buches; **beyond ~** für immer vorbei; **lost/gone beyond ~** für immer verloren/gegangen sein **b** (= *remembrance*) **powers of ~** Erinnerungsvermögen *nt*

recant [rɪˈkænt] **VT** *religious belief* widerrufen; *statement also* zurücknehmen **VI** widerrufen

recantation [ˌriːkænˈteɪʃən] N (*of religious belief*) Widerruf *m*; (*of statement also*) Zurücknahme *f*

recap¹ ['riːkæp] (*inf*) **N** kurze Zusammenfassung; **can we have a quick ~?** können wir kurz rekapitulieren *or* zusammenfassen? **VTI** rekapitulieren, kurz zusammenfassen

recap² [ˌriːˈkæp] (*US Aut*) **N** runderneuerter Reifen **VT** runderneuern

recapitulate [ˌriːkəˈpɪtjʊleɪt] **VT** rekapitulieren, kurz zusammenfassen; (*Mus*) *theme* wieder aufnehmen **VI** rekapitulieren, kurz zusammenfassen; (*Mus*) eine Reprise bringen

recapitulation ['riːkəˌpɪtjʊˈleɪʃən] N Rekapitulation *f*, kurze Zusammenfassung; (*Mus*) Reprise *f*

recapture [ˌriːˈkæptʃə] **VT** *animal* wieder einfangen; *prisoner* wieder ergreifen; *town, territory* wiedererobern; (*esp Sport*) *title etc* wiedergewinnen, wiedererlangen; (*fig*) *atmosphere, emotion, period* wieder wach werden lassen; **they ~d the spark that had originally united them** sie entzündeten den Funken, der einst da war, noch einmal; **to ~ the initiative** die Initiative wieder ergreifen **N** (*of animal*) Wiedereinfangen *nt*; (*of prisoner*) Wiederergreifung *f*; (*of town, territory*) Wiedereroberung *f*; (*esp Sport: of title etc*) Wiedererlangung *f*

recast [ˌriːˈkɑːst] **VT a** (*Metal*) neu gießen, umgießen **b** *play, film* eine neue Besetzung wählen für; *parts, roles* umbesetzen, neu besetzen **c** (= *rewrite*) umformen **N** (*Metal*) Neuguss *m*, Umguss *m*

recce [ˈrekɪ] **N, VI** (*dated Brit Mil sl*) *abbr of* **reconnaissance** *of* **reconnoitre**

recd *abbr of* **received** erh.

recede [rɪˈsiːd] **VI a** (*tide*) zurückgehen; (*fig*) sich entfernen; (*hope*) schwinden; **to ~ into the distance** in der Ferne verschwinden; **all hope is receding** jegliche Hoffnung schwindet **b** **if untreated, the gums ~** ohne Behandlung bildet sich das Zahnfleisch zurück; **his forehead ~s a bit** er hat eine leicht fliehende Stirn; **his hair is receding** er hat eine leichte Stirnglatze → *also* **receding c** (*price*) zurückgehen **d** **to ~ from** (*opinion, view etc*) abgehen von, aufgeben

receding [rɪˈsiːdɪŋ] **ADJ** *chin, forehead* fliehend; *hairline* zurückweichend; *hair* zurückweichend, dünn; **~ gums** Zahnfleischschwund *m*

receipt [rɪˈsiːt] ○ 20.5 **N a** *no pl* Empfang *m*; (*Comm*) Empfang *m*, Erhalt *m*, Eingang *m*; **on ~ of your remittance/the goods, we shall be pleased to ...** nach Empfang *etc* Ihrer Zahlung/der Waren werden wir gerne ...; **to pay on ~ (of the goods)** bei Empfang *etc* (der Waren) bezahlen; **I am in ~ of** (*on letter*) ich bin im Besitz (+*gen*); **~ stamp** Empfangsstempel *m* **b** (*Brit*: = *paper*) Quittung *f*, Beleg *m*; (= *receipt of posting*) Einlieferungsschein *m* **c** (*Comm, Fin*: = *money taken*) **~s** Einnahmen *pl*, Einkünfte *pl* **VT** *bill* quittieren

receipt book **N** Quittungsbuch *nt*

receiptor [rɪˈsiːtə] **N** (*esp US*) Empfänger(in) *m(f)*

receivable [rɪˈsiːvəbl] **ADJ** (*Jur*) zulässig; **accounts ~** (*Comm*) Außenstände *pl*; **bills ~** (*Comm*) Wechselforderungen *pl*

receive [rɪˈsiːv] **VT a** (= *get*) bekommen, erhalten; *punch* (ab)bekommen; *refusal, setback* erfahren; *impression* gewinnen, bekommen; *recognition* finden; (*esp Brit Jur*) *stolen goods* Hehlerei *f* (be)treiben mit; (*Tennis*) *ball, service* zurückschlagen; *sacrament* empfangen; **to ~ nothing but praise** nichts als Belobigungen hören; **he ~d nothing worse than a few bruises** er bekam nur ein paar blaue Flecke ab; **"received with thanks"** (*Comm*) „dankend erhalten"; **~d opinion** die allgemeine Meinung **b** *offer, proposal, news, new play etc, person* (*into group, the Church*) aufnehmen; **to ~ a warm welcome** herzlich empfangen werden; **given the welcome we ~d ...** so, wie wir empfangen worden sind, ...; **to ~ sb into one's family** jdn in seine Familie aufnehmen; **the play was well ~d** das Stück wurde gut aufgenommen **c** (*Telec, Rad, TV*) empfangen; **are you receiving me?** hören Sie mich? **VI a** (*form*) (*Besuch*) empfangen; **Mrs X ~s on Mondays** Frau X empfängt am Montagen **b** (*Jur*) Hehlerei *f* treiben **c** (*Tennis*) rückschlagen; **Borg to ~** Rückschläger Borg **d** (*Telec*) empfangen

received pronunciation [rɪˈsiːvdprəˌnʌnsɪˈeɪʃən] **N** hochsprachliche Aussprache

receiver [rɪˈsiːvə] ○ 27.3 **N a** (*of letter, goods*) Empfänger(in) *m(f)*; (*esp Brit Jur*: *of stolen property*) Hehler(in) *m(f)* **b** (*Fin, Jur*) **official ~** Konkursverwalter(in) *m(f)*; **to call in the ~** Konkurs anmelden **c** (*Telec*) Hörer *m*; **~ rest** Gabel *f* **d** (*Rad*) Empfänger *m* **e** (*Tennis*) Rückschläger(in) *m(f)*

receivership [rɪˈsiːvəʃɪp] **N to go into ~** in Konkurs gehen

receiving [rɪˈsiːvɪŋ] **N** (*esp Brit Jur*: *of stolen property*) Hehlerei *f*

receiving: receiving end **N** (*inf*) **to be on the ~ (of it)/of sth** derjenige sein, der es/etw abkriegt (*inf*); **receiving line** **N** (*US*) Empfangskomitee *nt*; **receiving set** **N** Empfangsgerät *nt*

recency [ˈriːsənsɪ] **N** Neuheit *f*

recension [rɪˈsenʃən] **N** Rezension *f*

recent [ˈriːsənt] **ADJ** kürzlich; *event, development, closure* jüngste(r, s), neueste(r, s); *news* neueste(r, s), letzte(r, s); *acquaintance, invention, edition, addition* neu; **the ~ improvement** die vor kurzem eingetretene Verbesserung; **their ~ loss** ihr vor kurzem erlittener Verlust; **a ~ decision** eine Entscheidung, die erst vor kurzem gefallen ist; **a ~ publication** eine Neuveröffentlichung; **his most ~ book** sein neuestes Buch; **he is a ~ acquaintance of mine** ich kenne ihn erst seit kurzem; **his ~ arrival** seine Ankunft vor kurzem; **her ~ trip** ihre erst kurz zurückliegende Reise; **he is a ~ arrival** er ist erst vor kurzem angekommen, er ist erst kurz hier; **in the ~ past** in jüngerer *or* jüngster Zeit (*geh*), erst vor kurzem; **in ~ years** in den letzten Jahren; **in ~ times** in letzter *or* jüngster (*geh*) Zeit; **of ~ date** neueren Datums; **in ~ history** in der jüngsten Vergangenheit; **~ developments** jüngste Entwicklungen, Entwicklungen in jüngster Zeit

recently [ˈriːsəntlɪ] **ADV** (= *a short while ago*) vor kurzem, kürzlich; (= *the other day also*) neulich; (= *during the last few days or weeks*) in letzter Zeit; **~ he has been doing it differently** seit kurzem macht er das anders; **as ~ as** erst; **quite ~ vor kurzem, erst kürzlich; until (quite) ~** (noch) bis vor kurzem; **he lived there until as ~ as last year** er hat bis letztes Jahr noch dort gelebt

receptacle [rɪˈseptəkl] **N** Behälter *m*

reception [rɪˈsepʃən] **○** 13 **N a** *no pl* (= *receiving, welcome*: *of person*) Empfang *m*; (*into group, of play, book etc*) Aufnahme *f*; **the play met with** *or* **had a very favourable ~** das Stück fand gute Aufnahme, das Stück wurde gut aufgenommen; **what sort of ~ did you get?** wie sind Sie empfangen *or* aufgenommen worden?; **to give sb a warm/chilly ~** jdm einen herzlichen/kühlen Empfang bereiten, jdn herzlich/kühl empfangen; **~ camp** Aufnahmelager *nt* **b** (= *party, ceremony*) Empfang *m* **c** (*esp Brit*: *in hotel etc*) der Empfang; **at/to ~** am/zum Empfang **d** (*Rad, TV*) Empfang *m* **e** (*Brit Sch*: *also* **reception class**) Anfängerklasse *f*

reception: reception area **N** Empfangsbereich *m*; **reception centre**, (*US*) **reception center** **N** Durchgangslager *nt*; **reception desk** **N** Empfang *m*, Rezeption *f*

receptionist [rɪˈsepʃənɪst] **N** (*in hotel*) Empfangschef *m*, Empfangsdame *f*; (*with firm*) Herr *m*/Dame *f* am Empfang, Empfangssekretärin *f*; (*at airport*) Bodenhostess *f*; (*at doctor's, dentist's etc*) Sprechstundenhilfe *f*

reception room **N** (*Brit*) Wohnzimmer *nt*; (*in hotel*) Aufenthaltsraum *m*

receptive [rɪˈseptɪv] **ADJ** *person, mind, market* aufnahmefähig; *audience* empfänglich; **~ to** empfänglich für; **to fall on ~ ears** auf offene Ohren treffen

receptiveness [rɪˈseptɪvnɪs], **receptivity** [ˌriːsepˈtɪvɪtɪ] **N** (*of person, mind, market*) Aufnahmefähigkeit *f*; (*of audience*) Empfänglichkeit *f*; **~ to** Empfänglichkeit *f* für

receptor [rɪˈseptə] **N a** (= *nerve*) Reizempfänger *m*, Rezeptor *m* **b** (*Rad*) Empfänger *m*

recess [rɪˈses] **N a** (= *cessation*) (*of Parliament*) (Sitzungs)pause *f*; (*of law courts*) Ferien *pl*; (*US Sch*) Pause *f* **b** (= *alcove*) Nische *f* **c** (= *secret place*) Winkel *m*; **in the (deepest) ~es of his mind** in den (tiefsten) Tiefen seines Geistes **VT** (= *set back*) in eine/die Nische stellen; *cupboard, cooker* einbauen; *windows* vertiefen; *lighting* versenken; (= *make a recess in*) *wall etc* eine Nische machen in (+*acc*), vertiefen

recession [rɪˈseʃən] **N a** *no pl* (*receding*) Zurückweichen *n*, Rückgang *m*; (*Eccl*) Auszug *m* **b** (*Econ*) Rezession *f*, (wirtschaftlicher) Rückgang

recessional [rɪˈseʃənl] (*Eccl*) **N** Schlusshymne *f* (*die während des Auszugs gesungen wird*) **ADJ** **~ hymn** Schlusshymne *f*

recessive [rɪˈsesɪv] **ADJ** zurückweichend; (*Econ, Biol*) rezessiv

recharge [ˌriːˈtʃɑːdʒ] **VT** *battery* aufladen; *gun* neu *or* wieder laden, nachladen; **to ~ one's batteries** (*fig*) auftanken **VI** sich wieder aufladen; **it ~s automatically** es lädt sich automatisch (wieder) auf

rechargeable [ˌriːˈtʃɑːdʒəbl] **ADJ** *battery* wieder aufladbar

recheck [ˌriːˈtʃek] **VT** nochmals prüfen *or* kontrollieren

recherché [rəˈʃeəʃeɪ] **ADJ** gewählt; *book, subject* ausgefallen; *expression* gesucht

rechristen [ˌriːˈkrɪsn] **VT** umtaufen; **it was ~ed Leningrad** es wurde in Leningrad umbenannt *or* umgetauft

recidivism [rɪˈsɪdɪvɪzəm] **N** Rückfälligkeit *f*

recidivist [rɪˈsɪdɪvɪst] **N** Rückfällige(r) *mf* **ADJ** rückfällig

recipe [ˈresɪpɪ] **N** Rezept *nt*; (*fig also*) Geheimnis *nt*; **that's a ~ for disaster** das führt mit Sicherheit in die Katastrophe; **a ~ for success** ein Erfolgsrezept *nt*

recipient [rɪˈsɪpɪənt] **N** Empfänger(in) *m(f)*; **Susan, as the ~ of his attentions** Susan, der seine Aufmerksamkeiten galten

reciprocal [rɪˈsɪprəkl] **ADJ** (= *mutual*) gegenseitig; *agreement* gegenseitig, wechselseitig, wechselwirksam; *measures* gegenseitig, im Gegenzug *pred*; *visit* gegenseitig, wechselseitig, untereinander *pred*; (= *done in return*) als Gegenleistung; (*Gram, Math*) reziprok; **the ~ relationship between these two phenomena** die Wechselbeziehung zwischen diesen zwei Phänomenen; **~ trade** Handel *m* untereinander **N** (*Math*) reziproker Wert, Reziproke *nt*

reciprocally [rɪˈsɪprəklɪ] **ADV** *admire, help* gegenseitig; *trade, correspond* untereinander, miteinander; (*Gram*) reziprok

reciprocate [rɪˈsɪprəkeɪt] **VT a** *smiles, wishes* erwidern; *help, kindness* erwidern, sich revanchieren für **b** (*Tech*) hin- und herbewegen; *piston* auf- und abbewegen **VI a** (= *reply*) sich revanchieren; **she ~d by throwing the saucepan at him** sie wiederum warf ihm den Topf nach **b** (*Tech*) hin- und hergehen; (*piston*) auf- und abgehen

reciprocating engine [rɪˈsɪprəkeɪtɪŋˈendʒɪn] **N** Kolbenmotor *m*

reciprocation [rɪˌsɪprəˈkeɪʃən] **N a** (*of help, kindness*) Erwiderung *f* (*of* +*gen*), Revanche *f* (*of* für) **b** (*Tech*) Hin und Her *nt*; (*of pistons*) Auf und Ab *nt*

reciprocity [ˌresɪˈprɒsɪtɪ] **N** (*of feelings, kindness etc*) Gegenseitigkeit *f*; (*of favours*) Austausch *m*; (*Pol*) Gegenseitigkeit *f*, Reziprozität *f* (*form*)

recital [rɪˈsaɪtl] **N a** (*of music, poetry*) Vortrag *m*, (= *piano recital etc*) Konzert *nt*; **song ~** Matinee *f*, Liederabend *m* **b** (= *account*) Schilderung *f*; (*of details*) Aufführung *f*, Aufzählung *f*

recitation [ˌresɪˈteɪʃən] **N** Vortrag *m*; **to give a ~ of sth** etw vortragen

recitative [ˌresɪtəˈtiːv] **N** Rezitativ *nt*

recite [rɪˈsaɪt] **VT a** *poetry* vortragen, rezitieren **b** *facts* hersagen; *details* aufzählen **VI** vortragen, rezitieren

reckless [ˈrekləs] **ADJ** *person, behaviour* leichtsinnig; *driver, driving* rücksichtslos; *speed* gefährlich; *attempt* gewagt; *disregard* leichtsinnig; **~ of the danger** (*liter*) ungeachtet der Gefahr (*liter*); **with ~ abandon** im selbstvergessenen Leichtsinn, mit risikofroher Hingabe

recklessly [ˈrekləslɪ] **ADV** *behave, disregard* leichtsinnig; *drive* rücksichtslos; *attempt* gewagt

recklessness ['reklɪsnɪs] N (of person) Leichtsinn m; (of behaviour) Leichtsinnigkeit f; (of driver, driving) Rücksichtslosigkeit f; (of attempt) Gewagtheit f

reckon ['rekən] **VT a** (= calculate) time, numbers, points, costs, area ausrechnen, berechnen; **he ~ed the cost to be £40.51** er berechnete die Kosten auf £ 40,51
b (= judge) rechnen, zählen (among zu); **she is ~ed (to be) a beautiful woman** sie gilt als schöne Frau
c (= think, suppose) glauben; (= estimate) schätzen; **what do you ~?** was meinen Sie?; **I ~ we can start** ich glaube, wir können anfangen; **I ~ he must be about forty** ich schätze, er müsste so um die vierzig sein; **he ~s himself to be one of the best ...** er hält sich für einen der besten ...
d (sl) (= like) gut finden (inf); (= think likely to succeed) große Chancen geben (+dat)
VI (= calculate) rechnen; **~ing from tomorrow** ab morgen gerechnet

▶ **reckon in** VT SEP einbeziehen, berücksichtigen

▶ **reckon on** VI +prep obj rechnen or zählen auf (+acc); **you can reckon on 30** Sie können mit 30 rechnen; **I was reckoning on doing that tomorrow** ich wollte das morgen machen; **I wasn't reckoning on having to do that** ich habe nicht damit gerechnet, dass ich das tun muss

▶ **reckon up** **VT** sep zusammenrechnen **VI** abrechnen (with mit)

▶ **reckon with** VI +prep obj rechnen mit; **if you insult him you'll have the whole family to reckon with** wenn Sie ihn beleidigen, müssen Sie mit der ganzen Familie rechnen; **he's a person to be reckoned with** er ist jemand, mit dem man rechnen muss

▶ **reckon without** VI +prep obj nicht rechnen mit; **he reckoned without the fact that ...** er hatte nicht damit gerechnet, dass ...; **you must reckon without my being there to help you** du musst damit rechnen, dass ich nicht da bin(, um dir zu helfen)

reckoner ['rekənə'] N = **ready reckoner**

reckoning ['rekənɪŋ] N **a** (= calculation) (Be)Rechnung f; (old: = bill, account) Rechnung f; **to be out in one's ~** sich ziemlich verrechnet haben; **the day of ~** der Tag der Abrechnung; **in your ~** Ihrer Meinung or Schätzung nach **b** (Naut) = **dead reckoning**

reclaim [rɪ'kleɪm] **VT a** land gewinnen; (by irrigation etc) kultivieren; **to ~ land from the sea** dem Meer Land abringen **b** (liter) person abbringen (from von) **c** (from waste) wiedergewinnen, regenerieren (from aus) **d** (= demand or ask back) rights, privileges, tax zurückverlangen; lost item, baggage abholen; **a campaign to ~ the streets** eine Kampagne für sichere Straßen **N a** past or beyond ~ rettungslos or für immer verloren **b** baggage or luggage ~ Gepäckausgabe f

reclaimable [rɪ'kleɪməbl] ADJ land nutzbar; by-products regenerierbar; money, tax rückverlangbar

reclamation [ˌreklə'meɪʃən] N **a** (of land) Gewinnung f; (by irrigation etc) Kultivierung f **b** (= recovery: of rights, privileges) Rückgewinnung f

recline [rɪ'klaɪn] **VT** arm zurücklegen (on auf +acc); head also zurücklehnen (on an +acc); seat zurückstellen **VI** (person) zurückliegen; (seat) sich verstellen lassen; **she was reclining on the sofa** sie ruhte auf dem Sofa; **reclining in his bath** im Bade liegend; **reclining figure** (Art) Liegende(r) mf

recliner [rɪ'klaɪnə'] N Ruhesessel m

reclining chair [rɪ'klaɪnɪŋ'tʃeə'] N Ruhesessel m

reclining seat [rɪ'klaɪnɪŋ'siːt] N verstellbarer Sitz; (in car, on boat) Liegesitz m

recluse [rɪ'kluːs] N Einsiedler(in) m(f)

recognition [ˌrekəg'nɪʃən] N **a** (= acknowledgement, also Pol) Anerkennung f; **in ~ of** in Anerkennung (+gen); **his ~ of these facts** dass er

diese Tatsachen akzeptierte; **to gain/receive ~** Anerkennung finden **b** (= identification) Erkennen nt; **the baby's ~ of its mother/mother's voice** dass das Baby seine Mutter/die Stimme seiner Mutter erkennt; **he/it has changed beyond or out of all ~** er/es ist nicht wieder zu erkennen

recognizable ['rekəgnaɪzəbl] ADJ erkennbar; **you're scarcely ~ with that beard** Sie sind mit dem Bart kaum zu erkennen; **Poland is no longer ~ as the country I knew in 1940** Polen ist nicht mehr das Land, das ich 1940 kannte

recognizably ['rekəgnaɪzəblɪ] ADV (= perceptibly) offensichtlich, erkennbar

recognizance [rɪ'kɒgnɪzəns] N (Jur) Verpflichtung f; (for debt) Anerkenntnis f; (= sum of money) Sicherheitsleistung f; **to be released on one's own ~** auf eigene Gefahr entlassen werden

recognizant [rɪ'kɒgnɪzənt] ADJ (form) **to be ~ of sth** etw anerkennen

recognize ['rekəgnaɪz] VT **a** (= know again) person, town, face, voice etc wieder erkennen; (= identify) erkennen (by an +dat); **you wouldn't ~ him/the house** etc Sie würden ihn/das Haus etc nicht wieder erkennen; **do you ~ this tune?** erkennen Sie die Melodie?; **I wouldn't have ~d him in that disguise** ich hätte ihn in der Verkleidung nicht erkannt
b (= acknowledge, also Pol) anerkennen (as, to be als); **she doesn't ~ me any more when she goes past** sie kennt mich nicht mehr, wenn sie mich trifft; **he doesn't even ~ my existence** er nimmt mich nicht einmal zur Kenntnis
c (= be aware) erkennen; (= be prepared to admit) zugeben, eingestehen; **you must ~ what is necessary** Sie müssen erkennen, was notwendig ist; **I ~ that I am not particularly intelligent** ich gebe zu, dass ich nicht besonders intelligent bin
d (US: = let speak) das Wort erteilen (+dat, an +acc)

recognized ['rekəgnaɪzd] ADJ anerkannt

recognizedly ['rekəgnaɪzɪdlɪ] ADV anerkanntermaßen

recoil [rɪ'kɔɪl] **VI a** (person) (from vor +dat) zurückweichen; (in fear) zurückschrecken; (in disgust) zurückschaudern; **he ~ed from (the idea of) doing it** ihm graute davor, das zu tun **b** (gun) zurückstoßen; (spring) zurückschnellen; **the gun will ~** das Gewehr hat einen Rückstoß **c** (fig: actions) **to ~ on sb** auf jdn zurückfallen, sich an jdm rächen **N** [rɪ'kɔɪl] (of gun) Rückstoß m; (of spring) Zurückschnellen nt no pl

recollect [ˌrekə'lekt] **VT** sich erinnern an (+acc), sich entsinnen (+gen) **VI** sich erinnern, sich entsinnen; **as far as I can ~** soweit ich mich erinnern kann

recollection [ˌrekə'lekʃən] N (= memory) Erinnerung f (of an +acc); **to the best of my ~** soweit ich mich erinnern kann; **his ~ of it is vague** er erinnert sich nur vage daran; **I have some/no ~ of it** ich kann mich schwach/nicht daran erinnern

recommence [ˌriːkə'mens] VTI wieder beginnen

recommend [ˌrekə'mend] ○ 2.1, 19.4 VT **a** (= advise, speak well of) empfehlen (as als); **what do you ~ for a cough?** was empfehlen or raten Sie gegen Husten?; **to ~ sb/sth to sb** jdm jdn/etw empfehlen; **to ~ doing sth** empfehlen, etw zu tun; **it is not to be ~ed** es ist nicht zu empfehlen; **to come highly ~ed** wärmstens empfohlen sein; **~ed speed** Richtgeschwindigkeit f; **~ed reading** empfohlene Lektüre; **~ed daily allowance** or **amount** empfohlene Tagesdosis or Tagesmenge **b** (= make acceptable) sprechen für; **she has much/little to ~ her** es spricht sehr viel/wenig für sie; **his manners do little to ~ him** seine Manieren sind nicht gerade eine Empfehlung für ihn; **this book has little/a great deal to ~ it** das Buch ist nicht gerade empfehlenswert/sehr empfehlenswert

c (old, liter. = entrust) child, one's soul empfehlen (to jdm)

recommendable [ˌrekə'mendəbl] ADJ empfehlenswert; course of action, measures also ratsam; **it is not a ~ wine** dieser Wein ist nicht zu empfehlen

recommendation [ˌrekəmen'deɪʃən] N Empfehlung f; **on the ~ of** auf Empfehlung von; **to make a ~** jemanden/etwas empfehlen; **letter of ~** Empfehlung f, Empfehlungsschreiben nt

recommendatory [ˌrekə'mendətərɪ] ADJ empfehlend

recommended price [ˌrekə'mendɪd'praɪs] N unverbindlicher Richtpreis

recompense ['rekəmpens] **N a** (= reward) Belohnung f; **as a ~** als or zur Belohnung; **in ~ for** als Belohnung für **b** (Jur, fig) Entschädigung f; (of loss) Wiedergutmachung f **VT a** (= reward) belohnen **b** (Jur, fig: = repay) person entschädigen; damage, loss wieder gutmachen

recompose [ˌriːkəm'pəʊz] VT **a** (= rewrite) umschreiben **b** (= calm) **to ~ oneself** sich wieder beruhigen

reconcilable ['rekənsaɪləbl] ADJ people versöhnbar; ideas, opinions miteinander vereinbar

reconcile ['rekənsaɪl] VT **a** people versöhnen, aussöhnen; differences beilegen; dispute schlichten; **they became** or **were ~d** sie versöhnten sich, sie söhnten sich aus
b (= make compatible) facts, ideas, theories, principles miteinander in Einklang bringen, miteinander vereinbaren; **to ~ sth with sth** etw mit etw in Einklang bringen, etw mit etw vereinbaren; **these ideas cannot be ~d with the plans** diese Ideen sind mit den Plänen unvereinbar; **how do you ~ that with the fact that you said no last week?** wie lässt sich das damit vereinbaren, dass Sie letzte Woche nein or Nein gesagt haben?
c (= make accept) **to ~ sb to sth** jdn mit etw versöhnen; **to ~ oneself to sth, to become ~d to sth** sich mit etw abfinden; **what ~d him to it was ...** was ihn damit versöhnte, war ...

reconciliation ['rekənsɪlɪ'eɪʃən] N (of persons) Versöhnung f, Aussöhnung f; (of opinions, principles) Vereinbarung f, Versöhnung f (esp Philos); (of differences) Beilegung f

reconciliatory [ˌrekən'sɪlɪətərɪ] ADJ versöhnlich, Versöhnungs-

recondite [rɪ'kɒndaɪt] ADJ abstrus

recondition [ˌriːkən'dɪʃən] VT generalüberholen; **a ~ed engine** ein Austauschmotor m

reconnaissance [rɪ'kɒnɪsəns] N (Aviat, Mil) Aufklärung f; **~ mission** Aufklärungseinsatz m; **to be on ~** bei einem Aufklärungseinsatz sein

reconnaissance: reconnaissance flight N Aufklärungsflug m; **reconnaissance patrol** N Spähtrupp m; **reconnaissance plane** N Aufklärer m, Aufklärungsflugzeug nt

reconnoitre, (US) **reconnoiter** [ˌrekə'nɔɪtə'] **VT** (Aviat, Mil) region auskundschaften, erkunden, aufklären **VI** das Gelände erkunden or aufklären

reconquer [ˌriː'kɒŋkə'] VT town, territory zurückerobern; enemy erneut or wieder besiegen

reconquest [ˌriː'kɒŋkwest] N (of town, territory) Zurückeroberung f; (of enemy) erneuter Sieg (of über +acc)

reconsider [ˌriːkən'sɪdə'] **VT** decision, judgement noch einmal überdenken; (= change) revidieren; facts neu erwägen; (Jur) case wieder aufnehmen; **to ~ one's position** seine Position überdenken; **won't you ~ your decision and come?** wollen Sie es sich (dat) nicht überlegen und doch kommen?; **I have ~ed my decision, I'd rather not accept** ich habe es mir noch einmal überlegt, ich lehne lieber ab **VI** ask him to ~ sagen Sie ihm, er soll es sich (dat) noch einmal überlegen; **there's still time to ~** es ist noch nicht zu spät, seine Meinung zu ändern or es sich anders zu überlegen

reconsideration ['riːkənsɪdə'reɪʃən] N (of decision, judgement) Überdenken nt; (of facts) erneute Erwägung; (*Jur, of case*) Wiederaufnahme *f*; **after ~, he decided ...** nach einiger Überlegung entschied er ...

reconstitute [ˌriːˈkɒnstɪtjuːt] VT **a** *assembly, committee* neu einrichten, rekonstituieren (*form*); (= *reconstruct*) wieder herstellen **b** *food* aus einem Konzentrat zubereiten; *solution in Wasser* auflösen

reconstitution [ˈriːkɒnstɪˈtjuːʃən] N **a** (*of assembly, committee*) Rekonstitution *f* (*form*) **b** (*of food*) Zubereitung *f* aus einem Konzentrat; (*of solution*) Auflösen *nt* in Wasser

reconstruct [ˌriːkənˈstrʌkt] VT rekonstruieren; *cities, building* wieder aufbauen; **to ~ one's life** (im Leben) noch einmal von vorn anfangen

reconstruction [ˌriːkənˈstrʌkʃən] N Rekonstruktion *f*; (*of city, building*) Wiederaufbau *m*

reconstructive [ˌriːkənˈstrʌktɪv] ADJ (*Med*) wiederherstellend; **~ surgery** Wiederherstellungschirurgie *f*

reconvene [ˌriːkənˈviːn] (*form*) VI (*parliament etc*) wieder zusammenkommen *or* -treten VT *committee, council etc* wieder einberufen

record [rɪˈkɔːd] VT **a** *facts, story, events* (*diarist, person*) aufzeichnen; (*documents, diary etc*) dokumentieren; (*in register*) eintragen; (= *keep minutes of*) protokollieren; *one's thoughts, feelings etc* festhalten, niederschreiben; *protest, disapproval* zum Ausdruck bringen; **these facts are not ~ed anywhere** diese Tatsachen sind nirgends festgehalten; **it's not ~ed anywhere** das ist nirgends dokumentiert *or* belegt; **to ~ sth photographically** etw im Bild festhalten; **to ~ one's vote** seine Stimme abgeben; **to ~ a verdict of accidental death** auf Tod durch Unfall befinden; **history ~s that ...** es ist geschichtlich dokumentiert, dass ...; **the author ~s that ...** der Verfasser berichtet, dass ...

b (*thermometer, meter etc*) verzeichnen, registrieren; (*needle*) aufzeichnen, registrieren; (*pen needle*) aufzeichnen

c (*on tape, cassette etc*) aufnehmen, aufzeichnen; (*person*) aufnehmen

VI (Tonband)aufnahmen machen; **he is ~ing at 5 o'clock** er hat um 5 Uhr eine Aufnahme; **his voice does not ~ well** seine Stimme lässt sich nicht gut aufnehmen; **the tape ~er won't ~** das Tonbandgerät nimmt nicht auf

N [ˈrekɔːd] **a** (= *account*) Aufzeichnung *f*; (*of attendance*) Liste *f*; (*of meeting*) Protokoll *nt*; (= *official document*) Unterlage *f*, Akte *f*; (*lit, fig: of the past, of civilization*) Dokument *nt*; (**public**) **~s** im Staatsarchiv gelagerte Urkunden; **a photographic ~** eine Bilddokumentation; **it's nice to have a photographic ~ of one's holidays** es ist nett, den Urlaub im Bild festgehalten zu haben; **to keep a ~ of sth** über etw (*acc*) Buch führen; (*official, registrar*) etw registrieren; (*historian, chronicler*) etw aufzeichnen; **to keep a personal ~ of sth** sich (*dat*) etw notieren; **it is on ~ that ...** es gibt Belege dafür, dass ...; (*in files*) es ist aktenkundig, dass ...; **there is no similar example on ~** es ist kein ähnliches Beispiel bekannt; **I'm prepared to go on ~ as saying that ...** ich stehe zu der Behauptung, dass ...; **he's on ~ as having said ...** es ist belegt, dass er gesagt hat, ...; **last night the PM went on ~ as saying ...** gestern Abend hat sich der Premier dahin gehend geäußert, dass ...; **to put sth on ~** etw schriftlich festhalten; **there is no ~ of his having said it** es ist nirgends belegt, dass er es gesagt hat; **to put** *or* **set the ~ straight** für klare Verhältnisse sorgen; **just to set the ~ straight** nur damit Klarheit herrscht; **for the ~** der Ordnung halber; (= *for the minutes*) zur Mitschrift; **this is strictly off the ~** dies ist nur inoffiziell; **(strictly) off the ~ he did come** ganz im Vertrauen: er ist doch gekommen

b (= *police record*) Vorstrafen *pl*; **~s** (= *files*) Strafregister *nt*; **he's got a ~** er ist vorbestraft; **~ of previous convictions** Vorstrafen *pl*; **he's got a clean ~, he hasn't got a ~** er ist nicht vorbestraft

c (= *history*) Vorgeschichte *f*; (= *achievements*) Leistungen *pl*; **to have an excellent ~** ausge-

zeichnete Leistungen vorweisen können; **the team with the best ~** die Mannschaft mit den besten Leistungen; **with a ~ like yours you should be able to handle this job** mit Ihren Voraussetzungen müssten Sie sich in dieser Stelle leicht zurechtfinden; **he has a good ~ of service** er ist ein verdienter Mitarbeiter; **service ~** (*Mil*) militärisches Führungszeugnis; **his attendance ~ is bad** er fehlt oft; **his past ~** seine bisherigen Leistungen; **to have a good school ~** ein guter Schüler/eine guter Schülerin sein; **to have a good safety ~** in Bezug auf Sicherheit einen guten Ruf haben; **to have a dubious ~ as far as sth is concerned** in Bezug auf etw (*acc*) einen zweifelhaften Ruf haben; **he's got quite a ~** (= *has done bad things*) er hat so einiges auf dem Kerbholz; **he left a splendid ~ of achievements behind him** er hat sehr viel geleistet; **to spoil one's ~** es sich (*dat*) verderben, sich (*dat*) ein Minus einhandeln (*inf*); **I've been looking at your ~, Jones** ich habe mir Ihre Akte angesehen, Jones

d (*Mus*) (Schall)platte *f*; (= *recording*) (*of voice, music etc*) Aufnahme *f*; (*of programme, speech*) Aufzeichnung *f*, Aufnahme *f*; **to make** *or* **cut a ~** eine Schallplatte machen

e (*Sport, fig*) Rekord *m*; **to beat** *or* **break the ~** den Rekord brechen; **to hold the ~** den Rekord halten *or* innehaben; **long-jump ~** Weitsprungrekord, Rekord im Weitsprung; **~ amount** Rekordbetrag *m*; **~ time** Rekordzeit *f*; **~ result** Rekordergebnis *nt*

f (*on seismograph etc*) Aufzeichnung *f*, Registrierung *f*

g (*Comput, in database*) Datensatz *m*

recordable [rɪˈkɔːdəbl] ADJ *music etc* für eine Aufnahme geeignet; *CD, cassette etc* bespielbar

record [ˈrekɔːd]: **record album** N Plattenalbum *nt*; **record breaker** N (*Sport*) Rekordbrecher(in) *m(f)*; **record-breaking** ADJ (*Sport, fig*) rekordbrechend, Rekord-; **a ~ achievement** eine Rekordleistung; **record cabinet** N Plattenschrank *m*; **record card** N Karteikarte *f*; **record changer** N Plattenwechsler *m*; **record company** N Plattenfirma *f*; **record dealer** N Schallplattenhändler(in) *m(f)*; **record deck** N Plattenspieler *m*

recorded [rɪˈkɔːdɪd] ADJ **a** *music, programme* aufgezeichnet; **~ programme** (*Brit*) *or* **program** (*US*) eine Aufzeichnung; **~ message** Ansage *f*, Bandansage *f* **b** *fact, occurrence* schriftlich belegt; *crime* angezeigt, gemeldet; **in all ~ history** seit unserer Geschichtsschreibung

recorded delivery N (*Brit*) eingeschriebene Sendung, Einschreiben *nt*; **by ~ post** (*Brit*) per Einschreiben

recorder [rɪˈkɔːdəʳ] N **a** (= *apparatus*) Registriergerät *nt*; **cassette ~** N Kassettenrekorder *m*; **tape ~** Tonbandgerät *nt* **b** (*Mus*) Blockflöte *f* **c** (*of official facts*) Berichterstatter(in) *m(f)*; (= *historian*) Chronist(in) *m(f)* **d** (*Brit Jur*) nebenher als Richter tätiger Rechtsanwalt

record holder N (*Sport*) Rekordhalter(in) *m(f)*, Rekordinhaber(in) *m(f)*

recording [rɪˈkɔːdɪŋ] N (*of sound*) Aufnahme *f*; (*of programme*) Aufzeichnung *f*

recording: **Recording Angel** N Engel, der gute und böse Taten aufschreibt; **recording artist** N Musiker(in) *m(f)*, der/die Schallplattenaufnahmen macht, Plattensänger(in) *m(f)*; **recording equipment** N Aufnahmegeräte *pl*; **recording session** N Aufnahme *f*; **recording studio** N Aufnahmestudio *nt*; **recording tape** N Tonband *nt*; **recording van** N (*Rad, TV*) Aufnahmewagen *m*

record library N Plattenverleih *m*; (= *collection*) Plattensammlung *f*

record player N Plattenspieler *m*

record token N Plattengutschein *m*

recount [rɪˈkaʊnt] VT (= *relate*) erzählen, wiedergeben

re-count [ˌriːˈkaʊnt] VT nachzählen N [ˈriːˌkaʊnt] (*of votes*) Nachzählung *f*

recoup [rɪˈkuːp] VT **a** (= *make good*) *money, amount* wieder einbringen *or* hereinbekommen; *losses* wieder gutmachen, wettmachen **b** (= *reimburse*) entschädigen; **to ~ oneself** sich entschädigen **c** (*Jur*) einbehalten

recourse [rɪˈkɔːs] N Zuflucht *f*; **to have ~ to sb** sich an jdn wenden; **to have ~ to sth** Zuflucht zu etw nehmen; **without ~ to his books** ohne seine Bücher zu konsultieren; **without ~** (*Fin*) ohne Regress

recover [rɪˈkʌvəʳ] VT *sth lost* wieder finden; *one's appetite, balance also* wiedergewinnen; *sth lent* zurückbekommen; *health* wiedererlangen; *goods, property, lost territory* zurückbekommen, zurückbekommen; (*police*) *stolen/missing goods* sicherstellen; *body, space capsule, wreck* bergen; (*Ind etc*) *materials* gewinnen; *debt* eintreiben, beitreiben; (*Jur*) *damages* Ersatz erhalten für; *losses* wieder gutmachen; *expenses* decken, wieder einholen; (*Comput*) *file* retten; **to ~ one's breath/strength** wieder zu Atem/Kräften kommen; **to ~ consciousness** wieder zu Bewusstsein kommen *or* gelangen, das Bewusstsein wiedererlangen (*geh*); **to ~ one's sight** wieder sehen können; **to ~ land from the sea** dem Meer Land abringen; **to ~ lost ground** (*fig*) aufholen; **to ~ oneself** *or* **one's composure** seine Fassung wiedererlangen; **to be quite ~ed** sich ganz erholt haben

VI **a** (*after shock, accident etc, St Ex, Fin*) sich erholen; (*from illness also*) genesen (*geh*); (*from falling*) sich fangen; (*regain consciousness*) wieder zu sich kommen

b (*Jur*) (den Prozess) gewinnen

re-cover [ˌriːˈkʌvəʳ] VT *chairs, pillow, umbrella* neu beziehen *or* überziehen; *book* neu einbinden

recoverable [rɪˈkʌvərəbl] ADJ (*Fin*) *debt* eintreibbar; *losses, damages* ersetzbar; *deposit* zurückzahlbar; *goods* rückgewinnbar, eintreibbar, wiedererlangbar

recovered memory N (*Psych*: = *thing remembered*) wieder gewonnene Erinnerung

recovery [rɪˈkʌvərɪ] N **a** (*of sth lost*) Wiederfinden *nt*; (*of one's appetite also*) Wiedergewinnung *f*; (*of sth lent*) Zurückbekommen *nt*; (*of health*) Wiedererlangung *f*; (*of goods, property, lost territory*) Zurückgewinnung *f*; (*of body, space capsule, wreck*) Bergung *f*; (*Ind etc, of materials*) Gewinnung *f*; (*of debt*) Eintreibung *f*; (*Jur, of damages*) Ersatz *m* (*of* für); (*of losses*) Wiedergutmachung *f*; (*of expenses*) Deckung *f*

b (*after shock, accident etc, St Ex, Fin*) Erholung *f*; (*from illness also*) Genesung *f* (*geh*); (*of consciousness*) Wiedererlangung *f*, Zusichkommen *nt*; (*Jur: = success in lawsuit*) Prozessgewinn *m*; (*Golf*) Schlag *m* vom Rough zum Fairway; **to be on the road** *or* **way to ~** auf dem Weg der Besserung sein; **he is making a good ~** er erholt sich gut; **beyond ~** nicht mehr zu retten; **to make a ~** (= *regain strength etc*) sich erholen; **to be in ~** (*from alcoholism etc*) eine Therapie machen

recovery: **recovery position** N (*Med*) stabile Seitenlage; **to put sb in the ~** jdn in die stabile Seitenlage bringen; **recovery room** N (*in hospital*) Wachstation *f*; **recovery service** N Abschleppdienst *m*; **recovery ship** N Bergungsschiff *nt*; **recovery team** N (*Aviat, Naut*) Bergungsmannschaft *f*, Rettungsmannschaft *f*; **recovery vehicle** N Abschleppwagen *m*

recreant [ˈrekrɪənt] (*liter*) N (= *coward*) Memme *f*; (= *traitor*) Verräter(in) *m(f)* ADJ (= *cowardly*) memmenhaft; (= *traitorous*) verräterisch

recreate [ˌriːkriːˈeɪt] VT (= *reproduce*) *atmosphere* wieder schaffen; *scene* nachschaffen; *love, friendship etc* wieder beleben

recreation [ˌrekrɪˈeɪʃən] N **a** (= *leisure*) Erholung *f*, Entspannung *f*; (= *pastime*) Hobby *nt*; **for ~ I go fishing** zur Erholung gehe ich angeln; **~ centre** (*Brit*) *or* **center** (*US*) Freizeitzentrum *nt*; **~ facilities** Möglichkeiten *pl* zur Freizeitgestaltung; **~ period** Freistunde *f* **b** (*Sch*) Pause *f*

recreational [ˌrekrɪˈeɪʃənəl] ADJ Freizeit-; **~ facilities** Freizeiteinrichtungen pl

recreational: recreational drug N Partydroge f; **recreational sport** N Freizeitsport m; **recreational vehicle** N (US) Caravan m

recreation ground N Freizeitgelände nt

recreation room N Freizeitraum m

recreative [ˈrekrɪˌeɪtɪv] ADJ erholsam, entspannend

recriminate [rɪˈkrɪmɪneɪt] VI Gegenbeschuldigungen vorbringen

recrimination [rɪˌkrɪmɪˈneɪʃən] N Gegenbeschuldigung f; (Jur) Gegenklage f; **(mutual) ~s** gegenseitige Beschuldigungen pl; **there's no point in all these ~s** es hat keinen Sinn, sich gegenseitig zu beschuldigen

rec room [ˈrekrʊm] N (US inf) abbr of **recreation room**

recrudesce [ˌriːkruːˈdes] VI (form) (wound) wieder aufbrechen; (illness) wieder ausbrechen; (problems) wieder beginnen

recruit [rɪˈkruːt] N (Mil) Rekrut(in) m(f) (to +gen); (to party, club) neues Mitglied (to in +dat); (to staff) Neue(r) mf (to in +dat) VT soldier rekrutieren; member werben; staff einstellen, anstellen; **to be ~ed from** (member, staff) sich rekrutieren aus; **he ~ed me to help** er hat mich dazu herangezogen VI (Mil) Rekruten ausheben or anwerben; (organization, club) Mitglieder werben; (employer) neue Leute einstellen

recruiting [rɪˈkruːtɪŋ] N (of soldiers) Rekrutierung f; (of members) Werben nt; (of staff) Einstellung f; **~ office** (Mil) Rekrutierungsbüro nt; **~ officer** Aushebungsoffizier m, Werbeoffizier m (Hist)

recruitment [rɪˈkruːtmənt] N (of soldiers) Rekrutierung f, Aushebung f; (of members) (An)werbung f; (of staff) Einstellung f

recruitment: recruitment agency N Personalagentur f; **recruitment consultant** N Personalberater(in) m(f); **recruitment drive** N Anwerbungskampagne f

recta [ˈrektə] pl of **rectum**

rectal [ˈrektəl] ADJ rektal (spec), des Mastdarms; **~ passage** Mastdarm m

rectangle [ˈrektæŋgl] N Rechteck nt

rectangular [rekˈtæŋgjʊlə] ADJ rechteckig; coordinates rechtwinklig

rectifiable [ˈrektɪfaɪəbl] ADJ a korrigierbar; instrument richtig einstellbar; omission nachholbar b (Chem, Math) rektifizierbar

rectification [ˌrektɪfɪˈkeɪʃən] N a (= correction) Korrektur f, Verbesserung f; (of statement, situation) Richtigstellung f, Berichtigung f; (of position, anomaly, mistake) Korrektur f; (of instrument) richtige Einstellung; (of omission) Nachholen nt, Wiedergutmachung f; (of problem) Behebung f b (Elec) Gleichrichtung f c (Chem, Math) Rektifikation f

rectifier [ˈrektɪfaɪə] N (Elec) Gleichrichter m

rectify [ˈrektɪfaɪ] VT a (= correct) korrigieren, verbessern; statement, situation richtig stellen, korrigieren; position, anomaly, mistake korrigieren; instrument richtig einstellen, korrigieren; omission nachholen, wieder gutmachen; problem beheben b (Elec) gleichrichten c (Chem, Math) rektifizieren

rectilineal [ˌrektɪˈlɪnɪəl], **rectilinear** [ˌrektɪˈlɪnɪə] ADJ geradlinig; **in a ~ direction** geradlinig

rectitude [ˈrektɪtjuːd] N Rechtschaffenheit f

rector [ˈrektə] N a (Rel) Pfarrer m (der Anglikanischen Kirche) b (Scot) (Sch) Direktor(in) m(f); (Univ) Rektor(in) m(f)

rectorship [ˈrektəʃɪp] N a (Rel) Zeit f als Pfarrer b (Scot, Sch) Direktorat nt; (Univ) Rektorat nt

rectory [ˈrektərɪ] N (= house) Pfarrhaus nt

rectum [ˈrektəm] N pl **-s** or **recta** Rektum nt (spec), Mastdarm m

recumbent [rɪˈkʌmbənt] ADJ (form) ruhend attr, liegend attr; **~ figure** (Art) liegende Figur, Liegende(r) mf; **~ bicycle** Liegefahrrad nt; **to be ~** liegen

recuperate [rɪˈkuːpəreɪt] VI sich erholen; (from illness also) genesen (geh) VT losses wettmachen, wieder gutmachen

recuperation [rɪˌkuːpəˈreɪʃən] N Erholung f; (from illness also) Genesung f (geh); (of losses) Wiedergutmachung f; **after ~, I decided ...** nachdem ich mich erholt hatte, entschied ich ...; **powers of ~** Heilkräfte pl

recuperative [rɪˈkuːpərətɪv] ADJ erholsam; **~ powers** Selbstheilungskräfte pl

recur [rɪˈkɜː] VI a (= happen again) wiederkehren; (error, event) sich wiederholen, wieder passieren; (opportunity) sich wieder bieten, sich noch einmal bieten; (problem, symptoms) wiederkehren, wieder auftreten; (idea, theme) wieder auftauchen; (dream) wiederkehren b (Math) sich periodisch wiederholen → **recurring** c (= come to mind again) wieder einfallen (to sb jdm); (thought, idea) wiederkommen (to sb jdm)

recurrence [rɪˈkʌrəns] N Wiederkehr f; (of error, event) Wiederholung f; (of problem, symptoms also) erneutes Auftreten f; (of idea, theme) Wiederauftauchen nt; (of dream) Wiederkehr f; **let there be no ~ of this** das darf nie wieder vorkommen

recurrent [rɪˈkʌrənt] ADJ a idea, theme, illness, symptom(s), dream, nightmare (ständig) wiederkehrend attr; error, problem häufig (vorkommend); event(s) sich wiederholend attr; expenses regelmäßig wiederkehrend b (Anat) sich zurückziehend

recurring [rɪˈkɜːrɪŋ] ADJ attr a = **recurrent** a b (Math) **four point nine three ~** vier Komma neun Periode drei

recurring decimal N (Math) periodische Dezimalzahl

recusant [ˈrekjʊzənt] ADJ (Rel Hist) der/die sich weigert, dem anglikanischen Gottesdienst beizuwohnen; (fig liter) renitent

recyclable [ˌriːˈsaɪkləbl] ADJ wieder verwertbar, recycelbar

recyclate [ˌriːˈsaɪklɪt] N wiedergewonnener Rohstoff

recycle [ˌriːˈsaɪkl] VT waste, paper etc wieder verwerten, wieder aufbereiten; **~d paper** Recyclingpapier nt; **made from ~d paper** aus Altpapier (hergestellt)

recycling [ˌriːˈsaɪklɪŋ] N Wiederaufbereitung f, Recycling nt

recycling bin N Recyclingbehälter m

recycling plant N Wiederaufbereitungsanlage f, Recyclingwerk nt

red [red] ADJ rot; **the lights are ~** (Aut) es ist rot; **deep ~** tiefrot; **~ as a beetroot** rot wie eine Tomate; **to go ~ in the face** rot anlaufen, einen roten Kopf bekommen; **was my face ~!** da habe ich vielleicht einen roten Kopf bekommen; **she turned ~ with embarrassment** sie wurde rot vor Verlegenheit; **there'll be some ~ faces in the town hall** das wird einigen Leuten im Rathaus sauer aufstoßen (inf); **nature ~ in tooth and claw** grausame Natur; **~ sky at night, shepherds' delight; ~ sky in the morning, shepherds' warning** (Prov) Abendrot verspricht dem Bauern Lohn und Brot, dahingegen Morgenröte verheißt dem Bauern arge Nöte; **better ~ than dead** lieber rot als tot

N (= colour) Rot nt; (Pol, = person) Rote(r) mf; (Billiards) Karambole f, roter Ball; (Roulette) Rot nt, Rouge nt; **to underline mistakes in ~** Fehler rot unterstreichen; **to go through the lights on ~, to go through on ~** bei Rot über die Ampel fahren; **to be (£100) in the ~** (mit £ 100) in den roten Zahlen or in den Roten (inf) sein; **to go into the ~** in die roten Zahlen kommen; **this pushed the company into the ~** das brachte or dadurch kam die Firma in die roten Zahlen; **to get out of the ~** aus den roten Zahlen or aus den Roten (inf) herauskommen; **to see ~** (fig) rotsehen; **~s under the bed** (Pol pej) verkappte Kommunisten pl, rote Wölfe pl im Schafspelz

red: red admiral N Admiral m; **red alert** N Alarmstufe f rot, höchste Alarmbereitschaft; **to be on ~** in höchster Alarmbereitschaft sein; **Red Army** N Rote Armee; **Red Army Faction** N Rote Armee Fraktion f; **redbaiting** [ˈredbaɪtɪŋ] N (US inf) Kommunistenhetze f; **red blood cell** N rotes Blutkörperchen, rote Blutzelle; **red-blooded** ADJ heißblütig; **redbreast** N Rotkehlchen nt; **redbrick university** N (Brit) um die Jahrhundertwende erbaute britische Universität; **red cabbage** N Rotkohl m, Rotkraut nt (S Ger, Aus), Blaukraut nt (S Ger, Aus); **redcap** N (Brit Mil sl) Militärpolizist(in) m(f); (US) Gepäckträger(in) m(f); (Orn) Stieglitz m; **red card** N (Ftbl) rote Karte; **to show sb the ~** (also fig) jdm die rote Karte zeigen; **red carpet** N (lit, fig) roter Teppich; **a ~ reception** ein Empfang m mit rotem Teppich; (fig also) ein großer Bahnhof; **to roll out the ~ for sb, to give sb the ~ treatment** (inf) den roten Teppich für jdn ausrollen, jdn mit großem Bahnhof empfangen; **red cedar** N Bleistiftzeder f, Virginischer Wacholder; **red cell** N (in blood) rote Zelle; **red cent** N (US inf) **not a ~** (= nothing) keinen roten Heller (inf); **Red China** N Rotchina nt; **redcoat** N (Brit Hist) Rotrock m (britischer Soldat z.B. im amerikanischen Unabhängigkeitskrieg); **red corpuscle** N rotes Blutkörperchen; **Red Crescent** N Roter Halbmond; **Red Cross** N Rotes Kreuz ATTR Rotkreuz-; **~ hospital** Rotkreuzkrankenhaus nt; **Red Cross Society** N (Internationales) Rotes Kreuz; **redcurrant** N (Brit) (rote) Johannisbeere; **red deer** N Rothirsch m; (pl) Rotwild nt

redden [ˈredn] VT röten; sky, foliage rot färben VI (face) sich röten; (person) rot werden; (sky, foliage) sich rot färben

reddish [ˈredɪʃ] ADJ rötlich; **~-brown** rotbraun

red duster N (Naut inf) = **Red Ensign**

redecorate [ˌriːˈdekəreɪt] VI (= paper) neu tapezieren; (= paint) neu streichen; **we'll have to ~** wir müssen das Haus/die Wohnung etc neu machen (inf) VT (= paper) neu tapezieren; (= paint) neu streichen

redecoration [riːˌdekəˈreɪʃən] N (action) (= papering) Neutapezieren nt; (= painting) Neustreichen nt; (result) (= papering) neue Tapeten pl; (= painting) neuer Anstrich

redeem [rɪˈdiːm] VT pawned object, trading stamps, coupons, bill etc einlösen (for gegen); promise, obligation einhalten, erfüllen; (Fin) debt abzahlen, löschen; mortgage tilgen, abzahlen; shares verkaufen; (US) banknote wechseln (for in +acc); one's honour, situation retten; (Rel) sinner erlösen; (= compensate for) failing, fault wettmachen, ausgleichen; **to ~ oneself** sich rein waschen; **to ~ sb from sin** jdn von seinen Sünden rein waschen or erlösen

redeemable [rɪˈdiːməbl] ADJ a debt tilgbar; pawned object, trading stamps, coupons, bill einlösbar; **~ against** einlösbar gegen; **~ for cash/goods** gegen Bargeld/Waren einzulösen b (Rel) erlösbar

Redeemer [rɪˈdiːmə] N (Rel) Erlöser m, Retter m, Heiland m

redeeming [rɪˈdiːmɪŋ] ADJ quality ausgleichend; **~ feature** aussöhnendes Moment; **the only ~ feature of this novel is ...** das Einzige, was einen mit diesem Roman aussöhnt, ist ...

redefine [ˌriːdɪˈfaɪn] VT neu definieren

redeliver [ˌriːdɪˈlɪvə] VT (= give back) wieder zurückgeben; prisoners etc wieder aushändigen or ausliefern

redemption [rɪˈdempʃən] N (of pawned object, trading stamps, coupons, bill etc) Einlösung f; (of promise, obligation) Einhaltung f, Erfüllung f; (Fin) (of debt) Abzahlung f, Löschung f; (of mortgage) Tilgung f; (of shares) Verkauf m; (US: of banknote) Wechsel m; (of one's honour, situation) Rettung f; (Rel) Erlösung f; **beyond** or **past ~** (fig) nicht mehr zu retten; **~ centre** (Brit) or **center** (US) ((Comm) Einlösestelle f

redemptive [rɪˈdemptɪv] ADJ (Rel) erlösend, rettend

Red Ensign N (Naut) britische Handelsflagge

redeploy [ˌriːdɪˈplɔɪ] VT troops umverlegen; workers anders einsetzen; staff umsetzen

redeployment [ˌriːdɪˈplɔɪmənt] N (of troops) Umverlegung f; (of workers) Einsatz m an einem anderen Arbeitsplatz; (of staff) Umsetzung f

redevelop [ˌriːdɪˈveləp] VT building, area sanieren

redevelopment [ˌriːdɪˈveləpmənt] N Sanierung f

redevelopment area N Sanierungsgebiet nt

red: red eye N (Phot) Rotfärbung der Augen auf Blitzlichtfotos, Rote-Augen-Effekt m; **redeye** (US, sl) **a** (= cheap whisky) Fusel m (inf), schlechter Whisky **b** (also **redeye flight**) Übernachtflug m; **red-eyed** ADJ mit geröteten or roten Augen; **red-faced** ADJ mit rotem Kopf; **Red Flag** N Rote Fahne; **red flag** N (on beach etc) rote Warnflagge or Signalflagge; **red giant** N (Astron) roter Riese or Riesenstern; **red grouse** N Rothuhn nt; **Red Guard** N Rote Garde; **red-haired** ADJ rothaarig; **red-handed** ADV **to catch sb ~** jdn auf frischer Tat ertappen; (esp sexually) jdn in flagranti erwischen (inf); **red hat** N (Rel, of cardinal) Kardinalshut m; **redhead** N Rothaarige(r) mf, Rotschopf m; **red-headed** ADJ rothaarig; **red heat** N Rotglut f; **to bring iron to ~** Eisen auf Rotglut erhitzen; **red herring** N (lit) Räucherhering m; (fig) Ablenkungsmanöver nt; (in thrillers, historical research) falsche Spur; **that's a ~** (= irrelevant) das führt vom Thema ab; **red-hot** ADJ **a** (lit) rot glühend; (= very hot) glühend heiß; (fig) telephone lines heißgelaufen; **~ favourite** ganz heißer or brandheißer Favorit; **he's a ~ favourite to win the race** er ist der heiße Favorit bei dem Rennen → also **red-hot poker b** (fig inf) (= very popular) heiß (inf); (= very skilled) toll (inf); (= very recent) news brandaktuell; (= ardent, burning) person leidenschaftlich, begeistert; attitude glühend, brennend, inständig **c** (= spicy) chilli scharf, beißend; **red-hot poker** N (Bot) Fackellilie f

redial [riːˈdaɪəl] (Telec) **VT/I** nochmals wählen **N automatic ~** automatische Wahlwiederholung

red: Red Indian N (dated) Indianer(in) m(f); **red ink** N (US: = losses) finanzielle Verluste pl, rote Zahlen pl; **to bleed ~** rote Zahlen schreiben

redirect [ˌriːdaɪˈrekt] VT letter, parcel umadressieren; (= forward) nachsenden; traffic umleiten; attention, efforts, resources umleiten, umverteilen

rediscounting [ˌriːdɪsˈkaʊntɪŋ] N Rediskontierung f

rediscover [ˌriːdɪsˈkʌvə] VT wieder entdecken

rediscovery [ˌriːdɪsˈkʌvərɪ] N Wiederentdeckung f

redistribute [ˌriːdɪˈstrɪbjuːt] VT wealth umverteilen, neu verteilen; (= reallocate) work neu zuteilen

redistribution [ˌriːdɪstrɪˈbjuːʃən] N (of wealth) Umverteilung f, Neuverteilung f; (of work) Neuzuteilung f

red: red lead N Bleirot nt, Bleimennige f; **red-letter day** N besonderer Tag, Tag, den man im Kalender rot anstreichen muss; **red light** N (lit) (= warning light) rotes Licht; (= traffic light) Rotlicht nt; **to go through the ~** (Mot) bei Rot über die Ampel fahren, die Ampel überfahren (inf); **to see the ~** (fig) die Gefahr erkennen; **the red-light district** die Strichgegend, der Strich (inf); (with nightclubs) das Rotlichtviertel; **redlining** [ˈredlaɪnɪŋ] N (US) die Praktik von Banken und Versicherungen, den Bewohnern heruntergekommener Stadtviertel Kredite, Hypotheken und den Abschluss von Versicherungen zu verweigern; **red man** N (at street crossing) rotes Licht; (as said to children) rotes Männchen; **red meat** N Rind-, Lamm- und Rehfleisch; **red mullet** N (rote) Meerasche; **redneck** N (US, inf) Prolet(in) m(f) (inf)

redness [ˈrednɪs] N Röte f

redo [riːˈduː] VT **a** (= do again) noch einmal machen, neu machen; hair in Ordnung bringen **b** = **redecorate**

redolence [ˈredəʊləns] N (liter) Duft m

redolent [ˈredəʊlənt] ADJ (liter) duftend; **~ of or with lavender** nach Lavendel duftend; **to be ~ of the 19th century/my youth** stark an das 19. Jahrhundert/meine Jugend erinnern

redouble [riːˈdʌbl] **VT a** efforts, zeal etc verdoppeln; attacks verstärken **b** (Bridge) rekontrieren **VI** (zeal, efforts) sich verdoppeln; (attacks) sich verstärken **N** (Bridge) Rekontra nt

redoubt [rɪˈdaʊt] N (Mil) Redoute f; (inside a fort) Kasematte f

redoubtable [rɪˈdaʊtəbl] ADJ (= formidable) task horrend; (= to be feared) person, teacher Respekt gebietend attr

redound [rɪˈdaʊnd] VI (form) **to ~ to sb's honour/advantage** jdm zur Ehre/zum Vorteil gereichen (geh); **to ~ to sb's credit** jdm hoch angerechnet werden; **to ~ upon** wieder treffen

red: red pepper N roter Paprika, rote Paprikaschote; **red pine** N Südkiefer f; (= wood) Redpine nt

redraft [ˌriːˈdrɑːft] **N** Neuentwurf m; (of speech also) Neufassung f; (of literary work) Umschrift f **VT** nochmals or neu entwerfen; literary work umschreiben

red rag N rotes Tuch; **it's like a ~ to a bull** das wirkt wie ein rotes Tuch

redress [rɪˈdres] **VT** one's errors, wrongs wieder gutmachen, sühnen; situation bereinigen; grievance beseitigen; balance wieder herstellen **N** (for errors, wrongs) Wiedergutmachung f; (for grievance) Beseitigung f; **to seek ~ for** Wiedergutmachung verlangen für; **he set out to seek ~ for these grievances** er wollte zu seinem Recht kommen; **there is no ~** das steht unumstößlich fest; **legal ~** Rechtshilfe f; **to have no ~ in law** keinen Rechtsanspruch haben; **but what ~ does a manager have against an employee?** aber welche Wege stehen dem Manager offen, gegen den Arbeitnehmer zu klagen?; **to gain ~** zu seinem Recht kommen

red: Red Riding Hood N (Little) **~** Rotkäppchen nt; **red salmon** N Pazifiklachs m; **Red Sea** N Rotes Meer; **red setter** N (roter) Setter; **redshank** N (Orn) Rotschenkel m; **red shift** N Rotverschiebung f; **redskin** N (pej) Rothaut f; **red snapper** N (roter) Schnapper; **red spider mite** N Rote Spinne, Rote Spinnmilbe; **Red Spot** N (Astron) roter Punkt; **Red Square** N Roter Platz; **red squirrel** N Eichhörnchen nt; **redstart** N (Orn) Rotschwanz m; **red tape** N (fig) Papierkrieg m (inf); (with authorities also) Behördenkram m (inf)

reduce [rɪˈdjuːs] **VT a** pressure, weight, swelling, risk, chances verringern, reduzieren; speed reduzieren, verlangsamen; authority schwächen; (= lower) standards, temperatures herabsetzen, reduzieren; prices ermäßigen, herabsetzen, reduzieren; taxes, costs senken; expenses, wages kürzen; value mindern; (= shorten) verkürzen; (in size) width, staff, drawing, photo verkleinern, reduzieren; scale of operations einschränken; output drosseln, reduzieren; (Cook) sauce einkochen lassen; (Mil etc, in rank) degradieren; **to ~ one's weight** abnehmen; **to ~ the strength of a solution** eine Lösung abschwächen; **to ~ speed** (Mot) langsamer fahren; **"reduce speed now"** (Mot) = langsam; **the facts may all be ~d to four main headings** die Tatsachen können alle auf vier Hauptpunkte reduziert werden **b** (in price) goods, item heruntersetzen, herabsetzen **c** (= change the form of, Chem) reduzieren; (Math) zerlegen (to in +acc); **to ~ sth to a powder** etw pulverisieren; **to ~ sth to its parts** etw in seine Einzelteile zerlegen; **to ~ sth to a common denominator** (Math, fig) etw auf einen gemeinsamen Nenner bringen; **to ~ an argument to a matter of principle** aus einem Argument eine Frage des Prinzips machen; **it has been**

~d to a mere ... es ist jetzt nur noch ein ...; **it has been ~d to nothing** es ist zu nichts zusammengeschmolzen; **he's ~d to a skeleton** er ist zum Skelett abgemagert; **to ~ sb to silence/despair/tears** jdn zum Schweigen/zur Verzweiflung/zum Weinen bringen; **to ~ sb to begging/to slavery** jdn zum Betteln/zur Sklaverei zwingen; **are we ~d to this!** so weit ist es also gekommen!; **to be ~d to submission** aufgeben müssen **d** (Med) joint wieder einrenken **VI** (esp US: = slim) abnehmen; **to be reducing** eine Schlankheitskur machen

reduced [rɪˈdjuːst] ADJ price, fare ermäßigt, reduziert; prices also, goods herabgesetzt, heruntergesetzt; scale, version kleiner; risk, demand, threat, role geringer; circumstances beschränkt; **the judge gave him a ~ sentence of five years** der Richter verurteilte ihn zu einer verkürzten Haftstrafe von fünf Jahren; **at a ~ price** zu einem ermäßigten or reduzierten Preis; **"reduced"** (on ticket) „ermäßigt"; **in ~ circumstances** in beschränkten (Lebens)umständen

reducer [rɪˈdjuːsə] N (Phot) Abschwächer m

reducible [rɪˈdjuːsəbl] ADJ (to auf +acc) (Chem, fig) reduzierbar; (Math) zerlegbar; drawing, scale verkleinerbar, reduzierbar; time verkürzbar; costs herabsetzbar; **to be ~ to sth** sich auf etw (acc) reduzieren lassen

reducing [rɪˈdjuːsɪŋ]: **reducing agent** N (Chem) Reduktionsmittel nt; **reducing diet** N Schlankheits-/Abmagerungskur f

reduction [rɪˈdʌkʃən] N **a** no pl (in sth etw gen) Reduzierung f, Reduktion f, Verringerung f; (in speed) Reduzierung f, Verlangsamung f; (in authority) Schwächung f; (in standards, temperatures) Herabsetzung f, Reduzierung f; (in prices) Ermäßigung f, Herabsetzung f, Reduzierung f; (in taxes, costs) Senkung f; (in expenses, wages) Kürzung f; (in value) Minderung f; (in size) Verkleinerung f; (= shortening) Verkürzung f; (in output) Drosselung f, Reduzierung f; (in scale of operations) Einschränkung f; (of goods, items) Herabsetzung f; (of fever) Senkung f; (of joint) Wiedereinrenken nt; **to make a ~ on an article** einen Artikel heruntersetzen; **~ for cash** Preisabschlag m bei Barzahlung; **~ of taxes** Steuersenkung f; **~ in rank** Degradierung f **b** (to another state, Chem) Reduktion f; (Math) Zerlegung f (to in +acc); **~ of sth to powder/to a pulp** Zermahlung f einer Sache (gen) zu Pulver/zu Brei **c** (= amount reduced) (in sth etw gen) (in pressure, temperature, output) Abnahme f, Rückgang m; (of speed) Verlangsamung f; (in size) Verkleinerung f; (in length) Verkürzung f; (in taxes) Nachlass m; (in prices) Ermäßigung f; (Jur: of sentence) Kürzung f; (of swelling) Rückgang m; **to sell (sth) at a ~** etw verbilligt verkaufen, etw zu ermäßigtem Preis verkaufen; **what a ~!** wie billig!; **~ in strength** Nachlassen nt der Kräfte **d** (= copy) Verkleinerung f

reductionism [rɪˈdʌkʃənɪzəm] N Reduktionismus m

reductive [rɪˈdʌktɪv] ADJ reduktiv (geh)

redundancy [rɪˈdʌndənsɪ] N **a** Überflüssigkeit f; (of style) Weitschweifigkeit f, Redundanz f (geh) **b** (Brit Ind) Arbeitslosigkeit f; **redundancies** Entlassungen pl; **the recession caused a lot of ~ or many redundancies** der Konjunkturrückgang brachte viel Arbeitslosigkeit mit sich; **he feared ~** er hatte Angst, seinen Arbeitsplatz zu verlieren

redundancy payment N (Brit Ind) Abfindung f

redundant [rɪˈdʌndənt] ADJ **a** überflüssig; land überschüssig; style zu wortreich, redundant (geh); **several ~ buildings have been demolished** mehrere Gebäude, die nicht mehr gebraucht werden, sind abgerissen worden **b** (Brit Ind, = out of work) arbeitslos; **to make sb ~** jdn entlassen, jdn freisetzen; **to become/to be made ~** den Arbeitsplatz verlieren; **he found himself ~** er war plötzlich ohne Arbeitsplatz

reduplicate [rɪ'dju:plɪkeɪt] **VT** wiederholen; (Ling) reduplizieren **ADJ** [rɪ'dju:plɪkɪt] (Ling) redupliziert

reduplication [rɪˌdju:plɪ'keɪʃən] **N** Wiederholung f; (Ling) Reduplikation f

reduplicative [rɪ'dju:plɪkətɪv] **ADJ** (Ling) reduplizierend

red: red wine N Rotwein m; **redwing** N Rotdrossel f; **redwood** N Redwood nt

redye [ˌri:'daɪ] **VT** **a** (= dye the same colour) nachfärben **b** (= dye a different colour) umfärben

re-echo [rɪ'ekəʊ] **VI** widerhallen **VT** echoen; **he ~ed his wife's opinion** er war wie das Echo seiner Frau

reed [ri:d] **N** **a** (Bot) Schilf(rohr) nt, Ried nt; **in the ~s** im Schilf or Ried; **a broken ~** (fig) ein schwankendes Rohr **b** (of wind instrument) Rohrblatt nt; (of harmonium) Durchschlagzunge f; (of organ) Zungenpfeife f; **~s** Rohrblattinstrumente pl

reed: reed basket N Korb m aus Schilfrohr; **reed bunting** N Rohrammer f; **reed instrument** N Rohrblattinstrument nt

re-edit [ˌri:'edɪt] **VT** neu herausgeben; book, text noch einmal redigieren; film, tape neu schneiden

reed: reed organ N Harmonium nt; **reed pipe** N Schalmei f; **reed stop** N Zungenregister nt

re-educate [ˌri:'edjʊkeɪt] **VT** umerziehen; **to ~ one's body** sich or seinen Körper umgewöhnen

re-education [ˈri:edjʊˈkeɪʃən] **N** Umerziehung f

reed warbler [ˈri:dˌwɔ:blə] N Rohrsänger m

reedy [ˈri:dɪ] **ADJ** (+er) schilfig; sound näselnd; music schnarrend; voice durchdringend; **~ instrument** Rohrblattinstrument nt

reef[1] [ri:f] **N** **a** (in sea) Riff nt **b** (Min) Ader f, Gang m

reef[2] (Naut) **N** Reff nt **VT** sail reffen

reefer [ˈri:fə] **N** (= jacket) Seemannsjacke f; (inf: = joint) Joint m (inf)

reef knot N Kreuzknoten m, Weberknoten m

reek [ri:k] **N** Gestank m **VI** stinken (of nach)

reeky [ˈri:kɪ] **ADJ** (+er) stinkig, stinkend

reel [ri:l] **N** **a** (of thread, wire etc) Rolle f, Spule f; (of film, magnetic tape) Spule f; (Fishing) (Angel)rolle f **b** (= dance) Reel m **VT** (Tech) thread aufspulen **VI** (person) taumeln; (drunk also) torkeln, schwanken; **he went ~ing down the street** er torkelte or schwankte die Straße hinunter; **the blow made him ~ or sent him ~ing** er taumelte unter dem Schlag; **my head is ~ing** mir dreht sich der Kopf; **the news made him or his mind ~** bei der Nachricht drehte sich ihm alles; **the news left us ~ing in disbelief** die Nachricht verschlug uns einfach die Sprache; **the whole country is still ~ing from the shock** das ganze Land ist noch tief erschüttert von diesem Schock; **economic problems sent markets ~ing** Wirtschaftsprobleme brachten die Börsen ins Wanken

▶ **reel in** VT sep (Fishing) einrollen; fish einholen; (fig) voters einfangen, an Land ziehen (inf)

▶ **reel off** VT sep list herunterrasseln (inf); names also herunterspulen (inf); (monotonously) herunterleiern (inf); thread abwickeln, abspulen

▶ **reel up** VT sep (Fishing) aufrollen, aufspulen

re-elect [ˌri:ɪ'lekt] **VT** wieder wählen

re-election [ˌri:ɪ'lekʃən] **N** Wiederwahl f

re-eligible [ˌri:'elɪdʒɪbl] **ADJ** wieder wählbar

reeling [ˈri:lɪŋ] **ADJ** head brummend (inf)

reel-to-reel [ˈri:ltə'ri:l] **ADJ** **~ (tape recorder)** Tonbandgerät nt, Tonbandmaschine f

re-embark [ˌri:ɪm'bɑ:k] **VT** wieder einschiffen **VI** sich wieder einschiffen; **to ~ on an enterprise** ein Unternehmen von neuem beginnen

re-embarkation [ˈri:ˌembɑ:'keɪʃən] **N** Wiedereinschiffung f

re-emerge [ˌri:ɪ'mɜ:dʒ] **VI** (object, swimmer) wieder auftauchen; (facts) (wieder) herauskommen

re-employ [ˌri:ɪm'plɔɪ] **VT** person wieder einstellen

re-enact [ˌri:ɪ'nækt] **VT** **a** (Jur) wieder in Kraft setzen **b** (= repeat) scene nachspielen; event, crime nachstellen

re-enactment [ˌri:ɪ'næktmənt] **N** (of law etc) Wiederinkraftsetzung f; (of scene) Nachspiel nt; (of event, crime) Nachstellen nt

re-engage [ˌri:ɪn'geɪdʒ] **VT** employee wieder einstellen; (Tech) gear wheels wieder ineinander greifen lassen; gear wieder einlegen; clutch wieder kommen lassen

re-enlist [ˌri:ɪn'lɪst] **VI** (Mil) sich wieder melden or verpflichten **VT** (Mil) neu verpflichten; **to ~ sb's help** jds Hilfe erneut in Anspruch nehmen

re-enter [ˌri:'entə] **VI** **a** (= walk in) wieder eintreten; (= drive in) wieder einfahren; (= penetrate: bullet etc) wieder eindringen; (= climb in) wieder einsteigen; (= cross border) wieder einreisen; (ship) wieder einlaufen **b** (= apply to) wieder auftreten **c** (for race, exam etc) sich wieder melden (for zu) **VT** **a** room wieder betreten; country wieder einreisen in (+acc); (Space) atmosphere wieder eintreten in (+acc); club etc wieder beitreten (+dat); politics wieder einsteigen in (+acc); society sich wieder eingliedern in (+acc); race sich wieder beteiligen an (+dat) **b** name (on list etc) wieder eintragen

re-entrant [ˌri:'entrənt] **N** Wiederholungskandidat(in) m(f)

re-entry [ˌri:'entrɪ] **N** **a** (also Space) Wiedereintritt m; (into country) Wiedereinreise f (into in +acc); (for exam) Wiederantritt m (for zu); **~ point** (Space) **point of ~** (Space) Wiedereintrittsstelle f; **a** = **into politics** ein Wiedereinstieg m in die Politik; **her ~ into society** ihre Wiedereingliederung in die Gesellschaft **b** (Jur) Wiederinbesitznahme f

re-erect [ˌri:ɪ'rekt] **VT** building, bridge wieder aufbauen; scaffolding also wieder aufstellen

re-establish [ˌri:ɪ'stæblɪʃ] **VT** order wieder herstellen; control wiedererlangen; diplomatic relations, dialogue wieder aufnehmen; custom wieder einführen; **this novel has ~ed him as a best-selling author** mit diesem Roman ist der Autor wieder auf die Bestsellerliste gekommen

re-establishment [ˌri:ɪ'stæblɪʃmənt] **N** (of order) Wiederherstellung f; (of custom) Wiedereinführung f; (of control) Wiedererlangen nt; (of diplomatic relations, dialogue) Wiederaufnahme f; (in a position, office) Wiedereinsetzung f

reeve[1] [ri:v] **N** **a** (Hist) Vogt m **b** (in Canada) ≈ Gemeindevorsteher(in) m(f)

reeve[2] **VT** (Naut, = thread) einscheren; (= fasten) festmachen

re-examination [ˈri:ɪgˌzæmɪ'neɪʃən] **N** Überprüfung f, erneute or nochmalige Prüfung; (of role) genaue Überprüfung; (Jur, of witness) erneute or nochmalige Vernehmung

re-examine [ˌri:ɪg'zæmɪn] **VT** überprüfen, erneut or nochmals prüfen; role nochmals genau ansehen; (Jur) witness erneut or nochmals vernehmen

re-export [ˌri:ɪk'spɔ:t] **VT** wieder ausführen **N** [ri:'ekspɔ:t] goods for **~** Waren pl zur Wiederausfuhr

re-exportation [ˌri:eks,pɔ:'teɪʃən] **N** Wiederausfuhr f

ref[1] [ref] **N** (Sport inf) abbr of **referee** Schiri m

ref[2] abbr of **reference (number)**

refashion [ˌri:'fæʃn] **VT** umgestalten, ummodeln (inf)

refectory [rɪ'fektərɪ] **N** (in college) Mensa f; (in monastery) Refektorium nt

refer [rɪ'fɜ:] **VT** **a** (= pass) matter, problem weiterleiten (to an +acc); decision übergeben (to sb jdm); **the case was ~red to arbitration** der Fall wurde einem Schiedsgericht übergeben; **it was**

~red to us for (a) decision es wurde uns (dat) zur Entscheidung übergeben; **I ~red him to the manager** ich verwies ihn an den Geschäftsführer; **the patient was ~red for tests** der Patient wurde zu Untersuchungen geschickt; **the doctor ~red him to a specialist** der Arzt überwies ihn an einen Spezialisten or schickte ihn zu einem Spezialisten; **to ~ sb to the article on ...** jdn auf den Artikel über (+acc) ... verweisen; **to ~ a cheque** (Brit) or **check** (US) **to drawer** (Comm) einen Scheck an den Aussteller zurücksenden **b** (Brit, Univ) thesis zur Änderung zurückgeben **VI** **a** **to ~ to** (= allude to) sprechen von; (= mention also) erwähnen; (words) sich beziehen auf (+acc); **I am not ~ring to you** ich meine nicht Sie; **what can he be ~ring to?** was meint er wohl?, wovon spricht er wohl?; **the letter ~s to you all** der Brief gilt euch allen; **~ring to your letter** (Comm) mit Bezug auf Ihren Brief **b** (= apply to) **to ~ to** (orders, rules) gelten für; (criticism, remark) sich beziehen auf (+acc) **c** (= consult) **to ~ to** (to notes, book) nachschauen in (+dat), konsultieren (geh); to person sich wenden an (+acc); **you must ~ to the original** Sie müssen aufs Original zurückgreifen

▶ **refer back** **VI** **a** (person, remark) sich beziehen (to auf +acc) **b** (= check back, consult again) zurückgehen (to zu) **VT** sep (= pass back) decision etc zurückgeben (to an +acc); case, matter zurückverweisen; **he referred me back to you** er hat mich an Sie zurückverwiesen

referee [ˌrefə'ri:] **N** **a** (Ftbl, Rugby, fig) Schiedsrichter(in) m(f); (Boxing) Ringrichter(in) m(f); (Judo, Wrestling) Kampfrichter(in) m(f) **b** (Jur) Schiedsrichter(in) m(f) **c** (Brit: = person giving a reference) Referenz f; **to be a ~ for sb** jdm als Referenz dienen **VT** (Sport, fig) Schiedsrichter(in) sein bei; match also (als Schieds-/Ring-/Kampfrichter(in)) leiten; (Ftbl also) pfeifen (inf) **VI** (Sport, fig) Schiedsrichter(in) sein, (den) Schiedsrichter/die Schiedsrichterin machen or spielen (inf); (Ftbl also) pfeifen (inf)

refereeing [ˌrefə'ri:ɪŋ] **N** (Sport) Schiedsrichterleistung f; (Boxing) Ringrichterleistung f; **~ is his vocation** er ist zum Schiedsrichter berufen

reference [ˈrefrəns] **☉** 19.2, 19.4 **N** **a** (= act of mentioning) Erwähnung f (to sb/sth jds/einer Sache); (= allusion, direct) Bemerkung f (to über +acc); (indirect) Anspielung f (to auf +acc); **to make (a) ~ to sth** etw erwähnen; **~ to any such delicate issue should be avoided** eine so delikate Sache sollte nicht erwähnt werden; **this was not said with ~ to you** diese Worte waren nicht auf dich gemünzt; **in** or **with ~ to** was ... anbetrifft; (Comm) bezüglich (+gen); **~ your letter ...** (Comm) mit Bezug auf Ihren Brief ... (form); **without ~ to age** ungeachtet des Alters; **without ~ to one's notes** ohne seine Aufzeichnungen zu Hilfe zu nehmen; **keep these details for (future) ~** bewahren Sie diese Einzelheiten als Beleg (für später) auf **b** no pl (= act of passing, of matter, problem) Weiterleitung f (to an +acc); (of decision) Übergabe f (to an +acc) **c** (= testimonial, also **references**) Referenz(en) f(pl), Zeugnis nt; **to give sb a good ~** jdm gute Referenzen or ein gutes Zeugnis ausstellen; **a banker's ~** eine Bankauskunft or -referenz; **I've been asked to give him a ~** man hat mich gebeten, ihm eine Referenz zu geben **d** (= note redirecting reader, in book, on map etc) Verweis m; (Comm) Zeichen nt → **cross-reference** **e** (= connection) **to have ~ to** in Beziehung stehen mit or zu; **this has no/little ~ to** das steht in keiner/in kaum einer Beziehung zu **f** (= authority, scope: of committee, tribunal) Zuständigkeitsbereich m → **term** **g** (esp US) = **referee** N c

reference: reference book N Nachschlagewerk nt; **reference library** N Präsenzbibliothek f; **reference number** N Aktenzeichen nt; (of subscriber etc) Nummer f

referendum [ˌrefəˈrendəm] N pl **referenda** [ˌrefəˈrendə] Volksentscheid m, Referendum nt; **to hold a ~** einen Volksentscheid durchführen, ein Referendum abhalten

referential [ˌrefəˈrenʃəl] ADJ sich beziehend (to auf +acc); **~ mark** Verweiszeichen nt

referral [rɪˈfɜːrəl] N (Med: to hospital, specialist etc) Überweisung f (to zu); (Jur: of case) Verweisung f (to an +acc); **~ letter, letter of ~** (Med) Überweisung f

refill [riːˈfɪl] VT nachfüllen, wieder füllen ◼N ['riːfɪl] (for fountain pen, lighter) Nachfüllpatrone f; (for ballpoint pen) Nachfüll- or Ersatzmine f; (for lipstick) Nachfüllstift m; (for propelling pencil) Ersatzmine f; (for notebook) Nachfüllblätter pl; **would you like a ~?** (inf, = drink) darf ich nachschenken?; **he wants another ~** er will noch einmal nachgeschenkt haben

refillable [riːˈfɪləbl] ADJ nachfüllbar; **~ pack** Nachfüllpackung f, Nachfüllpack m

refinancing [riːfaɪˈnænsɪŋ] N Refinanzierung f, Neufinanzierung f

refine [rɪˈfaɪn] VT ◼a metal, oil, sugar raffinieren ◼b language, manners, taste(s) verfeinern, kultivieren ◼c techniques, methods verfeinern, verbessern

▸**refine upon** VI +prep obj point, detail näher ausführen; method verbessern, verfeinern

refined [rɪˈfaɪnd] ADJ ◼a (= processed) metal, oil raffiniert, rein; foods veredelt; **~ sugar** Raffinade f; **~ flour** Auszugsmehl nt; **~ products** (St Ex, Econ) raffinierte/veredelte Produkte pl; **~ petroleum products** (St Ex, Econ) raffinierte Erdölprodukte pl ◼b (= sophisticated) taste fein; person, style fein, vornehm; model ausgeklügelt, raffiniert

refinement [rɪˈfaɪnmənt] N ◼a no pl (of metal, oil, sugar) Raffination f, Raffinierung f, Reinigung f ◼b no pl (of person, language, style) Vornehmheit f, Feinheit f; **a person of evident ~** ·ein offensichtlich kultivierter Mensch ◼c (= improvement: in technique, machine etc) Verfeinerung f, Verbesserung f (in sth +gen)

refinery [rɪˈfaɪnərɪ] N (metal, oil, sugar refinery) Raffinerie f

refit [riːˈfɪt] VT ship neu ausrüsten; factory neu ausstatten ◼VI (ship) neu ausgerüstet werden ◼N ['riːfɪt] (Naut) Neuausrüstung f

refitting [riːˈfɪtɪŋ], **refitment** [ˌriːˈfɪtmənt] N = **refit** N

reflate [riːˈfleɪt] VT (Econ) bewusst inflationieren, ankurbeln ◼VI (economy) sich beleben, angekurbelt werden; **they decided to ~** man beschloss, die Konjunktur anzukurbeln

reflation [riːˈfleɪʃən] N (Econ) Reflation f, Ankurbelung f der Konjunktur

reflationary [riːˈfleɪʃnərɪ] ADJ (Econ) reflationär

reflect [rɪˈflekt] VT ◼a (= cast back) light, image, heat, sound zurückwerfen, reflektieren; (surface of water, mirror) spiegeln, reflektieren; (fig) views, reality etc widerspiegeln; **to be ~ed in sth** (lit, fig) sich in etw (dat) spiegeln; **I saw him/myself ~ed in the mirror** ich sah ihn/mich im Spiegel; **the many difficulties ~ed in his report/attitude** die vielen Schwierigkeiten, die sich in seinem Bericht/seiner Haltung spiegeln; **~ing prism** Spiegelprisma nt; **to bask in ~ed glory** sich im Glanze eines anderen sonnen; **to ~ the fact that ...** die Tatsache widerspiegeln, dass ...; **his music ~s his love for her** in seiner Musik spiegelt sich seine Liebe zu ihr wider
◼b (= think) **I ~ed that thus was the way of the world** ich dachte bei mir, dass das eben der Lauf der Welt sei; **do you ever ~ that ...?** denken Sie je darüber nach, dass ...?
◼VI (= meditate) nachdenken, reflektieren (geh) (on, about über +acc)

▸**reflect (up)on** VI +prep obj etwas aussagen über (+acc); person also ein gutes/schlechtes Licht werfen auf (+acc); motives, reasons also in gutem/schlechtem Licht erscheinen lassen; reputation, sb's honour sich auswirken auf (+acc);

(unfavourably) schaden (+dat), ein schlechtes Licht werfen auf (+acc)

reflectingly [rɪˈflektɪŋlɪ] ADV = **reflectively**

reflecting telescope [rɪˈflektɪŋˈtelɪskəʊp] N Spiegelteleskop nt

reflection [rɪˈflekʃən] N ◼a no pl (= reflecting) Reflexion f; (by surface of lake, mirror) Spiegelung f; (fig) Widerspiegelung f
◼b (= image) Spiegelbild nt, Reflexion f; (fig) Widerspiegelung f; **to see one's ~ in a mirror** sich im Spiegel sehen; **a pale ~ of ...** ein matter Abglanz ... (gen)
◼c no pl (= consideration) Überlegung f; (= contemplation) Reflexion f, Betrachtung f; (up)on ~ wenn ich mir es recht überlege; **on further ~** bei genauerer Überlegung
◼d (= thoughts, comments) **~s on language** Reflexionen pl or Betrachtungen pl über die Sprache
◼e (= adverse criticism) **a ~ on his honour** ein Schatten m auf seiner Ehre; **this is a ~ on your taste** das zeigt, wie wenig Geschmack du hast; **this is no ~ on your ability** damit soll gar nichts über Ihr Können gesagt sein
◼f (Anat) Zurückbiegung f

reflective [rɪˈflektɪv] ADJ ◼a faculty, powers der Reflexion; person nachdenklich; expression nachdenklich, grübelnd; **to be in a ~ mood** in einer nachdenklichen Stimmung sein ◼b (Phys etc) surface reflektierend, spiegelnd; light reflektiert; clothing reflektierend ◼c (Gram) = **reflexive** ◼d **to be ~ of sth** (form, = in tune with) sich in Übereinstimmung mit etw befinden

reflectively [rɪˈflektɪvlɪ] ADV say, speak überlegt; **he scratched his chin ~** er kratzte sich nachdenklich am Kinn

reflectiveness [rɪˈflektɪvnɪs] N (of person) Nachdenklichkeit f

reflectivity [rɪflekˈtɪvɪtɪ] N (Phys) Reflexionsvermögen nt

reflector [rɪˈflektə'] N (on car, cycle) Rückstrahler m; (= telescope) Reflektor m

reflex ['riːfleks] ADJ (Physiol, Psych, Phys, fig) Reflex-; (Math) angle überstumpf; **~ action** (Physiol, Psych) Reflexhandlung f, Reflex m; **~ point** (Anat) Reflexzone f ◼N (Physiol, Psych, fig) Reflex m; (Phys, = image) Reflexion f → **condition** VT c

reflex camera N (Phot) Spiegelreflexkamera f

reflexion [rɪˈflekʃən] N = **reflection**

reflexive [rɪˈfleksɪv] (Gram) ADJ reflexiv ◼N Reflexiv nt

reflexively [rɪˈfleksɪvlɪ] ADV (Gram) reflexiv

reflexology [ˌriːflekˈsɒlədʒɪ] N (Med) Reflexologie f; (= practice) Reflexzonenmassage f

refloat [ˌriːˈfləʊt] VT ship (fig) business wieder flottmachen

reflux ['riːflʌks] N Rückfluss m

reforest [riːˈfɒrɪst] VT (US) = **reafforest**

reforestation [ˌriːfɒrɪsˈteɪʃən] N (US) = **reafforestation**

re-form [riːˈfɔːm] VT ◼a (= form again) wieder bilden; (Mil) ranks, troops neu formieren ◼b (= give new form) umformen, umgestalten (into zu) ◼VI sich wieder or erneut bilden; (Mil) sich neu formieren

reform [rɪˈfɔːm] N Reform f; (of person) Besserung f; **~ measures** Reformmaßnahmen pl; **~ school** (Brit dated, US) Besserungsanstalt f → **land reform** VT law, institutions, services, spelling system reformieren; society also verbessern; conduct, person bessern ◼VI (person) sich bessern

reformable [rɪˈfɔːməbl] ADJ person, conduct besserungsfähig

reformat [riːˈfɔːmæt] VT (Comput) disk neu formatieren

reformation [ˌrefəˈmeɪʃən] N (of person) Reformierung, Besserung f; **the Reformation** die Reformation

reformative [rɪˈfɔːmətɪv] ADJ effect reformierend; **~ fervour** Reformeifer m

reformatory [rɪˈfɔːmətərɪ] N Besserungsanstalt f

reformed [rɪˈfɔːmd] ADJ reformiert; person also gewandelt; (alcoholic, communist) ehemalig; (behaviour) gebessert; **he's a ~ character** er hat sich gebessert

reformer [rɪˈfɔːmə'] N (Pol) Reformer m; (Rel) Reformator m

reformism [rɪˈfɔːmɪzəm] N Reformismus m

reformist [rɪˈfɔːmɪst] ◼N Reformist m ◼ADJ reformistisch

refound [ˌriːˈfaʊnd] VT monastery etc wieder gründen

refract [rɪˈfrækt] VT brechen

refracting telescope [rɪˈfræktɪŋˈtelɪskəʊp] N Refraktor m

refraction [rɪˈfrækʃən] N Brechung f, Refraktion f (spec); **angle of ~** Brechungswinkel m

refractive [rɪˈfræktɪv] ADJ material, surface brechend

refractive index N Brechzahl f, Brechungsindex m

refractor [rɪˈfræktə'] N ◼a (Phys) brechendes Medium ◼b (= telescope) Refraktor m

refractoriness [rɪˈfræktərɪnɪs] N ◼a (of person) Eigensinn m, störrische Art ◼b (Med) Hartnäckigkeit f ◼c (Chem, Miner) Hitzebeständigkeit f

refractory [rɪˈfræktərɪ] ADJ ◼a person eigensinnig, störrisch ◼b (Med) hartnäckig ◼c (Chem, Miner) hitzebeständig

refrain[1] [rɪˈfreɪn] VI **please ~!** bitte unterlassen Sie das!; **he ~ed from comment** er enthielt sich eines Kommentars; **they ~ed from such actions** sie sahen von einem solchen Vorgehen ab; **I couldn't ~ from laughing** ich konnte mir das Lachen nicht verkneifen; **kindly ~ from saying that in front of the children** würden Sie das bitte nicht vor den Kindern sagen; **please ~ from smoking** bitte nicht rauchen!

refrain[2] N (Mus, Poet, fig) Refrain m

refrangible [rɪˈfrændʒəbl] ADJ brechbar

refresh [rɪˈfreʃ] VT (drink, bath, sleep, rest) erfrischen; (meal) stärken; **to ~ oneself** (with drink) eine Erfrischung zu sich (dat) nehmen; (with a bath) sich erfrischen; (with food) sich stärken; (with sleep, rest) sich ausruhen; **to ~ oneself with a glass of beer** zur Erfrischung ein Glas Bier trinken; **to ~ one's memory** sein Gedächtnis auffrischen; **let me ~ your memory** ich will Ihrem Gedächtnis nachhelfen

refresher [rɪˈfreʃə'] N ◼a (Brit, Jur) zusätzliches Anwaltshonorar ◼b (inf, = drink) Erfrischung f; **to have a ~** etwas trinken

refresher course N (Univ etc) Auffrischungskurs m

refreshing ADJ , **refreshingly** ADV [rɪˈfreʃɪŋ, -lɪ] (lit, fig) erfrischend

refreshment [rɪˈfreʃmənt] N ◼a (of mind, body) Erfrischung f; (through food) Stärkung f ◼b (= food, drink) (light) **~s** (kleine) Erfrischungen pl; **~ tent** Restaurationszelt nt; **~ room** Imbissstube f; (= cafeteria) Cafeteria f

refried beans [ˌriːfraɪdˈbiːnz] PL mexikanisches Bohnengericht (bei dem die Bohnen gekocht, gebraten, zerstampft und dann noch einmal gebraten werden)

refrigerant [rɪˈfrɪdʒərənt] ◼N Kühlmittel nt; (Med) kühlendes Mittel; (= fluid in fridge) Kältemittel nt ◼ADJ kühlend

refrigerate [rɪˈfrɪdʒəreɪt] VT (= chill) kühlen; (= freeze) tiefkühlen; **"refrigerate after opening"** „nach dem Öffnen kühl aufbewahren"

refrigeration [rɪˌfrɪdʒəˈreɪʃən] N (= chilling) Kühlung f; (= freezing) Tiefkühlung f

refrigerating [rɪˈfrɪdʒəreɪtɪŋ]: **refrigerating plant** N (Tech) Kühlanlage f; **refrigerating room** N Kühlraum m

refrigerator [rɪˈfrɪdʒəreɪtə'] N Kühlschrank m, Eisschrank m; (= cold room) Kühlraum m

refuel [ˌriːˈfjuːəl] VTI auftanken

refuelling, (US) **refueling** [ˌriːˈfjuːəlɪŋ] N Auftanken nt; **~ stop** Zwischenstopp m zum Auftanken

refuge ['refjuːdʒ] N **a** (lit, fig) Zuflucht f (from vor (+dat)); **place of ~** Zufluchtsort m; **a ~ for battered women** ein Frauenhaus nt; **to seek ~** Zuflucht suchen; **to seek ~ in silence** sich in Schweigen flüchten; **to take ~** Zuflucht nehmen (in in (+dat)), sich flüchten (in in (+acc)); **he took ~ in drink and drugs** er nahm Zuflucht zu Alkohol und Drogen; **she found ~ in books** Bücher waren ihre Zuflucht **b** (for climbers, pedestrians) Unterstand m

refugee [ˌrefjʊˈdʒiː] N Flüchtling m

refugee camp N Flüchtlingslager nt

refugee status N Flüchtlingsstatus m

refulgence [rɪˈfʌldʒəns] N (liter) Strahlen nt

refund [rɪˈfʌnd] **VT** money zurückzahlen, zurückerstatten; expenses erstatten; postage vergüten, zurückerstatten; **to ~ the difference** die Differenz erstatten **N** ['riːfʌnd] (of money) Rückzahlung f, Rückerstattung f; (of expenses) Erstattung f; (of postage) Vergütung f; **to get a ~ (on sth)** sein Geld (für etw) wiederbekommen; **they wouldn't give me a ~** man wollte mir das Geld nicht zurückgeben; **I'd like a ~ on this blouse, please** ich hätte gern mein Geld für diese Bluse zurück; **we will send (you) a ~** wir senden Ihnen das Geld zurück

refundable [rɪˈfʌndəbl] ADJ money, payment(s) zurückzahlbar, zurückerstattbar; **these expenses are ~** diese Ausgaben werden erstattet; **postage is ~** das Porto wird vergütet

refurbish [riːˈfɜːbɪʃ] VT image etc aufarbeiten, aufpolieren; furniture, house renovieren

refurnish [riːˈfɜːnɪʃ] VT neu möblieren

refusal [rɪˈfjuːzəl] N **a** Ablehnung f; (of offer) Ablehnung f, Zurückweisung f; (of food, permission, visa, permit) Verweigerung f; (to do sth) Weigerung f; **her ~ (of the invitation)** ihre Absage; **to meet with a ~, to get a ~** eine Absage erhalten; **to give (sb) a flat ~** jdm eine glatte Absage erteilen; **to give sb first ~ of sth** jdm etw zuerst or als Erstem anbieten; (with purchase) jdm das Vorkaufsrecht an etw (dat) einräumen; **to have (the) first ~ of sth** etw als Erster angeboten bekommen; **right of first ~** Vorkaufsrecht nt **b** (Showjumping) Verweigerung f

refuse¹ [rɪˈfjuːz] ❂ 9.3, 12.2 **VT** candidate, proposal, offer ablehnen; invitation also absagen; (stronger) abweisen, zurückweisen; visa, permit, permission, payment verweigern; **to ~ to do sth** sich weigern, etw zu tun, etw nicht tun wollen; **I ~ to believe it** ich weigere mich, das zu glauben, ich glaube das einfach nicht; **I ~ to be blackmailed** ich lasse mich nicht erpressen; **to be ~d sth** etw nicht bekommen; **he was ~d entry into Germany** ihm wurde die Einreise nach Deutschland verweigert; **he was ~d a visa** ihm wurde das Visum verweigert; **they were ~d permission (to leave)** es wurde ihnen nicht gestattet (wegzugehen); **he ~d food** er verweigerte die Nahrungsaufnahme; **he/his request was ~d** er/seine Bitte wurde abgelehnt; **she ~d him** sie wies ihn ab or zurück; **the horse ~d the fence** das Pferd hat am Hindernis verweigert **VI** ablehnen; (to do sth) sich weigern; (horse) verweigern

refuse² ['refjuːs] N Müll m; (= food waste) Abfall m; **household ~** Haus(halts)müll m; **garden ~** Gartenabfälle pl

refuse ['refjuːs] in cpds Müll-; **refuse bin** N Mülleimer m; **refuse chute** N Müllschlucker m; **refuse collection** N Müllabfuhr f; **refuse collector** N Müllwerker(in) m(f), Müllmann m (inf); **refuse destructor** N Müllvernichtungsanlage f; **refuse disposal** N Müllbeseitigung f; **refuse disposal service** N Müllabfuhr f; **refuse disposal unit** N Müllzerkleinerer m; **refuse dump** N Müllablageplatz m; **refuse lorry** N Müllwagen m

refusenik [rɪˈfjuːznɪk] N (inf) Verweigerer(in) m(f)

refutable [rɪˈfjuːtəbl] ADJ widerlegbar

refutation [ˌrefjʊˈteɪʃən] N Widerlegung f

refute [rɪˈfjuːt] VT widerlegen

-reg [redʒ] N (Brit, inf) abbr of **-registration Y-reg car** Auto nt mit dem Zulassungsbuchstaben Y (wobei der Buchstabe das Jahr der Erstanmeldung angibt)

reg. [redʒ] **N** (Brit, inf) abbr of **registration number** amtliches Kennzeichen **ADJ** abbr of **registered – no.** amtl. Kennzeichen

regain [rɪˈgeɪn] **VT** **a** (= gain back) wiedererlangen; lost time aufholen; control, confidence, title wiedergewinnen; territory zurückbekommen; **to ~ consciousness** das Bewusstsein wiedererlangen, wieder zu Bewusstsein kommen; **to ~ one's strength** wieder zu Kräften kommen; **to ~ one's health/fitness** wieder gesund/fit werden; **to ~ one's footing** seinen Halt wiederfinden; (fig) wieder auf die Beine kommen; **to ~ one's balance** das Gleichgewicht wiederfinden; **to ~ possession of sth** wieder in den Besitz einer Sache (gen) gelangen; **to ~ the lead** (in sport) wieder in Führung gehen; (in research etc) wieder an die Spitze gelangen; **to ~ weight** wieder zunehmen

b (= reach again) main road/firm ground wieder gelangen an (+acc)/auf (+acc)

regal ['riːgəl] ADJ königlich; (fig) hoheitsvoll

regale [rɪˈgeɪl] VT (with food, drink) verwöhnen; (with stories) ergötzen (geh)

regalia [rɪˈgeɪlɪə] PL Insignien pl; **she was in full ~** (hum) sie war in großer Gala or Aufmachung (hum)

regally ['riːgəlɪ] ADV königlich; say hoheitsvoll

regard [rɪˈgɑːd] ❂ 20.5, 21.2 **VT** **a** (= consider) betrachten; **to ~ sb/sth as sth** jdn/etw für etw halten, jdn/etw als betrachten; **to ~ sb/sth with favour** (Brit) or **favor** (US) jdn/etw wohlwollend betrachten; **to ~ sth with horror** mit Schrecken an etw (acc) denken; **to be ~ed as ... as ...** angesehen werden; **he is ~ed as a great poet** er wird als großer Dichter angesehen, er gilt als großer Dichter; **it's not generally ~ed as worth doing** es wird im Allgemeinen angenommen, dass sich das nicht lohnt; **we ~ it as worth doing** wir glauben, dass es sich lohnt(, das zu tun); **we don't ~ it as necessary** wir halten es nicht für notwendig; **she doesn't ~ it as her responsibility** sie betrachtet es nicht als ihre Verantwortung; **to ~ sb/sth highly** or **with great esteem** jdn/etw hoch schätzen or sehr achten; **he is highly ~ed** er ist hoch angesehen; **his work is highly ~ed** seine Arbeit wird sehr geschätzt

b (= concern) **as ~s that/my friend/your application** was das/meinen Freund/Ihren Antrag betrifft or anbelangt or angeht → also **regarding**

c (liter, = look at) betrachten

d (= heed) berücksichtigen; **without ~ing his wishes** ohne Rücksicht auf seine Wünsche **N** **a** (= attention, concern) Rücksicht f (for auf +acc); **to have some ~ for sb/sth** auf jdn/etw Rücksicht nehmen; **to show little/no ~ for sb/sth** wenig/keine Rücksichtnahme für jdn/etw zeigen; **with no ~ for his safety** ohne Rücksicht auf seine Sicherheit (zu nehmen); **without ~ to** or **for her views** ohne sich um ihre Ansichten zu kümmern; **without ~ to** or **for what people might think** ohne sich darum zu kümmern, was die Leute denken möchten

b **in this ~** diesbezüglich (form), in diesem Zusammenhang; **with** or **in ~ to** in Bezug auf (+acc)

c (= respect) Achtung f; **to hold sb in high ~** jdn achten or sehr schätzen; **to have a great ~ for sb** jdn hoch achten

d **regards** PL (in message) Gruß m; **to send sb one's ~s** jdn grüßen lassen; **give him my ~s** grüßen Sie ihn von mir; **(kindest) ~s, with kind ~s** mit freundlichen Grüßen **e** (liter, = look) Blick m

regardful [rɪˈgɑːdfʊl] ADJ (form) **~ of (one's) duty** seiner Pflicht (gen) bewusst, pflichtbewusst; **to be ~ of sb's feelings** jds Gefühle achten or respektieren

regarding [rɪˈgɑːdɪŋ] PREP in Bezug auf (+acc), bezüglich (+gen)

regardless [rɪˈgɑːdlɪs] **ADJ** **~ of** ohne Rücksicht auf (+acc), ungeachtet (+gen); **to do sth ~ of the consequences** etw ohne Rücksicht auf die Folgen tun; **~ of what it costs** egal, was es kostet; **~ of the fact that ...** ungeachtet dessen, dass ... **ADV** trotzdem; **he did it ~** er hat es trotzdem getan

regatta [rɪˈgætə] N Regatta f

regd abbr of **registered** reg.

regency ['riːdʒənsɪ] N Regentschaft f; **the Regency** (period) (Brit, Art etc) der Regency; **Regency furniture/style** (Brit Art etc) Regencymöbel pl/-stil m

regenerate [rɪˈdʒenəreɪt] **VT** **a** (= renew, re-create) erneuern; **to be ~d** sich erneuern, sich neu bilden, sich regenerieren; (fig: person: by holiday etc) sich erholen; (esp Rel) erneuert werden **b** (Elec) rückkoppeln **VI** (esp Sci) sich regenerieren **ADJ** [rɪˈdʒenərɪt] erneuert

regeneration [rɪˌdʒenəˈreɪʃən] N **a** (= renewal, re-creation) Erneuerung f; (fig: of person: by holiday etc) Erholung f **b** (Elec) Rückkoppelung f

regenerative [rɪˈdʒenərətɪv] ADJ **a** tissue sich regenerierend; (esp Rel) erneuernd; power, process regenerativ **b** (Elec) positiv rückgekoppelt

regent ['riːdʒənt] N Regent(in) m(f); (US, Univ) Mitglied nt des Universitäts- or Schulverwaltungsrats → **prince regent**

reggae ['regeɪ] N Reggae m

regicide ['redʒɪsaɪd] N (= act) Königsmord m; (= person) Königsmörder(in) m(f)

regime [reɪˈʒiːm] N **a** (Pol) Regime nt; (fig, = management, social system etc) System nt **b** = **regimen**

regimen ['redʒɪmen] N (Med) Kur f

regiment ['redʒɪmənt] **N** (Mil) Regiment nt; (fig) Kompanie f **VT** ['redʒɪment] (fig) reglementieren

regimental [ˌredʒɪˈmentl] **ADJ** (Mil) Regiments-; **~ commander** Regimentskommandeur m **N** **regimentals** PL (Mil) Uniform f; (of a particular regiment) Regimentsuniform f

regimentation [ˌredʒɪmenˈteɪʃən] N (fig) Reglementierung f

region ['riːdʒən] N (of country) Gebiet nt, Region f (also TV); (Admin) Bezirk m; (of body) Gegend f, Region f; (of atmosphere, sea) Bereich m; **the lower ~s** die Unterwelt; (of charts, football league) die untere Hälfte; **in the ~ of 5 kg** um die 5 kg

regional ['riːdʒənl] ADJ regional; **~ development** Gebietserschließung f; **~ television** Regionalfernsehen nt

regional council N (Scot, dated) ≈ Gemeinderat m

regionalism ['riːdʒənəlɪzəm] N Regionalismus m; (= division into regions) Einteilung f in Regionen; (= loyalty) Lokalpatriotismus m; (= word) nur regional verwendeter Ausdruck

regionalist ['riːdʒənəlɪst] **ADJ** regionalistisch **N** Regionalist(in) m(f)

register ['redʒɪstə] **N** **a** (= book) Register nt; (at school) Namensliste f; (in hotel) Gästebuch nt; (of members etc) Mitgliedsbuch nt; **to take the ~** die Namen aufrufen; **~ of births, deaths and marriages** Personenstandsbuch nt; **~ of wills** (US, person) Testamentsbeamte(r) m **b** (Tech, = recording device) Registriergerät nt; (for controlling airflow) Klappe f → **cash register** **c** (Mus) Register nt; (= organ stop) Registerzug m **d** (Ling) (Sprach)ebene f, Register nt (geh) **e** (Typ) Register nt **VT** **a** (authorities: = record formally) registrieren; (in book, files) eintragen; fact, figure erfassen; **he is ~ed (as) disabled/blind** er hat einen Schwerbehinderten-/Sehbehindertenausweis → **registered**

b (individual: = have recorded) birth, marriage, death, (Comm) company, trademark anmelden, eintragen lassen; vehicle, child at school etc, candidate anmelden; student einschreiben; **to ~ interest** sein Interesse anmelden; **to ~ a protest** Protest anmelden

c (= *indicate*) (*machine*) *speed, quantity, rainfall, temperature* registrieren; (*face, expression*) (*happiness, disapproval*) zum Ausdruck bringen; **his face ~ed surprise** die Überraschung zeigte sich in seinem Gesichtsausdruck; **he ~ed no emotion** er zeigte keine Gefühlsbewegung **d** (*Post*) *letter* einschreiben → **registered b e** (*Typ*) in Register bringen **f** (= *realize*) registrieren; **I ~ed the fact that he had gone** ich registrierte, dass er gegangen war **VI a** (*on electoral list etc*) sich eintragen; (*in hotel*) sich anmelden; (*student*) sich einschreiben, sich immatrikulieren; **to ~ with a doctor/dentist** sich bei einem Arzt/Zahnarzt auf die Patientenliste setzen lassen; **to ~ with the police** sich polizeilich melden; **to ~ for a course** sich für einen Kurs anmelden; (*Univ*) einen Kurs belegen
b (*inf,* = *be understood*) **it hasn't ~ed (with him)** er hat es noch nicht registriert

registered ['redʒɪstəd] **ADJ a** *student* eingeschrieben; *voter, company, name* eingetragen; *vehicle* amtlich zugelassen; **~ capital** Grundkapital *nt*, Nominalkapital *nt*; **a Y-registered car** (*Brit*) ein Auto *nt* mit den Zulassungsbuchstaben Y; **an American-registered ship** ein in Amerika registriertes Schiff **b** (*Post*) eingeschrieben, Einschreib-; **~ letter** eingeschriebener Brief, Einschreibbrief *m*; **by ~ post** per Einschreiben

registered: registered charity N eingetragene wohltätige Organisation; **Registered General Nurse** (*Brit*), **registered nurse** (*US*) N staatlich geprüfte Krankenschwester, staatlich geprüfter Pfleger; **registered office** N eingetragener (Gesellschafts)sitz; **registered shareholder** N Inhaber(in) *m(f)* von Namensaktien; **Registered Trademark** N eingetragenes Warenzeichen

register office N (*Brit*) = **registry (office)**

register ton N (*Naut*) Registertonne *f*

registrar [‚redʒɪ'strɑː] N (*Brit*) (*Admin*) Standesbeamte(r) *m*/-beamtin *f*; (*Univ*) höchster Verwaltungsbeamter, höchste Verwaltungsbeamtin, ≈ Kanzler(in) *m(f)*; (*Med*) Krankenhausarzt *m*/-ärztin *f*; **to be married by the ~** sich standesamtlich trauen lassen

registrar's office (*Brit Admin*) Standesamt *nt*

registration [‚redʒɪ'streɪʃən] N **a** (*by authorities,* = *formal recording*) Registrierung *f*; (*in books, files*) Eintragung *f*; (*of fact, figure*) Erfassung *f* **b** (*by individual, Comm*) Anmeldung *f*; (*of student*) Einschreibung *f*; **~ fee** Anmeldegebühr *f*; (*for evening class*) Kursgebühr *f*; (*Univ*) Einschreib(e)gebühr *f* **c** (= *indication, by machines*) Registrierung *f*; (*by face, expression*) Ausdruck *m* **d** (*Post, of letter*) Aufgabe *f* als Einschreiben; **~ fee** Einschreibegebühr *f*

registration: registration document N (*Brit Aut etc*) Kraftfahrzeugbrief *m*; **registration number** N (*Brit Aut etc*) Kraftfahrzeugkennzeichen *nt*, polizeiliches Kennzeichen; **registration office** N (*Brit*) = **registry (office)**; **registration plate** N (*Aut*) Nummernschild *nt*

registry ['redʒɪstrɪ] N Sekretariat *nt*; (*in church*) Sakristei *f*; (*Brit,* = *registry office*) Standesamt *nt*; **port of ~** Heimathafen *m*

registry office N (*Brit*) Standesamt *nt*; **to get married in a ~** standesamtlich heiraten

Regius ['riːdʒəs] ADJ (*Brit, Univ*) **~ professor** *Inhaber eines von einem Monarchen eingerichteten Lehrstuhls*

regorge [rɪ'ɡɔːdʒ] **VT** (*form*) erbrechen **VI** sich ergießen

regress [rɪ'ɡres] VI (*lit form:* = *move backwards*) sich rückwärts bewegen; (*fig: society*) sich rückläufig entwickeln; (*Biol, Psych, Med*) sich zurückentwickeln; **he is ~ing into childhood** er fällt wieder ins Kindesalter zurück

regression [rɪ'ɡreʃən] N (*lit form:* = *backward movement*) Rückwärtsbewegung *f*; (*fig: of society*) rückläufige Entwicklung *f*; (*Biol, Psych, Med*) Zurückentwicklung *f*; **his ~ into childhood** sein Rückfall *m* in die Kindheit

regressive [rɪ'ɡresɪv] ADJ regressiv; *trend* rückläufig; *behaviour, decision* rückschrittlich

regret [rɪ'ɡret] ⊘ 12.3, 18.1, 18.2, 20.6 **VT** bedauern; *one's youth, lost opportunity* nachtrauern (+*dat*); **I ~ that we will not be coming** ich bedauere, dass wir nicht kommen können; **to ~ the fact that ...** (die Tatsache) bedauern, dass ...; **I ~ to say that ...** ich muss Ihnen leider mitteilen, dass ...; **he is very ill, I ~ to say** er ist leider or bedauerlicherweise sehr krank; **we ~ to learn that ...** wir hören mit Bedauern, dass ...; **we ~ any inconvenience caused** für eventuelle Unannehmlichkeiten bitten wir um Verständnis; **it is to be ~ted that ...** es ist bedauerlich, dass ...; **you won't ~ it!** Sie werden es nicht bereuen; **this matter is much ~ted** dieser Vorfall hat großes Bedauern ausgelöst **N** Bedauern *nt no pl*; **to feel ~ for one's past youth** seiner vergangenen Jugend (*dat*) nachtrauern; **much to my ~** sehr zu meinem Bedauern; **I have no ~s** ich bereue nichts; **please give her my ~s that I cannot come** bitte, sagen Sie ihr, dass ich leider nicht kommen kann; **he sends his ~s** er lässt sich entschuldigen, er muss leider absagen

regretful [rɪ'ɡretfʊl] ADJ *look, attitude* bedauernd *attr*; **he was extremely ~ (about it)** es tat ihm sehr Leid, er bedauerte es sehr; **it is ~ that ...** es ist bedauerlich, dass ...

regretfully [rɪ'ɡretfʊlɪ] ADV **a** (= *with regret*) mit Bedauern; **very ~ I must announce ...** sehr zu meinem Bedauern muss ich bekannt geben, ... **b** (= *unfortunately, regrettably*) bedauerlicherweise, leider; **~, nationalism is flourishing in modern Europe** bedauerlicherweise or leider gedeiht heute in Europa der Nationalismus

regrettable [rɪ'ɡretəbl] ⊘ 14 ADJ bedauerlich

regrettably [rɪ'ɡretəblɪ] ADV **a** (= *unfortunately*) bedauerlicherweise, leider **b** (= *very*) bedauerlich; **~ few people came** bedauerlich wenige Leute kamen, leider kamen nur wenige Leute

regroup [riː'ɡruːp] **VT** umgruppieren, neu gruppieren **VI** sich umgruppieren, sich neu gruppieren

regrouping [riː'ɡruːpɪŋ] N Um- or Neugruppierung *f*

regt *abbr of* **regiment** Reg.

regular ['reɡjʊlə'] **ADJ a** (= *at even intervals*) *service, bus, pulse, reminders* regelmäßig; *footsteps, rhythm* gleichmäßig; *employment* fest, regulär; *way of life, bowel movements* geregelt; **~ flights** regelmäßige Flugverbindungen *pl*; **at ~ intervals** in regelmäßigen Abständen; **on a ~ basis** regelmäßig; **to be in ~ use** regelmäßig benutzt werden; **to be in** or **to have ~ contact with sb/sth** mit jdm/etw regelmäßig in Verbindung stehen or Kontakt haben; **to be ~ in one's habits** ein geregeltes Leben führen; **to eat ~ meals** regelmäßig essen; **to keep ~ hours** feste Zeiten haben; **his visits are as ~ as clockwork** nach seinen Besuchen kann man die Uhr stellen; **he has a ~ place in the team** er ist ein ordentliches Mannschaftsmitglied; **wanton violence is becoming a ~ feature of urban life** vorsätzliche Gewalt wird immer mehr zum Bestandteil städtischen Lebens; **eating fresh vegetables helps keep you ~** (*Med inf*) frisches Gemüse trägt zu einem regelmäßigen Stuhlgang bei; **I'm quite ~** (*in menstruation*) ich habe eine ziemlich regelmäßige Periode
b (= *habitual*) *size, price, time* normal; *listener, reader* regelmäßig; **our ~ cleaning woman** unsere normale Reinemachefrau; **~ customer** Stammkunde *m*/-kundin *f*; **~ pub** (*Brit*) seine Stammkneipe (*inf*); **to have a ~ partner** einen festen Partner haben; (*in relationship also*) in einer festen Beziehung leben; **it's past his ~ bedtime** es ist nach seiner normalen Schlafenszeit; **would you like ~ or large?** (*esp US*) möchten Sie normal oder extra or (*food also*) eine extragroße Portion?; **~ fries** (*esp US*) eine normale Portion Pommes frites
c (= *symmetrical, Gram*) regelmäßig; *surface* gleichmäßig; (*Geometry*) gleichseitig
d (= *permissible, accepted*) *action, procedure* rich-

tig; **~ procedure demands that ...** der Ordnung halber muss man ...; **it is quite ~ to apply in person** es ist ganz in Ordnung, sich persönlich zu bewerben
e (*Mil*) Berufs-, regulär; (*Police*) *forces, officer* regulär
f (*Rel*) **~ clergy** Ordensgeistlichkeit *f*
g (*esp US,* = *ordinary*) gewöhnlich; **he's just a ~ guy** er ist ein ganz normaler Typ (*inf*)
h (*inf,* = *real*) echt (*inf*); **he's a ~ idiot** er ist ein regelrechter Idiot
N a (*Mil*) Berufssoldat(in) *m(f)*, regulärer Soldat, reguläre Soldatin; (= *habitual customer etc*) Stammkunde *m*, Stammkundin *f*; (*in pub, hotel*) Stammgast *m*; **he's one of the ~s on that programme** er ist einer der Stammgäste dieser Sendung
b (*US,* = *gasoline*) Normalbenzin *nt*

regular army N Berufsarmee *f*, reguläre Armee

regular gas(oline) N (*US*) Normalbenzin *nt*

regularity [‚reɡjʊ'lærɪtɪ] N **a** (= *occurrence at even intervals*) Regelmäßigkeit *f*; (*of rhythm*) Gleichmäßigkeit *f*; (*of employment*) Festheit *f*; (*of way of life, bowel movements*) Geregeltheit *f* **b** (= *symmetry, Gram*) Regelmäßigkeit *f*; (*of surface*) Gleichmäßigkeit *f*; (*Geometry*) Gleichseitigkeit *f* **c** (= *permissibility: of action, procedure*) Richtigkeit *f*

regularize ['reɡjʊləraɪz] **VT** *breathing, service* regulieren; *situation, relationship* normalisieren; *menstrual period* regeln

regularly ['reɡjʊləlɪ] ADV **a** (= *frequently*) regelmäßig **b** (= *evenly, steadily*) *breathe, beat* regelmäßig, gleichmäßig **c** (= *at evenly spaced intervals*) in gleichmäßigen Abständen; **huge beeches, planted ~ along the avenue** riesige Buchen, die in gleichmäßigen Abständen die Allee säumen

regulate ['reɡjʊleɪt] **VT** (= *control*) regulieren; *flow, expenditure also, traffic, lifestyle* regeln; **to ~ the use of sth** den Gebrauch von etw begrenzen

regulation [‚reɡjʊ'leɪʃən] **N a** (= *regulating*) Regulierung *f*; (*of flow, expenditure also, traffic, lifestyle*) Regelung *f* **b** (= *rule*) Vorschrift *f*; (*of government etc*) Verordnung *f*, Vorschrift *f*; **the ~s of the society** die Satzung der Gesellschaft; **according to (the) ~s** laut Vorschrift/Satzung; **to be contrary to** or **against (the) ~s** gegen die Vorschrift(en)/Satzung verstoßen **ATTR** *boots, dress* vorgeschrieben; **army ~ boots** vorgeschriebene Armeestiefel *pl*

regulative ['reɡjʊlətɪv] ADJ regulativ, regulierend

regulator ['reɡjʊleɪtə'] N (= *instrument*) Regler *m*; (*in clock, watch*) Gangregler *m*; (*for manual adjustment*) Rücker *m*

regulatory [reɡjʊ'leɪtərɪ] ADJ Regulierungs-; **~ authority/body** Regulierungsbehörde *f*/-organ *nt*; **~ control** behördliche Kontrolle; **~ approval** Genehmigung *f* durch die Regulierungsbehörde

Regulo® ['reɡjʊləʊ] N **at ~ 4** auf Gasstufe 4

regurgitate [rɪ'ɡɜːdʒɪteɪt] **VT** wieder hochbringen, wieder von sich geben; (*fig*) *information, facts* wiederkäuen; **the young feed on ~d insects** die Jungen leben von vorverdauten Insekten

regurgitation [rɪ‚ɡɜːdʒɪ'teɪʃən] N Wiederhochbringen *nt*; (*fig: of information, facts*) Wiederkäuen *nt*

rehab ['riːhæb] *abbr of* **rehabilitation**

rehabilitate [‚riːə'bɪlɪteɪt] **VT a** *refugee, troops, the disabled* (in die Gesellschaft) eingliedern; *ex-criminal also* rehabilitieren; *drug addict, alcoholic* therapieren **b** (= *restore position to*) rehabilitieren; *reputation* wieder herstellen

rehabilitation ['riːə‚bɪlɪteɪʃən] N **a** (*of refugee, troops, the disabled*) Eingliederung *f* in die Gesellschaft; (*of ex-criminal*) Rehabilitation *f*; (*of drug addict, alcoholic*) Therapie *f* **b** (= *restoration of position*) Rehabilitation *f*; (*of reputation*) Wiederherstellung *f*

rehabilitation centre, *(US)* **rehabilitation center** N *(Admin)* Rehabilitationszentrum *nt*

rehash [ˌriːˈhæʃ] **VT** *literary material etc* aufbereiten **N** [ˈriːhæʃ] *(= action)* Aufbereitung *f*; *(= result)* Aufguss *m*

rehear [ˌriːˈhɪəʳ] **VT** **a** *(= hear again)* erneut anhören **b** *(Jur)* neu verhandeln, sich erneut befassen mit

rehearsal [rɪˈhɜːsəl] N **a** *(Theat, Mus)* Probe *f*; **the play is in ~** das Stück wird geprobt **b** *(= recital: of facts)* Aufzählung *f*

rehearse [rɪˈhɜːs] **VT** **a** *(Theat, Mus) play, concert* proben; *person* proben lassen; *argument* (wieder) anführen; **to ~ what one is going to say** einüben, was man sagen will **b** *(= recite)* aufzählen **VI** proben

reheat [ˌriːˈhiːt] **VT** aufwärmen

rehouse [ˌriːˈhaʊz] **VT** unterbringen

reify [ˈriːɪfaɪ] **VT** verdinglichen, reifizieren *(Philos)*

reign [reɪn] **N** *(lit, fig)* Herrschaft *f*; *(of monarch also)* Regentschaft *f*; **in the ~ of ...** während der Herrschaft ... *(+gen)*; **Queen Victoria had a long ~** Königin Viktoria übte eine lange Herrschaft aus; **the Reign of Terror** die Schreckensherrschaft **VI** *(lit, fig)* herrschen *(over über +acc)*; **silence ~s** es herrscht Ruhe → **supreme**

reigning [ˈreɪnɪŋ] **ADJ** *attr* regierend; *champion* amtierend; **the ~ beauty** die Schönheitskönigin

reimburse [ˌriːɪmˈbɜːs] **VT** *person* entschädigen; *loss* ersetzen; *expenses, costs* (zurück)erstatten, ersetzen; **to ~ sb for his expenses** jdm die Auslagen zurückerstatten

reimbursement [ˌriːɪmˈbɜːsmənt] **N** *(of person)* Entschädigung *f*; *(of loss)* Ersatz *m*; *(of expenses, costs)* (Rück)erstattung *f*

reimport [ˌriːɪmˈpɔːt] **VT** wieder einführen, reimportieren

reimportation [ˌriːɪmpɔːˈteɪʃən] **N** Wiedereinfuhr *f*

reimpose [ˌriːɪmˈpəʊz] **VT** *task, conditions* neu aufzwingen or auferlegen *(form)* *(on sb* jdm*)*; *sanctions, fine* erneut verhängen *(on* gegen*)*; *one's will, authority* erneut aufzwingen *(on sb* jdm*)*; **to ~ a tax on sth** etw erneut besteuern

rein [reɪn] **N** *(lit, fig)* Zügel *m*; **~s** *(for child)* Laufgurt *m*; **to hold the ~s** *(lit, fig)* die Zügel or das Heft in der Hand haben; **he kept the horse on a long/short ~** er ließ die Zügel lang/hielt die Zügel kurz; **to keep a tight ~ on sb/sth** *(lit, fig)* bei jdm/etw die Zügel kurz halten; **to give free ~ to sb/sth, to allow** or **give sb/sth free ~** *(fig)* jdm/einer Sache freien Lauf lassen; **to give sb free ~ to do sth** jdm freie Hand lassen, etw zu tun

▶ **rein back** **VT** *sep* zügeln **VI** zügeln

▶ **rein in** **VT** *sep horse* zügeln; *(fig) passions also* im Zaum halten; *spending, inflation* in Schranken halten; **to rein the horse in to a trot/canter** das Pferd im Trab/leichten Galopp gehen lassen; **to rein sb/oneself in** jdn/sich zügeln or bremsen **VI** zügeln

reincarnate [ˌriːɪnˈkɑːneɪt] **VT** reinkarnieren *(liter)*; **to be ~d** wieder geboren werden; **the belief that man is ~d (after death)** der Glaube an die Reinkarnation des Menschen or an die Wiedergeburt **ADJ** [ˌriːɪnˈkɑːnɪt] wieder geboren

reincarnation [ˌriːɪnkɑːˈneɪʃən] **N** die Wiedergeburt, die Reinkarnation

reindeer [ˈreɪndɪəʳ] **N** *pl* – Ren(tier) *nt*; **Rudolph the red-nosed ~** Rudolf Rotnase *m*

reinforce [ˌriːɪnˈfɔːs] **VT** *(lit, fig, Psych, Mil)* verstärken; *concrete also* armieren *(spec)*; *sb's demands, belief* stärken, stützen; *evidence, statement* stützen, bestätigen; *opinion* bestätigen; **to ~ sb's decision/determination** jdn in seiner Entscheidung/Absicht bestärken; **to ~ the message** der Botschaft *(dat)* mehr Nachdruck verleihen

reinforced concrete [ˌriːɪnfɔːstˈkɒŋkriːt] **N** Stahlbeton *m*

reinforcement [ˌriːɪnˈfɔːsmənt] **N** **a** *no pl (= act) (lit, fig, Psych, Mil)* Verstärkung *f*; *(of concrete also)* Armierung *f*; *(of sb's demands, beliefs)* Stärkung *f*, Stützung *f*; *(of evidence, statement)* Stützung *f*, Bestätigung *f*; *(of opinion)* Bestätigung *f*; **~ troops** *(Mil)* Verstärkungstruppen *pl* **b** *(= thing)* Verstärkung *f*; **~s** *(Mil, fig)* Verstärkung *f*

reinsert [ˌriːɪnˈsɜːt] **VT** wieder einfügen; *thermometer* wieder einführen; *coin* wieder einwerfen; *filing card* zurückstecken; *needle* wieder einstecken; *zip* wieder einsetzen

reinstate [ˌriːɪnˈsteɪt] **VT** *person* wieder einstellen *(in* in *+acc)*; *law and order* wieder herstellen *(in* in *+dat)*; *death penalty* wieder einführen

reinstatement [ˌriːɪnˈsteɪtmənt] **N** *(of person)* Wiedereinstellung *f*; *(of law and order)* Wiederherstellung *f*; *(of death penalty)* Wiedereinführung *f*

reinsurance [ˌriːɪnˈʃʊərəns] **N** Rückversicherung *f*

reinsure [ˌriːɪnˈʃʊəʳ] **VT** rückversichern; **to ~ one's car** *(with same company)* seine Autoversicherung verlängern

reintegrate [ˌriːˈɪntɪgreɪt] **VT** wieder eingliedern, wieder or erneut integrieren *(into* in *+acc)*

reintegration [ˈriːˌɪntɪˈgreɪʃən] **N** Wiedereingliederung *f*, Reintegration *f*

reintroduce [ˌriːɪntrəˈdjuːs] **VT** *measure, death penalty* wieder einführen; *(Parl) bill* erneut vorlegen; *(Zool) species* wieder heimisch machen

reinvent [ˌriːɪnˈvent] **VT** **to ~ the wheel** das Rad neu erfinden; **to ~ oneself** sich *(dat)* ein neues Image geben

reinvest [ˌriːɪnˈvest] **VT** reinvestieren

reissue [ˌriːˈɪʃuː] **VT** *book* neu auflegen; *stamps, recording, coins* neu herausgeben **N** *(of book)* Neuauflage *f*; *(of stamps, recording, coins)* Neuausgabe *f*

reiterate [ˌriːˈɪtəreɪt] **VT** wiederholen

reiteration [riːˌɪtəˈreɪʃən] **N** Wiederholung *f*

reiterative [riːˈɪtərətɪv] **ADJ** *comments* sich wiederholend *attr*; *style* repetitiv

reject [rɪˈdʒekt] **VT** **a** *damaged goods etc (customer)* ablehnen, zurückweisen; *(maker, producer)* aussortieren, ausscheiden **b** *(= turn down) application, request etc* ablehnen; *(stronger)* abweisen, zurückweisen; *candidate (through vote)* durchfallen lassen; *suitor, advances* abweisen, zurückweisen; *offer* ablehnen, ausschlagen; *criticism* zurückweisen; *plea* zurückweisen, abschlagen; *idea, possibility* verwerfen **c** *(Med) drug* nicht vertragen, ablehnen; *transplant* abstoßen; *(stomach) food* verweigern **N** [ˈriːdʒekt] *(Comm)* Ausschuss *m no pl*; **~ goods** Ausschussware *f*; **although this jacket's a ~ ...** obwohl dieses Jackett zweite Wahl ist, ...; **society's ~s** die Ausgestoßenen *pl*

rejection [rɪˈdʒekʃən] **N** **a** *(of damaged goods etc, by customer)* Ablehnung *f*, Zurückweisung *f*; *(by maker, producer)* Aussortierung *f*, Ausscheidung *f* **b** *(= turning down, of application, request, offer etc)* Ablehnung *f*; *(stronger)* Abweisung *f*, Zurückweisung *f*; *(of suitor, advances)* Abweisung *f*, Zurückweisung *f*; *(of criticism, plea)* Zurückweisung *f*; *(of idea, possibility)* Verwerfen *nt* **c** *(Med) (of drug)* Ablehnung *f*; *(of transplant)* Abstoßung *f*; *(of food by stomach)* Verweigerung *f*

rejection slip **N** Absage *f*

reject shop [ˈriːdʒekt-] **N** *Geschäft für Ausschussware*, Ramschladen *m (inf)*

rejig [riːˈdʒɪg] **VT** *(Brit, = redo)* neu machen; *system, structures* umkrempeln; *rules, wording* ummodeln *(inf)*

rejoice [rɪˈdʒɔɪs] **VT** *(liter) person* erfreuen **VI** sich freuen; *(= be jubilant)* jubeln; *(Rel)* jauchzen; **they ~d to see peace return to the country** sie jubilierten, dass wieder Frieden ins Land einkehrte; **~ in the Lord!** freut euch im Herrn!; **he ~s in the name of Marmaduke** *(hum)* er erfreut sich des Namens Marmaduke

rejoicing [rɪˈdʒɔɪsɪŋ] **N** Jubel *m*; **~s** Jubel *m*

rejoin¹ [riːˈdʒɔɪn] **VT** *person, regiment* sich wieder anschließen *(+dat)*; *party, club* wieder eintreten in *(+acc)*; **to ~ ship** *(Naut)* wieder aufs Schiff kommen; **then we ~ed the motorway** danach fuhren wir wieder auf die Autobahn

rejoin² [rɪˈdʒɔɪn] **VT** *(= reply)* erwidern; *(Jur)* duplizieren

rejoinder [rɪˈdʒɔɪndəʳ] **N** Erwiderung *f*; *(Jur)* Duplik *f*

rejuvenate [rɪˈdʒuːvɪneɪt] **VT** verjüngen; *(fig)* erfrischen

rekindle [ˌriːˈkɪndl] **VT** *(lit) fire, flame* wieder anzünden; *(fig) passions, love* wieder entzünden or entflammen; *tensions, enmities* wieder aufflammen lassen; *hope, interest* wieder erwecken; *debate* wieder entfachen; *affair* wieder aufleben lassen **VI** *(lit)* wieder aufflackern; *(fig, passion, love also)* wieder entflammen; *(tensions, enmities)* wieder aufflammen; *(hope, interest)* wieder erwachen

relapse [rɪˈlæps] **N** *(Med)* Rückfall *m*, Rückschlag *m*; *(fig, in economy)* Rückschlag *m*; *(into vice, crime)* Rückfall *m (into* in *+acc)*; **to have a ~** einen Rückfall haben **VI** *(Med)* einen Rückfall haben; *(economy)* einen Rückschlag erleiden; **to ~ (into crime/vice)** rückfällig werden

Relate [rɪˈleɪt] **N** *(Brit)* ≈ Eheberatungsstelle *f*

relate [rɪˈleɪt] **VT** **a** *(= recount) story* erzählen; *details* aufzählen; **strange to ~** so unglaublich es klingt **b** *(= associate)* in Verbindung or Beziehung or Zusammenhang bringen *(to, with* mit*)*; **to try to ~ events (to each other)** versuchen, die Dinge im Zusammenhang zu sehen; **it is often difficult to ~ cause and effect** der Zusammenhang zwischen Ursache und Wirkung ist oft schwer zu erkennen **VI** **a** *(= refer)* zusammenhängen *(to* mit*)* **b** *(= form relationship)* eine Beziehung finden *(to* zu*)*

related [rɪˈleɪtɪd] **ADJ** **a** *(in family)* verwandt *(to* mit*)*; **~ by** or **through marriage** angeheiratet, verschwägert; **he is ~ to the president by** or **through marriage** er ist durch Heirat mit dem Präsidenten verwandt **b** *(= connected)* zusammenhängend; *elements, languages, products* verwandt; *issues* (sach)verwandt; **to be ~ to sth** mit etw zusammenhängen, mit etw verwandt sein; **the two events are not ~** die beiden Ereignisse hängen nicht miteinander zusammen or haben nichts miteinander zu tun; **two closely ~ questions** zwei eng miteinander verknüpfte Fragen; **health-related problems** gesundheitliche Probleme *pl*; **earnings-related pensions** einkommensabhängige Renten *pl*

relating [rɪˈleɪtɪŋ] **ADJ ~ to** in Zusammenhang mit

relation [rɪˈleɪʃən] **N** **a** *(= person)* Verwandte(r) *mf*; **he's a/no ~ (of mine)** er ist/ist nicht mir verwandt; **what ~ is she to you?** wie ist sie mit Ihnen verwandt? **b** *(= relationship)* Beziehung *f*; **to bear a ~ to** in Beziehung stehen zu; **to bear no ~ to** in keinerlei Beziehung stehen zu, keinerlei Beziehung haben zu; **to bear little ~ to** wenig Beziehung haben zu; **in ~ to** *(= as regards)* in Bezug auf *(+acc)*; *(= compared with)* im Verhältnis zu **c relations** PL *(= dealings, ties, sexual relations)* Beziehungen *pl*; **to have business ~s with sb** geschäftliche Beziehungen zu jdm haben; **~s are rather strained** die Beziehungen sind etwas gespannt **d** *no pl (of story)* Erzählung *f*; *(of details)* Aufzählung *f*

relational [rɪˈleɪʃənəl] **ADJ** relational; **~ database** *(Comput)* relationale Datenbank

relationship [rɪˈleɪʃənʃɪp] **N** **a** *(in family)* Verwandtschaft *f (to* mit*)*; **what is your ~ (to** or **with him)?** wie sind Sie (mit ihm) verwandt? **b** *(= connection: between events etc)* Beziehung *f*, Verbindung *f*; *(= relations)* Verhältnis *nt*, Beziehungen *pl*; *(in business)* Verbindung *f*; **to have a (sexual) ~ with sb** ein Verhältnis *nt* mit jdm haben; **what kind of a ~ do you have with him?** *(is it good or bad?)* wie ist Ihr Verhältnis zu ihm?; (*on what footing?*) in welchem Verhältnis stehen Sie zu ihm?; **to have a good ~ with sb** ein gutes Verhältnis *or* gute Beziehungen zu jdm haben; **they have a good ~** sie haben ein gutes Verhältnis (zueinander); **we have a business ~** wir haben geschäftlich miteinander zu tun; **it is a strictly business ~** es ist eine rein geschäftliche Beziehung

relative ['relətɪv] **ADJ** **a** (= *comparative, not absolute, Sci*) relativ; **happiness is ~** Glück ist relativ; **~ to him, she is in a very happy position** verglichen mit ihm ist sie gut dran; **fuel consumption is ~ to speed** der Benzinverbrauch hängt von der Geschwindigkeit ab; **to live in ~ luxury** verhältnismäßig *or* relativ luxuriös leben; **with ~ ease** relativ leicht; **in ~ terms** vergleichsweise, relativ gesehen; **it's all ~** es ist alles relativ **b** (= *respective*) jeweilig; **the ~ merits of A and B** die jeweiligen Verdienste von A und B **c** (= *relating to*) **~ to** sich beziehend auf (+*acc*) **d** (*Gram*) Relativ-; **~ pronoun/clause** Relativpronomen *nt*/-satz *m* **e** (*Mus*) minor, major parallel **N a** (= *person*) relation **a b** (*Gram*, = *clause*) Relativsatz *m*; (= *pronoun*) Relativpronomen *nt*

relatively ['relətɪvlɪ] **ADV** relativ, verhältnismäßig; **~ speaking** relativ gesehen *or* betrachtet

relativism ['relətɪvɪzəm] **N** Relativismus *m*

relativist ['relətɪvɪst] **N** Relativist(in) *m(f)*

relativistic [ˌrelətɪˈvɪstɪk] **ADJ** relativistisch

relativity [ˌreləˈtɪvɪtɪ] **N** (*Phys, Philos*) Relativität *f*; **~ theory, the theory of ~** die Relativitätstheorie

relativize ['relətɪvaɪz] **VT** relativieren

relax [rɪˈlæks] **VT** lockern; *muscles also, person, one's mind* entspannen; *attention, effort* nachlassen in (+*dat*); **to ~ the bowels** (*Med*) den Stuhlgang fördern **VI** (sich) entspannen; (= *rest*) (sich) ausruhen; (= *calm down*) sich beruhigen; **let's just ~!** ganz ruhig!; **~!** reg dich nicht auf!, immer mit der Ruhe!; **his face ~ed into a smile** sein Gesicht entspannte sich zu einem Lächeln

relaxant [rɪˈlæksənt] **N** (*Med*) Relaxans *nt*

relaxation [ˌriːlækˈseɪʃən] **N a** (= *act of relaxing sth*) Lockerung *f*; (*of muscles also, person, one's mind*) Entspannung *f*; (*of attention, effort*) Nachlassen *nt* **b** (= *rest*) Entspannung *f*; (= *recreation*) Erholung *f*, Entspannung *f*; **you need some ~ after work** Sie sollten sich nach der Arbeit entspannen, Sie brauchen ein wenig Erholung nach der Arbeit; **reading is her form of ~** sie entspannt sich durch Lesen

relaxed [rɪˈlækst] **ADJ** locker; *person, smile, voice* gelöst, entspannt, ruhig; *atmosphere, surroundings* zwanglos, gelöst, gelockert; *throat* angegriffen; **to feel ~** (*physically*) entspannt sein; (*mentally*) sich wohl fühlen; **to stand in a ~ position** in einer zwanglosen Haltung dastehen; **to feel ~ about sth** etw ganz gelassen sehen

relaxing [rɪˈlæksɪŋ] **ADJ** entspannend; *climate* erholsam; **~ music** Musik, die (einen) entspannt

relay ['riːleɪ] **N a** (*of workers etc*) Ablösung *f*; (*of horses*) frisches Gespann; **to eat in ~s** in Schichten essen **b** (*Sport, also* **relay race**) Staffel *f*, Staffellauf *m* **c** (*Rad, TV*) Relais *nt* **VT a** (*Rad, TV etc*) *programme, signal* (weiter) übertragen **b** *message* ausrichten (*to sb* jdm); *information, details* weiterleiten (*to sb* an jdm)

re-lay [ˌriːˈleɪ] **VT** *carpet, cable* neu verlegen

release [rɪˈliːs] **VT a** *animal, person* freilassen; (*from prison*) entlassen; *employee, football player etc* freigeben; (= *rescue*) befreien; (*from obligation, vow*) entbinden, befreien; (*from pain*) erlösen; **to ~ sb from a debt** jdm eine Schuld erlassen; **can you ~ him for a few hours each week?** können Sie ihn für ein paar Stunden pro Woche freistellen?; **to ~ tension** (*emotional*) sich abreagieren; **to ~ one's anger on sb** seinen Ärger an jdm auslassen *or* abreagieren **b** (= *let go of*) loslassen; *handbrake* losmachen, lösen; (*Phot*) *shutter* auslösen; *bomb* abwerfen;

grip, clasp lösen; (*police*) *confiscated articles* freigeben; **to ~ the (foot)brake/clutch** den Fuß von der Bremse/Kupplung nehmen, die Kupplung kommen lassen; **to ~ one's hold** *or* **grip (on sth)** (etw) loslassen **c** (*Comm*, = *issue*) *film, goods* herausbringen; *record* veröffentlichen, herausbringen **d** (= *make known*) *news, statement* veröffentlichen; *figures also* bekannt geben **e** (= *emit*) *gas, energy* freisetzen; *smell* ausströmen; (= *let off: into atmosphere*) *pressure, steam* ablassen **f** (*Jur*) *property, title* aufgeben, verzichten auf (+*acc*) **N** (*of animal, person*) Freilassung *f*; (*from prison*) Entlassung *f*; (*of employee, football player etc*) Freigabe *f*; (= *rescue*) Befreiung *f*; (*from obligation, vow*) Entbindung *f*, Befreiung *f*; (*from pain*) Erlösung *f*; **death was a happy** *or* **welcome ~ for him** der Tod war eine Erlösung für ihn **b** (= *letting go*) Loslassen *nt*; (*of handbrake*) Lösen *nt*; (*Phot: of shutter*) Auslösen *nt*; (*of bomb*) Abwurf *m*; (*Police: of confiscated articles*) Freigabe *f*; (= *mechanism*) Auslöser *m* → **shutter** **c** (*Comm*: = *issuing, of film, goods*) Herausgeben *nt*; (*of record*) Veröffentlichung *f*, Herausbringen *nt*; (= *film*) Film *m*; (= *record*) Platte *f*; **this film is now on general ~** dieser Film ist nun überall zu sehen; **a new ~ from Michael Jackson** eine Neuerscheinung von Michael Jackson; **a new ~ from XYZ Films Inc** ein neuer Film der XYZ Filmgesellschaft **d** (*of news, statement*) Veröffentlichung *f*; (= *statement*) Verlautbarung *f* **e** (*of gas, energy*) Freisetzung *f* **f** (*Jur, of property, title*) Aufgabe *f* (*of* +*gen*), Verzicht *m* (*of auf* +*acc*)

release: release date **N a** (*of film*) Premieren- *or* Erstaufführungstag *m*; (*of record, book*) Erscheinungstag *m* **b** (*of prisoner*) Entlassungsdatum *nt*; **his first possible ~ is 2007** er kann frühestens 2007 entlassen werden; **release valve** **N** Entlastungsventil *nt*

relegate ['relɪɡeɪt] **VT a** (*lit, fig*: = *downgrade*) degradieren; (*Sport*) *team* absteigen lassen (*to* in +*acc*); *old toys, furniture* verbannen (*to* in +*acc*); **to be ~d** (*Sport*) absteigen; **~d to second place** (*fig*) an zweite Stelle abgeschoben *or* verbannt **b** (= *hand over*) *matter, question* weiterleiten (*to* an +*acc*)

relegation [ˌrelɪˈɡeɪʃən] **N a** (*lit, fig*: = *downgrading*) Degradierung *f*; (*Sport: of team*) Abstieg *m*; (*of old toys, furniture etc*) Verbannung *f* (*to* in +*acc*) **b** (= *handing over, of matter, question*) Weiterleitung *f* (*to* an +*acc*)

relent [rɪˈlent] **VI** (*person*) nachgeben; (*pace, pain*) nachlassen; (*weather*) sich bessern

relentless [rɪˈlentlɪs] **ADJ a** (= *uncompromising*) *attitude, opposition, person* unnachgiebig; **to be ~ in doing sth** etw unnachgiebig tun; **to be ~ in one's efforts to do sth** unnachgiebig in seinen Bemühungen sein, etw zu tun **b** (= *unrelenting*) *pain, cold, growth* nicht nachlassend; *search* unermüdlich; *progress* unaufhaltsam; **the ~ march of technology** der unaufhaltsame Fortschritt der Technik **c** (= *merciless*) erbarmungslos; *person also* unerbittlich

relentlessly [rɪˈlentlɪslɪ] **ADV a** (= *uncompromisingly*) *oppose, maintain* unnachgiebig **b** (= *unrelentingly*) *hurt, rain* unaufhörlich; **to push ~ forward** unaufhaltsam vorwärts drängen **c** (= *mercilessly*) unerbittlich, erbarmungslos

relet [ˌriːˈlet] **VT** neu vermieten

relevance ['reləvəns], **relevancy** ['reləvənsɪ] **N** Relevanz *f*; **to be of particular ~ (to sb)** (für jdn) besonders relevant sein; **what is the ~ of your question to the problem?** inwiefern ist Ihre Frage für das Problem relevant?; **to have no ~ to sth** irrelevant für *or* bei etw sein

relevant ['reləvənt] **ADJ** relevant (*to* für); *information, document, page also* entsprechend attr; *course, study also* sachbezogen; *authority, person* zuständig; *regulation* maßgeblich, entsprechend attr; *time, place* betreffend; *experience* erforderlich, entsprechend attr; **that is not ~** das ist

nicht relevant; **a course ~ to one's studies** ein studienbezogener Kurs; **a curriculum which is ~ to all pupils** ein Lehrplan, der für alle Schüler relevant ist; **the police are looking for any ~ information** die Polizei bittet um sachdienliche Hinweise; **applicants for the job need three years' ~ experience** Bewerber für die Stelle benötigen drei Jahre entsprechende (Berufs)Erfahrung

reliability [rɪˌlaɪəˈbɪlɪtɪ] **N** Zuverlässigkeit *f*; (*of person also*) Verlässlichkeit *f*; (*of firm, company*) Seriosität *f*, Vertrauenswürdigkeit *f*

reliable [rɪˈlaɪəbl] **ADJ** zuverlässig; *person also* verlässlich; *firm, company* seriös, vertrauenswürdig

reliably [rɪˈlaɪəblɪ] **ADV** zuverlässig; **I am ~ informed that …** ich weiß aus zuverlässiger Quelle, dass …

reliance [rɪˈlaɪəns] **N** (= *trust, confidence*) Vertrauen *nt* (*on auf* +*acc*); **to place ~ on sb/sth** sich auf jdn/etw (*acc*) verlassen; **his ~ on his memory rather than his notes always gets him into difficulties** er verlässt sich auf sein Gedächtnis statt auf seine Notizen und kommt dadurch immer in Schwierigkeiten

reliant [rɪˈlaɪənt] **ADJ** (= *dependent*) angewiesen (*on, upon auf* +*acc*) → **self-reliant**

relic ['relɪk] **N** Überbleibsel *nt*, Relikt *nt*; (*Rel*) Reliquie *f*; **a ~ of** *or* **from the past** ein Überbleibsel *nt* aus vergangener Zeit; **an old ~** (*pej inf*, = *person*) ein alter Knochen (*inf*); (= *car/wardrobe etc*) ein vorsintflutlicher Karren/Schrank etc (*pej inf*)

relief [rɪˈliːf] **N a** (*from anxiety, pain*) Erleichterung *f*; **to bring sb ~** (*drug*) jdm Erleichterung verschaffen; (*news*) jdn erleichtern; **that brought him some ~ from his headache** das hat seine Kopfschmerzen etwas gelindert; **that's a ~!** mir fällt ein Stein vom Herzen; **it was a ~ to find it** ich/er *etc* war erleichtert, als ich/er *etc* es fand; **it was a ~ to get out of the office** es war eine Wohltat, aus dem Büro wegzukommen **b** (*from monotony, boredom*) Abwechslung *f*; **to provide a little light/comic ~** für eine kleine Abwechslung/für etwas Humor sorgen **c** (= *assistance*) Hilfe *f*; **to come to sb's ~** jdm zu Hilfe kommen; **~ was available in the form of blankets and cups of tea** für Decken und heißen Tee war gesorgt; **to send ~ in the form of food** jdm mit Nahrungsmitteln zu Hilfe kommen; **~ of the poor** Armenfürsorge *f*; **to provide ~ for the poor** für die Armen sorgen; **to be on ~** (*US*) Fürsorge bekommen, von der Fürsorge leben **d** (*esp Mil*: = *act of relieving, replacement forces*) Entsatz *m*; (= *substitute*) Ablösung *f* **e** (*Art, Geog*) Relief *nt*; (*Typ*) Relief *nt*, Hochdruck *m*; **high/low ~** Hoch-/Flachrelief *nt*; **in ~** erhaben; **to stand out in ~** (*lit*) sich (deutlich) abheben; (*fig*) gegensätzlich sein; **to throw sth into ~** (*lit*) etw (deutlich) hervortreten lassen; (*fig*) etw hervorheben **f** (*Jur*) Rechtshilfe *f* (*of bei*) **ATTR a** (= *aid*) Hilfs-; **the ~ effort** die Hilfsaktion; (*in disaster*) die Rettungsaktion **b** (= *replacement*) *watchman, driver* zur Entlastung; **~ bus/train** Entlastungsbus/-zug *m* **c** (*Typ etc*) Relief-; **~ printing** Reliefdruck *m*

relief: relief agency **N** Rettungsorganisation *f*; **relief fund** **N** Hilfsfonds *m*; **relief map** **N** Reliefkarte *f*; **relief road** **N** Entlastungsstraße *f*; **relief supplies** **PL** Hilfsgüter *pl*; **relief troops** **PL** Entsatztruppen *pl*; **relief valve** **N** Ausgleichsventil *nt*; **relief workers** **PL** Rettungshelfer *pl*; (*in disaster*) Katastrophenhelfer *pl*

relieve [rɪˈliːv] **VT a** *person* erleichtern; (*of pain*) befreien von; **to feel ~d** erleichtert sein; **to be ~d at sth** bei etw erleichtert aufatmen; **he was ~d to learn that** er war erleichtert, als er das hörte; **to ~ sb's mind** jdn beruhigen **b** (= *take off burden, pain*) jdn von etw befreien; (*of duty, post, command*) jdn einer Sache (*gen*) entheben (*geh*); (*of coat, suitcase*) jdm etw abnehmen; (*hum*) *of wallet, purse etc* jdn um etw erleichtern (*hum*)

c (= *mitigate*) *anxiety* mildern, schwächen; *pain* lindern; (*completely*) stillen; *tension, stress* abbauen; *pressure, symptoms* abschwächen; *monotony* (= *interrupt*) unterbrechen; (= *liven things up*) beleben; *poverty* erleichtern; (*Med*) *congestion* abhelfen (+*dat*); (*completely*) beheben; **to ~ one's feelings** seinen Gefühlen Luft machen; **the black of her dress was ~d by a white collar** das Schwarz ihres Kleides wurde durch einen weißen Kragen etwas aufgelockert; **the new road ~s peak-hour congestion** die neue Straße entlastet den Berufsverkehr; **to ~ oneself** (*euph*) sich erleichtern

d (= *help*) *stricken country, refugees etc* helfen (+*dat*)

e (= *take over from, also Mil*) ablösen

f (*Mil*) *town* entsetzen, befreien

religion [rɪˈlɪdʒən] **N** Religion *f*; (= *set of beliefs*) Glaube(n) *m*; **the Christian ~** der christliche Glaube; **wars of ~** Glaubenskriege *pl*; **her name in ~** ihr Klostername *m*; **to get ~** (*pej inf*) fromm werden; **study of ~** Religionswissenschaft *f*; **it's an absolute ~ with him** (*fig*) **it's his ~** (*fig*) das ist ihm heilig

religiosity [rɪˌlɪdʒɪˈɒsɪti] **N** Frömmlertum *nt*

religious [rɪˈlɪdʒəs] **ADJ a** religiös; *order* geistlich; **~ freedom/war** Glaubens- or Religionsfreiheit *f*/-krieg *m*; **~ education** or **instruction** (*Sch*) Religionsunterricht *m*; **~ leader** Religionsführer(in) *m(f)* **b** (= *having religious beliefs*) *person* gläubig; (= *pious*) fromm; **she is a ~ maniac** or **lunatic** sie ist eine religiöse Fanatikerin **c** (*fig*, = *conscientious*) gewissenhaft; *silence* ehrfürchtig **N** Ordensmann *m*, Ordensfrau *f*; **the Religious** *pl* die Ordensleute *pl*

religiously [rɪˈlɪdʒəsli] **ADV a** *live* fromm, gottesfürchtig; *motivated* religiös; **India is a ~ diverse country** in Indien gibt es eine Vielfalt an Religionen **b** (*fig*, = *conscientiously*) gewissenhaft

religiousness [rɪˈlɪdʒəsnɪs] **N** (= *piety*) Frömmigkeit *f*; (*fig*, = *conscientiousness*) Gewissenhaftigkeit *f*

reline [riːˈlaɪn] **VT** *coat, jacket* neu füttern; *brakes* neu belegen

relinquish [rɪˈlɪŋkwɪʃ] **VT a** (= *give up*) *hope, habit, plan* aufgeben; *right, possessions, power, post* aufgeben, verzichten auf (+*acc*); *title* ablegen; **to ~ sth to sb** jdm etw abtreten or überlassen **b** (= *let go*) **to ~ one's hold on sb/sth** (*lit, fig*) jdn/etw loslassen; **he ~ed his hold on life** sein Lebenswille erstarb

relinquishment [rɪˈlɪŋkwɪʃmənt] **N** (*form, of claim, possessions etc*) Verzicht *m* (*of* auf +*acc*)

reliquary [ˈrelɪkwəri] **N** Reliquiar *nt*, Reliquienschrein *m*

relish [ˈrelɪʃ] **N a** (= *enjoyment*) Geschmack *m*, Gefallen *m* (*for* an +*dat*); **to do sth with (great) ~** etw mit (großem) Genuss tun; **he rubbed his hands with ~ at the prospect** er rieb sich (*dat*) beim Gedanken daran genüsslich die Hände; **he ate with (great) ~** er aß mit großem Genuss or Appetit; **he had no ~ for such activities** er fand an solchen Dingen keinen Geschmack or Gefallen **b** (*Cook*) Soße *f*; (= *spiciness*) Würze *f*; (*fig*, = *charm*) Reiz *m*; **tomato/fruit ~** Tomaten-/Obstchutney *nt*; **hunger is the best ~** (*prov*) Hunger ist der beste Koch (*prov*); **it had lost all ~ (for me)** (*fig*) das hatte für mich jeglichen Reiz verloren

VT genießen; *food, wine also* sich (*dat*) schmecken lassen; *idea, role, task* großen Gefallen finden an (+*dat*); **I don't ~ doing that** (= *enjoy*) das ist gar nicht nach meinem Geschmack; (= *look forward to*) darauf freue ich mich überhaupt nicht; **I don't ~ the thought of getting up at 5 a.m** der Gedanke, um 5 Uhr aufzustehen, behagt or schmeckt (*inf*) mir gar nicht

relive [riːˈlɪv] **VT** *life* noch einmal leben; *experience, one's childhood* noch einmal erleben or durchleben; *anguish* noch einmal durchleben or durchstehen

reload [riːˈləʊd] **VT** neu beladen; *gun* nachladen, neu laden

relocate [riːləʊˈkeɪt] **VT** umsiedeln, verlegen **VI** (*individual*) umziehen; (*company*) den Standort wechseln; **many companies are relocating out of London** viele Firmen verlegen ihren Standort nach außerhalb von London; **we will help you ~** wir helfen Ihnen beim Umzug or (*referring to company*) beim Standortwechsel

relocation [riːləʊˈkeɪʃən] **N** Umzug *m*; (*of company*) Standortwechsel *m*, (*of refugees etc*) Umsiedlung *f*; **~ allowance** Umzugsbeihilfe *f*

reluctance [rɪˈlʌktəns] **N a** Widerwillen *m*, Abneigung *f*; **to do sth with ~** etw widerwillig or ungern tun; **to make a show of ~** sich widerwillig geben **b** (*Phys*) magnetischer Widerstand

reluctant [rɪˈlʌktənt] **ADJ** unwillig, widerwillig; *admission, consent, praise* widerwillig; **he is ~ to do it** es widerstrebt ihm, es zu tun; **I'm ~ to go, as he may not even be there** ich gehe nur ungern, denn er ist vielleicht nicht einmal da; **he seems ~ to admit it** er scheint es nicht zugeben zu wollen; **he is a ~ soldier/student** er ist nur widerwillig Soldat/Student; **"reluctant sale"** „Notverkauf"

reluctantly [rɪˈlʌktəntli] **ADV** widerwillig

rely [rɪˈlaɪ] **VI to ~ (up)on sb/sth** sich auf jdn/etw verlassen; (= *be dependent on*) auf jdn/etw angewiesen sein; **she relied on the trains being on time** sie verließ sich darauf, dass die Züge pünktlich waren; **I ~ on him for my income** ich bin finanziell auf ihn angewiesen; **you can ~ (up)on my help** or **on me to help you** du kannst dich darauf verlassen, dass ich dir helfe; **she is not to be relied upon** man kann sich nicht auf sie verlassen

REM *abbr of* **rapid eye movement ~ sleep** REM-Phase *f*

remain [rɪˈmeɪn] **VI a** (= *be left*) bleiben; (= *be left over*) übrig bleiben; **much ~s to be done** es ist or bleibt noch viel zu tun; **nothing ~s to be said** es gibt or bleibt nichts mehr zu sagen; **all that ~s (for us) is to accept** wir brauchen jetzt nur noch anzunehmen or müssen nur noch zusagen or annehmen; (= *have no alternative*) es bleibt uns nichts anderes übrig, als anzunehmen; **all that ~s is for me to wish you every success** ich möchte Ihnen nur noch viel Erfolg wünschen; **all that ~s (for me/us etc to do) is to lock up** ich brauche/wir brauchen jetzt nur noch abzuschließen; **that ~s to be seen** das wird sich zeigen, das bleibt abzuwarten; **the fact ~s that he is wrong** das ändert nichts an der Tatsache, dass er Unrecht hat

b (= *stay*) bleiben; **~ seated!** bleiben Sie sitzen, behalten Sie Platz (*geh*); **to ~ silent** weiterhin schweigen; **to ~ behind/up** zurück-/aufbleiben; **let things ~ as they are** lassen wir alles so, wie es ist; (*talking to somebody else*) lassen Sie die Dinge so, wie sie sind; **it ~s the same** das bleibt sich gleich; **"I ~ yours faithfully John Smith"** „mit besten Grüßen verbleibe ich Ihr John Smith"

remainder [rɪˈmeɪndə] **N a** Rest *m* (*also Math*); **the ~** (= *remaining people*) der Rest, die übrigen (Leute); **for the ~ of the week** für den Rest der Woche, für die übrige Woche **b re-mainders** PL (*Comm*) Restbestände *pl*; (= *books*) Restbestände *pl*, Remittenden *pl* (*spec*) **c** (*Jur*) Erbanwartschaft *f* **VT** *books* als Remittenden abgeben

remaining [rɪˈmeɪnɪŋ] **ADJ** übrig, restlich; **the ~ four, the four ~** die übrigen vier, die vier Übrigen; **I have only one ~** ich habe nur noch einen/eine/eins (übrig)

remains [rɪˈmeɪnz] PL (*of meal*) Reste *pl*; (*of fortune, army*) Rest *m*; (*of building*) Überreste *pl*; (= *archaeological remains*) Ruinen *pl*; **his (mortal) ~** seine sterblichen Überreste; **human ~** menschliche Überreste *pl*

remake [riːˈmeɪk] *vb: pret, ptp* **remade** [riːˈmeɪd] **VT** wieder or nochmals machen; (*in new form*) neu machen; **to ~ a film** ein Thema neu verfil-

men **N** [ˈriːmeɪk] (*Film*) Neuverfilmung *f*, Remake *nt* (*spec*)

remand [rɪˈmɑːnd] **VT** (*Jur*) *case* vertagen; **to ~ sb (in custody/on bail)** jdn weiterhin in Untersuchungshaft behalten/unter Kaution halten; **to ~ sb to a higher court** jdn an eine höhere Instanz verweisen; **he was ~ed in custody/on bail** er blieb in Untersuchungshaft/unter Kaution; **the man ~ed in custody** der Untersuchungsgefangene **N** (*of person*) Aufrechterhaltung *f* der Untersuchungshaft/der Erhebung von Kaution (*of* gegen); (*form, of case*) Vertagung *f*; **to be on ~** in Untersuchungshaft sein; (= *on bail*) auf Kaution freigelassen sein

remand centre, remand home **N** (*Brit*) Untersuchungsgefängnis *nt* für Jugendliche

remand wing **N** Flügel *m* or Trakt *m* für Untersuchungsgefangene

remark [rɪˈmɑːk] **N a** (= *comment*) Bemerkung *f*; **I have a few ~s to make on that subject** ich habe einiges/nichts zu diesem Thema zu sagen; **to make** or **pass unkind ~s about sb/sth** abfällige Bemerkungen über jdn/etw machen; **~s were made** or **passed about our absence** man redete über unsere Abwesenheit **b** *no pl* (= *notice*) **worthy of ~** bemerkenswert; **without ~** unbemerkt **VT a** (= *say*) bemerken **b** (*old, liter, = notice*) bemerken, wahrnehmen **VI to ~ (up)on sth** über etw (*acc*) eine Bemerkung machen, sich zu etw äußern; **nobody ~ed on it** niemand hat etwas dazu gesagt; **everybody ~ed on it** alle haben ihre Bemerkungen dazu gemacht

remarkable [rɪˈmɑːkəbl] **ADJ** (= *notable*) bemerkenswert; *intelligence, talent, wit also* beachtlich; (= *extraordinary*) außergewöhnlich; (= *amazing*) *escape* wundersam; **to be ~ for sth** sich durch etw auszeichnen

remarkably [rɪˈmɑːkəbli] **ADV a** (= *notably*) bemerkenswert; (= *extraordinarily*) außergewöhnlich; **~ similar** bemerkenswert ähnlich; **a type of latex ~ similar to rubber** eine Latexart mit bemerkenswert ähnlichen Eigenschaften wie Gummi; **he looked ~ like his father** er sah seinem Vater bemerkenswert ähnlich; **~ little** erstaunlich wenig **b** (= *amazingly*) bemerkenswerterweise; **the factory had, ~, escaped the bombing** die Fabrik war wundersamerweise or wie durch ein Wunder dem Bombenangriff entkommen

remarriage [riːˈmærɪdʒ] **N** Wiederverheiratung *f* (*to* mit)

remarry [riːˈmæri] **VI** wieder heiraten

remediable [rɪˈmiːdɪəbl] **ADJ** *situation* rettbar; *fault, defect* behebbar

remedial [rɪˈmiːdɪəl] **ADJ** *attr* Hilfs-; (*Med*) Heil-; **~ action/measures** Hilfsmaßnahmen *pl*; **~ exercises** Heilgymnastik *f*; **~ treatment** (*Med*) Heilbehandlung *f*; **to teach ~ English/reading** einen Förderkurs in Englisch/im Lesen leiten; **~ education** fördernde Erziehung (*für lernschwache Schüler*); **~ teaching** Förder- or Hilfsunterricht *m*; **~ work** (*Sch*) Förderaufgaben *pl*; **~ class** Förderklasse *f*; **~ course** Förderkurs *m*; **she no longer needs ~ help** (*with learning*) sie benötigt keinen Förderunterricht mehr

remedy [ˈremədi] **N** (*Med, fig*) Mittel *nt* (*for* gegen); (= *medication*) Heilmittel *nt* (*for* gegen); (*Jur*) Rechtsmittel *nt*; **the situation is past** or **beyond ~** die Lage ist hoffnungslos verloren or irreparabel; **unless we can find a ~** wenn wir keinen Ausweg or keine Lösung finden **VT** (*Med*) heilen; (*fig*) *defect, fault, deficiency, problem* beheben; *situation* bessern; *abuse, evil* abhelfen (+*dat*); **his faults cannot be remedied** man kann ihn nicht von seinen Fehlern heilen; **the situation cannot be remedied** die Lage ist hoffnungslos

remember [rɪˈmembə] ⊙ 21.2, 26.1, 26.2 **VT a** (= *recall*) sich erinnern an (+*acc*); (= *bear in mind*) denken an (+*acc*); (= *learn*) *formula, facts, vocabulary* sich (*dat*) merken; **I ~ that he was very tall** ich erinnere mich (daran), dass er

sehr groß war; **I ~ her as a beautiful girl** ich habe sie als schönes Mädchen in Erinnerung; **I ~ her as a young girl** or **when she was young** ich erinnere mich noch, wie sie als kleines Mädchen war; **we must ~ that he's only a child** wir sollten bedenken or daran denken, dass er noch ein Kind ist; **to ~ to do sth** daran denken, etw zu tun; **I ~ doing it** ich erinnere mich daran, dass ich es getan habe; **I can't ~ the word at the moment** das Wort fällt mir im Moment nicht ein; **I've just ~ed his name** mir ist gerade sein Name wieder eingefallen; **don't you ~ me?** erinnern Sie sich nicht an mich?; **here's something to ~ me by** da hast du etwas, das dich (immer) an mich erinnern wird; **do you ~ when ...?** (reminiscing) weißt du noch, als ...?; (asking facts) weißt du (noch), wann ...?; **I don't ~ a thing about it** ich kann mich überhaupt nicht daran erinnern; (about lecture, book) ich weiß nichts mehr davon; **I can never ~ phone numbers** ich kann mir Telefonnummern einfach nicht merken; **we can't always ~ everything** wir können nicht immer an alles denken; **~ where/who you are!** denken Sie daran or bedenken Sie, wo/wer Sie sind!; **to ~ sb in one's prayers** jdn in sein Gebet einschließen; **to ~ sb in one's will** jdn in seinem Testament bedenken; **a night to ~** ein unvergesslicher Abend; **an occasion to ~** ein denkwürdiger Anlass **b** (= commemorate) the fallen, a battle gedenken (+gen)
c (Brit: = give good wishes to) **~ me to your mother** grüßen Sie Ihre Mutter von mir; **he asks to be ~ed to you** er lässt Sie grüßen
VI sich erinnern; **I can't ~** ich weiß das nicht mehr, ich habs vergessen; **not as far as I ~** soweit ich mich erinnere, nicht!; **if I ~ right(ly)** wenn ich mich recht erinnere or entsinne

remembrance [rɪ'membrəns] N **a** Erinnerung f (of an +acc); **in ~ of** zur Erinnerung an (+acc); **I have no ~ of that** ich habe keinerlei Erinnerung daran **b** (= keepsake) Andenken nt (of an +acc) **c** **remembrances** PL (old, form, = greetings) Empfehlungen pl

Remembrance Day N (Brit) ≈ Volkstrauertag m

remembrance service N Gedenkgottesdienst m

remigration [ˌriːmaɪˈɡreɪʃən] N Rückwanderung f, Rückkehr f

remind [rɪ'maɪnd] VT erinnern (of an +acc); **you are ~ed that ...** wir weisen darauf hin, dass ...; **to ~ sb to do sth** jdn daran erinnern, etw zu tun; **that ~s me!** da(bei) fällt mir was ein

reminder [rɪ'maɪndə'] N (= note, knot etc) Gedächtnisstütze f; **(letter of) ~** (Comm) Mahnung f; **as a ~ that ...** um dich/ihn etc daran zu erinnern, dass ...; **to give sb a ~ to do sth** jdn daran erinnern, etw zu tun; **his presence was a ~ of ...** seine Gegenwart erinnerte mich/dich etc an (+acc) ...; **a gentle ~** ein zarter Wink; **give him a gentle ~** weis ihn sachte darauf hin

remindful [rɪ'maɪndfʊl] ADJ (geh) erinnernd (of an +acc); **to be ~ of** sich erinnern an +acc

reminisce [ˌremɪ'nɪs] VI sich in Erinnerungen ergehen (about über +acc)

reminiscence [ˌremɪ'nɪsəns] N (= action) Zurückgehen nt (of zu); (= thought) Reminiszenz f, Erinnerung f (of an +acc)

reminiscent [ˌremɪ'nɪsənt] ○ 5.1 ADJ **a** **to be ~ of sth** an etw (acc) erinnern; **a style ~ of Shakespeare** ein an Shakespeare erinnernder Stil **b** (= reminiscing) person in Erinnerungen versunken or vertieft; smile erinnernd; style, chapter nostalgisch; **to be feeling ~, to be in a ~ mood** in nostalgischer Stimmung sein; **we listened to him speaking, quietly ~** tief in Erinnerungen versunken, hörten wir ihm zu

reminiscently [ˌremɪ'nɪsəntlɪ] ADV smile, sigh etc in der Erinnerung; **he talked ~ of the war** er erzählte von seinen Kriegserinnerungen

remiss [rɪ'mɪs] ADJ nachlässig; **he has been ~ in not doing it** es war nachlässig von ihm, das zu unterlassen

remissible [rɪ'mɪsɪbl] ADJ erlässlich, verzeihlich; (Rel) sin lässlich

remission [rɪ'mɪʃən] N (form) **a** (= cancelling, pardoning: of debt) Erlassen nt; (Brit Jur) (Straf-)Erlass m; (Rel) Nachlass m; **he got 3 years' ~ for good behaviour** (Brit) ihm wurden wegen guter Führung 3 Jahre erlassen **b** (= sending: of money) Überweisung f **c** (= postponement) Verschiebung f, Vertagung f; (of motion) Zurückverweisung f **d** (Jur: = transfer: of case) Verweisung f **e** (= becoming less) Nachlassen nt; (Med) Besserung f, Remission f (spec); **to be in ~** (patient) sich auf dem Wege der Besserung befinden; (illness) abklingen

remissness [rɪ'mɪsnɪs] N Nachlässigkeit f

remit¹ [rɪ'mɪt] (form) **VT** **a** (= cancel, pardon) debt, sentence, sins erlassen **b** (= send) money überweisen **c** (= postpone) verschieben, vertagen (to auf +acc, till bis); motion zurückverweisen **d** (Jur, = transfer) case verweisen (to an +acc) **VI** (= become less) nachlassen

remit² ['riːmɪt] N (form) Aufgabe f, Auftrag m; **that is outside our ~** das liegt außerhalb unseres Aufgabenbereiches

remittal [rɪ'mɪtl] N = remission b-d

remittance [rɪ'mɪtəns] N Überweisung f (to an +acc)

remittance advice N Überweisungsbescheid m

remittee [rɪmɪ'tiː] N (Comm) Überweisungsempfänger(in) m(f)

remittent [rɪ'mɪtənt] ADJ (Med) symptoms remittierend (spec); **~ fever** Wechselfieber nt

remitter [rɪ'mɪtə'] N (= sender) Überweiser(in) m(f)

remix ['riːmɪks] N (= record) Remix m

remnant ['remnənt] N Rest m; (fig, of splendour, custom) Überrest m; **the ~ of his fortune/~s of his former glory** was von seinem Vermögen/Ruhm übrig geblieben war

remnant day N (Comm) Resteverkaufstag m

remnant sale N (Comm) Resteausverkauf m

remodel [ˌriː'mɒdl] VT (also Art, Tech) umformen; nose richten; (fig) house, party, public services, society, constitution umgestalten

remold [ˌriː'məʊld] VT (US) = remould

remonstrance [rɪ'mɒnstrəns] N Protest m (with bei)

remonstrant [rɪ'mɒnstrənt] ADJ protestierend

remonstrate ['remənstreɪt] VI protestieren (against gegen); **to ~ with sb (about sth)** jdm Vorhaltungen (wegen etw) machen

remonstration [ˌremən'streɪʃən] N Protest m (against gegen)

remorse [rɪ'mɔːs] N Reue f (at, over über +acc); **he is completely without ~** er zeigt überhaupt keine Reue; **without ~** (= merciless) erbarmungslos

remorseful [rɪ'mɔːsfʊl] ADJ reumütig, reuig; **to feel ~** Reue spüren

remorsefully [rɪ'mɔːsfəlɪ] ADV reumütig, reuig

remorsefulness [rɪ'mɔːsfʊlnɪs] N Reue f; (of person also) Reumütigkeit f

remorseless [rɪ'mɔːslɪs] ADJ reu(e)los, ohne Reue; (fig, = merciless) unbarmherzig, erbarmungslos

remorselessly [rɪ'mɔːslɪslɪ] ADV reu(e)los, ohne Reue; (fig, = mercilessly) erbarmungslos, unbarmherzig, unerbittlich

remorselessness [rɪ'mɔːslɪsnɪs] N Reu(e)losigkeit f; (fig, = mercilessness) Unbarmherzigkeit f

remote [rɪ'məʊt] ADJ (+er) **a** (in place, = distant) entfernt, fern (geh) attr; (= isolated) entlegen, abgelegen; (Comput) rechnerfern; **in the ~st parts of Africa** in den abgelegensten Teilen Afrikas; **in a ~ spot** an einer entlegenen or abgelegenen Stelle; **a village ~ from the world** ein von der Welt abgeschiedenes Dorf
b (in time) past, future fern; **~ antiquity** die früheste Antike; **a ~ ancestor** (= man) ein Urahn m; (= woman) eine Urahne

c (= distanced, removed) relative, descendant, connection, relevance etc entfernt; **the government's statements seem ~ from the needs of the people** die Aussagen der Regierung scheinen weit von den Bedürfnissen der Bürger entfernt zu sein; **the union leaders have to beware of getting too ~ from their members** die Gewerkschaftsführer müssen aufpassen, sich nicht zu weit von der Basis zu entfernen
d (= aloof) unnahbar, unzugänglich
e (= slight) possibility, resemblance, risk entfernt; chance gering, winzig; **I haven't the ~st idea** ich habe nicht die leiseste Idee; **it could happen, although the odds are ~** das könnte passieren, obwohl es sehr unwahrscheinlich ist
f (= remote-controlled) handset zur Fernbedienung
N (Rad, TV: = remote control) Fernbedienung f

remote: remote access N (Telec, Comput) Fernzugriff m; **remote control** N Fernsteuerung f, Fernlenkung f; (Rad, TV) Fernbedienung f; **remote-control** ADJ device zur Fernbedienung; TV set mit Fernbedienung; **~ system** Fernbedienungssystem nt; **remote-controlled** ADJ model aeroplane etc ferngesteuert, ferngelenkt; gates fernbedient; **remote data entry** N (Comput) Datenfernverarbeitung f

remotely [rɪ'məʊtlɪ] ADV **a** (= vaguely) **to be ~ connected with sb/sth** entfernt mit jdm/etw zu tun haben; **it's just ~ possible** es ist gerade eben noch möglich; **if it's ~ possible** wenn es auch nur irgend möglich ist; **they're not even ~ similar** sie sind sich nicht im Entferntesten ähnlich; **he didn't say anything ~ interesting** er sagte nichts, was im Entferntesten interessant war; **avoid saying anything ~ likely to upset him** sag nichts, dass ihn im Geringsten aufregen könnte; **I've never seen anything ~ like it** ich habe noch nie irgendetwas Vergleichbares gesehen; **I'm not ~ interested in it/her** ich bin nicht im Geringsten daran/an ihr interessiert
b (= distantly) situated, related entfernt
c (= by remote control) **to ~ control/detonate sth** etw fernsteuern/fernzünden
d (= aloofly) say kühl, abweisend

remoteness [rɪ'məʊtnɪs] N **a** (in place, = distance) Ferne f; (= isolation) Abgelegenheit f **b** (in time) (weite) Ferne f **c** (= being distanced, removed: of connection, relevance etc) Entferntheit f; **the government's ~ from the people** die Bürgerferne der Regierung; **the government's ~ from the people's needs** die Unwissenheit der Regierung um die Bedürfnisse der Bürger; **his ~ from everyday life** seine Lebensfremdheit **d** (= aloofness) Unnahbarkeit f, Unzugänglichkeit f **e** (= slightness, of possibility, resemblance, risk) Entferntheit f; (of chance) Winzigkeit f

remote: remote pick-up N (Comput) Fernabfrage f (von Daten); **remote sensing** N Fernerkundung f; **~ satellite** Fernerkundungssatellit m, Radarsatellit m

remould, (US) **remold** [ˌriː'məʊld] VT **a** (Tech) tyre runderneuern **b** (fig) society umgestalten; team also ummodeln (inf) **N** ['riːməʊld] (= tyre) runderneuerter Reifen

remount [ˌriː'maʊnt] VT **a** horse, bicycle wieder besteigen; ladder wieder hinaufsteigen or -klettern **b** picture, photo wieder aufziehen **VI** wieder aufsitzen

removable [rɪ'muːvəbl] ADJ cover, attachment abnehmbar; trimming abtrennbar; lining abknöpfbar; stain entfernbar; (from container) herausnehmbar

removal [rɪ'muːvəl] N **a** (= taking off, taking away etc) (of cover, lid, attachments) Abnahme f, Entfernung f; (of splint, bandage, tie) Abnahme f; (of clothes) Ausziehen nt; (of stain) Entfernung f, Beseitigung f; (of buttons, trimmings) Abtrennung f; (of troops) Abzug m; **his ~ to hospital** seine Einlieferung ins Krankenhaus
b (= taking out, from container) Herausnehmen nt; (Med: of lung, kidney) Entfernung f; (of paragraph, word, item on list) Streichen nt; (Tech) Ausbau m

c (= *eradication, of threat, abuse, evil, difficulty, problem*) Beseitigung *f*; (*of tax, restrictions*) Aufhebung *f*; (*of objection, obstacle*) Ausräumung *f*; (*of doubt, suspicion, fear*) Zerstreuung *f*; (*euph, = killing*) Beseitigung *f*
d (*form*) (= *dismissal: of official*) Entfernung *f*
e (*Brit: = move from house*) Umzug *m*; **our ~ to this house/to York** unser Umzug in dieses Haus/nach York; **"Brown & Son, ~s"** „Spedition Brown & Sohn", „Brown & Sohn, Umzüge"

removal (*Brit*): **removal allowance** N Umzugsbeihilfe *f*; **removal expenses** PL Umzugskosten *pl*; **removal firm** N Spedition *f*; **removal man** N Möbelpacker *m*; **removal van** N Möbelwagen *m*

remove [rɪˈmuːv] **VT** **a** (= *take off, take away etc*) entfernen; *cover, lid, attachments* abnehmen, entfernen; *splint, bandage, tie* abnehmen; *clothes* ausziehen; *stain* entfernen, beseitigen; *buttons, trimmings* abtrennen; *lining* abknöpfen; *troops* abziehen; *weapons* abnehmen (*from* +*dat*); **to ~ sth from sb** jdm etw wegnehmen; **to ~ one's clothes** die Kleider ablegen; **to ~ sb to hospital** jdn ins Krankenhaus einliefern; **to ~ sb to the cells** jdn in die Zelle bringen; **to ~ a child from school** ein Kind von or aus der Schule nehmen; **he ~d himself to another room** er begab sich in ein anderes Zimmer
b (= *take out, from container*) herausnehmen (*from* aus); (*Med*) *lung, kidney* entfernen (*from* aus); *paragraph, word, item on list* streichen; (*Tech*) ausbauen (*from* aus)
c (= *eradicate*) *threat* beseitigen; *tax, restrictions* aufheben; *objection, obstacle* aus dem Weg schaffen or räumen; *difficulty, problem* beseitigen, ein Ende machen or setzen (+*dat*); *doubt, suspicion, fear* zerstreuen; *abuse, evil* abstellen, beseitigen; (*euph, = kill*) beseitigen; **to ~ all obstacles from one's path** (*fig*) alle Hindernisse aus dem Weg räumen
d (*form, = dismiss*) *official* entfernen
e (*form, to another house*) transportieren
f **to be far ~d from ...** weit entfernt sein von ...; **a cousin once/twice ~d** ein Cousin *m* im ersten/zweiten Grades; **I'm related to him, but several times ~d** (*inf*) ich bin mit ihm verwandt, aber um ein paar Ecken herum (*inf*)
VI (*form, = move house*) **to ~ to London/to larger premises** nach London/in größere Geschäftsräume (um)ziehen
N **a** **to be only a short ~ from ...** nicht weit entfernt sein von ...; **this is but one ~ from disaster** das kommt einer Katastrophe nahe; **it's a far ~ from ...** es ist weit entfernt von ...
b (*Brit, Sch*) Klasse *f* für lernschwache Schüler

remover [rɪˈmuːvə'] N **a** (*for nail varnish, stains etc*) Entferner *m* **b** (*Brit: = removal man*) Möbelpacker *m*

remunerate [rɪˈmjuːnəreɪt] VT (= *pay*) bezahlen, vergüten; (= *reward*) belohnen

remuneration [rɪˌmjuːnəˈreɪʃən] N Bezahlung *f*, Vergütung *f*; (= *reward*) Belohnung *f*

remunerative [rɪˈmjuːnərətɪv] ADJ lohnend, einträglich

renaissance [rɪˈneɪsɑ̃ːs] N (*liter*) Wiedergeburt *f*; (*of nature*) Wiedererwachen *nt*; **the Renaissance** (*Hist*) die Renaissance; **Renaissance man** der Renaissancemensch; (*fig*) der Humanist; (= *all-rounder*) Allroundtalent *nt*

renal [ˈriːnl] ADJ Nieren-, renal (*spec*); **~ failure** Nierenversagen *nt*

rename [ˌriːˈneɪm] VT umbenennen (*also Comput*), umtaufen; **Leningrad was ~d St Petersburg** Leningrad wurde in St. Petersburg umbenannt

renascence [rɪˈnæsns] N = **renaissance**

renascent [rɪˈnæsnt] ADJ (*liter*) wieder erwachend

rend [rend] pret, ptp **rent** VT (*liter*) *cloth* zerreißen; *armour* aufreißen; **to ~ sth from sb/sth** jdm/einer Sache etw entreißen; **a country rent by civil war** ein vom Bürgerkrieg zerrissenes Land; **a cry rent the air** ein Schrei drang durch

die Luft; **to ~ sb's heart** jdm das Herz zerreißen

render [ˈrendə'] VT **a** (*form, = give*) *service, help* leisten; *judgement, explanation* abgeben; *homage* erweisen; *decision, verdict* fällen; **~ unto Caesar the things which are Caesar's** (*Bibl, prov*) gebet dem Kaiser, was des Kaisers ist (*Bibl*); **to ~ thanks to sb/God** jdm/Gott Dank sagen or abstatten; **to ~ assistance** Hilfe leisten; **to ~ an account of one's expenditure** Rechenschaft über seine Ausgaben ablegen
b (*Comm*) **to ~ account** Rechnung legen or vorlegen; **(to) account ~ed £10** £ 10 laut früherer Rechnung
c (= *interpret, translate*) wiedergeben; (*in writing*) übertragen; *music, poem* vortragen
d (*form, = make*) machen; **his accident ~ed him helpless** das Unfall hat ihn hilflos gemacht
e (*also* **render down**) *fat* auslassen
f (*Build*) verputzen

▶ **render up** VT *sep fortress, prisoner* übergeben

rendering [ˈrendərɪŋ] N **a** Wiedergabe *f*; (*in writing*) Übertragung *f*; (*of piece of music, poem*) Vortrag *m* **b** (*esp Brit, Build*) Putz *m*

rendezvous [ˈrɒndɪvuː] **N** (= *place*) Treffpunkt *m*; (= *agreement to meet*) Rendezvous *nt* **VI** sich treffen (*with* mit)

rendition [renˈdɪʃən] N (*form*) = **rendering a**

renegade [ˈrenɪɡeɪd] **N** Renegat(in) *m(f)*, Abtrünnige(r) *mf* ADJ abtrünnig

renege [rɪˈniːɡ] VI nicht Wort halten; (*Cards*) nicht bedienen; **to ~ on a promise/an agreement** ein Versprechen/eine Übereinkunft brechen

renew [rɪˈnjuː] VT erneuern; *contract, passport etc* (*authority also*) verlängern; (*holder*) erneuern or verlängern lassen; *negotiations, discussions, diplomatic relations, attack, attempts* wieder aufnehmen; *one's strength* wieder herstellen; *fears* wieder wachrufen; *interest* wieder wecken; *supplies* auffrischen; **to ~ a library book** ein Buch verlängern lassen

renewable [rɪˈnjuːəbl] ADJ *contract, licence etc* erneuerbar, verlängerbar; *passport, bill of exchange* verlängerbar; *energy, resource* erneuerbar; (= *must be renewed*) zu erneuern/verlängern; **some library books are not ~** einige Bibliotheksbücher können nicht verlängert werden **N** **renewables** PL erneuerbare Energiequellen *pl*

renewal [rɪˈnjuːəl] N Erneuerung *f*; (*of contract, passport etc also*) Verlängerung *f*; (*of negotiations, discussions, diplomatic relations, attack, attempts*) Wiederaufnahme *f*; (*of interest*) Wiedererwachen *nt*; (*of one's strength*) Wiederherstellung *f*; (*of supplies*) Auffrischung *f*; **spiritual ~** geistige Erneuerung

renewed [rɪˈnjuːd] ADJ (= *new*) *fighting* erneut; *interest* erneut, neu; *pressure* erneut, wiederholt; **~ hope** neue Hoffnungen *pl*; **with ~ vigour** (*Brit*) or **vigor** (*US*) mit neuer Energie; **with ~ enthusiasm** mit neuem Schwung; **~ efforts** neue Anstrengungen *pl*; **~ strength** frische Kraft; **~ courage** frischer Mut; **~ outbreaks of rioting** erneute Krawalle *pl*; **to feel spiritually ~** sich wie ein neuer Mensch fühlen; **to make ~ efforts to do sth** erneute Anstrengungen unternehmen, etw zu tun

rennet [ˈrenɪt] N (*Cook*) Lab *nt*

renounce [rɪˈnaʊns] VT *title, right, violence* verzichten auf (+*acc*); *aufgeben*; *terrorism, religion, devil, faith* abschwören (+*dat*); (*Rel*) *world* entsagen (+*dat*); *opinions, cause, treaty* leugnen, abschwören (+*dat*); *friend* verleugnen; **to ~ the throne** auf den Thron verzichten **VI** (*Cards*) renoncieren

renouncement [rɪˈnaʊnsmənt] N = **renunciation**

renovate [ˈrenəʊveɪt] VT *building* renovieren; *painting, furniture* restaurieren

renovation [ˌrenəʊˈveɪʃən] N (*of building*) Renovierung *f*, Renovation *f*; (*of painting, furniture*) Restaurierung *f*

renown [rɪˈnaʊn] N guter Ruf, Ansehen *nt*; **of great ~** von hohem Ansehen, sehr berühmt; **a wine of ~** ein renommierter Wein

renowned [rɪˈnaʊnd] ADJ berühmt (*for* für)

rent[1] [rent] **N** (*for house, room*) Miete *f*; (*for farm, factory*) Pacht *f*; **for ~** (*US*) zu vermieten/verpachten/verleihen **VT** *house, room* mieten; *farm, factory* pachten; *TV, car etc* leihen; *video* sich (*dat*) ausleihen, ausleihen; **we don't own it, we only ~ it** es gehört uns (*dat*) nicht, wir haben es nur gemietet etc **b** (*also* **rent out**) *house, room* mieten; (= *rent farm, factory*) pachten; (= *rent TV etc*) leasen; (= *rent video*) ausleihen

rent[2] pret, ptp of **rend** N (*lit, fig*) Riss *m*; (*in rock*) Spalte *f*

rent-a-car N (*esp US*) **a** (*also* **rent-a-car company** or **service**) Autoverleih *m* **b** (= *hired car*) Leih- or Mietwagen *m*

rental [ˈrentl] N (= *amount paid, for house*) Miete *f*; (*for TV, car, boat etc also, video*) Leihgebühr *f*; (*for land*) Pacht *f*; (= *income from rents*) Miet-/Pacht-/Leihgebühreinnahmen *pl*; **~ car** Mietwagen *m*; **~ library** (*US*) Leihbücherei *f*

rent: rent boy N (*Brit inf*) Strichjunge *m* (*inf*), Stricher *m* (*inf*); **rent collector** N Mietkassierer(in) *m(f)*; **rent control** N Mietkontrolle *f*, Mieterschutz *m*; **rent-controlled** ADJ bewirtschaftet (*form*), mit gebundener Miete; **rent-free** ADJ ADV mietfrei; **rent man** N (*inf*) = **rent collector**; **rent rebate** N Mietrückzahlung *f*; (= *reduction*) Mietnachlass *m* or -ermäßigung *f*; **rent review** N Neufestsetzung *f* der Miete; **rent strike** N Mietstreik *m*; **to go on ~, to stage a ~** in den Mietstreik treten; **rent tribunal** N Mieterschiedsgericht *nt*

renumber [ˌriːˈnʌmbə'] VT umnummerieren

renunciation [rɪˌnʌnsɪˈeɪʃən] N (*of title, right, violence*) Verzicht *m* (*of* auf +*acc*), Aufgabe *f*; (*of terrorism*) Aufgabe *f*; (*of religion, devil, faith*) Abschwören *nt*; (*Rel: of world*) Entsagung *f*; (*of opinion, cause, treaty*) Leugnung *f*; (*of friend*) Verleugnung *f*

reoccupy [ˌriːˈɒkjʊpaɪ] VT *post, position* wieder innehaben or bekleiden; *house, hotel room etc* wieder belegen

reoffend [ˌriːəˈfend] VI erneut straffällig werden

reopen [ˌriːˈəʊpən] VT wieder öffnen, wieder aufmachen; *school, shop, theatre, fight, hostilities* wieder eröffnen; *debate, discussion, negotiations* wieder aufnehmen; (*Jur*) *case* wieder aufrollen, wieder aufnehmen **VI** wieder aufgehen; (*shop, theatre etc*) wieder eröffnen or aufmachen; (*school after holidays, negotiations*) wieder beginnen; (*case*) wieder aufgerollt werden; (*wound*) wieder aufgehen

reopening [ˌriːˈəʊpnɪŋ] N (*of shop etc*) Wiedereröffnung *f*; (*of school after holiday*) Wiederbeginn *m*; (*of negotiations, debate, case*) Wiederaufnahme *f*; **the ~ of old wounds** (*fig*) das Aufreißen alter Wunden

reorder [ˌriːˈɔːdə'] VT **a** *goods, supplies* nachbestellen; (*because first order is lost etc*) neu bestellen **b** (= *reorganize*) neu ordnen, umordnen; *books, people in a row* umstellen; *appointments* umlegen **VI** (= *reorder goods, supplies*) nachbestellen; (*because first order is lost etc*) neu bestellen

reorganization [riːˌɔːɡənaɪˈzeɪʃən] N Neu- or Umorganisation *f*; (*of furniture, books*) Umordnung *f*; (*of work, time*) Neueinteilung *f*; (*of essay*) Neuaufbau *m*; (*of one's life*) Neueinteilung *f*, Umorientierung *f*

reorganize [ˌriːˈɔːɡənaɪz] VT neu organisieren, umorganisieren; *furniture, books* umordnen; *work, time* neu einteilen; *essay* neu aufbauen; **to ~ one's life** sich (*dat*) sein Leben anders einteilen, sein Leben umorientieren **VI** (*Pol*) sich neu organisieren

Rep **a** *abbr of* **Republic** Rep. **b** *abbr of* **Republican** Rep., rep.

rep¹ [rep] **N** **a** *(Theat)* abbr of **repertory** Repertoire-Theater *nt* **b** *(Comm)* abbr of **representative** Vertreter(in) *m(f)* **VI** als Vertreter(in) arbeiten

rep² N *(Tex)* Rips *m*

repaid [ˌriːˈpeɪd] pret, ptp of **repay**

repaint [ˌriːˈpeɪnt] VT neu streichen

repair¹ [rɪˈpɛəʳ] **VT** *(lit, fig)* reparieren; *tyre also, clothes* flicken; *roof, wall also, road* ausbessern; *(fig) error, wrong, damage* wieder gutmachen; *image, relations* wieder herstellen
N **a** *(lit)* Reparatur *f*; *(of tyre also, clothes)* Flicken *nt*; *(of roof, wall also, road)* Ausbesserung *f*; *(fig: of relationship)* Kitten *nt*; **to be under ~** *(car, ship, machine)* in Reparatur sein; **to put sth in for ~** etw zur Reparatur bringen; **the road is under ~** an der Straße wird gerade gearbeitet; **beyond ~** nicht mehr zu reparieren/zu flicken/auszubessern; **damaged beyond ~** irreparabel, nicht mehr zu reparieren; **closed for ~s** wegen Reparaturarbeiten geschlossen; **"road ~s"** „Straßenbauarbeiten"; **"repairs while you wait"** „Sofortdienst", „Sofortreparaturen"
b *no pl (= condition)* **to be in good/bad ~** in gutem/schlechtem Zustand sein

repair² VI *(liter, = go)* sich begeben *(to nach)*

repairable [rɪˈpɛərəbl] ADJ *(lit, fig)* zu reparieren, reparabel; *tyre also, clothes* zu flicken; *roof, wall also, road* auszubessern *pred*; **is that ~?** lässt sich das reparieren/flicken?

repairer [rɪˈpɛərəʳ] N **watch/shoe ~** Uhr-/Schuhmacher(in) *m(f)*

repair: repair kit N Flickzeug *nt*; **repairman** N *(in house)* Handwerker *m*; **repair shop** N Reparaturwerkstatt *m*

repaper [ˌriːˈpeɪpəʳ] VT neu tapezieren

reparable [ˈrepərəbl] ADJ *damage* reparabel, wieder gutzumachen; *loss* ersetzbar

reparation [ˌrepəˈreɪʃən] N *(for damage)* Entschädigung *f*; *(usu pl: after war)* Reparationen *pl*; *(for wrong, misdeed)* Wiedergutmachung *f*; **to make ~ for sth** etw wieder gutmachen

reparative [rɪˈpærətɪv], **reparatory** [rɪˈpærətərɪ] ADJ *payments etc* wieder gutmachend, Entschädigungs-

repartee [ˌrepɑːˈtiː] N Schlagabtausch *m*; *(= retort)* schlagfertige Antwort; **to be good at ~** schlagfertig sein; **renowned for his ~** bekannt für seine Schlagfertigkeit

repartition [ˌriːpɑːˈtɪʃən] **N** **a** *(= distribution, partition)* Auf- or Verteilung *f* **b** *(= new distribution)* Neuverteilung *f* **VT** (neu) verteilen, aufteilen

repast [rɪˈpɑːst] N *(liter)* Mahl *nt (geh)*

repatriate [ˌriːˈpætrɪeɪt] **VT** in das Heimatland zurücksenden, repatriieren **N** [ˌriːˈpætrɪɪt] Repatriierte(r) *mf*

repatriation [ˈriːˌpætrɪˈeɪʃən] N Repatriierung *f*

repay [ˌriːˈpeɪ] pret, ptp **repaid** VT *money* zurückzahlen; *expenses* erstatten; *debt* abzahlen; *kindness* vergelten; *visit, compliment* erwidern; **if you lend me £2 I'll ~ it** or **you on Saturday** leih mir doch mal 2 Pfund, ich zahle sie dir am Samstag zurück; **I shall ~ my debt to you one day** *(fig)* ich werde es dir eines Tages vergelten or lohnen; **to ~ sb for his generosity** sich für jds Großzügigkeit revanchieren; **he repaid their kindness by stealing their camera** zum Dank für ihre Freundlichkeit hat er ihnen die Kamera gestohlen; **to be repaid for one's efforts** für seine Mühen belohnt werden; **how can I ever ~ you?** wie kann ich das jemals wieder gutmachen?; **she wants to ~ his faith in her** sie möchte das Vertrauen, das er in sie gesetzt hat, rechtfertigen

repayable [ˌriːˈpeɪəbl] ADJ rückzahlbar

repayment [ˌriːˈpeɪmənt] N *(of money)* Rückzahlung *f*; *(of effort, kindness)* Lohn *m*; **~s can be spread over 3 years** die Rückzahlung kann über 3 Jahre verteilt werden; **in ~** als Rückzahlung/Lohn

repayment mortgage N Tilgungshypothek *f*

repeal [rɪˈpiːl] **VT** *law* aufheben **N** Aufhebung *f*

repeat [rɪˈpiːt] ❂ 27.3 **VT** wiederholen; *(= tell to sb else)* weitersagen *(to sb jdm)*; **to ~ oneself** sich wiederholen; **he wasn't keen to ~ the experience** er war nicht darauf aus, die Erfahrung noch einmal zu machen; **he ~ed his lesson to the teacher** er sagte seine Lektion vor dem Lehrer auf; **to ~ an order** *(Comm)* nachbestellen; **this offer will never be ~ed!** dies ist ein einmaliges Angebot!
VI **a** *(= say again)* wiederholen; **~ after me** sprecht mir nach
b *(Mus)* wiederholen; **~!** *(conductor)* noch einmal!
c **radishes ~ on me** Radieschen stoßen mir auf
d *(gun, clock etc)* repetieren
e *(Math)* periodisch sein
N **a** *(Rad, TV)* Wiederholung *f*
b *(Mus, = section repeated)* Wiederholung *f*; *(= repeat sign)* Wiederholungszeichen *nt*
ADJ **~ business** Nachfolgeaufträge *pl*; **~ customer** Kunde, der/Kundin, die wiederkommt; *(= regular customer)* Stammkunde *m*, Stammkundin *f*

repeated ADJ , **repeatedly** ADV [rɪˈpiːtɪd, -lɪ] wiederholt

repeater [rɪˈpiːtəʳ] N *(= gun)* Repetier- or Mehrladegewehr *nt*; *(= watch)* Repetieruhr *f*

repeat function N *(Comput)* Wiederholungsfunktion *f*

repeating [rɪˈpiːtɪŋ] ADJ *(Math)* = **recurring b**

repeat: repeat mark N *(Mus)* Wiederholungszeichen *nt*; **repeat offender** N *(Jur)* Wiederholungstäter(in) *m(f)*; **repeat order** N *(Comm)* Nachbestellung *f*; **repeat performance** N *(Theat)* Wiederholungsvorstellung *f*; **he gave a ~** *(fig)* er machte es noch einmal; *(pej)* er machte noch einmal das gleiche Theater *(inf)*; **repeat prescription** N *(Med)* erneut verschriebenes Rezept, Folgerezept *nt*; **repeat sign** N *(Mus)* Wiederholungszeichen *nt*

repel [rɪˈpel] **VT** **a** *enemy, attack* zurückschlagen; *sb's advances, insects, flies* abwehren; *water* abstoßen **b** *(= disgust)* abstoßen **VI** *(= disgust)* abstoßen

repellent [rɪˈpelənt] **ADJ** **a** **~ to water** Wasser abstoßend **b** *(= disgusting)* abstoßend; *sight* widerlich, abstoßend; *smell* Ekel erregend, widerlich; **to be ~ to sb** Ekel erregend für jdn sein, auf jdn abstoßend wirken; **I find him ~** ich finde ihn abstoßend **N** *(= insect repellent)* Insektenschutzmittel *nt*

repelling [rɪˈpelɪŋ] ADJ = **repellent ADJ b**

repent [rɪˈpent] **VI** Reue empfinden *(of über +acc)* **VT** bereuen

repentance [rɪˈpentəns] N Reue *f*

repentant [rɪˈpentənt] ADJ *look, expression* reuig, reuevoll; **he was very ~** es reute ihn sehr; **to feel ~** Reue empfinden; **a ~ sinner** ein reuiger Sünder

repercussion [ˌriːpəˈkʌʃən] **N** **a** *(= consequence)* Auswirkung *f (on auf +acc)*; **~s** *pl (of misbehaviour etc)* Nachspiel *nt*; **that is bound to have ~s** das wird Kreise ziehen; **to have ~s on sth** sich auf etw *(acc)* auswirken **b** *(of shock)* Erschütterung *f*; *(of sounds)* Widerhall *m*

repertoire [ˈrepətwɑːʳ] N *(Theat, Mus)* Repertoire *nt*

repertory [ˈrepətərɪ] **N** **a** *(also* **repertory theatre)** Repertoire-Theater *nt*; **to act in ~, to play ~** Repertoire-Stücke spielen; **he was in ~** er spielte an einem Repertoire-Theater **b** *(= songs, plays)* = **repertoire**

repertory company N Repertoire-Ensemble *nt*

repetition [ˌrepɪˈtɪʃən] N Wiederholung *f*; **there are six ~s of the pattern** das Muster wiederholt sich sechsmal

repetitious [ˌrepɪˈtɪʃəs] ADJ sich wiederholend

repetitive [rɪˈpetɪtɪv] ADJ sich dauernd wiederholend; *work also* monoton; **to be ~** sich dauernd wiederholen; **standing in a production line is such ~ work** die Arbeit am Fließband ist äußerst eintönig

repetitive strain injury N Verletzung *f* durch wiederholte Belastung

rephrase [ˌriːˈfreɪz] VT neu formulieren, umformulieren

repine [rɪˈpaɪn] VI *(liter)* hadern *(geh) (at, against mit)*

replace [rɪˈpleɪs] **VT** **a** *(= put back)* zurücksetzen; *(on end, standing up)* zurückstellen; *(on its side, flat)* zurücklegen; **to ~ the receiver** *(Telec)* (den Hörer) auflegen **b** *(= provide or be substitute for)* person, thing, ingredient, goods (temporarily) vertreten; **the boss has ~d Smith with Jones** der Chef hat Smith durch Jones ersetzt **c** *(= renew)* components, parts austauschen, ersetzen

replaceable [rɪˈpleɪsəbl] ADJ *person* ersetzbar, zu ersetzen; *(= renewable)* components, parts also austauschbar

replacement [rɪˈpleɪsmənt] **N** **a** *(= substituting)* Ersatz *m*; *(by deputy)* Vertretung *f*; **~ cost** *(of equipment)* Wiederbeschaffungskosten *pl*; *(of personnel)* Wiederbesetzungskosten *pl* **b** *(= person or thing)* Ersatz *m*; *(= deputy)* Vertretung *f*; **~ engine** Austauschmotor *m*; **~ part** Ersatzteil *nt* **c** *(= putting back)* Zurücksetzen *nt*; *(on end, standing up)* Zurückstellen *nt*; *(on side, flat)* Zurücklegen *nt*; *(of receiver)* Auflegen *nt*

replant [ˌriːˈplɑːnt] VT *cabbages, trees etc* umpflanzen; *garden, field* neu bepflanzen

replay [ˈriːpleɪ] *(Sport)* **N** *(= recording)* Wiederholung *f*; *(= match also)* Wiederholungsspiel *nt* → **action replay** **VT** [ˌriːˈpleɪ] *match, game* wiederholen, nochmals austragen; **to ~ sth in one's mind** sich *(dat)* etw (immer) wieder vor Augen führen

replenish [rɪˈplenɪʃ] VT ergänzen; *(when badly depleted)* wieder auffüllen; *glass* auffüllen; *shelves* nachfüllen

replenishment [rɪˈplenɪʃmənt] N Ergänzung *f*; *(when badly depleted)* Wiederauffüllen *nt*; *(of glass)* Auffüllen *nt*; *(of shelves)* Nachfüllen *nt*

replete [rɪˈpliːt] ADJ *(form)* reichlich versehen or ausgestattet *(with mit)*; *(= well-fed)* person gesättigt

repletion [rɪˈpliːʃən] N *(form)* Sättigung *f*; **to eat to ~** essen, bis man gesättigt ist

replica [ˈreplɪkə] N *(of painting, statue)* Reproduktion *f*, Kopie *f*; *(of document)* Kopie *f*; *(of ship, building etc)* Nachbildung *f*; **she is a ~ of her sister** sie ist das Ebenbild ihrer Schwester

replicate [ˈreplɪkeɪt] VT *(= copy)* work, success wiederholen

reply [rɪˈplaɪ] ❂ 19.1, 19.4, 27.3, 27.5, 27.7 **N** *(written)* Antwort *f*; *(spoken also)* Erwiderung *f*; **in ~** (als Antwort) darauf; **in ~ to your letter** in Beantwortung Ihres Briefes *(form)*; **~ coupon** Antwortschein *m*; **to send a letter ~ paid** *(Brit)* einen Brief gebührenfrei senden; **~-paid envelope** *(Brit)* freigemachter Briefumschlag, Freiumschlag *m* **VT** **to ~ (to sb) that ...** (jdm) antworten, dass ... **VI** *(to sth auf etw +acc)* antworten; *(spoken also)* erwidern

repoint [ˌriːˈpɔɪnt] VT *(Build)* neu verfugen

repointing [ˌriːˈpɔɪntɪŋ] N *(Build)* Neuverfugung *f*

repopulate [ˌriːˈpɒpjʊleɪt] VT *area* neu besiedeln

report [rɪˈpɔːt] **N** **a** *(= account, statement)* Bericht *m* *(on über +acc)*; *(Press, Rad, TV)* Reportage *f*, Bericht *m* *(on über +acc)*; **to give a ~ on sth** Bericht über etw *(acc)* erstatten; *(Rad, TV)* eine Reportage über etw *(acc)* machen; **an official ~ on the motor industry** ein Gutachten *nt* über die Autoindustrie; **(school) ~** Zeugnis *nt*; **chairman's ~** Bericht *m* des Vorsitzenden
b *(= rumour)* **to know sth only by ~** etw nur vom Hörensagen kennen; **there are ~s that ...** es wird gesagt, dass ...
c *(= reputation)* Ruf *m*; **of good ~** von gutem Ruf
d *(of gun)* Knall *m*; **with a loud ~** mit lautem Knall

VT **a** *results, findings* berichten über (+*acc*); (= *announce officially*) melden; *losses* verzeichnen; **to ~ that ...** berichten, dass ...; **to ~ progress** einen Tätigkeitsbericht abgeben; **the papers ~ed the crime as solved** laut Presseberichten ist das Verbrechen aufgeklärt; **he is ~ed as having said ...** er soll gesagt haben ...; **it is ~ed that a prisoner has escaped, a prisoner is ~ed to have escaped** ein Gefangener wird als geflüchtet gemeldet or gilt als vermisst; **it is ~ed from the White House that ...** aus dem Weißen Haus wird berichtet or gemeldet, dass ...
b (*to sb* jdm) (= *notify authorities of*) *accident, crime, suspect, criminal, culprit* melden; (*to police*) melden, anzeigen; *one's position* angeben; **to ~ sb for sth** jdn wegen etw melden; **to ~ sb sick** jdn krankmelden; **~ed missing** als vermisst gemeldet; **nothing to ~** keine besonderen Vorkommnisse!
VI **a** (= *announce oneself*) sich melden; **~ to the director on Monday** melden Sie sich am Montag beim Direktor; **to ~ for duty** sich zum Dienst melden; **to ~ sick** sich krankmelden
b (= *give a report*) berichten, Bericht erstatten (*on* über +*acc*); (= *work as journalist*) Reporter(in) *m(f)* sein; **the committee is ready to ~** der Ausschuss hat seinen Bericht fertig; **this is Michael Brown ~ing (from Rome)** (*Rad, TV*) hier spricht Michael Brown (mit einem Bericht aus Rom)

▶ **report back** VI **a** (= *announce one's return*) sich zurückmelden **b** (= *give report*) Bericht erstatten (*to sb* jdm)

▶ **report to** VI +*prep obj* (*in organization*) unterstellt sein (+*dat*), unterstehen (+*dat*); **who do you report to?** wer ist Ihr Vorgesetzter?

reportable [rɪˈpɔːtəbl] ADJ *event* berichtenswert; (*Med*) *disease* anzeige- or meldepflichtig; *capital gains, income etc* steuerpflichtig

reportage [ˌrepɔːˈtɑːʒ] N Reportage *f*; (= *style*) Reporterstil *m*

report card N (*Sch*) Zeugnis(blatt) *nt*

reported [rɪˈpɔːtɪd] ADJ gemeldet

reportedly [rɪˈpɔːtɪdlɪ] ADV angeblich; **several houses were ~ destroyed** wie verlautet, sollen mehrere Häuser zerstört worden sein

reported speech N (*Gram*) indirekte Rede

reporter [rɪˈpɔːtəʳ] N **a** (*Press, Rad, TV*) Reporter(in) *m(f)*, Berichterstatter(in) *m(f)*; (*on the spot*) Korrespondent(in) *m(f)*; **special ~** Sonderberichterstatter(in) *m(f)* **b** (*Jur, Parl*, = *stenographer*) Stenograf(in) *m(f)*, Gerichtsschreiber(in) *m(f)* (*old*)

reporters' gallery [rɪˈpɔːtəzˈgælərɪ] N (*Jur, Parl*) Pressetribüne *f*

report generator N (*Comput*) Reportgenerator *m*

reporting [rɪˈpɔːtɪŋ]: **reporting restrictions** PL (*Brit, Jur*) Berichterstattungsbeschränkungen *pl* (*on* in Bezug auf +*acc*); **~ were not lifted** die Berichterstattungsbeschränkungen wurden nicht aufgehoben; **reporting structure** N Organisationsstruktur *f*

report stage N **the bill has reached the ~** (*Brit, Parl*) der Gesetzentwurf kommt nach seiner Beratung im Ausschuss zur Berichterstattung wieder vors Parlament

repose¹ [rɪˈpəʊz] N (*liter*, = *rest, peace*) Ruhe *f*; (= *composure*) Gelassenheit *f*; **in ~** in Ruhe **VI** (*form, liter*) **a** (= *rest, be buried*) ruhen **b** (= *be based*) beruhen (*upon* auf +*dat*)

repose² VT (*form, liter*) *trust, faith* setzen (*in* in or auf +*acc*)

repository [rɪˈpɒzɪtərɪ] N (= *warehouse*) Lager *nt*, Magazin *nt*; (*fig, of facts etc*) Quelle *f* (*of* für); (= *book, library*) Fundgrube *f* (*of* für); (*liter, of secret*) Hüter(in) *m(f)*

repossess [ˌriːpəˈzes] VT wieder in Besitz nehmen

repossession [ˌriːpəˈzeʃən] N Wiederinbesitznahme *f*

repot [ˌriːˈpɒt] VT *plant* umtopfen

repp N = **rep²**

reprehend [ˌreprɪˈhend] VT tadeln, rügen

reprehensible [ˌreprɪˈhensɪbl] ADJ verwerflich, tadelnswert

reprehensibly [ˌreprɪˈhensɪblɪ] ADV verwerflich

reprehension [ˌreprɪˈhenʃən] N **a** *no pl* (= *act*) Tadeln *nt*, Rügen *nt* **b** (= *rebuke*) Tadel *m*, Rüge *f*

represent [ˌreprɪˈzent] VT **a** darstellen; (= *stand for*) stehen für; (= *symbolize*) symbolisieren, darstellen; *opportunity* bedeuten; **he ~s all that is best in ...** er verkörpert das Beste (+*gen*) ...
b (= *act or speak for, Parl, Jur*) vertreten; **he ~s their firm in London** er vertritt or repräsentiert die Firma in London; **many countries were ~ed at the ceremony** viele Länder waren bei der Feier vertreten; **the foreign tourist should never forget that he ~s his country** ein Tourist sollte im Ausland nie vergessen, dass er sein Land repräsentiert
c (= *declare to be*) *person, event, risk etc* darstellen (*as* als); (*falsely*) hinstellen (*as* als); **it is exactly as ~ed in the advertisement** es ist genau, wie in der Anzeige dargestellt
d (= *set forth, explain*) vor Augen führen (*to sb* jdm)
e (*Theat*) *character, part* darstellen

re-present [ˌriːprɪˈzent] VT nochmals vorlegen

representation [ˌreprɪzenˈteɪʃən] N **a** (= *representing*) Darstellung *f*; (= *symbolizing*) Symbolisierung *f*; (= *acting or speaking for, Parl, Jur*) Vertretung *f*; (= *declaring to be sb/sth*) Darstellung *f*; (*falsely*) Darstellung *f* **b** (= *drawing, description, Theat*) Darstellung *f* **c** **representations** PL (*esp Pol*, = *remonstrations*) Vorstellungen *pl*, Vorhaltungen *pl*; **the ambassador made ~s to the government** der Botschafter wurde bei der Regierung vorstellig

representational [ˌreprɪzenˈteɪʃənəl] ADJ *art, picture* gegenständlich; **in ~ form** symbolisch; **a ~ party of** eine Vertretung (+*gen*)

representational system N (*Pol*) Repräsentativsystem *nt*

representative [ˌreprɪˈzentətɪv] ADJ **a** (*of* für) (= *typical*) *cross section, sample* repräsentativ; *attitude, game* typisch; (= *symbolic*) symbolisch **b** (= *acting for*) repräsentativ; **a ~ body** eine Vertretung **c** (*Parl*) *government* repräsentativ, parlamentarisch; **~ assembly** Abgeordnetenversammlung *f* **b** (*Comm*) Vertreter(in) *m(f)*; (*Jur*) Bevollmächtigte(r) *mf*, Beauftragte(r) *mf*; (*US, Pol*) Abgeordnete(r) *mf* → **house N b**; **authorized ~** Bevollmächtigte(r) *mf* → **house N b**

repress [rɪˈpres] VT *revolt, population, emotions, desires* unterdrücken; *laugh, sneeze* unterdrücken, zurückhalten; (*Psych*) verdrängen

repressed [rɪˈprest] ADJ unterdrückt; (*Psych*) verdrängt

repression [rɪˈpreʃən] N Unterdrückung *f*; (*Psych*) Verdrängung *f*

repressive [rɪˈpresɪv] ADJ repressiv

reprieve [rɪˈpriːv] N (*Jur*) Begnadigung *f*; (= *postponement*) Strafaufschub *m*; (*fig*) Gnadenfrist *f* **VT** **he was ~d** (*Jur*) er wurde begnadigt; (= *sentence was postponed*) seine Strafe wurde aufgeschoben; **the building/firm has been ~d for a while** das Gebäude/die Firma ist vorerst noch einmal verschont geblieben

reprimand [ˈreprɪmɑːnd] N Tadel *m*; (*official also*) Verweis *m* **VT** tadeln, maßregeln (*geh*)

reprint [ˌriːˈprɪnt] VT neu auflegen, neu abdrucken, nachdrucken N [ˈriːprɪnt] Neuauflage *f*, Nachdruck *m*

reprisal [rɪˈpraɪzəl] N (*for* gegen) Vergeltungsmaßnahme *f*; (*between companies, countries etc also*) Repressalie *f*; **to take ~s** zu Repressalien greifen; **as a ~ for** als Vergeltung für

reprivatization [ˈriːˌpraɪvətaɪˈzeɪʃən] N (*Econ*) Reprivatisierung *f*

reprivatize [ˌriːˈpraɪvətaɪz] VT (*Econ*) reprivatisieren

repro [ˈriːprəʊ] N (*inf*) *abbr of* **reproduction** Repro *f or nt*

reproach [rɪˈprəʊtʃ] ✪ 26.3 N **a** (= *rebuke*) Vorwurf *m*; **to heap ~s on sb** jdn mit Vorwürfen überhäufen; **a term of ~** ein Vorwurf *m*; **a look of ~** ein vorwurfsvoller Blick; **above or beyond ~** über jeden Vorwurf erhaben
b (= *discredit*) **to be a ~ to sb/sth** eine Schande für jdn/etw sein; **to bring ~ (up)on sb/sth** jdn/etw in schlechten Ruf bringen; **to bring ~ (up)on oneself** in schlechten Ruf kommen
VT Vorwürfe machen (+*dat*); **to ~ sb for his mistake** jdm einen Fehler vorwerfen; **to ~ sb for having done sth** jdm Vorwürfe dafür machen, dass er etw getan hat; **he has nothing to ~ himself for or with** er hat sich (*dat*) nichts vorzuwerfen

reproachful ADJ , **reproachfully** ADV [rɪˈprəʊtʃfʊl, -fəlɪ] vorwurfsvoll

reprobate [ˈreprəʊbeɪt] ADJ *action* ruchlos, verwerflich; *person* verkommen; (*Eccl*) verdammt N verkommenes Subjekt, Gestrauchelte(r) *mf* (*geh*); (*Eccl*) Verdammte(r) *mf*

reprobation [ˌreprəʊˈbeɪʃən] N Verdammung *f*

reprocess [ˌriːˈprəʊses] VT wieder verwerten; *sewage, atomic waste, fuel* wieder aufbereiten

reprocessing plant [ˌriːˈprəʊsesɪŋˈplɑːnt] N Wiederaufbereitungsanlage *f*

reproduce [ˌriːprəˈdjuːs] VT **a** (= *copy*) wiedergeben; (*mechanically, electronically*) reproduzieren; (*Typ*) abdrucken **b** (*Biol*) **to ~ its kind** sich or seine Art fortpflanzen **c** (*Theat*) *play* neu inszenieren **VI a** (*Biol*) sich fortpflanzen or vermehren **b** (*Typ*) **this picture won't ~ well** dieses Bild lässt sich nicht gut reproduzieren

reproducible [ˌriːprəˈdjuːsɪbəl] ADJ reproduzierbar

reproduction [ˌriːprəˈdʌkʃən] N **a** (= *procreation*) Fortpflanzung *f* **b** (= *copying*) Reproduktion *f*; (*of documents*) Vervielfältigung *f*; **sound ~** Klang- or Tonwiedergabe *f*; **this radio has good ~** das Radio gibt den Ton gut wieder **c** (= *copy*) Reproduktion *f*; (= *photo*) Kopie *f*; (= *sound reproduction*) Wiedergabe *f*

reproduction furniture N (moderne) Stilmöbel *pl*

reproductive [ˌriːprəˈdʌktɪv] ADJ Fortpflanzungs-

reproductive organ N Fortpflanzungsorgan *nt*

reproof¹ [ˈriːˈpruːf] VT *garment* frisch or neu imprägnieren

reproof² [rɪˈpruːf] N Tadel *m*, Rüge *f*

reproval [rɪˈpruːvəl] N **a** *no pl* (*act*) Tadeln *nt*, Rügen *nt* **b** = **reproof²**

reprove [rɪˈpruːv] VT *person, action* tadeln, rügen

reproving ADJ , **reprovingly** ADV [rɪˈpruːvɪŋ, -lɪ] tadelnd

reptile [ˈreptaɪl] N Reptil *nt*, Kriechtier *nt*; (*fig pej*) Kriecher *m* (*pej*) ADJ Reptilien-, reptilartig; **~ house** Reptilienhaus *nt*; **~ species** Reptilienart *f*

reptilian [repˈtɪlɪən] ADJ reptilartig; (*fig pej*) kriecherisch (*pej*) N Reptil *nt*, Kriechtier *nt*

republic [rɪˈpʌblɪk] N Republik *f*

republican [rɪˈpʌblɪkən] ADJ republikanisch N Republikaner(in) *m(f)*

republicanism [rɪˈpʌblɪkənɪzəm] N Republikanismus *m*

republication [ˈriːˌpʌblɪˈkeɪʃən] N (*of book*) Wieder- or Neuveröffentlichung *f*; (*of banns*) erneutes Aushängen

republish [ˌriːˈpʌblɪʃ] VT *book* wieder or neu veröffentlichen or herausbringen; *banns* wieder aushängen

repudiate [rɪˈpjuːdɪeɪt] VT *person* verstoßen; *authorship, debt, obligation* nicht anerkennen; *accusation, remarks, charge* zurückweisen

repudiation [rɪˌpjuːdɪˈeɪʃən] N (*of person*) Verstoßung *f*; (*of authorship, debt, obligation*) Nichtanerkennung *f*; (*of accusation, remarks, charge*) Zurückweisung *f*

repugnance [rɪˈpʌgnəns] N Widerwille *m*, Abneigung *f* (*towards, for* gegen)

repugnant [rɪˈpʌɡnənt] ADJ widerlich, abstoßend; (*stronger*) Ekel erregend; **to be ~ to sb**
jdm widerlich sein

repulse [rɪˈpʌls] **VT** (*Mil*) *enemy, attack* zurückschlagen, abwehren; (*fig*) *person, help, offer* abweisen, zurückweisen; **sb is ~d by sth** (*fig*) etw
stößt jdn ab, jd findet etw widerwärtig **N** (*Mil*)
Abwehr f, Zurückschlagen nt; (*fig*) Abweisung
f, Zurückweisung f

repulsion [rɪˈpʌlʃən] N **a** (= *distaste*) Widerwille
m (*for* gegen) **b** (*Phys*) Abstoßung f

repulsive [rɪˈpʌlsɪv] ADJ **a** (= *loathsome*) abstoßend, widerwärtig; **to be ~ to sb** für jdn abstoßend sein **b** (*Phys*) *forces* abstoßend, repulsiv

repulsively [rɪˈpʌlsɪvlɪ] ADV abstoßend, widerwärtig; **~ ugly** abstoßend hässlich

repulsiveness [rɪˈpʌlsɪvnɪs] N Widerwärtigkeit
f

repurchase [ˌriːˈpɜːtʃɪs] **N** Rückkauf m **VT** zurückkaufen

reputability [ˌrepjʊtəˈbɪlɪtɪ] N Ansehen nt; (*of
person also*) Ehrbarkeit f (*geh*); (*of firm*) Seriosität f

reputable [ˈrepjʊtəbl] ADJ ehrenhaft; *person* angesehen; *occupation* ordentlich, anständig; *dealer, firm* seriös

reputably [ˈrepjʊtəblɪ] ADV (= *well*) ordentlich;
behave ehrenhaft; *deal* seriös; **he is ~ established in the business world** er wird in der Geschäftswelt respektiert; **he is now ~ employed
as a gardener** er hat jetzt eine seriöse Anstellung als Gärtner

reputation [ˌrepjʊˈteɪʃən] N Ruf m, Name m; (=
bad reputation) schlechter Ruf; **what sort of ~
does she have?** wie ist ihr Ruf?; **he has a ~ for
being ...** er hat den Ruf, ... zu sein; **to have a ~
for honesty** als ehrlich gelten; **you don't want
to get (yourself) a ~, you know** du willst dich
doch sicherlich nicht in Verruf bringen; **she
was by ~ a good organizer** sie stand in dem
Ruf, Organisationstalent zu haben

repute [rɪˈpjuːt] **N** Ruf m, Ansehen nt; **to know
sb by ~** von jdm schon viel gehört haben; **to
be of high ~** einen guten Ruf genießen; **a restaurant of ~** ein angesehenes Restaurant; **a
house of ill ~** ein Haus von zweifelhaftem Ruf;
to be held in low ~ einen schlechten Ruf haben **VT** (*pass only*) **he is ~d to be ...** man sagt,
dass er ... ist; **to be ~d to be rich** als reich gelten; **he is ~d to be the best** er gilt als der Beste, er steht in dem Ruf, der Beste zu sein

reputed [rɪˈpjuːtɪd] ADJ angenommen; **the ~ father** (*Jur*) der vermutliche Vater

reputedly [rɪˈpjuːtɪdlɪ] ADV wie man annimmt;
he is ~ the best player in the world er gilt als
der beste Spieler der Welt

request [rɪˈkwest] **O** 10.1, 25.1 **N** Bitte f,
Wunsch m, Ersuchen nt (*geh*); **at sb's ~** auf jds
Bitte etc; **on/by ~** auf Wunsch; **no parking by ~**
bitte nicht parken; **to make a ~ for sth** um etw
bitten; **I have a ~ to make of or to you** ich habe
eine Bitte an Sie, ich muss eine Bitte an Sie
richten; (*record*) **~s** Plattenwünsche pl **VT** bitten um; *asylum also* nachsuchen um; (*Rad*) *record* sich (*dat*) wünschen; **to ~ silence** um Ruhe
bitten or ersuchen (*geh*); **to ~ sth of or from sb**
jdn um etw bitten or ersuchen (*geh*); **to ~ that
...** bitten, dass ...; **"you are ~ed not to smoke"**
„bitte nicht rauchen" → **presence, pleasure**

request: request programme, (*US*) **request
program** N (*Rad*) Wunschsendung f; **request
stop** N (*Brit*) Bedarfshaltestelle f

requiem [ˈrekwɪem] N Requiem nt

requiem mass N Totenmesse f

require [rɪˈkwaɪə] **O** 20.4 VT **a** (= *need*) brauchen, benötigen; *action, action* erfordern; (= *desire*) wünschen, mögen; **I have all I ~** ich habe
alles, was ich brauche; **the journey will ~ 3
hours** man braucht or benötigt 3 Stunden für
die Reise; **it ~s great care** das erfordert große
Sorgfalt; **it ~s repairing** es muss repariert werden; **what qualifications are ~d?** welche Qualifikationen werden verlangt or sind erforder-

lich?; **to be ~d to do sth** etw machen or tun
müssen; **that is not ~d** das ist nicht nötig or erforderlich; **if you ~ me** wenn Sie mich benötigen; **if ~d** falls notwendig or erforderlich; **when
(it is) ~d** auf Wunsch, wenn es gewünscht
wird; **as and when ~d** nach Bedarf; **dilute as
~d** nach Bedarf verdünnen

b (= *order*) verlangen; **to ~ sb to do sth** von
jdm verlangen, dass er etw tut; **you are ~d to
report to the boss immediately** Sie sollen sich
sofort beim Chef melden; **to ~ sth of sb** etw
von jdm verlangen; **as ~d by law** den gesetzlichen Bestimmungen gemäß or entsprechend

required [rɪˈkwaɪəd] ADJ erforderlich, notwendig; *date* vorgeschrieben; (= *desired*) gewünscht;
the ~ amount die benötigte Menge

required reading N (*Sch, Univ*) Pflichtlektüre
f

requirement [rɪˈkwaɪəmənt] N **a** (= *need*) Bedürfnis nt, Bedarf m no pl; (= *desire*) Wunsch
m, Anspruch m; **to meet sb's ~s** jds Bedürfnisse erfüllen, jds Wünschen (*dat*) entsprechen, jds Ansprüchen (*dat*) gerecht werden;
there isn't enough bread to meet the ~ es ist
nicht genügend Brot da, um den Bedarf zu decken **b** (= *condition, thing required*) Erfordernis
nt; **to fit the ~s** den Erfordernissen entsprechen

requisite [ˈrekwɪzɪt] **N** Artikel m; (= *necessary
thing*) **travel ~s** Reiseartikel pl
or -utensilien pl **ADJ** erforderlich, notwendig;
the ~ time die dazu erforderliche Zeit

requisition [ˌrekwɪˈzɪʃən] **N** Anforderung f; (=
act: of objects) Requisition f; **to make a ~ for sth**
etw anfordern **VT** *sb's services* anfordern; *supplies, food* requirieren; *building* beschlagnahmen,
requirieren

requital [rɪˈkwaɪtl] N (= *repayment*) Vergeltung f;
(= *revenge also*) Rache f

requite [rɪˈkwaɪt] VT **a** (= *repay*) *person* es vergelten (+*dat*); *action* vergelten; **~d love** erwi-
derte Liebe **b** (= *avenge*) *action* vergelten; *person* rächen

reran [ˌriːˈræn] pret of **rerun**

reread [ˌriːˈriːd] pret, ptp **reread** [ˌriːˈred] VT wieder or nochmals lesen

rerecord [ˌriːrɪˈkɔːd] VT *sound recording* überspielen; (*in recording studio*) mischen

reredos [ˈrɪədɒs] N Retabel nt

reroute [ˌriːˈruːt] VT *train, bus* umleiten; *electricity
etc also* umlenken

rerun [ˌriːˈrʌn] vb: pret **reran**, ptp **rerun** **VT** *film*
wieder or nochmals aufführen; *tape* wieder or
nochmals abspielen; *race, elections, programme,
event* wiederholen **N** [ˈriːrʌn] (*of film*) Wieder-
aufführung f; (*of tape*) Wiederabspielen nt; (*of
race, election, programme, event*) Wiederholung f

resale [ˈriːseɪl] N Weiterverkauf m; **"not for ~"**
„nicht zum Weiterverkauf bestimmt"; (*on free
sample*) „unverkäufliches Muster"; **~ value** Wie-
derverkaufswert m

resale price maintenance N (*Brit*) Preisbindung f

resat [ˌriːˈsæt] pret, ptp of **resit**

reschedule [ˌriːˈskedʒʊəl, (*esp Brit*) ˌriːˈʃedjuːl] VT
meeting etc neu ansetzen or festlegen; *date,
appointment* verlegen, verschieben (*for* auf
+*acc*); (*Econ, Fin*) die Rückzahlungsmodalitäten
ändern für

rescind [rɪˈsɪnd] VT *decision* rückgängig machen,
widerrufen; *judgement, contract also* annullieren;
law, act aufheben

rescission [ˌriːˈsɪʒən] N (*esp Jur, of judgement,
law, decision*) Aufhebung f, Annullierung f; (*of
contract etc*) Rücktritt m (*of* von); (*of purchase*)
Rückgängigmachung f

rescue [ˈreskjuː] **N** (= *saving*) Rettung f; (= *freeing*) Errettung f, Befreiung f; **~ was difficult** die
Rettung war schwierig; **to go/come to sb's ~**
jdm zu Hilfe kommen; **to the ~!** zu Hilfe!; **it
was Bob to the ~** Bob war unsere/seine etc
Rettung; **~ attempt/operation/party** Rettungsversuch m/-aktion f/-mannschaft f → **air-sea**

rescue **VT** (= *save*) retten; (= *free*) erretten, befreien; **you ~d me from a difficult situation** du
hast mich aus einer schwierigen Lage gerettet;
the ~d were taken to hospital die Geretteten
wurden ins Krankenhaus gebracht

rescuer [ˈreskjʊə] N (*who saves sb*) Retter(in)
m(f); (*who frees sb*) Befreier(in) m(f)

rescue services PL Rettungsdienst m

rescue worker N Bergungsarbeiter(in) m(f),
Rettungsarbeiter(in) m(f)

research [rɪˈsɜːtʃ] **N** Forschung f (*into, on* über
+*acc*); **a piece of ~** eine Forschungsarbeit; **to
do ~** forschen, Forschung betreiben; **to carry
out ~ into the effects of sth** Forschungen über
die Auswirkungen einer Sache (*gen*) anstellen
VT forschen, Forschung betreiben; **to ~ into** or
on sth etw erforschen, über etw (*acc*) forschen
or Forschung betreiben **VT** erforschen, untersuchen; **a well-researched book** ein Buch, das
auf solider Forschungsarbeit beruht; (*journalistic
investigation*) ein gut recherchiertes Buch

research in cpds Forschungs-; **research assistant** N wissenschaftlicher Assistent, wissenschaftliche Assistentin; **research budget** N
Forschungsetat m

researcher [rɪˈsɜːtʃə] N Forscher(in) m(f)

research: research establishment N For-
schungsstätte f; **research fellow** N (*Univ*) For-
schungsstipendiat(in) m(f); **research fellowship** N Forschungsstipendium nt; **research
student** N (*Univ*) Student, der Forschungen
für einen höheren akademischen Grad betreibt, ≈ Doktorand(in) m(f); **research worker** N Forscher(in) m(f)

reseat [ˌriːˈsiːt] VT **a** *chair* einen neuen Sitz geben (+*dat*); *trousers* einen neuen Hosenboden
anfertigen für **b** (*Tech*) *valve* neu einschleifen
c *person* umsetzen; **when everyone was ~ed** (=
had sat down again) als sich alle wieder gesetzt
hatten

resection [rɪˈsekʃən] N **a** (*Med*) Resektion f
b (*Surv*) Triangulation f

reselect [ˌriːsɪˈlekt] VT (*Pol*) wieder aufstellen

reselection [ˌriːsɪˈlekʃən] N , no pl (*Pol*) Wieder-
aufstellung f

resell [ˌriːˈsel] VT weiterverkaufen, wieder verkaufen

reseller [ˌriːˈselə] N Wiederverkäufer(in) m(f)

resemblance [rɪˈzembləns] **O** 5.3 N Ähnlichkeit f; **to bear a strong/a faint/no ~ to sb/sth**
starke/leichte/keine Ähnlichkeit mit jdm/etw
haben; **there's no ~ between them** es besteht
keine Ähnlichkeit zwischen ihnen, sie sind
sich (*dat*) nicht ähnlich

resemble [rɪˈzembl] VT ähneln, gleichen; **they ~
each other** sie ähneln or gleichen sich (*dat*) or
einander

resent [rɪˈzent] VT *remarks, behaviour* übel nehmen, sich ärgern über (+*acc*); *person* ein Res-
sentiment haben gegen; **he ~ed her for the rest
of his life** er nahm ihr das sein Leben lang
übel; **he ~ed my having** or **me for having got
the job** er nahm es mir übel, dass ich die Stelle
bekommen hatte; **he ~ed the fact that ...** er ärgerte sich darüber, dass ...; **they ~ed the way in
which ...** sie ärgerten sich darüber, wie ... or auf
welche Art und Weise ...; **to ~ sb's success** jdm
seinen Erfolg missgönnen; **I ~ that** das gefällt
mir nicht; **he may ~ my** or **me being here** es
könnte ihn ärgern, dass ich hier bin

resentful [rɪˈzentfʊl] ADJ *person, look* verärgert;
(= *jealous*) voller Ressentiments (*of* gegen); **to
be ~ at** or **about** or **of sth/of sb** über etw/jdn
verärgert sein, sich über etw/jdn ärgern; **to be
~ of sb's success** jdm seinen Erfolg nicht gönnen; **~ of the criticisms levelled at him** die an
ihm geübte Kritik übel nehmend; **he felt ~ a-
bout her promotion** er nahm es ihr übel, dass
sie befördert wurde; **to feel ~ toward(s)
sb for doing sth** es jdm übel nehmen, dass er/
sie etc etw getan hat; **he felt ~ toward(s) her for
not inviting him to the party** er nahm es ihr

übel, dass sie ihn nicht zu der Party eingeladen hatte

resentfully [rɪ'zentfəlɪ] ADV *say* ärgerlich; *look* verärgert, wütend; *behave* verärgert

resentment [rɪ'zentmənt] N Ärger *m no pl*, Groll *m no pl* (*of* über +*acc*)

reservation [ˌrezə'veɪʃən] N **a** (= *qualification of opinion*) Vorbehalt *m*; (*Philos*) Mentalreservation *f* (*spec*); **without ~** ohne Vorbehalt, vorbehaltlos; **with ~s** unter Vorbehalt(en); **to have ~s about sb/sth** Bedenken in Bezug auf jdn/etw haben **b** (= *booking*) Reservierung *f*; **to make a ~ at the hotel/on the boat** ein Zimmer im Hotel/einen Platz auf dem Schiff reservieren lassen; **how many ~s did you make?** für wie viel Personen haben Sie reservieren lassen?; **to have a ~ (for a room)** ein Zimmer reserviert haben **c** (= *area of land*) Reservat *nt*, Reservation *f*; **(central) ~** (*Brit: on motorway*) Mittelstreifen *m*

reservation(s) desk N Reservierungsschalter *m*

reserve [rɪ'zɜːv] ✪ 21.3 VT **a** (= *keep*) aufsparen, aufheben; **to ~ judgement/one's decision** mit einem Urteil/seiner Entscheidung zurückhalten; **to ~ the right to do sth** sich (*dat*) (das Recht) vorbehalten, etw zu tun; **to ~ oneself for sth** sich für etw schonen **b** (= *book in advance: client*) reservieren lassen; **the lady at the box office ~d 4 seats for us** die Dame an der Kasse hat uns 4 Plätze reserviert; **are you reserving these seats for anyone?** haben Sie diese Plätze für jemanden reserviert? N **a** (= *store*) (*of an* +*dat*) Reserve *f*, Vorrat *m*; (*Fin*) Reserve *f*; **to have great ~s of energy** große Kraftreserven haben; **cash ~** Barreserve *f*; **world ~s of copper** die Weltkupferreserven *pl*, die Weltreserven *pl* an Kupfer; **to have/keep sth in ~** etw in Reserve haben/halten **b** **without ~** ohne Vorbehalt, vorbehaltlos; **with great ~** unter *or* mit starken Vorbehalten **c** = *reserve price* **d** (= *piece of land*) Reservat *nt*, Reservation *f* **e** (= *coolness, reticence*) Reserve *f*, Zurückhaltung *f*; **he treated me with some ~** er behandelte mich etwas reserviert **f** (*Mil*, = *force*) Reserve *f*; (= *soldier*) Soldat(in) *m(f)* der Reserve; **the ~s** die Reserveeinheiten *pl* **g** (*Sport*) Reservespieler(in) *m(f)*

reserve *in cpds* Reserve-; **reserve currency** N Reservewährung *f*

reserved [rɪ'zɜːvd] ADJ **a** (= *reticent*) zurückhaltend, reserviert (*about* in Bezug auf +*acc*) **b** *room, seat* reserviert, belegt **c** (*Publishing*) **all rights ~** alle Rechte vorbehalten

reservedly [rɪ'zɜːvɪdlɪ] ADV zurückhaltend, reserviert

reserve: reserve fund N Rücklage *f*, Reservefonds *m*; **reserve list** N (*Brit Mil*) Reserveliste *f*; **reserve player** N Reservespieler(in) *m(f)*; **reserve price** N (*Brit*) Mindest- *or* Ausrufpreis *m*; **reserve tank** N Reservetank *m*; **reserve team** N Reserve(mannschaft) *f*

reservist [rɪ'zɜːvɪst] N (*Mil*) Reservist(in) *m(f)*

reservoir ['rezəvwɑː] N (*lit, for water*) Reservoir *nt*; (*for gas*) Speicher *m*; (*fig, of knowledge, facts, talent etc*) Fundgrube *f*

reset [ˌriː'set] *pret, ptp* **reset** VT **a** *precious stone* neu (ein)fassen; *watch* neu stellen (*to* auf +*acc*); (*for summer time etc*) umstellen (*for* auf +*acc*); *body clock* umstellen; *dial, gauge* zurückstellen (*to* auf +*acc*); *machine* neu *or* wieder einstellen; (*Comput*) rücksetzen; **~ switch** *or* **button** (*Comput*) Resettaste *f*; (*Typ*) *text* neu setzen **b** (*Med*) *limb, bone* wieder einrichten; *dislocated shoulder* wieder einrenken

resettle [ˌriː'setl] VT *refugees* umsiedeln; *land* neu *or* wieder besiedeln

resettlement [ˌriː'setlmənt] N (*of refugees*) Umsiedlung *f*; (*of land*) Neubesied(e)lung *f*

reshape [ˌriː'ʃeɪp] VT *dough, clay etc* umformen, neu formen; *text* umschreiben; *team* umgestalten; *policy* umstellen; **you can't ~ your body overnight** man kann nicht plötzlich eine andere

Figur bekommen; **to ~ itself** (*party*) sich neu formieren

reship [ˌriː'ʃɪp] VT *goods* wieder verschiffen; (= *transfer*) umladen (*to* auf +*acc*)

reshuffle [ˌriː'ʃʌfl] VT *cards* neu mischen; (*fig*) *Cabinet* umbilden; *board of directors* umbilden, umbesetzen N (*of cards*) erneutes Mischen; (*fig: of board*) Umbesetzung *f*, Umbildung *f*; **cabinet ~** (*Brit Pol*) Kabinettsumbildung *f*

reside [rɪ'zaɪd] VI **a** (*form:* = *live*) seinen Wohnsitz haben; (*monarch*) residieren **b** (*fig form*) **to ~ in sth** in etw (*dat*) liegen; **the power ~s with the President** die Macht liegt *or* ruht beim Präsidenten

residence ['rezɪdəns] N **a** (= *house*) Wohnhaus *nt*; (= *hostel: for students, nurses*) Wohnheim *nt*; (*of monarch, ambassador etc*) Residenz *f*; **the President's official ~** der Amtssitz des Präsidenten → **hall b** *no pl* (= *stay, living*) **country of ~** Aufenthaltsland *nt*; **place of ~** Wohnort *m*; **after 5 years' ~ in Britain** nach 5 Jahren Aufenthalt in Großbritannien; **to take up ~ in the capital** sich an der Hauptstadt niederlassen; **~ in the country is restricted to nationals** nur Staatsangehörige können im Land Wohnsitz nehmen (*form*); **to be in ~** (*monarch, governor etc*) anwesend sein; **poet etc in ~** (*Univ*) ansässiger Dichter *etc*; **the students are now in ~** das Semester hat angefangen

residence permit N Aufenthaltsgenehmigung *f*

residency ['rezɪdənsɪ] N **a** (*US*) = **residence b b** (*Brit*) Residenz *f* **c** (*of doctor*) Assistenzzeit *f* im Krankenhaus

resident ['rezɪdənt] N **a** Bewohner(in) *m(f)*; (*in town*) Einwohner(in) *m(f)*; (*of hospital*) Patient(in) *m(f)*; (*of prison*) Insasse *m*, Insassin *f*; (*in hotel*) Gast *m*; **"access restricted to ~s only"** „Anlieger frei"; **"parking for ~s only"** „Parkplatz nur für Mieter"; (*on road*) „Parken nur für Anlieger gestattet"; (*at hotel*) „Parkplatz nur für Gäste" **b** (= *doctor*) Anstaltsarzt *m*/-ärztin *f* ADJ **a** (*in country, town*) wohnhaft; (= *attached to institution*) ansässig, Haus-; **they are ~ in Germany** sie haben ihren Wohnsitz in Deutschland; **the ~ population** die ansässige Bevölkerung; **are you ~ in the hotel?** sind Sie Hotelgast/Hotelgäste?; **she is our ~ expert on ...** (*hum*) sie ist unsere Expertin vor Ort für ... **b** (*Zool*) *fox, badger etc* ortsansässig; **the ~ population** die ortsansässige Population **c** (*fig form*) wohnhaft

residential [ˌrezɪ'denʃəl] ADJ *job* im Haus; *college* mit einem Wohnheim verbunden; **~ requirements for voting** Meldevoraussetzungen zur Ausübung des Wahlrechts; **~ accommodation** Unterbringung *f* im Heim; **~ customer** (*for utilities*) Privathaushalt *m*; **~ development** Wohnungsbau *m*; **~ market** Häuser- und Wohnungsmarkt *m*, nichtgewerblicher Immobilienmarkt; **~ mortgage** Hypothek *f* für Wohneigentum; **~ property** Wohngebäude *nt*; **~ street** Wohnstraße *f*

residential: residential area N Wohngebiet *nt*, Wohngegend *f*; **residential care** N Heimpflege *f*; **residential home** N Wohnheim *nt*; (= *superior home*) Wohnstift *nt*

residents association N (*of area*) Bürgerinitiative *f*

residual [rɪ'zɪdjʊəl] ADJ restlich; (*Chem*) rückständig; **~ soil** (*Geol*) Alluvialboden *m*; (*by erosion*) Verwitterungsboden *m*; **~ risk** Restrisiko *nt* N (*Chem*) Rückstand *m*; (*Statistics, Math*) Abweichung *f*; **~s** (= *royalties*) Wiederholungsgage *f*

residuary [rɪ'zɪdjʊərɪ] ADJ restlich; (*Chem*) rückständig

residue ['rezɪdjuː] N **a** Rest *m*; (*Chem*) Rückstand *m* **b** (*Jur*) Nachlass *m* (*nach Abzug sämtlicher Verbindlichkeiten*)

residuum [rɪ'zɪdjʊəm] N (*Chem*) Rückstand *m*, Residuum *nt*; (*Jur*) = **residue b**

resign [rɪ'zaɪn] VT **a** (= *give up*) *office, post* zurücktreten von, abgeben; *claim, rights* aufgeben, verzichten auf (+*acc*); **he ~ed the leadership to his colleague** er übergab *or* überließ die Leitung seinem Kollegen; **to ~ one's commission** (*Mil*) seinen Abschied nehmen **b** **to ~ oneself to sth** sich mit etw abfinden; **to ~ oneself to doing sth** sich damit abfinden, etw zu tun → *also* **resigned** VI (*from public appointment, committee*) zurücktreten; (*employee*) kündigen; (*civil servant, clergyman*) sein Amt niederlegen; (*teacher*) aus dem Dienst ausscheiden; **to ~ from office** sein Amt niederlegen; **he ~ed from (his job with) "The Times"** er hat (seine Stelle) bei der „Times" gekündigt; **the Prime Minister was forced to ~** der Premierminister wurde zum Rücktritt gezwungen

resignation [ˌrezɪg'neɪʃən] N **a** (*from public appointment, committee*) Rücktritt *m*; (*of employee*) Kündigung *f*; (*of civil servant, clergyman*) Amtsniederlegung *f*; (*of teacher*) Ausscheiden *nt* aus dem Dienst; **to hand in** *or* **tender** (*form*) **one's ~** seinen Rücktritt/seine Kündigung einreichen/sein Amt niederlegen/aus dem Dienst ausscheiden **b** (= *mental state*) Resignation *f* (*to* gegenüber +*dat*), Ergebung *f* (*to* in +*acc*) **c** (*form, of right, claim etc*) Verzicht *m* (*of* auf +*acc*)

resigned [rɪ'zaɪnd] ADJ *person* resigniert; **to become ~ to sth** sich mit etw abfinden; **I was ~ to walking, when ...** ich hatte mich schon damit abgefunden, zu Fuß gehen zu müssen, als ...; **to be ~ to one's fate** sich in sein Schicksal ergeben haben; **to give a ~ shrug** resigniert die *or* mit den Achseln zucken

resignedly [rɪ'zaɪnɪdlɪ] ADV resigniert

resilience [rɪ'zɪlɪəns] N **a** (*of material*) Federn *nt* **b** (*fig, of person, nature*) Unverwüstlichkeit *f*; (*of economy*) Stabilität *f*

resilient [rɪ'zɪlɪənt] ADJ **a** *material* federnd *attr*; **to be ~** federn **b** (*fig*) *person, nature* unverwüstlich; *economy* nicht krisenanfällig, stabil; (*Comm*) *performance* robust

resin ['rezɪn] N Harz *nt*

resinous ['rezɪnəs] ADJ harzig

resist [rɪ'zɪst] VT **a** (= *oppose*) sich widersetzen (+*dat*); *arrest, sb's advances, enemy, attack* Widerstand leisten gegen, sich wehren gegen; *demand* sich wehren gegen; (*fig*) *proposal, change also* sich widersetzen (+*dat*), sich sträuben *or* wehren gegen **b** *temptation, sb, sb's charms, urge, impulse* widerstehen (+*dat*); **I couldn't ~ (eating) another piece of cake** ich konnte der Versuchung nicht widerstehen, noch ein Stück Kuchen zu essen **c** *wall, door* standhalten (+*dat*); **the lock ~ed my attempts at opening it** das Schloss widerstand meinen Versuchen, es zu öffnen; **to ~ corrosion** korrosionsbeständig sein VI **a** (= *be opposed*) sich widersetzen; (*faced with arrest, sb's advances, enemy, attack*) Widerstand leisten, sich wehren; (*fig, faced with proposal, change also*) sich sträuben *or* wehren **b** (*faced with temptation, sb, sb's charms*) widerstehen **c** (*wall, door*) standhalten

resistance [rɪ'zɪstəns] N (*to* gegen) Widerstand *m* (*also Elec, Phys, Mil*); (*Med*) Widerstandsfähigkeit *f*, Resistenz *f* (*geh*); **~ to water/heat** Wasser-/Hitzebeständigkeit *f*; **to meet with ~** auf Widerstand stoßen; **to offer no ~ (to sb/ sth)** (*to attacker, advances etc*) (jdm/gegen etw) keinen Widerstand leisten; (*to proposals*) sich (jdm/einer Sache) nicht widersetzen; **the (French) Resistance** (*Hist*) die Résistance; **the Resistance movement** (*Hist*) die Résistance → **line¹, passive resistance**

resistance fighter N Widerstandskämpfer(in) *m(f)*

resistant [rɪ'zɪstənt] ADJ *material, surface* strapazierfähig; (*Med*) immun (*to* gegen)

resister [rɪ'zɪstə] N Wehrdienstverweigerer *m*

resistor [rɪ'zɪstə] N (*Elec*) Widerstand *m*

resit [,riː'sɪt] *vb: pret, ptp* **resat** (*Brit*) **VT** *exam* wiederholen **VI** die Prüfung wiederholen **N** ['riːsɪt] Wiederholung(sprüfung) *f*

resize [,riː'saɪz] VT (*Comput*) *window* die Größe (+*gen*) verändern

reskill [,riː'skɪl] (*Ind*) **VI** umgeschult werden, sich umschulen lassen **VT** umschulen

resole [,riː'səʊl] VT neu besohlen

resolute ['rezəluːt] ADJ energisch, entschlossen; *answer, refusal* entschieden, bestimmt; **to take ~ action** energisch vorgehen; **to be ~ in sth** entschieden in etw (*dat*) sein; **to be ~ in doing sth** etw mit Entschlossenheit tun

resolutely ['rezəluːtlɪ] ADV *resist* entschieden; *refuse, answer also* bestimmt; *stare* entschlossen; *stride* entschlossen, resolut; **to be ~ opposed to sth** entschieden gegen etw sein; **to remain ~ committed to sth** sich weiterhin entschieden *or* entschlossen für etw einsetzen; **to stand ~ against** sich entschieden *or* entschlossen gegen etw wehren

resoluteness ['rezəluːtnɪs] N Entschlossenheit *f*; (*of refusal, answer*) Entschiedenheit *f*, Bestimmtheit *f*

resolution [,rezə'luːʃən] ✪ 8.1 N **a** (= *decision*) Beschluss *m*; (*esp Pol*) Resolution *f*; (*governing one's behaviour*) Vorsatz *m*; **good ~s** gute Vorsätze *pl* **b** *no pl* (= *resoluteness*) Entschlossenheit *f*, Bestimmtheit *f* **c** *no pl* (= *solving*: *of problem, puzzle*) Lösung *f* **d** (*Comput*) Auflösung *f* **e** (*Phys, Mus*) Auflösung *f* (*into* in +*acc*) **f** (*Med, of swelling*) Rückgang *m*

resolvable [rɪ'zɒlvəbl] ADJ *a problem, conflict, crisis* lösbar; *doubt* zerstreubar; **a dispute/an issue which is not ~** ein Streit *m*, der nicht beigelegt/ein Thema *nt*, das nicht geklärt werden kann **b** (*into elements*) zerlegbar; (= *convertible*) auflösbar

resolve [rɪ'zɒlv] **VT a** *problem, conflict, crisis* lösen; *doubt* zerstreuen; *dispute* beilegen; *differences, issue* klären
b (= *decide*) **to ~ that ...** beschließen, dass ...; **to ~ to do sth** beschließen, etw zu tun
c (= *break up: into elements*) zerlegen (*into* in +*acc*); (= *convert*) auflösen (*also Phys*) (*into* in +*acc*)
d (*Mus*) *chord, harmony* auflösen (*into* in +*acc*)
e (*Med*) zum Rückgang bringen **VI a** (= *decide*) **to ~ (up)on sth** etw beschließen
b (*into* in +*acc*) (= *break up*) zerfallen; (= *be converted*) sich auflösen **VR** (*into* in +*acc*) sich zerlegen lassen; (= *be converted*) sich auflösen
N a (= *decision*) Beschluss *m*; **to make a ~ to do sth** den Beschluss fassen, etw zu tun
b *no pl* (= *resoluteness*) Entschlossenheit *f*; **to do sth with ~** etw fest entschlossen tun

resolved [rɪ'zɒlvd] ADJ (fest) entschlossen

resolvedly [rɪ'zɒlvɪdlɪ] ADV (fest) entschlossen, entschieden

resonance ['rezənəns] N **a** Resonanz *f*; (*of voice*) voller Klang **b** (*fig*) **to have ~ for sb** für jdn von Bedeutung sein

resonant ['rezənənt] ADJ **a** *sound* voll; *voice* klangvoll; *laugh* schallend; *room* mit Resonanz; **~ with the sound of singing/a thousand voices** von Gesang/vom Klang von tausend Stimmen erfüllt **b** (*fig*) **to be ~ of sth** an etw (*acc*) erinnern; **to be ~ with tradition/history** reich an Tradition/Geschichte sein

resonate ['rezəneɪt] **VI a** widerhallen **b** (*fig*) **to ~ with sth** reich an etw (*dat*) sein; **that ~s with me** das bedeutet mir etwas

resonator ['rezəneɪtə'] N Resonator *m*

resorb [rɪ'zɔːb] VT resorbieren (*spec*), (wieder) aufsaugen

resort [rɪ'zɔːt] **N a** (= *recourse*) Ausweg *m*; (= *thing, action resorted to*) Rettung *f*, Ausweg *m*; **without ~ to violence** ohne Gewaltanwendung; **as a last ~** als Letztes; **in the last ~** im schlimmsten Fall, wenn alle Stricke reißen (*inf*); **you were my last ~** du warst meine letzte Rettung
b (= *place*) Urlaubsort *m*; **coastal ~** Seebad *nt*; **seaside ~** Seebad *nt*; **summer ~** Sommerurlaubsort *m*; **winter sports ~** Wintersportort *m* **›** **health resort, holiday resort**
VI a (= *have recourse*) **to ~ to sth** zu etw greifen; **to ~ to sb** sich an jdn wenden; **to ~ to violence** Gewalt anwenden, gewalttätig werden; **to ~ to begging/stealing/swearing** sich aufs Betteln/Stehlen/Fluchen verlegen
b (= *frequent*) **to ~ to a place** häufig an einem Ort verkehren

resound [rɪ'zaʊnd] VI (wider)hallen (*with* von); **my ears were still ~ing with the noise** mir tönten noch die Ohren von dem Lärm; **his name ~ed throughout the land** (*fig*) sein Name war in aller Munde

resounding [rɪ'zaʊndɪŋ] ADJ *noise, shout, thud, crack* widerhallend; *laugh, voice* schallend; (*fig*) *triumph, victory, failure* gewaltig; *success* durchschlagend; *defeat* haushoch; **~ silence** überwältigende Stille; **the response was a ~ "no"** die Antwort war ein überwältigendes „Nein"

resoundingly [rɪ'zaʊndɪŋlɪ] ADV **a** (= *convincingly*) *defeat* vernichtend; **to be ~ defeated** eine vernichtende Niederlage erleiden; **the play was ~ successful** das Stück war ein durchschlagender Erfolg **b** (= *loudly*) schallend

resource [rɪ'sɔːs] **N a resources** PL (= *wealth, supplies, money etc*) Mittel *pl*, Ressourcen *pl*; **financial ~s** Geldmittel *pl*; **mineral ~s** Bodenschätze *pl*; **natural ~s** Naturschätze *pl*; **human ~s** (= *workforce*) Arbeitskräfte *pl*; **~s in men and materials** Reserven *pl* an Menschen und Material; **he has no inner ~s** er weiß sich (*dat*) nicht zu helfen; **he has no ~s against boredom** er weiß sich (*dat*) gegen Langeweile nicht zu helfen; **left to his own ~s** sich (*dat*) selbst überlassen
b (= *expedient*) Ausweg *m*, Mittel *nt*; **as a last ~** als letzter Ausweg; **you are my last ~** du bist meine letzte Rettung **VT** (*Brit*) *project* mit den nötigen Mitteln *or* Ressourcen versorgen, finanzieren; (*with personnel*) personell ausstatten

resourced [rɪ'sɔːst] ADJ (*Brit*) **well-resourced** (*with materials*) gut ausgestattet; (*financially*) ausreichend finanziert; **under-resourced** (*with materials*) unzureichend ausgestattet; (*financially*) unzureichend finanziert; **the museum has always been under-resourced in both staff and finances** das Museum hatte immer schon zu wenig Personal und Geld

resourceful [rɪ'sɔːsfʊl] ADV *person* einfallsreich, findig; *scheme* genial

resourcefully [rɪ'sɔːsfəlɪ] ADV einfallsreich, findig

resourcefulness [rɪ'sɔːsfʊlnɪs] N Einfallsreichtum *m*, Findigkeit *f*; (*of scheme*) Genialität *f*

resourcing [rɪ'sɔːsɪŋ] N , *no pl* Verfügbarmachen *nt* von Ressourcen

respect [rɪ'spekt] ✪ 11.3 **N a** (= *esteem*) Respekt *m*, Achtung *f* (*for* vor +*dat*); **to have/show ~ for** Respekt *or* Achtung haben/zeigen vor (+*dat*); *for the law* achten; **I have the highest ~ for his ability** ich halte ihn für außerordentlich fähig; **to behave with ~** sich respektvoll verhalten; **to hold sb in (great) ~** jdn (sehr) achten; **he commands ~** er ist eine Respektsperson *or* (*public figure*) Respekt gebietende Persönlichkeit; **to command the ~ of the nation** dem Volk Respekt *or* Achtung abnötigen; **you should have a bit more ~ for his right hook** du solltest etwas mehr auf seinen rechten Haken achten
b (= *consideration*) Rücksicht *f* (*for* auf +*acc*); **to treat with ~** (*person*) rücksichtsvoll behandeln; *dangerous person etc* sich in Acht nehmen vor (+*dat*); *toys, clothes etc* schonend behandeln; **nitroglycerine should be treated with ~** Nitroglyzerin muss mit äußerster Vorsicht behandelt werden; **she has** *or* **shows no ~ for other people's feelings** sie nimmt keine Rücksicht auf die Gefühle anderer; **out of ~ for** aus Rücksicht auf (+*acc*); **with (due) ~, I still think that ...** bei allem Respekt, meine ich dennoch, dass ...
c (= *reference*) **with ~ to ..., in ~ of ...** was ... anbetrifft, in Bezug auf ... (+*acc*)
d (= *aspect*) Hinsicht *f*, Beziehung *f*; **in some/other ~s** in gewisser/anderer Hinsicht *or* Beziehung; **in many ~s** in vieler Hinsicht; **in this ~** in dieser Hinsicht *or* Beziehung; **in what ~?** in welcher Hinsicht *or* Beziehung?
e **respects** PL (= *regards*) Empfehlungen *pl* (*geh*), Grüße *pl*; **to pay one's ~s to sb** jdm seine Aufwartung machen; **give my ~s to** meine Empfehlung an (+*acc*) (*geh*); **to pay one's last ~s to sb** jdm die letzte Ehre erweisen
VT a (= *show respect for*) respektieren; *person, customs, the law, privacy, rights* respektieren, achten; *ability* anerkennen; **a ~ed company** eine angesehene Firma
b as ~s ... was ... anbelangt *or* betrifft

respectability [rɪ,spektə'bɪlɪtɪ] N (= *estimable quality, of person*) Ehrbarkeit *f*; (*of motives also*) Ehrenhaftigkeit *f*; (= *decent quality: of life, district, club*) Anständigkeit *f*; (= *socially approved quality, of person*) Angesehenheit *f*; (*of businessman, hotel*) Seriosität *f*; (*of clothes, behaviour*) Korrektheit *f*, Anständigkeit *f*

respectable [rɪ'spektəbl] ADJ **a** (= *estimable*) *person* ehrbar; *motives* ehrbar, ehrenhaft; (= *decent*) *life, district, club* anständig; (= *socially approved*) *person* angesehen, geachtet; *businessman, hotel* seriös; *clothes, behaviour* korrekt, anständig; **they are very ~ people** sie sind sehr ehrbare Leute; **he was outwardly ~ but ...** er wirkte sehr ehrbar, aber ...; **in ~ society** in guter Gesellschaft; **young people from ~ homes** junge Leute aus gutem Hause; **a perfectly ~ way to earn one's living** eine völlig akzeptable Art und Weise, seinen Lebensunterhalt zu verdienen; **the ~ face of capitalism** das ehrbare Gesicht des Kapitalismus; **that's not ~** das schickt *or* gehört sich nicht
b (= *large*) *size, income, sum* ansehnlich, beachtlich
c (= *fairly good*) *advantage* beträchtlich; *score, lead* beachtlich; **a ~ writer** ein ganz ordentlicher Schriftsteller; **she finished a ~ fourth** sie belegte einen beachtlichen *or* respektablen vierten Platz

respectably [rɪ'spektəblɪ] ADV **a** *dress, behave* anständig; **I'm a ~ married man** ich bin ein anständig verheirateter Mann **b** (= *fairly well*) **she finished ~ (in the race)** sie erzielte (im Rennen) ein beachtliches *or* respektables Ergebnis

respecter [rɪ'spektə'] N **the law is no ~ of persons** vor dem Gesetz sind alle gleich; **this disease is no ~ of persons** diese Krankheit macht vor niemandem halt; **he is no ~ of persons** er lässt sich von niemandem beeindrucken; **death is no ~ of wealth** der Tod nimmt keine Rücksicht auf Reichtum

respectful [rɪ'spektfʊl] ADJ respektvoll (*towards* gegenüber); **to be ~ of sth** etw respektieren; **to keep a ~ silence** respektvoll schweigen; **to follow sb at a ~ distance** jdm in angemessenem Abstand folgen

respectfully [rɪ'spektfəlɪ] ADV **a** respektvoll **b** (*in letters*) **I remain ~ yours** *or* **yours ~** ich verbleibe mit vorzüglicher Hochachtung Ihr ... (*form*)

respectfulness [rɪ'spektfʊlnɪs] N Respekt *m*; **~ of others** Rücksicht *f* auf andere

respecting [rɪ'spektɪŋ] PREP bezüglich (+*gen*)

respective [rɪ'spektɪv] ADJ jeweilig; **we took our ~ partners/glasses** wir nahmen jeder unseren Partner/unser Glas, wir nahmen unsere jeweiligen Partner/Gläser; **they each have their ~ merits** jeder von ihnen hat seine eigenen Vorteile

respectively [rɪ'spektɪvlɪ] ADV beziehungsweise; **the girls' dresses are green and blue ~** die Mädchen haben grüne beziehungsweise blaue Kleider; **and then allocate the funds ~** und die Mittel dann dementsprechend verteilen

respiration [,respɪ'reɪʃən] N (*Bot, Med*) Atmung *f*

respirator ['respɪreɪtə'] N (*Med*) Respirator *m*; (*Mil*) Atemschutzmaske *f*

respiratory [rɪ'spɪrətərɪ] ADJ Atem-, respiratorisch (*spec*); *infection, disease* der Atemwege; **~ problems** Atembeschwerden *pl*

respiratory: respiratory failure N respiratorische Insuffizienz (*spec*); **respiratory organs** PL Atmungsorgane *pl*; **respiratory system** N Atmungssystem *nt*; **respiratory tract** N Atemwege *pl*

respire [rɪ'spaɪəʳ] VTI (*Med, form*) atmen, respirieren (*spec*)

respite ['respaɪt] N **a** (= *rest*) Ruhepause *f* (*from* von); (= *easing off*) Nachlass *nt*; **without (a) ~** ohne Unterbrechung *or* Pause **b** (= *reprieve*) Aufschub *m*

resplendence [rɪ'splendəns] N (*of person*) Glanz *m*, Strahlen *nt*; (*of clothes*) Pracht *f*

resplendent [rɪ'splendənt] ADJ *person, face* glänzend, strahlend; *clothes* prächtig; **there he was, ~ in his new uniform** da war er, in seiner funkelnden neuen Uniform; **the stage, ~ in blue and gold** die Bühne in einer Pracht von Gold- und Blautönen

resplendently [rɪ'splendəntlɪ] ADV prächtig

respond [rɪ'spɒnd] VI **a** (= *reply*) antworten; **to ~ to a question** eine Frage beantworten, auf eine Frage antworten *or* erwidern; **to ~ to a toast** einen Toast erwidern **b** (= *show reaction*) (*to* auf +*acc*) reagieren; (*brakes, meter*) reagieren, ansprechen; **to ~ to an appeal** einen Appell beantworten; **to ~ to an appeal for money** einem Spendenaufruf folgen; **they ~ed well to the appeal for money** der Spendenaufruf fand ein großes Echo; **to ~ to a call** einem Ruf folgen; **the patient did not ~ to the treatment/his mother's voice** der Patient sprach auf die Behandlung nicht an/reagierte nicht auf die Stimme seiner Mutter; **the illness ~ed to treatment** die Behandlung schlug an

respondent [rɪ'spɒndənt] N (*Jur*) Scheidungsbeklagte(r) *mf*

responder [rɪ'spɒndəʳ] N (*Radar*) Antwortbake *f*, Responder *m* (*spec*)

response [rɪ'spɒns] N **a** (= *reply*) Antwort *f*, Erwiderung *f*; (*Eccl*) Antwort *f*; **in ~ (to)** als Antwort (auf +*acc*), in Erwiderung (+*gen*) (*geh*) **b** (= *reaction*) Reaktion *f*; **£50,000 was raised in ~ to the radio appeal** auf den Aufruf im Rundfunk hin gingen Spenden in Höhe von 50.000 Pfund ein; **we had hoped for a bigger ~ from the public** wir hatten uns größere Resonanz in der Öffentlichkeit erhofft; **my appeal met with no ~** meine Bitte fand kein Echo *or* keine Resonanz

response time N (*of machine, police, ambulance etc*) Ansprechzeit *f*

responsibility [rɪ,spɒnsə'bɪlɪtɪ] ✪ 18.3, 20.6 N **a** *no pl* Verantwortung *f*; **to put** *or* **place the ~ for sth on sb** jdm die Verantwortung für etw übertragen; **to take** *or* **assume (full) ~ (for sth)** die (volle) Verantwortung (für etw) übernehmen; **the management takes no ~ for objects left here** die Firma haftet nicht für liegen gelassene Gegenstände; **that's his ~** dafür ist er verantwortlich; **she's his ~** er hat die Verantwortung für sie; **it's not my ~ to do that** ich bin nicht dafür verantwortlich, das zu tun; **on one's own ~** auf eigene Verantwortung; **sense of ~** Verantwortungsgefühl *nt*; **~ payment** Verantwortlichkeitszuschlag *m* **b** (= *duty, burden*) Verpflichtung *f* (*to* für); **the responsibilities of state** die staatsmännischen Pflichten; **the responsibilities of office** die Dienstpflichten *pl*

responsible [rɪ'spɒnsəbl] ADJ **a** (*denoting cause*) verantwortlich; (= *to blame*) schuld (*for* an +*dat*); **bad workmanship was ~ for the failure** schlechte Arbeit war an dem Versagen schuld; **what's ~ for the hold-up?** woran liegt die Verzögerung?; **who is ~ for breaking the window?** wer hat das Fenster eingeschlagen? **b** (= *liable, answerable*) verantwortlich; **she is not ~ for her actions** sie ist für ihre Handlungen nicht voll verantwortlich; **to be ~ to sb for sth** jdm gegenüber für etw verantwortlich sein;

to be directly ~ to sb jdm unmittelbar unterstellt sein; **to hold sb ~ for sth** jdn für etw verantwortlich machen; **she is ~ for popularizing the sport** (*her task*) es ist ihre Aufgabe *or* sie ist dafür verantwortlich, die Sportart populärer zu machen; (*her merit*) es ist ihr zu verdanken, dass die Sportart populär geworden ist **c** (= *trustworthy*) *person, attitude* verantwortungsbewusst; *firm* seriös, zuverlässig **d** (= *involving responsibility*) *job* verantwortungsvoll

responsibly [rɪ'spɒnsəblɪ] ADV *act, behave* verantwortungsbewusst; *carry out one's duties* zuverlässig

responsive [rɪ'spɒnsɪv] ADJ **a** *person, audience* interessiert, mitgehend; *steering, brakes, motor* leicht reagierend *or* ansprechend; **to be ~ to sth** auf etw (*acc*) reagieren *or* ansprechen; **to be ~ to sb's needs** auf jds Bedürfnisse eingehen; **to be ~ to antibiotics** auf Antibiotika ansprechen; **he wasn't very ~ when I suggested it to him** er war nicht sehr begeistert, als ich ihm das vorschlug; **the pupils weren't very ~** die Schüler machten nicht richtig mit; **he wasn't very ~ (to my complaint)** er ging kaum darauf ein **b** (*form*, = *answering*) *smile, gesture* in Erwiderung; **the dog gave a ~ wag of his tail** der Hund reagierte mit einem Schwanzwedeln

responsiveness [rɪ'spɒnsɪvnɪs] N **because of the tremendous ~ of the audience** weil das Publikum so hervorragend mitging; **a class not noted for its ~** eine Klasse, die dafür bekannt ist, dass sie kaum mitmacht; **the ~ of the government** die Reaktionsfreudigkeit der Regierung; **they have improved the ~ of the steering** es ist ein leichteres Ansprechen der Steuerung erzielt worden; **I was somewhat surprised at their ~ to my suggestion/my needs** ich war über ihre positive Reaktion auf meinen Vorschlag/meine Bedürfnisse einigermaßen überrascht

rest¹ [rest] N **a** (= *relaxation*) Ruhe *f*; (= *pause*) Pause *f*, Unterbrechung *f*; (*in rest cure, on holiday etc*) Erholung *f*; **a day of ~** ein Ruhetag *m*; **to need ~** Ruhe brauchen; **I need a ~** ich muss mich ausruhen; (= *vacation*) ich brauche Urlaub; **to go to the mountains for a ~** zur Erholung in die Berge fahren; **to have** *or* **take a ~** (= *relax*) (sich) ausruhen; (= *pause*) (eine) Pause machen; **she took** *or* **had an hour's ~** (= *relaxation*) sie ruhte sich eine Stunde aus; (= *pause*) sie machte eine Stunde Pause; **take a ~!** (*inf*) hör doch auf!; **to have a good night's ~** sich ordentlich ausschlafen; **to give one's eyes a ~** seine Augen ausruhen; **to give sb/the horses a ~** jdn/die Pferde ausruhen lassen; **give it a ~!** (*inf*) hör doch auf! **b** **to be at ~** (= *peaceful*) ruhig sein; (*euph*, = *dead*) ruhen; **to lay to ~** (*euph*) zur letzten Ruhe betten; **to set at ~** (*fears, doubts*) beschwichtigen; **to put** *or* **set sb's mind at ~** jdn beruhigen; **you can set** *or* **put your mind at ~** Sie können sich beruhigen, Sie können beruhigt sein; **to come to ~** (*ball, car etc*) zum Stillstand kommen; (*bird, insect*) sich niederlassen; (*gaze, eyes*) hängenbleiben (*upon* an +*dat*) **c** (= *support*) Auflage *f*; (*of telephone*) Gabel *f*; (*Billiards*) Steg *m* → **armrest, footrest** **d** (*Mus*) Pause *f*; (*Poet*) Zäsur *f* VI **a** (= *lie down, take rest*) ruhen (*geh*); (= *relax, be still*) sich ausruhen; (= *pause*) Pause machen, eine Pause einlegen; (*on walk, in physical work*) rasten, Pause machen; (*euph*. = *be buried*) ruhen; **you must ~ for an hour** Sie sollten eine Stunde ausruhen; **she never ~s** sie arbeitet ununterbrochen; **he will not ~ until he discovers the truth** er wird nicht ruhen (und rasten), bis er die Wahrheit gefunden hat; **to ~ easy (in one's bed)** beruhigt schlafen; **to be ~ing** ruhen (*geh*); (*euph*, = *out of work*) ohne Engagement sein; **to let a field ~** einen Acker brachliegen lassen; **(the case for) the prosecution ~s** das Plädoyer der Anklage ist abgeschlossen; **to let a matter ~** eine Sache auf sich beruhen lassen; **let the matter ~!** lass es dabei!; **may he ~ in**

peace er ruhe in Frieden; **to ~ in the Lord** im Herrn ruhen **b** (= *remain: decision, authority, blame, responsibility etc*) liegen (*with* bei); **the matter must not ~ there** man kann die Sache so nicht belassen; **and there the matter ~s for the moment** und damit ist die Sache momentan erledigt; **(you may) ~ assured that …** Sie können versichert sein, dass … **c** (= *lean: person, head, ladder*) lehnen (*on* an +*dat*, *against* gegen); (= *be supported: roof etc*) ruhen (*on* auf +*dat*); (*fig: eyes, gaze*) ruhen (*on* auf +*dat*); (*fig: = be based, argument, case*) sich stützen (*on* auf +*acc*); (*reputation*) beruhen (*on* auf +*acc*); (*responsibility*) liegen, ruhen (*on* auf +*dat*); **her elbows were ~ing on the table** ihre Ellbogen waren auf den Tisch gestützt; **her head was ~ing on the table** ihr Kopf lag auf dem Tisch VT **a** *one's eyes* ausruhen; *voice* schonen; *horses* ausruhen lassen; **to ~ oneself** sich ausruhen; **to be ~ed** ausgeruht sein; **to feel ~ed** sich ausgeruht fühlen; **(may) God ~ his soul** Gott hab ihn selig!; **to ~ one's case** (*Jur*) das Plädoyer abschließen **b** (= *lean*) *ladder* lehnen (*against* gegen, *on* an +*acc*); *elbow* stützen (*on* auf +*acc*); (*fig*) *theory, suspicions* stützen (*on* auf +*acc*); **to ~ one's hand on sb's shoulder** jdm die Hand auf die Schulter legen; **to ~ one's head on the table** den Kopf auf den Tisch legen; **he ~ed his head against the wall** er lehnte den Kopf an die Wand

▶ **rest up** VI (*inf*) sich ausruhen

rest² N (= *remainder*) Rest *m*; **the ~ of the money/meal** der Rest des Geldes/Essens, das übrige Geld/Essen; **the ~ of the boys** der Rest der Jungen, die übrigen Jungen; **you go off and the ~ of us will wait here** ihr geht, und der Rest von uns wartet hier; **he was as drunk as the ~ of them** er war so betrunken wie der Rest *or* die übrigen; **she's no different from the ~** sie ist wie alle anderen; **all the ~ of the money** der ganze Rest des Geldes, das ganze übrige Geld; **all the ~ of the books** alle übrigen Bücher; **and all the ~ of it** (*inf*) und so weiter und so fort; **Mary, Jane and all the ~ of them** Mary, Jane und wie sie alle heißen; **the ~** im Übrigen

restart [,riː'stɑːt] VT *job, activity* wieder aufnehmen; *negotiations, career also* wieder beginnen *or* anfangen; *race* neu starten; *game* (*from beginning*) neu beginnen; (*after interruption*) fortsetzen; *engine, car* wieder anlassen; *machine* wieder anschalten; *economy* wieder ankurbeln; **to ~ work** wieder zu arbeiten anfangen VI wieder anfangen *or* beginnen; (*race*) von neuem beginnen; (*game*) (*from beginning*) neu beginnen; (*after interruption*) fortgesetzt werden; (*machine*) wieder starten; (*engine, car*) wieder anspringen

restate [,riː'steɪt] VT **a** (= *express again*) *reasons* wieder *or* erneut nennen; *problem, argument, theory* wieder *or* erneut vortragen; *case, one's position* wieder *or* erneut darstellen; (*Mus*) *theme* wieder aufnehmen **b** (= *express differently*) *case, one's position* neu darstellen

restatement [,riː'steɪtmənt] N **a** (= *expressing again, of reasons*) erneute Nennung; (*of problem, argument, theory*) erneuter Vortrag; (*of case, one's position*) erneute Darstellung; (*Mus, of theme*) Wiederaufnahme *f* **b** (= *expressing differently*) Umformulierung *f*; (*of case, one's position*) Neudarstellung *f*

restaurant ['restərɒnt] N Restaurant *nt*, Gaststätte *f*; **~ food/prices** Restaurantessen *nt*/-preise *pl*

restaurant car N (*Brit, Rail*) Speisewagen *m*

restaurateur [,restərə'tɜː] N Gastwirt *m*, Gastronom *m*

rest: rest cure N Erholung *f*; (*in bed*) Liegekur *f*; **rest day** N Ruhetag *m*

restful ['restfʊl] ADJ *occupation, pastime etc* erholsam; *atmosphere* gemütlich, entspannend; *lighting* beruhigend; *colour* ruhig; *place* friedlich; **she is very ~ to be with** es ist sehr gemütlich, mit ihr zusammen zu sein

rest home N Altersheim *nt*, Pflegeheim *nt*

resting place ['rɛstɪŋˌpleɪs] N Rastplatz *m*; (*euph*, = *grave*) Ruhestätte *f*

restitution [ˌrɛstɪ'tjuːʃən] N **a** (= *giving back*) Rückgabe *f*; (*of money*) Rückerstattung *f*, Rückgabe *f*; **to make ~ of sth** (*form*) etw zurückgeben/-erstatten; **~ of conjugal rights** (*Jur*) Wiederherstellung *f* der ehelichen Gemeinschaft **b** (= *reparation*) Schadenersatz *m*, Entschädigung *f*

restive ['rɛstɪv] ADJ **a** *horse* (= *stubborn*) störrisch; (= *nervous*) unruhig **b** (= *restless*) *person, manner* rastlos; *tribes* widerspenstig, aufsässig

restiveness ['rɛstɪvnɪs] N **a** (*of horse*, = *stubbornness*) störrische Art; (= *nervousness*) Unruhe *f* **b** (= *restlessness*) (*of person, manner*) Rastlosigkeit *f*; (*of tribes*) Widerspenstigkeit *f*, Aufsässigkeit *f*

restless ['rɛstlɪs] ADJ (= *unsettled*) *person, manner, sea, night* unruhig; *mind* ruhelos, unruhig; *energy* rastlos; (= *not wanting to stay in one place*) rastlos; **~ spirit** ruheloser Geist; **the natives are ~** (*hum*) es herrscht Unruhe im Land

restlessly ['rɛstlɪslɪ] ADV (= *in an unsettled manner*) unruhig; (= *not wanting to stay in one place*) rastlos

restlessness ['rɛstlɪsnɪs] N (= *unsettled manner*) Unruhe *f*; (= *not wanting to stay in one place*) Rastlosigkeit *f*

restock [ˌriː'stɒk] VT *shelves, fridge, bar* wieder auffüllen; *pond* wieder (mit Fischen) besetzen; *farm* den Viehbestand (+*gen*) erneuern

restorable [rɪ'stɔːrəbl] ADJ wiederherstellbar

restoration [ˌrɛstə'reɪʃən] N **a** (= *return*) Rückgabe *f* (*to* an +*acc*); (*of property*) Rückerstattung *f*, Rückgabe *f* (*to* an +*acc*); (*of confidence, order, calm, peace*) Wiederherstellung *f*; (*to office*) Wiedereinsetzung *f* (*to* in +*acc*) **b the Restoration** (*Hist*) die Restauration **c** (*of monument, work of art*) Restaurierung *f*

restorative [rɪ'stɔːrətɪv] ADJ stärkend N Stärkungsmittel *nt*

restore [rɪ'stɔː] VT **a** *sth lost, borrowed, stolen* (= *give back*) zurückgeben; (= *bring back*) zurückbringen; *confidence, order, calm, peace* wieder herstellen; **to ~ sb's health, to ~ sb to health** jds Gesundheit wieder herstellen, jdn wieder herstellen; **~d to health** wieder hergestellt; **to ~ freedom to sb** jdm die Freiheit wiedergeben; **to ~ sb to life** jdn ins Leben zurückrufen; **to ~ sth to its former condition** etw wieder herstellen; **the brandy ~d my strength** or **me** der Weinbrand hat mich wieder hergestellt **b** (*to former post*) wieder einsetzen (*to* in +*acc*); **to ~ sb to the throne** jdn als König(in) wieder einsetzen; **to ~ to power** wieder an die Macht bringen **c** (= *repair*) *building, painting, furniture, text* restaurieren

restorer [rɪ'stɔːrə] N (*Art*) Restaurator(in) *m(f)* → **hair restorer**

rest period N Erholungspause *f*

restrain [rɪ'streɪn] VT *person* zurückhalten; *prisoner* mit Gewalt festhalten; *animal, unruly children, madman* bändigen; *radicals* in Schranken halten; *sb's activities, power* einschränken; *emotions, laughter* unterdrücken; **to ~ inflation/prices** die Inflationsrate/Preisentwicklung aufhalten; **to exercise a ~ing influence** etwas mildernd einwirken (*on* auf +*acc*); **to ~ sb from doing sth** jdn davon abhalten, etw zu tun; **to ~ oneself** sich beherrschen

restrained [rɪ'streɪnd] ADJ *person, performance, response* zurückhaltend; *emotions* unterdrückt; *manner, words* beherrscht; *tone, voice, colour* verhalten; *criticism* maßvoll, gezügelt; **he was very ~ when he heard the news** er war sehr beherrscht, als er die Nachricht hörte

restraining order [rɪ'streɪnɪŋ-] N (*Jur*) Verbotsverfügung *f*; **to get a ~ (against sb)** eine gerichtliche (Verbots)verfügung (gegen jdn) erwirken

restraint [rɪ'streɪnt] N **a** (= *restriction*) Einschränkung *f*, Beschränkung *f*; **without ~** unbeschränkt; *develop* ungehemmt; **to put/keep sb under ~** (*Jur*) jdn in Haft nehmen/behalten **b** (= *moderation*) Beherrschung *f*; **to show a lack of ~** wenig Beherrschung zeigen; **he said with great ~ that ...** er sagte sehr beherrscht, dass ...; **to express oneself without ~** sich zwanglos ausdrücken; **wage ~** Zurückhaltung *f* bei Lohnforderungen **c** (= *head restraint*) Kopfstütze *f*

restrict [rɪ'strɪkt] VT **a** (= *limit*) beschränken (*to* auf +*acc*; *freedom, authority also* einschränken; *time, number also* begrenzen (*to* auf +*acc*); **to ~ sb's movements** jdn in seiner Bewegungsfreiheit einschränken; **all speakers are ~ed to three hours** die Redezeit ist auf drei Stunden beschränkt **b** (= *hinder*) **~ing clothes** beengende Kleidungsstücke

restricted [rɪ'strɪktɪd] ADJ **a** (= *limited*) *view* beschränkt, begrenzt; *diet* eingeschränkt; (*Admin, Mil*) *document, information* geheim; *locality* nur bestimmten Gruppen zugänglich; *admission* begrenzt; **within a ~ area** (= *within limited area*) auf begrenztem Gebiet **b** (= *hindered*) **I feel too ~ in jeans** ich fühle mich in Jeans zu beengt

restricted area N Sperrgebiet *nt*; (*Brit, Mot*) Strecke *f* mit Geschwindigkeitsbeschränkung

restriction [rɪ'strɪkʃən] N (*on sth* etw *gen*) Beschränkung *f*; (*of freedom, authority also*) Einschränkung *f*; (*on time, number also*) Begrenzung *f*; **to place ~s on sth** etw beschränken *or* einschränken; **~s of space** räumliche Beschränktheit; **without ~s** uneingeschränkt; **speed ~** (*Mot*) Geschwindigkeitsbegrenzung *f* or -beschränkung *f*; **price ~** Preisbeschränkung *f*

restrictive [rɪ'strɪktɪv] ADJ **a** (= *limiting*) restriktiv, einschränkend *attr*; *environment* beengend, restriktiv **b** (= *hindering*) *clothing* beengend, eng

restrictive practices PL (*Jur, Ind*) wettbewerbsbeschränkende Geschäftspraktiken *pl*

restring [ˌriː'strɪŋ] *pret, ptp* **restrung** [ˌriː'strʌŋ] VT *instrument* neu besaiten; *bow, racket* neu bespannen; *pearls* neu aufziehen

rest room N (*US*) Toilette *f*

restructure [ˌriː'strʌktʃə] VTI (*Comm, Ind*) umstrukturieren

restructuring [ˌriː'strʌktʃərɪŋ] N (*Comm, Ind*) Umstrukturierung *f*

rest stop N (*US Aut*) (= *place*) Rastplatz *m*; (= *break in journey*) Rast *f*

restyle [ˌriː'staɪl] VT (= *rearrange, remake*) umgestalten, umarbeiten; (= *realign*) neu ausrichten

result [rɪ'zʌlt] ⏣ 17.1 N **a** Folge *f*; **as a ~ he failed** folglich fiel er durch; **as a ~ of this** und folglich; **as a ~ of which he ...** was zur Folge hatte, dass er ...; **to be the ~ of** resultieren aus **b** (*of election, exam, race, Math etc*) Ergebnis *nt*, Resultat *nt*; (*good result*) Resultat *nt*; **~s** (*of test, experiment*) Werte *pl*; **I want to see ~s** ich möchte einen Erfolg or ein Resultat sehen; **to get ~s** (*person*) Erfolg or Resultate erzielen; **we had very good ~s with this** wir hatten damit großen Erfolg or sehr gute Resultate; **as a ~ of my inquiry** auf meine Anfrage (hin); **what was the ~?** (*Sport*) wie ist es ausgegangen?; **without ~** ergebnislos VI sich ergeben, resultieren (*from* aus); **from which it ~s that ...** woraus folgt, dass ...

▸ **result in** VI +*prep obj* führen zu; **this resulted in his being late** das führte dazu, dass er zu spät kam

resultant [rɪ'zʌltənt] ADJ resultierend, sich daraus ergebend N (*Phys*) Resultierende *f*

resume [rɪ'zjuːm] VT **a** (= *restart*) wieder aufnehmen; *activity also* weitermachen mit; *tale, account* wieder aufnehmen, fortfahren in (+*dat*); *journey* fortsetzen; **to ~ work** die Arbeit wieder aufnehmen; **well?, he ~d** nun?, fuhr er fort **b** *command, possession, role* wieder übernehmen; *name* wieder annehmen; **to ~ one's seat** seinen Platz wieder einnehmen; **to ~ possession of sth** etw wieder in Besitz nehmen **c** (= *sum up*)

zusammenfassen VI (*classes, work etc*) wieder beginnen

résumé ['reɪzjuːmeɪ] N Resümee *nt*, Zusammenfassung *f*; (*US*, = *curriculum vitae*) Lebenslauf *m*

resumption [rɪ'zʌmpʃən] N (*of activity*) Wiederaufnahme *f*; (*of command, possession*) erneute Übernahme *f*; (*of journey*) Fortsetzung *f*; (*of classes*) Wiederbeginn *m*

resurface [ˌriː'sɜːfɪs] VT *road* neu belegen VI (*diver, submarine, fig*) wieder auftauchen

resurge [rɪ'sɜːdʒ] VT wieder auferstehen; (*fig*: = *flare up again*) wieder erwachen or aufleben

resurgence [rɪ'sɜːdʒəns] N Wiederaufleben *nt*

resurgent [rɪ'sɜːdʒənt] ADJ wieder auflebend

resurrect [ˌrezə'rekt] VT **a** (*lit*) *person* wieder beleben; (*Rel*) auferstehen lassen; **to be ~ed** auferstehen **b** (*fig*) *law* wieder einführen; *ideology, institution* wieder ins Leben rufen; *custom, fashion, style, career* wieder beleben; *ideas, memories* wieder aufleben lassen; (*inf*) *old dress etc* ausgraben (*inf*); **to ~ the past** die Vergangenheit wieder heraufbeschwören

resurrection [ˌrezə'rekʃən] N **a** (*lit, of person*) Wiederbelebung *f*; **the Resurrection** (*Rel*) die Auferstehung **b** (*fig, of law*) Wiedereinführung *f*; (*of custom, fashion, style*) Wiederbelebung *f*; (*of ideas, memories*) Auflebenlassen *nt*

resuscitate [rɪ'sʌsɪteɪt] VT (*Med*) wieder beleben; (*fig*) beleben, neue Lebensgeister geben (+*dat*)

resuscitation [rɪˌsʌsɪ'teɪʃən] N (*Med*) Wiederbelebung *f*; (*fig*) Belebung *f*

resuscitator [rɪ'sʌsɪteɪtə] N (*Med*) Sauerstoffapparat *m*

retail ['riːteɪl] N Einzelhandel *m*, Kleinhandel *m*, Detailhandel *m* (*dated*); **~ and wholesale** Einzel- und Großhandel *m*; **to sell sth by ~** etw im Einzelhandel verkaufen VT **a** (= *sell*) *goods* im Einzel- or Kleinhandel or en detail (*dated*) verkaufen **b** (*fig*) *gossip* weitererzählen VI (*goods*) **to ~ at ...** im Einzelhandel ... kosten ADV im Einzelhandel; **to sell ~** im Einzelhandel or en detail (*dated*) verkaufen

retail *in cpds* Einzelhandels-; **retail banking** N Bankgeschäft *nt*; **retail business** N Einzel- or Kleinhandel *m*; (= *shop*) Einzelhandelsgeschäft *nt*; **retail chain** N Einzelhandelskette *f*; **retail dealer** N Einzelhändler(in) *m(f)*, Detailhändler(in) *m(f)* (*dated*)

retailer ['riːteɪlə] N Einzelhändler(in) *m(f)*, Kleinhändler(in) *m(f)*

retailing ['riːteɪlɪŋ] N der Einzelhandel

retail: retail outlet N Einzelhandelsverkaufsstelle *f*; **retail park** N (*Brit*) großes Einkaufszentrum, Shoppingcenter *nt*; **retail price** N Einzelhandelspreis *m*; **retail price index** N Einzelhandelspreisindex *m*; **retail sales** PL Einzelhandelsumsatz *m*; **retail trade** N Einzelhandel *m*

retain [rɪ'teɪn] VT **a** (= *keep*) behalten; *money, possession, person* zurück(be)halten; *custom* beibehalten, bewahren; *urine* zurückhalten; *colour* behalten; *flavour* beibehalten; *moisture* speichern; (*battery*) *charge* halten; (*dam*) *water* stauen; **to ~ water** (*soil, body*) Wasser speichern; (*sponge*) Wasser halten; **to ~ control of sth** etw weiterhin in der Gewalt haben; **to ~ power** weiter an der Macht bleiben; **to ~ the use of a limb/one's eyes** ein Glied/seine Augen noch gebrauchen können **b** (= *remember*) sich (*dat*) merken; (*computer*) *information* speichern **c** (= *engage*) *lawyer* beauftragen

retainer [rɪ'teɪnə] N **a** (*old*: = *servant*) Faktotum *nt* **b** (= *fee*) Vorschuss *m*

retaining [rɪ'teɪnɪŋ]: **retaining fee** N Vorschuss *m*; **retaining nut** N Befestigungsschraube *f*; **retaining wall** N Stützmauer *f*

retake [ˌriː'teɪk] *vb*: *pret* **retook**, *ptp* **retaken** [ˌriː'teɪkən] VT **a** (*Mil*) *town* zurückerobern; **he was ~n (prisoner)** er wurde wieder gefangen genommen **b** (*Film*) nochmals aufnehmen **c** (*Sport*) *penalty* wiederholen **d** *exam* wiederholen N ['riːteɪk] (*Film*) Neuaufnahme *f*; (*of exam*)

Wiederholung(sprüfung) *f*; **we need a ~ of that scene** wir müssen die Szene noch einmal filmen

retaliate [rɪˈtælɪeɪt] **VI** Vergeltung üben; (*for bad treatment, insults etc*) sich revanchieren (*against sb* an jdm); (*in battle*) zurückschlagen; (*Sport, in fight, with measures, in argument*) kontern; **he ~d by pointing out that ...** er konterte, indem er darauf hinwies, dass ...; **he ~d by kicking him on the shins** er hat sich mit einem Tritt gegen das Schienbein revanchiert; **then she ~d by calling him a pig** sie revanchierte sich damit *or* zahlte es ihm damit heim, dass sie ihn ein Schwein nannte; **how will the unions ~?** wie werden die Gewerkschaften kontern?

retaliation [rɪ,tælɪˈeɪʃən] **N** Vergeltung *f*; (*in fight also*) Vergeltungsschlag *m*; (*in argument, diplomacy etc*) Konterschlag *m*; **he was vicious** er hat sich auf üble Weise revanchiert; **in ~** zur Vergeltung; **that's my ~ for what you did to me** das ist meine Revanche für das, was Sie mir angetan haben; **in ~ for your unkindness** um mich für Ihre Unfreundlichkeit zu revanchieren; **policy of ~** Vergeltungspolitik *f*

retaliatory [rɪˈtælɪətərɪ] **ADJ** **~ measures** Vergeltungsmaßnahmen *pl*; **a ~ assassination** ein Vergeltungsmord *m*; **to take ~ action** zurückschlagen; (*Mil*) einen Vergeltungsschlag durchführen

retard [rɪˈtɑːd] **VT** *development* verlangsamen, verzögern; *explosion* verzögern; (*Aut*) *ignition* verzögern; (*Biol, Phys*) retardieren

retardant [rɪˈtɑːdənt] **N** (*Chem*) Verzögerungsmittel *nt*

retarded [rɪˈtɑːdɪd] **ADJ** zurückgeblieben; *growth, progress* verzögert; **mentally ~** geistig zurückgeblieben

retarded ignition **N** (*Aut*) Spätzündung *f*

retarget [,riːˈtɑːgɪt] **VT** *range of goods etc* neu ausrichten; *space vehicle etc* umdirigieren

retch [retʃ] **VI** würgen **N** Würgen *nt*

retching [ˈretʃɪŋ] **N** Würgerei *f*, Gewürge *nt*

ret(d) *abbr of* **retired** a. D.

retell [,riːˈtel] *pret, ptp* **retold** **VT** wiederholen; (*novelist*) *old legend* nacherzählen

retention [rɪˈtenʃən] **N** **a** Beibehaltung *f*; (*of possession*) Zurückhaltung *f*; (*of water*) Speicherung *f*; (*of facts*) Behalten *nt*; (*of information by computer*) Speicherung *f*; (*of lawyer*) Beauftragung *f*; (*Med: also* **retention of urine**) Harnverhaltung *f* **b** (= *memory*) Gedächtnis *nt*

retentive [rɪˈtentɪv] **ADJ** *memory* aufnahmefähig; **he is very ~** er hat ein gutes Gedächtnis; **moisture-retentive soil** Boden, der gut Feuchtigkeit speichert

retentiveness [rɪˈtentɪvnɪs] **N** (*of memory*) Aufnahmefähigkeit *f*; (*of person*) Merkfähigkeit *f*

rethink [,riːˈθɪŋk] *vb: pret, ptp* **rethought** [,riːˈθɔːt] **VT** überdenken **N** [ˈriːθɪŋk] (*inf*) Überdenken *nt*; **we'll have to have a ~** wir müssen das noch einmal überdenken

reticence [ˈretɪsəns] **N** Zurückhaltung *f*

reticent [ˈretɪsənt] **ADJ** zurückhaltend; **to be ~ about sth** in Bezug auf etw (*acc*) nicht sehr gesprächig sein

reticently [ˈretɪsəntlɪ] **ADV** zurückhaltend

reticle [ˈretɪkl] **N** (*Opt*) Messkreuz *nt*

reticulate [rɪˈtɪkjʊlɪt], **reticulated** [rɪˈtɪkjʊleɪtɪd] **ADJ** netzartig, retikular

retina [ˈretɪnə] **N** *pl* **-e** *or* **-s** [ˈretɪniː] Netzhaut *f*, Retina *f* (*spec*)

retinue [ˈretɪnjuː] **N** Gefolge *nt*

retire [rɪˈtaɪə] **VI** **a** (= *give up work*) aufhören zu arbeiten; (*civil servant, military officer*) in Pension gehen, sich pensionieren lassen, in den Ruhestand treten; (*soldier*) aus der Armee ausscheiden; (*singer, player etc*) (zu singen/spielen *etc*) aufhören; (*self-employed*) sich zur Ruhe setzen; **to ~ from business** sich zur Ruhe setzen, sich aus dem Geschäftsleben zurückziehen **b** (= *withdraw, Mil*) sich zurückziehen; (*Sport*) aufgeben; (*Ftbl, Rugby etc*) vom Feld gehen; (*jury*) sich zurückziehen; **to ~ into one's shell** sich

in sein Schneckenhaus verkriechen; **to ~ from public life** sich aus dem öffentlichen Leben zurückziehen

c (*old, form, = go to bed*) sich zurückziehen **VT** aus Altersgründen entlassen; *civil servant, military officer* pensionieren, in den Ruhestand versetzen; *soldier* verabschieden; (*Fin*) *bond* aus dem Verkehr ziehen

retired [rɪˈtaɪəd] **ADJ** **a** (= *no longer working*) *worker, employee* aus dem Arbeitsleben ausgeschieden (*form*); *civil servant, military officer* pensioniert, im Ruhestand; *soldier* aus der Armee ausgeschieden; **he is ~** er arbeitet nicht mehr; (*soldier*) er ist nicht mehr in der Armee; **~ people** Leute, die im Ruhestand sind; **a ~ worker/teacher/soldier** ein Rentner/pensionierter Lehrer/ehemaliger Soldat; **"occupation - ~"** „Beruf - Rentner/Pensionär/Veteran" **b** (= *secluded*) *life* zurückgezogen

retired list **N** (*Mil*) Liste *f* der aus dem aktiven Dienst Geschiedenen

retiree [,rɪtaɪˈriː] **N** Ruheständler(in) *m(f)*

retirement [rɪˈtaɪəmənt] **N** **a** (= *stopping work*) Ausscheiden *nt* aus dem Arbeitsleben (*form*); (*of civil servant, military officer*) Pensionierung *f*; (*of soldier*) Verabschiedung *f*; **~ at 60/65** Altersgrenze *f* bei 60/65; **to announce one's ~** sein Ausscheiden (aus seinem Beruf/seiner Stellung *etc*) ankündigen, sich pensionieren lassen wollen

b (= *period*) **how will you spend your ~?** was tun Sie, wenn Sie einmal nicht mehr arbeiten/wenn Sie pensioniert *or* im Ruhestand sind?; **to come out of ~** wieder zurückkommen **c** (= *seclusion*) Zurückgezogenheit *f*; **to live in ~** zurückgezogen leben **d** (*Mil*) Rückzug *m*; (*Sport*) Aufgabe *f*; (*Ftbl, Rugby etc*) Abgang *m* vom Spielfeld

retirement: retirement age **N** Rentenalter *nt*; (*of civil servant*) Pensionsalter *nt*; **to reach ~** das Rentenalter/Pensionsalter erreichen; **retirement benefit** **N** Altenhilfe *f*; **retirement home** **N** Seniorenheim *nt*; (*personal*) Alterswohnsitz *m*; **retirement pay** **N** Altersrente *f*; **retirement pension** **N** Altersruhegeld *nt* (*form*)

retiring [rɪˈtaɪərɪŋ] **ADJ** **a** (= *shy*) zurückhaltend **b** **~ age** Rentenalter *nt*; (*of civil servant*) Pensionsalter *nt*

retold [,riːˈtəʊld] *pret, ptp of* **retell**

retook [,riːˈtʊk] *pret of* **retake**

retort [rɪˈtɔːt] **N** **a** (= *answer*) scharfe Erwiderung *or* Antwort **b** (*Chem*) Retorte *f*; **~ stand** Retortenhalter *m or* -stand *m* **VT** scharf erwidern, zurückgeben **VI** scharf erwidern

retouch [,riːˈtʌtʃ] **VT** (*Art, Phot*) retuschieren

retrace [rɪˈtreɪs] **VT** *past, argumentation* zurückverfolgen; *development also* nachgehen (+*dat*), nachvollziehen; **to ~ one's path** *or* **steps** denselben Weg zurückgehen

retract [rɪˈtrækt] **VT** **a** (= *withdraw*) *offer* zurückziehen; *statement* zurücknehmen; *decision* zurücknehmen, rückgängig machen **b** (= *draw back*) *claws* einziehen; (*Aviat*) *undercarriage* einziehen **VI** **a** (= *withdraw*) einen Rückzieher machen **b** (*claws, undercarriage*) eingezogen werden

retractable [rɪˈtræktəbl] **ADJ** **a** *offer* zurückziehbar; *statement, decision* zurücknehmbar **b** *claws* einziehbar; (*Aviat*) *undercarriage* einziehbar

retraction [rɪˈtrækʃən] **N** **a** (= *act, of offer*) Rückzug *m*; (*of statement*) Rücknahme *f*; (*of decision*) Rückgängigmachung *f*; (= *thing retracted*) Rückzieher *m* **b** (*of claws, Aviat, of undercarriage*) Einziehen *nt*

retrain [,riːˈtreɪn] **VT** umschulen **VI** umlernen, umgeschult werden, sich umschulen lassen

retraining [,riːˈtreɪnɪŋ] **N** Umschulung *f*

retranslate [,riːtrænzˈleɪt] **VT** neu übersetzen

retranslation [,riːtrænzˈleɪʃən] **N** Neuübersetzung *f*

retransmit [,riːtrænzˈmɪt] **VT** weiterübertragen

retread [,riːˈtred] **VT** *tyre* die Laufflächen erneuern von [ˈriːtred] **N** (= *tyre*) runderneuerter Reifen

retreat [rɪˈtriːt] **N** **a** (*Mil*) Rückzug *m*; **to sound the ~** zum Rückzug blasen; **the army is in ~** die Armee befindet sich *or* ist auf dem Rückzug; **to make** *or* **beat a (hasty** *or* **swift) ~** (*Mil*) (schnell) den Rückzug antreten; (*fig*) (schleunigst) das Feld räumen; **his ~ into silence** seine Zuflucht zum Schweigen

b (= *place*) Zufluchtsort *m*, Zuflucht *f*; (= *hiding place*) Schlupfwinkel *m*; **this is my ~** hierhin ziehe ich mich zurück; **he has gone to his country ~** er hat sich aufs Land zurückgezogen **VI** **a** (*Mil*) den Rückzug antreten; (*in fear*) zurückweichen; (*flood, glacier*) zurückgehen, zurückweichen; **to ~ inside oneself** sich in sich selbst zurückziehen

b (*Chess*) zurückziehen **VT** (*Chess*) zurückziehen

retrench [rɪˈtrentʃ] **VT** *expenditure* einschränken, kürzen; *personnel* einsparen; *book* kürzen **VI** sich einschränken

▶ **retrench on** **VI** +*prep obj* = **retrench VT**

retrenchment [rɪˈtrentʃmənt] **N** (*of expenditure*) Einschränkung *f*, Kürzung *f*; (*of personnel*) Einsparung *f*

retrial [,riːˈtraɪəl] **N** (*Jur*) Wiederaufnahmeverfahren *nt*; **the case may go to a ~** es könnte zu einer Wiederaufnahme des Verfahrens kommen; **he requested a ~** er verlangte die Wiederaufnahme des Verfahrens

retribution [,retrɪˈbjuːʃən] **N** Vergeltung *f*; **in ~** als Vergeltung

retributive [rɪˈtrɪbjʊtɪv] **ADJ** Vergeltungs-, vergeltend; *justice* ausgleichend; **~ action** Vergeltungsaktion *f*

retrievable [rɪˈtriːvəbl] **ADJ** **a** (= *recoverable*) zurück-/hervor-/heraus-/herunterholbar; (= *rescuable*) rettbar; (*from wreckage etc*) zu bergen; *material from waste* rückgewinnbar; (*Comput*) *information, data* abrufbar; (*after a crash*) wiederherstellbar; *honour, position, money, investment* wiedererlangbar **b** *loss, error* wieder gutzumachen *pred*, wieder gutzumachend *attr*; *situation* zu retten

retrieval [rɪˈtriːvəl] **N** **a** (= *recovering*) Zurück-/Hervor-/Heraus-/Herunterholen *nt*; (= *rescuing*) Rettung *f*; (*from wreckage etc*) Bergung *f*; (*from waste*) Rückgewinnung *f*; (*Comput: of information*) Abfragen *nt*, Abrufen *nt*; (*after a crash*) Wiederherstellen *nt*; (*of honour, position, money, investment*) Wiedererlangen *nt*; (*of loss*) Wiedergutmachen *nt* **b** (= *setting to rights, of error*) Wiedergutmachung *f*; (*of situation*) Rettung *f*; **beyond ~** hoffnungslos **c** (*by dog*) Apportieren *nt*

retrieve [rɪˈtriːv] **VT** **a** (= *recover*) zurück-/hervor-/heraus-/herunterholen; (= *rescue*) retten; (*from wreckage etc*) bergen; *material from waste* zurückgewinnen; (*Comput*) *information, data* abrufen; (*after a crash*) wiederherstellen; *honour, position, money, investment* wiedererlangen; *loss* wieder gutmachen; **to ~ sth from oblivion** etw der Vergessenheit entreißen **b** (= *set to rights*) *error* wieder gutmachen; *situation* retten **c** (*dog*) apportieren **VI** (*dog*) apportieren

retriever [rɪˈtriːvə] **N** (= *breed*) Retriever *m*; **he is a good ~** er ist ein guter Apportierhund

retro [ˈretrəʊ] **N** (= *retrorocket*) Bremsrakete *f* **ADJ** (*Mus, Fashion*) Retro-; **~ music** Retromusik *f*

retro- *PREF* rück-, Rück-

retroactive [,retrəʊˈæktɪv] **ADJ** rückwirkend; **a ~ effect** eine Rückwirkung

retroactively [,retrəʊˈæktɪvlɪ] **ADV** rückwirkend

retroflected [ˈretrəʊˈflektɪd] **ADJ** *Zunge etc* zurückgebogen; (*Phon*) retroflex

retrograde [ˈretrəʊgreɪd] **ADJ** rückläufig; *order* umgekehrt; *policy* rückschrittlich; (*Phys, Biol, Astron*) rückläufig, retrograd (*spec*); **~ step** Rückschritt *m* **VI** (*Biol*) sich zurückentwickeln; (*Astron*) sich retrograd bewegen

retrogress [ˌretrəʊˈgres] VI (= *go backwards*) sich rückwärts bewegen; (= *deteriorate*) sich zurückentwickeln

retrogression [ˌretrəʊˈgreʃən] N (= *backward movement*) rückläufige Bewegung; (= *deterioration*) Rückentwicklung *f*

retrogressive [ˌretrəʊˈgresɪv] ADJ (= *moving backwards*) rückläufig; (*fig*) *plan, policy* rückschrittlich; (*Biol*) rückläufig; **~ step** Rückschritt *m*

retrorocket [ˈretrəʊˌrɒkɪt] N Bremsrakete *f*

retrospect [ˈretrəʊspekt] N **in ~, what would you have done differently?** was hätten Sie rückblickend *or* im Rückblick anders gemacht?; **everything looks different in ~** im Nachhinein *or* im Rückblick sieht alles anders aus

retrospection [ˌretrəʊˈspekʃən] N Zurückblicken *nt*

retrospective [ˌretrəʊˈspektɪv] **ADJ** *thought* rückblickend; *wisdom* im Nachhinein; (*Admin, Jur*) rückblickend; *pay rise* rückwirkend; **~ effect** Rückwirkung *f*; **a ~ exhibition** eine Retrospektive; **a ~ look (at)** ein Blick *m* zurück (auf +*acc*) ▶ N Retrospektive *f*

retrospectively [ˌretrəʊˈspektɪvlɪ] ADV **a** *act* rückwirkend **b** (= *in retrospect*) rückblickend, im Nachhinein; **to look ~ at sth** auf etw (*acc*) zurückblicken

retrovirus [ˈretrəʊˌvaɪrəs] N Retrovirus *nt or m*

retry [riːˈtraɪ] VT (*Jur*) *case* wieder aufnehmen, neu verhandeln; *person* neu verhandeln gegen, wieder vor Gericht bringen

retsina [retˈsiːnə] N Retsina *m*

retune [ˈriːˈtjuːn] **VT a** (*Mus*) neu stimmen **b** *engine, video recorder* neu einstellen **N the engine needs a ~** der Motor muss neu eingestellt werden

return [rɪˈtɜːn] ✪ 20.3, 21.3, 23.3 **VI** (*come back: person, vehicle*) zurück- *or* wiederkommen, zurück- *or* wiederkehren (*geh*); (*go back, person*) zurückgehen; (*vehicle*) zurückfahren; (*symptoms, doubts, fears*) wiederkommen, wieder auftreten; (*property:* = *pass back to*) zurückfallen (*to an* +*acc*); **to ~ to London/the town/the group** nach London/in die Stadt/zur Gruppe zurückkehren; **to ~ to school** wieder in die Schule gehen; **to ~ to (one's) work** (*after short pause*) wieder an seine Arbeit gehen; (*after strike*) die Arbeit wieder aufnehmen; **to ~ to a subject** auf ein Thema zurückkommen; **to ~ to one's old ways** in seine alten Gewohnheiten zurückfallen; **to ~ home** nach Hause kommen/gehen, heimkehren (*geh*); **his good spirits ~ed** seine gute Laune kehrte wieder; **to ~ to health** wieder gesund werden; **to ~ to dust** wieder zu Staub werden

VT a (= *give back*) *sth borrowed, stolen, lost* zurückgeben (*to sb* jdm); (= *bring or take back*) zurückbringen (*to sb* jdm); (= *put back*) zurücksetzen/-stellen/-legen; (= *send back*) (*to an* +*acc*) *letter etc* zurückschicken *or* -senden; (= *refuse*) *cheque* nicht einlösen; *ball* zurückschlagen/-werfen; *sound, light* zurückwerfen; *salute, visit, sb's love, compliment* erwidern; **to ~ sb's (phone) call** jdn zurückrufen; **to ~ a/sb's blow** zurückschlagen; **to ~ a book to the shelf/box** ein Buch auf das Regal zurückstellen/in die Kiste zurücklegen; **to ~ goods to the shop** Waren in das Geschäft zurückbringen; **to ~ thanks** (*form*) danksagen, Dank sagen; **to ~ thanks to sb** jdm danksagen *or* Dank sagen; **I hope to ~ your kindness** ich hoffe, dass ich mich einmal bei Ihnen revanchieren kann; **to ~ good for evil** Böses mit Gutem vergelten; **to ~ fire** (*Mil*) das Feuer erwidern; **to ~ hearts** (*Cards*) Herz nachspielen

b (= *reply*) erwidern, zurückgeben

c (= *declare*) *details of income* angeben; **to ~ a verdict of guilty (on sb)** (*Jur*) (jdn) schuldig sprechen, einen Schuldspruch (gegen jdn) fällen; **to ~ a verdict of murder on sb** (*Jur*) jdn des Mordes für schuldig erklären

d (*Fin*) *income* einbringen; *profit, interest* abwerfen

---

e (*Brit, Parl*) *candidate* wählen

N a (= *coming/going back, of person, vehicle, seasons*) Rückkehr *f*, Wiederkehr *f* (*geh*); (*of illness*) Wiederauftreten *nt*; **on my ~** bei meiner Rückkehr; **~ home** Heimkehr *f*; **~ to school** Schulbeginn *m*; **by ~ (of post)** (*Brit*) postwendend; **~ to work** (*after strike*) Wiederaufnahme *f* der Arbeit; **~ to health** Genesung *f*; **a ~ to one's old habits** ein Rückfall *m* in seine alten Gewohnheiten; **many happy ~s (of the day)!** herzlichen Glückwunsch zum Geburtstag! → **point**

b (= *giving back*) Rückgabe *f*; (= *bringing or taking back*) Zurückbringen *nt*; (= *putting back*) Zurücksetzen/-stellen/-legen *nt*; (= *sending back*) Zurückschicken *nt or* -senden *nt*; (= *refusal: of cheque*) Nichteinlösen *nt*; (*of ball*) Zurückschlagen *nt*/-werfen *nt*; (*of salute, compliment, sb's love*) Erwiderung *f*

c (*Brit: also* **return ticket**) Rückfahrkarte *f*; (*Aviat*) Rückflugticket *nt*

d (= *profit: from investments, shares*) (*on* aus) Einkommen *nt*; (*on capital*) Ertrag *m*, Gewinn *m*; (= *product: from land, mine etc*) Ertrag *m*; **~s** (= *profits*) Gewinn *m*; (= *receipts*) Einkünfte *pl*; **~ on capital** (*Fin*) Kapitalertrag *m*, Rendite *f*

e (*fig*, = *recompense*) **in ~** dafür; **in ~ for** für; **to do sb a favour /favor in ~** (*US*) sich bei jdm für einen Gefallen revanchieren

f (= *act of declaring, of verdict, election results*) Verkündung *f*; (= *report*) Bericht *m*; **the ~ of the jury** ≈ **das Urteil der Schöffen; the (election) ~s** das Wahlergebnis

g (*Brit, Parl, of candidate*) Wahl *f* (*to* in +*acc*)

h (*Sport*, = *game, match*) Rückspiel *nt*; (= *stroke*) Rückschlag *m*; (*Tennis*) Return *m*; (= *throw*) Rückwurf *m*; (= *return pass*) Rückpass *m*; **to make a good ~** den Ball gut zurückschlagen/-werfen

i (*Comm*. = *returned item*) zurückgebrachte Ware; (*Theat*) zurückgebrachte Karte; (= *book*) Remittende *f*

j (= *carriage return, Comput*) Return *nt*; (*on typewriter*) Rücklauftaste *f*

returnable [rɪˈtɜːnəbl] ADJ zur Rückgabe bestimmt; (= *reusable*) Mehrweg-; **~ bottle** Mehrwegflasche *f*; (*with deposit*) Pfandflasche *f*

returnee [rɪˈtɜːˈniː] N (*Pol*) Rückkehrer(in) *m(f)*

returner [rɪˈtɜːnə] N Wiedereinsteiger(in) *m(f)* (ins Berufsleben)

return: return fare N (*Brit*) Preis *m* für eine Rückfahrkarte *or* (*Aviat*) ein Rückflugticket *nt*; **return flight** N (*Brit*) Rückflug *m*; (*both ways*) Hin- und Rückflug *m*; **return half** N (*Brit: of ticket*) Abschnitt *m* für die Rückreise

returning: returning board [rɪˈtɜːnɪŋˌbɔːd] N (*US Pol*) Wahlausschuss *m*; **returning officer** [rɪˈtɜːnɪŋˈɒfɪsə] N (*Brit, Parl*) Wahlleiter(in) *m(f)*

return: return journey N (*Brit*) Rückreise *f*; (*both ways*) Hin- und Rückreise *f*; **return match** N (*Brit*) Rückspiel *nt*; **return pass** N (*Sport*) Rückpass *m*; **return ticket** N (*Brit*) Rückfahrkarte *f*; (*Aviat*) Rückflugticket *nt*; **return visit** N (*to person*) Gegenbesuch *m*; (*to place*) zweiter Besuch; **to make a ~ (to a place)** (an einen Ort) zurückkehren

reunification [riːˌjuːnɪfɪˈkeɪʃən] N Wiedervereinigung *f*

reunify [ˈriːˈjuːnɪfaɪ] VT wieder vereinigen

reunion [rɪˈjuːnjən] N **a** (= *coming together*) Wiedervereinigung *f* **b** (= *gathering*) Treffen *nt*, Zusammenkunft *f*; **a family/school ~** ein Familien-/Klassentreffen *nt*

reunite [ˌriːjuːˈnaɪt] **VT** wieder vereinigen; **they were ~d at last** sie waren endlich wieder vereint **VI** (*countries, parties*) sich wieder vereinigen; (*people*) wieder zusammenkommen

re-up [ˌriːˈʌp] VI (*US Mil inf*) sich weiterverpflichten, sich wieder verpflichten

reusable [ˌriːˈjuːzəbl] ADJ wieder verwendbar, wieder verwertbar

Rev [rev] *abbr of* **Reverend**

rev [rev] **N** *abbr of* **revolution** (*Aut*) Umdrehung *f*; **the number of ~s per minute** die Dreh- *or* Tourenzahl pro Minute; **4,000 ~s per minute**

4.000 Umdrehungen *or* Touren (*inf*) pro Minute; **~ counter** Drehzahlmesser *m*, Tourenzähler *m* **VI** (*driver*) den Motor auf Touren bringen; (*noisily*) den Motor aufheulen lassen; (*engine*) aufheulen **VT** *engine* aufheulen lassen

▶ **rev up** (*Aut*) = **rev VI b** (*inf*, = *prepare*) sich vorbereiten (*for* auf +*acc*) **VT** *sep* **a** (*Aut*) *engine* aufheulen lassen **b** (*Ind inf*) *production* ankurbeln **c to be revved up for sth** (*inf:* = *eager*) ganz wild auf etw (*acc*) sein

revaluation [riːˌvæljʊˈeɪʃən] N (*Fin*) Aufwertung *f*

revalue [ˈriːˈvæljuː] VT (*Fin*) aufwerten

revamp [ˈriːˈvæmp] VT (*inf*) *book, play, image* aufmotzen (*inf*); *company* auf Vordermann bringen (*inf*); (*Pol*) *party* auf Vordermann bringen (*inf*); *house, room* aufmöbeln

revanchist [rɪˈvæntʃɪst] ADJ revanchistisch

reveal [rɪˈviːl] VT **a** (= *make visible*) zum Vorschein bringen; (= *show*) zeigen; **stripping off the wallpaper ~ed an old frieze** unter der Tapete war ein alter Fries zum Vorschein gekommen; **a nightdress that ~ed her slender figure** ein Nachthemd, das ihre schlanke Gestalt abzeichnete; **a neckline that ~ed her bosom** ein Ausschnitt, der ihren Busen freigab

b (= *make known*) *truth, facts* enthüllen, aufdecken; *one's/sb's identity* zu erkennen geben, enthüllen; *name, details* preisgeben, verraten; *ignorance, knowledge* erkennen lassen; **to ~ the (full) extent of sth** etw völlig *or* in seinem vollen Umfang aufdecken *or* klarmachen; **I cannot ~ to you what he said** ich kann Ihnen nicht verraten, was er gesagt hat; **he ~ed himself as being ...** er verriet sich als ...; (*deliberately*) er gab sich als ... zu erkennen; **he could never ~ his feelings for her** er konnte seine Gefühle für sie nie zeigen; **what does this ~ about the motives of the hero?** was sagt das über die Motive des Helden aus?; **Nixon ~s all** Nixon packt aus (*inf*); **the doctor did not ~ to him how hopeless his situation was** der Arzt hat ihn nicht darüber aufgeklärt, wie hoffnungslos sein Zustand war

c (*Rel*) offenbaren (*to sb* jdm)

revealed religion [rɪˈviːldrɪˈlɪdʒən] N (*Rel*) Offenbarungsreligion *f*

revealing [rɪˈviːlɪŋ] ADJ **a** aufschlussreich; *insight also* verräterisch **b** *material, skirt etc* viel zeigend; *dress, neckline also* offenherzig (*hum*)

revealingly [rɪˈviːlɪŋlɪ] ADV *say* bezeichnenderweise; **he ~ remarked that he'd never read the book in question** er bemerkte, und das sagt schon einiges, dass er das fragliche Buch nie gelesen habe; **~, 60 per cent of purchasers are women** es ist sehr aufschlussreich *or* es lässt tief blicken, dass 60 Prozent der Käufer Frauen sind

reveille [rɪˈvælɪ] N (*Mil*) Reveille *f*, Wecksignal *nt*; **(the) ~ is at 6** um 6 Uhr ist Wecken

revel [ˈrevl] **VI a** (= *make merry*) feiern **b** (= *delight*) **to ~ in sth** etw in vollen Zügen genießen; **to ~ in doing sth** seine wahre Freude daran haben, etw zu tun; **like it? I ~ in it** gefallen? es macht mir Riesenspaß! **N revels** PL Feiern *nt*

revelation [ˌrevəˈleɪʃən] N Enthüllung *f*; (*Rel*) Offenbarung *f*; **(the book of) Revelations** die Offenbarung (des Johannes); **it was a ~ to me** das hat mir die Augen geöffnet; **what a ~!** unglaublich!

revelatory [ˌrevəˈleɪtərɪ] ADJ aufschlussreich

reveller, (*US*) **reveler** [ˈrevlə] N Feiernde(r) *m/f*

revelry [ˈrevlrɪ] N *usu pl* Festlichkeit *f*

revenge [rɪˈvendʒ] **N** Rache *f*; (*Sport*) Revanche *f*; **to take ~ on sb (for sth)** sich an jdm (für etw) rächen; **to take ~ on sb for sth** sich an jdm (für etw) Vergeltung üben; **to get one's ~** sich rächen, seine Rache bekommen; (*Sport*) sich revanchieren; **out of ~** aus Rache; **in ~ for** als Rache für; **~ is sweet** Rache ist süß **VT** *insult, murder, sb* rächen; **to ~ oneself** *or* **to be ~d (for sth)** (*für etw*) rächen; **to ~ oneself on sb (for sth)** sich (für etw) an jdm rächen

revengeful [rɪˈvendʒfʊl] ADJ rachsüchtig

revengefully [rɪˈvendʒfəlɪ] ADV rachsüchtig; *act* aus Rache

revenger [rɪˈvendʒəˈ] N Rächer(in) *m(f)*

revenue [ˈrevənjuː] N (*of state*) Staatseinkünfte *pl*, öffentliche Einnahmen *pl*; (= *tax revenue*) Steueraufkommen *nt*; (*of individual*) Einnahmen *pl*, Einkünfte *pl*; (= *department*) Finanzbehörde *f*, Fiskus *m* → **Inland Revenue, internal**

revenue: revenue investigator N Steuerfahnder(in) *m(f)*; **revenue officer** N Finanzbeamte(r) *m*/-beamtin *f*; **revenue stamp** N (*US*) Steuermarke *f*, Steuerbanderole *f*

reverb [rɪˈvɜːb] N (= *shaking effect*) Hall *m*; (= *echoing effect*) Echo *nt*

reverberant [rɪˈvɜːbərənt] ADJ *acoustics* nach- or widerhallend

reverberate [rɪˈvɜːbəreɪt] VI (*sound*) widerhallen, nachhallen; (*light, heat*) zurückstrahlen, reflektieren VT *sound, light, heat* zurückwerfen, reflektieren

reverberation [rɪˌvɜːbəˈreɪʃən] N (*of sound*) Widerhall *m*, Nachhall *m*; (*of light, heat*) Zurückstrahlen *nt*, Reflexion *f*

revere [rɪˈvɪəˈ] VT verehren

reverence [ˈrevərəns] N a Ehrfurcht *f*, Reverenz *f* (*geh*); (= *veneration*) Verehrung *f* (*for* für); **to have ~ for sb** jdn verehren; **to bow in ~** sich ehrfürchtig verneigen; **to treat sth with ~** etw ehrfürchtig behandeln; **to show ~** Ehrfurcht zeigen; **to show sb ~** jdm Ehrfurcht bezeigen; b **your Reverence** (Euer) Hochwürden c (*obs*, = *bow*) Reverenz *f* VT verehren

reverend [ˈrevərənd] ADJ **the Reverend Robert Martin** ≈ Pfarrer Robert Martin; **the Most Reverend John Smith** Erzbischof John Smith; **the Very Reverend John Smith** Dekan John Smith; **the Right Reverend John Smith** Bischof John Smith; **the Reverend Mother** die Mutter Oberin N (*inf*) ≈ Pfarrer *m*

reverent [ˈrevərənt] ADJ ehrfürchtig, ehrfurchtsvoll

reverential [ˌrevəˈrenʃəl] ADJ *awe, respect* ehrfürchtig; *bow, gesture etc* ehrerbietig; **in ~ tones** ehrfürchtig, ehrerbietig

reverently [ˈrevərəntlɪ] ADV ehrfürchtig, ehrfurchtsvoll

reverie [ˈrevərɪ] N (*liter*) Träumereien *pl*; **he drifted off into a ~** er verfiel ins Träumen

revers [rɪˈvɪəˈ] N *pl* - Revers *nt or m*

reversal [rɪˈvɜːsəl] N a (= *turning the other way round, of order, situation, procedure*) Umkehren *nt*; (*of objects, sentences, words*) Umstellen *nt*, Vertauschung *f*; (*of garment*) Wenden *nt*; (*of result*) Umkehren *nt*, Umdrehen *nt* b (*of verdict, judgement*) Umstoßung *f*; (*of decree*) Aufhebung *f*; (*of trend, process*) Umkehrung *f*; (*of policy*) Umkrempeln *nt*; (*of decision, surgical operation*) Rückgängigmachen *nt* c (= *setback*) Rückschlag *m*; **to suffer a ~** einen Rückschlag erleiden

reverse [rɪˈvɜːs] ADJ a (= *opposite*) umgekehrt; *direction* entgegengesetzt; (*Opt*) *image* seitenverkehrt; **in ~ order** in umgekehrter Reihenfolge; **in the ~ direction** in umgekehrter Richtung b **~ motion** *or* **action** (*Tech*, = *backwards*) Rückwärtsbewegung *f*; (= *opposite direction*) entgegengesetzte Bewegung N a (= *opposite*) Gegenteil *nt*; **quite the ~!** ganz im Gegenteil!; **he is the ~ of polite** er ist alles andere als höflich b (= *back*) Rückseite *f*; (*of cloth*) linke Seite c (= *setback, loss*) Rückschlag *m*; (= *defeat*) Niederlage *f*; **he suffered a ~ of fortune** sein Glück schlug um; **a ~ of fortune led to his losing all his wealth** sein Glück schlug um, und er verlor all seinen Reichtum d (*Aut*) Rückwärtsgang *m*; **in ~** im Rückwärtsgang; **to put a/the car into ~** den Rückwärtsgang einlegen; **to go into ~** in den Rückwärtsgang schalten

e **to do sth in ~** etw in umgekehrter Reihenfolge tun; **at this point the party's fortunes went into ~** (*fig*) zu diesem Zeitpunkt wendete sich das Schicksal der Partei f (*on typewriter*) Rückstelltaste *f*; (*on tape recorder*) Rücklauftaste *f* VT a (= *turn the other way round*) *order, situation, procedure* umkehren; *objects, sentences, words* umstellen, vertauschen; *garment* wenden; *result* umkehren, umdrehen; (*Phot*) *negative* umkehren; **to ~ one's direction** eine Kehrtwendung machen; **to ~ the order of sth** etw herumdrehen; **to ~ the charges** (*Brit Telec*) ein R-Gespräch führen; **~-charge call** (*Brit Telec*) R-Gespräch *nt*; **to ~ roles** die Rollen tauschen b (= *cause to move backwards*) *moving belt* rückwärts laufen lassen; **to ~ one's car into the garage/down the hill/into a tree** (*esp Brit*) rückwärts in die Garage fahren *or* setzen/den Berg hinunterfahren/gegen einen Baum fahren c *verdict, judgement* umstoßen, kassieren; *decree* aufheben; *trend, process* umkehren; *policy* völlig umstellen, umkrempeln; *decision, surgical operation* rückgängig machen; **lowering cholesterol levels can sometimes ~ coronary diseases** ein gesenkter Cholesterinspiegel kann bewirken, dass sich Herzgefäßerkrankungen zurückbilden VI (= *move backwards*) (*esp Brit*): *car, driver* zurücksetzen; (*dancer*) rückwärts tanzen; (*machine*) rückwärts laufen; **to ~ into the garage** (*esp Brit*) rückwärts in die Garage fahren

▶ **reverse out** VT *sep* (*Typ*) invertieren

reverse: reverse discrimination N (*US*) positive *or* umgekehrte Diskriminierung; **reverse gear** N (*Aut*) Rückwärtsgang *m*; **to put a/the car into ~** den Rückwärtsgang einlegen; **reverse racism** N umgekehrter Rassismus; **reverse video** N (*Comput*) invertierte Darstellung

reversibility [rɪˌvɜːsɪˈbɪlɪtɪ] N (*of decision*) Rückgängigmachung *f*; (*of process, Phys, Chem*) Umkehrbarkeit *f*; (*of operation etc*) Reversibilität *f*

reversible [rɪˈvɜːsəbl] ADJ *decision* rückgängig zu machen *pred*, rückgängig zu machend *attr*; *process* umkehrbar, reversibel; *operation, contraception* reversibel; *medical condition* heilbar, reversibel; (*Phys, Chem*) umkehrbar; **is vasectomy ~?** kann eine Sterilisation rückgängig gemacht werden?

reversible cloth N Doubleface *m or nt*

reversible jacket N Wendejacke *f*

reversing light [rɪˈvɜːsɪŋlaɪt] N Rückfahrscheinwerfer *m*

reversion [rɪˈvɜːʃən] N a (= *return to former state: of person*) Umkehr *f* (*to* zu); (*to bad state*) Rückfall *m* (*to* in +*acc*); **the ~ of this country to a republic** die Rückverwandlung dieses Landes in eine Republik; **~ to type** (*Biol*) (Arten)rückschlag *m*; **his ~ to type** das erneute Durchbrechen seiner alten Natur b (*Jur, of property*) Zurückfallen *nt* (*to* an +*acc*)

reversionary [rɪˈvɜːʃnərɪ] ADJ a (*Jur*) anwartschaftlich b (*Biol*) atavistisch (*spec*)

revert [rɪˈvɜːt] VI (= *return, to former state*) zurückkehren (*to* zu); (*to bad state*) zurückfallen (*to* in +*acc*); (*to topic*) zurückkommen (*to* auf +*acc*); (*to a dialect etc*) (zurück)verfallen (*to* in +*acc*); (*Jur: property*) zurückfallen (*to* an +*acc*); **he has ~ed back to childhood** er ist wieder ins Kindheitsalter zurückgefallen; **to ~ to type** (*Biol*) in der Art zurückschlagen; **he has ~ed to type** (*fig*) seine alte Natur ist wieder durchgebrochen; **fields ~ing to moorland/woodland** Felder, die wieder versumpfen/wieder zu Wäldern werden

review [rɪˈvjuː] N a (= *look back*) Rückblick *m*, Rückschau *f* (*of* über +*acc*); (= *report*) Überblick *m* (*of* über +*acc*); **I shall keep your case under ~** ich werde Ihren Fall im Auge behalten b (= *re-examination*) nochmalige Prüfung; **to do a ~ of sth** etw überprüfen; **the agreement comes up for ~ or comes under ~ next year** das Abkommen wird nächstes Jahr nochmals geprüft; **his salary is due for ~ in January** im Janu-

ar wird sein Gehalt neu festgesetzt; **there will be a ~ of the situation in 3 months' time** in 3 Monaten wird die Lage noch einmal überprüft c (*Mil*, = *inspection*) Inspektion *f*; **to hold a ~** eine Inspektion vornehmen d (*of book, film, play etc*) Kritik *f*, Besprechung *f*, Rezension *f* e (= *magazine*) Zeitschrift *f* VT a (= *look back at*) *one's life, the past etc* zurückblicken auf (+*acc*), überdenken b (= *re-examine*) *situation, case* erneut (über-)prüfen c (*Mil*) *troops* inspizieren, mustern d *book, play, film* besprechen, rezensieren e (*US, before exam*) wiederholen

review body N Untersuchungsausschuss *m*

review copy N (*of book*) Rezensionsexemplar *nt*

reviewer [rɪˈvjuːəˈ] N Kritiker(in) *m(f)*, Rezensent(in) *m(f)*

reviewing stand [rɪˈvjuːɪŋ-] N Ehrentribüne *f*

review panel N = **review body**

revile [rɪˈvaɪl] VT schmähen, verunglimpfen VI **to ~ against sb/sth** gegen jdn/etw schmähen

revisal [rɪˈvaɪzəl] N Nachprüfung *f*, nochmalige Durchsicht; (*Editing*) zweite Korrektur, Revision *f* (*spec*)

revise [rɪˈvaɪz] VT a (= *change*) *opinion, estimate, law* revidieren; **to ~ the constitution** die Verfassung überarbeiten b (= *correct*) *proof, text* revidieren, überarbeiten c (*Brit*, = *learn up*) wiederholen VI (*Brit*) (den Stoff) wiederholen

revised [rɪˈvaɪzd] ADJ a (= *amended*) *version, plan, procedure* überarbeitet, revidiert; *figure, estimate, schedule* revidiert; *offer* neu; **according to a ~ estimate** nach neuen Schätzungen b (*Typ*) *edition* überarbeitet; **the Revised Version** (*Brit*) die Bibelübersetzung (*von 1884*); **the Revised Standard Version** (*US*) die Bibelübersetzung (*von 1953*)

reviser [rɪˈvaɪzəˈ] N Bearbeiter(in) *m(f)*; (*of translations etc*) Korrektor(in) *m(f)*

revision [rɪˈvɪʒən] N a (*of opinion, estimate*) Überholen *nt*, Revidieren *nt* b (*of proofs*) Revision *f*, Überarbeitung *f* c (*Brit, for exam*) Wiederholung *f* (*des Stoffs*) d (= *revised version*) überarbeitete Ausgabe

revisionism [rɪˈvɪʒənɪzəm] N Revisionismus *m*

revisionist [rɪˈvɪʒənɪst] ADJ revisionistisch N Revisionist(in) *m(f)*

revisit [riːˈvɪzɪt] VT *place, person* wieder or nochmals besuchen; (*fig*) *argument, issue* nochmals zurückkommen auf (+*acc*)

revitalize [riːˈvaɪtəlaɪz] VT neu beleben

revival [rɪˈvaɪvəl] N a (= *bringing back, of custom, usage*) Wiedererwecken *nt*, Wiederauflebenlassen *nt*; (*of old ideas, affair*) Wiederaufnehmen *nt*, Wiederaufgreifen *nt*; (*from faint, fatigue*) Wiederbeleben *nt*, Wiederbelebung *f*; (*of play*) Wiederaufnahme *f*; (*of law*) Wiederinkrafttreten *nt* b (= *coming back, return: of custom, old ideas etc*) Wiederaufleben *nt*; (*from faint, fatigue*) Wiederbelebung *f*; **there has been a ~ of interest in ...** das Interesse an ... ist wieder wach geworden *or* ist wieder erwacht; **the dollar experienced a slight ~** der Dollar verzeichnete wieder einen leichten Aufschwung; **an economic ~** ein wirtschaftlicher Wiederaufschwung c (*Rel*) Erweckung *f*; **~ meeting** Erweckungsversammlung *f*

revivalism [rɪˈvaɪvəlɪzəm] N (*Rel*) Erweckungsbewegung *f*

revivalist [rɪˈvaɪvəlɪst] ADJ erneuernd; *meeting, spirit, preacher* der Erweckungsbewegung; **~ movement** Erweckungsbewegung *f*; **a ~ rock group** eine Revival-Rockband N Anhänger(in) *m(f)* der Erweckungsbewegung

revive [rɪˈvaɪv] VT *person* (*from fainting, from fatigue*) (wieder *or* neu) beleben, munter machen (*inf*); (*from near death*) wieder beleben; *economy* wieder beleben, wieder ankurbeln; *confidence* neu stärken; *memories* wieder lebendig werden lassen; *fashion, custom, usage, hatred, speculation,* *fears* wieder aufleben lassen; *friendship, old habit, word* wieder aufgreifen, wieder aufnehmen; *old play, talks, career* wieder aufnehmen; **a glass of brandy will ~ you** ein Glas Weinbrand wird Sie wieder beleben *or* wieder auf die Beine bringen; **to ~ interest in sth** neues Interesse an etw (*dat*) wecken; **to ~ the fortunes of sb/sth** jdm/ einer Sache wieder auf die Beine helfen **VI** (*person, from fainting*) wieder zu sich kommen; (*from fatigue*) wieder aufleben, wieder munter werden; (*hope, feelings*) wieder aufleben; (*business, trade*) wieder aufblühen

revivify [riːˈvɪvɪfaɪ] VT *person* wieder beleben, wieder munter machen; (= *restore to life*) wieder beleben

revocable [ˈrevəkəbl] ADJ widerruflich

revocation [ˌrevəˈkeɪʃən] N (*of law*) Aufhebung *f*; (*of order, promise*) Zurückziehen *nt*; (*of decision*) Widerruf *m*; (*of licence*) Entzug *m*

revoke [rɪˈvəʊk] VT *law* aufheben; *order, promise* zurückziehen; *decision* widerrufen, rückgängig machen; *licence* entziehen VI (*Cards*) nicht Farbe bekennen N (*Cards*) Nichtfarbebekennen *nt*

revolt [rɪˈvəʊlt] N Empörung *f*, Revolte *f*, Aufstand *m*; **to rise (up) in ~** einen Aufstand *or* eine Revolte machen, sich erheben; **to be in ~ (against)** rebellieren (gegen) **a** (= *rebel*) (*against* gegen) revoltieren, rebellieren **b** (= *be disgusted*) (*at, against* bei, gegen) (*one's nature, sensibilities*) sich empören; (*stomach*) rebellieren VT abstoßen, anekeln (*inf*); **I was ~ed by it** es hat mich angeekelt (*inf*) *or* abgestoßen

revolting [rɪˈvəʊltɪŋ] ADJ (= *repulsive, disgusting*) abstoßend; *meal, story* ekelhaft; (*inf*, = *unpleasant*) *weather, colour, dress* scheußlich, abscheulich; *person* widerlich

revoltingly [rɪˈvəʊltɪŋlɪ] ADV *dirty, ugly* ekelhaft; *sentimental* scheußlich

revolution [ˌrevəˈluːʃən] N **a** (*Pol, fig*) Revolution *f* **b** (= *turn*) (*around own axis*) Umdrehung *f*; (*of planet around sun*) Umlauf *m*; **4,000 ~s per minute** eine Drehzahl von 4.000 pro Minute

revolutionary [ˌrevəˈluːʃnərɪ] ADJ (*lit, fig*) revolutionär; **~ government** Revolutionsregierung *f*; **~ leader** Revolutionsführer(in) *m(f)* N Revolutionär(in) *m(f)*, Revoluzzer(in) *m(f)* (*pej*)

revolutionize [ˌrevəˈluːʃənaɪz] VT revolutionieren

revolvable [rɪˈvɒlvəbl] ADJ drehbar

revolve [rɪˈvɒlv] VT drehen VI sich drehen; **to ~ on an axis/around the sun** sich um eine Achse/um die Sonne drehen; **he thinks everything ~s around him** (*fig*) er glaubt, alles drehe sich nur um ihn

revolver [rɪˈvɒlvə] N Revolver *m*

revolving [rɪˈvɒlvɪŋ] *in cpds* Dreh-; **revolving chair** N Drehstuhl *m*; **revolving credit** N revolvierender Kredit; **revolving door** N **a** Drehtür *f* **b** (*fig*) **a ~ of highly paid executives** das Personalkarussell bei hoch dotierten Führungsposten; **~ between government and the private sector** das Hin und Her zwischen Regierung und privatem Sektor; **the ~ of justice system** der Drehtüreffekt in der Rechtsprechung; **revolving light** N Rundumleuchte *f*; **revolving pencil** N Drehbleistift *m*; **revolving restaurant** N Drehrestaurant *nt*; **revolving stage** N Drehbühne *f*

revue [rɪˈvjuː] N (*Theat*) Revue *f*; (*satirical*) Kabarett *nt*; **~ artist** Revuestar *m*, Kabarettist(in) *m(f)*

revulsion [rɪˈvʌlʃən] N **a** (= *disgust*) Abscheu *m*, Ekel *m* (*at* vor +*dat*) **b** (= *sudden change*) Umschwung *m*; (*reaction*) Empörung *f*

reward [rɪˈwɔːd] N Belohnung *f*; (= *money*) Entgelt *nt* (*form*); **as a ~ for helping me** als Belohnung für Ihre Hilfe; **EUR 1,000 ~** 1.000 EUR Belohnung; **~ offered for the return of ...** Finderlohn für ...; **the ~s of this job** die Vorzüge dieser Arbeit VT belohnen; **"finder will be ~ed"** „Finderlohn (ist) ausgesetzt"

rewarding [rɪˈwɔːdɪŋ] ADJ (*financially*) lohnend, einträglich; (*mentally, morally*) *experience* lohnend; *task, work* dankbar; *relationship* bereichernd; **this is a very ~ book/film** es lohnt sich wirklich, dieses Buch zu lesen/diesen Film zu sehen; **bringing up a child is ~** ein Kind großzuziehen ist eine dankbare *or* lohnende Aufgabe

rewind [ˌriːˈwaɪnd] *pret, ptp* **rewound** VT *thread* wieder aufwickeln; *watch* wieder aufziehen; *film, tape, video* zurückspulen; **~ button** Rückspultaste *f*

rewire [ˌriːˈwaɪə] VT neu verkabeln

reword [ˌriːˈwɜːd] VT *explanation, question* umformulieren, anders ausdrücken; *paragraph, sentence also* neu abfassen

rework [ˌriːˈwɜːk] VT (= *use again*) *theme* wieder verarbeiten; (= *revise*) neu fassen; *story* neu bearbeiten; *proposals* neu formulieren

rewound [ˌriːˈwaʊnd] *pret, ptp* **of rewind**

rewrite [ˌriːˈraɪt] *vb: pret* **rewrote** [ˌriːˈrəʊt] *ptp* **rewritten** [ˌriːˈrɪtn] VT (= *write out again*) neu schreiben; (= *recast*) umschreiben; **to ~ history** die Geschichte umschreiben; **to ~ the record books** einen neuen Rekord verzeichnen N [ˈriːraɪt] **this is just a ~ of his first novel** dies ist nur ein Neuaufguss *m* seines ersten Romans; **it needs a complete ~** es muss vollständig neu geschrieben werden

RGN (*Brit*) *abbr of* **Registered General Nurse**

Rh *abbr of* **rhesus** Rh

Rhaeto-Romanic [ˈriːtəʊrəʊˈmænɪk] N Rätoromanisch *nt*

rhapsodic [ræpˈsɒdɪk] ADJ (*Mus*) rhapsodisch; (*fig*) ekstatisch

rhapsodize [ˈræpsədaɪz] VI überschwänglich schwärmen (*over, about* von)

rhapsody [ˈræpsədɪ] N (*Mus*) Rhapsodie *f*; (*fig*) Schwärmerei *f*

rhd *abbr of* **right hand drive**

rhea [ˈriːə] N Nandu *m*, Pampasstrauß *m*

Rhenish [ˈrenɪʃ] ADJ *region, town* rheinisch; **~ wine** Rheinwein *m*

rhenium [ˈriːnɪəm] N (*Chem*) Rhenium *nt*

rheostat [ˈriːəʊstæt] N Regelwiderstand *m*, Rheostat *m* (*spec*)

rhesus [ˈriːsəs] N Rhesus *m*

rhesus: rhesus baby N Rhesus-geschädigtes Baby; **rhesus factor** N Rhesusfaktor *m*; **rhesus monkey** N Rhesusaffe *m*; **rhesus-negative** ADJ Rhesus negativ; **~ baby** Baby *nt* mit Rhesus negativ; **rhesus-positive** ADJ Rhesus positiv

rhetoric [ˈretərɪk] N Rhetorik *f*; (*pej*) Phrasendrescherei *f* (*pej*)

rhetorical [rɪˈtɒrɪkəl] ADJ rhetorisch; (*pej*) phrasenhaft, schwülstig (*pej*)

rhetorically [rɪˈtɒrɪkəlɪ] ADV (*pej*) schwülstig; *ask* rhetorisch

rhetorical question N rhetorische Frage

rhetorician [ˌretəˈrɪʃən] N Rhetoriker(in) *m(f)*; (*pej*) Phrasendrescher(in) *m(f)* (*pej*)

rheumatic [ruːˈmætɪk] N **a** (= *person*) Rheumatiker(in) *m(f)* **b** **rheumatics** SING Rheumatismus *m* ADJ *pains* rheumatisch; *joint* rheumakrank

rheumatic fever N rheumatisches Fieber, akuter Rheumatismus

rheumaticky [ruːˈmætɪkɪ] ADJ (*inf*, = *rheumatic*) *person* rheumatisch; **only now he realized how ~ he was becoming** er merkte erst jetzt, wie schlimm sein Rheuma geworden war; **~ hands/ fingers** Rheumahände *pl*/-finger *pl*; **~ ache/ pain** Rheumaschmerzen *pl*

rheumatism [ˈruːmətɪzəm] N Rheuma *nt*, Rheumatismus *m*

rheumatoid arthritis [ˈruːmətɔɪdɑːˈθraɪtɪs] N chronischer Rheumatismus, Gelenkrheumatismus *m*

rheumatologist [ˌruːməˈtɒlədʒɪst] N Rheumatologe *m*, Rheumatologin *f*

rheumatology [ˌruːməˈtɒlədʒɪ] N Rheumatologie *f*

rheumy [ˈruːmɪ] ADJ *eyes* wässrig

Rhine [raɪn] N Rhein *m*; **~ wine** Rheinwein *m*

Rhine: Rhineland N Rheinland *nt*; **Rhinelander** [ˈraɪnlændə] N Rheinländer(in) *m(f)*; **rhinestone** N Rheinkiesel *m*

rhino [ˈraɪnəʊ] N *abbr of* **rhinoceros**

rhinoceros [raɪˈnɒsərəs] N Nashorn *nt*, Rhinozeros *nt*

rhinoplasty [ˈraɪnəʊˌplæstɪ] N (*Med*) Nasenkorrektur *f*, Rhinoplastik *f* (*spec*)

rhizome [ˈraɪzəʊm] N Rhizom *nt*, Wurzelstock *m*

Rhodes [rəʊdz] N Rhodos *nt*; **in ~** auf Rhodos

Rhodesia [rəʊˈdiːʒə] N (*Hist*) Rhodesien *nt*

Rhodesian [rəʊˈdiːʒən] (*Hist*) ADJ rhodesisch N Rhodesier(in) *m(f)*

Rhodian [ˈrəʊdɪən] ADJ rhodisch, (von) der Insel Rhodos N Rhodier(in) *m(f)*

rhodium [ˈrəʊdɪəm] N (*Chem*) Rhodium *nt*

rhododendron [ˌrəʊdəˈdendrən] N Rhododendron *m or nt*

rhomb [rɒm] N Rhombus *m*

rhombic [ˈrɒmbɪk] ADJ rhombisch

rhomboid [ˈrɒmbɔɪd] N Rhomboid *nt* ADJ rhomboid

rhombus [ˈrɒmbəs] N Rhombus *m*

Rhone [rəʊn] N Rhone *f*

rhubarb [ˈruːbɑːb] N Rhabarber *m*; **"rhubarb, ~, ~"** (*Theat, hum*) „Rhabarbarhabarbarhabarba"

rhyme [raɪm] N **a** (= *rhyming word*) Reim *m*; **~ scheme** Reimschema *nt*; **without ~ or reason** ohne Sinn und Verstand; **there seems to be no ~ or reason to it**, that has no ~ or reason das hat weder Sinn noch Verstand **b** (= *poem*) Gedicht *nt*; **in ~** in Reimen *or* Versen; **to put into ~** in Reime *or* Verse bringen VT reimen VI **a** (*words*) sich reimen **b** (*pej*, = *write verse*) reimen, Verse schmieden

rhymester [ˈraɪmstə], **rhymer** [ˈraɪmə] N (*pej*) Verseschmied *m* (*pej*), Dichterling *m* (*pej*)

rhyming [ˈraɪmɪŋ] ADJ **~ couplets** Reimpaare *pl*; **~ dictionary** Reimwörterbuch *nt*

RHYMING SLANG

Rhyming slang ist eine Sonderform des Cockney-Slangs, in dem das gemeinte Wort durch einen Ausdruck ersetzt wird, der sich darauf reimt: z. B. „apples and pears" statt stairs. Für Leute, die damit nicht vertraut sind, kann das ziemlich verwirrend werden, vor allem dann, wenn das Reimwort weggelassen wird – so wird „butcher's hook", das für look steht, zu „butcher's", wie in „let's take a butcher's". Einige Ausdrücke des „rhyming slang" sind Teil der Umgangssprache geworden, z. B. „use your loaf", wobei loaf die Abkürzung von „loaf of bread" ist, das wiederum für head steht; kurz gesagt: „streng deinen Grips an" → COCKNEY

---

rhythm [ˈrɪðm] N Rhythmus *m*; **the ~ method (of contraception)** die Knaus-Ogino-Methode; **~ section** (*of band*) Rhythmusgruppe *f*; **~ and blues** Rhythm-and-Blues *m*

rhythmic(al) [ˈrɪðmɪk(əl)] ADJ rhythmisch; *breathing, pulse* gleichmäßig; **rhythmic gymnastics** rhythmische Gymnastik

rhythmically [ˈrɪðmɪkəlɪ] ADV rhythmisch; *breathe* gleichmäßig

RI *abbr of* **Religious Instruction**

rib [rɪb] N **a** (*Anat, Cook*) Rippe *f*; **to dig** (*esp Brit*) *or* **poke sb in the ~s** jdn in die Rippen stoßen **b** (*of leaf, ceiling, ship, shell*) Rippe *f*; (*of umbrella*) Speiche *f* **c** (*Knitting*) Rippen *pl*; **in ~** in Rippen VT (*inf* = *tease*) necken, foppen

RIBA [ˈriːbə] *abbr of* **Royal Institute of British Architects**

ribald ['rɪbəld, 'raɪbəld] ADJ deftig, zotig (pej); behaviour derb; company liederlich; **~ comments** Ferkeleien pl

ribaldry ['rɪbəldrɪ] N Ferkeleien pl, Schweinereien pl

riband ['rɪbənd] N (obs) = ribbon

ribbed [rɪbd] ADJ sole, condom, knitting gerippt; shell, ceiling mit Rippen

ribbon ['rɪbən] N **a** (for hair, dress) Band nt; (for typewriter) Farbband nt; (on medal) Ordensband nt; (fig, narrow strip) Streifen m **b** ribbons PL (= tatters) Fetzen pl; **to tear sth to ~s** etw zerfetzen or zerreißen; (fig) play etc etw in der Luft zerreißen

ribbon: ribbon development N (Brit) Zeilenbauweise f; **ribbon saw** N (Tech) Bandsäge f

rib cage N Brustkorb m

riboflavin ['raɪbəʊˈfleɪvɪn] N Riboflavin nt

ribonucleic acid ['raɪbəʊnjuːˈkliːɪkˈæsɪd] N Ribonukleinsäure f

rib-tickler N (hum inf) **it's a real ~** das ist die reinste Zwerchfellmassage (inf)

ribwort ['rɪbwɜːt] N Spitzwegerich m

rice [raɪs] N Reis m

rice in cpds Reis-; **ricefield** N Reisfeld nt; **rice growing** N Reis(an)bau m; **rice-growing** ADJ Reis anbauend; **rice paper** N Reispapier nt; **rice pudding** N (esp Brit) Milchreis m

ricer ['raɪsə'] N (esp US, Cook) Kartoffelpresse f

rice wine N Reiswein m

rich [rɪtʃ] ADJ (+er) **a** (= wealthy) reich; **~ and famous** reich und berühmt; **for ~er, for poorer** in guten wie in schlechten Zeiten; **to get ~ quick** schnell zu Reichtum gelangen **b** (= splendid) furniture, decoration, style, clothes prächtig; gift teuer; banquet üppig **c** food schwer; **~ tea biscuit** ≈ Butterkeks m; **a ~ diet** reichhaltige Kost **d** (= fertile) soil fruchtbar, fett; land fruchtbar, reich **e** (= abundant, plentiful) reich; **seaweed is a ~ source of iodine** Seetang ist eine reiche Jodquelle **f** (= intense) colour satt; sound, voice voll; wine schwer; smell kräftig, stark **g** (= full, eventful) life erfüllt; history, experience reich; **to be (all) the ~er for sth** durch etw bereichert sein **h** (inf, = amusing) köstlich; **that's ~!** (iro) das ist stark (inf) **i** (Aut) mixture fett **j** (= full of) **to be ~ in sth** (in resources etc) reich an etw (dat) sein; **~ in vitamins/protein** vitamin-/eiweißreich; **~ in corn/minerals** reich an Getreide/Bodenschätzen; **~ in detail** sehr detailliert; **~ in illustrations/examples** mit vielen Abbildungen/Beispielen; **to be ~ in spirit** ein gutes Herz haben; **the air was ~ with the scent of blossom** die Luft war von Blütenduft erfüllt **N a the ~** PL die Reichen pl; **the ~ and famous** die Reichen und Berühmten pl, die Schickeria f (iro) **b riches** PL Reichtümer pl; **natural ~es** natürliche Reichtümer pl

Richard ['rɪtʃəd] N Richard m; **~ (the) Lionheart** Richard Löwenherz

richly ['rɪtʃlɪ] ADV **a** (= ornately) dress, decorate prächtig **b** (= abundantly) illustrated reich; **to be ~ endowed with sth** mit etw reich ausgestattet sein **c** (= strongly) coloured, flavoured kräftig; scented kräftig, intensiv; **~ rewarding/satisfying** überaus lohnend/befriedigend; **a ~ textured narrative** eine üppig angelegte or ausgestattete Erzählung **d** (= thoroughly) **he ~ deserves it** er hat es mehr als verdient; **he was ~ rewarded** (lit) er wurde reich belohnt; (fig) er wurde reichlich belohnt

richness ['rɪtʃnɪs] N **a** (= wealthiness) Reichtum m **b** (of splendour, of furniture, decoration, style, clothes) Pracht f; (of banquet) Üppigkeit f **c** (of food) Schwere f; **the ~ of the food** die reichhaltige Kost **d** (= fertility: of soil, land) Fruchtbarkeit f **e** (= intensity, of colour) Sattheit f; (of

wine) Schwere f; (of smell) Stärke f; **the ~ of his voice** seine volle Stimme **f** (= fullness, of life) Erfülltheit f; (of history, experience) Reichtum m **g** (Aut, of mixture) Fettheit f **h** (in minerals, vitamins etc) Reichtum m (in an +dat)

Richter scale ['rɪktəˈskeɪl] N Richterskala f

rick¹ [rɪk] N Schober m

rick² N, VT = wrick

rickets ['rɪkɪts] N sing Rachitis f, die englische Krankheit

rickety ['rɪkɪtɪ] ADJ **a** furniture, stairs etc wack(e)lig; vehicle klapprig **b** (Med) rachitisch

rickrack ['rɪkræk] N, no pl (US) Zickzackbordüre f

rickshaw ['rɪkʃɔː] N Rikscha f

ricochet ['rɪkəʃeɪ] N Abprall m VI abprallen (off von); **the stone ~ed off the water** der Stein hüpfte auf dem Wasser

rictus ['rɪktəs] N (Anat, Zool) Sperrweite f

rid [rɪd] pret, ptp **rid** or **ridded** VT **to ~ of** (of pests, disease) befreien von; of bandits etc säubern von; **to ~ oneself of sb/sth** jdn/etw loswerden; of pests also sich von etw befreien; of ideas, prejudice etc sich von etw lösen; **to get ~ of sb/sth** jdn/etw loswerden; **to be ~ of sb/sth** jdn/etw los sein; **get ~ of it** sieh zu, dass du das loswirst; (= throw it away) schmeiß es weg (inf); **you are well ~ of him** ein Glück, dass du den los bist

riddance ['rɪdəns] N **good ~ (to bad rubbish)!** (inf) ein Glück, dass wir das/den etc los sind

ridden ['rɪdn] ptp of ride ADJ angst-ridden angsterfüllt; debt-ridden hoch verschuldet; disease-ridden von Krankheiten befallen; strife-ridden zerstritten; **~ with crime** mit hoher Kriminalität; **~ with intolerance** ohne die leiseste Spur von Toleranz

riddle¹ ['rɪdl] N (= sieve) (Schüttel)sieb nt VT **a** soil etc sieben; coal sieben, schütteln **b** **to ~ sb/sth with bullets** jdn/etw mit Kugeln durchlöchern; **~d with holes** völlig durchlöchert; **~d with woodworm** wurmzerfressen; **~d with cancer/corruption** vom Krebs/von der Korruption zerfressen; **~d with mistakes/contradictions** voller Fehler/Widersprüche

riddle² N Rätsel nt; **I'll ask you a ~** ich werde Ihnen ein Rätsel aufgeben; **to speak in ~s** in Rätseln sprechen

ride [raɪd] vb: pret **rode**, ptp **ridden** N **a** (in vehicle, on bicycle) Fahrt f; (on horse) Ritt m; (for pleasure) Ausritt m; **to go for a ~** eine Fahrt machen; (on horse) reiten gehen; **after a hard ~ across country** nach einer langen Überlandfahrt; (on horse) nach einem langen Ritt querfeldein; **he gave the child a ~ on his back** er ließ das Kind auf den Schultern reiten; **cycle/car/coach ~** Rad-/Auto-/Busfahrt f; **to go for a ~ in the car** mit dem Auto wegfahren, eine Fahrt (mit dem Auto) machen; **I just came along/went along for the ~** (fig inf) ich bin nur zum Vergnügen mitgekommen/mitgegangen; **to take sb for a ~** (in car etc) mit jdm eine Fahrt machen; (inf: = deceive) jdn anschmieren (inf); **he gave me a ~ into town** in his car er nahm mich im Auto in die Stadt mit; **it's my first ~ in a limousine/in a train** ich fahre zum ersten Mal in einer Limousine/in einem Zug; **can I have a ~ on your bike?** kann ich mal mit deinem Rad fahren?; **3 ~s on the merry-go-round** 3 Karussellfahrten; **that roller coaster is the scariest ~ I've ever been on** ich habe noch nie so viel Angst gehabt wie bei der Fahrt auf der Achterbahn; **to have a ~ in a helicopter** in einem Hubschrauber fliegen; **we had a ~ in a taxi/train** wir sind in einem Taxi/Zug gefahren; **it's an 80p ~ from the station** ab Bahnhof kostet die Fahrt 80 Pence; **the Ride of the Valkyries** der Ritt der Walküren **b** (= quality of ride) **this car gives a smooth/bumpy ~** mit diesem Auto fährt es sich sanft/unsanft **c** (= path for horses) Reitweg m **d** (sl: = lay) **to be a good ~** gut im Bett sein (inf)

VI **a** (on a horse etc, Sport) reiten (on auf +dat); **to go riding** reiten gehen; **the jockey was riding just under 65 kg** der Jockey brachte knapp 65 kg auf die Waage; **Peter Mandelson ~s again!** (fig hum) Peter Mandelson ist wieder da! **b** (= go in vehicle, by cycle etc) fahren; **he was riding on a bicycle** er fuhr mit einem Fahrrad; **to ~ on a bus/in a car/in a train/in a cart** in einem Bus/Wagen/Zug/Schubkarren fahren; **to ~ away** or **off/down** weg- or davon-/hinunterfahren **c** (fig, = float) **the seagull ~s on the wind** die Möwe lässt sich vom Wind tragen; **the moon was riding high in the sky** der Mond zog hoch am Himmel dahin; **he's riding high** (fig) er schwimmt ganz oben; **he was riding high in public opinion** in der öffentlichen Meinung stand er ganz oben; **to ~ at anchor** (ship) vor Anker liegen; **let's just have to let the matter** or **to let things ~ for a while** wir müssen einfach für eine Weile den Dingen ihren Lauf lassen; **... but I'll let it ~** ..., aber ich lasse es vorerst einmal **d** (horse) **to ~ well** gut laufen

VT **a** horse, donkey etc reiten mit or auf (+dat), reiten; bicycle, motorbike fahren mit, fahren; **I have never ridden a bicycle/a motorbike** ich bin noch nie Rad/Motorrad gefahren; **may I ~ your bike?** darf ich mit deinem Fahrrad fahren?; **he rode his horse away/back** etc er ritt weg/zurück etc; **he rode him hard** er ritt es scharf; **he rode the horse into the stable** er ritt das Pferd in den Stall; **Jason will be ridden by H. Martin** Jason wird unter H. Martin laufen; **to ~ two horses at the same time** (fig) auf zwei Hochzeiten tanzen; **to ~ a race** bei einem Rennen reiten; **to ~ a good race** (bei einem Rennen) gut reiten; **they had ridden 10 km** sie waren 10 km geritten/gefahren; **they had ridden all the way** sie waren den ganzen Weg geritten/gefahren; **he rode the land looking for ...** er durchritt/durchfuhr das ganze Land auf der Suche nach ...; **the birds riding the wind** die Vögel, die sich vom Wind tragen lassen; **the ship rode the waves** das Schiff trieb auf den Wellen; **the surfers rode the waves** die Surfer ritten auf den Wellen; **the party is riding the wave of public support** die Partei nutzt die Gunst der Öffentlichkeit; **witches ~ broomsticks** Hexen reiten auf einem Besen; **to ~ the storm** (lit, fig) den Sturm überstehen; **to ~ a horse to death** ein Pferd zu Tode reiten; **to ~ an argument to death** ein Argument totreden → also **ridden** **b** (US inf: = torment) piesacken (inf), schikanieren, zusetzen (+dat); **don't ~ him too hard** treibst nicht so toll mit ihm **c** (sl: = have sex with) reiten (sl)

▶**ride about** (Brit) or **around** VI (on horse etc) herumreiten; (in vehicle, on motorcycle) herumfahren; (on bicycle) herumradeln (inf), herumfahren

▶**ride behind** VI (on same horse, bicycle) hinten sitzen; (on different horse, bicycle) hinterherreiten, hinterherfahren

▶**ride down** VT sep **a** (= trample) umreiten **b** (= catch up with) einholen

▶**ride on** VI +prep obj (money, reputation) hängen an (+dat)

▶**ride out** VT sep überstehen; **to ride out the storm** (lit, fig) den Sturm überstehen VI (on horse) ausreiten, einen Ausritt machen

▶**ride up** VI **a** (horseman) heranreiten; (motorcyclist etc) heranfahren **b** (skirt etc) hochrutschen

rider ['raɪdə'] N **a** (= person, on horse) Reiter(in) m(f); (on bicycle, motorcycle) Fahrer(in) m(f) **b** (= addition) Zusatz m; (to document, will etc) Zusatzklausel f; (to bill) Allonge f; (to jury's verdict) zusätzliche Empfehlung; **I'd just like to add one ~ to that** zusätzlich (dazu) möchte ich noch eins sagen

ridge [rɪdʒ] N **a** (= raised strip, on fabric, cardboard etc) Rippe f; (on corrugated iron) Welle f; (on sand) Rippelmarke f; (on ploughed land) Grat *m*; (*in sea*: = *reef*) Riff *nt*; **a ~ of hills** eine Hügelkette; **a ~ of mountains** ein Höhenzug *m*; **a ~ of high pressure** (*Met*) ein Hochdruckkeil *m* **b** (*of hills, mountains*) Rücken *m*, Kamm *m*; (*pointed, steep*) Grat *m*; (*of roof*) First *m*; (*of nose*) Rücken *m* **VT** rocks, land, sand zerfurchen

ridge: ridgepole N (*of tent*) Firststange *f*; **ridge tent** N Firstzelt *nt*; **ridge tile** N Firstziegel *m*; **ridgeway** N (*Brit*) Gratweg *m*

ridgy ['rɪdʒɪ] ADJ *mountain passage etc* grat- or kammartig; (= *furrowed*) zerfurcht

ridicule ['rɪdɪkjuːl] **N** Spott *m*; **to hold sb/sth up to ~** sich über jdn/etw lustig machen; **she's an object of ~** alles macht sich über sie lustig; **to become an object of ~** der Lächerlichkeit preisgegeben werden **VT** verspotten, verlachen

ridiculous [rɪ'dɪkjʊləs] ADJ lächerlich; **don't be ~ red** keinen Unsinn; **to make oneself (look) ~** sich lächerlich machen; **to be made to look ~** der Lächerlichkeit preisgegeben werden; **to take sth to ~ extremes** or **lengths** etw bis ins Lächerliche or bis zur Lächerlichkeit übertreiben; **to go to ~ lengths (to do sth)** großen Aufwand betreiben(, um etw zu tun)

ridiculously [rɪ'dɪkjʊləslɪ] ADV lächerlich; **you're talking ~** du redest dummes Zeug; **~, he** blamed himself for the accident er gab sich lächerlicherweise selbst die Schuld an dem Unfall

ridiculousness [rɪ'dɪkjʊləsnɪs] N Lächerlichkeit *f*

riding ['raɪdɪŋ] N Reiten *nt*; **I enjoy ~** ich reite gern

riding in cpds Reit-; **riding breeches** PL Reithosen *pl*, Breeches *pl*; **a pair of ~** eine Reithose; **riding crop** N Reitgerte *f*; **riding habit** N Reitkostüm *nt*, Reitkleid *nt*; **riding jacket** N Reitjacke *f*; **riding light** N (*Naut*) Ankerlicht *nt*; **riding master** N Reitlehrer *m*; **riding whip** N Reitpeitsche *f*

Riesling ['riːzlɪŋ] N (= *variety of white wine*) Riesling *m*

rife [raɪf] ADJ **a** (= *widespread*) *disease, corruption* weit verbreitet; **to be ~** grassieren; (*rumour*) umgehen; **rumours** (*Brit*) or **rumors** (*US*) **are/ speculation is ~ that ...** es geht das Gerücht um/es wird spekuliert, dass ... **b** (= *full of*) **~ with** voll von, voller +*gen*; **the garden was ~ with weeds** der Garten strotzte vor Unkraut; **countries ~ with Aids** Länder mit einer hohen Aidsrate; **areas ~ with unemployment/violence** Gegenden mit hoher Arbeitslosigkeit/Gewaltkriminalität

riffle ['rɪfl] VT (*also* **riffle through**) *pages* blättern durch; *cards* mischen

riffraff ['rɪfræf] N Pöbel *m*, Gesindel *nt*

rifle[1] ['raɪfl] VT **a** *town* plündern; (*also* **rifle through**) *sb's pockets, drawer, till, house* durchwühlen **b** *ball, shot* donnern (*inf*)

rifle[2] N (= *gun*) Gewehr *nt* (*mit gezogenem Lauf*); (*for hunting*) Büchse *f*; **the Rifles** (*Mil*) die Schützen *pl*

rifle: rifle association N Schützenverein *m*; **rifle butt** N Gewehrkolben *m*; **rifle club** N Schützenverein *m*; **rifleman** N (*Gewehr-*)schütze *m*; **rifle practice** N (*Mil*) Schießübung *f*; **rifle range** N Schießstand *m*; **within ~ in** Schussweite (*eines Gewehrs*); **rifle shot** N Gewehrschuss *m*

rift [rɪft] N **a** Spalt *m* **b** (*fig: in friendship*) Riss *m*; (*Pol*) Spalt *m*, Riss *m*

rift: rift saw N (*Tech*) Gattersäge *f*; **rift valley** N Grabenbruch *m*

rig [rɪg] N **a** (*Naut*) Takelage *f*, Takelung *f* **b** (= *oil rig*) (Öl)förderturm *m*; (*offshore*) Ölbohrinsel *f* **c** (*inf, outfit: also* **rig-out**) Ausrüstung *f*; **in full ~** in großer Aufmachung, in voller Montur (*inf*) **d** (*inf*: = *articulated lorry*) Sattelschlepper *m* VT **a** (*Naut*) auftakeln **b** (*fig*) *election, market etc* manipulieren; **to ~ the vote** die Wahlergebnisse manipulieren; **it was ~ged!** das war Manipulation

▸ **rig out** VT *sep* (*inf,* = *equip*) ausstaffieren (*inf*); (= *dress*) auftakeln (*inf*)

▸ **rig up** VT *sep ship* auftakeln; *equipment* aufbauen; (*fig,* = *make*) improvisieren; (= *arrange*) arrangieren

rigger ['rɪgə'] N (*Naut*) Takler *m*

rigging ['rɪgɪŋ] N **a** (*Naut,* = *action*) Auftakeln *nt*; (= *ropes*) Tauwerk *nt* **b** (*inf, = dishonest interference*) Manipulation *f*, Schiebung *f* (*inf*)

right [raɪt] ⊘ 11.1, 13 ADJ **a** (= *just, fair, morally good*) richtig, recht (*S Ger*); **it isn't ~ to lie** es ist nicht richtig or recht zu lügen; **he thought it ~ to warn me** er hielt es für richtig, mich zu warnen; **it seemed only ~ to give him the money** es schien richtig, ihm das Geld zu geben; **it's only ~ (and proper)** es ist nur recht und billig; **it is only ~ to point out that ...** es ist nur recht und billig, wenn man darauf hinweist, dass ...; **to do the ~ thing by sb** sich jdm gegenüber anständig benehmen

b (= *true, correct*) *answer, solution, time, train* richtig; **to be ~** (*person*) recht haben; (*answer, solution*) richtig sein, stimmen; (*clock*) richtig gehen; **what's the ~ time?** wie viel Uhr ist es genau?; **you're quite ~** Sie haben ganz Recht; **how ~ you are!** (*inf*) da haben Sie ganz Recht; **you were ~ to refuse** or **in refusing** Sie hatten Recht, als Sie ablehnten; **my guess was ~** ich habe richtig geraten; **let's get it ~ this time!** mach es dieses Mal richtig; (*in reporting facts etc*) sag es dieses Mal richtig; **to put** or **set ~** (*error*) korrigieren; *clock* richtig stellen; *situation* wieder in Ordnung bringen; **I tried to put things ~ after their quarrel** ich versuchte, nach ihrem Streit wieder einzulenken; **to put** or **set sb ~** (= *correct*) jdn berichtigen

c (= *proper*) *clothes, document* richtig; **what's the ~ thing to do in this case?** was tut man da am besten?; **to come at the ~ time** zur rechten Zeit kommen; **to do sth the ~ way** etw richtig machen; **that is the ~ way of looking at it** das ist die richtige Einstellung; **the ~ man for the job** der rechte or richtige Mann für die Stelle; **Mr/Miss Right** (*inf*) der/die Richtige (*inf*); **we will do what is ~ for the country** wir werden tun, was für das Land gut ist; **to know the ~ people** die richtigen Leute kennen

d (= *well*) **the medicine soon put** or **set him ~** die Medizin hat ihn schnell wiederhergestellt or wieder auf die Beine gebracht; **I don't feel quite ~ today** ich fühle mich heute nicht ganz wohl; **to be as ~ as rain** (*Brit*) kerngesund sein; (*after accident*) keine Schramme abbekommen haben (*inf*); **to put the engine ~** den Motor reparieren; **the plumber put things ~** der Klempner brachte alles wieder in Ordnung; **to be in one's ~ mind** klar bei Verstand sein; **nobody in their ~ mind would ...** kein vernünftiger Mensch würde ...; **who in their ~ mind would ...?** welcher vernünftige Mensch würde ...?; **he's not ~ in the head** (*inf*) bei ihm stimmts nicht im Oberstübchen (*inf*) → **all right**

e (*phrases*) **~!, ~ oh!** (*Brit inf*) **~ you are!** (*Brit inf*) gut, schön, okay (*inf*); **~ on!** (*esp US inf*) super! (*sl*); **that's ~!** (= *correct, true*) das stimmt!; **that's ~, dear, put it on the table** schön, stell es bitte auf den Tisch; **so they came in the end – is that ~?** und so kamen sie schließlich – wirklich?; **~ enough!** (das) stimmt!; **it's a ~ mess in there** (*Brit inf*) das ist vielleicht ein Durcheinander hier (*inf*); **he's a ~ fool!** (*Brit inf*) er ist wirklich doof (*inf*); **you're a ~ one** (*Brit inf*) du bist mir der Richtige (*inf*)

f (= *opposite of left*) rechte(r, s); **~ hand** rechte Hand; **I'd give my ~ hand to know the answer** ich würde was drum geben, wenn ich die Antwort wüsste (*inf*); **on your ~ hand** rechter Hand, rechts

g **the ~ side of the material** die rechte Seite (des Stoffes)

ADV **a** (= *straight, directly*) direkt; (= *exactly*) genau; **~ in front/ahead of you** direkt or genau vor Ihnen; **go ~ on** gehen/fahren Sie geradeaus weiter; **~ away, ~ off** (= *immediately*) sofort, schnurstracks (*inf*); **~ off** (= *at the first attempt*) auf Anhieb (*inf*); **~ now** (= *at this very moment*)

in diesem Augenblick; (= *immediately*) sofort; **~ here** genau hier; **~ in the middle** genau or direkt in die/der Mitte; **~ at the beginning** gleich am Anfang; **I'll be ~ with you** ich bin gleich da; **it hit me ~ in the face** der Schlag traf mich genau or voll ins Gesicht

b (= *completely, all the way*) ganz; **~ round the house** ganz um das Haus herum; (*inside*) durch das ganze Haus; **~ through** (*drive, go*) mitten durch; **rotten ~ through** durch und durch verfault or (*fig*) verdorben

c (= *correctly*) richtig; **to guess ~** richtig raten; **you did ~ to refuse** es war richtig (von Ihnen) abzulehnen; **if everything goes ~** wenn alles klappt (*inf*); **nothing goes ~ for them** nichts klappt bei ihnen (*inf*), bei ihnen läuft alles schief (*inf*); **if I get you ~** (*inf*) wenn ich Sie (da) richtig verstehe; **I'll see you ~** (*inf*) ich werde aufpassen, dass Sie nicht zu kurz kommen (*inf*) → **serve**

d (*old, dial,* = *very*) sehr; **the Right Honourable John Smith MP** (*not old, dial*) der Abgeordnete John Smith

e (= *opposite of left*) rechts; **it is ~ of the bridge** es ist rechts von der Brücke; **turn ~** biegen Sie rechts ab; **~, left and centre** (*Brit*) or **center** (*US*) (= *everywhere*) überall; **to be cheated ~, left and centre** or **~ and left** (*inf*) von vorne bis hinten betrogen werden (*inf*); **to owe money ~, left and centre** (*Brit*) or **center** (*US, inf*) bei Gott und der Welt Schulden haben (*inf*)

N a *no pl* (*moral, legal*) Recht *nt*; **he doesn't know ~ from wrong** er kann Recht und Unrecht nicht auseinander halten; **I want to know the ~s and wrongs of it first** ich möchte erst beide Seiten kennen lernen; **to be in the ~** im Recht sein

b (= *entitlement*) Recht *nt*; (*to sth*) (An)recht *nt*, Anspruch *m*; (*to have*) **a ~ to sth** ein (An-)recht or einen Anspruch auf etw (*acc*) (haben); **to have a** or **the ~ to do sth** ein or das Recht haben, etw zu tun; **what ~ have you to say that?** mit welchem Recht sagen Sie das?; **by what ~?** mit welchem Recht?; **he is within his ~s** das ist sein gutes Recht; **by ~s** rechtmäßig, von Rechts wegen; **in one's own ~** selber, selbst; **the divine ~ (of kings)** das Gottesgnadentum → **civil rights**

c **rights** PL (*Comm*) Rechte *pl*; **to have the (sole) ~s to sth** die (alleinigen) Rechte an etw (*dat*) haben

d **to put** or **set sth to ~s** etw (wieder) in Ordnung bringen; **to put things** or **the world to ~s** die Welt verbessern; **to have sb bang** or **dead to ~s** (*esp liter.* = *have evidence against sb*) jdn festgenagelt haben (*inf*); (*inf*) (= *understand sb well*) jdn genau kennen; (= *describe sb well*) jdn genau so beschreiben, wie er/sie ist

e (= *not left*) rechte Seite; **to drive on the ~** rechts fahren; **to keep to the ~** sich rechts halten, rechts bleiben; **on my ~** rechts (von mir); **on** or **to the ~ of the church** rechts von der Kirche; **the Right** (*Pol*) die Rechte; **those to the ~ of him** (*Pol*) diejenigen, die weiter rechts stehen als er

VT **a** (= *return to upright position*) aufrichten **b** (= *make amends for*) *wrong* wieder gutmachen; **the problem should ~ itself** (*fig*) das Problem müsste sich von selbst lösen

right: rightabout ['raɪtəbaʊt] N (*Mil*) Kehrtwendung *f*; **right angle** N rechter Winkel; **at ~s (to)** rechtwinklig (zu); **right-angled** ADJ rechtwinklig; **right-angled triangle** N rechtwinkliges Dreieck; **right-click** (*Comput*) **VI** rechts klicken **VT** rechts klicken auf (+*acc*)

righteous ['raɪtʃəs] **ADJ a** rechtschaffen; (*pej*) selbstgerecht (*pej*) **b** *indignation, anger* gerecht **N** **the ~** (*Bibl*) die Gerechten *pl*

righteously ['raɪtʃəslɪ] ADV rechtschaffen

righteousness ['raɪtʃəsnɪs] N Rechtschaffenheit *f*

rightful ['raɪtfʊl] ADJ **a** *heir, owner, inheritance, role, place* rechtmäßig; **their ~ share** ihr rechtmäßiger Anteil, der ihnen zustehende Anteil **b** *punishment* gerecht

rightfully ['raɪtfəlɪ] ADV **a** rechtmäßig; **they must give us what is ~ ours** sie müssen uns geben, was uns rechtmäßig zusteht **b** *punish* gerechterweise

right: right-hand ADJ ~ *drive* rechtsgesteuert; ~ *side* rechte Seite; **right-handed** ADJ *person* rechtshändig; *punch, throw also* mit der rechten Hand; ADV rechtshändig; **right-hander** N (= *punch*) Rechte f; (= *person*) Rechtshänder(in) m(f); **right-hand man** N rechte Hand

rightie ['raɪtɪ] N (*inf*) = **righty**

rightist ['raɪtɪst] N (*Pol*) Rechte(r) mf ADJ rechtsorientiert

rightly ['raɪtlɪ] ✿ 11.1, 13, 26.3 ADV **a** (= *correctly*) richtig; **he said, ~, that ...** er sagte sehr richtig, dass ...; **quite ~** ganz recht; **they are ~ regarded as ...** sie werden zu Recht als ... angesehen; **if I remember ~** wenn ich mich recht erinnere

b (= *justifiably*) mit or zu Recht; **~ or wrongly** ob das nun richtig ist oder nicht; **and ~ so** und zwar mit Recht

c (*form*, = *properly*) richtig; **willpower can achieve great things when ~ applied** richtig eingesetzt, kann Willenskraft große Dinge erreichen

d (*inf*, = *really*) wirklich; **I can't ~ say** ich kann es wirklich nicht sagen; **I don't ~ know** ich weiß nicht genau

right: right-minded ADJ vernünftig; **right-of-centre**, (*US*) **right-of-center** ADJ (*Pol*) Mitte-rechts-; ~ **politician** Mitte-rechts-Politiker(in) m(f); **right of way** N (*across property*) Durchgangsrecht nt; (*Mot*, = *priority*) Vorfahrt(srecht) nt; **it's his ~** (*Mot*) **he has the ~** (*Mot*) er hat Vorfahrt

rights issue N (*St Ex*) Bezugsrechtsemission f

right: rightsizing N (*Comm*) Rightsizing nt; **right-thinking** ADJ vernünftig; **right-to-lifer** N (*US*) Abtreibungsgegner(in) m(f); **right triangle** N (*US*) rechtwinkliges Dreieck; **right wing** N **a** (*Pol*) rechter Flügel **b** **the ~** (*Ftbl, Hockey etc*) der rechte Flügel; **he's the ~** er ist (der) Rechtsaußen; **right-wing** ADJ (*Pol*) *government, party* rechtsgerichtet, rechtsorientiert; *politics, ideas* rechtsgerichtet, rechtslastig (*pej*); ~ **extremist** Rechtsextremist(in) m(f); ~ **extremism** Rechtsextremismus m; **right-winger** N (*Sport*) Rechtsaußen m; (*Pol*) Rechte(r) mf

righty ['raɪtɪ] N (*inf*) **a** (*Pol*) Rechte(r) mf **b** (*esp US*: = *right-handed person*) Rechtshänder(in) m(f)

rigid ['rɪdʒɪd] ADJ **a** (*lit*) *board, material, frame* starr, steif; ~ **with fear** starr or steif vor Angst; **to be ~ with anger** starr vor Wut sein; **to bore sb ~** jdn zu Tode langweilen; **to be bored ~** sich zu Tode langweilen; **the prison visit had shaken her ~** (*inf*) der Gefängnisbesuch hatte sie umgehauen (*inf*) **b** (*fig*) *person, character* strikt, streng, stur (*pej*); *discipline, principles* streng, strikt; (= *intolerant of others*) unbeugsam; *interpretation* genau, stur (*pej*); *specifications* genau festgelegt, strikt; *system* starr, unbeugsam; *timetable* fest, streng

rigidity [rɪ'dʒɪdɪtɪ] N **a** (*lit, of board, material, frame*) Starrheit f, Steifheit f **b** (*fig, of person, character*) Striktheit f, Strenge f, Sturheit f (*pej*); (*of discipline, principles*) Strenge f, Striktheit f; (= *intolerance of others*) Unbeugsamkeit f; (*of interpretation*) Genauigkeit f, Sturheit f (*pej*); (*of specifications*) Striktheit f; (*of system*) Starrheit f, Unbeugsamkeit f; (*of timetable*) Festigkeit f

rigidly ['rɪdʒɪdlɪ] ADV **a** (*lit*) *stand etc* starr, steif; **to stand ~ to** or **at attention** in Habachtstellung sein; **to sit ~ upright** steif aufrecht sitzen **b** (*fig*) *behave, treat* streng, strikt; *oppose* stur, strikt; (= *intolerantly of others*) unbeugsam

rigmarole ['rɪgmərəʊl] N Gelaber nt; (= *process*) Gedöns nt (*inf*); **to go through the whole** or **same ~ again** nochmal mit demselben Gelaber/Gedöns anfangen

rigor N (*US*) = **rigour**

rigor mortis ['rɪgə'mɔːtɪs] N die Toten- or Leichenstarre

rigorous ['rɪgərəs] ADJ **a** (= *strict*) *person, character, discipline, rule, structure, method* streng, strikt; *measures* rigoros; (= *thorough*) *book-keeping, work* peinlich genau; *analysis, tests* gründlich; **with ~ precision/accuracy** mit äußerster Präzision/peinlicher Genauigkeit; **they were ~ in controlling expenditure** sie nahmen es mit der Ausgabenkontrolle sehr genau; **he was a very ~ teacher** er war ein Lehrer, der es sehr genau nimmt; **he is ~ about quality** er ist sehr streng, wenn es um Qualität geht **b** (= *harsh*) *climate* streng

rigorously ['rɪgərəslɪ] ADV *enforce* rigoros; *test* gründlich, streng; *control* streng

rigour, (*US*) **rigor** ['rɪgə] N **a** *no pl* (= *strictness*) Strenge f, Striktheit f; **the full ~ of the law** die ganze Strenge des Gesetzes **b** **rigours** PL (*of climate, famine etc*) Unbilden pl

rigout ['rɪgaʊt] (*Brit inf*) = **rig** N **c**

rile [raɪl] VT (*inf*) ärgern, reizen

Riley ['raɪlɪ] N **to live the life of ~** (*Brit inf*) leben wie Gott in Frankreich (*inf*)

rill [rɪl] N (*poet*) Bächlein nt

rim [rɪm] N (*of cup, bowl*) Rand m; (*of hat also*) Krempe f; (*of spectacles also*) Fassung f; (*of wheel*) Felge f, Radkranz m

rime¹ [raɪm] N = **rhyme**

rime² (*liter*) (Rauh)reif m

rimless ['rɪmlɪs] ADJ *spectacles* randlos

rimmed [rɪmd] ADJ mit Rand; *wheel* mit Felge; **gold-rimmed spectacles** Brille f mit Goldfassung or -rand; **red-rimmed eyes** rot geränderte Augen

rind [raɪnd] N (*of cheese*) Rinde f; (*of bacon*) Schwarte f; (*of fruit*) Schale f

rinderpest ['rɪndəpɛst] N (*Vet*) Rinderpest f

ring¹ [rɪŋ] N **a** Ring m; (*for swimmer*) Schwimmring or -reifen m

b (= *circle*) Ring m; (*in tree trunk*) Jahresring m; **the ~s of Saturn** die Saturnringe pl; **to have (dark) ~s round** or **under one's eyes** (dunkle) Ringe unter den Augen haben; **to sit in a ~** im Kreis sitzen; **to run ~s round sb** (*inf*) jdn in die Tasche stecken (*inf*)

c (= *group, Pol*) Gruppe f; (*of dealers, spies*) Ring m

d (= *enclosure, at circus*) Manege f; (*at exhibition*) Ring m; (*Horse Racing*) Buchmacherring m; (= *boxing ring*) (Box)ring m

VT (= *surround*) umringen; (*in game: with hoop*) einen Ring werfen über (+*acc*); (= *put ring on* or *round*) *item on list etc* einkreisen, einen Kreis machen um; (*esp Brit*) *bird* beringen; *bear, bull* einen Nasenring verpassen (+*dat*); *tree* ringeln

ring² *vb: pret* **rang**, *ptp* **rung** N **a** (*sound*) Klang m; (= *ringing*) (*of bell, alarm bell*) Läuten nt; (*of electric bell, alarm clock, phone*) Klingeln nt; (= *metallic sound: of swords etc*) Klirren nt; (*of crystal*) Klang m; **there was a ~ at the door** es hat geklingelt or geläutet; **to hear a ~ at the door** die Türklingel hören; **give two ~s for the maid** für das Zimmermädchen zweimal läuten

b (*esp Brit, Telec*) Anruf m; **to give sb a ~** jdn anrufen

c (*fig*) Klang m; **his voice had an angry ~ (to it)** seine Stimme klang etwas böse; **that has the ~ of** or **a ~ of truth (to** or **about it)** das klingt sehr wahrscheinlich

d (= *set*) ~ **of bells** Glockenspiel nt

VT **a** (= *make sound*) klingen; (*bell, alarm bell*) läuten; (*electric bell*) läuten, klingeln; (*alarm clock, phone*) klingeln; (= *make metallic sound: swords etc*) klirren; (*crystal*) klingen; (*hammers*) schallen; **the (door)bell rang** es hat geläutet or geklingelt; **the bell rang for dinner** es hat zum Essen geläutet; **when the bell ~s** wenn es klingelt or läutet; (*church bell*) wenn die Glocke läutet; **to ~ for sb** (nach) jdm läuten; **to ~ for sth** für etw läuten; **you rang, sir?** (gnädiger Herr,) Sie haben geläutet?; **please ~ for attention** bitte läuten; **to ~ at the door** (an der Tür) klingeln or läuten

b (*esp Brit, Telec*) anrufen

c (= *sound, resound, words, voice*) tönen, schallen; (*music, singing*) erklingen (*geh*), tönen; **to ~**

false/true falsch/wahr klingen; **my ears are ~ing** mir klingen die Ohren; **the valley rang with their shouts** das Tal hallte von ihren Rufen wider (*geh*); **his words are still ~ing in my ears** seine Worte klingen mir noch im Ohr

VT **a** *bell* läuten; **to ~ the doorbell** (an der Tür) läuten or klingeln; **that/his name ~s a bell** (*fig inf*) das/sein Name kommt mir bekannt vor; **he/it ~s my bell** (*US, inf*) den/das find ich gut (*inf*); **to ~ the changes** (*lit: on bells*) (etw) im Wechsel läuten; (*fig*) alle Variationen durchspielen

b (*esp Brit: also* **ring up**) anrufen

▶ **ring back** (*esp Brit*) VT *sep* zurückrufen VI zurückrufen

▶ **ring down** VT *sep* **to ring down the curtain** (*Theat*) den Vorhang niedergehen lassen; **to ring down the curtain on sth** (*fig, on project*) einen Schlussstrich unter etw (*acc*) ziehen; **on era** den Vorhang über etw (*acc*) fallen lassen

▶ **ring in** VI **a** (*esp Brit, Telec*) sich telefonisch melden (*to in* +*dat*) **b** (*US*, = *clock in*) (zu Beginn der Arbeit) stempeln or stechen VT *sep* **to ring in the New Year** das neue Jahr einläuten

▶ **ring off** VI (*esp Brit, Telec*) aufhängen, (den Hörer) auflegen

▶ **ring out** VI **a** (*bell*) ertönen; (*shot*) knallen; (= *sound above others*) herausklingen **b** (*US*, = *clock out*) (am Ende der Arbeit) stempeln or stechen VT *sep* **to ring out the Old Year** das alte Jahr ausläuten

▶ **ring up** VT *sep* **a** (*esp Brit, Telec*) anrufen **b** **to ring up the curtain** (*Theat*) den Vorhang hochgehen lassen **c** (*cashier*) eintippen; (*Comm*) *sales, profits* einnehmen

ring: ring-a-ring-o'-roses N Ringelreihen m; **ring binder** N Ringbuch nt; **ringbolt** N Ringbolzen m; **ring circuit** N Ringverzweigung f; **ringdove** N Ringeltaube f

ringer ['rɪŋə] N **a** (= *bell-ringer*) Glöckner(in) m(f); **to be a dead ~ for sb** (*inf*) jdm aufs Haar gleichen

ring: ring exercise N (*Sport*) Übung f an den Ringen; **ring fence** N Umzäunung f; **ring-fence** ['rɪŋfɛns] VT einzäunen; *funding, assets* reservieren; **ring finger** N Ringfinger m

ringing ['rɪŋɪŋ] ADJ *bell* läutend; *voice, tone* schallend; *phrases, declaration* leidenschaftlich; *endorsement* klar, eindeutig; **in ~ tones** leidenschaftlich; ~ **tone** (*Brit, Telec*) Rufzeichen nt N **a** (*of bell*) Läuten nt; (*of electric bell also, alarm clock, phone*) Klingeln nt; (*in ears*) Klingen nt **b** (= *bell-ringing*) Glockenläuten nt

ringleader ['rɪŋˌliːdə] N Anführer(in) m(f)

ringlet ['rɪŋlɪt] N Ringellocke f, Korkenzieherlocke f

ring: ringmaster N Zirkusdirektor m; **ring-pull** N (*on can*) Dosenring m, Ringpull m; **ring-pull can** N Aufreißdose f, Ringpulldose f; **ring road** N (*Brit*) Umgehung(sstraße) f; **ringside** N **at the ~** am Ring; **ringside seat** N (*Boxing*) Ringplatz m; (*in circus*) Manegenplatz m; **to have a ~** (*fig*) einen Logenplatz haben; **ring spanner** N Ringschlüssel m; **ring-tailed** ADJ mit Ringelschwanz; **ringworm** N Scherpilzflechte f

rink [rɪŋk] N Eisbahn f; (= *roller-skating rink*) Rollschuhbahn f

rinse [rɪns] N **a** (= *act*) Spülung f; **to give sth a ~** (*clothes, hair*) etw spülen; *plates* etw abspülen; *cup, mouth* etw ausspülen; **have a ~** (*said by dentist*) bitte spülen **b** (*for hair*) Spülung f; (= *colorant*) Tönung f VT **a** *clothes, hair* spülen; *plates* abspülen; *cup, mouth, basin* ausspülen; **to ~ one's hands** sich (*dat*) die Hände abspülen; **to ~ the soap off one's hands** sich (*dat*) die Seife von den Händen abspülen **b** (= *colour with a rinse*) *hair* tönen

▶ **rinse down** VT *sep car, wall* abspülen

▶ **rinse out** VT *sep* **a** *hair, tint, colour, soap, cup* ausspülen, auswaschen; **to rinse out one's mouth** sich (*dat*) den Mund ausspülen **b** (= *wash quickly*) *clothes* auswaschen

Rio (de Janeiro) [ˈrɪəʊ(dədʒəˈnɪərəʊ)] N Rio (de Janeiro) nt

riot [ˈraɪət] **N a** (Pol) Aufstand m no pl, Aufruhr m no pl; (by mob, football fans etc) Krawall m, Ausschreitungen pl; (fig, = wild occasion) Orgie f; **there'll be a ~ if you announce that** wenn Sie das verkünden, gibt es einen Aufstand; **to run ~** (people) randalieren; (vegetation) wuchern; **his imagination runs ~** seine Fantasie or Phantasie geht mit ihm durch; **ivy had run ~ all over the house** Efeu hatte das ganze Haus überwuchert

b a ~ **of colour(s)** (Brit) or **color(s)** (US) eine Farbenexplosion, eine Farbenorgie; **a ~ of reds and blues** eine Explosion von Rot- und Blautönen; **a ~ of flowers** ein wildes Blumenmeer **c to be a ~** (inf) zum Schießen or Schreien sein (inf)

Vi randalieren; (= revolt) einen Aufruhr machen

riot: riot act N **a** (Hist) **the Riot Act** die Aufruhrakte **b** (fig) **to read sb the ~** jdm die Leviten lesen; **riot control** N , no pl Einsatz m bei Krawallen; **riot-control** ADJ equipment etc für den Einsatz bei Krawallen

rioter [ˈraɪətə] N Randalierer(in) m(f); (= rebel) Aufrührer(in) m(f)

riot gear N Schutzausrüstung f

rioting [ˈraɪətɪŋ] N Krawalle pl; (Pol also) Aufstände pl; ~ **in the streets** Straßenkrawalle or -schlachten pl

riotous [ˈraɪətəs] ADJ **a** person, crowd randalierend; living, behaviour, child wild **b** (inf, = wild, exuberant, boisterous) wild; (= hilarious) urkomisch (inf); **we had a ~ time** wir haben hoch her (inf); **a ~ success** ein Riesen- or Bombenerfolg (inf) m; **she burst into ~ laughter** sie brach in wildes Gelächter aus; **a ~ welcome** ein überschwängliches Willkommen

riotously [ˈraɪətəslɪ] ADV behave, live wild; **it was ~ funny** (inf) es war zum Schreien (inf)

riot: riot police N Bereitschaftspolizei f; **riot shield** N Schutzschild m; **riot squad** N Überfallkommando nt

RIP abbr of requiescat or requiescant in pace R.I.P.

rip [rɪp] **N** Riss m; (made by knife etc) Schlitz m **Vt** material, clothes einen Riss machen in (+acc); (stronger) zerreißen; (= vandalize) pictures etc zerschlitzen; **you've ~ped your jacket** du hast einen Riss in der Jacke, du hast dir die Jacke zerrissen; **to ~ sth down the middle** etw mitten durchreißen; **to ~ open** aufreißen; (with knife) aufschlitzen

Vi a (cloth, garment) reißen

b (inf) **the car ~s along** der Wagen rast dahin; **let her ~!** volle Pulle! (inf); **to let ~** loslegen (inf); **he let ~ (with) a stream of complaints** er hat einen Schwall Beschwerden vom Stapel gelassen (inf); **he let ~ at me** er ist auf mich losgegangen (inf)

▶ **rip down** VT sep herunterreißen; old buildings abreißen

▶ **rip into** VI +prep obj **a** (bullets etc) sich bohren in (+acc) **b** (fig inf: = criticize) zusammenstauchen (inf)

▶ **rip off** VT sep **a** (lit) abreißen (prep obj von); clothing herunterreißen; **he ripped off her dress** er riss ihr das Kleid vom Leib **b** (inf) object, goods mitgehen lassen (inf); bank, shop, house ausrauben; person abzocken (inf)

▶ **rip out** VT sep herausreißen (of aus)

▶ **rip through** VI +prep obj (explosion) erschüttern; (bullet) durchbohren

▶ **rip up** VT sep zerreißen; road aufreißen; floorboards herausreißen

riparian [raɪˈpɛərɪən] ADJ (form) Ufer-; ~ **right** Uferanliegerrecht nt

ripcord [ˈrɪpkɔːd] N Reißleine f

ripe [raɪp] ADJ (+er) **a** fruit, cheese, wine reif; (Anat) egg reif, gereift; (fig) lips voll **b** (fig, = mature) reif; **to live to a ~ old age** ein hohes Alter erreichen; **at the ~ old age of eighty** im

hohen or reifen Alter von achtzig Jahren **c** (= ready) **to be ~ for sth** für etw reif sein; **to be ~ for the picking** pflückreif sein; **the time is ~ for revolution** die Zeit ist reif für eine Revolution; **the time is ~ to begin afresh** die Zeit ist reif or es ist höchste Zeit, neu anzufangen; **when the time is ~** wenn die Zeit dafür reif ist **d** (inf, = pungent) smell durchdringend **e** (inf, = crude) language derb

ripen [ˈraɪpən] **Vt** (lit, fig) reifen lassen **Vi** reifen

ripeness [ˈraɪpnɪs] N Reife f

rip-off [ˈrɪpɔf] N (inf) Wucher m, Nepp m (inf); (= cheat) Schwindel m; (= copy: of film, song etc) Abklatsch m; **it's a ~** das ist Wucher or Nepp (inf)/Schwindel/nachgemacht or ein Abklatsch; **he'd been the victim of a ~** er war ausgenommen worden (inf)

riposte [rɪˈpɒst] **N** (= retort) scharfe Antwort, Gegenschlag m; (Fencing) Riposte f **Vi** (= retort) scharf erwidern, parieren; (Fencing) parieren und eine Riposte bringen

ripper [ˈrɪpə] N (= murderer) Frauenmörder m

ripping [ˈrɪpɪŋ] ADJ (dated Brit inf) herrlich, wunderbar

ripple [ˈrɪpl] **N a** (in water) kleine Welle; (of crops) sanftes Wogen no pl; **little ~s spread out across the water** das Wasser kräuselte sich; **the wind blew across the grass in ~s** das Gras wogte im Wind **b** (= noise) Plätschern nt; (of waves) Klatschen nt; **a ~ of laughter** ein kurzes Lachen; (girls') ein perlendes Lachen **Vi a** (= undulate, water) sich kräuseln; (crops) wogen **b** (= murmur, water) plätschern; (waves) klatschen **Vt** water kräuseln; corn wogen lassen; muscles spielen lassen

ripple: ripple effect N (= knock-on effect) Nachwirkungen pl; **ripple mark** N (on sand etc) Rippelmarke f

rip: rip-rap N (Build) Steinbettung f, Steinschüttung f; **rip-roaring** ADJ (inf) sagenhaft (inf); **ripsaw** [ˈrɪpsɔː] N (Tech) Spaltsäge f; **riptide** N Kabbelung f

rise [raɪz] ✪ 17.2 vb: pret **rose**, ptp **risen** **N a** (= increase) in sth etw gen) (in temperature, pressure, of tide, river) Anstieg m, Steigen nt no pl; (in number) Zunahme f; (in prices, bank rate) Steigerung f, Anstieg m; (St Ex) Aufschwung m; **a (pay) ~** (Brit) eine Gehaltserhöhung; **prices are on the ~** die Preise steigen; **there has been a ~ in the number of participants** die Zahl der Teilnehmer ist gestiegen; **a ~ in the population** ein Bevölkerungszuwachs m

b (= upward movement, of theatre curtain) Hochgehen nt, Heben nt; (of sun) Aufgehen nt; (Mus: in pitch) Erhöhung f (in +gen); (fig, to fame, power etc) Aufstieg m (to zu); **the ~ of the working classes** der soziale Aufstieg der Arbeiterklasse; **the ~ and fall of an empire** der Aufstieg und Niedergang eines Weltreichs; **to get a ~ out of sb** (inf) jdn zur Reaktion bringen; **to take the or a ~ out of sb** (dated inf) jdn auf den Arm nehmen (inf)

c (= inland hill) Erhebung f; (= slope) Steigung f **d** (= origin: of river) Ursprung m; **to give ~ to sth** etw verursachen; **to questions** etw aufwerfen; **to complaints** Anlass zu etw geben; **to speculation** zu etw führen; **to hopes, fears** etw aufkommen lassen

Vi a (= get up) (from sitting, lying) aufstehen, sich erheben (geh), um zu gehen; **to ~ from the table** vom Tisch aufstehen, sich vom Tisch erheben (geh); **to ~ in the saddle** sich im Sattel heben; **he rose from his sickbed to go and see her** er verließ das Krankenlager, um sie zu sehen; **~ and shine!** (inf) raus aus den Federn! (inf); **the horse rose on its hind legs** das Pferd stellte sich auf die Hinterbeine; (= reared up) das Pferd bäumte sich auf; **to ~ from the dead** (liter, Bibl) von den Toten auferstehen

b (= go up) steigen; (smoke, mist etc) (auf)steigen, emporsteigen; (prices, temperature, pressure etc) (an)steigen (to auf +acc); (balloon, aircraft, bird) (auf)steigen, sich heben (geh); (lift) hochfahren, nach oben fahren; (theatre curtain) hochgehen, sich heben; (sun, moon, bread,

dough) aufgehen; (wind, storm) aufkommen, sich erheben; (voice, in volume) sich erheben; (in pitch) höher werden; (swimmer, fish) hochkommen; (new buildings) entstehen; (fig, hopes) steigen; (anger) wachsen, zunehmen; (stomach) sich heben; **to ~ to the surface** an die Oberfläche kommen; **the fish are rising well** die Fische beißen gut; **he won't ~ to any of your taunts** er lässt sich von dir nicht reizen; **the idea rose in his mind** ihm kam der Gedanke; **the image rose in his mind** das Bild tauchte vor ihm auf; **I can't ~ to £100** ich kann nicht bis £ 100 gehen; **her spirits rose** ihre Stimmung hob sich; **his voice rose to screaming pitch** seine Stimme wurde kreischend or schrill; **to ~ to a crescendo** zu einem Crescendo anschwellen; **the colour** (Brit) or **color** (US) **rose in her cheeks** die Röte stieg ihr ins Gesicht

c (ground) ansteigen; (mountains, hills, castle) sich erheben; **the mountain ~s to 5,000 feet** der Berg erhebt sich auf 5.000 Fuß; **where the hills ~ against the sky** wo sich die Berge gegen den Himmel abheben

d (fig, in society, rank) **to ~ in the world** es zu etwas bringen; **to ~ to fame** Berümtheit erlangen; **to ~ from nothing** sich aus dem Nichts empor- or hocharbeiten; **he rose to be President/a captain** er stieg zum Präsidenten/Kapitän auf → **rank** [1]

e (= adjourn, assembly) auseinander gehen; (meeting) beendet sein; **the House rose at 2 a.m.** (Parl) das Haus beendete die Sitzung um 2 Uhr morgens; **Parliament will ~ on Thursday** das Parlament geht Donnerstag in Ferien

f (= originate: river) entspringen

g (also **rise up**) (= revolt: people) sich empören, sich erheben; (= rebel: one's soul etc) sich empören; **to ~ (up) in protest (at sth)** (people) sich protestierend (gegen etw) erheben; **to ~ (up) in anger (at sth)** (people) sich (gegen etw) empören; (soul, inner being etc) sich (gegen etw) auflehnen/zornig empören

▶ **rise above** VI +prep obj level of inflation etc ansteigen um mehr als; insults etc erhaben sein über (+acc), stehen über (+dat)

▶ **rise up** VI (person) aufstehen, sich erheben (geh); (mountain etc) sich erheben → also **rise VI g**

risen [ˈrɪzn] ptp of **rise** ADJ (Rel) **the ~ Lord** der Auferstandene; **Jesus Christ is ~!** Christ ist erstanden!

riser [ˈraɪzə] N **a** (= person) **to be an early ~** Frühaufsteher(in) m(f) sein, früh aufstehen; **to be a late ~** spät aufstehen, ein Langschläfer m/eine Langschläferin sein (inf) **b** (of stair) Setzstufe f **c** (for gas, water etc) Steigrohr nt, Steigleitung f

risibility [ˌrɪzɪˈbɪlɪtɪ] N (liter, = disposition) Lachlust f

risible [ˈrɪzɪbl] ADJ (liter, = laughable) lächerlich, lachhaft

rising [ˈraɪzɪŋ] **N a** (= rebellion) Erhebung f, Aufstand m **b** (of sun, star) Aufgehen nt, Aufgang m; (of barometer, prices, river) (An)steigen nt; (from dead) Auferstehung f; (of theatre curtain) Hochgehen nt; (of ground) Steigung f, Anstieg m; **the ~ and falling of ...** das Auf und Ab (+gen) ...

c (= adjournment: of Parliament etc) Auseinandergehen nt

ADJ a sun, star aufgehend; tide, barometer steigend; (= sloping) ground ansteigend; **the ~ sap** der aufsteigende Saft

b (= increasing) prices, inflation, stock market, currency steigend; unemployment steigend, zunehmend; crime zunehmend; wind aufkommend; hopes steigend; anger, fury wachsend; **the ~ tide of violence** die zunehmende Welle der Gewalt

c (fig) **a ~ young doctor** ein aufstrebender junger Arzt; **a ~ politician** ein kommender Politiker; **the ~ generation** die kommende Generation; **(the) ~ threes/fives** (Brit, Sch) die knapp Drei-/Fünfjährigen

ADV (inf) **she's ~ sixteen** sie ist fast sechzehn

rising damp N Bodenfeuchtigkeit f

risk [rɪsk] ○ 2.3, 16.2 **N** **a** Risiko nt; (in cpds) -gefahr f; **health/war** ~ Gesundheits-/Kriegsgefahr f; **to take** or **run ~s/a** ~ Risiken/ein Risiko eingehen; **to take** or **run the** ~ **of doing sth** das Risiko eingehen, etw zu tun; **you('ll) run the** ~ **of losing a lot of money** Sie laufen dabei Gefahr, eine Menge Geld zu verlieren; **there is no** ~ **of his coming** or **that he will come** es besteht keine Gefahr, dass er kommt; **at one's own** ~ auf eigene Gefahr, auf eigenes Risiko; **goods sent at sender's** ~ Warenversand m auf Risiko des Senders; **"cars parked at owners' ~"** „Parken auf eigene Gefahr"; **at the** ~ **of seeming stupid** auf die Gefahr hin, dumm zu scheinen; **at the** ~ **of his life** unter Einsatz seines Lebens; **children at** ~ gefährdete Kinder; **some jobs are at** ~ einige Stellen sind gefährdet; **to put sb at** ~ jdn gefährden; **to put sth at** ~ etw riskieren **b** (Insur) Risiko nt; **fire** ~ Feuerrisiko; **he's a bad accident** ~ bei ihm besteht ein hohes Unfallrisiko; **to be a good/bad (credit)** ~ (Fin) eine gute/schlechte Bonität haben → **security risk** **VT** **a** career, future, reputation, savings, life riskieren, aufs Spiel setzen → **neck** **b** defeat, quarrel, accident riskieren; (= venture) criticism, remark wagen, riskieren; **to** ~ **sb's wrath** riskieren, dass jd sehr erzürnt ist; **you'll** ~ **falling/losing your job** Sie riskieren dabei, hinzufallen/Ihre Stelle zu verlieren; **she won't** ~ **coming today** sie wird es heute nicht riskieren, zu kommen; **I'll** ~ **it** das riskiere ich, ich lasse es darauf ankommen

risk capital N Risikokapital nt

risk factor N Risikofaktor m

riskily ['rɪskɪlɪ] ADV riskant

riskiness ['rɪskɪnɪs] N Riskantheit f

risk: risk management N Absicherung f von Risiken; **risk sharing** N Risikoteilung f

risky ['rɪskɪ] ADJ (+er) **a** enterprise, deed, loan, investment, debt riskant; **it's** ~, **it's a** ~ **business** das ist riskant **b** joke, story pikant, gewagt

risotto [rɪ'zɒtəʊ] N Risotto m

risqué ['riːskeɪ] ADJ pikant, gewagt

rissole ['rɪsəʊl] N ≈ Frikadelle f

rite [raɪt] N Ritus m; **burial ~s** Bestattungsriten pl

rite of passage N (fig) Übergangsritual m, Rites pl de passage (Sociol); **a rite(s)-of-passage film** ein Film m über das Erwachsenwerden

ritual ['rɪtjʊəl] **ADJ** **a** rituell; ~ **abuse** ritueller Missbrauch; ~ **murder** Ritualmord m **b** (usu hum, = usual) comments üblich; visit üblich, gewohnheitsmäßig **N** Ritual nt; (pej also) Zeremoniell nt no pl; **the courtship** ~ **of frogs** das Paarungsverhalten der Frösche; **he went through the same old** ~ (fig) er durchlief dasselbe alte Ritual or Zeremoniell; **he went through the** ~ **of checking all the locks** er überprüfte nach dem üblichen Zeremoniell or Ritual, ob alles abgeschlossen war

ritualism ['rɪtjʊəlɪzəm] N Ritualismus m

ritualist ['rɪtjʊəlɪst] N Ritualist(in) m(f); (= expert) Ritualienforscher(in) m(f)

ritualistic [ˌrɪtjʊə'lɪstɪk] ADJ **a** (= pre-arranged) remarks üblich; **he came out with some** ~ **nonsense about** ... er kam mit den üblichen Blödsinn über ... (acc) losgelassen (inf) **b** (= ceremonial) rituell; ~ **abuse** ritueller Missbrauch

ritualize ['rɪtjʊəlaɪz] VT ritualisieren

ritually ['rɪtjʊəlɪ] ADV rituell

ritzy ['rɪtsɪ] ADJ (+er) (inf) nobel (inf), protzig (pej inf)

rival ['raɪvəl] **N** **a** (= competitor) Rivale m, Rivalin f (for um, to für); (in love also) Nebenbuhler(in) m(f) (old); (Comm) Konkurrent(in) m(f) **b** (= equal) **this collection of paintings has few ~s in the world** diese Gemäldesammlung hat in der Welt kaum ihresgleichen **ADJ** groups, fans, leaders rivalisierend; claims, plans, attraction konkurrierend; ~ **firm** Konkurrenzfirma f; ~ **bid** Konkurrenzangebot nt **VT** (in love, for affections) rivalisieren mit; (Comm) konkurrieren mit; **he can't** ~ **her in in-**

telligence er kann sich mit ihr in Bezug auf Intelligenz nicht messen; **his achievements** ~ **even yours** seine Leistungen können sich sogar mit deinen messen; **I can't** ~ **that** da kann ich nicht mithalten; **to** ~ **sth in significance** einer Sache (dat) die Bedeutung streitig machen

rivalry ['raɪvəlrɪ] N Rivalität f; (Comm) Konkurrenzkampf m

rive [raɪv] pret **rived**, ptp **riven** ['rɪvn] VT (old, liter) spalten; **~n by grief** (fig) von Schmerz zerrissen

river ['rɪvə] N Fluss m; (major) Strom m; **down** ~ fluss-/stromabwärts; **up** ~ fluss-/stromaufwärts; **the** ~ **Rhine** (Brit) **the Rhine** ~ (US) der Rhein; **~s of blood/lava** Blut-/Lavaströme pl → **sell**

river in cpds Fluss-; **river basin** N Flussbecken nt; **riverbed** N Flussbett nt; **riverboat** N Ausflugsschiff nt; **river fish** N Flussfisch m; **river fishing** N Flussangeln nt; **river head** N Flussquelle f

riverine ['rɪvəraɪn] ADJ (form, = of river) Fluss-; (= like river) flussartig; people am Fluss wohnend; ~ **estuary** Flussmündung f

river: river mouth N Flussmündung f; **river navigation** N Flussschifffahrt f; **river police** N Wasserschutzpolizei f; **riverside** **N** Flussufer nt; **on/by the** ~ am Fluss **ADJ** am Fluss (-ufer); **river traffic** N Flussschifffahrt f

rivet ['rɪvɪt] **N** Niete f **VT** (lit) nieten; two things vernieten; (fig) audience, attention fesseln; **his eyes were ~ed to the screen** sein Blick war auf die Leinwand geheftet; **it ~ed our attention** das fesselte uns or unsere Aufmerksamkeit; **~ed (to the spot) by fear** vor Angst wie festgenagelt; ~ **joint** Nietnaht f, Nietung f

riveter ['rɪvɪtə] N Nieter(in) m(f); (= tool) Nietmaschine f

riveting ['rɪvɪtɪŋ] ADJ (= gripping) fesselnd; **the book is a** ~ **read** das Buch ist spannender or fesselnder Lesestoff; **it's** ~ **stuff** es ist faszinierend

rivet(t)ing ['rɪvɪtɪŋ] N Nieten nt

Riviera [ˌrɪvɪ'eərə] N **the (French)/Italian** ~ die französische/italienische Riviera

rivulet ['rɪvjʊlɪt] N Flüsschen nt, Bach m

riyal [rɪ'jɑːl] N (Saudi Arabian) saudi-arabischer Riyal; (Yemeni) Jemen-Riyal m

RM (Brit) abbr of **Royal Marines**

rm abbr of **room** Zim.

RN **a** (Brit) abbr of **Royal Navy** **b** (US) abbr of **registered nurse**

RNA abbr of **ribonucleic acid** RNS f

RNAS (Brit) abbr of **Royal Naval Air Services**

RNLI (Brit) abbr of **Royal National Lifeboat Institution** ≈ DLRG f

RNR (Brit) abbr of **Royal Navy Reserve**

RNVR (Brit) abbr of **Royal Navy Volunteer Reserve**

roach [rəʊtʃ] N Plötze f; (inf, = cockroach) Schabe f

road [rəʊd] **N** **a** Straße f; **"road up"** (Brit) „Straßenbauarbeiten"; **"road narrows"** „Straßenverengung"; **by** ~ (send sth) per Spedition; (travel) mit dem Bus/Auto etc; **she lives across the** ~ **(from us)** sie wohnt gegenüber (von uns); **my car is off the** ~ **just now** ich kann mein Auto momentan nicht benutzen; **my car has never been/is never off the** ~ mein Auto war noch nie/ist nie in der Werkstatt; **I hope to put the car back on the** ~ **soon** ich hoffe, das Auto bald wieder fahren zu können; **this vehicle shouldn't be on the** ~ das Fahrzeug ist nicht verkehrstüchtig; **he is a danger on the** ~ er ist eine Gefahr für den Straßenverkehr; **to take to the** ~ sich auf den Weg machen, losfahren; (as tramp) Vagabund werden; **to be on the** ~ (= travelling) unterwegs sein; (theatre company) auf Tournee sein; (car) fahren; **is this the** ~ **to London?** geht es hier nach London?; **the London** ~ die Straße nach London; **"Westlands/London ~"** „Westlandsstraße/Londoner Straße"; **to have one for the** ~ (inf) zum Abschluss noch einen trinken; **gentleman of the** ~ Vagabund m **b** (fig) Weg m; **you're on the right** ~ (lit, fig)

Sie sind auf dem richtigen Weg; **on the** ~ **to ruin/success** auf dem Weg ins Verderben/zum Erfolg; **somewhere along the** ~ **he changed his mind** irgendwann hat er seine Meinung geändert; **you're in my** ~ (Brit dial inf) du bist mir im Weg; **(get) out of the ~!** (Brit dial inf) geh weg!; **any** ~ (Brit dial inf) = **anyhow** **c** **roads** PL (Naut) Reede f **d** (US) = **railroad**

ROADS

In Großbritannien und den USA hat man verschiedene Bezeichnungen für die unterschiedlichen Straßentypen.

In Großbritannien gibt es zwei Arten von Landstraßen: die wichtigeren, die unseren Bundesstraßen entsprechen (man nennt sie auch **trunk roads**), tragen die Bezeichnung **A roads**, die weniger wichtigen sind **B roads**. Einige der **A roads** können mehrere Fahrbahnen für beide Fahrtrichtungen haben: Diese werden dann **dual carriageways** genannt. Der amerikanische Ausdruck dafür ist **divided highway**.

Die Benutzung des britischen Pendants zu den Autobahnen, die **motorways**, ist kostenlos. In den USA heißt dieser Straßentyp allgemein **superhighway**, allerdings gibt es daneben noch einige ebenfalls gebräuchliche Bezeichnungen: die **interstate highways** verbinden mindestens zwei Staaten miteinander und sind manchmal gebührenfrei, meist kosten sie jedoch Maut, weshalb sie auch **toll roads** oder **turnpikes** heißen; **expressways** befinden sich normalerweise innerhalb oder in der Nähe von Städten; und **freeways** werden so genannt, weil sie gebührenfrei sind.

---

roadability [ˌrəʊdə'bɪlɪtɪ] N (US: of car) Fahreigenschaften pl

road in cpds Straßen-; **road accident** N Verkehrsunfall m; **roadblock** N Straßensperre f; **road book** N Straßenatlas m; **road conditions** PL Straßenzustand m; **road construction** N (US) Straßenbau m; **road-fund licence** N (Brit) ≈ Verkehrssteuer f; **road haulage** N (esp Brit) Spedition f; **road haulier**, (US) **road hauler** N Spediteur(in) m(f); (= company) Spedition f; **road hog** N (inf) Verkehrsrowdy m (inf); **roadholding (ability)** N Straßenlage f; (of tyres) Griffigkeit f; **roadhouse** N Rasthaus nt

roadie ['rəʊdɪ] N (inf) Roadie m (inf)

road: roadmaking N Straßenbau m; **road man** N (inf) Straßenbauarbeiter m; **road manager** N (of pop group) Roadmanager(in) m(f); **roadmender** N Straßenbauarbeiter(in) m(f); **road metal** N Straßenschotter m; **road movie** N Roadmovie nt; **road pricing** N (Brit) Straßenbenutzungsgebühren pl; **road race** N Straßenrennen nt; **road racer** N (= bicycle) Rennrad nt (für Straßenrennen); **road rage** N Aggressivität f im Straßenverkehr; **roadroller** N Straßenwalze f; **road safety** N Verkehrssicherheit f, Sicherheit f im Straßenverkehr; **road sense** N Verkehrssinn m; **road show** N (Theat) Tournee f; **roadside** **N** Straßenrand m; **along** or **by the** ~ am Straßenrand **ADJ** stall, toilet, pub an der Straße; **a** ~ **bomb** eine Bombe, die im Straßengraben versteckt ist; ~ **check** Straßenkontrolle f; ~ **ditch** Straßengraben m; ~ **repairs** (professional) Sofortdienst m; (done alone) Reparatur f am Straßenrand; **roadsign** N (Straßen)verkehrszeichen nt; **roadstead** N (Naut) Reede f

roadster ['rəʊdstə] N (old, = car) Vehikel nt (inf); (= bicycle) Drahtesel m (inf)

road: roadsweeper N (= person) Straßenkehrer(in) m(f); (= vehicle) Straßenkehrmaschine f; **road tax** N (Brit) Kraftfahrzeugsteuer f; **road test** N Straßentest m; **road-test** VT Probe fahren; **road traffic accident** N Verkehrsunfall m; **road transport** N Straßengüterverkehr m; **road trials** PL (= road-test) Straßentest m; (= rally) Straßenwettbewerb m; **road user** N Verkehrsteilnehmer(in) m(f); **roadway**

N Fahrbahn f; **roadwork** N (Sport) Straßentraining nt; **roadworks** PL (Brit) Straßenbauarbeiten pl; **roadworthiness** N (of car) Verkehrstüchtigkeit f, Verkehrssicherheit f; **roadworthy** ADJ verkehrstüchtig, -sicher

roam [rəʊm] **VI** streets, countryside wandern or ziehen durch; **to ~ the (seven) seas** die sieben Meere durchkreuzen; **to ~ the streets** (child, dog) (in den Straßen) herumstreunen; **to ~ the earth/world** durch die Welt ziehen **N** (herum-) wandern; (hum, hands) wandern, sich verirren

▶ **roam about** (Brit) or **around** **VI** herumwandern; (dogs, looters) herumstreunen **VI** +prep obj **to roam around the house** durch das Haus wandern; **to roam around the city/the streets** durch die Stadt/die Straßen streifen

roamer ['rəʊmə'] N Vagabund(in) m(f); (= dog) Herumstreuner m; (= child) Stromer m (inf)

roaming ['rəʊmɪŋ] **ADJ** person wandernd; animal also herumziehend; (fig) thoughts schweifend **N** Herumwandern nt; **this life of ~** dieses Vagabundenleben

roan [rəʊn] **ADJ** horse rötlich grau **N** Rotschimmel m

roar [rɔː'] **VI** (person, crowd, lion, bull) brüllen (with vor +dat); (fire in hearth) prasseln; (wind, engine, plane) heulen; (sea, waterfall) tosen; (thunder, forest fire) toben; (gun) donnern; **to ~ at sb** jdn anbrüllen; **the trucks ~ed past** die Lastwagen donnerten vorbei; **the car ~ed up the street** der Wagen donnerte die Straße hinauf; **he had them ~ing (with laughter)** sie brüllten vor Lachen

VT **a** (also **roar out**) order, song etc brüllen; **the fans ~ed their approval** die Fans grölten zustimmend

b engine aufheulen lassen

N **a** no pl (of person, crowd, lion, bull) Gebrüll nt; (of fire in hearth) Prasseln nt; (of wind, engine, plane) Heulen nt; (of sea, waterfall) Tosen nt; (of thunder, forest fire) Toben nt; (of gun, traffic) Donnern nt

b **~s of laughter** brüllendes Gelächter; **the ~s of the crowd/lion** das Brüllen der Menge/des Löwen

roaring ['rɔːrɪŋ] **ADJ** person, crowd, lion, bull brüllend; fire in hearth prasselnd; wind, engine, plane heulend; sea, waterfall tosend; thunder, forest fire tobend; gun, traffic, noise donnernd; **~ drunk** (inf) sternhagelvoll (inf); **the ~ Twenties** die wilden zwanziger Jahre or Zwanzigerjahre; **a ~ success** ein voller Erfolg, ein Bombenerfolg m (inf); **to do a ~ trade (in sth)** ein Riesengeschäft nt (mit etw) machen **N** = roar N a

Roaring Forties PL (Geog) **the ~** stürmischer Teil des Ozeans (zwischen dem 39. und 50. Breitengrad)

roast [rəʊst] **N** Braten m; **pork ~** Schweinebraten m **ADJ** pork, veal gebraten; potatoes in Fett im Backofen gebraten; **~ chicken** Brathähnchen nt; **~ beef** Roastbeef nt; **we had ~ pork** es gab Schweinebraten **VT** **a** meat braten; chestnuts, coffee beans, ore rösten; **to ~ oneself by the fire/in the sun** sich am Feuer/in der Sonne braten lassen; **to be ~ed alive** (fig) sich totschwitzen (inf); (by sun) gebraten werden (inf) → also **roasting** **b** (inf, = criticize) ins Gericht gehen mit (inf) **VI** (meat) braten; (inf, person) irrsinnig schwitzen (inf); (in sun) in der Sonne braten → also **roasting**

roaster ['rəʊstə'] N (= oven) Bratofen m, Bratröhre f; (= dish) Bräter m; (= coffee roaster) Röstapparat m; (for ore) Röstofen m; (= chicken) Brathähnchen nt; (= pig) Spanferkel nt

roasting ['rəʊstɪŋ] **N** **a** (lit) Braten nt **b** (inf, = criticism) Verriss m; (= telling-off) Standpauke f; **to give sb a ~** jdn verreißen; jdm eine Standpauke halten **ADJ** **a** (inf. = hot) days, weather knallheiß (inf) **b** (Cook) zum Braten; **~ chicken** Brathähnchen nt; **~ meat** Bratenfleisch nt

roasting: roasting bag N Bratschlauch m; **roasting tin, roasting tray** N Bräter m

rob [rɒb] VT person bestehlen; (more seriously) berauben; shop, bank ausrauben; orchard plün-

dern; **to ~ sb of sth** (lit, fig) jdn einer Sache (gen) berauben (geh), jdm etw rauben; (lit also) jdm etw stehlen; **I've been ~bed!** ich bin bestohlen worden!; (= had to pay too much) ich bin geneppt worden (inf); **to ~ the till** (Brit) die Ladenkasse ausräumen or plündern; **he was ~bed of the pleasure of seeing her** es war ihm nicht vergönnt, sie zu sehen; **the shock ~bed him of speech** er hat vor Schreck die Stimme verloren; (briefly also) der Schreck hat ihm die Sprache verschlagen; **our team was ~bed** (inf) das ist nicht fair(, wir hätten gewinnen müssen)

robber ['rɒbə'] N Räuber(in) m(f)

robbery ['rɒbərɪ] N Raub m no pl; (= burglary) Einbruch m (of in +acc); **~ with violence** (Jur) Raubüberfall m; **armed ~** bewaffneter Raubüberfall; **at that price it's sheer ~!** (inf) das ist der reinste Nepp (inf), das ist reiner Wucher (inf); **the bank ~** der Überfall auf die Bank

robe [rəʊb] **N** **a** (= garment, of office) Robe f, Talar m; (for priest) Rock m, Robe f; (for baby) langes Kleidchen; (esp US: for house wear) Morgenrock m, Haus- or Bademantel m; (obs, = gown) Kleid nt; **he was wearing his ~ of office** er war im Ornat; **ceremonial ~s** Festgewänder pl; **christening ~** Taufkleid nt **b** (US, = wrap) Decke f **VT** (lit) ankleiden, die Amtsrobe or den Ornat anlegen (+dat); **to ~ sb/sth in sth** (lit, fig) jdn/etw in etw (acc) kleiden **VI** (judge etc) die Amtsrobe or den Ornat anlegen

robin ['rɒbɪn] N Rotkehlchen nt → **round robin**

robinia [rə'bɪnɪə'] N (Bot) Robinie f, Scheinakazie f

robot ['rəʊbɒt] N Roboter m; (fig also) Automat m; **~ guidance, ~ pilot** Selbststeuerung f

robotics [rəʊ'bɒtɪks] N sing or pl Robotertechnik f, Robotik f

robust [rəʊ'bʌst] **ADJ** **a** (= strong, solid) person, material, toy, machine robust, widerstandsfähig; structure massiv, stabil; build kräftig, robust; economy robust, gesund; economic growth gesund; constitution robust; appetite, humour gesund, unverwüstlich; **to be in ~ health** sich bester Gesundheit erfreuen

b (= determined) attitude entschieden; speech, style markig; defence stark; **to put up or take a ~ defence** (Brit) or **defense** (US) **of sth** etw energisch verteidigen, für etw energisch eintreten

c (= vigorous) exercise hart; **he enjoyed more ~ recreations like rock climbing** er hatte Spaß an etwas aktiveren Sportarten wie Klettern

d (= intense) flavour kräftig; aroma kräftig, herzhaft; wine kernig

robustly ADV **a** (= strongly, solidly) robust **b** (= determinedly) energisch **c** flavoured kräftig, herzhaft

robustness [rəʊ'bʌstnɪs] **N** **a** (of person, material, toy, machine) Robustheit f, Widerstandsfähigkeit f; (of structure) Massivität f, Stabilität f; (of build) Kräftigkeit f, Robustheit f; (of economy) Robustheit f, Gesundheit f; (of economic growth) Gesundheit f; (of constitution) Kräftigkeit f **b** (of attitude) Entschiedenheit f; (of speech, style) Markigkeit f; (of defence) Stärke f **c** (of wine) Kernigkeit f

rock¹ [rɒk] **VT** **a** (= swing) schaukeln; (gently: = lull) wiegen; **to ~ a baby to sleep** ein Baby in den Schlaf wiegen; **~ed by the waves** von den Wellen hin und her geschaukelt

b (= shake) town erschüttern, zum Beben bringen; building ins Wanken bringen, erschüttern; ship hin und her werfen; (fig inf) person erschüttern; **to ~ the boat** (fig) für Unruhe sorgen

VI **a** (gently) schaukeln; **he was ~ing back and forth (in his chair)** er schaukelte (auf seinem Stuhl) vor und zurück

b (violently, building, tree, post) schwanken; (ship) hin und her geworfen werden; (ground) beben; **they ~ed with laughter** sie schüttelten sich or bebten vor Lachen

c (= rock and roll) rocken

N (= pop music) Rock m; (= dance) Rock n' Roll

m; **~-and-roll** Rock and Roll m, Rock n' Roll m; **to do the ~-and-roll** Rock n' Roll tanzen, rocken

rock² **N** **a** (= substance) Stein m; (= rock face) Fels(en) m; (Geol) Gestein nt; **caves hewn out of the ~** aus dem Fels(en) gehauene Höhlen; **hewn out of solid ~** aus massivem Stein/Fels gehauen; **built on ~** (lit, fig) auf Fels gebaut; **porous/volcanic ~** poröses/vulkanisches Gestein; **the study of ~s** Gesteinskunde f

b (large mass) Fels(en) m; (= boulder also) Felsbrocken m; (smaller) (großer) Stein m; **the Rock (of Gibraltar)** der Felsen von Gibraltar; **on the Rock** (inf) in Gibraltar; **to be caught between a ~ and a hard place** (inf) in der Klemme stecken or sitzen; **as solid as a ~** (structure) massiv wie ein Fels; firm, marriage unerschütterlich wie in Fels; **the ship went on the ~s** das Schiff lief (auf die Felsen) auf; **on the ~s** (inf, = with ice) mit Eis; (marriage etc) kaputt (inf); (= broke) bankrott; **"danger, falling ~s"** „Steinschlaggefahr"

c (inf, = diamond) Diamant m; **~s** (= jewels) Klunker pl (inf)

d no pl (Brit, = sweet) Zuckerstange f

e **to get one's ~s off** (sl) seinen Spaß haben (inf)

rock: rock bed N (Geol) Felsengrund m; **rock bottom** N der Tiefpunkt; **to be at ~** auf dem Nullpunkt or Tiefpunkt sein; **to reach or hit ~** den Nullpunkt or Tiefpunkt erreichen; **this is ~** (inf) schlimmer kann es nicht werden; **rock-bottom** ADJ (inf) interest rates niedrigste(r, s); **~ prices** Niedrigstpreise pl; **rock-bound** ADJ von Felsen umschlossen; **rock bun, rock cake** N ≈ Rosinenhäufchen nt; **rock carving** N Felszeichnung f; (= writing) Felsschrift f; (= action) Ritzen nt in Fels; **rock-climber** N (Felsen)kletterer(in) m(f); **rock climbing** N Klettern nt (im Fels); **rock club** N Rockklub m, Rockschuppen m (inf); **rock crystal** N Bergkristall m

rocker ['rɒkə'] **N** **a** (of cradle etc) Kufe f; **to be off one's ~** (inf) übergeschnappt sein (inf); **to go off one's ~** (inf) überschnappen (inf) **b** (sl, = person) Rocker(in) m(f) **c** (Aut: also **rocker arm**) Kipphebel m

rockery ['rɒkərɪ] N Steingarten m

rocket ['rɒkɪt] **N** **a** Rakete f **b** (Brit inf: = reprimand) Anschiss m (inf); **to get a ~** einen Anschiss bekommen (inf); **to give sb a ~** jdm einen Anschiss verpassen (inf) **VI** (prices) hochschießen, hochschnellen; **to ~ to fame** über Nacht berühmt werden; (person also) kometenhaft aufsteigen; **he went ~ing past my door** (inf) er zischte or schoss (wie ein geölter Blitz) an meiner Tür vorbei (inf)

rocket in cpds Raketen-; **rocket attack** N Raketenangriff m; **rocket fuel** N Raketentreibstoff m; **rocket launcher** N Raketenabschussgerät nt; (on plane) Raketenwerfer m; (multiple) Stalinorgel f; **rocket plane** N Raketenflugzeug nt; **rocket plane** N Raketenflugzeug nt; **rocket projector** N (Mil) Raketenwerfer m; **rocket propulsion** N Raketenantrieb m; **rocket range** N Raketenversuchsgelände nt; **within ~** mit Raketen zu erreichen

rocketry ['rɒkɪtrɪ] N Raketentechnik f; (= rockets) Raketen pl

rocket: rocket science N Raketentechnik f; **it's hardly ~** (inf) so schwer kann das das nicht sein; **rocket scientist** N Raketentechniker(in) m(f); **it doesn't take a ~ to ...** (inf) man muss kein Genie sein, um zu ...; **rocket ship** N Raketenträger m; (rocket-propelled) Raketenschiff nt; **rocket silo** N Raketensilo nt

rock: rock face N Felswand f; **rock fall** N Steinschlag m; **rock garden** N Steingarten m

Rockies ['rɒkɪz] PL **the ~** die Rocky Mountains pl

rocking ['rɒkɪŋ]: **rocking chair** N Schaukelstuhl m; **rocking horse** N Schaukelpferd nt

rock: rock lobster N (Zool) Gemeine Languste; **rock plant** N Steinpflanze f; **rock pool** N Wasserlache, die sich bei Ebbe zwischen Fel-

sen bildet; **rockrose** N Sonnenröschen *nt*; **rock salmon** N (*Brit*) Dorsch *m*; **rock salt** N Steinsalz *nt*; **rock star** N (*Mus*) Rockstar *m*; **rock-steady** ADJ *hand, camera, gun, car* ganz ruhig; *voice* ganz fest

rocky¹ ['rɒkɪ] ADJ (= *unsteady*) wackelig (*also fig inf*)

rocky² ADJ (+*er*) *mountain, hill* felsig; *road, path* steinig; ~ **outcrop** ausstreichendes Gestein (*spec*)

Rocky Mountains PL **the** ~ die Rocky Mountains *pl*

rococo [rəˈkəʊkəʊ] N Rokoko *nt* ADJ Rokoko-; ~ **period** Rokoko *nt*, Rokokozeit *f*

rod [rɒd] N a Stab *m*, Stange *f*; (= *switch*) Rute *f*, Gerte *f*; (*in machinery*) Stange *f*; (*for punishment, fishing*) Rute *f*; (*symbol of authority*) Stab *m*; **spare the** ~ **and spoil the child** (*prov*) wer mit der Rute spart, verzieht das Kind (*prov*); ~ **bacterium** Stäbchenbakterie *f* b (= *measure*) ≈ Rute *f* (5,5 *Yards*) c (*dated US, sl,* = *gun*) Schießeisen *nt* (*hum inf*)

rode [rəʊd] *pret of* **ride**

rodent ['rəʊdənt] N Nagetier *nt*

rodeo ['rəʊdɪəʊ] N Rodeo *nt*

rodomontade [ˌrɒdəmɒnˈteɪd] N (*liter*) Prahlerei *f*, Bramarbasieren *nt* (*geh*)

roe¹ [rəʊ] N *pl* -(s) (*species: also* **roe deer**) Reh *nt*; ~**buck** Rehbock *m*; ~ **deer** (*female*) Reh *nt*, Ricke *f* (*spec*)

roe² N *pl* - (*of fish*) Rogen *m*; **hard** ~ Rogen *m*; **soft** ~ Milch *f*; **herring** ~ Heringsrogen *m*

roentgen ['rɒntjən] N Röntgen *nt*

rogation [rəʊˈgeɪʃən] N (*Eccl,* = *litany*) Litanei *f*; (= *period: also* **Rogation** *or* **Rogation-tide**) Bittwoche *f*

Rogation Days PL (*Eccl*) Bitttage *pl*, Rogationstage *pl*

Rogation Sunday N (*Eccl*) (Sonntag *m*) Rogate *no art*

roger ['rɒdʒə'] INTERJ "roger" „verstanden"

rogue [rəʊg] N a (= *scoundrel*) Gauner(in) *m(f)*, Schurke *m*; (= *scamp*) Schlingel *m*; **you little** ~! du kleiner Gauner! b (*Zool*) Einzelgänger(in) *m(f)* ADJ a (*Zool*) ~ **male** ein Einzelgänger *m*; ~ **elephant** Einzelgänger(elefant) *m* b (= *maverick*) *person* einzelgängerisch; (= *criminal*) *person, organization* verbrecherisch, skrupellos c (= *abnormal, aberrant*) abnormal, entartet; (*Biol, Med*) *cell* aberrant, entartet; *satellite, rocket* fehlgeleitet; **a** ~ **firework flew into the crowd** ein fehlgezündeter Feuerwerkskörper flog in die Menge

roguery ['rəʊgərɪ] N , *no pl* (= *wickedness*) Gaunerei *f*, Schurkerei *f*; (= *mischief*) Spitzbüberei *f*

rogues' gallery ['rəʊgzˈgælərɪ] N (*Police inf*) Verbrecheralbum *nt*; **they look like a real** ~ sie sehen wie Gauner aus

roguish ['rəʊgɪʃ] ADJ spitzbübisch; (*old,* = *wicked*) schurkisch

roguishly ['rəʊgɪʃlɪ] ADV spitzbübisch; (*old,* = *wickedly*) schurkisch

roil [rɔɪl] (*esp US*) VI (= *churn: water*) strudeln VT (*fig*) in Aufruhr bringen; **to** ~ **the waters** für Unruhe sorgen

roister ['rɔɪstə'] VI (= *revel*) herumtollen

roisterer ['rɔɪstərə'] N Krawallmacher(in) *m(f)*

role [rəʊl] N (*Theat, fig*) Rolle *f*; **in the** ~ **of Ophelia** in der Rolle der Ophelia; ~ **reversal** (*Psych*) Rollentausch *m*

role model N (*Psych*) Rollenbild *nt*

role-playing ['rəʊlˌpleɪɪŋ] N Rollenspiel *nt*

roll [rəʊl] N a (*of paper, netting, film, hair etc*) Rolle *f*; (*of fabric*) Ballen *m*; (*of banknotes*) Bündel *nt*; (*of butter*) Röllchen *nt*; (*of flesh, fat*) Wulst *m*, Röllchen *nt*; **a** ~ **of paper** eine Rolle Papier; **a** ~ **of banknotes** ein Bündel *nt* Banknoten b (*Cook: also* **bread roll**) Brötchen *nt*; **ham/cheese** ~ Schinken-/Käsebrötchen *nt* → **sausage roll** *etc*

c (= *movement*) (*of sea, waves*) Rollen *nt*; (*of ship*) Schlingern *nt*, Rollen *nt*; (= *somersault, Aviat*) Rolle *f*; (*of person's gait*) Schaukeln *nt*, Wiegen *nt*; **to do a** ~ eine Rolle machen; **the ship gave a sudden** ~ das Schiff schlingerte plötzlich; **the dog was having a** ~ **on the grass** der Hund wälzte sich im Gras; **to have a** ~ **in the hay with sb** (*inf*) mit jdm ins Heu gehen (*inf*); **to be on a** ~ (*inf*) eine Glückssträhne haben

d (= *sound, of thunder*) Rollen *nt*; (*of drums*) Wirbel *m*; (*of organ*) Brausen *nt*

e (= *list, register*) Liste *f*, Register *nt*; (*of solicitors*) Anwaltsliste *f*; **we have 60 pupils on our** ~ bei uns sind 60 Schüler angemeldet; **to call the** ~ die Namensliste verlesen, die Namen aufrufen; ~ **of honour** (*Brit*) Ehrenliste *f*; (= *plaque*) Ehrentafel *f*; **to strike sb** *or* **sb's name off the** ~ jdn *or* jds Namen von der Liste streichen → **electoral roll**

VI a (*person, object*) rollen; (*from side to side: ship*) schlingern; (*presses*) laufen; (*Aviat*) eine Rolle machen; **to** ~ **over and over** rollen und rollen, kullern und kullern (*inf*); **the children/stones** ~**ed down the hill** die Kinder/Steine rollten *or* kugelten (*inf*) den Berg hinunter; **tears were** ~**ing down her cheeks** Tränen rollten *or* kullerten (*inf*) ihr über die Wangen; **the newspapers were** ~**ing off the presses** die Zeitungen rollten von den Druckerpressen; **heads will** ~! (*fig*) da werden die Köpfe rollen!; **to keep the show** ~**ing** (*Theat inf*) die Show in Gang halten; **can you keep the ball** *or* **things** ~**ing while I'm away?** (*inf*) können Sie den Laden in Schwung halten, solange ich weg bin? (*inf*); **the dog** ~**ed in the mud** der Hund wälzte sich im Schlamm; **he's** ~**ing in money** *or* **in it** (*inf*) er schwimmt im Geld (*inf*); **the words just** ~**ed off his tongue** die Worte flossen ihm nur so von den Lippen; **his eyes** ~**ed** (*during a fit*) er rollte mit den Augen; **to** ~ **with the punches** (*fig*) sich nicht aus dem Gleis werfen *or* bringen lassen; **he** ~**s from side to side as he walks** er hat einen schaukelnden Gang

b (= *sound, thunder*) rollen, grollen; (*drum*) wirbeln; (*organ*) brausen; (*echo*) rollen

c (*camera*) laufen

d (*Cine*) **the credits** ~**ed** der Abspann lief

VT a *barrel, hoop, ball, car* rollen; *umbrella* aufrollen; *cigarette* drehen; *pastry, dough* ausrollen; *metal, lawn, road* walzen; **to** ~ **one's eyes** die Augen rollen *or* verdrehen; **to** ~ **one's r's** das R rollen; **to** ~ **sth between one's fingers** etw zwischen den Fingern drehen; **to** ~ **one's own** (*cigarettes*) sich (*dat*) seine eigenen drehen; **to** ~ **wool into a ball** Wolle zu einem Knäuel aufwickeln; **the hedgehog** ~**ed itself into a ball** der Igel rollte sich zu einer Kugel zusammen; **he** ~**ed himself in a blanket** er wickelte sich in eine Decke; **it has a kitchen and a dining room** ~**ed into one** es hat eine Küche und Esszimmer in einem → *also* **rolled**

▶ **roll about** (*Brit*) *or* **around** VI (*balls*) herumrollen *or* -kugeln (*inf*); (*ship*) schlingern; (*person, dog*) sich herumwälzen, sich wälzen; (*inf, with laughter*) sich kugeln (vor Lachen) (*inf*)

▶ **roll along** VI a (*ball*) entlang- *or* dahinrollen; **we were rolling along enjoying the countryside** wir rollten dahin und genossen die Landschaft b (*inf,* = *arrive*) aufkreuzen (*inf*), eintrudeln (*inf*) VT *sep* rollen

▶ **roll away** VI (*ball, vehicle*) wegrollen; (*clouds, mist*) abziehen VT *sep trolley, table* wegrollen

▶ **roll back** VI zurückrollen; (*eyes*) nach innen rollen VT *sep object, carpet* zurückrollen; *sheet* zurückschlagen; **if only we could roll back the years** wenn wir nur die Uhr zurückdrehen könnten

▶ **roll by** VI (*vehicle, procession*) vorbeirollen; (*clouds*) vorbeiziehen; (*time, years*) dahinziehen

▶ **roll down** VI (*ball, person, tears*) hinunterrollen *or* -kugeln (*inf*) VT *sep cart* hinunterrollen; *window* herunterlassen

▶ **roll in** VI hereinrollen; (*letters, money, contributions, suggestions*) hereinströmen; (*inf, person*)

eintrudeln (*inf*) VT *sep barrel, trolley* hereinrollen

▶ **roll off** VI a (*vehicle, procession*) weg- *or* davonrollen b (= *fall off: object, person*) herunterrollen

▶ **roll on** VI weiterrollen; (*time*) verfliegen; **roll on the holidays!** (*Brit*) wenn doch nur schon Ferien wären! VT *sep stockings* (die Beine) hochrollen

▶ **roll out** VT *sep* a *barrel* hinausrollen b *pastry, dough* ausrollen; *metal* auswalzen c (*inf*) *sentence, verse* produzieren (*inf*) d (= *introduce*) *system in company etc* einführen VI hinausrollen

▶ **roll over** VI herumrollen; (*vehicle*) umkippen; (*person*) sich umdrehen; **the dog rolled over onto its back** der Hund rollte auf den Rücken VT *sep person, animal, object* umdrehen; *patient* auf die andere Seite legen

▶ **roll past** VI = **roll by**

▶ **roll up** VI a (*animal*) sich zusammenrollen (*into* zu) b (*inf.* = *arrive*) antanzen (*inf*) c (*at fairground etc*) **roll up!** treten Sie näher! VT *sep cloth, paper, map, umbrella* auf- *or* zusammenrollen; *sleeves, trouser legs* hochkrempeln

roll: rollbar N Überrollbügel *m*; **roll call** N (*Sch*) Namensaufruf *m*; (*Mil*) (Anwesenheits)appell *m*; **a** ~ **of sporting giants** ein Verzeichnis *nt* von Spitzensportlern; **roll collar** N Rollkragen *m*

rolled [rəʊld] ADJ *blanket, paper etc* zusammengerollt; *tobacco* gerollt, gedreht

rolled: rolled gold N Dubleegold *nt*; **rolled oats** PL Haferflocken *pl*; **rolled steel** N Walzstahl *m*

roller ['rəʊlə'] N a (*for pressing, smoothing*) Rolle *f*; (= *pastry roller*) Nudelholz *nt*; (*for lawn, road, Ind*) Walze *f*; (= *paint roller*) Rolle *f* b (*for winding sth round*) Rolle *f*; (= *hair roller*) (Locken)wickler *m*; **to put one's hair in** ~**s** sich (*dat*) die Haare aufdrehen *or* eindrehen; **with her** ~**s in** mit Lockenwicklern (im Haar) c (*for moving things*) Rolle *f*; (*log-shaped*) Rollklotz *m* d (= *wave*) Brecher *m*

roller: roller bandage N Rollbinde *f*; **roller bearing** N Rollenlager *nt*; **Rollerblade**® N Inliner *m*; **roller blind** N Springrollo *nt*; **roller coaster** N Achterbahn *f*, Berg-und-Tal-Bahn *f*; **an emotional** ~ eine gefühlsmäßige Berg-und-Tal-Fahrt; **roller skate** N Rollschuh *m*; **roller-skate** VI Rollschuh laufen; **he** ~**d down the street** er lief *or* fuhr mit seinen Rollschuhen die Straße entlang; **roller-skating** N Rollschuhlaufen *nt*; **roller towel** N Rollhandtuch *nt*

rollick ['rɒlɪk] VI (*also* **rollick about**) herumtollen

rollicking ['rɒlɪkɪŋ] ADJ *person* ausgelassen; *occasion, life* wild; ~ (**good**) **fun** Mordsspaß *m* (*inf*); **a** ~ **success** ein Mordserfolg *m* (*inf*); **to have a** ~ **time** richtig auf die Pauke hauen (*inf*) N (*Brit, inf,* = *telling-off*) **to get a** ~ runtergeputzt werden (*inf*); **to give sb a** ~ jdn runterputzen (*inf*)

rolling ['rəʊlɪŋ] ADJ a (= *swaying*) *motion* schwankend; *ship* schlingernd; *sea, waves* rollend, wogend; **to have a** ~ **gait** einen schaukelnden Gang haben; **to be** ~ **drunk** sturzbetrunken sein (*inf*) b (= *undulating*) *hills* gewellt; *landscape, countryside* wellig, hügelig; *lawns* wellig c (= *progressing*) *plan, programme* kontinuierlich; **three weeks of** ~ **strikes** dreiwöchige Streikmaßnahmen *pl*; ~ **news service** Nachrichtendienst *m* rund um die Uhr

rolling: rolling mill N (= *factory*) Walzwerk *nt*; (= *machine*) Walze *f*; **rolling pin** N Nudelholz *nt*, Teigrolle *f*; **rolling stock** N (*Rail*) rollendes Material, Fahrzeuge *pl*; **rolling stone** N **he's a** ~ er ist ein unsteter Bursche; **a** ~ **gathers no moss** (*Prov*) wer rastet, der rostet (*Prov*); **rolling train** N Walzstraße *f*

roll: rollmop (herring) N Rollmops *m*; **rollneck** N Rollkragen *m*; **rollneck(ed)** ADJ Rollkragen-; ~ **sweater** Rollkragenpullover *m*; **roll-on** N a Elastikschlüpfer *m* b (= *deodor-*

ant) (Deo)roller *m*; **roll-on/roll-off** ADJ Roll-on-roll-off-; **~ ferry** Roll-on-roll-off-Fähre *f*; **roll-out** N **a** (= *presentation of new aircraft*) Roll-out *m*; (*launch of new product*) (Produkt-)präsentation *f*, (Produkt)einführung *f* **b** (*of aircraft on runway*) Ausrollen *nt*; **rollover** N **a** (*Fin, of loan etc*) Laufzeitverlängerung *f* **b** (*US: cellphone*) Mitnehmen *nt* von nicht vertelefonierten Freiminuten in den Folgemonat **ATTR** (*Brit, in National Lottery*) **~ week** Woche mit Lotto-Jackpot, da es in der vorhergehenden Woche keinen Hauptgewinner gab → **jackpot** Jackpot *m*; **roll-top** N Rollladen *m*; **roll-top desk** N Rollschreibtisch *m*; **roll-up** N (*Brit inf*) Selbstgedrehte *f*; **to have a ~** sich (*dat*) eine drehen

Rolodex® ['rəʊlədeks] N Rolodex® *m*, Rotationskartei *f*

roly-poly ['rəʊlɪ'pəʊlɪ] **ADJ** (*inf*) kugelrund, mopsig (*inf*) N **a** (*Brit: also* **roly-poly pudding**) *mit Nierentalg hergestellter Strudel, der gebacken oder im Wasserbad gekocht wird* **b** (*inf, = plump child*) Rollmops *m* (*inf*), Pummel *m* (*inf*) **c** (*inf, = somersault*) Purzelbaum *m* (*inf*)

ROM [rɒm] N (*Comput*) *abbr of* **read only memory** ROM *m or nt*

romaine [ˌrəʊ'meɪn] N (*US*) Romagnasalat *m*, römischer Salat

Roman ['rəʊmən] N **a** Römer(in) *m(f)* **b** (*Typ: also* **Roman type**) Magerdruck *m* ADJ **a** römisch; **~ times** Römerzeit *f* **b** (= *Roman Catholic*) römisch-katholisch; **the ~ Church** die römische Kirche **c** **roman** (*Typ*) mager; **roman letters** Magerdruck *m*

roman à clef ['rəʊmã ˌnæ'kleɪ] N Schlüsselroman *m*

Roman: Roman alphabet N römisches Alphabet; **Roman arch** N romanischer Bogen; **Roman calendar** N römischer Kalender; **Roman candle** N Goldrausch *m*; **Roman Catholic** **ADJ** (römisch-)katholisch; **the ~ Church** die (römisch-)katholische Kirche **N** Katholik(in) *m(f)*, (Römisch-)Katholische(r) *mf*; **Roman Catholicism** N römisch-katholischer Glaube

romance [rəʊ'mæns] N **a** (= *book*) Fantasie- or Phantasieerzählung *f*, Roman *m*; (= *love story*) Liebesgeschichte *f* or -roman *m*; (= *adventure story*) Abenteuerroman *m*; (= *tale of chivalry*) Ritterroman *m*; (*no pl*: = *romantic fiction*) Liebesromane *pl*, (*fig*, = *lies*) Märchen *nt*; **it's pure ~** es ist das reinste Märchen **b** (= *love affair*) Romanze *f*; **it's quite a ~** das ist eine richtige Liebesgeschichte **c** *no pl* (= *romanticism*) Romantik *f*; **an air of ~ pervaded the village** ein romantischer Zauber umgab das Dorf; **the ~ of foreign lands** der Zauber ferner Länder **d** (*Mus*) Romanze *f* **e** **Romance** (= *Romance languages*) die romanischen Sprachen *pl* **ADJ** **Romance** (*language etc*) romanisch **VI** fantasieren, phantasieren, fabulieren **VT** eine Romanze haben mit

romancer [rəʊ'mænsə'] N (*fig*) Fantast(in) *m(f)*, Phantast(in) *m(f)*

Roman Empire N Römisches Reich

Romanesque [ˌrəʊmə'nesk] ADJ romanisch

Roman holiday N Spaß *m* auf Kosten anderer

Romania [rəʊ'meɪnɪə] N Rumänien *nt*

Romanian [rəʊ'meɪnɪən] **ADJ** rumänisch N **a** Rumäne *m*, Rumänin *f* **b** (= *language*) Rumänisch *nt*

Romanic [rəʊ'mænɪk] ADJ *language* romanisch

romanize ['rəʊmənaɪz] VT (*Hist*) romanisieren; (*Rel*) nach dem Katholizismus ausrichten

Roman: Roman law N römisches Recht; **Roman nose** N Römernase *f*; **Roman numeral** N römische Ziffer

Romansh [rəʊ'mænʃ] **ADJ** romantsch N Romantsch *nt*

romantic [rəʊ'mæntɪk] ADJ (*also Art, Liter, Mus: also* **Romantic**) romantisch; *person also* romantisch veranlagt; **~ comedy** romantische Komödie; **~ novel** Liebesroman *m*; **the Romantic movement** die Romantik; **they were very good friends but there was no ~ involvement** sie waren sehr enge Freunde, aber sie hatten keine Liebesbeziehung; **he played the ~ lead in several plays** er spielte in mehreren Stücken den romantischen Liebhaber N (*also Art, Liter, Mus: also* **Romantic**) Romantiker(in) *m(f)*

romantically [rəʊ'mæntɪkəlɪ] ADV romantisch; **to be ~ involved with sb** eine Liebesbeziehung mit jdm haben; **she was ~ linked with …** ihr wurde eine Beziehung mit … nachgesagt; **to be ~ inclined** romantisch veranlagt sein; **~, things are looking up** in Liebesdingen geht es aufwärts

romantic fiction N Liebesromane *pl*

romanticism [rəʊ'mæntɪsɪzəm] N (*Art, Liter, Mus: also* **Romanticism**) Romantik *f*; **his ~** sein romantisches Wesen

romanticist [rəʊ'mæntɪsɪst] N (*Art, Liter, Mus: also* **Romanticist**) Romantiker(in) *m(f)*

romanticize [rəʊ'mæntɪsaɪz] **VT** romantisieren, zu romantisch sehen **VI** fantasieren, phantasieren

romantic love N (*Liter*) romantische Liebe

Romany ['rəʊmənɪ] N **a** Roma *mf* **b** (*Ling*) die Zigeunersprache, Romani *nt* **ADJ** *language, culture* der Roma; **~ gypsy** Zigeuner(in) *m(f)*

Rome [rəʊm] N Rom *nt*; **when in ~ (do as the Romans do)** (*prov*) ≈ andere Länder, andere Sitten (*Prov*); **~ wasn't built in a day** (*Prov*) Rom ist auch nicht an einem Tag erbaut worden (*Prov*); **all roads lead to ~** (*Prov*) viele Wege führen nach Rom (*prov*); **the Church of ~** die römische Kirche

Romeo ['rəʊmɪəʊ] N Romeo *m*; (*fig*) Herzensbrecher *m*; **a Latin ~** ein Papagallo *m* (*inf*)

Romish ['rəʊmɪʃ] ADJ (*pej*) Katholen- (*pej*), papistisch (*pej*)

romp [rɒmp] N Tollerei *f*; (*hum: = sexual intercourse*) Nümmerchen *nt* (*inf*); **the play was just a ~** das Stück war reiner Klamauk; **to have a ~** herumtollen or -toben/ein Nümmerchen machen (*inf*) **VI** **a** (*children, puppies*) herumtollen or -toben; **he came ~ing up to me** er kam auf mich zugetollt **b** **to ~ home** (= *win*) spielend gewinnen; **to ~ away with the title** den Titel einstecken **c** **to ~ through sth** mit etw spielend fertig werden, etw mit der linken Hand erledigen

rompers ['rɒmpəz] PL (*also* **pair of rompers**) einteiliger Spielanzug

romping ADJ , **rompingly** ADV ['rɒmpɪŋ, -lɪ], **rompish** ADJ , **rompishly** ADV ['rɒmpɪʃ, -lɪ] (= *lively and boisterous*) ausgelassen, wild

rondeau ['rɒndəʊ], **rondel** ['rɒndəl] N (*Mus*) Rondeau *nt*; (*Liter also*) Rondel *nt*

rondo ['rɒndəʊ] N (*Mus*) Rondo *nt*

Roneo® ['rəʊnɪəʊ] **VT** (mit Matrize) kopieren N Kopie *f*

rood [ru:d] N **a** (*Archit*) Kruzifix *nt* **b** (*Brit, = measure*) Rute *f*, ≈ Viertelmorgen *m*

rood screen N Lettner *m* (*spec*)

roof [ru:f] N Dach *nt*; (*of car also*) Verdeck *nt*; (*of cave, tunnel*) Gewölbe *nt*; **the ~ of the mouth** der Gaumen; **the ~ of the world** das Dach der Welt; **a ~ of branches** ein Blätterdach *nt*; **without a ~ over one's head** ohne Dach über dem Kopf; **a room in the ~** ein Zimmer *nt* unter dem Dach; **to live under the same ~ as sb** mit jdm unter demselben Dach wohnen; **as long as you live under my ~** solange du deine Beine unter meinen Tisch streckst; **to go through the ~** (*inf, person*) an die Decke gehen (*inf*); (*prices etc*) untragbar werden → **hit, raise** **VT** *house* mit einem Dach decken; **flat-/red-roofed** mit flachem/rotem Dach

▶ **roof in** or **over** VT *sep* überdachen

roofer ['ru:fə'] N Dachdecker(in) *m(f)*

roof: roof garden N Dachgarten *m*; **roof guard** N Schneefang *m*

roofing ['ru:fɪŋ] N Material *nt* zum Dachdecken; (= *action*) Dachdecken *nt*; **~ felt** (*Brit*) or **paper** Dachpappe *f*

roof: roof lining N (*in car*) Himmel *m*; **roof rack** N Dach(gepäck)träger *m*; **rooftop** N Dach *nt*; **to shout** or **scream sth from the ~s** (*fig*) etw überall herumposaunen (*inf*), etw an die große Glocke hängen (*inf*)

rook [rʊk] N **a** (= *bird*) Saatkrähe *f* **b** (= *swindler*) Betrüger(in) *m(f)*, Gauner(in) *m(f)* **c** (*Chess*) Turm *m* **VT** (= *swindle*) übers Ohr hauen (*inf*), betrügen; **to ~ sb of £5** jdm £ 5 abgaunern **VI** (*Chess*) mit dem Turm ziehen

rookery ['rʊkərɪ] N Kolonie *f*

rookie ['rʊkɪ] N (*esp Mil sl*) Grünschnabel *m* (*inf*)

room [ru:m] N **a** (*in house, building*) Zimmer *nt*, Raum *m* (*geh*); (= *public hall, ballroom etc*) Saal *m*; (= *bedroom, also in hotel*) Zimmer *nt*; (= *office*) Büro *nt*; **the whole ~ laughed** alle im Zimmer lachten, der ganze Saal lachte; **"rooms to let"** „Zimmer zu vermieten"; **~ and board** Unterkunft mit Verpflegung; **they used to live in ~s** sie haben früher in möblierten Zimmern gewohnt; **I'll come to your ~** ich komme in deine Wohnung or auf deine Bude (*esp Univ inf*) **b** *no pl* (= *space*) Platz *m*; (*fig*) Spielraum *m*; **is there (enough) ~?** ist da genügend Platz?; **there is ~ for two (people)** es ist genügend Platz für zwei (Leute); **there is no ~ (for you/ that box)** es ist nicht genug Platz (für dich/die Kiste); **to make ~ for sb/sth** für jdn/etw Platz machen or schaffen; **there is still ~ for hope** es besteht immer noch Hoffnung; **there is little ~ for hope** es besteht wenig Hoffnung; **there is no ~ for doubt** es kann keinen Zweifel geben; **there is ~ for improvement in your work** Ihre Arbeit könnte um einiges besser sein; **~ for manoeuvre** (*Brit*) or **maneuver** (*US*) Spielraum *m* **VI** zur Untermiete wohnen; **~ing house** (*esp US*) Mietshaus *nt* (*mit möblierten Wohnungen*)

room: room clerk N (*US*) Empfangschef *m*, Empfangsdame *f*; **room divider** N Raumteiler *m*

-roomed [-ru:md] ADJ *suf* **a** **6-roomed house** ein Haus mit 6 Zimmern; **a two-roomed apartment** eine Zweizimmerwohnung

roomer ['ru:mə'] N (*US*) Untermieter(in) *m(f)*

roomful ['ru:mfʊl] N **there was quite a ~** das Zimmer war ganz schön voll; **a ~ of people** ein Zimmer voll(er) Leute

roominess ['ru:mɪnɪs] N Geräumigkeit *f*; (*of garment*) Weite *f*

room: roommate N (*Brit*) Zimmergenosse *m*, Zimmergenossin *f*; (*US*: = *flatmate*) Mitbewohner(in) *m(f)*; **room service** N Zimmerservice *m*, Etagendienst *m*; **room temperature** N Zimmertemperatur *f*; **wine at ~** Wein mit or auf Zimmertemperatur

roomy ['ru:mɪ] ADJ (+er) geräumig; *garment* weit

roost [ru:st] N (= *pole*) Stange *f*; (= *henhouse*) Hühnerhaus *nt* or -stall *m*; **at ~** auf der Stange; **to come home to ~** (*fig*) auf den Urheber zurückfallen → **cock, rule** **VI** (= *settle*) sich niederlassen; (= *sleep*) auf der Stange schlafen

rooster ['ru:stə'] N Hahn *m*

root [ru:t] N **a** (*of plant, hair, tooth*) Wurzel *f*; **~s** (*fig, of person*) Wurzeln *pl*; **by the ~s** mit der Wurzel; **to take ~** (*lit, fig*) Wurzeln schlagen; **her ~s are in Scotland** sie ist in Schottland verwurzelt; **she has no ~s** sie ist nirgends zu Hause; **to put down ~s in a country** in einem Land Fuß fassen; **~ and branch** (*fig*) mit Stumpf und Stiel → **grass-roots, pull up** **b** (*fig: = source: of evil, of trouble etc*) Wurzel *f*; **the ~ of the matter** der Kern der Sache; **to get to the ~(s) of the problem** dem Problem auf den Grund gehen; **that is** or **lies at the ~ of his behaviour** (*Brit*) or **behavior** (*US*) das ist der eigentliche Grund für sein Benehmen

c (Math, Ling) Wurzel f; (of equation) Lösung f; (Ling, = base form) Stamm m → **cube**, **square root**

VT plant Wurzeln schlagen lassen bei **VI** (plants etc) Wurzeln schlagen or fassen

▶ **root about** (Brit) or **around** VI herumwühlen (for nach)

▶ **root for** VI +prep obj team anfeuern; **to root for sb** jdm die Daumen drücken; (esp Sport: = cheer on) jdn anfeuern

▶ **root out** VT sep **a** (lit) = **root up b** (fig) (= remove) evil mit der Wurzel ausreißen; (= find) aufspüren, ausgraben (inf)

▶ **root up** VT sep plant herausreißen; (= dig up) ausgraben

root in cpds Wurzel-; **root beer** N (US) Art Limonade; **root-canal work**, **root-canal therapy** N (Dentistry) Wurzelkanalbehandlung f, Zahnwurzelbehandlung f; **root cause** N eigentlicher Grund; **root crop** N Wurzelgemüse nt no pl

rooted ['ruːtɪd] ADJ **a** (= grounded, based) verwurzelt; **to be ~ in sth** in etw (dat) verwurzelt sein **b** (= embedded) **(deeply) ~** (objection, conviction etc) tief sitzend attr, tief verwurzelt **c** **to be** or **stand ~ (to the spot)** (= immobile, frozen) wie angewurzelt dastehen

rooter ['ruːtə] N (esp US inf Sport) begeisterter Anhänger or Fan, begeisterte Anhängerin

rootless ['ruːtlɪs] ADJ plant wurzellos; (fig) person ohne Wurzeln; **a ~ existence** ein wurzelloses Leben, ein Leben ohne Wurzeln

root: root sign N (Math) Wurzelzeichen nt; **rootstock** N (Bot) Wurzelstock m; **root treatment** N (Dentistry) Wurzelbehandlung f; **root vegetable** N Wurzelgemüse nt; **root word** N (Ling) Wortwurzel f; (= base form) Wortstamm m

rope [rəʊp] N **a** Seil nt; (Naut) Tau nt; (of bell) Glockenstrang m; (= hangman's rope) Strang m, Strick m; **a ~ of pearls** eine Perlenschnur; **to give sb more/plenty of ~** (fig) jdm mehr/viel Freiheit lassen; **give him enough ~ and he'll hang himself** (fig) der dreht sich (dat) schon selbst seinen Strick; **I am at the end of my ~** (US inf) (= annoyed, impatient) mir reichts (inf); (= desperate) ich bin am Ende **b** (Mountaineering) Seil nt; **a ~ of climbers** eine Seilschaft; **to put on the ~s** anseilen; **to be on the ~** angeseilt sein; **there were three of them on the ~** sie waren zu dritt am Seil **c** **the ~s** (Boxing etc) die Seile pl; **to be on the ~s** (boxer) in den Seilen hängen; (inf) in der Klemme sein; **to know the ~s** (inf) sich auskennen; **to show sb the ~s** (inf) jdn in alles einweihen; **to learn the ~s** (inf) sich einarbeiten **VT a** box, case verschnüren; **to ~ sb to a tree** jdn an einen Baum binden; **to ~ sb's feet together** jdm die Füße zusammenbinden; **to ~ climbers (together)** Bergsteiger anseilen **b** (= lasso) mit dem Lasso fangen

▶ **rope in** VT sep **a** area (mit einem Seil) abgrenzen; cattle mit einem Seil einfrieden **b** (esp Brit fig) rankriegen (inf); **how did you get roped into that?** wie bist du denn da reingeraten? (inf); **I don't want to get roped into helping** ich will nicht, dass die mich zum Helfen rankriegen (inf)

▶ **rope off** VT sep area mit einem Seil abgrenzen

▶ **rope together** VT sep objects zusammenbinden; climbers aneinander seilen, anseilen

▶ **rope up** VI (climbers) sich anseilen VT sep anseilen

rope in cpds Seil-; **rope burn** N Reibungsverbrennung f (beim Umgang mit Seilen), Seilbrand m (spec); **rope ladder** N Strickleiter f; **ropemaker** N Seiler(in) m(f); **ropery** ['rəʊpərɪ] N Seilerei f

rope: rope sole N (aus Seil) geflochtene Sohle; **rope-soled** ADJ mit (aus Seil) geflochtener Sohle; **ropewalker** N Seiltänzer(in) m(f)

rop(e)y ['rəʊpɪ] ADJ (+er) (Brit inf, = bad) miserabel (inf); (= worn) mitgenommen; **the engine is a bit ~** der Motor pfeift auf dem letzten Loch (inf)

ropeyard ['rəʊpjɑːd] N Seilerei f

rosary ['rəʊzərɪ] N (Rel) Rosenkranz m; **to say the ~** den Rosenkranz beten

rose¹ [rəʊz] pret of **rise**

rose² N **a** Rose f; **wild ~** Wildrose f; **my life isn't all ~s** (inf) ich bin auch nicht auf Rosen gebettet; **life/marriage isn't all ~s** (inf) das Leben/die Ehe hat auch seine/ihre Schattenseiten; **an English ~** (fig) eine englische Schöne; **everything's coming up ~s** (inf) alles ist or läuft bestens (inf); **to come up smelling of ~s** (inf) gut dastehen; **that will put the ~s back in your cheeks** davon bekommst du wieder etwas Farbe im Gesicht; **under the ~** (fig liter) unter dem Siegel der Verschwiegenheit; **the Wars of the Roses** die Rosenkriege pl **b** (= nozzle) Brause f; (= rosette, Archit) Rosette f **c** (= colour) Rosarot nt, Rosenrot nt **ADJ** rosarot, rosenrot

rosé ['rəʊzeɪ] **ADJ** rosé N Rosé m

roseate ['rəʊzɪɪt] ADJ (liter) rosenfarben

rose in cpds Rosen-; **rosebay** N Oleander m; **rosebowl** N Rosenpokal m; **rosebud** N Rosenknospe f; **~ mouth** Rosenmund m; **rosebush** N Rosenstrauch m; **rose-coloured**, (US) **rose-colored** ADJ rosarot, rosenrot; **to see everything/life through ~ spectacles** (Brit) or **rose-colored glasses** (US) alles/das Leben durch die rosarote Brille sehen; **rose-cut** ADJ mit Rosetteschliff; **rose garden** N Rosengarten m; **rosehip** N Hagebutte f; **rosehip syrup** N Hagenbuttensirup m

rosemary ['rəʊzmərɪ] N Rosmarin m

rose: rose petal N Rosen(blüten)blatt nt; **rose-pink** ADJ rosarot N Rosarot nt; **rose quartz** N Rosenquarz m; **rose-red** ADJ rosenrot; **rosetree** N Rosenstrauch m

Rosetta stone [rəʊˈzetəˈstəʊn] N Stein m von Rosette

rosette [rəʊˈzet] N Rosette f

rose: rosewater N Rosenwasser nt; **rose window** N (Fenster)rosette f; **rosewood** N Rosenholz nt

Rosicrucian [rəʊzɪˈkruːʃən] N Rosenkreu(t)zer m ADJ der Rosenkreu(t)zer

rosin ['rɒzɪn] N Harz nt, Kolofonium nt, Kolophonium nt (esp Mus) VT mit Harz or Kolofonium or Kolophonium behandeln

ROSPA ['rɒspə] N (Brit) abbr of **Royal Society for the Prevention of Accidents** Königliche Gesellschaft für Unfallverhütung

roster ['rɒstə] N Dienstplan m → **duty roster**

rostrum ['rɒstrəm] N pl **rostra** ['rɒstrə] Tribüne f, Rednerpult nt; (for conductor) Dirigentenpult nt

rosy ['rəʊzɪ] ADJ (+er) **a** (= pink) rosarot; complexion, cheeks, face rosig **b** (fig, = hopeful) future, situation, view rosig; **to look ~** (situation, future) rosig aussehen; **to paint a ~ picture of sth** etw in den rosigsten Farben ausmalen

rot [rɒt] N **a** (in teeth, plants, wood) Fäulnis f no pl; **to stop the ~** (lit, fig) den Fäulnisprozess aufhalten; **then the ~ set in** (fig) dann setzte der Fäulnisprozess or Verfall ein **→ dry rot b** (inf, = rubbish) Quatsch m (inf), Blödsinn m (inf) VI (wood, material, rope) verrotten, faulen; (teeth, plant) verfaulen; (fig) verrotten; **to ~ in jail** im Gefängnis verrotten; **let him ~!** (inf) soll er doch vor die Hunde gehen! (inf) VT verfaulen lassen

▶ **rot away** VI verfaulen

rota ['rəʊtə] N **a** (Brit) Dienstplan m **b** (Eccl) Rota f

Rotarian [rəʊˈteərɪən] ADJ rotarisch N Rotarier(in) m(f)

rotary ['rəʊtərɪ] ADJ rotierend, Dreh-; **~ motion** Drehbewegung f; **~ iron** Heißmangel f

rotary: Rotary Club N Rotary Club m; **rotary engine** N Umlaufmotor m; **rotary plough**, (US) **rotary plow** N (Tech) **a** (also **rotary snow plough**) Schneefräse f **b** (Agr) Bodenfräse f; **rotary printer** N Rotationsdrucker m; **rotary (printing) press** N Rotationsmaschine f; **rotary pump** N Kreiselpumpe f

rotate [rəʊˈteɪt] VT **a** (around axis) drehen, rotieren lassen; (Math) rotieren lassen; (Comput) rotieren; head, body drehen **b** crops im Wechsel anbauen; work, jobs turnusmäßig erledigen **VI a** (around axis) sich drehen, rotieren; (Math) rotieren **b** (crops) im Wechsel angebaut werden; (people: = take turns) sich (turnusmäßig) abwechseln

rotating [rəʊˈteɪtɪŋ] ADJ (= revolving) rotierend, sich drehend; crops im Wechsel angebaut; presidency im Turnus wechselnd; **on a ~ basis** in einem gewissen Turnus

rotation [rəʊˈteɪʃən] N **a** no pl (around axis) Drehung f, Rotation f (also Math); (of crops) Wechsel m, Rotation f; (= taking turns) turnusmäßiger Wechsel; **in** or **by ~** abwechselnd im Turnus; **~ of crops**, **crop ~** Fruchtwechsel m **b** (= turn) (Um)drehung f, Rotation f

rotatory [rəʊˈteɪtərɪ] ADJ **a** rotierend; **~ motion** Drehbewegung f **b** schedule turnusmäßig; cultivation abwechselnd

Rotavator® ['rəʊtəveɪtə] N (Brit) = **Rotovator**

rote [rəʊt] N **by ~** (learn) auswendig; recite, teach mechanisch

rotgut ['rɒtˌgʌt] N (pej inf) Fusel m (inf)

rotisserie [rəʊˈtɪsərɪ] N (= spit) Grillspieß m; (= restaurant) Rotisserie f

rotogravure [ˌrəʊtəʊgrəˈvjʊə] N Kupferdruck m

rotor ['rəʊtə] N (Aviat, Elec, Aut) Rotor m

rotor: rotor arm N Verteilerfinger m; **rotor blade** N Flügelblatt nt

Rotovator® ['rəʊtəveɪtə] N (Brit) Bodenfräse f

rot-proof ['rɒtˌpruːf] ADJ fäulnissicher

rotten ['rɒtn] ADJ **a** vegetable, egg, tooth faul; wood morsch, faul; fruit faul, verdorben; (fig, = corrupt) korrupt, verdorben; **~ to the core** (fig) durch und durch verdorben; **~ apple** (fig) schwarzes Schaf; **there's always one ~ egg (in the basket)** (fig) es gibt immer ein schwarzes Schaf **b** (inf, = poor, incompetent) mies (inf); **she was a ~ driver** sie war eine miserable Fahrerin; **to be ~ at sth** in etw (dat) schlecht sein; **I was always ~ at drawing** ich konnte noch nie gut zeichnen **c** (inf, = dreadful, unpleasant) scheußlich (inf); weather mies (inf), scheußlich (inf); **what ~ luck!** so ein Pech!; **it's a ~ business** das ist eine üble Sache; **to have a ~ time** eine schlimme Zeit durchmachen; **what a ~ time you're having** was du zur Zeit aber auch alles durchmachen musst! (inf); **isn't it ~ about poor David?** ist das nicht furchtbar mit dem armen David? **d** (inf, = mean) gemein, eklig; **that was a ~ trick/a ~ thing to do** das war ein übler Trick/eine Gemeinheit; **that's a ~ thing to say** es ist gemein, so etwas zu sagen **e** (inf, = unwell) elend, mies (inf); **to feel ~** sich elend fühlen; **to look ~** schlecht aussehen **f** (inf, = guilty) **to feel ~ about doing sth** sich (dat) mies vorkommen, etw zu tun (inf) **g** (inf, = damned) verdammt (inf); **you can keep your ~ bike!** du kannst dein verdammtes or blödes Fahrrad behalten! (inf) **h** (inf) **to spoil ~ (something)** ~ jdn nach Strich und Faden verwöhnen (inf); **to fancy sb (something) ~** jdn wahnsinnig gern haben (inf)

rottenness ['rɒtnɪs] N (of vegetation, egg, fruit, tooth) Faulheit f; (of wood) Morschheit f, Faulheit f; (fig, = corruptness) Korruptheit f, Verdorbenheit f

rotter ['rɒtə] N (dated Brit inf) Lump m

rotting ['rɒtɪŋ] ADJ meat, food verfaulend; wood also modrig; carcass, bones also verwesend; teeth faul; fruit faulig

rotund [rəʊˈtʌnd] **ADJ** *person* rund(lich); *object* rund; *speech, literary style* bombastisch, hochtrabend; *voice* voll

rotunda [rəʊˈtʌndə] **N** Rotunde *f*, Rundbau *m*

rotundity [rəʊˈtʌndɪtɪ] **N** (*of person*) Rundlichkeit *f*; (*of object*) Rundheit *f*

rouble, (*US*) **ruble** [ˈruːbl] **N** Rubel *m*

roué [ˈruːeɪ] **N** (*dated*) Lebemann *m*

rouge [ruːʒ] **N** Rouge *nt* **VT** **to ~ one's cheeks** Rouge auflegen

rough [rʌf] **ADJ** (+er) **a** (= *uneven*) *ground* uneben; *path, road* uneben, holprig; *surface, skin, hands, cloth* rau; **~ edges** (*fig*) Ecken und Kanten *pl*
　b (= *harsh*) *sound* hart; *voice, tone* rauh; *taste, wine* sauer; *words* grob, hart; **to have ~ luck** schweres Pech haben; **to have a ~ tongue** (*fig*) eine scharfe Zunge haben; **he got the ~ side of her tongue** er bekam (von ihr) den Marsch geblasen
　c (= *coarse, unrefined*) *person* ungehobelt; *manners, speech* grob, roh
　d (= *violent*) *person, child* grob, roh; *treatment, handling* grob, hart; *life* wüst; *children's game* wild; *match, sport, work* hart; *neighbourhood, manners, pub* rau; *sea, weather, wind* rau, stürmisch; *sea crossing* stürmisch; **a ~ customer** (*inf*) ein übler Typ (*inf*); **to be ~ with sb** grob mit jdm umgehen, unsanft mit jdm umspringen (*inf*); **~ play** (*Sport*) Holzerei *f* (*inf*)
　e (*inf, = unpleasant*) **he had a ~ time (of it)** es ging ihm ziemlich dreckig (*inf*); **to be in for a ~ time (of it)** harten Zeiten entgegensehen; **the examiners gave him a ~ time** die Prüfer haben ihn ganz schön rangenommen (*inf*); **to make things ~ for sb** jdm Schwierigkeiten machen; **to be ~ on sb** grob mit jdm umspringen; **it's ~ on him** das ist hart für ihn; **things are ~ just now** die Dinge sind im Moment schlecht; **to have a ~ ride** es nicht leicht haben; **to get a ~ ride** Schwierigkeiten bekommen; **to give sb a ~ ride** jdm die Hölle heiß machen (*inf*); **he faces a ~ ride from the media** die Medien werden es ihm nicht leicht machen; **when the going gets ~ ...** wenn es hart wird, ...
　f (= *approximate, rudimentary*) *plan, calculation, estimate, translation* grob, ungefähr; *workmanship* schludrig; **~ sketch** Faustskizze *f*; **in its ~ state** im Rohzustand; **do your ~ work on the paper provided** mach deinen ersten Konzept auf dem dafür bereitgestellten Papier; **at a ~ guess** grob geschätzt; **to give sb a ~ idea** jdm einen groben Anhaltspunkt geben; **to have a ~ idea** eine vage Idee or eine ungefähre Ahnung haben
　g (= *basic, crude*) *shelter* notdürftig; *clothes* derb
　h (*inf, = unwell*) **to feel ~** sich mies fühlen (*inf*); **the engine sounds pretty ~** der Motor hört sich nicht gerade gut an
ADV *live* wüst; *play* wild; **to sleep ~** im Freien übernachten
N **a** unwegsames Gelände; (*Golf*) Rau *nt*; **~ or smooth?** (*Sport*) untere oder obere Seite? (*des Schlägers, die durch einen roten Faden gekennzeichnet ist; zum Bestimmen, wer anfängt*); **she likes a bit of ~** (*Brit inf: sexually*) sie mags gern heftig (*sl*)
　b (= *unpleasant aspect*) **to take the ~ with the smooth** das Leben nehmen, wie es kommt
　c (= *draft, sketch*) Rohentwurf *m*; **in (the) ~** im Rohzustand; **a diamond in the ~** ein Rohdiamant *m*
　d (= *person*) Rowdy *m*, Schläger *m*
VT **to ~ it** (*inf*) primitiv leben
▶ **rough out** **VT** *sep plan, drawing* grob entwerfen
▶ **rough up** **VT** *sep hair* zersausen, verstrubbeln (*inf*); (*inf*) *person* zusammenschlagen

roughage [ˈrʌfɪdʒ] **N** Ballaststoffe *pl*

rough: rough-and-ready **ADJ** *method, equipment, place* provisorisch; *work* zusammengehauen (*inf*), zusammengepfuscht (*inf*); *person* rau (-bein)ig; *measure, interpretation, attitude* grob; **rough-and-tumble** **N** (= *play*) Balgerei *f*; (= *fighting*) Keilerei *f*; **after the ~ of life in the navy** nach seinem wilden Leben in der Marine;

rough book **N** (*Sch*) Schmierheft *nt*; **roughcast** *vb: pret, ptp* **roughcast** **N** Rauputz *m* **VT** rau verputzen; **rough coat** **N** (*Archit*) Roh- or Rauputz *m*; **rough copy** **N** Konzept *nt*; **rough diamond** **N** (*lit*) Rohdiamant *m*; **he's a ~** er ist rau, aber herzlich; **rough draft** **N** Rohentwurf *m*, grober Entwurf; **rough-dry** **VT** einfach trocknen

roughen [ˈrʌfn] **VT** *ground* uneben machen; *skin, cloth* rau machen, rau werden lassen; *surface* aufrauhen **VI** **a** (*skin*) rau werden **b** (*sound*) hart werden; (*voice*) rau werden **c** (*treatment*) hart werden; (*neighbourhood*) verrohen; (*sea, wind, weather*) rau or stürmisch werden

rough: rough-hew **VT** *timber* grob behauen; **roughhouse** (*inf*) **N** Schlägerei *f* **VT** herumstoßen

roughing [ˈrʌfɪŋ] **N** (*Ice hockey*) übertriebene Härte

rough justice **N** willkürliche Urteile *pl*

roughly [ˈrʌflɪ] **ADV** **a** (= *not gently*) grob, roh; *play* rau; *answer, order* grob, hart **b** (= *crudely*) *make, sew, sketch, chop, slice* grob **c** (= *approximately*) ungefähr; **~ (speaking)** grob gesagt; **~ half** ungefähr die Hälfte; **~ equal** ungefähr gleich; **~ the same** ungefähr dasselbe; **~ similar** in etwa ähnlich; **to be ~ similar to sth** eine grobe Ähnlichkeit mit etw besitzen; **~ comparable** grob vergleichbar; **~ translated** grob übersetzt

roughneck [ˈrʌfˌnek] **N** (*inf*) **a** (= *thug*) Schläger *m* **b** (= *oil rig worker*) Ölbohrarbeiter(in) *m(f)*

roughness [ˈrʌfnɪs] **N** **a** (= *unevenness, of ground, path, road*) Unebenheit *f*; (*of surface, skin, hands, cloth*) Rauheit *f* **b** (= *harshness, of sound*) Härte *f*; (*of voice, tone*) Rauheit *f*; (*of wine*) saurer Geschmack; (*of words*) Grobheit *f* **c** (= *coarseness, of person*) Ungehobeltheit *f*; (*of manners, speech*) Grobheit *f*, Rohheit *f* **d** (= *violence, of person*) Grobheit *f*, Rohheit *f*; (*of treatment*) Grobheit *f*, Härte *f*; (*of children's game*) Wildheit *f*; (*of match, sport, work*) Härte *f*; (*of neighbourhood, manners, pub*) Rauheit *f*

rough: rough notebook **N** (*Sch*) Schmierheft *nt*; **rough paper** **N** Konzeptpapier *nt*; **roughrider** **N** Zureiter(in) *m(f)*; **roughshod** **ADV** **to ride ~ over sb/sth** rücksichtslos über jdn/etw hinweggehen; **rough-spoken** **ADJ** **to be ~** sich ungehobelt ausdrücken; **rough stuff** **N** Schlägereien *pl*, eine Schlägerei; **rough trade** **N** (*sl*) (*ohne feste Bindungsabsicht ausgewählter*) *homosexueller Geschlechtspartner mit grobem oder gewalttätigem Verhalten*

roulette [ruːˈlet] **N** Roulett(e) *nt*; **~ table/wheel** Roulettetisch *m*/-scheibe *f* → **Russian roulette**

Roumania *etc* [ruːˈmeɪnɪə] = **Romania** *etc*

round [raʊnd] **ADJ** (+er) **a** *rund*; (*Ling*) *vowel* gerundet; **~ arch** (*Archit*) Rundbogen *m*; **a ~ dozen** ein rundes Dutzend; **~ figure**, **~ number** runde Zahl; **in ~ figures, that will cost 20 million** es kostet rund (*gerechnet*) *or* runde 20 Millionen
　b (*dated*) (= *unequivocal*) *oath* kräftig; (= *considerable*) *sum* rund; *pace* flott; **in ~ terms** klar und deutlich
ADV (*esp Brit*) **there was a wall right ~** *or* **all ~** rings- or rundherum war eine Mauer; **you can't get through here, you'll have to go ~** Sie können hier nicht durch, Sie müssen außen herum gehen; **the long way ~** der Umweg, der längere Weg; **that's a long way ~** (*detour*) das ist ein großer Umweg; (*round field, town*) das ist eine ganz schöne Strecke; **for 5 km ~** im Umkreis von 5 km; **~ and ~** (= *in circles, round field etc*) rundherum; (= *all over the place*) überall herum; **I asked him ~ for a drink** ich lud ihn auf ein Glas Wein/Bier etc bei mir ein; **I'll be ~ at 8 o'clock** ich werde um 8 Uhr da sein; **spring will soon be ~ again** der Frühling steht bald wieder vor der Tür; **for the second time** zum zweiten Mal; **all (the) year ~** das ganze Jahr über or hindurch; **all ~** (*lit*) ringsherum; (*esp Brit fig: for everyone*) für alle; **drinks all ~!** (*esp Brit*)

eine Runde!; **taking things all ~, taken all ~** insgesamt gesehen, wenn man alles zusammennimmt; **this ought to make life much easier all ~** (*esp Brit*) damit müsste es insgesamt einfacher werden; **a pillar 2 m ~** eine Säule mit 2 m Umfang
PREP **a** (*esp Brit: of place etc*) um (... herum); **~ the table/fire** um den Tisch/das Feuer (herum); **~ her hat** das Band um ihren Hut; **all ~ the house** (*inside*) im ganzen Haus; (*outside*) um das ganze Haus herum; **~ and ~ the field** rings um das Feld herum; **to go ~ a corner/bend** um die Ecke/Kurve gehen/fahren *etc*; **if you're ~ this way** wenn Sie in der Gegend sind; **to look** *or* **see ~ a house** sich (*dat*) ein Haus ansehen; **to show sb ~ a town** jdm eine Stadt zeigen, jdn in einer Stadt herumführen; **they went ~ the cafés looking for him** sie gingen in alle Cafés, um nach ihm zu suchen; **to talk ~ a subject** um ein Thema herumreden; **she's 75 cm ~ the waist** um die Taille misst *or* ist sie 75 cm
　b (= *approximately*) ungefähr; **~ (about** (*esp Brit*)**) 7 o'clock** ungefähr um 7 Uhr; **~ (about** (*esp Brit*)**) £800** um die £ 800
N **a** (*circle etc*) Kreis *m*, Ring *m*; (*esp Brit: = slice of bread, meat etc*) Scheibe *f*; **a ~ of toast** (*esp Brit*) eine Scheibe Toast; **a ~ of beef sandwiches** (*esp Brit*) ein belegtes Brot mit Braten, eine Bratenschnitte
　b (= *delivery round*) Runde *f*; **~(s** (*of policeman, watchman, doctor*)**) Runde *f*; **to do** *or* **make one's ~(s)** seine Runde machen; **to be (out) on one's ~(s)** auf seiner Runde sein; **to go** *or* **make** *or* **do the ~s** (*visiting relatives etc*) die Runde machen; **to do the ~s of the clubs** *etc* (*inf*) durch die Klubs *etc* ziehen; **he does a paper ~** (*Brit*) er trägt Zeitungen aus; **the daily ~** (*fig*) die tägliche Arbeit, der tägliche Trott (*pej*); **her life was one long ~ of parties** ihr Leben war eine einzige Folge von Partys
　c **to go** *or* **do the ~s** (*story etc*) reihum gehen; **the story went the ~s of the club** die Geschichte ging im ganzen Verein reihum; **this coat has gone the ~s of the family** dieser Mantel ist durch die ganze Familie gegangen
　d (*Sport, of election, talks*) Runde *f*; (*Show-jumping*) Durchgang *m*; **a ~ (of drinks)** eine Runde; **a new ~ of negotiations** eine neue Verhandlungsrunde; **a ~ of ammunition** Ladung *f*; **10 ~s of bullets** 10 Schuss; **a ~ of 5 shots** eine Folge von 5 Schüssen; **a ~ of applause** Applaus *m*
　e (*Mus*) Kanon *m*
　f **in the ~** (= *as a whole*) insgesamt; **theatre in the ~** Arenatheater *nt*
VT **a** (= *make round*) runden
　b (= *go round*) *corner, bend* gehen/fahren um; *cape* umfahren, herumfahren um; *obstacle* herumgehen/-fahren um
▶ **round down** **VT** *sep price, number* abrunden
▶ **round off** **VT** *sep* **a** *edges etc* abrunden **b** (= *complete, perfect*) *list, series* voll machen; *speech, sentence, meal* abrunden; *debate, meeting, one's career* beschließen, abschließen; **and now, to round off, I would like to say ...** und zum Abschluss möchte ich nun sagen ...
▶ **round on** **VI** +*prep obj* (*verbally*) anfahren; (*in actions*) herumfahren zu
▶ **round out** **VT** *sep story etc* runden; *year* abschließen **VI** sich runden
▶ **round up** **VT** *sep* **a** (= *bring together*) *people* zusammentrommeln (*inf*); *cattle* zusammentreiben; *criminals* hochnehmen (*inf*); *facts* zusammentragen **b** *price, number* aufrunden
▶ **round upon** **VI** +*prep obj* = **round on**

roundabout [ˈraʊndəˌbaʊt] **ADJ** *answer, question* umständlich; **~ route** Umweg *m*; **we came a ~ way** *or* **by a ~ route** wir sind auf Umwegen gekommen, wir haben einen Umweg gemacht; **he has a ~ way of going about things** er geht sehr umständlich an die Dinge heran; **what a ~ way of doing things!** was haben nur so umständlich sein!; **by ~ means** auf Umwegen; **~ phrase** (*umständliche*) Umschreibung; **she gave a ~ reply** sie antwortete auf Umwegen; **to**

say sth in a ~ way etw auf Umwegen sagen N (*Brit, at fair*) Karussell *nt*; (*in children's playground*) Karussell *nt*; (*Mot*) Kreisverkehr *m*

round: round cell N (= *battery*) Knopfzelle *f*; **round-cheeked** ['raʊnd'tʃiːkt] ADJ mit runden Backen; **round dance** N Reigen *m*; (= *ballroom dance*) Rundtanz *m*

rounded ['raʊndɪd] ADJ **a** (= *curved*) rundlich; *edges* abgerundet; *hills* gerundet; *handwriting* rundlich; **(well-)rounded** (*bosom, figure*) wohlgerundet **b** (*fig, = complete*) *picture, character, individual, education, flavour* abgerundet; *film, book* in sich geschlossen; **(well-)rounded** (*sentences, style*) abgerundet **c a ~ tablespoon** (*Cook*) ein gehäufter Esslöffel **d** (= *resonant*) *tone* rund **e** (*Ling*) *vowel* rund

roundel ['raʊndl] N runde (Flugzeug)kokarde

roundelay ['raʊndɪleɪ] N (*Mus*) Lied *nt* mit Refrain

rounder ['raʊndə'] N (*Brit, Sport*) **to score a ~** einen Lauf machen

rounders ['raʊndəz] *sing* (*Brit, Sport*) ≈ Schlagball *m*

round: round-eyed ADJ großäugig; **round-faced** ADJ rundgesichtig, mit rundem Gesicht; **Roundhead** N (*Brit, Hist*) Rundkopf *m*; **roundhouse** N (*esp US, Rail*) Lokomotivschuppen *m*

roundly ['raʊndlɪ] ADV *condemn, criticize* rundum; *reject* rundweg, rundheraus; *defeat* klar, eindeutig

round-necked ['raʊnd'nekt] ADJ mit rundem Ausschnitt

roundness ['raʊndnɪs] N Rundheit *f*; (*of sound also*) Vollheit *f*; (*of vowel*) Gerundetheit *f*

round: round robin N **a** (= *petition*) gemeinsamer Antrag (*bei dem die Unterschriften (oft) im Kreis angeordnet sind*) **b** (*esp US, Sport*) Wettkampf *m*, in dem jeder gegen jeden spielt; **round-shouldered** ['raʊnd'ʃəʊldəd] ADJ mit runden Schultern; **to be ~** runde Schultern haben

roundsman ['raʊndzmən] N *pl* **-men** [-mən] (*Brit*) Austräger *m*; **milk ~** Milchmann *m*

round: Round Table N (*Hist*) (König Artus') Tafelrunde *f*; **round-table discussion/conference** N Diskussion *f*/Konferenz *f* am runden Tisch; **round-the-clock** ADJ (*Brit*) rund um die Uhr *not attr*; **round towel** N Rollhandtuch *nt*; **round trip** N Rundreise *f*; **round-trip ticket** N (*US*) Rückfahrkarte *f*; (*Aviat*) Hin- und Rückflugticket *nt*; **roundup** N **a** (= *act, of cattle*) Zusammentreiben *nt*; (*of people*) Zusammentrommeln *nt* (*inf*); (*of criminals*) Hochnehmen *nt* (*inf*); (*of facts*) Sammlung *f*, Zusammentragen *nt* **b** (= *group of cattle*) zusammengetriebene Herde; **a round-up of today's news** eine Zusammenfassung der Nachrichten vom Tage **c** (*US, = rodeo*) Rodeo *nt*; **roundworm** N Fadenwurm *m*

rouse [raʊz] VT **a** (*from sleep, daydream etc*) wecken **b** (= *stimulate*) *person* bewegen; *feeling, admiration, interest* wecken, wachrufen; *hatred, indignation* erregen; *suspicions* erwecken, erregen; **to ~ sb (to anger)** jdn reizen; **to ~ sb to passion** jds Leidenschaft entfachen; **to ~ sb to action** jdn zum Handeln bewegen; **to ~ sb out of his/her apathy** jdn aus seiner Apathie aufrütteln; **to ~ the masses** die Massen aufrütteln; **~ yourself!** raff dich auf! VI (= *waken*) wach werden; (= *become active*) lebendig werden

rousing ['raʊzɪŋ] ADJ *speech, sermon* zündend, mitreißend; *cheers, applause* stürmisch; *music* schwungvoll; *chorus* schallend; *reception* überschwänglich

roust [raʊst] VT (*US, from home, usual place on street: also* **roust out**) vertreiben; (= *call out*) kommen lassen; **to ~ sb out of bed, to ~ sb out** jdn aus dem Bett holen

roustabout ['raʊstəbaʊt] N **a** (*US Naut*) (= *deckhand*) Deckhelfer *m*; (*in dock*) Werft- or Hafenarbeiter *m* **b** (*US: = unskilled labourer*) Hilfsarbeiter *m* **c** (*Austral*) Helfer *m* beim Scheren

rout[1] [raʊt] N **a** (= *defeat*) Schlappe *f*; **to put to ~** in die Flucht schlagen **b** (*Jur, = mob*) Bande *f*, Rotte *f* VT (= *defeat*) in die Flucht schlagen

rout[2] VI (*pig: also* **rout about**) herumwühlen

▶ **rout out** VT *sep* (= *find*) aufstöbern; (= *force out*) (heraus)jagen (*of* aus)

route [ruːt, (*US*) raʊt] N **a** Strecke *f*, Route *f*; (*bus service*) Linie *f*; (*fig, in planning etc*) Weg *m*; **shipping ~s** Schifffahrtsstraßen *or* -wege; **air ~s** Flugwege; **what ~ does the 39 bus take?** welche Strecke *or* Route fährt der 39er-Bus?; **we live on a bus ~** wir wohnen an einer Buslinie; **the ~ to the coast goes through Easthampton** der Weg zur Küste führt durch Easthampton; **"all ~s"** (*Mot*) „alle Richtungen"; **~ map** Straßenkarte *f* **b** (*Mil*) Marschbefehl *m*; **~ march** Geländemarsch *m* **c** (*US, = delivery round*) Runde *f*; **he has a paper ~** er trägt Zeitungen aus **d** (*Med, of drug*) Weg *m* VT *train, coach, bus* legen; *telephone call* leiten; **my baggage was ~d through Amsterdam** mein Gepäck wurde über Amsterdam geschickt; **the train is ~d through Birmingham** der Zug wird durch Birmingham geführt *or* über Birmingham gelegt

routine [ruːˈtiːn] N **a** Routine *f* (*also Comput*); **business** *or* **office ~** Büroroutine *f*; **as a matter of ~** routinemäßig **b** (*Dancing, Skating*) Figur *f*; (*Gymnastics*) Übung *f*; **he gave me the old ~ about his wife not understanding him** er kam mit der alten Geschichte, dass seine Frau ihn nicht versteht ADJ Routine-, routinemäßig; **~ duties** tägliche Pflichten *pl*; **~ examination** Routineuntersuchung *f*; **~ flight** Routineflug *m*; **on a ~ basis** routinemäßig; **to be ~ procedure** Routine(sache) sein; **it was quite ~** es war eine reine Formsache; **reports of bloodshed had become almost ~** Berichte über Blutvergießen waren fast zur Gewohnheit geworden *or* waren fast an der Tagesordnung

routinely [ruːˈtiːnlɪ] ADV *use, torture* regelmäßig; *test* routinemäßig; *describe* üblicherweise

routinist [ruːˈtiːnɪst] N Gewohnheitsmensch *m*

roux [ruː] N Mehlschwitze *f*, Einbrenne *f*

rove [raʊv] VI (*person*) umherwandern *or* -ziehen; (*eyes*) umherwandern *or* -schweifen; **to ~ over sth** (*eyes*) über etw (*acc*) schweifen *or* wandern VT *countryside, streets* wandern *or* ziehen durch, durchwandern *or* -ziehen

rover ['raʊvə'] N **a** (= *wanderer*) Vagabund(in) *m(f)* **b** (*also* **Rover Scout**) Rover *m*

roving ['raʊvɪŋ] ADJ (= *itinerant*) *musicians* (herum)ziehend; *gang* vagabundierend; **he has a ~ eye** er riskiert gern ein Auge; **~ life** Vagabundenleben *nt* N Vagabundieren *nt no pl*

roving: roving ambassador N Botschafter(in) *m(f)* für mehrere Vertretungen; **roving commission** N weitläufiges Mandat; (= *travelling*) Reisemandat *nt*; **to have a ~ to do sth** eine umfassende Befugnis haben, etw zu tun; **roving reporter** N Reporter, der ständig unterwegs ist, rasender Reporter (*hum*)

row[1] [raʊ] N Reihe *f*; **4 failures in a ~** 4 Misserfolge hinter- *or* nacheinander; **arrange them in ~s** stell sie in Reihen auf

row[2] [raʊ] VI (*in boat*) rudern; **to ~ away/back** weg-/zurückrudern VT *boat* rudern; **to ~ across** jdn hinüberrudern; **to ~ stroke** Schlagmann sein N **I enjoy a ~** ich rudere gern; **to go for a ~** rudern gehen

row[3] [raʊ] N (*esp Brit inf*) **a** (= *noise*) Lärm *m*, Krach *m* (*inf*); **to make a** *or* **kick up a ~** Krach schlagen (*inf*) **b** (= *quarrel*) Streit *m*, Krach *m* (*inf*); **to have a ~ with sb** mit jdm Streit *or* Krach (*inf*) haben; **to start a ~** Streit anfangen **c** (= *scolding*) **to get a ~** Krach bekommen (*inf*); **to give sb a ~** jdn runtermachen (*inf*) VI (= *quarrel*) (sich) streiten

rowan ['raʊən] N (= *tree*) Eberesche *f*, Vogelbeere *f*; **~ berry** Vogelbeere *f*

rowboat ['rəʊbəʊt] N (*US*) Ruderboot *nt*

rowdiness ['raʊdɪnɪs] N (= *noisiness*) Lärmen *nt*; (= *disorderliness*) rüpelhaftes *or* flegelhaftes Benehmen

rowdy ['raʊdɪ] ADJ (+*er*) (= *noisy*) laut; *football fans* randalierend; *behaviour* grob, ungehobelt; *event, scene* gewalttätig; *party* ausufernd, chaotisch; **the party got a bit ~** die Party artete in Krawall aus N (*Brit*) Krawallmacher *m*; **football rowdies** Fußballrowdys *pl*

rowdyism ['raʊdɪɪzəm] N (*Brit*) Rowdytum *nt*

rower ['rəʊə'] N Ruderer *m*, Ruderin *f*

row house ['rəʊhaʊs] N (*US*) Reihenhaus *nt*

rowing[1] ['rəʊɪŋ] N Rudern *nt*

rowing[2] ['raʊɪŋ] N (*esp Brit: = quarrelling*) Streiterei *f*, Streitereien *pl*

rowing ['rəʊɪŋ]: **rowing boat** N (*Brit*) Ruderboot *nt*; **rowing club** N Ruderklub *or* -verein *m*

rowlock ['rɒlək] N (*esp Brit*) Dolle *f*

royal ['rɔɪəl] ADJ königlich; (*fig also*) fürstlich; **the ~ family** die königliche Familie, die Königsfamilie; **the ~ household** der königliche Haushalt; **~ enclosure** (*on racecourse*) abgeteilter Zuschauerbereich der königliche Familie **the ~ we** (*usu hum*) der Pluralis Majestatis; **the ~ road to freedom/success** etc (*fig*) der sichere Weg zur Freiheit/zum Erfolg *etc*; **he's a ~ pain (in the neck)** (*inf*) er geht einem tierisch auf die Nerven (*inf*) N **a** (*inf*) Angehörige(r) *mf* der königlichen Familie **b** (= *stag*) kapitaler Bock

royal: Royal Academy (of Arts) N (*Brit*) Königliche Akademie (*der Künste*); **Royal Air Force** N (*Brit*) Königliche Luftwaffe; **Royal Assent** N (*Brit*) **to receive** *or* **be given ~** die königliche Genehmigung bekommen; **royal blue** N Königsblau *nt*; **royal-blue** ADJ königsblau; **Royal Canadian Mounted Police** N *kanadische berittene Polizei*; **Royal Commission** N (*Brit*) königliche Untersuchungskommission; **royal correspondent** N Hofkorrespondent(in) *m(f)*; **Royal Engineers** N (*Brit, Mil*) Königliches Pionierkorps; **royal flush** N (*Cards*) Royal Flush *m*; **Royal Highness** N **Your/His ~** Eure/Seine Königliche Hoheit

royalism ['rɔɪəlɪzəm] N Royalismus *m*, Königstreue *f*

royalist ['rɔɪəlɪst] ADJ royalistisch, königstreu N Royalist(in) *m(f)*, Königstreue(r) *mf*

royal jelly N (*Med*) Gelée royale *nt*

royally ['rɔɪəlɪ] ADV **a** königlich; (**right**) **~** (*fig, = lavishly*) fürstlich, königlich **b** (*inf, = totally*) **to get ~ drunk** sich total besaufen (*inf*); **you have messed up ~** da hast du totalen Scheiß gebaut (*inf*)

royal: Royal Mail N (*Brit*) britischer Postdienst; **Royal Marines** PL (*Brit*) britische Marineinfanterie; **Royal Mint** N (*Brit*) Königliche Münzanstalt; **Royal Navy** (*Brit*) N Königliche Marine ATTR königliche Marine; **royal palace** N Königspalast *m*; **royal purple** N (*colour*) Purpur *m*; **Royal Society** N (*Brit*) Königliche Gesellschaft

---

ROYAL SHAKESPEARE COMPANY

Die **Royal Shakespeare Company** (oder auch nur **RSC**) ist ein britisches Theaterensemble, das 1960 in Shakespeares Geburtsort, Stratford-on-Avon, gegründet wurde. Sie hat gegenwärtig zwei Stammhäuser, eines in Stratford und das Barbican in London, und bringt selbstverständlich Stücke von Shakespeare, aber auch andere Klassiker und einige zeitgenössische Werke zur Aufführung. In den letzten Jahren ging die **RSC** jährlich für sechs Monate auf Tournee durch Großbritannien und konnte sich durch die ausgezeichnete Qualität ihrer Inszenierungen einen ausgezeichneten internationalen Ruf erwerben.

royalty [ˈrɔɪəltɪ] N **a** (= *dignity, rank*) das Königtum; (*collectively*: = *royal persons*) das Königshaus, die königliche Familie; **symbols of ~** Wahrzeichen *pl* der Königswürde; **he's ~** er gehört zur königlichen Familie **b** **royalties** PL (*on* auf +*acc*) (*from book, records*) Tantiemen *pl*; (*from patent*) Patent- or Lizenzgebühren *pl*

royal warrant N *königliche Urkunde für Hoflieferanten*

royal-watchers [ˈrɔɪəlˌwɒtʃəz] PL Hofbeobachter *pl*

rozzer [ˈrɒzə*ʳ*] N (*Brit, sl*) Bulle *m* (*sl*), Polyp *m* (*dated sl*)

RP *abbr of* **received pronunciation**

RPM (*Brit*) *abbr of* **resale price maintenance**

rpm *abbr of* **revolutions per minute** U/min

RR (*US*) *abbr of* **Railroad**

RSC (*Brit*) *abbr of* **Royal Shakespeare Company**

RSI *abbr of* **repetitive strain injury**

RSPB (*Brit*) *abbr of* **Royal Society for the Protection of Birds** ≈ Bund *m* für Vogelschutz

RSPCA (*Brit*) *abbr of* **Royal Society for the Prevention of Cruelty to Animals** ≈ Tierschutzverein *m*

RSVP *abbr of* **répondez s'il vous plaît** u. A. w. g.

RTA *abbr of* **road traffic accident** Verkehrsunfall *m*

Rt Hon (*Brit*) *abbr of* **Right Honourable**

rub [rʌb] N **a** Reiben *nt*; (*with duster etc*) Polieren *nt*; **to give sth a ~** etw reiben; *furniture, shoes, silver* etw polieren; **~-a-dub(-dub)!** (*inf*) rubbel-rubbel! (*inf*)
b (*fig*) **there's the ~!** da liegt der Hase im Pfeffer
VT reiben; (*with towel also*) frottieren; (= *polish*) polieren; (*Art*) *brass, inscription* durchzeichnen; **to ~ lotion into sth/oneself** etw/sich mit einer Lotion einreiben; **to ~ sth with sandpaper** etw (mit Sandpapier) abschmirgeln; **to ~ one's eyes** sich (*dat*) die Augen reiben; **to ~ one's hands (together) (in** or **with glee)** sich (*dat*) (vor Freude) die Hände reiben; **to ~ sth dry** etw trockenreiben or -rubbeln (*inf*); **to ~ noses** (*as greeting*) die Nasen aneinander reiben; **to ~ sb's nose in sth** (*fig*) jdm etw dauernd unter die Nase reiben or halten; **to ~ shoulders** (*esp Brit*) or **elbows** (*esp US*) **with all sorts of people** (*esp US*) mit allen möglichen Leuten in Berührung kommen; **to ~ sb the wrong way** (*US*) bei jdm anecken → **salt N a**
VI (*thing*) (*against* an +*dat*) reiben; (*collar*) scheuern; **you must have ~bed against some wet paint** da musst du an feuchte Farbe gekommen sein; **the cat ~bed against my legs/ the tree** die Katze strich mir um die Beine/ scheuerte sich am Baum

▶ **rub along** VI (*Brit inf*: = *manage*) sich durchschlagen (*inf*); **to rub along (together)** recht und schlecht miteinander auskommen

▶ **rub away** VT *sep* wegreiben

▶ **rub down** VT *sep* horse (= dry) abreiben; (= clean) striegeln; *person* abrubbeln (*inf*), abfrottieren; *wall, paintwork* (= clean) abwaschen; (= sandpaper) abschmirgeln

▶ **rub in** VT *sep* **a** *oil, lotion* einreiben (*prep obj*, -*to* in +*acc*); *butter* hinzureiben **b** (*fig*) sb's stupidity herumreiten auf (+*dat*); **he's always rubbing (it) in how rich he is** (*inf*) er reibt es uns/ ihnen *etc* immer unter die Nase, wie reich er ist (*inf*); **don't rub it in!** (= *don't keep mentioning*) reite nicht so darauf herum!; (= *don't keep alluding to*) musst du auch noch Salz in die Wunde streuen?

▶ **rub off** VT *sep* *dirt* abreiben; *writing* ausradieren; *tape* löschen; (*from blackboard*) aus- or wegwischen; *paint, gold-plating* abreiben; (*through wear*) abwetzen VI (*lit, fig*) abgehen; (*through wear also*) sich abwetzen; **to rub off on sb** (*fig*) auf jdn abfärben

▶ **rub out** VT *sep* stain etc herausreiben; (*with eraser*) ausradieren; (*inf*, = kill) auslöschen VI herausgehen; (*with eraser*) sich ausradieren lassen

▶ **rub up** VT *sep* **a** *vase, table* blank reiben, (auf)polieren **b** **to rub sb up the wrong way** (*Brit*) bei jdm anecken VI **the cat rubbed up against my leg** die Katze strich mir um die Beine; **to rub up against all sorts of people** (*esp Brit fig*) mit allen möglichen Leuten in Berührung kommen

rubber¹ [ˈrʌbə*ʳ*] N (= *material*) Gummi *m*; (*unprocessed, synthetic also*) Kautschuk *m* (*spec*); (*Brit*: = *eraser*) (Radier)gummi *m*; (*esp US sl*, = *contraceptive*) Gummi *m* (*inf*); **~s** (= *shoes*) Turnschuhe *pl*; (= *overshoes*) (Gummi)überschuhe *pl*; (= *clothing*) Ölzeug *nt* ADJ Gummi-; **~ goods** Gummiwaren; **is that a ~ cheque** (*Brit*) or **check** (*US*)? (*inf*) platzt der Scheck? (*inf*)

rubber² N (*Cards*) Rubber *m*, Robber *m*

rubber: rubber band N Gummiband *nt*; **rubber boat** N Schlauchboot *nt*; **rubber boot** N (*US*) Gummistiefel *m*; **rubber bullet** N Gummi(wucht)geschoss *nt*; **rubber coating** N Gummierung *f*; **rubber dinghy** N Schlauchboot *nt*

rubberize [ˈrʌbəraɪz] VT (= *cover*) mit Gummi überziehen; (= *impregnate*) gummieren

rubber: rubberneck (*esp US, inf*) N Gaffer(in) *m(f)* (*inf*) VI gaffen (*inf*); **rubber plant** N Gummibaum *m*; **rubber plantation** N Kautschukplantage *f*; **rubber stamp** N Stempel *m*; **rubber-stamp** VT (*lit*) stempeln; (*fig inf*) genehmigen; **rubber tree** N Kautschukbaum *m*; **rubber-tyred** [ˈrʌbəˌtaɪəd] ADJ mit Gummireifen

rubbery [ˈrʌbərɪ] ADJ **a** *material, skin* gummiartig; *meat* zäh, wie Gummi *pred*; (*hum*) *lips* wulstig **b** (= *weak*) *legs* gummiweich (*inf*)

rubbing [ˈrʌbɪŋ] N **a** (= *action*) Reiben *nt*; (*of collar*) Scheuern *nt*, Reiben *nt*; (*with towel*) Frottieren *nt*; (= *polishing*) Polieren *nt*; (*with sandpaper*) Schmirgeln *nt* **b** (*Art*) → **brass rubbing**

rubbing: rubbing alcohol N (*US*) Wundbenzin *nt*; **rubbing varnish** N Schleiflack *m*

rubbish [ˈrʌbɪʃ] (*esp Brit*) N **a** (= *waste material*) Abfall *m*, Abfälle *pl*; (= *household rubbish, in factory also*) Müll *m*; (*on building site*) Schutt *m*; (*fig*, = *trashy goods, record etc*) Mist *m*; **household ~** Hausmüll *m*; **garden ~** Gartenabfälle *pl*; **most modern furniture is ~** die meisten modernen Möbel sind nichts wert
b (*inf*: = *nonsense*) Quatsch *m* (*inf*), Blödsinn *m*; **don't talk ~!** red keinen Quatsch or Blödsinn! (*inf*); **he talked a lot** or **a load of ~** er hat eine Menge Blödsinn verzapft (*inf*); **(what a lot of) ~!** (so ein) Quatsch! (*inf*); **this book is ~** das Buch ist Quatsch (*inf*)
ATTR (*inf*) **a** = **rubbishy**
b (*inf*) **~ at it** ich bin zu blöd dazu (*inf*); **I'm ~ at doing it** ich krieg das (einfach) nicht hin (*inf*)
VT (*inf*) *person, idea* runtermachen (*inf*)

rubbish *in cpds* (*esp Brit*) Müll-; **rubbish bin** N Mülleimer *m*; **rubbish cart** N Müllwagen *m*; **rubbish chute** N Müllschlucker *m*; **rubbish collection** N Müllabfuhr *f*; **rubbish dump** N Müllabladeplatz *m*; (*in garden: also* **rubbish heap**) Abfallhaufen *m*; **rubbish tip** N Müllabladeplatz *m*

rubbishy [ˈrʌbɪʃɪ] ADJ (*Brit inf*) (= *worthless*) *goods* minderwertig, wertlos; *magazine, film* mies (*inf*); (= *nonsensical*) *ideas* blödsinnig; **~ shoes** Schuhe, die nichts taugen; **this is ~ stuff** (*article*) das taugt nichts, das ist Mist (*inf*); (*book, theory*) das ist Quatsch (*inf*)

rubble [ˈrʌbl] N Trümmer *pl*, (*smaller pieces*) Schutt *m*; (*Geol*) Geröll *nt*

rubdown [ˈrʌbˈdaʊn] N **to give sb/sth a ~** → **rub down**

rube [ruːb] N (*dated US, sl*) (Bauern)tölpel *m*

rubella [ruːˈbelə] N Röteln *pl*

Rubicon [ˈruːbɪkən] N **to cross the ~** den Rubicon überschreiten

rubicund [ˈruːbɪkənd] ADJ rot

rubidium [ruːˈbɪdɪəm] N (*Chem*) Rubidium *nt*

Rubik's cube® [ˈruːbɪksˈkjuːb] N Zauberwürfel *m*

ruble N (*US*) = **rouble**

rubric [ˈruːbrɪk] N (= *heading*) Überschrift *f*; (*Eccl*) (liturgische) Anweisungen *pl*; (*on exam paper*) Prüfungsanweisungen *pl*; **under the ~ ...** in der Rubrik ...

ruby [ˈruːbɪ] N (= *stone*) Rubin *m*; (*colour: also* **ruby red**) Rubinrot *nt* ADJ (= *ruby-coloured*) *wine, lips* rubinrot; (= *made of rubies*) Rubin-; **ring** Rubinring *m*

ruby-red [ˈruːbɪˈred] ADJ rubinrot

ruby wedding (anniversary) N vierzigster Hochzeitstag, Rubinhochzeit *f*

RUC *abbr of* **Royal Ulster Constabulary** *nordirische Polizeibehörde*

ruche [ruːʃ] N Rüsche *f*

ruched [ruːʃt] ADJ Rüschen-, gerüscht; **~ dress** Rüschenkleid *nt*; **~ and edged with lace** mit Rüschen und Spitzenbesatz

ruching [ˈruːʃɪŋ] N Rüschen *pl*

ruck¹ [rʌk] N **a** (*Racing*) Pulk *m*; **the (common) ~** (*fig*) die (breite) Masse; **to get out of the ~** (*fig*) von der breiten Masse absetzen **b** (*Rugby*) offenes Gedränge **c** (*Prison sl*, = *ruckus*) Krawall *m* (*inf*)

ruck² N (= *wrinkle*) Falte *f*

▶ **ruck up** VT *sep* seam zusammenziehen; *rug* verschieben; **his shirt is all rucked up** sein Hemd hat sich hochgeschoben VI (*seam*) sich zusammenziehen; (*shirt etc*) sich hochschieben; (*rug*) Falten schlagen

rucksack [ˈrʌksæk] N (*esp Brit*) Rucksack *m*

ruckus [ˈrʌkəs] N (*inf*) Krawall *m*

ruction [ˈrʌkʃən] N (*inf*) *usu pl* (= *dispute, scolding*) Krach *m no pl*; (= *uproar also*) Krawall *m no pl*; **there'll be ~s if you do that** es gibt Krach, wenn du das tust

rudder [ˈrʌdə*ʳ*] N (*Naut, Aviat*) Ruder *nt*

rudderless [ˈrʌdəlɪs] ADJ ohne Ruder; (*fig*) führungslos

ruddiness [ˈrʌdɪnɪs] N Röte *f*; **the ~ of his complexion** seine gesunde Gesichtsfarbe

ruddy [ˈrʌdɪ] ADJ (+*er*) **a** (= *red*) *face* rot; *complexion* gesund, rot; *sky, glow* rötlich **b** (*Brit, inf*, = *bloody*) verdammt (*inf*) ADV (*Brit, inf*, = *bloody*) verdammt (*inf*); **how could you be so ~ stupid?** wie konntest du nur so verdammt blöd sein? (*inf*)

rude [ruːd] ADJ (+*er*) **a** (= *impolite, bad-mannered*) unhöflich; (*stronger*) unverschämt; (= *rough, uncouth*) grob; **to be ~ to sb** unhöflich zu jdm sein; **it's ~ to stare** es gehört sich nicht, Leute anzustarren, man starrt andere Leute nicht an; **don't be so ~!** so was sagt man/tut man nicht!; **talk about ~!** der/die hat vielleicht einen Ton am Leib! (*inf*)
b (= *obscene, dirty*) unanständig, unflätig (*geh*); **to make a ~ gesture at sb** jdm gegenüber eine anstößige Geste machen; **to make a ~ noise** (*euph*) pup(s)en (*inf*)
c (= *harsh*) *shock* bös, hart; *blast, weather* wüst, rau; *reminder* unsanft → **awakening**
d (*liter*, = *crude, primitive*) primitiv; *fare* einfach, schlicht
e (*liter*, = *vigorous*) *strength* gewaltig; **he is in ~ health/strength** er strotzt (nur so) vor Gesundheit/Kraft

rudely [ˈruːdlɪ] ADV **a** (= *impolitely*) unhöflich; (*stronger*) unverschämt; (= *roughly, uncouthly*) grob; *push* rüde; **before I was so ~ interrupted** bevor ich so unhöflich unterbrochen wurde
b (= *obscenely*) unanständig **c** (= *harshly*) *awaken, remind, shatter* unsanft **d** (*liter*, = *crudely, primitively*) grob

▶ **rudeness** [ˈruːdnɪs] N **a** (= *impoliteness*) Unhöflichkeit *f*; (*stronger*) Unverschämtheit *f*; (= *roughness, uncouthness*) Grobheit *f* **b** (= *obscenity*) Unanständigkeit *f*, Unflätigkeit *f* (*geh*) **c** (= *harshness: of shock*) Härte *f*

rudiment ['ru:dɪmənt] N , **rudiments** PL **a** Anfangsgründe pl, Grundlagen pl **b** (Biol) Rudiment nt

rudimentary [ˌru:dɪ'mentərɪ] ADJ (= basic) principles elementar; equipment primitiv; language, system rudimentär; (Biol) rudimentär; ~ **knowledge** Grundkenntnisse pl; **in a ~ way** in einer primitiven Form or Art und Weise

rue[1] [ru:] VT (liter) bereuen; **to ~ the day that ...** den Tag verwünschen, an dem ...

rue[2] N (Bot) Raute f

rueful ['ru:fʊl] ADJ look reuig, reuevoll; situation beklagenswert

ruefully ['ru:fəlɪ] ADV reuevoll

ruff[1] [rʌf] N **a** (on dress etc, of bird, animal) Halskrause f **b** (= bird) Kampfläufer m

ruff[2] (Cards) N Trumpfen nt VTI trumpfen, stechen

ruffian ['rʌfɪən] N Rüpel m, Grobian m; (violent) Schläger m; **you little ~!** du kleiner Halbstarker!

ruffianism ['rʌfɪənɪzəm] N Rohheit f, Gewalttätigkeit f, Brutalität f

ruffle ['rʌfl] N (on dress) Rüsche f; (on water) Kräuseln nt no pl VTI **a** (= disturb) hair, feathers zerzausen; surface, water kräuseln; clothes verkrumpeln (inf); **the bird ~d (up) its feathers** der Vogel plusterte sich auf **b** (fig, = upset, disturb) aus der Ruhe bringen; (= annoy) verärgern, aufbringen; **to ~ sb's calm** jdn aus der Ruhe bringen; **to ~ sb's feathers** jdn aufregen

ruffled ['rʌfld] ADJ **a** (= flustered, perturbed) person aufgebracht; feelings erregt; **to smooth ~ feelings** erregte Gemüter besänftigen; **to smooth sb's ~ feathers** jdn besänftigen, jds erregtes Gemüt besänftigen **b** (= rumpled, dishevelled) bedclothes zerwühlt; hair zerzaust **c** shirt, skirt gekräuselt, gerafft

rug [rʌg] N **a** Teppich m; (esp rectangular) Läufer m; (valuable) Brücke f; (bedside) (Bett)vorleger m; **fireside ~** Kaminvorleger m; **to pull the ~ from under sb** (fig) jdm den Boden unter den Füßen wegziehen **b** (= blanket) (Woll)decke f

rugby ['rʌgbɪ] N (also **rugby football**) Rugby nt; ~ **footballer** Rugbyspieler(in) m(f)

rugby: Rugby League N Rugby nt (mit 13 (Profi)spielern pro Team); **rugby player** N Rugbyspieler(in) m(f); **rugby tackle** N Rugby-Tackling nt VT zu Boden bringen; **Rugby Union** N Rugby nt (mit 15 (Amateur)spielern pro Team)

rugged ['rʌgɪd] ADJ **a** (= rough, uneven) rau; country, landscape also wild; cliff, rocks, mountains zerklüftet; ground felsig; statue grob **b** (= tough-looking) man, face, features markig **c** (= tough: in character) personality rau; breed zäh, rau; determination wild; resistance verbissen; **a ~ test** eine harte Prüfung; ~ **individualism** rauer or knorriger Individualismus; **hill farmers are a ~ breed** Bergbauern sind ein rauer Menschenschlag **d** (= durable) machine widerstandsfähig; clothing strapazierfähig

ruggedness ['rʌgɪdnɪs] N **a** (= roughness, unevenness) Rauheit f; (of country, landscape also) Wildheit f; (of ground) Felsigkeit f; **the ~ of the cliffs** die zerklüfteten Klippen **b** (= tough appearance: of man, face, features) Markigkeit f

rugger ['rʌgə'] N (Brit, inf) = **rugby**

ruin ['ru:ɪn] N **a** no pl (of thing, person) Untergang m; (of event) Ende nt; (financial, social) Ruin m; **the palace was going to ~ or falling into ~** der Palast verfiel (zur Ruine); ~ **stared him in the face** (financial/social) er stand vor dem (finanziellen/gesellschaftlichen) Ruin **b** (= cause of ruin) Ende nt; (of person) Ruin m; **the ~ of my hopes** das Ende meiner Hoffnungen; **it will be the ~ of him** das wird ihn ruinieren; **you will be the ~ of me** du bist mein Ruin **c** (= ruined building) Ruine f; (fig, = person) Wrack nt; ~**s** (of building) Ruinen pl; (of reputation, beauty) Reste pl; (of hopes, career) Trümmer pl; **to be or lie in ~s** (lit) eine Ruine sein; (fig) zerstört sein; (life: financially, socially) ruiniert

sein VT **a** (= destroy) building zerstören; hopes also zunichte machen; chances, reputation, health, sb's life also ruinieren; (financially, socially) person ruinieren, zugrunde or zu Grunde richten; (= spoil) clothes, event, enjoyment, child, horse verderben; **they ~ed my birthday party** sie haben (mir) die Geburtstagsfeier verdorben

ruination [ˌru:ɪ'neɪʃən] N (of building, hopes) Zerstörung f; (of reputation, health, sb's life also, of person) Ruinierung f; **to be the ~ of sb** jds Ruin m sein

ruined ['ru:ɪnd] ADJ **a** building in Ruinen pred, zerfallen; city in Ruinen pred; **he visited ~ Warsaw** er besuchte das zerstörte or das in Ruinen liegende Warschau **b** (= wrecked) economy zugrunde or zu Grunde gerichtet, ruiniert; career ruiniert **c** (financially) ruiniert, erledigt

ruinous ['ru:ɪnəs] ADJ (financially) ruinös; price extrem; **to be in a ~ state or in ~ condition** (building) verfallen or baufällig sein

ruinously ['ru:ɪnəslɪ] ADV ~ **expensive** wahnsinnig teuer (inf)

rule [ru:l] N **a** (= regulation) Regel f; (Sport, Cards) (Spiel)regel f; (Admin) Vorschrift f, Bestimmung f; **the ~s of the game** die Spielregeln; **to play by the ~s** (lit, fig) die Spielregeln einhalten; **to bend or stretch the ~s** es mit den Regeln/Vorschriften nicht so genau nehmen; **running is against the ~s, it's against the ~s to run** Rennen ist nicht erlaubt; ~**s and regulations** Regeln und Bestimmungen; **it's a ~ that ...** es ist Vorschrift, dass ...; **that's the ~ of the road** (Mot) das ist im Straßenverkehr üblich; **the Franciscan ~** die Regeln des Franziskanerordens; **to work to ~** Dienst nach Vorschrift machen; **to do sth by ~** etw vorschriftsmäßig tun; **the ~ of three** (Math) der Dreisatz; **as a ~ of thumb** als Faustregel; ~ **book** Regelheft nt, Vorschriftenbuch nt; **to throw the ~ book at sb** (fig) jdn wegen jeder Kleinigkeit drankriegen (inf) **b** (= custom) Regel f; **I make it a ~ to get up early** ich habe es mir zur Regel gemacht, früh aufzustehen; **as a (general) ~** in der Regel; **ties are the ~ at the office** Krawatten sind im Büro die Regel; **violence is the ~ rather than the exception** Gewalt ist eher (die) Regel als (die) Ausnahme **c** (= authority, reign) Herrschaft f; (= period) Regierungszeit f; **the ~ of law** die Rechtsstaatlichkeit **d** (for measuring) Metermaß nt, Maßstab m; **a foot ~** (1 foot long) ein (30 cm langes) Lineal; (showing feet) ein Maßstab m mit Fußeinteilung; **folding ~** Zollstock m → **slide rule** VT **a** (= govern) beherrschen, regieren; (individual) beherrschen, herrschen über (+acc); (fig) passions, emotion beherrschen, zügeln; person beherrschen; **to ~ the roost** (fig) Herr im Haus sein (inf); **to be ~d by emotions** sich von Gefühlen beherrschen lassen; **if you would only be ~d by what I say** wenn du nur auf mich hören würdest; **I won't be ~d by what he wants** ich richte mich nicht nach seinen Wünschen; **he let his heart ~ his head** er ließ sich von seinem Herzen und nicht von seinem Verstand leiten **b** (Jur, Sport, Admin: = give decision) entscheiden; **his question was ~d out of order** seine Frage wurde als unzulässig abgewiesen; **the judge ~d the defence out of order** (Jur) der Richter rügte die Verteidigung **c** (= draw lines on) paper linieren; (= draw) line, margin ziehen; ~**d paper** liniertes Papier VI **a** (lit, fig: = reign) herrschen (over über +acc), regieren (over +acc) **b** (St Ex: = prices) notieren; **the prices ruling in London** die in London notierten Preise **c** (Jur) entscheiden (against gegen, in favour of für, on in +dat)

▶**rule off** VT sep einen Schlussstrich ziehen unter (+acc)

▶**rule out** 🕐 16.3 VT sep word, sentence einen Strich ziehen durch; (fig, = exclude, dismiss) ausschließen

ruler ['ru:lə'] N **a** (for measuring) Lineal nt **b** (= sovereign) Herrscher(in) m(f)

ruling ['ru:lɪŋ] ADJ **a** (in power) body, elite herrschend; **the ~ class** die herrschende Klasse; **the ~ party** die Regierungspartei **b** (= determining) factor ausschlaggebend; passion vorherrschend; (= prevalent) vor)herrschend; (Fin, St Ex) prices notiert; ~ **principle** leitendes Prinzip, Leitprinzip nt N (Admin, Jur) Entscheidung f; **to get a ~** einen Bescheid erhalten; **to give a ~** eine Entscheidung fällen

rum[1] [rʌm] N Rum m; ~ **toddy** Grog m

rum[2] ADJ (dated Brit, inf) komisch (inf); person also kauzig; **they're a ~ lot** das sind mir (so) die Rechten (inf)

Rumania etc [ru:'meɪnɪə] = **Romania** etc

rumba ['rʌmbə] N Rumba m or f

rumble ['rʌmbl] N **a** (of thunder) Grollen nt no pl; (of cannon) Donnern nt no pl; (of pipes) Knacken nt no pl; (of stomach) Knurren nt no pl; (of train, truck) Rumpeln nt no pl; **his stomach gave a ~** sein Magen knurrte **b** (inf, = fight) Schlägerei f VI (thunder) grollen; (cannon) donnern; (pipes) knacken; (stomach) knurren; (train, truck) rumpeln; **to ~ past/along/off** vorbei-/entlang-/davonrumpeln VT (Brit inf: = see through) swindle, trick, person durchschauen; **I soon ~d him or what he was up to** ich bin ihm bald auf die Schliche gekommen (inf)

rumble on VI (Brit: argument, controversy, scandal) weiter schwelen

rumble: rumble seat N Notsitz m; **rumble strip** N (Mot) akustische Schwelle

rumbling ['rʌmblɪŋ] N (of thunder) Grollen nt no pl; (of cannon) Donnern nt no pl; (of pipes) Knacken nt no pl; (of stomach) Knurren nt no pl; (of train, truck) Rumpeln nt no pl

rumbustious [rʌm'bʌstʃəs] ADJ derb

ruminant ['ru:mɪnənt] N Wiederkäuer m ADJ (lit) wiederkäuend; (fig) grübelnd

ruminate ['ru:mɪneɪt] VI (lit) wiederkäuen; (fig) grübeln (over, about, on über +acc) VT wiederkäuen

rumination [ˌru:mɪ'neɪʃən] N (lit) Wiederkäuen nt no pl; (fig) Grübeln nt no pl

ruminative ADJ , **ruminatively** ADV ['ru:mɪnətɪv, -lɪ] (fig) grübelnd

rummage ['rʌmɪdʒ] N **a to have a good ~ in sth** etw gründlich durchstöbern or durchwühlen; **to have a good ~ around** gründlich herumstöbern or herumwühlen **b** (= jumble) Ramsch m VI (also **rummage about, rummage around**) herumstöbern, herumwühlen (among, in in +dat, for nach)

rummage sale N (US) Ramschverkauf m

rummy ['rʌmɪ] N (Cards) Rommé nt, Rommee nt

rumour, (US) **rumor** ['ru:mə'] N Gerücht nt; ~ **has it that ...** es geht das Gerücht, dass ...; **as ~ has it** wie es Gerüchten zufolge heißt; **there are ~s of war** es gehen Kriegsgerüchte um VT **it is ~ed that ...** es geht das Gerücht, dass ...; (through gossip) man munkelt, dass ...; **he is ~ed to be in London** Gerüchten zufolge ist er in London; **he is ~ed to be rich** er soll angeblich reich sein; **his ~ed relationship with a model** die ihm nachgesagte Beziehung zu einem Model

rumour, (US) **rumor: rumour mill** ['ru:mə,mɪl] N (inf, pej) Gerüchteküche f (inf, pej); **rumour--monger** ['ru:mə,mʌŋgə'] N Gerüchtemacher(in) m(f), Klatschbase f (pej); **rumour--mongering** ['ru:mə,mʌŋgərɪŋ] N , no pl Klatscherei f (pej), Verbreitung f no pl von Gerüchten

rump [rʌmp] N (of animal) Hinterbacken pl; (of fowl) Bürzel m; (inf: of person) Hinterteil nt, Allerwerteste(r) m (hum); ~ **steak** Rumpsteak nt; **the Rump** (Brit, Hist) das Rumpfparlament (im 17. Jahrhundert in England)

Rumpelstiltskin ['rʌmpəl,stɪltskɪn] N Rumpelstilzchen nt

rumple ['rʌmpl] VT (*also* **rumple up**) *clothes, paper* zerknittern; *hair* verwuscheln, zerzausen

rumpled ['rʌmpld] ADJ *clothes, sheets* zerknittert; *person* unordentlich; *hair* zerzaust

rumply ['rʌmplɪ] ADJ *clothes, sheets etc* zerknittert

rumpus ['rʌmpəs] N (*inf, = noise*) Spektakel *nt* (*inf*), Krach *m*; (*= quarrel*) Krach *m* (*inf*); **to make a ~** (*= make noise*) einen Spektakel *or* Heidenlärm machen (*inf*); (*= complain*) Krach schlagen (*inf*); **to have a ~ with sb** sich mit jdm in die Haare geraten

rumpus room N (*US*) Spielzimmer *nt*

---

run [rʌn]
vb: pret **ran**, *ptp* **run**

1 NOUN	3 TRANSITIVE VERB
2 INTRANSITIVE VERB	4 PHRASAL VERBS

1 – NOUN

a = act of running Lauf *m* (*also Cricket, Baseball*); **to go for a 2-km run** einen 2-km-Lauf machen; **his run is slower than my walk** ich kann schneller gehen, als er laufen kann; **let the dog run** lass den Hund laufen; **he set off at a run** er rannte los; **he took the fence at a run** er nahm die Hürde im Lauf; **to break into a run** zu laufen *or* rennen anfangen; **to take a run at a hurdle** auf eine Hürde loslaufen; **to make a run for it** weglaufen, wegrennen; **he made a run for the door** er lief *or* rannte zur Tür; **he's had a good run** (*= long life*) er hatte ein langes Leben

♦ **on the run** (*from the police etc*) auf der Flucht; **at last we've got them on the run!** endlich haben wir sie in die Flucht geschlagen!; **to keep the enemy on the run** den Feind weiter zur Flucht zwingen; **the house and family keep you on the run** Haus und Familie halten einen ganz schön auf Trab (*inf*)

♦ **a good run for one's money** we'll give him **a good run for his money, he'll have a good run for his money** (*inf, in competition*) wir werden ihn auf Trab halten (*inf*); **these days has had a good run for its money** (*inf*) die Theorie hat sich lange gehalten

b = journey (*in vehicle*) Fahrt *f*; (*for pleasure*) Ausflug *m*; **to go for a run in the car** eine Fahrt/einen Ausflug im Auto machen

c = distance travelled (*in bus, boat, car*) Fahrt *f*; (*in plane*) Flug *m*; (*= route*) Strecke *f*; **it's a 30-minute run** es ist eine Fahrt von 30 Minuten; **the boat no longer does that run** das Schiff fährt die Strecke nicht mehr; **the ferries on the Dover-Calais run** die Fähren der Linie Dover-Calais; **the ships on the China run** die Schiffe der China-Linie; **bombing run** Bombenzielanflug *m*

♦ **in the long run** auf die Dauer; **it will be cheaper in the long run** es wird auf die Dauer billiger sein

♦ **in the short run** fürs Nächste; **this could be the best solution in the short run** dies könnte fürs Nächste die beste Lösung sein

d = use **to have the run of a place** einen Ort zur freien Verfügung haben; **to give sb the run of one's house** jdm sein Haus überlassen

e = series Folge *f*, Reihe *f*, Serie *f*; (*Cards*) Sequenz *f*; (*Theat*) Spielzeit *f*; (*of film*) Laufzeit *f*; **a run on the red** (*Roulette*) eine Serie von roten Zahlen; **when the London run was over** (*Theat*) als das Stück in London abgelaufen war; **the play had a long run** das Stück lief sehr lange; **a run of luck/of bad luck** eine Glücks-/Pechsträhne

f = great demand **run on** Ansturm *m* auf (*+acc*); (*St Ex, Fin*) Run *m or* Ansturm *m* auf (*+acc*); **there could be a run on the pound** es könnte einen Run *or* Ansturm auf das Pfund geben

g = type **the common run of athletes** der Durchschnittsathlet; **the usual run of illnesses** die normale Serie von Krankheiten

h = trend (*of market, opinion*) Tendenz *f*; (*of events*) Lauf *m*; **the ordinary run of things** der normale Gang der Dinge

i = track for sledging, skiing Bahn *f*; **ski run** Abfahrt(sstrecke) *f*

j = animal enclosure Gehege *nt*; (*for chickens*) Hühnerhof *m*

k = diarrhoea (*inf*) **the runs** der flotte Otto (*inf*), die Renneritis (*hum inf*)

l in stocking Laufmasche *f*

m Typ (*= printing run*) Auflage *f*

n Mus Lauf *m*

2 – INTRANSITIVE VERB

a laufen, rennen; (*in race*) laufen; **to run past/off** vorbei-/davonlaufen *or* -rennen; **she came running out** sie kam herausgelaufen *or* -gerannt; **to run down a slope** einen Abhang hinunterlaufen *or* -rennen; **run!** lauf!; **walk don't run!** du sollst gehen, nicht rennen!; **he's trying to run before he can walk** (*fig*) er sollte erst einmal langsam machen; **to run for the bus** zum Bus laufen *or* rennen; **she ran to meet him** sie lief *or* rannte ihm entgegen; **she ran to help him** sie kam ihm schnell zu Hilfe; **to run in the 100 metres** (*Brit*) *or* **meters** (*US*) die 100 Meter laufen; **eleven ran** (*Horse Racing*) elf (Pferde) waren am Start; **X, Y, Z also ran** (*Horse Racing*) X, Y, Z waren ebenfalls am Start; **this horse will run in the National** das Pferd startet im National → **also-ran**

b = flee davonlaufen, wegrennen; **to run for one's life** um sein Leben laufen *or* rennen; **run for it!** lauft *or* rennt, was ihr könnt!; **go on then, run to mummy!** na, lauf doch schon zu deiner Mutti!

c = go (*story, words*) gehen, lauten; (*tune*) gehen; **the rumour** (*Brit*) *or* **rumor** (*US*) **ran (a)round the office that ...** im Büro ging das Gerücht um, dass ...; **so the story runs** die Geschichte geht so; **the wording ran as follows** es hieß *or* lautete folgendermaßen; **the lyrics ran through my head** der Text ging mir durch den Kopf; **all the things I have to do keep running through my head** mir geht ständig durch den Kopf, was ich noch alles machen muss; **he ran down the list** er ging die Liste durch; **my thoughts ran on my sister** ich dachte an meine Schwester; **a shiver ran down her spine** ein Schauer lief ihr über den Rücken; **his eyes/fingers ran over the sculpture** seine Augen/Finger glitten über die Plastik

♦ **to run in the family** in der Familie liegen

d = stand as candidate kandidieren, sich aufstellen lassen; **to run for President** *or* **for the Presidency** für die Präsidentschaft kandidieren; **to run against sb** jds Gegenkandidat *m* sein

e = be **I'm running a bit late** ich bin ein bisschen spät dran; **all planes/trains are running late** alle Flugzeuge/Züge haben Verspätung; **the project is running late/to schedule** das Projekt hat sich verzögert/geht ganz nach Plan voran; **supplies are running low** die Vorräte sind knapp; **his blood ran cold** das Blut fror ihm in den Adern; **to be running scared** → **seed, short, wild, high**

♦ **to run dry** (*river*) austrocknen; (*pen*) leer werden; (*resources, funds*) ausgehen; (*conversation*) verstummen; **he ran dry of ideas** ihm gingen die Ideen aus; **their conversation ran dry** ihnen ging der Gesprächsstoff aus

♦ **to be running at** (*= stand*) betragen; **inflation is running at 20%** die Inflationsrate beträgt 20%; **interest rates are running at record levels/15%** die Zinssätze sind auf Rekordhöhe/stehen auf 15%

f = slide (*drawer, curtains, rope*) laufen, gleiten; (*vehicle*) rollen; **it runs on wheels** es läuft *or* fährt auf Rädern; **money just runs through his fingers** das Geld rinnt ihm (nur so) durch die Finger

g = flow (*water, tears, tap, nose, butter*) laufen; (*ink, river, electric current*) fließen; (*eyes*) tränen; (*sore, abscess*) eitern; (*paint, colour*) zerfließen, ineinander fließen; (*colour, dye in washing*) färben; **my shirt has run** mein Hemd hat gefärbt; **a heavy sea was running** die See ging hoch; **where the tide is running strongly** wo die Gezeiten sehr stark sind; **let the water run hot**

lass das Wasser laufen, bis es heiß kommt; **your bath is running** dein Badewasser läuft ein

♦ **to be running with** (*= saturated*) **the walls were running with damp** die Wände tropften vor Feuchtigkeit; **running with sweat** schweißüberströmt

♦ **to run into** (*= join*) **where the river runs into the sea** wo der Fluss ins Meer mündet; **the street runs into the square** die Straße mündet auf den Platz

h = continue, extend (*play, film, contract*) laufen; (*Jur: sentence*) laufen; (*Fin: interest rate*) gelten

♦ **to run into** (*with amounts, numbers*) **the expenditure runs into thousands of pounds** die Ausgaben gehen in die tausende *or* Tausende (von Pfund); **the book has run into three editions** das Buch hat schon drei Auflagen erreicht

♦ **to run and run** (*story, production*) noch lange laufen; (*debate*) noch lange fortgesetzt werden

i = sail **to run before the wind** vor dem Wind segeln; **to run onto the rocks** (auf die Felsen) auflaufen; **to run into port** in den Hafen einlaufen

j = provide service (*bus, train etc*) fahren, verkehren; **the train doesn't run on Sundays** der Zug fährt sonntags nicht; **no trains run there any more** dorthin gibt es keine Zugverbindung mehr

k = function (*machine, wheel*) laufen; (*factory*) arbeiten; (*fig, ceremony*) laufen; **when the central heating is running** wenn die Zentralheizung angeschaltet ist; **you mustn't leave the engine running** Sie dürfen den Motor nicht laufen lassen; **this model runs on diesel** dieses Auto fährt mit Diesel; **the radio runs off the mains/off batteries** das Radio läuft auf Netz/Batterie; **things are running smoothly** alles läuft glatt

l = extend in space (*road*) gehen, führen; (*mountains*) sich ziehen, sich erstrecken; (*river*) fließen; **he has a scar running across his chest** eine Narbe zieht sich quer über seine Brust; **a wall runs (a)round the garden** um den Garten zieht sich *or* läuft eine Mauer; **the railway line runs for 300 km** die Bahnlinie ist 300 km lang; **this theme runs through all his work** dieses Thema zieht sich durch sein ganzes Werk

m = unravel (*stocking*) eine Laufmasche bekommen; (*stitch*) laufen

n Comput (*software, computer*) laufen; **this software doesn't run under the new version** diese Software läuft nicht unter der neuen Version

3 – TRANSITIVE VERB

a subject: person *distance* laufen, rennen; *race* laufen; **he runs 3 km every day** er läuft jeden Tag 3 km; **the first race will be run at 2 o'clock** das erste Rennen findet um 2 Uhr statt; **to run errands** Botengänge machen; **to run the streets** (*child, dog*) sich auf der Straße herumtreiben; **to run sb/sth a close second** (*fig*) von jdm/etw nur knapp geschlagen werden; **to run sb close** (*Sport, fig*) nur knapp von jdm geschlagen werden → **mile**

b subject: events, disease, person **to run its/their course** seinen/ihren Lauf nehmen; **to run a temperature** *or* **a fever** Fieber haben; **he was running a high temperature** er hatte Fieber → **gauntlet**

c = pursue (*= hunt*) *fox, deer* treiben; (*= make run*) *person, animal* jagen; **they ran him out of the house** sie jagten ihn aus dem Haus; **to run sb off his feet** (*inf*) jdn ständig auf Trab halten (*inf*); **she is absolutely run off her feet** (*inf*) sie ist ständig auf Trab (*inf*); **to run sb into debt** jdn in Schulden stürzen → **earth, ground**[1]

d = cause to flow **to run water into a bath** Wasser in die Badewanne einlaufen lassen; **I'll run you a bath** ich lasse dir ein Bad einlaufen; **he runs his words together** bei ihm fließen alle Wörter ineinander über

e = transport *person, thing* fahren, bringen; **I'll run you to the station** ich fahre Sie zum Bahnhof

f = drive *vehicle* fahren; **he ran the car into the garage/a tree** er fuhr das Auto in die Garage/

gegen einen Baum; **he runs a Rolls** er fährt einen Rolls Royce

g ▢ buses, trains ▢ unterhalten; *extra buses, trains* einsetzen; **this company runs a bus service** diese Firma unterhält einen Busdienst; **they run trains to London every hour** es besteht stündlicher Zugverkehr nach London; **how many machines does this factory run?** wie viele Maschinen laufen in dieser Fabrik?

h ▢ horse ▢ laufen lassen

i ▢ candidate ▢ aufstellen

j ▢ = operate ▢ *machine, engine* betreiben; *computer* laufen lassen; *software* benutzen; *program* laden; (*person*) bedienen; **to run a radio off the mains** ein Radio auf Netz laufen lassen; **it would be cheaper to run the heating on gas** es wäre billiger, mit Gas zu heizen; **I can't afford to run a car** ich kann es mir nicht leisten, ein Auto zu unterhalten; **this car is cheap to run** dieses Auto ist billig im Unterhalt; **can you run SuperText 3 on your computer?** läuft Super-Text 3 auf deinem Computer?

k ▢ = conduct ▢ *experiment, test* durchführen

l ▢ = be responsible for ▢ (= *manage*) *business, hotel* führen, leiten; *shop* führen; *mine* führen, leiten; (= *organize*) *course of study, competition* veranstalten, durchführen; (= *be in charge of*) *course, competition, department, project* leiten; **a well-run hotel** ein gut geführtes Hotel; **he runs a small hotel in the village** er hat ein kleines Hotel im Dorf; **to run a house** einen Haushalt führen; **a house which is easy to run** ein Haus, das leicht in Schuss gehalten werden kann; **I want to run my own life** ich möchte mein eigenes Leben leben; **she's the one who really runs everything** sie ist diejenige, die den Laden schmeißt (*inf*); **I'm running this show!** (*inf*) ich bestimme, was gemacht wird

m ▢ = smuggle ▢ *guns etc* schmuggeln

n ▢ = move ▢ **to run one's fingers over the piano keys** die Finger über die (Klavier)tasten gleiten lassen; **to run one's finger down a list** mit dem Finger eine Liste durchgehen; **to run one's fingers/a comb through one's hair** sich (*dat*) mit den Fingern/einem Kamm durch die Haare fahren; **to run one's eye over a page** eine Seite überfliegen; **he ran the vacuum cleaner over the carpet** er ging mit dem Staubsauger über den Teppich

o ▢ = put ▢ *rope, road* führen; *piece of elastic, line, ditch* ziehen; *pipe, wires* (ver)legen; (*above ground*) führen; **to run a rope round a tree** ein Seil um einen Baum legen

p ▢ = thrust ▢ **he ran a sword into his side** er stieß ihm das Schwert in die Seite, er durchbohrte ihn mit dem Schwert

q ▢ = publish ▢ (*Press*) *article, series* bringen

r ▢ = present ▢ *film* zeigen, bringen; (*Comm*) *line* verkaufen; **the supermarket is running a new line in exotic fruit** im Supermarkt werden jetzt exotische Früchte angeboten

4 – PHRASAL VERBS

▶ **run about** (*Brit*) or **around** � (*lit, fig*) herumlaufen or -rennen; **to run around with sb** sich mit jdm herumtreiben; **I'm not going to run about** or **around after you cleaning up** ich putze doch nicht dauernd hinter dir her

▶ **run across** ▢ **a** (*lit*) hinüberlaufen or -rennen **b** (= *go to see*) kurz rüberlaufen or -rennen (*to zu*) ▢ +*prep obj* (= *meet*) *person* zufällig treffen; (= *find*) *object, reference* stoßen auf (+*acc*)

▶ **run after** ▢ **to come running after** hinterherlaufen or -rennen ▢ +*prep obj* nachlaufen or -rennen (+*dat*); **I'm not going to spend the rest of my days running after you!** (*fig*) ich denke gar nicht daran, nur immer für dich da zu sein!

▶ **run along** ▢ laufen, rennen; (= *go away*) gehen; **run along!** nun geht mal schön!

▶ **run around** ▢ = **run about**

▶ **run at** ▢ +*prep obj* zu- or loslaufen auf (+*acc*); (= *attack*) losstürzen auf (+*acc*)

▶ **run away** ▢ **a** (*child, animal*) weglaufen, wegrennen; (*person*) weglaufen; (*horse*) durch-

gehen; **to run away from home** von zu Hause weglaufen; **don't run away, I need your advice** (*inf*) gehen Sie nicht weg, ich möchte Sie um Rat fragen; **run away and play!** geht (mal schön) spielen **b** (*water*) auslaufen ▢ *sep water* auslaufen lassen

▶ **run away with** ▢ +*prep obj* (= *use up*) *funds, money, resources* verschlucken (*inf*), verbrauchen; (= *steal*) *money, object* durchgehen or durchbrennen mit (*inf*); (*Sport etc*: = *win easily*) *race, prize* spielend gewinnen; **don't run away with the idea that ...** (*fig*) kommen Sie nur nicht auf den Gedanken, dass ...; **he lets his imagination/enthusiasm run away with him** seine Fantasie or Phantasie/seine Begeisterung geht leicht mit ihm durch

▶ **run back** ▢ (*lit*) zurücklaufen, zurückrennen; **she'll come running back** sie wird reumütig zurückkommen ▢ *sep* **a** *person* zurückfahren or -bringen **b** (= *rewind*) *tape, film* zurückspulen

▶ **run down** ▢ **a** (*lit: person*) hinunterlaufen or -rennen **b** (*watch, clock*) ablaufen; (*battery*) leer werden; **to let stocks run down** das Lager leer werden lassen; (*deliberately*) die Vorräte abbauen ▢ *sep* **a** (= *knock down*) umfahren; (= *run over*) überfahren **b** (*Naut*) *ship* rammen; (*in battle*) versenken **c** (= *limit, reduce*) *factory, shop* (allmählich) auflösen; *department, stocks, staff* abbauen; *battery* zu stark belasten **d** (= *disparage*) schlecht machen, runtermachen (*inf*) **e** (= *pursue and capture*) *criminal, stag* zur Strecke bringen; *person* ausfindig machen

▶ **run in** ▢ (*lit*) hineinlaufen or -rennen ▢ *sep* **a** *car* einfahren **b** (*inf:* = *arrest*) sich (*dat*) schnappen

▶ **run into** ▢ +*prep obj* (= *meet*) zufällig treffen; (= *collide with*) rennen/fahren gegen; **to run into difficulties/trouble** Schwierigkeiten/Ärger bekommen; **to run into problems** auf Probleme stoßen; **to run into danger/debt** in Gefahr/Schulden geraten → *also* **run 2 h**

▶ **run off** ▢ = **run away** ▢ ▢ *sep* **a** *water* ablassen **b** (= *reproduce*) *copy* abziehen **c** (*Sport*) **to run off the heats** die Ausscheidungskämpfe durchführen **d** *excess weight* sich (*dat*) ablaufen or abrennen

▶ **run on** ▢ **a** (*lit*) weiterlaufen, weiterrennen **b** (*fig: in speaking*) **he does run on so!** er redet wie ein Buch!; **it ran on for four hours** das zog sich über vier Stunden hin **c** (*letters*) verbunden sein; (*words*) fortlaufend geschrieben sein; (*line of type*) ohne Absatz gedruckt sein **d** (*time*) weitergehen ▢ *sep letters* verbinden; *words* fortlaufend schreiben; *line of type* ohne Absatz drucken

▶ **run out** ▢ **a** (*person*) hinauslaufen or -rennen; (*rope, chain*) ablaufen; (*liquid*) herauslaufen; (*through leak*) auslaufen **b** (= *come to an end, lease, contract, period of time*) ablaufen; (*money, supplies*) ausgehen, zu Ende gehen; **my patience is finally running out** mir geht langsam die Geduld aus ▢ *sep* **a** *rope, chain* abwickeln **b** (*Cricket*) ausschlagen (*während der Schlagmann seinen Lauf macht*)

▶ **run out of** ▢ +*prep obj* **he ran out of supplies/money/patience** ihm gingen die Vorräte/ging das Geld/die Geduld aus; **she ran out of time** sie hatte keine Zeit mehr; **we're running out of time** wir haben nicht mehr viel Zeit

▶ **run over** ▢ **a** (*to neighbour etc*) kurz hinüberlaufen or hinübergehen or rübergehen (*inf*) **b** (*overflow: liquid, container*) überlaufen **c** (*Rad, TV etc*) **the play ran over by 10 minutes** das Stück hatte 10 Minuten Überlänge; **we're running over** wir überziehen ▢ +*prep obj story, part in play, details* durchgehen; *text, notes* durchsehen; **I'll run over your part with you** ich gehe Ihre Rolle kurz mit Ihnen durch ▢ *sep* (*in vehicle*) überfahren

▶ **run round** ▢ (*esp Brit*) kurz vorbeigehen; **to run round and see sb** kurz bei jdm vorbeigehen → *also* **run about**

▶ **run through** ▢ (*lit*) durchlaufen ▢ +*prep obj* **a** (= *use up*) *money, fortune* durchbringen **b** (= *rehearse*) *piece of music, play* durchspielen; *ceremony, part, list* durchgehen **c** = **run over** ▢ +*prep obj sep* **to run sb through (with a sword)** jdn (mit einem Schwert) durchbohren

▶ **run to** ▢ +*prep obj* **a** (= *afford*) **I can't run to a new car** ich kann mir kein neues Auto leisten; **the funds won't run to a party** die Finanzen reichen nicht für eine Party **b** (= *amount to*) **the poem runs to several hundred lines** das Gedicht geht über mehrere hundert Zeilen

▶ **run up** ▢ (*lit*, = *climb quickly*) hinauflaufen; (= *approach quickly*) hinlaufen or -rennen (*to zu*); **to run up against difficulties** auf Schwierigkeiten stoßen ▢ *sep* **a** *flag* hissen, hochziehen; **they ran the flag up (the mast)** sie hissten die Fahne **b** (= *incur*) machen; **to run up a bill** eine Rechnung zusammenkommen lassen; **to run up a debt** Schulden machen **c** (= *sew quickly*) schnell zusammennähen

run: runabout N (= *car*) kleiner Flitzer (*inf*); (= *boat*) kleines Motorboot; **runaround** N (*inf*) **to give sb the ~** jdn an der Nase herumführen (*inf*); **to get the ~ (from sb)** (von jdm) an der Nase herumgeführt werden (*inf*)

runaway ['rʌnəweɪ] N Ausreißer(in) *m(f)* ▢ ADJ *slave* entlaufen; *person, couple, horse* durchgebrannt (*inf*), ausgerissen; **a ~ car/train** ein Auto/ein Zug, das/der sich selbstständig gemacht hat; **the ~ child** der kleine Ausreißer; **they planned a ~ wedding** sie beschlossen, wegzulaufen und zu heiraten **b** (*fig, = unstoppable*) *winner* überragend; *inflation* unkontrollierbar; **a ~ success** ein Riesenerfolg *m*, ein voller Erfolg; **the ~ bestseller** der mit Abstand erfolgreichste Bestseller; **he had a ~ victory** er hatte einen sehr leichten Sieg; **she was the ~ winner of the championship** sie gewann die Meisterschaften mit großem Abstand

runback ['rʌnbæk] N (*Tennis*) Auslauf *m* hinter der Grundlinie

rundown ['rʌndaʊn] N **a** (*of factory, shop*) (allmähliche) Abbau *m* **b** (*of department, stock, personnel*) Abbau *m* **b** (*inf*, = *report*) Bericht *m*, Zusammenfassung *f*; **to give sb a ~ on sth** jdn über etw (*acc*) informieren, jdm einen Bericht über etw (*acc*) geben

run-down [ˌrʌn'daʊn] ADJ **a** (= *dilapidated*) heruntergekommen **b** (= *tired*) abgespannt **c** (= *inefficient*) *industry, service* heruntergekommen; *battery* leer

rune [ruːn] N Rune *f*; **to read the ~s** (*Brit, fig*) die Vorzeichen deuten

rung¹ [rʌŋ] *ptp of* **ring²**

rung² N (*of ladder, also fig*) Sprosse *f*; (*of chair*) Querstab *m*

runic ['ruːnɪk] ADJ runisch, Runen-; **~ symbol** Runenzeichen *nt*

run-in ['rʌnɪn] N (*inf*, = *argument*) Streit *m*

runner ['rʌnə*] N **a** (= *athlete*) Läufer(in) *m(f)*; (= *horse*) Rennpferd *nt*; (= *messenger*) Bote *m*, Botin *f*, Laufbursche *m*; (= *smuggler*) Schmuggler(in) *m(f)*; **(Bow Street) Runners** (*Brit, Hist*) ≈ Büttel *pl*; **it's a good ~, this car** (*inf*) das Auto läuft wirklich einwandfrei **b** (*on sledge, skate*) Kufe *f*; (*for curtain*) Vorhangröllchen *nt*; (*for drawer, machine part*) Laufschiene *f* **c** (= *carpet, for table*) Läufer *m* **d** (*Bot*) Ausläufer *m* **e** **to do a ~** (*Brit inf*) die Fliege machen (*sl*)

runner bean N (*Brit*) Stangenbohne *f*

runner-up ['rʌnər'ʌp] N Zweite(r), Zweitplazierte(r) *mf*; **the runners-up** die weiteren Plätze; (*in competition*) die weiteren Gewinner

running ['rʌnɪŋ] N **a** Laufen *nt*, Rennen *nt*; **~ style, style of ~** Laufstil *m*; **~ gear** Laufausrüstung *f*; **he started professional ~ eight years ago** er begann seine Laufkarriere vor acht Jahren; **to make the ~** (*lit, fig*) das Rennen machen; **to be in the ~ (for sth)** im Rennen (für etw) liegen; **out of the ~** aus dem Rennen; **to take up the ~** (*lit, fig*) sich an die Spitze setzen **b** (= *functioning: of machine, vehicle*) Laufen *nt*

c (= management, of business, hotel) Führung f, Leitung f; (of country, shop) Führung f; (of mine) Betrieb m; (of school, organization, newspaper) Leitung f; (= organization: of course, competition) Veranstaltung f, Durchführung f; (= being in charge: of course, competition, department, project) Leitung f

d (= maintenance: of machine) Unterhaltung f **e** (= smuggling) Schmuggel m

ADJ a (= flowing) water, stream fließend; tap, nose laufend; eyes tränend; ~ **sore** (Med) eiternde Wunde; (fig) Eiterbeule f; ~ **cold** schwerer Schnupfen; **hot and cold** ~ **water** fließend warmes und kaltes Wasser

b (= current) prices momentan

ADV hintereinander; **(for) five days** ~ fünf Tage hintereinander; **for the third year** ~ im dritten Jahr hintereinander; **sales have fallen for the third year** ~ die Verkaufszahlen sind seit drei Jahren rückläufig

running: running account N (Fin) laufendes Konto; **running battle** N (Mil) Gefecht, bei dem eine Seite immer weiter zurückgedrängt wird (fig) Kleinkrieg m; **to fight a** ~ (fig) einen Kleinkrieg führen; **running board** N Trittbrett nt; **running commentary** N (Rad, TV) fortlaufender Kommentar; **to give sb a** ~ **(on sth)** (fig) jdm fortlaufend Erläuterungen geben; **we don't need a** ~ (inf) wir brauchen keinen Kommentar; **running costs** PL Betriebskosten pl; (of car) Unterhaltskosten pl; **running expenses** PL laufende Kosten pl; **running head** N (Typ) Kolumnentitel m; **running joke** N it was a ~ **between them** es war ein ständiger Witz bei ihnen; **running jump** N Sprung m mit Anlauf; **to take a** ~ **at sth** mit Anlauf über etw (acc) springen; **go and take a** ~ (Brit inf) du kannst mich gern haben (inf); **running knot** N Schlaufenknoten m; **running light** N (Naut) Positionslampe f, Fahrlicht nt; **running mate** N (US, Pol) Kandidat für die Vizepräsidentschaft; **running order** N in ~ betriebsbereit; **running shoe** N Rennschuh m; **running speed** N (Tech) Umlaufgeschwindigkeit f; (Mot) Fahrgeschwindigkeit f; **running stitch** N (Sew) Vorstich m, Reihstich m; **running tally** N laufende Summe; **running text** N fortlaufender Text; **running time** N (of film) Laufzeit f; **running title** N = running head; **running total** N laufende Summe; **to keep a** ~ **of sth** (lit, fig) etw fortlaufend festhalten; **running track** N Aschenbahn f

runny ['rʌnɪ] ADJ (+er) egg, wax flüssig; nose laufend; eyes wässerig, tränend; honey, sauce, consistency dünnflüssig; **I've got a** ~ **nose** mir läuft die Nase, meine Nase läuft

run: runoff N (Sport) Entscheidungslauf m, Stechen nt; **run-of-the-mill** ADJ durchschnittlich, gewöhnlich; theme, novel Feld-Wald-Wiesen- (inf); **run-on (line)** N fortlaufende Zeile; **run-out** N (Ski) Auslauf m; **run-proof** ADJ tights etc laufmaschenfest

runt [rʌnt] N kleinstes Ferkel (eines Wurfes); (pej) Wicht m; (despicable) Fiesling m (inf)

run: run-through N Durchgehen nt; **let's have a final** ~ gehen wir das noch einmal durch; **to have a** ~ **of sth** etw durchgehen; **run-up** N (Sport) Anlauf m; (fig) Vorbereitungszeit f; **in the** ~ **to the election** in der Zeit vor der Wahl; **runway** N (Aviat) Start- und Landebahn f, Runway f or m

rupee [ruːˈpiː] N Rupie f

rupture ['rʌptʃə] **N** (lit, fig) Bruch m; (Pol, of relations) Abbruch m **VT** brechen; **to** ~ **oneself** (inf) sich (dat) einen Bruch heben (inf) **VI** brechen

ruptured ['rʌptʃəd] ADJ tank, pipe geplatzt; (Med) organ, tendon gerissen; blood vessel geplatzt

rural ['rʊərəl] ADJ **a** (= of the countryside) ländlich; poverty, crime auf dem Land; ~ **land** ländlicher Raum; ~ **development programme** or (US) **program** dünnflüssig Entwicklungsprogramm; ~ **worker** Landarbeiter(in) m(f); ~ **doctor** Landarzt m/-ärztin f; ~ **policeman** Dorfpolizist m; ~ **England** das ländliche England; **Ireland used to**

be largely a ~ **country** Irland war früher hauptsächlich ein Agrarstaat **b** (= rustic) landscape bäuerlich; accent dörflich

rural: rural depopulation N Abwanderung f der Landbevölkerung, Landflucht f; **rural deprivation** N Strukturschwäche f in ländlichen Gebieten; **rural district** N (Brit, Admin) Landbezirk m; **rural life** N Landleben nt; **rural planning** N Raumplanung f in ländlichen Gebieten; **rural population** N Landbevölkerung f

ruse [ruːz] N List f

rush¹ [rʌʃ] **N a** (= rapid movement, of crowd) Andrang m, Gedränge nt; (of air) Stoß m; (Mil, = attack) Sturm m; **he was caught in the** ~ **for the door** die zu Tür drängende Menge riss ihn mit; **they made a** ~ **for the door** sie drängten zur Tür; **there was a** ~ **for the empty seats** alles stürzte sich auf die leeren Sitze; **there's been a** ~ **on these goods** diese Waren sind rasend weggegangen; **we have a** ~ **on in the office just now** bei uns im Büro herrscht zur Zeit Hochbetrieb; **the Christmas** ~ der Weihnachtsbetrieb; **we've had a** ~ **of orders** wir hatten eine Flut von Aufträgen; **there was a** ~ **of water** Wasser strömte or schoss herein/heraus etc; **water streamed out in a** ~ das Wasser schoss in einem Schwall heraus; **a** ~ **of blood to the head** Blutandrang m im Kopf; **a** ~ **of panic** eine plötzliche Panik; **a** ~ **of emotion** eine Gefühlsaufwallung ~ **gold rush**

b (= hurry) Eile f; (stronger) Hetze f, Hast f; **the** ~ **of modern life** die Hetze des modernen Lebens; **to be in a** ~ in Eile sein; **I had a** ~ **to get here on time** ich musste ganz schön hetzen, um rechtzeitig hier zu sein; **I did it in a** ~ ich habe es sehr schnell or hastig gemacht; **what's (all) the** ~? wozu die Eile/Hetzerei?; **is there any** ~ **for this?** eilt das?; **it all happened in such a** ~ das ging alles so plötzlich

c rushes PL (Film) erste Kopie

VI (= hurry) eilen; (stronger) hetzen, hasten; (= run) stürzen; (wind) brausen; (water) schießen, stürzen; (= make rushing noise) rauschen; **they** ~**ed to help her** sie eilten ihr zu Hilfe; **I** ~**ed to her side** ich eilte an ihre Seite; **I'm** ~**ing to finish it** ich beeile mich, es fertig zu machen; **don't** ~, **take your time** überstürzen Sie nichts, lassen Sie sich Zeit; **you shouldn't just go** ~**ing into things** Sie sollten die Dinge nicht so überstürzen; **to** ~ **through** (book) hastig lesen; meal hastig essen; museum, town hetzen durch; work hastig erledigen; **to** ~ **past** (person) vorbeistürzen; (vehicle) vorbeischießen; **to** ~ **in/out/back** etc hinein-/hinaus-/zurückstürzen or -stürmen etc; **the ambulance** ~**ed to the scene** der Krankenwagen raste zur Unfallstelle; **to** ~ **to sb's defence** (Brit) or **defense** (US) (lit, fig) jdm zur Seite eilen; **to** ~ **into print** vorzeitig veröffentlichen; **the blood** ~**ed to his face** das Blut schoss ihm ins Gesicht; **memories** ~**ed into his mind** Erinnerungen schossen ihm durch den Kopf

VT a to ~ **sb to hospital** jdn schnellstens ins Krankenhaus bringen; **they** ~**ed more troops to the front** sie schickten eilends mehr Truppen an die Front; **they** ~**ed him out (of the room)** sie brachten ihn eilends aus dem Zimmer; **they** ~**ed the bill through Parliament** sie peitschten die Gesetzesvorlage durch das Parlament; **to** ~ **a book into print** ein Buch eilends in Druck geben

b (= force to hurry) hetzen, drängen; **don't** ~ **me!** hetz mich nicht; **he won't be** ~**ed** er lässt sich nicht drängen or hetzen; **to be** ~**ed off one's feet** dauernd auf Trab sein (inf); **to** ~ **sb off his feet** jdn dauernd auf Trab halten (inf); **to** ~ **sb into a decision** jdn zu einer hastigen Entscheidung treiben; **to** ~ **sb into doing sth** jdn dazu treiben, etw überstürzt zu tun

c (= charge at) stürmen; fence zustürmen auf (+acc); **the mob** ~**ed the line of policemen** der Mob stürmte auf den Polizeikordon zu; **to** ~ **one's fences** (fig) die Sache überstürzen

d (= do hurriedly) job, task hastig machen, schnell machen; (= do badly) schludern bei

(pej); **you can't** ~ **this sort of work** für solche Arbeit muss man sich (dat) Zeit lassen

e (inf, = charge exorbitantly) schröpfen (inf); **what were you** ~**ed for it?** wie viel haben sie dir dafür abgeknöpft? (inf)

▶ **rush about** (Brit) or **around** VI herumhasten or -hetzen

▶ **rush at** VI +prep obj **a** (lit) losstürzen auf (+acc), sich stürzen auf (+acc) **b** (fig) **he tends to rush at things** er neigt dazu, die Dinge überstürzt zu machen

▶ **rush down** VI (person) hinuntereilen; (very fast, also water etc) hinunterstürzen

▶ **rush out** **VI** hinauseilen; (very fast) hinausstürzen; **he rushed out and bought one** er kaufte sofort eines **VT** sep order eilends wegschicken; statement, book schnell(stens) veröffentlichen; troops, supplies eilends hintransportieren

▶ **rush through** VT sep order durchjagen; goods, supplies eilends durchschleusen; legislation, bill durchpeitschen; **they rushed medical supplies through to him** sie schickten eilends Medikamente zu ihm

▶ **rush up** **VI** (lit) hinaufeilen; (very fast) hinaufstürzen **VT** sep help, reinforcements eilends schicken

rush² N (Bot) Binse f; **in the** ~**es** im Schilf

rushed [rʌʃt] ADJ **a** (= hurried) meal hastig; decision übereilt **b** (= busy) gehetzt

rush: rush hour(s) N(PL) Hauptverkehrszeit f, Stoßzeit(en) f(pl), Rushhour f; **rush-hour traffic** Stoßverkehr m; **rush job** N eiliger Auftrag; (pej, = bad work) Schluderarbeit f (inf); **can you do a** ~ **for me?** können Sie das ganz schnell für mich machen?; **rushlight** N aus Binsen und Talg hergestellte Kerze; **rush mat, rush matting** N Binsenmatte f; **rush order** N (Comm) Eilauftrag m

rusk [rʌsk] N Zwieback m

russet ['rʌsɪt] **N a** (= colour) gelbliches Rotbraun **b** (= apple) Boskop m **ADJ** rostfarben

Russia ['rʌʃə] N Russland nt

Russian ['rʌʃən] **ADJ** russisch **N a** Russe m, Russin f **b** (Ling) Russisch nt; ~ **teacher** Russischlehrer(in) m(f)

Russian: Russian doll N russische Puppe; **Russian dressing** N pikant gewürzte Majonäse mit gehackten Salzgurken; **Russian Federation** N the ~ die Russische Föderation; **Russian leather** N Juchten nt; **Russian Orthodox** ADJ (Rel) russisch-orthodox; **the** ~ **Church** die russisch-orthodoxe Kirche; **Russian roulette** N russisches Roulette; **Russian salad** N russischer Salat

Russification [ˌrʌsɪfɪˈkeɪʃən] N Russifizierung f

Russky ['rʌskɪ] (pej) **N** Iwan m, Russki m; **the Russkies** der Iwan **ADJ** russisch

Russo- ['rʌsəʊ] PREF russisch-; ~**Japanese** russisch-japanisch

rust [rʌst] **N** Rost m; (Bot) Brand m; **covered in** ~ völlig verrostet **VI** (also **rust-coloured**) rostfarben **VT** (lit) rosten lassen **VI** rosten; (talent) verkümmern; (brain, language) (ein)rosten

▶ **rust in** VI (screw) einrosten

▶ **rust over** VI verrosten; **to be rusted over** verrostet sein

▶ **rust through** **VI** durchrosten **VT** sep durchrosten lassen

▶ **rust up** VI festrosten

rust: Rust Belt N (US) **the** ~ ≈ das Industriegebiet; **the** ~ **states of America's industrial heartland** die Staaten in Amerikas industriellem Zentrum; **rust bucket** N (inf, = car, boat) Rostlaube f (inf); **rust converter** N Rostumwandler m

rusted ['rʌstɪd] ADJ (esp US) rostig

rustic ['rʌstɪk] **N** Bauer m, Bäuerin f **ADJ a** (= rural) bäuerlich; furniture, style rustikal; ~ **novel** Bauernroman m **b** (pej, = crude) derb, bäurisch

rusticate ['rʌstɪkeɪt] VT **a** (*form, liter,* = *send to country*) aufs Land schicken; (= *make rustic*) bäurisch machen **b** (*Brit, Univ*) vorübergehend von der Universität verweisen

rusticity [rʌs'tɪsɪtɪ] N Ländlichkeit *f*

rustiness ['rʌstɪnɪs] N Rostigkeit *f*; (*fig*) eingerostete Kenntnisse *pl* (*of* in +*dat*)

rustle ['rʌsl] **N** Rascheln *nt*; (*of foliage*) Rauschen *nt* **VI** (*leaves, silk, papers*) rascheln; (*foliage, skirts*) rauschen; **the wind ~d through the leaves** der Wind rauschte in den Blättern; (*on the ground*) der Wind raschelte mit den Blättern **VT** **a** *paper, skirt, leaves on ground etc* rascheln mit; (*wind*) *leaves on tree* rauschen in (+*dat*) **b** (= *steal*) *cattle, sheep* klauen (*inf*)

▶ **rustle up** VT *sep* (*inf*) *meal* improvisieren (*inf*); *money* auftreiben; **can you rustle up a cup of coffee?** können Sie eine Tasse Kaffee beschaffen?

rustler ['rʌslə'] N (= *cattle thief*) Viehdieb(in) *m(f)*

rustling ['rʌslɪŋ] **ADJ** *noise, leaves, paper* raschelnd; *skirt* rauschend **N** **a** (*of leaves, paper*) Rascheln *nt*; (*of material*) Rauschen *nt* **b** (= *cattle theft*) Viehdiebstahl *m*

rust: **rust perforation** N Durchrosten *nt*; **rustproof** **ADJ** rostfrei **VT** einem Rostschutzverfahren unterziehen; **rustproofing** N (= *substance*) Rostschutzmittel *nt*; (*applied to surface etc*) Rostschutz *m*; **rust resistant** ADJ nicht rostend; **rust-through** N Durchrosten *nt*

rusty ['rʌstɪ] ADJ (+*er*) (*lit*) rostig; (*fig*) *mind, maths, language* eingerostet; *talent* verkümmert; **I'm a bit ~** ich bin etwas aus der Übung; **to get ~** (*lit*) verrosten; (*fig, person*) aus der Übung kommen; **~ brown** rostbraun

rut¹ [rʌt] (*Zool*) **N** Brunft *f*, Brunst *f* **VI** brunften, brunsten; **~ting call** Brunftschrei *m*; **~ting season** Brunftzeit *f*

rut² **N** (*in track, path*) Spur *f*, Furche *f*; (*fig:* = *routine*) Trott *m* (*inf*); **to be in a ~** (*fig*) im Trott sein (*inf*); **to get into a ~** (*fig*) in einen Trott geraten (*inf*); **to get out of a ~** (*fig*) aus dem Trott herauskommen (*inf*) **VT** furchen

rutabaga [ˌruːtəˈbeɪɡə] N (*US*) Steckrübe *f*

ruthenium [ruːˈθiːnɪəm] N (*Chem*) Ruthenium *nt*

ruthless ['ruːθlɪs] ADJ *person, deed* rücksichtslos; *cuts, treatment, self-analysis* schonungslos; *irony,* *sarcasm* unbarmherzig, schonungslos; **you'll have to be ~** man muss hart sein; **to be ~ in doing sth** etw ohne jede Rücksicht tun

ruthlessly ['ruːθlɪslɪ] ADV *suppress, crush* rücksichtlos, unbarmherzig; *criticize* schonungslos, unbarmherzig; **a ~ ambitious businessman** ein skrupellos ehrgeiziger Geschäftsmann

ruthlessness ['ruːθlɪsnɪs] N (*of person, deed*) Rücksichtslosigkeit *f*; (*of cuts, treatment*) Schonungslosigkeit *f*; (*of irony, sarcasm*) Unbarmherzigkeit *f*, Schonungslosigkeit *f*

RV **a** *abbr of* **Revised Version** **b** *abbr of* **recreational vehicle**

Rwanda [rʊˈændə] N Ruanda *nt*

Rwandan [rʊˈændən] **N** Ruander(in) *m(f)* **ADJ** ruandisch

rye [raɪ] N (= *grain*) Roggen *m*; (*US inf*) Roggenwhisky *m*, Rye(whisky) *m*; (= *bread*) Roggenbrot *nt*

rye: **rye bread** N Roggenbrot *nt*; **rye whisk(e)y** N Roggen- *or* Ryewhisky *m*

S

S, s [es] N S *nt*, s *nt*

S **a** abbr of **south** S **b** abbr of **Saint** St **c** abbr of **small**

s (*Brit, old*) abbr of **shilling**

's **a** he's *etc* = he is/has what's = what is/has/ does? **b** (*genitive*) John's book Johns Buch; my brother's car das Auto meines Bruders; at the Browns' bei den Browns; at the butcher's beim Fleischer **c** let's = let us

SA **a** abbr of **South Africa** **b** abbr of **South America** **c** abbr of **South Australia** **d** abbr of **Salvation Army**

sab [sæb] N (*Brit, inf*) Jagdsaboteur(in) *m(f)* (*bei Fuchsjagden*)

Sabbatarian [ˌsæbəˈtɛərɪən] N strenger Befürworter des Sonntagsgebots *or* (*Jewish*) Sabbatgebots

Sabbath [ˈsæbəθ] N Sabbat *m*; (*non-Jewish*) Sonntag *m* → **witch**

sabbatical [səˈbætɪkəl] ADJ **a** (*Rel*) Sabbat- **b** (*Univ*) he is on ~ leave er hat akademischen Urlaub *or* Forschungsurlaub **N** (*Univ*) akademischer Urlaub, Forschungsurlaub *m*; to have a/be on ~ Forschungsurlaub *or* akademischen Urlaub haben

sabbatical term N (*Univ*) ≈ Forschungssemester *nt*

sabbatical year N **a** (*Rel*) Sabbatjahr *nt* **b** (*Univ*) Forschungsjahr *nt*

sabbing [ˈsæbɪŋ] N (*Brit, inf*) Jagdsabotage *f* (*bei Fuchsjagden*)

saber N (*US*) = **sabre**

Sabine [ˈsæbaɪn] ADJ sabinisch **N** Sabiner(in) *m(f)*

sable [ˈseɪbl] **N** Zobel *m*; (= *fur*) Zobelfell *nt or* -pelz *m*; (*liter, = colour*) Schwarz *nt* ADJ (*liter, = black*) schwarz; ~ coat Zobelmantel *m*

sabot [ˈsæbəʊ] N Holzschuh *m*

sabotage [ˈsæbətɑːʒ] **N** Sabotage *f* **VT** (*lit, fig*) sabotieren

saboteur [ˌsæbəˈtɜː] N Saboteur(in) *m(f)*

sabre, (*US*) **saber** [ˈseɪbə] N Säbel *m*; **sabre: sabre cut** N Säbelhiebwunde *f*; (*duelling fraternity*) Schmiss *m*; **sabre-rattler** N Säbelrassler(in) *m(f)*; **sabre-rattling** N Säbelrasseln *nt*; **sabre-toothed tiger** N Säbelzahntiger *m*

sac [sæk] N (*Anat*) Sack *m*; (= *pollen sac*) Staubbeutel *m*

saccharin(e) [ˈsækərɪn] N Sa(c)charin *nt*

saccharine [ˈsækəriːn] ADJ Sa(c)charin-; (*fig liter*) zuckersüß; ~ sweetener Sa(c)charinsüßstoff *m*

sacerdotal [ˌsæsəˈdəʊtl] ADJ priesterlich

sachet [ˈsæʃeɪ] N Beutel *m*; (*of powder*) Päckchen *nt*; (*of shampoo, cream*) Briefchen *nt*; (= *lavender sachet*) Kissen *nt*

sack¹ [sæk] **N** **a** Sack *m*; **2 ~s of coal** 2 Säcke *or* Sack Kohlen; **to buy sth by the ~** etw sackweise *or* in Säcken kaufen; **like a ~ of potatoes** (*fig*) wie ein Mehlsack *m*; (= *dismissal*) **b** (*inf, = dismissal*) Entlassung *f*, Rausschmiss *m* (*inf*); **to get the ~** rausgeschmissen werden (*inf*), rausfliegen (*inf*); **to give sb the ~** jdn rausschmeißen (*inf*); **it's the ~ for him** er wird rausgeschmissen (*inf*),

er fliegt raus (*inf*) **c** (*inf, = bed*) **to hit the ~ sich in die Falle** *or* **Klappe hauen** (*sl*) **VT** **a** (= *put in sacks*) einsacken **b** (*inf, = dismiss*) rausschmeißen (*inf*), entlassen

sack² **N** (= *pillage*) Plünderung *f* **VT** plündern

sack³ N (*old*) Sherry *m*

sackbut [ˈsækbʌt] N (*Hist*) Posaune *f*

sackcloth [ˈsækklɒθ] N Sackleinen *nt*; in ~ and ashes in Sack und Asche

sackful [ˈsækfʊl] N Sack *m*; two ~s of potatoes zwei Sack Kartoffeln

sacking [ˈsækɪŋ] N **a** (= *material*) Sackleinen *nt* **b** (*inf, = dismissal*) Entlassung *f*

sack: sack race N (*as contest*) Sackhüpfen *nt*; **sack racing** N Sackhüpfen *nt*

sacral [ˈseɪkrəl] ADJ **a** (*Rel*) sakral **b** (*Anat*) Kreuzbein-; ~ vertebrae Kreuzbeinwirbel *pl*

sacrament [ˈsækrəmənt] N Sakrament *nt*; the (Blessed *or* Holy) Sacrament das heilige Sakrament; to receive the Holy Sacrament die heilige Kommunion *or* (*Protestant*) das heilige Abendmahl empfangen; the last ~s die Sterbesakramente *pl*

sacramental [ˌsækrəˈmentl] ADJ *vows, rites, significance* sakramental; ~ wine Opferwein *m*

sacred [ˈseɪkrɪd] ADJ **a** (= *holy*) heilig; *building* sakral; a statue ~ to Venus eine dem Venus geweihte Statue **b** (= *religious*) art, theme, rite sakral; *music, poetry* geistlich; ~ and profane geistlich und weltlich **c** (= *sacrosanct*) ~ duty heilige Pflicht; ~ to the memory of ... zum Gedenken *or* Andenken an (+*acc*) ...; these memories are ~ to me diese Erinnerungen sind mir heilig; she saw motherhood as woman's ~ calling sie sah Mutterschaft als die heilige Berufung einer jeden Frau an; is nothing ~? (*inf*) ist denn nichts mehr heilig?

sacred cow N (*lit, fig*) heilige Kuh

Sacred Heart N Herz *nt* Jesu

sacrifice [ˈsækrɪfaɪs] **N** (*lit, fig*) Opfer *nt*; (= *thing sacrificed also*) Opfergabe *f*; to make a ~ of sb/ sth jdn/etw opfern *or* zum Opfer bringen; to make ~s (*lit, fig*) Opfer bringen; what a ~ (to make)! welch ein Opfer!; the ~ of quality to speed wenn Qualität der Geschwindigkeit geopfert wird *or* zum Opfer fällt; to sell sth at a ~ (*inf*) etw mit Verlust verkaufen **VT** opfern (*sth to sb* jdm etw)

sacrificial [ˌsækrɪˈfɪʃəl] ADJ Opfer-; ~ rite Opferritus *m*, Opferritual *nt*

sacrificial lamb N Opferlamm *nt*

sacrilege [ˈsækrɪlɪdʒ] N Sakrileg *nt*; (*fig also*) Frevel *m*; that would be ~ das wäre ein Sakrileg *or* Frevel

sacrilegious [ˌsækrɪˈlɪdʒəs] ADJ (*lit*) gotteslästerlich, sakrilegisch (*geh*); (*fig*) frevelhaft, frevlerisch

sacristan [ˈsækrɪstən] N Sakristan(in) *m(f)*

sacristy [ˈsækrɪstɪ] N Sakristei *f*

sacrosanct [ˈsækrəʊˌsæŋkt] ADJ (*lit, fig*) sakrosankt

sacrum [ˈsækrəm] N Kreuzbein *nt*

SAD (*Med*) abbr of **seasonal affective disorder**

sad [sæd] ADJ (+*er*) **a** traurig; *loss* schmerzlich; *colour* trist; *disappointment* schlimm; *mistake, lack*

bedauerlich; to feel ~ traurig sein; he was ~ to see her go er war betrübt, dass sie wegging; it makes me ~ to think that ... der Gedanke betrübt mich, dass ...; to be ~ at heart (*liter*) zutiefst betrübt sein (*geh*); he left a ~der and wiser man er ging betrübt und geläutert weg; the ~ death of our father der schmerzliche Verlust unseres Vaters; how ~ for you! wie schrecklich für Sie!, wie traurig!; a ~ state of affairs eine traurige Angelegenheit; the ~ fact/truth is that ... die traurige Wahrheit ist, dass ...; ~ to say, ... (= *regrettably*) bedauerlicherweise ... **b** (*inf: = pathetic*) bedauernswert; what ~ people they must be if they have nothing better to do was für bedauernswerte Menschen, die nichts Besseres zu tun haben; she's a ~ case sie ist ein bedauernswerter Fall; it's pretty ~ stuff for a writer of his ability für einen Schriftsteller seines Formats ist das traurig

sadden [ˈsædn] VT betrüben

saddle [ˈsædl] **N** (*also of hill*) Sattel *m*; (*of meat*) Rücken *m*; to be in the ~ (*lit*) im Sattel sein; (*fig*) im Sattel sitzen **VT** **a** *horse* satteln **b** (*inf*) to ~ sb/oneself with sb/sth jdm/sich jdn/ etw aufhalsen (*inf*); to ~ sb/oneself with responsibilities jdm/sich Verantwortung aufbürden; to ~ sb/oneself with doubts jdn/sich mit Zweifeln belasten; to be/have been ~d with sb/ sth jdn/etw auf dem Hals *or* am Hals haben (*inf*); how did I get ~d with him? wie kommt es (nur), dass ich ihn am Hals habe?

▶ **saddle up** **VT** *sep* aufsatteln **VI** aufsatteln

saddle: saddle-backed ADJ *hill* sattelförmig; *pig, gull* mit sattelförmiger Markierung am Rücken; **saddlebag** N Satteltasche *f*; **saddlecloth** N Satteldecke *f*; **saddle horse** N Reitpferd *nt*

saddler [ˈsædlə] N Sattler(in) *m(f)*

saddle roof N Satteldach *nt*

saddlery [ˈsædlərɪ] N Sattlerei *f*; (= *articles*) Sattelzeug *nt*

saddle: saddle shoes PL (*US*) Sportschuhe *aus hellem Leder mit andersfarbigen Einsatz*; **saddle soap** N *Seife für die Behandlung von Sätteln*; **saddle sore** N wund gescheuerte Stelle; **saddle-sore** ADJ *person* wund geritten; to get ~ sich wund reiten

Sadducee [ˈsædjʊsiː] N Sadduzäer *m*

sad: sad-eyed ADJ traurig blickend *attr*; **sad-faced** ADJ traurig blickend *attr*, mit traurigem Gesichtsausdruck

sadism [ˈseɪdɪzəm] N Sadismus *m*

sadist [ˈseɪdɪst] N Sadist(in) *m(f)*

sadistic ADJ , **sadistically** ADV [səˈdɪstɪk, -əlɪ] sadistisch

sadly [ˈsædlɪ] ADV **a** (= *sorrowfully*) traurig; she will be ~ missed sie wird (uns/ihnen) allen sehr fehlen **b** (= *unfortunately*) bedauerlicherweise, leider; ~ (enough) he has ... bedauerlicherweise hat er ...; ~ for the dolphins, there are no regulations to protect them leider gibt es keine Bestimmungen zum Schutz der Delphine *or* Delfine **c** (= *regrettably, woefully*) bedauerlicherweise; he is ~ lacking in any sensitivity ihm fehlt absolut jegliches Feingefühl; the house had been

~ neglected es war traurig, wie vernachlässigt das Haus war; **to be ~ in need of sth** etw dringend benötigen *or* brauchen; **to be ~ mistaken** sich sehr *or* arg täuschen; **if you think you can hide the truth from us, you are ~ mistaken** wenn du glaubst, dass du uns die Wahrheit verheimlichen kannst, hast du dich sehr getäuscht

sadness ['sædnɪs] N Traurigkeit *f*; **our ~ at his death** unsere Trauer über seinen Tod

sadomasochism [ˌseɪdəʊ'mæsəʊkɪzəm] N Sadomasochismus *m*

sadomasochist [ˌseɪdəʊ'mæsəʊkɪst] N Sadomasochist(in) *m(f)*

s.a.e. abbr of **stamped addressed envelope**

safari [sə'fɑːrɪ] N Safari *f*; **to be/go on ~** eine Safari machen, auf Safari sein/gehen; **to go on ~ to Kenya** nach Kenia auf Safari fahren; **~ jacket** Safarijacke *f*; **~ park** Safaripark *m*

safarist [sə'fɑːrɪst] N Safariteilnehmer(in) *m(f)*

safe¹ [seɪf] N (for valuables) Safe *m or nt*, Panzerschrank *m*, Tresor *m*; (for meat) Fliegenschrank *m*

safe² ADJ (+er) **a** (= not in danger) sicher; (= out of danger) in Sicherheit; (= not injured) unverletzt; **to be ~ from sth/sb** vor jdm/etw sicher sein; **no girl is ~ with him** bei ihm ist kein Mädchen sicher; **to keep sth ~** etw sicher aufbewahren; **all the passengers/climbers are ~** alle Passagiere/Bergsteiger sind in Sicherheit *or* (not injured) sind unverletzt; **you're not ~ without a seat belt** es ist gefährlich *or* nicht sicher, ohne Gurt zu fahren; **~ journey!** gute Fahrt/Reise!; **~ journey home!** komm gut nach Hause!; **we've found him – is he ~?** wir haben ihn gefunden! – ist ihm etwas passiert?; **thank God you're ~** Gott sei Dank ist dir nichts passiert; **he was ~ at home all the time** er saß die ganze Zeit wohlbehalten zu Hause; **~ and sound** gesund und wohlbehalten; **the patient is ~ now** der Patient ist jetzt außer Gefahr; **my life's not ~ here** ich bin hier meines Lebens nicht sicher; **your reputation is ~** Ihr Ruf ist nicht in Gefahr; **the secret is ~ with me** bei mir ist das Geheimnis gut aufgehoben; **the thieves are now ~ in prison** die Diebe sind jetzt in sicherem Gewahrsam

b (= not likely to cause harm, not dangerous, not presenting risks) ungefährlich; (= stable, secure) building, roof etc sicher; **not ~** gefährlich; **this car is not ~ to drive** das Auto ist nicht verkehrssicher; **she is not ~ on the roads** sie ist eine Gefahr im Straßenverkehr; **is this beach ~ for bathing?** kann man an diesem Strand gefahrlos *or* ohne Gefahr baden?; **it is ~ to leave it open/tell him** man kann es unbesorgt *or* ohne weiteres auflassen/es ihm unbesorgt *or* ohne weiteres erzählen; **is it ~ to touch that/drive so fast/light a fire?** ist es auch nicht gefährlich, das anzufassen/so schnell zu fahren/ein Feuer anzumachen?; **it is ~ to eat/drink** das kann man gefahrlos essen/trinken; **the dog is ~ with children** der Hund tut Kindern nichts

c (= secure) place, hiding place sicher; **in a ~ place** an einem sicheren Ort

d (= reliable) job, contraceptive, driver sicher; mountain guide, method, player zuverlässig, verlässlich; **~ period** sichere *or* ungefährliche Zeit; **to be** *or* **have a ~ pair of hands** sicher und verlässlich sein; **in ~ hands** in sicheren Händen

e (= not likely to be/go wrong) investment, theory, choice, option sicher; policy vorsichtig, risikolos; estimate realistisch; **~ margin** Spielraum *m*; (Fin also) Reserve *f*; **it is ~ to assume** *or* **a ~ assumption that ...** man kann mit ziemlicher Sicherheit annehmen, dass ...; **it's a ~ guess** es ist so gut wie sicher; **they appointed a ~ man as headmaster** sie bestimmten einen gemäßigten Mann als Rektor; **he plays a ~ game (of tennis)** er spielt (Tennis) auf Sicherheit; **I think it's ~ to say ...** ich glaube, man kann wohl *or* ruhig sagen ...; **is it ~ to generalize?** kann man das ohne weiteres verallgemeinern?; **is it ~ to draw that conclusion?** kann man diesen Schluss so ohne weiteres ziehen?; **to be ~ in the knowl-**

edge that ... sich sicher fühlen, dass ...; **do you feel ~ just taking on three extra staff?** haben Sie keine Bedenken, wenn Sie nur drei extra Leute einstellen?; **just to be ~** *or* **on the ~ side** um ganz sicher zu sein, um sicherzugehen; **the ~st thing (to do) would be to wait here for her** das Sicherste wäre, hier auf sie zu warten; **it is a ~ bet that ...** man kann darauf wetten, dass ...; **to follow sb at a ~ distance** jdm in sicherem Abstand folgen; **better ~ than sorry** Vorsicht ist besser als Nachsicht (Prov)

f (= certain) **he is ~ to win/get the job** er wird sicher gewinnen/die Stelle sicher bekommen

safe: **safe area** N (Pol) Sicherheitszone *f*, Schutzzone *f*; **safe-blower, safe-breaker** N Schränker(in) *m(f)* (sl), Safeknacker(in) *m(f)* (inf); **safe-conduct** N freies *or* sicheres Geleit; (= document) Geleitbrief *m*; **safe-cracker** N (inf) Schränker(in) *m(f)* (sl), Safeknacker(in) *m(f)* (inf); **safe-deposit** N Tresorraum *m*; **safe-deposit box** N Banksafe *m or nt*; **safeguard** **N** Schutz *m*; **as a ~ against** zum Schutz gegen; **double-check these figures as a ~** überprüfen Sie diese Zahlen zur Sicherheit noch einmal **VT** schützen (against vor +dat); interests wahrnehmen **VI** **to ~ against sth** sich gegen etw absichern; **safe haven** N (fig) sicherer Zufluchtsort *or* Hafen; **safe house** N Zufluchtsort *m*; (police term for house used by terrorists) konspirative Wohnung; **safe keeping** N sichere Verwahrung; **to give sb sth for ~** jdm etw zur (sicheren) Aufbewahrung geben; **safelight** N (Phot) Dunkelkammerlicht *nt*

safely ['seɪflɪ] ADV (= unharmed) arrive, get home wohlbehalten, heil; (= without problems also) sicher, gut; (= without running risks) unbesorgt, gefahrlos; drive vorsichtig; (= solidly, firmly) sicher, fest; (= not dangerously) ungefährlich; **drive ~!** fahr vorsichtig!; **she held the door open until we were all ~ inside** sie hielt die Tür auf, bis wir alle sicher drinnen waren; **we can ~ estimate that ...** wir können mit einiger Sicherheit annehmen, dass ...; **I think I can ~ say/claim/assume ...** ich glaube, ich kann wohl *or* ruhig sagen/behaupten/annehmen ...; **I got ~ through the first interview** ich bin gut *or* heil durch das erste Interview gekommen; **the election is now ~ out of the way** die Wahlen haben wir jetzt zum Glück hinter uns; **money ~ deposited in the bank** sicher auf der Bank deponiertes Geld; **~ invested** sicher angelegt; **to put sth a-way** etw an einem sicheren Ort verwahren; **he put it ~ away in a drawer** er verwahrte es sicher in einer Schublade; **put it ~ out of the reach of the children** bringen Sie es vor den Kindern in Sicherheit; **he's ~ locked away in prison** er sitzt hinter Schloss und Riegel; **once the children are ~ tucked up in bed** wenn die Kinder erst mal im Bett sind; **he was ~ tucked up in bed** er lag wohlvermummt im Bett

safeness ['seɪfnɪs] N Sicherheit *f*

safe: **safe passage** N sicheres Geleit; **safe seat** N (Pol) ein sicherer Sitz; **safe sex** N Safersex *m*, Safer Sex *m*

safety ['seɪftɪ] N Sicherheit *f*; **in a place of ~** an einem sicheren Ort; **for ~'s sake** aus Sicherheitsgründen; **for his (own) ~** zu seiner (eigenen) Sicherheit; **to walk the streets in ~** unbehelligt ausgehen; **with complete ~** vollkommen sicher; **I can say with ~ that ...** ich kann mit Sicherheit behaupten, dass ...; **to play for ~** (Sport) auf Sicherheit spielen; (fig) sichergehen; **(there's) ~ in numbers** zu mehreren ist man sicherer; **to reach ~** in Sicherheit gelangen; **when we reached the ~ of the opposite bank** als wir sicher das andere Ufer erreicht hatten; **to leap to ~** sich in Sicherheit bringen; **to seek ~ abroad** sich ins Ausland in Sicherheit bringen; **the government must ensure the ~ of nuclear power plants** die Regierung muss die Betriebssicherheit von Atomkraftwerken gewährleisten

safety: **safety belt** N Sicherheitsgurt *m*; **safety binding** N (Ski) Sicherheitsbindung *f*; **safety buoy** N (Naut) Rettungsboje *f*; **safety car** N (Motor Racing) Sicherheitsauto *nt*; **safe-**

ty catch N (on gun) (Abzugs)sicherung *f*, Sicherungsbügel *m*; **was the ~ on/off?** war das Gewehr gesichert/entsichert?; **safety chain** N Sicherheitskette *f*; **safety curtain** N (Theat) eiserner Vorhang; **safety first** N to opt for ~ der Sicherheit den Vorrang geben; **~ campaign** Unfallverhütungskampagne *f*; **"safety first"** (as slogan) „Sicherheit geht vor"; **safety glass** N Sicherheitsglas *nt*; **safety harness** N Sicherheitsgurt *m*; **safety island** N (US, Aut) Verkehrsinsel *f*; **safety lamp** N Grubenlampe *f*; **safety lock** N Sicherheitsschloss *nt*; **safety margin** N Sicherheitsmarge *f*; **safety match** N Sicherheitszündholz *nt*; **safety measure** N Sicherheitsmaßnahme *f*; **safety net** N Sprung- *or* Sicherheitsnetz *nt*; **safety pin** N Sicherheitsnadel *f*; **safety precaution** N Sicherheitsvorkehrung *f*; **safety razor** N Rasierapparat *m*, Nassrasierer *m* (inf); **safety shot** N (Snooker) Safety *m*; **safety standards** PL Sicherheitsnormen *pl*; **safety switch** N (Elec etc) Sicherheitsschalter *m*; **safety valve** N Sicherheitsventil *nt*; (fig) Ventil *nt*

saffron ['sæfrən] **N** Safran *m*; (= colour) Safrangelb *nt* **ADJ** Safran-; (colour) safrangelb; **~ rice** Safranreis *m*

sag [sæg] **N** there's a bit of a ~ in the bed/ceiling das Bett/die Decke hängt etwas durch; **the ~ of her shoulders** ihre herabhängenden Schultern **VI** absacken; (in the middle) durchhängen; (shoulders) herabhängen; (breasts) schlaff herunterhängen; (production, rate) zurückgehen; (price, spirit) sinken; (conversation) abflauen; **don't ~, stand up straight** steh nicht so schlaff da (inf), stell dich gerade hin

saga ['sɑːgə] N Saga *f*; (= novel also) Generationsroman *m*; (fig) Geschichte *f*, Story *f* (inf)

sagacious ADJ, **sagaciously** ADV [sə'geɪʃəs, -lɪ] weise, klug

sagacity [sə'gæsɪtɪ] N Weisheit *f*, Klugheit *f*

sage¹ [seɪdʒ] **N** Weise(r) *m* **ADJ** (+er) weise

sage² N (Bot) Salbei *m*

sage green N Graugrün *nt*

sage-green ['seɪdʒ'griːn] ADJ graugrün

sagely ['seɪdʒlɪ] ADV weise

sageness ['seɪdʒnɪs] N Weisheit *f*

sagging ['sægɪŋ] ADJ **a** ceiling, beam, rope durchhängend; armchair durchgesessen **b** skin schlaff; **~ stomach/bosom/cheeks** Hängebauch *m*/-busen *m*/-backen *pl* **c** (fig) morale sinkend; **a drink will revive his ~ spirits** ein Drink wird seine Stimmung wieder heben

saggy ['sægɪ] ADJ (+er) mattress durchgelegen; sofa durchgesessen; garment ausgebeult; bottom, breasts schlaff; **if my breasts got ~** wenn ich einen Hängebusen bekäme

Sagittarian [ˌsædʒɪ'teərɪən] **N** Schütze *m* **ADJ** des Schützen

Sagittarius [ˌsædʒɪ'teərɪəs] N Schütze *m*; **he's (a) ~** er ist Schütze

sago ['seɪgəʊ] N Sago *m*

Sahara [sə'hɑːrə] N Sahara *f*; **the ~ Desert** die (Wüste) Sahara

sahib ['sɑːhɪb] N Sahib *m*

said [sed] pret, ptp of **say** ADJ (form) besagt

sail [seɪl] **N** **a** Segel *nt*; (of windmill) Flügel *m*; **under ~** mit aufgezogenen Segeln; **in** *or* **under full ~** mit vollen Segeln; **with all ~s set** mit gesetzten Segeln; **to make ~** (= hoist) Segel setzen; **to set** *or* **make ~ (for ...)** los- *or* abfahren (nach ...); (with sailing boat) absegeln (nach ...); **he set ~ from Dover** er fuhr von Dover los; (with sailing boat) er segelte von Dover ab *or* los **b** (= trip) Fahrt *f*; **it's 3 days' ~ from here** von hier aus fährt *or* (in yacht) segelt man 3 Tage; **to go for a ~** segeln gehen; **to take sb for a ~** mit jdm segeln gehen; **have you ever had a ~ in his yacht?** sind Sie schon einmal auf seiner Jacht gefahren *or* gesegelt? **c** (= boat) (Segel)schiff *nt*; (small) (Segel)boot *nt*; **20 ~** 20 Schiffe/Boote; **there was not a ~ in sight** kein einziges Schiff war zu sehen **VT** ship segeln mit; liner etc steuern; **they ~ed**

the ship to Cadiz sie segelten nach Cadiz; **he ~s his own yacht** er hat eine eigene Jacht; **to ~ the Atlantic** den Atlantik durchkreuzen; **to ~ the seas** die Meere befahren

VI **a** (*Naut*) fahren; (*with yacht*) segeln; **are you flying? – no, ~ing** fliegen Sie? – nein, ich fahre mit dem Schiff; **I went ~ing for a week** ich ging eine Woche segeln; **to ~ round the world** um die Welt segeln, die Erde umsegeln; **to ~ round a headland** eine Landzunge umfahren/umsegeln

b (= *leave*) (*for* nach) abfahren; (*yacht, in yacht*) absegeln; **passengers ~ing for New York** Passagiere nach New York

c (*fig*) (*glider, swan etc*) gleiten; (*moon, clouds*) ziehen; (*ball, object*) fliegen; **the plate ~ed past my head** der Teller segelte an meinem Kopf vorbei; **she ~ed past/out of the room** sie rauschte vorbei/aus dem Zimmer (*inf*); **she ~ed into the room** sie kam ins Zimmer gerauscht (*inf*); **she ~ed through all her exams** sie schaffte alle Prüfungen spielend *or* mit Leichtigkeit; **the week just ~ed by** (*inf*) die Woche verging wie im Flug

▶ **sail in** VI (*inf*, = *enter argument*) sich einschalten

▶ **sail into** VI *+prep obj* (*inf*) *person* anfahren; *discussion* sich einschalten in (*+acc*)

sail: sailable ['seɪləbl] ADJ (*Naut*) **a** *canal, river etc* schiffbar, befahrbar **b** *boat* segelfertig; **sailboard** **N** Windsurfbrett *nt* **VI** windsurfen; **sailboarder** N Windsurfer(in) *m(f)*; **sailboarding** N Windsurfen *nt*; **sailboat** N (*US*) Segelboot *nt*; **sailcloth** N Segeltuch *nt*; **sailfish** N Fächerfisch *m*

sailing ['seɪlɪŋ] N **a** Segeln *nt*; (*as sport*) Segeln *nt*, Segelsport *m* **b** (= *departure*) **when is the next ~ for Arran?** wann fährt das nächste Schiff nach Arran? → **plain**

sailing: sailing boat N (*Brit*) Segelboot *nt*; **sailing date** N Abfahrtstermin *m*; **sailing school** N Segelschule *f*; **sailing ship** N Segelschiff *nt*; **sailing time** N Abfahrtszeit *f*; **sailing vessel** N Segelschiff *nt*; **sailing yacht** ['seɪlɪŋjɔt] N Segeljacht *f*

sail maker N Segelmacher(in) *m(f)*

sailor ['seɪlə'] N **a** Seemann *m*; (*in navy*) Matrose *m*, Matrosin *f*; (= *sportsman*) Segler(in) *m(f)*; **~ suit** Matrosenanzug *m*; **hello ~** (*hum*) hallo Süßer **b** (*fig*) **to be a good/bad ~** seefest/nicht seefest sein

sailplane ['seɪlpleɪn] N Segelflugzeug *nt*

saint [seɪnt] **☉** 23.2 N **a** Heilige(r) *mf* **b** (*before name*) (*abbr* **St** [snt]) St John der heilige Johannes, Sankt Johannes, St. Johannes; **St Francis** der heilige Franziskus; **St Mark's (Church)** die Markuskirche **c** (*fig*) Heilige(r) *mf*; **she is a ~ to put up with that** sie muss ja eine Engelsgeduld haben, dass sie sich das gefallen lässt

sainted ['seɪntɪd] ADJ heilig gesprochen; **my ~ aunt!** (*inf*) heiliger Strohsack! (*inf*), heiliger Bimbam! (*inf*)

Saint Elmo's fire [snt'elməʊz,faɪə'] N (*Met*) Elmsfeuer *nt*

sainthood ['seɪnthʊd] N Heiligkeit *f*; **martyrs who were elevated to ~** Märtyrer, die in die Gemeinschaft der Heiligen aufgenommen wurden

saintliness ['seɪntlɪnɪs] N Heiligkeit *f*; (*fig pej, of person*) frömmlerisches Wesen; **the ~ of his smile** sein lammfrommes Lächeln

saintly ['seɪntlɪ] ADJ (*+er*) *image, figure, life* heilig; (*fig pej*) *person* frömmlerisch; *smile* lammfromm; **he stood there with a ~ look on his face** (*lit*) er hatte einen verklärten Gesichtsausdruck; (*iro*) er sah aus, als ob er kein Wässerchen trüben könnte

saint's day ['seɪntsdeɪ] N Heiligenfest *nt*, Tag *m* des/der Heiligen; **when is your ~?** wann ist Ihr Namenstag?

Saint Valentine's Day [snt'væləntaɪnz,deɪ] N Valentinstag *m* (*14. Februar*)

saith [seθ] (*old*) = **says**

---

sake¹ [seɪk] N **for the ~ of ...** um (*+gen*) ... willen; **for my ~** meinetwegen; (= *to please me*) mir zuliebe; **for your own ~** dir selbst zuliebe; **for your family's ~** um Ihrer Familie willen, Ihrer Familie wegen; **for the ~ of your career/my health** wegen deiner Karriere/meiner Gesundheit, deiner Karriere/meiner Gesundheit zuliebe; **for heaven's** *or* **Christ's ~!** (*inf*) um Gottes willen!; **for heaven's** *or* **Christ's ~ shut up** (*inf*) nun halt doch endlich die Klappe (*inf*); **for old times' ~** in Erinnerung an alte Zeiten; **for the ~ of those who ...** für diejenigen, die ...; **for whose ~ is the writer writing, his own or the public's?** für wen schreibt der Schriftsteller, (für) sich selbst oder den Leser?; **I'd do anything for your ~** für dich tue ich alles; (= *to keep you happy*) dir zuliebe tue ich alles; **I did it just for the ~ of having a new experience** ich habe es nur getan, um eine neue Erfahrung zu machen; **and all for the ~ of a few pounds** und alles wegen ein paar Pfund; **to talk for talking's ~** reden, nur damit etwas gesagt wird; **I do the job for its own ~** ich mache die Arbeit um ihrer selbst willen *or* ihrer selbst wegen

sake², **saki** ['sɑːkɪ] N (= *drink*) Sake *m*

sal *abbr* **of salary** Geh.

salaam [sə'lɑːm] **N** **INTERJ** Salem *m* **VI** sich mit Salem begrüßen

salable *etc* ADJ (*US*) = **saleable** *etc*

salacious [sə'leɪʃəs] ADJ schlüpfrig; *picture* aufreizend; *chuckle* anzüglich

salaciousness [sə'leɪʃəsnɪs] N Schlüpfrigkeit *f*; (*of picture*) aufreizende Darstellung; (*of chuckle*) Anzüglichkeit *f*

salad ['sæləd] N Salat *m*

salad: salad bar N Salatbüffet *nt*; **salad bowl** N Salatschüssel *f*; **salad cream** N ≈ Majonäse *f*, ≈ Mayonnaise *f*; **salad days** PL unschuldige Jugendtage *pl*; **in the ~ of his youth** als er noch jung und unschuldig war; **salad dressing** N Salatsoße *f*; **lettuce with ~** angemachter Salat; **salad oil** N Salatöl *nt*; **salad spinner** N (*Cook*) Salatschleuder *f*

salamander ['sælə,mændə'] N Salamander *m*; (*Myth*) Feuergeist *m*

salami [sə'lɑːmɪ] N Salami *f*

salami tactics PL (*inf*) Salamitaktik *f* (*inf*)

sal ammoniac [,sælə'məʊnɪæk] N Ammoniumsalz *nt*, Salmiak *m*

salaried ['sælərɪd] ADJ **~ post** Angestelltenposten *m*; **~ employee** Gehaltsempfänger(in) *m(f)*; **~ staff** Gehaltsempfänger *pl*

salary ['sælərɪ] **☉** 19.2 N Gehalt *nt*; **he earns a good ~** er hat ein gutes Gehalt; **what is his ~?** wie hoch ist sein Gehalt?

salary: salary account N Gehaltskonto *nt*; **salary earner** N Gehaltsempfänger(in) *m(f)*; **salary increase** N Gehaltserhöhung *f*; **salary package** N Gehalt *nt* (*einschließlich Sonderleistungen*), Gehaltspaket *nt*; **salary range** N Gehaltsrahmen *m*, Gehaltsspanne *f*; **salary scale** N Gehaltsskala *f*

sale [seɪl] N **a** (= *selling*) Verkauf *m*; **for ~** zu verkaufen; **to put sth up for ~** etw zum Verkauf anbieten; **is it up for ~?** steht es zum Verkauf?; **not for ~** nicht verkäuflich; **going cheap for a quick ~** umständehalber billig abzugeben; **to be on ~** verkauft werden; **on ~ at all bookshops** in allen Buchhandlungen erhältlich; **on a ~ or return basis** auf Kommission(sbasis)

b (*instance*) Geschäft *nt*; (*of insurance, bulk order*) Abschluss *m*; **~s** *pl* (= *turnover*) der Absatz; **how many ~s have you made?** wie viel (*Stück*) haben Sie verkauft?; (*of insurance etc*) wie viele Abschlüsse haben Sie gemacht?; **we've made no ~ to China** mit China haben wir keine Geschäfte abgeschlossen; **"no ~"** (*on till*) ≈ Nullbon

c sales SING (= *department*) Verkaufsabteilung *f*

d (*at reduced prices*) Rabattaktion *f*, Ausverkauf *m*; (*at end of season*) Schlussverkauf *m*; (= *clearance sale*) Räumungsverkauf *m*; **to go to the ~s** zum Ausverkauf gehen; **they've got a ~**

---

on da ist eine Rabattaktion; **in the ~, on ~** (*US*) im (Sonder)angebot; **to buy in** *or* **at the ~s** im Ausverkauf kaufen

e (= *auction, selling off*) Auktion *f*; **~ of work** Basar *m*

saleability, (*US*) **salability** ['seɪləbɪlɪtɪ] N **to ascertain the ~ of a product** feststellen, wie gut sich ein Produkt verkauft

saleable, (*US*) **salable** ['seɪləbl] ADJ (= *marketable*) absatzfähig; *skill* vermarktbar; *artist, idea* gut verkäuflich; (= *in saleable condition*) verkäuflich; **not in a ~ condition** nicht zum Verkauf geeignet

sale: sale and leaseback N Verkauf *m* mit Rückmiete; **sale price** N Ausverkaufspreis *m*; **saleroom** N Auktionsraum *m*

sales: sales check N Kassenbeleg *m*; **sales clerk** N (*US*) Verkäufer(in) *m(f)*; **sales conference** N Vertreterkonferenz *f*; **sales department** N Verkaufsabteilung *f*; **sales director** N Verkaufsdirektor(in) *m(f)*; **sales drive** N Verkaufskampagne *f*; **sales executive** N Verkaufsleiter(in) *m(f)*; **sales figures** PL Verkaufs- *or* Absatzziffern *pl*; **sales force** N Verkäufer *pl*; (= *sales reps*) Vertreter *pl*; **salesgirl**, **saleslady** N Verkäuferin *f*; **salesman** N Verkäufer *m*; (= *representative*) Vertreter *m*; **sales manager** N Verkaufsleiter(in) *m(f)*

salesmanship ['seɪlzmənʃɪp] N Verkaufstechnik *f*

sales: salespeople PL Verkaufspersonal *nt*; **salesperson** N Verkäufer(in) *m(f)*; **sales pitch** N Verkaufstechnik *or* -masche (*inf*) *f*; **to make one's ~** seine Ware anpreisen; (*fig inf*) seine Ideen verkaufen *or* anpreisen; **sales promotion** N Verkaufsförderung *f*; **sales rep** N (*inf*), **sales representative** N Vertreter(in) *m(f)*; **sales resistance** N Kaufunlust *f*; **to meet (with) ~** auf Absatzschwierigkeiten stoßen; **sales revenue** N Verkaufserlös *m*; **salesroom** N = **saleroom**; **sales slip** N Kassenzettel *m*, Bon *m*; (*received prior to payment*) Kaufbeleg *m*; **sales talk** N Verkaufsgespräch *nt*; **his ~ won me over** die Art, wie er die Ware angepriesen hat, hat mich überzeugt; **that's just ~** (*inf*) das ist nur Reklame; **sales target** N Verkaufsziel *nt*; **sales tax** N (*US*) Verkaufssteuer *f*; **sales volume** N Umsatz *m*; **saleswoman** N Verkäuferin *f*; (= *representative*) Vertreterin *f*

salicylic acid [,sælɪsɪlɪk'æsɪd] N (*Chem*) Salizylsäure *f*

salient ['seɪlɪənt] ADJ (*lit*) hervorstehend; (*fig*) hervorstechend; **the ~ points of his argument** die Hauptpunkte *pl* seiner Argumentation

salina [sə'laɪnə] N Salzsee *m*, Salzpfanne *f*, Salzsumpf *m*

saline ['seɪlaɪn] ADJ salzig

saline: saline drip N (*Med*, = *device*) Infusionsapparat *m* *or* Tropf *m* (*inf*) mit Kochsalzlösung; (= *liquid*) Kochsalzlösung *f*; **saline solution** N Salzlösung *f*

salinity [sə'lɪnɪtɪ] N Salzigkeit *f*; (= *content*) Salzgehalt *m*

saliva [sə'laɪvə] N Speichel *m*

salivary gland [sə'laɪvərɪˈglænd] N Speicheldrüse *f*

salivate ['sælɪveɪt] VI Speichel produzieren; (*animal*) geifern; (*old people, baby*) sabbern; (*with lust*) lüstern geifern; **to ~ over sth** (*fig*) von etw schwärmen

salivation [,sælɪ'veɪʃən] N Speichelfluss *m*

sallow ['sæləʊ] ADJ bleich, teigig; *colour* fahl

sallowness ['sæləʊnɪs] N Blässe *f*, Fahlheit *f*

sally ['sælɪ] **N** Ausbruch *m*; (*of troops*) Ausfall *m*; **to make a ~** (*troops*) einen Ausfall machen; (*fig: verbally*) eine Tirade loslassen; **I made a ~ into town** ich habe einen Trip in die Stadt gemacht **VI** (*old, hum*) **~ forth** (*Mil*) einen Ausfall machen; (= *rush out*) hinausstürmen; (= *set out*) sich aufmachen

Sally Army ['sælɪˈɑːmɪ] N (*Brit, inf*) = **Salvation Army**

salmon ['sæmən] **N** pl - Lachs m, Salm m; (= colour) Lachs(rosa) nt **ADJ** (colour) lachs(farben)

salmonella [,sælmə'nelə] N (also **salmonella poisoning**) Salmonellenvergiftung f

salmon: salmon leap N Lachssprung m; (man-made) Lachsleiter or -treppe f; **salmon pink** N Lachsrosa nt; **salmon-pink** ADJ lachsrosa; **salmon river** N Fluss in dem Lachse vorkommen; **salmon trout** N Lachsforelle f

salon ['sælɒn] N (all senses) Salon m

saloon [sə'luːn] N **a** Saal m; (Naut) Salon m **b** (Brit, Aut) Limousine f; (in motor racing) Tourenwagen m **c** (US dated) (= bar) Wirtschaft f; (in Westerns) Saloon m

saloon: saloon bar N (Brit) vornehmerer Teil eines Lokals; **saloon car** N (Brit) Limousine f

Salop ['sæləp] abbr of **Shropshire**

salopettes [,sælə'pets] PL (Ski) Lifthose f

salsa ['sælsə] N **a** (Mus) Salsa m **b** (Cook) Salsasoße f

salsify ['sælsɪfɪ] N Schwarzwurzel f

SALT [sɔːlt] abbr of **Strategic Arms Limitation Treaty** SALT

salt [sɔːlt] **N a** (Cook, Chem) Salz nt; (for icy roads) Streusalz nt; ~ **of the earth** (fig) Salz der Erde; **to be worth one's** ~ (fig) etwas taugen; **to take sth with a pinch** (Brit) or **grain** (US) **of** ~ (fig) etwas nicht ganz für bare Münze or nicht ganz so wörtlich nehmen; **to rub** ~ **into sb's wounds** (fig) Salz in jds Wunde streuen or reiben → **old salt**
b salts PL (= smelling salts) Riechsalz nt; (for bowels) salinisches Abführmittel; **that drink went through me like a dose of** ~**s** (inf) das Getränk hat mich richtig durchgeputzt (inf); **the new director went through the board like a dose of** ~**s** (inf) der neue Direktor hat im Vorstand mit eisernem Besen ausgekehrt
c (fig, = zest, flavour) Würze f
ADJ a (= salty) air salzig; ~ **water** Salzwasser nt
b (= salted) butter, meat, fish gesalzen; **it's very** ~ **es ist sehr salzig**
VT a (= cure) einsalzen; (= flavour) salzen
b (= grit) road mit Salz streuen

▸ **salt away** VT sep (inf) money auf die hohe Kante tun (inf)

saltcellar ['sɔːltselə] N Salzfässchen nt; (= shaker) Salzstreuer m

salted ['sɔːltɪd] ADJ nuts, butter, meat, fish gesalzen; **highly** ~ stark gesalzen; **lightly** or **slightly** ~ **butter** leicht gesalzene Butter; ~ **herrings** Salzheringe pl

salt: salt flats PL Salztonebene f; **salt-free** ADJ salzlos

saltiness ['sɔːltɪnɪs] N Salzigkeit f

salt: salt lake N Salzsee m; **salt lick** N Salzlecke f; **salt marsh** N Salzsumpf m; **salt mine** N Salzbergwerk nt

saltness ['sɔːltnɪs] N Salzigkeit f

salt: saltpan N Salzpfanne f; **saltpetre**, (US) **saltpeter** [,sɔːlt'piːtə] N Salpeter m; **salt shaker** N Salzstreuer m; **salt tax** N Salzsteuer f; **salt water** N Salzwasser nt; **saltwater** ADJ ~ **fish** Meeresfisch m; ~ **lake** Salzsee m; **saltworks** N sing or pl Saline f

salty ['sɔːltɪ] ADJ (+er) salzig; ~ **water** Salzwasser nt **b** (dated fig) language gesalzen; story scharf, gesalzen

salubrious [sə'luːbrɪəs] ADJ **a** (form) air, climate gesund **b** (inf) district, friends ersprießlich; **not a very** ~ **pub** eine recht zweifelhafte Kneipe

salubriousness [sə'luːbrɪəsnɪs], **salubrity** [sə'luːbrɪtɪ] N Heilsamkeit f, Bekömmlichkeit f, Zuträglichkeit f

salutary ['sæljʊtərɪ] ADJ **a** (= healthy) gesund **b** (= beneficial) advice nützlich; experience heilsam, lehrreich; effect günstig; **a** ~ **reminder that ...** eine heilsame or lehrreiche Erinnerung daran, dass ...

salutation [,sæljʊ'teɪʃən] N Begrüßung f; (in letters) Anrede f; **he raised his hand in** ~ er hob die Hand zum Gruß

salutatorian [səluːtə'tɔːrɪən] N (US) Student, der die Begrüßungsrede hält

salutatory [sə'luːtətərɪ] ADJ Begrüßungs-; ~ **oration** Begrüßungsansprache f

salute [sə'luːt] **N** Gruß m; (of guns) Salut m; **he raised his hand in** ~ er hob seine Hand zum Gruß; **to raise one's glass in** ~ sein Glas zu einem Toast hochheben; **flags were raised in** ~ zur Begrüßung wurden die Fahnen gehisst; **to stand at the** ~ salutieren; **a 21-gun** ~ 21 Salutschüsse; **to take the** ~ die Parade abnehmen; **he gave a smart** ~ er salutierte zackig **VT** (Mil) flag etc grüßen; person also salutieren vor (+dat); (fig liter, = welcome) begrüßen; courage bewundern, den Hut ziehen vor (+dat); **we** ~ **the glorious dead** wir gedenken der gefallenen Helden **VI** (Mil) salutieren, grüßen

salutories [sə'luːtərɪz] PL (US) Begrüßungsrede f (bei Semesterabschluss und Zeugnisüberreichung)

salvage ['sælvɪdʒ] **N** (= act) Bergung f; (= objects) Bergungsgut nt; (= payment) Bergelohn m; (= proceeds from salvaged goods) Wert m der geretteten Waren **VT** (from wreck, building) bergen (from aus); (fig) retten (from von); **to** ~ **sth from the fire** etw aus den Flammen retten; **to** ~ **one's pride/reputation** sich (dat) seinen Stolz/Ruf erhalten können; ~ **what you can** (lit, fig) rettet, was ihr retten könnt; **a few happy memories can be** ~**d from the marriage** ein paar glückliche Erinnerungen können aus den Trümmern der Ehe geborgen werden

salvage: salvage operation N Bergungsaktion f; (fig) Rettungsaktion f; **salvage tug** N Bergungsschlepper m; **salvage vessel** N Bergungsschiff nt

salvation [sæl'veɪʃən] N (= act of saving) Rettung f; (= state of being saved also, esp Rel) Heil nt; **he found** ~ **in the Church** er fand sein Heil in der Kirche; **he found** ~ **in his work** die Arbeit war seine Rettung; **the path to** ~ der Weg des Heils; **you were/that was my** ~ du warst/das war meine Rettung; **everyone has to work out his own** ~ jeder muss für sein eigenes Heil sorgen

Salvation Army **N** Heilsarmee f, **ATTR** hostel, band, meeting die Heilsarmee

salvationist [sæl'veɪʃənɪst] N Heilsprediger(in) m(f); (also **Salvationist**: = of Salvation Army) Angehörige(r) mf der Heilsarmee

salve¹ [sælv] VT (liter) = **salvage**

salve² **N** Salbe f; (fig liter) Balsam m; **as a** ~ **for his conscience** um sein Gewissen zu beruhigen **VT** (rare lit) (ein)salben; (fig) conscience beruhigen

salver ['sælvə] N Tablett nt

salvo ['sælvəʊ] N (of guns, fig) Salve f; **a** ~ **of applause** ein Beifallssturm m

sal volatile [,sælvə'lætəlɪ] N Riechsalz nt

Samaritan [sə'mærɪtən] N Samariter(in) m(f); **good** ~ (lit, fig) barmherziger Samariter

samarium [sə'mɛərɪəm] N (Chem) Samarium nt

samba ['sæmbə] **N** Samba f or m **VI** Samba tanzen

sambo ['sæmbəʊ] N (pej) Kaffer m

same [seɪm] ⚙ 5.4, 26.2, 26.3 **ADJ the** ~ **...** der/die/das gleiche ...; (= one and the same) der-/die-/dasselbe; **they were both wearing the** ~ **dress** sie hatten beide das gleiche Kleid an; **they both live in the** ~ **house** sie wohnen beide in demselben or im selben Haus; **they are all the** ~ sie sind alle gleich; **that's the** ~ **tie as I've got** so eine Krawatte habe ich auch, ich habe die gleiche Krawatte; **she just wasn't the** ~ **person** sie war ein anderer Mensch; **it's the** ~ **thing** das ist das Gleiche; **see you tomorrow,** ~ **time** ~ **place** bis morgen, gleicher Ort, gleiche Zeit or Ort und Zeit wie gehabt; **we sat at the** ~ **table as usual** wir saßen an unserem üblichen Tisch; **how are you?** – ~ **as usual** wie

gehts? – wie immer; **I've made the** ~ **mistake myself** den Fehler habe ich auch gemacht, ich habe den gleichen Fehler gemacht; **this** ~ **person** eben dieser Mensch; (Jur) besagte Person; **she was killed with this** ~ **knife** sie wurde mit eben or genau diesem Messer erstochen; **he is the** ~ **age as his wife** er ist (genau) so alt wie seine Frau; **it happened the** ~ **day** es ist am gleichen or selben Tag passiert; **if you can do the two jobs in the** ~ **day** wenn sie die beiden Arbeiten an einem Tag erledigen können; **(on) the very** ~ **day** genau am gleichen Tag; **it's the** ~ **old rubbish every night on TV** (inf) es gibt jeden Abend den gleichen Mist im Fernsehen (inf); ~ **difference** (inf) was ist der Unterschied?; **in the** ~ **way** (genau) gleich; (= by the same token) ebenso → **time**
PRON a the ~ der/die/das Gleiche, der-/die-/dasselbe; **I would do the** ~ **for you** ich würde das Gleiche für dich tun; **and I would do the** ~ **again** und ich würde es wieder tun; **he left and I did the** ~ er ist gegangen, und ich auch or ebenfalls; **they are one and the** ~ das ist doch dasselbe; (people) das ist doch ein und der-/dieselbe; **the (very)** ~ (form: = yes) genau; **is he that artist from New Orleans?– the very** ~ ist das dieser Künstler aus New Orleans?– genau der; **another drink? – thanks, I'll do the** ~ **again** noch etwas zu trinken? – ja bitte, das Gleiche noch mal; ~ **again, Joe** und noch einen, Joe; **she's much the** ~ sie hat sich kaum geändert; (in health) es geht ihr kaum besser; **he will never be the** ~ **again** er wird niemals mehr derselbe sein; **you're not the** ~ **any more** du bist nicht mehr der-/dieselbe; **I'm not the** ~ **as my brother** ich bin nicht so wie mein Bruder; **frozen chicken is not the** ~ **as fresh** tiefgefrorene Hähnchen sind kein Vergleich zu frischen; **it's always the** ~ es ist immer das Gleiche; **it comes** or **amounts to the** ~ das kommt or läuft aufs Gleiche hinaus
b no art (Comm) **for repairing chair: £10, for recovering** ~: **£25** Stuhlreparatur: £ 10, Beziehen: £ 25
c (in adverbial uses) **the** ~ gleich; **to pay/treat everybody the** ~ alle gleich bezahlen/behandeln; **things go on just the** ~ (as always) es ändert sich nichts; **it's not the** ~ **as before** es ist nicht wie früher; **I don't feel the** ~ **about it** ich sehe das nicht so; **I used to love you but I don't feel the** ~ **any more** ich habe dich mal geliebt, aber das ist jetzt anders; **I still feel the** ~ **about you** an meinen Gefühlen dir gegenüber hat sich nichts geändert; **if it's all the** ~ **to you** wenn es Ihnen egal ist; **it's all the** ~ **to me (what you do)** es ist mir egal(, was du tust)
d (phrases) **all** or **just the** ~ (= nevertheless) trotzdem; **thanks all the** ~ trotzdem vielen Dank; ~ **here** ich/wir auch; ~ **to you** (danke) gleichfalls; **you're an idiot –** ~ **to you** du bist ein Idiot – gleichfalls; **I'd have hit him, (the)** ~ **as you did** (inf) ich hätte ihn (an Ihrer Stelle) auch geschlagen; **we left our country the** ~ **as you did** wir haben unsere Heimat verlassen, wie Sie auch

same-day ['seɪmdeɪ] ADJ delivery am gleichen Tag; ~ **service** Erledigung f am gleichen Tag

sameness ['seɪmnɪs] N Eintönigkeit f

same-sex ['seɪmseks] ADJ couple, marriage, relationship gleichgeschlechtlich

samey ['seɪmɪ] ADJ (inf) eintönig, dasselbe in Grün (inf)

Samoa [sə'məʊə] N Samoa nt

Samoan [sə'məʊən] **ADJ** samoanisch **N a** Samoaner(in) m(f) **b** (Ling) Samoanisch nt

samovar [,sæmə'vɑː] N Samowar m

sampan ['sæmpæn] N Sampan m

sample ['sɑːmpl] **N** (= example) Beispiel nt (of für); (for tasting, fig: of talent, behaviour) Kostprobe f; (Comm, of cloth etc) Muster nt; (of commodities, urine, blood etc) Probe f; (Statistics) (Zufalls)stichprobe f, Sample nt; **that's a typical** ~ **of her cooking** genau so kocht sie immer; **up to** ~ (Comm) mustergetreu; **a representative** ~ **of the population** eine repräsentative Auswahl aus der Bevölkerung; **to take ~s of sb's blood** bei jdm Blutproben machen; **to take water ~s** Wasserproben entnehmen **ADJ** *attr* Probe-; (*esp Comm*) Muster-; **~ collection** Mustersammlung *f*; **a ~ section of the population** eine Auswahl aus der Bevölkerung **VT** *wine, food* probieren, kosten; *pleasures* kosten; *atmosphere* testen; **to ~ wines** eine Weinprobe machen; **the newspaper has ~d public opinion on this matter** die Zeitung hat die öffentliche Meinung in dieser Frage getestet

sample: sample book N Musterbuch *nt*; **sample bottle** N Probierflasche *f*; **sample pack** N Probepackung *f*

sampler ['sɑ:mplə'] N **a** (= *person*) Probierer(in) *m(f)* **b** (*Sew*) Stickmustertuch *nt* **c** (= *record*) Auswahlplatte *f*

sample survey N Stichprobenerhebung *f*

sampling ['sɑ:mplɪŋ] **N** (*of food*) Kostprobe *f*; (*of wine*) Weinprobe *f*; (*Statistics*) Stichprobenverfahren *nt* **ATTR** (*Statistics*) Stichproben-; **~ error** Fehler *m* im Stichprobenverfahren

Samson ['sæmsn] N (*lit*) Samson *m*; (*fig*) Herkules *m*

Samurai ['sæmjʊraɪ] **N** Samurai *m* **ATTR** Samurai-; **~ sword** Samuraischwert *nt*; **~ tradition** Tradition *f* der *or* bei den Samurai; **~ warrior** Samurai-Krieger *m*

sanatorium [,sænə'tɔ:rɪəm] N *pl* **sanatoria** [,sænə'tɔ:rɪə] (*Brit*) Sanatorium *nt*

sanctification [,sæŋktɪfɪ'keɪʃən] N (= *making holy*) Heiligung *f*; (= *consecrating*) Weihe *f*; (= *making binding: of vows*) Annahme *f*

sanctify ['sæŋktɪfaɪ] VT (= *make holy*) heiligen; (= *give quasi-moral sanction to also*) sanktionieren; (= *consecrate*) weihen; (= *make binding*) *vows* annehmen; **a custom sanctified by tradition** ein durch die Tradition geheiligter Brauch

sanctimonious [,sæŋktɪ'məʊnɪəs] ADJ frömmlerisch; **don't be so ~ about it** tu doch nicht so fromm

sanctimoniously [,sæŋktɪ'məʊnɪəslɪ] ADV frömmlerisch

sanctimoniousness [,sæŋktɪ'məʊnɪəsnɪs] N frömmlerisches Wesen; **the ~ of his remarks** seine frömmlerischen Bemerkungen

sanction ['sæŋkʃən] **N a** (= *permission, approval*) Zustimmung *f*; **to give one's ~ to sth** etw sanktionieren, seine Zustimmung zu etw geben; **rituals which have received the ~ of tradition** Rituale, die durch die Tradition sanktioniert sind **b** (= *enforcing measure*) Sanktion *f*; **to lift the ~s on a country** die Sanktionen gegen ein Land aufheben **VT a** sanktionieren **b** (*Pol: = impose sanctions on*) Sanktionen *pl* verhängen gegen

sanctions-busting ['sæŋkʃənz,bʌstɪŋ] N (*Pol*) Sanktionsbruch *m*

sanctity ['sæŋktɪtɪ] N Heiligkeit *f*; (*of rights*) Unantastbarkeit *f*; **a man of great ~** ein sehr heiliger Mann; **the ~ of (human) life** die Unantastbarkeit des (menschlichen) Lebens

sanctuary ['sæŋktjʊərɪ] N **a** (= *holy place*) Heiligtum *nt*; (= *altar sanctuary*) Altarraum *m* **b** (= *refuge*) Zuflucht *f*; **to seek ~ with** Zuflucht suchen bei **c** (*for animals*) Schutzgebiet *nt*

sanctum ['sæŋktəm] N **a** (= *holy place*) heiliger Ort **b** (*fig, = private place*) Allerheiligste(s) *nt*

sand [sænd] **N** Sand *m no pl*; **to be built on ~** (*fig*) auf Sand gebaut sein; **~s** (*of desert*) Sand *m*; (= *beach*) Sandstrand *m*; **the ~s are running out** (*fig*) die Zeit *or* Uhr läuft ab; **the ~s of time** (*fig*) die Zeit; **the shifting ~s of politics** der politische Flugsand **VT** (= *smooth*) schmirgeln; (= *sprinkle with sand*) streuen

▸ **sand down** VT *sep* (ab)schmirgeln

sandal ['sændl] N Sandale *f*

sandalled ['sændəld] ADJ **in her ~ feet** in *or* mit Sandalen

sandalwood ['sændlwʊd] N **ATTR** Sandelholz *nt* **ATTR** Sandelholz-; **~ oil** Sandelholzöl *nt*

sand: sandbag **N** Sandsack *m* **VT** mit Sandsäcken schützen; **sandbank** N Sandbank *f*; **sandbar** N Sandbank *f*; **sandblast** VT sandstrahlen; **sandblaster** N Sandstrahler *m*; **sandblasting** N Sandstrahlen *nt*; **sandbox** N (*Rail*) Sandstreuer *m*; (*Metal*) Sandform *f*; (*for playing*) Sandkasten *m*; **sandboy** N **as happy as a ~** (*Brit inf*) quietschvergnügt (*inf*); **sand castle** N Sandburg *f*; **sand dune** N Sanddüne *f*

sander ['sændə'] N (= *tool*) Rutscher *m*, Vibrationsschleifer *m*

sand: sand flea N Strandfloh *m*; (*harmful*) Sandfloh *m*; **sand fly** N Sandfliege *f*; **sand glass** N Sanduhr *f*; **sand hopper** N Sandhüpfer *m*

sandiness ['sændɪnɪs] N Sandigkeit *f*; **noted for the ~ of its beaches** berühmt für seine Sandstrände

S & L (*US, Fin*) *abbr of* **savings and loan association** Spar- und Darlehenskasse *f*

sand: sandlot ADJ (*US*) **~ baseball** *auf einem nicht als Spielfeld markierten Gelände und zum Spaß gespielter Baseball*; **sandman** N Sandmann *m*; **sand martin** N Uferschwalbe *f*; **sandpaper** **N** Sand- *or* Schmirgelpapier *nt* **VT** schmirgeln; **sandpaper down** VT *sep* abschmirgeln; **sandpiper** N Strandläufer *m*; **sandpit** N **a** (= *sand quarry*) Sandgrube *f* **b** (*Brit: in playground*) Sandkasten *m or* -kiste *f*; **sandshoe** N Stoffschuh *m*; (*for beach*) Strandschuh *m*; **sandstone** **N** Sandstein *m* **ADJ** Sandstein-, aus Sandstein; **~ building** Sandsteinbau *m*; **sandstorm** N Sandsturm *m*; **sand table** N (*Mil*) Sandkasten *m*

sandwich ['sænwɪdʒ] **N** Sandwich *nt*, Doppelschnitte *f or* -stulle *f* (*N Ger*); **open ~** belegtes Brot; **he has ~es for lunch** er isst Butterbrote *or* Sandwiches *or* Stullen (*N Ger*) zum Mittagessen; **he's the meat *or* filling in the ~** (*Brit, inf*) er ist das arme Opfer in der Mitte **VT** (*also* **sandwich in**) hineinzwängen; *car* einkeilen; **to be ~ed between two things/people** (*car, house*) zwischen zwei Dingen/Menschen eingekeilt sein; (*person also, small object*) zwischen zwei Dingen/Menschen eingezwängt sein; **~ed between two slices of bread** zwischen zwei Brotscheiben; **three pieces of wood, ~ed together** drei Stück Holz, die nebeneinander gequetscht sind

sandwich: sandwich bar N Snackbar *f*; **sandwich board** N Reklametafel *f*, Sandwich *nt* (*hum*); **sandwich cake** N Schichttorte *f*; **sandwich course** N Ausbildungsgang, *bei dem sich Theorie und Praxis abwechseln*; **sandwich man** N Plakatträger *m*, Sandwichmann *m*

sandy ['sændɪ] ADJ (+*er*) sandig; **~ beach** Sandstrand *m* **b** (*colour*) rötlich; *hair* rotblond

sand yacht N Strandsegler *m*

sane [seɪn] ADJ (+*er*) **a** (= *mentally healthy*) *person* normal; (*Med, Psych etc*) geistig gesund; (*Jur*) zurechnungsfähig; *world, society etc* gesund **b** (= *sensible*) *advice, policy, system, person, behaviour* vernünftig; **it's simply not ~ to ...** es ist doch verrückt, zu ...; **there is no ~ reason why ...** es gibt keinen vernünftigen Grund, weshalb ...

sang [sæŋ] *pret of* **sing**

sangfroid ['sɑ:ŋ'frwɑ:] N Gelassenheit *f*, Seelenruhe *f*

sangria [sæŋ'griːə] N Sangria *f*

sanguinary ['sæŋgwɪnərɪ] ADJ (*liter*) *battle* blutig; *person* blutrünstig; *expression etc* derb; **~ language** (*hum*) ≈ Fäkalsprache *f*

sanguine ['sæŋgwɪn] ADJ **a** (= *optimistic*) optimistisch; **to have a ~ nature *or* disposition** von Natur aus ein Optimist sein; **to be ~ about sth** in Bezug auf etw (*acc*) zuversichtlich sein; **he is ~ about his country's future** er ist voller Zuversicht was die Zukunft seines Landes betrifft; **I remain ~ about his chances** was seine Chancen betrifft, bin ich noch immer zuversichtlich; **~ that we shall succeed** zuversicht-

lich, dass wir Erfolg haben werden **b** **~ complexion** rote *or* gesunde (*euph*) Gesichtsfarbe

sanguinely ['sæŋgwɪnlɪ] ADV optimistisch; *say* zuversichtlich

sanguinity [sæŋ'gwɪnɪtɪ] N Optimismus *m*

sanies ['seɪnɪːz] N (*Med form*) Jauche *f*

sanitariness ['sænɪtrɪnɪs] N Hygiene *f*; **the ~ of conditions** die hygienischen Zustände; **the ~ of the toilets is not up to standard** bei den Toiletten lässt die Hygiene zu wünschen übrig

sanitarium [,sænɪ'tɛərɪəm] N (*US*) = **sanatorium**

sanitary ['sænɪtrɪ] ADJ hygienisch; *arrangements, services, installations* sanitär *attr*; *recommendations* in Bezug auf die Hygiene; *questions* der Hygiene; **~ regulations** Gesundheits- *or* Hygienebestimmungen *pl*

sanitary: sanitary belt N Bindengürtel *m*; **sanitary engineer** N (= *expert*) Sanitärtechniker(in) *m(f)*; (*euph: = dustman*) Entsorgungsfachmann *m*/-frau *f*; **sanitary engineering** N Sanitärtechnik *f*; **sanitary inspector** N Gesundheitsaufseher(in) *m(f)*; **sanitary napkin** N (*US*) Damenbinde *f*; **sanitary pad** N Damenbinde *f*; **sanitary protection** N (= *sanitary towels or tampons*) Binden und Tampons *pl*; **sanitary towel** N Damenbinde *f*

sanitation [,sænɪ'teɪʃən] N Hygiene *f*; (= *toilets etc*) sanitäre Anlagen *pl*; (= *sewage disposal*) Kanalisation *f*; **the ~ department** das Amt für Stadtreinigung

sanitation man N *pl* **sanitation men, sanitation worker** N (*US*) Stadtreiniger *m*, Müllmann *m*

sanitize ['sænɪtaɪz] VT **a** (*esp US*) keimfrei machen **b** *novel, film etc* von anstößigen Stellen reinigen *or* säubern

sanity ['sænɪtɪ] N **a** (= *mental balance*) geistige Gesundheit; (*esp of individual*) gesunder Verstand; (*Jur*) Zurechnungsfähigkeit *f*; **to lose one's ~** den Verstand verlieren; **to doubt sb's ~** an jds Verstand (*dat*) zweifeln; **the line between ~ and insanity** die Grenze zwischen gesundem und krankem Verstand **b** (= *sensibleness*) Vernünftigkeit *f*; **~ of judgement** ein gesundes Urteilsvermögen; **~ demands that it be done soon** die Vernunft gebietet, es bald zu tun; **to return to ~** Vernunft annehmen

sank [sæŋk] *pret of* **sink**[1]

San Marino [,sænmə'riːnəʊ] N San Marino *nt*

sanserif [,sɒnsə'riːf] **N** serifenlose Schrift; (= *character*) serifenloser Buchstabe **ADJ** serifenlos

Sanskrit ['sænskrɪt] **ADJ** sanskritisch **N** Sanskrit *nt*

Santa (Claus) ['sæntə('klɔːz)] N der Weihnachtsmann

sap[1] [sæp] N (*Bot*) Saft *m*; (*fig*) Lebenskraft *f*; **the ~ is rising** (*lit*) der Saft steigt; (*fig*) die Triebe erwachen

sap[2] **N** (*Mil*) Sappe *f* **VT a** (*Mil*) unterminieren, untergraben **b** (*fig*) untergraben; *confidence* untergraben, schwächen; **to ~ sb's strength** jdn entkräften, jds Kräfte angreifen; **to ~ sb's energy/enthusiasm** jdm die Energie/Begeisterung nehmen

sap[3] N (*inf*) Trottel *m* (*inf*)

sapling ['sæplɪŋ] N junger Baum

sapper ['sæpə'] N (*Mil*) Pionier *m*

Sapphic ['sæfɪk] ADJ sapphisch

sapphire ['sæfaɪə'] **N** Saphir *m*; (= *colour*) Saphirblau *nt* **ADJ** Saphir-; (*liter*) *sky* strahlend blau; **~ ring** Saphirring *m*

sappy ['sæpɪ] ADJ **a** *plant etc* saftig, voller Saft; (*fig*) kraftvoll, voller Energie **b** (*esp US = oversentimental*) *play, book, film* rührselig; (*inf, = silly, foolish*) einfältig, dämlich

saraband ['særəbænd] N Sarabande *f*

Saracen ['særəsn] **ADJ** sarazenisch, Sarazenen- **N** Sarazene *m*, Sarazenin *f*

Sarajevo [,sæ[r]ə'jeɪvəʊ] N Sarajevo *nt*

sarcasm ['sɑːkæzəm] N Sarkasmus *m*

sarcastic [sɑː'kæstɪk] ADJ sarkastisch; **he has a ~ tongue** er hat eine sarkastische Art; **are you being ~?** sind Sie jetzt sarkastisch?, das soll wohl ein Witz sein (*inf*); **to be ~ about sth** über etw (*acc*) sarkastische Bemerkungen machen

sarcastically [sɑː'kæstɪkəlɪ] ADV sarkastisch

sarcoma [sɑː'kəʊmə] N *pl* **-s** or **-ta** [-tə] (*Med*) Sarkom *nt*

sarcophagus [sɑː'kɒfəgəs] N *pl* **sarcophagi** [sɑː-'kɒfəgaɪ] Sarkophag *m*

sardine [sɑː'diːn] N Sardine *f*; **packed (in) like ~s** wie die Sardinen

Sardinia [sɑː'dɪnɪə] N Sardinien *nt*

Sardinian [sɑː'dɪnɪən] **ADJ** sardisch, sardinisch **N** Sarde *m*, Sardin *f*, Sardinier(in) *m(f)*

sardonic ADJ , **sardonically** ADV [sɑː'dɒnɪk, -əlɪ] süffisant; *grin, laugh also* sardonisch (*liter*)

sari ['sɑːrɪ] N Sari *m*

sarky ['sɑːkɪ] ADJ (+er) (*Brit, inf*) sarkastisch

sarnie ['sɑːnɪ] N (*Brit inf*) belegtes Brot, Sandwich *nt*

sarong [sə'rɒŋ] N Sarong *m*

sarsaparilla [ˌsɑːsəpə'rɪlə] N (= *plant*) Sarsaparille *f*; (= *drink*) dunkelbraunes Limonadengetränk aus Sarsaparillenwurzeln

sartorial [sɑː'tɔːrɪəl] ADJ **his ~ elegance** sein elegantes Aussehen, seine elegante Art, sich zu kleiden; **the very last word in ~ elegance** der letzte Schrei in der Herrenmode; **his unusual ~ preferences** seine Vorliebe für ungewöhnliche Kleidung; **~ styles** Herrenmoden *pl*

sartorially [sɑː'tɔːrɪəlɪ] ADV *dressed* elegant, stilvoll

SAS (*Brit*) abbr of **Special Air Service** Spezialeinheit der britischen Armee

SASE N (*US*) abbr of **self-addressed stamped envelope** adressierter und frankierter Rückumschlag

sash[1] [sæʃ] N Schärpe *f*

sash[2] N (= *sash window*) Schiebefenster *nt*; (= *cord*) Gewichtsschnur *f*

sashay ['sæʃeɪ] VI (*esp US, inf*) stolzieren; **I'll just ~ down to the bar** ich latsche mal eben zur Bar (*inf*)

sash: sash cord N Gewichtsschnur *f*; **sash saw** N Schlitzsäge *f*; **sash window** N Schiebefenster *nt*

Sask abbr of **Saskatchewan**

sass [sæs] (*US, inf*) **N** Frechheit *f* **VT** frech antworten (+*dat*)

sassafras ['sæsəfræs] N Sassafras *m*

Sassenach ['sæsənæx] (*Scot: pej, hum*) **N** Engländer(in) *m(f)* **ADJ** englisch

sassy ['sæsɪ] ADJ (+er) (*US, inf*) frech

SAT

Scholastic Aptitude Tests oder auch **SAT** sind Standardprüfungen, die US-Highschool--Schülerinnen und -Schüler ablegen, die ein College oder eine Universität besuchen wollen. Die Schwerpunkte des Examens bewerten die sprachlichen und mathematischen Fähigkeiten der Kandidaten, wobei eine ideale Punktzahl von 1600 erreicht werden kann; die durchschnittlich erreichte Punktzahl liegt bei 900. Die Ergebnisse, die so genannten „SAT scores", werden dann den Colleges zugesandt, bei denen sich die Studenten bewerben. Für die Aufnahme entscheidend sind neben diesen Ergebnissen auch die allgemeinen schulischen Leistungen an der Highschool. Der Test war als objektive und unvoreingenommene Bewertungsgrundlage gedacht, es wird aber bemängelt, dass er dem kulturellen Hintergrund von Schülern aus der Mittelklasse entgegenkommt. Der **SAT** kann beliebig oft wiederholt werden, allerdings wird jedes Mal eine Examensgebühr erhoben.

Sat *abbr of* **Saturday** Sa.

sat [sæt] *pret, ptp of* **sit**

Satan ['seɪtən] N Satan *m*

satanic [sə'tænɪk] ADJ **a** satanisch; **~ abuse** ritueller Missbrauch **b** (*fig*) teuflisch

Satanism ['seɪtənɪzəm] N Satanismus *m*, Satanskult *m*

satay ['sæteɪ] N *Fleischspießchen mit Erdnusssoße*

satchel ['sætʃəl] N Schultasche *f*, Schulranzen *m*

sate [seɪt] VT (*liter*) *appetite, desires* stillen (*geh*), befriedigen; **now that he was ~d** nun, da seine Lüste gestillt waren (*geh*); **a nation ~d with every luxury** ein Volk von jedem erdenklichen Luxus übersättigt; **to ~ oneself** (*with food*) sich sättigen (*on* an +*dat*) (*liter*); (*sexually*) seine Lust befriedigen

sateen [sæ'tiːn] N Baumwollsatin *m*

satellite ['sætəlaɪt] N Satellit *m*; (*natural also, fig*) Trabant *m*

satellite: satellite broadcasting N Satellitenfunk *m*; **satellite country** N Satellitenstaat *m*; **satellite dish** N Parabolantenne *f*, Satellitenantenne *f*; **satellite state** N Satellitenstaat *m*; **satellite telephone** N Satellitentelefon *nt*; **satellite television** N Satellitenfernsehen *nt*; **satellite town** N Satelliten- or Trabantenstadt *f*

satiate ['seɪʃɪeɪt] VT *appetite, desires, lust etc* stillen (*geh*); *person, animal* sättigen; (*to excess*) übersättigen; **we were ~d with food and drink** wir hatten unseren Hunger und Durst zur Genüge gestillt; **I'm quite ~d** (*liter, hum*) mein Bedarf ist gedeckt (*hum inf*), ich bin gesättigt (*hum, geh*)

satiation [ˌseɪʃɪ'eɪʃən] N Befriedigung *f*, Sättigung *f*; (*excessive*) Übersättigung *f*

satiety [sə'taɪətɪ] N Sättigung *f*; **they ate to ~** sie aßen sich satt

satin ['sætɪn] **N** Satin *m* **ADJ** Satin-; *skin* samtig; **~ dress** Satinkleid *nt*

satin: satin paper N satiniertes Papier, Atlaspapier *nt*; **satin stitch** N Plattstich *m*; **satinwood** N Satinholz *nt*

satiny ['sætɪnɪ] ADJ seidig; *skin* samtig

satire ['sætaɪə] N Satire *f* (*on* +*acc*); **the ~ in his voice** die Ironie in seiner Stimme

satirical [sə'tɪrɪkəl] ADJ *literature, film etc* satirisch; (= *mocking, joking*) ironisch

satirically [sə'tɪrɪkəlɪ] ADV satirisch; (= *mockingly, jokingly*) ironisch

satirist ['sætərɪst] N Satiriker(in) *m(f)*

satirize ['sætəraɪz] VT satirisch darstellen or (*written also*) beschreiben; **his novel ~s** or **in his novel he ~s contemporary American life** sein Roman ist eine Satire auf die zeitgenössische amerikanische Lebensart

satisfaction [ˌsætɪs'fækʃən] N **a** (= *act*) (*of person, needs, creditors, curiosity etc*) Befriedigung *f*; (*of debt*) Begleichung *f*, Tilgung *f*; (*of ambition etc*) Zufriedenstellung *f*; (*of conditions, contract*) Erfüllung *f* **b** Zufriedenheit *f* (*at* mit); **the ~ at** or **of having solved a difficult problem** die Genugtuung or das befriedigende Gefühl, ein schwieriges Problem gelöst zu haben; **to feel a sense of ~ at** etw Genugtuung über etw (*acc*) empfinden; **at least you have the ~ of seeing him pay** Sie haben wenigstens die Genugtuung, dass er zahlen muss; **she would not give him the ~ of seeing how annoyed she was** sie wollte ihm nicht die Genugtuung geben, ihren Ärger zu sehen; **he did it just for the ~ of seeing her suffer** er tat es nur, um sie leiden zu sehen; **we hope the meal was to your complete ~** wir hoffen, Sie waren mit dem Essen zufrieden or das Essen war zu Ihrer vollen Zufriedenheit ausgefallen (*form*); **has it been done to your ~?** sind Sie damit zufrieden?, ist es zu Ihrer Zufriedenheit erledigt worden? (*form*); **if anything in the hotel is not to your ~** sollte irgendetwas im Hotel nicht zu Ihrer Zufriedenheit sein; **our aim, your ~** bei uns ist der Kunde König; **the**

machine is guaranteed to give complete ~ wir garantieren mit diesem Gerät vollste Zufriedenheit; **it gives me much ~ to introduce ...** es ist mir eine besondere Freude, ... vorstellen zu können; **to get ~ out of sth** Befriedigung in etw (*dat*) finden; (= *find pleasure*) Freude *f* an etw (*dat*) haben; **I can't get any ~** ich bin unbefriedigt; **he gets ~ out of his job** seine Arbeit befriedigt ihn; **I get a lot of ~ out of listening to music** Musik gibt mir viel; **what ~ do you get out of climbing mountains?** was gibt Ihnen das Bergsteigen?; **he proved to my ~ that ...** er hat überzeugend bewiesen, dass ...; **he has shown to the examiners' ~ that ...** der Prüfungsausschuss hat befunden, dass er ...; **she has shown to the court's ~ that ...** sie hat dem Gericht überzeugend dargelegt, dass ... **c** (= *satisfying thing*) **your son's success must be a great ~ to you** der Erfolg Ihres Sohnes muss für Sie sehr befriedigend or eine große Freude sein; **one of her greatest ~s comes from her work with children** eines der Dinge, die sie am meisten befriedigt, ist ihre Arbeit mit Kindern; **it is no ~ to me to know that ...** es ist kein Trost (für mich) zu wissen, dass ...; **what ~ is that supposed to be!** das ist ein schwacher Trost **d** (= *redress*) Genugtuung *f*, Satisfaktion *f* (*old*); **to demand/obtain ~ from sb** Genugtuung or Satisfaktion (*old*) von jdm verlangen/erhalten; **to give sb ~** jdm Genugtuung or Satisfaktion (*old*) geben

satisfactorily [ˌsætɪs'fæktərɪlɪ] ADV zufrieden stellend; **does that answer your question ~?** ist damit Ihre Frage hinreichend beantwortet?; **was it done ~?** waren Sie damit zufrieden?; **he is progressing ~** er macht zufrieden stellende Fortschritte *pl*

satisfactory [ˌsætɪs'fæktərɪ] ADJ befriedigend, zufrieden stellend; *account, completion of contract* zufrieden stellend; (= *only just good enough*) ausreichend, hinlänglich *attr*; *reason* triftig, einleuchtend; *excuse* angemessen, annehmbar; (*in exams*) ausreichend, befriedigend; **to bring sth to a ~ conclusion** etw zufrieden stellend zum Abschluss bringen; **to be in a ~ condition** (*Med*) sich in einem zufrieden stellenden Zustand befinden; **work is proceeding at a ~ pace** die Arbeit geht zufrieden stellend voran; **how ~ do you find the new conditions?** wie sind Sie mit den neuen Verhältnissen zufrieden?; **his work is only just ~** seine Arbeit ist gerade noch annehmbar or (*Sch*) befriedigend; **this is just not ~!** das geht so nicht!; (= *not enough*) das reicht einfach nicht (aus)!; **it's hardly ~ being given only one hour's notice** das geht doch nicht, wenn einem nur eine Stunde vorher Bescheid gesagt wird; **an offer of 8% is simply not ~** ein Angebot von 8% reicht einfach nicht; **your attitude is not ~** Ihre Einstellung lässt zu wünschen übrig

satisfied ['sætɪsfaɪd] ADJ **a** (= *content*) *person, customer* zufrieden; **to be ~ with sth** mit etw zufrieden sein; **you'll have to be ~ with that** Sie werden sich damit zufrieden geben or begnügen or beschieden (*geh*) müssen; **not ~ with that he ...** damit noch immer nicht zufrieden, er ...; **(are you) ~?** (*iro*) (bist du) nun zufrieden?; **you've really upset her now, I hope you're ~** sie ist ganz außer sich, bist du jetzt zufrieden?; **with a ~ look on his face** mit einem zufriedenen Gesichtsausdruck **b** (= *certain*, = *convinced*) überzeugt; **to be ~ that ...** der Überzeugung sein, dass ...; **they were not ~ with the answers** sie waren mit den Antworten nicht zufrieden

satisfy ['sætɪsfaɪ] **VT a** (= *make contented*) befriedigen; *employer, customers etc* zufrieden stellen; (*meal*) *person* sättigen; *hunger* stillen; **that won't ~ the boss** damit wird der Chef nicht zufrieden sein; **nothing satisfies him** ihn kann nichts befriedigen; (= *always wants more*) er ist mit nichts zufrieden; **one glass of water didn't ~ him/his thirst** das eine Glas Wasser hat ihm nicht gereicht/hat seinen Durst nicht gelöscht **b** *needs, wishes, lust, demand, curiosity, person* befriedigen; (*sexually*) befriedigen; *hunger* stillen; *contract, conditions* erfüllen; *requirements* genügen (+*dat*); *ambitions* verwirklichen; **to do sth to ~ one's pride** etw nur aus reinem Stolz tun

c (= *convince*) überzeugen; **if you can ~ him that ...** wenn Sie ihn davon überzeugen können, dass ...; **X has satisfied the examiners that ...** X hat den Prüfungsausschuss so befunden, dass X ...; **X has satisfied the examiners in the following subjects** X hat in den folgenden Fächern die Prüfung bestanden

d (*Comm*) *debt* begleichen, tilgen; *claims* nachkommen (+*dat*); *creditors* befriedigen

e (*Math*) *equation* erfüllen

VR **to ~ oneself about sth** sich von etw überzeugen; **to ~ oneself that ...** sich davon überzeugen, dass ...

VI (*meal*) sättigen; **we aim to ~** wir bemühen uns, allen Wünschen zu entsprechen; **pleasures which no longer ~** Genüsse, die einen nicht mehr befriedigen

satisfying ['sætɪsfaɪɪŋ] ADJ befriedigend; *food, meal* sättigend; **a ~ experience** ein befriedigendes Erlebnis; **they had the ~ experience of seeing him fail** es tat ihnen gut, seinen Misserfolg zu erleben; **sounds which are very ~ to the ear** angenehme Klänge *pl*; **a cool ~ beer** ein kühles, durststillendes Bier

satsuma [ˌsæt'suːmə] N Satsuma *f*

saturate ['sætʃəreɪt] VT **a** (*with liquid*) (durch-)tränken; (*rain*) durchnässen; **I'm ~d** (*inf*) ich bin klatschnass (*inf*)

b (*Chem*) sättigen; **a ~d solution/colour** eine gesättigte Lösung/Farbe

c (*fig*) *market* sättigen; *airways* auslasten; **this area is ~d with a sense of history** dies ist eine geschichtsträchtige Gegend; **he ~d himself in French literature until the exam was over** er hat sich mit französischer Literatur voll gepfropft, bis die Prüfung vorbei war; **the government ~d the area with troops** die Regierung entsandte massenhaft Truppen in das Gebiet; **the area is ~d with troops** die Gegend wimmelt von Soldaten

saturation [ˌsætʃə'reɪʃən] N Sättigung *f*

saturation: saturation bombing N völliges Zerbomben; **saturation point** N Sättigungspunkt *m*; (*fig*) Sättigungsgrad *m*; **to have reached ~** seinen Sättigungsgrad erreicht haben

Saturday ['sætədɪ] N Samstag *m*, Sonnabend *m* (*esp N Ger*) → *also* **Tuesday**

Saturn ['sætən] N (*Astron, Myth*) Saturn *m*

saturnalia [ˌsætə'neɪlɪə] PL **a** **Saturnalia** Saturnalien *pl* **b** (*liter*, = *wild revelry*) wilde Feste *pl*, Freudenfeste *pl*

saturnine ['sætənaɪn] ADJ (*liter*) finster, düster

satyr ['sætə'] N Satyr *m*

sauce [sɔːs] N **a** Soße *f*, Sauce *f*; **white ~** Mehlsoße *f*; **what's ~ for the goose is ~ for the gander** (*Prov*) was dem einen recht ist, ist dem anderen billig (*prov*) **b** *no pl* (*inf*, = *cheek*) Frechheit *f*; **none of your ~!** werd bloß nicht frech! (*inf*) **c** (*US, inf*, = *alcohol*) Alk *m* (*sl*), Stoff *m* (*inf*); **to be on the ~** saufen (*inf*)

sauce: sauce boat N Sauciere *f*; **saucebox** N (*inf*) Frechdachs *m*

saucepan ['sɔːspən] N Kochtopf *m*

saucer ['sɔːsə'] N Untertasse *f*

saucily ['sɔːsɪlɪ] ADV **a** (= *cheekily*) frech **b** (= *suggestively*) *say, joke* aufreizend

sauciness ['sɔːsɪnɪs] N , *no pl* Frechheit *f*

saucy ['sɔːsɪ] ADJ (+*er*) **a** (= *cheeky*) frech; **don't be ~!** sei nicht so frech! **b** (= *suggestive*) *joke, humour* anzüglich, schlüpfrig; *picture, clothes* gewagt, aufreizend; **with her hat at a ~ angle** mit frech *or* keck aufgesetztem Hut

Saudi ['saʊdɪ] **N** (*inf*) = **Saudi Arabia** **ADJ** = **Saudi Arabian ADJ**

Saudi Arabia ['saʊdɪə'reɪbɪə] N Saudi-Arabien *nt*

Saudi Arabian ['saʊdɪə'reɪbɪən] **N** Saudi(-Araber) *m*, Saudi-Araberin *f* **ADJ** saudisch, saudi-arabisch

Saul [sɔːl] N Saul(us) *m*

sault [suː] N (*US*) (= *waterfall*) Wasserfall *m*; (*in river*) Stromschnelle *f*

sauna ['sɔːnə] N Sauna *f*; **to have a ~** in die Sauna gehen

saunter ['sɔːntə'] **N** Bummel *m*; **to have a ~ in the park** einen Parkbummel machen, durch den Park schlendern **VI** schlendern; **he ~ed up to me** er schlenderte auf mich zu; **she came ~ing in four hours late** sie tanzte vier Stunden zu spät an (*inf*); **to ~ out/away** hinaus-/wegschlendern

saunterer ['sɔːntərə'] N Bummler(in) *m(f)* (*inf*)

saurian ['sɔːrɪən] N Echse *f*; (= *dinosaur etc*) Saurier *m*

sausage ['sɒsɪdʒ] N **a** Wurst *f*; **you can't judge a ~ by its skin** (*prov*) man kann nicht nach dem Äußeren urteilen; **not a ~** (*Brit inf*) rein gar nichts (*inf*) **b** (*Brit, inf*, = *silly person*) Dummerchen *nt* (*inf*), Schäfchen *nt* (*inf*)

sausage: sausage dog N (*Brit, hum*) Dackel *m*; **sausage machine** N Wurstfüllmaschine *f*; (*fig hum*, = *school*) Bildungsfabrik *f*; **sausage meat** N Wurstbrät *nt*; **sausage roll** N ≈ Bratwurst *f* im Schlafrock

sauté ['saʊteɪ] **ADJ** **~ potatoes** Brat- *or* Röstkartoffeln *pl* **VT** *potatoes* rösten; (= *sear*) (kurz) anbraten

sauterne [saʊ'tɜːn] N Sauternes *m*

savable ['seɪvəbl] ADJ zu retten *pred*; *goal* haltbar, zu halten *pred*

savage ['sævɪdʒ] **ADJ** wild; *sport, fighter, punch, revenge* brutal; *custom* grausam; *animal* gefährlich; *competition* scharf, brutal (*inf*); *conflict* schwer, brutal; *war* grausam, brutal; (= *drastic, severe*) *cuts, measures* rigoros, hart, drastisch; *changes* drastisch; *criticism* schonungslos, brutal (*inf*); **the ~ people of New Guinea** die Wilden Neuguineas; **to put up a ~ fight** sich wütend *or* grimmig (*geh*) *or* wild (*inf*) verteidigen, sich verbissen wehren; **with a ~ snap of its jaws the crocodile ...** wütend biss das Krokodil ...; **the dog became a ~ beast** der Hund wurde zur reißenden Bestie; **the guard dogs are ~** die Wachhunde sind scharf *or* gefährlich; **to make a ~ attack on sb** brutal über jdn herfallen; (*fig*) jdn scharf angreifen; **he has a ~ temper** er ist ein äußerst jähzorniger Mensch; **he is in a ~ temper** er ist fuchsteufelswild (*inf*); **the critics were really ~ with her new play** die Kritiker haben ihr neues Stück wirklich schonungslos verrissen

N Wilde(r) *mf*

VT **a** (*animal*) anfallen; (*fatally*) zerfleischen

b (*fig*, = *criticize*) verreißen; *person also* (in der Luft) zerreißen

savagely ['sævɪdʒlɪ] ADV *attack, fight, punch* brutal; *bite* gefährlich; *reduce services* drastisch, rigoros; *criticize* schonungslos, brutal (*inf*); **he glared at her** ~ er warf ihr einen wilden Blick zu; **a ~ funny film** ein satirisch-humoriger Film; **the scenery was ~ beautiful** die Landschaft war von einer wilden Schönheit

savageness ['sævɪdʒnɪs] N Wildheit *f*; (*of sport, fighter, punch, revenge*) Brutalität *f*; (*of custom, war*) Grausamkeit *f*; (*of animal*) Gefährlichkeit *f*; (*of competition*) Schärfe *f*; (*of conflict*) Schwere *f*, Brutalität *f*; (= *severity, of cuts, measures*) Härte *f*; (*of criticism*) Schonungslosigkeit *f*

savagery ['sævɪdʒərɪ] N **a** (*of tribe, people*) Wildheit *f* **b** (= *cruelty*) Grausamkeit *f*; (*of attack*) Brutalität *f*; (*of treatment, prison life, cuts*) brutale Härte *f*; **the savageries committed ...** die Grausamkeiten *or* Gräueltaten *pl* ...

savanna(h) [sə'vænə] N Savanne *f*

save¹ [seɪv] N (*Ftbl etc*) Ballabwehr *f*; **what a ~!** eine tolle Parade!; **he made a fantastic ~** er hat den Ball prima abgewehrt *or* gehalten

VT **a** (= *rescue, Rel also*) retten; **to ~ sb from sth** jdn vor etw (*dat*) retten; **to ~ sb from disas-**

ter/ruin jdn vor einer Katastrophe/dem Ruin bewahren *or* retten; **he ~d me from falling/making that mistake** er hat mich davor bewahrt hinzufallen/den Fehler zu machen; **to ~ sth from sth** etw aus etw retten; **his goal ~d the match** sein Tor hat das Spiel gerettet *or* herausgerissen (*inf*); **to ~ the day** die Rettung sein; **God ~ the Queen** Gott schütze die Königin; **to ~ a building for posterity** ein Gebäude der Nachwelt erhalten; **to be ~d by the bell** (*inf*) gerade noch einmal davonkommen; **to ~ one's neck** *or* **ass** (*US sl*) *or* **butt** (*US inf*) seinen Kopf retten; **to ~ sb's neck** *or* **ass** (*US sl*) *or* **butt** (*US inf*) jdn rauspauken (*inf*), jdn retten

b (= *put by*) aufheben, aufbewahren, aufsparen; *money* sparen; (= *collect*) *stamps etc* sammeln; **~ some of the cake for me** lass mir etwas Kuchen übrig; **~ me a seat** halte mir einen Platz frei; **~ it for later, I'm busy now** (*inf*) spar dirs für später auf, ich habe jetzt zu tun (*inf*); **~ it!** (*inf*) spar dir das! (*inf*); **to ~ the best for last** das Beste bis zum Schluss aufheben

c (= *avoid using up*) *fuel, time, space, money* sparen; (= *spare*) *strength, eyes, battery* schonen; (= *save up*) *strength, fuel etc* aufsparen; **that will ~ you £20 a week** dadurch sparen Sie £ 20 die Woche; **going by plane will ~ you four hours on the train journey** der Flug spart dir vier Stunden Reisezeit im Vergleich zum Zug; **you don't ~ much by taking this short cut** Sie gewinnen nicht viel, wenn Sie diese Abkürzung nehmen; **he's saving himself for the big match** er schont sich für das große Spiel; **he's saving himself for the right woman** er spart sich für die Richtige auf

d (= *prevent*) *bother, trouble* ersparen; **at least it ~d the rain coming in** es hat wenigstens den Regen abgehalten; **it'll ~ a lot of hard work if we ...** es erspart uns (*dat*) sehr viel Mühe, wenn wir ...; **it ~d us having to do it again** das hat es uns (*dat*) erspart, es noch einmal machen zu müssen; **I've been ~d a lot of expense** mir blieben *or* mir wurden sehr viel Ausgaben erspart

e *goal* verhindern; *shot, penalty* halten; **well ~d!** gut gehalten!

f (*Comput*) sichern; **to ~ sth to disk** etw auf Diskette sichern *or* abspeichern

VI **a** (*with money*) sparen; **to ~ for sth** für *or* auf etw (*acc*) sparen; **~ as you earn** (*Brit = savings scheme*) Sparprogramm, bei dem der monatliche Beitrag unversteuert bleibt

b (*inf*: = *keep, food*) sich halten; (*news*) warten können

c (*Comput*) **the file won't ~** die Datei lässt sich nicht sichern *or* abspeichern

▶ **save up** **VI** sparen (*for* für, auf +*acc*) **VT sep** (= *not spend*) sparen; (= *not use*) aufheben, aufbewahren; **he's saving himself up for the big match** er schont sich für das große Spiel

save² [seɪv] **PREP** außer +*dat* **CONJ** **a** (*old, liter*) es sei denn (*geh*) **b** **~ that** nur dass

saveable ADJ = **savable**

saveloy ['sævɪlɔɪ] N Zervelatwurst *f*

saver ['seɪvə'] N **a** Retter(in) *m(f)*; **a ~ of lives** ein Lebensretter *m*, eine Lebensretterin **b** (*with money*) Sparer(in) *m(f)*

-saver N *suf* **it is a time-/money-/space-saver** es spart Zeit/Geld/Platz; **life-saver** Lebensretter(in) *m(f)*

saving ['seɪvɪŋ] **ADJ** **a** (= *redeeming*) **the one ~ feature of the scheme** das einzig Gute an dem Plan, das Einzige, was für den Plan spricht; **its/his ~ grace** was einen damit/mit ihm versöhnt

b sparsam; **she's not the ~ sort** sie ist nicht gerade sparsam

c **~ clause** Sicherheitsklausel *f*, einschränkende Klausel *f*

N **a** *no pl* (= *rescue, Rel*) Rettung *f*

b *no pl* (*of money*) Sparen *nt*; **to encourage ~** zum Sparen ermutigen

c (*of cost etc*, = *act*) Einsparung *f*; (= *amount saved*) Ersparnis *f*; **how much of a ~ is there?** wie viel wird eingespart?; **we must make ~s** wir müssen sparen; **a considerable ~ in time and money** eine beträchtliche Zeit- und Geldersparnis

d savings PL Ersparnisse *pl*; (*in account*) Spareinlagen *pl*; **post-office ~s** Postsparguthaben *nt*

PREP, CONJ = save²

-saving ADJ *suf* ... sparend; **time-/energy-saving** Zeit/Energie sparend; **life-saving** lebensrettend

savings *in cpds* Spar-; **savings account** N Sparkonto *nt*; **savings bank** N Sparkasse *f*; **savings bond** N (*US Fin*) (staatlicher) Sparbrief; **savings book** N Sparbuch *nt*; **savings certificate** N (*Brit Fin*) Sparbrief *m*; **savings deposit** N Spareinlage *f*; **savings stamp** N (*Brit*) Sparmarke *f*

saviour, (*US*) **savior** [ˈseɪvjəʳ] N Retter(in) *m(f)*; (*Rel also*) Erlöser *m*, Heiland *m*; **Our Saviour** unser Erlöser

savoir-faire [ˌsævwɑːˈfɛəʳ] N Gewandtheit *f*; (*in social matters*) gute Umgangsformen *pl*; **it's a question of ~** es ist nur eine Frage, wie man es anfasst

savor *etc* (*US*) = **savour** *etc*

savory [ˈseɪvərɪ] N (*Bot*) Bohnenkraut *nt*

savour, (*US*) **savor** [ˈseɪvəʳ] **N a** Geschmack *m*; **a ~ of garlic** ein Knoblauchgeschmack *m* **b** (*slight trace*) Spur *f*; **there is a ~ of pride in everything he says** in allem, was er sagt, schwingt ein gewisser Stolz mit **c** (= *enjoyable quality*) Reiz *m* **VT a** (*form*) kosten (*geh*), verkosten (*form*); *aroma (of food)* riechen **b** (*fig liter*) genießen, auskosten **VI to ~ of sth** (*fig liter*) etw ahnen lassen

savouriness, (*US*) **savoriness** [ˈseɪvərɪnɪs] N **a** (= *tastiness*) Schmackhaftigkeit *f*; **the ~ of the smells** die leckeren Gerüche **b** (= *spiciness*) Würzigkeit *f*, Pikantheit *f*; **the excessive ~ of all the food** das zu stark gewürzte Essen

savourless, (*US*) **savorless** [ˈseɪvəlɪs] ADJ geschmacklos

savoury, (*US*) **savory** [ˈseɪvərɪ] **ADJ a** (= *appetizing*) lecker **b** (= *not sweet*) pikant; **~ omelette** gefülltes Omelett; **~ biscuits** Salzgebäck *nt* **c** (*fig*) angenehm, ersprießlich; **that was not the most ~ adjective to have chosen** das war ja nicht gerade das feinste Adjektiv **N** (*Brit*) Häppchen *nt*; **would you like a sweet or a ~?** hätten Sie gern etwas Süßes oder etwas Pikantes oder Salziges?

savoy (cabbage) [səˈvɔɪ(ˈkæbɪdʒ)] N Wirsing (-kohl) *m*

savvy [ˈsævɪ] (*inf*) **N** (= *common sense*) Grips *m* (*inf*), Köpfchen *nt* (*inf*); (= *know-how*) Können *nt*, Know-how *nt*; **he hasn't got much ~** er hat keine Ahnung (*inf*) oder keinen Dunst (*inf*); **show a bit of ~!**, **use your ~!** streng mal dein Köpfchen *or* deinen Grips an (*inf*) **VT** kapieren (*inf*); **~?** kapiert? (*inf*), kapisko? (*dated sl*); **no ~** keine Ahnung (*inf*); (= *don't understand*) kapier ich nicht (*inf*)

saw¹ [sɔː] *pret of* **see¹**

saw² N Spruch *m*, Weisheit *f*

saw³ *vb: pret* **sawed**, *ptp* **sawed** *or* **sawn** **N** Säge *f*; **musical ~** singende Säge **VT a** (*lit*) sägen; **to ~ sth through** etw durchsägen; **to ~ sth in two** etw entzweisägen; **~ the wood into smaller logs** zersägen Sie das Holz in kleinere Scheite; **~n timber** (*esp Brit*) Schnittholz *nt* **b he/his arms ~ed the air** er schlug wild um sich, er fuchtelte mit den Armen (durch die Luft) **VI a** (*person, also*) sägen; (*wood*) sägen lassen **b to ~ away at the violin** auf der Geige herumsägen; **to ~ (away) at the meat** am Fleisch herumsäbeln (*inf*)

▶ **saw down** VT *sep* um- *or* absägen

▶ **saw off** VT *sep* absägen

▶ **saw up** VT *sep* zersägen (*into* in +*acc*)

saw: saw blade N Sägeblatt *nt*; **sawbones** N (*dated sl*) Medizinmann *m* (*inf*); **sawbuck** N (*US*) Sägebock *m*; (*sl*: = *banknote*) Zehndollarschein *m*; **sawdust** N Sägemehl *nt*; **sawfish**

N Sägefisch *m*; **sawhorse** N Sägebock *m*; **sawmill** N Sägewerk *nt*

sawn [sɔːn] *ptp of* saw³

sawn-off [ˈsɔːnˌɒf], (*US*) **sawed-off** [ˈsɔːdˌɒf] ADJ **~ shotgun** Gewehr *nt* mit abgesägtem Lauf

sawtooth N Sägezahn *m*

sawtoothed [ˈsɔːˈtuːθt] ADJ gezähnt

sawyer [ˈsɔːjəʳ] N Sägewerker(in) *m(f)*

sax [sæks] N (*inf*: = *saxophone*) Saxophon *nt*

saxhorn [ˈsækshɔːn] N (*Mus*) Saxhorn *nt*, Saxofon *nt*

saxifrage [ˈsæksɪfrɪdʒ] N Steinbrech *m*

Saxon [ˈsæksn] **N a** Sachse *m*, Sächsin *f*; (*Hist*) (Angel)sachse *m*/-sächsin *f* **b** (*Ling*) Sächsisch *nt* **ADJ** sächsisch; (*Hist*) (angel-)sächsisch

Saxony [ˈsæksənɪ] N Sachsen *nt*

saxophone [ˈsæksəfəʊn] N Saxophon *nt*, Saxofon *nt*

saxophonist [ˌsæksˈɒfənɪst] N Saxophonist(in) *m(f)*, Saxofonist(in) *m(f)*

---

say [seɪ]
vb: pret, ptp **said**
⚙ 1.1, 3.3, 6.3, 13

1 TRANSITIVE/INTRAN-SITIVE VERB	2 NOUN

1 – TRANSITIVE/INTRANSITIVE VERB

a sagen; **you can say what you like (about it/me)** Sie können (darüber/über mich) sagen, was Sie wollen; **I never thought I'd hear him say that** ich hätte nie gedacht, dass er das sagen würde; **that's not for him to say** es steht ihm nicht zu, sich darüber zu äußern; (= *to decide*) das kann er nicht entscheiden; **he looks very smart, I'll say that for him** er sieht sehr schick aus, das muss man ihm lassen; **if you see her, say I haven't changed my mind** wenn du sie siehst, sag ihr *or* richte ihr aus, dass ich es mir nicht anders überlegt habe; **I'm not saying it's the best, but ...** ich sage *or* behaupte ja nicht, dass es das Beste ist, aber ...; **though I say it myself** wenn ich das mal selbst sagen darf; **never let it be said that I didn't try** es soll keiner sagen können *or* mir soll keiner nachsagen, ich hätte es nicht versucht; **well, all I can say is ...** na ja, da kann ich nur sagen ...; **it tastes, shall we say, interesting** das schmeckt aber, na, sagen wir mal interessant; **you'd better do it – who says?** tun Sie das lieber – wer sagt das?; **well, what can I say?** na ja, was kann man da sagen?; **what does it mean? – I wouldn't like to say** was bedeutet das? – das kann ich auch nicht sagen; **having said that, I must point out ...** ich muss allerdings darauf hinweisen ...; **so saying, he sat down** und mit den Worten setzte er sich

♦ **to say for oneself** he didn't have much to say for himself er sagte *or* redete nicht viel; (*in defence*) er konnte nicht viel (zu seiner Verteidigung) sagen; **what have you got to say for yourself?** was haben Sie zu Ihrer Verteidigung zu sagen?

♦ **to say so** if you don't like it, say so wenn Sie es nicht mögen, dann sagen Sie es doch; **why didn't you say so?** warum haben Sie das denn nicht gesagt?; **do it this way – if you say so** machen Sie es so – wenn Sie meinen

b *giving instructions* he said to wait here er hat gesagt, ich soll/wir sollen *etc* hier warten

c = announce melden; **who shall I say?** wen darf ich melden?

d = recite *poem* aufsagen; *prayer, text* sprechen; **say after me ...** sprechen Sie mir nach ...

e = pronounce aussprechen; **he can't say his r's** er kann kein R aussprechen

f = indicate (*newspaper, dictionary, clock, horoscope*) sagen (*inf*); (*thermometer*) anzeigen, sagen (*inf*); (*law, church, Bible, computer*) sagen; **it says in the papers that ...** in den Zeitungen steht, dass ...; **what does the paper/this book/your horoscope etc say?** was steht in der Zeitung/diesem Buch/deinem Horoskop etc?; **the**

rules say that ... in den Regeln heißt es, dass ...; **what does the weather forecast say?** wie ist *or* lautet (*form*) der Wetterbericht?; **the weather forecast said that ...** es hieß im Wetterbericht, dass ..., laut Wetterbericht ...; **what does your watch say?** wie spät ist es auf Ihrer Uhr?, was sagt Ihre Uhr? (*inf*); **did the news say anything about the strike?** kam in den Nachrichten etwas über den Streik?; **they weren't allowed to say anything about it in the papers** sie durften in den Zeitungen nichts darüber schreiben

g = tell sagen; **it's hard to say what's wrong** es ist schwer zu sagen, was nicht stimmt; **what does that say about his intentions/the main character?** was sagt das über seine Absichten/die Hauptperson aus?; **that says a lot about his character/state of mind** das lässt tief auf seinen Charakter/Gemütszustand schließen; **these figures say a lot about recent trends** diese Zahlen sind in Bezug auf neuere Tendenzen sehr aufschlussreich; **and that's saying a lot** und das will schon etwas heißen; **that's not saying much** das will nicht viel heißen; **that doesn't say much for him** das spricht nicht für ihn; **that says a lot for him** das spricht für ihn; **there's no saying what might happen** es kann keiner vorhersagen; **there's something/a lot to be said for being based in London** es spricht einiges/viel für ein Zuhause *or (for a firm)* für einen Sitz in London

h = suppose **say it takes three men to ...** angenommen, man braucht drei Leute, um zu ...; **if it happens on, say, Wednesday?** wenn es am, sagen wir mal Mittwoch, passiert?

i *in suggestions* **what would you say to a whisky/game of tennis?** wie wärs mit einem Whisky/mit einer Partie Tennis?; **shall we say Tuesday/£50?** sagen wir Dienstag/£ 50?; **what did he say to your plan?** was hat er zu Ihrem Plan gesagt?; **I'll offer £500, what do you say to that?** ich biete £ 500, was meinen Sie dazu?; **what do you say we go now?** (*inf*) wie wärs *or* was hieltest du davon, wenn wir jetzt gingen?, was meinst du, sollen wir jetzt gehen?; **let's try again, what d'you say?** (*inf*) was meinste, versuchen wirs noch mal? (*inf*); **what do you say?** was meinst Sie?; **I wouldn't say no to a cup of tea** ich hätte nichts gegen eine Tasse Tee; **he never says no to a drink** er schlägt einen Drink nie aus, er sagt nie Nein *or* nein zu einem Drink

j *exclamatory* **well, I must say!** na, ich muss schon sagen!; **I say!** (*dated*) na so was!; (*to attract attention*) hallo!; **I say, thanks awfully, old man!** (*dated*) na vielen Dank, altes Haus! (*dated*); **say, what a great idea!** (*esp US*) Mensch, tolle Idee! (*inf*); **say, buddy!** (*esp US*) he, Mann! (*inf*); **I should say so!** das möchte ich doch meinen!; **you don't say!** (*also iro*) nein wirklich?, was du nicht sagst!; **well said!** (ganz) richtig!; **you('ve) said it!** Sie sagen es!; **you can say that again!** das kann man wohl sagen!; **say no more!** ich weiß Bescheid!; **says you!** (*inf*) das meinst auch nur du! (*inf*); **says who?** (*inf*) wer sagt das?; **and so say all of us** und wir stimmen alle zu

k *set expressions* **(it's) easier said than done** das ist leichter gesagt als getan; **no sooner said than done** gesagt, getan; **when all is said and done** letzten Endes; **they say ...,** it is said ...; heißt ...; **he is said to be very rich** er soll sehr reich sein, es heißt, er sei sehr reich; **a building said to have been built by ...** ein Gebäude, das angeblich von ... gebaut wurde *or* das von ... gebaut worden sein soll; **it goes without saying that ...** es versteht sich von selbst, dass ..., es ist selbstverständlich, dass ...; **that goes without saying** das ist selbstverständlich; **that is to say** das heißt; (*correcting also*) beziehungsweise; **that's not to say that ...** das soll nicht heißen, dass ...; **the plan sounded vague, not to say impractical** der Plan klang vage, um nicht zu sagen unpraktisch; **to say nothing of the noise/costs etc** von dem Lärm/den Kosten etc ganz zu schweigen *or* mal ganz abgesehen;

to say nothing of being ... davon, dass ich/er etc ... ganz zu schweigen or mal ganz abgesehen; **enough said!** genug!

2 – NOUN

a = opportunity to speak **let him have his say** lass ihn mal reden or seine Meinung äußern; **everyone should be allowed to have his say** jeder sollte seine Meinung äußern dürfen, jeder sollte zu Wort kommen; **you've had your say** Sie haben Ihre Meinung äußern können

b = right to decide etc Mitspracherecht nt (in bei); **to have no/a say in sth** bei etw nichts/etwas zu sagen haben, bei etw kein/ein Mitspracherecht haben; **I want more say in determining ...** ich möchte mehr Mitspracherecht bei der Entscheidung ... haben; **to have the last** or **final say (in sth)** (etw) letztlich entscheiden; (person also) das letzte Wort (bei etw) haben

sayest ['seɪəst] (obs) 2nd pers sing of **say**

saying ['seɪɪŋ] N Redensart f; (= proverb) Sprichwort nt; **as the ~ goes** wie man so sagt, wie es so schön heißt

say-so ['seɪsəʊ] N (inf, = assertion) Wort nt; (= authority) Plazet nt; **on whose ~?** wer sagt das? (inf), mit welchem Recht?

s/c abbr of **self-contained**

scab [skæb] N a (on cut) Schorf m, Grind m b (= scabies) Krätze f c (inf, = strikebreaker) Streikbrecher(in) m(f); **~ labour** (Brit) or **labor** (US) Streikbrecher pl VI a (inf) den Streik brechen b (wound) **to ~ over** Schorf bilden

scabbard ['skæbəd] N Scheide f

scabby ['skæbɪ] ADJ (+er) a skin, hands schorfig, grindig; knees verschorft b (= having scabies) räudig c (inf, = dilapidated) schäbig, oll (inf)

scabies ['skeɪbiːz] N Krätze f, Scabies f (spec); (of animal also) Räude f, Schäbe f

scabious ['skeɪbiəs] ADJ (= having scabies) räudig

scabrous ['skeɪbrəs] ADJ (= indecent) geschmacklos

scaffold ['skæfəld] N (on building) Gerüst nt; (for execution) Schafott nt

scaffolder ['skæfəldə'] N Gerüstbauer(in) m(f)

scaffolding ['skæfəldɪŋ] N Gerüst nt; **to put up ~** ein Gerüst aufbauen

scag [skæg] N (US Drugs sl) Schnee m (inf)

scalawag ['skæləwæg] N (US) = **scallywag**

scald [skɔːld] N Verbrühung f VT a oneself, skin etw verbrühen; **he was ~ed to death** er erlitt tödliche Verbrennungen; **like a ~ed cat** (Brit) wie von der Tarantel gestochen b instruments, vegetables abbrühen; milk abkochen

scalding ['skɔːldɪŋ] ADJ siedend; (inf: = very hot) siedend heiß; (fig) tears heiß ADV **~ hot** siedend heiß; skin, weather glühend heiß

scale¹ [skeɪl] N a (of fish, snake, skin) Schuppe f; (of rust) Flocke f; (of paint) Plättchen nt; (= kettle scale) Kesselstein m no pl; **to take the ~s from sb's eyes** jdm die Augen öffnen; **the ~s fell from his eyes** es fiel ihm wie Schuppen von den Augen VT a fish (ab)schuppen b **to ~ teeth** den Zahnstein entfernen VI (also **scale off**) sich schuppen; (paint, rust) abblättern

scale² N (pair of) **~s** pl, **~** (form) Waage f; **the Scales** (Astron) die Waage; **~-pan** Waagschale f; **he turns** or **tips the ~s at 80 kilos** er bringt 80 Kilo auf die Waage; **the extra votes have tipped** or **turned the ~s in favour** (Brit) or **favor** (US) **of Labour** die zusätzlichen Stimmen gaben den Ausschlag für die Labour Party VI wiegen

scale³ N a Skala f; (on thermometer etc) Skala f, Gradeinteilung f; (on ruler) (Maß)einteilung f; (fig) Leiter f; (= social scale) Stufenleiter f; (= list, table) Tabelle f; **~ of charges** Gebührenordnung f, Tarife pl; **he ranks at the top of the ~ of contemporary violinists** er steht an der Spitze der zeitgenössischen Geiger

b (= instrument) Messgerät nt

c (Mus) Tonleiter f; **the ~ of G** die G(-Dur)-Tonleiter

d (of map etc) Maßstab m; **on a ~ of 5 km to**

the cm in einem Maßstab von 5 km zu 1 cm; **what is the ~?** welchen Maßstab hat es?, in welchem Maßstab ist es?; **to be out of ~ (with sth)** im Maßstab nicht (zu etw) passen; **to draw sth to ~** etw maßstabgerecht or im Maßstab zeichnen; **(drawn/true) to ~** maßstabgerecht

e (fig, = size, extent) Umfang m, Ausmaß nt; **to entertain on a large/small ~** Feste im größeren/im kleineren Rahmen geben; **large stores buy on a different ~ from small ones** große Kaufhäuser kaufen in ganz anderen Mengen als kleine Geschäfte; **inflation on an unprecedented ~** Inflation von bisher nie gekanntem Ausmaß; **they differ enormously in ~** sie haben völlig verschiedene Größenordnungen; **small/large in ~** von kleinem/großem Umfang; **a house designed on a magnificent ~** ein in großem Stil or großzügig angelegtes Haus; **it's similar but on a smaller ~** es ist ähnlich, nur kleiner; **on a national ~** auf nationaler Ebene; **on a commercial ~** gewerbsmäßig

▶ **scale down** VT sep (lit) verkleinern; (fig) verringern; **a sort of scaled-down Parthenon** eine Art Parthenon im Kleinformat

▶ **scale up** VT sep (lit) vergrößern; (fig) erhöhen

scale⁴ VT mountain, wall erklettern

scale: scale drawing N maßstabgerechte or maßstabgetreue Zeichnung; **scale model** N maßstäbliches or maßstabgetreues Modell

scalene ['skeɪliːn] ADJ triangle ungleichseitig; cone schief

scaliness ['skeɪlɪnɪs] N Schuppigkeit f

scaling ladder ['skeɪlɪŋ'lædə'] N Sturmleiter f

scallion [skæliən] N (US) = **spring onion**

scallop ['skɒləp] N a (Zool) Kammmuschel f, Jakobsmuschel f (esp Cook); **~ shell** (for cooking) Muschelschale f b ['skæləp] (= loop) Bogen m, bogenförmige Verzierung; (on linenware) Feston m VT ['skæləp] (= decorate with loops) mit Bögen or mit einem Bogenrand versehen; linenware festonieren

scalloped ['skɒləpt] ADJ a mit einem Bogenrand; linenware festoniert; **~ edge** Bogen-/Festonrand m b ['skɒləp] (Cook) überbacken

scallywag ['skæliwæg] N (Brit inf) Schlingel m (inf), Strolch m (inf)

scalp [skælp] N a Kopfhaut f; (= Indian trophy) Skalp m; (Sport etc) Trophäe f; **she'll not have my ~ quite so easily** so leicht wird sie mich nicht besiegen; **to be after sb's ~** (fig) jdn fertig machen wollen (inf) VT skalpieren; (hum, barber) kahlscheren (hum); **you've really been ~ed** (hum) du bist wohl die Treppe runtergefallen (inf)

scalpel ['skælpəl] N Skalpell nt

scaly ['skeɪlɪ] ADJ (+er) a skin, creature schuppig; walls abblätternd b kettle, pipe verkalkt

scam [skæm] N (inf, = deception) Betrug m, Beschiss m (inf)

scamp¹ [skæmp] N (inf) Frechdachs m, Lausebengel m (inf)

scamp² VT work pfuschen or schludern (inf) bei

scamper ['skæmpə'] N **they can go for a ~ in the garden** sie können im Garten herumtollen VI (person, child, puppy) tollen; (rabbit) hoppeln; (squirrel, mice) huschen

scampi ['skæmpɪ] PL Scampi pl

scan [skæn] VT a (= search with sweeping movement) schwenken über (+acc); (person) seine Augen wandern lassen über (+acc); newspaper, book überfliegen; (= examine closely) horizon absuchen; (by radar) absuchen, abtasten; luggage durchleuchten; **he ~ned her face for a sign of emotion** er suchte in ihrem Gesicht nach Anzeichen einer Gefühlsregung

b (Med) ein Szintigramm machen von; (pregnant woman) einen Ultraschall machen bei

c (TV) abtasten, rastern

d verse in Versfüße zerlegen

VI (verse) einen richtigen Versmaß haben, sich reimen (inf); **he couldn't make it ~** er konnte es nicht ins richtige Versmaß bringen; **stressed differently so that the line ~s** anders betont,

um das richtige Metrum in der Zeile zu bekommen

N (Med) Scan m; (in pregnancy) Ultraschalluntersuchung f; (= picture) Ultraschallaufnahme f

▶ **scan in** VT sep (Comput) graphics einbinden, einfügen, scannen

scandal ['skændl] N a Skandal m; **the ~ of our overcrowded hospitals** unsere skandalös überfüllten Krankenhäuser; **to cause/create a ~** einen Skandal verursachen; (amongst neighbours etc) allgemeines Aufsehen erregen; **it's a ~!** (das ist) ein Skandal!; **it is a ~ that ...** es ist skandalös, dass ... b no pl (= gossip) Skandalgeschichten pl; (= piece of gossip) Skandalgeschichte f; **the latest ~** der neueste Klatsch

scandalize ['skændəlaɪz] VT schockieren; **she was ~d** sie war entrüstet or empört (by über +acc)

scandal: scandalmonger N Klatschmaul nt (inf), Lästerzunge f; **scandalmongering** N Klatschsucht f; (by press) Skandalsucht f

scandalous ['skændələs] ADJ skandalös; **~ talk** böswilliger Klatsch; **a ~ report/tale** eine Skandalgeschichte; **to reach ~ proportions** skandalöse Ausmaße annehmen

scandalously ['skændələslɪ] ADV skandalös; **to speak ~ of sb** böse or üble Gerüchte über jdn verbreiten; **her children are ~ neglected** es ist skandalös or ein Skandal, wie vernachlässigt ihre Kinder sind

scandal sheet N (pej inf) Skandalblatt nt (pej)

Scandinavia [ˌskændɪ'neɪvɪə] N Skandinavien nt

Scandinavian [ˌskændɪ'neɪvɪən] ADJ skandinavisch N Skandinavier(in) m(f)

scanner ['skænə'] N (Rad) Richtantenne f; (TV) Bildabtaster m; (Comput, = OCR reader, Med) Scanner m

scanning ['skænɪŋ] N (Comput, Rad, TV) Scannen nt, Abtastung f

scanning line N (TV) Rasterlinie f

scansion ['skænʃən] N (Poet) metrische Gliederung; (Sch) Zerlegung f in Versfüße

scant [skænt] ADJ (+er) wenig inv; satisfaction, attention, respect also, chance gering; success gering, mager; supply, grazing, amount dürftig, spärlich; **to do ~ justice to sth** einer Sache (dat) wenig or kaum gerecht werden; **to have ~ regard for sth** auf etw (acc) wenig Rücksicht nehmen; **to show ~ respect for sth** einer Sache (dat) wenig Respekt entgegenbringen, für etw wenig Respekt zeigen; **to pay ~ attention to sth** etw kaum beachten; **a ~ 3 hours** knappe or kaum 3 Stunden

scantily ['skæntɪlɪ] ADV spärlich; **~ clad** or **dressed** spärlich bekleidet

scantiness ['skæntɪnɪs], **scantness** ['skæntnɪs] N (of amount, supply, information, knowledge) Spärlichkeit f, Dürftigkeit f; (of piece of clothing) Knappheit f

scanty ['skæntɪ] ADJ (+er) amount, supply, information, knowledge spärlich, dürftig; vegetation, meal also kärglich; harvest also mager; hair schütter; piece of clothing knapp

scapegoat ['skeɪpgəʊt] N Sündenbock m; **to be a ~ for sth** für etw der Sündenbock sein; **to use sb/sth as a ~, to make sb/sth one's ~** jdm/einer Sache die Schuld zuschieben, VT die Schuld zuschieben (+dat)

scapula ['skæpjʊlə] N (Anat) Schulterblatt nt

scar [skɑː'] N (on skin, tree) Narbe f; (= scratch) Kratzer m; (= burn) Brandfleck m, Brandloch nt; (fig, emotional) Wunde f; (on good name) Makel m

VT furniture zerkratzen, Brandflecken hinterlassen auf (+dat); **to ~ the skin/a tree** auf der Haut/an einem Baum Narben/eine Narbe hinterlassen; **he was ~red for life** (lit) er behielt bleibende Narben zurück; (fig) er war fürs Leben gezeichnet; **her ~red face** ihr narbiges Gesicht; **the table was ~red with cigarette burns** der Tisch war mit Brandlöchern or Brandflecken von Zigaretten übersät; **his mind was ~red forever by this tragic occurrence** dieses tragische Ereignis hatte bei ihm tiefe Wunden hinterlassen ▣ **VI** Narben/eine Narbe hinterlassen

scarab ['skærəb] N Skarabäus m

scarce [skeəs] ADJ (+er) (= in short supply) knapp; (= rare) selten; **jobs** rar; **to make oneself ~** (inf) verschwinden (inf), abhauen (inf) ▣ **ADV** (old) = **scarcely**

scarcely ['skeəslɪ] ADV **a** kaum; **~ anybody** kaum einer or jemand; **~ anything** fast or beinahe nichts; **~ ever** kaum jemals, fast or beinahe nie; **with ~ a sound** fast lautlos; **I ~ know what to say** ich weiß nicht recht, was ich sagen soll; **~ had the car drawn to a halt when ...** das Auto war kaum zum Stehen gekommen, als ... **b** (= not really) wohl kaum; **you can ~ expect him to believe that** Sie erwarten doch wohl nicht or kaum, dass er das glaubt; **he's ~ the most polite of men** er ist nicht gerade or er ist wohl kaum der Höflichste

scarceness ['skeəsnɪs], **scarcity** ['skeəsɪtɪ] N (= shortage) Knappheit f; (= rarity) Seltenheit f; **because of the scarcity of talent among the singers/pupils** weil so wenige Sänger/Schüler wirklich begabt sind; **his pictures are expensive because of their ~** seine Bilder sind teuer, weil es so wenige davon gibt; **a scarcity of qualified people** ein Mangel m an qualifizierten Kräften; **in times of scarcity** in schlechten Zeiten; **there are many scarcities in wartime** in Kriegszeiten ist vieles knapp

scarcity value N Seltenheitswert m

scare [skeə'] ▣ **N** (= fright, shock) Schreck(en) m; (= general alarm) Panikstimmung f, Hysterie f (about in Bezug auf +acc, wegen); **to give sb a ~** jdm einen Schrecken einjagen; (= make sb jump also) jdn erschrecken; **the devaluation ~** die Abwertungshysterie; **to create** or **cause a ~** eine Panik auslösen ▣ **VI** einen Schrecken einjagen (+dat); (= worry) Angst machen (+dat); (= frighten physically) person, animal erschrecken; **birds** aufschrecken; **to be easily ~d** sehr schreckhaft sein; (= easily worried) sich (dat) leicht Angst machen lassen; (= timid) deer etc sehr scheu sein; **to ~ sb stiff** or **to death** or **out of his/her wits** (all inf) jdn zu Tode erschrecken (inf) ▣ **VI** **I don't ~ easily** ich bekomme nicht so schnell Angst

▶ **scare away** VT sep verscheuchen; **people** verjagen

▶ **scare off** VT sep **a** = **scare away b** (= put off) abschrecken (prep obj von)

scare: scare buying N Angstkäufe pl; **scarecrow** N (lit, fig) Vogelscheuche f

scared ['skeəd] ADJ **a** (= afraid) look, face, voice ängstlich, verängstigt; **he's a ~ man** er hat Angst; **to be ~ (of sb/sth)** (vor jdm/etw) Angst haben; **to be ~ stiff** or **to death** or **out of one's wits** (all inf) Todesängste ausstehen, fürchterliche Angst haben; **to be ~ to do sth** Angst haben, etw zu tun; **she was too ~ to speak** sie konnte vor Angst nicht sprechen; **she was always too ~ to speak in public** sie getraute sich nie, in der Öffentlichkeit zu sprechen; **he's ~ of telling her the truth** er getraut sich nicht, ihr die Wahrheit zu sagen **b** (= apprehensive) ängstlich; **to be ~ that ...** Angst haben, dass ..., befürchten, dass ...

scaredy-cat ['skeədɪ,kæt] N (inf) Angsthase m (inf)

scare: scarehead N (US) Sensationsschlagzeile f; **scaremonger** N (esp Brit) Panikmacher(in) m(f); **scaremongering** N (esp Brit) Panikmache(rei) f (inf); **scare story** N Schauergeschichte f; **scare tactics** PL Panikmache(rei) f (inf), Verängstigungstaktik f

scarf [skɑːf] N pl **scarves** Schal m; (= neck scarf) Halstuch nt; (= head scarf) Kopftuch nt; (round the shoulders) Schultertuch nt; **~ pin** Brosche f, Vorstecknadel f

scarfskin ['skɑːfskɪn] N (Anat) Oberhaut f

scarifying ['skeərɪfaɪɪŋ] ADJ (inf) beängstigend; **film** grus(e)lig (inf)

scarlatina [,skɑːlə'tiːnə] N Scharlach m

scarlet ['skɑːlɪt] ▣ **N** Scharlach(rot) nt ▣ **ADJ** (scharlach)rot, hochrot; **to turn** or **go ~** hochrot werden, rot anlaufen (inf); **he was ~ with rage** er war rot or knallrot (inf) vor Wut; **a ~ woman** (old, hum) eine verrufene or liederliche Frau

scarlet fever N Scharlach m, Scharlachfieber nt

scarp [skɑːp] N Abhang m

scarper ['skɑːpə'] VI (Brit, inf) abhauen (inf), verduften (inf)

scar tissue N vernarbtes Fleisch

scarves [skɑːvz] pl of **scarf**

scary ['skeərɪ] ADJ (+er) (inf) unheimlich; **film** grus(e)lig (inf); **it was pretty ~** da konnte man schon Angst kriegen (inf); **that's a ~ thought** das ist ein beängstigender Gedanke **b** (= nervous) horse, person schreckhaft; (= easily worried) ängstlich

scat¹ [skæt] INTERJ (inf) verschwinde!, verschwindet!

scat² (Jazz) ▣ **N** Scat m, rhythmisches Singen von Silben an Stelle von Worten ▣ **VI** Scat singen

scathing ['skeɪðɪŋ] ADJ bissig; remark also schneidend; attack scharf, schonungslos; look vernichtend; criticism beißend, vernichtend; **to be ~** bissige or schneidende Bemerkungen pl machen (about über +acc); **to make a ~ attack on sb/sth** jdn/etw scharf angreifen

scathingly ['skeɪðɪŋlɪ] ADV answer mit schneidendem Hohn; look vernichtend; criticize, attack scharf, schonungslos

scatology [skæ'tɒlədʒɪ] N (Med) Koprologie f (spec); (fig) Fäkalsprache f, Skatologie f (geh)

scatter ['skætə'] ▣ **N** = **scattering** ▣ **VT** **a** (= distribute at random) verstreuen; seeds, gravel streuen (on, onto auf +acc); (Phys) light streuen (on, onto auf +acc); money verschleudern; (= not group together) (unregelmäßig) verteilen; votes verteilen (between auf +acc); **to ~ sth around** or **about** etw überall umherstreuen or verstreuen; **to ~ sth with sth** etw mit etw bestreuen; **she knocked the table over, ~ing papers all over the room** sie stieß den Tisch um, und die Papiere flogen durch das ganze Zimmer **b** (= disperse) auseinander treiben; demonstrators, crowd also zerstreuen → also **scattered** ▣ **VI** sich zerstreuen (to in +acc); (in a hurry, in fear) auseinander laufen

scatter: scatterbrain N (inf) Schussel m (inf); **scatterbrained** ['skætə,breɪnd] ADJ schuss(e)lig (inf), zerfahren, flatterhaft; **scatter cushion** N (Sofa)kissen nt

scattered ['skætəd] ADJ population weit verstreut; objects, villages verstreut; trees einzeln stehend; clouds, showers, fighting vereinzelt; **my relatives are ~ all over the country** meine Verwandten sind über das ganze Land verstreut; **the books were ~ (about) all over the room** die Bücher lagen im ganzen Zimmer herum or verstreut; **a piano ~ with photographs** ein mit Fotos übersätes Klavier

scatter-gun ['skætəgʌn] ▣ **N** Schrotflinte f ▣ **ADJ** (fig) approach auf breiter Ebene, breit gefächert

scattering ['skætərɪŋ] N (of people) vereinzeltes Häufchen; (Phys, of light, waves) Streuung f; **a ~ of books/houses** vereinzelte Bücher pl/Häuser pl; **a thin ~ of snow on the hillside** dünner Schneefall auf dem Hügel

scatter rug N kleiner Teppich

scattershot ['skætəʃɒt] ADJ oberflächlich; **the money has been spent in a ~ fashion** das Geld ist nach dem Gießkannenprinzip or ziemlich willkürlich ausgegeben worden

scatty ['skætɪ] ADJ (+er) (inf) **a** (= scatterbrained) schusslig (inf), schusselig (inf) **b** (= mad) verrückt, närrisch (inf)

scavenge ['skævɪndʒ] **VT** (lit, fig) ergattern; **the scraps are ~d by hungry gulls** hungrige Möwen ergattern or holen sich (dat) die Essensreste; **the tramp ~d food from the piles of litter** der Landstreicher plünderte die Abfallhaufen **VI** (lit) Nahrung suchen; **to ~ for sth** nach etw suchen; **jackals live by scavenging** Schakale leben von Aas; **to ~ in the bins** die Abfalleimer plündern; **he's always scavenging around in scrapyards** er durchstöbert dauernd die Schrottplätze

scavenger ['skævɪndʒə'] N (= animal) Aasfresser m; (fig, = person) Aasgeier m

SCE abbr of **Scottish Certificate of Education** höherer Schulabschluss in Schottland

scenario [sɪ'nɑːrɪəʊ] N Szenar(ium) nt; (fig) Szenario nt

scene [siːn] **N** **a** (= place, setting) Schauplatz m; (of play, novel) Ort m der Handlung; **the ~ of the crime** der Tatort, der Schauplatz des Verbrechens; **the ~ of the battle was a small hill** die Schlacht fand an einem kleinen Hügel statt; **to set the ~** (lit, fig) den Rahmen geben; **the ~ is set in Padua** Ort der Handlung ist Padua, das Stück/der Roman etc spielt in Padua; **a change of ~ does you good** ein Tapetenwechsel m tut dir gut; **to come** or **appear on the ~** auftauchen, auf der Bildfläche erscheinen; **to disappear from the ~** von der Bildfläche verschwinden; **after the accident the police were first on the ~** nach dem Unfall war die Polizei als erste zur Stelle **b** (= description, incident) Szene f **c** (Theat) Szene f; **Act II, ~ i** Akt II, 1. Auftritt or Szene **d** (Theat, = scenery) Bühnenbild nt, Kulisse f; **the stagehands move the ~s** die Bühnenarbeiter wechseln die Kulissen; **behind the ~s** (lit, fig) hinter den Kulissen **e** (= sight) Anblick m; (= landscape) Landschaft f; (= tableau) Szene f; **~s of Parisian life** Szenen aus dem Pariser Leben; **favourite** (Brit) or **favorite** (US) Glasgow **~s** die beliebtesten Ansichten von Glasgow; **they left behind a ~ of destruction** sie hinterließen die Stätte der Verwüstung **f** (= fuss, argument) Szene f; **to make a ~** eine Szene machen **g** (inf: = area of activity) Szene f; **the London drug/pop** etc **~** die Londoner Drogen-/Popszene etc; **on the fashion ~** in der Modewelt; **that's not my ~** da steh ich nicht drauf (inf); **to know the ~** or **what the ~ is** wissen, was abgeht (sl); **it's a whole different ~ here** hier sieht alles ganz anders aus, hier läuft alles ganz anders (inf); **to make the ~** groß herauskommen (inf); **he knew he'd made the ~ when ...** er wusste, dass er es geschafft hatte, als ... (inf)

scene: scene change N Szenenwechsel m; **scene painter** N Bühnen- or Kulissenmaler(in) m(f)

scenery ['siːnərɪ] N **a** (= landscape) Landschaft f; **there was no ~ at all to look at** die Landschaft bot überhaupt nichts Sehenswertes; **do you like the ~?** gefällt Ihnen die Gegend?; **I'm tired of all the city ~** ich bin stadtmüde **b** (Theat) Bühnendekoration f, Kulissen pl

scene shifter N Kulissenschieber(in) m(f)

scenic ['siːnɪk] ADJ **a** (= of landscape) landschaftlich; **~ shots** (Phot) Landschaftsaufnahmen pl **b** (= picturesque) malerisch; **to take the ~ route** die landschaftlich schöne Strecke nehmen; (hum) einen kleinen Umweg machen **c** (= theatrical) bühnentechnisch; (Film) filmtechnisch; **~ effects** (Theat) Bühneneffekte pl; (Film) landschaftliche Effekte pl

scenic: scenic design N Szenenbild nt; **scenic designer** N Szenenbildner(in) m(f); **scenic railway** N Touristenbahnlinie f (durch landschaftlich schönes Gebiet), ≈ Berg- und Tal-Bahn f; (= roller coaster) Achterbahn f; **scenic road**, **scenic route** N landschaftlich schöne Strecke

scent [sent] **N** **a** (= smell) Duft m, Geruch m; **there was the ~ of danger in the air** es roch nach Gefahr **b** (= *perfume*) Parfüm *nt* **c** (*of animal*) Fährte *f*; **to be on the ~** (*lit, fig*) auf der Fährte *or* Spur sein (*of sb/sth* jdm/einer Sache); **to lose the ~** (*lit, fig*) die Spur *or* Fährte verlieren; **to put** *or* **throw sb off the ~** (*lit, fig*) jdn von der Spur *or* Fährte abbringen *or* ablenken **d** (= *sense of smell*) Geruchssinn *m*; (*fig*) (Spür)nase *f* **VT** **a** (= *smell, suspect*) wittern **b** (= *perfume*) parfümieren; **roses ~ed the air** der Duft von Rosen erfüllte die Luft

▶ **scent out** VT *sep* (*lit, fig*) aufspüren; *story* ausfindig machen

scent bottle N Parfümfläschchen *nt*

scented ['sentɪd] ADJ *soap, handkerchief* parfümiert; *flower, garden* duftend; **sweet ~** süß duftend; **~ candle** Duftkerze *f*; **~ oil** Duftöl *nt*

scent: scent gland N (*pleasant smell*) Duftdrüse *f*; (*unpleasant smell*) Stinkdrüse *f*; **scentless** ADJ *flower* duftlos, geruchlos; *shampoo etc* geruchsfrei, geruchsneutral; **scent spray** N Parfümzerstäuber *m*

scepter N (*US*) = **sceptre**

sceptic, (*US*) **skeptic** ['skeptɪk] N Skeptiker(in) *m(f)*

sceptical, (*US*) **skeptical** ['skeptɪkəl] ADJ skeptisch; **to be ~ about** *or* **of sth** über etw (*acc*) or in Bezug auf etw (*acc*) skeptisch sein; **he was ~ about it** er stand der Sache skeptisch gegenüber, er war skeptisch; **I'm ~ about how necessary this is** ich bin skeptisch *or* ich bezweifle, ob das nötig ist; **to have/adopt a ~ attitude toward(s) sth** eine skeptische Haltung gegenüber etw haben/einnehmen; **to cast a ~ eye on** *or* **over sth** einen skeptischen Blick auf etw (*acc*) werfen

sceptically, (*US*) **skeptically** ['skeptɪkəlɪ] ADV skeptisch

scepticism, (*US*) **skepticism** ['skeptɪsɪzəm] N Skepsis *f* (*about* gegenüber)

sceptre, (*US*) **scepter** ['septə'] N Zepter *nt*

sch *abbr of* **school** Sch.

schedule ['skedʒʊəl, (*esp Brit*) 'ʃedjuːl] **N** **a** (*of events*) Programm *nt*; (*of work*) Zeitplan *m*; (*of lessons*) Stundenplan *m*; (*esp US: = timetable*) Fahr-/Flugplan *m*; (*US, = list*) Verzeichnis *nt*; **production ~** Produktionsplan *m*, Fertigungsprogramm *nt*; **building ~** Bauprogramm *nt*; **what's on the ~ for today?** was steht für heute auf dem Programm?; **according to ~** planmäßig; (*work also*) nach Plan; **the train is behind ~** der Zug hat Verspätung; **the bus was on ~** der Bus war pünktlich, der Bus kam fahrplanmäßig an; **the building will be opened on ~** das Gebäude wird wie geplant eröffnet werden; **the work is up to ~** die Arbeit verläuft nach Zeitplan; **the work is ahead of/behind ~** wir/sie *etc* sind (mit der Arbeit) dem Zeitplan voraus/in Verzug or im Rückstand; **we are working to a very tight ~** unsere Termine sind sehr eng (*inf*) **b** (= *insurance, mortgage schedule*) Urkunde *f*; (*US, Jur, = appendix*) Anhang *m* **VT** planen; (= *put on programme, timetable*) ansetzen; (*US, = list*) aufführen; **the work is ~d for completion in 3 months** die Arbeit soll (nach dem *or* laut Zeitplan) in 3 Monaten fertig (gestellt) sein; **this is not ~d for this year** das steht für dieses Jahr nicht auf dem Programm; **this building is ~d for demolition** es ist geplant, dieses Gebäude abzureißen; **you are ~d to speak for 20 minutes** für Sie sind 20 Minuten Sprechzeit vorgesehen; **she is ~d to speak tomorrow** ihre Rede ist für morgen geplant *or* angesetzt; **trains/buses to New York will be ~d differently** die Abfahrtszeiten der Züge/Busse nach New York werden geändert; **the plane is ~d to take off at 2 o'clock** planmäßiger Abflug ist 2 Uhr; **the journey is ~d to last 7 hours** die Fahrt soll 7 Stunden dauern; **this stop was not ~d** dieser Aufenthalt war nicht eingeplant

scheduled ['skedʒʊəld, (*esp Brit*) 'ʃedjuːld] ADJ vorgesehen, geplant; *departure etc* planmäßig; **to make a ~ stop** einen planmässigen Halt machen; **on/before the ~ date** zum/vor dem ge-

planten *or* vorgesehenen Datum; **at the ~ time** zum vorgesehenen Zeitpunkt

scheduled: scheduled building N (*Brit, Archit*) denkmalgeschütztes *or* unter Denkmalschutz stehendes Gebäude; **scheduled flight** N (*not charter*) Linienflug *m*; (= *on timetable*) planmäßiger Flug; **scheduled territories** PL (*Brit Fin*) der Sterlingblock

schema ['skiːmə] N *pl* **-ta** ['skiːmətə] Darstellung *f*; (*Philos*) Schema *nt*

schematic ADJ , **schematically** ADV [skɪ'mætɪk, -əlɪ] schematisch

scheme [skiːm] **N** **a** (= *plan*) Plan *m*, Programm *nt*; (= *project*) Projekt *nt*; (= *insurance scheme*) Programm *nt*; (= *idea*) Idee *f*; **the ~ for the new bypass** das neue Umgehungsstraßenprojekt; **a ~ of work** ein Arbeitsprogramm *nt* or -plan *m*; **savings ~** Sparprogramm *nt* **b** (= *plot*) (raffinierter) Plan; (*esp political*) Komplott *nt*; (*at court, in firm etc*) Intrige *f*; **a ~ to overthrow the government** ein Komplott *m* gegen die Regierung, Pläne *pl*, die Regierung zu stürzen; **the CIA's ~s to discredit Castro** die Machenschaften *pl* des CIA, um Castro zu diskreditieren **c** (= *arrangement, layout, of town centre etc*) Anlage *f*; (*of room etc*) Einrichtung *f*; **the new road ~** das neue Straßensystem; **rhyme ~** Reimschema *nt*; **it doesn't fit into my ~ of things** es hat keinen Platz in meiner Betrachtungsweise; **in the grand ~ of things** im Ganzen gesehen **d** (*Brit: = housing scheme*) Siedlung *f* **VI** Pläne schmieden *or* aushecken (*inf*); (*in firm etc*) intrigieren; **to ~ for sth** auf etw (*acc*) hinarbeiten

schemer ['skiːmə'] N raffinierter Schlawiner; (*in firm etc*) Intrigant(in) *m(f)*, Ränkeschmied(in) *m(f)* (*geh*); **my mother's a real ~** meine Mutter schmiedet immer ganz raffinierte Pläne

scheming ['skiːmɪŋ] **N** raffiniertes Vorgehen, Tricks *pl* (*inf*); (*of politicians, businessmen etc*) Machenschaften *pl*, Schliche *pl*; (*at court, in firm etc*) Intrigen *pl*, Ränke *pl* (*liter*) **ADJ** *girl, methods, businessman* raffiniert, durchtrieben; *colleague, courtier* intrigant; *politician* gewieft (*inf*); **what's in your ~ little mind?** was führst du im Schild?; **her ~ mother-in-law** ihre hinterhältige Schwiegermutter

schemozzle [ʃɪ'mɒzl] N (*US inf*) Durcheinander *nt*

Schengen Agreement [ʃeŋə'griːmənt] N (*Pol*) Schengener Abkommen *nt*

scherzo ['skɛːtsəʊ] N Scherzo *nt*

schilling ['ʃɪlɪŋ] N (*Hist*) Schilling *m*

schism ['sɪzəm] N (*Eccl*) Schisma *nt*; (*general also*) Spaltung *f*

schismatic [sɪz'mætɪk] **ADJ** schismatisch **N** Schismatiker(in) *m(f)*

schist [ʃɪst] N Schiefer *m*

schizo ['skɪtsəʊ] (*inf*) **N** (= *schizophrenic*) Schizophrene(r) *mf*; (= *crazy person*) Verrückte(r) *mf* (*inf*) **ADJ** (= *schizophrenic*) schizophren; (= *crazy*) verrückt (*inf*)

schizoid ['skɪtsɔɪd] **ADJ** schizoid **N** Schizoide(r) *mf*

schizophrenia [ˌskɪtsəʊ'friːnɪə] N Schizophrenie *f*

schizophrenic [ˌskɪtsəʊ'frenɪk] **ADJ** *person, reaction* schizophren; **he has ~ tendencies** er neigt zur Schizophrenie; **a ~ illness** eine Art Schizophrenie **N** Schizophrene(r) *mf*

schizophrenically [ˌskɪtsəʊ'frenɪkəlɪ] ADV schizophren; **a ~ disturbed person** ein Mensch mit Bewusstseinsspaltung

schlemiel, schlemihl [ʃlə'miːl] N (*US inf*) Schlemihl *m*, Pechvogel *m*; (= *awkward person*) Tollpatsch *m* (*pej*)

schlep, schlepp [ʃlep] **N** (*US inf*) **VT** (= *lug*) schleppen, mit sich (herum)schleppen **VI** (= *traipse*) latschen (*inf*), sich schleppen; **to ~ through the traffic** sich durch den Verkehr quälen **N** **a** (= *strenuous journey*) ermüdende

Fahrt *or* Reise; (*on foot*) ermüdender Weg **b** = **schlepper**

schlepper ['ʃlepə'] N (*US inf, pej*) **a** (= *tedious person*) Langweiler(in) *m(f)* (*pej*) **b** (= *awkward person*) Tollpatsch *m* (*pej*), Umstandskrämer(in) *m(f)* (*inf, pej*) **c** (= *stupid person*) Trottel *m* (*inf, pej*)

schlock [ʃlɒk] N (*dated esp US sl*: = *trash*) Mist *m* (*inf*), Schund *m*

schlong [ʃlɒŋ] N (*US sl*) Schwanz *m* (*sl*)

schmal(t)z [ʃmɔːlts] N (*inf*) Schmalz *m* (*inf*)

schmal(t)zy ['ʃmɔːltsɪ] ADJ (*inf, = slushy*) schmalzig (*inf*)

schmear [ʃmɪə'] N (*US inf*) **the whole ~** das ganze Drumherum *or* Brimborium (*inf*)

schmo [ʃməʊ] N (*US, inf, = fool*) Bekloppte(r) *mf* (*inf*), Beknackte(r) *mf* (*sl*)

schmuck [ʃmʌk] N (*US, inf, = fool*) Beknackte(r) *mf* (*sl*)

schnap(p)s [ʃnæps] N Schnaps *m*

schnitzel ['ʃnɪtsəl] N (Wiener) Schnitzel *nt*

schnorkel ['ʃnɔː kl] N = **snorkel**

schnozzle ['ʃnɒzəl] N (*esp US, inf*) Zinken *m* (*inf*)

scholar ['skɒlə'] N **a** (= *learned person*) Gelehrte(r) *mf*; **the leading ~s of our time** die führenden Wissenschaftler unserer Zeit; **a famous Shakespeare ~** ein bekannter Shakespearekenner; **I'm no ~** ich bin ja kein Gelehrter **b** (= *student*) Student(in) *m(f)*, Schüler(in) *m(f)* **c** (= *scholarship holder*) Stipendiat(in) *m(f)*

scholarliness ['skɒlə lɪnɪs] N (*of person, work*) Gelehrtheit *f*, Gelehrsamkeit *f*; **the ~ of his interests** sein Interesse *nt* an hochgeistigen Dingen; **the ~ of his appearance** sein gelehrtes Aussehen

scholarly ['skɒlə lɪ] ADJ wissenschaftlich; (= *learned*) gelehrt; *interests* hochgeistig; **he's not at all ~** er hat keinen Hang zum Hochgeistigen; (*in his approach*) er geht überhaupt nicht wissenschaftlich vor; **his way of life was very ~** er führte das Leben eines Gelehrten

scholarship ['skɒlə ʃɪp] **N** **a** (= *learning*) Gelehrsamkeit *f*; **~ flourished during the Renaissance** die Gelehrsamkeit entfaltete sich in der Renaissance zur vollen Blüte **b** (= *money award*) Stipendium *nt*; **to win a ~ to Cambridge** ein Stipendium für Cambridge bekommen; **on a ~** mit einem Stipendium; **~ holder** Stipendiat(in) *m(f)*

scholastic [skə'læstɪk] ADJ **a** (= *relative to school*) schulisch, Schul-; (*Univ*) Studien-; **her ~ record** ihre schulischen Leistungen, ihre Schulleistungen; (*Univ*) ihre Studienleistungen; **the ~ profession** der Lehrberuf → *also* **SAT** **b** (= *relative to scholasticism*) scholastisch

scholasticism [skə'læstɪsɪzəm] N Scholastik *f*

school[1] [skuːl] **N** **a** Schule *f*; (*US, = college, university*) College *nt*, Universität *f*; **at ~** in der Schule/im College/an der Universität; **to go to ~** in die Schule/ins College/zur Universität gehen; **there's no ~ tomorrow** morgen ist schulfrei *or* keine Schule; **~ of art/dancing, art/dancing ~** Kunst-/Tanzschule *f*; **the ~ of life** die Schule des Lebens; **to be brought up in the ~ of hard knocks** durch bittere *or* schlechte Erfahrungen gelernt haben **b** (*Univ: = department*) Fachbereich *m*; (*of medicine, law*) Fakultät *f*; **School of Arabic Studies** Institut *nt* für Arabistik **c** (= *group of artists, philosophers etc*) Schule *f*; **Plato and his ~** Platon und seine Schüler (-schaft); **I'm not one of that ~** ich gehöre nicht zu den Leuten, die das meinen; **he adheres to another ~ of thought** er vertritt eine andere Lehrmeinung; **he's a diplomat of the old ~** er ist ein Diplomat der alten Schule **VT** lehren; *animal* dressieren; *one's temper* zügeln; **to ~ sb in a technique** jdn eine Technik lehren, jdn in einer Technik unterrichten *or* unterweisen; **he ~ed himself to control his temper** er hatte sich dazu erzogen, sich zu beherrschen

school² N (of fish) Schule f; (of herrings) Schwarm m

school in cpds Schul-; **school age** N schulpflichtiges Alter, Schulalter nt; **is he of ~ yet?** ist er schon schulpflichtig or im schulpflichtigen Alter?; **school bag** N Schultasche f; **school board** N (US) Schulbehörde f; (Brit) Schulaufsichtsrat m; **school book** N Schulbuch nt; **schoolboy** N Schuljunge m, Schüler m ADJ attr Pennäler-, Schuljungen-; ~ **prank** Pennäler-, Schuljungenstreich m; ~ **humour** or (US) **humor** Pennälerhumor m; **schoolchildren** PL Schüler pl, Schulkinder pl; **school days** PL Schulzeit f; **school dinner** N Schulessen nt; **school dropout** N Schulabbrecher(in) m(f)

schooled [sku:ld] ADJ to be ~ in sth in etw (dat) geschult sein; to be well ~ in sth sich in etw (dat) auskennen

school: school fees PL Schulgeld nt; **schoolgirl** N Schulmädchen nt, Schülerin f; **schoolhouse** N (= teacher's house) Lehrerhaus nt; (= school) Schulhaus nt

schooling ['sku:lɪŋ] N (= education) Ausbildung f; compulsory ~ was introduced in 1870 1870 wurde die Schulpflicht eingeführt; compulsory ~ lasts 11 years die (gesetzlich) vorgeschriebene Schulzeit dauert 11 Jahre

school: school-leaver N (Brit) Schulabgänger(in) m(f); **school-leaving age** N (Brit) Schulabgangsalter nt, Schulentlassungsalter nt; **schoolma'am**, **schoolmarm** N (pej) Schulmeisterin f (pej); **schoolmaster** N (dated) Lehrer m, Schulmeister m (dated); village ~ Dorfschullehrer m, Dorfschulmeister m (dated); **schoolmate** N (Brit) Schulkamerad(in) m(f), Schulfreund(in) m(f); **school meals** PL Schulessen nt; **schoolmistress** N (dated) Lehrerin f, Schulmeisterin f (dated); **school outing** N Schulausflug m; **school report** N Schulzeugnis nt; **schoolroom** N (in school) Klassenzimmer nt; (in private house) Schulzimmer nt; **school ship** N (Mil Naut) Schulschiff nt

schools inspector ['sku:lzɪnˌspektə'] N Schulinspektor(in) m(f)

school: schoolteacher N Lehrer(in) m(f); **school tie** N Schulkrawatte f → **old school tie**; **school uniform** N Schuluniform f; **school yard** N Schulhof m; **school year** N Schuljahr m

schooner ['sku:nə'] N **a** (= boat) Schoner m **b** (= sherry glass) großes Sherryglas; (US, Austral, = beer schooner) hohes Bierglas

schtick [ʃtɪk] N (US inf: = routine, act) Nummer f (inf)

schuss [ʃʊs] (Ski) N Schuss m VI (im) Schuss fahren

schwa [ʃwɑ:] N (Phon) Schwa nt

sciatic [saɪˈætɪk] ADJ Ischias-, ischiadisch (spec); ~ **nerve** Ischiasnerv m

sciatica [saɪˈætɪkə] N Ischias m or nt

science ['saɪəns] N **a** Wissenschaft f; (= natural science) Naturwissenschaft f; to study ~ Naturwissenschaften studieren; a man of ~ ein Wissenschaftler m; things that ~ cannot explain Dinge, die man nicht naturwissenschaftlich erklären kann; on the ~ side of the school im naturwissenschaftlichen Zweig der Schule; the ~ of cooking die Kochkunst; the ~ of life/astrology die Lehre vom Leben/von den Gestirnen **b** (= systematic knowledge or skill) Technik f; it wasn't luck that helped me to do it, it was ~! das war kein Zufall, dass mir das gelungen ist, das war Können!; there's a lot of ~ involved in that dazu gehört großes Können

science fiction N Sciencefiction f; ~ **novel** Zukunftsroman m, Sciencefictionroman m

science park N Forschungspark m

scientific [ˌsaɪənˈtɪfɪk] ADJ **a** (= of natural sciences) naturwissenschaftlich; apparatus, equipment wissenschaftlich; on a ~ basis auf wissen-

schaftlicher Grundlage; the ~ community die Wissenschaftlergemeinde; ~ officer wissenschaftlicher Mitarbeiter, wissenschaftliche Mitarbeiterin; ~ opinion die Expertenmeinung, die wissenschaftliche Lehrmeinung **b** (= systematic, exact) classification, methods, study wissenschaftlich; to be ~ about sth etw systematisch angehen; he is a keen but not ~ football player er ist ein begeisterter, doch technisch schwacher Fußballspieler; his ~ boxing technique seine gekonnte Boxtechnik

scientifically [ˌsaɪənˈtɪfɪkəlɪ] ADV **a** (= relating to natural sciences) naturwissenschaftlich; ~ (speaking), his work is ... vom wissenschaftlichen Standpunkt aus ist seine Arbeit ...; ~ proven wissenschaftlich erwiesen; ~ based auf wissenschaftlicher Basis; ~ trained wissenschaftlich ausgebildet **b** (= systematically, exactly) wissenschaftlich, systematisch; box, fence etc technisch gekonnt; he approaches sport very ~ der Sport wird bei ihm zur Wissenschaft

scientist ['saɪəntɪst] N (Natur)wissenschaftler(in) m(f)

scientology [ˌsaɪənˈtɒlədʒɪ] N Scientology f

sci-fi ['saɪfaɪ] N (inf) = science fiction

Scillies ['sɪlɪz], **Scilly Isles** ['sɪlɪˌaɪlz] PL Scillyinseln pl

scimitar ['sɪmɪtə'] N Krummschwert nt

scintillate ['sɪntɪleɪt] VI (diamonds, stars) funkeln; (fig: person, conversation) vor Geist sprühen

scintillating ['sɪntɪleɪtɪŋ] ADJ funkelnd attr; (fig, = witty, lively) wit, humour, performance sprühend attr; person, speech vor Geist sprühend attr; (= fascinating) information faszinierend; to be ~ funkeln; sprühen; vor Geist sprühen; faszinierend sein; in ~ form in Hoch- or Glanzform

scintillatingly ['sɪntɪleɪtɪŋlɪ] ADV ~ funny brillant komisch

scion ['saɪən] N **a** (Bot) Schössling m; (for grafting) (Pfropf)reis nt **b** (form) Nachkomme m, Nachfahr(in) m(f)

scissors ['sɪzəz] N **a** pl Schere f; a pair of ~ eine Schere **b** sing (Sport, also **scissors jump**) Schersprung m; (also **scissors hold**) Schere f

scissors-and-paste [ˌsɪzəzəndˈpeɪst] ADJ (Brit) a ~ job eine zusammengestückelte Arbeit (usu pej)

scissors kick N (Swimming, Ftbl) Scherenschlag m

sclerosis [sklɪˈrəʊsɪs] N Sklerose f → **multiple sclerosis**

sclerotic [sklɪˈrɒtɪk] ADJ (Med) blood vessel sklerotisch (spec), verkalkt; (fig) verkalkt (inf)

scoff¹ [skɒf] N verächtliche or abschätzige Bemerkung VI spotten; to ~ at sb/sth jdn/etw verachten; (verbally) sich verächtlich or abschätzig über jdn/etw äußern

scoff² (Brit inf) N (= food) Fressalien pl (inf); (= eating) Fresserei f (inf) VT futtern (inf), in sich (acc) hineinstopfen (inf); she ~ed the lot sie hat alles verputzt (inf) or verdrückt (inf)

scoffer ['skɒfə'] N Spötter(in) m(f)

scoffing ['skɒfɪŋ] N Spötterei f, verächtliche Bemerkungen pl ADJ spöttisch, verächtlich

scoffingly ['skɒfɪŋlɪ] ADV spöttisch, verächtlich

scold [skəʊld] VT (aus)schelten, ausschimpfen (for wegen); she ~ed him for coming home late sie schimpfte ihn aus, weil er so spät heimgekommen war VI schimpfen N (= person) Beißzange f (inf); (= woman also) Xanthippe f (inf)

scolding ['skəʊldɪŋ] N Schelte f no pl; (= act) Schimpferei f; to give sb a ~ jdn ausschimpfen, jdn (aus)schelten

scollop N = scallop N a

sconce [skɒns] N (with candles) Wandleuchter m; (electric) Wandleuchte f

scone [skɒn] N (Brit) brötchenartiges Buttergebäck

scoop [sku:p] N **a** (= instrument) Schaufel f; (for ice cream, potatoes etc) Portionierer m; (= ball

of ice cream, potato) Kugel f; in one ~ (lit, fig) auf einmal **b** (inf, = lucky gain) Fang m (inf) **c** (Press) Knüller m (inf), Scoop m (sl) VT **a** (with scoop) schaufeln; liquid schöpfen; he ~ed the ball into the air er löffelte den Ball in die Luft **b** The Times ~ed the other papers die Times ist den anderen Zeitungen zuvorgekommen **c** prize, jackpot, award gewinnen

▶ **scoop out** VT sep **a** (= take out) herausschaufeln; liquid herausschöpfen; the cat scooped out the goldfish with its paw die Katze hat den Goldfisch mit ihrer Pfote herausgefischt **b** (= hollow out) melon, marrow etc aushöhlen; hole graben

▶ **scoop up** VT sep aufschaufeln; liquid aufschöpfen; she scooped the child/cards/money up sie raffte das Kind/die Karten/das Geld an sich (acc)

scoop: scoop neck N U-Ausschnitt m; **scoop-necked** ['sku:pˈnekt] ADJ mit U-Ausschnitt

scoot [sku:t] VI (inf, = scram) abzischen (inf); (= walk quickly) rennen; ~ across and get it! komm rüber und hols dir! (inf)

scooter ['sku:tə'] N (Tret)roller m; (= motor scooter) (Motor)roller m

scope [skəʊp] N **a** (of topic, idea, investigation) Umfang m; (of law, measures) Reichweite f; (of sb's duties, department, tribunal) Kompetenzbereich m; **sth is within the ~ of sth** etw hält sich or bleibt im Rahmen einer Sache (gen); **sth is within the ~ of a department** etc etw fällt in den Kompetenzbereich einer Abteilung etc; **sth is beyond or outside the ~ of sth** etw geht über etw (acc) hinaus; **that's beyond the ~ of this department** das geht über den Kompetenzbereich dieser Abteilung hinaus; **it's not within the ~ of my authority to allow that** es würde meine Kompetenzen überschreiten, dies zu erlauben; **this project is more limited in ~** dieses Projekt ist auf einen engeren Rahmen begrenzt; **to be broad in ~** breit angelegt sein **b** (= extent of one's perception, grasp) Fassungsvermögen nt; (of talents, knowledge) Umfang m; **that job would be beyond my ~** diese Arbeit würde meine Fähigkeiten übersteigen; **that is beyond my ~** or **the ~ of my understanding** das übersteigt mein Fassungsvermögen; **that job is within his ~** diese Arbeit liegt im Bereich seiner Fähigkeiten **c** (= opportunity) Möglichkeit(en) f(pl); (to develop one's talents) Entfaltungsmöglichkeit f; (to use one's talents) Spielraum m; **there is ~ for improvement** es könnte noch verbessert werden; **there is ~ for further growth in the tourist industry** die Tourismusindustrie ist noch ausbaufähig or hat noch Entwicklungsmöglichkeiten; **there is little ~ for originality** es gibt wenig Spielraum für Originalität; **there is little ~ for reducing our costs** es gibt wenig Spielraum, um die Kosten zu senken; **to give sb ~ to do sth** jdm den nötigen Spielraum geben, etw zu tun; **the job gave him/his imaginative powers full ~** in diesem Beruf konnten sich seine Fähigkeiten/konnte sich seine Fantasie or Phantasie frei entfalten **d** (inf) = microscope, periscope etc

scorbutic [skɔːˈbjuːtɪk] ADJ skorbutisch

scorch [skɔːtʃ] N (also **scorch mark**) verbrannte or versengte Stelle, Brandfleck m VT versengen; **the sun ~ed our faces** die Sonne brannte auf unsere Gesichter VI **a** the sun ~ed down die Sonne brannte herunter **b** (= become scorched) that dress will ~ easily das Kleid kann man leicht versengen **c** (inf: = go fast) rasen (inf)

scorched earth policy [ˌskɔːtʃˈɜːθˈpɒlɪsɪ] N (Mil) Politik f der verbrannten Erde

scorcher ['skɔːtʃə'] N (inf) last summer was a real ~ im letzten Sommer war es wirklich heiß; phew, what a ~! das ist vielleicht eine Bullenhitze! (inf); his goal was quite a ~ das war ein scharfes Tor

scorching ['skɔːtʃɪŋ] ADJ (= very hot) sun, iron glühend heiß; day, weather brütend heiß, knallheiß (*inf*); *heat* sengend; (*inf*, = *very fast*) *speed* rasend; *driver* rasant; (*fig*, = *scathing*) gepfeffert (*inf*); **to set a ~ pace** (*Sport*) ein rasantes Tempo vorlegen **ADV** **the sun is ~ hot** die Sonne ist glühend heiß

score [skɔː'] **N** **a** (= *number of points*) (Punkte-)stand *m*; (*of game, Sport*) (Spiel)stand *m*; (= *final score*) Spielergebnis *nt*; **what was your ~ in the test?** wie viele Punkte hast du bei dem Test erreicht or gemacht? (*inf*) **England didn't get a very good ~** England hat nicht sehr gut abgeschnitten; (*in game, test also*) England hat nicht sehr viele Punkte erzielt; (*Ftbl etc also*) England hat nicht sehr viele Tore erzielt or geschossen; **the ~ was Rangers 3, Celtic 0** es stand 3:0 für Rangers (gegen Celtic); (= *final score*) Rangers schlug Celtic (mit) 3:0; **there was no ~ at half-time** zur Halbzeit stand es 0:0; **to keep (the) ~** (mit)zählen; (*officially*) Punkte zählen; (*on scoreboard*) Punkte anschreiben; **what's the ~?** wie steht es?; (*fig also*) wie sieht es aus? (*on mit*) (*inf*); **he doesn't know the ~** (*fig*) er weiß nicht, was gespielt wird (*inf*); **to make a ~ with sb** (*fig*) jdn stark beeindrucken

b (= *reckoning, grudge*) Rechnung *f*; **what's the ~?** was bin ich schuldig?, wie viel macht das?; **to pay off** or **settle old ~s** alte Schulden begleichen; **to have a ~ to settle with sb** mit jdm eine alte Rechnung zu begleichen haben

c (*Mus*, = *printed music*) Noten *pl*; (*esp of classical music*) Partitur *f*; (*of film, musical*) Musik *f*

d (= *line, cut*) Rille *f*, Kerbe *f*; (*on body*) Kratzer *m*; (= *weal*) Striemen *m*

e (= 20) zwanzig; **~s of ...** (= *many*) hunderte or Hunderte von ..., jede Menge ... (*inf*); **a ~ of people** zwanzig Leute; **3 ~ years and 10** (*old*) 70 Jahre; **~s and ~s** hunderte or Hunderte, jede Menge (*inf*); **~s of times** hundertmal, zigmal (*inf*); **by the ~** massenweise (*inf*)

f (= *reason, ground*) Grund *m*; **on that ~** aus diesem Grund, deshalb

VT **a** (= *win*) erzielen; *marks, points* erzielen, bekommen; *goals* schießen, erzielen; *runs* schaffen; (*Rugby*) *try* erzielen; (*Golf*) *hole-in-one* machen; **he ~d an advantage over his opponent** er war gegenüber seinem Gegner im Vorteil; **our last contestant ~d one hundred points** unser letzter Kandidat hat hundert Punkte; **each correct answer ~s five points** jede richtige Antwort zählt fünf Punkte; **to ~ a point off** or **over sb** (*fig*) auf jds Kosten (*acc*) glänzen, jdn ausstechen; **to ~ a hit with sb** jdn stark beeindrucken; **that remark ~d a hit** diese Bemerkung hat ins Schwarze getroffen

b (= *groove*) einkerben, Rillen/eine Rille machen in (+*acc*); (= *mark*) Kratzer/einen Kratzer machen in (+*acc*); (*Cook*) *fat, meat etc* einschneiden; **the wall is heavily ~d with lines** die Wand weist tiefe Rillen auf

c (*Mus*) schreiben; **the film was ~d by Michael Nyman** die Musik zu dem Film ist or stammt von Michael Nyman

d (*inf*) *drugs* sich (*dat*) beschaffen

VI **a** (= *win points etc*) einen Punkt erzielen or machen (*inf*); (*Ftbl etc*) ein Tor schießen; **to ~ well/badly** gut/schlecht abschneiden; (*in game, test etc also*) eine gute/keine gute Punktzahl erreichen; (*Ftbl etc also*) viele/wenig Tore schießen; **the batsman didn't ~ off the fast balls** der Schlagmann konnte die schnellen Bälle nicht verwandeln; **that's where he ~s** (*fig*) das ist sein großes Plus

b (= *keep score*) (mit)zählen

c (*inf: sexually*) **did you ~ (with her)?** hast du sie flachgelegt? (*sl*)

d (*inf*, = *obtain drugs*) sich (*dat*) Stoff beschaffen (*inf*)

▶**score off** **VT** *sep* (= *delete*) ausstreichen **VI** +*prep obj* **to score off sb** jdn als dumm hinstellen

▶**score out** or **through** **VT** *sep* aus- or durchstreichen

▶**score up** **VT** *sep* anschreiben (*to sb* für jdn); **score it up to me** (*fig*) eins zu null für mich (*inf*)

score: scoreboard **N** Anzeigetafel *f*; (*on TV*) Tabelle *f* der Spielergebnisse; **scorecard** **N** Spielprotokoll *nt*; (*Golf*) Zählkarte *f*; **score draw** **N** (*Brit, Ftbl*) Unentschieden *nt*; **scorekeeper** **N** (= *official, Sport*) Anschreiber(in) *m(f)*; (*in quiz etc*) Punktezähler(in) *m(f)*; **who's the ~?** wer zählt (mit)?; **scoreless** **ADJ** (*Sport*, = *without goals*) torlos; (= *without runs/points*) ohne dass ein Lauf/Punkt erzielt wurde; **Norway had held Holland to a ~ draw in Rotterdam** in Rotterdam hatte Norwegen gegen Holland null zu null gespielt; **the next six innings were ~** bei den nächsten sechs Innings wurde kein Lauf erzielt

scoreline ['skɔːlaɪn] **N** (*Brit Sport*) Endergebnis *nt*, Endstand *m*

scorer ['skɔːrə'] **N** **a** (*Ftbl etc*, = *player*) Torschütze *m*/-schützin *f*; **to be the top ~** die meisten Punkte machen; (*Ftbl etc*) die meisten Tore schießen; **Chelsea were the highest ~s** Chelsea schoss die meisten Tore; **he is the leading ~ in the competition** er hat die meisten Punkte or (*Ftbl*) Tore im Wettbewerb erzielt **b** = **scorekeeper**

score sheet **N** Spielberichtsbogen *m*, Protokoll *nt*

scoring ['skɔːrɪŋ] **N** Erzielen *nt* eines Punktes; (*Ftbl etc*) Torschuss *m*; (= *scorekeeping*) Zählen *nt*; **to open the ~** den ersten Punkt machen; (*Ftbl etc*) das erste Tor schießen; **rules for ~** Regeln über die Zählweise; **X did most of the ~** X erzielte die meisten Punkte; (*Ftbl etc*) X schoss die meisten Tore **ADJ** *suf* **a low-/high-scoring match** ein Spiel, in dem wenig/viele Punkte/Tore erzielt wurden; **he is Arsenal's top-scoring player** er hat die meisten Tore für Arsenal erzielt or geschossen, er ist Arsenals Torschützenkönig

scoring: scoring chance **N** (*Sport*) Torchance *f*; **scoring spree** **N** (*Sport*) Schützenfest *nt* (*inf fig*)

scorn ['skɔːn] **N** (= *disdain*) Verachtung *f*; (*verbal also*) Hohn *m*; **to laugh sb/sth to ~** jdn/etw höhnisch verlachen; **to pour** or **heap ~ on sb/ sth** jdn/etw verächtlich abtun; **to arouse sb's ~** jds Verachtung ernten **VT** (= *treat scornfully*) verachten; (*condescendingly*) verächtlich behandeln; (= *turn down*) *gift, advice* verschmähen; *idea* mit Verachtung von sich weisen; **to ~ to do sth** es für seiner (*gen*) unwürdig halten, etw zu tun; **to ~ sb as sth** jdn verächtlich als etw abtun

scornful ['skɔːnfʊl] **ADJ** verächtlich; *laughter also, person* spöttisch, höhnisch; **to be ~ of sb/sth** jdn/etw verachten; (*verbally*) jdn/etw verhöhnen; **to be ~ about sb/sth** sich über jdn/etw verächtlich äußern

scornfully ['skɔːnfʊlɪ] **ADV** verächtlich; *laugh also* spöttisch, höhnisch

scornfulness ['skɔːnfʊlnɪs] **N** Verachtung *f* (*of* für); **her ~ at the mere mention of his name** ihre verächtliche or höhnische Reaktion bei der bloßen Erwähnung seines Namens

Scorpio ['skɔːpɪəʊ] **N** Skorpion *m*; **he's (a) ~** er ist Skorpion

scorpion ['skɔːpɪən] **N** Skorpion *m*

Scot [skɒt] **N** Schotte *m*, Schottin *f*

Scotch [skɒtʃ] **ADJ** schottisch; **~ terrier** Scotchterrier *m*, Schottischer Terrier **N** **a** (= *Scotch whisky*) Scotch *m* **b** **the ~** *pl* die Schotten *pl*

scotch [skɒtʃ] **VT** *rumour* aus der Welt schaffen; *idea, plan* unterbinden, einen Riegel vorschieben (+*dat*); **the rain has ~ed that** der Regen hat uns (*dat*) einen Strich durch die Rechnung gemacht (*inf*)

Scotch: Scotch broth **N** (*Brit*) Gemüsesuppe mit Gerstengraupen und Hammelfleischbrühe; **Scotch egg** **N** (*Brit*) hart gekochtes Ei in Wurstbrät, paniert und ausgebacken; **Scotch fir** **N** Föhre *f*, (*gemeine*) Kiefer; **Scotch-man** **N** = **Scotsman**; **Scotch mist** **N** feuchter Nebel; **Scotch tape**® **N** Tesafilm® *m*; **Scotchwoman** **N** = **Scotswoman**

scot-free ['skɒt'friː] **ADV** ungeschoren; **to get off ~** ungeschoren davonkommen

Scotland ['skɒtlənd] **N** Schottland *nt*

Scots [skɒts] **ADJ** schottisch **N** (= *dialect*) Schottisch *nt*; **the ~** (= *people*) die Schotten *pl*

Scots: Scots law **N** schottisches Recht; **Scotsman** **N** Schotte *m*; **Scots pine** **N** Föhre *f*, (*gemeine*) Kiefer; **Scotswoman** **N** Schottin *f*

Scotticism ['skɒtɪsɪzəm] **N** schottischer Ausdruck

scotticize ['skɒtɪsaɪz] **VT** schottifizieren, verschotten (*hum*)

Scottie ['skɒtɪ] **N** **a** (*also* **Scottie dog**) Scotchterrier *m*, Schottischer Terrier **b** (*inf*: = *Scotsman*) Schotte *m*

Scottish ['skɒtɪʃ] **ADJ** schottisch **N** **a** (= *dialect*) Schottisch *nt* **b** **the ~** *pl* die Schotten *pl*

Scottish: Scottish Nationalism **N** schottischer Nationalismus; **Scottish National Party** **N** *schottische Partei, die sich für die Unabhängigkeit des Landes einsetzt*; **Scottish Office** **N** **the ~** das Ministerium für schottische Angelegenheiten; **Scottish Parliament** **N** **the ~** das schottische Parlament; **Scottish Secretary** **N** (*Brit, Pol*) Minister(in) *m(f)* für schottische Angelegenheiten

scoundrel ['skaʊndrəl] **N** (*dated*) Schurke *m*; (*inf*) Bengel *m*

scoundrelly ['skaʊndrəlɪ] **ADJ** (*dated*) schurkisch

scour¹ ['skaʊə'] **VT** scheuern **N** Scheuern *nt*; **give the pan a good ~** scheuern Sie den Topf gründlich

▶**scour away** or **off** **VT** *sep* abscheuern; *rust* abreiben

▶**scour out** **VT** *sep pan* ausscheuern; *borehole* durchspülen

scour² **VT** *area, town, shops* absuchen, abkämmen (*for* nach); *newspaper* durchkämmen (*for* nach)

▶**scour about** (*Brit*) or **around** **VI** herumsuchen (*for* nach)

scourer ['skaʊərə'] **N** Topfkratzer *m*; (= *sponge*) Scheuerschwamm *m*

scourge [skɜːdʒ] **N** (*lit, fig*) Geißel *f* **VT** **a** (*lit*) geißeln **b** (*fig*, = *punish*) (be)strafen; (= *devastate*) heimsuchen; (*verbally*) geißeln (*geh*)

scouring pad **N** = **scourer**

Scouse [skaʊs] **ADJ** Liverpooler **N** **a** (= *person*) Liverpooler(in) *m(f)* **b** (= *dialect*) Liverpooler Dialekt *m*

Scouser ['skaʊsə'] **N** (*Brit inf*) Liverpooler(in) *m(f)*

scout [skaʊt] **N** **a** (*Mil*, = *person*) Kundschafter(in) *m(f)*, Späher(in) *m(f)*; (= *ship, plane*) Aufklärer *m*

b (= *reconnaissance*) Erkundung *f*; (*Mil*) Aufklärung *f*; (= *search*) Suche *f*; **to have** or **take a ~ (a)round for sth** sich nach etw umsehen

c Scout (= *boy scout*) Pfadfinder *m*; (*US*, = *girl scout*) Pfadfinderin *f*

d (= *football scout etc*) Kundschafter(in) *m(f)*, Spion(in) *m(f)*; (= *talent scout*) Talentsucher(in) *m(f)*

e (*employed by motoring organization*) Pannenhelfer(in) *m(f)*

f (*Brit, Univ*) *Diener für die College-Studenten*

VI erkunden, auskundschaften; **they were ~ing inside enemy territory** sie waren auf Erkundung in feindlichem Gebiet; **to ~ for sth** nach etw Ausschau or Umschau halten; **he was ~ing for new talent** er war auf Talentsuche **VT** *area, country* erkunden

▶**scout about** (*Brit*) or **around** **VI** sich umsehen (*for* nach)

▶**scout out** **VT** *sep* aufstöbern; (*Mil*) auskundschaften

scout car **N** Aufklärungsfahrzeug *nt*; (*heavier*) Aufklärungs- or Spähpanzer *m*

scouting ['skaʊtɪŋ] **N** **a** Erkunden *nt*, Auskundschaften *nt*; (*Mil*) Aufklärung *f*; (= *looking*)

Suche f (for nach); (for talent) Talentsuche f **b** **Scouting** (= scout movement) Pfadfinderei f (inf), Pfadfindertum nt **ADJ** attr **Scouting** Pfadfinder-; **Scouting organization** Pfadfinderorganisation f

scout: scoutmaster N Gruppenführer m; **scout movement** N Pfadfinderbewegung f; **scout troop** N Pfadfindergruppe f

SCOW [skaʊ] N (Naut) Prahm m

scowl [skaʊl] N unmutiger Ausdruck, finsterer Blick, böses Gesicht; **to give sb a ~** jdn böse ansehen **VI** ein böses or finsteres Gesicht machen; **to ~ at sb** jdn böse ansehen; **what are you ~ing about or at?** warum machst du so ein böses Gesicht?

scowling ['skaʊlɪŋ] ADJ missmutig

SCR (Brit, Univ) abbr of **senior common room**

scrabble ['skræbl] VI (also **scrabble about** (Brit) or **around**) (herum)tasten; (among movable objects) (herum)wühlen; **the hens ~d (around) in the earth** die Hühner wühlten im Boden herum; **his mind ~d for alternatives** er suchte in seinem Hirn nach Alternativen N **Scrabble®** Scrabble® nt

scrag [skræg] N (also **scrag end**) Hals m VT (sl, = kill) abmurksen (inf)

scragginess ['skrægɪnɪs] N Magerkeit f; (of meat) minderwertige Qualität, Sehnigkeit f

scraggly ['skrægli] ADJ (+er) beard, hair zottig, zottelig; plant kümmerlich

scraggy ['skrægi] ADJ (+er) **a** (= scrawny) dürr; meat minderwertig, sehnig **b** (= unkempt, scanty) hair zottig, zerfranst; fur zottig

scram [skræm] VI (inf) abhauen (inf); **~!** verschwinde/verschwindet!

scramble ['skræmbl] N **a** (= climb) Kletterei f; **we went for a ~ in the hills** wir sind in den Bergen herumgeklettert

b (= mad dash) Gerangel nt, Gedrängel nt; **the ~ for the better-paid jobs** die Jagd nach den besser bezahlten Stellen

c (Motor sport) Querfeldeinrennen nt **VT** **a** pieces, letters (untereinander) mischen; **this will ~ your brain(s)** das verwirrt dein armes Hirn

b eggs verquirlen, verrühren

c (Telec) message chiffrieren, verschlüsseln; line an das Verschlüsselungsgerät anschließen

d (Mil) helicopter, crew schnell losschicken **VI** **a** (= climb) klettern; **to ~ out** herausklettern; **he ~d to his feet** er rappelte sich auf (inf); **to ~ through a hedge** durch eine Hecke kriechen or krabbeln (inf); **to ~ up sth** auf etw (acc) hinaufklettern or hinaufkraxeln (inf)

b (= struggle) **to ~ for sth** sich um etw balgen or raufen; for ball etc um etw kämpfen; for bargains, job, good site sich um etw drängeln; **to ~ to get sth** sich balgen or raufen, um etw zu bekommen; ball etc darum kämpfen, etw zu bekommen; bargains, job, good site sich drängeln, um etw zu bekommen

c (Aviat) einen Soforteinsatz fliegen; **~!** höchste Alarmstufe

scrambled egg(s) [ˌskræmbld'eg(z)] N(PL) Rührei(er) nt(pl)

scrambler ['skræmblə'] N **a** (Telec) Chiffriergerät nt **b** (= motorcyclist) Querfeldeinfahrer(in) m(f)

scrap¹ [skræp] N **a** (= small piece) Stückchen nt; (fig) bisschen no pl; (of papers, conversation, news) Fetzen m; (of truth) Fünkchen nt, Spur f; (of poetry) Fragment nt; **there isn't a ~ of food in the house** es ist überhaupt nichts zu essen or kein Bissen zu essen im Haus; **his few ~s of German** seine paar Brocken Deutsch; **his few ~s of knowledge** das bisschen Wissen, das er hat; **a few ~s of information** in paar magere Auskünfte; **it's a ~ of comfort** es ist wenigstens ein kleiner Trost; **not a ~!** nicht die Spur!; **not a ~ of evidence** nicht der geringste Beweis; **he was not a ~ of help** er war überhaupt keine Hilfe, er war nicht die geringste Hilfe

b (usu pl: = leftover) Rest m

c (= waste material) Altmaterial nt, Altwaren

pl; (= metal) Schrott m; (= paper) Altpapier nt; **these bits are ~** diese Sachen werden nicht mehr gebraucht; **are these notes ~?** können die Notizen weggeworfen werden?; **to sell a ship for ~** ein Schiff als Schrott or zum Verschrotten verkaufen; **what is your car worth as ~?** wie hoch ist der Schrottwert Ihres Autos? **VT** car, ship etc verschrotten; furniture, clothes ausrangieren; idea, plan etc fallenlassen; piece of work wegwerfen; **~ that** (inf, = forget it) vergiss es!

scrap² (inf) N Balgerei f; (verbal) Streiterei f; **to get into** or **have a ~ with sb** mit jdm in die Wolle geraten (inf) **VI** sich balgen; (verbal) sich streiten

scrap: scrapbook N Sammelalbum nt; **scrap dealer** N Altwarenhändler(in) m(f); (in metal) Schrotthändler(in), Altmetallhändler(in) m(f)

scrape [skreɪp] N **a** (= act) **to give sth a ~** (= make clean or smooth, potatoes, carrots etc) etw schaben; plate, wall, shoes etw abkratzen; dish, saucepan etw auskratzen; (= mark, graze) car etw schrammen; wall, gatepost etw streifen; arm, knee etw auf- or abschürfen

b (= mark, graze) Schramme f

c (= sound) Kratzen nt; **the ~ of his feet on the gravel** das Knirschen seiner Füße auf dem Kies

d (dated: = difficulty) Schwulitäten pl (inf); **to get into a ~** in Schwulitäten kommen (inf); **he gets into one ~ after another** er handelt sich (dat) dauernd Ärger ein (inf); **to get sb out of a ~** jdm aus der Patsche or Klemme helfen (inf) **VT** **a** (= make clean or smooth) potatoes, carrots etc schaben; plate, wall, shoes abkratzen; dish, saucepan auskratzen; **that's really scraping the (bottom of the) barrel** (fig) das ist wirklich das Letzte vom Letzten

b (= mark, graze) car schrammen; wall, gatepost streifen; arm, knee auf- or abschürfen; **the paint was ~d in the crash** der Lack bekam bei dem Unfall Kratzer

c (= grate against) kratzen an (+dat); **he ~d his bow across the violin** er kratzte mit dem Bogen auf der Geige; **he ~d his nail along the glass** er kratzte mit dem Nagel über das Glas

d (= make by scraping) hole scharren; **to ~ a living** gerade so sein Auskommen haben; **he ~d a living as a freelance reporter** er hielt sich als freier Reporter gerade so über Wasser (inf); **he was trying to ~ (up) an acquaintance with him** er versuchte mit allen Mitteln, seine Bekanntschaft zu machen **VI** **a** (= make clean) kratzen; **he ~d at the paint for hours** er kratzte stundenlang an der Farbe herum

b (= rub) streifen (against +acc); (= grate) kratzen (against an +dat); **the bird's broken wing ~d along the ground** der gebrochene Flügel des Vogels schleifte am Boden; **as he ~d past me** als er sich an mir vorbeizwängte; **the car just ~d past the gatepost** der Wagen fuhr um Haaresbreite am Torpfosten vorbei → bow²

c (= be economical) knapsen (inf), knausern

▶ **scrape along** VI sich schlecht und recht durchschlagen (inf) (on mit)

▶ **scrape away** VI herumkratzen (at an +dat) **VT** sep abkratzen

▶ **scrape by** VI (lit) sich vorbeizwängen; (fig) sich durchwursteln (inf) (on mit)

▶ **scrape in** VI **he just managed to scrape in** er ist gerade noch hineingerutscht (inf)

▶ **scrape off** VT sich abkratzen lassen **VT** sep abkratzen (prep obj von)

▶ **scrape out** VT sep auskratzen, ausschaben; eyes of potato, bad parts ausschneiden

▶ **scrape through** **VI** (lit, object) gerade so durchgehen; (person) sich durchzwängen; (in exam) durchkommen (inf) **VI** +prep obj narrow gap sich durchzwängen durch; exam durchrutschen durch (inf)

▶ **scrape together** VT sep leaves zusammenharken, zusammenrechen; money zusammen-

kratzen; people zusammenbringen, organisieren; support organisieren

▶ **scrape up** VT sep (lit) aufkratzen, zusammenkratzen; money auftreiben (inf); support organisieren

scraper ['skreɪpə'] N (= tool) Spachtel m; (at door) Kratzeisen nt

scrap heap N Schrotthaufen m; **to be thrown on the ~** (thing) zum Schrott geworfen werden; (person) zum alten Eisen geworfen werden; (idea) über Bord geworfen werden; **to end up on the ~** (person) beim alten Eisen landen; **at 55 you're on the ~** mit 55 gehört man zum alten Eisen

scrapings ['skreɪpɪŋz] PL (of food) Reste pl; (= potato scrapings) Schalen pl; (= carrot scrapings) Schababfälle pl, Schabsel pl; (= metal scrapings) Späne pl; **~ of old paint** abgekratzte alte Farbe

scrap: scrap iron N Alteisen nt; **scrap merchant** N Schrotthändler(in) m(f); **scrap metal** N Schrott m, Altmetall nt

scrappiness ['skræpɪnɪs] N (of knowledge) Lückenhaftigkeit f; **she apologized for the ~ of the meal** sie entschuldigte sich für das zusammengestoppelte Essen

scrappy ['skræpɪ] ADJ (+er) (= disjointed) zusammengestückelt, zusammengestoppelt (inf); knowledge lückenhaft; football match orientierungslos; **a ~ goal** ein Zufallstor nt

scrapyard ['skræpjɑːd] N (esp Brit) Schrottplatz m

scratch [skrætʃ] N **a** (= mark) Kratzer m

b (= act) **to give a dog a ~** einen Hund kratzen; **to have a ~** sich kratzen; **the dog enjoys a ~** der Hund kratzt sich gern

c (= sound) Kratzen nt no pl

d **to start from ~** (ganz) von vorn(e) anfangen; (Sport) ohne Vorgabe anfangen; **to start sth from ~** etw ganz von vorne anfangen; business etw aus dem Nichts aufbauen; **to learn a language/a new trade from ~** eine Sprache/einen neuen Beruf ganz von Anfang an or von Grund auf erlernen; **to be** or **come up to ~** (inf) die Erwartungen erfüllen, den Anforderungen entsprechen; **he/it is not quite up to ~ yet** (inf) er/es lässt noch zu wünschen übrig; **to bring sb up to ~** jdn auf Vordermann bringen (inf) **ADJ** attr **~ meal** improvisiert; crew, team zusammengewürfelt

b (= with no handicap) ohne Vorgabe

VT **a** (with nail, claw etc) kratzen; hole scharren; (= leave scratches on) zerkratzen; **the spots will get worse if you ~ them** die Pickel werden nur schlimmer, wenn du (daran) kratzt; **she ~ed the dog's ear** sie kratzte den Hund am Ohr; **to ~ sth away** etw abkratzen; **we ~ed our names in the wood** wir ritzten unsere Namen ins Holz; **to ~ a living** sich (dat) einen kümmerlichen Lebensunterhalt verdienen; **he ~ed a living from the soil** er konnte sich nur mühsam von den Erträgen des Bodens ernähren; **to ~ one's head** (lit, fig) sich am Kopf kratzen; **if you ~ my back, I'll ~ yours** (fig) eine Hand wäscht die andere; **to ~ the surface of sth** (fig) etw oberflächlich berühren

b **to ~ sth through** etw durchstreichen; **to ~ sb/sb's name off a list** jdn/jds Namen von or aus einer Liste streichen

c (Sport etc, = withdraw) streichen; horse zurückziehen

VI **a** (= make scratching movement/noise) kratzen; (in soil etc) scharren; (= scratch oneself) sich kratzen

b (= become scratched) **the new paint will ~ easily/won't ~** die neue Farbe bekommt leicht Kratzer/bekommt keine Kratzer

c (Sport) zurücktreten; **to ~ from** nicht antreten zu

▶ **scratch about** (Brit) or **around** VI (lit) herumscharren; (fig inf) sich umtun (inf) or umsehen (for nach)

▶ **scratch out** VT sep auskratzen; (= cross out) ausstreichen

▶ **scratch together** = **scratch up b**

▶**scratch up** VT *sep* **a** (*lit*) ausscharren **b** (*fig*) *money* zusammenkratzen; *team* zusammenbringen, auftreiben (*inf*)

scratch and sniff, **scratch 'n' sniff** ADJ ~ **card** Duftkarte *f*; **a** ~ **advertisement for perfume** eine Parfümwerbung mit einer Duftprobe zum Rubbeln

scratchcard ['skrætʃkɑːd] N (*Brit: for lottery etc*) Rubbellos *nt*

scratchily ['skrætʃɪlɪ] ADV kratzend

scratchiness ['skrætʃɪnɪs] N Kratzen *nt*

scratching ['skrætʃɪŋ] N (*Mus*, = *disc jockey technique*) Scratching *nt*

scratch: scratch line N (*US, in races*) Startlinie *f*; (*in jumping*) Absprunglinie *f*; (*in throwing*) Abwurflinie *f*; **scratch method** N (*Med*, = *test*) Skarifikation *f* (*spec*); (= *inoculation*) Ritzmethode *f*; **scratch 'n' sniff** ADJ = **scratch and sniff**; **scratch pad** N (*US, Comput*) Notizblock *m*; **scratch paper** N (*US*) Notizpapier *nt*; **scratch sheet** N (*US Horse Racing inf*) Rennzeitung *f*; **scratch test** N (*Med*) Kutanreaktionstest *m*, Einreibungstest *m*

scratchy ['skrætʃɪ] ADJ (+*er*) *sound, pen* kratzend *attr*; *record* zerkratzt; *feel, sweater* kratzig; **does his beard feel ~?** kratzt sein Bart?; **my old record-player has a rather ~ tone** mein alter Plattenspieler kracht ziemlich

scrawl [skrɔːl] N Krakelei *f*, Gekrakel *nt* (*inf*); (= *handwriting*) Klaue *f* (*inf*); (*inf*, = *message*) gekritzelte Nachricht; **the word finished in a ~** das Wort hörte mit einem Krakel aus VT hinschmieren (*inf*), hinkritzeln; **it's been ~ed all over with obscene messages** es war ganz voll geschmiert mit Obszönitäten VI krakeln (*inf*), schmieren

scrawny ['skrɔːnɪ] ADJ (+*er*) dürr

scream [skriːm] N **a** Schrei *m*; (*of saw, tyres*) Kreischen *nt*; (*of engines, siren*) Heulen *nt*; **there were ~s of laughter from the audience** das Publikum kreischte vor Lachen; **to let out** *or* **give a ~** einen Schrei ausstoßen; **a ~ of pain** ein Schmerzensschrei *m*; **a ~ of fear** ein Aufschrei *m*; **the car stopped with a ~ of tyres** das Auto hielt mit quietschenden *or* kreischenden Reifen an

b (*fig inf*) **to be a ~** zum Schreien sein (*inf*) VT *command* brüllen (*fig, headlines*) ausschreien; **to ~ sth at sb** jdm etw zuschreien; **you idiot, she ~ed at me** du Idiot, schrie sie mich an; **she ~ed insults at him** sie schrie ihm Beleidigungen ins Gesicht; **to ~ one's head off** (*inf*) sich (*dat*) die Lunge aus dem Leib *or* Hals schreien

VI schreien; (*saw, tyres*) kreischen; (*wind, engine, siren*) heulen; **to ~ at sb** jdn anschreien; **to ~ for sth** nach etw schreien; **to ~ in** *or* **with pain** vor Schmerzen schreien; **an ambulance ~ed past** ein Krankenwagen heulte vorbei; **newspaper headlines which ~ at you** (*fig*) Schlagzeilen, die einem entgegenschreien

▶**scream out** VI aufschreien; **to scream out for sth** (*lit, fig*) nach etw schreien VT *sep* ausschreien; (*person*) hinausschreien; *name* schreien, rufen; *warning* ausstoßen

screaming ['skriːmɪŋ] ADJ (*lit, fig*) schreiend; *saw, tyres* kreischend; *wind, engine, siren* heulend; (*inf*, = *bold*) *clothes* grell, in schreienden Farben N ~ **match** gegenseitige Anbrüllerei (*inf*); **to have a ~ match** sich gegenseitig anbrüllen (*inf*)

screamingly ['skriːmɪŋlɪ] ADV ~ **funny** (*inf*) zum Schreien komisch (*inf*)

scree [skriː] N Geröll *nt*; ~ **slope** Geröllhalde *f*, Geröllfeld *nt*

screech [skriːtʃ] N Kreischen *nt no pl*; (*of women, tyres, brakes also*) Quietschen *nt no pl*; (*of owl*) Schrei *m*; (*of whistle*) Schrillen *nt no pl*; **the car stopped with a ~ of brakes** das Auto hielt mit quietschenden Bremsen; **to give a ~ of anger/laughter** zornig/vor Lachen kreischen VT schreien; *high notes* quietschen VI kreischen; (*women, tyres, brakes also*) quietschen; **to**

~ **with pain** vor Schmerzen schreien; **to ~ with anger/laughter** zornig/vor Lachen kreischen; **to ~ with delight** vor Vergnügen quietschen; **jet planes ~ing over the housetops** Düsenflugzeuge, die heulend über die Hausdächer fliegen

screech owl N Schleiereule *f*

screed [skriːd] N Roman *m* (*inf*); **to write ~s (and ~s)** (*inf*) ganze Romane schreiben (*inf*)

screen [skriːn] N **a** (*protective*) Schirm *m*; (*for privacy etc*) Wandschirm *m*; (*as partition*) Trennwand *f*; (*against insects*) Fliegenfenster *nt*; (*against light*) Verdunklungsschutz *m*; (*fig, for protection*) Schutz *m*; (*of trees*) Wand *f*; (*of mist, secrecy*) Schleier *m*; (*of indifference*) Mauer *f*; ~ **of smoke** Rauchschleier *m*, Nebelwand *f*; **protected by a ~ of destroyers** durch eine Zerstörerflotte geschützt

b (*Film*) Leinwand *f*; (*TV*, = *radar screen*) (Bild-)schirm *m*; **stars of the ~** Filmstars *pl*; **to write for the ~** für den Film/das Fernsehen schreiben; **they are married off ~ as well as on** sie sind nicht nur im Film, sondern auch in Wirklichkeit *or* im wirklichen Leben verheiratet; **the big ~** die Leinwand; **the small ~** die Mattscheibe

c (*Comput*) Bildschirm *m*; **on ~** auf Bildschirm (*dat*); **to edit/work on** ~ am Bildschirm editieren/arbeiten; **to move forward a ~** einen Bildschirm vorrücken

d (= *sieve*) (Gitter)sieb *nt*

e (*in church*) Lettner *m*

f (*Cricket*) = **sight screen**

VT **a** (= *hide*) verdecken; (= *protect*) abschirmen; (*fig*) schützen (*from* vor +*dat*), abschirmen (*from* gegen); **to ~ the windows** (*with screen*) einen Schirm vor die Fenster stellen; (*with fabric*) die Fenster verhängen; (*against light*) die Fenster verdunkeln; (*against insects*) Fliegenfenster an den Fenstern anbringen; **to ~ sth from the enemy** etw vor dem Feind tarnen *or* verbergen; **he ~ed his eyes from the sun** er schützte die Augen vor der Sonne

b *TV programme* senden; *film* vorführen; **they gave permission for the conference to be ~ed** sie genehmigten die Vorführung der Filmaufzeichnungen von der Konferenz

c (= *sift*) sieben

d (= *investigate*) *applicants, security risks* überprüfen; *calls* überwachen; (*Med*) untersuchen

VI **to ~ for sth** (*Med*) auf etw (*acc*) untersuchen

▶**screen off** VT *sep* (durch einen Schirm/Vorhang/eine Wand *etc*) abtrennen

screen: screen actor N Filmschauspieler *m*; **screen actress** N Filmschauspielerin *f*

screenful ['skriːnfʊl] N (*Comput*) Bildschirm *m*

screening ['skriːnɪŋ] N **a** (*of applicants, security risks*) Überprüfung *f* **b** (*of film*) Vorführung *f*; (*TV*) Sendung *f*

screening room N (*Film*) Vorführraum *m*

screen: screen memory N (*Psych*) Deckerinnerung *f*; **screenplay** N Drehbuch *nt*; **screenprint** N Siebdruck *m* VT im Siebdruckverfahren drucken; **screen-printing** N Siebdruck *m*, Siebdruckverfahren *nt*; **screen saver** N (*Comput*) Bildschirmschoner *m*; **screen test** N Probeaufnahmen *pl*; **screen-test** VT Probeaufnahmen machen von; **screenwriter** N Drehbuchautor(in) *m(f)*; **screenwriting** N Drehbuchschreiben *nt*, Verfassen *nt* von Drehbüchern

screw [skruː] N **a** (*Mech*) Schraube *f*; **he's got a** ~ **loose** (*inf*) bei dem ist eine Schraube locker (*inf*); **to put** *or* **turn** *or* **tighten the ~s on sb** (*inf*) jdm die Daumenschrauben anlegen; **this is another turn of the** ~ das macht es noch schlimmer, das setzt sie/ ihn *etc* noch mehr unter Druck

b (*Naut, Aviat*) Schraube *f*, Propeller *m*

c (= *action*) Drehung *f*; **to give sth a ~** an etw (*dat*) drehen

d (*sl*: = *sexual intercourse*) Nummer *f* (*inf*); **he/ she is a good ~** er/sie vögelt gut (*inf*); **to have a ~** vögeln (*inf*), bumsen (*inf*)

e (*Brit inf*: = *wage*) **he earns a good ~** er verdient ganz schön viel Kohle (*inf*); **that's not a bad ~** bei dem Job stimmt die Kohle (*inf*)

f (*Brit sl*: = *prison officer*) Schließer(in) *m(f)* (*inf*) VT **a** (*using screws*) schrauben (*to* an +*acc*, *onto* auf +*acc*); **he ~ed his head round** er drehte seinen Kopf herum; **she ~ed her handkerchief into a ball** sie knüllte ihr Taschentuch zu einem Knäuel zusammen; **he ~ed his face into a smile** er verzog das Gesicht zu einem Lächeln

b (*inf*: = *put pressure on*) in die Mangel nehmen (*inf*); **to ~ sb for sth** etw aus jdm herausquetschen (*inf*)

c (*sl*: = *have intercourse with*) vögeln (*inf*), bumsen (*inf*); ~ **you!** (*sl*) leck mich am Arsch! (*vulg*), du kannst mich mal! (*inf*)

d (*inf*: = *rip off*) abzocken (*inf*); (= *cheat*) bescheißen (*sl*); **we're not out to ~ you for every penny you've got** wir wollen dich nicht abzocken (*inf*)

VI **a** (= *can be screwed*) sich schrauben lassen; (= *fasten with screw*) angeschraubt werden

b (*sl*: = *have intercourse*) vögeln (*inf*), bumsen (*inf*)

▶**screw down** VT *sep* an- *or* festschrauben

▶**screw in** VT *sep* (hin)einschrauben (*prep obj*, -*to* in +*acc*) VI (hin)eingeschraubt werden (*prep obj*, -*to* in +*acc*)

▶**screw off** VT *sep* abschrauben (*prep obj* von) VI abgeschraubt werden (*prep obj* von)

▶**screw on** VT *sep* anschrauben; **to screw sth on(to) sth** etw an etw (*acc*) schrauben; *lid, top* etw auf etw (*acc*) schrauben; **it was screwed on tightly** es war festgeschraubt; (*lid, top*) es war fest zugeschraubt; **to have one's head screwed on (the right way)** (*inf*) ein vernünftiger Mensch sein VI aufgeschraubt werden; (= *with screws*) angeschraubt werden

▶**screw out** VT *sep* herausschrauben (*of* aus); **to screw sth out of sb** (*esp Brit inf, money*) etw aus jdm herausquetschen (*inf*); *concessions* etw aus jdm herauspressen VI herausgeschraubt werden

▶**screw together** VT *sep* zusammenschrauben VI zusammengeschraubt werden

▶**screw up** VT *sep* **a** *screw, nut* anziehen **b** (= *crush*) *paper, material* zusammenknüllen, zerknüllen

c *eyes* zusammenkneifen; *face* verziehen; **to screw up one's courage** seinen ganzen Mut zusammennehmen; **to screw oneself up to do sth** sich aufraffen, etw zu tun

d (*inf*: = *spoil*) vermasseln (*inf*); **he's really screwed things up** er hat da wirklich Scheiße gebaut (*inf*)

e (*inf*: = *make uptight*) *sb* neurotisch machen; **he's so screwed up** der hat einen Schaden (*inf*); **to be screwed up about sth** sich wegen etw ganz verrückt machen; **to get screwed up about sth** sich in etw (*acc*) hineinsteigern

VI (*inf*: = *make a mess*) Scheiße bauen (*inf*) (*on sth bei* etw)

screw: screwball (*esp US, inf*) N Spinner(in) *m(f)* (*inf*) ADJ hirnverbrannt (*inf*); **screw cap** N Schraubverschluss *m or* -deckel *m*; (*Tech*) Überwurfmutter *f*; **screwdriver** N Schraubendreher *m*, Schraubenzieher *m* (*inf*)

screwed [skruːd] ADJ (*Brit, inf*, = *drunk*) voll (*inf*), hackezu (*sl*)

screw: screw nut N (*Tech*) Schraubenmutter *f*; **screw plug** N (*Tech*) Verschlussschraube *f*; **screw top** N Schraubverschluss *m*; **screw-topped** ['skruːtɒpt] ADJ mit Schraubverschluss; **screw-up** N (*inf*, = *muddle*) Chaos *nt* (*inf*); **it was one big ~** es war das totale Chaos (*inf*)

screwy ['skruːɪ] ADJ (+*er*) (*inf*) verrückt, bekloppt (*inf*); *person* komisch, schrullig; **you must be ~!** du bist wohl bekloppt (*inf*) *or* verrückt!

scribble ['skrɪbl] N Gekritzel *nt no pl*; (= *note*) schnell hingekritzelte Nachricht; **covered in ~(s)** voll gekritzelt VT hinkritzeln; **to ~ sth on sth** etw auf etw (*acc*) kritzeln; **paper ~d (over) with notes** mit Notizen voll gekritzeltes Papier;

to ~ sth down etw hinkritzeln **VI a** (= *write, draw untidily*) kritzeln; **the children ~d all over the wallpaper** die Kinder haben die ganze Tapete voll gekritzelt **b** (*inf*, = *write novel etc*) schreiben; **he ~s away all day at his novel** er schreibt den ganzen Tag an seinem Roman herum

scribbler ['skrɪblə'] N (*inf*) Schreiberling *m*

scribbling block ['skrɪblɪŋ,blɒk], **scribbling pad** ['skrɪblɪŋ,pæd] N (*Brit*) Schreibblock *m*, Notizblock *m*

scribe [skraɪb] N Schreiber(in) *m(f)*; (*Bibl*) Schriftgelehrte(r) *m*

scrimmage ['skrɪmɪdʒ] **N** (*US Ftbl*) Gedränge *nt*; (*Rugby*) offenes Gedränge; (*inf*, = *struggle*) Rangelei *f* (*inf*); **a ~ with the police** ein Handgemenge *nt* mit der Polizei **VI** sich drängen

scrimp [skrɪmp] VI sparen, knausern; **to ~ on sth** an etw (*dat*) sparen; **to ~ and save** geizen und sparen

scrimshank ['skrɪmʃæŋk] VI (*Brit Mil sl*) sich drücken (*inf*)

scrimshanker ['skrɪmʃæŋkə'] N (*Brit Mil sl*) Drückeberger(in) *m(f)* (*inf*)

script [skrɪpt] **N a** (= *style of writing*) Schrift *f*; (= *joined writing*) Schreibschrift *f*; (= *handwriting*) Handschrift *f*; (*Typ*, = *cursive*) Kursivdruck *m* **b** (*Sch, Univ*) (schriftliche) Arbeit **c** (*of play, documentary*) Text *m*; (= *screenplay*) Drehbuch *nt*; (*of talk etc*) (Manu)skript *nt* **VT** play, documentary den Text schreiben zu; *screenplay* das Drehbuch schreiben für; *talk etc* das (Manu-)skript schreiben für; **a ~ed conversation** ein vorbereitetes Gespräch

script girl N (*Film*) Scriptgirl *nt*

scriptorium [skrɪp'tɔːrɪəm] N pl **scriptoria** [skrɪp'tɔːrɪə] Schreibstube *f* (*eines Klosters*)

scriptural ['skrɪptʃərəl] ADJ Bibel-; **~ text** Bibeltext *m*; **that isn't strictly ~** das entspricht nicht genau der Bibel

scripture ['skrɪptʃə'] N **a** Scripture, the Scriptures die (Heilige) Schrift; **the Hindu ~s** die heiligen Schriften *or* Bücher der Hindus **b** (*Sch*) Religion *f*

scriptwriter ['skrɪpt,raɪtə'] N Textautor(in) *m(f)*; (*of screenplay*) Drehbuchautor(in) *m(f)*; (*of talk etc*) Verfasser(in) *m(f)* des (Manu)skripts

scrivener ['skrɪvənə'] N (*Hist*) Schreiber *m*

scrod [skrɒd] N (*US*) junger, kochfertig geschnittener Fisch

scrofula ['skrɒfjʊlə] N (*dated Med*) Skrofulose *f*, Skrofel *f*

scrofulous ['skrɒfjʊləs] ADJ (*dated Med*) skrofulös; (*depraved*) verkommen

scroll [skrəʊl] N **a** Schriftrolle *f*; (*decorative*) Schnörkel *m*; (= *volute, of violin*) Schnecke *f* **b** (*Comput*) Scrollen *nt* **VI** (*Comput*) scrollen

▶ **scroll down VT** sep vorrollen, vorscrollen **VI** vorrollen, vorscrollen

▶ **scroll up VT** sep zurückrollen, zurückscrollen **VI** zurückrollen, zurückscrollen

scroll saw N Laubsäge *f*

scrooch [skruːtʃ] VI (*esp US*) kauern; **to ~ down** sich hinkauern

Scrooge [skruːdʒ] N Geizhals *m*

scrotum ['skrəʊtəm] N (*Anat*) Hodensack *m*, Skrotum *nt* (*spec*)

scrounge [skraʊndʒ] (*inf*) **VI a** (= *sponge*) schnorren (*inf*) (*off, from* bei); **he ~d off his parents for years** er lag seinen Eltern jahrelang auf der Tasche (*inf*) **b** (= *hunt*) **to ~ around for sth** nach etw herumsuchen **VT** schnorren (*inf*), abstauben (*inf*) (*from, off* bei) **N** **to be on the ~** am Schnorren *or* Abstauben sein (*inf*); **he's always on the ~ for cigarettes** er schnorrt dauernd Zigaretten (*inf*)

scrounger ['skraʊndʒə'] N (*inf*) Schnorrer(in) *m(f)* (*inf*)

scrounging ['skraʊndʒɪŋ] N (*inf*) Schnorrerei *f* (*inf*)

scroungy ['skraʊndʒɪ] ADJ (*+er*) (*US, inf*) gammelig (*inf*)

scrub¹ [skrʌb] N Gebüsch *nt*, Gestrüpp *nt*; (*also* **scrubland**) Gestrüpp *nt*; (*tropical*) Busch(land *nt*) *m*

scrub² **N** Schrubben *nt* no pl; **to give sth a ~/a good ~** etw schrubben/gründlich abschrubben **VT** schrubben, scheuern; *vegetables* putzen; (*inf*, = *cancel*) abblasen (*inf*); *idea* abschreiben (*inf*); **to ~ oneself all over** sich von oben bis unten abschrubben; **to ~ off a dirty mark** einen Schmutzfleck wegschrubben **VI** **to ~ at sth** an etw (*dat*) herumreiben

▶ **scrub down VT** sep walls, person, oneself abschrubben

▶ **scrub out VT** sep pans etc ausscheuern

▶ **scrub up VI** (= *wash hands*) sich (*dat*) die Hände waschen *or* schrubben (*inf*)

scrubber ['skrʌbə'] N (*Brit, inf*) (billiges) Flittchen (*inf*)

scrubbing brush ['skrʌbɪŋ,brʌʃ] (*Brit*), **scrub brush** (*US*) N Scheuerbürste *f*

scrubby ['skrʌbɪ] ADJ (*+er*) bushes, beard struppig; *grass* buschig; *countryside* mit Buschwerk bewachsen; *chin* stoppelig

scrubland ['skrʌblænd] N → **scrub**

scrubwoman N (*US*) Scheuer- *or* Putzfrau *f*

scruff¹ [skrʌf] N **by the ~ of the neck** am Genick

scruff² N (*inf*: = *scruffy person*) (= *woman*) Schlampe *f* (*inf*); (= *man*) abgerissener Typ (*inf*)

scruffily ['skrʌfɪlɪ] ADV (*inf*) schlampig (*inf*)

scruffiness ['skrʌfɪnɪs] N (*inf, of person*) schlampiges *or* gammeliges Aussehen (*inf*); (*of city*) verlotterter Zustand (*inf*)

scruffy ['skrʌfɪ] ADJ (*+er*) (*inf*) gammelig (*inf*); *person, clothes also* schlampig (*inf*); *park, city* verlottert (*inf*), verwahrlost

scrum [skrʌm] N **a** (*Rugby*) Gedränge *nt*; **loose ~** offenes Gedränge; **set ~** Gedränge *nt* **b** (*of reporters, photographers etc*) Gedränge *nt*

scrum half N (*Rugby*) Gedrängehalbspieler(in) *m(f)*

scrummage ['skrʌmɪdʒ] N offenes Gedränge

scrump [skrʌmp] **VT** apples stehlen **VI** Äpfel stehlen

scrumptious ['skrʌmpʃəs] ADJ (*inf*) meal etc lecker; *girl* zum Anbeißen (*inf*)

scrumpy ['skrʌmpɪ] N (*Brit*) ≈ Most *m* (*S Ger, Aus, Sw*), starker Cider aus Südwestengland

scrunch [skrʌntʃ] **N** Knirschen *nt*; **the car came up the snowy road with a ~ of tyres** (*Brit*) or **tires** (*US*) die Reifen des Wagens knirschten auf der schneebedeckten Straße **VT** *nose* rümpfen; **to ~ sth (up) into a ball** etw zusammenknüllen **VI** (*gravel, snow*) knirschen; **his boots ~ed on the gravel** seine Stiefel knirschten auf dem Kies; **they ~ed through the fallen leaves** das Laub raschelte unter ihren Schritten; **he ~ed up his face** er verzog das Gesicht

scrunchie ['skrʌntʃɪ] N (*for hair*) Zopfkranz *m*, Zopfband *nt*

scruple ['skruːpl] **N** Skrupel *m*; **~s** (= *doubts*) (moralische) Bedenken *pl*; **to be without ~** keine Skrupel haben; **to have no ~s about sth** bei einer Sache keine Skrupel haben; **to have no ~s about doing sth** keine Skrupel haben, etw zu tun **VI** **I did not ~ to accept his offer** ich hatte keine Skrupel *or* Bedenken, sein Angebot anzunehmen

scrupulous ['skruːpjʊləs] ADJ person, organization gewissenhaft; *honesty, fairness* unbedingt, kompromisslos; *cleanliness* peinlich; *account* (peinlich) genau; **he can't afford to be too ~** er kann sich keine allzu großen Skrupel leisten; **he is not too ~ in his business dealings** er hat keine allzu großen Skrupel bei seinen Geschäften; **she is not too ~ in matters of cleanliness** sie nimmt es mit der Sauberkeit nicht so genau; **to be ~ in doing sth** etw sehr gewissenhaft tun; **to be ~ about sth** mit etw sehr gewissenhaft sein; **the kitchen staff are ~ about hy-**

giene das Küchenpersonal nimmt es mit der Hygiene sehr genau

scrupulously ['skruːpjʊləslɪ] ADV (= *honestly, conscientiously*) gewissenhaft; (= *honourably*) behave korrekt; (= *meticulously*) sorgfältig; *exact, clean* peinlich; *fair, careful* äußerst; **he's ~ careful about telling the truth** er nimmt es mit der Wahrheit äußerst *or* peinlichst genau; **the old church has been ~ maintained** die alte Kirche ist äußerst sorgfältig instand *or* in Stand gehalten worden

scrupulousness ['skruːpjʊləsnɪs] N (= *honesty, fairness*) Gewissenhaftigkeit *f*; (= *meticulousness*) (peinliche) Genauigkeit *f*

scrutineer [,skruːtɪ'nɪə'] N (*Brit, Pol*) Wahlprüfer(in) *m(f)*

scrutinize ['skruːtɪnaɪz] VT (= *examine*) (genau) untersuchen; (= *check*) genau prüfen; (= *stare at*) prüfend ansehen, mustern; **to ~ sth for sth** etw auf etw (*acc*) untersuchen *or* prüfen

scrutiny ['skruːtɪnɪ] N **a** (= *examination*) Untersuchung *f*; (= *checking*) (Über)prüfung *f*; (*of person*) Musterung *f*; (= *stare*) prüfender *or* musternder Blick; **everyone was subject to police ~** jeder wurde einer Überprüfung durch die Polizei unterzogen; **it does not stand up to ~** es hält keiner genauen Untersuchung *or* Prüfung stand **b** (*Pol*) Wahlprüfung *f*

SCSI ['skʌzɪ] (*Comput*) abbr of **Small Computer Systems Interface** SCSI

scuba ['skuːbə] N (*Schwimm*)tauchgerät *nt*

scuba: scuba dive VI tauchen mit Sauerstoffgerät; **scuba diver** N Sporttaucher(in) *m(f)*; **scuba diving** N Sporttauchen *nt*

scud [skʌd] VI flitzen; (*clouds*) jagen

scuff [skʌf] **VT** abwetzen; **don't ~ your feet like that!** schlurf nicht so! **VI** schlurfen; **the children ~ed through the pile of leaves** die Kinder raschelten *or* wateten durch den Laubhaufen **N a** (*also* **scuff mark**) abgewetzte Stelle **b** (*US*: = *slipper*) Pantolette *f*

scuffle ['skʌfl] **N** (= *skirmish*) Rauferei *f* (*inf*), Handgemenge *nt* **VI** (= *have skirmish*) sich raufen; (= *make noise*) poltern; **to ~ with the police** ein Handgemenge mit der Polizei haben

scull [skʌl] N (= *oar*) Skull *nt*; (= *boat*) Skullboot *nt* **VT** rudern **VI** rudern, skullen (*spec*)

scullery ['skʌlərɪ] N Spülküche *f*; **~ maid** Küchenmagd *f*

sculpt [skʌlpt] **VT = sculpture** VT **VI** bildhauern (*inf*); **he ~s for a living** er verdient sich (*dat*) seinen Lebensunterhalt als Bildhauer, er lebt vom Bildhauern (*inf*)

sculptor ['skʌlptə'] N Bildhauer(in) *m(f)*

sculptress ['skʌlptrɪs] N Bildhauerin *f*

sculptural ['skʌlptʃərəl] ADJ plastisch; (= *of statues*) bildhauerisch; **the ~ work on the cathedral** die Skulpturenarbeit der Kathedrale; **~ details** plastisch gearbeitete Details *pl*; **the ~ triumphs of Ancient Greece** die Meisterwerke der altgriechischen Bildhauerkunst

sculpture ['skʌlptʃə'] **N** (= *art*) Bildhauerkunst *f*, Skulptur *f*; (= *work*) Bildhauerei *f*; (= *object*) Skulptur *f*, Plastik *f* **VT** formen, arbeiten; (*in stone*) hauen, meißeln; (*in clay etc*) modellieren; **he ~d the tombstone out of marble** er haute den Grabstein in Marmor

sculptured ['skʌlptʃəd] ADJ **a** (*lit*) geformt; (*in stone*) gehauen, gemeißelt; **decorated with ~ flowers** mit plastisch gearbeiteten Blumen verziert **b** (*fig*) cheekbones, profile ausgeprägt, markant

scum [skʌm] N **a** (*on liquid*) Schaum *m*; (= *residue*) Rand *m*; **a pond covered in green ~** ein mit einer grünen Schleimschicht bedeckter Teich; **a greasy ~ floated on the soup** auf der Suppe schwamm eine Fettschicht **b** (*pej inf*) Abschaum *m*; (= *one individual*) Drecksau *f* (*inf*); **the ~ of the earth** der Abschaum der Menschheit

scumbag ['skʌmbæg] N (*inf*) Schleimscheißer *m* (*inf*)

scupper ['skʌpə'] **N** Speigatt *nt* **VT a** (*Naut*) versenken **b** (*Brit, inf,* = *ruin*) zerschlagen; **if he finds out, we'll be ~ed** wenn er das erfährt, sind wir erledigt (*inf*)

scurf [skɜːf] **N** Schuppen *pl*

scurrility [skʌˈrɪlɪtɪ] **N** (= *abusiveness*) Ehrenrührigkeit *f*; (*of person*) verleumderische Art; (= *abusive remark*) Verleumdung *f*, Verunglimpfung *f*; (= *indecency*) Zotigkeit *f*, Unflätigkeit *f*; (= *indecent remark*) zotige or unflätige Bemerkung

scurrilous ['skʌrɪləs] **ADJ** (= *abusive*) verleumderisch; *remark, attack, story also* ehrenrührig; (= *indecent*) unflätig, zotig

scurrilously ['skʌrɪləslɪ] **ADV** (= *abusively*) verleumderisch; (= *indecently*) unflätig, zotig

scurry ['skʌrɪ] **N** (= *hurry*) Hasten *nt*; (= *sound*) Trippeln *nt*; **there was a ~ to leave the room** alle hatten es eilig, das Zimmer zu verlassen **VI** (*person*) hasten; (*with small steps*) eilig trippeln; (*animals*) huschen; **to ~ along** entlanghasten/-trippeln/-huschen; **they all scurried out of the classroom** sie hatten es alle eilig, aus dem Klassenzimmer zu kommen; **to ~ for shelter** sich (*dat*) eilig einen Unterschlupf suchen; **she scurried through her work** hastig erledigte sie ihre Arbeit

scurvy ['skɜːvɪ] **N** Skorbut *m* **ADJ** (*obs*) *knave* schändlich

'scuse [skjuːz] **VT** (*inf*) = **excuse VT**

scut [skʌt] **N** Stummelschwanz *m*; (*of rabbit also*) Blume *f* (*Hunt*); (*of deer also*) Wedel *m* (*Hunt*)

scutcheon ['skʌtʃən] **N** = **escutcheon**

scutter ['skʌtə'] **N, VI** (*Brit inf*) = **scurry**

scuttle¹ ['skʌtl] **N** (= *coal scuttle*) Kohleneimer *m*

scuttle² **VI** (*person*) trippeln; (*animals*) hoppeln; (*spiders, crabs etc*) krabbeln; **she/it ~d off in a hurry** sie/es flitzte davon

scuttle³ (*Naut*) **N** Luke *f* **VT a** versenken **b** (*fig*) *treaty, agreement, talks* sprengen; *plans* kaputtmachen

scythe [saɪð] **N** Sense *f* **VT** (*mit der Sense*) mähen; **to ~ people down** Menschen niedermähen **VI** **to ~ through the crowd** durch die Menge pflügen; **the motorway ~s through the city** die Autobahn führt mitten durch die Stadt

Scythia ['sɪθɪə] **N** Skythien *nt*

SDI *abbr of* **strategic defence initiative** SDI *f*

SDP (*Brit*) *abbr of* **Social Democratic Party**

SE *abbr of* **south-east** SO

sea [siː] **N a** Meer *nt*, See *f*; **by ~** auf dem Seeweg; **to travel by ~** mit dem Schiff fahren; **a town by** or **on the ~** eine Stadt am Meer or an der See; (**out**) **at ~** auf See; **as I looked out to ~** als ich aufs Meer hinausblickte; **to be all at ~** (*fig*) nicht durchblicken (*with bei*) (*inf*); **I'm all at ~ about how to answer this question** ich habe keine Ahnung, wie ich die Frage beantworten soll; **that left him all at ~** er hatte überhaupt keinen Durchblick (*inf*); **to go to ~** zur See gehen; **to put to ~** in See stechen; **beyond the ~s** (*dated*) überm großen Meer (*old*), in Übersee

b (= *state of the sea*) See *f no pl*, Seegang *m*; **heavy/strong ~s** schwere/raue See

c (*fig*) Meer *nt*; **a ~ of faces** ein Meer von Gesichtern; **a ~ of flames** ein Flammenmeer

sea: sea air **N** Seeluft *f*; **sea anemone** **N** Seeanemone *f*; **sea animal** **N** Meerestier *nt*; **sea-based** **ADJ** *missiles* seegestützt; **sea bathing** **N** Baden *nt* im Meer; **sea battle** **N** Seeschlacht *f*; **seabed** **N** Meeresboden *m*, Meeresgrund *m* (*geh*); **sea bird** **N** Seevogel *m*; **seaboard** **N** (*US*) Küste *f*; **seaborne** **ADJ** *attack, landing* von See; *fruit, articles etc* auf dem Seeweg befördert; **~ goods** Seefrachtgüter *pl*; **~ trade** Seehandel *m*; **sea breeze** **N** Seewind *m*; **sea calf** **N** Meerkalb *nt*, Seehund *m*; **sea change** **N** totale Veränderung; **sea coast** **N** Meeresküste *f*; **sea cow** **N** Seekuh *f*; **sea cucumber** **N** Seegurke *f*, Seewalze *f*; **sea defences**, (*US*) **sea defenses** **PL** Hochwasserschutzmaßnahmen *pl*; **sea dog** **N** (*inf,* = *sailor*) Seebär *m*; (= *seal*)

Seehund *m*; **sea elephant** **N** Elefantenrobbe *f*, See-Elefant *m*, Seeelefant *m*; **seafarer** **N** Seefahrer(in) *m(f)*; **seafaring** **ADJ** *nation, people* seefahrend; *boat* hochseetüchtig; **~ man** Seefahrer *m*; **he has little ~ experience** er hat wenig Erfahrung auf See **N** Seefahrt *f*; **sea fight** **N** Seegefecht *nt*; **seafish** **N** See- or Meeresfisch *m*; **seafloor** **N** Meeresboden *m*; **sea fog** **N** Küstennebel *m*, Seenebel *m*; **seafood** **N** Meeresfrüchte *pl*; **~ restaurant** Fischrestaurant *nt*; **seafront** **N** (= *beach*) Strand *m*; (= *promenade*) Strandpromenade *f*; **sea god** **N** Meer(es)gott *m*; **sea goddess** **N** Meer(es)göttin *f*; **seagoing** **ADJ** *boat etc* hochseetüchtig; **~ nation** Seefahrernation *f*; **seagrass** **N** (*Bot*) Seegras *nt*; **sea green** **N** Meergrün *nt*; **sea-green** **ADJ** meergrün; **seagull** **N** Möwe *f*; **sea horse** **N** Seepferdchen *nt*; **sea kale** **N** See- or Strandkohl *m*

seal¹ [siːl] **N** (*Zool*) Seehund *m*; (= *sealskin*) Seal *m* **VI** Seehunde jagen; **to go ~ing** auf Seehundfang or -jagd gehen; **to go on a ~ing expedition** an einer Seehundjagd teilnehmen

seal² **N a** (= *impression in wax etc*) Siegel *nt*; (*against unauthorized opening*) Versiegelung *f*; (*of metal*) Plombe *f*; (= *die*) Stempel *m*; (= *ring*) Siegelring *m*; (= *decorative label*) Aufkleber *m*; **to be under ~** versiegelt sein; **under the ~ of secrecy** unter dem Siegel der Verschwiegenheit; **the ~ of the confessional** das Beichtgeheimnis; **~ of quality** Gütesiegel *nt*; **to put one's** or **the ~ of approval on sth** einer Sache (*dat*) seine offizielle Zustimmung geben; **to set one's ~ on sth** (*lit, fig*) unter etw (*acc*) sein Siegel setzen; **this set the ~ on their friendship** das besiegelte ihre Freundschaft; **as a ~ of friendship** zum Zeichen der Freundschaft

b (= *airtight closure*) Verschluss *m*; (= *washer*) Dichtung *f*

VT versiegeln; *envelope, parcel also* zukleben; (*with wax*) siegeln; *border* dichtmachen; *area* abriegeln; (= *make air-* or *watertight*) *joint, container* abdichten; *porous surface* versiegeln; (*fig,* = *settle, finalize*) besiegeln; **~ed envelope** verschlossener Briefumschlag; **~ed orders** versiegelte Order; **~ed train** plombierter Zug; **~ the meat before adding the stock** Poren (durch rasches Anbraten) schließen und dann Fleischbrühe hinzufügen; **my lips are ~ed** meine Lippen sind versiegelt; **this ~ed his fate** dadurch war sein Schicksal besiegelt; **to ~ victory** den Sieg besiegeln

▶ **seal in** **VT** *sep* einschließen; **this process seals all the flavour** (*Brit*) or **flavor** (*US*) **in** dieses Verfahren erhält das volle Aroma

▶ **seal off** **VT** *sep* absperren, abriegeln

▶ **seal up** **VT** *sep* versiegeln; *parcel, letter* zukleben; *crack, windows* abdichten

sea lane **N** (*Naut*) Seeweg *m*, Schifffahrtsweg *m*

sealant ['siːlənt] **N** Dichtungsmittel *nt*

sea: sea-launched ['siːˌlɔːnʃt] **ADJ** *missiles* seegestützt; **sea legs** **PL** **to get** or **find one's ~** (*inf*) standfest werden

sealer¹ ['siːlə'] **N** (= *boat*) Robbenfänger *m*; (= *person*) Robbenfänger(in) *m(f)*

sealer² (= *varnish*) (Ver)siegeler *m*

sea level **N** Meeresspiegel *m*; **above/below ~** über/unter dem Meeresspiegel

sealing ['siːlɪŋ]: **sealing ring** **N** Dichtungsring *m*; **sealing wax** **N** Siegelwachs *nt*

sea lion **N** Seelöwe *m*

seal: seal ring **N** Siegelring *m*; **sealskin** **N** Seehundfell *nt*, Seal *m*

Sealyham ['siːliəm] **N** Sealyhamterrier *m*

seam [siːm] **N a** Naht *f*; (= *scar*) Narbe *f*; (*Naut*) Fuge *f*; **are my ~s straight?** sitzen meine Nähte gerade?; **to come** or **fall apart at the ~s** (*lit, fig*) aus den Nähten gehen; **to be bursting at the ~s** (*lit, fig*) aus allen Nähten platzen (*inf*)

b (*Geol*) Flöz *nt* **VT** (= *sew, join*) nähen; (*fig,* = *mark with lines*) durchziehen

seaman ['siːmən] **N** *pl* **-men** [-mən] Seemann *m*

seaman: seaman-like **ADJ** seemännisch; **seamanship** **N** Seemannschaft *f*

sea mile **N** Seemeile *f*

seamless ['siːmlɪs] **a** **ADJ** *tube, stockings* nahtlos; *cardigan* ohne Nähte **b** (*fig*) **the ~ transition to democracy** der nahtlose Übergang zur Demokratie

seamstress ['semstrɪs] **N** Näherin *f*

seam welding **N** Nahtverschweißung *f*

seamy ['siːmɪ] **ADJ** (+*er*) *club, bar, person* heruntergekommen; *story, area, past* zwielichtig; *events, details* schmutzig; **the ~ side of life** die Schattenseite des Lebens

séance ['seɪɑ̃ːns] **N** spiritistische Sitzung, Séance *f*

sea: seapiece **N** (*Painting*) Seestück *nt*; **sea pink** **N** (gemeine) Grasnelke; **seaplane** **N** Wasserflugzeug *nt*; **seaport** **N** Seehafen *m*; **sea power** **N** Seemacht *f*; **seaquake** **N** Seebeben *nt*

sear [sɪə'] **VT a** (= *burn: hot metal, water etc*) verbrennen; (*pain*) durchzucken; (*Med* = *cauterize*) ausbrennen; (*Cook* = *brown quickly*) rasch anbraten; (*fig*) zutiefst treffen **b** (= *scorch, wither: sun, wind*) ausdörren, austrocknen

search [sɜːtʃ] **N** (= *hunt: for lost object, missing person etc*) Suche *f* (*for* nach); (= *examination: of cupboard, luggage, suspect etc*) Durchsuchung *f* (*of* +*gen*); (*esp Jur: of documents*) Nachforschungen *pl* (*of* über +*acc*); (*Comput*) Suchlauf *m*; **right of ~** Durchsuchungsrecht *nt*; **to go in ~ of sb/sth** auf die Suche nach jdm/etw gehen; **to carry out a ~ of a house** eine Haus(durch)suchung machen; **I found an interesting book in my ~** bei meiner Suche or beim Suchen habe ich ein interessantes Buch gefunden; **to do a ~ for sth** nach etw suchen; **they arranged a ~ for the missing child** sie veranlassten eine Suchaktion nach dem vermissten Kind; **to do a ~ (and replace) for sth** (*Comput*) etw suchen (und ersetzen)

VT (*for* nach) durchsuchen; *archives, records* suchen in (+*dat*), durchforschen; *conscience* erforschen; *memory, sb's face* durchforschen; **to ~ a place for sb/sth** einen Ort nach jdm absuchen/nach etw durch- or absuchen; **~ me!** (*inf*) was weiß ich? (*inf*); **if you ~ your heart ...** wenn Sie Ihr Herz fragen ...

VI (*also Comput*) suchen (*for* nach)

▶ **search about** (*Brit*) or **around** **VI** herumstöbern (*in* in +*dat*); (*in country etc*) (herum)suchen (*in* in +*dat*)

▶ **search out** **VT** *sep* heraussuchen; *person* ausfindig machen, aufspüren; *cause* herausfinden

▶ **search through** **VI** +*prep obj* durchsuchen; *papers, books* durchsehen

search: search-and-destroy **ADJ** (*Mil*) Vernichtungs-; **~ mission** Vernichtungsmission *f*; **search engine** **N** (*Comput*) Suchmaschine *f*

searcher ['sɜːtʃə'] **N** (*Customs etc*) Durchsuchungsbeamte(r) *m*, Durchsuchungsbeamtin *f*; **the ~s** (= *search party*) die Suchmannschaft *f*

search function **N** (*Comput*) Suchfunktion *f*

searching **ADJ** ['sɜːtʃɪŋ] *look* prüfend, forschend; *question* durchdringend, bohrend; *examination, test* gründlich; **his questions became more ~** er stellte tiefer gehende Fragen

searchingly ['sɜːtʃɪŋlɪ] **ADV** *look* prüfend, forschend

search: searchlight **N** Suchscheinwerfer *m*; **search operation** **N a** (*of police*) Fahndung *f* **b** (*Comput*) Suchlauf *m*; **search party** **N** Suchmannschaft *f*; **search tuning** **N** (*Rad*) Sendersuchlauf *m*; **search warrant** **N** Durchsuchungsbefehl *m*; **search word** **N** (*Comput*) Suchwort *nt*, Suchbegriff *m*

sea-rescue aircraft **N** Seerettungsflugzeug *nt*

searing ['sɪərɪŋ] **ADJ** *heat* glühend; *pain also* scharf; *wound* glühend heiß; (*fig*) (= *painful*) *grief, sense of loss* quälend; (= *forceful*) *indictment, attack* scharf; *documentary* eindringlich

sea: seascape **N** Seestück *nt*; **sea serpent** **N** Seeschlange *f*; **sea shanty** **N** Seemannslied *nt*; **seashell** N Muschel(schale) *f*; **seashore** N Strand *m*; **on the ~** am Strand; **the life found on the ~** die Strandflora und -fauna; **seasick** ADJ seekrank; **seasickness** N Seekrankheit *f*; **seaside** N **a** at the ~ am Meer; **to go to the ~** ans Meer fahren ATTR See-; *town* am Meer; **~ café** Strandcafé *nt*; **~ holidays** (*Brit*) Ferien *pl* am Meer; **seaside resort** N Seebad *nt*; **sea snake** N (*Zool*) Seeschlange *f*

season ['si:zn] N **a** (*of the year*) Jahreszeit *f*; **rainy/monsoon ~** Regen-/Monsunzeit *f*

b (= *social season, sporting season etc*) Saison *f*; **nesting/hunting ~** Brut-/Jagdzeit *f*; **the football ~** die Fußballsaison; **the strawberry ~** die Erdbeerzeit; **strawberries are in ~/out of ~ now** für Erdbeeren ist jetzt die richtige/nicht die richtige Zeit; **their bitch is in ~** ihre Hündin ist läufig; **in and out of ~** andauernd, jahrein (und) jahraus; **to go somewhere out of/in ~** an einen Ort fahren *or* gehen, wenn keine Saison/wenn Saison ist; **at the height of the ~** in der *or* zur Hochsaison; **the height of the London ~** der Höhepunkt der Londoner Saison; **the ~ of good will** (= *Christmas*) die Zeit der Nächstenliebe; **"Season's greetings"** „fröhliche Weihnachten und ein glückliches neues Jahr"

c (*Theat*) Spielzeit *f*; **they did a ~ at La Scala** sie spielten eine Saison lang an der Scala; **for a ~** eine Spielzeit lang; **a Dustin Hoffman ~, a ~ of Dustin Hoffman films** eine Serie von Dustin-Hoffman-Filmen

d (*of time*) **in due ~** zu gegebener Zeit; **in good ~** rechtzeitig; **if I might offer a word in ~** wenn ich dazu meinen Rat anbieten darf

VT **a** *food* würzen; (*fig*, = *temper*) durchsetzen **b** *wood* ablagern; (*fig*, = *inure*) troops stählen

seasonable ['si:zənəbl] ADJ **a** *dress, weather etc* der Jahreszeit entsprechend *attr*; **to be ~** der Jahreszeit entsprechen **b** (*form*, = *timely*) *advice, rebuke* zur rechten Zeit

seasonal ['si:zənl] ADJ jahreszeitlich bedingt; (*Econ*) Saison-, saisonbedingt; **~ fruit/vegetables** Früchte *pl*/Gemüse *nt* der Saison; **we eat whatever fruit is ~** wir essen das Obst, das gerade auf dem Markt ist

seasonal: seasonal adjustment N (*Econ, Pol*) Saisonbereinigung *f*; **seasonal affective disorder** N (*Med*) Winterdepression *f*

seasonally ['si:zənəlɪ] ADV **a** (*figures*) saisonbereinigt; **~ available fruit and vegetables** Obst und Gemüse *nt* der Saison

seasonal worker N Saisonarbeiter(in) *m(f)*

seasoned ['si:znd] ADJ **a** *food* gewürzt **b** *timber* abgelagert **c** (*fig*, = *experienced*) erfahren

seasoning ['si:znɪŋ] N (*Cook*) Gewürz *nt*; (*fig*) Würze *f*

season ticket N (*Rail*) Zeitkarte *f*; (*Theat*) Abonnement *nt*; **~ holder** Inhaber(in) *m(f)* einer Zeitkarte, Abonnent(in) *m(f)*

seat [si:t] N **a** (= *place to sit*) (Sitz)platz *m*; (= *actual piece of furniture*) Sitz *m*; (*usu pl*: = *seating*) Sitzgelegenheit *f*; **to have a front ~ at the opera** in der Oper in den vorderen Reihen sitzen; **an aircraft with 250 ~s** ein Flugzeug mit 250 Plätzen *or* Sitzen; **we'll have to borrow some ~s** wir werden uns wohl ein paar Stühle borgen müssen; **we haven't enough ~s** wir haben nicht genügend Sitzgelegenheiten; **to lose one's ~** seinen Platz verlieren *or* loswerden (*inf*); **will you keep my ~ for me?** würden Sie mir meinen Platz freihalten?; **I've booked two ~s** ich habe zwei Plätze reservieren lassen → **take**

b (*of chair etc*) Sitz *m*, Sitzfläche *f*; (*of trousers*) Hosenboden *m*; (= *buttocks*) Hinterteil *nt*; **he picked him up by the ~ of his pants** er packte ihn beim Hosenboden; **to fly by the ~ of one's pants** (*Aviat sl*) mit dem Hintern fliegen (*inf*); (*fig*) immer seinem Riecher folgen; **it's a ~-of--the-pants operation** (*inf*) es kommt dabei auf den richtigen Riecher an (*inf*)

c (*on committee, board of company*) Sitz *m*; **a ~ in Parliament** ein Sitz im Parlament, ein Mandat *nt*; **to win a ~** ein Mandat gewinnen; **his ~ is in Devon** sein Wahlkreis *m* ist in Devon

d (= *centre, of government, commerce etc*) Sitz *m*; (*of fire, trouble*) Herd *m*; **~ of emotions** Sitz der Gefühle; **~ of learning** Lehrstätte *f*

e (= *country seat, bishop's seat etc*) Sitz *m*

f (*of rider*) Sitz *m*; **to keep one's ~** im Sattel bleiben; **to lose one's ~** aus dem Sattel fallen

VT **a** *person etc* setzen; **to ~ oneself** sich setzen; **to be ~ed** sitzen; **please be ~ed** bitte, setzen Sie sich; **to remain ~ed** sitzen bleiben

b (= *have sitting room for*) **the car/table/sofa ~s 4** im Auto/am Tisch/auf dem Sofa ist Platz für 4 Personen; **the hall ~s 900** die Halle hat 900 Sitzplätze

c (*Tech*, = *fix in place*) einpassen

VI (*skirt etc*: = *go baggy*) ausbeulen, sich durchsitzen

seat: seat belt N Sicherheits- *or* Sitzgurt *m*; **to fasten one's ~, to put one's ~ on** sich anschnallen, seinen Sicherheitsgurt anlegen; **"fasten ~s"** „bitte anschnallen"; **seat cover** N (*Aut*) Sitzbezug *m*

-seater [-si:tə'] SUF N -sitzer *m*; **two-seater** Zweisitzer *m* ATTR -sitzig; **single-seater** (*racing car, plane*) einsitzig

seating ['si:tɪŋ] N Sitzgelegenheiten *pl*, Sitzplätze *pl*; **~ room** Platz *m* zum Sitzen

seating arrangements PL Sitzordnung *f*

seating plan N (*Theat etc*) Sitzplan *m*, Bestuhlungsplan *m*; (*at wedding etc*) Sitzordnung *f*

SEATO ['si:təu] *abbr* (*Hist*) of **South-East Asia Treaty Organization** SEATO *f*

sea: sea transport N Seetransport *m*; **sea trip** N Seereise *f*; **sea trout** N Meerforelle *f*; **sea turtle** N Meeresschildkröte *f*; **sea urchin** N Seeigel *m*; **sea view** N Seeblick *m*; **sea wall** N Deich *m*; **seaward** ADJ *direction, course* aufs Meer hinaus; **~ wind** Seewind *m*; **the ~ side of the quay** die seewärtige Seite des Kais ADV (*also* **seawards**) see- *or* meerwärts; **sea water** N Meer- *or* Seewasser *nt*; **seaway** N (= *route*) Seestraße *f*; (= *waterway*) Wasserweg *m or* -straße *f*; **seaweed** N (*Meeres*)alge *f*, (See-)tang *m*, Seegras *nt*; **seaworthy** ADJ seetüchtig

sebaceous [sɪ'beɪʃəs] ADJ Talg-

sebaceous glands PL Talgdrüsen *pl*

seborrhoea, (*US*) **seborrhea** [sebə'rɪə] N Seborrhö(e) *f*

sebum ['si:bəm] N Talg *m*

sec [sek] **a** *abbr of* **second(s)** Sek.; **wait a ~** (*inf*) Augenblick *or* Moment mal **b** *abbr of* **secretary**

secant ['si:kənt] N **a** Sekans *m* **b** (= *line*) Sekante *f*

secateurs [ˌsekə'tɜ:z] PL Gartenschere *f*

secede [sɪ'si:d] VI sich abspalten

secession [sɪ'seʃən] N Abspaltung *f*; (*US, Hist*) Sezession *f*

secessionism [sɪ'seʃənɪzəm] N Abspaltungsbestrebungen *pl*

secessionist [sɪ'seʃənɪst] ADJ Sezessions-, sezessionistisch; **~ movement** Sezessionsbewegung *f* N Sezessionist(in) *m(f)*

seclude [sɪ'klu:d] VT absondern

secluded [sɪ'klu:dɪd] ADJ *spot, house* abgelegen; *life* zurückgezogen, abgeschieden

seclusion [sɪ'klu:ʒən] N (= *act of secluding*) Absondern *nt*, Absonderung *f*; (= *being secluded*) Abgeschlossenheit *f*, Abgeschiedenheit *f*; (*of house, spot*) Abgelegenheit *f*; **in ~ from the world** in Weltabgeschiedenheit

second¹ ['sekənd] ADJ zweite(r, s); **the ~ floor** (*Brit*) der zweite Stock; (*US*) der erste Stock; **a ~ Goethe** ein zweiter Goethe; **every ~ house** jedes zweite Haus; **every ~ day/Thursday** jeden zweiten Tag/Donnerstag; **to be ~** Zweite(r, s) sein; **to be ~ to none** unübertroffen *or* unerreicht sein; **to be ~ only to sb/sth** nur von jdm/etw übertroffen werden; **in ~ place** (*Sport etc*) an zweiter Stelle; **to be** *or* **lie in ~ place** auf dem zweiten Platz sein *or* liegen; **to finish in ~ place** den zweiten Platz belegen; **in the ~ place** (= *secondly*) zweitens; **to be ~ in the queue** (*Brit*) *or* **line** (*US*) der/die Zweite in der

Schlange sein; **to be ~ in command** (*Mil*) stellvertretender Kommandeur sein; (*fig*) der zweite Mann sein; **~ violin** zweite Geige; **~ tenor** zweiter Tenor; **the ~ teeth** die zweiten *or* bleibenden Zähne, zweites Gebiss; **the Müllers' ~ car** der Zweitwagen der Müllers; **England's ~ city** die zweitwichtigste Stadt Englands; **his ~ self** sein zweites Ich; **she's like a ~ mother to me** sie ist wie eine Mutter zu mir; **will you have a ~ cup?** möchten Sie noch eine Tasse?; **I won't tell you a ~ time** ich sage dir das kein zweites Mal; **~ time around** beim zweiten Mal; **to give sb a ~ chance** jdm eine zweite *or* noch eine Chance geben; **you won't get a ~ chance** die Möglichkeit kriegst du so schnell nicht wieder (*inf*); **~ the thing he did was (to) get himself a drink** als Zweites holte er sich etwas zu trinken → **fiddle, wind¹**

ADV **a** (+*adj*) zweit-; (+*vb*) an zweiter Stelle; **the ~ largest house** das zweitgrößte Haus; **the ~ most common question** die zweithäufigste Frage, die am zweithäufigsten gestellte Frage; **the speaker against a motion always speaks ~** der Gegenredner spricht immer als Zweiter; **to come/lie ~** (*in race, competition*) Zweite(r) werden/sein; **to go** *or* **travel ~** (*by rail, bus etc*) zweiter Klasse fahren *or* reisen

b (= *secondly*) zweitens

VT *motion, proposal* unterstützen; **I'll ~ that!** (*at meeting*) ich unterstütze das; (*in general*) (genau) meine Meinung

N **a** (*of time, Math, Sci*) Sekunde *f*; (*inf*: = *short time*) Augenblick *m*; **just a ~!** (einen) Augenblick!; **it won't take a ~** es dauert nicht lange; **I'll only be a ~ (or two)** ich komme gleich; (= *back soon*) ich bin gleich wieder da; **at that very ~** genau in dem Augenblick

b (= *in order*) der/die/das Zweite; (*in race, class etc*) der/die Zweite; **to come a poor/good ~** einen schlechten/guten zweiten Platz belegen; **to come a poor ~ to sb/sth** erst an zweiter Stelle nach jdm/etw kommen; **Elizabeth the Second** Elizabeth die Zweite

c (*Aut*) **~ (gear)** der zweite Gang; **to put a/the car into ~** den zweiten Gang einlegen; **to drive in ~** im zweiten Gang *or* im Zweiten fahren

d (*Mus*: = *interval*) Sekunde *f*

e (*Brit, Univ*: = *degree*) mittlere Noten bei Abschlussprüfungen **he got an upper/a lower ~** ≈ er hat mit Eins bis Zwei/Zwei bis Drei abgeschnitten

f (*Sport, in duel*) Sekundant *m*; **~s out!** Ring frei!

g **seconds** PL (*inf*: = *second helping*) Nachschlag *m* (*inf*); **there aren't any ~s** es ist nichts mehr da; **can I have ~s?** kann ich noch etwas nachbekommen? **h** (*Comm*) **this is a ~** das ist zweite Wahl; **~s are much cheaper** Waren zweiter Wahl sind viel billiger

second² [sɪ'kɒnd] VT (*Brit*) abordnen, abstellen

secondarily ['sekəndrɪlɪ] ADV in zweiter Linie

secondary ['sekəndrɪ] ADJ **a** sekundär; *industry* verarbeitend; *reason* weniger bedeutend; **of ~ importance** von untergeordneter *or* sekundärer Bedeutung; **that was only ~ to our need to save money** das kam erst an zweiter Stelle nach der Notwendigkeit, Geld zu sparen; **~ character** (*Film, Theat*) Nebenfigur *f* **b** (= *higher*) *education* höher; **~ modern (school)** (*dated Brit*) ≈ Realschule *f*; **~ school** höhere Schule; **~ schooling** höhere Schulausbildung; **~ teacher** Lehrer(in) *m(f)* an einer höheren Schule; **subjects taught at ~ level** Unterrichtsfächer *pl* in höheren Schulen N (*inf*: = *school*) höhere Schule

secondary: secondary action N *Streik in nur indirekt beteiligten Firmen*; **secondary cancer** N Sekundärkrebs *m*; **secondary colour**, (*US*) **secondary color** N Mischfarbe *f*; **secondary feather** N Armschwinge *f*; **secondary host** N (*Biol*) Zwischenwirt *m*; **secondary infection** N Sekundärinfektion *f*; **secondary picketing** N *Aufstellung von Streikposten vor nur indirekt beteiligten Firmen*; **secondary road** N Nebenstraße *f*; **secondary sex(ual) characteristic** N sekundäres Geschlechtsmerkmal; **secondary smoking** N Passivrauchen *nt*; **secondary stress** N (*Gram*) Nebenton *m*

second: second ballot N (*Pol*) Stichwahl *f*; **second best** N Zweitbeste(r, s); **(the) ~ isn't good enough for him** das Beste ist gerade gut genug für ihn; **I won't settle for ~** ich gebe mich nicht mit dem Zweitbesten zufrieden ADV **to come off ~** es nicht so gut haben; (= *come off badly*) den kürzeren ziehen; **second-best** ADJ zweitbeste(r, s); **she always felt she was ~** sie hatte immer das Gefühl, zweite Wahl zu sein; **he was always ~ to his older brother** er stand immer im Schatten seines älteren Bruders; **that job was ~ for him** diese Stelle war eine Ausweichlösung für ihn; **second chamber** N zweite Kammer; **second childhood** N zweite Kindheit; **second class** N (*Rail, Post etc*) zweite Klasse; **second-class** ADJ a *travel, ticket, carriage, mail* zweiter Klasse *pred*; *status, education, treatment* zweitklassig; **~ degree** (*Brit, Univ*) = **second** [1] N e; **~ stamp** Briefmarke *für nicht bevorzugt beförderte Briefsendungen* **~ letter** *nicht bevorzugt beförderter Brief* b = **second-rate** ADV *travel* zweiter Klasse; **to send sth ~** etw mit nicht bevorzugter Post schicken; **second-class citizen** N Bürger(in) *m(f)* zweiter Klasse; **Second Coming** N Wiederkunft *f*; **second cousin** N Cousin *m*/Cousine *f* or Kusine *f* zweiten Grades; **second-degree** ADJ attr zweiten Grades; **second-degree burn** N Verbrennung *f* zweiten Grades

seconder ['sekəndə'] N Befürworter(in) *m(f)*

second: second-guess VT a (= *predict*) vorhersagen, prophezeien; **to ~ sb** vorhersagen, was jd machen/sagen wird b (*US:* = *criticize*) nachträglich or im Nachhinein kritisieren; **second hand** N (*of watch*) Sekundenzeiger *m*; **second-hand** ADJ gebraucht; *clothes* getragen, secondhand (*esp Comm*); (*fig*) *information, knowledge* aus zweiter Hand; **a ~ car** ein Gebrauchtwagen *m*; **~ dealer** Gebrauchtwarenhändler(in) *m(f)*; (*for cars*) Gebrauchtwagenhändler(in) *m(f)*; **~ value** Gebrauchtwert *m*; (*for books*) antiquarischer Wert; **~ bookshop** Antiquariat *nt*; **~ market** (*for cars*) Gebrauchtwagenmarkt *m*; **there is a thriving ~ market for this** das ist auch gebraucht sehr gefragt ADV gebraucht, aus zweiter Hand; **I only heard it ~** ich habe es nur aus zweiter Hand; **second language** N Zweitsprache *f*; **second lieutenant** N Leutnant *m*

secondly ['sekəndlɪ] ✪ 26.2 ADV zweitens; (= *secondarily*) an zweiter Stelle, in zweiter Linie

secondment [sɪ'kɒndmənt] N (*Brit*) Abordnung *f*; **to be on ~** abgeordnet sein

second: second mortgage N zweite Hypothek; **to take out a ~** eine zweite Hypothek aufnehmen; **second name** N Familienname *m*, Nachname *m*, Zuname *m*; **second nature** N zweite Natur; **to become ~ (to sb)** (jdm) in Fleisch und Blut übergehen; **second officer** N (*Mil*) zweiter Offizier; **second person** N (*Gram*) zweite Person; **the ~ singular/plural** die zweite Person Einzahl/Mehrzahl; **second-rate** ADJ (*pej*) zweitklassig, zweitrangig; **second sight** N zweites Gesicht; **you must have ~** du musst hellsehen können; **second string** N a (= *second possibility*) zweite Möglichkeit; **history/translation is my ~** ich kann jederzeit auf Geschichte/Übersetzungen als zweite Möglichkeit zurückgreifen; **to have a ~ to one's bow** zwei Eisen im Feuer haben b (*esp US Sport*) (= *player*) Ersatzspieler(in) *m(f)*, Reservespieler(in) *m(f)*; (= *team*) Ersatzmannschaft *f*, Reservemannschaft *f*; **second-string** ADJ (*esp US Sport*) Ersatz-, Reserve-; **~ team** Ersatzmannschaft *f*, Reservemannschaft *f*; **second thought** N with hardly or without a ~ ohne einen weiteren Gedanken, ohne lange or weiter darüber nachzudenken; **I didn't give him/it a ~** ich habe an ihn/daran überhaupt keinen Gedanken verschwendet; **to have ~s about sth** sich (*dat*) etw anders überlegen; **on ~s I decided not to** dann habe ich mich doch

dagegen entschieden; **on ~s maybe I'd better do it myself** vielleicht mache ich es, genau besehen, doch lieber selbst; **Second World War** N the ~ der Zweite Weltkrieg

secrecy ['si:krəsɪ] N (*of person,* = *ability to keep secrets*) Verschwiegenheit *f*; (= *secretiveness*) Geheimnistuerei *f*, Heimlichtuerei *f*; (*of event, talks*) Heimlichkeit *f*; **in ~** im Geheimen; **in strict ~** ganz im Geheimen; **there is no ~ about it** das ist kein Geheimnis → **swear**

secret ['si:krɪt] ADJ geheim; *pocket* versteckt; *drinker, admirer, ambition* heimlich; *ballot, vote* geheim; **a ~ door** eine verborgene Tür, eine Geheimtür; **the ~ ingredient** die geheimnisvolle Zutat; (*fig, of success etc*) die Zauberformel; **to keep sth ~ (from sb)** etw (vor jdm) geheim halten; **it's all highly ~** es ist alles streng geheim; **she was a ~ drug addict** sie verheimlichte ihre Drogensucht

N Geheimnis *nt*; **to keep sb/sth a ~ (from sb)** jdn/etw (vor jdm) geheim halten; **to tell sb a ~** jdm ein Geheimnis anvertrauen or (*give away*) verraten; **open ~** offenes Geheimnis; **in ~** im Geheimen; **I told you that in ~** or **as a ~** ich habe Ihnen das im Vertrauen erzählt; **they always met in ~** sie trafen sich immer heimlich; (*group etc*) sie hatten immer geheime Versammlungen; **she pretended to hate London, but in ~ she loved the city** sie gab vor, London zu hassen, aber insgeheim liebte sie die Stadt; **to be in on the ~** (in das Geheimnis) eingeweiht sein; **to let sb in on** or **into a ~** jdn in ein Geheimnis einweihen; **there's no ~ about it** das ist kein Geheimnis; **it's no ~ that ...** es ist kein Geheimnis, dass ...; **to keep a ~** ein Geheimnis für sich behalten; **can you keep a ~?** kannst du schweigen?; **to make no ~ of sth** kein Geheimnis or keinen Hehl aus etw machen; **the ~ of success** das Erfolgsgeheimnis; **the ~ of being a good teacher** das Geheimnis eines guten Lehrers; **I have no ~s from you** ich habe keine Geheimnisse vor dir

secret agent N Geheimagent(in) *m(f)*

secretaire [ˌsekrə'tɛə'] N (*Brit*) Sekretär *m*

secretarial [ˌsekrə'tɛərɪəl] ADJ *job, qualifications* als Sekretärin/Sekretär; **to do a ~ course** einen Sekretärinnenkurs machen, einen Kurs für Bürofachkräfte machen; **~ work** Sekretariatsarbeit *f*; **~ college** Schule *f* für Bürofachkräfte; **~ staff** Sekretärinnen und Schreibkräfte *pl*; (*of politician*) Stab *m*; **she joined his ~ staff** sie wurde Sekretärin bei ihm; **basic ~ skills** grundlegende Fertigkeiten *pl* als Bürofachkraft

secretarial agency N Personalvermittlung *f* für Bürokräfte

secretariat [ˌsekrə'tɛərɪət] N Sekretariat *nt*

secretary ['sekrətrɪ] N a Sekretär(in) *m(f)*; (*of society*) Schriftführer(in) *m(f)*; (*esp US, Pol,* = *minister*) Minister(in) *m(f)*; **~ to the board** Schriftführer(in) *m(f)* b (= *desk*) = **secretaire**

secretary: secretary bird N Sekretär *m*; **secretary-general** N *pl* secretaries-general, secretary-generals Generalsekretär(in) *m(f)*; **Secretary of State** N (*Brit*) Minister(in) *m(f)*; (*US*) Außenminister(in) *m(f)*; **secretaryship** N (= *office*) Amt *nt* des Schriftführers; (= *period*) Zeit *f* als Schriftführer

secret code N Geheimkode *m*

secrete [sɪ'kri:t] VT a (= *hide*) verbergen b (*Med*) absondern VI (*Med*) absondern

secretion [sɪ'kri:ʃən] N a (= *hiding*) Verbergen *nt* b (*Med,* = *act*) Absonderung *f*, Sekretion *f*; (= *substance*) Sekret *nt*

secretive[1] [sɪ'kri:tɪv] ADJ (*Med*) sekretorisch

secretive[2] ['si:krətɪv] ADJ *person (by nature)* verschlossen; (*in action*) geheimnistuerisch; *organization* verschwiegen, geheimnistuerisch; *smile, behaviour* geheimnisvoll; **to be ~ about sth** mit etw geheimnisvoll tun

secretively ['si:krətɪvlɪ] ADV geheimnisvoll; (= *in secret*) heimlich; **to behave ~** geheimnistuerisch sein

secretiveness ['si:krətɪvnɪs] N (= *character trait*) Verschlossenheit *f*; (= *secretive behaviour*) Ge-

heimnistuerei *f*; **the ~ of his smile/behaviour** sein geheimnisvolles Lächeln/Benehmen

secretly ['si:krətlɪ] ADV (= *in secrecy*) im Geheimen; *meet, marry, film* heimlich; (= *privately*) insgeheim, im Stillen; **he was ~ concerned** insgeheim war er beunruhigt

secretory [sɪ'kri:tərɪ] ADJ *gland etc* sekretorisch

secret: secret police N Geheimpolizei *f*; **secret service** N Geheimdienst *m*; **secret society** N Geheimgesellschaft *f*; **secret weapon** N (*lit, fig*) Geheimwaffe *f*

sect [sekt] N Sekte *f*

sectarian [sek'tɛərɪən] ADJ sektiererisch; *differences* konfessionell; **~ loyalties** konfessionelles Zugehörigkeitsgefühl; **~ violence** Gewalttätigkeiten *pl* mit konfessionellem Hintergrund N Sektierer(in) *m(f)*

sectarianism [sek'tɛərɪənɪzəm] N Sektierertum *nt*

section ['sekʃən] N a (= *part*) Teil *m*; (= *wing of building*) Trakt *m*; (*of book*) Abschnitt *m*; (*of document, law*) Absatz *m*; (*of motorway etc*) Abschnitt *m*; (*under construction*) Trakt *m*; (*of railway*) Streckenabschnitt *m*; (*of orange*) Stück *nt*; **the brass/string ~ of the orchestra** die Blechbläser *pl*/Streicher *pl* des Orchesters; **the sports ~** (*Press*) der Sportteil; **all ~s of the public** alle Teile der Öffentlichkeit; **the Indian ~ of the community** die Gruppe der Inder in der Gesellschaft

b (= *department, Mil*) Abteilung *f*; (*esp of academy etc*) Sektion *f*

c (= *diagram*) Schnitt *m*; **in ~** im Schnitt; **vertical/longitudinal ~** Quer-/Längsschnitt *m*

d (= *cutting: of rock, Med: of tissue*) Schnitt *m*; (*Med*) (= *operation*) Sektion *f*; (= *Caesarean section*) Kaiserschnitt *m*; **he took a horizontal ~ of the tissue** er machte einen Horizontalschnitt von dem Gewebe

VT a (= *cut to show a section*) einen Schnitt machen durch

b (= *divide into sections*) teilen

c (*Psych*) **to be ~ed** zwangseingewiesen werden

▶ **section off** VT sep abteilen; (= *cordon off*) absperren

sectional ['sekʃənl] ADJ a (= *in sections*) *road-building* abschnittsweise; *furniture, pipe, fishing rod* zerlegbar; **~ drawing** Darstellung *f* im Schnitt b *differences, rivalries* zwischen den Gruppen; *interests* partikularistisch

sectionalism ['sekʃənəlɪzəm] N Partikularismus *m*

sectionalize ['sekʃənəlaɪz] VI (= *subdivide*) unterteilen; **~d design** gegliederte Bauweise; (*according to different aspects*) nach lokalen Gesichtspunkten/Interessen einteilen

sector ['sektə'] N (*also Comput*) Sektor *m*

sectoral ['sektərəl] ADJ (*Econ*) sektorenspezifisch

secular ['sekjʊlə'] ADJ weltlich, säkular; *music, art* profan; *court, education* weltlich; *state* säkular; **~ priest** Weltgeistliche(r) *m(f)*

secularism ['sekjʊlərɪzəm] N Säkularismus *m*; (*of attitude*) Weltlichkeit *f*

secularization [ˌsekjʊlərar'zeɪʃən] N Säkularisation *f*; (*of education, court, Sunday also*) Säkularisierung *f*

secularize ['sekjʊləraɪz] VT säkularisieren

secure [sɪ'kjʊə'] ADJ (+er) a (= *safe*) sicher; (*emotionally*) geborgen; *existence, income* gesichert; **~ in the knowledge that ...** ruhig in dem Bewusstsein, dass ...; **to be ~ against** or **from sth** vor etw (*dat*) sicher sein; **to feel ~** sich sicher fühlen; (*emotionally*) sich geborgen fühlen; **to feel ~ about one's future** der Zukunft sicher entgegensehen; **to make sb feel ~** jdm das Gefühl der Sicherheit geben; **to be financially ~** finanziell abgesichert sein; **to be emotionally ~** emotional stabil sein

b (= *fastened*) *lock, door* gesichert; (= *firm, well-fastened*) *grip, knot, tile* fest; **is the window ~?** ist das Fenster fest zu?; **is the lid ~?** ist der Deckel fest drauf?; **to make a door/window/rope ~** eine Tür/ein Fenster/ein Seil sichern; **to make a tile ~** einen Ziegel befestigen

c (= *solid*) *base* sicher, solide; **to have a ~ foothold** (*fig*) festen Fuß gefasst haben; **on ~ ground** auf sicherem Boden

VT a (= *fasten, make firm*) festmachen; (= *tie up*) befestigen, festmachen; *window, door* fest zumachen; (*with chain, bolt etc*) sichern; *tile* befestigen; (= *make safe*) sichern (*from, against gegen*), schützen (*from, against* vor +*dat*)

b (= *obtain*) sich (*dat*) sichern; *majority of votes, order* erhalten; *profits, higher prices* erzielen; *share, interest in business* erwerben; (= *buy*) erstehen; *cook, employee* verpflichten; **to ~ sth for sb, to ~ sb sth** jdm etw sichern; **to ~ sb's services** jdn verpflichten; **their troops have now ~d the bridge/the airport** die Truppen haben jetzt die Brücke/den Flugplatz gegen feindliche Angriffe gesichert

c (= *guarantee*) sichern, garantieren; *loan* (ab-)sichern

secure accommodation N Sicherheitsverwahrung *f*

securely [sɪ'kjʊəlɪ] ADV (= *firmly*) fest; (= *safely*) sicher; **the prisoner was kept ~ in his cell** der Gefangene wurde streng gesichert in seiner Zelle gehalten; **~ established** fest etabliert

secureness [sɪ'kjʊənɪs] N **a** (= *safety*) Sicherheit *f*; (*emotional*) Geborgenheit *f* **b** (*of lock, door*) Sicherheit *f*

secure unit N Sicherheitsabteilung *f*

securities market [sɪ'kjʊərɪtɪz'mɑ:kɪt] M (*Fin*) Wertpapiermarkt *m*

security [sɪ'kjʊərɪtɪ] N **a** Sicherheit *f*; (*emotional*) Geborgenheit *f*; (= *security measures*) Sicherheitsvorkehrungen *or* -maßnahmen *pl*; **for ~** zur Sicherheit; **~ of tenure** Kündigungsschutz *m*; **airports have tightened their ~** die Flughäfen haben ihre Sicherheitsvorkehrungen verschärft; **in the ~ of one's own home** sicher im eigenen Heim; (*from emotional point of view*) in der Geborgenheit des eigenen Heims

b (= *security department*) Sicherheitsdienst *m*

c (*Fin*, = *guarantee*) Sicherheit *f*; (= *guarantor*) Bürge *m*, Bürgin *f*; **up to £500 without ~** bis zu £ 500 ohne Sicherheit; **to lend money on ~** Geld gegen Sicherheit leihen; **to stand ~ for sb** für jdn Bürge/Bürgin sein *or* Bürgschaft leisten

d **securities** PL (*Fin*) Effekten *pl*, (Wert)papiere *pl*

security in *cpds* Sicherheits-; **security adviser** N Sicherheitsberater(in) *m(f)*; **security blanket** N **a** (*around politicians etc*) Sicherheitsnetz *nt*; **to throw a ~ around sb/sth** jdm/etw mit einem Sicherheitsnetz umgeben **b** (*of child*) Kuscheldecke *f*; **security bond** N (*Fin*) Bürgschaftswechsel *m*; **security camera** N Überwachungskamera *f*; **security check** N Sicherheitskontrolle *f*; **security clearance** N Einstufung *f* als vertrauenswürdig *or* als kein Sicherheitsrisiko; **to have ~** kein Sicherheitsrisiko sein *or* darstellen; **Security Council** N Sicherheitsrat *m*; **security firm** N Wach- und Sicherheitsdienst *m*; **security force** N Sicherheitstruppe *f*; (*UN*) Friedenstruppe *f*; **security forces** PL Sicherheitskräfte *pl*; (*UN*) Friedensstreitmacht *f*; **security guard** N Wache *f*, Wächter(in) *m(f)*; (*for security checks*) Sicherheitsbeamte(r) *m*/-beamtin *f*; **security man** N Wache *f*, Wächter *m*; (*for security checks*) Sicherheitsbeamte(r) *m*; **one of the security men** einer der Sicherheitsleute; **security police** N Sicherheitspolizei *m*; **security precautions** PL Sicherheitsvorkehrungen *pl*; **security risk** N Sicherheitsrisiko *nt*; **security screening** N (*Pol*) Unbedenklichkeitsüberprüfung *f*; **security vetting** N Sicherheitsüberprüfung *f*

secy *abbr of* **secretary**

sedan [sɪ'dæn] N **a** (*also* **sedan chair**) Sänfte *f* **b** (*US, Aut*) Limousine *f*

sedate [sɪ'deɪt] **ADJ** (+*er*) gesetzt; *little girl, colour* ruhig; *furnishings, décor* gediegen; *life* geruhsam; *place* beschaulich; *party* ruhig, gesittet; *speed* gemächlich; *prose* bedächtig; **at a ~ pace** in gemessenem Tempo; **in a ~ manner** ruhig, gemessen **VT** Beruhigungsmittel geben (+*dat*), sedieren (*spec*); **he was heavily ~d** er stand stark unter dem Einfluss von Beruhigungsmitteln

sedately [sɪ'deɪtlɪ] ADV **a** (= *gently*) gemessen, ruhig; **he pulled ~ out of the driveway** er fuhr gemächlich aus der Auffahrt heraus **b** (= *conservatively*) *dressed, furnished* gediegen

sedateness [sɪ'deɪtnɪs] N Gesetztheit *f*; (*of little girl*) ruhige Art; (*of colour*) ruhiger Ton; (*of furnishings, décor*) Gediegenheit *f*; (*of life*) Geruhsamkeit *f*; (*of place*) Beschaulichkeit *f*; (*of prose*) Bedächtigkeit *f*

sedation [sɪ'deɪʃən] N Beruhigungsmittel *pl*; **to put sb under ~** jdm Beruhigungsmittel geben; **drugs used for ~** Drogen *pl* zur Beruhigung

sedative ['sedətɪv] **N** Beruhigungsmittel *nt*, Sedativum *nt* (*spec*) **ADJ** beruhigend, sedativ (*spec*)

sedentariness ['sedntərɪnɪs] N **a as a result of the ~ of the job** durch das dauernde Sitzen bei der Arbeit; **the excessive ~ of his daily life** das übermäßige tägliche Sitzen **b** (*of tribe*) Sesshaftigkeit *f*; (*of bird*) Verbleiben *nt* am Nistort

sedentary ['sedntərɪ] ADJ **a** *job, occupation* sitzend *attr*; **to lead a ~ life** sehr viel sitzen; **any job of a ~ nature** jede im Sitzen ausgeübte Tätigkeit **b** *tribe* sesshaft; **~ bird** Standvogel *m*

sedge warbler N Seggenrohrsänger *m*

sedge [sedʒ] N Riedgras *nt*, Segge *f*

sedgy ['sedʒɪ] ADJ **a** (*grown with sedge*) mit Riedgras bewachsen **b** (= *resembling sedge*) riedgrasartig

sediment ['sedɪmənt] N (Boden)satz *m*; (*in river*) Ablagerung *f*; (*in chemical solution*) Niederschlag *m*, Sediment *nt*

sedimentary [ˌsedɪ'mentərɪ] ADJ sedimentär; **~ rocks** Sedimentgestein *nt*

sedimentation [ˌsedɪmen'teɪʃən] N Ablagerung *f*, Sedimentation *f*

sedition [sə'dɪʃən] N Aufwiegelung *f*, Verhetzung *f*

seditious [sə'dɪʃəs] ADJ aufrührerisch, aufwieglerisch

seduce [sɪ'dju:s] VT verführen; **to ~ sb into doing sth** jdn zu etw verleiten, jdn dazu verleiten, etw zu tun; **to ~ sb (away) from his duty/a place** jdn seine Pflichten vergessen lassen/von einem Ort weglocken; **to ~ sb (away) from his wife** jdn seiner Frau abspenstig machen

seducer [sɪ'dju:sə'] N Verführer *m*

seducible [sɪ'dju:sɪbl] ADJ verführbar

seduction [sɪ'dʌkʃən] N Verführung *f*

seductive [sɪ'dʌktɪv] ADJ verführerisch; *salary, offer, suggestion* verlockend

seductively [sɪ'dʌktɪvlɪ] ADV verführerisch; *offer, suggest* verlockend

seductiveness [sɪ'dʌktɪvnɪs] N verführerische Art; **the ~ of the offer** etc das verlockende Angebot *etc*

seductress [sɪ'dʌktrɪs] N Verführerin *f*

sedulous ADJ , **sedulously** ADV ['sedjʊləs, -lɪ] unermüdlich, unentwegt

---

see¹ [si:]

pret **saw**, ptp **seen**

✪ 6.1, 6.2, 12.1, 15.2, 26.3

1 TRANSITIVE VERB	3 PHRASAL VERBS
2 INTRANSITIVE VERB	

1 – TRANSITIVE VERB

a sehen; **to see sb do sth** sehen, wie jd etw macht; **I've never seen him swim(ming)** ich habe ihn noch nie schwimmen sehen; **he was seen to enter the building** man hat ihn gesehen *or* er wurde gesehen, wie er das Gebäude betrat; **I saw it happen** ich habe gesehen, wie es passiert ist; **I've seen it done three times** das habe ich schon dreimal gesehen; **I wouldn't see you starve** ich würde doch nicht zusehen, wie du verhungerst; **I don't like to**

see people mistreated ich kann es nicht sehen, wenn Menschen schlecht behandelt werden; **I wouldn't like to see you unhappy** ich möchte doch nicht, dass du unglücklich bist; **see page 8** siehe Seite 8; **there was nothing to be seen** es war nichts zu sehen; **I don't know what she sees in him** ich weiß nicht, was sie an ihm findet; **we don't see much of them nowadays** wir sehen sie zurzeit nur selten; **I want to see a bit of the world** ich möchte etwas von der Welt sehen *or* kennen lernen; **I'll see him in hell first** (*inf*) ich denke nicht (im Schlaf) daran; **she won't see 40 again** sie ist gut und gern 40; **I/you must be seeing things** ich sehe/du siehst wohl Gespenster!; **I must be seeing things, if it isn't Peter!** ich glaub, ich seh nicht richtig, das ist doch der Peter!; **am I seeing things or is ...?** seh ich richtig, ist das nicht ...?; **I can't see my way to doing that** ich sehe mich nicht in der Lage, das zu tun; **I saw myself obliged to/faced with the need to ...** ich sah mich gezwungen, zu ...; **I suddenly saw myself being cheated** ich sah *or* erkannte plötzlich, dass man mich betrog

b = **check** nachsehen, gucken (*inf*); **I'll go and see who it is** ich gehe mal nachsehen *or* ich gucke (*inf*) mal(, wer das ist)

c = **go and see** *film, show, sights* sich (*dat*) ansehen; **worth seeing** sehenswert

d = **visit** besuchen; (*on business*) aufsuchen; **to call** *or* **go and see sb** jdn besuchen (gehen); **to see the doctor** zum Arzt gehen; **he is the man you ought to see about this** Sie sollten sich damit an ihn wenden

e = **meet, talk to, receive** (= *meet with*) sehen; (= *have a word with, talk to*) sprechen; (= *receive visit of*) empfangen; **the boss can't see you now, you can't see the boss now** Sie können den Chef jetzt nicht sprechen, Sie können jetzt nicht zum Chef (*inf*); **the boss/doctor will see you now** der Chef/der Herr Doktor ist jetzt frei; **what did he want to see you about?** weswegen wollte er Sie sprechen?; **I'll have to see my wife about that** das muss ich mit meiner Frau besprechen; **have you seen Personnel yet?** waren Sie schon bei der Personalabteilung?; **the minister saw the Queen yesterday** der Minister war gestern bei der Königin; **the Queen will see the minister tomorrow** die Königin wird den Minister morgen empfangen; **she refused to see us** sie wollte uns nicht empfangen *or* sehen; **there was only one applicant worth seeing** es war nur ein Bewerber dabei, den es sich anzusehen lohnte; **I shall be seeing them for dinner** ich treffe sie beim Abendessen; **see you (soon)!** bis bald!; **be seeing you!, see you later!** bis später!, bis nachher!; **see you on Sunday!** bis Sonntag!

f = **have relationship with** befreundet sein mit; **I'm not seeing anyone at the moment** ich habe zurzeit keinen Freund/keine Freundin

g = **accompany** begleiten, bringen; **to see sb to the door** jdn zur Tür bringen

h = **find out, know** we'll see if we can help mal sehen, ob wir helfen können; **we'll soon see who is right** wir werden ja bald sehen, wer Recht hat; **that remains to be seen** das wird sich zeigen; **let's just see what happens** wollen wir mal sehen *or* abwarten, was passiert; **I don't see any way I can help** ich sehe nicht, wie ich da helfen kann; **let me see if I can fix up something** ich werde mal sehen, ob sich etwas arrangieren lässt; **let me see if I can't find a better way** mal sehen, ob ich nicht etwas Besseres finden kann

i = **visualize** sich (*dat*) vorstellen; **I can't** *or* **don't see that working/him winning/myself living there** ich kann mir kaum vorstellen, dass das klappt/dass er gewinnt/dass ich da leben möchte; **I can't see myself in that job** ich glaube nicht, dass das eine Stelle für mich wäre; **can you see him as a father?** kannst du ihn dir als Vater vorstellen?; **he saw himself as a martyr** er sah sich als Märtyrer; **I can see it happening** ich sehe es kommen; **I can't see any chance of that happening** das halte ich für unwahrscheinlich *or* kaum möglich

j = experience erleben; **he lived to see the beginning of a new age** er hat den Anfang eines neuen Zeitalters miterlebt; **now I've seen everything!** ist das denn zu fassen?; **what impudence, I've never seen anything like it!** so eine Frechheit, so etwas habe ich ja noch nie gesehen or erlebt!; **it's seen a lot of hard wear** das ist schon sehr strapaziert worden

k = hear, notice sehen; **I see you still haven't done that/he's got married again** wie ich sehe, hast du das immer noch nicht gemacht/hat er wieder geheiratet

l = comprehend (= understand) verstehen; (= recognize) einsehen; (= realize) erkennen; **I don't see the importance of doing it/the need for the change** ich verstehe nicht or ich sehe nicht ein, warum das unbedingt gemacht werden muss/warum das geändert werden muss; **I can see that it might be a good thing** ich sehe ja ein, dass das eine gute Idee wäre; **I can see I'm going to be busy** ich sehe schon, ich werde viel zu tun haben; **I fail to or don't see how anyone could ...** ich begreife einfach nicht, wie jemand nur ... kann; **I don't see where the problem is** ich sehe das Problem nicht; **I see from this report that ...** ich ersehe aus diesem Bericht, dass ...; **(do you) see what I mean?** verstehst du(, wie ich meine)?; (= didn't I tell you!) siehst dus jetzt!; **I see what you mean** ich verstehe, was du meinst; (= you're quite right) ja, du hast Recht; **to make sb see sth** jdm etw klarmachen; **to make sb see reason** jdn zur Vernunft bringen; **I saw only too clearly that ...** ich erkannte nur zu deutlich, dass ...

m = consider problem sehen; **as I see it** so, wie ich das sehe; **this is how I see it** ich sehe das so; **that's how I see it** so sehe ich das jedenfalls; **try to see it my way** versuchen Sie doch einmal, es aus meiner Sicht zu sehen; **I don't see it that way** ich sehe das anders

n = ensure **see that it is done by tomorrow** sieh zu, dass es bis morgen fertig ist; **see that it doesn't happen again** sieh zu or pass auf, dass das nicht noch mal passiert; **I'll see you (all) right** (inf) ich werd dich nicht vergessen (inf)

o Cards **I'll see you** ich halte

2 – INTRANSITIVE VERB

a = have sight sehen

b = look sehen; **let me see, let's see** lassen Sie mich mal sehen; **can you see if I sit here?** können Sie (etwas) sehen, wenn ich hier sitze?; **it was so dark I couldn't see** es war so dunkel, ich konnte nichts sehen; **who was it? – I couldn't/didn't see** wer war das? – ich konnte es nicht sehen; **can you see to read?** ist es Ihnen hell genug zum Lesen?; **as far as the eye can see** so weit das Auge reicht; **see for yourself!** sieh doch selbst!; **now see here!** nun hören Sie mal her!

c = check, find out nachsehen, gucken (inf); **is he there? – I'll see** ist er da? – ich sehe mal nach or ich guck mal (inf); **I'll go and see** ich gehe mal nachsehen; **see for yourself!** sieh doch selbst (nach)!; **let me see** lassen Sie mich mal nachsehen

d = discover sehen; **will he come? – we'll soon see** kommt er? – das werden wir bald sehen or rausfinden (inf); **what kind of person is she? – you'll soon see for yourself** was für ein Mensch ist sie? – das werden Sie bald selbst sehen or feststellen; **you'll see!** du wirst es (schon) noch sehen!

e = understand verstehen; **as far as I can see ...** so wie ich das sehe ...; **it's all over, see?** es ist vorbei, verstehst du?; **it's logical, do you see?** es ist logisch, nicht wahr?; **he's dead, don't you see?** er ist tot, begreifst du das denn nicht?; **as I see from your report** wie ich aus Ihrem Bericht lese, wie ich aus Ihrem Bericht ersehe; **it's too late, (you) see** (explaining) weißt du, es ist zu spät; (= I told you so) siehst du, es ist zu spät!; **that's like this** es ist nämlich so; **(you) see, we can't do that** weißt du, das können wir nicht machen; **that's the way he is, (you) see** das ist eben seine Art(, weißt

du); **but this still has to be improved, you see** das muss natürlich noch verbessert werden; **and we went out, see, and saw this film, see, and ...** (dial) und wir sind weggegangen, weißte (inf) or nich (N Ger) or gell (S Ger), und haben uns den Film angesehen, weißte etc, und ...; **I see!** aha!; (after explanation) ach so!; (to keep conversation going, = I'm with you) ja; **yes, I see** ja, aha

f = consider **we'll see** (wir werden or wollen) mal sehen; **I don't know, I'll have to see** ich weiß nicht, ich muss mal sehen; **will you be there? – I'll see** bist du da? – mal sehen; **he said he'll see** er sagt, er will mal sehen; **let me see, let's see** warten Sie mal, lassen Sie mich mal überlegen

3 – PHRASAL VERBS

▶ **see about** VI +prep obj **a** (= attend to) sich kümmern um; **I'll have to see about getting the roof mended** ich muss mich darum kümmern, dass das Dach repariert wird; **he came to see about the TV** er kam, um sich (dat) den Fernseher anzusehen; **I've still a few things to see about** ich muss noch ein paar Dinge erledigen; **he came to see about the rent** er ist wegen der Miete gekommen; **we'd better see about going now** wir sehen besser zu, dass wir jetzt gehen

b (= consider) **I'll see about it** ich will mal sehen or schauen (esp S Ger); **we'll see about that!** (iro) das wollen wir mal sehen

▶ **see across** VT always separate hinüberbegleiten or -bringen (prep obj über +acc)

▶ **see after** VI +prep obj (esp US: = attend to) sich kümmern um

▶ **see in** VI (= look in) hineinsehen VT sep (= show in) hereinbringen; **to see the New Year in** das neue Jahr begrüßen

▶ **see into** VI +prep obj **a** house, room hineinsehen in (+acc); **to see into the future** in die Zukunft sehen or schauen; **to see into sb's mind** jds Gedanken lesen **b** (= investigate) untersuchen, prüfen, nachgehen (+dat)

▶ **see off** VT sep **a** (= bid farewell to) verabschieden; **are you coming to see me off (at the airport etc)?** kommt ihr mit mir (zum Flughafen etc)? **b** (= chase off) Beine machen (+dat) (inf); **see him off, boy!** verjag ihn! **c** (inf, = be better than) in die Tasche stecken (inf)

▶ **see out** VI (= look out) hinaussehen; **I can't see out of the window** ich kann nicht zum Fenster hinaussehen

VT sep **a** (= show out) hinausbringen or -begleiten (of aus); **I'll see myself out** ich finde (schon) alleine hinaus

b (= last to the end of) (coat, car) winter etc überdauern; (old man, invalid) wife, year etc überleben; **will he be fit enough to see out the game?** ist er fit genug, um das Spiel ganz durchzustehen?; **to see the Old Year out** das alte Jahr verabschieden

▶ **see over** or **round** (esp Brit) VI +prep obj house etc sich (dat) ansehen

▶ **see through** VI (lit) (hin)durchsehen (prep obj durch)

VI +prep obj (fig: = not be deceived by) durchschauen; **I can see right through you** ich habe dich durchschaut or erkannt

VT always separate **a** (= help through difficult time) beistehen (+dat); **to see sb through a bad time** jdm über eine schwierige Zeit hinweghelfen; **he had £100 to see him through the term** er hatte £ 100 für das ganze Semester; **I hope £10 will see you through** die £ 10 reichen dir hoffentlich

b job zu Ende bringen; (Parl) bill durchbringen

▶ **see to** VI +prep obj sich kümmern um; **these shoes need seeing to** mit den Schuhen muss etwas gemacht werden; **that cough needs seeing to** um den Husten muss man sich kümmern; **see to it that he doesn't forget** sieh zu, dass du/er das nicht vergisst; **I'll see to it** ich werde mich d(a)rum kümmern; **there's no chance now, the rain has seen to**

that es ist aussichtslos, dafür hat der Regen schon gesorgt

▶ **see up** VI +prep obj (= look up) hinaufsehen; **I could see up her skirt** ich konnte ihr unter den Rock sehen VT sep (= show up) heraufbringen

see² N Bistum nt; (Catholic also) Diözese f; (Protestant in Germany) Landeskirche f; **Holy See, See of Rome** Heiliger Stuhl

seed [si:d] N **a** (Bot, = one single) Samen m; (of grain, poppy, sesame etc) Korn nt; (within fruit) (Samen)kern m; (collective) Samen pl; (for birds) Körner pl; (= grain) Saat f, Saatgut nt; (liter, = sperm) Samen pl; (= offspring) Nachkommen pl; (fig, of unrest, idea etc) Keim m (of zu); **to go** or **run to ~** (vegetables) schießen; (flowers) einen Samenstand bilden; (fig: person) herunterkommen; **to sow the ~s of doubt (in sb's mind)** (bei jdm) Zweifel säen or den Keim des Zweifels legen; **he sowed the ~ from which ... developed** er hat den Keim gelegt, aus dem sich ... entwickelte; **I don't want to make a detailed proposal, just to sow the ~s** ich möchte keinen konkreten Vorschlag machen, ich möchte nur den Boden dafür bereiten

b (Sport) **to be the third ~** als Dritter platziert or gesetzt sein; **the number one ~** der/die als Nummer eins Gesetzte

VT **a** (= sow with seed) besäen

b (= extract seeds from) entkernen

c (Sport) setzen, platzieren; **~ed number one** als Nummer eins gesetzt; **~ed players** gesetzte or platzierte Spieler

VI (vegetables) schießen; (flowers) Samen entwickeln

VR **to ~ itself** (plant) sich aussäen

seed: seedbed N Saatbeet nt, Saatbett nt; **seed box** N Setzkasten m; **seedcake** N Kümmelkuchen m; **seedcase** N Samenkapsel f; **seed corn** N (Bot) Samenkorn nt; **they are eating their own ~** (fig) sie gehen aus Eingemachte (inf); **seed drill** N Sämaschine f

seediness ['si:dınıs] N (= disreputableness) Zwielichtigkeit f

seed: seed leaf N Keimblatt nt; **seedless** ADJ kernlos

seedling ['si:dlıŋ] N Sämling m

seed: seed pearl N Staubperle f; **seed plant** N Samenpflanze f; **seed potato** N Saatkartoffel f

seedsman ['si:dzmən] N pl **-men** [-mən] Samenhändler m

seed: seedtime N Saatzeit f; **seed tray** N = **seed box**

seedy ['si:dı] ADJ (+er) **a** (= disreputable) person, character zweifelhaft, zwielichtig; area, place zwielichtig **b** (inf: = unwell) **I feel ~** mir ist flau (inf), mir ist nicht gut; **to look ~** angeschlagen aussehen (inf), nicht gut aussehen

seeing ['si:ıŋ] N Sehen nt; **I'd never have thought it possible but ~ is believing** ich hätte es nie für möglich gehalten, aber ich habe es mit eigenen Augen gesehen; **look, ~ is believing, you can't deny it now** da haben Sie den Beweis vor Augen, jetzt können Sie es nicht mehr abstreiten CONJ **~ (that** or **as)** da

Seeing Eye Dog N (US) Blindenhund m

seek [si:k] pret, ptp **sought** VT **a** (= look for) suchen; fame, wealth erlangen wollen, streben nach; **to ~ sb's advice** jdn um Rat fragen; **the prosecutors are ~ing the death penalty** die Staatsanwaltschaft will die Todesstrafe; **the reason is not far to ~** der Grund liegt auf der Hand; **the quarrel is not of my ~ing** ich habe den Streit nicht gesucht; **~ time** (Comput) Zugriffszeit f **b** (liter, = attempt) suchen (geh); **to ~ to do sth** sich bemühen, etw zu tun; **those who sought his downfall** die(jenigen), die ihn zu Fall bringen wollten

▶ **seek after** VI +prep obj **a** (= look got) suchen
b → **sought-after**

▶ **seek for** VI +prep obj suchen nach; reforms, changes anstreben; **long-sought-for reforms/**

changes lang erstrebte Reformen *pl*/Veränderungen *pl*

▶ **seek out** VT *sep* ausfindig machen; *opinion* herausfinden; **seek him out, discover what he thinks** (*liter*) erforschen Sie ihn, finden Sie heraus, was er denkt (*geh*)

seeker ['siːkə'] N Suchende(r) *mf*; (= *pursuer*) Verfolger(in) *m(f)*; **to be a ~ of knowledge** auf der Suche nach Wissen *or* Erkenntnis sein; **~ of** *or* **after truth** Wahrheitssucher(in) *m(f)*

seem [siːm] ✪ 6.2, 26.2, 26.3 VI **a** (= *appear*) scheinen; **he ~s (to be) honest/a nice young man** er scheint ehrlich/ein netter junger Mann zu sein; **he ~ed nice enough** er schien ganz nett (zu sein); **he may ~ poor but ...** er mag arm scheinen *or* wirken, aber ...; **he ~s younger than he is** er wirkt jünger, als er ist; **that makes it ~ longer** dadurch wirkt es länger *or* kommt es einem länger vor; **he doesn't ~ (to be) able to concentrate** er scheint sich nicht konzentrieren zu können; **he is not what he ~s (to be)** er ist nicht (das), was er zu sein scheint; **things aren't always what they ~** vieles ist anders, als es aussieht; **I ~ to have heard that before** das habe ich doch schon mal gehört; **what ~s to be the trouble?** worum geht es denn?; (*doctor*) was kann ich für Sie tun?; **there ~s to be no solution** da scheint es keine Lösung zu geben; **it ~s to me that I'll have to do that again** mir scheint, ich muss das noch einmal machen; **he has left, it ~s** er ist anscheinend weggegangen, es scheint, er ist weggegangen; **we are not welcome, it ~s** wir sind anscheinend *or* scheinbar nicht willkommen; **so it ~s** es sieht (ganz) so aus; **he is, so it ~s, ...** er scheint ... zu sein; **it ~s** *or* **would ~ that he is coming after all** es sieht so aus, als ob er doch noch kommt, es scheint, er kommt doch noch; **it doesn't ~ that he'll be coming** es sieht nicht so aus, als ob er kommt; **if it ~s right to you** wenn Sie es für richtig halten; **it ~s** *or* **would ~ advisable** das scheint ratsam (zu sein); **how does it ~ to you?** was meinen SIE?; **how did she ~ to you?** wie fandst du sie?; **it ~s a shame to leave it unfinished** es ist doch irgendwie *or* eigentlich schade, das nicht fertig zu machen; **it just doesn't ~ right somehow** das ist doch irgendwie nicht richtig; **it would ~ that ...** es scheint fast so, als ob ...; **I can't ~ to do it** ich kann das anscheinend *or* scheinbar *or* irgendwie nicht

b **it only ~s like it** das kommt einem nur so vor; **I ~ to be floating in space** es kommt mir so vor, als ob ich schweben würde; **it all ~s so unreal to him/me** es kommt ihm/mir alles so unwirklich vor; **I ~ to remember that you had that problem before** es kommt mir so vor, als hätten Sie das Problem schon einmal gehabt

seeming ['siːmɪŋ] ADJ *attr* scheinbar

seemingly ['siːmɪŋlɪ] ADV scheinbar, anscheinend

seemliness ['siːmlɪnɪs] N Schicklichkeit *f*

seemly ['siːmlɪ] ADJ (+*er*) schicklich; **it isn't ~ (for sb to do sth)** es schickt sich nicht (für jdn, etw zu tun)

seen [siːn] *ptp of* **see** 1

seep [siːp] VI sickern; **to ~ through sth** durch etw durchsickern; **to ~ into sth** in etw (*acc*) hineinsickern

▶ **seep away** VI (*water*) versickern; (*strength*) schwinden

seepage ['siːpɪdʒ] N (*out of sth*) Aussickern *nt*; (*through sth*) Durchsickern *nt*; (*into sth*) Hineinsickern *nt*; **there is an excessive amount of ~** (*out of sth*) es läuft zu viel aus; (*into sth*) es dringt zu viel ein; (*Comm*) die Leckage ist zu groß

seer [sɪə'] N Seher(in) *m(f)*

seeress ['sɪəres] N Seherin *f*

seersucker ['sɪə,sʌkə'] N Krepp *m*, Seersucker *m*

seesaw ['siːsɔː] **N** Wippe *f*; (*fig, back and forth*) Hin und Her *nt*; (*up and down*) Auf und Ab *nt* **ADJ** schaukelnd; **~ changes** ständiges Hin und

Her **VI** wippen; (*fig, emotional states*) auf und ab gehen; (*prices, public opinion*) schwanken

seethe [siːð] VI (= *boil*) sieden; (= *surge*) schäumen; (= *be crowded*) wimmeln (*with* von); (= *be angry*) kochen (*inf*); **to ~ with anger** vor Wut schäumen *or* kochen (*inf*); **resentment ~d in him** er schäumte innerlich vor Groll; **the crowd ~d forward** die Menge drängte sich vor; **a seething mass of people** eine wogende Menschenmenge

see-through ['siːθruː] ADJ durchsichtig; **~ pack** Klarsichtpackung *f*

segment ['segmənt] **N** Teil *m*; (*of worm*) Glied *nt*, Segment *nt*; (*of orange*) Stück *nt*, Rippe *f*, Schnitz *m* (*dial*); (*of circle*) Abschnitt *m*, Segment *nt* **VT** [seg'ment] zerlegen, segmentieren **VI** [seg'ment] sich teilen

segmentation [,segmən'teɪʃən] N Zerlegung *f*, Segmentierung *f*; (*Biol*) Zellteilung *f*

segregate ['segrɪgeɪt] VT *individuals* absondern; *group of population* nach Rassen/Geschlechtern/Konfessionen trennen; *activities, facilities* nach gewissen Gesichtspunkten unterteilen; **to be ~d from sb/sth** von jdm/etw abgesondert sein; **~d** (*racially, church*) nur für Weiße/ Schwarze; *school also* mit Rassentrennung; *society* nach Rassen getrennt

segregation [segrɪ'geɪʃən] N Trennung *f*; **racial/ sexual ~** Rassen-/Geschlechtertrennung *f*

segregationist [segrɪ'geɪʃənɪst] N Befürworter(in) *m(f)* der Rassentrennung

segregative ['segrɪgeɪtɪv] ADJ sich absondernd, Trennungs-

segue ['segweɪ] (*Mus, fig*) **VI** **to ~ from/into** übergehen *or* überleiten von/in (+*acc*) **N** Übergang *m*

seine [seɪn] N Wade *f*

seismic ['saɪzmɪk] ADJ seismisch; (*fig*) *changes, events* kolossal, dramatisch; *forces* ungeheuer; **~ focus** Erdbebenherd *m*

seismograph ['saɪzməɡrɑːf] N Seismograf *m*

seismography [saɪz'mɒɡrəfɪ] N Seismologie *f*

seismologist [saɪz'mɒlədʒɪst] N Seismologe *m*, Seismologin *f*

seismology [saɪz'mɒlədʒɪ] N Seismologie *f*, Erdbebenkunde *f*

seize [siːz] **VT** **a** (= *grasp*) packen, ergreifen; (*as hostage*) nehmen; (= *confiscate*) beschlagnahmen; *passport* einziehen; *ship* (*authorities*) beschlagnahmen; (*pirates*) kapern; (= *capture*) *town* einnehmen; *train, building* besetzen; *criminal* fassen; **to ~ sb's arm, to ~ sb by the arm** jdn am Arm packen

b (*fig*) (= *lay hold of:* panic, fear, desire) packen, ergreifen; *power, leadership* an sich (*acc*) reißen; (= *leap upon*) *idea, suggestion* aufgreifen; *opportunity, initiative* ergreifen; **to ~ the moment** den günstigen Augenblick wahrnehmen; **to ~ the day** den Tag nutzen; **to ~ control of sth** etw unter Kontrolle bringen

VI = **seize up**

▶ **seize on** *or* **upon** VI +*prep obj* **a** (= *clutch at*) *idea, offer* stürzen auf (+*acc*); *excuse* beim Schopf packen **b** (= *pick out for criticism*) herausgreifen

▶ **seize up** VI **a** (*engine, brakes*) sich verklemmen **b** (*inf*) **my back seized up** es ist mir in den Rücken gefahren (*inf*); **she talks so much it's a miracle her jaw doesn't seize up** sie redet so viel, es ist ein Wunder, dass ihr Mundwerk nicht ausleiert (*inf*)

seizure ['siːʒə'] N **a** (= *confiscation*) Beschlagnahmung *f*; (*of passport*) Einzug *m*; (*of ship*) Beschlagnahme *f*; (*by pirates*) Kapern *nt*; (= *capture*) Einnahme *f*; (*of train, building*) Besetzung *f* **b** (*Med*) Anfall *m*; (= *apoplexy*) Schlaganfall *m*

seldom ['seldəm] ADV selten; **I ~ go there** ich gehe (nur) selten dorthin; **they are ~ seen** man sieht sie nur selten; **~ have I ...** ich habe selten ...; **~, if ever, does he do that** er tut das nur äußerst selten

select [sɪ'lekt] **VT** (aus)wählen; (*in buying also*) aussuchen; (*Sport*) auswählen; (*for football match*

etc) aufstellen; **~ed poems** ausgewählte Gedichte *pl* **VT** (aus)wählen; (*in buying also*) aussuchen; (*Sport*) auswählen; (*for football match etc*) aufstellen **ADJ** (= *exclusive*) exklusiv; (= *carefully chosen*) auserwählt, auserlesen; *tobacco* auserlesen; *fruit* ausgesucht; **a ~ few** eine kleine Gruppe Auserwählter

select committee N Sonderausschuss *m*

selection [sɪ'lekʃən] N **a** (= *choosing*) (Aus-) wahl *f*; (*Biol*) Auslese *f*, Selektion *f* **b** (= *person, thing selected*) Wahl *f*; (= *likely winner*) Tipp *m*; **to make one's ~** seine Wahl treffen; **~s from Rossini** ausgewählte Stücke *pl* von Rossini; **~s from Goethe** eine Auswahl aus Goethe; **~ committee** Auswahlkomitee *nt* **c** (= *range, assortment*) Auswahl *f* (*of an* +*dat*)

selective [sɪ'lektɪv] ADJ **a** wählerisch; *reader* kritisch, anspruchsvoll; **~ examination** Ausleseor Auswahlprüfung *f*; **~ process** Ausleseor Auswahlverfahren *nt*; **to be ~ in sth** in etw (*dat*) wählerisch sein; **he was very ~ in buying shoes** er war beim Schuhkauf sehr wählerisch; **we can't treat everything, we have to be ~** wir können nicht alles abhandeln, wir müssen eine Auswahl treffen *or* selektiv vorgehen *or* (*choose carefully*) wählerisch sein; **a more ~ approach to the available material ...** wenn Sie aus dem vorhandenen Material etwas kritischer auswählen würden ...; **a very ~ admission procedure** ein stark aussiebendes Aufnahmeverfahren; **the computer program has to be made more ~** man sollte mehr Wahlmöglichkeiten in das Computerprogramm einbauen; **~ school** Eliteschule *f*; **~ entry** (*Brit, Sch*) **~ admission** (*US, Sch*) selektives Aufnahmeverfahren; **~ breeding** (*Agr*) selektive Züchtung, Zuchtwahl *f*; **~ strike** (*Mil*) gezielter Angriff; (*Ind*) Schwerpunktstreik *m* **b** *radio* trennscharf, selektiv

selective attention N (*Psych*) selektives Aufnahmevermögen

selectively [sɪ'lektɪvlɪ] ADV wählerisch; *read also, operate* selektiv; **to read/buy ~** beim Lesen wählerisch/beim Einkaufen kritisch sein; **if you approach the material more ~** wenn Sie das Material besser auswählen *or* selektiver behandeln (*geh*); **he built up his collection very ~** er wählte bei der Zusammenstellung seiner Sammlung sorgfältig aus

selective memory N selektives Erinnerungsvermögen

selective service N (*US*) Wehrdienst *m*

selectivity [sɪlek'tɪvɪtɪ] N **a** Selektivität *f*; (*of reader, buyer*) kritisches Auswählen; **his collection shows great ~** seine Sammlung ist mit viel Sorgfalt ausgewählt; **to move toward(s) greater ~** ein kritischeres Bewusstsein entwickeln; **to show ~ in one's taste** einen anspruchsvollen Geschmack haben; **it diminishes the degree of ~** es verringert die (Aus)wahlmöglichkeiten *pl* **b** (*of radio*) Trennschärfe *f*, Selektivität *f*

selectman [sɪ'lektmən] N *pl* **-men** [-mən] (*US*) Stadtrat *m*, Stadträtin *f*

selector [sɪ'lektə'] N **a** (*Tech*) Wählschalter *m*; (= *lever*) Schaltgriff *m*; (= *knob*) Schaltknopf *m*; (*TV*) Programmtaste *f*; (*Rad*) Stationstaste *f*; (*on record-player*) Geschwindigkeitsregler *m*; (*Aut*) Schalthebel *m* **b** (*Sport*) jd, der die Mannschaftsaufstellung vornimmt

selenium [sɪ'liːnɪəm] N Selen *nt*

self [self] **N** *pl* **selves** Ich *nt*, Selbst *nt no pl*; (*esp Psych*, = *side of character*) Seite *f*; **he showed his true ~** er zeigte sein wahres Ich *or* Gesicht; **one's other/better ~** sein anderes/besseres Ich; **my whole ~ revolted at the idea** alles in mir lehnte sich gegen diese Idee auf; **he's quite his old ~ again, he's back to his usual ~** er ist wieder ganz der Alte (*inf*); **back to her usual cheerful ~** wieder fröhlich wie immer; **to be all ~** (*inf*) **to think of nothing but ~** nur an sich (*acc*) selbst denken; **with no thought of ~** ohne an sich (*acc*) selbst zu denken; **how is your good ~?** wie geht es Ihnen?

PRON (*Comm*) **pay ~** zahlbar an selbst; **a room**

for wife and ~ ein Zimmer für meine Frau und mich **ADJ** *attr lining* aus gleichem Material; **in a ~ colour** in uni

self: self-abandonment N (Selbst)aufopferung *f*, bedingungslose Hingabe; (*pej: to desire*) Zügellosigkeit *f*; **self-abasement** N Selbsterniedrigung *f*; **self-abnegation** N Selbstverleugnung *f*; **self-absorbed** ADJ mit sich selbst beschäftigt; **self-abuse** N (*euph*) Selbstbefleckung *f* (*euph*); **self-accusation** N Selbstanklage *f*; **self-accusing** ADJ selbstanklagend; **self-acting** ADJ selbsttätig; **self-activating** ADJ *bomb* selbstzündend; **self-addressed** ADJ *envelope* adressiert; **self-addressed stamped envelope** N (*US*) frankierter Rückumschlag; **self-adhesive** ADJ selbstklebend; **self-adjusting** ADJ selbstregulierend *attr; brakes* selbstnachstellend *attr;* **to be ~** sich selbst regulieren/nachstellen; **self-admiration** N Selbstbewunderung *f;* **self-advertisement** N Eigenreklame *f;* **self-aggrandizement** N Selbstverherrlichung *f;* **self-appointed** ADJ selbst ernannt; **he is the ~ spokesman of the group** er hat sich selbst zum Sprecher der Gruppe gemacht; **self-approval** N Selbstgefälligkeit *f;* **self-asserting** ADJ sich selbst behauptend; (*pej*) von sich selbst eingenommen; **self-assertion** N Durchsetzungsvermögen *nt;* (*pej*) Überheblichkeit *f,* Eingenommenheit *f* von sich selbst; **self-assertive** ADJ selbstbewusst; (*pej*) von sich selbst eingenommen; **self-assertiveness** ADJ Durchsetzungskraft *f;* (*pej*) Selbstverliebtheit *f* (*pej*); **self-assessment** N (*for tax*) Selbstveranlagung *f;* **self-assurance** N Selbstsicherheit *f;* **self-assured** ADJ selbstsicher; **self-aware** ADJ sich (*dat*) seiner selbst bewusst, selbstbewusst; **self-awareness** N Selbsterkenntnis *f,* Selbstbewusstsein *nt*

self-belief [selfbɪ'liːf] N Glaube *m* an sich (*acc*) selbst

self: self-cancelling ADJ *indicator* sich automatisch abschaltend *attr;* **self-catering** (*Brit*) **N** Selbstversorgung *f;* **to go ~** (*holidaymaker*) Urlaub *m* für Selbstversorger machen; (*hotel owner*) auf Selbstversorger umstellen **ADJ** für Selbstversorger; **self-censorship** N Selbstzensur *f;* **self-centred**, (*US*) **self-centered** ADJ egozentrisch, ichbezogen; **self-centredness**, (*US*) **self-centeredness** N Egozentrik *f,* Ichbezogenheit *f;* **self-certification** N (*Brit, Admin*) Krankmeldung *f* des Arbeitnehmers (*bei kurzer Abwesenheit anstelle eines ärztlichen Attests*); **self-cleaning** ADJ selbstreinigend; **self-closing** ADJ automatisch schließend, selbstschließend; **self-coloured**, (*US*) **self-colored** ADJ einfarbig, uni; **self-command** N Selbstbeherrschung *f;* **self-complacent** ADJ ; **self-complacently** ADV selbstgefällig; **self-composed** ADJ ruhig, gelassen; **self-conceit** N Eingebildetheit *f;* **self-conceited** ADJ ; **self-conceitedly** ADV eingebildet, dünkelhaft; **self-confessed** ADJ erklärt *attr;* **self-confidence** N Selbstvertrauen *nt,* Selbstbewusstsein *nt;* **self-confident** ADJ selbstbewusst, selbstsicher; **self-conscious** ADJ befangen, gehemmt; *piece of writing, style etc* bewusst; (*Philos, = self-aware*) selbstbewusst; **she walked to the door in a ~ way** sie wirkte gehemmt *or* verlegen, als sie zur Tür ging; **to be ~ about sth** (*about one's nose, looks etc*) sich (*dat*) einer Sache (*gen*) sehr bewusst sein; **self-consciously** ADV **a** (*= uncomfortably*) verlegen **b** (*= deliberately*) bewusst; **self-consciousness** N Befangenheit *f,* Gehemmtheit *f;* (*of piece of writing, style etc*) Bewusstheit *f;* (*Philos: = self-awareness*) Selbstbewusstsein *nt;* **self-contained** ADJ *person* distanziert; (*= self-sufficient*) selbstgenügsam **b** *flat* separat; *community* unabhängig; *place* in sich geschlossen; *economy* eigenständig; *group* geschlossen; **self-contradictory** ADJ sich (*dat*) selbst widersprechend *attr; alibi* widersprüchlich; **his argument is ~** seine Argumente widersprechen sich (*dat*); **self-control** N Selbstbeherrschung *f;*

self-controlled ADJ selbstbeherrscht; **self-correcting** ADJ selbstregulierend *attr; machine* mit Autokorrekturfunktion; **to be ~** sich selbst regulieren/korrigieren; **self-critical** ADJ selbstkritisch; **self-criticism** N Selbstkritik *f*

self: self-deceit, self-deception N Selbsttäuschung *f,* Selbstbetrug *m;* **self-defeating** ADJ sinnlos, unsinnig; *argument* sich selbst widerlegend *attr;* **the government's plan was ~** dieser Plan der Regierung hat das Gegenteil erzielt; **a ~ exercise** ein Eigentor *nt;* **self-defence**, (*US*) **self-defense** N Selbstverteidigung *f;* (*Jur*) Notwehr *f;* **to act in ~** in Notwehr handeln; **the noble art of ~** Boxen *nt;* **self-delusion** N Selbsttäuschung *f;* **self-denial** N Selbstzucht *f;* (*Rel*) Selbstverleugnung *f;* **self-denying** ADJ sich selbst einschränkend *attr;* (*Rel*) sich selbst verleugnend *attr;* **to be ~** sich einschränken/verleugnen; **self-deprecating** ADJ *person* bescheiden; *remark* sich selbst herabwürdigend *attr;* **to be ~** (*= person*) sich selbst abwerten; **Woody Allen's ~ humour** (*Brit*) *or* **humor** (*US*) Woody Allens Humor, der seine eigenen Schwächen offenbart; **self-destruct** **VI** sich selbst zerstören **ADJ** *attr* **~ button** Knopf *m* zur Selbstzerstörung; **self-destruction** N Selbstzerstörung *f;* (*of person, race*) Selbstmord *m;* **self-destructive** ADJ *behaviour, film star* selbstzerstörerisch; **she has a tendency to be ~** sie hat selbstzerstörerische Neigungen; **self-determination** N Selbstbestimmung *f* (*also Pol*); **self-discipline** N Selbstdisziplin *f;* **self-doubt** N Zweifel *m* an sich (*dat*) selbst; **self-dramatization** N **his tendency toward(s) ~** seine Neigung, sich in Szene zu setzen; **self-drive** ADJ (*Brit*) *car* für Selbstfahrer; **~ holiday** Ferienreise *f* mit dem eigenen Auto

self: self-educated ADJ autodidaktisch; **~ person** Autodidakt(in) *m(f);* **he is ~** er ist Autodidakt; **self-effacement** N Zurückhaltung *f;* **self-effacing** ADJ zurückhaltend; **self-employed** ADJ selbstständig; *artist* freischaffend; *journalist* freiberuflich; **on a ~ basis** freiberuflich; **self-esteem** N (*= self-respect*) Selbstachtung *f;* (*= conceit*) Selbstüberschätzung *f;* **to have high/low ~** sehr/wenig selbstbewusst sein; **self-evident** ADJ offensichtlich; (*= not needing proof*) selbstverständlich; **we'll need more money – that's ~** wir brauchen mehr Geld – das versteht sich von selbst; **self-evidently** ADV (*= obviously*) offensichtlich; **self-examination** N Selbstprüfung *f;* **self-explanatory** ADJ unmittelbar verständlich; **this word is ~** das Wort erklärt sich selbst; **self-expression** N Selbstdarstellung *f*

self: self-fertilization N Selbstbefruchtung *f;* **self-financing** ADJ selbstfinanzierend; **self-flagellation** N Selbstgeißelung *f;* **self-fulfilling** ADJ **a ~ prophecy** eine sich selbst bewahrheitende Voraussage, eine Selffulfilling Prophecy (*Sociol*); **to be ~** sich selbst bewahrheiten; **self-fulfilment**, (*US*) **self-fulfillment** N Erfüllung *f*

self: self-governed, self-governing ADJ selbstverwaltet, sich selbst verwaltend *attr;* **to become ~** eine eigene Regierung bekommen; **self-government** N Selbstverwaltung *f*

self: self-harming N Selbstverstümmelung *f;* **self-help** N Selbsthilfe *f;* **she never was one for ~** sie konnte sich noch nie selbst behelfen

self: self-image N Selbstbild *nt;* **self-importance** N Aufgeblasenheit *f;* **self-important** ADJ aufgeblasen; **self-imposed** ADJ selbst auferlegt; **his exile is ~** er hat sich (*dat*) sein Exil selbst auferlegt; **self-improvement** N Weiterbildung *f;* **self-incrimination** N Selbstbezichtigung *f;* **self-induced** ADJ *person* selbst auferlegt *attr;* **her miscarriage was ~** sie hat die Fehlgeburt selbst verursacht; **self-induction** N (*Elec*) Selbstinduktion *f;* **self-indulgence** N genießerische ADJ; (*in eating, drinking*) Maßlosigkeit *f;* **go on, take one, a little ~ never hurt anyone** nehmen Sie doch einen, jeder darf sich doch einmal gehen lassen *or* verwöhnen; **self-**

-indulgent ADJ genießerisch; (*in eating, drinking*) maßlos; **his columns grew ever more ~** er schrieb seine Spalten immer mehr zum eigenen Vergnügen; **be ~, have another slice** verwöhnen Sie sich, nehmen Sie noch ein Stück; **self-inflicted** ADJ *wounds* sich (*dat*) selbst zugefügt *or* beigebracht *attr; task, punishment* sich (*dat*) freiwillig auferlegt; **~ death** Selbstmord *m;* **his wounds are ~** er hat sich (*dat*) die Wunden selbst beigebracht; **self-interest** N (*= selfishness*) Eigennutz *m;* (*= personal advantage*) eigenes Interesse; **in our own ~** in unserem eigenen Interesse; **self-interested** ADJ (*= selfish*) eigennützig, auf sein eigenes Interesse bedacht; **self-invited** ADJ selbst eingeladen *attr;* **he is a ~ guest** er hat sich selbst eingeladen

selfish ['selfɪʃ] ADJ egoistisch, selbstsüchtig; **for ~ reasons** aus egoistischen Gründen

selfishly ['selfɪʃlɪ] ADV egoistisch, selbstsüchtig; **I was ~ glad that...** ich war egoistischerweise froh, dass ...

selfishness ['selfɪʃnɪs] N Egoismus *m,* Selbstsüchtigkeit *f*

self: self-justification N Rechtfertigung *f;* **he saw no reason for ~** er sah keinen Grund, sich zu rechtfertigen; **..., he said in ~** ..., sagte er zu seiner eigenen Rechtfertigung; **self-justifying** ADJ sachlich gerechtfertigt; **self-knowledge** N Selbsterkenntnis *f;* **self-laceration** N (*fig*) Selbstzerfleischung *f*

selfless ['selflɪs] ADJ selbstlos

selflessly ['selflɪslɪ] ADV selbstlos, in selbstloser Weise

selflessness ['selflɪsnɪs] N Selbstlosigkeit *f*

self: self-loader N Selbstlader *m;* **self-loading** ADJ **~ gun** Selbstlader *m;* **self-locking** ADJ von selbst schließend *attr; attachment* von selbst einrastend *attr;* **~ door** Tür mit Schnappschloss; **self-love** N Eigenliebe *f,* Selbstliebe *f* (*also Philos*)

self: self-made ADJ **~ man** Selfmademan *m;* **he's a ~ millionaire** er hat es aus eigener Kraft zum Millionär gebracht; **self-mockingly** ADV *say* voller Selbstironie; **self-murder** N Selbstmord *m;* **self-mutilation** N Selbstverstümmelung *f;* **self-neglect** [selfnɪ'glekt] N Vernachlässigung *f* seiner (*gen*) selbst; **as a result of his ~** weil er sich selbst vernachlässigt hat; **self-opinionated** ADJ rechthaberisch; *nonsense, drivel* selbstherrlich; **he's too ~ to change his mind** er ist viel zu sehr von sich selbst überzeugt, um seine Meinung zu ändern; **self-opinionatedness** N rechthaberisches und selbstherrliches Wesen; **this stream of ~** dieses selbstherrliche Gerede

self-parody N Selbstparodie *f*

self-perpetuating ADJ sich selbst erneuernd *or* erhaltend *attr;* **~ misery** sich ständig fortsetzendes Elend; **the system is ~** das System erhält sich selbst

self-perpetuation N Selbstperpetuierung *f*

self-pity N Selbstmitleid *nt*

self-pitying ADJ selbstbemitleidend

self-pollination N Selbstbestäubung *f*

self-portrait N Selbstporträt *or* -bildnis *nt*

self-possessed ADJ selbstbeherrscht

self-possession N Selbstbeherrschung *f*

self-praise N Eigenlob *nt*

self-preservation N Selbsterhaltung *f;* **the instinct for ~** der Selbsterhaltungstrieb

self-propagating ADJ *flower* sich selbst aussäend *attr; poverty, bad state of affairs* sich aus sich selbst weiterentwickelnd *attr*

self-propelled ADJ selbst angetrieben *attr,* mit Selbstantrieb

self-publicist N Selbstanpreiser(in) *m(f)*

self: self-raising, (*US*) **self-rising** ADJ *flour* selbsttreibend, *mit bereits beigemischtem Backpulver;* **self-realization** N Selbstverwirklichung *f;* **self-regard** N **a** (*= self-interest*) Eigennutz *m* **b** (*= self-esteem*) Selbstachtung *f;* **self-regulating** ADJ selbstregulierend *attr;*

this system is ~ dieses System reguliert sich selbst; **self-reliance** N Selbstständigkeit *f*; **self-reliant** ADJ selbstständig; **self-reproach** N Selbstvorwurf *m*; **all this** ~ diese Selbstvorwürfe *pl*; **self-respect** N Selbstachtung *f*; **have you no ~?** schämen Sie sich gar nicht?; **self-respecting** ADJ anständig; **no ~ person would ...** niemand, der etwas auf sich hält, würde ...; **self-restraint** N Selbstbeherrschung *f*; **self-righteous** ADJ selbstgerecht; **self-righteousness** N Selbstgerechtigkeit *f*; **self-righting** ADJ *boat* sich (von) selbst aufrichtend; **self-rising** ADJ (*US*) = **self-raising**; **self-rule** N Selbstbestimmung *f*, Selbstverwaltung *f*

self: self-sacrifice N Selbstaufopferung *f*; **it should not require too much** ~ das sollte kein zu großes Opfer sein; **self-sacrificing** ADJ aufopfernd; **selfsame** ADJ **the** ~ genau der/die/das gleiche ..., der-/die-/ dasselbe ...; **on the** ~ **day** noch am selben Tag; **self-satisfaction** N Selbstzufriedenheit *f*; (= *smugness*) Selbstgefälligkeit *f*; **self-satisfied** ADJ (= *smug*) selbstgefällig, selbstzufrieden; **self-sealing** ADJ *envelope, bag* selbstklebend; *fuel tank* selbstdichtend; **self-seeking** ADJ selbstsüchtig N Selbstsucht *f*; **self-service,** (*esp US*) **self-serve** ADJ Selbstbedienungs-; ~ **restaurant** Selbstbedienungsrestaurant *nt*; **the petrol station is now** ~ (*Brit*) **the gas station is now self-serve** (*US*) die Tankstelle hat jetzt auf Selbstbedienung umgestellt N Selbstbedienung *f*; **self-slaughter** N (*US Jur*) Selbstmord *m*; **self-starter** N (*Aut*) Selbstanlasser *m*; **self-styled** ADJ selbst ernannt; **self-sufficiency** N (*of person*) Selbstständigkeit *f*; (*emotional*) Selbstgenügsamkeit *f*; (*of country*) Autarkie *f*; (*of community*) Selbstversorgung *f*; **self-sufficient** ADJ *person* selbstständig; (*emotionally*) selbstgenügsam; *country* autark; **they are** ~ **in oil** sie können ihren Ölbedarf selbst decken; **a** ~ **community** eine Gemeinde, die sich selbst versorgen kann; **self-supplier** N Selbstversorger(in) *m(f)*; **self-supporting** ADJ *person* finanziell unabhängig; *structure* freitragend; *chimney* frei stehend; **the club is** ~ der Klub trägt sich selbst; **our commune is** ~ wir sind in unserer Kommune Selbstversorger; **self-sustaining** ADJ (*Econ*) *development, growth, economy* nachhaltig

self: self-tapping screw N selbstschneidende Schraube, Treibschraube *f*; **self-taught** ADJ *skills* selbst erlernt; **he is** ~ er hat sich (*dat*) das selbst beigebracht; (*intellectually*) er hat sich durch Selbstunterricht gebildet; **he's a** ~ **guitarist** er hat sich (*dat*) das Gitarrespielen selbst beigebracht; **a** ~ **man** ein Autodidakt *m*; **self-test** N (*of machine*) Selbsttest *m*; **to do a** ~ einen Selbsttest durchführen VI (*machine*) einen Selbsttest durchführen VI (*machine*) einen Selbsttest durchführen; **self-torture** N Selbstquälerei *f*

self: self-will N Eigenwilligkeit *f*, Eigensinn *m* (*pej*); **self-willed** ADJ eigenwillig, eigensinnig (*pej*); **self-winding** ADJ ~ *clock/watch* Automatikuhr *f*

sell [sel] *vb: pret, ptp* **sold** VI **a** *item, goods* verkaufen (*sb sth, sth to sb* jdm etw, etw an jdn); *insurance policy* abschließen (*to* mit); (*business*) *goods* verkaufen, absetzen; **I was sold this in Valencia** man hat mir das in Valencia verkauft; **the book sold 3,000 copies** von dem Buch wurden 3.000 Exemplare verkauft; **he could** ~ **a fridge to an Eskimo** er könnte einem Eskimo einen Eisschrank andrehen (*inf*) or aufschwatzen (*inf*); **to** ~ **insurance (for a living)** Versicherungsvertreter(in) *m(f)* sein; **to** ~ **one's life dearly** sein Leben teuer verkaufen; **he sold himself to the enemy** er hat sich an den Feind verkauft; **to** ~ **one's body** seinen Körper verkaufen; **to** ~ **one's soul to sb/sth** jdm/einer Sache seine Seele verschreiben; **modern man has sold his soul** der moderne Mensch hat seine Seele verloren; **what are you ~ing it for?** wie viel verlangen Sie dafür?, wie viel wollen Sie dafür haben?; **I can't remember what I sold it for** ich weiß nicht mehr, für wie viel ich es verkauft habe

b (= *stock*) führen, haben (*inf*); (= *deal in*) vertreiben

c (= *promote the sale of*) zugkräftig machen, einen guten Absatz verschaffen (+*dat*); **you need advertising to** ~ **your product** Sie müssen werben, um Ihr Produkt zu verkaufen or abzusetzen; **nothing will** ~ **this product, it's so bad** das Produkt ist so schlecht, dass es sich nicht verkaufen or an den Mann bringen (*inf*) lässt; **she finished up** ~**ing toothpaste on television** sie warb schließlich im Fernsehen für Zahnpasta

d (*inf*: = *gain acceptance for*) schmackhaft machen (*to sb* jdm), gewinnen für (*to sb* jdn); *religion* aufschwatzen (*inf*), verkaufen (*inf*) (*to sb* jdm); **you'll never** ~ **them that idea** dafür sind sie nicht zu haben; **I know I'll never be able to** ~ **it to him** ich weiß, dass ich ihn dafür nicht erwärmen kann or dass er dafür nicht zu haben ist; **to** ~ **oneself** (= *put oneself across*) sich profilieren (*to* bei), sich verkaufen (*to an* +*acc*)

e (*inf*: = *convince of the worth of*) **to** ~ **sb on sth** jdn von etw überzeugen; **to be sold on sb/sth** von jdm/etw begeistert sein; **how sold is he on the idea?** wie sehr hat es ihm diese Idee angetan? (*inf*)

f (*fig*, = *betray*) verraten; **to** ~ **sb down the river** (*inf*) jdn ganz schön verschaukeln (*inf*)

VI **a** (*person*) verkaufen (*to sb* an jdn); (*article*) sich verkaufen (lassen); **his book is** ~**ing well/won't** ~ sein Buch verkauft sich gut/lässt sich nicht verkaufen; **the house sold for £85,000** das Haus wurde für £ 85.000 verkauft; **what are they** ~**ing at** or **for?** wie viel kosten sie?; **the idea didn't** ~ (*fig*) die Idee kam nicht an, die Idee fand keinen Anklang

N **a** (*Comm inf*: = *sales appeal*) Zugkraft *f*, Attraktivität *f*

b (= *selling technique*) Verkaufstaktik or -methode *f* → **hard sell, soft sell**

c (*dated inf*, = *disappointment*) Reinfall *m*, Pleite *f* (*inf*)

▶ **sell off** VT *sep* verkaufen; (= *get rid of quickly, cheaply*) abstoßen; (*at auction*) versteigern

▶ **sell on** VT *sep* weiterverkaufen (*to an* +*acc*)

▶ **sell out** VI *sep* **a** (= *sell entire stock of*) ausverkaufen; **sorry, sold out** wir sind leider ausverkauft; **we're sold out of ice cream/size 10** wir haben kein Eis/keine Größe 10 mehr, das Eis/Größe 10 ist ausverkauft

b *share, interest* verkaufen, abgeben

c (*inf*, = *betray*) verraten (*to an* +*acc*)

VI **a** (= *sell entire stock*) alles verkaufen or absetzen; **this book/we sold out in two days** das Buch war/wir waren in zwei Tagen ausverkauft

b (*in business*) sein Geschäft/seine Firma/seinen Anteil *etc* verkaufen or abstoßen

c (*inf*, = *betray*) **the union leader sold out to the bosses** der Gewerkschaftsführer verkaufte die Arbeiter an die Bosse (*inf*); **he sold out to the right wing/the enemy** er hat sich an den rechten Flügel/den Feind verkauft

▶ **sell up** (*esp Brit*) VT *sep* zu Geld machen (*inf*); (*Fin*) zwangsverkaufen; **he was sold up by his creditors** die Gläubiger ließen seinen Besitz zwangsverkaufen VI sein Haus/seinen Besitz/ seine Firma *etc* verkaufen or zu Geld machen

sell-by date ['selbaɪdeɪt] N ≈ Haltbarkeitsdatum *nt*; **to be past one's** ~ (*hum inf*) seine besten Tage hinter sich (*dat*) haben

seller ['selə] N **a** Verkäufer(in) *m(f)*; **you should take faulty goods back to the** ~ du solltest fehlerhafte Ware (zum Händler) zurückbringen **b** (= *thing sold*) **big** ~ Verkaufsschlager *m*; **this book is a good/slow** ~ das Buch verkauft sich gut/schlecht; **the best/worst** ~ **we've had** das ist das bestgehende/am schlechtesten gehende Artikel, den wir je hatten

sellers' market N **it's a** ~ **in housing just now** zurzeit bestimmen die Verkäufer die Hauspreise

selling ['selɪŋ] N Verkauf *m*, Verkaufen *nt*; **they get a special training in** ~ sie werden besonders im Verkaufen ausgebildet

selling: selling point N Verkaufsanreiz *m*; **selling price** N Verkaufspreis *m*

sell-off ['selɒf] N Verkauf *m*

Sellotape® ['seləʊteɪp] (*Brit*) N Tesafilm® *m* VT **to sellotape (down)** mit Tesafilm® festkleben

sell: sellout N **a** (*inf*: = *betrayal*) fauler Kompromiss or Handel (*to* mit); (*of one's ideals etc*) Ausverkauf *m* (*to an* +*acc*) **b** (*Theat, Sport*) ausverkauftes Haus; **to be a** ~ ausverkauft sein (*Comm*) Verkaufsschlager *m*; **sell-through** ADJ *video* Verkaufs-

Seltzer (water) ['seltsə('wɔːtə')] N Selterswasser *nt*

selvage, selvedge ['selvɪdʒ] N Web(e)kante *f*

selves [selvz] *pl of* **self**

semantic ADJ, **semantically** ADV [sɪ'mæntɪk, -əlɪ] semantisch

semanticist [sɪ'mæntɪsɪst] N Semantiker(in) *m(f)*

semantics [sɪ'mæntɪks] N *sing* Semantik *f*; **the discussion got bogged down in** ~ die Diskussion blieb in Wortklaubereien stecken; **it's just a question of** ~ es ist nur eine Frage der Formulierung or (*interpretation*) Auslegung

semaphore ['seməfɔː'] N **a** (*Rail*) Semaphor *nt*, Signalmast *m* **b** (= *system*) Signalsprache *f*, Winken *nt*; **transmitted by** ~ durch optische Signale übermittelt; **to learn** ~ das Winkeralphabet lernen VT durch Winkzeichen signalisieren

semblance ['sembləns] N (*with def art*) Anschein *m* (*of* von); (*with indef art*) Anflug *m* (*of* von); **without a** ~ **of a smile** ohne den leisesten Anflug eines Lächelns; **to maintain some** ~ **of order** den Anschein von Ordnung wahren; **he had the** ~ **of an experienced lawyer** er erweckte den Anschein eines erfahrenen Anwalts; **I saw in him the** ~ **of his father** (*liter*) ich konnte in ihm die Ähnlichkeit mit seinem Vater erkennen; **it possessed some** ~ **of reality** (*liter*) es schien beinahe Wirklichkeit zu sein (*liter*)

semen ['siːmən] N Samenflüssigkeit *f*, Sperma *nt*

semester [sɪ'mestə'] N Semester *nt*

semi ['semɪ] N **a** (*Brit, inf*) = **semidetached b** (*inf*) = **semifinal c** (*US, inf*) = **semitrailer**

semi- PREF halb-, Halb-

semi: semiautomatic ADJ halbautomatisch N (= *weapon*) halbautomatische Waffe; **semibreve** N (*esp Brit*) ganze Note; **semicircle** N Halbkreis *m*; **semicircular** ADJ halbkreisförmig; ~ **canal** (*Anat*) Bogengang *m*; **semicolon** N Strichpunkt *m*, Semikolon *nt*; **semiconductor** N Halbleiter *m*; **semiconscious** ADJ halb bewusstlos; **he's only** ~, **but you can talk to him** er ist zwar noch nicht ganz bei Bewusstsein, Sie können aber mit ihm reden; **semidarkness** N Halbdunkel *nt*; **semidetached** (*Brit*) ADJ ~ **house** Doppelhaushälfte *f* N Doppelhaushälfte *f*; **semifinal** N Halb- or Semifinalspiel *nt*; ~**s** Halb- or Semifinale *nt*; **semifinalist** N Teilnehmer(in) *m(f)* am Halbfinale; **semi-finished** ADJ halbfertig, halb fertig; ~ **product** Halb(fertig)fabrikat *nt*

seminal ['semɪnl] ADJ **a** ~ **fluid** Samenflüssigkeit *f* **b** (= *embryonic*) keimhaft (*geh*); **to be present in a** ~ **state** im Keim vorhanden sein **c** (*form*, = *influential*) *book, author, text* einflussreich; *ideas* ertragreich; *event* grundlegend; **of** ~ **importance** von herausragender Bedeutung

seminar ['semɪnɑː'] N Seminar *nt*

seminarian [ˌsemɪ'neərɪən], **seminarist** ['semɪnərɪst] N Seminarist(in) *m(f)*

seminary ['semɪnərɪ] N Priesterseminar *nt*

semiofficial ['semɪə'fɪʃl] ADJ halbamtlich, halb amtlich, offiziös; *rule* halboffiziell

semiotic [semɪ'ɒtɪk] ADJ semiotisch

semiotics [semɪ'ɒtɪks] N *sing* Semiotik *f*

semi: semiprecious ADJ ~ **stone** Halbedelstein *m*; **semipro** ['semɪprəʊ] N (*inf*) = **semi-**

professional; **semiprofessional** ADJ **a** *job* überwiegend praktische Kenntnisse erfordernd; *musician etc* nebenberuflich **b** (*esp Sport*) halbprofessionell N (*esp Sport*) Halbprofi *m*, Feierabendprofi *m*; **semiquaver** N (*esp Brit*) Sechzehntel(note *f*) *nt*; **semiskilled** ADJ *worker* angelernt; ~ **job** Anlernberuf *m*; ~ **labour** (*Brit*) *or* **labor** (*US*) (= *workforce*) Angelernte *pl*; (= *work*) Arbeit *f* für Angelernte; **semi-skimmed milk** N (*Brit*) Halbfettmilch *f*, teilentrahmte Milch; **semisolid** ADJ halb fest N halb feste Substanz; **semisubmersible** N (= *oil rig*) schwimmende Bohrinsel, Halbtaucher *m*

Semite ['siːmaɪt] N Semit *m*, Semitin *f*

Semitic [sɪ'mɪtɪk] ADJ semitisch

semi: semitone N Halbton *m*; **semitrailer** N (*Brit*) Sattelschlepper *m*; (= *part*) Sattelauflieger *m*; **semivowel** N Halbvokal *m*

semolina [ˌseməˈliːnə] N Grieß *m*

sempiternal [ˌsempɪˈtɜːnl] ADJ (*liter*) immer während (*liter*)

sempstress ['sempstrɪs] N Näherin *f*

SEN (*Brit*) *abbr of* **State Enrolled Nurse** *staatlich geprüfte Krankenschwester, staatlich geprüfter Krankenpfleger*

Sen (*US*) *abbr of* **Senator**

senate ['senɪt] N Senat *m*

senator ['senɪtə'] N Senator(in) *m(f)*; (*as address*) Herr Senator/Frau Senatorin

senatorial [ˌsenəˈtɔːrɪəl] ADJ des/eines Senators

send [send] ○ 20.1, 20.3, 21.1, 21.3 *pret, ptp* **sent** VT **a** (= *dispatch*) schicken; *letter, messenger* schicken, senden; (= *send off*) *letter* abschicken; (*Rad*) *radio wave* ausstrahlen; *signal, SOS* senden; (*through wires*) übermitteln; **the satellite ~s signals (to us)** der Satellit sendet Signale aus/sendet uns Signale; **it ~s the wrong signal** *or* **message** (*fig*) das könnte falsch verstanden werden; **to ~ sb to prison/to his death** jdn ins Gefängnis/in den Tod schicken; **to ~ sb on a course/tour** jdn auf einen *or* zu einem Kurs/auf eine Tour schicken; **to ~ sb to university** jdn studieren lassen; **to ~ sb for sth** jdn nach etw schicken

b **she ~s her love/congratulations/apologies** *etc* sie lässt grüßen/ihre Glückwünsche ausrichten/sich entschuldigen *etc*; **~ him my love/ best wishes** grüßen Sie ihn von mir

c (= *propel, make go*) *arrow, ball* schießen; (*hurl*) schleudern; (*conveyor belt*) leiten, befördern; **he/ the explosion sent everything crashing to the ground** er/die Explosion ließ alles krachend zu Boden fallen; **the blow sent him sprawling** der Schlag schleuderte ihn zu Boden; **the fire sent everyone running out of the building** das Feuer ließ alle Gebäude fluchtartig verlassen; **the blue ball sent the red across the table** die blaue Kugel ließ die rote über den Tisch rollen; **the particle is sent off at an angle** das Teilchen fliegt schräg zur Seite weg; **his speech sent a wave of excitement through the audience** seine Rede ließ eine Woge der Aufregung durch die Zuschauer gehen; **the decision sent shock waves through the motor industry** die Entscheidung hat die Autobranche erschüttert; **the explosion had sent the spaceship off course** die Explosion hatte das Raumschiff vom Kurs abgebracht

d (= *cause to become, cause to go*) **this sent him into a real fury** das machte ihn fürchterlich wütend; **this sent him (off) into fits of laughter** das ließ ihn in einen Lachkrampf ausbrechen; **to ~ prices soaring** die Preise in die Höhe treiben; **to ~ shares soaring** Aktien in die Höhe schnellen lassen

e (*inf*) umhauen; **that tune/he ~s me** der Song/Typ haut mich um (*inf*), ich bin ganz hin und weg von dem Song/ihm (*sl*) → **sent**

f (*old*) geben; **~ her victorious** möge sie siegreich sein (*liter*)

VI **she sent to say that ...** sie ließ sagen *or* ausrichten *or* bestellen, dass ...; **the mail-order firm**

suddenly stopped **~ing** die Versandfirma lieferte plötzlich nicht mehr

▶ **send across** VT *sep* hinüberschicken; (*+prep obj*) schicken über (*+acc*)

▶ **send after** VT *sep* **to send sb after sb** jdn jdm nachschicken VI *+prep obj* **they sent after him** sie schickten ihm jemanden nach

▶ **send along** VT *sep* (*her-/hin*)schicken

▶ **send away** VT *sep* **a** (= *dispatch*) wegschicken, fortschicken; *letter etc* abschicken; **his parents sent him away to Europe/to school** seine Eltern schickten ihn nach Europa/ins Internat; **to send sth away to be mended** etw zur *or* in die Reparatur geben *or* schicken **b** **I had to send him away without an explanation** ich musste ihn ohne Erklärung weggehen lassen *or* wegschicken VI schreiben; **the number of people who sent away when they saw the TV advertisement** die Anzahl von Leuten, die auf die Fernsehreklame hin schrieben; **to send away for sth** etw anfordern

▶ **send back** VT *sep* zurückschicken; *food in restaurant* zurückgehen lassen VI **to send back for reinforcements** nach Verstärkung schicken, Verstärkung holen lassen

▶ **send down** VT *sep* **a** *temperature, prices* fallen lassen; (*gradually*) senken **b** (*Brit Univ: = expel*) relegieren **c** *prisoner* verurteilen (*for* zu)

▶ **send for** VI *+prep obj* **a** *person* kommen lassen; *doctor, police, priest* rufen; *help* herbeirufen; *reinforcements* herbeibeordern; *food* bringen lassen; (*person in authority*) *pupil, secretary, minister* zu sich bestellen; **I'll send for you/these books when I want you/them** ich lasse Sie rufen/ich schicke nach den Büchern, wenn ich Sie/sie brauche; **to send for sb to do sth** jdn herbeiholen *or* nach jdm schicken, um etw zu tun; **has the doctor been sent for yet?** ist der Arzt schon gerufen worden? **b** *copy, catalogue* anfordern, sich (*dat*) kommen lassen

▶ **send forth** VT *sep* (*liter*) aussenden (*geh*); *blossom* hervorbringen; *smell* verströmen (*geh*); *heat, light* ausstrahlen

▶ **send in** VT *sep* einschicken, einsenden; *person* hereinschicken; *troops* einsetzen VI = **send away** VI

▶ **send off** VT *sep* **a** *letter, parcel* abschicken **b** *children to school* wegschicken; **he sent his son off to Paris** er schickte seinen Sohn nach Paris **c** = **send away** VT b **d** (*Sport*) vom Platz stellen (*for* wegen); (*Ice hockey*) auf die Strafbank schicken; **he was sent off the pitch** er wurde vom Platz gestellt, er erhielt einen Platzverweis; **send him off, ref!** Platzverweis! **e** (= *see off*) verabschieden VI = **send away** VI

▶ **send on** VT *sep* **a** (= *forward*) *letter* nachschicken; (= *pass on*) *memo* weiterleiten **b** (*in advance*) *troops, luggage etc* vorausschicken **c** *substitute* aufs Feld schicken, einsetzen; *actor* auf die Bühne schicken

▶ **send out** VT *sep* **a** (*out of house, room*) hinausschicken (*of* aus); **he sent me out to the post office** er hat mich zur Post geschickt; **she sent me out to buy a paper** sie hat mich losgeschickt, um eine Zeitung zu kaufen; **the company started sending work out** die Firma hat angefangen, Arbeit außer Haus zu geben **b** (= *emit*) *rays, radio signals* aussenden; *light, heat, radiation* ausstrahlen, abgeben; *smoke* ausstoßen, abgeben **c** *leaflets, invitations, application forms* verschicken

▶ **send out for** VI *+prep obj* holen lassen VT *sep* **to send sb out for sth** jdn nach etw schicken

▶ **send up** VT *sep* **a** *rocket* hochschießen; *balloon* steigen lassen; *flare* in die Luft schießen; **I sent up a prayer of thanks** ich habe ein Dankgebet zum Himmel geschickt **b** *prices, temperature* hoch treiben, in die Höhe treiben; *pressure* steigen lassen **c** (= *destroy*) in die Luft gehen lassen; **to send sth up in flames** etw in Flammen aufgehen lassen **d** (*Brit, inf: = satirize*) verulken (*inf*) **e** (*US, inf: = send to prison*) hinter Gitter bringen (*inf*)

sender ['sendə'] N Absender(in) *m(f)*; **return to ~** zurück an Absender

send: sendoff N Abschied *m*, Verabschiedung *f*; **to give sb a good ~** jdn ganz groß verabschieden (*inf*); **send-up** N (*Brit, inf*) Verulkung *f* (*inf*); **to do a ~ of sb/sth** jdn/etw verulken (*inf*)

Senegal [ˌsenɪˈgɔːl] N Senegal *nt*

Senegalese [ˌsenɪgəˈliːz] ADJ senegalesisch N Senegalese *m*, Senegalesin *f*

senescence [sɪˈnesəns] N (*form*) Alterungsprozess *m*, Seneszenz *f* (*spec*)

senescent [sɪˈnesənt] ADJ (*form*) alternd

senile ['siːnaɪl] ADJ *person* senil; (*physically*) altersschwach; **~ decay** Altersabbau *m*; **he must be getting ~** er wird langsam senil *or* (*physically*) ein richtiger Tattergreis (*inf*)

senile dementia N (*Med*) senile Demenz (*spec*), Altersschwachsinn *m*

senility [sɪˈnɪlɪtɪ] N Senilität *f*; (*physical*) Altersschwäche *f*

senior ['siːnɪə'] ADJ (*in age*) älter; (*in rank*) vorgesetzt, übergeordnet; (*with longer service*) dienstälter; *rank, civil servant* höher; *officer* ranghöher; *position* höher, leitend; *designer, editor, executive, accountant etc* leitend; **at ~ level** (*in sport*) in einer höheren Altersgruppe; **he is ~ to me** (*in age*) er ist älter als ich; (*in rank*) er ist mir übergeordnet; (*in length of service*) er ist *or* arbeitet schon länger hier als ich; **~ section** ältere *or* höhere Altersgruppe; **the ~ management** die Geschäftsleitung; **~ consultant** Chefarzt *m*/-ärztin *f*; **~ pupil** Oberstufenschüler(in) *m(f)*; **my ~ officer** mein Vorgesetzter; **a very ~ officer** ein sehr hoher Offizier; **he's very/not very ~** er hat eine ziemlich hohe/keine sehr hohe Stellung; **can I speak to somebody more ~?** könnte ich bitte jemanden sprechen, der verantwortlich ist?; **J. B. Schwartz, Senior** J. B. Schwartz senior N (*Sch*) Oberstufenschüler(in) *m(f)*; (*US Univ*) Student(in) *m(f)* im 4./letzten Studienjahr; (*in club etc*) Senior(in) *m(f)*; **he is my ~** (*in age*) er ist älter als ich; (*in rank*) er ist mir übergeordnet; (*in length of service*) er ist *or* arbeitet schon länger hier als ich; **he is two years my ~, he is my ~ by two years** er ist zwei Jahre älter als ich

senior: senior citizen N älterer (Mit)bürger, ältere (Mit)bürgerin; **~ rail/bus pass** Seniorenpass *m*; **senior common room** N (*Brit, Univ*) Aufenthaltsraum *m* für Dozenten; **senior doctor** N Oberarzt *m*, Oberärztin *f*

seniority [ˌsiːnɪˈɒrɪtɪ] N (*in age*) (höheres) Alter; (*in rank*) (höhere) Position; (*Mil*) (höherer) Rang; (*in civil service etc*) (höherer) Dienstgrad; (*by length of service*) (längere) Betriebszugehörigkeit; (*in civil service etc*) (höheres) Dienstalter; **promotion on the basis of ~** Beförderung *f* nach Länge der Dienstzeit/Betriebszugehörigkeit

senior: senior nurse N Oberschwester *f*; (*male*) Oberpfleger *m*; **senior partner** N Seniorpartner(in) *m(f)*; **senior school**, (*US*) **senior high school** N Oberstufe *f*; **senior service** N (*Brit*) Kriegsmarine *f*

senna ['senə] N (= *drug*) Sennesblätter *pl*; (= *plant*) Sennespflanze *f*

sennight ['senɪt] N (*obs*) Woche *f*

sen(r) *abbr of* **senior** sen.

sensation [senˈseɪʃən] N **a** (= *feeling*) Gefühl *nt*; (*of heat, cold etc*) Empfindung *f*; (*of the external world*) Sinneseindruck *m*; **a/the ~ of falling** das Gefühl zu fallen; **a ~ of fear** ein Gefühl *nt* der Angst, ein Angstgefühl *nt*; **a ~ of hunger** ein Hungergefühl *nt*; **how can one describe the ~ of touching silk?** wie kann man beschreiben, was man beim Berühren von Seide empfindet?; **I felt a ~ of being watched** ich hatte das Gefühl, beobachtet zu werden **b** (= *great success*) Sensation *f*; **to cause** *or* **create a ~** (*großes*) Aufsehen erregen

sensational [senˈseɪʃənl] ADJ **a** sensationell, Aufsehen erregend; *newspaper, film, book* reißerisch aufgemacht, auf Sensation bedacht; *style, writing* reißerisch; *journalist* sensationsgierig *or* -lüstern (*inf*) **b** (*inf, = very good etc*) sagenhaft (*inf*)

sensationalism [sen'seɪʃnəlɪzəm] N (*of paper, reporter etc*) Sensationsmache f (*inf*); (*of reader*) Sensationsgier f; **the cheap ~ of his style** die billige Effekthascherei in seinem Stil

sensationalist [sen'seɪʃnəlɪst] ADJ Sensations-; *style also* sensationslüstern; **~ journalism/story** Sensationsjournalismus m/-geschichte f

sensationally [sen'seɪʃnəlɪ] ADV **a** (= *dramatically*) sensationell; *write, report* in einem reißerischen Stil **b** (= *amazingly*) sensationell, sagenhaft (*inf*); **a ~ successful movie** ein sensationell erfolgreicher Film; **our business has improved ~** unser Geschäft hat sich sensationell verbessert

sensation: sensation-seeker N sensationslüsterner Mensch; **sensation-seeking** ADJ sensationslüstern

sense [sens] **N a** (*bodily*) Sinn m; **~ of hearing** Gehörsinn m, Gehör nt; **~ of sight** Sehvermögen nt; **~ of smell** Geruchssinn m; **~ of taste** Geschmack(sinn) m; **~ of touch** Tastsinn m **b** **senses** PL (= *right mind*) Verstand m; **no man in his ~s ...** kein einigermaßen vernünftiger Mensch ...; **to frighten sb out of his ~s** jdn zu Tode erschrecken; **his ~s were deranged by ...** er war dicht ... völlig verstört; **to bring sb to his ~s** jdn zur Vernunft or Besinnung bringen; **to come to one's ~s** zur Vernunft or Besinnung kommen, Vernunft annehmen **c** (= *feeling*) Gefühl nt; **~ of duty** Pflichtbewusstsein or -gefühl nt; **~ of guilt** Schuldgefühl nt; **a ~ of pleasure** *etc* ein Gefühl der Freude *etc*; **a ~ of occasion** das Gefühl, dass etwas Besonderes stattfindet; **he has an exaggerated ~ of his own importance** er nimmt sich selbst übertrieben wichtig; **imbued with a ~ of history** von Geschichte durchtränkt (*liter*); **there's a ~ of insecurity in the country** in dem Land herrscht ein Gefühl der Unsicherheit; **a false ~ of security** ein falsches Gefühl der Sicherheit; **these buildings create a ~ of space** diese Gebäude vermitteln den Eindruck von Weite **d** (= *instinct, appreciation*) Sinn m; **his ~ for what is appropriate** sein Gefühl nt or Gespür nt dafür, was angebracht ist; **~ of colour** (*Brit*) *or* **color** (*US*)**/justice** Farben-/Gerechtigkeitssinn m **e** (= *good sense*) (**common**) **~** gesunder Menschenverstand; **haven't you ~ enough or e-nough ~ to stop when you're tired?** bist du nicht vernünftig genug aufzuhören, wenn du müde bist? **he had the (good) ~ to ...** er war so vernünftig or klug or gescheit und ...; **you should have had more ~ than to ...** du hättest vernünftiger sein sollen und nicht ...; **there is no ~ in that** das hat keinen Sinn, es ist zwecklos; **there's a lot of ~ in that** das hat Hand und Fuß, das ist ganz vernünftig; **what's the ~ of or in doing this?** welchen Sinn hat es denn, das zu tun?; **there is no ~ in doing that** es ist zwecklos or sinnlos, das zu tun; **there is no ~ in crying** es hat keinen Sinn zu heulen; **there's some ~ in what he says** was er sagt, ist ganz vernünftig; **there's some ~ in doing that** es wäre ganz vernünftig, das zu tun; **to be full of good ~** grundvernünftig sein; **to talk ~** vernünftig sein; **you're just not talking ~** du bist doch völlig unvernünftig; **now you're talking ~** das lässt sich schon eher hören; **he hasn't the ~ he was born with** er hat nicht für fünf Cent Verstand (*inf*); **to make sb see ~** jdn zur Vernunft bringen **f** **to make ~** (*sentence etc*) (einen) Sinn ergeben; (= *be sensible, rational etc*) sinnvoll or vernünftig sein, Sinn machen; **it doesn't make ~ doing it that way/spending** or **to spend all that money** es ist doch Unsinn or unvernünftig, es so zu machen/so viel Geld auszugeben; **why did he decide that? – I don't know, it doesn't make ~** warum hat er das beschlossen? – ich weiß es nicht, es ist mir unverständlich or es macht keinen Sinn; **the whole thing fails to**

make ~ to me die ganze Sache leuchtet mir nicht ein; **it makes good** *or* **sound ~** das scheint sehr vernünftig; **it makes good financial/political ~ to ...** aus finanzieller/politischer Sicht gesehen ist es sehr vernünftig, zu ...; **sometimes life just doesn't make ~** manchmal ergibt das Leben einfach keinen Sinn; **her conduct doesn't make ~ to me** ich werde aus ihrem Verhalten nicht schlau (*inf*); **he/his theory doesn't make ~** er/seine Theorie ist völlig unverständlich; **it all makes ~ now** jetzt wird einem alles klar; **it doesn't make ~, the jewels were there a minute ago** das ist ganz unverständlich, die Juwelen waren doch eben noch da; **to make ~ of sth** etw verstehen, aus etw schlau werden (*inf*); **you're not making ~** (*in explaining sth, in plans, intentions etc*) das ist doch Unsinn; (*in behaviour, attitude*) ich werde aus Ihnen nicht schlau (*inf*); **now you're making ~** (*in explaining sth*) jetzt verstehe ich, was Sie meinen; (*in plans, intentions etc*) das ist endlich eine vernünftige Idee **g** (= *meaning*) Sinn m no pl; **in the full** *or* **true ~ of the word** im wahrsten Sinn des Wortes; **it has three distinct ~s** es hat drei verschiedene Bedeutungen; **in what ~ are you using the word?** in welchem Sinn or welcher Bedeutung gebrauchen Sie das Wort?; **he is an amateur in the best ~** er ist Amateur im eigentlichen Sinn des Wortes; **in every ~ of the word** in der vollen Bedeutung des Wortes; **in the usual ~ of the word** im herkömmlichen Sinne des Wortes **h** (= *way, respect*) **in a ~** in gewisser Hinsicht, gewissermaßen; **in every ~** in jeder Hinsicht; **in what ~?** inwiefern?; **in one ~ what he claims is true** in gewisser Hinsicht hat er mit seiner Behauptung Recht **VT** fühlen, spüren; **I could ~ someone there in the dark** ich fühlte *or* spürte, dass da jemand in der Dunkelheit war

sense: sense datum N Sinnesdatum nt; **sense group** N (*Ling*) Sinngruppe f; (*Comput Ling: in SGML- or XML-text*) Bedeutungsgruppe f

senseless ['senslɪs] ADJ **a** (= *unconscious*) besinnungslos, bewusstlos; **to knock sb ~** jdn bewusstlos schlagen **b** (= *stupid*) unvernünftig, unsinnig; (= *futile*) waste, procedure sinnlos; **what a ~ thing to do/say** etc welch ein Unsinn

senselessly ['senslɪslɪ] ADV (= *pointlessly*) sinnlos; **a ~ cruel act** ein sinnloser Akt der Gewalt

senselessness ['senslɪsnɪs] N (= *stupidity*) Unvernunft f, Unsinnigkeit f; (= *futility*) Sinnlosigkeit f

sense organ N Sinnesorgan nt

sensibility [ˌsensɪ'bɪlɪtɪ] N (*to beauty etc*) Empfindsamkeit f; (= *artistic sensibility also*) Sensibilität f; (= *emotional sensibility, susceptibility to insult*) Empfindlichkeit f, Sensibilität f; **sensibilities** Zartgefühl nt

sensible ['sensəbl] ADJ **a** vernünftig; **be ~ about it** seien Sie vernünftig; **that's the ~ thing to do** das ist vernünftig **b** (*liter: = aware*) **to be ~ of sth** sich (*dat*) einer Sache (*gen*) bewusst sein **c** (*rare: = appreciable*) spürbar, merklich

sensibleness ['sensəblnɪs] N Vernünftigkeit f

sensibly ['sensəblɪ] ADV (= *reasonably*) vernünftig; **he very ~ ignored the question** er hat die Frage vernünftigerweise ignoriert; **~ priced** preisgünstig

sensitive ['sensɪtɪv] ADJ **a** (*emotionally*) *person* sensibel, empfindsam; (= *easily hurt*) empfindlich; (= *understanding*) einfühlsam; *novel, film, remark* einfühlend; **to be ~ about sth** in Bezug auf etw (*acc*) empfindlich sein; **she is very ~ to criticism/these things** sie reagiert sehr empfindlich auf Kritik/diese Dinge **b** (*physically*) *instruments, part of body, leaves, plants* empfindlich; (*Phot*) *emulsion, film* lichtempfindlich; (= *delicate*) *balance, adjustment* fein; (*fig*) *topic, issue* heikel, prekär; **~ to heat/light** wärme-/lichtempfindlich; **his wound is ~ to touch** seine Wunde tut weh, wenn man sie berührt; **he has access to some highly ~ information** er hat Zugang zu streng vertraulichen Informationen; **his visit comes at a ~ time** er

macht diesen Besuch zu einem schwierigen Zeitpunkt; **just how ~ are these figures?** inwiefern sind diese Zahlen als vertraulich zu behandeln?

sensitively ['sensɪtɪvlɪ] ADV **a** (= *sympathetically*) einfühlsam **b** (= *tastefully*) einfühlsam **c** (= *precisely*) genau; **the markets ~ register changes in consumer demand** der Markt reagiert empfindlich auf Nachfrageveränderungen

sensitiveness ['sensɪtɪvnɪs], **sensitivity** [ˌsensɪ'tɪvɪtɪ] N **a** (*emotional*) Sensibilität f, Empfindsamkeit f; (= *getting easily hurt*) Empfindlichkeit f; (= *understanding*) Einfühlsamkeit f; (*of novel, film, remark*) Einfühlungsvermögen nt **b** (*physical, of instrument, part of body etc*) Empfindlichkeit f; (*Phot: of emulsion, film*) Lichtempfindlichkeit f; (= *delicacy: of balance, adjustment*) Feinheit f; (*fig: of topic, issue*) heikle Natur; **sensitivity to heat/light** Wärme-/Lichtempfindlichkeit f; **an issue of great sensitivity** eine sehr heikle Angelegenheit

sensitize ['sensɪtaɪz] VT sensibilisieren

sensor ['sensə'] N Sensor m; (*non-electronic also*) Fühler m

sensorimotor ['sensərɪ'məʊtə'] ADJ sensomotorisch

sensory ['sensərɪ] ADJ sensorisch; **~ organ** Sinnesorgan nt

sensory deprivation N Reizabschirmung f, sensorische Deprivation (*spec*)

sensual ['sensjʊəl] ADJ sinnlich, wollüstig (*pej*); *person, life also* sinnesfreudig, lustbetont; **~ moments** Augenblicke pl der Lust

sensualism ['sensjʊəlɪzəm] N Sinnlichkeit f, Wollüstigkeit f (*pej*); (*Philos*) Sensualismus m

sensualist ['sensjʊəlɪst] N Genussmensch m, sinnlicher Mensch; Lüstling m (*pej*); (*Philos*) Sensualist(in) m(f)

sensuality [ˌsensjʊ'ælɪtɪ] N Sinnlichkeit f, Wollüstigkeit f (*pej*); (*of person also*) Sinnesfreudigkeit f

sensualize ['sensjʊəlaɪz] VT sinnlich machen, versinnlichen

sensually ['sensjʊəlɪ] ADV sinnlich, wollüstig (*pej*)

sensuous ADJ , **sensuously** ADV ['sensjʊəs, -lɪ] sinnlich, sinnenhaft

sensuousness ['sensjʊəsnɪs] N Sinnlichkeit f, Sinnenhaftigkeit f

sent [sent] pret, ptp of **send** ADJ (*inf*) look hingerissen (*inf*); **he's ~** er ist ganz weg (*inf*)

sentence ['sentəns] **N a** (*Gram*) Satz m; **~ structure** Satzbau m; (*of particular sentence*) Satzaufbau m, Satzstruktur f **b** (*Jur*) Strafe f; **to be under ~ of death** zum Tode verurteilt sein; **the judge gave him a 6-month ~** der Richter verurteilte ihn zu 6 Monaten Haft; **to pass ~ (on sb)** (über jdn) das Urteil verkünden; (*fig*) jdn verurteilen **VT** (*Jur*) verurteilen; **he was ~d to life imprisonment** er wurde zu lebenslänglichem Freiheitsentzug verurteilt

sententious ADJ , **sententiously** ADV [sen'tenʃəs, -lɪ] salbungsvoll

sententiousness [sen'tenʃəsnɪs] N **the ~ of the lecture/speaker** der salbungsvolle Vortrag/Redner; **..., he said with great ~** ..., sagte er salbungsvoll

sentience ['sentɪəns] N Empfindungsvermögen nt; **the ~ of approaching death** das Vorgefühl des nahenden Todes

sentient ['sentɪənt] ADJ empfindungsfähig

sentiment ['sentɪmənt] N **a** (= *feeling, emotion*) Gefühl nt **b** (= *sentimentality*) Sentimentalität f, Rührseligkeit f **c** (= *opinion*) Ansicht f, Meinung f; **what are your ~s on this?** was ist Ihre Meinung or Ansicht dazu?, wie denken Sie darüber?; **my ~s exactly!** genau meine Ansicht or Meinung! **d** (= *thought behind words or deeds*) Gedanke m

sentimental [ˌsentɪ'mentl] ADJ sentimental; *person, mood also* gefühlvoll; *novel, song, music also* gefühlsselig, kitschig (*pej*), schmalzig (*pej*); *val-*

ue gefühlsmäßig; **for ~ reasons** aus Sentimentalität; **to make a ~ visit to a place** einem Ort aus Sentimentalität einen Besuch abstatten; **a certain ~ attachment** eine gewisse gefühlsmäßige Bindung; **~ nonsense** Gefühlsduselei *f*

sentimentalism [ˌsentɪˈmentəlɪzəm] N Sentimentalität *f*

sentimentalist [ˌsentɪˈmentəlɪst] N Gefühlsmensch *m*, sentimentaler Mensch

sentimentality [ˌsentɪmenˈtælɪtɪ] N Sentimentalität *f*

sentimentalize [ˌsentɪˈmentəlaɪz] **VT** sentimental *or* gefühlvoll darstellen **VI** sentimental sein

sentimentally [ˌsentɪˈmentəlɪ] ADV *important, attached etc* gefühlsmäßig; *say, reminisce* sentimental; *sing, play music* gefühlvoll; *(pej)* sentimental, kitschig *(pej)*, schmalzig *(pej)*

sentinel [ˈsentɪnl] N Wache *f*; **to stand ~ over sth** *(liter)* über etw *(acc)* wachen *or* Wacht halten

sentry [ˈsentrɪ] N Wache *f*, Wachtposten *m*; **to be on ~ duty** auf Wache sein

sentry: sentry box N Wachhäuschen *nt*; **sentry go** N *(Mil)* Wachdienst *m*

sep *abbr of* **separate**

sepal [ˈsepəl] N Kelchblatt *nt*

separability [ˌsepərəˈbɪlɪtɪ] N Trennbarkeit *f*

separable [ˈsepərəbl] ADJ trennbar

separate [ˈseprət] ADJ **a** getrennt, gesondert *(from* von*)*; *organization, unit* gesondert, eigen *attr*; *two organizations, issues, parts* gesondert *attr*, voneinander getrennt, verschieden *attr*; *provisions, regulations* besondere(r, s) *attr*, separat, gesondert *attr*; *beds, rooms, accounts* getrennt; *account, bill, agreement, department* gesondert *attr*, extra *attr inv*; *entrance, toilet, flat* separat; *existence* eigen *attr*; **~ peace** Separat- *or* Sondervertrag *m*; **~ treaty** Sondervertrag *m*; **that is a ~ question/issue** das ist eine andere Frage, das ist eine Frage für sich; **on two ~ occasions** bei zwei verschiedenen Gelegenheiten; **on a ~ occasion** bei einer anderen Gelegenheit; **there will be ~ discussions on this question** diese Frage wird extra *or* separat *or* gesondert diskutiert; **they live ~ lives** sie gehen getrennte Wege; **a ~ sheet of paper** ein anderes Blatt Papier; *(= additional)* ein gesondertes *or* extra Blatt Papier; **this is quite ~ from his job** das hat mit seinem Beruf nichts zu tun; **to keep two things ~** zwei Dinge nicht zusammentun; *questions, issues* zwei Dinge auseinander halten; **always keep your chequebook** *(Brit)* **or checkbook** *(US)* **~ from your card** bewahren Sie Scheckbuch und Scheckkarte immer getrennt auf; **keep this book ~ from the others** halten Sie dieses Buch von den anderen getrennt

b *(= individual)* einzeln; **all the ~ sections/pieces/units/questions** alle einzelnen Abschnitte/Teile/Einheiten/Fragen; **everybody has a ~ cup/task** jeder hat eine Tasse/Aufgabe für sich *or* seine eigene Tasse/Aufgabe

N separates PL Röcke, Blusen, Hosen *etc*

VT [ˈsepəreɪt] trennen; *(Chem also)* scheiden; *milk* entrahmen; *(= divide up)* aufteilen *(into* in *+acc)*; **to ~ the good from the bad** die Guten von den Schlechten trennen *or* scheiden; **he can't ~ his private life from his work** er kann Privatleben und Arbeit nicht (voneinander) trennen, er kann das Privatleben nicht von der Arbeit trennen; **he is ~d from his wife** er lebt von seiner Frau getrennt

VI [ˈsepəreɪt] sich trennen; *(Chem also)* sich scheiden; **it ~s into four parts** es lässt sich in vier Teile auseinander nehmen; *(fig: problem etc)* es zerfällt in vier Teile

▶ **separate out VT** *sep* trennen *(from* von*)*, absondern *(from* von*)*, aussondern **VI** getrennt werden

separated [ˈsepəreɪtɪd] ADJ getrennt; *couple* getrennt lebend *attr*; **the couple are ~** das Paar lebt getrennt

separately [ˈseprətlɪ] ADV getrennt, gesondert, separat; *live* getrennt; *(= singly)* einzeln

separateness [ˈseprətnɪs] N Getrenntheit *f*, Gesondertheit *f*

separation [ˌsepəˈreɪʃən] N Trennung *f*; *(Chem also)* Scheidung *f*; *(of rocket etc)* Abtrennung *f* *(from* von*)*

separation allowance N Trennungsentschädigung *f*

separatism [ˈsepərətɪzəm] N Separatismus *m*

separatist [ˈsepərətɪst] ADJ separatistisch **N** Separatist(in) *m(f)*

separator [ˈsepəreɪtə] N Separator *m*

sepia [ˈsiːpjə] N Sepia *f* ADJ Sepia-; *(also* **sepia-coloured**) sepia(farben); **~ drawing** Sepiazeichnung *f*

sepoy [ˈsiːpɔɪ] N Sepoy *m*

sepsis [ˈsepsɪs] N Vereiterung *f*, Sepsis *f (spec)*

Sept *abbr of* **September** Sept.

September [sepˈtembə] **N** September *m*; **the first/tenth of ~** der erste/zehnte September; **on ~ 1st/19th** *(written)*, **on the 1st/19th of ~** *(written)*, **on the 1st/19th of ~** *(spoken)* am 1./19. September; **~ 3rd, 1990, 3rd ~ 1990** *(on letter)* 3. September 1990; **in ~** im September; **during ~** im September; **every** *or* **each ~** jeden September; **at the beginning/end of ~** Anfang/Ende September; **~ is a pleasant month** der September ist ein angenehmer Monat; **there are 30 days in ~** der September hat 30 Tage ADJ *attr* September-; *weather, mists etc also* septemberlich; **~ issue** *(of magazine etc)* Septemberausgabe *f*

septennial [sepˈtenɪəl] ADJ siebenjährig; *(= every seven years)* alle sieben Jahre stattfindend, siebenjährlich

septet, septette [sepˈtet] N Septett *nt*

septic [ˈseptɪk] ADJ vereitert, septisch; **the wound turned ~** die Wunde eiterte

septicaemia, *(US)* **septicemia** [ˌseptɪˈsiːmɪə] N Vergiftung *f* des Blutes, Septikämie *f (spec)*

septic shock N *(Med)* septischer Schock

septic tank N Faulbehälter *m*, Klärbehälter *m*

septuagenarian [ˌseptjʊədʒɪˈneərɪən] ADJ siebzigjährig **N** Siebzigjährige(r) *mf*; **to be a ~** ein(e) Siebziger(in) sein

Septuagesima [ˌseptjʊəˈdʒesɪmə] N Sonntag *m* Septuagesima

septuplet [sepˈtjuːplɪt] N *(= baby)* Siebenling *m*; *(Mus)* Septole *f*

sepulcher *(US)* = **sepulchre**

sepulchral [sɪˈpʌlkrəl] ADJ *(liter)* sepulkral *(liter)*; *(fig)* düster; **~ voice/silence** Grabesstimme *f*/-stille *f*; **in a ~ tone** mit Grabesstimme

sepulchre, *(US)* **sepulcher** [ˈsepəlkə] N Grabstätte *f*; **the Holy Sepulchre** das Heilige Grab → **whited sepulchre**

sequel [ˈsiːkwəl] N Folge *f (to* von*)*; *(of book, film)* Fortsetzung *f (to* von*)*; **it had a tragic ~** es hatte ein tragisches Nachspiel

sequence [ˈsiːkwəns] N **a** *(= order)* Folge *f*, Reihenfolge *f*; **~ of tenses/words** Zeiten-/Wortfolge *f*; **in ~** der Reihe nach; **to do sth in logical ~** etw in der logisch richtigen Reihenfolge tun **b** *(= things following)* Reihe *f*, Folge *f*; *(Mus, Cards, Eccl)* Sequenz *f*; *(Math)* Reihe *f* **c** *(Film, = dance sequence)* Sequenz *f*

sequencer [ˈsiːkwənsə] N *(Comput)* Ablaufsteuerung *f*

sequential [sɪˈkwenʃəl] ADJ *(form)* der Reihe nach, in regelmäßiger Folge; *(= following)* folgend; *(Comput)* sequenziell, sequentiell; **to be ~ to sth** auf etw *(acc)* folgen

sequester [sɪˈkwestə] VT **a** *(liter, = isolate)* abkapseln **b** *(Jur)* = **sequestrate**

sequestered [sɪˈkwestəd] ADJ **a** *(liter)* village abgeschieden; *spot* abgelegen; *life* zurückgezogen **b** *(Jur)* asset sequestriert

sequestrate [sɪˈkwestreɪt] VT *(Jur)* sequestrieren

sequestration [ˌsiːkweˈstreɪʃən] N *(Jur)* Sequestration *f*; *(in bankruptcy case also)* Zwangsverwaltung *f*

sequin [ˈsiːkwɪn] N Paillette *f*

sequined [ˈsiːkwɪnd] ADJ mit Pailletten besetzt

sequoia [sɪˈkwɔɪə] N Mammutbaum *m*, Sequoie *f*

seraglio [seˈrɑːlɪəʊ] N Serail *nt*

seraph [ˈseræf] N *pl* **-s** *or* **-im** Seraph *m*

seraphic [səˈræfɪk] ADJ verklärt, verzückt

seraphim [ˈseræfɪm] *pl of* **seraph**

Serb [sɜːb] N Serbe *m*, Serbin *f*

Serbia [ˈsɜːbɪə] N Serbien *nt*

Serbian [ˈsɜːbɪən] ADJ serbisch **N a** Serbe *m*, Serbin *f* **b** *(Ling)* Serbisch *nt*

Serbo-Croat [ˈsɜːbəʊˈkrəʊæt] **N a** *(Ling)* Serbokroatisch *nt* **b** **the ~s** *pl (= people)* die Serben und Kroaten

Serbo-Croatian [ˈsɜːbəʊkrəʊˈeɪʃən] ADJ serbokroatisch **N** **the Serbo-Croatians** PL die Serben und Kroaten

serenade [ˌserəˈneɪd] **N** Serenade *f* **VT** ein Ständchen *nt* bringen *(+dat)*

serenader [ˌserəˈneɪdə] N *jd, der ein Ständchen bringt*

serendipity [ˌserənˈdɪpɪtɪ] N Spürsinn *m (fig)*, mehr Glück als Verstand

serene [səˈriːn] ADJ gelassen; *sea* ruhig; *sky* heiter, klar; **His Serene Highness** seine Durchlaucht, Serenissimus

serenely [səˈriːnlɪ] ADV gelassen; **~ indifferent to the noise** gleichmütig dem Lärm gegenüber; **her face was ~ beautiful** ihr Gesicht war von einer gelassenen Schönheit

serenity [sɪˈrenɪtɪ] N Gelassenheit *f*; *(as title: also* **Serenity**) Durchlaucht *f*

serf [sɜːf] N Leibeigene(r) *mf*

serfdom [ˈsɜːfdəm] N Leibeigenschaft *f*; *(fig)* Knechtschaft *f*

serge [sɜːdʒ] N Serge *f*

sergeant [ˈsɑːdʒənt] N *(Mil)* Feldwebel(in) *m(f)*; *(Police)* Polizeimeister(in) *m(f)*; **~ at arms** *(Hist)* Waffenmeister *m*; *(Brit, Parl)* Exekutivbeamte(r) *m*/-beamtin *f* des Parlaments

sergeant first class N *(US)* Oberfeldwebel(in) *m(f)*

sergeant major N Oberfeldwebel(in) *m(f)*

serg(t) *abbr of* **sergeant**

serial [ˈsɪərɪəl] ADJ Serien-; *radio/TV programme* in Fortsetzungen; *writer* von Fortsetzungsromanen; *music* seriell; *(Comput)* printer, interface etc seriell; **published in ~ form** in Fortsetzungen veröffentlicht; **he is a ~ rapist** er ist ein Serientäter, der bereits mehrere Vergewaltigungen begangen hat; **~ drama** *(TV)* (Fernseh)serie *f*; **~ novel/story** Fortsetzungsroman *m*/-geschichte *f* **N** *(= novel)* Fortsetzungsroman *m*; *(in periodical)* Serie *f*; *(Rad)* Sendereihe *f* (in Fortsetzungen); *(TV)* Serie *f*; *(spec: = magazine)* (periodisch erscheinende) Zeitschrift; **it was published/broadcast as a ~** es wurde in Fortsetzungen veröffentlicht/gesendet

serialization [ˌsɪərɪəlaɪˈzeɪʃən] N *(Rad, TV)* Sendung *f* in Fortsetzungen; *(in magazines etc)* Fortsetzung(sreihe) *f*; *(= serializing)* Umarbeitung *f* in Fortsetzungen

serialize [ˈsɪərɪəlaɪz] VT in Fortsetzungen veröffentlichen; *(Rad, TV)* in Fortsetzungen senden; *(= put into serial form)* in Fortsetzungen umarbeiten

serial killer N Serienmörder(in) *m(f)*, Serienkiller(in) *m(f)*

serial killing N Serienmord *m*

serially [ˈsɪərɪəlɪ] ADV *publish, broadcast* in Fortsetzungen; *(= in order)* number fortlaufend; *(Mus, Comput)* seriell

serial: serial murder N Serienmord *m*; **serial number** N fortlaufende Nummer; *(on manufactured goods)* Fabrikationsnummer *f*; **serial port** N *(Comput)* serielle Schnittstelle; **serial rights** PL Rechte *pl* für die Veröffentlichung in Fortsetzungen

seriatim [ˌsɪərɪˈeɪtɪm] ADV *(form)* der Reihe nach

sericulture [ˌserɪˈkʌltʃə] N Seidenraupenzucht f

series [ˈsɪərɪz] N pl - **a** Serie f; (of books, lectures etc also, of films, talks, Math, Mus, Elec) Reihe f; (of events also, succession of things) Reihe f, Folge f; **a ~ of articles** eine Artikelserie or -reihe; **in ~** der Reihe nach; (Elec) in Reihe; (Comm) serienmäßig; publish als Serie **b** (Rad) Sendereihe f; (TV) Serie f

series-wound [ˈsɪəriːˌzwaʊnd] ADJ (Elec) in Serie or Reihe geschaltet

serif [ˈserɪf] N Serife f ADJ font serifenbetont

seriocomic(al) [ˌsɪərɪəʊˈkɒmɪk(l)] ADJ halb ernst, halb heiter

serious [ˈsɪərɪəs] ADJ **a** (= earnest) ernst; (= not frivolous) ernsthaft; consideration, discussion, conversation, doubts ernst, ernsthaft; point, matter, business ernst; newspaper, publication, interest ernsthaft, seriös; offer, suggestion ernst gemeint, seriös; attempt ernsthaft; contender ernst zu nehmend attr; **to be ~ about doing sth** etw im Ernst tun wollen; **I'm ~ (about it)** ich meine das ernst, das ist mein Ernst; **I'm deadly ~** es ist mir todernst (inf); **he is ~ about her** er meint es ernst mit ihr; **be ~ about your studies** du musst dein Studium ernst nehmen; **you can't be ~!** das meinst du doch nicht ernst!, das kann nicht dein Ernst sein!; **to give ~ thought** or **consideration to sth** sich (dat) etw ernsthaft or ernstlich überlegen, sich über etw (acc) ernsthafte Gedanken machen; **the ~ student of jazz will ...** wer sich ernsthaft mit Jazz beschäftigt, wird ...; **to earn ~ money** (inf) das große Geld verdienen

b (= critical) accident, flooding, deficiencies, loss schwer; mistake, injury schwer, schlimm; problem ernst, ernst zu nehmend attr; illness schwer, ernst; situation ernst, schlimm; patient's condition ernst, bedenklich; threat, shortage, lack ernst, ernstlich; deterioration bedenklich; **it's ~** das ist schlimm; **it's getting ~** es wird ernst; **inflation is getting ~** die Inflation nimmt ernste Ausmaße an

Serious Fraud Office N (Brit) Ermittlungsbehörde für schwere Betrugsfälle

seriously [ˈsɪərɪəslɪ] ◑ 12.2, 26.1 ADV **a** (= earnestly) ernst; talk, interested, work ernsthaft; (= not jokingly) im Ernst; **to take sb/sth ~** jdn/etw ernst nehmen; **to take oneself too ~** sich selbst zu wichtig nehmen; **do you ~ want to do that?** wollen Sie das wirklich or im Ernst tun?; **~ now/though ...** jetzt mal/aber mal ganz im Ernst ...; **but ~, ...** aber jetzt mal im Ernst ...; **~?** im Ernst?, ernsthaft?; **do you mean that ~?** meinen Sie das ernst?, ist das Ihr Ernst?; **he offered it quite ~** er hat das ernstlich angeboten; **a play that deals ~ with the issue of divorce** ein Stück, das sich auf ernsthafte Weise mit Scheidungsfragen befasst

b (= critically) wounded, damaged, ill, flooded schwer; worried ernstlich; deteriorate bedenklich; threaten ernsthaft; **he went ~ wrong** er hat einen schweren Fehler gemacht; **the takeoff went ~ wrong** beim Start ist etwas schlimm danebengegangen; **there is something ~ wrong with that** irgendetwas ist damit überhaupt nicht in Ordnung; **we are ~ short of water** bei uns herrscht schwerer or schlimmer Wassermangel

c (inf, = really) ehrlich (inf); **~ rich** (person) schwerreich; **I was beginning to get ~ annoyed** ich wurde langsam ernsthaft sauer (inf)

serious-minded [ˈsɪərɪəsˈmaɪndɪd] ADJ seriös, ernsthaft

seriousness [ˈsɪərɪəsnɪs] N **a** (= earnestness) Ernst m; (= lack of frivolity) Ernsthaftigkeit f; (of consideration, discussion, point, matter etc) Ernst m; (of newspaper, interest) Ernsthaftigkeit f, Seriosität f; (of offer, suggestion) Seriosität f; **in all ~** ganz im Ernst **b** (= critical nature, of accident, loss, mistake, injury, illness) Schwere f; (of problem, situation, patient's condition, threat, shortage) Ernst m; (of deterioration) Bedenklichkeit f

serjeant [ˈsɑːdʒənt] N = sergeant

sermon [ˈsɜːmən] N (Eccl) Predigt f; (= homily) Moralpredigt f; (= scolding) Strafpredigt f; **the Sermon on the Mount** die Bergpredigt

sermonize [ˈsɜːmənaɪz] VI Vorträge halten; (= reprove) Moralpredigten halten

serous [ˈsɪərəs] ADJ serös

serpent [ˈsɜːpənt] N **a** (liter) Schlange f (also fig) **b** (Mus) Serpent nt

serpentine [ˈsɜːpəntaɪn] ADJ lane, river gewunden, mit vielen Windungen; road also kurvenreich; garden verschlungen

Serps [sɜːps] N (Brit) abbr of **state earnings-related pension scheme** staatliche Rentenversicherung

serrated [seˈreɪtɪd] ADJ gezackt; leaves also gesägt; **~ knife** Sägemesser nt

serration [seˈreɪʃən] N Zacke f; (= edge) gezackter Rand; (on knife) Sägerand m; (of leaves) gesägter Rand

serried [ˈserɪd] ADJ **~ ranks** eng geschlossene Reihen pl

serum [ˈsɪərəm] N Serum nt

servant [ˈsɜːvənt] N (lit, fig) Diener(in) m(f); (also servant girl) Dienstmädchen nt; (domestic) Bedienstete(r) mf, Dienstbote m/-botin f; **to have ~s** Bedienstete or Diener haben; **~s' quarters** Gesinderäume pl (Hist), Dienstbotenräume pl; **your devoted** or **humble** or **obedient ~** (old) Ihr ergebenster or untertänigster Diener (old) → **public servant, civil servant**

serve [sɜːv] VT **a** (= work for) dienen (+dat); (= be of use) dienlich sein (+dat), nützen (+dat); **he ~d his country/the company well** er hat sich um sein Land/die Firma verdient gemacht; **he has ~d our cause faithfully** er hat sich um unsere Sache verdient gemacht, er hat unserer Sache treue Dienste geleistet; **if my memory ~s me right** wenn ich mich recht erinnere; **to ~ its purpose** seinen Zweck erfüllen; **to ~ sb's purpose** jds Zwecken (dat) dienen; **it ~s a variety of purposes** es hat viele verschiedene Verwendungsmöglichkeiten; **it ~s no useful purpose** es hat keinen praktischen Wert; **that will ~ my needs** das ist genau (das), was ich brauche; **this box has ~d us as a table** diese Kiste hat uns (dat) als Tisch gedient; **it has ~d us well** es hat uns gute Dienste geleistet; **his knowledge of history ~d him well** seine Geschichtskenntnisse kamen ihm sehr zugute

b (= work out) abdienen, ableisten; term of office durchlaufen; apprenticeship durchmachen; sentence verbüßen, absitzen (inf); **when he ~d his term as Prime Minister** während seiner Amtszeit als Premierminister

c (= supply:) transport, gas etc versorgen

d (in shop) bedienen; **to ~ sb with 5 kilos of potatoes** jdm 5 kg Kartoffeln bringen or geben; **are you being ~d?** werden Sie schon bedient?; **I'm being ~d, thank you** danke, ich werde schon bedient or ich bekomme schon (inf)

e (esp in restaurant) food, drink servieren; (= put on plate) aufgeben; guests bedienen; (waiter) bedienen, servieren (+dat); (= pour drink for) einschenken (+dat); wine etc einschenken; rations verteilen (to an +acc); **dinner is ~d** (butler) das Essen or es ist aufgetragen; (host, hostess) darf ich zu Tisch bitten?; **"serves three"** (on packet etc) „(ergibt) drei Portionen"

f Mass, Communion ministrieren bei

g (Tennis etc) ball aufschlagen; **to ~d a double fault** er hat einen Doppelfehler gemacht

h (Jur) zustellen (on sb jdm); **to ~ a summons on sb, to ~ sb with a summons** jdn vor Gericht laden; **the landlord ~d notice (to quit) on his tenants** (esp Brit) der Vermieter kündigte den Mietern

i (old: = treat) behandeln; **to ~ sb ill** jdm einen schlechten Dienst erweisen, jdm übel mitspielen; **(it) ~s you right!** (inf) das geschieht dir (ganz) recht!; **it ~s him right for being so greedy** (inf) das geschieht ihm ganz recht, was muss er auch so gierig sein!; **it would have ~d you right if ...** (inf) es wäre dir ganz recht geschehen, wenn ...

j (stallion etc) decken

VI **a** (= do duty) dienen; **to ~ on the jury** Geschworene(r) mf sein; **to ~ on a committee** einem Ausschuss angehören; **to ~ on the council** Ratsmitglied nt sein; **to ~ as chairman** das Amt des Vorsitzenden innehaben or bekleiden (form)

b (Mil) dienen

c (at table) aufgeben; (waiter, butler etc) servieren (at table bei Tisch); **is there anyone serving at this table?** bedient hier jemand?

d **to ~ as, to ~ for** dienen als; **it will ~ das** tuts; **it ~s to show/explain ...** das zeigt/erklärt ...; **these facts merely ~ to prove my point** diese Fakten dienen lediglich dazu, mein Argument zu beweisen

e (Eccl) ministrieren

f (Tennis etc) aufschlagen

N (Tennis etc) Aufschlag m; **whose ~ is it?** wer hat Aufschlag?

▶ **serve out** VT sep **a** food ausgeben; rations etc vergeben, verteilen **b** (= work out) time in army ableisten; apprenticeship beenden, abschließen; term of office ausüben; sentence absitzen

▶ **serve up** VT sep **a** food servieren; rations verteilen; **you can't serve this stuff up** (inf) so etwas kann man doch niemandem vorsetzen! **b** (inf, = present) servieren (inf); excuse auftischen

server [ˈsɜːvə] N **a** (= tray) Servierbrett nt **b** (= spoon/fork) Servierlöffel m, Vorlegelöffel m/-gabel f; (= pie server) Tortenheber m; (= fish server) Fischvorlegelöffel m; **salad** ~ Salatbesteck nt **c** (Tennis) Aufschläger(in) m(f); **he's a strong ~** er hat einen guten Aufschlag **d** (Eccl) Ministrant(in), Messdiener(in) m(f) **e** (Comput) Server m

servery [ˈsɜːvərɪ] N (Brit Cook) Anrichte f (meist als eigener Raum)

service [ˈsɜːvɪs] N **a** Dienst m; **his faithful ~** seine treuen Dienste; **~s to one's country/the Queen** (of soldier etc) Dienst an seinem Vaterland/für die Königin; **her ~s to industry/the country** (politician, industrialist) ihre Verdienste in der Industrie/um das Land; **he died in the ~ of his country** er starb in Pflichterfüllung für sein Vaterland; **he has ten years' ~ behind him** er hat zehn Jahre Dienstzeit hinter sich (dat); **to do sb a ~** jdm einen Dienst erweisen; **to do** or **see good ~** gute Dienste leisten; **this box did ~ as a table** diese Kiste hat schon als Tisch gedient; **to be of ~** nützlich sein; **to be of ~ to sb** jdm nützen; **it's of little ~ in an emergency** im Notfall nützt es wenig; **to be at sb's ~** jdm zur Verfügung stehen; (person also) jdm zu Diensten stehen; **can I be of ~ to you?** kann ich Ihnen behilflich sein?; **out of ~** außer Betrieb; **to need the ~s of a lawyer** einen Anwalt brauchen, einen Anwalt zuziehen müssen

b (= operation) Betrieb m; **to be out of ~** außer Betrieb sein; **to bring sth into ~** etw in Betrieb nehmen; **to come into ~** in Betrieb genommen werden; **"this number is not in ~"** (US Telec) „kein Anschluss unter dieser Nummer"

c (Mil) Militärdienst m; **to see ~ as a soldier/ sailor** beim Militär/in der Marine dienen; **when I was in the ~s** als ich beim Militär war; **the three ~s** die drei Waffengattungen

d (with adj attr: = branch, department etc) -dienst m; **telephone ~** Telekommunikation f; **telephone ~s** (= utility) Telekommunikationsdienste pl; **BT offers different telephone ~s** BT bietet eine Reihe von (Telekommunikations)dienstleistungen an; **medical ~(s)** ärztliche Versorgung

e (to customers) Service m; (in shop, restaurant etc) Bedienung f

f (= bus, train, plane service etc) Bus-/Zug-/Flugverbindung f; **to increase ~s in rural areas** den Verkehr or die Verkehrslage in ländlichen Gebieten verbessern; **there's no ~ to Oban on Sundays** sonntags besteht kein Zug-/Busverkehr nach Oban; **the number 12 (bus) ~** die Linie 12

g (= domestic service) Dienst m, Stellung f; **to be in ~ (with sb)** (bei jdm) in Stellung sein, in jds Dienst (dat) stehen; **to go into ~ (with sb)** (bei jdm) in Stellung gehen, in jds Dienst (acc) treten

h (Eccl) Gottesdienst m

i (of machines) Wartung f; (Aut: = major service) Inspektion f; **my car is in for/has had a ~** mein Auto wird/wurde gewartet, mein Auto ist/war zur Inspektion

j (= tea or coffee set) Service nt

k (Tennis) Aufschlag m; **to lose one's ~** seinen Aufschlag abgeben; **whose ~ is it?** wer hat Aufschlag?

l (Jur) Zustellung f

m **services** PL (commercial) Dienstleistungen pl; (gas, electricity, water) Versorgungsnetz nt; **all the ~s have been cut off** Gas, Wasser und Strom sind abgestellt worden

n **services** PL (Brit Mot) Tankstelle und Raststätte f

VT **a** car, machine warten; **to send a car to be ~d** ein Auto warten lassen; (major service) ein Auto zur Inspektion geben

b area bedienen; committee etc zuarbeiten (+dat); **to ~ sb's needs** jds Bedürfnissen gerecht werden

c cow, mare decken

d (Fin) loan, debt bedienen

serviceability [ˌsɜːvɪsəˈbɪlɪtɪ] N (= durability) Strapazierfähigkeit f; (= practicality) Zweckmäßigkeit f; (= usability) Brauchbarkeit f

serviceable [ˈsɜːvɪsəbl] ADJ (= durable) strapazierfähig; (= practical) praktisch, zweckmäßig; (= usable) brauchbar; (Tech) betriebsfähig

serviceableness [ˈsɜːvɪsəblnɪs] N Brauchbarkeit f, gute Verwendbarkeit f; (= durability) Strapazierfähigkeit f; (Tech) Betriebsfähigkeit f

service: service academy N (US, Mil) Militärakademie f; **service agreement** N Wartungsvertrag m; **service area** N (Brit) Tankstelle und Raststätte f; **service box** N (Elec) Hauptanschlusskasten m; **service break** N (Tennis) Break nt; **service bus** N Linienbus m; **service ceiling** N (Aviat) Dienstgipfelhöhe f; **service charge** N Bedienung f, Bedienungsgeld nt; (of bank) Bearbeitungsgebühr f; **service court** N (Tennis etc) Aufschlagfeld nt; **service department** N Kundendienstabteilung f; **service dress** N Dienstkleidung f; **service elevator** N (esp US) Lasten- or Warenaufzug m; **service engineer** N Servicemechaniker(in) m(f); **service entrance** N Dienstboteneingang m; **service family** N Familie f von Militärpersonal; **service flat** N (Brit) Appartement nt mit vollem Service (Portier, Hausmeister etc); **service game** N Aufschlagspiel m; **service hatch** N Durchreiche f; **service industry** N Dienstleistungsbranche f; **service life** N (Tech) Lebensdauer f; **service lift** N (Brit) Lasten- or Warenaufzug m; **service line** N (Tennis etc) Aufschlaglinie f; **serviceman** N Militärangehörige(r) m; **service module** N (Space) Versorgungsmodul nt; **service provider** N (Comput) Serviceprovider m; **service road** N (for access) Zufahrtsstraße f; (for works traffic) Versorgungsstraße f; (for delivery) Andienungsstraße f; **service sector** N (of economy) Dienstleistungssektor m; **service speed** N (Naut) Reisegeschwindigkeit f; **service station** N Tankstelle f (mit Reparaturwerkstatt); (Brit: = service area) Tankstelle und Raststätte f; **service switch** N (Elec) Hauptschalter m; **service tunnel** N Versorgungstunnel m; **servicewoman** N Militärangehörige f

servicing [ˈsɜːvɪsɪŋ] N **a** (Tech) Wartung f, Pflege f; **~ schedule** Wartungsplan m **b** (= supplying) Versorgung f

serviette [ˌsɜːvɪˈet] N (Brit) Serviette f; **~ ring** Serviettenring m

servile [ˈsɜːvaɪl] ADJ unterwürfig; obedience sklavisch

servility [sɜːˈvɪlɪtɪ] N Unterwürfigkeit f

serving [ˈsɜːvɪŋ] **ADJ** politician amtierend; (Mil) officer Dienst tuend attr, im Dienst; man im Dienst **N** (= helping of food) Portion f

serving: serving bowl N Servierschüssel f; **serving dish** N Servierplatte f; **serving girl** N Dienstmädchen nt; **serving hatch** N Durchreiche f; **serving spoon** N Vorlegelöffel m

servitude [ˈsɜːvɪtjuːd] N Knechtschaft f

servo [ˈsɜːvəʊ] **N** (inf) Servomechanismus m **ADJ** attr Servo-; ~(-assisted) **brakes** Servobremsen pl; **~mechanism** Servomechanismus m; **~ steering** Servolenkung f

sesame [ˈsesəmɪ] N **a** (Bot) Sesam m **b** **open ~!** Sesam, öffne dich!; **an open ~** (fig) ein Sesam-öffne-dich nt

sesame: sesame oil N Sesamöl nt; **sesame seed** N Sesamkorn nt; **~ roll** Sesambrötchen nt

sessile [ˈsesaɪl] ADJ (Bot) festgewachsen, sessil (spec)

session [ˈseʃən] N **a** (= meeting) Sitzung f; (Jur, Parl: = period) Sitzungsperiode f; (Parl: = term of office) Legislaturperiode f; **to be in ~** eine Sitzung abhalten; (Jur, Pol) tagen; **to go into secret ~** eine Geheimsitzung abhalten; **a ~ of talks/negotiations** Gespräche pl/Verhandlungen pl → **quarter sessions, court**

b (with psychiatrist etc: = period devoted to activity) Sitzung f; (at doctor's, dentist's) Behandlung f; (= discussion, meeting) Besprechung f; **recording ~** Aufnahme f; **photo ~** Fotosession f; **we're in for a long ~** das wird lange dauern; **I'll have a cleaning ~ tomorrow** (inf) morgen werde ich mal ausgiebig putzen (inf)

c (= academic year, Univ) Studienjahr nt; (Sch) Schuljahr nt; (= term) Semester/Trimester nt; (esp Sch) Halbjahr nt; (= division of course) Stunde f, Sitzung f (esp Univ); **the afternoon ~s begin ...** der Nachmittagsunterricht fängt ... an

session musician N Sessionmusiker(in) m(f)

sestet [sesˈtet] N (Mus) Sextett nt; (Poet) Sestine f

SET (Internet) abbr of **secure electronic transaction** SET m

set [set]
vb: pret, ptp **set**

1 NOUN	4 INTRANSITIVE VERB
2 ADJECTIVE	5 PHRASAL VERBS
3 TRANSITIVE VERB	

When the verb **set** is part of a fixed combination, eg **to set on fire, to set one's cap at,** look up the other word.

1 – NOUN

a of objects Satz m; (of two) Paar nt; (of underwear, cutlery, furniture, hairbrushes etc) Garnitur f; (= tea set etc) Service nt; (of tablemats etc) Set nt; (= chess or draughts set etc) Spiel nt; (= chemistry set etc) Bastelkasten m; (= painting set) Malkasten m; (= Meccano ®, construction set) Baukasten m; (of books, on one subject) Reihe f, Serie f; (by one author) gesammelte Ausgabe; (= gift or presentation set) Kassette f; (of rooms) Zimmerflucht f; **a set of tools** Werkzeug nt; **a set of teeth** ein Gebiss nt; **a complete set of Dickens' novels** eine Gesamtausgabe von Dickens

b = batch Reihe f; **he had a whole set of questions** er hatte eine ganze Menge or Reihe Fragen; **a strange set of ideas** eigenartige Ideen

c = group of people Kreis m; (pej) Bande f; (Brit, Sch: = stream) Kurs m; **the literary set** die Literaten pl; **the golfing set** die Golffreunde pl; **that set of people** dieser Personenkreis; **a nice set of people** nette Leute pl

d Math Reihe f; (in set theory) Menge f

e Sport (Tennis) Satz m; (Table Tennis) Spiel nt

f = part of concert Programmnummer f

g of play (Theat) Bühnenbild nt; (Film) Szenenaufbau m; **to be on the set** bei den Dreharbeiten

h = appliance (TV, radio etc) Gerät nt, Apparat m; (= headset) Paar nt; **set of headphones** Kopfhörer m

i Dancing Gruppe f; **to make up a set** eine Gruppe bilden; **they then move up the set** sie rücken (in der Gruppe) auf

j = position (of head, shoulders) Haltung f; **the set of sb's mouth** jds Mundstellung f

k = hairset Frisur f, Form f; **to have a shampoo and set** sich (dat) die Haare waschen und legen lassen

l of wind Richtung f

m Hunt Vorstehen nt; **to make a dead set at sb** (dated, = try to attract) sich an jdn ranmachen (inf)

n US = **sett**

2 – ADJECTIVE

a = likely

♦ **to be set to** he is set to become the new champion ihm werden die besten Chancen auf den Meistertitel eingeräumt; **the talks are set to continue all week** die Gespräche werden voraussichtlich die ganze Woche über andauern

b = ready fertig, bereit

♦ **all set are we all set?** sind wir alle fertig or bereit?; **all set?** alles klar?; **to be all set for sth** für etw gerüstet or auf etw (acc) vorbereitet sein; (= mentally prepared) auf etw (acc) eingestellt sein; **to be all set to do sth** (= have made all the arrangements) sich darauf eingerichtet haben, etw zu tun; (= mentally prepared) fest entschlossen or drauf und dran sein, etw zu tun; **we're all set to go** wir sind so weit or startklar; **with their cameras all set** mit schussbereiten Kameras

c = rigid starr; face starr, unbeweglich; expression feststehend; forms starr, fest; habit, custom fest; **to be set in one's ways** in seinen Gewohnheiten festgefahren sein

d = fixed time, place festgesetzt, bestimmt, ausgemacht (inf); **one of my set tasks is ...** eine der mir übertragenen Aufgaben ist es ...; **set hours for studying** feste Zeiten zum Lernen; **his set purpose was to ...** er war fest entschlossen, zu ...; **set menu** Tageskarte f; **set lunch/meal** Tagesgericht nt; **set speech** Standardrede f; **set phrase** feststehender Ausdruck

♦ **set piece** (in novel, play) Standardszene nt; (in exam) Pflichtstück nt; (in football match etc) Standardsituation f; (= fireworks) Feuerwerksbild nt

e = prescribed festgesetzt, fest; task bestimmt; essay topic vorgegeben, bestimmt; **set book(s)** Pflichtlektüre f; **set song** Pflichtstück nt

f = resolved entschlossen; **to be set on sth** zu etw entschlossen sein; **to be set on doing sth** entschlossen sein, etw zu tun; **to be dead set on sth/doing sth** etw auf Biegen oder Brechen haben/tun wollen; **to be (dead) set against sth/doing sth/sb doing sth** (absolut) gegen etw sein/dagegen sein, etw zu tun/dagegen sein, dass jd etw tut; **she is far too set on getting her own way** sie will immer nur ihren eigenen Kopf durchsetzen

3 – TRANSITIVE VERB

a = place stellen; (on its side, flat) legen; (deliberately, carefully) setzen; **to set the chairs by the window** die Stühle ans Fenster setzen or stellen; **he set the stones carefully on top of each other** er setzte or legte die Steine vorsichtig aufeinander; **to set the child on his feet** das Kind auf die Beine stellen; **I set him on his way** (lit) ich schickte ihn los; (fig) ich habe ihm zu einem guten Anfang verholfen; **I set him/his books above all others** ich schätze ihn/seine Bücher höher ein als alle anderen; **to set a value/price on sth** (lit, fig) einen Wert/Preis für etw festsetzen; **to set a high value on sth** einer Sache (dat) großen Wert beimessen, etw hoch bewerten

♦ **to set free to set sb free** jdn freilassen

♦ **to set right to set sth/things right** etw/die Dinge in Ordnung bringen; **to set sb right (about sth)** jdn (in Bezug auf etw acc) berichtigen

♦ **to set straight to set sb straight** jdn berichtigen

b = cause **to set sth going/in motion** etw in Gang/Bewegung bringen; **what set the dog barking?** warum bellt der Hund?

♦ **to set sb doing sth** jdn dazu veranlassen, etw zu tun; **that set me thinking** das veranlasste mich nachzudenken

♦ **to set sb to doing** or **to do sth** jdn etw tun lassen; **to set oneself to doing** or **to do sth** sich daranmachen, etw zu tun

c ‖ = regulate ‖ *timer, controls* einstellen (*at* auf +*acc*); *clock* stellen (*by* nach, *to* auf +*acc*); *trap, snare* (*lit*) aufstellen; (*fig*) stellen (*for* sb jdm)

d ‖ = prescribe, impose ‖ *target, limit etc* festsetzen, festlegen; *task, question* stellen (*sb* jdm); *homework* aufgeben; *exam, exam questions* zusammenstellen; *book for exam* vorschreiben; **Hamlet has not been set this year** Hamlet steht dieses Jahr nicht auf dem Lehrplan; **to set sb a problem** (*lit*) jdm ein Problem aufgeben; (*fig*) jdn vor ein Problem stellen; **he was set a target** ihm wurde ein Soll vorgeschrieben; **England was set 75 to win** (*Sport*) England brauchte 75 (Punkte), um zu gewinnen

e ‖ = arrange ‖ *time, date* festsetzen, ausmachen (*inf*), anberaumen (*form*); *place* bestimmen, ausmachen (*inf*); **to set the date (of the wedding)** die Hochzeit festsetzen; **the attack was set for midnight** der Angriff war für Mitternacht geplant

f ‖ = establish ‖ *record* aufstellen; *fashion* bestimmen

g ‖ = mount ‖ *gem* fassen (*in* in +*dat*); *piece of jewellery* besetzen (*with* mit); *windowpane* einsetzen (*in* in +*acc*)

h ‖ = embed firmly ‖ einlegen (*in* in +*acc*); (*in ground*) einlassen (*in* in +*acc*); **to set stones in concrete** Steine einzementieren

i ‖ = locate ‖ **to be set in the valley** im Tal liegen; **a house set on a hillside** ein am Berghang gelegenes Haus; **his eyes were set wide apart** er hatte weit auseinander liegende Augen; **the book is set in Rome** das Buch spielt in Rom; **he set the book in 19th century France/in Rome** er wählte das Frankreich des 19. Jahrhunderts/Rom als Schauplatz für sein Buch; **she set the action in the 16th century/in Vienna** sie verlegte die Handlung ins 16. Jahrhundert/nach Wien

j ‖ = lay with cutlery ‖ *table* decken; **to set places for 14** für 14 decken, 14 Gedecke auflegen

k ‖ = station ‖ *guard* aufstellen; **to set a guard on sb/sth** jdn/etw bewachen lassen

l ‖ = make solid ‖ *jam* fest werden lassen, gelieren lassen; *concrete* hart werden lassen; *dye* fixieren

m ‖ bone ‖ (*Med*) einrichten; *dislocated joint* einrenken

n ‖ hair ‖ legen, eindrehen

o ‖ Typ ‖ setzen, absetzen (*spec*)

p ‖ set expressions ‖ **to set sth to music** etw vertonen; **to set a dog/the police on sb** einen Hund/die Polizei auf jdn ansetzen or hetzen

4 – INTRANSITIVE VERB

a ‖ = go down ‖ (*sun, moon*) untergehen; **his star is setting** (*fig*) sein Stern ist im Sinken

b ‖ = harden ‖ (*jelly, cement*) hart or fest werden; (*jam*) fest werden, gelieren; (*bone*) zusammenwachsen

c ‖ dye ‖ farbbeständig werden

d ‖ Dancing ‖ **to set to one's partner** sich dem Partner zuwenden

e ‖ Hunt ‖ vorstehen

5 – PHRASAL VERBS

▶ **set about** **VI** +*prep obj* **a** (= begin) sich machen an (+*acc*), anfangen; (= tackle) anfassen, anpacken (*inf*), anstellen (*inf*); **to set about doing sth** (= begin) sich daranmachen, etw zu tun; **how do I set about getting a loan?** wie fasse or packe (*inf*) ich es an, um ein Darlehen zu bekommen? **b** (= attack) herfallen über (+*acc*)

▶ **set against** **VT** *sep* +*prep obj* **a** (= influence against) einnehmen gegen; (= cause trouble between) Zwietracht säen zwischen (+*dat*); **to set oneself against sth** sich einer Sache (*dat*) entgegenstellen; **the civil war set friend against friend/father against son** der Bürgerkrieg ließ

Freunde/Väter und Söhne zu Feinden werden → *also* **set 2 c** **b** (= balance against) gegenüberstellen (+*dat*); **his story must be set against the evidence of the police** man muss seine Darstellung den Aussagen der Polizei gegenüberhalten

▶ **set apart** **VT** *sep* **a** (= distinguish) abheben, unterscheiden; **he felt set apart from the other boys** er fühlte, dass er nicht so war wie die anderen Jungen **b** (= save) *money* beiseite legen, auf die Seite legen; *time* einplanen

▶ **set aside** **VT** *sep* **a** *newspaper, book etc* zur Seite legen; *work, money* beiseite legen; *time* einplanen; *land, room* reservieren; *plans* aufschieben; *differences, quarrels, hostilities* beiseite schieben, begraben; *dislike* vergessen; *mistrust, bitterness* sich hinwegsetzen von; *formality* verzichten auf (+*acc*); *rules, protest* übergehen, außer Acht lassen **b** (*Jur*) aufheben; *will* für nichtig or ungültig erklären

▶ **set back** **VT** *sep* **a** (= place at a distance) zurücksetzen; **the house is set back from the road** das Haus liegt etwas von der Straße ab or liegt nicht direkt an der Straße **b** (= retard) verzögern, behindern; (*by a certain length of time*) zurückwerfen; **the plans have been set back (by) 2 years** die Pläne sind um 2 Jahre zurückgeworfen **c** (*inf*, = cost) kosten; **the dinner set me back £35** das Essen hat mich £ 35 gekostet or ärmer gemacht (*inf*)

▶ **set down** **VT** *sep* **a** (= put down) *suitcase, passenger* absetzen **b** (in writing) (schriftlich) niederlegen **c** (= attribute) zuschreiben (*to* dat) **d** (= classify as) **to set sb/sth down as sth** jdn/etw für etw halten

▶ **set forth** **VT** *sep* (= expound) *theory, plan* darlegen **VI** (*liter*) ausziehen (*old*)

▶ **set in** **VI** (= start) einsetzen; (*panic*) ausbrechen; (*night*) anbrechen; (*Med, gangrene, complications*) sich einstellen; **the rain has set in** es hat sich eingeregnet **VT** *sep* **a** (*Typ*, = indent) einrücken **b** (*Sew*) *sleeve* einsetzen; *pocket* einarbeiten (*into* in +*acc*)

▶ **set off** **VT** *sep* **a** (= ignite) *bomb, firework* losgehen lassen **b** (= start) führen zu; *speculation, quarrel* auslösen; **that set us all off laughing** das brachte uns (*acc*) alle zum Lachen; **to set sb off on a new line of thought** jdn auf einen neuen Gedanken bringen; **her remark set him off on a story** auf ihre Bemerkung hin erzählte er eine Geschichte; **don't set him off!** lass ihn nur nicht damit anfangen!; **that really set him off** daraufhin legte er richtig los or war er nicht mehr zu bremsen (*inf*) **c** (= offset) **to set sth off against sth** etw einer Sache (*dat*) gegenüberstellen **d** (= enhance) hervorheben; **to set sth off from sth** etw von etw abheben **VI** (= depart) sich auf den Weg machen, aufbrechen; (*car, in car*) losfahren; **to set off on a journey** eine Reise antreten; **to set off for Spain** nach Spanien abfahren; **the police set off in pursuit** die Polizei nahm die Verfolgung auf

▶ **set on** **VT** *sep* +*prep obj dogs* hetzen or ansetzen auf → **eye** **VI** +*prep obj* → **set upon**

▶ **set out** **VT** *sep* **a** (= display) ausbreiten; (= arrange) *chess pieces* aufstellen; *printed matter, essay* anordnen, anlegen; (= state) darlegen, darstellen **VI** → **set off VI b** (= intend) beabsichtigen; (= start) sich daranmachen

▶ **set to** **VI** (= start working, fighting) loslegen (*inf*); (= start eating) reinhauen (*inf*); **they set to and repaired it** sie machten sich an die Arbeit und reparierten es **VI** +*prep obj* **to set to work** sich an die Arbeit machen; **to set to work doing** or **to do sth** beginnen, etw zu tun

▶ **set up** **VI** (= establish oneself) **to set up as a doctor** sich als Arzt niederlassen; **to set up in business** sein eigenes Geschäft aufmachen; **to set up for oneself** sich selbstständig machen **VT** *sep* **a** (= place in position) *statue, post* aufstellen; (= assemble, get ready) *tent, stall, apparatus* aufbauen; (*Typ*) einrichten; (*fig*, = arrange) *meeting* arrangieren, vereinbaren; *robbery* pla-

nen, vorbereiten; **to set sth up for sb** etw für jdn vorbereiten **b** (= establish) gründen; *school, office, system* einrichten; *inquiry* veranlassen, anordnen; *record* aufstellen; **to set sb up in business** jdm zu einem Geschäft verhelfen; **to set sb up in an apartment** jdm eine Wohnung einrichten; **to set sb up as sth** (es) jdm ermöglichen, etw zu werden; **to set oneself up as sth** sich aufspielen als; **to be set up for life** für sein ganzes Leben ausgesorgt haben; **to be well set up** sich gut stehen; **to set up camp** die Zelte or das Lager aufschlagen; **they've set up home in Glasgow/Spain** sie haben sich in Glasgow/Spanien niedergelassen → **house, shop c** (= restore to health) gut tun (+*dat*); **a weekend at the seaside will set you up again** ein Wochenende am Meer wird dich schon wieder auf die Beine bringen **d** (= raise) *cry, protest, cheer* anstimmen; **to set up a commotion** allgemeinen Aufruhr auslösen or hervorrufen; (= make noise) Krach machen **e** (= cause) *infection, reaction* auslösen, verursachen **f** (*inf*, = frame) **to set sb up** jdm etwas anhängen; **I've been set up** das will mir einer anhängen (*inf*) or in die Schuhe schieben **g** (*inf*, = rig) **the fight had been set up** der Kampf war von vornherein eine abgekartete Sache

▶ **set upon** **VI** +*prep obj* überfallen; (*animal*) anfallen

set: **setback** N Rückschlag *m*; **set designer** N (*Theat*) Bühnenbildner(in) *m(f)*; **setdown** N **a** (*fig*: = damper) Dämpfer *m* (*inf, fig*) **b** (= dressing-down) Rüffel *m* (*inf*); **set-in** ADJ *sleeve* eingesetzt; *pocket* eingearbeitet; **set-piece specialist** N (*Ftbl*) Freistoß- or Eckballspezialist(in) *m(f)*; **set point** N Set- or Satzpunkt *m*; **set square** N Zeichendreieck *nt*

sett, (*US*) **set** [set] N (= badger's den) Bau *m*

settee [seˈtiː] N Couch *f*, Sofa *nt*

setter [ˈsetə] N **a** (= typesetter) Setzer(in) *m(f)* **b** (= dog) Setter *m*

set theory N Mengenlehre *f*

setting [ˈsetɪŋ] N **a** (of sun, moon) Untergang *m* **b** (= background, atmosphere) Rahmen *m*; (= environment, surroundings) Umgebung *f*; (of novel etc) Schauplatz *m*; **a film with a medieval ~** ein Film, der im Mittelalter spielt **c** (of jewel) Fassung *f* **d** (= place setting) Gedeck *nt* **e** (= position on dial etc) Einstellung *f* **f** (= musical arrangement) Vertonung *f* **g** (*Hairdressing*) Legen *nt*

setting lotion N (Haar)festiger *m*

setting-up [ˈsetɪŋˈʌp] N (of machine etc) Aufstellen *nt*, Montage *f*; (*Comput: of program etc*) Installation *f*

setting-up exercises PL (*US Sport*) Gymnastik *f*, gymnastische Übungen *pl*

settle¹ [ˈsetl] N (Wand)bank *f*

settle² **VT** **a** (= decide) entscheiden; (= sort out) regeln, erledigen; *problem, question, points* klären; *dispute, differences, quarrel* beilegen, schlichten; *doubts* ausräumen, beseitigen; *date, place* vereinbaren, ausmachen (*inf*); *venue* festlegen or -setzen; *deal* abschließen; *price* sich einigen auf (+*acc*), aushandeln; *terms* aushandeln; **the result of the game was ~d in the first half** das Ergebnis des Spiels stand schon in der ersten Halbzeit fest; **when my future is ~d** wenn sich meine Zukunft entschieden hat; **to ~ one's affairs** seine Angelegenheiten in Ordnung bringen; **to ~ an estate** (*Jur*) die Verteilung des Nachlasses regeln; **to ~ a case out of court** einen Fall außergerichtlich klären; **that's ~d then** damit das ist also klar or geregelt; **that ~s it** damit wäre der Fall (ja wohl) erledigt; (*angry*) jetzt reichts

b (= pay) *bill* begleichen, bezahlen; *account* ausgleichen

c (= calm) *nerves, stomach* beruhigen; **we need rain to ~ the dust** wir brauchen Regen, damit sich der Staub setzt

d (= *place carefully*) legen; (*in upright position*) stellen; (= *make comfortable for sleep etc*) child, invalid versorgen; *pillow* zurechtlegen; **to ~ oneself comfortably in an armchair** es sich (*dat*) in einem Sessel bequem machen; **she ~d her head back against the headrest** sie lehnte ihren Kopf zurück an die Kopfstütze; **to ~ oneself to doing sth** sich daranmachen, etw zu tun; **she ~ one's gaze on sb/sth** seinen Blick auf jdm/etw ruhen lassen

e (= *establish: in house*) unterbringen; **to get one's daughter ~d with a husband** seine Tochter verheiraten *or* unter die Haube bringen (*inf*)

f **to ~ sb into a house/job** jdm helfen, sich häuslich einzurichten/sich in eine Stellung einzugewöhnen; **we'd just ~d the children into a new school** wir hatten die Kinder gerade in einer neuen Schule gut untergebracht → **settle in VT**

g (= *colonize*) land besiedeln; (= *set up*) people ansiedeln

h (*form*) **to ~ money/property on sb** jdm Geld/Besitz überschreiben *or* übertragen; (*in will*) jdm Geld/Besitz vermachen; **to ~ an annuity on sb** für jdn eine Rente aussetzen

i (*inf*, = *put an end to*) **I'll soon ~ his nonsense** ich werde ihm schon die Flausen austreiben; **I'll soon ~ him** dem werd ichs geben (*inf*); (*verbally also*) dem werd ich was erzählen (*inf*); **that ~d him!** da hatte er sein Fett weg (*inf*)

VI **a** (= *put down roots*) sesshaft werden; (*in country, town, profession*) sich niederlassen; (*as settler*) sich ansiedeln; (*in house*) sich häuslich niederlassen, sich einrichten; (= *feel at home*) (*in house, town, country*) sich einleben (*into* in +*dat*); (*in job, surroundings*) sich eingewöhnen (*into* in +*dat*); **to ~ into a way of life** sich an einen Lebensstil gewöhnen; **to ~ into a habit** sich (*dat*) etw angewöhnen; **as he ~d into middle age** als er älter und reifer wurde

b (= *become less variable: weather*) beständig werden; **the wind ~d in the east** der Wind kam schließlich aus Osten

c (= *become calm, child, matters, stomach*) sich beruhigen; (*panic, excitement*) sich legen; (= *become less excitable or restless*) zur Ruhe kommen, ruhiger werden; **he couldn't ~ to anything** er konnte sich auf nichts konzentrieren

d (= *come to rest, sit down, person, bird, insect*) sich niederlassen *or* setzen; (*dust*) sich setzen *or* legen; (= *sink slowly, subside, building, walls*) sich senken; (*ground, liquid, sediment, coffee grounds*) sich setzen; (*wine*) sich beruhigen; **to ~ comfortably in an armchair** es sich (*dat*) in einem Sessel gemütlich *or* bequem machen; **the boat ~d in the water** das Boot hörte auf zu schaukeln; **fog/silence ~d over the city** Nebel/Stille legte sich über die Stadt *or* breitete sich über der Stadt aus; **gloom ~d over the meeting** eine bedrückte Stimmung breitete sich in der Versammlung aus → **dust**

e (*Jur*) **to ~ (out of court)** sich vergleichen

f (= *pay*) bezahlen → *also* **settle with**

▶**settle back** VI sich (gemütlich) zurücklehnen

▶**settle down VI** **a** → **settle² VI a** **it's time he settled down** es ist Zeit, dass er ein geregeltes Leben anfängt *or* dass er zur Ruhe kommt; **to marry and settle down** heiraten und sesshaft *or* häuslich werden; **to settle down at school/in a new house** sich an einer Schule/in einem Haus einleben; **to settle down in a new job** sich in einer neuen Stellung eingewöhnen; **he ought to settle down with a steady job** er sollte sich (*dat*) endlich eine feste Stellung suchen; **they have settled down in Spain** sie haben sich in Spanien niedergelassen; **settle down, children!** ruhig, Kinder!

b → **settle² VI c**

c **to settle down to work** sich an die Arbeit machen *or* setzen; **to settle down for a chat** sich zu einem Schwatz zusammensetzen; **to settle down for the night** sich schlafen legen; **to settle down to watch TV** es sich (*dat*) vor dem Fernseher gemütlich machen

---

VT *sep* **a** (= *calm down*) beruhigen

b *baby* hinlegen; *patient* versorgen; **to settle oneself down to work** sich an die Arbeit machen *or* setzen; **to settle oneself down to finish the job** sich daranmachen, die Arbeit fertig zu machen; **the cat settled itself down for the night** die Katze kuschelte sich zum Schlafen zurecht; **the campers settled themselves down for the night** die Zeltenden richteten alles für die Nacht her

▶**settle for** VI +*prep obj* sich zufrieden geben mit; **I'd settle for a diamond necklace** ich wäre schon mit einem Diamanthalsband zufrieden; **I think I'll settle for this one** ich glaube, ich nehme doch das da; **she won't settle for anything less** mit weniger gibt sie sich nicht zufrieden; **he was glad to settle for a bronze medal** er war schon mit einer Bronzemedaille zufrieden

▶**settle in VI** (*in house, town*) sich einleben; (*in job, school*) sich eingewöhnen; **how are you settling in?** haben Sie sich schon eingelebt/eingewöhnt? **VT** *sep* **to settle sb in** jdm helfen, sich einzuleben/sich einzugewöhnen

▶**settle on** *or* **upon** VI +*prep obj* sich entscheiden für; (= *decide, settle*) sich entschließen zu; (= *agree on*) sich einigen auf (+*acc*)

▶**settle up VI** (be)zahlen; **to settle up with sb** (*lit, fig*) mit jdm abrechnen **VT** *sep* bill bezahlen

▶**settle with VI** +*prep obj* (*lit, fig*) abrechnen mit; +*prep obj* **a** debt etc abrechnen mit; **to settle one's account with sb** (*lit, fig*) mit jdm abrechnen **b** (= *come to agreement with*) **to settle sth with sb** sich mit jdm auf etw (*acc*) einigen

settled ['setld] ADJ *weather* beständig; *way of life* geregelt; *opinions* fest; *procedure* feststehend, festgelegt; **to be ~** in geregelten Verhältnissen leben, etabliert sein; (*in place*) sesshaft sein; (= *have permanent job etc*) festen Fuß gefasst haben; (*in a house*) sich häuslich niedergelassen haben; (= *be less restless*) ruhiger *or* gesetzter sein; **to feel ~** sich wohl fühlen; **I don't feel very ~ at the moment** ich hänge zurzeit in der Luft (*inf*), ich fühle mich zurzeit verunsichert

settlement ['setlmənt] ◑ 20.7 N **a** (*act, = deciding*) Entscheidung *f*; (= *sorting out*) Regelung *f*, Erledigung *f*; (*of problem, question etc*) Klärung *f*; (*of dispute, differences etc*) Beilegung *f*, Schlichtung *f*; (*of estate*) Regelung *f*; (*of bill, claim*) Bezahlung *f*; (*of account*) Ausgleich *m*; (= *contract, agreement etc*) Übereinkunft *f*, Übereinkommen *nt*; **an out-of-court ~, a ~ out of court** (*Jur*) ein außergerichtlicher Vergleich; **to reach a ~** sich einigen, einen Vergleich treffen; **the terms of the ~** (*Jur*) die Bedingungen des Übereinkommens; **this payment is made in ~ of all claims** mit dieser Zahlung werden alle Forderungen beglichen; **in ~ of our account** zum Ausgleich unseres Kontos; **~ discount** Skonto *nt or m*

b (= *settling of money*) Übertragung *f*, Überschreibung *f* (*on* +*acc*); (*esp in will*) Vermächtnis *nt*; (*of annuity, income*) Aussetzung *f*; (= *document, agreement*) Schenkungsvertrag *m*; **he receives £10,000 by the ~** auf ihn wurden £ 10.000 übertragen *or* überschrieben, ihm wurden £ 10.000 vermacht

c (*of building*) Senkung *f*; (*of sediment*) Absetzen *nt*

d (= *colony, village*) Siedlung *f*, Niederlassung *f*; (= *act of settling persons*) Ansiedlung *f*; (= *colonization*) Besiedlung *f*

e (*US: also* **settlement house**, = *institution*) Wohlfahrtseinrichtung *f*; (= *building*) Gemeindezentrum *nt*

settlement day N (*Econ*) Abrechnungstag *m*

settler ['setlə'] N Siedler(in) *m(f)*

settling day ['setlɪŋ,deɪ] N (*Econ*) Abrechnungstag *m*

set-to ['settuː] N (*Brit inf*) Krach *m*, Streiterei *f* (*inf*); **to have a ~ with sb** sich mit jdm in die Wolle kriegen (*inf*)

set-top box ['settɒpˈbɒks] N (*TV*) Digitalreceiver *m*, d-box® *f*

---

setup ['setʌp] N **a** (*inf*, = *situation*) Umstände *pl*; (= *way of organizing things*) Organisation *f*, Drum und Dran *nt* (*inf*); **it's a funny ~** das sind (vielleicht) komische Zustände!; **what's the ~ here?** wie verhält sich *or* läuft (*inf*) das hier (alles)?; **she didn't quite understand the ~** sie verstand die Sachlage nicht ganz **b** (= *equipment*) Geräte *pl*, Instrumente *pl* **c** (*US, for drinks*) Zubehör *nt* für Cocktails etc **d** (*inf*, = *rigged contest*) abgekartete Sache

setup file N (*Comput*) Einrichtungsdatei *f*, Setupdatei *f*

seven ['sevn] ADJ sieben; **to sail the ~ seas** die sieben Meere befahren; **he's got the ~-year itch** (*inf*) er ist im verflixten siebenten Jahr **N** Sieben *f* → *also* **six**

sevenfold ['sevnfəʊld] ADJ siebenfach ADV um das Siebenfache

seventeen ['sevn'tiːn] ADJ siebzehn **N** Siebzehn *f* → *also* **sixteen**

seventeenth ['sevn'tiːnθ] ADJ siebzehnte(r, s); **a ~ part** ein Siebzehntel *nt* **N** (= *fraction*) Siebzehntel *nt*; (*of series*) Siebzehnte(r, s)

seventh ['sevnθ] ADJ siebte(r, s); **a ~ part** ein Siebtel *nt*; **Seventh-Day Adventist** Adventist(in) *m(f)* vom Siebenten Tag **N** (= *fraction*) Siebtel *nt*; (*in series*) Siebte(r, s); (*Mus, = interval*) Septime *f*; (= *chord*) Septimenakkord *m* → *also* **sixth**

seventhly ['sevnθlɪ] ADV siebtens

seventieth ['sevntɪθ] ADJ siebzigste(r, s) **N** (= *fraction*) Siebzigstel *nt*; (*in series*) Siebzigste(r, s)

seventy ['sevntɪ] ADJ siebzig **N** Siebzig *f*

seventy-eight [,sevntɪ'eɪt] N Achtundsiebzig *f*; (= *record*) Achtundsiebziger(platte) *f*, 78er-Platte *f*

sever ['sevə'] **VT** (= *cut through*) durchtrennen; (*violently*) durchschlagen; (= *cut off*) abtrennen; (*violently*) abschlagen; (*fig, = break off*) ties lösen; *relations, links, friendship* abbrechen; *communications* unterbrechen; (= *divide*) nation teilen; **the wires were ~ed in the storm** beim Sturm sind die Leitungen (durch)gerissen; **to ~ sb from sb/sth** jdn von jdm/etw trennen; **to ~ sth from sth** etw von etw abtrennen **VI** (durch)reißen

several ['sevrəl] ADJ **a** (= *some*) einige, mehrere; (= *different, diverse, various*) verschiedene; **I went with ~ others** ich ging mit einigen *or* ein paar anderen zusammen; **I've seen him ~ times/~ times** ich habe ihn einige Male gesehen/schon mehrmals *or* mehrere Male gesehen; **there are ~ ways of doing it** das kann man auf mehrere *or* verschiedene Arten machen; **I'll need ~ more** ich brauche noch einige **b** (*dated*: = *respective*) jeweilig; **they went their ~ ways** jeder ging seinen Weg, sie gingen ihrer Wege (*old*) **PRON** einige; **~ of the houses** einige (der) Häuser; **~ of us** einige von uns

severally ['sevrəlɪ] ADV einzeln

severance ['sevərəns] N (= *cutting through*) Durchtrennen *nt*; (*violently*) Durchschlagen *nt*; (= *cutting off*) Abtrennen *nt*; (*violently*) Abschlagen *nt*; (*fig*: = *breaking off of ties*) Lösen *nt*; (*of relations, links, friendship*) Abbruch *m*; (*of communications*) Unterbrechung *f*

severance pay N Abfindung *f*

severe [sɪ'vɪə'] ADJ (+*er*) **a** (= *grave, grievous*) defeat, hardship, damage, pressure schwer; *illness, injury, blow, loss* schwer, schlimm; *pain* stark, heftig; *problem* schwer, ernsthaft; *consequence* schwerwiegend, schwer wiegend; **to have a ~ cold** eine schwere Erkältung haben

b (= *strict*) critic, law, punishment, test hart; *penalty* schwer(wiegend), schwer (wiegend); *discipline* streng, eisern; *reprimand, criticism* scharf

c (= *harsh*) weather conditions schwer, schwierig; *winter* streng, hart; *frost, drought* schwer, schlimm; *storm* schwer, stark

d (= *grim, serious*) person, manner streng; *expression* ernst; **to be ~ with sb** streng mit jdm sein; **to be ~ on sb** hart über jdn urteilen

e (= *austere*) clothes, appearance, hairstyle, architecture, style streng

severely [sɪ'vɪəlɪ] ADV **a** (= *gravely, badly*) *defeat, affect, damage, injure, disabled* schwer; *disrupt, limit* stark; *strain* schwer, äußerst; **a ~ ill child** ein schwer krankes Kind **b** (= *strictly*) *punish* hart; *criticize, reprimand* scharf; **to be ~ critical of sth** sich äußerst kritisch über etw (*acc*) äußern **c** (= *grimly, seriously*) streng **d** (= *austerely*) *dress* streng

severeness [sɪ'vɪənɪs] N = **severity**

severity [sɪ'verɪtɪ] N (= *strictness, of person, appearance, style*) Strenge *f*; (= *harshness, of critic, law, winter also, punishment, competition, test*) Härte *f*; (*of criticism*) Schärfe *f*; (= *seriousness, of expression, warning*) Ernst *m*; (*of illness, injury, blow, crime, storm, loss*) Schwere *f*; (*of pain, storm*) Stärke *f*, Heftigkeit *f*; (*of weather*) Rauheit *f*; **the ~ of the cold/drought** die große *or* schwere Kälte/Dürre; **the ~ of the frost** der starke *or* schwere Frost; **severities** Härten *pl*

Seville [sə'vɪl] N Sevilla *nt*

Seville orange N Bitterorange *f*, Pomeranze *f*

sew [səʊ] *pret* sewed, *ptp* sewn VT nähen; **to ~ sth on/under/together** etw an-/auf-/zusammennähen VI nähen

▶ **sew up** VT *sep* **a** (*lit*) nähen (*also Med*); *opening* zunähen; **to sew sth up in sth** etw in etw (*acc*) einnähen **b** (*fig*) unter Dach und Fach bringen; **it's all sewn up** es ist unter Dach und Fach; **we've got the game all sewn up** das Spiel ist gelaufen (*inf*)

sewage ['sjuːɪdʒ] N Abwasser *nt*; **~ sludge** Klärschlamm *m*

sewage: sewage disposal N Abwasserbeseitigung *f*; **sewage farm** N Rieselfeld *nt*; **sewage works** N *sing or pl* Kläranlage *f*

sewer[1] ['səʊə'] N Näher(in) *m(f)*

sewer[2] ['sjʊə'] N (= *pipe*) Abwasserleitung *f or* -rohr *nt*; (= *main sewer*) Abwasserkanal *m*; (*fig, = smelly place*) Kloake *f*; (= *evil place*) Sündenpfuhl *m*, Kloake *f* (*liter*); **~ gas** Faulschlammgas *nt*; **~ rat** Wanderratte *f*; **he has a mind like a ~** (*inf*) er hat eine schmutzige *or* dreckige (*inf*) Fantasie *or* Phantasie

sewerage ['sjʊərɪdʒ] N Kanalisation *f*; (= *service*) Abwasserbeseitigung *f*; (= *sewage*) Abwässer *pl*

sewing ['səʊɪŋ] N (= *activity*) Nähen *nt*; (= *piece of work*) Näharbeit *f*

sewing: sewing basket N Nähkorb *m*; **sewing box** N Nähkästchen *nt*; **sewing machine** N Nähmaschine *f*

sewn [səʊn] *ptp* of **sew**

sex [seks] N **a** (*Biol*) Geschlecht *nt*; **what ~ is the baby?** welches Geschlecht hat das Baby? **b** (= *sexuality*) Sexualität *f*, Sex *m*; (= *sexual intercourse*) Sex *m* (*inf*), Geschlechtsverkehr *m* (*form*); **to teach pupils (about) ~** Schüler aufklären; **to have ~** (Geschlechts)verkehr haben ADJ *attr* Geschlechts-, Sexual-; **~ hygiene** Sexualhygiene *f*; **~ film/scandal** Sexfilm/-skandal *m* VT das Geschlecht (+*gen*) bestimmen

sexagenarian [ˌseksədʒɪ'neərɪən] ADJ sechzigjährig; **~ members of the club** Clubmitglieder, die in den Sechzigern sind N Sechzigjährige(r) *mf*; **to be a ~** in den Sechzigern sein

Sexagesima [ˌseksə'dʒesɪmə] N Sonntag *m* Sexagesima

sex: sex aid N sexuelles Hilfsmittel; **sex-and-shopping** ADJ **~ novel** (*Brit*) *Roman der Trivialliteratur, in dessen Mittelpunkt Sex und Luxusartikel stehen*; **sex appeal** N Sexappeal *m*; **sex change** N Geschlechtsumwandlung *f*; **to have a ~** sich einer Geschlechtsumwandlung unterziehen ATTR **~ operation** (Operation *f* zur) Geschlechtsumwandlung *f*; **sex crime** N Trieb- *or* Sexualverbrechen *nt*; **sex discrimination** N Diskriminierung *f* aufgrund *or* auf Grund des Geschlechts; **sex drive** N Geschlechts- *or* Sexualtrieb *m*

sexed [sekst] ADJ **to be highly ~** einen starken Geschlechtstrieb haben → **oversexed**, **undersexed**

sex: sex education N Sexualerziehung *f*; **sex god** N Sexgott *m*; **sex goddess** N Sexgöttin

f; **sex hormone** N Geschlechts- *or* Sexualhormon *nt*

sexily ['seksɪlɪ] ADV aufreizend, sexy (*inf*)

sex industry N Sexindustrie *f*

sexism ['seksɪzəm] N Sexismus *m*

sexist ['seksɪst] N Sexist(in) *m(f)* ADJ sexistisch

sex: sex killing N Sexualmord *m*; **sex kitten** N (*inf*) Sexkätzchen *nt* (*inf*), Sexmieze *f* (*inf*); **sexless** ADJ geschlechtslos; **sex life** N Geschlechtsleben *nt*; (*of people also*) Liebesleben *nt*; **sexlinked** ADJ geschlechtsgebunden; **sex maniac** N (= *criminal*) Triebverbrecher(in) *or* -täter(in) *m(f)*; **he/she is a ~** (*inf*) er/sie ist ganz verrückt nach *or* ganz wild auf Sex (*inf*); **you're a ~** (*inf*) du denkst aber auch nur an Sex; **sex manual** N (*inf*) **sex object** N Sex(u-al)objekt *nt*, Lustobjekt *nt*; **sex offender** N Sexualtäter(in) *m(f)*; **sex organ** N Geschlechts- *or* Sexualorgan *nt*; **sex partner** N Sexualpartner(in) *m(f)*

sexpert ['sekspɜːt] N (*hum*) Experte *m*/Expertin *f* in Sachen Sex (*inf*), Sexperte *m* (*hum*), Sexpertin *f* (*hum*)

sexploit ['seksplɔɪt] N (*hum*) Liebesabenteuer *nt*

sexploitation [ˌseksplɔɪ'teɪʃən] N Kommerzialisierung *f* des Sex

sex: sexpot N (*inf, = woman*) Sexbombe *f* (*inf*); **to be a real ~** unheimlich sexy sein (*inf*); **sex scene** N (*Film, Theat*) Sexszene *f*; **sex shop** N Sexshop *m*, Sexladen *m*; **sex show** N Sexshow *f*; **sex-starved** ADJ (*inf*) sexhungrig; **sex symbol** N Sexsymbol *nt*

sextant ['sekstənt] N Sextant *m*

sextet(te) [seks'tet] N Sextett *nt*

sex therapy N Sexualtherapie *f*

sex therapist N Sexualtherapeut(in) *m(f)*

sextillion [sek'stɪljən] N (*Brit*) Sextillion *f*; (*US*) Trilliarde *f*

sexton ['sekstən] N Küster *m*

sex tourism N Sextourismus *m*

sextuplet [seks'tjuːplɪt] N (= *baby*) Sechsling *m*; (*Mus*) Sextole *f*

sexual ['seksjʊəl] ADJ **a** *performance, preference, violence* sexuell; **~ crime** Sexualdelikt *nt*, Sexualverbrechen *nt*; **his ~ exploits** seine Liebesabenteuer *pl*; **his/her ~ politics** seine/ihre Haltung zu Fragen der Sexualität; **~ services** sexuelle Dienste *pl* **b** (*Physiol*) Sexual-; **~ characteristics** Geschlechtsmerkmale *pl*; **~ cycle** Sexualzyklus *m*; **~ maturity** Geschlechtsreife *f*

sexual: sexual abuse N sexueller Missbrauch; **sexual equality** N Gleichberechtigung *f* (der Geschlechter); **sexual harassment** N sexuelle Belästigung; **sexual health** N Sexualhygiene *f*; **sexual intercourse** N Geschlechtsverkehr *m*

sexuality [ˌseksjʊ'ælɪtɪ] N Sexualität *f*

sexually ['seksjʊəlɪ] ADV **a** sexuell; **~ mature** geschlechtsreif; **~ transmitted diseases** durch Geschlechtsverkehr übertragene Krankheiten; **to be ~ harassed** sexuell belästigt werden; **to be ~ attracted to sb** sich zu jdm sexuell hingezogen fühlen **b** (= *according to gender*) **~ segregated groups** nach Geschlechtern getrennte Gruppen

sexual: sexual offence, (*US*) **sexual offense** N Sexualstraftat *f*; **sexual organ** N Geschlechts- *or* Sexualorgan *nt*; **sexual orientation** N sexuelle Orientierung; **sexual partner** N Sexual- *or* Intimpartner(in) *m(f)*; **sexual reproduction** N geschlechtliche Vermehrung; **sexual stereotyping** N traditionelle *or* klischeehafte Zuordnung der Geschlechterrollen

sex worker N (*euph*) Prostituierte *f*

sexy ['seksɪ] ADJ (+*er*) **a** (*inf*) *person, clothes* sexy *inv usu pred* (*inf*); *smile, pose also* aufreizend; *joke, film* erotisch; **the sexiest girl in the class** das Mädchen in der Klasse, das am meisten Sexappeal hat **b** (*inf, = exciting*) geil (*sl*)

Seychelles [seɪ'ʃelz] PL Seychellen *pl*

SF **a** *abbr of* **science fiction** **b** (*Irl Pol*) *abbr of* **Sinn Féin**

SFO (*Brit*) *abbr of* **Serious Fraud Office**

s.g. *abbr of* **specific gravity**

sgraffito [sgræ'fiːtəʊ] N Sgraffito *nt*

sgt *abbr of* **sergeant**

sh [ʃ] INTERJ sch(t)

shabbily ['ʃæbɪlɪ] ADV (*lit, fig*) schäbig

shabbiness ['ʃæbɪnɪs] N Schäbigkeit *f*

shabby ['ʃæbɪ] ADJ (+*er*) (*lit, fig*) schäbig; **they were ~-genteel** sie gehörten zur verarmten Oberschicht; **that was a ~ trick!** das war ein schäbiger *or* mieser Trick!

shack [ʃæk] N Hütte *f*, Schuppen *m* VI (*inf*) **to ~ up with sb** mit jdm zusammenziehen; **to ~ up together** zusammenziehen

shackle ['ʃækl] N **a** *usu pl* Kette *f*, Fessel *f* (*also fig*) **b** (*Tech*) Schäkel *m* VT in Ketten legen; **they were ~d together/to the wall** sie waren aneinander gekettet/an die Wand (an)gekettet; **to ~ sb with sth** (*fig*) jdn mit etw belasten; **to be ~d by sth** (*fig*) an etw (*acc*) gebunden sein; **to be ~d with sth** die Belastung einer Sache (*gen*) haben

shad [ʃæd] N Alse *f*

shade [ʃeɪd] N **a** Schatten *m*; **30° in the ~** 30 Grad im Schatten; **to give** *or* **provide ~** Schatten spenden; **the ~s of night** (*liter*) der Schatten der Nacht (*liter*); **to put sb/sth in the ~** (*fig*) jdn/etw in den Schatten stellen

b (= *lampshade*) (Lampen)schirm *m*; (= *eye shade*) Schild *nt*, Schirm *m*; (*esp US, = blind*) Jalousie *f*; (= *roller blind*) Springrollo *nt*; (*outside house*) Markise *f*; **~s** (*inf*: = *sunglasses*) Sonnenbrille *f*

c (*of colour*) (Farb)ton *m*; (*fig, of opinion*) Schattierung *f*; (*of meaning*) Nuance *f*; **turquoise is a ~ of blue** Türkis ist ein blauer Farbton; **a brighter ~ of red** ein leuchtenderer Rotton; **a new ~ of lipstick** ein neuer Farbton für Lippenstift; **~-card** Farb(en)probe *f*; **of all ~s and hues** (*lit*) in den verschiedensten Farben, in allen Schattierungen; (*fig*) aller Schattierungen

d (= *small quantity*) Spur *f*; **it's a ~ long/too long** es ist etwas lang/etwas *or* eine Spur zu lang

e (*liter, = ghost*) Schatten *m*; **the ~s** (*Myth*) die Bewohner *pl* des Schattenreiches; (= *Hades*) das Reich der Schatten, das Schattenreich; **~s of Professor Jones!** (*inf*) wie mich das an Professor Jones erinnert!

VT **a** (= *cast shadow on*) Schatten werfen auf (+*acc*), beschatten (*geh*); (= *protect from light, sun*) abschirmen; *lamp, window* abdunkeln; **that part is ~d by a tree** der Teil liegt im Schatten eines Baumes; **to be ~d from the sun** im Schatten liegen *or* sein; (*protected against sun*) vor der Sonne geschützt sein; **he ~d his eyes with his hand** er hielt die Hand vor die Augen(, um nicht geblendet zu werden); **to ~ the truth** die Wahrheit beschönigen

b (= *darken with lines*) schraffieren; (*for artistic effect*) schattieren; **to ~ sth in** etw ausschraffieren; (= *colour in*) etw ausmalen; **to ~ one colour** (*Brit*) *or* **color** (*US*) **into another** eine Farbe langsam in die andere übergehen lassen

c (*inf*) (= *narrowly win*) *game* knapp gewinnen; (= *narrowly defeat*) *opponent* knapp besiegen

VI (*lit, fig*) übergehen; **to ~ off** allmählich blasser werden; **blue that ~s (off) into black** Blau, das in Schwarz übergeht

shadeless ['ʃeɪdlɪs] ADJ schattenlos

shadiness ['ʃeɪdɪnɪs] N Schattigkeit *f*; (*fig*) Zwielichtigkeit *f*

shading ['ʃeɪdɪŋ] N (= *shaded area*) Schraffierung *f*, Schraffur *f*; (*Art*) Schattierung *f*

shadow ['ʃædəʊ] N **a** (*lit, fig*) Schatten *m* (*also Med, Art*); (= *growth of beard*) Anflug *m* von Bartstoppeln; (*fig, = threat*) (Be)drohung *f*; **in the ~** im Schatten; **in the ~s** im Dunkel; **the valley of the ~ of death** das finstere Tal des Todes; **sb lives under the ~ of sth** etw liegt *or* lastet wie ein Schatten auf jdm; **to be in sb's ~** (*fig*) in jds Schatten (*dat*) stehen; **to be afraid**

of one's own ~ (fig) sich vor seinem eigenen Schatten fürchten; **to wear oneself to a ~** sich aufreiben, sich zugrunde or zu Grunde richten; **to be just a ~ of one's former self** nur noch ein Schatten seiner selbst sein; **to chase ~s** (fig) einem Phantom or Schatten nachjagen

b (= trace) Spur f; **a ~ of hope** ein Hoffnungsschimmer m; **without a ~ of a doubt** ohne den geringsten Zweifel

c (= person following sb) Schatten m; **to put a ~ on sb** jdn beschatten lassen (inf)

ATTR (Brit, Pol) Schatten-; **~ government** Schattenregierung f; **~ Foreign Secretary** Schattenaußenminister(in) m(f), Außenminister(in) m(f) des Schattenkabinetts

VT **a** (= darken) Schatten werfen auf (+acc); (fig) überschatten; **the room is ~ed by a high wall** das Zimmer liegt im Schatten einer hohen Mauer

b (= follow) beschatten (inf)

shadow: **shadow-boxing** N (lit, fig) Schattenboxen nt; **shadow cabinet** N (Brit Pol) Schattenkabinett nt; **shadow minister** N (Brit, Pol) Schattenminister(in) m(f); **shadow printing** N (Comput) Schattendruck m

---

SHADOW CABINET

Im politischen Leben Großbritanniens spielt das **Shadow Cabinet**, das Schattenkabinett der stärksten Oppositionspartei, eine wichtige Rolle. Jeder Regierungsposten hat seine Entsprechung im Schattenkabinett, so gibt es z. B. einen Schatten-Innenminister, **Shadow Home Secretary**, und einen Schatten-Finanzminister, **Shadow Chancellor**. Die Schattenminister haben die Aufgabe, die Regierungspolitik in ihren jeweiligen Verantwortungsbereichen infrage zu stellen und die Politik ihrer Partei öffentlich zu vertreten → CABINET

---

shadowy ['ʃædəʊɪ] ADJ schattig; (= blurred) outline, form schattenhaft, verschwommen; (= vague) thought, fear unbestimmt, vage; **a ~ figure** (lit) eine schemenhafte Gestalt; (fig) eine undurchsichtige Gestalt; **the ~ world of espionage** die dunkle Welt der Spionage; **a ~ existence** ein undurchsichtiges Dasein

shady ['ʃeɪdɪ] ADJ (+er) **a** place schattig; tree, hat Schatten spendend **b** (inf, = of dubious honesty) zwielichtig, zweifelhaft; **he has a ~ past** er hat eine dunkle Vergangenheit; **to be on the ~ side of the law** dunkle Geschäfte treiben; **on the ~ side of forty** (US, inf) vierzig vorbei (inf); **there's something ~ about it** da ist etwas faul dran (inf)

shaft [ʃɑːft] **N** **a** Schaft m; (of tool, golf club etc) Stiel m; (of cart, carriage) Deichsel f; (of light) Strahl m; (Mech) Welle f; (liter, = arrow) Pfeil m; (= spear) Speer m; (fig, = remark) Spitze f; **~s of wit** geistreiche Spitzen pl; **the ~s of Cupid** Amors Pfeile pl **b** (of lift, mine etc) Schacht m **VT** (sl) **a** (= have sex with) stoßen (vulg) **b** (= trick, cheat) aufs Kreuz legen (inf)

shag¹ [ʃæg] **N** **a** (= tobacco) Shag m **b** (of carpet etc) Flor m; **~~pile carpet** langfloriger Teppich

shag² N (Orn) Krähenscharbe f

shag³ (Brit sl) **N** **a** (= intercourse, partner) Nummer f (inf); **to have a ~** eine Nummer machen (inf) **VT** **a** (= have sex) bumsen (inf) **b** **to be ~ged out** voll am Ende sein (sl) **VI** bumsen (inf)

shaggy ['ʃægɪ] ADJ (+er) (= long-haired) zottig; (= unkempt) zottelig; **~ carpet** zotteliger Teppich

shaggy dog story N breit gewalzte Geschichte mit schwacher Pointe

shagreen [ʃæ'griːn] N Chagrin(leder) nt

Shah [ʃɑː] N Schah m

shake [ʃeɪk] vb: pret **shook**, ptp **shaken** **N** **a** (= act of shaking) Schütteln nt; **to give a rug a ~** einen Läufer ausschütteln; **give the paint a (good) ~** die Farbe (gut) durchschütteln; **to give sb/oneself a good ~** jdn/sich kräftig schütteln; **with a ~ of her head** mit einem Kopfschütteln; **with a ~ in his voice** mit zittriger Stimme

b (= milkshake) Milchshake m **c** (inf, = moment) Minütchen nt (inf); **in two ~s (of a lamb's tail)** in zwei Sekunden

d **to be no great ~s** (inf) nicht umwerfend sein (at in +dat)

e **the ~s** pl (inf) der Tatterich (inf); (esp with fear) das Zittern; **he's got the ~s** er hat einen Tatterich (inf); (due to alcoholism also) ihm zittern die Hände; (esp with fear) er hat das große Zittern (inf); (esp with cold, emotion) er zittert am ganzen Körper

VT **a** person, head, object schütteln; building erschüttern; cocktail durchschütteln; **"shake well before using"** „vor Gebrauch gut schütteln"; **to be ~n to pieces** total durchgeschüttelt werden; **she shook the door handle which seemed to have stuck** sie rüttelte an der Türklinke, die zu klemmen schien; **to ~ pepper on a steak** Pfeffer auf ein Steak streuen; **to ~ one's fist at sb** jdm mit der Faust drohen; **to ~ oneself/itself free** sich losmachen; **to ~ hands** sich (dat) die Hand geben; (for longer time, in congratulations etc) sich (dat) die Hand schütteln; **to ~ hands with sb** jdm die Hand geben/schütteln; **I'd like to ~ him by the hand** ihm würde ich gern die Hand schütteln or drücken; **English people don't often ~ hands** Engländer geben sich (dat) selten die Hand; **~ hands** (to dog) (gib) Pfötchen; (to child) gib mal die Hand; **to ~ a leg** (inf, = hurry) Dampf machen (inf); (dated: = dance) das Tanzbein schwingen (dated); **he has more medals than you can ~ a stick at** (inf) er hat jede Menge Medaillen (inf)

b (= weaken) faith, foundation of society erschüttern; evidence, reputation, courage, resolve ins Wanken bringen; **to ~ the foundations of sth** die Grundfesten einer Sache (gen) erschüttern; **society was ~n to its very core** die Gesellschaft wurde bis in ihre Grundfesten erschüttert

c (= shock, amaze) erschüttern; **to ~ the world** die Welt erschüttern; **that shook him!** da war er platt (inf); **it shook me rigid** (inf) da war ich schwer geschockt (inf); **it was a nasty accident, he's still rather badly ~n** es war ein schlimmer Unfall, der Schreck sitzt ihm noch in den Knochen; **she was badly ~n by the news** die Nachricht hatte sie sehr mitgenommen or erschüttert

d (inf) = shake off

VI wackeln, (voice) zittern; (earth, voice) beben; **the whole boat shook as the waves struck it** das ganze Boot wurde vom Aufprall der Wellen erschüttert; **the trees shook in the wind** die Bäume schwankten im Wind; **to ~ like a leaf** zittern wie Espenlaub; **to ~ with fear/cold** vor Angst/Kälte zittern; **he was shaking all over** er zitterte am ganzen Körper; **to ~ with laughter** sich vor Lachen schütteln; **to ~ in one's shoes** (inf) das große Zittern kriegen (inf); **~!** (inf) ~ **on it!** (inf) Hand drauf!; **~!** (= me too) da können wir uns ja die Hand reichen!; **they shook on the deal** sie bekräftigten das Geschäft mit Handschlag

▶**shake down** **VT** sep **a** fruit herunterschütteln **b** (US, inf, = extort money from) ausnehmen (inf); **to shake sb down for 500 dollars** jdn um 500 Dollar erleichtern (inf) **c** (US, inf, = search) absuchen, durchsuchen (for nach) **VI** (inf) **a** (= sleep) kampieren, sein Lager aufschlagen **b** (= settle, people) sich eingewöhnen; (machinery) sich einlaufen; (situation) sich einspielen

▶**shake off** VT sep dust, snow, pursuer abschütteln; visitor, cold, image, illness, feeling loswerden; **to shake the dust (of a place) off one's feet** (fig) den Staub (eines Ortes) von seinen Schuhen schütteln

▶**shake out** **VT** sep **a** (lit) herausschütteln; tablecloth, rug ausschütteln; **she took off her hat and shook out her long hair** sie nahm den Hut ab und schüttelte sich (dat) die langen Haare zurecht **b** (fig, out of complacency etc) aufrütteln (of aus) **VI** (Mil, = spread out) ausschwärmen

▶**shake up** **VT** sep **a** bottle, liquid schütteln **b** (= upset) erschüttern; **he was badly shaken up by the accident** der Unfall hat ihm einen schweren Schock versetzt; **she's still a bit**

shaken up sie ist immer noch ziemlich mitgenommen **c** management, recruits auf Zack bringen (inf); ideas revidieren; system umkrempeln (inf); country, industry wachrütteln; **your ideas could do with a bit of shaking up** deine Ansichten müssten an und für sich mal wieder revidiert werden; **to shake things up** die Dinge in Bewegung bringen

shakedown ['ʃeɪkdaʊn] N (= bed) Lager nt, Notbett nt; (US inf) (= extortion) Gaunerei f; (= search) Razzia f (inf), Durchsuchung f; **he slept on a ~ in the living room** er hatte sein Lager im Wohnzimmer aufgeschlagen, er kampierte im Wohnzimmer; **to give a room a ~** ein Zimmer nt auf den Kopf stellen; **~ cruise** Probefahrt f

shaken ['ʃeɪkən] ptp of shake

shake-out ['ʃeɪkaʊt] N (inf) Gesundschrumpfung f (inf)

shaker ['ʃeɪkə'] N (= cocktail shaker) Mixbecher m, Shaker m; (= flour/salt shaker) Mehl-/Salzstreuer m

Shakespearean, **Shakespearian** [ʃeɪk'spɪərɪən] ADJ shakespearesch, shakespearisch; **~ actor** Shakespeare-Schauspieler m; **a tragedy of ~ proportions** eine Tragödie, die eines Shakespeare würdig ist or wäre **N** Shakespeareforscher(in) m(f)

shake-up ['ʃeɪkʌp] N (inf, = reorganization) Umbesetzung f; **to give a department etc a good ~** (= revitalization) eine Abteilung etc auf Zack bringen (inf); (= reorganization) eine Abteilung etc umbesetzen or umorganisieren

shakily ['ʃeɪkɪlɪ] ADV wackelig; talk, say mit zittriger Stimme; walk mit wackeligen Schritten; write, pour etc zitterig

shakiness ['ʃeɪkɪnɪs] N (of chair) Wackeligkeit f; (of evidence) Fragwürdigkeit f, Unsicherheit f; (of voice, hands, writing) Zitterigkeit f; (of knowledge) Unsicherheit f; (of sb's French) Holprigkeit f; **the ~ of their position** ihre wackelige Position

shaking ['ʃeɪkɪŋ] N Zittern nt; **to give sb/sth a good ~** jdn/etw kräftig schütteln; (fig) jdn kräftig treten; **a nasty experience, it gave me a ~** ein unangenehmes Erlebnis, das sitzt mir immer noch in den Knochen

shako ['ʃækəʊ] N Tschako m

shaky ['ʃeɪkɪ] ADJ (+er) chair, position wackelig; evidence fragwürdig, unsicher; voice, hands, writing zitt(e)rig; knowledge unsicher, wackelig; **in rather ~ French** in ziemlich holprigem Französisch; **to be ~ on one's legs** wackelig auf den Beinen sein; **to feel ~** (physically) sich ganz schwach fühlen; (from nerves) sich zitt(e)rig fühlen; **I still feel a bit ~ about this theory** diese Theorie sitzt bei mir noch nicht; **to get off to a ~ start** (fig) einen unsicheren or holprigen Anfang nehmen; **to be on ~ ground** (fig) sich auf schwankendem or unsicherem Boden bewegen

shale [ʃeɪl] N Schiefer m

shale oil N Schieferöl nt

shall [ʃæl] ⊕ 3.3 pret **should** MODAL AUX VB **a** (future) I/we ~ or I'll/we'll go to France this year ich werde/wir werden dieses Jahr nach Frankreich fahren, ich fahre/wir fahren dieses Jahr nach Frankreich; **~ do** (inf) wird gemacht (inf); **no, I ~ not** or **I shan't** nein, das werde ich nicht tun or das tue ich nicht; **yes, I ~** jawohl, das werde ich tun or das tue ich!

b (determination, obligation) **you ~ pay for this!** dafür sollst or wirst du büßen!; **but I say you ~ do it!** aber ich sage dir, du wirst das machen!; **the directors ~ not be disturbed** (form) die Direktoren dürfen nicht gestört werden; **the court ~ rise** das Gericht muss sich erheben; (command) erheben Sie sich!; **thou shalt not kill** (Bibl) du sollst nicht töten; **the manufacturer ~ deliver ...** (in contracts etc) der Hersteller liefert ...; **I want to go too – and so you ~** ich will auch mitkommen – aber gewiss doch or (in fairy stories) es sei!

c (in questions, suggestions) **what ~ we do?** was sollen wir machen?, was machen wir?; **let's go**

in, ~ we? komm, gehen wir hinein!; **~ I go now?** soll ich jetzt gehen?; **I'll buy 3, ~ I?** soll ich 3 kaufen?, ich kaufe 3, oder?

shallot [ʃəˈlɒt] N Schalotte f

shallow [ˈʃæləʊ] ADJ flach; *water also* seicht; *soil* dünn; (*Physiol*) *breathing* flach; (*fig*) oberflächlich; *talk, person, novel* seicht, oberflächlich; **in the ~ end of the pool** am flachen *or* niedrigen Ende des Beckens; **his body was buried in a ~ grave** seine Leiche wurde verscharrt N **shallows** PL seichte *or* flache Stelle (im Wasser), Untiefe f

shallowly [ˈʃæləʊlɪ] ADV *breathe* flach

shallowness [ˈʃæləʊnɪs] N Flachheit f; (*of water also*) Seichtheit f; (*of soil*) Dünne f; (*Physiol: of breathing*) Schwäche f; (*fig, of talk, person, novel*) Seichtheit f, Oberflächlichkeit f

shalom [ʃæˈlɒm] INTERJ schalom!

shalt [ʃælt] (*obs*) 2nd pers sing of **shall**

sham [ʃæm] N **a** (= *pretence*) Heuchelei f; **he's not really sorry, it's all a big ~** es tut ihm nicht wirklich Leid, er heuchelt nur *or* das ist geheuchelt; **their marriage had become a ~** ihre Ehe war zur Farce geworden *or* bestand nur noch zum Schein; **his life seemed a ~** sein Leben erschien ihm als Lug und Trug; **this diamond is a ~** dieser Diamant ist nicht echt

b (= *person*) Scharlatan m; **you don't really feel anything, you big ~!** du empfindest überhaupt nichts, du Heuchler!

ADJ *diamonds, oak etc* unecht, imitiert; *politeness etc* vorgetäuscht, geheuchelt; *person* betrügerisch; **a ~ marriage** eine Scheinehe; **a ~ deal** ein Scheingeschäft nt; **a ~ battle** ein Scheingefecht nt

VT vortäuschen, vorgeben; *illness also* simulieren; *emotions, sympathy* heucheln

VI so tun; (*esp with illness*) simulieren; (*with feelings*) heucheln; **he's just ~ming** er tut nur so

shamanism [ˈʃæmənɪzəm] N Schamanismus m

shamble [ˈʃæmbl] VI trotten; (*people also*) latschen (*inf*); **every morning he ~s in half an hour late** er kommt jeden Morgen eine halbe Stunde zu spät angelatscht (*inf*)

shambles [ˈʃæmblz] N *sing* heilloses Durcheinander; (*esp of room etc*) Tohuwabohu nt; **the room was a ~** im Zimmer herrschte das reinste Tohuwabohu *or* ein heilloses Durcheinander; **the economy/country is in a ~** die Wirtschaft/das Land befindet sich in einem Chaos; **they left the house in a ~** sie hinterließen das Haus wie ein Schlachtfeld; **the game was a ~** das Spiel war das reinste Kuddelmuddel (*inf*); **he made a ~ of that job** da hat er vielleicht einen Mist gebaut! (*inf*)

shambolic [ʃæmˈbɒlɪk] ADJ (*inf*) chaotisch (*inf*)

shame [ʃeɪm] ✪ 14, 18.2 N **a** (= *feeling of shame*) Scham f; (= *cause of shame*) Schande f; **to feel ~ at sth** sich für etw schämen; **he hung his head in ~** er senkte beschämt den Kopf; (*fig*) er schämte sich; **to bring ~ upon sb/oneself** jdm/sich Schande machen; **he is without ~** er hat keinerlei Schamgefühl, ihm fehlt jegliches Schamgefühl; **she is beyond all (sense of) ~** sie hat jegliches Schamgefühl verloren; **she has no ~, dancing around like that** dass sie sich nicht schämt so herumzutanzen; **have you no ~?** schämst du dich (gar) nicht?; **to put sb/sth to ~** (*lit*) jdm/etw Schande machen; (*fig*) jdn/etw in den Schatten stellen; **by working so hard he puts us to ~** er arbeitet so schwer, dass er uns alle beschämt; **to my (eternal) ~** zu meiner (ewigen) Schande; **I'll never forget the ~ of it** ich werde nie vergessen, wie ich mich schämte; **the ~ of it all** die Schande *or* Schmach; **the ~ of it!** was für eine Schande!, diese Schande!; **the street is the ~ of the town** die Straße ist der Schandfleck *or* die Schande dieser Stadt; **for ~!** schäm dich!/schämt euch!; **she didn't! for ~!** nein! sie sollte sich schämen!; **~ on you!** du solltest dich/ihr solltet euch schämen!

b (= *pity*) **it's a ~ you couldn't come** schade, dass du nicht kommen konntest; **it's a (great)**

~ we have to leave so early es ist (so) schade *or* ein Jammer, dass wir schon so früh gehen müssen; **what a ~!** (das ist aber) schade!, wie schade!; **what a ~ he ...** schade, dass er ...; **nice legs, ~ about the face** (*inf*) hübsche Beine, aber über den Rest schweigen wir lieber ⟶ **crying**

VT Schande machen (+*dat*); (*fig, by excelling*) in den Schatten stellen; **he ~d us by working so hard** er hat uns alle durch sein hartes Arbeiten beschämt; **by giving so much he ~d me into making a bigger contribution** dadurch, dass er so viel gab, fühlte ich mich moralisch gezwungen, mehr zu spenden; **see if you can ~ him into changing his mind** appelliere an sein besseres Ich, dann überlegt er es sich vielleicht anders

shamefaced [ˈʃeɪmˈfeɪst] ADJ , **shamefacedly** [ˈʃeɪmˈfeɪsɪdlɪ] ADV betreten

shamefacedness [ˈʃeɪmˈfeɪstnɪs] N Betretenheit f

shameful [ˈʃeɪmfʊl] ADJ schändlich; *experience, secret* peinlich; **another ~ day for the pound** noch ein schmachvoller Tag für das Pfund Sterling; **how ~!** was für eine Schande!; **what ~ prices/behaviour!** diese Preise sind/dieses Benehmen ist eine Schande; **there is nothing ~ about it** das ist doch keine Schande

shamefully [ˈʃeɪmfəlɪ] ADV schändlich; **he is ~ ignorant** es ist eine Schande, wie wenig er weiß

shamefulness [ˈʃeɪmfʊlnɪs] N Ungeheuerlichkeit f

shameless [ˈʃeɪmlɪs] ADJ schamlos; **are you completely ~?** hast du gar kein Schamgefühl?; **he was quite ~ about it** er schämte sich überhaupt nicht; **he was quite ~ about lying to his parents** er belog seine Eltern schamlos

shamelessly [ˈʃeɪmlɪslɪ] ADV schamlos; **a ~ sentimental film** ein unverhohlen sentimentaler Film

shamelessness [ˈʃeɪmlɪsnɪs] N Schamlosigkeit f

shaming [ˈʃeɪmɪŋ] ADJ beschämend

shammer [ˈʃæmə] N Schwindler(in) m(f), Heuchler(in) m(f); (*of illness*) Simulant(in) m(f)

shammy (leather) [ˈʃæmɪ(ˈleðə)] N Ledertuch nt, Fensterleder nt

shampoo [ʃæmˈpuː] N **a** (= *liquid*) Shampoo nt, Schampon nt; (*for hair also*) Haarwaschmittel nt; (= *act of washing*) Reinigung f; (*of hair*) Waschen nt; **to give the carpet a ~** den Teppich reinigen *or* schamponieren; **~ and set** Waschen und Legen; **to have a ~ and set** sich (*dat*) die Haare waschen und legen lassen VT *person* die Haare waschen (+*dat*); *hair* waschen; *dog* das Fell waschen (+*dat*); *carpet, upholstery* reinigen, schamponieren; **to have one's hair ~ed** sich (*dat*) die Haare waschen lassen

shamrock [ˈʃæmrɒk] N Klee m; (= *leaf*) Kleeblatt nt

shandy [ˈʃændɪ] N (*Brit*) Bier nt mit Limonade; **lemonade ~** Alsterwasser nt (*N Ger*), Radlermaß nt (*S Ger*)

shanghai [ʃæŋˈhaɪ] VT (*Naut*) schanghaien; **to ~ sb into doing sth** (*fig inf*) jdn zwingen, etw zu tun

shank [ʃæŋk] N **a** (= *part of leg, of person*) Unterschenkel m; (*of horse*) Unterarm m; (*of beef*) Hachse f; **~s** (*inf, = legs*) Hachsen pl (*inf*); **(to go) on Shanks' pony** auf Schusters Rappen (reiten) **b** (*of anchor, key etc*) Schaft m; (*of spoon*) Stiel m

shan't [ʃɑːnt] *contr of* **shall not ~!** (*inf*) will nicht! (*inf*)

shantung [ʃænˈtʌŋ] N Schantungseide f

shanty¹ [ˈʃæntɪ] N (= *hut*) Baracke f, Hütte f

shanty² N (*Mus*) Seemannslied nt, Shanty nt

shantytown [ˈʃæntɪˌtaʊn] N Slum(vor)stadt f, Bidonville f

SHAPE [ʃeɪp] N *abbr of* **Supreme Headquarters Allied Powers Europe** Hauptquartier der alliierten Streitkräfte in Europa während des 2. Weltkriegs

shape [ʃeɪp] N **a** (= *geometrical form, outline*) Form f; **what ~ is it?** welche Form hat es?; **it's rectangular etc in ~** es ist rechteckig *etc*; **that dress hasn't much/has lost its ~** das Kleid hat keine richtige Form/hat keine Form verloren; **she's the right ~ for a model** sie hat die richtige Figur für ein Mannequin; **to hammer metal into ~** Metall zurechthämmern *or* -schlagen; **to knock sth out of ~** etw zerbeulen; **to take ~** (*lit*) Form bekommen; (*fig*) Gestalt *or* Konturen annehmen; **a flowerbed in the ~ of a circle** ein Blumenbeet in der Form eines Kreises; **government action took the ~ of a ban** die Regierung griff mit einem Verbot ein; **help in the ~ of a donation** Hilfe in Form einer Spende; **of all ~s and sizes, of every ~ and size** aller Art, jeder Art, in allen Variationen; **I don't accept gifts in any ~ or form** ich nehme überhaupt keine Geschenke an; **we do not know the ~ of things to come** wir wissen nicht, wie sich die Zukunft gestalten wird; **this may be the ~ of things to come** so könnte das vielleicht in Zukunft sein

b (= *unidentified figure*) Gestalt f; (= *object*) Form f

c (= *guise*) Gestalt f; **in human ~** in Menschengestalt, in menschlicher Gestalt

d (*fig, = order, condition*) **to be in good/bad ~** (*sportsman*) in Form/nicht in Form sein; (*mentally, healthwise*) in guter/schlechter Verfassung sein, gut/schlecht drauf sein (*inf*); (*things*) in gutem/schlechtem Zustand sein; (*business*) gut/schlecht in Schuss sein (*inf*), in gutem/schlechtem Zustand sein; **what sort of ~ is your boxer in?** wie fit ist Ihr Boxer?; **to be out of ~** (*physically*) nicht in Form sein; **what sort of ~ was the business in?** in welchem Zustand war das Unternehmen?; **to get sb/a business into ~** jdn/ein Geschäft *or* Unternehmen auf Vordermann bringen (*inf*); **to get a house into ~** ein Haus in Ordnung bringen; **to get one's affairs into ~** seine Angelegenheiten ordnen

e (= *mould, for hats*) Hutform f; (*for dressmaking*) Schneiderpuppe f; (*Cook*) Form f; (*for cutting*) Ausstecher m

VT (*lit*) *stone, wood etc* bearbeiten; *clay etc* formen (*into* zu); (*fig*) *character, ideas* formen, prägen; *future, development, market, one's life* gestalten; **he ~d the wood/stone into the desired form** er verlieh dem Holz/Stein die gewünschte Form; **the factors which ~ one's life** die Faktoren, die das Leben prägen *or* bestimmen; **those who ~ the course of history** die(jenigen), die den Lauf der Geschichte bestimmen; **those who have helped ~ our society** die(jenigen), die unsere Gesellschaft mitgeformt haben; **we must ~ our strategy according to our funds** wir müssen unsere Strategie nach den zur Verfügung stehenden Mitteln ausrichten

VI sich entwickeln

▶ **shape up** VI to shape up well sich gut entwickeln, viel versprechend sein; **he is shaping up nicely as a goalkeeper** er ist ein viel versprechender Torwart; **things are shaping up well** es sieht sehr gut aus

shaped [ʃeɪpt] ADJ geformt; **an oddly ~ hat** ein Hut mit einer komischen Form; **~ like a ...** in der Form einer/eines ...

-shaped [-ʃeɪpt] ADJ *suf* -förmig; **egg-/pear-shaped** ei-/birnenförmig

shapeless [ˈʃeɪplɪs] ADJ formlos; (= *ugly*) unförmig

shapelessly [ˈʃeɪplɪslɪ] ADV unförmig

shapelessness [ˈʃeɪplɪsnɪs] N Formlosigkeit f; (= *ugliness*) Unförmigkeit f

shapeliness [ˈʃeɪplɪnɪs] N (*of figure*) Wohlproportioniertheit f; (*of legs, bust*) Wohlgeformtheit f

shapely [ˈʃeɪplɪ] ADJ (+*er*) *figure, woman* wohlproportioniert; *legs, bust* wohlgeformt; *car* formschön

shard [ʃɑːd] N (Ton)scherbe f

share¹ [ʃɛə] ✪ 12.1, 26.3 N **a** (= *portion*) Anteil m (*in or of an* +*dat*); **we want fair ~s for all** wir wollen, dass gerecht geteilt wird; **I want my**

fair ~ ich will meinen (An)teil, ich will, was mir zusteht; **he didn't get his fair ~** er ist zu kurz gekommen; **I've had more than my fair ~ of bad luck** ich habe mehr (als mein Teil an) Pech gehabt; **I'll give you a ~ in the profits** ich beteilige Sie am Gewinn; **in equal ~s** zu gleichen Teilen; **your ~ is £5** du bekommst £ 5, du musst £ 5 bezahlen; **how much is my ~?** wie groß ist mein Anteil?; **he came in for his full ~ of criticism** er hat sein Teil an Kritik abbekommen; **to fall to sb's ~** (liter) jdm zufallen (liter); **to go ~s** (inf) teilen; **to bear one's ~ of the cost** seinen Anteil an den Kosten tragen; **to take one's ~ of the proceeds** sich (dat) seinen Anteil am Gewinn nehmen; **to take one's ~ of the blame** sich mitschuldig erklären; **to pay one's ~** seinen (An)teil bezahlen; **to have a ~ in sth** an etw (dat) beteiligt sein; **I had no ~ in that** damit hatte ich nichts zu tun

b (Fin, general) (Geschäfts)anteil m; (in a public limited company) Aktie f; **to hold ~s in a company** (Geschäfts)anteile pl/Aktien pl eines Unternehmens besitzen

VT (= divide) teilen; (= have in common also) gemeinsam haben; **responsibility** gemeinsam tragen; **we ~ the same birthday** wir haben am gleichen Tag Geburtstag; **they ~ a room** sie teilen ein Zimmer, sie haben ein gemeinsames Zimmer; **I do not ~ that view** diese Ansicht teile ich nicht

VI a teilen; **there was only one room free so we had to ~** es gab nur noch ein freies Zimmer, also mussten wir es uns teilen; **children have to learn to ~** Kinder müssen lernen, mit anderen zu teilen; **to ~ and ~ alike** (brüderlich) mit (den) anderen teilen

b **to ~ in sth** sich an etw (dat) beteiligen; in **profit** an etw (dat) beteiligt werden; in **enthusiasm** etw teilen; in **success, sorrow** an etw (dat) Anteil nehmen

▶ **share out** VT sep verteilen

share² N (Agr) (Pflug)schar f

share: share broker N (esp Brit) Effekten- or Börsenmakler(in) m(f); **share capital** N Aktienkapital nt; **share certificate** N Aktienzertifikat nt; **sharecropper** N (US, Agr) (Farm-)pächter(in) m(f) (der/die Pacht in Form eines Ernteanteils zahlt); **shareholder** N Aktionär(in) m(f); **shareholding** N Beteiligung f; **share index** N Aktienindex m; **share issue** N (St Ex) Aktienemission f; **share option** N Aktienoption f; **share-out** N Verteilung f; (St Ex) (Dividenden)ausschüttung f

shareware [ɔɔ] N (Comput, Internet) Shareware f

share warrant N (Fin) (auf den Inhaber lautendes) Aktienzertifikat

shark [ʃɑːk] N **a** Hai(fisch) m **b** (inf, = swindler) Schlitzohr nt (inf); **loan/property ~** Kredit-/Grundstückshai m (inf)

sharp [ʃɑːp] ADJ (+er) **a** knife, blade etc scharf; needle, point etc spitz

b (= clear-cut, not blurred) outline, photo, contrast scharf; **to come into ~ focus** (fig inf) aufs Korn genommen werden

c (= observant, keen) eyes, wits, glance, mind scharf; nose gut, empfindlich; observation, remark scharfsinnig, schlau; (= intelligent) person schlau, gewieft (inf), auf Draht (inf); child schlau, aufgeweckt; **that was pretty ~ of you** das war ganz schön schlau or clever (inf) von dir; **keep a ~ watch for him/the train** pass gut auf, ob du ihn/den Zug siehst

d (= sudden, intense) whistle, cry durchdringend, schrill; drop in prices steil; frost, contrast scharf; shower, desire, pain heftig; hunger nagend (geh), groß; **after a short, ~ struggle** nach kurzem, heftigem Kampf; **be ~ about it!** (inf) (ein bisschen) dalli! (inf), zack, zack! (inf)

e (= acute) angle spitz; bend, turn by car scharf

f (pej, = cunning) person gerissen, raffiniert, clever (inf); trick etc raffiniert; **~ practice** unsaubere Geschäfte pl; **that was a pretty ~ move** das war ein raffinierter Schachzug

g (= harsh, fierce) tongue, retort, tone of voice

scharf; person schroff; temper hitzig

h (= acidic, pungent) taste scharf; apple sauer; wine herb, sauer (pej); (fig, = biting) air schneidend kalt; wind beißend

i (Mus) note (= too high) zu hoch; (= raised a semitone) (um einen Halbton) erhöht; **you played F natural instead of F ~** du hast f statt fis gespielt; **her voice goes ~ on the higher notes** sie singt die höheren Töne zu hoch

j (inf, = stylish) person, clothes toll (inf), todschick (inf); piece of driving clever (inf); **he's a ~ dresser** er zieht sich immer todschick an (inf)

ADV (+er) **a** (Mus) zu hoch

b (= punctually) pünktlich, genau; **at 5 o'clock ~** Punkt 5 Uhr

c look ~! dalli! (inf), zack, zack! (inf); **if you don't look ~** ... wenn du nicht schnell machst ...; **to pull up ~** plötzlich anhalten; **to turn ~ left** scharf nach links abbiegen

N (Mus) Kreuz nt

sharp-edged [ʃɑːpˈedʒd] ADJ knife, outline etc scharf; piece of furniture etc scharfkantig

sharpen [ˈʃɑːpən] VT **a** knife schleifen, schärfen, wetzen; razor wetzen; pencil spitzen; (fig) appetite anregen; wits schärfen; sensation erhöhen; **to ~ one's claws** (lit, fig) seine Krallen wetzen **b** (Mus, by a semitone) (um einen Halbton) erhöhen; (= raise pitch) höher singen/spielen/stimmen **VI her voice ~ed** (in fear, anxiety etc) ihre Stimme wurde schrill

sharp end N **at the ~** (fig) in vorderster Front

sharpener [ˈʃɑːpnə] N Schleifgerät nt; (in rod shape) Wetzstahl m; (= pencil sharpener) (Bleistift)spitzer m

sharper [ˈʃɑːpə] N Gauner(in) m(f); (= card sharper) Falschspieler(in) m(f)

sharp: sharp-eyed ADJ scharfsichtig; **to be ~** scharfe or gute Augen haben; **it was ~ of you to see that** du hast ja Augen wie ein Luchs; **sharp-featured** ADJ mit scharfen (Gesichts-)zügen

sharpish [ˈʃɑːpɪʃ] ADV (Brit inf) schnell, fix (inf)

sharpness [ˈʃɑːpnɪs] N (of knife, blade etc) Schärfe f; (of needle, point etc) Spitzheit f

b (of outline, photo, contrast) Schärfe f

c (= keenness, of eyes, wits, mind) Schärfe f; (of nose) Empfindlichkeit f; (of observation, remark) Scharfsinnigkeit f; (= intelligence, of person) Schläue f, Gewieftheit f (inf); (of child) Aufgewecktheit f

d (= suddenness, intensity, of whistle, cry) Schrillheit f; (of frost, contrast) Schärfe f; (of desire, pain) Heftigkeit f; (of hunger) Größe f; **because of the unexpected ~ of the drop in prices** wegen des unerwartet steilen Preissturzes

e (= acuteness, of angle) Spitzheit f; (of bend, turn by car) Schärfe f

f (pej, = shrewdness) Gerissenheit f, Raffiniertheit f, Cleverness f (inf)

g (= fierceness) (of tongue, retort, tone of voice) Schärfe f; (of person) Schroffheit f; (of temper) Hitzigkeit f

h (= acidity, pungency, of taste) Schärfe f; (of apple) Säure f; (of wine) Herbheit f; **there is a ~ in the air** es ist sehr frisch

sharp: sharpshooter N (esp US) Scharfschütze m, Scharfschützin f; **sharp-sighted** ADJ = sharp-eyed; **sharp-tempered** ADJ hitzig; **sharp-tongued** ADJ scharfzüngig; **sharp-witted** ADJ scharfsinnig

shat [ʃæt] pret, ptp of shit¹

shatter [ˈʃætə] VT **a** (lit) zertrümmern, zerschmettern; hopes, dreams zunichte machen; nerves zerrütten; **he hurled a brick at the window, ~ing it into a thousand pieces** er schleuderte einen Ziegel gegen das Fenster, das in tausend Stücke zersplitterte or zersprang; **the blast ~ed all the windows** durch die Explosion zersplitterten alle Fensterscheiben; **to ~ sth against a wall** etw gegen eine Wand schmettern; **his hopes were ~ed** seine Hoffnungen hatten sich zerschlagen

b (Brit fig inf: = exhaust) erledigen (inf); (mentally) mitnehmen; **how are you? – ~ed!** wie gehts? – ich bin total kaputt or erledigt (inf);

she was absolutely ~ed by the divorce die Scheidung hatte sie schwer mitgenommen

c (Brit inf: = flabbergast) erschüttern; **I've won the pools? I'm ~ed!** ich habe im Toto gewonnen? ich bin platt! (inf)

VI zerbrechen, zerspringen; (windscreen) (zer-)splittern

shattering [ˈʃætərɪŋ] ADJ **a** blow wuchtig, gewaltig; explosion gewaltig; defeat vernichtend; **it had a ~ effect on the economy** es wirkte sich verheerend auf die Wirtschaft aus

b (fig inf: = exhausting) erschöpfend, anstrengend; (psychologically) niederschmetternd; **a ~ blow to his ego** ein schwerer Schlag für sein Ich; **I had a ~ day at the office** der Tag im Büro hat mich wahnsinnig geschlaucht (inf), ich bin total erledigt vom Büro (inf); **the divorce was a ~ experience for her** die Scheidung hat sie unheimlich mitgenommen (inf)

c (inf, = flabbergasting) news, realization erschütternd; effect umwerfend (inf); **this new film is a ~ experience** dieser neue Film ist ein umwerfendes Erlebnis (inf); **it must have been absolutely ~ for you to have found out that ...** das war bestimmt entsetzlich für Sie, als Sie erfuhren, dass ...

shatterproof [ˈʃætəpruːf] ADJ splitterfest or -frei

shave [ʃeɪv] vb: pret shaved, ptp shaved or shaven

N Rasur f; **to have a ~** sich rasieren; (at a barber's) sich rasieren lassen; **this new razor gives you a good ~** dieser neue Rasierapparat rasiert gut; **a close ~** (lit) eine glatte Rasur; **to have a close ~** (fig) gerade noch davonkommen, mit knapper Not davonkommen, gerade noch Glück haben; **that was a close ~** das war knapp **VT** face, legs rasieren; leather (ab)falzen; wood hobeln; (= graze) streifen **VI** (person) sich rasieren; (razor) rasieren, schneiden

▶ **shave off** VT sep beard sich (dat) abrasieren; sb's beard abrasieren; wood abhobeln; **she has shaved four seconds off the world record** sie hat den Weltrekord um vier Sekunden verbessert

shave foam N (US) Rasierschaum m

shaven [ˈʃeɪvn] ADJ head etc kahl geschoren; **~-headed** kahl geschoren

shaver [ˈʃeɪvə] N **a** (= razor) Rasierapparat m **b** (inf) young ~ junger Bengel (inf); (as address) junger Freund

shaver point, (US) **shaver outlet** N Steckdose f für Rasierapparate

Shavian [ˈʃeɪvɪən] ADJ shawsch

shaving [ˈʃeɪvɪŋ] N **a** Rasieren nt **b** shavings PL Späne pl

shaving in cpds Rasier-; **shaving brush** N Rasierpinsel m; **shaving cream** N Rasiercreme f; **shaving foam** N Rasierschaum m; **shaving gel** N Rasiergel nt; **shaving mug** N Rasierschale f; **shaving point** N Steckdose f für Rasierapparate; **shaving soap, shaving stick** N Rasierseife f; **shaving tackle** N Rasierzeug nt

shawl [ʃɔːl] N (round shoulders) (Umhänge)tuch nt; (tailored) Umhang m; (covering head) (Kopf-)tuch nt

she [ʃiː] PRON sie; (of boats, cars etc) es; **~ who ...** (liter) diejenige, die ...; **it is ~** (form) sie ist es N Sie f

she- PREF weiblich; **~bear** weiblicher Bär, Bärin f

s/he PRON (= he or she) er/sie

sheading [ˈʃiːdɪŋ] N (Brit) Verwaltungsbezirk m (der Isle of Man)

sheaf [ʃiːf] N pl sheaves (of wheat, corn) Garbe f; (of arrows etc, papers, notes) Bündel nt

shear [ʃɪə] pret sheared, ptp shorn **VT** sheep scheren; wool (ab)scheren **or** shorn **VI a** (Mech: = fracture) **the metal plate had ~ed** in der Metallplatte hatte sich ein Riss gebildet

▶**shear off** **VT** sep sheep's wool abscheren; **the ship had its bows shorn off in the collision** beim Zusammenstoß wurde dem Schiff der Bug abrasiert **VI** (= break off) abbrechen

shearer ['ʃɪərə'] N (Schaf)scherer(in) m(f)

shearing ['ʃɪərɪŋ] N (Schaf)schur f; **~s** Schur- or Scherwolle f

shearing: shearing machine N Schermaschine f; **shearing time** N Schurzeit f, Zeit f der Schafschur

shears [ʃɪəz] PL (große) Schere; (for hedges) Heckenschere f; (for metal) Metallschere f

shearwater ['ʃɪəwɔːtə'] N Sturmtaucher m

sheath [ʃiːθ] N (for sword etc) Scheide f; (Bot) (Blatt)scheide f; (on cable) Mantel m, Armierung f; (= contraceptive) Gummischutz m, Kondom m or nt; (= dress) Futteralkleid nt; **the cat withdrew its claws into their ~s** die Katze zog die Krallen ein; **the wing-sheath of an insect** die Flügeldecke eines Insekts

sheathe [ʃiːð] VT sword, knife in die Scheide stecken; claws einziehen; cables armieren; **to ~ sth in metal** etw mit Metall verkleiden; **she was ~d in a red dress** sie steckte in einem roten Kleid

sheathing ['ʃiːðɪŋ] N (on roof, house) Verkleidung f; (on ship also) Beschlag m; (with wood) Verschalung f; (on cables) Armierung f, Bewehrung f

sheath knife N Fahrtenmesser nt

sheaves [ʃiːvz] pl of sheaf

shebang [ʃə'bæŋ] N (inf) **the whole ~** die ganze Chose (inf), der ganze Kram (inf)

shebeen [ʃɪ'biːn] N (Ir) Kaschemme f, Spelunke f

shed¹ [ʃed] pret, ptp shed **VT** **a** leaves, hair etc verlieren; horns abwerfen; clothes ausziehen, ablegen; **the dancer slowly ~ another layer** die Tänzerin schälte sich langsam aus einer weiteren Hülle; **to ~ its skin** sich häuten; **to ~ its load** (lorry) seine Ladung verlieren; **you should ~ a few pounds** Sie sollten ein paar Pfund abnehmen or abspecken

 b tears, blood vergießen; **he ~ his blood** sein Blut floss; (= died also) sein Blut wurde vergossen; **why should I ~ my blood?** warum sollte ich Leib und Leben einsetzen?; **I won't ~ any tears over him** ich weine ihm keine Träne nach

 c burden, leader, reputation loswerden; cares, ideas ablegen; friend fallen lassen; jobs abbauen; **an actress who ~ husbands like a snake ~s skins** eine Schauspielerin, die die Ehemänner wechselt wie andere das Hemd

 d light, perfume verbreiten; **to ~ light on sth** (fig) erhellen, Licht auf etw (acc) werfen **VI** (dog, cat etc) sich haaren

shed² N Schuppen m; (industrial also) Halle f; (= cattle shed) Stall m; (= night shelter etc) Unterstand m → watershed

she'd [ʃiːd] contr of she would of she had

sheen [ʃiːn] N Glanz m

sheep [ʃiːp] N pl - (lit, fig) Schaf nt; **to count ~** Schäfchen zählen; **to separate the ~ from the goats** die Schafe von den Böcken trennen; **to make ~'s eyes at sb** jdn anhimmeln; **you might as well be hanged for a ~ as a lamb** (prov) wennschon, dennschon

sheep: sheep-dip N Desinfektionsbad nt für Schafe; (for mange) Räudebad nt; **sheepdog** N Hütehund m; **sheepdog trials** PL Gehorsamkeits- und Geschicklichkeitsprüfungen pl für Hütehunde; **sheep farm** N Schaffarm f; **sheep farmer** N Schafzüchter(in) m(f); **sheep farming** N Schafzucht f; **sheepfold** N Schafhürde f

sheepherder ['ʃiːp,hɜːdə'] N (US) Schäfer(in) m(f)

sheepish ['ʃiːpɪʃ] ADJ verlegen; **I felt a bit ~ about it** das war mir ein bisschen peinlich

sheepishly ['ʃiːpɪʃlɪ] ADV verlegen

sheep: sheep run N Schafweide f; **sheepshearer** N (= person) Schafscherer(in) m(f); **sheepshearing** N Schafschur f; **sheepskin** N **a** Schaffell nt; **~ (jacket)** Schaffelljacke f **b**

(US, inf, = diploma) Pergament nt; **sheepwalk** N (Brit) Schafweide f

sheer [ʃɪə'] ADJ (+er) **a** (= absolute) rein; nonsense, madness rein, glatt; stupidity rein, schier; **by ~ force of personality** aufgrund or auf Grund seiner Persönlichkeit; **by ~ chance** rein zufällig; **by ~ hard work** durch nichts als harte Arbeit; **the ~ impossibility of doing that** die schiere Unmöglichkeit, das zu tun; **it was ~ hell** es war die (reinste) Hölle (inf)

 b (= steep) cliff, drop steil, jäh (geh); **there is a ~ drop of 200 feet** es fällt 200 Fuß steil or senkrecht ab

 c cloth etc (hauch)dünn, (hauch)zart; **~ nylon stockings** hauchdünne Nylonstrümpfe pl **ADV** steil, jäh (geh); (= vertically) senkrecht **VI** (Naut) ausscheren

▶**sheer away** VI **a** (ship, plane) ausweichen **b** (= avoid) **to sheer away from sb/sth** jdm/einer Sache ausweichen

▶**sheer off** VI **a** (ship) ausscheren **b** (person: = make off) sich davonmachen

sheerness ['ʃɪənɪs] N (of cliffs) Steilheit f

sheet¹ [ʃiːt] N **a** (for bed) (Bett)laken nt, Leinor Betttuch nt; (= waterproof sheet) Gummidecke f; (for covering furniture) Tuch nt; **between the ~s** (inf) im Bett (inf); **the furniture was covered with (dust)sheets** die Möbel waren verhängt

 b (of paper, inf: = newspaper) Blatt nt; (big, as of wrapping paper, stamps etc, Typ) Bogen m; **~ of music** Notenblatt nt; **~s** (Brit sl: = money) Kohle f (inf)

 c (of plywood, metal) Platte f; (of glass) Scheibe f, Platte f; (= baking sheet) (Back)blech nt; (Geol) Schicht f; (of water, ice etc) Fläche f; (of flame) Flammenmeer nt; **a ~ of ice covered the lake** eine Eisschicht bedeckte den See; **the ~ of water covering the lawn** das Wasser, das auf dem Rasen stand; **like a glasslike ~ of water** der See, eine spiegelblanke Wasserfläche; **a huge ~ of flame engulfed the building** das Gebäude ging in einem Flammenmeer unter; **the rain was coming down in ~s** es regnete in Strömen

▶**sheet down** VI (Brit inf) **it's sheeting down** (= raining hard) es regnet in Strömen; (snow) es schneit in dicken Flocken

sheet² N (Naut, = rope) Schot f, (Segel)leine f; **he's three ~s to or in the wind** (dated inf) er ist voll wie eine Strandhaubitze (dated inf)

sheet: sheet anchor N Notanker m; (fig) Rettungsanker m; **sheet anchor man** N Eckpfeiler m; **sheetbend** N Schotstek m; **sheet copper** N Kupferblech nt; **sheet feed** N (Comput) Einzelblatteinzug m; **sheet glass** N Flach- or Scheibenglas nt; **sheet ice** N Glatteis nt

sheeting ['ʃiːtɪŋ] N (= cloth) Leinen nt; (= metal etc) Verkleidung f; (= wood) Verschalung f; **plastic ~** Plastiküberzug m

sheet: sheet iron N Eisenblech nt; **sheet lightning** N Wetterleuchten nt; **sheet metal** N Walzblech nt; **sheet music** N Notenblätter pl

sheik(h) [ʃeɪk] N Scheich m

sheik(h)dom ['ʃeɪkdəm] N Scheichtum nt

sheila ['ʃiːlə] N (Austral, inf) Biene f (inf), Puppe f (inf)

shekel ['ʃekl] N Sekel m, Schekel m; **~s** (inf) Moneten pl (dated sl)

sheldrake ['ʃeldreɪk] N Brandente f

shelf [ʃelf] N pl shelves **a** Brett nt, Bord nt; (for books) Bücherbrett or -bord nt; **shelves** (= unit of furniture) Regal nt; **to buy sth off the ~** etw als Handelsware kaufen; **to be on the ~** (girl) eine alte Jungfer sein, sitzen geblieben sein; (worker) zum alten Eisen gehören; **she was left on the ~** sie ist eine alte Jungfer geworden, sie ist sitzen geblieben **b** (= ledge of rock etc, on rock face) Gesims nt, (Fels-)vorsprung m; (under water) (Felsen)riff nt, Felsbank f; (= sandbank) Sandbank f, Untiefe f

shelf: shelf life N (lit) Lagerfähigkeit f; (fig) Dauer f; **to have a long/short ~** (fig) sich lange/kurz halten; **shelf mark** N Standortzeichen nt; **shelf room** N Platz m in den Regalen; **shelf-warmer** N (hum) Ladenhüter m (inf)

shell [ʃel] **N** **a** (of egg, nut, mollusc) Schale f; (on beach) Muschel f; (of pea etc) Hülse f; (of snail) (Schnecken)haus nt; (of tortoise, turtle, insect) Panzer m; (= pastry shell) Form f; **to come out of one's ~** (fig) aus seinem Schneckenhaus kommen, aus sich (dat) herausgehen; **to retire into one's ~** (fig) sich in sein Schneckenhaus verkriechen; **I'm just an empty ~** (fig) ich bin nur noch eine leere Hülse

 b (= frame, of building) Mauerwerk nt, Mauern pl; (unfinished) Rohbau m; (= ruin) Gemäuer nt, Ruine f; (of car, unfinished) Karosserie f; (gutted) Wrack nt; (of ship) Gerippe nt, Rumpf m; (gutted) Wrack nt

 c (Mil) Granate f; (esp US, = cartridge) Patrone f

 d (= boat) Rennruderboot nt **VT** **a** peas etc enthülsen; eggs, nuts schälen; **~ed prawns** geschälte Garnelen

 b (Mil) (mit Granaten) beschießen; **the town is still being ~ed** die Stadt steht immer noch unter Beschuss

▶**shell out** (inf) **VT** sep blechen (inf) **VI** **to shell out for sth** für etw blechen (inf)

she'll [ʃiːl] contr of she will of she shall

shellac [ʃə'læk] vb: pret, ptp shellacked **N** Schellack m **VT** **a** mit Schellack behandeln **b** (US sl, = defeat utterly) fertig machen (inf); (= beat) vermöbeln (inf); **to get a ~king** eins auf die Schnauze kriegen (inf); (= beating also) eine Tracht Prügel kriegen

shell: shell company N (Comm) Firmenmantel m; **shellfire** N Granatfeuer nt; **shellfish** N Schaltier(e) nt(pl); (Cook) Meeresfrüchte pl; **shell-hole** N Granattrichter m

shelling ['ʃelɪŋ] N Granatfeuer nt (auf +acc)

shell: shell program N (Comput) Shellprogramm nt; **shellproof** ADJ bombensicher; **shell shock** N Kriegsneurose f; **shell-shocked** ADJ to be ~ (lit) unter einer Kriegsneurose leiden; (fig) verstört sein; **shell suit** N modischer leichter Jogginganzug

shelter ['ʃeltə'] **N** (= protection) Schutz m; (= place) Unterstand m; (= air-raid shelter) (Luftschutz)keller or -bunker m; (= bus shelter) Wartehäuschen nt; (= mountain shelter) (Berg- or Schutz)hütte f; (for the night) Obdach nt (liter), Unterkunft f; **a ~ for homeless people** ein Obdachlosenheim or -asyl nt; **under the ~ of the rock** im Schutze des Felsens; **when the ship reached ~** als das Schiff eine sichere or schützende Stelle erreichte; **to take ~** sich in Sicherheit bringen; (from rain, hail etc) sich unterstellen; **to seek ~** Schutz suchen; **to run for ~** Zuflucht suchen; **to give sb ~** jdn beherbergen; **to provide ~ for sb** jdm Schutz bieten; (= accommodation) jdn beherbergen; **the peasants offered the guerrillas ~** die Bauern boten den Partisanen Zuflucht

 VT schützen (from vor +dat); criminal verstecken; **to ~ sb from blame** jdn gegen Vorwürfe in Schutz nehmen; **to ~ sb from harm** jdn vor Schaden bewahren; **the police think he's ~ing someone** die Polizei glaubt, dass er jemanden deckt; **parents ~ing their children from harsh reality** Eltern, die ihre Kinder vor der rauen Wirklichkeit behüten

 VI **there was nowhere to ~** man konnte nirgends Schutz finden; (from rain etc) man konnte sich nirgends unterstellen; **a good place to ~** eine Stelle, wo man gut geschützt ist; **we ~ed in a shop doorway** wir stellten uns in einem Ladeneingang unter; **we ~ed behind the rocks** wir stellten uns zum Schutz hinter die Felsen; **to ~ behind a friend/one's reputation** (fig) sich hinter einem Freund/seinem Ansehen verstecken

sheltered ['ʃeltəd] ADJ place geschützt; life behütet; **~ from the wind** windgeschützt

sheltered: sheltered housing N (for the elderly) Wohnungen pl für Senioren; (for the disa-

bled) Wohnungen *pl* für Behinderte; **sheltered workshop** N beschützende Werkstätte, Behindertenwerkstatt *f*

sheltie, shelty [ʃeltɪ] N (= *Shetland pony*) Sheltie *nt*; (= *Shetland sheepdog*) Sheltie *m*

shelve [ʃelv] **VI** (= *slope*) abfallen **VT** **a** *room* mit Regalen versehen, Regale einbauen in (+*acc*) **b** *problem* aufschieben; *plan, project* ad acta legen

shelves [ʃelvz] *pl* of **shelf**

shelving [ʃelvɪŋ] N Regale *pl*; (= *material also*) Bretter *pl*

shemozzle [ʃɪˈmɒzl] N (*US inf*) = **schemozzle**

shenanigans [ʃəˈnænɪɡənz] PL (*inf*, = *tomfoolery*) Faxen *pl* (*inf*), Mumpitz *m* (*inf*); (= *goings-on*) Dinger *pl* (*inf*), Sachen *pl* (*inf*); (= *trickery*) üble Tricks *pl* (*inf*), Dinger *pl* (*inf*)

shepherd [ʃepəd] **N** **a** Schäfer *m*, (Schaf)hirt *m*; **the Good Shepherd** der Gute Hirte **b** (*US*) = **German sheepdog** **VT** führen

shepherd: shepherd boy N Hütejunge *m*; **shepherd dog** N Schäferhund *m*

shepherdess [ʃepədɪs] N Schäferin *f*

shepherd's [ʃepədz]: **shepherd's pie** N Auflauf aus Hackfleisch und Kartoffelbrei; **shepherd's plaid** N *schwarzweiß or schwarz-weiß karierter Wollstoff*; **shepherd's-purse** N (*Bot*) Hirtentäschel(kraut) *nt*

sherbet [ʃɜːbət] N **a** (= *powder*) Brausepulver *nt*; (= *drink*) Brause *f*, Sorbet *m or nt*; (*US*, = *water ice*) Fruchteis *nt*

sherd [ʃɜːd] N = **shard**

sheriff [ʃerɪf] N Sheriff *m*; (*Scot*) Friedensrichter(in) *m(f)*

Sherpa [ʃɜːpə] N Sherpa *m*

sherry [ʃerɪ] N Sherry *m*

she's [ʃiːz] *contr of* **she is** *of* **she has**

Shetland [ʃetlənd] N , **Shetland Islands** [ʃetləndˈaɪləndz] PL Shetlandinseln *pl*

Shetland pony N Shetlandpony *nt*

Shetlands [ʃetləndz] PL Shetlandinseln *pl*

shew [ʃəʊ] VTI (*old*) *ptp* **shewn** [ʃəʊn] → **show**

shibboleth [ʃɪbəleθ] N (= *custom*) Gepflogenheit *f*, Konvention *f*; (= *catchword*) Losung *f*, Parole *f*, Schibboleth *nt* (*rare, liter*)

shield [ʃiːld] **N** (*Mil, Her*) Schild *m*; (*Zool also*) Panzer *m*; (= *sporting trophy also*) Trophäe *f*; (*on machine*) Schutzschirm *or* -schild *m*; (= *eyeshield, radiation shield*) Schirm *m*; (*fig*) Schutz *m*; **riot ~** Schutzschild *m*; **God is our ~** Gott ist unser Schild **VT** schützen (*sb from* jdn vor etw *dat*); *industry* absichern, abschirmen; **she tried to ~ him from the truth** sie versuchte, ihm die Wahrheit zu ersparen

shift [ʃɪft] **N** **a** (= *change*) Änderung *f*; (*in policy, opinion*) Wandel *m*, Änderung *f*; (*Ling*) Verschiebung *f*; (*Mus*) Lagenwechsel *m*; (*from one place to another*) Verlegung *f*; **a ~ of scene** eine Szenenwechsel *m*; **a ~ in direction** eine Richtungsänderung *f*; **a ~ in public opinion** ein Meinungsumschwung *m* in der Bevölkerung; **a ~ of or in emphasis** eine Gewichtsverlagerung; **a population ~** eine Bevölkerungsverschiebung; **this shows a ~ away from the government** dies lässt eine für die Regierung ungünstige Tendenz erkennen; **a new ~ toward(s) liberalism** ein neuer Trend zum Liberalismus

b (*Aut*, = *gear shift*) Schaltung *f*

c (= *period at work, group of workers*) Schicht *f*; **to work (in) ~s** in Schichten arbeiten

d (= *stratagem*) List *f*, Kniff *m*; (= *expedient*) Ausweg *m*; **to make ~ with/without sth** sich mit/ohne etw behelfen

e (= *dress*) Hemdkleid *nt*; (*old*: = *undergarment*) Hemd *nt*

VT **a** (= *move*) (von der Stelle) bewegen; *screw, nail* loskriegen, rauskriegen; *lid* abkriegen; *cork* rauskriegen; *furniture* verrücken; *head, arm* wegnehmen; (*from one place to another*) verlagern, verschieben; *offices etc* verlegen; *rubble, boulder* wegräumen; **to ~ scenery** Kulissen schieben; **to ~ sb from an opinion** jdn von einer Mei-

nung abbringen; **he stood ~ing his weight from foot to foot** er trat von einem Fuß auf den anderen; **to ~ one's gaze** seinen Blick abwenden; **to ~ the blame onto somebody else** die Verantwortung auf jemand anders schieben; **to ~ sth to another room** etw in ein anderes Zimmer schaffen; **~ the table over to the wall** rück den Tisch an die Wand (rüber)!; **can you ~ your car back a bit?** können Sie ein Stück zurücksetzen?; **they ~ed him to Munich** sie haben ihn nach München versetzt; **we'll ~ all this junk out of the cupboard** wir räumen das ganze Gerümpel aus dem Schrank

b (*inf*, = *get rid of*) loswerden

c (*US, Aut*) **to ~ gears** schalten

d (*inf*) *food* verputzen (*inf*); *drink* schlucken (*inf*)

VI **a** (= *move*) sich bewegen; (*ballast, cargo*) sich verlagern; (*scene*) wechseln; (*wind*) umspringen; (*from one's opinion*) abgehen; **he ~ed out of the way** er ging aus dem Weg; **he was ~ing about in his chair** er rutschte auf seinem Stuhl hin und her; **~ over, you're taking up too much room** rück mal rüber, du nimmst zu viel Platz weg!; **he ~ed onto his back** er drehte sich auf den Rücken; **he refused to ~** (*fig*) er war nicht umzustimmen

b (*Aut*) schalten

c (*Brit inf*, = *move quickly*: *cars, runners*) flitzen (*inf*), rasen; **that's really ~ing!** das nenne ich Tempo!

d (= *manage*) **to ~ for oneself** sich (*dat*) (selbst) behelfen

shifter [ʃɪftə] N **a** (*Theat*) Kulissenschieber(in) *m(f)* **b** (*US Aut, bicycle*) Schalthebel *m*

shiftily [ʃɪftɪlɪ] ADV zwielichtig, nicht ganz sauber (*inf*); *glance* verstohlen; *reply* ausweichend; *behave* verdächtig

shiftiness [ʃɪftɪnɪs] N Zwielichtigkeit *f*; (*of person, character also*) Fragwürdigkeit *f*; (*of glance*) Verstohlenheit *f*; (*of reply*) Ausweichen *nt*; **there was a certain ~ in his manner** sein Verhalten hatte etwas Verdächtiges

shifting sands [ʃɪftɪŋˈsændz] PL **a** (*Geol*) Flugsand *m* **b** (*Naut*) Treibsand *m*

shift key N (*on typewriter*) Umschalttaste *f*; (*Comput*) Shifttaste *f*

shiftless [ʃɪftlɪs] ADJ träge, energielos

shiftlessness [ʃɪftlɪsnɪs] N Trägheit *f*, Energielosigkeit *f*

shift: shift lever N (*esp US*; *Aut, bicycle*) Schalthebel *m*; **shift lock** N (*on typewriter*) Umschaltfeststeller *m*; **shiftwork** N Schichtarbeit *f*; **to do ~** Schicht arbeiten, Schichtarbeit machen; **shiftworker** N Schichtarbeiter(in) *m(f)*

shifty [ʃɪftɪ] ADJ (+*er*) zwielichtig, nicht ganz sauber (*inf*); *person, character also* fragwürdig; *glance* verstohlen; *eyes* verschlagen; *reply* ausweichend; **there was something ~ about ...** mit ... war etwas faul (*inf*); **he has a ~ look in his eye** er hat so einen unsicheren Blick; **a ~ expression came over his face** sein Gesicht nahm einen gerissenen Ausdruck an; **a ~ little man** ein verdächtiger kleiner Kerl

shiitake [ʃiːˈtɑːkeɪ] N *pl* **shiitake** (*Bot*) Shitakepilz *m*

Shiite [ʃiːaɪt] **N** Schiit(in) *m(f)* ADJ schiitisch

shillelagh [ʃəˈleɪlə] N (*Ir*) (Schlehdorn- *or* Eichen)knüppel *m*

shilling [ʃɪlɪŋ] N (*Brit, old, Africa etc*) Shilling *m*

shilly-shally [ʃɪlɪʃælɪ] VI (*esp Brit inf*) unschlüssig sein; **stop ~ing** lass das Fackeln; **you've shilly-shallied long enough** du hast lange genug gezögert

shimmer [ʃɪmə] **N** Schimmer *m* **VI** schimmern

shimmy [ʃɪmɪ] **N** Shimmy *m* **VI** sich schieben; (= *dance the shimmy*) den Shimmy tanzen

shin [ʃɪn] **N** Schienbein *nt*; (*of meat*) Hachse *f*; **to kick sb on the ~** jdn vors Schienbein treten **VI** **to ~ up/down** (geschickt) hinauf-/hinunterklettern

shinbone [ʃɪnbəʊn] N Schienbein *nt*

shindig [ʃɪndɪɡ] N (*inf*) Remmidemmi *nt* (*inf*)

shindy [ʃɪndɪ] N (*inf*) Radau *m* (*inf*); (= *noise also, dispute*) Krach *m* (*inf*)

shine [ʃaɪn] *vb*: *pret, ptp* **shone** **N** Glanz *m*; **to give one's shoes a ~** seine Schuhe polieren *or* blank putzen; **~, sir?** Schuhe putzen, der Herr?; **to have a ~** glänzen; **to put a ~ on sth** etw blank polieren; (*fig*) einer Sache (*dat*) (den richtigen) Glanz geben; **to take the ~ off sth** (*lit, fig*) einer Sache (*dat*) den Glanz nehmen; **she's taken a real ~ to Oxford/my brother** (*inf*) Oxford/mein Bruder hat es ihr wirklich angetan → **rain**

VT **a** *pret, ptp usu* **shined** (= *polish*: *also* **shine up**) blank putzen; *shoes* polieren

b (= *direct a light*) **to ~ a light on sth** etw beleuchten; **~ the torch this way!** leuchte einmal hierher!; **don't ~ it in my eyes!** blende mich nicht!

VI **a** (*lit*) leuchten; (*stars, eyes, face*) leuchten, glänzen; (*metal, nose, paint*) glänzen; (*moon, sun, lamp*) scheinen; (*glass*) blitzblank sein; **to ~ like a beacon** (*fig*) wie ein Licht in der Dunkelheit sein *or* leuchten; (*hum: face, nose*) wie ein Lampion leuchten

b (*fig*: = *excel*) glänzen; **to ~ at/in sth** bei/in etw (*dat*) glänzen; **he doesn't exactly ~ at sports/his work** er ist keine *or* nicht gerade eine Leuchte im Sport/bei der Arbeit

▶ **shine down** VI herabscheinen (*on* auf +*acc*)

▶ **shine out** VI **a** (*light*) the light shining out from the windows across the lawn das durch die Fenster auf den Rasen fallende Licht; **a light (suddenly) shone out from the darkness** in der Dunkelheit blitzte (plötzlich) ein Licht auf; **the sun shone out from behind a cloud** die Sonne schien hinter einer Wolke hervor; **he thinks the sun shines out of her arse** (*Brit*) *or* **ass** (*US*) (*sl*) für ihn ist sie (einfach) die Größte (*inf*) **b** (*fig, qualities*) **his courage shines out** sein Mut ragt heraus

shiner [ʃaɪnə] N (*inf*, = *black eye*) Veilchen *nt* (*sl*)

shingle¹ [ʃɪŋɡl] **N** **a** (= *tile*) Schindel *f*; (*US inf*: = *signboard*) Schild *nt*; **to put up one's ~** (*US*) ein Geschäft eröffnen; (*doctor, lawyer*) sich niederlassen **b** (= *hairstyle*) Herrenschnitt *m*, Bubikopf *m* **VT** *roof etc* mit Schindeln decken **b** *hair* einen Herrenschnitt *or* Bubikopf machen (+*dat*)

shingle² N , *no pl* (= *pebbles*) Kiesel *m*, Kieselsteine *pl*; (= *shingle beach*) Kiesel(strand) *m*

shingles [ʃɪŋɡlz] N *sing* (*Med*) Gürtelrose *f*

shingly [ʃɪŋɡlɪ] ADJ *beach* steinig, voller Kieselsteine

shin guard [ʃɪnɡɑːd] N Schienbeinschützer *m*

shininess [ʃaɪnɪnɪs] N Glanz *m*

shining [ʃaɪnɪŋ] ADJ (*lit, fig*) leuchtend; *light* strahlend; *metal, paint, hair* glänzend; *car* blitzend, blitzblank; **a ~ light** (*fig*) eine Leuchte; **~ white** leuchtend *or* strahlend weiß; **he's my knight in ~ armour** (*Brit*) *or* **armor** (*US*) er ist mein Märchenprinz

Shinto [ʃɪntəʊ] (*Rel*) **N** Schintoismus *m* ADJ schintoistisch

Shintoism [ʃɪntəʊɪzəm] N (*Rel*) Schintoismus *m*

shinty [ʃɪntɪ] N *dem Hockey ähnliches Spiel*

shiny [ʃaɪnɪ] ADJ (+*er*) glänzend; *elbows, trousers also* blank

ship [ʃɪp] **N** **a** Schiff *nt*; **the good ~ Venus** die gute Venus; **on board ~** an Bord; **to take ~ (for)** (*liter*) sich einschiffen (nach); **when my ~ comes home or in** (*fig*) wenn ich das große Los ziehe; **~ of the line** Kriegsschiff *nt*; **~ of the desert** Wüstenschiff *nt*; **the great ~ of state** das Staatsschiff

b (*US inf*, = *plane*) Maschine *f*; (= *spaceship*) (Raum)schiff *nt*

VT **a** (= *take on board*) an Bord nehmen; *mast* setzen; **to ~ oars** die Riemen einlegen; **to ~ water** leck sein; **we're ~ping water** unser Boot leckt *or* ist leck

b (= *transport*) versenden; *coal, grain etc* verfrachten; (*esp by sea*) verschiffen

VI (= *take employment*) anheuern

▶**ship off** VT sep versenden; coal, grain etc verfrachten; (esp by ship) verschiffen; **they shipped their sons off to boarding school** sie steckten ihre Söhne ins Internat (inf)

▶**ship out** VT sep versenden; coal, grain etc verfrachten; **to ship supplies out to sb** jdn (per Schiff) mit Vorräten versorgen

ship: ship biscuit N (US) Schiffszwieback m; **shipboard** N on ~ an Bord (eines/des Schiffes) ADJ an Bord (eines/des Schiffes); **a ~ romance** eine Romanze an Bord; **shipborne aircraft** [ˈʃɪpbɔːˈnɛəkrɑːft] N (Naut, Aviat) Bordflugzeug nt; **shipbreaker** N Schiffsverschrotter m; **shipbuilder** N Schiffbauer(in) m(f); **a firm of ~s** eine Schiffbaufirma; **shipbuilding** N Schiffbau m; **ship canal** N (See)kanal m; **ship chandler** N Schiffsausrüster(in) m(f); **shipload** N Schiffsladung f; **the tourists were arriving by the ~** (inf) ganze Schiffsladungen von Touristen kamen an; **shipmaster** N (Naut) (Handels)kapitän m; **shipmate** N Schiffskamerad(in) m(f)

shipment [ˈʃɪpmənt] N Sendung f; (of coal, grain, tractors) Transport m; (= transporting by sea) Verschiffung f; (= taking on board) Verladen nt

shipowner [ˈʃɪpəʊnə^r] N Schiffseigner(in) m(f); (of many ships) Reeder(in) m(f)

shipper [ˈʃɪpə^r] N (= company) Speditionsfirma f

shipping [ˈʃɪpɪŋ] N no pl a Schifffahrt f; (= ships) Schiffe pl; **the Suez Canal has been reopened to ~** der Suezkanal ist wieder für die Schifffahrt or für den Schiffsverkehr geöffnet b (= transportation) Verschiffung f; (by rail etc) Versand m ADJ attr ~ **business** Reederei- or Schifffahrtsgeschäft nt; ~ **costs** Frachtkosten pl; ~ **documents** Versanddokumente pl, Warenbegleitpapiere pl

shipping: shipping agent N Reeder(in) m(f); **shipping case** N Versandkiste f or -behälter m; **shipping clerk** N Expedient(in) m(f), Angestellte(r) mf in der Versandabteilung; **shipping company** N Schifffahrtsgesellschaft f or -linie f, Reederei f; **shipping forecast** N (Met) Seewetterbericht m; **shipping lane** N Schifffahrtsstraße f; **shipping line** N = **shipping company**; **shipping losses** PL Verluste pl von or an Schiffen; **shipping office** N (= agent's office) Büro nt einer Reedereivertretung; (= place where seamen get jobs) Heuerbüro nt; **shipping route** N Schifffahrtslinie f

ship's: ship's articles PL Heuervertrag m, Schiffsartikel pl; **ship's biscuit** N Schiffszwieback m; **ship's company** N (Schiffs)besatzung f; **ship's doctor** N Schiffsarzt m/-ärztin nt; **ship's manifest** M (for goods) Ladeverzeichnis nt; (for passengers) Passagierliste f

shipshape [ˈʃɪpʃeɪp] ADJ, ADV tipptopp (inf); **to get everything ~** alles tipptopp machen (inf); **we'll soon have you ~ again, said the doctor** (inf) Sie werden bald wieder auf dem Damm sein, sagte der Arzt (inf); ~ **and Bristol fashion** in bester Ordnung

ship's papers PL Schiffspapiere pl

ship: ship-to-shore radio N Seefunk m; **shipway** N (= support) Stapel m; (= ship canal) (See)kanal m, Schifffahrtsweg m; **shipwreck** N (lit, fig) Schiffbruch m; (fig also) Scheitern nt; **in the ~** bei dem Schiffbruch VT (lit) schiffbrüchig werden lassen; (fig) zum Scheitern bringen, scheitern lassen; **to be ~ed** (lit) schiffbrüchig sein; (fig) Schiffbruch erleiden, scheitern; **shipwright** N Schiffbauer(in) m(f); **shipyard** N (Schiffs)werft f

shire [ˈʃaɪə^r] N (Brit, old) Grafschaft f

shire horse N Zugpferd nt

shirk [ʃɜːk] VT sich drücken vor (+dat), ausweichen (+dat) VI sich drücken; **you're ~ing!** du willst dich drücken!

shirker [ˈʃɜːkə^r] N Drückeberger(in) m(f)

shirking [ˈʃɜːkɪŋ] N Drückebergerei f

shirr [ʃɜː^r] VT kräuseln

shirring [ˈʃɜːrɪŋ] N Kräuselarbeit f; ~ **elastic** Gummizug m

shirt [ʃɜːt] N (men's) (Ober)hemd nt; (Ftbl) Hemd nt, Trikot nt; (women's) Hemdbluse f; **keep your ~ on** (Brit inf) reg dich nicht auf!; **to put one's ~ on a horse** (inf) den letzten Cent or sein letztes Hemd auf ein Pferd setzen; **to lose one's ~ on a horse** (inf) den letzten Cent or sein letztes Hemd bei einer Pferdewette verlieren; **I'm putting my ~ on him to get the job** (inf) ich gehe jede Wette ein, dass er die Stelle bekommt; **he'd give you the ~ off his back** (inf) er würde einem sein letztes Hemd geben; **he'll have the ~ off your back!** (inf) er zieht dich aus bis aufs letzte Hemd! (inf)

shirt: shirt collar N Hemdkragen m; **shirt front** N Hemdbrust f

shirting [ˈʃɜːtɪŋ] N Hemdenstoff m

shirtsleeve [ˈʃɜːtsliːv] ADJ hemdsärmelig; **it's real ~ weather now** jetzt kann man wirklich in Hemdsärmeln gehen N **shirtsleeves** PL Hemdsärmel pl; **in his/their ~s** in Hemdsärmeln

shirt-tail [ˈʃɜːtteɪl] N Hemd(en)schoß m

shirtwaister [ˈʃɜːtweɪstə^r], (US) **shirtwaist** [ˈʃɜːtweɪst] N Hemdblusenkleid nt

shirty [ˈʃɜːtɪ] ADJ (+er) (esp Brit inf) sauer (inf), verärgert (as characteristic) griesgrämig (inf); **he got pretty ~ about it** er wurde ganz schön sauer (inf); **now don't get ~ with me!** nun werd nicht gleich sauer! (inf)

shit¹ [ʃɪt] vb: pret, ptp **shat** (sl) N a (= excrement) Scheiße f (vulg); **to have a ~** scheißen (vulg); **to have the ~s** Dünnschiss haben (inf) b (= person) Arschloch nt (vulg) c (= nonsense) Scheiße f (inf), Scheiß m (inf); **that film/idea/singer is ~** dieser Film/diese Idee/dieser Sänger ist Scheiße (inf); **don't give me that ~!** erzähl mir nicht solche Scheiße (inf) or solchen Scheiß (inf)! d **shits** PL (= state of fear) Schiss m (sl), Muffensausen nt (inf); **to have/get the ~s** Schiss (sl) or Muffensausen (inf) haben/kriegen; **it gives me the ~s** da krieg ich Schiss (sl) e **to be up ~ creek (without a paddle)** bis zum Hals in der Scheiße stecken (vulg); **to be in the ~ or in deep ~** in der Scheiße stecken (vulg); **I don't give a ~** das ist mir scheißegal (inf); **tough ~!** Scheiße auch! (inf) ADJ attr Scheiß- (inf), beschissen (inf); **a ~ film** ein Scheißfilm m (inf), ein beschissener Film (inf) VI scheißen (vulg); **to ~ on sb** (= inform) jdn verpfeifen (inf); **all offenders will be shat on from a great height** (hum) wer nicht spurt, wird unheimlich zusammengeschissen (inf) or zur Sau gemacht (inf); **it's time to ~ or get off the pot** (US fig) komm endlich zu Potte oder lass es ganz bleiben (inf) VT **to ~ bricks or a brick** sich (dat) (vor Angst) in die Hosen scheißen (vulg) VR **to ~ oneself** sich voll scheißen (vulg); (with fear) sich (dat) vor Angst in die Hosen scheißen (vulg) INTERJ Scheiße (inf)

shit² N (sl: = drugs) Shit m (sl)

shitake [ʃiˈtɑːkeɪ] N pl **-ke** (Bot) Shitakepilz m

shite [ʃaɪt] N, ADJ, VIR, INTERJ (Brit sl) = **shit¹**

shit: shitface N (sl) = **shithead**; **shitfaced** ADJ (sl) (with alcohol) stockbesoffen (sl) (with drugs) high (inf); **shithead** N (sl) Scheißkerl m (inf), Scheißtyp m (inf); **shit-hot** ADJ (Brit sl: = very good) geil (sl), krass (sl); **shithouse** N (sl: = lavatory) Scheißhaus nt (sl); **this ~ of a country** dieses Scheißland (inf); **shitless** ADJ **to be scared ~** (sl) sich (dat) vor Angst in die Hosen scheißen (vulg)

shitty [ˈʃɪtɪ] ADJ (+er) (inf) beschissen (inf); **to feel ~** sich beschissen fühlen (inf)

shitwork [ˈʃɪtwɜːk] N , no pl (US sl) Scheißarbeit f (inf)

shiver¹ [ˈʃɪvə^r] N a (of cold) Schauer m; (of horror) Schauder m, Schauer m; **a ~ of cold** ein kalter Schauer; **a ~ ran down my spine** es lief mir kalt den Rücken hinunter; **a little ~ of fear ran down my spine** ein Angstschauer überlief

mich; **the sight sent ~s down my spine** bei dem Anblick lief es mir kalt den Rücken hinunter or überliefes mich kalt; **his touch sent ~s down her spine** es durchzuckte sie bei seiner Berührung b (fig) **to get the ~s** eine Gänsehaut kriegen; **it gives me the ~s** ich kriege davon eine Gänsehaut VI zittern (with vor +dat); (with fear also) schaudern

shiver² N Splitter m, Scherbe f VTI zersplittern, zerbrechen

shivering [ˈʃɪvərɪŋ] N Schau(d)er m; ~ **bout** or **fit** Schüttelfrost m

shivery [ˈʃɪvərɪ] ADJ **to feel ~** frösteln; **the 'flu made him a bit ~** wegen seiner Grippe fröstelte er leicht

shlep [ʃlep] VT, VI, N (US, inf) = **schlep**

shlepper [ˈʃlepə^r] N (US, inf) = **schlepper**

shlock [ʃlɒk] N (dated esp US sl) = **schlock**

shmear [ʃmɪə^r] N (US inf) = **schmear**

shmo [ʃməʊ] N (US, inf) = **schmo**

shmuck [ʃmʌk] N (US, inf) = **schmuck**

shoal¹ [ʃəʊl] N (= shallow place) Untiefe f; (= sandbank) Sandbank f

shoal² N (of fish) Schwarm m; **in ~s** (letters, applications etc) massenweise, in Massen; (people) in hellen Scharen; ~**s of letters** Unmengen pl von Briefen, eine Briefflut

shock¹ [ʃɒk] N a (of explosion, impact) Wucht f; (of earthquake) (Erd)stoß m b (Elec) Schlag m; (Med) (Elektro)schock m; **to get a ~** einen Schlag bekommen c (= emotional disturbance) Schock m, Schlag m; (= state) Schock(zustand) m; **to suffer from ~** einen Schock (erlitten) haben; **to be in (a state of) ~** unter Schock stehen; **the ~ killed him** den Schock hat er nicht überlebt; **rabbits can die of ~** für ein or bei einem Kaninchen kann ein Schock tödlich sein; **a feeling of ~ spread through the town** Entsetzen nt verbreitete sich in der Stadt; **our feeling is one of ~** wir sind zutiefst bestürzt; **a ~ to one's system** ein Kreislaufschock; **it comes as a ~ to hear that ...** mit Bestürzung höre ich/hören wir, dass ...; **to give sb a ~** jdn erschrecken; **it gave me a nasty ~** es hat mir einen bösen Schreck(en) eingejagt; **to get the ~ of one's life** den Schock seines Lebens kriegen; **I got the ~ of my life when I heard ...** ich dachte, mich trifft der Schlag, als ich hörte ... (inf); **he is in for a ~!** (inf) der wird sich wundern (inf) VT (= affect emotionally) erschüttern, bestürzen; (= make indignant) schockieren, schocken (inf); **to be ~ed by sth** über etw (acc) erschüttert or bestürzt sein; (morally) über etw (acc) schockiert or geschockt (inf) sein; **she is easily ~ed** sie ist leicht or schnell schockiert; **he was ~ed when they took his passport away** es hat ihn geschockt, dass man ihm den Pass abgenommen hat (inf); **to ~ sb into doing sth** jdm eine solche Angst einjagen, dass er etw tut; **to ~ sb into action/out of his/her etc complacency** jdn zum Handeln/aus seiner Selbstzufriedenheit aufrütteln VI (film, writer etc) schockieren, schocken (inf)

shock² N (Agr) Garbenbündel nt, Hocke f

shock³ N (also **shock of hair**) (Haar)schopf m

shock absorber [ˈʃɒkəbˌzɔːbə^r] N Stoßdämpfer m

shocked [ʃɒkt] ADJ erschüttert, bestürzt; (= indignant, outraged) schockiert, empört; (= amazed) geschockt (inf); **to be ~** (Med) unter Schock stehen, in einem Schockzustand sein; **the patient is badly ~** der Patient hat einen schweren Schock (erlitten)

shocker [ˈʃɒkə^r] N (inf) Reißer m (inf), Schocker m (inf); **he told me a ~ about conditions in jail** er erzählte mir eine Schauergeschichte über die Zustände im Gefängnis; **it's a ~** das hat einen um (inf); **I have a ~ of a cold** ich habe eine grausige (inf) or entsetzliche Erkältung; **he's a ~** er ist ein ganz Schlimmer (hum)

shockheaded [ˈʃɒkˌhedɪd] ADJ **to be ~** strubbeliges or zotteliges Haar haben, ein Struwwelpeter sein (inf)

shock-horror [ˈʃɒkˈhɒrə] ADJ **~ story** (Press, hum) Horrorgeschichte f

shocking [ˈʃɒkɪŋ] ADJ **a** (= outrageous) schockierend; (= upsetting) news, report erschütternd, schockierend; **it may be ~ to the older generation** es mag für die ältere Generation schockierend sein; **the ~ truth** die grausame Wahrheit; **~ pink** knallrosa (inf), pink (Fashion) **b** (inf: = very bad) entsetzlich, furchtbar; state schockierend; **I'm ~ at spelling** meine Rechtschreibung ist entsetzlich; **what a ~ thing to say/way to behave!** wie kann man bloß so etwas Schreckliches sagen/sich bloß so schrecklich benehmen!; **isn't it ~!** es ist doch furchtbar!

shockingly [ˈʃɒkɪŋlɪ] ADV **a** (= badly) schrecklich, furchtbar; **to behave ~ (toward(s) sb)** (jdm gegenüber) haarsträubend or miserabel benehmen **b** (= extremely) entsetzlich, schrecklich **c** (= disturbingly) erschreckend; **suddenly and ~** auf plötzliche und erschreckende Weise

shock: shock jock N (esp US, inf) Radio-Diskjockey, der seine kontroversen (meist rechtsradikalen) Ansichten provokativ vertritt; **shockproof** ADJ stoßfest or -sicher; **shock tactics** PL (Mil) Stoß- or Durchbruchstaktik f; (fig) Schocktherapie f; **shock therapy**, **shock treatment** N Schocktherapie or -behandlung f; **shock troops** PL Stoßtruppen pl; **shock value** N Schockwirkung f; **shock wave** N (lit) Druckwelle f; (fig) Erschütterung f, Schock m no pl

shod [ʃɒd] pret, ptp of **shoe**

shoddily [ˈʃɒdɪlɪ] ADV schäbig

shoddiness [ˈʃɒdɪnɪs] N Schäbigkeit f; (of work) Schludrigkeit f; (of goods) Minderwertigkeit f

shoddy [ˈʃɒdɪ] ADJ (+er) schäbig; work schludrig; goods minderwertig; service schlampig, schludrig; **a ~ attempt** ein schluderiger Versuch N (= cloth) Shoddy nt or m

shoe [ʃuː] vb: pret, ptp shod N **a** Schuh m; **I wouldn't like to be in his ~s** ich möchte nicht in seiner Haut stecken; **to put oneself in sb's ~s** sich in jds Lage (acc) versetzen; **to step into or fill sb's ~s** an jds Stelle (acc) treten or rücken; **where the ~ pinches** (fig) wo mich/uns der Schuh drückt; **if the ~ fits(, wear it)** (US prov) wem die Jacke passt(, der soll sie sich (dat) anziehen) **b** (= horseshoe) (Huf)eisen nt **c** (= brake shoe) Bremsschuh m **d** (for electric power cable) (Gleit)schuh m; (for mast) Schuh m; (on sledge) Beschlag m VT horse beschlagen; **to be well-shod** (of person) gut beschuht sein (hum, geh)

shoe: shoeblack N Schuhputzer m; **shoebox** N (lit: for shoes) Schuhkarton m; (fig: = small flat) Schuhkarton m (inf fig); **shoebrush** N Schuhbürste f; **shoe cream** N Schuhcreme f, Schuhkrem(e) f; **shoehorn** N VT Schuhanzieher m, Schuhlöffel m; **to ~ oneself/sth into sth** sich/etw in etw (acc) zwängen; **shoelace** N Schnürsenkel m; **shoe leather** N Schuhleder nt; **to wear out one's ~** seine Schuhe auftragen; **save ~ by taking the bus** fahr mit dem Bus und schone deine Schuhsohlen; **shoeless** ADJ ohne Schuhe; **shoemaker** N Schuhmacher(in) m(f), Schuster(in) m(f); **shoemender** N (Flick)schuster(in) m(f); **shoe polish** N Schuhcreme f; **shoe repairer** N (= person) Schuster(in) m(f); (= shop) Schuhreparaturdienst m; **shoeshine** N (US) Schuh(e)putzen nt; **to have a ~** sich (dat) die Schuhe putzen lassen; **shoeshine boy** N Schuhputzer m; **shoe shop** N Schuhgeschäft nt; **shoe size** N Schuhgröße f; **what ~ are you?** welche Schuhgröße haben Sie?; **act your age, not your ~** (inf) stell dich nicht so kindisch an; **shoestring** N **a** (US, = shoelace) Schnürsenkel m, Schnürband m (fig) **to live on a ~** von der Hand in den Mund leben; **the project is run on a ~** das Projekt wird mit ganz wenig Geld

finanziert; **shoestring budget** N Minibudget nt (inf); **shoetree** N (Schuh)spanner m

shone [ʃɒn] pret, ptp of **shine**

shoo [ʃuː] INTERJ sch; (to dog etc) pfui; (to child) husch VT **to ~ sb away** jdn verscheuchen or wegscheuchen; **I ~ed the children into the garden** ich scheuchte die Kinder in den Garten

shoo-in [ˈʃuːɪn] N (US, inf) todsicherer Tipp (inf)

shook¹ [ʃʊk] pret of **shake**

shook² N (of corn) Garbenbündel nt, Hocke f

shoot [ʃuːt] vb: pret, ptp shot N **a** (Bot) Trieb m; (esp sprouting from seed, potato etc) Keim m; (out of ground: of bushes, trees) Schössling m, Schoss m; (= young branch) Reis nt **b** (= hunting expedition) Jagd f; (= shooting party) Jagdgesellschaft f; (= competition) (Wett)schießen nt; (= land) (Jagd)revier nt, Jagd f **c** (= photographic assignment) Fotosession f VT **a** (Mil etc) shoot; bullet, gun abfeuern **b** person, animal (= hit) anschießen; (= wound seriously) niederschießen; (= kill) erschießen; **to ~ sb dead** jdn erschießen; **he shot himself** er hat sich erschossen; **he shot himself in the foot** er schoss sich (dat) in den Fuß; (fig inf) er hat ein Eigentor geschossen (inf); **he was shot in the leg** er wurde ins Bein getroffen; **the bird had been shot in the wing** dem Vogel war ein Flügel durchschossen worden; **he was fatally shot in the neck** ihn traf ein tödlicher Genickschuss; **you'll get me shot** (fig inf) du bringst mich um Kopf und Kragen (inf); **you'll get shot for doing that!** (fig inf) das kann dich Kopf und Kragen kosten! (inf); **people have been shot for less!** (hum inf) es sind schon Leute für weniger an den Galgen gekommen! (inf); **it was like ~ing fish in a barrel** es war ein ungleicher Wettkampf **c** (= throw, propel) schleudern; **to ~ a question at sb** eine Frage auf jdn abfeuern; **to ~ a glance at sb, to ~ sb a glance** jdm einen (schnellen) Blick zuwerfen; **to ~ a line** (inf) aufschneiden, sich wichtig tun (to sb bei jdm) **d** **to ~ the bolt** den Riegel vorlegen; **to ~ one's bolt** (fig) sein Pulver verschießen; **to ~ the rapids** über die Stromschnellen jagen; **to ~ the lights** eine Ampel (bei Rot) überfahren; **to ~ the breeze** (inf) einfach daherreden (inf) **e** (Sport) schießen; (US, sl, = play) craps, pool spielen; **to ~ dice** würfeln, Würfel spielen **f** (Phot) film, scene drehen; snapshot schießen; subject aufnehmen **g** (inf, = inject) drug drücken (sl) VI **a** (with gun) schießen; (as hunter) jagen; **to ~ to kill** gezielt schießen; (police) einen gezielten Todesschuss/gezielte Todesschüsse abgeben; **don't ~!** nicht schießen!; **stop or I'll ~!** stehen bleiben oder ich schieße!; **to ~ at sb/sth** auf jdn/etw schießen; **to ~ straight** genau schießen; **to ~ wide** danebenschießen; **to ~ from the hip** aus der Hüfte schießen; **~!** (fig inf, = ask away etc) schieß los!; **to ~ for the moon** sich (dat) Großes vornehmen **b** (= move rapidly) schießen (inf); **to ~ ahead/into the lead** an die Spitze vorpreschen; **he shot ahead of the other boys in maths** er ließ die anderen Jungen in Mathe weit hinter sich (dat); **the car shot along the track** der Wagen schoss or jagte die Piste entlang; **he shot down the stairs** er schoss or jagte die Treppe hinunter; **to ~ by** or **past** vorbeischießen or -jagen; **to ~ in** (he)reingeschossen kommen; **to ~ to fame/stardom** auf einen Schlag berühmt/zum Star werden **c** (Sport) schießen; **to ~ at goal** aufs Tor schießen **d** (pain) **the pain shot up his leg** der Schmerz durchzuckte sein Bein; **~ing pains** stechende Schmerzen pl **e** (Bot) treiben **f** (Phot) knipsen (inf); (Film) drehen

▶ **shoot away** VI **a** (= move rapidly) davonschießen, losjagen **b** (= shoot continuously) schießen; **we shot away at them for two hours** wir beschossen sie zwei Stunden lang; **shoot away!** (fig inf) schieß los! VT sep wegschießen

▶ **shoot down** VT sep plane abschießen; (fig inf) person fertig machen (inf); suggestion abschmettern (inf); argument in der Luft zerreißen; **the plane was shot down in flames** die Maschine wurde in Brand geschossen und stürzte ab; **his plan was shot down in flames** (fig) sein Plan wurde in der Luft zerrissen

▶ **shoot off** VI **a** (= rush off) davonschießen, losjagen (inf) **b** (sl, = ejaculate) abspritzen (sl) VT sep abschießen; gun etc also abfeuern; **to shoot one's mouth off** (inf, indiscreetly) tratschen (inf); (boastfully) das Maul aufreißen (inf); **he'll start shooting his mouth off to the police** er wird bei der Polizei anfangen zu quatschen (inf)

▶ **shoot out** VI (= emerge swiftly) herausschießen (of aus) VT sep **a** (= put out swiftly) hand etc blitzschnell ausstrecken; tongue etc hervor- or herausschnellen (lassen); (inf, = eject) an die Luft setzen (inf), raussetzen (inf); **they were shot out of the car** sie wurden aus dem Auto geschleudert **b** **to shoot it out** sich (dat) ein (Feuer)gefecht liefern; **the cowboys shot it out** die Cowboys machten die Sache mit ihren Colts aus (inf); **nobody dared to shoot it out with Bad Jake** keiner wagte es, sich mit Bad Jake zu schießen (inf)

▶ **shoot up** VI **a** (hand, prices, temperature) in die Höhe schnellen; (= grow rapidly, children, plant) in die Höhe schießen; (new towns, buildings etc) aus dem Boden schießen **b** (Drugs inf) sich (dat) einen Schuss setzen (inf) VT sep **a** **to shoot up a town** (inf) in einer Stadt herumballern (inf) or -knallen (inf); **the aerodrome was shot up** das Flugfeld wurde heftig beschossen; **he was badly shot up in the war** er ist im Krieg übel zusammengeschossen worden **b** (inf) drug drücken (sl)

shooter [ˈʃuːtə] N (inf, = gun) Knarre f (sl), Kanone f (sl)

shooting [ˈʃuːtɪŋ] N **a** (= shots) Schießen nt; (by artillery) Feuer nt; **was there any ~?** gab es Schießereien? **b** (= murder, execution) Erschießung f; **there was a ~ last night** gestern Nacht ist jemand erschossen worden; **"new outbreak of ~s in Beirut"** "Schießereien in Beirut wieder aufgeflammt"; **the police are investigating the ~** die Polizei untersucht die Schiesserei **c** (Sport: Ftbl etc, with guns) Schießen nt **d** (Hunt) Jagen nt, Jagd f; (= shooting rights) Jagdrecht(e) nt(pl); (= land) Jagd f, Jagdrevier nt; **there is good ~ in Scotland** in Schottland kann man gut jagen; **to go ~** auf die Jagd gehen; **good ~!** Weidmannsheil! **e** (Film) Drehen nt; **~ was interrupted** die Dreharbeiten wurden unterbrochen

shooting: shooting box N Jagdhütte f; **shooting brake** N (dated Aut) Kombiwagen m; **shooting club** N Schießklub m; **shooting gallery** N Schießstand m, Schießbude f; **shooting iron** N (US, inf) Schießeisen nt (hum inf), Knarre f (sl); **shooting jacket** N Jagdrock m; **shooting lodge** N = shooting box; **shooting match** N Wett- or Preisschießen nt; **the whole ~** (inf) der ganze Laden (inf); **shooting party** N Jagdgesellschaft f; **shooting range** N Schießplatz m; **shooting rights** PL Jagdrecht(e) nt(pl); **shooting script** N (Film) Drehplan m; **shooting star** N Sternschnuppe f; **shooting stick** N Jagdstuhl m; **shooting war** N offener or heißer Krieg

shoot-out [ˈʃuːtaʊt] N Schießerei f

shop [ʃɒp] N **a** (esp Brit) Geschäft nt, Laden m; (= large store) Kaufhaus m; **I have to go to the ~s** ich muss einkaufen gehen; **~!** Bedienung!; **to set up ~** ein Geschäft or einen Laden eröffnen; **to shut up** or **close up ~** zumachen, schließen; **you've come to the wrong ~** (fig inf) da sind Sie an der falschen Adresse; **all over the ~** (Brit inf) in der ganzen Gegend herum (inf); **to talk ~** über die or von der Arbeit reden; (esp of professional people) fachsimpeln; **no ~, please!** keine Fachsimpelei, bitte!

b (= *workshop*) Werkstatt *f*; (= *workers*) Arbeiter *pl*, Arbeiterschaft *f* **c** (*Brit*: = *shopping*) **to do one's weekly ~** seinen wöchentlichen Einkauf erledigen ◾**VI** einkaufen, Einkäufe machen; **to go ~ping** einkaufen, Einkäufe machen; **we spend Saturday mornings ~ping** samstags vormittags gehen wir einkaufen; **~ at Macfarlane's!** kaufen Sie bei Macfarlane!; **to ~ for fish** Fisch kaufen gehen ◾**VT** (*Brit, inf*) **to ~ sb (to sb)** jdn (bei jdm) verpfeifen (*inf*)

▶**shop around** VI (*lit, fig*) sich umsehen (*for* nach)

shop: shop assistant N (*esp Brit*) Verkäufer(in) *m(f)*; **shopbreaker** N Einbrecher(in) *m(f)*; **shopbreaking** N Ladeneinbruch *m*; **shopfitter** N Geschäftsausstatter(in) *m(f)*; **shopfittings** PL Ladeneinrichtungen *pl*; **shop floor** N **a** (= *place*) Produktionsstätte *f*; (*for heavier work*) Werkstatt *f*; **the manager's son started off working on the ~** der Sohn des Direktors hat zunächst in der Fabrik angefangen; **on the ~** in der Werkstatt *etc*, bei *or* unter den Arbeitern **b** (= *workers*) Arbeiter *pl*, Leute *pl* in der Produktion; **shop-floor gossip** Klatsch *m or* Tratsch *m* unter den Arbeitern; **shop front** N (*esp Brit*) Ladenfassade *f*; **shopgirl** N (*Brit*) Ladenmädchen *nt*; **shopgrifting** [ˈʃɒpˌgrɪftɪŋ] N (*US*) *die Praxis, etw zu kaufen und innerhalb von 30 Tagen gegen Gelderstattung wieder zurückzugeben*; **shop hours** PL (*esp Brit*) Öffnungszeiten *pl*; **shop-in-shop** N Shop-in-Shop *m*; **shopkeeper** N (*esp Brit*) Ladenbesitzer(in) *m(f)*, Geschäftsinhaber(in) *m(f)*; **a nation of ~s** ein Krämervolk *nt*; **shopkeeping** [ˈʃɒpˌkiːpɪŋ] N Betrieb *m* eines (Laden)geschäfts; **shoplifter** N Ladendieb(in) *m(f)*; **shoplifting** N Ladendiebstahl *m*

shopper [ˈʃɒpəʳ] N Käufer(in) *m(f)*; **she's a good ~** sie kann gut einkaufen; **the streets were thronged with ~s** in den Straßen drängten sich die Kauflustigen

shopping [ˈʃɒpɪŋ] N (= *act*) Einkaufen *nt*; (= *goods bought*) Einkäufe *pl*; **she had her ~ in a plastic bag** sie hatte ihre Einkäufe in einer Plastiktüte; **to do one's ~** einkaufen, Einkäufe machen

shopping: shopping bag N Einkaufstasche *f*; **shopping basket** N Einkaufskorb *m*; **shopping cart** N (*US*) = **shopping trolley**; **shopping centre**, (*US*) **shopping center** N Einkaufszentrum *nt*; **shopping list** N Einkaufszettel *m*; **a ~ of requests/demands** eine (Wunsch)liste von Bitten/Forderungen; **shopping mall** N Shoppingcenter *nt*; **shopping precinct** N Ladengegend *f*, Ladenbereich *m*; **shopping spree** N Einkaufsbummel *m*; **shopping street** N Einkaufsstraße *f*; **shopping trolley** N (*Brit*) Einkaufswagen *m*

shop: shopsoiled ADJ (*Brit*) *clothes, furniture, wallpaper* angestaubt, angeschmutzt; *goods, material* leicht beschädigt; **shop steward** N (gewerkschaftlicher) Vertrauensmann (*im Betrieb*); **shoptalk** N Reden *nt* über die Arbeit; (*of professional people also*) Fachsimpelei *f*; **shopwalker** N (*Brit*) Aufsichtsperson *f* (*form*), Aufsicht *f*; **shop window** N (*lit, fig*) Schaufenster *nt*; **shopworn** ADJ *goods, furniture etc* leicht beschädigt

shore¹ [ʃɔːʳ] N **a** (= *seashore, lake shore*) Ufer *nt*, Gestade *nt* (*liter*); (= *beach*) Strand *m*; **these ~s** (*fig*) dieses Land, diese Gestade *pl* (*liter*); **he returned to his native ~** er kehrte zurück zu heimatlichen Gefilden; **a house on the ~s of the lake** ein Haus am Seeufer; **no invader has since set foot on these ~s** seitdem hat kein Eroberer mehr diesen Boden betreten **b** (= *land*) Land *nt*; **on ~** an Land

shore² N (*Min, Naut*) Stützbalken *m*, Strebe *f* ◾**VT** (*also* **shore up**) (ab)stützen; (*fig*) stützen

shore: shore dinner N (*US*) Meeresfrüchte *pl*; **shore leave** N (*Naut*) Landurlaub *m*; **shoreline** N Wasserlinie *f*, Uferlinie *f*; **shore pass** N (*Naut*) Landurlaubsschein *m*; **shore patrol** N (*US*) Küstenstreife *f*, Küstenpatrouille *f* (*der*

US-Marine); **shoreward(s)** ADJ **~ wind** Seewind *m*; **in a ~ direction** in Richtung Küste *or* Land, landwärts ◾ADV landwärts, zum Land (hin)

shoring [ˈʃɔːrɪŋ] N **a** (= *supporting beams*) Stützbalken *pl* **b** (*supporting of wall etc*) Abstützen *nt*

shorn [ʃɔːn] ptp of **shear** ADJ **a** **to be ~ of sth** einer Sache (*gen*) entkleidet sein **b** *sheep* geschoren; *head* (kahl) geschoren; **her ~ locks** ihr kurz geschorenes Haar

short [ʃɔːt] ADJ (+er) **a** kurz; *steps, person* klein; *waist* (*of dress*) hoch; **a ~ way off** nicht weit entfernt; **to be ~ in the leg** (*person*) kurze Beine haben; (*trousers*) zu kurz sein; **to be in ~ trousers** in kurzen Hosen herumlaufen; (*fig*) ein kleiner Junge sein; **~ back and sides** kurzer Haarschnitt; **a ~ time ago** vor kurzer Zeit, vor kurzem; **in a ~ time** *or* **while** in Kürze, in kurzer Zeit; **time is getting/is ~** die Zeit wird/ist knapp; **to take the ~ view** die Sache auf kurze Sicht betrachten; **in ~ order** (*US, inf*) sofort; **~ drink** Kurze(r) *m* (*inf*), Schnaps *m* **b** (*Ling*) *vowel, syllable* kurz; (= *unstressed*) unbetont **c** (= *brief*) kurz; **~ and sweet** schön kurz, kurz und ergreifend (*iro*); **the ~ answer is that he refused** kurz gesagt, er lehnte ab; **in ~** kurz gesagt; **she's called Pat for ~** sie wird kurz *or* einfach Pat genannt; **Pat is ~ for Patricia** Pat ist die Kurzform für Patricia **d** (= *curt*) *reply* knapp; (= *rude*) barsch, schroff; *manner, person* schroff, kurz angebunden (*inf*); **to have a ~ temper** unbeherrscht sein; **his ~ temper** seine Unbeherrschtheit; **to be ~ with sb** jdn schroff behandeln, jdm gegenüber kurz angebunden sein (*inf*) **e** (= *insufficient*) zu wenig *inv*; *rations* knapp; **to be in ~ supply** knapp sein; (*Comm*) beschränkt lieferbar sein; **to be ~** (= *in short supply*) knapp sein; (*shot, throw*) zu kurz sein, nicht weit genug sein; **we are (five/£3) ~**, we are (**five/£3**) wir haben (fünf/£ 3) zu wenig; **it's five/£3 ~** es fehlen fünf/£ 3; **we are seven ~** uns (*dat*) fehlen sieben; **we are ~ of books/staff** wir haben zu wenig Bücher/Personal; **we are not ~ of volunteers** wir haben genug Freiwillige, uns fehlt es nicht an Freiwilligen; **to be ~ of time** wenig Zeit haben; **I'm a bit ~ (of cash)** (*inf*) ich bin etwas knapp bei Kasse (*inf*); **he's one sandwich ~ of a picnic** (*hum inf*) **he's** one *or* several **cards ~ of a full deck** (*US hum inf*) er hat sie nicht alle beisammen (*inf*); **we are £2,000 ~/not far ~ of our target** wir liegen £ 2.000/(nur) knapp unter unserem Ziel; **not far** *or* **much ~ of £100** nicht viel weniger als £ 100, beinahe £ 100, knapp unter £ 100; **he is not far ~ of his fiftieth birthday now** er ist jetzt knapp unter fünfzig, ihm fehlt nicht mehr viel bis zu seinem fünfzigsten Geburtstag; **to be ~ on experience/examples** wenig Erfahrung/Beispiele haben; **to give sb ~ change** jdm zu wenig herausgeben *or* zu wenig Wechselgeld geben → **breath, measure** **f** (*Fin*) *sale* ohne Deckung, ungedeckt; *loan, bill* kurzfristig; **~ stock** auf Baisse gekaufte Aktien **g** *pastry* mürbe ◾ADV **a** (= *below the expected amount*) **to fall ~** (*arrow etc*) zu kurz landen; (*shot*) zu kurz sein; (*supplies etc*) nicht ausreichen; **that's where the book falls ~** daran fehlt es dem Buch; **to fall ~ of sth** etw nicht erreichen; *of expectations* etw nicht erfüllen; **it fell 10 feet ~ of the target** es fehlten 10 Fuß zum Ziel, es war 10 Fuß zu kurz; **it falls far ~ of what we require** das bleibt weit hinter unseren Bedürfnissen zurück; (*in quantity*) das bleibt weit unter unseren Bedürfnissen; **production has fallen ~ by 100 tons** die Produktion ist um 100 Tonnen zu niedrig; **to go ~** (*of money/food etc*) zu wenig (Geld/zu essen *etc*) haben; **we never went ~** wir hatten immer genügend; **the parents went ~ of food so that the children could eat** die Eltern haben an sich (*dat*) selbst gespart, damit die Kinder zu essen hatten; **they never let the children go ~** sie ließen es den Kindern an nichts fehlen;

we are running ~ (of water/time) wir haben nicht mehr viel (Wasser/Zeit); **I'm running ~ of ideas** mir gehen die Ideen aus; **my patience is running ~** meine Geduld ist bald zu Ende; **sugar/water is running ~** Zucker/Wasser ist knapp; **to sell sb ~** (*in shop*) jdm zuwenig geben; (= *betray, cheat*) jdn betrügen; **to sell oneself ~** (*inf*) sein Licht unter den Scheffel stellen, sich unter Wert verkaufen; **to sell ~** (*Fin*) ungedeckt *or* ohne Deckung verkaufen **b** (= *abruptly, suddenly*) plötzlich, abrupt; **to pull up** *or* **stop ~** (*while driving*) plötzlich *or* abrupt anhalten; (*while walking also*) plötzlich *or* abrupt stehen bleiben; **to stop ~** (*while talking*) plötzlich *or* unvermittelt innehalten; **to stop sb ~** jdn unterbrechen; **to stop sth ~** etw abbrechen; **I'd stop ~ of murder** vor Mord würde ich Halt machen; **he stopped ~ of actually calling me a liar** er ging nicht so weit, mich tatsächlich einen Lügner zu nennen; **to be caught ~** (*inf*, = *unprepared*) überrascht werden; (= *without money, supplies*) zu knapp (dran) sein; (= *need the toilet*) dringend mal müssen (*inf*); **to catch sb ~** (*inf*) jdn in einer Verlegenheit antreffen; **to be caught ~ by sth** auf etw (*acc*) nicht vorbereitet sein **c** **~ of** (= *except*) außer (+*dat*); **it is nothing ~ of robbery** das ist glatter Diebstahl; **nothing ~ of a revolution can ...** nur eine Revolution kann ...; **it's little ~ of madness** das grenzt an Wahnsinn; **it's little ~ of murder** das ist ja schon fast Mord; **I don't see what you can do ~ of asking him yourself** ich sehe keine andere Möglichkeit, außer dass Sie ihn selbst fragen; **~ of telling him a lie ...** außer ihn zu belügen ... ◾**N** (= *short circuit*) Kurzschluss, Kurze(r) (*inf*) *m*; (*inf*, = *short drink*) Kurze(r) *m* (*inf*); (= *short film*) Kurzfilm *m*; **to have/get sb by the ~ and curlies** (*Brit inf*) jdn am Wickel haben/kriegen (*inf*) → **long²** ◾**VT** (*Elec*) kurzschließen ◾**VI** (*Elec*) einen Kurzschluss haben

shortage [ˈʃɔːtɪdʒ] N (*of goods, objects*) Knappheit *f no pl* (*of an* +*dat*); (*of people*) Mangel *m no pl* (*of an* +*dat*); **the housing ~** die Wohnungsknappheit; **a ~ of staff** ein Mangel *m* an Arbeitskräften, ein Personalmangel *m*; **in times of ~** in Zeiten der Knappheit; **there are always ~s** irgend etwas ist immer knapp; **there's no ~ of advice** es fehlt nicht an guten Ratschlägen

short: short arse N (*Brit sl*) Knirps *m* (*inf*); **shortbread** N Shortbread *nt*, ≈ Butterkeks *m*; **shortcake** N (*Brit*: = *shortbread*) Butterkeks *m*; (*US*, = *sponge*) Biskuittörtchen *nt*; **strawberry ~** Erdbeertörtchen *nt*; **short-change** VT **to ~ sb** (*lit*) jdm zu wenig Wechselgeld geben, jdm zu wenig herausgeben; (*fig inf*) jdn übers Ohr hauen (*inf*); **short circuit** N Kurzschluss *m*; **short-circuit** ◾**VT** kurzschließen; (*fig*, = *bypass*) umgehen ◾**VI** einen Kurzschluss haben; **shortcoming** N (*esp pl*) Mangel *m*; (*of person*) Fehler *m*; (*of system*) Unzulänglichkeit *f*, Mangel *m*; **shortcrust** N (*also* **shortcrust pastry**) Mürbeteig *m*; **short cut** N Abkürzung *f*; (*fig*) Schnellverfahren *nt*; (= *easy solution*) Patentlösung *f*; **there's no ~ to success** der Erfolg fällt einem nicht in den Schoß; **short-dated** ADJ (*Fin*) *stock* kurzfristig; *bonds, gilts* mit kurzer Laufzeit

shorten [ˈʃɔːtn] ◾**VT** **a** (= *make shorter*) verkürzen; *life, name* abkürzen; *dress, rope* kürzer machen, kürzen; *book, programme, letter, syllabus etc* kürzen; *odds* verringern; *sail* reffen **b** *pastry* Fett beigeben (+*dat*) ◾**VI** (*evenings, days*) kürzer werden; (*odds*) sich verringern

shortening [ˈʃɔːtnɪŋ] N (*Cook*) (Back)fett *nt*

short: shortfall N Defizit *nt*; **short-haired** ADJ kurzhaarig; **shorthand** N Kurzschrift *f*, Stenografie *f*; **in ~** in Kurzschrift; **to write ~** stenografieren; **to take sth down in ~** etw stenografieren; **short-handed** ADJ **to be ~** zu wenig Personal haben; **shorthand notebook** N Stenoblock *m*; **shorthand notes** PL stenografische Notizen *pl*; **shorthand typist** N Stenotypist(in) *m(f)*; **shorthand writer** N

Stenograf(in) *m(f)*; **short haul** N Nahtransport *m*; **short-haul jet** N Kurzstreckenflugzeug *nt*; **shorthorn** N Kurzhornrind *nt*, Shorthorn *nt*; ~ **cattle** Kurzhornrinder *pl*

shortie [ˈʃɔːtɪ] N **a** (*inf: also* **shortie nightie**) Shorty *nt*, kurzes Nachthemd **b** = **shorty**

shortish [ˈʃɔːtɪʃ] ADJ **a** ziemlich kurz; *person* ziemlich klein **b** (= *scarce*) ziemlich knapp

short: short list N (*esp Brit*) Auswahlliste *f*; **to be on the** ~ in der engeren Wahl sein; **short-list** VT (*esp Brit*) **to** ~ **sb** jdn in die engere Wahl nehmen *or* ziehen; **he has not been** ~**ed** er ist nicht in die engere Wahl gekommen; **short-lived** ADJ (*lit, fig*) kurzlebig; *protests, attempts* nicht lange andauernd; **to be** ~ (*success, happiness*) von kurzer Dauer sein

shortly [ˈʃɔːtlɪ] ADV **a** (= *soon*) bald, in Kürze; *after, before, afterwards* kurz **b** (= *briefly*) kurz **c** (= *curtly*) barsch

shortness [ˈʃɔːtnɪs] N **a** Kürze *f*; (*of person*) Kleinheit *f*; ~ **of sight** Kurzsichtigkeit *f*; ~ **of breath** Kurzatmigkeit *f* **b** (= *curtness*) Schroffheit *f*, Barschheit *f* **c** (*of supplies, money*) Knappheit *f*

short: short-order ADJ (*US*) *cook, waiter* im Schnellimbiss; ~ **dishes** Schnellgerichte *pl*; **short pastry** N Mürbeteig *m*; **short-range** ADJ mit geringer *or* kurzer Reichweite; *walkie-talkie* für den Nahbereich; (*fig*) *plans* kurzfristig; ~ **missile/aircraft** Kurzstreckenrakete *f*/-flugzeug *nt*; ~ **weapon** Nahkampfwaffe *f*; ~ **weather forecast** Wetterbericht *m* für die nächsten Tage

shorts [ʃɔːts] PL **a** (= *short trousers*) Shorts *pl*, kurze Hose(n *pl*) **b** (*esp US*, = *underpants*) Unterhose *f*

short: short sharp shock N (*Brit*, = *punishment*) *kurze, aber harte Gefängnisstrafe*; **short-sighted** ADJ , **short-sightedly** ADV (*lit, fig*) kurzsichtig; **short-sightedness** N (*lit, fig*) Kurzsichtigkeit *f*; **short ski** N Kurzski *m*; **short-sleeved** ADJ kurzärmelig; **short-staffed** ADJ **to be** ~ zu wenig Personal haben; (*in a bad temper*) gereizt; **to be** ~ **with sb** mit jdm ungeduldig sein; **short-stay** ADJ (*Brit*) *hospital ward* Kurzzeitstation *f*; ~ **car park** Kurzzeitparkplatz *m*; ~ **visa** Visum *nt* für einen Kurzaufenthalt; **short-stay parking** N (*Brit*) Kurzparken *nt*; **short term** N **in the** ~ auf kurze Frist gesehen, vorläufig; **plans for the** ~ kurzfristige Pläne; **in the** ~ auf kurze Sicht; **short-term** ADJ kurzfristig; ~ **memory** Kurzzeitgedächtnis *nt*; **to take a** ~ **view** kurzfristig denken; **banks took a** ~ **view that was harmful to small firms** die kurzsichtige Einstellung der Banken schadete den Kleinunternehmen; **on a** ~ **basis** kurzfristig ADV kurzfristig; **short-term contract** N Kurzzeitvertrag *m*; **he was engaged on a** ~ er wurde mit Kurzzeitvertrag eingestellt; **short time** N Kurzarbeit *f*; **to be on** ~, **to work** ~ kurzarbeiten, Kurzarbeit haben; **short ton** N *Tonne von 2000 Pounds = 907,18 kg*; **short-waisted** ADJ *person* mit kurzer Taille; *coat* hoch tailliert; **to be** ~ eine kurze/hohe Taille haben; **short wave** N Kurzwelle *f*; **short-wave** ADJ *transmission* auf Kurzwelle; **a** ~ **radio** ein Kurzwellenempfänger *m*; **short-winded** ADJ (= *breathless*) kurzatmig

shorty [ˈʃɔːtɪ] N (*inf*) Kleine(r) *mf*, Knirps *m* (*inf*)

shot¹ [ʃɒt] *pret, ptp of* **shoot** N **a** (*from gun, bow etc*) Schuss *m*; **to fire** *or* **take a** ~ **at sb/sth** ein Schuss auf jdn/etw abfeuern *or* abgeben; **a** ~ **across the bows** (*lit, fig*) ein Schuss *m* vor den Bug; **to exchange** ~**s** sich (*dat*) einen Schusswechsel liefern; **the first** ~**s in the election campaign** (*fig*) die ersten scharfen Schüsse im Wahlkampf; **to call the** ~**s** (*fig*) das Sagen haben (*inf*) → **long shot, parting**

b (= *projectile*) Kugel *f*; (*no pl*: = *lead shot*) Schrot *m*, Schrotkugeln *pl*

c (= *person*) Schütze *m*, Schützin *f* → **big shot**

d (= *attempt*) Versuch *m*; **at the first** ~ auf Anhieb; **to take** *or* **have a** ~ (**at it**) (= *try*) es (mal) versuchen; (= *guess*) (auf gut Glück) raten; **I had a** ~ **at water-skiing** ich habe auch mal versucht, Wasserski zu laufen; **it's your** ~ du bist dran; **to give sth one's best** ~ (*inf*) sich nach Kräften um etw bemühen → **dark**

e (= *space shot*) (Raum)flug *m*; (= *launch*) Start *m*

f like a ~ (*inf*, = *quickly, run away, be off*) wie der Blitz (*inf*); *do sth, agree* sofort

g (= *injection*) Spritze *f*; (= *immunization*) Impfung *f*; (*of alcohol*) Schuss *m*; **he gave him a** ~ **of morphine** er gab ihm eine Morphiumspritze; **a** ~ **of rum** ein Schuss *m* Rum; **to give a company a** ~ **in the arm** (*fig*) einer Firma eine Finanzspritze geben

h (*Phot*) Aufnahme *f*; **out of** ~ nicht im Bild

i (*Sport, Ftbl, Hockey etc*) Schuss *m*; (= *throw*) Wurf *m*; (*Tennis, Golf*) Schlag *m*; **to take a** ~ **at goal** aufs Tor schießen

j (*shot-putting*) **the** ~ (= *discipline*) Kugelstoßen *nt*; (= *weight*) die Kugel; **to put the** ~ kugelstoßen

shot² ADJ **a** (= *variegated*) durchzogen, durchschossen (*with* mit); *silk* eingeschossen, changierend; **to be** ~ **through with sth** (*lit, with colour etc*) von etw durchzogen sein; (*fig*) *with emotion etc* von etw durchdrungen sein; **his hair is** ~ **through with silver** sein Haar ist von silbernen Strähnen durchzogen **b** (*Brit inf*: = *rid*) **to be/get** ~ **of sb/sth** jdn/etw los sein/loswerden

c (= *destroyed*) **my nerves are totally** ~ ich bin mit den Nerven fertig *or* am Ende; **her confidence was** ~ **to pieces** ihr Vertrauen war völlig zerstört

shot: shotgun N Schrotflinte *f*; **shotgun wedding** N Mussheirat *f*; **shot put** N (= *event*) Kugelstoßen *nt*; (= *throw*) Wurf *m*, Stoß *m*; **shot-putter** N Kugelstoßer(in) *m(f)*; **shot tower** N Schrotturm *m*

should [ʃʊd] ⚙ *1.1, 2.1, 14, 15.2, 26.1 pret of* **shall** MODAL AUX VB **a** (*expressing duty, advisability, command*) **I/he** ~ **do that** ich/er sollte das tun; **you** ~**n't do that** Sie sollten das nicht tun; **I** ~ **have done it** ich hätte es tun sollen *or* müssen; **I** ~**n't have done it** ich hätte es nicht tun sollen *or* dürfen; **all is as it** ~ **be** alles ist so, wie es sein sollte *or* muss; **which is as it** ~ **be** und so soll(te) es auch sein; **he** ~ **know that it's wrong to lie** er sollte *or* müsste wissen, dass man nicht lügen darf; **you really** ~ **see that film** den Film sollten *or* müssen Sie wirklich sehen; **you** ~ **have seen his face** (*inf*) du hättest sein Gesicht sehen sollen!; ~ **I go too?** – **yes you** ~ sollte ich auch gehen? – ja, das sollten Sie schon; **was it a good film?** – **I** ~ **think it was** war der Film gut? – und ob; **he's coming to apologize** – **I** ~ **think so** er will sich entschuldigen – das möchte ich auch meinen *or* hoffen; **... and I** ~ **know** ... und ich müsste es ja wissen; **how** – **I know?** woher soll ich das wissen?

b (*expressing probability*) **he** ~ **be there by now** er müsste eigentlich schon da sein; **they** ~ **arrive tomorrow** sie müssten morgen ankommen; **this** ~ **be enough** das müsste eigentlich reichen; **why** ~ **he suspect me?** warum sollte er mich verdächtigen?; **this book** ~ **help you** dieses Buch wird Ihnen bestimmt helfen; **this** ~ **be good!** (*inf*) das wird bestimmt gut!

c (*in tentative statements*) **I** ~**n't like to say** das möchte ich nicht gern sagen; **I** ~ **hardly have called him an idiot** ich hätte ihn wohl kaum einen Idioten genannt; **I** ~ **think there were about 40** ich würde schätzen, dass etwa 40 dort waren; ~ **I open the window?** soll ich das Fenster aufmachen?; **I** ~ **like to disagree** da möchte ich widersprechen; **I** ~ **like to know** ich wüsste gern, ich möchte gern wissen; **I** ~ **like to apply for the job** ich würde mich gern um die Stelle bewerben; **thanks, I** ~ **like to** danke, gern

d (*expressing surprise*) **who** – **I see/**~ **it be but Anne!** und wen sehe ich/und wer war's?

Anne!; why ~ **he want to know/do that?** warum will er das wohl wissen/machen?; **why** – **he have done it, if ...?** warum hat er es dann gemacht, wenn ...?

e (*subjunc, conditional*) **I/he** ~ **go if ...** ich/er würde gehen, wenn ...; **we** – **have come if ...** wir wären gekommen, wenn ...; **it seems unbelievable that he** ~ **have failed/be so young** es scheint unglaublich, dass er versagt hat/so jung ist; **I don't see why he** ~**n't have paid by now** ich verstehe nicht, warum er bis jetzt noch nicht bezahlt hat; **if they** ~ **send for me** wenn *or* falls sie nach mir schicken sollten; **if he** ~ **come**, ~ **he come** falls er kommen sollte, sollte er kommen; ~ **it not be true** sollte das nicht wahr sein; **I** ~**n't be surprised if he comes** *or* **came** *or* **were to come** ich wäre nicht *or* keineswegs überrascht, wenn er kommen würde *or* wenn er käme; **I** ~**n't (do that) if I were you** ich würde das an Ihrer Stelle nicht tun; **I** ~**n't worry about it** ich würde mir darüber keine Gedanken machen; **it is necessary that he** ~ **be told** es ist nötig, dass man es ihm sagt; **unless he** ~ **change his mind** falls er es sich (*dat*) nicht anders überlegt

shoulder [ˈʃəʊldə] N **a** (*of person, animal*) Schulter *f*; (*of bird*) Schultergürtel *m*; (*of meat*) Bug *m*; (*of pork*) Schulter *f*, Schulterstück *nt*; (*of garment*) Schulter(partie) *f*; **to shrug one's** ~**s** mit den Schultern *or* Achseln zucken; **to have broad** ~**s** (*lit*) breite Schultern haben; (*fig also*) einen breiten Rücken *or* Buckel (*inf*) haben; **to put one's** ~ **to the wheel** (*fig*) sich ins Zeug legen; **to cry on sb's** ~ sich an jds Brust (*dat*) ausweinen; **a** ~ **to cry on** jemand, bei dem man sich ausweinen kann; ~ **to** ~ Schulter an Schulter → **cold, rub, straight**

b (*of mountain*) Schulter *f*; (*of road*) Seitenstreifen *m*, Bankett *nt*; (*US*: = *hard shoulder*) Seitenstreifen *m*; (*of vase, bottle*) Ausbuchtung *f*

VT **a** (*lit*) *load, case, person* schultern, auf die Schulter nehmen; (*fig*) *responsibilities, blame, task* auf sich (*acc*) nehmen; *expense* tragen; ~ **arms!** (*Mil*) das Gewehr über!; **the fans** ~**ed him off the pitch** die Fans trugen ihn auf den Schultern vom Platz

b (= *push*) (mit der Schulter) stoßen; **to** ~ **sb aside** (*lit*) jdn zur Seite stoßen; (*fig*) jdn beiseite drängen; **to** ~ **one's way through (the crowd)** sich durch die Menge drängen *or* boxen

shoulder: shoulder bag N Umhängetasche *f*; **shoulder blade** N Schulterblatt *nt*; **shoulder flash** N (*Mil*) Dienstgradabzeichen *nt*, Schulterstück *nt*; **shoulder-high** ADV schulterhoch; **his hands were raised** ~ er hatte seine Hände schulterhoch erhoben; **to carry sb** ~ jdn auf den Schultern tragen; **to stand** ~ **to sb** jdm bis an die Schultern reichen ADJ *pred* schulterhoch, schulterhohe(r, s) *attr*; **shoulder holster** N Schulterholster *nt*; **shoulder-length** ADJ *hair* schulterlang; **shoulder loop** N Dienstgradabzeichen *nt*; **shoulder pad** N Schulterpolster *nt*; **shoulder strap** N (*Mil*) Schulterklappe *f*; (*of dress*) Träger *m*; (*of satchel, bag etc*) (Schulter)riemen *m*

shouldn't [ˈʃʊdnt] *contr of* **should not**

shout [ʃaʊt] N Ruf *m*, Schrei *m*; **a** ~ **of protest** ein Protestruf *m*; **a** ~ **of joy/pain** ein Freuden-/Schmerzensschrei *m*; ~**s of applause** Beifallsrufe *pl*; ~**s of laughter** Lachsalven *pl*, brüllendes Gelächter *nt*; **to give a** ~ einen Schrei ausstoßen; **to give sb a** ~ jdm zurufen; **give me a** ~ **when you're ready** (*inf*) sag Bescheid, wenn du fertig bist; **his voice rose to a** ~ seine Stimme steigerte sich bis zum Brüllen; **it's my** ~ (*Brit inf*) (= *turn*) ich bin dran; (*for food, drink*) ich zahle

VT **a** schreien, (= *call*) rufen; *order* brüllen; *protest, disapproval etc* laut(stark) kundtun; **to** ~ **abuse at sb** (*in* laut) beschimpfen; **to** ~ **a warning to sb** jdm eine Warnung zurufen

b (*inf*: = *buy as treat*) **to** ~ **sb sth** jdm etw spendieren (*inf*)

VI **a** (= *call out*) rufen; (*very loudly*) schreien; (*angrily, commanding*) brüllen; **to** ~ **for sb/sth** nach jdm/etw rufen; **she** ~**ed for Jane to come** sie rief, Jane solle kommen; **to** ~ **at sb** mit jdm schreien; (*abusively*) jdn anschreien; **don't ~!** schrei nicht (so)!; **to ~ to sb** jdm zurufen; **he ~ed to me to open the door** er rief mir zu, ich sollte die Tür öffnen; **to ~ for help** um Hilfe rufen; **to ~ for joy** einen Freudenschrei ausstoßen; **to ~ with laughter** vor Lachen brüllen; **it was nothing to ~ about** (*inf*) es war nicht umwerfend

VR **to ~ oneself hoarse** sich heiser schreien

▶ **shout down** VT *sep person* niederbrüllen; *play* ausbuhen

▶ **shout out** VI einen Schrei ausstoßen; (*in pain, rage, protest*) aufschreien; **to shout out in despair/pain** verzweifelt/vor Schmerz aufschreien, einen Verzweiflungs-/Schmerzensschrei ausstoßen; **shout out when you're ready** ruf, wenn du fertig bist **VT** *sep* ausrufen; *order* brüllen

shouting [ˈʃaʊtɪŋ] N (= *act*) Schreien *nt*; (= *sound*) Geschrei *nt*; **it's all over bar the ~** (*inf*) es ist so gut wie gelaufen (*inf*)

shouting match N it turned into a ~ sie brüllten sich nur noch gegenseitig an

shove [ʃʌv] **N** Schubs(er) *m* (*inf*), Stoß *m*; **to give sb a ~** jdn schubsen (*inf*) or stoßen; **to give sth a ~** etw rücken; *door* gegen etw stoßen; *ball* etw anstoßen; *car* etw anschieben; **one more ~** noch einmal schieben, noch einen Ruck

VT **a** (= *push*) schieben; (*with one short push*) stoßen, schubsen (*inf*); (= *jostle*) drängen; **stop shoving me** hör auf zu drängeln or mich zu schubsen (*inf*); **to ~ sb against a wall** jdn gegen die Wand stoßen; **to ~ sb off the pavement** jdn vom Bürgersteig herunterschubsen (*inf*), jdn vom Bürgersteig herunterdrängen; **to ~ one's way forward** sich nach vorn durchdrängen; **to ~ a door open** eine Tür aufstoßen **b** (*inf*, = *put*) **to ~ sth on(to) sth** etw auf etw (*acc*) werfen (*inf*); **to ~ sth in(to)/between sth** etw in etw (*acc*)/zwischen etw (*acc*) stecken; **he ~d his head out of the window** er steckte seinen Kopf aus dem Fenster; **he ~d a book into my hand** er drückte mir ein Buch in die Hand **VI** stoßen; (*to move sth*) schieben; (= *jostle*) drängeln

▶ **shove about** (*Brit*) or **around** VT *sep* (*inf*) herumstoßen

▶ **shove away** VT *sep* (*inf*) wegstoßen, wegschubsen (*inf*)

▶ **shove back** VT *sep* (*inf*) *chair etc* zurückschieben; *sb, plate* zurückstoßen, zurückschubsen (*inf*); (= *replace*) zurücktun (*inf*); (*into pocket etc*) wieder hineinstecken

▶ **shove down** VT *sep* (*inf*, = *put*) hinlegen, hinwerfen (*inf*); (= *write*) hinschmieren (*inf*), aufschreiben

▶ **shove off** VT *sep* (*Naut*) vom Ufer abstoßen **VI** **a** (*in boat*) ablegen **b** (*inf*, = *leave*) abschieben (*inf*)

▶ **shove on** VT *sep* (*inf*) *coat* anziehen; *hat* aufsetzen; *record* auflegen

▶ **shove out** VT *sep boat* abstoßen; *person* rausschmeißen (*inf*); **to shove sb out of office** (*inf*) jdn rausschmeißen (*inf*)

▶ **shove over** (*inf*) **VT** *sep* rüberwerfen (*inf*), rüberschmeißen (*inf*) **VI** (*also* **shove up**) rutschen

shove-halfpenny [ˈʃʌvˌheɪpnɪ] N *Spiel, bei dem Münzen in auf einer Platte vorgezeichnete Felder gestoßen werden*

shovel [ˈʃʌvl] **N** Schaufel *f*; (*with long handle also*) Schippe *f*; (*on power shovel*) Löffel *m*; (= *power shovel*) Löffelbagger *m*; **a ~ of coal** eine Schaufel Kohle **VT** schaufeln; *coal, snow also* schippen; **to ~ food into one's mouth** (*inf*) Essen in sich (*acc*) hineinschaufeln; **to ~ snow off a path** einen Pfad von Schnee freischaufeln

shoveler [ˈʃʌvələ^r] N (*Orn*) Löffelente *f*

shovelful [ˈʃʌvlfʊl] N Schaufel *f*; **a ~ of coal** eine Schaufel Kohle

show [ʃəʊ] ⊙ 26.2 *vb: pret* **showed**, *ptp* **shown** **N** **a** (= *display*) **a fine ~ of roses** eine Rosenpracht; **~ of force** Machtdemonstration *f*; **there was a strong ~ of resistance** es gab starken Widerstand; **the demonstration was a ~ of sympathy** die Demonstration war eine Solidaritätsbekundung; **~ of hands** Handzeichen *nt*, Hand(er)heben *nt* **b** (= *outward appearance*) Schau *f*; (= *trace*) Spur *f*; (*of hatred, affection*) Kundgebung *f*; **it's just for ~** das ist nur zur Schau da; (= *pretence*) das ist nur Schau (*inf*); **to do sth for ~** etw tun, um Eindruck zu schinden (*inf*) or zu machen; **it's all done for ~** das ist alles nur dazu da, um Eindruck zu machen; **to make a great ~ of being impressed/overworked/pleased** sich (*dat*) ganz den Anschein geben, beeindruckt/überarbeitet/erfreut zu sein; **they made a great ~ of their wealth** sie protzten mit ihrem Reichtum (*inf*); **without any ~ of emotion** ohne irgendwelche Gefühle zu zeigen; **it was all ~** es war alles nur Schau (*inf*); **to be fond of ~** gerne prunken **c** (= *exhibition*) Ausstellung *f*; **dog/fashion ~** Hunde-/Modenschau *f*; **to be on ~** ausgestellt or zu sehen sein **d** (*Theat*) Aufführung *f*; (*TV, variety or pop show*) Show *f*; (*Rad*) Sendung *f*; (*Film*) Vorstellung *f*; **to go to a ~** (*esp Brit: in theatre*) ins Theater gehen; (*US: in movie theater*) ins Kino gehen; **the ~ must go on** es muss trotz allem weitergehen; **on with the ~!** anfangen!; (= *continue*) weitermachen!; **to stop the ~** (*lit*) die Aufführung unterbrechen; **he stopped the ~ with his marvellous medley of old hits** (*fig*) der Höhepunkt der Show war sein wunderbares Medley alter Hits → **steal e** (*esp Brit, inf*) **(jolly) good ~!** (*dated*) ausgezeichnet!, bravo!; **bad ~!** (*dated*) schwaches Bild (*inf*); (= *what a pity*) so ein Pech!; **to put up a good/poor ~** eine gute/schwache Leistung zeigen; **it's a pretty poor ~ when ...** das ist vielleicht traurig or ein schwaches Bild (*inf*), wenn ... **f** (*inf*, = *undertaking, organization*) Laden *m* (*inf*); **he runs the ~** er schmeißt hier den Laden (*inf*); **to give the (whole) ~ away** alles verraten **VT** **a** (= *display*) zeigen; (*at exhibition*) ausstellen, zeigen; (= *demonstrate*) *dog* vorführen; *slides, film* zeigen, vorführen; *passport, ticket* vorzeigen; **to ~ sb sth, to ~ sth to sb** jdm etw zeigen; **~ me how to do it** zeigen Sie mir, wie man das macht; **it's been ~n on television** das kam im Fernsehen; **the film was first ~n in 1988** der Film wurde 1988 uraufgeführt; **to ~ one's face** sich zeigen; **he had nothing to ~ for it** er hatte am Ende nichts vorzuweisen; **he has nothing to ~ for all his effort** seine ganze Mühe hat nichts gebracht; **I'll ~ him!** (*inf*) dem werd ichs zeigen! (*inf*); **that ~ed him!** (*inf*) dem habe ichs aber gezeigt! (*inf*) → **hand, heel** [1] **b** (= *register*) (an)zeigen; *loss, profit* haben, verzeichnen; *rise in numbers* aufzeigen; (*thermometer, speedometer*) stehen auf (+*dat*); (*calendar*) zeigen; **it ~s that ...** es zeigt, dass ...; **as ~n in the illustration** wie in der Illustration dargestellt; **the roads are ~n in red** die Straßen sind rot (eingezeichnet); **what time does your watch ~?** wie spät ist es nach Ihrer Uhr?; **the dial will ~ red if ...** der Zeiger zeigt auf Rot, wenn ... **c** (= *indicate*) zeigen; (= *prove*) beweisen; *kindness, favour* erweisen; *courage* zeigen, beweisen; *loyalty, taste, tact, intelligence* beweisen; *respect* bezeigen; *proof* erbringen; **to ~ one's gratitude** sich dankbar zeigen; **this ~s him to be a thief** das beweist, dass er ein Dieb ist; **I hope I have ~n how silly it is** ich habe hoffentlich (auf)gezeigt, wie dumm das ist; **it all** or **just goes to ~ that ...** das zeigt doch nur, dass ... **d** (= *reveal*) zeigen; **the housing market is ~ing signs of life** auf dem Immobilienmarkt tut or rührt sich (wieder) (et)was (*inf*); **it ~ed signs of having been used** man sah, dass es gebraucht worden war; **to ~ signs of wear** Abnutzungserscheinungen *pl* aufweisen; **to ~ signs of tiredness** Ermüdungserscheinungen *pl* zeigen; **~ a leg!** (*Brit inf*) raus aus den Federn!

(*inf*); **he's beginning to ~ his age** man sieht ihm allmählich das Alter an; **that dress ~s her bra** bei dem Kleid sieht man ihren BH; **the carpet ~s the dirt** auf dem Teppich sieht man den Schmutz **b** (= *direct*) zeigen; **to ~ sb the way** jdm den Weg zeigen; **to ~ sb in/out** jdn hereinbringen/hinausbringen or -begleiten; **to ~ sb out of a room** jdn hinausbegleiten, jdn aus dem Zimmer begleiten; **to ~ sb into a room** jdn hereinbringen, jdn ins Zimmer bringen; **to ~ sb to his seat/the door** jdn an seinen Platz/an die or zur Tür bringen; **to ~ sb over** or **(a)round the house** jdm das (ganze) Haus zeigen; **they were ~n over** or **(a)round the factory** ihnen wurde die Fabrik gezeigt, sie wurden in der Fabrik herumgeführt

VI **a** (= *be visible*) zu sehen sein, sichtbar sein; (*petticoat etc*) vorsehen, rausgucken (*inf*); (*film*) gezeigt werden, laufen; (*exhibit: artist*) ausstellen; **the dirt doesn't ~** man sieht den Schmutz nicht; **his anger ~ed in his eyes** man konnte ihm seinen Ärger von den Augen ablesen; **don't let your anger ~** lassen Sie sich (*dat*) den Ärger nicht anmerken!; **the tulips are beginning to ~** die Tulpen kommen langsam heraus; **the pregnancy** or **she is now beginning to ~** man sieht or merkt jetzt allmählich, dass sie schwanger ist; **it only ~s when ...** (= *be visible*) man sieht es nur, wenn ...; (= *be noticed*) man merkt es nur, wenn ...; **to ~ through** durchkommen; **the house ~s through the gap** durch den Spalt kann man das Haus sehen; **he didn't ~** (*inf*) er hat sich nicht blicken lassen (*inf*) **b** (= *prove*) **it just goes to ~!** da sieht mans mal wieder! **c** (*Horse Racing*) sich platzieren

VR **to ~ oneself** sich blicken lassen (*inf*); **to ~ oneself to be incompetent** sich (als) unfähig erweisen; **he ~ed himself to be a coward** es zeigte sich, dass er ein Feigling war; **it ~s itself in his speech** das merkt man an seiner Sprache

▶ **show off** VI angeben (*to, in front of* vor +*dat*) **VT** *sep* **a** (= *flaunt*) *knowledge, medal* angeben mit; *new car, son* vorführen (*to sb* jdm); *wealth* protzen mit (*inf*) **b** (= *enhance*) *beauty, picture* hervorheben; *figure* betonen; **to show sth off to its best advantage** etw (richtig) zur Geltung bringen; **the dress shows her off to great advantage** das Kleid ist sehr vorteilhaft für sie

▶ **show up** VI **a** (= *be seen*) zu sehen or zu erkennen sein; (= *stand out*) hervorstechen; **the stain shows up** man sieht den Fleck; **the tower showed up clearly against the sky** der Turm zeichnete sich deutlich gegen den Himmel ab; **to show up well/badly** (*fig*) eine gute/schlechte Figur machen **b** (*inf*: = *turn up*) auftauchen, sich blicken lassen (*inf*) **VT** *sep* **a** (= *highlight*) (deutlich) erkennen lassen; **the bright light showed up the faded wallpaper** in dem hellen Licht konnte man sehen, wie verblichen die Tapete war **b** (= *reveal*) *flaws, bad condition, errors* zum Vorschein bringen; *sb's character, intentions* deutlich zeigen; *impostor, fraud* aufdecken; *person* bloßstellen; **my question showed him up to be a liar** meine Frage entlarvte ihn als Lügner **c** (= *shame*) blamieren; **his bad manners show his parents up** mit seinen schlechten Manieren blamiert er seine Eltern; **he always gets drunk and shows her up** er betrinkt sich immer und bringt sie dadurch in eine peinliche Situation; **to show oneself up** sich blamieren **d** (= *direct*) heraufbringen

show: **show bill** N Werbe- or Reklameplakat *nt*; **show biz** N (*inf*) = **show business**; **showboat** N (*esp US*) *Dampfer auf dem eine Schauspieltruppe etc Vorstellungen gibt*; **show business** N Showbusiness *nt*, Showgeschäft *nt*; **to be in ~** im Showgeschäft (tätig) sein; **~ personalities** Persönlichkeiten *pl* aus dem Showgeschäft; **showcase** **N** Schaukasten *m*, Vitrine *f*; (*fig*) Schaufenster *nt* **VT** *sb's work, talents* präsentieren, vorstellen; **show-**

down N (inf) Kraftprobe f, Show-down m, Showdown m (inf); **there was a ~ between the two rivals** zwischen den Rivalen kam es zur Kraftprobe; **to have a ~ with sb** sich mit jdm auseinander setzen

shower ['ʃaʊə'] **N a** (of rain etc) Schauer m; (of arrows, stones, blows, bullets etc) Hagel m; (of curses, questions) Schwall m; **a ~ of sparks** ein Funkenregen m; **~ of water** Dusche f, Wasserstrahl m
  b (= shower bath) Dusche f; **to take** or **have a ~** (sich) duschen); **to send sb to the ~s** (US inf) (Sport) jdn vom Feld schicken; (fig) jdn rausschmeißen (inf); **his bad language earned him a trip to the ~s** (US fig inf) weil er ständig Kraftausdrücke benutzte, wurde er rausgeschmissen (inf)
  c (Brit fig inf) Blödmänner pl (inf); **what a ~!** so ein lausiges Volk! (inf)
  d (US inf: = party) Party, auf der jeder ein Geschenk für den Ehrengast mitbringt (for bride-to-be) ≈ Polterabend m; **baby ~** Party vor Geburt eines Babys, auf der jeder ein Geschenk für das Baby mitbringt
  VT to ~ sb with sth, to ~ sth on sb (curses) etw auf jdn niederregnen lassen; blows etw auf jdn niederprasseln or niederhageln lassen; praise, affection, honours, presents jdn mit etw überschütten or überhäufen; **the broken pipe ~ed water on the passers-by** das Wasser aus dem kaputten Rohr bespritzte die Passanten; **to ~ abuse on sb, to ~ sb with abuse** einen Schwall von Beschimpfungen gegen jdn loslassen
  VI a (= wash) duschen, brausen (dated)
  b (= descend: also **shower down**) niedergehen auf (+acc)

shower: shower attachment N Brauseaufsatz m; **shower base** N Duschwanne f; **shower bath** N Dusche f; **shower cabinet** N Duschkabine f; **shower cap** N Duschhaube f; **shower cubicle** N = shower stall; **shower curtain** N Duschvorhang m; **shower gel** N Duschgel nt; **showerproof** ADJ regenfest; **shower stall** N Duschkabine f

showery ['ʃaʊərɪ] ADJ regnerisch

show: show flat N (Brit) Musterwohnung nt; **showgirl** N Revuegirl nt; **showground** N Ausstellungsgelände nt; (for circus) Zirkusgelände nt; **show home, show house** N (Brit) Musterhaus nt

showily ['ʃaʊɪlɪ] ADV protzig (inf); furnished also, produced bombastisch; behave theatralisch; **~ dressed** aufgeputzt

showiness ['ʃaʊɪnɪs] N Protzigkeit f (inf); (of person) auffallende Art; (as regards clothes) Aufgeputztheit f; (of manner) theatralische Art; (of ceremony, décor) bombastische Art; (of colour) Auffälligkeit f; (of production) Effekthascherei f

showing ['ʃaʊɪŋ] N **a** (= exhibition) Ausstellung f **b** (= performance) Aufführung f; (of film) Vorstellung f; (of programme) Ausstrahlung f **c** (= standard of performance) Leistung f; **to make a good/poor ~** eine gute/schwache Leistung zeigen; **on his present ~** mit seinen jetzigen Leistungen; **on present ~** so, wie die Dinge zurzeit stehen **d** **on his own ~** nach eigenen Angaben

showing-off ['ʃaʊɪŋ'ɒf] N Angeberei f

show: show-jumper N Springreiter(in) m(f); **showjumping** N Springen nt, Springreiten nt

showman ['ʃaʊmən] N pl **-men** [-mən] Showman m; (fig) Schauspieler m

showmanship ['ʃaʊmənʃɪp] N (of person) Talent nt für effektvolle Darbietung; (of act) effektvolle Darbietung; (fig) Talent nt sich in Szene zu setzen; **he knows nothing about ~** er hat keine Ahnung, wie man etwas effektvoll darbietet or in Szene setzt; **it's just ~** das ist reine Schau or Effekthascherei

shown [ʃaʊn] ptp of **show**

show: show-off N (inf) Angeber(in) m(f); **showpiece** N Schaustück nt; (= fine example) Paradestück nt; **showplace** N (= tourist attrac-

tion) Sehenswürdigkeit f; **showroom** N Ausstellungsraum m; **in ~ condition** in makellosem Zustand; **show stopper** N (inf) Publikumshit m (inf); (fig) Clou m des Abends/der Party etc; **show-stopping** ADJ attr (inf) performance, product fantastisch, phantastisch (inf); **~ number** Publikumshit m; **show tent** N Ausstellungszelt nt; **showtime** N (Theat, TV) Vorstellungsbeginn m; **it's close to ~ now** die Vorstellung fängt gleich an; **show trial** N Schauprozess m; **show window** N Schaufenster nt, Auslage f

showwoman ['ʃaʊwʊmən] N pl **-women** [-wɪmɪn] Showfrau f; (fig) Schauspielerin f

showy ['ʃaʊɪ] ADJ (+er) protzig (inf); person auffallend; (as regards clothes) protzig angezogen (inf); manner theatralisch; ceremony, décor bombastisch; colour grell, auffällig; production bombastisch, auf Schau (inf) or Effekte gemacht

shrank [ʃræŋk] pret of **shrink**

shrapnel ['ʃræpnl] N Schrapnell nt

shred [ʃred] **N** (= scrap) Fetzen m; (of paper also) Schnipsel m, Schnippel m (inf); (of vegetable, meat) Stückchen nt; (fig) Spur f; (of truth) Fünkchen nt; **~ of cloth** Stofffetzen m; **not a ~ of evidence** keinerlei Beweis; **without a ~ of clothing on** splitter(faser)nackt; **to be** or **hang in ~s** zerfetzt sein; **her dress hung in ~s** ihr Kleid hing ihr in Fetzen vom Leib; **his reputation was in ~s** sein (guter) Ruf war ruiniert; **to tear sth to ~s** etw total zerreißen, etw in Stücke reißen; (fig) etw verreißen; argument etw total zerpflücken; **to tear sb to ~s** (fig) keinen guten Faden an jdm lassen
  VT a food zerkleinern, schnitzeln; (= grate) carrots raspeln; cabbage hobeln; paper zerstückeln, schnitzeln; (in shredder) schreddern; piece of clothing zerkleinern
  b (= tear) in kleine Stücke reißen; (with claws) zerfetzen

shredder ['ʃredə'] N **a** Schredder m, Shredder m, Zerkleinerungsmaschine f; (esp for wastepaper) Papierwolf m, Reißwolf m **b** (= grater) Reibe f; (in electric mixer) Gemüseschneider m

shredding machine ['ʃredɪŋmə'ʃiːn] N = shredder a

shrew [ʃruː] N Spitzmaus f; (fig) Xanthippe f; **"The Taming of the Shrew"** (Liter) „Der Widerspenstigen Zähmung"

shrewd [ʃruːd] ADJ (+er) person gewitzt, klug, clever (inf); businessman also, plan, move clever (inf), raffiniert, geschickt; investment, argument taktisch geschickt, klug; assessment, observer scharf, genau; smile verschmitzt, wissend; eyes schlau; mind scharf; glance durchdringend, prüfend; **I can make a ~ guess** ich kann ja mal raten; **that was a ~ guess** das war gut geraten; **I have a ~ idea that ...** ich habe so das bestimmte Gefühl, dass ...; **I have a ~ idea of what he'll say** ich kann mir gut denken, was er sagen wird; **to be ~ enough to do sth** schlau or clever (inf) genug sein, etw zu tun; **a ~ judge of character** ein guter Menschenkenner; **to have a ~ suspicion that ...** den stillen Verdacht hegen, dass ...; **to have a ~ understanding of sth** in Bezug auf etw (acc) Durchblick haben

shrewdly ['ʃruːdlɪ] ADV geschickt, clever (inf); look wissend; observe klug; **he ~ realized that ...** schlauerweise erkannte er, dass ...; **he ~ guessed that/what ...** er hat gut geraten, dass/was ...; **~, he decided ...** gewitzt or clever (inf) wie er ist, hat er beschlossen ...; **... he said ~ ...** sagte er schlau or clever (inf)

shrewdness ['ʃruːdnɪs] N (of person) Gewitztheit f, Klugheit f, Cleverness f (inf); (of businessman also, plan, move) Raffiniertheit f, Geschicktheit f; (of investment, argument) Klugheit f; (of assessment, observer) Schärfe f, Genauigkeit f; (of guess) Treffsicherheit f

shrewish ['ʃruːɪʃ] ADJ zänkisch, boshaft, giftig

shrewishly ['ʃruːɪʃlɪ] ADV giftig

shrewishness ['ʃruːɪʃnɪs] N Boshaftigkeit f, Giftigkeit f

shriek [ʃriːk] **N** (schriller) Schrei; (of whistle) schriller Ton; (of brakes, hinges) Quietschen nt no pl; **a ~ of pain/horror** ein Schmerzens-/ Schreckensschrei m; **~s of laughter** kreischendes Lachen; **to give a ~** einen schrillen Schrei ausstoßen **VT** kreischen, schreien **VI** aufschreien; **to ~ at sb** jdn ankreischen; **to ~ with pain/horror** vor Schmerz/Entsetzen schreien; **to ~ with laughter** vor Lachen quietschen; **to ~ out** aufschreien, einen Schrei ausstoßen

shrift [ʃrɪft] N **to give sb/sth short ~** jdn/etw kurz abfertigen

shrike [ʃraɪk] N Würger m

shrill [ʃrɪl] **ADJ** (+er) schrill; criticism, speech scharf; demand lautstark **VI** schrillen **VT** kreischen, schrill schreien

shrillness ['ʃrɪlnɪs] N Schrillheit f

shrilly ['ʃrɪlɪ] ADV schrill; (fig, = fiercely) lautstark; **what are you doing?, she demanded ~** was tust du da?, fragte sie mit einer schrillen Stimme

shrimp [ʃrɪmp] **N** Garnele f, Krevette f; **that ~ of a child** der kleine Steppke (inf) **to go ~-ing** vi Krevetten- or Garnelenfang gehen; **~-ing net** Reuse f (für den Garnelenfang)

shrine [ʃraɪn] N Schrein m; (= sacred place also) Heiligtum nt; (= tomb) Grabstätte f; (= chapel) Grabkapelle f; (= altar) Grabaltar m; **to worship at sb's ~** (fig inf) jdm zu Füßen liegen

shrink [ʃrɪŋk] vb: pret shrank, ptp shrunk **VT** einlaufen lassen; **the fabric is shrunk before it is used** der Stoff wird vor Gebrauch gewaschen, damit er danach nicht mehr einläuft; **to ~ a part on** (Tech) ein Teil aufschrumpfen
  VI a (= get smaller) kleiner werden, schrumpfen; (clothes etc) einlaufen; (metal etc) sich zusammenziehen, schrumpfen; (wood) schwinden; (fig, popularity) abnehmen, schwinden; (trade) zurückgehen; **to ~ away to nothing** auf ein Nichts zusammenschrumpfen
  b (fig, = recoil) zurückschrecken; **to ~ from doing sth** davor zurückschrecken, etw zu tun; **to ~ from saying sth** sich davor scheuen, etw zu sagen; **to ~ from the truth** vor der Wahrheit die Augen verschließen; **to ~ back** zurückweichen; **to ~ away from sb** vor jdm zurückweichen
  N (inf) Seelenklempner(in) m(f) (inf), Psychiater(in) m(f)

shrinkage ['ʃrɪŋkɪdʒ] N (of material, clothes) Einlaufen nt; (of wood) Schwund m; (of metal) Schrumpfung f; (fig: of tourism, economic growth etc) Schrumpfung f, Rückgang m; (Comm) Schwund m, Einbußen pl; **there will be ~ with this material** dieser Stoff läuft noch ein

shrinking [ɔɔ] ADJ **a** (= decreasing) schrumpfend, abnehmend **b** (= shy) scheu

shrinking violet [ʃrɪŋkɪŋ'vaɪəlɪt] N (inf: = shy person) schüchternes Pflänzchen

shrinkproof ['ʃrɪŋkpruːf], **shrink-resistant** ['ʃrɪŋkrɪ'zɪstənt] ADJ nicht einlaufend

shrink-wrap ['ʃrɪŋkræp] VT einschweißen

shrink-wrapping ['ʃrɪŋkræpɪŋ] N (= process) Einschweißen nt; (= material) Klarsichtfolie f

shrive [ʃraɪv] pret shrove, ptp shriven VT (old) die Beichte abnehmen (+dat)

shrivel ['ʃrɪvl] **VT** plants (frost, dryness) welk werden lassen; (heat) austrocknen; skin, fruit runzlig werden lassen; nylon zusammenschrumpfen lassen **VI** kleiner werden, schrumpfen; (balloon, nylon) zusammenschrumpfen; (plants) welk werden; (through heat) austrocknen; (fruit, skin) runzlig werden → also **shrivelled**

▶ **shrivel away** VI zusammenschrumpfen; (leaves) verwelken, vertrocknen; (nylon) zusammenschmelzen; (worries, problems) sich in Luft auflösen

▶ **shrivel up** **VT** sep = shrivel VT **VI a** = shrivel VI **b** (fig) **I just want to shrivel up when he looks at me like that** wenn er mich so ansieht, möchte ich am liebsten in den Boden versinken; **he just shrivelled up when the boss questioned him** bei den Fragen des Chefs wurde er ganz klein

shrivelled, (US) **shriveled** ['ʃrɪvld] ADJ (= withered) vegetation verwelkt, verdorrt; person verwelkt; body part verrunzelt, runz(e)lig; fruit verschrumpelt; **a ~ old lady** eine kleine, vertrocknete alte Dame

shriven ['ʃrɪvn] ptp of **shrive**

shroud [ʃraʊd] N a Leichentuch nt, Totenhemd nt b (fig) Schleier m; **a ~ of smoke** Rauchschwaden pl; **a ~ of secrecy** der Schleier eines Geheimnisses c **shrouds** PL (Naut) Wanten pl VT a (lit) in ein Leichentuch hüllen b (fig) hüllen; **the whole thing is ~ed in mystery** die ganze Angelegenheit ist von einem Geheimnis umgeben

shrove [ʃrəʊv] pret of **shrive**

Shrove Monday N Rosenmontag m

Shrovetide ['ʃrəʊvtaɪd] N Fastnacht f (die drei Tage vor Aschermittwoch)

Shrove Tuesday N Fastnachtsdienstag m

shrub [ʃrʌb] N Busch m, Strauch m

shrubbery ['ʃrʌbərɪ] N (= shrub bed) Strauchrabatte f; (= shrubs) Büsche pl, Sträucher pl, Buschwerk nt; **the ball got lost in the ~** der Ball ging im Gebüsch verloren

shrubby ['ʃrʌbɪ] ADJ strauchartig

shrug [ʃrʌg] N Achselzucken nt no pl; **to give a ~** mit den Schultern or Achseln zucken; **a ~ of despair** ein verzweifeltes Achselzucken VT shoulders zucken (mit); **she ~ged herself out of the coat** sie schüttelte ihren Mantel ab

▶ **shrug off** VT sep mit einem Achselzucken abtun; coat abschütteln; **he simply shrugged the whole affair off** er hat die ganze Sache einfach von sich abgeschüttelt

shrunk [ʃrʌŋk] ptp of **shrink**

shrunken ['ʃrʌŋkən] ADJ (ein)geschrumpft; old person geschrumpft; profits, savings zusammengeschrumpft

shrunken head N Schrumpfkopf m

shtoom [ʃtʊm] ADJ (inf, = quiet) **to keep ~ about sth** über etw (acc) die Klappe halten (inf)

shtuck [ʃtʊk] ADJ (inf) angeschmiert (inf); **to be in (dead) ~** angeschmiert sein (inf)

shuck [ʃʌk] N (US) Schale f; (of corn, peas) Hülse f VT a (= shell) schälen; peas enthülsen b (inf) **he ~ed his jacket** er warf seine Jacke ab

▶ **shuck off** VT SEP (US inf) garment abwerfen, abstreifen; **to shuck off one's clothes** seine Kleidung abstreifen

shucks [ʃʌks] INTERJ (US) verflixt, Mist (inf); (= rubbish) Unsinn, Quatsch (inf); **~, I'm sorry** Mist!, tut mir Leid (inf); **~ to you** (inf) bätsch! (inf)

shudder ['ʃʌdə'] N Schauer m, Schauder m; **to give a ~** (person) sich schütteln, erschaudern (geh); (ground) beben; **she gave a ~ of revulsion** sie schüttelte sich vor Ekel; **the dying man gave a last great ~** ein letztes Zucken lief durch den Körper des Sterbenden; **a ~ ran through her/his body** ein Schauer überlief sie; **she realized with a ~ that ...** schaudernd erkannte sie, dass ...; **a ~ of fear/cold** ein Angst-/Kälteschauer m; **with a ~ of anticipation/pleasure** zitternd or bebend vor Erwartung/Freude; **a ~ went through the building as the heavy truck passed by** das Gebäude bebte, als der schwere Lastwagen vorbeifuhr; **with a ~ the old car moved into second gear** der alte Wagen vibrierte, als der zweite Gang eingelegt wurde; **that gives me the ~s** (inf) da läuft mir kalt den Buckel runter (inf); **he gives me the ~s** (inf) er ist mir unheimlich VI (person) schaudern, schauern; (house, ground) beben, zittern; (car, train) rütteln, geschüttelt werden; **her whole body was ~ing** sie zitterte am ganzen Körper; **the train ~ed to a halt** der Zug kam rüttelnd zum Stehen; **I ~ to think** mir graut, wenn ich nur daran denke

shudderingly ['ʃʌdərɪŋlɪ] ADV (with fear etc) schaudernd; (with cold) zitternd; **the rocket climbed ~ into the sky** die Rakete stieg zitternd zum Himmel auf

shuffle ['ʃʌfl] N a Schlurfen nt no pl; **to walk with a ~** schlurfen b (= dance) Shuffle m c (Cards) **to give the cards a ~** die Karten mischen d (= change round) Umstellung f; (of jobs) Umbesetzung f; **the latest ~ of the cabinet** die letzte Kabinettsumbildung; **to get lost in the ~** (people) in der Menge untergehen; (things) verloren gehen VT a **he ~d his feet as he walked** er schlurfte beim Gehen; **he sat there shuffling his feet** er saß da und scharrte mit den Füßen b cards mischen; **he ~d the papers on his desk** er durchwühlte die Papiere auf seinem Schreibtisch c (fig, = change round) cabinet umbilden; jobs umbesetzen; **top men are ~d around quite often** die Männer an der Spitze werden oft von einem Ressort ins andere versetzt VI a (= walk) schlurfen; **the dancers ~d around on the floor** die Tänzer schoben sich über die Tanzfläche; **he just ~s through life** er lässt sich einfach treiben b (Cards) mischen

▶ **shuffle off** VT sep skin, dress abstreifen; (fig) worries, fear ablegen; responsibility abwälzen, abschieben (onto auf +acc); **to shuffle off this mortal coil** (euph) die sterbliche Hülle ablegen or abstreifen

shuffling ['ʃʌflɪŋ] ADJ walk, steps, sound schlurfend; **the ~ movement of a badger** das Watscheln eines Dachses

shun [ʃʌn] VT meiden; publicity, light scheuen; **to be ~ned by the world** ausgestoßen sein

'shun [ʃʌn] INTERJ (Mil) Achtung

shunt [ʃʌnt] N Stoß m; (inf: = car crash) Crash m (sl); **they gave the wagon a ~ into the siding** sie schoben or rangierten den Waggon auf das Abstellgleis; **to give sth a ~** etw anstoßen, einer Sache (dat) einen Stoß geben VT a (Rail) rangieren, verschieben; **they ~ed the train off the main line** sie schoben den Zug auf ein Nebengleis b (inf) person schieben; (out of the way) abschieben; **to ~ sb from one place to another** jdn herumschubsen (inf); **our department then has to ~ the papers back for signing** unsere Abteilung muss die Papiere dann zur Unterschrift zurückverfrachten (inf); **they ~ed him off to boarding school** sie schoben ihn ins Internat ab c (inf, = crash) car einen Unfall bauen mit (inf) VI (Rail, train) rangiert or verschoben werden; (person) rangieren; **a line of trucks ~ed past** eine Reihe Güterwagen schob sich vorbei

shunter ['ʃʌntə'] N (Brit Rail) Rangierer m

shunting ['ʃʌntɪŋ] N (Rail) Rangieren nt; **~ engine** Rangierlokomotive f

shunting yard N Rangier- or Verschiebebahnhof m

shush [ʃʊʃ] INTERJ pst, sch VT beruhigen, zum Schweigen bringen; **the teacher ~ed the excited children** der Lehrer brachte die aufgeregten Kinder mit einem „Pst!" zum Schweigen VI **still sein; oh ~, will you!** oh halt still! (inf)

shut [ʃʌt] vb: pret, ptp **shut** VT a (= close) eyes, door, box etc zumachen, schließen; sportsground schließen; penknife, book, wallet zumachen, zuklappen; **they ~ the office at 6** das Büro wird um 18.00 Uhr geschlossen; **the strike ~ the factory for a week** der Streik legte die Fabrik für eine Woche still; **~ your eyes** mach die Augen zu; **to ~ one's ears/eyes to sth** vor etw (dat) die Ohren/Augen verschließen; **to ~ one's mind to sth** sich einer Sache (dat) verschließen; **he ~ his mind to thoughts of the past** Gedanken an die Vergangenheit schob er weit von sich; **~ your mouth or face!** (inf) **~ it!** (inf) halts Maul! (inf) b **to ~ sb/sth in(to) sth** jdn/etw in etw (dat) einschließen; **she was ~ in the cellar as a punishment** sie wurde zur Strafe im Keller eingesperrt; **to ~ one's fingers in the door** sich (dat) die Finger in der Tür einklemmen

VI (door, window, box) schließen, zugehen; (shop, factory) schließen, geschlossen werden, zumachen (inf); (sportsground) geschlossen werden; (eyes) sich schließen; **the suitcase just won't ~** der Koffer will einfach nicht zugehen; **it ~s very easily** es lässt sich ganz leicht schließen or zumachen; **when do the shops ~?** wann schließen die Geschäfte?, wann machen die Geschäfte zu? (inf); **the door ~ in the wind** der Wind schlug die Tür zu ADJ geschlossen, zu pred (inf); **sorry sir, we're ~** tut mir leider geschlossen; **the door swung ~** die Tür schlug zu; **to find the door swung ~** vor verschlossener Tür stehen; **~ in his dungeon** in seinem Kerker eingeschlossen; **~ in his own little world** abgekapselt in seiner eigenen kleinen Welt; **the ~ mind of a reactionary** die Verbohrtheit eines Reaktionärs; **his mind is ~ to anything new** er verschließt sich allem Neuen

▶ **shut away** VT sep (= put away) wegschließen; (in sth) einschließen (in in +dat); (= keep locked away) books, papers etc unter Verschluss halten; (safely) verwahren; persons verborgen halten; **to keep sb shut away from sth** jdn von etw fern halten; **he was shut away in a mental hospital** er wurde in eine Nervenklinik gesteckt; **to shut oneself away** sich zurückziehen

▶ **shut down** VT sep shop, factory zumachen (inf), schließen; reactor abschalten; operations stilllegen; **Heathrow is completely shut down** Heathrow ist vollkommen zu or dicht (inf) VI (shop, factory etc) zumachen (inf), schließen; (reactor) sich abschalten; (engine) sich ausschalten; (resort) Betrieb einstellen; **the television service shuts down at midnight** um Mitternacht ist Sendeschluss im Fernsehen

▶ **shut in** VT sep einschließen (also fig), einsperren (inf) (prep obj, -to in +dat); **close the door and shut the heat in** schließe die Tür, damit die Wärme drinnen bleibt

▶ **shut off** VT sep a gas, water, electricity abstellen; light, engine ab- or ausschalten; street (ab-) sperren; **the kettle shuts itself off** der Wasserkessel schaltet von selbst ab b (= isolate) (ab-) trennen; **I feel very shut off on this island** ich fühle mich auf dieser Insel sehr abgeschlossen; **I feel shut off from my friends/civilization** ich komme mir von meinen Freunden/der Zivilisation abgeschnitten vor; **to shut oneself off (from sth)** sich abkapseln (von etw) VI abschalten; **the heater shuts off automatically** das Heizgerät schaltet (sich) automatisch ab

▶ **shut out** VT sep a person, oneself aussperren (of aus); view versperren; light, world nicht hereinlassen (of in +acc); **the child was shut out of the house** das Kind war ausgesperrt; **don't shut the sun out** lass doch die Sonne herein; **draw the curtains to shut out the light** zieh die Vorhänge zu, damit das Licht nicht hereinfällt; **the trees shut out the light** die Bäume nehmen das Licht weg; **she closed the door to shut out the noise/draught** (Brit) or **draft** (US) sie schloss die Tür, damit kein Lärm hereinkam/damit es nicht zog b (fig) foreign competition ausschalten; memory loswerden, unterdrücken; (= censor) foreign news etc unterdrücken; **I can't shut her out of my life** ich kann sie nicht von meinem Leben ausschließen c (US, Sport) opponent nicht zum Zuge kommen lassen; **they shut the opponents out with two hits** sie schalteten ihre Gegner mit zwei Treffern aus; **they shut them out 1-0** sie warfen sie mit 1:0 aus dem Rennen

▶ **shut to** VT sep ganz or richtig zumachen; (not quite closed) anlehnen; **the door wasn't shut to** die Tür war nicht ganz zu

▶ **shut up** VT sep a house verschließen → **shop** b (= imprison) einsperren; **you can't spend your whole life shut up in libraries** Sie können sich doch nicht Ihr ganzes Leben lang in Bibliotheken vergraben c (inf, = silence) zum Schweigen bringen; **that'll soon shut him up** das wird ihm schon den Mund stopfen (inf);

every time I try to say something she always tries to shut me up jedes Mal, wenn ich etwas sagen will, fährt sie mir über den Mund **VI** (*inf*) den Mund *or die* Klappe halten (*inf*); **shut up!** halt die Klappe! (*inf*)

shut: shutdown N Stillegung *f*; (*of schools, factory*) Schließung *f*; (*TV, Rad*) Sendeschluss *m*; **shuteye** N (*inf*) Schlaf *m*; **I need some ~** ich brauche etwas Schlaf *or* ein paar Stunden Schlaf; **shut-in** ADJ **a** (*US, = confined to the house/bed*) ans Haus/Bett gefesselt **b** ~ **feeling** ein Gefühl *nt* des Eingeschlossenseins **N** (*US*) he is ~ er ist ans Haus/ans Bett gefesselt; **shut-off** **N** (*of gas, water*) Abstellen *nt*; **we regret the temporary water ~ yesterday** wir bedauern, dass wir gestern vorübergehend das Wasser abstellen mussten **a** ~ **feeling** ein Gefühl des Abgeschlossenseins *or* Abgeschnittenseins **b** ~ **switch** (*of electricity, engine*) Hauptschalter *m*; **shut-out** N (*US Sport*) Zu-null-Niederlage *f*, Zu-null-Sieg *m*

shutter ['ʃʌtə] **N** (Fenster)laden *m*; (*Phot*) Verschluss *m*; **to put up the ~s** (*lit*) die (Fenster)läden zumachen; (*fig*) den Laden dichtmachen (*inf*) **VT** ~ **the windows** mach die (Fenster)läden zu

shutterbug ['ʃʌtəbʌg] N (*esp US inf*) Fotonarr *m*/-närrin *f* (*inf*)

shuttered ['ʃʌtəd] ADJ **a** (*= with shutters*) house mit (Fenster)läden; door, window mit Läden **b** (*= with closed shutters*) house, room mit geschlossenen (Fenster)läden; **the people watched from behind ~ windows** die Leute sahen hinter den geschlossenen (Fenster)läden zu **c** (*fig*) **a ~ look** ein verschlossener Blick

shutter release N (*Phot*) Auslöser *m*

shuttle ['ʃʌtl] **N a** (*of loom, sewing machine*) Schiffchen *nt* **b** (*= shuttle service*) Pendelverkehr *m*; (*plane/train etc*) Pendelflugzeug *nt*/-zug *m etc*; **c** (*= space shuttle*) Raumtransporter *m*, Spaceshuttle *m* **c** (*= shuttlecock*) Federball *m* **VT** passengers, goods hin- und hertransportieren; **to ~ sb around** jdn herumschieben; **the form was ~d around between different departments** das Formular wurde in den verschiedenen Abteilungen herumgereicht **VI** (*people*) pendeln; (*goods*) hin- und hertransportiert werden; (*forms*) herumgereicht werden

shuttle: shuttle bus N Shuttlebus *m*, Pendelbus *m*; **shuttlecock** N Federball *m*; **shuttle diplomacy** N Pendeldiplomatie *f*; **shuttle service** N Pendelverkehr *m*

shy[1] [ʃaɪ] ADJ (+er) **a** schüchtern; *animal* scheu; **don't be ~** nur keine Hemmungen! (*inf*); **to be ~ of/with sb** Hemmungen vor/gegenüber jdm haben; **to be ~ of** *or* **about doing sth** Hemmungen haben, etw zu tun; **to feel ~** schüchtern sein; **don't be ~ of telling me if there's anything you need** sagen Sie mir ruhig, wenn Sie etwas brauchen; **to make sb ~** jdn verschüchtern → **fight b** (*esp US inf: = short*) **we're 3 dollars ~** wir haben 3 Dollar zu wenig; **two days ~ of his 95th birthday** zwei Tage vor seinem 95. Geburtstag **VI** (*horse*) scheuen (*at vor +dat*)

▶ **shy away** VI (*horse*) zurückscheuen; (*person*) zurückweichen; **to shy away from sb** vor jdm zurückweichen; **to shy away from etw** etw (*dat*) zurückschrecken; **he shies away from accepting responsibility** er scheut sich, Verantwortung zu übernehmen

shy[2] **N** (*= throw*) Wurf *m*; **to have** *or* **take a ~ at sth** nach etw werfen; **to have a ~ at sth** (*fig*) sich an etw (*dat*) versuchen; **I'll have a ~ at it** ich kanns ja mal versuchen; **to have a ~ at doing sth** etw zu tun versuchen **VT** werfen

Shylock ['ʃaɪlɒk] N (*fig: = mean person*) Geizhals *m*; (*dated: = moneylender*) Wucherer *m*, Wucherin *f*

shyly ['ʃaɪlɪ] ADV smile, say schüchtern

shyness ['ʃaɪnɪs] N Schüchternheit *f*; (*esp of animals*) Scheu *f*; **his ~ at meeting people** seine Schüchternheit, wenn er andere Leute kennen lernt; **her ~ of strangers** ihre Scheu vor Fremden

shyster ['ʃaɪstə] N (*US inf*) Gauner(in) *m(f)*; (*= lawyer*) Rechtsverdreher(in) *m(f)* (*inf*)

Siam [saɪˈæm] N Siam *nt*

Siamese [ˌsaɪəˈmiːz] ADJ siamesisch **N a** Siamese *m*, Siamesin *f* **b** (*Ling*) Siamesisch *nt* **c** (*= cat*) Siamkatze *f*, siamesische Katze

Siamese cat N Siamkatze *f*, Siamesische Katze

Siamese twins PL siamesische Zwillinge *pl*

Siberia [saɪˈbɪərɪə] N Sibirien *nt*

Siberian [saɪˈbɪərɪən] ADJ sibirisch **N** Sibirier(in) *m(f)*, Sibirer(in) *m(f)*

sibilant ['sɪbɪlənt] ADJ zischend; *hiss* scharf; ~ **sound** (*Phon*) Zischlaut *m* **N** (*Phon*) Zischlaut *m*

sibling ['sɪblɪŋ] N Geschwister *nt* (*form*)

sibyl ['sɪbɪl] N (*lit*) Sibylle *f*; (*fig*) Prophetin *f*, Weissagerin *f*

sibylline ['sɪbɪlaɪn] ADJ (*lit*) sibyllinisch; (*fig*) prophetisch

sic [sɪk] ADV sic

Sicilian [sɪˈsɪlɪən] ADJ sizilianisch **N a** Sizilianer(in) *m(f)* **b** (*Ling*) Sizilianisch *nt*

Sicily ['sɪsɪlɪ] N Sizilien *nt*

sick [sɪk] ✪ 7.3 **N** (*= vomit*) Erbrochene(s) *nt* **ADJ** (+er) **a** (*= ill*) krank (*also fig*); **the ~** die Kranken *pl*; **to be (off) ~** (wegen Krankheit) fehlen; **to fall** *or* **take ~, to be taken ~** krank werden; **to call in** *or* **phone in** (*esp Brit*) ~ sich (telefonisch) krankmelden; **she's off ~ with tonsillitis** sie ist wegen einer Mandelentzündung krankgeschrieben; **he's as ~ as a parrot** *or* **dog** (*inf*) ihm ist kotzübel (*sl*); **he was ~ at heart** (*liter*) er war von Kummer verzehrt (*liter*)

b (*= vomiting or about to vomit*) **to be ~** brechen, sich übergeben, kotzen (*sl*); (*esp cat, baby, patient*) spucken; **he was ~ all over the carpet** er hat den ganzen Teppich voll gespuckt *or* voll gekotzt (*sl*); **I think I'm going to be ~** ich glaube, ich muss kotzen (*sl*) *or* mich übergeben; **I felt ~** mir war schlecht *or* übel; **to feel ~ to one's stomach** sich im Magen schlecht fühlen; **I get ~ in aeroplanes** im Flugzeug wird mir immer schlecht *or* übel; **that smell/that food makes me ~** bei dem Geruch/von dem Essen wird mir übel *or* schlecht; **to make sb ~** (*fig inf*) jdn (ganz) krank machen (*inf*); **it's enough to make you ~** (*inf*) das reicht, damit einem schlecht wird; **it makes me ~ to think that ...** wenn ich daran denke, dass ...; **it makes you ~ the way he's always right** (*inf*) es ist zum Weinen *or* zum Kotzen (*sl*), dass er immer Recht hat; **to be ~ at sth** (*fig, = disgusted*) von etw angewidert sein; (*= upset*) wegen etw geknickt sein; **to feel ~ about sth** (*fig*) von etw angewidert sein; **I am worried ~, I am ~ with worry** mir ist vor Sorge ganz schlecht; **~ with envy** grün vor Neid

c (*inf, = fed up*) **to be ~ of sth/sb** etw/jdn satt haben; **to be ~ of doing sth** es satt haben, etw zu tun; **I'm ~ and tired of it** ich habe davon die Nase (gestrichen) voll (*inf*), ich habe es gründlich satt; **to be ~ and tired of doing sth** es Leid sein, etw zu tun; **I'm ~ of the sight of her** ich habe ihren Anblick satt; **I get ~ of listening to her complaining** ich habe es langsam satt, immer ihr Gejammer hören zu müssen

d (*inf*) geschmacklos; *joke* makaber, geschmacklos; *person* abartig, pervers; ~ **humour** schwarzer Humor; **he has a ~ mind** er ist abartig; **a comedy about life in Dachau, how ~ can you get!** eine Komödie über das Leben in Dachau, das ist schon pervers!

▶ **sick up** VT *sep* erbrechen

sick: sickbag N Spucktüte *f*; **sickbay** N Krankenrevier *nt*; **sickbed** N Krankenlager *nt*; **sick building syndrome** N gesundheitliche Probleme aufgrund eines schlechten Raumklimas

sicken ['sɪkn] **VT** (*= turn sb's stomach*) anekeln, anwidern; (*= upset greatly*) erschüttern, krank machen (*inf*); (*= disgust*) anwidern; **what they

saw in the camp ~ed them sie waren entsetzt über das, was sie im Lager sahen; **it ~s me the way he treats her** es macht mich krank, wie er sie behandelt (*inf*); **doesn't it ~ you?** das ist doch unerträglich *or* zum Kotzen (*sl*) **VI a** (*= feel ill*) **to ~ at sth** sich vor etw (*dat*) ekeln **b** (*= become ill*) krank werden; **he's definitely ~ing for something** er wird bestimmt krank; **you must be ~ing for something** (*lit iro*) ist mit dir was nicht in Ordnung?; **he's ~ing for a virus** bei ihm ist ein Virus im Anzug **c** **to ~ of sth** einer Sache (*gen*) müde (*geh*) werden *or* sein, etw satt haben

sickener ['sɪknə] N (*inf*) **a** (*thing*) ekelhafte Sache, Brechmittel *nt* (*fig inf*) **b** (*= obnoxious person*) Ekel *nt* (*fig*)

sickening ['sɪknɪŋ] ADJ (*lit*) Ekel erregend; *smell, sight also* widerlich; (*= upsetting*) erschütternd; (*= disgusting, annoying*) ekelhaft, zum Kotzen (*sl*); *treatment* abscheulich; *cruelty* widerlich; *delays, price increase* unerträglich; *person* ekelhaft; **his ~ habit of always being right** seine unerträgliche Angewohnheit, immer Recht zu haben; **the most ~ thing I've ever seen** das Widerlichste, was ich je gesehen habe; **we're going to be late again – how ~** wir kommen schon wieder zu spät – es ist einfach furchtbar

sickeningly ['sɪknɪŋlɪ] ADV (*lit*) Ekel erregend; (*fig*) unerträglich; ~ **sweet** widerlich süß; **his English is ~ good** es ist schon unerträglich, wie gut sein Englisch ist; **we had all that ~ good weather during the exams** es war richtig gemein, dass wir ausgerechnet während der Prüfungszeit so schönes Wetter hatten; **now it's all ~ obvious** das schreit ja schon zum Himmel

sick headache N ≈ Migräneanfall *m*, ≈ Migräne *f*

sickie ['sɪkɪ] N (*Brit, Austral, inf*) Krankentag *m*; **to take a ~** einen Tag krankfeiern (*inf*)

sickle ['sɪkl] N Sichel *f*

sick leave N **to be on ~** krankgeschrieben sein; **employees are allowed six weeks' ~ per year** Angestellte dürfen insgesamt sechs Wochen pro Jahr wegen Krankheit fehlen; **he has three months' ~ because of his accident** aufgrund *or* auf Grund seines Unfalls hat er drei Monate Genesungsurlaub; **he only gets two weeks' paid ~** im Krankheitsfall wird sein Gehalt nur zwei Wochen (lang) weitergezahlt

sickle-cell anaemia, (*US*) **sickle-cell anemia** ['sɪklsɛlǝˈniːmɪǝ] N Sichelzellenanämie *f*

sickliness ['sɪklɪnɪs] N (*of person, appearance*) Kränklichkeit *f*; (*of complexion, light*) Blässe *f*; (*of smell, taste, food, sentimentality, colour*) Widerlichkeit *f*, Ekelhaftigkeit *f*; (*of smile*) Mattheit *f*; (*of grin*) Schwachheit *f*

sick list N (*because of illness*) Krankenliste *f*; (*because of injury*) Verletztenliste *f*; **to be on the ~** (*Mil, Sport*) auf der Kranken-/Verletztenliste stehen; **he's off the ~** (*inf*) er ist wieder im Einsatz (*inf*)

sickly ['sɪklɪ] ADJ (+er) *person, appearance* kränklich; *complexion, light* blass; *smell, taste, food, sentimentality, colour* widerlich, ekelhaft; *smile* matt; *grin* schwach; *climate* ungesund; ~ **sweet smell** unangenehm süßer Geruch; ~ **sweet smile** übersüßes *or* zuckersüßes Lächeln

sick-making ['sɪkmeɪkɪŋ] ADJ (*inf*) grässlich

sickness ['sɪknɪs] N (*Med*) Krankheit *f* (*also fig*); (*= nausea*) Übelkeit *f*; (*= vomiting*) Erbrechen *nt*; (*of joke, book, film*) Geschmacklosigkeit *f*; **there is ~ on board** an Bord geht eine Krankheit um; **in ~ and in health** in guten und in schlechten Zeiten *or* Tagen; **the ~ of his mind** seine Abartigkeit

sickness benefit N (*Brit*) Krankengeld *nt*

sick note N (*Brit inf*) Krankmeldung *f*

sicko ['sɪkǝʊ] (*esp US inf*) **N** Kranke(r) *mf*, Irre(r) *mf* (*pej*) **ADJ** *person, group* krank, irr (*pej*)

sick: sick-out N (US, Ind) geschlossene Krankmeldung der Mitarbeiter einer Firma; **sick pay** N Gehalts- or (for workers) Lohnfortzahlung f im Krankheitsfall; **sickroom** N Krankenzimmer nt; **sick ward** N (of prison etc) Krankenabteilung f or -station f

side [saɪd] **N** **a** (= wall, vertical surface, of car, box, hole, ditch) Seite f; (of cave, artillery trench, mining shaft, boat, caravan) Wand f; (of cliff, mountain) Hang m; **the ~s of the hill** die Berghänge pl
b (= flat surface, line: of triangle, cube, coin, paper, material, record) Seite f; **this ~ up!** (on parcel etc) oben!; **right/wrong ~** (of cloth) rechte/linke Seite; **this pillowcase is right/wrong ~ out** dieser Kopfkissenbezug ist rechts/links (herum)
c (= edge) Rand m; **at the ~ of the road** am Straßenrand; **the body was found on the far ~ of the wood** die Leiche wurde am anderen Ende des Waldes gefunden; **at** or **on the ~ of his plate** auf dem Tellerrand
d (= not back or front, area to one side) Seite f; **by/at the ~ of sth** seitlich von etw; **the destroyer rammed the ~ of the boat** der Zerstörer rammte das Boot seitlich; **to drive on the left(-hand) ~** auf der linken Straßenseite fahren; **the path goes down the ~ of the house** der Weg führt seitlich am Haus entlang; **it's this/the other ~ of London** (out of town) es ist auf dieser/auf der anderen Seite Londons; (in town) es ist in diesem Teil/am anderen Ende von London; **the south/respectable ~ of Glasgow** der südliche/vornehme Teil Glasgows; **the debit/credit ~ of an account** die Soll-/Habenseite eines Kontos; **the enemy attacked them on** or **from all ~s** der Feind griff sie von allen Seiten an; **this statement was attacked on** or **from all ~s** diese Behauptung wurde von allen angegriffen; **he moved over** or **stood to one ~** er trat zur Seite; **the car moved to one ~ of the road and stopped** der Wagen fuhr seitlich heran und hielt; **he stood to one ~ and did nothing** (lit) er stand daneben und tat nichts; (fig) er hielt sich raus; **to put sth on one ~** etw beiseite or auf die Seite legen; (shopkeeper) etw zurücklegen; **I'll put that issue on one ~** ich werde diese Frage vorerst zurückstellen; **to take sb to** or **on one ~** jdn beiseite nehmen; **just this ~ of the boundary** (lit) (noch) diesseits der Grenze; (fig) gerade an der Grenze; **on the other ~ of the boundary** jenseits der Grenze; **this ~ of Christmas** vor Weihnachten; **just this ~ of legal** (inf) am Rande der Legalität; **just this ~ of the line between sanity and madness** gerade an der Grenze zum Wahnsinn; **with one's head on one ~** mit zur Seite geneigtem Kopf; **from ~ to ~** hin und her; **to shake one's head from ~ to ~** den Kopf schütteln
e **to be on the safe ~** sichergehen; **we'll take an extra £50 just to be on the safe ~** wir werden vorsichtshalber or für alle Fälle £ 50 mehr mitnehmen; **to get on the right ~ of sb** jdn für sich einnehmen; **to stay on the right ~ of sb** es (sich dat) mit jdm nicht verderben; **to get on the wrong ~ of sb** es (sich dat) mit jdm verderben; **to be on the right/wrong ~ of 40** noch nicht 40/über 40 sein; **on the right ~ of the law** auf dem Boden des Gesetzes; **only just on the right ~ of the law** an der Grenze der Legalität; **to make a bit (of money) on the ~** (inf) sich (dat) etwas nebenher or nebenbei verdienen (inf); **to have a bit on the ~** (inf) einen Seitensprung machen; (for longer) noch nebenher etwas laufen haben (inf); **I'm not going to be your bit on the ~** (inf) ich will nicht deine Nebenfrau/dein Nebenmann sein (inf)
f (of person, Anat) Seite f; **~ of bacon** Speckseite f; **by sb's ~** neben jdm; **~ by ~** nebeneinander, Seite an Seite; **to stand/sit ~ by ~ with sb** direkt neben jdm stehen/sitzen; **to fight ~ by ~ with sb** Seite an Seite mit jdm kämpfen; **I'll be by your ~** (fig) ich werde Ihnen zur Seite stehen; **to hold one's ~s** (with laughter) sich (dat) den Bauch halten (vor Lachen) → **split**
g (= branch, of family) Seite f; (of business, school) Zweig m; **the Catholic/intellectual ~ of**

the family der katholische Teil/die Intelligenz der Familie; **on one's father's/mother's ~** väterlicher-/mütterlicherseits; **there's French blood on the paternal/maternal ~** von väterlicher/mütterlicher Seite ist französisches Blut da
h (= aspect) Seite f; **there are always two ~s to every story** alles hat seine zwei Seiten; **let's hear your ~ of the story** erzählen Sie mal Ihre Version (der Geschichte); **the management's ~ of the story was quite different** die Geschichte hörte sich vonseiten or von Seiten des Managements ganz anders an; **to hear both ~s of the question** bei einer Frage beide Seiten (an-) hören; **the bright/seamy ~ of life** die Sonnen-/Schattenseite des Lebens; **to look on the bright ~** (= be optimistic) zuversichtlich sein; (= look on the positive side) die positive Seite betrachten; **you don't know his cruel ~** Sie kennen ihn nicht von seiner grausamen Seite
i (a bit) **on the large/high/formal** etc **~** etwas groß/hoch/förmlich etc; (for somebody) etwas zu groß/hoch/förmlich etc; **he errs on the ~ of generosity** er ist eher etwas zu großzügig
j (= team etc, Sport, in quiz) Mannschaft f; (fig) Seite f; **there are two ~s in the dispute** in dem Streit stehen sich zwei Parteien gegenüber; **the management ~ refused to give in** die Managementseite weigerte sich nachzugeben; **with a few concessions on the government ~** mit einigen Zugeständnissen vonseiten or von Seiten der Regierung; **to change ~s** sich auf die andere Seite schlagen; (Sport) die Seiten wechseln; **to take ~s** parteiisch sein; **to take ~s with sb** für jdn Partei ergreifen; **he's on our ~** er steht auf unserer Seite; **whose ~ are you on?** (supporting team) für wen sind Sie?; (playing for team) bei wem spielen Sie mit?; (in argument) zu wem halten Sie eigentlich? → **angel**
k (dated inf: = superiority) **there's no ~ to him** er sitzt nicht auf dem hohen Ross; **to put on ~** sich aufplustern
ADJ attr (= on one side) Seiten-; (= not main) Neben-; **~ door** Seiten-/Nebentür f; **~ road** Seiten-/Nebenstraße f
VI to ~ with/against sb Partei für/gegen jdn ergreifen

side: side aisle N (of church) Seitenschiff nt; **side arm** N an der Seite getragene Waffe f; (sword etc) Seitenwaffe f; **sideboard** N Anrichte f, Sideboard nt; **sideboards** (Brit), **sideburns** PL Koteletten pl; (longer) Backenbart m; **sidecar** N Beiwagen m; (esp Sport) Seitenwagen m

-sided [-saɪdɪd] ADJ suf -seitig; **one-sided** einseitig; **double-sided** doppelseitig

side: side dish N Beilage f; **side drum** N kleine Trommel; **side effect** N Nebenwirkung f; **side elevation** N Seitenansicht f, Seitenriss m; **side face** N Seitenansicht f, Profil nt; **side glance** N (lit, fig) Seitenblick m; **side horse** N (apparatus gymnastics) Seitpferd nt; **side impact protection system** N (Aut) Seitenaufprallschutz m; **side issue** N Randproblem nt; **that's just a ~** das ist Nebensache; **sidekick** N (inf) Kumpan(in) m(f) (inf), Kumpel m (inf); (= assistant) Handlanger(in) m(f) (pej); **the rancher and his ~s** der Farmer und seine Leute; **sidelight** N (Brit Aut) Parklicht nt, Parkleuchte f; (incorporated in headlight) Standlicht nt; **that was an interesting ~ on his character** das warf ein neues Licht auf seinen Charakter; **sideline** **N** (= extra business) Nebenerwerb m; **it's just a ~** das läuft so nebenher (inf); **to do sth as a ~** etw nebenher or nebenbei tun **VT to be ~d** (Sport, fig) aus dem Rennen sein; **sidelines** PL Seitenlinien pl; **the trainer sat on the ~** der Trainer saß am Spielfeldrand; **to keep to the ~** (fig) im Hintergrund bleiben; **to be** or **stand** or **sit on the ~** (fig) unbeteiligter Außenstehender or Zuschauer sein; **sidelong** ADJ **a ~ glance** ein Seitenblick m; **to give sb a ~ glance** jdn kurz aus den Augenwinkeln anblicken; **to glance ~ at sb** jdn kurz aus den Augenwinkeln anblicken; **side netting** N (Sport: of goal) Außennetz m; **side-on** ADJ **~ collision** or **crash** Seitenaufprall m; **~**

view Seitenansicht f; **side order** N (Cook) Beilage f

sidereal [saɪˈdɪərɪəl] ADJ (spec) siderisch

side: side-saddle **N** Damensattel m **ADV** im Damensattel or Damensitz **ADJ** rider im Damensattel; **she was a wonderful ~ rider** sie ritt vorzüglich im Damensattel; **side salad** N Salat m (als Beilage); **sideshow** N Nebenvorstellung f; (= exhibition) Sonderausstellung f; **sideslip** N (Aviat) Slippen nt, Seitenrutsch m

sidesman [ˈsaɪdzmən] N pl **-men** [-mən] ≈ Kirchendiener m

side: side-splitting ADJ urkomisch, zum Totlachen (inf); **side step** N Schritt m zur Seite; (Dancing) Seitenschritt m; (Sport) Ausfallschritt m; (fig, = dodge) Ausweichmanöver nt; **a master of the dribble and ~** ein Meister im Dribbeln und Ausweichen; **sidestep** **VT** tackle, punch (seitwärts) ausweichen (+dat); person ausweichen (+dat); (fig) ausweichen (+dat), umgehen **VI** (seitwärts or zur Seite) ausweichen; (fig) ausweichen, ausweichende Antworten geben; **side street** N Seitenstraße f; **sidestroke** N Seitenschwimmen nt; **to do the ~** seitenschwimmen; **sideswipe** N Puff m (inf); (fig) Seitenhieb m (at gegen); **to take a ~ at sb** (lit) jdm einen Puff geben (inf); (verbally) jdm einen Seitenhieb versetzen; **side table** N Beistelltisch m; **sidetrack** **N** (esp US) = **siding** **VT** ablenken; **I got ~ed onto something else** ich wurde durch irgendetwas abgelenkt; (from topic) ich wurde irgendwie vom Thema abgebracht or auf ein anderes Thema gebracht; **she's easily ~ed** sie lässt sich leicht ablenken; **side view** N Seitenansicht f; **to have a ~ of sth** etw von der Seite sehen; **I just caught a ~ of her head** ich konnte sie nur kurz im Profil sehen; **sidewalk** N (US) Bürgersteig m, Gehsteig m, Trottoir nt (S Ger); **sidewalk artist** N (US) Pflastermaler(in) m(f); **sidewalk café** N (US) Straßencafé nt; **sidewall** N Seitenwand f; **sideward** ADJ = **sidewards** ADJ **a**

sidewards [ˈsaɪdwədz] **ADJ** (= to one side) movement zur Seite; glance von der Seite; **to give sb/sth a ~ glance** jdn/etw von der Seite ansehen **ADV** (= to one side) move zur Seite, seitwärts; look at sb von der Seite

sideways [ˈsaɪdweɪz] **ADJ** **a** (= to one side) movement zur Seite; glance von der Seite **b** (in career) **the Justice Minister's recent ~ move to education** die kürzliche Versetzung des Justizministers in das Bildungsressort **ADV** **a** (= to one side) move zur Seite, seitwärts; look at sb von der Seite; **it goes in ~** es geht seitwärts hinein; **he was knocked ~ by it** (fig inf) es hat ihn umgehauen (inf) **b** (= side on) sit seitlich; **~ on** seitlich (to sth zu etw) **c** (in career) **to move ~** sich auf gleichem Niveau verändern

side: sidewheeler [ˈsaɪdˌwiːlə] N (US: = paddle steamer) Raddampfer m; **side wind** N Seitenwind m; **side whiskers** PL Backenbart m; **sidewinder** N **a** (US: = blow) Haken m **b** (= rattlesnake) Seitenwinder m, gehörnte Klapperschlange

sidewise [ˈsaɪdwaɪz] ADJ, ADV = **sidewards**

siding [ˈsaɪdɪŋ] N Rangiergleis nt; (= dead end) Abstellgleis nt

sidle [ˈsaɪdl] VI (sich) schleichen; **to ~ away** (sich) wegschleichen; **he must have ~d off** er muss sich verdrückt haben (inf); **to ~ up to sb** sich an jdn heranschleichen

SIDS [sɪdz] (Med) abbr of **sudden infant death syndrome**

siege [siːdʒ] N (of town) Belagerung f; (by police) Umstellung f; **to be under ~** belagert werden; (by police) umstellt sein; **to lay ~ to a town** eine Stadt belagern; **to lay ~ to a house** ein Haus umstellen; **he attempted to lay ~ to her emotions** er versuchte, ihr Herz zu erobern

siege mentality N Bunkermentalität f

sienna [sɪˈenə] **N** (= earth) Sienaerde f; (= colour) Ockergelb nt; **raw ~** Ockergelb nt; **burned ~** gebrannte Siena **ADJ** ockergelb; **raw ~** ockergelb; **burned ~** siena(braun), rotbraun

sierra [sɪˈerə] N Sierra f

Sierra Leone [sɪˈerəlɪˈəʊn] N Sierra Leone f

siesta [sɪˈestə] N Siesta f; **to have** or **take a ~** Siesta halten or machen

sieve [sɪv] **N** Sieb nt; **to have a memory** or **brain like a ~** (inf) ein Gedächtnis wie ein Sieb haben (inf) **VT** = **sift VT a**

sift [sɪft] **VT a** (lit) sieben; coal schütteln; **~ the sugar onto the cake** den Kuchen mit Zucker besieben **b** (fig, = search) sichten, durchgehen; (= separate) trennen **VI** (fig) sieben; **to ~ through the evidence** das Beweismaterial durchgehen; **a ~ing process** ein Siebeverfahren nt

▶ **sift out** VT sep **a** stones, seed, wheat aussieben **b** (fig) herausfinden, herauskristallisieren; (= eliminate) absondern; applicants aussieben

sifter [ˈsɪftə] N Sieb nt

sigh [saɪ] **N** (of person) Seufzer m; (of wind, = murmur) Säuseln nt no pl; (= moan) Seufzen nt no pl (liter); **a ~ of relief** ein Seufzer m der Erleichterung → **breathe** **VI** seufzen; (wind, = murmur) säuseln; (= moan) seufzen (liter); **to ~ with relief** erleichtert aufatmen; **to ~ with pleasure** vor Vergnügen seufzen; **to ~ for sb/sth** sich nach jdm/etw sehnen **VT** seufzen

sighing [ˈsaɪɪŋ] N (of person) Seufzen nt; (of wind, = murmuring) Säuseln nt; (= moaning) Seufzen nt (liter)

sight [saɪt] **N a** (= faculty) Sehvermögen nt; **the gift of ~** die Gabe des Sehens; **long/short ~** Weit-/Kurzsichtigkeit f; **to have long/short ~** weit-/kurzsichtig sein; **to lose/regain one's ~** sein Augenlicht verlieren/wiedergewinnen; **he has very good ~** er sieht sehr gut; **~ is the most valuable sense** das Auge ist das wertvollste Sinnesorgan **b** (= glimpse, seeing) **it was my first ~ of Paris** das war das Erste, was ich von Paris gesehen habe; **to hate sb at first ~** or **on ~** jdn vom ersten Augenblick an nicht leiden können; **at first ~ I hated him, but then ...** zuerst konnte ich ihn gar nicht leiden, aber dann ...; **at first ~ it seemed easy** auf den ersten Blick erschien es einfach; **to shoot at ~** sofort schießen; **he played the music by ~** er hat vom Blatt gespielt; **love at first ~** Liebe auf den ersten Blick; **at the ~ of the police they ran away** als sie die Polizei sahen, rannten sie weg; **to know sb by ~** jdn vom Sehen kennen; **to catch ~ of sb/sth** jdn/etw entdecken or erblicken; **if I catch ~ of you round here again ...** wenn du mir hier noch einmal unter die Augen kommst, ...; **don't let me catch ~ of you with her again** ich möchte dich nicht noch einmal mit ihr erwischen; **to get a ~ of sb/sth** jdn/etw zu sehen or zu Gesicht bekommen; **we had a glorious ~ of the mountains** wir hatten einen herrlichen Blick auf die Berge; **to lose ~ of sb/sth** (lit, fig) jdn/etw aus den Augen verlieren; **don't lose ~ of the fact that ...** Sie dürfen nicht außer Acht lassen, dass ... → **second sight** **c** (= sth seen) Anblick m; **the ~ of blood/her makes me sick** wenn ich Blut/sie sehe, wird mir übel; **that is the most beautiful ~ I've ever seen** das ist das Schönste, was ich je gesehen habe; **I hate** or **can't bear the ~ of him/his greasy hair** ich kann ihn/seine fettigen Haare (einfach) nicht ausstehen; **to be a ~ to see** or **behold** ein herrlicher Anblick sein; (funny) ein Bild or Anblick für die Götter sein (inf); **what a horrible ~!** das sieht ja furchtbar aus!; **it was a ~ for sore eyes** es war eine wahre Augenweide; **you're a ~ for sore eyes** es ist schön, dich zu sehen **d** (inf) **to be** or **look a ~** (= funny) zum Schreien aussehen (inf); (horrible) fürchterlich aussehen; **he looks a ~** der sieht vielleicht aus (inf); **what a ~ you are!** wie siehst du denn aus! **e** (= range of vision) Sicht f; **to be in** or **within ~** in Sicht or in Sichtweite sein; **land in ~!** Land in Sicht!; **our goal is in ~** unser Ziel ist in greifbare Nähe gerückt; **we are in ~ of victory** unser Sieg liegt in greifbarer Nähe; **we came in ~ of the coast** die Küste kam in Sicht; **at last we were in ~ of land** endlich war Land in Sicht;

to keep sb in ~ jdn im Auge behalten; **to keep out of ~** sich verborgen halten; **to keep sb/sth out of ~** jdn/etw nicht sehen lassen; **keep out of my ~!** lass dich bloß bei mir nicht mehr sehen or blicken; **to be out of** or **lost to ~** nicht mehr zu sehen sein, außer Sicht sein; **the minute I was out of ~ of the school** sobald ich von der Schule aus nicht mehr zu sehen war; **when he's out of our ~** wenn wir ihn nicht sehen; **somewhere out of ~ a cat was mewing** irgendwo miaute eine (unsichtbare) Katze; **don't let the children out of your ~** lass die Kinder nicht aus den Augen; **darling, I'll never let you out of my ~ again** Schatz, ich lasse dich nie mehr fort; **she dropped out of ~ after her first movie** nach ihrem ersten Film geriet sie in Vergessenheit; **to be lost to ~** nicht mehr zu sehen sein; **out of ~, out of mind** (Prov) aus den Augen, aus dem Sinn (Prov) **f** (Comm) **payable at ~** zahlbar bei Sicht; **30 days' ~** 30 Tage nach Sicht; **~ unseen** unbesehen, ohne Besicht (form); **we need to have ~ of the document first** das Dokument muss uns (dat) zuerst vorliegen **g** (fig, = opinion) **in sb's ~** in jds Augen (dat); **in the ~ of God** vor Gott **h** usu pl (of city etc) Sehenswürdigkeit f; **to see the ~s of a town** etc eine Stadt etc besichtigen **i** (on telescope etc) Visiereinrichtung f; (on gun) Visier nt; **to set one's ~s too high** (fig) seine Ziele zu hoch stecken; **to lower one's ~s** (fig) seine Ansprüche herabsetzen or herunterschrauben; **to set one's ~s on sth** (fig) ein Auge auf etw (acc) werfen; **to have sb/sth in** or **within one's ~s** (fig) jdn/etw im Fadenkreuz haben **j** (= aim, observation) **to take a ~ with a gun** etc **at sth** etw mit einem Gewehr etc anvisieren **k** (inf) **not by a long ~** bei weitem nicht; **a ~ better/cheaper** einiges besser/billiger; **he's a damn ~ cleverer than you think** er ist ein ganzes Ende gescheiter als du meinst (inf) **l** (inf) **out of ~** sagenhaft (sl), der Wahnsinn (inf) **VT a** (= see) sichten (also Mil); person ausmachen **b** gun (= provide with sights) mit Visier versehen; (= adjust sights) richten

sight bill, sight draft N Sichtwechsel m

sighted [ˈsaɪtɪd] ADJ sehend

-sighted ADJ suf (Med, fig) -sichtig; **far-sighted** weitsichtig; **short-sighted** kurzsichtig

sighting [ˈsaɪtɪŋ] N Sichten nt; **at the first ~ of land** zum ersten Mal Land gesichtet wurde; **another ~ of the monster was reported** das Ungeheuer soll erneut gesehen or gesichtet worden sein

sightless [ˈsaɪtlɪs] ADJ person erblindet, blind; **~ since birth** von Geburt an blind; **worms are completely ~** Würmer haben kein Sehvermögen (form), Würmer können überhaupt nicht sehen; **with ~ eyes** mit blicklosen (geh) or toten Augen

sightlessness [ˈsaɪtlɪsnɪs] N Blindheit f

sightline [ˈsaɪtlaɪn] N Sicht f

sightly [ˈsaɪtlɪ] ADJ ansehnlich

sight: sight-read VTI vom Blatt spielen/lesen/singen; **sightscreen** N (Cricket) Sichtblende f hinter dem Tor; **sightseeing N** Besichtigungen pl; **I hate ~** ich hasse Sightseeing; **~ in Ruritania** eine Rundreise durch Ruritanien; (= list of sights) Sehenswürdigkeiten pl von Ruritanien; **to go ~** auf Besichtigungstour gehen **ADJ ~ tour** Rundreise f; (in town) (Stadt)rundfahrt f; **~ tourists** Touristen pl (auf Besichtigungstour); **sightseer** N Tourist(in) m(f); **sight test** N Sehtest m

sign [saɪn] **N a** (with hand etc) Zeichen nt; **he nodded as a ~ of recognition** er nickte zum Zeichen, dass er mich/ihn etc erkannt hatte; **to give sb a ~** jdm ein Zeichen geben; **to make a ~ to sb** jdm ein Zeichen machen or geben; **he gave** or **made me a ~ to stay** er gab mir durch ein Zeichen zu verstehen, ich solle bleiben; **he made a rude ~** er machte eine unverschämte Geste

b (= indication, Med) Anzeichen nt (of für, +gen); (= evidence) Zeichen nt (of von, +gen); (= trace) Spur f; **a sure/good/bad ~** ein sicheres/gutes/schlechtes Zeichen; **it's a ~ of the times** es ist ein Zeichen unserer Zeit; **it's a ~ of a true expert** daran erkennt man den wahren Experten; **at the slightest/first ~ of disagreement** beim geringsten/ersten Anzeichen von Uneinigkeit; **there is no ~ of their agreeing** nichts deutet darauf hin, dass sie zustimmen werden; **to show ~s of sth** Anzeichen für etw erkennen lassen; **he shows ~s of doing it** es sieht so aus, als ob es tun würde; **our guest showed no ~(s) of leaving** unser Gast machte keine Anstalten zu gehen; **the rain showed no ~(s) of stopping** nichts deutete darauf hin, dass der Regen aufhören würde; **he gave no ~ of having heard** er ließ nicht erkennen, ob er es gehört hatte; **there was no ~ of life** in the village es gab keine Spur or kein Anzeichen von Leben im Dorf; **there was no ~ of him/the book anywhere** von ihm/von dem Buch war keine Spur zu sehen; **is there any ~ of him yet?** ist er schon zu sehen? **c** (= road sign, inn sign, shop sign) Schild nt **d** (= written symbol) Zeichen nt; (Astron, Astrol) (Tierkreis)zeichen nt **VT a** **to ~ one's name** unterschreiben; **to ~ one's name in a book** sich in ein Buch eintragen; **he ~s himself J.G. Jones** er unterschreibt mit J. G. Jones **b** letter, contract, cheque unterschreiben, unterzeichnen (form); picture, book signieren; **to ~ the guest book** sich ins Gästebuch eintragen; **to ~ the register** sich eintragen; **~ed, sealed** (unterschrieben und) besiegelt; **~ed, sealed and delivered** unter Dach und Fach, fix und fertig (inf); **~ed copy** handsigniertes Exemplar **c** football player etc unter Vertrag nehmen, einstellen **d** (= use sign language in) programme, performance in die Gebärdensprache übersetzen **VI a** (= signal) **to ~ to sb to do sth** jdm ein Zeichen geben, etw zu tun **b** (with signature) unterschreiben; **Fellows has just ~ed for United** Fellows hat gerade bei United unterschrieben **c** (= use sign language) die Gebärdensprache benutzen

▶ **sign away** VT sep verzichten auf (+acc); **she felt she was signing away her life** sie hatte den Eindruck, ihr Leben abzuschreiben; **I'm not going to sign my life away with a mortgage** ich werde mich nicht ein Leben lang mit einer Hypothek belasten

▶ **sign for** VI +prep obj den Empfang (+gen) bestätigen

▶ **sign in** **VT** sep person eintragen; **to sign sb in at a club** jdn als Gast in einen Klub mitnehmen **VI** sich eintragen

▶ **sign off** **VI** (Rad, TV) sich verabschieden; (in letter) Schluss machen **VT** +prep obj **to sign off (the dole)** (Brit) eine Arbeit aufnehmen

▶ **sign on** **VT** sep = **sign up** VT **VI a** = **sign up** VI **b** (Brit: for unemployment benefit etc) **to sign on (for unemployment benefit)** (= apply) sich arbeitslos melden; **he's still signing on** er ist immer noch arbeitslos, er bezieht immer noch Arbeitslosenunterstützung **c** (disc jockey etc) sich melden **VI** +prep obj **to sign on (the dole)** (Brit) sich arbeitslos melden

▶ **sign out** **VI** sich austragen; **to sign out of a hotel** (aus einem Hotel) abreisen **VT** sep austragen

▶ **sign over** VT sep überschreiben (to sb jdm)

▶ **sign up** **VT** sep (= employ, enlist) verpflichten; workers, employees anstellen; mercenaries anwerben; sailors anheuern **VI** sich verpflichten; (mercenaries) sich melden (with zu); (employees, players) sich einschreiben (sailors) anheuern; (for evening class etc) sich einschreiben

signal[1] [ˈsɪgnl] **N a** (= sign) Zeichen nt; (as part of code) Signal nt; (= message) Nachricht f; **to**

give the ~ for sth das Zeichen/Signal zu etw geben; **to make a ~ to sb** jdm ein Zeichen geben

b (= *apparatus, Rail*) Signal *nt*; **the ~ is at red** das Signal steht auf Rot

c (*Telec*) Signal *nt*

d (*Brit, Mil*) **Signals** ≈ Fernmelder *pl, Angehörige der britischen Fernmeldetruppe Royal Corps of Signals*

VT **a** (= *indicate*) anzeigen; *arrival, future event, spring etc* ankündigen; **to ~ sb to do sth** jdm ein Zeichen geben, etw zu tun; **the policeman ~led** (*Brit*) or **~ed** (*US*) **the cars on** der Polizist gab den Autos das Zeichen weiterzufahren; **he ~led** (*Brit*) or **~ed** (*US*) **that he was going to turn left** er zeigte an, dass er (nach) links abbiegen wollte; **the train was ~led** (*Brit*) or **~ed** (*US*) **onto another line** der Zug wurde durch Signale auf ein anderes Gleis gewiesen or geleitet; **to ~ one's intention to do sth** anzeigen, dass man vorhat, etw zu tun

b *message* signalisieren

VI ein Zeichen geben; **he ~led** (*Brit*) or **~ed** (*US*) **to the waiter** winkte dem Ober; **he ~led for his bill** (*Brit*) **he ~ed for the check** (*US*) er winkte zum Zeichen, dass er zahlen wollte; **the driver didn't ~** der Fahrer hat kein Zeichen gegeben or hat nicht angezeigt; **the general ~led** (*Brit*) or **~ed** (*US*) **for reinforcements** der General forderte Verstärkung an

signal² ADJ *attr* (*liter*) *victory, courage* beachtlich, bemerkenswert; *success, contribution* beachtlich; *failure, stupidity* eklatant (*geh*)

signal: signal box N Stellwerk *nt*; **signal flag** N Signalflagge *f*

signalize ['sɪɡnəlaɪz] VT kennzeichnen

signal lamp N Signallampe *f*

signaller, (*US*) **signaler** ['sɪɡnələ] N (*Mil*) Fernmelder(in) *m(f)*, Funker(in) *m(f)*

signalling, (*US*) **signaling** ['sɪɡnəlɪŋ] N (*Mil*) Nachrichtenübermittlung *f*

signally ['sɪɡnəlɪ] ADV (*liter*) *successful, ineffective* bemerkenswert; *stupid* eklatant; **he has ~ failed** er hat eindeutig versagt; **he has ~ failed to provide evidence** er hat es eindeutig nicht geschafft, Beweise vorzulegen

signal: signalman N (*Rail*) Stellwerkswärter *m*; (*Mil*) Fernmelder *m*, Funker *m*; **signal-red** ADJ signalrot; **signal tower** N (*US Rail*) Stellwerk *nt*

signatory ['sɪɡnətərɪ] ADJ Signatar-; **the ~ countries of an agreement** die Signatarstaaten eines Abkommens **N** (= *person*) Unterzeichner(in) *m(f)*, Signatar(in) *m(f)* (*form*); **the signatories of** or **to the EC treaty** die Signatarstaaten des EG-Vertrags

signature ['sɪɡnətʃə] N **a** Unterschrift *f*; (*of artist*) Signatur *f* **b** (*Mus*) Vorzeichnung *f* **c** (*Typ*) Signatur *f*

signature tune N (*Brit*) Erkennungsmelodie *f*

signboard ['saɪnbɔːd] N Schild *nt*; (= *hoarding*) Anschlagtafel *f*

signer ['saɪnə] N Unterzeichner(in) *m(f)*

signet ring ['sɪɡnɪt,rɪŋ] N Siegelring *m*

significance [sɪɡ'nɪfɪkəns] N Bedeutung *f*; (*of action also*) Tragweite *f*; (*of one special event also*) Wichtigkeit *f*; **what is the ~ of this?** was bedeutet das?, welche Bedeutung hat das?; **of no ~** belanglos, bedeutungslos; **to attach great ~ to sth** einer Sache (*dat*) große Bedeutung beimessen; **he attaches great ~ to us arriving on time** er legt großen Wert darauf, dass wir pünktlich sind

significant [sɪɡ'nɪfɪkənt] ADJ **a** (= *considerable, having consequence*) bedeutend; (= *important*) wichtig; **is it of any ~ interest?** ist das von wesentlichem Interesse?; **to be ~ to or for sth** in eine bedeutende or wichtige Rolle in etw (*dat*) spielen; **statistically ~** statistisch signifikant or bedeutsam; **politically/historically ~** politisch/ historisch bedeutend

b (= *meaningful*) bedeutungsvoll; *look* viel sagend, bedeutsam; *sigh, tone of voice* bedeutungsvoll; **it is ~ that ...** es ist bezeich-

nend, dass ...; **he wondered whether her glance was ~** er fragte sich, ob ihr Blick etwas zu bedeuten habe; **to be ~ of sth** (*liter*) ein (An)zeichen *nt* für etw sein

significantly [sɪɡ'nɪfɪkəntlɪ] ADV **a** (= *considerably*) bedeutend; **it is not ~ different** das ist kaum anders, da besteht kein wesentlicher Unterschied **b** (= *meaningfully*) bedeutungsvoll; *look* vielsagend, bedeutsam; **~, she refused** bezeichnenderweise weigerte sie sich ab; **he was ~ absent** er fehlte bezeichnenderweise

signification [ˌsɪɡnɪfɪ'keɪʃən] N **a** (= *meaning*) Sinn *m*, Bedeutung *f* **b** (= *indication*) Bezeichnung *f*; **a ~ of one's intentions** eine Absichtsbekundung or -erklärung

signify ['sɪɡnɪfaɪ] **VT** **a** (= *mean*) bedeuten **b** (= *indicate*) andeuten, erkennen lassen **VI** (*dated*) **it/he doesn't ~** das/er spielt keine Rolle

signing ['saɪnɪŋ] N **a** (*of document*) Unterzeichnen *nt* **b** (*of football player, pop star etc*) Untervertragnahme *f*; (= *football player, pop star etc*) neu unter Vertrag Genommene(r) *mf* **c** (= *sign language*) Gebärdensprache *f*

sign: sign language N Zeichensprache *f*; (*for deaf also*) Gebärdensprache *f*; **sign painter** N Plakat- or Schildermaler(in) *m(f)*; **signpost** **N** Wegweiser *m* **VT** *way* beschildern; *diversion, special route* ausschildern; **signposting** N Beschilderung *f*; (*of special route, diversion*) Ausschilderung *f*; **signwriter** N Schriften- or Schildermaler(in) *m(f)*

Sikh [siːk] N Sikh *mf*

silage ['saɪlɪdʒ] N Silage *f*, Silofutter *nt*

silence ['saɪləns] **N** Stille *f*; (= *quietness also*) Ruhe *f*; (= *absence of talk also, of letters etc*) Schweigen *nt*; (*on a particular subject*) (Still)schweigen *nt*; **~!** Ruhe!; **in ~** still; (= *not talking also*) schweigend; **there was ~** alles war still; **there was a short ~** es herrschte für kurze Zeit Stille; **the conversation was full of awkward ~s** die Unterhaltung kam immer wieder ins Stocken; **to break the ~** die Stille durchbrechen; **he broke his ~** er brach sein Schweigen; **a minute's** (*Brit*) or **moment's** (*US*) **~** eine Schweigeminute

VT (*lit, fig*) zum Schweigen bringen; **to ~ sb's tongue** jdn zum Schweigen bringen

silencer ['saɪlənsə] N (*on gun, Brit: on car*) Schalldämpfer *m*; (= *whole fitting on car*) Auspufftopf *m*

silent ['saɪlənt] ADJ **a** still; (= *not talking also*) schweigsam; *engine, machine etc* (= *running quietly*) ruhig; **to fall** or **become ~** still werden; (*people also, guns*) verstummen; **to keep** or **remain ~** still sein or bleiben, sich still verhalten; **be ~!** sei still!; **the guns are ~** die Waffen schweigen; **ovarian cancer is a ~ killer** Eierstockkrebs tötet auf leise or unbemerkte Art; **his father was the strong ~ type** sein Vater war ein schweigsamer, willensstarker Typ

b (= *not giving comment*) **to be ~** schweigen; **to be ~ about** or **on sth** über etw (*acc*) schweigen or Stillschweigen bewahren; **the law is ~ on this point** das Gesetz schweigt zu diesem Punkt; **to keep** or **remain ~** nichts sagen, sich nicht äußern; **he kept completely ~ when questioned** er sagte kein einziges Wort or überhaupt nichts, als man ihn verhörte; **everyone kept ~** keiner sagte etwas; **you have the right to remain ~** Sie haben das Recht zu schweigen; **to give sb the ~ treatment** jdn mit Schweigen strafen; **a ~ witness** ein stummer Zeuge, eine stumme Zeugin

c (= *quiet, wordless*) *protest* still; *agreement, disapproval* (still)schweigend *attr*; **~ demonstration** Schweigemarsch *m*

d (*Film*) **~ film** (*esp Brit*) or **movie** (*esp US*) Stummfilm *m*; **the ~ era** die Stummfilmzeit

e (*Ling*: = *not pronounced*) **~ letter** stummer Buchstabe; **the "k" is ~ in the word "knee"** das Wort „knee" hat ein stummes „k"; **~ "h"** stummes „h"

PL **the silents** (*Brit Film*) die Stummfilme *pl*

silently ['saɪləntlɪ] ADV lautlos, (= *without talking*) schweigend; (= *with little noise*) leise

silent: silent majority N **the ~** die schweigende Mehrheit; **silent partner** N (*US Comm*) stiller Teilhaber or Gesellschafter; **silent vigil** N Mahnwache *f*

Silesia [saɪ'liːzɪə] N Schlesien *nt*

Silesian [saɪ'liːzɪən] ADJ schlesisch **N** Schlesier(in) *m(f)*

silhouette [ˌsɪluː'et] **N** Silhouette *f*; (= *picture*) Schattenriss *m*, Scherenschnitt *m* **VT** **to be ~d against sth** sich (als Silhouette) gegen or von etw abzeichnen

silica ['sɪlɪkə] N Kieselerde *f*

silica gel N Kieselgel *nt*

silicate ['sɪlɪkɪt] N Silikat *nt*, Silicat *nt*

siliceous [sɪ'lɪʃəs] ADJ kiesig

silicon ['sɪlɪkən] N Silizium *nt*

silicon chip N Siliziumchip *nt*

silicone ['sɪlɪkəʊn] N Silikon *nt*; **~ treatment** Silikonbehandlung *f*; **~ (breast) implants** Silikonimplantate *pl*, Silikon(brust)einlagen *pl*

Silicon Valley N Silicon Valley *nt*

silicosis [ˌsɪlɪ'kəʊsɪs] N (*Med*) Staublunge *f*, Silikose *f* (*spec*)

silk [sɪlk] **N** **a** Seide *f*; (= *silk dress*) Seidene(s) *nt*, Seidenkleid *nt*; **dressed in beautiful ~s** in herrliche Seidengewänder gekleidet; **dressed in ~s and satins** in Samt und Seide (gekleidet) **b** (*Brit, Jur, = barrister*) Kronanwalt *m*/-anwältin *f*; (= *gown*) Seidengewand *nt*; **to take ~** Kronanwalt werden **c** **silks** PL (= *racing colours*) (Renn)farben *pl* **ADJ** Seiden-, seiden; **~ tie** Seidenkrawatte *f*; **the dress is ~** das Kleid ist aus Seide; **you can't make a ~ purse out of a sow's ear** (*Prov*) aus einem Ackergaul kann man kein Rennpferd machen (*prov*)

silken ['sɪlkən] ADJ (*old*: = *of silk*) seiden; (= *like silk*) seidig; *manner* glatt; *voice* (bedrohlich) sanft

silk hat N Zylinder *m*

silkiness ['sɪlkɪnɪs] N (= *appearance*) seidiger Glanz; (= *feeling*) seidige Weichheit; (*of voice*) Sanftheit *f*; (*of manner*) Glätte *f*

silk: silk moth N Seidenspinner *m*; **silk screen** N Seidensieb *nt*; (*also* **silk-screen printing**) Seidensiebdruck *m*; **silk stocking** N Seidenstrumpf *m*; **silk-stocking** ADJ (*US*) vornehm; **silkworm** N Seidenraupe *f*

silky ['sɪlkɪ] ADJ (+*er*) seidig; *voice* samtig; *manner* glatt; *movements* weich; **~ smooth/soft** seidenweich

sill [sɪl] N Sims *m* or *nt*; (= *windowsill*) (Fenster-) sims *m* or *nt*; (*esp of wood*) Fensterbrett *nt*; (= *doorsill*) Schwelle *f*; (*on car*) Türleiste *f*

sillabub N = **syllabub**

silliness ['sɪlɪnɪs] N Albernheit *f*; **no ~ while we're out, children!** macht keine Dummheiten, wenn wir nicht da sind!

silly ['sɪlɪ] ADJ (+*er*) albern, dumm, doof (*inf*); **don't be ~** (= *do silly things*) mach keinen Quatsch (*inf*); (= *say silly things*) red keinen Unsinn; (= *ask silly questions*) frag nicht so dumm; **that was ~ of you, that was a ~ thing to do** das war dumm (von dir); **I've done a ~ thing and come without the key** ich war so dumm, ohne Schlüssel zu kommen, ich Dussel bin ohne Schlüssel gekommen (*inf*); **it was a ~ thing to say** es war dumm, das zu sagen; **I hope he doesn't do anything ~** ich hoffe, er macht keine Dummheiten; **I know it's ~ to feel jealous** ich weiß, es ist dumm, eifersüchtig zu sein; **he was ~ to resign** es war dumm von ihm zurückzutreten; **I feel ~ in this hat** mit diesem Hut komme ich mir albern or lächerlich vor; **to make sb look ~** jdn lächerlich machen; **that remark of yours made him look/left him looking a bit ~** nach dieser Bemerkung von dir stand er ziemlich dumm da; **to knock sb ~** (*inf*) jdn windelweich schlagen (*inf*); **to laugh oneself ~** (*inf*) sich dumm und dämlich lachen (*inf*); **to worry sb ~** (*inf*) jdn vor Sorge (ganz) krank machen; **to drink oneself ~** (*inf*) seinen Verstand versaufen (*inf*); **to be bored ~** (*inf*) zu Tode gelangweilt sein; **to bore sb ~** (*inf*) jdn zu Tode langweilen; **to pay a ~ price for sth** (*inf, high* price) für etw einen sündhaft teuren Preis bezahlen; (low price) für etw einen Spottpreis bezahlen; ~ **money** (inf) Wahnsinnssummen pl (inf)

N (Brit: also **silly-billy**) Dussel m (inf); **you big** ~ du Dummerchen (inf); **don't be such a** ~ sei nicht albern

silly season N närrische Zeit; (Brit Press) Saure-Gurken-Zeit f

silo ['saɪləʊ] N Silo nt; (for missile) (Raketen)silo nt

silt [sɪlt] **N** Schwemmsand m; (= river mud) Schlick m **VT** (also **silt up**) mit Schlick/Schwemmsand füllen **VI** (also **silt up**) verschlammen

silty ['sɪltɪ] ADJ verschlammt, schlammig

Silurian [saɪ'ljuːrɪən] ADJ (Geol) silurisch

silvan ['sɪlvən] ADJ (liter) = **sylvan**

silver ['sɪlvə'] **N a** (= metal) Silber nt **b** (= coins) Silber(geld) nt, Silbermünzen pl; **£10 in** ~ £ 10 in Silber **c** (= tableware, articles) Silber nt **d** (= colour) Silber nt **ADJ** Silber-, silbern; ~ **jewellery** (Brit) or **jewelry** (US) Silberschmuck m; **to be born with a** ~ **spoon in one's mouth** (prov) mit einem silbernen Löffel im Mund geboren sein (prov) **VT** metal, mirror versilbern; **old age had** ~**ed his hair** das Alter hatte sein Haar silbergrau werden lassen

silver: silver birch N Weißbirke f; **silver disc** N (Brit Mus) silberne Schallplatte; **silver fir** N Weiß- or Silbertanne f; **silverfish** N Silberfischchen nt; **silver foil** N (= kitchen foil) Alu(minium)folie f; (= silver paper) Silberpapier nt; **silver fox** N Silberfuchs m; **silver-grey**, (US) **silver-gray** ADJ silbergrau; hair silberweiß; **silver-haired** ADJ silberhaarig; **he is** ~ er hat silberweißes Haar

silveriness ['sɪlvərɪnɪs] N silbriger Schimmer; (of sound, voice) silberheller Klang

silver: silver jubilee N 25jähriges Jubiläum; **silver lining** N (fig) Silberstreifen f (am Horizont), Lichtblick m (fig); **silver medal** N Silbermedaille f; **silver medallist**, (US) **silver medalist** N (Sport) Silbermedaillengewinner(in) m(f); **silver nitrate** N Silbernitrat nt; **silver oxide** N Silberoxid nt; **silver oxide battery** N Silberoxidbatterie f; **silver paper** N Silberpapier nt; **silver plate** N (= plating) Silberauflage f, Versilberung f; (= articles) versilberte Sachen pl; **is that** ~? ist das versilbert?; **silver-plate** VT versilbern; **silver-plating** N Versilberung f; (= layer also) Silberauflage f; **silver screen** N Leinwand f; **silver service** N (in restaurant) Servieren nach allen Regeln der Kunst; **silverside** N (Cook) quer geschnittenes Stück aus der Rindskeule; **silversmith** N Silberschmied(in) m(f); **silversmith's (shop)** N Silberschmiede f; **silver standard** N Silberstandard m; **silver surfer** N (inf) Internetbenutzer(in) m(f) in fortgeschrittenem Alter; **silver-tongued** ADJ (liter) wort- or redegewandt; **silverware** N Silber nt, Silberzeug nt (inf); (in shop also) Silberwaren pl; **silver wedding** N Silberhochzeit f

silvery ['sɪlvərɪ] ADJ silbern, silbrig; sound, voice silberhell; ~ **grey** (Brit) or **gray** (US) silbergrau; ~ **white** silberweiß

silviculture ['sɪlvɪkʌltʃə'] N Waldbau m

SIM (Telec) abbr of subscriber identification module SIM; ~ **card** SIM-Karte f

simian ['sɪmɪən] **ADJ** (form) der Affen; appearance affenartig **N** Affe m

similar ['sɪmɪlə'] ADJ ähnlich (also Math); amount, size fast or ungefähr gleich; **to be** ~ **to sb/sth** jdm/einer Sache ähnlich sein; **this is** ~ **to what happened before** etwas Ähnliches ist schon einmal geschehen; **she and her sister are very** ~, **she is very** ~ **to her sister** ihre Schwester und sie sind sich sehr ähnlich, sie ähnelt ihrer Schwester sehr; **to be** ~ **in appearance to sth** eine ähnliche Erscheinung wie etw haben; **they are very** ~ **in appearance/character** sie ähneln sich sehr im äußerlich/charakterlich sehr; ~ **in size** ungefähr or fast gleich groß; **to taste** ~ **to**

sth ähnlich wie etw schmecken; **they are of a** ~ **age** sie sind etwa gleich alt; **in a** ~ **way** ähnlich; (= likewise) genauso, ebenso

similarity [ˌsɪmɪ'lærɪtɪ] N Ähnlichkeit f (to mit)

similarly ['sɪmɪləlɪ] ADV ähnlich; (= equally) genauso, ebenso; **a** ~ **pained expression** ein ähnlich qualvoller Ausdruck; ~, **you could maintain** ... genauso gut könnten Sie behaupten ...

simile ['sɪmɪlɪ] N Gleichnis nt; **his use of** ~ sein Gebrauch m von Gleichnissen

similitude [sɪ'mɪlɪtjuːd] N (liter) Ähnlichkeit f

simmer ['sɪmə'] **N to be on the** ~ (Cook) auf kleiner Flamme kochen; **to keep sth on the** ~ (lit) etw auf kleiner Flamme kochen lassen; (fig) etw nicht zur Ruhe kommen lassen **VT** auf kleiner Flamme kochen lassen **VI** auf kleiner Flamme kochen; (fig, with rage) kochen (inf); (with excitement) fiebern

▶ **simmer down** VI sich beruhigen, sich abregen (inf)

simnel cake ['sɪmnlkeɪk] N (Brit) marzipanüberzogener Früchtekuchen

simonize ['saɪmənaɪz] VT polieren

simony ['saɪmənɪ] N (old Eccl) Simonie f

simp [sɪmp] N (US inf, pej) Simpel m (pej)

simper ['sɪmpə'] **N** ... **she said with a** ~ ..., sagte sie mit säuselnder Stimme **VI** (= smile) geziert or albern lächeln; (= talk) säuseln **VT** säuseln

simpering ['sɪmpərɪŋ] ADJ geziert, albern

simperingly ['sɪmpərɪŋlɪ] ADV geziert, albern; talk säuselnd

simple ['sɪmpl] ADJ (+er) **a** (= uncomplicated, easy) einfach; **the camcorder is** ~ **to use** der Camcorder ist einfach zu bedienen; **it's as** ~ **as ABC** es ist kinderleicht; **"chemistry made** ~" „Chemie leicht gemacht" **b** (= plain, not elaborate) einfach; decor, dress schlicht, einfach; **in** ~ **terms** in einfachen Worten; **in** ~ **language** in einfacher Sprache; **the** ~ **fact** or **truth is** ... es ist einfach so, dass ...; **the** ~ **fact that** ... die schlichte Tatsache, dass...; **for the** ~ **reason that** ... aus dem einfachen or schlichten Grund, dass ...; **it's a** ~ **matter of money** es ist schlicht und einfach eine Frage des Geldes; **it's a** ~ **matter of finding adequate finance** es geht ganz einfach darum, angemessene finanzielle Mittel zu finden **c** (= unsophisticated, unworldly) einfach, schlicht; **I'm a** ~ **soul** ich bin ein einfacher Mensch; **she likes the** ~ **life** sie mag das einfache Leben or einen einfachen Lebensstil; **the** ~ **things in** or **of life** die einfachen Dinge des Lebens or im Leben **d** (= foolish, mentally deficient) einfältig **e** (Chem, Med, Math, Ling) einfach; (Biol, Bot) life form primitiv, einfach

simple: simple contract N (Jur) formloser Vertrag; **simple fracture** N (Med) einfacher Bruch; **simple interest** N (Fin) Kapitalzinsen pl; **simple majority** N einfache Mehrheit; **simple-minded** ADJ einfältig; **simple-mindedness** N Einfältigkeit f, Einfalt f; **Simple Simon** ['sɪmpl'saɪmən] N (= simpleton) Einfaltspinsel m (inf pej); **simple time** N (Mus) gerader Takt

simpleton ['sɪmpltən] N Einfaltspinsel m

simplex ['sɪmpleks] N (Ling) Simplex nt

simplicity [sɪm'plɪsɪtɪ] N **a** Einfachheit f; (= unworldliness, lack of sophistication: of decor, dress) Schlichtheit f, Einfachheit f; **it's** ~ **itself** das ist das Einfachste, das ist die einfachste Sache der Welt **b** (= foolishness) Einfalt f, Einfältigkeit f

simplifiable ['sɪmplɪfaɪəbl] ADJ zu vereinfachend attr, zu vereinfachen pred, simplifizierbar

simplification [ˌsɪmplɪfɪ'keɪʃən] N Vereinfachung f, Simplifizierung f

simplified ['sɪmplɪfaɪd] ADJ vereinfacht

simplify ['sɪmplɪfaɪ] VT vereinfachen, simplifizieren

simplistic [sɪm'plɪstɪk] ADJ simpel, simplistisch (geh); **or am I being** ~? oder sehe ich das zu einfach?

simply ['sɪmplɪ] ADV einfach; (= merely) nur, bloß; **but you** ~ **must!** aber du musst einfach!; **to put it** ~ ... um es einfach auszudrücken ...; **very** ~, **he was short of money** er war schlicht und einfach knapp bei Kasse; **not** ~ ... **but also** ... nicht (einfach) nur ..., sondern auch ...; **he was known** ~ **as Jay** er war einfach als Jay bekannt; **he is quite** ~ **the best** er ist ganz einfach der Beste

simulate ['sɪmjʊleɪt] VT **a** (= feign) vortäuschen; illness simulieren; **to** ~ **sth** (material) etw imitieren; (animal, person) sich als etw tarnen; ~**d leather** Lederimitation f; ~**d sheepskin** falsches Schafsfell **b** (= reproduce) conditions simulieren

simulation [ˌsɪmjʊ'leɪʃən] N **a** Vortäuschung f; (= simulated appearance) Imitation f; (of animals) Tarnung f; **his** ~ **of pain** seine simulierten Schmerzen **b** (= reproduction) Simulation f

simulator ['sɪmjʊleɪtə'] N Simulator m

simulcast ['sɪmʊlkɑːst] VT gleichzeitig in Fernsehen und Hörfunk übertragen **N** gleichzeitige Übertragung in Fernsehen und Hörfunk

simultaneity [ˌsɪmʊltə'nɪətɪ] N Gleichzeitigkeit f, Simultan(e)ität f (geh)

simultaneous [ˌsɪml'teɪnɪəs] ADJ gleichzeitig, simultan (geh); ~ **interpreting/translation** Simultandolmetschen nt/-übersetzung f

simultaneous equation N (Math) Simultangleichung f

simultaneously [ˌsɪml'teɪnɪəslɪ] ADV gleichzeitig, zur gleichen Zeit, simultan (geh); ~ **with sb/sth** zur gleichen Zeit wie jd/etw

sin [sɪn] **N** (Rel, fig) Sünde f; **to live in** ~ (inf) in wilder Ehe leben; (Rel) in Sünde leben; **I've been chosen to organize the office party, for my** ~**s** (hum) man hat mich drangekriegt, ich darf die Büroparty organisieren (inf); **is that your work/family?** – **yes for my** ~**s** (hum) haben Sie das gemacht/ist das Ihre Familie? – ja, leider; **to cover a multitude of** ~**s** (hum) viele Schandtaten verdecken; **this hat is covering a multitude of** ~**s, she said** (hum) aber fragen Sie bloß nicht, wie es unter dem Hut aussieht!, sagte sie; **isn't it a** ~! ist das nicht unerhört or eine Schande! **VI** sündigen (against gegen, an +dat), sich versündigen (against an +dat); (against principles, standards etc) verstoßen (gegen); **he was more** ~**ned against than** ~**ning** er hat mehr Unrecht erlitten als begangen

Sinai ['saɪneɪaɪ] N Sinai m; ~ **Peninsula** Sinaihalbinsel f; **Mount** ~ der Berg Sinai

sin bin N (inf: Ice Hockey) Strafbank f

since [sɪns] ✪ 21.1 **ADV** (= in the meantime) inzwischen; (= up to now) seitdem; **ever** ~ seither; **a long time** ~, **long** ~ schon lange; **he died long** ~ er ist schon lange tot; **not long** ~ erst vor kurzem; **I've never heard it before or** ~ ich habe das weder vorher noch nachher je wieder gehört
PREP seit; **ever** ~ **1900** (schon) seit 1900; **he had been living there** ~ **1900** er lebte da schon seit 1900; **I've been coming here** ~ **1992** ich komme schon seit 1992 hierher; **he left in June,** ~ **when we have not heard from him** er ging im Juni fort und seitdem haben wir nichts mehr von ihm gehört; **it's a long time** ~ **then** das ist schon lange her; **how long is it** ~ **the accident?** wie lange ist der Unfall schon her?; ~ **when?** (inf) seit wann denn das? (inf)
CONJ a (time) seit(dem); **ever** ~ **I've known him** seit(dem) ich ihn kenne **b** (= because) da

sincere [sɪn'sɪə'] ADJ aufrichtig; person also offen; intention also ernst, ehrlich; **a** ~ **friend** ein wahrer Freund; **to be** ~ **about sth** in Bezug auf etw (acc) aufrichtig sein; **to be** ~ **in one's desire to do sth** or **in wanting to do sth** den aufrichtigen Wunsch haben, etw zu tun; **it is our** ~ **hope that** ... wir hoffen aufrichtig, dass ...

sincerely [sɪn'sɪəlɪ] ADV aufrichtig; *intend also* ernsthaft; **her ~ held religious beliefs** ihre ehrlich *or* aufrichtig gemeinte religiöse Überzeugung; **yours ~** (*Brit*) mit freundlichen Grüßen, hochachtungsvoll (*form*)

sincerity N Aufrichtigkeit *f*; (*of person also*) Offenheit *f*; (*of intention also*) Ernsthaftigkeit *f*; **in all ~** in aller Offenheit; **I was acting in all ~ when ...** ich habe es ganz aufrichtig *or* ehrlich gemeint, als ...

sine [saɪn] N (*Math*) Sinus *m*

sinecure ['saɪnkjʊə'] N Pfründe *f*, Sinekure *f* (*geh*); **this job is no ~!** diese Arbeit ist kein Ruheposten

sine die [ˌsaɪnɪ'daɪiː, 'siːneɪ'diːeɪ] ADV **to adjourn ~** auf unbestimmte Zeit vertagen

sine qua non [ˌsɪnɪkwɑː'nəʊn] N unerlässliche Voraussetzung, Conditio sine qua non *f* (*to, for* für)

sinew ['sɪnjuː] N **a** Sehne *f* **b** **sinews** PL (*fig*) Kräfte *pl*, Stärke *f*

sinewy ['sɪnjʊɪ] ADJ sehnig; (*fig*) *plant, tree* knorrig; *prose style* kraftvoll, kernig

sinfonia [sɪn'fəʊnɪə] N (= *symphony*) Sinfonie *f*, Symphonie *f*; (= *overture*) Opernsinfonia *f*; (= *orchestra*) Sinfonie- *or* Symphonieorchester *nt*, Sinfoniker *pl*, Symphoniker *pl*

sinfonietta [ˌsɪnfəʊn'etə] N (= *music*) Sinfonietta *f*; (= *orchestra*) kleines Sinfonie- *or* Symphonieorchester

sinful ['sɪnfʊl] ADJ sündig; *person, act, thought also* sündhaft (*geh*); *waste* sündhaft (*geh*); **it is ~ to ...** es ist eine Sünde, zu ...

sinfully ['sɪnfəlɪ] ADV sündig, sündhaft (*geh*)

sinfulness ['sɪnfʊlnɪs] N Sündigkeit *f*, Sündhaftigkeit *f* (*geh*)

sing [sɪŋ] *vb*: *pret* **sang**, *ptp* **sung** **N** **to have a (good) ~** (tüchtig) singen **VT** **a** *song* singen; **to ~ a child to sleep** ein Kind in den Schlaf singen; **to ~ the praises of sb/sth** ein Loblied auf jdn/etw singen; **to ~ one's own praises** sich selber loben **b** (*poet*) besingen, singen von **VI** singen; (*ears*) dröhnen; (*kettle*) summen; **they are ~ing from the same hymn sheet** *or* **song sheet** (*Brit fig*) sie sagen alle das Gleiche *or* dasselbe

▶ **sing along** VI mitsingen

▶ **sing away** **VI** (*person, bird*) (ununterbrochen) singen; (*kettle*) summen; (*to oneself*) vor sich (*acc*) hin trällern **VT** *sep troubles* fortsingen

▶ **sing of** VI +*prep obj* singen von (*poet*), besingen

▶ **sing out** **VI** **a** (= *sing loudly, person, bird*) laut *or* aus voller Kehle singen; (*voice*) erklingen, tönen; (*kettle*) summen; **come on, sing out, let's hear you** na los, singt mal tüchtig, wir wollen was hören (*inf*); **their voices sang out through the church** ihr Singen tönte durch die Kirche **b** (*inf*: = *shout*) schreien (*inf*) **VT** *sep words, tune* singen, hervorbringen; (= *shout out*) (mit singender Stimme) ausrufen; **to sing one's heart out** sich (*dat*) die Seele aus dem Leib singen

▶ **sing up** VI lauter singen

sing. *abbr of* **singular** Sing.

singable ['sɪŋəbl] ADJ sangbar (*geh*); **that tune is (not/very) ~** diese Melodie lässt sich (nicht/sehr) gut singen

Singapore [ˌsɪŋgə'pɔː'] N Singapur *nt*

Singaporean [ˌsɪŋgə'pɔːrɪən] ADJ *person, culture* singapurisch; **he is ~** er ist Singapurer **N** (= *person*) Singapurer(in) *m(f)*

singe [sɪndʒ] **VT** sengen; *clothes also* versengen; (*slightly*) ansengen; *hairs, eyebrows* absengen **VI** versengt/angesengt werden, sengen **N** (*on clothes etc*) versengte/angesengte Stelle; **there's a slight ~ on the sleeve** der Ärmel ist leicht angesengt

singer ['sɪŋə'] N Sänger(in) *m(f)*

singer-songwriter [ˌsɪŋə'sɒŋraɪtə'] N Liedermacher(in) *m(f)*

Singhalese [ˌsɪŋgə'liːz] **ADJ** singhalesisch; **he is ~** er ist Singhalese **N** **a** Singhalese *m*, Singhalesin *f* **b** (*Ling*) Singhalesisch *nt*

singing ['sɪŋɪŋ] N Singen *nt*; (*of person, bird also*) Gesang *m*; (*in the ears*) Dröhnen *nt*; (*of kettle*) Summen *nt*; **he teaches ~** er gibt Sing- *or* Gesangsstunden, er gibt Singen (*inf*); **do you like my ~?** gefällt dir, wie ich singe?, gefällt dir mein Gesang?

singing: singing lesson N Gesangstunde *f*; **singing telegram** N *durch eine Agentur persönlich übermittelter, in Gesangsform vorgetragener Geburtstagsgruß etc*; **singing voice** N Singstimme *f*

single ['sɪŋgl] **ADJ** **a** (= *one only*) einzige(r, s); **not a ~ one spoke up** nicht ein Einziger äußerte sich dazu; **every ~ day was precious** jeder (einzelne) Tag war kostbar; **I've missed the bus every ~ day this week** diese Woche habe ich jeden Tag den Bus verpasst; **every ~ book I looked at** (aber auch) jedes Buch, das ich mir ansah; **with a ~ voice they cried out for reform** wie mit einer Stimme riefen sie nach Reformen; **not a ~ thing** überhaupt nichts; **the ~ most expensive product** das teuerste Produkt; **in a ~ day** in einem einzigen Tag; **in a ~ gulp** mit einem einzigen Schluck; **in ~ figures** in einstelligen Zahlen

b (= *not double etc*) einzeln; (*Typ*) einfach; *carburettor* einfach; (*Brit*) *ticket* einfach; **a ~-tank aqualung** ein Pressluftatmer *m* mit nur einer Sauerstoffflasche

c (= *not married*) unverheiratet, ledig; **marital status? – ~** Familienstand? – ledig; **he was tired of the ~ life** er hatte das Junggesellendasein satt; **~ people** Ledige *pl*, Unverheiratete *pl*; **I'm a ~ man/girl** ich bin ledig; **the ~ homeless** die allein stehenden Obdachlosen

N **a** (*Cricket*) Schlag *m* für einen Lauf; (*Baseball*) Lauf *m* zum ersten Mal; (*Golf*) Zweier *m*

b (*Brit*: = *ticket*) Einzelfahrschein *m*, Einzelfahrkarte *f*; (= *room*) Einzelzimmer *nt*; (= *record*) Single *f*; (= *bank note*) Einpfund-/Eindollarschein *m*; **a ~/two ~s to Xanadu** (*Brit*) einmal/zweimal einfach nach Xanadu

c (= *unmarried person*) Single *m*

▶ **single out** VT *sep* (= *choose*) auswählen; *victim, prey* sich (*dat*) herausgreifen; **a** (= *distinguish, set apart*) herausheben (*from* über +*acc*); **to single sb out for special attention** jdm besondere Aufmerksamkeit zuteil werden lassen; **you couldn't single any one pupil out as the best** es wäre unmöglich, einen einzelnen Schüler als den besten hinzustellen

single: single-action ADJ (*Mil*) **~ rifle** Einzelfeuergewehr *nt*; **single-barrelled**, (*US*) **single-barreled** [ˌsɪŋgl'bærld] ADJ *gun* mit einem Lauf; **single bed** N Einzelbett *nt*; **single-blind** ADJ **~ experiment** (*Pharm, Psych*) Blindversuch *m*; **single-breasted** ADJ *jacket* einreihig; **~ suit** Einreiher *m*; **single-cell(ed)** ADJ (*Biol*) einzellig; **single-chamber** ADJ (*Pol*) Einkammer-; **~ parliament** Einkammerparlament *nt*; **single combat** N Nah- *or* Einzelkampf *m*; (*esp of knights etc*) Kampf *m* Mann gegen Mann, Zweikampf *m*; **single cream** N (*Brit*) Sahne *f* (*mit geringem Fettgehalt*); **single currency** N einheitliche Währung, Einheitswährung *f*; **single-decker** N (*Brit*) einstöckiger Omnibus/einstöckige Straßenbahn, Eindecker *m*; **single-density** ADJ (*Comput*) *disk* mit einfacher Dichte; **singledom** ['sɪŋgldəm] N Singledasein *nt or* -leben *nt*; **single-drive** ADJ *computer* mit Einzellaufwerk; **single-engined** ADJ *plane* einmotorig; **single-entry book-keeping** N einfache Buchführung; **single European currency** N einheitliche europäische Währung, europäische Einheitswährung *f*; **single European market** N Europäischer Binnenmarkt; **single file** N **in ~** im Gänsemarsch; **single-handed** **ADJ** (ganz) allein *pred*; *achievement* allein *or* ohne (fremde) Hilfe vollbracht; *arrest* allein *or* ohne (fremde) Hilfe durchgeführt; *struggle* einsam **ADV** (*also* **single-handedly**) ohne Hilfe, im Alleingang; **to sail ~ (a)round the world** ganz allein *or* als Einhandsegler(in) um

die Welt fahren; **single honours** N (*Brit Univ*) Abschluss *m* in einem Einzelfach; **singlehood** ['sɪŋlhʊd] N Singledasein *nt or* -leben *nt*; **single-lens reflex (camera)** N (einäugige) Spiegelreflexkamera; **single-line** ADJ eingleisig; *track* einspurig; **single malt (whisky)** N Single Malt (Whisky) *m*; **single-masted** ADJ einmastig; **~ ship** Einmaster *m*; **single-minded** ADJ zielbewusst, zielstrebig, beharrlich; *devotion* unbeirrbar; **his ~ pursuit of money** sein ausschließlich auf Geld gerichtetes Streben; **to be ~ in** *or* **about doing sth** zielstrebig darin sein, etw zu tun; **single-mindedly** ADV zielstrebig; **he was ~ interested in science** er interessierte sich einzig und allein für Naturwissenschaften; **single-mindedness** N Zielstrebigkeit *f*, Beharrlichkeit *f*; (*of devotion*) Unbeirrbarkeit *f*; **single mother** N allein erziehende Mutter

singleness ['sɪŋglnɪs] N **~ of purpose** Zielstrebigkeit *f*; **his ~ of purpose caused him to neglect his family** er ging so vollkommen in der Sache auf, dass er seine Familie vernachlässigte

single: single parent N allein Erziehende(r) *mf*, Alleinerziehende(r) *mf*; **I as a ~ ...** ich als allein erziehende Mutter/allein erziehender Vater ...; **single-parent** ADJ **a ~ family** eine Familie mit nur einem Elternteil, eine Einelternfamilie; **single-party** ADJ Einparteien-; **~ system** Einparteiensystem *nt*; **single-phase** ADJ einphasig, Einphasen-; **~ power** Einphasenstrom *m*; **single price** N Einheitspreis *m*; **single room** N Einzelzimmer *nt*

singles ['sɪŋglz] N *sing or pl* (*Sport*) Einzel *nt*; **the ~ finals** das Finale im Einzel; **~ is more tiring** Einzel sind anstrengender

singles bar N Singles-Bar *f*

single-seater [ˌsɪŋgl'siːtə'] N Einsitzer *m*

single-sex ['sɪŋgl'seks] ADJ *education* nach Geschlechtern getrennt; **a ~ class** eine reine Jungen-/Mädchenklasse; **a ~ school** eine reine Jungen-/Mädchenschule

singles holiday N (*Brit*) Urlaub *m* für Singles

single-sided ['sɪŋgl'saɪdɪd] ADJ (*Comput*) *disk* einseitig

single-space ['sɪŋgl'speɪs] VTI (*Typ, Comput*) mit einzeiligem Abstand schreiben

single-storey, (*US*) **single-story** ['sɪŋgl'stɔːrɪ] ADJ einstöckig

singlet ['sɪŋglɪt] N (*Brit, Sport*) ärmelloses Trikot; (= *underclothing*) (ärmelloses) Unterhemd, Trikohemd *nt*

singleton ['sɪŋgltən] N (*Cards*) Single *nt* (*einzige Karte einer Farbe*)

single: single-tongue VTI mit einfachem Zungenschlag spielen; **single-tonguing** N der einzelne Zungenschlag; **single-track** ADJ einspurig; (*Rail also*) eingleisig; **to have a ~ mind** nur eine einzige Sache im Kopf haben; **Single Transferable Vote** N (*Pol*) *modifiziertes Mehrheitswahlrecht, bei dem die Stimme auf einen anderen Kandidaten übertragen wird, falls der gewünschte Kandidat ausscheidet*

singly ['sɪŋglɪ] ADV einzeln; (= *solely*) einzig, nur

singsong ['sɪŋsɒŋ] **ADJ** the **~** Welsh accent der walisische Singsang; **in his ~ voice** mit *or* in seinem Singsang **N** Liedersingen *nt no indef art, no pl*; **we often have a ~ after a few drinks** nachdem wir etwas getrunken haben, singen wir oft zusammen

singular ['sɪŋgjʊlə'] **ADJ** **a** (*Gram*) im Singular, singularisch (*form*); **a ~ noun** ein Substantiv *nt* im Singular; **~ ending** Singularendung *f*; **~ form** Singular *m* **b** (= *odd*) sonderbar, eigenartig; **how very ~!** das ist aber sehr sonderbar *or* eigenartig! **c** (= *outstanding*) einzigartig, einmalig **N** (*Gram*) the **~** im Singular

singularity [ˌsɪŋgjʊ'lærɪtɪ] N (= *oddity*) Sonderbarkeit *f*, Eigenartigkeit *f*

singularly ['sɪŋgjʊləlɪ] ADV **a** außerordentlich; *appropriate, unattractive* (ganz) besonders, überaus; **he was ~ unimpressed** er war ganz und gar nicht beeindruckt; **he has ~ failed to a- chieve this** er ist mit seinem Versuch, dies zu erreichen, vollkommen gescheitert; **hey are ~ lacking in originality** es fehlt ihnen ganz und gar an Originalität **b** (*dated, = strangely*) sonderbar, eigenartig

Sinhalese [sɪnhəˈliːz] ADJ, N = **Singhalese**

sinister [ˈsɪnɪstə'] ADJ **a** unheimlich; *person, night, scheme* finster, unheimlich; *music, look* düster; *fate* böse; *forces* dunkel; *development, motives* unheilvoll; **a ~ organization** eine in dunkle Machenschaften verwickelte Organisation **b** (*Her*) linke(r, s)

sink¹ [sɪŋk] *pret* **sank**, *ptp* **sunk** **VT** **a** *ship, object* versenken

b (*fig, = ruin*) *theory* zerstören; *hopes* zunichte machen, zerstören; **now we're sunk!** (*inf*) jetzt sind wir geliefert (*inf*)

c *shaft* senken, teufen (*spec*); *hole* ausheben; **to ~ a post in the ground** einen Pfosten in den Boden einlassen; **they sank a pipe under the riverbed** sie versenkten ein Rohr unter dem Flussbett → **well¹**

d (*Brit inf*) *drink* hinunterschütten (*inf*), hinunterspülen (*inf*)

e *teeth, claws* schlagen; **I'd like to ~ my teeth into a juicy steak** ich möchte in ein saftiges Steak reinbeißen (*inf*)

f *differences* begraben

g **to ~ money into sth** Geld in etw (*acc*) stecken

h *golf ball* einlochen; *billiard ball* in das Loch treiben

i (*= lower*) *eyes, voice, value of currency* senken; **he sank his head in his hands** er stützte den Kopf auf die Hände

j **to be sunk in thought** in Gedanken versunken sein; **to be sunk in a book** in ein Buch vertieft sein; **sunk in depression/despair** völlig deprimiert/verzweifelt

VI **a** *person, object* untergehen; (*ship*) untergehen, sinken; **to ~ to the bottom** auf den Grund sinken; **he was left to ~ or swim** (*fig*) er war ganz auf sich allein angewiesen; **if I go down I'll make sure you all ~ with me** wenn es mich erwischt, werde ich euch alle mitreißen

b (*= go down, subside*) sinken; (*sun*) versinken; (*voice*) sich senken; (*building, land etc*) sinken, absinken; **the building is gradually ~ing into the mud** das Gebäude versinkt allmählich im Schlamm; **he sank up to his knees in the mud** er sank bis zu den Knien im Schlamm ein; **to ~ (down) into a chair** in einen Sessel (nieder)sinken; **to ~ back into the cushions** in die Kissen versinken; **the flames sank lower and lower** das Feuer fiel immer mehr in sich zusammen; **the sun sank beneath the horizon** die Sonne versank am Horizont; **the record has sunk to the bottom of the charts** die Platte ist ans Ende der Liste gerutscht; **to ~ to one's knees** auf die Knie sinken; **to ~ out of sight** versinken; **to ~ into a deep sleep/into depression** in tiefen Schlaf/in Depressionen versinken; **my spirits** *or* **my heart sank at the sight of the work** beim Anblick der Arbeit verließ mich der Mut; **the sick man is ~ing fast** der Kranke verfällt zusehends

c (*= deteriorate, lessen: output, shares, standards*) sinken; **to ~ into insignificance** zur Bedeutungslosigkeit herabsinken; **to ~ deeper into recession** immer tiefer in die Rezession geraten; **she has sunk in my estimation** sie ist in meiner Achtung gesunken

▸ **sink away** VI (*seabed, ground*) abfallen

▸ **sink in** **VI** **a** (*into mud etc*) einsinken (*prep obj, -to* in +*acc*) **b** (*inf, = be understood*) kapiert werden (*inf*); **it's only just sunk in that it really did happen** ich kapiere/er kapiert *etc* erst jetzt, dass das tatsächlich passiert ist (*inf*); **can't you get this to sink in?** kannst du das denn nicht in deinen dicken Schädel bekommen? (*inf*); **repeat each line so that the words sink in** wiederhole jede Zeile, damit dus dir merkst (*inf*) **VT** *sep stakes, pylons etc* einlassen (*prep obj, -to* in +*acc*)

sink² N Ausguss *m*; (*in kitchen also*) Spülbecken *nt*; **~ unit** Spültisch *m*, Spüle *f*; **~ of iniquity** Sündenpfuhl *m*, Stätte *f* des Lasters → **kitchen sink**

sinker [ˈsɪŋkə'] N (*Fishing*) Senker *m*, Senkgewicht *nt* → **hook N d**

sinking [ˈsɪŋkɪŋ] **N** (*of ship*) Untergang *m*; (*deliberately*) Versenkung *f*; (*of shaft*) Senken *nt*, Abteufen *nt* (*spec*); (*of well*) Bohren *nt* **ADJ** (*Fin*) *currency* fallend; **a ~ ship** (*lit, fig*) ein sinkendes Schiff; **with (a) ~ heart** schweren Herzens; **he realized with a ~ heart that ...** das Herz wurde ihm schwer, als er merkte, dass ...; **~ feeling** flaues Gefühl (im Magen) (*inf*); **I got a horrible ~ feeling when I realized ...** mir wurde ganz anders, als ich erkannte ...

sinking fund N (*Fin*) Tilgungsfonds *m*

sinless [ˈsɪnlɪs] ADJ *person* ohne Sünde, frei von Sünde; *life also* sündenfrei

sinner [ˈsɪnə'] N Sünder(in) *m(f)*

Sinn Fein [ʃɪnˈfeɪn] N (*Ir Pol*) Sinn Fein *f*

Sino- [ˈsaɪnəʊ-] PREF chinesisch-, sino- (*form*); **~American** chinesisch-amerikanisch, sinoamerikanisch (*form*)

sinologist [ˌsaɪˈnɒlədʒɪst] N Sinologe *m*, Sinologin *f*

sinology [ˌsaɪˈnɒlədʒɪ] N Sinologie *f*

sinuosity [ˌsɪnjʊˈɒsɪtɪ] N (*liter*) Schlangenbewegungen *pl*; (*of river*) Windungen *pl*; (*fig*) Gewundenheit *f*

sinuous [ˈsɪnjʊəs] ADJ (*lit, fig*) gewunden; *motion of snake* schlängelnd *attr*; *dancing etc* geschmeidig, schlangenartig; **the river follows a ~ course through the trees** der Fluss windet sich *or* schlängelt sich zwischen den Bäumen hindurch

sinuously [ˈsɪnjʊəslɪ] ADV gewunden; *dance etc* geschmeidig, schlangenartig

sinus [ˈsaɪnəs] N (*Anat*) Sinus *m* (*spec*); (*in head*) (Nasen-)nebenhöhle *f*, Stirnhöhle *f*

sinusitis [ˌsaɪnəˈsaɪtɪs] N Stirnhöhlenkatarr(h) *m*, Sinusitis *f*

Sioux [suː] **N** Sioux *mf* **ADJ** Sioux-, der Sioux; **~ chief** Siouxhäuptling *m*

sip [sɪp] **N** Schluck *m*; (*very small*) Schlückchen *nt* **VT** in kleinen Schlucken trinken; (*suspiciously, daintily*) nippen an (+*dat*); (*= savour*) schlürfen **VI** **to ~ at sth** an etw (*dat*) nippen

siphon [ˈsaɪfən] **N** Heber *m*; (*= soda siphon*) Siphon *m* **VT** absaugen; (*into tank*) (mit einem Heber) umfüllen

▸ **siphon off** VT *sep* **a** (*lit*) abziehen, absaugen; *petrol* abzapfen; (*into container*) (mit einem Heber) umfüllen *or* abfüllen **b** (*fig*) *staff, money* abziehen; *profits* abschöpfen

▸ **siphon out** VT *sep liquid* mit einem Heber herausleiten

SIPS *abbr of* **side impact protection system**

sir [sɜː'] N **a** (*in direct address*) mein Herr (*form*), Herr X; **no, ~** nein(, Herr X); (*Mil*) nein, Herr Leutnant/General *etc*; **you will apologize, ~!** (*dated*) dafür werden Sie sich entschuldigen (müssen); **Sir** (*to editor of paper*) *not translated* **Dear Sir (or Madam), ...** Sehr geehrte (Damen und) Herren!; **my dear** *or* **good ~!** (*dated*) mein (lieber) Herr! (*dated*) **b** (*= knight etc*) Sir *m* **c** (*Sch inf: = teacher*) er (*Sch sl*); **please ~!** er X!; **I'll tell ~** ich sags ihm

sire [ˈsaɪə'] **N** **a** (*Zool*) Vatertier *nt*, Vater *m*; (*= stallion*) Deck- *or* Zuchthengst *m*, Beschäler *m* (*form*) **b** (*old: to monarch etc*) Sire Majestät *f*, Sire *m* **c** (*old, poet: = father, forebear*) Erzeuger *m*, Ahn *m* **VT** zeugen; **the horse A, ~d by B** Pferd A, Vater B; **he ~d 49 children** (*hum*) er hat 49 Kinder in die Welt gesetzt

siren [ˈsaɪərən] N (*all senses*) Sirene *f*

siriasis [sɪˈraɪəsɪs] N (*Med*) Sonnenstich *m*

sirloin [ˈsɜːlɔɪn] N (*Cook*) Lendenfilet *nt*

sirocco [sɪˈrɒkəʊ] N Schirokko *m*

sirrah [ˈsɪrə] N (*obs*) Bube *m* (*obs*)

sirup N (*US*) = **syrup**

sis [sɪs] N (*inf*) Schwesterherz *nt* (*inf*)

sisal [ˈsaɪsəl] N Sisal *m*

siskin [ˈsɪskɪn] N (*Orn*) Zeisig *m*

sissified [ˈsɪsɪfaɪd] ADJ weibisch, wie ein Weib

sissy [ˈsɪsɪ] (*inf*) **N** Waschlappen *m* (*inf*), Memme *f* **ADJ** weibisch; **a ~ man** ein Waschlappen *m* (*pej, inf*); **poetry is ~ stuff** Gedichte sind Weiberkram (*inf*)

sister [ˈsɪstə'] N **a** Schwester *f*; (*in trade union*) Kollegin *f*; (*= ship*) Schwesterschiff *nt*; **to be ~ to** (*form*) *or* **the ~ of sb** jds Schwester sein **b** (*= nun*) (Ordens)schwester *f*; (*before name*) Schwester *f* **c** (*Brit, = senior nurse*) Oberschwester *f*

sister *in cpds* Schwester-; **sister city** N (*US*) = **twin town**; **sister company** N Schwesterfirma *f or* -gesellschaft *f*; **sisterhood** [ˈsɪstəhʊd] N **a** Schwesterschaft *f*; **she emphasized the ~ of women all over the world** sie betonte, dass alle Frauen der ganzen Welt Schwestern seien **b** (*Eccl*) Schwesternorden *m* **c** (*= association of women*) Frauenvereinigung *f*; **sister-in-law** N *pl* **sisters-in-law** Schwägerin *f*

sisterly [ˈsɪstəlɪ] ADJ schwesterlich

Sistine [ˈsɪstiːn] ADJ Sixtinisch

Sisyphus [ˈsɪsɪfəs] N Sisyphus *m*

sit [sɪt] *vb: pret, ptp* **sat** **VI** **a** (*= be sitting*) sitzen (*in/on* in/auf +*dat*); (*= sit down*) sich setzen (*in/on* in/auf +*acc*); **~!** (*to dog*) sitz!; **a place to ~** ein Sitzplatz; **~ by/with me** setz dich zu mir/neben mich; **to ~ for a painter** für einen Maler Modell sitzen; **to ~ for an exam** (*Brit*) eine Prüfung ablegen (*form*) *or* machen; **to ~ on one's hands** (*fig*) untätig zusehen; **to be ~ting pretty** (*fig inf*) gut dastehen (*inf*); **don't just ~ there, do something!** sitz nicht nur tatenlos da (herum), tu (endlich) was! → **still¹**

b (*assembly*) tagen; (*= have a seat*) einen Sitz haben; **he ~s for Liverpool** (*Brit, Parl*) er ist der Abgeordnete für Liverpool; **to ~ in parliament/on a committee** einen Sitz im Parlament/in einem Ausschuss haben

c (*object: = be placed, rest*) stehen; **the car sat in the garage** das Auto stand in der Garage; **the package is ~ting in the hall** das Päckchen liegt im Flur; **this food ~s heavy on the stomach** dieses Essen liegt schwer im Magen

d (*bird: = hatch*) sitzen, brüten; **the hen is ~ting on two eggs** das Huhn brütet zwei Eier aus, das Huhn sitzt auf zwei Eiern

e (*fig: clothes*) sitzen (*on sb* bei jdm)

f **how ~ the wind?** (*liter*) wie steht der Wind?

g (*inf*) = **baby-sit**

VT **a** (*also* **sit down**) setzen (*in* in +*acc*, *on* auf +*acc*); (*= place*) *object* stellen; **to ~ a child on one's knee** sich (*dat*) ein Kind auf die Knie setzen; **the table/car ~s 5 people** (*= accommodate*) an dem Tisch/in dem Auto haben 5 Leute Platz

b *horse* sitzen auf (+*dat*); **to ~ a horse well** gut zu Pferde sitzen

c (*Brit*) *examination* ablegen (*form*), machen **VR** **to ~ oneself down** sich gemütlich niederlassen *or* hinsetzen; **~ you down** (*dial*) setz dich hin

N **to have a ~** sitzen

▸ **sit about** (*Brit*) *or* **around** VI herumsitzen

▸ **sit back** VI (*lit, fig*) sich zurücklehnen; (*fig, = do nothing, not take action*) die Hände in den Schoß legen

▸ **sit by** VI (*tatenlos*) dasitzen, (*tatenlos*) herumsitzen

▸ **sit down** VI **a** (*lit*) sich (hin)setzen; **to sit down in a chair** sich auf einen Stuhl setzen **b** (*fig*) **to take sth sitting down** etw einfach hinnehmen

▸ **sit for** VI **a** (*Brit*) *exam* machen **b** (*Brit*) die Prüfung machen für **c** (*Brit, Parl*) *constituency* vertreten, Abgeordnete(in) *m(f)* sein für **d** (*Art*) **to sit for one's portrait** sich porträtieren lassen

▸ **sit in** VI **a** (*demonstrators*) ein Sit-in machen *or* veranstalten **b** (*= take place of*) **to sit in for sb** jdn vertreten **c** (*= attend as visitor*) dabei sein, dabeisitzen (*on sth* bei etw) **d** (= *stay in*) zu Hause or im Haus sitzen

▶ **sit on** **VI** (= *continue sitting*) sitzen bleiben **VI** +prep obj **a** *committee, panel, jury* sitzen in (+*dat*); **I was asked to sit on the committee** man bat mich, Mitglied des Ausschusses zu werden **b** (= *not deal with*) sitzen auf (+*dat*) **c** (*inf, = suppress*) *idea, invention, product* unterdrücken, nicht hochkommen lassen; *person* einen Dämpfer aufsetzen (+*dat*) (*inf*); **to get sat on** (= *suppressed*) unterdrückt werden; (= *rebuked*) eins draufkriegen (*inf*)

▶ **sit out** **VI** draußen sitzen **VT** *sep* **a** (= *stay to end*) *play, film, meeting* bis zum Schluss or Ende (sitzen) bleiben bei, bis zum Schluss or Ende durch- or aushalten (*pej*); *storm* auf das Ende (+*gen*) warten; *problem* aussitzen; *war* durchstehen; **we'd better sit it out** wir bleiben besser bis zum Ende (hier) **b** *dance* auslassen; **I'll sit this one out** ich setze diesmal aus; **to sit out a round** (*in game*) eine Runde aussetzen

▶ **sit through** VI +prep obj durchhalten, aushalten (*pej*)

▶ **sit up** **VI** **a** (= *be sitting upright*) aufrecht sitzen; (= *action*) sich aufrichten, sich aufsetzen; **to sit up (and beg)** (*dog etc*) Männchen machen (*inf*) **b** (= *sit straight*) aufrecht or gerade sitzen; **sit up!** setz dich gerade hin!, sitz gerade!; **to make sb sit up (and take notice)** (*fig inf*) jdn aufhorchen lassen **c** (= *not go to bed*) aufbleiben, aufsitzen (*dated*); **she sat up with the sick child** sie wachte bei dem kranken Kind; **to sit up and wait for sb** aufbleiben und auf jdn warten **d** **to sit up to the table** sich an den Tisch setzen **VT** *sep* aufrichten, aufsetzen; *doll also, baby* hinsetzen

▶ **sit upon** VI +prep obj = **sit on** VI +prep obj

sitar [sɪˈtɑː] N Sitar *m*

sitcom [ˈsɪtkɒm] N (*inf*) Situationskomödie *f*

sit-down [ˈsɪtdaʊn] **N** (*inf, = rest*) Verschnaufpause *f* (*inf*) **ADJ** *attr* **to stage a ~ strike** einen Sitzstreik abhalten; **a ~ meal** eine richtige Mahlzeit

site [saɪt] **N** **a** Stelle *f*, Platz *m*; (*Med, of infection*) Stelle *f* **b** (*Archeol*) Stätte *f* **c** (= *building site*) (Bau)gelände *nt*, Baustelle *f*; **missile ~** Raketenbasis *f*; **~ foreman** Polier *m*; **~ office** (Büro *nt* der) Bauleitung *f* **d** (= *camping site*) Campingplatz *m* **VT** legen, anlegen; **to be ~d** liegen, (gelegen) sein; **a badly ~d building** ein ungünstig gelegenes Gebäude

sit-in [ˈsɪtɪn] N Sit-in *nt*; **to hold** or **stage a ~** ein Sit-in veranstalten

siting [ˈsaɪtɪŋ] N Legen *nt*; **the ~ of new industries away from London is being encouraged** man fördert die Errichtung neuer Betriebe außerhalb Londons; **the ~ of the buildings here was a mistake** es war ein Fehler, die Gebäude hier zu errichten

sit spin N (*Figure Skating*) Sitzpirouette *f*

sitter [ˈsɪtə] N (*Art*) Modell *nt*; (= *baby-sitter*) Babysitter(in) *m(f)*; (= *bird*) brütender Vogel; (*Sport sl*) todsicherer Ball (*inf*)

sitting [ˈsɪtɪŋ] **ADJ** sitzend; *bird* brütend; *conference* tagend, in Sitzung; **to be in a ~ position** aufsitzen; **to get into a ~ position** sich aufsetzen; **there is ~ room only** es gibt nur Sitzplätze **N** (*of committee, parliament, for portrait*) Sitzung *f*; **they have two ~s for lunch** sie servieren das Mittagessen in zwei Schüben; **the first ~ for lunch is at 12 o'clock** die erste Mittagessenzeit ist um 12 Uhr; **at one** or **a single ~** (*fig*) auf einmal

sitting: sitting duck N (*fig*) leichte Beute; **sitting member** N (*Brit, Parl*) (derzeitiger) Abgeordneter, (derzeitige) Abgeordnete; **sitting room** N (*esp Brit*) (= *lounge*) Wohnzimmer *nt*; (*in guest house etc*) Aufenthaltsraum *m*; **sitting target** N (*lit, fig*) leichte Beute; **sitting tenant** N (*Brit*) (derzeitiger) Mieter, (derzeitige) Mieterin

situate [ˈsɪtjʊeɪt] VT legen

situated [ˈsɪtjʊeɪtɪd] ADJ gelegen; *person* (*financially*) gestellt, situiert (*geh*); **it is ~ in the High Street** es liegt an der Hauptstraße; **a pleasantly ~ house** ein Haus in angenehmer Lage; **he is well ~ to appreciate the risks** er ist sehr wohl (dazu) in der Lage, die Risiken abzuschätzen

situation [sɪtjʊˈeɪʃən] N **a** (= *state of affairs*) Lage *f*, Situation *f*; (*financial, marital etc*) Lage *f*, Verhältnisse *pl*; (*in play, novel*) Situation *f*; **to save the ~** die Lage or Situation retten; **a 2-0 ~** eine 2:0-Situation **b** (*of house etc*) Lage *f* **c** (= *job*) Stelle *f*; **"situations vacant"** (*Brit*) „Stellenangebote"; **"situations wanted"** (*Brit*) „Stellengesuche"

situation comedy N Situationskomödie *f*

Situationism [sɪtjʊˈeɪʃənɪzəm] N (*Philos*) Situationismus *f*

Situationist [sɪtjʊˈeɪʃənɪst] (*Philos*) **ADJ** situationistisch **N** Situationist(in) *m(f)*

sit-up [ˈsɪtʌp] N (*Sport*) Sit-up *m*; **~s** Rumpfheben *nt*

sitz bath [ˈzɪtsbɑːθ] N Sitzbadewanne *f*

six [sɪks] **ADJ** sechs; **she is ~ (years old)** sie ist sechs (Jahre alt); **at (the age of) ~** im Alter von sechs Jahren, mit sechs Jahren; **it's ~ (o'clock)** es ist sechs (Uhr); **there are ~ of us** wir sind sechs; **it cost ~ pounds** es kostete sechs Pfund; **~ and a half/quarter** sechseinhalb/-einviertel; **in ~-eight time** (*Mus*) im Sechsachteltakt; **to be ~ foot under** (*hum*) sich (*dat*) die Radieschen von unten besehen (*hum*); **it's ~ (of one) and half a dozen (of the other)** (*inf*) das ist Jacke wie Hose (*inf*), das ist gehupft wie gesprungen (*inf*) **N** **a** (*Math, = figure, mark, tram*) Sechs *f*; (= *bus*) Sechser *m*; **~ and a half/quarter** Sechseinhalb/-einviertel *f* **b** (*Cards, on dice, Golf*) Sechs *f*; (*Cricket*) Sechserschlag *m*; (= *team of six*) Sechsermannschaft *f*; **to divide sth into ~** etw in sechs Teile teilen; **we divided up into ~es** wir teilten uns in Sechsergruppen auf; **they are sold in ~es** sie werden in Sechserpackungen verkauft; **to be at ~es and sevens** (*things*) wie Kraut und Rüben durcheinander liegen (*inf*); (*person*) völlig durcheinander sein; **to knock sb for ~** (*Brit inf*) jdn umhauen (*inf*)

six: Six Counties PL **the ~** (*Brit*) *die sechs Grafschaften Nordirlands*; **six-day race** N , **six days** PL (*inf, Cycling etc*) Sechstagerennen *nt*; **sixfold** **ADJ** sechsfach **ADV** um das Sechsfache; **six-footer** N ≈ über 1,80 (*gesprochen: einsachtzig*) sein; **six-gun** N (*US, inf*) = **six-shooter**; **six hundred** **ADJ** sechshundert **N** Sechshundert *f*

sixish [ˈsɪksɪʃ] ADJ um sechs herum

six: six million ADJ, N sechs Millionen; **six-pack** N **a** Sechserpackung *f* **b** (*Brit inf, = muscles*) Muskelpaket *nt* (*inf*); **sixpence** N (*Brit old: = coin*) Sixpencestück *m*; **sixpenny** **ADJ** für Sixpence **N** (= *stamp*) Sixpence-Marke *f*; **six-shooter** N (*US, inf*) sechsschüssiger Revolver

sixteen [ˈsɪksˈtiːn] **ADJ** sechzehn **N** Sechzehn *f*

sixteenth [ˈsɪksˈtiːnθ] **ADJ** sechzehnte(r, s); **a ~ part** ein Sechzehntel *nt*; **a ~ note** (*esp US Mus*) eine Sechzehntelnote, ein Sechzehntel *nt* **N** **a** (= *fraction*) Sechzehntel *nt*; (*in series*) Sechzehnte(r, s) **b** (= *date*) **the ~** der Sechzehnte

sixth [sɪksθ] **ADJ** sechste(r, s); **a ~ part** ein Sechstel *nt*; **he was** or **came ~** er wurde Sechster; **he was ~ from the end/left** er war der Sechste von hinten/von links **N** **a** (= *fraction*) Sechstel *nt*; (*in series*) Sechste(r, s); **Charles the Sixth** Karl der Sechste **b** (= *date*) **the ~** der Sechste; **on the ~** am Sechsten; **the ~ of September, September the ~** der sechste September **c** (*Mus, = interval*) Sexte *f*; (= *chord*) Sextakkord *m* **d** (*Brit*) = **sixth form** **ADV** **he did it ~** (= *the sixth person he did it*) er hat es als Sechster gemacht; (= *the sixth thing he did*) er hat es als Sechstes or an sechster Stelle gemacht

sixth: sixth form N (*Brit*) Abschlussklasse *f*, ≈ Prima *f*; **sixth-former** N (*Brit*) Schüler(in)

m(f) der Abschlussklasse, ≈ Primaner(in) *m(f)*; **sixth grade** N (*US, Sch*) *sechstes Schuljahr (unmittelbar vor Eintritt in die Junior Highschool)*

sixthly [ˈsɪksθlɪ] ADV sechstens, als Sechstes

six thousand **ADJ** sechstausend **N** Sechstausend *f*

sixth sense N sechster Sinn

sixtieth [ˈsɪkstɪɪθ] **ADJ** sechzigste(r, s); **a ~ part** ein Sechzigstel *nt* **N** (= *fraction*) Sechzigstel *nt*; (*in series*) Sechzigste(r, s)

sixty [ˈsɪkstɪ] **ADJ** sechzig; **~-one** einundsechzig **N** Sechzig *f*; **the sixties** die sechziger Jahre or Sechzigerjahre *pl*; **to be in one's sixties** in den Sechzigern sein; **to be in one's late/early sixties** Ende/Anfang sechzig sein; **~-one** Einundsechzig *f* → *also* **six**

sixty-fourth note [ˈsɪkstɪˈfɔːθnəʊt] N (*esp US Mus*) Vierundsechzigstel(note *f*) *nt*

sixty-four thousand dollar question N (*hum*) Hunderttausendmarkfrage *f* (*hum*)

sixtyish [ˈsɪkstɪɪʃ] ADJ um die Sechzig (*inf*), ungefähr sechzig

six: six-yard box N (*Ftbl*) Fünfmeterraum *m*; **six-year-old** **ADJ** sechsjährig *attr*, sechs Jahre alt *pred*; *war* schon sechs Jahre dauernd **N** Sechsjährige(r) *mf*

sizable ADJ = **sizeable**

size¹ [saɪz] **N** (*all senses*) Größe *f*; (*of problem, operation also*) Ausmaß *nt*; **collar/hip/waist ~** Kragen-/Hüft-/Taillenweite *f*; **shoe/dress ~** Schuh-/Kleidergröße *f*; **bra ~** BH-Größe *f*; **it's the ~ of a brick** es ist so groß wie ein Ziegelstein; **he's about your ~** er ist ungefähr so groß wie du; **what ~ is it?** wie groß ist es?; (*clothes, shoes, gloves etc*) welche Größe ist es?; **it's quite a ~** es ist ziemlich groß; **it's two ~s too big** es ist zwei Nummern zu groß; **to cut sth to ~** etw auf die richtige Größe zurechtschneiden; **do you want to try it for ~?** möchten Sie es anprobieren, ob es Ihnen passt?; **try this one for ~** (*fig inf*) wie wärs denn damit?; **that's about the ~ of it** (*inf*) ja, so ungefähr kann man es sagen **VT** größenmäßig ordnen

▶ **size up** VT *sep* abschätzen; **I can't quite size him up** ich werde aus ihm nicht schlau

size² [saɪz] **N** (*Grundier*)leim *m* **VT** grundieren

sizeable [ˈsaɪzəbl] **ADJ** ziemlich groß, größer; *car, estate, jewel also* ansehnlich; *sum, problem, difference* also beträchtlich

sizeably [ˈsaɪzəblɪ] ADV beträchtlich

-size(d) [-saɪz(d)] ADJ *suf* -groß; **medium-size(d)** mittelgroß, von mittlerer Größe; **life-size(d)** lebensgroß

sizzle [ˈsɪzl] **VI** brutzeln **N** Brutzeln *nt*, Brutzelei *f*

sizzler [ˈsɪzlə] N (*inf*) glühend heißer Tag

sizzling [ˈsɪzlɪŋ] **ADJ** *fat, bacon* brutzelnd; (*inf*) *temperatures* siedend; *weather* brütend heiß; *performance* erregend **ADV** **~ hot** kochend heiß; **it was a ~ hot day** (*inf*) es war knallheiß (*inf*)

skate¹ [skeɪt] N (= *fish*) Rochen *m*

skate² **N** (= *shoe*) Schlittschuh *m*; (= *blade*) Kufe *f*; **put** or **get your ~s on** (*fig inf*) mach/macht mal ein bisschen dalli! (*inf*) → **ice skate**, **roller skate** **VI** Eis laufen, Schlittschuh laufen; (= *figure-skate*) Eiskunst laufen; (= *roller-skate*) Rollschuh laufen; **he ~d across the pond** er lief (auf Schlittschuhen) über den Teich; **she ~d up to him** sie lief auf ihn zu; **the next couple to ~** das nächste Paar auf dem Eis

▶ **skate (a)round** or **over** VI +prep obj links liegen lassen; *difficulty, problem* einfach übergehen

skateboard [ˈskeɪtbɔːd] N Skateboard *nt*, Rollbrett *nt*

skateboarder [ˈskeɪtbɔːdə] N Skateboardfahrer(in) *m(f)*

skateboarding [ˈskeɪtbɔːdɪŋ] N Skateboardfahren *nt*

skateboard park N Skateboardanlage *f*

skatepark [ˈskeɪtpɑːk] N Skateboardanlage *f*

skater ['skeɪtə'] N (= ice-skater) Eisläufer(in) m(f), Schlittschuhläufer(in) m(f); (= figure-skater) Eiskunstläufer(in) m(f); (= roller-skater) Rollschuhläufer(in) m(f)

skate sailing N (Sport) Eissegeln nt

skating ['skeɪtɪŋ] N (= ice-skating) Eislauf m, Schlittschuhlauf m; (= figure-skating) Eiskunstlauf m; (= roller-skating) Rollschuhlauf m

skating: skating exhibition N (Sport) Schaulaufen nt; **skating rink** N Eisbahn f; (for roller--skating) Rollschuhbahn f

skedaddle [skɪ'dædl] VI (inf) Reißaus nehmen (inf), türmen (inf); ~! weg mit dir/euch!, verzieh dich/verzieht euch!

skeet shooting ['skiːtʃuːtɪŋ] N (Sport) Skeetschießen nt, Tontaubenschießen nt

skein [skeɪn] N (of wool etc) Strang m; (of geese) Schwarm m; (of evidence, lies etc) Geflecht nt

skeletal ['skelɪtl] ADJ person bis aufs Skelett abgemagert; appearance wie ein Skelett; shapes of trees etc skelettartig; ~ **muscles** Skelettmuskulatur f; ~ **remains** Teile pl eines Gerippes; **the ~ system** das Skelett

skeleton ['skelɪtn] **N** (lit, fig) Skelett nt; (esp of ship) Gerippe nt; **a ~ in one's cupboard** (Brit) or **closet** (US) ein dunkler Punkt (seiner Vergangenheit); (of public figure) eine Leiche im Keller **ADJ** plan, outline etc provisorisch

skeleton: skeleton crew N Not- or Minimalbesatzung f; **skeleton key** N Dietrich m; **skeleton service** N Notdienst m; **skeleton staff** N Notbesetzung f

skep [skep] N (old, = basket) Korb m; (= bee skep) Bienenkorb m

skeptic etc (US) = **sceptic** etc

sketch [sketʃ] **N** (Art, Liter) Skizze f; (Mus) Impression f; (Theat) Sketch m; (= draft, design also) Entwurf m **VT** (lit, fig) skizzieren **VI** Skizzen machen

▶ **sketch in** VT sep (= draw) (grob) einzeichnen; (verbally) umreißen

▶ **sketch out** VT sep (= draw) grob skizzieren; (= outline also) umreißen

sketch: sketch block N Skizzenblock m; **sketchbook** ['sketʃbʊk] N Skizzenbuch nt

sketchily ['sketʃɪlɪ] ADV flüchtig, oberflächlich

sketchiness ['sketʃɪnɪs] N Flüchtigkeit f, Oberflächlichkeit f; (= insufficiency) Unzulänglichkeit f

sketching ['sketʃɪŋ] N (Art) Skizzenzeichnen nt

sketch map N Kartenskizze f

sketch pad N Skizzenblock m

sketchy ['sketʃɪ] ADJ (+er) (= inadequate) knowledge, account flüchtig, oberflächlich; outline skizzenhaft; (= incomplete) record bruchstückhaft

skew [skjuː] **N on the ~** schief; (= on the diagonal) schräg **ADJ** (lit, fig) schief; (= diagonal) schräg **VT** (= turn round) umdrehen; (= make crooked) krümmen; (fig, = distort) verzerren **VI** **the car ~ed off the road** der Wagen kam von der Straße ab; **the ball ~s to the right** der Ball hat einen Rechtsdrall

skewbald ['skjuːbɔːld] **N** Schecke mf **ADJ** scheckig

skewer ['skjuə'] **N** Spieß m **VT** aufspießen

skewwhiff, skewwiff [skjuː'wɪf] ADJ, ADV (Brit inf) schief

ski [skiː] **N** Ski m; (Aviat) Kufe f **VI** Ski laufen or fahren; **they ~ed down the slope** sie fuhren (auf ihren Skiern) den Hang hinunter

ski in cpds Ski-; **skibob** N Skibob m; **ski boot** N Skistiefel or -schuh m; **ski circuit, ski circus** N Skizirkus m

skid [skɪd] **N a** (= sliding movement: Aut etc) Schleudern nt; **to steer into/against a ~** mit-/gegensteuern; **to go into a ~** ins Schleudern geraten or kommen; **to correct a ~, to pull out of a ~** das Fahrzeug abfangen or wieder in seine Gewalt bekommen; **to stop with a ~** schleudernd zum Stehen kommen

b (on wheel) Rolle f
c (= runner) Gleiter m; (of plane, sledge etc) Gleitkufe f
d skids PL (fig) **he was on** or **hit the ~s** (inf) es ging abwärts mit ihm; **her marriage/career is on the ~s** (inf) ihre Ehe/Karriere ist ins Schleudern geraten; **to put the ~s under sb/sb's plans** (inf) jdn/jds Pläne zu Fall bringen, jdm die Suppe versalzen (inf)
VI (car, objects) schleudern; (person) ausrutschen; **to ~ across the floor** über den Boden rutschen or schlittern; **the car ~ded into a tree** der Wagen schleuderte gegen einen Baum

skid: skidlid N (sl) Sturzhelm m; **skidmark** N Reifenspur f; (from braking) Bremsspur f; **skidpan** N Schleuderstrecke f; **skidproof** ADJ tyre etc rutschfest; **skid row** N (esp US, inf) (Kaschemmen- und) Pennergegend f (inf); **to be on** or **in ~** heruntergekommen sein; **he ended up in ~** er ist als Penner geendet (inf)

skier ['skiːə'] N Skiläufer(in) m(f), Skifahrer(in) m(f)

skiff [skɪf] N Skiff nt; (Sport) Einer m

skiffle ['skɪfl] N Skiffle m; ~ **group** Skifflegroup f

ski-flying ['skiːflaɪŋ] N Skifliegen nt

skiing ['skiːɪŋ] N Skilaufen nt, Skifahren nt; **to go ~** Ski laufen or Ski fahren gehen

ski: ski jump N (= action) Skisprung m; (= place) Sprungschanze f; **ski-jumping** N Skispringen nt

skilful, (US) **skillful** ['skɪlfʊl] ADJ geschickt; piano-playing etc also gewandt; sculpture, painting etc kunstvoll; job fachgerecht

skilfully, (US) **skillfully** ['skɪlfəlɪ] ADV geschickt; play the piano also gewandt; paint, sculpt etc kunstvoll

skilfulness, (US) **skillfulness** ['skɪlfʊlnɪs] N = **skill a**

ski lift N Skilift m

skill [skɪl] N **a** no pl (= skilfulness) Geschick nt, Geschicklichkeit f; (of sculptor etc) Kunst(fertigkeit) f; **his ~ at billiards** sein Geschick nt beim Billard; **her ~ in persuading people** ihre Fähigkeit, andere zu überreden **b** (= acquired technique) Fertigkeit f; (= ability) Fähigkeit f; **to learn new ~s** etwas Neues lernen; **it's a ~ that has to be acquired** so etwas muss gelernt sein

Skillcentre ['skɪlsentə'] N (Brit) staatliches Ausbildungs- und Umschulungszentrum

skilled [skɪld] ADJ (= skilful) geschickt, gewandt (at in +dat); (= trained) ausgebildet; (= requiring skill) fachmännisch; **he's ~ in persuading people** er versteht es, andere zu überreden; **a man ~ in diplomacy** ein geschickter Diplomat

skilled worker N Facharbeiter(in) m(f)

skillet ['skɪlɪt] N Bratpfanne f

skillful etc (US) = **skilful** etc

skill shortage N (Econ) Mangel m an qualifizierten Fachkräften

skim [skɪm] **VT a** (= remove floating matter) abschöpfen; milk entrahmen; (fig) profits absahnen (inf) **b** (= pass low over) streifen or streichen über (+acc); (fig, = touch on) berühren; **he ~med stones across the water** er ließ Steine übers Wasser hüpfen or springen; **he ~med his hat across the room** er schleuderte seinen Hut quer durchs Zimmer; **the book merely ~s the surface of the problem** das Buch berührt das Problem nur an der Oberfläche **c** (= read quickly) überfliegen **VI** (across, over über +acc) (= move quickly) fliegen; (aircraft also) rasch gleiten; (stones) springen, hüpfen

▶ **skim off** VT sep abschöpfen; (fig) absahnen (inf); **to skim the cream off the milk** die Milch entrahmen; **to skim the cream off sth** (fig) Geld von etw absahnen (inf)

▶ **skim through** VI +prep obj book etc überfliegen

skimmed milk [ˌskɪmd'mɪlk], (US) **skim milk** N Magermilch f

skimmer ['skɪmə'] N **a** Schaumlöffel m **b** (Orn) Scherenschnabel m

skimp [skɪmp] **VT** food, material sparen an (+dat), knausern mit; work hudeln bei (inf), nachlässig erledigen; details zu kurz kommen lassen **VI** sparen (on an +dat), knausern (on mit)

skimpily ['skɪmpɪlɪ] ADV dürftig; live, eat also kärglich; dressed spärlich

skimpy ['skɪmpɪ] ADJ (+er) dürftig; meal also kärglich; clothes knapp

skin [skɪn] **N a** Haut f; **to be soaked to the ~** bis auf die Haut nass sein; **he's nothing but ~ and bone(s) nowadays** er ist nur noch Haut und Knochen; **that's no ~ off his nose** (esp Brit inf) das braucht ihn nicht zu stören; **that's no ~ off my nose** (esp Brit inf) das juckt mich nicht (inf); **to get inside the ~ of a part** (Theat) in einer Rolle aufgehen; **all men/women are brothers/sisters under the ~** im Grunde sind alle Menschen gleich; **to save one's own ~** die eigene Haut retten; **to jump out of one's ~** (inf) erschreckt hochfahren; **to get under sb's ~** (inf, = irritate) jdm auf die Nerven gehen (inf); (= fascinate, music, voice) jdm unter die Haut gehen; (person) jdn faszinieren; (= understand) jdn verstehen; **I've got you under my ~** du hast mirs angetan; **to have a thick/thin ~** (fig) ein dickes Fell (inf)/eine dünne Haut haben; **by the ~ of one's teeth** (inf) mit knapper Not, mit Ach und Krach (inf)

b (= hide) Haut f; (= fur) Fell nt
c (= oilskins) Ölhaut f, Ölzeug nt
d (for wine etc) Schlauch m
e (of fruit etc) Schale f; (of grape, tomato) Haut f, Schale f
f (on sausage etc) Haut f, Darm m
g (on milk etc) Haut f
h (for duplicating) Matrize f
i (= skinhead) Skin m
j (Drugs inf: = cigarette paper) Zigarettenpapier nt (zum Rauchen von Drogen)
VT a animal häuten; fruit schälen; grapes, tomatoes enthäuten; **there's more than one way to ~ a cat** (inf) es gibt nicht nur einen Weg; **to ~ sb alive** (inf) jdm den Kopf abreißen (hum inf) **eye**
b (= graze) knee abschürfen

▶ **skin up** VI (Drugs inf) sich (dat) einen Joint drehen (inf)

skin: skin care N Hautpflege f; **skin-deep** ADJ → **beauty**; **skin disease** N Hautkrankheit f; **skin-diver** N Sporttaucher(in) m(f); **skin diving** N Sporttauchen nt; **skin flick** N (US inf) Porno(film) m; **skinflint** N (inf) Geizkragen m (inf); **skin food** N Nahrung f für die Haut

skinful ['skɪnfʊl] N (Brit inf) **to have had a ~** einen über den Durst getrunken haben, einen sitzen haben (inf)

skin: skin game N (US, inf) Schwindel m; **skin graft** N Hauttransplantation or -verpflanzung f; **skinhead** **N** Skin(head) m **ADJ** attr Skin(head)-; ~ **gang** Skin(head)bande f; **skinless** ADJ sausage ohne Haut or Darm; chicken breast ohne Haut

-skinned [-skɪnd] ADJ suf -häutig; **fair-skinned** hellhäutig; **dark-skinned** dunkelhäutig

skinner ['skɪnə'] N (removing skins) Abdecker(in) m(f); (preparing skins) Gerber(in) m(f)

skinny ['skɪnɪ] ADJ (+er) (of person, legs, arms dünn; sweater eng anliegend attr, hauteng

skinny: skinny-dip VI (inf) nackt baden; **skinny dipping** N (inf) Nacktbaden nt; **to go ~** nackt baden; **skinny-rib** ADJ Rippen-; ~ **sweater** Rippenpullover m

skin patch N (Med) Hautfleck m

skint [skɪnt] ADJ (Brit, inf) **to be ~** pleite or blank sein (inf)

skin: skin test N Hauttest m; **skintight** ADJ hauteng

skip¹ [skɪp] **N** Hüpfer m; (in dancing) Hüpfschritt m; **she gave a little ~ of pleasure** sie machte einen Freudensprung

VI a hüpfen; (*with rope*) seilhüpfen, seilspringen; **she came ~ping up to us** sie kam auf uns zugesprungen; **she was ~ping** (*with rope*) sie sprang Seil

b (= *move from subject to subject*) springen **c** (*inf*, = *abscond, flee*) abhauen (*inf*), türmen (*inf*)

VT a (= *omit, miss*) school, church etc schwänzen (*inf*); *generation, passage, chapter etc* überspringen, auslassen; (*Comput, printer*) überspringen; **my heart ~ped a beat** mein Herzschlag setzte für eine Sekunde aus; **to ~ lunch** das Mittagessen ausfallen lassen; **to ~ bail** (*inf*) die Kaution verfallen lassen (*und nicht vor Gericht erscheinen*); **~ it!** ist ja auch egal!

b (*US*) **to ~ rope** seilhüpfen, seilspringen **c** (*US inf*) **to ~ town** aus der Stadt verschwinden (*inf*); **to ~ the country** über die Grenze fliehen

▶ **skip about** (*Brit*) or **around** **VI** (*lit*) herumhüpfen; (*fig: author, speaker*) springen

▶ **skip across** **VI** (*inf*) rüberspringen (*inf*); **skip across to the other office** spring doch mal rüber ins andere Büro! (*inf*)

▶ **skip off** **VI** (*inf*) abhauen (*inf*)

▶ **skip over** **VT** (*inf*) = **skip across** **VI** +*prep obj* (= *pass over*) überspringen

▶ **skip through** **VI** +*prep obj book* durchblättern

skip² **N a** (*Build*) Container *m*, Bauschuttmulde *f* (*form*); (*Min*) Förderkorb *m* **b** = **skep**

skip³ **N** (*Sport*) Kapitän *m*

ski: **ski pants** **PL** Skihose *f*; **ski pass** **N** Skipass *m*; **skiplane** **N** Flugzeug *nt* mit Schneekufen; **ski pole** **N** = **ski stick**

skipper ['skɪpə'] **N** Kapitän(in) *m(f)*; **aye, aye ~!** jawohl, Käpt'n! **the team was ~ed by X** Kapitän(in) der Mannschaft war X

skipping ['skɪpɪŋ] **N** Seilhüpfen *nt*, Seilspringen *nt*

skipping rope **N** (*Brit*) Hüpf- or Sprungseil *nt*

ski: **ski rack** **N** Skiträger *m*; **ski resort** **N** Skiort *m*

skirl [skɜ:l] **N the ~ of the bagpipes** das Pfeifen der Dudelsäcke

skirmish ['skɜ:mɪʃ] **N** (*Mil*) Gefecht *nt*, Plänkelei *f*; (= *scrap, fig*) Zusammenstoß *m* **VI** (*Mil*) kämpfen; (= *scrap, also fig*) zusammenstoßen

skirmisher ['skɜ:mɪʃə'] **N** Kämpfende(r) *mf*

skirt [skɜ:t] **N a** Rock *m*; (*of jacket, coat*) Schoß *m* **b** (*inf*: = *woman*) Braut *f* (*sl*); **a bit of ~** eine Braut (*sl*) **VT a** (*also* **skirt around**) umgehen; (= *encircle*) umgeben

skirting (board) ['skɜ:tɪŋ(,bɔ:d)] **N** (*Brit*) Fußleiste *f*

ski: **ski run** **N** Skipiste *f*; **ski school** **N** Skischule *f*; **ski stick** **N** Skistock *m*; **ski suit** **N** Skianzug *m*

skit [skɪt] **N** (satirischer) Sketch (*on* über +*acc*), Parodie *f* (*on* +*gen*)

ski: **ski touring** **N** Skitouren *nt*; **ski tow** **N** Schlepplift *m*

skitter ['skɪtə'] **VI** rutschen

skittish ['skɪtɪʃ] **ADJ** (= *playful*) übermütig, schelmisch; (= *flirtatious*) *woman* neckisch, kokett; (= *nervous*) *horse, investor* unruhig

skittishly ['skɪtɪʃlɪ] **ADV** (= *playfully*) übermütig, schelmisch; (= *flirtatiously: of woman*) neckisch, kokett; (= *nervously: of horse*) unruhig

skittishness ['skɪtɪʃnɪs] **N** (= *playfulness*) Übermütigkeit *f*, Übermut *m*; (= *flirtatiousness: of woman*) Neckereien *pl*; (= *nervousness: of horse*) Unruhe *f*

skittle ['skɪtl] **N** (*Brit*) Kegel *m*; **to play ~s** kegeln; **~ alley** Kegelbahn *f*

skive [skaɪv] (*Brit, inf*) **N to be on the ~** blaumachen (*inf*); (*from school etc*) schwänzen (*inf*); **to have a good ~** sich (*dat*) einen schönen Tag machen (*inf*), sich vor der Arbeit drücken (*inf*) **VI** blaumachen (*inf*); (*from school etc*) schwänzen (*inf*)

▶ **skive off** **VI** (*Brit, inf*) sich abseilen (*sl*), sich drücken (*inf*)

skiver ['skaɪvə'] **N** (*Brit, inf*) fauler Bruder (*inf*), faule Schwester (*inf*)

skivvy ['skɪvɪ] **N** (*Brit, inf*) Dienstmagd *f*

skua ['skju:ə] **N** Skua *f*, Große Raubmöwe

skulduggery [skʌl'dʌgərɪ] **N** (*inf*) üble Tricks *pl* (*inf*); **a bit of ~** ein übler Trick (*inf*); **what ~ are you planning?** (*hum*) na, was für Schandtaten hast du denn vor?

skulk [skʌlk] **VI** (= *move*) schleichen, sich stehlen; (= *lurk*) sich herumdrücken

▶ **skulk off** **VI** sich davonschleichen, sich davonstehlen

skull [skʌl] **N** Schädel *m*; **I couldn't get it into his thick ~** (*inf*) das wollte einfach nicht in seinen Schädel (*inf*); **~ and crossbones** Totenkopf *m*

skullcap ['skʌlkæp] **N** Kipa *f*

skunk [skʌŋk] **N a** Skunk *m*, Stinktier *nt*; (*inf*, = *person*) Schweinehund *m* (*inf*) **b** (*inf*: = *marijuana*) Pot *nt* (*sl*)

sky [skaɪ] **N** Himmel *m*; **under the open ~** unter freiem Himmel; **in the ~** am Himmel; **the ~'s the limit!** nach oben hin keine Grenzen gesetzt; **out of a clear (blue) ~** aus heiterem Himmel; **to praise sb to the skies** jdn in den Himmel heben, jdn über den grünen Klee loben (*inf*)

sky: **sky advertising** **N** Luftwerbung *f*; **sky blue** **N** Himmelblau *nt*; **sky-blue** **ADJ** himmelblau; **skycap** **N** (*US*) Gepäckträger(in) *m(f)*; **skydiver** **N** Fallschirmspringer(in) *m(f)*; **skydiving** **N** Fallschirmspringen *nt*

Skye terrier ['skaɪ'terɪə'] **N** Skyeterrier *m*

sky: **sky-high** **ADJ a** *prices* schwindelnd hoch; *confidence* unermesslich **b** (= *tall*) himmelhoch **ADV** zum Himmel; **mortgage rates went ~** die Hypothekenzinsen stiegen in Schwindel erregende Höhen; **to blow a bridge ~** (*inf*) eine Brücke in die Luft sprengen (*inf*); **to blow a theory ~** (*inf*) eine Theorie zum Einsturz bringen; **skyjack** ['skaɪdʒæk] **VT** entführen **N** Flugzeugentführung *f*; **skyjacker** **N** Luftpirat(in) *m(f)*, Flugzeugentführer(in) *m(f)*; **skylark** **N** Feldlerche *f* **VI** (*inf*, = *frolic*) tollen; (= *fool around*) blödeln (*inf*); **skylarking** **N** (*inf*) Tollen *nt*; (= *fooling around*) Blödelei *f* (*inf*); **skylight** **N** Oberlicht *nt*; (*in roof also*) Dachfenster *nt*; **skyline** **N** (= *horizon*) Horizont *m*; (*of building, hills etc*) Silhouette *f*; (*of city*) Skyline *f*, Silhouette *f*; **sky pilot** **N** (*Mil sl*) Schwarzrock *m* (*inf*); **skyrocket** **N** (Feuerwerks)rakete *f* **VI** (*prices, expenses, blood pressure*) in die Höhe schießen **VT** in die Höhe schießen lassen; **skyscape** ['skaɪskeɪp] **N** Wolkenlandschaft *f*; **skyscraper** **N** Wolkenkratzer *m*

skyward(s) ['skaɪwəd(z)] **ADJ** zum or gen (*geh*) Himmel gerichtet **ADV** zum or gen (*geh*) Himmel

sky: **skyway** **N** Luftweg *m*; **skywriting** **N** Himmelsschrift *f*

slab [slæb] **N** (*of wood etc*) Tafel *f*; (*of stone, concrete etc*) Platte *f*; (*in mortuary*) Tisch *m*; (= *slice*) dicke Scheibe; (*of cake, bread*) großes Stück; (*of chocolate*) Tafel *f*

slack [slæk] **ADJ** (+*er*) **a** (= *not tight*) locker **b** (= *lazy*) bequem, träge; *student* verbummelt; (= *negligent*) nachlässig, schlampig (*inf*); **they are very ~ in renewing contracts** das Erneuern der Verträge wird sehr nachlässig gehandhabt; **to be ~ in one's work** in Bezug auf seine Arbeit nachlässig sein **c** (= *not busy*) (*Comm*) *market* flau; *period, season* ruhig; **business is ~** das Geschäft geht schlecht **d** (= *slow*) *water* träge; *wind* flau **N a** (*of rope etc*) durchhängendes Teil (*des Seils/Segels etc*), Lose(s) *nt* (*spec*); **to take up the ~ (on a rope/sail)** ein Seil/Segel straffen or spannen; **there is too much ~** das Seil/Segel hängt zu sehr durch; **to cut sb some ~** (*fig inf*) mit jdm nachsichtig sein **b** (= *coal*) Grus *m* **VI** bummeln

▶ **slack off** **VI** = **slacken off** **b**

slacken ['slækn] **VT a** (= *loosen*) lockern **b** (= *reduce*) vermindern, verringern **VI a** (= *become loose*) sich lockern **b** (*speed*) sich verringern; (*rate of development*) sich verlangsamen; (*wind, demand, market*) abflauen, nachlassen

▶ **slacken off** **VI a** (= *diminish*) nachlassen; (*wind*) abflauen, nachlassen; (*work, trade*) abnehmen **b** (*person*, = *relax*) nachlassen; (*for health reasons*) sich schonen

▶ **slacken up** **VI** = **slacken off b**

slackening ['slæknɪŋ] **N** (= *loosening*) Lockern *nt*; (= *reduction*) Abnahme *f*; (*of rate of development, speed*) Verlangsamung *f*; (*of wind, efforts, market*) Abflauen *nt*; **there is no ~ off in the demand** die Nachfrage ist nicht zurückgegangen

slacker ['slækə'] **N** Bummelant(in) *m(f)*

slackly ['slæklɪ] **ADV** (= *loosely, floppily*) schlaff; *hold* locker; *hang* schlaff, lose **b** (= *carelessly, sloppily*) schlampig

slackness ['slæknɪs] **N a** (*of rope, reins*) Schlaffheit *f*, Durchhängen *nt* **b** (= *laziness*) Bummelei *f*; (= *negligence*) Nachlässigkeit *f*, Schlampigkeit *f* (*inf*) **c** (*of business, market etc*) Flaute *f*

slacks [slæks] **PL** Hose *f*

slacksuit ['slæksu:t] **N** (*US*) **a** (*for leisure*) Freizeitanzug *m* **b** (= *pantsuit*) Hosenanzug *m*

slag [slæg] **N a** Schlacke *f* **b** (*Brit sl*: = *woman*) Schlampe *f* (*inf*) **VT** (*Brit inf*, = *run down*) mies machen (*inf*), runtermachen (*inf*)

▶ **slag off** **VT** *sep* (*Brit inf*, = *run down*) mies machen (*inf*), runtermachen (*inf*)

slag heap **N** Schlackenhalde *f*

slain [sleɪn] *ptp of* **slay**

slake [sleɪk] **VT a** (*liter*, = *quench*) stillen **b** *lime* löschen; **~d lime** gelöschter Kalk, Löschkalk *m*

slalom ['slɑ:ləm] **N** Slalom *m*

slam [slæm] **N a** (*of door etc*) Zuschlagen *nt*, Zuknallen *nt no pl*; (*of fist etc*) Aufschlagen *nt no pl*; **with a ~** mit voller Wucht

b (*Cards*) Schlemm *m*; **little** *or* **small ~** Kleinschlemm *m* → *also* **grand slam**

VT a (= *close violently*) zuschlagen, zuknallen; **to ~ the door** (*inf*) die Tür zuschlagen; **to ~ sth shut** etw zuknallen; **to ~ the door in sb's face** jdm die Tür vor der Nase zumachen; **to ~ home a bolt** einen Riegel vorwerfen

b (*inf*, = *put, throw etc with force*) knallen (*inf*); **he ~med his fist into my face** er knallte mir die Faust ins Gesicht (*inf*); **she ~med her fist on the table** sie knallte mit der Faust auf den Tisch (*inf*); **to ~ the brakes on** (*inf*) auf die Bremse latschen (*inf*)

c (*inf*, = *defeat*) vernichtend schlagen, am Boden zerstören

d (*inf*, = *criticize harshly*) verreißen; *person* herunterputzen (*inf*), mies machen (*inf*)

VI a (*door, window*) zuschlagen, zuknallen **b** **to ~ into/against sth** in etw (*acc*)/gegen etw knallen

▶ **slam down** **VT** *sep* (= *put down violently*) hinknallen (*inf*); *phone* aufknallen (*inf*); *window* zuknallen; **to slam sth down on the table** etw auf den Tisch knallen

slam dancing **N** Slamdancing *nt*

slam-dunk ['slæmdʌŋk] (*US, Basketball*) **N** Slam Dunk *m* **VT** *ball* kraftvoll im Korb versenken **VI** einen Slam Dunk spielen

slammer ['slæmə'] **N** (*inf*, = *prison*) Knast *m* (*inf*), Bau *m* (*inf*)

slander ['slɑ:ndə'] **N** Verleumdung *f* **VT** verleumden

slanderer ['slɑ:ndərə'] **N** Verleumder(in) *m(f)*

slanderous ['slɑ:ndərəs] **ADJ** verleumderisch

slang [slæŋ] **N** Slang *m*; (= *army slang, schoolboy slang etc*) Jargon *m*; **street ~** Straßenjargon *m*; **gipsy ~** Zigeunersprache *f* **ADJ** Slang-; **expression** Slangausdruck *m* **VT** (*esp Brit, inf*) **to ~ sb** jdn beschimpfen; **to ~ sth** über etw (*acc*) schimpfen

slanging match ['slæŋɪŋ,mætʃ] N (*Brit*) Wettschimpfen *nt*; **they were having a** ~ sie beschimpften sich um die Wette (*inf*)

slangy ADJ (*+er*), **slangily** ADV ['slæŋɪ, -lɪ] salopp

slant [slɑːnt] **N a** Neigung *f*, Schräge *f*; **to be on a** ~ sich neigen, schräg sein; **his handwriting has a definite** ~ **to the right/left** er schreibt stark nach rechts/links **b** (*fig*: = *bias, leaning*) Tendenz *f*, Neigung *f*; (*of newspaper article*) Anstrich *m*; **these newspapers have a right-wing** ~ diese Zeitungen sind rechtsgerichtet *or* haben einen Rechtsdrall; **to put a** ~ **on sth** etw biegen **VT** verschieben; *report* färben; **the book is ~ed toward(s) women** das Buch ist auf Frauen ausgerichtet **VI** (*road*) sich neigen; **the light ~ed in through the window** das Licht fiel schräg durch das Fenster herein; **her eyes ~ up at the corners** ihre Augen sind schräg gestellt

slanted ['slɑːntɪd] ADJ (*fig*) gefärbt

slant-eyed ['slɑːntˈaɪd] ADJ (*pej*) schlitzäugig (*pej*)

slanting ['slɑːntɪŋ] ADJ schräg

slantways ['slɑːntweɪz], **slantwise** ['slɑːntwaɪz] ADV quer

slap [slæp] **N** Schlag *m*, Klaps *m*; **to give sb a** ~ jdm einen Klaps geben; **a** ~ **across the face** (*lit*) eine Ohrfeige; **a** ~ **in the face** (*fig*) ein Schlag *m* ins Gesicht; **to give sb a** ~ **on the back** (*anerkennend*) auf den Rücken klopfen; (*fig*) jdn loben; ~ **and tickle** (*hum inf*) Balgerei *f* (*inf*), Kalberei *f* (*inf*); **to give sb a** ~ **on the wrist** (*fig inf*) jdn zurechtweisen, jdm einen Anpfiff geben (*inf*); **a £1,000 fine to him is just a** ~ **on the wrist** eine Geldstrafe von £ 1.000 ist für ihn allenfalls ein kleiner Denkzettel **ADV** (*inf*) direkt; **to run** ~ **into sb/sth** mit jdm/etw zusammenknallen (*inf*); ~ **in the middle of the beach** mitten auf dem Strand **VT a** (= *hit*) schlagen; **to** ~ **sb's face, to** ~ **sb on** *or* **round the face** jdm ohrfeigen, jdm ins Gesicht schlagen, jdm eine runterhauen (*inf*); **to** ~ **sb on the back** jdm auf den Rücken klopfen; **to** ~ **one's knee(s)** sich (*dat*) auf die Schenkel schlagen **b** (= *put noisily*) knallen (*on*(*to*) auf +*acc*) **c** (*inf*, = *put carelessly*) **a piece of cheese ~ped between two slices of bread** ein Stück Käse zwischen zwei Scheiben Brot geklatscht (*inf*)

▸ **slap down** VT *sep* (*inf*) **a** (= *put down*) hinknallen **b** (*fig*) **to slap sb down** jdm eins aufs Dach *or* auf den Deckel geben (*inf*); **to be slapped down** eins aufs Dach *or* auf den Deckel bekommen (*inf*)

▸ **slap on** VT *sep* (*inf*) **a** (= *apply carelessly*) *paint, make-up* draufklatschen (*inf*) **b** (= *put on top*) draufklatschen (*inf*); (*fig*) *tax, money* draufhauen (*inf*); **to slap an injunction/a fine on sb** jdm eine einstweilige Verfügung/eine Geldstrafe verpassen (*inf*)

slap: **slap-bang** ADV (*esp Brit inf*) mit Karacho (*inf*); **it was** ~ **in the middle** es war genau in der Mitte; **to run** ~ **into sb/sth** mit jdm/etw zusammenknallen (*inf*); **slapdash** ADJ flüchtig, schludrig (*pej*); **slaphappy** ADJ (*inf*) unbekümmert; **slaphead** N (*inf*) Glatzkopf *m* (*inf*); **slapjack** N (*US*) ≈ Pfannkuchen *m*

slapper ['slæpə'] N (*Brit inf*) Flittchen *nt* (*inf*)

slap: **slapstick** N Klamauk *m* (*inf*); ~ **comedy** Slapstick *m* (*inf*); **slap-up meal** N (*Brit inf*) Schlemmermahl *nt* (*inf*)

slash [slæʃ] **N a** (= *action*) Streich *m*; (= *wound*) Schnitt *m* **b** (*Sew*) Schlitz *m*; **a black velvet dress with ~es of red silk** ein schwarzes Samtkleid mit roten Seidenschlitzen **c** (*Typ*) Schrägstrich *m* **d** (*Brit inf*) **to go for a** ~ schiffen gehen (*sl*); **to have a** ~ schiffen (*sl*) **VT a** (= *cut*) zerfetzen; *face, tyres, throat* aufschlitzen; *undergrowth* abhauen, wegschlagen; (*with sword*) hauen auf (+*acc*), schlagen; **to** ~

sb with a knife jdn durch Messerstiche verletzen; **to** ~ **sth to ribbons** etw zerfetzen; **he ~ed the air with his sword** er ließ das Schwert durch die Luft sausen → **wrist** **b** (*inf*, = *reduce drastically*) *price* radikal herabsetzen; *workforce* drastisch reduzieren; *estimate, budget* zusammenstreichen (*inf*); **to** ~ **the odds** die Chance(n) erheblich reduzieren **c** (*Sew*) mit Schlitzen versehen; **~ed sleeves** Schlitzärmel *pl*; **~ed doublet** Schlitzwams *nt* **VI** **to** ~ **at sb/sth** nach jdm/etw schlagen

▸ **slash off** VT *sep* abschlagen; **to slash £500 off the budget** £ 500 aus dem Etat streichen

slash-and-burn [,slæʃən'bɜːn] ADJ ~ **farming** Brandrodung *f*

slasher film ['slæʃə,fɪlm], **slasher movie** ['slæʃə,muːvɪ] N (*inf*) Horrorfilm mit Szenen, in denen Menschen mit Messern, Rasierklingen etc *verletzt werden*

slashing ['slæʃɪŋ] ADJ *blow* zerschmetternd; *attack also* scharf; *criticism* vernichtend

slat [slæt] N Leiste *f*; (*wooden also*) Latte *f*; (*in grid etc*) Stab *m*

slate [sleɪt] **N a** (= *rock*) Schiefer *m*; (= *roof slate*) Schieferplatte *f*; (= *writing slate*) (Schiefer-)tafel *f*; **put it on the** ~ (*Brit inf*) schreiben Sie es mir an; **to have a clean** ~ (*fig*) eine reine Weste haben, nichts auf dem Kerbholz haben (*inf*); **to start with a clean** ~ (*fig*) einen neuen Anfang machen; **to wipe the** ~ **clean** (*fig*) reinen Tisch machen **b** (*US, Pol*) (Kandidaten)liste *f* **ADJ** Schiefer-, schief(e)rig; **the roof is** ~ das Dach ist aus Schiefer **VT a** *roof* (mit Schiefer) decken **b** (*esp US*, = *propose*) vorschlagen; (= *schedule*) ansetzen; **it is ~d to start at nine** es ist für neun Uhr angesetzt **c** (*Brit inf*, = *criticize harshly*) *play, performance* verreißen; *person* zusammenstauchen (*inf*)

slate: **slate-blue** ADJ blaugrau; **slate-coloured** ADJ schiefergrau, schieferfarben; **slate-grey**, (*US*) **slate-gray** ADJ schiefergrau; **slate pencil** N Griffel *m*; **slate quarry** N Schieferbruch *m*

slater ['sleɪtə'] N Dachdecker(in) *m(f)*, Schieferdecker(in) *m(f)* (*rare*)

slate roof N Schieferdach *nt*

slating ['sleɪtɪŋ] N (*Brit inf*) Verriss *m*; **to give sb a** ~ jdn zusammenstauchen (*inf*); **to get a** ~ zusammengestaucht werden (*inf*); (*play, performance etc*) verrissen werden

slatted ['slætɪd] ADJ → **slat** aus Leisten/Latten/Stäben bestehend; **a** ~ **fence** ein Lattenzaun *m*

slattern ['slætən] N Schlampe *f*

slatternly ['slætənlɪ] ADJ liederlich, schlampig

slaty ['sleɪtɪ] ADJ *material* schief(e)rig; (*in colour*) schieferfarben; ~ **blue eyes** graublaue Augen *pl*

slaughter ['slɔːtə'] **N** (*of animals*) Schlachten *nt no pl*; (*of persons*) Gemetzel *nt no pl*, Abschlachten *nt no pl* (*liter*); **the Slaughter of the Innocents** (*Bibl*) der Mord der Unschuldigen Kinder; **the** ~ **on the streets** das Töten auf den Straßen **VT** schlachten; *persons* (*lit*) abschlachten; (*fig*) fertig machen (*inf*)

slaughterer ['slɔːtərə'] N (*lit*) Schlachter(in) *m(f)*; (*fig*) Schlächter(in) *m(f)*

slaughterhouse ['slɔːtəhaʊs] N Schlachthof *m*, Schlachthaus *nt*

Slav [slɑːv] ADJ slawisch **N** Slawe *m*, Slawin *f*

slave [sleɪv] **N** Sklave *m*, Sklavin *f*; **to be a** ~ **to sb/sth** jds Sklave/Sklavin von etw sein **VI** sich abplagen, schuften (*inf*); **to** ~ **(away) at sth** sich mit etw herumschlagen; **to** ~ **over a hot stove** (den ganzen Tag) am Herd stehen; **he was slaving over his homework** er schlug sich mit seinen Hausaufgaben herum

slave: **slave-driver** N (*lit, fig*) Sklaventreiber(in) *m(f)*; **slave labour**, (*US*) **slave labor** N **a** (= *work*) Sklavenarbeit *f* **b** (= *work force*) Sklaven *pl*; **he uses** ~ seine Leute müssen wie

die Sklaven arbeiten; **slave market** N (*Hist*) Sklavenmarkt *m*

slaver¹ ['sleɪvə'] N (= *ship*) Sklavenschiff *nt*; (= *person*) Sklavenhändler(in) *m(f)*

slaver² ['slævə'] **VI** speicheln (*geh*), geifern; **the dog ~ed at the mouth** der Hund hatte Schaum vor dem Maul; **he began to** ~ **at the thought of food** bei dem Gedanken ans Essen lief ihm das Wasser im Munde zusammen; **to** ~ **over sb/sth** nach jdm/etw geifern **N** Speichel *m*, Geifer *m*

slavery ['sleɪvərɪ] N Sklaverei *f*; (= *condition*) Sklavenleben *nt*; (*fig*: = *addiction*) sklavische Abhängigkeit (*to von*); **she was tired of domestic** ~ sie hatte es satt, sich immer im Haushalt abrackern zu müssen

slave: **slave ship** N Sklavenschiff *nt*; **slave trade** N Sklavenhandel *m*; **slave trader** N = **slaver¹**

slavey ['sleɪvɪ] N (*dated Brit, inf*) (Dienst)mädchen *nt*

Slavic ['slɑːvɪk] ADJ slawisch **N** das Slawische

slavish ADJ , **slavishly** ADV ['sleɪvɪʃ, -lɪ] sklavisch

slavishness ['sleɪvɪʃnɪs] N sklavische Abhängigkeit; (= *submissiveness*) Unterwürfigkeit *f*; **the** ~ **with which she imitated him** die sklavische Art, in der sie ihn nachahmte

Slavonian [slə'vəʊnɪən] ADJ slawonisch **N** Slawone *m*, Slawonin *f*

Slavonic [slə'vɒnɪk] ADJ slawisch **N** das Slawische

slaw [slɔː] N (*US*) Krautsalat *m*

slay [sleɪ] *pret* **slew**, *ptp* **slain** VT erschlagen; (*with gun etc, esp US*, = *kill*) ermorden; **this will** ~ **you** (*inf*) da lachst du dich tot! (*inf*); **he really ~s me** (*inf*) ich könnte mich über ihn totlachen (*inf*)

slayer ['sleɪə'] N (*liter*) Mörder(in) *m(f)*, Töter(in) *m(f)* (*old liter*)

slaying ['sleɪɪŋ] N (*esp US*, = *murder*) Mord *m*; **an increasing number of ~s** eine Zunahme von Mordfällen

SLD (*Brit, Pol*) *abbr of* **Social and Liberal Democrats**

sleaze [sliːz] N (*inf*, = *depravity*) Verderbtheit *f*; (*esp Pol*: = *corruption*) Skandalgeschichten *pl*

sleazebag ['sliːzbæg] N (*pej inf*) Dreckskerl *m* (*pej inf*)

sleazo ['sliːzəʊ] N (*inf*, = *sleazy person*) schmierige Type (*inf*)

sleazy ['sliːzɪ] ADJ (*+er*) (*inf*) schäbig

sledge [sledʒ], (*esp US*) **sled** [sled] **N** Schlitten *m* **VI** Schlitten fahren

sledge(hammer) ['sledʒ(,hæmə')] N Vorschlaghammer *m*; **to use a sledgehammer to crack a nut** (*fig*) mit Kanonen auf Spatzen schießen

sleek [sliːk] ADJ (*+er*) *hair, fur, animal* geschmeidig, glatt; (*of general appearance*) gepflegt; *car also* schnittig, elegant; *behaviour* aalglatt (*pej*), glatt **VT** glätten; (*cat*) lecken

sleekness ['sliːknɪs] N (*of hair, fur, animal*) Geschmeidigkeit *f*; (*of general appearance*) Gepflegtheit *f*; (*of car*) Schnittigkeit *f*, Eleganz *f*

sleep [sliːp] *vb*: *pret, ptp* **slept** **N** Schlaf *m*; **to go to** ~ (*person, limb*) einschlafen; **to drop off to** ~ (*person*) einschlafen; **I couldn't get to** ~ **last night** ich konnte letzte Nacht nicht einschlafen; **try and get some** ~ versuche, etwas zu schlafen; **to have a** ~ (etwas) schlafen; **to have a good night's** ~ sich richtig ausschlafen, richtig schlafen; **to put sb to** ~ (*person, cocoa etc*) jdn zum Schlafen bringen; (*drug*) jdn einschläfern; **to put an animal to** ~ (*euph*) ein Tier einschläfern; **that film sent me to** ~ während des Films bin ich eingeschlafen; **to walk in one's** ~ schlafwandeln; **to talk in one's** ~ im Schlaf sprechen **VT a** **to** ~ **the day away** den ganzen Tag verschlafen; **to** ~ **the** ~ **of the just** den Schlaf des Gerechten schlafen; **to** ~ **the** ~ **of the dead** *or* **the last** ~ den ewigen *or* letzten Schlaf schlafen (*liter*)

b (= *accommodate*) unterbringen; **the house ~s 10** in dem Haus können 10 Leute schlafen *or* übernachten

VI schlafen; **to ~ like a log** *or* **top** *or* **baby** wie ein Klotz *or* wie ein Murmeltier schlafen; **to ~ late** lange schlafen; **to ~ right round the clock** rund um die Uhr schlafen; **the village slept** (*liter*) das Dorf schlief (*geh*); **you must have been ~ing** (*fig*) da musst du geschlafen haben

▶ **sleep around** VI (*inf*) mit jedem schlafen (*inf*)

▶ **sleep in** VI **a** (= *lie in*) ausschlafen; (*inf, = oversleep*) verschlafen **b** (= *live in*) im Hause wohnen

▶ **sleep off** VT *sep* (*inf*) hangover etc ausschlafen; **to sleep it off** seinen Rausch ausschlafen; *cold etc* sich gesund schlafen; **to sleep off one's lunch** ein Verdauungsschläfchen *nt* halten

▶ **sleep on** **VI** (= *continue sleeping*) weiterschlafen **VI** +*prep obj problem etc* überschlafen; **let's sleep on it** schlafen wir erst einmal darüber, überschlafen wir die Sache erst einmal

▶ **sleep out** VI **a** (*in open air*) draußen *or* im Freien schlafen **b** (*hotel staff: = live out*) außer Haus wohnen

▶ **sleep through** **VI** durchschlafen **VI** +*prep obj* weiterschlafen bei; **to sleep through the alarm (clock)** den Wecker verschlafen

▶ **sleep together** VI zusammen schlafen

▶ **sleep with** VI +*prep obj* schlafen mit

sleep disturbance N Schlafstörung *f*, Einschlaf- *or* Durchschlafstörung *f*

sleeper ['sliːpə'] N **a** (= *person*) Schlafende(r) *mf*, Schläfer(in) *m(f)*; **to be a heavy/light ~** einen festen/leichten Schlaf haben **b** (*Brit Rail, = on track*) Schwelle *f* **c** (*Brit Rail, = train*) Schlafwagenzug *m*; (= *coach*) Schlafwagen *m*; (= *berth*) Platz *m* im Schlafwagen; **I've booked a ~** ich habe Schlafwagen gebucht **d** (*esp Brit: = earring*) einfacher Ohrring, der das Zuwachsen des Loches im Ohrläppchen verhindern soll **e** (= *spy*) abgeschalteter Agent, abgeschaltete Agentin **f** **sleepers** PL (*US: = child's pyjamas*) einteiliger Schlafanzug

sleepily ['sliːpɪlɪ] ADV *ask, smile, blink* verschlafen

sleepiness ['sliːpɪnɪs] N **a** (= *drowsiness*) Müdigkeit *f*, Schläfrigkeit *f* **b** (*fig: of place, atmosphere*) Verschlafenheit *f*

sleeping ['sliːpɪŋ] ADJ schlafend; **Sleeping Beauty** Dornröschen *nt* N Schlafen *nt*; **between ~ and waking** zwischen Schlaf und Wachen

sleeping: sleeping accommodation N Schlafgelegenheit *f*; **sleeping bag** N Schlafsack *m*; **sleeping car** N Schlafwagen *m*; **sleeping draught**, (*US*) **sleeping draft** N Schlaftrunk *m*; **sleeping partner** N (*Brit*) stiller Teilhaber *or* Gesellschafter; **sleeping pill** N Schlaftablette *f*; **sleeping policeman** N (= *traffic bump*) (fahrdynamische) Schwelle, Bodenschwelle *f*; **sleeping quarters** PL Schlafräume *pl*, Schlafsaal *m*; **sleeping sickness** N Schlafkrankheit *f*; **sleeping tablet** N Schlaftablette *f*

sleepless ['sliːplɪs] ADJ schlaflos

sleeplessness ['sliːplɪsnɪs] N Schlaflosigkeit *f*

sleep: sleepover N Übernachtung *f* (*bei Freunden, Bekannten etc*); **sleepwalk** VI schlafwandeln; **he was ~ing** er hat *or* ist geschlafwandelt; **sleepwalker** N Schlafwandler(in) *m(f)*; **sleepwalking** **N** Schlafwandeln *nt* **ATTR** schlafwandlerisch; **sleepwear** ['sliːpwɛə'] N Nachtwäsche *f*

sleepy ['sliːpɪ] ADJ (+*er*) **a** (= *drowsy*) *person, voice etc* müde, schläfrig; (= *not yet awake*) verschlafen; **to be/look ~** müde sein/aussehen; **I feel very ~ by midnight** gegen Mitternacht bin ich schon sehr müde **b** (= *inactive*) *person* lahm (*inf*), müde; *place, atmosphere* verschlafen; *climate* schläfrig machend; *afternoons* schläfrig

sleepyhead ['sliːpɪhɛd] N (*inf*) Schlafmütze *f* (*inf*)

sleet [sliːt] N Schneeregen *m* **VI** **it was ~ing** es gab Schneeregen

sleeve [sliːv] N **a** (*on garment*) Ärmel *m*; **to roll up one's ~s** (*lit*) sich (*dat*) die Ärmel hochkrempeln; (*fig*) die Ärmel aufkrempeln (*inf*); **to have sth up one's ~** (*fig inf*) etw in petto haben *or* auf Lager haben → **laugh** **b** (*for record, on book*) Hülle *f* **c** (*Tech*) Muffe *f*, Manschette *f*

-sleeved [-sliːvd] ADJ *suf* -ärmelig; **long-sleeved** langärmelig; **short-sleeved** kurzärmelig

sleeveless ['sliːvlɪs] ADJ ärmellos

sleigh [sleɪ] N (Pferde)schlitten *m*; **~ bell** Schlittenglocke *f*; **~ ride** Schlittenfahrt *f*

sleighing ['sleɪɪŋ] N Schlittenfahren *nt*

sleight [slaɪt] N **~ of hand** Fingerfertigkeit *f*; **by ~ of hand** durch Taschenspielertricks

slender ['slɛndə'] ADJ schlank; *hand, waist also* schmal; *resources, income* knapp, mager; *chance, hope* schwach, gering; *excuse, profit margin* dürftig, schwach; *lead, majority* knapp, gering

slenderize ['slɛndəraɪz] VT (*US*) schlank machen

slenderly ['slɛndəlɪ] ADV **~ built** *or* **made** schlank

slenderness ['slɛndənɪs] N Schlankheit *f*; (*of hand, waist also*) Schmalheit *f*; (*fig*) (*of chance, hope*) Schwäche *f*; (*of excuse*) Dürftigkeit *f*; (*of lead, majority*) Knappheit *f*; **the ~ of his income** sein geringes Einkommen

slept [slɛpt] *pret, ptp of* **sleep**

sleuth [sluːθ] (*inf*) **N** Spürhund *m* (*inf*) **VI** Detektiv spielen

slew[1], (*US*) **slue** [sluː] (*also* **slew round**) **VT** *crane, lorry* (herum)schwenken; *head* drehen; **to ~ sth to the left** etw nach links schwenken **VI** (herum)schwenken; **to ~ to the left/right** nach links/rechts schwenken

slew[2], (*US*) **slue** N (*inf*) Haufen *m* (*inf*)

slew[3] *pret of* **slay**

slewed [sluːd] ADJ *pred* (*inf*) voll (*inf*), besoffen (*inf*); **to get ~** sich voll laufen lassen (*inf*)

slice [slaɪs] **N** **a** (*lit*) (*of cake, lemon, meat etc*) Scheibe *f*; (*of bread*) Scheibe *f*, Schnitte *f* **b** (*fig: = portion, of population, profits*) Teil *m*; (*of land*) Stück *nt*; **a ~ of life in contemporary Paris** ein Ausschnitt *m* aus dem Leben im heutigen Paris; **a ~ of luck** eine Portion Glück; **that was a ~ of luck!** das war ein glücklicher Zufall **c** (*esp Brit, = food server*) Wender *m*; **cake ~** Tortenheber *m* **d** (*Sport*) angeschnittener Ball; **to put a bit of ~ on the ball** den Ball etwas anschneiden **VT** **a** (= *cut*) durchschneiden; *bread, meat etc* (in Scheiben) schneiden; **to ~ sth in two** etw durchschneiden, etw in zwei Teile schneiden **b** *ball* (an)schneiden **VI** **a** (= *cut*) schneiden; **to ~ through sth** etw durchschneiden **b** (*Sport*) schneiden

▶ **slice off** VT *sep* **a** abschneiden; **he sliced off the top of his egg** er köpfte sein Ei (*inf*) **b** *money, time* wegnehmen; **he sliced £1000 off the total cost** er hat die Gesamtkosten noch um £ 1000 gesenkt; **he sliced 4 seconds off the world record** er hat den Weltrekord um 4 Sekunden unterboten

▶ **slice up** VT *sep* (ganz) in Scheiben schneiden; *bread, meat, sausage also* aufschneiden; (= *divide*) aufteilen

sliced [slaɪst] ADJ (in Scheiben) geschnitten; *loaf, bread, sausage* (auf)geschnitten; **he/it is the best thing since ~ bread** (*inf*) so jemanden/etwas hat die Welt schon lange nicht mehr gesehen (*inf*)

slicer ['slaɪsə'] N (= *cheese-slicer, cucumber-slicer etc*) Hobel *m*; (= *machine, = bread-slicer*) Brot(schneide)maschine *f*, Brotschneider *m*; (= *bacon-slicer*) ≈ Wurstschneidemaschine *f*

slick [slɪk] **ADJ** (+*er*) **a** (*often pej, = clever*) gewieft (*inf*), clever (*inf*); *answer, solution* glatt; *show, performance, translation, style* glatt, professionell; **a ~ novel** ein glatt *or* professionell geschriebener Roman; **a ~ customer** ein ganz gewiefter Kerl (*inf*) **b** *hair* geschniegelt **c** (*US, = slippery*) glatt, schlüpfrig **N** **a** (= *oil slick*) (Öl)teppich *m*, Schlick *m* **b** (*US, inf, = glossy*) Hochglanzmagazin *nt* **c** (= *racing tyre*) Slick *m* (*inf*)

▶ **slick back** VT *sep* **to slick one's hair back** sich (*dat*) die Haare anklatschen (*inf*); **the slicked-back hairstyles of the 50s** die geschniegelten Frisuren der 50er Jahre

slicker ['slɪkə'] N (*US*) **a** (= *coat*) Regenjacke *f* **b** (*inf, = swindler*) Gauner *m* (*inf*), Ganove *m* (*inf*) **c** → **city slicker**

slickly ['slɪklɪ] ADV (*often pej: = cleverly*) gewieft (*inf*), clever (*inf*); *answer, perform, write, translate* glatt

slickness ['slɪknɪs] N **a** (*often pej: = cleverness*) Gewieftheit *f* (*inf*), Cleverness *f* (*inf*); (*of performance, style, writing*) Glattheit *f*; **we were impressed by the ~ with which he answered** wir waren davon beeindruckt, wie glatt er antwortete **b** (*of appearance*) geschniegeltes Aussehen

slide [slaɪd] *vb: pret, ptp* **slid** [slɪd] **N** **a** (= *place for sliding, chute*) Rutschbahn *f*; (*in playground, for logs etc*) Rutsche *f* **b** (*fig, = fall, drop*) Abfall *m*; **the ~ in share prices** der Preisrutsch bei den Aktien; **his slow ~ into alcoholism** sein langsamer Abstieg zum Alkoholiker **c** (= *landslide*) Rutsch *m*, Rutschung *f* (*spec*) **d** (*of trombone*) Zug *m*; (= *sequence of notes*) Schleifer *m* **e** (*Tech, = part*) gleitendes Teil, Schlitten *m* **f** (*esp Brit, for hair*) Spange *f* **g** (*Phot*) Dia *nt*, Diapositiv *nt* (*form*); (= *microscope slide*) Objektträger *m*; **a lecture with ~s** ein Diavortrag *m*, ein Lichtbildervortrag *m* **VT** (= *push*) schieben; (= *slip*) gleiten lassen; **he slid the gun into the holster** er ließ den Revolver ins Halfter gleiten; **to ~ the drawer (back) into place** die Schublade (wieder) zurückschieben **VI** **a** (= *slip*) rutschen; **to ~ down the banisters** das Treppengeländer hinunterrutschen; **suddenly it all slid into place** plötzlich passte alles zusammen **b** (= *move smoothly: machine part etc*) sich schieben lassen; **it slid into its place** es glitt *or* rutschte an die richtige Stelle **c** (*person*) schleichen; **he slid into the room** er kam ins Zimmer geschlichen **d** (*fig*) **the days slid past** die Tage schwanden dahin (*geh*); **to ~ into bad habits** (allmählich) in schlechte Gewohnheiten verfallen; **to let sth ~** etw schleifen lassen, etw vernachlässigen; **to let things ~** die Dinge laufen *or* schleifen lassen

slide: slide area N *Gebiet, in dem es zu Rutschungen kommt* "slide area" (*road sign*) „Vorsicht Erdrutschgefahr"; **slide bar** N (*Tech*) Gleitschiene *f*; **slide control** N Schieberegler *m*; **slide fastener** N (*US*) Reißverschluss *m*; **slide film** N Diafilm *m*; **slide projector** N Diaprojektor *m*; **slide rule** N Rechenschieber *m*; **slide show** N Diavortrag *m*; **slide tackle** N (*Ftbl*) Grätsche *f*

sliding ['slaɪdɪŋ] ADJ *part* gleitend

sliding: sliding door N Schiebetür *f*; **sliding roof** N Schiebedach *nt*; **sliding scale** N gleitende Skala; **sliding seat** N verschiebbarer Sitz, Schiebesitz *m*; (*in rowing boat*) Rollsitz *m*; **sliding tackle** N (*Ftbl*) Grätsche *f*

slight [slaɪt] **ADJ** (+*er*) **a** *person, build* zierlich; **to be of ~ build** eine schlanke *or* zierliche Figur haben **b** (= *small, trivial*) leicht; *change, possibility* geringfügig; *importance, intelligence* gering; *error* leicht, klein; *problem* klein; *pain* leicht, schwach; *acquaintance* flüchtig; **the wound is only ~** es ist nur eine leichte Verwundung; **the wall's at a ~ angle** die Mauer ist leicht *or* etwas geneigt; **to have a ~ cold** eine leichte Erkältung haben; **to a ~ extent** in geringem Maße; **he showed some ~ optimism** er zeigte gewisse Ansätze von Optimismus; **just the ~est bit short** ein ganz kleines bisschen zu kurz; **it doesn't make the ~est bit of differ-ence** es macht nicht den geringsten or mindesten Unterschied; **I wasn't the ~est bit inter-ested** ich war nicht im Geringsten or Mindesten or mindesten interessiert; **nobody showed the ~est interest** niemand zeigte auch nur das geringste Interesse; **the ~est optimism** das geringfügigste Zeichen von Optimismus; **the ~est criticism/possibility** die geringste Kritik/Möglichkeit; **he is upset by at the ~est thing** er ist wegen jeder kleinsten Kleinigkeit gleich verärgert; **I haven't the ~est idea** ich habe nicht die geringste or leiseste (inf) Ahnung; **I don't have the ~est idea (of) what he's talking about** ich habe nicht die geringste or leiseste Ahnung, wovon er redet; **not in the ~est** nicht im Geringsten or Mindesten or mindesten (geh); **without the ~est difficulty** ohne die kleinste or mindeste Schwierigkeit; **without the ~est hint of embarrassment** ohne das geringste Anzeichen von Verlegenheit; **to do sth at the ~est provocation** etw bei der geringsten Provokation tun

N (= affront) Affront m (on gegen); **a ~ on one's/sb's character** eine persönliche Kränkung or Beleidigung

VT (= offend) kränken, beleidigen; (= ignore) ignorieren; **to feel ~ed** gekränkt or beleidigt sein

slighting ['slaɪtɪŋ] ADJ (= offensive) kränkend; (= disparaging) behaviour geringschätzig; remark abschätzig, abfällig

slightingly ['slaɪtɪŋlɪ] ADV speak abschätzig, abfällig; treat geringschätzig

slightly ['slaɪtlɪ] ADV **a** ~ **built** or **made** (person) zierlich **b** (= to a slight extent) etwas, ein klein(es) bisschen; know flüchtig; smell leicht, etwas; ~ **injured** leicht verletzt; **he hesitated ever so** ~ er zögerte fast unmerklich

slightness ['slaɪtnɪs] N **a** (of person, build) Zierlichkeit f **b** (= triviality) Geringfügigkeit f; (of acquaintance) Flüchtigkeit f

slim [slɪm] **ADJ** (+er) **a** schlank; ankle, waist etc schmal; volume schmal, dünn **b** resources, prof-its mager; excuse, hope schwach; chances gering; majority knapp **VI** eine Schlankheitskur machen **VT** schlank(er) machen; (fig) demands etc schrumpfen

▸ **slim down VT** sep **a** person abnehmen lassen, schlank(er) machen **b** (fig) business etc verschlanken; budget kürzen **VI a** (= person) abnehmen, abspecken (inf) **b** (fig, business etc) verschlanken, abspecken (inf)

slimdown ['slɪmdaʊn] N (of firm/company) Gesundschrumpfung f

slime [slaɪm] N Schleim m; **trail of** ~ Schleimspur f

slimeball ['slaɪmbɔːl] N (esp US, pej inf) schmie-rige Type (inf), Ekeltyp m (pej inf)

sliminess ['slaɪmɪnɪs] N (of liquid, secretion) Schleimigkeit f; (of stone, wall) Glitschigkeit f; (of hands) Schmierigkeit f; (fig: of person, smile) Schleimigkeit f, Öligkeit f

slimline ['slɪmlaɪn] ADJ diary dünn; mobile phone flach; figure schlank

slimmer ['slɪmə'] N Kalorienzähler(in) m(f) (hum); **special meals for ~s** spezielle Gerichte für Leute, die abnehmen wollen

slimming ['slɪmɪŋ] **ADJ** schlank machend attr; **crispbread/black is** ~ Knäckebrot/schwarz macht schlank; **to be on a** ~ **diet** eine Schlankheitskur machen; ~ **foods** kalorien-arme Nahrungsmittel pl **N** Abnehmen nt; **is** ~ **really worth it?** lohnt es sich wirklich abzunehmen?

slimming club N Diätklub m, Schlankheitsklub m

slimming pill N Schlankheitspille f

slimnastics [ɔɔ] N **a** sing (= discipline) Schlankheitsgymnastik f **b** pl (= exercises) Schlankheitsgymnastik f

slimness ['slɪmnɪs] N **a** Schlankheit f; (of ankle, waist etc) Schmalheit f; (of volume) Dünne f **b**

(of resources, profits) Magerkeit f; (of majority) Knappheit f; **because of the ~ of their chances** weil ihre Chancen so gering waren

slimy ['slaɪmɪ] ADJ (+er) liquid, secretion schleimig; stone, wall glitschig; hands schmierig; (fig) schleimig; smile, person ölig, schleimig

sling [slɪŋ] vb: pret, ptp **slung N a** (Med) Schlinge f; **to have one's arm in a** ~ den Arm in der Schlinge tragen **b** (for hoisting) Schlinge f, Schlaufe f; (for rifle) (Trag)riemen m; (for baby) (Baby)tragetuch nt, (Baby)trageschlinge f; **to carry a rifle/baby in a** ~ ein Gewehr am Riemen/ein Baby in einer or der Schlinge tragen **c** (= weapon) Schleuder f; ~**s and arrows** (fig) Missgeschicke pl **VT a** (= throw) schleudern; (inf) schmeißen (inf); **to ~ sth away** etw wegschleudern/weg-schmeißen (inf); **to ~ sth over to sb** (inf) jdm etw zuschmeißen (inf); **he slung the box onto his back** er warf sich (dat) die Kiste auf den Rücken; **to ~ one's hook** (Brit, fig inf) Leine zie-hen (inf) **b** (= hoist with a sling) in einer Schlinge hoch-ziehen **c** (= hang) aufhängen

▸ **sling out** VT sep (inf) rausschmeißen (inf)

sling: slingback **ADJ** ~ **shoes** Slingpumps pl; (= sandals) Sandaletten pl **N** ~**s** Slings pl, Slingpumps pl; **sling bag** N (US) Schulterta-sche f; **slingshot** N (US) (Stein)schleuder f

slink [slɪŋk] pret, ptp **slunk** VI schleichen; **to ~ a-way** or **off** sich davonschleichen; **to ~ along the wall** sich an der Wand entlangdrücken; **to ~ off with one's tail between one's legs** (fig inf) mit eingezogenem Schwanz abziehen (inf)

slinky ADJ (+er), **slinkily** ADV ['slɪŋkɪ, -lɪ] (inf) aufreizend; walk etc also katzenhaft

slip [slɪp] **N a** (= slide) **she had a nasty** ~ sie ist ausgerutscht und bös gefallen **b** (= mistake) Ausrutscher m, Patzer m; **to make a (bad)** ~ sich (übel) vertun (inf), einen (ganz schönen) Bock schießen (inf); **a ~ of the pen** ein Flüchtigkeitsfehler m; **a ~ of the tongue** ein Versprecher m; **it was just a ~ of the pen** da habe ich mich nur verschrieben; **there's many a ~ ('twixt cup and lip)** (Prov) man soll den Tag nicht vor dem Abend loben (Prov), zwischen Lipp und Kelchesrand (schwebt der finstern Mächte Hand) (liter) **c to give sb the ~** (inf: = escape) jdm entwi-schen **d** (= pillow slip) Kissenbezug m **e** (= undergarment) Unterrock m; **waist** ~ Halb-unterrock m; **full-length** ~ Unterkleid nt **f** (= paper) Zettel m; ~**s of paper** Zettel pl; **withdrawal** ~ Auszahlungsschein m; **sales** ~ Kassenzettel m **g** (inf: = person) **a (mere) ~ of a girl** (= slightly built) ein zierliches Persönchen; (= young) eine halbe Portion (inf) **h** (Hort, for planting) Steckling m; (for grafting) Reis nt **i** (Cricket, = position/area) Position/Gebiet ne-ben dem Torwächter (= fielder) Eckmann m **j slips** PL (Theat) Bühnenloge f **k** (Pottery) geschlämmter Ton **l** (Aviat, = side-slip) Schlipp m **VT a** (= move smoothly) schieben; (= slide) glei-ten or rutschen lassen; **to ~ sth across to sb** jdm etw zuschieben; (unobtrusively) jdm etw zuschmuggeln; **she ~ped the dress over her head** sie streifte sich (dat) das Kleid über den Kopf; **to ~ one's arm round sb's waist** jdm den Arm um die Taille legen; **to ~ sb sth** (inf) jdn reinlegen (inf); **to ~ sb some money** (inf) jdm etwas Geld zustecken (inf) **b** (= escape from) sich losreißen von; **the dog ~ped its lead** der Hund schlüpfte aus seinem Halsband; **the boat had ~ped its moorings** das Boot hatte sich losgerissen; **to ~ anchor** (Naut) den Anker kappen (form); **it/his birthday ~ped my mind** or **memory** ich habe es/seinen Ge-burtstag vergessen or verschwitzt (inf) **c** (= loose) losmachen; **he ~ped the dog from**

its chain er machte den Hund (von der Kette) los **d** (Med) **to ~ a disc** sich (dat) einen Band-scheibenschaden zuziehen; **a ~ped disc** ein Bandscheibenschaden m **e** (Aut) clutch schleifen lassen **f to ~ a stitch** eine Masche (ungestrickt) ab-heben **VI a** (= slide, person) (aus)rutschen; (feet, tyres) (weg)rutschen; (= become loose: knot, nut) sich lösen; (Aut: clutch) schleifen; **the knife ~ped** das Messer rutschte ab; **it ~ped from her hand** es rutschte ihr aus der Hand; **the beads ~ped through my fingers** die Perlen glitten durch meine Finger; **money ~s through her fingers** das Geld rinnt ihr (nur so) durch die Finger; **to let sth ~ through one's fingers** sich (dat) etw entgehen lassen; **the police let the thief ~ through their fingers** die Polizei ließ sich (dat) den Dieb in letzter Minute durch die Finger schlüpfen; **suddenly everything ~ped into place** plötzlich passte alles zusammen **b** (= move quickly) schlüpfen; (= move smoothly) rutschen; **I'll ~ round to the shop** ich spring schnell zum Laden; **the motorcycle ~s through the traffic** das Motorrad schlängelt sich durch den Verkehr **c to let (it) ~ that ...** fallen lassen, dass ...; **he let ~ an oath** ihm entfuhr ein Fluch; **to let a secret ~** ein Geheimnis ausplaudern; **to let a chance ~** eine Gelegenheit vorübergehen las-sen **d** (= decline: standards, morals etc) fallen; **you're ~ping!** (inf) du lässt nach (inf)

▸ **slip away** VI sich wegschleichen, sich weg-stehlen; (time) verstreichen, vergehen; (chances) (allmählich) schwinden; (opportunity) dahin-schwinden; **her life was slipping away from her** ihr Leben schwand dahin

▸ **slip back** VI **a** (= return unobtrusively) unbe-merkt zurückgehen; (quickly) schnell zurückge-hen **b** (= deteriorate, production) zurückgehen; (patient) einen Rückfall haben

▸ **slip by** VI (= pass unobtrusively, person) sich vorbeischleichen or vorbeischmuggeln (prep obj an +dat); (mistake) durchgehen; (years) verflie-gen, nur so dahinschwinden

▸ **slip down** VI (= fall) ausrutschen, ausgleiten; (= go down) hinunterlaufen; **this wine slips down easily** dieser Wein rutscht or kullert so schön (die Kehle hinunter) (inf)

▸ **slip in** VI (= enter unobtrusively) (sich) hineinschleichen; (burglar also, mistake) sich einschlei-chen **VT to ~ sth into sb's pocket** jdm etw in die Tasche gleiten lassen; **to slip a coin into a slot** eine Münze einwerfen; **she slipped the car into first gear** sie legte den ers-ten Gang ein **b** (= mention casually) einfließen lassen

▸ **slip off** VI sich wegschleichen, sich wegstehlen **VT** sep clothes, shoes ausziehen, abstreifen

▸ **slip on** VT sep schlüpfen in (+acc); dress, gloves also überstreifen, überziehen; ring aufzie-hen; lid drauftun (prep obj auf +acc); **he slipped the ring onto her finger** er steckte ihr den Ring an den Finger

▸ **slip out** VI **a** (= leave unobtrusively) kurz weg-gehen or rausgehen **b** (= be revealed) heraus-kommen; **the secret slipped out** das Geheim-nis ist ihm/ihr etc herausgerutscht

▸ **slip past** VI = slip by

▸ **slip up** VI (inf, = err) sich vertun (inf), (einen) Schnitzer machen (over, in bei); **you really slipped up there!** da hast du aber wirklich Murks gemacht (inf); **he usually slips up on spelling** meistens stolpert er über die Recht-schreibung (inf)

slip: slipcase N Schuber m; **slipcover** N (esp US) Schonbezug m; **slipknot** N Schlippstek m (spec); **slip-ons** PL (also **slip-on shoes**) Slip-per pl; **slipover** N Pullunder m

slippage ['slɪpɪdʒ] N **a** (Mech) Schlupf m, Spiel nt **b** (fig) Rückstand m; **to prevent** ~ um Rückstände zu vermeiden

slipper ['slɪpəʳ] N (= *bedroom slipper*) Pantoffel *m*, Hausschuh *m*; (= *dancing slipper*) Pumps *m*, Slipper *m*

slipperiness ['slɪpərɪnɪs] N **a** Schlüpfrigkeit *f*; (*of rope, road, ground, shoes*) Glätte *f*; (*of fish, mud*) Glitschigkeit *f* **b** (*pej inf, of person*) Glätte *f*, aalglatte Art

slippery ['slɪpərɪ] ADJ **a** schlüpfrig; *rope, road, ground* glatt, rutschig; *shoes* glatt; *fish, mud* glitschig; **the roads were ~ with ice** die Straßen waren eisglatt; **my hands were ~ with sweat** meine Hände waren ganz glitschig vor lauter Schweiß; **to be on ~ ground** (*fig*) sich auf unsicherem Boden bewegen; **he's on the ~ slope** (*fig*) er ist auf der schiefen Bahn; **it's a ~ slope** (*fig*) das ist ein gefährlicher Weg **b** (*pej inf*) *person* glatt, windig (*inf*); **a ~ customer** ein aalglatter Kerl (*inf*); **he's as ~ as they come** *or* **as an eel** er ist aalglatt

slippy ['slɪpɪ] ADJ (*inf*) **a** (= *slippery*) glatt **b** (*esp Brit*) **to look ~** einen Zahn zulegen (*inf*) (*about sth* bei etw); **... and look ~ (about it)!** ... und zwar flott *or* ein bisschen dalli! (*inf*)

slip-resistant ADJ *sole, socks etc* rutschfest, rutschsicher

slip road ['slɪprəʊd] N (*Brit*) Zufahrtsstraße *f*; (*for entering motorway*) (Autobahn)auffahrt *f*; (*for leaving motorway*) (Autobahn)ausfahrt *f*

slipshod ['slɪpʃɒd] ADJ schludrig

slip: slipsole ['slɪpsəʊl] N (*for shoes*) Einlegesohle *f*; **slipstream** N (*Aviat*) Sog *m*; (*Aut*) Windschatten *m*; **slip-up** N (*inf*) Schnitzer *m*; (*more serious*) Patzer *m*; **there's been a ~ somewhere** da muss irgendetwas schief gelaufen sein; **slipway** N (*Aut*) Ablaufbahn *f*, Gleitbahn *f*

slit [slɪt] vb: pret, ptp **slit** N Schlitz *m*; (*in castle wall also*) Schießscharte *f* VT (auf)schlitzen; **to ~ a sack open** einen Sack aufschlitzen; **to ~ sb's throat** jdm die Kehle aufschlitzen

slit-eyed ['slɪt'aɪd] (*pej*) schlitzäugig

slither ['slɪðəʳ] VI rutschen; (*snake*) gleiten; **to ~ about on the ice** auf dem Eis herumschlittern *or* -rutschen

slit: slit pocket N Durchgrifftasche *f*; **slit trench** N Splittergraben *m*

sliver ['slɪvəʳ] N (*of wood, glass etc*) Splitter *m*; (= *thin slice*) Scheibchen *nt*

Sloane (Ranger) ['sləʊn('reɪndʒəʳ)] N (*dated Brit inf*) *wohlhabendes (weibliches) Mitglied der gehobenen Mittelklasse*

slob [slɒb] N (*inf*) Drecksau *f* (*inf*)

slob out VI (*inf*) herumfaulenzen

slobber ['slɒbəʳ] N Sabber *m* (*inf*) VI sabbern, sabbeln (*also fig*); (*dog*) geifern; **to ~ over sb** (*fig inf*) von jdm schwärmen; (= *kiss*) jdn abküssen; **to ~ over sth** (*fig inf*) etw anschmachten; (*dirty old man etc*) sich an etw (*dat*) aufgeilen (*sl*)

slobbery ['slɒbərɪ] ADJ nass; **the newspaper is all ~** die Zeitung ist ganz voll gesabbert (*inf*)

sloe [sləʊ] N (= *fruit*) Schlehe *f*; (= *tree*) Schlehdorn *m*; **~ gin** Schlehdornschnaps *m*

sloe-eyed ['sləʊ'aɪd] ADJ *person* dunkeläugig

slog [slɒg] (*inf*) N **a** (= *effort*) Schinderei *f*, Plackerei *f* (*inf*); **it's a long ~ to the top of the hill** es ist eine ganz schöne Schinderei *or* Plackerei (*inf*), bis man oben ist **b** (= *stroke*) wuchtiger Schlag; **to take a ~ at sb/sth** auf jdn/etw (ein-)dreschen VT *ball* dreschen (*inf*); *opponent* hart schlagen *or* treffen VI **a** **to ~ at sth** (= *hit*) auf etw (*acc*) (ein)dreschen (*inf*); (= *work*) an etw (*dat*) schuften (*inf*); **to ~ away (at sth)** sich (mit etw) abrackern (*inf*) **b** (= *walk*) **to ~ on/along** sich weiter/dahinschleppen

slogan ['sləʊgən] N Slogan *m*; (= *motto*) Motto *nt*, Wahlspruch *m*; (*political*) Parole *f*, Slogan *m*; **advertising ~** Werbeslogan *m*, Werbespruch *m*

sloganeering [sləʊgə'nɪərɪŋ] N *Einsatz von Werbe- bzw. Wahlslogans*

slogger ['slɒgəʳ] N (*Brit inf*) Arbeitstier *nt* (*inf*)

slo-mo [ˌsləʊ'məʊ] (*inf*) abbr of **slow motion**

sloop [sluːp] N Slup *f*, Schlup *f*

slop [slɒp] VI **a** (= *spill*) (über)schwappen; **to ~ over (into sth)** überschwappen (in etw *acc*) **b** **to ~ around** (= *splash*) herumschwappen (*inf*); (*fig inf, in slippers etc*) herumschlurfen VT **a** (= *spill*) verschütten; (= *pour out*) schütten **b** (*inf: sentimental*) rühreliges Zeug, Schmalz *m* **b** (= *tasteless food: also* **slops**) Schlabber *m* (*inf*) **c** (*usu pl,* = *waste*) Schmutzwasser *nt*, Abwasser *nt*; (= *swill*) Schweinetrank *m*

▶ **slop out** VI (*in prison etc*) den/die Toiletteneimer (aus)leeren

slop basin, slop bowl N Abgussschale *f* (*Teil des Teeservice, in das Teereste gegossen werden*)

slope [sləʊp] N **a** (= *angle*) Neigung *f*; (*esp downwards*) Gefälle *nt*; (*of roof*) Schräge *f* **b** (= *sloping ground*) (Ab)hang *m*; **on a ~** am Hang; **halfway up the ~** auf halber Höhe; **there is a ~ down to the town** es fällt zur Stadt hin ab; **he broke his leg on the (ski) ~s** er hat sich das Bein *or* Bein gebrochen **c** (*Mil*) **with his rifle at the ~** mit geschultertem Gewehr VT neigen, schräg (an)legen; **~ arms!** (*Mil*) schultert Gewehr! VI **a** (*writing*) geneigt sein; (*road, garden, floor, roof, ground*) sich neigen; **the picture is sloping to the left/right** das Bild hängt schief; **his handwriting ~s to the left/backwards** seine Handschrift ist nach links/nach hinten geneigt **b** (*inf,* = *move casually*) schlendern (*inf*)

▶ **slope away** VI **a** (*ground, roof*) abfallen **b** (*inf: = slip away*) abziehen (*inf*)

▶ **slope down** VI sich neigen, abfallen

▶ **slope off** VI (*inf*) abziehen (*inf*)

▶ **slope up** VI **a** (*road etc*) ansteigen **b** (*inf: person*) herschlendern; **to slope up to sb** auf jdn zuschlendern

sloping ['sləʊpɪŋ] ADJ *hill, road* (*upwards*) ansteigend; (*downwards*) abfallend; *roof, floor* schräg, geneigt; *shoulders* abfallend; *garden, field etc* am Hang; (= *not aligned*) schief

slop pail N Eimer *m* für Schmutzwasser

sloppily ['slɒpɪlɪ] ADV (*inf: = carelessly*) schlampig (*inf*); *work* nachlässig, schlud(e)rig (*inf*); **to write/talk ~** nachlässig *or* schlampig (*inf*) schreiben/sprechen

sloppiness ['slɒpɪnɪs] N (*inf*) **a** (= *carelessness*) Schlampigkeit *f* (*inf*); (*of work, writing*) Nachlässigkeit *f*, Schlud(e)rigkeit *f* (*inf*) **b** (= *sentimentality: of film, book*) Rührseligkeit *f*

slopping out ['slɒpɪŋ'aʊt] N (*in prison etc*) *Ausleeren von Toiletteneimern in Gefängnissen*

sloppy ['slɒpɪ] ADJ (+*er*) (*inf*) **a** (= *careless*) schlampig (*inf*); *work, writing* nachlässig, schlud(e)rig (*inf*) **b** (= *sentimental*) rührselig; *film, novel also* schmalzig

sloppy joe N (= *pullover*) Schlabberpullover *m* (*inf*)

slopshop ['slɒpʃɒp] N (*pej*) Laden *m* mit billiger Konfektionsware

slosh [slɒʃ] (*inf*) VT **a** (*Brit,* = *hit*) *person* eine schmieren (+*dat*) (*inf*); *ball* dreschen **b** (= *splash*) klatschen; **don't ~ the milk around** schwapp nicht so mit der Milch herum VI **a** **to ~ (around)** (*liquid*) (herum)schwappen; **to ~ through mud/water** durch Matsch/Wasser waten

sloshed [slɒʃt] ADJ pred (*Brit inf*) blau (*inf*), voll (*inf*); **to get ~** sich besaufen (*inf*)

slot [slɒt] N (= *opening*) Schlitz *m*; (= *groove*) Rille *f*; (*Comput*) Slot *m*, Steckplatz *m*; (*for aircraft to land etc*) Slot *m*; (*inf,* = *place*) Plätzchen *nt* (*inf*); (*TV*) (gewohnte) Sendezeit; **do we have a ~ for this in our range?** können wir das in unser Programm einbauen?

▶ **slot in** VT *sep* hineinstecken; **to slot sth into sth** etw in etw (*acc*) stecken; **to slot sb/sth in** (*fig*: = *fit in*) jdn/etw dazwischenschieben; **to slot sb into the firm** jdn in der Firma unterbringen; **to slot in commercials** Werbespots

einbauen VI sich einfügen lassen; **suddenly everything slotted into place** plötzlich passte alles zusammen

▶ **slot together** VI (*parts, object*) sich zusammenfügen lassen; (*fig, pieces of mystery etc*) sich zusammenfügen, zusammenpassen VT *sep parts, object* zusammenfügen

sloth [sləʊθ] N **a** (= *laziness*) Trägheit *f*, Faulheit *f* **b** (*Zool*) Faultier *nt*

slothful ['sləʊθfʊl] ADJ faul; *person, life also* träge

slothfully ['sləʊθfəlɪ] ADV faul

slothfulness ['sləʊθfʊlnɪs] N Trägheit *f*, Faulheit *f*

slot machine N Münzautomat *m*; (*for gambling*) Spielautomat *m*

slot meter N Münzzähler *m*

slotted spoon ['slɒtɪd'spuːn] N Schaumlöffel *m*

slouch [slaʊtʃ] N **a** (= *posture*) krumme Haltung; (*of shoulders*) Hängen *nt*; (= *gait*) latschiger Gang (*inf*); **to walk with a ~** latschen, latschig gehen (*inf*) **b** (*inf,* = *incompetent or lazy person*) Niete *f* (*inf*); **to be no ~ at sth** etw ganz schön gut können (*inf*) VI (= *stand, sit*) herumhängen, sich lümmeln (*inf*); (= *move*) latschen; **to ~ off** davonzockeln (*inf*); **he was ~ed over his desk** er hing über seinem Schreibtisch, er war über seinen Schreibtisch gebeugt; **he sat ~ed on a chair** er hing auf einem Stuhl

slouch hat N Schlapphut *m*

slough¹ [slaʊ] N (*liter*) Morast *m*; (= *swamp also*) Sumpf *m* (*also fig liter*); **to sink into the Slough of Despond** (*liter*) in tiefe Verzweiflung stürzen (*liter*)

slough² [slʌf] N (*Zool*) abgestreifte Haut; (*Med*) Schorf *m* VT (*snake*) *skin* abstreifen; **it ~s (off) its skin** sie häutet sich

▶ **slough off** VT *sep skin, cells* abstreifen; *habits, cares* abwerfen, abschütteln; (*hum*) *husband* den Laufpass geben (+*dat*)

Slovak ['sləʊvæk] ADJ slowakisch N **a** Slowake *m*, Slowakin *f* **b** (*Ling*) Slowakisch *nt*

Slovakia [sləʊ'vækɪə] N die Slowakei

Slovak Republic N Slowakische Republik, die Slowakei

sloven ['slʌvn] N Schlampe *f* (*pej inf*); (= *man*) Schlamper *m* (*inf*)

Slovene ['sləʊviːn] ADJ slowenisch N **a** Slowene *m*, Slowenin *f*, Slowenier(in) *m(f)* **b** (*Ling*) Slowenisch *nt*

Slovenia [sləʊ'viːnɪə] N Slowenien *nt*

Slovenian [sləʊ'viːnɪən] ADJ, N = **Slovene**

slovenliness ['slʌvnlɪnɪs] N Schlampigkeit *f*; (*of person, work also*) Schlud(e)rigkeit *f* (*inf*)

slovenly ['slʌvnlɪ] ADJ schlud(e)rig (*inf*), schlampig (*inf*); *appearance, person also* verlottert (*inf*)

slow [sləʊ] ADJ (+*er*) **a** langsam; **it's ~ work** das braucht seine Zeit; **he's a ~ learner/reader** er lernt/liest langsam; **it was ~ going** es ging nur langsam voran; **to get off to a ~ start** (*race*) schlecht vom Start kommen; (*project*) nur langsam in Gang kommen; **at (a) ~ speed** mit langsamer Geschwindigkeit; **this method is ~ but sure** dieses Verfahren ist langsam, aber sicher; **to be ~ to do sth** sich (*dat*) mit etw Zeit lassen; **to be ~ in doing sth** sich (*dat*) Zeit damit lassen, etw zu tun; **not to be ~ to do sth** *or* **in doing sth** etw prompt erledigen; **he is ~ to make up his mind** er braucht lange, um sich zu entscheiden; **he is ~ to anger** er wird nicht so leicht wütend; **they were ~ to act** sie ließen sich (*dat*) Zeit; **to be (20 minutes) ~** (*clock*) (20 Minuten) nachgehen

b (= *stupid*) *person* langsam, begriffsstutzig → **uptake**

c (= *dull*) *person, place, event* langweilig

d (*Comm*: = *slack*) flau; **business is ~** das Geschäft ist flau *or* geht schleppend

e (= *unhurried*) ruhig; **life there is ~** das Leben dort ist ruhig

f (= *slowing down movement*) *surface, track, pitch*

langsam; (*because of rain etc*) schwer; (= *slow-burning*) *fire* langsam brennend; **bake in a ~ oven** bei schwacher Hitze backen

ADV (*+er*) langsam; **to go ~** (*driver*) langsam fahren; (*workers*) einen Bummelstreik machen; **~-spoken** langsam sprechend; **"slow"** (*on sign*) „langsam fahren"

VI sich verlangsamen; (= *drive/walk more slowly*) langsamer fahren/gehen; (*inflation*) abnehmen; **to ~ to a stop/standstill** langsam zum Halten/zum Stillstand kommen

VT verlangsamen; **he ~ed his horse to a walk** er ließ sein Pferd langsamer gehen; **he ~ed his speed to 30 miles an hour** er verminderte seine Geschwindigkeit auf 30 Meilen pro Stunde

▶ **slow down** *or* **up** **VI** sich verlangsamen; (= *drive/walk more slowly*) langsamer fahren/gehen; (*worker*) langsamer arbeiten; (*inflation*) abnehmen; **if you don't slow down** *or* **up you'll make yourself ill** Sie müssen zurückstecken, sonst werden Sie krank; **my mind has slowed down** ich werde immer langsamer im Denken **VT** *sep* (*lit*) verlangsamen; *engine* drosseln; *machine* herunterschalten; (*fig*) *project* verzögern, verlangsamen; **to slow the car down** langsamer fahren; **you just slow me up** *or* **down** du hältst mich nur auf; **we should slow things down** *or* **up** wir sollten etwas langsamer machen (*inf*)

slow: slow-acting ADJ *poison* langsam wirkend; (*Tech also*) träge (ansprechend); *medicine, therapy* Langzeit-; **slow-burning** ADJ *candle* langsam herunterbrennend; *fire also* langsam brennend; (*fig*) *rage, anger* schwelend; **~ stove** Dauerbrandofen *m*; **slowcoach** N (*Brit inf*) Langweiler(in) *m(f)*; (*mentally*) Transuse *f* (*inf*); **slow cooker** N Reiskocher *m*; **slowdown** N **a** (= *slowing*) Verlangsamung *f* (*in, of +gen*) **b** (*US*, = *go-slow*) Bummelstreik *m*; **slow film** N unempfindlicher Film; **slow fuse** N Zündschnur *f*; **slow handclap** N rhythmisches Klatschen (*zum Zeichen des Protests*); **to give sb the/a ~** durch Klatschen gegen jdn protestieren; **slow lane** N (*Aut*) Kriechspur *f*; **life in the ~** (*fig*) das ruhige *or* gemächliche Leben

slowly [ˈsləʊlɪ] ADV langsam; **~ but surely** langsam aber sicher

slow: slow march N Trauermarsch *m*; **slow match** N (*Mil Hist*) Zündschnur *f*, Lunte *f*; **slow motion** N Zeitlupe *f*; **in ~** in Zeitlupe; **slow-motion** ADJ **a ~ shot** eine Einstellung in Zeitlupe; **slow-moving** ADJ sich (nur) langsam bewegend; *traffic* kriechend; *river* langsam fließend; *bureaucracy* träge, schwerfällig; *plot* langatmig; *film* langsam

slowness [ˈsləʊnɪs] N **a** Langsamkeit *f*; **their ~ to act** ihr Zaudern **b** (= *stupidity: of person*) Begriffsstutzigkeit *f*; **~ of mind** Begriffsstutzigkeit *f* **c** (= *inactivity: of party, film, plot*) Lahmheit *f*, Langweiligkeit *f* **d** (*Comm: = slackness*) Flaute *f* **e** (*slowing down movement*) (*of surface, track, pitch*) Langsamkeit *f*; (*because of rain etc*) Schwere *f*

slow: slow poison N schleichendes Gift; **slowpoke** N (*US, inf*) = **slowcoach**; **slow puncture** N (*esp Brit*) langsam Luft ablassendes Loch *nt* in einem Reifen; **slow train** N (*Brit*) Personenzug *m*, Bummelzug *m* (*inf*); **slow virus** N Slow-Virus *m*; **slow-witted** ADJ begriffsstutzig, schwer von Begriff; **slowworm** N Blindschleiche *f*

sludge [slʌdʒ] N Schlamm *m*, Matsch *m* (*inf*); (= *sediment*) schmieriger Satz

slue N, VTI (*US*) = **slew¹**, **slew²**

slug¹ [slʌg] N Nacktschnecke *f*; **~s and snails** Schnecken *pl* (mit und ohne Gehäuse)

slug² N **a** (= *bullet*) Kugel *f* **b** (*Typ, = piece of metal*) Reglette *f*; (= *line*) (Setzmaschinen)zeile *f* **c** (*inf*) **a ~ of whisky** ein Schluck *m* Whisky

slug³ (*inf*, = *hit*) **VT** (eine) knallen (*+dat*) (*inf*) **N** gehöriger *or* tüchtiger Schlag (*inf*); **to give sb a ~** jdm eine knallen (*inf*)

slugabed [ˈslʌgəbed] N Langschläfer(in) *m(f)*

sluggard [ˈslʌgəd] N Faulpelz *m*

sluggardly [ˈslʌgədlɪ] ADJ faul, träge

slugger [ˈslʌgəʳ] N (*inf*) Schläger(in) *m(f)* (*inf*); (*Baseball*) Schmetterer *m*

sluggish [ˈslʌgɪʃ] ADJ (= *indolent, also Med*) träge; *engine, car* lahm, langsam; *temperament* phlegmatisch; *steps* schwerfällig; *river* träge; *business* flau; *market, stock exchange* flau, lustlos

sluggishly [ˈslʌgɪʃlɪ] ADV *move, flow* träge; *walk* schwerfällig; (*Comm*) flau, lustlos

sluggishness [ˈslʌgɪʃnɪs] N (= *indolence, also Med*) Trägheit *f*; (*of engine, car*) Lahmheit *f*; (*of temperament*) Phlegma *nt*; (*of steps, pace*) Schwerfälligkeit *f*; (*of river*) Trägheit *f*; **the ~ of the market** die Flaute am Markt; **the ~ of the business** die geschäftliche Flaute

sluice [sluːs] **N** Schleuse *f*; (*Min*) (Wasch)rinne *f*; **to give the car/wall a ~ down** Wasser über das Auto/gegen die Wand schütten; (*with hose*) das Auto/die Wand abspritzen **VT** *ore* waschen; **to ~ sth (down)** etw abspritzen **VI** **to ~ out** herausschießen

sluice: sluicegate [ˈsluːsgeɪt] N Schleusentor *nt*; **sluiceway** N (Schleusen)kanal *m*

slum [slʌm] **N** (*usu pl: = area*) Slum *m*, Elendsviertel *nt*; (= *house*) Elendsquartier *nt*; **to live in the ~s** in den Slums leben **VI** (*also* **go slumming**) sich unters gemeine Volk mischen **VTI** (*inf: also* **slum it**) primitiv leben; **we don't often see you (a)round here – I'm ~ming (it)** du lässt dich doch sonst kaum hier sehen! – ich misch mich eben mal unters gemeine Volk mischen

slumber [ˈslʌmbəʳ] (*liter*) **N** Schlummer *m* (*geh*), Schlaf *m*; **~s** Schlummer *m*, Träume *pl*; (*fig: intellectual etc*) Dornröschenschlaf *m*; **to disturb sb's ~s** jds Schlummer stören **VI** schlummern (*geh*)

slumb(e)rous [ˈslʌmb(ə)rəs] ADJ (*liter*, = *sleepy*) schläfrig; (= *inducing sleep*) einschläfernd, einlullend

slumber party N (*esp US*) Party, bei der Jugendliche im Elternhaus eines Teilnehmers feiern und anschließend auch dort schlafen

slum: slum children PL Slumkinder *pl*; **slum clearance** N ≈ (Stadt)sanierung *f*, Beseitigung *f* der Slums; **slum dweller** N Slumbewohner(in) *m(f)*

slummy [ˈslʌmɪ] ADJ (*+er*) (*inf*) verwahrlost; **~ district** Slumgegend *f*

slump [slʌmp] **N** (*in sth* etw *gen*) (*in numbers, popularity, morale etc*) (plötzliche) Abnahme; (*in production, sales*) Rückgang *m*; (= *state*) Tiefstand *m*; (*Fin*) Sturz *m*, Baisse *f* (*spec*); (*of prices*) plötzliches Absinken; **~ in prices** Preissturz *m* (*of* bei); **the 1929 Slump** die Weltwirtschaftskrise von 1929 **VI a** (*also* **slump off**, *Fin, Comm, prices*) stürzen, fallen; (*sales, production*) plötzlich zurückgehen; (*fig, morale etc*) sinken, fallen **b** (= *sink*) fallen, sinken; **to ~ into a chair** sich in einen Sessel fallen *or* plumpsen (*inf*) lassen; **he was ~ed over the wheel** er war über dem Steuer zusammengesackt; **he was ~ed on the floor** er lag in sich (*dat*) zusammengesunken auf dem Fußboden

slum schools PL Schulen *pl* in den Slums

slung [slʌŋ] *pret, ptp of* **sling**

slunk [slʌŋk] *pret, ptp of* **slink**

slur [slɜːʳ] **N a** Makel *m*, Schandfleck *m*; (= *insult*) Beleidigung *f*; **to cast a ~ on sb/sth** jdn/etw in schlechtes Licht erscheinen lassen; (*person*) jdn/etw verunglimpfen; **it is no ~ on him to say that ...** es geht nicht gegen ihn, wenn man sagt, dass ... **b** (*Mus, = mark*) Bindebogen *m*; (= *notes*) Bindung *f* **c** **to speak with a ~** unartikuliert sprechen **VT a** (= *pronounce indistinctly*) undeutlich artikulieren; *words, syllable* (halb) verschlucken, verschleifen **b** (*Mus*) binden, gebunden spielen/singen

▶ **slur over** VI +prep obj hinweggehen über (+acc)

slurp [slɜːp] **VTI** (*inf*) schlürfen **N** Schlürfen *nt*; **to drink sth with a ~** etw schlürfen

slurred [slɜːd] **ADJ** undeutlich; (*Mus*) *note* gebunden **ADV** (*Mus*) gebunden

slush [slʌʃ] N (= *watery snow*) (Schnee)matsch *m*; (= *mud*) Matsch *m*, Morast *m*; (*inf, = sentimental nonsense*) Kitsch *m*

slush fund N Schmiergelder *pl*, Schmiergeldfonds *m*

slush pile N (*Publishing inf*) unaufgefordert eingesandte Manuskripte

slushy [ˈslʌʃɪ] ADJ (*+er*) *snow* matschig; *mud, path also* morastig; (*inf, = sentimental*) kitschig

slut [slʌt] (*inf*) N (liederliche) Schlampe (*inf*)

sluttish [ˈslʌtɪʃ] ADJ liederlich

sly [slaɪ] **ADJ** (*+er*) **a** (= *cunning*) schlau, gerissen; *person, look also* verschlagen **b** (= *mischievous*) *look, wink* verschmitzt; *humour* versteckt **N** **on the ~** heimlich, still und leise (*hum*), ganz heimlich

slyboots [ˈslaɪbuːts] N pl **-boots** (*inf*) Schlauberger(in) *m(f)* (*inf, hum*)

slyly [ˈslaɪlɪ] ADV **a** (= *cunningly*) schlau; *say, look at* listig **b** (= *mischievously*) *look, wink* verschmitzt

slyness [ˈslaɪnɪs] N **a** (= *cunning*) Schlauheit *f*, Gerissenheit *f*; (*of person, look also*) Verschlagenheit *f* **b** (= *mischievousness: of look*) Verschmitztheit *f*

smack¹ [smæk] **N** (= *taste*) (leichter) Geschmack (*of* nach), Spur *f* (*of* von); (= *smell*) (leichter) Geruch (*of* nach), Hauch *m* (*of* von); (*fig*) Spur *f* (*of* von) **VI** **to ~ of** (= *taste*) leicht schmecken nach; (= *smell*) leicht riechen nach; (*fig*) riechen nach

smack² **N a** (klatschender) Schlag; (= *slap also*) fester Klaps; (= *sound*) Klatschen *nt*; **to give a child a (hard) ~** ein Kind eine knallen (*inf*); **you'll get a ~** du fängst gleich eine (*inf*); **a ~ in the eye** (*fig*) ein Schlag *m* ins Gesicht; **to have a ~ at sth** (*esp Brit, fig inf*) an etw (*acc*) rangehen (*inf*), etw mal probieren (*inf*) **b** (*inf: = kiss*) **to give sb a ~ on the cheek** jdn einen Schmatz auf die Backe geben (*inf*) **VT** (= *slap*) knallen (*inf*); **to ~ a child** einem Kind eine runterhauen (*inf*); **to ~ sb's face** jdn ins Gesicht schlagen (*inf*); **to ~ one's hands (together)** in die Hände klatschen; **to ~ one's thigh** sich (*dat*) auf den Schenkel klatschen; **I'll ~ your bottom, you'll get a ~ed bottom** ich versohl dir gleich den Hintern! (*inf*) → **lip** **ADV** (*inf*) direkt; **he kissed her ~ on the lips** er gab ihr einen Schmatzer (*inf*); **she ran ~ into the door** sie rannte rums! gegen die Tür (*inf*); **~ in front of sth** genau vor etw (*dat*); **to be ~ in the middle of sth** mittendrin in etw (*dat*) sein; **the office was ~ in the middle of the building site** das Büro befand sich mitten auf der Baustelle; **~ on 4 o'clock** Punkt 4 Uhr

smack³ N (*Naut*) Schmack(e) *f*

smack⁴ N (*inf: = heroin*) Heroin *nt*

smacker [ˈsmækəʳ] N **a** (*inf: = kiss*) Schmatzer *m* (*inf*) **b** (= *blow*) Klaps *m* **c** (= *money*) Pfund *nt*; Dollar *m*

smackhead [ˈsmækhed] N (*sl*) Heroinfixer(in) *m(f)*

smacking [ˈsmækɪŋ] N Tracht *f* Prügel; **to give sb a good ~** jdn tüchtig verdreschen (*inf*)

small [smɔːl] **ADJ** (*+er*) **a** klein; *supply, stock* klein, gering; *waist* schmal; (= *not much*) *reason, desire* wenig, gering; *effort* gering; **~ in size** von geringer Größe, klein; **a ~ number of people** eine geringe Anzahl von Leuten; **the ~est possible number of books** so wenig Bücher wie möglich; **to have a ~ appetite** keinen großen Appetit haben; **it's written with a ~ "e"** es wird mit kleinem „e" geschrieben; **~ shareholder** Kleinaktionär(in) *m(f)*; **no ~ success** ein beachtlicher Erfolg; **to feel ~** (*fig*) sich (ganz) klein (und hässlich) vorkommen; **to look ~** (*fig*) schlecht aussehen *or* dastehen; **he/it made me feel pretty ~** da kam ich mir ziemlich klein vor; **to be of ~ concern to sb** jdn nur wenig betreffen

b (= *unimportant, minor*) klein; *present, sum*

klein, bescheiden; *importance, consequence* gering; **a few ~ matters/problems** ein paar Kleinigkeiten; **to be of no ~ consequence** nicht unbeträchtliche Folgen haben; **this is no ~ matter** das ist keine Kleinigkeit; **to help/contribute in a ~ way** bescheidene Hilfe/einen bescheidenen Beitrag leisten; **to start in a ~ way** bescheiden *or* klein anfangen

c (= *quiet*) *voice* leise; **to say sth in a ~ voice** etw mit leiser Stimme sagen

d (*fig*, = *mean, petty*) *person* kleinlich

N **a** **the ~ of the back** das Kreuz

b **smalls** PL (*Brit, inf*) Unterwäsche *f*

ADV **to chop sth up ~** etw klein hacken

small: small ads PL (*Brit*) Kleinanzeigen *pl*; **small arms** PL Handfeuerwaffen *pl*; **small beer** N (*old*) Dünnbier *nt*; **he's very ~** (*inf*) er ist ein kleiner Fisch (*inf*); **small-bore** ADJ kleinkalibrig; **small business** N Kleinunternehmen *nt*; **small businessman** N Kleinunternehmer *m*; **small capitals** PL Kapitälchen *pl*; **small change** N Kleingeld *nt*; **small claims court** N Zivilgericht *nt* (*für Bagatellfälle*); **small fry** PL (= *unimportant people*) kleine Fische *pl* (*inf*); **smallholder** N Kleinbauer *m*, Kleinbäuerin *f*; **smallholding** N kleiner Landbesitz; **small hours** PL früher Morgen; **in the** (**wee**) **~** in den frühen Morgenstunden; **small intestine** N Dünndarm *m*

smallish [ˈsmɔːlɪʃ] ADJ (eher) kleiner; **he is ~** er ist eher klein; **a ~ number of sth/people** eine geringe Anzahl an etw (*dat*)/von Leuten

small: small letter N Kleinbuchstabe *m*; **small-minded** ADJ *person, attitude* engstirnig; **small-mindedness** N Engstirnigkeit *f*

smallness [ˈsmɔːlnɪs] N Kleinheit *f*; (*of sum, present*) Bescheidenheit *f*; (= *pettiness*) Kleinlichkeit *f*

small: small potatoes PL (*esp US fig inf*) kleine Fische *pl* (*inf*); **smallpox** N Pocken *pl*, Blattern *pl* (*old*); **smallpox vaccination** N Pockenimpfung *f*; **small print** N **the ~** das Kleingedruckte; **in ~** klein gedruckt; **small-scale** ADJ *map, model* in verkleinertem Maßstab; *project, study* klein angelegt; *war, conflict* begrenzt; **~ farmers** Kleinbauern *pl*; **~ industry** Kleinindustrie *f*; **~ integration** (*Comput*) niedriger Integrationsgrad; **small screen** N (*TV*) **on the ~** auf dem Bildschirm; **small-sized** ADJ klein; **small talk** N oberflächliche Konversation, Smalltalk *m*, Small Talk *m*; **she has no ~** oberflächliche *or* höfliche Konversation liegt ihr nicht; **to make ~** plaudern, Smalltalk *or* Small Talk machen; **to engage in** *or* **make ~ with sb** höflich mit jdm Konversation machen; **small-time** ADJ (*inf*) mickerig (*inf*), armselig; *crook* klein; **~ politician/reporter** Schmalspurpolitiker(in) *m(f)*/-reporter(in) *m(f)*; **small-town** ADJ Kleinstadt-, kleinstädtisch; **~ life** Kleinstadtleben *nt*; **~ America** die amerikanische Provinz

---

SMALL TOWN

In den USA wird mit dem Begriff **small town** jede Ortschaft mit bis zu 10.000 Einwohnern bezeichnet. Das Wort **village** wird in den Vereinigten Staaten für eine Kleinstadt selten verwendet, da der Begriff mit Europa oder auch der Dritten Welt assoziiert wird. Eine **small town** ist in der Vorstellung der Amerikaner normalerweise mit positiven Werten verbunden, wie Freundlichkeit, Ehrlichkeit, Höflichkeit, Nachbarschaftshilfe und Vaterlandsliebe. Allerdings kann **small town** manchmal auch negative Seiten repräsentieren: so versteht man unter „small-town attitudes" vorurteilsbehaftete und engstirnige Ansichten.

---

smarm [smɑːm] (*Brit, inf*) **VT** **to ~ one's hair down** sich (*dat*) das Haar anklatschen (*inf*) *or* an den Kopf kleben **VI** **to ~ up to sb** sich an jdn heranschmeißen (*inf*); **to ~ one's way into sb's confidence** sich in jds Vertrauen (*acc*) einschleichen **N** Kriecherei *f*

smarmy [ˈsmɑːmɪ] ADJ (+*er*) (*Brit inf*, = *greasy*) schmierig; (= *ingratiating*) kriecherisch (*pej*); *voice* einschmeichelnd

smart [smɑːt] ADJ (+*er*) **a** schick; *person, clothes, car* schick, flott; *society* fein; (= *not shabby*) *appearance* gepflegt; **a ~-looking girl** ein flott aussehendes Mädchen; **a ~-looking garden** ein gepflegter Garten; **the ~ set** die Schickeria (*inf*)

b (= *bright, clever*) clever (*inf*), schlau, gewitzt; *thief, trick* raffiniert, clever (*inf*); (*pej*) *person, answer* superklug, neunmalklug (*pej inf*); (*Comput, Mil*) intelligent; **that wasn't very ~ (of you)** das war nicht besonders intelligent (von dir); **to get ~** (*US inf*) sich am Riemen reißen (*inf*); (= *get cheeky*) frech kommen (*with* +*dat*); **he thinks it's ~ to criticize his parents** er kommt sich toll vor, wenn er seine Eltern kritisiert

c (= *quick*) (blitz)schnell; *pace, work* rasch, flott (*inf*); *work* schnell, fix (*inf*); **and look ~ (about it)!** und zwar ein bisschen fix *or* plötzlich! (*inf*)

N Schmerz *m* (*also fig*); (*of ointment, from wound also*) Brennen *nt*

VI brennen; **it will make the cut ~** es wird in der Schnittwunde brennen; **to ~ under sth** (*fig*) unter etw (*dat*) leiden; **he is still ~ing after the criticism** die Kritik tut ihm immer noch weh; **to ~ from sth** (*from blow etc*) von etw brennen; (*fig*) unter etw (*dat*) leiden; **to ~ over sth** über etw (*acc*) gekränkt sein

smart: smart alec(k) N (*inf*) Schlauberger(in) *m(f)* (*inf*), Besserwisser(in) *m(f)*; **smart-alec(k)** ADJ (*inf*) besserwisserisch, superschlau (*inf*); *child* neunmalklug (*pej inf*); **smartarse** [ˈsmɑːtɑːs], (*US*) **smartass** [ˈsmɑːtæs] (*sl*) **N** Klugscheißer(in) *m(f)* (*inf*) ADJ klugscheißerisch (*inf*); **smart bomb** N intelligente Bombe; **smart card** N Chipkarte *f*; **smart drug** N bewusstseinsverändernde Droge

smarten [ˈsmɑːtn] (*also* **smarten up**) **VT** *house, room* herausputzen; *appearance* (her)richten, aufmöbeln (*inf*); **to ~ oneself up** (= *dress up*) sich in Schale werfen (*inf*); (= *generally improve appearance*) mehr Wert auf sein Äußeres legen; **you'd better ~ up your ideas** (*inf*) du solltest dich am Riemen reißen (*inf*) **VI** (= *dress up*) sich in Schale werfen (*inf*); (= *improve appearance*) sich herausmachen; (*pace*) schneller *or* flotter (*inf*) werden

smartly [ˈsmɑːtlɪ] ADV **a** (= *elegantly*) schick; *dress* schick, flott **b** (= *cleverly*) clever (*inf*), schlau, gewitzt; (*pej*) superschlau (*inf*), neunmalklug (*pej inf*) **c** (= *quickly*) (blitz)schnell, fix (*inf*); *walk* rasch

smart money N (*Fin*) Investitionsgelder *pl*; **the ~ is on him winning** Insider setzen darauf, dass er gewinnt

smartness [ˈsmɑːtnɪs] N **a** (= *elegance, of person, clothes, car*) Schick *m*; (*of appearance*) Gepflegtheit *f* **b** (= *brightness, cleverness*) Cleverness *f* (*inf*), Schlauheit *f*, Gewitztheit *f*; (*of thief, trick*) Raffiniertheit *f*; (*pej, of person*) Besserwisserei *f* (*pej*); (*of answer*) Vorwitzigkeit *f* **c** (= *quickness*) Schnelligkeit *f*, Fixheit *f* (*inf*); (*of pace*) Raschheit *f*

smarty(-pants) [ˈsmɑːtɪ(ˌpænts)] N *sing* (*inf*) Schlaumeier(in) *m(f)*, Schlauberger(in) *m(f)* (*inf*)

smash [smæʃ] **VT** **a** (= *break into pieces*) zerschlagen; *window* einschlagen; **I ~ed my glasses** mir ist die Brille kaputtgegangen; **I ~ed my knee** ich habe mir das Knie aufgeschlagen

b (= *defeat or destroy*) zerschlagen; *rebellion, revolution* niederschlagen, zerschlagen; *opponent* zerschmettern; *record* haushoch schlagen; *business* ruinieren

c (= *strike, also Tennis*) schmettern; **he ~ed his fist into his face** er schlug ihm mit der Faust ins Gesicht; **he ~ed him on the nose** er schlug ihm auf die Nase; **he ~ed his way through the mob** er musste sich (*dat*) gewaltsam einen Weg durch den Mob bahnen; **to ~ one's way into a building** gewaltsam in ein Gebäude eindringen **VI** **a** (= *break*) zerschlagen, zerbrechen; **it ~ed into a thousand pieces** es (zer)sprang in tausend Stücke

b (= *crash*) prallen; **the car ~ed into the wall** das Auto krachte gegen die Mauer; **the terrified animal ~ed through the fence** das verängstigte Tier durchbrach das Gatter; **the plane ~ed into the houses** das Flugzeug raste in eine Häusergruppe; **the ship ~ed onto the rocks** das Schiff prallte gegen die Felsen; **the sound of the waves ~ing against the rocks** das Geräusch der gegen die Felsen klatschenden Wellen

N **a** (= *noise*) Krachen *nt*; (*of waves*) Klatschen *nt*; **there was a ~** es hat gekracht *or* (*of broken glass*) gescheppert

b (= *collision*) Unfall *m*; (*esp with another vehicle*) Zusammenstoß *m*; **rail ~** Zugunglück *nt*

c (= *blow*) Schlag *m*; (*Tennis*) Smash *m*, Schmetterball *m*

d (*inf*: = *success*: *also* **smash hit**) Riesenhit *m* ADV (*inf*) mit Karacho (*inf*)

▶ **smash in** VT *sep* einschlagen; **the firemen had to smash their way in** die Feuerwehrleute mussten gewaltsam eindringen; **to smash sb's face in** (*inf*) Hackfleisch aus jdm machen (*inf*)

▶ **smash up** VT *sep* zertrümmern; *face* übel zurichten; *car* kaputtfahren (*inf*), kaputtgehen; **the capsule completely smashed up on landing** die Kapsel zerschellte bei der Landung

smash-and-grab (raid) [ˌsmæʃənˈgræb(reɪd)] N Schaufenstereinbruch *m*

smashed [smæʃt] ADJ *pred* (*inf*) total zu (*inf*)

smasher [ˈsmæʃə] N (*esp Brit inf*) toller Typ (*inf*); (= *woman also*) Klassefrau *f* (*inf*); **to be a ~** eine Wucht (*inf*) *or* (ganz große) Klasse sein (*inf*)

smash hit N (*inf*) Superhit *m* (*inf*); **her new boyfriend was a ~ with her family** ihr neuer Freund kam bei ihrer Familie unwahrscheinlich gut an (*inf*)

smashing [ˈsmæʃɪŋ] ADJ (*esp Brit, inf*) klasse *inv*, Klasse *pred*, dufte (*all inf*); **isn't it ~!** unheimlich dufte! (*inf*)

smash-up [ˈsmæʃʌp] N (*Brit: Aut, Rail*) übler Unfall; (*esp with another vehicle*) Karambolage *f*

smatterer [ˈsmætərə] N Stümperer *m* (*pej*), Stümperin *f* (*pej*)

smattering [ˈsmætərɪŋ] N **a ~ of French** ein paar Brocken Französisch

smear [smɪə] **N** verschmierter Fleck; (*fig*) Beschmutzung *f*, Verleumdung *f*; (*Med*) Abstrich *m*; **he had ~s of blood/grease on his hands** er hatte blut-/fettbeschmierte Hände; **this left a ~ on the institution** das hinterließ einen Fleck auf dem guten Namen der Institution; **he angrily repudiated their ~s** empört wies er ihre Verleumdungen zurück

VT **a** *grease, ointment* schmieren; (= *spread*) verschmieren; (= *mark, make dirty*) beschmieren; *face, body* einschmieren; **don't ~ the paint** verschmiere die Farbe nicht!

b (*fig*) *person* verunglimpfen; *sb's reputation, name* beschmutzen, besudeln; *organization* in den Schmutz ziehen

VI (*glass*) verschmieren; (*print*) verschmiert *or* verwischt werden; (*ballpoint pen*) schmieren; (*paint, ink*) verlaufen

smear: smear campaign N Verleumdungskampagne *f*; **smear tactics** PL Verleumdungstaktiken *pl*; **smear test** N (*Med*) Abstrich *m*; **smear word** N Schimpfwort *nt*

smeary [ˈsmɪərɪ] ADJ (+*er*) *glass* verschmiert; *clothes* schmierig; (= *likely to smear*) *paint, ink* schmierend

smell [smel] *vb*: *pret, ptp* **smelt** (*esp Brit*) *or* **smelled** **N** (= *sense of smell, odour*) Geruch *m*; (*unpleasant also*) Gestank *m*; (*fragrant also*) Duft *m*; **it has a nice ~** es riecht gut *or* angenehm; **there's a funny ~ in here** hier riecht es komisch; **to have** *or* **take a ~ at sth** an etw (*acc*) riechen *or* (*dog etc*) schnuppern

VT **a** (*lit*) riechen; **can** *or* **do you ~ burning?** riechst du, dass etwas brennt *or* (*Cook*) anbrennt?; **first he ~s the wine** zunächst einmal riecht er an dem Wein

b (*fig*) *danger* wittern; **to ~ trouble** Ärger *or* Stunk (*inf*) kommen sehen; **to ~ a rat** (*inf*)

Lunte or den Braten riechen, etw spitzkriegen; **aha, I can ~ a rat** (inf) da scheint mir doch etwas faul zu sein!

VI riechen; (unpleasantly also) stinken; (fragrantly also) duften; **that ~s!** (lit, fig) das stinkt!; **to ~ of sth** (lit, fig) nach etw riechen; **his breath ~s** er riecht aus dem Mund, er hat Mundgeruch; **can fish ~?** können Fische riechen?

▶**smell out** VT sep **a** rabbit, traitor etc aufspüren; plot aufdecken **b** these onions are smelling the house out! die Zwiebeln verpesten das ganze Haus!

smelling bottle ['smelɪŋˌbɒtl] N Riechfläschchen nt

smelling salts ['smelɪŋˌsɔːlts] PL Riechsalz nt

smelly ['smelɪ] ADJ (+er) übel riechend, stinkend; **it's ~ in here** hier drin stinkt es; **~ cheese** (inf) Stinkkäse m (inf); **you've got ~ feet** deine Füße stinken; **come here, ~!** komm her, du kleines Stinktier! (inf)

smelt[1] [smelt] (esp Brit) pret, ptp of **smell**

smelt[2] VT ore schmelzen; (= refine) verhütten

smelt[3] N pl -(s) (= fish) Stint m

smelter ['smeltə] N (= furnace) Schmelzhütte f, Schmelzerei f; (= person) Schmelzer(in) m(f)

smidgen, smidgin ['smɪdʒən] N (inf) **just a ~ for me** für mich nur ein (klitzekleines (inf)) bisschen

smile [smaɪl] **N** Lächeln nt; **there was a sarcastic ~ on his face** ein sarkastisches Lächeln ging über sein Gesicht; **to be all ~s** übers ganze Gesicht strahlen; **she gave a little ~** sie lächelte schwach or ein bisschen; **to give sb a ~** jdm zulächeln; **come on, give me a ~** lach doch mal!; **take that ~ off your face!** hör auf, so zu grinsen!

VI lächeln; **we tried to make the baby ~** wir versuchten, das Baby zum Lachen zu bringen; **come on, ~** lach mal!; **~ for the camera!** bitte recht freundlich!; **he's always smiling** er lacht immer; **keep smiling!** keep smiling!; **he kept smiling through all his troubles** trotz aller Schwierigkeiten ließ er den Kopf nicht hängen; **to ~ at sb** jdn anlächeln; (cheerful person) jdn anlachen; **to ~ at sth** über etw (acc) lächeln; **to ~ at danger** der Gefahr (dat) ins Gesicht lachen; **to ~ with pleasure/relief** etc vor Freude/Erleichterung etc strahlen; **fortune ~d on him** (liter) ihm lachte das Glück

VT **she ~d her thanks** sie lächelte dankbar; **he ~d a bitter ~** er lächelte bitter

smiley ['smaɪlɪ] ADJ **a** face, eyes, person freundlich **b** (on computer bulletin boards etc) **~ badge** Smileybutton m; **~ symbol** Smileysymbol nt **N** (on computer bulletin boards etc) Smiley nt

smiling ADJ , **smilingly** ADV ['smaɪlɪŋ, -lɪ] lächelnd

smirch [smɜːtʃ] (liter) **N** Schmutz- or Schandfleck m, Makel m (geh) **VT** beflecken (liter), besudeln (geh)

smirk [smɜːk] **N** Grinsen nt **VI** grinsen, süffisant lächeln

smite [smaɪt] pret smote, ptp smitten VT (old, liter) schlagen; **he smote off his head** er schlug or hieb ihm den Kopf ab; **the sound of gunfire smote our ears** der Lärm von Schüssen schlug an unsere Ohren; **and the Lord shall ~ them down** und der Herr wird sie zerschmettern

smith [smɪθ] N Schmied(in) m(f)

smithereens [ˌsmɪðə'riːnz] PL **to smash sth to ~** etw in tausend Stücke schlagen; **in ~** in tausend Stücken

smithery ['smɪθərɪ] N Schmiedekunst f, Schmiedehandwerk nt; (= single piece of work) Schmiedearbeit f

---

SMITHSONIAN INSTITUTION

Die **Smithsonian Institution** ist der weltweit größte Museumskomplex, der sich in Washington, DC befindet und von der US-Regierung als ein Zentrum für Wissenschaft und Künste unterstützt wird. Der amerikanische Kongress gründete das Institut 1846 mit den finanziellen Mitteln, die der englische Wissenschaftler James Smithson den Vereinigten Staaten zur Förderung der Wissenschaften hinterlassen hatte. Mittlerweile umfasst es eine Sammlung von rund 100 Millionen Kunstwerken und anderen Ausstellungsstücken in 14 Museen, wie zum Beispiel dem **National Air and Space Museum**, dem **National Museum of American History**, dem **National Museum of the American Indian**, der **National Gallery of Art** und der **National Portrait Gallery**. Das **Smithsonian** wird im Volksmund auch „the nation's attic" genannt, weil sich dort wie auf einem Speicher alles Mögliche ansammelt. Es hat sogar einen Zoo und führt Forschungen in allen Wissenschaftsbereichen durch.

---

smithy ['smɪðɪ] N Schmiede f

smitten ['smɪtn] ptp of **smite** ADJ **to be ~ with the plague** von der Pest heimgesucht werden; **to be ~ with remorse/fear** von Reue/Angst geplagt werden; **to be ~ with pity** von Mitleid ergriffen sein; **he's really ~ with her** (inf) er ist wirklich vernarrt in sie; **he's really ~ this time** (inf) diesmal hats ihn erwischt (inf); **I've never seen him so ~** (inf) ich habe ihn noch nie so vernarrt gesehen; **to be ~ with sth** (= captivated) von etw begeistert sein; **do you like it? – I'm not ~ with it** gefällt es dir? – ich bin nicht erpicht darauf

smock [smɒk] **N** Kittel m; (as top) Hänger m **VT** smoken

smocking ['smɒkɪŋ] N Smokarbeit f

smog [smɒg] N Smog m

smoggy ['smɒgɪ] ADJ (+er) city, sky, air versmogt

smoke [smǝʊk] **N** **a** Rauch m; **there's no ~ without fire, where there's ~ there's fire** (prov) wo Rauch ist, da ist auch Feuer (prov); **to go up in ~** in Rauch (und Flammen) aufgehen; (fig) sich in Wohlgefallen auflösen; (inf: = get angry) in die Luft gehen (inf); **it's all ~ and mirrors** (US) das ist nur Blendwerk

b (inf: = cigarette etc) was zu rauchen (inf); **have you got a ~?** hast du was zu rauchen? (inf); **it's a good ~, this tobacco** dieser Tabak raucht sich gut; **~s** Glimmstengel pl (dated inf)

c (= act) **to have a ~** eine rauchen; **I'm dying for a ~** ich muss unbedingt eine rauchen; **the condemned were allowed a final ~** die Verurteilten durften eine letzte Zigarette rauchen

VT **a** tobacco, pipe, cigarette, cannabis rauchen **b** bacon, fish etc räuchern

VI rauchen; (oil lamp etc) qualmen; **to ~ like a chimney** wie ein Schlot rauchen; **do you mind if I ~?** stört es (Sie), wenn ich rauche?

▶**smoke out** VT sep ausräuchern; (= fill with smoke) einräuchern, einnebeln (inf)

smoke: smoke alarm N Rauchmelder m; **smoke bomb** N Rauchbombe f

smoked [smǝʊkt] ADJ bacon, fish geräuchert, Räucher-

smoke detector N Rauchmelder m

smoke-dried ['smǝʊkdraɪd] ADJ geräuchert

smoked: smoked glass M Rauchglas nt; **smoked glasses** PL Gläser pl aus Rauchglas; **smoked salmon** N Räucherlachs m

smoke: smoke-filled ['smǝʊkfɪld] ADJ room verraucht, verqualmt; **smoke-free** ['smǝʊkfriː] ADJ zone rauchfrei; **smoke hood** N (on plane) Sauerstoffmaske f

smokeless ['smǝʊklɪs] ADJ zone rauchfrei; fuel rauchlos

smoker ['smǝʊkǝ] N **a** (= person) Raucher(in) m(f); **to be a heavy ~** stark rauchen, starker Raucher sein; **~'s cough** Raucherhusten m **b** (Rail) Raucherabteil nt, Raucher m **c** (= entertainment) Herrenabend m

smoke: smoke ring N (Rauch)ring m; **smokeroom** N Rauchsalon m, Rauchzimmer nt; **smoke screen** N Nebelwand f, Rauchvorhang m; (fig) Deckmantel m, Vorwand m; **a ~ of words** ein Schwall m von Worten; **his answer was just a ~** seine Antwort war nur ein Ablenkungsmanöver nt; **smoke signal** N Rauchzeichen nt; **smokestack** N Schornstein m; **~ industries** Schornsteinindustrien pl

smoking ['smǝʊkɪŋ] ADJ rauchend **N** Rauchen nt; **"no ~"** „Rauchen verboten"

smoking: smoking compartment, (US) **smoking car** N Raucherabteil nt; **smoking gun** N (esp US, fig) entscheidender Beweis; **smoking jacket** N Rauchjacke f, Hausjacke f; **smoking room** N Rauchzimmer nt

smoky ['smǝʊkɪ] ADJ (+er) chimney, fire rauchend; room, atmosphere verraucht; (= stained by smoke) verräuchert; (= like smoke) flavour rauchig; colour rauchfarben; **~ glass** Rauchglas nt

smoky: smoky bacon N Räucherschinken m; **smoky blue** ADJ rauchblau; **smoky grey**, (US) **smoky gray** ADJ rauchgrau

smolder VI (US) = **smoulder**

smooch [smuːtʃ] (inf) **VI** knutschen (inf) **N to have a ~** rumknutschen (inf)

smoochy ['smuːtʃɪ] ADJ (+er) (inf) music, record schmusig (inf), zum Knutschen (inf), romantisch

smooth [smuːð] ADJ (+er) **a** (in texture, surface etc) glatt; sea ruhig, glatt; road, surface glatt, eben; outline sanft; skin glatt, weich; hair weich; **as ~ as silk** weich wie Seide, seidenweich; **as ~ as glass** spiegelglatt; worn ~ (steps) glatt getreten; knife abgeschliffen; tyre abgefahren; **this razor gives you a really ~ shave** dieser Apparat rasiert wirklich sanft

b (in consistency) paste sämig; sauce glatt; **whisk sauce until ~** Soße glatt rühren

c motion, flight, crossing ruhig; flow gleichmäßig; gear change weich, leicht; takeoff, landing glatt; breathing gleichmäßig; **the car came to a ~ stop** der Wagen kam glatt or ruhig zum Stehen; **he is a very ~ driver** er ist ein sehr angenehmer, ruhiger Fahrer; **to ensure a ~ fit** damit es genau passt

d (= trouble-free) transition, functioning reibungslos, glatt; relations reibungslos; **the bill had a ~ passage through Parliament** der Gesetzentwurf kam glatt durchs Parlament; **we want the move to the new offices to be as ~ as possible** wir wollen, dass der Umzug in die neuen Büroräume so reibungslos wie möglich verläuft

e (= not harsh in taste) flavour, coffee mild; whisky weich; beer süffig

f style of writing glatt, flüssig; tones sanft; diction flüssig, geschliffen; **the ~, relaxing voice of the hypnotist** die sanft beruhigende Stimme des Hypnotiseurs

g (= polite: often pej) manners glatt; person glatt, aalglatt (pej); (= unruffled) kühl, cool (inf); **to be a ~ talker** schönreden können; **he's too ~ to be sincere** er ist bestimmt nicht ehrlich, er redet zu schön; **a ~ operator** ein Schlawiner m (inf)

h (inf) restaurant, furniture, car, person gepflegt

i (Tennis) glatt

N to give sth a ~ etw glatt streichen → **rough N**

VT surface glätten, glatt machen; dress, hair glätten, glatt streichen; wood glatt hobeln; (fig) feelings besänftigen, beruhigen; **to ~ one's skirt over one's knees** sich den Rock über den Knien glatt streichen; **to ~ cream into sb's skin** Creme auf jds Haut streichen; **to ~ the way for sb/sth** jdm/einer Sache den Weg ebnen

▶**smooth away** VT sep glätten; (fig) fears besänftigen

▶**smooth back** VT sep hair zurückstreichen

▶**smooth down** **VT** sep glatt machen; feathers, hair, dress glatt streichen; (fig) person, feelings besänftigen **VI** (fig) sich beruhigen

▶**smooth out** VT sep (= make smooth) crease, surface glätten; (fig) difficulty, differences ausräumen, aus dem Weg räumen

▶**smooth over** VT sep (fig) quarrel in Ordnung bringen, geradebiegen (inf); **to smooth things over** die Sache geradebiegen (inf)

smooth: smoothbore ADJ glatt N Gewehr *nt* mit glattem Lauf; **smooth-faced** ADJ zarthäutig; *(fig)* scheinheilig

smoothly ['smu:ðlɪ] ADV **a** *shave* sanft **b** *land, change gear* weich; *drive* ruhig; *fit* genau; **to run ~** *(engine)* ruhig laufen **c** (= *without problems*) **to go ~** glatt über die Bühne gehen; **to run ~** *(event)* reibungslos verlaufen; **~ running organization** reibungslos laufende Organisation **d** *flowing prose* flüssige Prosa; **the music passes ~ from one mood to another** die Musik fließt unmerklich von einer Stimmung in die andere über **e** *talk* schön; *behave* aalglatt *(pej)*; **he handled the situation very ~** er hat die Lage sehr kühl gemeistert

smoothness ['smu:ðnɪs] N **a** *(of texture etc)* Glätte *f; (of sea)* Ruhe *f; (of road, surface)* Ebenheit *f; (of skin)* Glätte *f,* Weichheit *f;* **it has the ~ of silk** es ist seidenweich **b** *(in consistency) (of paste)* Sämigkeit *f; (of sauce)* Weichheit *f* **c** *(of motion, flight, crossing)* Ruhe *f; (of gear change)* Weichheit *f; (of takeoff, landing)* Sanftheit *f; (of breathing, flow)* Gleichmäßigkeit *f; (of fit)* Genauigkeit *f* **d** (= *ease: of transition, functioning, relations)* Reibungslosigkeit *f* **e** *(in taste, of whisky etc)* Weichheit *f; (of coffee)* Milde *f* **f** *(of style of writing, diction)* Flüssigkeit *f; (of tones)* Sanftheit *f* **g** *(pej, of manners, salesman)* Glätte *f; (of person)* (aal)glatte Art *(pej)*

smooth: smooth-running ADJ *engine, car* ruhig laufend; *convention etc* reibungslos verlaufend; **smooth-shaven** ADJ *man, face* glatt rasiert; **smooth-spoken, smooth-tongued** ADJ *(pej)* schönredend *(pej)*, schönrednerisch *(pej)*; **smooth-talk** VT *(pej)* überreden *(into* zu); **to ~ sb into doing sth** jdn dazu überreden etw zu tun

smoothy ['smu:ðɪ] N *(inf)* Schönling *m;* (= *smooth talker)* Schönredner *m; (pej)* Lackaffe *m (inf)*

smorgasboard ['smɔːgəsbɔːd] N *aus vielen Speisen bestehendes kaltes Büfett/Buffet* **a** (= *of) (fig)* eine Vielzahl *or* große Auswahl an *+dat or* von

smote [sməʊt] *pret of* **smite**

smother ['smʌðəʳ] VT **a** (= *stifle)* person, fire, weeds* ersticken; *(fig) criticism, yawn, laughter* unterdrücken; **to ~ sb with affection** jdn mit seiner Liebe erdrücken **b** (= *cover)* bedecken, überschütten; **fruit ~ed in cream** Obst, das in Sahne schwimmt; **~ed in dust** völlig eingestaubt; **she ~ed his face with kisses** sie bedeckte sein Gesicht mit Küssen, sie erstickte ihn fast mit ihren Küssen VI ersticken

smother-love ['smʌðəˌlʌv] N *(inf)* übertriebene Mutterliebe

smoulder, *(US)* **smolder** ['sməʊldəʳ] VI *(lit, fig)* glimmen, schwelen; *(fig)* *model, actress etc* Sexappeal *m* ausstrahlen; **his eyes were ~ing with anger** seine Augen glühten vor Zorn; **she was ~ing with rage** der Zorn schwelte in ihr

smouldering, *(US)* **smoldering** ['sməʊldərɪŋ] ADJ **a** *fire* schwelend; *embers, cigarette* glimmend **b** (= *suppressed)* anger, resentment, hatred* schwelend **c** (= *passionate)* eyes* feurig; **a ~ look** ein glühender Blick

SMP *(Brit)* abbr of **Statutory Maternity Pay** gesetzliches Erziehungsgeld

SMS *(Telec)* abbr of **Short Message Service** SMS

smudge [smʌdʒ] N **a** Fleck *m; (of ink)* Klecks *m* **b** *(US,* = *fire)* (qualmendes) Feuer *(gegen Insekten)* VT *ink, lipstick, paint* verwischen; **he had chocolate ~d all over his face** er hatte sich *(dat)* das ganze Gesicht mit Schokolade voll geschmiert VI verlaufen, verschmieren

smudgy ['smʌdʒɪ] ADJ *(+er)* verschmiert; *outline* verwischt, verschwommen

smug [smʌg] ADJ *(+er)* selbstgefällig; *grin, remark also* süffisant; **~ satisfaction** eitle Selbstzufriedenheit

smuggle ['smʌgl] VT *(lit, fig)* schmuggeln; **to ~ sb/sth in** jdn/etw einschmuggeln, jdn einschleusen; **to ~ sb/sth out** jdn/etw herausschmuggeln, jdn herausschleusen VI schmuggeln

smuggler ['smʌgləʳ] N Schmuggler(in) *m(f)*

smuggling ['smʌglɪŋ] N Schmuggel *m*

smuggling ring N Schmuggelring *m*

smugly ['smʌglɪ] ADV selbstgefällig; *grin, say also* süffisant; **he is ~ self-confident** er ist eitel selbstzufrieden

smugness ['smʌgnɪs] N Selbstgefälligkeit *f*

smut [smʌt] N **a** (= *piece of dirt)* Rußflocke *f;* **there's a ~ on your nose/in your eye** du hast da was an der Nase/im Auge; **~s from the stove** Ruß *m* aus dem Ofen **b** *(fig)* Schmutz *m;* **to talk ~** Schweinereien erzählen **c** *(Bot)* Brand *m*

smuttiness ['smʌtɪnɪs] N *(fig)* Schmutz *m; (of joke, language)* Anstößigkeit *f,* Unflätigkeit *f*

smutty ['smʌtɪ] ADJ *(+er) (lit, fig)* schmutzig

snack [snæk] N Kleinigkeit *f* (zu essen), Imbiss *m;* **to have a ~** eine Kleinigkeit essen, einen Imbiss zu sich *(dat)* nehmen; **we just have a ~ for lunch** mittags essen wir nicht viel *or* groß *(inf)*; **too many ~s between meals ...** wenn man zwischen den Mahlzeiten zu viel isst ...

snack bar N Imbissstube *f*

snaffle¹ ['snæfl] N *(also* **snaffle bit**) Trense *f*

snaffle² VT *(Brit, inf)* sich *(dat)* unter den Nagel reißen *(inf)*

▸ **snaffle up** VT sep *(Brit, inf)* bargain* wegschnappen *(inf)*

snafu [snæ'fuː] *(US, sl)* N Schlamassel *m (inf)* VT total durcheinander bringen

snag [snæg] N **a** (= *hidden difficulty)* Haken *m,* Schwierigkeit *f;* **there's a ~** die Sache hat einen Haken; **what's the ~?** woran liegt es?, was ist das Problem?; **to run into** *or* **hit a ~** in Schwierigkeiten *(acc)* kommen **b** (= *flaw in clothes etc)* gezogener Faden **c** *(in water)* Baumstumpf *m* (im Wasser) VT *thread* sich *(dat)* einen Faden ziehen; **I ~ged my tights** ich habe mir an den Strumpfhosen einen Faden gezogen VI Fäden ziehen

snail [sneɪl] N Schnecke *f;* **edible ~** Weinbergschnecke *f;* **at a ~'s pace** im Schneckentempo

snail lane N *(US Aut)* Kriechspur *f*

snail mail N *(hum)* Schneckenpost *f (inf, im Gegensatz zur elektronischen Post)*

snake [sneɪk] N Schlange *f;* **a ~ in the grass** *(fig,* = *woman)* eine listige Schlange; *(= man)* ein heimtückischer Kerl VI sich schlängeln

snake: snakebite N **a** Schlangenbiss *m* **b** (= *drink)* Getränk aus Cidre und Bier; **snake charmer** N Schlangenbeschwörer(in) *m(f);* **snake fence** N *(esp US)* Scherengitter *nt;* **snakepit** N Schlangengrube *f;* **snakeskin** N Schlangenhaut *f;* (= *leather)* Schlangenleder *nt* ADJ Schlangenleder-, aus Schlangenleder; **~ boots** Schlangenlederstiefel *pl*

snaky ['sneɪkɪ] ADJ *windings* schläng(e)lig; *movements* schlangenartig

snap [snæp] N **a** (= *sound)* Schnappen *nt; (with fingers)* Schnippen *nt,* Schnalzen *nt; (of sth breaking)* Knacken *nt;* (= *click)* Klicken *nt; (of whip)* Knall *m* **b** (= *fastener)* Druckknopf *m* **c** *(Phot)* Schnappschuss *m* **d** *(Cards)* ≈ Schnippschnapp *nt* **e** *(inf,* = *vigour)* Schwung *m;* **put a bit of ~ into it** mach ein bisschen zackig! *(inf)* **f** *(Brit:* = *biscuit)* Plätzchen *nt* **g cold ~** Kälteeinbruch *m* **h** *(US, inf,* = *cinch)* **it's a ~** das ist ein Kinderspiel *or* ein Klacks *(inf)* ADJ **a** *attr* plötzlich, spontan; **~ vote** Blitzabstimmung *f* **b** *(US inf:* = *easy)* kinderleicht ADV **to go ~** (= *make sound)* schnapp machen; *(sth breaking)* knacken; (= *break)* (knackend) entzweibrechen INTERJ **I bought a green one – ~!** *(Brit inf)* ich

hab mir ein grünes gekauft – ich auch! VT **a** *fingers* schnipsen *or* schnalzen mit; *whip* knallen mit; **to ~ a book shut** ein Buch zuklappen; **to ~ a purse shut** ein Portemonnaie zuschnappen lassen; **he ~ped the lid down** er ließ den Deckel runterklappen; **to ~ sth into place** etw einschnappen lassen; **to ~ one's fingers at sb/sth** *(fig)* auf jdn/etw pfeifen *(inf)* **b** (= *break)* zerbrechen, entzweibrechen; *bone* brechen **c** *(also* **snap out)* **to ~ an order** bellend etwas befehlen; **she ~ped a few words at the children** sie pfiff die Kinder an **d** *(Phot)* knipsen VI **a** (= *click)* (zu)schnappen, einschnappen; (= *crack, break)* entzweibrechen, zerbrechen; *(of whip)* knallen; **to ~ shut** zuschnappen; **my patience finally ~ped** dann ist mir aber der Geduldsfaden gerissen **b** (= *speak sharply)* bellen *(inf)*, schnappen *(inf)*; **to ~ at sb** jdn anpfeifen *or* anschnauzen *(inf)*; **there's no need to ~** du brauchst nicht gleich so zu schnauzen! **c** *(of dog, fish etc, fig)* schnappen *(at nach)* **d** **to ~ to attention** zackig Haltung annehmen; **~ to it!** mach 'n bisschen zackig! *(inf)* **e** *(inf,* = *crack up)* durchdrehen *(inf)*; **something ~ped (in him)** da hat (bei ihm) etwas ausgehakt *(inf)*

▸ **snap off** VT sep (= *break off)* abbrechen; (= *bite off)* abbeißen; **to snap sb's head off** *(fig inf)* jdm ins Gesicht springen *(inf)* VI (= *break off)* abbrechen

▸ **snap out** VT sep **a** *order* brüllen, bellen **b** **to snap sb out of sth** jdn aus etw herausreißen VI **to snap out of sth** sich aus etw herausreißen, mit etw Schluss machen; **it's time he snapped out of this depression** es wird höchste Zeit, dass er aus dieser Depression rauskommt; **snap out of it!** reiß dich zusammen *or* am Riemen! *(inf)*; (= *cheer up)* Kopf hoch!

▸ **snap up** VT sep *(lit, fig)* wegschnappen

snap: snap decision N plötzlicher Entschluss; **snapdragon** N Löwenmaul *nt;* **snap fastener** N Druckknopf *m;* **snap hook** N Karabinerhaken *m;* **snap lock** N Schnappschloss *nt*

snapper ['snæpəʳ] N (= *fish)* Schnapper *m*

snappish ['snæpɪʃ] ADJ *(lit, fig)* bissig

snappiness ['snæpɪnɪs] N *(lit, fig)* Bissigkeit *f*

snappy ['snæpɪ] ADJ *(+er)* **a** *(inf,* = *quick)* flott *(inf)*, zackig *(inf)*; **and be ~ about it!, and make it ~!** und zwar ein bisschen flott *or* dalli! *(inf)* **b** *(lit, fig)* dog, person* bissig **c** *(inf)* translation* kurz und treffend; *phrase* zündend **d** *(inf:* = *fashionable)* flott, schick; **he's a ~ dresser** er kleidet sich sehr modebewusst

snap: snap ring N Karabinerhaken *m;* **snapshot** N Schnappschuss *m*

snare¹ [snɛəʳ] N *(lit, fig:* = *trap)* Falle *f; (fig also)* Fallstrick *m* VT *(lit, fig)* (ein)fangen

snare² N **a** *(of drum)* Schnarrsaite *f* **b** (= *snare drum)* kleine Trommel

snarl¹ [snɑːl] N Knurren *nt no pl;* **..., he said with a ~** ..., sagte er knurrend VI knurren; **to ~ at sb** jdn anknurren

snarl² N *(in wool)* Knoten *m,* verhedderte Stelle VT *wool* verheddern

▸ **snarl up** *(inf)* VT sep *traffic, system* durcheinander bringen; *plan also* vermasseln *(inf)*; **traffic always gets snarled up at the bridge** an der Brücke ist der Verkehr immer chaotisch; **I got snarled up in a traffic jam** ich bin im Verkehr stecken geblieben VI *(traffic)* chaotische Formen annehmen

snarl-up ['snɑːlʌp] N *(Brit inf, in traffic)* (Verkehrs)chaos *nt; (in system, on switchboard etc)* Kuddelmuddel *nt (inf)*; **~s** ein großes Kuddelmuddel *(inf)*; **the ~s at rush-hour periods** das Chaos in den Stoßverkehrszeiten

snatch [snætʃ] N **a** (= *act)* Griff *m* **b** *(Brit inf:* = *robbery)* Raub *m;* (= *kidnapping)* Entführung *f* **c** (= *snippet)* Stück *nt,* Brocken *m; (of conversa-*

tion) Fetzen *m*; (*of music*) ein paar Takte; **to do sth in ~es** etw in Etappen tun

 d (*Weightlifting*) Reißen *nt*

 e (*US, sl, = female genitals*) Möse *f* (*vulg*)

 VT **a** (= *grab*) greifen; **to ~ sth from sb** jdm etw entreißen; **to ~ hold of sth** nach etw greifen, etw packen; **to ~ sth out of sb's hand** jdm etw aus der Hand reißen

 b *some sleep etc* ergattern; **to ~ a quick meal** schnell etwas essen; **the Ferrari ~ed the lead on the last lap** der Ferrari riss in der letzten Runde die Führung an sich; **to ~ an opportunity** eine Gelegenheit ergreifen *or* beim Schopf packen; **they ~ed a quick kiss** sie gaben sich (*dat*) schnell einen Kuss; **he ~ed a kiss while she wasn't looking** als sie gerade wegsah, stahl er ihr einen Kuss; **to ~ defeat from the jaws of victory** einen sicheren Sieg in eine Niederlage verwandeln; **they ~ed victory from the jaws of defeat with a goal in the last minute** mit einem Tor in der letzten Minute konnten sie aus der Niederlage noch einen Sieg machen

 c (*inf*) (= *steal*) *money* klauen (*inf*); *handbag* aus der Hand reißen; (= *kidnap*) entführen

 VI greifen (*at* nach); **don't ~!** nicht grapschen! (*inf*); **to ~ at an opportunity** nach einer Gelegenheit greifen

▸ **snatch away** VT *sep* wegreißen (*sth from sb* jdm etw); **death snatched him away from us** der Tod hat ihn uns (*dat*) entrissen

▸ **snatch up** VT *sep* schnappen; **he snatched up his camera** er schnappte sich (*dat*) seine Kamera; **the mother snatched her child up** die Mutter riss ihr Kind an sich (*acc*)

snatcher ['snætʃə'] N (*esp Brit*) Handtaschenräuber(in) *m(f)*; (*esp US*) Kidnapper(in) *m(f)*

snatch squad N (*Brit*) Greifertrupp *m* (*inf*)

snazzy ADJ (+*er*), **snazzily** ADV ['snæzɪ, -lɪ] (*dated inf*) flott

sneak [sniːk] **N** Schleicher(in) *m(f)*; (*dated Brit Sch inf*) Petzer *m*, Petze *f* (*Sch inf*) **VT** **he ~ed a cake off the counter** er klaute *or* stibitzte einen Kuchen vom Tresen (*inf*); **to ~ sth into a room** etw in ein Zimmer schmuggeln; **to ~ a look at sb/sth** auf jdn/etw schielen **VI** **a** **to ~ about** herumschleichen; **to ~ away** *or* **off** sich wegschleichen *or* -stehlen; **to ~ in** sich einschleichen; **to ~ past sb** (sich) an jdm vorbeischleichen; **to ~ up on sb** sich an jdn heranschleichen **b** (*dated Brit Sch inf, = tell tales*) petzen (*inf*); **to ~ on sb** jdn verpetzen (*inf*)

sneakers ['sniːkəz] PL (*esp US*) Freizeitschuhe *pl*, Leisetreter *pl* (*hum*), Schleicher *pl* (*hum*)

sneaking ['sniːkɪŋ] ADJ *attr* geheim *attr*; *suspicion also* leise; **to have a ~ feeling that ...** ein schleichendes Gefühl haben, dass ...

sneak preview N (*of film etc*) Vorschau *f*; (*of new car etc*) Vorbesichtigung *f*

sneak thief N Langfinger *m* (*inf*), Einschleichdieb(in) *m(f)*

sneaky ['sniːkɪ] ADJ (+*er*) (*pej inf*) gewieft (*inf*), raffiniert; **there's something ~ about it** da ist was faul dran

sneer [snɪə'] **N** (= *expression*) spöttisches *or* höhnisches Lächeln; (= *remark*) spöttische *or* höhnische Bemerkung **VI** spotten; (= *look sneering*) spöttisch *or* höhnisch grinsen; **adolescents often ~ at what they cannot understand** Jugendliche spotten oft über das, was sie nicht verstehen können; **to ~ at sb** jdn verhöhnen; (*facially also*) jdn auslachen

sneerer ['snɪərə'] N Spötter(in) *m(f)*

sneering ADJ , **sneeringly** ADV ['snɪərɪŋ, -lɪ] höhnisch, spöttisch

sneeze [sniːz] **N** Nieser *m*; **~s** Niesen *nt* **VI** niesen; **not to be ~d at** nicht zu verachten; **when America ~s, Britain catches a cold** wenn Amerika niest, bekommt Großbritannien einen Schnupfen

sneezing ['sniːzɪŋ] N Niesen *nt*

snick [snɪk] **N** (= *small cut*) Kerbe *f* **VT** (*with razor*) schneiden; (*with knife*) schnitzen; (*with*

tweezers) zupfen; (*Cricket*) *ball* auf Kante schlagen

snicker ['snɪkə'] N, VI = **snigger**

snide [snaɪd] ADJ abfällig

sniff [snɪf] **N** Schniefen *nt no pl* (*inf*); (*disdainful*) Naserümpfen *nt no pl*; (*of dog*) Schnüffeln *nt no pl*; **we never even got a ~ of the money** wir haben das Geld noch nicht mal von weitem zu sehen bekommen; **have a ~ at this** riech mal hieran; **at the first ~ of danger, he backed out** sobald er Gefahr witterte, zog er sich zurück

 VT (= *test by smelling*) riechen, schnuppern an (+*dat*) (*inf*); *air* riechen, schnuppern; *smelling salts* einziehen; *glue* einatmen, schnüffeln (*inf*); *drugs* sniffen (*sl*); *snuff* schnupfen; (*fig, = detect*) wittern, riechen; **the dogs ~ed each other** die Hunde beschnupperten sich; **~ these flowers** riech mal an den Blumen

 VI (*person*) schniefen (*inf*); (*dog*) schnüffeln, schnuppern; **to ~ at sth** (*lit*) an etw (*dat*) schnuppern; (*fig*) die Nase über etw (*acc*) rümpfen; **not to be ~ed at** nicht zu verachten

▸ **sniff around** (*inf*) **VI** (*for information*) herumschnüffeln (*inf*) **VI** +*prep obj* **a** *room etc* herumschnüffeln in (+*dat*) (*inf*) **b** *girlfriend etc* herumhängen bei (*inf*)

▸ **sniff out** VT *sep* (*lit, fig inf*) aufspüren; *crime, plot* aufdecken

▸ **sniff round** VI, VI +*prep obj* (*esp Brit*) = **sniff around**

sniffer dog ['snɪfədɒg] N Spürhund *m*

sniffle ['snɪfl] N, VI = **snuffle**

sniffy ['snɪfɪ] ADJ (+*er*) (*inf, = disdainful*) naserümpfend; (= *put out*) verschnupft, eingeschnappt (*inf*); **she was rather ~ about the plan** sie hat über den Plan nur die Nase gerümpft

snifter ['snɪftə'] N (*dated inf*) Kurze(r) *m* (*inf*); **to have a ~** einen Kurzen trinken *or* nehmen (*inf*)

snigger ['snɪgə'] **N** Kichern *nt*, Gekicher *nt*; **to give a ~** loskichern **VI** kichern (*at, about* wegen)

snip [snɪp] **N** **a** (= *cut, cutting action*) Schnitt *m*; (= *sound*) Schnipsen *nt no pl*, Klappern *nt no pl* **b** (*of cloth*) Stück *nt*; (*of paper*) Schnipsel *m*, Schnippel *m or nt* (*inf*); (*from newspaper*) Ausschnitt *m* **c** (*esp Brit, inf, = bargain*) Geschäft *nt*, günstiger Kauf; **at only £2 it's a real ~** für nur £ 2 ist es unheimlich günstig **d** (*US, inf, = insignificant person*) Würstchen *nt* (*pej inf*)

 VT schnippeln (*inf*); **to ~ sth off** etw abschnippeln (*inf*) **VI** **to ~ at** schnippeln an (+*dat*) (*inf*)

snipe [snaɪp] **N** *pl* - (*Orn*) Schnepfe *f* **VI** **to ~ at sb** (*lit, fig*) aus dem Hinterhalt auf jdn schießen

sniper ['snaɪpə'] N Heckenschütze *m*/-schützin *f*; **~-fire** Heckenschützenfeuer *nt*

snippet ['snɪpɪt] N Stückchen *nt*; (*of paper also*) Schnipsel *m or nt*; (*of information*) (Bruch)stück *nt*; **~s of (a) conversation** Gesprächsfetzen *pl*

snippy ['snɪpɪ] ADJ (*US inf*) *person, tone* schnippisch, kurz angebunden; **to be in a ~ mood** kurz angebunden sein

snitch [snɪtʃ] (*inf*) **VT** klauen (*inf*) **VI** **to ~ on sb** über jdn plaudern (*inf*) *or* klatschen

snivel ['snɪvl] VI heulen, flennen (*inf*)

sniveller ['snɪvlə'] N Jammerer *m*

snivelling, (*US*) **sniveling** ['snɪvlɪŋ] ADJ heulend, flennend (*inf*) **N** Geheul(e) *nt* (*inf*), Geflenne *nt* (*inf*)

snob [snɒb] N Snob *m*; **~ appeal** *or* **value** Snobappeal *m*

snobbery ['snɒbərɪ] N Snobismus *m*

snobbish ADJ ['snɒbɪʃ] snobistisch, versnobt (*inf*); **place für Snobs; to be ~ about sth** bei etw wählerisch sein

snobbishly ['snɒbɪʃlɪ] ADV snobistisch, versnobt (*inf*)

snobbishness ['snɒbɪʃnɪs] N Snobismus *m*, Versnobtheit *f* (*inf*)

snog [snɒg] (*Brit, inf*) **N** Knutscherei *f* (*inf*); **to have a ~ with sb** mit jdm rumknutschen (*inf*) **VI** rumknutschen (*inf*) **VT** abknutschen (*inf*)

snood [snuːd] N Haarnetz *nt*

snook [snuːk] N → **cock** VT b

snooker ['snuːkə'] **N** Snooker *nt* **VT** **to ~ sb** jdn sperren; **to be ~ed** (*Brit fig inf*) festsitzen (*inf*); **I've ~ed myself** (*fig inf*) ich habe mich festgefahren

snoop [snuːp] **N** **a** = **snooper** **b** (= *act*) **I'll have a ~ around** ich gucke mich mal (ein bisschen) um **VI** schnüffeln; **to ~ about** (*Brit*) *or* **around** herumschnüffeln

snooper ['snuːpə'] N Schnüffler(in) *m(f)*

snoopy ADJ , **snoopily** ADV ['snuːpɪ, -lɪ] (*inf*) neugierig

snootily ['snuːtɪlɪ] ADV (*inf*) hochnäsig, von oben herab

snooty ['snuːtɪ] ADJ (+*er*) (*inf*) hochnäsig

snooze [snuːz] **N** Schläfchen *nt*, Nickerchen *nt*; **to have a ~** Schläfchen machen; **~ button** (*on alarm clock*) Schlummertaste *f* **VI** dösen, ein Nickerchen machen

snore [snɔː'] **N** Schnarchen *nt no pl* **VI** schnarchen

snorer ['snɔːrə'] N Schnarcher(in) *m(f)*

snoring ['snɔːrɪŋ] N Schnarchen *nt*

snorkel ['snɔːkl] **N** Schnorchel *m* **VI** schnorcheln; **to go ~ling** schnorcheln gehen

snorkelling, (*US*) **snorkeling** ['snɔːkəlɪŋ] N Schnorcheln *nt*

snort [snɔːt] **N** Schnauben *nt no pl*; (*of person also*) Prusten *nt no pl*; (*of boar*) Grunzen *nt no pl*; **with a ~ of rage** wutschnaubend; **he gave a ~ of contempt/rage** er schnaubte verächtlich/vor Wut; **to give a ~ of laughter** losprusten **VI** schnauben; (*person also*) prusten; (*boar*) grunzen **VT** **a** (*person*) schnauben **b** *drugs* sniffen (*sl*)

snot [snɒt] N (*inf*) Rotz *m* (*inf*)

snotty ['snɒtɪ] ADJ (+*er*) (*inf*) **a** *handkerchief* rotzig (*inf*); *child* rotznäsig (*inf*); **~ nose** Rotznase *f* (*inf*) **b** (*fig, = snooty*) rotzig (*inf*), pampig (*inf*)

snotty-nosed ['snɒtɪ'nəʊzd] ADJ rotznäsig (*inf*)

snout [snaʊt] **N a** (*of animal*) Schnauze *f*; (*of pig also, of insect*) Rüssel *m*; (*of person*) Rüssel *m* (*inf*), Zinken *m* (*inf*) **b** (*sl, = informer*) Spitzel *m* **c** (*Brit, inf, = tobacco*) Knaster *m* (*inf*)

snow [snəʊ] **N a** Schnee *m*; (= *snowfall*) Schneefall *m*; **new ~** Neuschnee *m*; **the ~s that lie on the plains** der Schnee in der Ebene; **the heavy ~s last winter** die heftigen Schneefälle im letzten Winter; **as white as ~** schneeweiß, blütenweiß; **as pure as the driven ~** engelrein **b** (*TV*) Geflimmer *nt*, Schnee *m* **c** (*sl, = cocaine or heroin*) Schnee *m* (*inf*) **VI** schneien

▸ **snow in** VT *sep* (*usu pass*) **to be** *or* **get snowed in** einschneien; **we are snowed in** wir sind eingeschneit

▸ **snow off** VT *sep* (*usu pass*) **to be snowed off** wegen Schnee abgesagt werden *or* ausfallen

▸ **snow under** VT *sep* (*inf, usu pass*) **to be snowed under** (*with work*) reichlich eingedeckt sein; (*with requests*) überhäuft werden

▸ **snow up** VT *sep* (*usu pass*) = **snow in**

snow: snowball **N** Schneeball *m*; (= *drink*) Snowball *m*; **he doesn't stand a ~'s chance in hell** (*Brit inf*) seine Chancen sind gleich null **VT** Schneebälle werfen auf (+*acc*) **VI** eskalieren; **we must take action now otherwise things will ~ and get out of control** wir müssen jetzt etwas unternehmen, sonst wachsen uns die Dinge über den Kopf; **opposition to the referendum just ~ed** die Opposition gegen die Volksabstimmung wuchs lawinenartig an; **snowball effect** N Schneeballeffekt *m*; **snow bank** N (*esp US*) Schneeverwehung *f*, Schneewehe *f*; **snow-blind** ADJ schneeblind; **snow blindness** N Schneeblindheit *f*; **snowboard** ['snəʊbɔːd] **N** Snowboard *nt* **VI** snowboarden, Snowboard fahren; **snowboarder** N Snowboarder(in) *m(f)*; **snowboarding** N Snowboarding *nt*, Snowboardfahren *nt*; **snowbound** ADJ eingeschneit; **snow cannon** N (*Ski*) Schneekanone *f*; **snowcapped** ADJ schneebedeckt; **snowcat** N (Ski) Pistenwalze f; **snow chains** PL Schneeketten pl; **snow-clad** (poet), **snow-covered** ADJ verschneit; **snow-cuffs** PL Schneegamaschen pl; **snowdrift** N Schneewehe f; **snowdrop** N Schneeglöckchen nt; **snowfall** N Schneefall m; **snowfield** N Schneefeld nt; **snowflake** N Schneeflocke f; **snow goggles** PL Schneebrille f; **snow goose** N Schneegans f; **snow guard** N (on roof) Schneefang m; **snow-in-summer** N (Bot) Hornkraut nt; **snow job** N (inf) freundliches Gerede; (= to do a ~ on sb jdn einzuwickeln versuchen (inf pej); **snow leopard** N Schneeleopard m; **snow line** N Schneegrenze f; **snowman** N Schneemann m → **abominable**; **snowmobile** N Schneemobil nt; **snowplough**, (US) **snowplow** N (also Ski) Schneepflug m; **snowshed** N (US) Schneedach nt; **snowshoe** N Schneeschuh m; **snowslide** N (US) Schneerutsch m; **snowstorm** N Schneesturm m; **snowsuit** N gefütterter Overall; **snow tyre**, (US) **snow tire** N Winterreifen m; **Snow White** N Schneewittchen nt; **snow-white** ADJ schneeweiß; hair, beard also schlohweiß

snowy ['snəʊɪ] ADJ (+er) **a** weather, region schneereich; hills verschneit; **it was very ~ yesterday** gestern hat es viel geschneit **b** (= white as snow) schneeweiß

snowy owl N Schneeeule f

SNP abbr of **Scottish National Party**

snub [snʌb] **N** Brüskierung f; **to give sb a ~** jdn brüskieren, jdn vor den Kopf stoßen; subordinate, pupil etc (verbally) jdm über den Mund fahren; **to get a ~ from sb** von jdm brüskiert or vor den Kopf gestoßen werden **VT a** person brüskieren, vor den Kopf stoßen; subordinate, pupil (verbally) über den Mund fahren (+dat); suggestion, proposal kurz abtun; offer, request, plea ablehnen; talks bewusst fernbleiben (+dat) **b** (= ignore, not greet) schneiden

snub: snub nose N Stupsnase f; **snub-nosed** ADJ stumpfnasig; person also stupsnasig

snuff [snʌf] **N a** Schnupftabak m; **to take ~** schnupfen **b** **to be/come up to ~** (dated inf) mithalten können (inf) **VT** candle (= extinguish: also **snuff out**) auslöschen; (= trim wick) putzen, schnäuzen (old); (fig) revolt ersticken; hopes zunichte machen, zerschlagen; **to ~ out sb's life** jds Lebenslicht auslöschen; **to ~ it** (Brit, inf: = die) abkratzen (sl)

snuffbox ['snʌfbɒks] N Schnupftabakdose f, Tabatiere f (geh)

snuffer ['snʌfə'] N Kerzenlöscher m; **~s** Lichtputzschere f

snuffle ['snʌfl] **N** Schniefen nt no pl; **to have the ~s** (inf) einen leichten Schnupfen haben **VI** (person, animal) schnüffeln; (with cold, from crying also) schniefen (inf)

snuff movie N brutaler (Porno)film, in dem tatsächlich gestorben wird

snug [snʌg] **ADJ** (+er) (= cosy, comfortable) behaglich, gemütlich; (= cosy and warm) bed, garment, room etc mollig warm, behaglich warm; (= sheltered) spot, harbour geschützt; (= close-fitting) gut sitzend attr; (= tight) eng; **to be ~ in bed/in one's sleeping bag** im Bett/Schlafsack mollig or behaglich warm haben; **I was as ~ as a bug in a rug** (Brit inf) es war urgemütlich; **it is a good ~ fit** es passt gut **N** (Brit, in pub) kleines Nebenzimmer

snuggle ['snʌgl] **VI** sich schmiegen, sich kuscheln; **to ~ down in bed** sich ins Bett kuscheln; **to ~ up (to sb)** sich (an jdn) anschmiegen or ankuscheln; **I like to ~ up with a book** ich mache es mir gern mit einem Buch gemütlich; **to ~ into sb/sth** sich an jdm ankuscheln/in etw (acc) einkuscheln; **the cottages ~d in the valley** die Häuschen schmiegten sich ins Tal **VT** an sich (acc) schmiegen

snugly ['snʌglɪ] ADV **a** (= cosily) gemütlich, behaglich; **~ tucked in**, **~ tucked up (in bed)** mollig warm eingepackt (im Bett) **b** (= tightly) close fest; fit gut

snugness ['snʌgnɪs] N (= cosiness, comfort) Behaglichkeit f, Gemütlichkeit f; (= cosiness and warmth) mollige or behagliche Wärme; (= sheltered nature) Geschütztheit f; (= closeness of fit: of garment) guter Sitz

So abbr of **south** S

so [səʊ] **ADV a** so; **so much tea** so viel Tee; **so many flies** so viele Fliegen; **he was so stupid (that)** er war so or dermaßen or derart dumm(, dass); **he's so quick I can't keep up with him** er ist so schnell, dass ich nicht mithalten kann; **not so ... as ... wie**; **he is not so fast a runner as you** er ist kein so schneller Läufer wie Sie, er kann nicht so schnell laufen wie Sie; **I am not so stupid as to believe that** or **that I believe that** so dumm bin ich nicht, dass ich das glaube(n würde); **he was so stupid as to tell her** er war so dumm und hat es ihr gesagt; **would you be so kind as to open the door?** wären Sie bitte so freundlich und würden die Tür öffnen?; **so great a writer as Shakespeare** ein so großer Dichter wie Shakespeare; **he's not been so well recently** in letzter Zeit geht es ihm nicht so sonderlich; **how are things? – not so bad!** wie gehts? – nicht schlecht!; **not so as you'd notice** aber das fällt kaum auf

b (emphatic) glad, sorry, sure, rich, hurt so; pleased, relieved, hope, wish sehr; love so sehr; hate so sehr, derart; **that's so true** das ist ja so wahr, das ist wirklich wahr; **I'm so very tired** ich bin ja so müde; **it's not so very difficult** es ist gar nicht so schwer; **it would be so much better/nicer** etc es wäre so viel besser/netter etc; **so much the better/worse (for sb)** umso besser/schlechter (für jdn); **that's so kind of you** das ist wirklich sehr nett von Ihnen; **I so hope you're right!** ich hoffe (wirklich) sehr, dass Sie Recht haben!

c (replacing longer sentence) da, es; **I hope so** hoffentlich; (emphatic) hoffe ich doch sehr; **I think so** ich glaube schon; **I never said so** das habe ich nie gesagt; **I told you so** ich habe es dir doch or ja gesagt; **I told you so yesterday** das habe ich dir gestern gesagt; **why should I do it? – because I say so** warum muss ich das tun? – weil ich es sage, darum; **I didn't say so** das habe ich nicht gesagt; **can I go/will you do it? – I suppose so** darf ich gehen/machen Sie es? – na ja, meinetwegen; **is that right/can I do it like that? – I suppose so** stimmt das/kann ich es so machen? – ich glaube schon; **so I see** ja, das sehe ich; **please, do so** bitte(, tun Sie es ruhig); **perhaps so** vielleicht; **it may be so** es kann schon sein; **so be it** nun gut; **if so** wenn ja; **he said he would finish it this week, and so he did** er hat gesagt, er würde es diese Woche fertig machen und das hat er auch (gemacht); **how** or **why so?** wieso or warum das?; or **so they say** oder so heißt es jedenfalls; **he's a millionaire, or so he says** er ist Millionär, zumindest or jedenfalls behauptet er das; **it is so!** (contradiction) doch!; **so it is!** (contradiction) und ob (ich das kann)!, doch!; **I didn't say that – you did so** das habe ich nicht gesagt – doch, das hast du (sehr wohl gesagt)!; **you've got the papers? – yes, that's so** haben Sie die Papiere? – jawohl; **that is so** das stimmt; **if that's so** wenn das stimmt; **he's coming by plane – is that so?** er kommt mit dem Flugzeug – ach so, ja?, tatsächlich?; **you're a fool – is that so?** du bist ein Idiot – ach, wirklich?; **... – so it is/I have/he did** etc ... – (ja) tatsächlich?; **he's a nice chap – so he is** er ist ein netter Kerl – ja, wirklich or ja, das ist er auch

d (= thus, in this way) so; **perhaps it was better so** vielleicht war es auch besser so; **so it was that** ... so kam es, dass ...; **and so it was** und so war es auch; **by so doing he has ...** dadurch hat er ..., indem er das tat, hat er ...; **bother them!** he exclaimed, and so saying walked out zum Kuckuck! rief er, und damit ging er hinaus; **... and so to bed ...** und dann ins Bett; **and so on** or **forth** und so weiter

e (unspecified amount) **how high is it? – oh, a-**bout so high (accompanied by gesture) wie hoch ist das? – oh, ungefähr so; **so much per head** so viel pro Kopf; **they looked like so many gypsies** sie sahen wie so viele andere Zigeuner auch aus; **how long will it take? – a week or so** wie lange dauert das? – ungefähr eine Woche or so eine Woche; **50 or so** etwa 50

f (= likewise) auch; **so am/would/do/could** etc **I** ich auch; **he's wrong and so are you** ihr irrt euch beide; **as A is to B, so D is to E** A verhält sich zu B wie D zu E

g he walked past and didn't so much as look at me er ging vorbei, ohne mich auch nur anzusehen; **he didn't say so much as thank you** er hat nicht einmal danke gesagt; **I haven't so much as a penny** ich habe keinen Cent; **so much for that!** (inf) das wärs ja wohl gewesen! (inf); **so much for him!** (inf) das war ja wohl nichts mit ihm! (inf); **so much for his/her help** (inf) schöne Hilfe! (inf); **so much for his ambition to be a doctor/for our new car** aus der Traum vom Arztwerden/vom neuen Auto; **so much for his promises** und er hat solche Versprechungen gemacht → **ever**, **far** ADV **a**, **just** [1], **long** [2] ADV **a, c**, **more** N, **PRON b**, **quite a**

CONJ a (expressing purpose) damit; **so (that) you don't have to do it again** damit Sie es nicht noch einmal machen müssen; **we hurried so as not to be late** wir haben uns beeilt, um nicht zu spät zu kommen

b (expressing result, = therefore) also; **it rained (and) so we couldn't go out** es regnete, also konnten wir nicht weggehen or und deshalb konnten wir nicht weggehen; **he refused to move so (that) finally the police had to carry him away** er weigerte sich wegzugehen, so dass or sodass ihn die Polizei schließlich wegtragen musste; **he was standing in the doorway so (that) no-one could get past** er stand in der Tür, so dass or sodass niemand vorbeikonnte; **I told him to leave and so he did** ich habe ihm gesagt, er solle gehen und das hat er auch getan; **so I told him he could get lost** (inf) da habe ich ihm gesagt, er kann or könnte mir den Buckel runterrutschen; **so, far from helping us, he** ... nicht nur, dass er uns nicht geholfen hat, sondern ...; **so you see ...** wie du siehst ...

c (in questions, exclamations) also; **so you're Spanish?** Sie sind also Spanier(in)?; **so you're leaving?** Sie gehen also?; **so you lost it, did you?** du hast es also verloren, wie?; **so you did do it!** du hast es also doch gemacht!; **so there you are!** hier steckst du also!; **so what did you do?** und was haben Sie (da) gemacht?; **so (what)?** (inf) (na) und?; **so what if you don't do it?** (inf) (na) und wenn dus nicht machst?; **I'm not going, so there!** (inf) ich geh nicht, fertig, aus!

soak [səʊk] **VT a** (= wet) durchnässen **b** (= steep) einweichen (in in +dat); **to ~ oneself in sth** (fig) sich in etw (acc) vertiefen **c** (inf: the rich etc) schröpfen; **to ~ sb for sth** jdn um etw angehen **VI a** (= steep) **leave it to ~** weichen Sie es ein; (in dye) lassen Sie die Farbe einziehen; **to ~ in a bath** sich einweichen (inf) **b** (= penetrate) rain has ~ed through the ceiling der Regen ist durch die Decke gesickert; **the coffee was ~ing into the carpet** der Kaffee saugte sich in den Teppich **N a** (= act of soaking) **give the washing a good ~** lassen Sie die Wäsche gut einweichen; **the sheets are in** ~ die Laken sind eingeweicht; **the garden needs a ~** der Garten muss gründlich bewässert werden; **I had a long ~ in the bath** ich habe lange in der Wanne gelegen **b** (inf, = drunkard) Schluckbruder m (inf), Säufer(in) m(f)

▶ **soak in** VI (stain, dye etc) einziehen; **to leave sth to soak in** etw einziehen lassen

▶ **soak off** **VT** sep ablösen **VI** sich (ab)lösen (+prep obj von)

▶ **soak out** **VT** sep mark, stain durch Einweichen entfernen **VI** beim Einweichen herausgehen

▶**soak up** VT *sep liquid* aufsaugen; *sunshine* genießen; *alcohol* in sich (*acc*) hineinkippen; *sound, money, resources* schlucken; (*fig*) *atmosphere* in sich (*acc*) hineinsaugen; *information* aufsaugen

soaked [səʊkt] ADJ **a** (= *drenched*) *person, garment* durchnässt; **her dress was ~** ihr Kleid war klatschnass (*inf*) *or* völlig durchnässt; **his T-shirt was ~ in sweat** sein T-Shirt war schweißgetränkt; **to get ~** völlig durchnässt werden; **to be ~ to the skin, to be ~ through** bis auf die Haut nass sein **b** (*fig*, = *steeped*) **to be ~ in sth** (*person*) in etw (*dat*) ganz aufgehen; (*performance etc*) von etw durchdrungen sein

soaking ['səʊkɪŋ] **ADJ** *person* klitschnass, patschnass; *object also* triefend **ADV** **~ wet** triefend nass, klitschnass **N** (= *steeping*) Einweichen *nt no indef art*; **to get a ~** patschnass werden; **to give sth a ~** etw einweichen

so-and-so ['səʊənsəʊ] N (*inf*) **a** (= *unspecified person*) Soundso *no art*; **~ up at the shop** Herr/Frau Soundso im Laden **b** (*pej*) **he's a real/an old ~** das ist ein gemeiner Kerl; **you old ~** du bist vielleicht einer/eine

soap [səʊp] **N** **a** (= *substance*) Seife *f* **b** (= *soap opera*) Seifenoper *f* (*inf*), Soap *f* (*inf*) **VT** einseifen, abseifen

soap: soapbox N (*lit:* = *packing case*) Seifenkiste *f*; (*fig:* = *platform*) Apfelsinenkiste *f*; (*as cart*) Seifenkiste *f*; **to get up on one's ~** (*fig*) Volksreden *pl* halten; **soapbox derby** N Seifenkistenrennen *nt*; **soapbox evangelist** N Wanderprediger(in) *m(f)*; **soapbox orator** N Volksredner(in) *m(f)*; **soap bubble** N Seifenblase *f*; **soapdish** N Seifenschale *f*; **soap dispenser** N Seifenspender *m*; **soap flakes** PL Seifenflocken *pl*; **soap opera** N (*TV, Rad:* *inf*) Seifenoper *f* (*inf*), Soap-Opera *f* (*inf*); **soap powder** N Seifenpulver *nt*; **soapstone** N Speckstein *m*; **soapsuds** PL Seifenschaum *m*

soapy ['səʊpɪ] ADJ (*+er*) **a** *taste, smell* seifig; **~ water** Seifenwasser *nt* **b** (*pej*, = *sentimental*) rührselig

soar [sɔː] VI **a** (*rise: also* **soar up**) aufsteigen; **to ~ (up) into the sky** zum Himmel steigen **b** (*fig, building, tower*) hochragen; (*price, cost, profit*) hochschnellen; (*ambition, popularity, reputation, hopes*) einen Aufschwung nehmen; (*morale, spirits*) einen Aufschwung bekommen; **the tower/hill ~ed above the town** der Turm/Hügel ragte über die Stadt hinaus

soaraway ['sɔːrəweɪ] ADJ (*inf*) *success* fantastisch (*inf*); *career* steil; **~ sales** explosionsartig ansteigende Verkaufszahlen *pl*

soaring ['sɔːrɪŋ] ADJ **a** *bird, plane* aufsteigend, in die Luft steigend; *tower* hoch aufragend; *imagination, ideas, ambition* hochfliegend; *popularity, reputation* schnell zunehmend; *prices* in die Höhe schnellend; *inflation* unaufhaltsam; *unemployment* hochschnellend; *pride, hopes* wachsend; **I watched the lark's ~ flight** ich sah, wie sich die Lerche in die Lüfte schwang; **the ~ crime rate** die schnell zunehmende Verbrechensrate **b** (*liter*) *voice, music* sich erhebend

sob [sɒb] **N** Schluchzer *m*, Schluchzen *nt no pl*; **to give a ~** (auf)schluchzen; **..., he said with a ~** ..., sagte er schluchzend **VI** schluchzen (*with* vor +*dat*); **~, ~** (*inf*) schluchz, schluchz **VT** schluchzen; **to ~ oneself to sleep** sich in den Schlaf weinen

▶**sob out** VT *sep information* schluchzend hervorstoßen; *story* schluchzend erzählen; **to sob one's heart out** sich (*dat*) die Seele aus dem Leib weinen

s.o.b. (*esp US, sl*) abbr of **son of a bitch**

sobbing ['sɒbɪŋ] **N** Schluchzen *nt* **ADJ** schluchzend

sober ['səʊbə] ADJ **a** (= *not drunk*) nüchtern; **to be as ~ as a judge** stocknüchtern sein (*inf*) **b** (= *sedate, serious*) *life, expression, mood, occasion, person* ernst; (= *sensible, moderate*) *opinion* vernünftig; *assessment, statement, advice, facts* nüchtern **c** (= *not bright or showy*) schlicht, dezent; *colour, suit* gedeckt

▶**sober down** VI ruhiger werden

▶**sober up** **VT** *sep* (*lit*) nüchtern machen; (*fig*) zur Vernunft bringen **VI** (*lit*) nüchtern werden; (*fig*) ruhiger werden; (*after laughing, joking etc*) sich beruhigen

sober-headed [ˌsəʊbə'hedɪd] ADJ nüchtern, vernünftig

sobering ['səʊbərɪŋ] ADJ *effect, experience, thought* ernüchternd

soberly ['səʊbəlɪ] ADV nüchtern; *behave* vernünftig; *dress, furnish* schlicht, dezent

sober-minded [ˌsəʊbə'maɪndɪd] ADJ nüchtern, vernünftig

soberness ['səʊbənɪs] N = **sobriety**

sobersides ['səʊbəsaɪdz] N (*dated inf*) Fadian *m* (*inf*)

sobriety [sə'braɪɪtɪ] N **a** (= *not being drunk*) Nüchternheit *f*; **she maintained her ~ for 7 years** sie hat 7 Jahre lang nicht getrunken **b** (= *seriousness, sedateness*) Solidität *f*; (*of dress etc*) Schlichtheit *f*, Dezentheit *f*; (*of colour*) Gedecktheit *f*

sobriquet ['səʊbrɪkeɪ], **soubriquet** N Spitzname *m*

sob: sob sister N (*esp US, inf*) Briefkastentante *f* (*inf*); **sob story** N (*inf*) rührselige Geschichte (*inf*); **sob stuff** N (*inf*) Schmalz *m* (*inf*); (= *book, film*) Tränendrüsendrücker *m* (*inf*); (= *heartrending tale*) todtraurige Geschichte (*inf*)

Soc *abbr of* **Socialist** Soz.

SOC *abbr of* **society** Ges.

so-called [ˌsəʊ'kɔːld] ADJ so genannt, (= *supposed*) angeblich

soccer ['sɒkə] N Fußball *m*; **~ player** (*US*) Fußballer(in) *m(f)*, Fußballspieler(in) *m(f)*

sociability [ˌsəʊʃə'bɪlɪtɪ] N Geselligkeit *f*

sociable ['səʊʃəbl] ADJ **a** (= *gregarious*) gesellig; (= *friendly*) freundlich; **... just to be ~** ..., man möchte sich ja nicht ausschließen; **I'm not feeling very ~ today** mir ist heute nicht nach Geselligkeit (zumute *or* zu Mute); **they eat together because it's ~** sie essen aus Gründen der Geselligkeit zusammen

sociably ['səʊʃəblɪ] ADV *say* freundlich; **he didn't behave very ~** er war nicht gerade umgänglich

social ['səʊʃəl] **ADJ** **a** (= *relating to community*, = *Admin, Pol*) sozial; *structure, development, conditions, evil* gesellschaftlich, sozial; *order/system* Gesellschafts- *or* Sozialordnung *f*/-system *nt*; **~ reform/legislation/policy** Sozialreform *f*/-gesetzgebung *f*/-politik *f*; **to suffer from ~ deprivation** sozial benachteiligt sein; **~ justice** soziale Gerechtigkeit; **~ programme** Sozialprogramm *nt*; **~ research** Sozialforschung *f*; **~ spending** die Sozialausgaben *pl*; **to have a ~ conscience** ein soziales Gewissen haben; **to be a ~ outcast/misfit** ein sozialer Außenseiter/eine soziale Außenseiterin sein; **the norms of ~ behaviour** die gesellschaftlichen Normen *pl*; **~ skills** soziale Fähigkeiten *pl*

b *engagements, pleasures, ambitions, life, equal, superior, event, activities* gesellschaftlich; *visit* privat; *relationship* sozial; *behaviour* in Gesellschaft; *distinctions, advancement, rank, status* sozial, gesellschaftlich; **~ snobbery** Standesdünkel *m*; **to be sb's ~ inferior/superior** gesellschaftlich unter/über jdm stehen; **a room for ~ functions** ein Gesellschaftsraum *m*; (*larger*) ein Saal *m* für Gesellschaften; **there isn't much ~ life around here** hier in der Gegend wird gesellschaftlich nicht viel geboten; **how's your ~ life these days?** (*inf*) und was treibst du so privat? (*inf*); **a job which leaves no time for one's/a ~ life** ein Beruf, bei dem man keine Freizeit *or* kein Privatleben hat; **to have an active** *or* **a good ~ life** ein ausgefülltes Privatleben haben; **to broaden** *or* **widen one's ~ circle** seinen Bekanntenkreis erweitern; **to be a ~ drinker/smoker** nur in Gesellschaft trinken/rauchen; **a ~ acquaintance** ein Bekannter, eine Bekannte; **this isn't a ~ call** *or* **visit** dies ist kein privater Besuch; **to have**

~ contact with sb privaten Kontakt mit jdm pflegen

c (= *gregarious*) *evening, person* gesellig; (= *living in groups*) *animals, bees, ants etc* gesellig lebend, sozial; **~ gathering** (*form*) geselliges Beisammensein; **man is a ~ animal** der Mensch ist ein Gesellschaftswesen

N geselliger Abend

social: social administration N Sozialverwaltung *f*; **social anthropologist** N Sozialanthropologe *m*/-anthropologin *f*; **social anthropology** N Sozialanthropologie *f*; **Social Chapter** N (*Pol*) Sozialcharta *f*; **Social Charter** N (*Pol*) Sozialcharta *f*; **social class** N gesellschaftliche Klasse, Gesellschaftsklasse *f*; **social climber** N Emporkömmling *m* (*pej*), sozialer Aufsteiger, soziale Aufsteigerin; **social club** N Verein *m*, Klub *m* für geselliges Beisammensein; **social column** N Gesellschaftsspalte *f*; **social contract** N (*Hist*) der Gesellschaftsvertrag; **social democracy** N Sozialdemokratie *f*; **social democrat** N Sozialdemokrat(in) *m(f)*; **social democratic** ADJ sozialdemokratisch; **the Social Democratic Party** (*Brit*) die sozialdemokratische Partei; **social disease** N **a** (*euph:* = *VD*) Geschlechtskrankheit *f* **b** (*caused by social conditions*) Volksseuche *f*; **social engineering** N (*Sociol*) Steuerung *f* des Sozialverhaltens; **social exclusion** N sozialer Ausschluss; **social fund** N Sozialfonds *m*; **social history** N Sozialgeschichte *f*; **social housing** N (*Brit*) Sozialwohnungen *pl*; **social insurance** N Sozialversicherung *f*

socialism ['səʊʃəlɪzəm] N Sozialismus *m*

socialist ['səʊʃəlɪst] **ADJ** sozialistisch; **the Socialist Republic of ...** die Sozialistische Republik ...; **Socialist Workers' Party** Sozialistische Arbeiterpartei **N** Sozialist(in) *m(f)*

socialistic [ˌsəʊʃə'lɪstɪk] ADJ (*esp pej*) sozialistisch angehaucht

socialist realism N (*Art, Liter*) sozialistischer Realismus

socialite ['səʊʃəlaɪt] N (*inf*) Angehörige(r) *mf* der Schickeria *or* der feinen Gesellschaft; (= *man also*) Salonlöwe *m* (*inf*); **a London ~** eine Figur der Londoner Gesellschaft

socialization [ˌsəʊʃəlaɪ'zeɪʃən] N (*Pol*) Vergesellschaftung *f*, Sozialisierung *f*; (*Sociol, Psych*) Sozialisation *f*

socialize ['səʊʃəlaɪz] **VT** sozialisieren; *means of production* vergesellschaften **VI** **to ~ with sb** (= *meet socially*) mit jdm gesellschaftlich verkehren; (= *chat to*) sich mit jdm unterhalten; **I don't ~ much these days** ich komme zurzeit nicht viel unter die Leute; **she ~s a lot** sie hat ein reges gesellschaftliches Leben

socially ['səʊʃəlɪ] ADV **a** (*relating to community*) gesellschaftlich; *deprived, structured etc* sozial; **~ acceptable/unacceptable** gesellschaftlich akzeptabel/unakzeptabel; **~ aware** sozialbewusst, gesellschaftlich bewusst; **~ inferior** gesellschaftlich auf einer niedrigeren Stufe stehend; **~ prominent** gesellschaftlich bedeutend **b** (*as opposed to professionally etc*) gesellschaftlich; *meet* privat; **to mix ~ with sb** privaten Umgang mit jdm haben; **to know sb ~** jdn privat kennen

social: social realism N (*Art, Liter*) **a** sozialer Realismus **b** = **socialist realism**; **social science** N Sozialwissenschaft *f*; **social scientist** N Sozialwissenschaftler(in) *m(f)*; **social secretary** N persönlicher Sekretär, persönliche Sekretärin; (*of club*) Veranstaltungsbeauftragte(r) *mf*; **social security** N (*Brit*) Sozialhilfe *f*; (*US*) Sozialversicherungsleistungen *pl*; (= *scheme*) Sozialversicherung *f*; **to be on ~** (*Brit*) Sozialhilfeempfänger(in) sein; (*US*) Sozialversicherungsleistungen erhalten; **~ benefits** Sozialleistungen *pl*; **~ payments** (*Brit*) Sozialhilfe *f*; (*US*) Sozialversicherungsbezüge *pl*; **~ taxes** Sozialabgaben *pl*; **the ~ budget** der Sozialhaushalt; **~ minister** (*Brit*) Minister(in) *m(f)* für Soziales; **Social Security Administration** (*US*) Sozialversicherungsbehörde *f*; (= *social security office*) Sozialamt *nt*

SOCIAL SECURITY NUMBER

Die **social security number**, die Sozialversicherungsnummer, ist in den USA zu einer wichtigen landesweiten Identifikationshilfe geworden. Sie setzt sich aus neun Zahlen zusammen und war ursprünglich nur bei der Aufnahme eines Beschäftigungsverhältnisses oder für den Bezug von Sozialhilfe nötig. Seit 1987 bekommen Kinder gleich bei der Geburt eine **social security number** zugeteilt. Die Nummer wird auf Bankschecks gedruckt, einige Staaten benutzen sie für den Führerschein und Colleges und Universitäten als Immatrikulationsnummer.

social: social services PL Sozialdienste pl, soziale Einrichtungen pl; **social studies** N sing or pl ≈ Gemeinschaftskunde f; **social welfare** N soziales Wohl; **~ programme** Sozialfürsorgeprogramm nt; **~ system** (soziales) Wohlfahrtssystem; **social work** N Sozialarbeit f; **~ training** Sozialhelferausbildung f; **social worker** N Sozialarbeiter(in) m(f)

societal [sə'saɪətl] ADJ gesellschaftlich

society [sə'saɪətɪ] N **a** (= social community) die Gesellschaft; **modern industrial ~** die moderne Industriegesellschaft **b** (= company) Gesellschaft f; **I enjoy her ~** (esp liter) ich bin gerne in ihrer Gesellschaft; **everyone needs human ~** jeder braucht die Gesellschaft anderer Menschen **c** (= high society) die Gesellschaft; **London ~** die Londoner Gesellschaft, die gesellschaftlichen Kreise Londons; **to go into ~** in die Gesellschaft eingeführt werden; **the years she spent in ~** die Jahre, die sie in gesellschaftlichen or feinen Kreisen verbracht hat **d** (= club, organization) Verein m; (learned, Comm) Gesellschaft f; (debating, history, dramatic etc, Sch) Arbeitsgemeinschaft f; (Univ) Klub m; **cooperative ~** Genossenschaft f; **Society of Jesus** Gesellschaft Jesu

society in cpds Gesellschafts-; **society column** N Gesellschaftsspalte f; **society gossip** N Gesellschaftsklatsch m; **society man** N Mann m der Gesellschaft; **society wedding** N Hochzeit f in den besseren Kreisen

socio- [ˌsəʊsɪəʊ-] PREF sozio-; **socioeconomic** sozioökonomisch; **socioeconomic grouping** sozioökonomische Gruppe; **sociolinguistic** soziolinguistisch; **sociolinguistics** Soziolinguistik f

sociological ADJ [ˌsəʊsɪə'lɒdʒɪkəl] soziologisch

sociologically [ˌsəʊsɪə'lɒdʒɪkəlɪ] ADV soziologisch; **~ speaking** in soziologischer Hinsicht

sociologist [ˌsəʊsɪ'ɒlədʒɪst] N Soziologe m, Soziologin f

sociology [ˌsəʊsɪ'ɒlədʒɪ] N Soziologie f

sociopolitical [ˌsəʊsɪəʊpə'lɪtɪkəl] ADJ sozialpolitisch

sock[1] [sɒk] N Socke f, Socken m (inf); (knee-length) Kniestrumpf m; (= insole) Einlegesohle f; (= wind sock) Wind- or Luftsack m; **to pull one's ~s up** (Brit inf) sich am Riemen reißen (inf); **put a ~ in it!** (Brit, inf) hör auf damit!; **to work ones ~s off** (inf) bis zum Umkippen arbeiten (inf); **this will knock** or **blow your ~s off** (inf) das wird dich umhauen; **this film knocks the ~s off most other science fiction films** (inf) dieser Film stellt die meisten anderen Sciencefictionfilme in den Schatten

sock[2] N (inf) Schlag m (mit der Faust); **to give sb a ~ on the jaw/in the eye** jdm eine aufs Kinn/aufs Auge verpassen (inf); **that's a ~ in the eye for her!** (fig inf) das hat es ihr ordentlich gegeben! VT (inf, = hit) hauen (inf); **~ him one!** knall ihm eine! (inf), hau ihm eine rein! (inf); **he ~ed her right in the eye** er verpasste ihr eine aufs Auge

socket ['sɒkɪt] N **a** (of eye) Augenhöhle f; (of joint) Gelenkpfanne f; (of tooth) Zahnhöhle f; **to pull sb's arm out of its ~** jdm den Arm auskugeln **b** (Elec) Steckdose f; (for light bulb) Fassung f; (Mech) Sockel m, Fassung f

socket: socket joint N (Anat, Tech) Kugelgelenk nt; **socket wrench** N (Tech) Steckschlüssel m

socko ['sɒkəʊ] (US, inf) N (= great success) Bombenerfolg m (inf) ADJ (= great) bombig (inf)

Socrates ['sɒkrətiːz] N Sokrates m

Socratic [sɒ'krætɪk] ADJ sokratisch

sod[1] [sɒd] N (= turf) Grassode f; **beneath the ~** (liter) unter dem grünen Rasen (liter)

sod[2] (Brit, inf) N (mean, nasty) Sau f (inf); **the poor ~s** die armen Schweine (inf); **you stupid ~** blöde Sau! (inf); **~ him/you** der kann/du kannst mich mal (inf) or mal am Arsch lecken (vulg)!

▶ **sod off** VI (Brit, inf) Leine ziehen (inf), **sod off!** zieh Leine, du Arsch! (vulg)

soda ['səʊdə] N **a** (Chem) Soda nt; (= sodium oxide) Natriumoxid nt; (= caustic soda) Ätznatron nt **b** (= drink) Soda(wasser) nt

soda: soda biscuit, (US) **soda cracker** N Kräcker m; **soda bread** N mit Backpulver gebackenes Brot; **soda crystals** PL (Wasch-) soda nt; **soda fountain** N (dated US: serving drinks etc) Theke f; **soda pop** N (US inf) Limo f (inf)

sod all N (Brit inf: = nothing) rein gar nichts; **how much did he give you? – ~** wie viel hat er dir gegeben? – rein gar nichts (inf)

soda: soda siphon N Siphon m; **soda water** N Sodawasser nt

sodden ['sɒdn] ADJ durchnäßt, triefnaß; ground durchnäßt, durchweicht; **to be ~ with drink** sinnlos betrunken sein

sodding ['sɒdɪŋ] (Brit inf) ADJ verflucht (inf), Scheiß- (inf); **what a ~ nuisance** verdammte Scheiße (inf); **what the ~ hell is going on?** was zum Teufel geht hier vor? (inf) ADV verdammt (inf), verflucht (inf); **I'll ~ murder you if you do that!** verdammt noch mal, ich bring dich um, wenn du das tust! (inf)

sodium ['səʊdɪəm] N Natrium nt

sodium: sodium bicarbonate N Natron nt, doppeltkohlensaures Natrium; **sodium carbonate** N Natriumkarbonat nt, Soda nt; **sodium chloride** N Natriumchlorid nt, Kochsalz nt; **sodium hydroxide** N Natriumhydroxid nt, Ätznatron nt; **sodium nitrate** N Natriumnitrat nt

Sodom ['sɒdəm] N Sodom nt; **~ and Gomorrha** Sodom und Gomorr(h)a

sodomite ['sɒdəmaɪt] N jd, der Analverkehr betreibt

sodomize ['sɒdəmaɪz] VT sodomisieren

sodomy ['sɒdəmɪ] N Analverkehr m

Sod's law [ˌsɒdz'lɔː] N (inf) „Gesetz", demzufolge eine Sache, die schief gehen kann, auch bestimmt schief gehen wird **after all that it didn't work – that's ~, isn't it?** am Ende hat es noch nicht mal funktioniert – das musste ja so kommen

sofa ['səʊfə] N Sofa nt, Couch f; **~ bed** Sofabett nt, Schlafcouch f

soft [sɒft] ADJ (+er) **a** weich; meat zart; (pej, = flabby) muscle schlaff; **a book in ~ covers** ein kartoniertes Buch; **~ cheese** Weichkäse m; **~ margarine** ungehärtete Margarine; **~ ice cream** Softeis nt **b** (= smooth) skin zart; surface glatt; material, velvet weich; hair seidig; **as ~ as silk** or **velvet** seiden- or samtweich **c** (= gentle, not harsh) sanft; (= subdued) light, sound gedämpft, sanft; music gedämpft; (= not loud) leise; rain, breeze, tap, pressure leicht; fold, curve sanft; pleat zart; line weich; **a ~ landing** (lit, fig) eine weiche Landung **d** (Ling) consonant weich **e** (= weak) character, government schwach; treatment nachsichtig; (= lenient) teacher, parent nachsichtig, gutmütig; judge, sentence, punishment mild(e); **to be ~ with** or **on sb** jdm gegenüber nachgiebig sein; with children also jdm alles durchgehen lassen; **to be (too) ~ on sth** (zu) nachgiebig mit etw sein; **to go ~ (on sth)** (einer

Sache (dat) gegenüber) zu nachgiebig sein; **to have a ~ heart** ein weiches Herz haben; **to be as ~ as shit** (sl) ein Weichei sein (sl) **f** (= not tough) verweichlicht; liberalism gemäßigt; **he thinks it's ~ for a boy to play the violin** er hält es für unmännlich, wenn ein Junge Geige spielt; **to make sb ~** jdn verweichlichen; **the ~ left** (Pol) die gemäßigte Linke **g** (= easy) job, life bequem; **he has a ~ time of it** er hats leicht or bequem; **that's a ~ option** das ist der Weg des geringsten Widerstandes **h** (= kind, warm) smile warm; **he had another, ~er side to him** er hatte noch eine andere, gefühlvollere Seite **i** (Econ) currency weich; prices instabil; stocks, economy, growth schwach; market nachgiebig **j** drink alkoholfrei; drug, pornography weich; **~ porn film/magazine** weicher Porno; **~ porn actress** Softpornodarstellerin f **k** (Typ, Comput) return, hyphen weich **l** (Brit inf: = foolish) doof (inf), nicht ganz richtig im Kopf (inf); **he's ~ (in the head)** er ist nicht ganz richtig im Kopf (inf); **you must be ~!** du spinnst wohl! (inf); **I must be going ~** ich fange wohl an zu spinnen (inf) **m** (inf, = feeling affection) **to be ~ on sb** für jdn schwärmen; **to have a ~ spot for sb** eine Schwäche für jdn haben

soft: softball N Softball m; **soft-boiled** ADJ egg weich (gekocht); **soft centre** N (= chocolate) Praline f (mit Cremefüllung); **soft-centred** ADJ mit Cremefüllung; **soft coal** N Stein- or Fettkohle f; **soft-core** ADJ pornography weich; **soft-cover** ADJ **a ~ book** ein Taschenbuch nt

soften ['sɒfn] VT weich machen; water also enthärten; light, sound, colour dämpfen; effect, sb's anger, reaction, impression, tone mildern; outline weicher machen; image weich zeichnen; voice sanfter machen; resistance, opposition, sb's position, stance schwächen; demands, impact abschwächen VI (material, person, heart) weich werden; (voice, look) sanft werden; (anger, resistance) nachlassen; (outlines) weicher werden

▶ **soften up** VT sep **a** (lit) weich machen **b** (fig) person, opposition milde stimmen; (by flattery etc) schmeicheln (+dat); customer kaufwillig stimmen; (by bullying) einschüchtern, weich machen; enemy, resistance zermürben; enemy position schwächen; prisoner weich machen VI (material) weich werden; (person, attitude) nachgiebiger werden; **to soften up on sb** jdm gegenüber nachgiebig or schwach werden

softener ['sɒfnə] N Weichmacher m; (for water also) Enthärtungsmittel nt; (= fabric softener) Weichspüler m, Weichspülmittel nt

softening ['sɒfnɪŋ] N **a** (lit) Weichmachen nt; **~ of the brain** (Med) Gehirnerweichung f **b** (fig, of person) Erweichen nt; (of anger, resistance) Nachlassen nt; **there has been a ~ of his attitude** er ist nachgiebiger geworden

soft: soft focus N (Film, Phot) Weichzeichnung f; **a photo taken in ~** ein Foto mit weichen Kontrasten; **soft-focus lens** N Weichzeichner m; **soft-footed** ADJ tiger, person auf leisen Sohlen schleichend attr; tread leise, lautlos; **to be ~** leise gehen; **soft fruit** N (Brit) Beerenobst nt; **soft furnishings** PL (Brit) Vorhänge, Teppiche, Kissen etc; **softhead** N (inf) Schwachkopf m (inf); **soft-headed** ADJ (inf) doof (inf); **soft-hearted** ADJ weichherzig; **soft-heartedness** N Weichherzigkeit f

softie ['sɒftɪ] N (inf, too tender-hearted) gutmütiger Trottel (inf); (sentimental) sentimentaler Typ (inf); (effeminate, cowardly) Schlappschwanz m (inf), Weichling m (inf); **I know I'm an old ~ but ...** ich bin ja ein gutmütiger Typ or Mensch, aber ...

softly ['sɒftlɪ] ADV **a** (= gently, tenderly) sanft; (= not loud) leise; rain, blow leicht, sanft; **her hair falls ~ round her shoulders** ihr Haar fällt weich auf die Schultern; **a ~ blowing breeze** ein sanfter or schwacher Wind; **~ whipped cream** leicht geschlagene Sahne; **to be ~ spoken** eine angenehme Stimme haben; **~ lit** gedämpft beleuchtet **b** (= *leniently*) nachsichtig

softly-softly [ˌsɒftlɪˈsɒftlɪ] **ADJ** (*Brit*: = *careful*) *approach* vorsichtig; *style* taktvoll **ADV** sachte; **~ works best** man sollte behutsam vorgehen

softness [ˈsɒftnɪs] **N a** Weichheit *f*; (*of meat*) Zartheit *f*; (*of muscle*) Schlaffheit *f* **b** (= *smoothness, of skin*) Zartheit *f*; (*of surface*) Glätte *f*; (*of material, velvet*) Weichheit *f*; (*of hair*) Seidigkeit *f* **c** (= *gentleness*) Sanftheit *f*; (*of light*) Gedämpftheit *f*; (*of music*) leiser Klang; (*of rain, breeze, pressure*) Sanftheit *f*, Leichtheit *f* **d** (*Ling, of consonant*) Weichheit *f* **e** (= *weakness, of character, government*) Schwäche *f*; (*of treatment*) Nachsichtigkeit *f*; (= *leniency, of teacher, parent*) Gutmütigkeit *f*; (*of judge, punishment*) Milde *f* **f** (= *ease: of life, job*) Bequemlichkeit *f*

soft: soft option N **to take the ~** den Weg des geringsten Widerstands gehen; **soft palate** N weicher Gaumen, Gaumensegel *nt*; **soft pedal** N (*Mus; on piano*) Dämpfer *m*, Pianopedal *nt*; **soft-pedal** **VT** (*Mus*) note, passage mit Dämpfer spielen; (*fig inf*) demands etc herunterschrauben **VI** zurückstecken; **soft sell** N Softsell *m*, weiche Verkaufstaktik; **he's very good at the ~** er kann die Leute sehr gut auf sanfte Art *or* auf die sanfte Tour (*inf*) überreden; **soft-shelled** ADJ weichschalig; **soft shoulder** N (*of road*) unbefestigtes Bankett; **soft-soap** (*Brit fig*) **N** Schmeichelei *f* **VT** einseifen (*inf*), um den Bart gehen (+*dat*); **they ~ed him into doing it** sie sind ihm so lange um den Bart gegangen, bis er es getan hat (*inf*); **soft-spoken** ADJ person leise sprechend *attr*; **to be ~** eine angenehme Stimme haben; **soft target** N leichte Beute; (*Mil*) leichtes Ziel; **soft top** N (*esp US, Aut*) Kabriolett *nt*; **soft toy** N (*Brit*) Stofftier *nt*; **soft verges** PL (*Brit, Aut*) nicht befahrbare Bankette; (*on sign*) Seitenstreifen nicht befahrbar; **software** N Software *f*; **software company** N Softwarehaus *nt*; **software-controlled** ADJ softwaregesteuert; **software package** N Softwarepaket *nt*; **softwood** N Weichholz *nt*

softy N (*inf*) = softie

SOGAT [ˈsəʊɡæt] (*Brit old*) abbr of **Society of Graphical and Allied Trades** *britische Grafikergewerkschaft*

sogginess [ˈsɒɡɪnɪs] N triefende Nässe; (*of soil*) Aufgeweichtheit *f*; (*of food*) Matschigkeit *f* (*inf*); (*of cake, bread*) Klitschigkeit *f*

soggy [ˈsɒɡɪ] ADJ (+*er*) durchnässt, triefnass; *soil, compost* durchweicht; *food, vegetables* matschig (*inf*); *cake, bread* klitschig; **a ~ mess** eine Matsche

soi-disant [ˌswɑːˈdiːzɑːŋ] ADJ sogenannt, angeblich

soigné [ˈswɑːnjeɪ] ADJ gepflegt, soigniert (*geh*)

soil¹ [sɔɪl] N (= *earth, ground*) Erde *f*, Erdreich *nt*, Boden *m*; **cover it with ~** bedecken Sie es mit Erde; **native/foreign/British ~** heimatlicher/fremder/britischer Boden, heimatliche/fremde/britische Erde; **the ~** (*fig*, = *farmland*) die Scholle; **a son of the ~** ein mit der Scholle verwachsener Mensch

soil² **VT** (*lit*) beschmutzen, schmutzig machen; (*fig*) *reputation* beschmutzen, beflecken; *honour* beflecken; *oneself* besudeln; **the baby has ~ed its nappy** das Baby hat eine schmutzige Windel *or* hat in die Windel gemacht; **to ~ one's hands** (*lit, fig*) sich (*dat*) die Hände schmutzig *or* dreckig (*inf*) machen **VI** schmutzig werden, verschmutzen

soilage [ˈsɔɪlɪdʒ] N (*Agr*) Grünfutter *nt*

soil conservation N Bodenschutz *m*

soiled [sɔɪld] ADJ schmutzig, verschmutzt; *goods* verschmutzt; *sanitary towel* gebraucht; **~ linen** Schmutzwäsche *f*

soil pipe N Abflussrohr *nt*

soirée [ˈswɑːreɪ] N (*form*) Soirée *f* (*geh*)

soixante-neuf [ˌswæsɑːntˈnɜːf] N Neunundsechzig *nt no art*, Soixante-neuf *nt no art*

sojourn [ˈsɒdʒɜːn] **N** (*liter*) Aufenthalt *m*; (= *place*) Aufenthaltsort *m* **VI** (ver)weilen (*liter*) (*in* in +*dat*)

sojourner [ˈsɒdʒənə] N (*geh*) Gast *m*, Besucher(in) *m(f)*

solace [ˈsɒlɪs] **N** Trost *m* **VT** trösten

solar [ˈsəʊlə] ADJ Sonnen-, Solar-; **~ activity** Sonnenaktivität *f*; **~ calendar** Sonnenkalender *m*; **~ heat** Sonnenwärme *f*; **~ power/radiation** Sonnenkraft *f*/-strahlung *f*; **~ year** Sonnenjahr *nt*

solar: solar battery N Sonnen- *or* Solarbatterie *f*; **solar cell** N Solarzelle *f*; **solar collector** N Sonnenkollektor *m*; **solar eclipse** N Sonnenfinsternis *f*; **solar energy** N Sonnenenergie *f*; **solar flare** N Sonneneruption *f*; **solar heating** N Solarheizung *f*

solarium [səʊˈlɛərɪəm] **N** *pl* **solaria** [səʊˈlɛərɪə] Solarium *nt*

solar: solar panel N Sonnenkollektor *m*; **solar plexus** N Solarplexus *m* (*spec*), Magengrube *f*; **solar-powered** ADJ durch Sonnenenergie angetrieben, mit Sonnenenergie betrieben; **solar system** N Sonnensystem *nt*; **solar wind** N Sonnen- *or* Solarwind *m*

sold [səʊld] pret, ptp of **sell**

solder [ˈsəʊldə] **N** Lötmittel *nt*, Lötzinn *nt* **VT** löten; (= *solder together*) verlöten; **~ed joint** Lötstelle *f*

soldering iron [ˈsəʊldərɪŋaɪən] N Lötkolben *m*

soldier [ˈsəʊldʒə] **N a** Soldat(in) *m(f)*; **~ of fortune** Söldner(in) *m(f)*; **to play (at) ~s** Soldaten *or* Krieg spielen; **old ~** altgedienter Soldat; (*fig*) alter Kämpe; **old ~s never die(, they just fade away)** (*prov*) manche Leute sind nicht totzukriegen (*inf*) **b** (*Zool*) Soldat *m* **VI** Soldat(in) sein, (in der Armee) dienen; **after 6 years of ~ing** nach 6 Jahren Dienst in der Armee; **tired of ~ing** des Soldatenlebens müde

▶**soldier on** VI unermüdlich weitermachen; **two of them soldiered on to the top** zwei kämpften sich bis zum Gipfel vor

soldierly [ˈsəʊldʒəlɪ] ADJ soldatisch

soldiery [ˈsəʊldʒərɪ] N Soldaten *pl*, Soldateska *f* (*pej geh*)

sole¹ [səʊl] **N** Sohle *f* **VT** besohlen

sole² N (= *fish*) Seezunge *f*

sole³ ADJ *reason, responsibility, owner, ownership* alleinig; *use* ausschließlich; **with the ~ exception of ...** mit alleiniger Ausnahme +*gen* ...; **for the ~ purpose of ...** einzig und allein zu dem Zweck +*gen* ..., zum alleinigen *or* einzigen Zweck +*gen* ...; **he is the ~ remaining candidate** er ist der einzige (noch) verbleibende *or* noch übrige Kandidat; **~ heir** Alleinerbe *m*/-erbin *f*; **their ~ surviving daughter** ihre einzige überlebende Tochter

sole: sole agency N Alleinvertretung *f*; **sole agent** N Alleinvertreter(in) *m(f)*; **sole beneficiary** N (*Jur*) Alleinbegünstigte(r) *m(f)*

solecism [ˈsɒlɪsɪzəm] N (*linguistic*) Solözismus *m* (*geh*), Fehler *m*; (*in behaviour etc*) Fauxpas *m*

-soled [-səʊld] ADJ suf mit ... Sohlen; **soft-soled** mit weichen Sohlen; **rubber-soled** mit Gummisohlen

solely [ˈsəʊllɪ] ADV (einzig und) allein, nur; **he is ~ responsible** er allein trägt die Verantwortung, er ist allein verantwortlich; **they are not ~ to blame** man kann ihnen nicht die alleinige Schuld geben; **~ because of this ...** nur *or* allein deswegen ...

solemn [ˈsɒləm] ADJ feierlich; *face, mood, music also, person, plea, warning* ernst; *architecture* ehrwürdig, erhaben; *promise, duty, oath* heilig; (= *drab*) *colour* trist; **in a ~ tone** mit feierlicher Stimme; **I give you my ~ word** ich verspreche es hoch und heilig

solemnity [səˈlemnɪtɪ] N Feierlichkeit *f*; (*of face, mood, music also, person, plea, warning*) Ernst *m*; (*of architecture*) Ehrwürdigkeit *f*, Erhabenheit *f*; (*of promise, duty, oath*) heiliger Ernst; (*of colour*) Tristheit *f*; **with great ~** feierlich (und würdig)

solemnization [ˌsɒləmnaɪˈzeɪʃən] N feierlicher Vollzug

solemnize [ˈsɒləmnaɪz] VT feierlich begehen; *marriage* (feierlich) vollziehen

solemnly [ˈsɒləmlɪ] ADV feierlich; *walk* gemessenen Schrittes, würdevoll; *look, warn, plead* ernst; *say* ernsthaft; *promise* hoch und heilig; *swear* bei allem, was einem heilig ist; **I do ~ swear to tell the truth** (*Jur*) ich schwöre feierlich, die Wahrheit zu sagen

solenoid [ˈsəʊlənɔɪd] N Magnetspule *f*; **~ switch** Magnetschalter *m*

sole: sole rights PL Alleinrechte *pl*; **sole trader** N Einzelunternehmer(in) *m(f)*, Einzelkaufmann *m*/-kauffrau *f*

sol-fa [ˌsɒlˈfɑː] N Solmisation *f*

solicit [səˈlɪsɪt] **VT** *support, money, donations* erbitten, bitten um; *person* anflehen, inständig bitten; *business, sympathy* werben um; *news, advice, help* bitten um; (*prostitute*) customers ansprechen; **to ~ sb for sex** (*prostitute*) jdm Sex anbieten; **to ~ sb for sth** jdn um etw bitten, etw von jdm erbitten; **to ~ custom** um Kunden werben **VI** (*prostitute*) Kunden anwerben, zur Unzucht auffordern (*form*)

solicitation [səˌlɪsɪˈteɪʃən] N (*form*) Flehen *nt no pl* (*geh*)

soliciting [səˈlɪsɪtɪŋ] N Aufforderung *f* zur Unzucht

solicitor [səˈlɪsɪtə] N (*Jur, Brit*) Rechtsanwalt *m*/-anwältin *f* (*der/die normalerweise nicht vor Gericht plädiert*); (*US*) Justizbeamte(r) *m*/-beamtin *f*; **Solicitor General** (*Brit*) zweiter Kronanwalt, zweite Kronanwältin; (*US*) ≈ Generalstaatsanwalt *m*/-anwältin *f*

solicitous [səˈlɪsɪtəs] ADJ (*form*, = *concerned*) besorgt (*about* um); (= *eager*) dienstbeflissen; **to be ~ of sb** um jdn besorgt sein

solicitously [səˈlɪsɪtəslɪ] ADV (*form*) besorgt; (= *eagerly*) eifrig

solicitude [səˈlɪsɪtjuːd] N (*form*) Besorgtheit *f*

solid [ˈsɒlɪd] **ADJ a** (= *firm, not liquid*) fuel, food, substance fest; **~ body** Festkörper *m*; **to be frozen ~** hart gefroren sein; **to be stuck ~** fest sitzen; **the pudding is rather ~** der Nachtisch ist ziemlich schwer

b (= *pure, not hollow, not broken*) block, gold, oak, rock massiv; *matter* fest; *crowd, traffic etc* dicht; *stretch, row, line* ununterbrochen; *queue, line of people etc* geschlossen; *layer* dicht, dick; *week* ganz; (= *heavily-built*) person stämmig; **~ ball/tyre** Vollgummiball *m*/-reifen *m*; **the square was packed ~ with cars** die Autos standen dicht an dicht auf dem Platz; **the room was ~ with people** der Raum war mit Leuten voll gedrängt; **the garden was a ~ mass of colour** der Garten war ein einziges Farbenmeer; **they worked for two ~ days** sie haben zwei Tage ununterbrochen gearbeitet, sie haben zwei volle Tage gearbeitet; **we had a week of ~ rain** wir hatten eine Woche lang Dauerregen *m*; **he was 6 ft of ~ muscle** er war fast 2 Meter groß und bestand nur aus Muskeln; **a man of ~ build** ein kräftig *or* massiv gebauter Mann; **a ~ gold bracelet** ein Armband *nt* aus massivem Gold

c (= *stable, secure*) bridge, house, car stabil; *furniture, piece of work, character* solide; *foundations, ground* fest; *business, firm* gesund, solide, reell; (= *worthy*) place respektabel; (= *powerful*) grip kraftvoll; (= *competent*) performance solide; **he's a good ~ worker** er ist ein solider *or* guter Arbeiter; **he's a good ~ sort** er ist ein verlässlicher Kerl; **he is a ~ citizen** er ist ein grundsolider Bürger

d *reason, argument* handfest, stichhaltig; *grounds* gut, fundiert; **it makes ~ good sense** das leuchtet durchaus ein; **~ common sense** gesunder Menschenverstand

e (= *unanimous*) vote einstimmig; *support* voll, geschlossen; **to be ~ on sth** (*accept/reject*) etw einstimmig *or* geschlossen annehmen/ablehnen; **we are ~ behind you/that proposal** wir stehen voll und ganz hinter Ihnen/diesem Vorschlag; **we are ~ for peace** wir sind hundertprozentig für den Frieden; **Newtown is ~ for Labour** Newtown wählt fast ausschließlich Labour

f (= *valuable, substantial*) *education, knowledge, grounding* solide; *relationship* stabil; *meal* kräftig, nahrhaft

g (= *not hyphenated*) **to be written ~** zusammengeschrieben werden

h (*dated US, inf,* = *excellent*) prima *inv* (*inf*)

ADV **a** (= *completely*) völlig; **the main streets were jammed ~** die Hauptstraßen waren völlig verstopft; **flights to Israel are booked ~** Flüge nach Israel sind voll or total ausgebucht

b (= *without a break*) pausenlos; **for eight hours ~** acht Stunden lang ununterbrochen

N a fester Stoff; **~s and liquids** feste und flüssige Stoffe *pl*, (*Sci*) Festkörper und Flüssigkeiten *pl*

b (*Geometry*) Körper *m*

c **solids** PL (= *food*) feste Nahrung *no pl*; (= *sewage*) Feststoffe *pl*

solidarity [ˌsɒlɪˈdærɪtɪ] N Solidarität *f*

solid: solid figure N (*Geometry*) Körper *m*; **solid fuel** N fester Brennstoff; (*for rockets*) Feststoff *m*; **solid geometry** N Raumlehre *f*

solidification [səˌlɪdɪfɪˈkeɪʃən] N Festwerden *nt*, Verfestigung *f*; (*of planet, lava etc*) Erstarrung *f*; (*of metal also*) Erhärtung *f*; (*of blood*) Gerinnung *f*; (*fig, of support*) Festigung *f*

solidify [səˈlɪdɪfaɪ] **VI** fest werden, (*planet, lava etc*) erstarren; (*metal also*) hart werden; (*blood*) gerinnen; (*fig: support*) sich festigen **VT** fest werden lassen; *lava* erstarren lassen; *metal also* hart werden lassen; *blood* gerinnen lassen; (*fig*) *support* festigen

solidity [səˈlɪdɪtɪ] N **a** (*of substance*) Festigkeit *f* **b** (= *stability, of bridge, house, car*) Stabilität *f*; (*of furniture also, piece of work, character*) solide Art; (*of foundations*) Festigkeit *f* **c** (= *unanimity, of vote*) Einstimmigkeit *f*; (*of support*) Geschlossenheit *f*

solidly [ˈsɒlɪdlɪ] ADV **a** (= *firmly*) *stuck, secured* fest; (= *hard*) hart; **~ built** (*house*) fest or solide gebaut; *person* kräftig or massiv gebaut; **to be ~ based on sth** fest auf etw (*dat*) beruhen **b** *reasoned, argued* stichhaltig **c** (= *uninterruptedly*) *work* ununterbrochen **d** (= *unanimously*) *vote* einstimmig; *support* geschlossen; **to be ~ behind sb/sth** geschlossen hinter jdm/etw stehen **e** (= *thoroughly*) *Republican, Conservative* durch und durch; **a ~ middle-class neighbourhood** eine durch und durch bürgerliche Nachbarschaft

solid-state [ˌsɒlɪdˈsteɪt] ADJ Festkörper-; (*Elec*) Halbleiter-; **~ laser** Halbleiterlaser *m*

solid-state physics N Festkörperphysik *f*

soliloquize [səˈlɪləkwaɪz] **VI** monologisieren; (= *talk to oneself*) Selbstgespräche führen **VT** zu sich selbst sagen

soliloquy [səˈlɪləkwɪ] N Monolog *m* (*also Theat*), Zwiegespräch *nt* mit sich selbst

solipsism [ˈsɒlɪpsɪzəm] N Solipsismus *m*

solipsist [ˈsɒlɪpsɪst] N Solipsist(in) *m(f)*

solipsistic [ˌsɒlɪpˈsɪstɪk] ADJ solipsistisch

solitaire [ˌsɒlɪˈtɛəʳ] N (= *game*) Patience *f*; (= *gem*) Solitär *m*

solitariness [ˈsɒlɪtərɪnɪs] N (*of task*) Einsamkeit *f*; (*of life*) Abgeschiedenheit *f*

solitary [ˈsɒlɪtərɪ] ADJ **a** (= *alone, secluded*) *life, person* einsam; *place* abgelegen, einsam; **a few ~ houses** ein paar einzelne or vereinzelte Häuser; **to take a ~ walk** allein einen Spaziergang machen; **do you enjoy this ~ life?** gefällt Ihnen das Leben so allein?; **in ~ splendour** in einsamer Pracht; **a ~ person** ein Einzelgänger *m*, eine Einzelgängerin; **I'm not a ~ drinker** ich trinke nicht gern allein; **she ate a ~ dinner** sie nahm ein einsames Mahl

b (= *sole*) *case, example, goal* einzig; **with the ~ exception of ...** mit alleiniger Ausnahme von ...; **not a ~ one** kein Einziger

N (= *solitary confinement*) Einzelhaft *f*

solitary confinement N Einzelhaft *f*; **to be put/kept** *or* **held in ~** in Einzelhaft genommen/ gehalten werden

solitude [ˈsɒlɪtjuːd] N Einsamkeit *f*; (*of place also*) Abgelegenheit *f*

solo [ˈsəʊləʊ] **N** Solo *nt*; **piano ~** Klaviersolo *nt* **ADJ** Solo-; **a ~ goal** ein im Alleingang geschossenes Tor; **~ album** Soloalbum *nt*; **~ artist** Solokünstler(in) *m(f)*; **~ flight** Solo- or Alleinflug *m*; **~ passage** (*Mus*) Solopassage *f*; **~ performance** (*Mus*) Solo *nt*; (*Theat*) Solovorstellung *f* **ADV** allein; (*Mus*) solo; **to go ~** (*musician etc*) eine Solokarriere einschlagen; **to fly ~** einen Alleinflug machen

soloist [ˈsəʊləʊɪst] N Solist(in) *m(f)*

Solomon [ˈsɒləmən] N Salomo(n) *m*; **the ~ Islands** die Salomonen *pl*, die Salomon-Inseln *pl*

solstice [ˈsɒlstɪs] N Sonnenwende *f*, Solstitium *nt* (*spec*)

solubility [ˌsɒljʊˈbɪlɪtɪ] N **a** Löslichkeit *f* **b** (*of problem*) Lösbarkeit *f*

soluble [ˈsɒljʊbl] ADJ **a** löslich, auflösbar; **~ in water** wasserlöslich; **fat-soluble** fettlöslich **b** *problem* lösbar

solution [səˈluːʃən] ✿ 26.3 N **a** Lösung *f* (*to +gen*); (*of crime*) Aufklärung *f*; **a problem incapable of ~** ein unlösbares Problem **b** (*Chem,* = *liquid*) Lösung *f*; (= *act*) Auflösen *nt*

solvable [ˈsɒlvəbl] ADJ = **soluble b**

solve [sɒlv] VT *problem, equation* lösen; *mystery* enträtseln; *crime, murder* aufklären; **that problem remains to be ~d** dieses Problem muss noch geklärt werden

solvency [ˈsɒlvənsɪ] N (*Fin*) Zahlungsfähigkeit *f*, Solvenz *f*

solvent [ˈsɒlvənt] **ADJ** **a** (*Chem*) lösend **b** (*Fin*) zahlungsfähig, solvent **N** (*Chem*) Lösungsmittel *nt*

solvent: solvent abuse N (*Brit form*) Lösungsmittelmissbrauch *m*; **solvent abuser** N (*Brit form*) Schnüffler(in) *m(f)* (*inf*); **solvent agent** N Lösungsmittel *nt*

solvent agent N Lösungsmittel *nt*

Som (*Brit*) *abbr of* **Somerset**

Somali [səˈmɑːlɪ] **ADJ** somali; *person, culture, institution* somalisch; **he is ~** er ist Somalier **N** **a** Somali *mf*, Somalier(in) *m(f)* **b** (*Ling*) Somali *nt*

Somalia [səˈmɑːlɪə] N Somalia *nt*

Somaliland [səˈmɑːlɪlænd] N Somaliland *nt*

somatic [səˈmætɪk] ADJ somatisch

sombre, (*US*) **somber** [ˈsɒmbəʳ] ADJ **a** (= *dark*) dunkel; (= *gloomy*) düster **b** (= *grave, serious*) *prospect* trüb, düster; *message* trüb, traurig; *news* traurig; *face* düster; *person* düster, finster; *music* trist, trauervoll; **in ~ mood** in trüber or düsterer Stimmung

sombrely, (*US*) **somberly** [ˈsɒmbəlɪ] ADV *say* traurig, düster; *watch* finster; *dress* trist

sombreness, (*US*) **somberness** [ˈsɒmbənɪs] N **a** (= *darkness*) Dunkelheit *f*; (= *gloominess*) Düsterkeit *f* **b** (*of mood*) Trübheit *f*; (*of news*) trauriger Charakter; (*of face*) Düsterkeit *f*; (*of person*) finsteres or düsteres Wesen; (*of music*) trauervoller or trister Klang

sombrero [sɒmˈbrɛərəʊ] N Sombrero *m*

some [sʌm] **ADJ** **a** (*with plural nouns*) einige; (= *a few, emph*) ein paar; (= *any: in* "if" *clauses, questions*) *meist nicht übersetzt* **if you have ~ questions** wenn Sie Fragen haben; **did you bring ~ records?** hast du Schallplatten mitgebracht?; **~ records of mine** einige meiner Platten; **would you like ~ more biscuits?** möchten Sie noch (ein paar) Kekse?; **take ~ nuts** nehmen Sie sich (*dat*) doch (ein paar) Nüsse; **~ few people** einige wenige Leute; **~ suggestions, please!** Vorschläge bitte!

b (*with singular nouns*) etwas, *meist nicht übersetzt* (= *a little, emph*) etwas, ein bisschen; **there's ~ ink on your shirt** Sie haben Tinte auf dem Hemd; **would you like ~ cheese?** möchten

Sie (etwas) Käse?; **~ more (tea)?** noch etwas (Tee)?; **leave ~ cake for me** lass mir ein bisschen or etwas Kuchen übrig; **did she give you ~ money/sugar?** hat sie Ihnen Geld/Zucker gegeben?; **have you got ~ money?** haben Sie Geld?; **it was (of) ~ help** es war eine gewisse Hilfe; **we played ~ golf** wir haben ein bisschen Golf gespielt

c (= *certain, in contrast*) manche(r, s); **~ people say ...** manche Leute sagen ...; **~ people just don't care** es gibt Leute, denen ist das einfach egal; **there are ~ things you just don't say** es gibt (gewisse or manche) Dinge, die man einfach nicht sagt; **~ questions were really difficult** manche (der) Fragen waren wirklich schwierig; **~ work is very rewarding** manche Arbeit ist sehr lohnend; **~ butter is salty** manche Buttersorten sind salzig; **~ in ~ ways** in gewisser Weise

d (*vague, indeterminate*) irgendein; **~ book/man or other** irgendein Buch/Mann; **~ woman rang up** da hat eine Frau angerufen; **~ woman, whose name I forget ...** eine Frau, ich habe ihren Namen vergessen, ...; **~ idiot of a driver** irgend so ein Idiot von (einem) Autofahrer; **at ~ place in Africa** irgendwo in Afrika; **in ~ way or another** irgendwie; **or ~ such** oder so etwas Ähnliches; **or ~ such name** oder so ein ähnlicher Name; **(at) ~ time last week** irgendwann letzte Woche; **~ time or other** irgendwann einmal; **~ other time** ein andermal; **~ day** eines Tages; **~ day next week** irgendwann nächste Woche

e (*intensifier*) ziemlich; (*in exclamations*) vielleicht ein (*inf*); **it took ~ courage** dazu brauchte man schon (einigen) or ziemlichen Mut; **(that was) ~ argument/party!** das war vielleicht ein Streit/eine Party! (*inf*); **that's ~ whisky** das ist vielleicht ein Whisky! (*inf*); **it's ~ size!** das ist vielleicht ein Ding!; **this might take ~ time** das könnte einige Zeit dauern; **quite ~ time** ganz schön lange (*inf*), ziemlich lange; **to speak at ~ length** ziemlich lange sprechen; **it's ~ distance from the house** es ist ziemlich weit vom Haus entfernt

f (*iro*) vielleicht ein (*inf*); **~ experts!** das sind vielleicht Experten! (*inf*); **~ help you are/this is** du bist/das ist mir vielleicht eine Hilfe (*inf*); **~ people!** Leute gibts!

PRON **a** (= *some people*) einige; (= *certain people*) manche; (*in* "if" *clauses, questions*) welche; **~ ..., others ...** manche ..., andere ...; **~ of my friends** einige or manche meiner Freunde; **there are still ~ who will never understand** es gibt immer noch Leute, die das nicht begreifen werden; **~ of them were late** einige kamen zu spät

b (*referring to plural nouns,* = *a few*) einige; (= *certain ones*) manche; (*in* "if" *clauses, questions*) welche; **~ of these books** einige dieser Bücher; **~ of them have been sold** einige sind verkauft worden; **I've only seen ~ of the mountains** ich habe nur ein paar von den Bergen gesehen; **they're lovely, try ~** die schmecken gut, probieren Sie mal; **I've still got ~** ich habe noch welche; **he took ~** er hat welche genommen; **tell me if you see ~** sagen Sie mir Bescheid, wenn Sie welche sehen; **would you like ~?** möchten Sie welche?

c (*referring to singular nouns,* = *a little*) etwas; (= *a certain amount, in contrast*) manches; (*in* "if" *clauses, questions*) welche(r, s); **here is the milk, if you feel thirsty drink ~** hier ist die Milch, wenn du Durst hast, trinke etwas; **I drank ~ of the milk** ich habe (etwas) von der Milch getrunken; **I drank ~ of the milk but not all** ich habe etwas von der Milch getrunken, aber nicht alles; **have ~!** nehmen Sie sich (*dat*), bedienen Sie sich; **it's lovely cake, would you like ~?** das ist ein sehr guter Kuchen, möchten Sie welchen?; **try ~ of this cake** probieren Sie doch mal diesen Kuchen; **would you like ~ money/tea? – no, I've got ~** möchten Sie Geld/ Tee? – nein, ich habe Geld/ich habe noch; **have you got money? – no, but he has ~** haben Sie Geld? – nein, aber er hat welches; **~ of it had been eaten** einiges (davon) war gegessen worden; **he only believed/read ~ of it** er hat es nur teilweise geglaubt/gelesen; **~ of his speech was excellent** manches *or* einiges in seiner Rede war ausgezeichnet; **~ of his work is good** manches, was er macht, ist gut

d **this is ~ of the oldest rock in the world** dies gehört zum ältesten Gestein der Welt; **~ of the finest poetry in the English language** einige der schönsten Gedichte in der englischen Sprache; **this is ~ of the finest scenery in Scotland** dies ist eine der schönsten Landschaften Schottlands

ADV **a** ungefähr, etwa, zirka; **~ 20 people** ungefähr 20 Leute; **~ few difficulties** einige Schwierigkeiten

b (*US inf*) (= *a little*) etwas, ein bisschen; (= *a lot*) viel; **it sure benefited us** ~ das hat uns ziemlich zu schaffen gemacht; **he's travelling** ~ er fährt schnell; **I really drank ~ last night** ich habe gestern Abend ganz schön was getrunken (*inf*); **that's going ~** das ist ganz schön schnell (*inf*)

somebody ['sʌmbədɪ] **PRON** jemand; (*dir obj*) jemand(en); (*indir obj*) jemandem; **~ else** jemand anders; **~ or other** irgendjemand; **~ knocked at the door** es klopfte jemand an die Tür; **we need ~ German** wir brauchen einen Deutschen; **everybody needs ~ to talk to** jeder braucht einen, mit dem er sprechen kann; **~ or other** irgendjemand; **you must have seen ~** Sie müssen doch irgendjemand(en) gesehen haben **N** **to be (a)** ~ etwas vorstellen, wer (*inf*) *or* jemand sein; **he thinks he's ~ now** er bildet sich (*dat*) ein, er wäre jetzt jemand *or* wer (*inf*)

someday ['sʌmdeɪ] **ADV** eines Tages

somehow ['sʌmhaʊ] **ADV** irgendwie; **it must be done ~ or other** es muss irgendwie gemacht werden; **~ (or other) I never liked him** irgendwie habe ich ihn nie gemocht *or* nie leiden können

someone ['sʌmwʌn] **PRON = somebody PRON**

someplace ['sʌmpleɪs] **ADV** (*US, inf*) *be* irgendwo; *go* irgendwohin; **~ else** (*be*) woanders; *go* woandershin

somersault ['sʌməsɔːlt] **N** Purzelbaum *m*; (*Sport, fig*) Salto *m*; **to do** *or* **turn a ~** einen Purzelbaum schlagen; (*Sport*) einen Salto machen; (*car*) sich überschlagen, einen Salto machen (*inf*); (*stomach*) einen Satz machen **VI** (*person*) einen Purzelbaum schlagen; (*Sport*) einen Salto machen; (*car*) sich überschlagen, einen Salto machen (*inf*); **the car ~ed into a lamppost** das Auto hat sich überschlagen und ist gegen einen Laternenpfahl geprallt

something ['sʌmθɪŋ] **PRON** **a** etwas; **~ nice/ unpleasant/serious** *etc* etwas Nettes/Unangenehmes/Ernstes *etc*; **~ or other** irgendetwas, irgendwas; **did you say ~?** hast du (et)was gesagt?; **~ of the kind** so (et)was (Ähnliches); **that's ~ I don't know** das weiß ich nicht; **there's ~ I don't like about him** irgendetwas *or* irgendwas gefällt mir an ihm nicht; **do you want to make ~ of it?** willst du dich mit mir anlegen? (*inf*); **there's ~ in what you say** an dem, was du sagst, ist (schon) was dran; **well, that's ~** (das ist) immerhin etwas; **he's ~ to do with the Foreign Office** er ist irgendwie beim Außenministerium; **she's called Rachel ~** sie heißt Rachel Soundso *or* Sowieso; **there were thirty ~** es waren etwas über dreißig; **three hundred and ~** dreihundert und ein paar (Zerquetschte (*inf*)); **we left at five ~** wir sind etwas nach fünf gegangen

b (*inf*, = *something special or unusual*) **it was ~ else** (*esp US*) *or* **quite ~** das war schon toll (*inf*); **it's quite ~ to be Prime Minister at 44** es will schon was heißen, mit 44 Premierminister zu sein; **what a beautiful dress! that's really ~** so ein schönes Kleid! ganz große Klasse! (*inf*)

c **or ~** (*inf*) oder so (was); **are you drunk or ~?** (*inf*) bist du betrunken oder was? (*inf*); **she's called Maria or ~ like that** sie heißt Maria oder so ähnlich

N **a little ~** (= *present etc*) eine kleine Aufmerksamkeit, eine Kleinigkeit; **a certain ~** ein gewisses Etwas; **that certain ~ that makes all the dif-**

ference das gewisse Etwas, auf das es ankommt

ADV **a** **~ over 200** etwas über 200, etwas mehr als 200; **~ like 200** ungefähr 200, um die 200 herum; **you look ~ like him** du siehst ihm irgendwie ähnlich; **this is ~ like the one I wanted** so (et)was Ähnliches wollte ich haben; **now that's ~ like a rose!** das nenne ich eine Rose!; **another £500, now that's ~ like** it noch £ 500 und wir kommen der Sache schon näher

b **it's ~ of a problem** das ist schon ein Problem; **I feel ~ of a stranger here** ich fühle mich hier irgendwie fremd; **he's ~ of a musician** er ist ein recht guter Musiker; **~ of a surprise** eine ziemliche Überraschung; **~ of a drunkard** ein ziemlicher Säufer

c (*Brit dial*) **they tease her ~ chronic** sie ziehen sie immer ganz furchtbar auf; **the weather was ~ shocking** das Wetter war einfach schrecklich

-something [-sʌmθɪŋ] **SUF** **he's twenty-something** er ist in den Zwanzigern *or* zwischen zwanzig und dreißig; **thirty-somethings** Leute *pl* in den Dreißigern *or* zwischen dreißig und vierzig; **most American twenty-somethings**, **most twenty-something Americans** die meisten Amerikaner in den Zwanzigern *or* zwischen zwanzig und dreißig

sometime ['sʌmtaɪm] **ADV** irgendwann; **~ or other it will have to be done** irgendwann muss es gemacht werden; **write to me ~ soon** schreib mir (doch) bald (ein)mal; **~ before tomorrow** bis morgen, heute noch; **~ next year** irgendwann nächstes Jahr *or* im nächsten Jahr **ADJ** *attr* (*form*) ehemalig, früher, einstig

sometimes ['sʌmtaɪmz] **ADV** manchmal

someway ['sʌmweɪ] **ADV** (*US*) irgendwie

somewhat ['sʌmwɒt] **ADV** ein wenig; **more than ~!** mehr als das!, und ob! (*inf*); **more than ~ disappointed/late** *etc* ganz schön enttäuscht/ verspätet *etc*; **the system is ~ less than perfect** das System funktioniert irgendwie nicht ganz; **it was ~ of a mystery** es war irgendwie rätselhaft; **~ of a surprise/disappointment** eine ziemliche *or* arge Überraschung/Enttäuschung; **~ of a drunkard** ein arger Trinker; **~ to my surprise ...** ziemlich überraschend für mich ...

somewhere ['sʌmweə'] **ADV** *be* irgendwo; *go* irgendwohin; **~ else** irgendwo anders, anderswo, irgendwo anders hin, anderswohin; **to take one's business ~ else** seine Geschäfte woanders machen; **from ~** von irgendwo, irgendwoher; **from ~ else** von irgendwo anders, anderswoher; **I left it ~ or other** ich habe es irgendwo liegen/stehen lassen; **I know ~ where ...** ich weiß, wo ...; **I needed ~ to live in London** ich brauchte irgendwo in London eine Unterkunft; **we just wanted ~ to go after school** wir wollten bloß einen Ort, wo wir nach der Schule eingehen können; **it's about ~ or around ~** es ist hier irgendwo; **~ about or a-round here** irgendwo hier in der Nähe; **~ nice/ cheap** irgendwo, wo es nett/billig ist; **the ideal place to go is ~ like New York** am besten fährt man in eine Stadt wie New York; **he went to live in Cumbria or ~ like that** er zog nach Cumbria oder so; **somebody ~ must know where she is** irgendjemand irgendwo muss wissen, wo sie ist; **don't I know you from ~?** kenne ich Sie nicht von irgendwoher?

b (*fig*) **the temperature was ~ about 40° C** die Temperatur betrug ungefähr 40° C *or* war um die 40° (*inf*); **~ about £50 or in the region of £50** etwa £ 50 *or* (die) £ 50 herum; **she is ~ in her fifties** sie muss in den Fünfzigern sein; **~ between midnight and one o'clock** irgendwann zwischen Mitternacht und ein Uhr; **the truth lies ~ in the middle** die Wahrheit liegt irgendwo dazwischen; **~ between 10,000 and 20,000 people** irgendwo zwischen 10.000 und 20.000 Leute; **now we're getting ~** jetzt kommen wir voran

somnambulism [sɒm'næmbjʊlɪzəm] **N** Nacht- *or* Schlafwandeln *nt*, Mondsüchtigkeit *f*, Somnambulismus *m* (*spec*)

somnambulist [sɒm'næmbjʊlɪst] **N** Nacht- *or* Schlafwandler(in) *m(f)*, Mondsüchtige(r) *mf*, Somnambule *mf* (*spec*)

somnolence ['sɒmnələns] **N** Schläfrigkeit *f*; **the heavy ~ of this summer's day** die bleierne Schwere dieses Sommertages

somnolent ['sɒmnələnt] **ADJ** **a** (= *sleepy*) schläfrig **b** (= *causing sleep*) einschläfernd

son [sʌn] **N** (*lit, fig*) Sohn *m*; (*as address*) mein Junge; **Son of God/Man** Gottes-/Menschensohn *m*; **the ~s of men** (*liter*) die Menschen; **he's his father's ~** er ist ganz der Vater; **~ of a bitch** (*esp US sl*) Scheißkerl *m* (*inf*), Hurensohn *m* (*vulg*); (= *thing*) Scheißding *nt* (*inf*); **~ of a gun** (*esp US, inf*) Schlawiner *m* (*inf*)

sonant ['səʊnənt] (*Ling, Phon*) **N** Sonant *m*, stimmhafter Laut **ADJ** stimmhaft

sonar ['səʊnɑː'] **N** Sonar(gerät) *nt*, Echolot *nt*

sonata [sə'nɑːtə] **N** Sonate *f*

sonata form **N** (*Mus*) Sonatenform *f*

sonatina [ˌsɒnə'tiːnə] **N** (*Mus*) Sonatine *f*

sonde [sɒnd] **N** (*Tech*) Sonde *f*

son et lumière [ˌsɒneɪ'luːmɪeə'] **N** Son et Lumière *nt*

song [sɒŋ] **N** **a** Lied *nt*; (= *modern folk song, blues song*) Song *m*; **give us a ~!** sing uns etwas vor!; **one of Brecht's ~s** ein Brecht-Song *m*; **to burst into ~** ein Lied anstimmen; **~-and-dance act** Gesangs- und Tanznummer *f*; **Song of Songs**, **Song of Solomon** Lied *nt* der Lieder, Hohelied *nt* Salomos

b (= *singing, bird song*) Gesang *m*

c (*Brit fig inf*) **to make a ~ and dance about sth** eine Haupt- und Staatsaktion aus etw machen (*inf*); **to be on a ~** (*Brit*) in Hochform sein; **to sell/buy sth for a ~** etw für einen Apfel und ein Ei *or* für ein Butterbrot verkaufen/kaufen; **it was going for a ~** das gab es für einen Apfel und ein Ei

song: songbird **N** Singvogel *m*; **songbook** **N** Liederbuch *nt*; **song cycle** **N** Liederzyklus *m*; **songless** **ADJ** Bird nicht singend *attr*; **song sheet** **N** Liedblatt *nt*, Liederzettel *m*; **songsmith** **N** (*liter*) Texter(in) *m(f)*

songster ['sɒŋstə'] **N** Sänger *m*

songstress ['sɒŋstrɪs] **N** Sängerin *f*

song: song thrush **N** Singdrossel *f*; **songwriter** **N** Texter(in) *m(f)* und Komponist(in) *m(f)*; (*of modern ballads*) Liedermacher(in) *m(f)*

sonic ['sɒnɪk] **ADJ** Schall-

sonic: sonic barrier **N** Schallmauer *f*; **sonic boom** **N** Überschallknall *m*; **sonic depth finder** **N** Echolot *nt*

son-in-law ['sʌnɪnlɔː] **N** *pl* **sons-in-law** Schwiegersohn *m*

sonnet ['sɒnɪt] **N** Sonett *nt*; **~ form** Sonettform *f*

sonny ['sʌnɪ] **N** (*inf*) Junge *m*; **~ Jim** (*inf*) mein Junge *m*

sonority [sə'nɒrɪtɪ] **N** Klangfülle *f*

sonorous ['sɒnərəs] **ADJ** volltönend, sonor (*geh*); *language, poem* klangvoll; *snore* laut

sonorously ['sɒnərəslɪ] **ADV** volltönend, sonor (*geh*); **the French horns echoing ~ in the background** das volle Echo der Hörner im Hintergrund

sonorousness ['sɒnərəsnɪs] **N** Klangfülle *f*

sons-in-law *pl of* **son-in-law**

soon [suːn] **ADV** **a** (= *in a short time from now*) bald; (= *early*) früh; (= *quickly*) schnell; **it will ~ be Christmas** bald ist Weihnachten; **~ after his death** kurz nach seinem Tode; **~ afterwards** kurz *or* bald danach; **how ~ can you be ready?** wann kannst du fertig sein?; **how ~ would you like it back?** wann *or* bis wann möchtest du es wiederhaben?; **we got there too ~** wir kamen zu früh an; **Friday is too ~** Freitag ist zu früh; **all too ~** viel zu schnell; **we were none too ~** wir kamen gerade rechtzeitig; **as ~ as** sobald; **as ~ as possible** so schnell wie möglich; **when can I have it? – as ~ as you like** wann kann ichs kriegen? – wann du willst!; **please reply**

~est bitte antworten Sie schnellstmöglich **b I would just as ~ not go** (= *prefer not to*) ich würde lieber nicht gehen; (= *don't mind*) es ist mir egal, wenn ich nicht gehe; **I would (just) as ~ you didn't tell him** es wäre mir lieber, wenn du es ihm nicht erzählen würdest

sooner ['suːnə] ADV **a** (*time*) früher, eher; **~ or later** früher oder später; **the ~ the better** je eher or früher, desto besser; **no ~ had we arrived than ...** wir waren gerade or kaum angekommen, da ...; **in 5 years or at his death, whichever is the ~** in 5 Jahren bzw. bei seinem Tode, je nachdem, was früher eintrifft; **no ~ said than done** gesagt, getan **b** (*preference*) lieber; **I would ~ not do it** ich würde es lieber nicht tun; **which would you ~?** was möchtest du lieber?

soot [sʊt] N Ruß *m*; **black as ~** rußschwarz

sooth [suːθ] N **in ~** (*obs, liter*) wahrlich (*obs*)

soothe [suːð] **VT** beruhigen; *pain* lindern, mildern **VI** beruhigen; (= *relieve pain*) lindern; **an ointment which ~s** eine schmerzlindernde Salbe

soothing ['suːðɪŋ] ADJ beruhigend, besänftigend; (= *pain-relieving*) schmerzlindernd; *massage* wohltuend; *bath* entspannend; **he put a ~ hand on my shoulder** er legte mir beruhigend or besänftigend die Hand auf die Schulter

soothingly ['suːðɪŋlɪ] ADV *say, whisper* beruhigend, besänftigend; **she rubbed his bruised arm ~** sie rieb ihm den Arm, um den Schmerz zu lindern; **the old house was ~ familiar** das alte Haus war auf beruhigende Weise vertraut

soothsayer ['suːθseɪə] N (*old*) Wahrsager(in) *m(f)*

soothsaying ['suːθseɪɪŋ] N (*old*) Wahrsagerei *f*

sooty ['sʊtɪ] ADJ (*+er*) rußig; **buildings covered with a ~ deposit** mit einer Rußschicht bedeckte Gebäude; **a dull ~ black** ein trübes, rußfarbenes Schwarz; **~ particles** Rußpartikel *pl*

sop [sɒp] N **a** (= *food*) eingetunktes Brotstück **b** (*to pacify*) Beschwichtigungsmittel *nt*; **they're just offering you that as a ~ to keep you quiet** sie bieten euch das nur an, damit ihr ruhig bleibt; **as a ~ to his conscience** als Trostpflaster für sein (schlechtes) Gewissen

▶ **sop up** VT *sep gravy etc* aufnehmen

sophism ['sɒfɪzəm] N Sophismus *m*

sophist ['sɒfɪst] N Sophist(in) *m(f)*

sophistic(al) [sə'fɪstɪk(əl)] ADJ sophistisch

sophisticate [sə'fɪstɪkɪt] N **the ~s who haunt the fashionable restaurants** die Schickeria, die sich in den richtigen Restaurants zeigt

sophisticated [sə'fɪstɪkeɪtɪd] ADJ **a** (= *worldly, cultivated*) kultiviert; *cabaret act, audience* anspruchsvoll, niveauvoll; *restaurant* niveauvoll; *hairdo* gepflegt, elegant; *dress* raffiniert, schick; **she's a very ~ young lady considering she's only twelve** für eine Zwölfjährige ist sie schon sehr weit; **she thinks she looks more ~ with a cigarette holder** sie glaubt, mit einer Zigarettenspitze mehr darzustellen **b** (= *complex, advanced*) hoch entwickelt; *techniques* raffiniert; *method* durchdacht; *device* ausgeklügelt **c** (= *subtle, refined*) subtil; *prose, style, discussion* anspruchsvoll; *plan* ausgeklügelt, raffiniert; *system, approach* differenziert, komplex; *mind* differenziert; **the conversation was too ~ for me** mir war die Unterhaltung zu hochgestochen; **politically ~** politisch anspruchsvoll

sophistication [səfɪstɪ'keɪʃən] N **a** (= *worldliness*) Kultiviertheit *f*; (*of manners, taste also*) Feinheit *f*; (*of cabaret act, audience*) Gepflegtheit *f*, (*of person, restaurant also*) Gepflegtheit *f*, Eleganz *f*; (*of dress*) Raffiniertheit *f*, Schick *m* **b** (= *complexity*) hoher Entwicklungsstand or -grad; (*of techniques*) Raffiniertheit *f*; (*of method*) Durchdachtheit *f*; (*of device*) Ausgeklügeltheit *f* **c** (= *subtlety, refinement*) Subtilität *f*; (*of mind*) Differenziertheit *f*; (*of prose, style*) hohe Ansprüche *pl*; (*of discussion*) hohes Niveau; (*of plan*)

Ausgeklügeltheit *f*, Raffiniertheit *f*; (*of system, approach*) Komplexheit *f*

sophistry ['sɒfɪstrɪ] N Sophisterei *f*

Sophocles ['sɒfəkliːz] N Sophokles *m*

sophomore ['sɒfəmɔː] N (*US*) Student(in) im zweiten Jahr

soporific [sɒpə'rɪfɪk] ADJ einschläfernd **N** (= *drug*) Schlafmittel *nt*

sopping ['sɒpɪŋ] ADJ (*also* **sopping wet**) durchnässt, triefend; *person* klitschnass

soppy ['sɒpɪ] ADJ (*Brit inf*) (= *sentimental*) *book, song* schmalzig (*inf*); *person* sentimental; *look* schmachtend; (= *effeminate*) weibisch

soprano [sə'prɑːnəʊ] **N** Sopran *m*; (= *person also*) Sopranist(in) *m(f)*; (= *voice also*) Sopranstimme *f*; (= *part*) Sopranpartie *f*, Sopran *m*; **to sing ~** Sopran singen **ADJ** Sopran-; **~ saxophone** Sopransaxophon or -saxofon *nt* **ADV** im Sopran

Sorb [sɔːb] N Sorbe *m*, Sorbin *f*

sorbet ['sɔːbeɪ] N Sorbet *nt* or *m*, Fruchteis *nt*; **lemon ~** Zitronensorbet *nt* or *m*

sorbic acid [sɔːbɪk'æsɪd] N (*Chem*) Sorbinsäure *f*

sorcerer ['sɔːsərə] N Hexenmeister *m*, Hexer *m*

sorceress ['sɔːsəres] N Hexe *f*

sorcery ['sɔːsərɪ] N Hexerei *f*

sordid ['sɔːdɪd] ADJ eklig; *place, room also* verkommen, heruntergekommen; *motive* schmutzig, niedrig, gemein; *conditions, life, story* elend, erbärmlich; *crime* gemein; *affair* schmutzig; **he considers it ~ to discuss money** er hält es für unfein, über Geld zu sprechen; **spare me the ~ details** erspar mir die schmutzigen Einzelheiten

sordidness ['sɔːdɪdnɪs] N Ekligkeit *f*; (*of place, room also*) Verkommenheit *f*; (*of motive*) Schmutzigkeit *f*, Niedrigkeit *f*, Gemeinheit *f*; (*of conditions, life, story*) Elend *nt*, Erbärmlichkeit *f*; (*of crime*) Gemeinheit *f*; (*of affair*) Schmutzigkeit *f*

sore [sɔː] **ADJ** (*+er*) **a** (= *hurting*) weh, schlimm (*inf*); (= *inflamed*) wund, entzündet; **to have a ~ throat** Halsschmerzen haben; **my eyes are ~** mir tun die Augen weh; **my wrist feels ~** mein Handgelenk schmerzt (*geh*) or tut weh; **to have ~ muscles** Muskelkater haben; **to have a ~ head** (*esp US, Scot*) Kopfschmerzen haben; **I've got ~ feet after all that walking** meine Füße tun nach all dem Wandern weh; **I'm ~ all over** mir tut alles weh; **where are you ~?** wo tut es (dir/Ihnen) weh?, was tut (dir/Ihnen) weh?; **to be ~ at heart** (*liter*) betrübt sein (*geh*); **her heart was ~** (*liter*) ihr war weh ums Herz (*liter*) **b** (*fig*) **a ~ point** ein wunder Punkt; **a ~ subject** ein heikles Thema **c** (*esp US inf*: = *angry, upset*) verärgert, sauer (*inf*) (*about sth* über etw *acc*, *at sb* über jdn); **now don't get ~ at me** werd doch nicht gleich sauer! (*inf*) **d** (= *great*) **to be in ~ need of sth** etw unbedingt or dringend brauchen; **in ~ distress** (*liter*) in arger Not (*liter*) **ADV** (*obs, = greatly*) arg (*old*), gar sehr (*obs*); **and when they saw the angel they were ~ afraid** (*Bibl*) und als sie den Engel sahen, fürchteten sie sich sehr **N** (*Med*) wunde Stelle; (*caused by friction*) wunde or wund gescheuerte Stelle; **open ~** offene Wunde; **to open old ~s** (*fig*) alte Wunden öffnen

sorehead ['sɔːhed] N (*US, inf*) Brummbär *m* (*inf*)

sorely ['sɔːlɪ] ADV *tempted* sehr, arg (*S Ger, Aus, Sw*); *needed* dringend; *missed* schmerzlich; (*liter*) *afflicted, troubled, offended* zutiefst; *wounded* schwer; **he has been ~ tested** or **tried** seine Geduld wurde auf eine sehr harte Probe gestellt; **to be ~ lacking** bedauerlicherweise fehlen

soreness ['sɔːnɪs] N **a** (= *ache*) Schmerz *m*; (= *rawness*) Wundsein *nt* **b** (*inf, = anger*) Verärgerung *f* (*at* über +*acc*)

sorghum ['sɔːgəm] N Sorghum *nt*

sororicide [sə'rɒrɪsaɪd] N Schwestermord *m*; (= *person*) Schwestermörder(in) *m(f)*

sorority [sə'rɒrɪtɪ] N (*US, Univ*) Studentinnenvereinigung *f*

SORORITY/FRATERNITY

An vielen amerikanischen Colleges und Universitäten gibt es Studentenverbindungen, für Frauen **sororities**, für Männer **fraternities**. Mitglied kann man nur nach persönlicher Einladung werden. Die Hauptaktivitäten bestehen aus Freizeitveranstaltungen wie Partys, aber auch Spendenaktionen für gemeinnützige Zwecke oder Veranstaltungen, mit denen das Prestige der eigenen Verbindung angehoben werden soll. Die **sororities** und **fraternities** haben normalerweise einen Namen, der sich aus zwei oder drei Buchstaben des griechischen Alphabets zusammensetzt: z. B. „Kappa Kappa Gamma sorority" oder „Sigma Chi fraternity". Heutzutage stehen die Verbindungen in dem Ruch, elitär und diskriminierend zu sein. Außerdem werden die geheimen Aufnahmeriten kritisiert, bei denen die Kandidaten verschiedenen seelischen und körperlichen Prüfungen, dem so genannten **hazing**, unterworfen werden.

---

sorrel ['sɒrəl] **N a** (*Bot*) Großer Sauerampfer; (= *wood-sorrel*) Sauerklee *m* **b** (= *horse*) Fuchs *m* **ADJ** *horse* rotbraun

sorrow ['sɒrəʊ] ✪ 24.4 **N** (*no pl*: = *sadness*) Traurigkeit *f*; (*no pl*: = *grief*) Trauer *f*, Kummer *m*; (= *trouble, care*) Sorge *f*, Kümmernis *f*; (= *affliction, suffering*) Leiden *nt*; **more in ~ than in anger** eher aus Betrübnis als aus Zorn; **to my (great) ~** zu meinem größten Kummer; **this was a matter of real ~ to me** das hat mir großen Kummer bereitet; **a feeling of ~** ein Gefühl von Traurigkeit, ein wehes Gefühl (*liter*); **to drown one's ~s** seine Sorgen ertränken; **the ~s of their race** die Leiden ihres Volkes **VI** sich grämen (*geh*) (*at, over, for* über +*acc*)

sorrowful ADJ , **sorrowfully** ADV ['sɒrəʊ fʊl, -fəlɪ] traurig

sorry ['sɒrɪ] ✪ 18.1, 18.2 ADJ (*+er*) **a** *pred* (= *sad*) traurig; **I was ~ to hear that** es tat mir Leid, das zu hören or das hören zu müssen; **we were ~ to hear about your mother's death** es tat uns Leid, dass deine Mutter gestorben ist; **he wasn't in the least bit ~ to hear the news** es war ihm egal, was passiert war; **I can't say I'm ~ he lost** es tut mir wirklich nicht Leid, dass er verloren hat; **I'm ~ I did it** es tut mir nicht Leid, es getan zu haben; **this work is no good, I'm ~ to say** diese Arbeit taugt nichts, das muss ich leider sagen; **to be** or **feel ~ for sb/oneself** jdn/sich selbst bemitleiden; **I feel ~ for the child** das Kind tut mir Leid; **I feel ~ for him having to ...** es tut mir Leid, dass er ... muss; **I'm only ~ I didn't do it sooner** es tut mir nur Leid, dass ich es nicht eher getan habe; **don't feel ~ for me, I don't need your pity!** du brauchst mich nicht zu bedauern, kein Mitleid, bitte!; **you'll be ~ (for this)!** das wird dir noch Leid tun! **b** (*in apologizing, = repentant*) **~!** Entschuldigung!, Verzeihung!; **I'm/he's ~** es tut mir/ihm Leid; **I'm so ~!** entschuldige(n Sie) bitte!; **can you lend me £5? – ~** kannst du mir £ 5 leihen? – bedaure, leider nicht; **~?** (= *pardon*) wie bitte?; **he's from England, ~ Scotland** er ist aus England, nein, Entschuldigung, aus Schottland; **to say ~ (to sb for sth)** sich (bei jdm für etw) entschuldigen; **I'm ~ to hurt you** es tut mir Leid, dass ich dir wehtun muss; **I'm ~ but ...** (es) tut mir Leid, aber ...; **I'm ~ about that vase/your dog** es tut mir Leid um die Vase/um Ihren Hund; **I'm ~ about Thursday, but I can't make it** es tut mir Leid wegen Donnerstag, aber ich kann nicht; **I'm ~ about (what happened on) Thursday** es tut mir Leid wegen Donnerstag **c** (= *pitiful*) *condition, plight* traurig; *sight, figure* jämmerlich, traurig; *excuse* faul; **to be in a ~ state** (*person*) in einer jämmerlichen Verfassung sein; (*object*) in einem jämmerlichen Zustand sein

sort [sɔːt] **N** **a** (= *kind*) Art *f*; (= *species, type, model*) Sorte *f*, Art *f*; **a ~ of** eine Art (+*nom*), so ein/eine; **this ~ of house** diese Art Haus, so ein Haus; **an odd ~ of novel** ein komischer Roman; **I felt a ~ of shame** ich schämte mich irgendwie; **a silly ~ of smile** so ein albernes Grinsen; **I have a ~ of idea that ...** ich habe das *or* so ein Gefühl, dass ...; **what ~ of** was für ein; **what ~ of (a) man is he?** was für ein Mensch ist er?; **he's not the ~ of man to do that** er ist nicht der Mensch, der das täte; **this ~ of thing** so etwas; **all ~s of things** alles Mögliche; **people of all ~s** alle möglichen Leute; **he's a painter of a ~ *or* of ~s** er ist Maler, sozusagen; **it's coffee of a ~ *or* of ~s** das ist Kaffee oder so etwas Ähnliches; **something of the ~** (irgend) so (et)was; **he's some ~ of administrator** er hat irgendwie in der Verwaltung zu tun; **he's got some ~ of job with ...** er hat irgendeinen Job bei ...; **nothing of the ~!** von wegen!; **you'll do nothing of the ~!** von wegen!, das wirst du schön bleiben lassen!; **that's the ~ of person I am** ich bin nun mal so!; **I'm not that ~ of girl** ich bin nicht so eine

b (= *person*) **he's a good ~** er ist ein prima Kerl; **she sounds a good ~** sie scheint in Ordnung zu sein; **he's not my ~** er ist nicht mein Typ; **I don't trust his ~** solchen Leuten traue ich nicht; **I know your ~** euch Brüder kenn ich! (*inf*); **your ~ never did any good** du und deinesgleichen, ihr habt noch nie etwas zustande gebracht; **it takes all ~s (to make a world)** es gibt so 'ne und solche

c **to be out of ~s** (*Brit*) nicht ganz auf der Höhe *or* auf dem Damm (*inf*) sein

d (*Comput*) Sortieren *nt*, Sortiervorgang *m*; **to do a ~** sortieren

ADV **~ of** (*inf*) irgendwie; **it's ~ heavy** es ist irgendwie schwer (*inf*); **is it tiring?** – **~ of** ist das anstrengend? – irgendwie schon; **it's ~ of finished** es ist eigentlich schon fertig; **aren't you pleased?** – **~ of** freust du dich nicht? – doch, eigentlich schon; **is this how he did it?** – **well, ~ of** hat er das so gemacht? – ja, so ungefähr

VT **a** (*also Comput*) sortieren; **to ~ the ripe tomatoes from the unripe ones** die reifen und die unreifen Tomaten aussortieren; **to ~ sth on sth** (*Comput*) etw nach etw sortieren

b (= *solve, organize*) **to get sth ~ed** etw auf die Reihe bekommen; **everything is now ~ed** es ist jetzt alles (wieder) in Ordnung

VI **a** **to ~ through sth** etw durchsehen

b (*Comput*) sortieren

▶ **sort out** VT *sep* **a** (= *arrange*) sortieren, ordnen; (= *select*) aussortieren, aussuchen; **to sort sth out from sth** etw von etw trennen; **to sort red apples out from green ones** rote und grüne Äpfel aussortieren

b (= *straighten out*) *muddle* in Ordnung bringen; *problem* lösen; *situation* klären; **the problem will sort itself out** das Problem wird sich von selbst lösen *or* erledigen; **to sort oneself out** zur Ruhe kommen, sich (*dat*) über sich (*acc*) selbst klar werden; **you must come and visit us once we've sorted ourselves out** wenn wir uns erst mal richtig eingerichtet haben, musst du uns unbedingt besuchen

c (*esp Brit inf*) **to sort sb out** sich (*dat*) jdn vorknöpfen (*inf*)

sorta ['sɔːtə] ADV (*inf*) = **sort of** → **sort** ADV

sort code N (*Banking*) Bankleitzahl *f*

sorter ['sɔːtə'] N (= *person*) Sortierer(in) *m(f)*; (= *machine*) Sortiermaschine *f*; (*Post:* = *person*) Briefverteiler(in) *m(f)*

sortie ['sɔːtɪ] N (*Mil*) Ausfall *m*; (*Aviat*) (Einzel-)einsatz *m*, Feindflug *m*; **a ~ into town/banking** ein Ausflug *or* Abstecher *m* in die Stadt/ins Bankwesen

sorting office ['sɔːtɪŋˌɒfɪs] N (*Brit*) Sortierstelle *f*

SOS N SOS *nt*

so-so ['səʊ'səʊ] ADJ PRED, ADV (*inf*) soso, so la la

sot [sɒt] N (*pej*) Säufer *m*, Trunkenbold *m* (*dated*)

sottish ['sɒtɪʃ] ADJ dem Trunk ergeben; *grin* benebelt

sotto voce ['sɒtəʊ'vəʊtʃɪ] ADV leise; (= *conspiratorially*) mit unterdrückter Stimme; (*Mus*) sotto voce

sou [suː] N (*inf*) **I haven't a ~** ich habe keinen Cent

sou' [saʊ] (*Naut*) abbr of **south**

soubrette [suː'bret] N (*dated*) Soubrette *f* (*dated*)

soubriquet ['suːbrɪkeɪ] N = **sobriquet**

Soudanese ADJ, N = **Sudanese**

sou'easter [saʊ'iːstə'] N (*Naut*, = *wind*) Südost (-wind) *m*

soufflé ['suːfleɪ] N Soufflé *nt*, Souflee *nt*

sough [saʊ] (*liter*) **N** Rauschen *nt* **VI** (*wind*) rauschen

sought [sɔːt] *pret, ptp* of **seek**

sought-after ['sɔːtɑːftə'] ADJ begehrt; **much ~** viel begehrt; *rare object* gesucht

soul [səʊl] N **a** Seele *f*; **upon my ~!** (*dated*) **(God) bless my ~!** meiner Treu (*dated*), na so was!; **All Souls' Day** Allerheiligen *nt*; **God rest his ~!** Gott hab ihn selig! → **body a**

b (= *inner being*) Innerste(s), Wesen *nt*; **he may not be a brilliant intellect, but he has a beautiful ~** er ist vielleicht kein großer Geist, aber er hat innere Werte; **he loved her with all his ~** er liebte sie von ganzem Herzen; **he loved her with all his heart and with all his ~** er liebte sie mit jeder Faser seines Herzens; **the priest urged them to search their ~s** der Priester drängte sie, ihr Gewissen zu erforschen; **a little humility is good for the ~** ein bisschen Bescheidenheit tut der Seele gut; **the ~ of the city has been destroyed by modernization** durch die Modernisierung ist die Stadt in ihrem innersten Wesen zerstört worden; **to have a ~ above sth** etw (*acc*) hoch erhaben sein; **the music lacks ~** der Musik fehlt echter Ausdruck; **poetry is the ~ of civilization** die Dichtkunst ist die Seele der Zivilisation

c (= *finer feelings*) Herz *nt*, Gefühl *nt*; **complete lack of ~** vollkommene Gefühllosigkeit; **a musician of considerable technical skill, but lacking ~** ein Musiker von beachtlichem technischem Können, aber ohne echtes Gefühl; **you've got to have ~** (*US, sl*) du musst Feeling haben (*inf*); **~ brother** Bruder *m*; **~ sister** Schwester *f*; **he's a ~ brother** er ist einer von uns

d (= *person*) Seele *f*; **3,000 ~s** 3.000 Seelen (*geh*); **poor ~!** (*inf*) Ärmste(r)!; **how is she, the wee ~?** wie gehts denn unsrer Kleinen?; **he's a good ~** er ist ein guter Mensch; **she's a kind** *or* **kindly ~** sie ist eine gute Seele; **she's a simple ~** sie hat ein schlichtes Gemüt; **not a ~** keine Menschenseele; **there wasn't a living ~ about** keine Menschenseele war zu sehen; **the ship was lost with all ~s** das Schiff ging mit (der ganzen Besatzung und) allen Passagieren unter

e **he's the ~ of generosity/discretion** er ist die Großzügigkeit/Diskretion in Person

f (*Mus*) Soul *m*

soul-destroying ['səʊldɪˌstrɔɪɪŋ] ADJ geisttötend; *factory work etc* nervtötend

soulful ['səʊlfʊl] ADJ *look* seelenvoll; *person, song* gefühlvoll; *eyes* ausdrucksstark

soulfully ['səʊlfəlɪ] ADV *sing, write* gefühlvoll; *look* voll Gefühl

soulless ['səʊllɪs] ADJ *person* seelenlos; *work also* eintönig; *place* gottverlassen; *system* herzlos, seelenlos; *music* eintönig; *eyes* leer; *existence* eintönig, öde

soul; soul mate N Seelenfreund(in) *m(f)*; **soul music** N Soul *m*, Soulmusik *f*; **soul-searching** N Gewissensprüfung *f*; **soul-stirring** ADJ *speech, music* bewegend

---

sound¹ [saʊnd] **ADJ** (+*er*) **a** (= *in good condition*) *person, animal, tree, constitution, lungs* gesund; *condition, building, chassis* einwandfrei; **to be as ~ as a bell** kerngesund sein; **to be ~ in wind and limb** gesund und munter sein; **to be of ~ mind** (*esp Jur*) bei klarem Verstand sein, im Vollbesitz seiner geistigen Kräfte sein (*Jur*); **the windows were broken, but the frames were ~** die Fensterscheiben waren zerbrochen, aber die Rahmen waren heil

b (= *valid, good, dependable*) solide; *argument, analysis* fundiert, solide; *economy, currency* stabil; *person, goalkeeper* verlässlich; *idea* gesund, vernünftig; *basis* solide; *move* vernünftig; *advice* wertvoll, vernünftig; **he's ~ on financial policy** er hat gründliche Kenntnisse in der Finanzpolitik; **a ~ scholar** ein ernst zu nehmender Gelehrter; **that's ~ sense** das ist vernünftig

c (= *thorough*) gründlich, solide; *beating* gehörig; *defeat* vernichtend

d (*Jur*) *decision* rechtmäßig; *claim* berechtigt

e (= *deep*) *sleep* tief, fest; **I'm a very ~ sleeper** ich schlafe sehr tief *or* fest, ich habe einen gesunden Schlaf

ADV (+*er*) **to be ~ asleep** fest schlafen; **I shall sleep the ~er for it** ich werde nur umso besser schlafen

sound² [saʊnd] **N** **a** (= *noise*) Geräusch *nt*; (*Ling*) Laut *m*; (*Phys*) Schall *m*; (*Mus, of instruments*) Klang *m*; (*verbal, TV, Rad, Film*) Ton *m*; (*of band etc*) Sound *m*; **don't make a ~ still!**; **the speed of ~** (die) Schallgeschwindigkeit; **within ~ of** in Hörweite (+*gen*); **to the ~(s) of the national anthem** zu den Klängen der Nationalhymne; **French has a soft ~** die französische Sprache hat einen weichen Klang; **would you still recognize the ~ of Karin's voice?** würdest du Karins Stimme immer noch erkennen?; **not a ~ was to be heard** man hörte keinen Ton; **the ~(s) of laughter** Gelächter *nt*; **we heard the ~ of voices on the terrace** wir hörten Stimmen auf der Terrasse; **vowel ~** Vokallaut *m*; **~ and fury** leerer Schall

b (= *impression*) **I don't like the ~ of it** das klingt gar nicht gut; **from the ~ of it he had a hard time** es hört sich so an *or* es klingt, als sei es ihm schlecht gegangen; **his remarks had a familiar ~** seine Bemerkungen klangen vertraut

VT **a** (= *produce sound from*) **~ your horn** hupen!; **the trumpeter ~ed a high note** der Trompeter spielte einen hohen Ton; **to ~ the alarm** (*mechanism*) die Alarmanlage auslösen; **to ~ the retreat** zum Rückzug blasen; **to ~ the "r" in "cover"** das „r" in „cover" aussprechen; **his speech ~ed a note of warning** in seiner Rede klang eine Warnung an; **I think we need to ~ a note of warning** ich finde, wir sollten eine vorsichtige Warnung aussprechen

b (= *test by tapping, Med*) abklopfen

VI **a** (= *emit sound*) erklingen, ertönen; **feet ~ed in the corridor** im Flur waren Schritte zu hören; **a gun ~ed a long way off** in der Ferne hörte man einen Schuss

b (= *give aural impression*) klingen, sich anhören; **it ~s hollow** es klingt hohl; **the children happy** es hört sich so an, als ob die Kinder Spaß haben; **he ~s angry** es hört sich so an, als wäre er wütend; **he ~ed depressed on the phone** am Telefon klang er deprimiert; **he ~s French (to me)** er hört sich (für mich) wie ein Franzose an

c (= *seem*) sich anhören; **that ~s very odd** das hört sich sehr seltsam an; **he ~s like a nice man** er scheint ein netter Mensch zu sein; **it ~s like a sensible idea** das klingt ganz vernünftig; **how does it ~ to you?** wie findest du das?

▶ **sound off** VI (*inf*) sich verbreiten *or* auslassen (*about* über +*acc*); **don't listen to him, he's just sounding off** hör nicht auf ihn, er spielt sich nur auf!

sound³ VT (*Naut*) loten, ausloten; (*Met*) messen; **~ing line** Lot *nt*, Senkblei *nt*; **~ing balloon** Versuchs- *or* Registrierballon *m*

▶ **sound out** VT *sep person* aushorchen, ausfragen; *intentions, opinions* herausfinden, herausbekommen; **to sound sb out about** or **on sth** bei jdm in Bezug auf etw (*acc*) vorfühlen

sound⁴ N (*Geog*) Meerenge *f*, Sund *m*

sound: sound-absorbing [ˈsaʊndəbˌsɔːbɪŋ] ADJ schalldämpfend or -schluckend; **sound archives** PL Tonarchiv *nt*; **sound barrier** N Schallmauer *f*; **sound bite** N Soundclip *m*, Tonclip *m*; **soundboard** N = **sounding board** a; **soundbox** N (*Mus*) Schallkörper *m*, Schallkasten *m*; **sound card** N (*Comput*) Soundkarte *f*; **sound check** N (*Mus*) Soundcheck *m*; **sound effects** PL Toneffekte *pl*; **sound engineer** N Toningenieur(in) *m(f)*; **sound film** N Tonfilm *m*; **sound hole** N Schallloch *nt*

sounding [ˈsaʊndɪŋ] N (*Naut*) Loten *nt*, Peilung *f*; **to take ~s** (*lit*) Lotungen vornehmen; (*fig*) sondieren

sounding board [ˈsaʊndɪŋˌbɔːd] N **a** (*on instrument*) Resonanzboden *m*; (*over platform etc*) Schalldeckel *m* **b** (*fig*) Resonanzboden *m*; **he used the committee as a ~ for his ideas** er benutzte den Ausschuss, um die Wirkung seiner Vorschläge zu sondieren

sound insulation N Schalldämmung *f*

soundless [ˈsaʊndlɪs] ADJ lautlos

soundlessly [ˈsaʊndlɪslɪ] ADV (= *silently*) move geräuschlos; *weep* lautlos; *laugh* tonlos; (= *inaudibly*) unhörbar

soundly [ˈsaʊndlɪ] ADV *built, made* solide; *argue, reason, invest, play also* vernünftig; *thrash* tüchtig, gehörig; *defeat* vernichtend; *condemn* rundum; *train* gründlich; *based* fest; **our team was ~ beaten** unsere Mannschaft wurde eindeutig or klar geschlagen; **to sleep ~** (tief und) fest schlafen

sound motion picture N (*US*) Tonfilm *m*

soundness [ˈsaʊndnɪs] N **a** (= *good condition*) gesunder Zustand; (*of building, chassis*) guter Zustand **b** (= *validity, dependability*) Solidität *f*; (*of argument, analysis*) Fundiertheit *f*, Solidität *f*; (*of economy, currency*) Stabilität *f*; (*of idea, advice, move, policy*) Vernünftigkeit *f*; (*of person, goalkeeper*) Verlässlichkeit *f* **c** (= *thoroughness*) Gründlichkeit *f*, Solidität *f* **d** (*Jur, of decision, claim*) Rechtmäßigkeit *f* **e** (*of sleep*) Tiefe *f*

sound: sound pollution N Umweltverschmutzung *f* durch Lärm, Lärmbelästigung *f*; **soundproof** ADJ schalldicht ▮VT▮ schalldicht machen, schalldämmen; **soundproofing** N Schallisolierung *f*; **sound quality** N Tonqualität *f*; **sound recording** N Tonaufnahme *f*, Tonaufzeichnung *f*; **sound shift** N Lautverschiebung *f*; **sound technician** N (*Radio, TV*) Tontechniker(in) *m(f)*; **soundtrack** N Tonspur *f*; (= *sound, recording*) Ton *m*, Filmmusik *f*; **sound wave** N Schallwelle *f*

soup [suːp] N Suppe *f*; **to be in the ~** (*inf*) in der Tinte or Patsche sitzen (*inf*)

▶ **soup up** VT *sep* (*inf*) *car, engine* (hoch)frisieren (*inf*)

soupçon [ˈsuːpsɔ̃ːŋ] N (*of spice etc*) Spur *f*; (*of irony etc*) Anflug *m*; (*of melancholy*) Hauch *m*, Spur *f*; **sauce? – just a ~** Soße? – (ja bitte, nur) ganz wenig

soup: soup kitchen N Volksküche *f*; (*for disaster area etc*) Feldküche *f*; **soup plate** N Suppenteller *m*, tiefer Teller; **soup spoon** N Suppenlöffel *m*; **soup tureen** N Suppenterrine *f*

sour [ˈsaʊə] ADJ (+*er*) **a** *fruit, soil* sauer; *wine, vinegar* säuerlich; **whisky ~** (*esp US*) Whisky mit Zitrone

b (= *bad*) *milk* sauer; *smell* streng, säuerlich; **to go** or **turn ~** (*lit*) sauer werden; **to go** or **turn ~ (on sb)** (*fig, relationship, marriage*) jdn anöden; (*plan, investment*) sich als Fehlschlag erweisen; **things began to turn ~** die Dinge begannen einen negativen Verlauf zu nehmen

c (*fig*) *person, expression* verdrießlich, griesgrämig; *remark* bissig; **he's feeling ~ about being demoted** er ist über seine Absetzung verbittert; **it's just ~ grapes** die Trauben sind zu sauer or hängen zu hoch; **it sounds like ~ grapes to me** das kennt man: die Trauben sind zu sauer or hängen zu hoch

▮VT▮ *milk* sauer or dick werden lassen; *soil* sauer

or kalkarm machen; (*fig*) *person* verdrießlich or griesgrämig machen; *relationship, atmosphere* vergiften; *success* verderben

▮VI▮ (*milk*) sauer or dick werden; (*soil*) sauer or kalkarm werden; (*fig, person*) verbittern, griesgrämig werden; (*atmosphere, mood, relationship*) sich verschlechtern

source [sɔːs] N **a** (*of river, light, information*) Quelle *f*; (*of troubles, problems etc*) Ursache *f*, Ursprung *m*; **a ~ of vitamin C** eine Vitamin-C-Quelle *f*; **they tried to trace the ~ of the gas leak** sie versuchten, das Leck in der Gasleitung ausfindig zu machen; **he is a ~ of embarrassment to us** er bringt uns ständig in Verlegenheit; **~ of supply** Bezugsquelle *f*; **to have its ~ in sth** seine Ursache or seinen Ursprung in etw (*dat*) haben; **I have it from a good ~ that ...** ich habe es aus sicherer Quelle, dass ...; **at ~** (*tax*) unmittelbar, direkt; **these rumours must be stopped at ~** diese Gerüchte darf man gar nicht erst aufkommen lassen; **~s** (*in book etc*) Quellen *pl*, Literaturangaben *pl*; **from reliable ~s** aus zuverlässiger Quelle

▮VT▮ (*Comm*) beschaffen; **furniture ~d from all over the world** Möbel aus der ganzen Welt

source: sourcebook N Quellenwerk *nt*, Quellensammlung *f*; **source code** N (*Comput*) Quellcode *m*; **source file** N (*Comput*) Quelldatei *f*, Ursprungsdatei *f*; **source language** N Ausgangssprache *f*; **source material** N Quellenmaterial *nt*

sourdough [ˈsaʊədəʊ] N Sauerteig *m*

sour(ed) cream [ˌsaʊə(d)ˈkriːm] N saure Sahne, Sauerrahm *m*

sour-faced [ˈsaʊəfeɪst] ADJ (*inf*) vergrätzt (*inf*)

sourly [ˈsaʊəlɪ] ADV (*fig*) verdrießlich, griesgrämig

sourness [ˈsaʊənɪs] N (*of lemon, milk*) saurer Geschmack; (*of wine, vinegar also, of smell*) Säuerlichkeit *f*; (*of soil*) saure Beschaffenheit; (*fig, of person, expression*) Verdrießlichkeit *f*, Griesgrämigkeit *f*, Verbitterung *f*; (*of remark*) Bissigkeit *f*

sourpuss [ˈsaʊəpʊs] N (*inf*) Miesepeter *m* (*inf*)

sousaphone [ˈsuːzəfəʊn] N Sousaphon *nt*, Sousafon *nt*

souse [saʊs] VT **a** (= *cover with water etc*) nass machen; *fire* löschen; **he ~d himself with water** er übergoss sich mit Wasser **b** (= *pickle*) *fish* einlegen, marinieren **c** **to be ~d** (*inf*) sternhagelvoll sein (*inf*); **to get ~d** (*inf*) sich voll laufen lassen (*inf*)

soutane [suːˈtæn] N (*Eccl*) Soutane *f*

south [saʊθ] ▮N▮ Süden *m*; **in the ~ of** im Süden +*gen*; **to the ~ of** im Süden or südlich von; **from the ~** aus dem Süden; (*wind*) aus Süden; **to veer to the ~** in südliche Richtung or nach Süden drehen; **the wind is in the ~** es ist Südwind; **the South of France** Südfrankreich *nt*; **which way is ~?** in welcher Richtung ist Süden?; **down ~** (*be, live*) unten im Süden; *go* runter in den Süden

▮ADJ▮ südlich; (*in names*) Süd-; **South German** süddeutsch; **~ London** Süd-London *nt*; **South Wales** Südwales *nt*; **the MP for Coventry South** der Abgeordnete für (den Wahlkreis) Coventry Süd

▮ADV▮ im Süden; (= *towards the south*) nach Süden, gen Süden (*liter*), südwärts (*liter, Naut*); (*Met*) in südliche Richtung; **to be further ~** weiter südlich sein; **~ of** südlich or im Süden von

south *in cpds* Süd-; **South Africa** N Südafrika *nt*; **South African** ADJ südafrikanisch; **he's ~** er ist Südafrikaner ▮N▮ Südafrikaner(in) *m(f)*; **South America** N Südamerika *nt*; **South American** ADJ südamerikanisch; **he's ~** er ist Südamerikaner ▮N▮ Südamerikaner(in) *m(f)*; **South Atlantic** N Südatlantik *m*; **South Australia** N Südaustralien *nt*; **southbound** ADJ (in) Richtung Süden; **South Carolina** N Südkarolina *nt*, South Carolina *nt*; **South Dakota** N Süddakota *nt*, South Dakota *nt*; **southeast** ▮N▮ Südosten *m*, Südost *m* (*esp Naut*); **from the ~** aus dem Südosten; (*wind*) von Südosten; **in the ~** im Südosten ▮ADJ▮ süd-

östlich; (*in names*) Südost-; **~ wind** Südost (-wind) *m*, Wind *m* aus Südost or südöstlicher Richtung; **~ London** Südostlondon *nt* ▮ADV▮ nach Südosten; **~ of** südöstlich von; **Southeast Asia** N Südostasien *nt*; **southeaster** N (*esp Naut*) Südostwind *m*, Südost *m*; **southeasterly** ADJ *direction* südöstlich; *wind also* aus Südost ▮N▮ (= *wind*) Südostwind *m*; **southeastern** ADJ südöstlich, im Südosten; **~ England** Südostengland *nt*; **southeastward(s)** ADV nach Südosten

southerly [ˈsʌðəlɪ] ADJ südlich; *course also* nach Süden; *wind* aus Süden or südlicher Richtung ▮ADV▮ nach Süden, südwärts (*esp Naut*) ▮N▮ Südwind *m*

southern [ˈsʌðən] ADJ südlich; (*in names*) Süd-; (= *Mediterranean*) südländisch; **~ people** Südländer *pl*; **a ~ belle** eine Schönheit aus dem Süden; **Southern Africa** das südliche Afrika; **Southern Europe** Südeuropa *nt*; **Southern England** Südengland *nt*; **Southern States** (*US*) Südstaaten *pl*

Southern Cross N Kreuz *nt* des Südens

southerner [ˈsʌðənə] N Bewohner(in) *m(f)* des Südens, Südengländer(in) *m(f)*/-deutsche(r) *mf etc*; (*from the Mediterranean*) Südländer(in) *m(f)*; (*US*) Südstaatler(in) *m(f)*

Southern Ireland N (*Pol*) (Süd)irland *nt, die* Republik Irland

southern lights PL Südlicht *nt*

southernmost [ˈsʌðənməʊst] ADJ südlichste(r, s)

south: south-facing ADJ *wall, window* nach Süden gerichtet; *garden* nach Süden gelegen; **~ slope** Südhang *m*; **South Korea** N Südkorea *nt*; **South Korean** ADJ südkoreanisch ▮N▮ Südkoreaner(in) *m(f)*; **South Pacific** N Südpazifik *m*; **southpaw** N (*Boxing*) Linkshänder(in), Rechtsausleger(in) *m(f)*; **South Pole** N Südpol *m*; **South Sea Islands** PL Südseeinseln *pl*; **South Seas** PL Südsee *f*; **south-south-east** ▮N▮ Südsüdosten *m*, Südsüdost *m* (*esp Naut*) ▮ADJ▮ südsüdöstlich ▮ADV▮ nach Südsüdost(en); **south-south-west** ▮N▮ Südsüdwesten *m*, Südsüdwest *m* (*esp Naut*) ▮ADJ▮ südsüdwestlich ▮ADV▮ nach Südsüdwest(en); **~ of** südsüdwestlich von; **South Vietnam** N Südvietnam *nt*; **southward(s)** ADJ südlich ▮ADV▮ nach Süden, südwärts; **southwest** ▮N▮ Südwesten *m*, Südwest *m* (*esp Naut*); **in the ~** im Südwesten; **from the ~** aus dem Südwesten; (*wind*) von Südwesten ▮ADJ▮ Südwest-, südwestlich; **~ wind** Südwestwind *m* ▮ADV▮ nach Südwest(en); **~ of** südwestlich von; **South West Africa** N Südwestafrika *nt*; **southwester** N (*esp Naut*) Südwest(wind) *m*; **southwesterly** ADJ *direction* südwestlich; *wind also* aus Südwest ▮N▮ Südwestwind *m*; **southwestern** ADJ südwestlich, im Südwesten; **southwestward(s)** ADV nach Südwesten; **South Yorkshire** N Süd-Yorkshire *nt*

souvenir [ˌsuːvəˈnɪə] N Andenken *nt*, Souvenir *nt* (*of an* +*acc*)

sou'wester [saʊˈwestə] N **a** (= *hat*) Südwester *m* **b** (*Naut: = wind*) Südwest(wind) *m*

sovereign [ˈsɒvrɪn] ▮N▮ (= *monarch*) Souverän *m*, Herrscher(in) *m(f)*; (*Brit, old: = coin*) 20-Shilling-Münze *f* ▮ADJ▮ **a** (= *supreme*) höchste(r, s), oberste(r, s); *state, power* souverän; *contempt* tiefste(r, s), äußerste(r, s); **the ~ power of the Pope** die Oberhoheit des Papstes; **our ~ Lord the King** (*old*) unser gnädiger Herr, der König **b** **a ~ remedy** (*lit, fig*) ein Allheilmittel *nt* (*for* gegen) **c** (*Fin*) **~ debt** Staatsschulden *pl*; **~ lending** staatliche Kreditaufnahme

sovereignty [ˈsɒvrəntɪ] N Oberhoheit *f*, Oberherrschaft *f*; (= *right of self-determination*) Souveränität *f*; **the ~ of papal decrees** die unumschränkte Gültigkeit der päpstlichen Erlasse

soviet [ˈsəʊvɪət] ▮N▮ Sowjet *m*; **the Soviets** (= *people*) die Sowjets; **the Supreme Soviet** der Oberste Sowjet ▮ADJ▮ *attr* sowjetisch, Sowjet-; **~ power** Sowjetmacht *f*; **~ citizen** Sowjetbürger(in) *m(f)*

sovietize ['səʊvɪətaɪz] VT sowjetisieren

Sovietologist [ˌsəʊvɪə'tɒlədʒɪst] N Sowjetologe m, Sowjetologin f

Soviet: Soviet Republic N Sowjetrepublik f; **Soviet Russia** N Sowjetrussland nt; **Soviet Union** N Sowjetunion f

sow¹ [səʊ] pret sowed, ptp sown or sowed VT **a** corn, plants säen; seed aussäen; (Mil) mine legen; **to ~ the garden with grass** im Garten Gras (aus)säen; **this field has been ~n with barley** auf diesem Feld ist Gerste gesät; **to ~ mines in a strait** eine Meerenge verminen **b** (fig) **to ~ (the seeds of) hatred/discord** Hass/Zwietracht säen; **to ~ (the seeds of) anarchy** zur Anarchie anstiften; **to ~ the wind and reap the whirlwind** (prov) wer Wind sät, wird Sturm ernten (Prov); **as you ~ so shall you reap** (prov) was der Mensch sät, das wird er ernten (Prov) → **seed**

sow² [saʊ] N **a** (= pig) Sau f; (of wild boar) (Wild)sau f; (of badger) Dächsin f **b** (Tech, = block of iron) Massel f; (= channel) Masselgraben m

sower ['səʊə'] N (= person) Säer(in) m(f), Sämann m; (= machine) Sämaschine f; **a ~ of doubt** ein Mensch, der Zweifel verbreitet

sowing ['səʊɪŋ] N (= action) (Aus)säen nt, Aussaat f; (= quantity sown) Saat f; **the ~ of a field** die Aussaat auf einem Feld

sown [səʊn] ptp of **sow¹**

sox [sɒks] pl (US Comm inf) = **socks**

soya ['sɔɪə], **soy** [sɔɪ] N Soja f; **~ flour** Sojamehl nt

soya bean N Sojabohne f

soya sauce N Sojasoße f

soybean ['sɔɪbiːn] N (US) = **soya bean**

sozzled ['sɒzld] ADJ (Brit, inf) **to be ~** einen sitzen haben (inf); **to get ~** beschwipst werden

SP abbr of **starting price a** (Horse Racing) Starterquote f **b** (inf, = information) **what's the SP on him?** was erzählt man sich so über ihn?; **to give sb the SP on sb/sth** jdm Infos über jdn/ etw geben (inf)

spa [spaː] N (= town) (Heil- or Mineral)bad nt, Kurort m; (= spring) (Heil- or Mineral)quelle f

space [speɪs] N **a** Raum m (also Phys); (= outer space) der Weltraum, das Weltall; **time and ~** Zeit und Raum; **to stare or gaze into ~** ins Leere starren; **to give sb some ~** (fig) jdm Freiraum gewähren → **outer space**
b no pl (= room) Platz m, Raum m; (Typ, between letters) Spatien pl; (between lines) Durchschuss m; **to take up a lot of ~** viel Platz wegnehmen or einnehmen; **to clear/leave some ~ for sb/sth** für jdn/etw Platz schaffen/lassen; **to buy/sell ~** (Press) Platz für Anzeigen kaufen/ verkaufen; (TV) Sendezeit kaufen/verkaufen; **parking ~** Platz m zum Parken
c (= gap, empty area) Raum m; (between objects, words, lines) Zwischenraum m; (Mus: on stave) Zwischenraum m; (= parking space) Lücke f; **to leave a ~ for sb/sth** für jdn/etw Platz lassen; **there was a (blank) ~ at the end of the document** am Ende des Dokuments war Platz gelassen; **please answer in the ~ provided** bitte an der dafür vorgesehenen Stelle beantworten; **to leave an empty ~ in a room** eine Lücke in einem Zimmer hinterlassen; **indent the line a few ~s** rücken Sie die Zeile ein paar Stellen ein; **the wide open ~s** das weite, offene Land **d** (Typ, = piece of metal, between words) Spatienkeil m; (between lines) Reglette f
e (of time) Zeitraum m; **in a short ~ of time** in kurzer Zeit; **in the ~ of one hour/three generations** innerhalb einer Stunde/von drei Generationen
VT (also **space out**) in Abständen verteilen; chairs also in Abständen aufstellen; seedlings also in Abständen setzen; visits verteilen; words Zwischenraum or Abstand lassen zwischen (+dat); (Typ) spatiieren (spec); **~ them out more, ~ them further out or further apart** lassen Sie etwas mehr Zwischenraum or Abstand (dazwischen); **houses ~d (out) along the road** Häuser, die sich entlang der Straße verteilen; **well**
~d-out houses genügend weit auseinander gebaute Häuser; **to ~ payments** nach und nach zahlen; **to ~ the children (out)** (when planning a family) in vernünftigen (Zeit)abständen Kinder bekommen → **spaced out**

space in cpds (Welt)raum-; **space age** N (Welt)raumzeitalter nt; **space-age** ADJ attr des Raumzeitalters; **space bar** N (Typ) Leertaste f; **space blanket** N Rettungsdecke f, (Alu)isoliermatte f; **space-borne** ADJ **a** (Welt)raum-; **~ satellite** Weltraumsatellit m **b** (= via satellite) über Satellit, Satellen-; **~ television** Satellitenfernsehen nt; **space cadet** N (US, inf) **to be a ~** ständig zugedröhnt or auf dem Trip sein (inf); **space capsule** N (Welt-) raumkapsel f; **space carrier** N Raumtransporter m; **space character** N (Comput, Typ) Leerzeichen nt, Zwischenraumzeichen nt; **spacecraft** N Raumfahrzeug nt; (unmanned) Raumkörper m; **space debris** N Weltraummüll m

spaced out [ˌspeɪst'aʊt] ADJ (inf, = confused etc) geistig weggetreten (inf); (= on drugs) high (inf)

space: space fiction N Zukunftsromane pl über den Weltraum; **space flight** N Weltraumflug m; **space heater** N (esp US) Heizgerät nt; **space helmet** N Astronautenhelm m; **Space Invaders®** N SING Space Invaders pl; **space key** N (Typ) Leertaste f; **space lab(oratory)** N Weltraumlabor nt; **spaceman** N (Welt)raumfahrer m; **space platform** N Raumstation f; **spaceport** N Raumflugzentrum nt; **space probe** N Raumsonde f; **space programme**, (US) **space program** N Raumfahrtprogramm nt

spacer ['speɪsə'] N = **space-bar**

space: space race N Wettlauf m im All; **space rocket** N Weltraumrakete f; **space-saving** ADJ equipment, gadget Platz sparend; furniture also Raum sparend; **space science** N Raumforschung f; **space scientist** N Raumforscher(in) m(f); **space-seller** N (Press) Anzeigenakquisiteur(in) m(f); (TV) Werbungspromoter(in) m(f); **spaceship** N Raumschiff nt; **space shot** N (= launching) Abschuss m eines Raumfahrzeugs/-körpers; (= flight) Raumflug m; **space shuttle** N Raumfähre f; **space sickness** N Weltraumkrankheit f; **space station** N (Welt)raumstation f; **spacesuit** N Raumanzug m; **space-time (continuum)** N Raum-Zeit-Kontinuum nt; **space travel** N die Raumfahrt; **space vehicle** N Raumfahrzeug nt; **space walk** N Weltraumspaziergang m **VI** im Weltraum spazieren gehen; **spacewoman** N (Welt)raumfahrerin f; **space writer** N (Press) Korrespondent(in) m(f) (der/die nach der Länge seiner/ihrer Artikel bezahlt wird)

spacey ['speɪsɪ] ADJ (inf) music trancehaft, sphärisch; person ausgeflippt (inf)

spacing ['speɪsɪŋ] N Abstände pl; (between two objects) Abstand m; (also **spacing out**) Verteilung f; (of payments) Verteilung f über längere Zeit; **single/double ~** (Typ) einzeiliger/zweizeiliger Abstand

spacious ['speɪʃəs] ADJ geräumig; garden, park weitläufig

spaciousness ['speɪʃəsnɪs] N Geräumigkeit f; (of garden, park) Weitläufigkeit f

spade [speɪd] N **a** (= tool) Spaten m; (= children's spade) Schaufel f; **to call a ~ a ~** (Brit prov) das Kind beim Namen nennen (Prov) **b** (Cards) Pik nt; **the Queen/two of Spades** die Pikdame/Pikzwei; **to play in ~s** Pik spielen; **~s are trumps** Pik ist Trumpf **c** (pej sl) Nigger m (pej sl)

spadeful ['speɪdfʊl] N **a ~ of earth** ein Spaten m or eine Schaufel (voll) Erde; **by the ~** spaten- or schaufelweise

spadework ['speɪdwɜːk] N (fig) Vorarbeit f

spag bol [ˌspæg'bɒl] N (Brit inf) Spag(h)etti pl

spaghetti [spə'getɪ] N Spag(h)etti pl; (fig inf, = cabling) Kabelgewirr nt, Kabelsalat m (inf)

spaghetti: spaghetti bolognaise N Spag(h)etti pl Bolognese; **spaghetti junction** N
(inf) Autobahnknoten(punkt) m; **spaghetti western** N (inf) Italowestern m

Spain [speɪn] N Spanien nt

spake [speɪk] (obs) pret of **speak**

Spam® [spæm] N Frühstücksfleisch nt

spam VT (Comput sl) (zu)spammen (sl), mit Werbung bombardieren (inf) or zumüllen (sl)

spamming ['spæmɪŋ] N (Comput sl) Spamming nt (sl), Bombardierung f mit Werbung (inf)

span¹ [spæn] N **a** (of hand) Spanne f; (= wingspan, of bridge etc) Spannweite f; (= arch of bridge) (Brücken)bogen m; **a single-span bridge** eine eingespannte Bogenbrücke
b (= time span) Zeitspanne f, Zeitraum m; (of memory) Gedächtnisspanne f; (of attention) Konzentrationsspanne f; (= range) Umfang m; **for a ~ of several months** einige Monate lang; **the whole ~ of world affairs** die Weltpolitik in ihrer ganzen Spannweite
c (of oxen) Gespann nt
d (old: = measurement) Spanne f
VT (rope, rainbow) sich spannen über (+acc); (bridge also) überspannen; (plank) führen über (+acc); years, globe, world umspannen; (Mus) octave etc greifen; (= encircle) umfassen; (in time) sich erstrecken über (+acc), umfassen

span² (old) pret of **spin**

spangle ['spæŋgl] N Paillette f **VT** mit Pailletten besetzen; **~d with stars/flowers** mit Sternen/Blumen übersät

spangly ['spæŋglɪ] ADJ paillettenbesetzt

Spaniard ['spænjəd] N Spanier(in) m(f)

spaniel ['spænjəl] N Spaniel m

Spanish ['spænɪʃ] ADJ spanisch; **he is ~** er ist Spanier; **she is ~** sie ist Spanierin **N a the ~** die Spanier pl **b** (Ling) Spanisch nt

Spanish: Spanish America N die spanischsprachigen Länder Mittel- und Südamerikas; **Spanish-American** N spanischsprachiger Lateinamerikaner, spanischsprachige Lateinamerikanerin ADJ spanisch-amerikanisch; **Spanish chestnut** N Edelkastanie f; **Spanish Civil War** N **the ~** der Spanische Bürgerkrieg; **Spanish fly** N , no pl Spanische Fliege; **Spanish guitar** N spanische Gitarre; **Spanish Main** N Karibik f; **Spanish moss** N (US) Spanisches Moos, Greisenbart m; **Spanish omelette** N Omelett nt mit Piment, Paprika und Tomaten; **Spanish onion** N Gemüsezwiebel f

spank [spæŋk] N Klaps m; **to give sb a ~** jdm einen Klaps geben; (= spanking) jdm den Hintern versohlen **VT** versohlen; **to ~ sb's bottom** jdm den Hintern versohlen **VI to ~ along** dahinjagen, dahinrasen

spanker ['spæŋkə'] N **a** (Naut, = sail) Besan m **b** (dated inf, = horse) Renner m; **a real ~** (= blow) ein Schlag, der nicht von Pappe war (inf)

spanking ['spæŋkɪŋ] N Tracht f Prügel; **to give sb a ~** jdm eine Tracht Prügel verpassen, jdm den Hintern versohlen ADJ **a** (= brisk) pace scharf, schnell; **at a ~ pace** in schnellem Tempo **b** (= splendid) **in ~ condition** in hervorragendem Zustand ADV (dated inf, = exceedingly) **~ new** funkelnagelneu; **~ clean** blitzsauber

spanner ['spænə'] N (Brit) Schraubenschlüssel m; **to put or throw a ~ in the works** (fig) jdm Knüppel or einen Knüppel zwischen die Beine werfen; **that's a real ~ in the works** das ist wirklich ein Hemmschuh

span roof N Satteldach nt

spar¹ [spaː] N (Naut) Rundholz nt

spar² VI (Boxing) sparren, ein Sparring nt machen; (fig) sich kabbeln (inf) (about um)

spar³ N (Miner) Spat m

spare [speə'] ADJ **a** den/die/das man nicht braucht, übrig pred; (= surplus) überzählig, übrig pred; **~ bed** Gästebett nt; **have you any ~ string?, have you any string ~?** kannst du mir (einen) Bindfaden geben (, hast du)? **can you give me a ~ for him?**; **I can give you a racket/pencil, I have a ~ one** ich kann dir einen Schläger/Bleistift geben, ich habe noch einen *or* ich habe einen übrig; **take a ~ pen in case that one doesn't work** nehmen Sie noch einen Füller mit, falls dieser nicht funktioniert; **take some ~ clothes** nehmen Sie Kleider zum Wechseln mit; **it's all the ~ cash I have** mehr Bargeld habe ich nicht übrig; **if you have any ~ cash** wenn Sie Geld übrig haben; **should you have any ~ time** *or* **a ~ minute** sollten Sie Zeit (übrig) haben; **when you have a ~ minutes** *or* **a few minutes** wenn Sie mal ein paar freie Minuten haben *or* ein paar Minuten übrig haben; **we have two ~ seats** wir haben zwei Plätze übrig; **I still have one ~ place in the car** ich habe noch einen Platz im Auto (frei); **there are two seats (going) ~** es sind noch zwei Plätze frei

b (= *thin*) hager; (= *meagre*) dürftig

c **to drive sb ~** (*inf*) jdn wahnsinnig machen (*inf*); **to go ~** durchdrehen (*inf*), wild werden (*inf*)

N Ersatzteil *nt*; (= *tyre*) Reserverad *nt*

VT a *usu neg* (= *grudge, use sparingly*) sparen mit; *expense, pains, effort* scheuen; **don't ~ the horses** (*hum*) steig aufs Gas (*inf*); **we must ~ no effort in trying to finish this job** wir dürfen keine Mühe scheuen, um diese Arbeit zu erledigen; **there was no expense ~d in building this hotel** beim Bau dieses Hotels ist an nichts gespart worden *or* hat man keine Kosten gescheut; **no expense ~d** es wurden keine Kosten gescheut; **she doesn't ~ herself** sie schont sich nicht; **~ the rod and spoil the child** (*prov*) wer mit der Rute spart, verzieht das Kind (*Prov*)

b (= *give*) *money etc* übrig haben; *space, room* frei haben; *time* (übrig) haben; **to ~ sb sth** jdm etw überlassen *or* geben; *money* jdm etw geben; **can you ~ the time to do it?** haben Sie Zeit, das zu machen?; **I can ~ you five minutes** ich habe fünf Minuten Zeit für Sie (übrig); **can you ~ a penny for a poor old man?** haben Sie einen Groschen für einen armen alten Mann?; **there is none to ~** es ist keine(r, s) übrig; **to have sth to ~** etw übrig haben; **there's enough and to ~** es ist mehr als genug da; **to have a few minutes/hours to ~** ein paar Minuten/Stunden Zeit haben; **I got to the theatre/airport with two minutes to ~** ich war zwei Minuten vor Beginn der Vorstellung im Theater/vor Abflug am Flughafen

c (= *do without*) *person, object* entbehren, verzichten auf (+*acc*); **I can't ~ him/it** ich kann ihn/es nicht entbehren, ich kann auf ihn/es nicht verzichten, ich brauche ihn/es unbedingt; **can you ~ this for a moment?** brauchst du das gerade?, kannst du das im Moment entbehren?; **if you can ~ it** wenn Sie es nicht brauchen; **to ~ a thought for sb/sth** an jdn/etw denken

d (= *show mercy to*) verschonen; (= *refrain from upsetting*) *sb, sb's feelings* schonen; **the fire ~d nothing** nichts blieb vom Feuer verschont; **the soldiers ~d no-one** die Soldaten verschonten keinen; **if we're ~d** wenn wir (dann) noch leben; **to ~ sb's life** jds Leben verschonen

e (= *save*) **to ~ sb/oneself sth** jdm/sich etw ersparen; **~ me the gory details** verschone mich mit den grausigen Einzelheiten; **to ~ him any embarrassment** um ihn nicht in Verlegenheit zu bringen; **he has been ~d the ordeal of seeing her again** es blieb ihm erspart, sie noch einmal sehen zu müssen

sparely ['speəlɪ] ADV **~ built** schlank gebaut

spare: spare part N Ersatzteil *nt*; **spare-part surgery** N (*inf*) Ersatzteilchirurgie *f* (*inf*); **sparerib** N Rippchen *nt*, Spare Rib *no art*; **spare room** N Gästezimmer *nt*; **spare time** N (= *leisure time*) Freizeit *f*; **spare tyre**, (*US*) **spare tire** N Ersatzreifen *m*; (*fig inf*) Rettungsring *m* (*hum inf*); **spare wheel** N (*esp Brit*) Ersatzrad *nt*

sparing ['speərɪŋ] ADJ sparsam; **to be ~ with one's time** mit seiner Zeit geizen *or* knausern; **to be ~ in one's praise** mit Lob geizen; **to be ~ of words** nicht viel sagen, wortkarg sein

sparingly ['speərɪŋlɪ] ADV sparsam; *spend, drink, eat* in Maßen; **to use sth ~** mit etw sparsam umgehen; **these plants should be watered more ~** diese Pflanzen sollten mäßiger gegossen werden

spark [spɑːk] **N a** (*from fire, Elec*) Funke *m*; (*fig, = glimmer*) Fünkchen *nt*, Funke(n) *m*; **not a ~ of life** kein Fünkchen Leben, kein Lebensfunke; **a ~ of interest** ein Fünkchen *or* Funke(n) Interesse; **a few ~s of wit toward(s) the end of the speech** ein paar geistreiche Bemerkungen am Ende der Rede; **when the ~s start to fly** (*fig*) wenn die Fetzen anfangen zu fliegen **b** (*dated inf, = person*) Stutzer *m* (*dated*); **a bright ~** (*iro*) ein Intelligenzbolzen *m* (*iro*); (*clumsy*) ein Tollpatsch *m*

VT (*also* **spark off**) entzünden; *explosion* verursachen; (*fig*) auslösen; *quarrel* entfachen; *interest, enthusiasm* wecken; **to ~ a fire** ein Feuer entzünden *or* entfachen; (*by accident*) ein Feuer auslösen *or* verursachen **VI** Funken sprühen; (*Elec*) zünden

spark: spark coil N Zündspule *f*; **spark gap** N Funkenstrecke *f*

sparking plug ['spɑːkɪŋplʌg] N Zündkerze *f*

sparkle ['spɑːkl] **N** Funkeln *nt*, Glitzern *nt*; (*of eyes*) Funkeln *nt*; **he has no ~, he lacks ~** ihm fehlt der (rechte) Schwung **VI** funkeln, glitzern; (*eyes*) blitzen, funkeln (*with* vor +*dat*); (*fig: person*) vor Leben(sfreude) sprühen; (*with intelligence, wit etc*) brillieren; **her eyes ~d with excitement** ihre Augen blitzten vor Erregung; **she was so happy she really ~d** sie sprühte geradezu vor Glück; **his conversation ~d (with wit)** seine Unterhaltung sprühte vor Geist

sparkler ['spɑːklə] N **a** (= *firework*) Wunderkerze *f* **b** (*inf, = diamond*) Klunker *m* (*inf*)

sparkling ['spɑːklɪŋ] ADJ *lights* glänzend, funkelnd; *eyes* funkelnd; *wit* sprühend; (= *lively*) *person* vor Leben sprühend; (= *scintillating*) *performance* brilliant; (= *witty*) *person, speech, conversation* vor Geist sprühend; (= *bubbling*) *lemonade etc* perlend; *wine* perlend, moussierend; *cider* kohlensäurehaltig; **~ (mineral) water** Mineralwasser *nt* mit Kohlensäure, Selterswasser *nt*; **~ wine** (*as type*) Schaumwein *m*, Sekt *m*; (= *slightly sparkling*) Perlwein *m*; **in ~ form** in glänzender Form; **the car was ~ (clean)** das Auto blitzte vor Sauberkeit

ADV funkelnd, blitzend; **~ clean floors and walls** blitzsaubere Fußböden und Wände

sparkly ['spɑːklɪ] ADJ (*inf*) funkelnd; **her eyes were ~** ihre Augen funkelten

spark plug N Zündkerze *f*

sparring ['spɑːrɪŋ] **: sparring match** N (*lit*) Sparringkampf *m*; (*fig*) (Wort)geplänkel *nt*, Wortgefecht *nt*; **sparring partner** N (*lit*) Sparringpartner(in) *m(f)*; (*fig also*) Kontrahent(in) *m(f)*

sparrow ['spærəʊ] N Sperling *m*, Spatz *m*; **house ~** Haussperling *m*

sparrowgrass ['spærəʊgrɑːs] N (*inf*) Spargel *m*

sparrowhawk ['spærəʊhɔːk] N (*European*) Sperber *m*; (*N American*) amerikanischer Falke

sparse [spɑːs] ADJ spärlich; *covering, vegetation also* dünn; *hair* dünn, schütter; *furnishings, data, resources* dürftig

sparsely ['spɑːslɪ] ADV spärlich; *wooded also, populated* dünn; *furnished also* dürftig; **a hillside ~ covered with trees** ein Hang mit spärlichem Baumwuchs

sparseness ['spɑːsnɪs] N Spärlichkeit *f*; (*of furnishings also*) Dürftigkeit *f*; (*of population*) geringe Dichte

Sparta ['spɑːtə] N Sparta *nt*

Spartan ['spɑːtən] ADJ (*fig: also* **spartan**) spartanisch N Spartaner(in) *m(f)*

spasm ['spæzəm] N (*Med*) Krampf *m*, Spasmus *m* (*spec*); (*of asthma, coughing, fig*) Anfall *m*; **~s of coughing** krampfartige Hustenanfälle *pl*; **there was a ~ of activity** es entwickelte sich fieberhafte Aktivität; **they play well in ~s** sie spielen ab und zu ganz gut

spasmodic [spæz'mɒdɪk] ADJ (*Med*) krampfartig, spasmisch, spasmodisch; (*fig, = occasional*) sporadisch; *growth* schubweise; **his generosity was ~** er hatte Phasen *or* Anfälle von Großzügigkeit

spasmodically [spæz'mɒdɪkəlɪ] ADV (*Med*) krampfartig; (*fig*) sporadisch, hin und wieder; *grow in Schüben*, schubweise

spastic ['spæstɪk] ADJ spastisch; (*pej sl*) schwach (*inf*) N Spastiker(in) *m(f)*

spasticity [spæ'stɪsɪtɪ] N spastische Lähmung

spat¹ [spæt] N (*of oyster etc*) Muschellaich *m* VI (*oyster etc*) laichen

spat² N Halbgamasche *f*

spat³ N (*inf: = quarrel*) Knatsch *m* (*inf*), Krach *m* (*inf*) VI (*US, inf: = quarrel*) zanken, streiten

spat⁴ *pret, ptp of* **spit¹**

spate [speɪt] N (*of river*) Hochwasser *nt*; (*fig, of letters, orders etc*) Flut *f*; (*of burglaries, accidents*) Serie *f*; (*of words, abuse*) Schwall *m*; **the river is in (full) ~** der Fluss führt Hochwasser; **a ~ of words** ein Wortschwall *m*; **a ~ of excited talk** aufgeregtes Stimmengewirr

spatial ADJ , **spatially** ADV ['speɪʃəl, -ɪ] räumlich

spatiotemporal [ˌspeɪʃɪəʊ'tempərəl] ADJ räumlich-zeitlich

spatter ['spætə] VT bespritzen; **to ~ water over sb, to ~ sb with water** jdn nass spritzen; **a wall ~ed with blood** eine blutbespritzte Wand VI **to ~ over sth** etw voll spritzen; **it ~ed all over the room** es verspritzte im ganzen Zimmer; **the rain ~ed (down) on the roof** der Regen klatschte aufs Dach N (= *mark*) Spritzer *pl*; (= *sound: of rain*) Klatschen *nt*; **a ~ of rain** ein paar Tropfen Regen; **a ~ of applause** kurzer Beifall

spatula ['spætjʊlə] N Spachtel *m*; (*Med*) Spatel *m*

spavin ['spævɪn] N Spat *m*

spavined ['spævɪnd] ADJ *horse* spatkrank

spawn [spɔːn] **N a** (*of fish, shellfish, frogs*) Laich *m* **b** (*of mushrooms*) Fadengeflecht *nt* VI laichen **VT** (*fig*) hervorbringen, erzeugen; **bad living conditions ~ crime** schlechte Wohnverhältnisse sind Brutstätten des Verbrechens

spawning ['spɔːnɪŋ] **N** Laichen *nt* ADJ **a** *fish* laichend, Laich-; **~ time** Laichzeit *f* **b** (= *sprawling*) sich stark ausbreitend *or* vermehrend

spawning ground ['spɔːnɪŋgraʊnd] N Laichplatz *m*

spay [speɪ] VT *cat, dog* sterilisieren

SPCA *abbr of* **Society for the Prevention of Cruelty to Animals** ≈ Tierschutzverein *m*

speak [spiːk] *pret* **spoke** *or* (*obs*) **spake**, *ptp* **spoken** *or* (*obs*) **spoke** **VT a** (= *utter*) sagen; *one's thoughts* aussprechen, äußern; *one's lines* aufsagen; **to ~ one's mind** seine Meinung sagen; **nobody spoke a word** niemand sagte ein Wort, keiner sagte etwas; **his eyes spoke his love** sein Blick verriet seine Liebe → **volume** **b** *language* sprechen; **English spoken here** man spricht Englisch

VI a (= *talk, be on speaking terms*) sprechen, reden (*about* über +*acc*, von); (= *converse*) reden, sich unterhalten (*with* mit); (*fig, guns, drums*) sprechen, ertönen; **to ~ to** *or* **with sb** mit jdm sprechen *or* reden; **did you ~?** haben Sie etwas gesagt?; **to ~ in a whisper** flüstern; **~, don't shout** nun schrei nicht so doch nicht (so)!; **they don't ~ (to one another)** sie reden *or* sprechen nicht miteinander; **I'm not ~ing to you** mit dir rede *or* spreche ich nicht mehr; **she never spoke to me again** seitdem hat sie nie wieder mit mir geredet *or* gesprochen; **to ~ to oneself** Selbstgespräche führen; **I'll ~ to him about it** (*euph, = admonish*) ich werde ein Wörtchen mit ihm reden; **I'll have to ~ to my lawyer about it** das muss ich mit meinem Anwalt besprechen; **~ when you're spoken to** antworte, wenn man mit dir redet *or* spricht; **servants should only ~ when spoken to** Diener sollten nur dann etwas sagen, wenn man sie anspricht; **I don't know him to ~ to** ich kenne ihn nicht näher; **music**

~s directly to the soul Musik spricht die Seele an; **~ing dictionaries ...** da or wo wir gerade von Wörterbüchern sprechen ..., apropos Wörterbücher ...; **not to ~ of ...** ganz zu schweigen von ...; **it's nothing to ~ of** es ist nicht weiter erwähnenswert, es ist nichts weiter; **no money/ trees** etc **to ~ of** so gut wie kein Geld/keine Bäume etc; **to ~ ill of sb/sth** über jdn/etw schlecht reden; **to ~ well of sb/sth** jdn/etw loben, (nur) Gutes über jdn/etw sagen; **he is well spoken of** er genießt große Achtung; **so to ~** sozusagen, eigentlich; **roughly ~ing** grob gesagt; **strictly ~ing** genau genommen; **legally/ biologically ~ing** rechtlich/biologisch gesehen; **generally ~ing** im Allgemeinen; **~ing personally ...** wenn Sie mich fragen ..., was mich betrifft ...; **~ing as a member of the club I have ...** als Mitglied des Vereins habe ich ...; **to ~ down to sb** jdn von oben herab behandeln

b (= make a speech) reden (on zu), sprechen (on zu); (= give one's opinion) sich äußern (on, to zu); **to ~ in public** in der Öffentlichkeit reden; **to ~ in the debate** in der Debatte das Wort ergreifen; **to ask sb to ~** jdm das Wort erteilen; **Mr X will ~ next** als Nächster hat Herr X das Wort; **then Geoffrey rose to ~** dann stand Geoffrey auf, um das Wort zu ergreifen

c (Telec) **~ing!** am Apparat!; **Jones ~ing!** (hier) Jones!; **who is that ~ing?** wer ist da, bitte?; (on extension phone, in office) wer ist am Apparat?

d (fig: = suggest) zeugen (of von); **their appearance ~s of poverty** ihre Erscheinung verrät Armut or zeugt von Armut

N suf **Euro-speak** Eurojargon m

▶ **speak against** VI +prep obj (in debate) sprechen gegen, sich aussprechen gegen; (= criticize) etwas sagen gegen, kritisieren

▶ **speak for** VI +prep obj **a** (in debate) unterstützen

b **to speak for sb** (= on behalf of) in jds Namen (dat) sprechen; (= in favour of) ein gutes Wort für jdn einlegen; **he speaks for the miners/delegation** er ist der Sprecher der Bergleute/Abordnung; **I know I speak for all of us** ich bin sicher, dass ich im Namen aller spreche; **speaking for myself ...** was mich angeht ...; **let her speak for herself** lass sie selbst reden; **speak for yourself!** (= I don't agree) das meinst auch nur du!; (= don't include me) du vielleicht!; **I can speak for his honesty** ich kann mich für seine Ehrlichkeit verbürgen; **that speaks well for him** das spricht für ihn; **to speak well/badly for sth** ein Beweis m/nicht gerade ein Beweis m für etw sein

c **to speak for itself** (= be obvious) für sich sprechen, alles sagen

d **to be spoken for** (dated: girl) versprochen sein (old), vergeben sein (hum); **the chair had already been spoken for** (hum) der Stuhl war schon reserviert; **that's already spoken for** (hum) das ist schon vergeben

▶ **speak out** VI (audibly) deutlich sprechen; (= give one's opinion) seine Meinung deutlich vertreten; **to speak out in favour of sth** für etw eintreten; **to speak out against sth** sich gegen etw aussprechen

▶ **speak up** VI **a** (= raise one's voice) lauter sprechen or reden; (= talk loudly) laut (und verständlich) sprechen or reden; **speak up!** sprich lauter!; **if you want anything speak up** sag, wenn du etwas willst **b** (fig) seine Meinung sagen or äußern; **don't be afraid to speak up** sagen Sie ruhig Ihre Meinung, äußern Sie sich ruhig; **to speak up for sb/sth** für jdn/etw eintreten; **what's wrong? speak up!** was ist los? heraus mit der Sprache!

speakeasy ['spiːkiːzɪ] N (US) Mondscheinkneipe f (inf, Lokal, in dem während der Prohibition Alkohol ausgeschenkt wurde)

speaker ['spiːkə'] N **a** (of language) Sprecher m; **all ~s of German, all German ~s** alle, die Deutsch sprechen, alle Deutsch Sprechenden; (esp native speakers) alle Deutschsprachigen **b** Sprecher(in) m(f); (in lecture, = public speaker) Redner(in) m(f); **the last** or **previous ~** der Vor-

redner; **our ~ today is ...** der heutige Referent ist ...; **he's a good/poor ~** er ist ein guter/ schlechter Redner **c** (= loudspeaker) Lautsprecher m; (on hi-fi etc) Box f **d** (Parl) **Speaker** Sprecher(in) m(f); **Mr Speaker** ≈ Herr Präsident

SPEAKER/SPEAKER OF THE HOUSE

Im britischen Parlamentssystem hat der **Speaker** die Aufgabe, im **House of Commons** die Ordnung aufrechtzuerhalten und zu garantieren, dass alle Mitglieder die Geschäftsordnung befolgen. Der **Speaker**, der nicht Mitglied der Regierungspartei sein muss, wird zur Eröffnung eines neuen Parlaments gewählt. Sobald er oder sie im Amt ist, spricht der **Speaker** nur noch in seiner offiziellen Funktion und muss absolut unparteiisch sein. Die Parlamentsmitglieder beginnen ihre Reden stets mit „Mister/Madam Speaker". In den Vereinigten Staaten ist der **Speaker of the House** der Vorsitzende des Repräsentantenhauses, der zudem der Vorsitzende der Partei ist, die die Mehrheit stellt. Er ist selbst Mitglied des **House of Representatives** und wird von seiner eigenen Partei gewählt. Er ist nicht nur für die Einhaltung der Geschäftsordnung zuständig, sondern fungiert zugleich als Sprecher seiner Partei. Der **Speaker of the House** steht direkt nach dem Vizepräsidenten in der Präsidentennachfolge.

speaking ['spiːkɪŋ] **N** (= act of speaking) Sprechen nt; (= speeches) Reden pl; **the art of ~** die Redekunst **ADJ** attr doll sprechend, Mama- (inf); (fig) likeness verblüffend; **to be within ~ distance** nahe genug sein, dass man sich verständigen kann; **I have a ~ engagement later today** ich muss heute noch eine Rede halten

-speaking ADJ suf -sprechend; (with native language also) -sprachig; **English-speaking** Englisch sprechend, englischsprachig

speaking: speaking clock N (Brit) telefonische Zeitansage; **speaking part, speaking role** N (Film, Theat) Sprechrolle f; **speaking terms** PL **to be on ~ with sb** mit jdm sprechen or reden; **speaking trumpet** N (old) Hörrohr nt; **speaking tube** N Sprachrohr nt; **speaking voice** N Sprechstimme f

spear [spɪə'] **N** Speer m; (= leaf) Lanzettenblatt nt; (of grass) Halm m; (of grain) Keim m; **broccoli ~s** Brokkoliköpfe pl; **asparagus ~s** Stangen pl Spargel **VT** aufspießen; (= wound, kill) durchbohren; (= catch with spear) mit Speeren fangen; **he ~ed him through the arm** er durchbohrte ihm den Arm; **he ~ed the meat with his fork** er spießte das Fleisch auf die Gabel

spear: spear carrier N **a** (Theat) Statist(in) m(f) **b** (pej = henchman) Handlanger(in) m(f) (pej); **spearhead** **N** **a** (of spear) Speerspitze f; (Mil) Angriffsspitze f **b** (fig, = thing) Bahnbrecher m (of für); (= person) Bahnbrecher(in) m(f) (of für) **VT** (lit, fig) anführen; **spearman** N Speerträger m; **spearmint** N (= plant, flavour) Grüne Minze; **~ chewing gum** Spearmintkaugummi m

spec [spek] N (inf) **on ~** auf Verdacht, auf gut Glück

special ['speʃəl] ADJ **a** besondere(r, s); (= specific) purpose, use, person, case bestimmt, speziell; (= exceptional) friend, favour, occasion speziell; **I have no ~ person in mind** ich habe eigentlich an niemanden Bestimmtes gedacht; **in this one ~ instance** in diesem einen Fall; **take ~ care of it** passen Sie besonders gut darauf auf; **nothing ~** nichts Besonderes; **he expects ~ treatment** er will besonders behandelt werden, er will eine besondere Behandlung haben (inf); **this is rather a ~ day for me** heute ist ein ganz besonderer Tag für mich; **he uses the word in a ~ way** er gebraucht das Wort in einer speziellen Bedeutung; **he's a very ~ person to her, he's very ~ to her** er bedeutet ihr sehr viel; **you're extra ~!** (inf) du bist was ganz Besonderes! (inf); **what's so ~ about her/the house?** was ist

denn an ihr/an dem Haus so besonders?; **what's so ~ about that?** na und? (inf), das ist doch nichts Besonderes!; **I do that my own ~ way** ich mache das ganz auf meine (eigene) Weise; **everyone has his ~ place** jeder hat seinen eigenen Platz; **to feel ~** sich als etwas ganz Besonderes vorkommen; **make him feel ~** seien Sie besonders nett zu ihm

b (= out of the ordinary) Sonder-, besondere(r, s); **~ permission** Sondererlaubnis f; **~ legislation** Sondergesetzgebung f; **~ feature** (Press) Sonderartikel m

c (= specialized) speziell, Spezial-; **~ subject** Spezialfach nt

d (inf, = separate) place, book etc gesondert **N** (= constable) Hilfspolizist(in) m(f); (TV, Rad) Sonderprogramm nt; (= train) Sonderzug m; (Cook) Tagesgericht nt; (= edition) Sonder- or Extraausgabe f; **chef's ~** Spezialität f des Küchenchefs

special: special agent N (= spy) Agent(in) m(f); **special bargain** N (Comm) Sonderangebot nt, Schnäppchen nt (inf); **Special Branch** N (Brit) Sicherheitspolizei f, Sicherheitsdienst m; **special case** N (also Jur) Sonderfall m; **special character** N (Comput) Sonderzeichen nt; **special constable** N Hilfspolizist(in) m(f); **special correspondent** N (Press) Sonderberichterstatter(in) m(f); **special delivery** N Eilzustellung f; **a special-delivery letter** ein Eilbrief m; **by ~** durch Eilzustellung, per Eilboten (inf); **special drawing rights** PL Sonderziehungsrechte pl; **special edition** N Sonderausgabe f; **special envoy** N Sondergesandte(r) mf; **special investigator** N Sonderbeauftragte(r) mf, Untersuchungsbeamte(r) m/-beamtin f

specialism ['speʃəlɪzəm] N (= specializing) Spezialisierung f; (= special subject) Spezialgebiet nt

specialist ['speʃəlɪst] **N** Spezialist(in) m(f), Fachmann m, Fachfrau f (in für); (Med) Facharzt m/-ärztin f; **a ~ in tropical diseases** ein Facharzt or Spezialist für Tropenkrankheiten **ADJ** attr Fach-; **~ dictionary** Fach- or Spezialwörterbuch nt; **it's ~ work** dazu braucht man einen Fachmann

specialist knowledge N Fachwissen nt

speciality [ˌspeʃɪˈælɪtɪ], (US) **specialty** ['speʃəltɪ] N Spezialität f; (= special area) Spezialgebiet nt; **to make a ~ of sth** sich auf etw (acc) spezialisieren; **to make a ~ of doing sth** sich darauf spezialisieren, etw zu tun; **a ~ of the house** eine Spezialität des Hauses

specialization [ˌspeʃəlaɪˈzeɪʃən] N Spezialisierung f (in auf +acc); (= special subject) Spezialgebiet nt

specialize ['speʃəlaɪz] **VI** sich spezialisieren (in auf +acc); **we ~ in ...** wir haben uns auf ... (acc) spezialisiert **VT the species/tail has been ~d** die Art/der Schwanz hat sich gesondert entwickelt

specialized ['speʃəlaɪzd] ADJ spezialisiert; **a ~ knowledge of biology** Fachkenntnisse pl in Biologie

special licence N (Brit) (Ehe)dispens f (des Erzbischofs von Canterbury)

specially ['speʃəlɪ] ADV besonders; (= specifically) extra; (= for a particular purpose) speziell, extra; **a ~ difficult task** eine besonders schwierige Aufgabe; **I had it ~ made** ich habe es extra machen lassen; **we asked for it ~** wir haben es extra darum gebeten; **he brought it ~ for me** er hat es extra or eigens für mich gebracht; **they were all pretty girls, ~ the two sisters** die Mädchen waren alle hübsch, besonders or insbesondere die beiden Schwestern; **we would ~ like to see the orchard** wir würden besonders gern den Obstgarten sehen; **don't go to the post office ~/~ for me** gehen Sie deswegen/meinetwegen nicht extra zur Post

special: special messenger N Expressbote m/-botin f; (Mil) Kurier(in) m(f); **special needs** PL (Brit) **children with ~, ~ children** behinderte Kinder pl, Kinder pl mit Behinderungen; **~ teacher** Behindertenlehrer(in) m(f),

Sonderschullehrer(in) *m(f)*; **special offer** N Sonderangebot *nt*; **special pleading** N *(Jur)* Beibringung *f* neuen Beweismaterials; *(fig)* Berufung *f* auf einen Sonderfall; **special prosecutor** N *(US)* Sonderstaatsanwalt *m/*-anwältin *f*; **special relationship** N *(Pol)* besondere Beziehungen *pl (with mit)*; **special school** N *(Brit)* Sonderschule *f*; *(for physically handicapped)* Behindertenschule *f*

specialty ['speʃəltɪ] N *(US)* = **speciality**

specie ['spiːʃiː] N , *no pl* Hartgeld *nt*, Münzgeld *nt*

species ['spiːʃiːz] N *pl* - Art *f*; *(Biol also)* Spezies *f*; **the human ~** der Mensch

specific [spə'sɪfɪk] **ADJ** **a** *(= definite)* bestimmt, speziell; *(= precise) statement, instructions* genau; *example* ganz bestimmt; **9.3, to be ~** 9,3, um genau zu sein; **can you be a bit more ~?** können Sie sich etwas genauer äußern?; **to be ~ about sth** sich spezifisch zu etw äußern; **he was quite ~ on that point** er hat sich zu diesem Punkt recht spezifisch geäußert; **nothing ~** nichts Spezielles

b **to be ~ to sb/sth** *(= peculiar)* auf jdn/etw zutreffen

c *(Biol, Chem, Phys, Med)* spezifisch

N **a** *(old Med)* Spezifikum *nt*

b **specifics** PL nähere *or* genauere Einzelheiten *pl*; **to get down to ~s** zu den Einzelheiten kommen

-specific [spə'sɪfɪk] ADJ *suf* -spezifisch; **country--specific** landesspezifisch; **job-specific** berufsspezifisch, berufsbezogen

specifically [spə'sɪfɪkəlɪ] ADV *warn, order, state, mention* ausdrücklich; *(= specially) designed, request* speziell; *(= precisely)* genau; *(= in particular)* im Besonderen; **~, we need three** wir brauchen genau drei; **can you define that more ~?** können Sie das etwas genauer definieren?

specification [ˌspesɪfɪ'keɪʃən] N **a** *(= specifying)* Angabe *f*; **his ideas need more ~** seine Ideen müssen noch genauer ausgeführt werden **b** *(= detailed statement, of requirements)* genaue Angabe, Aufstellung *f*; *(for patent)* (genaue) Beschreibung; *(= design, for car, machine)* (detaillierter) Entwurf; *(for building)* Bauplan *m*; **~s** *pl* genaue Angaben *pl*; *(of car, machine)* technische Daten *or* Angaben *pl*; *(of new building)* Raum- und Materialangaben *pl*, Baubeschreibung *f*; **the new ~ includes ...** *(= model)* die neue Ausführung hat auch ... **c** *(= stipulation)* Bedingung *f*; *(for building)* Vorschrift *f*

specific: specific character N *(Biol)* Artmerkmal *nt*; **specific gravity** N *(Chem, Phys)* spezifisches Gewicht, Wichte *f*; **specific heat** N *(Chem, Phys)* spezifische Wärme

specified ['spesɪfaɪd] ADJ *(= particular) amount, number* bestimmt; *period* vorgeschrieben; *price* vorgegeben; **at a ~ time** zu einer bestimmten Zeit

specify ['spesɪfaɪ] **VT** angeben; *(= list individually or in detail)* spezifizieren, (einzeln) aufführen; *(= stipulate)* vorschreiben; *(blueprint, contract etc)* vorsehen; **in the specified order** in der angegebenen *or* vorgeschriebenen Reihenfolge; **to ~ how to do sth** genauer *or* näher ausführen, wie etw gemacht werden soll **VI** genaue Angaben machen; **unless otherwise specified** wenn nicht anders angegeben

specimen ['spesɪmɪn] **N** Exemplar *nt*; *(of urine, blood etc)* Probe *f*; *(= sample)* Muster *nt*; **a beautiful *or* fine ~** ein Prachtexemplar *nt*; **if that's a ~ of your work** wenn das eine Probe deines Könnens ist **b** **you're a pretty poor ~** *(inf)* du hast ja nicht viel zu bieten *(inf)* **ADJ** *attr* Probe-; **~ page** Probeseite *f*; **a ~ copy** ein Beleg- *or* Probeexemplar *nt*; **a ~ signature** eine Unterschriftenprobe

specious ['spiːʃəs] ADJ *argument, proposal, logic* vordergründig bestechend; *excuse* fadenscheinig; *claim* unfundiert, fadenscheinig; *charm, phrases* leer; *nonsense* hohl

speciousness ['spiːʃəsnɪs] N *(of argument)* Vordergründigkeit *f*; *(of excuse)* Fadenscheinigkeit *f*; *(of claim)* Unfundiertheit *f*

speck [spek] **N** Fleck *m*; *(of blood, paint, mud also)* Spritzer *m*; *(of dust)* Körnchen *nt*; *(of soot)* Flocke *f*, Flöckchen *nt*; *(of gold, colour etc)* Sprenkel *m*; *(= small portion, of drink etc)* Tropfen *m*, Tröpfchen *nt*; *(of sugar, butter)* kleines bisschen; *(fig, of truth, confidence)* Fünkchen *nt*, Quäntchen *nt*; **a ~ on the horizon** ein Punkt *m or* Pünktchen *nt* am Horizont **VT** **to be ~ed with black** schwarze Fleckchen haben; *(bird, eyes etc)* schwarz gesprenkelt sein; **his face was ~ed with dirt** er hatte Schmutzflecken im Gesicht; **to be ~ed with blood** blutbespritzt sein

speckle ['spekl] **N** Sprenkel *m*, Tupfer *m*, Tupfen *m* **VT** sprenkeln; **to be ~d with sth** mit etw gesprenkelt sein; **to be ~d with brown** braun gesprenkelt sein

speckless ADJ , **specklessly** ADV ['speklɪs, -lɪ] fleckenlos, sauber, rein

specs [speks] PL **a** *(inf)* Brille *f* **b** abbr of **specifications**

spectacle ['spektəkl] **N** **a** *(= show)* Schauspiel *nt*; **a sad ~** ein trauriger Anblick; **to make a ~ of oneself** unangenehm auffallen **b** **spectacles** PL *(also* **pair of spectacles)** Brille *f*

spectacle case N Brilletui *or* -futteral *nt*

spectacled ['spektəkld] ADJ bebrillt; *(Zool)* brillenähnlich gezeichnet

spectacular [spek'tækjʊlə'] **ADJ** sensationell; *improvement, success* also spektakulär; *scenery* atemberaubend; *sight* sensationell, atemberaubend; *failure* spektakulär **N** *(Theat)* Show *f*

spectacularly [spek'tækjʊləlɪ] ADV **a** *(= stunningly)* überwältigend **b** *(= dramatically) successful* sensationell; *improve, fail* also spektakulär; *good, bad* unglaublich; **he was ~ wrong** er hat einen Riesenfehler gemacht; **to do ~ well/badly** unglaublich gut/schlecht abschneiden

spectate [spek'teɪt] VI *(inf: esp Sport)* zuschauen *(at bei)*

spectator [spek'teɪtə'] N Zuschauer(in) *m(f)*

spectator sport N Publikumssport *m*

specter N *(US)* = **spectre**

spectogram ['spektəʊgræm] N Spektogramm *nt*

spectra ['spektrə] *pl of* **spectrum**

spectral ['spektrəl] ADJ **a** *(of ghosts)* geisterhaft, gespenstisch **b** *(of the spectrum)* spektral, Spektral-; **~ colour** Spektralfarbe *f*

spectre, *(US)* **specter** ['spektə'] N Gespenst *nt*; *(fig)* (Schreck)gespenst *nt*; **the ~ of a woman in white** die Erscheinung einer Frau in Weiß

spectrograph ['spektrəʊgræf] N Spektrograph *m*

spectroscope ['spektrəʊskəʊp] N Spektroskop *nt*

spectroscopic [ˌspektrəʊ'skɒpɪk] ADJ spektroskopisch

spectroscopic analysis N Spektralanalyse *f*

spectrum ['spektrəm] N *pl* **spectra** Spektrum *nt*; *(fig, = range also)* Palette *f*, Skala *f*; **~ analysis** Spektralanalyse *f*

specula ['spekjʊlə] *pl of* **speculum**

speculate ['spekjʊleɪt] VI **a** *(= meditate, ponder)* (nach)grübeln, nachdenken *(on über +acc)*; *(= conjecture)* Vermutungen anstellen, spekulieren *(about, on über +acc)*; **I ~ that ...** ich vermute, dass ... **b** *(Fin)* spekulieren *(in mit, on an +dat)*

speculation [ˌspekjʊ'leɪʃən] N *(all senses)* Spekulation *f* *(on über +acc)*; *(= guesswork also)* Vermutung *f*; **it is the subject of much ~** darüber sind viele Spekulationen *or* Vermutungen angestellt worden; **it's pure ~** das ist reine Vermutung

speculative ['spekjʊlətɪv] ADJ **a** spekulativ *(esp Philos)*; *approach, suggestions, ideas* rein theoretisch; *expression, look* grüblerisch **b** *(Fin)* Spekulations-; **~ gain** Spekulationsgewinn *m*; **~ builder** Bauspekulant(in) *m(f)*; **~ building** Bauspekulation *f*; **~ investor** Investitionsspeku-

lant(in) *m(f)*; **a ~ venture** ein Spekulationsvorhaben *nt*

speculatively ['spekjʊlətɪvlɪ] ADV **a** spekulativ, theoretisch; *look, say* grüblerisch **b** *(= tentatively)* vorsichtig **c** *(Fin)* spekulativ; **to invest ~ in sth** etw spekulativ anlegen

speculator ['spekjʊleɪtə'] N *(also Fin)* Spekulant(in) *m(f)*

speculum ['spekjʊləm] N *pl* **specula** *(Med)* Spekulum *nt*; *(in telescope)* Metallspiegel *m*

sped [sped] *pret, ptp of* **speed**

speech [spiːtʃ] **N** **a** *no pl* *(= faculty of speech)* Sprache *f*; *(= act of speaking)* Sprechen *nt*; *(= manner of speaking)* Sprechweise *f*; **to be slow of ~** langsam sprechen; **his ~ was very indistinct** er sprach sehr undeutlich; **he expresses himself better in ~ than in writing** er drückt sich mündlich besser aus als schriftlich; **to burst into ~** in einen Redeschwall ausbrechen; **to lose/recover the power of ~** die Sprache verlieren/zurückgewinnen; **~ is silver, silence is golden** *(prov)* Reden ist Silber, Schweigen ist Gold *(Prov)*; **freedom of ~** Redefreiheit *f*

b *(= language)* Sprache *f*; **in dockers' ~** in der Sprache der Hafenarbeiter

c *(= oration, Theat)* Rede *f* *(on, about über +acc)*; *(in court)* Plädoyer *nt*; **to give *or* make a ~** eine Rede halten; **the actor had three ~es** der Schauspieler hat dreimal gesprochen; **the chairman invited ~es from the floor** der Vorsitzende forderte das Publikum zu Meinungsäußerungen auf; **the ~ from the throne** die Thronrede

d *(Brit, Gram)* **direct/indirect** *or* **reported ~** direkte/indirekte Rede → **figure**, **part**

e *(US: Sch, Univ: = study of speech)* Sprechkunde *f*

speech: speech act N Sprechakt *m*; **speech bubble** N *(in comic, cartoon)* Sprechblase *f*; **speech community** N Sprachgemeinschaft *f*; **speech day** N *(Brit)* Schulfeier *f*; **speech defect** N Sprachfehler *m*

speechify ['spiːtʃɪfaɪ] VI salbadern, Volksreden halten

speechifying ['spiːtʃɪfaɪɪŋ] N Volksreden *pl*, Schwätzerei *f*

speechless ['spiːtʃlɪs] ADJ **a** *(= at a loss for words)* sprachlos *(with vor)*; *anger* stumm; **everybody was ~ at this** darüber waren alle völlig sprachlos; **his remark left me ~** seine Bemerkung machte mich sprachlos *or* verschlug mir die Sprache; **she stared at him in ~ disbelief** sie starrte ihn sprachlos vor Verblüffung an **b** *(lit: = dumb)* stumm; **to be ~** nicht sprechen können

speechlessly ['spiːtʃlɪslɪ] ADV wortlos; *(from surprise, shock etc)* sprachlos

speechlessness ['spiːtʃlɪsnɪs] N **a** Sprachlosigkeit *f* **b** *(lit)* Stummheit *f*; *(= loss of speech)* Sprachverlust *m*

speech: speechmaking N *(= making speeches)* Redenhalten *nt*; *(pej, = speechifying)* Schwätzerei *f*, Gelabere *nt* *(inf)*; **speech organ** N Sprechwerkzeug *nt*; **speech pattern** N Sprechmuster *nt*; **speech recognition** N Spracherkennung *f*; **speech sound** N Sprachlaut *m*; **speech synthesizer** N Sprachsynthesizer *m*; **speech therapist** N Sprachtherapeut(in) *m(f)*, Logopäde *m*, Logopädin *f*; **speech therapy** N Sprachtherapie *f*, Logopädie *f*; *(= treatment)* logopädische Behandlung; **speech writer** N Ghostwriter(in) *m(f)* *(inf)*, Redenschreiber(in) *m(f)*

speed [spiːd] *vb: pret, ptp* **sped** *or* **speeded** **N** **a** Geschwindigkeit *f*; *(= esp fast speed)* Schnelligkeit *f*; *(of moving object or person)* Tempo *nt*, Geschwindigkeit *f*; **at ~** äußerst schnell; **at high/low ~** mit hoher/niedriger Geschwindigkeit; **at full *or* top ~** mit Höchstgeschwindigkeit; **at a ~ of 50 mph** mit einer Geschwindigkeit *or* einem Tempo von 50 Meilen pro Stunde; **the ~ of light/sound** die Licht-/Schallgeschwindigkeit; **at the ~ of light** mit Lichtgeschwindigkeit; **walking ~** Schritttempo *nt*; **to**

pick up or **gather** ~ beschleunigen, schneller werden; (fig, development) sich beschleunigen; (person) schneller werden; **to lose** ~ (an) Geschwindigkeit verlieren; **to be up to** ~ (inf: = informed) auf dem neuesten Stand sein; **to bring a factory/system up to** ~ eine Fabrik/ein System auf den neuesten Stand bringen; **to bring sb up to** ~ (inf) jdn auf den neuesten Stand bringen; **what** ~ **were you doing?** wie schnell sind Sie gefahren?; **her typing/shorthand** ~ **is good** sie kann schnell Maschine schreiben/stenografieren; **what is her typing/shorthand** ~**?** wie viele Anschläge/Silben (pro Minute) schreibt sie?; **with all possible** ~ so schnell wie möglich; **with such** ~ so schnell; **full** ~ **ahead!** (Naut) volle Kraft voraus!

b (Aut, Tech: = gear) Gang m; **three-speed bicycle** Fahrrad mit Dreigangschaltung; **a three-speed gear** ein Dreiganggetriebe nt

c (Phot, = film speed) Lichtempfindlichkeit f; (= shutter speed) Belichtungszeit f

d (inf: = drug) Speed nt (sl)

VT **to** ~ **sb on his way** (person) jdn verabschieden; (iro) jdn hinauskomplimentieren; (good wishes etc) jdn auf seinem Weg begleiten; **if you fetch the visitors' coats it may** ~ **them on their way** wenn du die Mäntel der Gäste holst, machen sie sich vielleicht auf den Weg; **God** ~ **you!** (old) Gott (sei) mit dir! (old)

VI **a** pret, ptp **sped** (= move quickly) jagen, flitzen; (arrow) sausen, flitzen; **the years sped by** die Jahre verflogen or vergingen wie im Fluge; **God** ~ (old) Gott mit dir (old)

b pret, ptp **speeded** (Aut, = exceed speed limit) zu schnell fahren, die Geschwindigkeitsbegrenzung überschreiten

▸ **speed along** pret, ptp **speeded** or **sped along** **VT** sep work etc beschleunigen; person antreiben; **to speed things along** die Dinge vorantreiben **VI** entlangjagen or -flitzen (+prep obj +acc); (work) vorangehen

▸ **speed off** pret, ptp **speeded** or **sped off** VI davonjagen; (car also) davonbrausen; (person also) davonflitzen

▸ **speed up** pret, ptp **speeded up** **VI** (car, driver etc) beschleunigen; (person) Tempo zulegen, schneller machen; (work, production etc) schneller werden; **their pace speeded up** ihr Tempo wurde schneller; **with practice you'll speed up** wenn du erst mehr Übung hast, wirst du schneller **VT** sep beschleunigen; person antreiben, auf Trab bringen (inf); **that speeded me up** das hat mir Antrieb gegeben; **tell her to speed up that coffee** (inf) sag ihr, sie soll sich mit dem Kaffee beeilen

speed: speedboat N Renn- or Schnellboot nt; **speed bump** N Bodenschwelle f; **speed camera** N (Police) Blitzgerät nt; **speed cop** N (inf) weiße Maus (inf), Verkehrsbulle m (inf); **speed counter** N (esp Aut) Drehzahlmesser m

speeder ['spiːdə'] N Temposünder(in) m(f) (inf), Raser(in) m(f) (inf)

speed freak N **a** (inf) Geschwindigkeitsfreak m (inf) **b** (Drugs inf) Speedabhängige(r) m(f) (sl)

speedily ['spiːdɪlɪ] ADV schnell; reply, return prompt

speediness ['spiːdɪnɪs] N Schnelligkeit f

speeding ['spiːdɪŋ] N Geschwindigkeitsüberschreitung f; **to get a** ~ **fine** eine Geldstrafe wegen Geschwindigkeitsüberschreitung bekommen

speed: speed limit N Geschwindigkeitsbegrenzung f; **a 30 mph** ~ eine Geschwindigkeitsbegrenzung von 50 km/h; **speed merchant** N (inf) Raser m (inf); **Nicholas is a real** ~ Nicholas fährt wie der Henker (inf)

speedo ['spiːdəu] N (Brit, inf) Tacho m (inf)

speedometer [spɪ'dɒmɪtə'] N Geschwindigkeitsmesser m, Tachometer m

speed: speed ramp N (Mot) Bodenschwelle f; **speed-read** VTI diagonal lesen, quer lesen;

speed skater N Eisschnellläufer(in) m(f); **speed skating** N Eisschnelllauf m

speedster ['spiːdstə'] N (inf, = car) Flitzer m; (= person) Raser(in) m(f) (inf)

speed: speed table N (US Mot) Bodenschwelle f; **speed trap** N Radarfalle f (in bei), Beschleunigung f (in +gen); (in research) Vorantreiben nt (in +gen); (in rate of inflation) Steigerung f (in +gen); **speedway** N (Sport) Speedwayrennen nt; (= track) Speedwaybahn f **b** (US, = racetrack) Rennstrecke f; (= expressway) Schnellstraße f; **speedwell** N (Bot) Ehrenpreis m or nt, Veronika f; **speedwriting** N Schnellschreiben nt

speedy ['spiːdɪ] ADJ (+er) schnell; answer, service also prompt; remedy schnell wirkend; **we wish Joan a** ~ **recovery** wir wünschen Joan eine rasche Genesung; **to bring sth to a** ~ **conclusion** etw schnell zu Ende bringen; **to bring a** ~ **end to sth** etw schnell beenden

speleologist [ˌspiːlɪ'ɒlədʒɪst] N Höhlenkundler(in) m(f)

speleology [ˌspiːlɪ'ɒlədʒɪ] N Höhlenkunde f, Speläologie f (spec)

spell[1] [spel] N (lit, fig) Zauber m; (= incantation) Zauberspruch m; **to be under a** ~ (lit) unter einem Zauber stehen, verzaubert or verhext sein; (fig) wie verzaubert sein; **to put a** ~ **on sb, to cast a** ~ **on** or **over sb, to put sb under a** ~ (lit) jdn verzaubern or verhexen; (fig) jdn in seinen Bann ziehen, jdn verzaubern; **to be under sb's** ~ (fig) in jds Bann (dat) stehen; **to break the** ~ (lit, fig) den Bann brechen, den Zauber lösen

spell[2] N (= period) Weile f, Weilchen nt; for a ~ eine Weile, eine Zeit lang; **cold/hot** ~ Kälte-/Hitzewelle f; **dizzy** ~ Schwächeanfall m; **a short** ~ **of sunny weather** eine kurze Schönwetterperiode; **we had** or **spent a** ~ **in Chile** wir hielten uns eine Zeit lang in Chile auf; **to do a** ~ **on the assembly line/as a waitress** sich kurzzeitig am Fließband/als Serviererin betätigen; **he did** or **had a** ~ **in prison** er hat eine Zeit lang (im Gefängnis) gesessen; **to take a** ~ **at the wheel** eine Zeit lang or ein Weilchen das Steuer übernehmen; **they're going through a bad** ~ sie machen eine schwierige Zeit durch

spell[3] pret, ptp **spelt** (esp Brit) or **spelled** **VI** (in writing) (orthografisch) richtig schreiben; (aloud) buchstabieren; **they can't** ~ sie kann keine Rechtschreibung; **children should learn to** ~ Kinder sollten richtig schreiben lernen **VT** **a** (in writing) schreiben; (aloud) buchstabieren; **how do you** ~ **"onyx"?** wie schreibt man „Onyx"?; **how do you** ~ **your name?** wie schreibt sich Ihr Name?, wie schreiben Sie sich?; **what do these letters** ~**?** welches Wort ergeben diese Buchstaben? **b** (= denote) bedeuten; **it** ~**s disaster (for us)** das bedeutet Unglück (für uns)

▸ **spell out** VT sep (= spell aloud) buchstabieren; (= read slowly) entziffern; (= explain) verdeutlichen, klarmachen; **to spell sth out for sb** jdm etw klarmachen; **he needs everything spelled out to him** man muss ihm alles überdeutlich machen; **do I have to spell it out for you?** (inf) muss ich noch deutlicher werden?

spellbinder ['spelbaɪndə'] N fesselnder Redner/Sänger etc, fesselnde Rednerin/Sängerin etc; (= film) fesselnder Film, Knüller m (inf); **to be a** ~ das Publikum fesseln

spellbinding ['spelbaɪndɪŋ] ADJ fesselnd

spellbound ['spelbaund] ADJ, ADV (fig) wie verzaubert, gebannt; (lit) princess, castle verzaubert; **to hold sb** ~ jdn fesseln; (person also) jdn in seinen Bann schlagen

spell: spell-check (Comput) **N** Rechtschreibprüfung f **VT** die Rechtschreibung (+gen) prüfen; **spellchecker** N (Comput) Rechtschreibprüfung f

speller ['spelə'] N **to be a good/bad** ~ in Rechtschreibung gut/schlecht sein

spelling ['spelɪŋ] N Rechtschreibung f, Orthografie f; (of a word) Schreibweise f; (= activity)

Rechtschreiben nt; (Sch, = lesson) Rechtschreibunterricht m; **the correct** ~ **is ...** die richtige Schreibweise ist ...

spelling: spelling bee N (Sch) Buchstabierwettbewerb m; **spelling book** N Fibel f; **spelling check** N (Comput) Rechtschreibprüfung f; **spelling mistake** N (Recht)schreibfehler m, orthografischer Fehler; **spelling pronunciation** N buchstabengetreue Aussprache

spelt[1] [spelt] N (Bot) Spelz(weizen) m, Dinkel m

spelt[2] (esp Brit) pret, ptp of **spell**[3]

spelunker [spɪ'lʌŋkə'] N Hobbyhöhlenforscher(in) m(f)

spend [spend] pret, ptp **spent** **VT** **a** (= use) money ausgeben (on für); energy, strength verbrauchen; time brauchen; **I've spent all my strength** ich habe meine ganze Kraft aufgebraucht; **we spent a lot of time in useless discussion** wir haben sehr viel Zeit mit nutzlosen Diskussionen vertan; **I've spent three hours on this job** ich habe drei Stunden für diese Arbeit gebraucht; **time well spent** sinnvoll genutzte Zeit

b (= pass) time, holiday, evening etc verbringen; **he** ~**s all his spare time on his car/with his friends** er verbringt jede freie Minute an seinem Auto/mit seinen Freunden; **I spent the night with her/in a hotel** ich habe bei ihr/in einem Hotel übernachtet; **I** ~ **my weekends sleeping** ich verschlafe meine Wochenenden; **he** ~**s his time reading** er verbringt seine Zeit mit Lesen

c ~ **money/time/effort on sth** (= devote to) Geld/Zeit/Mühe für etw aufbringen or in etw (acc) investieren; **I spent a lot of effort on that** das hat mich viel Mühe gekostet

d (= exhaust) **to have spent itself** (anger, fury) sich erschöpft or gelegt haben; **the storm had spent itself** or **its fury** der Sturm hatte sich ausgetobt or gelegt → also **spent**

VI Geld ausgeben; **he was** ~**-ing somewhat too freely** er gab das Geld mit vollen Händen aus

spender ['spendə'] N **he is a big/free** ~ bei ihm sitzt das Geld locker; **the Arabs are the big** ~**s nowadays** heutzutage haben die Araber das große Geld; **the last of the big** ~**s** (iro) ein echter Großkapitalist (hum)

spending ['spendɪŋ] N , no pl Ausgaben pl; **government** ~ **cuts** Kürzungen pl im Etat

spending: spending money N Taschengeld nt; **spending power** N Kaufkraft f; **spending spree** N Großeinkauf m; **to go on a** ~ groß einkaufen gehen

spendthrift ['spendθrɪft] **ADJ** verschwenderisch **N** Verschwender(in) m(f)

spent [spent] pret, ptp of **spend** ADJ ammunition, cartridge, match verbraucht; bullets also verschossen; person erschöpft; **to be/look** ~ erschöpft sein/aussehen; (= prematurely aged) müde und verbraucht sein/aussehen; **as a poet he was** ~ **at 25** mit 25 war seine dichterische Schaffenskraft verbraucht; **to be a** ~ **force** nichts mehr zu sagen haben; (movement) sich totgelaufen haben; (ideology) keine Zugkraft mehr haben; **they collapsed, their energy** ~ ihre ganze Energie verbraucht, brachen sie zusammen; **he held her down until her fury was** ~ er hielt sie fest, bis ihre Wut erschöpft war

sperm [spɜːm] N Samenfaden m, Spermatozoon nt, Spermium nt; (= fluid) Samenflüssigkeit f, Sperma nt

spermaceti [ˌspɜːmə'setɪ] N Spermazet nt, Walrat nt

spermary ['spɜːmərɪ] N (Anat) Keimdrüse f

spermatic [spɜː'mætɪk] ADJ Samen-

spermatic cord N Samenstrang m

spermatozoon [ˌspɜːmætəʊ'zəʊɒn] N pl **spermatozoa** [ˌspɜːmætə'zəʊə] Spermatozoon nt, Spermium nt

sperm bank N Samenbank f

sperm cell N Samenzelle f

sperm count N Spermienzahl f

spermicidal [ˌspɜːmɪˈsaɪdəl] ADJ spermizid

spermicide [ˈspɜːmɪsaɪd] N Spermizid nt

sperm: sperm oil N Walratöl nt; **sperm whale** N Pottwal m

spew [spjuː] VI **a** (inf: = vomit) brechen, spucken; **it makes me ~** (fig) es kotzt mich an (sl) **b** (= flow: also **spew forth** (form) or **out**) sich ergießen (geh); (esp liquid) hervorsprudeln VT **a** (also **spew up**) (inf: = vomit) erbrechen, ausspucken; blood spucken, speien **b** (fig: also **spew out**) flames spucken, speien; lava auswerfen, spucken; waste water etc ablassen; **the popular press ~s (out) lies** die Boulevardpresse überschüttet ihre Leser mit Lügen

sphagnum [ˈsfægnəm] N Torf- or Bleichmoos nt

sphere [sfɪə] N **a** Kugel f; (= heavenly sphere) Gestirn nt (geh); (old Astron) Sphäre f (old); **the celestial ~** (poet) das Himmelszelt (poet); **to be a ~** kugelförmig sein → **music b** (fig) Sphäre f, Welt f; (of person, personal experience) Bereich m; (of knowledge etc) Gebiet nt, Feld nt; (= social etc circle) Kreis m; **in the ~ of politics** in der Welt der Politik; **his ~ of interest/influence** sein Interessen-/Einflussbereich; **~ of activity** (= job, specialism) Wirkungskreis m; **that's outside my ~** das geht über meinen Horizont; (= not my responsibility) das ist nicht mein Gebiet

spherical [ˈsferɪkəl] ADJ (in shape) kugelförmig, (kugel)rund; (Math, Astron) sphärisch

sphericity [sfəˈrɪsɪtɪ] N Kugelform f or -gestalt f

spheroid [ˈsfɪərɔɪd] N (Geometry) Rotationsellipsoid nt

sphincter [ˈsfɪŋktə] N (Anat) Schließmuskel m, Sphinkter m (spec)

sphinx [sfɪŋks] N Sphinx f

sphinxlike [ˈsfɪŋkslaɪk] ADJ sphinxhaft

spice [spaɪs] N **a** Gewürz nt; **~ rack** Gewürzbord or -regal nt; **~ trade** Gewürzhandel m; **mixed ~** Gewürzmischung f **b** (fig) Würze f; (= trace: of irony, humour) Anflug m, Hauch m; **the ~ of life** die Würze des Lebens; **stories with some ~** pikante Geschichten pl VT (lit, fig) würzen

spiced [spaɪst] ADJ (Cook) savoury dish würzig; sweet dish aromatisch; **~ wine** Glühwein m; **highly ~** pikant (gewürzt); **delicately ~** delikat gewürzt

spiciness [ˈspaɪsɪnɪs] N (= quality) Würzigkeit f, Würze f; (= taste) Würze f; (fig) Pikanterie f; **because of its ~** weil das so stark gewürzt ist

spick-and-span [ˌspɪkənˈspæn] ADJ house etc blitzsauber, tipptopp in Ordnung pred; **to look ~** (person) wie aus dem Ei gepellt aussehen; (house) blitzsauber sein

spicy [ˈspaɪsɪ] ADJ (+er) würzig; sauce, food also stark gewürzt; (fig) story etc pikant; language kräftig

spider [ˈspaɪdə] N **a** Spinne f; **~'s web** Spinnwebe f, Spinnengewebe nt, Spinnennetz nt **b** (inf, = wheelbrace) Kreuzschlüssel m **c** (for roofrack) elastisches Befestigungsband

spider: spider crab N Spinnenkrabbe f or -krebs m; **spiderman** N (inf) **a** (= building worker) Gerüstbauer m **b** (= steeplejack) Schornsteinarbeiter m; **spider monkey** N Klammeraffe m; **spider plant** N Grünlilie f; **spiderweb** N (US) Spinnwebe f, Spinnengewebe nt, Spinnennetz nt

spidery [ˈspaɪdərɪ] ADJ writing krakelig; outline, drawing, pattern fein, spinnwebartig; limbs etc spinnenhaft

spiel [ʃpiːl] N (inf) Sermon m (inf), Blabla nt (inf); (= tall story, excuse) Geschichte f (inf)

spiffing [ˈspɪfɪŋ] ADJ (dated inf) famos (dated inf)

spigot [ˈspɪgət] N (on cask) Spund m, Zapfen m; (in tap) Abschlusskörper m; (US, = faucet) Hahn m

spike [spaɪk] N **a** (on wall, railing, helmet etc) Spitze f; (= nail) Nagel m; (on plant) Stachel m; (on shoe, tyre etc) Spike m; (for receipts, wastepa-

per etc) Dorn m; **~ heel** Pfennigabsatz m → also **spikes b** (Bot) Ähre f **c** (Elec) Spannungsspitze f **d** (= hair) (Igel)schnitt m VT **a** (lit: = pierce) aufspießen; (with weapon) durchbohren **b** (fig, = frustrate) rumours den Boden entziehen (+dat); plans ruinieren; **the editor ~d the story** (Press) der Redakteur ließ die Story in einer Schublade verschwinden; **to ~ sb's guns** (Brit inf) jdm den Wind aus den Segeln nehmen **c** (= lace) einem Schuss zusetzen (+dat); **~d with rum** mit einem Schuss Rum

spiked [spaɪkt] ADJ shoe mit Spikes; stick mit Dornen versehen; railings mit Spitzen; drink mit Schuss; **~ hair** Igel(schnitt) m; **~ helmet** Pickelhaube f

spikes [spaɪks] PL (inf, = running shoes) Spikes pl

spiky [ˈspaɪkɪ] ADJ (+er) **a** (= having spikes) railings, top of wall mit Metallspitzen; bush, animal stach(e)lig; branch dornig **b** (= like spikes) grass spitz, stach(e)lig; flower mit spitzen Blütenblättern; plant spitzblättrig; leaf spitz; hair hoch stehend; writing steil **c** (fig) person empfindlich, leicht eingeschnappt (inf)

spilehole [ˈspaɪlhəʊl] N (of barrel) Spundloch nt

spill¹ [spɪl] vb: pret, ptp **spilt** (esp Brit) or **spilled** N **a** (= spilled liquid etc) Lache f; oil ~ Ölkatastrophe f **b** (= fall) Sturz m; **to have a ~** stürzen VT **a** (= water, sand, salt etc) verschütten; **to ~ sb's blood** jds Blut vergießen; **to ~ the beans** alles ausplaudern, plaudern; **to ~ the beans about sth** etw ausplaudern **b** (horse) abwerfen; **the lorry ~ed its load onto the road** die Ladung fiel vom Lastwagen herunter auf die Straße VI verschüttet werden; (large quantity) sich ergießen; (tears) strömen, laufen; (fig: people) strömen; **the milk ~ed all over the carpet** die Milch war auf dem ganzen Teppich verschüttet; **light ~ed into the room** Licht strömte ins Zimmer; **light ~ed under the door** Licht drang durch den Türspalt herein

▶ **spill out** VI (of aus) (liquid) herausschwappen; (grain) herausrieseln; (money, jewels) herausfallen; (fig: people) (heraus)strömen; **clothes were spilling out of the drawer** Kleidungsstücke quollen aus der Schublade hervor VT sep ausschütten; (by accident) verschütten

▶ **spill over** VI (liquid) überlaufen; (grain etc, assembly) überquellen; (fig, population) sich ausbreiten (into auf +acc); (meeting) sich hinziehen (into bis in +acc)

spill² N (of wood) (Kien)span m; (of paper) Fidibus m

spillage [ˈspɪlɪdʒ] N (act) Verschütten nt; (= quantity) verschüttete Menge, Spillage f (Comm)

spillikin [ˈspɪlɪkɪn] N **a** (old: = spill) Kienspan m **b spillikins** PL (= game) Mikado nt

spillover [ˈspɪləʊvə] N Überschuss m

spillway [ˈspɪlweɪ] N Überlaufrinne f

spilt [spɪlt] (esp Brit) pret, ptp of **spill¹**

spin [spɪn] vb: pret **spun** or (old) **span**, ptp **spun** N **a** (= revolution) Drehung f; (= washing machine programme) Schleudern nt no pl; **to give sth a ~** etw (schnell) drehen; spinning top etw treiben; (in washing machine) etw schleudern; **to be in a (flat) ~** (Brit fig inf) am Rotieren or Durchdrehen sein (inf) (about wegen); **to send sb/sth into a (flat) ~** (Brit fig inf) jdn/etw zum Rotieren bringen (inf) **b** (on ball) Dreh m, Drall m; (Billiards) Effet m; **to put ~ on the ball** dem Ball einen Drall/Effet geben; (with racquet) den Ball anschneiden **c** (inf: = interpretation) **to put a new/different etc ~ on sth** etw neu/anders etc interpretieren **d** (Aviat) Trudeln nt no pl; **to go into a ~** zu trudeln anfangen **e** (dated, = trip) Spritztour f; **to go for a ~** eine Spritztour machen VT **a** (person, spider) spinnen; **to ~ a web of**

deceit ein Lügengewebe spinnen → **yarn b** (= turn) wheel drehen; (fast) herumwirbeln; top tanzen lassen, treiben; (in washing machine) schleudern; (= toss) ball, coin (hoch)werfen; (Sport) ball einen Drall/Effet geben (+dat); (with racquet) (an)schneiden; **he's just ~ning his wheels** (US fig inf) er tritt nur Wasser (inf) VI **a** (person) spinnen **b** (= revolve) sich drehen; (fast) (herum)wirbeln; (plane etc) trudeln; (in washing machine) schleudern; **to ~ round and round** sich im Kreis drehen; (dancer) im Kreis herumwirbeln; **the ball spun into the air/past him** der Ball flog wirbelnd in die Luft/an ihm vorbei; **the car spun out of control** der Wagen begann, sich unkontrollierbar zu drehen; **to send sb/sth ~ning** jdn/etw umwerfen; **my head is ~ning** mir dreht sich alles; **the wine makes my head ~** von dem Wein dreht sich mir alles; **the noise made his head ~** ihm schwirrte der Kopf von dem Lärm

▶ **spin along** VI (= move quickly) (dahin)rasen, (dahin)sausen

▶ **spin (a)round** VI (= revolve) sich drehen; (very fast) (herum)wirbeln; (in surprise) herumwirbeln, herumfahren VT sep (schnell) drehen; (very fast) herumwirbeln

▶ **spin out** VT sep (inf) money, food strecken (inf); holiday, meeting in die Länge ziehen; story ausspinnen

spina bifida [ˌspaɪnəˈbɪfɪdə] N offene Wirbelsäule, Spina bifida f (spec) ADJ attr baby mit einer offenen Wirbelsäule

spinach [ˈspɪnɪtʃ] N Spinat m

spinal [ˈspaɪnl] ADJ Rücken-, Rückgrat-, spinal (spec); **~ injury** Rückgratverletzung f

spinal: spinal column N Wirbelsäule f; **spinal cord** N Rückenmark nt; **spinal fluid** N Rückenmark(s)flüssigkeit f; **spinal marrow** N Rückenmark nt; **spinal meningitis** N Spinalmeningitis f

spin bowler N (Cricket) Werfer, der dem Ball einen Drall gibt

spindle [ˈspɪndl] N (for spinning, Mech) Spindel f

spindleshanks [ˈspɪndlʃæŋks] N (inf) **a** pl (= legs) Streichholzbeine pl (inf), Stelzen pl (inf) **b** sing (= person) Langbein nt (inf)

spindly [ˈspɪndlɪ] ADJ (+er) legs, arms, plant spindeldürr (inf); chairs zierlich

spin: spin doctor N (Pol inf) PR-Berater(in) m(f); **spin-drier** N (Brit) (Wäsche)schleuder f; **spindrift** N Gischt f; **spin-dry** VTI schleudern; **spin-dryer** N = **spin-drier**

spine [spaɪn] N **a** (Anat) Rückgrat nt; (of book) (Buch)rücken m; (of mountain range) (Gebirgs-) grat m **b** (= spike) Stachel m; (of plant) Dorn m, Stachel m

spine: spine-chiller N (inf) Gruselgeschichte f, Gruselfilm m; **spine-chilling** ADJ (inf) schaurig, gruselig; noise also unheimlich

spineless [ˈspaɪnlɪs] ADJ **a** (Anat) wirbellos; (fig) person ohne Rückgrat; compromise, refusal feige; **don't be so ~** beweisen Sie mal, dass Sie Rückgrat haben! **b** (Zool) stachellos; (Bot) dornenlos, stachellos

spinelessly [ˈspaɪnlɪslɪ] ADV (fig) feige

spinet [spɪˈnet] N **a** Spinett nt **b** (US) Kleinklavier nt

spine-tingling [ˈspaɪntɪŋglɪn] ADJ (= frightening) schaurig, Schauder erregend; (= moving) ergreifend

spinnaker [ˈspɪnəkə] N (Naut) Spinnaker m

spinner [ˈspɪnə] N **a** (of cloth) Spinner(in) m(f) **b** (inf) = **spin-drier c** (Fishing) Spinnköder m **d** (Cricket) Werfer, der den Bällen einen Drall gibt

spinney [ˈspɪnɪ] N (Brit) Dickicht nt

spinning [ˈspɪnɪŋ] N Spinnen nt

spinning in cpds Spinn-; **spinning jenny** N Jennymaschine f; **spinning mill** N Spinnerei f; **spinning top** N Kreisel m; **spinning**

wheel N Spinnrad nt; **spinning works** N sing or pl Spinnerei f, Spinnstoffabrik f

spin-off ['spɪnɒf] N (= side-product) Nebenprodukt nt; **~ effect** Folgewirkung f

spinster ['spɪnstə'] N Unverheiratete f, Ledige f; (pej) alte Jungfer (pej); **Mary Jones, ~** die ledige Mary Jones; **to be a ~** unverheiratet or ledig or eine alte Jungfer (pej) sein

spinsterhood ['spɪnstəhʊd] N (old) Ehelosigkeit f, Jungfernstand m (old); **she preferred ~** sie wollte lieber unverheiratet bleiben

spinsterish ['spɪnstərɪʃ] ADJ (pej) altjüngferlich (pej)

spiny ['spaɪnɪ] ADJ (+er) stach(e)lig; plant also dornig; **~ lobster** (Zool) Languste f, Stachelhummer m

spiracle ['spɪrəkl] N (of shark, ray etc) Atemloch nt; (of insect also) Stigma nt (spec); (of whale, dolphin) Spritzloch nt

spiral ['spaɪərəl] **ADJ** spiralförmig, spiralig; shell also gewunden; spring Spiral-; / movement, descent in Spiralen; **a ~ curve** eine Spirale; **~ nebula** Spiralnebel m **N** (lit, fig) Spirale f; **price/inflationary ~** Preis-/Inflationsspirale f **VI** (also **spiral up**) sich (hoch)winden; (smoke also, missile etc) spiralförmig or in einer Spirale aufsteigen; (prices) (nach oben) klettern

▶ **spiral down** VI spiralförmig or in einer Spirale herunterkommen; (staircase also) sich abwärts winden

spirally ['spaɪərəlɪ] ADV in einer Spirale, spiralförmig

spiral staircase N Wendeltreppe f

spirant ['spaɪərənt] N (Ling, Phon) Spirans m, Spirant m, Reibelaut m

spire [spaɪə'] N (of church) Turmspitze f, Turm m

spired ['spaɪəd] ADJ spitz (zulaufend), zugespitzt; church mit Spitzturm

spirit ['spɪrɪt] N **a** (= soul) Geist m; **the life of the ~** das Seelenleben; **he was troubled in ~** (liter) etwas lastete auf seiner Seele (geh); **I'll be with you in ~** im Geiste werde ich bei euch sein; **the ~ is willing (but the flesh is weak)** der Geist ist willig, (aber das Fleisch ist schwach) **b** (= supernatural being, ghost) Geist m **c** (= leading person, of age, movement etc) Geist m; (of party, enterprise) Kopf m **d** no pl (= courage) Mut m, Schneid m; (= vitality, enthusiasm) Elan m, Schwung m; **a man of ~** (= courageous) ein mutiger Mensch; **a horse with plenty of ~** ein feuriges Pferd; **to break sb's ~** jdn brechen, jds Mut brechen; **to sing with ~** mit Inbrunst singen; **to reply with ~** mutig antworten; **to put ~ into sth** Leben in eine Sache bringen **e** (= mental attitude: of country, group of people, doctrine, reform etc) Geist m; (= mood) Stimmung f; **Christmas ~** (Rel) weihnachtlicher Geist; (= mood) weihnachtliche Stimmung; **a ~ of optimism/rebellion** eine optimistische/rebellische Stimmung; **to do sth in a ~ of optimism/humility** voll Optimismus/voller Demut tun; **in a ~ of forgiveness/revenge** aus einer vergebenden/rachsüchtigen Stimmung heraus; **Christian ~** Christlichkeit f; **the ~ of the age** der Zeitgeist; **he has the right ~** er hat die richtige Einstellung; **to enter into the ~ of sth** bei etw mitmachen or dabei sein; **when the ~ moves him** wenn es ihn überkommt; **that's the ~!** (inf) so ists recht! (inf) **f** no pl (= intention) Geist m; **the ~ of the law** der Geist or Sinn des Gesetzes; **to take sth in the right/wrong ~** etw richtig/falsch auffassen; **to take sth in the ~ in which it was intended** etw so nehmen, wie es gemeint war; **the ~ in which it is done** wie es getan wird

g **spirits** PL (= state of mind) Stimmung f, Laune f; (= courage) Mut m; **to be in high ~** bester Laune sein; **to be in good/low ~s** guter/schlechter Laune sein; **to be out of ~s** niedergeschlagen sein; **to keep up one's ~s** den Mut nicht verlieren; **my ~s rose** ich bekam (neuen) Mut; **her ~s fell** ihr sank der Mut; **to raise or lift sb's ~s** jdn aufmuntern; **to revive sb's ~s**

jds Lebensgeister wieder erwecken **h** **spirits** PL (= alcohol) Branntwein m, Spirituosen pl, geistige Getränke pl **i** (Chem) Spiritus m; **~s of ammonia** Salmiakgeist m; **~(s) of turpentine** Terpentinöl nt **VT** **to ~ sb/sth away or off** jdn/etw verschwinden lassen or wegzaubern; **to ~ sb out of a room** etc jdn aus einem Zimmer etc wegzaubern

spirited ['spɪrɪtɪd] ADJ temperamentvoll; horse also feurig; book, performance lebendig; (= courageous) person, reply, attack, attempt etc beherzt, mutig; **to make a ~ defence of sth** etw mutig verteidigen

spiritedly ['spɪrɪtɪdlɪ] ADV say beherzt; defend mutig

spiritedness ['spɪrɪtɪdnɪs] N Temperament nt; (of horse also) Feurigkeit f; (of performance) Lebendigkeit f; (= courage) (of person, reply, attempt etc) Beherztheit f, Mut m; (of defence) Mut m

spirit gum N Mastix(gummi) m

spiritism ['spɪrɪtɪzəm] N Spiritismus m

spiritistic ADJ , **spiritistically** ADV [,spɪrɪˈtɪstɪk, -əlɪ] spiritistisch

spirit lamp N Petroleumlampe f

spirit level N Wasserwaage f

spirit rapping ['spɪrɪt,ræpɪŋ] N Geisterklopfen nt (in spiritistischer Sitzung)

spirit stove N Spirituskocher m

spiritual ['spɪrɪtjʊəl] **ADJ** geistig; person spirituell; expression vergeistigt; (Eccl) geistlich; **~ life** Seelenleben nt; **my ~ home** meine geistige Heimat; **Lords ~** geistliche Lords (im Oberhaus); **the ~ world** die spirituelle Welt **N** (Mus) Spiritual nt

spiritualism ['spɪrɪtjʊəlɪzəm] N Spiritismus m

spiritualist ['spɪrɪtjʊəlɪst] N Spiritist(in) m(f)

spirituality [,spɪrɪtjʊˈælɪtɪ] N Geistigkeit f

spiritually ['spɪrɪtjʊəlɪ] ADV geistig; **~, he is ...** in geistiger Hinsicht ist er ...

spirituous ['spɪrɪtjʊəs] ADJ (form) alkoholisch, spirituos (rare)

spit[1] [spɪt] vb: pret, ptp **spat** **N** **a** (= action) (Aus)spucken nt; (= saliva) Spucke f; **there was just a ~ of rain** es tröpfelte nur; **to give sth a bit of ~ and polish** (inf) etw wienern (inf); **it needs a bit of ~ and polish** (inf) es müsste einmal tüchtig geputzt werden (inf); **a ~ and sawdust club** (Brit inf) eine (echte) Spelunke **b** (inf, = image) = **spitting image** **VT** spucken, speien (geh); curses ausstoßen (at gegen) **VI** spucken, speien (geh); (fat) spritzen; (fire) zischen; (person: verbally, cat) fauchen, zischen; **to ~ at sb** jdn anspucken, jdn anspeien (geh); jdn anfauchen, jdn anzischen; **to ~ in sb's face/eye** jdm ins Gesicht spucken; (fig) auf jdn pfeifen (inf); **it is ~ting (with rain)** (Brit) es tröpfelt; **she's spitting in the wind if she thinks that'll work** (inf) da hat sie sich verrechnet, wenn sie denkt, dass das funktionieren wird; **fighting the system is like ~ting in the wind** (inf) gegen das System anzukämpfen hat sowieso keine Wirkung

▶ **spit out** VT sep ausspucken, ausspeien (geh); words ausstoßen; **spit it out!** (fig inf) spucks aus! (inf), heraus mit der Sprache!

spit[2] **N** **a** (Cook) (Brat)spieß m; **on the ~** am Spieß **b** (of land) Landzunge f **VT** meat (auf-)spießen

spite [spaɪt] ✿ 26.2 **N** **a** (= ill will) Boshaftigkeit f, Gehässigkeit f; **to do sth out of ~** etw aus reiner Boshaftigkeit tun **b** **in ~ of** (= despite) trotz (+gen); **it was a success/we went in ~ of him** dennoch war es ein Erfolg/gingen wir hin; **he did it in ~ of himself** er konnte nicht anders; **in ~ of the fact that he ...** obwohl er ...; **in ~ of that I'll still go** ich gehe trotzdem **VT** ärgern; **she just does it to ~ me** sie tut es nur

mir zum Trotz, sie tut es nur, um mich zu ärgern

spiteful ['spaɪtfʊl] ADJ boshaft, gemein; (= gloating also) schadenfroh, gehässig

spitefully ['spaɪtfəlɪ] ADV boshaft, gemein; (= gloatingly) gehässig; **~ she told him ...** voll Bosheit erzählte sie ihm ...; (= gloatingly) voll Schadenfreude erzählte sie ihm ...

spitefulness ['spaɪtfʊlnɪs] N Boshaftigkeit f, Gemeinheit f; (= gloating) Schadenfreude f, Gehässigkeit f

spitfire ['spɪtfaɪə'] N Feuer speiender Drache; (= woman also) Giftnudel f (inf)

spitroast ['spɪtrəʊst] VT am Spieß braten; **with ~ pieces of lamb** mit Lammstücken vom Spieß

Spitsbergen ['spɪts,bɜːgən] N Spitzbergen nt

spitting: **spitting distance** N (inf) **to be within ~ of a place** nur einen Steinwurf von einem Ort entfernt sein; **spitting image** N (inf) Ebenbild nt; **to be the ~ of sb** jdm wie aus dem Gesicht geschnitten sein, jdm zum Verwechseln ähnlich sehen

spittle ['spɪtl] N Speichel m, Spucke f

spittoon [spɪˈtuːn] N Spucknapf m

spiv [spɪv] N (Brit, inf) schmieriger Typ (inf)

spivvy ['spɪvɪ] ADJ (Brit, inf) person schmierig (inf); tie, suit etc ordinär

splash [splæʃ] **N** **a** (= spray) Spritzen nt no pl; (= noise) Platschen nt no pl, Platscher m (inf); **he dived in with a ~** es spritzte/platschte, als er hineinsprang; **it made a ~ as it hit the water** das Wasser spritzte nach allen Seiten, als es hineinfiel; (noise) es fiel platschend ins Wasser; **to make a ~** (fig) Furore machen; (news) wie eine Bombe einschlagen; (book) einschlagen **b** (= sth splashed) Spritzer m; (esp in drink etc) Schuss m; (of colour, light) Tupfen m; (= patch) Fleck m; **~es of paint** Farbspritzer pl **VT** **a** water etc spritzen; (= pour) gießen; person, object bespritzen; **to ~ sb with water, to ~ water over sb** jdn mit Wasser bespritzen; **to ~ paint on sth** etw mit Farbe bespritzen; (with brush) Farbe auf etw (acc) klatschen (inf); **to ~ one's way through a stream** platschend einen Bach durchqueren **b** (Press inf) story groß rausbringen (inf); **the story was ~ed all over the papers** die Geschichte wurde in allen Zeitungen groß rausgebracht (inf) **VI** (liquid) spritzen; (rain, waves) klatschen; (tears) tropfen; (when diving, walking etc) platschen; (when playing) plan(t)schen

▶ **splash about** (Brit) or **around** **VI** herumspritzen; (in water) herumplan(t)schen; (while walking) herumplatschen **VT** sep water herumspritzen mit; (fig inf) money um sich werfen mit (inf); story groß aufziehen or rausbringen (inf)

▶ **splash down** VI **a** (Space) wassern **b** (rain) herunterrinnen (prep obj an +dat)

▶ **splash out** VI (Brit inf) tüchtig in die Tasche greifen (inf); (on reception, giving presents etc) sich nicht lumpen lassen (inf); **to splash out on sth** sich (dat) etw spendieren (inf)

▶ **splash up** **VT** sep spritzen **VI** (water, mud) aufspritzen

splash: **splashback**, **splashboard** N Spritzschutz m; **splashdown** N (Space) Wasserung f; **splash guard** N (US, Aut) Schmutzfänger m; **splash water** N (Tech) Schwall- or Spritzwasser nt

splashy ['splæʃɪ] ADJ (US inf) protzig, auffällig

splat [splæt] **N** Platschen nt **ADV** **to go ~ into sth** gegen etw platschen

splatter ['splætə'] **N** Spritzen nt no pl; (of rain) Prasseln nt no pl; (= sth splattered) Fleck m; (of ink, paint etc) Klecks m; (Art, = splatter technique) Spritztechnik f **VI** spritzen; (ink, paint also) klecksen; (rain) prasseln **VT** bespritzen; (with ink, paint etc) beklecksen; **to ~ sb with mud** jdn mit Schlamm bespritzen

splay [spleɪ] **VT** **a** (= spread out) legs, fingers, toes spreizen; feet nach außen stellen; **the wheels are ~ed** die Räder stehen nach außen, die Räder haben negativen Sturz **b** (*Tech*) pipe weiten; *window frame* ausschrägen **vi** nach außen gehen; (*pillars also*) sich nach außen biegen; (*window frame*) ausgeschrägt sein; **he was ~ed out on the ground** er lag auf der Erde und hatte alle viere von sich gestreckt **N** (*Archit*) Ausschrägung *f*

splay: splayfoot N nach außen gestellter Fuß; **splayfooted** ADJ mit nach außen gestellten Füßen; **to be ~** nach außen gehen

spleen [spliːn] N (*Anat*) Milz *f*; (*fig*) Zorn *m*, Rage *f* → **vent** VT

splendid ['splendɪd] ADJ **a** (= *excellent*) hervorragend; *rider etc, chance, idea, amusement* glänzend, ausgezeichnet; **(that's simply) ~!** (das ist ja) ausgezeichnet! **b** (= *magnificent*) *clothes, sunset, music* herrlich; *occasion, scale, villain* großartig

splendidly ['splendɪdlɪ] ADV **a** (= *magnificently*) *dressed* prächtig; *restored* herrlich **b** (= *excellently*) hervorragend, glänzend, ausgezeichnet; **everything is going ~** alles klappt wunderbar **c** (= *outrageously*) unerhört; **he is ~ arrogant** er ist unerhört arrogant

splendidness ['splendɪdnɪs] N **a** (= *magnificence*) Glanz *m*, Pracht *f* **b** (= *excellence*) Großartigkeit *f*

splendiferous [splen'dɪfərəs] ADJ (*dated inf*) fabelhaft

splendour, (*US*) **splendor** ['splendə] N Pracht *f no pl*; (*of music, achievement*) Großartigkeit *f*; **the ~s of the Roman Empire** der Glanz *or* die Pracht des Römischen Reiches

splenetic [splɪ'netɪk] ADJ **a** (*Anat*) Milz-; **~ cell** Milzzelle *f* **b** (*liter*, = *peevish*) unwirsch; **his ~ outbursts** seine Galligkeit

splice [splaɪs] **N** Verbindung *f*; (*of ropes also*) Spleiß *m* (*spec*); (*of tapes, film also*) Klebung *f*; (*of wood also*) Fuge *f* **VT** *ropes* spleißen (*spec*); *tapes, film* (zusammen)kleben; *pieces of wood etc* verfugen; **to ~ sth together** etw zusammenfügen; **to get ~d** (*inf*) sich verehelichen (*hum*)

splicer ['splaɪsə] N (*for films*) Klebepresse *f*

spliff [splɪf] N (*inf*: = *joint*) Joint *m* (*inf*)

splint [splɪnt] **N** Schiene *f*; **to put a ~ on sb/sth** jdn/etw schienen; **to be in ~s** geschient sein **VT** schienen

splinter ['splɪntə] **N** Splitter *m* **VT** (zer)splittern; (*with axe*) *wood* zerhacken; (*fig*) *party* spalten **VI** (zer)splittern; (*fig: party*) sich spalten; **to ~ off** absplittern; (*fig*) sich abspalten

splinter: splinter group N Splittergruppe *f*; **splinter party** N (*Pol*) Splitterpartei *f*; **splinterproof** ADJ splitterfrei

splintery ['splɪntərɪ] ADJ splitt(e)rig

split [splɪt] vb: pret, ptp **split** **N** **a** Riss *m* (*in* in +*dat*); (*esp in wall, rock, wood*) Spalt *m* (*in* in +*dat*) **b** (*fig*: = *division*) Bruch *m* (*in* in +*dat*), Entzweiung *f* (+*gen*); (*Pol, Eccl*) Spaltung *f* (*in* +*gen*); **there is a ~ in the party over ...** die Partei ist in der Frage (+*gen*) ... gespalten; **there is a three-way ~ in the party over ...** die Partei zerfällt in der Frage (+*gen*) ... in drei Lager, die Partei ist in der Frage (+*gen*) ... dreigeteilt; **a three-way ~ of the profits** eine Drittelung des Gewinns; **I want my ~** (*inf*) ich will meinen Schnitt (*inf*) **c** (= *distinction: in meaning*) Aufteilung *f* **d** *pl* **the ~s** Spagat *m*; **to do the ~s** (einen) Spagat machen **e** (*inf*: = *sweet*) (*also* **banana split**) (Bananen)split *m*; **jam/cream ~** *mit Marmelade/Sahne gefülltes Gebäckstück* **f** (*esp US*: = *bottle*) kleine Flasche **ADJ** gespalten (*on, over* in +*dat*) **VT** **a** (= *cleave*) (zer)teilen; *wood, atom* spalten; *stone* zerbrechen; *fabric, garment* zerreißen, zerschlitzen; *seam* aufplatzen lassen; **the sea had ~ the ship in two** in dem Sturm zerbrach das Schiff in zwei Teile; **to ~ hairs** (*inf*) Haarspalterei treiben (*inf*); **to ~ one's sides (laughing)** (*inf*) vor Lachen fast platzen; **to ~ sth open** etw

aufbrechen; **his lip had been ~ open** seine Lippe war aufgeplatzt; **he ~ his head open when he fell** er hat sich (*dat*) beim Fallen den Kopf aufgeschlagen **b** (= *divide*) spalten; (= *share*) *work, costs, roles etc* (sich *dat*) teilen; **to ~ sth into three parts** etw in drei Teile aufteilen; **to ~ the vote** die Abstimmung zum Scheitern bringen; **a party ~ three ways** eine in drei Lager gespaltene Partei; **to ~ one's vote** *or* (*US*) **ticket** panaschieren; **they ~ the profit three ways** sie haben den Gewinn gedrittelt *or* in drei Teile geteilt; **to ~ the difference** (*fig*: in *argument etc*) sich auf halbem Wege einigen; (*lit, with money etc*) sich (*dat*) die Differenz teilen **VI** **a** (*wood, stone*) (entzwei)brechen; (*hair*) sich spalten; (*trousers, seam etc*) platzen; (*fabric*) zerreißen; (*ship*) auseinander brechen; **to ~ open** aufplatzen, aufbrechen; **to ~ at the seams** (*lit*) an den Nähten aufplatzen; (*fig*) aus allen *or* den Nähten platzen; **my head is ~ting** (*fig*) mir platzt der Kopf **b** (= *divide*) sich teilen; (*people*) sich aufteilen; (*Pol, Eccl*) sich spalten (*on, over* wegen) **c** (*inf*: = *leave*) abhauen (*inf*) **d** (*Brit inf*, = *tell tales*) **to ~ on sb** jdn verpfeifen (*inf*)

▶ **split off** **VT** *sep* abtrennen (*prep obj* von); (*with axe also*) abspalten (*prep obj* von); (= *break*) abbrechen (*prep obj* von) **VI** abbrechen; (*rock also*) sich lösen; (*fig*) sich trennen (*from* von)

▶ **split up** **VT** *sep money, work* (auf)teilen; *meanings* aufteilen; *party, organization* spalten; *meeting* ein Ende machen (+*dat*); *two people* trennen; *crowd* zerstreuen **VI** zerbrechen; (= *divide*) sich teilen; (*meeting, crowd*) sich spalten; (*partners*) sich voneinander trennen

split: split decision N (*Boxing*) nicht einstimmige Entscheidung; **split ends** PL gespaltene Haarspitzen *pl*, Spliss *m*; **split infinitive** N (*Gram*) getrennter Infinitiv; **split-level** ADJ (*Archit*) mit versetzten Geschossen; **split peas** PL getrocknete (halbe) Erbsen *pl*; **split-pea soup** N Erbsensuppe *f*; **split personality** N (*Psych*) gespaltene Persönlichkeit; **split pin** N (= *cotter pin*) Splint *m*; (*on envelope*) Musterklammer *f*; **split screen** N (*Comput*) geteilter Bildschirm; **split second** N Bruchteil *m* einer Sekunde; **in a ~** in Sekundenschnelle; **split-second** ADJ **~ timing** Abstimmung *f* auf die Sekunde; (*of actor*) Gefühl *nt* für den richtigen Moment; **split time** N (*Sport*) Zwischenzeit *f*

splitting ['splɪtɪŋ] **N** Zerteilung *f*; (*of wood*) Spalten *nt*; **the ~ of the atom** die Kernspaltung **ADJ** *headache* rasend, heftig; **there was a ~ sound** (*of wood*) es klang, als ob etwas zerbräche; (*of cloth*) es klang, als ob etwas zerrisse

split-up ['splɪtʌp] N (*of friends*) Bruch *m* (*of* zwischen +*dat*); (*of partners*) Trennung *f* (*of* +*gen*); (*of party*) Spaltung *f* (*of* +*gen*)

▶ **splurge (out) on** VI +*prep obj* (*inf*) sich in Unkosten stürzen mit

splodge [splɒdʒ], (*US*) **splotch** [splɒtʃ] **N** Fleck *m*, Klecks *m*; (*of cream etc*) Klacks *m* **VT** *clothes* bespritzen; (*with paint, ink also*) beklecksen; *mud* spritzen; *paint* klecksen

splodgy ['splɒdʒɪ], **splotchy** ['splɒtʃɪ] ADJ fleckig, schmutzig

splurge [splɜːdʒ] N (*inf*, = *shopping spree*) Kauforgie *f* (*pej inf*); **to go on a ~** groß einkaufen gehen; **a big ~ on publicity** eine groß aufgemachte Werbekampagne; **we had a big ~ on the reception** unser Empfang war ein Riesentamtam (*inf*)

splutter ['splʌtə] **N** (*of engine*) Stottern *nt*; (*of fire*) Zischen *nt*; (*of sausages*) Zischen *nt*; (*while talking*) Prusten *nt no pl* **VI** (*person*, = *spit*) prusten, spucken; (= *stutter*) stottern; (*engine*) stottern; (*fire, lamp, fat*) zischen; (*sausages*) brutzeln, zischen; **to ~ with indignation** vor Entrüstung prusten **VT** (*hervor*)stoßen; **that's not true, he ~ed** das ist nicht wahr, platzte er los

spoil [spɔɪl] vb: pret, ptp **spoilt** (*Brit*) *or* **spoiled** **N** *usu pl* Beute *f no pl*; (*fig*, = *profits also*) Gewinn *m*; **the ~s of war** die Kriegsbeute; **~s of**

office Vergünstigungen *pl* im Amt
VT **a** (= *ruin, detract from*) verderben; *town, looks etc* verschandeln; *peace of mind* zerstören; *life* ruinieren; (*Brit*) *ballot papers* ungültig machen; **to ~ the party** (*fig*) ein Spaßverderber sein; **to ~ sb's fun** jdm den Spaß verderben; **it ~ed our evening** das hat uns (*dat*) den Abend verdorben; **if you eat now you'll ~ your lunch** wenn du jetzt etwas isst, verdirbst du dir den Appetit fürs Mittagessen; **~ed ballot papers** (*Brit*) ungültige Stimmzettel *pl* **b** *person* verwöhnen; *children* verwöhnen, verziehen; **to ~ sb for sth** (*inf*) jdn für etw verderben; **to be ~ed for choice** eine übergroße Auswahl haben, die Qual der Wahl haben **VI** **a** (*food*) verderben **b** **to be ~ing for trouble/a fight** Ärger/Streit suchen

spoilage ['spɔɪlɪdʒ] N (*Comm*) verdorbene Ware, Verderb *m* (*von Waren*); (*Printing*) Makulatur *f*

spoiler ['spɔɪlə] N **a** (*Aut, Aviat*) Spoiler *m* **b** (= *person*) Spielverderber(in) *m(f)*; (*Press*) *Publikation, die zur gleichen Zeit wie ein Konkurrenzprodukt erscheint*

spoilsman ['spɔɪlzmən] N *pl* **-men** [-mən] (*US, Pol*) **a** (= *supporter*) Befürworter(in) *m(f)* der Ämterpatronage **b** (= *profiteer*) Profiteur(in) *m(f)* der Ämterpatronage

spoilsport ['spɔɪlspɔːt] N (*inf*) Spielverderber(in) *m(f)* (*inf*)

spoils system N (*US, Pol*) Ämterpatronage *f*, Filzokratie *f* (*inf*)

spoilt [spɔɪlt] (*Brit*) pret, ptp of **spoil** ADJ *child* verwöhnt, verzogen; *meal* verdorben; *ballot papers* ungültig

spoke[1] [spəʊk] N Speiche *f*; **to put a ~ in sb's wheel** (*Brit inf*) jdm Knüppel zwischen die Beine werfen (*inf*)

spoke[2] pret of **speak**

spoken ['spəʊkən] ptp of **speak** ADJ *language* gesprochen; **his ~ English is better than ...** er spricht Englisch besser als ...; **~-voice record** Sprechplatte *f*; **the ~ word** das gesprochene Wort

spokeshave ['spəʊkʃeɪv] N Schabhobel *m*, Speichenhobel *m*

spokesman ['spəʊksmən] N *pl* **-men** [-mən] Sprecher *m*; **to act as (a) ~ for a group** als Sprecher einer Gruppe auftreten

spokesperson ['spəʊkspɜːsən] N Sprecher(in) *m(f)*

spokeswoman ['spəʊkswʊmən] N *pl* **-women** [-wɪmɪn] Sprecherin *f*

spoliation [ˌspəʊlɪ'eɪʃən] N (*liter*) Plünderung *f*

spondee ['spɒndiː] N Spondeus *m*

spondulicks, **spondulix** [spɒn'duːlɪks] PL (*hum inf*) Piepen *pl* (*inf*)

sponge [spʌndʒ] **N** **a** (*also Zool*) Schwamm *m*; **contraceptive ~** (empfängnisverhütendes) Schwämmchen *nt* → **throw in b** (= *sponging*) **to give sth a ~** (*floor*) etw wischen; *car* etw waschen; *walls* etw abwaschen; *table* etw abwischen **c** (*Cook*, *also* **sponge cake**) Rührkuchen *m*; (*fatless*) Biskuit(kuchen) *m*; (= *sponge mixture*) Rührteig *m*, Biskuitmasse *f*; **jam ~** Biskuit(kuchen) mit Marmeladenfüllung **VT** **a** (= *clean*) abwischen; *wound* abtupfen **b** (*inf*: = *scrounge*) schnorren (*inf*) (*from* bei)

▶ **sponge down** VT *sep person* (schnell) waschen; *walls also* abwaschen; *horse* abreiben

▶ **sponge off** VT *sep stain, liquid* abwischen

▶ **sponge off** *or* **on** VI +*prep obj* (*inf*) **to sponge off** *or* **on sb** jdm auf der Tasche liegen (*inf*)

▶ **sponge out** VT *sep* (= *remove*) *stain* herausreiben, herausmachen; (= *clean out*) *drawer* auswaschen; *wound* austupfen

▶ **sponge up** VT *sep* aufwischen

sponge: sponge bag N (*Brit*) Waschbeutel *m*, Kulturbeutel *m*; **sponge bath** N (*esp US*) **to give sb a ~** jdn (gründlich) waschen; **sponge cake** N Rührkuchen *m*; (*fatless*) Biskuit(kuchen) *m*; **sponge-down** N kurze Wäsche; **to give sb/sth a ~** jdn/etw kurz abwaschen; **sponge pudding** N Mehlpudding *m*

sponger ['spʌndʒə'] N (*inf*) Schmarotzer(in) *m(f)*, Schnorrer(in) *m(f)* (*inf*)

sponginess ['spʌndʒɪnɪs] N Nachgiebigkeit *f*, Weichheit *f*; (*of pudding*) Lockerheit *f*; (*of skin etc*) Schwammigkeit *f*

spongy ['spʌndʒɪ] ADJ (*+er*) nachgiebig, weich; (= *light*) *pudding* locker; *skin etc* schwammig

sponsor ['spɒnsə'] **N** **a** Förderer *m*, Förderin *f*; (*for membership*) Bürge *m*, Bürgin *f*; (*for event*) Schirmherr(in) *m(f)*; (*Rad, TV, Sport etc*) Geldgeber(in) *m(f)*, Sponsor(in) *m(f)*; (*for fund-raising*) Spender(in) *m(f)*; (*Parl, of bill*) Befürworter(in) *m(f)*; **to stand ~ for sb** jdn fördern, für jdn bürgen
b (= *godparent*) Pate *m*, Patin *f*; **to stand ~ for a child** Pate/Patin eines Kindes sein
VT **a** unterstützen; (*financially*) fördern, unterstützen, sponsern; *event* sponsern, die Schirmherrschaft übernehmen (*+gen*); *future member* bürgen für; *membership, bill* befürworten, empfehlen; (*Rad, TV*) *programme* sponsern; (*Sport*) *event* sponsern; **he ~ed him (at) 5p a mile** (*Brit*) er verpflichtete sich, ihm 5 Pence pro Meile zu geben
b (*as godparent*) die Patenschaft (*+gen*) übernehmen

sponsored ['spɒnsəd] ADJ (*Brit: for charity etc*) *walk, silence etc* gesponsert

sponsorial [spɒn'sɔːrɪəl] ADJ Paten-

sponsorship ['spɒnsəʃɪp] N **a** Unterstützung *f*; (*financial also*) Förderung *f*, Sponsern *nt*; (*of future member*) Bürgschaft *f*; (*of membership, bill*) Befürwortung *f*, Empfehlung *f*; (*Rad, TV: of programme*) Finanzierung *f*; (*Sport, of event*) Finanzierung *f*; **he got into the club under my ~** durch *or* auf meine Empfehlung kam er in den Klub **b** Patenschaft *f*

spontaneity [ˌspɒntə'neɪɪtɪ] N Spontaneität *f*; (*of style*) Ungezwungenheit *f*

spontaneous [spɒn'teɪnɪəs] ADJ spontan; *style* ungezwungen

spontaneous: spontaneous abortion N spontaner Abort; **spontaneous combustion** N Selbstentzündung *f*; **spontaneous generation** N Urzeugung *f*, Abiogenese *f* (*spec*)

spontaneously [spɒn'teɪnɪəslɪ] ADV spontan; (= *voluntarily also*) von sich aus, von selbst; **to combust ~** sich selbst entzünden

spontaneous remission N (*Med*) Spontanheilung *f*

spoof [spuːf] (*inf*) **N** **a** (= *parody*) Parodie *f* (*of* auf *+acc*) **b** (= *hoax*) Ulk *m* (*inf*), (April-)scherz *m* (*inf*) **ADJ** *attr poem, programme etc* parodiert; *version* verballhornt **VT** **a** (= *parody*) *novel* parodieren; *poem also* verballhornen

spook [spuːk] (*inf*) **N** **a** Gespenst *nt* **b** (*US*: = *spy*) Spion(in) *m(f)* **VT** (*esp US*, = *frighten*) einen Schrecken einjagen (*+dat*)

spooky ['spuːkɪ] ADJ (*+er*) (*inf*) **a** gespenstisch, gruselig (*inf*) **b** (= *strange*) sonderbar; **it was really ~** das war wirklich ein sonderbares *or* eigenartiges Gefühl; **to bear a ~ resemblance to sb/sth** eine unheimliche Ähnlichkeit mit jdm/etw haben

spool [spuːl] **N** (*Phot, on sewing machine*) Spule *f*; (*on fishing line*) Rolle *f*; (*for thread*) (Garn)rolle *f*; (*of thread*) Rolle *f* **VT** (*Comput*) spulen

spooler ['spuːlə'] N (*Comput*) (Drucker)spooler *m*

spoon [spuːn] **N** Löffel *m* → **silver VT** löffeln **VI** (*dated inf*) schmusen, poussieren (*dated inf*)

▶ **spoon out** VT *sep* (löffelweise) ausschöpfen

▶ **spoon up** VT *sep* löffeln; (= *eat up*) auslöffeln; *spillage* auflöffeln

spoon: spoon bait N (*Angling*) Blinker *m*; **spoonbill** ['spuːnbɪl] N Löffler *m*, Löffelreiher *m*; **spoon chisel** N (*Tech*) Hohlmeißel *m*

spoonerism ['spuːnərɪzəm] N lustiger Versprecher

spoon-feed ['spuːnfiːd] *pret, ptp* **spoon-fed** ['spuːnfed] VT *baby, invalid* füttern; (*fig, = do thinking for*) gängeln; (= *supply with*) füttern (*inf*)

spoonful ['spuːnful] N Löffel *m*; **a ~ of soup** ein Löffel Suppe

sporadic [spə'rædɪk] ADJ sporadisch; (= *occasional also*) gelegentlich; **we heard ~ gunfire** wir hörten gelegentlich Schüsse

sporadically [spə'rædɪkəlɪ] ADV sporadisch; (= *occasionally also*) gelegentlich; **snow fell ~** es fiel vereinzelt Schnee

spore [spɔː'] N Spore *f*

sporran ['spɒrən] N Felltasche *f* (*über dem Schottenrock getragen*)

sport [spɔːt] **N** **a** (= *games collectively*) Sport *m no pl*; (= *type of sport*) Sportart *f*; **to be good at ~(s)** gut im Sport sein, sportlich sein; **tennis is my ~** Tennis ist mein Lieblingssport; **the ~ of kings** der königliche Sport, der Pferderennsport; **to offer good ~** gute Jagd-/Angelmöglichkeiten *pl* bieten; **outdoor ~s** Sport *m* im Freien; **indoor ~s** Hallensport *m*
b **sports** PL (*also* **sports meeting**) Sportveranstaltung *f*
c (= *amusement*) Spaß *m*; **to do sth in ~** etw zum Spaß tun; **it was great ~** es hat großen Spaß gemacht; **to say sth in ~** etw aus *or* im *or* zum Spaß sagen; **to make ~ of sb/sth** (*old*) sich über jdn/etw lustig machen
d (*inf*: = *person*) feiner *or* anständiger Kerl (*inf*); (*Austral*) Junge *m*; **to be a (good) ~** alles mitmachen; **they are such good ~s** mit ihnen kann man Pferde stehlen (*inf*); **he's a good ~, he doesn't mind losing** er ist kein Spielverderber, er macht sich nichts daraus, wenn er verliert; **be a ~!** sei kein Spielverderber!, sei nicht so! (*inf*)
e (*Biol, Zool*) Spielart *f*, Abart *f*
VT *tie, dress* anhaben; (= *show off*) *ring etc* protzen mit; *black eye, pink etc hair, beard* herumlaufen mit (*inf*)
VI (= *frolic*) (herum)tollen; (*kitten*) (herum)spielen
ADJ *attr* (*US*) = **sports**

sport car N (*US*) Sportwagen *m*

sporting ['spɔːtɪŋ] ADJ **a** *person, interests* sportlich; **~ events** Wettkämpfe *pl*; **~ gods** Sportidole *pl*; **~ goods** Sportartikel *pl*; **~ gun** Sportwaffe *f*; **~ injury** Sportverletzung *f*; **~ organization** Sportverband *m*; **a great ~ man** ein großer Sportsmann; **~ editor** (*US*) Sportredakteur(in) *m(f)*; **the ~ world** die Welt des Sports
b (= *sportsmanlike*) sportlich; (*fig*) *offer, solution* fair; (= *decent*) anständig; **it's ~ of you to ...** es ist anständig von dir, zu ...; **to give sb a ~ chance** jdm eine faire Chance geben; **there is a ~ chance that ...** die Chancen stehen nicht schlecht, dass ...; **to have a ~ chance of winning** eine faire Siegchance haben; **~ spirit** Sportsgeist *m*

sportingly ['spɔːtɪŋlɪ] ADV fair; (= *decently*) anständig; **he ~ gave him a start** er gab ihm fairerweise einen Vorsprung

sportive ADJ , **sportively** ADV ['spɔːtɪv, -lɪ] (*liter*) fidel, launig (*liter*)

sports [spɔːts], (*US also*) **sport** *in cpds* Sport-; **sports bra** N Sport-BH *m*; **sports car** N Sportwagen *m*; **sportscast** N Sportübertragung *or* -sendung *f*; **sports centre**, (*US*) **sports center** N Sportzentrum *nt*; **sports commentator**, (*esp US*) **sportscaster** N Sportreporter(in) *m(f)*, (*Sport*)kommentator(in) *m(f)*; **sports coat** N = **sports jacket**; **sports day** N (*Brit*) (Schul)sportfest *nt*; **sports department** N Sportabteilung *f*; **sports field**, **sports ground** N (*Brit*) Sportplatz *m*; **sports jacket** N Sportjackett *nt*, Sakko *m or nt*; **sportsman** [-mən] N (= *player*) Sportler *m*; (= *hunter*) Jäger *m*; **~ of the year** Sportler *m* des Jahres; **sportsmanlike** [-mənlaɪk] ADJ sportlich; (*fig*) *behaviour, act etc* fair; **sportsmanship** [-mənʃɪp] N (= *skill*) Sportlichkeit *f*; (= *fairness also*) sportliches Verhalten, Fairness *f*; **sports medicine** N Sportmedizin *f*; **sports page** N Sportseite *f*; **sportsperson** N Sportler(in) *m(f)*; **sports**

programme, (*US*) **sports program** N Sportprogramm *nt*; **sports section** N (*of newspaper*) Sportteil *m*; **sportswear** N (*for sport*) Sportkleidung *f*; (= *leisure wear*) Freizeitkleidung *f*; **sportswoman** N Sportlerin *f*; **~ of the year** Sportlerin *f* des Jahres; **sports writer** N Sportjournalist(in) *m(f)*

sporty ['spɔːtɪ] ADJ (*+er*) (*inf*) **a** *person* sportbegeistert, sportlich; *clothes, car* sportlich **b** (= *jaunty*) flott

spot [spɒt] **N** **a** (= *dot*) Tupfen *m*, Punkt *m*; (*on dice*) Punkt *m*; (*Zool, Bot*) Fleck *m*, Punkt *m*; (= *stain*) (*on fruit*) Fleck *m*; (*fig, on reputation, good name*) Makel *m* (*on* an *+dat*); **a dress with ~s** ein getupftes *or* gepunktetes Kleid; **~s of blood/grease** Blut-/Fettflecken *pl*; **~s of ink** Tintenkleckse *or* -flecke *pl*; **to knock ~s off sb/ sth** (*fig inf*) jdn in den Schatten stellen, jdn in die Tasche stecken (*inf*); **to see ~s before one's eyes** Sternchen sehen; **without a ~ (or stain)** (*fig liter*) makellos
b (*Med etc*) Fleck *m*; (= *pimple*) Pickel *m*; (= *place*) Stelle *f*; **to break out** *or* **come out in ~s** Flecken/Pickel bekommen
c (= *place*) Stelle *f*; (= *point*) Punkt *m*; **this is the ~ where Rizzio was murdered** an dieser Stelle *or* hier ist Rizzio ermordet worden; **a pleasant ~** ein schönes Fleckchen (*inf*); **on the ~** (= *at the scene*) an Ort und Stelle; (= *at once*) auf der Stelle, sofort; **our man on the ~** unser Mann am Ort (des Geschehens) *or* vor Ort; **on-the-spot investigation** (= *at the scene*) Untersuchung *f* an Ort und Stelle; (= *immediate*) sofortige Untersuchung; **an on-the-spot report** ein Bericht vom Ort des Geschehens; **an on-the-spot fine** eine sofort *or* auf der Stelle zu bezahlende Geldstrafe
d (*Brit, inf,* = *small quantity*) **a/the ~ of** ein/das bisschen; **we had a ~ of rain/a few ~s of rain** wir hatten ein paar Tropfen Regen; **there was a ~ of trouble/bother** es gab etwas Ärger; **we're in a ~ of bother** wir haben Schwierigkeiten; **why don't you do a ~ of work?** warum arbeiten Sie nicht mal ein bisschen?; **after a ~ of bother** nach einigen Schwierigkeiten; **would you like a ~ of lunch?** möchten Sie eine Kleinigkeit zu Mittag essen?
e (= *characteristic*) Punkt *m*, Stelle *f*; **weak ~** schwache Stelle
f (= *difficulty*) Klemme *f*; **to be in a (tight) ~** in der Klemme sitzen (*inf*), in Schwulitäten sein (*inf*); **to put sb in a** *or* **on the ~** jdn in Verlegenheit *or* Schwulitäten (*inf*) bringen
g (*in show*) Nummer *f*; (*Rad, TV*) (ein paar Minuten) Sendezeit *f*; (*for advertisement*) Werbespot *m*; (= *announcement*) Kurzmeldung *f*; **he's got a ~ on that show** er tritt in dieser Show auf; **a three-minute TV ~** drei Minuten Sendezeit im Fernsehen, ein dreiminütiger Werbespot im Fernsehen
h **spots** PL (*Comm*) Lokowaren *pl* (*spec*), sofort lieferbare Waren *pl*
i (*Billiards, on table*) Marke *f*; (*also* **spot ball**) Spielball *m*
j (*esp Theat, inf, = spotlight*) Scheinwerfer *m*
VT **a** (= *notice, see*) entdecken, sehen; (= *pick out*) *signs, difference, opportunity* erkennen; (*trends, talent, gap*) entdecken; *mistake, bargain* finden; (*Mil,* = *pinpoint*) ausmachen; **to ~ a winner** (*lit, fig*) richtig tippen (*inf*)
b (= *stain*) bespritzen
c (*Billiards*) *ball* auf die Marke(n) setzen
VI **a** (*Brit*) **it's ~ting (with rain)** es tröpfelt
b (= *stain*) Flecken bekommen, schmutzen

spot: spot business N (*Comm*) Lokogeschäft *nt*; **spot cash** N sofortige Bezahlung; **for ~** gegen sofortige Bezahlung; **spot check** N Stichprobe *f*; **spot-check** NT stichprobenweise untersuchen (*for* auf *+acc*); *motorists* Stichproben machen bei (*for* in Bezug auf *+acc*); **spot fine** N Bußgeld *nt* (*das sofort an Ort und Stelle bezahlt werden muss*); **spot goods** PL sofort lieferbare Waren *pl*, Lokowaren *pl* (*spec*); **spot height** N Höhenangabe *f*

spotless ['spɒtlɪs] ADJ *person, house, clothes* tadellos *or* makellos sauber, pikobello (*inf*); (*fig*) *reputation* makellos, untadelig; **~ white** strahlend weiß

spotlessly ['spɒtlɪslɪ] ADV ~ **clean** blitzsauber

spotlessness ['spɒtlɪsnɪs] N (*of person, house etc*) tadellose *or* makellose Sauberkeit; (*fig, of reputation*) Makellosigkeit *f*, Untadeligkeit *f*

spot: spotlight *vb: pret, ptp* **spotlighted** **N** (= *lamp, in TV studio etc*) Scheinwerfer *m*; (*small, in room etc*) Spot *m*, Strahler *m*; (= *light*) Scheinwerferlicht *nt*, Rampenlicht *nt* (*also fig*); (*on car etc*) Suchscheinwerfer *m*; **to be in the ~** (*lit*) im Scheinwerferlicht *or* Rampenlicht stehen; (*fig*) im Rampenlicht der Öffentlichkeit stehen; **to turn the ~ on sb/sth** (*lit*) die Scheinwerfer auf jdn/etw richten; (*fig*) die Aufmerksamkeit auf jdn/etw lenken; **to come under the ~** (*fig*) ins Rampenlicht der Öffentlichkeit geraten **VT** anstrahlen; (*fig*) aufmerksam machen auf (+*acc*); **spot market** N Spotmarkt *m*, Kassamarkt *m*; **spot news** N Kurznachrichten *pl*; **spot-on** ADJ (*Brit, inf*) *answer, analysis* exakt, haarscharf richtig (*inf*); **~!** richtig!, genau!; **his guess was ~** er hat es haarscharf getroffen; **spot price** N (*St Ex*) Kassapreis *m*; **spot remover** N Fleck(en)entferner *m*; **spot survey** N Stichprobenuntersuchung *f*

spotted ['spɒtɪd] ADJ gefleckt; (= *with dots*) getüpfelt; *material* getüpfelt, getupft; (= *marked, stained*) fleckig; **~ with brown** braun gefleckt; **blue material ~ with white** blauer Stoff mit weißen Tupfen; **~ with blood** blutbespritzt; **~ with paint/mould** mit Farb-/Schimmelflecken

spotted: spotted dick N (*Brit*) ≈ Kochpudding *m* mit Rosinen; **spotted flycatcher** N (*Orn*) Grauer Fliegenschnäpper; **spotted hyena** N Tüpfelhyäne *f*

spotter ['spɒtə'] N **a** (*Aviat: also* **spotter plane**) Aufklärer *m* → **train spotter b** (*US, inf, = detective*) Detektiv(in) *m(f)*

spot test N Stichprobe *f*

spottiness ['spɒtɪnɪs] N (*Med*) Fleckigkeit *f*, Flecken *pl*, fleckige Haut; (= *pimples*) Pickeligkeit *f* (*inf*), Pickel *pl*, pickelige Haut

spotty ['spɒtɪ] ADJ (+*er*) (= *stained*) fleckig; (*Med*) fleckig, voller Flecken; (= *pimply*) pick(e)lig, voller Pickel

spot-weld ['spɒtweld] VTI punktschweißen

spousal ['spaʊzl] ADJ (*esp US*) ehelich

spouse [spaʊs] N (*form*) Gatte *m*, Gattin *f*

spout [spaʊt] **N** **a** Ausguss *m*, Tülle *f*; (*on teapot, cup*) Schnabel *m*, Ausguss *m*; (*on gargoyle, guttering*) Speirohr *nt*; (*on pump, tap*) Ausflussrohr *nt*; (*on pipe*) Ausfluss *m*; (*on watering can*) Rohr *nt*; **up the ~** (*Brit inf: plans, building, schedule etc*) im Eimer (*inf*); **she's up the ~** (*Brit inf, = pregnant*) sie hat 'nen dicken Bauch (*inf*)

b (*of whale: also* **spout-hole**) Spritzloch *nt*, Atemloch *nt*

c (= *jet of water etc*) Fontäne *f*; (*Met, = water spout*) Wasserhose *f*

VT **a** (= *gush, fountain etc*) (heraus)spritzen; (*whale*) ausstoßen, spritzen; (*volcano, gargoyle*) speien

b (*inf, = declaim*) *poetry, speeches* vom Stapel lassen (*inf*), loslassen (*at sb auf jdn*) (*inf*); *words* hervorsprudeln; *figures* herunterrasseln (*inf*); *nonsense* von sich geben

VI **a** (*water, fountain etc, whale*) spritzen (*from aus*); (*gargoyle*) speien; **to ~ out (of sth)** (aus etw) hervorspritzen; (*lava*) (aus etw) ausgespien werden; **to ~ up (from sth)** (aus etw) hochspritzen *or* herausschießen

b (*fig inf, = declaim*) palavern (*inf*), salbadern (*pej*); **to ~ (forth) about sth** über etw (*acc*) salbadern

sprain [spreɪn] **N** Verstauchung *f* **VT** verstauchen; **to ~ one's wrist/ankle** sich (*dat*) das Handgelenk/den Fuß verstauchen

sprang [spræŋ] *pret of* **spring**

sprat [spræt] N Sprotte *f*; **to set** *or* **use a ~ to catch a mackerel** (*prov*) mit der Wurst nach der Speckseite werfen (*Prov*)

sprawl [sprɔːl] **N** (= *posture*) Lümmeln *nt no pl* (*inf*), Flegeln *nt no pl* (*inf*); (= *mass: of buildings, town etc*) Ausbreitung *f*; **urban ~** wild wuchernde Ausbreitung des Stadtgebietes; **in the urban ~** in der riesigen Stadtlandschaft

VI (*person, = fall*) der Länge nach hinfallen; (= *lounge*) (herum)lümmeln (*inf*), sich hinflegeln; (*plant, town*) (wild) wuchern; **he was ~ing (out) on the floor** er lag ausgestreckt auf dem Fußboden; **she was ~ing in a chair** sie hatte sich in einem Sessel breit gemacht; **to send sb ~ing** jdn zu Boden werfen, jdn der Länge nach umwerfen

VT **to be ~ed over sth/on sth** (*body*) ausgestreckt auf etw (*dat*) liegen; **his legs were ~ed over the arm of the chair** seine Beine hingen zwanglos über die Sessellehne

sprawling ['sprɔːlɪŋ] ADJ **a** *city, suburbs* wild wuchernd; *house* großflächig; *grounds* ausgedehnt; *figure* hingeflegelt; *body* ausgestreckt; *handwriting* riesig **b** *novel* ausufernd

spray¹ [spreɪ] N (= *bouquet*) Strauß *m*; (= *buttonhole*) Spray *m*; (= *shoot, twig*) Zweig *m*; (= *brooch*) Brosche *f* (*in Form eines Sträußchens*)

spray² **N** **a** Sprühnebel *m*, Sprühregen *m*; (*of sea*) Gischt *m*; **the ~ from the lorries makes it difficult to see** die Lastwagen spritzen so, dass man kaum etwas sehen kann

b (= *implement*) Sprühdose *f*, Sprühflasche *f*; (= *insecticide spray, for irrigation*) Spritze *f*, Sprühgerät *nt*; (= *scent spray*) Zerstäuber *m*; (*on shower*) Brause *f*, Duschkopf *m*

c (= *preparation, Med, hairspray etc*) Spray *m or nt*

d (= *act of spraying*) (Be)sprühen *nt*; **to give sth a ~** etw besprühen; (*with paint, insecticide*) etw spritzen; (*with hairspray etc*) etw sprayen

VT *plants, insects etc* besprühen; *garden, crops* (*with paint, insecticide*) spritzen; *hair* sprayen; *room* aussprühen; *bullets* regnen lassen; *water, paint, foam* spritzen; *champagne* verspritzen; *graffiti* sprühen; *perfume* zerstäuben, (ver)sprühen; **to ~ insecticide on plants** Pflanzen (mit Insektenmittel) spritzen; **to ~ sth with water/bullets** etw mit Wasser besprühen/mit Kugeln übersäen

VI sprühen; (*water, mud*) spritzen; **to ~ out** heraussprühen/-spritzen; **to ~ against sth** gegen etw spritzen

spray: spray artist N Sprayer(in) *m(f)*; **spray can** N Sprühdose *f*

sprayer ['spreɪə'] N = **spray²** N **b**

spray: spray gun N Spritzpistole *f*; **spray-on** ['spreɪɒn] ADJ **a** (*lit*) zum Aufsprühen; ~ **furniture polish** Möbelpolitur *f* zum Aufsprühen **b** (*hum inf*) *jeans, dress etc* knalleng; **spray-paint** ['spreɪpeɪnt] VT sprühen (*on auf +acc, an +acc*)

spread [spred] *vb: pret, ptp* **spread** **N** **a** (*of wings*) Spannweite *f*, Flügelspanne *f*; (= *range, of marks*) Verteilung *f*, Streuung *f*; (*of prices*) Spanne *f*; (*of ideas, interests*) Spektrum *nt*; (= *distribution: of wealth*) Verteilung *f*; (= *scope: of theory, ideas*) Umfang *m*; **middle-age ~** Füllidkeit *f*, Altersspeck *m* (*inf*); **Gerry's beginning to suffer from middle-age ~** Gerry setzt langsam Speck an (*inf*)

b (= *growth*) Ausbreitung *f*, Verbreitung *f*; (*spatial*) Ausdehnung *f*; **the ~ of nuclear weapons** die zunehmende Verbreitung von Atomwaffen

c (*inf, of food etc*) Festessen *nt*, Festschmaus *m*; **that was an excellent ~** das war prima, was du *etc* da aufgetischt hast

d (= *cover*) Decke *f*

e (*for bread*) (Brot)aufstrich *m*; **anchovy ~** Sardellenpaste *f*; **cheese ~** Streichkäse *m*

f (*Press, Typ, = two pages*) Doppelseite *f*; **a full-page/double ~** eine ganz-/zweiseitige Anzeige; **a picture ~** ein ganzseitiger Bildbericht; **the centre ~ of a paper** die Mittelseite einer Zeitung

VT **a** (= *open or lay out: also* **spread out**) *rug, nets, hay, wings, arms* ausbreiten; *fan* öffnen; *goods* ausbreiten, auslegen; *hands, legs* spreizen;

the peacock ~ its tail der Pfau schlug ein Rad; **he was lying with his arms and legs ~ out** er lag mit ausgestreckten Armen und Beinen da; **the fields were ~ (out) below us** die Felder breiteten sich unter uns aus; **the view which was ~ (out) before us** die Sicht, die sich uns bot; **the yacht ~ its sails** die Segel des Bootes blähten sich

b *bread, canvas, surface* bestreichen; *butter, paint etc* (ver- *or* auf)streichen; *table* decken; ~ **the paint evenly** verteilen Sie die Farbe gleichmäßig; **he ~ the plaster over the wall** er verstrich den Gips an der Wand; **to ~ a cloth/blanket over sth** ein Tuch/eine Decke über etw (*acc*) breiten; **the table was ~ with food** der Tisch war reichlich *or* üppig gedeckt

c (= *distribute: also* **spread out**) *forces, writing, objects, payments, risk* verteilen; *sand, fertilizer, muck* streuen; (*in time*) verteilen (*over über +acc*); **our resources are ~ very thin** unsere Mittel sind maximal beansprucht

d (= *disseminate*) *news, knowledge, panic, disease, smell* verbreiten; *rumour* ausstreuen, verbreiten; **I'll ~ the news to everyone in the office** ich werde es allen im Büro mitteilen

VI **a** (= *extend, spatially*) sich erstrecken, sich ausdehnen (*over, across über +acc*); (*with movement, weeds, liquid, fire, smile, industry*) sich ausbreiten (*over, across über +acc*); (*towns, settlements*) sich ausdehnen; (*knowledge, fear etc, smell*) sich verbreiten; (*disease, trouble, fire*) sich verbreiten, um sich greifen; **the course ~s over four months** der Kurs erstreckt sich über vier Monate; **to ~ to sth** etw erreichen; (*disease etc*) auf etw (*acc*) übergreifen; **to ~ into sth** sich in etw (*acc*) erstrecken; (*in time*) sich bis in etw (*acc*) erstrecken; **under the ~ing trees** unter den ausladenden Bäumen; **he's worried about his ~ing stomach** er macht sich Sorgen, weil er in die Breite geht (*inf*) → **wildfire**

b (*butter etc*) sich streichen *or* schmieren (*inf*) lassen

VR **to ~ oneself** (*physically*) sich ausstrecken; (= *spread one's things*) sich ausbreiten; (*in speech, writing*) sich verbreiten

▸ **spread about** (*Brit*) *or* **around** VT *sep news, rumours, disease* verbreiten, unters Volk bringen (*inf*); *toys, seeds etc* verstreuen

▸ **spread out** **VT** *sep* = **spread** VT **a, c** **VI** **a** (*countryside etc*) sich ausdehnen **b** (*troops, runners*) sich verteilen

spread-eagle ['spred,iːgl] VT **to be** *or* **lie ~d** mit ausgestreckten Armen und Beinen daliegen, alle viere von sich (*dat*) strecken (*inf*); **the policeman outlined the ~d body** der Polizist zeichnete die Umrisse des ausgestreckt daliegenden Toten

spreader ['spredə'] N **a** Spachtel *m*; (*for butter etc*) Messer *nt* **b** (*Agr, = muck spreader*) (Stall-)miststreuer *m*

spreadsheet ['spredʃiːt] N (*Comput*) Tabellenkalkulation *f*, Spreadsheet *nt*; (= *software*) Tabellenkalkulations- *or* Spreadsheetprogramm *nt*

spree [spriː] N **spending** *or* **shopping ~** Großeinkauf *m*; **drinking/gambling ~** Zech-/Spieltour *f* (*inf*); **killing ~** (*of gunman*) Amoklauf *m*; **to go/be on a ~** (*drinking*) eine Zechtour machen; (*spending*) groß einkaufen gehen/groß einkaufen

sprig [sprɪg] N Zweig *m*; **embroidered with ~s of heather** mit Heidekrautzweigen bestickt

sprightliness ['spraɪtlɪnɪs] N (*of person, tune*) Munterkeit *f*, Lebhaftigkeit *f*; (*of old person*) Rüstigkeit *f*; (*of walk, dance*) Schwung *m*

sprightly ['spraɪtlɪ] ADJ (+*er*) *person, tune* munter, lebhaft; *old person* rüstig; *walk, dance* schwungvoll

spring [sprɪŋ] *vb: pret* **sprang** *or* (*US*) **sprung**, *ptp* **sprung** **N** **a** (*lit, fig liter, = source*) Quelle *f*; **~s** (*fig liter, = origins*) Ursprung *m*

b (= *season*) Frühling *m*, Frühjahr *nt*, Lenz *m* (*poet*); **in (the) ~** im Frühling, im Frühjahr; **~ is in the air** der Frühling liegt in der Luft, der Lenz hält seinen Einzug (*poet*); **in the ~ of his**

life im Frühling seines Lebens, im Lenz des Lebens (*poet*)

c (= *leap*) Sprung *m*, Satz *m*; **to make a ~ at sb/sth** sich auf jdn/etw stürzen

d (*Mech*) Feder *f*; (*in mattress, seat etc*) (Sprung)feder *f*; **~s** (*Aut*) Federung *f*

e no pl (= *bounciness, of chair*) Federung *f*; (*of wood, grass etc*) Nachgiebigkeit *f*, Elastizität *f*; **to walk with a ~ in one's step** mit federnden Schritten gehen; **the news put an extra ~ in his step** die Nachricht beflügelte seine Schritte

ADJ attr **a** (*seasonal*) Frühlings-; **a ~ day** ein Frühlingstag *m*

b (= *with springs*) gefedert; **~ mattress** Federkernmatratze *f*

VT **a** (= *leap over*) überspringen, springen über (+*acc*)

b (= *put springs in*) federn

c (= *cause to operate*) auslösen; *mine* explodieren lassen; *lock, mousetrap etc* zuschnappen lassen; **to ~ a leak** (*pipe*) (plötzlich) undicht werden; (*ship*) (plötzlich) ein Leck bekommen; **to ~ sth on sb** (*fig, idea, decision*) jdn mit etw konfrontieren; **to ~ a piece of news on sb** jdn mit einer Neuigkeit überraschen; **to ~ a surprise on sb** jdn völlig überraschen

d (*inf, = free*) rausholen (*inf*)

VI **a** (= *leap*) springen; (= *be activated*) ausgelöst werden; (*mousetrap*) zuschnappen; **to ~ at sb** jdn anspringen; **to ~ out at sb** auf jdn losspringen; **to ~ open** aufspringen; **to be poised to ~** (*lit, fig*) sprungbereit sein; **to ~ into the saddle** sich in den Sattel schwingen; **to ~ to one's feet** aufspringen; **to ~ out of bed** aus dem Bett hüpfen; **tears sprang to her eyes** ihr schossen die Tränen in die Augen; **his hand sprang to his gun** er griff (schnell) zur Waffe; **an oath sprang to his lips** ein Fluch drängte sich auf seine Lippen (*geh*); **to ~ into action** aktiv werden; (*police, fire brigade etc*) in Aktion treten; **to ~ to attention** (*Mil*) Haltung annehmen; **to ~ to arms** zu den Waffen eilen; **to ~ into view** plötzlich in Sicht kommen; **to ~ to mind** einem einfallen; **to ~ to sb's aid/defence** jdm zu Hilfe eilen; **he sprang to fame** er wurde plötzlich berühmt; **to ~ (in)to life** (plötzlich) lebendig werden; **the debate sprang (in)to life** es kam plötzlich Leben in die Debatte

b (= *issue: also* **spring forth**, *liter, water, blood*) (hervor)quellen (*from aus*); (*fire, sparks*) sprühen (*from aus*); (*shoot*) (hervor)sprießen (*from aus*); (*from family etc*) abstammen (*from von*); (*fig, idea*) entstehen (*from aus*); (*interest, irritability etc*) herrühren (*from von*); **where did you ~ from?** (*inf*) wo kommst du denn her?; **to ~ into existence** (plötzlich *or* rasch) entstehen

▶ **spring back** VI (*person*) zurückspringen; (*in fear*) zurückschrecken; (*object*) zurückschnellen

▶ **spring up** VI (*plant*) hervorsprießen; (*weeds*) aus dem Boden schießen; (*person*) hoch- *or* aufspringen; (*wind*) aufkommen; (*building, settlement*) aus dem Boden schießen; (*fig, suspicion, friendship*) erwachen; (plötzlich) entstehen; (*firm, magazine*) entstehen; (*problem, rumour*) auftauchen

spring: **spring balance** N Federwaage *f*; **spring binder** N Klemmhefter *m*; **springboard** N (*lit, fig*) Sprungbrett *nt*

springbok ['sprɪŋbɒk] N Springbock *m*

spring: **spring chicken** N Stubenküken *nt*; **he's no ~** (*fig inf*) er ist nicht mehr feucht hinter den Ohren (*inf*); **spring-clean** VT gründlich putzen; **to ~ a house** (in einem Haus) Frühjahrsputz machen **VI** Frühjahrsputz machen; **spring-cleaning** N Frühjahrsputz *m*

springer (spaniel) ['sprɪŋə'-] N Springerspaniel *m*

spring fever N **a** (= *energetic feeling*) Frühlingsgefühle *pl*; **it must be ~!** das muss der Frühling sein!, es muss am Frühling liegen! **b** (= *lassitude*) Frühjahrsmüdigkeit *f*

springform ['sprɪŋfɔːm] N (*also* **springform pan**, *Cook*) Springform *f*

springiness ['sprɪŋɪnɪs] N Elastizität *f*; (*of turf, wood, grass, track also*) Nachgiebigkeit *f*; (*of*

springboard also) Sprungkraft *f*; (*of bed*) Federung *f*; **the ~ of his step** sein federnder Gang

spring: **springless** ADJ ungefedert; **springlike** ADJ frühlingshaft; **spring-loaded** ADJ mit einer Sprungfeder; **to be ~** eine Sprungfeder haben; **spring mattress** N Federkernmatratze *f*; **spring onion** N (*Brit*) Frühlingszwiebel *f*; **spring roll** N Frühlingsrolle *f*; **spring tide** N Springflut *f*; **springtide** N (*poet*: = *springtime*) Lenz *m* (*poet*); **springtime** N Frühlingszeit *f*, Frühjahr *nt*; (*fig*) Frühling *m*, Lenz *m* (*poet*); **spring water** N Quellwasser *nt*; **spring wheat** N Sommerweizen *m*

springy ['sprɪŋɪ] ADJ (+*er*) *step* federnd; *plank, turf, grass also* nachgiebig, elastisch; *rubber, wood, plastic etc, hair* elastisch; *bed* weich gefedert

sprinkle ['sprɪŋkl] **VT** *water* sprenkeln, sprengen; *lawn, plant* besprengen; (*with holy water*) besprengen; *salt, dust, sugar etc* streuen; *dish, cake* bestreuen; **a lawn ~d with daisies** ein mit Gänseblümchen durchzogener Rasen; **his hair was ~d with grey** sein Haar war grau meliert; **churches/pubs are ~d throughout the town** man findet Kirchen/Gasthäuser über die ganze Stadt verstreut; **~d with quotations** mit Zitaten durchsetzt **N** (*of liquid, vinegar*) ein paar Spritzer; (*of salt etc*) Prise *f*

sprinkler ['sprɪŋklə'] N **a** (*Hort, Agr*) Berieselungsapparat *m*, Sprinkler *m*; (*in garden also*) (Rasen)sprenger *m*; (*for firefighting*) Sprinkler *m*; (*on watering can etc*) Sprenger *m*, Gießkannenkopf *m*; (*on shower*) Brause *f* **b** (= *sugar sprinkler*) Streudose *f*, Streuer *m* **b** (*Eccl*) Weihwasserwedel *m*

sprinkler: **sprinkler head** N Sprinkler *m*; (*on watering can*) Sprenger *m*, Gießkannenkopf *m*; (*on shower*) Brause *f*; **sprinkler system** N Berieselungsanlage *f*; (*for firefighting also*) Sprinkleranlage *f*

sprinkling ['sprɪŋklɪŋ] N (*of rain, dew etc*) ein paar Tropfen; (*of sugar etc*) Prise *f*; (*fig, of humour, comedy etc*) Anflug *m*; (*of common sense*) Spur *f*; **there was a ~ of grey in his hair** ein paar graue Fäden durchzogen sein Haar; **there was a ~ of young people** es waren ein paar vereinzelte junge Leute da; **a ~ of freckles** ein paar Sommersprossen; **to give sth a ~** (*with water*) etw besprengen *or* besprenkeln

sprinkling can N (*US*) Gießkanne *f*

sprint [sprɪnt] **N** Lauf *m*; (= *race*) Sprint *m*; (= *burst of speed*) Spurt *m*, Sprint *m*; **the 100-m ~** der 100-m-Lauf; **she made a ~ for the bus** sie sprintete *or* spurtete zum Bus; **a ~ finish** ein Endspurt *m*; **he has a good ~ finish** er legt einen guten Endspurt vor **VI** (*in race*) sprinten; (= *dash*) rennen

sprinter ['sprɪntə'] N Kurzstreckenläufer(in) *m(f)*, Sprinter(in) *m(f)*

sprit [sprɪt] N Spriet *nt*

sprite [spraɪt] N Kobold *m* (*also Comput: icon*); **water/wood ~** Wasser-/Waldgeist *m*

spritsail ['sprɪtsəl] N Sprietsegel *nt*

spritzer ['sprɪtsə'] N (Wein)schorle *f*, Gespritzte(r) *m*

sprocket ['sprɒkɪt] N **a** (= *tooth*) Zahn *m* **b** (= *sprocket wheel*) Kettenrad *nt*; (*on bicycle*) Kettenzahnrad *nt*, Zahnkranz *m*; (*Film*) Greifer *m*; (*on printer etc*) Stachelrad *m*

sprog [sprɒg] (*Brit, inf*) **N** **a** (= *baby, child*) Balg *nt* (*pej inf*), Gör *nt* (*inf*); **how are the ~s?** was macht der Nachwuchs? (*inf*) **b** (*Mil*) Rekrut(in) *m(f)*

sprout [spraʊt] **N** **a** (= *shoot, of plant*) Trieb *m*; (*of tree also*) Schössling *m*, Trieb *m*; (*from seed*) Keim *m*

b (= *Brussels sprout*) (Rosenkohl)röschen *nt*; **~s** *pl* Rosenkohl *m*

VT *leaves, buds, shoots etc* treiben; *horns etc* entwickeln; *seeds, wheat etc* keimen lassen; (*inf*) *beard* sich (*dat*) wachsen lassen; **the town is ~ing new buildings** in der Stadt sprießen neue Gebäude hervor; **he suddenly started ~ing**

hairs on his chest er bekam plötzlich Haare auf der Brust

VI **a** (= *grow*) wachsen, sprießen; (*seed, wheat etc*) keimen; (*potatoes, trees etc*) Triebe *pl* bekommen

b (*lit, fig: also* **sprout up**, *plants*) emporschießen, sprießen; (*new sects, new buildings*) wie die Pilze aus dem Boden schießen

spruce[1] [spruːs] N (*also* **spruce fir**) Fichte *f*

spruce[2] ADJ (+*er*) *person* proper, gepflegt; *men's clothes* flott, schmuck (*dated*); *women, children, women's clothes, appearance* adrett; *building* schmuck; *lawn, flower beds* gepflegt; **he was looking very ~** er sah geschniegelt und gebügelt aus

▶ **spruce up** VT sep *child* herausputzen; *house, garden* auf Vordermann bringen (*inf*); *image* aufpolieren; **to spruce oneself up** (*in general*) sein Äußeres pflegen; (= *get dressed up*) sich in Schale werfen; (*woman*) sich schönmachen; **he looks much better now that he has spruced himself up** so gepflegt sieht er wesentlich besser aus; **all spruced up** (*children, men*) geschniegelt und gestriegelt; (*women*) schön zurechtgemacht; (*house*) auf Hochglanz

sprucely ['spruːslɪ] ADV *dressed* (*man*) flott, schmuck (*dated*); (*woman, child*) adrett; *painted, decorated etc* schmuck; *laid out* sauber und ordentlich; **~ kept gardens** gepflegte Gärten

spruceness ['spruːsnɪs] N (*of person, appearance*) Gepflegtheit *f*

sprung [sprʌŋ] ptp of **spring** ADJ gefedert; **a well-sprung mattress** eine gut gefederte Matratze

spry [spraɪ] ADJ rüstig

SPUC (*Brit*) abbr of **Society for the Protection of the Unborn Child** *Gesellschaft zum Schutz des ungeborenen Lebens*

spud [spʌd] N (*inf, = potato*) Kartoffel *f*; **~-bashing** (*Brit Mil sl*) Küchendienst *m*

spume [spjuːm] N (*liter*) Gischt *f*

spun [spʌn] pret, ptp of **spin** ADJ *gold, silver, silk* gesponnen; **~ sugar** (= *candyfloss*) Zuckerwatte *f*

spunk [spʌŋk] N **a** (*inf*) Mumm *m* (*inf*), Courage *f* **b** (*vulg, = semen*) Saft *m* (*sl*)

spunky ['spʌŋkɪ] ADJ (+*er*) (*inf*) couragiert

spur [spɜː'] **N** **a** Sporn *m*; (*fig*) Ansporn *m*, Antrieb *m* (*to* für); **he urged the horse on with his ~s** er gab dem Pferd die Sporen; **to win** *or* **earn one's ~s** (*fig*) sich (*dat*) die Sporen verdienen; **this might act as a ~ to the players** das könnte ein Ansporn für die Spieler sein; **this was a new ~ to his ambition** das gab seinem Ehrgeiz neuen Antrieb *or* Ansporn

b **on the ~ of the moment** ganz spontan; **a ~-of-the-moment decision** ein spontaner Entschluss *m*

c (*Geog*) Vorsprung *m*

d (*Zool*) Sporn *m*

e (*Rail*) Nebengleis *nt*, Rangiergleis *nt*

VT **a** *horse* die Sporen geben (+*dat*)

b (= *urge on: also* **spur on**) (vorwärts) treiben, vorantreiben; (*fig*) anspornen; **~red (on) by greed/ambition** von Habgier/vom Ehrgeiz getrieben **VI** (*also* **spur on**) galoppieren, sprengen (*dated*)

spurge [spɜːdʒ] N (*Bot*) Wolfsmilch *f*; **~ laurel** Lorbeerseidelbast *m*

spurious ['spjʊərɪəs] ADJ *claim, claimant* unberechtigt; *document, account* falsch; *anger, interest, affection* nicht echt; *argument* fadenscheinig; **on the ~ grounds that ...** mit den fadenscheinigen Begründung, dass ...

spuriousness ['spjʊərɪəsnɪs] N (*of claim, claimant*) mangelnde Berechtigung; (*of document, account*) Falschheit *f*; (*of anger, interest, affection*) mangelnde Echtheit; (*of argument*) Fadenscheinigkeit *f*

spurn [spɜːn] VT verschmähen

spurned [spɜːnd] ADJ *offer, gift* zurückgewiesen; *lover* abgewiesen; *love* verschmäht

spurred [spɜːd] ADJ gespornt

spurt [spɜːt] **N** **a** (= *flow*) Strahl *m*; **~s of flame** Stichflammen **b** (= *burst of speed*) Spurt *m*; **a**

final ~ (*lit, fig*) ein Endspurt *m*; **to put a ~ on** (*lit, fig*) einen Spurt vorlegen; **there was a ~ of activity** es brach plötzlich Aktivität aus; **in a sudden ~ of energy** in einer plötzlichen Energieanwandlung; **to work in ~s** (nur) sporadisch arbeiten **VI** **a** = *gush*: *also* **spurt out**) (heraus)spritzen (*from* aus) **b** (= *run*) spurten **VT** **the wound ~ed blood** aus der Wunde spritzte Blut; **the pipe ~ed water** aus dem Rohr spritzte das Wasser

spur: spur track N (*Rail*) Nebengleis *nt*, Rangiergleis *nt*; **spur wheel** N Stirnrad *nt*

Sputnik ['spʊtnɪk] N Sputnik *m*

sputter ['spʌtə'] **VI** zischen; (*in frying pan*) brutzeln; (*tap*) spritzen; (*engine*) stottern; (*in speech*) sich ereifern (*about* über +*acc*); **he was ~ing with rage** er geiferte (vor Zorn); **the candle ~ed out** die Kerze ging flackernd aus; **to ~ to a halt** (*lit, fig*) stotternd zum Stillstand kommen

sputum ['spju:təm] N (*Med*) Auswurf *m*, Sputum *nt* (*spec*)

spy [spaɪ] **N** **a** Spion(in) *m(f)*; (= *police spy*) Spitzel *m*; **~ in the cab** (*inf*, = *tachograph*) Fahrtenschreiber *m* **VT** **a** sehen, erspähen (*geh*); **finally I spied him coming** endlich sah ich ihn kommen; **I ~ with my little eye something ...** ≈ ich sehe was, was du nicht siehst, und ... **VI** spionieren; **Spionage treiben; to ~ into sth** in etw (*dat*) herumspionieren; **to ~ on sb** jdn bespitzeln; **on neighbours** jdm nachspionieren; **I Spy** (= *game*) ≈ ich sehe was, was du nicht siehst

▶ **spy out** VT *sep* ausfindig machen; **to spy out the land** (*Mil*) die Gegend auskundschaften; (*fig*) die Lage peilen

spy: spy case N Spionagefall *m*; **spycatcher** N (*inf*) Geheimdienstler(in) *m(f)* (*inf*); **spy glass** N Fernglas *nt*; **spy hole** N Guckloch *nt*, Spion *m*; **spy master** N Chefagent *m*, Agentenführer *m*; **spy plane** N Spionageflugzeug *nt*; **spy ring** N Spionagering *m*, Agentenring *m*; **spy satellite** N Spionagesatellit *m*; **spy story** N Spionagegeschichte *f*

Sq *abbr of* **Square**

sq *abbr of* **square sq m** qm, m²

squab [skwɒb] N **a** (*Orn*) Jungtaube *f* **b** (*Aut*) Bank *f*

squabble ['skwɒbl] **N** Zank *m*, Streit *m*; **~s** Zankereien *pl*, Streitigkeiten *pl* **VI** (sich) zanken, (sich) streiten (*about, over* um)

squabbler ['skwɒblə'] N Streithammel *m* (*inf*)

squabbling ['skwɒblɪŋ] N Zankerei *f*, Streiterei *f*

squad [skwɒd] N (*Mil*) Korporalschaft *f*; (= *special unit of police etc*) Kommando *nt*; (= *police department*) Dezernat *nt*; (*of workmen*) Trupp *m*; (*Sport, fig*) Mannschaft *f*

squad car N (*US*) Streifenwagen *m*

squaddie ['skwɒdɪ] N (*Brit, inf*: = *private soldier*) Gefreite(r) *mf*; **the pub was full of ~s** die Kneipe war voller Soldaten

squadron ['skwɒdrən] N (*of cavalry*) Schwadron *f*; (*Aviat*) Staffel *f*; (*Naut*) Geschwader *nt*

squadron leader N (*Brit, Aviat*) Luftwaffenmajor(in) *m(f)*

squalid ['skwɒlɪd] ADJ *room, house* schmutzig und verwahrlost; *existence, conditions* elend, erbärmlich; *motive, manoeuvres, deed, idea etc* gemein, niederträchtig; *experience* übel; *dispute, gossip* entwürdigend; *affair* schmutzig

squalidly ['skwɒlɪdlɪ] ADV *live* in elenden *or* erbärmlichen Verhältnissen; *behave, treat sb* gemein, niederträchtig

squall [skwɔ:l] **N** **a** (= *storm*) Bö(e) *f*; (*fig*) Gewitter *nt*, Sturm *m*; **there are ~s ahead** (*fig*) wir gehen stürmischen Zeiten entgegen **b** (= *cry*) Schrei *m* **VI** schreien

squally ['skwɔ:lɪ] ADJ (+*er*) stürmisch; *wind also* böig

squalor ['skwɒlə'] N Schmutz *m*; (= *moral squalor*) Verkommenheit *f*; **the ~ of the conditions** die elenden *or* erbärmlichen Verhältnisse; **to live in ~** in unbeschreiblichen Zuständen leben

squander ['skwɒndə'] VT verschwenden, vergeuden (*on* an +*acc*); *opportunity* vertun

square [skwɛə'] **N** **a** (= *shape, Geometry, on graph paper*) Quadrat *nt*; **a 6 metre ~** 6 Meter im Quadrat **b** (*piece of material, paper etc*) (= *perfect square*) Quadrat *nt*; (= *rectangle*) Viereck *nt*; (*on chessboard etc*) Feld *nt*; (*on paper*) Kästchen *nt*, Karo *nt*; (*in crossword*) Kästchen *nt* (= *check on material etc*) Karo *nt*; (= *head square*) Kopftuch *nt*; **form yourselves into a ~** stellen Sie sich im Viereck auf; **cut it in ~s** schneiden Sie es quadratisch *or* in Quadrate zu; **to go back to ~ one** (*fig*) **to start (again) from ~ one** (*fig*) noch einmal von vorne anfangen; **we're back to ~ one** jetzt sind wir wieder da, wo wir angefangen haben **c** (*in town*) Platz *m*; (*US: of houses*) Block *m*; (*Mil* = *barrack square*) (Kasernen)platz *m* **d** (*Math*) Quadrat(zahl *f*) *nt*; **the ~ of 3 is 9** 3 hoch 2 *or* 3 (im) Quadrat ist 9 **e** (*Tech*) Winkelmaß *nt*; (= *set square*) Zeichendreieck *nt*; (= *T-square*) Reißschiene *f*; **to be on the ~** (*fig inf*, = *above board*) in Ordnung sein **f** (*Mil*, = *battle formation*) Karree *nt* **g** (*inf*, = *conventional person*) Spießer(in) *m(f)* (*inf*); **to be a ~** von (vor)gestern sein **ADJ** (+*er*) **a** (*in shape*) quadratisch; *picture, lawn etc* viereckig, quadratisch; *nib* viereckig; *block of wood etc* vierkantig; **to be a ~ peg in a round hole** am falschen Platz sein **b** (= *forming right angle*) *angle* recht; *corner* rechtwinklig; *shoulder* eckig; *chin, jaw* kantig, eckig; *build* vierschrötig; **~ bracket** eckige Klammer **c** (*Math*) Quadrat-; **3 ~ kilometres** 3 Quadratkilometer; **3 metres ~** 3 Meter im Quadrat; **there wasn't a ~ inch of space left** es war kein Zentimeter Platz mehr **d** *attr* (= *complete*) *meal* anständig, ordentlich **e** (= *fair*) *deal* gerecht, fair; *dealings, game, person* ehrlich; **to give sb a ~ deal** jdn gerecht *or* fair behandeln; **to get a ~ deal** fair behandelt werden; **I'll be ~ with you** ich will ehrlich *or* offen mit dir sein **f** (*fig*, = *even*) **to be ~** (*accounts etc*) in Ordnung sein; **to get ~ with sb** mit jdm abrechnen; **we are (all) ~** (*Sport*) wir stehen beide/alle gleich; (*fig*) jetzt sind wir quitt; **he wanted to be ~ with his creditors** er wollte mit seinen Gläubigern im Reinen sein; **we can start again all ~** wir sind wieder quitt **g** (*inf*, = *conventional*) überholt, verstaubt; *person, ideas* spießig (*inf*); **he's ~** er ist von (vor)gestern; **be there or be ~!** das kann man sich nicht entgehen lassen! **ADV** (+*er*) **a** (= *at right angles*) rechtwinklig; **~ with sth** im rechten Winkel *or* senkrecht zu etw **b** (= *directly*) direkt, genau; **to hit sb ~ in the chest** jdn voll in die Brust treffen; **to look sb ~ in the eye** jdm direkt in die Augen schauen; **to be ~ in the middle of sth** mitten in etw (*dat*) drin sein; **he kissed her ~ on the mouth** er küsste sie direkt auf den Mund **c** (= *parallel*) **to stand ~** gerade stehen; **he turned to face me ~ on** er wandte sich mir voll zu; **to be ~ with** *or* **to sth** parallel zu etw ausgerichtet sein **d** (= *honestly*) ehrlich, fair → **fair**¹ **VT** **a** (= *make square*) quadratisch machen; (= *make a right angle*) rechtwinklig machen; **to ~ one's shoulders** die Schultern straffen; **to ~ a block of wood** (= *cut square*) einen Holzklotz vierkantig zuschneiden; **to try to ~ the circle** die Quadratur des Kreises versuchen; **he ~d the ball to Gascoigne** er spielte einen Querpass auf Gascoigne; **to ~ a match** in einem Spiel gleichziehen **b** (*Math*) *number* quadrieren; **3 ~d is 9** 3 hoch 2 *or* 3 (im) Quadrat ist 9 **c** (= *adjust*) *debts* begleichen; *creditors* abrechnen mit; (= *reconcile*) in Einklang bringen; **to ~ one's accounts** abrechnen (*with* mit); **to ~ sth with one's conscience** etw mit seinem Gewissen vereinbaren *or* in Einklang bringen; **I'll ~ it**

with the porter (*inf*) ich mache das mit dem Portier ab (*inf*) **d** (*inf*, = *bribe*) schmieren (*inf*) **VI** übereinstimmen

▶ **square off** **VT** *sep* **a** (= *make square*) *corner* rechtwinklig machen **b** (= *draw squares on*) in Quadrate einteilen **VI** (*esp US*) in Kampfstellung gehen, Kampfstellung annehmen

▶ **square up** VI **a** (*boxers, fighters*) in Kampfstellung gehen, Kampfstellung annehmen; **to square up to sb** sich vor jdm aufpflanzen (*inf*); (*boxer*) vor jdm in Kampfstellung gehen; (*fig*) jdm die Stirn bieten; **to square up to sth** sich einer Sache (*dat*) stellen **b** (*lit, fig, = settle*) abrechnen

square: square-bashing N (*Brit Mil sl*) Drill *m*; **square bracket** N eckige Klammer; **square-built** ADJ *woman* stämmig *or* breit gebaut; *man* vierschrötig; *house* quadratisch gebaut; **square-cut** ADJ (*in a perfect square*) quadratisch; (= *rectangular*) rechteckig

squared [skwɛəd] ADJ *paper* kariert

square: square dance N Squaredance *m*; **squarehead** ['skwɛəhɛd] N (*US inf*) **a** (= *stupid person*) Holzkopf *m* (*pej*) **b** (*pej*: = *person of Germanic or Scandinavian origin*) Quadratschädel *m* (*pej*); **square-jawed** ADJ mit kantigem Kinn; **square knot** N (*US*) Kreuzknoten *m*

squarely ['skwɛəlɪ] ADV **a** (= *directly*) direkt, genau; (*fig*, = *firmly*) fest; **to hit sb ~ in the stomach** jdn voll in den Magen treffen; **~ in the middle of sth** genau in der Mitte von etw; **to place the blame for sth ~ on sb** jdm voll und ganz die Schuld an etw (*dat*) geben; **to face sb/sth ~** jdm/einer Sache tapfer entgegentreten; **we must face this ~** wir müssen dieser Sache (*dat*) (fest) ins Auge sehen **b** (= *honestly*) ehrlich; (= *fairly*) gerecht, fair; **to deal ~ with sb** jdn gerecht *or* fair behandeln **c** **~ built** stämmig *or* breit gebaut

square: square measure N Flächenmaß *nt*; **square number** N Quadratzahl *f*; **square-rigged** ADJ voll getakelt; **square-rigger** N (*Naut*) Rahsegler *m*; **square root** N Quadratwurzel *f*, zweite Wurzel; **to work out the ~ of sth** die zweite Wurzel *or* Quadratwurzel aus etw ziehen; **square sail** N Rahsegel *nt*; **square shooter** N (*US, inf*) ehrlicher Kerl (*inf*); **square-shouldered** ADJ mit eckigen Schultern; **square-toed** ADJ *shoes* mit breiter Kappe

squash¹ [skwɒʃ] **N** **a** (*Brit*, = *fruit concentrate*) Fruchtsaftkonzentrat *nt*, Squash *nt*; (= *drink*) Fruchtsaft *m*; **a glass of orange ~** ein Glas Orangensaft **b** (*Brit*) (= *crowd*) (Menschen)menge *f*; (= *crush*) Gedränge *nt*; **it's a bit of a ~** es ist ziemlich eng **VT** **a** (*also* **squash up**) zerdrücken, zerquetschen; *box etc* zusammendrücken; **to be ~ed to a pulp** zu Brei gequetscht *or* zerquetscht werden; **my hat was ~ed flat** *or* **in** mein Hut war völlig zerdrückt **b** (*fig*) (*inf*: = *silence*) *person* über den Mund fahren (+*dat*); (= *quash*) *protest, argument, proposal* vom Tisch fegen (*inf*); *hopes* vernichten; **I felt completely ~ed** ich kam mir ganz klein und hässlich vor (*inf*) **c** (= *squeeze*) quetschen; **to ~ sb in** jdn einquetschen; **to ~ sth in** etw hineinquetschen; **to be ~ed up against sb** gegen jdn gequetscht *or* gepresst werden; **to be ~ed together** eng zusammengepresst *or* -gequetscht sein **VI** **a** (= *get squashed*) zerdrückt *or* zerquetscht werden **b** (= *squeeze*) sich quetschen; **to ~ in** sich hinein-/hereinquetschen; **could you ~ up?** könnt ihr etwas zusammenrücken?; (*one person*) kannst du dich etwas kleiner machen?

squash² N (*Sport*: *also* **squash rackets** *or* (*esp US*) **racquets**) Squash *nt*; **~ courts** *pl* Squashhalle *f*

squash³ N , *no pl* (*US*) (Pâtisson)kürbis *m*

squash court N Squashplatz *m*

squasher ['skwɒʃə'] N Squasher(in) *m(f)*

squash racket, (*esp US*) **squash racquet** N Squash-Schläger *m*

squashy ['skwɒʃɪ] ADJ (*+er*) matschig; *cushion* weich

squat [skwɒt] **ADJ** (*+er*) gedrungen, kompakt; *chair* niedrig; *figure*, *person* gedrungen **VI a** (*person*) hocken, kauern; (*animal*) hocken **b** (*also* **squat down**) sich (hin)hocken *or* (hin-) kauern **c** (*on land*) sich (illegal) ansiedeln; **to ~ (in a house)** ein Haus besetzt haben, sich in einem Haus eingenistet haben (*inf*); **they are not tenants, they're just ~ting** das sind keine Mieter, das sind Hausbesetzer N (*inf*, = *place*) Unterschlupf *m* (*für Hausbesetzer*); **after their ~ in that house ...** nachdem sie sich in dem Haus eingenistet hatten ... (*inf*), nachdem sie das Haus als Unterschlupf benutzt hatten ...

squatter ['skwɒtə'] N (*on land*) Squatter(in) *m(f)*, illegaler Siedler, illegale Siedlerin; (*in house*) Hausbesetzer(in) *m(f)*

squat thrust N Stützstrecke *f*

squaw [skwɔː] N (*pej*) Squaw *f*

squawk [skwɔːk] **N** heiserer Schrei; (*fig inf*: = *complaint*) Protest *m*; **he let out a ~** er kreischte auf; **the ~s of the hens** das aufgeregte Gackern der Hühner **VI** (*bird*, *person*) schreien, kreischen; (*fig inf*: = *complain*) protestieren

squeak [skwiːk] **N** (*of hinge, wheel etc, shoe, pen*) Quietschen *nt no pl*; (*of person*) Quiekser *m*; (*of small animal*) Quieken *nt no pl*; (*of mouse, bird*) Piepsen *nt no pl*; (*fig inf*: = *sound*) Pieps *m* (*inf*), Mucks *m* (*inf*); **she gave a ~ of delight** sie quiekste entzückt; **to give a ~ of protest** schwach protestieren; **the door opened with a ~** die Tür ging quietschend auf **VI** (*door, hinge, shoes etc*) quietschen; (*person*) quieksen; (*small animal*) quieken, quieksen; (*mouse, bird*) piepsen **VT** quieksen

▶ **squeak by** *or* **through** VI (*inf*: = *narrowly succeed*) gerade so durchkommen (*inf*)

squeaky ['skwiːkɪ] ADJ (*+er*) quietschend; *voice* piepsig

squeaky-clean [ˌskwiːkɪ'kliːn] ADJ (*inf*) absolut sauber (*inf*), blitzsauber (*inf*); **the ~ brigade** die Saubermänner *pl* (*inf*)

squeal ['skwiːl] **N** Schrei *m*; (*of person, tyre, brakes*) Kreischen *nt no pl*; (*of protest*) (Auf-) schrei *m*; (*of pig*) Quieken *nt no pl*; **with a ~ of brakes/tyres** mit kreischenden Bremsen/Reifen; **a ~ of pain** ein Schmerzensschrei *m*; **~s of protest** Protestgeschrei *nt*; **~s/a ~ of laughter** schrilles Gelächter **VI a** (= *screech*) (*person*) schreien, kreischen; (*brakes, tyres*) kreischen, quietschen; (*pig, puppy*) quieksen; (*fig inf*) jammern; **to ~ in pain** vor Schmerz aufheulen *or* kreischen; **to ~ with delight** vor Wonne quietschen; **to ~ with laughter** laut auflachen; **to ~ for sb** nach jdm schreien; **to ~ for help** um Hilfe schreien **b** (*inf*: = *confess, inform, criminal*) singen (*inf*) (*to* bei); (*schoolboy etc*) petzen (*inf*) (*to* bei) **VT** schreien, kreischen

squeamish ['skwiːmɪʃ] ADJ *person* (= *easily nauseated*) empfindlich, heikel (*dial*); (= *easily shocked*) zart besaitet, empfindlich; **I felt a bit ~** (= *sick*) mir war leicht übel; **it gave me a ~ feeling in my stomach** mein Magen revoltierte; **I felt a bit ~ about telling him the bad news** mir war gar nicht wohl dabei, dass ich ihm die schlechte Nachricht mitteilen musste; **I'm not ~** (= *not easily nauseated*) mir wird nicht so schnell schlecht *or* übel; (= *not easily shocked*) ich bin nicht so zart besaitet *or* empfindlich; (= *not nervous about unpleasant things*) ich bin ja nicht zimperlich; **don't be so ~** sei nicht so zimperlich; **this book is not for the ~** das Buch ist nichts für zarte Gemüter

squeamishness ['skwiːmɪʃnɪs] N (= *nausea*) Übelkeit *f*; (= *disgust*) Ekel *m*; (= *prudishness*) Zimperlichkeit *f*; **his ~ when he sees blood** die Übelkeit, die ihn beim Anblick von Blut überkommt; **you have to overcome your ~** (= *prudishness, reluctance*) Sie dürfen nicht so zimper-

lich sein; (= *disgust*) Sie müssen Ihren Ekel überwinden

squeegee ['skwiːdʒiː] N (Gummi)wischer *m*; (*Phot*) Rollenquetscher *m*

squeegee merchant N (*inf*) jd, der unaufgefordert die Scheiben von vor Ampeln etc wartenden Autos putzt

squeeze [skwiːz] **N a** (= *act of squeezing*) Drücken *nt no pl*, Pressen *nt no pl*; (= *hug*) Umarmung *f*; (*of hand*) Händedruck *m*; (*in bus etc*) Gedränge *nt*; **to give sth a ~** etw drücken, etw pressen; *lemon, sponge* etw ausdrücken; **to give sb a ~** jdn an sich (*acc*) drücken; **to give sb's hand a ~** jdm die Hand drücken; **it was a tight ~** es war fürchterlich eng; **getting into that dress was a bit of a ~** es war nicht so leicht, mich in das Kleid zu zwängen
b (= *amount*) Spritzer *m*; **put a ~ of toothpaste on the brush** drücken Sie etwas Zahnpasta auf die Bürste
c (= *credit squeeze*) Kreditbeschränkung *f*
d **to put the ~ on sb** (*inf*) jdm die Daumenschrauben ansetzen (*inf*)
e (*inf*: = *romantic partner*) Freund *m*, Freundin *f*
VT drücken; *sponge, tube* ausdrücken; *orange* auspressen, ausquietschen; (= *squash*) *person, hand* einquetschen; (*fig*: = *restrict*) *person, economy, business etc* unter Druck setzen; *profits, costs* drücken; **to ~ one's eyes shut** die Augen fest zudrücken; **to ~ clothes into a case** Kleider in einen Koffer zwängen; **to ~ liquid out of** *or* **from sth** Flüssigkeit aus etw (heraus)pressen; **to ~ out water/juice** Wasser/Saft herauspressen (*from* aus); **he ~d the trigger** er drückte ab; **to ~ out a tear** eine Träne zerdrücken; **to ~ sth dry** (*lit*) etw auswringen; (*fig*) das Letzte aus etw herausholen; **to ~ sb dry** (*fig*) jdn ausbluten; **to ~ money/information** *etc* **out of sb** Geld/Informationen *etc* aus jdm herausquetschen; **to ~ the rich** die Reichen schröpfen; **to be ~d to death** erdrückt werden; **I'll see if we can ~ you in** vielleicht können wir Sie noch unterbringen; **we'll ~ another song in before the interval** wir schaffen vor der Pause noch ein Lied
VI **you should be able to ~ through** wenn du dich klein machst, kommst du durch; **to ~ in/ out** sich hinein-/hinausdrängen; **to ~ past sb** sich an jdm vorbeidrücken; **to ~ onto the bus** sich in den Bus hineinzwängen; **to ~ through a crowd/hole** sich durch eine Menge/ein Loch zwängen; **to ~ (through) underneath a fence** sich unter einem Zaun durchzwängen; **you'll have to ~ up a bit** Sie müssen ein bisschen zusammenrücken

squeeze: squeeze-bottle ['skwiːzˌbɒtl] N (Plastik)spritzflasche *f*; **squeeze-box** ['skwiːzbɒks] N (*inf*) Quetschkommode *f* (*inf*)

squeezer ['skwiːzə'] N Presse *f*

squeezy ['skwiːzɪ] ADJ (*+er*) (*inf*) nachgiebig

squelch [skweltʃ] **N** quatschendes Geräusch (*inf*); **I heard the ~ of his footsteps in the mud** ich hörte, wie er quatschend (*inf*) *or* platschend durch den Schlamm lief; **the tomato hit the floor with a ~** die Tomate schlug mit einem satten Platsch auf den Boden auf **VT a** **to ~ one's way through sth** durch etw p(l)atschen **b** (*inf*) *speculation, protest* unterdrücken **VI** patschen, platschen; (*shoes, mud*) quatschen

squib [skwɪb] N (= *firework*) Knallfrosch *m* → **damp**

squid [skwɪd] N Tintenfisch *m*

squiffy ['skwɪfɪ] ADJ (*+er*) (*Brit, inf*) angesäuselt (*inf*)

squiggle ['skwɪgl] **N** Schnörkel *m* **VT** **to ~ a line under sth** eine Wellenlinie unter etw (*acc*) machen

squiggly ['skwɪglɪ] ADJ (*+er*) schnörkelig; **~ tail** Ringelschwanz *m*

squillion ['skwɪlɪən] N (*inf*) Myriade *f* usu *pl*, Abermillionen *pl*; **~s of pounds** Abermillionen Pfund

squinch [skwɪntʃ] (*US*) **VT** *eyes* zusammenkneifen **VI** blinzeln, die Augen zusammenkneifen

squint [skwɪnt] **N a** (*Med*) Schielen *nt no pl*; **to have a ~** leicht schielen; **he has a terrible ~ in his left eye** er schielt furchtbar auf dem linken Auge **b** (*inf*, = *look*) Blick *m*; (= *sidelong glance*) Seitenblick *m*; **to have** *or* **take a ~ at sb/ sth** einen Blick auf jdn/etw werfen; (*obliquely*) jdn/etw von der Seite ansehen, nach jdm/etw schielen **VI a** schielen; (*in strong light etc*) blinzeln; **to ~ at sb/sth** nach jdm/etw schielen; (*quickly*) einen kurzen Blick auf jdn/etw werfen **ADJ** (= *crooked*) schief

squint-eyed [ˌskwɪnt'aɪd] ADJ *person* schielend *attr*; **to be ~** schielen

squire ['skwaɪə'] **N a** (*esp Brit*, = *landowner*) Gutsherr *m*, ≈ Junker *m* (*Hist*); **right, ~** (*Brit, inf*) jawohl, der Herr (*dated*), in Ordnung, Chef (*inf*); **the ~ of the manor** der Herr des Gutes **b** (*Hist*, = *knight's attendant*) Knappe *m* **c** (*dated*, = *escort*) Kavalier *m* (*dated*) **VT** (*dated*) begleiten, eskortieren (*dated*)

squirearchy ['skwaɪərɑːkɪ] N Gutsbesitzer *pl*, ≈ Landjunkertum *nt* (*Hist*)

squirm [skwɜːm] **N** Winden *nt*; **to give a ~** sich winden **VI** sich winden; (*in distaste*) schaudern; (*with embarrassment*) sich (drehen und) winden; (*from discomfort*) hin und her rutschen; **blood/ that joke makes me ~** bei Blut/diesem Witz dreht sich in mir alles herum

squirrel ['skwɪrəl] **N** Eichhörnchen *nt* **ADJ** *attr* Eichhörnchen-; **~ fur** Eichhörnchenpelz *m*

squirt [skwɜːt] **N a** Spritzer *m* **b** (= *implement*) Spritze *f* **c** (*pej inf*, = *person*) Fatzke *m* (*inf*); (*small*) Pimpf *m* (*inf*) **VT** *liquid* spritzen; *object, person* bespritzen; **to ~ water at sb, to ~ sb with water** jdn mit Wasser bespritzen **VI** spritzen

squirt gun N (*US*) Spritzpistole *f*, Wasserpistole *f*

squish [skwɪʃ] VT (*inf*) zermatschen (*inf*)

squishy ['skwɪʃɪ] ADJ (*+er*) (*inf*) matschig (*inf*)

squit [skwɪt] N (*Brit inf*) **a** (= *small or insignificant person*) kleiner Scheißer (*inf*) **b** (= *diarrhoea*) **the ~s** (*sl*) die Scheißerei (*sl*), Durchfall *m*

Sr *abbr of* **senior** sen., Sr

SRC (*Brit*) *abbr of* **Students' Representative Council**

Sri Lanka [ˌsriː'læŋkə] N Sri Lanka *nt*

Sri Lankan [ˌsriː'læŋkən] **ADJ** sri-lankisch; **he/ she is ~** er/sie ist aus Sri Lanka **N** Sri-Lanker(in) *m(f)*, Sri Lanker(in) *m(f)*

SRN (*Brit*) *abbr of* **State Registered Nurse**

SS *abbr of* **steamship**

SSE *abbr of* **south-south-east** SSO

SST N (*US*) *abbr of* **supersonic transport** Überschallflugzeug *nt*

SSW *abbr of* **south-south-west** SSW

st (*Brit*) *abbr of* **stone(s)**

St. a *abbr of* **Street** Str. **b** *abbr of* **Saint** hl., St. **c** *abbr of* **Strait**

stab [stæb] **N a** (*with knife etc, wound, of pain*) Stich *m*; **~ wound** Stichwunde *f*; **to feel a ~ of pain** einen stechenden Schmerz empfinden; **to feel a ~ of guilt** ein schlechtes Gewissen haben, Gewissensbisse haben; **she felt a ~ of jealousy** plötzlich durchfuhr sie Eifersucht; **he felt a ~ of alarm/panic** plötzlich bekam er Angst/verspürte er Panik; **he felt a ~ of pity** das Mitleid schnitt ihm in die Seele; **a ~ in the back** (*fig*) ein Dolchstoß *m*
b (*inf*, = *try*) Versuch *m*; **to have a ~ at sth** etw probieren
VT *person* einen Stich versetzen (+*dat*); (*several times*) einstechen auf (+*acc*); (= *wound seriously*) niederstechen; *food* durchstechen; **to ~ sb (to death)** jdn erstechen; (*with dagger also*) jdn erdolchen; **to ~ sb with a knife, to ~ a knife into sb** jdn mit einem Messerstich, mit Messerstichen verletzen; **he ~bed his penknife into the desk** er stach sein Taschenmesser in den Tisch; **he was ~bed through the arm/heart** der Stich

traf ihn am Arm/ins Herz; **to ~ a knife into sth** ein Messer in etw (*acc*) hineinstoßen; **to ~ a fork into sth** mit einer Gabel in etw (*acc*) hineinstechen; **to ~ sb in the back** (*lit*) jdm in den Rücken stechen; (*fig*) jdm in den Rücken fallen; **he ~bed the air with his finger** er fuchtelte in der Luft herum (*inf*)

VI **to ~ at sb/sth** (*with knife etc*) nach jdm/etw stechen; (*with finger*) auf jdn/etw zeigen

stabbing ['stæbɪŋ] **N** Messerstecherei *f* **ADJ** *pain* stechend; *fear, memory* durchdringend; **~ incident** Messerstecherei *f*

stability [stə'bɪlɪtɪ] **N** Stabilität *f*; (*of relationship also, of job*) Beständigkeit *f*; (**mental**) **~** (seelische) Ausgeglichenheit

stabilization [ˌsteɪbəlaɪ'zeɪʃən] **N** Stabilisierung *f*

stabilize ['steɪbəlaɪz] **VT** (*Fin, Naut, Aviat*) stabilisieren **VI** sich stabilisieren

stabilizer ['steɪbəlaɪzəʳ] **N** (*Naut, Chem*) Stabilisator *m*; (*Aviat*) Stabilisierungsfläche *f*; (*US Aviat*) Höhenflosse *f*; (*on bicycle*) Stützrad *nt*

stable¹ ['steɪbl] **ADJ** (+*er*) stabil; *ladder, structure also* sicher; *relationship also, of job* beständig, dauerhaft; *character* gefestigt; (*Psych, Med*) *condition, blood pressure* stabil; *weight* konstant; **mentally ~** ausgeglichen, innerlich gefestigt

stable² **N** (= *building*) Stall *m*; (= *group of race-horses*) (Renn)stall *m*; **riding ~s** Reitstall *m*; **to be out of the same ~** (*fig*) aus dem gleichen Stall stammen; **to close** or **shut** or **lock the ~ door after the horse has bolted** (*prov*) den Brunnen erst zudecken, wenn das Kind hineingefallen ist (*prov*) **VT** (= *put in stable*) in den Stall bringen; (= *keep in stable*) im Stall halten; **he ~s his horses with the trainer** seine Pferde stehen im Stall des Trainers

stable: **stableboy** **N** Stallbursche *m*; **stable companion** **N** = **stablemate**; **stable door** **N** quer geteilte Tür; **stablelad** (*Brit*), **stableman** **N** Stallbursche *m*; **stablemate** **N** (= *horse*) Pferd *nt* aus demselben Stall

stabling ['steɪblɪŋ] **N** Stallungen *pl*, Ställe *pl*

stab wound **N** Stichwunde *f*

staccato [stə'kɑːtəʊ] **ADJ, ADV** (*Mus*) staccato, stakkato; (*fig*) abgehackt

stack [stæk] **N** **a** (= *pile*) Haufen *m*; (*neatly piled*) Stoß *m*, Stapel *m*; (*of rifles*) Pyramide *f*; **to be in the ~** (*Aviat*) kreisen, Warteschleifen *pl* ziehen (*over* über +*dat*)

b (*inf,* = *lots*) Haufen *m* (*inf*); **~s** jede Menge (*inf*); **~s of time/helpers** jede Menge (*inf*) Zeit/Hilfskräfte

c (*in library: also* **stacks**) Magazin *nt*

d = **chimney stack, smokestack**

e (*Geol*) Felssäule *f*

VT **a** (= *pile up*) stapeln; *shelves* einräumen; **to ~ up** aufstapeln

b (*Aviat*) **incoming planes had to be ~ed** ankommende Maschinen mussten kreisen or Warteschleifen ziehen

c (*US, Cards*) packen, *beim Mischen betrügen*; **the cards** or **odds are ~ed against us** (*fig*) wir haben einen großen Chancen

VI sich stapeln lassen; **~ing chairs** Stühle, die sich (gut) stapeln lassen

stacked [stækt] **ADJ** (*inf*) **to be (well) ~** einen großen or üppigen Vorbau haben (*inf*), Holz vor der Hütte haben (*inf*)

stacker ['stækəʳ] **N** (*for printer*) Ablage *f*

stadium ['steɪdɪəm] **N** *pl* **-s** or **stadia** ['steɪdɪə] Stadion *nt*

staff [stɑːf] **N** **a** (= *personnel*) Personal *nt*; (*Sch, Univ*) Kollegium *nt*, Lehrkörper *m* (*form*); (*of one department, on one project*) Mitarbeiterstab *m*; **all the ~ support this idea** die ganze Belegschaft or (*Sch, Univ*) das ganze Kollegium unterstützt diesen Vorschlag; **we have a large ~** wir haben viel Personal/ein großes Kollegium/ einen großen Mitarbeiterstab; **we don't have enough ~ to complete the project** wir haben nicht genügend Mitarbeiter, um das Projekt zu beenden; **editorial ~** Redaktion *f*, Redaktionsstab *m*; **administrative ~** Verwaltungsstab *m*,

Verwaltungspersonal *nt*; **a member of ~** ein Mitarbeiter *m*, eine Mitarbeiterin; (*Sch*) ein Kollege *m*, eine Kollegin; **my fellow members of ~** meine Kollegen; **we have 30 women on the ~** bei uns sind 30 Frauen angestellt; **to be on the ~** zum Personal/Kollegium/Mitarbeiterstab gehören; **are you ~?** (*inf*) arbeiten Sie hier?; **he joined the** or **our ~ in 1996** er arbeitet seit 1996 bei uns; **he has left our ~** er arbeitet nicht mehr hier

b *pl* **-s** or (*old*) **staves** (= *stick, symbol of authority*) Stab *m*; (= *flagstaff*) Stock *m*; (*fig liter:* = *support*) Stütze *f*; **~ of office** Amtsstab *m*; **the ~ of life** das wichtigste Nahrungsmittel

c (*Mil:* = *general staff*) Stab *m*

d *pl* **staves** (*Mus*) Notenlinien *pl*, Notensystem *nt*

VT *department* Mitarbeiter finden für; *hospital, shop, hotel* mit Personal besetzen, Personal finden für; *school* mit Lehrpersonal besetzen; **the kitchens are ~ed by foreigners** das Küchenpersonal besteht aus Ausländern

staff: **staff association** **N** ≈ Betriebsrat *m*; **staff canteen** **N** (Betriebs)kantine *f*; **staff college** **N** Generalstabsakademie *f*

staffed [stɑːft] **ADJ** *hospital, hotel* mit Personal besetzt; *railway station* bemannt; **to be well ~** gut besetzt sein, ausreichend Personal haben

staffer ['stɑːfəʳ] **N** (*esp US*) Mitarbeiter(in) *m(f)*

staffing ['stɑːfɪŋ] **N** Stellenbesetzung *f*

staffing: **staffing costs** **PL** Personalkosten *pl*; **staffing problem** **N** Problem *nt* mit der Stellenbesetzung

staff: **staff notation** **N** Notenschrift *f*; **staff nurse** **N** (*Brit*) (voll)ausgebildete Krankenschwester, Vollschwester *f* (*inf*); **staff officer** **N** Stabsoffizier(in) *m(f)*; **staff problem** **N** Personalproblem *nt*; **staffroom** **N** Lehrerzimmer *nt*; **staff training** **N** betriebliche Ausbildung

stag [stæg] **N** **a** (*Zool,* = *deer*) Hirsch *m*; (= *male animal*) Bock *m*, Bulle *m* **b** (*Brit, Fin*) Spekulant(in) *m(f)* (*der/die junge Aktien aufkauft*) **c** (*inf*) Mann, der solo ist (*inf*) **ADJ** *film, weekend etc* für Männer **ADV** **to go ~** solo ausgehen (*inf*)

stag beetle **N** Hirschkäfer *m*

stage [steɪdʒ] **N** **a** (*Theat, fig*) Bühne *f*; **the ~** (= *profession*) das Theater, die Bühne; **to be on/ go on/leave the ~** (*as career*) beim Theater sein/ zum Theater gehen/das Theater verlassen; **to go on ~** (*actor*) die Bühne betreten; (*play*) anfangen; **to come off ~**, **to leave the ~** von der Bühne abtreten; **to put a play on the ~** ein Stück aufführen or auf die Bühne bringen; **to write for the ~** Theater- or Bühnenstücke schreiben; **to adapt a novel for the ~** einen Roman fürs Theater bearbeiten; **to hold** or **dominate the ~** (*lit, fig*) die Szene beherrschen; **the ~ was set** (*lit*) das Bühnenbild war aufgebaut; (*fig*) alles war vorbereitet; **to set the ~ for sth** (*fig*) den Weg für etw bereiten; **the ~ was set for a confrontation** die Situation war reif für eine Auseinandersetzung

b (= *platform in hall*) Podium *nt*

c (= *period*) Stadium *nt*; (*of process, operation, development*) Phase *f*; **at this ~ such a thing is impossible** zum gegenwärtigen Zeitpunkt ist das unmöglich; **at this ~ in the negotiations** an diesem Punkt der Verhandlungen; **at this ~ in the game** (*fig*) zu diesem Zeitpunkt; **in the early/final ~(s)** im Anfangs-/Endstadium; **an early ~ in its history** ganz zu Anfang seiner Geschichte; **what ~ is your thesis at?** wie weit sind Sie mit Ihrer Dissertation?; **we have reached a ~ where ...** wir sind an einem Punkt angelangt, wo ...; **I'm at the talking ~ with the club** ich befinde mich mit dem Klub gerade in Gesprächen; **to go through a difficult ~** eine schwierige Phase durchmachen; **to be at the experimental ~** im Versuchsstadium sein

d (= *part of journey, race etc*) Abschnitt *m*, Etappe *f*; (= *fare stage*) Teilstrecke *f*, Fahrzone *f*; (= *actual bus stop*) Zahlgrenze *f*; **in** or **by** (*easy*) **~s** (*lit*) etappenweise; (*fig also*) Schritt für Schritt

e (= *section of rocket*) Stufe *f*; **a three-stage rocket** eine dreistufige Rakete

f (*old inf,* = *stagecoach*) Postkutsche *f*

VT *play* aufführen, auf die Bühne bringen; *competition, event* durchführen; *accident, scene, coup* inszenieren; *welcome* arrangieren; *demonstration, strike, protest etc* veranstalten; **to ~ a recovery** sich erholen; **to ~ a comeback** sein Come-back or Comeback machen; **the play is ~d in the 19th century** das Stück spielt im 19. Jahrhundert

stage: **stage box** **N** Bühnen- or Proszeniumsloge *f*; **stage career** **N** Bühnen- or Theaterkarriere *f*; **stagecoach** **N** Postkutsche *f*; **stagecraft** **N** dramaturgisches Können; (*of actor*) schauspielerisches Können; **stage design** **N** Bühnenbild *f*; **stage designer** **N** Bühnenbildner(in) *m(f)*; **stage direction** **N** Bühnen- or Regieanweisung *f*; **stage director** **N** Regisseur(in) *m(f)*; **stage door** **N** Bühneneingang *m*; **stage effect** **N** Bühneneffekt *m*; **stage fright** **N** Lampenfieber *nt*; **to have an attack of ~** Lampenfieber haben; **stage hand** **N** Bühnenarbeiter(in) *m(f)*; **stage-manage** **VT** (*lit*) Inspizient sein bei; (*fig*) *demonstration, argument* inszenieren; **stage manager** **N** Inspizient(in) *m(f)*; **stage name** **N** Künstlername *m*; **stage play** **N** Bühnenstück *n*

stager ['steɪdʒəʳ] **N** **old ~** alter Hase (*inf*)

stage: **stage race** **N** (*Cycling*) Etappenrennen *nt*; **stage rights** **PL** Aufführungs- or Bühnenrechte *pl*; **stage set** **N** Bühnenbild *nt*; **stage setting** **N** Bühnenbild *nt*; **stage-struck** **ADJ** theaterbesessen; **to be ~** unbedingt zum Theater wollen; **stage whisper** **N** Bühnenflüstern *nt*; **to say sth in a ~** etw hörbar flüstern; **stage win** **N** (*Cycling*) Etappensieg *f*

stagey **ADJ** = **stagy**

stagflation [stæg'fleɪʃən] **N** (*Econ*) Stagflation *f*

stagger ['stægəʳ] **VI** schwanken, taumeln; (*because of illness, weakness*) wanken; (*drunkenly*) torkeln; **he was ~ing along the street** er taumelte die Straße entlang **VT** **a** (*fig,* = *amaze*) *news etc*) den Atem verschlagen (+*dat*), umhauen (*inf*); **he was ~ed to hear of his promotion** die Nachricht von seiner Beförderung verschlug ihm die Sprache or haute ihn um (*inf*); **you ~ me!** da bin ich aber platt! (*inf*) **b** *hours, holidays* staffeln, stufen; *seats, spokes* versetzt anordnen, versetzen **N b** **to give a ~** taumeln, schwanken; **with a ~** taumelnd, schwankend **b** **staggers** *sing* or *pl* (*Vet*) (Dumm)koller *m*

staggered ['stægəd] **ADJ** **a** (= *amazed*) verblüfft, platt (*inf*) **b** *working hours etc* gestaffelt, gestuft; **they work ~ hours** ihre Arbeitszeit ist gestaffelt; **a ~ junction** eine Kreuzung mit versetzt angeordneten Straßen; **a ~ start** ein versetzter Start; (*in time*) ein zeitlich gestaffelter Start

staggering ['stægərɪŋ] **ADJ** **a** **to be a ~ blow (to sb/sth)** ein harter or schwerer Schlag (für jdn/etw) sein **b** (= *amazing*) atemberaubend, umwerfend

staggeringly ['stægərɪŋlɪ] **ADV** (= *amazingly*) umwerfend, erstaunlich; *beautiful, successful* umwerfend; **~ high prices** unglaublich hohe Preise

stag: **staghound** **N** Jagdhund *m* (*für die Hirschjagd*); **stag hunt**, **stag hunting** **N** Hirschjagd *f*

stagily ['steɪdʒɪlɪ] **ADV** *dressed, made up* auffallend

staginess ['steɪdʒɪnɪs] **N** auffällige Art

staging ['steɪdʒɪŋ] **N** **a** (= *production*) Inszenieren *nt*; (= *scenery etc*) Inszenierung *f* **b** (= *stage*) Bühne *f*

staging area **N** (*esp Mil, of troops*) Bereitstellungsraum *m*; (= *assembly point*) Auffangsraum *m*

stagnancy ['stægnənsɪ] **N** Stagnieren *nt*; (*of trade also*) Stagnation *f*, Stocken *nt*

stagnant ['stægnənt] **ADJ** (= *still, not moving*) *air, water* (still)stehend *attr*, gestaut; (= *foul, stale*) *water* abgestanden; *air* verbraucht; *trade* stagnierend, stockend; *mind* träge; **the economy/ market is ~** die Wirtschaft/der Markt stagniert

stagnate [stægˈneɪt] VI (= *not circulate*) stagnieren; (= *become foul, water*) abstehen; (*air*) verbraucht werden; (*trade*) stagnieren, stocken; (*person*) verdummen; (*mind*) einrosten

stagnation [stægˈneɪʃən] N Stagnieren *nt*; (*of trade also*) Stagnation *f*, Stocken *nt*; (*of air*) Stau *m*; (*of person*) Verdummung *f*; (*of mind*) Verlangsamung *f*

stag: stag night N Saufabend *m* (*inf*) des Bräutigams mit seinen Kumpeln (*am Vorabend der Hochzeit*); **stag party** N **a** Herrenabend *m* **b** = **stag night**

stagy [ˈsteɪdʒɪ] ADJ (*+er*) theatralisch; *appearance* auffallend

staid [steɪd] ADJ (*+er*) seriös, gesetzt; *community* respektabel; *place, product* seriös; *colour* gedeckt

staidly [ˈsteɪdlɪ] ADV gesetzt; *dressed* gedeckt

staidness [ˈsteɪdnɪs] N Gesetztheit *f*

stain [steɪn] N **a** (*lit*) Fleck *m*; (*fig*) Makel *m*; **a blood ~** ein Blutfleck *m*; **a grease ~** ein Fettfleck *m*; **a mud ~** ein Schlammspritzer *m*; **~ remover** Fleckenentferner *m*; **without a ~ on his character** ohne (einen) Makel **b** (= *colorant*) (Ein)färbemittel *nt*; (= *woodstain*) Beize **VT** beflecken; (= *colour*) einfärben; (*with woodstain*) beizen **VI a** (= *leave a stain*) Flecken hinterlassen **b** (= *become stained*) fleckig werden, Flecken bekommen

stained [steɪnd] ADJ *fingers, teeth* gefärbt; *clothes, floor* fleckig, befleckt (*geh*); *glass* bunt, bemalt; *reputation* befleckt; **~-glass window** Buntglasfenster *nt*, farbiges Glasfenster; **~ with blood** blutbefleckt; **the white shirt was ~ crimson with blood** das weiße Hemd hatte dunkelrote Blutflecken

staining [ˈsteɪnɪŋ] N **a** (= *change in colour*) (Ver)färbung *f*; (= *soiling*) Verschmutzung *f* **b** (*esp Tech*: = *dyeing*) Färben *nt*; (*of wood*) Beizen *nt*

stainless [ˈsteɪnlɪs] ADJ **a** *character* tadellos **b** (= *rust-resistant*) rostfrei

stainless steel N rostfreier (Edel)stahl; **"stainless steel"** „rostfrei"; **~ cutlery** rostfreies Besteck

stair [stɛəʳ] N **a** (= *step*) Stufe *f* **b** *usu pl* (= *stairway*) Treppe *f*; **at the top of the ~s** oben an der Treppe; **below ~s** (*Brit, dated*) beim (Haus)personal → **flight** [1]

stair: stair carpet N Treppenläufer *m*; **staircase** N Treppe *f*; **stair lift** N Treppenlift *m*; **stair rod** N Teppichstab *m*; **stairway** N Treppe *f*; **stairwell** N Treppenhaus *nt*

stake [steɪk] N **a** (= *post*) Pfosten *m*, Pfahl *m*; (*for vampires*) Pfahl *m*; (*for plant*) Stange *f*; (*for animal*) Pflock *m* → **pull up**
b (= *place of execution*) Scheiterhaufen *m*; **to die at the ~** auf dem Scheiterhaufen sterben, verbrannt werden; **he was ready to go to the ~ or be burned at the ~ for his principles** er war bereit, sich für seine Prinzipien ans Kreuz nageln zu lassen
c (= *bet*) Einsatz *m*; (= *financial interest*) Anteil *m*; **to be at ~** auf dem Spiel stehen; **he has a lot at ~** er hat viel zu verlieren; **to have a ~ in sth** (*in business*) einen Anteil an etw (*dat*) haben; *in the future* von etw betroffen werden; **he has a big ~ in the success of the plan** für ihn hängt viel vom Erfolg des Planes ab; **that's precisely the issue at ~** genau darum geht es; **the issue at ~ is not ...** es steht nicht zur Debatte, ob ...
d **stakes** PL (= *prize*) Gewinn *m*; **the Newmarket ~s** der Große Preis von Newmarket; **to raise the ~s** (*lit, fig*) den Einsatz erhöhen **VT a** *animal* anpflocken
b (*also* **stake up**) *plant* hochbinden; *fence* abstützen
c (= *bet, risk*) setzen (*on* auf +*acc*); (*esp US*: = *back financially*) finanziell unterstützen; **to ~ one's life on sth** seine Hand für etw ins Feuer legen; **to ~ one's reputation on sth** sein Wort

für etw verpfänden; **to ~ a/one's claim to sth** sich (*dat*) ein Anrecht auf etw (*acc*) sichern

▶ **stake off** *or* **out** VT *sep land* abstecken

▶ **stake out** VT *sep place* umstellen; *person* überwachen

stakeholder [ˈsteɪkhəʊldəʳ] N Teilhaber(in) *m(f)*

stakeholder society N Teilhabergesellschaft *f*

stakeout [ˈsteɪkaʊt] N Überwachung *f*

stalactite [ˈstæləktaɪt] N Stalaktit *m*

stalagmite [ˈstæləgmaɪt] N Stalagmit *m*

stale [steɪl] ADJ (*+er*) **a** (= *old, musty*) alt; *cake* trocken; *bread, biscuit* altbacken; (*in smell*) muffig; *water, beer, wine* abgestanden, schal; *air* verbraucht; *cigarette smoke* kalt; **to go ~** (*food*) verderben; **to smell ~** muffig riechen **b** (*fig*) *news* veraltet; *joke* abgedroschen; *idea* abgegriffen; *athlete, pianist etc* ausgepumpt, verbraucht; **to be ~** (*person*) alles nur noch routinemäßig machen; **to become ~** (*relationship*) an Reiz verlieren; (*situation*) langweilig werden; **I'm getting ~** ich mache langsam alles nur noch routinemäßig; **don't let yourself get ~** pass auf, dass du nicht in Routine verfällst

stalemate [ˈsteɪlmeɪt] N (*Chess*) Patt *nt*; (*fig*) Patt(situation *f*) *nt*, Sackgasse *f*; **to reach ~** (*lit*) ein Patt erreichen; (*fig*) in eine Sackgasse geraten; **to end in (a) ~** (*lit*) mit (einem) Patt enden, patt enden; (*fig*) in einer Sackgasse enden **VT** (*Chess*) patt setzen; (*fig*) matt setzen; *negotiations* zum Stillstand bringen

staleness [ˈsteɪlnɪs] N **a** (*lit, of beer, water etc*) Schalheit *f*, Abgestandenheit *f*; (*of bread, biscuit*) Altbackenheit *f*; (*of taste, smell*) Muffigkeit *f*; **the ~ of the air made them sleepy** die verbrauchte Luft machte sie schläfrig **b** (*fig, of joke*) Abgedroschenheit *f*; **the ~ of the news** die veraltete Nachricht; **he practised to the point of ~** er übte, bis er langsam alles nur noch routinemäßig machte

stalk[1] [stɔːk] **VT** *game* sich anpirschen an (+*acc*); *person* sich anschleichen an (+*acc*); (*animal*) beschleichen, sich heranschleichen an (+*acc*); **evil ~ed the streets** (*liter*) das Böse ging in den Straßen um **VI a** (= *walk haughtily*) stolzieren **b** (*Hunt*) pirschen; **to go ~ing** auf die Pirsch gehen

stalk[2] N (*of plant, leaf*) Stiel *m*; (= *cabbage stalk*) Strunk *m*; **his eyes came out on ~s** (*inf*) er bekam Stielaugen (*inf*)

stalker [ˈstɔːkəʳ] N **a** (*Hunt*) Pirschjäger(in) *m(f)* **b** (= *pursuer*) jd, der die ständige Nähe zu einer von ihm verehrten (*meist prominenten*) *Person* sucht oder sie mit Anrufen, Briefen *etc* belästigt

stalking [ˈstɔːkɪŋ] N **a** (*Hunt*) Pirschjagd *f* **b** (*Jur*) das Verfolgen und Belästigen einer (*meist prominenten*) *Person*

stalking-horse [ˈstɔːkɪŋhɔːs] N (*fig,* = *person*) Strohmann *m*/-frau *f*; (= *pretext*) Vorwand *m*

stall [stɔːl] N **a** (*in stable*) Box *f*, Bucht *f*; (*old,* = *stable*) Stall *m*
b (*at market etc*) Stand *m*
c **stalls** PL (*Brit: Theat, Film*) Parkett *nt*; **in the ~s** im Parkett
d (*Eccl*) Kirchenstuhl *m*; **~s** Chorgestühl *nt*
e (*Aviat*) überzogener Flug; **to do a ~ turn** (*Aviat*) ein Flugzeug auffangen und neu starten **VT a** *horse, cow* einstellen
b (*Aut*) abwürgen; (*Aviat*) überziehen
c (*also* **stall off**) *person* hinhalten; *decision, process, bill* hinauszögern; *talks* verzögern **VI a** (*engine*) absterben; (*Aviat*) überziehen
b (= *delay*) Zeit schinden; **stop ~ing!** hören Sie auf auszuweichen *or* drum herumzureden (*inf*)!; **to ~ over a decision** eine Entscheidung hinauszögern; **to ~ for time** versuchen, Zeit zu gewinnen *or* zu schinden (*inf*)

stall-feed [ˈstɔːlfiːd] VT *cattle etc* in Boxen mästen

stalling speed N (*Aviat*) kritische Geschwindigkeit

stallion [ˈstæljən] N Hengst *m*; (*for breeding*) Zuchthengst *m*

stalwart [ˈstɔːlwət] ADJ **a** (*in spirit*) treu, unentwegt; *supporter* treu, getreu; *belief* unerschütterlich **b** (*in build*) kräftig, robust **N** (= *supporter*) (getreuer) Anhänger; **the party leader and his ~s** der Parteichef und seine Getreuen

stalwartly [ˈstɔːlwətlɪ] ADV *fight, oppose* tapfer, unentwegt; *support* treu; *believe* unerschütterlich; *built* kräftig

stamen [ˈsteɪmən] N Staubgefäß *nt*

stamina [ˈstæmɪnə] N Stehvermögen *nt*, Durchhaltevermögen *nt*

stammer [ˈstæməʳ] **N** Stottern *nt*; **to speak with a ~** stottern; **he has a bad ~** er stottert stark **VT** (*also* **stammer out**) stammeln **VI** stottern; **to start ~ing** ins Stottern geraten

stammerer [ˈstæmərəʳ] N Stotterer *m*, Stotterin *f*

stammering [ˈstæmərɪŋ] N (*act*) Stottern *nt*, Stammeln *nt*; (= *stammered speech*) Gestotter(e) *nt*, Gestammel(e) *nt*

stammeringly [ˈstæmərɪŋlɪ] ADV stammelnd, stotternd

stamp [stæmp] **N a** (= *postage stamp*) (Brief-) marke *f*, (Post)wertzeichen *nt* (*form*); (= *insurance stamp, revenue stamp etc*) Marke *f*; (= *trading stamp*) (Rabatt)marke *f*; (= *charity stamp, airmail stamp, sticker*) Aufkleber *m*; **to collect (postage) ~s** Briefmarken *pl* sammeln; **to save (trading) ~s** Rabattmarken sammeln
b (= *rubber stamp, die, impression*) Stempel *m*
c (*fig*) **a man of his ~** im Mann seines Schlags; **to bear the ~ of the expert/of authenticity** den Stempel des Experten/die Züge der Echtheit tragen **VT a** **to ~ one's foot** (mit dem Fuß) (auf-) stampfen; **he ~ed the turf back into place** er stampfte die Sode wieder an ihrem Platz fest
b (= *put postage stamp on*) freimachen, frankieren; **a ~ed addressed envelope** ein frankierter Rückumschlag
c *paper, document etc* (*with rubber stamp*) stempeln; (*with embossing machine*) prägen; *name, pattern* aufstempeln, aufprägen (*on* auf +*acc*); (*fig*) ausweisen (*as* als) **VI** (= *walk*) sta(m)pfen, trampeln; (*disapprovingly, in dancing*) (mit dem Fuß) (auf)stampfen; (*horse*) aufstampfen; **he was ~ing about the house** er trampelte im Haus herum; **to ~ in/out** hinein-/hinausstapfen; **you ~ed on my foot** Sie haben mir auf den Fuß getreten

▶ **stamp on** **VT** *sep pattern, design* aufprägen; **to stamp a pattern on sth** auf etw (*acc*) ein Muster (auf)prägen; **to be stamped on sb's memory** sich jdm eingeprägt haben; **the new leader has stamped his personality on the party** der neue Vorsitzende hat der Partei seine Persönlichkeit aufgeprägt *or* seinen Stempel aufgedrückt; **to stamp one's personality on sth** einer Sache (*dat*) seine Autorität aufzwingen **VI** +*prep obj* (= *put one's foot on*) treten auf (+*acc*); (*fig*) im Keim ersticken; **to stamp on the brakes** (*lit*) auf die Bremse treten; (*fig*) die Notbremse ziehen

▶ **stamp out** **VT** *sep* **a** *fire* austreten; (*fig,* = *eradicate*) *epidemic, crime, practice* ausrotten; *opposition* unterdrücken, zunichte machen; *trouble* niederschlagen; *rebels* unschädlich machen **b** (= *punch or cut out*) *pattern, shape* ausstanzen **c** *rhythm* (mit)stampfen **VI** heraustrampeln, heraussta(m)pfen

stamp: stamp album N Briefmarkenalbum *nt*; **stamp collecting** N Briefmarkensammeln *nt*; **stamp collection** N Briefmarkensammlung *f*; **stamp collector** N Briefmarkensammler(in) *m(f)*; **stamp dealer** N Briefmarkenhändler(in) *m(f)*; **stamp duty** N (*Brit*) (Stempel)gebühr *f*

stampede [stæmˈpiːd] **N** (*of horses, cattle*) wilde Flucht *f*; (*of people*) Massenandrang *m*, Massenansturm *m* (*on* auf +*acc*); (= *rush*) wilde *or* panikartige Flucht; **the exodus turned into a ~** der Exodus geriet zur Panik **VT** *cattle, horses, crowd in* (wilde *or* helle) Panik versetzen; **to ~**

sb into doing sth (*fig*) jdn dazu drängen, etw zu tun; **let's not be ~d** (*fig*) wir wollen uns nicht kopfscheu machen lassen **VI** durchgehen; (*crowd*) losstürmen (*for* auf +*acc*)

stamping ground ['stæmpɪŋ‚graʊnd] N = stomping ground

stamp machine N Briefmarkenautomat *m*

stance [stæns] N (= *posture, Sport*) Haltung *f*; (= *mental attitude etc*) Einstellung *f*; (*Cricket, Golf etc also*) Stand *m*; **to take up a ~** (*lit*) in Stellung gehen; (*fig*) eine Haltung einnehmen

stand [stænd] **☼** 7.3 *vb*: *pret, ptp* **stood** **N** **a** (= *position*) Platz *m*, Standort *m*; **my ~ is that ...** ich stehe auf dem Standpunkt, dass ..., ich vertrete die Einstellung, dass ...; **to take a ~ (on a matter)** (*zu einer Angelegenheit*) eine Einstellung vertreten; **to take a firm ~** einen festen Standpunkt vertreten (*on* zu)
b (*Mil*, = *resistance*) Widerstand *m*; (= *battle*) Gefecht *nt*; **to make a ~** (*lit, fig*) sich widersetzen, Widerstand leisten; **that was their last ~** das war ihr letztes Gefecht
c (= *taxi stand*) Stand *m*
d (*Brit Theat*) Gastspiel *nt*; (*of pop group etc*) Konzert *nt*
e (= *furniture, lamp stand, music stand*) Ständer *m*
f (= *market stall etc*) Stand *m*
g (= *band stand*) Podium *nt*
h (*Brit Sport*) Tribüne *f*; (*US, Jur*) Zeugenstand *m*; (**we sat**) **in the ~** (wir saßen) auf der Tribüne; **to take the ~** (*Jur*) in den Zeugenstand treten
i (*esp US: Forest*) (Baum)bestand *m*
VT **a** (= *place*) stellen → **stead, head**
b (= *withstand*) *pressure, close examination etc* (= *object*) standhalten (+*dat*); (*person*) gewachsen sein (+*dat*); *test* bestehen; *climate* vertragen; *heat, noise* ertragen, aushalten; *loss, cost* verkraften; **the wall could ~ another coat of paint** (*inf*) die Wand könnte noch einen Anstrich vertragen
c (*inf*, = *put up with*) *person, noise, interruptions etc* aushalten; **I can't ~ him/it** (= *don't like*) ich kann ihn/das nicht ausstehen; **I can't ~ being kept waiting** ich kann es nicht leiden *or* ausstehen, wenn man mich warten lässt; **I can't ~ it any longer** ich halte das nicht mehr (länger) aus
d (*Brit inf*, = *treat*) **to ~ sb a drink/a meal** jdm einen Drink/ein Essen spendieren
e **to ~ trial** vor Gericht stehen (*for* wegen)
VI **a** (= *be upright*) stehen; (= *get up*) aufstehen; **all ~!** alles aufstehen!; **don't just ~ there(, do something)!** stehen Sie nicht nur (dumm) rum, tun Sie was! (*inf*); **to ~ still** still stehen; **we stood talking** wir standen da und unterhielten uns; **~ and deliver!** (*old, hum*) anhalten, her mit dem Zeug! (*inf*) → **attention, ease**
b (= *measure, person*) groß sein; (*tree etc*) hoch sein
c (= *be situated*) stehen; **it has stood there for 600 years** es steht da schon seit 600 Jahren
d (= *remain unchanged*) stehen; (*fig*) bestehen (bleiben)
e **to ~ as a candidate** kandidieren → *also* **stand for a**
f (= *continue to be valid, offer, argument, promise*) gelten; (*objection, contract*) gültig bleiben; (*decision, record, account*) stehen; **the theory ~s or falls by** *or* **on this** damit steht und fällt die Theorie
g (= *be at a certain level, thermometer, record*) stehen (*at* auf +*dat*); (*sales*) liegen (*at* bei)
h (*fig*, = *be in a position*) **to ~ to lose/gain a lot** wir können sehr viel verlieren/gewinnen; **he ~s to make a lot of money** er wird wohl eine Menge Geld (dabei) verdienen; **what do we ~ to gain by it?** was springt für uns dabei heraus? (*inf*), was bringt uns (*dat*) das ein?
i (*fig*, = *be placed*) **how do we ~?** wie stehen wir?; **I'd like to know where I ~ (with him)** ich möchte wissen, woran ich (bei ihm) bin; **where do you ~ with him?** wie stehen Sie sich mit ihm?; **where do you ~ on this issue?** welchen

Standpunkt vertreten Sie in dieser Frage?; **as things ~** nach Lage der Dinge; **as it ~s** so wie die Sache aussieht; **to ~ alone** (= *be best*) unerreicht sein; **to ~ accused of sth** einer Sache (*gen*) angeklagt sein
j (*fig*, = *be, continue to be*) **to ~ firm** *or* **fast** festbleiben; **to ~ ready** sich bereithalten; **to ~ in need of help** Hilfe brauchen; **to ~ together** zusammenhalten; **to ~ (as) security for sb** für jdn bürgen; **nothing now ~s between us** es steht nichts mehr zwischen uns

▶ **stand about** (*Brit*) *or* **around** VI herumstehen

▶ **stand apart** VI (*lit*) abseits stehen; (*fig*) sich fern halten; **to stand apart from the others** abseits stehen

▶ **stand aside** VI (*lit*) zur Seite treten; (*fig*, = *withdraw*) zurücktreten; (= *play no part*) (tatenlos) danebenstehen

▶ **stand back** VI (= *move back*) zurücktreten; (= *be situated at a distance*) zurückstehen, abliegen, zurückliegen; (*fig*, = *distance oneself*) Abstand nehmen; (= *play no part*) (tatenlos) danebenstehen; **to stand back and do nothing** tatenlos zusehen

▶ **stand by** VI **a** (= *remain uninvolved*) (unbeteiligt) danebenstehen; **to stand by and do nothing** tatenlos zusehen **b** (= *be on alert*) sich bereithalten; **to stand by for further news** auf weitere Nachrichten warten **VI** +*prep obj* **to stand by a promise/sb** ein Versprechen/zu jdm halten

▶ **stand down** VI **a** (= *retire, withdraw*) zurücktreten **b** (*Jur*) den Zeugenstand verlassen **c** (*Mil*) aufgelöst werden

▶ **stand for** VI +*prep obj* **a** (= *be candidate for*) kandidieren für, sich zur Wahl stellen für; **to stand for Labour** für Labour kandidieren; **to stand for (the post of) chairman** für den Posten des Vorsitzenden kandidieren; **to stand for election** (in einer Wahl) kandidieren, sich zur Wahl stellen; **to stand for re-election** sich zur Wiederwahl stellen; **to stand for election to sth** für etw kandidieren; **she is standing for election to Parliament** sie kandidiert in den Parlamentswahlen **b** (= *be abbreviation for, represent*) stehen für, bedeuten **c** (= *put up with*) hinnehmen, sich (*dat*) gefallen lassen

▶ **stand in** VI einspringen

▶ **stand off** VI (*Naut*) seewärts anliegen

▶ **stand out** VI **a** (= *project*) hervorstehen; (*land, balcony*) herausragen **b** (= *contrast, be noticeable*) hervorstechen, auffallen; **to stand out against sth** sich gegen etw *or* von etw abheben; **to stand out from the others** hervorstechen, auffallen; (= *hold out*) **to stand out against sth** weiterhin gegen etw Widerstand leisten; **to stand out for sth** auf etw (*acc*) bestehen

▶ **stand over** VI (*work, project*) liegen bleiben; **to let sth stand over** etw liegen lassen **VI** +*prep obj* (= *supervise*) auf die Finger sehen (+*dat*); **I can't work with you standing over me** ich kann nicht arbeiten, wenn du mir (dauernd) über die Schulter siehst

▶ **stand to** VI (*Mil*) in Bereitschaft *or* in Waffen stehen

▶ **stand up** **VI** **a** (= *get up*) aufstehen; (= *be standing*) stehen; **stand up straight!** stell dich gerade hin; **to stand up and be counted** sich zu seiner Meinung *or* seinen Überzeugungen bekennen **b** (= *be valid, argument*) überzeugen; (*Jur*) bestehen **c** **to stand up for sb/sth** für jdn/etw eintreten; **to stand up to sth** (*to test, pressure, object*) einer Sache (*dat*) standhalten; (*person*) einer Sache (*dat*) gewachsen sein; *to hard wear* etw vertragen *or* aushalten; **to stand up to sb** sich jdm gegenüber behaupten **VT** *sep* **a** (= *put upright*) hinstellen **b** (*inf*) *boyfriend, sb* versetzen

stand-alone ['stændəl(ə)un] N (*Comput*) eigenständiges Gerät, Stand-alone-Gerät *nt*

standard ['stændəd] **N** **a** (= *average, established norm*) Norm *f*; (= *criterion*) Maßstab *m*; (*usu pl*: = *moral standards*) (sittliche) Maßstäbe *pl*; **to set**

a good ~ Maßstäbe setzen; **to be above/below ~** über/unter der Norm sein *or* liegen; **to be up to ~** den Anforderungen genügen; **his (moral) ~s are abysmally low** er hat eine erschreckend niedere Moral; **to conform to society's ~s** den Wertvorstellungen der Gesellschaft entsprechen; **he sets himself very high ~s** er stellt hohe Anforderungen an sich (*acc*) selbst; **by any ~(s)** egal, welche Maßstäbe man anlegt; **by today's ~(s)** aus heutiger Sicht
b (= *degree, level*) Niveau *nt*; **~ of living** Lebensstandard *m*; **~ of culture** kulturelles Niveau; **first-year university ~** Wissensstand *m* des ersten Studienjahrs; **of high/low ~** von hohem/niedrigem Niveau
c (*Measurement*) (Maß)einheit *f*, Standard *m*; (= *monetary standard*) (Währungs)standard *m*; **these coins don't contain enough silver to conform to the monetary ~** diese Münzen enthalten weniger Silber, als dem Münzfuß entspräche
d (= *flag*) Flagge *f*, Fahne *f*; (*on car*) Stander *m*; (= *royal standard*) (königliche) Standarte *f*
e (= *pole*) Mast *m*
f (*Hort*) (Hoch)stamm *m*; **~ rose** Stammrose *f*
g (= *piece of popular music*) Klassiker *m*
ADJ **a** (= *usual, customary*) üblich; (*Comm*) Standard-, (handels)üblich; (= *average*) *performance, work* durchschnittlich; (= *widely referred to*) Standard-; **~ model** Standardmodell *nt*; **~ weight** Normalgewicht *nt*; **such requirements are not ~** solche Forderungen sind nicht die Norm *or* Regel; **to be ~ practice** üblich sein
b (*Ling*) (allgemein) gebräuchlich; **~ English** korrektes Englisch; **~ German** Hochdeutsch *nt*; **that word is hardly ~** dieses Wort ist ziemlich ungebräuchlich

standard: standard-bearer N Fahnenträger(in) *m(f)*; (*fig also*) Bannerträger(in) *m(f)* (*old*); **standard class** N (*Rail*) zweite Klasse; **standard deviation** N Standardabweichung *f*; **Standard Grade** N (*Scot, Sch*) ≈ Realschulabschluss *m*; **standard-issue** ADJ zur Standardausrüstung gehörend; (*Mil*) standardmäßig; **to be standard issue** Standardausführung sein; **a ~ shirt** (= *ordinary*) ein ganz normales Hemd, ein Nullachtfünfzehnhemd *nt* (*pej inf*)

standardization [‚stændədaɪ'zeɪʃən] N (*of education, style, approach*) Vereinheitlichung *f*; (*of format, sizes*) Normung *f*, Standardisierung *f*

standardize ['stændədaɪz] **VT** *education, style, approach* vereinheitlichen; *format, sizes etc* normen, standardisieren **VI** **to ~ on sth** etw standardmäßig verwenden

standard lamp N Stehlampe *f*

standard time N Standardzeit *f*

stand-by ['stændbaɪ] **N** **a** (= *person*) Ersatz *m*, Ersatzperson *f*; (*Sport*) Ersatz- *or* Auswechselspieler(in) *m(f)*; (= *thing*) Reserve *f*; (*Aviat*, = *plane*) Entlastungsflugzeug *nt*; (= *ticket*) Stand-by-Ticket *nt*; (= *passenger*) Passagier, der mit einem Stand-by-Ticket reist **b** (= *state of readiness*) **on ~** in Bereitschaft; (= *ready for action*) in Einsatzbereitschaft; **to be on 24-hour ~** 24 Stunden Bereitschaftsdienst haben **attr** (*Mil, Sport*) Reserve-, Ersatz-; **~ plane** Entlastungsflugzeug *nt*; **~ player** Ersatz- *or* Reservespieler(in) *m(f)*; **~ ticket** Stand-by-Ticket *nt*

stand-down ['stænddaʊn] N (*Mil*) Feuerpause *f* **b** (*in firm etc*: = *work stoppage*) (vorübergehende) Arbeitseinstellung *f or* -niederlegung *f*

standee [stæn'diː] N (*esp US*) jd, der steht oder einen Stehplatz hat

stand-in ['stændɪn] N (*Film, Theat*) Ersatz *m*

standing ['stændɪŋ] **N** **a** (*social*) Rang *m*, (gesellschaftliche) Stellung *f*; (*professional*) Position *f*; (*financial*) (finanzielle) Verhältnisse *pl*; (= *repute*) Ruf *m*, Ansehen *nt*; **of high ~** von hohem Rang; (= *repute*) von hohem Ansehen; **a man of some ~** ein angesehener Mann; **what is his ~ locally?** was hält man in der Gegend von ihm?; **to be in good ~ with sb** gute Beziehungen zu jdm haben
b (= *duration*) Dauer *f*; **a treaty of only six months'** ein Vertrag, der erst seit sechs Mo-

naten besteht; **her husband of five years'** ~ ihr Mann, mit dem sie seit fünf Jahren verheiratet ist; **of long** ~ alt, langjährig; *relationship, agreement etc also* von langer Dauer

ADJ *attr* **a** (= *established, permanent*) ständig; *rule, custom* bestehend; *army* stehend; **it's a ~ joke** das ist schon zu einem Witz geworden; **the ~ orders of an association** die Geschäftsordnung einer Gesellschaft

b (= *from a standstill*) aus dem Stand; (= *erect*) *corn* auf dem Halm (stehend); ~ **ticket** Stehplatzkarte *f*; ~ **room only** nur Stehplätze; **to give sb a ~ ovation** jdm eine stehende Ovation darbringen; **to receive a ~ ovation** eine stehende Ovation erhalten, stürmischen Beifall ernten

standing: standing charge N Grundgebühr *f*, Grundpreis *m*; **standing committee** N ständiger Ausschuss; **standing order** N (*Brit Fin*) Dauerauftrag *m*; **to pay sth by** ~ etw per Dauerauftrag bezahlen; **standing start** N (*Sport*) stehender Start; **from a** ~ mit stehendem Start; **standing stone** N Menhir *m*; **circle of ~s** Steinkreis *m*

stand: standoff N (= *stalemate*) Patt *nt*, Pattsituation *f*; **standoffish** ADJ , **standoffishly** ADV [ˌstænd'ɒfɪʃ, -lɪ] (*inf*) distanziert; **standoffishness** N (*inf*) Distanziertheit *f*; **standpipe** N Steigrohr *nt*; **standpoint** N Standpunkt *m*; **from the ~ of the teacher** vom Standpunkt des Lehrers (aus) gesehen; **standstill** N Stillstand *m*; **to be at a ~** (*plane, train*) stehen; (*machines, traffic*) stillstehen; (*trade, factory, production*) ruhen; **to bring production to a ~** die Produktion lahm legen *or* zum Erliegen bringen; **to come to a ~** (*person*) stehen bleiben, anhalten; (*vehicle*) zum Stehen kommen, anhalten; (*traffic, machines*) zum Stillstand kommen; (*industry etc*) zum Erliegen kommen; **stand-up** ADJ *attr meal* im Stehen; ~ **buffet** Stehbüffet *nt*; ~ **collar** Stehkragen *m*; ~ **comedian** Bühnenkomiker(in) *m(f)*, Alleinunterhalter(in) *m(f)*; ~ **comedy** Stand-up Comedy *f*; ~ **fight** Schlägerei *f* N (*inf*) (= *comedy*) Stand-up Comedy *f*; (= *comedian*) Bühnenkomiker(in) *m(f)*, Alleinunterhalter(in) *m(f)*

stank [stæŋk] *pret of* **stink**

stannic ['stænɪk] ADJ Zinn-

stannic sulphide N Zinnsulfid *nt*

stanza ['stænzə] N Strophe *f*

staple¹ ['steɪpl] N Klammer *f*; (*for paper*) Heftklammer *f*; (*for wires, cables etc*) Krampe *f* VT heften; *wire* mit Krampen befestigen; **to** ~ **sth together** etw zusammenheften

staple² ADJ Haupt-; ~ **diet** Grund- *or* Hauptnahrung *f*; ~ **subject** Hauptthema *nt* N **a** (= *main product*) Hauptartikel *m*; (= *main element*) Ausgangsmaterial *nt*; (= *main food*) Hauptnahrungsmittel *nt* **b** (*of cotton*) Rohbaumwolle *f*; (*of wool*) Rohwolle *f*

staple gun N Tacker *m*

stapler ['steɪplə'] N Heftgerät *nt*

star ['stɑː'] N **a** Stern *m*; (= *asterisk, Sch*) Sternchen *nt*; **the Stars and Stripes** das Sternenbanner; **to be born under a lucky** ~ unter einem glücklichen Stern geboren sein; **you can thank your lucky ~s that ...** Sie können von Glück sagen, dass ...; **it's (all) in the ~s** es steht (alles) in den Sternen; **to see ~s** Sterne sehen; **to have ~s in one's eyes** sich (*dat*) optimistische Hoffnungen machen; **a three-star general** (*US, Mil*) ein Dreisternegeneral *m* **b** (= *person*) Star *m* ADJ *attr* Haupt-; ~ **attraction** Hauptattraktion *f*; ~ **performer/player** Star *m* VT **a** (= *mark with stars*) mit einem Stern/mit Sternen versehen; (*fig, scatter*) übersäen **b** (*Film etc*) **to** ~ **sb** (*film*) jdn in der Hauptrolle zeigen; **a film ~ring Greta Garbo** ein Film mit Greta Garbo (in der Hauptrolle); **~ring ...** in der Hauptrolle/den Hauptrollen ... VI (*Film etc*) die Hauptrolle spielen *or* haben

star: star billing N **to get** ~ auf Plakaten groß herausgestellt werden; **starboard** ['stɑːbəd] N

Steuerbord *nt*; **to** ~ (*direction*) (nach) Steuerbord; (*place*) (nach) Steuerbord ADJ Steuerbord-; ~ **side** Steuerbordseite *f* ADV (nach) Steuerbord; **star boat** N (*Naut*) Starboot *nt*; **starburst** N (*liter*) Sternregen *m*

starch [stɑːtʃ] N Stärke *f*; **low in** ~ stärkearm VT stärken

starchily ['stɑːtʃɪlɪ] ADV (*fig*) steif

starchiness ['stɑːtʃɪnɪs] N (*fig*) Steifheit *f*, Förmlichkeit *f*

starch-reduced [ˌstɑːtʃrɪ'djuːst] ADJ stärkereduziert

starchy ['stɑːtʃɪ] ADJ (+*er*) stärkehaltig; (*fig*) steif

star cloud N (*Astron*) Sternnebel *m*

star-crossed ['stɑːkrɒst] ADJ **they were** ~ **lovers** ihre Liebe stand unter einem Unstern

stardom ['stɑːdəm] N Berühmtheit *f*, Ruhm *m*; **where he hoped to find** ~ wo er hoffte, ein Star zu werden

stardust ['stɑːdʌst] N **a** (*Astron*) Sternnebel *m* **b** (= *naïvely romantic quality*) **there was** ~ **in her eyes** in ihrem Blick lag etwas Naiv-Romantisches **c** (= *charisma*) Ausstrahlung *f* eines Stars

stare [steə'] N (starrer) Blick; **the village idiot looked at me with a vacant** ~ der Dorftrottel sah mich mit stierem Blick an; **to give sb a** ~ jdn anstarren

VT **the answer was staring us in the face** die Antwort lag klar auf der Hand; **to** ~ **death/defeat in the face** dem Tod/der Niederlage ins Auge blicken; **defeat was staring us in the face** wir blickten der Niederlage ins Auge

VI (*vacantly etc*) (vor sich hin) starren; (*cow, madman*) stieren, glotzen (*inf*); (*in surprise*) große Augen machen; (*eyes*) weit aufgerissen sein; **he ~d in disbelief** er starrte ungläubig; **it's rude to** ~ es ist unhöflich, andere Leute anzustarren; **to** ~ **at sb/sth** jdn/etw anstarren; (*cow, madman also*) jdn/etw anstieren *or* anglotzen (*inf*); **don't** ~ **(at me)!** starr (mich) nicht so (an)!; **to** ~ **at sb in horror/amusement/disbelief** *etc* jdn entsetzt/verblüfft/ungläubig *etc* anstarren; **to** ~ **after sb** jdm nachstarren *or* hinterherstarren

▶ **stare down** *or* **out** VT *sep* **they were trying to stare each other down** *or* **out** sie versuchten, sich so lange gegenseitig anzustarren, bis einer aufgab; **I bet I can stare you down** *or* **out** wetten, dass du zuerst wegguckst (*inf*); **the teacher just sat there and stared him down** *or* **out** der Lehrer saß da und fixierte ihn

starer N Gaffer(in) *m(f)* (*inf*)

star: starfish N Seestern *m*; **stargazer** N (*hum inf*) Sterngucker(in) *m(f)* (*hum inf*)

staring ['steərɪŋ] ADJ starrend *attr*; ~ **eyes** starrer Blick

stark [stɑːk] ADJ (+*er*) *realism, contrast, ignorance, poverty, warning* krass; *reality, truth, terror, fact* nackt; *clothing, simplicity* schlicht; *madness* rein, schier, hell; *reminder, message also* überdeutlich; *choice, silhouette* hart; *landscape, cliffs, branches* nackt, kahl; *light bulb* grell; *colour* eintönig; (= *glaring*) grell; *black* trist; *white* nackt; **in** ~ **terms** in harten Worten, unverblümt ADV ~ **raving** *or* **staring mad** (*inf*) total verrückt (*inf*); ~ **naked** splitter(faser)nackt (*inf*)

starkers ['stɑːkəz] ADJ *pred* (*Brit inf*) splitter(faser)nackt (*inf*); *children also* nackig (*inf*)

starkly ['stɑːklɪ] ADV *lit* grell; *described* krass, schonungslos; *different, apparent* vollkommen; ~ **dressed in black** in tristes Schwarz gekleidet; ~ **trees** ~ **silhouetted against the winter sky** Bäume, die sich hart gegen den Winterhimmel abhoben; **to contrast** ~ **with sth** (*fig*) sich krass von etw unterscheiden; **to be** ~ **exposed** schonungslos aufgedeckt sein; **a** ~ **beautiful region** eine karge und zugleich schöne Gegend

starkness N (*of clothing*) Schlichtheit *f*; (*of colour*) Eintönigkeit *f*; (*glaring*) Grellheit *f*; (*of truth, contrast*) Härte *f*, Krassheit *f*; (*of landscape*) Nacktheit *f*, Kahlheit *f*

starless ['stɑːlɪs] ADJ sternenlos

starlet ['stɑːlɪt] N (Film)sternchen *nt*, Starlet *nt*

starlight ['stɑːlaɪt] N Sternenlicht *nt*

starling ['stɑːlɪŋ] N Star *m*

star: starlit ADJ *sky, night* stern(en)klar; *woods, hills* von Sternen beschienen; **star part** N Hauptrolle *f*; **star prize** N (*in competition*) Hauptpreis *m*

starred [stɑːd] ADJ mit (einem) Sternchen bezeichnet

starriness ['stɑːrɪnɪs] N (*of night, sky*) Stern(en)klarheit *f*; (*of eyes*) Leuchten *nt*, Strahlen *nt*

star role N = star part

starry ['stɑːrɪ] ADJ (+*er*) *night* stern(en)klar; *eyes* strahlend, leuchtend; ~ **sky** Sternenhimmel *m*

starry-eyed [ˌstɑːrɪ'aɪd] ADJ *idealist* romantisch, blauäugig; (= *naively trusting*) arglos, blauäugig; **to go all** ~ glänzende Augen kriegen

star: star shell N Leuchtkugel *f*, Leuchtgeschoss *nt*; **star sign** N Sternzeichen *nt*; **star-spangled** ADJ (*liter*) *sky* stern(en)übersät (*liter*); **star-spangled banner** N **The Star-spangled Banner** das Sternenbanner; **starstruck** ADJ überwältigt; **star-studded** ['stɑːstʌdɪd] ADJ **a** (*liter*) *night* sternenklar, voller Sterne; *sky* sternenklar, sternenübersät (*liter*) **b** (*fig*) ~ **cast/audience** Starbesetzung *f*/-publikum *nt*; **star system** N **a** (*Astron*) Sternsystem *nt* **b** (*Film*) **the** ~ *Engagement bekannter Schauspieler, um den Erfolg durchschnittlicher Filme zu garantieren*

START [stɑːt] *abbr of* **Strategic Arms Reduction Treaty** START(-Vertrag) *m*

start¹ [stɑːt] N **to give a** ~ zusammenfahren; (= *start up*) aufschrecken; (*horse*) scheuen; **to give sb a** ~ jdn erschrecken, jdm einen Schreck(en) einjagen; **to wake with a** ~ aus dem Schlaf hochschrecken; **he looked up with a** ~ er blickte erschreckt hoch → **fit² VI a** (= *jump nervously*) zusammenfahren; (= *start up*) aufschrecken; **to** ~ **from one's chair** aus dem Stuhl hochfahren; **to** ~ **out of one's sleep** aus dem Schlaf hochschrecken **b** **tears ~ed to his eyes** Tränen traten ihm in die Augen; **his eyes were ~ing out of his head** die Augen traten ihm fast aus dem Kopf VT *pheasant etc* aufscheuchen (*from aus*)

start² ⊙ 20.4, 26.1 N **a** (= *beginning*) Beginn *m*, Anfang *m*; (= *departure*) Aufbruch *m*; (*of race*) Start *m*; (*of rumour, trouble, journey*) Ausgangspunkt *m*; **at the** ~ am Anfang, zu Beginn; (*Sport*) am Start; **for a** ~ (= *to begin with*) fürs Erste; (= *firstly*) zunächst einmal; **from the** ~ von Anfang an; **from** ~ **to finish** von Anfang bis Ende, von vorn bis hinten (*inf*); **to get off to a good** *or* **flying** ~ gut vom Start wegkommen; (*fig*) einen glänzenden Start haben; **to get off to a bad** ~ schlecht vom Start wegkommen; (*fig*) einen schlechten Start haben; **to get sb off to a good** ~ jdm einen guten Start verschaffen; **to get sth off to a good** ~ etw gut anlaufen lassen; **to give sb a (good)** ~ **in life** jdm eine (gute) Starthilfe geben; **the review gave the book a good** ~ die Rezension war eine gute Starthilfe für das Buch; **to make a** ~ **(on sth)** (mit etw) anfangen; **to make an early** ~ frühzeitig aufbrechen; **to make a** ~ **for home** sich auf den Heimweg machen; **to make a new** ~ **(in life)** (noch einmal) von vorn anfangen

b (= *advantage, Sport*) Vorsprung *m* (*over* vor +*dat*)

VT **a** (= *begin*) anfangen mit; *argument, career, new life, negotiations* beginnen, anfangen; *new job, journey* antreten; **to** ~ **work** anfangen zu arbeiten; **he ~ed life as a miner** er hat als Bergmann angefangen; **don't** ~ **that again!** fang nicht schon wieder (damit) an!; **to** ~ **smoking** das Rauchen *or* mit dem Rauchen anfangen; **he ~ed coming late** er fing an, zu spät zu kommen; **you ~ed it!** du hast angefangen!

b (*runners*) starten zu; (= *cause to begin*) *runners, race* starten; *rumour* in Umlauf setzen; *conversation* anfangen, anknüpfen; *fight* anfangen; *war* anfangen, auslösen; *blaze, collapse, chain reaction* auslösen; *coal fire etc* anzünden; (*arsonist*) legen;

(= *found*) *enterprise, newspaper* gründen, starten (*inf*); **to ~ sb thinking** jdn nachdenklich machen; **to ~ sb on a subject** jdn auf ein Thema bringen; **to ~ sb in business/on a career** jdm zu einem Start im Geschäftsleben/zu einer Karriere verhelfen; **the discovery ~ed a new line of research** mit der Entdeckung kam eine neue Forschungsrichtung in Gang; **I don't want to ~ anything but ...** ich will keinen Streit anfangen, aber ...; **just to ~ you getting used to it** nur damit Sie sich erst mal daran gewöhnen; **as soon as she ~ed the baby** (*inf*) sobald sich das Baby angekündigt hatte; **when she wore the first miniskirt she didn't realize what she was ~ing** als sie den ersten Minirock trug, war ihr nicht bewusst, was sie damit auslösen würde; **look what you've ~ed now!** da hast du was Schönes angefangen! (*inf*)

c *car* starten; *engine* anlassen, starten; *clock* in Gang setzen; *machine, motor* starten, anwerfen

d **to ~ a horse in a race** eine Nennung für ein Pferd abgeben

VI (= *begin*) anfangen, beginnen; (*car, engine*) anspringen, starten; (*plane*) starten; (= *move off*) anfahren; (*bus, train*) abfahren; (*boat*) ablegen; (*rumour*) in Umlauf kommen; (*violins, cellos etc*) einsetzen; **~ing from Tuesday** ab Dienstag; **to ~ for home** (nach Hause) losfahren; **to ~ for work** zur Arbeit gehen/fahren; **to ~ for London** nach London losfahren; **to ~ (off) with** (= *firstly*) erstens, erst einmal; (= *at the beginning*) **what shall we have to ~ (off) with?** was nehmen wir als Vorspeise?; **I'd like soup to ~ (off) with** ich möchte erst mal eine Suppe; **to ~ after sb** jdn verfolgen; **to get ~ed** anfangen; (*on journey*) aufbrechen; **he finds it difficult to get ~ed in the morning** er kommt morgens nur schwer in Schwung or Gang; **to ~ on a task/journey/the food** sich an eine Aufgabe/auf eine Reise/ans Essen machen; **to ~ talking** or **to talk** zu sprechen beginnen or anfangen; **he ~ed by saying ...** er sagte zunächst ...; **don't you ~!** fang du nicht auch noch an!

▸ **start back** VI sich auf den Rückweg machen; **we started back for home** wir machten uns auf den Heimweg; **the rocket started back to earth** die Rakete trat die Rückkreise zur Erde an

▸ **start in** VI (*inf*) **a** (= *begin to scold*) loslegen (*inf*), vom Leder ziehen (*inf*) (*on sb* gegen jdn) **b** **to start in on sth** sich an etw (*acc*) machen

▸ **start off** **VI** (= *begin*) anfangen; (= *begin moving: person*) losgehen; (*on journey*) aufbrechen; (= *run*) loslaufen; (= *drive*) losfahren; (*esp Sport*) starten; (= *begin talking etc*) anfangen, loslegen (*inf*) (*on* mit); **to start off with** = **start²** VI

VT *sep* anfangen; **to start sb off (talking)** jdm das Stichwort geben; **to start the baby off (crying)** das Baby zum Schreien bringen; **whatever you do, don't start her off** sieh bloß zu, dass sie nicht damit anfängt; **to start the dog off (barking)** da fing der Hund an zu bellen; **to start sb off on sth** jdn auf etw (*acc*) bringen; **a few stamps to start you off** ein paar Briefmarken für den Anfang; **I'll play a few bars to start you off** ich spiele ein paar Takte, um Sie einzustimmen

▸ **start out** VI (= *begin*) (zunächst) beginnen or anfangen; (= *begin a journey*) aufbrechen (*for* nach); **we started out on a long journey** wir machten uns auf eine lange Reise; **I'm starting out on a new career** ich fange eine neue Berufslaufbahn an; **we started out with great hopes for the future** wir hatten mit großen Zukunftshoffnungen begonnen

▸ **start over** VI (*esp US*) noch (ein)mal von vorn anfangen

▸ **start up** **VI** **a** (= *move suddenly*) **a rabbit started up out of the undergrowth** ein Kaninchen schoss aus dem Unterholz hervor; **he started up in bed at the noise** bei dem Geräusch schreckte er or fuhr er im Bett hoch

b (= *begin*) (*music etc*) anfangen; (*machine*) angehen (*inf*), in Gang kommen; (*motor*) anspringen; (*siren*) losheulen; **when I started up in**

business als ich als Geschäftsmann anfing; **he started up by himself when he was 21** er machte sich mit 21 selbstständig

VT *sep* **a** (= *cause to function*) anmachen (*inf*), in Gang bringen; *engine also* anlassen, starten; *machine also* anwerfen

b (= *begin*) eröffnen; *business also* anfangen; *conversation* anfangen, anknüpfen; (*amongst other people*) in Gang bringen

starter ['staːtəʳ] N **a** (*Sport*) Starter(in) *m(f)* (*also horse*); (= *competitor*) Teilnehmer(in) *m(f)*; **to be under ~'s orders** auf das Startkommando warten; (*fig*) in den Startblöcken sitzen

b (*Aut etc, = self-starter*) Starter *m*, Anlasser *m* **c** (*inf, = person*) **to be a late ~** ein Spätzünder *m* sein (*inf*); (*child*) ein Spätentwickler *m* sein; **to be a late ~ with girls** ein Spätzünder *m* sein, was Mädchen betrifft (*inf*); **he was a late ~ in the presidential race** er beteiligte sich erst spät an den Präsidentschaftswahlen; **she is a slow ~ in the morning** sie kommt morgens nur langsam in Schwung

d (*Brit inf, = first course*) Vorspeise *f*

e **for ~s** (*inf*) für den Anfang (*inf*)

starter: starter home N *Immobilienobjekt für Erstkäufer*; **starter pack** N (*Comm*) Erstausstattung *f*, Startpaket *nt*

starting ['staːtɪŋ] *in cpds* (*Sport*) Start-; **starting block** N Startblock *m*; **to be fast/slow off the ~s** schnell/langsam aus den Startblöcken wegkommen; **starting gate** N Startmaschine *f*; **starting grid** N Start(platz) *m*; **starting gun** N Startpistole *f*; **starting handle** N Anlasserkurbel *f*; **starting point** N (*lit, fig*) Ausgangspunkt *m*; **starting post** N Startpflock *m*; **starting price** N (*Horse Racing*) letzter Kurs vor dem Start; **starting stalls** PL (*Brit: horse racing*) Startmaschine *f*

startle ['staːtl] **VT** erschrecken; *animal also* aufschrecken; **I was ~d to see how old he looked** ich stellte entsetzt fest, wie alt er aussah **VI** **she ~s easily** sie ist sehr schreckhaft

startling ['staːtlɪŋ] ADJ *news, clarity, revelation* überraschend; (= *bad*) alarmierend, bestürzend; *coincidence, resemblance, contrast, change* erstaunlich; *colour, originality* aufregend, erregend; *dress, blue* aufregend; *discovery, claim, success, results* aufregend, sensationell

startlingly ['staːtlɪŋlɪ] ADV *simple, alike* überraschend; *dressed, beautiful* aufregend; *different* verblüffend; **nothing ~ new/original** nichts besonders or allzu Neues/Originelles

start-up ['staːtʌp] N (*of machine, new business*) Start *m*; **100 new ~s a week** (= *new businesses*) 100 Neugründungen pro Woche; **~ costs** (*of business, project*) Startkosten *pl*; **Start-Up Scheme** (*Brit*) *Existenzgründungsprogramm für Arbeitslose*

star turn N (*esp Brit*) Sensation *f*, Hauptattraktion *f*

starvation [staːˈveɪʃən] N (*act*) Hungern *nt*; (*of besieged people*) Aushungern *nt*; (= *condition*) Hunger *m*; **to die of ~** verhungern, hungers or den Hungertod sterben (*geh*); **to live on a ~ diet** Hunger leiden; **the prisoners were kept on a ~ diet for months** man ließ die Gefangenen monatelang fast verhungern; **to go on a ~ diet** (*hum*) eine Hungerkur machen; **~ wages** Hungerlohn *m*, Hungerlöhne *pl*

starve [staːv] VT **a** (= *deprive of food*) hungern lassen; (*also* **starve out**) aushungern; (= *kill: also* **starve to death**) verhungern lassen, hungers sterben lassen (*geh*); **to ~ oneself** hungern; **to ~ a town into surrender** eine Stadt durch Aushungern zur Kapitulation zwingen; **he ~d his way through college** er hat sich (*dat*) das Studium vom Mund abgespart

b (*fig*) **to ~ sb of sth** jdm etw vorenthalten or verweigern; **to be ~d of oxygen** Sauerstoffmangel haben; **to be ~d of capital/graduates** an akutem Kapital-/Akademikermangel leiden; **to be ~d of affection** unter Liebesentzug erfahren, an Liebesentzug leiden **VI** hungern; (= *die: also* **starve to death**) verhungern; **I'm simply starving!** (*inf*) ich sterbe vor Hunger!

(*inf*); **you must be starving!** du musst doch halb verhungert sein! (*inf*); **to ~ for sth** (*fig*) nach etw hungern

▸ **starve out** VT *sep garrison etc* aushungern

starveling ['staːvlɪŋ] N (*dated*) Hungerleider *m*

starving ['staːvɪŋ] ADJ (*lit*) hungernd *attr*; (*fig*) hungrig

Star Wars N *sing* Sternenkrieg *m*, Krieg *m* der Sterne

stash [stæʃ] VT (*inf: also* **stash away**) bunkern (*sl*); *money* beiseite schaffen

stasis ['steɪsɪs] N Stauung *f*, Stase *f* (*spec*); (*Liter*) Stillstand *m*

state [steɪt] **N** **a** (= *condition*) Zustand *m*; **~ of health/mind/war/siege** Gesundheits-/Geistes-/Kriegs-/Belagerungszustand *m*; **married/single ~** Ehe-/Ledigenstand *m*; **to be in a ~ of weightlessness** sich im Zustand der Schwerelosigkeit befinden; **the ~ of the nation** die Lage der Nation; **the present ~ of the economy** die gegenwärtige Wirtschaftslage; **in a liquid/solid ~** in flüssigem/festem Zustand; **where animals live in their natural ~** wo Tiere im Naturzustand leben; **in a good/bad ~** in gutem/ schlechtem Zustand; **he's in no (fit) ~ to do that** er ist auf gar keinen Fall in der Verfassung, das zu tun; **what a ~ of affairs!** was sind das für Zustände!; **look at the ~ of your hands!** guck dir bloß mal deine Hände an!; **my papers are in such a ~!** meine Papiere sind in einem furchtbaren Durcheinander!; **the room was in a terrible ~** im Zimmer herrschte ein fürchterliches Durcheinander

b (*inf, = anxiety*) **to get into a ~ (about sth)** (*inf*) wegen etw durchdrehen (*inf*); **to be in a terrible ~** (*inf*) in heller Aufregung or ganz durchgedreht (*inf*) sein

c (= *rank*) Stand *m*, Rang *m*; **~ of bishop** Bischofswürde *f*

d (= *pomp*) Aufwand *m*, Pomp *m*; **to be received in great ~** mit großem Staat empfangen werden; **to travel in ~** aufwendig or aufwändig or pompös reisen; **to lie in ~** (feierlich) aufgebahrt sein

e (*Pol*) Staat *m*; (= *federal state*) (Bundes)staat *m*; (*in Germany, Austria*) (Bundes)land *nt*; **the States** die (Vereinigten) Staaten; **the State of Florida** der Staat Florida; **a ~ within a ~** ein Staat im Staate; **affairs of ~** Staatsangelegenheiten *pl*

VT darlegen, vortragen; *name, price, amount* nennen, angeben; *preference, purpose* angeben; *opposition, intention* anmelden; **to ~ that ...** feststellen or erklären, dass ...; **to ~ one's case** seine Sache vortragen; **it must be clearly ~d in the records ...** es muss aus den Akten einwandfrei hervorgehen, ...; **to ~ the case for the prosecution** (*Jur*) die Anklage vortragen; **the theme is ~d in the first few bars** das Thema wird in den ersten paar Takten vorgestellt; **unless otherwise ~d** wenn nicht anders angegeben; **as ~d in my letter I ...** wie in meinem Brief erwähnt, ... ich ...

state *in cpds* Staats-; *control, industry* staatlich; (*US etc*) des Bundes- or Einzelstaates, bundesstaatlich; **state-aided** ADJ staatlich gefördert; **state apartment** N Prunksaal *m*; **state bank** N Staatsbank *f*; **statecraft** N die Staatskunst

stated ['steɪtɪd] ADJ **a** (= *declared*) *sum, date* angegeben, genannt; *limits* bestimmt **b** (= *fixed, regular*) *times, amount* fest(gesetzt); **at ~ intervals** in den festgelegten Abständen; **on the date ~** zum festgesetzten Termin

state: State Department N (*US*) Außenministerium *nt*; **state education** N staatliche Erziehung; (= *system*) staatliches Erziehungs- or Bildungswesen; **state-funded** ADJ staatlich finanziert; **state funding** N staatliche Finanzierung; **state funeral** N Staatsbegräbnis *nt*

statehood ['steɪthʊd] N Eigenstaatlichkeit *f*; **to achieve ~** ein eigener or selbstständiger Staat werden; **when was Alaska granted ~?** wann wurde Alaska zum Bundesstaat erklärt?

state: statehouse N (US) Parlamentsgebäude nt, Kapitol nt; **stateless** ADJ staatenlos; **~ person** Staatenlose(r) mf; **statelessness** N Staatenlosigkeit f

statelet ['steɪtlɪt] N (Pol) Splitterstaat m

stateliness ['steɪtlɪnɪs] N (of person, bearing) Würde f; (of pace, walk) Gemessenheit f; (of palace) Pracht f

stately ['steɪtlɪ] ADJ (+er) person, bearing würdevoll; progress gemessen; palace, tree prächtig; **~ home** herrschaftliches Anwesen, Schloss nt

statement ['steɪtmənt] N **a** (= putting forward: of thesis etc) Darstellung f; (of problem) Darlegung f; **a clear ~ of the facts** eine klare Feststellung der Tatsachen
b (= that said) Feststellung f; (= claim) Behauptung f; (Mus, of theme) Vorstellen nt; (= official, Government statement) Erklärung f, Stellungnahme f; (in court, to police) Aussage f; (written) Protokoll nt, Aussage f; **to make a ~ to the press** eine Presseerklärung abgeben
c (Philos) Behauptung f, These f; (Logic) Satz m; (Gram) Feststellung f
d (Fin) Rechnung f; (also **bank statement**) Kontoauszug m ▶ VT (= assess) **to ~ a child** Lernschwierigkeiten bei einem Kind offiziell feststellen; **~ed children** Kinder, bei denen offiziell eine Lernschwäche festgestellt wurde

state: state occasion N Staatsanlass m, Staatsfeierlichkeit f; **state-of-the-art** ADJ hochmodern, dem neuesten Stand der Technik entsprechend attr; **to be ~** dem neuesten Stand der Technik entsprechen; **~ technology** Spitzentechnologie f

---

---

state: state-owned ADJ staatseigen; **State Registered Nurse** N (Brit) staatlich anerkannte Krankenschwester, staatlich anerkannter Krankenpfleger; **stateroom** N (Naut) Kabine f; (US, Rail) Privat(schlafwagen)abteil nt; **state school** N (Brit) öffentliche Schule; **state secret** N Staatsgeheimnis nt; **state's evidence** N (US) Aussage f eines Kronzeugen; **to turn ~** als Kronzeuge auftreten; **stateside** (US, inf) ADJ in den Staaten (inf); newspaper aus den Staaten (inf) ▶ ADV nach Hause, nachhause (Aus, Sw); **when I'm back ~** ... wenn ich wieder zu Hause in den Staaten bin, ...

statesman ['steɪtsmən] N pl **-men** [-mən] Staatsmann m

statesmanlike ['steɪtsmənlaɪk], **statesmanly** ['steɪtsmənlɪ] ADJ staatsmännisch

statesmanship ['steɪtsmənʃɪp] N Staatskunst f; **act of ~** staatsmännische Handlungsweise f

---

---

stateswoman ['steɪtswʊmən] N pl **-women** Staatsmännin f

state: state trooper N (US) Staatspolizist(in) m(f); **state visit** N Staatsbesuch m; **state-wide** ADJ (US) im ganzen Bundesstaat, landesweit

static ['stætɪk] ADJ **a** (Phys) statisch; **~ electricity** Reibungselektrizität f, statische Aufladung
b (= not moving or changing) konstant; (= stationary) feststehend attr; condition, society statisch; **if the development of a civilization remains ~** ... wenn eine Kultur sich nicht mehr weiterentwickelt, ...; **their relationship became ~** ihre Beziehung stagnierte, ihre Beziehung trat auf der Stelle ▶ N (Phys) Reibungselektrizität f; (Rad also) atmosphärische Störungen pl

statics ['stætɪks] N sing Statik f

station ['steɪʃən] N **a** Station f; (= police station, fire station) Wache f; (= space station) (Raum)station f; (US, = gas station) Tankstelle f → **work station**
b (= railway station, bus station) Bahnhof m; (= stop) Station f
c (Mil, = post) Stellung f, Posten m; **border ~** Grenzstellung f; **naval ~** Flottenstützpunkt m
d (esp Austral, = ranch) Farm f; **sheep/cattle ~** Schaf-/Rinderzuchtfarm f; **~ hand** Farmgehilfe m/-gehilfin f
e (Rad, TV) Sender m, Sendestation f; (= channel) Sender m
f (= position) Platz m; **to take up (one's) ~** sich (auf)stellen, seinen Platz einnehmen; **the Stations of the Cross** die Stationen pl des Kreuzwegs
g (= rank) Stand m, Rang m; **~ in life** Stellung f (im Leben), Rang m; **to marry below/above one's ~** nicht standesgemäß/über seinem Stand heiraten; **he has got ideas above his ~** er hat Ideen, die jemandem aus seinem Stand gar nicht zukommen ▶ VT (auf)stellen, postieren; (Mil) stationieren; bicycle, train abstellen

station agent N (US) = **stationmaster**

stationary ['steɪʃənərɪ] ADJ (= not moving) car parkend attr, haltend attr; (= not movable) fest (stehend attr); **to be ~** (vehicles) stehen; (traffic, fig) stillstehen; **to remain ~** sich nicht bewegen; (traffic) stillstehen

station break N (US Radio, TV) Pausenzeichen nt

stationer ['steɪʃənə] N Schreibwarenhändler(in) m(f); **~'s (shop)** Schreibwarenhandlung f

stationery ['steɪʃənərɪ] N (= notepaper) Briefpapier nt; (= writing materials) Schreibwaren pl; **office ~** Büromaterial nt

station: station house N (US, Police) (Polizei)wache f, (Polizei)revier nt; **stationmaster** N Bahnhofsvorsteher(in), Stationsvorsteher(in) (dated) m(f); **station police** N Bahnpolizei f; **station selector** N (Rad) Sendereinstellung f; **station wagon** N (US) Kombi(wagen) m

statist ['steɪtɪst] ADJ (Pol) staatlich

statistic [stə'tɪstɪk] N Statistik f

statistical [stə'tɪstɪkəl] ADJ statistisch

statistically [stə'tɪstɪkəlɪ] ADV statistisch; **~ speaking** statistisch gesehen

statistician [stætɪ'stɪʃən] N Statistiker(in) m(f)

statistics [stə'tɪstɪks] N **a** sing Statistik f **b** pl (= data) Statistiken pl → **vital statistics**

stator ['steɪtə] N (Elec) Stator m

statuary ['stætjʊərɪ] (form) ADJ statuarisch (geh); **~ art** Plastik f **b** (Art) Plastik f, Bildhauerei f; (= statues) Plastiken pl, Statuen pl

statue ['stætjuː] N Statue f, Standbild nt; **Statue of Liberty** Freiheitsstatue f

statuesque [stætjʊ'esk] ADJ standbildhaft, statuesk (liter); **a woman with ~ looks** eine Frau von klassischer Schönheit

statuette [stætjʊ'et] N Statuette f

stature ['stætʃə] N **a** Wuchs m; (esp of man) Statur f; **of short ~** von kleinem Wuchs **b** (fig) Format nt

status ['steɪtəs] N Stellung f; (= legal status, social status also) Status m; **equal ~** Gleichstellung f; **marital ~** Familienstand m; **many people who merely desire ~** viele Menschen, die bloß nach Prestige streben; **unsupported statements have no ~ in law** unbewiesene Behauptungen sind rechtlich irrelevant; **the idea that possession brings ~** die Vorstellung, dass Besitz das Prestige erhöht

status: status-conscious ADJ statusbewusst; **status line** N (Comput) Statuszeile f

status quo [steɪtəs'kwəʊ] N Status quo m

status: status report N Zwischenbericht m; **status symbol** N Statussymbol nt

statute ['stætjuːt] N Gesetz nt; (of organization) Satzung f, Statut nt; **by ~** gesetzlich, statutarisch, satzungsgemäß

statute: statute-barred ['stætjuːtbɑːd] ADJ (US Jur) verjährt; **statute book** N (esp Brit) Gesetzbuch nt; **to put sth on the ~** etw zum Gesetz machen or erheben; **to be on the ~** geltendes Recht sein; **statute law** N Gesetzesrecht nt, Statute Law nt; **statute mile** N britische Meile

statutorily ['stætjʊtərəlɪ] ADV (= legally) gesetzlich; **broadcasting needs to be regulated ~** Rundfunk und Fernsehen müssen gesetzlich geregelt werden; **refugee families are ~ homeless** Flüchtlingsfamilien sind rechtlich gesehen heimatlos

statutory ['stætjʊtərɪ] ADJ gesetzlich; holiday also, quarantine gesetzlich vorgeschrieben; (in organization) satzungsgemäß, statutarisch; right verbrieft; punishment (vom Gesetz) vorgesehen; **~ maternity pay** (Brit) gesetzliches Erziehungsgeld; **~ nuisance** Ruhestörung f; **this is ~** das ist Gesetz

statutory rape N (US) Unzucht f mit Minderjährigen

staunch¹ [stɔːntʃ] ADJ (+er) ally, friend unerschütterlich; Catholic, loyalist etc überzeugt; member, supporter ergeben, getreu; support standhaft; **to be ~ in one's belief** fest or unerschütterlich im Glauben sein

staunch² VT flow stauen; bleeding stillen; **to ~ a wound** die Blutung einer Wunde stillen

staunchly ['stɔːntʃlɪ] ADV treu, standhaft; oppose entschieden; defend standhaft; Catholic streng

staunchness ['stɔːntʃnɪs] N (of Catholic, loyalist) Überzeugtheit f; (of member, supporter) Treue f; (of support) Unerschütterlichkeit f

stave [steɪv] N **a** (of barrel) (Fass)daube f; (= rung) (Leiter)sprosse f; (= stick) Knüppel m, Knüttel m (old) **b** (Mus, = staff) Notenlinien pl **c** (Liter, = stanza) Strophe f, Vers m

▶ **stave in** pret, ptp **staved** or **stove in** VT sep eindrücken; head einschlagen ▶ VI eingedrückt werden

▶ **stave off** VT sep **a** attack zurückschlagen; threat, crisis, cold abwehren; defeat, disaster, bankruptcy abwenden; hunger, boredom lindern **b** (= delay) person hinhalten; crisis, day hinausschieben

stave rhyme N (Poet) Stabreim m

staves [steɪvz] pl of **staff** N **b, d**

stay¹ [steɪ] N **a** Aufenthalt m; **come for a longer ~ next year** komm nächstes Jahr für länger; **a short ~ in hospital** ein kurzer Krankenhausaufenthalt
b (Jur) Aussetzung f; **~ of execution** Ausset-

zung f, Vollstreckungsaufschub m; (fig) Galgenfrist f; (of death penalty) Hinrichtungsaufschub m

VT **a** (old, liter, = stop) Einhalt gebieten (+dat) (geh); hunger stillen; **to ~ one's/sb's hand** sich/jdn zurückhalten

b (Jur) order, sentence aussetzen

c **to ~ the course** (lit, fig) durchhalten

d **to ~ the night (with sb/in a hotel)** (bei jdm/in einem Hotel) übernachten

VI **a** (= remain) bleiben; **to ~ for** or **to supper** zum Abendessen bleiben; **to have come to ~** (fashion etc) sich halten; **is unemployment here to ~?** ist die Arbeitslosigkeit nun ein Dauerzustand?; **if it ~s fine** wenn es schön bleibt; **if he can ~ with the others** wenn er mit den anderen mithalten kann; **~ with it!** nicht aufgeben! → **put²**

b (= reside) wohnen; (at youth hostel etc) übernachten; **to ~ at a hotel** im Hotel wohnen or übernachten; **I ~ed in Italy for a few weeks** ich habe mich ein paar Wochen in Italien aufgehalten; **when I/Goethe was ~ing in Italy** als ich/Goethe in Italien war or weilte (liter); **where are you ~ing?** wo wohnen Sie?; **he is ~ing at Chequers for the weekend** er verbringt das Wochenende in Chequers; **he went to ~ in the country for a while** er ist für einige Zeit aufs Land gefahren; **we would ~ at a different resort each year** wir waren jedes Jahr an einem anderen Urlaubsort; **it's a nice place to ~ in the summer** dort kann man gut den Sommer verbringen; **my brother came to ~ for a week** mein Bruder ist für eine Woche gekommen; **my brother came to ~** mein Bruder ist zu Besuch gekommen

c (old, = wait) ~! stehen bleiben!; **~, wanderer!** halt inne, Wanderer! (old, liter)

▶ **stay away** VI (from von) wegbleiben; (from person) sich fern halten; **to stay away from a girl** von einem Mädchen die Finger lassen; **he can't stay away from the pub** ihn zieht es immer wieder in die Kneipe (inf)

▶ **stay behind** VI zurückbleiben; (Sch, as punishment) nachsitzen; **I stayed behind after the party** ich blieb nach der Party noch da

▶ **stay down** VI (= keep down) unten bleiben; (Sch) wiederholen; **nothing I eat stays down** alles, was ich esse, kommt wieder hoch

▶ **stay in** VI (at home) zu Hause bleiben; (in position, in book etc) drinbleiben; (Sch) nachsitzen; **he had to stay in as a punishment** (at home) er kriegte zur Strafe Stubenarrest or Hausarrest

▶ **stay off** **VI** **a** (rain) ausbleiben **VI** +prep obj **a** (= not go on) nicht betreten **b** **to stay off work/school** nicht zur Arbeit/Schule gehen; **to stay off the bottle** (inf) die Flasche nicht anrühren (inf)

▶ **stay on** VI (lid etc) draufbleiben; (light) anbleiben; (people) (noch) bleiben; **he stayed on for another year** er blieb noch ein Jahr; **to stay on at school** (in der Schule) weitermachen; **to stay on as manager** (weiterhin) Geschäftsführer bleiben

▶ **stay out** VI draußen bleiben; (esp Brit: on strike) weiterstreiken; (= not come home) wegbleiben; **to stay out of sth** sich aus etw heraushalten; **he never managed to stay out of trouble** er war dauernd in Schwierigkeiten; **you stay out of this!** halt du dich da raus!

▶ **stay up** VI **a** (person) aufbleiben; **don't stay up for me!** bleib nicht meinetwegen auf! **b** (tent, fence, pole) stehen bleiben; (picture, decorations) hängen bleiben; (swimmer) oben bleiben; (roof) draufbleiben; **his trousers won't stay up** seine Hosen rutschen immer **c** (at university) (an der Uni) bleiben **d** **he's still staying up with the front runners** er liegt immer noch auf gleicher Höhe mit den Läufern an der Spitze

stay² N **a** (= guy-rope) Stütztau nt, Halteseil nt; (Naut) Stag nt; **the ~ of one's old age** (fig) die Stütze seines Alters **b** **stays** pl (old, = corsets) Korsett nt

stay-at-home ['steɪəthəʊm] **N** Stubenhocker(in) m(f) **ADJ** attr stubenhockerisch

stayer ['steɪə'] N (= horse) Steher m; (= person) beständiger or ausdauernder Mensch

staying power ['steɪɪŋˌpaʊə'] N Stehvermögen nt, Durchhaltevermögen nt, Ausdauer f

stay-in strike ['steɪɪnˌstraɪk] N (Brit) Sitzstreik m

St Bernard [sənt'bɜːnəd] N Bernhardiner m

STD **a** (Brit, Telec) abbr of **subscriber trunk dialling** der Selbstwählferndienst; **~ code** Vorwahl(nummer) f **b** abbr of **sexually transmitted disease** Geschlechtskrankheit f; **~ clinic** Sprechstunde f/Praxis f für Geschlechtskrankheiten

stead [sted] N **in his ~** an seiner Stelle or statt (liter, form); **to stand sb in good ~** jdm zugute or zustatten kommen

steadfast ['stedfəst] ADJ fest; look also unverwandt; person also standhaft, unerschütterlich; refusal also standhaft; belief also unerschütterlich; **to remain ~ in faith** in seinem Glauben nicht schwanken; **the sky was a ~ blue** (poet) der Himmel war von einem wolkenlosen Blau

steadfastly ['stedfəstlɪ] ADV fest; look unverwandt; adhere, refuse standhaft, unerschütterlich; **to be ~ loyal to sb** jdm unerschütterlich treu sein; **to ~ maintain one's innocence** unerschütterlich auf seiner Unschuld beharren; **to remain ~ at one's post** beharrlich auf seinem Posten bleiben

steadfastness ['stedfəstnɪs] N Festigkeit f; (of look also) Unverwandtheit f; (of person also) Standhaftigkeit f, Unerschütterlichkeit f; (of refusal also) Standhaftigkeit f; (of belief also) Unerschütterlichkeit f

Steadicam® ['stedɪkæm] N (Film) Steadicam® nt

steadily ['stedɪlɪ] ADV **a** (= firmly) ruhig; balanced fest; gaze fest, unverwandt **b** (= constantly) ständig; rain ununterbrochen; **the atmosphere in the country is getting ~ more tense** die Stimmung im Land wird immer gespannter **c** (= reliably) zuverlässig, solide **d** (= regularly) gleichmäßig, regelmäßig

steadiness ['stedɪnɪs] N (= stability) Festigkeit f; (of hand, eye) Ruhe f; (= regularity) Stetigkeit f; (of gaze) Unverwandtheit f; (of character) Zuverlässigkeit f, Solidität f

steady ['stedɪ] ADJ (+er) **a** (= firm, not wobbling) hand, nerves, eye ruhig; gaze fest, unverwandt; (= composed) voice fest; **with a ~ hand** mit ruhiger Hand; **~ on one's legs/feet** fest or sicher auf den Beinen; **to hold sth ~** etw ruhig halten; ladder etw festhalten; **the chair is not very ~** der Stuhl ist wacklig

b (= constant) wind, progress, demand etc ständig, stet (geh); drizzle ununterbrochen; temperature beständig; income geregelt; **at a ~ pace** in gleichmäßigem Tempo; **at a ~ 70** ständig mit 70

c (= reliable, regular) worker zuverlässig, solide; **he plays a ~ game** er ist ein zuverlässiger Spieler

d job, boyfriend fest

ADV ~! (= carefully, gently) vorsichtig!; (Naut) Kurs halten!; ~ **(on)!, ~ the buffs!** immer mit der Ruhe! (inf), sachte! (inf); **to go ~ (with sb)** (inf) mit jdm (fest) gehen (inf); **they're going ~** (inf) sie gehen fest miteinander, sie sind fest zusammen

N (inf) fester Freund (inf), feste Freundin (inf)

VT plane, boat wieder ins Gleichgewicht bringen; (= stabilize) nerves, person beruhigen; (in character) **to ~ oneself** festen Halt finden; **she had a ~ing influence on him** durch ihren Einfluss wurde er ausgeglichener

VI sich beruhigen; (person, voice) ruhig(er) werden; **her breathing steadied** ihr Atem wurde ruhiger

steady-going ['stedɪˌɡəʊɪŋ] ADJ gleich bleibend, ausgeglichen; service to a good cause etc unerschütterlich; family man etc solide, gesetzt

steady-state theory [ˌstedɪ'steɪtˌθɪərɪ] N (Phys) Gleichgewichtstheorie f

steak [steɪk] N Steak nt; (of fish) Filet nt; **a ham/bacon ~** eine Scheibe gebackener Schinken/Speck; **~ and kidney pie** Fleischpastete f mit Nieren; **~ dinner** Steakmenü nt

steak: steakhouse N Steakhouse nt; **steak knife** N Steakmesser nt; **steak tartare** N Tatarbeefsteak nt

steal [stiːl] vb: pret **stole**, ptp **stolen** **VT** object, idea, kiss, heart stehlen; **to ~ sth from sb** jdm etw stehlen; **to ~ sb's girlfriend** jdm die Freundin ausspannen (inf); **to ~ the show** die Schau stehlen; **to ~ the limelight from sb** jdm die Schau stehlen; **to ~ sb's thunder** jdm den Wind aus den Segeln nehmen; **Labour have stolen the Tories' clothes** Labour hat sich der Politik der Tories bemächtigt; **the baby stole all the attention** das Kind zog die ganze Aufmerksamkeit auf sich; **to ~ a glance at sb** verstohlen zu jdm hinschauen

VI **a** (= thieve) stehlen

b (= move quietly etc) sich stehlen, (sich) schleichen; **to ~ away** or **off** sich weg- or davonstehlen; **to ~ into a room** sich in ein Zimmer stehlen; **to ~ up on sb** sich an jdn heranschleichen; **old age was ~ing up on her** das Alter machte sich allmählich bei ihr bemerkbar; **the mood/feeling which was ~ing over the country** die Stimmung, die sich allmählich im Land verbreitete; **he could feel happiness ~ing over him** er fühlte, wie ihn ein Glücksgefühl überkam; **to ~ home** (Baseball) ungehindert zur Ausgangsbase vorrücken

N (US, inf, = bargain) Geschenk nt (inf); **it's a ~!** das ist (ja) geschenkt! (inf)

stealth [stelθ] N List f; (of fox also) Schläue f; **by ~** durch List

Stealth bomber N (Aviat) Tarn(kappen)bomber m, Stealthbomber m

stealthily ['stelθɪlɪ] ADV verstohlen

stealthiness ['stelθɪnɪs] N Verstohlenheit f

stealthy ['stelθɪ] ADJ (+er) verstohlen; footsteps verhalten

steam [stiːm] **N** Dampf m; (from swamp also) Dunst m; **driven by ~** dampfgetrieben; **full ~ ahead** (Naut) volle Kraft voraus; (fig) mit Volldampf voraus; **to get** or **pick up ~** (lit) feuern, Dampf aufmachen (dated); (fig) in Schwung kommen; **to let off ~** (lit, fig) Dampf ablassen; **to run out of ~** (lit) Dampf verlieren; (fig) Schwung verlieren; **he ran out of ~** ihm ist die Puste ausgegangen (inf); **the ship went on under its own ~** das Schiff fuhr mit eigener Kraft weiter; **under one's own ~** (fig) allein, ohne Hilfe

VT dämpfen; food also dünsten; **to ~ open an envelope** einen Briefumschlag über Dampf öffnen; **~ed pudding** Kochpudding m

VI **a** (= give off steam) dampfen

b (= move) dampfen; **we were ~ing along at 12 knots** wir fuhren mit 12 Knoten; **the ship ~ed into the harbour** das Schiff kam in den Hafen gefahren; **the ship ~ed out** das Schiff dampfte ab; **the runner came ~ing round the last bend** (inf) der Läufer kam mit Volldampf um die letzte Kurve (inf)

▶ **steam ahead** VI (inf, project, work) gut vorankommen

▶ **steam off** **VT** sep stamp, label über Dampf ablösen; excess flab sich (dat) abschwitzen **VI** abfahren; (train also) losdampfen

▶ **steam over** VI (window) beschlagen

▶ **steam up** **VT** sep window beschlagen lassen; **to be (all) steamed up** (ganz) beschlagen sein; (fig inf) (ganz) aufgeregt sein; **to get (all) steamed up** (ganz) beschlagen; (fig inf) sich aufregen, hochgehen (inf); **look at you, all steamed up about nothing** deine ganze Aufregung war umsonst **VI** beschlagen

steam: steam blower N (Tech) Dampf(strahl)-gebläse nt, Dampfstrahler m; **steamboat** N Dampfschiff nt, Dampfer m; **steam-driven** ADJ mit Dampfantrieb, dampfgetrieben; **steam engine** N Dampflok f; (stationary) Dampfmaschine f

steamer ['sti:mə'] N (= ship) Dampfer m; (Cook) Dampf(koch)topf m

steam: steam fitter N Heizungsinstallateur(in) m(f); **steam gauge**, (US) **steam gage** N (Tech) Dampfdruckmesser m; **steam hammer** N Dampfhammer m; **steam heating** N Dampfheizung f

steaming ['sti:mɪŋ] ADJ (inf) **a** (= angry) person, letter wütend **b** (Scot, = drunk) voll (inf), breit (inf)

steam: steam iron N Dampfbügeleisen nt; **steam radio** N (hum) Dampfradio nt (hum); **steamroller** N Dampfwalze f **VT** road glatt walzen; (fig) person überfahren; **they ~ed their way into the next round** sie bahnten sich unaufhaltsam den Weg in die nächste Runde; **to ~ a bill through parliament** (fig) ein Gesetz im Parlament durchpeitschen **ADJ** ~ **tactics** Holzhammermethode f (inf); **steam room** N Saunaraum m; (in Turkish bath) Dampfraum m; **steamship** N Dampfschiff nt, Dampfer m; **steamship company** N Dampfschifffahrtsgesellschaft f; **steamship line** N Schifffahrtslinie f, Dampferlinie f; **steam-shovel** N Löffelbagger m; **steam turbine** N Dampfturbine f

steamy ['sti:mɪ] ADJ (+er) dampfig, dunstig; jungle, swamp dunstig; room, atmosphere dampfig, voll Dampf; window, mirror beschlagen; (fig) affair, novel heiß; **it is so ~ in here** hier ist vielleicht ein Dampf!

stearin ['stɪərɪn] N Stearin nt

steed [sti:d] N (liter) Ross nt

steel [sti:l] **N** Stahl m; (= sharpener) Wetzstahl m; (for striking spark) Feuerstahl m; **he felt cold ~ between his ribs** er spürte den kalten Stahl zwischen den Rippen; **a man of ~** ein stahlharter Mann; **as hard as ~** stahlhart, so hart wie Stahl → **nerve** **ADJ** attr Stahl-; ~ **manufacture** Stahlproduktion f **VT** **to ~ oneself** sich wappnen (for gegen); (physically) sich stählen (for für); **to ~ oneself to do sth** allen Mut zusammennehmen, um etw zu tun; **to ~ oneself against sth** sich gegen etw hart machen or verhärten; **he ~ed his troops for the battle** er machte seiner Truppe Mut für den Kampf; (physically) er stählte seine Truppe für den Kampf

steel in cpds Stahl-, stahl-; **steel band** N Steelband f; **steel cable** N Stahlseil nt; **steel-clad** ADJ stahlgepanzert; **steel girder** N (Tech) Stahlträger m; **steel grey**, (US) **steel gray** N Stahlgrau nt **ADJ** stahlgrau; **steel guitar** N Hawaiigitarre f; **steel helmet** N (Mil) Stahlhelm m; **steel mill** N Stahlwalzwerk nt; **steel-plated** ADJ mit Stahlüberzug; (for protection) stahlgepanzert; **steel wool** N Stahlwolle f; **steel worker** N (Eisen- und) Stahlarbeiter(in) m(f); **steelworks** N sing or pl Stahlwerk nt

steely ['sti:lɪ] ADJ (+er) grip stahlhart; smile, expression hart; gaze hart, stählern; eyes stählern; determination eisern, ehern; (= grim) person knallhart; ~ **blue/grey** stahlblau/-grau

steelyard ['sti:lja:d] N Handwaage f

steely-eyed ['sti:lɪˌaɪd] N mit hartem or stählernem Blick

steep¹ [sti:p] ADJ (+er) **a** steil; fall tief; **it's a ~ climb** es geht steil hinauf; **there's been a ~ drop in the value of the pound** das Pfund ist stark gefallen **b** (fig inf) demand, price unverschämt; bill gepfeffert (inf), gesalzen (inf); **that's pretty ~!** das ist allerhand!; **it seems a bit ~ that ...** es ist ein starkes Stück, dass ...

steep² **VT** **a** (in liquid) eintauchen; (in marinade, dye) ziehen lassen; dried food, washing einweichen **b** (fig) **to be ~ed in sth** von etw durchdrungen sein; **~ed in history** geschichtsträchtig; **~ed in vice/prejudice** durch und durch verdorben/voreingenommen; **a scholar ~ed in the classics** ein Gelehrter, der sich in die Klassiker versenkt hat **VI** **to leave sth to ~** etw einweichen; (in marinade, dye) etw ziehen lassen

steepen ['sti:pən] **VT** steiler machen **VI** (slope) steiler werden; (ground) ansteigen; (fig) slump zunehmen

steeple ['sti:pl] N Kirchturm m

steeple: steeplechase N (for horses) Jagdrennen nt, Hindernisrennen nt; (for runners) Hindernislauf m; **steeplechaser** N (= horse) Steepler m; (= jockey) Reiter(in) m(f) in einem Jagdrennen; (= runner) Hindernisläufer(in) m(f); **steeplejack** N Turmarbeiter(in) m(f)

steeply ['sti:plɪ] ADV steil

steepness ['sti:pnɪs] N **a** Steile f, Steilheit f **b** (fig inf) Unverschämtheit f

steer¹ [stɪə'] **VT** (lit, fig) lenken; car also, ship steuern; person also lotsen; **to ~ a steady course** (lit, fig) einen geraden Kurs steuern; **to ~ a course through sth** (lit, fig) durch etw hindurchsteuern; **this car is easy to ~** der Wagen lässt sich leicht lenken **VI** (in car) lenken; (in ship) steuern; **to ~ due north** Kurs nach Norden halten; **~ left a bit** lenken or (in ship) steuern Sie etwas nach links; **to ~ for sth** auf etw (acc) zuhalten; (Naut) etw ansteuern, auf etw (acc) Kurs halten; (fig) auf etw (acc) zusteuern → **clear**

steer² N junger Ochse

steerage ['stɪərɪdʒ] N Zwischendeck nt

steerageway ['stɪərɪdʒweɪ] N Steuerkraft f

steering ['stɪərɪŋ] N (in car etc) Lenkung f; (Naut) Steuerung f

steering: steering column N Lenksäule f; **steering-column lock** N (Aut) Lenkerschloss nt; **steering committee** N Lenkungsausschuss m; **steering gear** N (of plane) Leitwerk nt; (of boat) Ruderanlage f; **steering lock** N Lenkradschloss nt; **steering wheel** N Steuer(rad) nt; (of car also) Lenkrad nt; **steering-wheel lock** N (Aut) Lenkradschloss nt

steersman ['stɪəzmən] N pl **-men** [-mən] Steuermann m

stein [ʃtaɪn] N Maßkrug m

stele ['sti:lɪ] N (Archeol) Stele f

stellar ['stelə'] ADJ stellar

stem [stem] ❂ 17.2 **N** **a** (of plant) Stiel m; (of woody plant, shrub) Stamm m; (of grain) Halm m; (fig, of family tree) Hauptlinie f, Hauptzweig m **b** (of glass) Stiel m; (of pipe) Hals m; (Mus: of note) (Noten)hals m; (in watch) Welle f; (of thermometer) Röhre f **c** (of word) Stamm m **d** (Naut) Vordersteven m; **from ~ to stern** von vorne bis achtern **VT** (= check, stop) aufhalten; flow of sth, tide, flood, losses, exodus also eindämmen; bleeding, decline also zum Stillstand bringen; inflation also, flow of words Einhalt gebieten (+dat) **VI** **to ~ from sth** (= result from) von etw kommen, von etw herrühren; (= have as origin) aus etw (her)stammen, auf etw (acc) zurückgehen; **what does this increase in inflation ~ from?** welche Ursachen hat diese Zunahme der Inflation?

stem christie [stem'krɪstɪ] N (Ski) Kristianiaschwung m

stem ginger N kandierter Ingwer

stemmed [stemd] ADJ Stiel-; ~ **glass** Stielglas nt

stem parallel N (Ski) (ausgestemmter) Parallelschwung m

stem turn N Stemmbogen m

stench [stentʃ] N Gestank m; ~ **trap** Geruchsverschluss m

stencil ['stensl] **N** Schablone f; (Printing: for duplicating) Matrize f **VT** mit Schablonen zeichnen; (Printing) auf Matrize schreiben

sten gun ['stengʌn] N (Mil) leichtes Maschinengewehr

steno ['stenəʊ] N (US, inf) = **stenographer, stenography**

stenographer [ste'nɒgrəfə'] N (US form) Stenograf(in) m(f)

stenography [ste'nɒgrəfɪ] N (form) Stenografie f

stentorian [sten'tɔ:rɪən] ADJ schallend; voice Stentor- (geh)

step [step] N **a** (= pace, in dancing) Schritt m; **to take a ~** einen Schritt machen; **~ by ~** (lit, fig) Schritt für Schritt; **we followed his ~s in the snow** wir folgten seinen Fußstapfen im Schnee; **he watched my every ~** (fig) er beobachtete mich auf Schritt und Tritt; **to watch one's ~** Acht geben; (fig also) sich vorsehen; **to be** or **stay one ~ ahead of sb** (fig) jdm einen Schritt voraussein **b** **to be in ~** (lit) im Gleichschritt or Tritt sein (with mit); (in dancing) im Takt sein (with mit); (fig) im Gleichklang sein (with mit); **to be out of ~** (lit) nicht im Tritt or im gleichen Schritt sein (with mit); (in dancing) nicht im gleichen Takt sein (with wie); (fig) nicht im Gleichklang sein (with mit); **to get out of ~** (lit) aus dem Schritt or Tritt kommen; (in dancing) aus dem Takt kommen; (fig) von der gemeinsamen Linie abkommen; **to keep in ~** (lit) Tritt halten; (fig) Schritt halten; **to break ~** (lit) aus dem Tritt kommen; (fig) aus dem Schritt kommen; **to fall into ~** (lit) in Gleichschritt fallen (with mit); (fig) in den gleichen Takt kommen (with wie) **c** (Brit: = distance) **it's (quite) a good ~ (to the village)** es ist ein ziemlich weiter Weg (bis zum Dorf), es ist ziemlich weit (bis zum Dorf); **it's only a few ~s** es sind nur ein paar Schritte **d** (= move) Schritt m; (= measure) Maßnahme f, Schritt m; **the first ~ is to form a committee** als Erstes muss ein Ausschuss gebildet werden; **it's a great ~ forward** es ist ein großer Schritt nach vorn; **that would be a ~ back/in the right direction for him** das wäre für ihn ein Rückschritt/ein Schritt in die richtige Richtung; **one can't take a single ~ without having to consult somebody** man kann (rein) gar nichts unternehmen, ohne fragen zu müssen; **to take ~s to do sth** Maßnahmen ergreifen, (um) etw zu tun; **to take legal ~s** gerichtlich vorgehen **e** (in process, experiment) Abschnitt m, Stufe f; (in learning, course) Stufe f, Lernschritt m **f** (= stair, fig, in scale, hierarchy) Stufe f; **~s** (outdoors) Treppe f; **mind the ~** Vorsicht Stufe **g** **steps** PL (Brit: = stepladder: also **pair of steps**) Tritt- or Stufenleiter f **h** (= step aerobics) Steppaerobic nt **VT** **a** (old) dance tanzen **b** (= arrange in steps) terrassenförmig anlegen, abstufen **c** ~ **two paces to the left** treten Sie zwei Schritte nach links **VI** gehen; **to ~ into/out of sth** (house, room, puddle) in etw (acc)/aus etw treten; (train, dress in etw (acc)/aus etw steigen; **to ~ on(to) sth** (plane, train) in etw (acc) steigen; (platform, ladder auf etw (acc) steigen; **to ~ on sth** (object, toy) auf etw (acc) treten; **he ~ped on my foot** er ist mir auf den Fuß getreten; **to ~ over sb/sth** über jdn/etw steigen; **please mind where you ~** geben Sie Acht, wo Sie hintreten; **~ this way, please** hier entlang, bitte!; **he ~ped into the road** er trat auf die Straße; **he ~ped into his father's job/shoes** er übernahm die Stelle seines Vaters; **to ~ into sb's boots** (Brit, Sport) in jds Fußstapfen treten; **to ~ on board** an Bord gehen; **to ~ inside** hineintreten; **to ~ outside** hinaustreten; (for fight) (mal eben) vor die Tür gehen; **~ on it!** mach mal ein bisschen (schneller)! (inf); (in car) gib Gas!

▶ **step aside** VI **a** (lit) zur Seite treten **b** (fig) Platz machen; **to step aside to make way for sb** jdm Platz machen

▶ **step back** VI **a** (lit) zurücktreten **b** (fig) **to step back from sth** von etw Abstand gewinnen; **let us step back into the 18th century** versetzen wir uns einmal ins 18. Jahrhundert zurück

▶ **step down** VI **a** (lit) hinabsteigen **b** (fig) **to step down for sb** or **in favour of sb** jdm Platz machen, zu jds Gunsten zurücktreten; **he decided to step down and not stand for the presidency** er beschloss, seine Kandidatur für das Amt des Präsidenten zurückzuziehen **c** (= *resign*) zurücktreten); **to step down as president/chairman** vom Amt des Präsidenten/Vorsitzenden zurücktreten

▶ **step forward** VI vortreten; (*fig*) sich melden

▶ **step in** VI **a** (*lit*) eintreten (*-to, +prep obj* in *+acc*); **she suddenly stepped into a totally new world** sie fand sich plötzlich in einer ganz neuen Welt wieder **b** (*fig*) eingreifen, einschreiten; (*interferingly*) dazwischenkommen

▶ **step off** VI *+prep obj* (*off bus, plane, boat*) aussteigen (*prep obj* aus); **to step off the pavement** vom Bürgersteig treten

▶ **step out** **VT** *sep* (= *measure*) abschreiten **VI a** (= *go out*) hinausgehen **b** (= *walk briskly*) zügig or schnell gehen, forsch ausschreiten (*liter*); (= *speed up*) schneller gehen **c** **to be stepping out with sb** (*dated*) mit jdm gehen

▶ **step up** **VT** *sep* steigern; *efforts also, security, campaign, speed, criticism, support, activities* verstärken; *pressure also, demands, volume, numbers, pace* erhöhen; *fight* steigern; **to step up a gear** (*fig*) eine Stufe höher schalten **VI a** (= *come forward*) vortreten; **to step up to sb** auf jdn zugehen/zukommen; **step up, ladies and gentlemen** treten Sie näher, meine Damen und Herren; **he stepped up onto the stage** er trat auf die Bühne; **he stepped up another rung** er stieg eine Sprosse höher **b** (= *increase*) zunehmen; (*rate, volume*) ansteigen

step- PREF Stief-; **stepbrother** Stiefbruder *m*; **stepchild** Stiefkind *nt*; **stepdaughter** Stieftochter *f*; **stepfather** Stiefvater *m*; **stepmother** Stiefmutter *f*

step aerobics N *sing* Steppaerobic *nt*

step-by-step ['stɛpbaɪˈstɛp] ADJ schrittweise

step-down ['stɛpdaʊn] ADJ (*Elec*) heruntertransformierend

Stephen ['stiːvn] N Stephan *m*

step: stepladder ['stɛpˌlædə'] N Stufenleiter *f*, Trittleiter *f*; **step-off** ['stɛpɒf] N Steilabhang *m*; **steppe** [stɛp] N Steppe *f*; **stepper motor** ['stɛpəˌməʊtə'] N Schrittmotor *m*; **stepping stone** ['stɛpɪŋˌstəʊn] N (Tritt)stein *m*; (*fig*) Sprungbrett *nt*; **step pyramid** N Stufenpyramide *f*; **stepson** ['stɛpsʌn] N Stiefsohn *m*; **step-up** ['stɛpʌp] **N** (*inf*, = *increase*) Anstieg *m*, Zunahme *f* (*in +gen*) **ADJ** (*Elec*) herauftransformierend; **stepwise** ['stɛpwaɪz] ADJ, ADV schritt- or stufenweise; **stereo** ['stɛrɪəʊ] **N** Stereo *nt*; (= *record-player*) Stereoanlage *f*; **in ~** in Stereo; **on the ~** auf dem einen Stereogerät **ADJ** Stereo-; **~ unit** Stereoanlage *f*; **stereophonic** [ˌstɛrɪəˈfɒnɪk] ADJ stereophon, stereofon; **stereophony** [stɛrɪˈɒfənɪ] N Stereophonie *f*, Stereofonie *f*, Raumklang *m*; **stereoscope** ['stɛrɪəˌskəʊp] N Stereoskop *nt*; **stereoscopic** [ˌstɛrɪəˈskɒpɪk] ADJ stereoskopisch; **stereotype** ['stɛrɪəˌtaɪp] **N a** (*fig*) Klischee (-vorstellung *f*), Stereotyp *nt*; (= *stereotype character*) stereotype Figur *f*; **the ~ of the Englishman** der typische Engländer **b** (*Typ*, = *plate*) Stereotypplatte *f*; (= *process*) Plattendruck *m* **ATTR** stereotyp; *ideas, thinking also* klischeehaft **VT a** (*fig*) *character* klischeehaft zeichnen or darstellen; **the plot of the Western has become ~d** die Handlung des Westerns ist zu einem Klischee geworden; **I don't like being ~d** ich lasse mich nicht gern in ein Klischee zwängen **b** (*Typ*) stereotypieren; **stereotyped** ['stɛrɪəˌtaɪpt] ADJ **a** = **stereotype** attr; **stereotypical** [ˌstɪərɪəˈtɪpɪkl] ADJ stereotyp; **sterile** ['stɛraɪl] ADJ **a** *animal, soil* unfruchtbar; *person* steril, unfruchtbar; (*fig*, = *fruitless*) ergebnislos, unfruchtbar **b** (= *germ-free*) steril, keimfrei; (*fig*) steril; **sterility** [stɛˈrɪlɪtɪ] N **a** (*of animal, soil*) Unfruchtbarkeit *f*; (*of person also*) Sterilität *f*; (*fig*, = *fruitlessness also*) Ergebnislosigkeit *f* **b** (= *absence of contamination, fig*) Sterilität *f*; **sterilization** [ˌstɛrɪlaɪˈzeɪʃən] N Sterilisierung *f*, Sterilisation *f*; (*of person also*) Sterilisation *f*; **sterilize** ['stɛrɪlaɪz] VT *person, instruments* sterilisieren; **sterilizer** ['stɛrɪlaɪzə'] N (*for instruments*) Sterilisator *m*; **sterling** ['stɜːlɪŋ] **ADJ a** (*Fin*) Sterling-; **in pounds ~** in Pfund Sterling **b** (*fig*) gediegen; *character* lauter **c** **~**

cutlery Silberbesteck *nt* **N a** *no art* (= *money*) das Pfund Sterling, (*das englische Pfund*) in ~ in Pfund Sterling **b** (= *silver*) (Sterling)silber *nt* **ADJ** *attr* aus (Sterling)silber; **sterling area** N Sterlinggebiet *nt*, Sterlingblock *m*; **sterling silver** N Sterlingsilber *nt*; **stern**[1] [stɜːn] N (*Naut*) Heck *nt*; (*fig hum, of person*) Hinterteil *nt*; **the ~ of the ship** das Achterschiff; **stern**[2] ADJ (*+er*) (= *strict*) streng; *words also, character, warning* ernst; (= *tough*) *test* hart; *opposition* stark, hart; **with a ~ face** mit strenger Miene; **made of ~er stuff** aus härterem Holz geschnitzt; **sternly** ['stɜːnlɪ] ADV **a** (= *severely*) *say, rebuke* ernsthaft; *look* streng; *warn* ernst; **a ~ worded statement** eine streng formulierte Aussage; **to deal ~ with sb/sth** streng mit jdm/etw umgehen **b** (= *firmly*) *forbid* streng; *oppose, resist* eisern; **sternmost** ['stɜːnməʊst] ADJ achterste(r, s); **sternness** ['stɜːnnɪs] N Strenge *f*; (*of words also, character, warning*) Ernst *m*; **sternum** ['stɜːnəm] N Brustbein *nt*, Sternum *nt* (*spec*); **sternway** ['stɜːnweɪ] N (*Naut*) Heckfahrt *f*; **sternwheeler** ['stɜːnˌwiːlə'] N Heckraddampfer *m*; **steroid** ['stɪərɔɪd] N Steroid *nt*; **stertorous** ['stɜːtərəs] ADJ (*liter*) *breathing* röchelnd, rasselnd; **stet** [stɛt] (*Typ*) **INTERJ** stehen lassen (*Punkte unter falscher Korrektur*) **VT** die Korrektur (*+gen*) rückgängig machen; **stethoscope** ['stɛθəskəʊp] N Stethoskop *nt*; **stetson** ['stɛtsən] N Stetson *m*, Texashut *m*; **stevedore** ['stiːvɪdɔː'] N Stauer *m*, Schauermann *m*; **stew** [stjuː] **N a** Eintopf *m* → **Irish stew b** (*inf*) **to be in a ~ (over sth)** (*über etw acc*) *or* wegen etw) (ganz) aufgeregt sein **c** (*obs*, = *brothel*) Bordell *nt* **VT a** *meat* schmoren; **~ed apples** Apfelkompott *nt*; **the tea was ~ed** der Tee war bitter geworden **b** **to be ~ed** (*inf*, = *drunk*) voll sein (*inf*); **to get ~ed** sich voll laufen lassen (*inf*) **VI** (*meat*) schmoren; (*fruit*) dünsten; (*inf: tea*) bitter werden; **to let sb ~** or **to leave sb to ~ (in his/her own juice)** jdn (im eigenen Saft) schmoren lassen; **steward** ['stjuːəd] N Steward *m*; (*on estate etc*) Verwalter(in) *m(f)*; (*at dance, meeting*) Ordner(in) *m(f)*; (= *bouncer*) Türsteher(in) *m(f)*; (= *shop steward*) (gewerkschaftlicher) Vertrauensmann (*im Betrieb*); **stewardess** [ˌstjuːəˈdɛs] N Stewardess *f*; **stewardship** ['stjuːədʃɪp] N Verwaltung *f*; (= *rank, duties*) Verwalteramt *nt*

stewing ['stjuːɪŋ]: **stewing pan** N Kasserolle *f*, Bratentopf *m*; **stewing steak** N (*Brit*) Rindfleisch *nt* für Eintopf

stewpot N Schmortopf *m*

St. Ex. *abbr of* **Stock Exchange**

stick[1] [stɪk] **N a** Stock *m*; (= *twig*) Zweig *m*; (= *conductor's baton*) Taktstock *m*; (= *hockey stick*) Schläger *m*; (= *drumstick*) Schlegel *m*; **it was used as a ~ to beat us with** (*fig*) es wurde gegen uns verwendet; **he might try to use the vote as a ~ to beat striking coal miners with** vielleicht versucht er, die Abstimmung als Peitsche gegen die streikenden Bergarbeiter einzusetzen; **to give sb the ~, to take the ~ to sb** jdm eine Tracht Prügel geben; **to give sb/sth some/a lot of ~** (*Brit inf*, = *criticize*) jdn/etw heruntermachen (*inf*) or herunterputzen (*inf*); **to take (a lot of) ~** (*Brit inf*) viel einstecken (müssen); **just a few ~s of furniture** nur ein paar Möbelstücke; **to carry a big ~** (*fig*) Macht haben; **they adopted the policy of the big ~** sie holten den großen Knüppel raus (*inf*); **to get hold of the wrong end of the ~** (*fig inf*) etw falsch verstehen → **carrot**

b (*of sealing wax, celery, rhubarb, dynamite*) Stange *f*; (*of chalk, shaving soap*) Stück *nt*; (*Aviat*, = *joystick*) Steuerknüppel *m*; (*of bombs*) Bombenladung *f* für Reihenabwurf; (*Typ*) Winkelhaken *m*; **a ~ deodorant** ein Deodorant ~, **a ~ of deodorant** ein Deostift *m*; **a ~ of rock** eine Zuckerstange

c (*Brit inf*: = *person*) Kerl *m* (*inf*); **he's/she's a funny old ~** er/sie ist ein komischer Kauz; **he's/she's such a dry old ~** er/sie ist ein solcher Stockfisch

d **the ~s** (*Horse Racing inf*) die Hürden *pl*

e **in the ~s** (= *backwoods*) in der hintersten or finsteren Provinz **VT** *plants* stützen

stick[2] *pret, ptp* **stuck** **VT a** (*with glue etc*) kleben; **to ~ a stamp on sth** eine Briefmarke auf etw (*acc*) kleben; **please ~ the posters to the walls with pins** bitte die Poster mit Stecknadeln an den Wänden befestigen; **is this glue strong enough to ~ it?** wird dieser Klebstoff das halten?; **to ~ the blame on sb** jdm die Schuld zuschieben

b (= *pin*) stecken; **he stuck a badge on his lapel** er steckte sich (*dat*) ein Abzeichen ans Revers; **he stuck a badge on her** er steckte ihr ein Abzeichen an

c (= *jab*) *knife, sword etc* stoßen; **he stuck a knife into her arm** er stieß ihr ein Messer in den Arm; **he stuck a pin into his finger** (*accidentally*) er hat sich (*dat*) mit einer Nadel in den Finger gestochen → *also* **stick in**

d *pig* (ab)stechen; **he stuck him with his bayonet** er spießte ihn mit dem Bajonett auf

e (*inf*: = *place, put*) tun (*inf*); (*esp in sth*) stecken (*inf*); **~ it on the shelf** tus ins or aufs Regal; **he stuck his head round the corner** er steckte seinen Kopf um die Ecke; **to ~ one's hat on** sich (*dat*) den Hut aufsetzen; **he stuck a drink in my hand and a record on the turntable** er drückte mir ein Glas in die Hand und legte eine Platte auf; **you know where you can ~ that** (*inf*) du kannst mich am Arsch lecken! (*vulg*); **I'll tell him where he can ~ his job!** (*inf*) den Job kann er sich (*dat*) sonst wohin stecken (*inf*)

f (= *decorate*: *with pearls*) besetzen

g (*Brit, inf*: = *tolerate*) aushalten; *pace, pressure of work* durchhalten; **I can't ~ him/that** ich kann ihn/das nicht ausstehen (*inf*); **I can't ~ it any longer!** ich halte das nicht mehr (länger) aus!

h **to ~ sb with sth** (*inf*) (= *lumber*) jdm etw aufladen or aufhalsen (*inf*); (*with bill*) jdm etw andrehen

VI a (*glue, burr etc*) kleben (*to an +dat*); **to make a charge ~** genügend Beweismaterial haben; **you'll never make it ~!** damit kommen Sie nie durch!; **how do they hope to make the charge ~?** wie wollen sie das (je) beweisen?; **the name seems to have stuck to her** der Name scheint ihm/ihr geblieben zu sein

b (= *become caught, wedged etc*) stecken bleiben; (*drawer, window*) klemmen; **the word "please" seems to ~ in his throat** sie scheint das Wort „bitte" nicht über die Lippen bringen zu können → **stuck**

c (*sth pointed*) stecken (*in in +dat*); **it stuck in my foot** das ist mir im Fuß stecken geblieben

d (*Cards*) halten

e (= *project*) **his toes are ~ing through his socks** seine Zehen kommen durch die Socken; **we could see Manfred's head ~ing over the wall** wir sahen Manfreds Kopf über die Mauer gucken (*inf*); **a narrow finger of land ~ing into German territory** ein schmaler Landstreifen, der in deutsches Gebiet hineinragt

f (= *stay*) bleiben; (*slander*) haften bleiben; **to ~ in sb's mind** jdm im Gedächtnis bleiben; **to make sth ~ in one's mind** sich (*dat*) etw einprägen; **a teacher must be able to make things ~** der Lehrer muss den Stoff so bringen, dass er haftenbleibt

▶ **stick around** VI (*inf*) dableiben; **stick around!** warts ab!; **he decided to stick around Bonn** er beschloss, noch in Bonn zu bleiben

▶ **stick at** VI *+prep obj* **a** (= *persist*) bleiben an (*+dat*) (*inf*); **to stick at it** dranbleiben (*inf*) **b** (= *stop at*) zurückschrecken vor (*+dat*); **he will stick at nothing** er macht vor nichts halt

▶ **stick by** VI *+prep obj sb* halten zu; *promise* stehen zu; *rules, principles* sich halten an

▶ **stick down** VT *sep* **a** (= *glue*) ankleben; *envelope* zukleben **b** (*inf*, = *put down*) abstellen; (= *write down*) aufschreiben

▶ **stick in** **VT** *sep* **a** (= *glue*) *stamps etc* einkleben; **to stick stamps in(to) an album** Briefmarken in ein Album kleben **b** (= *put in*) hineinstecken; *knife etc* hineinstechen; **to stick sth**

in(to) sth etw in etw (*acc*) stecken; (= *prick*) *knife, pin etc* mit etw in etw (*acc*) stechen; **he stuck his knife in(to) the table** er stieß das Messer in den Tisch; **she stuck a knife in(to) him** sie stieß ihm ein Messer in den Leib 🔲 (*knife, arrow*) stecken (bleiben)

▶ **stick on** 🔲 *sep* **a** *label, cover* aufkleben (*prep obj* auf +*acc*) **b** (= *add*) *money* draufschlagen; (+*prep obj*) aufschlagen auf (+*acc*) 🔲 **a** (*label etc*) kleben, haften (*prep obj* an +*dat*) **b** (*inf: on horse*) oben bleiben; **to stick on the horse** auf dem Pferd bleiben

▶ **stick out** 🔲 vorstehen (*of* aus); (*ears, hair*) abstehen; (*fig:* = *be noticeable*) auffallen; **his head was sticking out of the turret** sein Kopf sah aus dem Turm vor 🔲 *sep* **a** herausstrecken **b** (= *not give up*) durchhalten; **I decided to stick it out a bit longer** ich beschloss, noch ein bisschen länger durchzuhalten

▶ **stick out for** 🔲 +*prep obj* sich stark machen für

▶ **stick to** 🔲 +*prep obj* **a** (= *adhere to*) bleiben bei; (= *remain faithful to*) *principles etc* treu bleiben (+*dat*); (= *follow*) *rules, timetable, plan, policy, diet* sich halten an (+*acc*) **b** **the photographers stuck to her wherever she went** die Fotografen hefteten sich ihr überall an die Fersen **c** (= *persist with*) *task* bleiben an (+*dat*); **to stick to one's knitting** (*fig*) bei seinem Leisten bleiben

▶ **stick together** 🔲 zusammenkleben; (*fig: partners etc*) zusammenhalten

▶ **stick up** 🔲 *sep* **a** (*with tape etc*) zukleben **b** (*inf,* = *raise*) **stick 'em up!** Hände hoch!; **stick up your hand if you want to go** Hand hoch, wer gehen will; **three pupils stuck up their hands** drei Schüler meldeten sich **c** (*inf,* = *rob*) *bank* überfallen **d** (*inf*) **she just stuck up her nose and marched off** sie stolzierte erhobenen Hauptes weg; **don't stick your nose up at my cooking** rümpf bloß nicht die Nase über meine Kochkünste 🔲 (*nail etc*) vorstehen; (*hair*) abstehen; (*collar*) hochstehen

▶ **stick up for** 🔲 +*prep obj sb, one's principles* eintreten für; **to stick up for oneself** sich behaupten

▶ **stick with** 🔲 +*prep obj* bleiben bei; (= *remain loyal to*) halten zu; *the leaders* mithalten mit

stick: stick celery N Stangensellerie *m*; **stick control** N (*Aviat*) Knüppelsteuerung *f*

sticker ['stɪkə'] N **a** (= *label*) Aufkleber *m*; (= *price sticker*) Klebeschildchen *nt* **b** (*inf,* = *determined person*) **he's a ~** er ist zäh

stick figure N Strichmännchen *nt*

stickiness ['stɪkɪnɪs] N (*lit*) Klebrigkeit *f*; (*of atmosphere, weather*) Schwüle *f*; (*of air*) Stickigkeit *f*; **the ~ of the situation** die heikle Situation

sticking ['stɪkɪŋ]: **sticking plaster** N (*Brit*) Heftpflaster *nt*; **sticking point** N **the main ~ (in the discussion) was ...** der kontroverseste Punkt (in der Diskussion) war ...

stick insect N Gespenstheuschrecke *f*

stick-in-the-mud ['stɪkɪnðə,mʌd] (*inf*) 🔲 Muffel *m* (*inf*) 🔲 rückständig; *parents etc* also muffelig (*inf*)

stickleback ['stɪklbæk] N Stichling *m*

stickler ['stɪklə'] N **to be a ~ for sth** es mit etw peinlich genau nehmen

stick: stick-on ADJ zum Aufkleben; **~ label** Klebeetikett *nt*; **stick-out** (*US inf*) ADJ herausragend, Star- 🔲 Star *m* (*among* unter +*dat*); **stick pin** N (*US*) Krawattennadel *f*; **stick-to-it-ive** [stɪk'tuːɪtɪv] ADJ (*US inf*) zäh, hartnäckig; **stick-to-it-ive-ness** [stɪk'tuːɪtɪvnɪs] N (*US inf*) Zähigkeit *f*, Hartnäckigkeit *f*; **stickum** ['stɪkəm] N (*US inf*) Klebstoff *m*, Kleister *m*; **stick-up** N (*inf*) Überfall *m*

sticky ['stɪkɪ] ADJ (+*er*) **a** klebrig; *paint* feucht; *atmosphere, weather* schwül; *air* stickig; (= *sweaty*) *hands* feucht, verschwitzt; **I'm all hot and ~** ich bin total verschwitzt; **to have ~ eyes** verklebte Augen haben; **to be ~ with blood/sweat** blut-/schweißverklebt sein; **~ bun** ≈ Krapfen

m; **~ label** Klebeetikett *nt*; **~ tape** (*Brit*) Klebeband *nt*
 b (*fig inf*) *problem, person* schwierig; *situation, moment* heikel; **he was a bit ~ about it** er hat dabei Schwierigkeiten gemacht; **we had a ~ time in the discussion** wir hatten in der Diskussion ein paar heikle Augenblicke; **to go through a ~ patch** eine schwere Zeit durchmachen; **to find the going ~** sich schwer tun; **to come to a ~ end** ein böses Ende nehmen; **to be** or **to bat on a ~ wicket** in der Klemme sein; **he's got ~ fingers** (*Brit fig*) er hat lange Finger (*inf*)

stiff [stɪf] ADJ (+*er*) **a** steif; *corpse* starr, steif; *brush, bristles* hart; *dough, paste* fest
 b *resistance, drink, dose* stark; *fight* zäh, hart; *sentence, challenge, competition* hart; *opposition* stark, heftig; *breeze* steif; *climb, test* schwierig; *examination, task* schwer, schwierig; *penalty, punishment* schwer; *price, demand* hoch; **that's a bit ~** das ist ganz schön happig (*inf*)
 c *door, lock, drawer* klemmend
 d **to be ~ with cold** steif gefroren sein; **to go ~ with terror** in Angststarre verfallen; **to be (as) ~ as a board** or **poker** steif wie ein Brett sein
 e *smile* kühl; *bow, person, manner, atmosphere* steif
 ADV steif
 🔲 (*inf*) Leiche *f*

stiff: stiff arm N (*US*) **to give sb the ~** jdn mit ausgestrecktem Arm wegstoßen; **stiff-arm** VT (*US*) **to ~ sb** jdn mit ausgestrecktem Arm wegstoßen

stiffen ['stɪfn] (*also* **stiffen up**) 🔲 steif machen; *shirt etc* stärken, steifen; (*disease*) *limb* steif werden lassen; *resistance etc* verstärken 🔲 steif werden; (*fig: resistance*) sich verhärten; (*breeze*) auffrischen; **when I said this she ~ed (up)** als ich das sagte, wurde sie ganz starr

stiffener ['stɪfnə'] N (*for collar*) Kragenstäbchen *nt*; (= *starch etc*) Stärke *f*

stiffening ['stɪfnɪŋ] N Einlage *f*

stiffly ['stɪflɪ] ADV steif; *starched* kräftig

stiff-necked [,stɪf'nekt] ADJ (*fig*) halsstarrig

stiffness ['stɪfnɪs] N **a** Steifheit *f*; (*of corpse also*) Starre *f*; (*of brush*) Härte *f*; (*of dough, paste*) Festigkeit *f* **b** (*of resistance, opposition, dose*) Stärke *f*; (*of fight*) Zähigkeit *f*; (*of sentence, challenge, competition*) Härte *f*; (*of breeze*) Steifheit *f*; (*of climb, test, task*) Schwierigkeit *f*; (*of penalty, punishment*) Schwere *f*; (*of price, demand*) Höhe *f* **c** (*of door, lock, drawer*) Klemmen *nt* **d** (*of person, bow, manner*) Steifheit *f*

stifle ['staɪfl] 🔲 (= *suffocate*) ersticken; (*fig*) *laugh, cough* also, *rage, opposition* unterdrücken; **the heat nearly ~d them** sie sind fast umgekommen vor Hitze 🔲 ersticken

stifling ['staɪflɪŋ] ADJ **a** *fumes, smoke* erstickend; *heat* drückend; **it's ~ in here** es ist ja zum Ersticken hier drin (*inf*) **b** (*fig*) beengend; *situation* erdrückend; *atmosphere* stickig

stigma ['stɪgmə] N **a** *pl* **-s** (= *mark of shame*) Brandmal *nt*, Stigma *nt* **b** *pl* **-ta** [stɪg'mɑːtə] Wundmal *nt*; (*Rel*) Stigmatisierung *f* **c** *pl* **-s** (*Bot*) Narbe *f*, Stigma *nt*

stigmatize ['stɪgmətaɪz] VT **a** (*Rel*) stigmatisieren **b** **to ~ sb as sth** jdn als etw brandmarken

stile [staɪl] N (*Zaun*)übertritt *m*

stiletto [stɪ'letəʊ] N (*esp Brit*) **a** (= *knife*) Stilett *nt* **b** (*also* **stiletto heel**) Bleistift- or Pfennigabsatz *m*, Stilettoabsatz *m* **c** (*also* **stiletto-heeled shoe**) Schuh *m* mit Bleistift- or Pfennigabsatz

still¹ [stɪl] ADJ, ADV (+*er*) **a** (= *motionless*) bewegungslos; *person* bewegungs- or reglos; *sea, waters* ruhig; **to keep ~** stillhalten, sich nicht bewegen; **to hold sth ~** etw ruhig or still halten; **to be ~** (*vehicle, measuring needle etc*) stillstehen; **to lie ~** still or reglos daliegen; **to stand/sit ~** still stehen/sitzen; **my heart stood ~** mir stockte das Herz; **time stood ~** die Zeit stand still; **his hands were never ~** seine Hände ruhten nie; **~ waters run deep** (*Prov*) stille Wasser sind tief (*Prov*)

 b (= *quiet, calm*) still; **be ~!** (*US*) sei still!; **a ~ small voice** ein leises Stimmchen
 ADJ *wine* nicht moussierend; *drink* ohne Kohlensäure; **a ~ photograph** ein Standfoto *nt*
 🔲 **a** Stille *f*; **in the ~ of the night** in der nächtlichen Stille, in der Stille der Nacht **b** (*Film*) Standfoto *nt*; **~(s) photographer** Fotograf(in) *m(f)*
 VT (*liter,* = *calm*) beruhigen; *anger* besänftigen; *sounds* zum Verstummen bringen; *passion, pain* abklingen lassen, stillen; **to ~ sb's fears** jdm die Furcht nehmen
 🔲 sich legen; **the roar of the crowd ~ed to a murmur** der Lärm der Menge legte sich zu einem Murmeln

still² ADV **a** (*temporal*) noch; (*for emphasis, in exasperation, used on its own*) immer noch; (*in negative sentences*) noch immer, immer noch; (= *now as in the past*) nach wie vor; **is he ~ coming?** kommt er noch?; **she is ~ in the office** sie ist noch im Büro; (*with emphasis*) sie ist immer noch im Büro; **do you mean you ~ don't believe me?** willst du damit sagen, dass du mir immer noch nicht or noch immer nicht glaubst?; **it ~ hasn't come** es ist immer noch nicht gekommen; **I will ~ be here** ich werde noch da sein; **will you ~ be here at 6?** bist du um 6 noch da?; **the results have ~ to be published** die Ergebnisse müssen (erst) noch veröffentlicht werden; **the problems were ~ to come** die Probleme sollten erst noch kommen; **there are ten weeks ~ to go** es bleiben noch zehn Wochen; **there will ~ be objections, no matter ...** es wird nach wie vor Einwände geben, egal ...
 b (*esp US inf: also* **still and all**: = *nevertheless, all the same*) trotzdem; **~, it was worth it** es hat sich trotzdem gelohnt; **~, he's not a bad person** na ja, er ist eigentlich kein schlechter Mensch; **~, he is my brother** er ist trotz allem mein Bruder; **rich but ~ not happy** reich und doch nicht glücklich; **~, at least we didn't lose anything** na ja, wir haben wenigstens nichts dabei verloren; **~ what can you expect?** was kann man auch anderes erwarten?
 c (*with comp*) noch; **~ better** noch besser; **better ~, do it this way** oder ... noch besser, mach es so; **~ more (so)** because ... und umso mehr, als ..., und umso mehr, weil ...; **more serious ~** or **~ more serious is ...** noch ernster ist ...; **worse ~, ...** schlimmer noch, ... CONJ (und) dennoch

still³ N Destillierapparat *m*; (= *small distillery*) Brennerei *f*

still: stillbirth N Totgeburt *f*; **stillborn** ADJ (*lit, fig*) tot geboren; **the child was ~** das Kind war eine Totgeburt, das Kind kam tot zur Welt; **still hunt** N **a** (*Hunt*) Pirschjagd *f* **b** (*US inf fig*) heimliche Jagd (*for* auf +*acc*); **still life** N *pl* **still lifes** Stillleben *nt*; **still-life** ADJ *attr* **a ~ picture/composition** ein Stillleben *nt*

stillness ['stɪlnɪs] N **a** (= *motionlessness*) Unbewegtheit *f*; (*of person*) Reglosigkeit *f* **b** (= *quietness*) Stille *f*, Ruhe *f*

still room N (= *pantry*) Vorratskammer *f*

stilt [stɪlt] N Stelze *f*; (*Archit*) Pfahl *m*; **a house built on ~s** ein Pfahlbau *m*

stilted ['stɪltɪd], **stiltedly** ['stɪltɪd, -lɪ] gestelzt, gespreizt

stiltedness ['stɪltɪdnɪs] N Gestelztheit *f*, Gespreiztheit *f*

Stilton® ['stɪltən] N Stilton *m*

stimulant ['stɪmjʊlənt] 🔲 Stimulans *nt*, Anregungsmittel *nt*; (*fig*) Ansporn *m* ADJ anregend, belebend

stimulate ['stɪmjʊleɪt] VT **a** (= *excite*) *body, circulation, mind* anregen; (*cold shower, coffee etc*) *sb* beleben; (*Med*) stimulieren; *nerve* reizen; (*sexually*) erregen, stimulieren; (*fig*) *person* animieren, anspornen; (*mentally, intellectually*) stimulieren; *sb's interest* erregen; **to ~ sb to do sth** jdn anspornen or dazu animieren, etw zu tun; **to ~ sb into activity** jdn aktiv werden lassen **b** (= *increase*) *economy, sales etc* ankurbeln; *growth, production, market* stimulieren; (= *incite*) *response* hervorrufen; *criticism* anregen zu; **to ~ invest-ments** Investitionen anlocken

stimulating ['stɪmjʊleɪtɪŋ] ADJ anregend; *drug also* stimulierend; *bath, shower, walk, music* bele-bend; *prospect* ermunternd, animierend, beflü-gelnd; *experience (physically)* erfrischend, ermun-ternd; *(mentally)* stimulierend; **intellectually ~** intellektuell anregend *or* stimulierend; **visually ~** visuell anregend; **sexually ~** sexuell erregend

stimulation [ˌstɪmjʊ'leɪʃən] N **a** *(act, physical, mental)* Anregung *f*; *(from shower, walk etc)* bele-bende Wirkung; *(Med)* Stimulation *f*; *(sexual)* Stimulieren *nt*, Erregen *nt*; *(= state)* Angeregt-heit *f*, Erregung *f*; *(sexual)* Erregung *f*; *(fig: = in-centive)* Anreiz *m*, Ansporn *m*; *(intellectual)* Sti-mulation *f* **b** *(of economy, sales etc)* Ankurbe-lung *f (to +gen)*; *(of criticism)* Anregung *f (of zu)*; *(of response)* Hervorrufen *nt*

stimulative ['stɪmjʊlətɪv] ADJ anregend, bele-bend; *(esp Physiol)* stimulierend; **to have a ~ ef-fect on the economy** konjunkturbelebend wir-ken

stimulus ['stɪmjʊləs] N *pl* **stimuli** ['stɪmjʊlaɪ] An-reiz *m*, Ansporn *m*; *(= inspiration)* Anregung *f*, Stimulus *m*; *(Physiol)* Reiz *m*; *(Psych)* Stimulus *m*; **it gave the trade new ~** das hat dem Handel neuen Aufschwung gegeben

stimy VT **= stymie**

sting [stɪŋ] *vb: pret, ptp* **stung** N **a** *(Zool, Bot: = organ, of insect)* Stachel *m*; *(of jellyfish)* Brennfa-den *m*; *(of nettle)* Brennhaar *nt* **b** *(of insect: = act, wound)* Stich *m*; *(of nettle, jel-lyfish, = act)* Brennen *nt*; *(= wound)* Quaddel *f* **c** *(= pain, from needle etc)* Stechen *nt*, stechen-der Schmerz; *(of antiseptic, ointment, from nettle etc)* Brennen *nt*; *(of whip)* brennender Schmerz; **there might be a bit of a ~** das brennt jetzt vielleicht ein bisschen; **we felt the ~ of the hail on our faces** wir spürten den Hagel wie Na-deln im Gesicht **d** *(fig, of remark, irony)* Stachel *m*; *(of attack, criticism etc)* Schärfe *f*; **a ~ of remorse** Gewis-sensbisse *pl*; **to take the ~ out of sth** etw ent-schärfen; *(out of remark, criticism also)* einer Sache *(dat)* den Stachel nehmen; **to have a ~ in its tail** *(story, film)* ein unerwartet fatales Ende nehmen; *(remark)* gesalzen sein; **death, where now thy ~?** Tod, wo ist dein Stachel?
VT **a** *(insect)* stechen; *(jellyfish)* verbrennen; **she was stung by the nettles** sie hat sich an den Nesseln verbrannt **b** **the hail stung our faces** der Hagel stach uns wie mit Nadeln im Gesicht **c** *(comments, sarcasm etc)* treffen, schmerzen; *(remorse, conscience)* quälen; **he was stung by their insults** ihre Beleidigungen haben ihn sehr getroffen *or* geschmerzt; **to ~ sb into doing sth** jdn antreiben, etw zu tun; **he was stung into replying** er ließ sich dazu hinreißen zu antwor-ten; **to ~ sb into action** jdn aktiv werden las-sen **d** *(inf)* **to ~ sb for sth** jdn bei etw ausnehmen *(inf)* or schröpfen *(inf)*; **could I ~ you for a fiv-er?** kann ich dir einen Fünfer abknöpfen? *(inf)*
VI **a** *(insect)* stechen; *(nettle, jellyfish etc)* bren-nen; *(= burn: eyes, cut, ointment etc)* brennen; **smoke makes your eyes ~** Rauch brennt in den Augen **b** *(hail etc)* wie mit Nadeln stechen **c** *(comments, sarcasm etc)* schmerzen

stingaree ['stɪŋəriː] N *(US, Austral)* Stachelro-chen *m*

stinger ['stɪŋə'] N **a** *(= cocktail)* Stinger *m* **b** *(US, = insect)* stechendes Insekt **c** *(US, inf, = re-mark)* Stichelei *f*, Spitze *f*

stingily ['stɪndʒɪlɪ] ADV *(inf)* knauserig *(inf)*, knickerig *(inf)*; **he ~ donated a mere 20p** knauserig *or* knickerig, wie er ist, hat er nur 20 Pence gespendet *(inf)*

stinginess ['stɪndʒɪnɪs] N *(inf, of person, govern-ment)* Geiz *m*, Knauserigkeit *f (inf)*, Knickerig-keit *f (inf)*; *(of sum, portion, donation)* Schäbig-keit *f*, Popeligkeit *f (inf)*

stinging ['stɪŋɪŋ] ADJ **a** *pain, sensation, blow* ste-chend; *cut, slap, ointment* brennend; *rain* peit-schend; *wind* scharf **b** *(fig) comment* stechend, schneidend; *attack* scharf N *(= sensation)* Ste-chen *nt*

stinging nettle N Brennnessel *f*

stingray ['stɪŋreɪ] N Stachelrochen *m*

stingy ['stɪndʒɪ] ADJ *(+er) (inf) person, government* geizig, knauserig *(inf)*, knickerig *(inf)*; *sum, por-tion, donation* schäbig, popelig *(inf)*; **to be ~ with sth** mit etw knausern

stink [stɪŋk] *vb: pret* **stank**, *ptp* **stunk** N **a** *(lit: = unpleasant smell)* Gestank *m* (of nach); *(fig, of corruption etc)* (Ge)ruch *m* **b** *(inf, = fuss, scan-dal)* Knatsch *(inf)*, Stunk *(inf) m*; **to kick up** *or* **make a ~** Stunk machen *(inf)* VI **a** *(lit: = smell unpleasant)* stinken; **it ~s in here** hier (drin) stinkts; **it ~s to high heaven** das stinkt zum Himmel *(inf)* **b** *(fig inf, = be bad)* sauschlecht *or* miserabel sein *(inf)*; **the idea ~s** das ist eine sauschlechte *or* miserable Idee *(inf)*; **the whole business ~s** die ganze Sache stinkt *(inf)*

▶ **stink out** VT *sep (Brit)* **a** *(inf) room* verstän-kern *(inf)* **b** *fox etc* ausräuchern

▶ **stink up** VT *sep (US inf) room* verstänkern *(inf)*

stink bomb N Stinkbombe *f*

stinker ['stɪŋkə'] N *(inf, = person)* Ekel *nt*, Fies-ling *m (inf)*; *(= problem, question)* harter Bro-cken, harte Nuss; *(= letter)* gesalzener *or* gehar-nischter Brief; **that problem/meeting was a ~** das war ein ganz verzwicktes *(inf)* Problem/ei-ne äußerst schwierige Besprechung

stinking ['stɪŋkɪŋ] ADJ **a** *(lit)* stinkend **b** *(inf)* beschissen *(inf)*; **you can keep your ~ money!** du kannst dein Scheißgeld behalten! *(inf)*; **I've got a ~ cold** ich habe eine Mordserkältung *(inf)* ADV *(inf)* **~ rich** *(Brit)* stinkreich *(inf)*

stinko ['stɪŋkəʊ] ADJ *(inf: = extremely drunk)* sturzbesoffen *(inf)*

stinky ['stɪŋkɪ] ADJ *(+er) (inf, = smelly)* stinkend

stint [stɪnt] N **a** *(= allotted amount of work)* Ar-beit *f*, Aufgabe *f*; *(= share)* Anteil *m*, Teil *nt or m (of an +dat)*; **to do one's ~** *(= daily work)* sei-ne Arbeit leisten *or* tun; *(= one's share)* sein(en) Teil beitragen *or* tun; **a 2-hour ~** eine 2-Stun-den-Schicht; **he did a five-year ~ on the oil rigs** er hat fünf Jahre auf Ölplattformen gearbeitet; **my ~ was from 3 to 6/lasted two hours** ich war von 3 bis 6/zwei Stunden lang dran; **he has done his ~ of washing up** er hat seinen (An)teil am Abwaschen geleistet; **would you like to do a ~ at the wheel?** wie wärs, wenn du auch mal fahren würdest?; **that was a long ~** das hat vielleicht lange gedauert!; **I've finished my ~ for today** für heute habe ich genug getan; **he does a ~ in the gym/at the computer every day** er betätigt sich jeden Tag eine Weile in der Turn-halle/am Computer **b** **without ~** ohne Einschränkung VT sparen mit, knausern mit; **to ~ sb of sth** jdm gegenüber mit etw knausern; *of praise, re-ward* jdm etw vorenthalten; **to ~ oneself (of sth)** sich (mit etw) einschränken VI **to ~ on sth** mit etw sparen *or* knausern

stipend ['staɪpend] N *(esp Brit: for official, clergy-man)* Gehalt *nt*; *(US: for student)* Stipendium *nt*

stipendiary [staɪ'pendɪərɪ] ADJ *official, magis-trate, duty* nicht ehrenamtlich; **~ allowance** Ge-halt *nt*, Bezüge *pl*

stipple ['stɪpl] VT *picture* in der Tupfentechnik malen; *paint* tupfen, in Tupfen auftragen VI die Tupfentechnik anwenden N Tupfen *pl*; *(= tech-nique)* Tupfentechnik *f*

stipulate ['stɪpjʊleɪt] VT **a** *(= make a condition)* zur Auflage machen, verlangen **b** *delivery date, amount, price* festsetzen; *size, quantity* vorschrei-ben, festsetzen; *conditions* stellen, fordern, sti-pulieren *(geh)*

stipulation [ˌstɪpjʊ'leɪʃən] N **a** *(= condition)* Auflage *f*; **with** *or* **on the ~ that ...** unter der Be-dingung *or* mit der Auflage, dass ... **b** *(= act of stipulating, of delivery date, amount, price, size,*

quantity) Festsetzung *f*; *(of conditions)* Stellen *nt*, Fordern *nt*, Stipulation *f (geh)*

stipulator ['stɪpjʊleɪtə'] N *(Jur)* Vertragspartei *f*, Kontrahent(in) *m(f)*

stir [stɜː'] N **a** *(lit)* Rühren *nt*; **to give sth a ~** etw rühren; *tea etc* etw umrühren **b** *(fig, = excitement)* Aufruhr *m*; **to cause** *or* **create a ~** Aufsehen erregen VT **a** *tea, paint, soup* umrühren; *cake mixture* rühren; **~ sugar into the mixture** den Zucker darunterrühren; **he sat there thoughtfully ~ring his tea** er saß da und rührte gedankenverloren in seinem Tee; **to ~ the pot** *(fig)* die Sache am Kochen halten **b** *(= move)* bewegen; *limbs* rühren; *water, waves* kräuseln; **come on, ~ yourself, we're late** *(inf)* komm, beweg dich, wir sind ohnehin schon spät dran; **if you want to pass the exam you'd better ~ yourself** wenn du die Prüfung beste-hen willst, solltest du dich besser ranhalten *(inf)* **c** *(fig) emotions* aufwühlen; *passion, controversy, memories* wachrufen; *imagination* anregen; *curios-ity* anstacheln, erregen; *blood* in Wallung verset-zen; *(= incite) person* anstacheln; *(= move) person, heart* rühren, bewegen; **to ~ sb to do sth** jdn bewegen, etw zu tun; *(= incite)* jdn dazu ansta-cheln, etw zu tun; **to ~ sb into action** jdn zum Handeln bewegen; **to ~ sb to pity** an jds Herz *(acc)* rühren, jds Mitleid erregen; **we were all ~red by the speech** wir waren alle von der Re-de tief bewegt VI **a** *(= move)* sich regen; *(person)* sich rühren, sich regen; *(leaves, curtains, animal etc)* sich be-wegen; *(emotion, anger etc)* wach werden; *(pity, love)* sich rühren, wach werden **b** *(inf, through gossip etc)* stänkern *(inf)*; **he's al-ways ~ring** er muss immer stänkern *(inf)*

▶ **stir up** VT *sep* **a** *liquid, mixture* umrühren; *cream* rühren, schlagen; *mud* aufwühlen **b** *(fig) curiosity, attention, anger, controversy* erregen; *memories, the past* wachrufen; *opposition, discord* entfachen, erzeugen; *hatred* schüren; *revolution, revolt* anzetteln; *mob* aufstacheln; *lazy person* aufrütteln; **to stir up trouble** Unruhe stiften; **to stir sb up to do sth** jdn dazu anstacheln, etw zu tun; **that'll stir things up** das kann heiter werden!; **he's always trying to stir things up a-mong the workers** er versucht immer, die Ar-beiter aufzuhetzen

stir-fry ['stɜːfraɪ] N Pfannengericht *nt* VT *(unter Rühren)* kurz anbraten

stirrer ['stɜːrə'] N *(Brit inf, = gossipmonger etc)* Stänkerer *m*, Stänkerin *f (inf)*; *(= troublemaker)* Scharfmacher(in) *m(f) (inf)*, Agitator(in) *m(f)*

stirring ['stɜːrɪŋ] ADJ *speech, music, scene, poetry* bewegend; *(stronger)* aufwühlend; *victory* bewe-gend; *days, times* bewegt N *(= development)* **a ~ of interest** ein sich regendes Interesse; **there were ~s of unease/discontent** Unbehagen/Un-zufriedenheit machte sich breit; **the first ~s of sth** die ersten Anzeichen *pl* von etw

stirrup ['stɪrəp] N Steigbügel *m (also Anat)*

stirrup: stirrup cup N Abschiedstrunk *m*; **stirrup pump** N Handspritze *f*

stitch [stɪtʃ] N **a** Stich *m*; *(in knitting etc)* Ma-sche *f*; *(= kind of stitch, in knitting etc)* Muster *nt*; *(in embroidery)* Stichart *f*; **to put a few ~es in sth** etw mit ein paar Stichen nähen; **to put ~es in a wound** eine Wunde nähen; **he had to have ~es** er musste genäht werden; **he needed ~es in his arm** sein Arm musste genäht werden; **to have the ~es taken out** die Fäden gezogen be-kommen; **a ~ in time saves nine** *(Prov)* was du heute kannst besorgen, das verschiebe nicht auf morgen *(Prov)* **b** *(inf, = piece of clothing)* **she hadn't a ~ on** sie war splitter(faser)nackt *(inf)*; **I haven't a ~ to wear** ich habe überhaupt nichts anzuziehen **c** *(= pain)* Seitenstiche *pl* **d** **to be in ~es** *(inf, from laughing)* sich schiefla-chen *(inf)*; **the story had us all in ~es** wir ha-ben uns alle darüber schiefgelacht *(inf)*; **he had us all in ~es** er brachte uns alle furchtbar zum Lachen *(inf)*

VT (*Sew, Med*) nähen; *book* (zusammen)heften, broschieren; (= *mend*) *hole, tear* zunähen, stopfen; (= *embroider*) sticken

VI nähen (*at* an +*dat*); (= *embroider*) sticken (*at* an +*dat*)

▶ **stitch down** VT *sep* festnähen

▶ **stitch on** VT *sep* aufnähen; *button* annähen

▶ **stitch up** VT *sep* **a** *seam, wound, patient* nähen; (= *mend*) *hole etc* zunähen, stopfen; (= *sew up*) *hem* hochnähen **b** (*Brit inf*: = *frame*) **I've been stitched up** man hat mich reingelegt (*inf*); (= *something has been foisted on me*) man hat mir das untergejubelt (*inf*) **c** (*Brit inf*) *agreement* zusammenstoppeln (*inf*)

stitching ['stɪtʃɪŋ] N (= *seam*) Naht *f*; (*ornamental*) Zierstiche *pl*, Ziernaht *f*; (= *embroidery*) Stickerei *f*; (*of book*) Broschur *f*

stitching: stitching machine N Stepp- *or* Heftmaschine *f*; **stitching needle** N Heft- *or* Stücknadel *f*

stitch-up ['stɪtʃʌp] N (*Brit, inf*) abgekartete Sache

stoat [stəʊt] N Wiesel *nt*

stock [stɒk] N **a** (= *supply*) Vorrat *m* (*of* an +*dat*); (*Comm*) Bestand *m* (*of* an +*dat*); **~ of knowledge** Wissensschatz *m*; **~ of information** Informationsmaterial *nt*; **to lay in a ~ of wood/candles** *etc* sich (*dat*) einen Holz-/Kerzenvorrat *etc* anlegen; **to have sth in ~** etw vorrätig haben; **to be in ~/out of ~** vorrätig/nicht vorrätig sein; **to keep sth in ~** etw auf Vorrat haben; **to get sth from ~** etw vom Lager holen; **to take ~** (*Comm*) Inventur machen; (*fig*) Bilanz ziehen; **to take ~ of sb** jdn abschätzen; **to take ~ of sth** (*of situation, prospects*) sich (*dat*) klar werden über etw (*acc*); (*of one's life*) Bilanz aus etw ziehen; **surplus ~** Überschuss *m*; **the ~ was auctioned** die Bestände wurden versteigert **b** (= *livestock*) Viehbestand *m*; **some good ~** schönes Vieh **c** (*Cook*) Brühe *f* **d** (*Fin*, = *capital raised by company*) Aktienkapital *nt*; (= *shares held by investor*) Anteil *m*; (= *government stock*) Staatsanleihe *f*; **to have** *or* **hold ~ in oil companies** Ölaktien haben; **~s and shares** (Aktien und) Wertpapiere *pl*, Effekten *pl* **e** (*Hort, of tree, plant*) Stamm *m*; (*of vine, rose*) Stock *m*; (*for grafting onto*) Wildling *m*, Unterlage *f*; (*for supplying grafts*) das Edelreis liefernde Pflanze **f** (*Bot*) Levkoje *f* **g** (= *tribe, race etc*) Stamm *m*; (= *descent*) Abstammung *f*, Herkunft *f*; (*Ling*) (Sprach)familie *f*, (Sprach)gruppe *f*; **to be** *or* **come of good ~** guter Herkunft sein; **to be from good farming ~** aus einer alten Bauernfamilie stammen **h** (= *handle*) Griff *m*; (*of rifle*) Schaft *m* **i** **to be on the ~s** (*ship*) im Bau sein; (*book etc*) in Arbeit sein **j** **stocks** **PL** (*Hist: for punishment*) Stock *m* **k** (= *neckcloth*) Halsbinde *f* **l** (*Rail*) rollendes Material **m** (*US, Theat*) **to play in summer ~** bei den Sommeraufführungen mitwirken; **this play is in their ~** dieses Stück gehört zu ihrem Repertoire

ADJ *attr* (*Comm, fig*) Standard-; **~ size** Standardgröße *f*; **~ response** Standardantwort *f*

VT **a** (*shop etc*) *goods* führen **b** (= *provide with stock*) *cupboard* füllen; *shop, library* ausstatten; *pond, river* (mit Fischen) besetzen; *farm* mit einem Viehbestand versehen

▶ **stock up** **VI** sich eindecken (*on* mit); (*squirrel etc*) einen Vorrat anlegen; **I must stock up on rice, I've almost run out** mein Reis ist fast alle, ich muss meinen Vorrat auffüllen **VT** *sep shop, larder etc* auffüllen; *library* anreichern; *farm* den Viehbestand (+*gen*) vergrößern; *lake, river* den Fischbestand vergrößern in (+*dat*)

stockade [stɒˈkeɪd] N (= *fence*) Palisade *f*; (= *area*) Einfriedung *f*, Umzäunung *f*

stock: stockbreeder N Viehzüchter(in) *m(f)*; **stockbreeding** N Viehzucht *f*; **stockbroker** N Börsenmakler(in) *m(f)*; **the ~ belt** (*Brit*) = die

reichen Villenvororte *pl*; **stockbroking** N Effektenhandel *m*, Wertpapierhandel *m*; **stock car** N **a** (*for racing*) Stockcar *m* (*frisierter, verstärkter Serienwagen*) **b** (*US, Rail*, = *cattle truck*) Viehwag(g)on *m*, Viehwagen *m*; **stock-car racing** N Stockcarrennen *nt*; **stock certificate** N (*esp US; Econ, Fin*) Aktienzertifikat *nt*; **stock character** N (*Theat*) Typ *m* (im Rollenfach); **stock company** N **a** (*Fin*) Aktiengesellschaft *f* **b** (*US, Theat*) Repertoiretheater *nt*; **stock corporation** N (*esp US; Econ*) **a** (= *incorporated company*) Kapitalgesellschaft *f* **b** (= *public company*) Aktiengesellschaft *f*; **stock cube** N Brüh- *or* Suppenwürfel *m*; **stock dividend** N (*esp US; Econ, Fin*) Dividende *f* in Form von Gratisaktien; **stock exchange** N Börse *f*; **stock farmer** N Viehhalter(in) *m(f)*; **stock farming** N Viehzucht *f*, Viehhaltung *f*; **stockfish** N Stockfisch *m*; **stockholder** N (*US*) Aktionär(in) *m(f)*; **stockholding** N **a** (*Comm*, = *storage*) Lagerhaltung *f*; (= *stock stored*) Lagerbestand *m* **b** *usu pl* (*Fin*) Aktienbestand *m*

stockily ['stɒkɪlɪ] ADV **~ built** stämmig

stockiness ['stɒkɪnɪs] N Stämmigkeit *f*

stockinet(te) [ˌstɒkɪˈnet] N (Baumwoll)trikot *m*

stocking ['stɒkɪŋ] N Strumpf *m*; (*knee-length*) Kniestrumpf *m*; (*of horse*) Fessel *f*; **in one's ~(ed) feet** in Strümpfen

stocking: stocking filler N kleines Geschenk (*für den Weihnachtsstrumpf*); **stocking mask** N Strumpfmaske *f*; **stocking stitch** N glatt rechts gestricktes Muster; **in ~** glatt rechts gestrickt

stock in trade [ˌstɒkɪnˈtreɪd] N (= *tools, materials, also fig*) Handwerkszeug *nt*; **that joke is part of his ~** den Witz hat er ständig auf Lager

stockist ['stɒkɪst] N (*Brit*) (Fach)händler(in) *m(f)*; (= *shop*) Fachgeschäft *nt*

stock: stockjobber N (*Brit*) Börsenhändler(in) *m(f)*; (*US, pej*) Börsenspekulant(in) *m(f)*; **stock list** N **a** (*Comm*) Warenliste *f* **b** (*Fin*) Börsenzettel *m*; **stockman** N **a** (*US, Austral*) Viehzüchter *m*; (= *farmhand*) Farmarbeiter *m* **b** (*US, in shop etc*) Lagerist *m*, Lagerverwalter *m*; **stock market** N Börsenmarkt *m*, Börse *f*; **stock option** N (*esp US; Econ*) Aktienbezugsrecht *nt* (*für Betriebsangehörige*); **stockpile** **N** Vorrat *m* (*of* an +*dat*); (*of weapons*) Lager *nt*; **the nuclear ~** das Atomwaffenlager, das Kernwaffenarsenal **VT** Vorräte an (+*dat*) ... anlegen; (*pej*) horten; **to ~ weapons** Waffenlager *or* Waffenarsenale anlegen; **stockpiling** ['stɒkˌpaɪlɪŋ] N Vorratsbildung *f*; **stock play** N (*Theat*) gängiges Repertoirestück; **stock room** N Lagerraum *m*, Lager *nt*; **stock-still** ADJ, ADV **to be/stand ~** stockstill sein/stehen; **stocktaking** N Inventur *f*; (*fig*) Bestandsaufnahme *f*; **stocktaking sale** N Ausverkauf *m* wegen Inventur, ≈ Jahresschlussverkauf *m*; **stock warrant** N (*esp US Fin*) (auf den Inhaber lautendes) Aktienzertifikat

stocky ['stɒkɪ] ADJ (+*er*) stämmig

stockyard ['stɒkjɑːd] N Viehhof *m*, Schlachthof *m*

stodge [stɒdʒ] N (*inf*) Pampe *f* (*inf*)

stodgy ['stɒdʒɪ] ADJ (+*er*) *food* pampig (*inf*), schwer; *style* schwerfällig; *subject* trocken; *book* schwer verdaulich; *person* langweilig, fad

stog(e)y, stogie ['stəʊgɪ] N (*US, inf*: = *cigar*) Zigarillo *nt*

Stoic ['stəʊɪk] N (*Philos*) **N** Stoiker *m* **ADJ** stoisch

stoic ['stəʊɪk] **N** Stoiker(in) *m(f)* **ADJ** stoisch

stoical ADJ , **stoically** ADV ['stəʊɪkə l, -ɪ] stoisch

Stoicism ['stəʊɪsɪzəm] N (*Philos*) Stoizismus *m*

stoicism ['stəʊɪsɪzəm] N (*fig*) Stoizismus *m*, stoische Ruhe, Gleichmut *m*

stoke [stəʊk] VT *furnace* (be)heizen, beschicken (*spec*); *fire* schüren; (*fig*) *inflation, fears, conflict, speculation* anheizen, schüren

▶ **stoke up** **VT** *sep furnace* (be)heizen, beschicken (*spec*); *fire* schüren; (*fig*) *conflict, pressure, inflation, violence* anheizen, schüren **VI** (= *eat*) sich satt essen (*on* an +*dat*); (= *drink*) tanken (*inf*)

stoke: stokehold N (*Naut*) Heizraum *m*; **stokehole** N **a** (*Naut*) Heizraum *m* **b** (*in furnace*) Schürloch *nt*

stoker ['stəʊkə] N Heizer(in) *m(f)*; (= *device*) Beschickungsanlage *f*

stole¹ [stəʊl] N Stola *f*

stole² *pret of* **steal**

stolen ['stəʊlən] *ptp of* **steal** ADJ gestohlen; *pleasures* heimlich; **~ goods** gestohlene Waren *pl*, Diebesgut *nt*; **to receive ~ goods** Hehler *m* sein; **he was charged with receiving ~ goods** er wurde wegen Hehlerei angeklagt *or* der Hehlerei bezichtigt

stolid ['stɒlɪd] ADJ *person* phlegmatisch, stur (*pej*); *indifference* stumpf; *determination, silence* beharrlich, stur (*pej*)

stolidly ['stɒlɪdlɪ] ADV phlegmatisch, stur (*pej*); *remain silent, work* beharrlich, stur (*pej*); **he is ~ British** er ist durch und durch ein Brite

stolidness ['stɒlɪdnɪs] N (*of person*) Phlegma *nt*, Sturheit *f* (*pej*); **the ~ of his manner** sein Phlegma *nt*, seine sture Art (*pej*)

stoma ['stəʊmə] N *pl* **-ta** (*Bot*) Stoma *nt* (*spec*)

stomach ['stʌmək] **N** (= *abdomen*) Magen *m*; (= *belly, paunch*) Bauch *m*; (*fig*, = *appetite*) Lust *f* (*for* auf +*acc*), Interesse *nt* (*for* an +*dat*); **to lie on one's ~** auf dem Bauch liegen; **hold your ~ in** zieh den Bauch ein!; **to have a pain in one's ~** Magen-/Bauchschmerzen haben; **to hit sb in the ~** jdn in die Magengrube/Bauchgegend schlagen *or* (*bullet etc*) treffen; **on an empty ~** (*drink, take medicine etc*) auf leeren *or* nüchternen Magen; **on an empty/full ~** (*swim, drive etc*) mit leerem *or* nüchternem/vollem Magen; **an army marches on its ~** (*prov*) mit leerem Magen kann man nichts Ordentliches zustande *or* zu Stande bringen; **I feel sick to my ~** (*fig*) mir ist speiübel; **I have no ~ for that** das ist mir zuwider; (*for party, journey etc*) mir ist nicht danach (zumute); **he doesn't have the ~ for it** (= *guts*) dazu hat er nicht den Mumm (*inf*); **to have a strong ~** eine guten Magen haben

VT (*inf*) *behaviour, rudeness, cruelty* vertragen; *person, film, music etc* ausstehen

stomach *in cpds* Magen-; **stomach ache** N Magenschmerzen *pl*; **stomach pump** N Magenpumpe *f*; **stomach trouble** N Magenbeschwerden *pl*; **stomach upset** N Magenverstimmung *f*

stomata [stəʊˈmɑːtə] *pl of* **stoma**

stomp [stɒmp] VI stapfen

stomping ground ['stɒmpɪŋgraʊnd] N Gefilde *nt usu pl*; **his old ~** seine alten Jagdgründe *pl*; **we were far from our usual ~** wir waren weit entfernt von unseren heimatlichen Gefilden; **it is a favourite ~ for collectors** es ist ein beliebter Tummelplatz für Sammler; **it's the ~ of a lot of students** es ist ein beliebter Studententreff

stone [stəʊn] **N** **a** Stein *m*; **a heart of ~** ein Herz aus Stein; **a ~'s throw from the station** nur einen Steinwurf *or* Katzensprung vom Bahnhof entfernt; **to leave no ~ unturned** nichts unversucht lassen; **to have a ~ in one's kidney/gall bladder** einen Nieren-/Gallenstein haben; **to be set** *or* **cast** *or* **carved in ~** (*fig*) in Stein gemeißelt sein **b** (*Brit*: = *weight*) britische Gewichtseinheit = *6,35 kg*

ADJ Stein-, aus Stein; **~ building** Steinbau *m*

VT **a** (= *throw stones at*) mit Steinen bewerfen; (= *kill*) steinigen; **~ the crows!** (*Brit, inf*) jetzt brat mir einer einen Storch! (*inf*) **b** (*esp Brit*) *fruit* entsteinen **c** (*inf*) **to be ~d** (*out of one's mind*) total zu sein (*inf*)

stone: Stone Age N Steinzeit *f*; **stone-blind** ADJ stockblind (*inf*); **stone-broke** ADJ (*US, inf*) = **stony-broke**; **stone circle** N (*Brit*) Steinkreis *m*; **stone coal** N (*Miner*) Anthrazit *m*; **stone-cold** ADJ eiskalt ADV ~ **sober** stocknüchtern (*inf*); **stone crusher** N (*Tech*) Steinbrechmaschine *f*; **stone-dead** ADJ mausetot (*inf*); **to kill sb/sth** ~ jdm/einer Sache den Garaus machen (*inf*); **stone-deaf** ADJ stocktaub (*inf*); **stone fruit** N Steinfrucht *f*; (*as collective*) Steinobst *nt*; **stone marten** N (*Zool*) Stein- or Hausmarder *m*; **stonemason** N Steinmetz *m*; **stone pit, stone quarry** N Steinbruch *m*; **stonewall** VI (*fig, esp Parl*) obstruieren; (*in answering questions*) ausweichen; (*Sport*) mauern (*sl*); **stonewaller** [ˈstəʊnˈwɔːlə] N (*Pol*) Obstruktionspolitiker(in) *m(f)*; **stoneware** N Steingut *nt* ADJ *attr* aus Steingut; **stone-washed** ADJ *jeans* stone-washed; **stonework** N Mauerwerk *nt*

stonily [ˈstəʊnɪlɪ] ADV (*fig*) mit steinerner Miene, starr

stoniness [ˈstəʊnɪnɪs] N (*of ground etc*) Steinigkeit *f*; (*fig, of look etc*) Versteinertheit *f*

stoning [ˈstəʊnɪŋ] N Steinigen *nt*, Steinigung *f*

stonking [ˈstɒŋkɪŋ] ADJ (*dated Brit inf*) irre gut (*dated inf*) ADV irre (*dated inf*); **to have a ~ good time** sich irre gut amüsieren (*sl*)

stony [ˈstəʊnɪ] ADJ (+er) *ground, beach* steinig; *texture* steinartig; (*fig*) *glance, silence* steinern; *person, welcome* kalt; *face* undurchdringlich

stony: stony-broke ADJ (*Brit, inf*) völlig abgebrannt (*inf*), total blank *or* pleite (*inf*); **stony-faced** [ˈstəʊnɪˈfeɪst] ADJ (= *solemn*) ernst; (= *impassive*) mit steinerner Miene; **stony-hearted** ADJ kaltherzig

stood [stʊd] *pret, ptp* of **stand**

stooge [stuːdʒ] N (*inf*) Handlanger(in) *m(f)*; (= *comedian's stooge*) Stichwortgeber(in) *m(f)*

stook [stuːk] N Hocke *f*

stool [stuːl] N **a** (= *seat*) Hocker *m*; (= *milking stool*) Schemel *m*; (*folding*) Stuhl *m*; **to fall between two ~s** sich zwischen zwei Stühle setzen; (= *be neither one thing nor the other*) weder dem einen noch dem anderen gerecht werden **b** (*esp Med*, = *faeces*) Stuhl *m*

stool pigeon N **a** (*lit, fig*, = *decoy*) Lockvogel *m* **b** (*inf*, = *informer*) Spitzel *m* (*inf*)

stoop[1] [stuːp] N Gebeugtheit *f*; (= *deformity*) krummer Rücken, Buckel *m*; **to walk with a ~** gebeugt gehen; **to have a ~** einen Buckel *or* einen krummen Rücken haben VT beugen; *head* (*to avoid sth*) einziehen VI sich beugen *or* neigen (*over* über +*acc*); (*also* **stoop down**) sich bücken; (= *have a stoop, walk with a stoop*) gebeugt gehen; **~ing shoulders** krumme Schultern *pl*; **to ~ to sth** (*fig*) sich zu etw herablassen *or* hergeben; **to ~ to doing sth** (*fig*) sich dazu herablassen *or* hergeben, etw zu tun

stoop[2] N (*US*) Treppe *f*

stooping [ˈstuːpɪŋ] ADJ gebückt, gebeugt, krumm

stop [stɒp] N **a** (= *act of stopping*) Halt *m*, Stoppen *nt*; **the signal is at ~** das Signal steht auf Halt *or* Stop; **to bring sth to a ~** (*lit*) etw anhalten *or* stoppen, einer Sache *dat* ein Ende machen; (*fig*) *project, meeting, development* einer Sache (*dat*) ein Ende machen; *conversation* etw verstummen lassen; **to come to a ~** (*car, machine*) anhalten, stoppen; (*traffic*) stocken; (*fig, meeting, rain*) aufhören; (*research, project*) eingestellt werden; (*conversation*) verstummen; **to come to a dead/sudden ~** (*vehicle*) abrupt anhalten *or* stoppen; (*traffic*) völlig/plötzlich zum Erliegen kommen; (*rain*) ganz plötzlich aufhören; (*research, project, meeting*) ein Ende/ein abruptes Ende finden; (*conversation*) völlig/abrupt verstummen; **when the aircraft has come to a complete ~** wenn die Maschine völlig zum Stillstand gekommen ist; **to make a ~** (*bus, train, tram*) (an)halten; (*plane, ship*) (Zwischen)station machen; **to put a ~ to sth** einer Sache (*dat*) einen Riegel vorschieben **b** (= *stay*) Aufenthalt *m*; (= *break*) Pause *f*; (*Aviat, for refuelling etc*) Zwischenlandung *f*; **to have a ~ for coffee** eine Kaffeepause machen;

to have a ~ Halt machen; **we had** *or* **made three ~s** wir haben dreimal Halt gemacht; **to work for eight hours without a ~** acht Stunden ohne Unterbrechung arbeiten

c (= *stopping place*) Station *f*; (*for bus, tram, train*) Haltestelle *f*; (*for ship*) Anlegestelle *f*; (*for plane*) Landeplatz *m*

d (*Brit*: = *punctuation mark*) Punkt *m*

e (*Mus, of wind instruments*) (Griff)loch *nt*; (*on organ: also* **stopknob**) Registerzug *m*; (= *organ pipe*) Register *nt*; **to pull out all the ~s** (*fig*) alle Register ziehen

f (= *stopper, for door, window*) Sperre *f*; (*on typewriter*) Feststelltaste *f*

g (*Phot*: = *f number*) Blende *f*

h (*Phon*) Verschlusslaut *m*; (= *glottal stop*) Knacklaut *m*

VT **a** (= *stop when moving*) *person, vehicle, clock* anhalten; *ball* stoppen; *engine, machine etc* abstellen; *blow* abblocken, auffangen; (= *stop from going away, from moving on*) *runaway, thief etc* aufhalten; *attack, enemy, progress* aufhalten, hemmen; *traffic* (= *hold up*) aufhalten; (= *bring to complete standstill*) zum Stehen *or* Erliegen bringen; (*policeman*) anhalten; (= *keep out*) *noise, light* abfangen, auffangen; **~ thief!** haltet den Dieb!; **to ~ a bullet** (*be shot*) eine Kugel verpasst kriegen (*inf*); **to ~ sb dead** *or* **in his tracks** jdn urplötzlich anhalten lassen; (*in conversation*) jdn plötzlich verstummen lassen

b (= *stop from continuing*) *activity, rumour, threat, crime* ein Ende machen *or* setzen (+*dat*); *nonsense, noise* unterbinden; *match, conversation, work* beenden; *development* aufhalten, (*temporarily*) unterbrechen; *flow of blood* stillen, unterbinden; *progress, inflation* aufhalten, hemmen; *speaker, speech* unterbrechen; *production* zum Stillstand bringen; (*temporarily*) unterbrechen; **he was talking and talking, we just couldn't ~ him** er redete und redete, und wir konnten ihn nicht dazu bringen, endlich aufzuhören; **the referee ~ped play** der Schiedsrichter hat das Spiel abgebrochen; (*temporarily*) der Schiedsrichter hat das Spiel unterbrechen lassen; **this will ~ the pain** das hilft gegen die Schmerzen

c (= *cease*) aufhören mit; **to ~ doing sth** aufhören, etw zu tun, etw nicht mehr tun; **she never ~s talking** sie redet ununterbrochen *or* in einer Tour (*inf*); **to ~ smoking** mit dem Rauchen aufhören; (*temporarily*) das Rauchen einstellen; **I'm trying to ~ smoking** ich versuche, das Rauchen aufzugeben *or* nicht mehr zu rauchen; **~ saying that** nun sag das doch nicht immer; **~ it!** lass das!, hör auf!; **I just can't ~ it** ich kann es nicht sein lassen

d (= *suspend*) stoppen; *payments, production, fighting* einstellen; *leave, cheque, water supply, wages* sperren; *privileges* unterbinden; *subsidy, allowances, grant etc* streichen; *battle, negotiations, proceedings* abbrechen; (= *cancel*) *subscription* kündigen; (*temporarily*) *delivery, newspaper* abbestellen; **the money was ~ped out of his wages** (*Brit*) das Geld wurde von seinem Lohn einbehalten

e (= *prevent from happening*) *sth* verhindern; (= *prevent from doing*) *sb* abhalten; **to ~ oneself** sich beherrschen, sich bremsen (*inf*); **can't you ~ him?** können Sie ihn nicht davon abhalten?; **there's no ~ping him** (*inf*) er ist nicht zu bremsen (*inf*); **there's nothing ~ping you** *or* **to ~ you** es hindert Sie nichts, es hält Sie nichts zurück **f** (*in participial construction*) **to ~ sb (from) doing sth** jdn davon abhalten *or* (*physically*) daran hindern, etw zu tun; (= *put a stop to*) dafür sorgen, dass jd etw nicht mehr tut *or* dass jd aufhört, etw zu tun; **to ~ sth (from) happening** (= *prevent, put a stop to*) (es) verhindern, dass etw geschieht; **that will ~ it (from) hurting** (= *prevent*) dann wird es nicht wehtun; (= *put a stop to*) dann wird es nicht mehr wehtun; **how can we ~ the baby (from) crying?** (= *prevent*) was können wir tun, damit das Baby nicht schreit?; **that'll ~ the gas (from) escaping/the pipe (from) leaking** dass wird verhindern, dass Gas entweicht/das Rohr leckt; **to ~ the thief (from) escaping** den Dieb an der Flucht hindern; **it will ~ you from worrying** dann brau-

chen Sie sich (*dat*) keine Sorgen zu machen; **to ~ oneself from doing sth** sich zurückhalten und etw nicht tun

g (= *block*) verstopfen; (*with cork, bung, cement etc*) zustopfen (*with* mit); (= *fill*) *tooth* plombieren, füllen; (*fig*) *gap* füllen, stopfen; *leak of information* stopfen; (*Mus*) *string* greifen; *finger hole* zuhalten; **to ~ one's ears with cotton wool/one's fingers** sich (*dat*) Watte/die Finger in die Ohren stecken

VI **a** (= *halt*) anhalten; (*train, car*) (an)halten, stoppen; (*traveller, driver, hiker*) Halt machen; (*pedestrian, clock, watch*) stehen bleiben; (*engine, machine*) nicht mehr laufen; **~ right there!** halt!, stopp!; **we ~ped for a drink at the pub** wir machten in der Kneipe Station, um etwas zu trinken; **to ~ at nothing (to do sth)** (*fig*) vor nichts Halt machen(, um etw zu tun); **to ~ dead** *or* **in one's tracks** plötzlich *or* abrupt *or* auf der Stelle stehen bleiben → **short**

b (= *finish, cease*) aufhören; (*heart*) aufhören zu schlagen, stehen bleiben; (*production, payments, delivery*) eingestellt werden; (*programme, show, match, film*) zu Ende sein; **to ~ doing sth** aufhören, etw zu tun, etw nicht mehr aufhören; **ask him to ~** sag ihm, er soll aufhören; **he ~ped in mid sentence** er brach mitten im Satz ab; **I will not ~ until I find him/convince you** ich gebe keine Ruhe, bis ich ihn gefunden habe/dich überzeugt habe; **if you had ~ped to think** wenn du nur einen Augenblick nachgedacht hättest; **~ to think before you speak** erst denken, dann reden; **he never knows when** *or* **where to ~** er weiß nicht, wann er aufhören muss *or* Schluss machen muss

c (*Brit inf*: = *stay*) bleiben (*at* in +*dat*, *with* bei); **to ~ for** *or* **to ~ to supper** zum Abendessen bleiben

▶ **stop behind** VI (*inf*) (noch) dableiben, länger bleiben; (*Sch, as punishment*) nachsitzen

▶ **stop by** VI kurz vorbeikommen *or* vorbeischauen; **to stop by sb's house** bei jdm hereinschauen (*inf*)

▶ **stop down** VI (*Phot*) abblenden, eine niedrigere Blende einstellen

▶ **stop in** VI (*Brit inf*) drinbleiben (*inf*); (*Sch, as punishment*) nachsitzen, dableiben

▶ **stop off** VI (kurz) Halt machen (*at sb's place* bei jdm); (*on travels also*) Zwischenstation machen (*at* in +*dat*); **let's stop off and pick up a pizza on the way home** lass uns kurz auf dem Heimweg eine Pizza mitnehmen

▶ **stop on** VI (*Brit inf*) (noch) dableiben, länger bleiben; **to stop on at school** in der Schule weitermachen

▶ **stop out** VI (*inf*) wegbleiben, streiken

▶ **stop over** VI kurz Halt machen; (*on travels*) Zwischenstation machen (*in* in +*dat*); (*Aviat*) zwischenlanden

▶ **stop up** VT *sep* verstopfen; *crack, hole also* zustopfen VI **a** (*inf*, = *stay up*) aufbleiben **b** (*Phot*) eine größere Blende einstellen

stop: stop-and-go traffic [ˈstɒpnˌɡəʊˈtræfɪk] N Stop-and-go-Verkehr *m*; **stop bit** N (*Comput*) Stopbit *nt*; **stop button** N Halteknopf *m*; **stopcock** N Absperrhahn *m*; **stopgap** N (= *thing*) Notbehelf *m*; (= *scheme*) Notlösung *f*; (= *person*) Lückenbüßer(in) *m(f)*; **stopgap measure** N Überbrückungsmaßnahme *f*; **stop-go** ADJ *attr* ~ **policies** Politik *f* des ewigen Hin und Her; **stoplight** N (= *brakelight*) Bremslicht *nt*, Stopplicht *nt*; (*esp US*, = *traffic light*) rotes Licht; **stop-loss order** [ˈstɒplɒsˌɔːd] N (*St Ex*) Stop-loss-Auftrag *m*; **stop-motion camera** [ˈstɒpˌməʊʃənˈkæmərə] N Zeitrafferkamera *f*; **stopover** N Zwischenstation *f*; (*Aviat*) Zwischenlandung *f*; **to have** *or* **make a ~** Zwischenstation/Zwischenlandung machen; **stopover ticket** N (*Aviat*) Rundreiseticket *nt*

stoppage [ˈstɒpɪdʒ] N **a** (*in work, game*) Unterbrechung *f*; (*in traffic*) Stockung *f*; (*in production etc, temporary, because of mechanical problems*) Unterbrechung *f*; (*for longer time, because of strike etc*) Stopp *m*; (= *strike*) Streik *m* **b** (*of pay, leave, cheque*) Sperrung *f*; (*of delivery, supplies etc*)

Stopp m; (= deduction) Abzug m **c** (= blockage) Verstopfung f, Stau m

stop payment N (Fin: for cheques etc) Zahlungssperre f

stopper ['stɒpə'] **N** (= plug) Stöpsel m; (= cork also) Pfropfen m **VT** verstöpseln

stopping ['stɒpɪŋ] N ~ **and starting** (in driving) stückchenweises Vorwärtskommen, Stop-and-go-Verkehr m; (in work) ständige Unterbrechungen pl

stopping: stopping place N (of bus, train etc) Haltestelle f; **this is an ideal** ~ das ist ein idealer Platz zum Haltmachen; **stopping train** N (esp Brit) Personenzug m

stop: stop press N (esp Brit, = space) Spalte f für letzte Meldungen; (= news) letzte Meldungen pl; **stop sign** N Stoppschild nt; **stop-watch** N Stoppuhr f

storable ['stɔːrəbl] **ADJ** goods etc lagerfähig, Lager- N lagerfähige Ware

storage ['stɔːrɪdʒ] N (of goods, food) Lagerung f; (of books, documents, in household) Aufbewahrung f; (of water, electricity, data) Speicherung f, Speichern nt; (= cost) Lagergeld nt; **to put sth into** ~ etw unterstellen, etw (ein)lagern → **cold storage**

storage: storage battery N Akkumulator m; **storage capacity** N (of computer) Speicherkapazität f; **storage charge** N Lagergeld nt; **storage device** N (Comput) Speichereinheit f; **storage heater** N (Nachtstrom)speicherofen m; **storage problems** PL Lagerungsprobleme pl; (in house) Probleme pl mit der Aufbewahrung, Platzmangel m; **storage space** N Lagerraum m; (in house) Schränke und Abstellräume pl; **storage tank** N Vorratstank m

store [stɔː'] **N** **a** (= stock) Vorrat m (of an +dat); (fig) Fülle f, Schatz m, Reichtum m (of an +dat); **~s** pl (= supplies) Vorräte pl, Bestände pl; **to lay in a ~ of food/coal** einen Lebensmittel-/Kohlenvorrat anlegen; **to have** or **keep sth in** ~ etw lagern, einen Vorrat von etw haben; (in shop) etw auf Lager or etw vorrätig haben; **to be in** ~ **for sb** jdm bevorstehen, auf jdn warten; **to have a surprise in** ~ **for sb** für jdn eine Überraschung auf Lager haben; **that's a treat in** ~ **(for you)** da habt ihr noch was Schönes vor euch, das ist etwas, worauf ihr euch freuen könnt; **what has the future in** ~ **for us?** was wird uns (dat) die Zukunft bringen?; **to set great/little** ~ **by sth** viel/wenig von etw halten, einer Sache (dat) viel/wenig Bedeutung beimessen; **a vast** ~ **of knowledge** ein großer Wissensschatz

b (= place) Lager nt; **he is** or **works in the ~s** er ist im Lager tätig; **to put one's furniture in** ~ seine Möbel unterstellen or (ein)lagern

c (Comput) (Daten)speicher m

d (= large shop, book store) Geschäft nt; (= department store) Kaufhaus nt, Warenhaus nt; (esp US, = shop) Laden m

ADJ attr (US) clothes von der Stange; bread aus der Fabrik

VT lagern; documents aufbewahren; furniture unterstellen; (in depository) einlagern; information, electricity, heat, energy speichern; (in one's memory) sich (dat) merken; (= equip, supply) larder etc auffüllen; **the cellar can** ~ **enough coal for the winter** der Keller hat genügend Platz für die Winterkohle; **to** ~ **sth away** etw verwahren; **squirrels** ~ **away nuts for the winter** Eichhörnchen legen einen Vorrat von Nüssen für den Winter an; **to** ~ **sth up** einen Vorrat an etw (dat) anlegen; (fig) einen anstauen; surprise etw auf Lager haben; **to** ~ **up trouble for sb/oneself** jdm/sich Ärger bereiten; **hatred ~d up over years** jahrelang angestauter Hass

VI (fruit, vegetables) sich lagern or aufbewahren lassen

store: store card N Kundenkreditkarte f; **store detective** N Kaufhausdetektiv(in) m(f); **storefront** ['stɔːfrʌnt] N (esp US) Ladenfront f; **storehouse** N Lager(haus) nt; (fig) Fundgrube f, Schatzkammer f; **storekeeper** N (in storehouse) Lagerverwalter(in) m(f), Lage-

---

rist(in) m(f); (esp US, = shopkeeper) Ladenbesitzer(in) m(f), Geschäftsinhaber(in) m(f); **storeman** N Lagerverwalter m, Lagerist m; (esp US, = shopkeeper) Ladenbesitzer m; **storeroom** N Lagerraum m; (for food) Vorratskammer f

storey, (esp US) **story** ['stɔːrɪ] N pl **-s** or (US) **stories** Stock(werk nt) m, Etage f; **a nine-storey building** ein neunstöckiges Gebäude, ein Gebäude mit neun Stockwerken or Etagen; **on the second** ~ im zweiten Stock(werk), auf der zweiten Etage; (US) im ersten Stock(werk), auf der ersten Etage; **he fell from the third-storey window** er fiel aus dem Fenster des dritten or (US) zweiten Stock(werk)s or der dritten or (US) zweiten Etage

-storeyed, (esp US) **-storied** [-'stɔːrɪd] ADJ suf -stöckig; **an eight-storeyed building** ein achtstöckiges Gebäude

stork [stɔːk] N Storch m

storm [stɔːm] **N** **a** Unwetter nt; (= thunderstorm) Gewitter nt; (= strong wind) Sturm m; **there is a** ~ **blowing** es stürmt; **come in and out of the** ~ kommen Sie herein ins Trockene; **to brave the** ~ dem Unwetter/Gewitter/Sturm trotzen; (fig) das Gewitter über sich (acc) ergehen lassen; **a** ~ **in a teacup** (Brit fig) ein Sturm im Wasserglas

b (fig, of abuse, insults) Flut f (of von); (of applause, indignation, criticism) Sturm m (of +gen); (of blows, arrows, missiles) Hagel m (of von); (= outcry) Aufruhr m; ~ **of protest** Proteststurm m; ~ **and stress** Sturm und Drang m

c **to take sth/sb by** ~ (Mil, fig) etw/jdn im Sturm erobern

VI **a** (= talk angrily) toben, wüten (at gegen); **he ~ed on for an hour about the government** er schimpfte eine Stunde lang wütend über die Regierung

b (= move violently) stürmen; **to** ~ **out of/into a room** aus einem/in ein Zimmer stürmen

c (esp US, Met) stürmen

storm: storm-beaten ADJ sea sturmgepeitscht; **stormbound** ADJ vom Sturm aufgehalten; **storm centre**, (US) **storm center** N Sturmzentrum nt; (fig) Unruheherd m; **storm cloud** N (lit, fig) Gewitterwolke f; **storm cone** N Sturmkegel m; **storm door** N äußere Windfangtür; **storm force** N Windstärke f; **storm-force** ADJ wind mit Sturmstärke wehend

stormily ['stɔːmɪlɪ] ADV (lit, fig) stürmisch; protest, reply, answer, react hitzig, heftig

storminess ['stɔːmɪnɪs] N (of reaction, temper) Heftigkeit f; **the** ~ **of the weather** das stürmische Wetter; **the** ~ **of his reception** sein stürmischer Empfang

storming ['stɔːmɪŋ] ADJ (inf: = impressive) performance, comeback stürmisch

storm: storm lantern N Sturmlaterne f; **storm-lashed** ADJ sea sturmgepeitscht; **storm petrel** N Sturmschwalbe f; **stormproof** ADJ sturmsicher; **storm signal** N Sturmsignal nt; **storm-tossed** ADJ (liter) sturmgepeitscht (liter); **storm trooper** N (NS) SA-Mann m; **storm troopers** PL (Sonder-)einsatzkommando nt; **storm troops** PL Sturmtruppe f; **storm warning** N Sturmwarnung f; **storm window** N äußeres Doppelfenster

stormy ['stɔːmɪ] ADJ (+er) (lit, fig) stürmisch; discussion also, temper hitzig; protests heftig; **he has a** ~ **temper** er ist jähzornig; ~ **waters** (fig) turbulente Zeiten pl

stormy petrel N Sturmschwalbe f; (fig) Unglücksbote m/-botin f

story¹ ['stɔːrɪ] N **a** (= tale) Geschichte f; (esp Liter) Erzählung f; (= joke) Witz m; **it's a long** ~ das ist eine lange Geschichte; **the** ~ **of her life** ihre Lebensgeschichte; **that's the** ~ **of my life** (inf) das plagt mich mein ganzes Leben lang! (inf); (said as a response) wem sagen Sie das! (inf); **that's another** ~ das ist eine andere Geschichte; **the** ~ **goes that ...** man erzählt sich,

---

dass ...; **his** ~ **is that ...** er behauptet, dass ...; **according to your** ~ dir zufolge; **I've heard his (side of the)** ~ ich habe seine Version gehört; **the full** ~ **still has to be told** die ganze Wahrheit muss noch ans Licht kommen; **that's not the whole** ~ das ist nicht die ganze Wahrheit; **your school marks tell their own** ~ deine Zeugnisnoten sprechen für sich; **to cut a long story short** um es kurz zu machen, kurz und gut; **it's the (same) old** ~ es ist das alte Lied; **but it's a different** ~ **now** aber jetzt sieht die Sache anders aus

b (Press, = event) Geschichte f; (= newspaper story) Artikel m; **it'll make a good** ~ das gibt einen guten Artikel

c (= plot) Handlung f

d (inf, = lie) Märchen nt; **to tell stories** Märchen erzählen

story² N (US) = storey

story: storyboard N (TV, Film) Storyboard nt; **storybook** **N** Geschichtenbuch nt **ADJ** attr castles, romance etc märchenhaft; ~ **ending** Ende nt wie im Märchen, Happyend nt, Happy-End nt; **story line** N Handlung f; **storyteller** N **a** (= narrator) Geschichtenerzähler(in) m(f) **b** (inf, = liar) Lügenbold m; **storytelling** N , no pl (spoken) Geschichtenerzählen nt; (written) Erzählkunst f

stoup [stuːp] N (Eccl) Weihwasserbecken nt

stout [staʊt] **ADJ** (+er) **a** (= corpulent) man untersetzt, korpulent; woman füllig; **to get** or **grow** ~ untersetzter/fülliger werden **b** (= strong) stick, horse etc kräftig; door, rope, wall, gate stark; shoes fest; coat dick **c** (= brave) heart tapfer; person beherzt; fellow, resistance beherzt, tapfer, mannhaft (liter); refusal, denial entschieden; belief fest; defence hartnäckig; opposition zäh; support solide; ~ **fellow!** (dated inf) tapferer Kerl! **d** (Brit) Stout m, dunkles, obergäriges Bier (= sweet stout) Malzbier nt

stouthearted ADJ , **stoutheartedly** ADV [ˌstaʊt'hɑːtɪd, -lɪ] tapfer, unerschrocken, mannhaft (liter)

stoutish ['staʊtɪʃ] ADJ person etc ziemlich dick, korpulent (geh, euph)

stoutly ['staʊtlɪ] ADV (= strongly) made solide; (= resolutely) resist, defend, fight tapfer, beherzt, mannhaft (liter); believe, maintain fest, steif und fest (pej); resist, refuse, deny entschieden; ~ **built** (person) stämmig, kräftig (gebaut); wall, door stark, kräftig; house solide gebaut; ~ **Catholic** etc gut katholisch etc

stoutness ['staʊtnɪs] N **a** (= corpulence) Untersetztheit f, Korpulenz f; (of woman) Fülligkeit f **b** (= sturdiness, of stick, horse) Kräftigkeit f; (of door, rope, wall, gate) Stärke f; (of shoes) Festigkeit f **c** (= resoluteness, of heart) Tapferkeit f; (of resistance also) Beherztheit f, Mannhaftigkeit f (liter); (of refusal, denial) Entschiedenheit f; (of belief) Festigkeit f

stove [staʊv] N Ofen m; (for cooking) Herd m; **electric/gas** ~ Elektro-/Gasherd m

stove: stove enamel N Einbrennlack m; **stovepipe** N Ofenrohr nt; **stovepipe hat** N (inf) Angströhre f (inf), Zylinder m

stow [staʊ] VT **a** (Naut) cargo verladen, (ver-)stauen; ship (be)laden **b** (= put away: also **stow away**) verstauen (in in +dat); **he ~ed the money (away) behind the clock** er versteckte das Geld hinter der Uhr **c** (inf, = desist) ~ **it!** hör auf!

▶ **stow away** VI als blinder Passagier fahren

stowage ['staʊɪdʒ] N (= stowing) (Be)laden nt, Stauen nt; (= space) Stauraum m; (= charge) Staugeld nt, Staugebühr f

stowaway ['staʊəweɪ] N blinder Passagier

strabismus [strə'bɪzməs] N (Med) Schielen nt

straddle ['strædl] **VT** (standing) breitbeinig or mit gespreizten Beinen stehen über (+dat); (sitting) rittlings sitzen auf (+dat); (jumping) grätschen über (+acc); (fig) differences überbrücken; two continents, border überspannen; periods gehen über; **he ~d the fence/horse** etc er saß rittlings auf dem Zaun/Pferd etc; **to ~ the border/ river** sich über beide Seiten der Grenze/beide Ufer des Flusses erstrecken; **to ~ an issue** (US, inf) in einer Frage zwischen zwei Lagern schwanken **N** (Sport) Grätsche f; (in high jump) Schersprung m

strafe [strɑːf] VT unter Beschuss nehmen; (with shells also) mit Granaten bewerfen; (with bombs) bombardieren

straggle ['stræɡl] VI **a** (= spread untidily, houses, trees) verstreut liegen; (hair) (unordentlich) hängen; (plant) (in die Länge) wuchern, in die Höhe schießen; **the town ~s on for miles** die Stadt zieht sich über Meilen hin **b** **to ~ behind** zurückbleiben, hinterherzockeln (inf); **to ~ behind the leader** in weitem Abstand hinter dem Führer zurückbleiben or hinterherzockeln (inf); **to ~ along the road** die Straße entlangbummeln or -zockeln (inf); **to ~ in/out** vereinzelt kommen/gehen; **stop straggling** bleibt beieinander

straggler ['stræɡlə] N Nachzügler(in) m(f)

straggling ['stræɡlɪŋ] ADJ **a** children, cattle etc weit verteilt; group of people ungeordnet; (= straggling behind) zurückgeblieben, hinterherzottelnd (inf); village sich lang hinziehend; houses zerstreut liegend; group, row of houses auseinander gezogen **b** (inf: also **straggly**) hair unordentlich, zottig; beard zottig; plant hochgeschossen; handwriting krakelig

straight [streɪt] **ADJ** (+er) **a** gerade; shot, pass direkt; stance, posture aufrecht; hair glatt; skirt, trousers gerade geschnitten; **your tie isn't ~** deine Krawatte sitzt schief; **the picture isn't ~** das Bild hängt schief; **your hem isn't ~** dein Saum ist nicht gerade; **to pull sth ~** etw geradeziehen; **is my hat on ~?** sitzt mein Hut gerade?; **please put the picture ~** bitte hängen Sie das Bild gerade hin; **hold yourself ~!** halte dich gerade!; **as ~ as a die** (Brit) kerzengerade; road schnurgerade; (= honest) grundehrlich; **to keep a ~ face, to keep one's face** ernst bleiben, das Gesicht nicht verziehen; **with a ~ face** ohne die Miene zu verziehen; **~ left/right** (Boxing) gerade Linke/Rechte
b (= clear) thinking klar; **to get things ~ in one's mind** sich (dat) der Dinge klar werden
c (= frank) answer, talking, question offen, direkt; piece of advice offen, ehrlich; denial, refusal direkt, ohne Umschweife; (= honest) person, dealings ehrlich; **to be ~ with sb** offen und ehrlich zu jdm sein; **to keep sb ~** dafür sorgen, dass jd ehrlich bleibt or nicht auf die schiefe Bahn gerät (inf); **to play a ~ bat** (Brit fig) ein faires Spiel spielen; **~ arrow** (US inf) biederer Mensch; (= man also) Biedermann m (inf)
d (= plain, straightforward) drink pur; (Pol) fight direkt; yes or no, choice, exam pass einfach; **~ A's** glatte Einsen pl; **she's a ~ A student** sie hat alles Einsen; **to vote the ~ ticket** (US, Pol) seine Stimme einer einzigen Partei (dat) geben; **he's a ~ Democrat** er ist ein hundertprozentiger Demokrat; **to have a ~ choice between ...** nur die Wahl zwischen ... haben
e (= continuous) ununterbrochen; **for the third ~ day** (US) drei Tage ohne Unterbrechung; **the ~ line of succession to the throne** die Thronfolge in der direkten Linie; **our team had ten ~ wins** unsere Mannschaft gewann zehnmal hintereinander or in ununterbrochener Folge; **in ~ sets/games** (win) ohne Satz-/Spielverlust; (lose) ohne Satz-/Spielgewinn, in aufeinander folgenden Sätzen/Spielen
f (Theat) production konventionell; actor ernsthaft; **a ~ play** ein reines Drama
g pred (in order) house, room ordentlich; paperwork in Ordnung; **to be (all) ~** in Ordnung sein; (fig: = clarified also) (völlig) geklärt sein; **now we're ~** jetzt haben wir die Sache geklärt; (= tidy) jetzt ist alles in Ordnung; **to put things ~** (= tidy) alles in Ordnung bringen; (= clarify) alles klären; **let's get this ~** das wollen wir mal klarstellen; **and get this ~** und damit wir uns richtig verstehen; **to put** or **set sb ~ about sth** jdm etw klarmachen; **if I give you a**

fiver, **then we'll be ~** (inf) wenn ich dir einen Fünfer gebe, sind wir quitt
h (inf, = heterosexual) hetero (inf); (= conventional) etabliert, spießig (pej)
i (Drugs inf) clean (inf); **I've been ~ for three years now** ich bin jetzt seit drei Jahren clean (inf)
ADV **a** hold, walk, fly, shoot, grow gerade; sit up, stand up aufrecht, gerade; hit genau; leap at, aim for direkt; above genau, direkt; across direkt; **~ through sth** glatt durch etw; **he came ~ at me** er kam direkt or geradewegs auf mich zu; **it went ~ up in the air** es flog senkrecht in die Luft; **to look ~ ahead** geradeaus sehen; **the town lay ~ ahead of us** die Stadt lag direkt or genau vor uns; **the airport is ~ ahead** der Flughafen ist geradeaus; **go ~ ahead with your plan** führen Sie Ihren Plan wie vorgesehen durch; **to drive ~ on** geradeaus weiterfahren; **he drove ~ into a tree** er fuhr direkt or voll (inf) gegen einen Baum; **the arrow went ~ to the target** der Pfeil traf genau ins Ziel; **to go ~** (criminal) keine krummen Sachen (mehr) machen (inf)
b (= directly) direkt; **I went ~ home** ich ging direkt or sofort nach Hause; **to look sb ~ in the eye** jdm direkt or genau in die Augen sehen
c (= immediately) sofort; **~ after this** sofort or unmittelbar danach; **~ away** or **off** sofort, gleich, auf der Stelle; **he said ~ off that ...** er sagte ohne Umschweife or sofort, dass ...; **to come ~ to the point** sofort or gleich zur Sache kommen
d (= clearly) think, see klar
e (= frankly) offen, rundheraus, ohne Umschweife; **I'll give it to you ~, you're fired** ich sage es Ihnen rundheraus or ohne Umschweife, Sie sind entlassen; **~ out** (inf) unverblümt (inf), rundheraus; **to give** or **tell sb sth/it ~ from the shoulder** jdm etw/es jdm unverblümt or ohne Umschweife sagen; **~ up, I got fifty quid for it** (inf) echt, ich habe fünfzig Pfund dafür gekriegt; **I got fifty quid for it ~ up?** (inf) ich habe fünfzig Pfund dafür gekriegt – echt? (inf)
f (Theat) play, produce konventionell
g drink pur
N **a** (= straight part) (on race track) Gerade f; (on road, Rail) gerade Strecke; **the final ~** die Zielgerade; **in the ~** auf der Geraden; **the ~ and narrow** der Pfad der Tugend; **to keep sb on the ~ and narrow** dafür sorgen, dass jd ehrlich bleibt or nicht auf die schiefe Bahn gerät; **to stay on** or **keep to the ~ and narrow** auf dem Pfad der Tugend bleiben
b (= straight line) Gerade f; **to cut sth on the ~** etw gerade (ab)schneiden; cloth etw am Faden(lauf) entlang schneiden
c (inf, = heterosexual) Hetero m (inf)

straight: straight angle N gestreckter Winkel, Winkel m von 180°; **straight arrow** N (US inf fig) grundanständiger Kerl; **straightaway** (US) **N** Gerade f; (on road, Rail) gerade Strecke **ADV** = straight ADV c; **straight edge** N Lineal nt

▶ **straighten** ['streɪtn] **VT** **a** (= make straight) back, legs etc gerade machen; picture gerade hinhängen; road, river begradigen; hat gerade aufsetzen; tablecloth, sheet, rope, clothes, tie gerade ziehen; wire gerade biegen; one's shoulders straffen; hair glätten **b** (= tidy) in Ordnung bringen **VI** (road, plant etc) gerade werden; (hair) glatt werden; (person) sich aufrichten **VR** **to ~ oneself** sich aufrichten

▶ **straighten out** **VT** sep **a** (= make straight) legs etc gerade machen; road begradigen; wire gerade biegen; rope gerade ziehen; hair glätten **b** (= put right) problem, situation klären; one's ideas ordnen; one's affairs, the economy in Ordnung bringen; misunderstanding (auf)klären; person (by discipline) auf die richtige Bahn bringen; **to straighten oneself out** ins richtige Gleis kommen; **the problem will soon straighten itself out** das Problem wird sich bald von selbst erledigen; **to straighten things out** die Sache geradebiegen or in Ordnung

bringen; (= clarify) Klarheit in die Sache bringen **VI** (road etc) gerade werden; (hair) glatt werden

▶ **straighten up** **VI** sich aufrichten **VT** sep **a** (= make straight) gerade machen; papers ordentlich hinlegen; picture gerade hinhängen; hat gerade aufsetzen; lines begradigen; **to straighten oneself up** sich aufrichten **b** (= tidy) in Ordnung bringen, aufräumen

straight: straight-faced ['streɪt'feɪst] **ADV** ohne die Miene zu verziehen **ADJ** **to be ~** keine Miene verziehen; **straight flush** N (Cards) Straightflush m; **straightforward** ADJ (= honest) person aufrichtig; explanation, look also offen, freimütig; (= simple) question, problem, situation, choice einfach; process unkompliziert; instructions einfach, verständlich; **I'm a ~ soldier** ich bin ein einfacher Soldat; **straightforwardly** ADV answer offen, freimütig; behave aufrichtig; **everything went ~** alles verlief nach Plan; **straightforwardness** N (= frankness, of person) Aufrichtigkeit f; (of explanation, look also) Offenheit f, Freimütigkeit f; (= simplicity) (of question, problem, situation, choice) Einfachheit f; (of process) Unkompliziertheit f; (of instructions) Einfachheit f, Verständlichkeit f; **straight-from-the-shoulder** [ˌstreɪtfrəmðə'ʃəʊldə] ADJ remark etc unverblümt; **straight-laced** ADJ = strait-laced; **straight man** N (Theat) Stichwortgeber für einen Komiker; **straight-out** **ADJ** (esp US, inf) resentment, threat unverblümt (inf), offen; opposition also kompromisslos; refusal, murder glatt (inf); **he's a ~ Democrat** er ist durch und durch Demokrat **ADV** (inf) unverblümt (inf), rundheraus; **straight run** N (Cards) Sequenz f; **straightway** ADV (liter) sogleich (liter)

strain[1] [streɪn] **N** **a** (Mech) Belastung f, Beanspruchung f; (on rope, arch) Spannung f, Belastung f; (on beams, floor) Druck m; **the ~ on a rope** die Seilspannung; **can you take some of the ~?** können Sie mal mit festhalten/mit ziehen?; **to put a (great) ~ on sth** etw (stark) belasten; **to show signs of ~** Zeichen pl von Überlastung or Überbeanspruchung zeigen; **to take the ~ off sth** etw entlasten
b (fig, mental, economic etc) Belastung f (on für); (= effort) Anstrengung f; (= pressure, of job etc also) Beanspruchung f (of durch); (of responsibility) Last f; **to be under a lot of ~** großen Belastungen ausgesetzt sein; **to suffer from (nervous) ~** (nervlich) überlastet sein, im Stress sein; **I find her/it a bit of a ~** ich finde sie/das ziemlich anstrengend; **to put a (great) ~ on sb/ sth** jdn/etw stark belasten; **to put too great a ~ on sb/sth** jdn/etw überlasten; **to show signs of ~** Zeichen pl von Überlastung or Überanstrengung zeigen; **to take the ~ off sb/sth** jdn/ etw entlasten; **the ~ of six hours at the wheel** die Anstrengung, sechs Stunden am Steuer zu sitzen
c (= muscle-strain) (Muskel)zerrung f; (on eyes, heart etc) Überanstrengung f (on +gen); **back ~** überanstrengter Rücken
d **strains** PL (of instrument, tune) Klänge pl; **to the ~s of** zu den Klängen (+gen)
VT **a** (= stretch) spannen
b (= put strain on) rope, beams, relationship, faith, budget belasten; nerves, patience, resources strapazieren; (= put too much strain on) überlasten; meaning, word dehnen; **it ~s my nerves** das zerrt an meinen Nerven; **to ~ one's ears/eyes to ...** angestrengt lauschen/gucken, um zu ...; **to ~ every nerve** jeden Nerv anspannen; **to ~ oneself** sich anstrengen; (excessively) sich überanstrengen; **don't ~ yourself!** (iro inf) überanstrenge dich bloß nicht!, reiß dir bloß kein Bein aus! (inf)
c (Med) muscle zerren; ankle, arm, neck verrenken; back, eyes, voice anstrengen, strapazieren; (excessively) überanstrengen; heart belasten; (excessively) überlasten
d (= filter) (durch)sieben, (durch)seihen; (= pour water off) vegetables abgießen; **to ~ off water** Wasser abgießen; **to ~ out solids** feste Stoffe aussieben

VI (= *exert effort*) sich anstrengen, sich abmühen; (= *pull*) zerren, ziehen; (*fig: = strive*) sich bemühen, streben; **to ~ to do sth** sich anstrengen *or* abmühen, etw zu tun; **to ~ at sth** sich mit etw abmühen; (= *pull*) an etw (*dat*) zerren *or* ziehen; **to ~ at the leash** (*dog*) an der Leine zerren; (*fig*) aufmucken, aufmüpfig werden (*inf*); **to ~ after sth** nach etw streben, sich um etw bemühen; **to ~ against sb** sich an jdn drücken; **to ~ against sth** sich gegen etw stemmen; **to ~ at a gnat and swallow a camel** (*prov*) Mücken seihen und Kamele verschlucken

strain² **N** **a** (= *streak*) Hang *m*, Zug *m*; (*hereditary*) Veranlagung *f*; **a ~ of madness** eine Veranlagung zum Wahnsinn **b** (= *style*) Anflug *m*; **there is a humorous ~ in his writing** seine Schriften haben einen humorvollen Anflug *or* Zug **c** (= *breed, of animal*) Rasse *f*; (*of plants*) Sorte *f*; (*of virus etc*) Art *f*; (*old: = race*) Geschlecht *nt* (*old*)

strained [streɪnd] **ADJ** **a** (= *unnatural*) *expression, performance, style* unnatürlich, gekünstelt; *laugh, smile, conversation* gezwungen; *economic situation, relationship* angespannt; *meeting* steif; *voice, relations, atmosphere, nerves* (an)gespannt; **he looked rather ~** er sah ziemlich abgespannt aus **b** *liquids* durchgesiebt, durchgeseiht; *solids* ausgesiebt; *vegetables* abgegossen **c** *muscle* gezerrt; *back, eyes* überanstrengt, strapaziert; **to have a ~ ankle** sich (*dat*) den Knöchel verrenkt haben

strainer ['streɪnə'] **N** **a** (*Cook*) Sieb *nt* **b** (*Tech*) Filter *m*

strait [streɪt] **N** **a** (*Geog*) Meerenge *f*, Straße *f*; **the ~s of Dover/Gibraltar** die Straße von Dover/Gibraltar **b** **straits** PL (*fig*) Nöte *pl*, Schwierigkeiten *pl*; **to be in dire** *or* **desperate ~s** in großen Nöten sein, in einer ernsten Notlage sein

straitened ['streɪtnd] **ADJ** *means* beschränkt; *circumstances also* bescheiden, dürftig; **in these ~ times** in diesen harten Zeiten

strait: **straitjacket** *n* (*lit, fig*) Zwangsjacke *f*; **strait-laced** [ˌstreɪt'leɪst] **ADJ** prüde, puritanisch, spießig (*inf*)

strand¹ [strænd] **N** (*liter, = beach*) Gestade *nt* (*liter*) **VT** *ship, fish* stranden lassen; *person (in place)* verschlagen, geraten lassen; (*without money, help etc*) seinem Schicksal überlassen; **to be ~ed** (*ship, fish, shipwrecked person*) gestrandet sein; (*person*) festsitzen; (*with out money also*) auf dem Trockenen sitzen (*inf*); **to leave sb ~ed** jdn seinem Schicksal überlassen

strand² **N** Strang *m*; (*of hair*) Strähne *f*; (*of thread, wool*) Faden *m*; (*of wire*) Litze *f*; (*of vine etc*) Ranke *f*; (*of beads*) Schnur *f*; (*fig, in melody etc*) Melodienfolge *f*; (*in story*) Handlungsfaden *m*; **a three-strand necklace** eine dreireihige Halskette

strange [streɪndʒ] **ADJ** (*+er*) **a** seltsam, sonderbar, merkwürdig; **to think/find it ~ that ...** es seltsam finden, dass ...; **~ as it may seem ...** so seltsam es auch scheinen mag, ...; **for some reason** aus irgendeinem unerfindlichen *or* seltsamen Grund; **the ~ thing is (that) ...** das Seltsame ist, dass...; **he told me the ~st story** er erzählte mir eine sehr seltsame *etc* Geschichte; **by a ~ chance** *or* **coincidence** durch einen seltsamen Zufall; **~ to say** so seltsam es klingen mag; **I feel a bit ~** (= *odd*) mir ist etwas seltsam **b** (= *unfamiliar*) *country, surroundings, bed* fremd; (= *unusual, unaccustomed*) *work, activity* nicht vertraut, ungewohnt; **don't talk to ~ men** sprich nicht mit fremden Männern; **I felt rather ~ at first** zuerst fühlte ich mich ziemlich fremd; **I feel ~ in a skirt** ich komme mir in einem Rock komisch vor (*inf*); **to be ~ to sb** jdm fremd *or* unbekannt sein; **the boys are ~ to the school** die Schule ist den Jungen noch nicht vertraut *or* noch fremd

strangely ['streɪndʒlɪ] **ADV** (= *oddly*) seltsam, sonderbar, merkwürdig; *act, behave also* komisch (*inf*); **~ enough** seltsamerweise, sonderbarerweise, merkwürdigerweise; **to be ~ rem-**

iniscent of sb/sth seltsam an jdn/etw erinnern; **~ named** seltsam benannt

strangeness ['streɪndʒnɪs] **N** **a** (= *oddness*) Seltsamkeit *f*, Merkwürdigkeit *f* **b** (= *unfamiliarity*) Fremdheit *f*; (*of work, activity*) Ungewohntheit *f*

stranger ['streɪndʒə'] **N** Fremde(r) *mf*; **he's a complete ~ to me** ich kenne ihn überhaupt nicht; **I'm a ~ here myself** ich bin selbst fremd hier; **he is no ~ to London** er kennt sich in London aus; **he is no ~ to misfortune** Leid ist ihm nicht fremd; **to be a ~ to this kind of work** mit dieser Art von Arbeit nicht vertraut sein; **hullo, ~!** (*inf*) hallo, lange nicht gesehen; **you're quite a ~ here** (*inf*) man kennt dich ja gar nicht mehr; **the little ~** (*hum*) der kleine Neuankömmling

Strangers' Gallery **N** (*Brit, Parl*) Besuchergalerie *f*

strangle ['stræŋgl] **VT** (= *murder*) erwürgen, erdrosseln, strangulieren (*form*); (*fig*) *cry, economy, originality* ersticken; *protests* abwürgen, ersticken; **this collar is strangling me** (*inf*) dieser Kragen schnürt mir den Hals zu *or* ein

strangled ['stræŋgld] **ADJ** *voice, sound, laugh, cry* erstickt; **in a ~ voice** mit erstickter Stimme

stranglehold ['stræŋgl.həʊld] **N** (*lit*) Würgegriff *m*, Manschette *f*; (*fig*) absolute Machtposition (*on* gegenüber); **they have a ~ on us** (*fig*) sie haben uns in der Zange

strangler ['stræŋglə'] **N** Würger(in) *m(f)*

strangling ['stræŋglɪŋ] **N** **a** (= *murder*) Mord *m* durch Erwürgen **b** (= *act of strangling*) Erwürgen *nt*, Erdrosseln *nt*; (*fig*) Ersticken *nt*

strangulate ['stræŋgjʊleɪt] **VT** (*Med*) abschnüren, abbinden

strangulation [ˌstræŋgjʊ'leɪʃən] **N** **a** (= *being strangled*) Ersticken *nt*; (= *act of strangling*) Erwürgen *nt*, Erdrosseln *nt*; **death was due to ~** der Tod trat durch Ersticken ein **b** (*Med*) Abschnürung *f*, Abbindung *f*

strap [stræp] **N** **a** Riemen *m*; (*esp for safety*) Gurt *m*; (*in bus etc*) Schlaufe *f*, Lasche *f*; (*on ski pants etc*) Steg *m*; (= *watch strap*) Band *nt*; (= *shoulder strap*) Träger *m*; **to give sb the ~** jdn verprügeln, jdn züchtigen **VT** **a** (= *fasten with strap*) festschnallen (*to an* +*dat*); **to ~ sth onto sth** etw auf etw (*acc*) schnallen; **he ~ped on his rucksack** er schnallte (sich *dat*) den Rucksack auf; **to ~ sb/ sth down** jdn/etw festschnallen; **to ~ on one's watch** sich (*dat*) die Uhr umbinden; **to ~ on one's belt** sich (*dat*) den Gürtel umschnallen; **to ~ sb/oneself in** (*in car, plane*) jdn/sich anschnallen **b** (*Med: also* **strap up**) bandagieren; *dressing* festkleben **c** (= *punish*) *person* verprügeln, züchtigen **d** (*inf*) **to be ~ped (for cash)** (= *broke*) pleite *or* blank sein (*inf*)

strap: **strap-hang** VI (*inf*) **I had to ~** ich musste stehen; **straphanger** N (*inf: = commuter*) Pendler(in) *m(f)*; **straphanging** N (*inf: = commuting*) Pendeln *nt*; **strapless** **ADJ** trägerlos, schulterfrei; **strapline** N (*Press*) Schlagzeile *f*

strapping ['stræpɪŋ] **ADJ** (*inf*) stramm; *woman also* drall

strappy ['stræpɪ] **ADJ** (*inf*) **~ sandals** Riemchensandalen *pl*; **~ dress** Kleid *nt* mit Spag(h)ettiträgern

Strasbourg ['stræzbɜːg] **N** Straßburg *nt*

strata ['strɑːtə] *pl of* **stratum**

stratagem ['strætɪdʒəm] **N** (*Mil*) Kriegslist *f*; (= *artifice*) List *f*

strategic [strə'tiːdʒɪk] **ADJ** strategisch; (= *strategically important*) strategisch wichtig; (*fig*) taktisch, strategisch; **to put sth in a ~ position** etw in eine strategisch günstige Position bringen

strategically [strə'tiːdʒɪkəlɪ] **ADV** strategisch; (*fig also*) taktisch; **to be ~ placed** eine strategisch günstige Stellung haben; **a few ~ placed plants will brighten up any room** ein paar

Pflanzen an der richtigen Stelle machen jedes Zimmer freundlicher; **~, his move was a mistake** strategisch gesehen war das falsch

strategist ['strætɪdʒɪst] **N** Stratege *m*, Strategin *f*; (*fig also*) Taktiker(in) *m(f)*

strategy ['strætɪdʒɪ] **N** **a** (*Mil*) Strategie *f*; (*Sport, fig*) Taktik *f*, Strategie *f*; (= *art of strategy, Mil*) Kriegskunst *f*; (*fig*) Taktieren *nt*

stratification [ˌstrætɪfɪ'keɪʃən] **N** (*lit, fig*) Schichtung *f*; (= *stratifying also*) Schichtenbildung *f*; (*Geol*) Stratifikation *f*

stratified ['strætɪfaɪd] **ADJ** (*Geol*) geschichtet, schichtförmig; **~ rock** Schichtgestein *nt*

stratify ['strætɪfaɪ] **VT** schichten; (*Geol also*) stratifizieren; **a highly stratified society** eine vielschichtige Gesellschaft **VI** (*Geol*) Schichten bilden, sich aufschichten; (*fig*) Schichten herausbilden, in Schichten zerfallen

stratosphere ['strætəʊsfɪə'] **N** Stratosphäre *f*; **to send sth into the ~** (*fig*) etw astronomisch ansteigen lassen

stratospheric [ˌstrætəʊs'ferɪk] **ADJ** stratosphärisch

stratum ['strɑːtəm] **N** *pl* **strata** (*Geol, fig*) Schicht *f*

stratus ['strɑːtəs] **N** (*Met*) Stratus *m*, Schichtwolke *f*

straw [strɔː] **N** **a** (= *stalk*) Strohhalm *m*; (*collectively*) Stroh *nt* *no pl*; **it's the last ~, it's the ~ that breaks the camel's back** (*prov*) das ist der letzte Tropfen, der das Fass zum Überlaufen bringt (*prov*); **that's the last** *or* **final ~!** (*inf*) das ist der Gipfel! (*inf*); **it's a ~ in the wind** das ist ein Vorzeichen; **to clutch** *or* **grasp at ~s** sich an einen Strohhalm klammern; **to draw the short ~** den kürzeren ziehen; **man of ~** Strohmann *m*; (*in politics*) Marionette *f*, (= *set-up opponent*) Scheingegner(in) *m(f)* → **drowning** **b** (= *drinking straw*) Trink- *or* Strohhalm *m* **ADJ** *attr* Stroh-; *basket* aus Stroh; **~ mat** Strohmatte *f*

straw bale N Strohballen *m*

strawberry ['strɔːbərɪ] **N** (= *plant, fruit*) Erdbeere *f*

strawberry *in cpds* Erdbeer-; **strawberry blonde** **N** Rotblonde(r) *mf*; **she's a ~** sie hat rotblondes Haar **ADJ** rotblond; **strawberry jam** N Erdbeermarmelade *f*; **strawberry mark** N (*rotes*) Muttermal

straw: **straw boss** N (*US, inf*) Pro-forma-Vorgesetzte(r) *mf*; **straw-coloured**, (*US*) **straw-colored** ADJ strohfarben, strohfarbig; *hair* strohblond; **straw hat** N Strohhut *m*; **straw man** N Strohmann *m*; (*in politics*) Marionette *f*, (= *set-up opponent*) Scheingegner(in) *m(f)*; **straw mattress** N Strohsack *m*; **straw poll**, **straw vote** N Probeabstimmung *f*; (*in election*) Wählerbefragung *f*

stray [streɪ] **VI** (*also* **stray away**) sich verirren, abirren; (*also* **stray about**) (umher)streunen; (*fig: thoughts, speaker*) abschweifen; **to ~ (away) from sth** (*lit, fig*) von etw abkommen; **to ~ from a path** von einem Weg abkommen; **to ~ from the path of virtue** vom rechten Weg *or* vom Pfad der Tugend abkommen; **the cattle ~ed into the road** die Rinder haben sich auf die Straße verirrt; **they ~ed into the enemy camp** sie verirrten sich ins feindliche Lager **ADJ** *child, bullet, cattle* verirrt; *cat, dog etc* streunend *attr*; (= *ownerless*) herrenlos; (= *isolated*) *remarks, houses, cases, hairs* vereinzelt; (= *single*) *remark, success* einzeln; (= *occasional*) gelegentlich; *thoughts* flüchtig **N** **a** (= *dog, cat*) streunendes Tier; (*ownerless*) herrenloses Tier; **that cat's a ~** das ist eine herrenlose Katze → **waif** **b** **strays** PL (*Rad*) (atmosphärische) Störungen *pl*

streak [striːk] **N** Streifen *m*; (*of light*) Strahl *m*; (*fig, = trace*) Spur *f*; (*of jealousy, meanness etc*) Zug *m*; (*of madness, humour*) Anflug *m*; **~s** (*in hair*) Strähnchen *pl*, Strähnen *pl*; **~ of lightning** Blitz(strahl) *m*; **there was a ~ of blood on his arm** eine Blutspur zog sich über seinen Arm;

there is a ~ of Spanish blood in her sie hat spanisches Blut in den Adern; **his lucky** ~ seine Glückssträhne; **a winning/losing** ~ eine Glücks-/Pechsträhne; **he's got a mean** ~ er hat einen gemeinen Zug (an sich (*dat*)); **he went past like a ~ (of lightning)** er sauste vorbei wie der Blitz

VT streifen; **to be** ~**ed** gestreift sein; **the sky was** ~**ed with red** der Himmel hatte rote Streifen; **to have one's hair** ~**ed** sich (*dat*) Streifen ins Haar färben lassen; **hair** ~**ed with blonde/grey** Haar mit blonden/grauen Strähnen; ~**ed with dirt** schmutzverschmiert; ~**ed with tears** tränenverschmiert; **rock** ~**ed with quartz** von Quarzadern durchzogener Stein

VI **a** (*lightning*) zucken; (*inf, = move quickly*) flitzen (*inf*); **to ~ along/past** entlang-/vorbeiflitzen (*inf*)

b (*= run naked*) blitzen, flitzen

streaker ['striːkəʳ] N Blitzer(in) *m(f)*, Flitzer(in) *m(f)*

streaky ['striːkɪ] ADJ (*+er*) *glass, face* verschmiert; *window, mirror* streifig; *pattern* gestreift; *hair* strähnig; ~ **bacon** (*Brit*) durchwachsener Speck

stream [striːm] **N** **a** (*= small river*) Bach *m*, Flüsschen *nt*; (*= current*) Strömung *f*; **to go with/against the** ~ (*lit, fig*) mit dem/gegen den Strom schwimmen

b (*= flow, of liquid, air, people, cars*) Strom *m*; (*of light, tears*) Flut *f*; (*of words, excuses, abuse*) Schwall *m*, Flut *f*; ~ **of consciousness** (*Liter*) Bewusstseinsstrom *m*

c (*Brit, Sch*) Leistungsgruppe *f*

d (*Tech*) **to be/come on** ~ (*oil well*) in Betrieb sein/genommen werden; (*oil*) fließen/zu fließen anfangen

VT **a** (*liter*) **the walls** ~**ed water** von den Wänden rann das Wasser; **his face** ~**ed blood** Blut rann *or* strömte ihm übers Gesicht

b (*Brit, Sch*) in (Leistungs)gruppen einteilen

VI **a** (*= flow, liquid*) strömen, fließen, rinnen; (*eyes: because of cold, gas etc*) tränen; (*air, sunlight*) strömen, fluten; (*people, cars etc*) strömen; **the wound was** ~**ing with blood** Blut strömte *or* rann aus der Wunde; **the walls were** ~**ing with water** die Wände trieften vor Nässe; **her eyes were/face was** ~**ing with tears** Tränen strömten ihr aus den Augen/übers Gesicht; **his nose was** ~**ing** (*Brit*) seine Nase lief

b (*= wave: flag, hair*) wehen

▶ **stream down** VI (*liquid*) in Strömen fließen; (*+prep obj*) herunterströmen; (*cars*) in Strömen herunterfahren; (*hair*) wallend herunterfallen (*prep obj* über *+acc*); **the rain was streaming down** es regnete in Strömen; **tears streamed down her face** Tränen rannen *or* strömten *or* liefen über ihr Gesicht

▶ **stream in** VI hereinströmen

▶ **stream out** VI hinausströmen (*of* aus); (*liquid also*) herausfließen (*of* aus); **her hair streamed out behind her** ihre Haare wehten nach hinten

▶ **stream past** VI vorbeiströmen (*prep obj* an *+dat*); (*cars*) in Strömen vorbeifahren (*prep obj* an *+dat*); **the cars kept streaming past** der Strom der Autos brach nicht ab

streamer ['striːməʳ] N (*= flag*) Banner *nt*; (*made of paper*) Papier- *or* Luftschlange *f*; (*made of cloth, as decoration*) Band *nt*; ~ **headline** (*US*) Balkenüberschrift *f*

stream feed N (*on photocopier*) automatischer Papiereinzug

streaming ['striːmɪŋ] **N** (*Brit, Sch*) Einteilung *f* in Leistungsgruppen **ADJ** *nose, windows* triefend; *eyes also* tränend; **I have a** ~ **cold** (*Brit*) ich habe einen fürchterlichen Schnupfen

streamlet ['striːmlət] N (*poet*) Bächlein *nt*, Rinnsal *nt* (*liter*)

streamline ['striːmlaɪn] VT *racing car, aeroplane* windschlüpfig machen, Stromlinienform geben (*+dat*); (*fig*) rationalisieren

streamlined ['striːmlaɪnd] ADJ *wing* windschlüpfig; *car, plane also* stromlinienförmig; (*fig*) rationalisiert

street [striːt] N **a** Straße *f*; **in** *or* **on the** ~ auf der Straße; **to live in** *or* **on a** ~ in einer Straße wohnen; **the man/woman in the** ~ (*fig*) der Mann/die Frau auf der Straße; **it's right up my** ~ (*Brit fig inf*) das ist genau mein Fall (*inf*); **to be** ~**s ahead of sb** (*fig inf*) jdm haushoch überlegen sein (*inf*); ~**s apart** (*fig*) grundverschieden; **he's not in the same** ~ **as her** (*fig inf*) zwischen ihm und ihr ist ein himmelweiter Unterschied (*inf*); **to take to the** ~**s** (*demonstrators*) auf die Straße gehen; **to go on the** ~**s** (*inf*) auf den Strich gehen (*inf*); **a woman of the** ~**s** ein Mädchen *nt* von der Straße, ein Straßenmädchen *nt* → **man**

b (*inf, = residents*) Straße *f*

street in *cpds* Straßen-; **street Arab** N (*Brit dated liter*) Gassenkind *nt*; **streetball** N Streetball *nt*; **street battle** N Straßenschlacht *f*; **streetcar** N (*US*) Straßenbahn *f*; **street cleaner** N (*esp US*) Straßenkehrer(in) *m(f)*, Straßenfeger(in) *m(f)*; **street cred** (*Brit inf*), **street credibility** N Glaubwürdigkeit *f*; **as an undercover agent in the Bronx you need** ~ als Geheimagent in der Bronx muss man sich dem Milieu anpassen können; **this jacket does nothing for my** ~ dieses Jackett versaut mein ganzes Image (*inf*); **street crime** N Straßenkriminalität *f*; **street door** N Tür *f* zur Straße hin; **street fighter** N Straßenkämpfer(in) *m(f)*; **street fighting** N Straßenkämpfe *pl*; **street furniture** N (*= benches, road signs, cycle stands etc*) Stadtmöbel *pl*, urbanes Mobiliar; **street lamp** N Straßenlaterne *f*; **street level** N **at** ~ zu ebener Erde; **street life** N (*inf*) Leben *nt* auf der Straße; **street light** N Straßenlaterne *f*; **street lighting** N Straßenbeleuchtung *f*; **street map** N Stadtplan *m*, Straßenplan *m*; **street market** N Straßenmarkt *m*; **street musician** N Straßenmusikant(in) *m(f)*; **street party** N Straßenfest *nt*; **street people** PL Obdachlose *pl*; **street plan** N Straßen- *or* Stadtplan *m*; **street smart** ADJ (*esp US inf: = streetwise*) gewieft (*inf*), clever (*inf*); **street sweeper** N (*= person*) Straßenkehrer(in) *m(f)* *or* -feger(in) *m(f)*; (*= machine*) Kehrmaschine *f*; **street theatre**, (*US*) **street theater** N Straßentheater *nt*; **street urchin** N Straßen- *or* Gassenjunge *m*; **street vendor** N Straßenverkäufer(in) *m(f)*; **streetwalker** N Prostituierte *f*, Straßenmädchen *nt*; **streetwise** ADJ gewieft (*inf*), clever (*inf*)

strength [streŋθ] **N** **a** (*lit, fig*) Stärke *f*; (*of person, feelings*) Kraft *f*; (*of table, bolt, nail, wall*) Stabilität *f*; (*of material, character*) Stärke *f*, Festigkeit *f*; (*of conviction, shoes*) Festigkeit *f*; (*of views*) Überzeugtheit *f*; (*of imagination*) Lebhaftigkeit *f*; (*of reason, argument, evidence*) Überzeugungskraft *f*; (*of plea, protest*) Eindringlichkeit *f*; (*of letter*) geharnischte *or* starke Ausdrucksweise; (*of measure*) Drastik *f*; ~ **of character/will** *or* **mind** Charakter-/Willensstärke *f*; **to increase in** *or* **gain** ~ stärker werden; **on the** ~ **of sth** auf Grund einer Sache (*gen*); **he decided to be a writer on the** ~ **of selling one short story** er beschloss, Schriftsteller zu werden, nachdem er eine einzige Kurzgeschichte verkauft hatte; **his** ~ **failed him** seine Kräfte versagten, ihn verließen die Kräfte; **to be beyond sb's** ~ über jds Kräfte (*acc*); **to save one's** ~ mit seinen Kräften haushalten *or* Haus halten; **you don't know your own** ~! du weißt gar nicht, wie stark du bist!; **to argue from a position of** ~ von einer starken Position aus argumentieren; **to go from** ~ **to** ~ einen Erfolg nach dem anderen erzielen *or* haben; **he was a great** ~ **to me** er war mir eine große Stütze

b (*= health, of constitution*) Robustheit *f*, Kräftigkeit *f*; (*of eyes, heart*) Stärke *f*; **the patient is recovering his** ~ der Patient kommt wieder zu Kräften; **when she has her** ~ **back** wenn sie wieder bei Kräften ist

c (*of colour*) Kräftigkeit *f*, Intensität *f*; (*of acid, bleach*) Stärke *f*; (*of diluted solution*) Konzentration *f*

d (*= numbers*) (An)zahl *f*; (*Mil*) Stärke *f*; **to be at full** ~ vollzählig sein; **to bring sth up to** ~

etw vollzählig machen; **to be up to/below** *or* **under** ~ (die) volle Stärke/nicht die volle Stärke haben; **to turn out in** ~ in großer Zahl kommen, zahlreich erscheinen; **the police were there in** ~ ein starkes Polizeiaufgebot war da

e (*of currency*) Stärke *f*; (*of market prices*) Stabilität *f*; (*of economy*) Gesundheit *f*

strengthen ['streŋθən] **VT** stärken; *material, shoes, building, grip, resolve also* verstärken; *eyesight* verbessern; *muscles, patient* stärken, kräftigen; *person* (*lit*) Kraft geben (*+dat*); *currency, market* festigen; *effect* vergrößern; **to ~ sb's hand** (*fig*) jdn bestärken *or* ermutigen; **this only** ~**ed her determination** das bestärkte sie nur in ihrem Entschluss **VI** stärker werden; (*wind, desire also*) sich verstärken; **the** ~**ing economy** die sich verbessernde Wirtschaftslage

strenuous ['strenjʊəs] ADJ **a** (*= exhausting*) anstrengend; *march, game* anstrengend, ermüdend **b** (*= energetic*) *attempt, supporter, support* unermüdlich, energisch; *attack, effort, denial* hartnäckig; *opposition, conflict, protest* heftig

strenuously ['strenjʊəslɪ] ADV **a** *exercise* anstrengend **b** (*= vigorously*) *deny* entschieden; *oppose* energisch, entschieden; *object* nachdrücklich

strep throat ['strep'θrəʊt] N (*esp US, inf*) Halsentzündung *f*

streptococcus [ˌstreptəʊ'kɒkəs] N *pl* **streptococci** [ˌstreptəʊ'kɒksaɪ] Streptokokkus *m*

stress [stres] ❂ 26.3 **N** **a** (*= strain*) Belastung *f*, Stress *m*; (*Med*) Überlastung *f*, Stress *m*; **the** ~**es and strains of modern life** die Belastungen *or* der Stress des heutigen Lebens; **times of** ~ Krisenzeiten *pl*, Zeiten *pl* großer Belastung; **to be under** ~ großen Belastungen ausgesetzt sein; (*as regards work*) unter Stress stehen, im Stress sein; **to put sb under great** ~ jdn großen Belastungen aussetzen; **to break down under** ~**/the** ~ unter Stress *or* bei Belastung/unter dem Stress *or* unter der Belastung zusammenbrechen

b (*= accent*) Betonung *f*, Ton *m*; (*fig, = emphasis*) Akzent *m*, (Haupt)gewicht *nt*; **to put** *or* **lay** (**great**) ~ **on sth** großen Wert auf etw (*acc*) legen, einer Sache (*dat*) großes Gewicht beimessen; *fact, detail* etw (*besonders*) betonen

c (*Mech*) Belastung *f*; (*= pressure*) Druck *m*; (*= tension*) Spannung *f*; **the** ~ **acting on the metal** die Belastung, der das Metall ausgesetzt ist

VT **a** (*lit, fig, = emphasize*) betonen; *innocence* beteuern; *good manners, subject* großen Wert legen auf (*+acc*); *fact, detail* hervorheben, betonen

b (*Mech*) belasten, beanspruchen

stressed [strest] ADJ **a** *syllable, word* betont **b** (*= under stress*) *person* gestresst, über(be)lastet

stressed out ADJ gestresst; **what are you getting so** ~ **about?** worüber regst du dich so auf? (*inf*)

stress fracture N Spannungsriss *m*

stressful ['stresfʊl] ADJ anstrengend, stressig; **a** ~ **situation** eine angespannte Lage

stress mark N Akzent *m*, Betonungszeichen *nt*

stretch [stretʃ] **N** **a** (*= act of stretching*) Strecken *nt*, Dehnen *nt*; **to have a** ~ sich strecken *or* dehnen; (*person also*) sich recken; **to be at full** ~ (*lit: material*) bis zum Äußersten gedehnt sein; (*fig, person*) mit aller Kraft arbeiten; (*factory etc*) auf Hochtouren arbeiten (*inf*); (*engine, production, work*) auf Hochtouren laufen; **by no** ~ **of the imagination** beim besten Willen nicht; **not by a long** ~ bei weitem nicht

b (*= elasticity*) Elastizität *f*, Dehnbarkeit *f*; **a fabric with plenty of** ~ ein stark dehnbares *or* sehr elastisches Material; **there's not much** ~ **left in this elastic** das Gummi ist ziemlich ausgeleiert

c (*= expanse, of road etc*) Strecke *f*, Stück *nt*; (*on racecourse*) Gerade *f*; (*of wood, river, countryside etc*) Stück *nt*; (*of journey*) Abschnitt *m*, Teil *m*; **a straight** ~ **of road** eine gerade Strecke; **that** ~ **of water is called …** dieser Gewässerlauf heißt ...; **in that ~ of the river** in dem Teil des Flusses; **for a long ~** über eine weite Strecke

d (= *stretch of time*) Zeit *f*, Zeitraum *m*, Zeitspanne *f*; **for a long ~ of time** für (eine) lange Zeit, lange Zeit; **for hours at a ~** stundenlang; **three days at a ~** drei Tage an einem Stück *or* ohne Unterbrechung; **to do a ~** (*inf, in prison*) im Knast sein (*inf*)

ADJ *attr* dehnbar, elastisch; **~ trousers** Stretchhose *f*

VT a (= *extend, lengthen*) strecken; (= *widen*) *jumper, gloves also, elastic, shoes* dehnen; (= *spread*) *wings, blanket etc* ausbreiten; (= *tighten*) *rope, canvas* spannen; **to become ~ed** ausleiern; **a curtain was ~ed across the room** ein Vorhang war quer durchs Zimmer gezogen; **she ~ed a tarpaulin over the woodpile** sie breitete eine Plane über den Holzstoß; **to ~ sth tight** etw straffen, etw straff ziehen; *cover* etw stramm ziehen; **to ~ one's legs** (= *go for a walk*) sich (*dat*) die Beine vertreten (*inf*); **to ~ one's neck** den Hals recken

b (= *make go further*) *meal, money* strecken; (= *use fully*) *resources* voll (aus)nutzen; *credit* voll beanspruchen; *athlete, student etc* fordern; *one's abilities* bis zum Äußersten fordern; **to ~ one's imagination** seine Fantasie anstrengen; **to ~ sb/ sth to the limit(s)** jdn/etw bis zum äußersten belasten; **to be fully ~ed** (*esp Brit, person*) voll ausgelastet sein; **he ~ed his lead to 10 points** er baute seinen Vorsprung auf 10 Punkte aus

c (= *strain*) *meaning, word* äußerst weit fassen; *truth, law, rules* es nicht so genau nehmen mit; **this clause/law could be ~ed to allow ...** diese Klausel/dieses Gesetz könnte so weit gedehnt werden, dass sie/es ... zulässt; **to ~ a point** ein Auge zudrücken, großzügig sein; **that's ~ing it too far/a bit (far)** das geht zu weit/fast zu weit

VI (*after sleep etc*) sich strecken; (= *be elastic*) sich dehnen, dehnbar sein; (= *extend: time, area, authority, influence*) sich erstrecken (*to* bis, *over* über +*acc*); (= *be enough: food, money, material*) reichen (*to* für); (= *become looser*) weiter werden; (= *become longer*) länger werden; **the rope won't ~ to that post** das Seil reicht nicht bis zu dem Pfosten (hinüber); **to ~ to reach sth** sich recken, um etw zu erreichen; **he ~ed a-cross and touched her cheek** er reichte herüber und berührte ihre Wange; **to ~ back to** zurückreichen bis; **the fields ~ed away into the distance** die Felder dehnten sich bis in die Ferne aus; **the years ~ed (out) ahead of him** die Jahre dehnten sich vor ihm aus; **a life of misery ~ed (out) before her** vor ihr breitete sich ein Leben voll Kummer und Leid aus; **the protests ~ed into their second week** die Proteste dauerten bereits die zweite Woche an; **I can't ~ to that** so viel kann ich mir nicht erlauben; **our funds won't ~ to that** das lassen unsere Finanzen nicht zu

VR a (*after sleep etc*) sich strecken

b (= *strain oneself*) sich verausgaben; **if only he'd ~ himself a little** wenn er sich nur etwas anstrengen würde

▶**stretch out VT** *sep arms, wings, blanket* ausbreiten; *leg, hand* ausstrecken; *foot* vorstrecken; *rope* spannen; *meeting, discussion, essay, story* ausdehnen; **to stretch oneself out (on the ground)** sich auf den Boden legen **VI** (*inf*: = *lie down*) sich hinlegen; (*countryside*) sich ausbreiten; (*in time*) sich erstrecken, sich hinziehen (*over* über +*acc*); **her arm stretched out** sie streckte den Arm aus; **he stretched out on the bed** er legte sich (ausgestreckt) aufs Bett

stretcher ['stretʃə] N **a** (*Med*) (Trag)bahre *f* **b** (*for shoes, gloves*) Spanner *m*; (*Art, for canvas*) Rahmen *m*

▶**stretcher off VT** *sep* auf einer (Trag)bahre wegtragen *or* abtransportieren

stretcher: stretcher-bearer N Krankenträger(in) *m(f)*; **stretcher case** N Kranke(r) *mf*/Verletzte(r) *mf*, der/die nicht gehen kann; (*Mil*) Schwerverwundete(r) *mf*, schwer Verwundete(r) *mf*; **by the time I've finished this work I'll be a ~** (*hum*) bis ich diese Arbeit fertig

habe, bin ich krankenhausreif (*inf*); **stretcher party** N Team *nt* von Krankenträgern

stretch: stretch limo N (*inf*) Großraumlimousine *f*; **stretch mark** N Dehnungsstreifen *m*; (*in pregnancy*) Schwangerschaftsstreifen *m* *or* -narbe *f*; **stretch nylon** N Stretchnylon *nt*, Helanca® *nt*; (*esp for ski pants*) Lastex *nt*

stretchy ['stretʃɪ] ADJ (+*er*) elastisch, dehnbar

strew [stru:] *pret* **strewed**, *ptp* **strewed** *or* **strewn** [stru:n] VT (= *scatter*) verstreuen; *flowers, gravel, sand* streuen; (= *cover with*) *floor etc* bestreuen; **to ~ one's clothes around (the room)** seine Kleider im Zimmer verstreuen; **dresses were ~n about the room** Kleider lagen im ganzen Zimmer verstreut herum; **the floor was ~n with ...** ... lagen überall auf dem Boden verstreut

strewth [stru:θ] INTERJ (*inf*) = **struth**

striated [straɪ'eɪtɪd] ADJ (*form, = striped*) gestreift; (= *furrowed*) gefurcht; (*Geol*) mit Schliffen *or* Schrammen

striation [straɪ'eɪʃən] N (*form, = stripes*) Streifen *pl*; (= *furrows*) Furchen *pl*, Furchung *f*; (*Geol*) Schliffe *pl*, Schrammen *pl*

stricken ['strɪkən] (*old*) *ptp of* **strike** ADJ (*liter, = wounded*) verwundet; (= *afflicted*) leidgeprüft, schwer geprüft; (*with grief*) schmerzerfüllt, gramgebeugt (*liter*); (= *ill*) leidend (*geh*); *ship, plane* in Not; (= *horrified*) *person* wie vom Blitz getroffen *or* vom Donner gerührt; *expression* niedergeschlagen; **~ with guilt/fear etc** von Schuld/Angst etc erfüllt, von Angst ergriffen; **~ in years** hochbetagt (*geh*); **to be ~ by** *or* **with illness** leidend sein (*geh*); **to be ~ with blindness** mit Blindheit geschlagen sein (*geh*); **to be ~ by drought/famine** von Dürre/Hungersnot geplagt *or* heimgesucht werden

-stricken ADJ *suf* (*with emotion*) -erfüllt; (*by catastrophe*) von ... heimgesucht; **grief-stricken** schmerzerfüllt; **panic-stricken** von Panik ergriffen

strict [strɪkt] ADJ (+*er*) **a** (= *stern, severe*) *law, parent, principles, judge etc* streng; *order, ban, discipline* strikt, streng; *obedience* absolut, strikt; *Catholic* strenggläubig; **they're very ~ about timekeeping** es wird streng auf Pünktlichkeit geachtet

b (= *precise*) streng; *accuracy, neutrality, secrecy* absolut, streng; *translation, meaning* genau; **in the ~ sense of the word** genau genommen; **in ~ confidence** streng vertraulich; **in (the) ~est confidence** in strengster Vertraulichkeit, strengstens vertraulich; **there is a ~ time limit on that** das ist zeitlich genau begrenzt; **in ~ order of precedence** streng nach Rangordnung

strictly ['strɪktlɪ] ADV **a** streng; **smoking is ~ forbidden** Rauchen ist streng *or* strengstens verboten

b (= *precisely*) genau; (= *absolutely*) absolut, streng; **to be ~ accurate** um ganz genau zu sein; **our relationship was ~ business** unser Verhältnis war rein geschäftlich; **~ in confidence** ganz im Vertrauen; **~ personal** privat; **confidential** streng vertraulich; **"strictly private"** „streng vertraulich"; **~ speaking** genau genommen; **not ~ true** nicht ganz richtig; **~ between ourselves/between you and me** ganz unter uns; **unless ~ necessary** wenn nicht unbedingt erforderlich; **fox-hunting is ~ for the rich** Fuchsjagden sind ausschließlich etwas für reiche Leute; **the car park is ~ for the use of residents** der Parkplatz ist ausschließlich für Anwohner vorgesehen

strictness ['strɪktnɪs] N **a** Strenge *f*; (*of order, discipline*) Striktheit *f*, Strenge *f* **b** (= *preciseness*) Genauigkeit *f*

stricture ['strɪktʃə] N **a** *usu pl* (*form: = criticism*) (scharfe) Kritik *no pl*; **to make** *or* **pass ~s upon sb** jdn (scharf) kritisieren **b** (*Med*) Verengung *f*, Striktur *f* (*spec*)

stride [straɪd] *vb: pret* **strode**, *ptp* **stridden** ['strɪdn] **N** (= *step*) Schritt *m*; (= *gait also*) Gang *m*; (*fig*) Fortschritt *m*; **to get into** *or* **hit one's ~** (*fig*) in Schwung *or* in Fahrt kommen; **to take sth in one's ~** (*Brit*) *or* **in ~** (*US*) mit etw spielend

fertig werden; *exam, interview* etw spielend schaffen; **to put sb off his/her ~** jdn aus dem Konzept bringen; **he took everything in his ~** es schien alles spurlos an ihm vorüberzugehen zu sein

VI schreiten (*geh*), mit großen Schritten gehen; **to ~ along** ausschreiten (*geh*); **to ~ away** *or* **off** sich mit schnellen Schritten entfernen, davonschreiten (*geh*); **to ~ up to sb** (mit großen Schritten) auf jdn zugehen, auf jdn zuschreiten (*geh*); **to ~ up and down** auf- und abgehen *or* -schreiten (*geh*)

stridency ['straɪdənsɪ] N (*of sound, voice*) Schrillheit *f*, Durchdringlichkeit *f*; (*of colour*) Grellheit *f*; (*of person*) Streitbarkeit *f*; (*of protest, criticism, tone*) Schärfe *f*; (*of demand*) Stärke *f*

strident ['straɪdənt] ADJ *sound, voice* schrill, durchdringend; *colour* grell; *person* streitbar; *criticism, tone* scharf; *demand, protest, nationalism, attack* lautstark

stridently ['straɪdəntlɪ] ADV *talk etc* schrill, durchdringend; *object, protest* scharf, lautstark; *demand, behave* lautstark; **a ~ anti-American approach** eine scharf antiamerikanische Haltung

strife [straɪf] N Unmut *m* (*geh*), Unfriede *m*; (*in family, between friends*) Zwietracht *f* (*geh*); **party ~** Zwietracht *f* (*geh*) *or* Zwistigkeiten *pl* in der Partei; **internal ~** innere Kämpfe *pl*; **civil/industrial ~** Auseinandersetzungen *pl* in der Bevölkerung/Industrie; **to cease from ~** (*liter*) allen Zwist begraben (*geh*)

strife-torn ['straɪftɔ:n], **strife-ridden** ['straɪfrɪdn] ADJ *country* konfliktgeschüttelt; *party* zerstritten

strike [straɪk] *vb: pret* **struck**, *ptp* **struck** *or* (*old*) **stricken** **N** **a** Streik *m*, Ausstand *m*; **official/ unofficial ~** offizieller/wilder Streik; **to be on ~** streiken, im Ausstand sein; **to be on official/ unofficial ~** offiziell/wild streiken; **to come out on ~, to go on ~** in den Streik *or* Ausstand treten; **to bring sb out on ~** jdn zum Streik veranlassen → **hunger strike**

b (= *discovery of oil, gold etc*) Fund *m*; **a big oil ~** ein großer Ölfund; **to make a ~** fündig werden; **a lucky ~** ein Treffer *m*, ein Glücksfall *m*

c (*Baseball*) verfehlter Schlag; (*Tenpin Bowling*) Strike *m*, alle zehne; **to get a ~** alle zehne werfen, abräumen (*inf*); **to have the ~** (*Cricket*) schlagen; **three ~s and you're out** wenn du zum Ball dreimal verfehlst, bist du draußen; **it/she has two ~s against it/her** (*esp US, inf*) es/sie hat zwei Nachteile

d (*Fishing*) **he got three ~s** drei haben angebissen

e (*Mil, = attack*) Angriff *m*

f (= *act of striking*) Schlag *m*

VT **a** (= *hit*) schlagen; *door* schlagen an *or* gegen (+*acc*); *nail, table* schlagen auf (+*acc*); *metal, hot iron etc* hämmern; (*stone, blow, bullet etc*) treffen; (*snake*) beißen; (*pain*) durchzucken, durchfahren; (*misfortune, disaster*) treffen; (*disease*) befallen; **to ~ one's fist on the table, to ~ the table with one's fist** mit der Faust auf den Tisch schlagen; **to ~ sb/sth a blow** jdm/ einer Sache einen Schlag versetzen; **who struck the first blow?** wer hat zuerst (zu)geschlagen?; **to ~ a blow for sth** (*fig*) eine Lanze für etw brechen; **to ~ a blow (at sth)** (*fig*) einen Schlag (gegen etw) führen; **to be struck by lightning** vom Blitz getroffen werden; **he struck his forehead in surprise** er schlug sich (*dat*) überrascht an die Stirn; **to ~ 38 (per minute)** 38 Ruderschläge (pro Minute) machen

b (= *collide with, meet*) *person* stoßen gegen; (*spade*) stoßen auf (+*acc*); (*car*) fahren gegen; *ground* aufschlagen *or* auftreffen auf (+*acc*); (*ship*) auflaufen auf (+*acc*); (*sound, light*) *ears, eyes* treffen; (*lightning*) *person* treffen; *tree* einschlagen in (+*acc*), treffen; **to ~ one's head against sth** mit dem Kopf gegen etw stoßen, sich (*dat*) den Kopf an etw (*acc*) stoßen; **to ~ problems** (*fig*) in Schwierigkeiten geraten; **a terrible sight struck my eyes** plötzlich sah ich etwas Schreckliches

c (= *sound*) *instrument* zu spielen anfangen; *string, chord, note* anschlagen; (*clock*) schlagen; **to ~ the keys** (*of piano, typewriter*) in die Tasten greifen; **to ~ the hour** die volle Stunde schlagen; **to ~ 4** 4 schlagen; **that struck a familiar note** das kam mir/ihm *etc* bekannt vor → **note**

d (*Hort*) *cutting* schneiden; (*plant*) *roots* schlagen

e (= *occur to*) in den Sinn kommen (+*dat*); **to ~ sb as cold/unlikely** *etc* jdm kalt/unwahrscheinlich *etc* vorkommen; **that ~s me as a good idea** das kommt mir als eine gute Idee vor; **has it ever struck you that ...?** (= *occurred to you*) haben Sie je daran gedacht, dass ...?; (= *have you noticed*) ist Ihnen je aufgefallen, dass ...?; **it ~s me that ...** (= *I have the impression*) ich habe den Eindruck, dass ...; (= *I am noticing*) mir fällt auf, dass ...; **it struck me how ...** (= *occurred to me*) mir ging plötzlich auf, wie ...; (= *I noticed*) mir fiel auf, wie ...; **the funny side of it struck me later** erst später ging mir auf, wie lustig das war; **a thought struck me** mir kam plötzlich ein Gedanke

f (= *impress*) beeindrucken; **to be struck by sth** von etw beeindruckt sein; **how does it ~ you?** wie finden Sie das?, was halten Sie davon?; **how does she ~ you?** welchen Eindruck haben Sie von ihr?; **she struck me as being very competent** sie machte auf mich einen sehr fähigen Eindruck → *also* **struck**

g (= *produce, make*) *coin, medal* prägen; (*fig*) *agreement, truce* sich einigen auf (+*acc*), aushandeln; *pose* einnehmen; **to ~ a light** Feuer machen; **to ~ a match** ein Streichholz anzünden; **to ~ sparks** Funken schlagen; **to be struck blind/deaf/dumb** blind/taub/stumm werden, mit Blindheit/Taubheit/Stummheit geschlagen werden (*geh*); **to ~ fear** *or* **terror into sb/sb's heart** jdn mit Angst *or* Schrecken erfüllen; **~ a light!** (*inf*) ach du grüne Neune! (*inf*), hast du da noch Töne! (*inf*)

h (= *find*) *gold, oil, correct path* finden, stoßen auf (+*acc*); **to ~ it rich** das große Geld machen → **oil**; **to ~ gold** (*fig*) auf eine Goldgrube stoßen → **oil**

i (= *make*) *path* hauen

j (= *take down*) *camp, tent* abbrechen; (*Naut*) *flag, sail* einholen, streichen; *mast* kappen, umlegen; (*Theat*) *set* abbauen

k (= *remove*) streichen; **to be struck** *or* (*US*) **stricken from a list/the record** von einer Liste/aus dem Protokoll gestrichen werden

VI **a** (= *hit*) treffen; (*lightning*) einschlagen; (*snake*) zubeißen; (*tiger*) die Beute schlagen; (*attack, Mil etc*) zuschlagen, angreifen; (*disease*) zuschlagen; (*panic*) ausbrechen; **to ~ against sth** gegen etw stoßen; **to ~ at sb/sth** (*lit*) nach jdm/etw schlagen; (*fig: at democracy, existence*) an etw (*dat*) rütteln; **they struck at his weakest point** sie trafen ihn an seinem wundesten Punkt; **to ~ at the roots of sth** etw an der Wurzel treffen; **to be/come within striking distance of sth** einer Sache (*dat*) nahe sein; **to put sb within striking distance of sth** jdn in Reichweite von etw bringen; **to come within striking distance of doing sth** nahe daran sein, etw zu tun; **they were within striking distance of success** der Erfolg war für sie in greifbarer Nähe; **the snake struck at me** die Schlange fuhr auf mich los → **home**, **iron**

b (*clock*) schlagen; **when midnight ~s** wenn es Mitternacht schlägt

c (*workers*) streiken

d (*match*) zünden, angehen

e (*Naut*, = *run aground*) auflaufen (*on* auf +*acc*)

f (*Fishing*) anbeißen

g **inspiration struck** er/sie *etc* hatte eine Eingebung; **to ~ on a new idea** eine neue Idee haben, auf eine neue Idee kommen

h (= *take root*) Wurzeln schlagen

i (= *go in a certain direction*) **to ~ across country** querfeldein gehen; **to ~ into the woods** sich in die Wälder schlagen; **the sun struck through the mist** die Sonne brach durch den Dunst

▶ **strike back VI** zurückschlagen; (*fig also*) sich wehren, sich zur Wehr setzen; **to strike back at sb** jds Angriff (*acc*) erwidern; (*fig*) sich gegen jdn wehren *or* zur Wehr setzen **VT** *sep* zurückschlagen

▶ **strike down** VT *sep* niederschlagen; (*God*) *enemies* vernichten; (*fig*) zu Fall bringen; (*US*) *law* abschaffen; **to be struck down** niedergeschlagen werden; (*by illness*) getroffen werden; (*by blow*) zu Boden gestreckt werden; **he was struck down in his prime** er wurde in seiner Blüte dahingerafft

▶ **strike off VT** *sep* **a** (= *cut off*) abschlagen **b** (= *remove*) (*from list*) (aus)streichen; *solicitor* die Lizenz entziehen (+*dat*); *doctor* die Zulassung entziehen (+*dat*); (*from price*) abziehen (*prep obj* von); **to be struck off** (*Brit Med, Jur*) die Zulassung verlieren **c** (= *print*) drucken; **to strike off a proof** einen Bürstenabzug machen **VI** (= *set off*) sich auf den Weg machen; (*road etc also*) abbiegen

▶ **strike out VI** **a** (= *hit out*) schlagen; **to strike out wildly** *or* **blindly** wild um sich schlagen; **to strike out at sb** (*lit, fig*) jdn angreifen **b** (= *change direction*) zuhalten (*for, towards* auf +*acc*); (= *set out*) sich aufmachen, losziehen (*inf*) (*for* zu); **to strike out for home** sich auf den Heimweg machen; **to strike out on one's own** (*lit*) allein losziehen; (*fig*) eigene Wege gehen; **to strike out in a new direction** (*fig*) neue Wege gehen **c** (*Baseball*) „aus" sein; (*US fig*) nicht durchkommen **VT** *sep* (aus)streichen; **to strike sth out of the record** etw aus dem Protokoll streichen

▶ **strike through** VT *sep* durchstreichen

▶ **strike up VI** (*band etc*) einsetzen, anfangen (zu spielen) **VT** *insep* **a** (*band*) *tune* anstimmen; **strike up the band!** Musik! **b** *friendship* schließen, anknüpfen; *conversation, relationship* anfangen

strike: strike action N Streikmaßnahmen *pl*; **strike ballot** N Urabstimmung *f*; **strike-bound** ADJ bestreikt, vom Streik betroffen; **strikebreaker** N Streikbrecher(in) *m(f)*; **strikebreaking** N Streikbruch *m*; **strike call** N Aufruf *m* zum Streik; **strike force** N (*Mil*) Kampftruppe *f*; **strike fund** N Streikkasse *f*; **strike leader** N Streikführer(in) *m(f)*; **strike pay** N Streikgeld *nt*; **strike-prone** ADJ streikanfällig

striker ['straɪkə] N **a** (= *worker*) Streikende(r), Ausständige(r) *mf* **b** (*Ftbl*) Stürmer(in) *m(f)*

striking ['straɪkɪŋ] ADJ **a** (= *arresting*) *contrast, colour, resemblance etc* auffallend, bemerkenswert; *difference* verblüffend, erstaunlich; *person* bemerkenswert; *looks* umwerfend; *appearance, beauty* eindrucksvoll; **a ~ example of sth** ein hervorragendes Beispiel für etw **b** *attr worker* streikend **c** *attr clock* mit Schlagwerk; **the ~ clock keeps me awake** das Schlagen der Uhr lässt mich nicht schlafen; **~ mechanism** Schlagwerk *nt*

striking distance N (*of missile etc*) Reichweite *f*

strikingly ['straɪkɪŋlɪ] ADV *similar, evident, bold* auffallend; *different* unübersehbar; *attractive* bemerkenswert; *modern* verblüffend; *demonstrate* unmissverständlich; *contrast* deutlich; **more ~, ...** was noch mehr ins Auge fällt, dass ...

Strimmer® ['strɪmə] N Rasentrimmer *m*

strine [straɪn] N (*hum inf*) *australisches Englisch*

string [strɪŋ] *vb: pret, ptp* **strung** **N** **a** (*pl rare*: = *cord*) Schnur *f*, Kordel *f*, Bindfaden *m*; (*on apron etc*) Band *nt*; (*on anorak, belt*) Kordel *f*; (*of puppet*) Faden *m*, Schnur *f*, Draht *m*; **to have sb on a ~** (*fig inf*) jdn am Gängelband haben (*inf*); **to pull ~s** (*fig*) Fäden ziehen, Beziehungen spielen lassen; **without ~s, with no ~s attached** ohne Bedingungen; **a relationship with no ~s attached** eine völlig lockere Beziehung; **he wants a girlfriend but no ~s attached** er möchte eine Freundin, will sich aber in keiner Weise gebunden fühlen

b (= *row, of beads, onions etc*) Schnur *f*; (*of racehorses etc*) Reihe *f*; (*of people*) Schlange *f*; (*of vehicles*) Kette *f*, Schlange *f*; (*fig: = series*) Reihe *f*; (*of lies, curses*) Haufen *m*, Serie *f*

c (*of musical instrument, tennis racquet etc*) Saite *f*; (*of bow*) Sehne *f*; **a twelve-string guitar** eine zwölfsaitige Gitarre; **to have two ~s** *or* **a second ~** *or* **more than one ~ to one's bow** zwei Eisen im Feuer haben → **second string a**

d **strings** PL (= *instruments*) **the ~s** die Streichinstrumente *pl*; (= *players*) die Streicher *pl*; **he plays in the ~s** er ist Streicher, er gehört zu den Streichern

e (*Bot*) Faden *m*

f (*Comput: of characters*) Zeichenfolge *f*

VT **a** (= *put on string*) aufreihen, auffädeln, aufziehen

b *violin etc, tennis racquet* (mit Saiten) bespannen, besaiten; *bow* spannen → **highly strung**

c *beans* abfasern, (die) Fäden (+*gen*) abziehen

d (= *space out*) aufreihen; **they strung lights in the trees** sie haben Lampen in die Bäume gehängt

▶ **string along** (*inf*) **VT** *sep* **to string sb along** jdn hinhalten **VI** (= *go along, play along with*) sich anschließen (*with* +*dat*)

▶ **string out VI** sich verteilen; **the children strung out behind the teacher** die Kinder gingen in weiten Abständen hinter dem Lehrer her **VT** *sep lanterns, washing* aufhängen; *guards, posts* verteilen

▶ **string together** VT *sep words, sentences* aneinander reihen; **she can't even string two sentences together** sie bringt keinen vernünftigen Satz zusammen; **she can't string her thoughts together coherently** sie ist unfähig, zusammenhängend zu denken

▶ **string up** VT *sep* **a** (= *suspend with string*) aufhängen; (*inf*, = *hang*) aufknüpfen (*inf*) **b** → **strung-up**

string: string bag N (*esp Brit*) Einkaufsnetz *nt*; **string band** N Streichorchester *nt*; **string bass** N Kontrabass *m*; **string bean** N (*esp US*, = *bean*) grüne Bohne; (*fig*, = *person*) Bohnenstange *f* (*hum inf*)

stringed [strɪŋd] ADJ **~ instrument** Saiteninstrument *nt*; (*played with bow also*) Streichinstrument *nt*

stringency ['strɪndʒənsɪ] N (*of standards, law, reforms, discipline*) Strenge *f*; (*of rules, testing, training etc also*) Härte *f*, Schärfe *f*; **economic ~** strenge Sparmaßnahmen *pl*

stringent ['strɪndʒənt] ADJ *standards, laws, discipline, reforms* streng; *rules, testing, training etc also* hart; *measures* hart, scharf; *market* gedrückt; **~ economies** strenge Sparmaßnahmen *pl*; **they have to practise ~ economy** sie müssen eisern sparen

stringently ['strɪndʒəntlɪ] ADV *control* streng; *enforce, train also* hart; *deal with* energisch; *economize* eisern

stringer ['strɪŋə] N (*Press sl*) Lokalreporter(in) *m(f)*

string: string instrument N Saiteninstrument *nt*; (*played with bow also*) Streichinstrument *nt*; **string player** N Streicher(in) *m(f)*; **string-puller** N Drahtzieher *m*; **string-pulling** N Spielenlassen *nt* von Beziehungen; **string quartet** N Streichquartett *nt*; **string tie** N schmale Krawatte; **string vest** N Netzhemd *nt*

stringy ['strɪŋɪ] ADJ (+*er*) *meat* sehnig, zäh, faserig; *vegetable* faserig, voller Fäden; *person* sehnig; *plant, seaweed, root* lang und dünn; *hair* strähnig

strip [strɪp] **N** **a** (= *narrow piece*) Streifen *m*; (*of metal*) Band *nt* → **comic strip**, **tear off**

b (*Brit, Sport*) Trikot *nt*, Dress *m*

c (*US*: = *main street*) Hauptgeschäftsstraße *f*

d (*inf*, = *airstrip*) Start-und-Lande-Bahn *f*, Piste (*inf*) *f*

e (*inf*, = *striptease*) **to do a ~** strippen (*inf*)

VT **a** (= *remove clothes etc from*) *person* ausziehen; *bed* abziehen; *wall* (= *remove paint from*) abkratzen; (= remove paper from) die Tapeten abziehen von; floor abziehen, abschleifen; paint abbeizen; wallpaper abziehen; (= remove contents from) ausräumen; **to ~ sb naked** or **to the skin** jdn bis auf die Haut ausziehen, jdn nackt ausziehen; **to ~ a house of its contents** ein Haus ausräumen; **to ~ a room of all its pictures** alle Bilder aus einem Zimmer entfernen; **to ~ sth from** or **off sth** etw von etw entfernen; **to ~ a tree of fruit** einen Baum abernten; **the wind ~ped the leaves from** or **off the trees** der Wind wehte die Blätter von den Bäumen; **to ~ the bark from the trees** Bäume schälen or entrinden; **~ped of sth** ohne etw; **~ped of official language, this means ...** in einfachen Worten heißt das ...

b (fig, = deprive of) berauben (of +gen); **he was ~ped of his titles** seine Titel wurden ihm aberkannt

c (Tech) (= damage) gear kaputtmachen (inf), beschädigen; screw überdrehen; (= dismantle) engine, car, gun auseinander nehmen, zerlegen; **to ~ the thread (off a screw)** eine Schraube überdrehen

VI (= remove clothes) sich ausziehen; (at doctor's) sich freimachen; (= perform striptease) strippen (inf); **to ~ naked** sich bis auf die Haut ausziehen, sich ganz ausziehen; **to ~ to the waist** den Oberkörper freimachen; **~ped to the waist** mit nacktem Oberkörper

▶ **strip away** VT SEP layer of dirt, turf, bark ablösen, abziehen; (fig) pretence, hypocrisy abwerfen, über Bord werfen (inf)

▶ **strip down** **VT** sep engine auseinander nehmen, zerlegen **VI** **to strip down to one's underwear** sich bis auf die Unterwäsche ausziehen

▶ **strip off** **VT** sep clothes ausziehen; berries, leaves abmachen (prep obj von); (wind) herunterwehen (prep obj von); paper abziehen (prep obj von); buttons, ornaments entfernen, abmachen (prep obj von); fruit skin, bark abschälen, ablösen (prep obj von); **to strip off the leaves** die Blätter vom Zweig entfernen **VI** **a** (= take one's clothes off) sich ausziehen; (at doctor's) sich freimachen; (in striptease) strippen (inf) **b** (bark) sich abschälen lassen; (paper) sich ablösen lassen

strip: **strip cartoon** N (Brit) Comic(strip) m; **strip club** N Stripteaseklub m; **strip cropping** N (Agr) Streifenpflanzung f

stripe [straɪp] N **a** Streifen m **b** (Mil) (Ärmel-)streifen m, Winkel m; **to gain** or **get/lose one's ~s** befördert/degradiert werden **c** (old: = stroke) Schlag m, Hieb m **d** (US: = kind, of politics) Färbung f, Richtung f; (of character, opinion) Art f, Schlag m **e** **stripes** PL (US, inf, = prison uniform) Sträflingsanzug m (inf)

striped [straɪpt] ADJ gestreift; **~ with ...** mit ... Streifen; **to be ~ with grey** graue Streifen haben, grau gestreift sein

strip: **strip farming** N (Agr) Streifenpflanzung f, Streifenflurwirtschaft f; **strip light** N (esp Brit) Neonröhre f; **strip lighting** N (esp Brit) Neonlicht nt or -beleuchtung f

stripling ['strɪplɪŋ] N (liter) Bürschchen nt; (pej also) Grünschnabel m

strip: **strip mill** N Walzwerk nt; **strip mine** N (US) Tagebau m; **strip mining** N (US) Abbau m über Tage

strippagram ['strɪpəgræm] N durch eine Angestellte einer Agentur persönlich übermittelter Geburtstagsgruß etc mit Striptease

stripped-down ['strɪptdaʊn] ADJ car etc ohne Extras pred

stripper ['strɪpə] N **a** (= performer) Stripperin f, Stripteasetänzerin f; **male ~** Stripper m, Stripteasetänzer m **b** (= paint stripper) Farbentferner m; (= wallpaper stripper) Tapetenlöser m

strip: **strip poker** N Strippoker nt; **strip-search** **N** Leibesvisitation f **VT** einer Leibesvisitation (dat) unterziehen; **he was ~ed** er musste sich einer Leibesvisitation unterziehen; **strip show** N Strip(tease)show f, Striptease m or nt; **striptease** **N** Striptease m or nt; **to do**

a ~ strippen (inf), einen Striptease machen **ADJ** attr Striptease-; **~ act** Stripteasenummer f

stripy ['straɪpɪ] ADJ (+er) (inf) gestreift

strive [straɪv] pret **strove**, ptp **striven** ['strɪvn] VI (= exert oneself) sich bemühen; (= fight) kämpfen; **to ~ to do sth** bestrebt or bemüht sein, etw zu tun; **to ~ for** or (old) **after sth** etw anstreben, nach etw streben; **to ~ against sth** gegen etw (an)kämpfen; **to ~ with sb/sth** mit jdm/etw ringen or kämpfen

strobe [strəʊb] **ADJ** stroboskopisch **N** stroboskopische Beleuchtung

stroboscope ['strəʊbəskəʊp] N Stroboskop nt

stroboscopic [ˌstrəʊbəˈskɒpɪk] ADJ stroboskopisch

strode [strəʊd] pret of **stride**

stroke [strəʊk] **N** **a** (= blow) Schlag m, Hieb m; **a ~ of lightning** ein Blitz(schlag) m **b** (Cricket, Golf, Rowing, Tennis) Schlag m; (Billiards) Stoß m; (Swimming, = movement) Zug m; (= type of stroke) Stil m; **they are rowing (at) a fast ~** sie rudern mit hoher Schlagzahl; **to put sb off his ~** (fig) jdn aus dem Takt or Konzept bringen

c (Rowing: = person) Schlagmann m **d** (of pen, brush etc) Strich m; (fig, of work) Schlag m; (in diplomacy, business) Schachzug m; **he doesn't do a ~ (of work)** er tut keinen Schlag (inf), er rührt keinen Finger (inf); **a ~ of genius** ein genialer Einfall; **a ~ of luck** ein Glücksfall m; **we had a ~ of luck** wir hatten Glück; **with one ~ of the pen** (lit, fig) mit einem Federstrich; **at a** or **one ~** mit einem Schlag **e** (of clock) Schlag m; **on the ~ of twelve** Punkt zwölf (Uhr) **f** (of piston) Hub m; **two-stroke engine** Zweitaktmotor m **g** (Med) Schlag m; **to have a ~** einen Schlag(-anfall) bekommen **h** (= caress) Streicheln nt no pl; **to give sb/sth a ~** jdn/etw streicheln; **with gentle ~s** mit sanftem Streicheln; **different ~s for different folks** (esp US, inf) jedem Tierchen sein Pläsierchen (hum inf)

VT **a** cat, hand, hair, face streicheln; **he ~d his chin** er strich sich (dat) übers Kinn; **to ~ one's hair down** sich (dat) das Haar glattstreichen **b** **to ~ a boat (to victory)** als Schlagmann (ein Boot zum Sieg) rudern

stroke play N (Golf) Zählspiel nt; **stroke-play tournament** Zählspielturnier nt

stroll [strəʊl] **N** Spaziergang m, Bummel m; **to go for** or **have** or **take a ~** einen Spaziergang or Bummel machen

VI spazieren, bummeln; **to ~ along/around** herumspazieren or -bummeln or -schlendern; **to ~ along the road** die Straße entlangspazieren or -bummeln or -schlendern; **to ~ around the house** um das Haus herumspazieren; **to ~ around the town** durch die Stadt bummeln; **to ~ up to sb** auf jdn zuschlendern; **to ~ in(to the room)** (ins Zimmer) hineinspazieren or -schlendern; **to ~ out (of the room)** (aus dem Zimmer) herausspazieren or -schlendern; **to ~ up and down (the road)** die Straße auf und ab spazieren or bummeln or schlendern

stroller ['strəʊlə] N **a** (= walker) Spaziergänger(in) m(f) **b** (esp US, = pushchair) Sportwagen m

strolling ['strəʊlɪŋ] ADJ attr actor, minstrel fahrend

strong [strɒŋ] **ADJ** (+er) **a** stark; (physically) person, material, kick, hands kräftig, stark; grip, voice kräftig; table, bolt, nail, wall stabil, solide; shoes fest; (= strongly marked) features ausgeprägt; **you need a ~ stomach to be a nurse** als Krankenschwester muss man allerhand verkraften können

b (= healthy) kräftig; person, constitution robust, kräftig; teeth, eyes, eyesight, heart, nerves gut; **when you're ~ again** wenn Sie wieder bei Kräften sind; **he's getting ~er every day** er wird mit jedem Tag wieder kräftiger

c (= powerful, effective) stark; character, convic-

tion, views fest; country mächtig; candidate, case aussichtsreich; influence, temptation groß, stark; reason, argument, evidence überzeugend; protest, plea energisch; measure drastisch; letter geharnischt, in starken Worten abgefasst; (Liter) plot, sequence, passage, performance gut, stark (inf); **to have ~ feelings/views about sth** in Bezug auf etw (acc) stark engagiert sein; **I didn't know you had such ~ feelings about it** ich habe nicht gewusst, dass Ihnen so viel daran liegt or dass Ihnen das so viel bedeutet; (against it) ich habe nicht gewusst, dass Sie so dagegen sind; **she has very ~ feelings about him** sie hat sehr viel für ihn übrig; (as candidate etc) sie hält sehr viel von ihm; (against him) sie ist vollkommen gegen ihn; **to have ~ feelings for** or **about sth** eine starke Bindung an etw (acc) haben; **we need a ~ hand to fight crime** wir müssen das Verbrechen mit starker Hand bekämpfen; **his ~ point** seine Stärke; **to protest in ~ terms** energisch protestieren; **I had a ~ sense of déjà-vu** ich hatte ganz den Eindruck, das schon einmal gesehen zu haben; **there is a ~ possibility that ...** es ist überaus wahrscheinlich, dass ...

d (in numbers) stark; **a group 20 ~** eine 20 Mann starke Gruppe **e** (= capable) gut, stark (inf); **he is ~ in/on sth** etw ist seine Stärke or starke Seite **f** (= enthusiastic, committed) begeistert; supporter, Catholic, socialist überzeugt; belief, faith unerschütterlich, stark; **he's very ~ for Smith** (inf) er ist (ein) Smith-Fan (inf) **g** food deftig; smell, perfume etc stark; (= pungent, unpleasant) smell, taste streng; (of butter) ranzig; colour, light kräftig; acid, bleach stark; solution konzentriert; **a ~ drink** ein harter Drink **h** accent, verb, rhyme stark; syllable etc betont **i** (Fin) market, economy gesund; price stabil; currency stark

ADV (+er) **a** (inf) **to be going ~** (old person, thing) gut in Schuss sein (inf); (runner) gut in Form sein; (party, rehearsals) in Schwung sein (inf); **that's (coming it) a bit ~!** das ist ein starkes Stück!; **he pitched it pretty ~** (inf) er drückte sich ziemlich drastisch aus **b** (Fin) in einer starken Position

strong: **strong-arm** (inf) **ADJ** tactics etc brutal; **~ man** Schläger m **VT** (esp US, = beat up) zusammenschlagen; (= intimidate) unter Druck setzen; **they were ~ed into paying** sie wurden so unter Druck gesetzt, dass sie zahlten; **strongbox** N (Geld)kassette f; **strong breeze** N (Met) starke Winde pl, Windstärke 6; **strong gale** N (Met) Windstärke 9; **stronghold** N (= castle, fortress) Festung f; (= town etc) Stützpunkt m; (fig) Hochburg f

strongly ['strɒŋlɪ] ADV **a** (physically) stark; kick, grip, shine kräftig; fight, attack heftig; built solide, stabil; (person) kräftig; marked stark **b** (mentally) influence, suspect, tempt, interest stark; desire sehr; believe fest; **to feel ~ about sb/sth** → strong ADJ c **c** (= powerfully) stark; protest, defend heftig, energisch; plead inständig; support kräftig; sense zutiefst; answer, worded in starken Worten; **~ anti-American** stark antiamerikanisch; **he spoke ~ against it** er sprach sich entschieden dagegen aus; **I ~ advise you ...** ich möchte Ihnen dringend(st) raten ...; **I feel very ~ that ...** ich vertrete entschieden die Meinung, dass ...; **he is a man with ~ held views** er ist ein Mann mit sehr festen Ansichten; **to be ~ recommended** besonders or nachdrücklich empfohlen werden; **to be ~ in favour of sth** etw sehr or stark befürworten; **to be ~ opposed to** or **against sth** etw scharf ablehnen; **to be ~ critical of sb/sth** eine sehr kritische Haltung gegenüber jdm/etw haben; **to react ~ to sth** heftig auf etw (acc) reagieren

d (= markedly) **her accent sounded ~ northern** sie hatte einen auffallend norddeutschen/-englischen etc Akzent; **vegetables featured ~ on the menu** auf der Speisekarte war Gemüse besonders stark vertreten; **to smell/taste ~ of sth** stark nach etw riechen/schmecken

strongman ['strɒŋmæn] N *pl* **-men** [-men] (*lit*, *fig*) starker Mann

strong-minded ADJ , **strong-mindedly** ADV [ˌstrɒŋ'maɪndɪd, -lɪ] willensstark

strong-mindedness [ˌstrɒŋ'maɪndɪdnɪs] N Willensstärke *f*

strong: strong point N Stärke *f*; **strongroom** N Tresorraum *m*, Stahlkammer *f*; **strong-willed** [ˌstrɒŋ'wɪld] ADJ willensstark, entschlossen, (*pej*) eigensinnig, trotzig

strontium ['strɒntɪəm] N Strontium *nt*

strop [strɒp] N Streichriemen *m* VT abziehen

strophe ['strəʊfɪ] N Strophe *f*

stroppiness ['strɒpɪnɪs] N (*Brit inf*) Fuchtigkeit *f* (*inf*); (*of answer, children*) Pampigkeit *f* (*inf*); (*of bouncer etc*) Aggressivität *f*; (*of official*) Sturheit *f*

stroppy ['strɒpɪ] ADJ (+er) (*Brit inf*) fuchtig (*inf*); *answer, children* pampig (*inf*); *bouncer etc* aggressiv; (= *obstinate*) *official* stur; **to be ~ about doing sth** fuchtig/pampig sein, weil man etw tun soll (*inf*); **don't get ~ with me** (= *aggressive*) werd jetzt nicht pampig (*inf*); (= *obstinate, uncooperative*) mach nicht so auf stur (*inf*)

strove [strəʊv] *pret of* **strive**

struck [strʌk] *pret, ptp of* **strike** ADJ **a** *pred* **to be ~ with sb/sth** (= *impressed*) von jdm/etw begeistert *or* angetan sein; **I wasn't very ~ with him** er hat keinen großen Eindruck auf mich gemacht; **to be ~ on sb/sth** (= *keen*) auf jdn/etw stehen (*inf*), auf jdn/etw versessen sein **b** *attr* (*US*, = *striking*) *workers* streikend; *factory, employers* vom Streik betroffen, bestreikt

structural ['strʌktʃərəl] ADJ **a** strukturell, Struktur-; (*of building*) *alterations, damage, requirements* baulich; **~ material** Baumaterial *nt*; **~ part** Bauteil *nt*; **the bridge suffered ~ damage** die Struktur der Brücke wurde beschädigt **b** (= *weight-bearing*) *wall, beam* tragend **c** (*fig*, = *essential*) essenziell, essentiell, notwendig

structural: structural analysis N (*Gram*) Strukturanalyse *f*; **structural defect** N Konstruktionsfehler *m*; **structural engineer** N Konstrukteur(in) *m(f)*; **structural engineering** N Bautechnik *f*; **structural fault** N Konstruktionsfehler *m*; **structural formula** N (*Chem*) Strukturformel *f*

structuralism ['strʌktʃərəlɪzəm] N der Strukturalismus

structuralist ['strʌktʃərəlɪst] N Strukturalist(in) *m(f)* ADJ *attr* strukturalistisch

structurally ['strʌktʃərəlɪ] ADV strukturell; **~ the novel is excellent** vom Aufbau her ist der Roman ausgezeichnet; **~ sound** sicher; **the building is ~ unsound** das Gebäude weist bautechnische Mängel auf; **~ the building is in good condition** was das rein Bauliche betrifft, ist das Haus in gutem Zustand

structural: structural steel N Konstruktionsstahl *m*; **structural survey** N Bauzustandsgutachten *nt*; **structural unemployment** N strukturelle Arbeitslosigkeit

structure ['strʌktʃə] N **a** (= *organization*) Struktur *f*; (*Liter*) Aufbau *m*; (*Tech, of bridge, car etc*) Konstruktion *f*; **bone ~** Knochenbau *m* **b** (= *thing constructed*) Konstruktion *f* VT strukturieren; *essay, argument* aufbauen, gliedern; *layout, life* gestalten

structured ['strʌktʃəd] ADJ *programme* strukturiert; *approach* durchdacht; *essay* sorgfältig gegliedert; *society* durchorganisiert, strukturiert; **highly ~** (*society*) stark gegliedert; *novel etc* sorgfältig (auf)gebaut *or* gegliedert

strudel ['ʃtruːdl] N (*esp US*) Strudel *m*

struggle ['strʌgl] N (*lit, fig*) Kampf *m* (*for* um); (*fig*, = *effort*) Anstrengung *f*; **without a ~** kampflos; **to put up a ~** sich wehren; **the ~ for survival/existence** der Überlebens-/Daseinskampf; **the ~ to feed her seven children** der Kampf, ihre sieben Kinder zu ernähren; **the ~ to find somewhere to live** der Kampf *or* die Schwierigkeiten, bis man eine Wohnung gefunden hat; **it is/was a ~** es ist/war mühsam; **she finds life a ~** sie findet das Leben mühsam; **I had a ~ to**

persuade him es war gar nicht einfach, ihn zu überreden

VI **a** (= *contend*) kämpfen; (*in self-defence*) sich wehren; (= *writhe*) sich winden; (*financially*) in Schwierigkeiten sein, krebsen (*inf*); (*fig*, = *strive*) sich sehr bemühen *or* anstrengen, sich abmühen; **the police were struggling with the burglar** zwischen der Polizei und dem Einbrecher gab es ein Handgemenge; **to ~ to do sth** sich sehr anstrengen, etw zu tun; **to ~ for sth** um etw kämpfen, sich um etw bemühen; **to ~ against sb/sth** gegen jdn/etw kämpfen; **to ~ with sb** mit jdm kämpfen; **to ~ with sth** (*with problem, difficulty, question*) sich mit etw herumschlagen; *with injury, mortgage, debts, feelings* mit etw zu kämpfen haben; *with doubts, one's conscience* mit etw ringen; *with luggage, language, subject, homework, words* sich mit etw abmühen; **to ~ with life** es im Leben nicht leicht haben; **this firm/team/family is struggling** diese Firma/Mannschaft/Familie hat (schwer) zu kämpfen; **are you struggling?** hast du Schwierigkeiten?; **can you manage? – I'm struggling** schaffst dus? – mit Müh und Not; **he was struggling to make ends meet** er hatte seine liebe Not durchzukommen

b (= *move with difficulty*) sich quälen; **to ~ to one's feet** mühsam aufstehen *or* auf die Beine kommen, sich aufrappeln (*inf*); **to ~ to get up** sich hochquälen; **he ~d through the tiny window** er zwängte sich durch das kleine Fenster; **to ~ on** (*lit*) sich weiterkämpfen; (*fig*) weiterkämpfen; **to ~ along/through** (*lit, fig*) sich durchschlagen *or* -kämpfen

► **struggling** ['strʌglɪŋ] ADJ *artist, musician, actor* am Hungertuch nagend *attr*

strum [strʌm] VT *tune, chord* klimpern; *guitar* klimpern auf (+*dat*); **to ~ out a song** ein Liedchen klimpern VI klimpern (*on* auf +*dat*)

strumpet ['strʌmpɪt] N (*old*) Hure *f*, Dirne *f*

strung [strʌŋ] *pret, ptp of* **string**

strung-up [ˌstrʌŋ'ʌp] ADJ **to be ~** nervös *or* gespannt sein (*about sth* wegen etw)

strut¹ [strʌt] VI stolzieren; **to ~ about (the yard)** (auf dem Hof) herumstolzieren; **to ~ past** vorbeistolzieren VT **to ~ one's stuff** (*inf*) zeigen, was man drauf hat; (*sexually*) zeigen, was man hat N angeberischer Gang, Stolzieren *nt*; **to walk with a ~** stolzieren

strut² N (*horizontal*) Strebe *f*; (*sloping also*) Stütze *f*; (*vertical*) Pfeiler *m*

struth [struːθ] INTERJ (*Brit, inf*) heiliger Strohsack (*inf*)

strychnine ['strɪkniːn] N Strychnin *nt*

stub [stʌb] N (*of candle, pencil, tail*) Stummel *m*; (*of cigarette etc*) Kippe *f*; (*of cheque, ticket*) Abschnitt *m*; (*of tree*) Stumpf *m* VT **to ~ one's toe (on** *or* **against sth)** sich (*dat*) den Zeh (an etw *dat*) stoßen, mit dem Zeh an *or* gegen etw (*acc*) stoßen; **to ~ out a cigarette** eine Zigarette ausdrücken

stub axle N Achszapfen *m*

stubble ['stʌbl] N , *no pl* Stoppeln *pl*; **a field of ~** ein Stoppelfeld *nt*

stubbly ['stʌblɪ] ADJ (+er) Stoppel-; *face* stoppelig; **~ beard** Stoppelbart *m*; **~ field** Stoppelfeld *nt*

stubborn ['stʌbən] ADJ **a** (= *obstinate*) *person, insistence* stur; *animal, child* störrisch; **to be ~ about sth** stur auf etw (*dat*) beharren; **she has a ~ streak** sie kann sehr stur sein **b** (= *persistent*) *refusal, resistance, campaign, stain etc* hartnäckig; **in ~ silence** stur schweigend **c** *lock, material* widerspenstig; *essay, argument* widerspenstig

stubbornly ['stʌbənlɪ] ADV **a** *refuse* stur; *insist* störrisch; *say* trotzig, starrköpfig **b** (= *persistently*) hartnäckig; **interest rates have remained ~ high** die Zinsen sind unbeirrt hoch geblieben

stubbornness ['stʌbənnɪs] N **a** (= *obstinacy, of person*) Sturheit *f*; (*of animal, child*) störrische Art **b** (*of refusal, resistance*) Hartnäckigkeit *f* **c** (*of lock*) Widerspenstigkeit *f*; (*of cough*) Hartnäckigkeit *f*

stubby ['stʌbɪ] ADJ (+er) *revolver etc* kurz; *tail* stummelig; *pencil, vase* kurz und dick; *person* gedrungen, stämmig, untersetzt; *legs* kurz und stämmig; **~ fingers** Wurstfinger *pl* (*inf*); **~ wings** Stummelflügel *pl*

stucco ['stʌkəʊ] N *pl* **-(e)s** Stuck *m*; (*also* **stucco work**) Stuckarbeit *f*, Stukkatur *f* ADJ *attr* Stuck-; **~ ceiling** Stuckdecke *f* VT mit Stuck verzieren

stuck [stʌk] *pret, ptp of* **stick²** ADJ **a** (= *baffled*) (*on, over* mit) **to be ~** nicht klarkommen, nicht zurechtkommen; **to get ~** nicht weiterkommen **b** (= *wedged*) **to be ~** (*door etc*) verkeilt sein; **to get ~** stecken bleiben **c** (= *trapped, stranded*) **to be ~** festsitzen; **to be ~ in a traffic jam** im Stau festsitzen **d** (*inf*) **he/she is ~ for sth** es fehlt ihm/ihr an etw (*dat*), ihm/ihr fehlt etw; **I'm a bit ~ for cash** ich bin ein bisschen knapp bei Kasse; **he wasn't exactly ~ for something to say** man kann nicht gerade sagen, dass ihm der Gesprächsstoff fehlte; **to be ~ for sb** jdn dringend brauchen **e** (*Brit inf*) **to get ~ into sb** jdn richtig in die Mangel nehmen (*inf*); **to get ~ into sth** sich in etw (*acc*) richtig reinknien (*inf*); **Stephen got ~ into his steak** Stephen nahm sein Steak in Angriff; **get ~ in!** schlag zu! (*inf*) **f** (*inf*, = *infatuated*) **to be ~ on sb** in jdn verknallt sein (*inf*) **g** (*inf*) **to be ~ with sb/sth** mit jdm/etw dasitzen, jdn/etw am Hals haben (*inf*) **h** **to squeal like a ~ pig** wie am Spieß schreien

stuck-up [ˌstʌk'ʌp] ADJ (*inf*) *person, attitude, voice* hochnäsig; **to be ~ about sth** sich (*dat*) viel auf etw (*acc*) einbilden

stud¹ [stʌd] N **a** (= *nail*) Beschlagnagel *m*; (*decorative*) Ziernagel *m*; (*Brit*: *on boots*) Stollen *m*; **reflector ~** Katzenauge *nt* **b** (= *collar stud*) Kragenknopf *m* **c** (= *earring*) Ohrstecker *m* VT (*usu pass*) übersäen; (*with jewels*) (dicht) besetzen; **their family tree is ~ded with generals** in ihrem Stammbaum wimmelt es von Generälen

stud² N (= *group of horses, for breeding*) Gestüt *nt*, Zucht *f*; (*for racing etc*) Stall *m*; (= *stallion*) (Zucht)hengst *m*; (*inf*, = *man*) Hengst *m* (*inf*); **the stallion is at ~** der Hengst wird zur Zucht benutzt; **to put to ~** zu Zuchtzwecken verwenden

studbook ['stʌdbʊk] N Gestüt- *or* Zuchtbuch *nt*

student ['stjuːdənt] N (*Univ*) Student(in) *m(f)*, Studierende(r) *mf*; (*esp US, at school, night school*) Schüler(in) *m(f)*; **he is a ~ of French life/human nature** er studiert die französische Lebensart/die menschliche Natur; **he is a ~ of French** *or* **a French ~** (*Univ*) er studiert Französisch; (*Sch*) er lernt Französisch; **medical/law ~s** Medizin-/Jurastudenten *pl* ADJ *attr* Studenten-; *activities, protest movement* studentisch; **~ driver** (*US*) Fahrschüler(in) *m(f)*; **~ nurse** Krankenpflegeschüler(in) *m(f)*

student: student body N Studentenschaft *f*; **student card** N Studentenausweis *m*; **student loan** N Studentendarlehen *nt*; **studentship** N (*Brit*, = *grant*) Stipendium *nt*; **student(s') union** N (*Brit*) **a** (= *organization*) Studentenorganisation an britischen Universitäten, die sich um soziale Belange der Studenten kümmert (*esp political*) Studentenbund *m* **b** (= *building*) Gebäude *nt* der Student(s') Union/des Studentenbundes; **student teacher** N Referendar(in) *m(f)*; **student unrest** N Studentenunruhen *pl*

stud: stud farm N Gestüt *nt*; **stud horse** N Zuchthengst *m*

studied ['stʌdɪd] *pret, ptp of* **study** ADJ (= *carefully considered*) *reply* (gut) durchdacht, wohl überlegt; *simplicity* bewusst, ausgesucht; *prose, style* kunstvoll; (= *deliberate*) berechnet; *calm, politeness* gewollt; *insult* beabsichtigt, bewusst; *avoidance* sorgfältig; *pose* einstudiert; *elegance* gekünstelt; *voice* gewählt; **to maintain a ~ silence** wohl überlegt schweigen

studio ['stjuːdɪəʊ] N (*all senses*) Studio *nt*; (*of painter, photographer also*) Atelier *nt*; (= broadcasting *studio also*) Senderaum *m*

studio: studio apartment N Studiowohnung *f*; **studio audience** N Publikum *nt* im Studio; **studio couch** N Schlafcouch *f*; **studio flat** N (*Brit*) = **studio apartment**

studious ['stjuːdɪəs] ADJ *person* fleißig, eifrig; *life, habits, appearance* gelehrsam; *turn of mind* lernbegierig; *attention, piece of work, research* gewissenhaft, sorgfältig; *avoidance* gezielt, sorgsam; *politeness* bewusst; *effort* eifrig, beflissen (*geh*); **a ~ atmosphere** eine eifrige Lernatmosphäre

studiously ['stjuːdɪəslɪ] ADV fleißig, eifrig; (= *painstakingly*) sorgsam, sorgfältig; *polite* bewusst; *avoid* gezielt, sorgsam; (= *deliberately*) absichtlich, bewusst; **to remain ~ neutral** sorgsam auf Neutralität bedacht sein

studiousness ['stjuːdɪəsnɪs] N (*of person*) Lerneifer *m*, Fleiß *m*

study ['stʌdɪ] ✪ 26.2 **N** **a** (= *studying, branch of study, esp Univ*) Studium *nt*; (*at school*) Lernen *nt*; (*of situation, evidence, case*) Untersuchung *f*; (*of nature*) Beobachtung *f*; **the ~ of cancer** die Krebsforschung; **the ~ of Chinese** das Chinesischstudium; **African studies** (*Univ*) afrikanische Sprache und Kultur, Afrikanistik *f*; **modern French studies** französische Sprache und Landeskunde; **to make a ~ of sth** etw untersuchen; (*academic*) etw studieren; **to spend one's time in ~** seine Zeit mit Studieren/Lernen verbringen; **fond of ~** lernbegierig; **during my studies** während meines Studiums; **his face was a ~** (*inf*) sein Gesicht war sehenswert → **brown study**

  b (= *piece of work*) Studie *f* (*of über* +*acc*); (*Art, Phot*) Studie *f* (*of* +*gen*); (*Liter, Sociol*) Untersuchung *f* (*of über* +*acc*); (*Mus*) Etüde *f*

  c (= *room*) Arbeits- or Studierzimmer *nt*

  VT studieren; (*Sch*) lernen; *nature also, stars* beobachten; *author, particular tune, text etc* sich befassen mit; (= *research into*) erforschen; (= *examine*) untersuchen; *clue, evidence* prüfen, untersuchen

  VI studieren; (*esp Sch*) lernen; **to ~ to be a teacher/doctor** ein Lehrerstudium/Medizinstudium machen; **to ~ for an exam** sich auf eine Prüfung vorbereiten, für eine Prüfung lernen; **to ~ under sb** bei jdm studieren

study: study group N Arbeitsgruppe or -gemeinschaft *f*; **study hall** N Studien- or Lesesaal *m*; **study tour** N Informationsreise *f*; **study visit** N Studienreise *f*

stuff [stʌf] **N** **a** Zeug *nt*; **black/sweet** *etc* ~ schwarzes/süßes *etc* Zeug; **the ~ that dreams are made of** der Stoff, aus dem die Träume sind; **the ~ of tragedy** echte Tragik; **show him what kind of ~ you're made of** zeig ihm, aus welchem Holz du geschnitzt bist; **there was a lot of rough ~** es ging ziemlich rau zu; **there is some good ~ in that book** in dem Buch stecken ein paar gute Sachen; **it's poor/good** ~ das ist schlecht/gut; **this tea is strong ~** der Tee ist ziemlich stark; **this book is strong ~** das Buch ist starker Tobak; **I can't read his ~** ich kann sein Zeug nicht lesen; **his later ~ is less original** seine späteren Sachen sind weniger originell; **he brought me some ~ to read/to pass the time** er hat mir etwas zum Lesen/zur Unterhaltung mitgebracht; **books and ~** Bücher und so (*inf*); **and ~ like that** und so was (*inf*); **all that ~ about how he wants to help us** all das Gerede, dass er uns helfen will; **~ and nonsense** Quatsch *m* (*inf*), Blödsinn *m*; **all this ~ about Father Christmas** (*inf*) all der Quatsch vom Weihnachtsmann (*inf*)

  b (*inf*) **she's a nice bit of ~** die ist nicht ohne (*inf*); **a drop of the hard ~** ein Schluck von dem scharfen Zeug; **that's the ~!** so ists richtig!, weiter so!; **to do one's ~** seine Nummer abziehen (*inf*); **go on, do your ~!** nun mach mal or doch! (*inf*); **he did his ~ well** er hat seine Sache gut gemacht; **to know one's ~** wissen,

wovon man redet, sich auskennen → **hot stuff**

  c (= *possessions*) Zeug *nt*, Sachen *pl*

  d (*inf* = *drugs*) Stoff *m* (*inf*)

  e (*old* = *cloth*) Material *nt*, Stoff *m*

  VT **a** (= *fill*) *container, room, person* voll stopfen; *hole* zustopfen, verstopfen; *contents, object, books* (hinein)stopfen (*into* in +*acc*); (*into envelope*) stecken (*into* in +*acc*); **to ~ sb with food** jdn mit Essen voll stopfen, jdn mästen (*inf*); **to ~ one's face** (*inf*) sich vollstopfen (*inf*); **to ~ sth away** etw wegstecken; **he ~ed it away in his pocket** er stopfte es in seine Tasche; **he ~ed some money in my hand** er drückte mir Geld in die Hand; **to ~ one's fingers into one's ears** sich (*dat*) die Finger in die Ohren stecken; **to be ~ed up (with a cold)** verschnupft sein, eine verstopfte Nase haben; **my nose is ~ed up** ich habe eine verstopfte Nase

  b (*Cook*) füllen

  c *cushion etc* füllen; *toy* ausstopfen; (*in taxidermy*) ausstopfen; **a ~ed toy** ein Stofftier *nt*

  d (*Brit, inf*) ~ **it** (= *be quiet*) halts Maul! (*inf*), Schnauze! (*inf*); **get ~ed!** du kannst mich mal (*inf*)!; **I told him to ~ it** ich sagte, er kann mich mal (*inf*); **you can ~ your job** *etc* du kannst deinen blöden Job *etc* behalten (*inf*); ~ **him!** der kann mich mal! (*inf*); ~ **the tax reform!** ich scheiß auf die Steuerreform! (*sl*)

  VI (*inf*: = *eat*) sich voll stopfen (*inf*)

  VR **to ~ oneself (with food/on cakes)** sich (mit Essen/Kuchen) voll stopfen (*inf*)

stuffed shirt ['stʌft'ʃɜːt] N (*inf*) Stockfisch *m* (*inf*)

stuffily ['stʌfɪlɪ] ADV (= *narrow-mindedly*) spießig; (= *prudishly*) prüde; (= *stiffly*) steif, gezwungen; (= *dully*) langweilig

stuffiness ['stʌfɪnɪs] N **a** (*of room, atmosphere*) Stickigkeit *f*, Dumpfheit *f* **b** (*of person*, = *narrow-mindedness*) Spießigkeit *f*; (= *prudishness*) Prüderie *f*, Zimperlichkeit *f*

stuffing ['stʌfɪŋ] N (*of pillow, quilt, Cook*) Füllung *f*; (*of furniture*) Polstermaterial *nt*; (*in taxidermy, toys*) Füllmaterial *nt*, Stopfmaterial *nt*; **to knock the ~ out of sb** (*inf*) jdn fertig machen (*inf*), jdn schaffen (*inf*)

stuffy ['stʌfɪ] ADJ (+er) **a** *room, atmosphere* stickig, dumpf; **it's a bit ~ in here** es ist etwas stickig hier drinnen **b** (= *narrow-minded*) spießig; (= *prudish*) prüde, zimperlich **c** (= *stiff*) steif; *atmosphere* gezwungen, steif; (= *dull*) langweilig, öde, fad **d** (= *blocked*) *nose* verstopft

stultify ['stʌltɪfaɪ] **VT** lähmen; *mind, person* verkümmern or verdummen lassen; **to become stultified** verkümmern, verdummen **VI** verkümmern, verdummen

stultifying ['stʌltɪfaɪɪŋ] ADJ lähmend; *boredom, inactivity also* abstumpfend; **to have a ~ effect on sb** jdn verkümmern lassen

stumble ['stʌmbl] **N** Stolpern *nt no pl, no indef art* (*in speech etc*) Stocken *nt no pl, no indef art* **VI a** (*lit, fig*) stolpern; (*in speech*) stocken; **to ~ against sth** gegen etw stoßen; **to ~ on sth** (*lit*) über etw (*acc*) stolpern; (*fig*) auf etw (*acc*) stoßen; **he ~d through a waltz/his speech** stockend or holperig spielte er einen Walzer/hielt er seine Rede

stumbling block ['stʌmblɪŋblɒk] N (*fig*) Hürde *f*, Hindernis *nt*, Problem *nt*; **to be a ~ to sth** einer Sache (*dat*) im Weg stehen

stumer ['stjuːmə'] N (*Brit inf*) **a** (= *counterfeit*) Fälschung *f* **b** (= *cheque*) wertloser Scheck **c** (= *failure*) Misserfolg *m*

stump [stʌmp] **N a** ADJ (*of tree, limb, tooth*) Stumpf *m*; (*of candle, pencil, tail, cigar*) Stummel *m*; (*Cricket*) Stab *m*; **to stir one's ~s** (*inf*) sich rühren, sich regen

  b (*US, Pol*, = *platform*) Rednertribüne *f*; ~ **speaker** Wahlredner(in) *m(f)*; **to go out on the ~s** (öffentlich or vor Ort) als Redner auftreten

  VT a (*Cricket*) ausschalten (*durch Umwerfen der Stäbe*)

  b (*fig inf*) **you've got me ~ed** da bin ich überfragt; **I'm ~ed by that problem, that problem's got me ~ed** ich bin mit meiner Weisheit or

meinem Latein am Ende (*inf*); **to be ~ed for an answer** um eine Antwort verlegen sein

  c (*US, Pol*) **to ~ the country** Wahl(kampf)reisen durch das Land machen

  VI (*inf*) stapfen; **to ~ along/about** entlang-/herumstapfen

▶ **stump up** (*Brit, inf*) **VT** insep springen lassen (*inf*), lockermachen (*inf*) **VI** blechen (*inf*) (*for sth* für etw)

stumpy ['stʌmpɪ] ADJ (+er) *pencil, candle* stummelig (*inf*), kurz; *person* stämmig, untersetzt; *tree* klein und gedrungen; *legs* kurz; *building* gedrungen; **a ~ tail** ein Stummelschwanz *m*

stun [stʌn] VT **a** (= *make unconscious*) betäuben; (*noise also*, = *daze*) benommen machen; (*fig*, = *shock*) fassungslos machen; (= *amaze*) erstaunen, verblüffen; **he was ~ned by the news** (*bad news*) er war über die Nachricht fassungslos or wie gelähmt; (*good news*) die Nachricht hat ihn überwältigt; **he was ~ned by his good fortune** er war sprachlos über sein Glück

stun bullet N Wuchtgeschoss *nt*

stung [stʌŋ] *pret, ptp of* **sting**

stun grenade N Blendgranate *f*

stunk [stʌŋk] *ptp of* **stink**

stunned [stʌnd] ADJ (= *unconscious*) betäubt; (= *dazed*) benommen; (*fig*, = *shocked*) fassungslos; (= *amazed*) sprachlos; **there was a ~ silence** benommenes Schweigen breitete sich aus; **I sat in ~ silence/disbelief** ich saß sprachlos/fassungslos da

stunner ['stʌnə'] N (*inf*, = *thing*) Wucht *f* (*inf*); (= *woman*) tolle Frau, tolles Weib (*inf*); (= *man*) toller Mann or Kerl (*inf*)

stunning ['stʌnɪŋ] ADJ (*lit*) *blow* wuchtig, betäubend; (*fig*) *news, victory* fantastisch, phantastisch, toll (*inf*); *dress, girl, effect, view, display, looks* atemberaubend; *defeat, shock* überwältigend

stunningly ['stʌnɪŋlɪ] ADV atemberaubend, fantastisch, phantastisch; *beautiful* überwältigend; *simple* erstaunlich

stunt[1] [stʌnt] N Kunststück *nt*, Nummer *f*; (= *publicity stunt, trick*) Gag *m*; (*Aviat*) Kunststück *nt*; **to do ~s** (= *be stuntman*) Stuntman sein, doubeln; **he does most of his own ~s** gefährliche Szenen spielt er meist selbst

stunt[2] VT (*lit, fig*) *growth, development* hemmen; *trees, mind etc* verkümmern lassen

stunt double N (*Film*) Double *nt*

stunted ['stʌntɪd] ADJ *plant, mind* verkümmert; *child* unterentwickelt; **the ~ growth of these trees** der verkümmerten Bäume; **his ~ growth** seine Verwachsenheit; **~ development** Unterentwicklung *f*

stunt: stunt flying N Kunstflug *m*; **stunt kite** N Drachen *m* (*mit dem Flugmanöver vorgeführt werden können*); **stuntman** N Stuntman *m*, Double *nt*

stupefaction [ˌstjuːpɪˈfækʃən] N Verblüffung *f*; **he looked at me in ~** er sah mich verblüfft or voller Verblüffung an

stupefy ['stjuːpɪfaɪ] VT benommen machen; (*fig*, = *amaze, surprise*) verblüffen; **to be stupefied by drink** vom Alkohol benommen sein

stupefying ['stjuːpɪfaɪɪŋ] ADJ betäubend; (*fig*, = *amazing*) verblüffend

stupendous [stjuːˈpendəs] ADJ fantastisch, phantastisch; *effort* enorm

stupendously [stjuːˈpendəslɪ] ADV fantastisch, phantastisch; *hard* enorm; *boring* ungeheuer

stupid ['stjuːpɪd] **ADJ** **a** dumm; (= *foolish also, boring, wretched*) blöd(e) (*inf*); **don't be ~** sei nicht so blöd (*inf*); **I've done a ~ thing** ich habe etwas ganz Dummes or Blödes (*inf*) gemacht; **you ~ idiot!** du blöder Idiot! or **you ~ little man!** Sie Blödmann! (*inf*); **take that ~ look off your face** guck nicht so dumm or blöd (*inf*)!; **that was ~ of you** das war dumm (von dir); **that was a ~ thing to do** das war dumm; **it was ~ of me (to say anything)** es war blöd von mir (etwas zu sagen); **I was ~ to do that** es war dumm von mir, das zu tun; **you would be ~ to move**

to **London** du wärst ja dumm or blöd (*inf*), wenn du nach London ziehen würdest; **to make sb look ~** jdn blamieren; **to be so ~** or **to be ~ enough as to do sth** dumm genug sein, etw zu tun; **it is the ~est thing I've ever done/ heard** das ist das Dümmste, was ich jemals getan/gehört habe

b (= *stupefied*) benommen, benebelt; **to drink oneself ~** sich sinnlos betrinken; **the blow knocked him ~** der Schlag hat ihn völlig benebelt; **to be ~ with tiredness** ganz benommen vor lauter Müdigkeit sein; **to bore sb ~** jdn zu Tode langweilen; **to laugh oneself ~** sich dumm und dämlich lachen (*inf*)

ADV (*inf*) **to talk ~** Quatsch reden (*inf*); **to act ~** sich dumm stellen

N (*inf*, = *person*) Blödmann *m* (*inf*), Dummkopf *m* (*inf*)

stupidity [stjuːˈpɪdɪtɪ] N Dummheit *f*; (= *silliness also*) Blödheit *f* (*inf*)

stupidly [ˈstjuːpɪdlɪ] ADV (= *unintelligently*) dumm; (= *foolishly also*) blöd (*inf*); say dummerweise; stare dumm; grin albern; **~ I'd forgotten my keys** dummerweise hatte ich meine Schlüssel vergessen; **he ~ refused** er war so dumm or blöd (*inf*) abzulehnen; **he had told the boss several ~ obvious lies** er hatte dem Chef einige dummdreiste Lügen erzählt

stupor [ˈstjuːpə] N Benommenheit *f*; **he lay/sat there in a ~** er lag/saß benommen or apathisch or teilnahmslos da; **to be in a drunken ~** sinnlos betrunken or im Vollrausch sein

sturdily [ˈstɜːdɪlɪ] ADV **a** stabil; **~ built** (*person*) kräftig or stämmig gebaut; chair, ship etc stabil gebaut **b** (*fig*) unerschütterlich, standhaft; say resolut, bestimmt; independent unerschütterlich

sturdiness [ˈstɜːdɪnɪs] N **a** (of person, body, plant) Kräftigkeit *f*, Stämmigkeit *f*; (of material) Robustheit *f*; (of building, ship, car) Stabilität *f* **b** (fig, of opposition) Unerschütterlichkeit *f*, Standhaftigkeit *f*

sturdy [ˈstɜːdɪ] ADJ (+er) **a** person, body, plant kräftig, stämmig; material robust; building, ship, car stabil; **~ shoes** festes Schuhwerk *nt* **b** (fig) opposition unerschütterlich, standhaft

sturgeon [ˈstɜːdʒən] N Stör *m*

stutter [ˈstʌtə] **N** (of person, engine) Stottern *nt* no pl; (of guns) Trommeln *nt*; **he has a bad ~** er stottert sehr; **to say sth with a ~** etw stotternd sagen, etw stottern **VI a** stottern; **he was ~ing with embarrassment** er stotterte vor Verlegenheit; **she ~ed out an apology** sie entschuldigte sich stotternd **b** (= *advance slowly*) **to ~ on/a-long** entlangstottern; (fig, reform) sich dahinquälen **VT** stottern; **she ~ed an apology** sie entschuldigte sich stotternd

stutterer [ˈstʌtərə] N Stotterer *m*, Stotterin *f*

stuttering [ˈstʌtərɪŋ] N Stottern *nt*

sty [staɪ] N (lit, fig) Schweinestall *m*

sty(e) [staɪ] N (Med) Gerstenkorn *nt*

Stygian [ˈstɪdʒɪən] ADJ (liter) gloom, darkness stygisch (liter)

style [staɪl] **N a** (Art, Mus, Liter, personal etc) Stil *m*; **~ of painting** Malstil *m*; **the ~ of his writing** sein Stil *m*; **~ of life** Lebensstil *m*; **~ of management** Führungsstil *m*; **a poem in the Romantic ~** ein Gedicht im Stil der Romantik; **he won in fine ~** er gewann souverän or überlegen; **in his own inimitable ~** (iro) in seiner unnachahmlichen Art or Manier, auf die ihm typische Art; **that house is not my ~** so ein Haus ist nicht mein Stil; **hillwalking is not his ~** Bergwanderungen liegen ihm nicht; **that's the ~** (inf) so ists richtig

b (= *elegance*) Stil *m*; **the man has (real) ~** der Mann hat Klasse or Format; **in ~** stilvoll; **to do things in ~** etw im großen Stil tun; **to celebrate in ~** groß feiern; **to get married in ~** eine Hochzeit großen Stils or im großen Stil feiern

c (= *sort, type*) Art *f*; **a new ~ of house/car** etc ein neuer Haus-/Autotyp etc; **just the ~ of car I like** ein Auto, wie es mir gefällt

d (Fashion) Stil *m* no pl, Mode *f*; (= cut) Schnitt *m*; (= hairstyle) Frisur *f*; **these coats are available in two ~s** diese Mäntel gibt es in zwei verschiedenen Schnittarten or Macharten; **I want something in that ~** ich hätte gern etwas in der Art or in dem Stil; **all the latest ~s** die neue(ste) Mode, Mode im neue(ste)n Stil; **the latest ~s in shoes** die neue(ste)n Schuhmoden **e** (= *style of address*) Anrede *f*; (= title) Titel *m* **f** (Bot) Griffel *m*

VT a (= *designate*) nennen **b** (= design) entwerfen; interior etc gestalten; hair stylen; **a smartly ~d dress** ein elegant geschnittenes Kleid; **it is ~d for comfort, not elegance** es ist auf Bequemlichkeit und nicht Eleganz zugeschnitten

-style [staɪl] ADJ suf nach ... Art, auf (+acc) ... Art; **American-style fried chicken** Brathähnchen nach amerikanischer Art; **cowboy-style** auf Cowboyart, nach Art der Cowboys; **Swedish-style furniture/design** Möbel/Design im schwedischen Stil; **Western-style democracy** Demokratie nach westlichem Vorbild; **to dress 1920s-style** sich im Stil der zwanziger Jahre or Zwanzigerjahre kleiden; **the old-style cricketer** der Cricketspieler der alten Schule

stylebook [ˈstaɪlbʊk] N (Typ) Stilvorschriften pl; (Fashion) Modeheft *nt*; (for hairstyles) Frisurenheft *nt*

style sheet N (Comput, Typ) Dokumentvorlage *f*; (Editing) Stilblatt *nt*

styli [ˈstaɪlaɪ] pl of **stylus**

styling [ˈstaɪlɪŋ] N (of car etc) Design *nt*; (of dress) Machart *f*, Schnitt *m*; (of hair) Schnitt *m*; **~ mousse** Schaumfestiger *m*

stylish [ˈstaɪlɪʃ] ADJ **a** (= *elegant*) person elegant; car, hotel, district also vornehm; furnishings, film, performer, design stilvoll; performance kunstvoll; wedding großen Stils; way of life großartig, im großen Stil **b** (= *fashionable*) clothes modisch

stylishly [ˈstaɪlɪʃlɪ] ADV **a** (= *elegantly*) elegant; furnished stilvoll; live im großen Stil; travel mit allem Komfort **b** (= *fashionably*) dress modisch

stylishness [ˈstaɪlɪʃnɪs] N **a** (= *elegance*) (of person) Eleganz *f*; (of car, hotel, district also) Vornehmheit *f*; (of furnishings) stilvolle Art; (of wedding etc) groß angelegter Stil **b** (= *fashionableness*) modische Finesse

styli [ˈstaɪlaɪ] PL of **stylus**

stylist [ˈstaɪlɪst] N **a** (Fashion) Modeschöpfer(in) *m(f)*, Modestylist(in) *m(f)*; (= hair stylist) Friseur *m*, Friseuse *f*, Coiffeur *m* (geh), Coiffeuse *f* (geh) **b** (Liter, Sport) Stilist(in) *m(f)*

stylistic [staɪˈlɪstɪk] ADJ stilistisch; **~ device** Stilmittel *nt*

stylistically [staɪˈlɪstɪkəlɪ] ADV radical, surprising, conventional stilistisch; **~, it lacks polish** stilistisch gesehen or vom Stil her fehlt es am letzten Schliff

stylistics [staɪˈlɪstɪks] N sing Stilistik *f*

stylite [ˈstaɪlaɪt] N Säulenheilige(r) *m*, Stylit *m* (spec)

stylize [ˈstaɪlaɪz] VT stilisieren

stylized [ˈstaɪlaɪzd] ADJ picture, performance, design stilisiert; gesture abstrakt, stilisiert

stylus [ˈstaɪləs] N pl **styli a** (on record player) Nadel *f* **b** (= writing instrument) Griffel *m*, Stilus *m* (Hist)

stymie [ˈstaɪmɪ] VT (fig inf) matt setzen (inf); **to be ~d** aufgeschmissen sein (inf)

styptic [ˈstɪptɪk] **N** blutstillendes Mittel **ADJ** effect blutstillend

styptic pencil N Blutstillstift *m*

Styria [ˈstɪrɪə] N (part of Austria) Steiermark *f*

Styrofoam® [ˈstaɪrəfəʊm] N (US) Styropor® *nt*

Suabian [ˈsweɪbɪən] ADJ, N = **Swabian**

suave ADJ, **suavely** ADV [swɑːv, -lɪ] weltmännisch, aalglatt (pej)

suaveness [ˈswɑːvnɪs], **suavity** [ˈswɑːvɪtɪ] N Gewandtheit *f*, aalglatte Art (pej)

sub [sʌb] abbr **a** of sub-edit of sub-editor **b** of submarine **c** of subscription **d** of substitute

sub- PREF (= under, subordinate, inferior) Unter-, unter-; (esp with foreign words) Sub-, sub-; **subgroup** Untergruppe *f*; **subalpine** subalpin

subagency [ˈsʌbˌeɪdʒənsɪ] N **a** (Comm etc) Unteragentur *f*; (US) Nebenstelle *f* **b** (Jur) Nebenvollmacht *f*

subaltern [ˈsʌbltən] N (Brit, Mil) Subalternoffizier(in) *m(f)*

sub: subaqua [sʌbˈækwə] ADJ attr unter Wasser; **~ club** Taucherklub *m*; **subaquatic** [ˌsʌbəˈkwætɪk] ADJ Unterwasser-; **subarctic** ADJ subarktisch; **subatomic** ADJ particle subatomar; **subbasement** N Kellergeschoss *nt*, Kellergeschoß *nt* (Aus, Sw); **subcategory** N Subkategorie *f*, Untergruppe *f*; **subclass** N Unterabteilung *f*; **subclassify** VTI unterteilen; **subcommittee** N Unterausschuss *m*; **subcompact** N (US, Aut) Kleinstwagen *m*; **subconscious** ADJ unterbewusst **N** das Unterbewusstsein; **in his ~** im Unterbewusstsein; **subconsciously** ADV im Unterbewusstsein; **subcontinent** N Subkontinent *m*; **subcontract** VT (vertraglich) weitervergeben (to an +acc); **subcontractor** N Unterkontrahent(in) *m(f)*, Subunternehmer(in) *m(f)*; **subculture** N Subkultur *f*; **subcutaneous** ADJ subkutan; **subdivide** VT unterteilen **VI** sich aufteilen; **subdivision** N (= act) Unterteilung *f*; (= subgroup) Unterabteilung *f*; **subdominant** **N** Subdominante *f* **ADJ** **~ chord** Subdominantakkord *m*

subdue [səbˈdjuː] VT rebels, country unterwerfen; enemy also besiegen; rioters überwältigen; demonstrations niederschlagen; (fig) anger, desire unterdrücken, zähmen; noise, light, high spirits dämpfen; animals, children bändigen; pain lindern; wilderness zähmen

subdued [səbˈdjuːd] ADJ (= quiet) colour, lighting, voice, response gedämpft; manner, person ruhig, still; mood, atmosphere gedrückt; (= submissive) voice, manner, person fügsam, gehorsam, gefügig; (= repressed) feelings, excitement unterdrückt; **lunch was a ~ affair** die Stimmung während des Mittagessens war gedrückt

sub: subedit VTI (esp Brit) redigieren; **subeditor** N (esp Brit) Redakteur(in) *m(f)*; **subentry** N (Book-keeping) Nebenposten *m*; **subfamily** N (esp Biol) Unterfamilie *f*; **sub-frame** N (of car) Zwischenrahmen *m*, Nebenrahmen *m*; **subgrade** N (of road etc) Unterbau *m*; **subhead** (inf), **subheading** N Untertitel *m*; **subhuman** ADJ treatment, person unmenschlich; **they were treated as if they were ~** sie wurden behandelt, als seien sie Untermenschen

subject [ˈsʌbdʒɪkt] ⊘ 26.2 **N a** (Pol) Staatsbürger(in) *m(f)*; (of king etc) Untertan *m*, Untertanin *f*

b (Gram) Subjekt *nt*, Satzgegenstand *m* **c** (= topic, Mus) Thema *nt*; **the ~ of the picture is ...** das Thema or Sujet (geh) des Bildes ist ...; **he paints urban ~s** er malt städtische Motive; **to change the ~** das Thema wechseln; **on the ~ of ...** zum Thema (+gen) ...; **while we're on the ~** da wir gerade beim Thema sind; **while we're on the ~ of mushrooms** wo wir gerade von Pilzen reden, apropos Pilze; **that's off the ~** das gehört nicht zum Thema

d (= discipline, Sch, Univ) Fach *nt*; (= specialist subject) (Spezial)gebiet *nt*

e (= reason) Grund *m*, Anlass *m* (for zu)

f (= object) Gegenstand *m* (of +gen); (in experiment, = person) Versuchsperson *f*, Versuchsobjekt *nt*; (= animal) Versuchstier *nt*, Versuchsobjekt *nt*; (esp Med, for treatment) Typ *m*; **he is the ~ of much criticism** er wird stark kritisiert, er ist Gegenstand häufiger Kritik; **he's a good ~ for treatment by hypnosis** er lässt sich gut hypnotisch behandeln; **the survey team asked 100 ~s** die Meinungsforscher befragten 100 Personen

g (Philos, = ego) Subjekt *nt*, Ich *nt* **h** (Phot) Objekt *nt*

ADJ a (= conquered) unterworfen

b **~ to** (= under the control of) unterworfen

(+*dat*); **provinces ~ to foreign rule** Provinzen *pl* unter Fremdherrschaft; **to be ~ to sth** (*to law, constant change, sb's will*) einer Sache (*dat*) unterworfen sein; *to illness* für etw anfällig sein; *to consent, approval* von etw abhängig sein; **northbound trains are ~ to delays** bei Zügen in Richtung Norden muss mit Verspätung gerechnet werden; **prices/opening times are ~ to change** *or* **alteration without notice** Preisänderungen/Änderungen der Öffnungszeiten sind vorbehalten; **all these plans are ~ to last minute changes** all diese Pläne können in letzter Minute noch geändert werden; **~ to flooding** überschwemmungsgefährdet; **to be ~ to taxation** besteuert werden; **~ to correction** vorbehaltlich Änderungen; **all offers are ~ to availability** alle Angebote nur so weit verfügbar; **~ to confirmation in writing** vorausgesetzt, es wird schriftlich bestätigt; **~ to certain conditions** unter bestimmten Bedingungen
▪ **VT** [səbˈdʒekt] **a** (= *subjugate*) unterwerfen; *terrorists, guerrillas* zerschlagen
b to ~ sb to sth (*to questioning, analysis, treatment*) jdn einer Sache (*dat*) unterziehen; *to test* also jdn einer Sache (*dat*) unterwerfen; *to torture, suffering, heat, ridicule, criticism* jdn einer Sache (*dat*) aussetzen; **to ~ sb to insults** jdn beschimpfen; **to ~ sb to criticism** jdn unter Kritik nehmen, jdn kritisieren
▪ **VR** [səbˈdʒekt] **to ~ oneself to sth** (*to insults, suffering*) etw hinnehmen; (*to criticism, ridicule*) sich einer Sache (*dat*) aussetzen; (*to examination, test, questioning*) sich einer Sache (*dat*) unterziehen
subject: subject catalogue N Schlagwortkatalog *m*; **subject heading** N Überschrift *f*; (*in index*) Rubrik *f*; **subject index** N Sachregister *nt*

subjection [səbˈdʒekʃən] N **a** (= *state*) Abhängigkeit *f*; **to keep a people in ~** ein Volk unterdrücken **b** (= *act*) Unterwerfung *f*; (*of terrorists, guerrillas etc*) Zerschlagung *f* **c** **the ~ of sb to sth** → **subject** VT b

subjective [səbˈdʒektɪv] ADJ **a** subjektiv **b** (*Gram*) **~ case** Nominativ *m*

subjectively [səbˈdʒektɪvlɪ] ADV subjektiv

subjectivism [səbˈdʒektɪvɪzəm] N Subjektivismus *m*

subjectivity [ˌsʌbdʒekˈtɪvɪtɪ] N Subjektivität *f*

subject matter [ˈsʌbdʒɪktmætəʳ] N (= *theme*) Stoff *m*; (= *content*) Inhalt *m*

subjoin [ˌsʌbˈdʒɔɪn] VT hinzufügen (*to dat*), beilegen (*to gen*), beifügen (*to dat*)

sub judice [ˌsʌbˈdʒuːdɪsɪ] ADJ (*Jur*) **to be ~** verhandelt werden

subjugate [ˈsʌbdʒʊgeɪt] VT unterwerfen

subjugation [ˌsʌbdʒʊˈgeɪʃən] N Unterwerfung *f*

subjunctive [səbˈdʒʌŋktɪv] **ADJ** konjunktivisch; **the ~ verb/mood/form** der Konjunktiv ▪ **N** (= *mood, verb*) Konjunktiv *m*

sub: sublease **N** (= *contract, on farm etc*) Unterpachtvertrag *m* (*on für*); (*on house etc*) Untermietvertrag *m* (*on für*); **they have a ~ on that house** das Haus ist an sie untervermietet worden ▪ **VT** *land* unter- *or* weiterverpachten (*to an* +*acc*); *house* unter- *or* weitervermieten (*to an* +*acc*); **she has ~d the flat from the tenants** sie hat die Wohnung in Untermiete; **sublessee** [ˌsʌbleˈsiː] N (*of house*) Untermieter(in) *m(f)*; (*of land*) Unterpächter(in) *m(f)*; **sublessor** [ˌsʌbleˈsɔː] N (*of house*) Untervermieter(in) *m(f)*; (*of land*) Unterverpächter(in) *m(f)*; **sublet** pret, ptp **sublet** **VT** *house, room* unter- *or* weitervermieten (*to an* +*acc*) ▪ **VI** untervermieten; **subletting** N Untervermietung *f*; **sublieutenant** N (*esp Brit*) Leutnant *m* zur See

sublimate [ˈsʌblɪmeɪt] ▪ **N** (*Chem*) Sublimat *nt* ▪ **VT** (*Chem, Psych*) sublimieren

sublimation [ˌsʌblɪˈmeɪʃən] N Sublimierung *f*

sublime [səˈblaɪm] ADJ **a** *poetry, beauty, scenery, thoughts, feelings* erhaben; *achievement, courage, genius* also überragend; **that's going from the ~ to the ridiculous** (*inf*) das nenne ich tief sinken (*inf*) **b** (*iro, = extreme*) *ignorance* vollendet; *impertinence, confidence* unglaublich; *indifference,*

contempt herablassend **c** (*inf, = delightful*) reizend

sublimely [səˈblaɪmlɪ] ADV erhaben; *unaware, ignorant* ergreifend (*iro*), vollkommen; *foolish, drunk, simple* unglaublich; **~ beautiful** von erhabener Schönheit; **~ romantic** von erhabener Romantik; **a ~ contented expression on his face** ein überglücklicher Gesichtsausdruck; **~ contemptuous/indifferent, he ...** mit souveräner Verachtung/Gleichgültigkeit ... er ...

subliminal [ˌsʌbˈlɪmɪnl] ADJ (*Psych*) unterschwellig

subliminal advertising N Schleichwerbung *f*

subliminal message N unterschwellige *or* an das Unterbewusstsein gerichtete Botschaft

sublimity [səˈblɪmɪtɪ] N (*liter*) Erhabenheit *f*

submachine gun [ˌsʌbməˈʃiːngʌn] N Maschinenpistole *f*

submarginal [ˌsʌbˈmɑːdʒɪnl] ADJ (*Agr*) *land* nicht (mehr) rentabel

submarine [ˈsʌbməriːn] ▪ **N** **a** Unterseeboot *nt*, U-Boot *nt* **b** (*US, inf, = sandwich*) Jumbosandwich *nt* (*inf*) ▪ **ADJ** *life, equipment, cable* unterseeisch, submarin; **~ base** U-Boot-Stützpunkt *m*

submariner [sʌbˈmærɪnəʳ] N U-Boot-Fahrer(in) *m(f)*

submenu [ˈsʌbˌmenjuː] N (*Comput*) Untermenü *nt*

submerge [səbˈmɜːdʒ] ▪ **VT** untertauchen; (= *flood*) überschwemmen; **to ~ sth in water** etw in Wasser (*acc*) (ein)tauchen; **to ~ oneself in sth** (*fig*) ganz in etw (*acc*) versinken ▪ **VI** (*diver, submarine*) tauchen

submerged [səbˈmɜːdʒd] ADJ *rocks* unter Wasser; *wreck* gesunken; *city* versunken; (*Pol: = underprivileged*) unterdrückt; (*Psych*) verdrängt; **to be half ~** halb versunken sein; **the house was completely ~** das Haus stand völlig unter Wasser; **she was ~ in work** sie ist erstickt in Arbeit

submersible [səbˈmɜːsəbl] ADJ versenkbar; *submarine* tauchfähig ▪ **N** Tauchboot *nt*

submersion [səbˈmɜːʃən] N Untertauchen *nt*; (*of submarine*) Tauchen *nt*; (*by flood*) Überschwemmung *f*; **~ in liquid** Eintauchen *nt* in Flüssigkeit; **prolonged ~ in water** langes Liegen im Wasser

submission [səbˈmɪʃən] N **a** (= *yielding*) Unterwerfung *f* (*to unter* +*acc*); (= *submissiveness*) Gehorsam *m*; (*Sport*) Aufgabe *f*; **to force sb into ~** jdn zwingen, sich zu ergeben; **to starve sb into ~** jdn aushungern **b** (= *presentation*) Eingabe *f*; (= *documents submitted*) Vorlage *f*; **to make a ~ to sb** jdm eine Vorlage machen *or* unterbreiten; **his ~ to the appeals tribunal** seine Berufung **c** (= *contention*) Einwurf *m* (*to* gegenüber); **it is our ~ that ...** wir behaupten, dass ...

submissive [səbˈmɪsɪv] ADJ demütig, gehorsam; unterwürfig (*pej*) (*to* gegenüber); **~ to authority** autoritätsgläubig

submissively [səbˈmɪsɪvlɪ] ADV *bow, kneel* demütig; *behave* unterwürfig

submissiveness [səbˈmɪsɪvnɪs] N Demut *f*, Gehorsam *m*, Unterwürfigkeit *f* (*pej*) (*to* gegenüber)

submit [səbˈmɪt] ▪ **VT** **a** (= *put forward*) vorlegen (*to* +*dat*); *application, claim etc* einreichen (*to* bei); **to ~ that ...** (*esp Jur*) behaupten, dass ...; **to ~ an entry to a competition** (= *participate*) an einem Wettbewerb teilnehmen
b (= *refer*) verweisen (*to an* +*acc*); **to ~ sth to scrutiny/tests** *etc* etw einer Prüfung/Tests (*dat*) *etc* unterziehen; **to ~ sb to heat/cold** *etc* jdn der Hitze/Kälte (*dat*) *etc* aussetzen
▪ **VI** (= *yield*) sich beugen, nachgeben; (*Mil*) sich ergeben (*to* +*dat*); (*Sport*) aufgeben; **to ~ to sth** (*to sb's orders, judgement, God's will*) sich einer Sache (*dat*) beugen *or* unterwerfen; *to inspection* sich einer Sache (*dat*) unterziehen; *to indignity* sich etw gefallen lassen, etw erdulden; *to demands, pressure* einer Sache (*dat*) nachgeben; **to ~ to blackmail/questioning** sich erpressen/verhören lassen
▪ **VR to ~ oneself to sth** (*to examination, opera-*

tion, questioning etc) sich einer Sache (*dat*) unterziehen

subnormal [ˌsʌbˈnɔːməl] ADJ *intelligence, temperature* unterdurchschnittlich; *person* minderbegabt; (*inf*) schwachsinnig; **educationally ~** lernbehindert; **mentally ~** minderbemittelt

subordinate [səˈbɔːdnɪt] **ADJ** *officer* rangniedriger; *rank, position, importance, role* untergeordnet; **to be ~ to sb/sth** jdm/einer Sache untergeordnet sein; **to be ~ in importance to** weniger wichtig sein als; **~ in rank** rangniedriger (*to* als) ▪ **N** Untergebene(r) *mf* ▪ **VT** [səˈbɔːdɪneɪt] unterordnen (*to dat*)

subordinate clause N (*Gram*) Nebensatz *m*

subordinating conjunction [səˈbɔːdɪneɪtɪŋkənˈdʒʌŋkʃən] N (*Gram*) unterordnende Konjunktion

subordination [səˌbɔːdɪˈneɪʃən] N (= *subjection*) Unterordnung *f* (*to unter* +*acc*)

suborn [sʌˈbɔːn] VT (*Jur*) *witness* beeinflussen

subplot [ˈsʌbˌplɒt] N Nebenhandlung *f*

subpoena [səˈpiːnə] (*Jur*) ▪ **N** Vorladung *f*; **to serve a ~ on sb** jdn vorladen ▪ **VT** *witness* vorladen; *documents* unter Strafandrohung verlangen *or* fordern; **he was ~ed to give evidence** er wurde als Zeuge vorgeladen

sub: subpolar ADJ subpolar; **sub-postmaster/-postmistress** N (*Brit*) Poststellenleiter(in) *m(f)*; **sub-post office** N (*Brit*) Poststelle *f*; **sub rosa** [sʌbˈrəʊzə] (*form*) **ADJ** geheim, sub rosa (*geh*) ▪ **ADV** im Geheimen, sub rosa (*geh*); **subroutine** N (*Comput*) Unterroutine *f*, Unterprogramm *nt*

subscribe [səbˈskraɪb] ✿ 12.1 ▪ **VT** *money* zeichnen (*form*); (*to appeal*) spenden (*to* für); **to ~ one's signature** *or* **name to a document** (*form*) ein Dokument (unter)zeichnen
▪ **VI** **a** (= *contribute, promise to contribute*) spenden, geben (*to* +*dat*); **to ~ to an appeal** sich an einer Spendenaktion beteiligen; **to ~ for a book** ein Buch vorbestellen; **to ~ for shares in a company** Aktien einer Gesellschaft zeichnen **b** (*to e-mail list*) sich anmelden; **to ~ to a magazine** *etc* eine Zeitschrift *etc* abonnieren **c** (= *support*) **to ~ to sth** (*to proposal*) etw gutheißen, etw billigen; *to opinion, theory* sich einer Sache (*dat*) anschließen

subscriber [səbˈskraɪbəʳ] N (*to paper*) Abonnent(in) *m(f)*; (*to fund*) Spender(in) *m(f)*, Zeichner(in) *m(f)* (*form*); (*Telec*) Teilnehmer(in) *m(f)*; (*to opinion*) Befürworter(in) *m(f)*; (*of shares*) Zeichner(in) *m(f)*; **~ trunk dialling** (*Brit*) der Selbstwählferndienst

subscript [ˈsʌbskrɪpt] ADJ *character, number* tiefgestellt

subscription [səbˈskrɪpʃən] N Subskription *f* (*form*), Zeichnung *f* (*form*); (= *money subscribed*) Beitrag *m*; (*to newspaper, concert etc*) Abonnement *nt* (*to* +*gen*); **to take out a ~ to sth** etw abonnieren; **to pay one's ~ (to a club)** seinen (Vereins)beitrag bezahlen; **by public ~** mit Hilfe von *or* durch Spenden; **by ~** durch Subskription(en) *f(pl)*

subscription rate N Abonnements- *or* Bezugspreis *m*

subsection [ˈsʌbˌsekʃən] N Unterabteilung *f*; (*Jur*) Paragraf *m*

subsequent [ˈsʌbsɪkwənt] ADJ (nach)folgend, anschließend; (*in time*) später, anschließend; **~ to** (*form*) im Anschluss an (+*acc*)

subsequently [ˈsʌbsɪkwəntlɪ] ADV (= *afterwards*) später, anschließend; *alter, add etc* also nachträglich; (= *from that time*) von da an

subserve [səbˈsɜːv] VT (*form*) dienen (+*dat*), dienlich *or* förderlich sein (+*dat*) (*form*)

subservience [səbˈsɜːvɪəns] N (*pej*) Unterwürfigkeit *f* (*to* gegenüber); (*form*) Unterworfenheit *f* (*to unter* +*acc*)

subservient [səbˈsɜːvɪənt] ADJ (*pej*) unterwürfig (*to* gegenüber); (*form*) unterworfen (*to* +*dat*)

subserviently [səbˈsɜːvɪəntlɪ] ADV unterwürfig

subset [ˈsʌbset] N (*Math*) Teilmenge *f*

subside [səb'saɪd] VI **a** (*flood, river*) sinken; (*land, building, road*) sich senken, absacken (*inf*); **the lorry ~d into the mud** der Lastwagen sank im Schlamm ein; **to ~ into a chair** auf einen Stuhl sinken **b** (*storm, wind*) abflauen, nachlassen, sich legen; (*anger, excitement, laughter, noise*) nachlassen, abklingen; (*fever*) sinken

subsidence [səb'saɪdəns] N Senkung *f*, Absacken *nt* (*inf*); **there's a lot of ~ in the area** in der Gegend senkt sich das Erdreich; **"danger: ~"** „Achtung: Bodensenkung"; **we can't get a mortgage because of the ~** wir bekommen keine Hypothek, weil sich das Gelände senkt

subsidiarity [sʌb,sɪdɪ'ærɪtɪ] N (*Pol*) Subsidiarität *f*; (*principle*) Subsidiaritätsprinzip *nt*

subsidiary [səb'sɪdɪərɪ] ADJ untergeordnet; *question* zusätzlich; *importance* nebensächlich; **~ role** Nebenrolle *f*; **~ subject** Nebenfach *nt*; **~ company** Tochtergesellschaft *f*; **to be ~ to sth** einer Sache (*dat*) untergeordnet sein N Tochtergesellschaft *f*

subsidization [,sʌbsɪdaɪ'zeɪʃən] N Subventionierung *f*

subsidize ['sʌbsɪdaɪz] VT *company etc* subventionieren; *housing* finanziell unterstützen; (*inf*) *sb's habits* subventionieren; *person* unterstützen

subsidized ['sʌbsɪdaɪzd] ADJ *prices, food, exports* subventioniert; *housing* finanziell unterstützt

subsidy ['sʌbsɪdɪ] N Subvention *f*, Zuschuss *m*; **there is a ~ on butter** Butter wird subventioniert *or* bezuschusst; **rent ~** Wohnungsbeihilfe *f*; **housing subsidies** (*for building, renovation etc*) Wohnungsbaubeihilfen *pl*

subsist [səb'sɪst] VI (*form*) sich ernähren, leben (*on von*)

subsistence [səb'sɪstəns] N (= *living*) Leben *nt* (*on von*); (= *means of subsistence*) Existenz *f*, (Lebens)unterhalt *m*; **on £11 is impossible** es ist unmöglich, von £ 11 zu leben; **rice is their chief means of ~** sie ernähren sich hauptsächlich von Reis

subsistence: subsistence allowance N Unterhaltszuschuss *m*; **subsistence farmer** N Bauer, der nur für den Eigenbedarf anbaut; **subsistence farming** N Ackerbau *m* für den Eigenbedarf, Subsistenzwirtschaft *f*; **subsistence level** N Existenzminimum *nt*; **at ~** auf dem Existenzminimum; **subsistence wage** N Minimallohn *m*

sub: subsoil N Untergrund *m*; **subsonic** ADJ Unterschall-; **~ speed** Unterschallgeschwindigkeit *f*; **subspecies** N Unterart *f*, Subspezies *f*

substance ['sʌbstəns] N **a** Substanz *f*, Materie *f*, Stoff *m*; **what is this ~?** was ist das für eine Substanz?; **he rubbed a yellow ~ on the wound** er strich eine gelbe Masse auf die Wunde **b** *no pl* (= *subject matter*) Substanz *f*, Gehalt *m*; (= *essence*) Kern *m*; **in ~** im Wesentlichen; **I agree with the ~ of his proposals** im Wesentlichen stimme ich seinen Vorschlägen zu **c** *no pl* (= *weight, importance*) Gewicht *nt*; **the book lacks ~** das Buch hat keine Substanz; **there is some ~ in his claim** seine Behauptung ist nicht unfundiert **d** *no pl* **a man of ~** ein vermögender Mann

substance abuse N Drogen- und Alkoholmissbrauch *m*

substandard [,sʌb'stændəd] ADJ *work, goods* minderwertig; *quality also, housing* unzulänglich; *worker* unterdurchschnittlich; (*Ling*) nicht korrekt

substantial [səb'stænʃəl] ADJ **a** *person, cloth* kräftig; *furniture, building, firm* solide; *rope* stark; *book* umfangreich; *meal, dish* reichhaltig **b** (= *considerable*) *income, loss, gain, amount* beträchtlich, erheblich; *part, majority, contribution, improvement* wesentlich; (= *rich*) *landowner, businessman* vermögend, kapitalkräftig **c** (= *weighty, important*) bedeutend; *proof, argument* überzeugend, stichhaltig; *difference* wesentlich, bedeutend; **to be in ~ agreement** im Wesentlichen übereinstimmen **d** (= *real, material*) körperlich, wesenhaft

substantially [səb'stænʃəlɪ] ADV **a** (= *solidly*) solide; (= *considerably*) erheblich, beträchtlich, wesentlich; **~ built** (*house*) solide gebaut; *person* kräftig gebaut **b** (= *essentially, basically*) im Wesentlichen; **to remain ~ unchanged** größtenteils *or* im Wesentlichen unverändert bleiben

substantiate [səb'stænʃɪeɪt] VT erhärten, untermauern

substantiation [səb,stænʃɪ'eɪʃən] N Erhärtung *f*, Untermauerung *f*; **as yet this theory lacks ~** diese Theorie ist bisher noch nicht erhärtet; **in ~ of** zur Erhärtung (+*gen*)

substantival [,sʌbstən'taɪvəl] ADJ (*Gram*) substantivisch

substantive ['sʌbstəntɪv] ADJ **a** *evidence, argument* überzeugend, stichhaltig **b** (= *considerable*) *contribution, improvement* beträchtlich, wesentlich, bedeutend **c** **~ motion** endgültige Formulierung des Antrags **d** (*Gram*) = **substantival** N (*Gram*) Substantiv *nt*, Hauptwort *nt*

substantivize ['sʌbstəntɪ,vaɪz] VT substantivieren

substation ['sʌb,steɪʃən] N (*Elec*) Umspann(ungs)werk *nt*

substitute ['sʌbstɪtjuːt] N Ersatz *m no pl*; (= *representative also*) Vertretung *f*; (*Sport*) Ersatzspieler(in) *m(f)*, Auswechselspieler(in) *m(f)*; **to find a ~ for sb** für jdn Ersatz finden; **to use sth as a ~** etw als Ersatz benutzen; **coffee ~** Kaffee-Ersatz *m*, Kaffeeersatz *m*; **various coffee ~s** verschiedene Sorten Kaffee-Ersatz; **there's no ~ for ...** es gibt keinen Ersatz für ..., ... kann man durch nichts ersetzen ADJ *attr* Ersatz-; **~ drug** Ersatzdroge *f* VT **to ~ A for B** B durch A ersetzen; (*Sport also*) B gegen A austauschen *or* auswechseln; **~ 3 for X** setze für X 3 ein, substituiere 3 für X VI **to ~ for sb** jdn vertreten, für jdn einspringen; **to ~ for sth** etw ersetzen

substitute teacher N (*US*) Aushilfslehrer(in) *m(f)*

substitution [,sʌbstɪ'tjuːʃən] N Ersetzen *nt* (*of X for Y* von Y durch X); (*Sport*) Austausch *m* (*of X for Y* von Y gegen X); (*Math*) Substitution *f*, Einsetzen *nt* (*of X for Y* von X für Y); **the ~ of margarine for butter** der Gebrauch von Margarine statt Butter

substrate ['sʌbstreɪt] N (*Chem*) Substrat *nt*

substratum ['sʌb,strɑːtəm] N *pl* **substrata** ['sʌb,strɑːtə] Substrat *nt*; (*Geol*) Untergrund *m*; (*Sociol*) Substratum *nt*

substructure ['sʌb,strʌktʃə] N Unterbau *m*; (*fig also*) Grundlage *f*; (*Build*) Fundament *nt*; (*of bridge*) Widerlager *nt*

subsume [səb'sjuːm] VT **to ~ sth under sth** etw unter etw (*dat*) zusammenfassen *or* subsumieren (*geh*)

subsystem ['sʌbsɪstəm] N Untersystem *nt*

subteen ['sʌb'tiːn] N (*esp US*) Kind *nt*

sub-teenage ['sʌb'tiːneɪdʒ] ADJ *attr* (*esp US*) *drinking etc* von Kindern; *fans* im Kindesalter

subtenancy [,sʌb'tenənsɪ] N **during his ~ of the flat/farm** während er Untermieter in der Wohnung/Unterpächter des Bauernhofes war

subtenant [,sʌb'tenənt] N (*of flat etc*) Untermieter(in) *m(f)*; (*of land*) Unterpächter(in) *m(f)*

subtend [səb'tend] VT gegenüberliegen (+*dat*)

subterfuge ['sʌbtəfjuːdʒ] N (= *trickery*) Täuschung *f*, List *f*; (= *trick*) Trick *m*, List *f*; **to resort to ~** zu einer List greifen; **to be incapable of ~** (zu) keiner Falschheit *or* List fähig sein

subterranean [,sʌbtə'reɪnɪən] ADJ unterirdisch; (*fig*) *force, power* verborgen

subterraneous ADJ, **subterraneously** ADV [,sʌbtə'reɪnɪəs, -lɪ] = **subterranean**

subtitle ['sʌbtaɪtl] N Untertitel *m* (*also Film*) VT film mit Untertiteln versehen; *book etc* einen Untertitel geben (+*dat*); **the film is ~d in English** der Film hat englische Untertitel; **the book is ~d ...** das Buch hat den Untertitel ...

subtle ['sʌtl] ADJ **a** (= *delicate, gentle*) fein; *irony, distinction* fein, subtil (*geh*); *perfume, flavour* zart, fein; *hint, allusion* zart, leise; *charm* leise, unaufdringlich **b** (= *ingenious, not obvious*) *remark, argument, point* scharfsinnig, spitzfindig; *problem* subtil; *pressure* sanft; *design, construction, proof* raffiniert, fein ausgedacht *or* ausgetüftelt (*inf*); **he has a very ~ mind** er ist ein sehr subtiler Denker (*geh*); **be ~ about it** gehen Sie mit Zartgefühl vor **c** (= *quick at seeing fine distinctions*) *observer, critic* aufmerksam, subtil (*geh*)

subtlety ['sʌtltɪ] N **a** (= *delicacy*) Feinheit *f*; (*of irony, distinction also*) Subtilität *f* (*geh*); (*of perfume, flavour also, hint, allusion*) Zartheit *f*; (*of charm*) Unaufdringlichkeit *f* **b** (= *sophistication, of remark, argument, point*) Scharfsinn(igkeit *f*) *m*, Spitzfindigkeit *f*; (*of problem*) Subtilität *f*; (*of design, construction, proof*) Raffiniertheit *f*; **his methods lack ~** seinen Methoden fehlt (die) Finesse *or* Subtilität (*geh*); **the subtleties of the novel** die Feinheiten *pl* des Romans; **~ is wasted on him** feine Andeutungen nützen bei ihm nichts **c** (= *discriminative powers, of observer, critic*) Aufmerksamkeit *f*, Subtilität *f* (*geh*)

subtly ['sʌtlɪ] ADV fein; *flavoured also* delikat; *argue, reply* scharfsinnig, subtil (*geh*); *analyse, think* scharfsinnig; (= *slightly*) *change* geringfügig; (= *indirectly*) *imply* unterschwellig, indirekt; *achieve one's ends* auf raffinierte Weise; **~ different** auf subtile Weise verschieden *or* unterschiedlich; **he ~ suggested** er schlug geschickt vor; **it's just very ~ wrong** es ist schwer zu fassen, was falsch daran ist

subtotal ['sʌbtəʊtl] N Zwischen- *or* Teilsumme *f*

subtract [səb'trækt] VTI abziehen, subtrahieren (*from von*)

subtraction [səb'trækʃən] N Subtraktion *f*; (*act also*) Abziehen *nt*

subtrahend ['sʌbtrə,hend] N (*Math, form*) Subtrahend *m*

subtropical [,sʌb'trɒpɪkəl] ADJ subtropisch

subtropics [,sʌb'trɒpɪks] PL Subtropen *pl*

subtype ['sʌbtaɪp] N Unterart *f*

suburb ['sʌbɜːb] N Vorort *m*; **in the ~s** am Stadtrand

suburban [sə'bɜːbən] ADJ *area, community* vorstädtisch; (*pej*) spießig, kleinbürgerlich; **the area is becoming increasingly ~** die Gegend nimmt immer mehr vorstädtischen Charakter an; **~ line** (*Rail*) Vorortbahn *f*; **~ street** Vorortstraße *f*; **in ~ London** in Londons Vorstädten; **~ sprawl** Vorstädte *pl*

suburbanite [sə'bɜːbənaɪt] N Vorstädter(in) *m(f)*, Vorstadtbewohner(in) *m(f)*

suburbia [sə'bɜːbɪə] N (*usu pej*) die Vororte *pl*; **to live in ~** am Stadtrand wohnen; **that's typical of ~!** typisch Spießbürger!

subvention [səb'venʃən] N Subvention *f*

subversion [səb'vɜːʃən] N, *no pl* Subversion *f*; (*of rights, freedom etc*) Untergrabung *f*, Unterminierung *f*; **the US was accused of ~ in Chile** die USA wurden subversiver *or* umstürzlerischer Tätigkeiten in Chile beschuldigt; **~ is rife in the army** die Armee ist voll(er) subversiver Elemente

subversive [səb'vɜːsɪv] ADJ subversiv, umstürzlerisch; **~ elements** subversive Elemente *or* Kräfte *pl* N Umstürzler(in) *m(f)*, Subversive(r) *mf*

subvert [səb'vɜːt] VT *government* zu stürzen versuchen; *faith, morals etc* untergraben, unterminieren; *constitution, state authority, socialism* unterwandern; *person* zum Umsturz anstacheln

subway ['sʌbweɪ] N Unterführung *f*; (*for cars also*) Tunnel *m*; (*esp US, Rail*) U-Bahn *f*

subzero [,sʌb'zɪərəʊ] ADJ *temperature* unter null, unter dem Nullpunkt

succeed [sək'siːd] **a** (= *be successful, person*) erfolgreich sein, Erfolg haben; (*plan etc*) gelingen, erfolgreich sein; **to ~ in business/in a plan** geschäftlich/mit einem Plan erfolgreich sein; **I**

~ed in doing it es gelang mir, es zu tun; **you'll only ~ in making things worse** damit erreichst du nur, dass alles noch schlimmer wird; **nothing ~s like success** (prov) nichts ist so erfolgreich wie der Erfolg; **if at first you don't ~(, try, try, try again)** (Prov) wirf die Flinte nicht gleich ins Korn (prov)

b (= come next) **to ~ to an office** in einem Amt nachfolgen; **he ~ed to his father's position** er wurde (der) Nachfolger seines Vaters, er trat die Nachfolge seines Vaters an (geh); **to ~ to the throne** die Thronfolge antreten; **there ~ed a period of peace** (form) es folgte eine Zeit des Friedens

VT (= come after, take the place of) folgen (+dat), folgen auf (+acc); (person also) Nachfolger(in) m(f) +gen; **to ~ sb in a post/in office** jds Nachfolger werden, jds Stelle/Amt (acc) übernehmen; **who ~ed James I?** wer kam nach or folgte auf Jakob I.?

succeeding [sək'siːdɪŋ] ADJ folgend; **~ generations** spätere or nachfolgende Generationen pl

success [sək'ses] ✪ 23.5 N Erfolg m; **without ~** ohne Erfolg, erfolglos; **wishing you every ~ in your exams** mit besten Wünschen für eine erfolgreiche Prüfung; **to make a ~ of sth** mit or bei etw Erfolg haben, mit or bei etw erfolgreich sein; **they made a ~ of their marriage** ihre Ehe war ein Erfolg; **to be a ~ with sb** bei jdm ankommen; **the new car is not a ~** das neue Auto ist nicht gerade ein (durchschlagender) Erfolg; **the plan was a ~** der Plan war erfolgreich or ein voller Erfolg; **to meet with ~** Erfolg haben, erfolgreich sein; **~ story** Erfolgsstory f; (= person) Erfolg m

successful [sək'sesfʊl] ADJ erfolgreich; **to reach a ~ conclusion** zu einem erfolgreichen Abschluss kommen; **after ~ completion** nach erfolgreicher Beendigung; **to be ~** erfolgreich sein, Erfolg haben (in mit, bei); **to be entirely ~** ein voller Erfolg sein; **I was ~ in doing it** es gelang mir, es zu tun; **to be ~ in one's efforts** mit seinen Bemühungen Erfolg haben; **to be ~ at doing sth** etw erfolgreich tun; **unfortunately your application has not been ~** Ihre Bewerbung war leider nicht erfolgreich; **to be ~ as a doctor** ein erfolgreicher Arzt sein

successfully [sək'sesfəlɪ] ADV erfolgreich, mit Erfolg

succession [sək'seʃən] N **a** Folge f, Serie f; (with no intervening period) (Aufeinander)folge f, Kette f; **a ~ of visitors** eine Kette or Serie von Besuchern; **life is a ~ of joys and sorrows** das Leben ist ein steter Wechsel von Kummer und Freude; **in ~** nacheinander, hintereinander; **in quick** or **rapid ~** in rascher Folge, schnell hintereinander

b (to post) Nachfolge f; (to throne) Thronfolge f; (to title, estate) Erbfolge f; **his ~ to the office** seine Amtsübernahme; **his ~ to the title** seine Übernahme des Titels; **her ~ to the throne** ihre Thronbesteigung; **in ~ to sb** als jds Nachfolger(in) m(f), in jds Nachfolge (dat) (geh); **fourth in (line of) ~ to the throne** an vierter Stelle in der Thronfolge → **apostolic**

succession state N Nachfolgestaat m

successive [sək'sesɪv] ADJ aufeinander folgend attr; **four ~ days** vier Tage nacheinander or hintereinander, vier aufeinander folgende Tage; **on four ~ days** an vier aufeinander folgenden Tagen; **for the third ~ time** zum dritten Mal hintereinander; **he was sacked from three ~ jobs** er wurde nacheinander or hintereinander aus drei verschiedenen Stellen hinausgeworfen

successively [sək'sesɪvlɪ] ADV nacheinander, hintereinander; **~ higher levels of unemployment** sukzessiv höhere Arbeitslosenraten

successor [sək'sesə'] N Nachfolger(in) m(f) (to +gen); (to throne) Thronfolger(in) m(f)

succinct [sək'sɪŋkt] ADJ knapp, kurz und bündig pred

succinctly [sək'sɪŋktlɪ] ADV kurz und bündig, in kurzen or knappen Worten or Zügen; **write in knappem** or **gedrängtem Stil; as he very ~ put it** wie er so treffend bemerkte

succinctness [sək'sɪŋktnɪs] N Knappheit f, Kürze f; **with great ~** kurz und bündig, in kurzen Worten; **write** in knappem Stil

succour, (US) **succor** ['sʌkə'] (liter) **N** Beistand m **VT** beistehen (+dat)

succotash ['sʌkətæʃ] N (US Cook) Mais-Bohnen-Eintopf m

succubus ['sʌkjʊbəs] N pl **succubi** ['sʌkjʊbaɪ] Sukkubus m

succulence ['sʌkjʊləns] N Saftigkeit f

succulent ['sʌkjʊlənt] ADJ peach, steak saftig; (Bot) plant, stem fleischig, sukkulent (spec) **N** (Bot) Fettpflanze f, Sukkulente f (spec)

succumb [sə'kʌm] VI erliegen (to +dat); (to threats) sich beugen (to +dat)

such [sʌtʃ] ADJ **a** (= of that kind) solche(r, s); **~ a person** so or solch ein Mensch, ein solcher Mensch; **~ a book** so ein Buch, ein solches Buch; **~ people/books** solche Leute/Bücher; **many/few/all ~ people/books** viele/wenige/all solche Leute/Bücher; **all ~ books are very expensive** solche Bücher sind sehr teuer; **do you have ~ a book?** haben Sie so ein Buch?; **~ a thing** so etwas, so was (inf); **have you got ~ a thing as ...?** haben Sie so etwas wie ...?; **there's ~ a thing as divorce** es gibt so etwas wie eine Scheidung; **I said no ~ thing** das habe ich nie gesagt; **no ~ thing** nichts dergleichen; **I'll/you'll do no ~ thing** ich werde mich/du wirst dich hüten; **there's no ~ thing as a unicorn** so etwas wie ein Einhorn gibt es nicht; **... or some ~ idea** ... oder so etwas, ... oder so was in der Richtung (inf), ... oder so ähnlich; **... or some ~ name/place** ... oder so (ähnlich); **he was ~ a one/just ~ another** er war einer von ihnen/ auch (so) einer; **in ~ a case** in einem solchen Fall; **men/books ~ as these, ~ men/books as these** Männer/Bücher wie diese, solche Männer/Bücher; **writers ~ as Agatha Christie, ~ writers as Agatha Christie** (solche) Schriftsteller wie Agatha Christie; **he's not ~ a fool as you think** er ist nicht so dumm, wie Sie denken; **I'm not ~ a fool as to believe that** or **that I'd believe that** ich bin nicht so dumm or kein solcher Dummkopf, dass ich das glaube; **~ people as attended** die(jenigen), die anwesend waren; **I'll give you ~ books/money as I have** was ich an Büchern/Geld habe, gebe ich Ihnen

b (= so much, so great etc) **he's ~ a liar** er ist so or solch ein Lügner, er ist ein derartiger or solcher Lügner; **he did it in ~ a way that ...** er machte es so, dass ...; **~ wealth!** welch (ein) Reichtum!; **~ beauty!** welche Schönheit!; **he's always in ~ a hurry** er hat es immer so eilig

c pred **his surprise was ~ that ..., ~ was his surprise that ...** seine Überraschung war so groß, dass ..., er war so überrascht, dass ...; **his manner was ~ that ...** er benahm sich so, dass ...; **her speech was ~ that ...** ihre Rede war so gehalten, dass ...

d → **such-and-such**

ADV so, solch (geh); **nobody else makes ~ a good cup of tea as you** niemand kocht so guten Tee wie du; **it's ~ a long time ago** es ist so lange her

PRON **rabbits and hares and ~** Kaninchen, Hasen und dergleichen; **~ being the case ...** in diesem Fall ...; **~ was not my intention** dies war nicht meine Absicht; **~ is not the case** dies ist nicht der Fall; **~ is life!** so ist das Leben!; **those and ~ as those** (hum inf) die oberen zehntausend (hum); **may all ~ perish!** mögen sie alle verderben!; **as ~** an sich; **~ as?** (wie) zum Beispiel?; **~ as it is** so, wie es nun mal ist; **the food, ~ as there was of it ...** das Essen, so weit vorhanden ..., was an Essen da war, ...; **I'll give you ~ as I have** ich gebe Ihnen, was ich habe

such-and-such ['sʌtʃən'sʌtʃ] (inf) ADJ **~ a time/ town** die und die Zeit/Stadt **N** Soundso nt

suchlike ['sʌtʃ,laɪk] (inf) ADJ solche **PRON** dergleichen

suck [sʌk] **N** **to have a ~** (at straw) saugen, ziehen (at an +dat); (at lemonade etc) nuckeln (inf), ziehen (at an +dat); (at lollipop) lutschen

(at an +dat); **to give ~ (to a baby)** (old) (ein Baby) stillen

VT saugen; breast, straw saugen an (+dat); sweet, pastille lutschen; lollipop lutschen an (+dat); thumb lutschen or nuckeln (inf) an (+dat); **to ~ one's teeth** mit den Zähnen saugen; **to ~ the juice out of sth** den Saft aus etw heraussaugen; **to ~ sb's blood** (lit) jdm das Blut aussaugen; (fig) jdn bis aufs Blut aussaugen; **to ~ sb dry** (fig) jdn bis aufs Blut aussaugen; **go and teach your grandmother to ~ eggs** (prov) da will das Ei wieder klüger sein als die Henne (prov); **~ it and see** (fig) Probieren geht über Studieren (Prov)

VI **a** (at an +dat) saugen; (at dummy) nuckeln (inf); (at lollipop) lutschen; (at thumb) lutschen, nuckeln (inf); (at pipe, through straw) ziehen; **he always makes a ~ing noise with his soup** er schlürft seine Suppe immer

b (US, inf, = be very bad) **this city ~s** diese Stadt ist echt Scheiße (inf)

▶ **suck down** VT sep hinunterziehen

▶ **suck in** VT sep liquid, dust aufsaugen; air (ventilator) ansaugen; (person) in tiefen Zügen einatmen; cheeks, stomach einziehen; (fig) knowledge, facts (in sich acc) aufsaugen; imports anlocken

▶ **suck off** VT sep (vulg) **to suck sb off** jdm einen (ab)lutschen (vulg)

▶ **suck under** VT sep hinunterziehen; (completely) verschlingen

▶ **suck up** **VT** sep liquid, dust aufsaugen; **the child sucked up his milk** das Kind trank seine Milch (mit einem Strohhalm) aus **VI** (inf) **to suck up to sb** vor jdm kriechen

sucker ['sʌkə'] N **a** (= rubber sucker, Zool) Saugnapf m; (Bot) unterirdischer Ausläufer; (on creeper) Häkchen nt **b** (US, inf, = lollipop) Lutscher m; **all-day ~** Dauerlutscher m **c** (inf, = fool) Trottel m (inf); **to be a ~ for sth** (immer) auf etw (acc) hereinfallen; (= be partial to sth) eine Schwäche für etw haben; **to be had for a ~** zum Narren gehalten werden, für dumm verkauft werden; **he's looking for some ~ who'll lend him £200** er sucht einen Dummen, der ihm £ 200 leiht

sucker punch N (Boxing, fig inf) Überraschungsschlag m

sucking: **sucking calf** ['sʌkɪŋ,kɑːf] N Milchkalb nt; **sucking pig** ['sʌkɪŋ,pɪg] N Spanferkel nt

suckle ['sʌkl] **VT** child stillen; animal säugen **VI** saugen, trinken

suckling ['sʌklɪŋ] N (old) Säugling m; (= animal) Jungtier nt; **out of the mouths of babes and ~s** (Bibl) aus dem Mund von Kindern und Säuglingen; (fig) Kindermund tut Wahrheit kund (Prov)

suckling pig N Spanferkel nt

sucrose ['suːkrəʊz] N Sa(c)charose f, pflanzlicher Zucker

suction ['sʌkʃən] N Saugwirkung f; (caused by air or water currents) Sog m

suction pad N Saugnapf m

suction pump N Saugpumpe f

Sudan [sʊ'dɑːn] N (the) **~** der Sudan

Sudanese [ˌsuːdə'niːz] ADJ sudanesisch, sudanisch; **he is ~** er ist Sudanese **N** Sudanese m, Sudanesin f

sudden ['sʌdn] ADJ plötzlich; movement also jäh, abrupt; drop, silence also jäh; (= unexpected) bend, change of direction unerwartet; **there was a ~ bend** da war plötzlich eine Kurve, da war eine unerwartete Kurve; **this is all so ~** das kommt alles so plötzlich **N** **all of a ~** (ganz) plötzlich, urplötzlich (inf)

sudden: **sudden death** N (Ftbl: at end of drawn game) Sudden Death m, Spielverlängerung bis zum entscheidenden Tor **sudden-death (overtime)** (US, Sport) Sudden Death m, Spielverlängerung bis zum entscheidenden Punktgewinn **sudden-death (play-off)** (Sport) Ausscheidungsrunde f; **sudden infant death syndrome** N (Med) plötzlicher Kindstod

suddenly ['sʌdnlɪ] ADV plötzlich, auf einmal; *move also* jäh, abrupt; **he had died ~ of a heart attack** er war ganz plötzlich an einem Herzanfall gestorben

suddenness ['sʌdnnɪs] N Plötzlichkeit f; *(of movement also)* Jähheit f, Abruptheit f

Sudetenland [suː'deɪtən,lænd] N Sudetenland nt

sudorific [,sjuːdə'rɪfɪk] *(Med, Pharm)* ADJ schweißtreibend N schweißtreibendes Mittel

suds [sʌdz] PL Seifenwasser nt or -lauge f; (= *lather*) (Seifen)schaum m; *(US, inf, = beer)* Bölkstoff m *(sl)*

sudser ['sʌdzə'] N *(esp US inf)* a (= *soap opera*) Seifenoper f b *(Film: = tear-jerker)* Schmachtfetzen m *(inf)*

sudsy ['sʌdzɪ] ADJ Seifen-; **~ water** Seifenwasser nt

sue [suː] VT a *(Jur)* verklagen, (gerichtlich) belangen; **to ~ sb for sth** jdn auf etw *(acc)* or wegen etw verklagen; **to ~ sb for divorce** gegen jdn die Scheidung einreichen; **to ~ sb for damages** jdn auf Schadenersatz verklagen; **I'll ~ you for every penny you've got** ich werde (vor Gericht) den letzten Cent aus dir herausholen b *(liter: = ask)* bitten, anflehen *(for* um) VI a *(Jur)* klagen, einen Prozess anstrengen, Klage erheben; **to ~ for divorce** die Scheidung einreichen b *(liter)* **to ~ for peace** um Frieden bitten

suede [sweɪd] N Wildleder nt; *(soft, fine also)* Velours(leder) nt ADJ Wildleder-, aus Wildleder; *(of finer quality also)* Velours(leder)-, aus Velours(leder); **~ boots** Wildleder-/Velours(leder)stiefel pl

suet ['suːɪt] N Nierenfett nt, Nierentalg m; **~ pudding** *(sweet)* im Wasserbad gekochte Süßspeise, zu der Nierenfett verwendet wird *(savoury)* mit Nierenfett zubereitete Pastete

Suetonius [swiː'təʊnɪəs] N Sueton(ius) m

suety ['suːɪtɪ] ADJ talgig

Suez ['suːɪz] N Sues nt, Suez nt

Suez Canal N Sueskanal m, Suezkanal m

suffer ['sʌfə'] VT a (= *undergo, be subjected to*) pain, injuries, heart attack, loss, setback, damage, hardship erleiden; hunger leiden; headache, stress, effects etc leiden unter or an *(+dat)*; shock haben; **to ~ defeat/death** eine Niederlage/den Tod erleiden *(geh)*; **the pound ~ed further losses** das Pfund musste weitere Einbußen hinnehmen; **she ~ed quite a blow** sie hat einen Schicksalsschlag erlitten; **her popularity ~ed a decline** ihre Beliebtheit hat gelitten b (= *tolerate*) dulden, ertragen; **he doesn't ~ fools gladly** Dummheit ist ihm ein Gräuel c *(liter: = allow)* zulassen, dulden; **to ~ sth to be done** zulassen or dulden, dass etw geschieht; **~ the little children to come unto me** *(Bibl)* lasset die Kindlein zu mir kommen *(Bibl)* VI *(physically, mentally, fig)* leiden *(from* unter *+dat, from illness an +dat)*; *(as punishment, in hell etc)* büßen; **he was ~ing from shock** er hatte einen Schock (erlitten); **your health/work will ~** deine Gesundheit/Arbeit wird darunter leiden; **the runners are clearly ~ing in this heat** die Hitze macht den Läufern sichtlich zu schaffen; **the regiment ~ed badly** das Regiment erlitt schwere Verluste; **the town ~ed badly in the raids** die Stadt wurde bei den Luftangriffen schwer in Mitleidenschaft gezogen; **how I ~ed!** was ich alles durchgemacht habe!; **to ~ for one's sins** für seine Sünden büßen; **you'll ~ for this!** das wirst du büßen!; **we will see that you don't ~ from the changes** wir werden zusehen, dass Ihnen aus den Umstellungen keine Nachteile entstehen

sufferable ['sʌfərəbl] ADJ erträglich

sufferance ['sʌfərəns] N Duldung f; **on ~** *(nur or stillschweigend)* geduldet; **he's allowed to sleep here on ~ only** es wird nur geduldet, dass er hier schläft

sufferer ['sʌfərə'] N *(Med)* Leidende(r) mf *(from* an *+dat)*; **diabetes ~s, ~s from diabetes** Diabe-

teskranke pl, an Diabetes Leidende pl; **he's been a ~ from arthritis for several years** er leidet seit mehreren Jahren an Arthritis; **the ~s from the earthquake** die Erdbebenopfer pl; **my fellow ~s at the concert** meine Leidensgenossen bei dem Konzert

suffering ['sʌfərɪŋ] N Leiden nt; (= *hardship, deprivation*) Leid nt no pl

suffice [sə'faɪs] *(form)* VI genügen, (aus)reichen VT genügen *(+dat)* *(geh)*; sb also zufrieden stellen; **~ it to say ...** es reicht wohl, wenn ich sage, ...

sufficiency [sə'fɪʃənsɪ] N (= *adequacy*) Hinlänglichkeit f; **to have a ~** genügend haben

sufficient [sə'fɪʃənt] ADJ genügend, ausreichend, genug inv; maturity, temperature genügend attr, ausreichend; reason, condition, explanation, translation hinreichend; funds ausreichend, hinreichend; evidence ausreichend; **is that ~ reason for his dismissal?** ist das Grund genug or ein ausreichender Grund, ihn zu entlassen?; **to be ~** genügen, ausreichen, genug sein; **thank you, that's ~** danke, das genügt or reicht; **I think you have drunk quite ~** ich glaube, Sie haben genug getrunken; **we haven't got ~ to live on** wir haben nicht genug zum Leben; **~ unto the day (is the evil thereof)** *(Prov)* der morgige Tag wird für sich selber sorgen

sufficiently [sə'fɪʃəntlɪ] ADV genug; **~ good/warm etc** gut/warm etc genug pred, genügend or ausreichend gut/warm etc; **a ~ large number** eine ausreichend große Anzahl

suffix ['sʌfɪks] N *(Ling)* Suffix nt, Nachsilbe f; *(in code etc)* Zusatz m VT anfügen, anhängen *(to* an *+acc)*

suffocate ['sʌfəkeɪt] VT *(lit, fig)* ersticken; **his obsessive jealousy/he is suffocating me** seine krankhafte Eifersucht/er erdrückt mich; **he felt ~d in that environment** er hatte das Gefühl, in dieser Umgebung zu ersticken; **he was ~d by the smoke** er erstickte am Rauch VI *(lit, fig)* ersticken

suffocating ['sʌfəkeɪtɪŋ] ADJ *(lit)* erstickend attr; heat drückend attr, brütend attr; room stickig; *(fig)* relationship, atmosphere erdrückend attr; **it's ~ in here** es ist stickig hier drinnen, hier erstickt man fast; **intellectually ~** geisttötend

suffocation [,sʌfə'keɪʃən] N *(lit, fig)* Ersticken nt

suffragan ['sʌfrəgən] ADJ Suffragan-; **~ bishop** Suffraganbischof m N Suffragan(bischof) m

suffrage ['sʌfrɪdʒ] N Wahl- or Stimmrecht nt; *(form, = vote)* Stimme f; **universal ~** das allgemeine Wahlrecht; **female ~** das Frauenstimmrecht

suffragette [,sʌfrə'dʒet] N Suffragette f

suffuse [sə'fjuːz] VT erfüllen; *(light)* durchfluten; **~d with light** in Licht getaucht, lichtdurchflutet *(geh)*; **eyes ~d with tears** Augen voller Tränen, tränenerfüllte Augen; **a blush ~d her face** eine Röte überzog ihr Gesicht

sugar ['ʃʊgə'] N a Zucker m b *(inf, = term of affection)* (meine) Süße, (mein) Schatz, Schätzchen nt *(all inf)* VT zuckern, süßen; *(fig)* criticism etc versüßen, mildern; **to ~ the pill** die bittere Pille versüßen

sugar in cpds Zucker-; **sugar basin** N Zuckerdose f; **sugar beet** N Zuckerrübe f; **sugar bowl** N Zuckerdose f; **sugar candy** N Kandis(zucker) m; *(US, = sweet)* Bonbon nt or m; **sugar cane** N Zuckerrohr nt; **sugar-coated** ADJ mit Zucker überzogen; **sugar-coating** N a *(Cook)* Zuckerguss m b *(fig)* Beschönigen nt, Beschönigung f; **sugar cube** N Zuckerwürfel m; **sugar daddy** N *(inf)* **she's looking for a ~** sie sucht einen alten Knacker, der sie aushält *(inf)*; **sugar diabetes** N Zuckerkrankheit f, Diabetes m *(spec)*, Zucker m *(inf)*

sugared ['ʃʊgəd] ADJ gezuckert; words (honig-) süß; **~ almonds** Zuckermandeln pl

sugar: sugar-free ADJ ohne Zucker; **sugar loaf** N Zuckerhut m; **Sugar Loaf Mountain** der

Zuckerhut; **sugar maple** N Zuckerahorn m; **sugarplum** N Bonbon nt or m, Süßigkeit f; **~ fairy** Zuckerfee f; **sugar shaker** N Zuckerstreuer m; **sugar tongs** PL Zuckerzange f

sugary ['ʃʊgərɪ] ADJ taste süß; (= *full of sugar*) zuckerig; *(fig pej)* style, music, sentiment etc süßlich; film zuckersüß

suggest [sə'dʒest] ✪ 1.1, 1.2 VT a (= *propose*) candidate, place, idea etc vorschlagen; **I ~ that we go, I ~ going** ich schlage vor, zu gehen or (dass) wir gehen; **what do you ~ we do?** was schlagen Sie vor?; **are you ~ing I should tell a deliberate lie?** soll das heißen, dass ich bewusst lügen soll?; **I am ~ing nothing of the kind** das habe ich nicht gesagt b (= *put forward for consideration*) explanation, theory nahe legen, vorbringen; **I ~ (to you) that ...** *(esp Jur)* ich möchte (Ihnen) nahe legen, dass ... c (= *insinuate, hint at*) andeuten; *(unpleasantly)* unterstellen; **what are you trying to ~?** worauf wollen Sie hinaus?, was wollen Sie damit sagen?; **I'm not trying to ~ that he's lying** ich will damit nicht unterstellen or sagen, dass er lügt d (= *indicate, facts, data, sb's action*) andeuten, hindeuten auf *(+acc)*; *(evoke, music, poem)* denken lassen an *(+acc)*; *(symbolism, colours)* andeuten; **it certainly ~s complicity** das deutet zweifellos auf Mittäterschaft hin; **the symptoms would ~ an operation** die Symptome lassen eine Operation angeraten erscheinen e *(Psych)* **to ~ sth to sb** jdm etw suggerieren VR *(idea, thought, plan)* sich aufdrängen, sich anbieten

suggestibility [sə,dʒestɪ'bɪlɪtɪ] N Beeinflussbarkeit f

suggestible [sə'dʒestɪbl] ADJ person beeinflussbar

suggestion [sə'dʒestʃən] ✪ 1.1, 1.2 N a (= *proposal, recommendation*) Vorschlag m, Anregung f; **my ~ is that ...** mein Vorschlag lautet ..., ich schlage vor, dass ...; **following your ~** auf Ihren Vorschlag or Ihre Anregung hin; **Rome was your ~** Rom war deine Idee; **John was his ~ as candidate** er schlug John als Kandidaten vor; **I'm open to ~s** Vorschläge sind or jeder Vorschlag ist willkommen b (= *theory, explanation*) Vermutung f; **he made the ~ that ...** er äußerte die Vermutung, dass ...; **that theory was Professor Higgins' ~** die Theorie stammt von Professor Higgins c (= *insinuation, hint*) Andeutung f, Anspielung f; *(unpleasant)* Unterstellung f; **I resent that ~** ich weise diese Unterstellung zurück; **there is no ~ that he was involved** (= *nobody is suggesting it*) niemand deutet an or unterstellt, dass er beteiligt war; (= *no indication*) es gibt keinen Hinweis darauf or Anhaltspunkt dafür, dass er beteiligt war d (= *trace*) Spur f; **with a ~ of irony in his voice** mit einer Spur or einem Anflug von Ironie in der Stimme e (= *impression*) Eindruck m, Vorstellung f; **to create a ~ of depth** um den Eindruck von Tiefe zu erwecken f (also **indecent suggestion**) unsittlicher Antrag g *(Psych)* Suggestion f

suggestions box N Kasten m für Verbesserungsvorschläge, Kummerkasten m *(inf)*

suggestive [sə'dʒestɪv] ADJ a **to be ~ of sth** an etw *(acc)* denken lassen, auf etw *(acc)* hindeuten; (= *create impression of*) den Eindruck von etw erwecken or vermitteln; (= *be indicative of*) auf etw *(acc)* hindeuten b *(Psych)* suggestiv c (= *indecent*) joke, remark etc zweideutig, anzüglich; movements, gesture, clothing aufreizend; **sexually ~** sexuell aufreizend

suggestively [sə'dʒestɪvlɪ] ADV viel sagend, anzüglich; move, dance aufreizend

suggestiveness [sə'dʒestɪvnɪs] N Zweideutigkeit f, Anzüglichkeit f; **the ~ of her dancing** ihr aufreizendes Tanzen

suicidal [,sɔɪ'saɪdl] ADJ selbstmörderisch; **she was ~** sie war selbstmordgefährdet; **to have ~**

tendencies zum Selbstmord neigen; **I feel ~ this morning** ich möchte heute Morgen am liebsten sterben; **it would be ~ (for them) to do that** (fig) es wäre glatter Selbstmord (für sie), das zu tun

suicide ['sʊɪsaɪd] N Selbstmord m, Freitod m (euph), Suizid m (spec); (= person) Selbstmörder(in) m(f); **to commit ~** Selbstmord begehen; **to contemplate ~** sich mit Selbstmordgedanken tragen; **~ squad** Selbstmordkommando nt

suicide: suicide attempt, suicide bid N Selbstmord- or Suizidversuch m; **suicide bomber** N Selbstmordattentäter(in) m(f); **suicide bombing** N Selbstmordanschlag m; **suicide note** N Abschiedsbrief m; **suicide pact** N Selbstmordabkommen nt

sui generis [,suːaɪˈdʒenərɪs] ADJ sui generis (geh), einzig(artig)

suit [suːt] ⊙ 7.4, 11.3 N a Anzug m; (woman's) Kostüm nt; **~ of clothes** Garnitur f (Kleider); **they bought him a new ~ of clothes** sie kleideten ihn von Kopf bis Fuß neu ein; **~ of armour** Rüstung f

b (Jur) Prozess m, Verfahren nt; **to bring a ~ (against sb for sth)** (wegen etw gegen jdn) Klage erheben or einen Prozess anstrengen; **he lost his ~** er hat seinen Prozess verloren

c (Cards) Farbe f; **short ~** kurze Farbe; **long/ strong ~** lange/starke Farbe; (fig) starke Seite, Stärke f; **to follow ~** (lit) Farbe bedienen; (fig) jds Beispiel (dat) folgen

d (inf, = business executive) Businessman m, Businessfrau f

e (old, liter, in marriage) Werbung f; **to press one's ~** seiner Werbung (dat) Nachdruck verleihen

f (form, = request) Anliegen nt (form), Bitte f; **to press one's ~** seinem Anliegen or seiner Bitte Nachdruck verleihen

VT a (= be convenient, pleasing to, arrangement, date, price) passen (+dat); (climate, food) bekommen (+dat); (occupation, job) gefallen (+dat); **~s me!** (inf) ist mir recht (inf), mir solls recht sein (inf); **that ~s me fine!** (inf) das ist mir recht; **that would ~ me nicely** (time, arrangement) das würde mir gut (in den Kram (inf)) passen; (house, job etc) das wäre genau das Richtige für mich; **when would it ~ you to come?** wann würde es Ihnen passen?, wann wäre es Ihnen recht?; **I know what ~s me best** ich weiß, was für mich das Beste ist

b **to be ~ed for/to** (= be suitable, right for) geeignet sein für; **he is very well ~ed to the job** er eignet sich sehr gut für die Stelle; **he is not ~ed to be a doctor** er eignet sich nicht zum Arzt; **they are well ~ed (to each other)** sie passen gut zusammen

c (clothes, hairstyle) (gut) stehen (+dat), passen zu; **you ~ a beard/fringe** ein Bart/Pony steht dir gut; **such behaviour hardly ~s you** so ein Benehmen steht dir nicht an

d (= adapt) anpassen (to +dat); **to ~ one's style to the audience** sich dem Publikumsgeschmack anpassen, sich nach dem Publikum richten; **~ing the action to the word he ...** er setzte seine Worte in die Tat um und ...

e (= please) gefallen (+dat), zufrieden stellen; **you can't ~ everybody** man kann es nicht jedem recht machen; **we try to ~ every taste** wir versuchen, etwas für jeden Geschmack zu finden or jedem Geschmack gerecht zu werden

VR he ~s himself er tut, was er will or was ihm passt; **you can ~ yourself whether you come or not** du kannst kommen oder nicht, ganz wie du willst; **~ yourself!** wie du willst!, mach, was du willst!; **I like to be able to ~ myself** ich möchte gern tun und lassen können, was ich will

VI (= be suitable) passen

suitability [,suːtəˈbɪlɪtɪ] N Angemessenheit f; (of person for job) Eignung f; **they discussed his ~ as a husband for their daughter** sie diskutierten darüber, ob er sich als Ehemann für ihre Tochter eignete; **the ~ of a film for children** ob ein Film für Kinder geeignet ist

suitable ['suːtəbl] ADJ (= convenient, practical, right for the purpose) geeignet, passend; (= socially, culturally appropriate to the occasion) angemessen; **to be ~ for sb** (date, place) jdm passen; (film, job) für jdn geeignet sein; (hairstyle, clothes) das Richtige für jdn sein; **she's not ~ for him** sie passt nicht zu ihm; **to be ~ for sth** für etw geeignet sein, sich für etw eignen; (socially) einer Sache (dat) angemessen sein; **none of the dishes is ~ for freezing** keines der Rezepte eignet sich zum Einfrieren; **the most ~ man for the job** der am besten geeignete Mann für den Posten; **would 8 o'clock be a ~ time?** würde Ihnen etc 8 Uhr passen?; **Tuesday is the most ~ day** Dienstag ist der günstigste or beste Tag, Dienstag passt am besten; **quality machinery ~ to the task** Qualitätsmaschinen, die der Aufgabe gewachsen sind; **animals that are ~ as pets** Tiere, die als Haustiere geeignet sind; **you're not ~ to be parents** Sie eignen sich nicht als Eltern; **we couldn't find anything ~** wir konnten nichts Passendes or Geeignetes finden; **to be considered ~** als geeignet angesehen werden; **eminently ~** überaus passend; **to make sth ~ for sth** für etw passend machen

suitableness ['suːtəblnɪs] N = **suitability**

suitably ['suːtəblɪ] ADV angemessen; (behave also, apologize) geziemend (geh), wie es sich gehört; **he was ~ impressed** er war gehörig beeindruckt; **I'm ~ impressed** ich bin ja auch beeindruckt; **~ refreshed** ausreichend erfrischt; **to look ~ embarrassed** überaus verlegen aussehen; **a ~ elegant room** ein Raum von angemessener Eleganz; **we camped ~ close to the hills** wir zelteten in günstiger Nähe der Berge

suitcase N Koffer m; **to live out of a ~** aus dem Koffer leben

suite [swiːt] N (of retainers) Gefolge nt; (of furniture) Garnitur f; (= chairs and sofa) Sitzgarnitur f; (of rooms) Suite f, Zimmerflucht f; (Mus) Suite f; **bedroom ~** Schlafzimmergarnitur or -einrichtung f; **3-piece ~** dreiteilige Sitzgarnitur

suiting ['suːtɪŋ] N (= fabric) Anzugstoff m

suitor ['suːtə'] N a (old, of woman) Freier m (old) b (Jur) Kläger(in) m(f)

sulfa etc (US) = **sulpha** etc

sulk [sʌlk] VI schmollen, eingeschnappt sein, beleidigt sein; (photo model) einen Schmollmund machen N Schmollen nt; **to have a ~** schmollen, den Eingeschnappten/die Eingeschnappte spielen; **she was in the ~s all day** sie schmollte den ganzen Tag; **to go into a ~** sich in den Schmollwinkel zurückziehen, einschnappen

sulkily ['sʌlkɪlɪ] ADV say, look beleidigt

sulkiness ['sʌlkɪnɪs] N Schmollen nt; **the ~ of his expression** sein eingeschnappter or schmollender Gesichtsausdruck

sulky[1] ['sʌlkɪ] ADJ (+er) answer eingeschnappt, beleidigt; person, expression also schmollend; silence beleidigt; **to be/look ~ about sth** wegen etw beleidigt sein/aussehen; **~ mouth** Schmollmund m

sulky[2] N (Sport) Sulky nt

sullen ['sʌlən] ADJ a (= morose) mürrisch, missmutig, verdrießlich; behaviour unfreundlich, mürrisch; silence mürrisch b (liter) landscape, sky etc düster, finster

sullenly ['sʌlənlɪ] ADV mürrisch, missmutig

sullenness ['sʌlənnɪs] N a (of person) Missmutigkeit f, Verdrießlichkeit f b (liter, of landscape, sky) Düsterkeit f

sully ['sʌlɪ] VT reputation besudeln; **to ~ one's hands by doing sth** (fig) sich (dat) die Hände schmutzig machen, indem man etw tut

sulpha, (US) **sulfa** ['sʌlfə] ADJ **~ drug** Sulfonamid nt

sulphate, (US) **sulfate** ['sʌlfeɪt] N Sulfat nt, schwefelsaures Salz

sulphide, (US) **sulfide** ['sʌlfaɪd] N Sulfid nt

sulphite, (US) **sulfite** ['sʌlfaɪt] N Sulfit nt

sulphonamide, (US) **sulfonamide** [sʌlˈfɒnəmaɪd] N Sulfonamid nt

sulphur, (US) **sulfur** ['sʌlfə'] N Schwefel m

sulphur dioxide, (US) **sulfur dioxide** N Schwefeldioxid nt

sulphuretted, (US) **sulfuretted** ['sʌlfjʊˌretɪd] ADJ geschwefelt; **~ hydrogen** Schwefelwasserstoff m

sulphuric, (US) **sulfuric** [sʌlˈfjʊərɪk] ADJ Schwefel-

sulphuric acid, (US) **sulfuric acid** N Schwefelsäure f

sulphurize, (US) **sulfurize** ['sʌlfjʊˌraɪz] VT schwefeln

sulphurous, (US) **sulfurous** ['sʌlfərəs] ADJ schwefelig, schwefelhaltig; **~ acid** schwefelige Säure

sultan ['sʌltən] N Sultan m

sultana [sʌlˈtɑːnə] N a (= person) Sultanin f b (Brit: = fruit) Sultanine f

sultanate ['sʌltənɪt] N Sultanat nt

sultriness ['sʌltrɪnɪs] N (lit) Schwüle f; (fig) Heißblütigkeit f; (of look) Glut f

sultry ['sʌltrɪ] ADJ weather, atmosphere schwül; woman heißblütig, temperamentvoll; voice, beauty, look glutvoll

sum [sʌm] N a (= total) Summe f; **that was the ~ (total) of his achievements** das war alles, was er geschafft hatte; **the ~ total of my ambitions** das Ziel meiner Wünsche b (of money) Betrag m, Summe f c (esp Brit, = calculation) Rechenaufgabe f; **to do ~s (in one's head)** (im Kopf) rechnen; **I was bad at ~s** ich war schlecht im Rechnen d (form, = essence) **in ~** mit einem Wort, zusammengefasst

▶ **sum up** VT sep a (= review, summarize) zusammenfassen b (= evaluate rapidly) ab- or einschätzen, taxieren; **she summed me up at a glance** sie taxierte mich mit einem Blick VI (also Jur) zusammenfassen, resümieren; **to sum up, we can say that ...** zusammenfassend or als Resümee können wir feststellen, dass ...; **the judge hasn't summed up yet** der Richter hat sein Resümee noch nicht gegeben

sumac(h) ['suːmæk] N (= plant) Sumach m, Gerberstrauch m; (= preparation) Schmack m

Sumatra [suːˈmɑːtrə] N Sumatra nt

Sumatran [suːˈmɑːtrən] ADJ von/aus Sumatra N Bewohner(in) m(f) von Sumatra

Sumerian [suːˈmɪərɪən] ADJ sumerisch N a Sumerer(in) m(f) b (Ling) Sumerisch nt

summa cum laude [sʊmɑːkʊmˈlaʊdeɪ] ADV (US) summa cum laude

summarily ['sʌmərɪlɪ] ADV (= briefly) knapp, kurz gefasst; (= fast, without ceremony) kurz und bündig, ohne viel Federlesen(s); (Jur) punish, try summarisch; read flüchtig, kursorisch (geh); execute unverzüglich, auf der Stelle

summarize ['sʌməraɪz] VT zusammenfassen

summary ['sʌmərɪ] N Zusammenfassung f; (Sci also) Abriss m; **here is a ~ of the main points of the news** hier ein Überblick m über die wichtigsten Meldungen; **he gave us a short ~ of the film** er gab uns eine kurze Inhaltsangabe des Films; **~ of contents** Inhaltsangabe f ADJ a (= brief) account knapp, gedrängt, kurz gefasst; **in ~ form** in Zusammenfassung b (= fast, without ceremony) treatment kurz, knapp; perusal flüchtig; (Jur) trial, punishment summarisch; dismissal fristlos; **the court dealt out ~ justice** das Gericht sprach Recht im Schnellverfahren; **~ procedure** Schnellverfahren nt

summary execution N Hinrichtung f im Schnellverfahren

summary offence N (Jur) ≈ Übertretung f

summation [sʌˈmeɪʃən] N (= act) Addition f; (= total) Summe f; (= summary) Zusammenfassung f; (US, Jur) Plädoyers pl; in ~ zusammenfassend

summer ['sʌmə'] N Sommer m; **in (the) ~** im Sommer; **two ~s ago** im Sommer vor zwei Jahren; **a girl of seventeen ~s** (liter) ein Mädchen von siebzehn Lenzen (liter); **a ~'s day** ein Sommertag m ADJ attr Sommer-; **~ resort** Ferien- or Urlaubsort m (für die Sommersaison)

VI den Sommer verbringen; (*birds also*) über-sommern

summer: summer camp N Sommerlager *nt*; **summer collection** N (*Fashion*) Sommerkollektion *f*; **summer fallow** N (*Agr*) Sommerbrache *f*; **summer holidays** PL (*esp Brit*) Sommerferien *pl*, Sommerurlaub *m*; **summerhouse** N Gartenhaus *nt*, (Garten)laube *f*; **summer house** N (*US*) Ferienhaus *nt*/-wohnung *f*; **summer lightning** N Wetterleuchten *nt*; **summer sales** PL Sommerschlussverkauf *m*

summersault N, VI = **somersault**

summer: summer school N Sommerkurs *m*; **summertime** N Sommer *m*, Sommer(s)zeit *f*; (= *daylight-saving time*) Sommerzeit *f*; **summerweight** ADJ sommerlich; ~ **coat** Sommermantel *m*

summery ['sʌmərɪ] ADJ sommerlich

summing-up [sʌmɪŋ'ʌp] N (*Jur*) Resümee *nt*

summit ['sʌmɪt] N (*lit*) Gipfel *m*; (*fig also*) Höhepunkt *m*; (= *summit conference*) Gipfelkonferenz *f*, Gipfel *m* **ADJ** *attr* (*Pol*) Gipfel-; **at** ~ **level** auf Gipfelebene

summiteer [ˌsʌmɪ'tɪə] N Gipfelteilnehmer(in) *m(f)*, Teilnehmer(in) *m(f)* an der Gipfelkonferenz

summit meeting N Gipfeltreffen *nt*

summit talks PL Gipfelgespräche *pl*

summon ['sʌmən] VT **a** *servant etc* (herbei)rufen, kommen lassen, herbeizitieren; *police, fire brigade etc* (herbei)rufen; *help* holen; *members* zusammenrufen; *meeting, Parliament* einberufen; **to** ~ **sb to do sth** (= *order*) jdn auffordern, etw zu tun; **the King** ~**ed his ministers** der König rief seine Minister zusammen; **he was** ~**ed back** er wurde zurückgerufen; **to be** ~**ed into sb's presence** zu jdm befohlen or zitiert (*iro*) werden; **a bell** ~**ed them to their work** eine Glocke rief sie zur Arbeit

b (*Jur*) vorladen; ~ **the next witness!** rufen Sie den nächsten Zeugen (auf)!

c to ~ **the courage/strength to do sth** den Mut/die Kraft aufbringen, etw zu tun

▶ **summon up** VT *sep courage* zusammennehmen, zusammenraffen; *strength* aufbieten; *enthusiasm, energy* aufbieten, aufbringen; *sympathy, image, memories* heraufbeschwören; **summoning up all his strength he lifted it up** unter Aufbietung aller Kräfte hob er es hoch

summons ['sʌmənz] **N a** (*Jur*) Vorladung *f*; **to take out a** ~ **against sb** jdn vorladen lassen, jdn vor Gericht laden **b** (= *order to appear etc*) Aufruf *m*, Aufforderung *f*; **he received a** ~ **to see the boss** er wurde zum Chef gerufen, er wurde aufgefordert, zum Chef zu kommen **VT** (*Jur*) vorladen

sumo ['suːməʊ] N Sumo *nt*; ~ **wrestler** Sumoringer *m*

sump [sʌmp] N (*Brit Aut*) Ölwanne *f*; (*Min*) Sumpf *m*

sumptuary ['sʌmptjʊərɪ] ADJ den Aufwand betreffend

sumptuous ['sʌmptjʊəs] ADJ (= *splendid*) luxuriös; (= *costly*) aufwändig, kostspielig; *food etc* üppig, verschwenderisch

sumptuously ['sʌmptjʊəslɪ] ADV (= *splendidly*) luxuriös; (= *expensively*) aufwändig, kostspielig

sumptuousness ['sʌmptjʊəsnɪs] N (= *opulence*) Luxus *m*; (= *expensiveness*) Aufwand *m*, Kostspieligkeit *f*; (*of meal etc*) Üppigkeit *f*

Sun abbr of **Sunday** So.

sun [sʌn] **N** Sonne *f*; **I've got the** ~ **in my eyes** die Sonne scheint mir in die Augen, die Sonne blendet mich; **he was up with the** ~ er stand in aller Frühe auf; **to have a touch of the** ~ einen Sonnenstich haben (*also fig*); **you've caught the** ~ dich hat die Sonne erwischt; **he's tried everything under the** ~ er hat alles Menschenmögliche versucht; **a place in the** ~ (*fig*) ein Platz an der Sonne; **there's nothing new under the** ~ (*prov*) es ist alles schon einmal da gewesen (*Prov*) **VT** der Sonne aussetzen **VR** sich sonnen

sun: sunbaked ADJ ausgedörrt; **sun bath** N Sonnenbad *nt*; **sunbathe** VI in der Sonne liegen, sonnenbaden; **sunbather** N Sonnenbeter(in) *m(f)* (*hum*); **all the** ~**s in the park** all die Leute, die sich im Park sonnen or die im Park in der Sonne liegen; **sunbathing** N Sonnenbaden *nt*; **sunbeam** N Sonnenstrahl *m*; **sun bed** N Sonnenbank *f*

sun: sun blind N (= *awning*) Markise *f*; (= *venetian blind*) Jalousie *f*; **sun block** N Sonnenschutzcreme *f*, Sunblockcreme *f*; **sun bonnet** N Sonnenhut *m*; **sunburn** N Bräune *f*; (*painful*) Sonnenbrand *m*; **sunburnt** ADJ sonnengebräunt, sonnenverbrannt; (*painfully*) von der Sonne verbrannt; **to get** ~ braun werden; (*painfully*) (einen) Sonnenbrand bekommen; **sunburst** N **a** (*US*) plötzlicher Sonnenschein **b** (= *pattern*) Sonnenrad *nt*

sundae ['sʌndeɪ] N Eisbecher *m*

sun dance N Sonnenanbetungstanz *m*

Sunday ['sʌndɪ] **N** Sonntag *m*; **a month of** ~**s** (*inf*) ewig (lange), eine Ewigkeit; **not** or **never in a month of** ~**s** (*inf*) nie im Leben → *also* **Tuesday ADJ** *attr* Sonntags-; *trading* am Sonntag; ~ **(news)paper** Sonntagszeitung *f*

Sunday: Sunday best N Sonntagskleider *pl*, Sonntagsstaat *m* (*old, hum*); **Sunday driver** N Sonntagsfahrer(in) *m(f)*; **Sunday-go-to-meeting** ADJ (*US inf*) Sonntags-; ~ **clothes** Sonntagskleider *pl*, Sonntagnachmittagsausgehkleider *pl* (*hum*); **Sunday painter** N Sonntagsmaler(in) *m(f)*

Sunday school N Sonntagsschule *f*

sun deck N Sonnendeck *nt*

sunder ['sʌndə] (*liter*) **VT** brechen; *chains* sprengen; (*fig*) *connection* abbrechen **VI** brechen; (*fig*) sich trennen

sun: sundew N (*Bot*) Sonnentau *m*; **sundial** N Sonnenuhr *f*; **sundown** N (*Brit*) Sonnenuntergang *m*; **at/before** ~ bei/vor Sonnenuntergang; **sundowner** N **a** (*Austral, inf*, = *tramp*) Penner *m* (*inf*), Vagabund *m* **b** (= *drink*) Abendtrunk

m; **sun-drenched** ADJ *beaches* sonnenüberflutet, in Sonne getaucht; **sundress** N leichtes Sonnenkleid; **sun-dried** ADJ *fruit* an or in der Sonne getrocknet

sundry ['sʌndrɪ] **ADJ** verschiedene **PRON all and** ~ jedermann **N sundries** PL Verschiedenes (+*sing vb*)

sun: sunfast ADJ (*esp US*) lichtecht; **sunflower** N Sonnenblume *f*

sung [sʌŋ] *ptp of* **sing**

sun: sunglasses PL Sonnenbrille *f*; **sun-god** N Sonnengott *m*; **sun-goddess** N Sonnengöttin *f*; **sun hat** N Sonnenhut *m*; **sun helmet** N Tropenhelm *m*

sunk [sʌŋk] *ptp of* **sink**[1]

sunken ['sʌŋkən] ADJ *wreck, ship* gesunken, versunken; *treasure* versunken; *garden* abgesenkt; *bath* eingelassen; *cheeks* eingefallen, hohl; *eyes* eingesunken

sun: Sun King N Sonnenkönig *m*; **sun-kissed** ADJ (*liter*) von der Sonne geküsst; **sun lamp** N Höhensonne *f*; **sunless** ADJ *garden* ohne Sonne; *room also* dunkel; *day also* trübe; **sunlight** N Sonnenlicht *nt*; **in the** ~ in der Sonne, im Sonnenlicht; **sunlit** ADJ *room, day* sonnig; *fields etc also* sonnenbeschienen; **sun lounge** N Wintergarten *m*, Glasveranda *f*; **sun lounger** N Sonnenliege *f*

sunnily ['sʌnɪlɪ] ADV heiter; *smile also* sonnig

sunny ['sʌnɪ] ADJ (+*er*) *place, room, day etc* sonnig; (*fig*) *smile, disposition also, answer, face* heiter; *person* fröhlich; ~ **intervals** (*Met*) Aufheiterungen *pl*; **on the** ~ **side of the house** auf der Sonnenseite (des Hauses); ~~**side up** (*egg*) nur auf einer Seite gebraten; **the outlook is** ~ (*Met*) die Wetteraussichten sind gut; (*fig*) die Aussichten sind rosig; **to look on the** ~ **side (of things)** die Dinge von der angenehmen Seite nehmen; **to be on the** ~ **side of forty** noch nicht vierzig sein, unter vierzig sein

sun: sun parlor N (*US*) Wintergarten *m*, Glasveranda *f*; **sun porch** N Veranda *f*; **sunray** N Sonnenstrahl *m* **ADJ** *attr* ~ **lamp** Höhensonne *f*; ~ **treatment** Ultraviolettbehandlung *f*; **sun-ripened** ADJ *fruit, vegetables* sonnengereift; **sunrise** N Sonnenaufgang *m*; **at** ~ bei Sonnenaufgang; **sunrise industry** N Zukunftsindustrie *f*; **sunroof** N (*of car*) Schiebedach *nt*; (*of hotel etc*) Sonnenterrasse *f*; **sunscald** ['sʌnskɔːld] N (*Bot*) Sonnen- or Rindenbrand *m*; **sunscreen** N Sonnenschutzmittel *nt*; **sunseeker** N Sonnenhungrige(r) *mf*; **sunset** N Sonnenuntergang *m*; **at** ~ bei Sonnenuntergang; **sunshade** N (*lady's, over table*) Sonnenschirm *m*; (= *awning*) Markise *f*, Sonnenblende *f*; **sunshine** N **a** Sonnenschein *m*; **hours of** ~ Sonnenstunden *pl*; **a daily average of 5 hours'** ~ durchschnittlich 5 Stunden Sonne täglich **b** (*inf*, = *person*) mein Lieber, meine Liebe; **sunshine roof** N (*Brit*) Schiebedach *nt*; **sunspot** N **a** Sonnenfleck *m* **b** (*inf, for holiday*) Ferienparadies *nt*; **sunstroke** N Sonnenstich *m*; **to get** ~ einen Sonnenstich bekommen; **sunstruck** ADJ **to be** ~ einen Sonnenstich haben; **sunsuit** N Spiel- or Sonnenanzug *m*; **suntan** N Sonnenbräune *f*; **to get a** ~ braun werden; ~ **lotion/oil** Sonnenöl *nt*; **suntanned** ADJ braun gebrannt; **suntrap** N sonniges Eckchen; **sunup** N (*US*) Sonnenaufgang *m*; **at** ~ bei Sonnenaufgang; **sun-worship** N (*lit, fig*) Sonnenanbetung *f*; **sun-worshipper** N (*lit, fig*) Sonnenanbeter(in) *m(f)*

sup [sʌp] **VT** (*esp N Engl, Scot*) trinken **VI** (*old*: = *dine*) zu Abend essen; **to** ~ **off** or **on sth** etw zu Abend essen; **he that** ~**s with the devil must have a long spoon** (*Prov*) wer den Teufel zum Freund hat, kommt leicht in die Hölle (*Prov*) **N** (= *drink*) Schluck *m*

▶ **sup up** (*esp N Engl, Scot*) **VT** *sep* austrinken **VI** austrinken

super[1] ['suːpə] ADJ (*dated esp Brit inf*) fantastisch, phantastisch, sagenhaft, klasse *inv* (*inf*); ~! Klasse! (*inf*); **we had a** ~ **time** es war große

Klasse (*inf*) or fantastisch or phantastisch or sagenhaft

super² N **a** (*inf*) abbr of **superintendent** Aufseher(in) *m(f)*; (*of police*) ≈ Kommissar(in) *m(f)* **b** (*Theat, Film*) abbr of **supernumerary** Statist(in) *m(f)*

super- PREF super-, Super-

superable ['suːpərəbl] ADJ überwindbar, überwindlich

superabound [ˌsuːpərə'baʊnd] VI **a** im Überfluss vorhanden sein **b** eine Überfülle haben (*in/with an +dat*)

superabundance [ˌsuːpərə'bʌndəns] N (*of an +dat*) großer Reichtum; (= *excessive amount*) Überfluss *m*, Überschuss *m*; (*of enthusiasm*) Überschuss *m*

superabundant [ˌsuːpərə'bʌndənt] ADJ überreichlich

superadd [ˌsuːpər'æd] VT (noch) hinzufügen (*to* zu); **to be ~ed** noch dazukommen (*to* zu)

superannuate [ˌsuːpə'rænjʊeɪt] VT (*esp Brit*) pensionieren, in den Ruhestand versetzen

superannuated [ˌsuːpə'rænjʊeɪtɪd] ADJ (*esp Brit*) pensioniert, im Ruhestand; (*fig inf*) veraltet, überholt

superannuation [ˌsuːpəˌrænjʊ'eɪʃən] N (*esp Brit*) (= *act*) Pensionierung *f*, Versetzung *f* in den Ruhestand; (= *state*) Pension *f*, Ruhestand *m*; (= *pension*) Rente *f*; (*for civil servants, teachers*) Ruhegehalt *nt* (*form*); **~ contribution** Beitrag *m* zur Altersversicherung

superb [suː'pɜːb] ADJ großartig; *design, painting also* meisterhaft; *quality, food also* vorzüglich, superb (*dated, geh*)

superblock ['suːpəblɒk] N (*US*) durchgeplantes, meist autofreies Stadtviertel mit Geschäften, Sozial- und Freizeiteinrichtungen

superbly [suː'pɜːblɪ] ADV *play, perform* großartig; **~ fit/self-confident** ungemein fit/selbstbewusst; **~ well** großartig, hervorragend

superbness [suː'pɜːbnɪs] N Großartigkeit *f*; (*of quality, food also*) Vorzüglichkeit *f*

Superbowl ['suːpəˌbəʊl] N (*US*) Superbowl *m*, jährlich ausgetragenes American-Football-Turnier zwischen den Spitzenreitern der beiden großen nationalen Ligen in den USA

super: superbug N (*inf*) gegen Antibiotika resistenter Krankheitserreger, Superbazillus *m* (*inf*); **supercargo** N pl **-es** Frachtaufseher *m*; **supercharged** ADJ *gas* vorverdichtet; *engine* aufgeladen; (*fig*) *atmosphere* gereizt; **supercharger** N Lader *m*

supercilious ADJ , **superciliously** ADV [ˌsuːpə'sɪlɪəs, -lɪ] hochnäsig

superciliousness [ˌsuːpə'sɪlɪəsnɪs] N Hochnäsigkeit *f*

super: supercomputer N Supercomputer *m*; **superconductor** N (*Phys, Tech*) Supraleiter *m*; **supercool** VT unterkühlen; **super-duper** [ˌsuːpə'duːpə'] ADJ (*hum inf*) ganz toll (*inf*); **super-duty** ADJ (*Tech*) Höchstleistungs-, für höchste Beanspruchung; **superego** N Über-ich *nt*

superelevation [ˌsuːpərelɪ'veɪʃən] N (*of bend*) Überhöhung *f*

supererogation [ˌsuːpərerə'geɪʃən] N (*form*) Mehrleistung *f*, Supererogation (*form*) *f*; (*Eccl*) freiwillige Gebete *pl*, gute Werke *pl*; **an act of ~** eine Mehrleistung or Supererogation (*form*)

superficial [ˌsuːpə'fɪʃəl] ADJ *person, behaviour, injury, treatment, knowledge* oberflächlich; *characteristics, resemblance* äußerlich

superficiality [ˌsuːpəfɪʃɪ'ælɪtɪ] N (*of person, behaviour, injury, treatment, knowledge*) Oberflächlichkeit *f*; (*of characteristics, resemblance*) Äußerlichkeit *f*

superficially [ˌsuːpə'fɪʃəlɪ] ADV *discuss, examine* oberflächlich; *similar, different* äußerlich; **~ this may be true** oberflächlich gesehen mag das stimmen

superfine ['suːpəfaɪn] ADJ *clay, sugar* sehr fein; *distinction* übertrieben fein

superfluity [ˌsuːpə'fluːɪtɪ] N Überfluss *m*; **his ~ of style**, **the ~ of his style** sein verschwenderischer Stil

superfluous [suː'pɜːfluəs] ADJ überflüssig; *style* verschwenderisch; **it is ~ to say …** es ist überflüssig, zu sagen …

superfluously [suː'pɜːfluəslɪ] ADV überflüssigerweise; **… he added ~** … fügte er überflüssigerweise hinzu

super: superglue N Sekundenkleber *m*; **supergrass** N (*Brit inf, = informant*) Kronzeuge *m* (*inf*), Kronzeugin *f* (*inf*), Topinformant(in) *m(f)*; **supergroup** N (*Mus*) Supergruppe *f*; **superheat** VT überhitzen; **superheavyweight** (*Boxing*) **N a** (= *weight category*) Superschwergewicht *nt* **b** (= *boxer*) Superschwergewichtler(in) *m(f)* **ADJ** Superschwergewichts-; **superhero** N Superheld *m*; **superhighway** N (*US*) ≈ Autobahn *f*; **the information ~** die Datenautobahn; **superhuman** ADJ übermenschlich

superimpose [ˌsuːpərɪm'pəʊz] VT **to ~ sth on sth** etw auf etw (*acc*) legen; (*Phot*) etw über etw (*acc*) fotografieren; (*Film*) etw über etw (*acc*) filmen; (*Geol*) etw über etw (*acc*) lagern; (*fig*) etw über etw überlagern; **by superimposing one image on another** indem man zwei Bilder aufeinander legt; **the images were ~d** die Bilder hatten sich überlagert

superintend [ˌsuːpərɪn'tend] VT beaufsichtigen, überwachen

superintendence [ˌsuːpərɪn'tendəns] N (Ober)aufsicht *f*

superintendent [ˌsuːpərɪn'tendənt] N Aufsicht *f*; (*US: in building*) Hausmeister(in) *m(f)*; (*in swimming pool*) Bademeister(in) *m(f)*; (*of hostel, Sunday school etc*) Leiter(in) *m(f)*; (*of police, Brit*) ≈ Kommissar(in) *m(f)*; (*US*) ≈ Polizeipräsident(in) *m(f)*

superior [suː'pɪərɪə'] ✪ 5.2 **ADJ a** (= *better*) *quality, equipment* besser (*to* als); *intellect, ability, skill, technique* überlegen (*to sb/sth* jdm/einer Sache); **he thinks he's so ~** er hält sich für so überlegen or für so viel besser **b** (= *excellent*) *work(manship), technique* großartig, hervorragend; *craftsman* ausgezeichnet; *intellect* überragend; **goods of ~ quality, ~ quality goods** Waren *pl* bester Qualität **c** (= *higher in rank etc*) höher; **~ officer** Vorgesetzte(r) *mf*; **~ court** höheres Gericht; **to be ~ to sb/sth** einer Sache übergeordnet sein, höher stehen als jd/etw **d** (= *greater*) *forces* stärker (*to* als); *strength* größer (*to* als); **they were ~ to us in number(s)** sie waren uns zahlenmäßig überlegen **e** (= *snobbish*) *person, manner* überheblich; *tone, smile* überlegen; (= *smart*) *restaurant, clientele* fein, vornehm **f** (*Typ*) *figure, letter* hochgestellt; **~ number** Hochzahl *f* **N a** (*in rank*) Vorgesetzte(r) *mf* **b** (*in ability*) Überlegene(r) *mf*; **to be sb's ~** jdm überlegen sein; **he has no ~s when it comes to that** was das anbelangt, ist ihm keiner überlegen **c** (*Eccl*) **Father Superior** Vater Superior *m*; **Mother Superior** Mutter Superiorin or Oberin *f*

superiority [suːˌpɪərɪ'ɒrɪtɪ] N **a** (*of cloth etc*) bessere Qualität; (*of technique, ability etc*) Überlegenheit *f*; **its ~ as a holiday resort** seine bessere Klasse als Ferienort **b** (= *excellence*) Großartigkeit *f*; (*of intellect*) überragende Eigenschaft **c** (*in rank*) höhere Stellung, höherer Rang **d** (*in numbers etc*) Überlegenheit *f* **e** (= *conceitedness*) Überheblichkeit *f*; (*of tone, smile*) Überlegenheit *f*; **~ complex** Superioritätskomplex *m*

superlative [suː'pɜːlətɪv] **ADJ** (= *excellent*) überragend, unübertrefflich; *happiness* größte(r, s), höchste(r, s); *indifference* höchste(r, s); (*Gram*) superlativisch, im Superlativ; (= *exaggerated*) *style* überschwänglich **N** Superlativ *m*; **to speak in ~s** zu Superlativen greifen

superlatively [suː'pɜːlətɪvlɪ] ADV (= *excellently*) überragend, unübertrefflich; *happy, fit* höchst; **~ well** überragend (gut)

superman ['suːpəmæn] N pl **-men** [-men] Übermensch *m*; **Superman** (*in comics*) Supermann *m*

supermarket ['suːpəˌmɑːkɪt] N Supermarkt *m*

supernatural [ˌsuːpə'nætʃərəl] **ADJ** übernatürlich; **the ~ world** die Welt des Übernatürlichen **N the ~** das Übernatürliche

supernormal [ˌsuːpə'nɔːməl] ADJ übermenschlich

supernova [ˌsuːpə'nəʊvə] N pl **-s** or **-e** [-'nəʊviː] Supernova *f*

supernumerary [ˌsuːpə'njuːmərərɪ] **ADJ** zusätzlich; (= *superfluous*) überzählig **N** Zusatzperson *f*, Supernumerar *m* (*form*); (*Theat, Film*) Statist(in) *m(f)*

superpower ['suːpəˌpaʊə'] N (*Pol*) Supermacht *f*

supersaver ['suːpəˌseɪvə'] N Supersparangebot *nt*, Superschnäppchen *nt* (*inf*); (*Brit Rail, also* **supersaver ticket**) Fahrkarte *f* zum Supersparpreis

superscribe [ˌsuːpə'skraɪb] VT *one's name etc* obenan setzen; *document etc* beschriften, überschreiben

superscript ['suːpəˌskrɪpt] ADJ *character, number* hochgestellt

supersede [ˌsuːpə'siːd] VT ablösen; *person, belief also* an die Stelle treten von

supersize ['suːpəsaɪz] **N** Riesenformat *nt*, Übergröße *f* **ADJ** übergroß, riesig

supersonic [ˌsuːpə'sɒnɪk] ADJ Überschall-; **at ~ speed** mit Überschallgeschwindigkeit; **~ travel** Reisen *nt* mit Überschallgeschwindigkeit

superstar ['suːpəstɑː'] N (Super)star *m*

superstate ['suːpəsteɪt] N Superstaat *m*

superstition [ˌsuːpə'stɪʃən] N Aberglaube *m* no pl; **this is a ~** das ist Aberglaube

superstitious [ˌsuːpə'stɪʃəs] ADJ abergläubisch; **~ belief** Aberglaube *m*; **to be ~ about sth** in Bezug auf etw (*acc*) abergläubisch sein

superstitiously [ˌsuːpə'stɪʃəslɪ] ADV abergläubisch

superstitiousness [ˌsuːpə'stɪʃəsnɪs] N Aberglaube *m*, Abergläubigkeit *f*

superstore ['suːpəstɔː'] N Großmarkt *m* (*für Endverbraucher*)

superstratum [ˌsuːpə'strɑːtəm] N pl **-strata** [-'strɑːtə] (*Geol*) obere Schicht; (*Ling*) Superstrat *nt*

superstructure ['suːpəˌstrʌktʃə'] N Überbau *m* (*also Sociol*); (*of ship*) Aufbauten *pl*

supertanker ['suːpəˌtæŋkə'] N Super- or Riesentanker *m*

supertax ['suːpətæks] N Höchststeuer *f*

Super Tuesday N (*US, Pol*) ein Dienstag im März eines Jahres in dem Präsidentenwahlen stattfinden, an dem in 20 Staaten Vorwahlen abgehalten werden

supervene [ˌsuːpə'viːn] VI dazwischenkommen, hinzukommen

supervise ['suːpəvaɪz] **VT** beaufsichtigen; *work also* überwachen **VI** Aufsicht führen, die Aufsicht haben

supervision [ˌsuːpə'vɪʒən] N Aufsicht *f*; (= *action*) Beaufsichtigung *f*; (*of work*) Überwachung *f*, Beaufsichtigung *f*; **under the ~ of** unter der Aufsicht von

supervision order N (*Brit, Jur*) gerichtliche Verfügung der Aufsicht

supervisor ['suːpəvaɪzə'] N (*of work*) Aufseher(in) *m(f)*, Aufsicht *f*; (*of research*) Leiter(in) *m(f)*; (*Brit Univ*) ≈ Tutor(in) *m(f)*; (*for PhD*) Doktorvater *m*/-mutter *f*

supervisory ['suːpəvaɪzərɪ] ADJ *role* beaufsichtigend, überwachend; **in a ~ post** in einer Aufsichtsposition; **in his ~ capacity** in seiner Eigenschaft als Aufsichtsperson; **~ staff** Aufsichtspersonal *nt*; **~ powers** Kontrollbefugnis *f*

supervisory board N (*Comm, Ind*) Aufsichtsrat *m*

supervisory body N Aufsichtsgremium *nt*

superwoman ['su:pə,wʊmən] *pl* **-women** [-wɪm-ɪn] N Superfrau *f*

supine ['su:paɪn] ADJ zurückliegend *attr; person* (*lit*) ausgestreckt; (*fig*) entspannt; (*fig liter*) lethargy träge, gleichgültig; **in a ~ position** auf dem Rücken liegend; **to be/lie ~** auf dem Rücken liegen N (*Gram*) Supinum *nt*

supper ['sʌpə'] N (= *evening meal*) Abendessen *nt,* Abendbrot *nt,* Abendmahl *nt* (*liter*); (= *late evening snack*) (später) Imbiss; **they were at ~** sie waren beim Abendessen; **to have ~** zu Abend essen, Abendbrot essen

supper: **supper club** N (*US*) Luxusnachtklub *m;* **suppertime** N Abendessenszeit *f,* Abendbrotzeit *f;* **at ~** zur Abendbrotzeit; **when is ~?** wann wird zu Abend gegessen?

supplant [sə'plɑːnt] VT ablösen, ersetzen; (*forcibly*) verdrängen; (*by ruse*) *rival* ausstechen

supple ['sʌpl] ADJ (*+er*) *body, material etc* geschmeidig, elastisch; *person* beweglich; *shoes* weich; *mind, intellect* beweglich, flexibel; **to keep oneself/one's fingers ~** sich/seine Finger beweglich halten

supplement ['sʌplɪmənt] N a Ergänzung *f* (*to +gen*); (*of book*) Ergänzungsband *m* (*to* zu); (= *at end of book*) Anhang *m,* Nachtrag *m;* (= *food supplement*) Zusatz *m;* **a ~ to his pension** eine Aufbesserung seiner Rente; **family income ~s** Kindergeld *nt* b (= *colour supplement etc*) Beilage *f,* Magazin *nt* VT ergänzen; *income also* aufbessern

supplemental [,sʌplɪ'mentəl] ADJ (*esp US*) zusätzlich

supplementary [,sʌplɪ'mentərɪ] ADJ zusätzlich, ergänzend; (*Med*) *vitamins* ergänzend; **to be ~ to sth** etw ergänzen; **~ food** Zusatznahrung *f;* **~ volume** Ergänzungsband *m*

supplementary: **supplementary angle** N Supplement- *or* Ergänzungswinkel *m;* **supplementary benefit** N (*Brit*) ≈ Sozialhilfe *f;* **to be on ~** ≈ Sozialhilfe beziehen; **supplementary question** N (*Parl*) Zusatzfrage *f*

suppleness ['sʌplnɪs] N (*of body, material etc*) Geschmeidigkeit *f,* Elastizität *f;* (*of person*) Beweglichkeit *f;* (*of shoes*) Weichheit *f;* (*of mind, intellect*) Beweglichkeit *f,* Flexibilität *f*

suppliant ['sʌplɪənt], **supplicant** ['sʌplɪkənt] ADJ flehend *attr;* N Flehende(r) *mf,* Bittsteller(in) *m(f)*

supplicate ['sʌplɪkeɪt] VT (*form*) flehen

supplication [,sʌplɪ'keɪʃən] N Flehen *nt no pl*

supplier [sə'plaɪə'] N (*Comm*) Lieferant(in) *m(f)*

supply [sə'plaɪ] N a (= *supplying*) Versorgung *f;* (*Comm:* = *delivery*) Lieferung *f* (*to* an *+acc*); (*Econ*) Angebot *nt;* **electricity ~** Stromversorgung *f;* **the ~ of blood to the brain** die Versorgung des Gehirns mit Blut; **~ and demand** Angebot und Nachfrage (*+pl vb*) b (= *what is supplied*) Lieferung *f;* **to cut off the ~** (*of gas, water etc*) das Gas/Wasser abstellen; **our wholesaler has cut off our ~** unser Großhändler hat die Lieferungen eingestellt; **where does the badger get its food ~?** woher bekommt der Dachs seine Nahrung? c (= *stock*) Vorrat *m;* **supplies** *pl* (= *food*) Vorräte *pl;* (*for expedition also, for journey*) Proviant *m;* **a good ~ of coal** ein guter Kohlenvorrat; **to get** *or* **lay in supplies** *or* **a ~ of sth** sich (*dat*) einen Vorrat an etw (*dat*) anlegen *or* zulegen; **a month's ~** ein Monatsbedarf *m;* **to be in short ~** knapp sein; **to be in good ~** reichlich vorhanden sein; **our supplies are running out** unser Vorrat geht *or* unsere Vorräte gehen zu Ende; **fresh supplies** (*Mil*) Nachschub *m;* **office supplies** Bürobedarf *m,* Büromaterial *nt;* **medical supplies** Arzneimittel *pl;* (*including bandages*) Ärztebedarf *m;* **electrical supplies** Elektrowaren *or* -artikel *pl* d (= *supply teacher*) Aushilfslehrer(in) *m(f);* **to be on ~** aushilfsweise *or* vertretungsweise unterrichten e (*Parl*) (Militär- und Verwaltungs)etat *m* VT a *material, food, tools etc* sorgen für; (= *deliver*) *goods, information, answer, details* liefern; *clue,*

evidence, gas, electricity liefern; (= *put at sb's disposal*) stellen; **pens and paper are supplied by the firm** Schreibmaterial wird von der Firma gestellt b (*with* mit) *person, army, city* versorgen; (*Comm*) beliefern; **she supplies the humour in the office** sie sorgt für (den) Humor im Büro; **this supplied me with the chance ...** das gab mir die Chance ...; **we were not supplied with a radio** wir hatten kein Radio c (= *satisfy, make good*) *need* befriedigen; *want, deficiency* abhelfen (*+dat*); (*Comm*) *demand* decken

supply: **supply base** N Vorratslager *nt;* **supply day** N (*Parl*) *Tag, an dem der Haushaltsplan vorgelegt wird;* **supply depot** N Versorgungslager *nt;* **supply industry** N Zulieferungsindustrie *f;* **supply lines**, **supply routes** PL (*Mil, fig*) Versorgungslinien *pl;* **supply ship** N Versorgungsschiff *nt;* **supply-side economics** N *sing or pl* Angebotswirtschaft *f;* **supply teacher** N (*Brit*) Aushilfslehrer(in) *m(f);* **supply train** N Versorgungszug *m*

support [sə'pɔːt] N 11.2, 12.2, 13, 26.3 a (*lit*) Stütze *f;* **to give ~ to sb/sth** jdn/etw stützen; **the ceiling will need some kind of ~** die Decke muss irgendwie abgestützt werden; **the bridge ~s** die Stützpfeiler *pl* der Brücke; **to lean on sb for ~** sich auf jdn stützen b (*fig, no pl:* = *moral, financial backing*) Unterstützung *f;* (= *person*) Stütze *f;* **in ~ of** zur Unterstützung (*+gen*); **in ~ of an allegation** zur Untermauerung *or* Stützung einer Behauptung; **to speak in ~ of sb/sth** etw/jdn unterstützen; **to depend on sb for financial ~** auf jds finanzielle Unterstützung angewiesen sein; **our ~ comes from the workers** wir stützen uns auf die Arbeiterschaft ATTR (*Mil etc*) Hilfs- VT a (*lit*) stützen; (= *bear the weight of*) tragen; **it is ~ed on 4 columns** es wird von 4 Säulen getragen *or* gestützt b (*fig*) unterstützen (*also Comput*); *plan, motion, sb's application* befürworten, unterstützen; *party, cause* eintreten für, unterstützen; (= *give moral support to*) beistehen (*+dat*), Rückhalt geben (*+dat*); (= *corroborate*) *claim, theory* erhärten, untermauern; (*financially*) *family* unterhalten; *party, orchestra* finanziell unterstützen; **he ~s Arsenal** er ist Arsenal-Anhänger *m;* **which team do you ~?** für welche Mannschaft bist du?; **without his family to ~ him** ohne die Unterstützung seiner Familie; **Burton and Taylor, ~ed by X and Y** Burton und Taylor, mit X und Y in den Nebenrollen; **his parents ~ed him through university** seine Eltern haben ihn während seines Studiums finanziell unterstützt c (= *endure*) *bad behaviour, tantrums* dulden, ertragen VR (*physically*) sich stützen (*on* auf *+acc*); (*financially*) seinen Unterhalt (selbst) bestreiten

supportable [sə'pɔːtəbl] ADJ erträglich

support act N (*Mus*) Vorgruppe *f*

support band N Vorgruppe *f*

supporter [sə'pɔːtə'] N Anhänger(in) *m(f);* (*of theory, cause, opinion also*) Befürworter(in) *m(f);* (*Sport also*) Fan *m;* **~s' club** Fanklub *m*

support group N Selbsthilfegruppe *f*

supporting [sə'pɔːtɪŋ] ADJ a *documents* zur Unterstützung; **~ group** Vorgruppe *f;* **~ role** (*lit, fig*) Nebenrolle *f;* **with full ~ cast** mit vielen anderen (bedeutenden) Darstellern; **with full ~ programme** mit vollem Nebenprogramm b (*Tech,* = *load-bearing*) stützend, tragend; **~ wall** Stützwand *f*

supporting: **supporting actor** N (*Film, Theat*) Nebendarsteller *m;* **supporting actress** N (*Film, Theat*) Nebendarstellerin *f;* **supporting evidence** N Beweise *pl;* **supporting film** N Vorfilm *m*

supportive [sə'pɔːtɪv] ADJ stützend *attr;* (*fig*) unterstützend *attr;* **if his parents had been more ~** wenn seine Eltern ihn mehr unterstützt hätten; **try to be more ~ (of her/me)** du solltest

versuchen, sie/mich mehr zu unterstützen; **to be ~ of sb/sth** jdn/etw unterstützen

supportiveness [sə'pɔːtɪvnɪs] N Unterstützung *f*

support tights PL Stützstrumpfhose *f*

support troops PL Hilfstruppen *pl*

suppose [sə'pəʊz] ✪ 1.1, 26.3 VT a (= *imagine*) sich (*dat*) vorstellen; (= *assume*) annehmen; **let us ~ we are living in the 8th century** stellen wir uns einmal vor, wir lebten im 8. Jahrhundert; **let us ~ that X equals 3** angenommen, X sei gleich 3; **even supposing it were** *or* **was true** (sogar) angenommen, dass es wahr ist, angenommen, es sei wahr; **always supposing he comes** immer vorausgesetzt, (dass) er kommt; **~ they could see us now!** wenn sie uns jetzt sehen könnten! b (= *believe, think*) annehmen, denken; **I ~ he'll come** ich nehme an, (dass) er kommt, er wird wohl *or* vermutlich kommen; **I don't ~ he'll come** ich glaube kaum, dass er kommt; **I ~ he won't come** ich denke, er wird nicht kommen, er wird wohl nicht kommen; **I ~ that's the best thing, that's the best thing, I ~** das ist *or* wäre vermutlich das Beste; **he's rich, I ~** er muss wohl reich sein; **you're coming, I ~?** ich nehme an, du kommst?; **I don't ~ you could lend me a pound?** Sie könnten mir nicht zufällig ein Pfund leihen?; **do you ~ we could have dinner some evening?** meinen Sie, wir könnten einmal abends zusammen essen gehen?; **will he be coming? – I ~ so** kommt er? – ich denke *or* glaube schon; **you ought to be leaving – I ~ so** du solltest jetzt gehen – stimmt wohl; **don't you agree with me? – I ~ so** bist du da nicht meiner Meinung? – na ja, schon; **I don't ~ so** ich glaube kaum; **isn't he coming? – I ~ not** kommt er nicht? – ich glaube kaum; **so you see, it can't be true – I ~ not** da siehst du selbst, es kann nicht stimmen – du wirst wohl Recht haben; **he can't very well refuse, can he? – I ~ not** er kann wohl kaum ablehnen, oder? – eigentlich nicht; **I never ~d him (to be) a hero** ich habe ihn nie für einen Helden gehalten; **he is generally ~d to be rich** er gilt als reich; **he's ~d to be coming** er soll (angeblich) kommen; **and he's ~d to be an expert!** und der soll (angeblich) (ein) Experte sein! c (*modal use in pass:* = *ought*) **to be ~d to do sth** etw tun sollen; **he's the one who's ~d to do it** er müsste es eigentlich tun; **you're ~d to be in bed** du solltest eigentlich im Bett sein, du gehörst eigentlich ins Bett; **he isn't ~d to find out** er darf es nicht erfahren; **you're not ~d to (do that)** das darfst du nicht tun; **I am ~d to start work here today** ich soll hier heute anfangen; **you're ~d to report to the police** Sie müssen sich bei der Polizei melden d (*in imper:* = *I suggest*) **~ we have a go?** warum versuchen wir es nicht einmal?; **~ we buy it?** wie wäre es, wenn wir es kauften?; **~ you have a wash?** wie wärs, wenn du dich mal wäschst? e (= *presuppose*) voraussetzen; **that ~s unlimited resources** das setzt unbegrenzte Vorräte voraus

supposed [sə'pəʊzd] ADJ vermutet; *date of birth, site of temple, author also* mutmaßlich; *insult, glamour* angeblich

supposedly [sə'pəʊzɪdlɪ] ADV angeblich; **the atom was ~ indivisible** das Atom galt als unteilbar

supposing [sə'pəʊzɪŋ] CONJ angenommen; **but ~ ...** aber wenn ...; **~ he can't do it?** und wenn er es nicht schafft?; **even ~ that ...** sogar wenn ...; **always ~ ...** immer unter der Annahme, dass ...

supposition [,sʌpə'zɪʃən] N (*no pl:* = *hypothesizing*) Mutmaßung *f,* Spekulation *f;* (= *thing supposed*) Annahme *f;* **based on (a) pure ~** auf reiner Spekulation beruhend; **going on the ~ that you are right** vorausgesetzt, dass Sie Recht haben

suppository [sə'pɒzɪtərɪ] N Zäpfchen *nt,* Suppositorium *nt* (*spec*)

suppress [sə'pres] VT **a** *feelings, smile, dissent, views, symptoms, protest* unterdrücken; *appetite* zügeln; *information, evidence* zurückhalten **b** (*Elec*) entstören

suppressant [sə'presnt] N (*Med*) *Medikament zur Unterdrückung bestimmter Körperfunktionen* **appetite** ~ Appetitzügler *m*

suppression [sə'preʃən] N **a** (*of feelings, smile, dissent, views, symptoms, protest*) Unterdrückung *f*; (*of appetite*) Zügelung *f*; (*of information, evidence*) Zurückhalten *nt* **b** (*Elec*) Entstörung *f*

suppressive [sə'presɪv] ADJ Unterdrückungs-, repressiv

suppressor [sə'presəˈ] N (*Elec*) Entstörungselement *nt*

suppurate ['sʌpjʊəreɪt] VI eitern

suppuration [ˌsʌpjʊə'reɪʃən] N Eiterung *f*

supra- ['suːprə-] PREF über-; (*esp with foreign words*) supra-; **supranational** überstaatlich, supra- or übernational

supremacy [sʊ'preməsɪ] N Vormachtstellung *f*; (*Pol, Eccl, fig*) Supremat *nt* or *m*; **air/naval ~** Luft-/Seeherrschaft *f*

supreme [sʊ'priːm] ADJ **a** (= *highest in authority*) höchste(r, s); *court, Soviet* oberste(r, s) **b** (= *very great*) *courage, indifference etc* äußerste(r, s), größte(r, s); **with ~ indifference** äußerst or völlig unbeteiligt **c** (= *ultimate*) **to make the ~ sacrifice** das höchste Opfer bringen; **the ~ moment of the opera** der Höhepunkt der Oper ADV **to rule** or **reign ~** (*monarch*) absolut herrschen; (*champion, justice*) unangefochten herrschen; (*silence*) überall herrschen

Supreme Being N höchstes Wesen

supreme commander N Oberbefehlshaber(in) *m(f)*

supremely [sʊ'priːmlɪ] ADV *confident, self-satisfied, indifferent* zutiefst; *important, elegant* überaus; ~ **gifted** hoch begabt, überaus begabt; **she does her job ~ well** sie macht ihre Arbeit außerordentlich gut

supremo [sʊ'priːməʊ] N (*Brit inf*) Oberboss *m* (*inf*)

Supt abbr of **Superintendent**

surcharge ['sɜːtʃɑːdʒ] N Zuschlag *m*; (*postal*) Nachporto *nt*, Strafporto *nt* (*inf*); **for a small ~** gegen einen geringen Aufschlag VT Zuschlag erheben auf (+*acc*); **he was ~d** er musste Zuschlag bezahlen

surd [sɜːd] N (*Math*) irrationaler Ausdruck

sure [ʃʊəˈ] ✪ 15.1, 16.1 ADJ (+*er*) **a** (= *reliable, steady, safe*) *hand, touch, marksman, footing, knowledge* sicher; *criterion, proof, facts* eindeutig; *method, remedy, friend* zuverlässig, verlässlich; *understanding* genau; **his aim was ~** er traf sicher ins Ziel; **in the ~ knowledge that ...** in der Gewissheit, dass ...
b (= *definite*) sicher; **it is ~ that he will come** es ist sicher, dass er kommt, er kommt ganz bestimmt; **it's ~ to rain** es regnet ganz bestimmt; **he was ~ to see her again** es war sicher, dass er sie wiedersehen würde; **be ~ to tell me** sag mir auf jeden Fall Bescheid; **be ~ to turn the gas off** vergiss nicht, das Gas abzudrehen; **be ~ to go and see her** du musst sie unbedingt besuchen; **you're ~ of a good meal/of success** ein gutes Essen/der Erfolg ist Ihnen sicher; **I want to be ~ of seeing him** ich möchte ihn auf jeden Fall sehen; **to make ~** (= *check*) nachsehen, kontrollieren; **to make ~ to do sth** nicht vergessen, etw zu tun; **make ~ you get the leads the right way round** achten Sie darauf, dass die Kabel richtig herum sind; **make ~ you take your keys** denk daran, deine Schlüssel mitzunehmen; **it's best to make ~** sicher ist sicher; **to make ~ of one's facts** sich der Fakten (*gen*) versichern; **to make ~ of a seat** sich (*dat*) einen Platz sichern; **I've made ~ that there's enough coffee for everyone** ich habe dafür gesorgt, dass genug Kaffee für alle da ist; ~ **thing!** (*esp US, inf*) klare Sache! (*inf*); **he's a ~ thing for president** (*esp US, inf*) er ist ein todsicherer Tipp für die Präsidentschaft; **he'll quit for ~** er kündigt ganz sicher; **I'll find**

out for ~ ich werde das genau herausfinden; **do you know for ~?** wissen Sie das ganz sicher?; **to be ~!** Mensch!, tatsächlich!; **and there he was, to be ~** (*esp Ir*) und da war er doch tatsächlich!
c (= *positive, convinced*) sicher; **I'm ~ she's right** ich bin sicher, sie hat Recht; **do you want to see that film? – I'm not ~** willst du diesen Film sehen? – ich bin mir nicht sicher; **I'm perfectly ~** ich bin (mir da) ganz sicher; **to be ~ about sth** sich (*dat*) einer Sache (*gen*) sicher sein; **I'm not so ~ about that** da bin ich nicht so sicher; **to be ~ about** or **of one's facts** seiner Fakten sicher sein; **to be ~ about** or **of sb** (= *confident*) sich bei jdm or über jdn sicher sein; **to be ~ of oneself** (*dat*) seiner Sache sicher sein; (= *generally self-confident*) selbstsicher sein; **I'm ~ I don't know, I don't know, I'm ~** ich habe keine Ahnung; **I'm not ~ how/why ...** ich bin (mir) nicht sicher or ich weiß nicht genau, wie/warum ...
ADV **a** (*inf*) **will you do it? – ~!** machst du das? – klar! (*inf*); **that meat was ~ tough** or ~ **was tough** das Fleisch war vielleicht zäh!; **know what I mean? – ~ do** du weißt, was ich meine? – aber sicher or aber klar (*inf*); **that's ~ pretty** (*US*) das ist doch schön, nicht?
b and ~ enough he did come und er ist tatsächlich gekommen; **he'll come ~ enough** er kommt ganz bestimmt, er kommt schon; **it's blood ~ enough** es ist tatsächlich Blut
c as ~ as ~ can be (*inf*) **as ~ as I'm standing here** (*inf*) garantiert, todsicher (*inf*)

sure: sure-fire ADJ (*inf*) todsicher (*inf*), bombensicher (*inf*); **sure-footed** ADJ (tritt)sicher; (*fig: = confident*) selbstsicher

surely ['ʃʊəlɪ] ADV **a** bestimmt, sicher; ~ **you don't mean it?** das meinen Sie doch bestimmt or sicher nicht (so)?; ~ **he's come(, hasn't he?)** er ist doch bestimmt gekommen(, oder?); ~ **he hasn't come(, has he?)** er ist doch bestimmt or sicher nicht gekommen(, oder?); ~ **not!** das kann doch nicht stimmen!; ~ **someone must know the answer** irgendjemand muss doch die Antwort wissen; **there must ~ be something we can do** irgendetwas müssen wir doch (sicher) tun können; **I can't – oh, ~ you can** ich kann (es) nicht – aber sicher kannst du das!; **but ~ you can't expect us to believe that** Sie können doch wohl nicht erwarten, dass wir das glauben!; ~ **if a equals b, then c must ...** also, wenn a gleich b ist, dann muss c doch sicherlich ...; ~ **to God** or **goodness** (*inf*) sicherlich
b (*esp US, = gladly*) gern, mit Vergnügen
c (= *inevitably, with certainty*) zweifellos
d (= *undoubtedly*) **he is an artist, just as ~ as** Rembrandt was er ist ein Künstler, genauso wie Rembrandt einer war
e (*confidently*) mit sicherer Hand; **slowly but ~** langsam aber sicher

sureness ['ʃʊənɪs] N **a** (= *positiveness, conviction*) Überzeugung *f*, Sicherheit *f* **b** (= *reliability, steadiness, sure-footedness*) Sicherheit *f*; (*of method, cure, sb's judgement*) Verlässlichkeit *f*, Zuverlässigkeit *f*; ~ **of touch** (*Sport*) Treffsicherheit *f*; (*fig*) glückliche Hand

surety ['ʃʊərətɪ] N **a** (= *sum*) Bürgschaft *f*, Sicherheit *f* **b** (= *person*) Bürge *m*, Bürgin *f*; **to stand ~ for sb** für jdn bürgen; **he was granted bail with a ~ of £5,000** er wurde gegen Hinterlegung einer Kaution von £ 5.000 auf freien Fuß gesetzt **b** (*obs, = certainty*) Sicherheit *f*, Gewissheit *f*; **of a ~** gewiss, sicherlich

surf [sɜːf] N Brandung *f* VI surfen VT **to ~ the waves** surfen, wellenreiten; **to ~ the Net** (*inf*) im Netz or (Inter)net surfen (*inf*)

surface ['sɜːfɪs] N **a** (*lit, fig*) Oberfläche *f*; (*of road*) Decke *f*, Belag *m*; **on the ~ it seems that ...** oberflächlich sieht es so aus, als ob ...; **on the ~ he is friendly enough** nach außen hin ist er sehr freundlich **b** (*Math, of cube etc*) Fläche *f* **c** (*Min*) **at/on/up to the ~** über Tage *pl* (*Aviat*) Tragfläche *f* ADJ attr **a** oberflächlich; ~ **texture** Oberflächenstruktur *f* **b** (= *not by air*) *travel* auf dem Land-/Seeweg **c** (*Min*) *worker,*

job über Tage VT **a** *road* mit einem Belag versehen; *wall* verblenden **b** *submarine* auftauchen lassen VI (*lit, fig*) auftauchen

surface: surface area N Fläche *f*; (*Math*) Flächeninhalt *m*; **surface dressing** N (*on roads, = method*) Straßenreparatur *f* mit Rollsplitt; (= *material*) Rollsplitt *m*; **surface grammar** N Oberflächengrammatik *f*; **surface mail** N Post *f* auf dem Land-/Seeweg; **by ~** auf dem Land-/Seeweg; **surface-mounted** ADJ oberflächenmontiert; **surface noise** N Rauschen *nt*; **surface structure** N (*Ling*) Oberflächenstruktur *f*; **surface tension** N Oberflächenspannung *f*; **surface-to-air** ADJ attr Boden-Luft-; ~ **missile** Boden-Luft-Rakete *f*; **surface-to-surface** ADJ attr Boden-Boden-; ~ **missile** Boden-Boden--Rakete *f*; **surface vessel** N Schiff *nt* (*im Gegensatz zu Unterseeboot*)

surfacing ['sɜːfɪsɪŋ] N **what did they use as ~ for the roads/walls?** was für ein Material wurde für den Straßenbelag/als Wandbelag verwendet?

surfboard ['sɜːfbɔːd] N Surfbrett *nt*

surfeit ['sɜːfɪt] N Übermaß *nt*, Zuviel *nt* (*of an* +*dat*) VT *sb, oneself* übersättigen, überfüttern (*on, with* mit)

surfer ['sɜːfəˈ] N Surfer(in) *m(f)*, Wellenreiter(in) *m(f)*; (*on Internet*) (Net-)Surfer(in) *m(f)*

surfing ['sɜːfɪŋ] N Surfen *nt*, Surfing *nt*, Wellenreiten *nt*; **a good ~ beach** ein guter Strand zum Surfen or Wellenreiten

surge [sɜːdʒ] N **a** (*of sea*) Wogen *nt*; (*of floodwater*) Schwall *m*; (*Elec*) Spannungsstoß *m*; **a ~ of people** eine wogende Menschenmenge; **there was a ~ of sympathy for him** es gab eine Sympathiewelle für ihn; **he felt a sudden ~ of rage** er fühlte, wie die Wut in ihm aufstieg; **a ~ in demand/exports** ein rascher Nachfrage-/Exportanstieg
VI (*sea*) branden; (*floods, river*) anschwellen; (*demand, exports*) rasch ansteigen; **blood ~d to her head** ihr schoss das Blut ins Gesicht; **they ~d toward(s)/(a)round him** sie drängten auf ihn zu/umdrängten ihn; **people ~d in/out** eine Menschenmenge flutete herein/heraus; **to ~ a-head/forward** vorpreschen

surgeon ['sɜːdʒən] N Chirurg(in) *m(f)*; (*Mil*) Stabsarzt *m*/-ärztin *f*; (*Naut*) Marinearzt *m*/-ärztin *f* → **dental surgeon**, **veterinary surgeon**

surgeon general N (*Mil*) Sanitätsinspekteur(in) *m(f)*; (*US*) ≈ Gesundheitsminister(in) *m(f)*

surgery ['sɜːdʒərɪ] N **a** Chirurgie *f*; **to have ~** operiert werden; **to need (heart) ~** (am Herzen) operiert werden müssen; **to undergo major heart ~** sich einer größeren Herzoperation unterziehen; ~ **is the only solution** Operieren ist die einzige Lösung; **a fine piece of ~** eine großartige chirurgische Leistung **b** (*Brit, = room*) Sprechzimmer *nt*; (= *consultation*) Sprechstunde *f*; ~ **hours** Sprechstunden *pl*; **when is his ~?** wann hat er Sprechstunde?

surgical ['sɜːdʒɪkəl] ADJ *treatment, removal* operativ; *technique, instrument, training, skill, hospital* chirurgisch; ~ **corset** Stützkorsett *nt*; ~ **gloves** OP-Handschuhe *pl*, Chirurgenhandschuhe *pl*; ~ **goods shop** orthopädisches Fachgeschäft; ~ **intervention** chirurgischer Eingriff; ~ **strike** (*Mil*) gezielter Angriff; ~ **team** OP-Team *nt*, Chirurgenteam *nt*; ~ **ward** chirurgische Station, Chirurgie *f* (*inf*)

surgical: surgical appliance N Stützapparat *m*; **surgical boot** N orthopädischer Schuh; **surgical gown** N OP-Kleidung *f*

surgically ['sɜːdʒɪkəlɪ] ADV *treat, remove* operativ; ~, **we have advanced a long way** wir haben in der Chirurgie große Fortschritte gemacht

surgical mask N OP-Maske *f*

surgical spirit N (*Brit*) Wundbenzin *nt*

surgicenter ['sɜːdʒɪˌsentəˈ] N (*US Med*) Poliklinik *f*

surging ['sɜːdʒɪŋ] ADJ *water, corn, crowd* wogend; *price, power, demand, exports, imports* rasch ansteigend

Surinam, **Suriname** [ˌsʊərɪˈnæm] N Suriname *nt*

surliness [ˈsɜːlɪnɪs] N Verdrießlichkeit *f*, Missmutigkeit *f*

surly [ˈsɜːlɪ] ADJ (+er) verdrießlich, mürrisch, missmutig

surmise [ˈsɜːmaɪz] N Vermutung *f*, Mutmaßung *f* **VT** [sɜːˈmaɪz] vermuten, mutmaßen; **I ~d as much** das hatte ich (schon) vermutet; **as one could ~ from his book** wie man nach seinem Buch vermuten *or* mutmaßen konnte

surmount [sɜːˈmaʊnt] VT **a** *difficulty, obstacle* überwinden **b** (*esp Archit, Her etc*) **~ed by sth** von *or* mit etw gekrönt

surmountable [sɜːˈmaʊntəbl] ADJ überwindlich, zu überwinden

surname [ˈsɜːneɪm] N Nachname *m*, Familienname *m*; **what is his ~?** wie heißt er mit Nachnamen?

surpass [sɜːˈpɑːs] VT **a** (= *be better than*) übertreffen **b** (= *exceed*) *comprehension* hinausgehen über (+*acc*); **to ~ all expectations** alle Erwartungen übertreffen **VR** sich selbst übertreffen

surpassing [sɜːˈpɑːsɪŋ] ADJ (*liter*) *beauty* unvergleichlich

surplice [ˈsɜːpləs] N Chorrock *m*, Chorhemd *nt*

surplus [ˈsɜːpləs] N Überschuss *m* (*of an* +*dat*); **a balance of trade ~** ein Überschuss *m* in der Handelsbilanz ADJ überschüssig; (*of countable objects*) **~ value** Mehrwert *m*; Army **~ boots** Stiefel *pl*; **sale of ~ stock** Verkauf *m* von Lagerbeständen; **have you any ~ sheets I could borrow?** hast du Laken übrig, die ich mir borgen könnte?; **it is ~ to (my) requirements** das benötige ich nicht; **~ store** *Geschäft, das billig Lagerbestände verkauft*

surprise [səˈpraɪz] ☼ 15.2, 16.1, 16.2 N Überraschung *f*; **in ~** voller Überraschung, überrascht; **much to my ~, to my great ~** zu meiner großen Überraschung; **with a look of ~** mit überraschtem Gesicht; **it was a ~ (for *or* to me) to find that …** ich war überrascht, als ich entdeckte, dass …; **it came as a ~ to us** wir waren überrascht, es hat uns überrascht; **what a ~!** was für eine Überraschung!; **to give sb a ~** jdn überraschen; **to take sb by ~** jdn überraschen; **~, ~, it's me!** rate mal, wer hier ist?; **~, ~!** (*iro*) was du nicht sagst! **ATTR** Überraschungs-, überraschend; **~ attack** Überraschungsangriff *m*; **~ success** Überraschungserfolg *m*; **~ winner** Überraschungssieger(in) *m(f)* **VT** überraschen; (= *catch unawares also*) *army, sentry* überrumpeln; *thief* (auf frischer Tat) ertappen; **you ~ me!** (*also iro*) das überrascht mich!; **I was ~d to hear it** ich war überrascht, das zu hören; **I wouldn't be ~d if … es** würde mich nicht wundern, wenn …; **don't be ~d if he refuses** wundern Sie sich nicht, wenn er ablehnt; **it's nothing to be ~d at** das ist nicht weiter verwunderlich; **I'm ~d at *or* by his ignorance** ich bin überrascht über seine Unkenntnis; **I'm ~d you didn't think of that** es wundert mich, dass du nicht daran gedacht hast; **go on, ~ me!** lass mich überraschen!; **he ~d me into agreeing** er hat mich so verblüfft, dass ich zugestimmt habe

surprising [səˈpraɪzɪŋ] ADJ überraschend, erstaunlich; **there's nothing ~ about that** das ist nicht weiter verwunderlich; **it's hardly ~ he said no** es ist kaum verwunderlich, dass er nein *or* Nein gesagt hat

surprisingly [səˈpraɪzɪŋlɪ] ADV *big, successful* überraschend; **~ (enough), he was right** er hatte erstaunlicherweise Recht; **and then ~ he left** und dann ist er überraschenderweise *or* zu unserer/ihrer *etc* Überraschung gegangen; **not ~ it didn't work** wie zu erwarten (war), hat es nicht geklappt

surreal [səˈrɪəl] ADJ unwirklich

surrealism [səˈrɪəlɪzəm] N Surrealismus *m*

surrealist [səˈrɪəlɪst] ADJ surrealistisch N Surrealist(in) *m(f)*

surrealistic [səˌrɪəˈlɪstɪk] ADJ **a** surrealistisch **b** (= *surreal*) unwirklich

surrender [səˈrendə] **VI** sich ergeben (*to* +*dat*); (*to police*) sich stellen (*to* +*dat*); **I ~!** ich ergebe mich! **VT** (*Mil*) übergeben; *firearms also, control, power, title, lead* abgeben; *goods, suspect* ausliefern; *insurance policy* einlösen; *lease* kündigen; *claim, right, hope* aufgeben **VR to ~ oneself to sth** sich einer Sache (*dat*) hingeben; *to fate* sich in etw (*acc*) ergeben **N a** (*Mil, = capitulation*) Kapitulation *f* (*to vor* +*dat*) **b** (= *handing over*) Übergabe *f* (*to an* +*acc*); (*of control, power, title, lead*) Abgabe *f*; (*of suspect*) Auslieferung *f*, Aushändigung *f* (*to an* +*acc*); (*of insurance policy*) Einlösen *nt*; (*of lease*) Kündigung *f*; (*of claim, right, hope*) Aufgabe *f*, Preisgabe *f*; **~ value** (*Insur*) Rückgabe- *or* Rückkaufswert *m*

surreptitious [ˌsʌrəpˈtɪʃəs] ADJ heimlich; *whisper, glance, kiss also* verstohlen; **he made a few ~ changes** er machte heimlich ein paar Änderungen

surreptitiously [ˌsʌrəpˈtɪʃəslɪ] ADV heimlich

surrey [ˈsʌrɪ] N (*US*) zweisitzige Kutsche

surrogacy [ˈsʌrəgəsɪ] N Leihmutterschaft *f*

surrogate [ˈsʌrəgɪt] N (= *substitute*) Ersatz *m*, Surrogat *nt* (*geh*); (*Brit, Eccl*) ≈ Weihbischof *m* **ATTR** Ersatz-; **~ bishop** ≈ Weihbischof *m*

surrogate: surrogate family N Ersatzfamilie *f*; **surrogate mother** N Leihmutter *f*; **surrogate motherhood** N Leihmutterschaft *f*

surround [səˈraʊnd] N (*esp Brit*) Umrandung *f*; (= *floor round carpet*) Ränder *pl*; **the ~s** die Umgebung **VT** umgeben; (*Mil*) umstellen, umzingeln; **she was ~ed by children/suitors** sie war von Kindern umgeben/von Verehrern umgeben *or* umschwärmt

surrounding [səˈraʊndɪŋ] ADJ umliegend; **in the ~ countryside** in der Umgebung *or* Umgegend; **in the ~ darkness** in der Dunkelheit, die mich/ihn *etc* umgab; **~ tissue** (*Med*) Bindegewebe *nt*

surroundings [səˈraʊndɪŋz] PL Umgebung *f*; **the ~ of Glasgow** die Umgebung von Glasgow

surround sound N (*TV, Radio*) Surround-Sound *m*; (= *sytem*) Surround-Sound-System *nt*

surtax [ˈsɜːtæks] N Steuerzuschlag *m*

surtitle [ˈsɜːtaɪtl] N (*in opera etc*) Übertitel *m*

surveillance [sɜːˈveɪləns] N Überwachung *f*, Observation *f* (*form*); **to be under ~** überwacht *or* observiert (*form*) werden; **to keep sb under ~** jdn überwachen *or* observieren (*form*)

survey [ˈsɜːveɪ] N **a** (*Surv, of land, coast*) Vermessung *f*; (= *report*) (Vermessungs)gutachten *nt*; (*of house*) Begutachtung *f*; (= *report*) Gutachten *nt*; **they are doing a ~ for a new motorway** sie führen Vermessungsarbeiten für eine neue Autobahn durch; **to have a ~ done on a house** ein Gutachten über ein Haus erstellen lassen **b** (= *inquiry*) Untersuchung *f* (*of, on* über +*acc*); (*by opinion poll, market research etc*) Umfrage *f* (*of, on* über +*acc*) **c** (= *comprehensive look, review, of surroundings, countryside*) Musterung *f* (*of* +*gen*), Überblick *m* (*of* über +*acc*); (*of subject, recent development*) Überblick *m* **VT** [sɜːˈveɪ] **a** (= *look at*) *countryside, person, prospects, plans* betrachten, sich (*dat*) ansehen; (*esp appraisingly*) begutachten; *person, goods* mustern; **to ~ the situation** (*lit, fig*) die Lage peilen; **he is monarch of all he ~s** er beherrscht das Land, soweit er blicken kann **b** (= *study*) *prospects, developments* untersuchen; *institutions* einer Prüfung (*gen*) unterziehen; (= *take general view of*) *events, trends* einen Überblick geben über (+*acc*) **c** (*Surv*) *site, land* vermessen; *building* inspizieren

surveying [sɜːˈveɪɪŋ] N **a** (*of site, land*) Vermessung *f*; (*of building*) Inspektion *f* **b** (= *profes-*

sion) Landvermessung *f*; (*of buildings*) Inspektion *f* von Gebäuden

surveyor [sɜːˈveɪə] N (= *land surveyor*) Landvermesser(in) *m(f)*; (= *building surveyor*) Bauinspektor(in) *m(f)*, Baugutachter(in) *m(f)*

survival [səˈvaɪvəl] N **a** Überleben *nt*; (*of customs, usages*) Weiterleben *nt*; **the ~ of the fittest** das Überleben der Stärkeren; **his ~ as prime minister seems unlikely** es ist unwahrscheinlich, dass er sich als Premierminister halten kann; **~ bag** Expeditionsschlafsack *m* **b** (= *relic*) Überbleibsel *nt* (*of, from aus*)

survival instinct N Überlebensinstinkt *m*

survivalist [səˈvaɪvəlɪst] N Überlebenskünstler(in) *m(f)*

survival kit N Überlebensausrüstung *f*

survive [səˈvaɪv] **VI** (*person, animal etc*) überleben, am Leben bleiben; (*in job*) sich halten (können); (*house, treasures, book, play*) erhalten bleiben; (*custom, religion*) weiterleben, fortbestehen; **only five copies ~ or have ~d** nur fünf Exemplare sind erhalten; **will this play ~ despite the critics?** wird sich das Stück trotz der Kritiken halten?; **you'll ~** (*iro*) das wirst du schon überleben!; **he ~d to tell the tale** er hat als Zeuge überlebt; (*hum*) er hat es überlebt (*hum*) **VT** überleben; *experience, accident also* (lebend) überstehen; (*house, objects*) *fire, flood* überstehen; (*inf*) *heat, boredom etc* aushalten; **to ~ the ages** die Jahrhunderte überdauern; **he was ~d by his wife** seine Frau überlebte ihn

surviving [səˈvaɪvɪŋ] ADJ **a** (= *still living*) noch lebend; **the oldest ~ member of the family** das älteste noch lebende Mitglied der Familie **b** (= *remaining*) noch existierend; **the largest ~ shipyard** die größte noch produzierende Werft

survivor [səˈvaɪvə] N Überlebende(r) *mf*; (*Jur*) Hinterbliebene(r) *mf*; (*of abuse etc*) Opfer *nt*; **he's a ~** (*fig, in politics etc*) er ist ein Überlebenskünstler; **she is the sole ~ of the winning team** sie ist die einzige noch lebende Vertreterin der siegreichen Mannschaft

Susan [ˈsuːzn] N Susanne *f*

susceptibility [səˌseptəˈbɪlɪtɪ] N **a** no pl **~ to sth** (*to charms, flattery etc*) Empfänglichkeit *f* für etw; (*to attack*) Ausgesetztsein *nt* (*to sth* gegenüber etw); (*to rheumatism, colds*) Anfälligkeit *f* für etw; **~ to pain** Schmerzempfindlichkeit *f*; **~ to treatment** Behandelbarkeit *f*; **~ to unkind remarks** Empfindlichkeit *f* in Bezug auf unfreundliche Bemerkungen; **his ~ to her tears/pleas** dass er sich durch ihre Tränen/Bitten erweichen lässt/ließ **b** **susceptibilities** PL (= *sensibilities*) Feingefühl *nt*

susceptible [səˈseptəbl] ADJ **a** (= *impressionable*) beeindruckbar, leicht zu beeindrucken *pred*; **~ to sth** (*to charms, flattery etc*) für etw empfänglich; *to kindness, suggestion, influence etc* einer Sache (*dat*) zugänglich; *to attack* einer Sache (*dat*) ausgesetzt; *to rheumatism, colds* für etw anfällig; **~ to pain** schmerzempfindlich; **~ to treatment** behandelbar; **he's very ~ to remarks about his big nose** er reagiert sehr empfindlich auf Anspielungen auf seine große Nase; **he was ~ to her tears/pleas** er ließ sich durch ihren Tränen/Bitten erweichen **b** (*form*) **to be ~ of proof** beweisbar sein; **to be ~ of interpretation** Interpretationssache sein

suspect [ˈsʌspekt] ADJ verdächtig, suspekt N [ˈsʌspekt] Verdächtige(r) *mf* **VT** [səˈspekt] *a person* verdächtigen (*of sth* einer Sache *gen*), in Verdacht haben; *plot, swindle* vermuten, ahnen, argwöhnen (*geh*); **I ~ her of having stolen it/written it** ich habe sie im Verdacht *or* ich verdächtige sie, es gestohlen/geschrieben zu haben; **he is ~ed of being a member of this sect, he is a ~ed member of this sect** er steht im Verdacht *or* man verdächtigt ihn, Mitglied dieser Sekte zu sein; **the ~ed bank robber/terrorist** *etc* der mutmaßliche Bankräuber/Terrorist *etc*; **he ~s nothing** er ahnt nichts; **does he ~ anything?** hat er

Verdacht geschöpft?
b (= *doubt*) *truth* bezweifeln, anzweifeln; *motive* argwöhnisch sein gegenüber
c (= *think likely*) vermuten; **I ~ed as much** das habe ich doch vermutet *or* geahnt, das habe ich mir doch gedacht; **a ~ed case of measles** ein Fall, bei dem Verdacht auf Masern besteht; **he was taken to hospital with a ~ed heart attack** er wurde mit dem Verdacht auf Herzinfarkt ins Krankenhaus eingeliefert; **~ed cases of child abuse** mögliche Fälle von Kindesmissbrauch
VI [sə'spekt] einen Verdacht haben

suspend [sə'spend] VT **a** (= *hang*) (auf)hängen (*from* an +*dat*); (*Chem*) suspendieren; **to be ~ed in sth** in etw (*dat*) hängen; (*Chem*) in etw (*dat*) suspendiert sein; **to hang ~ed from sth/in sth** von/in etw (*dat*) hängen
b (= *stop, defer*) *publication, payment* (zeitweilig) einstellen; *campaign, talks, judgement* aussetzen; *flights* aufschieben; **he was given a ~ed sentence** seine Strafe wurde zur Bewährung ausgesetzt; **to be in a state of ~ed animation** im Zustand vorübergehender Leblosigkeit sein; **to ~ one's disbelief** (*Theat*) sich verzaubern lassen
c *person* suspendieren; *member, pupil, student* zeitweilig ausschließen; (*Sport*) sperren; *licence* zeitweilig einziehen; *law, privileges* aussetzen; *constitution* zeitweilig außer Kraft setzen; **to ~ sb from duty** jdn (vom Dienst) suspendieren

suspender [sə'spendə'] N *usu pl* **a** (*Brit, for stockings*) Strumpfhalter *m*, Straps *m*; (*for socks*) Sockenhalter *m*; **~ belt** Strumpf(halter)gürtel *m* **b** (*US*) **suspenders** PL Hosenträger *pl*

suspense [sə'spens] N (*in book, film etc*) Spannung *f*; **the ~ is killing me** ich bin gespannt wie ein Regenschirm (*hum inf*); **to keep sb in ~** jdn in Spannung halten, jdn auf die Folter spannen (*inf*); **to wait in ~** gespannt *or* voller Spannung warten

suspense account N Interimskonto *nt*

suspenseful [sə'spensfʊl] ADJ spannend

suspenser [sə'spensə'] N (*inf*) Thriller *m*, spannender Film

suspension [sə'spenʃən] N **a** (*of publication, payment*) zeitweilige Einstellung; (*of flights*) Aufschub *m*; (*of campaign, talks, judgement*) Aussetzung *f*; (*of prison sentence*) Aussetzung *f* (*zur Bewährung*) **b** (*of person*) Suspendierung *f*; (*of member, pupil, student*) zeitweiliger Ausschluss; (*Sport*) Sperrung *f*; (*of licence*) zeitweiliger Einzug; (*of laws, privileges*) Aussetzen *nt* **c** (*Aut*) Federung *f*; (*of wheels*) Aufhängung *f* **d** (*Chem*) Suspension *f* **e** (*Mus*) **to be in ~** suspendiert sein, gehalten werden

suspension: suspension bridge N Hängebrücke *f*; **suspension file** N Hängemappe *f*; **suspension point** N (*Typ*) Auslassungspunkt *m*

suspensory [sə'spensərɪ] ADJ (*Anat*) Aufhänge-; **~ ligament** Aufhängeband *nt*

suspicion [sə'spɪʃən] N **a** Verdacht *m no pl*, Argwohn *m no pl* (*geh*); **to arouse sb's ~s** jds Verdacht *or* Argwohn (*geh*) erregen; **I have a ~ that ...** ich habe den Verdacht *or* das Gefühl, dass ...; **to have one's ~s about sth/sb** seine Zweifel bezüglich einer Sache (*gen*)/bezüglich einer Person (*gen*) haben; **my ~s were right** mein Verdacht hat sich bestätigt; **to be above (all) ~** über jeden Verdacht erhaben sein; **to be under ~** unter Verdacht stehen; **to arrest sb on ~/on ~ of murder** jdn wegen Tatverdachts/ Mordverdachts festnehmen; **to be open to ~** sich verdächtig machen; **~ fell on him** der Verdacht fiel auf ihn; **to view sb/sth with ~** jdn/ etw argwöhnisch *or* misstrauisch betrachten
b (= *trace, touch*) Hauch *m*, Spur *f*

suspicious [sə'spɪʃəs] ADJ **a** (= *feeling suspicion*) argwöhnisch, misstrauisch (*of* gegenüber); **you have a ~ mind** Sie sind aber misstrauisch; **to be ~ about sth** etw mit Misstrauen *or* Argwohn (*geh*) betrachten **b** (= *causing suspicion*) verdächtig; **there were no ~ circumstances** es gab keine verdächtigen Umstände; **he died in ~ circumstances** er starb unter verdächtigen *or*

zweifelhaften Umständen; **the police are treating her death as ~** die Polizei betrachtet ihren Tod als nicht natürlich

suspiciously [sə'spɪʃəslɪ] ADV **a** (= *with suspicion*) *examine, glance, ask* argwöhnisch, misstrauisch **b** (= *causing suspicion*) *behave, act* verdächtig **c** (= *probably*) verdächtig; **it looks ~ like measles to me** das sieht mir verdächtig nach Masern aus; **it sounds ~ as though ...** es hört sich verdächtig danach an, als ob ...

suspiciousness [sə'spɪʃəsnɪs] N **a** (= *feeling suspicion*) Verdacht *m*, Argwohn *m* (*geh*) **b** (= *causing suspicion*) Verdächtigkeit *f*

suss [sʌs] VT (*Brit, inf*) **a** (= *suspect*) *plan* kommen hinter (+*acc*) (*inf*); **to ~ it** dahinter kommen (*inf*); **as soon as he ~ed what was going on** sobald er dahinter kam, was da gespielt wurde (*inf*) **b to ~ sb out** jdm auf den Zahn fühlen (*inf*); **I can't ~ him out** bei ihm blicke ich nicht durch (*inf*); **I've got him ~ed (out)** ich habe ihn durchschaut; **to ~ sth out** etw herausbekommen (*inf*); **to ~ things out** die Lage peilen (*inf*)

sussed [sʌst] ADJ (*Brit inf, = knowledgeable*) bewandert; (= *clever*) clever

sustain [sə'steɪn] VT **a** (= *support*) *load, weight* aushalten, tragen; *life* erhalten; *family* unterhalten; *charity* unterstützen; (= *nourish*) *body* bei Kräften halten; **not enough to ~ life** nicht genug zum Leben; **that isn't enough food to ~ you** das wird Ihnen nicht reichen; **his love has ~ed her over the years** seine Liebe hat ihr über die Jahre hinweg viel Kraft gegeben
b (= *keep going, maintain*) *pretence, argument, theory, effort, veto, interest, support* aufrechterhalten; *growth, position* beibehalten; (*Mus*) *note* (aus)halten; (*Theat*) *accent, characterization* durchhalten; (*Jur*) *objection* stattgeben (+*dat*); **objection ~ed** Einspruch stattgegeben → *also* **sustained**
c (= *receive*) *injury, damage, loss* erleiden; **to ~ an attack** angegriffen werden

sustainable [sə'steɪnəbl] ADJ *aufrechtzuerhalten pred*, aufrechtzuerhaltend *attr*; *development, recovery, agriculture, forestry* nachhaltig; *resources* erneuerbar; *growth* nachhaltig, kontinuierlich; *level, situation, argument* haltbar; *position* vertretbar

sustained [sə'steɪnd] ADJ *effort etc* ausdauernd; *applause also, attack, pressure* anhaltend; (*Mus*) *note* (aus)gehalten; (*Econ*) *economic growth, recovery, recession* anhaltend

sustaining [sə'steɪnɪŋ] ADJ *food* nahrhaft, kräftig

sustaining pedal N (*Mus*) Fortepedal *nt*

sustaining program N (*US, Rad, TV*) nichtkommerzielle *or* nicht kommerzielle Sendung

sustenance ['sʌstɪnəns] N (= *food and drink*) Nahrung *f*; (= *nutritive quality*) Nährwert *m*; **to get one's ~ from sth** sich von etw ernähren

susurration [ˌsjuːsə'reɪʃən] N (*liter*) Säuseln *nt* (*liter*)

suture ['suːtʃə'] N (*Med*) Naht *f* **VT** (ver)nähen

SUV N (*esp US Aut*) *abbr of* **sport utility vehicle** Sport-utility-Fahrzeug *nt*, geländegängige Limousine

suzerainty ['suːzəreɪntɪ] N Suzeränität *f*

svelte [svelt] ADJ (= *slender*) grazil; (= *sophisticated*) vornehm, elegant

Svengali [sven'ɡɑːlɪ] N *jd, der den Willen anderer, normalerweise mit finsteren Absichten, beherrscht*

SVGA (*Comput*) *abbr of* **super video graphics array** SVGA *nt*

SW *abbr* **a** *of* **south-west** SW **b** *of* **short wave** KW

swab [swɒb] N **a** (*Med*) Tupfer *m*; (= *specimen*) Abstrich *m*; **to take a ~** einen Abstrich machen **b** (*Naut*) Mop *m* **VT a** (*Med*) *wound etc* (ab)tupfen **b** (*Naut*: *also* **swab down**) wischen

Swabia ['sweɪbɪə] N Schwaben *nt*

Swabian ['sweɪbɪən] ADJ schwäbisch **N a** Schwabe *m*, Schwäbin *f* **b** (*Ling*) Schwäbisch *nt*

swacked [swækt] ADJ (*esp US inf*) **a** (*from alcohol*) blau (*inf*) **b** (*from taking drugs*) high (*inf*)

swaddle ['swɒdl] VT *baby* wickeln (*in* in +*acc*); **swaddling clothes** (*esp Bibl*) Windeln *pl*

swag [swæɡ] N (*inf*) Beute *f*

swagger ['swæɡə'] **N** (= *gait*) Stolzieren *nt*; (= *behaviour*) Angeberei *f*, Großtuerei *f*; **to walk with a ~** stolzieren **VI a** (= *strut*) stolzieren; **he ~ed down the street/over to our table** er stolzierte die Straße hinunter/zu unserem Tisch herüber **b** (= *boast, act boastfully*) angeben

swaggerer ['swæɡərə'] N Großtuer(in) *m(f)*

swaggering ['swæɡərɪŋ] **ADJ a** *gait, manner* forsch **b** (= *boastful*) großtuerisch, angeberisch **N** Großtuerei *f*, Angeberei *f*; **his ~ about** sein Herumstolzieren *nt*

swagger stick N Offiziersstöckchen *nt*

Swahili [swɑː'hiːlɪ] N (= *African language*) Suaheli *nt*

swain [sweɪn] N (*old, = suitor*) Freier *m*; (= *lad*) Bursch(e) *m*

SWALK [swɔːlk] *abbr of* **sealed with a loving kiss** (*auf Briefumschlägen*)

swallow[1] ['swɒləʊ] **N** Schluck *m* **VT** *food, drink* (hinunter)schlucken; (*fig*) *story, evidence, insult* schlucken; **to ~ one's tongue** (*Med*) sich an seiner Zunge verschlucken; **to ~ one's pride** seinen Stolz schlucken; **to ~ sth whole** (*lit*) etw ganz schlucken; (*fig*) etw ohne weiteres schlucken; **that's a bit hard to ~** das glaubt ja kein Mensch (*inf*); **to ~ one's words** (= *speak indistinctly*) seine Worte verschlucken; (= *remain silent*) hinunterschlucken, was er/sie *etc* sagen wollte; (= *retract*) seine Worte zurücknehmen → **bait** **VI** schlucken; **to ~ hard** (*fig*) kräftig schlucken

▶ **swallow down** VT *sep* hinunterschlucken

▶ **swallow up** VT *sep* (*fig*) verschlingen; **the mist/darkness seemed to swallow them up** der Nebel/die Dunkelheit schien sie zu verschlucken; **I wished the ground would open and swallow me up** ich hätte vor Scham in den Boden versinken können

swallow[2] N (= *bird*) Schwalbe *f*; **one ~ doesn't make a summer** (*prov*) eine Schwalbe macht noch keinen Sommer (*Prov*)

swallow: swallow dive N Schwalbensprung *m*; **swallowtail** N (= *butterfly*) Schwalbenschwanz *m*; **swallow-tailed coat** ['swɒləʊteɪld'kəʊt] N Schwalbenschwanz *m*

swam [swæm] *pret of* **swim**

swamp [swɒmp] **N** Sumpf *m* **VT** unter Wasser setzen, überschwemmen; (*fig, = overwhelm*) überschwemmen; **to be ~ed with sth** mit etw überschwemmt werden

swamp: swamp buggy N Sumpffahrzeug *nt*; **swamp fever** N Sumpffieber *nt*; **swampland** N Sumpfland *nt*, Sumpf *m*

swampy ['swɒmpɪ] ADJ (+*er*) sumpfig; **to become ~** versumpfen

swan [swɒn] **N** Schwan *m* **VI** (*Brit inf*) **to ~ off** abziehen (*inf*); **to ~ around New York** in New York herumziehen (*inf*); **to ~ around (the house)** zu Hause herumschweben (*inf*)

swan dive N (*US*) Schwalbensprung *m*

swank [swæŋk] (*esp Brit inf*) **N a** (= *boastfulness*) Angabe *f*, Protzerei *f* (*inf*); (= *ostentation*) Schau *f* (*inf*); **it's just a lot of ~** das ist doch nur Angabe/Schau **b** (= *person*) Angeber(in) *m(f)* **VI** angeben (*about* mit); **to ~ around** protzen (*inf*), große Töne spucken (*inf*)

swanky ['swæŋkɪ] ADJ (+*er*) (*esp Brit, inf*) *manner, words, party* großspurig; *car, restaurant, house etc* protzig (*inf*); *neighbourhood* hochnäsig

swannery ['swɒnərɪ] N Schwanenteich *m*

swan's-down ['swɒnzˌdaʊn] N (= *feathers*) Schwanendaunen *pl*; (= *fabric*) *wolliges Material*

swan: swan song N (fig) Schwanengesang m; **swan-upping** [ˌswɒnˈʌpɪŋ] N feierliche Zeichnung der jungen Schwäne

swap [swɒp] **N** Tausch m, Tauschhandel m; **~s** (= stamps) Tauschmarken pl; **it's a fair ~** das ist ein fairer Tausch; **to do a ~ (with sb)** (mit jdm) tauschen **VT** stamps, cars, houses etc tauschen; stories, reminiscences, addresses, insults austauschen; **to ~ sth for sth** etw für etw eintauschen; **to ~ places with sb** mit jdm tauschen; **to ~ sides** die Seiten wechseln; **I'll ~ you!** (inf) ich tausch mit dir (inf) **VI** tauschen

swap meet N (US, Comm) Tauschbörse f

SWAPO [ˈswɑːpəʊ] abbr of **South-West Africa People's Organization** SWAPO f

swap shop N Tauschbörse f

sward [swɔːd] N (obs, poet) Rasen m

swarm [swɔːm] **N** (of insects, birds) Schwarm m; (of people also) Schar f; **the sightseeers came in ~s** die Touristen kamen scharenweise or in Scharen **VI** (bees, flies, people) schwärmen; **the place was ~ing with insects/people** es wimmelte von Insekten/Leuten; **the main street was ~ing (with people)** (inf) auf der Hauptstraße herrschte Hochbetrieb (inf); **tourists were ~ing everywhere** es wimmelte überall von Touristen; **children ~ed all round the car** Kinder schwärmten um das Auto herum

▶ **swarm up** VI +prep obj hinauf- or hochklettern

swarthiness [ˈswɔːðɪnɪs] N (of skin) Dunkelheit f; (of person also) Dunkelhäutigkeit f, dunkle Farbe

swarthy [ˈswɔːðɪ] ADJ (+er) skin dunkel; person also dunkelhäutig

swashbuckler [ˈswɒʃˌbʌklə'] N verwegener Kerl

swashbuckling [ˈswɒʃˌbʌklɪŋ] ADJ person, manner, performance verwegen; **a ~ film** ein Mantel-und-Degen-Film m

swastika [ˈswɒstɪkə] N Hakenkreuz nt; (= religious symbol also) Swastika f

swat [swɒt] **VT** fly totschlagen; table schlagen auf (+acc) **VI** **to ~ at a fly** nach einer Fliege schlagen **N** **a** (= blow) Schlag m **b** (= fly swat) Fliegenklatsche f

swatch [swɒtʃ] N (Textil)muster nt; (= collection of samples) Musterbuch nt

swath [swɔːθ] N Schwade f; **to cut a ~ through sth** eine Bahn durch etw schneiden

swathe [sweɪð] **N** = swath **VT** wickeln (in in +acc); (in bandages also) umwickeln (in mit); **to ~ oneself in sth** sich in etw (acc) einwickeln or einhüllen, etw um sich wickeln

swatter [ˈswɒtə'] N (= fly swatter) Fliegenklatsche f

sway [sweɪ] **N** **a** (= movement, of trees) Sichwiegen nt; (of hanging object) Schwingen nt; (of building, mast, bridge etc, unsteady person) Schwanken nt; (of train, boat) Schaukeln nt; (of hips) Wackeln nt; (fig) Schwenken nt; **the graceful ~ of the dancer's body** das anmutige Wiegen der Tänzerin **b** (= ruling, rule) Macht f (over über +acc); **to bring a city/a people under one's ~** sich (dat) eine Stadt/ein Volk unterwerfen; **to hold ~ over sb/a nation** jdn/ein Volk beherrschen or in seiner Macht haben **VI** (trees) sich wiegen; (hanging object) schwingen; (building, mast, bridge, unsteady person) schwanken; (train, boat) schaukeln; (hips) wackeln; (fig) schwenken; **she ~s as she walks** sie wiegt beim Gehen die Hüften; **the drunk ~ed up the road** der Betrunkene schwankte die Straße entlang; **to ~ between two alternatives** zwischen zwei Alternativen schwanken **VT** **a** hips wiegen; (wind) hin und her bewegen **b** (= influence) beeinflussen; (= change sb's mind) umstimmen

sway bar N (US Aut) Stabilisator m

Swaziland [ˈswɑːzɪlænd] N Swasiland nt

swear [swɛə'] vb: pret **swore**, ptp **sworn** **VT** **a** allegiance, love, revenge schwören; oath leisten, schwören; **I ~ it!** ich kann das beschwören!

b (Jur) witness, jury vereidigen; **to ~ sb to secrecy** jdn schwören lassen, dass er nichts verrät; **I've been sworn to secrecy** ich habe schwören müssen, dass ich nichts sage **VI** **a** (= use solemn oath) schwören; **to ~ on the Bible** auf die Bibel schwören; **to ~ by all one holds dear** schwören bei allem, was einem lieb ist; **to ~ to sth** etw beschwören; **to ~ blind** or (US) **up and down that ...** (inf) Stein und Bein schwören, dass ... (inf)

b (= use swearwords) fluchen (about über +acc); **to ~ at sb/sth** jdn/etw beschimpfen **N** **to have a (good) ~** (tüchtig) fluchen

▶ **swear by** VI +prep obj (inf) schwören auf (+acc)

▶ **swear in** VT sep witness, jury, president vereidigen

▶ **swear off** VI +prep obj (inf) abschwören (+dat)

swearing [ˈswɛərɪŋ] N Fluchen nt

swearing-in [ˌswɛərɪŋˈɪn] N Vereidigung f

swearword [ˈswɛəwɜːd] N Fluch m, Kraftausdruck m

sweat [swet] **N** **a** Schweiß m no pl; (on walls) (Kondens)wasser nt; **drops/beads of ~** Schweißtropfen pl/-perlen pl; **his face was running with ~** Schweiß rann ihm von der Stirn; **by the ~ of one's brow** (fig) im Schweiße seines Angesichts (liter); **to be in a ~** (lit, fig) schwitzen; **to get into a ~ about sth** (fig) wegen etw ins Schwitzen geraten or kommen; **no ~** (inf) kein Problem

b (inf, = work) **what a ~ that was!** das war eine Heidenarbeit! (inf); **we had a real ~ to do it** wir haben dabei wirklich geschuftet (inf); **that's too much ~ for me** das ist mir zu anstrengend **VI** (person, animal, wall) schwitzen (with vor +dat); (fig inf, = work hard) sich abrackern (inf) (over mit); (= worry) zittern, schwitzen (inf) (with vor +dat); **to ~ like a pig** (inf) wie ein Affe schwitzen (inf) **VT** horse, athlete schwitzen lassen; (pej) worker für einen Hungerlohn arbeiten lassen; recruit schleifen (inf); **to ~ buckets** (inf) wie ein Affe schwitzen (inf); **to ~ blood** (with worry) Blut und Wasser schwitzen; (with effort, work) sich abrackern (inf)

▶ **sweat out** VT sep **a** illness, fever herausschwitzen **b** **to sweat it out** (fig inf) durchhalten; (= sit and wait) abwarten

sweatband [ˈswetbænd] N Schweißband nt

sweated [ˈswetɪd] ADJ worker völlig unterbezahlt, ausgebeutet; goods für einen Hungerlohn hergestellt; **~ labour** billige Arbeitskräfte pl; **it was ~ labour!** (inf) das war Ausbeutung

sweater [ˈswetə'] N Pullover m

sweat gland N Schweißdrüse f

sweating system [ˈswetɪŋˌsɪstəm] N (economy based on exploitation) Ausbeutungssystem nt

sweat: sweat lodge N Schwitzhütte f; **sweat pants** PL (esp US) Jogginghose f; **sweatshirt** N Sweatshirt nt; (Sport) Trainingspullover m; **sweatshop** N (pej, hum inf) Ausbeuterbetrieb m (pej); **sweatsuit** N (Sport) Trainingsanzug m

sweaty [ˈswetɪ] ADJ (+er) hands schweißig; brow schweißbedeckt; body, person, socks verschwitzt; weather, day, work zum Schwitzen; place heiß; **to get ~** ins Schwitzen geraten; **digging is ~ work** beim Graben kommt man leicht ins Schwitzen; **a hot and ~ job** eine heiße und schweißtreibende Arbeit; **to have a ~ smell** nach Schweiß riechen; **~ feet** Schweißfüße pl

Swede [swiːd] N Schwede m, Schwedin f

swede [swiːd] N (esp Brit) Kohlrübe f, Steckrübe f

Sweden [ˈswiːdn] N Schweden nt

Swedish [ˈswiːdɪʃ] **ADJ** schwedisch; **he is ~** er ist Schwede; **she is ~** sie ist Schwedin **N** **a** (Ling) Schwedisch nt **b** **the ~** die Schweden pl

Swedish mile N schwedische Meile (10 km)

Sweeney [ˈswiːnɪ] N (Brit inf) Überfallkommando nt (inf)

sweep [swiːp] vb: pret, ptp **swept** **N** **a** **to give the floor a ~** den Boden kehren or fegen; **the chimney needs a ~** der Schornstein muss gekehrt or gefegt werden

b (= chimney sweep) Schornsteinfeger(in) m(f), Kaminkehrer(in) m(f)

c (of arm, pendulum) Schwung m; (of sword) Streich m; (of dress) Rauschen nt no pl; (of oars) Durchziehen nt no pl; (of light, radar) Strahl m; **in one ~** (fig) auf einen Schwung; **with a ~ of her skirts** mit rauschenden Gewändern; **to make a ~ for mines** nach Minen suchen; **the police made a ~ of the district** die Polizei hat die Gegend abgesucht; **to make a clean ~** (fig) gründlich aufräumen, gründlich Ordnung schaffen; **the Russians made a clean ~ of the athletic events** die Russen haben beim Leichtathletikkampf tüchtig abgeräumt (inf) or alle Preise eingesteckt

d (= range) Bereich m; (of gun) Schussbereich m

e (= curve, line, of road, river) Bogen m; (of facade, contour, hair) Schwung m; **a wide ~ of country** eine sich weit ausdehnende Landschaft; **a beautiful ~ of hills** herrliche Berge pl

f = sweepstake

VT **a** floor, street, chimney kehren, fegen; room (aus)kehren, (aus)fegen; dust, snow wegfegen; **to ~ a path through the snow** einen Weg durch den Schnee bahnen; **to ~ sth under the carpet** (fig) etw unter den Teppich kehren

b (= scan, move searchingly over) absuchen (for nach); (bullets) streichen über (+acc); minefield, sea durchkämmen; mines räumen; **to ~ a channel clear of mines** einen Kanal von Minen säubern

c (= move quickly over, wind, skirt) fegen über (+acc); (waves) deck, sand etc überrollen, überschwemmen; (glance) gleiten über (+acc); (fig, wave of protest, violence, fashion) überrollen; (disease) um sich greifen in (+dat)

d (= remove with sweeping movement, wave) spülen, schwemmen; (current) reißen; (wind) fegen; person reißen; **to ~ sth off the table/onto the floor** etw vom Tisch/zu Boden fegen; **the crowd swept him into the square** er wurde von der Menge zum Platz hin mitgerissen; **he swept the obstacles from his path** er stieß die Hindernisse aus dem Weg; **the army swept the enemy before them** die Armee jagte die feindlichen Truppen vor sich hin

e (= triumph) große Triumphe feiern in (+dat); **to ~ the polls** (Pol) die Wahlen haushoch gewinnen; **to ~ all before one** (fig) alle in die Tasche stecken (inf); **to ~ the board** (fig) alle Preise/Medaillen gewinnen, abräumen (inf) **VI** **a** (with broom) kehren, fegen → **broom**

b (= move, person) rauschen; (vehicle, plane, quickly) schießen; (majestically) gleiten; (skier) fegen; (road, river) in weitem Bogen führen; **panic/the disease swept through Europe** Panik/die Krankheit griff in Europa um sich or breitete sich in Europa aus; **the tornado swept across the fields** der Wirbelsturm fegte über die Felder

▶ **sweep along** **VI** dahin- or entlangrauschen; (majestically) dahin- or entlanggleiten **VT** sep (lit, fig) mitreißen

▶ **sweep aside** VT sep (lit, fig) wegfegen, beiseitefegen

▶ **sweep away** **VI** = sweep off **VT** sep dust, leaves etc wegfegen; (storm also, avalanche) wegreißen; (flood etc) wegspülen, wegschwemmen; (fig) old laws aufräumen mit; work, accomplishments zunichte machen; doubts zerstreuen; opposition vernichten

▶ **sweep down** **VI** hinunterrauschen; (car, plane) hinunterschießen; (majestically) hinuntergleiten; (road, hill) in sanftem Bogen abfallen; **to sweep down on sb** sich auf jdn stürzen, über jdn herfallen **VT** sep abkehren, abfegen

▶ **sweep off** **VI** davonrauschen; (car, plane) davonschießen; (majestically) davongleiten; (skier) davonfegen **VT** sep vase, clock herunterfegen; **to sweep sb off somewhere** jdn irgendwohin entführen; **the children were swept off to bed** die

Kinder wurden schleunigst ins Bett gesteckt (*inf*) *or* geschickt; **to sweep sb off his/her feet** (*lit*) jdn umreißen; (*fig*) *audience* jdn begeistern; **he swept her off her feet** (*fig*) sie hat sich Hals über Kopf in ihn verliebt (*inf*)

▶ **sweep out** **VI** (*inf*) hinausrauschen; (*car*) herausschießen; (*majestically*) hinausgleiten; **to sweep out of a room** aus einem Zimmer rauschen **VT** *sep room* auskehren, ausfegen; *dust* hinauskehren *or* -fegen

▶ **sweep up** **VI** **a** (*with broom*) zusammenkehren *or* -fegen; **to sweep up after sb** hinter jdm herfegen **b** (= *move*) **the car swept up to the house** der Wagen rollte aufs Haus zu; **she swept up in a Rolls Royce** sie rollte in einem Rolls Royce vor; **a broad driveway sweeps up to the manor** ein breiter Zufahrtsweg schwingt sich zum Herrenhaus hinauf **VT** *sep* zusammenkehren *or* -fegen; (= *collect up*) *objects* zusammenraffen; *person* hochreißen; *hair* hochbinden

sweepback ['swiːpbæk] N (*Aviat*) Pfeilform *f*

sweeper ['swiːpə] N **a** (= *road sweeper*) Straßenkehrer(in) *m(f)* *or* -feger(in) *m(f)*; (= *machine*) Kehrmaschine *f*; (= *carpet sweeper*) Teppichkehrer *m* **b** (*Ftbl*) Ausputzer(in) *m(f)*

sweep hand N Sekundenzeiger *m*

sweeping ['swiːpɪŋ] **ADJ** **a** *gesture, stroke, curve* weit ausholend; *bow, curtsey, lines* schwungvoll; *glance* streifend; *staircase* geschwungen; *lawn* ausgedehnt; *view* weit **b** (*fig*) *change, reduction* radikal, drastisch; *statement* pauschal; *victory* überragend, glänzend; **to make a ~ condemnation of sth** etw in Bausch und Bogen verdammen **N** (= *cleaning*) Kehren *nt*, Fegen *nt*

sweepingly ['swiːpɪŋlɪ] **ADV** *gesture* schwungvoll; *speak* verallgemeinernd; *condemn* in Bausch und Bogen

sweepings ['swiːpɪŋz] PL Kehricht *m*, Dreck *m*; (*fig, of society etc*) Abschaum *m*

sweepstake ['swiːpsteɪk] N (= *race*) Rennen, in dem die Pferdebesitzer alle Einsätze machen, Sweepstake *nt or m*; (= *prize*) aus allen Einsätzen gebildeter Preis (= *lottery*) Wette, bei der die Preise aus den Einsätzen gebildet werden

sweet [swiːt] **ADJ** (+*er*) **a** süß; **to like ~ things** gern Süßes essen; **to have a ~ tooth** gern Süßes essen, naschhaft sein
b (= *fresh*) *food, water* frisch; *air, breath* rein, frisch; *soil* nicht sauer; (= *fragrant*) *smell* süß; **the air was ~ with the scent of roses** die Luft war erfüllt vom Duft der Rosen
c (*fig*) süß; (= *kind*) lieb; **that's very ~ of you** das ist sehr lieb von dir; **that car/horse is a ~ little runner** das Auto/Pferd läuft prächtig; **to be ~ on sb** (*dated inf*) in jdn vernarrt sein; **to keep sb ~** (*inf*) jdn bei Laune halten; **the water tasted ~ to him** (*liter*) das Wasser schmeckte (ihm) so gut; **success was doubly ~ to him** er genoss den Erfolg doppelt; **once he caught the ~ smell of success** als erst der Erfolg lockte; **at his own ~ will** (*iro*) wie es ihm gerade passt *or* einfällt; **in his own ~ way** (*iro*) auf seine unübertroffene Art; **~ Fanny Adams** *or* **FA** (*Brit inf*) nix (*inf*), nicht die Bohne (*inf*) → **dream, nothing**
N **a** (*Brit* = *candy*) Bonbon *nt*
b (*Brit* = *dessert*) Nachtisch *m*, Dessert *nt*; **for ~** zum *or* als Nachtisch *or* Dessert
c **yes, (my) ~** (*inf*) ja, (mein) Schätzchen *or* Liebling
d **sweets** PL (*fig*: = *pleasures*) Freuden *pl*; **once he had tasted the ~s of success** nachdem er einmal erfahren hatte, wie süß der Erfolg sein kann

sweet: sweet-and-sour ADJ süßsauer; **sweetbread** N Bries *nt*; **sweetbrier** N Weinrose *f*; **sweet chestnut** N Edelkastanie *f*; **sweetcorn** N Mais *m*

sweeten ['swiːtn] **VT** *coffee, sauce* süßen; *air, breath* reinigen; (*fig*) *temper* bessern; *task* versüßen; *deal, terms* schmackhaft machen; **to ~ sb** (*inf*) jdn gnädig stimmen; (*inf*: = *bribe*) jdn schmieren (*inf*); **to ~ the pill** die bittere Pille

versüßen **VI** (*temper*) sich bessern; (*person*) gute Laune bekommen

sweetener ['swiːtnə] N (*Cook*) Süß(ungs)mittel *nt*; (*esp artificial*) Süßstoff *m*; (*inf, to make sth more acceptable*) Anreiz *m*; (*inf, = bribe*) Schmiergeld *nt*

sweetening ['swiːtnɪŋ] N (*Cook*) Süßungsmittel *nt*; (*artificial*) Süßstoff *m*

sweetheart ['swiːthɑːt] N Schatz *m*, Liebste(r) *mf*; **soon they were ~s** (*dated*) bald waren sie ein Pärchen; **Vera Lynn, the Forces' ~** Vera Lynn, der Liebling der Armee

sweet herbs PL Küchen- *or* Gewürzkräuter *pl*

sweetie ['swiːtɪ] N **a** (*inf*: also **sweetie-pie**) **yes, ~** ja, Schatzi (*inf*) *or* Süße(r); **she's/he's a ~** sie/er ist ein Engel *or* ist süß (*inf*) **b** (*Brit baby-talk*: = *candy*) Bonbon *m*

sweetish ['swiːtɪʃ] ADJ *taste, smell* süßlich

sweetly ['swiːtlɪ] **ADV** **a** *sing, play* süß; *say* süßlich; *smile also, answer* lieb; **the engine was running ~** der Motor ist prächtig gelaufen; **he chipped the equalizer ~ into the net** er hat den Ausgleichstreffer wunderschön ins Netz gesetzt; **rather ~, he offered to drive me there** er bot an, mich hinzufahren, was wirklich süß *or* lieb von ihm war **b** *innocent* niedlich; *seductive* sanft, auf sanfte Art **c** *scented, fragrant* süßlich; **to smell ~ of sth** süßlich nach etw duften; **the ~ acid smell of peat smoke** der süßlich scharfe Geruch des Torfrauches

sweet: sweetmeat N (*old*) Leckerei *f*; **sweet-natured** ADJ lieb

sweetness ['swiːtnɪs] N (*lit*) Süßigkeit *f*, Süße *f*; (*fig*) Süße *f*; (*of smile, nature*) Liebenswürdigkeit *f*; (*of person*) liebe Art; (= *freshness, of food, water*) Frische *f*; (*of air, breath*) Reinheit *f*, Frische *f*; **now all is ~ and light** (*usu iro*) nun herrscht eitel Freude und Sonnenschein

sweet: sweet pea N Gartenwicke *f*; **sweet potato** N Süßkartoffel *f*, Batate *f*; **sweet-scented** ADJ süß duftend; **sweet shop** N (*Brit*) Süßwarenladen *m* *or* -geschäft *nt*; **sweet-smelling** ADJ süß riechend; **sweet talk** N (*inf*) süße Worte *pl*; **sweet-talk** VT (*inf*) **to ~ sb into doing sth** jdn mit süßen Worten dazu bringen, etw zu tun; **sweet-tempered** ADJ verträglich; **sweet tooth** N (*inf, fig*) Vorliebe *f* für Süßigkeiten; **she has a ~** sie isst gerne Süßigkeiten, sie ist eine Naschkatze (*inf*); **sweet trolley** N (*Brit*) Dessertwagen *m*; **sweet william** N Bartnelke *f*

swell [swel] **vb**: *pret* **swelled**, *ptp* **swollen** *or* **swelled** **N** **a** (*of sea*) Wogen *nt no pl*; (= *wave*) Woge *f*; **there was a heavy ~** es herrschte hoher Seegang *or* schwere See
b (*dated inf*, = *stylish person*) feine Dame, feiner Herr; (= *important person*) hohes Tier; (*of high society*) Größe *f*; **the ~s** *pl* die feinen Leute
c (*Mus*, = *sound*) Crescendo *nt*; (= *control, knob*) Schweller *m*; (= *mechanism*) Schwellwerk *nt*
ADJ (*inf*) **a** (*dated*, = *stylish*) fein, vornehm; *house, restaurant* nobel (*inf*), vornehm
b (*esp US, dated*, = *excellent*) klasse (*inf*), prima (*inf*)
VT *ankle, river, sound etc* anschwellen lassen; *stomach* (auf)blähen; *wood* (auf)quellen; *sail* blähen; *numbers, population* anwachsen lassen; *sales* steigern; **to be swollen with pride** stolzgeschwellt sein; **your praise will only ~ her head** dein Lob wird ihr nur zu Kopf steigen
VI **a** (*ankle, arm, eye etc*: also **swell up**) (an-)schwellen; (*balloon, air bed, tyre*) sich füllen; **to ~ (up) with rage** vor Wut rot anlaufen; **to ~ (up) with pride** vor Stolz anschwellen; **the children's bellies had swollen with hunger** die Bäuche der Kinder waren vom Hunger (auf-) gebläht
b (*river, lake, sound etc*) anschwellen; (*sails: also* **swell out**) sich blähen; (*wood*) quellen; (*in size, number: population, debt etc*) anwachsen; **the crowd ~ed to 2000** die Menschenmenge wuchs auf 2000 an; **the cheers ~ed to a roar** der Jubel schwoll zu einem Begeisterungssturm an; **the debt had swollen to a massive sum** die Schuld

war zu einer riesigen Summe angewachsen → *also* **swollen**

swell box N (*Mus*) Schwellwerk *nt*

swellhead ['swelhed] N (*dated esp US inf*) aufgeblasener Typ (*inf*)

swell-headed ['swelˌhedɪd] **ADJ** (*inf*) aufgeblasen (*inf*)

swelling ['swelɪŋ] **N** **a** Verdickung *f*; (*Med*) Schwellung *f* **b** (= *act, of ankle, arm, eye, sound*) Anschwellen *nt*; (*of sails*) Blähen *nt*; (*of wood*) Quellen *nt*; (*of population, debt etc*) Anwachsen *nt* **ADJ** *attr ankle etc* (an)schwellend; *sails* gebläht; *sound* anschwellend; *numbers* steigend, anwachsend, zunehmend; *line, curve* geschwungen; **her ~ breasts** die Wölbung ihrer Brüste

swelter ['sweltə] **VI** (vor Hitze) vergehen, verschmachten (*inf*)

sweltering ['sweltərɪŋ] **ADJ** *day, weather* glühend heiß; *heat* glühend; **it's ~ in here** (*inf*) hier verschmachtet man ja! (*inf*)

swept [swept] *pret, ptp of* **sweep**

swept: sweptback ADJ *wing* pfeilförmig; **swept volume** N (*Tech, Aut etc*) Hubraum *m*; **sweptwing** ADJ *aircraft* mit pfeilförmigen Flügeln

swerve [swɜːv] **N** Bogen *m*; (*of road, coastline also*) Schwenkung *f*; (*of car etc also*) Schlenker *m* (*inf*); (= *spin on ball*) Effet *m*; **with a ~ he avoided his opponent** er wich seinem Gegner mit einer geschickten Bewegung aus
VI einen Bogen machen; (*car, driver*) ausschwenken; (*boxer*) ausweichen; (*horse*) ausbrechen; (*ball*) im Bogen fliegen; (*fig, from truth*) abweichen; (*from chosen path*) abschwenken; **to ~ round sth** einen Bogen um etw machen; **the road ~s (round) to the right** die Straße schwenkt nach rechts; **he ~d in behind me** er schwenkte plötzlich hinter mir ein; **the car ~d in and out of the traffic** der Wagen schoss im Slalom durch den Verkehrsstrom
VT *car etc* herumreißen; *ball* anschneiden

swift [swɪft] **ADJ** (+*er*) schnell; *movement, steps also* flink; *reaction, reply also, revenge* prompt; *runner also* flink, flott; *pace* flott, rasch; **to take ~ action** schnell handeln; **~ of foot** (*liter*) schnellfüßig; **to be ~ to anger** jähzornig sein; **to be ~ to do sth** etw schnell tun **N** (= *bird*) Mauersegler *m*

swift: swift-flowing ADJ schnell fließend; **swift-footed** ADJ (*liter*) schnellfüßig

swiftly ['swɪftlɪ] **ADV** schnell; *react* schnell, unverzüglich, prompt; **events have moved ~** die Ereignisse haben sich überstürzt; **time passes ~** die Zeit vergeht wie im Flug; **a ~ flowing river** ein schnell dahinfließender Fluss; **to act ~** to do sth rasch handeln, etw eine zu tun; **~ followed by ...** rasch gefolgt von ...

swiftness ['swɪftnɪs] N Schnelligkeit *f*; (*of movement, steps also*) Flinkheit *f*; (*of reaction, reply also*) Promptheit *f*; (*of pace*) Raschheit *f*; **the ~ of the current** die reißende Strömung

swig [swɪg] (*inf*) **N** Schluck *m*; **to have** *or* **take a ~ of beer** einen Schluck Bier trinken; **to have** *or* **take a ~ from a bottle** einen Schluck aus einer Flasche trinken; **have a ~ of this** nimm Sie mal einen Schluck (davon) (*inf*); **to down a drink in one ~** das Glas in einem Zug leeren **VT** (*also* **swig down**) heruntergippen (*inf*)

swill [swɪl] **N** **a** (= *animal food*) (Schweine)futter *nt*; (= *garbage, slops, solid*) Abfälle *pl*; (*liquid*) Schmutzwasser *nt*; (*fig pej*) (Schweine)fraß *m* (*inf*); (*liquid*) Abwaschwasser *nt* **b** (= *cleaning*) **to give sth a ~ (out/down)** = swill VT **a** (*esp Brit*: *also* **swill out**) auswaschen; *cup, dish* ausschwenken; **to ~ sth down** etw abspülen; *floor etc* waschen **b** (*inf*) *beer etc* kippen (*inf*); **he ~ed it down with beer** er hat es mit Bier runtergespült (*inf*) **c** **to ~ sth round** etw (herum)schwenken

swim [swɪm] **vb**: *pret* **swam**, *ptp* **swum** **N** **a** **after a 2 km ~** nach 2 km Schwimmen, nachdem ich/er *etc* 2 km geschwommen war; **it's a long ~** es ist weit (zu schwimmen); **that was a nice ~** das (Schwimmen) hat Spaß gemacht!; **I like**

or enjoy a ~ ich gehe gern (mal) schwimmen, ich schwimme gern (mal); **to have a ~** schwimmen

b (*inf*) **to be in the/out of the ~** up to date/nicht mehr up to date sein; (= *socially active*) mitmischen (*inf*)/den Anschluss verloren haben **VT** schwimmen; *river, Channel* durchschwimmen **VI** schwimmen; **to ~ back** zurückschwimmen; **we shall have to ~ for it** wir werden schwimmen müssen; **the room swam before my eyes** das Zimmer verschwamm vor meinen Augen; **my head is ~ming** mir dreht sich alles, mir ist ganz schwummrig (*inf*)

swim bladder [ˈswɪmˌblædə²] N Schwimmblase *f*

swimmer [ˈswɪmə²] N Schwimmer(in) *m(f)*

swimming [ˈswɪmɪŋ] N Schwimmen *nt*; **do you like ~?** schwimmen Sie gern? **ADJ** (= *dizzy*) *feeling* schwummrig (*inf*)

swimming *in cpds* Schwimm-; **swimming bath** N *usu pl* (*Brit*) Schwimmbad *nt*; **swimming cap** N (*Brit*) Badekappe *f*, Bademütze *f*; **swimming costume** N (*Brit*) Badeanzug *m*; **swimming gala** N Schwimmfest *nt*; **swimming instructor** N Schwimmlehrer(in) *m(f)*

swimmingly [ˈswɪmɪŋlɪ] ADV (*inf*) glänzend; **to go ~** (*inf*, = *like clockwork*) wie geschmiert gehen *or* laufen (*inf*); **they got along ~** sie verstanden sich glänzend

swimming: swimming pool N Schwimmbad *nt*; (*outdoor also*) Freibad *nt*; (*indoor also*) Hallenbad *nt*; **swimming ring** N Schwimmring *m*; **swimming things** PL Badesachen *pl*, Badezeug *nt*; **swimming trunks** PL (*Brit*) Badehose *f*

swimsuit [ˈswɪmsuːt] N Badeanzug *m*

swindle [ˈswɪndl] **N** Schwindel *m*, Betrug *m*; **it's a ~!** das ist (der reinste) Schwindel! **VT** *person* beschwindeln, betrügen; **to ~ sb out of sth** (= *take from*) jdm etw abschwindeln *or* abgaunern (*inf*); (= *withhold from*) jdn um etw beschwindeln *or* betrügen

swindler [ˈswɪndlə²] N Schwindler(in) *m(f)*, Gauner(in) *m(f)* (*inf*)

swine [swaɪn] N **a** *pl* - (*old, form*) Schwein *nt* → **pearl²** N **b** *pl* -s (*pej inf*, = *man*) (gemeiner) Hund (*inf*); (= *woman*) gemeine Sau (*sl*); **this translation is a ~** diese Übersetzung ist wirklich gemein (*inf*)

swine: swine fever N Schweinepest *f*; **swineherd** N (*old*) Schweinehirt(in) *m(f)*

swing [swɪŋ] *vb: pret, ptp* **swung** **N** **a** (= *movement*) Schwung *m*; (*to and fro*) Schwingen *nt*; (*of needle*) Ausschlag *m*; (= *distance*) Ausschlag *m*, Schwung(weite *f*) *m*; (*Boxing etc*: = *blow*) Schwinger *m*; (*Golf, Skiing etc*) Schwung *m*; (*fig, Pol*) (*Meinungs*)umschwung *m*; **to take a ~ at sb** nach jdm schlagen; **the golfer took a big ~ at the ball** der Golfer holte weit aus und schlug den Ball; **my ~ is too short** ich hole nicht weit genug aus; **a ~ in opinion** ein Meinungsumschwung *m*

b (= *rhythm*) Schwung *m*; (= *kind of music, dance*) Swing *m*; **to walk with a ~** schwungvoll gehen; **to go with a ~** (*fig*) ein voller Erfolg sein (*inf*); **to be in full ~** voll im Gang sein; **to get into the ~ of sth** (*of new job, married life etc*) sich an etw (*acc*) gewöhnen; **to get into the ~ of things** (*inf*) reinkommen (*inf*)

c (= *seat for swinging*) Schaukel *f*; **to give sb a ~** jdn anstoßen *or* anschubsen (*inf*); **to have a ~** schaukeln; **what you win or gain on the ~s (you lose on the roundabouts)** (*prov*) was man auf der einen Seite gewinnt, verliert man auf der anderen; **it's ~s and roundabouts** (*Brit inf*) es ist gehupft wie gesprungen

d (*esp US*, = *scope, freedom*) **he gave his imagination full ~** er ließ seiner Fantasie *or* Phantasie (*dat*) freien Lauf; **he was given full ~ to make decisions** man hat ihm bei allen Entscheidungen freie Hand gelassen **VT** **a** *object* schwingen; (*to and fro*) hin und

her schwingen; (*on swing, hammock*) schaukeln; *arms, legs* (*vigorously*) schwingen (mit); (= *dangle*) baumeln mit; *propeller* einen Schwung geben (+*dat*); **to ~ a child** ein Kind schaukeln; **to ~ one's hips** sich in den Hüften wiegen; **to ~ the lead** (*Brit, inf*) sich drücken (*inf*) → **cat**

b (= *move*) schwingen; **he swung his axe at the tree/at me** er schwang die Axt gegen den Baum/gegen mich; **he swung his racket at the ball** er holte mit dem Schläger aus; **to ~ a door open/shut** eine Tür aufstoßen/zustoßen; **he swung the case (up) onto his shoulder** er schwang sich (*dat*) die Kiste auf die Schulter; **he swung himself over the stream/wall/up into the saddle** er schwang sich über den Bach/über die Mauer/in den Sattel

c (= *influence*) *election, decision, voters* beeinflussen; *opinion* umschlagen lassen; *person* umstimmen, herumkriegen (*inf*); **his speech swung the decision in our favour** seine Rede ließ die Entscheidung zu unseren Gunsten ausfallen; **what swung it for me was the fact that ...** (*inf*) was dann letzten Endes den Ausschlag gegeben hat, war, dass ...; **to ~ it (so that ...)** (*inf*) es so drehen *or* deichseln (*inf*)(, dass ...); **he managed to ~ it in our favour** es gelang ihm, es zu unseren Gunsten zu drehen (*inf*); **he managed to ~ the deal** (*inf*) er hat das Geschäft gemacht (*inf*)

d (*turn: also* **swing round**) *plane, car* herumschwenken **VI** **a** (*object*) schwingen; (*to and fro*) (hin und her) schwingen; (= *pivot*) sich drehen; (*on swing*) schaukeln; (*arms, legs:* = *dangle*) baumeln; **he was left ~ing by his hands** er hing *or* (*dangerously*) baumelte nur noch an den Händen; **he swung at me with his axe** er schwang die Axt gegen mich; **the golfer swung at the ball** der Golfer holte aus

b (= *move: into saddle, along rope etc*) sich schwingen; **to ~ from tree to tree** sich von Baum zu Baum schwingen; **to ~ open** aufschwingen; **to ~ shut** zuschlagen; **to ~ into action** in Aktion treten; **the car swung into the square** der Wagen schwenkte auf den Platz ein; **opinion/the party has swung to the right** die Meinung/die Partei hat einen Rechtsschwenk gemacht

c (*music, tune*) Schwung haben; **the town/club began to ~** in der Stadt/im Klub kam Stimmung auf (*inf*); **London really swung in the sixties** in den sechziger Jahren war in London schwer was los (*inf*)

d (*inf*, = *be hanged*) **he'll ~ for it** dafür wird er baumeln (*inf*); **I'll ~ for him (yet)** ich bring ihn noch um (*inf*); **he's not worth ~ing for** es lohnt sich nicht, sich an ihm die Hände schmutzig zu machen (*inf*)

▶ **swing across** VI hinüberschwingen; (*hand-over-hand*) sich hinüberhangeln; (+*prep obj*) schwingen über (+*acc*); (*person, animal*) schwingen über (+*acc*); (*hand-over-hand*) sich hangeln über (+*acc*)

▶ **swing (a)round** **VI** (*person*) sich umdrehen, herumfahren (*inf*); (*car, ship, plane, crane*) herumschwenken (*needle*) ausschlagen; (*fig: voters, opinion*) umschwenken **VT** *sep* herumschwenken; *voters* umstimmen; *opinion* umschlagen lassen

▶ **swing back** **VI** zurückschwingen; (*opinion*) zurückschlagen **VT** *sep* zurückschwingen; *opinion* zurückschlagen lassen

▶ **swing to** VI (*door*) zuschlagen

swing: swingback N (*fig*) Rückfall *m* (*to in* +*acc*), Rückkehr *f* (*to zu*); **swingball** N (*Brit*) = tetherball; **swing band** N (*Mus*) Swingband *f*; **swing-bin** N Mülleimer *m* mit Schwingdeckel; **swingboat** N Schiffsschaukel *f*; **swing bridge** N Drehbrücke *f*; **swing door** N (*Brit*) Pendeltür *f*

swingeing [ˈswɪndʒɪŋ] ADJ (*Brit*) *blow, penalty, punishment* hart; *attack* scharf; *defeat* vernichtend; *taxation, price increases, fee, charge* extrem hoch; *cuts* extrem

swinger [ˈswɪŋə²] N (*inf*) lockerer Typ (*inf*)

swinging [ˈswɪŋɪŋ] ADJ *step* schwungvoll; *movement* schaukelnd; *music* Swing-, swingend; (*fig inf*) *person* locker (*inf*); **~ door** (*US*) Pendeltür *f*; **~ London** Swinging London *nt*; **London was a ~ place then** in London war damals wirklich was los (*inf*); **the ~ sixties** die flotten sechziger Jahre, die „swinging sixties" (*sl*)

swinging single N (*US*) flotter Single

swing: swing seat N Hollywoodschaukel *f*; **swing shift** N (*US, Ind inf*) **a** (= *period*) Spätschicht *f* **b** (= *workers*) Spätschicht *f*; **swing vote** N (*esp US, Pol*) Stimmenanteil *m* der Wechselwähler; **swing voter** N (*esp US, Pol*) Wechselwähler(in) *m(f)*; **swing-wing** ADJ *aircraft* mit ausfahrbaren Tragflächenteilen

swinish [ˈswaɪnɪʃ] ADJ (*fig*) gemein

swipe [swaɪp] **N** (= *blow*) Schlag *m*; **to take** *or* **make a ~ at sb/sth** nach jdm/etw schlagen; (*fig*: = *criticize*) gegen jdn/etw ausholen **VT** **a** *person, ball etc* schlagen; **he ~d the wasp with the towel** er schlug mit dem Handtuch auf die Wespe **b** (*inf*, = *steal*) mopsen (*inf*), klauen (*inf*) **c** *credit card* einlesen, durchziehen; *entry card* durchziehen **VI** **to ~ at sb/sth** nach jdm/etw schlagen

swipe card N Magnetstreifenkarte *f*

swirl [swɜːl] **N** Wirbel *m*; (= *whorl in pattern also*) Spirale *f*; **the ~ of the dancers' skirts** die wirbelnden Röcke der Tänzerinnen; **she put a ~ of cream on the cake** sie spritzte ein Sahnehäufchen auf den Kuchen **VT** *water, dust etc* wirbeln; **to ~ sth along** (*river*) etw wirbelnd mitreißen; **he ~ed his partner round the room** er wirbelte seine Partnerin durchs Zimmer **VI** wirbeln; **to ~ around** herumwirbeln

swish [swɪʃ] **N** (*of whip, cane*) Zischen *nt*, Sausen *nt*; (*of grass*) Rascheln *nt*; (*of skirts, water*) Rauschen *nt*; (*of tyres*) Pfeifen *nt*, Zischen *nt*; (*of windscreen wipers*) Wischen *nt* **ADJ** (+*er*) (*esp Brit, inf*: = *smart*) (tod)schick **VT** *cane* zischen *or* sausen lassen; *tail* schlagen mit; *skirt* rauschen mit; *water* schwenken; **she ~ed water round the bowl** sie schwenkte die Schüssel mit Wasser aus **VI** (*whip, cane*) zischen, sausen; (*grass*) rascheln; (*skirts*) rauschen, rascheln; (*water*) rauschen; (*tyres*) zischen, pfeifen; (*windscreen wipers*) wischen

Swiss [swɪs] **ADJ** Schweizer, schweizerisch; **he is ~** er ist Schweizer; **she is ~** sie ist Schweizerin; **the ~-German part of Switzerland** die deutsch(sprachig)e Schweiz; **the ~ Guard** die Schweizergarde; **a ~ Guard** ein Schweizer *m*; **~ steak** (*US, Cook*) paniertes Steak mit Tomaten und Zwiebeln **N** Schweizer(in) *m(f)*; **the ~** *pl* die Schweizer *pl*

Swiss: Swiss army knife N Schweizer Offiziersmesser *nt*, Schweizermesser *nt*; **Swiss cheese** N Schweizer Käse *m*; **her argument has more holes than ~** (*esp US*) ihre Argumentation hat mehr Löcher als ein Schweizer Käse; **~ plant** Fensterblatt *nt*, Philodendron *m or nt*; **Swiss franc** N Schweizer Franken *m*; **Swiss French** N **a** (= *person*) Welschschweizer(in) *m(f)* **b** (*Ling*) Schweizer Französisch *nt*; **Swiss German** N **a** (= *person*) Deutschschweizer(in) *m(f)* **b** (*Ling*) Schweizerdeutsch *nt*, Schwyzerdütsch *nt*; **Swiss roll** N (*Brit*) Biskuitrolle *f*

switch [swɪtʃ] **N** **a** (*Elec etc*) Schalter *m* **b** (*US, Rail*) Weiche *f* **c** (= *change*) Wechsel *m*; (*in plans, policies*) Änderung *f*, Umstellung *f* (*in* +*gen*); (*in opinion*) Änderung *f* (*in* +*gen*); (= *exchange*) Tausch *m*; **to make a ~** tauschen **d** (= *stick, cane*) Rute *f*, Gerte *f*; (= *riding whip*) Gerte *f* **e** (*of hair*) falscher Zopf **VT** **a** (= *change, alter*) wechseln; *direction, plans* ändern; *allegiance* übertragen (*to auf* +*acc*); *attention, conversation* lenken (*to auf* +*acc*); **to ~ schools** die Schule wechseln; **to ~ sides** die Seiten wechseln; **to ~ channels** auf einen anderen Kanal umschalten; **to ~ parties/jobs** zu einer anderen Partei/anderen Stelle überwechseln **b** (= *move*) *production* verlegen; *object* umstellen **c** (= *exchange*) tauschen; (= *transpose: also*

switch over, switch round *objects, letters in word, figures in column* vertauschen; **I ~ed hats with him** ich tauschte meinen Hut mit ihm; **we ~ed hats** wir tauschten die Hüte; **to ~ A for B** A für *or* gegen B (ein)tauschen; **to ~ A and B (over)** A und B vertauschen

d (*Elec*) (um)schalten; **~ the radio to another programme** schalten Sie auf ein anderes Radioprogramm um

e *tail, cane* schlagen mit

f (*esp US, Rail*) rangieren

VI a (= *change: also* **switch over**) (über)wechseln (*to zu*); (*Elec, TV, Rad*) umschalten (*to auf* +*acc*); (= *exchange: also* **switch round, switch over**) tauschen; **to ~ (over) from Y to Z** von Y auf Z (*acc*) (über-) wechseln; **we've ~ed (over) to gas** wir haben auf Gas umgestellt; **the wind ~ed to the east** der Wind hat (sich) nach Osten gedreht; **he ~ed to another line of attack** er wechselte seine Angriffstaktik; **she ~ed to being in favour of it** sie änderte ihre Meinung und war auf einmal dafür

b (*Rail*) rangieren

▶ **switch (a)round VT** *sep* (= *swap round*) vertauschen; (= *rearrange*) umstellen **VI** = **switch VI a**

▶ **switch back VI** (*to original plan, product, allegiance etc*) zum Alten zurückkehren, auf das Alte zurückgreifen; (*Elec, Rad, TV*) zurückschalten (*to zu*) **VT** *sep heater, cooker* zurückschalten (*to auf* +*acc*); **to switch the light back on** das Licht wieder anschalten

▶ **switch off VT** *sep* **a** *light* ausschalten; *radio, TV* aus- *or* abschalten; *machine, engine* abschalten; *gas, water supply* abstellen; **the oven switches itself off** der Backofen schaltet sich selbsttätig ab *or* aus **b** (*inf*) **(can't somebody) switch him off for goodness' sake!** (*inf*) kann den denn niemand abstellen, um Himmels willen **VI a** (*light*) ausschalten; (*radio, TV also, machine, engine*) abschalten; (*gas, water supply*) abstellen; **the TV won't switch off** der Fernseher lässt sich nicht aus- *or* abschalten **b** (*inf: person*) abschalten

▶ **switch on VT** *sep* **a** *gas, water* anstellen; *machine* anschalten; *radio, TV, light* einschalten; *engine* anlassen; **please leave the TV switched on** lass den Fernseher bitte an

b (*inf*) *person* (= *interest*) munter machen, begeistern; (*emotionally, by drugs*) antörnen (*sl*), high machen (*inf*); (*sexually*) auf Touren bringen (*inf*); **switched on** begeistert; (*emotionally, on drugs*) high (*inf*); (*sexually*) auf Touren (*inf*); (= *up-to-date*) in (*inf*); **to be switched on to jazz** auf Jazz stehen (*inf*)

VI (*gas, water*) anstellen; (*machine*) anschalten; (*radio, TV, light*) einschalten; (*engine*) anlassen; **the cooker will switch on at 10 o'clock** der Herd schaltet sich um 10 Uhr an *or* ein

▶ **switch over VI** = **switch VI a VT** *sep* **a** = **switch VT c b** (*TV, Rad*) **to switch the programme over** auf ein anderes Programm umschalten

▶ **switch through** VT *sep* (*Telec*) durchstellen (*to zu*), verbinden (*to mit*)

switch: **switchback** N (*US*) Berg- und Talbahn *f*; (*Brit, = roller-coaster also*) Achterbahn *f*; **switchblade** N (*US*) Schnappmesser *nt*; **switchboard** N (*Telec, = exchange*) Vermittlung *f*; (*in office etc*) Zentrale *f*; (= *actual panel, Elec*) Schalttafel *f*; **switchboard operator** N (*in office*) Telefonist(in) *m(f)*; **switch box** N (*Elec*) Schaltkasten *m*; **switch clock** N (*Tech*) Schaltuhr *f*

switcheroo [ˌswɪtʃəˈruː] N (*esp US, inf*) Kehrtwendung *f*; **to pull a ~** eine Kehrtwendung machen

switch: **switchgear** N , *no pl* (*Elec*) Schaltgerät *nt*; **switch-hit** VI (*Baseball*) beidhändig schlagen; **switch-hitter** N (*Baseball*) beidhändiger Hitter; **switchman** N (*US, Rail*) Weichensteller *m*; **switch-over** N Wechsel *m* (*to auf* +*acc, zu*); (= *exchange*) Tausch *m*; (*of letters, figures etc*) Vertauschung *f*; **switch-round** N Tausch *m*; (*of letters, figures etc*) Vertauschung *f*; (= *re-*

arrangement) Umstellen *nt*; **switch yard** N (*US, Rail*) Rangierbahnhof *m*

Switzerland [ˈswɪtsələnd] N die Schweiz; **to ~** in die Schweiz; **French-/German-/Italian-speaking ~** die französische/deutsche/italienische Schweiz, die französisch-/deutsch-/italienischsprachige Schweiz

swivel [ˈswɪvl] **N** Drehgelenk *nt attr* Dreh-; **~ base** (*of monitor etc*) Schwenksockel *m*; **~ chair** Drehstuhl *m* **VT** (*also* **swivel round**) (herum-) drehen **VI** (*also* **swivel round**) sich drehen; (*person*) sich herumdrehen

swivel bridge N (*Tech*) Drehbrücke *f*

swivelling [ˈswɪvəlɪŋ] ADJ schwenkbar

swizz [swɪz], **swizzle** [ˈswɪzl] N (*Brit inf, = swindle*) Bauernfängerei *f* (*inf*); (= *disappointment*) Gemeinheit *f* (*inf*)

swizzle stick N Sektquirl *m*

swollen [ˈswəʊlən] *ptp of* **swell** ADJ *ankle, face, glands etc* (an)geschwollen; *stomach* aufgedunsen, aufgebläht; *wood* verquollen, gequollen; *sails* gebläht; *river* angeschwollen, angestiegen; *numbers* (an)gestiegen, angewachsen; **her eyes were ~ with tears** ihre Augen waren verweint; **he has a ~ head** (*fig*) er ist so aufgeblasen

swollen-headed [ˌswəʊlənˈhedɪd] ADJ aufgeblasen (*inf*)

swollen-headedness [ˌswəʊlənˈhedɪdnɪs] N Aufgeblasenheit *f* (*inf*)

swoon [swuːn] **N** (*old*) Ohnmacht *f*; **to fall into a ~** in Ohnmacht fallen *or* sinken (*geh*); **to be in a ~** ohnmächtig sein **VI** (*old: = faint*) in Ohnmacht fallen, ohnmächtig werden; (*fig: over pop star etc*) beinahe ohnmächtig werden (*over sb/ sth* wegen jdm/einer Sache)

swoop [swuːp] VI (*lit: also* **swoop down**, *bird*) herabstoßen, niederstoßen (*on auf* +*acc*); (*plane*) einen Sturzflug machen; (*fig, police*) einen Überraschungsangriff machen (*on auf* +*acc*) *or* landen (*on bei*); (*person*) sich stürzen (*on auf* +*acc*); **the plane ~ed low over the village** das Flugzeug flog im Tiefflug über das Dorf hinweg; **the police ~ed on 8 suspects** die Polizei schlug überraschend bei 8 Verdächtigen zu; **they're just waiting to ~** die lauern nur darauf zuzuschlagen **N** (*of bird, plane*) Sturzflug *m*; (*by police*) Razzia *f* (*on in* +*dat, on sb* bei jdm); **to make a ~** (*bird*) herabstoßen (*on auf* +*acc*); **at** *or* **in one (fell) ~** auf einen Schlag

swoosh [swuːʃ] **VI** rauschen; (*air*) brausen; (*tyres in rain*) sirren; (*skirts, curtains*) rauschen **N** Rauschen *nt*; (*of air*) Brausen *nt*; (*of tyres in rain etc*) Pfeifen *nt*, Sirren *nt*; (*of skirts, curtains*) Rauschen *nt*

swop N, VTI = **swap**

sword [sɔːd] N Schwert *nt*; **to cross ~s with sb** (*lit, fig*) mit jdm die Klinge(n) kreuzen; **by fire and (the) ~** mit Feuer und Schwert; **those that live by the ~ die by the ~** (*prov*) wer das Schwert ergreift, der soll durchs Schwert umkommen

sword *in cpds* Schwert-; **sword and sorcery** N (*Liter*) *Sciencefiction mit mittelalterlichen Themen*; **swordbearer** N Schwertträger *m*; **sword cane** N Stockdegen *m*; **sword dance** N Schwert(er)tanz *m*; **swordfish** N Schwertfisch *m*; **swordplay** N (Schwert)fechten (*nt*); **swordpoint** N **at ~** mit vorgehaltener Klinge

swordsman [ˈsɔːdzmən] N *pl* **-men** [-mən] Schwertkämpfer *m*; (= *fencer*) Fechter *m*

swordsmanship [ˈsɔːdzmənʃɪp] N Fechtkunst *f*

sword: **swordstick** N Stockdegen *m*; **sword swallower** N Schwertschlucker(in) *m(f)*

swore [swɔː] *pret of* **swear**

sworn [swɔːn] *ptp of* **swear** ADJ *enemy* eingeschworen; **~ statement/testimony** (*Jur*) eidliche Aussage, Aussage *f* unter Eid

swot [swɒt] (*Brit, inf*) **VI** büffeln (*inf*), pauken (*inf*); **to ~ up (on) one's maths** Mathe pauken (*inf*); **to ~ at sth** etw pauken (*inf*) *or* büffeln (*inf*) **VT** büffeln (*inf*), pauken (*inf*) **N** (*pej, = person*) Streber(in) *m(f)*

swotter [ˈswɒtə] N (*Brit, inf*) Büffler(in) *m(f)* (*inf*), Streber(in) *m(f)* (*inf, pej*)

swotting [ˈswɒtɪŋ] N (*Brit, inf*) Büffeln (*inf*), Pauken (*inf*) *nt*; **to do some ~** büffeln (*inf*), pauken (*inf*)

swum [swʌm] *ptp of* **swim**

swung [swʌŋ] *pret, ptp of* **swing** ADJ (*Typ*) **~ dash** Tilde *f*

sybarite [ˈsɪbəraɪt] N (*form*) Genussmensch *m*

sybaritic [ˌsɪbəˈrɪtɪk] ADJ (*form*) *person* genusssüchtig; *way of life* schwelgerisch

sycamore [ˈsɪkəmɔː] N Bergahorn *m*; (*US: = plane tree*) nordamerikanische Platane; (= *wood*) Ahorn *m*

sycophancy [ˈsɪkəfənsɪ] N Kriecherei *f*, Speichelleckerei *f* (*inf*)

sycophant [ˈsɪkəfənt] N Kriecher(in) *m(f)*, Speichellecker(in) *m(f)* (*inf*)

sycophantic [ˌsɪkəˈfæntɪk] ADJ kriecherisch, unterwürfig

syllabary [ˈsɪləbərɪ] N Syllabar *nt*, Silbentabelle *f*

syllabic [sɪˈlæbɪk] ADJ silbisch

syllabification [sɪˌlæbɪfɪˈkeɪʃən] N Silbentrennung *f*

syllable [ˈsɪləbl] N Silbe *f*; **a two-syllable(d) word** ein zweisilbiges Wort; **in words of one ~** (*hum*) in einfachen Worten

syllabub [ˈsɪləbʌb] N (= *dessert*) Obstspeise mit Sahne

syllabus [ˈsɪləbəs] N *pl* **-es** *or* **syllabi** [ˈsɪləbaɪ] (*esp Brit: Sch, Univ*) Lehrplan *m*; (*of club etc*) Programm *nt*; **the Syllabus (of Errors)** (*Eccl*) der Syllabus (von Zeitirrtümern)

syllogism [ˈsɪlədʒɪzəm] N Syllogismus *m*

syllogistic [ˌsɪləˈdʒɪstɪk] ADJ syllogistisch

syllogize [ˈsɪlədʒaɪz] VI syllogistisch folgern

sylph [sɪlf] N (*Myth*) Sylphe *mf*; (*fig, = girl*) Sylphide *f*, Nymphe *f*

sylphid [ˈsɪlfɪd] N Sylphide *f*

sylphlike [ˈsɪlflaɪk] ADJ *figure etc* grazil, sylphidenhaft

sylvan, silvan [ˈsɪlvən] ADJ (*liter*) Wald-; *shade* des Waldes; *surroundings* waldig; **~ goddess** Waldgöttin *f*

symbiosis [ˌsɪmbɪˈəʊsɪs] N Symbiose *f*

symbiotic [ˌsɪmbɪˈɒtɪk] ADJ symbiotisch

symbol [ˈsɪmbəl] N Symbol *nt*, Zeichen *nt* (*of für*)

symbolic(al) [sɪmˈbɒlɪk(əl)] ADJ symbolisch (*of für*); **to be ~ of sth** etw symbolisieren, ein Symbol für etw sein; **symbolic logic** mathematische Logik

symbolically [sɪmˈbɒlɪkəlɪ] ADV *represent* symbolisch; **~ important** von symbolischer Bedeutung

symbolism [ˈsɪmbəlɪzəm] N Symbolik *f*; (*Art, Liter, = movement*) Symbolismus *m*

symbolist [ˈsɪmbəlɪst] **N** Symbolist(in) *m(f)* **ADJ** symbolistisch

symbolization [ˌsɪmbəlaɪˈzeɪʃən] N Symbolisierung *f*

symbolize [ˈsɪmbəlaɪz] VT symbolisieren

symmetrical ADJ , **symmetrically** ADV [sɪˈmetrɪkəl, -lɪ] symmetrisch

symmetry [ˈsɪmɪtrɪ] N Symmetrie *f*

sympathetic [ˌsɪmpəˈθetɪk] ADJ **a** (= *showing pity*) mitfühlend, teilnahmsvoll; (= *understanding*) verständnisvoll; (= *well-disposed*) wohlwollend, wohlgesonnen (*geh*); *look, smile* verbindlich, freundlich; **to be** *or* **feel ~ to(wards) sb** (= *showing pity*) mit jdm mitfühlen; (= *understanding*) jdm Verständnis entgegenbringen, für jdn Verständnis haben; (= *being well-disposed*) mit jdm sympathisieren; **he was most ~ when I told him all my troubles** er zeigte sehr viel Mitgefühl für all meine Sorgen; **a ~ ear** ein offenes Ohr

b (= *likeable*) sympathisch

c (*Physiol, Phys*) sympathisch; **~ vibration** Mitschwingung *f*; ~ **string** mitschwingende Saite, Bordunsaite *f*; ~ **magic** Sympathiezauber *m*

sympathetically [ˌsɪmpəˈθetɪkəlɪ] ADV (= *showing pity*) mitfühlend; (= *with understanding*) verständnisvoll; (= *well-disposed*) wohlwollend; **to be ~ inclined toward(s) sb/sth** jdm/einer Sache wohlwollend gegenüberstehen; **to respond/vibrate ~** (*Phys etc*) mitreagieren/-schwingen

sympathize [ˈsɪmpəθaɪz] VI (= *feel compassion*) mitfühlen, Mitleid haben (*with* mit); (= *understand*) Verständnis haben (*with* für); (= *agree*) sympathisieren (*with* mit) (*esp Pol*); (= *express sympathy*) sein Mitgefühl aussprechen; (*on bereavement*) sein Beileid aussprechen; **to ~ with sb over sth** (= *feel sorry*) mit jdm in einer Sache mitfühlen können; **to ~ with sb's views** jds Ansichten teilen; **to ~ with sb's problems** mit jdm mitfühlen; **I really do ~** (= *have pity*) das tut mir wirklich Leid; (= *understand your feelings*) ich habe wirklich vollstes Verständnis; **I ~ with you** *or* **with what you say/feel, but ...** ich teile Ihre Ansichten/Gefühle, aber ..., ich kann Ihnen das nachfühlen, aber ...; **to ~ with sb in his bereavement/grief** jds Verlust/Schmerz teilen; (= *express sympathy*) jdm sein Beileid/Mitgefühl aussprechen

sympathizer [ˈsɪmpəθaɪzə'] N Mitfühlende(r) *mf*; (*at death also*) Kondolierende(r) *mf*; (*with cause*) Sympathisant(in) *m(f)*

sympathy [ˈsɪmpəθɪ] ✪ 24.4 N **a** (= *pity, compassion*) Mitgefühl *nt*, Mitleid *nt* (*for* mit); (*at death*) Beileid *nt*; **to feel** *or* **have ~ for sb** Mitgefühl *or* Mitleid mit jdm haben; **a letter of ~** ein mitfühlender Brief, ein Beileidsbrief *m*; **you have our deepest** *or* **heartfelt ~** *or* **sympathies** wir fühlen mit Ihnen, (unser) aufrichtiges *or* herzliches Beileid; **you have my ~!** (*hum*) herzliches Beileid (*hum*); **my sympathies are with her family** mir tut ihre Familie Leid; **to express one's ~** sein Mitgefühl aussprechen, sein Beileid aussprechen; **you won't get any ~ from me** erwarte kein Mitleid von mir
b (= *understanding*) Verständnis *nt*; (= *fellow feeling, agreement*) Sympathie *f*; **to be in/out of ~ with sb/sth** mit jdm/etw einhergehen/nicht einhergehen; **the sympathies of the crowd were with him** (*in match, discussion*) die Zuschauer waren auf seiner Seite; **he has Democratic sympathies** er sympathisiert mit den Demokraten; **politically there was a lack of ~ between them** sie verstanden sich politisch nicht gut; **to come out** *or* **strike in ~** (*Ind*) in Sympathiestreik treten; **the dollar fell and the pound fell in ~** der Dollar fiel und das Pfund fiel mit; **to resonate/vibrate in ~** mitklingen/-schwingen

sympathy strike N Sympathiestreik *m*

symphonic [sɪmˈfɒnɪk] ADJ sinfonisch, symphonisch

symphonic poem N sinfonische *or* symphonische Dichtung

symphony [ˈsɪmfənɪ] N Sinfonie *f*, Symphonie *f*; **a ~ of colours** (*liter*) eine Sinfonie von Farben, eine Farbensinfonie

symphony orchestra N Sinfonie- *or* Symphonieorchester *nt*; **the London Symphony Orchestra** die Londoner Symphoniker *pl*

symposium [sɪmˈpəʊzɪəm] N *pl* **-s** *or* **symposia** [sɪmˈpəʊzɪə] Symposium *nt*, Symposion *nt*

symptom [ˈsɪmptəm] N (*lit, fig*) Symptom *nt*

symptomatic [ˌsɪmptəˈmætɪk] ADJ symptomatisch (*für*)

symptomize [ˈsɪmptəmaɪz] VT symptomatisch sein für

synaesthesia, (*US*) **synesthesia** [ˌsɪnəsˈθiːzɪə] N , *no pl* Synästhesie *f*

synagogue [ˈsɪnəgɒg] N Synagoge *f*

synapse [ˈsaɪnæps] N (*Physiol*) Synapse *f*

sync [sɪŋk] N (*Film, TV inf*) *abbr of* **synchronization in ~** synchron; **out of ~** nicht synchron; **to be in ~ with the lights** (*Mot, inf*) grüne Welle haben (*inf*)

synchro [ˈsɪŋkrəʊ] (*Aut inf*) *abbr of* **synchromesh** N Synchrongetriebe *nt* ATTR **~ gearbox** Getriebe *nt* mit Synchroneinrichtung

synchromesh [ˈsɪŋkrəʊˌmeʃ] N Synchrongetriebe *nt*

synchronic [sɪŋˈkrɒnɪk] ADJ (*Ling*) synchronisch

synchronization [ˌsɪŋkrənaɪˈzeɪʃən] N Abstimmung *f*; (*Film*) Synchronisation *f*; (*of clocks*) Gleichstellung *f*; (*of actions*) Zusammenfall *m*, gleichzeitiger Ablauf; (*of movements*) Übereinstimmung *f*

synchronize [ˈsɪŋkrənaɪz] VT abstimmen (*with* auf +*acc*); *two actions, movements* aufeinander abstimmen; (*Film*) synchronisieren (*with* mit); *clocks* gleichstellen (*with* mit); **~ (your) watches!** Uhrenvergleich!; **~d swimming** Synchronschwimmen *nt* VI (*Film*) synchron sein (*with* mit); (*clocks*) gleich gehen; (*actions*) zusammenfallen, gleichzeitig ablaufen (*with* mit); (*movements*) in Übereinstimmung sein (*with* mit)

synchronous [ˈsɪŋkrənəs] ADJ gleichzeitig; (*Comput*) synchron

syncopate [ˈsɪŋkəpeɪt] VT (*Mus*) synkopieren; (*Ling also*) zusammenziehen

syncopation [ˌsɪŋkəˈpeɪʃən] N Synkope *f*; (= *act*) Synkopierung *f*

syncope [ˈsɪŋkəpɪ] N (*Ling, Med*) Synkope *f*

syncretism [ˈsɪŋkrɪtɪzəm] N (*Ling*) Synkretismus *m*

syndicalism [ˈsɪndɪkəlɪzəm] N Syndikalismus *m*

syndicate [ˈsɪndɪkɪt] N Interessengemeinschaft *f*; (*for gambling*) Wettgemeinschaft *f*; (*Comm*) Syndikat *nt*, Verband *m*; (*Press*) (Presse)zentrale *f*; (= *crime syndicate*) Ring *m* VT [ˈsɪndɪkeɪt] (*Press*) an mehrere Zeitungen verkaufen; **there are several ~d articles in this newspaper** mehrere Artikel dieser Zeitung stammen aus einer Pressezentrale

syndrome [ˈsɪndrəʊm] N (*Med*) Syndrom *nt*; (*fig, Sociol*) Phänomen *nt*

synecdoche [sɪˈnekdəkɪ] N Synekdoche *f*

synergistic ADJ , **synergistically** ADV [ˌsɪnəˈdʒɪstɪk, -əlɪ] (*Med, Pharm, Physiol*) synergistisch, zusammenwirkend; **~ effect** (*Econ*) Synergieeffekt *m*

synergy [ˈsɪnədʒɪ] N Synergie *f*

synesthesia [ˌsɪnəsˈθiːzɪə] N (*US*) = **synaesthesia**

synod [ˈsɪnəd] N Synode *f*

synodal [ˈsɪnədl], **synodic** [sɪˈnɒdɪk], **synodical** [sɪˈnɒdɪkl] ADJ **a** (*Rel*) synodal **b** (*Astron*) *month* synodisch

synonym [ˈsɪnənɪm] N Synonym *nt*

synonymous [sɪˈnɒnɪməs] ADJ synonym, synonymisch; **his name was ~ with sex** sein Name war gleichbedeutend mit Sex

synonymy [sɪˈnɒnɪmɪ] N Synonymik *f*

synopsis [sɪˈnɒpsɪs] N *pl* **synopses** [sɪˈnɒpsiːz] Abriss *m* der Handlung; (*of article, book*) Zusammenfassung *f*

synoptic [sɪˈnɒptɪk] ADJ zusammenfassend; **~ view** Überblick *m*, Übersicht *f*; **Synoptic Gospels** die Evangelien des Markus, Matthäus und Lukas; **~ chart** (*Met*) synoptische Karte

syntactic(al) [sɪnˈtæktɪk(əl)] ADJ syntaktisch

syntax [ˈsɪntæks] N Syntax *f*; (*of sentence also*) Satzbau *m*; **~ error** (*Comput*) Syntaxfehler *m*

synthesis [ˈsɪnθəsɪs] N *pl* **syntheses** [ˈsɪnθəsiːz] Synthese *f*; (= *artificial production also*) Synthetisieren *nt*

synthesize [ˈsɪnθəsaɪz] VT synthetisieren; *speech* synthetisch bilden; *theories etc* zusammenfassen

synthesizer [ˈsɪnθəˌsaɪzə'] N (*Mus*) Synthesizer *m*

synthetic [sɪnˈθetɪk] ADJ **a** synthetisch; **~ fibre** Kunstfaser *f*; **~ smile** künstliches *or* gekünsteltes Lächeln **b** (*Ling, Philos*) synthetisch N Kunststoff *m*, synthetischer Stoff; **~s** Synthetik *f*

synthetically [sɪnˈθetɪkəlɪ] ADV synthetisch, künstlich; (*fig*) *smile* gekünstelt

syphilis [ˈsɪfɪlɪs] N Syphilis *f*

syphilitic [ˌsɪfɪˈlɪtɪk] ADJ syphilitisch N Syphilitiker(in) *m(f)*

syphon N = **siphon**

Syracuse [ˈsaɪərəkjuːz] N (= *town in Sicily*) Syrakus *nt*

Syria [ˈsɪrɪə] N Syrien *nt*

Syrian [ˈsɪrɪən] ADJ syrisch N Syr(i)er(in) *m(f)*

syringa [sɪˈrɪŋgə] N (*Bot*) Falscher Jasmin, Pfeifenstrauch *m*; (= *lilac*) Flieder *m*, Syringe *f*

syringe [sɪˈrɪndʒ] (*Med*) N Spritze *f* VT (aus-) spülen

syrup, (*US also*) **sirup** [ˈsɪrəp] N Sirup *m* (*also Med*); (= *preservative also*) Saft *m*; **~ of figs** Feigensaft *m*; **fruit ~** Fruchtsirup *m*; **cough ~** (*Med*) Hustensaft *or* -sirup *m*

syrupy, (*US also*) **sirupy** [ˈsɪrəpɪ] ADJ sirupartig, sirupähnlich; (*pej*) *smile, voice* zucker- *or* honigsüß; (= *sentimental*) *voice, song* schmalzig

system [ˈsɪstəm] N **a** System *nt*; **new teaching ~s** neue Lehrmethoden *pl*; **the democratic ~ of government** das demokratische (Regierungs-) system; **the Pitman ~ of shorthand** die Kurzschriftmethode nach Pitman
b (= *working whole*) System *nt*; **digestive ~** Verdauungsapparat *m*; **respiratory ~** Atmungsapparat *m*; **it's good for the ~** das ist gesund; **to pass through the ~** den Körper auf natürlichem Wege verlassen; **to be absorbed into the ~** aufgenommen werden; **it was a shock to his ~** er hatte schwer damit zu schaffen; **to get sth out of one's ~** (*fig inf*) sich (*dat*) etw von der Seele schaffen, etw loswerden (*inf*); **it's all ~s go!** (*inf*) jetzt heißt es: volle Kraft voraus!
c (= *established authority*) **the ~** das System; **you can't beat** *or* **buck the ~** gegen das System kommst du *or* kommt man einfach nicht an
d (*Comput*, = *machine, operating system*) System *nt*; **~ disk** Systemdiskette *f*; **~ software** Systemsoftware *f*

systematic [ˌsɪstəˈmætɪk] ADJ systematisch; *liar, cruelty* ständig; **he works in a ~ way** er arbeitet mit System; **on a ~ basis** systematisch

systematically [ˌsɪstəˈmætɪkəlɪ] ADV systematisch

systematization [ˌsɪstəmətaɪˈzeɪʃən] N Systematisierung *f*

systematize [ˈsɪstəmətaɪz] VT systematisieren

system: system building N (*Archit*) Systembauweise *f*; **system crash** N (*Comput*) Systemzusammenbruch *m*; **system error**, **system fault** N (*Comput*) Systemfehler *m*

systemic [sɪˈstemɪk] ADJ systemisch

systems: systems analysis N Systemanalyse *f*; **systems analyst** N Systemanalytiker(in) *m(f)*; **systems disk** N (*Comput*) Systemdiskette *f*; **systems manager** N Systemmanager(in) *m(f)*; **systems software** N Systemsoftware *f*

systole [ˈsɪstəlɪ] N (*Physiol*) Systole *f*

systolic [sɪˈstɒlɪk] ADJ (*Physiol*) *blood pressure* systolisch

T

T, t [tiː] N T nt, t nt; **it suits him to a T** es ist genau das Richtige für ihn; **that's him to a T** das ist er, wie er leibt und lebt; **that's it to a T** genau so ist es; **he got him to a T** er hat ihn haargenau getroffen

TA **a** (*Brit*) *abbr of* **Territorial Army** **b** (*US*) *abbr of* **teaching assistant**

ta [tɑː] INTERJ (*Brit, inf*) danke

tab¹ [tæb] **N** **a** (= *loop on coat etc*) Aufhänger *m*; (*on back of boot, book*) Schlaufe *f*; (= *fastener on coat etc*) Riegel *m*; (= *name tab, of owner*) Namensschild *nt*; (*of maker*) Etikett *nt*; (*on collar*) Verschluss(riegel) *m*; (*Mil*) Spiegel *m*; (*on shoulder, pocket*) Klappe *f*, Patte *f*; (*on filing cards*) Tab *m*, Reiter *m*; **to keep ~s on sb/sth** (*inf*) jdn/etw genau im Auge behalten **b** (*Aviat*) Klappe *f* **c** (*esp US, inf,* = *bill*) Rechnung *f*; **to pick up the ~** (*also Brit*) die Rechnung übernehmen **d** (*Drugs inf*) Pappe *f* (*sl*), Paper *nt* (*sl*), Ticket *nt* (*sl*)

tab² (*Comput etc*) **N** Tab *m*; (*on typewriter*) Tabulator *m*; **to set the ~s** tabulieren **VT** **columns** tabulieren

tabard ['tæbəd] N (*of knight, herald*) Heroldsrock *m*, Wappenrock *m*, Tappert *m*; (*Fashion*) ärmelloser, an den Seiten offener Kasak

Tabasco® [təˈbæskəʊ] N Tabasco® *m*, Tabascosoße *f*

tabby ['tæbɪ] **N** **a** (*also* **tabby cat**) getigerte Katze; (= *female cat*) (weibliche) Katze **b** (*inf,* = *old maid*) Tantchen *nt* (*inf*)

tabernacle ['tæbənækl] N (= *church*) Gotteshaus *nt*; (= *receptacle*) Tabernakel *m or nt*; **the Tabernacle** (*Bibl*) die Stiftshütte

tab key N Tabtaste *f*; (*on typewriter*) Tabulatortaste *f*

table ['teɪbl] **N** **a** Tisch *m*; (= *banquet table*) Tafel *f*; **at the ~** am Tisch; **at ~** bei Tisch; **to sit at ~** sich zu Tisch setzen; **to sit down at a ~** sich an einen Tisch setzen; **he was sitting at the Mayor's ~** er saß am Bürgermeistertisch; **who was on your ~?** wer saß an Ihrem Tisch or bei Ihnen am Tisch?; **to eat at sb's ~** seine Beine or Füße unter jds Tisch strecken (*inf*); **to be under the ~** (= *drunk*) unter dem Tisch liegen; **to drink sb under the ~** jdn unter den Tisch trinken; **the motion is on the ~** (*Brit, Parl*) der Antrag liegt vor; **on the ~** (*US:* = *postponed*) zurückgestellt, aufgeschoben; **to turn the ~s (on sb)** (gegenüber jdm) den Spieß umdrehen or umkehren **b** (= *people at a table*) Tisch *m*, Tischrunde *f*; **the whole ~ laughed** der ganze Tisch or die ganze Runde lachte **c** (*of figures, prices etc, Sport*) Tabelle *f*; (= *log table*) Logarithmentafel *f*; (**multiplication**) **~s** Einmaleins *nt*; (*up to 10*) kleines Einmaleins; (*from 11 to 20*) großes Einmaleins; **to say one's three/five times ~** das Einmaldrei/Einmalfünf aufsagen; **~ of contents** Inhaltsverzeichnis *nt* **d** (*Bibl:* = *tablet*) Tafel *f* **e** (*Geog*) **water ~** Grundwasserspiegel *m* **f** (= *tableland*) Tafelland *nt*, Plateau *nt*, Hochebene *f*

VT **a** motion, amendment, resolution einbringen **b** (*US,* = *postpone*) bill zurückstellen **c** (= *put in tabular form*) tabellarisieren (*form*), in einer Tabelle zusammenstellen

tableau ['tæbləʊ] N pl **-s** or **-x** ['tæbləʊ(z)] (*Art, Theat*) Tableau *nt*; (*fig*) Bild *nt*, Szene *f*

table: **table clamp** N Tisch(tuch)klammer *f*; **tablecloth** N Tischdecke *f* or -tuch *nt*; **table dancing** N (*on table*) Striptease *m* auf einem Tisch; **table d'hôte** [ˌtɑːblˈdəʊt] N Tagesmenü or -gedeck *nt*; **table d'hôte menu** N Tageskarte *f*; **table-hop** VI (*inf, in restaurant etc*) von einem Tisch zum andern gehen; **table lamp** N Tischlampe *f*; **tableland** N Tafelland *nt*, Plateau *nt*, Hochebene *f*; **table licence** N Schankerlaubnis *f* bei Abgabe von Speisen; **table-lifting** N Anheben *nt* von Tischen; **table lighter** N Tischfeuerzeug *nt*; **table linen** N, no pl Tischwäsche *f*; **table manners** PL Tischmanieren *pl*; **table mat** N Untersetzer *m*; (*of cloth*) Set *nt*; **Table Mountain** N Tafelberg *m*; **table napkin** N Serviette *f*; **table-rapping** N Tischrücken *nt*; **table salt** N Tafelsalz *nt*; **tablespoon** N Esslöffel *m*; **tablespoonful** N Esslöffel *m* (voll)

tablet ['tæblɪt] **N** **a** (*Pharm*) Tablette *f* **b** (*of paper*) Block *m*; (*of wax, clay*) Täfelchen *nt*; (*of soap*) Stückchen *nt* **c** (*on wall etc*) Tafel *f*, Platte *f*

table: **table talk** N, no pl Tischgespräch *nt*; **table tennis** N Tischtennis *nt*; **table top** N Tischplatte *f*; **table-turning** N Drehen *nt* von Tischen; **tableware** N, no pl Tafelgeschirr *nt* und -besteck *nt*; **table water** N Tafelwasser *nt*; **table wine** N Tafelwein *m*

tabloid ['tæblɔɪd] N (*also* **tabloid newspaper**) bebilderte, kleinformatige Zeitung (*pej*) Boulevardzeitung *f*, Revolverblatt *nt* (*inf*); **~ journalism** Sensations- or Boulevardpresse *f*

---

taboo, tabu [təˈbuː] **N** Tabu *nt*; **to be a ~** tabu sein, unter einem Tabu stehen **ADJ** tabu; **~ words** Tabuwörter *pl* **VT** für tabu erklären, tabu(sier)eren

tabo(u)ret ['tæbuːreɪ] N (*Sew*) Stickrahmen *m*

tabu N, ADJ, VT = **taboo**

---

tabular ['tæbjʊlə] ADJ tabellenförmig, tabellarisch; **in ~ form** in Tabellenform, tabellarisch

tabulate ['tæbjʊleɪt] VT tabellarisch aufzeichnen or darstellen, tabellarisieren

tabulation [ˌtæbjʊˈleɪʃən] N tabellarische Aufstellung, Tabellarisierung *f*

tabulator ['tæbjʊleɪtə] N (*on typewriter*) Tabulator *m*

tache [tæʃ] N (*Brit inf*) Schnurrbart *m*, Oberlippenbart *m*

tachograph ['tækəʊgrɑːf] N (*Brit*) Fahrtenschreiber *m*, Tachograf *m*

tachometer [tæˈkɒmɪtə] N Drehzahlmesser *m*

tachycardia [ˌtækɪˈkɑːdɪə] N Herzjagen *nt*, Tachykardie *f* (*spec*)

tacit ['tæsɪt] ADJ stillschweigend

tacitly ['tæsɪtlɪ] ADV accept, support, acknowledge, approve or stillschweigend; **it was ~ understood that ...** es bestand ein stillschweigendes Einvernehmen darüber, dass ...

taciturn ['tæsɪtɜːn] ADJ schweigsam, wortkarg

taciturnity [ˌtæsɪˈtɜːnɪtɪ] N Schweigsamkeit *f*, Wortkargheit *f*

tack¹ [tæk] **N** **a** (= *nail*) kleiner Nagel; (*esp with small head*) Stift *m*; (*for shoes*) Tä(c)ks *m*; (*esp US,* = *drawing pin*) Reiß- or Heftzwecke *f*, Reißnagel *m* **b** (*Brit, Sew*) Heftstich *m* **c** (*Naut:* = *course*) Schlag *m*; (*fig*) Richtung *f*, Weg *m*; **to be on the port/starboard ~** auf Backbord-/Steuerbordbug segeln; **they are on a new/different ~** (*fig*) sie haben eine neue/andere Richtung eingeschlagen; **to be on the right/wrong ~** (*fig*) auf der richtigen/falschen Spur sein, richtig/falsch liegen (*inf*); **to try another ~** (*fig*) es anders versuchen **d** (*Naut,* = *zigzag*) Aufkreuzen *nt*; **to make a ~ toward(s) land** landwärts kreuzen **e** (*for horse*) Sattel- und Zaumzeug *nt*

VT **a** (*with nail*) annageln (*to an +dat or acc*); (*with clip, pin*) feststecken (*to an +dat*) **b** (*Brit, Sew*) heften

VI **a** (*Naut*) aufkreuzen; **to ~ to port** mit Backbordbug kreuzen **b** (*Brit, Sew*) heften

▶ **tack about** VI (*Naut*) wenden

▶ **tack down** VT sep festnageln; (*Brit, Sew*) festheften

▶ **tack on** VT sep annageln (-*to an +acc or dat*); (*with drawing pin*) anstecken (-*to an +acc or dat*); (*with clips*) anheften, anstecken (-*to an +acc or dat*); (*Sew*) anheften; (*fig*) anhängen (-*to +dat*)

▶ **tack together** VT sep (*with nails*) zusammennageln; (*with clips*) zusammenstecken or -heften; (*Sew*) zusammenheften

▶ **tack up** VT sep **a** picture etc anpinnen; (*with drawing pins*) mit Reißzwecken aufhängen; (*Brit*) hem heften **b** horse satteln

tack² N (*Naut,* = *biscuits*) Schiffszwieback *m*

tack³ N (*inf*) = **tackiness²**

tackiness¹ ['tækɪnɪs] N (*of paint etc*) Klebrigkeit *f*

tackiness² N (*inf*) Billigkeit *f*; (*of area, bar*) heruntergekommener Zustand; (*of clothes, food, colour scheme*) Geschmacklosigkeit *f*

tacking ['tækɪŋ] N **a** (*Brit, Sew*) Heften *nt* **b** (*Naut*) Aufkreuzen *nt*

tacking stitches PL (*Brit Sew*) Heftstiche *pl*

tacking thread N (*Brit Sew*) Heftfaden *m*

tackle ['tækl] **N** **a** (= *lifting gear*) Flaschenzug *m*; (*Naut*) Talje *f*, Takel *nt*, Zugwinde *f* **b** (*Naut*, = *rigging*) Tauwerk *nt* **c** (= *equipment*) Ausrüstung *f*, Zeug *nt* (*inf*); **fishing ~** Angelausrüstung *f or* -zeug *nt* (*inf*) **d** (*Sport*) Angriff *m*, Tackling *nt* **VT** **a** (*physically, Sport*) angreifen, angehen (*geh*); (*Rugby*) fassen; (*verbally*) zur Rede stellen (*about* wegen) **b** (= *undertake*) *job* in Angriff nehmen; *new challenge* sich versuchen an (+*dat*); *problem* angehen, anpacken (*inf*); (= *manage to cope with*) bewältigen, fertig werden mit; *blaze, fire* bekämpfen; **could you ~ another ice cream?** (*inf*) schaffst du noch ein Eis? (*inf*); **I don't know how to ~ it** ich weiß nicht, wie ich es anfangen soll **VI** angreifen

tack-weld VTI (*Tech*) heftschweißen

tacky¹ ['tækɪ] ADJ (+*er*) klebrig; **the paint is still ~** die Farbe klebt noch

tacky² ADJ (+*er*) (*inf*) billig; *area, bar* heruntergekommen; *clothes, food, colour scheme* geschmacklos

tact [tækt] N , *no pl* Takt *m*

tactful ['tæktfʊl] ADJ taktvoll; **to be ~ about sth** etw mit Feingefühl behandeln; **it was not the most ~ way to put it/of saying it** es war nicht besonders taktvoll, es so auszudrücken; **to be ~ with sb** taktvoll mit jdm umgehen

tactfully ['tæktfəlɪ] ADV taktvoll

tactfulness ['tæktfʊlnɪs] N Takt *m*; (*of person*) Feingefühl *nt*

tactic ['tæktɪk] N Taktik *f*

tactical ['tæktɪkəl] ADJ (*Mil, fig*) taktisch

tactically ['tæktɪkəlɪ] ADV (*Mil, fig*) taktisch

tactical voting N (*Brit Pol*) taktisches Wahlverhalten

tactician [tæk'tɪʃən] N (*Mil, fig*) Taktiker(in) *m(f)*

tactics ['tæktɪks] N *sing* (= *art, science, Mil*) Taktik *f*; (*fig also*) Taktiken *pl*

tactile ['tæktaɪl] ADJ **a** Tast-, taktil (*spec*); (= *tangible*) greifbar, fühlbar; (*form,* = *gained by touching*) stimulation, experience durch Berührung erfolgend; **~ sense** Tastsinn *m*; **~ organ** Tastorgan *nt*; **she is a very ~ person** sie ist ein Mensch, der gern Körperkontakt hat; **a more ~ society** eine Gesellschaft, in der Körperkontakte eine größere Rolle spielen **b** (= *interesting to touch*) **a ~ fabric** angenehm anzufühlende Stoffe

tactless ['tæktlɪs] ADJ taktlos; **it was ~ of me to ask** es war taktlos *or* eine Taktlosigkeit von mir, zu fragen

tactlessly ['tæktlɪslɪ] ADV taktlos

tactlessness ['tæktlɪsnɪs] N Taktlosigkeit *f*

tactual ['tæktjʊəl] ADJ taktil (*spec*); **~ pleasure** Berührungslust *f*

tactually ['tæktjʊəlɪ] ADV (= *by touch*) durch Berühren *or* Fühlen; **to be ~ pleasing** sich angenehm anfühlen; **~ oriented** berührungsorientiert

tad [tæd] N , *no pl* (*inf*) **a** **~** ein bisschen, etwas; **a ~ big/small** etwas *or* ein bisschen (zu) groß/klein

Tadjikistan [tɑːdʒɪkɪ'stɑːn] N = **Tajikistan**

tadpole ['tædpəʊl] N Kaulquappe *f*

Tadzhikistan [tɑːdʒɪkɪ'stɑːn] N = **Tajikistan**

taffeta ['tæfɪtə] N Taft *m*

taffrail ['tæfreɪl] N (*Naut*) Heckreling *f*

Taffy ['tæfɪ] N (*inf*) Waliser(in) *m(f)*

taffy ['tæfɪ] N (*US*) Toffee *nt*

tag [tæg] **N** **a** (= *label*) Schild(chen) *nt*; (*on clothes, with maker's name*) Etikett *nt*; (*with owner's name*) Namensschild(chen) *nt*; (= *loop*) Aufhänger *m*; (= *electronic tag*) elektronische Mar-

kierung; (*fig,* = *description*) Bezeichnung *f*; **the cattle had metal ~s in their ears** die Rinder hatten Blechmarken in den Ohren **b** (= *hackneyed phrase*) stehende Redensart **c** (*Gram,* = *question tag*) Bestätigungsfrage *f* **d** (= *game*) Fangen *nt* **e** = **tag wrestling** **VT** **a** *specimen* mit Schildchen versehen; *cattle* (mit Blechmarke) zeichnen; *garment, goods* etikettieren; (*with price*) auszeichnen; (*with owner's name*) (mit Namensschildchen) zeichnen; *suitcase* mit einem Anhänger versehen; *offender* (*with electronic tag*) mit einer elektronischen Markierung versehen; (*fig,* = *describe*) bezeichnen **b** (*US, Mot inf*) einen Strafzettel verpassen (+*dat*) **VI** **to ~ behind** *or* **after sb** hinter jdm hertrotten *or* -zockeln (*inf*)

▶ **tag along** VI (*unwillingly, unwanted*) mittrotten (*inf*) *or* -zockeln (*inf*); **to tag along behind sb** hinter jdm herzockeln (*inf*) *or* -trotten (*inf*); **why don't you tag along?** (*inf*) warum kommst/geht du nicht mit?

▶ **tag on** **VI** sich anhängen (*to* an +*acc*) **VT** *sep* (= *attach*) anhängen (*to* an +*acc*), befestigen (*to* an +*dat*); (= *add as afterthought*) anhängen (*to* an +*acc*)

▶ **tag together** VT *sep* (= *fasten*) zusammenheften

Tagalog [tə'gɑːlɒg] N (*Ling*) Tagal *nt*

tag end N = **fag end**

tagliatelle [ˌtæljə'telɪ] N (*Cook*) Tagliatelle *pl*, Bandnudeln *pl*

tagmeme ['tægmiːm] N (*Ling*) Tagmem *nt*

tagmemics ['tægmemɪks] N (*Ling*) Tagmemik *f*

tag: tag question N Bestätigungsfrage *f*; **tag rope** N (*Sport*) Seil *nt* (*beim tag wrestling*); **tag sale** N (*US*) privater Verkauf von Haushaltsgegenständen und Trödel; **tag wrestler** N Ringer(in) *m(f)* (*beim tag wrestling*); **tag wrestling** N Ringkampf zwischen 2 Ringerpaaren, wobei immer 2 auf der Matte sind, während die 2 Auswechselkämpfer an den Seilen warten

tahini [tə'hiːnɪ] N , *no pl* Tahina *f*, Sesampaste *f*

Tahiti [tɑː'hiːtɪ] N Tahiti *nt*

Tahitian [tɑː'hiːʃən] ADJ tahitisch **N** **a** Tahitianer(in) *m(f)* **b** (*Ling*) Tahitisch *nt*

t'ai chi [ˌtaɪ'tʃiː] N Tai-Chi *nt*

taiga ['taɪgə] N Taiga *f*

tail [teɪl] **N** **a** (*of animal*) Schwanz *m*; (*hum inf, of person*) Hinterteil *nt* (*inf*), Allerwerteste(r) *m* (*hum inf*); **with his ~ between his legs** (*fig*) wie ein geprügelter Hund, mit eingezogenem Schwanz (*inf*); **to turn ~** ausreißen, die Flucht ergreifen; **he was right on my ~** er saß mir direkt im Nacken **b** (*of aeroplane, kite, procession, list*) Schwanz *m*; (*of comet*) Schweif *m*; (*of shirt*) Zipfel *m*; (*of jacket, coat*) Schoß *m*; (*of letter*) Schleife *f*; (*Mus, of note*) Notenhals *m* **c** (*inf,* = *person following sb*) Schatten *m* (*inf*), Beschatter(in) *m(f)* (*inf*); **to put a ~ on sb** jdn beschatten lassen **d** (*inf*) **they were out looking for ~** sie hielten nach Weibern (*inf*) *or* Bräuten (*sl*) Ausschau; **a nice piece of ~** ein geiler Arsch (*sl*) **e** **~s** PL (*on coin*) Rück- *or* Zahlseite *f*; **~s I win!** bei Zahl gewinne ich; **it came down ~s** die Zahl kam nach oben **f** **tails** PL (= *jacket*) Frack *m*, Schwalbenschwanz *m* (*inf*); **"tails (will be worn)"** „Frackzwang" *m* **VT** **a** *person, suspect* beschatten (*inf*); *car etc* folgen (+*dat*) **b** = **top¹**

▶ **tail after** VI +*prep obj* hinterherzockeln (+*dat*) (*inf*)

▶ **tail away** VI = **tail off a**

▶ **tail back** VI (*Brit: traffic*) sich gestaut haben

▶ **tail off** VI **a** (= *diminish*) abnehmen, schrumpfen; (*interest*) abflauen, abnehmen,

schwinden; (*sounds*) sich verlieren, schwächer werden; (*sentence*) mittendrin abbrechen; **his voice tailed off into silence** seine Stimme wurde immer schwächer, bis sie schließlich verstummte **b** (= *deteriorate*) sich verschlechtern, nachlassen; **the article tailed off into a jumble of figures** der Artikel war zum Schluss nur noch ein Gewirr von Zahlen

tail: tailback N (*Brit*) Rückstau *m*; **tailboard** N Ladeklappe *f*; **tail coat** N Frack *m*

-tailed [-teɪld] ADJ *suf* -schwänzig; **short-tailed** kurzschwänzig

tail: tail end N Ende *nt*; (*of procession also*) Schwanz *m* (*inf*); **to come in at** *or* **on the ~** (*of discussion etc*) erst am Ende dazukommen; (*of race*) den Schwanz bilden; **tail feather** N Schwanzfeder *f*; **tail fin** N (*Aut*) Heckflosse *f*; **tailgate** **N** (*of car*) Hecktür *f*; (*of lorry*) Ladeklappe *f* **VI** (*inf*) zu dicht auffahren, schieben (*inf*) **VT** (*inf*) **to ~ sb** dicht hinter jdm herfahren; **tail gun** N Heckkanone *f*; **tail gunner** N Heckschütze *m/*-schützin *f*; **tail-heavy** ADJ (*Aviat*) *plane* schwanzlastig; **tail-hopping** N (*Ski*) Sprungwedeln *nt*; **tailless** ADJ schwanzlos; **tail-light** N (*Aut*) Rücklicht *nt*; (*Aviat*) Hecklicht *nt*

tailor ['teɪlə] **N** Schneider(in) *m(f)* **VT** **a** *dress etc* schneidern; **the dress was ~ed to show off her figure** das Kleid war so geschnitten, dass es ihre Figur betonte **b** (*fig*) *plans, insurance, holiday, message, policy, testimony* zuschneiden (*to* auf +*acc*); *products, salary structure* abstimmen (*to* auf +*acc*); **~ed to meet his needs** auf seine Bedürfnisse abgestimmt

tailored ['teɪləd] ADJ **a** (= *classically styled*) klassisch; (= *made by tailor*) vom Schneider gemacht; **a well-tailored suit** ein gut gearbeiteter Anzug; **his personally ~ clothes** seine für ihn persönlich gefertigten Kleider

tailoring ['teɪlərɪŋ] N Verarbeitung *f*; (= *profession*) Schneiderei *f*; **this is a nice piece of ~** das ist sehr gut gearbeitet

tailor-made [ˌteɪlə'meɪd] ADJ **a** maßgeschneidert, nach Maß gearbeitet; **~ suit** Maßanzug *m*; **~ costume** Schneiderkostüm *nt* **b** (*fig*) *role, holiday* maßgeschneidert (*for* für), zugeschnitten (*for* auf +*acc*); *car* nach Kundenwünschen ausgelegt; **the job was ~ for him** die Stelle war ihm wie auf den Leib geschnitten; **she seemed ~ for the part** sie schien für die Rolle wie geschaffen

tailor-make [ˌteɪlə'meɪk] VT **the company can ~ your entire trip** die Firma kann Ihre ganze Reise für Sie persönlich zusammenstellen; **you can ~ running to suit your needs** Sie können das Dauerlaufen auf Ihre eigenen Bedürfnisse zuschneiden; **the therapist will ~ the session for you** der Therapeut stimmt die Sitzung auf Ihre persönlichen Bedürfnisse ab

tailor's ['teɪləz] **tailor's chalk** N Schneiderkreide *f*; **tailor's dummy** N (*lit*) Schneiderpuppe *f*; (*fig inf*) Ölgötze *m* (*inf*); **tailor's-tack**, **tailor-tack** N Schlinge *f* beim Durchschlagen eines Musters

tail: tailpiece N **a** Anhang *m*, Anhängsel *nt* (*inf*) **b** (*Aviat*) Heck *nt* **c** (*on violin*) Saitenhalter *m* **d** (*Typ*) Schlussvignette *f*; **tailpipe** N (*US*) Auspuffrohr *nt*; **tailplane** N (*Aviat*) Höhenleitwerk *nt*; **tail section** N (*Aviat*) hinterer Bereich; **tail side** N (*of coin*) Zahlseite *f*; **tailskid** N **a** (*Aviat*) Schwanzsporn *m* **b** (*Aut*) Schleudern *nt no pl* der Hinterräder; **to go into a ~** mit den Hinterrädern herumrutschen *or* schleudern; **tailspin** N (*Aviat*) Trudeln *nt*; **tail unit** N (*Aviat*) Schwanzstück *nt*; **tail wheel** N (*Aviat*) Spornrad *nt*; **tailwind** N Rückenwind *m*

taint [teɪnt] **N** **a** (*lit, of food etc*) Stich *m*; **meat free from ~** einwandfreies Fleisch **b** (*fig,* = *blemish*) Makel *m*; (= *trace*) Spur *f*; **a ~ of madness** eine Anlage zum Irrsinn; **the hereditary ~** die krankhafte Erblanlage; **the ~ of sin** der Makel der Sünde; **a nasty ~ of fascism** ein übler faschistischer Beigeschmack **VT** **a** *food* verderben **b** *air, atmosphere* verderben, verpesten **c** *(fig) reputation* beflecken, beschmutzen

tainted ['teɪntɪd] ADJ **a** *(fig) money* unsauber; *evidence* unsauber, manipuliert; *reputation* beschmutzt; **not ~ by prejudice** von Vorurteilen unbelastet; **to be ~ with sth** mit etw belastet *or* behaftet sein; **to become ~ with racism** den Ruch des Rassismus erhalten **b** (= *contaminated*) *food* verdorben; *blood* infiziert; *air* verpestet, verunreinigt; **to become ~** (*food*) schlecht werden, verderben

Taiwan [taɪˈwɑːn] N Taiwan *nt*

Taiwanese [ˌtaɪwɑːˈniːz] ADJ taiwanisch N Taiwaner(in) *m(f)*

Tajikistan [tɑːˌdʒiːkɪˈstɑːn] N Tadschikistan *nt*

---

take [teɪk]
vb: pret **took**, *ptp* **taken**

1 TRANSITIVE VERB	3 NOUN
2 INTRANSITIVE VERB	4 PHRASAL VERBS

When **take** is part of a set combination, eg **to take sb by surprise, to take one's time, to take a bath,** look up the other word.

1 – TRANSITIVE VERB

a = remove, steal nehmen; (= *take away with one*) mitnehmen; (= *remove from its place*) wegnehmen; **to take sth from a drawer** etw aus einer Schublade nehmen; **I took it by mistake** ich habe es aus Versehen mitgenommen; **the thieves took everything** die Einbrecher haben alles mitgenommen; **that man has taken my wallet** der Mann hat mir meine Brieftasche weggenommen *or* gestohlen; **how much did he take off you for that?** wie viel hat er dir dafür abverlangt *or* abgenommen?

b = accompany (= *carry, transport*) bringen; (= *take along with one*) *person, things* mitnehmen; **let me take your case** komm, ich nehme *or* trage deinen Koffer; **you can't take it with you when you die** wenn du tot bist, nützt es dir auch nichts mehr

♦ **to take sb somewhere I'll take you to the station** ich bringe Sie zum Bahnhof; **I'll take you (with me) to the party** ich nehme dich zur Party mit; **he took me a new way to the coast** er ist mit mir eine neue Strecke zur Küste gefahren; **to take sb to the cinema** jdn ins Kino mitnehmen; **I'll take you for a meal** (*Brit*) ich lade Sie zum Essen ein; **to take sb on a trip** mit jdm eine Reise machen; **this bus will take you to the town hall** der Bus fährt zum Rathaus; **this road will take you to Paris** diese Straße führt *or* geht nach Paris; **if it won't take you out of your way** wenn es kein Umweg für Sie ist; **what takes you to London this time?** was führt Sie diesmal nach London?; **his ability took him to the top of his profession** seine Begabung brachte ihn in seinem Beruf bis an die Spitze

c = get hold of nehmen; **to take sb's arm/hand** jds Arm/Hand nehmen; **to take sb by the throat** jdn am Kragen (*inf*) *or* an der Kehle packen; **to take a knife by the handle** ein Messer am Griff (an)fassen *or* beim Griff nehmen; **take three eggs** (*Cook*) man nehme drei Eier

♦ **to be taken ... to be taken sick** *or* **ill** krank werden; **she has been taken ill with pneumonia** sie hat eine Lungenentzündung bekommen

d = capture *person* fassen, fangen; *animal* fangen; *town, country etc* einnehmen, erobern; *ship* kapern; (*Chess etc*) schlagen, nehmen; (*Cards*) trick machen; **to take sb prisoner** jdn gefangen nehmen; **they took 200 prisoners** sie machten 200 Gefangene; **to be taken alive** lebend gefasst werden

e = accept, receive nehmen; *job, dye, perm* annehmen; *command, lead, second position, role* übernehmen; *phone call* entgegennehmen, annehmen; **take that!** da!; (= *hold that*) halt mal; **I won't take less than £200** ich verkaufe es nicht unter £ 200; **would you take an offer?** kann ich Ihnen ein Angebot machen?; **she took**

---

paying guests sie vermietete Zimmer an Gäste; **to take things as they come** die Dinge nehmen, wie sie kommen; **to take a bet** eine Wette annehmen; **I wouldn't take a bet on it** darauf würde ich keine Wette eingehen; **take it from me!** das können Sie mir glauben; **take it from me, he'll never ...** eines können Sie mir glauben, er wird nie ...; **he took the blow on his left arm** der Schlag traf ihn am linken Arm; (*in defence*) er wehrte den Schlag mit dem linken Arm ab; **to take sb into partnership** jdn zu seinem Partner machen; **to take sb into the business** jdn ins Geschäft aufnehmen; **will it take a British plug?** passt da ein englischer Stecker (rein)?; **the school only takes boys/private pupils** die Schule nimmt nur Jungen/Privatschüler (auf); **he takes (private) pupils** er gibt (Privat)stunden

♦ **take it or leave it (you can)** take it or leave it ja oder nein(, ganz wie Sie wollen); **I can take it or leave it** ich mache mir nicht besonders viel daraus

f = occupy, possess sich (*dat*) nehmen; **take a seat/chair!** setzen Sie sich doch!; **take your seats!** nehmen Sie Ihre Plätze ein!; **this seat is taken** dieser Platz ist besetzt; **to take a wife** (*old*) sich (*dat*) eine Frau nehmen (*old*); **he took her** (*sexually*) er nahm sie; **take your partners for a waltz** führen Sie Ihre Partnerinnen zum Walzer

g = buy, rent (*esp Brit*) nehmen; (= *buy regularly*) *newspaper* immer nehmen *or* kaufen; (*on subscription*) beziehen, bekommen; **I'll take a pound of apples** ich nehme ein Pfund Äpfel; **I think I'll take the steak** ich glaube, ich nehme das Steak

h = gain *prize, honours etc* bekommen; *game, match* gewinnen; **the shop takes £10,000 a week** (*Brit*) das Geschäft nimmt £ 10.000 pro Woche ein

i = sit exam machen, ablegen; *driving test* machen; **to take a PhD** promovieren, den Doktor machen (*inf*); **he took his degree in 1995** er hat 1995 Examen gemacht *or* sein Examen abgelegt

j = teach *lesson* halten, geben; *subject* unterrichten, geben; *class* unterrichten, halten; **he takes 25 classes a week** er hat *or* gibt 25 Wochenstunden; **who takes you for Latin?** (*Brit*) **who are you taking for Latin?** (*US*) bei wem habt ihr Latein?, wer unterrichtet *or* gibt bei euch Latein?

k = study, learn *course, French* machen; (*as optional subject*) wählen; *lessons, private tuition* nehmen

l = organize *census, poll* durchführen; *church service* (ab)halten; **to take (the chair at) a meeting** den Vorsitz bei einer Versammlung führen; **he takes a scout troop in the evenings** abends hat er eine Pfadfindergruppe

m = go on *walk, stroll* machen; *trip* unternehmen

n = travel by *taxi, train* nehmen, fahren mit; *motorway, country roads* nehmen, fahren auf (+*dat*); **to take the plane** fliegen; **to take the next bus** den nächsten Bus nehmen; **we took a wrong turning** (*Brit*) *or* **turn** (*US*) wir sind falsch abgebogen

o = consume *drink, food* zu sich (*dat*) nehmen; *drugs, pill, medicine* nehmen; (*on directions for use*) einnehmen; **to take sugar in one's tea** den Tee mit Zucker trinken; **to take a sip/a drink** ein Schlückchen/einen Schluck trinken; **do you take sugar?** nehmen Sie Zucker?; **to take a meal** (*old*) (etwas) essen, speisen (*geh*); **I took tea with her** (*dated form*) ich war bei ihr zum Tee; **they took tea together once a week** (*old*) sie trafen sich einmal wöchentlich zum Tee; **they took coffee on the veranda** sie tranken den Kaffee auf der Veranda; **will you take coffee or tea?** möchten Sie Kaffee oder Tee?; **not to be taken (internally)** (*Med*) nur zur äußerlichen Anwendung

p Film, Phot *photo* machen; (= *shoot*) drehen; **he took the whole group** er nahm die ganze Gruppe auf

q = write down *letter, dictation* aufnehmen; *address, details, particulars* (sich *dat*) aufschreiben;

(sich *dat*) notieren; **to take notes** sich (*dat*) Notizen machen

r = measure *temperature, pulse* messen; **to take sb's measurements** bei jdm Maß nehmen; **to take the measurements of a room** ein Zimmer ausmessen; **to take sb's temperature/pulse** jds Temperatur *or* bei jdm Fieber/den Puls messen

s = tolerate sich (*dat*) gefallen lassen; *alcohol, climate* vertragen; *long journey* aushalten; *emotional experience, shock* fertig werden mit, verkraften; (*thing*) aushalten; **I can take it** ich kanns verkraften, ich werde damit fertig; **I just can't take any more** ich bin am Ende; **I just can't take it any more** das halte ich nicht mehr aus; **I won't take any nonsense!** ich dulde keinen Unsinn!

t = respond to *news, blow* aufnehmen, reagieren auf (+*acc*); *person* nehmen; **she never knows how to take him** sie weiß nie, woran sie bei ihm ist; **she took his death very badly** sein Tod hat sie sehr mitgenommen

u = understand auffassen, verstehen; **I would take that to mean ...** ich würde das so auffassen *or* verstehen ...; **how am I meant to take that?** wie soll ich das auffassen *or* verstehen?; **she took what he said as a compliment** sie hat das, was er sagte, als Kompliment aufgefasst; **do you take my meaning?** verstehen Sie mich?, verstehen Sie, was ich meine?

v = assume annehmen; **to take sb/sth for** *or* **to be ...** jdn/etw für ... halten; **how old do you take him to be?** für wie alt halten Sie ihn?, wie alt schätzen Sie ihn?; **what do you take me for?** wofür hältst du mich eigentlich?; **may I take it that ...?** darf ich annehmen, dass ... ?; **I take it you don't want to come** ich nehme an, du willst nicht mitkommen, du willst wohl nicht mitkommen

w = consider *case, example* nehmen; **take (the case of) England in the 17th century** nehmen Sie zum Beispiel England im 17. Jahrhundert; **taking everything together, it's been a very successful day** alles in allem (genommen,) war es ein sehr erfolgreicher Tag; **taking one year with another** wenn man die Jahre zusammen betrachtet

x = extract entnehmen (*from* +*dat*); **he takes his examples from real life** seine Beispiele sind aus dem Leben gegriffen; **to take a quotation from a text** eine Stelle aus einem Text zitieren

y = require brauchen; *clothes size* haben; **the journey takes 3 hours** die Fahrt dauert 3 Stunden; **the wound took five weeks to heal** es dauerte fünf Wochen, bis die Wunde verheilt war; **I took a long time over it** ich habe lange dazu gebraucht

♦ **it takes it takes five hours/men ...** man braucht *or* benötigt fünf Stunden/Leute ...; **it takes me five hours ...** ich brauche fünf Stunden ...; **it took ten men to complete the job** zehn Leute waren nötig *or* es wurden zehn Leute benötigt, um diese Arbeit zu erledigen; **it took him two hours to write a page, it took two hours for him to write a page** er brauchte zwei Stunden, um eine Seite zu schreiben; **it took a lot of courage/intelligence** dazu gehörte viel Mut/Intelligenz; **it takes more than that to make me angry** deswegen werde ich noch lange nicht wütend; **it takes time** es braucht (seine) Zeit, es dauert (eine Weile); **it took a long time** es hat lange gedauert; **it took me a long time** ich habe lange gebraucht; **it won't take long** das dauert nicht lange; **it won't take long to convince him** er ist schnell *or* leicht überzeugt; **that'll take some explaining** das wird schwer zu erklären sein; **it takes some believing** das kann man kaum glauben

♦ **what it takes she's got what it takes** (*inf*) sie ist nicht ohne (*inf*), die bringts (*sl*); (= *is capable also*) sie kann was (*inf*); **it's a difficult job but he's got what it takes** (*inf*) es ist eine schwierige Arbeit, aber er hat das Zeug dazu

z = support *weight* aushalten; **the bridge can take 5 tons** die Brücke hat eine Höchstbelastung von 5 Tonnen

aa = have capacity or room for *people, books* Platz haben für; *gallons* fassen; **the road can take**

3,500 cars an hour die Straße bewältigt eine Verkehrsdichte von 3.500 Autos pro Stunde

bb = negotiate *obstacle* nehmen; *hurdle, fence* überspringen; *bend, corner (person)* nehmen; (*car*) fahren um; *hill* hinauffahren

cc = sing, dance, play etc **let's take it from the beginning of Act 2** fangen wir mit dem Anfang vom zweiten Akt an; **let's take that scene again** die Szene machen wir noch einmal; **the orchestra took that passage too quickly** das Orchester hat die Stelle zu schnell gespielt; **the director took her through her lines** der Regisseur ging die Rolle mit ihr durch

dd Math (= *subtract*) abziehen (*from* von)

ee Gram stehen mit; (*preposition*) *case* gebraucht werden mit, haben (*inf*); **verbs that take "haben"** Verben, die mit „haben" konjugiert werden; **this word takes the accent on the first syllable** dieses Wort wird auf der ersten Silbe betont

ff illness (*old, dial*) bekommen; **to take a cold** sich erkälten

2 – INTRANSITIVE VERB

a = take hold (*fire*) angehen; (*dye, perm, graft*) angenommen werden; (*vaccination*) anschlagen; (*plant*) anwachsen; (*seeds*) kommen; (*fish: = bite*) anbeißen; (*fig, gimmick*) ankommen (*inf*); (*novel, idea*) Anklang finden; **the ink won't take on this paper** dieses Papier nimmt die Druckfarbe nicht an

b = become **she took ill** (*inf*) sie wurde krank

c = detract **that doesn't take from his merit** das tut seinen Verdiensten keinen Abbruch, das schmälert seine Verdienste nicht; **that takes from its usefulness/attraction** das vermindert den Gebrauchswert/die Anziehungskraft

3 – NOUN

a Film Aufnahme *f*; **after several takes they ...** nachdem sie die Szene mehrmals gedreht hatten, ... sie ...

b = catch (*Hunt*) Beute *f*; (*Fishing*) Fang *m*

c = takings (*US, inf*) Einnahmen *pl*

4 – PHRASAL VERBS

▶ **take aback** VT *sep* überraschen; **I was completely taken aback** mir hatte es völlig den Atem verschlagen, ich war völlig perplex

▶ **take after** VI *+prep obj* nachschlagen (*+dat*); (*in looks*) ähneln (*+dat*), ähnlich sein (*+dat*)

▶ **take along** VT *sep* mitnehmen

▶ **take apart** VT *sep* auseinander nehmen; (= *dismantle also*) zerlegen; (*fig inf*) *person, team etc* auseinander nehmen

▶ **take (a)round** VT *sep* mitnehmen; (= *show around*) herumführen

▶ **take aside** VT *sep* beiseite nehmen

▶ **take away** VI **to take away from sth** etw schmälern; *from merit, reputation also* einer Sache (*dat*) Abbruch tun; *from worth* etw mindern *or* verringern; *from pleasure, fun etc* etw beeinträchtigen

VT *sep* **a** (= *subtract*) abziehen; **6 take away 2** 6 weniger 2

b (= *remove*) *child, thing, privilege* wegnehmen (*from sb* jdm); (*from school etc*) nehmen (*from* aus); (= *lead, transport, carry away*) weg- *or* fortbringen (*from* von); *prisoner* abführen (*to* in *+acc*); **to take sb/sth away (with one)** jdn/etw mitnehmen; **to take away sb's pain/freedom etc** jdm die Schmerzen/Freiheit *etc* nehmen; **they've come to take him away** sie sind da, um ihn abzuholen; **"not to be taken away"** (*on library book*) „nicht für die Ausleihe"; **what takes you away so early?** warum müssen Sie denn schon so früh gehen?

c *food* mitnehmen; **pizza to take away** Pizza zum Mitnehmen

d from the 15th bar, take it away! noch mal von Takt 15, los!

▶ **take back** VT *sep* **a** (= *reclaim, get back*) sich (*dat*) zurückgeben lassen; *toy etc* wieder wegnehmen; (*fig = retract*) *threat, statement* zurücknehmen

b (= *return*) zurückbringen; **he took us back (home)** er brachte uns (nach Hause) zurück, er brachte uns wieder heim

c (= *agree to receive again*) *thing* zurücknehmen; *employee* wieder einstellen; *husband* wieder aufnehmen; *boyfriend* wieder gehen mit; *tenant* wieder vermieten an (*+acc*)

d (= *remind*) **to take sb back to his childhood** jdn in seine Kindheit zurückversetzen; **this photograph/that takes me back** dieses Foto/das ruft Erinnerungen wach; **that takes me back fifteen years** das erinnert mich an die Zeit vor fünfzehn Jahren

▶ **take down** VT *sep* **a** (*lit, off high shelf etc*) herunternehmen; *curtains, decorations* abnehmen; *Christmas cards* wegräumen; *picture* abhängen; *flag* einholen; **to take one's trousers down** seine Hose herunterlassen

b (= *dismantle*) *scaffolding etc* abbauen; *tent* abbrechen, abbauen; *railing, gate* entfernen

c (= *write down*) (*sich dat*) notieren *or* aufschreiben; *notes* (*dat*) machen; *letter* aufnehmen; *speech, lecture* mitschreiben; **anything you say will be taken down and ...** alles, was Sie sagen, wird festgehalten und ...; **take this down please** notieren Sie bitte, bitte schreiben Sie

d (= *humble*) einen Dämpfer geben (*+dat*) → peg

▶ **take home** VT *sep* £400 **per week** netto verdienen *or* bekommen

▶ **take in** VT *sep* **a** (= *bring in*) *thing, person* hereinbringen *or* -nehmen; *harvest* einbringen; **I'll take the car in(to work) on Monday** ich fahre am Montag mit dem Auto (zur Arbeit); **when are you taking the car in (to the garage)?** wann bringen Sie das Auto in die Werkstatt?; **to take a lady in to dinner** eine Dame zu Tisch führen

b (= *receive in one's home*) *refugee* (bei sich) aufnehmen, beherbergen; *child, stray dog* zu sich nehmen, ins Haus nehmen; (*for payment*) *student* (Zimmer) vermieten an (*+acc*); **she takes in lodgers** sie vermietet (Zimmer)

c (= *receive*) *money* einnehmen; **to take in laundry/sewing** Wasch-/Näharbeiten übernehmen

d (= *make narrower*) *dress* enger machen; **to take in sail** die Segel reffen

e (*usu insep*: = *include, cover*) einschließen; **the lecture took in all the more recent developments** der Vortrag berücksichtigte auch alle neueren Entwicklungen

f (= *note visually*) *surroundings, contents* wahrnehmen, registrieren (*inf*); *area, room* überblicken; (= *grasp, understand*) *meaning, lecture* begreifen; *impressions, sights* aufnehmen; *situation* erfassen; **the children were taking it all in** die Kinder haben alles mitbekommen *or* mitgekriegt (*inf*); **his death was so sudden that she couldn't take it in** sein Tod kam so plötzlich, dass sie es gar nicht fassen konnte

g (= *deceive*) hereinlegen; **to be taken in** hereingelegt werden; **to be taken in by sb/sth** auf jdn/etw hereinfallen; **to be taken in by appearances** sich vom äußeren Schein täuschen lassen

h (= *go to*) *film, party, town* (noch) mitnehmen (*inf*)

▶ **take off** VI **a** (*plane, passengers*) starten, abfliegen; (*plane: = leave the ground*) abheben; (*Sport*) abspringen; (*fig, project, sales*) anlaufen; (*film, product*) ankommen; (*career*) abheben

b (*inf, = leave*) sich absetzen, sich davonmachen (*inf*)

VT *sep* **a** (= *remove, cut off*) *beard, hat, lid* abnehmen (*prep obj* von); *tablecloth, bedspread* herunternehmen, entfernen (*prep obj* von); *pillowcases etc* abziehen (*prep obj* von); *coat, gloves etc* (*sich dat*) ausziehen; *leg, limb* abnehmen, amputieren; (= *withdraw*) *play* absetzen; *food from menu, train, bus* streichen (*prep obj* von); *service, tax* abschaffen; (= *remove from duty, job*) *detective, journalist etc* abziehen (*prep obj* von); *waitress, driver* ablösen; **to take sth off sb** jdm etw abnehmen; **double deckers have been taken off this route** Doppeldecker werden auf dieser

Strecke nicht mehr eingesetzt; **to take the receiver off (the hook)** den Hörer abnehmen, den Hörer von der Gabel nehmen; **he took her dress off** er zog ihr das Kleid aus; **she took her dress off** sie zog ihr Kleid aus, sie zog (*sich dat*) das Kleid aus; **he took his/her clothes off** er zog sich/sie aus; **would you like to take your coat off?** möchten Sie ablegen?; **he had two inches taken off (his hair)** er hat sich (*dat*) die Haare 5 cm kürzer schneiden lassen; **please take a little off the top** bitte oben etwas kürzer; **the barber took too much off** der Friseur hat zu viel abgeschnitten; **the 5 o'clock train has been taken off today/for the summer** der 5-Uhr-Zug ist heute ausgefallen/ wurde den Sommer über (vom Fahrplan) gestrichen

b (= *deduct*) abziehen (*prep obj* von); (*from price*) 5%, 50p nachlassen; **he took 50p off (the price)** er hat 50 Pence nachgelassen, er hat es 50 Pence billiger gemacht

c (= *lead away, go away with*) mitnehmen; (*under arrest etc*) abführen; **he was taken off to hospital** er wurde ins Krankenhaus gebracht; **to take oneself off** (*inf*) sich auf den Weg machen

d (*from ship, wreck*) von Bord holen; (*from island, mountain*) herunterholen (*prep obj* von)

e (= *have free*) *week, Monday* frei nehmen; **to take time off (work)** sich (*dat*) freinehmen; **to take a day off (work)** einen Tag frei nehmen

f (*Brit* = *imitate*) nachmachen

g *+prep obj* (*in phrases*) **to take sb's mind off sth** jdn von etw ablenken; **to take the weight off one's feet** seine Beine ausruhen; **to take sb/sth off sb's hands** jdm jdn/etw abnehmen; **to take years/ten years off sb** jdn um Jahre/ zehn Jahre verjüngen

▶ **take on** VI **a** (*inf, = become upset*) sich aufregen

b (= *become popular: song, fashion etc*) sich durchsetzen

VT *sep* **a** (= *undertake*) *job, work* an- *or* übernehmen; *responsibility* auf sich (*acc*) nehmen *or* laden, übernehmen; *sick person, backward child* sich annehmen (*+gen*); *bet* annehmen; **when he married her he took on more than he bargained for** als er sie heiratete, hat er sich (*dat*) mehr aufgeladen *or* aufgebürdet, als er gedacht hatte; **he took on the fundraising** er hat es übernommen, das Geld aufzutreiben

b (*Sport etc*: = *accept as opponent*) antreten gegen; *union, shop steward* sich anlegen mit; **I could take on someone twice your size** ich könnte es mit einem zweimal so großen wie Sie; **I'll take you on at tennis** ich werde gegen Sie im Tennis antreten; **I bet you £50 – OK, I'll take you on** ich wette mit Ihnen um £ 50 – gut, die Wette gilt

c (= *employ*) einstellen, anstellen; *apprentice* annehmen

d (= *take aboard*) *passengers* (*coach, train etc*) aufnehmen; (*plane, ship*) an Bord nehmen, übernehmen; *cargo, stores* (über)nehmen, laden; *fuel* tanken

e (= *assume*) *colour, aspect, expression* bekommen, annehmen; **her face/eyes took on a doleful expression** ihr Gesicht nahm/ihre Augen nahmen einen traurigen Ausdruck an; **his face took on a greenish tinge** sein Gesicht verfärbte sich grün *or* bekam einen grünen Schimmer; **he took on an air of importance** er gab sich (*dat*) eine gewichtige Miene

▶ **take out** VT *sep* **a** (= *bring or carry out*) (hinaus)bringen (*of* aus); (*out of garage*) *car* herausfahren (*of* aus); (*for drive etc*) *car, boat* wegfahren mit; **the current took the boat out to sea** die Strömung trieb das Boot aufs Meer hinaus

b (*to theatre etc*) ausgehen mit, ausführen; **to take the children/dog out (for a walk)** mit den Kindern/dem Hund spazieren gehen *or* einen Spaziergang machen, den Hund ausführen; **to take sb out for a drive** mit jdm eine Autofahrt machen; **to take sb out** *to or* **for dinner/to the opera** jdn zum Essen/in die Oper einladen *or* ausführen; **he has been taking her out for sev-**

eral months er geht schon seit einigen Monaten mit ihr

c (= *pull out, extract*) herausnehmen; *tooth* ziehen; *appendix etc* herausnehmen, entfernen; *nail, screw* herausziehen (*of* aus); **to take sth out of sth** etw aus etw (heraus)nehmen; **take your hands out of your pockets** nimm die Hände aus der Tasche

d (= *cause to disappear*) *stain* entfernen (*from* aus); **cold water will take the stain out of the tablecloth** mit kaltem Wasser geht der Fleck aus dem Tischtuch heraus

e (= *withdraw from bank etc*) abheben

f (= *deduct*) **take it out of the housekeeping** nimm es vom Haushaltsgeld; **to take time out from sth** von etw (eine Zeit lang) Urlaub nehmen; **to take time out from doing sth** etw eine Zeit lang nicht tun

g (= *procure*) *insurance* abschließen; *mortgage* aufnehmen; **to take out a licence** eine Lizenz erwerben, sich (*dat*) eine Lizenz geben lassen → **patent, subscription, summons**

h **to take sb out of himself** jdn auf andere Gedanken bringen

i (*inf*) **to take sth out on sb** etw an jdm auslassen (*inf*) *or* abreagieren (*inf*); **to take it out on sb** sich an jdm abreagieren

j (= *tire*) **to take it/a lot out of sb** jdn ziemlich/sehr schlauchen (*inf*)

k (*Mil, fig, Sport*) außer Gefecht setzen; *village* angreifen

l (*inf.* = *kill*) beseitigen

m (*US*) = **take away VT c**

▶**take over** **VI** (= *assume government*) an die Macht kommen; (*military junta etc*) die Macht ergreifen; (*party*) an die Regierung kommen; (*new boss etc*) die Leitung übernehmen; (*in a place: tourists, guests etc*) (*inf*); **to take over (from sb)** jdn ablösen; **can you take over?** können Sie mich/ihn *etc* ablösen?; **he's ill so I have to take over** da er krank ist, muss ich (für ihn) einspringen; **his wife has taken over completely** seine Frau führt das Regiment; **the next shift takes over at 6 o'clock** die nächste Schicht übernimmt um 6 Uhr; **the Martians have taken over** die Marsmenschen haben die Erde/Stadt *etc* besetzt

VT *sep* **a** (= *take control or possession of*) übernehmen; **tourists take Edinburgh over in the summer** im Sommer machen sich die Touristen in Edinburgh breit (*inf*); **she took over the whole show** (*inf*) sie riss das Regiment an sich

b (= *escort or carry across*) *person* hinüberbringen; (+*prep obj*) bringen über (+*acc*); (*in boat*) übersetzen; (*to visit town, people etc*) mitnehmen (*to* nach, *to sb* zu jdm)

c **to take sb over sth** (= *show round*) jdn durch etw führen, jdm etw zeigen; (= *tell about*) *facts* etw mit jdm durchgehen

▶**take round** **VT** *sep* (*esp Brit*) **a** **I'll take it round (to her place or to her)** ich bringe es zu ihr **b** (= *show round*) führen (*prep obj* durch)

▶**take to** **VI** +*prep obj* **a** (= *form liking for*) *person* mögen, sympathisch finden; **sb takes to a game/subject/place** ein Spiel/Fach/Ort sagt jdm zu; **the children soon took to their new surroundings** den Kindern gefiel es bald in der neuen Umgebung; **I'll never take to it** dafür werde ich mich nie erwärmen *or* begeistern können; **I don't know how she'll take to him/it** ich weiß nicht, wie sie auf ihn/darauf reagieren wird; **I don't take kindly to that** ich kann das nicht leiden; **I don't take kindly to you doing that** ich kann es nicht leiden, wenn Sie das tun

b (= *form habit of*) **to take to doing sth** anfangen, etw zu tun; **to take to drink** zu trinken anfangen, sich (*dat*) das Trinken angewöhnen; **to take to drugs** anfangen, Drogen zu nehmen; **she took to telling everyone that ...** sie erzählte allen Leuten, dass ...

c (= *escape to*) *woods, hills* sich flüchten *or* zurückziehen in (+*acc*), Zuflucht suchen in (+*dat*); **to take to the boats** sich in die Boote retten; **to take to one's bed** sich ins Bett legen → **heel**[1]

▶**take up** **VI** (= *continue*) (*person*) weitermachen; **chapter 3 takes up where chapter 1 left off** das dritte Kapitel schließt thematisch ans erste an

VT *sep* **a** (= *raise, lift*) aufnehmen; *carpet, floorboards* hochnehmen; *road* aufreißen; *dress* kürzer machen, kürzen; *pen* zur Hand nehmen, greifen zu; **take up your bed and walk** (*Bibl*) nimm dein Bett und wandle

b (= *lead or carry upstairs etc*) *invalid, child* hinaufbringen; *visitor* (mit) hinaufnehmen; *thing* hinauftragen

c (*vehicles*) *passengers* mitnehmen, einsteigen lassen

d (= *occupy*) *time, attention* in Anspruch nehmen, beanspruchen; *space* einnehmen

e (= *absorb*) (in sich *acc*) aufnehmen; *esp liquids* aufsaugen

f *matter, point* (= *raise*) besprechen, zur Sprache bringen; (= *go into*) eingehen auf (+*acc*); **I'll take that up with the headmaster** das werde ich beim Rektor zur Sprache bringen *or* mit dem Rektor besprechen; **I'd like to take up the point you made earlier on** ich möchte auf das eingehen, was Sie vorhin sagten

g (= *start doing as hobby*) *photography, archaeology* zu seinem Hobby machen; *a hobby* sich (*dat*) zulegen; *a language* (anfangen zu) lernen; **to take up painting/pottery/the guitar** anfangen zu malen/zu töpfern/Gitarre zu spielen

h (= *adopt*) *cause* sich einsetzen für, verfechten; *idea* aufgreifen; *case* sich annehmen (+*gen*); **to take up an attitude** eine Haltung einnehmen; **to take up a person** (*as protégé*) sich eines Menschen annehmen; **to take up a position** (*lit*) eine Stellung einnehmen; (*fig*) eine Haltung einnehmen

i (= *accept*) *challenge, invitation* annehmen; *suggestion* aufgreifen

j (= *start*) *job, employment* annehmen; *new job, post* antreten; *one's duties* übernehmen; *career* einschlagen; **he left to take up a job as a headmaster** er ist gegangen, um eine Stelle als Schulleiter zu übernehmen; **to take up residence** sich niederlassen (*at, in* in +*dat*); (*in house*) einziehen (*in* in +*acc*); (*sovereign etc*) Residenz beziehen (*in* in +*dat*)

k (= *continue*) *story* aufnehmen; *conversation* fortfahren mit, weiterführen; (= *join in*) *chorus, chant* einstimmen in (+*acc*); **the crowd took up the cry** die Menge nahm den Schrei auf

l **to take sb up on his/her invitation/offer** von jds Einladung/Angebot Gebrauch machen; **to take sb up on his/her promise** jdn beim Wort nehmen; **I'll take you up on that** ich werde davon Gebrauch machen; (*on promise etc*) ich nehme Sie beim Wort

m (= *question, argue with*) **I would like to take you up on that** ich möchte gern etwas dazu sagen; **he took me up on that point** dagegen hatte er etwas einzuwenden; **I would like to take you up on what you said about strikes** zu ihrer Bemerkung über Streiks hätte ich noch etwas zu sagen

n (*Fin*) **to take up an option** Bezugsrecht ausüben; **to take up a bill** einen Wechsel einlösen; **to take up shares** Aktien beziehen

o *collection* durchführen

p **to be taken up with sb/sth** mit jdm/etw sehr beschäftigt sein

▶**take upon** **VT** +*prep obj* **he took that job upon himself** er hat das völlig ungebeten getan; **he took it upon himself to answer for me** er meinte, er müsse für mich antworten

▶**take up with** **VI** +*prep obj* *person* sich anfreunden mit; **to take up with bad company** in schlechte Gesellschaft geraten

---

take: takeaway (*esp Brit*) **N** **a** (= *meal*) Essen *nt* zum Mitnehmen; **let's get a ~** wir können uns ja etwas (zu essen) holen *or* mitnehmen **b** (= *restaurant*) Imbissstube *f* **ADJ** *attr food* zum Mitnehmen; **the ~ menu is quite different** für Gerichte zum Mitnehmen gibt es eine andere Speisekarte; **takedown** (*esp US*) **ADJ** *gun etc* zerlegbar, auseinander nehmbar **N** **a** (=

taking apart) Zerlegen *nt* **b** (= *gadget*) (leicht) zerlegbares Gerät **c** (*Wrestling*) Niederwurf *m* **d** (*inf:* = *police raid or arrest*) Razzia *f*, Polizeiaktion *f*; **take-home pay** **N** Nettolohn *m*; **take-in** **N** (*inf*) Schwindel *m*

taken ['teɪkən] *ptp of* **take** **ADJ** **to be ~ with sb/sth** (= *attracted by*) von jdm/etw angetan sein; **she wasn't very ~ with him/it** sie war nicht sehr von ihm/davon angetan

take: takeoff **N** **a** (*Aviat*) Start *m*, Abflug *m*; (= *moment of leaving ground*) Abheben *nt*; (*Sport*) Absprung *m*; (= *place*) Absprungstelle *f or* -brett *nt*; **the plane was ready for ~** das Flugzeug war startbereit *or* flugklar; **at ~** beim Start *or* Abheben; **to be cleared for ~** Starterlaubnis haben/bekommen **b** (*Brit:* = *imitation*) Parodie *f*, Nachahmung *f*; **to do a ~ of sb** jdn nachahmen *or* nachmachen (*inf*); **takeout** (*esp US*) **ADJ** *meal* zum Mitnehmen; *restaurant etc* mit Straßenverkauf **N** **a** (= *takeaway food*) Essen *nt* zum Mitnehmen **b** (= *takeaway restaurant*) Restaurant *nt* mit Straßenverkauf; **takeover** **N** (*Comm*) Übernahme *f*; **takeover bid** **N** Übernahmeangebot *nt*

taker ['teɪkə] **N** (*Betting*) Wettende(r) *mf*; (*at auction, fig*) Interessent(in) *m(f)*; **any ~s?** wer wettet?; (*at auction*) wer bietet?; (*fig*) wer ist daran interessiert?; **there were no ~s** (*Betting*) niemand wettete, niemand schloss eine Wette ab; (*at auction*) es wurden keine Angebote gemacht, niemand bot; (*fig*) niemand war daran interessiert

take-up ['teɪkʌp] **N** (*esp Brit*) **a** Inanspruchnahme *f*; **there is a very low ~ of housing benefit** nur wenige nehmen Wohngeld in Anspruch **b** (*Tech, of tape etc*) Aufwickeln *nt*, Aufspulen *nt*; **the rate of ~** die Aufwickel- *or* Aufspulgeschwindigkeit; **~ spool** Aufwickelspule *f*

taking ['teɪkɪŋ] **N** **a** **it's yours for the ~** das können Sie (umsonst) haben **b** **takings** PL (*Comm*) Einnahmen *pl* **c** (*Mil, of town*) Einnahme *f*, Eroberung *f* **d** (*old:* = *distress*) Aufregung *f*, Erregung *f*; **to be in a ~** aufgeregt *or* erregt sein **ADJ** *manners, ways* einnehmend, gewinnend; *person* sympathisch, anziehend

taking: taking away **N** Wegnahme *f*; **taking over** **N** Übernahme *f*

talc [tælk] **N** (*also* **talcum**) ['tælkəm] **a** Talk *m* **b** (*also* **talcum powder**) Talkumpuder *m*; (*esp perfumed*) (Körper)puder *m* **VT** pudern

tale [teɪl] **N** **a** Geschichte *f*; (*Liter*) Erzählung *f*; **Tales of King Arthur** Artussagen *pl*; **he had quite a ~ to tell** er hatte einiges zu erzählen, der hatte vielleicht was zu erzählen (*inf*); **I bet he/that bed could tell a ~ or two** (*inf*) er/das Bett könnte bestimmt so einiges erzählen; **it tells its own ~** das spricht für sich; **at least he lived to tell the ~** zumindest hat er die Sache überlebt; **thereby hangs a ~** das ist eine lange Geschichte; **I've heard a fine ~ about you** (*iro*) von dir hört man ja schöne Geschichten!

b **to tell ~s** petzen (*inf*) (*to* +*dat*); (*dated:* = *fib*) flunkern; **to tell ~s out of school** (*inf*) aus der Schule plaudern; **to tell ~s about sb** jdn verpetzen (*inf*) (*to* bei)

tale-bearing ['teɪlbɛərɪŋ] **N** = **tale-telling**

talent ['tælənt] **N** **a** Begabung *f*, Talent *nt*; **to have a ~ for drawing/mathematics** Begabung *f* zum Zeichnen/für Mathematik haben; **a painter of great ~** ein hoch begabter *or* sehr talentierter Maler **b** (= *talented people*) Talente *pl* **c** (*inf,* = *girls*) Bräute *pl* (*sl*); (= *boys*) Typen *pl* (*sl*), Jungs *pl* (*inf*); **they went to inspect the local ~** sie zogen los, um zu sehen, wie die Bräute dort waren (*sl*) **d** (*Hist*) Talent *nt*

talent competition, talent contest **N** Talentwettbewerb *m*

talented ['tæləntɪd] **ADJ** *person* begabt, talentiert

talent: talent scout **N** Talentsucher(in) *m(f)*; **talent show** **N** Talentwettbewerb *m*; **talent spotter** **N** Talentsucher(in) *m(f)* (*inf*)

talesman ['teɪlzmən] **N** *pl* **-men** [-mən] (*Jur*) Ersatzgeschworene(r) *mf*

tale: tale-teller N *(Sch)* Petzer(in) *m(f)* *(inf)*; **tale-telling** N *(Sch)* Petzerei *f* *(inf)*

Taliban ['talıban] N Taliban *f*

talisman ['tælızmən] N *pl* **-s** Talisman *m*

talk [tɔːk] **Ⅰ** **a** Gespräch *nt* *(also Pol)*; *(= conversation)* Gespräch *nt*, Unterhaltung *f*; *(esp heart-to-heart)* Aussprache *f*; **to have a ~** ein Gespräch führen/sich unterhalten/sich aussprechen *(with sb about sth* mit jdm über etw *acc)*; **could I have a ~ with you?** könnte ich Sie mal sprechen?; **to hold** *or* **have ~s** Gespräche führen; **to have a friendly ~** with sb mit jdm nett unterhalten, mit jdm plaudern; *(giving advice, warning)* mit jdm (mal) in aller Freundschaft reden; **I have enjoyed our ~** ich habe mich gern mit Ihnen unterhalten; **to meet for ~s** sich zu Gesprächen treffen **b** *no pl (= talking)* Reden *nt*, Rederei *f*; *(= rumour)* Gerede *nt*; **he's all ~** er ist ein fürchterlicher Schwätzer; *(and no action)* er führt bloß große Reden; **there is some ~ of his returning** es heißt, er kommt zurück; **there is too much ~ of going on strike in this factory** in dieser Fabrik wird zu viel vom Streiken geredet; **it's the ~ of the town** es ist Stadtgespräch; **she's the ~ of the town** sie ist zum Stadtgespräch geworden **c** *(= lecture)* Vortrag *m*; **to give a ~** einen Vortrag halten *(on* über +acc); **a series of ~s** eine Vortragsreihe; **her ~ on the dangers ...** ihre (kurze) Rede über die Gefahren ... **Ⅵ a** *(= speak)* sprechen, reden *(of* von, *about* über +acc); *(= have conversation)* reden, sich unterhalten *(of, about* über +acc); *(bird, doll, child)* sprechen; **to ~ to** *or* **with sb** mit jdm sprechen *or* reden *(about* über +acc); *(= converse also)* sich mit jdm unterhalten *(about* über +acc); *(= reprimand also)* mit jdm ein ernstes Wort reden; **could I ~ to Mr Smith please?** kann ich bitte Herrn Smith sprechen?; **don't ~ silly!** *(inf)* red keinen Stuss! *(inf)*, red nicht so blöd (daher)! *(inf)*; **it's easy** *or* **all right for you to ~** *(inf)* du hast gut reden *(inf)*; **don't (you) ~ to me like that!** wie redest du denn mit mir?; **who do you think you're ~ing to?** was meinst du denn, wen du vor dir hast?; **that's no way to ~ to your parents!** so redet man doch nicht mit seinen Eltern!; **hey, that's no way to ~** hör mal, sag doch so was nicht!; **he sat there without ~ing** er saß da und sagte kein Wort; **~ to me!** erzähl mir was!; **to get/be ~ing to sb** mit jdm ins Gespräch kommen/im Gespräch sein; **I'm not ~ing to you** *(= we're on bad terms)* mit dir spreche *or* rede ich nicht mehr; *(= I mean somebody else)* ich spreche nicht mit dir; **he knows/doesn't know what he's ~ing about** er weiß (schon)/weiß (doch) nicht, wovon er spricht, er hat (davon) ziemlich Ahnung *(inf)*/(doch) überhaupt keine Ahnung; **you can ~!** *(inf)* du kannst gerade reden!; **to keep sb ~ing** jdn (mit einem Gespräch) hinhalten; **to ~ to oneself** Selbstgespräche führen; **now you're ~ing!** das lässt sich schon eher hören! **b** *(= mention)* sprechen, reden; **he's been ~ing of going abroad** er hat davon gesprochen *or* geredet, dass er ins Ausland fahren will; **~ing of salaries/films ...** da *or* wo *(inf)* wir gerade von Gehältern/Filmen sprechen ...; **~ about impertinence/rude/hot!** so was von Frechheit/unverschämt/heiß! *(inf)* **c** *(= chatter)* reden, schwatzen; **stop ~ing!** sei/seid ruhig! **d** *(= gossip)* reden, klatschen; **everyone was ~ing about them** sie waren in aller Munde; *(because of scandal also)* alle haben über sie geredet *or* geklatscht; **to get oneself ~ed about** von sich reden machen; *(because of scandal)* ins Gerede kommen **e** *(= reveal secret)* reden; **the spy refused to ~** der Spion schwieg beharrlich *or* weigerte sich zu reden; **to make sb ~** jdn zum Reden bringen; **OK, Kowalski, ~!** O.K. *or* o.k., Kowalski, raus mit der Sprache! *(inf)* **f** **we're ~ing about at least £2,000/3 months** es geht um mindestens £ 2.000/3 Monate, wir müssen mit mindestens £ 2.000/3 Monaten

rechnen; **what sort of sum are we ~ing about?** um welche Summe geht es? **Ⅶ a** *(= speak)* a language, slang sprechen; *nonsense* reden; **~ sense!** red keinen solchen Unsinn!; **he simply wasn't ~ing sense** er hat bloß Unsinn geredet *or* verzapft *(inf)* **b** *(= discuss)* politics, cricket, business reden über *(+acc) or* von, sich unterhalten über *(+acc)*; **we're ~ing big money/serious crime** *etc* here *(inf)* hier gehts um große Geld/um schlimme Verbrechen *etc (inf)*; **we have to ~ business for a while** wir müssen mal kurz etwas Geschäftliches besprechen; **then they got down to ~ing business** dann sind sie zum geschäftlichen Teil übergegangen; **let's ~ business** kommen wir zur Sache; **now you're ~ing business** das lässt sich schon eher hören → **shop** **c** *(= persuade)* **to ~ sb/oneself into doing sth** jdn überreden *or* jdn/sich dazu bringen, etw zu tun; *(against better judgement)* jdm/sich einreden, dass man etw tut; **he ~ed himself into believing she was unfaithful** er hat sich eingeredet, sie sei ihm nicht treu; **to ~ sb out of sth/doing sth** jdn von etw abbringen/davon abbringen, etw zu tun, jdm etw ausreden/jdm etw ausreden, etw zu tun **d** *(= achieve by talking)* **he ~ed himself out of that job** durch sein Reden hat er sich *(dat)* diese Stelle verscherzt; **you won't be able to ~ your way out of this** jetzt können Sie sich nicht mehr herausreden; **he ~ed himself out of trouble** er redet sich *(geschickt)* heraus; **he ~ed himself into this situation** er hat sich selbst durch sein Reden in diese Lage gebracht; **to ~ sb into a better humour** jdn in eine bessere Laune bringen; **to ~ sb out of his bad temper** jdm die schlechte Laune vertreiben **e** **to ~ oneself hoarse** sich heiser reden → **head**

▶ **talk at** VI +prep obj person einreden auf *(+acc)*

▶ **talk away** **Ⅵ** ununterbrochen reden, schwatzen; **we talked away for hours** wir haben stundenlang geschwatzt *or* uns stundenlang unterhalten **Ⅶ** sep **a** *(= spend talking)* im Gespräch verbringen; **we talked the evening away** wir haben den ganzen Abend lang geredet, wir haben den Abend im Gespräch verbracht **b** *debts, problems etc* wegdiskutieren

▶ **talk back** VI *(= be cheeky)* frech antworten *(to sb* jdm)

▶ **talk down** **Ⅵ** **to talk down to sb** mit jdm herablassend *or* von oben herab reden *or* sprechen **Ⅶ** sep **a** *(= reduce to silence)* über den Haufen reden *(inf)*, niederreden **b** *(Aviat)* pilot, plane zur Landung einweisen **c** *(esp Brit: in negotiations)* herunterhandeln **d** *(= play down)* herunterspielen

▶ **talk on** VI weiterreden; **they talked on and on** sie reden und redeten

▶ **talk out** VT sep **a** *(= discuss)* problems, differences ausdiskutieren **b** *(Parl)* **to talk out a bill** die rechtzeitige Verabschiedung eines Gesetzes verschleppen

▶ **talk over** VT sep **a** *question, problem* bereden *(inf)*, besprechen; **let's talk it over quietly** wir wollen jetzt einmal in aller Ruhe darüber reden **b** *(= persuade)* = **talk round** VT

▶ **talk round** **Ⅶ** *always separate (Brit)* umstimmen; **I talked her round to my way of thinking** ich habe sie zu meiner Anschauung bekehrt **Ⅵ** +prep obj *(esp Brit)* problem, subject herumreden um

▶ **talk through** VT SEP **a** *(= discuss)* besprechen, durchsprechen **b** *(= explain)* besprechen; **to talk sb through sth** jdm etw erklären

▶ **talk up** VT SEP **a** *(in negotiations)* heraufreden **b** *(= play up)* heraufspielen

talkative ['tɔːkətıv] ADJ *person* gesprächig, redselig

talkativeness ['tɔːkətıvnıs] N Gesprächigkeit *f*, Redseligkeit *f*

talkback ['tɔːkbæk] N *(= device)* Gegensprechanlage *f*; *(= talking)* Anweisungen *pl* im Hintergrund

talked-of ['tɔːktɒv] ADJ *much* **~** berühmt; *plans also* viel besprochen; **his much ~ brilliance was apparent** seine viel gerühmte Brillanz wurde offensichtlich

talker ['tɔːkəʳ] N Redner(in) *m(f)*; **the parrot was a good ~** der Papagei konnte gut sprechen; **he's just a ~** er ist ein Schwätzer *m*

talkfest ['tɔːkfest] N *(US inf)* lange Diskussion, großes Palaver *(inf)*

talkie ['tɔːkı] N *(dated inf)* Tonfilm *m*

talking ['tɔːkıŋ] N Reden *nt*, Sprechen *nt*; **no ~ please!** bitte Ruhe!, Sprechen verboten!; **I'll let you do the ~** ich überlasse das Reden Ihnen; **he did all the ~** er übernahm das Reden; **his constant ~ will drive me mad** sein dauerndes Gerede *or* Geschwätz macht mich noch verrückt; **that's enough ~!** Ruhe jetzt!, Schluss mit dem Reden!

talking: talking bird N sprechender Vogel; **talking book** N *(for the blind etc)* Hörbuch *nt*; **talking doll** N sprechende Puppe, Sprechpuppe *f*; **talking head** N *(TV)* Kopfaufnahme *f*, Brustbild *nt*; **talking picture** N *(old)* Tonfilm *m*; **talking point** N Gesprächsthema *nt*; **talking shop** N *(esp Brit pej inf)* Quasselbude *f* *(inf)*; **talking-to** N *(inf)* Standpauke *f* *(inf)*; **to give sb a good ~** jdm eine Standpauke halten *(inf)*

talk: talk radio N Talkradio *nt*; **talk show** N Talkshow *f*

tall [tɔːl] ADJ *(+er)* **a** *person* groß, lang *(inf)*; **~ and slim** groß und schlank; **how ~ are you?** wie groß sind Sie?; **he is 6 ft ~** er ist 1,80 m groß; **she's 5 cm ~er than me, she's ~er than me by 5 cm** sie ist 5 cm größer als ich; **to stand 6 ft ~** *(person)* 1,80 m groß sein; **a 6 ft ~ man** ein 1,80 m großer Mann; **to feel ten foot** *or* **feet ~** *(inf)* riesig stolz sein *(inf)*; *(after compliment also)* um einen halben Meter wachsen *(inf)*; **to stand ~** aufrecht dastehen; **to walk ~** stolz einhergehen **b** *building, tree, grass, glass, window* hoch; *mast* lang, hoch **c** *(inf)* **that's a ~ order** das ist ganz schön viel verlangt; *(indignant also)* das ist eine Zumutung; **a ~ story** *or* **tale** ein Märchen *nt* *(inf)*

tallboy ['tɔːlbɔı] N *(Brit)* hohe Schlafzimmerkommode

tallish ['tɔːlıʃ] ADJ *person* ziemlich groß; *building* ziemlich hoch

tallness ['tɔːlnıs] N **a** *(of person)* Größe *f*, Länge *f* *(of building, tree, grass)* Höhe *f*; *(of mast also)* Länge *f*

tallow ['tæləʊ] N Talg *m*, Unschlitt *m* *(old)*; **~ candle** Talglicht *nt*

tallowy ['tæləʊı] ADJ talgig

tall ship N Klipper *m*; **~s race** Klipperregatta *f*

tally ['tælı] **Ⅰ** **a** *(Hist, = stick)* Kerbholz *nt* **b** *(= count, account)* **to keep a ~ of** Buch führen über *(+acc)* **c** *(= result of counting, number)* (An)zahl *f*; **what's the ~?** wie viel ist/sind es? **Ⅶ** übereinstimmen; *(reports etc also)* sich decken; **they don't ~** sie stimmen nicht (miteinander) überein **Ⅶ** *(also* **tally up**) zusammenrechnen *or* -zählen

tally clerk N Kontrolleur(in) *m(f)*

tally-ho [ˌtælɪˈhəʊ] INTERJ halali N Halali *nt*

tally trade N *(Brit Comm)* Teilzahlungsgeschäft *nt*

Talmud ['tælmuːd] N Talmud *m*

talon ['tælən] N Kralle *f*, Klaue *f*; *(fig, of person)* Kralle *f*

tamable ADJ = **tameable**

tamarind ['tæmərınd] N *(= tree, fruit)* Tamarinde *f*

tamarisk ['tæmərısk] N Tamariske *f*

tambour ['tæmˌbʊəʳ] N **a** *(old Mus)* Trommel *f* **b** *(on desk etc)* Rouleau *nt*, Rollo *nt*

tambourine [ˌtæmbəˈriːn] N Tamburin *nt*

tame [teɪm] **ADJ** *(+er)* **a** *animal* zahm; **the village has its own ~ novelist** *(hum)* der Ort hat seinen dorfeigenen Schriftsteller *(inf)*; **I'll get my ~ lawyer to do that** *(hum)* ich beauftrage meinen treuen Rechtsanwalt damit **b** *(= dull) person, life, adventure, answer, shot, tennis service etc* lahm *(inf)*; *story, criticism, joke* zahm, lahm *(inf)* **VT** *animal, person* zähmen, bändigen; *passion* (be)zähmen, zügeln; *garden, inflation, unions, deficit* unter Kontrolle bringen

tameable [ˈteɪməbl] **ADJ** zähmbar

tamely [ˈteɪmlɪ] **ADV** *(= meekly)* zahm; *agree, accept, surrender* lahm

tameness [ˈteɪmnɪs] **N a** *(of animal)* Zahmheit *f*, *(of person, life, adventure etc)* Lahmheit *f* *(inf)*; *(of film, criticism, joke etc also)* Zahmheit *f*; *(of shot)* Lahmheit *f*, Zahmheit *f*

tamer [ˈteɪmə] **N** *(of animals)* Bändiger(in) *m(f)*, Dompteur(in) *m(f)*

taming [ˈteɪmɪŋ] **N** Zähmung *f*, Bändigung *f*; **"The Taming of the Shrew"** „Der Widerspenstigen Zähmung"

tam-o'-shanter [ˌtæməˈʃæntə], **tammy** [ˈtæmɪ] **N** (schottische) Baskenmütze

tamp [tæmp] **VT a** *(= block up)* drill hole etc (ver)stopfen **b** *(= ram down)* earth (fest)stampfen; **to ~ (down) tobacco in a pipe** die Pfeife (fest) stopfen

Tampax® [ˈtæmpæks] **N** Tampon *m*

tamper [ˈtæmpə] **N** *(for soil etc)* Stampfer *m*; *(for tobacco)* Stopfer *m*

▸ **tamper with VI** *+prep obj* herumhantieren an *(+dat)*; *(with evil intent)* sich *(dat)* zu schaffen machen an *(+dat)*; *plan, schedule, elections, system* herumpfuschen an *(+dat)* *(inf)*; *document, evidence* verfälschen; *(Jur)* *witness* beeinflussen; *(= bribe)* bestechen; **the car had been tampered with** jemand hatte sich am Auto zu schaffen gemacht

tamper-evident, tamper-proof ADJ *food* sicherheitsverpackt, mit Sicherheitsverpackung, gegen unbefugte Eingriffe gesichert, Sicherheits-

tampon [ˈtæmpən] **N** Tampon *m*

tan [tæn] **N a** *(= suntan)* Bräune *f*; **to get a ~** braun werden; **she's got a lovely ~** sie ist schön braun; **what a ~!** du bist/er ist *etc* aber schön braun! **b** *(= colour)* Hellbraun *nt* **ADJ a** *skins* gerben; **to ~ sb's hide** *(fig inf)* jdm das Fell gerben **b** *(sun)* face, body etc bräunen, braun werden lassen **VI** braun werden; **she ~s easily** sie wird schnell braun

tandem [ˈtændəm] **N a** *(= cycle)* Tandem *nt*; **the horses were in ~** die Pferde liefen hintereinander im Gespann; **in ~ (with)** *(fig)* zusammen (mit) **ADV** hintereinander im Gespann

tang [tæŋ] **N** *(= smell)* scharfer Geruch; *(= taste)* starker Geschmack; **the fish has a salty ~** der Fisch schmeckt salzig

tanga [ˈtæŋgə] **N** *(= bikini, briefs)* Tanga *m*

tangent [ˈtændʒənt] **N** *(Math)* Tangente *f*; **to go off at a ~** *(fig)* (plötzlich) vom Thema abkommen *or* abschweifen; **he went off at a ~ about flowers** er schweifte plötzlich ab und fing an, über Blumen zu reden

tangential [tænˈdʒənʃəl] **ADJ** *(Math)* tangential; **this is merely ~ to the problem** dies berührt das Problem nur am Rande

tangentially [tænˈdʒənʃəlɪ] **ADV** *(form, = indirectly)* indirekt; **the question was only touched on ~** die Frage wurde nur am Rande gestreift

tangerine [ˌtændʒəˈriːn] **N** *(also* **tangerine orange**) Mandarine *f* **ADJ** *(colour)* stark orange, rötlich orange

tangibility [ˌtændʒɪˈbɪlɪtɪ] **N** Greifbarkeit *f*

tangible [ˈtændʒəbl] **ADJ a** *(lit)* greifbar, berührbar **b** *(fig)* result greifbar; *proof* handfest; *assets* handfest, real

tangibly [ˈtændʒəblɪ] **ADV** greifbar; **he would prefer to be rewarded more ~** ihm wäre etwas Handfesteres als Belohnung lieber; **the evi-**

dence **~ supports his claim** die Beweise unterstützen seine Behauptung nachhaltig

Tangier(s) [tænˈdʒɪə(z)] **N** Tanger *nt*

tangle [ˈtæŋgl] **N a** *(lit)* Gewirr *nt*; **the string was in a ~** die Schnur hatte sich verheddert; **the ~s in her hair** ihr verheddertes Haar; **to get into a ~** sich verheddern **b** *(fig, = muddle)* Wirrwarr *m*, Durcheinander *nt*; **to get into a ~** sich verheddern; **I'm in such a ~ with my tax forms** ich komme bei meinen Steuerformularen überhaupt nicht klar; **she has got herself into an emotional ~** sie hat sich gefühlsmäßig verstrickt **c** *(fig, = trouble)* Ärger *m*, Schwierigkeiten *pl*; **she's in a real ~ this time** diesmal hat sie sich aber böse hineingeritten; **he got into a ~ with the police** er ist mit der Polizei aneinander geraten, er hat Schwierigkeiten mit der Polizei gehabt **VT** *(lit, fig)* verwirren, durcheinander bringen; *wool, string also* verheddern; *hair* durcheinander bringen; **to get ~d** *(lit, fig)* sich verheddern; *(ropes)* sich verknoten; **a ~d web** ein Gespinst *nt*

▸ **tangle up VT** *sep* *(lit, fig)* verwirren, durcheinander bringen; *wool, string also* verheddern; **to get tangled up** durcheinander geraten; *(wool etc also)* sich verheddern; *(ropes)* sich verknoten; *(person, in talking, explaining etc)* sich verstricken *or* verheddern; *(= become involved)* verwickelt *or* verstrickt werden; **the string got all tangled up in the machine** die Schnur hat sich in der Maschine verheddert; **she got tangled up with a married man** sie hat sich mit einem verheirateten Mann eingelassen

▸ **tangle with VI** *+prep obj* *(inf)* aneinander geraten mit; **I'm not tangling with him** mit ihm lass ich mich *(doch)* nicht ein

tangly [ˈtæŋlɪ] **ADJ** *(+er)* *(= confused)* verwickelt, verworren

tango [ˈtæŋgəʊ] **N** Tango *m* **VI** Tango tanzen; **they ~ed across the room** sie tanzten im Tangoschritt durch das Zimmer; **it takes two to ~** *(fig inf)* es gehören immer zwei dazu

tangy [ˈtæŋɪ] **ADJ** *(+er)* taste scharf, streng; *smell also* durchdringend

tank [tæŋk] **N a** *(= container)* Tank *m*; *(esp for water)* Wasserspeicher *m*; *(of boiler)* Kessel *m*; *(Naut, for water supply)* Kessel *m*; *(in submarines)* Tauchtank *m*; *(Rail, in engine)* Kessel *m*; *(for diver. = oxygen tank)* Flasche *f*; *(Phot)* Wanne *f*; **fill up the ~, please** *(Aut)* volltanken, bitte **b** *(Mil)* Panzer *m*, Tank *m* **c** *(US, inf)* Kittchen *nt* *(inf)*, Knast *m* *(inf)*

▸ **tank along VI** *(inf, = move fast, car)* dahinbrettern *(inf)*; *(runner)* dahinsausen *(inf)*

▸ **tank up VI a** *(ship, plane)* auftanken; *(car, driver)* voll tanken, auftanken **b** *(Brit inf, = get drunk)* sich voll laufen lassen *(inf)* **VT** *sep* a *ship, plane* auftanken; *car* voll tanken, auftanken **b** *(Brit inf)* **to get tanked up** sich voll laufen lassen *(inf)* *(on* mit); **to be tanked up** voll sein *(inf)*

tankage [ˈtæŋkɪdʒ] **N a** *(= storage capacity of tank)* Fassungsvermögen *nt* **b** *(= storage fee)* Gebühr *f* für Lagerung *(in einem Tank)*; *(= storage)* Lagerung *f* *(in einem Tank)* **c** *(Agr, = meat and bone meal)* Tierkörpermehl *nt* *(als Dünger oder Futtermittelzusatz)*

tankard [ˈtæŋkəd] **N** *(esp Brit)* Humpen *m*; *(for beer also)* Seidel *nt*

tank car N *(Rail)* Kesselwagen *m*

tanker [ˈtæŋkə] **N a** *(= boat)* Tanker *m*, Tankschiff *nt* **b** *(= vehicle)* Tankwagen *m*

tank farm N *(US)* Tanklager *nt*

tank farming N Pflanzenanbau *m* in Hydrokultur

tankful [ˈtæŋkfʊl] **N a** Tank *m* (voll) **b** *(Brit, inf, = drink)* **he's had a ~** der ist total voll *(inf)*

tank: tank top N Pullunder *m*; **tank town N** *(US)* Wasser(auffüll)station *f*; *(fig)* Kuhnest *nt* *(inf)*; **tank trap N** Panzersperre *f*; **tank truck**

N *(esp US)* Tankwagen *m*; **tank wagon**, *(Brit)* **tank waggon N** *(Rail)* Kesselwagen *m*

tanned [tænd] **ADJ a** *person* braun (gebrannt) **b** *skins* gegerbt

tanner¹ [ˈtænə] **N** Gerber(in) *m(f)*

tanner² **N** *(old Brit, inf)* Sixpence *m*

tannery [ˈtænərɪ] **N** Gerberei *f*

tannic [ˈtænɪk] **ADJ** Gerb-

tannic acid N Tannin *nt*

tannin [ˈtænɪn] **N** Tannin *nt*

tanning [ˈtænɪŋ] **N a** *(of hides)* Gerben *nt*; *(= craft)* Gerberei *f* **b** *(= punishment)* Tracht *f* Prügel; **to give sb a ~** jdm das Fell gerben

Tannoy® [ˈtænɔɪ] **N** Lautsprecheranlage *f*; **over** *or* **on the ~** über den Lautsprecher

tansy [ˈtænzɪ] **N** Rainfarn *m*

tantalize [ˈtæntəlaɪz] **VT** reizen; *(= torment also)* quälen; **to be ~d** Tantalusqualen ausstehen

tantalizing [ˈtæntəlaɪzɪŋ] **ADJ** *smell, promise* verlockend, verführerisch; *behaviour, glimpse also* aufreizend; **he spoke with ~ slowness** er sprach aufreizend langsam; **it is ~ to think that ...** es ist zum Verrücktwerden, zu denken, dass ... *(inf)*

tantalizingly [ˈtæntəlaɪzɪŋlɪ] **ADV** verlockend, verführerisch; **success was ~ close** der Erfolg schien zum Greifen nahe

tantamount [ˈtæntəmaʊnt] **ADJ** **to be ~ to sth** einer Sache *(dat)* gleichkommen, auf etw *(acc)* hinauslaufen

tantrum [ˈtæntrəm] **N** Wutanfall *m*, Koller *m* *(inf)*; **to have** *or* **throw a ~** einen Koller *or* Wutanfall bekommen; **she drove off in a ~** sie fuhr wütend weg

Tanzania [ˌtænzəˈnɪə] **N** Tansania *nt*

Tanzanian [ˌtænzəˈnɪən] **ADJ** tansanisch **N** Tansanier(in) *m(f)*

Taoism [ˈtaʊɪzəm] **N** Taoismus *m*

tap¹ [tæp] **N a** *(esp Brit)* Hahn *m*; **the hot/cold ~** der Kaltwasser-/Heißwasserhahn; **don't leave the ~s running** lass das Wasser nicht laufen!, dreh die Hähne zu!; **on ~** *(lit, beer etc)* vom Fass; *(fig)* zur Hand; **he has plenty of ideas on ~** er hat immer Ideen auf Lager *(inf)* **b** *(of phones)* Abhören *nt*, Abhöraktion *f* **VT a** *cask, barrel* anzapfen, anstechen; *tree* anzapfen; **to ~ a pine for resin** einer Kiefer *(dat)* Harz abzapfen **b** *(fig)* resources, market erschließen; **to ~ an electric current** eine Stromleitung anzapfen; **to ~ telephone wires** Telefonleitungen anzapfen; **the wires are ~ped here** die Leitung hier wird abgehört; **to ~ sb for money/a loan** *(inf)* jdn anzapfen *(inf)*, jdn anpumpen *(inf)*; **he tried to ~ me for information** er wollte mich aushorchen

▸ **tap into VI** *+prep obj* *(= gain access to)* system, network anzapfen; *(= exploit)* fear, enthusiasm ausnutzen

tap² **N a** *(= light knock)* Klopfen *nt* **b** *(= light touch)* Klaps *m*, leichter Schlag; **to give sb a ~ on the shoulder** jdn *or* jdm auf die Schulter klopfen **c** **taps SING OR PL** *(Mil)* Zapfenstreich *m* **VT** klopfen; **he ~ped me on the shoulder** er klopfte mir auf die Schulter; **to ~ in a nail** einen Nagel einschlagen; **he ~ped his foot impatiently** er klopfte ungeduldig mit dem Fuß auf den Boden; **he ~ped his fingers impatiently on the table** er trommelte ungeduldig (mit den Fingern) auf den Tisch **VI** klopfen; **to ~ on** *or* **at the door** sachte an die Tür klopfen *or* pochen *(geh)*, leise anklopfen; **she sat ~ping away at the typewriter** sie klapperte auf der Schreibmaschine herum; **he ~ped with his fingers on the table** er trommelte mit den Fingern auf den Tisch

▸ **tap out VT** *sep* a *pipe* ausklopfen **b** *rhythm* klopfen; **to tap out a message (in Morse)** eine Nachricht morsen

tap: tap dance N Stepptanz *m*; **tap-dance VI** steppen; **tap-dancer N** Stepptänzer(in) *m(f)*, Stepper(in) *m(f)*; **tap-dancing N** Steppen *nt*

tape [teɪp] **N** **a** Band nt; (= sticky paper) Klebeband nt; (= Sellotape ® etc) Kleb(e)streifen m, Tesafilm® m; (= ticker-tape, computer tape etc) Lochstreifen m; (Sport) Zielband nt; **to break** or **breast the ~** (Sport) durchs Ziel gehen **b** (magnetic) (Ton)band nt, Magnetband nt; **on ~** auf Band; **to put** or **get sth on ~** etw auf Band aufnehmen; **to make a ~ of sth** etw auf Band aufnehmen **VT** **a** parcel (mit Kleb(e)streifen/Klebeband) verkleben or zukleben; **to ~ together two documents** zwei Dokumente mit Kleb(e)streifen/Klebeband zusammenkleben **b** (= tape-record) song, message (auf Band) aufnehmen; (= video-tape) show (auf Video) aufnehmen **c** (inf) **I've got the situation ~d** ich habe die Sache im Griff (inf); **I've got him ~d** ich kenne mich mit ihm aus

▶ **tape back** VT sep (mit Kleb(e)streifen/Klebeband) zurückkleben

▶ **tape down** VT sep (mit Kleb(e)streifen/Klebeband) festkleben

▶ **tape on** VT sep (mit Kleb(e)streifen/Klebeband) ankleben or -heften; **to tape sth on(to) sth** etw auf etw (acc) kleben

▶ **tape over** (Recording) **VI** +prep obj überspielen **VT** sep **to tape A over B** B mit A überspielen

▶ **tape up** VT sep sth broken mit Kleb(e)streifen/Klebeband zusammenkleben; parcel mit Kleb(e)streifen/Klebeband verkleben; gap, windows, mouth zukleben

tape: tape cassette N Tonbandkassette f; **tape deck** N Tapedeck nt; **tape head** N Tonkopf m; **tape measure** N Maßband nt, Bandmaß nt

taper ['teɪpə] **N** (= candle) (dünne) Kerze **VT** end of plank, stick etc zuspitzen; edge abschrägen; hair spitz zuschneiden; pair of trousers (nach unten) verengen **VI** sich verjüngen; (vase) sich verjüngen; (trousers) nach unten enger werden; (hair) (im Nacken) spitz zulaufen; **to ~ to a point** spitz zulaufen

▶ **taper off** VI (lit) spitz zulaufen, sich zuspitzen; (vase) sich verjüngen; (road, trousers) sich verengen **b** (fig: = decrease gradually) langsam aufhören; (numbers) langsam zurückgehen; (production) langsam auslaufen **VT** sep edge abschrägen; end of plank, stick etc zuspitzen; (fig) production zurückschrauben; (= bring to an end) langsam auslaufen lassen

tape: tape reader N (Comput) Lochstreifenleser m; **tape-record** VT auf Band aufnehmen; **tape recorder** N Tonbandgerät nt; (= cassette recorder) Kassettenrekorder m; **tape recording** N Bandaufnahme f

tapered ['teɪpəd] ADJ spitz zulaufend; **~ trousers** Hosen, die unten enger werden

tapering ['teɪpərɪŋ] ADJ spitz zulaufend

tape streamer N (Comput) Streamer m

taper tap N (Tech) Gewindebohrer m

tapestry ['tæpɪstrɪ] N Wand- or Bildteppich m; (= fabric) Gobelin m; **~-making** Tapisserie f; **it's all part of life's rich ~** das gibt alles dem Leben mehr Würze

tapeworm ['teɪpwɜːm] N Bandwurm m

tapioca [ˌtæpɪˈəʊkə] N Tapioka f

tapir ['teɪpə] N Tapir m

tappet ['tæpɪt] N (Aut) Stößel m

tapping ['tæpɪŋ] N **a** (of barrel) Anzapfen nt, Anstich m; (of beer etc from barrel) Abzapfen nt **b** (of telephone etc) Anzapfen nt **c** (Med) Punktieren nt **d** (fig, of funds etc) Erschließen nt **e** (Tech) Gewindebohren nt or -schneiden nt; **~ drill** Gewindebohrer m

tap: taproom N Schankstube f, Schenke f, Schänke f; **taproot** N (Bot) Pfahlwurzel f

tapster ['tæpstə] N (old) Schankkellner(in) m(f), Zapfer(in) m(f)

tap water N Leitungswasser nt

tar¹ [tɑː] **N** Teer m **VT** road, fence teeren; **they are all ~red with the same brush** (fig) sie sind alle vom gleichen Schlag; **to ~ and feather sb** jdn teeren und federn

tar² N (old Naut sl) Teerjacke f (hum), Seemann m

tarantella [ˌtærənˈtelə] N Tarantella f

tarantula [təˈræntjʊlə] N Tarantel f

tarboard ['tɑːbɔːd] N Dach- or Teerpappe f

tarbrush ['tɑːbrʌʃ] N **a touch of the ~** (pej inf) schwarzes Blut

tardily ['tɑːdɪlɪ] ADV arrive, offer, send verspätet; discover zu spät

tardiness ['tɑːdɪnɪs] N **a** (of person) Säumigkeit f (geh) **b** (US: = lateness) Zuspätkommen nt; (of train etc) Verspätung f

tardy ['tɑːdɪ] ADJ (+er) **a** (= belated) reply, arrival, offer to help (reichlich) spät; person säumig (geh); **to be ~ in doing sth** etw erst reichlich spät tun **b** (US: = late) **to be ~** (person) zu spät kommen; (train etc) Verspätung haben; **the train was ~ (in arriving at New York)** der Zug kam mit Verspätung (in New York) an

tare¹ [teə] N (Bot) Wicke f

tare² N (Comm) Tara f; (of vehicle) Leergewicht nt

target ['tɑːgɪt] **N** **a** (= person, object, Mil) Ziel nt; (Sport: = board) Ziel- or Schießscheibe f; (fig, of joke, criticism etc) Zielscheibe f; **he was a ~ for racial abuse** er war Zielscheibe rassistischer Pöbeleien; **she was the ~ of a violent attack** sie war das Ziel eines brutalen Angriffs or Überfalls; **his shot was off/on ~** (Mil) sein Schuss ist danebengegangen/hat getroffen; (Ftbl etc) sein Schuss war ungenau/sehr genau; **the bombs were on/off ~** die Bomben haben getroffen/sind daneben niedergegangen; **Apollo III is on ~ for the moon** Apollo III ist auf direktem Kurs zum Mond; **they were at least 12 km off ~** sie hatten das Ziel um mindestens 12 km verfehlt **b** (= objective, goal) Ziel nt; (in production) (Plan)soll nt; **production ~** Produktionssoll nt no pl; **production is above/on/below ~** das Produktionssoll ist überschritten/erfüllt/nicht erfüllt; **the government met its ~ for reducing unemployment** die Regierung hat mit der Abnahme der Arbeitslosigkeit ihren Plan erfüllt; **he set a ~ for spending** er setzte eine Höchstgrenze für die Ausgaben fest; **we set ourselves the ~ of £10,000** wir haben uns £ 10.000 zum Ziel gesetzt; **to be on ~** auf Kurs sein; **the project is on ~ for completion** das Projekt ist auf dem besten Weg, planmäßig fertig zu werden; **we're on ~ for £10,000** alles läuft nach Plan, um auf £ 10.000 zu kommen; **to stay on ~** den Kurs halten; **to be behind ~** hinter dem Soll zurückliegen **VT** sich (dat) zum Ziel setzen; group, audience als Zielgruppe haben, abzielen auf (+acc); area, resources abzielen auf (+acc); **to ~ 500 tons per day** 500 Tonnen pro Tag anspielen

target: targetable ['tɑːgɪtəbl] ADJ (Mil) warhead etc aufs Ziel einstellbar or programmierbar; **target area** N Zielbereich m, Zielgebiet nt; **target cost** N Richtkosten pl, Plankosten pl; **target date** N angestrebter Termin; **target figure** N Richtsumme f, Plansumme f; **we have a ~ of 100,000 visitors** wir nehmen uns (dat) 100.000 Besucher zum Ziel gesetzt; **target group** N Zielgruppe f; **target language** N Zielsprache f; **target market** N Zielmarkt m; **target practice** N (Mil) Zielschießen nt

targetting ['tɑːgɪtɪŋ] N (= setting targets) Zielsetzung f; **the ~ of teenagers as customers** das Ansteuern von Teenagern or das Abzielen auf Teenager als Kunden

tariff ['tærɪf] **N** **a** (esp Brit) (Gebühren)tarif m; (in hotels) Preisverzeichnis nt, Preisliste f **b** (Econ, = tax) Zoll m; (= table) Zolltarif m

tariff reform N (Econ) Zolltarifreform f; (Hist) Einführung f von Schutzzöllen

tariff walls PL (Econ) Zollschranken pl

tarmac ['tɑːmæk] **N** **a** Tarmac® Makadam m; (generally) Asphalt m, Makadam m (spec) **b** (esp Brit, Aviat) Rollfeld nt **VT** road (generally) asphaltieren, makadamisieren (spec)

tarmacadam [ˌtɑːməˈkædəm] N Makadam m

tarn [tɑːn] N kleiner Berg- or Gebirgssee

tarnish ['tɑːnɪʃ] **VT** metal stumpf werden lassen; **the silver was ~ed by exposure to air** das Silber war an der Luft angelaufen **b** (fig) reputation, glory beflecken; ideals, image trüben, den Glanz nehmen (+dat) **VI** (metal) anlaufen **N** Beschlag m; **to prevent ~** das Anlaufen verhindern

taro ['tɑːrəʊ] N Taro m

tarot card ['tærəʊkɑːd] N Tarockkarte f

tarp [tɑːp] N (US, inf) = tarpaulin

tar paper N (US) Dachpappe f, Teerpappe f

tarpaulin [tɑːˈpɔːlɪn] **N** **a** (= waterproof sheet) Plane f; (Naut) Persenning f **b** **tarpaulins** PL (= clothes) Ölzeug nt

tarpon ['tɑːpɒn] N Atlantischer Tarpon, Silberkönig m

tarragon ['tærəgən] N Estragon m

tarry¹ ['tɑːrɪ] ADJ teerig

tarry² ['tærɪ] **VI** (old, liter) **a** (= remain) verweilen (old, liter) **b** (= delay) säumen (old, liter), zögern

tarsus ['tɑːsəs] N Tarsus m

tart¹ [tɑːt] ADJ (+er) **a** flavour, wine herb, sauer (pej); fruit sauer **b** (fig) remark, manner scharf; humour beißend; person schroff

tart² N (Cook) Obstkuchen m, Obsttorte f; (individual) Obsttörtchen nt; **apple ~** Apfelkuchen m/-törtchen nt; **jam ~** Marmeladenkuchen m/-törtchen nt

tart³ N (Brit inf, = prostitute) Nutte f (inf); (= loose woman) Flittchen nt (pej inf); (pej, = woman) Schachtel f (inf)

▶ **tart up** VT sep (esp Brit, inf) aufmachen (inf); oneself auftakeln (inf), aufdonnern (inf); **there she was, all tarted up** da stand sie, aufgetakelt wie eine Fregatte (inf)

tartan ['tɑːtən] **N** (= pattern) Schottenkaro nt; (= material) Schottenstoff m; **what's your ~?** welches Clanmuster tragen Sie? **ADJ** skirt etc im Schottenkaro or -muster

Tartar ['tɑːtə] N Tatar(in) m(f); **to catch a ~** (fig) sich (dat) etwas Übles einhandeln

tartar¹ ['tɑːtə] N (fig) Tyrann(in) m(f)

tartar² N (of wine) Weinstein m; (in kettle) Kesselstein m; (on teeth) Zahnstein m

tartare ['tɑːtɑː] ADJ → steak

tartaric acid [tɑːˌtærɪkˈæsɪd] N Weinsäure f

tartar sauce N ≈ Remouladensoße f

Tartary ['tɑːtərɪ] N Tatarei f

tartlet ['tɑːtlɪt] N (Brit) Törtchen nt

tartly ['tɑːtlɪ] ADV speak scharf; **a ~ flavoured tomato relish** ein scharf gewürztes Tomatenchutney

tartness ['tɑːtnɪs] N **a** (of flavour, wine) Herbheit f, Säure f (pej); (of fruit) Säure f **b** (fig, of remark, manner) Schärfe f; (of humour) Beißende(s) nt; (of person) Schroffheit f

tash [tæʃ] N (Brit, inf) = tache

task [tɑːsk] **N** **a** Aufgabe f; **to set** or **give sb a ~** jdm eine Aufgabe stellen or geben; **it is the ~ of the politician to ...** es ist Aufgabe des Politikers zu ...; **to take sb to ~** jdn ins Gebet nehmen, sich (dat) jdn vornehmen (inf) (for, about wegen) **VT** = tax VT b

task: task force N Sondereinheit f, Spezialeinheit f; **taskmaster** N (strenger) Arbeitgeber; **he's a hard ~** er ist ein strenger Meister; **task time** N (US Econ) Zeitnorm f

Tasmania [tæzˈmeɪnɪə] N Tasmanien nt

Tasmanian [tæzˈmeɪnɪən] **ADJ** tasmanisch **N** Tasmanier(in) m(f)

Tasman Sea [ˌtæzmənˈsiː] N Tasmansee f

tassel ['tæsəl] N Quaste f, Troddel f

tasselled ['tæsəld] ADJ mit Quasten or Troddeln verziert

taste [teɪst] **N** **a** (= *sense*) Geschmack(sinn) *m*; **to be sweet to the ~** süß schmecken, einen süßen Geschmack haben

b (= *flavour*) Geschmack *m*; **I don't like the ~** das schmeckt mir nicht; **her cooking has no ~** ihr Essen schmeckt nach nichts; **a ~ of onions** ein Zwiebelgeschmack; **to leave a bad ~ in the mouth** (*lit, fig*) einen üblen Nachgeschmack hinterlassen

c (= *small amount*) Kostprobe *f*, Versucherchen *nt* (*inf*); (*fig, as an example*) Kostprobe *f*; (*of sth in the future*) Vorgeschmack *m*; **would you like some? – just a ~** möchten Sie etwas? – nur eine Idee; **to have a ~ (of sth)** (*lit*) (etw) probieren *or* kosten; (*fig*) eine Kostprobe (von etw) bekommen; (*of sth to come*) einen Vorgeschmack (von etw) haben; **two years in the army will give him a ~ of discipline** zwei Jahre bei der Armee werden ihm zeigen *or* werden ihn spüren lassen, was Disziplin ist; **to give sb a ~ of the whip** jdn die Peitsche *or* Knute spüren lassen; **he gave them a ~ of his bad temper** er gab ihnen eine (Kost)probe seiner schlechten Laune; **a ~ of what was to come** ein Vorgeschmack dessen, was noch kommen sollte

d (= *liking*) Geschmack *m no pl*; **to have a ~ for sth** eine Vorliebe für etw haben; **to acquire** *or* **develop a ~ for sth** Geschmack an etw (*dat*) finden; **it's an acquired ~** das ist etwas für Kenner; **she has expensive ~s in hats** was Hüte anbelangt, hat sie einen teuren Geschmack; **my ~ in music has changed over the years** mein musikalischer Geschmack hat sich mit der Zeit geändert; **to be to sb's ~** nach jds Geschmack sein; **it is a matter of ~** das ist Geschmack(s)sache; **there is no accounting for ~s** über Geschmack lässt sich (nicht) streiten; **~s differ** die Geschmäcker sind verschieden; **sweeten to ~** (*Cook*) nach Geschmack *or* Bedarf süßen; **her novels are too violent for my ~** ihre Romane enthalten für meinen Geschmack zu viel Gewalt

e (= *discernment*) Geschmack *m*; **she has very good ~ in furniture** was Möbel anbelangt, hat sie einen sehr guten Geschmack; **she has no ~ at all when it comes to choosing friends** sie ist nicht sehr wählerisch in der Auswahl ihrer Freunde; **a man of ~** ein Mann mit Geschmack; **in good ~** geschmackvoll; **in bad ~** geschmacklos; **to be in doubtful ~** von zweifelhaftem Geschmack zeugen; **that joke shows very poor ~** dieser Witz ist geschmacklos; **the house is furnished in impeccable ~** das Haus ist, was Geschmack betrifft, tadellos eingerichtet

VT **a** (= *perceive flavour of*) schmecken; *blood* lecken; **I can't ~ anything** ich schmecke überhaupt nichts; **I can't ~ anything wrong in** ich kann nichts Besonderes schmecken; **once you've ~d real champagne** wenn Sie einmal echten Sekt getrunken haben; **I've never ~d caviar** ich habe noch nie Kaviar gekostet (*geh*) *or* gegessen; **wait till you ~ this** warten Sie mal, bis Sie das probiert haben; **he hadn't ~d food for a week** er hatte seit einer Woche nichts zu sich genommen

b (= *take a little*) versuchen, probieren, kosten

c (= *test*) *wine* probieren; *food products* probieren; (*official*) prüfen; **~ the sauce before adding salt** schmecken Sie die Soße ab, bevor Sie Salz beigeben

d (*fig*) *power, freedom, success, victory* erfahren, erleben; **once the canary had ~d freedom …** als der Kanarienvogel erst einmal Geschmack an der Freiheit gefunden hatte …

VI **a** (*food, drink*) schmecken; **to ~ good** *or* **nice** (gut) schmecken; **it ~s all right to me** ich schmecke nichts; (= *I like it*) ich finde, das schmeckt nicht schlecht; **to ~ of sth** nach etw schmecken

b **to ~ of** (*liter*) erfahren; **those who have ~d of the knowledge of Zen** diejenigen, denen die Weisheit des Zen zuteil geworden ist (*geh*)

taste bud N Geschmacksknospe *f*

tasteful ADJ , **tastefully** ADV ['teɪstfʊl, -fəlɪ] geschmackvoll

tastefulness ['teɪstfʊlnɪs] N guter Geschmack

tasteless ['teɪstlɪs] ADJ (*lit, fig*) geschmacklos; *food also* fade

tastelessly ['teɪstlɪslɪ] ADV *furnished, decorated* geschmacklos; **~ inappropriate** geschmacklos und unangebracht; **~ extravagant** geschmacklos extravagant; **her ordeal was handled ~ in the press** ihre Tortur wurde in der Presse geschmacklos behandelt

tastelessness ['teɪstlɪsnɪs] N (*lit, fig*) Geschmacklosigkeit *f*; (*of food also*) Fadheit *f*

taster ['teɪstə'] N **a** (*of wine, tobacco*) Prüfer(in) *m(f)*, Probierer(in) *m(f)*; (*of tea*) Schmecker(in) *m(f)*; (*as bodyguard*) Vorkoster(in) *m(f)* **b** (*esp Brit fig*) Vorgeschmack *m*; **this is just a ~ of what's to come** dies ist nur ein kleiner Vorgeschmack von dem, was noch kommt

tastily ['teɪstɪlɪ] ADV schmackhaft

tastiness ['teɪstɪnɪs] N Schmackhaftigkeit *f*

tasty ['teɪstɪ] ADJ (+er) *dish* schmackhaft; **a ~ morsel** (*lit*) ein Leckerbissen *m*; **his new girlfriend is very ~** (*inf*) seine neue Freundin ist zum Anbeißen (*inf*)

tat¹ [tæt] **VI** Okkispitze *or* Schiffchenspitze machen **VT** in Okkispitze *or* Schiffchenspitze arbeiten; **she ~ted a strip of lace** sie stellte eine Spitze in Okkiarbeit her

tat² N → **tit²**

ta-ta [tæ'tɑː] INTERJ (*Brit, inf*) tschüss (*inf*), ata ata (*baby-talk*)

tattered ['tætəd] ADJ *clothes, person* zerlumpt; *book, sheet* zerfleddert, zerfetzt; (*fig*) *pride, reputation* angeschlagen; *nerves* zerrüttet

tatters ['tætəz] PL Lumpen *pl*, Fetzen *pl*; **to be in ~** in Fetzen sein *or* hängen; **his jacket hung in ~** sein Jackett war zerrissen *or* hing ihm in Fetzen vom Leib; **his reputation/confidence was in ~** sein Ruf/Selbstbewusstsein war sehr angeschlagen *or* hatte sehr gelitten

tattie, tatty ['tætɪ] N (*Scot, inf*) Kartoffel *f*

tattily ['tætɪlɪ] ADV (*inf*) *dressed* schäbig; *produced, manufactured* schlampig (*inf*)

tattiness ['tætɪnɪs] N Schmuddeligkeit *f*; (*of clothes*) Schäbigkeit *f*

tatting ['tætɪŋ] N Okki- *or* Schiffchenspitze *f*, Frivolitätenarbeit *f*

tattle ['tætl] **VI** tratschen (*inf*), klatschen **N** Geschwätz *nt*, Gerede *nt*; **office ~** Büroklatsch *m or* -tratsch *m* (*inf*)

tattler ['tætlə'] N Klatschmaul *nt* (*pej sl*), Klatschbase *f* (*inf*)

tattoo¹ [tə'tuː] **VT** tätowieren **N** Tätowierung *f*

tattoo² N **a** (*Brit: = military pageant*) Musikparade *f* **b** (*Mil, on drum or bugle*) Zapfenstreich *m*; **to beat** *or* **sound the ~** den Zapfenstreich blasen; **to beat a ~ on the table** (*with one's fingers*) auf den Tisch trommeln

tattooer [tə'tuːə'], **tattooist** [tə'tuːɪst] N Tätowierer(in) *m(f)*

tatty¹ ['tætɪ] ADJ (+er) (*esp Brit inf*) schmuddelig; *clothes* schäbig

tatty² ['tætɪ] N (*Scot, inf*) = **tattie**

taught [tɔːt] pret, ptp of **teach**

taunt [tɔːnt] **N** Spöttelei *f*, höhnische Bemerkung; **he paid no attention to their ~s of "traitor"** er kümmerte sich nicht darum, dass sie ihn als Verräter verhöhnten **VT** *person* verspotten, aufziehen (*inf*) (*about* wegen); **to ~ sb with racial abuse** jdn mit rassistischen Beschimpfungen verhöhnen

taunting ADJ , **tauntingly** ADV ['tɔːntɪŋ, -lɪ] höhnisch, spöttisch

Taurean [tɔː'rɪən] N (*Astrol*) Stier *m*

Taurus ['tɔːrəs] N (*Astron, Astrol*) Stier *m*; **he's (a) ~** er ist Stier

taut [tɔːt] ADJ (+er) **a** *rope* straff (gespannt); *skin* straff; *muscles* stramm, gestrafft; **to hold sth ~** etw straff halten; **to be stretched ~** straff gespannt sein; **to pull sth ~** etw stramm ziehen;

~ round thighs pralle Oberschenkel *pl* **b** (*fig, = tense*) *nerves, situation* (an)gespannt; *person, voice* angespannt; *look* gespannt; **his face was ~ with anger** sein Gesicht war vor Wut verzogen

c (*fig, = precise, economical*) *style, prose* knapp **d** (= *lean*) *person* schlank; *body* straff

tauten ['tɔːtn] **VT** *rope* spannen, straff anziehen, straffen; *sail* straffen; *muscle, body* anspannen **VI** sich spannen *or* straffen, straff werden

tautly ['tɔːtlɪ] ADV **a** *stretch* straff **b** (*fig: = precisely, economically*) knapp

tautness ['tɔːtnɪs] N (*of skin, rope*) Straffheit *f*; (*of muscles*) Strammheit *f*; (*fig, of atmosphere*) Gespanntheit *f*; (*of nerves*) Anspannung *f*; (*of style*) Knappheit *f*

tautological [ˌtɔːtə'lɒdʒɪkəl], **tautologous** [tɔː'tɒləgəs] ADJ tautologisch, doppelt gemoppelt (*inf*)

tautology [tɔː'tɒlədʒɪ] N Tautologie *f*, weißer Schimmel (*inf*)

tavern ['tævən] N (*old*) Taverne *f*, Schänke *f*, Schenke *f* (*old*)

tawdrily ['tɔːdrɪlɪ] ADV billig und geschmacklos; **~ dressed** aufgedonnert

tawdriness ['tɔːdrɪnɪs] N (*of jewellery, decorations etc*) ordinäre Protzigkeit; (*of story, idea*) Geschmacklosigkeit *f*; **the ~ of her appearance** ihre billige und geschmacklose Aufmachung

tawdry ['tɔːdrɪ] ADJ (+er) *clothes* billig und geschmacklos; *hat, splendour, decorations* ordinär; *person, appearance* aufgedonnert; *story, idea* geschmacklos; **all this cheap and ~ jewellery** all dieser billige Flitterkram

tawny ['tɔːnɪ] ADJ (+er) gelbbraun, goldbraun; **~ brown** gelbbraun; **~ port** bräunlicher Portwein, Tawny-Portwein *m*

tawny owl N Waldkauz *m*; **Tawny Owl** (*in Brownies*) Helferin *f* der Wichtelmutter

tax [tæks] **N** **a** (*Fin, Econ*) Steuer *f*; (*on a company's profit*) Abgabe *f*; (= *import tax*) Gebühr *f*; **before ~** brutto, vor Abzug der Steuern; **after ~** netto, nach Abzug der Steuern; **profits before/after ~** Brutto-/Nettoverdienst *m*; **that's done for ~ purposes** das wird aus steuerlichen Gründen getan; **free of ~** steuer-/abgaben-/gebührenfrei; **to put a ~ on sb/sth** jdn/etw besteuern, jdn/etw mit einer Steuer belegen; **the heavy ~ on the rich** die hohe Besteuerung der Reichen; **the ~ on alcohol/cars** etc die Getränke-/Kraftfahrzeugsteuer *etc*

b (*fig*) Belastung *f* (*on sth +gen*, *on sb* für jdn) **VT** **a** (*Fin, Econ*) besteuern; *country* mit Steuern belegen; **this government is going to ~ us all out of existence** diese Regierung zieht uns den letzten Cent aus der Tasche (*inf*)

b (*fig*) *brain, imagination, nerves, patience etc* strapazieren; *strength* stark beanspruchen; *savings, resources* angreifen, schmälern

c (*liter, = accuse*) **to ~ sb with sth** jdn einer Sache (*gen*) beschuldigen *or* bezichtigen *or* zeihen (*liter*)

tax abatement N Steuernachlass *m*

taxability [ˌtæksə'bɪlɪtɪ] N (*subject to tax*) Steuerpflichtigkeit *f*; (*of income*) Besteuerungsfähigkeit *f*; (*Jur*) Gebührenpflichtigkeit *f*

taxable ['tæksəbl] ADJ *person* steuerpflichtig; *income also* (be)steuerbar (*form*); *goods* besteuert, abgabenpflichtig

tax: tax advantage N Steuervorteil *m*; **tax adviser** N Steuerberater(in) *m(f)*; **tax allowance** N Steuervergünstigung *f*; (= *tax-free income*) Steuerfreibetrag *m*

taxation [tæk'seɪʃən] N Besteuerung *f*; (= *taxes also*) Steuern *pl*; **money acquired from ~** Steuereinnahmen *or* -einkünfte *pl*; **exempt from ~** nicht besteuert; *goods, income also* steuerfrei; **subject to ~** steuerpflichtig

tax: tax avoidance N Steuerumgehung *f*; **tax bill** N (*Brit inf*) Steuerbescheid *m*; **tax bracket** N Steuergruppe *f or* -klasse *f*; **tax burden** N Steuerlast *f*; **tax code, tax coding** N Steuerkennziffer *f*; **tax collecting** N Steuereinziehung *f*; **tax collector** N Finanz- *or* Steuerbeamte(r) *m*/-beamtin *f*; (*Bibl, Hist*) Zöllner *m*; **tax credit** N (auf Steuerschuld) anrechenbarer Betrag (*aus Verlusten bei Aktienverkauf etc*); **tax cut** N Steuersenkung *f*; **tax-deductible** ADJ (steuerlich *or* von der Steuer) absetzbar; *mortgage* steuerbegünstigt; **tax demand** N Steuerbescheid *m*; **tax disc** N (*Brit: on vehicle*) Steuermarke *f or* -plakette *f*; **tax dodge** N Trick *m* um Steuern zu umgehen; **tax dodger, tax evader** N Steuerhinterzieher(in) *m(f)*; (*who goes abroad*) Steuerflüchtling *m*; **tax evasion** N Steuerhinterziehung *f*; (*by going abroad*) Steuerflucht *f*; **tax-exempt** ADJ (*US*) *person* steuerbefreit; *business* abgabenfrei; *income, status* steuerfrei; **tax exile** N Steuerexil *nt*; (= *person*) Steuerflüchtling *m*; **tax fairness** N Steuergerechtigkeit *f*; **tax form** N Steuerformular *nt*; **tax-free** ADJ, ADV steuerfrei; **tax haven** N Steuerparadies *nt*

taxi ['tæksɪ] **N** Taxi *nt*; **to go by ~** mit dem Taxi fahren **VI** (*Aviat*) rollen; **the plane ~ed to a halt** das Flugzeug rollte aus

taxi: taxicab N (*esp US*) Taxi *nt*; **taxi dancer** N (*US*) Tanzdame *f*

taxidermist ['tæksɪdɜːmɪst] N Präparator(in) *m(f)*, Tierausstopfer(in) *m(f)*

taxidermy ['tæksɪdɜːmɪ] N Taxidermie *f*

taxi: taxi driver N Taxifahrer(in) *m(f)*; **taximeter** N Fahrpreisanzeiger *m*, Taxameter *m* (*form*)

tax: tax incentive N Steueranreiz *m*; **tax inspector** N (*Brit*) Finanzbeamte(r) *mf*

taxi: taxiplane N (*US*) Lufttaxi *nt*; **taxi rank** (*Brit*), **taxi stand** N (*esp US*) Taxistand *m*; **taxiway** N (*Aviat*) Rollbahn *f*

tax: tax loophole N Steuerschlupfloch *nt*; **tax loss** N Steuerausfall *m*; **taxman** ['tæksmæn] N Steuer- *or* Finanzbeamte(r) *m*; **the ~ gets 35%** das Finanzamt bekommt 35%; **taxonomy** [tæk'sɒnəmɪ] N Taxonomie *f*

tax: taxpayer N Steuerzahler(in) *m(f)*; **tax rebate** N Steuervergütung *f or* -rückzahlung *f*; **tax refund** N Steuer(rück)erstattung *f*; **tax relief** N Steuervergünstigung *f*; **~ of 5%** ein Steuernachlass *m* von 5%; **it qualifies for ~** das ist steuerbegünstigt; **tax return** N Steuererklärung *f*; **tax revenue** N Steueraufkommen *nt*; **tax shelter** N a (= *tax avoidance*) steuersparende Maßnahme b (*minimalized tax*) Steuerbegünstigung *f*; **tax structure** N Steuersystem *nt*; **tax system** N Steuerwesen *nt*, Steuer- *or* Besteuerungssystem *nt*; **tax write-off** N Steuerabschreibung *f*; **tax year** N Steuerjahr *nt*

TB *abbr of* **tuberculosis** Tb *f*, Tbc *f*

tba *abbr of* **to be arranged** *of* **to be announced** Einzelheiten werden noch bekannt gegeben

T-bar ['tiːbɑː] N Bügel *m*; (= *lift*) Schlepplift *m*; (*Tech*) T-Träger *m*

tbc *abbr of* **to be confirmed** noch zu bestätigen

T-bone steak ['tiːbəʊn'steɪk] N T-Bone-Steak *nt*

tbs(p) *abbr of* **tablespoonful(s)** *of* **tablespoon(s)** Essl.

TCP® N (*Brit*) *mildes Antiseptikum*

TD *abbr of* **touchdown**

T.D. (*US*) *abbr of* **Treasury Department**

tea [tiː] **N** a (= *substance, drink*) Tee *m*; **to make (the) ~** (den) Tee machen; **a cup of ~** eine Tasse Tee; **not for all the ~ in China** nicht um alles Gold der Welt b (*also* **tea plant**) Tee (-strauch) *m* c (*Brit*) (= *afternoon tea*) ≈ Kaffee und Kuchen; (= *meal*) Abendbrot *nt*; **we have ~ at five** wir essen um 5 Uhr Abendbrot *or* zu Abend

tea: tea bag N Teebeutel *m*; **tea ball** N (*esp US*) Tee-Ei *nt*, Teeei *nt*; **tea biscuit** N Butterkeks *m*; **tea boy** N Stift *m*; **tea break** N (*esp Brit*) Pause *f*; **tea caddy** N (*esp Brit*) Teebüchse *f or* -dose *f*; (= *dispenser*) Teespender *m*; **teacake** N (*Brit*) Rosinenbrötchen *nt*; **teacart** N (*US*) Teewagen *m*, Servierwagen *m*

---

teach [tiːtʃ] *vb: pret, ptp* **taught** **VT** *subject, person* unterrichten, lehren (*geh*); *animal* abrichten; **to ~ sth to sb, to ~ sb sth** jdm etw beibringen; (*teacher*) jdn in etw (*dat*) unterrichten, jdm Unterricht in etw (*dat*) geben; **to ~ sb to do sth** jdm beibringen, etw zu tun; **the accident taught me to be careful** durch diesen Unfall habe ich gelernt, vorsichtiger zu sein; **to ~ sb how to do sth** jdm zeigen, wie man etw macht, jdm etw beibringen; **you can't ~ somebody how to be happy** man kann niemanden lehren, glücklich zu sein; **he ~es French** er unterrichtet *or* gibt (*inf*) *or* lehrt (*geh*) Französisch; **who taught you to drive?** bei wem haben Sie Fahren gelernt?; **to ~ school** (*US*) Lehrer(in) sein/werden; **to ~ oneself sth** sich (*dat*) etw beibringen; **I taught myself to ride a bike** ich habe mir das Radfahren (selbst) beigebracht; **let that ~ you not to ...** lass dir diese eine Lehre sein, nicht zu ...; **that'll ~ him a thing or two!** da werden ihm die Augen aufgehen, da wird er erst mal sehen (*inf*); **it taught me a thing or two** es war sehr lehrreich, da habe ich einiges gelernt; **that'll ~ him!** das hat er nun davon!; **make her pay, that'll ~ her** lass sie bezahlen, das wird ihr eine Lehre sein; **that'll ~ you to break the speed limit/not to pay your insurance** das hast du (nun) davon, dass du die Geschwindigkeitsbegrenzung überschritten/die Versicherung nicht bezahlt hast; **I'll ~ you to speak to me like that!** ich werde dir schon austreiben (*inf*) *or* werde dich lehren, so mit mir zu sprechen!; **you can't ~ him anything about that** darüber können Sie ihm nichts Neues mehr erzählen

VI unterrichten, Unterricht geben; **he wants to ~** er möchte Lehrer werden; **he can't ~** (= *not allowed*) er darf nicht unterrichten; (= *no ability*) er gibt keinen guten Unterricht

N (*esp US inf*: = *teacher: as address*) Herr *m*, Frau *f*

teachability [ˌtiːtʃə'bɪlɪtɪ] N (*of pupil*) Lernfähigkeit *f*; (*of subject*) Lehrbarkeit *f*

teachable ['tiːtʃəbl] ADJ *animal, child* lernfähig; **music is a very ~ subject** Musik ist ein Fach, das sich gut unterrichten *or* lehren (*geh*) lässt; **this is not a ~ skill** diese Fertigkeit kann man niemandem beibringen; **things in life which are not ~** Dinge, die man niemandem beibringen kann

teacher ['tiːtʃə] N Lehrer(in) *m(f)*; *university* ~s Hochschullehrer *pl*, Lehrkräfte *pl* an (den) Universitäten (*form*); ~s of English, English ~s Englischlehrer *pl*; **she is a German ~** sie ist Deutschlehrerin

teacher-training [ˌtiːtʃə'treɪnɪŋ] N Lehrer(aus)-bildung *f*; (*for primary teachers*) Studium *nt or* Ausbildung *f* an einer pädagogischen Hochschule; (*for secondary teachers*) Referendarausbildung *f*; **~ course** Lehrerausbildung *f*; **~ college** (*for primary teachers*) pädagogische Hochschule; (*for secondary teachers*) Studienseminar *nt*

tea chest N (*Brit*) Kiste *f*

teach-in ['tiːtʃɪn] N Teach-in *nt*

teaching ['tiːtʃɪŋ] N a das Unterrichten *or* Lehren (*geh*); (*as profession*) der Lehrberuf; **to take up ~** den Lehrberuf ergreifen (*form*), Lehrer werden; **she enjoys ~** sie unterrichtet gern; **he is no good at ~** er ist kein guter Lehrer b (= *doctrine: also* **teachings**) Lehre *f*; **his ~ on this subject was somewhat vague** seine Ausführungen zu diesem Thema waren ziemlich vage

teaching: teaching aid N Lehr- *or* Unterrichtsmittel *nt*; **teaching diploma** N Lehrbefugnis *f*; **teaching hospital** N Ausbildungskrankenhaus *nt*; **teaching machine** N Lernmaschine *f*, Lehrmittel *nt* für den programmierten Unterricht; **teaching profession** N Lehrberuf *m*; (= *all teachers*) Lehrer *pl*; **teaching staff** N Lehrerkollegium *nt*, Lehrkörper *m* (*form*)

tea: tea cloth N (*Brit*) Geschirrtuch *nt*; **tea cosy**, (*US*) **tea cozy** N Teewärmer *m*; **teacup** N a Teetasse *f* → **storm** N a b (*also* **teacupful**) Tasse *f* (voll); **tea dance** N Tanztee

---

m; **tea garden** N Gartencafé *nt*; **teahouse** N Teehaus *nt*

teak [tiːk] N (= *wood*) Teak(holz) *nt*; (= *tree*) Teakbaum *m*

teakettle ['tiːketl] N Wasserkessel *m*

teal [tiːl] N *pl* - Krickente *f*

tea: tea lady N (*Brit*) *Frau, die in Büros etc für die Angestellten Tee zubereitet*; **tea leaf** N a Teeblatt *nt* → **read** ¹ VT b b (*Brit, inf,* = *thief*) Langfinger *m* (*inf*)

team [tiːm] **N** a Team *nt*; (*Sport*) Team *nt*, Mannschaft *f*; **football ~** Fußballmannschaft *f or* -elf *f*; **they work as a ~** sie arbeiten im *or* als Team; **they make a good ~** sie sind ein gutes Team *or* (*two also*) Gespann, sie arbeiten gut zusammen; **research ~** Forschungsgruppe *f or* -gemeinschaft *f or* -team *nt*; **a ~ of scientists** eine Gruppe *or* ein Team *nt* von Wissenschaftlern b (*of horses, oxen etc*) Gespann *nt* **VT** *horses, oxen* zusammenspannen; (*fig*) zusammentun

▶ **team up** **VI** (*people*) sich zusammentun (*with* mit); (= *join group*) sich anschließen (*with sb* jdm, an jdn); **I see that John and Mary have teamed up** John und Mary sehen jetzt (anscheinend) miteinander (*inf*) **VT** *sep* zusammenschließen

team: team captain N Mannschaftskapitän *m*; **team effort** N Teamarbeit *f*; **team game** N Mannschaftsspiel *nt*; **team leader** N Teamleiter(in) *m(f)*; **team-mate** N Mannschaftskamerad(in) *m(f)*; **team member** N Teammitglied *nt*; (*Sport also*) Mannschaftsmitglied *nt*; **team spirit** N Gemeinschaftsgeist *m*; (*Sport*) Mannschaftsgeist *m*

teamster ['tiːmstə] N a (*US*, = *truck driver*) Lastwagenfahrer(in) *m(f)*, LKW-Fahrer(in) *m(f)* b (*old Agr*) Fuhrmann *m*

teamwork ['tiːmwɜːk] N Gemeinschaftsarbeit *f*, Teamarbeit *f*, Teamwork *nt*

tea: tea party N Teegesellschaft *f*; **teapot** N Teekanne *f*

tear¹ [tɛə] *vb: pret* **tore**, *ptp* **torn** **VT** a *material, paper, dress* zerreißen; *flesh* verletzen, aufreißen; *hole* reißen; **I've torn a muscle** ich habe mir einen Muskel gezerrt; **the nail tore a gash in his arm** er hat sich (*dat*) an dem Nagel eine tiefe Wunde am Arm beigebracht; **to ~ sth in two** etw (in zwei Stücke *or* Hälften) zerreißen, etw in der Mitte durchreißen; **to ~ sth to pieces** etw in Stücke reißen; **the critics tore the play to pieces** die Kritiker haben das Stück total verrissen; **to ~ sth open** etw aufreißen; **that's torn it!** (*Brit fig inf*) das hat alles verdorben! b (= *pull away*) reißen; **the wind tore the tent from the pole** der Wind riss das Zelt von der Stange; **her child was torn from her/from her arms** das Kind wurde ihr entrissen/ihr aus den Armen gerissen; **he tore it out of my hand** er riss es mir aus der Hand; **to ~ one's hair (out)** sich (*dat*) die Haare raufen c (*fig, usu pass*) **a country torn by war** ein vom Krieg zerrissenes Land; **a heart torn with remorse** ein von Reue gequältes Herz; **to be torn between two things/people** zwischen zwei Dingen/Menschen hin und her gerissen sein; **she was completely torn** sie war innerlich zerrissen **VI** a (*material etc*) (zer)reißen; **her coat tore on a nail** sie zerriss sich (*dat*) den Mantel an einem Nagel; **~ along the dotted line** an der gestrichelten Linie abtrennen b (= *move quickly*) rasen; **to ~ past** vorbeirasen **N** (*in material etc*) Riss *m*

▶ **tear along** VI entlangrasen; **he tore along the street** er raste die Straße entlang *or* hinunter

▶ **tear apart** VT *sep place, house* völlig durcheinander bringen; *meat, flesh, country* zerreißen; **it tore me apart to leave you** es hat mir schier das Herz zerrissen, dich zu verlassen

▶ **tear at** VI +*prep obj* zerren an (+*dat*); **he tore at the walls of his cell** er verkrallte sich in die

Wände seiner Zelle; **the thorns tore at her hands** die Dornen zerkratzten ihr die Hände

▶ **tear away** VI davonrasen VT *sep wrapping* abreißen, wegreißen (*from* von); **to tear away sb's mask** jdm die Maske vom Gesicht reißen; **to tear sth away from sb** jdm etw wegreißen *or* entreißen (*geh*); **if you can tear yourself away from the paper** wenn du dich von der Zeitung losreißen kannst; **if you can tear him away from the party** wenn du ihn von der Party wegkriegen *or* loseisen kannst (*inf*)

▶ **tear down** VI hinunterrasen (*prep obj +acc*) VT *sep poster* herunterreißen; *house* abreißen, abbrechen; *trade barriers* abbauen

▶ **tear into** VI *+prep obj* **a** (*shell, rocket*) ein Loch reißen in (+*acc*); (*animals*) *deer etc* zerfleischen; *food* sich hermachen über (+*acc*); (*saw*) *wood* sich fressen durch **b** (= *attack physically*) herfallen über (+*acc*) **c** (= *attack verbally*) abkanzeln, zur Schnecke machen (*inf*); (*critic*) keinen guten Faden lassen an (+*dat*)

▶ **tear off** VI **a** (= *rush off*) wegrasen; **he tore off down the street** er raste die Straße hinunter **b** (*the carbon tears off*) die Durchschrift lässt sich abtrennen VT *sep label, wrapping, calendar leaf* abreißen; *cover* wegreißen; *clothes* herunterreißen; **please tear off this part and complete** bitte hier abtrennen und ausfüllen; **he tore a strip off me** (*Brit inf*) **he tore me off a strip** (*Brit inf*) er hat mich zur Minna *or* Schnecke gemacht (*inf*)

▶ **tear out** VI hinausrasen, wegrasen; **he tore out through the front door** er raste *or* rannte zur Vordertür hinaus VT *sep* (her)ausreißen (*of* aus); **the tree was torn out by the roots** der Baum wurde entwurzelt

▶ **tear up** VI angerast kommen; **he tore up the hill/road** er raste den Berg hinauf/die Straße entlang VT *sep* **a** *paper etc* zerreißen **b** (*fig, = cancel*) *contract, agreement* aufkündigen **c** (= *pull from ground*) *post, stake, plant* (her)ausreißen **d** (= *break surface of*) *ground* aufwühlen; *road* aufreißen

tear² [tɪəʳ] N Träne *f*; **in ~s** in Tränen aufgelöst; **wet with ~s** tränenfeucht; **there were ~s in her eyes** ihr standen Tränen in den Augen; **the news brought ~s to her eyes** als sie das hörte, stiegen ihr die Tränen in die Augen; **you are bringing ~s to my eyes** (*iro*) mir kommen die Tränen (*iro*); **the ~s were running down her cheeks** ihr Gesicht war tränenüberströmt; **smiling bravely through her ~s** unter Tränen tapfer lächelnd; **to laugh till the ~s come** Tränen lachen; **to weep ~s of joy** Freudentränen weinen *or* vergießen → **shed** ¹, **burst**

tearaway ['tɛərəweɪ] N (*Brit inf*) Rabauke *m* (*inf*); **I used to be a bit of a ~** ich war ein ziemlicher Rabauke (*inf*)

tear drop N Träne *f*

tearful ['tɪəfʊl] ADJ *look* tränenfeucht; *face* tränenüberströmt; *farewell, reunion* tränenreich; **he looked at her with ~ eyes** er sah sie mit Tränen in den Augen an; **to become ~** zu weinen anfangen; **she is a ~ person** ihr kommen leicht die Tränen; **there were a few ~ moments** es gab ein paar tränenvolle Augenblicke; **..., she said in a ~ voice** ..., sagte sie unter Tränen

tearfully ['tɪəfəlɪ] ADV *look* mit Tränen in den Augen; *say* unter Tränen

tear gas N Tränengas *nt*

tearing ['tɛərɪŋ] ADJ (*dated*) **to be in a ~ hurry** es fürchterlich *or* schrecklich eilig haben

tear: tear-jerker N (*inf*) Schmachtfetzen *m* (*inf*); **to be a ~** ein Schmachtfetzen sein (*inf*), auf die Tränendrüsen drücken (*inf*); **tear-jerking** ADJ (*inf*) **to be ~** (*film etc*) auf die Tränendrüsen drücken (*inf*)

tear-off ['tɛərɒf] ADJ *sheet, form* zum Abtrennen *or* Abreißen; **~ calendar** Abreißkalender *m*

tea: tearoom N (*Brit*) Teestube *f*, Café *nt*; **tea rose** N Teerose *f*

---

tear-stained ['tɪəsteɪnd] ADJ *face, person* verweint, verheult (*pej inf*), tränenverschmiert; *pillow, handkerchief* nass geweint

tease [tiːz] VT **a** *person* necken; *animal* reizen; (= *torment*) quälen; (= *make fun of: because of stutter etc*) aufziehen, hänseln (*about* wegen); (= *pull leg, have on*) auf den Arm nehmen (*inf*), veralbern (*inf*)
b = **tease out a**
c (= *raise nap on*) *cloth* kämmen
d (= *backcomb*) *hair* toupieren
e (= *ease gently*) **he ~d the red into the pocket/the rope through the crack** er manipulierte die rote Kugel ins Loch/schob das Seil geschickt durch den Spalt
VI **a** **give it back to her, don't ~** gib es ihr zurück und neck sie nicht, gibs ihr zurück und neck sie nicht **b** (= *joke*) Spaß machen
N (*inf, = person*) Scherzbold *m* (*inf*); **don't be a ~, give it back to her** neck sie nicht, gibs ihr zurück; **he's a real ~** ihm sitzt der Schalk im Nacken (*hum*), er ist ein kleiner Schäker (*inf*); **she's/he's just a ~** (*sexually*) sie/er geilt einen nur auf (*inf*)

▶ **tease out** VT *sep* **a** *fibres* kardieren, karden; *wool* krempeln, kämmen; *flax* hecheln; *tangles* auskämmen **b** (*fig*) *significant factors etc* herausdestillieren; *meaning* herauslesen; **to tease sth out of sth** etw aus etw herauspusseln (*inf*); **he managed to tease the information out of her** er hat ihr die Auskunft abgelockt

teasel ['tiːzl] N **a** (*Bot*) Karde *f* **b** (*Tech*) Karde *f*, Krempel *f*

teaser ['tiːzəʳ] N **a** (= *difficult question*) harte Nuss (*inf*); (= *riddle*) Denksportaufgabe *f* **b** (= *person*) Schelm *m*, Schäker(in) *m(f)* (*inf*); **don't be such a ~, tell me** neck mich nicht so, sags schon; **he's a real ~** ihm sitzt der Schalk im Nacken (*hum*); **she's/he's just a ~** (*sexually*) sie/er geilt einen nur auf (*inf*)

tea: tea service, tea set N Teeservice *nt*; **teashop** N Teestube *f*

teasing ['tiːzɪŋ] ADJ *voice, manner* neckend; *expression, smile* neckisch; (= *making fun*) hänselnd N (*of person*) Neckerei *f*; (*of animal*) Reizen *nt*; (= *tormenting*) Quälerei *f*; (= *mockery*) Hänselei *f*; (= *joking*) Veralbern *nt*

teasingly ['tiːzɪŋlɪ] ADV **a** (= *provocatively*) herausfordernd **b** (= *playfully*) neckend **c** (*sexually*) betörend, verführerisch

tea: teaspoon N **a** Teelöffel *m* **b** (*also* **teaspoonful**) Teelöffel *m* (voll); **tea strainer** N Teesieb *nt*

teat [tiːt] N (*of animal*) Zitze *f*; (*of woman*) Brustwarze *f*; (*Brit, on baby's bottle*) (Gummi)sauger *m*

tea: tea table N (*esp Brit*) **to lay the ~** den Tisch zum Tee/fürs Abendessen decken; **at the ~** beim Tee/Abendessen; **teatime** N (*Brit*) (*for afternoon tea*) Teestunde *f*; (= *mealtime*) Abendessen *nt*; **when is ~ in your house?** wann trinkt ihr Tee/esst ihr zu Abend?; **we'll talk about it at ~** wir werden uns beim Tee/beim Abendessen darüber unterhalten; **I'll meet you at ~** ich treffe Sie am späten Nachmittag; **tea towel** N (*Brit*) Geschirrtuch *nt*; **tea tray** N Tablett *nt*, Teebrett *nt*; **tea trolley** N Teewagen *m*, Servierwagen *m*; **tea urn** N Teebereiter *m*; **tea wagon** N (*US*) Teewagen *m*, Servierwagen *m*

teazel N = **teasel**

TEC N (*Brit*) abbr of **Training and Enterprise Council** staatliche Einrichtung zur Förderung der Zusammenarbeit zwischen Berufsschulen und Unternehmen

tech [tek] (*Brit*) abbr of **technical college**

techie ['tekɪ] N (*inf*) Technikfreak *m* (*inf*)

technical ['teknɪkəl] ADJ **a** (= *concerning technology and technique*) technisch; **~ hitch** technische Schwierigkeit, technisches Problem
b (*of particular branch*) fachlich, Fach-; *problems, vocabulary* fachspezifisch; *details* formal; **~ journal** Fachzeitschrift *f*; **~ dictionary** Fachwörterbuch *nt*; **~ term** Fachausdruck *m*, Terminus technicus *m* (*geh*); **~ terminology** Fachsprache

---

f; **~ question** (*Jur*) Verfahrensfrage *f*; **for ~ reasons** (*Jur*) aus verfahrenstechnischen Gründen; **the judgment was quashed on a ~ point** (*Jur*) das Urteil wurde aufgrund *or* auf Grund eines Verfahrensfehlers aufgehoben; **the book is a bit too ~ for me** in dem Buch sind mir zu viele Fachausdrücke; **he uses very ~ language** er benutzt sehr viele Fachausdrücke; **am I getting too ~ for you?** benutze ich zu viele Fachausdrücke?; **a 2L 54, if you want to be ~** ein 2L 54, um den Fachausdruck zu gebrauchen; **that's true, if you want to be ~** das stimmt schon, wenn mans genau nimmt

technical: technical college N (*esp Brit*) technische Fachschule; **technical defeat** N (*Mil*) rein formale Niederlage; **technical drawing** N technische Zeichnung; **technical institute** N technisches Institut

technicality [ˌteknɪˈkælɪtɪ] N **a** *no pl* **the ~ of the language** die Fülle von Fachausdrücken; **the ~ of his style** (= *complex style*) die formale Komplexität seines Stils; (= *technical terms*) sein Fachjargon *m* (*pej*), seine Fachterminologie **b** (= *technical detail, difficulty*) technische Einzelheit; (*fig, Jur*) Formsache *f*; **because of a ~** aufgrund *or* auf Grund einer Formsache; **that's just a ~** das ist bloß ein Detail

technical knockout N (*Boxing*) technischer K.o.

technically ['teknɪkəlɪ] ADV **a** technisch; **~, Windows is a graphical user interface** technisch gesehen ist Windows eine grafische Benutzeroberfläche **b** (= *concerned with specialist field*) vom Fachlichen her gesehen; **he spoke very ~** er benutzte sehr viele Fachausdrücke; **~ speaking** (= *in technical language*) fachsprachlich **c** (= *strictly speaking*) **you're right** genau genommen haben Sie recht; **~ speaking** (= *strictly speaking*) streng genommen

technical: technical offence N Verstoß *m*; **technical school** N (*Brit*) Gewerbeschule *f*, Fachschule *f*; (*US*: = *technical college*) technische Fachschule; **technical sergeant** N (*US*) Oberfeldwebel *m*

technical support N (*Comput*) (technischer) Support

technician [tekˈnɪʃən] N Techniker(in) *m(f)*; (= *skilled worker*) Facharbeiter(in) *m(f)*

Technicolor® ['teknɪˌkʌləʳ] N Technicolor® *nt*

technique [tekˈniːk] N Technik *f*; (= *method*) Methode *f*

techno ['teknəʊ] N (*Mus*) Techno *m*

technocracy [tekˈnɒkrəsɪ] N Technokratie *f*

technocrat ['teknəʊkræt] N Technokrat(in) *m(f)*

technocratic [ˌteknəʊˈkrætɪk] ADJ technokratisch

technological [ˌteknəˈlɒdʒɪkəl] ADJ technologisch; *details, information* technisch; **the ~ age** das Technologiezeitalter

technologically [ˌteknəˈlɒdʒɪklɪ] ADV (= *technically*) *advanced, backward, oriented* technologisch; **~, these cars are nothing new** vom technologischen Standpunkt aus (gesehen) ist an diesen Autos nichts Neues

technologist [tekˈnɒlədʒɪst] N Technologe *m*, Technologin *f*

technology [tekˈnɒlədʒɪ] N Technologie *f*; **the ~ of printing** die Technik des Druckens, die Drucktechnik; **computer/communications ~** Computer-/Kommunikationstechnik *f*, Computer-/Kommunikationstechnologie *f*; **University/College of Technology** Technische Universität/Fachhochschule; **the age of ~** das technische Zeitalter, das Zeitalter der Technik; **~ transfer** Technologietransfer *m*

technophobe ['teknəʊfəʊb] N Technikfeind *m*

technophobia [ˌteknəʊˈfəʊbɪə] N Technikfeindlichkeit *f*, Technophobie *f*

technophobic [ˌteknəʊˈfəʊbɪk] ADJ technikfeindlich

techy ADJ = **tetchy**

tectonics [tekˈtɒnɪks] N *sing* (*Geol*) Tektonik *f*

Ted [ted] N *dim of* **Edward**

ted [ted] N (*dated Brit inf*) Halbstarke(r) *m*

tedder ['tedə'] N Heuwender *m*

Teddy ['tedɪ] N *dim of* **Edward**

teddy (bear) N Teddy(bär) *m*

teddy boy N Halbstarke(r) *m*; (*referring to style of dress*) Teddyboy *m*

tedious ['tiːdɪəs] ADJ langweilig, öde; *behaviour* ermüdend; **such lists are ~ to read** solche Listen lesen sich langweilig

tediously ['tiːdɪəslɪ] ADV langweilig; **a ~ long journey** eine lange und langweilige Reise; **~ repetitive** sich ewig wiederholend

tediousness ['tiːdɪəsnɪs] N Lang(e)weile *f*; **his ~** seine Langweiligkeit

tedium ['tiːdɪəm] N Lang(e)weile *f*

tee¹ [tiː] (*Golf*) **N** Tee *nt* **VT** *ball* auf das Tee legen

▶ **tee off** VI einen Ball vom (ersten) Abschlag spielen

▶ **tee up** **VI** den Ball auf das Tee legen, aufteen (*spec*) **VT** *sep* auf das Tee legen

tee² N = T

tee-hee ['tiː'hiː] INTERJ (*giggle*) hihi; (*snigger*) ätsch

teem [tiːm] VI **a** (*with people, insects etc*) wimmeln (*with* von); (*with mistakes, information etc*) strotzen (*with* vor); **his mind was ~ing with ideas** in seinem Kopf wimmelte es nur so von Ideen **b** (= *pour*) **it's ~ing with rain** es regnet *or* gießt (*inf*) in Strömen; **he watched the rain ~ing down** er sah zu, wie der Regen vom Himmel strömte

teeming ['tiːmɪŋ] ADJ **a** *streets* von Menschen wimmelnd; *crowd* wuselnd; **the world's ~ millions** die Millionen und Abermillionen von Menschen (auf der Erde) **b** (= *pouring*) *rain* strömend

teen [tiːn] ADJ *esp US movie, magazine* für Teenager; *boy, girl* im Teenageralter; *pregnancy* im Teenageralter; **~ crime** Jugendkriminalität *f*; **the ~ years** die Teenagerjahre *pl*

teenage ['tiːneɪdʒ] ADJ Teenager-; *child, son, boy, girl* halbwüchsig, im Teenageralter; *pregnancy, suicide* unter Teenagern; **the ~ years** die Teenagerjahre *pl*

teenaged ['tiːneɪdʒd] ADJ im Teenageralter; **she is the mother of two ~ daughters** sie ist Mutter zweier Töchter im Teenageralter; **~ boy/girl** Teenager *m*

teenager ['tiːneɪdʒə'] N Teenager *m*

teener ['tiːnə'] N (*US*) = **teenager**

teens [tiːnz] PL **a** Teenageralter *nt*; **to be in one's ~** im Teenageralter sein; **to reach one's ~** ins Teenageralter kommen; **he is still in/barely out of his ~** er ist noch keine/knapp über zwanzig (Jahre alt) **b** (*inf*, = *teenagers*) Teenager *pl*

teenybopper ['tiːnɪˌbɒpə'] N Teenager *m*, Teeny *m* (*inf*); (= *girl also*) Pipimädchen *nt* (*pej inf*)

teeny(weeny) ['tiːnɪ('wiːnɪ)] ADJ (*inf*) winzig (klein), klitzeklein (*inf*); **just a ~ drop** nur ein ganz klein wenig

tee shirt N = **T-shirt**

teeter ['tiːtə'] VI **a** (= *balance unsteadily*) taumeln, schwanken; **to ~ on the brink** *or* **edge of sth** (*lit*) am Rand von etw taumeln; (*fig*) am Rand von etw sein **b** (*US*: = *seesaw*) wippen, schaukeln

teeterboard ['tiːtəˌbɔːd], **teeter-totter** ['tiːtəˌtɒtə'] N (*US*) Wippe *f*

teeth [tiːθ] *pl of* **tooth**

teethe [tiːð] VI zahnen

teething ['tiːðɪŋ] N Zahnen *nt*

teething: teething ring N Beißring *m*; **teething troubles** PL (*Brit fig*) Kinderkrankheiten *pl*

teetotal [ˌtiː'təʊtl] ADJ *person* abstinent; *party etc* ohne Alkohol; **to be ~** abstinent sein, Antialkoholiker(in) *m(f)* sein

teetotaler N (*US*) = **teetotaller**

teetotalism [ˌtiː'təʊtəlɪzəm] N Abstinenz *f*

teetotaller, (*US*) **teetotaler** [ˌtiː'təʊtlə'] N Abstinenzler(in) *m(f)*, Nichttrinker(in) *m(f)*, Antialkoholiker(in) *m(f)*

TEFL *abbr of* **Teaching of English as a Foreign Language**

TEFL, TESL, TESOL, ELT

TEFL (**Teaching of English as a Foreign Language**) und **EFL** (**English as a Foreign Language**) sind Begriffe, die sich auf das Englisch beziehen, das Menschen aus nicht englischsprachigen Ländern gelehrt, bzw. von diesen gelernt wird.

TESL (**Teaching of English as a Second Language**) und **ESL** (**English as a Second Language**) betreffen dagegen Englisch, das von Menschen gelernt wird, die in einem englischsprachigen Land leben, deren Muttersprache allerdings nicht Englisch ist, wie dies z. B. bei ethnischen Minderheiten der Fall ist. Im ESL-Unterricht wird versucht, den kulturellen Hintergrund und die Muttersprache der Schüler in den Lernprozess mit einzubeziehen.

TESOL (**Teaching of English as a Second** or **Other Language**) ist der allgemeine amerikanische Begriff sowohl für **TEFL** als auch für **TESL**. **ESOL** (**English for Speakers of Other Languages**) ist das Äquivalent zu **EFL** und **ESL**.

ELT (**English Language Teaching**) ist der allgemeine Begriff für das Unterrichten von Englisch als Fremd- oder zweite Sprache.

Teflon® ['teflɒn] N Teflon® *nt*

Tehran [teə'rɑːn] N Teheran *nt*

tel *abbr of* **telephone (number)** Tel.

telebanking [ˈtelɪˌbæŋkɪŋ] N Homebanking *nt*, Telebanking *nt*

telecamera [ˈtelɪˌkæmərə] N Fernsehkamera *f*

telecast ['telɪkɑːst] **N** Fernsehsendung *f* **VT** im Fernsehen übertragen *or* senden

telecaster ['telɪkɑːstə'] N Fernsehjournalist(in) *m(f)*

telecommunications [ˌtelɪkəmjuːnɪ'keɪʃənz] **a** *pl* Fernmeldewesen *nt* **b** *sing* (= *science*) Fernmeldetechnik *f*

telecommute ['telɪkəmjuːt] VI Telearbeit machen

telecommuter ['telɪkəmjuːtə'] N jd, der Telearbeit macht

telecommuting ['telɪkəmjuːtɪŋ] N Telearbeit *f*

teleconference ['telɪkɒnfərəns] N Telekonferenz *f*

teleconferencing ['telɪkɒnfərənsɪŋ] N Telekonferenzschaltung *f*

Telecopier® ['telɪˌkɒpɪə'] N Fernkopierer *m*, Telekopierer *m*

telecopy ['telɪkɒpɪ] N Fernkopie *f*, Telekopie *f*

telecottage ['telɪkɒtɪdʒ] N (*esp Brit*) (ländliches) Computerzentrum (*für jedermann*); (*for teleworking*) Telearbeit-Center *nt*

telediagnosis ['telɪˌdaɪəg'nəʊsɪs] N (*Med*) Ferndiagnose *f*

telegram ['telɪgræm] N Telegramm *nt*

telegrammatic [ˌtelɪgrə'mætɪk] ADJ im Telegrammstil

telegraph ['telɪgrɑːf] **N** **a** (= *apparatus*) Telegraf *m* **b** (= *message*) Telegramm *nt* **VT** telegrafisch übermitteln; *message also* telegrafieren; *person* telegrafieren (+*dat*); (*fig*) *one's intentions, plans etc* offenlegen **VI** telegrafieren

telegraphese [ˌtelɪgrɑː'fiːz] N Telegrammstil *m*

telegraphic [ˌtelɪ'græfɪk] ADJ telegrafisch; *address, style, speech* Telegramm-; **by ~ transfer** per Telegramm

telegraphically [ˌtelɪ'græfɪkəlɪ] ADV (= *concisely*) knapp; **she writes almost ~** sie schreibt fast im Telegrammstil

telegraphist [tɪ'legrəfɪst] N Telegrafist(in) *m(f)*

telegraph: telegraph pole N (*Brit*) Telegrafenmast *m or* -stange *f*; **telegraph wire** N Telegrafendraht *m or* -leitung *f*; (*under ground*) Telegrafenkabel *nt*

telegraphy [tɪ'legrəfɪ] N Telegrafie *f*

telekinesis [ˌtelɪkɪ'niːsɪs] N Telekinese *f*

telemarketing ['telɪmɑːkɪtɪŋ] N Telemarketing *nt*, Telefonverkauf *m*

telemessage ['telɪmesɪdʒ] N (*Brit*) Telegramm *nt*

telemeter ['telɪmiːtə'] N Entfernungsmesser *m*, Telemeter *nt*

telemetry [te'lemɪtrɪ] N Telemetrie *f*, Fernmessung *f*

teleological [ˌtelɪə'lɒdʒɪkl] ADJ teleologisch

teleology [ˌtelɪ'ɒlədʒɪ] N Teleologie *f*

teleordering ['telɪˌɔːdərɪŋ] N Teleordern *nt*

telepathic [ˌtelɪ'pæθɪk] ADJ telepathisch; **you must be ~!** du musst ja ein Hellseher sein!; **I'm not ~!** ich kann doch keine Gedanken lesen! (*inf*)

telepathically [ˌtelɪ'pæθɪkəlɪ] ADV *influence, communicate* telepathisch

telepathist [tɪ'lepəθɪst] N Telepath(in) *m(f)*; (= *believer in telepathy*) Telepathiegläubige(r) *mf*

telepathy [tɪ'lepəθɪ] N Telepathie *f*

telephone ['telɪfəʊn] **N** Telefon *nt*, Fernsprecher *m* (*form*); **there's somebody on the ~ for you, you're wanted on the ~** Sie werden am Telefon verlangt; **are you on the ~?** (*Brit*) **have you got a ~?** haben Sie Telefon?; (= *can you be reached by telephone?*) sind Sie telefonisch zu erreichen?; **he's on the ~** (= *is using the telephone*) er telefoniert gerade; (= *wants to speak to you*) er ist am Telefon; **by ~** telefonisch; **I've just been on the ~ to him** ich habe eben mit ihm telefoniert; **I'll get on the ~ to her** ich werde sie anrufen; **we arranged it by ~** *or* **over the ~** wir haben es telefonisch vereinbart; **I heard a strange noise down the ~** ich hörte ein merkwürdiges Geräusch im Telefon; **to shout down the ~** ins Telefon brüllen
VT anrufen; *message, reply* telefonisch mitteilen *or* übermitteln; **he ~d the news (through) to his mother** er rief seine Mutter an, um ihr die Nachricht mitzuteilen; **would you ~ the office to say ...** würden Sie im Büro *or* das Büro anrufen und sagen ...; **~ this number for further information** weitere Informationen unter folgender Telefonnummer, für weitere Informationen rufen Sie bitte diese Nummer an
VI anrufen, telefonieren; (= *make telephone call*) telefonieren; **to ~ for an ambulance/a taxi** einen Krankenwagen/ein Taxi rufen

▶ **telephone back** VTI *sep* = **phone back**

▶ **telephone in** VTI = **phone in**

telephone *in cpds* Telefon-, Fernsprech- (*form*); **telephone answering machine** N Anrufbeantworter *m*; **telephone banking** N Telefonbanking *nt*; **telephone bill** N Telefonrechnung *f*; **telephone book** N Telefonbuch *nt*; **telephone box**, (*US*) **telephone booth** N Telefonzelle *f*; **telephone call** N Telefongespräch *nt*, Telefonanruf *m*; **telephone charges** PL Telefongebühren *pl*; **telephone directory** N Telefonbuch *nt*; **telephone exchange** N (*esp Brit*) Fernsprechamt *nt*, Vermittlungsstelle *f* (*form*); **telephone kiosk** N Telefonzelle *f*, Sprechzelle *f* (*form*); **telephone line** N Telefonleitung *f*; **telephone message** N telefonische Nachricht; **telephone network** N Telefonnetz *nt*; **telephone number** N Telefonnummer *f*, Rufnummer *f* (*form*); **~s** (*fig inf*, = *large amount*) riesige Summen *pl*; **telephone operator** N (*esp US*) Telefonist(in) *m(f)*; **telephone sex** N Telefonsex *m*; **~ line** Telefonsexdienst *m*; **telephone subscriber** PL Fernsprechteilnehmer(in) *m(f)*

telephonic [ˌtelɪ'fɒnɪk] ADJ telefonisch; **~ technology** Telefontechnik *f*

telephonically [tɪlɪˈfɒnɪkəlɪ] ADV fernsprech-technisch; (= by telephone) telefonisch

telephonist [tɪˈlefənɪst] N (Brit) Telefonist(in) m(f)

telephony [tɪˈlefənɪ] N Fernsprechwesen nt

telephotograph [ˌtelɪˈfəʊtəɡrɑːf] N (Telec) durch Bildtelegrafie übertragenes Foto

telephoto (lens) [ˈtelɪˌfəʊtəʊ(ˈlenz)] N Teleobjektiv nt

teleport [ˈtelɪpɔːt] VT (Sci-Fi) teleportieren

teleprinter [ˈtelɪˌprɪntə'] N Fernschreiber m

Teleprompter® [ˈtelɪˌprɒmptə'] N (esp US) Teleprompter m

telerecord [ˌtelɪrɪˈkɔːd] VT fürs Fernsehen aufzeichnen

telerecording [ˌtelɪrɪˈkɔːdɪŋ] N Fernsehaufzeichnung f

telesales [ˈtelɪseɪlz] N sing or pl Telefonverkauf m, Verkauf m per Telefon

telescope [ˈtelɪskəʊp] **N** Teleskop nt, Fernrohr nt **VI** (also **telescope together**, train carriages) sich ineinander schieben; (aerial, umbrella) sich ineinander schieben lassen VT (also **telescope together**) ineinander schieben; umbrella, aerial zusammenschieben; (fig) komprimieren

telescopic [ˌtelɪˈskɒpɪk] ADJ aerial etc ausziehbar, zusammenschiebbar; view teleskopisch; ~ **arm** Teleskoparm m

telescopic: telescopic lens N Fernrohrlinse f; **telescopic sight** N Zielfernrohr nt; **telescopic umbrella** N Taschenschirm m, Knirps® m

teleshopping [ˈtelɪˌʃɒpɪŋ] N Teleshopping nt

Teletext® [ˈtelɪtekst] N Videotext m

telethon [ˈtelɪˌθɒn] N sehr lange Fernsehsendung, in deren Verlauf Spenden für wohltätige Zwecke gesammelt werden, Fernsehspendenaktion f

Teletype® [ˈtelɪtaɪp] N (US, = apparatus) Fernschreiber m; (= message) Fernschreiben nt, Telex nt

teletypewriter [ˌtelɪˈtaɪpraɪtə'] N (US) Fernschreiber m

televangelism [ˌtelɪˈvændʒəlɪzəm] N , no pl (esp US) Bekehrungssendungen im Fernsehen

televangelist [ˌtelɪˈvændʒəlɪst] N (esp US) Fernsehevangelist(in) m(f)

televise [ˈtelɪvaɪz] VT (im Fernsehen) senden or übertragen; **~d debate** Fernsehdebatte f

television [ˈtelɪˌvɪʒən] N Fernsehen nt; (= set) Fernseher m, Fernsehapparat m; **to watch ~** fernsehen; **to be on ~** im Fernsehen kommen; **have you ever been on ~?** bist du schon einmal im Fernsehen gewesen?; **what's on ~ tonight?** was gibt es heute Abend im Fernsehen?; **jobs in ~** Stellen pl beim Fernsehen

television in cpds Fernseh-; **television camera** N Fernsehkamera f; **television licence** N (Brit) Bescheinigung über die Entrichtung der Fernsehgebühren **to pay one's ~** die Fernsehgebühren bezahlen; **television personality** N bekannte Fernsehpersönlichkeit; **television rights** PL Übertragungsrechte pl, Fernsehrechte pl; **television screen** N Bildschirm m, Mattscheibe f (inf); **television set** N Fernsehapparat m, Fernsehgerät nt, Fernseher m; **television studio** N Fernsehstudio nt; **television viewer** N Fernsehzuschauer(in) m(f)

televisual [ˌtelɪˈvɪʒʊəl] ADJ Fernseh-, TV-; **to make ~ history** Fernsehgeschichte or TV-Geschichte machen

telework [ˈtelɪwɜːk] VI Telearbeit machen

teleworker [ˈtelɪwɜːkə'] N Telearbeiter(in) m(f)

teleworking [ˈtelɪwɜːkɪŋ] N , no pl Telearbeit f

telex [ˈteleks] **N** Telex nt; (= message also) Fernschreiben nt **VT** message telexen, per Telex mitteilen; person ein Telex schicken (+dat)

tell [tel] pret, ptp told **VT a** (= relate) story, experiences, adventures erzählen (sb sth, sth to sb jdm etw acc); (= inform, say, announce) sagen (sb

sth jdm etw acc); **to ~ lies** lügen; **to ~ tales** petzen (inf); **to ~ fortunes** wahrsagen; **to ~ sb's fortune** jdm wahrsagen, jdm die Zukunft deuten; **to ~ the future** wahrsagen, die Zukunft deuten; **to ~ sb a secret** jdm ein Geheimnis anvertrauen or (give away) verraten; **to ~ sb about** or **of sth** jdm von etw erzählen; **I told my friend/boss about what had happened** ich erzählte meinem Freund/berichtete meinem Chef, was geschehen war; **... or so I've been told** ... so hat man es mir jedenfalls gesagt or erzählt; **I can't ~ you how pleased I am** ich kann Ihnen gar nicht sagen, wie sehr mich das freut; **you can't ~ her anything** (= she can't keep a secret) man kann ihr (aber auch) nichts sagen or anvertrauen; (= she's a know-all) sie lässt sich (dat) nichts sagen; **to ~ sb the way** jdm den Weg sagen; **could you ~ me the way to the station, please?** könn(t)en Sie mir bitte sagen, wie ich zum Bahnhof komme?; **don't let me have to ~ you that again** ich will dir das nicht noch einmal sagen müssen; **(I'll) ~ you what, let's go to the cinema** weißt du was, gehen wir doch ins Kino!; **don't ~ me you can't come!** sagen Sie bloß nicht, dass Sie nicht kommen können!; **I won't do it, I ~ you!** und ich sage dir, das mache ich nicht!; **let me ~ you that ...** ich kann Ihnen sagen, dass ..., lassen Sie sich von mir sagen, dass ...; **it was cold, I can ~ you** ich kann dir sagen, das war vielleicht kalt!; **I told you so** ich habe es (dir) ja gesagt; **~ me another!** nicht möglich!, wers glaubt! (inf); **that ~s all I need to know** das sagt mir alles; **that ~s me a lot** das sagt mir allerlei

b (= distinguish, discern) erkennen; **to ~ the time** die Uhr kennen; **to ~ the time by the sun** die Zeit an der Sonne ablesen; **to ~ the difference** den Unterschied sehen/fühlen/schmecken etc; **you can ~ that he's clever/getting worried** man sieht or merkt, dass er intelligent ist/sich Sorgen macht; **we couldn't ~ much from his letter** wir konnten aus seinem Brief nicht viel entnehmen; **you can't ~ whether it's moving** man kann nicht sagen or sehen, ob es sich bewegt; **I couldn't ~ if he had been in a fight or had just fallen** ich hätte nicht sagen können, ob er in einem Kampf verwickelt oder nur hingefallen war; **it was impossible to ~ where the bullet had entered** es war unmöglich festzustellen, wo die Kugel eingetreten war; **to ~ sb/sth by sth** jdn/etw an etw (dat) erkennen; **I can't ~ butter from margarine** ich kann Butter nicht von Margarine unterscheiden; **to ~ right from wrong** wissen, was Recht und Unrecht ist, Recht von Unrecht unterscheiden → **apart**

c (= know, be sure) wissen; **how can I ~ that?** wie soll ich das wissen?; **how could I ~ that?** wie hätte ich das wissen können?; **how can I ~ that he will do it?** wie kann ich sicher sein, dass er es tut?

d (= order) sagen (sb jdm); **we were told to bring sandwiches with us** es wurde uns gesagt, dass wir belegte Brote mitbringen sollten; **~ him to stop singing** sagen Sie ihm, er soll aufhören zu singen; **don't you ~ me what to do!** Sie haben mir nicht zu sagen, was ich tun soll!; **I told you not to do that** ich habe dir doch gesagt, du sollst das nicht tun!; **do as** or **what you are told!** tu, was man dir sagt!

e (old: = count) **to ~ one's beads** den Rosenkranz beten

VI +indir obj es sagen (+dat); **I won't ~ you again** ich sage es dir nicht noch einmal; **you know what? – don't ~ me, let me guess** weißt du was? – sags mir nicht, lass mich raten; **she wouldn't be told** sie hat sich (ja) nichts sagen lassen; **you're ~ing me!** das kann man wohl sagen!, wem sagen Sie das!

VI a (= discern, be sure) wissen; **as** or **so far as one can ~** soweit man weiß; **who can ~?** wer weiß?; **how can I ~?** (= how should I know) woher soll ich das wissen?; **how will I be able to ~?** wie kann ich das erkennen or wissen?; **no-one can/could ~** niemand kann/konnte das sagen, das weiß/wusste keiner; **you never can ~, you can never ~** man kann nie wissen

b (= talk, tell tales of) sprechen; **his face told of his sorrow** aus seinem Gesicht sprach Kummer; **that would be ~ing!** das kann ich nicht verraten; **promise you won't ~** du musst versprechen, dass du nichts sagst

c (= have effect) sich bemerkbar machen; **his age told against him** (in applying for job) sein Alter war ein Nachteil für ihn; (in competition) sein Alter machte sich bemerkbar; **character always ~s in the end** zum Schluss schlägt doch die Veranlagung durch; **a boxer who makes every punch ~** ein Boxer, bei dem jeder Schlag sitzt

▶ **tell off** VT sep **a** (inf, = scold) ausschimpfen, schelten (for wegen); **he told me off for being late** er schimpfte (mich aus), weil ich zu spät kam **b** (Mil etc) abkommandieren (for zu)

▶ **tell on** VI +prep obj **a** (inf, = inform on) verpetzen (inf) **b** (= have a bad effect on) sich bemerkbar machen bei; **the pressure is beginning to tell on her** der Druck, der auf ihr lastet, macht sich langsam bemerkbar

teller [ˈtelə'] N **a** (in bank) Kassierer(in) m(f) **b** (= vote counter) Stimmenauszähler(in) m(f) **c** (of story) Erzähler(in) m(f)

telling [ˈtelɪŋ] **ADJ** (= effective) wirkungsvoll; argument also schlagend; blow (lit, fig) empfindlich; (= revealing) aufschlussreich; blush verräterisch **N a** (= narration) Erzählen nt; **it loses a lot in the ~** das kann man gar nicht so schön erzählen **b there is no ~ what he may do** man kann nicht sagen or wissen, was er tut; **there's no ~** das lässt sich nicht sagen; **there's no ~ how long the talks could last** es lässt sich nicht absehen, wie lange die Gespräche dauern werden; **there's never any ~ with him** bei ihm lässt sich das nie sagen

telling-off [ˌtelɪŋˈɒf] N (Brit inf) Standpauke f (inf); **to give sb a good ~** jdn kräftig ausschimpfen, jdm eine (kräftige) Standpauke halten (inf); **to get a good ~** kräftig ausgeschimpft werden, eine Standpauke bekommen (inf)

telltale [ˈtelteɪl] **N a** (Brit) Petzer m, Petze f **b** (Tech) Kontrolllicht nt, Kontrolllampe f **ADJ** attr verräterisch

tellurium [teˈlʊərɪəm] N (Chem) Tellur nt

telly [ˈtelɪ] N (Brit, inf) Fernseher m, Glotze f (inf); **on ~** im Fernsehen; **to watch ~** fernsehen → also television

temazepam [tɪˈmæzɪpæm] N zu den Benzodiazepinen gehörendes Schlafmittel

temerity [tɪˈmerɪtɪ] N Kühnheit f, Unerhörtheit f (pej)

temp[1] **a** abbr of temporary **b** abbr of temperature Temp

temp[2] [temp] **N** Aushilfskraft m **VI** als Aushilfskraft arbeiten

temper [ˈtempə'] **N a** (= disposition) Wesen nt, Naturell nt; (= angry mood) Wut f; **~ tantrum** Wutanfall m; **to be in a ~** wütend sein; **to be in a good/bad ~** guter/schlechter Laune sein; **he was not in the best of ~s** er war nicht gerade bester Laune; **she's got a quick ~** sie kann sehr jähzornig sein; **she's got a terrible/foul/vicious ~** sie kann sehr unangenehm/ausfallend/tückisch werden; **what a ~ that child has!** was dieses Kind für Wutanfälle hat!; **to be in a (bad) ~ with sb/over** or **about sth** auf jdn/wegen einer Sache (gen) wütend sein; **to lose one's ~** die Beherrschung verlieren (with sb bei jdm); **to keep one's ~** sich beherrschen (with sb bei jdm); **~, ~!** aber, aber, wer wird denn gleich so zornig werden!; **to fly into a ~** einen Wutanfall bekommen, in die Luft gehen (inf); **a fit of ~** ein Wutanfall m; **to put sb in a ~, to get sb's ~ up** jdn zur Weißglut bringen, jdn wütend machen; **he has quite a ~** er kann ziemlich aufbrausen; **to be out of ~** (old) verstimmt sein, übel gelaunt sein; **I hope he can control his ~** ich hoffe, er kann sich unter Kontrolle halten **b** (of metal) Härte f, Härtegrad m **VT a** metal tempern **b** (old Mus) temperieren (old)

c *(fig) action, passion* mäßigen; *criticism* mildern; *enthusiasm* zügeln; **to ~ justice with mercy** bei aller Gerechtigkeit Milde walten lassen; **to be ~ed by concern/realism** mit Fürsorge/Realismus vermischt sein

tempera ['tempərə] N Temperafarbe *f*; **to paint in ~** in Tempera malen

temperament ['tempərəmənt] N **a** (= *disposition*) Veranlagung *f*; *(of a people)* Temperament *nt*; **his ~ isn't suited to that job** er ist von seiner Veranlagung her nicht für diese Stelle geeignet; **he has an artistic ~** er ist eine Künstlernatur; **their ~s are quite different** sie sind völlig unterschiedlich veranlagt; **he has a happy ~** er hat ein fröhliches Wesen or Naturell **b** *no art* (= *temper, excitability*) Temperament *nt*; **she was given to fits of ~** sie war launisch

temperamental [,tempərə'mentl] ADJ **a** temperamentvoll, launenhaft *(pej)*; **~ outburst** Temperamentsausbruch *m* **b** *machine, car* launisch *(hum)*; **to be ~** Mucken haben *(inf)*, launisch sein *(hum)* **c** (= *caused by temperament*) *inability, unsuitability* veranlagungsmäßig; *laziness etc* angeboren

temperamentally [,tempərə'mentəlɪ] ADV **a** *behave etc* temperamentvoll, launenhaft *(pej)* **b** *(of machine, car)* launisch *(hum)* **c** (= *as regards disposition*) charakterlich, veranlagungsmäßig; **to be ~ averse to sth** einer Sache *(dat)* vom Temperament her abgeneigt sein

temperance ['tempərəns] N **a** (= *moderation*) Mäßigung *f*; *(in speech etc)* Zurückhaltung *f*; *(in eating, drinking)* Maßhalten *nt*, Mäßigung *f* **b** (= *teetotalism*) Enthaltsamkeit *f*, Abstinenz *f*

temperance: temperance hotel N alkoholfreies Hotel; **temperance movement** N Temperenzler- or Temperenzbewegung *f*; **temperance society** N Temperenzverein *m* or -gesellschaft *f*

temperate ['tempərɪt] ADJ **a** *climate* gemäßigt; *forest* mit gemäßigtem Klima; *(Bot, Zool) plant, animal* in gemäßigten Klimazonen beheimatet; **the Temperate Zone** die gemäßigte Klimazone **b** *person, language* gemäßigt; *(in eating, demands)* maßvoll

temperature ['temprɪtʃə'] N Temperatur *f*; *(Med, above normal temperature also)* Fieber *nt*; **water boils at a ~ of 100° C** Wasser kocht bei einer Temperatur von 100° C; **to take sb's ~** jds Temperatur messen, bei jdm Fieber messen; **he has a ~** er hat Fieber; **he has a slight/high ~**, **he's running a slight/high ~** er hat erhöhte Temperatur/hohes Fieber; **he has a ~ of 39° C** er hat 39° Fieber

temperature: temperature chart N *(Med)* Fiebertabelle *f*; (= *curve of graph*) Fieberkurve *f*; **temperature gauge** N Temperaturanzeiger *m*; **temperature-sensitive** ADJ temperaturempfindlich

tempered ['tempəd] ADJ **a** *steel* gehärtet **b** *(Mus)* temperiert

-tempered ADJ *suf* ... gelaunt; **good-tempered** gut gelaunt; **bad-tempered** schlecht gelaunt

tempest ['tempɪst] N *(liter)* Sturm *m* *(also fig)*, Unwetter *nt*; **it was a ~ in a teapot** *(US)* es war ein Sturm im Wasserglas

tempestuous [tem'pestjʊəs] ADJ **a** *(lit liter) winds* stürmisch; *sea* tobend, stürmisch **b** *(fig)* stürmisch; *argument, rage* heftig; *speech* leidenschaftlich

tempestuously [,tem'pestjʊəslɪ] ADV *(lit liter, fig)* heftig

tempestuousness [,tem'pestjʊəsnɪs] N *(lit liter, fig)* Heftigkeit *f*; *(of sea)* Aufgewühltheit *f*

temping agency ['tempɪŋ,eɪdʒənsɪ] N Zeitarbeitsunternehmen *nt*

Templar ['templə'] N *(also* **Knight Templar***)* Tempelherr *m*, Templer *m*

template, templet ['templɪt] N Schablone *f*; *(fig)* Vorlage *f*

temple[1] ['templ] N *(Rel)* Tempel *m*

temple[2] N *(Anat)* Schläfe *f*

templet N = **template**

tempo ['tempəʊ] N *(Mus, fig)* Tempo *nt*

temporal ['tempərəl] ADJ **a** zeitlich; *(Gram)* Zeit-, temporal; **~ adverb** Zeitadverb *nt* **b** *(Rel)* weltlich

temporal bone N Schläfenbein *nt*

temporarily ['tempərərɪlɪ] ADV vorübergehend, für einige Zeit

temporariness ['tempərərɪnɪs] N vorübergehender Charakter

temporary ['tempərərɪ] ADJ vorübergehend; *job also* für kurze Zeit, befristet; *arrangement also, method, building, road surface* provisorisch; *powers* zeitweilig, befristet; *licence* zeitlich begrenzt; **our new secretary is only ~** unsere neue Sekretärin ist nur vorübergehend or für einige Zeit hier; **I'm only here for a ~ stay** ich bin nur für kurze Zeit hier; **she is a ~ resident here** sie wohnt hier nur vorübergehend; **~ worker** Zeitarbeiter(in) *m(f)*; **~ staff** Zeitpersonal *nt*; **~ injunction** *(Jur)* einstweilige Verfügung **N** Aushilfe *f*, Aushilfskraft *f*

temporize ['tempəraɪz] VI (= *delay*) ausweichen (um Zeit zu gewinnen), Verzögerungstaktiken anwenden; **to ~ with sb** jdn hinhalten

temporizer ['tempəraɪzə'] N Verzögerungstaktiker *m*

tempt [tempt] VT **a** (= *entice*) in Versuchung führen; *(successfully)* verführen, verleiten; **to ~ sb to do** or **into doing sth** jdn dazu verleiten or verführen, etw zu tun; **don't ~ me** bring or führ mich nicht in Versuchung!; **one is ~ed to believe that ...** man möchte fast glauben, dass ...; **I am very ~ed to accept** ich bin sehr versucht anzunehmen; **try and ~ her to eat a little** versuchen Sie, ob Sie sie nicht dazu bringen können, etwas zu essen; **may I ~ you to have a little more wine?** kann ich Sie noch zu etwas Wein überreden?; **are you sure you won't come? – no, I won't be ~ed!** willst du bestimmt nicht mitkommen? – nein, ich bleibe hart; **to ~ fate** or **providence** *(fig)* sein Schicksal herausfordern; *(in words)* den Teufel an die Wand malen **b** *(Rel)* versuchen, in Versuchung führen; **the devil ~s us** der Teufel führt uns in Versuchung

temptation [temp'teɪʃən] N Versuchung *f* *(also Rel)*, Verlockung *f*; **to put ~ in sb's way** jdn in Versuchung führen; **lead us not into ~** *(Bibl)* führe uns nicht in Versuchung *(Bibl)*; **to yield to** or **give way to ~** der Versuchung erliegen

tempter ['temptə'] N Versucher *m*, Verführer *m*; **the Tempter** *(Rel)* der Versucher

tempting ['temptɪŋ] ADJ verlockend, verführerisch; **it is ~ to say that ...** es ist verlockend zu sagen, dass ...

temptingly ['temptɪŋlɪ] ADV verlockend, verführerisch

temptress ['temptrɪs] N Verführerin *f*

ten [ten] ADJ zehn; **the Ten Commandments** die Zehn Gebote; **~ to one he won't come** (ich wette) zehn gegen or zu eins, dass er nicht kommt; **nine out of ~ people would agree with you** neun von zehn Leuten würden Ihnen zustimmen; **a packet of ~ (cigarettes)** eine Zehnerpackung (Zigaretten) **N** Zehn *f*; **~s** *(Math)* Zehner *pl*; **to count in ~s** in Zehnern zählen; **you can only buy them in ~s** man kann sie nur in Zehnerpackungen kaufen → *also* **six**

tenability [,tenə'bɪlɪtɪ] N *(Mil: of position)* Haltbarkeit *f*; *(fig, of opinion, theory also)* Vertretbarkeit *f*

tenable ['tenəbl] ADJ **a** *(Mil) position* haltbar; *(fig) opinion, theory* haltbar, vertretbar **b** *pred* **a post ~ for life** eine Lebensstellung, eine Stelle auf Lebenszeit; **a post ~ for two years** eine auf zwei Jahre befristete Stelle

tenacious [tɪ'neɪʃəs] ADJ zäh, hartnäckig; *character, person also* beharrlich; *memory* unschlagbar; **to be ~ in doing sth** etw hartnäckig or eisern tun; **the disease had a ~ hold on ...** die Krankheit hielt ... in eisernem Griff; **to be ~ of sth** *(form)* zäh an etw *(dat)* festhalten; **to be ~ of life** *(form)* **to have a ~ hold on life** zäh am Leben hängen

tenaciously [tɪ'neɪʃəslɪ] ADV zäh, hartnäckig; **she held ~ to her principles** sie hielt zäh an ihren Prinzipien fest; **the dog held on ~ to the bone** der Hund hielt den Knochen zäh fest; **he clung ~ to it** er hielt zäh am Leben fest

tenacity [tɪ'næsɪtɪ] N Zähigkeit *f*, Hartnäckigkeit *f*; *(of character, person also)* Beharrlichkeit *f*; **the ~ of his grip** sein eiserner Griff; **his ~ of purpose** seine zielstrebige Beharrlichkeit

tenancy ['tenənsɪ] N **right/conditions of ~** Mietrecht *nt*/-bedingungen *pl*; *(of farm)* Pachtrecht *nt*/-bedingungen *pl*; **during his ~** während er (dort) Mieter/Pächter ist/war; **period of ~** Dauer *f* des Miet-/Pachtverhältnisses

tenant ['tenənt] **N** Mieter(in) *m(f)*; *(of farm)* Pächter(in) *m(f)* **VT** *(form) house* zur Miete wohnen in (+*dat*); *premises* gemietet haben; *farm* in Pacht haben

tenant farmer N Pächter(in) *m(f)*

tenantry ['tenəntrɪ] N , *no pl* *(of estate)* Pächter *pl*; *(of building, premises)* Mieter *pl*; **the law of ~** das Mietrecht; *(of farm)* das Pachtrecht

tend[1] [tend] VT sich kümmern um; *sheep* hüten; *sick person* pflegen; *land* bestellen; *machine* bedienen

tend[2] VI **a** **to ~ to be/do sth** (= *have a habit of being/doing sth*) gewöhnlich or gern etw sein/tun, die Tendenz haben, etw zu sein/tun; *(person also)* dazu neigen or tendieren, etw zu sein/tun; **the lever ~s to stick** der Hebel bleibt oft hängen; **I ~ to believe him** ich neige or tendiere dazu, ihm zu glauben; **that would ~ to suggest that ...** das würde gewissermaßen darauf hindeuten, dass ... **b** **to ~ toward(s)** (= *be directed, lead, line*) führen or streben *(geh)* nach; *(measures, actions etc)* führen zu, anstreben; (= *incline, person, views, designs etc*) neigen or tendieren or eine Tendenz haben zu; *(prices, colours)* tendieren or eine Tendenz haben zu; **his opinion is ~ing in our direction** seine Meinung tendiert in unsere Richtung

tendency ['tendənsɪ] N Tendenz *f* *(geh)*; (= *physical predisposition*) Neigung *f*; **artistic tendencies** künstlerische Neigungen *pl*; **to have a ~ to be/do sth** gern or gewöhnlich etw sein/tun; *(person, style of writing also)* dazu neigen or tendieren, etw zu sein/zu tun; **he had an annoying ~ to forget things** er hatte die ärgerliche Angewohnheit, alles zu vergessen; **there is a ~ for prices to rise in autumn** gewöhnlich steigen die Preise im Herbst; **a strong upward ~** *(St Ex)* eine stark steigende Tendenz

tendentious ADJ , **tendentiously** ADV [ten'denʃəs, -lɪ] tendenziös

tendentiousness [ten'denʃəsnɪs] N tendenziöse Färbung

tender[1] ['tendə'] N **a** Hüter(in) *m(f)*; *(of sick person)* Pfleger(in) *m(f)*; **machine ~** Maschinenwart *m* **b** *(Naut, Rail)* Tender *m*

tender[2] **VT** *money, services, shares* (an)bieten, geben; *thanks, apology* aussprechen; *resignation* einreichen; **"please ~ exact fare"** „bitte Fahrgeld abgezählt bereithalten" **VI** *(Comm)* sich bewerben *(for* um*)* **N** *(Comm)* Angebot *nt*; **to invite ~s for a job** Angebote *pl* für eine Arbeit einholen; **to put work out to ~** Arbeiten *pl* ausschreiben; **to put in a ~ for sth** ein Angebot für etw machen or einreichen; **we won the ~** wir haben die Ausschreibung gewonnen; **~ documents** Ausschreibungsunterlagen *pl*; **~ price** Angebotspreis *m*; **call for ~** Ausschreibung *f*

tender[3] ADJ **a** (= *sore, easily hurt*) *spot, bruise* empfindlich; *skin, plant* zart, empfindlich; *(fig) subject* heikel; **at the ~ age of 7** im zarten Alter von 7 Jahren; **she left home at a very ~ age** sie verließ sehr früh ihr Elternhaus; **my arm still feels ~** mein Arm ist noch sehr empfindlich; **~ to the touch** berührungsempfindlich; **she is a ~ plant** *(fig)* sie ist ein zartes Pflänzchen

b _meat_ zart; **cook the carrots for about 10 minutes or until ~** die Möhren etwa 10 Minuten lang kochen oder bis sie weich sind **c** (= _affectionate_) _person, voice, look_ zärtlich, liebevoll; _memories_ lieb, zärtlich; _heart_ gut; _gesture_ sanft; _kiss, embrace_ zärtlich; **~ loving care** Liebe und Zuneigung _f_; **he gave her a ~ smile** er lächelte sie zärtlich an; **to bid sb a ~ farewell** liebevoll(en) _or_ zärtlich(en) Abschied von jdm nehmen; **in sb's ~ care** in jds Obhut; **to leave sb to sb's ~ mercies** (_iro_) jdn jds liebevollen Händen anvertrauen

tender: tenderfoot N Neuling _m_; **tenderhearted** ADJ gutherzig; **tenderheartedness** N Gutherzigkeit _f_

tendering ['tendərɪŋ] N , _no pl_ (_Comm_) Angebotsabgabe _f_

tenderize ['tendəraɪz] VT _meat_ zart _or_ weich machen; (_by beating_) klopfen

tenderizer ['tendəraɪzə'] N Mürbesalz _nt_; (= _hammer_) Fleischklopfer _m_

tenderloin ['tendəlɔɪn] N Lendenstück _nt_

tenderly ['tendəlɪ] ADV zärtlich, liebevoll

tenderness ['tendənɪs] N **a** (= _soreness_) Empfindlichkeit _f_ **b** (_of meat_) Zartheit _f_ **c** (= _affection, of person, voice, look_) Zärtlichkeit _f_; (_of heart_) Güte _f_

tendon ['tendən] N Sehne _f_

tendril ['tendrɪl] N Ranke _f_; (_of hair_) Ringellocke _f_

tenement ['tenɪmənt] N **a** (_also_ **tenement house**) Mietshaus _nt_, Mietskaserne _f_ (_pej_) **b** (_Jur_) Mietbesitz _m_; (= _farm_) Pachtbesitz _m_

Tenerife [ˌtenə'riːf] N Teneriffa _nt_

tenet ['tenət] N Lehrsatz _m_; (_Rel_) Glaubenssatz _m_

tenfold ['tenfəʊld] ADJ zehnfach ADV zehnfach, um das Zehnfache; **to increase ~** sich verzehnfachen

ten-gallon hat [ˌtengælnˈhæt] N Cowboyhut _m_

tenish ['tenɪʃ] ADJ (so) um zehn herum (_inf_)

tenner ['tenə'] N (_Brit inf_) Zehner _m_ (_inf_)

tennis ['tenɪs] N Tennis _nt_

tennis _in cpds_ Tennis-; **tennis ball** N Tennisball _m_; **tennis club** N Tennisklub _m_, Tennisverein _m_; **tennis court** N Tennisplatz _m_; **tennis elbow** N (_Med_) Tennisarm _m_; **tennis player** N Tennisspieler(in) _m(f)_; **tennis racket**, **tennis racquet** N Tennisschläger _m_; **tennis shoe** N Tennisschuh _m_

tenon ['tenən] N Zapfen _m_; **~ joint** Zapfenverbindung _f_

tenon saw N Zapfenschneidsäge _f_

tenor ['tenə'] N **a** (= _voice, person_) Tenor _m_; **to sing ~** Tenor singen **b** (= _purport_) Tenor _m_; (_of theory_) Tendenz _f_; (= _general nature, of life_) Stil _m_; (_of events_) (Ver)lauf _m_ ADJ (_Mus_) Tenor-; **~ voice** Tenorstimme _f_; **~ saxophone** Tenorsaxophon _nt_, Tenorsaxofon _nt_

tenor clef N (_Mus_) Tenorschlüssel _m_

ten: tenpence N zehn Pence; (_also_ **tenpenny piece**) Zehnpencestück _nt_; **tenpin bowling**, (_US_) **tenpins** N Bowling _nt_

tense[1] [tens] N (_Gram_) Zeit _f_, Tempus _nt_; **present ~** Gegenwart _f_; **past ~** Vergangenheit _f_; **future ~** Zukunft _f_

tense[2] ADJ (+_er_) _rope_ gespannt, straff; _muscles_ (an)gespannt; _neck_ verspannt; _person, expression, bearing_ (_through stress, worry etc_) angespannt; (_through nervousness, fear etc_) verkrampft; _voice_ nervös; _silence, atmosphere_ gespannt; _situation_ (an)gespannt; _time_ spannungsgeladen; _negotiations_ spannungsgeladen; _relations_ angespannt; (= _thrilling_) _scene_ spannungsgeladen; **~ headache** Spannungskopfschmerz _m_; **to grow** _or_ **become** _or_ **get ~** (_person_) nervös werden; **to make sb ~** jdn in Anspannung versetzen; **I've been feeling rather ~ all day** ich bin schon den ganzen Tag so nervös; **in a voice ~ with emotion** mit erregter Stimme; **things are getting rather ~** die Lage wird gespannter

VT anspannen; **to ~ oneself to do sth** sich darauf konzentrieren, etw zu tun VI sich (an)spannen, sich straffen

▶ **tense up** VI (_person, muscle_) sich anspannen VT _sep muscle_ anspannen

tensely ['tenslɪ] ADV (_lit_) _stretch_ straff; (_fig_) _listen, sit_ angespannt; _speak, wait_ (= _nervously_) nervös; (= _excitedly_) gespannt

tenseness ['tensnɪs] N **a** (= _tautness, of rope_) Gespanntheit _f_, Straffheit _f_; (_of muscles_) (An)gespanntheit _f_ **b** (_of person, expression, bearing, through stress, worry etc_) Angespanntheit _f_; (_through nervousness, fear etc_) Verkrampftheit _f_; (_of voice_) Nervosität _f_; (_of atmosphere, situation_) Gespanntheit _f_; (_of negotiations_) Spannungsgeladenheit _f_; (_of relations_) Angespanntheit _f_ **c** (= _excitement: of scene_) Spannung(sgeladenheit) _f_

tensile ['tensaɪl] ADJ dehnbar, spannbar; **high ~ steel** Spannstahl _m_; **high ~ wire** besonders zugfester Draht

tensile: tensile load N Zugbelastung _f_; **tensile strength** N Zugfestigkeit _f_; **tensile stress** N Zugspannung _f_

tension ['tenʃən] N **a** (_lit_) Spannung _f_; (_of muscle_) Anspannung _f_; (_Knitting_) Festigkeit _f_; (_Sew_) Spannung _f_; **to check the ~** (_Knitting_) eine Maschenprobe machen **b** (= _nervous strain_) nervliche Belastung, Anspannung _f_ **c** (_in relationship_) Spannungen _pl_

tensor (muscle) ['tensɔ:'-] N Tensor _m_

tenspot ['tenspɒt] N (_US, inf_) Zehner _m_ (_inf_)

tent [tent] N Zelt _nt_

tentacle ['tentəkl] N (_Zool_) Tentakel _m or nt_ (_spec_); (_of octopus etc also_) Fangarm _m_; (_of snail also_) Fühler _m_; (_fig_) Klaue _f_

tentative ['tentətɪv] ADJ (= _not definite, provisional_) vorläufig; _offer_ unverbindlich; (= _hesitant_) _player, movement_ vorsichtig; _conclusion, suggestion_ vorsichtig, zögernd; _smile_ zögernd; **this proposal** _or_ **suggestion is only ~** das ist ja nur ein Vorschlag; **we've a ~ arrangement to play tennis tonight** wir haben halb abgemacht, heute Abend Tennis zu spielen

tentatively ['tentətɪvlɪ] ADV (= _hesitantly_) _smile_ zögernd; (= _gingerly_) vorsichtig; (= _provisionally_) _agree_ vorläufig; **he ~ suggested a weekend in Brighton** er machte den Vorschlag, eventuell ein Wochenende in Brighton zu verbringen

tent: tent bed N Feldbett _nt_; **tent city** N Zeltstadt _f_

tented ['tentɪd] ADJ _attr_ **a** (= _with tents_) _field_ mit Zelten (belegt); **~ camp** Zeltlager _nt_ **b** (= _draped_) _room, ceiling_ drapiert, verhangen

tenterhooks ['tentəhʊks] PL **to be on ~** wie auf glühenden Kohlen sitzen (_inf_); **to keep sb on ~** jdn zappeln lassen

tenth [tenθ] ADJ (_in series_) zehnte(r, s); **a ~ part** ein Zehntel _nt_ N (= _fraction_) Zehntel _nt_; (_in series_) Zehnte(r, s); (_Mus_) Dezime _f_ → _also_ **sixth**

tenthly ['tenθlɪ] ADV zehntens

tent peg N Zeltpflock _m_, Hering _m_

tent pole N Zeltstange _f_

tenuity [te'njʊɪtɪ] N (_liter_) = **tenuousness**

tenuous ['tenjʊəs] ADJ **a** (_lit_) _thread_ dünn, fein; _cobweb_ zart, fein; _air_ dünn; _gas_ flüchtig **b** (_fig_) _connection, argument, relationship_ schwach; (= _insecure_) _position_ unsicher; _supply line_ anfällig; **he kept a ~ hold on life** er hatte nur noch einen schwachen Lebenswillen; **to have a ~ grasp of sth** etw nur ansatzweise verstehen; **a ~ lead** eine mögliche Spur

tenuously ['tenjʊəslɪ] ADV (= _slightly_) schwach, leicht; **another world, connected to reality only ~** eine andere Welt, nur schwach mit der Realität verbunden

tenuousness ['tenjʊəsnɪs] N **a** (_lit, of thread_) Dünne _f_, Feinheit _f_; (_of cobweb_) Zartheit _f_, Feinheit _f_; (_of air_) Dünne _f_; (_of gas_) Flüchtigkeit _f_ **b** (_fig, of connection, argument, relationship_) Schwäche _f_; (= _insecurity of position_) Unsicherheit _f_

tenure ['tenjʊə'] N **a** (= _holding of office_) Anstellung _f_; (= _period of office_) Amtszeit _f_ **b** (_of property_) **during her ~ of the house/farm** während sie das Haus/die Farm innehatte; **laws governing land ~** Landpachtgesetze _pl_

tepee ['ti:pi:] N Tipi _nt_

tepid ['tepɪd] ADJ (_lit, fig_) lau(warm)

tepidity [te'pɪdɪtɪ], **tepidness** ['tepɪdnɪs] N (_lit, fig_) Lauheit _f_

tequila [tɪ'ki:lə] N Tequila _m_

tercentenary [ˌtɜ:sen'ti:nərɪ] N (= _anniversary_) dreihundertster Jahrestag; (= _celebration_) Dreihundertjahrfeier _f_, dreihundertjähriges Jubiläum ATTR für den dreihundertsten Jahrestag; **~ celebrations** Dreihundertjahrfeier _f_

tercet ['tɜ:sɪt] N (_Poet_) Terzine _f_; (_Mus_) Triole _f_

tergiversate ['tɜ:dʒɪvəseɪt] VI (_form, hum_) dauernd seine Gesinnung ändern

tergiversation [ˌtɜ:dʒɪvə'seɪʃən] N _usu pl_ (_form, hum_) (ständiger) Gesinnungswandel _no pl_

term [tɜ:m] N **a** (= _period of time_) Dauer _f_, Zeitraum _m_; (_of contract_) Laufzeit _f_; (= _limit_) Frist _f_; **~ of government** Regierungszeit _f_; **~ of office** Amtsdauer _or_ -zeit _f_; **~ of imprisonment** Gefängnisstrafe _f_; **~ of service** (_Mil_) Militärdienstzeit _f_; **to set a ~ (of three years) for sth** etw (auf drei Jahre) befristen; **elected for a three-year ~** auf _or_ für drei Jahre gewählt; **the contract is nearing its ~** der Vertrag läuft bald ab; **in the long/short ~** auf lange/kurze Sicht; **at ~** (_Fin_) bei Fälligkeit; (_Med_) zur rechten Zeit; **to carry a baby to ~** ein Kind (voll) austragen **b** (_Sch, three in one year_) Trimester _nt_; (_four in one year_) Vierteljahr _nt_, Quartal _nt_; (_two in one year_) Halbjahr _nt_; (_Univ_) Semester _nt_; **end-of-term exam** Examen _nt_ am Ende eines Trimesters _etc_; **during** _or_ **in ~(-time)** während der Schulzeit; (_Univ_) während des Semesters; **out of ~(-time)** in den Ferien **c** (= _expression_) Ausdruck _m_; **in simple ~s** in einfachen Worten; **a legal ~** ein juristischer (Fach)ausdruck _or_ Terminus (_geh_); **he spoke of her in the most flattering ~s** er äußerte sich sehr schmeichelhaft über sie; **a contradiction in ~s** ein Widerspruch in sich **d** (_Math, Logic_) Term _m_; **~ in parentheses** Klammerausdruck _m_; **to express one thing in ~s of another** eine Sache mit einer anderen erklären; **in ~s of production we are doing well** was die Produktion betrifft, stehen wir gut da; **in ~s of money** geldlich, finanziell; **in ~s of time** zeitlich **e** **terms** PL (= _conditions_) Bedingungen _pl_; **~s of surrender/service/sale/payment** Kapitulations-/Arbeits-/Verkaufs-/Zahlungsbedingungen _pl_; **~s of reference** (_of committee etc_) Aufgabenbereich _m_; (_of thesis etc_) Themenbereich _m_; **to buy sth on credit/easy ~s** etw auf Kredit/auf Raten kaufen; **the hotel offered reduced ~s in winter** das Hotel bot ermäßigte Winterpreise an; **on what ~s?** zu welchen Bedingungen?; **not on any ~s** unter gar keinen Umständen; **to accept sb on his/her own ~s** jdn nehmen, wie er/sie ist; **on equal ~s** auf gleicher Basis; **to come to ~s (with sb)** sich (mit jdm) einigen; **to come to ~s with sth** sich mit etw abfinden **f** **terms** PL (= _relations_) **to be on good/bad ~s with sb** gut/nicht (gut) mit jdm auskommen; **to be on friendly ~s with sb** auf freundschaftlichem Fuß mit jdm stehen; **they are not on speaking ~s** sie reden nicht miteinander; **what sort of ~s are they on?** wie ist ihre Beziehung? VT nennen, bezeichnen

termagant ['tɜ:məgənt] N Furie _f_

terminal ['tɜ:mɪnl] ADJ **a** (= _final_) End-; (_Med, = incurable_) _illness, patient_ unheilbar; (= _for the dying_) _care_ für Sterbende; (= _dire_) _problem_ fatal; **~ stage** (_of illness etc_) Endstadium _nt_; **he's a ~ case** er ist unheilbar krank; **to be in ~ decline** sich in unaufhaltsamem Niedergang befinden **b** (_inf, = utter_) _boredom_ endlos; _stupidity_ bodenlos; _adolescent_ ewig; _workaholic_ extrem **c** (_Bot, Anat, = on extremity_) am Ende befindlich N **a** (_Rail_) Endbahnhof _m_; (_for tramway, buses_)

Endstation *f*; (= *container terminal*) Containerterminal *m*; **air** *or* **airport** ~ (Flughafen)terminal *m*, Flughafengebäude *nt*; **cargo** ~ Frachtterminal *m*; **ferry** ~ Fährterminal *m*; **passenger** ~ Passagierterminal *m*; **railway** (*Brit*) *or* **railroad** (*US*) ~ Zielbahnhof *m*; **sea** ~ Seehafenanleger *m*

b (*Elec*) Pol *m*

c (*Comput*) Terminal *nt*

terminal bonus N (*Insur*) Zusatzdividende *f* (*fällig bei Vertragsablauf*)

terminal building N Terminal *m or nt*

terminally ['tɜːmɪnəlɪ] ADV **a** ~ **ill** unheilbar krank; **the** ~ **ill** die Todkranken *pl* **b** (= *utterly*) *boring* endlos; ~ **stupid** (*inf*) saublöd (*inf*); ~ **unfashionable** heillos unmodern

terminal: terminal station N (*Rail*) Endbahnhof *m*; **terminal velocity** N (*Phys*) Endgeschwindigkeit *f*; **terminal voltage** N (*Elec*) Klemmenspannung *f*; **terminal ward** N Sterbestation *f*

terminate ['tɜːmɪneɪt] VT beenden, beschließen; *contract, lease etc* lösen; *pregnancy* unterbrechen; *employment* kündigen; *relationship, conversation, friendship, life* beenden VI enden; (*contract, lease*) ablaufen; **most plural nouns ~ in "s"** die meisten Substantive enden im Plural auf „s"

termination [ˌtɜːmɪ'neɪʃən] N **a** Ende *nt*; (= *bringing to an end*) Beendigung *f*; (*of contract, lease etc = expiry*) Ablauf *m*, Erlöschen *nt*; (= *cancellation*) Lösung *f*; ~ **of pregnancy** Schwangerschaftsabbruch *m* **b** (*Gram*) Endung *f*

terminological [ˌtɜːmɪnə'lɒdʒɪkəl] ADJ terminologisch

terminology [ˌtɜːmɪ'nɒlədʒɪ] N Terminologie *f*; **all the technical ~ in the article** all die Fachausdrücke in dem Artikel

term insurance N (zeitlich) befristete Versicherung

terminus ['tɜːmɪnəs] N (*Rail, bus*) Endstation *f*

termite ['tɜːmaɪt] N Termite *f*

term money N (*Fin*) Festgeld *nt*

tern [tɜːn] N (*Zool*) Seeschwalbe *f*

ternary ['tɜːnərɪ] ADJ ternär

Terpsichorean [ˌtɜːpsɪkə'rɪən] ADJ (*form, hum*) *skill etc* im Tanzen; ~ **art** Tanzkunst *f*

terrace ['terəs] N **a** (= *patio*) Terrasse *f* **b** (*on hillside*) Terrasse *f*; ~ **cultivation** Terrassenfeldbau *m* **c** **terraces** PL (*Brit, Sport*) Ränge *pl* **d** (*Brit, = row of houses*) Häuserreihe *f*; (*as street name*) Weg *m* VT *garden, hill* in Terrassen anlegen, stufenförmig anlegen

terraced ['terəst] ADJ **a** *hillside etc* terrassenförmig *or* stufenförmig angelegt; *garden* in Terrassen angelegt **b** (*esp Brit*) *street* mit Reihenhäusern; ~ **house** Reihenhaus *nt*

terracing ['terəsɪŋ] N , *no pl* **a** (*on land*) Terrassen *pl* **b** (*Brit, Sport*) Ränge *pl*

terracotta [ˌterə'kɒtə] N Terrakotta *f* ATTR Terrakotta-, aus Terrakotta; ~ **floor** Terrakottaboden *m*

terra firma [ˌterə'fɜːmə] N fester Boden; **to be on ~ again** wieder festen Boden unter den Füßen haben

terrain [te'reɪn] N Terrain *nt* (*esp Mil*), Gelände *nt*; (*fig*) Boden *m*

terrapin ['terəpɪn] N Sumpfschildkröte *f*

terrarium [tə'reərɪəm] N (*for plants*) Pflanzenschale *f* (*in Kugelform*); (*for animals*) Terrarium *nt*

terrazzo [te'rætsəʊ] N Terrazzo *m*

terrestrial [tɪ'restrɪəl] ADJ **a** (= *of land*) Land-; ~ **animal** Landtier *nt*, auf dem Land lebendes Tier; ~ **plant** Landpflanze *f* **b** (= *of the planet Earth*) terrestrisch, irdisch; *life* irdisch; (*Brit*) *TV channel, television, broadcasting* terrestrisch; ~ **globe** Erdball *m*, Globus *m* **c** (= *worldly*) *problems* irdisch, weltlich N Erdbewohner(in) *m(f)*

terrible ['terəbl] ADJ **a** schrecklich, furchtbar; **he is ~ at golf** er spielt furchtbar (*inf*) *or* furchtbar schlecht Golf; **I feel ~** (= *feel ill*) mir

ist fürchterlich schlecht; (= *feel guilty*) es ist mir furchtbar peinlich; **to sound ~** (= *ill*) sich schrecklich anhören; **I sound ~ on tape** auf Band klinge ich furchtbar **b** (*inf, = absolute*) *fool* furchtbar

terribleness ['terəblnɪs] N Schrecklichkeit *f*, Fürchterlichkeit *f*

terribly ['terəblɪ] ADV **a** (= *very*) *important, difficult* schrecklich (*inf*); *disappointed, sorry* furchtbar; (= *very much*) *suffer* fürchterlich, furchtbar; **I'm not ~ good with money** ich kann nicht besonders gut mit Geld umgehen; **I miss him ~** ich vermisse ihn ganz furchtbar **b** (= *badly*) *behave* schrecklich, furchtbar; *play, sing* schrecklich, fürchterlich

terrier ['terɪə] N Terrier *m*

terrific [tə'rɪfɪk] ADJ *shame, nuisance, shock* unheimlich (*inf*); *person, success, idea, party* also sagenhaft (*inf*), klasse *inv* (*inf*); *speed, heat, strength, generosity* unwahrscheinlich (*inf*); **that's ~ news** das sind tolle Nachrichten (*inf*); **to look ~** (*person*) klasse aussehen (*inf*); **to have a ~ time** viel Spaß haben; **~!** (*also iro*) prima! (*inf*), toll! (*inf*)

terrifically [tə'rɪfɪkəlɪ] ADV (*inf, = very*) unheimlich (*inf*); (= *very well*) unheimlich (gut) (*inf*); **the party went ~** die Party war klasse (*inf*)

terrified ['terɪfaɪd] ADJ *person, animal* verängstigt; *look* also angstvoll; **to be ~ of sth** vor etw schreckliche Angst haben; **he was ~ when/in case ...** er hatte fürchterliche Angst, als .../davor, dass ...; **you look ~** du hast Angst, das sieht man!

terrify ['terɪfaɪ] VT *person* fürchterliche *or* schreckliche Angst machen *or* einjagen (+*dat*), in Angst *or* Schrecken versetzen; **flying terrifies him** er hat schreckliche Angst vor dem Fliegen; **my driving terrifies her** wenn ich Auto fahre, bekommt sie es mit der Angst zu tun

terrifying ['terɪfaɪɪŋ] ADJ *film, story* Grauen erregend; *thought, sight* entsetzlich; *speed* Angst erregend, Furcht erregend

terrifyingly ['terɪfaɪɪŋlɪ] ADV entsetzlich; **he came ~ close to disaster** er kam dem Unheil schrecklich nahe

terrine [te'riːn] N Pastete *f*

territorial [ˌterɪ'tɔːrɪəl] ADJ territorial; ~ **sovereignty** Gebietshoheit *f*; ~ **integrity** territoriale Unverletzlichkeit *f*; ~ **possessions** Territorialbesitz *m*; ~ **rights** Hoheitsrechte *pl*; ~ **behaviour** (*of animal*) Revierverhalten *nt*; **a strongly ~ bird** ein Vogel mit ausgeprägtem Territorial- *or* Revierverhalten N (*esp Brit*) **Territorial** Soldat *m* der Heimatschutztruppe; **the Territorials** (*Brit*) die Heimatschutztruppe

Territorial Army N (*Brit*) Territorialheer *nt*

TERRITORIAL ARMY

Die **Territorial Army** (abgekürzt auch **TA**) ist eine britische Organisation freiwilliger Armeereservisten. Die Mitglieder sind Zivilisten, die in ihrer Freizeit Militärübungen absolvieren und in Kriegs- oder Krisenzeiten zur Unterstützung der regulären Armee zur Verfügung stehen. Als Gegenleistung erhalten die Freiwilligen regelmäßige Bezüge.

---

territorial waters PL Territorialgewässer *pl*

territory ['terɪtərɪ] N (Staats)gebiet *nt*, Territorium *nt*; (*in US, Austral*) Territorium *nt*; (*of animals*) Revier *nt*, Territorium *nt*; (*Comm: of agent etc*) Bezirk *m*; (*fig*) Revier *nt*, Gebiet *nt*; **uncharted territories** (*lit*) unerforschte Gebiete *pl*; (*fig*) unerforschtes Terrain *nt*; **the occupied territories** die besetzten Gebiete; **that comes *or* goes with the ~** das gehört einfach dazu; **such problems have become familiar ~** solche Probleme sind allgegenwärtig geworden

terror ['terə] N **a** *no pl* (= *great fear*) panische Angst (*of* vor +*dat*); **in ~** in panischer Angst; **to be in ~ of one's life** um sein Leben bangen; **it held no ~ for him** er schreckte nicht davor zurück; **reign of ~** (*Hist, fig*) Terror- *or* Schre-

ckensherrschaft *f*; **the IRA ~ campaign** die Terrorkampagne der IRA

b (= *cause of terror, terrible event*) Schrecken *m*; **he was the ~ of the other boys** er terrorisierte die anderen Jungen; **the headmaster was a ~ to boys who misbehaved** der Rektor war der Schrecken aller Jungen, die sich schlecht benahmen

c (*inf, = person*) Teufel *m*; (= *child*) Ungeheuer *nt*; **a ~ with the ladies** ein Weiberheld *m* (*inf*)

terrorism ['terərɪzəm] N Terrorismus *m*; (= *acts of terrorism*) Terror *m*; **an act of ~** ein Terrorakt *m*

terrorist ['terərɪst] N Terrorist(in) *m(f)* ADJ *attr* terroristisch; ~ **attack** Terroranschlag *m*

terrorize ['terəraɪz] VT terrorisieren

terror-stricken ['terəˌstrɪkən], **terror-struck** ['terəˌstrʌk] ADJ starr vor Schreck(en)

terry ['terɪ]: **terry cloth** N (*US*) Frottee *nt or m*; **terry towel** N (*Brit*) Frotteetuch *nt*, Frottier(hand)tuch *nt*; **terry towelling** N (*Brit*) Frottee *nt or m*

terse [tɜːs] ADJ (+*er*) knapp; **he was very ~** er war sehr kurz angebunden

tersely ['tɜːslɪ] ADV knapp, kurz; *say, answer* kurz (angebunden); **to dismiss sth ~** etw kurzerhand verwerfen

terseness ['tɜːsnɪs] N Knappheit *f*; (*of reply also, person*) Kürze *f*, Bündigkeit *f*

tertiary ['tɜːʃərɪ] ADJ tertiär; ~ **education** (*Brit*) Universitätsausbildung *f*

tertiary: tertiary burns PL Verbrennungen *pl* dritten Grades; **tertiary colour** N Mischfarbe *f*; **Tertiary period** N (*Geol*) Tertiär *nt*

Terylene® ['terəliːn] N Terylen(e)® *nt*, ≈ Trevira® *nt*, ≈ Diolen® *nt*

TESL *abbr of* **Teaching of English as a Second Language** → **TEFL**

TESOL *abbr of* **Teaching of English as a Second or Other Language** → **TEFL**

tessellated ['tesɪleɪtɪd] ADJ Mosaik-; ~ **floor** Mosaik(fuß)boden *m*

test [test] N **a** (*Sch*) Klassenarbeit *f*; (*Univ*) Klausur *f*; (*short*) Kurzarbeit *f*, Test *m*; (= *intelligence test, psychological test etc*) Test *m*; (= *driving test*) (Fahr)prüfung *f*; **he gave them a vocabulary ~** er ließ eine Vokabel- *or* Wörterarbeit schreiben; (*orally*) er hat sie Vokabeln abgefragt; **this is a ~ of public opinion** damit wird die öffentliche Meinung ausgelotet; **to put sb/sth to the ~** jdn/etw auf die Probe stellen; **to stand the ~** die Probe bestehen; **their marriage didn't stand up to the ~ of separation** ihre Ehe hat die Trennung nicht verkraftet; **to stand the ~ of time** die Zeit überdauern; **that was a real ~ of character/his endurance** das war eine wirkliche Charakterprüfung/Belastungsprobe für ihn; **to pass one's ~** (*Aut*) die (Fahr)prüfung bestehen; **to fail one's ~** (*Aut*) (durch die (Fahr)prüfung) durchfallen

b (*on vehicle, product, weapon etc*) Test *m*; (= *check*) Kontrolle *f*

c (= *chemical test*) Test *m*, Untersuchung *f*; **a skin ~** ein Hauttest; **to do a ~ for sugar** einen Zuckertest machen, eine Untersuchung auf Zucker machen; **the samples were sent for ~s** die Proben wurden zur Untersuchung geschickt

d (*Brit*) = **test match**

ADJ *attr* Test-; ~ **model** Testmodell *nt*

VT **a** (= *examine, check*) testen, prüfen; (*Sch*) *pupil* prüfen; (*orally*) abfragen; *person, intelligence* testen; (*fig*) auf die Probe stellen; **the teacher ~ed them on that chapter** der Lehrer fragte sie das Kapitel ab; **to ~ sb for a job** jds Eignung für eine Stelle prüfen *or* testen; **to ~ sb/sth for accuracy** jdn/etw auf Genauigkeit prüfen; **I just wanted to ~ your reaction** ich wollte nur mal sehen, wie du reagierst

b (*chemically*) *gold* prüfen; *water, contents of stomach etc* untersuchen; **to ~ sth for sugar** etw auf seinen Zuckergehalt untersuchen; **the blood samples were sent for ~ing** *or* **to be ~ed** die Blutproben wurden zur Untersuchung geschickt

VI Tests/einen Test machen; (*chemically also*) untersuchen (*for auf +acc*); **~ing, ~ing one, two, three!** eins, zwei, drei; **we are ~ing for a gas leak/loose connection** wir überprüfen die Leitung auf eine undichte Stelle, wir überprüfen, ob irgendwo Gas austritt/ein Anschluss locker ist

▶ **test out** VT *sep* ausprobieren (*on bei or an +dat*)

testament ['testəmənt] N **a** (*old*) Testament *nt*, letzter Wille **b** (*Bibl*) **Old/New Testament** Altes/Neues Testament *nt*

testamentary [ˌtestə'mentərɪ] ADJ testamentarisch

testator [te'steɪtəʳ] N Erblasser(in) *m(f)* (*form*)

testatrix [te'steɪtrɪks] N Erblasserin *f* (*form*)

test: test ban N Versuchsverbot *nt*; **test ban treaty** N Teststoppabkommen *nt*; **test-bed** N Prüfstand *m*; **test card** N (*TV*) Testbild *nt*; **test case** N Musterfall *m*; **test cricket** N (*Brit: Cricket*) internationales Kricket, Testkricket *nt*; **test drive** N Probefahrt *f*; **test-drive** VT *car* probefahren

testee [te'sti:] N **a** (*Psych etc*) Testperson *f* **b** (*Sch etc*) Prüfling *m*

tester ['testəʳ] N (*of product etc*) Prüfer(in) *m(f)*; (*= machine*) Prüfgerät *nt*

testes ['testi:z] PL Testikel *pl*, Hoden *pl*

test: test flight N Test- *or* Probeflug *m*; **test-fly** VT Test fliegen

testicle ['testɪkl] N Testikel *m*, Hoden *m*

testify ['testɪfaɪ] VI **to ~ that …** (*Jur*) bezeugen, dass … **VI** (*Jur*) eine Zeugenaussage machen, aussagen; **to ~ against/for sb** gegen/für jdn aussagen; **to ~ to sth** (*= speak for*) etw bezeugen (*also Jur*); (*= be sign of*) to sincerity, efforts etc von etw zeugen, ein Zeichen für etw sein

testily ['testɪlɪ] ADV *say* unwirsch, gereizt

testimonial [ˌtestɪ'məʊnɪəl] N **a** (*= character recommendation*) Referenz *f* **b** (*= gift*) Geschenk *nt* als Zeichen der Anerkennung *or* Wertschätzung (*geh*) **c** (*Sport*) Gedenkspiel *nt*

testimony ['testɪmənɪ] N Aussage *f*; **he gave his ~** er machte seine Aussage; **to bear ~ to sth** etw bezeugen; **accept this gift as ~ of** *or* **to my friendship** nehmen Sie dieses Geschenk als Zeichen *or* Beweis meiner Freundschaft

testiness ['testɪnɪs] N Gereiztheit *f*

testing ['testɪŋ] ADJ hart; **I had a ~ time** es war hart (für mich)

testing ground N Test- *or* Versuchsgebiet *nt*; (*fig*) Versuchsfeld *nt*

test: test-market VT auf dem Markt testen; **test marketing** N Markttest *m*; **test match** N (*Brit*) Testmatch *nt*; (*Kricket also*) internationales Kricketmatch; (*Rugby also*) internationales Rugbymatch

testosterone [te'stɒstərəʊn] N Testosteron *nt*

test: test paper N (*Sch*) Klassenarbeit *f*; (*Chem*) Reagenzpapier *nt*; **test pattern** N (*US*) = test card; **test piece** N (*of handwork*) Prüfungsstück *nt*; (*Mus*) Stück *nt* zum Vorspielen; **test pilot** N Testpilot(in) *m(f)*; **test print** N (*Phot*) Probeabzug *m*; **test results** PL (*Med etc*) Testwerte *pl*; **test stand** N (*Tech*) Prüfstand *m*; **test tube** N Reagenzglas *nt*; **test-tube baby** N Kind *nt* aus der Retorte, Retortenbaby *nt*

testy ['testɪ] ADJ (*+er*) unwirsch, gereizt

tetanus ['tetənəs] N Wundstarrkrampf *m*, Tetanus *m*; **~ injection** Tetanusspritze *f*

tetchily ['tetʃɪlɪ] ADV *say* gereizt

tetchiness ['tetʃɪnɪs] N (*esp Brit inf*) (*on particular occasion*) Gereiztheit *f*; (*as general characteristic*) Reizbarkeit *f*

tetchy, techy ['tetʃɪ] ADJ (*+er*) (*esp Brit inf*) (*on particular occasion*) gereizt; (*as general characteristic*) reizbar

tête-à-tête [ˌteɪtɑː'teɪt] ADJ, ADV unter vier Augen **N** Tete-a-tete *nt*, Tête-à-tête *nt*

---

tether ['teðəʳ] **N** (*lit*) Strick *m*; (*= chain*) Kette *f*; **he was at the end of his ~** (*Brit fig inf*, = annoyed, impatient) ihm hats gereicht (*inf*); (*= desperate*) er war am Ende (*inf*) **VT** (*also* **tether up**) *animal* anbinden, festbinden

tetherball ['teðɔːbɔːl] N (*US*) Spiel, bei dem ein Ball, der an einem an einer Stange befestigten Seil hängt, geschlagen wird, so dass sich das Seil um die Stange herumwickelt

tetrachloride [ˌtetrə'klɔːraɪd] N Tetrachlorid *nt*

tetrahedron [ˌtetrə'hiːdrən] N Tetraeder *nt*

tetrameter [te'træmɪtəʳ] N (*Liter*) Tetrameter *m*

tetrapod ['tetrəpɒd] N Tetrapode *m* (*spec*), Vierfüßer *m*

Teuton ['tjuːtɒn] N Teutone *m*, Teutonin *f*

Teutonic [tjʊ'tɒnɪk] ADJ (*Hist, hum*) teutonisch

Texan ['teksən] **N** Texaner(in) *m(f)* **ADJ** texanisch

Texas ['teksəs] N Texas *nt*

text [tekst] **N a** Text *m*; **to restore a ~** den Originaltext wieder herstellen **b** (*of sermon*) Text *m* **VT** **to ~ sb** (*on mobile phone*) jdm eine Textnachricht schicken

textbook ['tekstbʊk] **N** Lehrbuch *nt* **ADJ** ~ **case** Paradefall *m*; ~ **landing** Bilderbuchlandung *f*

text editor N (*Comput*) Texteditor *m*

textile ['tekstaɪl] **ADJ** Textil-; ~ **industry** Textilindustrie *f* **N** Stoff *m*; **~s** Textilien *pl*, Textilwaren *pl*

text (*Comput*): **text input** N Texteingabe *f*; **text message** N Textnachricht *f*, SMS *f*; **text messaging** N (*Telec*) SMS-Messaging *nt*, SMS-Versand *m*; **text processing** N Textverarbeitung *f*; **text processor** N (*software also*) Textsystem *nt*; (*= software also*) Textsystem *nt*

textual ['tekstjʊəl] ADJ Text-; ~ **analysis** Textanalyse *f*

texture ['tekstʃəʳ] N (*stoffliche*) Beschaffenheit, Textur *f*; (*of dough also*) Konsistenz *f*; (*of food*) Substanz *f*, Textur *f*; (*of material, paper*) Griff *m* und Struktur, Textur *f*; (*fig, of music, poetry etc*) Gestalt *f*; **the ~ of velvet** wie sich Samt anfühlt; **the smooth ~ of silk makes it pleasant to wear** es ist angenehm, Seide zu tragen, weil sie so anschmiegsam ist; **a sculptor interested in ~** ein Bildhauer, der an der Materialgestalt *or* -beschaffenheit interessiert ist; **the ~ of one's life** seine Lebensqualität

textured ['tekstʃəd] ADJ strukturiert, texturiert (*form*)

TGIF (*hum*) *abbr of* **thank God it's Friday**

T-girder N (*Tech*) T-Träger *m*

TGWU (*Brit*) *abbr of* **Transport and General Workers' Union** Transportarbeitergewerkschaft

Thai [taɪ] **ADJ** thailändisch **N a** Thailänder(in) *m(f)*, Thai *mf* **b** (*= language*) Thai *nt*; (*= language family*) Tai *nt*

Thailand ['taɪlænd] N Thailand *nt*

thalidomide [θə'lɪdəʊmaɪd] N Contergan® *nt*, Thalidomid *nt*; ~ **baby** Contergankind *nt*

thallium ['θælɪəm] N (*Chem*) Thallium *nt*

Thames [temz] N Themse *f*; **he'll never set the ~ on fire** (*prov*) er hat das Pulver auch nicht erfunden (*prov*)

than [ðæn, (*weak form*) ðən] **❂** 5.2, 5.3 CONJ als; **I'd rather do anything ~ that** das wäre das Letzte, was ich tun wollte; **no sooner had I sat down ~ he began to talk** kaum hatte ich mich hingesetzt, als er auch schon anfing zu reden; **who better to help us ~ he?** wer könnte uns besser helfen als er? → **more, other adj c, rather**

thank [θæŋk] **❂** 20.2, 20.4, 22 VT **a** danken (*+dat*); sich bedanken bei; **I'll never be able to ~ him (enough) for what he has done** ich kann ihm nie genug dafür danken, was er für mich getan hat; **I don't know how to ~ you** ich weiß nicht, wie ich Ihnen danken soll

b (*phrases*) **he won't ~ you for it** er wird es Ihnen nicht danken; **I'll ~ you to mind your own business** ich wäre Ihnen dankbar, wenn Sie

---

sich nicht einmischen würden; **he has his brother/he only has himself to ~ for this** das hat er seinem Bruder zu verdanken/sich selbst zuzuschreiben

c ~ **you** danke (schön); ~ **you very much** vielen Dank; **no** ~ **you** nein, danke; **yes,** ~ **you** ja, bitte *or* danke; ~ **you for coming – not at all,** ~ **YOU!** vielen Dank, dass Sie gekommen sind – ich danke IHNEN *or* ICH habe zu danken; ~ **you for the present** vielen Dank für Ihr Geschenk; ~ **you for nothing** (*iro*) vielen Dank auch!; **to say** ~ **you** danke sagen (*to sb* jdm), sich bedanken (*to* bei)

d ~ **goodness** *or* **heavens** *or* **God** (*inf*) Gott sei Dank! (*inf*)

thankee ['θæŋki:] INTERJ (*dial*) = thank you → thank c

thankful ['θæŋkfʊl] ADJ dankbar (*to sb* jdm); **to be ~ to sb for sth** jdm für etw dankbar sein; **to be ~ to sb for doing sth** jdm dankbar sein, dass er/sie etw getan hat; **we were ~ to be alive** wir waren dankbar, noch am Leben zu sein; **I'm only ~ that it didn't happen** ich bin bloß froh, dass es nicht passiert ist

thankfully ['θæŋkfəlɪ] ADV dankbar, voller Dankbarkeit; ~**, no real harm has been done** zum Glück ist kein wirklicher Schaden entstanden; ~ **for my family I wasn't hurt** zum Glück für meine Familie war ich unverletzt

thankfulness ['θæŋkfʊlnɪs] N Dankbarkeit *f*

thankless ['θæŋklɪs] ADJ undankbar; **a ~ task** eine undankbare Aufgabe

thank-offering ['θæŋkˌɒfərɪŋ] N (*lit*) Dankopfer *nt*; (*fig*) Dankesgabe *f*

thanks [θæŋks] **❂** 17.1, 22 **PL a** Dank *m*; **to accept sth with ~** etw dankend *or* mit Dank annehmen; **and that's all the ~ I get** und das ist jetzt der Dank dafür; **to give ~ to God** Gott danksagen *or* Dank sagen; ~ **be to God** (*Eccl*) Dank sei Gott

b ~ **to** wegen (*+gen*); (*with positive cause also*) dank (*+gen*); ~ **to his coming early …** weil er so früh kam, …; **it's all ~ to you that we're so late** bloß deinetwegen kommen wir so spät; **it was no ~ to him that …** ich hatte/wir hatten es nicht ihm zu verdanken, dass …; **you managed it then – yes, no ~ to you** du hast es also doch geschafft – ja, und das habe ich ganz bestimmt nicht dir zu verdanken

INTERJ (*inf*) danke (*for* für); **many ~** vielen *or* herzlichen Dank (*for* für); ~ **a lot** *or* **a million** vielen *or* tausend Dank; (*iro*) (na,) vielen Dank (*inf*); ~ **for nothing!** (*iro*) vielen Dank auch!; **will you have some more? – no ~/yes,** ~ etwas mehr? – nein/ja, danke

thanksgiving ['θæŋksgɪvɪŋ] N Dankbarkeit *f*

Thanksgiving (Day) N (*US*) Thanksgiving Day *m*

THANKSGIVING

Thanksgiving Day oder auch einfach nur **Thanksgiving** ist ein Feiertag in den USA, der auf den vierten Donnerstag im November fällt. Er erinnert an das erste Erntedankfest der Pilgrim Fathers, als diese im Jahre 1621 ihre erste erfolgreiche Ernte auf amerikanischem Boden feierten. Deshalb darf bei keinem traditionellen Thanksgiving-Festessen der Truthahnbraten und der Kürbiskuchen fehlen. Bei einem solchen Essen versammelt sich häufig die gesamte Familie, wofür auch lange Anreisen in Kauf genommen werden. In Kanada gibt es am zweiten Montag im Oktober einen ähnlichen Feiertag (allerdings ohne den historischen Hintergrund der Pilgrim Fathers) → PILGRIM FATHERS

thank you N Dankeschön *nt*; **he grabbed the book without even a thank-you** er riss das Buch ohne ein Dankeschön *nt* oder ohne ein Wort *nt* des Dankes an sich; **thank-you letter** N Dankschreiben *nt*

that[1] [ðæt, (*weak form*) ðət] **DEM PRON** *pl* **those a** das; **what is ~?** was ist das?; **they all say ~**

das sagen alle; **~ is Joe (over there)** das (dort) ist Joe; **who is ~?** wer ist das?; **who is ~ speaking?** wer spricht (denn) da?; (on phone) wer ist am Apparat?; **~'s what I say** or **think too** das finde ich auch; **if she's as unhappy/stupid** etc **as (all) ~** wenn sie so or derart unglücklich/ dumm etc ist; **she's not as stupid as all ~** so dumm ist sie nun auch (wieder) nicht; **I didn't think she'd get/be as angry as ~** ich hätte nicht gedacht, dass sie sich so ärgern würde; **... and all ~ ...** und so (inf); **like ~** so; **with luck/talent like ~ ...** bei solchem or so einem (inf) Glück/ Talent ...; **just like ~** einfach so; **~'s got ~/him out of the way** so, das wäre geschafft/den wären wir los; **~ is (to say)** das heißt; **oh well, ~'s ~** nun ja, damit ist der Fall erledigt; **there, ~'s ~** so, das wärs; **you can't go and ~'s ~** du darfst nicht gehen, und damit hat sichs or und damit basta (inf); **well, ~'s ~ then** das wärs dann also; **so ~ was ~** damit hatte sichs; **~'s it!** das ist es!; (= the right way) gut so!, richtig!; (= finished) so, das wärs!; (= the last straw) jetzt reichts!; **will he come? – ~ he will** (dial) kommt er? – (der?) bestimmt

b (after prep) **after/before/below/over ~** danach/davor/darunter/darüber; **and ... at ~** und dabei ...; (= on top of that) und außerdem ...; **you can get it in any supermarket and quite cheaply at ~** man kann es in jedem Supermarkt, und zwar ganz billig, bekommen; **my watch is broken already and it was my good one at ~** meine Uhr ist schon kaputt und dabei war es meine gute; **what do you mean by ~?** (not understanding) was wollen Sie damit sagen?; (amazed, annoyed) was soll (denn) das heißen?; **as for ~** das betrifft or angeht; **if things have** or **if it has come to ~** wenn es (schon) so weit gekommen ist; **with ~ she got up and left/burst into tears** damit stand sie auf und ging/brach sie in Tränen aus → **leave**

c (opposed to "this" and "these") das (da), jenes (old, geh); **I prefer this to ~** dies ist mir lieber als das (da); **~'s the one I like, not this one** das (dort) mag ich, nicht dies (hier)

d (followed by rel pron) **this theory is different from ~ which ...** diese Theorie unterscheidet sich von derjenigen, die ...; **~ which we call ~** das, was wir ... nennen

DEM ADJ pl **those a** der/die/das, jene(r, s); **what was ~ noise?** was war das für ein Geräusch?; **~ child/dog!** dieses Kind/dieser Hund!; **~ poor girl!** das arme Mädchen!; **I only saw him on ~ one occasion** ich habe ihn nur bei dieser einen Gelegenheit gesehen; **~ morning I had put on my green dress** an jenem Morgen hatte ich mein grünes Kleid an(gezogen); **everyone agreed on ~ point** alle waren sich in dem Punkt einig; **I like ~ one** ich mag das da

b (in opposition to this) der/die/das; **I'd like ~ one, not this one** ich möchte das da, nicht dies hier; **she was rushing this way and ~** sie rannte hierhin und dorthin

c (with poss) **~ dog of yours!** Ihr Hund, dieser Hund von Ihnen (inf); **what about ~ plan of yours now?** wie steht es denn jetzt mit Ihrem Plan?, was ist denn nun mit Ihrem Plan?

DEM ADV (inf) so; **he was at least ~ much taller than me** er war mindestens (um) so viel größer als ich; **it's not ~ good/cold** etc SO gut/kalt etc ist es auch wieder nicht; **it's not ~ good a film** SO ein guter Film ist es nun auch wieder nicht; **he was ~ angry** er hat sich DERart(ig) geärgert

that² REL PRON a der/die/das, die; **all/nothing/ everything** etc **~ ...** alles/nichts/alles etc, was ...; **the best/cheapest** etc **~ ...** das or was ...; **fool ~ I am** ich Idiot; **the girl ~ I told you about** das Mädchen, von dem ich Ihnen erzählt habe; **no-one has come ~ I know of** meines Wissens or soviel ich weiß, ist niemand gekommen

b (with expressions of time) **the minute ~ he came the phone rang** genau in dem Augenblick, als er kam, klingelte das Telefon; **the day ~ we spent on the beach was one of the hottest** der Tag, den wir am Strand verbrach-

ten, war einer der heißesten; **the day ~ ...** an dem Tag, als ...

that³ CONJ a dass; **she promised ~ she would come** sie versprach zu kommen; **he said ~ it was wrong** er sagte, es sei or wäre (inf) falsch, er sagte, dass es falsch sei or wäre (inf); **not ~ I want to do it** nicht (etwa), dass ich das tun wollte → **so b** (in exclamations) **~ things** or **it should come to this!** dass es so weit kommen konnte!; **oh ~ I could only see you again** (liter) oh, dass ich dich doch wiedersehen könnte! (liter) **c** (obs, liter, = in order that) auf dass (old)

thatch [θætʃ] **N a** (= straw) Stroh nt; (= reed) Reet nt; (= roof) Stroh-/Reetdach nt **b** (inf, = hair) Mähne f **VT** roof mit Stroh/Reet decken

thatched [θætʃt] **ADJ** → **thatch N a** cottage mit Stroh-/Reetdach, stroh-/reetgedeckt; **~ roof** Stroh-/Reetdach nt; (= roofing) ein Stroh-/Reetdach haben, mit Stroh/Reet gedeckt sein

thatcher [ˈθætʃə] N Dachdecker(in) m(f)

Thatcherism [ˈθætʃərɪzəm] N Thatcherismus m

Thatcherite [ˈθætʃəraɪt] **N** Thatcher-Anhänger(in) m(f), Thatcherist(in) m(f) **ADJ** thatcheristisch

thatching [ˈθætʃɪŋ] N → **thatch N a** (= act, skill) Stroh-/Reetdachdecken nt; (= roofing) Stroh-/ Reetdach nt

thaw [θɔː] **VT** auftauen (lassen); ice, snow also tauen lassen; (= make warm) person, hands aufwärmen; (fig, make friendly) person auftauen or warm werden lassen; relations entspannen **VI** (lit, fig) auftauen; (ice, snow) tauen; (person: = become warmer) auftauen, sich aufwärmen; **it is ~ing** es taut **N** (lit, fig) Tauwetter nt; **before the ~/a ~ sets in** bevor das Tauwetter einsetzt; **there's been a ~ in relations between ...** die Beziehungen zwischen ... sind aufgetaut

▶ **thaw out VI** (lit, fig) auftauen **VT** sep (lit) frozen food etc auftauen (lassen); person, hands aufwärmen; (fig) person aus der Reserve locken; **it took several whiskies to thaw him out** (inf) er brauchte mehrere Whiskys, bis er auftaute or warm wurde

the [ðə, (vor Vokalen auch, zur Betonung auch) ðiː] **DEF ART a** der/die/das; **in ~ room** im or in dem Zimmer; **on ~ edge** am or an dem Rand; **he went up on(to) ~ stage** er ging aufs or auf das Podium; **to play ~ piano/guitar** Klavier/Gitarre spielen; **all ~ windows** all die or alle Fenster; **have you invited ~ Browns?** haben Sie die Browns or (with children) die Familie Brown eingeladen?; **in ~ 20s** in den zwanziger Jahren or Zwanzigerjahren pl; **Henry ~ Eighth** Heinrich der Achte; **how's ~ leg/wife?** (inf) wie gehts dem Bein/Ihrer Frau? (inf)

b (with adj used as n) das, die; (with comp or superl) der/die/das; **~ Good** das Gute; **~ poor/ rich** die Armen pl/Reichen pl; **translated from ~ German** aus dem Deutschen übersetzt; **she was ~ prettiest/prettiest** sie war die Hübschere/ Hübscheste

c (denoting whole class) der/die/das; **~ elephant is in danger of extinction** der Elefant ist vom Aussterben bedroht

d (distributive use) **80p ~ pound** 80 Pence das or pro Pfund; **by ~ hour** pro Stunde; **~ car does thirty miles to ~ gallon** das Auto braucht eine Gallone auf dreißig Meilen, das Auto verbraucht 11 Liter auf 100km

e [ðiː] (stressed) der/die/das; **it's THE restaurant in this part of town** das ist DAS Restaurant in diesem Stadtteil

ADV (with comp adj or adv) **all ~ more/better/ harder** umso mehr/besser/schwieriger; **~ more he has ~ more he wants** je mehr er hat, desto mehr will er; **(all) ~ more so because ...** umso mehr, als ... → **better²**, **worse**

theatre, (US) **theater** [ˈθɪətəʳ] **N a** Theater nt; **to go to the ~** ins Theater gehen; **what's on at the ~?** was wird im Theater gegeben? **b** no pl (= theatrical business, drama) Theater nt; **he's always been keen on (the) ~** er war schon immer theaterbegeistert; **he has been in (the) ~ all his life** er war sein Leben lang beim Theater; **not all Shaw's plays are good ~** nicht alle Stücke

von Shaw eignen sich für die Bühne **c** (Brit, = operating theatre) Operationssaal m **d** (= scene of events) Schauplatz m; **~ of war** Kriegsschauplatz m; **~ of operations** Schauplatz m der Handlungen

theatre, (US) **theater**: **theatre company** N Theaterensemble nt; (touring) Schauspiel- or Theatertruppe f; **theatre critic** N Theaterkritiker(in) m(f); **theatregoer**, (US) **theatergoer** N Theaterbesucher(in) m(f)

theatreland [ˈθɪətəlænd] N (Brit) Theatergegend f; **in ~** in der Theatergegend

theatre nuclear weapon N (Mil) taktische Atomwaffe

theatre nurse N (Brit, Med) Op-Schwester f

theatrical [θɪˈætrɪkəl] **ADJ a** Theater-; **~ production** Theaterproduktion f **b** (pej) behaviour etc theatralisch; **there was something very ~ about him** er hatte etwas sehr Theatralisches an sich **N theatricals** PL Theaterspielen nt; **most people have taken part in ~s** die meisten Menschen haben schon mal Theater gespielt

theatrical agent N Theateragent(in) m(f)

theatrical company N Theater- or Schauspieltruppe f

theatricality [θɪˌætrɪˈkælɪt] N theatralische Art

theatrically [θɪˈætrɪkəlɪ] **ADV a** schauspielerisch; **~ it was a disaster** vom Theaterstandpunkt war das eine Katastrophe **b** (pej) behave, speak theatralisch

theatrical producer N Theaterproduzent(in) m(f)

thee [ðiː] PRON (old, dial: objective case of thou, dir only, with prep +acc) Euch (obs), dich (also Eccl); (indir obj, with prep +dat) Euch (obs), dir (also Eccl); **God be with ~** Gott sei mit dir; **for ~ and thine** für dich und die deinen or Deinen

theft [θeft] N Diebstahl m

their [ðɛəʳ] **POSS ADJ a** ihr **b** (inf, = belonging to him or her) seine(r, s); **everyone knows ~ rights nowadays** jeder kennt heutzutage seine Rechte → also **my POSS ADJ**

theirs [ðɛəz] **POSS PRON a** ihre(r, s); **~ is not to reason why** es ist nicht an ihnen zu fragen; **~ is the Kingdom of Heaven** ihrer ist das Himmelreich **b** (inf, = belonging to him or her) seine(r, s) → also **mine¹ POSS PRON**

theism [ˈθiːɪzəm] N Theismus m

theist [ˈθiːɪst] N Theist(in) m(f)

theistic [θiːˈɪstɪk] ADJ theistisch

them [ðem, (weak form) ðəm] **PERS PRON** pl **a** (dir obj, with prep +acc) sie; (indir obj, with prep +dat) ihnen; **both of ~ saw me** beide haben mich gesehen; **neither of ~ saw me** keiner von beiden hat mich gesehen; **give me a few of ~** geben Sie mir ein paar davon; **none of ~** keiner/keinen (von ihnen); **he's one of ~** das ist einer von ihnen; (= homosexual) er ist andersrum (inf) **b** (emph) sie; **~ and us** (inf) sie or die (inf) und wir; **it's ~** sie sinds; **it's ~ who did it** SIE or DIE haben es gemacht **c** (dial, incorrect) **~ as wants to** die, die wollen **ADJ** (incorrect) diese

thematic ADJ , **thematically ADV** [θɪˈmætɪk, -əlɪ] thematisch

theme [θiːm] ✪ 26.2 N **a** (= subject) Thema nt **b** (US, Sch, = essay) Aufsatz m **c** (Mus) Thema nt; (Film, TV) Thema nt, Melodie f (from aus)

themed [θiːmd] **ADJ** (esp Brit) place thematisch gestaltet; event thematisch ausgerichtet

theme: **theme music** N (Film) Titelmusik f; (TV) Erkennungsmelodie f; **theme park** N Themenpark m; **theme pub** N (Brit) Lokal, das einem bestimmten Thema entsprechend ausgestattet ist, Themenkneipe f; **theme restaurant** N erlebnisgastronomisches Restaurant, Themenrestaurant nt; **theme song** N (Film) Titelsong m; (TV) Erkennungssong m; (of opera) Leitmotiv nt; **theme tune** N = **theme music**

themselves [ðəm'selvz] PERS PRON pl **a** (*reflexive*) sich **b** (*emph*) selbst; **the figures ~** die Zahlen selbst or an sich → *also* **myself**

then [ðen] ADV **a** (= *next, afterwards*) dann; **and ~ what happened?** und was geschah dann? **b** (= *at this particular time*) da; (= *in those days*) damals; **it was ~ 8 o'clock** da war es 8 Uhr; **I was/will be in Paris ~** ich war da (gerade) in Paris/werde da in Paris sein; **he did it ~ and there or there and ~** er hat es auf der Stelle getan → **now** **c** (*after prep*) **from ~ on(wards)** von da an; **before ~** vorher, zuvor; **but they had gone by ~** aber da waren sie schon weg; **we'll be ready by ~** bis dahin sind wir fertig; **since ~** seitdem, seit der Zeit; **between now and ~** bis dahin; **(up) until ~ I had never tried it** bis dahin hatte ich es nie versucht **d** (= *in that case*) dann; **I don't want that – ~ what DO you want?** ich will das nicht – was willst du denn?; **what are you going to do, ~?** was wollen Sie dann tun?; **but ~ that means that ...** das bedeutet ja aber dann, dass ...; **all right, ~** also or dann meinetwegen; **so it's true ~** dann ist es (also) wahr, es ist also wahr; (**so**) **I was right ~** ich hatte also Recht; **you don't want it ~?** Sie wollen es also nicht?, dann wollen Sie es (also) nicht?; **where is it ~?** wo ist es denn? **e** (= *furthermore, and also*) dann, außerdem; (**and**) **~ there's my aunt** und dann ist da noch meine Tante; **but ~ ... also** ... auch; **but ~ he's my son** aber er ist (eben) auch mein Sohn; **but ~ again he is my friend** aber andererseits ist er mein Freund **f** (*phrases*) **now ~, what's the matter?** na, was ist denn los?; **come on ~** nun komm doch ADJ *attr* damalig; **the ~ Prime Minister** der damalige Premierminister

thence [ðens] ADV **a** (*old*: = *from that place*) von dannen (*old*), von dort or da (weg) **b** (*old, = from that time*) **which dated from ~** was aus der (damaligen) Zeit stammt; **they met again a week ~** sie trafen eine Woche darauf wieder zusammen **c** (*form, = for that reason*) infolgedessen

thenceforth [ˌðens'fɔːθ], **thenceforward** [ˌðens'fɔːwəd] ADV von da an, von der Zeit an

theocracy [θɪ'ɒkrəsɪ] N Theokratie f

theocratic [ˌθɪə'krætɪk] ADJ theokratisch

theodolite [θɪ'ɒdəlaɪt] N Theodolit m

theologian [θɪə'ləʊdʒən] N Theologe m, Theologin f

theological [θɪə'lɒdʒɪkəl] ADJ theologisch; **~ college** Priesterseminar nt; **~ student** Theologiestudent(in) m(f)

theology [θɪ'ɒlədʒɪ] N Theologie f

theorem ['θɪərəm] N Satz m (*also Math*), Theorem nt (*geh, spec*)

theoretic(al) [θɪə'retɪk(əl)] ADJ theoretisch

theoretically [θɪə'retɪkəlɪ] ADV theoretisch

theoretician [θɪərə'tɪʃən], **theorist** ['θɪərɪst] N Theoretiker(in) m(f)

theorize ['θɪəraɪz] VI theoretisieren

theorizer ['θɪəraɪzə'] N Theoretiker(in) m(f)

theory ['θɪərɪ] N Theorie f; **in ~** theoretisch, in der Theorie; **~ of colour/evolution** Farben-/Evolutionslehre or -theorie f; **he has a ~ that ...** er hat die Theorie, dass ...; **well, it's a ~** das ist eine Möglichkeit; **he always goes on the ~ that ...** er geht immer davon aus, dass ...

theosophical [θɪə'sɒfɪkəl] ADJ theosophisch

theosophist [θɪ'ɒsəfɪst] N Theosoph(in) m(f)

theosophy [θɪ'ɒsəfɪ] N Theosophie f

therapeutic(al) [ˌθerə'pjuːtɪk(əl)] ADJ therapeutisch; **to be therapeutic** therapeutisch wirken

therapeutic community N Therapiegruppe f

therapeutics [ˌθerə'pjuːtɪks] N *sing* Therapeutik f

therapeutic touch N Therapie f durch Handauflegen

therapist ['θerəpɪst] N Therapeut(in) m(f)

therapy ['θerəpɪ] N Therapie f

there [ðeə'] ADV **a** dort, da; (*with movement*) dorthin, dahin; **look, ~'s Joe/~'s Joe coming** guck mal, da ist/kommt Joe; **it's under/over/in ~** es liegt dort or da drunter/drüben/drin; **put it under/over/in/on ~** stellen Sie es dort or da drunter/rüber or hinüber/rein or hinein/drauf or hinauf; **let's stop ~** hören wir doch da auf; (*travelling*) halten wir doch da or dort an; **~ and back** hin und zurück; **so ~ we were** da waren wir nun also; **is Gordon ~ please?** (*on telephone*) ist Gordon da?; **to be ~ for sb** (*inf*: = *supportive*) für jdn da sein **b** (*fig*, = *on this point*) da; **~ you are wrong** da irren Sie sich; **you've got me ~** da bin ich überfragt; **I've got you ~** da or jetzt habe ich Sie **c** (*in phrases*) **~ is/are** es or da ist/sind; (= *there exists/exist* also) es gibt; **~ were three of us** wir waren zu dritt; **~ is a mouse in the room** es ist eine Maus im Zimmer; **~ was once a castle here** hier war or stand einmal eine Burg; **~ is a chair in the corner** in der Ecke steht ein Stuhl; **~ is dancing afterwards** danach ist Tanz, danach wird getanzt; **is ~ any beer?** ist Bier da?; **~'s a book I want to read** da ist ein Buch, das ich lesen möchte; **afterwards ~ was coffee** anschließend gab es Kaffee; **is ~ any wine left? – well, ~ was** ist noch Wein da? – gerade war noch welcher da; **~ isn't any food/time/paint, is ~? – yes ~ is** es gibt wohl nichts zu essen/dazu haben wir wohl keine Zeit/das hat wohl keinen Sinn, oder? – doch!; **~ seems to be no-one at home** es scheint keiner zu Hause zu sein; **~ appears to be a flaw in your argument** da scheint ein Fehler in Ihrer Beweisführung zu sein; **how many mistakes were ~?** wie viele Fehler waren es?; **~ is a page missing** es or da fehlt eine Seite; **~ comes a time when ...** es kommt eine Zeit, wo ...; **~ being no alternative solution** da es keine andere Lösung gibt; **~ will be an opportunity for shopping** es wird Gelegenheit zum Einkaufen geben; **God said: let ~ be light, and ~ was light** und Gott sprach: es werde Licht! und es ward Licht; **hi ~!** hallo!; **you go again** (*inf*) jetzt gehts schon wieder los; **now ~'s a real woman** das ist eine richtige Frau; **~'s gratitude for you!** (*iro*) da haben Sie Ihren Dank!; **~'s a good idea!** (das ist) eine gute Idee!; **so ~!** ätsch!; **~ you are** (*giving sb sth*) hier(, bitte)!; (*on finding sb*) da sind Sie ja!; **~ you we are, you see, I knew he'd say that** na, sehen Sie, ich habe es ja gewusst, dass er das sagen würde; **wait, I'll help you ... ~ you are!** warten Sie, ich helfe Ihnen, ... so(, das wärs)!; **you press the switch and ~ you are!** Sie brauchen nur den Schalter zu drücken, das ist alles; **I can't dance, but ~ again, I never could** ich kann nicht tanzen, aber das habe ich eigentlich noch nie gekonnt INTERJ **~! ~!** na, na!; **stop crying now, ~'s a good boy** hör auf zu weinen, na komm; **drop it, ~'s a good dog** lass das fallen, komm, sei brav; **now ~'s a good boy, don't tease your sister** komm, sei ein braver Junge und ärgere deine Schwester nicht; **hey, you ~!** (*inf*) he, Sie da!; **hurry up ~** (*inf*) Beeilung!, Tempo, Tempo! (*inf*); **make way ~** Platz da!, machen Sie mal Platz!; **~, take this to your mother** da, bring das deiner Mutter; **but ~, what's the good of talking about it?** was solls, es hat doch keinen Zweck, darüber zu reden; **~! I knew it would break!** da! ich habs ja gewusst, dass es kaputtgehen würde!

thereabouts [ˌðeərə'baʊts] ADV **a** (*place*) dort in der Nähe, dort irgendwo **b** (*quantity, degree*) **five pounds/fifteen or ~** so um die fünf Pfund/fünfzehn (herum); **four o'clock or ~** so um vier Uhr herum (*inf*); **is it ten dollars I owe you? – ~** schulde ich dir nicht zehn Dollar? – so ungefähr

thereafter [ˌðeər'ɑːftə'] ADV (*form*) danach, darauf (*geh*)

thereby [ˌðeə'baɪ] ADV dadurch, damit; **and ~ hangs a tale** und da gibt es eine Geschichte dazu

therefore ['ðeəfɔː'] **○** 17.1, 26.1, 26.3 ADV deshalb, daher; (*as logical consequence*) also; **so – I was wrong** ich hatte also Unrecht; **we can deduce, ~, that ...** wir können also or daher folgern, dass ...

therein [ðeər'ɪn] ADV (*form*) **a** (= *in that particular*) darin, in dieser Hinsicht; **~ lies the problem** darin liegt das Problem **b** (= *in that place*) darin, dort

thereof [ˌðeər'ɒv] ADV (*form*) davon; **this town and the citizens ~** diese Stadt und deren Bürger; **a charge of ten pounds per hour or part ~** eine Gebühr von zehn Pfund pro angefangene Stunde

thereon [ˌðeər'ɒn] ADV (*form, = on that*) darauf; (= *on that subject*) darüber

there's [ðeəz] *contr of* **there is** *of* **there has**

thereto [ˌðeə'tuː] ADV (*form*) damit; **official business and all expenses related ~** offizielle Geschäfte und alle damit verbundenen Ausgaben

thereunder [ˌðeər'ʌndə'] ADV (*form*) darunter

thereupon [ˌðeərə'pɒn] ADV **a** (= *then, at that point*) darauf(hin) **b** (*form, = on that subject*) darüber; (= *on that*) darauf

therewith [ˌðeə'wɪθ] ADV (*form*) **a** (= *with that*) damit **b** (= *thereupon*) darauf

therm [θɜːm] N (*Brit*) 100.000 Wärmeeinheiten (*ca. 10⁸ Joules*)

thermal ['θɜːml] ADJ **a** (*Phys*) Wärme-; *neutron, reactor, equilibrium* thermisch; **~ expansion** Wärmeausdehnung f; **~ power station** Wärmekraftwerk nt **b** *clothing* Thermo-; **~ socks** Thermosocken pl; **~ blanket** Aluminiumdecke f; **~ underwear** Thermounterwäsche f **N** **a** (*Aviat, Met*) Thermik f *no pl* **b** **thermals** PL (*inf, = thermal underwear*) Thermounterwäsche f

thermal: thermal barrier N (*Phys, Aviat*) Temperatur- or Hitzebarriere f; **thermal baths** PL Thermalbäder pl; **thermal conductivity** N Wärmeleitfähigkeit f; **thermal imager** N Thermograf m; **thermal imaging** N Thermografie f; **thermal imaging system** N Thermografiesystem nt; **thermal paper** N Thermopapier nt; **thermal printer** N (*Comput*) Thermodrucker m; **thermal spa** N Thermalbad nt; **thermal spring** N Thermalquelle f; **thermal transfer** N Thermotransfer m; **thermal unit** N Wärmeeinheit f

thermic ['θɜːmɪk] ADJ thermisch

thermionic [ˌθɜːmɪ'ɒnɪk] ADJ thermionisch, glühelektrisch; **~ valve** (*Brit*) or **tube** (*US*) Glühelektronenröhre f

thermistor ['θɜːmɪstə'] N (*Tech*) Heißleiter m, Thermistor m

thermo [θɜːməʊ-]: **thermodynamic** ADJ thermodynamisch; **thermodynamics** PL Thermodynamik f; **thermoelectric** ADJ thermoelektrisch; **thermoelectricity** N Thermoelektrizität f

thermomat N Isomatte f

thermometer [θə'mɒmɪtə'] N Thermometer nt

thermo: thermonuclear ADJ thermonuklear; **~ war** Thermonuklearkrieg m; **~ strike** Thermonuklearschlag m; **~ weapon** Thermonuklearwaffe f; **thermopile** N Thermosäule f; **thermoplastic** ADJ thermoplastisch **N** Thermoplast m

Thermos® [θɜːmɒs] N (*also* **Thermos flask** or (*US*) **bottle**) Thermosflasche f

thermostat ['θɜːməstæt] N Thermostat m

thermostatic [ˌθɜːmə'stætɪk] ADJ thermostatisch; **~ regulator/switch** Temperaturregler m/-schalter m

thermostatically [ˌθɜːmə'stætɪkəlɪ] ADV thermostatisch

thermotherapy [ˌθɜːmə'θerəpɪ] N (*Med*) Thermotherapie f (*spec*), Wärmebehandlung f

thesaurus [θɪ'sɔːrəs] N Thesaurus m

these [ðiːz] ADJ, PRON diese → **this**

thesis ['θiːsɪs] N pl **theses** ['θiːsiːz] **a** (= *argument*) These f **b** (*Univ, for PhD*) Dissertation f, Doktorarbeit f (*inf*); (*for diploma*) Diplomarbeit f

thespian ['θespɪən] (liter, hum) ADJ dramatisch; ~ **art** Schauspielkunst f N Mime m, Mimin f

they [ðeɪ] PERS PRON pl **a** sie; ~ **are very good people** es sind sehr gute Leute; **it is** ~ (form) sie sind es; ~ **who** diejenigen, die or welche, wer (+sing vb) **b** (= people in general) ~ **say that ...** man sagt, dass ...; ~ **are going to build a new road** man will or sie wollen eine neue Straße bauen; ~ **are thinking of changing the law** es ist beabsichtigt, das Gesetz zu ändern **c** (inf) **if anyone looks at this closely,** ~ **will notice ...** wenn sich das jemand näher ansieht, wird er bemerken ...

they'd [ðeɪd] contr of **they had** of **they would**

they'd've ['ðeɪdəv] contr of **they would have**

they'll [ðeɪl] contr of **they will**

they're [ðɛə'] contr of **they are**

they've [ðeɪv] contr of **they have**

thiamine ['θaɪəmiːn] N Thiamin nt

thick [θɪk] ADJ (+er) **a** dick; thread, legs, arms dick, stark; lips dick, voll; **a wall three feet** ~ eine drei Fuß dicke or starke Wand; **to give sb a** ~ **ear** (Brit inf) jdm ein paar hinter die Ohren hauen (inf); **you'll get a** ~ **ear in a minute** (Brit inf) du kriegst gleich ein paar hinter die Ohren!; (inf); **the shelves were** ~ **with dust** auf den Regalen lag dick der Staub; **to have a** ~ **head** einen Brummschädel haben (inf), einen dicken Kopf haben (inf) **b** hair, smoke dick, dicht; forest, hedge, beard dicht; liquid, sauce, syrup etc dick(flüssig); mud dick; darkness tief; night undurchdringlich; crowd dicht(gedrängt); air schlecht, dick (inf); (= airless) atmosphere schwer; (= unclear) voice träge; accent stark, breit; **they are** ~ **on the ground** (inf) die gibt es wie Sand am Meer (inf); **the hedgerows were** ~ **with wild flowers** die Hecken strotzten von wilden Blumen; **the streets are** ~ **with people/traffic** die Straßen sind voller Menschen/Verkehr; **his voice was** ~ **with a cold/emotion/fear/drink** er sprach mit belegter/bewegter/angstvoller Stimme/schwerer Zunge; **the air is pretty** ~ **in here** hier ist eine Luft zum Schneiden, hier ist sehr schlechte Luft; **the air is** ~ **with rumours** Gerüchte liegen in der Luft **c** (Brit inf: = stupid) person dumm, doof (inf); **to get sth into or through sb's** ~ **head** etw in jds dicken Schädel bekommen (inf); **as** ~ **as a brick** or **as two (short) planks** dumm wie ein Brett (inf), strohdoof (inf) **d** (inf, = intimate) **they are very** ~ sie sind dicke Freunde (inf); **to be very** ~ **with sb** mit jdm eine dicke Freundschaft haben (inf) **e** (inf: = much) **that's a bit** ~! das ist ein starkes Stück (inf) N **a** **in the** ~ **of the crowd** mitten in der Menge; **to be in the** ~ **of the fighting** im dicksten Kampfgetümmel stecken; **in the** ~ **of it** mittendrin; **he likes to be in the** ~ **of things** er ist gern bei allem voll dabei; **to stick together through** ~ **and thin** zusammen durch dick und dünn gehen **b** (of finger, leg) dickste Stelle; **the** ~ **of the calf** die Wade ADV (+er) spread, lie, cut dick; grow dicht; **the snow lay** ~ es lag eine dichte Schneedecke; **his blows fell** ~ **and fast** seine Schläge prasselten nieder; **offers of help poured in** ~ **and fast** es kam eine Flut von Hilfsangeboten; **they are falling** ~ **and fast** sie fallen um wie die Fliegen (inf); **the jokes came** ~ **and fast** die Witze kamen Schlag auf Schlag; **to lay it on** ~ (inf) (zu) dick auftragen (inf); **that's laying it on a bit** ~ (inf) das ist ja wohl etwas übertrieben

thicken ['θɪkən] VT sauce etc eindicken VI **a** (fog, hair, crowd, forest) dichter werden; (smoke, darkness) sich verdichten; (sauce, mixture) dick werden **b** (fig: plot, mystery) immer verwickelter or undurchsichtiger werden; **aha, the plot** ~**s!** aha, jetzt wirds interessant!

thickener ['θɪkənə'], **thickening** ['θɪkənɪŋ] N (for sauces) Bindemittel nt

thicket ['θɪkɪt] N Dickicht nt

thick: **thick-flowing** ADJ dickflüssig; **thickhead** N (inf) Dummkopf m; **thickheaded** ADJ (inf) dumm, doof (inf); **thickheadedness** N (inf) Dummheit f, Doofheit f (inf)

thickie ['θɪkɪ] N (Brit inf) Dummkopf m, Doofkopf m (inf), Doofi m (inf)

thick-lipped ['θɪkˈlɪpt] ADJ mit dicken or wulstigen Lippen, mit Wulstlippen

thickly ['θɪklɪ] ADV **a** spread, paint, cut dick; populated, crowded, wooded dicht **b** (= deeply) lie dick; **to be** ~ **covered with sth** dick mit etw bedeckt sein; **to be** ~ **carpeted** mit einem dicken Teppich ausgelegt sein; **snow was falling** ~ dichter Schnee fiel; **the** ~ **falling snow** der dicht fallende Schnee **c** speak (with a cold) mit belegter Stimme; (with drink) mit schwerer Zunge; (with emotion) bewegt; (with fear) angstvoll

thickness ['θɪknɪs] N **a** Dicke f; (of wall, thread, legs, arms also) Stärke f; **the** ~ **of his lips** seine dicken or wulstigen Lippen; **it is sold in three different** ~**es** es wird in drei verschiedenen Dicken or Stärken verkauft **b** (of hair, fog, beard) Dicke f; (of forest, hedge, beard) Dichte f; (of liquid, sauce, syrup etc) Dickflüssigkeit f; (of accent) Stärke f; **the** ~ **of his voice** (through cold) seine belegte Stimme; (through drink) seine schwere Zunge; (through emotion) seine bewegte Stimme; (through fear) seine bebende Stimme **c** (= layer) Lage f, Schicht f

thicko ['θɪkəʊ] N (inf) = thickie

thick: **thickset** ADJ gedrungen; hedge dicht; **thick-skinned** ADJ (lit) dickhäutig; (fig) dickfellig

thick-witted ADJ , **thick-wittedly** ADV dumm, begriffsstutzig

thicky ['θɪkɪ] N (inf) = thickie

thief [θiːf] N pl **thieves** [θiːvz] Dieb(in) m(f); **to set a** ~ **to catch a** ~ (prov) einen vom Fach benutzen; **to be as thick as thieves** (Brit inf) dicke Freunde sein (inf)

thieve [θiːv] VTI stehlen

thievery ['θiːvərɪ] N (= theft) Diebstahl m

thieving ['θiːvɪŋ] ADJ magpie diebisch; **keep your** ~ **hands off my cigarettes** lass die Finger weg von meinen Zigaretten (inf); **this** ~ **lot** (inf) diese Räuberbande (inf) N (= thefts) Stehlen nt, Diebstähle pl

thievish ['θiːvɪʃ] ADJ diebisch attr

thievishness ['θiːvɪʃnɪs] N diebische Art

thigh [θaɪ] N (Ober)schenkel m

thigh: **thighbone** N Oberschenkelknochen m; **thigh-length** ADJ boots übers Knie reichend; coat kurz

thimble ['θɪmbl] N Fingerhut m

thimbleful ['θɪmblfʊl] N (fig) Fingerhut m (voll)

thimble printer N (Comput) Thimbledrucker m

thin [θɪn] ADJ (+er) **a** (= not fat) dünn; **as** ~ **as a rake** (Brit) or **rail** (US) dünn wie eine Bohnenstange **b** (= not thick) paper, slice, string, wall, blood, dress dünn; liquid dünn(flüssig); (= narrow) column schmal **c** (= sparse) hair, grass dünn, schütter; eyebrows schütter, licht; vegetation gering, spärlich, kümmerlich (pej); population, crowd klein, kümmerlich (pej); **his hair is getting quite** ~ sein Haar lichtet sich; **he's a bit** ~ **on top** bei ihm lichtet es sich oben schon ein wenig; **to be** ~ **on the ground** (fig) dünn gesät sein **d** (= not dense) fog leicht; air dünn; **to vanish into** ~ **air** (fig) sich in Luft auflösen; **the agent simply vanished into** ~ **air** der Agent schien sich einfach in Luft aufgelöst zu haben; **to appear out of** ~ **air** aus dem Nichts auftauchen **e** (fig, = weak, poor) voice, smile schwach, dünn; excuse schwach, fadenscheinig; disguise, story line, plot schwach; trading, profits gering; **a majority** eine knappe Mehrheit; **she had a** ~ **time of it** (dated inf) es war nicht gerade schön für sie; **to give sb a** ~ **time of it** (dated inf) jdm das Leben schwer machen

ADV (+er) spread, cut dünn; lie dünn, spärlich VT paint, sauce, ozone layer verdünnen; trees, ranks lichten; hair ausdünnen; blood dünner werden lassen

VI (fog, crowd) sich lichten; (hair also) schütter werden; (ozone layer) dünner werden; (population) abnehmen

▶ **thin down** VI dünner werden; (person also) abnehmen, schlanker werden VT sep paint, sauce verdünnen

▶ **thin out** VI (fog) sich lichten, schwächer werden; (crowd) kleiner werden; (audience) sich lichten; (hair) sich lichten, schütter werden; **the trees started thinning out** die Bäume lichteten sich VT sep hair ausdünnen; seedlings also verziehen; forest lichten; population verkleinern

thine [ðaɪn] (old, dial) POSS PRON der/die/das deine or Deine; **for thee and** ~ für dich und deinen or Deinen → **mine**[1] POSS ADJ (only before vowel) Euer/Eure/Euer (obs), dein/deine/dein (also Eccl)

thing [θɪŋ] N **a** (= any material object) Ding nt; **a** ~ **of beauty/great value** etwas Schönes/sehr Wertvolles; **she likes sweet** ~**s** sie mag Süßes or süße Sachen; **what's that** ~? was ist das?; **I don't have a** ~ **to wear** ich habe nichts zum Anziehen **b** **things** PL (= clothes, equipment, belongings) Sachen pl; **have you got your swimming** ~**s?** hast du dein Badezeug or deine Badesachen dabei?; **they washed up the breakfast** ~**s** sie spülten das Frühstücksgeschirr **c** (non material: = affair, subject) Sache f; **you know, it's a funny** ~ wissen Sie, es ist schon seltsam; **the odd/best** ~ **about it is ...** das Seltsame/Beste daran ist, ...; **it's a good** ~ **I came** nur gut, dass ich gekommen bin; **it's a bad/strange** ~ **but ...** es ist schlecht/seltsam, aber ...; **to make a big** ~ **of** or **about sth** viel Lärm um etw machen; **to make a big** ~ **of** or **about doing sth** eine große Sache daraus machen, dass man etw tut; **he's on to** or **onto a good** ~ (inf) er hat da was Gutes aufgetan (inf); **he's got a good** ~ **going there** (inf) der hat da was Gutes laufen (inf); **what a (silly)** ~ **to do** wie kann man nur so was (Dummes) tun!; **you take the** ~ **too seriously** Sie nehmen die Sache or das zu ernst; **there is one/one other** ~ **I want to ask you** eines/und noch etwas möchte ich Sie fragen; **and there's another** ~, **why didn't you ...?** und noch etwas, warum haben Sie nicht ...?; **it's one** ~ **to talk about it, it's another to do it** es ist eine Sache, davon zu reden, eine völlig andere, es dann auch zu tun; **the** ~**s you do/say!** was du so machst/sagst!; **I must be hearing/seeing** ~**s!** ich glaube, ich höre/sehe nicht richtig, ich glaube, ich spinne! (inf); **all the** ~**s I meant to say/do** alles, was ich sagen/tun wollte; **which** ~**s in life do you value most?** was or welche Dinge im Leben bewerten Sie am höchsten?; **to expect great** ~**s of sb/sth** Großes or große Dinge von jdm/etw erwarten; **I must think** ~**s over** ich muss mir die Sache or das überlegen; ~**s are going from bad to worse** es wird immer schlimmer; **as** ~**s stand at the moment, as** ~**s are ...** so wie die Dinge im Moment liegen; **how are** ~**s (with you)?** wie gehts (bei) Ihnen?; **since that's how** ~**s are ...** wenn das so ist ..., in dem Fall ...; **it's bad enough as** ~**s are** es ist schon schlimm genug; ~**s aren't what they used to be** es ist alles nicht mehr so wie früher; **to talk of one** ~ **and another** von diesem und jenem reden; **taking one** ~ **with another** im Großen und Ganzen, alles in allem; **it's been one** ~ **after the other** (going wrong) es kam eins zum anderen; **if it's not one** ~ **it's the other** es ist immer irgendetwas; **(what) with one** ~ **and another I haven't had time to do it yet** ich bin einfach noch nicht dazu gekommen; **it's neither one** ~ **nor the other** es ist weder das eine noch das andere; **one** ~ **led to another** eins führte zum anderen; **for one** ~ **it doesn't make sense** erst einmal ergibt das überhaupt keinen Sinn; **not to see/understand a** ~ (absolut) nichts sehen/verstehen; **not to know a** ~ (absolut) nichts wissen, keine Ahnung haben; **to tell sb a ~ or two** jdm einiges erzählen; **he knows a ~ or two** er hat etwas auf dem Kasten (*inf*); **he knows a ~ or two about cars** er kennt sich mit Autos aus; **it's just one of those ~s** so was kommt eben vor (*inf*); **in all ~s** in allem → **teach**

d (= *person, animal*) Ding *nt*; **poor little ~** das arme (kleine) Ding!; **you poor ~!** du Arme(r)!; **she's a funny old ~** sie ist ein komisches altes Haus (*inf*); **I say, old ~** (*dated inf*) na, du altes Haus (*inf*); **lucky ~!** der/die Glückliche/du Glückliche(r)!; **he looks quite the ~** er sieht (richtig) nach etwas aus

e (= *what is suitable, best*) **that's just the ~ for me** das ist genau das Richtige für mich; **that's not the ~ to do** so was macht or tut man nicht; **his behaviour isn't quite the ~** (*dated*) sein Benehmen ist nicht gerade berückend (*inf*); **the latest ~ in ties** der letzte Schrei in der Krawattenmode; **the ~ to do now would be ...** was wir jetzt machen sollten, wäre ...; **that would be the honourable ~ to do** es wäre nur anständig, das zu tun

f (*in phrases*) **I'm not at my best first ~ in the morning** so früh am Morgen bin ich nicht gerade in Hochform; **I'll do that first ~ in the morning** ich werde das gleich or als Erstes morgen früh tun; **I'll do it first ~** ich werde das zuerst or als Erstes tun; **last ~ at night** vor dem Schlafengehen; **painting is his ~** das Malen liegt ihm (*inf*); **the ~ is to know when ...** man muss wissen, wann ...; **yes, but the ~ is ...** ja, aber ...; **the ~ is we haven't got enough money** die Sache ist die, wir haben nicht genug Geld; **the ~ is, you see, he loves her** das Problem ist, dass er sie liebt; **yes but the ~ is it won't work** ja, aber das Dumme ist, es funktioniert nicht; **to do one's own ~** (*inf*) tun, was man will; **when Michael Jackson starts doing his ~** (*inf*) wenn Michael Jackson seine Schau abzieht (*inf*); **she's got this ~ about Sartre/dogs** (*inf*, = *can't stand*) sie kann Sartre/Hunde einfach nicht ausstehen; (= *is fascinated by*) sie hat einen richtigen Sartre-/Hundefimmel (*inf*); **she's got a ~ about spiders** (*inf*) bei Spinnen dreht sie durch (*inf*); **he's got a ~ about her** (*inf*, = *can't stand*) er kann sie nicht ausstehen; (= *is infatuated with*) er ist verrückt nach ihr

g (**all**) **~s German/mystical/mechanical** alles Deutsche/Geheimnisvolle/Mechanische

h (*inf, for forgotten name of person*) Dings(bums) *mf* (*inf*)

thingummybob ['θɪŋəmɪˌbɒb], **thingamajig** ['θɪŋəmɪˌdʒɪg], **thingummy** ['θɪŋəmɪ] N Dings (-da) *nt or* (*for people*) *mf*, Dingsbums *nt or* (*for people*) *mf*

think [θɪŋk] ✪ 6.2, 16.1, 26.2 *vb*: pret, ptp **thought** Ⅵ denken; **to ~ to oneself** sich (*dat*) denken; **I was just sitting there ~ing to myself** ich saß so in Gedanken da; **~ before you speak/act** denk nach or überleg, bevor du sprichst/handelst; **do animals ~?** können Tiere denken?; **to act without ~ing** unüberlegt handeln; (= *stupidly also*) unbedacht handeln; **~ again!** denk noch mal nach; **so you ~ I'll give you the money? well, you'd better ~ again!** du denkst also, ich gebe dir das Geld? Das hast du dir (wohl) gedacht!; **it makes you ~** es macht or stimmt einen nachdenklich; **I need time to ~** ich brauche Zeit zum Nachdenken; **it's so noisy you can't hear yourself ~** bei so einem Lärm kann doch kein Mensch denken; **now let me ~** lass (mich) mal überlegen or nachdenken; **stop and ~ before you make a big decision** denke in aller Ruhe nach, bevor du eine schwerwiegende or schwer wiegende Entscheidung triffst; **it's a good idea, don't you ~?** es ist eine gute Idee, findest or meinst du nicht auch?; **just ~** stellen Sie sich (*dat*) bloß mal vor; **just ~, you too could be rich** stell dir vor or denk dir nur, auch du könntest reich sein; **where was it? ~, man, ~!** wo war es?, denk doch mal nach!; **listen, I've been ~ing, ...** hör mal, ich habe mir überlegt ...; **sorry, I just wasn't ~ing** Entschuldigung, da habe ich geschlafen (*inf*); **you just didn't ~, did you?**

da hast du dir nichts gedacht, oder?; **you just don't ~, do you?** (*about other people*) du denkst auch immer nur an dich; (*about consequences*) was denkst du dir eigentlich? → **big**

Ⅵ **a** (= *believe*) denken; (= *be of opinion*) glauben, meinen, denken; **I ~ you'll find I'm right** ich glaube or denke, Sie werden zu der Überzeugung gelangen, dass ich Recht habe; **I ~ it's too late** ich glaube, es ist zu spät; **I ~ I can do it** ich glaube or denke, dass ich es schaffen kann; **well, I THINK it was there!** nun, ich glaube zumindest, dass es da war!; **and what do you ~?** asked the interviewer und was meinen Sie or und was ist Ihre Meinung? fragte der Interviewer; **you never know what he's ~ing** ich weiß nie, was er (sich) denkt; **I ~ you'd better go/accept/be careful** ich denke, Sie gehen jetzt besser/Sie stimmen lieber zu/Sie wären besser vorsichtig; **well, I THINK he'll understand** na ja, ich nehme zumindest an, dass er das verstehen wird; **I ~ so** ich denke or glaube (schon); **I ~ so too** das meine or denke ich auch; **I don't ~ so, I shouldn't ~ so, I ~ not** ich denke or glaube nicht; **I'll take this one then – I ~ not, Mr Green** dann nehme ich dieses – das glaube ich kaum, Herr Green; **I should ~ so!** das will ich (aber) auch gemeint haben; **I should ~ not!** das will ich auch nicht hoffen; **I hardly ~/~ it likely that ...** ich glaube kaum/ich halte es nicht für wahrscheinlich, dass ...; **I wasn't even ~ing** daran habe ich nicht einmal gedacht; **one would have thought there was an easier answer** man sollte eigentlich meinen, dass es da eine einfachere Lösung gäbe; **one would have thought you could have been more punctual** man könnte eigentlich erwarten, dass Sie etwas pünktlicher kommen; **one would have thought they'd have grasped it by now** man sollte eigentlich erwarten, dass sie das inzwischen begriffen haben; **what do you ~ I should do?** was glauben Sie, soll ich tun?, was soll ich Ihrer Meinung nach tun?; **well, what do you ~, shall we leave now?** nun, was meinst du, sollen wir jetzt gehen?; **I ~ I'll go for a walk** ich glaube, ich mache einen Spaziergang; **do you ~ you can manage?** glauben Sie, dass Sie es schaffen?

b (= *consider*) **you must ~ me very rude** Sie müssen mich für sehr unhöflich halten; **he ~s he's intelligent, he ~s himself intelligent** er hält sich für intelligent, er meint, er ist or sei intelligent; **they are thought to be rich** man hält sie für reich; **I wouldn't have thought it possible** das hätte ich nicht für möglich gehalten

c (= *imagine*) sich (*dat*) denken, sich (*dat*) vorstellen; **I don't know what to ~** ich weiß nicht, was ich davon halten soll; **that's what you ~!** denkste! (*inf*); **that's what he ~s** hat der eine Ahnung! (*inf*); **who do you ~ you are!** für wen hältst du dich eigentlich!, wofür hältst du dich eigentlich?; **you can't ~ how pleased I am to see you** Sie können sich (*dat*) (gar) nicht denken or vorstellen, wie froh ich bin, Sie zu sehen; **I can't ~ what he means!** ich kann mir (gar) nicht denken, was er meint; (*iro also*) was er damit bloß meinen kann or meint?; **anyone would ~ he was dying** man könnte beinahe glauben, er läge im Sterben; **one or you would ~ they'd already met** man könnte (geradezu) glauben or denken, sie seien alte Bekannte; **who would have thought it?** wer hätte das gedacht?; **to ~ that she's only ten!** wenn man bedenkt or sich (*dat*) vorstellt, dass sie erst zehn ist

d (= *reflect*) **to ~ how to do sth** sich (*dat*) überlegen, wie man etw macht; **I was ~ing (to myself) how ill he looked** ich dachte mir (im Stillen), dass er sehr krank aussah; **I never thought to ask you** ich habe gar nicht daran gedacht, Sie zu fragen

e (= *expect, intend: often neg or interrog*) **I didn't ~ to see you here** ich hätte nicht gedacht or erwartet, Sie hier zu treffen or dass ich Sie hier treffen würde; **I thought as much, I thought so** das habe ich mir schon gedacht

f **to ~ one's way out of a difficulty** sich (*dat*) einen Ausweg aus einer Schwierigkeit überlegen; **you'll ~ yourself into a rage again** du stei-

gerst dich (nur) wieder in eine Wut hinein

Ⓝ **have a ~ about it and let me know** denken Sie mal darüber nach or überlegen Sie es sich (*dat*) einmal, und geben Sie mir dann Bescheid; **to have a good ~** gründlich nachdenken; **you've got another ~ coming** (*Brit inf*) da irrst du dich aber gewaltig (*inf*), da bist du aber auf dem Holzweg (*inf*)

▶ **think about** ✪ 6.1, 6.3, 15.3 Ⅵ +*prep obj* **a** (= *reflect on*) idea, suggestion nachdenken über (+*acc*); **OK, I'll think about it** okay, ich überlege es mir; **what are you thinking about?** woran denken Sie gerade?; **it's worth thinking about** das ist überlegenswert, das wäre zu überlegen; **to think twice about sth** sich (*dat*) etw zweimal überlegen; **that'll give him something to think about** das wird ihn zu denken geben

b (*in progressive tenses*: = *half intend to*) daran denken, vorhaben; **I was thinking about coming to see you** ich habe vorgehabt or daran gedacht, Sie zu besuchen; **we're thinking about a holiday in Spain** wir denken daran, in Spanien Urlaub zu machen

c → **think of a, b, f**

▶ **think ahead** Ⅵ vorausdenken; (= *anticipate*: *driver etc*) Voraussicht walten lassen

▶ **think back** Ⅵ sich zurückversetzen (*to in* +*acc*)

▶ **think of** ✪ 6.1, 12.2, 14, 25.2 Ⅵ +*prep obj* **a** (= *consider, give attention to*) denken an (+*acc*); **I've too many things to think of just now** ich habe gerade zu viel um die Ohren (*inf*); **I've enough things to think of as it is** ich habe sowieso schon den Kopf voll or schon genug um die Ohren (*inf*); **he has his family to think of** er muss an seine Familie denken; **he thinks of nobody but himself** er denkt bloß an sich; **what was I thinking of!** (*inf*) was habe ich mir da(bei) bloß gedacht!; **come to think of it** wenn ich es mir recht überlege

b (= *remember*) denken an (+*acc*); **will you think of me sometimes?** wirst du manchmal an mich denken?; **I can't think of her name** ich kann mich nicht an ihren Namen erinnern, ich komme nicht auf ihren Namen

c (= *imagine*) sich (*dat*) vorstellen, bedenken, sich (*dat*) denken; **and to think of her going there alone!** und wenn man bedenkt or sich (*dat*) vorstellt, dass sie ganz allein dorthin gehen will/geht/ging; **think of the cost of all that!** stell dir bloß vor or denk dir bloß, was das alles kostet; **just think of him in a kilt!** stellen Sie sich (*dat*) ihn mal in einem Schottenrock vor!

d (= *entertain possibility of*) **she'd never think of getting married** sie denkt gar nicht daran zu heiraten; **he'd never think of such a thing** so etwas würde ihm nicht im Traum einfallen; **would you think of lowering the price a little?** würden Sie unter Umständen den Preis etwas ermäßigen?

e (= *devise, suggest*) solution, idea, scheme sich (*dat*) ausdenken; **who thought of that idea?** wer ist auf diese Idee gekommen or verfallen?; **who thought of that plan?** wer hat sich diesen Plan ausgedacht?; **the best thing I can think of is to go home** ich halte es für das Beste, nach Hause zu gehen; **shoes for dogs? what will they think of next!** Schuhe für Hunde! was sie sich wohl (nächstens) noch alles einfallen lassen!

f (= *have opinion of*) halten von; **what do you think of it/him?** was halten Sie davon/von ihm?; **to think well or highly of sb/sth** eine gute or hohe Meinung von jdm/etw haben, viel von jdm/etw halten; **to think little or not to think much of sb/sth** wenig or nicht viel von jdm/etw halten; **I told him what I thought of him** ich habe ihm gründlich die or meine Meinung gesagt; **he is very well thought of in his own town** in seiner Heimatstadt hält man große Stücke auf ihn

▶ **think on** Ⅵ +*prep obj* (*old, dial*) = **think about a**

▶ **think out** VT *sep* plan durchdenken; (= *come up with*) solution sich (*dat*) ausdenken; **a person**

who likes to think things out for himself ein Mensch, der sich (*dat*) seine eigene Meinung bildet

▶ **think over** VT *sep offer, suggestion* nachdenken über (+*acc*), sich (*dat*) überlegen; **can I think it over?** darf ich darüber nachdenken?, kann ich es mir noch mal überlegen?

▶ **think through** VT *sep* (gründlich) durchdenken

▶ **think up** VT *sep* sich (*dat*) ausdenken; **who thought up that idea?** wer ist auf die Idee gekommen?

thinkable ['θɪŋkəbl] ADJ denkbar

thinker ['θɪŋkə'] N Denker(in) *m(f)*

thinking ['θɪŋkɪŋ] ADJ denkend; **he's not really a ~ man, he prefers action** er ist kein Denker, sondern ein Macher; **all ~ men will agree with me** alle vernünftigen Menschen werden mit mir übereinstimmen; **the ~ man's/woman's pin-up** das Pin-up für den gebildeten Mann/die gebildete Frau; **to put one's ~ cap on** scharf überlegen or nachdenken; **~ time** Bedenkzeit *f*; **~ process** Denkprozess *m* or -vorgang *m*; **~ patterns** Denkmuster *pl*
N **to do some hard ~ about a question** sich (*dat*) etwas gründlich überlegen, etwas genau durchdenken; **to my way of ~** meiner Meinung nach; **that might be his way of ~** das mag seine Meinung sein; **this calls for some quick ~** hier muss eine schnelle Lösung gefunden werden

think: **think-piece** N (*Press*) ausführlicher Kommentar; **think-tank** N Expertenkommission *f*

thin-lipped ['θɪnlɪpt] ADJ dünnlippig; *smile* dünn

thinly ['θɪnlɪ] ADV **a** (= *in thin slices or layers*) dünn **b** (= *sparsely*) dünn; *wooded, attended* spärlich **c** (= *lightly*) *clad* leicht, dünn **d** (*fig*) *veiled, disguised* kaum, dürftig; *smile* schwach

thinner ['θɪnə'] N Verdünner *m*, Verdünnungsmittel *nt*

thinness ['θɪnnɪs] N **a** Dünnheit *f*, Dünnigkeit *f*; (*of dress, material*) Leichtheit *f*; (*of liquid*) Dünnflüssigkeit *f*; (*of paper, line, thread*) Feinheit *f*; (*of column of print*) geringe Breite **b** (*of person*) Magerkeit *f* **c** (= *sparseness*) **the ~ of his hair** sein schütterer or spärlicher Haarwuchs; **the ~ of the grass** das spärlich wachsende Gras **d** (= *lack of density: of air*) Dünnheit *f* **e** (*fig, of voice, smile*) Schwachheit *f*; (*of excuse, disguise, plot*) Dürftigkeit *f*; (*of trading*) Schlaffheit *f*; (*of profits*) geringe Höhe; (*of majority*) Knappheit *f* → **thin**

thin-skinned ['θɪnskɪnd] ADJ (*fig*) empfindlich, dünnhäutig

third [θɜːd] ADJ **a** (*in series*) dritte(r, s); **to be ~** Dritte(r, s) sein; **in ~ place** (*Sport etc*) an dritter Stelle; **in the ~ place** (= *thirdly*) drittens; **~ time around** beim dritten Mal; **she was** or **came ~ in her class** sie war die Drittbeste in der Klasse; **he was** or **came ~ in the race** er machte or belegte den dritten Platz beim Rennen; **~ time lucky** beim dritten Anlauf gelingt's!; **the ~ finger** (*Anat*) der Ringfinger
b (*of fraction*) **a ~ part** ein Drittel *nt*
N **a** (*of series*) Dritte(r, s); (= *fraction*) Drittel *nt* → *also* **sixth**
b (*Mus*) Terz *f*
c (*Aut*, = *third gear*) dritter Gang; **to be in ~** im dritten Gang sein; **to change/go into ~** in den dritten Gang wechseln/gehen
d (*Brit, Univ*) Drei *f*; **he got a ~** er bestand (sein Examen) mit „Befriedigend"

third: **third-class** ADV dritter Klasse ADJ **a** (*lit*) dritter Klasse; (*fig*) drittklassig; **~ degree** (*Brit, Univ*) Abschluss *m* mit „Befriedigend" **b** (*US, Post*) *mail, stamp* dritter Klasse; **third degree** N **to give sb the ~** (*lit*) (beim Verhör) Stufe drei einschalten; (*fig*) jdn in die Zange nehmen; **third-degree burn** N (*Med*) Verbrennung *f* dritten Grades; **third estate** N der dritte Stand, das Bürgertum

thirdly ['θɜːdlɪ] ○ 26.2 ADV drittens

third: **third party** N Dritte(r) *mf*, dritte Person; **third-party** ADJ *attr* Haftpflicht-; **~ insurance** Haftpflichtversicherung *f*; **~, fire and theft (insurance)** ≈ Teilkaskoversicherung *f* ADV **insured ~** in einer Haftpflichtversicherung, haftpflichtversichert; **third person** ADJ in der dritten Person N **the ~ singular/plural** (*Gram*) die dritte Person Singular/Plural; **third-rate** ADJ drittklassig, drittrangig; **third reading** N (*Parl*) dritte Lesung; **Third World** N Dritte Welt ATTR der Dritten Welt

thirst [θɜːst] N Durst *m*; **~ for knowledge** Wissensdurst *m*; **~ for adventure** Abenteuerlust *f*; **he's got a real ~ on him** (*inf*) er hat einen noblen Durst (am Leibe) (*inf*); **to die of ~** verdursten VI **a** (*old*) **I ~** es dürstet *or* durstet mich **b** (*fig*) **to ~ for revenge/knowledge** *etc* nach Rache/Wissen *etc* dürsten; **the plants were ~ing for water** die Pflanzen dürsteten nach Wasser

thirstily ['θɜːstɪlɪ] ADV (*lit*) *drink* durstig; (*fig*) begierig

thirsty ['θɜːstɪ] ADJ (+*er*) **a** durstig; **to be/feel ~** Durst haben; **it made me ~** das machte mich durstig, das machte mir Durst; **to get ~** durstig werden, Durst bekommen; **~ for praise** begierig auf Lob; **~ for love/revenge/knowledge/blood** nach Liebe/Rache/Wissen/Blut dürstend *or* lechzend (*old, hum*); **the land is ~ for rain** das Land dürstet nach Regen **b** (*fig inf*) *car* mit hohem Benzinverbrauch, durstig (*inf*) **c** (= *causing thirst*) **it's ~ work** diese Arbeit macht durstig

thirteen ['θɜːˈtiːn] ADJ dreizehn N Dreizehn *f*

thirteenth ['θɜːˈtiːnθ] ADJ (*in series*) dreizehnte(r, s); **a ~ part** ein Dreizehntel *nt* N (*in series*) Dreizehnte(r, s); (= *fraction*) Dreizehntel *nt* → *also* **sixth**

thirtieth ['θɜːtɪθ] ADJ (*in series*) dreißigste(r, s); **a ~ part** ein Dreißigstel *nt* N (*in series*) Dreißigstel *nt* → *also* **sixth**

thirty ['θɜːtɪ] ADJ dreißig; **~-one/two** ein-/zweiunddreißig; **a ~-second note** (*US, Mus*) Zweiunddreißigstel *nt* N Dreißig *f*; **the thirties** (= *era*) die dreißiger Jahre *or* Dreißigerjahre; **one's thirties** (= *age*) die Dreißiger → *also* **sixty**

thirtyish ['θɜːtɪʃ] ADJ um die dreißig

this [ðɪs] DEM PRON *pl* **these** dies, das; **what is ~?** was ist das dies?; **who is ~?** wer ist das?; **~ is John** das *or* dies ist John; **these are my children** das *or* dies sind meine Kinder; **~ is where I live** hier wohne ich; **~ is what he showed me** dies *or* das (hier) hat er mir gezeigt; **do you like ~?** gefällt dir das?; **I prefer ~** ich mag das hier *or* dies(es) lieber; **~ is to certify that ...** hiermit wird bestätigt, dass ...; **~ under/in front of etc ~** darunter/davor *etc*; **it ought to have been done before ~** es hätte schon vorher getan werden sollen; **with ~ he left us** damit *or* mit diesen Worten verließ er uns; **what's all ~?** was soll das?; **what's all I hear about your new job?** was höre ich da so (alles) über deine neue Stelle?; **~ and that** mancherlei; **we were talking of ~ and that** wir haben von diesem und jenem *or* über dies und das geredet; **~, that and the other** alles Mögliche; **will you take ~ or that?** nehmen Sie dieses hier oder das hier?; **it was like ~** es war so; **~ is Friday the 13th** heute ist Freitag der 13.; **but ~ is May** aber es ist doch Mai!; **and now ~!** und jetzt (auch noch) dies *or* das!; **~ is Mary (speaking)** hier (ist) Mary; **~ is what I mean!** das meine ich (ja)!; **~ is it!** (= *now*) jetzt!; (*showing sth*) das da!, das ist er/sie/es!; (= *exactly*) genau!

DEM ADJ *pl* **these** diese(r, s); **~ week** diese Woche; **~ month** diesen Monat; **~ year** dieses Jahr; **~ evening** heute Abend; **~ time last week** letzte Woche um diese Zeit; **~ coming week** jetzt die (kommende) Woche; **~ time** diesmal, dieses Mal; **these days** heutzutage; **all ~ talk** dieses ganze Gerede, all das *or* dies Gerede; **to run ~ way and that** hin und her rennen; **I have been waiting for you ~ past half-hour** ich habe bereits die letzte halbe Stunde auf dich gewartet; **~ boy of yours!** also, Ihr Junge!; **I met ~ guy**

who ... (*inf*) ich habe (so) einen getroffen, der ...; **~ friend of hers** dieser Freund von ihr (*inf*), ihr Freund
DEM ADV so; **it was ~ long** es war so lang; **~ far** (*time*) bis jetzt; (*place*) so weit, bis hierher; **~ much is certain** so viel ist sicher, eins steht fest

thistle ['θɪsl] N Distel *f*

thistledown ['θɪsldaʊn] N Distelwolle *f*; **as light as ~** federleicht

thither ['ðɪðə'] ADV (*old*) dorthin, dahin → **hither**

tho' [ðəʊ] *abbr of* **though**

thole [θəʊl] N (*Naut*) Dolle *f*, Riemenauflage *f*

Thomist ['təʊmɪst] N Thomist(in) *m(f)* ADJ thomistisch

thong [θɒŋ] N **a** (*of whip*) Peitschenschnur *f*, Peitschenriemen *m*; (= *fastening*) Lederriemen *m* **b** (*US:* = *flip-flop*) Badelatsche *f* (*inf*), Gummilatsche *f* (*inf*) **c** (= *G-string*) Tangaslip *m*

thoracic [θɔːˈræsɪk] ADJ Brust-, thorakal (*spec*); **~ vertebra** Brustwirbel *m*

thorax ['θɔːræks] N Brustkorb *m*, Brustkasten *m*, Thorax *m* (*spec*)

thorium ['θɔːrɪəm] N (*Chem*) Thorium *nt*

thorn [θɔːn] N Dorn *m*; (= *shrub*) Dornbusch *m*, Dornenstrauch *m*; **to be a ~ in sb's flesh** *or* **side** (*fig*) jdm ein Dorn im Auge sein

thorn apple N Stechapfel *m*

thornless ['θɔːnlɪs] ADJ ohne Dornen

thorny ['θɔːnɪ] ADJ (+*er*) (*lit*) dornig, dornenreich; (*fig*) haarig

thorough ['θʌrə] ADJ gründlich; *knowledge also* umfassend, solide; *contempt also* bodenlos; *success* voll, durchschlagend; *fool, rascal* ausgemacht; **to do a ~ job** gründliche Arbeit leisten; **to have/get a ~ grounding in sth** eine solide Basis in etw haben/bekommen; **to be ~ in doing sth** etw gründlich machen; **she's a ~ nuisance** sie ist wirklich eine Plage; **it's a ~ nuisance** das ist wirklich lästig

thorough: **thorough bass** N (*Mus*) Generalbass *m*; **thoroughbred** N reinrassiges Tier; (= *horse*) Vollblut(pferd) *nt*, Vollblüter *m* ADJ reinrassig; **~ horse** Vollblut(pferd) *nt*; **~ dog** Rassehund *m*; **thoroughfare** N Durchfahrts- or Durchgangsstraße *f*; **it's the most famous ~ of this town** es ist die berühmteste Straße dieser Stadt; **this isn't a public ~** das ist keine öffentliche Verkehrsstraße; **"no ~"** (*cul-de-sac*) „Sackgasse"; (*not open to public*) „Durchfahrt verboten"; **thoroughgoing** ADJ *changes* gründlich; *revision* grundlegend, tief greifend; *measure, reform* durchgreifend; *believer* eingefleischt; **to be a ~ professional** durch und durch Profi sein; **he is a ~ rascal** er ist ein Spitzbube durch und durch

thoroughly ['θʌrəlɪ] ADV **a** gründlich, von Grund auf **b** (= *extremely*) durch und durch, von Grund auf; *convinced* völlig, vollkommen; **we ~ enjoyed our meal** wir haben unser Essen von Herzen genossen; **I ~ enjoyed myself** es hat mir aufrichtig Spaß gemacht; **I ~ agree** ich stimme voll und ganz zu; **I'm ~ ashamed** ich schäme mich zutiefst, ich bin zutiefst beschämt; **a ~ nasty person** ein Scheusal durch und durch; **~ modern** durch und durch modern; **~ boring** ausgesprochen langweilig

thoroughness ['θʌrənɪs] N Gründlichkeit *f*; (= *carefulness*) Sorgfältigkeit *f*, Sorgfalt *f*; (*of knowledge*) Umfang *m*, Solidität *f*

Thos *abbr of* **Thomas**

those [ðəʊz] *pl of* **that** DEM PRON das (da) *sing*; **what are ~?** was ist das (hier) da?, was sind das für Dinger? (*inf*); **whose are ~?** wem gehören diese da?; **~ are my suggestions** das *or* dies sind meine Vorschläge; **on top of ~** darauf; (= *moreover*) darüber hinaus; **above ~** darüber; **after ~** danach; (*place*) dahinter; **~ are the ones I want** ich möchte diese dort; **~ who want to go, may** wer möchte, kann gehen, diejenigen, die gehen möchten, können das tun (*form*); **one of ~ who** einer/eine von denen *or* denjenigen, die ...; **there are ~ who say ...** einige sagen ...

DEM ADJ diese *or* die (da), jene (*old, liter*); **what are ~ men doing?** was machen diese Männer da?; **on ~ two occasions** bei diesen beiden Gelegenheiten; **it was just one of ~ days/things** das war wieder so ein Tag/so eine Sache; **he is one of ~ people who ...** er ist einer von den Leuten *or* von denjenigen, die ...; **~ dogs!** also, diese Hunde!; **~ sons of yours!** also, deine Söhne!

thou [ðaʊ] PERS PRON (*old, to friend, servant etc*) Er/Sie (*obs*); (*to stranger*) Ihr (*obs*); (*Rel*) du; (*Brit: dial*) du

though [ðəʊ] ✪ 15.2 CONJ **a** (= *in spite of the fact that*) obwohl, obgleich, obschon; **even ~** obwohl *etc*; **~ poor she is generous** obwohl sie arm ist, ist sie großzügig; **strange ~ it may seem ...** so seltsam es auch scheinen mag ..., mag es auch noch so seltsam scheinen ... (*geh*); **important ~ it may be/is ...** so wichtig es auch sein mag/ist, auch wenn es noch so wichtig ist ...; **~ I say it** *or* **so myself** auch wenn ich es selbst sage **b** (*liter*: = *even if*) **I will go (even) ~ it may cost me my life** ich werde gehen und sollte es mich (auch) das Leben kosten *or* und koste es das Leben (*liter*); **~ it take forever** (*liter*) und dauerte es auch ewig (*liter*) **c as ~** als ob

ADV a (= *nevertheless*) doch; **he didn't/did do it ~** er hat es aber (doch) nicht/aber doch gemacht; **I'm sure he didn't do it ~** ich bin aber sicher, dass er es nicht gemacht hat; **nice day – rather windy ~** schönes Wetter! – aber ziemlich windig! **b** (= *really*) **but will he ~?** tatsächlich?, wirklich? **c** (*inf*) **hot, isn't it? – isn't it ~!** warm, was? – allerdings!

thought [θɔ:t] *pret, ptp of* **think** N **a** *no pl* (= *act or process of thinking*) Denken *nt*; **to spend hours in ~** stundenlang in Gedanken (vertieft) sein; **to be lost in ~** ganz in Gedanken sein, gedankenverloren sein (*geh*); **to take ~** (*old*) denken; **logical ~** logisches Denken; **in ~** in Gedanken **b** (= *idea, opinion*) Gedanke *m*; (*sudden*) Einfall *m*; **she hasn't a ~ in her head** sie hat nichts im Hirn *or* Kopf; **the ~s of Chairman Mao** die Gedanken des Vorsitzenden Mao; **he didn't express any ~s on the matter** er hat keine Ansichten zu diesem Thema geäußert; **that's a ~!** (= *amazing*) man stelle sich das mal vor!; (= *problem to be considered*) das ist wahr!; (= *good idea*) das ist eine (gute) Idee *or* ein guter Gedanke *or* Einfall; **what a ~!** was für ein Gedanke *or* eine Vorstellung!; **a ~ has just occurred to me, I've just had a ~** (*inf*) mir ist gerade ein Gedanke gekommen, mir ist gerade etwas eingefallen; **don't give it another ~** machen Sie sich (*dat*) keine Gedanken darüber; (= *forget it*) denken Sie nicht mehr daran; **his one ~ was ...** sein einziger Gedanke war ...; **to have no ~ of doing sth** gar nicht vorhaben *or* gar nicht daran denken, etw zu tun; **it's a shame it doesn't fit, but it's the ~ that counts** ist ein Jammer, dass es nicht passt, aber es war gut gemeint; **it's the ~ that counts, not how much you spend** es kommt nur auf die Idee an, nicht auf den Preis; **to collect one's ~s** sich sammeln, seine Gedanken zusammennehmen; **her ~s were elsewhere** sie war in Gedanken woanders; **the mere** *or* **very ~ of it** der bloße Gedanke (daran), die bloße Vorstellung **c** *no pl* (= *body of ideas*) Denken *nt*; **modern ~** das moderne Denken, das Denken der Moderne **d** *no pl* (= *care, consideration*) Nachdenken *nt*, Überlegung *f*; **to give some ~ to sth** sich (*dat*) Gedanken über *or* etw machen, etw bedenken *or* überlegen; **after much ~** nach langer Überlegung *or* langem Überlegen; **to act without ~** gedankenlos *or* ohne Überlegung handeln; **without ~ for sb/oneself/sth** ohne an jdn/sich selbst/etw zu denken, ohne Rücksicht auf jdn/sich selbst/etw; **he has no ~ for his parents' feelings** er nimmt keine Rücksicht auf

die Gefühle seiner Eltern; **I never gave it a moment's ~** ich habe mir nie darüber Gedanken gemacht **e** **a ~** (= *a little*) eine Idee, ein Ideechen *nt* (*inf*); **with a ~ more tact** mit einer Idee *or* einer Spur mehr Takt

thought: thought blocking N (*Psych*) Denkhemmung *f*; **thought experiment** N Gedankenexperiment *nt*

thoughtful ['θɔːtfʊl] ADJ **a** (= *full of thought*) expression, person nachdenklich, gedankenvoll, grüblerisch; *remark, analysis, book* gut durchdacht, wohl überlegt; *present* gut ausgedacht; *silence* nachdenklich **b** (= *considerate*) rücksichtsvoll; (= *attentive, helpful*) aufmerksam; **to be ~ of sb's comfort/needs** an jds Wohlbefinden/Bedürfnisse denken; **to be ~ of/toward(s) sb** jdm gegenüber aufmerksam/rücksichtsvoll sein; **to be ~ of others** auf andere Rücksicht nehmen; **it was very ~ of you to ...** es war sehr aufmerksam von Ihnen, zu ...

thoughtfully ['θɔːtfəlɪ] ADV **a** *say, look* nachdenklich **b** (= *with much thought*) mit viel Überlegung; **a ~ written book** ein wohl durchdachtes Buch **c** (= *considerately*) rücksichtsvoll; (= *attentively, helpfully*) aufmerksam; **she ~ provided rugs** sie war so aufmerksam, Decken bereitzustellen, aufmerksamerweise hatte sie Decken bereitgestellt

thoughtfulness ['θɔːtfʊlnɪs] N **a** (*of expression, person*) Nachdenklichkeit *f*; (*of remark, analysis*) Tiefgang *m* **b** (= *consideration*) Rücksicht(nahme) *f*; (= *attentiveness, helpfulness*) Aufmerksamkeit *f*; **his ~ for his parents** seine Aufmerksamkeit/Rücksichtnahme seinen Eltern gegenüber

thoughtless ['θɔːtlɪs] ADJ **a** (= *inconsiderate*) person gedankenlos, rücksichtslos; (= *inattentive, unhelpful*) gedankenlos, unachtsam; **he's very ~ of** *or* **about/to(wards) other people** er ist sehr gedankenlos/rücksichtslos anderen gegenüber; **how ~ of you!** wie rücksichtslos von dir!; **it was ~ of her (to tell him)** es war gedankenlos von ihr(, es ihm zu erzählen) **b** (= *without reflection*) gedankenlos, unüberlegt, unbesonnen; **~ of the danger, he leapt** ungeachtet der Gefahr sprang er

thoughtlessly ['θɔːtlɪslɪ] ADV **a** (= *inconsiderately*) *act, behave* rücksichtslos **b** (= *unthinkingly*) gedankenlos, unüberlegt; **he had ~ taken it with him** er hatte es aus Gedankenlosigkeit mitgenommen

thoughtlessness ['θɔːtlɪsnɪs] N **a** (= *lack of consideration*) Gedankenlosigkeit *f*, Rücksichtslosigkeit *f*; (= *inattentiveness, unhelpfulness*) Unaufmerksamkeit *f* **b** (= *lack of reflection*) Gedankenlosigkeit *f*, Unüberlegtheit *f*

thought: thought process N Gedankengang *m*; **thought-provoking** ADJ *film, book, article, idea* zum Nachdenken anregend; **thought reader** N Gedankenleser(in) *m(f)*; **thought reading** N Gedankenlesen *nt*; **thought transference** N Gedankenübertragung *f*

thousand ['θaʊzənd] ADJ tausend; **a ~** (ein)tausend; **two ~** zweitausend; **a ~ times** tausendmal; **a ~ and one/two** tausend(und)eins/-zwei; **I died a ~ deaths** (*inf*, = *was embarrassed*) ich wäre fast in den Boden versunken; (= *was afraid*) ich habe tausend Ängste ausgestanden; **I have a ~ and one (different) things to do** (*inf*) ich habe tausenderlei *or* tausend Dinge zu tun; **Thousand Island dressing** Thousand-Islands-Dressing *nt* **N** Tausend *nt*; **the ~s** (*Math*) die Tausender *pl*; **there were ~s of people present** es waren tausende *or* Tausende (von Menschen) anwesend; **the year three ~** das Jahr dreitausend; **people arrived in their ~s** die Menschen kamen zu tausenden *or* Tausenden

thousandfold ['θaʊzəndfəʊld] (*liter*) ADJ tausendfach ADV **a** ~ tausendfach, tausendfältig

thousandth ['θaʊzənθ] ADJ (*in series*) tausendste(r, s); **a** *or* **one ~ part** ein Tausendstel *nt* **N** (*in series*) Tausendste(r, s); (= *fraction*) Tausendstel *nt* → *also* **sixth**

thraldom, (*US*) **thralldom** ['θrɔːldəm] N (*liter*) Knechtschaft *f*; **to be in ~ to her beauty** (*fig*) ihre Schönheit hatte ihn in ihren Bann geschlagen

thrall [θrɔːl] N (*liter*) **a** (= *slave*) Leibeigene(r) *m*, Sklave *m* (*also fig*), Knecht *m* **b** (= *condition*) **to be in ~ to sb/sth** in jds Bann (*dat*)/Bann einer Sache (*gen*) stehen

thrash [θræʃ] VT **a** (= *beat*) verprügeln, verdreschen; *donkey etc* einschlagen auf (+*acc*); **to ~ the (living) daylights out of sb** (*inf*) jdn grün und blau schlagen **b** (*Sport inf*) *opponent* (vernichtend) schlagen **c** (= *move wildly*) *arms* schlagen mit, fuchteln mit; *legs* strampeln mit; **he ~ed his arms (about)** angrily er schlug wütend (mit den Armen) um sich **d** (*Agr*) = **thresh VI** **to ~ about** *or* **around** um sich schlagen; (*in bed*) sich herumwerfen; (*fish*) zappeln; **the branches ~ed against the panes** die Zweige schlugen gegen die Fensterscheiben **N** (*dated Brit, inf, = party*) Party *f*

▸ **thrash out** VT *sep differences, deal, terms, details* ausdiskutieren; **to thrash things out** die Sache durchdiskutieren

thrashing ['θræʃɪŋ] N **a** (= *beating*) Prügel *pl*, Schläge *pl*, Dresche *f* (*inf*); **to give sb a good ~** jdm eine ordentliche Tracht Prügel verpassen **b** (*Sport inf*) komplette Niederlage; **to give sb a ~** jdn vernichtend schlagen

thrash metal N (*Mus*) Thrash Metal *nt*

thread [θred] N **a** (*of cotton, wool etc*) Faden *m*; (*Sew*) Garn *nt*, Faden *m*; (= *strong thread*) Zwirn *m*; **to hang by a ~** (*fig*) an einem (seidenen *or* dünnen) Faden hängen **b** (*fig, of story*) (roter) Faden; **to follow the ~ of a conversation** dem Gedankengang eines Gespräches folgen; **he lost the ~ of what he was saying** er hat den Faden verloren; **to pick up the ~s of one's story/a conversation** den (roten) Faden/den Gesprächsfaden wieder aufnehmen; **to gather up** *or* **pick up the ~s of one's career/life** alte Fäden wieder anknüpfen **c** (*Tech, of screw*) Gewinde *nt* **d** (*fig*) (= *thin line: of light*) Strahl *m*, Streifen *m* **e** (*E-mail*) Subject *m* **VT a** *needle* einfädeln; *beads* aufreihen, auffädeln (*on* auf +*acc*); *necklace* aufziehen; **~ed with silver** von Silber(fäden) durchzogen, mit Silber(fäden) durchsetzt **b** **to ~ one's way through the crowd/trees** *etc* sich durch die Menge/zwischen den Bäumen *etc* hindurchschlängeln; **he ~ed the ball through to Gascoigne** er spitzelte den Ball zu Gascoigne durch **c** (*Tech*) *screw* mit einem Gewinde versehen **VI** **he ~ed through the crowd** er schlängelte sich durch die Menge (hindurch)

threadbare ['θredbeəʳ] ADJ abgewetzt, fadenscheinig; *clothes also* abgetragen; *carpet also* abgelaufen; (*fig*) *argument* fadenscheinig; *joke* abgedroschen; *idea* veraltet

threaded ['θredɪd] ADJ (*Tech*) Gewinde-, mit Gewinde; **~ bolt** Gewindebolzen *m*

thread mark N Silberfaden *m* (*in Banknoten*)

threat [θret] N **a** Drohung *f*; **is that a ~?** soll das eine Drohung sein?; **to make a ~** drohen, eine Androhung machen (*against sb* jdm); **under ~ of sth** unter Androhung von etw; **he is under ~ of expulsion** ihm wurde der Ausschluss angedroht **b** (= *danger*) Bedrohung (*to* +*gen*), Gefahr *f* (*to* für); **this war is a ~ to civilization** dieser Krieg stellt eine Gefahr für die Zivilisation *or* eine Bedrohung der Zivilisation dar

threaten ['θretn] VT **a** *person* bedrohen, drohen (+*dat*); *revenge, violence* androhen, drohen mit; **don't you ~ me!** von Ihnen lasse ich mir nicht drohen!; **to ~ to do sth** (an)drohen, etw zu tun; **to ~ sb with sth** jdm etw androhen, jdm mit etw drohen; **to ~ sb with a weapon** jdn mit der Waffe bedrohen; **to ~ legal action** mit rechtlichen Schritten drohen **b** (= *put in danger*) bedrohen, gefährden; **the rain ~ed to spoil the harvest** der Regen drohte, die Ernte zu zerstören

c (*Met, = give warning of*) **the sky ~s rain** der Himmel sieht (bedrohlich) nach Regen aus; **it's ~ing to rain** es sieht (bedrohlich) nach Regen aus **VI** (*danger, storm etc*) drohen, im Anzug sein

threatened [ˈθrɛtnd] ADJ **a** **he felt ~** er fühlte sich bedroht **b** (*= endangered, under threat*) species, jobs gefährdet **c** (*= presaged*) angedroht

threatening [ˈθrɛtnɪŋ] ADJ drohend; *weather, clouds also, situation* bedrohlich; **a ~ letter/phone call** ein Drohbrief *m*/-anruf *m*; **~ behaviour** Drohungen *pl*; **to find sb ~** sich von jdm bedroht fühlen

threateningly [ˈθrɛtnɪŋlɪ] ADV drohend; **the sky darkened ~** der Himmel verfinsterte sich bedrohlich

three [θriː] **ADJ** drei **N** (*= figure, bus, Cards*) Drei *f*; **~'s a crowd** drei Leute sind schon zu viel, bei dreien ist einer zu viel → also **six**

three: three-act play N Dreiakter *m*; **three--colour**, (*US*) **three-color** ADJ (*Phot*) Dreifarben-; **~ printing** Dreifarbendruck *m*; **three--cornered** ADJ **~ contest** or **fight** Kampf *m* mit drei Beteiligten or Parteien, Dreieckskampf *m*; **~ hat** Dreispitz *m*; **three-D N to be in ~** dreidimensional or 3-D sein **ADJ** (*also* **three--dimensional**) dreidimensional, 3-D-; **~ movie** 3-D-Film *m*; **three-decker** N **a** (*Naut*) Dreidecker *m* **b** (*= sandwich*) Doppelsandwich *nt*; **three-dimensional** ADJ dreidimensional; (*= realistic*) *character* ausgereift; **threefold** ADJ, ADV dreifach; **three-fourths** N (*US*) = **three--quarters**; **three-legged** ADJ dreibeinig; **~ race** (*Sport*) Wettlauf, bei dem zwei an einem Bein zusammengebunden werden; **three-master** N Dreimaster *m*; **threepence** N (*Brit, old*) Dreipennystück *nt*; **threepenny** (*Brit, old*) Dreipennystück *nt*; **threepenny bit** N (*Brit, old*) Dreipennystück *nt*; **threepenny opera** N Dreigroschenoper *f*; **threepenny piece** N (*Brit, old*) = **threepenny bit**; **three-phase** ADJ Dreistufen-; (*Elec*) Dreiphasen-; **~ circuit** Dreiphasenschaltung *f*; **~ plan/programme** Dreistufenplan *m*/-programm *nt*; **three-piece suit** N (*man's*) Anzug *m* mit Weste; (*lady's*) dreiteiliges Ensemble; **three-piece suite** N (*esp Brit*) dreiteilige Polster- or Sitzgarnitur; **three--pin plug** N Stecker *m* mit drei Kontakten; **three--ply** **N** (*= wool*) Dreifachwolle *f*; (*= wood*) dreischichtiges Spanholz **ATTR** *wood* dreischichtig; **~ wool** Dreifachwolle *f*; **three-point landing** N (*Aviat*) Dreipunktlandung *f*; **three-point turn** N (*Aut*) Wenden *nt* in drei Zügen; **three--quarter** N (*Sport*) Dreiviertelspieler(in) *m(f)* **ATTR** dreiviertel-; **~ length** dreiviertellang; **~ portrait** Halbbild *nt*; **three-quarters** **N** drei Viertel *pl*; **~ of an hour** eine Dreiviertelstunde **ADV** drei viertel, zu drei Vierteln; **three-ring circus** N (*US sl*) Affenzirkus *m*; **threescore** ADJ sechzig; **threesome** N Trio *nt*, Dreiergruppe *f*; (*Golf*) Dreier *m*; **in a ~** zu dritt; **three-speed** ADJ attr = **gears** Dreigangschaltung *f*; **three-way** ADJ *discussion* mit drei Parteien; **~ catalyst** Dreiwegkatalysator *m*; **a ~ split** eine Dreiteilung; **there's a ~ tie for the lead** es gibt drei punktgleiche Spitzenanwärter; **three-wheeler** N (*Aut*) dreirädriges Auto; (*= tricycle*) Dreirad *nt*

THREE Rs

Die **three Rs** sind „reading, writing and arithmetic" - Lesen, Schreiben, Rechnen - die allgemein wichtigsten Fähigkeiten, die man durch Erziehung und Bildung erlernen kann. Der Ausdruck nimmt von der ironisch-falschen Schreibweise „reading, 'riting and 'rithmetic" und wird häufig in öffentlichen Diskussionen über den sich abzeichnenden Niedergang des Bildungsniveaus angeführt.

---

threnody [ˈθrɛnədɪ] N (*Liter*) Threnodie *f*
thresh [θrɛʃ] VTI dreschen
thresher [ˈθrɛʃə] N **a** (*Agr, = machine*) Dreschmaschine *f*; (*= person*) Drescher(in) *m(f)* **b** (*= thresher shark*) Drescherhai *m*

threshing [ˈθrɛʃɪŋ] N Dreschen *nt*
threshing floor N Dreschboden *m*, Tenne *f*
threshing machine N Dreschmaschine *f*
threshold [ˈθrɛʃhəʊld] N (*lit, fig, Psych*) Schwelle *f*; (*of door also*) Türschwelle *f*; **on the ~** an der Schwelle; **we are on the ~ of a great discovery** wir stehen unmittelbar an der Schwelle zu einer großen Entdeckung; **to have a high/low pain ~** eine hohe/niedrige Schmerzschwelle haben

threw [θruː] pret of **throw**
thrice [θraɪs] ADV (*old*) dreimal; **he is ~ blessed** er ist dreifach or dreifältig gesegnet
thrift [θrɪft] N Sparsamkeit *f*
thriftily [ˈθrɪftɪlɪ] ADV **a** sparsam, wirtschaftlich, haushälterisch **b** (*US*) **his business is do-ing ~** sein Geschäft floriert
thriftiness [ˈθrɪftɪnɪs] N **a** Sparsamkeit *f*, Wirtschaftlichkeit *f* **b** (*US, = prosperity*) Gedeihen *nt*
thriftless [ˈθrɪftlɪs] ADJ verschwenderisch
thriftlessness [ˈθrɪftlɪsnɪs] N Verschwendung(ssucht) *f*
thrifty [ˈθrɪftɪ] ADJ (*+er*) **a** (*= careful, economical*) sparsam, wirtschaftlich, haushälterisch **b** (*US, = thriving*) blühend

thrill [θrɪl] **N** Erregung *f*; **all the ~s and spills of the circus** all die Sensationen und der Nervenkitzel des Zirkus; **a ~ of joy** eine freudige Erregung; **a ~ of horror** ein Entsetzensschauder *m*; **she heard his voice with a ~ of excitement** sie hörte seine Stimme, und Erregung durchfuhr sie; **it gave me quite a ~, it was quite a ~ for me** es war ein richtiges Erlebnis; **what a ~!** wie aufregend!; **he gets a ~ out of hunting** Jagen hat für ihn einen ganz besonderen Reiz; **the real ~ comes at the end of the book** die eigentliche Sensation kommt erst am Ende des Buches; **that's how he gets his ~s** das erregt ihn; **this will give you the ~ of a lifetime** das wird DAS Erlebnis deines Lebens (sein); **go on, give us a ~!** (*inf*) nun lass uns mal was sehen (*inf*) **VT** *person* (*story, crimes*) mitreißen, fesseln, packen; (*experience*) eine Sensation sein für; (*sb's touch, voice etc*) freudig erzittern lassen; (*sexually*) erregen; **I was quite ~ed by the sight of the Alps** ich war ganz hingerissen beim Anblick der Alpen; **I was ~ed to get your letter** ich habe mich riesig über deinen Brief gefreut; **the thought of going to America ~ed her** der Gedanke an eine Amerikareise versetzte sie in freudige Erregung; **to be ~ed to bits** (*inf*) sich freuen wie ein Kind; (*esp child*) ganz aus dem Häuschen sein vor Freude **VI** **she ~ed at the sound of his voice/to his touch** ein freudiger Schauer durchlief sie, als sie seine Stimme hörte/bei seiner Berührung

thriller [ˈθrɪlə] N Reißer *m* (*inf*); (*= whodunnit*) Krimi *m*, Thriller *m*
thrilling [ˈθrɪlɪŋ] ADJ aufregend; *book, film* spannend, fesselnd; *sensation* überwältigend, hinreißend; *music* hinreißend, mitreißend; *experience, victory* überwältigend, umwerfend (*inf*); (*sexually*) erregend; **we had a ~ time** es war richtig aufregend
thrillingly [ˈθrɪlɪŋlɪ] ADV spannungsgeladen; **~ new** aufregend neu
thrive [θraɪv] pret **throve** (*old*) or **thrived**, ptp **thriven** (*old*) or **thrived** VI (*= be in good health*: *animal, plant*) (gut) gedeihen; (*child also*) sich gut or prächtig entwickeln; (*= do well, business*) blühen, florieren; (*businessman*) erfolgreich sein
▶ **thrive on** VI +prep obj **the baby thrives on milk** mit Milch gedeiht das Baby prächtig; **this plant thrives on sun and light** bei Sonne und Licht gedeiht or entwickelt sich diese Pflanze prächtig; **he thrives on criticism/praise** Kritik/Lob bringt ihn erst zur vollen Entfaltung; **like it? I thrive on it** ob mir das gefällt? ich brauche das
thriven [ˈθrɪvən] (*old*) ptp of **thrive**

thriving [ˈθraɪvɪŋ] ADJ **a** *plant* prächtig gedeihend, kräftig; *person, city, community* blühend; *child* gut gedeihend; **he's ~!** ihm gehts prächtig!; (*child*) er blüht und gedeiht! **b** *business, economy, night life* florierend, blühend; *businessman* erfolgreich
thro' [θruː] abbr of **through**
throat [θrəʊt] N (*external*) Kehle *f*; (*internal also*) Rachen *m*; **to grab sb by the ~** jdn bei or an der Kehle or Gurgel packen; **to cut sb's ~** jdm die Kehle or Gurgel durchschneiden; **to cut one's own ~** (*fig*) (*dat*) selbst das Wasser abgraben; **my ~ is really dry** ich habe einen völlig trockenen Hals or eine ganz trockene Kehle; **I've a fishbone stuck in my ~** mir ist eine Gräte im Hals stecken geblieben; **the doctor looked down her ~** der Arzt sah ihr in den Hals; **cancer of the ~** Kehlkopfkrebs *m*; **to clear one's ~** sich räuspern; **they've been pouring drink down my ~ all evening** (*inf*) sie haben den ganzen Abend lang Alkohol in mich hineingeschüttet (*inf*); **to ram or force one's ideas down sb's ~** (*inf*) jdm seine eigenen Ideen aufzwingen; **the words stuck in my ~** die Worte blieben mir im Halse stecken; **it sticks in my ~** (*fig*) das geht mir gegen den Strich (*inf*)
throat microphone N Kehlkopfmikrofon *nt*
throaty [ˈθrəʊtɪ] ADJ (*+er*), **throatily** ADV [ˈθrəʊtɪ, -lɪ] kehlig, rau
throb [θrɒb] **VI** (*engine*) klopfen, hämmern; (*drums, gunfire*) dröhnen; (*heart, pulse*) pochen, klopfen; (*painfully: wound*) pochen, pulsieren, klopfen; (*very strongly*) hämmern; (*fig: with life, activity*) pulsieren (*with* vor +*dat*, mit); **my head was still ~bing (with pain)** ich hatte immer noch dieses Pochen im Kopf; **my head is ~bing** ich habe rasende Kopfschmerzen; **a street ~bing with people** eine Straße, die von Menschen wimmelt **N** (*of engine*) Klopfen *nt*, Hämmern *nt*; (*of drums, gunfire*) Dröhnen *nt*; (*of heart, pulse, wound*) Klopfen *nt*, Pochen *nt*, Hämmern *nt*; **the ~ of life** der Pulsschlag des Lebens
throbbing [ˈθrɒbɪŋ] **N** (*of engine*) Klopfen *nt*, Hämmern *nt*; (*of drums, gunfire*) Dröhnen *nt*; (*of heart, pulse*) Pochen *nt* **ADJ** **a** *pain* pulsierend; *headache, head* pochend **b** *music* hämmernd **c** (*fig: = pulsating*) *place, nightlife* pulsierend
throes [θrəʊz] PL **a** **the ~ of childbirth** die (Geburts)wehen *pl*; **in the ~ of death** im Todeskampf, in Todesqualen *pl*; **to be in the final ~ of sth** (*fig*) in den letzten Zügen einer Sache (*gen*) liegen **b** (*fig*) Wirren *pl*; **we are in the ~ of moving** wir stecken mitten im Umzug; **I was in the ~ of composition** ich war völlig vertieft in meine Kompositionen; **in the ~ of inspiration** in künstlerischer Versunkenheit
thrombosis [θrɒmˈbəʊsɪs] N Thrombose *f*
thrombus [ˈθrɒmbəs] N Thrombus *m* (*form*), Blutpfropf *m*
throne [θrəʊn] **N** Thron *m*; (*Eccl*) Stuhl *m*; **to come to the ~** den Thron besteigen; **to swear allegiance to the ~** der Krone den Treueid leisten; **the power of the ~** die Macht der Krone **VT** (*he is*) **~d in glory** (*Eccl*) er sitzet or thronet in Herrlichkeit
throne room N Thronsaal *m*; (*hum*) Klo *nt* (*inf*)
throng [θrɒŋ] **N** (*of people*) Scharen *pl*, Menschenmenge *f*; (*of angels*) Heerschar *f* **VI** sich drängen; **to ~ round sb/sth** sich um jdn/etw drängen or scharen; **to ~ toward(s) sb/sth** sich zu jdm/etw drängen, zu jdm/etw strömen **VT** belagern; **people ~ed the streets** die Menschen drängten sich in den Straßen; **to be ~ed with** wimmeln von or mit
throttle [ˈθrɒtl] **VT** **a** (*lit*) *person* erdrosseln, erwürgen **b** (*fig*) *feeling* ersticken, unterdrücken; *opposition* ersticken, unterbinden; *economy* drosseln; **to ~ the press** die Presse knebeln **c** (*Tech*) = **throttle back** **N** **a** (*on engine*) Drossel *f*; (*Aut etc, = lever*) Gashebel *m*; (*= valve*) Drosselklappe *f*; **at full ~** mit Vollgas; **to open/close the ~** die Drossel öffnen/schließen; (*Aut*

etc) Gas geben/zurücknehmen **b** (*hum*, = *throat*) Kehle *f*

▶ **throttle back** *or* **down** **VT** *sep* drosseln **VI** Gas zurücknehmen, den Motor drosseln

through, (*US*) **thru** [θruː] **PREP** **a** (*place*) durch; **he couldn't get ~ the hedge** er konnte nicht durch die Hecke durchkommen *or* (hin)durchschlüpfen; **to listen ~ the door** durch die (geschlossene) Tür mithören, lauschen; **he was shot ~ the head** er bekam einen Kopfschuss; **he went right ~ the red light** er ist bei Rot einfach durchgefahren; **he has come ~ many hardships** er hat viel Schweres durchgemacht; **we're ~ that stage now** wir sind jetzt durch dieses Stadium hindurch; **to be halfway ~ a book** ein Buch halb *or* zur Hälfte durchhaben (*inf*); **that happens halfway/three-quarters of the way ~ the book** das passiert in der Mitte/im letzten Viertel des Buches **b** (*time*) **all ~ his life** sein ganzes Leben lang; **he won't live ~ the night** er wird die Nacht nicht überleben; **he worked ~ the night** er hat die Nacht durchgearbeitet; **he lives there ~ the week** er wohnt da während *or* unter (*dial*) der Woche *or* die Woche über; **he slept ~ the film** er hat den ganzen Film über *or* hindurch *or* lang geschlafen; **all ~ the autumn** den ganzen Herbst über *or* hindurch **c** (*US*, = *up to and including*) bis (einschließlich); **Monday ~ Friday** von Montag bis (einschließlich) Freitag **d** (= *means, agency*) durch; **~ the post** (*Brit*) *or* **mail** (*US*) mit der Post, per Post; **it happened ~ no fault of mine** *or* **my own** es geschah nicht durch meine Schuld; **absent ~ illness** abwesend wegen Krankheit; **~ neglect** durch Nachlässigkeit; **to act ~ fear** aus Angst handeln; **he spoke ~ an interpreter** er wurde gedolmetscht **ADV** (*time, place*) durch; **he's a liar/gentleman ~ and ~** er ist durch und durch verlogen/ein Gentleman; **to sleep all night ~** die ganze Nacht durchschlafen; **did you stay right ~?** (*Brit*) sind Sie bis zum Schluss geblieben?; **they stayed ~ until Thursday** (*Brit*) sie blieben bis Donnerstag (da); **he knew all ~ what I was getting at** er wusste die ganze Zeit (über), worauf ich hinauswollte; **to let sb ~** jdn durchlassen; **to be wet ~** durch und durch *or* bis auf die Haut nass sein; **to read sth ~** etw durchlesen; **he's ~ in the other office** er ist (drüben) in einem anderen Büro; **the train goes ~ to Berlin** der Zug fährt bis nach Berlin durch **ADJ** *pred* **a** (= *finished*) **to be ~ with sb/sth** mit jdm/etw fertig sein (*inf*); **we're ~** (= *have finished relationship*) es ist (alles) aus zwischen uns; (= *have finished job*) wir sind fertig; **I'm ~ with him** der ist für mich gestorben *or* erledigt, ich bin fertig mit ihm (*all inf*); **I'm ~ with that kind of work** ich habe genug von dieser Arbeit; **you're ~, Kowalski, fired** wir sind mit Ihnen fertig, Kowalski, Sie fliegen!; **are you ~?** sind Sie fertig? **b** (*Brit, Telec*) **to be ~ (to sb/London)** mit jdm/London verbunden sein; **to get ~ (to sb/London)** zu jdm/nach London durchkommen; **you're ~, caller** Ihre Verbindung!, Ihr Gespräch!

through: through coach N (*Rail*) Kurswagen *m* (for *nach*); (= *bus*) direkte Busverbindung; **through flight** N Direktflug *m*; **through freight** N Durchgangsfracht *f*; **through-hole** ADJ (*Comput*) durchkontaktiert

throughout [θruːˈaʊt] **PREP** **a** (*place*) überall in (+*dat*); **~ the country** im ganzen Land; **~ the world** in der ganzen Welt **b** (*time*) den ganzen/die/das ganze ... hindurch *or* über; **~ his life** sein ganzes Leben lang **ADV** **a** (= *in every part*) **the house is carpeted ~** das Haus ist ganz *or* überall mit Teppichboden ausgelegt; **a house with electric light ~** ein Haus, das in jedem Raum elektrisches Licht hat; **a block of flats with water and gas ~** im Wohnblock mit Wasser und Gas in allen Wohnungen; **the coat is lined ~** der Mantel ist ganz gefüttert **b** (*time*) die ganze Zeit hindurch *or* über

through: throughput N (*Ind, Comput*) Durchsatz *m*; **through ticket** **N can I get a ~ to London?** kann ich bis London durchlösen?; **through traffic** N Durchgangsverkehr *m*; **through train** N durchgehender Zug; **throughway** N (*US*) Schnellstraße *f*

throve [θrəʊv] (*old*) *pret of* **thrive**

throw [θrəʊ] *vb: pret* **threw**, *ptp* **thrown** **N** **a** (*of ball, javelin, dice*) Wurf *m*; **it's your ~** du bist dran; **have another ~** werfen Sie noch einmal; **to lose the ~** (*dice*) den Wurf verlieren; **a 30-metre ~** ein Wurf von 30 Metern; **the first ~ went to the German** (*Wrestling*) der Deutsche brachte seinen Gegner als erster zu Boden; **at 10 dollars a ~** zu 10 Dollar das Stück **b** (*for covering furniture*) Überwurf *m* **VT** **a** *ball, stone* werfen; *water* schütten; **to ~ the dice** würfeln; **to ~ a six** eine Sechs würfeln; **to ~ sth to sb** jdm etw zuwerfen; **~ me those keys** werfen Sie mir die Schlüssel herüber; **to ~ sth at sb** etw nach jdm werfen; *mud, paint etc* jdn mit etw bewerfen; **to ~ a ball 20 metres** einen Ball 20 Meter weit werfen; **to ~ sth across the room** etw (quer) durchs Zimmer werfen; **to ~ sb across the ring** jdn durch den Ring schleudern; **he threw himself to the floor** er warf sich auf den Boden *or* zu Boden; **to ~ oneself at sb** (*physically*) sich auf jdn werfen *or* stürzen; (*fig*) sich jdm an den Hals werfen *or* schmeißen (*inf*); **to ~ oneself into the job** sich in die Arbeit stürzen; **to ~ one's voice** seine Stimme zum Tragen bringen; **to ~ money at sth** etw mit Geld überhäufen; **to ~ one's hat** *or* **cap into the ring** (*fig*) sich anbieten **b** (= *send to ground*) *rider* abwerfen; *opponent* zu Boden werfen *or* bringen; **to be ~n from the saddle** aus dem Sattel geworfen werden **c** (= *put hastily*) werfen; **to ~ a coat over sb** jdm einen Mantel überwerfen **d** (*fig*, = *cast*) **to ~ a glance at sb/sth** einen Blick auf jdn/etw werfen; **to ~ an angry look at sb/sth** jdm/einer Sache einen wütenden Blick zuwerfen; **to ~ light** *dated* geben; **to ~ sb off the scent** *or* **trail** jdn von der Spur abbringen; **to ~ sb into prison** jdn ins Gefängnis werfen; **to ~ the blame on sb** jdm die Schuld zuschieben *or* in die Schuhe schieben; **to ~ doubt on sth** etw in Zweifel ziehen; **he threw his troops into action** er warf seine Truppen ins Gefecht **e** *switch, lever* betätigen **f** (*inf*, = *disconcert*) aus dem Konzept bringen **g** *party* geben, schmeißen (*inf*) **h** *fit* bekommen, kriegen (*inf*) **i** (*inf*: = *deliberately lose*) *match, game* absichtlich verlieren **j** *vase* töpfern, drehen; *silk* zwirnen **k** (*snake*) **to ~ its skin** sich häuten **l** (*animal*: = *give birth to*) werfen **VI** werfen; (= *throw dice*) würfeln

▶ **throw about** (*Brit*) *or* **around** VT *always separate* **a** (= *scatter*) verstreuen; (*fig*) *money, name, words* um sich werfen mit **b** (= *toss*) herumwerfen; *one's arms* fuchteln mit; *one's legs* strampeln mit; **to throw oneself around** (*in bed, on floor*) sich hin und her werfen, sich herumwerfen; **to throw a ball around** ein bisschen Ball spielen; **he was thrown around in the car/accident** er wurde im Auto hin und her geschleudert/bei dem Unfall herumgeschleudert

▶ **throw away** VT *sep* **a** (= *discard*) *rubbish* wegwerfen **b** (= *waste*) verschenken; *money* verschwenden (*on sth* auf *or* für etw, *on sb* an jdn), vergeuden (*on sth* für etw, *on sb* an jdn); **you are throwing yourself away on him** Sie sind zu schade für ihn, Sie verschwenden sich an ihn (*geh*); **to throw one's life away** sein Leben wegwerfen **c** (= *say casually*) *remark* nebenbei machen, beiläufig sagen

▶ **throw back** **VI** (*Biol*) **a type which throws back to an earlier species** ein Typ, der Merkmale einer früheren Art aufweist **VT** *sep* **a** (= *send back*) *ball, enemy* zurückwerfen **b** (*backwards*) *head, bedclothes* zurückwerfen;

curtains aufreißen; **to throw oneself back** zurückweichen, zurückspringen **c** (*fig*) **to be thrown back upon sth** auf etw (*acc*) wieder angewiesen sein, auf etw (*acc*) zurückgreifen müssen; **the crisis threw them back on their own resources** durch die Krise waren sie wieder auf sich selbst angewiesen **d** **I don't want you throwing that back at me** ich möchte nicht, dass du mir meine eigenen Worte/Taten wieder vorhältst

▶ **throw down** VT *sep* **a** (*from a roof, the stairs etc*) herunterwerfen; **throw down your guns!** werfen Sie die Waffen weg!; **to throw oneself down on the floor** sich zu Boden werfen, sich auf den Boden fallen lassen; **to throw oneself down on the sofa** sich aufs Sofa fallen lassen; **it's throwing it down** (*inf*, = *raining*) es gießt (in Strömen) **b** (*fig*) **to throw down a challenge to sb** jdn herausfordern

▶ **throw in** VT *sep* **a** *extra* (gratis) dazugeben; **with a tour of London thrown in** mit einer Gratistour durch London extra **b** (*Sport*) *ball* einwerfen **c** (*fig*) **to throw in one's hand** aufgeben, sich geschlagen geben; **to throw in the sponge** (*Brit*) *or* **towel** das Handtuch werfen (*inf*) **d** (= *say casually*) *remark* einwerfen (*to in* +*acc*)

▶ **throw off** VT *sep* **a** (= *get rid of*) *clothes* abwerfen; *disguise, habits* ablegen; *pursuer* abschütteln; *cold* loswerden; **to throw off the yoke of tyranny** die Ketten der Tyrannei sprengen **b** (= *emit*) *sparks, smell* abgeben, von sich geben

▶ **throw on** VT *sep clothes* sich (*dat*) überwerfen

▶ **throw open** VT *sep* **a** *door, window* aufreißen; *arms* ausbreiten; *stately home etc* (öffentlich) zugänglich machen (*to* für); **the doors were thrown open to the public** die breite Öffentlichkeit hatte Zutritt

▶ **throw out** VT *sep* **a** (= *discard*) *rubbish etc* wegwerfen **b** (= *reject*) *suggestion, bill* (*Parl*) ablehnen, verwerfen (*geh*); *case* verwerfen **c** *person* hinauswerfen, rauswerfen (*inf*) (*of* aus); **to be thrown out of work** entlassen werden; **automation has thrown a lot of people out of work** die Automation hat viele Menschen arbeitslos gemacht *or* vielen Menschen ihren Arbeitsplatz genommen **d** (= *utter*) *hint* machen; *idea* äußern; **to throw out a challenge to sb** jdn herausfordern **e** (*plant*) *suckers, shoots* treiben; (*fire etc*) *heat* abgeben **f** *one's chest* herausdrücken **g** (= *make wrong*) *calculations etc* über den Haufen werfen (*inf*), durcheinander bringen; **to throw sb out in his calculations** jdn bei seinen Berechnungen durcheinander bringen

▶ **throw over** VT *sep plan* über den Haufen werfen (*inf*); *girlfriend* sitzen lassen (*for wegen*)

▶ **throw together** VT *sep* **a** (= *put hastily together*) *ingredients* zusammenwerfen; *clothes* zusammenpacken; (= *make quickly*) hinhauen; *essay* hinhauen (*inf*), runterschreiben (*inf*) **b** (= *bring together*) *people* (*fate etc*) zusammenführen; (*friends etc*) zusammenbringen

▶ **throw up** **VI** (*inf*) sich übergeben, brechen; **it makes you want to throw up** da kann einem schlecht werden, da kommt einem das Kotzen (*sl*) **VT** *sep* **a** *ball, hands* hochwerfen; *dust* aufwirbeln; *stones* aufspritzen lassen **b** (= *abandon*) *job* aufgeben; *opportunity etc* verschenken; **I feel like throwing everything up** ich würde am liebsten alles hinwerfen (*inf*) **c** (= *vomit up*) von sich (*dat*) geben, ausbrechen **d** (= *produce*) hervorbringen; *problems, questions* aufwerfen; **the meeting threw up several good ideas** bei der Versammlung kamen ein paar gute Ideen zutage; **the new politicians thrown up by the war** die neuen Politiker, die der Krieg hervorgebracht hat **e** *building etc* aus dem Boden stampfen

throw: throwaway **ADJ** **a** (= *casual*) *remark* achtlos gemacht; *style* unauffindlich, leger; **a ~**

line eine hingeworfene Bemerkung **b** (= *disposable*) Wegwerf-, zum Wegwerfen; **~ wrapping** Wegwerf- or Einwegverpackung *f*; **~ society** Wegwerfgesellschaft *f* **c** (= *cheap*) **~ prices** Schleuderpreise *pl* **N throwaways** PL Einwegprodukte *pl*; **throwback** N **a** he's a **~ to his Irish ancestors** bei ihm kommen seine irischen Vorfahren wieder durch **b** (*fig*, = *return*) Rückkehr *f* (to zu); (= *revival*) Neubelebung *f* (to gen)

throw-down ['θrəʊdaʊn] N (*Ftbl*) Schiedsrichterball *m*

thrower ['θrəʊə'] N Werfer(in) *m(f)*; **he's not a very good ~** er kann nicht sehr gut werfen

throw-in ['θrəʊɪn] N (*Sport*) Einwurf *m*

thrown [θrəʊn] ptp of **throw**

thru PREP, ADV, ADJ (*US*) = **through**

thrum [θrʌm] **VI** guitar klimpern auf (+*dat*), schlagen; *tune* klimpern (*auf der Gitarre etc*); **he ~med the desk with his fingers, he ~med his fingers on the desk** er trommelte mit seinen Fingern auf der Schreibtischplatte **VI** (*on guitar*) klimpern; (*air conditioning*) summen

thrupenny ['θrʌpni] ADJ, N (*Brit*, *inf*) = **threepenny**

thruppence ['θrʌpəns] N (*Brit*, *inf*) = **threepence**

thrush[1] [θrʌʃ] N (*Orn*) Drossel *f*

thrush[2] N (*Med*) Soor *m* (*spec*), Schwämmchen *nt*; (*of vagina*) Pilzkrankheit *f*; (*Vet*, *in horses*) Strahlfäule *f*

thrust [θrʌst] vb: pret, ptp **thrust** **N** **a** Stoß *m*; (*of knife*) Stich *m*, Stoß *m*; (*fig, of intellect*) Stoßkraft *f* **b** (*Tech*) Druckkraft *f*; (*in rocket, turbine*) Schub *m*, Schubkraft *f* **c** (*Mil*: *also* **thrust forward**) Vorstoß *m* **d** (*fig, of speech, article etc*) Tenor *m*; **I get the general ~ of what you're saying** ich weiß, worauf es Ihnen ankommt **VI** **a** (= *push, drive*) stoßen; **the tree ~ its branches upward** der Baum streckte seine Äste in den Himmel; **to ~ one's hands into one's pockets** die Hände in die Tasche stecken or stopfen (*inf*); **she ~ her books into the box** sie stopfte ihre Bücher in die Kiste; **she ~ the money into his hands** sie drückte ihm das Geld in die Hand **b** (*fig*) **to ~ oneself upon sb** sich jdm aufdrängen; **I had the job ~ upon me** die Arbeit wurde mir aufgedrängt or aufgezwungen; **and some have greatness ~ upon them** und einigen wird Größe auferlegt or aufgebürdet; **to ~ one's way through a crowd** sich durch die Menge drängen or schieben; **to ~ one's way to the front** sich nach vorne vordrängen, sich nach vorne kämpfen **VI** stoßen (*at* nach); (*with knife*) stechen (*at* nach); (*Fencing*) einen Ausfall machen, ausfallen (*at* gegen)

▶ **thrust aside** VT sep beiseite schieben; *person also* beiseite or zur Seite drängen; (*fig*) *objection also* zurückweisen

▶ **thrust forward** VT sep **to thrust sb forward** (*lit*) jdn vorschieben; (*fig*) sich für jdn stark machen; **to thrust oneself forward** (*lit*) sich vorschieben, sich nach vorne durchdrängeln; (*fig*) sich einsetzen; (*pej*) sich in den Vordergrund drängen

▶ **thrust out** VT sep *leg* ausstrecken; *hand also* hinstrecken; *head, breasts* vorstrecken; *chest* herausdrücken, wölben; **she thrust her head out (of the window)** sie streckte den Kopf (zum Fenster) hinaus; **the goalie thrust out his legs** der Torwart streckte die Beine vor

▶ **thrust past** VI sich vorbeidrängen (*prep obj* an +*dat*)

thrust bearing N Drucklager *nt*

thruster ['θrʌstə'] N (= *directional rocket*) (Fein-) steuerrakete *f*

thrustful ['θrʌstfʊl], **thrusting** ADJ *person, behaviour* energisch, zielstrebig, resolut; (*pej*) (etwas) zu zielstrebig

thrustfulness ['θrʌstfʊlnɪs] N energische Art, Zielstrebigkeit *f*, Resolutheit *f*; (*pej*) (etwas) zu große Zielstrebigkeit

thrusting ['θrʌstɪŋ] ADJ = **thrustful**

thrust: thrust performance N (*Aviat, Tech*) Schubleistung *f*; **thrust weapon** N Stich- or Stoßwaffe *f*

thruway ['θruːweɪ] N (*US*) Schnellstraße *f*

Thu *abbr of* **Thursday** Do.

thud [θʌd] **N** dumpfes Geräusch; **the ~ of his footsteps** seine dumpfen Schritte; **he fell to the ground with a ~** er fiel mit einem Plumps (*inf*) or einem dumpfen Aufschlag zu Boden; **the ~ of the waves against the hull** das dumpfe Schlagen der Wellen gegen den Schiffsrumpf **VI** dumpf aufschlagen; (= *move heavily*) stampfen; **the blow ~ded against his chin** dumpf klatschte der Schlag gegen sein Kinn; **a ~ding noise** ein dumpfes Geräusch; **with ~ding heart** mit pochendem Herzen; **the heavy door ~ded shut** mit einem dumpfen Knall fiel die Tür zu

thug [θʌɡ] N Schlägertyp *m*

thuggish ['θʌɡɪʃ] ADJ *person, behaviour* gewalttätig; **to be ~ in dealing with sb** mit jdm brutal umgehen

thulium ['θjuːlɪəm] N (*Chem*) Thulium *nt*

thumb [θʌm] **N** Daumen *m*; **to be under sb's ~** unter jds Pantoffel (*dat*) or Fuchtel (*dat*) stehen; **she has him under her ~** sie hat ihn unter ihrer Fuchtel; **to be all ~s** zwei linke Hände haben; **he gave me the ~s up/down** er gab mir zu verstehen, dass alles in Ordnung war/dass es nicht in Ordnung war; **the idea was given the ~s up/down** für den Vorschlag wurde grünes/rotes Licht gegeben; **it sticks out like a sore ~** das springt einem direkt ins Auge; **he sticks out like a sore ~** (= *doesn't fit in*) er ist auffallend anders **VI** **a** (*inf*) **to ~ a ride** or **lift** per Anhalter fahren; **let's ~ a lift with this lorry** wir wollen versuchen, diesen Lastwagen anzuhalten **b** **to ~ one's nose at sb/sth** jdm/einer Sache eine lange Nase machen; (*fig*) auf jdn/etw pfeifen **c** **a well ~ed book** ein Buch mit abgegriffenen Seiten

▶ **thumb through** VI +*prep obj book* durchblättern; *card index* durchgehen, durchsehen

thumber ['θʌmə'] N (*inf*) Anhalter(in) *m(f)*, Tramper(in) *m(f)*

thumb: thumb index N Daumenregister *nt*, Daumenindex *m*; **thumbnail** N Daumennagel *m*; **thumbnail sketch** N (= *drawing*) kleine Skizze; (= *description*) kurze Skizze, kurze Zusammenfassung; **thumbprint** N Daumenabdruck *m*; **thumbscrew** N (*Tech*) Flügelschraube *f*; (*torture*) Daumenschraube *f*; **to put the ~s on sb** (*fig*) jdm die Daumenschrauben anlegen; **thumbstall** N Daumenkappe *f*, Daumenschützer *m*, Fingerling *m*; **thumb-sucking** N Daumenlutschen *nt*; **thumbtack** N (*US*) Reißnagel *m*, Reiß- or Heftzwecke *f*

thump [θʌmp] **N** (= *blow*) Schlag *m*; (= *noise*) (dumpfes) Krachen, Bums *m* (*inf*) **VT** *table* klopfen or schlagen auf (+*acc*); *door* klopfen or schlagen an (+*acc*); (*esp Brit inf*) *person* verhauen (*inf*); (*repeatedly*) trommeln auf/an (+*acc*); (*accidentally*) *one's head* sich (*dat*) anschlagen or anhauen (*inf*); (*dog*) *tail* klopfen mit; **he ~ed his fist on the desk** er donnerte die Faust auf den Tisch; **he ~ed his chest** er schlug sich (*dat*) auf die Brust; **he ~ed the box down on my desk** er knallte die Schachtel auf meinen Tisch; **the prisoners started ~ing their stools on the floor** die Gefangenen schlugen mit ihren Hockern auf den Boden; **I ~ed him (one) on the nose** (*esp Brit inf*) ich habe ihm eins auf die Nase verpasst (*inf*); **I'll ~ you (one) if you don't shut up** (*esp Brit inf*) wenn du nicht gleich den Mund hältst, knallts (*inf*) **VI** (*person*) schlagen; *(heart)* heftig schlagen or pochen; (= *move heavily*) stapfen; (*object*: = *fall loudly*) plumpsen (*inf*); **he ~ed on the door/table** er schlug gegen or an die Tür/auf den

Tisch; **ask the people upstairs to stop ~ing around** sag den Leuten über uns, sie sollen aufhören herumzutrampeln

▶ **thump out** VT sep *tune* hämmern

thumping ['θʌmpɪŋ] ADJ (*inf*: *also* **thumping great**) kolossal, enorm

thunder ['θʌndə'] **N** **a** Donner *m*; **a long roll of ~** ein langer rollender Donner, ein langes Donnergrollen; **there is ~ in the air** es liegt ein Gewitter *nt* in der Luft **b** (*fig, of applause*) Sturm *m*; (*of cannons*) Donnern *nt*, Dröhnen *nt*; (*of waves*) Tosen *nt*; **a ~ of applause** ein Beifallssturm *m* → **steal VI** (*lit, fig*) donnern; (*guns, hooves also*) dröhnen; (*applause also*) brausen; (*waves, sea*) tosen, brausen; **the horses came ~ing up to the gate** die Pferde kamen aufs Tor zugeprescht; **the senator ~ed against them** der Senator wetterte gegen sie **VT** (= *shout*) brüllen, donnern, mit Donnerstimme brüllen

▶ **thunder out** VT sep *order* mit donnernder Stimme geben; *tune* donnern **VI** (*guns*) losdonnern; **his voice thundered out** er donnerte los

▶ **thunder past** VI (*train, traffic*) vorbeidonnern

thunder: thunderbolt N (*lit*) Blitz *m*, Blitz und Donner; **the news came like a ~** (*fig*) die Nachricht schlug wie der Blitz ein or kam wie ein Donnerschlag; **thunderclap** N Donnerschlag *m*; **thundercloud** N Gewitterwolke *f*

thunderer ['θʌndərə'] N **the Thunderer** (*Myth*) der Blitzeschleuderer

thunderhead ['θʌndəhed] N (*esp US*, *Met*) Kumulonimbusspitze *f*

thundering ['θʌndərɪŋ] ADJ **a** (= *loud*) applause, chords donnernd; *waterfall* tosend **b** (= *forceful, direct*) voice, question donnernd **c** (*inf*, = *real*) verteufelt (*inf*), verflixt (*inf*); **a ~ success** ein Bombenerfolg *m* (*inf*); **to be in a ~ rage** vor Wut kochen or schäumen **ADV** (*inf*, = *really*) **a ~ great lorry** ein großer, donnernder Laster; **~ great nuisance** ein Riesenärgernis *nt* (*inf*); **~ good music** verdammt gute Musik (*inf*)

thunderous ['θʌndərəs] ADJ stürmisch; *voice, explosion, knock* donnernd; *volley, header* krachend

thunder: thunderstorm N Gewitter *nt*; **thunderstruck** ADJ (*fig*) wie vom Donner gerührt

thundery ['θʌndərɪ] ADJ *weather, showers* gewitterig

thurible ['θjʊərɪbl] N (*Eccl*) (Weih)rauchfass *nt*, Räucherfass *nt*

Thuringia [θjʊə'rɪndʒɪə] N Thüringen *nt*

Thurs *abbr of* **Thursday** Do.

Thursday ['θɜːzdɪ] N Donnerstag *m* → *also* **Tuesday**

thus [ðʌs] ✿ 26.3 ADV **a** (= *in this way*) so, auf diese Art; **you must hold it ~** Sie müssen das so halten; **~ it was that ...** so kam es, dass ... **b** (= *consequently*) folglich, somit **c** (+*ptp or adj*) reassured, encouraged etc solchermaßen (*geh*), derart (*geh*); **~ far** so weit; **~ far and no further** so weit und keinen Schritt weiter

thwack [θwæk] **N** (= *blow*) Schlag *m*; (= *noise*) Klatschen *nt*, Bums *m* (*inf*) **VT** schlagen; (*waves*) klatschen gegen; **he ~ed his cane on the table** er ließ seinen Stock auf den Tisch heruntersausen **VI** schlagen (*against* gegen); (*waves, cane*) klatschen

thwart[1] ['θwɔːt] VT vereiteln; *plan also* durchkreuzen; *robbery, attack also* verhindern; **he was ~ed** ihm wurde ein Strich durch die Rechnung gemacht; **to ~ sb in sth** jdm etw vereiteln; **to ~ the will of the people** gegen den Willen des Volkes handeln; **to be ~ed at every turn** überall auf Hindernisse stoßen; **~ed!** wieder nichts!

thwart[2] N (*Naut*) Ruderbank *f*, Ducht *f*

thy [ðaɪ] POSS ADJ (*old, dial*) *before vowel* **thine** Euer/Eure/Euer (*obs*); (*dial, to God*) dein/deine/dein

thyme [taɪm] N Thymian *m*

thyroid ['θaɪrɔɪd] N (*also* **thyroid gland**) Schilddrüse *f* ADJ Schilddrüsen-; **~ hormone** Schilddrüsenhormon *nt*

thyself [ðaɪ'self] PERS PRON (old, dial) **a** (reflexive dir obj with prep +acc) Euch (obs); (dial, to God) dich; (indir obj with prep +dat) Euch (obs); (dial, to God) dir **b** (emph) Ihr selbst (obs), du selbst (obs); (acc) Euch selbst (obs), dich selbst; (dat) Ihnen selbst (obs), dir selbst

tiara [tɪ'ɑːrə] N Diadem nt; (of pope) Tiara f

Tiber ['taɪbə] N Tiber m

Tibet [tɪ'bet] N Tibet nt

Tibetan [tɪ'betən] ADJ tibetanisch, tibetisch; **he is ~** er ist Tibeter **N** ▶ Tibeter(in) m(f), Tibetaner(in) m(f) **b** (Ling) Tibetisch nt

tibia ['tɪbɪə] N pl -s or -e ['tɪbɪiː] Schienbein nt, Tibia f (spec)

tic [tɪk] N (Med) Tick m, nervöses Zucken

tich, **titch** [tɪtʃ] N (Brit, inf) Knirps m; **hey, ~!** he, Kleine(r)!

tichy, **titchy** [tɪtʃɪ] ADJ (+er) (Brit, inf: also **tichy little**) person winzig, knirpsig (inf); things klitzeklein (inf), winzig

tick¹ [tɪk] **N a** (of clock etc) Ticken nt
b (Brit inf, = moment) Augenblick m, Sekunde f, Minütchen nt (inf); **half a ~** eine Sekunde; **are you ready yet? – half a ~** or **two ~s!** bist du schon fertig? – sofort; **I'll be ready in a ~** or **two ~s** im sofort fertig (inf); **he did it in two ~s** er hat es in Sekundenschnelle or im Handumdrehen getan
c (esp Brit, = mark) Häkchen nt, Haken m; **to put a ~ against a name/an answer** einen Namen/eine Antwort abhaken
VI a (clock) ticken; **the minutes ~ed by** or **past/away** die Minuten vergingen or verstrichen **b** (inf) **what makes him ~?** was geht in ihm vor?
VT (Brit) name abhaken; box, answer ankreuzen

▶ **tick off** VT sep (Brit) **a** name etc abhaken **b** (inf, = scold) ausschimpfen (inf), anpfeifen (inf); **he got ticked off for doing it** er wurde angepfiffen (inf) or er bekam einen Rüffel or Anpfiff (inf), weil er das getan hat

▶ **tick over** VI **a** (= idle: engine) im Leerlauf sein; **the engine is ticking over nicely** der Motor läuft ganz gut or ruhig **b** (fig: business etc) ganz ordentlich laufen; (pej) auf Sparflamme sein (inf); **to keep things ticking over** die Sache in Gang halten

tick² N (Zool) Zecke f

tick³ N (Brit, inf) **on ~** auf Pump (inf)

tick⁴ N (Tex: = cover, for mattress) Matratzenbezug m; (for pillow etc) Inlett nt

ticker ['tɪkə'] N (inf) **a** (= heart) Pumpe f (inf) **b** (= watch) Zwiebel f (dated hum inf), Wecker m (inf)

ticker tape N Lochstreifen m; **~ welcome/parade** Konfettibegrüßung f/-parade f

ticket ['tɪkɪt] N **a** (= rail ticket, bus ticket) Fahrkarte f, Fahrschein m; (= plane ticket) Ticket nt, Flugkarte f, Flugschein m; (Theat, for football match etc) (Eintritts)karte f; (= cloakroom ticket) Garderobenmarke f; (for dry cleaner's, cobbler etc) Abschnitt m, Zettel m; (= luggage office ticket) (Gepäck-)schein m; (= raffle ticket) Los nt; (= lottery ticket) Lottoschein m; (= price ticket) Preisschild nt; (for car park) Parkschein m; **admission by ~ only** Einlass nur gegen Eintrittskarten
b (US, Pol) Wahlliste f; **he's running on the Democratic ~** er kandidiert für die Demokratische Partei → **split, straight**
c (Jur) Strafzettel m; **to give sb a ~** jdm einen Strafzettel geben or verpassen (inf)
d (dated Brit, inf) **that's just the ~!** das ist famos! (dated inf)

ticket: ticket agency N (Theat) Vorverkaufsstelle f (für Karten etc) Verkaufsstelle f; **ticket barrier** N (Brit, Rail) Fahrkartensperre f; **ticket-cancelling machine**, (US) **ticket-canceling machine** ['tɪkɪt,kænsəlɪŋməʃiːn] N (Fahrschein)entwerter m; **ticket collector** N (Rail, on train) Schaffner(in) m(f); (in station) Bahnsteigschaffner(in) m(f), Fahrkartenkontrolleur(in) m(f); **ticketholder** N (Theat etc) jd,

der eine Eintrittskarte hat **~s only through this door** (Theat etc) Eingang nur für Besucher mit Eintrittskarten; **ticket inspector** N (Fahrkarten)kontrolleur(in) m(f); **ticket machine** N (public transport) Fahrkartenautomat m; (in car park) Parkscheinautomat m; **ticket office** N (Rail) Fahrkartenschalter m, Fahrkartenausgabe f; (Theat) Kasse f; **ticket tout** N Kartenschwarzhändler(in) m(f); **ticket window** N (Rail) (Fahrkarten)schalter m; (Theat) Kasse f

ticking ['tɪkɪŋ] N **a** (for mattress) Matratzendrell m; (for pillows etc) Inlett nt **b** (of clock) Ticken nt

ticking cover N Matratzenbezug m

ticking-off [,tɪkɪŋ'ɒf] N (Brit, inf) Rüffel m, Anpfiff m (inf); **he needs a good ~** dem muss man mal den Marsch blasen (inf)

tickle ['tɪkl] **VT a** (lit) kitzeln; **to ~ sb's ribs** jdn in der Seite kitzeln; **to ~ sb's toes** jdn an den Zehen kitzeln; **this wool ~s my skin** diese Wolle kratzt or juckt (auf der Haut)
b (fig inf) person (= please) schmeicheln (+dat) und freuen; (= amuse) belustigen, amüsieren; **to be ~d** sich gebauchpinselt fühlen (inf); **here's a little story that might ~ your imagination** eine kleine Geschichte, die Sie wohl recht amüsant finden werden; **that story really ~d me** diese Geschichte fand ich wirklich köstlich; **to be ~d pink** or **to death** sich wie ein Schneekönig freuen (inf); **to ~ the ivories** (inf) auf den Tasten klimpern → **fancy**
VI kitzeln; (wool) kratzen, jucken; **stop it, that ~s** aufhören, das kitzelt; **my ear is tickling** mein Ohr juckt
N Kitzeln nt; **he gave the baby a little ~** er kitzelte das Baby ein bisschen; **to have a ~ in one's throat** einen Hustenreiz haben; **I didn't get a ~ all day** (Fishing) es hat den ganzen Tag keiner (an)gebissen

tickler ['tɪklə'] N (inf) kitz(e)lige Angelegenheit

ticklish ['tɪklɪʃ] ADJ (lit) kitz(e)lig; (fig) situation also heikel; (= touchy) empfindlich; **~ cough** Reizhusten m

tick: tick-over N (Brit, Aut) Leerlauf m; **ticktack** N Zeichensprache f der Buchmacher; **ticktack man** N Buchmachergehilfe m; **tick-tack-toe** N (US) Tic Tac Toe nt, Kinderspiel mit Nullen und Kreuzen; **ticktock** N (= sound) ticktack; (baby-talk, = clock) Ticktack f

ticky-tacky ['tɪkɪ,tækɪ] (US, inf) ADJ house, hotel heruntergekommen **N**, no pl (= building material) minderwertiges Baumaterial; (= goods) Schund m, Ramsch m (inf)

tidal ['taɪdl] ADJ Tide-, Gezeiten-; **waters** den Gezeiten unterworfen; **this river is not ~** in diesem Fluss gibt es keine Gezeiten, das ist kein Tidefluss

tidal: tidal atlas N Gezeitenatlas m; **tidal barrier**, **tidal barrage** N Staudamm m, Staumauer f; **tidal basin** N Tidebecken m; **tidal current** N Gezeitenstrom m; **tidal harbour** N Tidehafen m; **tidal inlet** N Priel m; **tidal lift** N Tidenhub m; **tidal power plant**, **tidal power station** N Tide- or Gezeitenkraftwerk nt; **tidal wave** N (lit) Flutwelle f; **a great ~ of enthusiasm swept over the country** (fig) eine Welle der Begeisterung ging durch das Land

tidbit ['tɪdbɪt] N (US) = **titbit**

tiddler ['tɪdlə'] N (Brit) **a** (= fish) winziger Fisch **b** (inf, = child) Knirps m; **she teaches ~s** sie unterrichtet die ganz Kleinen

tiddly ['tɪdlɪ] ADJ (+er) (Brit inf) **a** (= tiny) winzig, klitzeklein (inf); **a ~ little scratch** ein klitzekleiner (inf) or winzig kleiner Kratzer **b** (= tipsy) angesäuselt (inf), beschwipst; **she gets ~ on half a glass of sherry** sie bekommt von einem halben Glas Sherry schon einen Schwips

tiddlywinks ['tɪdlɪwɪŋks] N Floh(hüpf)spiel nt; **to play ~** Flöhhüpfen spielen

tide [taɪd] N **a** (lit) Gezeiten pl, Tide f (N Ger); **(at) high ~** (bei) Hochwasser nt or Flut f; **(at) low ~** (bei) Niedrigwasser nt or Ebbe f; **the rise and fall of the ~** Ebbe f und Flut f, der Tiden-

hub (spec); **we'll sail on the next ~** wir fahren mit der nächsten Flut; **the ~ is in/out** es ist Flut/Ebbe, es ist Hochwasser/Niedrigwasser (form); **the ~ comes in very fast** die Flut kommt sehr schnell; **the ~s are influenced by the moon** Ebbe und Flut or die Gezeiten werden vom Mond beeinflusst; **stranded by the ~** in der Ebbe/Flut gestrandet; **until the ~ turns** bis zum Gezeitenwechsel, bis die Flut/Ebbe einsetzt
b (fig: = trend) **the ~ of history** der Lauf der Geschichte; **the ~ of public opinion** der Trend der öffentlichen Meinung; **carried away by the ~ of events** vom Strom der Ereignisse mitgerissen; **to go** or **swim against/with the ~** gegen den/mit dem Strom schwimmen; **the ~ has turned** das Blatt hat sich gewendet; **the ~ of the battle turned** das Glück (der Schlacht) wendete sich → **turn, time**
c (old: = time) Zeit f

▶ **tide over** VT always separate **that will tide me over until tomorrow** damit werde ich bis morgen auskommen; **is that enough to tide you over?** reicht Ihnen das vorläufig?

tide: tide-bound ADJ boat etc von der Ebbe am Auslaufen gehindert; **tide gate** N Seeschleuse f; **tideland** N (US) Watt nt; **tidemark** N Flutmarke f; (man-made) Pegelstand m; (hum, on neck, in bath) schwarzer Rand; **tide race** N Gezeitenstrom m; **tidewater** N Flut f; (US, = lowlands) Watt nt; **tideway** N Priel m

tidily ['taɪdɪlɪ] ADV ordentlich

tidiness ['taɪdɪnɪs] N (of person) Ordentlichkeit f; (of appearance) Gepflegtheit f; (of room) Aufgeräumtheit f; (of desk) Ordnung f; (of handwriting, schoolwork) Sauberkeit f

tidings ['taɪdɪŋz] PL (old, liter) Kunde f (old, liter), Botschaft f (liter), Nachricht f

tidy ['taɪdɪ] **ADJ** (+er) **a** (= orderly) ordentlich; appearance gepflegt, ordentlich; room aufgeräumt; desk ordentlich; handwriting, schoolwork sauber; **to look ~** (person) ordentlich or gepflegt aussehen; (room) ordentlich aussehen; **she has very ~ habits** sie ist ein sehr ordentlicher or ordnungsliebender Mensch; **to teach sb ~ habits** jdn zur Ordnung erziehen; **to keep sth ~** etw in Ordnung halten; **to get a room ~** ein Zimmer aufräumen; **she's very ~ in her dress** sie ist immer sehr ordentlich gekleidet; **to make oneself ~** sich zurechtmachen; **to have a ~ mind** klar or logisch denken
b (inf, = considerable) ordentlich (inf), ganz schön (inf); **a ~ sum** eine ordentliche Stange Geld (inf)
VT hair in Ordnung bringen; room also aufräumen; (also **tidy up**) drawer, desk aufräumen **N** Behälter m

▶ **tidy away** VT sep wegräumen, aufräumen

▶ **tidy out** VT sep entrümpeln, ausmisten (inf)

▶ **tidy up** VI **a** (= clear away) aufräumen, Ordnung machen **b** (= clean oneself) sich zurechtmachen **VT** sep books, room aufräumen, in Ordnung bringen; drawer, desk aufräumen; piece of work in Ordnung bringen; **to tidy oneself up** sich zurechtmachen; **to tidy up the loose ends** die Fäden vernähen

tidy: tidy-out N Entrümpelung f; **the cupboards could do with a ~** die Schränke müssten mal entrümpelt or ausgemistet (inf) werden; **tidy-up** N Aufräumen nt; **this room needs a ~** dieses Zimmer muss aufgeräumt werden; **go and give yourself a ~** mach dich ein bisschen zurecht

tie [taɪ] N **a** (esp US: also **neck tie**) Krawatte f, Schlips m (inf), Binder m (dated form)
b (Archit, Build, also **tie beam**) Binderbalken m, Bundbalken m; (= tie piece) Stichbalken m; (Mus) Haltebogen m; (US Rail) Schwelle f; (= cord) Schnur f
c (fig, = bond) Band nt (liter), Beziehung f, (Ver)bindung f; **~s of friendship** freundschaftliche Beziehungen or Bande (liter) pl; **the blood ~** Blutsbande pl; **business ~s** Geschäftsverbindungen pl; **he's investigating the ~s between Pasternak and Rilke** er untersucht die Beziehung zwischen Pasternak und Rilke; **family ~s**

familiäre Bindungen *pl*
d (= *hindrance*) Belastung *f* (*on* für); **family ~s** familiäre Bindungen *or* Fesseln *pl*; **I don't want any ~s** ich will keine Bindung, ich will mich nicht gebunden fühlen
e (*Sport etc, = result*) Unentschieden *nt*; (= *match etc ending in a draw*) unentschiedenes Spiel; **the match ended in a ~** das Spiel endete mit einem Unentschieden; **the result of the competition was a ~** der Wettkampf ging unentschieden aus; **there was a ~ for second place** es gab zwei zweite Plätze
f (*Brit esp Ftbl*: = *match*) Spiel *nt*
VT **a** (= *fasten*) binden (*to an +acc*), befestigen (*to an +dat*); **~ the string round the tree** binde die Schnur um den Baum; **my hands are ~d** (*fig*) mir sind die Hände gebunden
b (= *knot*) *shoelace, tie, ribbon* binden; **to ~ a knot in sth** einen Knoten in etw (*acc*) machen; **to ~ a bow in a ribbon** *or* **a ribbon in a bow** ein Band zu einer Schleife binden
c (*fig, = unite, link*) verbinden
d (= *restrict*) *person* binden (*to an +acc*)
e (*Sport*) **the match was ~d** das Spiel ging unentschieden aus
f **~d** (*Mus, notes*) gebunden
VI **a** (*ribbon etc*) **it won't ~ properly** es lässt sich nicht richtig binden; **it ~s at the back** es wird hinten (zu)gebunden
b (*Sport*) unentschieden spielen; (*in competition, vote*) gleich stehen; **they ~d for first place** (*Sport, competition*) sie teilten sich den ersten Platz; (*Sch*) sie waren mit (den gleichen Noten) die Klassenbesten

▸ **tie back** VT *sep hair, roses, door* zurückbinden

▸ **tie down** VT *sep* **a** (*lit*) festbinden (*to an +dat*); *huts, tents* verankern (*to in +dat*); *horse* fesseln **b** (*fig, = restrict*) binden (*to an +acc*); *meaning* genau bestimmen; **to tie sb/oneself down to sth** jdn/sich auf etw (*acc*) festlegen; **to tie oneself down to doing sth** sich verpflichten, etw zu tun; **marriage/owning property ties you down** durch die Ehe/durch Eigentum ist man gebunden; **she's tied down because of the children, the children tie her down** durch die Kinder ist sie sehr gebunden

▸ **tie in** VI dazu passen; **to tie in with sth** zu etw passen, dazu passen; **it all ties in** das passt alles zusammen; **the new evidence didn't tie in** das neue Beweismaterial passte nicht ins Bild **VT** *sep plans* verbinden, in Einklang bringen

▸ **tie on** VT *sep* anbinden, festbinden; **to tie sth on(to) sth** etw an etw (*dat*) anbinden

▸ **tie up** VI **a** now **it all ties up** jetzt passt alles zusammen; **it all ties up with his marital problems** das hängt alles mit seinen Eheproblemen zusammen
b (*Naut*) festmachen
VT *sep* **a** *parcel* verschnüren; *shoelaces* binden **b** *boat* festmachen; *animal* festbinden, anbinden (*to an +dat*); *prisoner, hands etc* fesseln **c** (= *settle*) *deal, arrangements etc* unter Dach und Fach bringen → **loose d** (*Fin*) *capital* (fest) anlegen, festlegen **e** (= *link*) **to be tied up with sth** mit etw zusammenhängen; **are you still tied up with that firm?** haben Sie noch Verbindungen zu der Firma? **f** (= *keep busy*) beschäftigen; *machines* auslasten; **he's tied up all tomorrow** er ist morgen den ganzen Tag belegt *or* beschäftigt; **he's tied up with the manager at the moment** er hat momentan beim Betriebsleiter zu tun **g** (= *obstruct, hinder*) *production etc* stilllegen

tie: **tie beam** N (*Archit*) Spannbalken *m*; **tie-break, tiebreaker** N (*Tennis, in quiz etc*) Tie-break *m*, Tie-Break *m*; **tie clip** N Krawattennadel *f*

tied [taɪd]: **tied cottage** N (*Brit*) Gesindehaus *nt*; **tied house** N (*Brit*: = *pub*) Brauereigaststätte *f*, brauereieigene Gaststätte

tie: **tie-dye** VT nach dem Bindebatikverfahren färben; **tie-in** N **a** (= *connection, relationship*) Verbindung *f*, Beziehung *f*, Zusammenhang *m* **b** (*US, = sale*) Kopplungsgeschäft *nt* **ATTR** **~ e-**

dition (*of book*) Begleitbuch *nt*, Buch *nt* zum Film/zur Serie; **tie line** N (*Telec*) Direktverbindung *f*; **tie-on** ADJ *attr cover, cushion* zum Anbinden *or* Festbinden; **tiepin** N Krawattennadel *f*, Schlipsnadel *f* (*inf*)

tier [tɪəʳ] N (*of cake*) Etage *f*, Stufe *f*; (*of amphitheatre*) Reihe *f*; (*Theat, of stadium*) Rang *m*; (*fig, in hierarchy etc*) Stufe *f*, Rang *m*; **a cake with three ~s** ein dreistöckiger Kuchen; **a three-tier hierarchy** eine dreigestufte Hierarchie; **to arrange sth in ~s** etw stufenförmig aufbauen

tiered [tɪəd] ADJ gestuft; **a three-tiered cake** ein dreistöckiger Kuchen

tie: tie rod N (*Aut*) Lenkspurstange *f*; **tie-up** N **a** (= *connection*) Verbindung *f* **b** (*US, = stoppage*) Stillstand *m*; **there is a ~ in transportation** der Verkehr steht still *or* ist lahm gelegt

tiff [tɪf] N (*inf*) Krach *m* (*inf*); **he's had a ~ with his girlfriend** er hat mit seiner Freundin Krach gehabt (*inf*)

tiger [ˈtaɪgəʳ] N Tiger *m*

tiger: tiger cat N Tigerkatze *f*; (= *striped domestic cat*) getigerte (Haus)katze; **tiger economy** N schnell wachsende Wirtschaft *f*; (= *tiger state*) Tigerstaat *m*; **tiger lily** N Tigerlilie *f*; **tiger moth** N Bärenspinner *m*; **tiger shark** N Tigerhai *m*

tight [taɪt] ADJ (+*er*) **a** (= *close-fitting*) *clothes* eng; *join* dicht; **these jeans/shoes are too ~** diese Jeans/Schuhe sind zu eng
b (= *stiff, difficult to move*) *screw, bolt* festsitzend, unbeweglich; **the tap is (too) ~** der Hahn ist zu fest zu; **the cork/screw/bolt is (too) ~** der Korken/die Schraube/der Bolzen sitzt fest; **the drawer/window is a bit ~** die Schublade/das Fenster klemmt ein bisschen *or* geht schwer auf
c (= *firm*) *screw* fest angezogen; *tap, window* dicht; *lid, embrace* fest; *control, discipline, security* streng; *organization* straff; **to have/keep a ~ hold of sth** (*lit*) etw gut festhalten; **to keep a ~ hold on the reins** (*fig*) die Zügel fest in der Hand haben; **to keep a ~ lid on sth** (*fig*) etw streng unter Kontrolle halten; **to run a ~ ship** (*lit, fig*) ein strenges Regiment führen
d (= *taut*) *rope, skin* straff; *knot* fest (angezogen); **she wears her hair in a ~ bun** sie trägt ihr Haar in einem festen Knoten; **to be as ~ as a drum** straff sein; (*inf*: = *drunk*) sturzbetrunken sein (*inf*)
e (= *leaving little space*) eng; *weave* eng, dicht; **~ curls** kleine Locken; **things are getting rather ~ in this office** es wird ziemlich eng im Büro; **it's a ~ space for lorries** es ist eng hier für Lastwagen
f (= *leaving little time*) *timing etc* knapp; *schedule* knapp bemessen; **4 o'clock is a bit ~ for me** 4 Uhr ist ein bisschen knapp für mich
g (= *difficult*) *situation* schwierig; **in a ~ corner** *or* **spot** (*fig*) in der Klemme (*inf*); **things are getting a bit ~ for him round here** es wird langsam brenzlig für ihn (*inf*); **things were ~** die Lage war schwierig
h (= *close*) *race, match* knapp
i (= *tense*) *voice* fest; *lips* zusammengepresst; *mouth* verkniffen; *smile* verkrampft; *throat* zusammengeschnürt; *muscle* verspannt
j (= *constricted*) *chest, stomach* zusammengeschnürt; **a ~ feeling in the chest** ein beengtes Gefühl in der Brust
k (= *close, close-knit*) eng; **the Common Market is a ~ federation of states** der gemeinsame Markt ist ein enger Staatenbund
l (= *sharp*) *bend* eng
m (*Fin*) *budget, money* knapp
n (*inf, = miserly*) knick(e)rig (*inf*), geizig; **to be ~ with one's money** geizig mit seinem Geld sein
o (*inf*: = *drunk*) voll (*inf*), blau (*inf*); **to get ~** blau werden (*inf*)
ADV (+*er*) *hold, shut, screw, fasten* fest; *stretch* straff; **the suitcase/train was packed ~ with ...** der Koffer/Zug war voll gestopft mit ...; **he kept his mouth shut ~** er schwieg eisern; (*at*

dentist etc) er hielt den Mund fest geschlossen; **to hold sb/sth ~** jdn/etw festhalten; **to do sth up ~** etw festmachen *or* gut befestigen; **to pull sth ~** etw festziehen *or* stramm ziehen; **to stretch sth ~** etw straff spannen; **to sit ~** sich nicht rühren; **sleep ~!** schlaf(t) gut!; **hold ~!** festhalten!; **she held ~ to her assertion** sie blieb felsenfest bei ihrer Behauptung
ADJ *suf* -dicht; **watertight** wasserdicht; **airtight** luftdicht

tightarsed [ˈtaɪtɑːst], (*US*) **tightassed** [ˈtaɪtæst] ADJ (*sl*) *person, behaviour* verbohrt (*inf*), stur (*inf*); (= *miserly*) knick(e)rig (*inf*)

tighten [ˈtaɪtn] (*also* **tighten up**) **VT** **a** *knot* fester machen, anziehen; *screw* anziehen; (= *retighten*) nachziehen; *muscles* anspannen; *lips* verkneifen; *rope* straffen, anziehen; (= *stretch tighter*) straffer spannen; **to ~ one's grip** (*lit*) fester zugreifen; (*fig*) die Schraube fester ziehen; **to ~ one's grip on sth** (*lit*) etw fester halten; (*fig*) etw besser unter Kontrolle bringen; **to ~ the steering in a car** die Lenkung an einem Auto nachziehen
b (*fig*) *rules, security, control, law, procedures, restrictions* verschärfen; **to ~ the screw on sth/a country** den Druck auf etw (*acc*)/ein Land verstärken → **belt**
VI (*rope*) sich spannen, sich straffen; (*knot*) sich zusammenziehen; **whenever he's angry his mouth ~s** immer wenn er wütend ist, wird sein Mund schmal und verkniffen

▸ **tighten up** **VI** **a** = **tighten VI b** (*in discipline*) strenger werden, härter durchgreifen; **they've tightened up on security** sie haben die Sicherheitsvorkehrungen verschärft **VT** *sep* **a** = **tighten VT a b** *organization, procedure* straffen; *discipline, controls* verschärfen

tight: tightfisted [ˌtaɪtˈfɪstɪd] ADJ knauserig, knickerig (*inf*); **to be ~** die Hand auf der Tasche halten; **tight-fitting** ADJ eng anliegend; **tightknit** ADJ *community* eng (miteinander) verbunden *or* verwachsen; **tight-lipped** ADJ **a** (*lit*) mit schmalen Lippen; (= *silent*) verschwiegen, verschlossen; **he kept a ~ silence** er wahrte absolutes *or* eisernes Schweigen; **to be ~ about sth** sich nicht zu etw äußern **b** (= *angry*) *person* verbissen; *expression* abweisend; *smile* verkniffen; **~ disapproval** verbissene Ablehnung

tightly [ˈtaɪtlɪ] ADV **a** (= *closely*) *hold* fest; **~ fitting** eng anliegend **b** (= *securely*) *closed, bound* fest; *wrapped* eng; **a ~ knit community** eine eng verbundene Gemeinschaft; **behind ~-closed doors** hinter fest verschlossenen Türen **c** (= *tautly*) *stretch* stramm, straff **d** (= *compactly*) dicht; **~ packed** dicht gedrängt; **a ~ packed crowd** eine dicht gedrängte Menge **e** (= *rigorously*) *scharf*, streng, rigoros; **~ controlled** streng kontrolliert; **a ~-guarded border** eine streng bewachte Grenze

tightness [ˈtaɪtnɪs] N **a** (*of clothes*) enges Anliegen; (*of join*) Dichtheit *f*
b (= *stiffness: of screw, bolt*) Festsitzen *nt*, Unbeweglichkeit *f*; **the ~ of the drawer/window** das Klemmen der Schublade/des Fensters
c (= *firmness: of screw, tap*) fester Sitz; (*of window*) Dichtheit *f*; (*of control, discipline, security*) Strenge *f*; (*of organization*) Straffheit *f*; **the ~ of his embrace** seine feste Umarmung
d (= *tautness, of rope, skin*) Straffheit *f*; (*of knot*) Festigkeit *f*
e (= *crowdedness*) Enge *f*; (*of weave also*) Dichte *f*
f (*of schedule*) Knappheit *f*
g (= *closeness: of race, match*) Knappheit *f*
h (= *constriction: in chest, stomach*) Beengtheit *f*
i (*inf, = miserliness*) Knick(e)rigkeit *f* (*inf*), Geiz *m*
j (*inf, = drunkenness*) Besoffenheit *f* (*inf*)

tightrope [ˈtaɪtrəʊp] N Seil *nt*; **to walk a ~** (*fig*) einen Balanceakt vollführen

tightrope act N (*lit, fig*) Balanceakt *m*

tightrope walker N Seiltänzer(in) *m(f)*

tights [taɪts] PL (*Brit*) Strumpfhose *f*; **a pair of ~** ein Paar *nt* Strumpfhosen, eine Strumpfhose

tightwad ['taɪtwɒd] N (US) Geizhals m, Geizkragen m (inf)

tigress ['taɪɡrɪs] N Tigerin f

tilapia [tɪ'læpɪə] N Tilapia m, Buntbarsch m

tilde ['tɪldə] N Tilde f

tile [taɪl] **N** (on roof) (Dach)ziegel m; (= ceramic tile) Fliese f; (on wall) Kachel f, Fliese f; (= lino tile, cork tile, polystyrene tile etc) Platte f, Fliese f; (= carpet tile) (Teppich)fliese f; **to have a night on the ~s** (Brit inf) einen draufmachen (inf) **VT** roof (mit Ziegeln) decken; floor mit Fliesen/Platten auslegen; wall kacheln, mit Platten bedecken; bathroom kacheln, Fliesen anbringen in (+dat)

tiled [taɪld] ADJ floor gefliest; path mit Platten ausgelegt; wall, room, fireplace gekachelt; **~ roof** Ziegeldach nt

tiler ['taɪə'] N **a** (for roof) Dachdecker(in) m(f) **b** (for floor) Fliesen- or Plattenleger(in) m(f)

tiling ['taɪlɪŋ] N **a** (= action, of roof) (Dach)decken nt; (of floor) Fliesenlegen nt; (of wall) Kacheln nt, Belegen nt mit Platten; **the ~ of the floor ...** das Legen der Bodenfliesen ... **b** (= tiled surface, on roof) Ziegel pl; (on floor) Fliesen pl, Platten pl; (on wall) Kacheln pl, Fliesen pl, Platten pl

till¹ [tɪl] PREP, CONJ = **until**

till² N (Brit, = cash register) Kasse f; (= drawer, in bank) Geldkasse f, Geldkasten m; (in shop) Ladenkasse f; **pay at the ~** an der Kasse bezahlen; **to be caught with one's hand in the ~** (fig) beim Griff in die Kasse ertappt werden

till³ VT (Agr) bestellen

tillable ['tɪləbl] ADJ (= Agr) land anbaufähig

tillage ['tɪlɪdʒ] N (= act) Bestellen nt; (= land) bestelltes Land

tiller¹ ['tɪlə'] N (Naut) Ruderpinne f; **at the ~** am Ruder; **to take the ~** das Ruder übernehmen

tiller² N (Agr) Landmann m (old); **~ of the soil** (liter) Ackersmann m (old), Bebauer m der Scholle (liter)

tilt [tɪlt] **N** **a** (= slope) Neigung f; **the sideways ~ of his head** seine schräge Kopfhaltung; **if you increase the (angle of) ~ of the conveyor belt ...** wenn Sie das Fließband schräger stellen ...; (sideways also) wenn Sie das Fließband weiter kippen ...; **to have a ~** sich neigen; **the wall has developed rather a dangerous ~** die Wand neigt sich ziemlich gefährlich; **the bird's/plane's wings have a slight downward ~** die Flügel des Vogels/Flugzeugs neigen sich leicht nach unten **b** (Hist, = tournament) Turnier nt; (= thrust) Stoß m; **to have a ~ at sb/sth** (fig) jdn/etw aufs Korn nehmen → **full** **VT** **a** kippen, schräg stellen; head (seitwärts) neigen **b** (fig) argument kippen; **to ~ the balance of power toward(s)/against sb** das Kräftegleichgewicht zugunsten/zuungunsten von jdm verschieben **VI** **a** (= slant) sich neigen; **this part of the machine ~s** dieser Teil der Maschine lässt sich kippen **b** (fig) **to ~ at sb/sth** jdn/etw attackieren → **windmill**

▶ **tilt back** **VI** sich nach hinten neigen **VT** sep nach hinten neigen; chair also, machine part nach hinten kippen

▶ **tilt forward** **VI** sich nach vorne neigen; (machine part) nach vorn kippen **VT** sep nach vorne neigen; chair also, machine part nach vorne kippen

▶ **tilt over** **VI** (= lean) sich neigen; (= fall) (um-)kippen **VT** sep (= slant) neigen, schräg stellen; barrel, chair kippen

▶ **tilt up** **VI** nach oben kippen; **the back of the truck tilts up** die Ladefläche des Lastwagens kippt **VT** sep bottle kippen; kaleidoscope schräg nach oben halten

tilth [tɪlθ] N **a** (= topsoil) (Acker)krume f **b** (= cultivated land) Ackerland nt

tilting ['tɪltɪŋ] ADJ schwenkbar, kippbar

tilting train [,tɪltɪŋ'treɪn] N Neigezug m

Tim [tɪm] N abbr of **Timothy** (Brit, Telec) der Zeitservice

timber ['tɪmbə'] **N** **a** Holz nt; (for building) (Bau)holz nt; (= land planted with trees) (Nutz-)wald m; **to put land under ~** Land mit Bäumen bepflanzen; **standing ~** Nutzwald m; **~!** Baum fällt! **b** (= beam) Balken m; (esp Naut) Spant nt **c** (Hunt) (Holz)zäune und -gatter pl **d** (US, = character) **a man of that ~** ein Mann dieses Kalibers; **a woman of presidential ~** eine Frau, die das Zeug zum Präsidenten hat **VT** house mit Fachwerk versehen; gallery (in mine) abstützen, verzimmern

timbered ['tɪmbəd] ADJ **a** **~ house** Fachwerkhaus nt **b** (= wooded) bewaldet

timber: timber-framed ADJ Fachwerk-; **~ house** Fachwerkhaus nt; **timber framing** N Fachwerk nt

timbering ['tɪmbərɪŋ] N (inside house) Gebälk nt, Balkenwerk nt; (outside house) Fachwerk nt; (Naut) Spanten pl; (Min) Stützbalken pl; (= material) (Bau)holz nt

timber: timberland N (US) Waldland nt; **timber line** N Baumgrenze f; **timberman** ['tɪmbəmən] N Holzfäller m; **timber mill** N Sägemühle f, Sägewerk nt; **timber tree** N Nutzholzbaum m; **timber wolf** N Timberwolf m; **timberwork** N (= beams) Gebälk nt, Balkenwerk nt; (= timber framing) Fachwerk nt; **timberyard** N (Brit) Holzlager nt

timbre, (US) **timber** ['tɪmbə'] N Timbre nt; (Phon) Tonqualität f

---

time [taɪm]

1 NOUN	2 TRANSITIVE VERB

1 – NOUN

a Zeit f; **how time flies!** wie die Zeit vergeht!; **only time will tell whether ...** es muss sich erst herausstellen, ob ...; **it takes time to do that** das erfordert or braucht (seine) Zeit; **to take (one's) time (over sth)** sich (dat) (bei etw) Zeit lassen; **it took me all my time to finish** ich bin gerade noch fertig geworden; **in (the course of) time** mit der Zeit; **in (next to or less than) no time** im Nu, in Handumdrehen; **at this (present) point or moment in time** zu diesem or zum gegenwärtigen Zeitpunkt; **to have a lot of/no time for sb/sth** viel/keine Zeit für jdn/etw haben; (fig: = be for/against) viel/nichts für jdn/etw übrig haben; **to find time (for sb/sth)** Zeit (für jdn/etw) finden; **to make time (for sb/sth)** sich (dat) Zeit (für jdn/etw) nehmen; **time is on our side** die Zeit arbeitet für uns; **he lost no time in telling her** er verlor keine Zeit und sagte es ihr sofort; **there is no time to lose** es gibt keine Zeit (mehr) zu verlieren; **my time is my own** ich kann frei über meine Zeit verfügen; **in or given time** mit der Zeit; **in one's own/the company's time** in or während der Freizeit/Arbeitszeit; **don't rush, do it in your own time** nur keine Hast, tun Sie es, wie Sie es können; **time is money** (prov) Zeit ist Geld (prov); **time and tide wait for no man** (Prov) das Rad der Zeit hält niemand auf (Prov); **for some time past** seit einiger Zeit; **I don't know what she's saying half the time** (inf) meistens verstehe ich gar nicht, was sie sagt; **in two weeks' time** in zwei Wochen; **for a time** eine Zeit lang; **not before time** (Brit) das wurde auch (langsam) Zeit; **to do time** (inf, in prison) sitzen (inf); **to make time with sb** (dated esp US inf: = have sex with) es mit jdm treiben (inf)

♦ **all the time** (= always) immer; (= all along) die ganze Zeit; **I get them mixed up all the time** ich verwechsle sie immer; **I knew that all the time** das wusste ich die ganze Zeit

♦ **in good time to be in good time** rechtzeitig dran sein; **let me know in good time** sagen Sie mir rechtzeitig Bescheid; **all in good time** alles zu seiner Zeit

♦ **in one's own good time** he'll let you know **in his own good time** er wird Ihnen Bescheid sagen, wenn er so weit ist; **he does everything in his own good time** er lässt sich bei nichts hetzen

♦ **a long time (for) a long time** lange; **I'm going away for a long time** ich fahre für or auf längere Zeit weg; **it's a long time (since ...)** es ist schon lange her(, seit ...); **what a (long) time you have been!** du hast (aber) lange gebraucht!

♦ **a short time (for) a short time** kurz; **a short time later** kurz darauf; **a short time ago** vor kurzem; **in a short time they were all gone** nach kurzer Zeit waren alle gegangen

♦ **for the time being** (= provisionally) vorläufig; (= temporarily) vorübergehend

♦ **time on one's hands to have time on one's hands** viel freie Zeit haben; **too many people who have time on their hands** zu viele Leute, die zu viel freie Zeit haben; **having time on my hands I went into a café** da ich (noch) Zeit hatte, ging ich ins Café

b by clock **what time is it?, what's the time?** wie spät es ist?, wie viel Uhr ist es?; **what time do you make it?** wie spät haben Sies?; **my watch keeps good time** meine Uhr geht genau; **the time is 2.30** es ist 2.30 Uhr, die Zeit: 2.30 Uhr; **it's 2 o'clock local time** es ist 2.00 Uhr Ortszeit; **what was his time?** (in race) welche Zeit hatte er?; **the winning time was ...** die Zeit des Siegers war ...; **it's time (for me/us etc) to go, it's time I was/we were etc going, it's time I/we etc went** es wird Zeit, dass ich gehe/wir gehen etc; **it's time for tea** es ist Teezeit; **time gentlemen please!** Feierabend! (inf), bitte, trinken Sie aus, wir schließen gleich

♦ **the time of day to pass the time of day (with sb)** (mit jdm) über Belanglosigkeiten reden; **I wouldn't even give him the time of day** ich würde ihm nicht einmal guten or Guten Tag sagen

♦ **to tell the time** (person) die Uhr kennen; (instrument) die Uhrzeit anzeigen; **can you tell the time?** kennst du die Uhr?

♦ **to make good time** gut or schnell vorankommen; **if we get to Birmingham by 3 we'll be making good time** wenn wir um 3 Uhr in Birmingham sind, sind wir ziemlich schnell

♦ **about time it's about time he was here** (he has arrived) es wird (aber) auch Zeit, dass er kommt; (he has not arrived) es wird langsam Zeit, dass er kommt; **(and) about time too!** das wird aber auch Zeit!

♦ **ahead of time** zu früh; **we are ahead of time** wir sind früh dran

♦ **behind time** zu spät; **we are behind time** wir sind spät dran

♦ **at + time at any time during the day** zu jeder Tageszeit; **not at this time of night!** zu dieser nachtschlafenden Zeit or Stunde!; **at one time** früher, einmal; **at any time** jederzeit; **come (at) any time** du kannst jederzeit kommen; **at the same time** (lit) gleichzeitig; **they arrived at the same time as us** sie kamen zur gleichen Zeit an wie wir; **but at the same time, you must admit that ...** aber andererseits müssen Sie zugeben, dass ...; **it was hard, but at the same time you could have tried** es war schwierig, aber Sie hätten es trotzdem versuchen können

♦ **in/on time** rechtzeitig; **to be in time for sth** rechtzeitig zu etw kommen; **on time** pünktlich; **the trains are on time** die Züge fahren pünktlich

♦ **to time the trains are running to time** die Züge fahren pünktlich

c = moment, season Zeit f; **there's a time and a place for everything** alles zu seiner Zeit; **this is hardly the time or the place to ...** dies ist wohl kaum die rechte Zeit oder der rechte Ort, um ...; **this is no time for quarrelling** or **to quarrel** jetzt ist nicht die Zeit, sich zu streiten; **well, this is a fine time to tell me that** (iro) Sie haben sich (dat) wahrhaftig eine gute Zeit ausgesucht, um mir das zu sagen; **there are times when ...** es gibt Augenblicke, wo or da (geh) ...; **at the** or **that time** damals, zu der Zeit, seinerzeit; **at this (particular) time, at the present**

time zurzeit; **sometimes ..., (at) other times ...** (manch)mal ..., (manch)mal ...; **from that time on** von der Zeit an, von da an; **since that time** seit der Zeit; **this time last year/week** letztes Jahr/letzte Woche um diese Zeit; **to choose** or **pick one's time** sich (dat) einen günstigen Zeitpunkt aussuchen; **to die before one's time** zu früh sterben; **my time is (almost) up** meine or die Zeit ist (gleich) um; (fig: = life) meine Zeit ist gekommen

♦ **time + come the time has come (to do sth)** es ist an der Zeit(, etw zu tun); **the time has come for us to leave** es ist Zeit für uns zu gehen; **when the time comes** wenn es so weit ist; **when her time comes** (of pregnant woman) wenn es (mit dem Baby) so weit ist; **when my time comes** (= when I die) wenn meine Zeit gekommen ist; **when the time comes for you to be the leader** wenn Sie an der Reihe sind, die Führung zu übernehmen

♦ **at + times** manchmal; **at all times** jederzeit, immer; **at various times in the past** schon verschiedene Male or verschiedentlich

♦ **between times** (inf) zwischendurch

♦ **by the time** by the time it had finished als es zu Ende war; **by the time we arrive, there's not going to be anything left** bis wir ankommen, ist nichts mehr übrig

♦ **by that time** by that time we knew da or inzwischen wussten wir es; **by that time we'll know** dann or bis dahin wissen wir es

♦ **by this time** inzwischen; **by this time next year/tomorrow** nächstes Jahr/morgen um diese Zeit

♦ **from time to time** dann und wann, von Zeit zu Zeit

♦ **such time until such time as ...** so lange bis ...; **until such time as you apologize** solange du dich nicht entschuldigst, bis du dich entschuldigst

♦ **time of this time of the day/year** diese Tages-/Jahreszeit; **at this time of the week/month** zu diesem Zeitpunkt der Woche/des Monats; **it's my** or **the time of the month** (= period) ich habe meine or die Tage (inf)

♦ **time to now's the time to do it** jetzt ist der richtige Zeitpunkt or die richtige Zeit, es zu tun; **now's my/your etc time to do it** jetzt habe ich/hast du etc Gelegenheit, es zu tun

d [= occasion] **this time** diesmal, dieses Mal; **every** or **each time ...** jedes Mal, wenn ...; **many a time, many times** viele Male; **many's the time I have heard him say ...** ich habe ihn schon oft sagen hören ...; **for the last time** zum letzten Mal; **and he's not very bright at the best of times** und er ist ohnehin or sowieso nicht sehr intelligent; **the time before** das letzte or vorige Mal; **the time before last** das vorletzte Mal; **time and (time) again, time after time** immer wieder, wieder und wieder (geh); **I've told you a dozen times ...** ich habe dir schon x-mal gesagt ...; **nine times out of ten** — neun von zehn Malen ...; **she comes three times a week** sie kommt dreimal pro Woche or in der Woche

♦ **at a time** they came in one/three etc at a time sie kamen einzeln/immer zu dritt etc herein; **four at a time** vier auf einmal; **for weeks at a time** wochenlang

♦ **a time** (Brit) he pays me £10 a time er zahlt mir jedes Mal £ 10; **rides on the roundabout cost £2 a time** eine Fahrt auf dem Karussell kostet £ 2

♦ **(the) next time** nächstes Mal, das nächste Mal; **(the) next time I see you** wenn ich dich nächstes Mal or das nächste Mal sehe

♦ **(the) last time** letztes Mal, das letzte Mal; **(the) last time he was here** letztes Mal or das letzte Mal, als er hier war

e [Math] **2 times 3 is 6** 2 mal 3 ist 6; **it was ten times as big as** or **ten times the size of ...** es war zehnmal so groß wie ...; **our profits are rising four times faster than our competitors'** unsere Gewinne steigen viermal so schnell wie die unserer Konkurrenten

f [= rate] **Sunday is (paid) double time/time and a half** sonntags gibt es 100%/50% Zuschlag

g [= era] Zeit f; **this is the greatest problem of our time** das ist das größte Problem unserer Zeit; **in my time** zu meiner Zeit; **it happened before my time** das war vor meiner Zeit; **of all time** aller Zeiten; **time was when ...** es gab Zeiten, da ...; **he is ahead of his time** or **before his time** er ist seiner Zeit (weit) voraus; **in Victorian times** im Viktorianischen Zeitalter; **in olden times** in alten Zeiten; **times are hard** die Zeiten sind hart or schwer; **when times are hard** in harten or schweren Zeiten; **times change** die Zeiten ändern sich; **times are changing** es kommen andere Zeiten; **times are changing for the better/worse** es kommen bessere/schlechtere Zeiten; **times have changed for the better/worse** die Zeiten haben sich gebessert/verschlechtert

♦ **the times to be behind the times** rückständig sein, hinter dem Mond leben (inf); (= be out of touch) nicht auf dem Laufenden sein; **to keep up with the times** mit der Zeit gehen; (= keep in touch) auf dem Laufenden bleiben

h [= experience] **to have the time of one's life** eine herrliche Zeit verbringen, sich glänzend amüsieren; **what a time we had** or **that was!** das war eine Zeit!; **what times we had!, what times they were!** das waren (noch) Zeiten!; **to have an easy/a hard time** es leicht/schwer haben; **we had an easy/a hard time getting to the finals** es war leicht für uns/wir hatten Schwierigkeiten, in die Endrunde zu kommen; **was it difficult? – no, we had an easy time (of it)** war es schwierig? – nein, (es war) ganz leicht; **he didn't have an easy time of it in the operating theatre** er war im Operationssaal schlimm dran; **to have a bad/rough time** wenig mitmachen; **to give sb a bad/rough etc time (of it)** jdm das Leben schwer machen; **we had such a bad time with the travel agency** wir hatten solches Pech mit dem Reisebüro; **the goalkeeper had a rough time** der Torwart hatte schwer zu kämpfen

♦ **a good time** we had a good time es war (sehr) schön, es hat uns (dat) gut gefallen; **he doesn't look as though he's having a good time** es scheint ihm hier nicht besonders gut zu gefallen; **have a good time!** viel Vergnügen or Spaß!; **to show sb a good time** jdn ausführen; **she'll give you a good time for £30** bei ihr kannst du dich für £ 30 amüsieren

i [= rhythm] Takt m; **(to be) in time (with)** im Takt (sein) (mit); **(to be) out of time** aus dem Takt (sein); **you're singing out of time (with the others)** du singst nicht im Takt (mit den anderen); **3/4 time** Dreivierteltakt m; **to keep time** (= beat time) den Takt angeben or schlagen; (= keep in time) (den) Takt halten

2 – TRANSITIVE VERB

a [= choose time of] **to time sth perfectly** genau den richtigen Zeitpunkt für etw wählen; **you must learn to time your requests a little more tactfully** du musst lernen, deine Forderungen zu einem geeigneteren Zeitpunkt vorzubringen; **he timed his arrival to coincide with ...** er legte seine Ankunft so, dass sie mit ... zusammenfiel; **you timed that well** du hast dir den richtigen Zeitpunkt (dafür) ausgesucht; **the bomb is timed to explode at ...** die Bombe ist so eingestellt, dass sie um ... explodiert

b [= measure time of] (with stopwatch) stoppen; speed messen; **to time sb (over 1000 metres)** jdn (auf 1000 Meter) stoppen, jds Zeit (auf or über 1000 Meter) nehmen; **time how long it takes you** sieh auf die Uhr, wie lange du brauchst; **time yourself** sieh auf die Uhr, wie lange du brauchst; (with stopwatch) stopp, wie lange du brauchst; **to time an egg** auf die Uhr sehen, wann man ein Ei kocht; **a computer that times its operator** ein Computer, der die Zeit misst, die sein Operator braucht

time: time and motion expert N Fachmann m/Fachfrau f für Zeitstudien, ≈ REFA-Fachmann m/-Fachfrau f; **time and motion study** N Zeitstudie f, Bewegungsstudie f; **time bargain** N (Brit St Ex) Termingeschäft nt; **time bomb** N (lit, fig) Zeitbombe f; **time capsule** N Kassette f mit Zeitdokumentationen; **timecard** N (for workers) Stechkarte f; **time change** N Zeitumstellung f; **time check** N (general) Zeitkontrolle f; (Rad, TV) Zeitvergleich m; **time clock** N Stechuhr f; **time-consuming** ADJ zeitraubend; **time credit** N (flex(i)-time) Zeitguthaben f; **time debit** N (flex(i)time) Fehlzeit f; **time delay** N (gen, Telec) Zeitverzögerung f; (in bank) Zeitschloss nt; **time-delay** ADJ mechanism, safe mit Zeitschloss; **time deposit** N (Fin) Festgeld nt, Termingeld nt; **time difference** N Zeitunterschied m; **time exposure** N Langzeitbelichtung f; (= photograph) Langzeitaufnahme f; **time fault** N (Show-jumping) Zeitfehler m; **time-release** ADJ (Pharm) = time-release; **time frame, time-frame** N Zeitrahmen m, zeitlicher Rahmen; **to set a ~ for sth** den Zeitrahmen or zeitlichen Rahmen für etw festlegen; **time fuse,** (US) **time fuze** N Zeitzünder m; **time-honoured,** (US) **time-honored** ADJ althergebracht, altehrwürdig; **timekeeper** N (Sport) Zeitnehmer(in) m(f); **to be a good/bad ~** (watch) richtig or genau/nicht richtig gehen; (Brit: employee) immer/nie das Zeitsoll erfüllen; **timekeeping** N (in sports) Zeitnahme f, Zeitmessung f; (in factories etc) Zeitkontrolle f; (of worker) Erfüllung f des Zeitsolls; **bad ~** (Brit) ständiges Zuspätkommen; **time-lag** N Zeitdifferenz f; (= delay) Zeitverschiebung f; **cultural/technical ~** Unterschied m in der kulturellen/technischen Entwicklung; **time-lapse** ADJ camera für Zeitrafferaufnahmen; **~ photography** Zeitraffertechnik f

timeless ['taɪmlɪs] ADJ zeitlos; (= everlasting) immer während

timelessly ['taɪmlɪslɪ] ADV zeitlos; (= eternally) immerfort

timelessness ['taɪmlɪsnɪs] N Zeitlosigkeit f; (= eternal nature) Unvergänglichkeit f

time limit N zeitliche Begrenzung; (for the completion of a job) Frist f; **to put a ~ on sth** etw befristen

timeliness ['taɪmlɪnɪs] N Rechtzeitigkeit f; **the ~ of his warning soon became apparent** man merkte bald, dass seine Warnung genau zum richtigen Zeitpunkt erfolgt war

time lock N Zeitschloss nt

timely ['taɪmlɪ] ADJ rechtzeitig; **~ advice** ein Rat zur rechten Zeit; **that was very ~** das war genau zur rechten Zeit

time: time machine N Zeitmaschine f; **time money** N (Fin) Festgeld nt; **time-out** N (US) **a** (Ftbl, Basketball) Auszeit f **b** (= break) **to take ~** Pause machen; **timepiece** N Uhr f, Chronometer nt (geh)

timer ['taɪməʳ] N Zeitmesser m; (= switch) Schaltuhr f; (= person) Zeitnehmer(in) m(f)

time: time-release ADJ (Pharm) mit Depotwirkung; **~ drug** Depotpräparat nt; **time-saver** N **to be a ~** Zeit sparen; **time-saving** ADJ Zeit sparend; **timescale** N (in novel, drama etc) zeitlicher Rahmen; (= perception of time) Zeitmaßstab m; **to think on a different ~** einen anderen Zeitbegriff haben; **time-sensitive** ADJ project, information, money transfers etc zeitabhängig, zeitgebunden; **time-served** ADJ apprentice ausgelernt; **timeserver** N Opportunist m, Gesinnungslump m (pej inf); **timeserving** Ⓝ Opportunismus m, Gesinnungslumperei f (pej inf); Ⓐ opportunistisch; **timeshare** Ⓝ Wohnung f/Haus nt etc auf Timesharingbasis; Ⓐ attr salesman, company, apartment, holiday Timesharing-; development, resort für Timesharingurlauber; **a ~ week** eine Woche auf Timesharingbasis; **timesharing** N Teilnehmerrechensystem nt, Timesharing nt; **time sheet** N Stundenzettel m, Arbeitszeitkontrollliste f (form); **time signal** N (Brit) Zeitzeichen nt; **time signature** N Taktvorzeichnung f; **time span** N Zeitspanne f; **time switch** N Schaltuhr f, Zeitschalter m; **timetable** N (Transport) Fahrplan m; (Brit Sch) Stundenplan m; **to have a busy ~** ein volles Programm haben; **what's on**

the **~?** was steht auf dem Programm?; **time-tested** ADJ (alt)bewährt; **time travel** N Zeitreise f, Reise f durch die Zeit; **time traveller** N Zeitreisende(r) mf; **time trial** N Zeitrennen nt; **time unit** N (Telec) Zeiteinheit f; **time warp** N (Sci-Fi, fig) Zeitverzerrung f; **we're entering a ~** wir werden in eine andere Zeit versetzt; **time-waster** N (pej) **to be a ~** (activity) eine Zeitverschwendung sein; (person) seine Zeit verschwenden; **calls from ~s** nicht ernst gemeinte Anrufe pl; **"no ~s"** (in ad) „nur ernst gemeinte Angebote"; **time-wasting** N (Sport) Bummelei f; **timeworker** N nach Zeit bezahlter Arbeiter, nach Zeit bezahlte Arbeiterin; **timeworn** ADJ stones verwittert; (through use) abgetreten; cliché, joke abgedroschen; **time zone** N Zeitzone f

timid ['tɪmɪd] ADJ scheu, ängstlich; person, behaviour, words also schüchtern, zaghaft; measure zaghaft; **to be ~ about doing sth** etw nur zögernd tun

timidity [tɪ'mɪdɪtɪ] N Scheu f, Ängstlichkeit f; (of person, behaviour, words also) Schüchternheit f, Zaghaftigkeit f; (of measure) Zaghaftigkeit f

timidly ['tɪmɪdlɪ] ADV say, ask zaghaft; enter, approach schüchtern, ängstlich

timidness ['tɪmɪdnɪs] N = **timidity**

timing ['taɪmɪŋ] N **a** (= choice of time) Wahl f des richtigen Zeitpunkts (of für), Timing nt; (Tennis, Ftbl) Timing nt; **it's all a question of ~** es ist eine Frage der (Wahl) des richtigen Zeitpunkts or des Timings; **perfect ~, I'd just opened a bottle** ihr kommt gerade richtig, ich habe eben eine Flasche aufgemacht; **the ~ of the statement was wrong/excellent** die Erklärung kam zum falschen/genau zum richtigen Zeitpunkt; **what's the ~ for the reform?** wie sieht der Zeitplan für die Reform aus?; **the actors' ~ was terrible** die Schauspieler zeigten eine erbärmliche Synchronisierung; **to improve one's ~** sein Timing verbessern; **the dancer showed a good sense of ~** der Tänzer bewies ein gutes Gefühl fürs Timing **b** (Aut, = mechanism) Steuerung f; (= adjustment) Einstellung f; **~ mechanism** Steuermechanismus m **c** (= measuring of time) Zeitnahme f, Zeitmessung f (of bei); (of race, runners etc) Stoppen nt

timorous ['tɪmərəs] ADJ furchtsam, ängstlich, scheu

Timothy ['tɪməθɪ] N Timotheus m

timpani ['tɪmpənɪ] PL (Mus) Timpani pl, Kesselpauken pl

timpanist ['tɪmpənɪst] N Timpanist(in) m(f), Paukist(in) m(f)

tin [tɪn] N **a** Blech nt; (Chem, = metal) Zinn nt **b** (esp Brit, = can) Dose f, Büchse f; **a ~ of beans** eine Dose or Büchse Bohnen; **a ~ of biscuits** eine Dose Kekse VT **a** (= coat with tin) verzinnen **b** (esp Brit, = can) in Dosen or Büchsen konservieren

tin can N **a** (Blech)dose f, (Blech)büchse f **b** (US, Naut inf, = destroyer) Zerstörer m

tincture ['tɪŋktʃə'] N **a** (Pharm, Her) Tinktur f; **~ of iodine** Jodtinktur f **b** (fig, = tinge) Spur f, Andeutung f VT views, opinions einen Anstrich or Beigeschmack geben (+dat) (with von); **to be ~d with sth** einen Anstrich or Beigeschmack von etw haben

tinder ['tɪndə'] N Zunder m

tinderbox ['tɪndəbɒks] N Zunderbüchse f; **to be (like) a ~** wie Zunder brennen; (country etc) ein Pulverfass sein

tine [taɪn] N (of fork) Zinke f; (of antlers) Ende nt, Sprosse f

tinfoil ['tɪnfɔɪl] N (= wrapping) Stanniolpapier nt; (= aluminium foil) Aluminiumfolie f

ting [tɪŋ] VT bell läuten; **to ~ the bell** klingeln; **he ~ed his knife against the glass, he ~ed the glass with his knife** er schlug mit dem Messer an das Glas, dass es klirrte VI (bell) klingen N Klingen nt; **to give the bell a (quick) ~** (kurz) klingeln

ting-a-ling [ˌtɪŋə'lɪŋ] N Kling(e)ling nt INTERJ kling(e)ling

tinge [tɪndʒ] N **a** (of colour) Hauch m, Spur f; **a ~ of red** ein (leichter) Rotstich, ein Hauch m von Rot **b** (fig: = hint, trace) Spur f; (of sadness) Anflug m, Spur f VT **a** (= colour) (leicht) tönen; **lavender water ~d with pink** Lavendelwasser, das leicht rosa getönt ist **b** (fig) **to ~ sth with sth** einer Sache (dat) eine Spur von etw geben; **~d with ...** mit einer Spur von ...; **our happiness was ~d with sorrow** unser Glück war getrübt

tingle ['tɪŋgl] VI prickeln, kribbeln (inf) (with vor +dat); (with blows) leicht brennen (with von); **to ~ with excitement** vor Aufregung beben, ganz kribbelig sein (inf) N Prickeln nt, Kribbeln nt (inf); (from blows) leichtes Brennen; **she felt a ~ of excitement** sie war ganz kribbelig (inf); **a ~ of excitement ran up her spine** ihr lief (vor Aufregung) ein Schauer über den Rücken

tingling ['tɪŋglɪŋ] N Prickeln nt, Kribbeln nt (inf); (from blows) leichtes Brennen ADJ (with cold, freshness, excitement) prickelnd; (with blows) brennend

tingly ['tɪŋglɪ] ADJ prickelnd; **my arm feels (all) ~** ich habe ein prickelndes Gefühl im Arm, mein Arm kribbelt (inf); **I feel ~ all over** es kribbelt mich überall (inf); (with excitement) es prickelt mir unter der Haut, ich bin ganz kribbelig (inf)

tin: tin god N (fig) Bonze m; (= idol) Abgott m, Abgöttin f; **tin hat** N (inf) Stahlhelm m, steifer Hut (inf); **tinhorn** N (dated US, sl) Angeber(in) m(f) (inf)

tinker ['tɪŋkə'] N (Brit pej) Kesselflicker m; **you little ~!** (inf) du kleiner Stromer or Zigeuner! (inf); **not to give a ~'s curse** or **cuss** or **damn about sb/sth** (inf) sich keinen feuchten Kehricht um jdn/etw scheren (inf); **not to be worth a ~'s curse** or **cuss** or **damn** (inf) keinen Pfifferling wert sein (inf); (person) keinen Schuss Pulver wert sein (inf) VI **a** (also **tinker about**) herumbasteln (with, on an +dat) **b** (unskilfully) **to ~ with sth** an etw (dat) herumpfuschen

tinkle ['tɪŋkl] VT zum Klingen bringen; **he ~d the bell** er klingelte (mit der Glocke) VI **a** (bells etc) klingen, bimmeln (inf); (on piano) klimpern; (breaking glass, ice cubes) klirren **b** (inf: = to urinate) pinkeln (inf) N Klingen nt no pl, Bimmeln nt no pl (inf); (of breaking glass, ice cubes) Klirren nt no pl; **to give sb a ~** (Brit, inf, on telephone) jdn anbimmeln (inf)

tinkling ['tɪŋklɪŋ] N (of bells etc) Klingen nt, Bimmeln nt (inf); (of piano) Klimpern nt; (of broken glass, ice cubes) Klirren nt ADJ bells klingend, bimmelnd (inf); piano klimpernd; broken glass, ice cubes klirrend

tin: tin lizzie N (inf, = car) Klapperkiste f; **tin mine** N Zinnmine f, Zinnbergwerk nt

tinned [tɪnd] ADJ (esp Brit) peas, fruit etc aus der Dose; **~ meat** Dosen- or Büchsenfleisch nt

tinnery ['tɪnərɪ] N (Brit) Konservenfabrik f

tinny ['tɪnɪ] ADJ (+er) sound blechern; instrument blechern klingend; taste nach Blech; (pej) typewriter etc schäbig; **these cars are so ~** diese Autos bestehen fast nur aus Blech

tin: tin-opener N (esp Brit) Dosen- or Büchsenöffner m; **Tin Pan Alley** N die Schlagerindustrie; (= district) das Zentrum der Schlagerindustrie; **tin plate** N Zinnblech nt; **tin-plate** VT verzinnen; **tinpot** ADJ (esp Brit, inf) mickrig (inf); **~ dictator** Westentaschendiktator(in) m(f) (inf)

tinsel ['tɪnsəl] N **a** (= foil) Girlanden pl aus Rauschgold etc; (on dress) Lamé nt, Lamee nt **b** (pej) Talmi nt (geh), Tand nt (geh)

Tinseltown ['tɪnsəltaʊn] N (usu pej) Hollywood nt

tin: tinsmith N Blechschmied(in) m(f); **tin soldier** N Zinnsoldat m

tint [tɪnt] N Ton m; (= product for hair) Tönung(smittel nt) f; **~s of purple** Violetttöne pl VT hair tönen

tintack ['tɪntæk] N Tapeziernagel m

tinted ['tɪntɪd] ADJ hair, spectacles, glass getönt

tintinnabulation [ˌtɪntɪnæbju'leɪʃən] N (liter, form) Klingeln nt or Geläut nt (von Glocken)

tin whistle N Blechflöte f

tiny ['taɪnɪ] ADJ (+er) winzig, sehr klein; baby, child sehr or ganz klein; **~ little** winzig klein; **a ~ mind** (pej) ein winziger Verstand, ein Zwergenverstand m

tip¹ [tɪp] N Spitze f; (of cigarette) Filter m; **to stand on the ~s of one's toes** auf Zehenspitzen stehen; **it's on the ~ of my tongue** es liegt mir auf der Zunge; **it was on the ~ of my tongue to tell her what I thought of her** ich war fast so weit, ihr zu sagen, was ich von ihr hielt; **it's just the ~ of the iceberg** (fig) das ist nur die Spitze des Eisbergs → **fingertip, wingtip** VT (= put tip on) **to ~ sth with copper/steel** etc etw mit einer Kupfer-/Stahlspitze versehen; **copper/steel-tipped** mit Kupfer-/Stahlspitze; **~ped** (cigarette) mit Filter

tip² N **a** (= gratuity) Trinkgeld nt; **what do your ~s amount to?** wie viel Trinkgeld bekommen Sie (insgesamt)?; **£100 a week, plus ~s** £ 100 pro Woche, plus Trinkgeld(er); **50p is sufficient as a ~** 50 Pence Trinkgeld reichen **b** (= warning) Wink m, Tipp m; (= advice) Tipp m, Hinweis m, Ratschlag m; (Racing) Tipp m; **if you take my ~** wenn Sie meinen Tipp or Wink beachten **c** (= tap) **to give the ball a ~** den Ball nur antippen VT **a** (= give gratuity to) Trinkgeld geben (+dat); **to ~ sb £3** jdm £ 3 Trinkgeld geben **b** (Racing) tippen auf (+acc), setzen auf (+acc); **he ~ped Golden Boy for the 3.30** er setzte or tippte im 3.30-Uhr-Rennen auf Golden Boy; **to be ~ped for success** (Brit) als sicherer Erfolgskandidat gelten; **they are ~ped to win the competition/election** (Brit fig) sie sind die Favoriten in dem Wettbewerb/in der Wahl; **you ~ped a winner** (lit, fig) da hast du auf das richtige Pferd gesetzt **c** (= tap, with fingers) tippen or schnipsen an (+acc); (with bat, racket) antippen; **to ~ one's hat (to sb)** an den Hut tippen VI **Americans ~ better** Amerikaner geben mehr Trinkgeld

▶ **tip off** VT sep einen Tipp or Wink geben +dat (about über +acc); **he tipped off the police as to her whereabouts** er verriet der Polizei, wo sie war (inf); **they've been tipped off** man hat ihnen einen Tipp or Wink gegeben

tip³ VT (= tilt, incline) kippen; (= overturn) umkippen; (= pour) liquid kippen, schütten; (= empty) load, sand, rubbish schütten; books, clothes etc schmeißen; **to ~ sth backwards/forwards** etw nach hinten/vorne kippen or neigen; **to ~ a load into a ship** eine Ladung in ein Schiff leeren or kippen; **he ~s the scales at 70kg** er bringt 70 kg auf die Waage; **it ~ped the scales in his favour** (fig) das hat für ihn den Ausschlag gegeben; **to ~ the balance** (fig) den Ausschlag geben; **~ the case upside down** dreh die Kiste um, stell die Kiste auf den Kopf; **to ~ sb off his chair** jdn vom Stuhl kippen; **to ~ one's hat over one's eyes** sich (dat) den Hut über die Augen ziehen/schieben VI (= incline) kippen; (= dump rubbish) Schutt abladen; **the boat ~ped to and fro** das Boot schaukelte auf und ab; **"no ~ping", "tipping prohibited"** „Schutt abladen verboten" N **a** (Brit, for rubbish) Müllkippe f; (for coal) Halde f; (inf, = untidy place) Saustall m (inf) **b** **to give sth a ~** etw (um)kippen

▶ **tip back** VI (chair, person, mirror) nach hinten (weg)kippen VT sep nach hinten kippen; head nach hinten neigen; person nach hinten legen

▶ **tip out** VT sep auskippen; liquid, sand also ausschütten; load, objects, rubbish abladen, ausleeren; **they tipped him out of bed** sie kippten ihn aus dem Bett VI (liquid) herauslaufen; (sand) herausrutschen; (load, objects, rubbish also) herausfallen

▶ **tip over** VT sep (= overturn) umkippen VI (= overturn) umkippen

▶ **tip up** VT sep (= tilt) kippen; (= overturn) umkippen VI (= tilt) kippen; (= overturn) umkippen; (folding seat) hochklappen

tip-and-run raid [ˌtɪpənˈrʌn,reɪd] N (Mil) Blitzangriff m mit sofortigem Rückzug

tip-off ['tɪpɒf] N (inf) Tipp m, Wink m

tipper ['tɪpə] N **a** (also **tipper lorry** (Brit), **tipper truck**) Kipplaster m, Kipper m **b** (= person) **he's a generous ~** er gibt großzügig Trinkgeld

tipper lorry, tipper truck (US) N (Mot, Tech) Kipper m, Kippfahrzeug nt

tippet ['tɪpɪt] N (old, woman's) Schultertuch nt; (Eccl) Stola f

Tipp-Ex® ['tɪpeks] N Tipp-Ex® nt VT **to ~ (out)** mit Tipp-Ex® löschen

tipple ['tɪpl] (esp Brit inf) N **he enjoys a ~** er trinkt ganz gerne mal einen; **gin is his ~** er trinkt am liebsten Gin VI (ganz schön) süffeln (inf), picheln (inf)

tippler ['tɪplə] N (esp Brit inf) Schluckspecht m (inf)

tippy-toe ['tɪpɪtəʊ] VI, N (US, inf) = tiptoe

tipsily ['tɪpsɪlɪ] ADV beschwipst, angesäuselt (inf)

tipsiness ['tɪpsɪnɪs] N Beschwipstheit f

tipstaff ['tɪpstɑːf] N (Brit, Jur) ≈ Ordnungsbeamte(r) m/-beamtin f

tipster ['tɪpstə] N jd, der bei Pferderennen Wetttipps verkauft

tipsy ['tɪpsɪ] ADJ (+er) beschwipst, angesäuselt (inf); **to be ~** beschwipst or angesäuselt (inf) sein, einen Schwips haben

tipsy cake N mit Alkohol getränkter Kuchen

tip: tiptoe VI auf Zehenspitzen gehen N **on ~** auf Zehenspitzen; **they stood on ~** sie standen auf Zehenspitzen; **they raised themselves on ~** sie stellten sich auf die Zehenspitzen; **tiptop** ADJ (inf, = first-rate) tipptopp (inf) pred, erstklassig; **tip-up lorry** (Brit), **tip-up truck** N Kipplaster m, Kipper m; **tip-up seat** N Klappsitz m

tirade [taɪˈreɪd] N Tirade f, Schimpfkanonade f

tire¹ [taɪə] VT ermüden, müde machen VI **a** (= become fatigued) ermüden, müde werden **b** (= become bored) **to ~ of sb/sth** jdn/etw satt haben, einer Sache (gen) müde (geh) or überdrüssig (geh) werden; **she never ~s of talking about her son** sie wird es nie müde, über ihren Sohn zu sprechen

▶ **tire out** VT sep (völlig) erschöpfen

tire² (US) = tyre

tired ['taɪəd] ADJ **a** (= fatigued) müde; cliché abgegriffen; **~ out** völlig erschöpft; **~ and emotional** (hum inf, = drunk) nicht mehr ganz nüchtern

b **to be ~ of sb/sth** jds/einer Sache (gen) müde or überdrüssig sein (geh), jdn/etw leid sein, jdn/etw satt haben; **to get ~ of sb/sth** jdn/etw satt bekommen; **I'm ~ of telling you** ich habe es satt, dir das zu sagen; **I'm ~ of people making money out of me** ich habe es satt, dass Leute mich finanziell ausnutzen; **to be ~ to death (of sth)** (inf) die Nase (von etw) gestrichen voll haben (inf); **you make me ~!** du regst mich auf!

c (= old) müde; **a ~, worn-out organization** eine müde, verbrauchte Organisation; **a ~ lettuce leaf** ein schlaffes Salatblatt

d (pej, = boring, stale) langweilig; **another one of his ~ excuses** wieder eine seiner langweiligen Ausreden; **their advertising is getting rather ~** ihrer Werbung fehlt allmählich der Schwung or Pep (inf)

tiredly ['taɪədlɪ] ADV müde; say also mit müder Stimme

tiredness ['taɪədnɪs] N Müdigkeit f; **~ had got the better of him** (die) Müdigkeit hatte ihn

übermannt; **the accident was a result of (his) ~** (seine) Übermüdung war die Unfallursache

tireless ['taɪəlɪs] ADJ unermüdlich; patience also unerschöpflich; **to be ~ in sth** unermüdlich in etw (dat) sein

tirelessly ['taɪəlɪslɪ] ADV work, campaign unermüdlich

tirelessness ['taɪəlɪsnɪs] N Unermüdlichkeit f

tiresome ['taɪəsəm] ADJ (= irritating) lästig; (= boring) langweilig

tiresomeness ['taɪəsəmnɪs] N (= irritating nature) Lästigkeit f; (= boringness) Langweiligkeit f

tiring ['taɪərɪŋ] ADJ anstrengend, ermüdend; **looking after 6 children under 5 is ~** es ist sehr anstrengend or es macht (einen) sehr müde, auf 6 Kinder unter 5 Jahren aufzupassen; **this is ~ work/a ~ job** diese Arbeit ist anstrengend

tiro N = tyro

Tirol N = Tyrol

'tis [tɪz] (Poet, dial) contr of **it is** es ist

tissue ['tɪʃuː] N **a** (Anat, Bot, fig) Gewebe nt; **a ~ of lies** ein Lügengewebe nt, ein Lügengespinst nt **b** (= handkerchief) Papier(taschen)tuch nt **c** (also **tissue paper**) Seidenpapier nt

tissue cell N Gewebezelle f

tissue culture N Gewebekultur f

tit¹ [tɪt] N (= bird) Meise f

tit² N **~ for tat** wie du mir, so ich dir, Auge um Auge(, Zahn um Zahn); **it was ~ for tat** es ging Auge um Auge(, Zahn um Zahn)

tit³ N (sl) **a** (= breast) Titte f (sl); **~ and bum press** (Brit, hum) Arsch-und-Titten-Presse f (hum sl); **he/it gets on my ~s** er/das geht mir auf den Sack (sl) **b** (esp Brit pej inf: = stupid person) (blöde) Sau (sl); **I felt a right ~** ich kam mir total bescheuert vor (inf)

Titan ['taɪtən] N (Myth) Titan m

titan ['taɪtən] N (fig) Titan(in) m(f), Gigant(in) m(f)

titanic [taɪˈtænɪk] ADJ **a** (= huge) gigantisch **b** (Chem) Titan-; **~ oxide** Titandioxid nt

titanium [tɪˈteɪnɪəm] N (Chem) Titan nt

titbit ['tɪtbɪt], (US) **tidbit** ['tɪdbɪt] N **a** Leckerbissen m **b** (= piece of information) Pikanterie f

titch [tɪtʃ] N (Brit, inf) = tich

titchy ['tɪtʃɪ] ADJ (Brit, inf) = tichy

titfer ['tɪtfə] N (Brit, inf, = hat) Deckel m (inf)

tithe [taɪð] N usu pl Zehnte m; **to pay ~s** den Zehnten bezahlen or abgeben

titillate ['tɪtɪleɪt] VT person, senses anregen, angenehm erregen; interest erregen; **it ~s the palate** es kitzelt den Gaumen

titillation [ˌtɪtɪˈleɪʃən] N (of person, senses) Anregung f, angenehme Erregung; (of interest) Erregen nt; **such ~ is not for the serious-minded** solcher Kitzel ist nichts für ernsthaft gesinnte Menschen

titivate ['tɪtɪveɪt] (old, hum) VI sich fein machen VT oneself, hair etc, restaurant herausputzen, verschönern

titivation [ˌtɪtɪˈveɪʃən] N (old, hum) Verschönerung f

title ['taɪtl] N **a** Titel m (also Sport); (of chapter) Überschrift f; (Film) Untertitel m; (= form of address) Anrede f; **what ~ do you give a bishop?** wie redet or spricht man einen Bischof an? **b** (Jur, = right) (Rechts)anspruch m (to auf +acc), Titel m (spec); (= document) Eigentumsurkunde f

title bout N (Boxing) Titelkampf m

titled ['taɪtld] ADJ person, classes mit (Adels)titel; **is he ~?** hat er einen Titel?

title: title deed N Eigentumsurkunde f; **title fight** N Titelkampf m; **titleholder** N (Sport) Titelträger(in) m(f), Titelinhaber(in) m(f); **title page** N (Typ) Titelseite f; **title part, title role** N (Theat, Film) Titelrolle f

titmouse ['tɪtmaʊs] N Meise f

titrate ['taɪtreɪt] VT (Chem) titrieren

titter ['tɪtə] VT kichern N Kichern nt, Gekicher nt

tittie ['tɪtɪ] N (inf) = titty

tittle ['tɪtl] N → jot

tittle-tattle ['tɪtlˌtætl] N Geschwätz nt; (= gossip also) Klatsch m, Tratsch m (inf) VI quatschen, schwatzen; (= gossip also) klatschen, tratschen (inf)

titty ['tɪtɪ] N **a** (inf, = breast) Brüstchen nt (inf) **b** **that's tough ~** (inf) das ist Pech (inf); **that's tough ~ for you** (inf) da hast du wohl Pech gehabt (inf), dumm gelaufen (inf)

titular ['tɪtjʊlə] ADJ **a** possessions zum Titel gehörend **b** (= without real authority) nominell; (Univ) degree Ehren-; **~ bishop** Titularbischof m

tizzy ['tɪzɪ], **tizwoz** ['tɪzwɒz] N (inf) **to be in a ~** höchst aufgeregt sein; **to get into a ~** sich schrecklich aufregen

T-junction ['tiːdʒʌŋkʃən] N (Brit) T-Kreuzung f; **"T-junction ahead"** „Achtung Vorfahrtsstraße"

TLC (inf) abbr of **tender loving care**

TLS (Brit) abbr of **Times Literary Supplement** von der Times herausgegebene Literaturbeilage

TM abbr of **trademark** Wz

TNT abbr of **trinitrotoluene** TNT nt

---

to [tuː]

1 PREPOSITION	3 ADVERB
2 ADJECTIVE	

1 – PREPOSITION

a = in direction of, towards zu; **to go to the station** zum Bahnhof gehen; **to go to the doctor('s)/greengrocer's** etc zum Arzt/Gemüsehändler etc gehen; **to go to the opera/concert** etc in die Oper/ins Konzert etc gehen; **to go to France/London** nach Frankreich/London fahren; **to go to Switzerland** in die Schweiz fahren; **to go to school** zur Schule or in die Schule gehen; **to go to bed** ins or zu Bett gehen; **to the left** nach links; **to the west** nach Westen; **he came up to where I was standing** er kam dahin or zu der Stelle, wo ich stand; **to fall to the ground** auf den Boden or zu Boden fallen; **to turn a picture/one's face to the wall** ein Bild/sich mit dem Gesicht zur Wand drehen; **hold it up to the light** halte es gegen das Licht

b = as far as, until bis; **to count (up) to 20** bis 20 zählen; **there were (from) 40 to 60 people** es waren 40 bis 60 Leute da; **it's 90 kms to Paris** bis nach Paris sind es 90 km; **it's correct to a millimetre** es stimmt bis auf den Millimeter; **8 years ago to the day** auf den Tag genau vor 8 Jahren; **to this day** bis auf den heutigen Tag; **they perished to a man** sie kamen alle bis auf den letzten Mann ums Leben

c = in in (+dat); **I have never been to Brussels/India** ich war noch nie in Brüssel/Indien

d = secure to **he nailed it to the wall/floor** etc er nagelte es an die Wand/auf den Boden etc; **they tied him to the tree** sie banden ihn am Baum fest; **they held him to the ground** sie hielten ihn am Boden

e with indirect object **to give sth to sb** jdm etw geben; **a present from me to you** ein Geschenk für dich von mir or von mir an dich; **who did you give it to?** wem haben Sie es gegeben?; **I said to myself ...** ich habe mir gesagt ...; **he was muttering/singing to himself** er murmelte/sang vor sich hin; **what is it to you?** was geht dich das an?; **he is kind to everyone** er ist zu allen freundlich; **it's a great help to me** das ist eine große Hilfe für mich; **he has been a good friend to us** er war uns (dat) ein guter Freund; **"To ... "** (on envelope etc) „An (+acc) ..."; **to pray to God** zu Gott beten

f in toasts auf (+acc); **to drink to sb** jdm zutrinken; **to drink to sb's health** auf jds Wohl (acc) trinken

g = next to (with position) **bumper to bumper** Stoßstange an Stoßstange; **close to sb/sth** nahe bei jdm/etw; **at right angles to the wall** im rechten Winkel zur Wand; **parallel to the wall**

parallel zur Wand; **to the west (of)/the left (of)** westlich/links (von)

h with expressions of time vor; **20 (minutes) to 2** 20 (Minuten) vor 2; **at (a) quarter to 2** um Viertel vor 2; **25 to 3** 5 (Minuten) nach halb 3; **it was five to when we arrived** es war fünf vor, als wir ankamen

i = in relation to zu; **A is to B as C is to D** A verhält sich zu B wie C zu D; **by a majority of 10 to 7** mit einer Mehrheit von 10 zu 7; **they won by 4 goals to 2** sie haben mit 4:2 (spoken: vier zu zwei) Toren gewonnen

j = per pro; (in recipes, when mixing) auf (+acc); **one person to a room** eine Person pro Zimmer

k Math **3 to the 4th, 3 to the power of 4** 3 hoch 4

l = concerning **what do you say to the idea?** was hältst du von der Idee?; **what would you say to a beer?** was hältst du von einem Bier?; **there's nothing to it** (= it's very easy) es ist nichts dabei; **that's all there is to it** das ist alles; **to repairing television £30** (Comm) (für) Reparatur eines Fernsehers £ 30

m = according to **to the best of my knowledge** nach bestem Wissen; **it's not my taste** das ist nicht nach meinem Geschmack

n = accompanied by **to sing to the guitar** zur Gitarre singen; **to sing sth to the tune of ...** etw nach der Melodie von ... singen; **to dance to a tune/a band** zu einer Melodie/den Klängen or der Musik eines Orchesters tanzen

o = of **ambassador to America/the King of France** Botschafter in Amerika/am Hofe des Königs von Frankreich; **secretary to the director** Sekretärin des Direktors

p = producing **to everyone's surprise** zu jedermanns Überraschung

q infinitive **to begin to do sth** anfangen, etw zu tun; **he decided to come** er beschloss zu kommen; **I want to do it** ich will es tun; **I want him to do it** ich will, dass er es tut

r conditional use of infinitive **to see him now, one would never think ...** wenn man ihn jetzt sieht, würde man nicht glauben, ...

s infinitive expressing purpose, result **to eat/work to live** essen/arbeiten, um zu leben; **I did it to help you** ich tat es, um dir zu helfen; **to get to the point, ...** um zur Sache zu kommen, ...; **well, not to exaggerate ...** ohne zu übertreiben, ...; **I arrived to find she had gone** als ich ankam, war sie weg; **never to be found again** und wurde nie wieder gefunden

t omitting verb **I don't want to** ich will nicht; **I'll try to** ich werde es versuchen; **you have to** du musst; **I'd love to** sehr gerne; **we didn't want to but we were forced to** wir wollten nicht, aber wir waren dazu gezwungen; **I intended to (do it), but I forgot (to)** ich wollte es tun, aber ich habe es vergessen; **buy it, it would be silly not to** kaufe es, es wäre dumm, es nicht zu tun; **he often does things one doesn't expect him to** er macht oft Dinge, die man nicht von ihm erwartet

u set structures

♦ **noun/pronoun + to + infinitive he is not the sort to do that** er ist nicht der Typ, der das täte, er ist nicht der Typ dazu; **I have done nothing to deserve this** ich habe nichts getan, womit ich das verdient hätte; **there's no-one to help us** es ist niemand da, der uns helfen könnte; **who is he to order you around?** wer ist er denn, dass er dich so herumkommandiert?; **he was the first to arrive** er kam als Erster an, er war der Erste, der ankam; **who was the last to see her?** wer hat sie zuletzt gesehen?; **there is much to be done** es gibt viel zu tun; **what is there to do here?** was gibt es hier zu tun?; **now is the time to do it** jetzt ist die (beste) Zeit, es zu tun; **the book is still to be written** das Buch muss noch geschrieben werden

♦ **adjective + to + infinitive to be ready to do sth** (= willing) bereit sein, etw zu tun; **are you ready to go at last?** bist du endlich fertig?; **it's hard to understand** es ist schwer zu

verstehen; **it's impossible to believe** das kann man einfach nicht glauben; **you are foolish to try it** du bist dumm, das überhaupt zu versuchen; **is it good to eat?** schmeckt es gut?; **it's too heavy to lift** es ist zu schwer zum Heben; **too young to marry** zu jung zum Heiraten; **he's too old to be still in short trousers** er ist schon so alt und trägt noch kurze Hosen

2 – ADJECTIVE

door (= ajar) angelehnt; (= shut) zu

3 – ADVERB

to and fro hin und her; walk auf und ab

toad [təʊd] N Kröte f; (fig, = repulsive person) Ekel nt

toad-in-the-hole [ˌtəʊdɪnðəˈhəʊl] N Teigspeise mit Würsten

toadstool [ˈtəʊdstuːl] N (nicht essbarer) Pilz; **poisonous ~** Giftpilz m

toady [ˈtəʊdɪ] **N** (pej) Kriecher(in) m(f), Speichellecker(in) m(f) **VI** Rad fahren (pej inf); **to ~ to sb** vor jdm kriechen

to and fro ADV hin und her

toast¹ [təʊst] **N** Toast m; **a piece of ~** ein Toast m, eine Scheibe Toast; **on ~** auf Toast; **as warm as ~** (fig) mollig warm **VT** bread toasten; (on open fire, in oven) rösten; **to ~ one's feet by the fire** sich (dat) die Füße am Feuer wärmen **VI** (bread etc) sich toasten/rösten lassen; (inf: person) braten (inf), rösten (inf)

toast² **N** **a** Toast m, Trinkspruch m; **to drink a ~ to sb** auf jdn trinken; **to propose a ~** einen Toast or Trinkspruch ausbringen (to auf +acc); **they raised their glasses in a ~ (to him)** sie hoben ihre Gläser (um auf ihn zu trinken) **b** **she was the ~ of the town** sie war der gefeierte Star der Stadt **VT** **to ~ sb/sth** auf jds Wohl or jdn/etw trinken; **we ~ed the victory in champagne** wir haben unseren Sieg mit Champagner gefeiert or begossen (inf)

toasted cheese [ˌtəʊstɪdˈtʃiːz] N (Brit) überbackener Käsetoast

toasted teacakes [ˌtəʊstɪdˈtiːkeɪks] PL (Brit) getoastete Rosinenbrötchen

toaster [ˈtəʊstə] N Toaster m

toastie [ˈtəʊstɪ] N (Brit) Toastschnitte f, getoastetes Sandwich

toasting fork [ˈtəʊstɪŋfɔːk] N Gabel f zum Brotrösten

toastmaster [ˈtəʊstmɑːstə] N jd, der bei Diners Toasts ankündigt oder ausbringt und Tischreden ansagt

toast rack N Toastständer m

toasty [ˈtəʊstɪ] **N** = toastie **ADJ** (inf: also **toasty warm**) mollig warm (inf)

tobacco [təˈbækəʊ] N Tabak m

tobacco: tobacco jar N Tabak(s)dose f; **tobacco leaf** N Tabakblatt nt

tobacconist [təˈbækənɪst] N Tabak(waren)händler(in) m(f); (= shop) Tabak(waren)laden m; **at the ~'s** im Tabak(waren)laden

tobacco: tobacco plantation N Tabakplantage f; **tobacco pouch** N Tabak(s)beutel m

to-be [təˈbiː] ADJ zukünftig; **the bride-to-be** die zukünftige Braut; **the husband-to-be** der zukünftige Mann; **the mother-to-be** die werdende Mutter

toboggan [təˈbɒgən] **N** Schlitten m, Rodel (-schlitten) m; **~ run** Schlitten- or Rodelbahn f **VI** Schlitten fahren, rodeln; **to ~ down a slope** mit dem Schlitten einen Hang hinunterfahren; **to go ~ing** Schlitten fahren, rodeln

toby jug [ˈtəʊbɪdʒʌg] N Figurkrug m

toccata [təˈkɑːtə] N Tokkata f

tocsin [ˈtɒksɪn] N (old) Alarmglocke f, Alarm m

tod [tɒd] N (Brit, inf) **on one's ~** ganz allein

today [təˈdeɪ] ADV, N **a** heute; **a week/fortnight ~** heute in einer Woche/zwei Wochen; **he's been here a week ~** heute ist er eine Woche da; **a year ago ~** heute vor einem Jahr; **~ is**

Monday, **it's Monday ~** heute ist Montag; **from ~** von heute an, vom heutigen Tag an, ab heute; **later** ~ später (am Tag); **~'s paper/news** die heutige Zeitung/heutigen Nachrichten, die Zeitung/Nachrichten von heute; **what's ~'s date?** welches Datum ist heute?, der Wievielte ist heute?; **~'s rate** (Fin) der Tageskurs; **here ~ and gone tomorrow** (fig) heute hier und morgen da; **our yesterdays, our ~s and our tomorrows** unsere Vergangenheit, unsere Gegenwart und unsere Zukunft

b (= these days) heutzutage; **the cinema ~** das Kino (von) heute; **the world/youth/writers of ~** die Welt/Jugend/Schriftsteller von heute; **~'s world/youth** die heutige Welt/Jugend, die Welt/Jugend von heute; **live for ~ and let tomorrow take care of itself** lebe dem Heute und lass das Morgen morgen sein

toddle [ˈtɒdl] VI **a** (child) wackelnd laufen; **the little boy ~d into the room** der kleine Junge kam ins Zimmer gewackelt **b** (inf, = walk) gehen; (= leave: also **toddle off**) abzwitschern (inf); **well, I'd better be toddling (off)** ich zwitschere wohl besser mal ab (inf); **could you just ~ down to the shops and ...** könntest du mal zu den Geschäften runtergehen und ... N (inf) **to go for a ~** an die Luft gehen

toddler [ˈtɒdlə] N Kleinkind nt

toddy [ˈtɒdɪ] N Grog m

todger [ˈtɒdʒə] N (Brit, sl) Schniedel m (inf)

to-do [təˈduː] N (inf) Theater nt (inf), Gedöns nt (inf); **she made quite a ~ about it** sie machte viel Wind or vielleicht ein Theater or Gedöns darum (inf); **what a ~!** so ein Theater! (inf); **what's all the ~?** was soll denn das ganze Theater or Getue or Gedöns? (inf)

toe [təʊ] **N** Zehe f, Zeh m; (of sock, shoe) Spitze f; **to tread or step on sb's ~s** (lit) jdm auf die Zehen treten; (fig) jdm ins Handwerk pfuschen (inf); **with so many of us we'll be treading on each other's ~s** wir sind so viele, dass wir uns gegenseitig ins Gehege kommen; **to be on one's ~s** (fig) auf Zack sein (inf); **to keep sb on his ~s** (fig) jdn auf Zack halten (inf); **to go or stand ~ to ~ with sb** (esp US, fig) jdm offen gegenübertreten; **there are scenes in the film that make your ~s curl** in dem Film sind Szenen, da bekommt man das kalte Grausen (inf) **VT** (fig) **to ~ the line** sich einfügen, spuren (inf); **to ~ the party line** (Pol) sich nach der Parteilinie richten

toe: toecap N (Schuh)kappe f; **toeclip** N (on bicycle) Rennbügel m

-toed [-təʊd] ADJ suf -zehig; **two-toed** zweizehig, mit zwei Zehen

toe-dance [ˈtəʊdɑːns] VI (US) auf den Spitzen tanzen

TOEFL abbr of **Test of English as a Foreign Language** TOEFL-Test m, englische Sprachprüfung für ausländische Studenten

toe: toehold N Halt m für die Fußspitzen; (fig) Einstieg m; **toe-in** N Vorlauf m; **toenail** N Zehennagel m; **toe-piece** N (on shoe, Ski) Zehenteil nt; **toerag** N (pej inf) Arsch m (vulg); **toe shoe** N (US) Spitzenschuh m

toff [tɒf] N (Brit, inf) feiner Pinkel (inf)

toffee [ˈtɒfɪ] N (= substance) (Sahne)karamell m; (= sweet) Toffee nt, (weiches) Karamellbonbon; **he can't sing for ~** (inf) er kann überhaupt nicht singen, er kann nicht die Bohne singen (inf)

toffee: toffee apple N kandierter Apfel; **toffee-nosed** ADJ (Brit, inf) eingebildet, hochnäsig

tofu [ˈtəʊfuː] N Tofu nt

tog [tɒg] N (Brit: = measure of insulation) Maß für die Wärmeableitung von Bettdecken etc

toga [ˈtəʊgə] N Toga f

together [təˈgeðə] **ADV** **a** zusammen; **to do sth ~** etw zusammen tun; (= with one another) discuss, play, dance etc also etw miteinander tun; (= jointly) try, achieve, do research etc also etw gemeinsam tun; **to sit/stand** etc **~** zusammensitzen/-stehen *etc*, beieinander sitzen/stehen *etc*; **to be (all) ~** (*people*) (alle) zusammen *or* beieinander *or* miteinander sein; **to tie/fit/glue** *etc* **two things ~** zwei Dinge zusammenbinden/-setzen/-kleben *etc*; **we're in this ~** wir hängen da alle *or* (*two people*) beide zusammen drin (*inf*); **they were both in it ~** sie waren beide zusammen *or* miteinander daran beteiligt; **just you and me ~** nur wir beide zusammen; **to go ~** (= *match*) zusammenpassen

b (= *at the same time*) zusammen; **all ~ now** jetzt alle zusammen; **you're not ~** (*Mus*) ihr seid im Takt auseinander

c (= *continuously*) **for hours ~** stundenlang; **can't you sit still for two minutes ~!** kannst du nicht mal zwei Minuten (lang) still sitzen?

d **~ with** (zusammen) mit
ADJ (*inf*) cool (*inf*); **she's more ~ now** sie ist jetzt besser beieinander (*inf*)

togetherness [təˈɡeðənɪs] N (*physical*) Beisammensein *nt*; (*mental, emotional*) Zusammengehörigkeit *f*; **a feeling** *or* **sense of ~** ein Gefühl *nt* der Zusammengehörigkeit, ein Zusammengehörigkeitsgefühl *nt*

toggle [ˈtɒɡl] **N** Knebel *m*; (*on clothes*) Knebelknopf *m*; (*on tent*) Seilzug *m* **VI** (*Comput*) hin- und herschalten

toggle key N (*Comput*) Umschalttaste *f*

toggle switch N Kipp(hebel)schalter *m*

Togo [ˈtəʊɡəʊ] N Togo *nt*

Togoland [ˈtəʊɡəʊlænd] N Togo *nt*

togs [tɒɡz] PL (*inf*) Sachen *pl*, Klamotten *pl* (*inf*), Zeug *nt*

▶ **tog up** VT *sep* (*inf*) **to tog oneself up**, **to get togged up** sich in Schale werfen (*inf*); (*for tennis etc*) seine Kluft anlegen; **to be togged up in one's best clothes** seine besten Sachen anhaben (*inf*)

toil [tɔɪl] **VI** **a** (*liter*, = *work*) sich plagen, sich abmühen (*at, over* mit) **b** (= *move with effort*) sich schleppen; **to ~ up a hill** sich einen Berg hinaufschleppen **N** (*liter*, = *work*) Mühe *f*, Plage *f* (*geh*); **after months of ~** nach monatelanger Mühe *or* Plage

toiler [ˈtɔɪlə] N Schwerarbeiter(in) *m(f)*

toilet [ˈtɔɪlɪt] N (= *lavatory*) Toilette *f*, Klosett *nt* (*dated*); **to go to the ~** (*esp Brit*) auf die Toilette gehen; **she's in the ~/~s** sie ist auf *or* in der Toilette; **to put sth down the ~** etw in die Toilette werfen; **the cat's done the ~ on the carpet** die Katze hat auf den Teppich gemacht (*inf*) **b** (*old*) Toilette *f* (*geh*)

toilet *in cpds* Toiletten-; **toilet bag** N (*Brit*) Kulturbeutel *m*, Toilettentasche *f*; **toilet bowl** N Toilettenbecken *nt*; **toilet brush** N Klobürste *f* (*inf*); **toilet case** N = **toilet bag**; **toilet humour** N Gossenhumor *m*; **toilet paper** N Toilettenpapier *nt*; **toilet requisites** PL Toilettenartikel *pl*

toiletries [ˈtɔɪlɪtrɪz] PL Toilettenartikel *pl*

toilet: toilet roll N Rolle *f* Toilettenpapier; **toilet seat** N Toilettensitz *m*, Brille *f* (*inf*); **toilet set** N (= *brush and comb*) Toilettengarnitur *f*; (= *bathroom set*) Badezimmergarnitur *f*; **toilet soap** N Toilettenseife *f*; **toilet tissue** N Toilettenpapier *nt*; **toilet training** N Erziehung *f* zur Sauberkeit; **has he started his ~ yet?** geht er schon auf den Topf?; **toilet water** N Duftwasser *nt*, Eau de Toilette *nt*

toils [tɔɪlz] PL (*old, lit*) Netze *pl*; (*fig*) Maschen *pl*, Schlingen *pl*

toilsome [ˈtɔɪlsəm] ADJ (*liter*) mühselig, mühsam

to-ing and fro-ing [ˌtuːɪŋənˈfrəʊɪŋ] N (*esp Brit*) Hin und Her *nt*

Tokay [təˈkaɪ] N (= *wine*) Tokaier *m*

token [ˈtəʊkən] ✪ 22 **N a** (= *sign*) Zeichen *nt*; **as a ~ of**, **in ~ of** als *or* zum Zeichen (+*gen*); **by the same ~** ebenso; (*with neg*) aber auch; **... then by the same ~ you can't object to ...** dann können Sie aber auch nichts gegen ... einwenden

b (= *chip: for gambling, jukebox etc*) Spielmarke *f*

---

c (*Brit*: = *voucher, gift token*) Gutschein *m*
ATTR Schein-, Alibi-; *pro forma*; **~ gesture** leere Geste; **it was just a ~ offer** das hat er/sie *etc* nur pro forma *or* nur so zum Schein angeboten; **~ payment** symbolische Bezahlung; **~ resistance** Scheinwiderstand *m*; **~ strike** Warnstreik *m*; **~ fine** symbolische Strafe; **the one ~ black** der/die Alibischwarze; **the one ~ woman** die Alibifrau

Tokyo [ˈtəʊkɪəʊ] N Tokio *nt*

told [təʊld] *pret, ptp of* **tell**; **there were 50 people there all ~** es waren insgesamt *or* alles in allem 50 Leute da

tolerable [ˈtɒlərəbl] ADJ (*lit*) *pain, noise level etc* erträglich; (*fig*, = *not too bad also*) annehmbar, leidlich, passabel (*inf*); **to keep sth at a ~ level** etw im erträglichen Rahmen *or* im Rahmen des Erträglichen halten; **how are you? – ~** wie gehts dir? – ganz leidlich *or* passabel (*inf*); **to be ~ to sb** für jdn annehmbar sein

tolerably [ˈtɒlərəblɪ] ADV ziemlich; **~ well** ganz leidlich *or* annehmbar, ziemlich gut; **they are ~ well-educated** sie sind leidlich gebildet *or* (*rather well*) ziemlich gebildet

tolerance [ˈtɒlərəns] **N a** Toleranz *f*, Duldsamkeit *f* (*of, for, towards* gegenüber); (*towards children, one's juniors*) Nachsicht *f* (*of* mit); **racial ~** Toleranz in Rassenfragen; **I have no ~ for such behaviour** für solch ein Benehmen habe ich kein Verständnis **b** (*Med, Tech*) Toleranz *f*; **to work to fine ~s** mit kleinen *or* engen Toleranzen arbeiten

tolerant [ˈtɒlərənt] ADJ **a** (*of, towards, with* gegenüber) tolerant, duldsam; (*towards children, one's juniors*) nachsichtig; **the Lord is ~ of our mistakes** der Herr sieht uns unsere Schwächen nach; **to adopt a more ~ attitude to** *or* **toward(s) sth** einer Sache (*dat*) toleranter gegenüberstehen **b** (*Tech, Med*) **to be ~ of heat** hitzebeständig sein; **to be ~ to light** Licht vertragen können; **to be ~ to a drug** ein Medikament (gut) vertragen

tolerantly [ˈtɒlərəntlɪ] ADV *smile* nachsichtig; *wait, listen* geduldig

tolerate [ˈtɒləreɪt] ✪ 14 VT **a** *pain, noise, weather etc* ertragen; *drug* vertragen **b** *person* tolerieren; *behaviour, injustice etc* dulden, tolerieren, hinnehmen; *idea* tolerieren; **he can ~ anything except intolerance** er kann alles tolerieren, nur keine Intoleranz; **it is not to be ~d** so etwas kann man nicht dulden *or* hinnehmen; **I won't ~ this disobedience!** ich dulde diesen Ungehorsam nicht!

toleration [ˌtɒləˈreɪʃən] N Duldung *f*, Tolerierung *f*

toll[1] [təʊl] **VI** läuten; **for whom the bell ~s** wem die Stunde schlägt **VT** *bell* läuten **N** Läuten *nt*; (= *single stroke*) Glockenschlag *m*

toll[2] **N a** (= *bridge toll, road toll*) Maut *f*, Zoll *m*, Benutzungsgebühr *f*; (*US, Telec*) (Fernsprech)gebühr *f*; **~ charge** Maut *f*, Mautgebühr *f*; (*US, Telec*) (Fernsprech)gebühr *f* **b** (= *deaths, loss etc*) **the ~ on the roads** die Zahl der Verkehrsopfer; **the ~ of the floods continues to rise** (*in terms of people*) die Zahl der Opfer der Flutkatastrophe steigt ständig weiter; (*in terms of property*) das Ausmaß der Flutschäden wird immer größer; **the earthquake took a heavy ~ of human life** das Erdbeben forderte *or* kostete viele Menschenleben; **the ~ of the war** der Blutzoll des Krieges

toll: tollbar N Zahlschranke *f*, Mautschranke *f*; **tollbooth** N Zahlstelle *f*, Mautstelle *f*; **toll bridge** N gebührenpflichtige Brücke, Mautbrücke *f*; **toll call** N (*US*) Ferngespräch *nt*; **toll-free** (*US Telec*) **ADJ** *number, call* gebührenfrei **ADV** *call* gebührenfrei; **tollgate** N Schlagbaum *m*, Mautschranke *f*; **tollhouse** N Mauthaus *nt*

tolling [ˈtəʊlɪŋ] N *, no pl* Läuten *nt*

toll: tollkeeper N Mautner(in) *m(f)* (*esp Aus*); **toll plaza** N (*US: Mot*) (Reihe *f* von) Mauthäuschen *pl*; **toll road** N Mautstraße *f*, gebührenpflichtige Straße

toluene [ˈtɒljuiːn] N (*Chem*) Toluol *nt*

Tom [tɒm] N *dim of* **Thomas** **any ~, Dick or Harry** (*inf*) jeder x-Beliebige; **you don't have to invite every ~, Dick and Harry** (*inf*) du brauchst ja nicht gerade Hinz und Kunz einzuladen (*inf*); **it's not every ~, Dick and Harry who can afford this** nicht jeder kann sich (*dat*) so was leisten

tom [tɒm] N (= *cat*) Kater *m*

tomahawk [ˈtɒməhɔːk] N Tomahawk *m*

tomato [təˈmɑːtəʊ, (*US*) təˈmeɪtəʊ] N *pl* **-es** Tomate *f*

tomato *in cpds* Tomaten-; **tomato juice** N Tomatensaft *m*; **tomato ketchup** N (Tomaten-)ket(s)chup *m or nt*; **tomato puree** N Tomatenmark *nt*; **tomato sauce** N Tomatensoße *f*; (= *ketchup*) (Tomaten)ket(s)chup *m or nt*

tomb [tuːm] N (= *grave*) Grab *nt*; (= *building*) Grabmal *nt*

tomb chamber N Grabkammer *f*

tombola [tɒmˈbəʊlə] N Tombola *f*

tomboy [ˈtɒmbɔɪ] N Wildfang *m*; **she is a real ~** sie ist ein richtiger Junge *or* Wildfang

tomboyish [ˈtɒmbɔɪɪʃ] ADJ *girl* jungenhaft

tomboyishness [ˈtɒmbɔɪɪʃnɪs] N Jungenhaftigkeit *f*

tombstone [ˈtuːmstəʊn] N Grabstein *m*

tomcat [ˈtɒmkæt] N **a** Kater *m* **b** (*US, fig inf*, = *woman-chaser*) Schürzenjäger *m* (*inf*)

tome [təʊm] N dickes Buch, Wälzer *m* (*inf*)

tomfool [ˈtɒmˈfuːl] **N** Blödian *m* **ADJ** *attr* blöd(sinnig)

tomfoolery [tɒmˈfuːlərɪ] N Blödsinn *m*, Unsinn *m*

Tommy [ˈtɒmɪ] N *dim of* **Thomas** (*Brit Mil sl*) Tommy *m* (*sl*)

tommy: Tommy gun N Maschinenpistole *f*; **tommyrot** N (*dated inf*) dummes Zeug, Mumpitz *m* (*dated*)

tomography [təˈmɒɡrəfɪ] N Tomografie *f*

tomorrow [təˈmɒrəʊ] ADV, N morgen; (= *future*) Morgen *nt*; **~ week, a week ~** morgen in einer Woche; **a fortnight ~** morgen in zwei Wochen; **he'll have been here a week ~** morgen ist er eine Woche da; **a year ago ~** morgen vor einem Jahr; **the day after ~** übermorgen; **~ morning/lunchtime/afternoon/evening** morgen früh/Mittag/Nachmittag/Abend; **late/early ~** morgen spät/früh; **~ is Monday, it's Monday ~** morgen ist Montag; **(as) from ~** ab morgen, von morgen an, vom morgigen Tag an; **see you ~!** bis morgen!; **~'s paper** die morgige Zeitung, die Zeitung von morgen; **the article will be in ~'s paper** der Artikel wird morgen in der Zeitung sein; **will ~ do?** (*early enough*) reicht es noch bis morgen?, hat es noch bis morgen Zeit?; (*convenient*) ist es morgen recht?; **~ is another day** (*prov*) morgen ist auch noch ein Tag (*prov*); **~ may never come** wer weiß, was morgen ist; **~ never comes** (*prov*) es heißt immer „morgen, morgen, nur nicht heute"; **who knows what ~ will bring?** wer weiß, was das Morgen bringt?; **a brighter ~** eine bessere Zukunft; **the science of ~** die Wissenschaft von morgen; **the stars of ~** die Stars von morgen; **~'s problems** die Probleme von morgen; **like there was no ~** als wenn es kein morgen (mehr) gäbe; *eat, drink* was das Zeug hält (*inf*)

tom: Tom Thumb N der Däumling; **tomtit** N (Blau)meise *f*; **tom-tom** N Tamtam *nt*

ton [tʌn] **N a** (britische) Tonne; **she/it weighs a ~** (*fig inf*) das wiegt ja eine Tonne → **appendix b tons** PL (*inf*: = *lots*) jede Menge (*inf*); **to have ~s of time/friends/money** *etc* jede Menge (*inf*) *or* massenhaft (*inf*) Zeit/Freunde/Geld *etc* haben **c** (*inf, of speed*) **to do a ~** mit hundertsechzig Sachen fahren (*inf*)

tonal [ˈtəʊnl] ADJ klanglich, Klang-; (*Mus*: = *regarding form*) tonal; (*Art*) farblich, Farb-; **~ variation** Klangvariation *f*; (*in colours*) Farbstufung *f*; **~ effects** (*in music*) Klangeffekte *pl*; (*in painting*) Farbeffekte *pl*; **~ music** tonale Musik; **~ value** (*Phot*) Farbwert *m*

tonality [təʊˈnælɪtɪ] N (*Mus*) Tonalität *f*; (*of voice*) Klang *m*; (*of poem*) Tonart *f*; (*of painting*) Farbkomposition *f*

tone [təʊn] **N a** (*of sound*, = tone of voice, *Phon*) Ton *m*; (= *quality of sound*) Klang *m*; **the soft ~s of a flute** die sanften Töne einer Flöte; **the soft ~s of her voice** der sanfte Klang ihrer Stimme; **... he said in a friendly ~** ... sagte er in freundlichem Ton; **I don't like your ~ (of voice)** mir gefällt dein Ton nicht; **don't speak to me in that ~ (of voice)** in diesem Ton kannst du mit mir nicht reden

b (*of colour*) (Farb)ton *m*

c (*fig*, = *mood, character*) Ton *m*; **what was the ~ of his letter?** wie war denn der Ton seines Briefes?; **the new people have lowered/raised the ~ of the neighbourhood** die neuen Leute haben dem Ansehen *or* Ruf des Viertels geschadet/das Ansehen *or* den Ruf des Viertels verbessert; **of course, Trevor had to lower the ~ (of the conversation)** Trevor musste natürlich auffallend werden

d (*Mus*) Ton *m*; (*US*, = *note*) Note *f*

e (*Physiol*) Tonus *m* (*spec*)

VT a (*Phot*, = *tint*) einfärben, tonen (*spec*)

b *body, muscles* in Form bringen

VI (*colours*) (im Farbton) harmonieren

▸ **tone down** VT *sep* (*lit, fig*) abmildern; *colour also* abschwächen; *criticism also, language, demands* mäßigen

▸ **tone in** VI (im Farbton) harmonieren

▸ **tone up** VT *sep muscles* kräftigen; *person, body* in Form bringen; **cycling keeps you toned up** Radfahren hält einen in Form

tone: tone arm N Tonarm *m*; **tone colour**, (*US*) **tone color** N (*Mus*) Klangfarbe *f*; **tone control** N Klangfarbeneinstellung *f*, Tonblende *f*

-toned [təʊnd] ADJ *suf* **sepia-toned** sepiafarben; **pastel-toned drawings** Zeichnungen *pl* in Pastelltönen; **high-toned philosophising** hochtrabendes Philosophieren; **a beautiful silver-toned voice** eine schöne, silbern klingende Stimme

tone: tone-deaf ADJ nicht in der Lage, Tonhöhen zu unterscheiden; **he's ~** er hat kein Gehör für Tonhöhen; **tone language** N Tonsprache *f*, Tonhöhensprache *f*

toneless [ˈtəʊnlɪs] ADJ tonlos; *music* eintönig; *colour* stumpf

tonelessly [ˈtəʊnlɪslɪ] ADV *reply* tonlos; *sing* eintönig

tone poem N Tongedicht *nt*

toner [ˈtəʊnə] N **a** (*for printer, copier*) Toner *m*

b (= *cosmetic*) Tönung *f*

toner cartridge N Tonerpatrone *f*

toner cassette N Tonerkassette *f*

tone row, tone series (*US*) N (*twelve-tone music*) Reihe *f*

tongs [tɒŋz] PL Zange *f*; (= *curling tongs, Hist*) Brennschere *f*; (*electric*) Lockenstab *m*; **a pair of ~** eine Zange

tongue [tʌŋ] **N a** Zunge *f*; **to put** *or* **stick one's ~ out at sb** jdm die Zunge herausstrecken; **to lose/find one's ~** (*fig*) die Sprache verlieren/wieder finden; **to hold one's ~** den Mund halten; **to have a ready ~** schlagfertig sein, nicht auf den Mund gefallen sein; **to have a sharp ~** eine scharfe Zunge haben; **keep a civil ~ in your head!** werden Sie nicht ausfallend!; **I can't get my ~ round it** dabei breche ich mir fast die Zunge ab → **slip, tip, tongue-in-cheek**

b (*liter*, = *language*) Sprache *f*; (*old Bibl*) Zunge *f*; **the gift of ~s** (*Bibl*) die Gabe, in fremden Zungen zu reden

c (*of shoe*) Zunge *f*, Lasche *f*; (*of bell*) Klöppel *m*; (*of land*) (Land)zunge *f*; (*of wood*) Spund *m*, Zapfen *m*; **a ~ of fire licked the building** eine Flamme züngelte an dem Gebäude empor

VT (*Mus*) *note* (mit der Zunge) stoßen

tongue: tongue-and-groove joint N Anschlitzzunge *f*, Spundung *f*; **tongue-in-cheek** ADJ *attr*, **tongue in cheek¹** ADJ *pred humour,*

approach ironisch; *remark* ironisch gemeint; **tongue in cheek²** ADV nicht ganz ernst gemeint; **tongue-lashing** N **to give sb a ~** jdm gehörig die Meinung sagen; **to get a ~** gehörig die Meinung gesagt bekommen; **tongue-tied** ADJ **to be ~** keinen Ton herausbringen; **she sat there ~** sie saß da und brachte keinen Ton heraus; **tongue twister** N Zungenbrecher *m*

tonguing [ˈtʌŋɪŋ] N (*Mus*) Zungenschlag *m* → **double-tonguing**

tonic [ˈtɒnɪk] **N a** (*Med*) Tonikum *nt*; (= *hair tonic*) Haarwasser *nt*; (= *skin tonic*) Lotion *f*; **it was a real ~ to see him again** (*fig*) es hat richtig gut getan, ihn wiederzusehen **b** ~ **(water)** Tonic(water) *nt*; **gin and ~** Gin *m* (mit) Tonic *f* **c** (*Mus*) Tonika *f*, Grundton *m*; **sol-fa** Solmisation *f* ADJ **a** (*Med*) stärkend, kräftigend, tonisch (*spec*); ~ **wine** Stärkungswein *m* **b** (*Phon*) *syllable, stress* tontragend **c** (*Mus*) *note* tonisch

tonicity [təʊˈnɪsɪtɪ] N (*of muscles*) Tonus *m* (*spec*), Spannungszustand *m*

tonight, (*US*) **tonite**: (*inf*) [təˈnaɪt] **ADV** (= *this evening*) heute Abend; (= *during the coming night*) heute Nacht; **see you ~!** bis heute Abend!

N (= *this evening*) der heutige Abend; (= *the coming night*) die heutige Nacht; ~**'s party** die Party heute Abend; **I'm looking forward to ~** ich freue mich auf heute Abend *or* auf den heutigen Abend; ~ **is the night we've been looking forward to** heute ist der Abend, auf den wir uns gefreut haben; ~ **is a night I'll remember all my life** an den heutigen Abend/an heute Nacht werde ich mich mein ganzes Leben lang erinnern; ~**'s weather:** heute Nacht wird es klar, aber kalt sein; ~**'s paper** die heutige Abendzeitung, die Abendzeitung von heute

tonnage [ˈtʌnɪdʒ] N Tonnage *f*

tonne [tʌn] N Tonne *f*

tonneau [ˈtɒnəʊ] N (*Aut*) **a** (*of car*) hinterer Teil (*mit Rücksitzen/Rückbank*) **b** (*also* **tonneau cover**) Verdeck *nt*

-tonner [-ˈtɒnə] N *suf* (*inf*) -tonner *m*; **two-tonner** Zweitonner *m*

tonsil [ˈtɒnsl] N Mandel *f*; **to have one's ~s out** sich (*dat*) die Mandeln herausnehmen lassen

tonsillectomy [ˌtɒnsɪˈlektəmɪ] N Mandeloperation *f*

tonsillitis [ˌtɒnsɪˈlaɪtɪs] N Mandelentzündung *f*

tonsorial [tɒnˈsɔːrɪəl] ADJ (*hum, rare form*) Barbier- (*hum*); ~ **artist** Barbier *m*

tonsure [ˈtɒnsə] **N** Tonsur *f* **VT** scheren, die Tonsur erteilen (+*dat*) (*spec*)

ton-up [ˈtʌnʌp] ADJ (*inf*) ~ **kids** Motorradrocker *pl* (*inf*)

too [tuː] ADV **a** (+*adj or adv*) zu; **that's ~/not ~ difficult a question to answer** diese Frage ist zu/nicht zu schwer zu beantworten; ~ **much** zu viel *inv*; ~ **many** zu viele; **he's had ~ much to drink** er hat zu viel getrunken; **you can have ~ much of a good thing** allzu viel ist ungesund (*prov*); **it's ~ much for her** es ist zu viel für sie; **don't worry ~ much** mach dir nicht zu viel Sorgen; ~ **much!** (*inf*) geil! (*sl*), Klasse! (*inf*); ~ **right!** (*inf*) das kannst laut sagen (*inf*)

b (= *very*) zu; **all ~ ...** allzu ...; **only ~ ...** nur zu ...; **none ~ ...** gar nicht ..., keineswegs ...; **not ~ ...** nicht zu ...; **not any ~ ...** nicht allzu ...; **he wasn't ~ interested** er war nicht allzu interessiert; **I'm not/none ~ sure** ich bin nicht ganz/gar nicht *or* keineswegs sicher; **(that's) ~ kind of you** (*iro*) (das ist) wirklich zu nett von Ihnen; **none ~ soon** keineswegs zu früh; **all ~ soon** allzu früh

c (= *also*) auch; **HE can swim ~, he ~ can swim** er kann AUCH schwimmen, auch ER kann schwimmen

d (= *moreover, into the bargain*) auch noch; **it was really cheap, and it works ~!** es war wirklich billig, und es funktioniert sogar *or* auch noch!; **they asked for a price reduction ~!** sie wollten auch noch einen Preisnachlass!

toodle-pip [ˌtuːdlˈpɪp] INTERJ (*dated Brit, inf*) tschau (*inf*)

took [tʊk] *pret of* **take**

tool [tuːl] **N a** Werkzeug *nt*; (= *gardening tool*) (Garten)gerät *nt*; ~**s** Werkzeuge *pl*; (= *set*) Werkzeug *nt*; **that's one of the ~s of the trade** das gehört zum Handwerkszeug; **to have the ~s for the job** das richtige *or* nötige Werkzeug haben **b** (*fig*, = *person*) Werkzeug *nt* **c** (*sl*, = *penis*) Ding *nt* (*inf*), Apparat *m* (*sl*) **VT** *book, leather* punzen

▸ **tool along** VI (*inf*) dahinbrausen (*inf*)

▸ **tool up** VT factory (mit Maschinen) ausrüsten **VI** (*factory*) (mit Maschinen) ausgerüstet werden (*for* für)

tool: toolbag N Werkzeugtasche *f*; **toolbar** N (*Comput*) Symbolleiste *f*; **toolbox, tool chest** N Werkzeugkasten *m*

tooling [ˈtuːlɪŋ] N Punzarbeit *f*

tool: toolkit N Werkzeug(ausrüstung *f*) *nt*; **tool-maker** N Werkzeugmacher(in) *m(f)*; **tool-making** ADJ *attr* Werkzeugbau-; ~ **firm** Werkzeughersteller *m*, Werkzeugbaufirma *f*; **tool shed** N Geräteschuppen *m*

toot [tuːt] **VT** **to ~ a horn** auf dem Horn blasen *or* (*child's trumpet*) tuten; (*in car, on bicycle*) auf die Hupe drücken, hupen; **to ~ a whistle** pfeifen, auf der Pfeife blasen **VI** (*in car, on bicycle*) hupen; (*train*) (*ship*) tuten **N** (*in car, on bicycle*) Hupen *nt*; (*of train*) Pfiff *m*, Pfeifsignal *nt*; **give a quick ~** (*on car horn*) drück mal kurz auf die Hupe

tooth [tuːθ] **N** *pl* **teeth a** (*of person, animal*) Zahn *m*; **to have a ~ out/filled** sich (*dat*) einen Zahn ziehen/plombieren lassen; **to get one's teeth into sth** (*lit*) etw zwischen die Zähne bekommen; (*fig*) sich in etw (*dat*) festbeißen; **armed to the teeth** bis an die Zähne bewaffnet; **to show one's teeth** die Zähne zeigen (*also fig*) *or* fletschen; **to fight ~ and nail** bis aufs Blut kämpfen; **in the teeth of the wind** gegen den Wind; **in the teeth of all opposition** ungeachtet allen Widerstands; **to lie through** *or* **in one's teeth** das Blaue vom Himmel herunterlügen; **I'm fed up to the (back) teeth with that** (*inf*) *or* **sick to the (back) teeth of that** (*inf*) ich habe die Nase gestrichen voll davon (*inf*), es hängt mir zum Hals heraus (*inf*); **to give a law/ an organization some teeth** (*fig*) einem Gesetz/ einer Organisation Wirksamkeit verleihen; **selling a car these days is like pulling teeth** (*esp US*) ein Auto zu verkaufen ist heutzutage ein mühsames Geschäft

b (*of zip, wheel etc*) Zahn *m*; (*of comb, rake*) Zinke *f*, Zahn *m*

tooth in cpds Zahn-; **toothache** N Zahnweh *nt*, Zahnschmerzen *pl*; **toothbrush** N Zahnbürste *f*; **toothbrush moustache** N Bürste *f*; **tooth decay** N Karies *f*, Zahnverfall *m*

toothed [tuːθt] ADJ gezahnt, mit Zähnen; ~ **wheel** Zahnrad *nt*

tooth: tooth fairy N *Fantasiefigur, die die Milchzähne der Kinder einsammelt und ihnen dafür eine Münze gibt*; **toothless** ADJ zahnlos; (*fig*, = *powerless*) body zahnlos, ohne Biss; *law, agreement* wirkungslos; **a ~ tiger** (*fig*) ein Papiertiger *m*; **toothpaste** N Zahnpasta *or* -creme *f*; **toothpick** N Zahnstocher *m*; **tooth powder** N Zahnpulver *nt*; **toothsome** ADJ schmackhaft, wohlschmeckend

toothy [ˈtuːθɪ] ADJ (*+er*) **she's a bit ~** sie hat ein ziemliches Pferdegebiss (*pej inf*); **he gave me a ~ smile** er lachte mich an und zeigte dabei seine Zähne/Zahnlücken

toothypeg [ˈtuːθɪpeg] N (*baby-talk*) Beißerchen *nt* (*baby-talk*)

tootle [ˈtuːtl] (*esp Brit inf*) VI **a** (*on whistle etc*: *also* **tootle away**) vor sich hin dudeln (*inf*) **b** (= *drive*) juckeln (*inf*); (= *go*) trotten, zotteln; **I'll just ~ (down) to the shops** ich geh bloß mal eben (runter) einkaufen (*inf*); **it's time I was tootling off** es wird Zeit, dass ich abzottele (*inf*) **N to give a ~ on the car horn** hupen; **to give a ~ on a whistle** auf einer Flöte herumdudeln (*inf*)

▶ **tootle along** VI (*dated inf*) dahinzuckeln (*inf*); **I'd better tootle along now** ich zottele jetzt mal lieber ab (*inf*); **I thought I'd tootle along to the party** (*inf*) ich zottel mal mit zu der Party (*inf*)

too-too ['tuː'tuː] ADJ *pred* (*dated inf*: = *marvellous*) pfundig (*inf*); (*iro*, = *affected*) affig (*inf*) ADV (= *excessively*) zu

toots [tuːts] N (*inf*) Schätzchen *nt* (*inf*)

tootsy ['tʊtsɪ] N (*baby-talk*) Füßchen *nt*

top¹ [tɒp] N **a** (= *highest part*) oberer Teil; (*of spire, pyramid, cone etc, fig, of league, company etc*) Spitze *f*; (*of mountain*) Gipfel *m*; (*of tree*) Krone *f*, Spitze *f*; (*of pine tree*) Wipfel *m*, Spitze *f*; (*of branch*) oberes Ende *nt*; (*of wave*) Kamm *m*; (*of carrots, radishes*) Ende *nt*; (= *leafy part*) Kraut *nt*; (= *detachable part*: *of cupboard etc*) Aufsatz *m*; (= *head end*: *of table, bed, sheet*) Kopfende *nt*, oberes Ende *nt*; (*of road, beach*) oberes Ende *nt*; **which is the ~?** wo ist oben?; **the ~ of the tree/page/ list/wall** *etc* **is ...** der Baum/die Seite/Liste/ Wand *etc* ist oben ...; **the ~ of the milk** die Rahmschicht (auf der Milch); **at the ~** oben; **at the ~ of the page/list** oben auf der Seite/Liste; **at the ~ of the league/pile** oben in der Tabelle/im Stapel; **at the ~ of the stairs/wall/hill/tree** oben an der Treppe/Wand/am Berg/Baum; **at the ~ of the table/road** am oberen Ende des Tisches/der Straße; **to be (at the) ~ of the class** Klassenbeste(r) *or* -erste(r) sein, der/die Beste in der Klasse sein; **to come out at the ~ of the list** Erste(r) sein; **near the ~** (ziemlich) weit oben; **he's near the ~ in English** in Englisch gehört er zu den Besten; **the liquid was cloudy near the ~** die Flüssigkeit war oben wolkig; **she bashed the ~ of her head on the luggage rack** sie schlug sich (*dat*) den Kopf an der Gepäckablage an; **he looked over the ~ of his spectacles** er sah über den Brillenrand (hinweg); **he curled his fingers over the ~ of the window** er klammerte sich mit den Fingern an den oberen Fensterrand; **she fell from the ~ of the stairs to the bottom** sie fiel die ganze Treppe von oben bis unten hinunter; **five lines from the ~** in der fünften Zeile von oben; **from ~ to toe** von Kopf bis Fuß; **from ~ to bottom** von oben bis unten; **the system is rotten from ~ to bottom** das System ist von vorn bis hinten schlecht (*inf*); **to scream at the ~ of one's voice** aus vollem Hals *or* aus Leibeskräften brüllen; **they were talking at the ~(s) of their voices** sie haben sich in voller Lautstärke unterhalten; **to be at the ~ of the ladder** *or* **the tree** (*fig*) auf dem Gipfel (des Erfolgs) sein; **go to the ~ of the class** (*inf*) du bist gar nicht so dumm!; **off the ~ of my head** (*fig*) grob gesagt; (*with figures*) über den Daumen gepeilt (*inf*); **just a quick comment please, off the ~ of your head** bitte einen kurzen Kommentar, ganz spontan; **to talk off the ~ of one's head** (*inf*) nur so daherreden; **to go over the ~** (*in trenches*) aus dem Schützengraben klettern; (= *exaggerate*) zu viel des Guten tun; **that's a bit over the ~** das ist ein bisschen übertrieben, das geht ein bisschen zu weit; **I find him a bit over the ~** ich finde, er übertreibt es ein bisschen; **he's over the ~** (= *past his best*) er ist auf dem absteigenden Ast; **on the pops** (*record*) Spitzenreiter *m* (in der Hitparade); **the ~ of the morning to you!** (*Ir*) grüß Gott! (*S Ger, Aus*), (schönen) guten Morgen! → **bill³**

b (= *upper surface*) Oberfläche *f*; **to be on ~** oben sein *or* liegen; (*fig*) obenauf sein; **it was on ~ of/on the ~ of the cupboard etc** es war auf/oben auf dem Schrank/Stapel *etc*; **put it on ~ of/the ~ of the cupboard etc** leg es oben auf den Schrank *etc*; **to go up on ~** (*on boat*) an Deck gehen; **seats on ~!** (*in bus*) oben sind noch Sitzplätze!; **to see London from the ~ of a bus** London vom Oberdeck eines Busses aus sehen; **on ~ of** (*in addition to*) zusätzlich zu; **things are getting on ~ of me** die Dinge wachsen mir über den Kopf; **then, on ~ of all that ...** und dann, um das Maß voll zu machen ...; **and, on ~ of that ...** und zusätzlich ..., und außerdem ...; **it's just one thing on ~ of another**

es kommt eines zum anderen; **he didn't see it until he was right on ~ of it** er sah es erst, als er ganz nah dran war; **he felt he was on ~ of the situation** er hatte das Gefühl, die Situation im Griff *or* unter Kontrolle zu haben; **to come out on ~** sich durchsetzen; (*over rival*) die Oberhand gewinnen

c (*inf, of body*) Oberkörper *m*; **to blow one's ~** in die Luft *or* an die Decke gehen (*inf*), aus der Haut fahren (*inf*); **she's rather big round the ~** sie ist oben herum ganz schön füllig (*inf*)

d (= *working surface*) Arbeitsfläche *f*

e (= *bikini top*) Oberteil *nt*; (= *blouse*) Top *nt*

f (= *lid, of jar, suitcase*) Deckel *m*; (*of bottle*) Verschluss *m*; (*of pen*) Hülle *f*; (*of car*) Dach *nt*; **hard ~** (*Aut*) Hardtop *nt*; **soft ~** (*Aut*) Weichverdeck *nt*

g (*Aut, = top gear*) höchster Gang; **in ~** im vierten/fünften, im höchsten Gang

h (*inf, = big top*) Großzelt *nt*, Zirkuszelt *nt*

i (*inf*) **to be (the) ~s** klasse *or* Klasse sein (*inf*), spitze *or* Spitze sein (*inf*)

j (*Naut*) Mars *m*

ADJ (= *upper*) obere(r, s); (= *highest*) oberste(r, s); *branches, note, honours, price* höchste(r, s); (= *best*) Spitzen-, Top-; *pupil, school, marks* beste(r, s); ~ **athlete** Spitzenathlet(in) *m(f)*; **he was the ~ seed** er war an erste Stelle gesetzt; ~ **job** Spitzenjob *m*; ~ **prices** Höchstpreise *pl*; **today's ~ story** die wichtigste Meldung von heute; **on the ~ floor** im obersten Stockwerk; **a ~-floor flat** eine Dachgeschosswohnung; **he's out of the ~ drawer** (*fig*) er gehört zu den oberen zehntausend; **the ~ end of the market** das obere Marktsegment; **the car has a ~ speed of 120** das Auto hat eine Höchstgeschwindigkeit von 120; **at ~ speed** mit Höchstgeschwindigkeit; **in ~ form** in Höchstform; **to be ~** (*Sch*) Beste(r) *or* Erste(r) sein; **the ~ men in the party/government/firm** die Partei-/Regierungs-/Unternehmensspitze; **the newspaper for ~ people** die Zeitung für Führungskräfte; **the ~ people** (*in a company*) die Leute an der Spitze; (*in society*) die oberen zehntausend; **the Top Ten** (*Mus*) die Top Ten *pl*

ADV **a** **to come ~** (*Sch*) Beste(r) werden **b** ~**s** (*inf*) höchstens, maximal; **it'll take an hour ~s** das dauert höchstens *or* maximal eine Stunde

VT **a** (= *cover, cap*) bedecken; ~**ped by a dome** gekrönt von einer Kuppel; **fruit ~ped with cream** Obst mit Sahne darauf

b (= *reach top of*) *just as the car/he* ~**ped the hill** gerade, als das Auto/er oben auf dem Berg angekommen war *or* den Gipfel des Berges erreicht hatte

c (= *be at top of*) **his name ~ped the list** sein Name stand ganz oben auf der Liste *or* an der Spitze der Liste → **bill³**

d (= *be higher than, fig, = surpass*) übersteigen; **that ~s the lot** (*inf*) das übertrifft alles; **and to ~ it all ...** (*inf*) und um das Maß voll zu machen ...

e **to ~ a tree/radish/carrot** die Spitze eines Baumes/das Ende eines Rettichs/einer Mohrrübe abschneiden; **to ~ and tail gooseberries** (*Brit*) Stachelbeeren putzen

f **to ~ oneself** (*inf*) sich umbringen

▶ **top off** VT *sep* **a** abrunden **b** (*US*) = **top up**

▶ **top out** VT *sep* **to top out a building** den letzten Stein legen; **topping out ceremony** ≈ Richtfest *nt*

▶ **top up** VT *sep* (*Brit*) *glass, battery, tank, account* auffüllen; *pension, income* ergänzen; **to top up the oil** Öl nachfüllen; **can I top you up?** (*inf*) darf ich dir nachschenken?

top² N Kreisel *m*; **to sleep like a ~** wie ein Murmeltier schlafen

topaz ['təʊpæz] N Topas *m*

top: topcoat N **a** (= *overcoat*) Mantel *m*; (*for men also*) Überzieher *m* **b** (= *coat of paint*) Deckanstrich *m*, letzter Anstrich *m*; **top copy** N Original *nt*; **top dog** N (*fig*) **he always has to be ~** er muss immer das Sagen haben; **top dollar** N (*esp US, inf*) **to pay ~ for sth** Höchst-

preise für etw bezahlen; **top-dollar prices** Höchstpreise *pl*; **top-down** ADJ *approach, view, analysis* von oben nach unten; **top-dress** VT (*Agr*) mit Kopfdünger düngen; **top dressing** N (*Agr*) Kopfdünger *m*

topee ['təʊpiː] N Tropenhelm *m*

top: top-fermented ADJ obergärig; **top-flight** ADJ Spitzen-, erstklassig; ~ **football** Spitzenfußball *m*; **top-full** ADJ *glass etc* randvoll; **top gear** N höchster Gang; **to be in ~** (*lit*) im höchsten Gang sein; (*fig*) auf Hochtouren sein; **top hat** N Zylinder *m*; **top-hatted** [tɒp'hætɪd] ADJ mit Zylinder; **top-heavy** ADJ (*lit, fig*) kopflastig; **she's a ~** (*hum inf*) sie hat einen ziemlichen Vorbau (*inf*); **the army is ~ with officers** die Armee hat zu viele hohe Offiziere (*dated*), erstklassig **top-hole** ADJ, INTERJ (*dated inf*) famos (*dated*), erstklassig

topi ['təʊpiː] N = **topee**

topiary ['təʊpɪərɪ] N (*Hort*) Formschnitt *m*

topic ['tɒpɪk] N Thema *nt*; ~ **of conversation** Gesprächsthema *nt*

topical ['tɒpɪkəl] ADJ **a** *problem, speech, event* aktuell; **he made a ~ remarks/allusions** er ging kurz auf aktuelle Geschehnisse ein/ spielte kurz auf aktuelle Geschehnisse an **b** (= *according to subject*) ~ **index** Sachregister *nt*

topicality [ˌtɒpɪ'kælɪtɪ] N (*of problem, event*) Aktualität *f*

topically ['tɒpɪkəlɪ] ADV **a** aktuell **b** (= *according to subject*) nach Sachgebieten

topic sentence N (*US, Gram*) Einleitungssatz *m*

top: topknot N Dutt *m*; **topless** ADJ oben ohne, Oben-ohne-; **pictures of ~ women** Bilder von Frauen oben ohne; ~ **waitress** Oben-ohne-Bedienung *f*; ~ **model** Oben-ohne-Modell *nt*; ~ **bar** Oben-ohne-Bar *f*, Toplessbar *f* ADV *sunbathe, pose, dance* oben ohne; **to go ~** oben ohne gehen; **top-level** ADJ Spitzen-; *inquiry, negotiations* auf höchster Ebene; ~ **meeting** Spitzentreffen *nt*; **top light** N (*Phot, Painting*) Oberlicht *nt*; **top-line** ADJ *actor etc* prominent; *news* wichtigste(r, s); *hotel etc* erstklassig, renommiert; **top loader** N (= *washing machine*) Toplader *m*; **top management** N Spitzenmanagement *nt*; **topmast** N (*Naut*) Toppmast *m*, Marsstenge *f*; **topmost** ADJ oberste(r, s); **on the ~ floor** im obersten Stockwerk; **top-notch** ADJ (*inf*) eins a (*inf*), prächtig; **top-of-the-range, top-of-the-line** ADJ *attr* Spitzen-, der Spitzenklasse; ~ **model** Spitzenmodell *nt*

topographer [tə'pɒgrəfə'] N Topograf(in) *m(f)*, Vermessungsingenieur(in) *m(f)*

topographic(al) [ˌtɒpə'græfɪk(əl)] ADJ topografisch

topography [tə'pɒgrəfɪ] N Topografie *f*

topological [ˌtɒpə'lɒdʒɪkəl] ADJ topologisch

topology [tə'pɒlədʒɪ] N Topologie *f*

toponym ['tɒpənɪm] N Ortsname *m*

topper ['tɒpə'] N (*inf*, = *hat*) Angströhre *f* (*inf*)

topping ['tɒpɪŋ] ADJ (*dated Brit, inf*) famos (*dated*) N (*Cook*) **with a ~ of cream/nuts** *etc* mit Sahne/Nüssen *etc* (oben) darauf; **recipes for various different ~s for ice cream** verschiedene Rezepte, wie man Eis überziehen kann; **artificial cream ~** Schlagschaum *m*

topping-out (ceremony) ['tɒpɪŋaʊt('serɪmə-nɪ)] N (*Build*) Richtfest *nt*

topple ['tɒpl] VI wackeln; (= *fall*) fallen; (*fig, from power*) gestürzt werden VT umwerfen; (*from a height*) hinunterkippen *or* -werfen; (*fig*) *government etc* stürzen; **to ~ sb from power** jdn stürzen *or* entmachten

▶ **topple down** VI umfallen; (*thing also*) umkippen; (*group of objects*) runterpurzeln; (*from chair, top of stairs etc*) hinunterfallen; (+*prep obj*) hinunterfallen; **they all came toppling down** sie kamen alle runtergepurzelt

▶ **topple over** VI schwanken und fallen (*prep obj* über +*acc*)

top: top-ranked ADJ *attr* (*Sport*) Spitzen-; **~ player** Spitzenspieler(in) *m(f)*; **~ Miami** das Spitzenteam Miami; **top-ranking** ADJ von hohem Rang; *civil servant, officer also* hohe(r); *personality* hoch gestellt; *tennis player etc* der Spitzenklasse; **~ author** Spitzenautor(in) *m(f)*; **top-rated** ADJ *attr* führend

TOPS [tɒps] N (*Brit*) *abbr of* **Training Opportunities Scheme** Umschulungsprogramm *für Arbeitnehmer*

tops [tɒps] ADJ (*Brit sl*) **to be ~** cool sein (*sl*)

top: topsail N (*Naut*) Marssegel *nt*; **top-secret** ADJ streng geheim; **top-shelf** ADJ (*Brit*) *magazine* pornographisch; **topside** N (*Brit: of beef*) Oberschale *f* ADV (*Naut*) **to go ~** an Deck gehen; **topsoil** N (*Agr*) Ackerkrume *f*; **topspin** N Topspin *m*; **top station** N Bergstation *f*

topsy-turvy [ˌtɒpsɪˈtɜːvɪ] (*inf*) ADJ (*lit, = upside down*) umgedreht; (*= in disorder*) kunterbunt durcheinander *pred*; (*fig*) auf den Kopf gestellt; **it's a ~ world** es ist eine verkehrte Welt; **the room was all ~** alles im Zimmer war kunterbunt durcheinander ADV **to turn sth ~** (*lit, fig*) etw auf den Kopf stellen; *plans etc* über den Haufen werfen

top-up [ˈtɒpʌp] (*Brit*) N (*inf*) **the oil needs a ~** es muss Öl nachgefüllt werden; **would you like a ~?** darf man dir noch nachschenken? ADV Zusatz-; **~ loan** Zusatzdarlehen *nt*

toque [təʊk] N Toque *f*

tor [tɔː] N (*esp in names*) Berg *m*

Torah [ˈtɔːrə] N Thora *f*

torch [tɔːtʃ] N (*lit, fig*) Fackel *f*; (*Brit: = flashlight*) Taschenlampe *f*; (*= blowlamp*) Schweißbrenner *m*; **the ~ of learning** die Fackel der Wissenschaft; **to carry a ~ for sb** nach jdm schmachten; **to carry the ~ of** *or* **for sth** ein eifriger Verfechter einer Sache (*gen*) sein VT (*= to set fire to*) anstecken, anzünden

torch: torch battery N (*Brit*) Taschenlampenbatterie *f*; **torchbearer** N (*lit, fig*) Fackelträger(in) *m(f)*; **torchlight** N Licht *nt* der Fackel/Taschenlampe; **torchlight procession** N Fackelzug *m*

tore [tɔː] *pret of* **tear**[1]

toreador [ˈtɒrɪədɔː] N Torero *m*

torment [ˈtɔːment] N Qual *f*; (*inf, = person*) Quälgeist *m*; **to be in ~, to suffer ~(s)** Qualen leiden VT [tɔːˈment] quälen; (*= annoy, tease*) plagen; **~ed by remorse** von Reue gequält *or* geplagt

tormentor [tɔːˈmentə] N Peiniger(in) *m(f)*

torn [tɔːn] *ptp of* **tear**[1]

tornado [tɔːˈneɪdəʊ] N *pl* **-es** Tornado *m*

torpedo [tɔːˈpiːdəʊ] N *pl* **-es** Torpedo *m* VT torpedieren

torpedo boat N Torpedoboot *nt*

torpedo tube N Torpedoausstoßrohr *nt*

torpid [ˈtɔːpɪd] ADJ (*= lethargic*) träge; (*= apathetic*) abgestumpft; (*Zool*) torpid

torpidity [tɔːˈpɪdɪtɪ], **torpor** [ˈtɔːpə] N (*= lethargy*) Trägheit *f*; (*= apathy*) Abgestumpftheit *f*; (*Zool*) Torpidität *f*

torque [tɔːk] N (*Mech*) Drehmoment *nt*

torque spanner N (signalgebender) Drehmomentenschlüssel

torrent [ˈtɒrənt] N (*= river*) reißender Strom *m*; (*fig, of lava*) Strom *m*; (*of words, insults*) Sturzbach *m*, Schwall *m*, Flut *f*; **the rain came down in ~s** der Regen kam in wahren Sturzbächen herunter; **a ~ of abuse** ein Schwall *m* von Beschimpfungen

torrential [tɒˈrenʃəl] ADJ *rain* sintflutartig

torrid [ˈtɒrɪd] ADJ (*lit, fig*) heiß; *heat, air, sun* sengend; **to have a ~ time** (*= stressful*) eine anstrengende Zeit durchmachen

torsion [ˈtɔːʃən] N Drehung *f*, Torsion *f* (*spec*); **degree of ~** Drehbeanspruchung *f*, Torsionsschwingung *f* (*spec*)

torso [ˈtɔːsəʊ] N Körper *m*; (*Art*) Torso *m*

tort [tɔːt] N (*Jur*) Delikt *nt*

tortilla [tɔːˈtiːə] N Tortilla *f*

tortilla chip N Tortilla Chip *m*

tortoise [ˈtɔːtəs] N Schildkröte *f*

tortoiseshell [ˈtɔːtəʃel] N **a** Schildpatt *m*; (*esp for spectacle frames*) Horn *nt* **b** (*also* **tortoiseshell cat**) Schildpattkatze *f*

tortuous [ˈtɔːtjʊəs] ADJ (*lit*) *path* gewunden; (*fig*) verwickelt; *methods also, person, journey* umständlich

torture [ˈtɔːtʃə] N Folter *f*; (*fig*) Qual *f*; **instrument of ~** Folterwerkzeug *nt*; **it was sheer ~!** (*inf*) es war eine wahre Qual *or* Folter VT **a** (*lit*) foltern **b** (*fig, = torment*) quälen, peinigen (*geh*) **c** (*fig, = distort*) verzerren; *language* vergewaltigen; **~d language** verkrampfte Sprache; **~d steel** grotesk verbogener Stahl; **her hair had been ~d into elaborate curls** ihr Haar war mühsam in kunstvolle Locken gedreht

torture chamber N Folterkammer *f*

torturer [ˈtɔːtʃərə] N (*lit*) Folterknecht *m*; (*fig, = tormentor*) Peiniger(in) *m(f)*

torturous [ˈtɔːtʃərəs] ADJ qualvoll

Tory [ˈtɔːrɪ] (*Brit, Pol*) N Tory *m*, Konservative(r) *mf* ADJ konservativ, Tory-; **the ~ government** die Tory-Regierung, die konservative Regierung

Toryism [ˈtɔːrɪɪzəm] N (*Brit, Pol*) Konservativismus *m*

tosh [tɒʃ] N (*dated Brit, inf*) dummes Zeug

toss [tɒs] N **a** (*= throw*) Wurf *m*; **to take a ~** (*from horse*) abgeworfen werden; **with a proud ~ of her head** mit einer stolzen Kopfbewegung **b** (*of coin*) Münzwurf *m*; **to win/lose the ~** (*esp Sport*) die Seitenwahl gewinnen/verlieren; **there is no point in arguing the ~ (with me)** (*Brit*) es hat keinen Sinn, (mit mir) darüber zu streiten *or* (mit mir) herumzustreiten; **there'll always be somebody who'll want to argue the ~** (*Brit*) es gibt immer einen, der Einwände hat; **I don't give a ~ about ...** (*Brit inf*) ... ist mir völlig schnuppe (*inf*) VT **a** (*= throw*) *ball* werfen; *salad* anmachen; *pancake* wenden (*durch Hochwerfen*); *rider* abwerfen; **to ~ sth to sb** jdm etw zuwerfen; **~ it** (*US, rubbish*) schmeiß *or* wirf es weg; **~ it over!** wirf es herüber, schmeiß mal her (*inf*); **to ~ sth aside** etw zur Seite werfen; **to ~ sb aside** jdn fallen lassen; **~ing the caber** Baumstammwerfen *nt*; **to be ~ed by a bull** auf die Hörner genommen werden; **to be ~ed by a horse** vom Pferd (ab)geworfen werden **b** (*= move*) schütteln, zerren an (*+dat*); **the boat, ~ed by the wind ...** das Boot, vom Wind hin und her geworfen, ...; **to ~ one's head** den Kopf zurückwerfen *or* hochwerfen; **to ~ one's hair** das Haar nach hinten werfen **c** **to ~ a coin** eine Münze (zum Losen) hochwerfen; **we settled it by ~ing a coin** wir haben eine Münze hochgeworfen und es ausgeknobelt; **to ~ sb for sth** mit jdm (durch Münzenwerfen) um etw knobeln; **I'll ~ you for it** lass uns darum knobeln VI **a** (*ship*) rollen; (*corn*) wogen; (*plumes*) flattern; **to ~ and turn (in bed)** sich (im Bett) hin und her wälzen *or* hin und her werfen[2] **b** (*with coin*) (durch Münzenwerfen) knobeln; **to ~ for sth** um etw knobeln

▶ **toss about** (*Brit*) *or* **around** VI sich heftig hin und her bewegen; (*person*) sich hin und her werfen VT *sep* (*= move*) hin und her schütteln, durchschütteln; *boat* schaukeln; (*= throw*) *ball* herumwerfen; (*fig*) *ideas* zur Debatte stellen

▶ **toss away** VT *sep* wegwerfen

▶ **toss back** VT *sep head* zurückwerfen, hochwerfen; *drink* hinunterstürzen, (runter)kippen (*inf*)

▶ **toss off** VT *sep* **a** *drink* hinunterstürzen, (runter)kippen (*inf*) **b** *clothes* abstreifen **c** (*inf, = produce quickly*) *essay* hinhauen (*inf*); *remark* hinwerfen **d** (*sl, = masturbate*) einen runterholen (*+dat*) (*inf*) VI (*sl*) sich (*dat*) einen runterholen (*inf*)

▶ **toss out** VT *sep rubbish* wegschmeißen (*inf*), wegwerfen; *person* hinauswerfen, rausschmeißen (*inf*); *comment, rules, idea* verwerfen

▶ **toss up** VI knobeln (*for* um) VT *sep* werfen; **to toss sth up (into the air)** etw hochwerfen, etw in die Luft werfen

tosser [ˈtɒsə] N (*Brit sl*) Wichser *m* (*sl*)

tosspot [ˈtɒspɒt] N **a** (*sl*) = **tosser** **b** (*old inf, = drunkard*) Säufer(in) *m(f)* (*inf*)

toss-up [ˈtɒsʌp] N (*lit*) Knobeln *nt* durch Münzenwerfen; **it was a ~ whether ...** (*inf*) es war völlig offen, ob ...

tot [tɒt] N **a** (*= child: also* **tiny tot**) Steppke (*inf*), Knirps (*inf*) *m* **b** (*esp Brit, of alcohol*) Schlückchen *nt*

▶ **tot up** VT *sep* (*esp Brit, inf*) zusammenzählen, zusammenrechnen

total [ˈtəʊtl] ADJ (*= complete*) völlig, absolut; (*= comprising the whole*) Gesamt-; *war, eclipse* total; *disaster* absolut, total; **~ sum/amount** Gesamtsumme *f*; **the ~ cost** die Gesamtkosten *pl*; **~ income** Gesamteinkommen *nt*; **what is the ~ number of rooms you have?** wie viele Zimmer haben Sie (insgesamt)?; **a ~ population of 650,000** eine Gesamtbevölkerung von 650.000; **the ~ effect of all this worry was ...** im Endeffekt haben seine Sorgen bewirkt, dass ...; **a ~ stranger** ein völlig Fremder; **to be in ~ disagreement** völlig verschiedener Meinung sein; **to be in ~ ignorance (of sth)** (von etw) überhaupt nichts wissen; **the silence was ~** es herrschte völlige *or* vollkommene *or* totale Stille; **my bewilderment was ~** meine Verwirrung war vollkommen *or* komplett N Gesamtmenge *f*; (*= money, figures*) Endsumme *f*; **a ~ of 50 people** insgesamt 50 Leute; **this brings the ~ to £100** das bringt die Gesamtsumme auf £ 100; **the true jobless ~ was 4 million** die wahre Arbeitslosenzahl belief sich auf insgesamt 4 Millionen; **in ~** (*= in all*) insgesamt → **grand, sum** VT **a** (*= amount to*) sich belaufen auf (*+acc*); **the visitors ~led 5000** insgesamt kamen 5000 Besucher; **prizes ~ling £3000** Preise im Gesamtwert von £ 3000 **b** (*= add: also* **total up**) zusammenzählen, zusammenrechnen **c** (*US, inf, = wreck*) *car* zu Schrott fahren

total allergy syndrome N , *no pl* multiallergisches Syndrom

totalitarian [ˌtəʊtælɪˈtɛərɪən] ADJ totalitär

totalitarianism [ˌtəʊtælɪˈtɛərɪənɪzəm] N Totalitarismus *m*

totality [təʊˈtælɪtɪ] N Gesamtheit *f*, Totalität *f* (*esp Philos*); (*Astron*) totale Finsternis

totalizator [ˈtəʊtəlaɪˌzeɪtə], **totalizer** [ˈtəʊtəlaɪzə] N (*Horse-racing*) Totalisator *m*

totally [ˈtəʊtəlɪ] ADV völlig, total

total recall N (*Psych*) lückenlose Erinnerung

tote[1] [təʊt] N (*Brit inf*) **the ~** der Totalisator

tote[2] VT (*inf, = carry*) *sth heavy* schleppen; *gun* bei sich haben; **to ~ sth around** etw herumschleppen; **gun-/camera-toting people** Leute, die immer ein Gewehr/eine Kamera mit sich herumschleppen

tote bag N (*US*) (Einkaufs)tasche *f*

tote board N Totalisator *m*

totem [ˈtəʊtəm] N Totem *nt*

totemism [ˈtəʊtəmɪzəm] N Totemismus *m*

totem pole N Totempfahl *m*

totter [ˈtɒtə] VI **a** (*= wobble before falling*) wanken, schwanken; (*= stagger*) taumeln, unsicher gehen; (*old man, baby*) tapsen; (*invalid*) schwanken, taumeln; **to ~ about** *or* **around** herumwanken/-taumeln/-tapsen **b** (*fig*) schwanken; (*economy*) kränkeln; **the country was ~ing on the brink of war** das Land befand sich am Rande eines Krieges

tottering [ˈtɒtərɪŋ] ADJ schwankend, wankend; *person also* taumelnd; *regime* bröckelig; *economy, government* wack(e)lig, kränklich; **a ~ monarch** ein Monarch auf einem wackeligen Thron

tottery ['tɒtərɪ] ADJ wack(e)lig; *person* tatterig; **a ~ old man** ein Tattergreis *m* (*inf*)

totty ['tɒtɪ] N (*Brit, inf*) Weiber *pl* (*inf*); **a nice piece of ~** ein tolles Weib (*inf*)

toucan ['tu:kən] N Tukan *m*, Pfefferfresser *m*

touch [tʌtʃ] **N** **a** (= *sense of touch*) (Tast)gefühl *nt*; **to be cold/soft to the ~** sich kalt/weich anfühlen

b (= *act of touching*) Berühren *nt*, Berührung *f*; (*of pianist, typist, piano, typewriter*) Anschlag *m*; **she thrilled to the ~** es durchzuckte sie, als er sie berührte; **it opens at a ~** es öffnet sich auf Fingerdruck; **at the ~ of a button** auf Knopfdruck; **the wheel responds to the slightest ~** das Lenkrad reagiert sofort *or* reagiert auf jede Bewegung; **braille is read by ~** Blindenschrift wird durch Abtasten gelesen

c (= *skill*) Hand *f*; (= *style*) Stil *m*; **the ~ of a master** die Hand eines Meisters; **it has the ~ of genius/the professional ~** es hat etwas Geniales/Professionelles *or* einen genialen/professionellen Anstrich; **he's losing his ~** er wird langsam alt; **to have the right ~ with sb/sth** mit jdm/etw umgehen können; **a personal ~** eine persönliche Note

d (= *stroke, Art*) Strich *m*; (*fig*) Einfall *m*; **a book with humorous ~es** ein stellenweise humorvolles Buch; **a nice ~** eine hübsche Note; (*gesture*) eine nette Geste; **to put the final** *or* **finishing ~es to sth** letzte Hand an etw (*acc*) legen, einer Sache (*dat*) den letzten Schliff geben; **the house lacks a woman's ~** es fehlt eine Frau im Haus

e (= *small quantity*) Spur *f*; (*esp of irony, sadness etc*) Anflug *m*; **a ~ of flu** eine leichte Grippe; **a ~ of fever** leichtes Fieber; **a ~ of spring** ein Hauch *m* (von) Frühling; **he gave the horse a ~ of the whip** er ließ das Pferd die Peitsche fühlen *or* spüren; **it is a ~ expensive** (*esp Brit*) es ist eine Spur zu teuer → **sun**

f (= *communication*) **to be in (constant) ~ with sb** mit jdm in (ständiger) Verbindung stehen; **they were in ~ with us yesterday** sie haben sich gestern mit uns in Verbindung gesetzt; **to be/keep in ~ with (political) developments** (politisch) auf dem Laufenden sein/bleiben; **I'll be in ~!** ich lasse von mir hören!, ich melde mich!; **keep in ~!** lass wieder einmal von dir hören!; **to be out of ~ with sb** keine Verbindung mehr zu jdm haben; **to be completely out of ~ (with sth)** (in Bezug auf etw *acc*) überhaupt nicht auf dem Laufenden sein; **you can get in ~ with me at this number** Sie können mich unter dieser Nummer erreichen; **you ought to get in ~ with the police** Sie sollten sich mit der Polizei in Verbindung setzen; **to lose ~ (with sb)** den Kontakt (zu jdm) verlieren; **to lose ~ (with sth)** (in Bezug auf etw *acc*) nicht mehr auf dem Laufenden sein; **a husband and wife who have lost ~ with each other** ein Ehepaar, das sich fremd geworden ist *or* sich entfremdet hat; **I'll put you in ~ with Mr Brown** ich werde Sie mit Herrn Brown in Verbindung bringen

g (*Ftbl*) Aus *nt*; (*Rugby*) Aus *nt*, Mark *f*; **in ~** im Aus/in der Mark; **to kick for ~** (*Rugby*) ins Aus *or* in die Mark treten; **to kick sth into ~** (*Brit, fig*) etw zurückstellen, etw auf Eis legen

h (*inf*) **to make a ~** Geld schnorren (*inf*); **he's usually good for a ~** ihn kann man normalerweise gut anpumpen (*inf*) *or* anzapfen (*inf*); **to be an easy** *or* **soft ~** leicht anzupumpen (*inf*) *or* anzuzapfen (*inf*) sein

VT **a** (= *be in or make contact with*) berühren; (= *get hold of*) anfassen; (= *press lightly*) piano keys anschlagen, leicht drücken; (= *strike lightly*) harp strings streichen über (+*acc*); (= *brush against*) streifen; **she was so happy, her feet hardly ~ed the ground** (*fig*) sie war so glücklich, dass sie in den Wolken schwebte; **to ~ glasses** anstoßen; **don't ~ that!** fass das nicht an!; **he ~ed his hat to me** er tippte (zum Gruß) an den Hut; **the speedometer needle ~ed 100** die Tachonadel ging auf 100; **I was ~ing 100 most of the way** ich fuhr fast immer 100; **once I ~ed 100** einmal habe ich 100 geschafft

b (= *lay hands on*) anrühren, anfassen; **the police/tax authorities can't ~ me** die Polizei/das Finanzamt kann mir nichts anhaben; **the paintings weren't ~ed by the fire** die Gemälde blieben vom Feuer verschont

c *food, drink* anrühren; *capital* herankommen an (+*acc*) (*inf*); (= *use*) antasten; **I haven't ~ed the piano for months** ich habe seit Monaten nicht mehr Klavier gespielt

d (= *equal*) herankommen an (+*acc*), erreichen; **there's nothing to ~ hot lemon for a cold** bei einer Erkältung geht nichts über heiße Zitrone

e (= *deal with*) *problem etc* anrühren; **everything he ~es turns to gold** ihm gelingt einfach alles; **I wouldn't ~ those shares** ich würde meine Finger von den Aktien lassen; **an ordinary detergent won't ~ dirt like that** ein normales Reinigungsmittel wird mit diesem Schmutz nicht fertig; **I asked them not to ~ my desk** ich bat darum, nicht an meinen Schreibtisch zu gehen

f (= *concern*) berühren, betreffen

g (= *move emotionally*) rühren, bewegen; (= *affect*) berühren; (= *wound*) *pride* treffen; **deeply ~ed** tief gerührt *or* bewegt; **to ~ sb's heart** jds Herz (an)rühren

h (*Brit inf*) **to ~ sb for a loan** jdn um einen Kredit angehen; **he ~ed me for £10** er hat mich um £ 10 angepumpt (*inf*)

i **his hair was ~ed with grey** sein Haar war von Grau durchzogen

VI (= *come into contact*) sich berühren; (*estates etc* = *be adjacent also*) aneinander stoßen, aneinander grenzen; **don't ~!** Finger weg!; **"please do not ~"** „bitte nicht berühren"

▶ **touch at** VI +prep obj (*Naut*) anlaufen

▶ **touch down** **VI** **a** (*Aviat, Space*) aufsetzen **b** (*Rugby, US Ftbl*) einen Versuch erzielen **VT** *sep ball* niederlegen

▶ **touch in** VT *sep details, shading etc* einfügen

▶ **touch off** VT *sep explosion, argument, fire, flood* auslösen

▶ **touch up** VT *sep* **a** *colour, make-up* auffrischen; *picture, paintwork* ausbessern; *photo* retuschieren; *essay, article* ausbessern **b** (*Brit inf*) *woman, man* betatschen (*inf*), befummeln (*inf*)

▶ **touch (up)on** VI +prep obj *subject* kurz berühren, antippen; **he barely touched on the question** er hat die Frage kaum berührt

touch-and-go [ˌtʌtʃənˈgəʊ] ADJ **to be ~** riskant *or* prekär sein; **it's ~ whether ...** es steht auf des Messers Schneide, ob ...; **he won eventually but it was ~ for a while** er gewann schließlich, aber es stand eine Zeit lang auf des Messers Schneide; **it's ~ if we'll make it** es ist noch vollkommen offen, ob wir es schaffen; **after his operation it was ~** nach der Operation hing sein Leben an einem Faden

touchdown ['tʌtʃdaʊn] N **a** (*Aviat, Space*) Aufsetzen *nt* **b** (*Rugby, US Ftbl*) Versuch *m*, Niederlegen des Balles im Malfeld des Gegners

touché [tuːˈʃeɪ] INTERJ (*Fencing*) Treffer; (*fig inf*) eins zu null für dich (*inf*)

touched [tʌtʃt] ADJ pred **a** (= *moved*) gerührt, bewegt **b** **to be a bit ~** (*inf*, = *mad*) einen leichten Stich haben (*inf*)

touch football N (*US*) sanftere Art des Football, bei der der Gegner berührt wird, anstatt zu Fall gebracht zu werden

touchiness ['tʌtʃɪnɪs] N Empfindlichkeit *f* (*on* in Bezug auf +*acc*); (= *irritability also*) leichte Reizbarkeit; **because of the ~ of this subject** weil dieses Thema so heikel ist

touching ['tʌtʃɪŋ] ADJ rührend, bewegend PREP (*form*) bezüglich (*form*)

touchingly ['tʌtʃɪŋlɪ] ADV rührend, bewegend; **she is ~ naive** sie ist rührend naiv; **~, his daughter has supported him throughout** seine Tochter hat ihn in rührender Weise während der ganzen Zeit unterstützt

touch: **touch judge** N (*Rugby*) Seitenrichter(in) *m(f)*; **touchline** N (*esp Brit Sport*) Seitenlinie *f*, Auslinie *f*; **touchpaper** N Zündpapier *nt*; **to light the (blue) ~** (*fig*) für helle Auf-

regung sorgen; **touchscreen** ['tʌtʃskriːn] N (*Comput*) Touchscreen *m*, Berührungsbildschirm *m*; **touch-sensitive** ADJ berührungsempfindlich; **~ screen** Touch-Screen *m*; **~ switch** Kontaktschalter *m*; **touchstone** N (*fig*) Prüfstein *m*; **touch system** N (*Typing*) Zehnfingersystem *nt*; **touch-tone** ADJ *telephone* Tonwahl-; **touch-type** VI blind schreiben; **touch-typing** N Blindschreiben *nt*; **touch-up paint** N Tupflack *m*

touchy ['tʌtʃɪ] ADJ empfindlich (*about* in Bezug auf +*acc*); (= *irritable also*) leicht reizbar; *subject* heikel, kitzlig (*inf*)

touchy-feely ['tʌtʃɪ'fiːlɪ] ADJ (*pej*) sentimental; **she is very ~** sie hat gern viel Körperkontakt; **a ~ song** eine zuckersüße Schnulze (*inf*)

tough [tʌf] **ADJ** (+*er*) **a** zäh; (= *resistant*) widerstandsfähig; *cloth* strapazierfähig; *membrane* widerstandsfähig; *skin* rau; (*towards others*) hart, knallhart (*inf*); *bargaining, negotiator, opponent, fight, struggle, lesson* hart; *district, city* hart, rau; **as ~ as leather** zäh wie Leder (*inf*); **(as) ~ as old boots** (*Brit hum inf*) *or* **shoe leather** (*US hum inf*) zäh wie Leder (*inf*); **he'll get over it, he's pretty ~** er wird schon darüber hinwegkommen, er ist hart im Nehmen (*inf*); **to get ~ (with sb)** (*physically*) grob werden (mit jdm *or* gegen jdn), handgreiflich werden (gegen jdn); (*fig*) hart durchgreifen (gegen jdn); **~ guy** (*inf*) (knall)harter Kerl *or* Bursche (*inf*); **getting him to agree took some ~ talking** er musste ganz schön bearbeitet werden, damit er zustimmte

b (= *difficult*) *task, problem* hart; *journey* strapaziös, anstrengend; *choice* schwierig; *competition* hart, zäh; **it was ~ going** (*lit, fig*) es war eine Strapaze *or* ein Schlauch *m* (*inf*); **to have a ~ time of it** nichts zu lachen haben; **I had a ~ time controlling my anger** es fiel mir schwer, meinen Zorn unter Kontrolle zu halten; **it's a ~ job being Prime Minister** Premierminister zu sein, ist eine schwierige Aufgabe *or* ein harter Job (*inf*); **it's ~ when you have kids** es ist schwierig, wenn man Kinder hat; **it must have been ~ being** *or* **to be a child in the war** für ein Kind muss die Zeit während des Krieges sehr schwer gewesen sein; **she's a ~ customer** sie ist zäh wie Leder (*inf*)

c (= *strict*) *policy, controls* hart; **to take a ~ line with sb/on sth** bei jdm/einer Sache eine starre Haltung einnehmen

d (*inf:* = *unfortunate*) hart; **that's pretty ~!** das ist ganz schön hart!; **it was ~ on the others** das war hart für die anderen; **~ (luck)!** Pech!; **~ luck on Taylor** Pech für Taylor; **~ shit** (*sl*) Scheißpech *nt* (*inf*)

N (*inf*) Schlägertyp *m* (*pej inf*), (knall)harter Bursche (*inf*)

ADV (+*er*) (*inf*) **to treat sb ~** jdn hart rannehmen; **to talk ~** große Sprüche machen; **to act ~** hart durchgreifen; **to hang ~** unnachgiebig festhalten

▶ **tough out** VT *always separate* **to tough it out** hartnäckig auf seine Standpunkt beharren

toughen ['tʌfn] **VT** **a** *glass, metal* härten **b** (*fig*) *person* zäh *or* hart machen; (*esp physically*) abhärten; *laws, rules, terms, sanctions* verschärfen; **to ~ one's stance (on sth)** einen härteren Standpunkt beziehen (in Bezug auf etw *acc*); **they will have to ~ their policy** sie müssen einen härteren politischen Kurs einschlagen **VI** (*glass, metal*) aushärten, hart werden; (*meat*) zäh werden; (*attitude*) sich verhärten

▶ **toughen up** **VT** *sep person* hart *or* zäh machen, stählen (*geh*); *muscles* trainieren; *sportsman also* fit machen; *regulations* verschärfen **VI** hart *or* zäh werden; (*attitude*) sich verhärten; **to toughen up on sth** härter gegen etw vorgehen

toughie ['tʌfɪ] N (*inf:* = *ruffian*) Raubein *nt* (*inf*); (= *child*) Rabauke *m* (*inf*); (= *problem, question*) harte Nuss *f*; **she thinks she's a ~ and can take it** sie hält sich für hart genug, das auszuhalten

tough love N (*esp US inf*) liebevolle, aber strenge Haltung

toughly ['tʌflɪ] ADV *made robust; built also* stabil; *say* fest; **~ worded** geharnischt; **to behave ~** (= *like a tough guy*) den harten Mann spielen *or* markieren (*inf*); (= *decisively*) hart auftreten

tough-minded [tʌf'maɪndɪd] ADJ störrisch

toughness ['tʌfnɪs] N **a** (*of meat etc*) Zähheit *f*; (*of person*) Zähigkeit *f*; (= *resistance*) Widerstandsfähigkeit *f*; (*of cloth*) Strapazierfähigkeit *f*; (*of skin*) Rauheit *f*; (*of bargaining, negotiator, opponent, fight, struggle, lesson*) Härte *f*; (*of district, city*) Rauheit *f* (= *difficulty*) Schwierigkeit *f*, (*of journey*) Strapazen *pl* **c** (= *harshness: of policy, controls*) Härte *f*

toupee ['tu:peɪ] N Toupet *nt*

tour [tʊə] N **a** (= *journey, walking tour etc*) Tour *f*; (*by bus, car etc also*) Fahrt *f*, Reise *f*, Tour *f*; (*of town, building, exhibition etc*) Rundgang *m* (*of* durch); (*also* **guided tour**) Führung *f* (*of* durch); (*by bus*) Rundfahrt *f* (*of* durch); **to go on a ~ of Scotland** auf eine Schottlandreise gehen; **to make a ~ of Germany** eine Deutschlandreise machen; **he took us on a ~ of the Highlands** er machte mit uns eine Reise durch die Highlands

b (*also* **tour of inspection**) Runde *f* (*of* durch); (*esp on foot*) Rundgang *m* (*of* durch); **he had a 3-year ~ (of duty) in Africa** er wurde für drei Jahre nach Afrika versetzt; **leave between ~s (of duty)** Urlaub *m* zwischen zwei Versetzungen; **to make a ~ of the site/house** einen Rundgang durch das Gelände/das Haus machen

c (*Theat*) Gastspielreise *f*, Tournee *f* (*of* durch); (*Sport*) Tournee *f*; **to go/be on ~** auf Gastspielreise *or* Tournee gehen/sein; **to take a company/play on ~** mit einer Truppe/einem Stück auf Gastspielreise *or* Tournee gehen

VT *country, district etc* fahren durch; (*on foot*) ziehen durch; (= *travel around*) bereisen; **to ~ the world** um die Welt reisen, eine Weltreise machen

b (= *visit*) *town, building, exhibition* einen Rundgang machen durch, besichtigen; (*by bus etc*) eine Rundfahrt machen durch

c (*Theat, Sport*) Tournee machen durch

VI a (*on holiday*) eine Reise *or* Tour *or* Fahrt machen; **we're ~ing (around)** wir reisen herum; **to go ~ing** eine Tour machen

b (*Theat, Sport*) eine Tournee machen; **to go/be ~ing** auf Tournee gehen/sein

tour de force ['tʊədə'fɔ:s] N Glanzleistung *f*

tour director N (*US*) Reiseleiter(in) *m(f)*

Tourette('s) syndrome [tʊə'ret(s)ˌsɪndrəʊm] N Tourettesyndrom *nt*

tour guide N Reiseleiter(in) *m(f)*

touring ['tʊərɪŋ] N (Herum)reisen *nt*, (Herum-)fahren *nt*

touring: touring club N Touring-Club *m*; **touring company** N (*Theat*) Tourneetheater *nt*; **touring holiday** N (*Brit*) Reiseurlaub *m*; **touring party** N Reisegruppe *f*; **touring team** N Gastmannschaft *f*

tourism ['tʊərɪzəm] N Fremdenverkehr *m*, Tourismus *m*

tourist ['tʊərɪst] N (= *person*) Tourist(in) *m(f)*, Fremde(r) *mf*; (*Sport*) Gast *m*; (= *tourist class*) Touristenklasse *f*; **to travel ~** in der Touristenklasse reisen ATTR Touristen-; **~ season** Reisesaison *or* -zeit *f*; **~ traffic** Reiseverkehr *m*

tourist: tourist class N Touristenklasse *f* ADV *travel, fly* in der Touristenklasse; **tourist-class** ADJ *ticket, fare, passenger* der Touristenklasse; **tourist guide** N Fremdenführer(in) *m(f)*; **tourist information centre** N (*Brit*) Touristen-Informationsbüro *nt*, Touristen-Informationszentrum *nt*; **tourist office** N Fremdenverkehrsbüro *nt*; **tourist trade** N Fremdenverkehrsgewerbe *nt*

touristy ['tʊərɪstɪ] ADJ (*pej*) auf Tourismus getrimmt; *resorts, shops, souvenirs* für Touristen; **to do ~ things** das machen, was man so als Tourist tut

tour manager N (*Sport, Mus*) Tourmanager(in) *m(f)*, Tourneeleiter(in) *m(f)*

tournament ['tʊənəmənt] N (*Sport etc, also Hist*) Turnier *nt*

tournedos [tʊə'neɪdəʊ] N (*Cook*) Tournedos *nt*

tourney ['tʊənɪ] N (*Hist, US, Sport*) Turnier *nt*

tourniquet ['tʊənɪkeɪ] N Aderpresse *f*, Tourniquet *nt* (*spec*)

tour operator N Reiseveranstalter *m*

tousle ['taʊzl] VT *hair* zerzausen; (*affectionately also*) zausen

tousled ['taʊzld] ADJ *hair* zerzaust, wuschelig (*inf*); **~ head** Wuschelkopf *m* (*inf*)

tout [taʊt] (*inf*) N (= *tipster*) Wettberater(in) *m(f)*; (*esp Brit:* = *spy*) Schnüffler(in) *m(f)* (*inf*), Spion(in) *m(f)* (*inf*); (= *ticket tout*) (Karten-)schwarzhändler(in) *m(f)*; (*for business*) Kundenfänger(in) *m(f)*

VT (*Racing*) *horse* als Favorit angeben, als heißen Tipp nennen; (= *spy*) *stables* ausspionieren (*inf*); *horse* herumschnüffeln bei (*inf*); (= *sell: also* **tout around**) *information* anbieten; *tickets* anbieten, schwarz verkaufen (*inf*); *ideas* propagieren (den Leuten) aufschwatzen (*inf*)

VI (*Racing,* = *offer tips*) Wetttipps (gegen Honorar) verteilen; (= *spy*) herumspionieren, herumschnüffeln (*inf*); **to ~ for business** (aufdringlich) Reklame machen; **to ~ for customers** auf Kundenfang sein (*inf*), Kunden schleppen (*inf*)

touter ['taʊtə] N Kundenfänger(in) *m(f)*

tow[1] [təʊ] N Werg *nt*, Hede *f*

tow[2] N **to take a car in ~** ein Auto abschleppen; **to take a yacht in ~** eine Jacht schleppen *or* ins Schlepptau nehmen; **to give sb/a car a ~** (*in car*) jdn/ein Auto abschleppen; (*to start*) jdn/ein Auto anschleppen; **do you want a ~?** soll ich Sie abschleppen/anschleppen?; **to give a yacht a ~** eine Jacht schleppen *or* ins Schlepptau nehmen; **"on ~"** ≈ „Fahrzeug wird abgeschleppt"; **in ~** (*fig*) im Schlepptau **VT** *boat, glider* schleppen; *car also* abschleppen; (*to start*) anschleppen; *trailer, caravan* ziehen; **he was ~ing a huge dog behind him** er zog *or* schleifte einen riesigen Hund hinter sich (*dat*) her

▶ **tow away** VT *sep car* (gebührenpflichtig) abschleppen

towage ['təʊɪdʒ] N **a** (*of ships*) Bugsieren *nt*, Schleppen *nt*; (*of cars*) Abschleppen *nt* **b** (= *fee, for ships*) Schlepp- *or* Bugsiergebühr *f*; (*for cars*) Abschleppgebühr *f*; **~ charges** (*for ships*) Schlepp- *or* Bugsiergebühren *pl*; (*for cars*) Abschleppgebühren *pl*, Abschleppkosten *pl*

toward [tə'wɔ:d] ADJ (*form,* = *favourable*) angemessen

toward(s) [tə'wɔ:d(z)] PREP **a** (= *in direction of*) (*with verbs of motion*) auf (+*acc*) ... zu; **they walked ~ the town** sie gingen auf die Stadt zu; **we sailed ~ China** wir segelten in Richtung China; **it's further north, ~ Dortmund** es liegt weiter im Norden, Richtung Dortmund; **~ the south** nach *or* gen (*liter*) Süden; **he turned ~ her** er wandte sich ihr zu; **with his back ~ the wall** mit dem Rücken zur Wand; **you should read with your back ~ the light** Sie sollten mit dem Rücken zum Licht lesen; **on the side (facing) ~ the sea** zum Meer hin; **a hotel facing ~ the sea** ein Hotel mit Blick aufs Meer; **they are working ~ a solution** sie arbeiten auf eine Lösung hin; **if it helps ~ finding a solution** wenn es dazu beiträgt, eine Lösung zu finden; **~ a better understanding of ...** zum besseren Verständnis von ...; **I gave him some money ~ a car** ich gab ihm etwas Geld als Beitrag zu seinem Auto

b (= *in relation to*) ... (*dat*) gegenüber; **what are your feelings ~ him?** was empfinden Sie ihm gegenüber?, was empfinden Sie für ihn?

c (= *ten o'clock*) gegen zehn Uhr; **~ the end of the 60's/the year** gegen Ende der sechziger Jahre *or* Sechzigerjahre/des Jahres

tow: towbar N Anhängerkupplung *f*; **towboat** N Schleppschiff *nt*, Schlepper *m*; **towcar** N (*esp US*) Abschleppwagen *m*

towel ['taʊəl] N Handtuch *nt* → **throw in** VT (mit einem Handtuch) (ab)trocknen

▶ **towel down** VT *sep* (ab)trocknen, trockenreiben

towel dispenser N Handtuchautomat *m*

towelling ['taʊəlɪŋ] N Frottee(stoff) *m*

towel rail N Handtuchhalter *m*

tower ['taʊə] N **a** Turm *m* **b** (*fig:* = *person*) **a ~ of strength** eine Stütze, ein starker (Rück)halt **c** (*Comput*) Tower *m* **VI** ragen

▶ **tower above** *or* **over** VI +*prep obj* **a** (*buildings etc*) emporragen über (+*acc*) **b** (*lit, fig: people*) überragen

▶ **tower up** VI hinaufragen, emporragen

tower block N (*Brit*) Hochhaus *nt*

towering ['taʊərɪŋ] ADJ **a** *building* hochragend, alles überragend; *mountain* (steil) aufragend; *tree* hoch gewachsen; **the boy stood before the ~ figure of his father** der Schüler stand vor der hoch aufragenden Gestalt seines Vaters **b** (*fig:* = *magnificent*) *achievement, presence, talent* überragend; *performance* hervorragend; **a ~ rage** eine rasende *or* unbändige Wut; **one of the ~ giants of literature** eine der einsamen Größen der Literatur, ein Titan *m* der Literatur

tower system N (*Comput*) Towersystem *nt*

towheaded ['təʊhedɪd] ADJ flachsblond

towline ['təʊlaɪn] N (*Aut*) Abschleppseil *nt*; (*Naut, for glider*) Schleppseil *nt*

town [taʊn] N **a** Stadt *f*; **the ~ of Brighton** (die Stadt) Brighton; **to go into** *or* **down ~** in die Stadt gehen; **to live in ~** in der Stadt wohnen; **guess who's in ~** rate mal, wer zurzeit hier in (der Stadt) ist?; **he's out of ~** er ist nicht in der Stadt, er ist außerhalb; **~ and gown** (*Univ*) (die) Bevölkerung und (die) Studenten; **to have a night on the ~** (*inf*) die Nacht durchmachen; **you didn't know? but it's all over ~** du hattest keine Ahnung? das ist doch stadtbekannt; **it's all over ~ now that he has ...** es hat sich herumgesprochen, dass er ...; **to go to ~ on sth** (*fig inf,* = *go to great trouble with*) sich (*dat*) bei etw einen abbrechen (*inf*); (*to please*) sich bei etw in Zeug legen; (= *exaggerate*) etw übertreiben; **you've really gone to ~ on this essay** bei diesem Aufsatz sind Sie wirklich ins Detail gegangen; **John's really gone to ~ on his new house** John hat bei seinem neuen Haus wirklich keine Kosten gescheut

b (*Brit:* = *London*) London *nt*; **to go up to ~** nach London gehen *or* fahren; **he is out of ~** er ist nicht in London

town: town centre, (*US*) **town center** N Stadtmitte *f*, (Stadt)zentrum *nt*, Stadtinnere(s) *nt*; **town clerk** N Stadtdirektor(in) *m(f)*, Stadtschreiber(in) *m(f)* (*old, Sw*); (*of bigger town*) Oberstadtdirektor(in) *m(f)*; **town council** N Stadtrat *m*; **town councillor**, (*US*) **town councilor** N Stadtrat *m*, Stadträtin *f*; **town crier** N (*Hist*) Ausrufer(in) *m(f)*; **town dweller** N (*Brit*) Städter(in) *m(f)*, Stadtbewohner(in) *m(f)*

townee ['taʊni:] N (*pej*) Städter(in) *m(f)*, Stadtmensch *m*; (*Univ*) Bewohner einer Universitätsstadt, der nicht der Universität angehört

towner ['taʊnə] N (*esp US*) Stadtbewohner(in) *m(f)*, Stadtmensch *m*

town: town gas N Stadtgas *nt*; **town hall** N Rathaus *nt*; **town house** N Stadthaus *nt*, Haus *nt* in der Stadt; (= *type of house*) Reihenhaus *nt*

townie ['taʊni:] N = **townee**

town: town life N Stadtleben *nt*, Leben *nt* in der Stadt; **town meeting** N (*US Pol*) Gemeindeversammlung *f*; **town planner** N Stadt- *or* Städteplaner(in) *m(f)*; **town planning** N Stadtplanung *f*, Städteplanung *f*; **townscape** N Stadtbild *nt*, Stadtlandschaft *f*; (*Art*) Stadtansicht *f*

townsfolk ['taʊnzfəʊk] PL Städter *pl*, Stadtmenschen *pl*, Stadtbevölkerung *f*; (= *citizens*) Bürger *pl*

township ['taʊnʃɪp] N (Stadt)gemeinde *f*; (*US*) Verwaltungsbezirk *m*; (*US Surv*) 6 Meilen großes Gebiet; (*in South Africa*) Township *f*

towns: townsman N Städter *m*, Stadtmensch *m*; (= *citizen*) Bürger *m*; **my fellow townsmen** meine (lieben) Mitbürger; **townspeople** PL Städter *pl*, Stadtmenschen *pl*; (= *citizens*) Bürger *pl*; **townswoman** N Bürgerin *f*; **the townswomen of Paisley** die Bewohnerinnen *or* Bürgerinnen *pl* von Paisley; **townswomen's guild** *Frauenvereinigung mit gesellschaftlichen Aufgaben*

tow: towpath N Treidelpfad *m*; **towplane** N Schleppflugzeug *nt*; **towrope** N = **towline**; **tow start** N (*Aut*) Anschleppen *nt*; **to give sb a** ~ jdn anschleppen; **tow truck** N (*US*) Abschleppwagen *m*

toxaemia, (*US*) **toxemia** [tɒk'siːmɪə] N Blutvergiftung *f*, Sepsis *f* (*spec*)

toxic ['tɒksɪk] ADJ giftig, Gift-, toxisch; *effects* schädlich; **to be** ~ **to sb/sth** für jdn/etw schädlich sein

toxicity [tɒk'sɪsɪtɪ] N Giftigkeit *f*, Giftgehalt *m*

toxicological [ˌtɒksɪkə'lɒdʒɪkəl] ADJ toxikologisch

toxicology [ˌtɒksɪ'kɒlədʒɪ] N Toxikologie *f*

toxic shock syndrome N toxisches Schocksyndrom

toxic waste N Giftmüll *m*

toxin ['tɒksɪn] N Giftstoff *m*, Toxin *nt*

toy [tɔɪ] ⚙ 8.2 N Spielzeug *nt*; ~**s** Spielsachen *pl*, Spielzeug *nt*; (*in shops also*) Spielwaren *pl*; **it's not a** ~! das ist kein (Kinder)spielzeug! VI **to** ~ **with an object/idea** *etc* mit einer Sache/ Idee *etc* spielen; **to** ~ **with one's food** mit dem Essen (herum)spielen

toy *in cpds* Spielzeug-; **toy boy** N (*inf*) jugendlicher Liebhaber; **he looks like my ideal** ~ so was Junges wie er wäre ideal zum Vernaschen (*inf*); **toy car** N Spielzeugauto *nt*; **toy dog** N Zwerghund *m*; (*made of material*) Stoffhund *m*; **toy poodle** N Zwergpudel *m*; **toyshop** N Spielzeug- *or* Spielwarenladen *m*; **toytown** ADJ (*esp Brit pej*) (*childish*) kindisch; (= *worthless*) wertlos; ~ **money** Spielgeld *nt*; ~ **revolutionary** Möchtegern-Revoluzzer(in) *m(f)*

trace[1] [treɪs] N a (= *sign*) Spur *f*; **I can't find any** ~ **of your file** Ihre Akte ist spurlos verschwunden; **there's no** ~ **of it** keine Spur davon; **to vanish without** ~ spurlos verschwinden; **to sink without** ~ spurlos *or* ohne Spur versinken *or* untergehen; (*fig also*) sang- und klanglos untergehen; **to lose all** ~ **of sb/sth** jdn/etw aus den Augen verlieren

b (= *small amount*) (*of poison, spice*) Spur *f*; (*of irony etc*) Hauch *m*, Spur *f*

VT a (= *draw*) zeichnen; (= *copy*) nachziehen, nachzeichnen; (*with tracing paper*) durchpausen, abpausen; **he** ~**d his name in the sand** er malte seinen Namen in den Sand

b (= *follow trail of*) *trail, progress, developments* verfolgen; *steps* folgen (+*dat*); **to** ~ **a phone call** einen Anruf zurückverfolgen; **we** ~**d it to a house in Soho** ihre Spur führte zu einem Haus in Soho

c (= *find*) ausfindig machen, auffinden; **I can't** ~ **your file** ich kann Ihre Akte nicht finden

▶ **trace back** VI zurückgehen (*to* auf +*acc*) VT *sep descent* zurückverfolgen; *rumour* auf seinen Ursprung zurückverfolgen; *neurosis, problem etc* zurückführen (*to* auf +*acc*); **he can trace his family back to Henry VIII** seine Familie lässt sich bis zu Heinrich VIII. zurückverfolgen; **we traced the story back to one of the secretaries** wir fanden heraus, dass die Geschichte von einer der Sekretärinnen in die Welt gesetzt worden war

▶ **trace out** VT *sep* (= *copy*) nachzeichnen; (*with tracing paper*) durchpausen (*onto* auf +*acc*); (= *draw*) zeichnen; **we traced out the route on the map** wir zeichneten die Route auf der Karte ein

trace[2] N (*of harness*) Zuggurt *m*, Zugriemen *m* → **kick over**

traceable ['treɪsəbl] ADJ a (= *can be found*) auffindbar b **to be** ~ **to sth** sich auf etw (*acc*) zurückführen lassen

trace element, **trace mineral** N Spurenelement *nt*

tracer ['treɪsə'] N a (*Mil: also* **tracer bullet**) Leuchtspurgeschoss *nt* b (*Med*) Isotopenindikator *m* c (= *inquiry form*) Suchzettel *m*, Laufzettel *m*

tracery ['treɪsərɪ] N (*Archit*) Maßwerk *nt*; (= *pattern: of threads, branches etc*) Filigranmuster *nt*

trachea [trə'kɪə] N Luftröhre *f*; (*of insects*) Trachea *f*

tracheotomy [ˌtrækɪ'ɒtəmɪ] N Luftröhrenschnitt *m*

trachoma [trə'kəʊmə] N Körnerkrankheit *f*, (hartnäckige) Bindehautentzündung

tracing ['treɪsɪŋ] N (= *drawing*) Durchpausen *nt*, Durchzeichnen *nt*; (= *result*) Pause *f*

tracing: tracing file N Suchkartei *f*; **tracing paper** N Pauspapier *nt*; **tracing service** N Suchdienst *m*

track [træk] N a (= *trail*) Fährte *f*, Spur *f*; (*of tyres*) (Fahr)spur *f*; **to be on sb's** ~ jdm auf der Spur sein; **you can't expect to keep** ~ **of your friends if you never write to them** du kannst nicht erwarten, Kontakt zu deinen Freunden zu behalten, wenn du nie schreibst; **to keep** ~ **of sb/sth** (= *watch, follow*) jdn/etw im Auge behalten; (= *keep up to date with*) über jdn/etw auf dem Laufenden bleiben; **I can't keep** ~ **of his movements** *or* **of him** ich weiß nie, wo er sich gerade aufhält; **how do you keep** ~ **of the time without a watch?** wie können Sie wissen, wie spät es ist, wenn Sie keine Uhr haben?; **I can't keep** ~ **of your girlfriends** du hast so viele Freundinnen, da komme ich nicht mit (*inf*); **no-one can keep** ~ **of the situation** niemand hat mehr einen Überblick über die Lage; **to lose** ~ **of sb/sth** (= *lose contact with, lose sight of*) jdn/etw aus den Augen verlieren; (= *lose count of, be confused about*) über Leute/etw den Überblick verlieren; (= *not be up to date with*) über jdn/etw nicht mehr auf dem Laufenden sein; **we lost** ~ **of time** wir haben die Zeit ganz vergessen, wir haben einfach nicht auf die Uhr *or* Zeit geachtet; **he lost** ~ **of what he was saying** er hat den Faden verloren; **I lost** ~ **of what he was saying** ich habe nicht (mehr) mitbekommen, was er gesagt hat

b (*fig*) **we must be making** ~**s** (*inf*) wir müssen uns auf die Socken (*inf*) *or* auf den Weg machen; **to make** ~**s for home** sich auf den Nachhauseweg machen; **he made** ~**s for London** er ging/fuhr nach London; **he stopped dead in his** ~**s** er blieb abrupt stehen; **to stop sth (dead) in its** ~**s** etw abrupt zum Stillstand bringen; **to stop sb (dead) in his/her** ~**s** jdn abrupt zum Stillstand bringen; **to cover (up) one's** ~**s** seine Spuren verwischen

c (= *path*) Weg *m*, Pfad *m*; **to throw sb off the** ~ (*fig*) jdn aus der Bahn bringen *or* werfen; **to be on** ~ (*fig*) auf Kurs sein; **to be on the right** ~ (*fig*) auf der richtigen Spur sein; **to be on the wrong** ~ (*fig*) auf dem falschen Weg sein, auf dem Holzweg sein (*inf*); **to get the economy back on** ~ die Wirtschaft wieder auf Kurs bringen

d (= *course, of hurricane*) Weg *m*; (*of comet*) (Lauf)bahn *f*; (*of rocket*) Bahn *f*, Kurs *m*

e (*Rail*) Gleise *pl*; (*US*, = *platform*) Bahnsteig *m*; **a new section of** ~ eine neue (Gleis)strecke; **the** ~ **to Paisley** die Bahnstrecke nach Paisley; **"keep off the** ~**"** „Betreten der Gleise verboten"; **two miles of new** ~ zwei Meilen neuer Gleise *or* Schienen; **to leave the** ~(**s**) entgleisen; **double/single** ~ **line** zwei-/eingleisige Strecke; **to be born on the wrong side of the** ~**s** (*US, fig*) aus niedrigem Milieu stammen

f (*Sport*) Rennbahn *f*; (*Athletics*) Bahn *f*; (*Motorsport*) Piste *f*, Bahn *f*; (= *circuit*) Rennstrecke *f*; (*Cycling*) Radrennbahn *f*

g (*on tape, diskette, CD*) Spur *f*; (= *song etc*) Stück *nt*; **four-track tape recorder** Vierspurgerät *nt*

h (*also* **caterpillar track**) Raupenkette *f*

i (*Aut, between wheels*) Spur(weite) *f*

VT a (= *follow*) *person, animal* verfolgen; *move-*

ments folgen (+*dat*); (*Space*) *rocket* die Flugbahn (+*gen*) verfolgen

b (*US*) **the children** ~**ed dirt all over the carpet** die Kinder hinterließen überall auf dem Teppich Schmutzspuren

VI a (= *follow trail*) Fährten lesen

b (*Aut*) spurgenau laufen

c (*Film, TV*) fahren

d (= *move*) (*hurricane etc*) ziehen; (*stylus*) sich bewegen

▶ **track down** VT *sep* aufspüren (*to* in +*dat*); *thing* aufstöbern, auftreiben (*inf*), finden; *reference, source of infection* ausfindig machen

▶ **track in** VI (*Film, TV*) heranfahren (*on* an +*acc*)

track: track and field N Leichtathletik *f*; **track-and-field** ADJ Leichtathletik-; ~ **events** Leichtathletikwettbewerbe *pl*; **track athletics** N *sing* Laufdisziplinen *pl*; **trackball** (*Comput, in laptop*) Trackball *m*; (*in mouse*) Rollkugel *f*

tracked [trækt] ADJ ~ **vehicle** Ketten- *or* Raupenfahrzeug *nt*

tracker ['trækə'] N (= *Indian etc*) Fährtenleser *m*; (*Hunt*) Tracker *m*

tracker dog N Spürhund *m*

track event N Laufwettbewerb *m*

tracking ['trækɪŋ] N Verfolgen *nt*

tracking station N Bodenstation *f*

tracklayer ['trækˌleɪə'] N a (= *caterpillar (vehicle)*) Raupenfahrzeug *nt or* -schlepper *m* b (*US Rail*) Streckenarbeiter(in) *m(f)*

tracklaying vehicle [ˌtrækleɪɪŋ'viːɪkl] N Kettenfahrzeug *nt*

trackless ['træklɪs] ADJ a *vehicle* ohne Ketten b *forest* weglos

trackless surgery N Schlüssellochchirurgie *f*

track: track maintenance N (*Rail*) Streckenwartung *f*; **track meeting**, (*US*) **track meet** N Leichtathletikwettbewerb *or* -wettkampf *m*; **track race** N Rennen *nt*; (*Athletics also*) Lauf *m*; **track racing** N Laufwettbewerb *m*; (*Motorsport*) Rennen *nt*; (*Cycling*) Radrennen *nt*; **track record** N (*fig*) **what's his** ~? was hat er vorzuweisen?; **to have a good/poor** ~ gute/schlechte Leistungen vorweisen können; **he's got a pretty good** ~ er hat einiges vorzuweisen; **they've got an abysmal** ~ **for delivering on schedule** sie stehen nicht gerade im Ruf, pünktlich zu liefern; **track rod** N Spurstange *f*; **track shoe** N Rennschuh *m*; **tracksuit** N Trainingsanzug *m*

tract[1] [trækt] N a (*of land*) Gebiet *nt*; **narrow** ~ Streifen *m* b (*respiratory*) Wege *pl*; (*digestive*) Trakt *m*

tract[2] N Traktat *nt*, Schrift *f*

tractability [ˌtræktə'bɪlɪtɪ] N (*lit: of metal*) Formbarkeit *f*, Bearbeitbarkeit *f*; (*fig*) (*of child, animal, disposition*) Fügsamkeit *f*, Lenkbarkeit *f*; (*of problem*) (leichte) Lösbarkeit

tractable ['træktəbl] ADJ (*lit*) *metal etc* leicht zu bearbeiten, formbar; (*fig*) *child, animal, disposition* fügsam, lenkbar; *problem* leicht lösbar

traction ['trækʃən] N Zugkraft *f*, Ziehkraft *f*, Zugleistung *f*; (*of wheels*) Bodenhaftung *f*; (*Med*) Streckverband *m*; **in** ~ im Streckverband

traction engine N Zugmaschine *f*, Dampftraktor *m*

tractor ['træktə'] N a Traktor *m*, Trecker *m*, Zugmaschine *f* b (*of truck*) Sattelschlepper *m*

tractor: tractor driver N Traktorfahrer(in) *m(f)*, Traktorist(in) *m(f)*; **tractorfeed** ['træktəfiːd] N (*Comput*) Traktor *m*; **tractor-trailer** [ˌtræktə'treɪlə'] N (*Aut*) Sattelzug *m*

trad [træd] (*inf*), **trad jazz** N Traditional *m*, Oldtime *m*

trade [treɪd] N a (= *commerce*) Handel *m*, Gewerbe *nt*; (= *hotel trade, catering trade*) die Geschäfte *nt*; (= *turnover: of shop, hotel etc*) die Geschäfte *pl*; **he used to be in** ~ er war Geschäftsmann; **how's** ~? wie gehen die Geschäfte?; **to do** ~ **with sb** mit jdm Handel treiben; **to do a good**

~ gute Geschäfte machen; **to do a brisk ~ in sth** einen reißenden Absatz an etw (*dat*) haben

b (= *line of business*) Branche *f*, Geschäftszweig *m*; **he's in the wool** ~ er ist in der Wollbranche, er ist im Wollhandel tätig; **what ~ are you in?** in welcher Branche sind Sie (tätig)?; **he's in the** ~ er ist in der Branche, er ist vom Fach; **as we call it in the** ~ wie es in unserer Branche heißt

c (= *job*) Handwerk *nt*; **he's a bricklayer by** ~ er ist Maurer von Beruf; **a lawyer by** ~ (*hum*) ein gelernter Rechtsanwalt (*hum*); **to put sb to a** ~ (*old*) jdn ein Handwerk erlernen lassen

d (= *people*) Geschäftsleute *pl*, Branche *f*; **special terms for the** ~ Vergünstigungen *pl* für Leute aus der Branche; **to sell to the** ~ an Gewerbetreibende verkaufen

e (= *exchange*) Tauschgeschäft *nt*, Tauschhandel *m*

f the Trades PL (*Geog*) der Passat

VT tauschen; **to ~ sth for sth else** etw gegen etw anderes (ein)tauschen; **to ~ secrets** Geheimnisse austauschen; **to ~ places (with sb)** (*lit*) (mit jdm) die Plätze wechseln, (*fig*) (mit jdm) tauschen

VI a (*Comm*) Handel treiben, handeln; **to ~ in sth** mit etw handeln; **to ~ with sb** mit jdm Geschäfte machen *or* Handel treiben

b (*US, inf*) einkaufen (*at* bei)

ADV to get sth ~ etw zum Großhandelspreis bekommen

▶ **trade in** VT *sep* in Zahlung geben (*for* für)

▶ **trade up** VI **to trade up to a bigger house** sich ein größeres Haus kaufen; **he traded up to a more powerful car** er kaufte sich ein Auto mit mehr Leistung

▶ **trade (up)on** VI +*prep obj* ausnützen

trade: trade agreement N Handelsabkommen *nt*; **trade balance** N Handelsbilanz *f*; **trade barrier** N Handelsschranke *f*; **trade cycle** N (*Brit*) Konjunkturzyklus *m*; **trade deficit** N Handelsdefizit *nt*; **Trade Descriptions Act** N *Gesetz über die korrekte Beschreibung von Waren*; **trade directory** N Branchenverzeichnis *nt*, Firmenverzeichnis *nt*; **trade discount** N Händlerrabatt *m*; **trade disputes** N Arbeitsstreitigkeiten *pl*; **trade fair** N Handelsmesse *f*; **trade figures** PL Handelsziffern *pl*; **trade gap** N Außenhandelsdefizit *nt*; **trade-in** N Altgerät *nt*; (= *car*) in Zahlung gegebenes Auto; **we offer £50 as a** ~ **if you buy a new cooker** beim Kauf eines neuen Herds nehmen wir Ihren alten für £ 50 in Zahlung; **we will take your old car as a** ~ wir nehmen Ihren alten Wagen in Zahlung; **ATTR** ~ **value** Gebrauchtwert *m*; **they don't give very good** ~ **terms** sie bezahlen nicht sehr viel für Altgeräte/Gebrauchtwagen; **trade margin** N Handelsspanne *f*; **trademark** N (*lit*) Warenzeichen *nt*; **honesty was his** ~ er war für seine Ehrlichkeit bekannt; **trade mission** N Handelsreise *f*; **trade name** N Handelsname *m*; **trade-off** N **there's always a** ~ etwas geht immer verloren; **there's bound to be a** ~ **between speed and quality** es gibt entweder Einbußen bei der Schnelligkeit oder bei der Qualität; **trade paper** N Fachzeitschrift *f*, Fachblatt *nt*; **trade press** N Fachpresse *f*; **trade price** N Großhandelspreis *m*

trader ['treɪdə'] N **a** (= *person*) Händler(in) *m(f)* **b** (= *ship*) Handelsschiff *nt*

trade route N Handelsweg *m*, Handelsstraße *f*

tradescantia [ˌtrædə'skæntɪə] N Tradeskantie *f*

trade: trade school N Gewerbe- *or* Berufsschule *f*; **trade secret** N (*lit, fig*) Betriebsgeheimnis *nt*

trades: tradesman N (= *delivery man*) Lieferant *m*; (= *shopkeeper*) Händler *m*, Ladenbesitzer *m*; (= *plumber, electrician etc*) Handwerker *m*; ~**'s entrance** Lieferanteneingang *m*; **tradespeople** PL Geschäftsleute *pl*, Händler *pl*; **trades union** N (*Brit*) = **trade union Trades Union Congress** (britischer) Gewerkschaftsbund; **trades-**

woman N (= *shopkeeper*) Händlerin *f*, Ladenbesitzerin *f*; (= *plumber, electrician etc*) Handwerkerin *f*

trade: trade union N (*Brit*) Gewerkschaft *f*; **trade unionism** N (*Brit*) Gewerkschaftsbewegung *f*; **trade unionist** N (*Brit*) Gewerkschaft(l)er(in) *m(f)*; **trade war** N Handelskrieg *m*; **trade wind** N Passat *m*

trading ['treɪdɪŋ] N Handel *m*, Handeln *nt* (*in* mit); ~ **was brisk at the Stock Exchange today** der Handel an der Börse war heute lebhaft; **there was heavy** ~ **in ...** ... wurde(n) verstärkt gehandelt

trading *in cpds* Handels-; **trading account** N Geschäftskonto *nt*; **trading centre**, (*US*) **trading center** N Handelszentrum *nt*; **trading company** N Handelsgesellschaft *f*; **trading estate** N Industriegelände *nt*; **trading floor** N (*St Ex*) Börsenparkett *nt*; **trading licence**, (*US*) **trading license** N Gewerbeerlaubnis *f*, Gewerbeschein *m*; **trading loss** N Betriebsverlust *m*; **trading partner** N Handelspartner(in) *m(f)*; **trading post** N Laden *m*; **trading profits** PL Geschäfts- *or* Handelsgewinn *m*; **trading results** PL Betriebsergebnis *nt*; **trading stamp** N Rabattmarke *f*

tradition [trə'dɪʃən] N Tradition *f*; **village** ~**s** Dorfbräuche *pl or* -traditionen *pl or* -brauchtum *nt*; **it has become a** ~ **for the chairman to propose the first toast** es ist jetzt so üblich *or* ist zum festen Brauch geworden, dass der Vorsitzende den ersten Toast ausbringt; **according to** ~ **he ...,** ~ **has it that he ...** es ist überliefert, dass er ...; **there is a** ~ **in the village that Queen Mary slept here** im Dorf erzählt man sich, dass Königin Mary dort übernachtet hat; **in the French** ~ in der französischen Tradition; **in the best** ~ **(of ...)** nach bester Tradition (+*gen* ...)

traditional [trə'dɪʃənl] ADJ **a** traditionell; *story, custom also* alt; *virtues also* überkommen; **it's** ~ **for us to spend New Year's Day at my mother's** es ist bei uns so üblich *or* Brauch, dass wir den Neujahrstag bei meiner Mutter verbringen; **in the** ~ **way** auf traditionelle Weise; **the** ~ **way of doing sth** die traditionelle Weise, etw zu tun; **this custom is** ~ **to Somerset** dieser Brauch hat in Somerset Tradition **b** (= *conventional*) **to be** ~ **in one's outlook** eine konservative Auffassung haben

traditionalism [trə'dɪʃnəlɪzəm] N Festhalten *nt* am Alten, Traditionalismus *m*

traditionalist [trə'dɪʃnəlɪst] **N** Traditionalist(in) *m(f)* **ADJ** traditionsgebunden, an Traditionen hängend *or* festhaltend

traditional jazz N Traditional Jazz *m*, Oldtime-Jazz *m*

traditionally [trə'dɪʃnəlɪ] ADV traditionell; (= *customarily*) üblicherweise, normalerweise; **they have** ~ **voted Conservative** sie haben schon immer konservativ gewählt; **it's** ~ **a holiday** es ist schon immer ein Feiertag gewesen; **turkey is** ~ **eaten at Christmas** es ist Tradition *or* ein Brauch, Weihnachten Truthahn zu essen

traditional medicine N Schulmedizin *f*

trad jazz N = **trad**

traduce [trə'djuːs] VT (*liter*) verleumden

traducer [trə'djuːsə'] N (*liter*) Ehrabschneider(in) *m(f)* (*geh*)

traffic ['træfɪk] **N a** Verkehr *m*; (*Aviat*) Flug- *or* Luftverkehr *m*; **a policeman was directing** ~ ein Polizist regelte den Verkehr; ~ **coming into London is advised to avoid Putney Bridge** Fahrern in Richtung Innenstadt London wird empfohlen, Putney Bridge zu meiden

b (= *business: of port, airport*) Umschlag *m*; ~ **in steel** Stahlumschlag *m*; **freight** ~ Frachtumschlag *m*

c (*usu pej*, = *trading*) Handel *m* (*in* mit); (*in pornography*) Vertrieb *m* (*in* von); (*in illegal alcohol*) Schieberei *f* (*in* von)

VI (*usu pej*) handeln (*in* mit); (*in drugs also*) dealen (*inf*) (*in* mit); (*in pornography*) vertreiben (*in +acc*); (*in illegal alcohol*) verschieben (*in acc*)

trafficability [ˌtræfɪkə'bɪlɪtɪ] N (*esp US*) **a** (*Econ*) Marktfähigkeit *f* **b** (*of road*) Passierbarkeit *f*

trafficator ['træfɪkeɪtə'] N (*dated Brit*) (Fahrt-)richtungsanzeiger *m* (*form*)

traffic *in cpds* Verkehrs-; **traffic calming** N Verkehrsberuhigung *f*; **traffic circle** N (*US*) Kreisverkehr *m*; **traffic control tower** N (*Aviat*) Kontrollturm *m*, Tower *m*; **traffic cop** N (*US, inf*) Verkehrspolizist(in) *m(f)*; **traffic court** N (*US, Jur*) Verkehrsgericht *nt*; **traffic diversion** N Umleitung *f*; **traffic duty** N Verkehrsdienst *m*; **to be on** ~ Verkehrsdienst haben; **traffic-guidance system** N Verkehrsleitsystem *nt*; **traffic hold-up** N = **traffic jam**; **traffic indicator** N (*Brit*) (Fahrt)richtungsanzeiger *m* (*form*); (*flashing*) Blinker *m*; **traffic island** N Verkehrsinsel *f*; **traffic jam** N Verkehrsstockung *or* -stauung *f*

trafficker ['træfɪkə'] N (*usu pej*) Händler(in) *m(f)*, Schieber(in) *m(f)* (*pej*); (*in drugs also*) Dealer(in) *m(f)* (*inf*)

trafficking ['træfɪkɪŋ] N Handel *m* (*in* mit); (*in illegal alcohol*) Schieberei *f* (*in* von); (*in pornography*) Vertrieb *m* (*in* von)

traffic: traffic lights PL , (*US*) **traffic light** N Verkehrsampel *f*; **traffic offender** N Verkehrssünder(in) *m(f)*; **traffic planning** N Verkehrsplanung *f*; **traffic police** PL Verkehrspolizei *f*; **traffic policeman** N Verkehrspolizist *m*; **traffic sign** N Verkehrszeichen *nt or* -schild *nt*; **traffic signals** PL = **traffic lights**; **traffic warden** N (*Brit*) ≈ Verkehrspolizist(in) *m(f)* ohne polizeiliche Befugnisse; (*woman*) ≈ Politesse *f*

tragedian [trə'dʒiːdɪən] N (= *writer*) Tragiker *m*, Tragödiendichter *m*; (= *actor*) Tragöde *m* (*geh*), Darsteller *m* tragischer Rollen

tragedienne [trəˌdʒiːdɪ'en] N (= *writer*) Tragikerin *f*, Tragödiendichterin *f*; (= *actress*) Tragödin *f* (*geh*), Darstellerin *f* tragischer Rollen

tragedy ['trædʒɪdɪ] N (= *tragic incident*) Tragödie *f*; (*Theat also*) Trauerspiel *nt*; (*no pl*: = *tragicness*) Tragische(s) *nt*; **he often acts in** ~ er tritt oft in Tragödien auf; **six killed in bus crash** – tragischer Busunfall forderte sechs Todesopfer; **the** ~ **of it is that ...** das Tragische daran ist, dass ...; **it is a** ~ **that ...** es ist (wirklich) tragisch *or* ein Unglück, dass ...

tragic ['trædʒɪk] ADJ tragisch; **the** ~ **and the comic** (*Theat*) das Tragische und das Komische; ~ **actor** Tragöde *m*; ~ **actress** Tragödin *f*

tragically ['trædʒɪkəlɪ] ADV ~, **he was killed** tragischerweise kam er ums Leben; **she was** ~ **unaware of what had happened** tragischerweise wusste sie nicht, was geschehen war; **her career ended** ~ **at the age of 19** ihre Karriere endete tragisch, als sie 19 Jahre alt war; **her husband's** ~ **short life/early death** das tragisch kurze Leben/der tragisch frühe Tod ihres Mannes; **he died** ~ **young** es war tragisch, dass er so jung starb; **the operation went** ~ **wrong** die Operation nahm einen tragischen Verlauf; **don't take it too** ~! nehmen Sie es nicht zu tragisch!

tragicomedy ['trædʒɪ'kɒmɪdɪ] N Tragikomödie *f*

tragicomic ['trædʒɪ'kɒmɪk] ADJ tragikomisch

trail [treɪl] **N a** Spur *f*; (*of meteor*) Schwanz *m*, Schweif *m*; ~ **of blood** Blutspur *f*; ~ **of smoke** Rauchfahne *f*; ~ **of dust** Staubwolke *f*; **the hurricane left a** ~ **of destruction** der Hurrikan hinterließ eine Spur der Verwüstung

b (= *track*) Fährte *f*, Spur *f*; **hot on the** ~ dicht auf den Fersen; **to be on the** ~ **of an animal** die Spur eines Tieres verfolgen; **the police are on his** ~ die Polizei ist ihm auf der Spur

c (= *path*) Weg *m*, Pfad *m*; (= *nature trail etc*) (Wander)weg *m*

d (*Ski, cross-country*) Loipe *f*

VT a (*esp Brit*: = *follow*) *person* folgen (+*dat*), verfolgen; **to** ~ **an animal** ein Tier *or* die Spur eines Tieres verfolgen

b (= *drag*) schleppen, schleifen; **the bird** ~**ed its broken wing** der Vogel zog seinen gebrochenen Flügel nach

c (*US,* = *tow*) ziehen, schleppen **d** *team, rival* zurückliegen hinter (+*dat*); **we are ~ing them by 4 points** wir liegen 4 Punkte hinter ihnen (zurück) **VI a** (*on floor*) schleifen **b** (*plant*) sich ranken; **a house with ivy ~ing round the windows** ein Haus mit efeuumrankten Fenstern **c** (= *walk*) zuckeln, trotten **d** (= *be behind*) (*in competition etc*) weit zurückliegen, hinterherhinken; (*Sport*) weit zurückgefallen sein; **our team is ~ing by 3 points** unsere Mannschaft ist mit 3 Punkten im Rückstand

▶ **trail along VI** entlangzuckeln; **the child trailed along behind his mother** das Kind trottete *or* zuckelte hinter der Mutter her **VT** entlangschleppen *or* -schleifen; **the child trailed his coat along behind him** das Kind schleifte *or* schleppte seinen Mantel hinter sich (*dat*) her

▶ **trail away** *or* **off VI** (*voice*) sich verlieren (*into* in +*dat*), verhallen; **his voice trailed off into silence** er verstummte

▶ **trail behind VI** hinterhertrotten *or* -zuckeln (+*prep obj* hinter +*dat*); (*in competition etc*) zurückgefallen sein (+*prep obj* hinter +*acc*) **VT** *sep* hinter sich (*dat*) herziehen

trailblazer ['treɪlbleɪzə'] N (*fig*) Wegbereiter(in) *m(f)*, Bahnbrecher(in) *m(f)*

trailblazing ['treɪlbleɪzɪŋ] ADJ (*fig*) bahnbrechend

trailer ['treɪlə'] N **a** (*Aut*) Anhänger *m*; (*esp US, of lorry*) Sattelauflieger *m* **b** (*US*) Wohnwagen *m*, Caravan *m* **c** (*Bot*) Hängepflanze *f* **d** (*Film, TV*) Trailer *m*

trailer camp N Platz *m* für Wohnwagen *or* Caravans

trailing ['treɪlɪŋ] ADJ **a** (*Bot*) hängend; **~ plant** Hängepflanze *f* **b** (*Aviat*) **~ edge** Hinterkante *f*, Achterkante *f*

trail mix N *Trockenfrüchte und Nüsse,* ≈ Studentenfutter *nt*

train¹ [treɪn] N **a** (*Rail*) Zug *m*; **to go/travel by ~** mit dem Zug *or* der (Eisen)bahn fahren/reisen; **a ~ journey** eine Bahn- *or* Zugfahrt; **to take** *or* **catch** *or* **get the 11 o'clock ~** den Elfuhrzug nehmen; **to change ~s** umsteigen; **on the ~** im Zug **b** (= *line*) Kolonne *f*; (*of people*) Schlange *f*; (*of camels*) Karawane *f*; (= *retinue*) Gefolge *nt*; **in his ~** in seinem Gefolge; **the war brought famine in its ~** der Krieg brachte eine Hungersnot mit sich; **to set** *or* **put sth in ~** (*esp Brit form*) etw einleiten *or* in Gang setzen; **to be in ~** (*esp Brit form*) im Gang(e) sein **c** (*of events*) Folge *f*, Kette *f*; **he interrupted my ~ of thought** er unterbrach meinen Gedankengang **d** (*of dress*) Schleppe *f* **e** **~ of gunpowder** Pulverspur *f*

train² **VT a** *person* ausbilden; *staff* weiterbilden; *child* erziehen; *animal* abrichten, dressieren; *mind* schulen; (*Sport*) trainieren; **to ~ sb as sth** jdn als *or* zu etw ausbilden; **to ~ oneself to do sth** sich dazu erziehen, etw zu tun; **to ~ sb to be assertive** jdm Bestimmtheit anerziehen; **to ~ an animal to do sth** ein Tier dazu abrichten, etw zu tun; **this dog has been ~ed to kill** dieser Hund ist aufs Töten abgerichtet; **a lion ~ed to do tricks** ein dressierter Löwe, der Kunststücke macht; **she has her husband well ~ed** (*hum*) sie hat ihren Mann gut dressiert (*hum*) **b** (= *aim*) *gun, telescope* richten (*on* auf +*acc*) **c** *plant* wachsen lassen (*over* über +*acc*); **she ~ed her roses along/up the trellis** sie ließ ihre Rosen am Gitter entlang-/hochwachsen **VI a** (*esp Sport*) trainieren (*for* für) **b** (= *study*) ausgebildet werden; **he ~ed as a teacher** er hat eine Lehrerausbildung gemacht, er ist ausgebildeter Lehrer; **where did you ~?** wo haben Sie Ihre Ausbildung erhalten?, wo sind Sie ausgebildet worden?

▶ **train up VT** *sep* (*esp Brit*) heranbilden (*to* zu); *team* trainieren

train: train accident N Zugunglück *nt*, Zugsunglück *nt* (*Aus*); **trainbearer** N Schleppenträger(in) *m(f)*; **train driver** N Zug- *or* Lokführer(in) *m(f)*

trained [treɪnd] ADJ *worker* gelernt; *nurse, teacher* ausgebildet; *animal* dressiert; *dog* abgerichtet, dressiert; *mind, ear* geschult; *eye* geübt, geschult; *voice* ausgebildet; **to be highly/specially ~** hoch qualifiziert/speziell ausgebildet sein; **to be ~ for sth** für etw ausgebildet sein; **a well-trained child** ein gut erzogenes Kind

trainee [treɪ'ni:] N Auszubildende(r) *mf*; (*academic, technical*) Praktikant(in) *m(f)*; (= *nurse*) Krankenpflegeschüler(in) *m(f)*, Schwesternschülerin *f*; (*management*) Trainee *m*; **I am a ~** ich bin *or* ich befinde mich in der Ausbildung

trainee: trainee manager N Managementtrainee *m*; **trainee mechanic** N Schlosserlehrling *m*; **trainee nurse** N Krankenpflegeschüler(in) *m(f)*, Schwesternschülerin *f*; **trainee teacher** N (*in primary school*) ≈ Praktikant(in) *m(f)*; (*in secondary school*) ≈ Referendar(in) *m(f)*

trainer ['treɪnə'] N **a** (*Sport, of racehorse*) Trainer(in) *m(f)*; (*of animals*) Dresseur(in) *m(f)*; (*in circus*) Dompteur *m*, Dompteuse *f* **b** (*Brit:* = *shoe*) Turnschuh *m*

trainer plane N (*Aviat*) Schulflugzeug *nt*

train ferry N Eisenbahnfähre *f*

training ['treɪnɪŋ] N **a** Ausbildung *f* (*also Mil*); (*of staff*) Schulung *f*; (*of animal*) Dressur *f*, Abrichten *nt*; **it's good ~ for the mind** es ist eine gute Denkschulung **b** (*Sport*) Training *nt*; **to be in ~** im Training stehen *or* sein, trainieren; (= *be fit*) gut in Form sein, fit *or* durchtrainiert sein; **to be out of ~** nicht in Form sein, aus dem Training sein; **to go into ~** das Training beginnen, anfangen zu trainieren

training: Training and Enterprise Council N (*Brit*) *staatliches Programm zur Förderung der Zusammenarbeit zwischen Berufsschulen und Unternehmen;* **training area** N (*Mil*) Truppenübungsplatz *m*; **training camp** N Trainingslager *nt*; **training centre**, (*US*) **training center** N Lehr- *or* Ausbildungszentrum *nt*; **training college** N (*for teachers*) pädagogische Hochschule; **training course** N Ausbildungskurs *m*; **training ground** N (*Sport, fig*) Trainingsgelände *nt*; **training injury** N (*Med, Sport*) Trainingsverletzung *f*; **training manual** N Lehrbuch *nt*; **Training Opportunities Scheme** N (*Brit*) *Umschulungsprogramm für Arbeitnehmer;* **training period** N Ausbildungsdauer *f*; **training plane** N Schulflugzeug *nt*; **training scheme** N Ausbildungsprogramm *nt*; **training session** N (*Sport*) Trainingseinheit *f*; **training ship** N Schulschiff *nt*; **training shoes** PL (*Brit*) Turnschuhe *pl*

train: trainload N (*of goods*) Zugladung *f*; **~s of holidaymakers** (*Brit*) *or* **vacationers** (*US*) ganze Züge voller Urlauber; **soldiers were sent there by the ~** ganze Zugladungen Soldaten wurden hingeschickt; **trainman** N (*US*) Eisenbahner *m*; (= *brakeman*) Bremser *m*; **train oil** N Tran *m*; **train service** N Zugverkehr *m*; (*between two places*) (Eisen)bahnverbindung *f*; **train set** N (Spielzeug)eisenbahn *f*; **trainsick** ADJ **he gets ~** ihm wird beim Zugfahren schlecht *or* übel; **trainsickness** N **I've never suffered from ~** mir ist beim Zugfahren noch nie schlecht *or* übel geworden; **train spotter** N Eisenbahnfan *m*; (*Brit pej inf:* = *nerd*) Schwachkopf *m* (*inf*); **trainspotting** N *Hobby, bei dem Züge begutachtet und deren Nummern notiert werden;* **train surfing** N S-Bahn-Surfen *nt*

traipse [treɪps] (*inf*) **VI** latschen (*inf*); **to ~ (a)round the shops** in den Geschäften rumlatschen (*inf*); **to ~ (a)round the shops for sth** die Geschäfte nach etw abklappern (*inf*) **N** **it's a long ~** da muss man lange latschen (*inf*)

trait [treɪt, treɪ] N Eigenschaft *f*; (*of particular person also*) Charakter- *or* Wesenszug *m*

traitor ['treɪtə'] N Verräter(in) *m(f)*; **to be a ~ to one's country** sein Vaterland verraten; **to turn ~** zum Verräter werden

traitorous ['treɪtərəs] ADJ *behaviour, action* verräterisch; *coward also* treulos

traitorously ['treɪtərəslɪ] ADV in verräterischer Weise

traitress ['treɪtrɪs] N Verräterin *f*

trajectory [trə'dʒektərɪ] N Flugbahn *f*

tram [træm] N **a** (*esp Brit*) Straßenbahn *f*, Tram(bahn) *f* (*S Ger, Sw, Aus*); **Blackpool still has ~s** in Blackpool gibt es noch Straßenbahnen; **to go by ~** mit der Straßenbahn fahren; **I saw her on a ~** ich habe sie in einer Straßenbahn gesehen **b** (*Min*) Grubenbahn *f*

tram: tramcar N (*esp Brit*) Straßenbahn *f*; (= *single car*) Straßenbahnwagen *m*; **tram driver** N (*esp Brit*) Straßenbahnfahrer(in) *m(f)*; **tramline** N (*esp Brit*) (= *track*) Straßenbahnschiene *f*; (= *route*) Straßenbahnlinie *f*; **~s** (*Tennis*) Linien *pl* des Doppelspielfelds

trammel ['træməl] **VT** einengen; **to feel ~led by sth** sich durch etw behindert *or* eingeengt fühlen **N** **trammels** PL Fesseln *pl*

tramp [træmp] N **a** (= *walk heavily, trudge*) stapfen, mit schweren Schritten gehen, stampfen; **the soldiers ~ed along for hours** die Soldaten marschierten stundenlang (mit schweren Schritten); **I've been ~ing (a)round town all day** ich bin den ganzen Tag in der Stadt herumgestiefelt (*inf*); **to ~ up and down the platform** auf dem Bahnsteig auf und ab marschieren **b** (= *hike*) marschieren, wandern; (*vagabond*) umherziehen; **he ~ed all over Europe** er wanderte in ganz Europa umher **VT a** (= *spread by walking*) herumtreten; **don't ~ that mud into the carpet** tritt den Dreck nicht in den Teppich **b** (= *walk*) *streets* latschen durch (*inf*) **N a** (= *vagabond*) Landstreicher(in) *m(f)*, Tramp *m*; (*in town*) Stadtstreicher(in) *m(f)* **b** (= *sound*) Stapfen *nt*, schwere Schritte *pl* **c** (= *walk*) Wanderung *f*; **it's a long ~** es ist ein weiter Weg **d** (*Naut*) Trampdampfer *m* **e** (*inf,* = *loose woman*) Flittchen *nt* (*pej*)

▶ **tramp down VT** *sep* feststampfen, festtreten; *corn, flowers etc* platt treten, niedertrampeln

▶ **tramp in VT** *sep* festtreten, in den Boden treten

trample ['træmpl] **VT** niedertrampeln, niedertreten, zertrampeln; **to ~ sth underfoot** (*lit, fig*) auf etw (*dat*) herumtrampeln; **she ~s her husband underfoot** (*fig*) ihr Mann hat bei ihr nichts zu sagen (*inf*); **he was ~d to death by a bull** er wurde von einem Bullen zu Tode getrampelt; **to ~ sth into the ground** etw in den Boden treten *or* trampeln **N** stapfen, trampeln; **he lets his wife ~ all over him** (*fig*) er lässt sich (*dat*) von seiner Frau auf dem Kopf herumtanzen **N** Getrampel *nt*, Trampeln *nt*

▶ **trample about** (*Brit*) *or* **around VI** herumtrampeln

▶ **trample down VT** *sep* heruntertreten, niedertreten

▶ **trample on VI** +*prep obj* herumtreten auf (+*dat*); **several children were trampled on** mehrere Kinder wurden getreten; **to trample on sb** (*fig*) jdn herumschikanieren; **to trample on sb's feelings** (*fig*) auf jds Gefühlen herumtrampeln, jds Gefühle mit Füßen treten

trampoline ['træmpəlɪn] N Trampolin *nt*

tramp steamer N Trampdampfer *m*

tram: tramride N (*esp Brit*) Straßenbahnfahrt *f*; **tramway** N (*esp Brit*) Straßenbahn *f*; (= *route*) Straßenbahnstrecke *f*

trance [trɑːns] N Trance *f*; (*Med*) tiefe Bewusstlosigkeit *f*; **to go into a ~** in Trance verfallen; **to put sb into a ~** jdn in Trance versetzen; **she's been going about in a ~ for the past few days** die letzten paar Tage ist sie wie in Trance *or* im Tran (*inf*) durch die Gegend gelaufen

tranche [trɑːnʃ] N (*of shares, cash*) Tranche *f*

tranny ['trænɪ] N **a** (Brit, inf) Transistor m (inf), Kofferradio nt **b** (inf: = transvestite) Transvestit m

tranquil ['træŋkwɪl] ADJ ruhig, friedlich, still; life friedlich, ohne Aufregung; mind, appearance ruhig, gelassen; music ruhig, sanft; person gelassen, ausgeglichen

tranquillity, (US) **tranquility** [træŋ'kwɪlɪtɪ] N Ruhe f, Friedlichkeit f, Stille f; (of life) Friede m; (of mind) Gelassenheit f; (of music) Sanftheit f; (of person) Gelassenheit f, Ausgeglichenheit f; **the ~ of the home** die friedliche Atmosphäre des Hauses; **he was soothed by the ~ of the music** die sanfte Musik beruhigte ihn

tranquillize, (US) **tranquilize** ['træŋkwɪlaɪz] VT beruhigen

tranquillizer, (US) **tranquilizer** ['træŋkwɪlaɪzə'] N Beruhigungstablette f, Beruhigungsmittel nt

tranquillizing dart, (US) **tranquilizer dart** Betäubungspfeil m

tranquillizing dart ['træŋkwɪlaɪzɪŋˈdɑːt] N Betäubungspfeil m

tranquilly ['træŋkwɪlɪ] ADV say, gaze gelassen; rest, sleep ruhig

trans- [trænz-] PREF trans-, Trans-

transact [træn'zækt] VT abwickeln; business also abschließen, durchführen; deal abschließen

transaction [træn'zækʃən] N **a** (= act) Abwicklung f; (= deal) Abschluss m; **~ of business** Geschäftsbetrieb m; **the bank will be closed for the ~ of business at 3 p.m.** die Bank hat or ist ab 15.00 Uhr geschlossen **b** (= piece of business) Geschäft nt; (Fin, St Ex) Transaktion f **c transactions** PL (of society) Sitzungsbericht m

transalpine ['trænz'ælpaɪn] ADJ transalpin

transatlantic ['trænsət'læntɪk] ADJ transatlantisch, Transatlantik-; customs auf der anderen Seite (des Atlantiks); cousins, fashion, accent etc (= American) amerikanisch; (= British) britisch; **~ flight** Transatlantikflug m; **a ~ phone call** ein Anruf m aus/nach Übersee

transceiver [træn'siːvə'] N Sender-Empfänger m, Sende-Empfangsgerät nt

transcend [træn'send] VT übersteigen, überschreiten, hinausgehen über (+acc); (Philos) transzendieren

transcendence [træn'sendəns], **transcendency** [træn'sendənsɪ] N Erhabenheit f; (Philos) Transzendenz f

transcendent [træn'sendənt] ADJ (Philos) transzendent; (= supreme) hervorragend, alles übersteigend, überragend

transcendental [ˌtrænsen'dentl] ADJ überirdisch; (Philos) transzendental; vision transzendierend; **~ meditation** transzendentale Meditation; **~ number** (Math) transzendente Zahl, Transzendente f

transcendentalism [ˌtrænsen'dentəlɪzəm] N transzendentale Philosophie, Transzendentalismus m

transcontinental ['trænz,kɒntɪ'nentl] ADJ transkontinental

transcribe [træn'skraɪb] VT manuscripts abschreiben, transkribieren; (from shorthand) (in Langschrift) übertragen; speech, proceedings, interview etc niederschreiben, mitschreiben; (Mus) transkribieren; **to ~ sth phonetically** etw in phonetische (Um)schrift übertragen

transcript ['trænskrɪpt] N **a** (of court proceedings) Protokoll nt; (of tapes) Niederschrift f; (= copy) Kopie f, Abschrift f **b** (US, = academic record) Abschrift f (Studienunterlagen)

transcription [træn'skrɪpʃən] N (Mus, Phon) Transkription f; (= copy, of shorthand notes) Abschrift f; (= act) Abschrift f, Abschreiben nt; (of speech, proceedings) Niederschrift f, Protokoll nt; (Rad, TV, = recording) Aufnahme f; **phonetic ~** Lautschrift f, phonetische (Um)schrift

transducer [ˌtrænz'djuːsə'] N Umformer m, Umwandler m

transept ['trænsept] N Querschiff nt, Transept nt (spec)

trans-European ['trænsˌjʊərə'piːən] ADJ trans-europäisch; journey quer durch Europa

transfer [træns'fɜː'] VT (= move) übertragen (to auf +acc); prisoner überführen (to in +acc), verlegen (to nach); premises, soldiers verlegen (to in +acc, to town nach); soldier, employee versetzen (to in +acc, to town, country nach); (Sport) player transferieren (to zu), abgeben (to an +acc); (Fin) funds, money überweisen (to auf +acc), transferieren (to nach); account verlegen; stocks transferieren (to nach); (Jur) property übertragen, überschreiben (to über +acc); right übertragen (to auf +acc); **he ~red the bigger engine into his old car** er baute den größeren Motor in sein altes Auto ein; **to ~ one's concentration from one task to another** seine Konzentration von einer Aufgabe auf eine andere umstellen; **he ~red his capital into gold shares** er investierte sein Kapital in Goldaktien, er legte sein Kapital in Goldaktien an; **he ~red the money from the box to his pocket** er nahm das Geld aus der Schachtel und steckte es in die Tasche; **the magician had somehow ~red the rabbit from the hat to the box** der Zauberer hatte das Kaninchen irgendwie aus dem Hut in die Kiste praktiziert; **she ~red her affections to another man** sie schenkte ihre Zuneigung einem anderen; **~red charge call** (Brit, Telec) R-Gespräch nt

VI **a** (= move) überwechseln (to zu); (to new system, working conditions) umstellen (to auf +acc); **he can easily ~ from one language to another** er kann leicht von einer Sprache auf eine andere überwechseln or umschalten

b (Fin) umsteigen (into auf +acc); **just before the crash he ~red into government bonds** gerade rechtzeitig vor dem Zusammenbruch stieg er auf Regierungsanleihen um

c (in travelling) umsteigen (to in +acc); (Univ) das Studienfach wechseln, umsatteln (inf) (from ... to ... auf +acc)

N ['trænsfɜː'] **a** (= act) Übertragung f; (of prisoner) Überführung f; (of premises, troops) Verlegung f; (of employee) Versetzung f; (Sport: of player) Transfer m, Wechsel m; (Fin: of funds, money) Überweisung f; (of account) Verlegung f; (of stocks) Transfer m; (Jur, of property) Überschreibung f; (of right) Übertragung f; **he asked for a ~** (soldier, employee) er bat um Versetzung; (footballer) er bat, auf die Transferliste gesetzt zu werden **b** (= person transferred) **he's a ~ from another regiment** er ist von einem anderen Regiment hierher versetzt or verlegt worden; **he's a ~ from Chelsea** er ist von Chelsea hierher gewechselt; **Chelsea's latest ~** Chelseas jüngste Neuerwerbung

c (= picture) Abziehbild nt

d (in travelling) Umsteigen nt

e (= transfer ticket) Umsteige(fahr)karte f

transferable [træns'fɜːrəbl] ADJ übertragbar; money, stocks transferierbar; **"not ~"** „nicht übertragbar"; **the ticket/prize is not ~** die Fahrkarte/der Preis ist nicht übertragbar

transfer desk N (Aviat) Transitschalter m

transference ['trænsfərəns] N **a** (Psych) Übertragung f **b** (Jur: of holdings, real estate) Übertragung f, Überschreibung f (to sb auf jdn); (Fin: of money) Transfer m

transfer: transfer fee N (Ftbl) Transfersumme f; **transfer list** N (Ftbl) Transferliste f; **transfer lounge** N (Aviat) Transitraum m; **transfer passenger** N (esp Aviat) Transitreisende(r) mf; **transfer payments** N (staatliche) Unterstützungszahlungen pl; **transfer picture** N Abziehbild nt; **transfer rate**, **transfer speed** N (Comput: of data) Übertragungsgeschwindigkeit f; **transfer ticket** N Umsteige(fahr)karte f

transfiguration [ˌtrænsfɪgəˈreɪʃən] N **a** Verklärtheit f; (= transformation) Wandel m, Wandlung f **b** (Rel) **Transfiguration** Verklärung f Jesu, Transfiguration f

transfigure [træns'fɪgə'] VT verklären; (= transform) verwandeln

transfix [træns'fɪks] VT **a** (= fix) annageln, feststecken (to an +acc); butterflies aufspießen **b** (fig) **to be** or **stand ~ed with horror** starr vor

Entsetzen sein; **he stood as though ~ed (to the ground)** er stand da wie angewurzelt

transform [træns'fɔːm] VT umwandeln, umformen, umgestalten (into zu); ideas, views (von Grund auf) verändern; person, life, country, caterpillar verwandeln; (Phys) umwandeln, verwandeln (into in +acc); (Elec) (um)wandeln, umformen (into in +acc), transformieren (into in +acc); **the old house was ~ed into three luxury apartments** das alte Haus wurde in drei Luxuswohnungen umgebaut; **when she came out of the hairdresser's she was ~ed** als sie aus dem Friseursalon kam, sah sie wie umgewandelt aus; **a coat of paint ~ed the dull old room** ein Anstrich ließ den langweiligen alten Raum in neuem Glanz erstrahlen

transformation [ˌtrænsfə'meɪʃən] N Umwandlung f, Umformung f; (of ideas, views etc) (grundlegende) Veränderung f; (of person, caterpillar etc) Verwandlung f; (Phys, Elec) Umwandlung f; (Ling) Umformung f, Transformation f; **~ scene** (Theat) Verwandlungsszene f

transformational [ˌtrænsfə'meɪʃənl] ADJ (Ling) Transformations-; **~ grammar** Transformationsgrammatik f

transformer [træns'fɔːmə'] N (Elec) Transformator m

transfuse [træns'fjuːz] VT (Med) blood übertragen; (fig) erfüllen, durchdringen

transfusion [træns'fjuːʒən] N **a** (also **blood transfusion**) Blutübertragung f, (Blut)transfusion f; **to give sb a ~** jdm eine Blutübertragung or (Blut)transfusion geben; (**blood**) **~ service** Blutspendedienst m **b** (fig) **a ~ of public money** eine Finanzspritze aus öffentlichen Geldern für ...; **it was like a ~ of new life into their friendship** es war, als ob ihre Freundschaft von neuem Leben durchdrungen or erfüllt würde

transgress [træns'gres] VT standards verstoßen gegen, verletzen; law also überschreiten VI sündigen; **to ~ against the Lord** gegen Gottes Gebote sündigen or verstoßen

transgression [træns'greʃən] N **a** (of law) Verstoß m, Verletzung f, Überschreitung f **b** (= sin) Sünde f, Verstoß m

transgressor [træns'gresə'] N Übeltäter(in) m(f), Missetäter(in) m(f); (= sinner) Sünder(in) m(f)

tranship [træn'ʃɪp] VT umladen, umschlagen

transhipment [træn'ʃɪpmənt] N Umladung f

transhumance [træns'hjuːməns] N (Agr) Transhumanz f

transience ['trænzɪəns], **transiency** ['trænzɪənsɪ] N (of life) Kürze f, Vergänglichkeit f; (of grief, joy) Kurzlebigkeit f, Vergänglichkeit f; (of interest) Kurzlebigkeit f, Flüchtigkeit f

transient ['trænzɪənt] ADJ **a** life kurz; grief, joy, pleasure kurzlebig, vergänglich, vorübergehend; interest kurzlebig, flüchtig, vorübergehend; **the ~ nature of sth** die Kurzlebigkeit von etw **b** (US) **~ population** nicht ansässiger or nicht ansässiger Teil der Bevölkerung eines Ortes N (US) Durchreisende(r) mf

transistor [træn'zɪstə'] N **a** (Elec) Transistor m **b** (also **transistor radio**) Transistorradio nt, Kofferradio nt, Transistor m (inf)

transistorize [træn'zɪstəraɪz] VT transistorisieren, transistorieren; **~d** transistorisiert

transit ['trænzɪt] N Durchfahrt f, Transit m; (of goods) Transport m; **the books were damaged in ~** die Bücher wurden auf dem Transport beschädigt; **passengers in ~ for New York** Transitreisende pl nach New York; **goods in ~ for New York** Güter pl für den Weitertransport nach New York; **they are stationed here in ~** sie sind hier zwischendurch stationiert

transit: transit camp N Durchgangslager nt; **transit desk** N Transitschalter m; **transit freight** N Transitfracht f

transition [træn'zɪʃən] N Übergang m (from ... to von ... zu); (of weather) Wechsel m, Umschwung m; (Mus, = act) Übergang m; (= passage) Überleitung f; **period of ~, ~ period** Übergangsperiode or -zeit f; **~ stage** Übergangsstadium nt

transitional [trænˈzɪʃənl] ADJ Übergangs-; (= provisional) arrangements, costs vorläufig; **~ government** Übergangsregierung f; **~ relief** vorrübergehende Entlastung

transition element N (Chem) Übergangselement nt

transitive [ˈtrænzɪtɪv] ADJ transitiv; **~ verb** transitives Verb, Handlungsverb nt, Transitiv(um) nt

transitively [ˈtrænzɪtɪvlɪ] ADV transitiv

transitivity [ˌtrænzɪˈtɪvɪtɪ] N transitive Eigenschaft or Funktion

transit lounge N Warteraum m, Transitraum m

transitory [ˈtrænzɪtərɪ] ADJ life kurz; grief, joy kurzlebig, vergänglich, vorübergehend; interest kurzlebig, flüchtig; **~ period** Übergangsperiode f; **the ~ nature of sth** die Kurzlebigkeit von etw

transit: transit passenger N Durchgangsreisende(r) mf, Transitreisende(r) mf; **Transit (van)**® N (Brit) Lieferwagen m, Transporter m; **transit visa** N Durchreisevisum nt, Transitvisum nt

translatable [trænzˈleɪtəbl] ADJ übersetzbar

translate [trænzˈleɪt] **VT** **a** (lit) text, novel übersetzen; **to ~ a text from German (in)to English** einen Text aus dem Deutschen ins Englische übersetzen; **it is ~d as ...** es wird mit ... übersetzt
b (fig) übertragen; **to ~ feelings into action** Gefühle in die Tat umsetzen; **to ~ a novel into a film** aus einem Roman einen Film machen; **could you ~ that into cash terms?** lässt sich das geldmäßig ausdrücken?
c (Eccl) bishop in eine andere Diözese berufen; (Rel, to heaven) aufnehmen
d (rare, = transfer) übertragen; person versetzen
VI **a** (lit) übersetzen; **it ~s well (into English)** es lässt sich gut (ins Englische) übersetzen or übertragen
b (fig) übertragbar sein; **the novel didn't ~ easily into screen terms** es war nicht einfach, aus dem Roman einen Film zu machen; **how does that ~ into cash?** was kommt geldmäßig dabei heraus?

translation [trænzˈleɪʃən] N **a** (= act, translated work) Übersetzung f (from aus); (of work of literature also, fig) Übertragung f; **to do a ~ of sth** von etw eine Übersetzung machen or anfertigen; **errors in ~** Übersetzungsfehler pl; **it loses (something) in ~** es verliert (etwas) bei der Übersetzung; **a ~ problem** ein Übersetzungsproblem nt; **he is not good at ~** er kann nicht gut übersetzen; **~ table** (Comput) Umsetzungs- or Übersetzungstabelle f **b** (Eccl) Berufung f in eine andere Diözese; (to heaven) Himmelfahrt f

translator [trænzˈleɪtə'] N Übersetzer(in) m(f)

transliterate [trænzˈlɪtəreɪt] VT transliterieren

transliteration [ˌtrænzlɪtəˈreɪʃən] N Transliteration f

translucence [trænzˈluːsns], **translucency** [trænzˈluːsnsɪ] N Lichtdurchlässigkeit f, Durchsichtigkeit f

translucent [trænzˈluːsnt], **translucid** [trænzˈluːsɪd] ADJ glass etc lichtdurchlässig; skin durchsichtig; **~ glass** Milchglas nt; **a prose of ~ clarity** eine Prosa von brillanter Klarheit

transmigrate [ˌtrænzmaɪˈgreɪt] VI (Rel) wieder geboren werden

transmigration [ˌtrænzmaɪˈgreɪʃən] N (Rel) (Seelen)wanderung f, Transmigration f (spec); **the ~ of souls** die Seelenwanderung; **the ~ of a human soul into an animal body** die Wiedergeburt einer menschlichen Seele in einem Tierleib

transmissible [trænzˈmɪsəbl] ADJ übertragbar

transmission [trænzˈmɪʃən] N **a** (= transmitting) Übertragung f; (through heredity) Vererbung f; (of news) Übermittlung f; (of heat) Leitung f; (= programme) Sendung f **b** (Aut) Getriebe nt

transmission: transmission belt N (Tech) Treibriemen f; **transmission error** N (Comput) Übertragungsfehler m; **transmission gear** N (Tech) Wechselgetriebe nt; **transmission shaft** N Kardanwelle f

transmit [trænzˈmɪt] **VT** (= convey) message übermitteln; sound waves übertragen; information, knowledge vermitteln, übermitteln; illness übertragen; (by heredity) vererben; heat etc leiten; radio/TV programme, picture übertragen, senden **VI** senden; Programme pl ausstrahlen

transmitter [trænzˈmɪtə'] N (Tech) Sender m; (in telephone) Mikrofon nt, Mikrophon nt

transmitting [trænzˈmɪtɪŋ]: **transmitting set** N Sender m; **transmitting station** N (of broadcasting company) Sendestation f; (general) Sendestelle f

transmogrification [ˌtrænzmɒgrɪfɪˈkeɪʃən] N (hum) wunderbare Wandlung (hum)

transmogrify [trænzˈmɒgrɪfaɪ] VT (hum) auf wunderbare Weise verwandeln or umwandeln (hum)

transmutable [trænzˈmjuːtəbl] ADJ verwandelbar

transmutation [ˌtrænzmjuːˈteɪʃən] N Verwandlung f, Umwandlung f; (Biol) Umbildung f, Transmutation f

transmute [trænzˈmjuːt] VT umwandeln, verwandeln (into in +acc); metal verwandeln (into in +acc)

transoceanic [ˌtrænzəʊʃɪˈænɪk] ADJ travel nach Übersee; countries überseeisch; migration über den Ozean

transom [ˈtrænsəm] N (= transom window) Oberlicht nt; (= cross-piece) Querbalken m

transpacific [ˌtrænzpəˈsɪfɪk] ADJ über den Pazifik; countries jenseits des Pazifik

transparency [trænsˈpærənsɪ] N **a** Transparenz f, Durchsichtigkeit f **b** (of lies, excuses etc) Durchschaubarkeit f **c** (of system, institution) Transparenz f **d** (Phot) Dia(positiv) nt; **colour** (Brit) or **color** (US) **~** Farbdia nt

transparent [trænsˈpærənt] ADJ **a** durchsichtig, lichtdurchlässig, transparent; blouse durchsichtig; **to be ~ to light** lichtdurchlässig sein **b** (fig: = obvious) lie, intentions durchschaubar, durchsichtig; personality durchschaubar; guilt, meaning klar, eindeutig, offensichtlich; **it became ~ that ...** es wurde offensichtlich, dass ...; **you're so ~** du bist so leicht zu durchschauen; **to be ~ to sb** für jdn leicht durchschaubar sein **c** (= open) system, institution transparent

transparently [trænsˈpærəntlɪ] ADV **a** (= blatantly) lie durchschaubar, offensichtlich, offenkundig; **it was ~ obvious that ...** es war ganz offensichtlich or ganz klar zu erkennen, dass ...; **it had been organized, pretty ~, as a public relations exercise** es war ganz unverhohlen zu Werbezwecken veranstaltet worden **b** (= unambiguously) offensichtlich, offenkundig; **he had been ~ honest with her about his intentions** er hatte ihr seine Absichten ganz offen dargelegt

transpiration [ˌtrænspɪˈreɪʃən] N (Anat) Schweißabsonderung f, Transpiration f; (Bot) Transpiration f, Ausdunstung f

transpire [trænsˈpaɪə'] **VI** **a** (= become clear) sich herausstellen; (slowly) durchsickern **b** (= happen) passieren (inf) **c** (Anat) schwitzen, transpirieren (geh) **d** (Bot) Feuchtigkeit abgeben or verdunsten, transpirieren (spec) **VT** (Bot) moisture verdunsten, abgeben

transplant [trænsˈplɑːnt] **VT** **a** (Hort) umpflanzen, umsetzen, verpflanzen **b** (Med) verpflanzen, transplantieren (spec) **c** (fig) people verpflanzen; **his wealth ~ed him into a new world** sein Reichtum versetzte ihn in eine neue Welt **N** [ˈtrænsplɑːnt] (= operation) Verpflanzung f, Transplantation f; (= organ) Transplantat nt, transplantiertes or verpflanztes Organ; **to have a ~** sich einer Organverpflanzung unterziehen

transplantation [ˌtrænsplɑːnˈteɪʃən] N (Hort) Umpflanzung f, Verpflanzung f; (Med) Transplantation f, Verpflanzung f

transpolar [trænsˈpəʊlə'] ADJ über den (Nord-/Süd)pol or das Polargebiet; **the ~ route** die Polroute

transponder [trænsˈpɒndə'] N (Tech) Transponder m, Antwortsender m

transport [ˈtrænspɔːt] **N** **a** (of goods) Transport m, Beförderung f; (of troops) Transport m; **road ~** Straßentransport m or Transport m per Straße, Beförderung f or Transport m per Bahn, (Eisen)bahntransport m; **Ministry of Transport** (Brit) Verkehrsministerium nt
b (= vehicle) have you got your own **~?** hast du einen fahrbaren Untersatz? (inf), bist du motorisiert?; **public ~** öffentliche Verkehrsmittel pl; **what are we going to do about ~?** wie lösen wir die Transportfrage?; **~ will be provided** für An- und Abfahrt wird gesorgt
c (Mil, = ship) (Truppen)transporter m; (= plane) Transportflugzeug nt
d (US, = shipment) (Schiffs)fracht f, Ladung f
e (liter) **~(s) of delight** freudige Entzückung or (Rel) Entrückung (liter); **it sent her into ~s of delight** es erfüllte sie mit freudigem Entzücken (liter)
VT [trænˈspɔːt] **a** goods befördern, transportieren; people befördern
b (Hist) convict deportieren
c (liter) **to be ~ed by joy** freudig entzückt sein (liter)

transportable [trænˈspɔːtəbl] ADJ transportabel, transportierbar

transportation [ˌtrænspɔːˈteɪʃən] N **a** Beförderung f, Transport m; (= means) Beförderungsmittel nt; (public) Verkehrsmittel nt; (= cost) Transport- or Beförderungskosten pl; **Department of Transportation** (US) Verkehrsministerium nt **b** (Hist, of criminal) Deportation f

transport café N (Brit) Fernfahrerlokal nt

transporter [trænˈspɔːtə'] N (Brit: = car transporter) Transporter m; (= transporter crane) Verladebrücke f; (in factory) Transportband nt

transport: transport line N (in factory) Transportband nt; **transport plane** N Transportflugzeug nt; **transport ship** N (Truppen-)transporter m; **transport system** N Verkehrswesen nt

transpose [trænsˈpəʊz] VT (= move) übertragen; (= switch round) vertauschen, umstellen; (Mus) transponieren

transposition [ˌtrænspəˈzɪʃən] N Umstellung f, Vertauschung f; (Mus) Transponierung f

transputer [trænsˈpjuːtə'] N (Comput) Transputer m

transsexual [trænsˈseksjʊəl] N Transsexuelle(r) mf

transship [trænsˈʃɪp] VT = **tranship**

transshipment [trænsˈʃɪpmənt] N = **transhipment**

transubstantiate [ˌtrænsəbˈstænʃɪeɪt] VT (Rel) verwandeln

transubstantiation [ˈtrænsəbˌstænʃɪˈeɪʃən] N (Rel) Wandlung f, Transsubstantiation f (spec)

transverse [ˈtrænzvɜːs] ADJ Quer-; muscles transversal; position horizontal; engine quer stehend; **~ beam** Querbalken m; **~ section** Querschnitt m

transversely [trænzˈvɜːslɪ] ADV quer; divided diagonal

transvestism [trænzˈvestɪzəm] N Transves(ti)tismus m

transvestite [trænzˈvestaɪt] N Transvestit(in) m(f)

trap [træp] **N** **a** (for animal, fig) Falle f; **to set or lay a ~ for an animal** eine Falle für ein Tier (auf)stellen; **to set a ~ for sb** (fig) jdm eine Falle stellen; **be careful of this question, there is a ~ in it** pass bei dieser Frage auf, da ist ein Haken dabei; **to be caught in a ~** (lit, fig) in der Falle sitzen; **the lawyer had caught him in a ~** er war dem Rechtsanwalt in die Falle gegangen; **to fall into a ~** in die Falle gehen; **to fall into the ~ of doing sth** den Fehler begehen, etw zu tun

b (*in greyhound racing*) Box *f*; (*Shooting*) Wurftaubenanlage *f*, Wurfmaschine *f*

c (*in drainpipe*) Siphon *m*, Geruchsverschluss *m*

d (*Brit*: = *vehicle*) zweirädriger Pferdewagen

e (*also* **trap door**) Falltür *f*; (*Theat*) Versenkung *f*

f (*inf*, = *mouth*) Klappe *f* (*inf*), Fresse *f* (*vulg*), Schnauze *f* (*inf*); **shut your ~!** (halt die) Klappe! (*inf*), halt die Fresse (*vulg*) *or* Schnauze (*inf*)!; **keep your ~ shut about this** darüber hältst du aber die Klappe (*inf*), halt ja die Schnauze! (*inf*)

VT a *animal* (mit einer Falle) fangen

b (*fig*) *person* in die Falle locken; **he realized he was ~ped** er merkte, dass er in der Falle saß; **to ~ sb into saying sth** jdn dazu bringen, etw zu sagen; **I was ~ped into saying I would organize the party** ich hatte mich darauf eingelassen, die Party zu organisieren; **she ~ped him into marriage** sie hat ihn geködert (*inf*), sie hat ihn ins Netz gelockt

c (= *block off, leave no way of escape*) in die Enge treiben; **the miners are ~ped** die Bergleute sind eingeschlossen; **the ship was ~ped in the port by the storm** das Schiff saß wegen des Sturms im Hafen fest; **to be ~ped in the snow** im Schnee festsitzen; **the soldiers found themselves ~ped at the end of the gully** am Ende des Hohlweges stellten die Soldaten fest, dass sie in der Falle saßen; **he feels ~ped in his marriage** er fühlt sich in seiner Ehe als Gefangener; **I get this ~ped feeling** ich fühle mich wie gefangen *or* im Gefängnis *or* eingeschlossen; **my arm was ~ped behind my back** mein Arm war hinter meinem Rücken eingeklemmt

d (= *catch*) *ball* stoppen; **to ~ one's finger/one's foot in the door** sich (*dat*) den Finger/Fuß in der Tür einklemmen; **to ~ a nerve** sich (*dat*) einen Nerv (ein)klemmen

e *gas, liquid* stauen; **pools of water lay ~ped among the rocks as the tide receded** als die Flut zurückging, blieben Wasserpfützen zwischen den Felsen zurück

VI (*trapper*) Trapper sein

trap door N Falltür *f*; (*Theat*) Versenkung *f*

trapeze [trəˈpiːz] N (*in circus*) Trapez *nt*

trapeze artist N Trapezkünstler(in) *m(f)*

trapezium [trəˈpiːzɪəm] N (*Brit*) Trapez *nt*; (*US*) Trapezoid *nt*

trapezoid [ˈtræpɪzɔɪd] N (*Brit*) Trapezoid *nt*; (*US*) Trapez *nt*

trapper [ˈtræpəʳ] N Fallensteller(in) *m(f)*, Trapper(in) *m(f)*

trappings [ˈtræpɪŋz] PL **a** (*of admiral, chieftain etc*) Rangabzeichen *pl*; (*of horse*) Schmuck *m* **b** (*fig*) äußere Aufmachung, äußeres Drum und Dran (*inf*); **~ of office** Amtsinsignien *pl*; **shorn of all its ~** aller Ausschmückungen entkleidet; **he surrounded himself with all the ~ of power** er umgab sich mit allen Insignien der Macht

Trappist [ˈtræpɪst] N (*also* **Trappist monk**) Trappist *m*

trappy [ˈtræpɪ] ADJ (+er) *ground etc* tückisch

trapse VI = **traipse**

trapshooting [ˈtræpʃuːtɪŋ] N Wurftaubenschießen *nt*

trash [træʃ] N **a** (*US*, = *refuse*) Abfall *m* **b** (= *goods*) Schund *m*, Ramsch *m* (*inf*), billiges Zeug; (= *book, play etc*) Schund *m*; (= *pop group etc*) Mist *m* (*inf*); **don't talk ~** red nicht so einen Quatsch (*inf*) **c** (*pej inf*, = *people*) Gesindel *nt*, Pack *nt*; → **like her** Gesindel wie sie; **she/he is ~** sie/er taugt nichts → **white trash VT a** (*inf*) *place* verwüsten; *car* (= *crash*) zu Schrott fahren; (= *vandalize*) kaputt machen (*inf*) **b** (*esp US, inf*, = *criticize*) verreißen, schlecht machen

trash: trash can N (*US*) Abfalleimer *m*; **trashman** [ˈtræʃmən] N (*US*) Müllmann *m*

---

trashy [ˈtræʃɪ] ADJ (+er) *goods* minderwertig, wertlos; *play* minderwertig; *pop group* billig; *place* schäbig; **~ novel** Schundroman *m*; **clothes for teenagers are often ~** Teenagerkleidung ist oft Schund *or* billiges Zeug

trattoria [ˌtrætəˈriːə] N Trattoria *f*

trauma [ˈtrɔːmə] N (*Psych*) Trauma *nt*, seelischer Schock

traumatic [trɔːˈmætɪk] ADJ traumatisch; **it is ~ to lose one's job** seine Arbeit zu verlieren ist eine traumatische Erfahrung

traumatize [ˈtrɔːmətaɪz] VT (*Med, Psych*) traumatisieren

travail [ˈtræveɪl] N **a** *usu pl* (= *toils*) Mühen *pl*; **after all the ~s of Watergate** nach den schweren Belastungen durch die Watergate-Affäre **b** (*old, liter*: = *exhausting labour*) Plackerei *f*, Mühsal *f* **c** (*old*: = *childbirth*) (Geburts)wehen *pl* **VI a** (*old, liter*: = *toil*) sich plagen (*old*); **he ~ed in the depths of despair** er litt in tiefer Verzweiflung **b** (*old*: *in childbirth*) in den Wehen liegen, Wehen haben

travel [ˈtrævl] **VI a** (= *make a journey*) reisen; **they have ~led** (*Brit*) *or* **~ed** (*US*) **a lot** sie sind viel gereist, sie haben viele Reisen gemacht; **he ~s to work by car** er fährt mit dem Auto zur Arbeit; **she is ~ling** (*Brit*) *or* **~ing** (*US*) **to London tomorrow** sie fährt morgen nach London; **the President is ~ling** (*Brit*) *or* **~ing** (*US*) **to Paris tomorrow** der Präsident reist morgen nach Paris; **they have ~led** (*Brit*) *or* **~ed** (*US*) **a long way** sie haben eine weite Reise *or* lange Fahrt hinter sich (*dat*); (*fig*) sie haben es weit gebracht (*im* Leben); **they ~led** (*Brit*) *or* **~ed** (*US*) **for 6 hours/300 kms** sie fuhren 6 Stunden lang/300 km; **to ~ (a)round the world** eine Reise um die Welt machen; **to ~ around a country** ein Land durchreisen *or* bereisen

b (= *go, move*) sich bewegen; (*sound, light*) sich fortpflanzen; **light ~s at ...** die Lichtgeschwindigkeit beträgt ...; **we were ~ling** (*Brit*) *or* **~ing** (*US*) **at 80 kph** wir fuhren 80 km/h; **the parts ~ along the conveyor belt** die Teile werden vom Förderband weiterbefördert; **the electricity ~s along the wire** der Strom fließt durch den Draht; **you were ~ling** (*Brit*) *or* **~ing** (*US*) **too fast** Sie sind zu schnell gefahren; **he was certainly ~ling** (*Brit*) *or* **~ing** (*US*)! (*inf*) er hatte vielleicht einen Zahn drauf! (*inf*); **wow! that's ~ling** (*Brit*) *or* **~ing** (*US*)! (*inf*) Mann, das ist aber schnell!

c (*Comm*) Vertreter(in) *m(f)* sein; **he ~s for a Berlin insurance firm** er ist Vertreter einer Berliner Versicherungsgesellschaft

d (*wine sales*) **some wines do not ~ well** manche Weine vertragen den Transport nicht; **his humour** (*Brit*) *or* **humor** (*US*) **~s well** sein Humor kommt auch anderswo gut an

e (= *pass*) **his eye ~led** (*Brit*) *or* **~ed** (*US*) **over the scene** seine Augen wanderten über die Szene

f (*Tech*) sich hin- und herbewegen; **as the piston ~s from A to B** während sich der Kolben von A nach B bewegt; **it doesn't ~ freely** es bewegt sich schwer; **the sliding doors don't ~ freely** diese Schiebetüren gleiten nicht gut

g (*Basketball*) einen Schrittfehler machen

VT *area* bereisen; *distance* zurücklegen, fahren; *route* fahren

N a *no pl* (= *travelling*) Reisen *nt*; **to be fond of ~** gerne reisen; **~ was difficult in the 18th century** im 18. Jahrhundert war das Reisen beschwerlich

b **travels** PL (*in country*) Reisen *pl*; (*hum, in town, building*) Ausflüge *pl*, Gänge *pl*; **if you meet him on your ~s** wenn Sie ihm auf einer Ihrer Reisen begegnen; **he's off on his ~s again tomorrow** er verreist morgen wieder

c (*Tech*) Weg *m*; (*of instrument's needle etc*) Ausschlag *m*; (*of piston*) Hub *m*

travel: travel agency N Reisebüro *nt*; **travel agent** N Reisebürokaufmann *m*/-kauffrau *f*; (*of package tours*) Reiseveranstalter(in) *m(f)*; **~('s)** (= *travel agency*) Reisebüro *nt*; **travel allowance** N Reisekostenzuschuss *m*

---

travelator [ˈtrævəleɪtəʳ] N Rollband *nt*, Fahrband *nt*

travel: travel brochure N Reiseprospekt *m*; **travel bureau** N Reisebüro *nt*; **travel card** N (*Brit, for a week*) Wochenkarte *f*; (*for a month*) Monatskarte *f*; (*for a year*) Jahreskarte *f*; **travel companion** N Reisebegleiter(in) *m(f)*, Reisegefährte *m*/-gefährtin *f*; **travel expenses** PL (*esp US*) Reisekosten *pl or* -spesen *pl*; **travel insurance** N Reiseversicherung *f*

travelled, (*US*) **traveled** [ˈtrævld] ADJ well-travelled (*person*) weit gereist; *route* viel befahren; **widely ~** weit gereist

traveller, (*US*) **traveler** [ˈtrævləʳ] N **a** Reisende(r) *mf*; **I am a poor ~** ich vertrage das Reisen nicht **b** (*also* **commercial traveller**) Vertreter(in) *m(f)*, Handelsreisende(r) *mf*

traveller's cheque, (*US*) **traveler's check** N Reisescheck *m*, Travellerscheck *m*

travelling, (*US*) **traveling** [ˈtrævlɪŋ] N Reisen *nt*; **I hate ~** ich reise sehr ungern, ich hasse das Reisen

travelling, (*US*) **traveling**: **travelling bag** N Reisetasche *f*; **travelling circus** N Wanderzirkus *m*; **travelling clock** N Reisewecker *m*; **travelling crane** N Lauf- *or* Rollkran *m*; **travelling exhibition** N Wanderausstellung *f*; **travelling expenses** PL Reisekosten *pl*; (*on business*) Reisespesen *pl*; **travelling people** PL fahrendes Volk; **travelling rug** N Reisedecke *f*; **travelling salesman** N Vertreter *m*, Handelsreisende(r) *m*; **travelling scholarship** N Auslandsstipendium *nt*; **travelling theatre** N Wandertheater *nt*, Tourneetheater *nt*

travel: travel literature N Reisebeschreibung *f*; **travel novel** N Reisebeschreibung *f*

travelogue, (*US*) **travelog** [ˈtrævəlɒg] N (= *film*) filmischer Reisebericht; (= *slides*) Lichtbildervortrag *m* (über eine Reise); (= *lecture*) Reisebericht *m*

travel: travel-sick ADJ reisekrank; **travel-sickness** N Reisekrankheit *f*; **travel-sickness pill** N Pille *f* gegen Reisekrankheit; **travel-weary**, **travel-worn** ADJ von der Reise ermüdet *or* erschöpft

traverse [ˈtrævɜːs] **VT a** (= *cross*) *land* durchqueren; (*bridge, person*) *water* überqueren; **to ~ the globe** den Erdball bereisen; **the searchlight ~d the sky from east to west** der Suchscheinwerfer leuchtete den Himmel von Osten nach Westen ab

b (= *cross and recross*) **the searchlight ~d the sky** der Suchscheinwerfer leuchtete den Himmel ab

c (= *extend over*) *period* überdauern

d (*Mountaineering*) *ice, slope* queren, traversieren

VI (*Mountaineering, Ski*) sich quer zum Hang bewegen, (den Hang) traversieren

N (*on mountain, = movement*) Queren *nt*, Traversieren *nt*; (= *place*) Quergang *m*; (*Archit*) Querbalken *m*, Traverse *f*

travesty [ˈtrævɪstɪ] **N** (*Liter*) Travestie *f*; **a ~ of justice** ein Hohn *m* auf die Gerechtigkeit; **the elections were a ~** die Wahlen waren ein Hohn *m or* eine Farce **VT** ins Lächerliche ziehen, travestieren (*esp Liter*)

trawl [trɔːl] **N** (*also* **trawl net**) Schleppnetz *nt*, Trawl *nt*; (*US: also* **trawl line**) Grundleine *f* **VI a to ~ (for fish)** mit dem Schleppnetz fischen; (*US*) mit einer Grundleine fischen **b** (*esp Brit*) **to ~ for players/lawyers** Spieler/Rechtsanwälte fischen **VT a** *fish* mit dem Schleppnetz fangen; **they ~ed the sea-bottom** sie fischten mit Schleppnetzen auf dem Meeresboden; **they ~ed the net along the sea-bottom** sie schleppten das Netz über den Meeresboden **b** (*esp Brit*) *world, streets, bars, files, Internet* durchkämmen

trawler [ˈtrɔːləʳ] N (= *boat*) Fischdampfer *m*, Trawler *m*

trawlerman [ˈtrɔːləmən] N *pl* **-men** [-mən] Trawlerfischer *m*

trawling ['trɔːlɪŋ] N Dampfer- or Trawlfischerei f

tray [treɪ] N Tablett nt; (= tea tray) Teebrett nt, Servierbrett nt; (of cakes, small) Platte f; (big) Brett nt; (for display) Auslagekästchen nt; (= baking tray) (Back)blech nt; (for pencils etc) (Feder)schale f; (for papers, mail) Ablage f; (of street vendor etc) Bauchladen m; (= drawer) (Schub-) fach nt; (in suitcase, trunk) Einsatz m; (Phot, = ice tray) Schale f; (for ash) Kasten m; (in bird cage) Schublade f

tray cloth N Deckchen nt (für ein Tablett)

treacherous ['tretʃərəs] ADJ **a** person, action verräterisch **b** (= unreliable) trügerisch, irreführend; **my memory is rather ~ now** mein Gedächtnis lässt mich neuerdings ziemlich im Stich **c** (= dangerous) tückisch; corner gefährlich; weather conditions, ice trügerisch; journey gefahrvoll

treacherously ['tretʃərəslɪ] ADV **a** (= disloyally) verräterisch, in verräterischer Weise **b** (= unreliably) trügerisch, irreführend; **at times he can be ~ convincing** er wirkt manchmal gefährlich überzeugend **c** (= dangerously) tückisch; **rocks hidden ~ beneath the surface** Felsen, die gefährlich dicht unter der Wasseroberfläche liegen; **in ~ bad conditions** unter gefährlich schlechten Bedingungen

treacherousness ['tretʃərəsnɪs] N **a** (= disloyalty) **the ~ of these generals** diese verräterischen Generäle **b** (= unreliability: of memory etc) Unzuverlässigkeit f **c** (of road/weather conditions) Tücke f, Gefährlichkeit f; **because of the ~ of the snow** wegen der trügerischen Schneeverhältnisse

treachery ['tretʃərɪ] N Verrat m; (of weather) Tücke f; **an act of ~** Verrat m, eine verräterische Tat

treacle ['triːkl] N (Brit) Sirup m

treacle pudding N im Dampfbad gekochter, mit Sirup angereicherter Teig

treacle tart N Kuchen mit Überzugmasse aus Sirup

treacly ['triːklɪ] ADJ (+er) (lit) sirupartig; (fig) voice honig- or zuckersüß; song, sentiment schmalzig

tread [tred] vb: pret **trod**, ptp **trodden** N **a** (= act) **over the years the ~ of feet has worn the steps away** über die Jahre sind die Stufen völlig ausgetreten **b** (= gait, noise) Schritt m, Tritt m; **to walk with a heavy/springy ~** mit schweren/hüpfenden Schritten gehen, einen schweren/hüpfenden Gang haben; **I could hear his ~ on the stairs** ich konnte seine Schritte auf der Treppe hören **c** (of stair) Stufe f **d** (of shoe, tyre) Profil nt, Lauffläche f VI **a** (= walk) gehen **b** (= bring foot down) treten (on auf +acc); **mind you don't ~ on it!** passen Sie auf, dass Sie nicht darauf treten!; **will you ~ on that cigarette end?** könnten Sie den Zigarettenstummel austreten?; **he trod on my foot** er trat mir auf den Fuß; **to ~ on sb's heels** (lit) jdm auf die Fersen treten; (fig) jdm (dat) hängen; **to ~ softly or lightly** leise or leicht auftreten; **to ~ carefully** (lit) vorsichtig gehen; (fig) vorsichtig vorgehen; **to ~ in sb's footsteps** (fig) in jds Fuß(s)tapfen (acc) treten VI path (= make) treten; (= follow) gehen; **he's ~ing the same path as his father** (fig) er hat den gleichen Weg wie sein Vater eingeschlagen; **to ~ a fine line between ...** sich vorsichtig zwischen ... bewegen; **it got trodden underfoot** es wurde zertreten; **to ~ grapes** Trauben stampfen; **he trod his cigarette into the sand** er trat seine Zigarette in den Sand aus; **to ~ water** Wasser treten; (fig) auf der Stelle treten; **to ~ the boards** (Theat) auf der Bühne or den Brettern stehen; **don't ~ that earth into the carpet** treten Sie die Erde nicht in den Teppich

▶ **tread down** VT sep festtreten

▶ **tread in** VT sep festtreten

▶ **tread out** VT sep fire, cigarette austreten

treadle ['tredl] N (of sewing machine) Tretkurbel f, Pedal nt; (of lathe also) Fußhebel m VI treten

treadmill ['tredmɪl] N (lit) Tretwerk nt; (fig) Tretmühle f; (in gym) Laufband nt

treas. abbr of treasurer

treason ['triːzn] N Verrat m (to an +dat); **an act of ~** Verrat m

treasonable ['triːzənəbl], **treasonous** ['triːzənəs] ADJ verräterisch; **it was ~ to do such a thing** so etwas zu tun, war Verrat

treasure ['treʒə] N (lit) Schatz m; (fig also) Kostbarkeit f; (= dear person) Schatz m; **many ~s of modern art** viele moderne Kunstschätze; **she's a real ~** sie ist eine Perle or ein Juwel nt VT (hoch) schätzen, zu schätzen wissen; **he really ~s his books** seine Bücher bedeuten ihm sehr viel; **I shall ~ this memory** ich werde das in lieber Erinnerung behalten

▶ **treasure up** VT sep horten, ansammeln, anhäufen; (in memory) aufbewahren

treasure: treasure chest N (lit) Schatztruhe f; (fig) Fundgrube f; ~ **house** N (lit) Schatzkammer f; ~ **of knowledge** eine Fundgrube des Wissens; **treasure hunt** N Schatzsuche f

treasurer ['treʒərə] N (of club) Kassenwart(in) m(f), Kassenverwalter(in) m(f); (= city treasurer) Stadtkämmerer m/-kämmerin f; (of business) Leiter(in) m(f) der Finanzabteilung; (of king) Schatzmeister(in) m(f)

treasure trove N Schatzfund m; (= market) Fundgrube f; (= collection, source) Schatzhöhle f

treasury ['treʒərɪ] N **a** (Pol) **the Treasury** (Brit) **the Treasury Department** (US) das Finanzministerium **b** (of society) Kasse f **c** (= anthology) Schatzkästlein nt, Schatzgrube f

---

TREASURY

Her/His Majesty's Treasury, allgemein bekannt als **the Treasury**, ist das britische Finanzministerium, das vom Staat dem Gebiet der Wirtschaftsstrategie Kompetenzen besitzt. Seine Rechnungsbehörde ist das Schatzamt, **Exchequer**, das für Einnahme und Ausgabe der öffentlichen Finanzmittel verantwortlich ist. Der Schatzkanzler, das für die Finanzen zuständige Kabinettsmitglied (**Chancellor of the Exchequer**) hat seinen offiziellen Wohnsitz direkt neben dem des Premierministers, nämlich in 11 Downing Street.
In den USA steht dem **Department of Treasury**, dem Finanzministerium, der **Secretary of the Treasury** vor, zu dessen Kompetenzbereich auch der Schutz des Präsidenten, der Zoll, die Finanzbehörde - **Internal Revenue Service (IRS)** - die Verschuldung der Öffentlichen Hand und außerdem Alkohol, Tabakwaren und Feuerwaffen gehören → BUDGET

---

treasury: Treasury Bench N (Brit) Regierungsbank f (im Parlament); **Treasury bill** N kurzfristiger Schatzwechsel; **treasury bond** N (US) Schatzobligation f; **treasury note** N (US) Schatzanweisung f or -wechsel m

treat [triːt] VT **a** (= behave towards) person, animal behandeln; (= handle) books behandeln, umgehen mit **b** (= consider) betrachten (as als); **you should ~ your work more seriously** Sie sollten Ihre Arbeit ernster nehmen **c** (Med) behandeln; **which doctor is ~ing you?** bei welchem Arzt sind Sie in Behandlung?, welcher Arzt behandelt Sie?; **the doctor is ~ing him for nervous exhaustion** er ist wegen Nervenüberlastung in Behandlung **d** (= process) behandeln (with mit); leather bearbeiten, behandeln (with mit); sewage klären; wastepaper verarbeiten **e** subject behandeln; (esp scientifically, philosophically) abhandeln **f** (= pay for, give) einladen; **to ~ sb to sth** jdn zu etw einladen, jdm etw spendieren; (to drink, ice cream also) jdm etw ausgeben; **I'm ~ing you** ich lade Sie ein; **to ~ oneself to sth** sich (dat) etw gönnen; **he ~ed his wife to a weekend in Paris** er spendierte seiner Frau ein Wochenen-

---

de in Paris; **he ~ed us to a preview of the exhibition** er machte uns (dat) eine Freude und zeigte uns die Ausstellung vorher; **for once she ~ed us to the sight of her knees** endlich einmal gönnte sie uns den Anblick ihrer Knie; **he ~ed us to a display of his temper** (iro) er gab uns (dat) eine Kostprobe seiner Launenhaftigkeit

VI (= deal) **to ~ with sb for sth** mit jdm über etw (acc) Verhandlungen führen, mit jdm um or über etw (acc) verhandeln; **the general decided to ~ for peace** der General entschloss sich, Friedensverhandlungen zu führen

N **a** (= special outing, present) besondere Freude; **tomorrow we're going on our Christmas ~** morgen machen wir unsere Weihnachtsfeier (inf); **children's ~** Kinderfest nt, Kindernachmittag m; **I thought I'd give myself a ~** ich dachte, ich gönne mir mal etwas; **I'm taking them to the circus as a ~** ich mache ihnen eine Freude und lade sie in den Zirkus ein or nehme sie in den Zirkus mit; **it's my ~** das geht auf meine Kosten or Rechnung, ich lade Sie ein; **I want to give them a ~** ich möchte ihnen eine besondere Freude machen; **our uncle's ~ was to give us tickets for the opera** unser Onkel hat uns (dat) Opernkarten spendiert; **that was a ~!** das war ein Genuss!; **what a ~ to have a quiet afternoon** das ist ein Genuss or tut gut, mal einen ruhigen Nachmittag zu verbringen; **there's a ~ in store** es gibt etwas, worauf ihr uns noch freuen können; **this time you can carry the bags as a ~!** (iro) dieses Mal darfst du ausnahmsweise die Taschen tragen; **it's a (real) ~ to see you again** was für eine Freude, Sie mal wiederzusehen! **b** (inf) **it's coming on a ~** es macht sich prima (inf); **it worked a ~** es klappte or lief wie am Schnürchen (inf) or wie eine Eins (inf)

▶ **treat of** VI +prep obj (form) handeln von, behandeln

treatise ['triːtɪz] N Abhandlung f (on über +acc)

treatment ['triːtmənt] N **a** Behandlung f; **their ~ of foreigners** ihre Art, Ausländer zu behandeln; **to give sb the ~** (inf, violently, sexually) es jdm ordentlich besorgen (inf); **during his two-day interview, they gave him the full ~** (inf) bei seinem zweitägigen Einstellungsgespräch wurde er ganz schön in die Mangel genommen (inf); **she went to the beauty parlour and they really gave her the ~** (inf) sie ging in den Schönheitssalon und wurde dort nach allen Regeln der Kunst bearbeitet (inf); **when the foreign delegates visited the factory, they were given the full ~** (inf) als die ausländischen Delegierten die Firma besichtigten, wurde ein enormes Tamtam gemacht (inf) or eine große Schau abgezogen (inf) **b** (Med) Behandlung f; **there are many ~s for ...** es gibt viele Behandlungsarten or Heilverfahren für ...; **to be having ~ for sth** wegen etw in Behandlung sein **c** (= processing) Behandlung f; (of sewage) Klärung f; (of wastepaper) Verarbeitung f **d** (of subject) Behandlung f, Bearbeitung f

treaty ['triːtɪ] N Vertrag m

treaty port N Vertragshafen m

treble¹ ['trebl] ADJ dreifach; **it's in ~ figures** es ist eine dreistellige Summe; ~ **chance (pools)** eine Variante des Fußballtotos mit dreifacher Gewinnchance ADV **they had ~ our numbers** sie waren dreimal so viele wie wir; **clothes are ~ the price** Kleider kosten dreimal so viel VT verdreifachen VI sich verdreifachen N (on dartboard etc) Dreifache(s) nt; (Brit, Sport: = three victories/trophies etc) Hattrick m

treble² N (Mus: = boy's voice) (Knaben)sopran m; (= highest part) Oberstimme f; (of piano) Diskant m; (= child's speaking voice) Diskantstimme f ADJ ~ **voice** (Knaben)sopranstimme f

treble clef N (Mus) Violinschlüssel m

treble recorder N Altblockflöte f

trebly ['treblɪ] ADV dreifach; **the child was ~ dear to him** er liebte das Kind dreimal mehr

tree [triː] **N** **a** Baum *m*; **an oak ~** eine Eiche; **a cherry ~** ein Kirschbaum *m*; **rose ~** Rosenstämmchen *nt*; **~ of knowledge** Baum *m* der Erkenntnis; **~ of life** Baum *m* des Lebens; **money doesn't/good teachers don't grow on ~s** das Geld fällt/gute Lehrer fallen nicht vom Himmel; **to be up a ~** (inf) in der Patsche or Tinte or Klemme sitzen (inf); **he's at the top of the ~** (fig inf) er ist ganz oben (an der Spitze); **he's out of his ~** (inf) (= drunk) er ist total zu (inf); (= crazy) er tickt nicht richtig (inf) **b** (= family tree) Stammbaum *m* **c** (= shoe tree) Spanner *m*, Leisten *m* **d** (Rel, = cross) Kreuz *nt* **VT** auf einen Baum jagen or treiben

tree in cpds Baum-; **tree-covered** ADJ baumbestanden; **tree fern** N Baumfarn *m*; **tree frog** N Laub- or Baumfrosch *m*; **tree house** N Baumhaus *nt*; **tree hugger** N (esp US, hum inf) Umweltapostel *m* (hum inf), Umweltfreak *m* (hum inf); **treeless** ADJ baumlos; **tree line** N Baumgrenze *f*; **above/below the ~** oberhalb/unterhalb der Baumgrenze; **tree-lined** ADJ baumbestanden, von Bäumen gesäumt (geh); **tree ring** N (Bot) Jahresring *m*; **tree structure** N (Comput) Baumstruktur *f*; **tree surgeon** N Baumchirurg(in) *m(f)*; **treetop** N Baumkrone *f*, Wipfel *m*; **tree trunk** N Baumstamm *m*

trefoil ['trefɔɪl] N (Bot) Klee *m*; (symbol of Girl Guide movement) Kleeblatt *nt*; (Archit) Dreipass *m*

trek [trek] **VI** trecken; (inf) latschen (inf); **they ~ked across the desert** sie zogen durch die Wüste; **I had to ~ up to the top floor** ich musste bis ins oberste Stockwerk latschen (inf) **N** Treck *m*, Zug *m*; (inf) anstrengender Weg or Marsch

Trekkie ['trekɪ] N (inf) Trekkie *m*, Fan der Fernsehserie „Raumschiff Enterprise"

trekking ['trekɪŋ] N Trekking *nt*, Trecking *nt*

trellis ['trelɪs] **N** Gitter *nt*; (for plants also) Spalier *nt* **VT** (= furnish with trellis) mit einem Gitter or Spalier versehen; vines etc am Spalier ziehen

trelliswork ['trelɪswɜːk] N Rankspalier *nt*

tremble ['trembl] **VI** (person, hand etc) zittern (with vor); (voice also) beben (with vor); (ground, building) beben, zittern; **I ~ to think what might have happened** mir wird angst or ich zittere, wenn ich daran denke, was hätte geschehen können; **to ~ for sb/sth** um jdn/etw zittern or bangen **N** Zittern *nt*, Beben *nt*; **to be all of a ~** (inf) am ganzen Körper zittern, das große Zittern haben (inf)

trembling ['tremblɪŋ] **ADJ** hands zitternd; voice, lip also bebend **N** (of person, hand) Zittern *nt*; (of voice, ground, building) Beben *nt* → **fear N a**

trembling: trembling grass N Zittergras *nt*; **trembling poplar** N Zitterpappel *f*, Espe *f*

tremendous [trəˈmendəs] **ADJ a** gewaltig, enorm; size, number, crowd riesig, enorm; storm, explosion gewaltig, ungeheuer stark; **he's a ~ eater** er isst unglaublich viel; **a ~ success** ein Riesenerfolg *m* **b** (= very good) klasse, prima, toll (all inf); **we had a ~ time** wir haben uns prima or ganz toll amüsiert (inf); **he's a ~ person** er ist ein toller Mensch (inf), er ist klasse or prima (all inf); **she has done a ~ job** sie hat fantastische or phantastische Arbeit geleistet

tremendously [trəˈmendəslɪ] **ADV** sehr; fat, tall, long etc also enorm; relieved, upset, grateful, dangerous also ungeheuer, äußerst; pretty also äußerst; intelligent, difficult also enorm, äußerst; **it was ~ good** es war einfach prima or umwerfend gut or sagenhaft (inf); **they enjoyed themselves ~** sie haben sich prächtig or prima or ausgezeichnet amüsiert (inf)

tremolo ['tremələʊ] N (Mus) Tremolo *nt*

tremor ['tremə*] N Zittern *nt*, Beben *nt*; (Med) Tremor *m*; (of emotion) Zittern *nt*, Zucken *nt*; (= earth tremor) Beben *nt*, Erschütterung *f*; **a ~ of fear** ein Schaudern *nt*; **without a ~** völlig ruhig, unbewegt

tremulous ['tremjʊləs] **ADJ** (= trembling) voice zitternd, bebend; hand zitternd; handwriting zittrig; breath bebend; (= timid) smile, person zaghaft, schüchtern; request zaghaft

tremulously ['tremjʊləslɪ] **ADV** (= timidly) zaghaft, ängstlich

trench [trentʃ] **N** Graben *m*; (Mil) Schützengraben *m*; **in the ~es** (Mil) im Schützengraben **VT** Gräben *pl* ziehen in (+dat); (Mil) Schützengräben *pl* ausheben in (+dat)

trenchancy ['trentʃənsɪ] N (of language) Treffsicherheit *f*; (of style) Prägnanz *f*; (of satire, statement) Bissigkeit *f*; (of view, speech) Pointiertheit *f*; (of wit, criticism) Schärfe *f*

trenchant ['trentʃənt] **ADJ** language treffsicher; style prägnant; satire beißend; view, speech pointiert; wit, criticism scharf; statement bissig; **to be ~ on** or **about sth** in Bezug auf etw (acc) kein Blatt vor den Mund nehmen

trenchantly ['trentʃəntlɪ] **ADV** say, observe scharf; **he made his point ~** er argumentierte sicher; **a ~ witty remark** eine scharfe, geistreiche Bemerkung

trench coat N Trenchcoat *m*, Regenmantel *m*

trencher ['trentʃə*] N (Tech) Grabenbagger *m* **b** (old: = platter) Tran(s)chierbrett *nt*

trencherman ['trentʃəmən] N pl **-men** [-mən] **good/poor ~** guter/schlechter Esser

trench: trench mortar N (Mil) Granatwerfer *m*; **trench warfare** N Stellungskrieg *m*, Grabenkrieg *m*

trend [trend] **N** **a** (= tendency) Tendenz *f*, Richtung *f*, Trend *m*; **the ~ toward(s) violence** der Trend or die Tendenz zur Gewalttätigkeit; **upward ~** steigende Tendenz, Aufwärtstrend *m*; **the downward ~ in the birth rate** die Rückläufigkeit or der Abwärtstrend der Geburtenrate; **the ~ away from materialism** die zunehmende Abkehr vom Materialismus; **to set a ~** eine neue Richtung setzen, richtungweisend sein **b** (= fashion) Mode *f*, Trend *m*; **that is the ~/the latest ~ among young people** das ist bei jungen Leuten jetzt Mode/der letzte Schrei (inf); **to follow a ~** einem Trend folgen; (fashion) eine Mode mitmachen **c** (Geog) Verlauf *m* **VI** verlaufen (towards nach); **prices are ~ing upwards** die Preise haben eine steigende Tendenz; **his views are ~ing toward(s) the anarchistic** seine Auffassungen neigen or tendieren zum Anarchismus

trendily ['trendɪlɪ] **ADV** modern; **to dress ~** sich nach der neuesten Mode kleiden

trendiness ['trendɪnɪs] N (of person) Modebewusstsein *nt*; (of ideas etc) Modernität *f*; **the ~ of her clothes** ihre modische Kleidung

trend: trendsetter N Trendsetter(in) *m(f)*; **trendsetting** **N** Entwicklung *f* neuer Trends **ADJ** trendsetzend; (in fashion also) Mode machend

trendy ['trendɪ] **ADJ** (+er) modern, in pred (inf); image modisch, schick; **to be ~** als schick gelten, große Mode sein; **it's no longer ~ to smoke** Rauchen ist nicht mehr in (inf), Rauchen ist aus der Mode geraten; **a restaurant where all the ~ people go** ein Restaurant, in dem sich die Schickeria trifft; **this is a ~ club** dieser Klub ist zur Zeit in (inf) **N** (inf) Schickimicki *m* (inf); **the trendies** die Schickeria sing; **he looks a real ~** der macht vielleicht auf modern!

trepan [trɪˈpæn] **VT** (Med) trepanieren **N** Trepan *m*

trepidation [ˌtrepɪˈdeɪʃən] N Bangigkeit *f*, Beklommenheit *f*, Ängstlichkeit *f*; **full of ~ he knocked on the door** voll ängstlicher Erwartung klopfte er an die Tür; **a look of ~** ein banger or beunruhigter or ängstlicher Blick; **a feeling of ~** ein beklommenes Gefühl, ein Gefühl der Bangigkeit or Verzagtheit; **I am writing, not without some ~, to tell you …** nicht ohne ein Gefühl der Beklommenheit teile ich Ihnen mit …

trespass ['trespəs] **VI** **a** (on property) unbefugt betreten (on sth etw acc); **"no ~ing"** „Betreten verboten"; **you're ~ing** Sie dürfen sich hier nicht aufhalten **b** **to ~ (up)on sb's rights/area of responsibility** in jds Rechte/Verantwortungsbereich (acc) eingreifen; **to ~ (up)on sb's privacy** jds Privatsphäre verletzen; **to ~ (up)on sb's kindness/time** jds Freundlichkeit/Zeit überbeanspruchen **c** (Bibl) **as we forgive them that ~ against us** wie wir vergeben unseren Schuldigern **N** **a** (Jur) unbefugtes Betreten **b** (Bibl) **forgive us our ~es** vergib uns unsere Schuld

trespasser ['trespəsə*] N Unbefugte(r) *mf*; **"trespassers will be prosecuted"** „widerrechtliches Betreten wird strafrechtlich verfolgt"; **the farmer found a ~ on his land** der Bauer fand einen Eindringling auf seinem Land

tress [tres] N (liter) Locke *f* (liter)

tressed [trest] **ADJ** hair (= plaited) geflochten; (= curly) gelockt

trestle ['tresl] N (Auflage)bock *m*

trestle: trestle bridge N Bockbrücke *f*; **trestle table** N auf Böcken stehender Tisch; (decorator's) Tapeziertisch *m*

trews [truːz] **PL** (Scot) eng anliegende Hose im Schottenkaro; (Brit inf, = trousers) Hose *f*; **a pair of ~** eine Hose

Triad ['traɪæd] N (= Chinese secret society) Triade *f*

triad ['traɪæd] N Triade *f*, Trias *f*; (Mus) Dreiklang *m*; (Chem) dreiwertiges Element

trial ['traɪəl] **N** **a** (Jur) (Gerichts)verfahren *nt*, Prozess *m*; (= actual hearing) (Gerichts)verhandlung *f*; **to be on ~** angeklagt sein, unter Anklage stehen; **he goes on ~ tomorrow** seine Verhandlung ist morgen; **to be on ~ for theft** des Diebstahls angeklagt sein, wegen Diebstahls unter Anklage stehen; **to be on ~ for one's life** wegen eines mit Todesstrafe bedrohten Verbrechens angeklagt sein; **to stand ~ (for sth)** (wegen etw) vor Gericht stehen; **at the ~** bei or während der Verhandlung; **to bring sb to ~** jdn vor Gericht stellen, jdm den Prozess machen; **the case comes up for ~ next month** der Fall wird nächsten Monat verhandelt; **~ by jury** Schwurgerichtsverfahren *nt*; **~ by television/the media** (fig) Vorverurteilung *f* durch das Fernsehen/die Medien **b** (= test) Versuch *m*, Probe *f*, Erprobung *f*; **~s** (of machine, aeroplane) Test(s) *m(pl)*, (Über)prüfung *f*; (Sport) Qualifikationsspiel *nt*; **horse ~s** Querfeldeinrennen *nt*; **to give sth a ~** etw ausprobieren; **the manager has promised to give me a ~ as a clerk** der Betriebsleiter hat versprochen, mir eine Chance als Büroangestellter zu geben; **to take sb/sth on ~** jdn/etw zur Probe nehmen, jdn/etw probeweise nehmen; **to put sb/sth to the ~** jdn/etw testen or auf die Probe stellen; **to be on a ~** (= new product etc) getestet werden; **the new clerk is on ~** der neue Büroangestellte ist auf Probe eingestellt; **~ of strength** Kraftprobe *f*; **by ~ and error** durch Ausprobieren; **a system of ~ and error** ein System der empirischen Lösung **c** (= hardship) Widrigkeit *f*, Unannehmlichkeit *f*; (= nuisance) Plage *f*, Problem *nt* (to für); **he's a ~ to his mother** er macht seiner Mutter sehr viel Kummer; **~s and tribulations** Aufregungen *pl*, Schwierigkeiten *pl*, Drangsale *pl* (liter)

trial: trial-and-error method N Trial-and-Error-Methode *f*, empirische Methode; **trial balance** N Saldenbilanz *f*, Probebilanz *f*; **trial basis** N **to employ sb on a ~** jdn auf Probe einstellen; **trial flight** N Testflug *m* or *nt*; **trial judge** N Richter(in) *m(f)* der ersten Instanz, Hauptverhandlungsrichter(in) *m(f)*; **trial lawyer** N (US, Jur) Prozessanwalt *m*, Prozessanwältin *f*; **trial marriage** N Ehe *f* auf Probe; **trial offer** N Einführungsangebot *nt*; **trial order** N Probeauftrag *m*; **trial package** N Probepackung *f*; **trial period** N (for people) Probezeit *f*; (for goods) Probezeit *f*, Zeit, die man etw zur Probe oder Prüfung hat; **trial run** N Generalprobe *f*; (with car etc) Versuchsfahrt *f*, Probefahrt *f*; (of machine) Probelauf *m*; **give the new method**

a ~ probieren Sie diese neue Methode einmal aus *or* durch

triangle ['traɪæŋgl] N Dreieck *nt*; (= *set square*) (Zeichen)dreieck *nt*; (*Mus*) Triangel *m*; (*fig*: = *relationship*) Dreiecksbeziehung *f*

triangular [traɪ'æŋgjʊlə'] ADJ **a** (*Math*) dreieckig **b** ~ **relationship** Dreiecksverhältnis *nt*; ~ **contest** Dreipersonenwettkampf *m*; (*between nations*) Dreinationenwettkampf *m*

triangulate [traɪ'æŋgjʊlɪt] ADJ (*Math*) triangulär (*form*) VT [traɪ'æŋgjʊleɪt] in Dreiecke einteilen; (*Surv*) triangulieren

triangulation station [traɪˌæŋgjʊ'leɪʃənˌsteɪʃən] N (*Surv*) Vermessungspunkt *m*

tribal ['traɪbəl] ADJ Stammes-; ~ **chief** Stammeshäuptling *m*; ~ **region/settlement** Stammesgebiet *nt*/-siedlung *f*; ~ **rituals** Stammesrituale *pl*; ~ **loyalties** Stammestreue *f*; **Celtic society was basically** ~ die Gesellschaftsordnung der Kelten war stammesgebunden; **to be divided on** *or* **along** ~ **lines** (*lit*) nach Stammeszugehörigkeit geteilt sein; (*fig*) in feindliche Lager gespalten sein

tribalism ['traɪbəlɪzəm] N Stammesstruktur *f*

tribe [traɪb] N **a** Stamm *m*; (*Bot, Zool*) Gattung *f* **b** (*fig inf*) Korona *f*

tribesman ['traɪbzmən] N *pl* **-men** [-mən] Stammesangehörige(r) *m*

tribeswoman ['traɪbzwʊmən] N *pl* **-women** [-wɪmɪn] Stammesangehörige *f*

tribulation [ˌtrɪbjʊ'leɪʃən] N Kummer *m no pl*; ~**s** Sorgen *pl*; (*less serious*) Kümmernisse *pl*; **to bear one's** ~**s bravely** sein Leid *nt* tapfer tragen → **trial**

tribunal [traɪ'bjuːnl] N Gericht *nt*; (= *inquiry*) Untersuchungsausschuss *m*; (*held by revolutionaries etc, fig*) Tribunal *nt*

tribune[1] ['trɪbjuːn] N (*Hist*) (Volks)tribun *m*

tribune[2] N (= *platform*) Tribüne *f*

tributary ['trɪbjʊtərɪ] ADJ **a** *state* tributpflichtig **b** ~ **river** Nebenfluss *m*; ~ **valley** Seitental *nt* N **a** (= *state*) tributpflichtiger Staat **b** (= *river*) Nebenfluss *m*

tribute ['trɪbjuːt] N **a** (*Hist*, = *payment*) Tribut *m* **b** (= *admiration*) Tribut *m*; **to pay** ~ **to sb/sth** jdm/einer Sache (den schuldigen) Tribut zollen; **they stood in silent** ~ **in them** sie zollten ihm (stehend) ihren stillen Tribut; **after their performance** ~**s came flooding in** nach ihrer Vorstellung wurde sie mit Ehrungen überschüttet; **to be a** ~ **to one's parents/school** seinen Eltern/seiner Schule (alle) Ehre machen

trice[1] [traɪs] N (*Brit*) **in a** ~ im Handumdrehen, im Nu

trice[2] VT (*Naut*: *also* **trice up**) *sail* aufholen

Tricel® ['traɪsel] N Tricel *nt*

triceps ['traɪseps] N *pl* **-(es)** Trizeps *m*

trichina [trɪ'kaɪnə] N *pl* **-e** [-iː] Trichine *f*

trichinosis [ˌtrɪkɪ'nəʊsɪs] N Trichinenkrankheit *f*, Trichinose *f*

trick [trɪk] N **a** (= *ruse*) Trick *m*; **be careful, it's a** ~ pass auf, das ist eine Falle!; **be careful with this question, there's a** ~ **in it** sei vorsichtig bei dieser Frage, sie enthält eine Falle!; **he knows a** ~ **or two** (*inf*) der kennt sich aus, der weiß, wie der Hase läuft; **he never misses a** ~ (*inf*) er lässt sich (*dat*) nichts entgehen; **he knows all the** ~**s of the trade** er ist ein alter Hase; (= *is crafty*) er ist mit allen Wassern gewaschen; **he is full of** ~**s** (*child, footballer etc*) er steckt voller Tricks; (*salesman, politician etc*) er hat es faustdick hinter den Ohren; **it's a** ~ **of the light** da täuscht das Licht *nt* **b** (= *mischief*) Streich *m*; **to play a** ~ **on sb** jdm einen Streich spielen; **unless my eyes are playing** ~**s on me** wenn meine Augen mich nicht täuschen; **a dirty** ~ ein ganz gemeiner Trick; **he's up to his (old)** ~**s again** jetzt macht er wieder seine (alten) Mätzchen (*inf*); **how's** ~**s?** (*Brit inf*) wie gehts? **c** (= *skilful act*) Kunststück *nt*; **to teach a dog to do** ~**s** einem Hund Kunststücke beibringen; **once you get the** ~ **of adjusting it** wenn du

einmal den Dreh *or* Trick heraushast, wie man das einstellt; **there's a special** ~ **to it** da ist ein Trick dabei; **that should do the** ~ (*inf*) das müsste eigentlich hinhauen (*inf*) → **dog**

d (= *habit*) Eigenart *f*; **to have a** ~ **of doing sth** die Eigenart haben, etw zu tun; **he has a** ~ **of always arriving as I'm pouring out the tea** er hat eine merkwürdige Art, immer gerade dann zu erscheinen, wenn ich den Tee einschenke; **history has a** ~ **of repeating itself** die Geschichte hat die merkwürdige Eigenschaft, sich immer zu wiederholen

e (*Cards*) Stich *m*; **to take a** ~ einen Stich machen

f (*inf, of prostitute*) Nummer *f* (*inf*); **to turn a** ~ es einem Kunden machen *or* besorgen (*sl*)

ATTR *cigar, spider, glass* als Scherzartikel VT mit einem Trick betrügen, hereinlegen (*inf*); **I've been** ~**ed!** ich bin hereingelegt *or* übers Ohr gehauen (*inf*) worden!; **to** ~ **sb into doing sth** jdn (mit einem Trick *or* mit List) dazu bringen, etw zu tun; **he** ~**ed the old lady into giving him her life savings** er hat die alte Dame mit einem Trick um all ihre Ersparnisse betrogen; **to** ~ **sb out of sth** jdn um etw prellen, jdm etw abtricksen (*inf*)

▶ **trick out** VT *sep* herausputzen; **tricked out in her Sunday best** in ihrem Sonntagsstaat; **tricked out in all one's finery** in vollem Staat

trick cyclist N Kunstradfahrer(in) *m(f)*; (*Brit fig inf*) Klapsdoktor *m* (*inf*)

trickery ['trɪkərɪ] N Tricks *pl* (*inf*); **a piece of** ~ ein Trick *m*; **financial** ~ Finanztrickserei *f* (*inf*); **beware of verbal** ~ **in the contract** passen Sie auf, dass im Vertragstext nicht irgendwelche Fallen enthält!

trickiness ['trɪkɪnɪs] N **a** (= *difficulty*) Schwierigkeit *f*; (= *fiddliness*) Kniffligkeit *f* **b** (*of situation*) Schwierigkeit *f*, Kitzligkeit *f* (*inf*); **the** ~ **of the present industrial situation ...** die heikle *or* kitzlige (*inf*) augenblickliche Lage in der Industrie ... **c** (= *slyness*) Durchtriebenheit *f*, Gerissenheit *f*

trickle ['trɪkl] VI **a** (*liquid*) tröpfeln, tropfen; **tears** ~**d down her cheeks** Tränen kullerten ihr über die Wangen; **the rain** ~**d down his neck** der Regen tropfte ihm in den Kragen; **if you don't fix the leak the water will all** ~ **away/out** wenn Sie die undichte Stelle nicht abdichten, tropft das ganze Wasser heraus; **the sand** ~**d through his fingers** der Sand rieselte ihm durch die Finger

b (*fig*) *people/escapees* **began to** ~ **in/out/back** die Leute/Flüchtlinge begannen, vereinzelt herein-/hinaus-/zurückzukommen; **the ball** ~**d into the net** der Ball trudelte (langsam) ins Netz; **reports/donations are beginning to** ~ **in** so langsam trudeln die Berichte/Spenden ein (*inf*)

VT *liquid* tröpfeln, träufeln, tropfenweise gießen N **a** (*of liquid*) Tröpfeln *nt*; (= *stream*) Rinnsal *nt*

b (*fig*) **a steady** ~ **of people gradually filled the lecture hall** der Hörsaal füllte sich langsam aber stetig mit Leuten; **news reports have dwindled to a mere** ~ Berichte *pl* kommen *or* (*secretively*) sickern nur noch ganz selten durch; **arms deliveries have shrunk to a** ~ die Waffenlieferungen sind spärlich geworden; **we cut their supplies to a** ~ wir haben ihren Nachschub drastisch reduziert

trickle: trickle charger N (*Elec*) Kleinlader *m*; **trickle-down** N (*Econ*) *Wirtschaftstheorie, nach der sich der Reichtum einiger positiv auf die Gesamtgesellschaft auswirkt*

trick: trick or treat N *Spiel zu Halloween, bei dem Kinder von Tür zu Tür gehen und von den Bewohnern entweder Geld oder Geschenke erhalten oder ihnen einen Streich spielen*; **trick photography** N Trickfotografie *f*; **trick question** N Fangfrage *f*; **to ask sb a** ~ jdm eine Falle stellen

trickster ['trɪkstə'] N Schwindler(in) *m(f)*, Betrüger(in) *m(f)*

tricksy ['trɪksɪ] ADJ (+*er*) (*inf*) = **tricky c**

tricky ['trɪkɪ] ADJ (+*er*) **a** (= *difficult*) schwierig; (= *fiddly*) knifflig; **he is a very** ~ **person to get on with** es ist äußerst schwierig, mit ihm auszukommen; **warts can be** ~ **to get rid of** Warzen loszuwerden kann schwierig sein; **it is going to be** ~ **explaining** *or* **to explain his absence** es wird nicht einfach sein, seine Abwesenheit zu erklären; **it's** ~ **for me to give you an answer now** es ist nicht einfach für mich, Ihnen jetzt darauf zu antworten

b (= *requiring tact*) *situation, problem* heikel, kitzlig

c (= *sly, crafty*) *person, plan* durchtrieben, gerissen; *question* schwierig, knifflig (*inf*); **a** ~ **customer** ein schwieriger Typ

tricolour, (*US*) **tricolor** ['trɪkələ'] N Trikolore *f*

tricorn ['traɪkɔːn] N Dreispitz *m*

tricot ['triːkəʊ] N (*Tex*) Trikot *m*

tricuspid [traɪ'kʌspɪd] ADJ trikuspidal (*spec*)

tricycle ['traɪsɪkl] N Dreirad *nt*

trident ['traɪdənt] N Dreizack *m*

Tridentine [traɪ'dentaɪn] ADJ Tridentinisch

tried [traɪd] ADJ erprobt, bewährt

tried-and-tested ['traɪdəndˈtestɪd], **tried and tested** ADJ *method* erprobt, bewährt; *recipe, technology* bewährt, ausgereift; *product* getestet; *system* bewährt; **the airbag technology is tried and tested** die Airbagtechnologie hat sich vielfach bewährt

triennial [traɪ'enɪəl] ADJ (= *lasting 3 years*) dreijährig; (= *every 3 years*) dreijährlich, alle drei Jahre stattfindend

triennially [traɪ'enɪəlɪ] ADV alle drei Jahre, dreijährlich

triennium [traɪ'enɪəm] N Zeitraum *m* von drei Jahren

trier ['traɪə'] N **to be a** ~ sich (*dat*) (ernsthaft) Mühe geben

trifle ['traɪfl] N **a** Kleinigkeit *f*; (= *trivial matter*) Lappalie *f*, Kleinigkeit *f*; **the merest** ~ **upsets her** die geringste *or* kleinste Kleinigkeit regt sie auf; **I'm so sorry – a** ~, **don't let it worry you** es tut mir außerordentlich Leid – das ist doch nicht der Rede wert, machen Sie sich deswegen keine Sorgen! **b** (= *small amount*) Kleinigkeit *f*; **have some more cake – just a** ~, **thank you** noch etwas Kuchen? – bloß ein ganz kleines Stückchen, bitte; **a** ~ **hot/small** *etc* ein bisschen heiß/klein *etc*; **a** ~ **too ...** ein wenig *or* eine Spur zu ... **c** (*Brit Cook*) Trifle *nt*

▶ **trifle away** VT *sep* vergeuden

▶ **trifle with** VI +*prep obj person* zu leicht nehmen; *affections, food* spielen mit; **he is not a person to be trifled with** mit ihm ist nicht zu spaßen

trifling ['traɪflɪŋ] ADJ unbedeutend, geringfügig

trifoliate [traɪ'fəʊlɪɪt] ADJ dreiblättrig

trigger ['trɪgə'] 🔧 17.2 N (*of gun*) Abzug(shahn) *m*, Drücker *m* (*inf*); (*of bomb*) Zünder *m*; (*of cine camera, machine*) Auslöser *m*; (*Elec*) Trigger *m*; **to pull the** ~ abdrücken; **to be quick on the** ~ schnell abdrücken VT (*also* **trigger off**) auslösen; *bomb* zünden

trigger: trigger finger N Zeigefinger *m*; **my** ~**'s itching** es juckt mich abzudrücken; **trigger grip** N Pistolengriff *m*; **trigger guard** N Abzugsbügel *m*; **trigger-happy** ADJ (*inf*) schießfreudig (*inf*), schießwütig (*pej*); (*hum*) *photographer* knipswütig (*inf*)

trigonometric(al) [ˌtrɪgənə'metrɪk(əl)] ADJ trigonometrisch

trigonometry [ˌtrɪgə'nɒmɪtrɪ] N Trigonometrie *f*

trihedron [ˌtraɪ'hiːdrən] N Dreiflächner *m*, Trieder *nt*

trike [traɪk] N (*inf*) *abbr of* **tricycle**

trilateral [ˌtraɪ'lætərəl] ADJ dreiseitig; *conference, agreement also* trilateral

trilby ['trɪlbɪ] N (*also* **trilby hat**) weicher Filzhut

trilingual [traɪ'lɪŋgwəl] ADJ dreisprachig

trill [trɪl] **N** **a** (of bird) Trillern nt; (of voice) Tremolo nt **b** (Mus) Triller m **c** (Phon) Rollen nt, rollende Aussprache **VT** **a** (birds) trillern, tirilieren (geh); (person) trällern **b** (Mus) note trillern **c** (Phon) consonant rollen, rollend aussprechen **VI** **a** (bird) trillern, tirilieren (geh); (person) trällern **b** (Mus) trillern

trillion [ˈtrɪljən] **N** Billion f; (dated Brit) Trillion f; **there were ~s of them there** (fig) es waren Millionen und Abermillionen da

trilogy [ˈtrɪlədʒɪ] **N** Trilogie f

trim [trɪm] **ADJ** (+er) **a** sauber; appearance gepflegt, sauber; hair, haircut gepflegt; **he keeps his lawn/garden/house very ~** sein Rasen/Garten/Haus ist immer sehr gepflegt
b (= slim) person schlank; waist schmal; **to stay ~ in Form bleiben; she has a ~ figure** sie hat eine schlanke Figur
N **a** (Brit: = condition) Zustand m, Verfassung f; (= fitness) Form f; **in good ~** (house, car etc) in gutem Zustand; (person) gut in Form; **to get into ~** sich trimmen, sich in Form bringen; **in fighting ~** kampfbereit
b **to give sth a ~** etw schneiden; tree, hedge, beard also etw stutzen; **your hair needs a ~** du musst dir die Haare etwas nachschneiden lassen; **just a ~, please** nur etwas kürzen or nachschneiden, bitte
c (Aut, outside) Zierleisten pl; (inside) Innenausstattung f
d (Naut) Trimm m, Gleichgewichtslage f; **in/out of ~** (ship) in/nicht in Trimm or Gleichgewichtslage
e (Aviat) Trimm m, Fluglage f
f (= edging) Rand m; (= decoration) Bordüre f
g (inf: of book) Format nt
VT **a** (= cut) hair nachschneiden; beard, hedge, branch stutzen; dog trimmen; wick, roses beschneiden; piece of wood (with knife/saw/plane) zurechtschneiden/-sägen/-hobeln; **to ~ the fat** (lit) das Fett weg- or abschneiden; (fig) sich bescheiden
b (fig: = cut down) budget, essay kürzen; interest rates (etwas) senken; staff reduzieren
c (= decorate) dress besetzen; Christmas tree schmücken
d boat, plane trimmen; sails richtig stellen
e (US inf) (= defeat) schlagen; (= cheat) übers Ohr hauen (inf)

▶ **trim away** VT sep weg- or abschneiden; details etc entfernen

▶ **trim back** VT sep hedge, roses zurückschneiden; costs senken; staff reduzieren

▶ **trim down** VT sep wick, budget, essay kürzen (to auf +acc); hedge (zurecht)stutzen; roses zurückschneiden; **to trim down one's figure** etwas für seine Figur tun

▶ **trim off** VT sep bits of beard, ends of branch abschneiden; rough edges (with knife/saw/plane/file) abschneiden/-sägen/-hobeln/-feilen; fat ab- or wegschneiden; **they have trimmed 1p off income tax** sie haben den Einkommensteuersatz um 1p gesenkt

trimaran [ˈtraɪməræn] **N** Dreirumpfboot nt, Trimaran m

trimester [trɪˈmestə'] **N** Trimester nt

trimming [ˈtrɪmɪŋ] **N** **a** (on clothes) Besatz m; **~s** Verzierung(en) f(pl) **b** **trimmings** PL (= cuttings) Abfälle pl; (of paper also) (Papier-)schnitzel pl, Schnipsel pl (inf) **c** **trimmings** PL (= accessories) Zubehör nt; **the car costs £20,000 with all the ~s** das Auto kostet £ 20.000 mit allen Extras or mit allem Zubehör; **roast beef with all the ~s** Roastbeef mit allem Drum und Dran (inf) or mit allen Beilagen

trimness [ˈtrɪmnɪs] **N** (of hair, lawn etc) Gepflegtheit f, gepflegtes Aussehen; (of figure) Schlankheit f

trimonthly [traɪˈmʌnθlɪ] **ADJ** dreimonatlich, vierteljährig, Vierteljahres- **N** periodical, journal Vierteljahresschrift f

trim: trim size N (of book) Format nt; **trim trail** N Trim-dich-Pfad m

Trinidad [ˈtrɪnɪdæd] **N** Trinidad nt

trinitrotoluene [traɪˌnaɪtrəʊˈtɒljʊiːn] **N** Trinitrotoluol nt

Trinity [ˈtrɪnɪtɪ] **N** **a** Trinität f, Dreieinigkeit f, Dreifaltigkeit f **b** (= Trinity term) Sommertrimester nt

Trinity Sunday N Trinitatis(fest) nt, Dreieinigkeitsfest nt, Dreifaltigkeitsfest nt

trinket [ˈtrɪŋkɪt] **N** Schmuckstück nt; (= ornament) Schmuckgegenstand m; **the ~s hanging from her bracelet** die Anhänger an ihrem Armband

trinket box N Schmuckkästchen nt

trinketry [ˈtrɪŋkɪtrɪ] **N** billiger or wertloser Schmuck

trinomial [traɪˈnəʊmɪəl] **ADJ** trinomisch, dreigliedrig **N** Trinom nt

trio [ˈtriːəʊ] **N** Trio nt

trip [trɪp] **N** **a** (= journey) Reise f; (= excursion) Ausflug m, Tour f; (esp shorter) Trip m; **let's go on a ~ to the seaside** machen wir doch einen Ausflug ans Meer!, fahren wir doch ans Meer!; **when was your last ~ to the dentist's?** wann waren Sie zuletzt beim Zahnarzt?; **that's his fifth ~ to the bathroom already!** er geht jetzt schon zum fünften Mal auf die Toilette! (inf); **he is away on a ~** er ist verreist or auf Reisen; **she's away on a ~ to Canada** sie macht zurzeit eine Reise nach Kanada; **to take a ~ (to)** eine Reise machen (nach), verreisen (nach)
b (inf: on drugs) Trip m (inf); **to go on a ~** auf einen Trip or auf die Reise gehen (inf)
c (= stumble) Stolpern nt; **that was a nasty ~** da sind Sie aber übel gestolpert
d (esp Sport) Beinstellen nt; **he didn't fall, it was a ~** er ist nicht (von selbst) hingefallen, man hat ihm ein Bein gestellt
e (= mistake) Fehler m, Ausrutscher m (inf)
f (Mech) Auslösung f
VI **a** (= stumble) stolpern (on, over über +acc)
b (= trip up VI **b**
c (= skip) trippeln; **to ~ in/out** hinein-/hinaustrippeln; **a phrase which ~s off the tongue** ein Ausdruck, der einem leicht von der Zunge geht; **the notes should come ~ping off the tongue** die Töne müssen richtig perlend kommen
VT **a** (= make fall) stolpern lassen; (deliberately) ein Bein stellen (+dat); **I was ~ped** jemand hat mir ein Bein gestellt → also **trip up** VT **b**
b (Mech) lever betätigen; mechanism auslösen
c (old: = dance) tanzen; **to ~ the light fantastic** (hum) das Tanzbein schwingen (inf)

▶ **trip over** VI stolpern (+prep obj über +acc)

▶ **trip up** **VI** **a** (lit) stolpern **b** (fig) sich vertun **VT** sep **a** (= make fall) stolpern lassen; (deliberately) zu Fall bringen **b** (fig: = cause to make a mistake etc) stellen (+dat), aufs Glatteis führen; **he was trying to trip me up with his ad-libbing** er versuchte, mich mit seinem Improvisieren aus dem Konzept zu bringen; **question six managed to trip most of the candidates up** die meisten Prüflinge sind über die sechste Frage gestolpert

tripartite [ˌtraɪˈpɑːtaɪt] **ADJ** agreement, talks dreiseitig; **~ division** Dreiteilung f

tripe [traɪp] **N** **a** (Cook) Kaldaunen pl, Kutteln pl (S Ger, Aus, Sw) **b** (fig inf) Quatsch m, Stuss m (inf)

triphammer [ˈtrɪpˌhæmə'] **N** Aufwerfhammer m

triplane [ˈtraɪpleɪn] **N** Dreidecker m

triple [ˈtrɪpl] **ADJ** dreifach **ADV** dreimal so viel; **it's ~ the distance** es ist dreimal so weit; **at ~ the speed** mit dreifacher Geschwindigkeit; **it costs ~ what it used to** es kostet dreimal so viel wie früher, es kostet das Dreifache von früher **N** Dreifache(s) nt **VT** verdreifachen **VI** sich verdreifachen

triple: triple-digit ADJ (esp US) number dreistellig; **triple glazing** N Dreifachverglasung f; **triple jump** N Dreisprung m

triplet [ˈtrɪplɪt] **N** **a** (= baby) Drilling m **b** (Mus) Triole f; (Poet) Dreireim m

triple time N (Mus) Dreiertakt m

Triplex® [ˈtrɪpleks] **N** Verbundglas nt

triplicate [ˈtrɪplɪkɪt] **N** **in ~** in dreifacher Ausfertigung **ADJ** in dreifacher Ausfertigung **VT** [ˈtrɪplɪkeɪt] document dreifach or in drei Exemplaren ausfertigen

triply [ˈtrɪplɪ] **ADV** dreimal; **~ expensive** dreimal so teuer

tripod [ˈtraɪpɒd] **N** (Phot) Stativ nt; (Hist) Dreifuß m

tripos [ˈtraɪpɒs] **N** Abschlussexamen nt (an der Universität Cambridge)

tripper [ˈtrɪpə'] **N** (esp Brit inf) Ausflügler(in) m(f) → **day-tripper**

tripping [ˈtrɪpɪŋ] **ADJ** walk trippelnd; notes perlend; metre fließend

tripping device N (Mech) Auslösemechanismus m

trippingly [ˈtrɪpɪŋlɪ] **ADV** walk trippelnd; **grand phrases roll ~ off his tongue** ihm kommen große Worte über die Lippen

trippy [ˈtrɪpɪ] **ADJ** (inf) ausgeflippt (inf)

trip: trip recorder N (Aut) Tageszähler m; **trip switch** N (Elec) Sicherheitsschalter m

triptych [ˈtrɪptɪk] **N** Triptychon nt

triptyche [ˈtrɪptiːk] **N** (Aut: = customs document) Triptyk nt, Triptik nt

tripwire [ˈtrɪpwaɪə'] **N** Stolperdraht m

trireme [ˈtraɪriːm] **N** Triere f, Trireme f

trisect [traɪˈsekt] **VT** in drei Teile teilen, dreiteilen; angle in drei gleiche Teile teilen

trisection [traɪˈsekʃən] **N** Dreiteilung f; (of angle) Einteilung f in drei gleiche Teile

trisyllabic [ˌtraɪsɪˈlæbɪk] **ADJ** dreisilbig

trisyllable [ˌtraɪˈsɪləbl] **N** dreisilbiges Wort

trite [traɪt] **ADJ** (+er) (= trivial, banal) banal, nichts sagend; (= hackneyed) abgedroschen; **it would be ~ to say that ...** es wäre banal zu sagen, dass ...

tritely [ˈtraɪtlɪ] **ADV** **a ~ obvious remark** eine Binsenweisheit; **nobody is perfect, he said ~** er machte die banale Bemerkung: niemand ist vollkommen

triteness [ˈtraɪtnɪs] **N** (= banality) Banalität f; (= hackneyed quality) Abgedroschenheit f

tritium [ˈtrɪtɪəm] **N** Tritium nt

triumph [ˈtraɪʌmf] **N** **a** Triumph m; **in ~** triumphierend, im Triumph; **shouts of ~** Triumphgeschrei nt; **to score a ~ over sb/sth** einen Triumph über jdn/etw erzielen **b** (Hist, = procession) Triumphzug m **VI** (= win) den Sieg davontragen (over über +acc); **to ~ over sb/sth** über jdn/etw triumphieren; **they ~ed over incredible odds** sie setzten sich gegen unglaubliche Widerstände durch; **we've made it! he ~ed** wir habens geschafft!, triumphierte er

triumphal [traɪˈʌmfəl] **ADJ** triumphal

triumphal arch N Triumphbogen m

triumphant [traɪˈʌmfənt] **ADJ** (= victorious) siegreich; (= rejoicing) triumphierend; moment triumphal; **to be ~ (over sth)** triumphieren (über etw acc); **to emerge ~** triumphieren; **to be or prove a ~ success** ein triumphaler Erfolg sein; **he was ~ in his success** er jubelte triumphierend or triumphierte über seinen Erfolg; **in our ~ hour** in unserer Stunde des Triumphs

triumphantly [traɪˈʌmfəntlɪ] **ADV** triumphierend; **it was a ~ successful expedition** die Expedition war ein triumphaler Erfolg

triumvir [traɪˈʌmviːr] **N** (Hist) Triumvir m

triumvirate [traɪˈʌmvɪrɪt] **N** (Hist) Triumvirat nt

triune [ˈtraɪjuːn] **ADJ** (Rel) dreieinig

trivalent [ˌtraɪˈveɪlənt] **ADJ** (Chem) dreiwertig

trivia [ˈtrɪvɪə] **PL** belangloses Zeug; **the ~ of daily life** die Trivialitäten des täglichen Lebens

trivial [ˈtrɪvɪəl] **ADJ** **a** trivial; objection, loss, details, matters geringfügig, belanglos, trivial; mistake belanglos; **look, your health is not something ~** hör mal, mit der Gesundheit ist nicht zu spaßen!; **the ~ round** das triviale Einerlei **b** person oberflächlich

triviality [ˌtrɪvɪˈælɪtɪ] N Trivialität f; (of objection, loss, details, matters also) Geringfügigkeit f, Belanglosigkeit f

trivialization [ˌtrɪvɪəlaɪˈzeɪʃən] N Trivialisierung f

trivialize [ˈtrɪvɪəlaɪz] VT trivialisieren

Trivial Pursuit® N Trivial Pursuit® nt

trochaic [trəˈkeɪɪk] ADJ trochäisch

trochee [ˈtrəʊkiː] N Trochäus m

trod [trɒd] pret of **tread**

trodden [ˈtrɒdn] ptp of **tread**

troglodyte [ˈtrɒɡlədaɪt] N Höhlenmensch m, Troglodyt m (liter); (fig: = recluse) Einsiedler(in) m(f)

troika [ˈtrɔɪkə] N Troika f

troilism [ˈtrɔɪlɪzəm] N , no pl (form) Troilismus m

Trojan [ˈtrəʊdʒən] N (Hist) Trojaner(in) m(f), Troer(in) m(f); **to work like a ~** (fig) wie ein Pferd arbeiten; **he's a real ~** (fig) er ist wirklich eine treue Seele **ADJ** trojanisch; (fig) übermenschlich

Trojan Horse N (lit, fig) Trojanisches Pferd

Trojan War N Trojanischer Krieg

troll[1] [trəʊl] N (Myth) Troll m

troll[2] VI (inf, = walk) laufen

trolley [ˈtrɒlɪ] N a (Brit: = cart, four wheels) Handwagen m; (in supermarket) Einkaufswagen m; (in station) Gepäckwagen m, Ladekasten m; (for passengers) Kofferkuli m; (two wheels, for golf clubs) Caddy m; (in station, factory etc) Sackkarre f

b (Brit: = tea trolley) Teewagen m c (Brit Rail) Lore f, Förderkarren m; (hand-driven) Draisine f, Dräsine f d (Elec, = trolley pole) Kontaktarm m, Stromabnehmerstange f; (= trolley-wheel) Kontaktrolle f, Rollenstromabnehmer m e (= passenger vehicle) = **trolleybus** (US: = trolley car) Straßenbahn f f **to be off one's ~** (Brit inf) nicht mehr alle Tassen im Schrank haben (inf)

trolley: trolleybus N Obus m, Oberleitungsomnibus m (form), Trolleybus m (dated); **trolley car** N (US) Straßenbahn f; **trolley pole** N Kontaktarm m, Stromabnehmerstange f

trollop [ˈtrɒləp] N (dated: = prostitute) leichtes Mädchen, Straßenmädchen nt; (pej) Schlampe f

trombone [trɒmˈbəʊn] N (Mus) Posaune f

trombonist [trɒmˈbəʊnɪst] N Posaunist(in) m(f)

troop [truːp] N a (Mil, of cavalry) Trupp m; (= unit) Schwadron f b **troops** PL (Mil) Truppen pl; **a dozen of our best ~s** zwölf unserer besten Soldaten; **200 ~s** 200 Soldaten c (of Scouts) Stamm m d (of people) Horde f (pej), Schar f VI **to ~ out/in** hinaus-/hineinströmen; **to ~ upstairs** nach oben strömen; **to ~ past sth** an etw (dat) vorbeiziehen; **to ~ away or off** abziehen (inf); **to ~ up** herbeiströmen VT (Brit Mil) **to ~ the colours** die Fahnenparade abhalten; **the colours being ~ed today** die Fahnen bei der heutigen Parade; **the ~ing of the colours** die Fahnenparade

troop carrier [ˈtruːpˌkærɪə] N (= vehicle) Truppentransporter m

troop-carrying vehicle [ˈtruːpˌkærɪŋˈviːɪkl̩] N (Brit Mil) Mannschaftswagen m

trooper [ˈtruːpə] N (Mil) berittener Soldat, Kavallerist m; (US, = state trooper) Staatspolizist(in) m(f); **to swear like a ~** (Brit inf) wie ein Kutscher fluchen

troop: troop reduction N Truppenabbau m; **troopship** N (Truppen)transportschiff nt; **trooptrain** N Truppentransportzug m; **troop withdrawal** N Truppenabzug m

trope [trəʊp] N (Liter) Trope f

trophy [ˈtrəʊfɪ] N (Hunt, Mil, Sport) Trophäe f

trophy wife N (pej inf) junge, gut aussehende Gattin eines erfolgreichen Mannes **she denies that she is a ~** sie streitet ab, dass ihr Mann sie nur wegen ihrer Jugend und ihres Aussehens geheiratet hat

tropic [ˈtrɒpɪk] N a Wendekreis m; **Tropic of Cancer/Capricorn** Wendekreis m des Krebses/Steinbocks b **tropics** PL Tropen pl

tropical [ˈtrɒpɪkəl] ADJ tropisch, Tropen-; **~ diseases** Tropenkrankheiten pl; **the heat was ~** es herrschte tropische Hitze

tropical medicine N Tropenmedizin f

tropical rainforest N tropischer Regenwald

tropism [ˈtrəʊpɪzəm] N (Biol) Tropismus m

tropopause [ˈtrɒpəpɔːz] N (Met) Tropopause f

troposphere [ˈtrɒpəsfɪə] N (Met) Troposphäre f

trot [trɒt] N a (= pace) Trab m; **to go at a ~** traben; **to go for a ~** einen Ausritt machen; **I've been on the ~ all day** (fig inf) ich bin schon den ganzen Tag auf Trab b (inf) **for five days on the ~** fünf Tage lang in einer Tour; **he won three games on the ~** er gewann drei Spiele hintereinander c (inf: = diarrhoea) **the ~s** die Renneritis (hum inf) VI (horse, person) traben; (pony) zockeln; (small child) trippeln; **he ~ted obediently (a)round the shops after her** er zottelte folgsam hinter ihr her durch die Geschäfte VT horse traben lassen

▶ **trot along** VI (horse, person) traben; (pony) zockeln; (small child) trippeln; (= go away) abmarschieren; **to trot along behind sb** hinter jdm hertraben etc

▶ **trot away** or **off** VI → **trot** VI davon- or wegtraben/-zockeln/-trippeln

▶ **trot out** VI → **trot** VI hinaustraben/-zockeln/-trippeln VT sep excuses, theories, names, list aufwarten or kommen mit

▶ **trot round** VI (esp Brit = go quickly) hinüberlaufen; **to trot round to the grocer's** zum Kaufmann laufen

troth [trəʊθ] N (old) → **plight**[1]

trotter[1] [ˈtrɒtə] N (= horse) Traber m

trotter[2] N (of animal) Fuß m; **pigs' ~s** (Cook) Schweinsfüße pl

trotting race [ˈtrɒtɪŋˌreɪs] N (horse racing) Trabrennen nt

troubadour [ˈtruːbədɔː] N Troubadour m

trouble [ˈtrʌbl̩] ⊘ 2.3, 17.2 N a Schwierigkeiten pl; (bothersome) Ärger m; **did you have any ~ (in) getting it?** hatten Sie Schwierigkeiten es zu bekommen?; **to be in ~** in Schwierigkeiten sein; **you'll be in ~ for this** da bekommen Sie Ärger or Schwierigkeiten; **to be in ~ with sb** mit jdm Schwierigkeiten or Ärger haben; **to get into ~** in Schwierigkeiten geraten; (with authority) Schwierigkeiten or Ärger bekommen (with mit); **to get sb into ~** jdn in Schwierigkeiten bringen (with mit); **to get a girl into ~** (euph) ein Mädchen ins Unglück bringen; **to get out of ~** aus den Schwierigkeiten herauskommen; **to get sb out of ~** jdm aus seinen Schwierigkeiten heraushelfen; **to keep** or **stay out of ~** nicht in Schwierigkeiten kommen, sauber bleiben (inf); **now we're out of ~** jetzt sind wir aus den Schwierigkeiten heraus; **the children are never out of ~** die Kinder stellen dauernd etwas an; **to make ~** (= cause a row etc) Krach schlagen (inf), Ärger machen; **to make ~ for sb/oneself** (with authority) jdn/sich selbst in Schwierigkeiten bringen; **that's/you're asking for ~** das kann ja nicht gut gehen; **are you looking for ~?** Sie wollen wohl Ärger?; **to look for ~, to go around looking for ~** sich (dat) Ärger einhandeln; **there'll be ~ if he finds out** wenn er das erfährt, gibts Ärger or Trouble (inf); **here comes ~** (inf) jetzt geht es los! (inf), jetzt gibt es Ärger or Trouble! (inf); **what's the ~?** was ist los?; (to sick person) wo fehlts?; **the ~ is that ...** das Problem ist, dass ...; **that's the ~** das ist das Problem; **family/money ~s** Familien-/Geldsorgen pl; **his ~s are not yet over** seine Sorgen or Probleme sind noch nicht vorbei

b (= bother, effort) Mühe f; **it's no ~ (at all)** das mache ich doch gern; **thank you – (it was)**

no ~ vielen Dank – (das ist) gern geschehen; **it's no ~ to do it properly** man kann es genauso gut ordentlich machen; **it's not worth the ~** das ist nicht der Mühe wert; **she's/it's more ~ than she's/it's worth** sie/es macht mehr Ärger or Umstände als sie/es wert ist; **nothing is too much ~ for her** nichts ist ihr zu viel; **to go to the ~ (of doing sth), to take the ~ (to do sth)** sich (dat) die Mühe machen(, etw zu tun); **to go to/to take a lot of ~ (over** or **with sth)** sich (dat) (mit etw) viel Mühe geben; **you have gone to a lot of ~ over the food** Sie haben sich (dat) solche Umstände mit dem Essen gemacht; **he went to enormous ~** er hat alles nur Erdenkliche getan; **to put sb to the ~ of doing sth** jdn bemühen, etw zu tun; **to put sb to a lot of ~** jdm viel Mühe machen

c (= nuisance) **to be a ~ (to sb)** (jdm) Mühe machen; (dependent person also) (jdm) zur Last fallen; **the child is nothing but ~ to his parents** das Kind macht seinen Eltern nur Sorgen; **he's been no ~ at all** (of child) er war ganz lieb

d (Med: = illness) Leiden nt; (fig) Schaden m; **heart/back ~** Herz-/Rückenleiden nt; **my back is giving me ~** mein Rücken macht mir zu schaffen; **engine ~** (ein) Motorschaden m

e (= unrest, upheaval) Unruhe f; **labour** (Brit) or **labor** (US) **~s** Arbeiterunruhen pl; **there's ~ at the factory/in Iran** in der Fabrik/im Iran herrscht Unruhe; **he caused/made ~ between them** er hat Unruhe zwischen ihnen gestiftet → **stir up**

VT a (= worry) beunruhigen; (= disturb, grieve) bekümmern; **to be ~d by sth** wegen etw besorgt or beunruhigt/bekümmert sein; **he's ~d with a bad back** er leidet an Rückenschmerzen b (= bother) bemühen, belästigen; **I'm sorry to ~ you, but could you tell me if ...** entschuldigen Sie die Störung, aber könnten Sie mir sagen, ob ...; **may I ~ you for a light?** darf ich Sie um Feuer bitten?; **will it ~ you if I smoke?** stört es Sie, wenn ich rauche?; **I shan't ~ you with the details** ich werde Ihnen die Einzelheiten ersparen; **we are ~d with mice just now** wir werden zurzeit von Mäusen geplagt; **I'll ~ you to remember who you're speaking to!** (iro) würden Sie bitte daran denken, mit wem Sie sprechen!

c (= take the trouble) **to ~ to do sth** sich bemühen, etw zu tun; **please don't ~ yourself** bitte bemühen Sie sich nicht; **don't ~ to write until you've settled down** schreib erst, wenn du dich eingelebt hast; **if you had ~d to ask, you might have found out the truth** wenn du dir die Mühe gemacht und gefragt hättest, hättest du wahrscheinlich die Wahrheit erfahren; **oh, don't ~ to apologize!** (iro) bemüh dich nicht, dich zu entschuldigen

VI sich bemühen

troubled [ˈtrʌbl̩d] ADJ a person, look, sleep unruhig, beunruhigt; (= grieved) bekümmert; mind, conscience aufgewühlt; water aufgewühlt; (= unsettled) relationship, marriage gestört; life schwer; times, area, country, region unruhig; **the ~ waters of industrial relations** die gestörte Beziehung zwischen Arbeitgebern und Arbeitnehmern → **oil** b (Ind, Fin) company, bank, industry in Schwierigkeiten pred; **financially ~** in finanziellen Nöten

trouble: trouble-free ADJ period, process, car problemlos; relationship also reibungslos; area ruhig; machine störungsfrei; **troublemaker** N Tunichtgut m; (deliberate) Unruhestifter(in) m(f); **troubleproof** ADJ störungsfrei; **troubleshooter** N Störungssucher(in) m(f); (Pol, Ind, = mediator) Vermittler(in) m(f); **~s** (Pol etc, = organization) Krisenfeuerwehr f; **troublesome** ADJ (= bothersome) lästig; person, problem schwierig; **the most ~ boy in the school** der schwierigste Junge in der Schule; (= troublemaker) der größte Störenfried in der Schule; **don't be ~!** sei nicht so schwierig!; **trouble spot** N Unruheherd m; (in system) Störung f

troublous [ˈtrʌbləs] ADJ (liter) unruhig

trough [trɒf] N a (= container) Trog m; **drinking ~** Wassertrog m b (= depression) Furche f, Rille *f*; (*between waves, on graph*) Tal *nt*; (*Met*) Trog *m*; **~ of depression** Tiefdrucktrog *m*

trounce [traʊns] VT verprügeln; (*Sport*) vernichtend schlagen

trouncing ['traʊnsɪŋ] N Prügel *pl* (*also Sport*); **to give sb a ~** jdm Prügel verpassen

troupe [tru:p] N (*Theat*) Truppe *f*

trouper ['tru:pə'] N (*Theat*) Mime *m*, Mimin *f* (*dated*); **an old ~** (*fig*) ein alter Hase; **he/she is a real ~** er/sie packt immer mit an

trouser ['traʊzə'] (*esp Brit*): **trouser clip** N Hosenklammer *f*; **trouser leg** N Hosenbein *nt*; **trouser press** N Hosenpresse *f*

trousers ['traʊzɪz] PL (*esp Brit*) (*also* **pair of trousers**) Hose *f*; **she was wearing ~** sie hatte Hosen *or* eine Hose an; **to wear the ~** (*fig inf*) die Hosen anhaben (*inf*); **to be caught with one's ~ down** (*inf, lit: sexually*) in flagranti erwischt werden (*inf*); (*fig*) überrumpelt werden; (*= unprepared*) sich unvorbereitet erwischen lassen

trouser suit N (*Brit*) Hosenanzug *m*

trousseau ['tru:səʊ] N Aussteuer *f*

trout [traʊt] N Forelle *f*; **~ fishing** Forellenfang *m*, Forellenangeln *nt*; **silly old ~!** (*inf*) blöde alte (Zimt)ziege (*inf*)

trove [trəʊv] N = **treasure trove**

trowel ['traʊəl] N Kelle *f*; **to lay sth on with a ~** (*Brit inf*) bei etw dick auftragen

Troy [trɔɪ] N (*Hist*) Troja *nt* → **Helen**

troy [trɔɪ] N (*also* **troy weight**) Troygewicht *nt*

truancy ['traʊənsɪ] N (Schule)schwänzen *nt*, unentschuldigtes Fehlen (in der Schule) (*form*), (Schul)schwänzerei *f* (*inf*)

truancy officer N Sozialarbeiter, der sich um Schulschwänzer kümmert

truant ['truənt] N (Schul)schwänzer(in) *m(f)*; **to play ~ (from sth)** (bei etw) unentschuldigt fehlen, (etw) schwänzen (*inf*) VI schwänzen (*inf*)

truce [tru:s] N (*Mil, fig*) Waffenstillstand *m*; (*Mil, interrupting fighting*) Waffenruhe *f*; **~!** Friede!

truck[1] [trʌk] N a (*esp Brit Rail*) Güterwagen *m* b (*= barrow*) Karren *m*, Wagen *m*; (*for luggage*) Gepäckkarren *m*; (*motorized*) Elektrokarren *m* c (*= lorry*) Last(kraft)wagen *m*; (*= van, pick-up*) Lieferwagen *m* VT (*US*) transportieren, spedieren VI (*US*) Lastwagen fahren

truck[2] N a (*fig: = dealings*) **to have no ~ with sb/sth** mit jdm/etw nichts zu tun haben b (*Hist: = payment*) **~ (system)** Trucksystem *nt* (*spec*); **they were paid in ~** sie wurden in Waren bezahlt c (*US: = garden produce*) Gemüse *nt* (*für den Verkauf angebaut*)

truckage ['trʌkɪdʒ] N (*US, = transport*) Transport *m*, Spedition *f*; (*= charge*) Transportkosten *pl*

truckage company N Spedition(sfirma) *f*, Transportunternehmen *nt*

truck driver N Lastwagenfahrer(in) *m(f)*

trucker ['trʌkə'] N a (*esp US, = truck driver*) Lastwagenfahrer(in) *m(f)*; (*= haulage contractor*) Spediteur(in) *m(f)* b (*US: = farmer*) Gemüsegärtner(in) *m(f)*

truck (*US*): **truck farm** N Gemüsefarm *f*; **truck farmer** N Gemüsegärtner(in) *m(f)*; **truck garden** N Gemüsegärtnerei *f*

trucking ['trʌkɪŋ] N (*esp US*) Spedition *f*, Transport *m*

truckle ['trʌkl] VI klein beigeben (*to sb* jdm gegenüber)

truckle bed N niedriges Rollbett

truck: **truckload** N Wagenladung *f*; **they came by the ~** sie kamen in ganzen Wagenladungen; **truckman** N Lastwagenfahrer *m*; **truckstop** N (*US*) Fernfahrerlokal *nt*

truculence ['trʌkjʊləns] N Trotzigkeit *f*, Aufsässigkeit *f*

truculent ['trʌkjʊlənt] ADJ trotzig, aufsässig

trudge [trʌdʒ] VI **to ~ in/out/along** *etc* hinein-/hinaus-/entlangtrotten *etc*; **to ~ through the mud** durch den Matsch stapfen; **we ~d**

(a)round the shops wir sind durch die Geschäfte getrottet *or* gelatscht (*inf*) VT **streets, town** trotten durch; (*looking for sth*) abklappern N mühseliger Marsch

true [tru:] ⚙ 26.1, 26.3 ADJ a (*= not false*) *story, news, rumour, statement* wahr; **to come ~** (*dream, wishes*) Wirklichkeit werden, wahr werden; (*prophecy*) sich verwirklichen; (*fears*) sich bewahrheiten; **to make sth come ~** etw wahr werden lassen; **it is ~ that ...** es stimmt, dass ..., es ist wahr *or* richtig, dass ...; **that's ~** das stimmt, das ist wahr; **can it be ~ (that he didn't know)?** kann es stimmen *or* sein(, dass er das nicht wusste)?; **it is ~ to say that ...** es ist richtig, dass ...; **~!** richtig!; **too ~!** (das ist nur) zu wahr!, wie wahr!; **it is only too ~ that ...** es ist nur allzu wahr, dass ...; **we mustn't generalize, (it's) ~, but ...** wir sollten natürlich nicht verallgemeinern, aber ...; **that's wrong! – ~, but ...** das ist falsch! – stimmt *or* richtig, aber ...; **is it ~ about Harry?** stimmt es, was man über Harry sagt?; **the reverse is ~** ganz im Gegenteil; **the reverse is ~ for ...** für ... trifft das Gegenteil zu; **he's got so much money it's not ~!** (*inf*) es ist unfassbar, wie viel Geld er hat!

b (*= accurate*) *description, report, account* wahrheitsgetreu; *likeness* (lebens)getreu; *copy* getreu; *aim* genau; **the ~ meaning of** die wahre Bedeutung (*+gen*); **in the ~ sense (of the word)** im wahren Sinne (des Wortes)

c (*= real, genuine*) *feeling, friendship, friend, Christian, heir, opinion* wahr, echt; *reason* wirklich; *leather, antique* echt; **the frog is not a ~ reptile** der Frosch ist kein echtes Reptil; **spoken like a ~ football fan** so spricht ein wahrer Fußballfan; **in a ~ spirit of friendship/love** im wahren Geist der Freundschaft/Liebe; **~ love** die wahre Liebe; (*= person*) Schatz *m*, Herzallerliebste(r) *mf* (*old*); **the path of ~ love ne'er did run smooth** (*prov*) die Pfade der Liebe sind gewunden; **what is the ~ situation?** wie verhält es sich wirklich?; **in ~ life** im wirklichen Leben; **the one ~ God** der einzige wahre Gott; **the True Cross** (*Rel*) das wahre Kreuz

d (*= faithful*) *friend, follower* treu; **to be ~ to sb** jdm treu sein/bleiben; **to be ~ to one's word/promise** (treu) zu seinem Wort/Versprechen stehen, seinem Wort treu bleiben; **to be ~ to oneself** sich selbst treu bleiben; **to thine own self be ~** (*liter*) bleibe dir selbst treu; **twelve good men and ~** zwölf ehrbare Männer; **~ to life** lebensnah; (*Art*) lebensecht; **the horse ran ~ to form** das Pferd lief erwartungsgemäß; **~ to type** erwartungsgemäß; *dog* artgetreu

e *wall, surface* gerade; *join* genau; *circle* rund

f (*Phys*) tatsächlich; **~ north** der eigentliche *or* tatsächliche *or* geografische Norden

g (*= applicable*) **to be ~ for sb/sth** für jdn/etw wahr sein; **to be ~ of sb/sth** auf jdn/etw zutreffen; **the same is** *or* **holds ~ for ...** dasselbe gilt auch für ..., dasselbe trifft auch auf ... (*acc*) zu

h (*Mus*) *note* richtig; *voice* rein

N **out of ~** (*upright, beam, wheels*) schief; *join* verschoben

ADV *aim* genau; *sing* richtig; **to breed ~** sich reinrassig fortpflanzen; **he speaks ~** (*old*) er spricht die Wahrheit; **they speak ~r than they know** (*old*) sie kommen der Wahrheit näher, als ihnen bewusst ist → **ring**[2]

▶ **true up** VT *sep machinery* genau einstellen; *beam* genau einrichten; *wheel* einrichten; **to true up the edges of the planks** die Bretterkanten plan machen

true: **true blue** N (*Brit*: = Tory) echter Tory, waschechte Tory (*inf*); **true-blue** ADJ waschecht (*inf*), echt; **true-born** ADJ echt, gebürtig; (*= legitimate*) rechtmäßig; **true-bred** ADJ wahr, echt; *cattle* reinrassig; **true-hearted** ADJ getreu, aufrichtig; **true-life** ADJ *attr* aus dem Leben gegriffen; **true rib** N wahre Rippe

truffle ['trʌfl] N Trüffel *f or m*

trug [trʌg] N Korb *m*

truism ['tru:ɪzəm] N (*= obvious truth*) Binsenwahrheit *f*; (*= platitude*) Plattitüde *f*, Gemeinplatz *m*

truly ['tru:lɪ] ADV a (*= truthfully, genuinely*) wirklich, wahrhaftig; **(really) ~?** wirklich und wahrhaftig?; **he did it, ~ he did!** er hat es wirklich und wahrhaftig getan!; **the only man she had ever ~ loved** der einzige Mann, den sie je wahrhaft geliebt hat; **I am ~ sorry** es tut mir aufrichtig Leid; **it can ~ be said that ...** es lässt sich wahrhaftig sagen, dass ...; **~ amazing/terrible** wirklich erstaunlich/furchtbar → **well**[2] b (*= faithfully*) *serve, love* treu; *reflect* wahrheitsgetreu

trump[1] [trʌmp] N (*Cards, fig*) Trumpf *m*; (*dated inf, = person*) prima Kerl *m* (*dated inf*); **spades are ~s** Pik ist Trumpf; **what's ~s?** was ist Trumpf?; **to hold all the ~s** (*fig*) alle Trümpfe in der Hand halten; **he's absolutely ~s** (*dated inf*) er ist große Klasse (*inf*); **to come** *or* **turn up ~s** (*Brit inf*) sich als Sieger erweisen VT (*Cards*) stechen; (*fig*) übertrumpfen

▶ **trump up** VT *sep* erfinden

trump[2] N (*liter*) Trompete *f*; **at the Last Trump** wenn die Posaunen des Jüngsten Gerichts erklingen

trump card N (*Cards*) Trumpfkarte *f*; (*fig*) Trumpf *m*; **to play one's ~** (*lit, fig*) seinen Trumpf ausspielen

trumped-up ['trʌmptʌp] ADJ *charge* erfunden

trumpery ['trʌmpərɪ] N Plunder *m no pl*; (*= ornaments*) Kitsch *m*; (*= jewellery*) Flitterkram *m*; (*= nonsense*) Unsinn *m* ADJ billig; *ornaments also* kitschig

trumpet ['trʌmpɪt] N a (*Mus*) Trompete *f* → **blow**[2] b (*of elephant*) Trompeten *nt no pl* c (*of flower*) Trompete *f*; (*= hearing trumpet*) Hörrohr *nt*; (*= speaking trumpet*) Sprachrohr *nt*, Megaphon *nt*, Megafon *nt* VT (*rare: also* **trumpet forth**) hinaustrompeten VI (*elephant*) trompeten

trumpet call N Trompetensignal *nt*

trumpeter ['trʌmpɪtə'] N Trompeter(in) *m(f)*

trumpeting ['trʌmpɪtɪŋ] N (*of elephant*) Trompeten *nt*

trumpet major N Stabstrompeter *m*

truncate [trʌŋ'keɪt] VT kürzen, beschneiden; (*Comput*) *number* abschneiden; *process* abbrechen ADJ ['trʌŋkeɪt] *cone* stumpf; *leaf* abgestumpft

truncated [trʌŋ'keɪtɪd] ADJ *tree* gestutzt; *article, speech, version* gekürzt; *presidency* verkürzt; *cone* stumpf; *leaf* abgestumpft

truncation [trʌŋ'keɪʃən] N Kürzung *f*, Beschneidung *f*; (*Comput*) (*of number*) Abschneiden *nt*; (*of process*) Abbruch *m*

truncheon ['trʌntʃən] N (Gummi)knüppel *m*; (*esp of riot police*) Schlagstock *m*

trundle ['trʌndl] VT (*= push*) rollen; (*= pull*) ziehen VI **to ~ in/along/down** hinein-/entlang-/hinunterzockeln; (*= clatter*) hinein-/entlang-/hinunterrumpeln

trundle bed N (*US*) Rollbett *nt*

trunk [trʌŋk] N a (*of tree*) Stamm *m*; (*of body*) Rumpf *m* b (*of elephant*) Rüssel *m* c (*= case*) Schrankkoffer *m* d (*US, Aut*) Kofferraum *m* e **trunks** PL (*for swimming*) Badehose *f*; (*for sport*) Shorts *pl*; (*dated Brit: = underwear*) Unterhose *f*; **a pair of ~s** eine Badehose; (*for sport*) Shorts *pl*; (*Brit: = underwear*) eine Unterhose

trunk: **trunk call** N (*Brit, Telec*) Ferngespräch *nt*; **trunk hose** N (*Hist*) Pluderhose *f*; **trunk line** N (*Rail*) Hauptstrecke *f*; (*Telec*) Fernleitung *f*; **trunk road** N (*Brit*) Fernstraße *f*

truss [trʌs] N a (*Brit, = bundle*) Bündel *nt*, Garbe *f* b (*Build, of bridge*) Fachwerk *nt*; (*of roof*) Gespärre *nt*; (*= single beam*) Dachsparren *m*; (*vertical*) Dachbalken *m* c (*Med*) Bruchband *nt* VT a (*= tie*) *hay* bündeln; *person* fesseln b (*Cook*) *chicken etc* dressieren c (*Build*) (ab)stützen

▶ **truss up** VT *sep* (*Cook*) *chicken etc* dressieren; (*inf*) *person* fesseln

trust [trʌst] N a (*= confidence, reliance*) Vertrauen *nt* (*in* zu); **I have every ~ in him** ich habe volles Vertrauen zu ihm; **to put** or **place one's ~ in sb** Vertrauen in jdn setzen; **to take sth on ~** etw einfach glauben; **to give sb sth on ~** (= *without payment*) jdm etw auf sein ehrliches Gesicht hin (*inf*) or im guten Glauben geben; **position of ~** Vertrauensstellung f

b (= *charge*) Verantwortung f; **to commit sth to sb's ~** jdm etw anvertrauen

c (*Jur, Fin*) Treuhand(schaft) f; (= *property*) Treuhandeigentum nt; (= *charitable fund*) Fonds m, Stiftung f; **to hold sth in ~ for sb** etw für jdn treuhänderisch verwalten; **all his money was tied up in a ~** sein ganzes Geld wurde treuhänderisch verwaltet

d (*Comm: also* **trust company**) Trust m
e (*Brit: also* **trust hospital**) *finanziell eigenverantwortliches, vom staatlichen Gesundheitswesen getragenes Krankenhaus*

VT a (= *have confidence in*) trauen (+*dat*); *person* (ver)trauen (+*dat*); *words* glauben; **to ~ sb to do sth** (= *believe him honest etc*) jdm vertrauen, dass er etw tut; (= *believe him capable*) jdm zutrauen, dass er etw tut; **don't you ~ me?** vertraust du mir nicht?; **to ~ sb with sth, to ~ sth to sb** jdm etw anvertrauen; **I don't ~ her with my boyfriend** ich traue ihr mit meinem Freund nicht; **can he be ~ed not to lose it?** kann man sich darauf verlassen, dass er es nicht verliert?; **can we ~ him to go shopping alone?** können wir ihn allein einkaufen gehen lassen?; **you can't ~ a word he says** man kann ihm kein Wort glauben; **I wouldn't ~ him (any) farther than I can throw him** ich traue ihm nicht über den Weg (*inf*)

b (*iro inf*) **~ you/him!** typisch!; **~ him to break it!** er muss es natürlich kaputtmachen
c (= *hope*) hoffen; **I ~ not** hoffentlich nicht, ich hoffe nicht; **you're going to help, I ~** du wirst doch hoffentlich mithelfen

VI a (= *have confidence*) vertrauen; **to ~ in sb** auf jdn vertrauen

b (= *rely on*) **to ~ to sth** sich auf etw (*acc*) verlassen, auf etw (*acc*) vertrauen; **to ~ to luck** or **chance** sich auf sein Glück verlassen; **I'll have to ~ to luck to find it** ich kann nur hoffen, dass ich es finde

trust: trust account N Treuhandkonto nt; **trust company** N (*Econ, Fin*) Treuhandgesellschaft f, Treuhandbank f

trusted ['trʌstɪd] ADJ *method* bewährt; *friend, servant* getreu

trustee [trʌs'tiː] N **a** (*of estate*) Treuhänder(in) m(f), Vermögensverwalter(in) m(f) **b** (*of institution*) Kurator(in) m(f), Verwalter(in) m(f); **~s** Vorstand m; **Trustee Savings Bank** ≈ Sparkasse f

trusteeship [trʌs'tiːʃɪp] N **a** Treuhandschaft f
b (*of a territory*) Treuhandschaft f, Mandat nt
c (*also* **trusteeship territory**) Treuhandgebiet nt, Mandat(sgebiet) nt

trustful ['trʌstfʊl] ADJ *look, expression* vertrauensvoll; *person also* gutgläubig, arglos

trustfully ['trʌstfəlɪ] ADV vertrauensvoll

trust fund N Treuhandvermögen nt, Stiftungsgelder pl

trusting ['trʌstɪŋ] ADJ *person, nature* arglos, gutgläubig; *relationship* vertrauensvoll; *face* arglos

trustingly ['trʌstɪŋlɪ] ADV vertrauensvoll; *look* arglos

trust territory N (*Pol*) Treuhandgebiet nt

trustworthiness ['trʌst,wɜːðɪnɪs] N (*of person*) Vertrauenswürdigkeit f; (*of statement, account*) Glaubhaftigkeit f, Glaubwürdigkeit f

trustworthy ['trʌst,wɜːðɪ] ADJ *person* vertrauenswürdig; *statement, account* glaubhaft, glaubwürdig

trusty ['trʌstɪ] ADJ (+*er*) (*liter, hum*) getreu (*liter*); **~ steed** (*dated*) treues Ross N (= *prisoner*) vertrauenswürdiger Häftling

truth [truːθ] N pl **-s** [truːðz] f **a** no pl Wahrheit f; **you must always tell the ~** du musst immer die Wahrheit sagen; **to tell the ~ ...,** **to tell ...** um ehrlich zu sein ..., um die Wahrheit zu sagen ...; **the ~ of it** or **the matter is that ...** die

Wahrheit ist dass ..., in Wahrheit ...; **there's no ~ or** or **not a word of ~ in what he says** es ist kein Wort wahr von dem, was er sagt; **there's some ~ in that** es ist etwas Wahres daran, da ist etwas Wahres dran (*inf*); **the ~, the whole ~ and nothing but the ~** (*Jur*) die Wahrheit, die reine Wahrheit und nichts als die Wahrheit; **in ~** in Wahrheit, in Wirklichkeit; **~ will out** (*prov*) die Wahrheit wird ans Licht kommen, die Sonne wird es an den Tag bringen (*prov*)

b (= *belief, fact*) Wahrheit f → **home truth**

truth drug N Wahrheitsdroge f

truthful ['truːθfʊl] ADJ *person* ehrlich; *statement* ehrlich, wahrheitsgetreu; **to be ~ about it** ehrlich sein

truthfully ['truːθfəlɪ] ADV ehrlich; *answer, say also, explain* wahrheitsgemäß, der Wahrheit entsprechend

truthfulness ['truːθfʊlnɪs] N Ehrlichkeit f, Aufrichtigkeit f; (*of statement*) Wahrheit f

truth serum N Wahrheitsdroge f

truth-value N (*Logic*) Wahrheitswert m

try [traɪ] N **a** (= *attempt*) Versuch m; **to have a ~** es versuchen; **let me have a ~** lass mich mal versuchen!, lass mich mal! (*inf*); **to have a ~ at doing sth** (sich daran) versuchen, etw zu tun, (es) probieren, etw zu tun; **have another ~ (at it)** versuchs noch mal; **I'll give it a ~** (= *will attempt it*) ich werde es mal versuchen; (= *will test it out*) ich werde es ausprobieren; **I'll give him a ~** ich werde ihm eine Chance geben; **it was a good ~** das war schon ganz gut; **it's worth a ~** es ist einen Versuch wert; **at the first ~** beim ersten Versuch, auf Anhieb; **can I have a ~ at your bicycle?** kann ich mal dein Rad ausprobieren?

b (*Rugby*) Versuch m; **to score a ~** einen Versuch erzielen

VT a (= *attempt*) versuchen; **you have only tried two questions** du hast dich nur an zwei Fragen versucht (*inf*), du hast nur zwei Fragen zu beantworten versucht; **to ~ one's hardest** or **one's best** sein Bestes tun or versuchen; **do ~ to understand** bitte versuche doch zu verstehen!; **I've given up ~ing to help him** ich habe es aufgegeben, ihm helfen zu wollen; **it's ~ing to snow** (*inf*) es sieht aus, als würde es schneien; **the sun's ~ing to come out** es sieht so aus, als wollte die Sonne rauskommen; **to ~ one's hand at sth** etw probieren, **I'll ~ anything once** ich probiere alles einmal; **just you ~ it!** (= *you dare*) versuch das bloß!

b (= *try out*) *new detergent, bicycle etc* ausprobieren; *job applicant* eine Chance geben (+*dat*), es versuchen mit (*inf*); *glue, aspirin* es versuchen mit; (= *try to buy* or *get sth at*) *newsagent, next door* es versuchen (bei); (= *try to open*) *door, window* ausprobieren; **I can't shut this case – ~ sitting on it** ich kriege diesen Koffer nicht zu – setz dich doch mal drauf! (*inf*); **you could ~ seeing whether John would help** Sie könnten doch John mal um Hilfe angehen; **I've tried everything** ich habe alles versucht or probiert; **~ whether ...** probieren Sie mal, ob dieser/diese etc passt; (*fig inf*) wie wärs denn damit? (*inf*); **to ~ one's strength** seine Kraft erproben

c (= *sample, taste*) *beer, olives* probieren

d (= *test*) *courage, patience* auf die Probe stellen; (= *strain*) *eyes* anstrengen; **he was tried and found wanting** (*liter*) er wurde gewogen und zu leicht befunden; **(just) ~ me!** (*inf*) wetten?, wetten dass?; **they have been sorely tried** sie sind schwer geprüft (worden); **these things are sent to ~ us** ja, ja, das Leben ist nicht so einfach → **tried-and-tested**

e (*Jur*) *person* vor Gericht stellen; *case* verhandeln; **he is being tried for theft** er steht wegen Diebstahls vor Gericht

VI versuchen; **~ and arrive on time** versuch mal, pünktlich zu sein; **~ as he might, he didn't succeed** sosehr er es auch versuchte or sosehr er sich auch bemühte, er schaffte es einfach nicht; **he didn't even ~** er hat sich (*dat*) überhaupt keine Mühe gegeben; (= *didn't at-*

tempt it) er hat es überhaupt nicht versucht; **you can't say I didn't ~** du kannst nicht sagen, ich hätte es nicht versucht → **succeed**

▸ **try for** VI +*prep obj* sich bemühen um

▸ **try on** VT *sep* **a** *clothes* anprobieren; *hat* aufprobieren **b** (*fig inf*) **to try it on with sb** probieren, wie weit man bei jdm gehen kann, jdn provozieren; **the policeman warned the thief not to try anything on** der Polizist warnte den Dieb, keine Mätzchen (*inf*) or Dummheiten zu machen; **he's just trying it on** er probiert nur, wie weit er gehen or wie weit er es treiben kann; **don't you try it on with me, or I'll tell my husband** versuchs nicht bei or mit mir, sonst sag ichs meinem Mann

▸ **try out** VT *sep* ausprobieren (*on* bei, an +*dat*); *person* eine Chance geben (+*dat*), einen Versuch machen mit VI **two of their players are trying out for Arsenal** zwei ihrer Spieler machen bei Arsenal ein Probetraining

▸ **try over** VT *sep* (*Mus*) *piece* proben

trying ['traɪɪŋ] ADJ schwierig, anstrengend; *work, day, time* anstrengend, aufreibend; *experience* schwer; **it has been a ~ time for them recently** sie haben es in letzter Zeit sehr schwer gehabt; **how ~!** wie ärgerlich!

try: try-on N (*inf*) **do you think he'll do what he threatened? – no, it was just a ~** glaubst du, er wird seine Drohung wahr machen? – nein, er wollte uns nur auf den Arm nehmen (*inf*); **tryout** N (*of machine etc*) Erprobung f; (*of car*) Probefahrt f; (*Ftbl etc*) Probespiel nt; (*of applicant*) Probezeit f; (*of actor*) Probevortrag m; **to give sb a ~** jdm eine Chance geben; **to give sth a ~** etw ausprobieren

tryst [trɪst] N (*old*) Stelldichein nt (*dated*)

trysting place ['trɪstɪŋ,pleɪs] N (*old*) Stelldichein nt (*dated*)

tsar [zɑː] N Zar m

tsarevitch ['zɑːrəvɪtʃ] N Zarewitsch m

tsarina [zɑːˈriːnə] N Zarin f

tsarist ['zɑːrɪst] N Zarist(in) m(f) ADJ zaristisch

tsetse (fly) ['tsetsɪ('flaɪ)] N Tsetsefliege f

T-shirt ['tiːʃɜːt] N T-Shirt nt

tsp(s) abbr of **teaspoonful(s)** or **teaspoon(s)** Teel.

T-square ['tiːskweə'] N Reißschiene f

t-storm ['tiːstɔːm] N (*US: inf*) Gewitter nt

tsunami [tsʊˈnɑːmɪ] N (= *tidal wave*) Tsunami m

TT abbr **a** of **teetotal** **b** of **teetotaller** **c** (*Mot*) of **Tourist Trophy** *jährlich auf der Insel Man abgehaltenes Motorradrennen* **d** (*Agr*) of **tuberculin-tested** or **telegraphic transfer** telegrafische Geldüberweisung

TU (*Brit*) abbr of **Trade Union** Gew.

tub [tʌb] N **a** Kübel m; (*for rainwater*) Tonne f, Traufe f; (*for washing*) Zuber m, Bottich m, Trog m; (*of ice cream, margarine*) Becher m **b** (*esp US inf, = bath tub*) Wanne f **c** (*inf, = boat*) Kahn m

tuba ['tjuːbə] N Tuba f

tubby ['tʌbɪ] ADJ (+*er*) (*inf*) dick; *woman* mollig, rundlich; *child* pummelig, kugelrund; *man* rundlich; **he is getting quite ~** er gibt immer mehr in die Breite, er wird immer runder

tube [tjuːb] N **a** (= *pipe*) Rohr nt; (*of rubber, plastic*) Schlauch m; (= *speaking tube*) Sprachrohr nt; (= *torpedo tube*) Rohr nt; **to go down the ~s** (*fig inf*) den Bach runtergehen (*inf*) **b** (= *container, of toothpaste, paint, glue*) Tube f; (*of sweets*) Röhrchen nt, Rolle f **c** (*Brit: = London underground*) U-Bahn f; **to travel by ~** mit der U-Bahn fahren **d** (*Elec, TV, US, Rad*) Röhre f; **the ~** (*US, inf*) die Röhre (*inf*) **e** (*Anat*) Röhre f; (= *Fallopian tube*) Eileiter m; **the bronchial ~s** die Bronchien pl

tubeless ['tjuːblɪs] ADJ *tyre* schlauchlos

tuber ['tjuːbə'] N (*Bot*) Knolle f

tubercle ['tjuːbɜːkl] N (*Bot*) Knoten m, Knötchen nt; (*Med also*) Tuberkel m

tubercular [tjʊˈbɜːkjʊlə'] ADJ tuberkulös

tuberculin [tjʊˈbɜːkjʊlɪn] N Tuberkulin *nt*; **~-tested** tuberkulingetestet

tuberculosis [tjʊˌbɜːkjʊˈləʊsɪs] N Tuberkulose *f*

tuberculous [tjʊˈbɜːkjʊləs] ADJ tuberkulös

tube station N (*Brit*) U-Bahnstation *f*

tube train N (*Brit*) U-Bahnzug *m*

tubing [ˈtjuːbɪŋ] N Schlauch *m*

tub: tub-thumper N (*pej*) Demagoge *m*, Demagogin *f*, Volksredner(in) *m(f)*; **tub-thumping** (*esp Brit*) **N** Demagogie *f* **ADJ** demagogisch

tubular [ˈtjuːbjʊlə] ADJ röhrenförmig; **~ furniture/scaffolding** Stahlrohrmöbel *pl*/-gerüst *nt*

tubular bells N Glockenspiel *nt*

TUC (*Brit*) *abbr of* **Trades Union Congress** ≈ DGB *m*

tuck [tʌk] **N** **a** (*Sew*) Saum *m*; (*ornamental*) Biese *f*; **to put a ~ in sth** einen Saum in etw (*acc*) nähen
b (*Brit Sch inf*, = *food*) Süßigkeiten *pl*
VT **a** (= *put*) stecken; **he ~ed his umbrella under his arm** er steckte *or* klemmte (*inf*) sich (*dat*) den Regenschirm unter den Arm; **the bird's head was ~ed under its wing** der Vogel hatte den Kopf unter den Flügel gesteckt; **he ~ed his coat (a)round the shivering child** er legte seinen Mantel fest um das frierende Kind; **she sat with her feet ~ed under her** sie saß mit untergeschlagenen Beinen da
b (*Sew*) Biesen *pl* steppen in (+*acc*); **a ~ed bodice** ein Oberteil mit Biesen
VI **your bag will ~ under the seat** du kannst deine Tasche unter dem Sitz verstauen

▶ **tuck away** VT *sep* **a** (= *hide*) wegstecken; **he tucked it away in his pocket** er steckte es in die Tasche; **the hut is tucked away among the trees** die Hütte liegt versteckt zwischen den Bäumen **b** (*inf*, = *eat*) **he can certainly tuck it away!** er kann ganz schön was wegputzen (*inf*); **I can't think where he tucks it all away** ich weiß nicht, wo er das alles lässt (*inf*)

▶ **tuck in** **VI** (*Brit inf*) zulangen, reinhauen (*inf*); **tuck in!** langt zu!, haut rein! (*inf*); **to tuck into sth** sich (*dat*) etw schmecken lassen **VT** *sep* **a** *flap etc* hineinstecken, reinstecken (*inf*); *sheet also* an den Seiten feststecken; **to tuck one's shirt in(to) one's trousers**, **to tuck one's shirt in** das Hemd in die Hose stecken; **tuck your tummy in!** zieh den Bauch ein! **b** **to tuck sb in** jdn zudecken; **to tuck sb into bed** jdn ins Bett stecken

▶ **tuck up** VT *sep* **a** *skirt, hair* hochnehmen; *sleeve* hochkrempeln; *legs* unterschlagen **b** (*Brit*) **to tuck sb up (in bed)** jdn zudecken

tuck box N (*Brit*) Schachtel mit Süßigkeiten

tucker[1] [ˈtʌkə] N (*old: Fashion*) Schultertuch *nt* → **bib**

tucker[2] VT (*US, inf*) fertig machen (*inf*)

tucker[3] N (*esp Austral*) Proviant *m*

tucker-bag [ˈtʌkəbæg] N (*esp Austral*) Provianttasche *f*

tuck-in [tʌkɪn] N (*inf*) Essen *nt*; **to have a (good) ~** kräftig zulangen, ordentlich futtern (*inf*) *or* reinhauen (*inf*)

tuck shop N (*Brit*) Bonbonladen *m*

Tudor [ˈtjuːdə] **ADJ** Tudor-; **~ period** Tudorzeit *f* **N** Tudor *mf*

Tue(s) *abbr of* **Tuesday** Di.

Tuesday [ˈtjuːzdɪ] N Dienstag *m*; **on ~** (am) Dienstag; **on ~s, on a ~** dienstags, an Dienstagen (*form*); **I met her on a ~** ich habe sie an einem Dienstag kennen gelernt; **on ~ morning/evening** (am) Dienstag Morgen/Abend, am Dienstagmorgen/-abend; **on ~ mornings/evenings** dienstags *or* Dienstag morgens/abends; **I'll never forget that ~ evening** diesen Dienstagabend werde ich nie vergessen; **last/next/this ~** Dienstag letzter/nächster/dieser Woche, letzten/nächsten/diesen Dienstag; **a year (ago) last/next ~** letzten/nächsten Dienstag vor einem Jahr; **~'s newspaper** die Zeitung vom Dienstag; **our ~ meeting** (*this week*) unser Treffen am Dienstag; (*every week*) unser dienstägli-

ches Treffen, unser Dienstagstreffen; **~ December 5th** (*in letter*) Dienstag, den 5. Dezember

tuffet [ˈtʌfɪt] N (*old*) kleiner Hügel, Buckel *m*

tuft [tʌft] N Büschel *nt*; **a ~ of hair** ein Haarbüschel *nt*; **a ~ of feathers** ein Federbusch *m*

tufted [ˈtʌftɪd] ADJ (*Orn*) mit Federbusch; (*Bot*) büschelförmig

tufted duck N Reiherente *f*

tufty [ˈtʌftɪ] ADJ büschelig

tug [tʌg] **VT** zerren, ziehen; *vessel* (ab)schleppen; **she ~ged his sleeve** sie zog an seinem Ärmel; **she ~ged a tuft of his hair out by the roots** sie zog *or* riss ihm ein Büschel Haare aus **VI** ziehen, zerren (*at* an +*dat*) → **heartstrings** **N** **a** (= *pull*) **to give sth a ~** an etw (*dat*) ziehen; **I felt a ~ on my sleeve** ich spürte, wie mich jemand am Ärmel zog; **parting with it was quite a ~** es fiel mir *etc* sehr schwer, mich *etc* davon zu trennen **b** (*also* **tugboat**) Schlepper *m*, Schleppkahn *m*

tug: tug-of-love N Tauziehen um das Kind/ die Kinder bei einer Ehescheidung; **tug-of--war** N (*Sport, fig*) Tauziehen *nt*

tuition [tjʊˈɪʃən] N Unterricht *m*; **extra ~** Nachhilfeunterricht *m*

tulip [ˈtjuːlɪp] N Tulpe *f*; **~ tree** Tulpenbaum *m*

tulle [tjuːl] N Tüll *m*

tumble [ˈtʌmbl] **N** **a** (= *fall*) Sturz *m*; **to take a ~** stürzen, straucheln; (*fig*) fallen **b** (= *mess*) Durcheinander *nt* **VI** **a** (= *fall*) straucheln, (hin)fallen; (= *move quickly*) stürzen; (*fig: prices*) fallen; **he ~d off his bicycle** er stürzte vom Fahrrad; **to ~ out of/into bed** aus dem Bett/ ins Bett fallen; **to ~ over sth** über etw (*acc*) fallen *or* stolpern **b** (*inf*: = *realize*) **to ~ to sth** etw kapieren (*inf*) **c** (*gymnast*) Bodenakrobatik machen **VT** **a** (= *make fall*) fallen lassen; (= *make untidy*) **to ~ sb's hair** jdm das Haar zerzausen, durcheinander bringen

▶ **tumble about** (*Brit*) *or* **around** VI durcheinander purzeln; (*children, kittens etc*) herumpurzeln; **the clothes tumbled about in the drier** die Wäsche wurde im Trockenautomaten durcheinander gewirbelt

▶ **tumble down** VI **a** (= *fall down, person*) hinfallen, stürzen; (*object*) herunterfallen; (*building*) einstürzen; **to tumble down the stairs** die Treppe hinunterfallen **b** (= *move quickly*) **they came tumbling down the stairs** sie kamen die Treppe heruntergestürzt

▶ **tumble in** VI (= *come in*) hereinpurzeln

▶ **tumble out** VI (= *go out*) hinauspurzeln

▶ **tumble over** VI umfallen, umkippen

tumble: tumbledown ADJ verfallen, baufällig; **tumble drier, tumble dryer** N Trockenautomat *m*, Heißlufttrockner *m*, Trockner *m* (*inf*)

tumbler [ˈtʌmblə] N **a** (= *glass*) (Becher)glas *nt*, Tumbler *m* **b** (*in lock*) Zuhaltung *f* **c** (= *acrobat*) Bodenakrobat(in) *m(f)* **d** (= *toy*) Stehaufmännchen *nt* **e** (= *tumble drier*) Trockenautomat *m*, Trockner *m* (*inf*) **f** (*Orn*) Tümmler *m*

tumbleweed [ˈtʌmblˌwiːd] N Steppenläufer *m* *or* -hexe *f*

tumbrel, tumbril [ˈtʌmbrəl] N (*Hist*) Karren *m*

tumescence [tuːˈmesns] N (*form*) Schwellung *f*

tumescent [tjuːˈmesnt] ADJ (*form*) anschwellend

tumid [ˈtjuːmɪd] ADJ (*Med*) geschwollen; (*fig*) *style* geschwollen; *speech* schwülstig

tummy [ˈtʌmɪ] N (*inf*) Bauch *m*, Bäuchlein *nt* (*baby-talk*); **those green tomatoes will give you a sore ~** von diesen grünen Tomaten kriegst du Bauchschmerzen *or* Bauchweh

tummy tuck N (*Med inf*) Fettabsaugung *f* am Bauch

tumour, (*US*) **tumor** [ˈtjuːmə] N Geschwulst *f*, Tumor *m*; **a ~ on the brain, a brain ~** ein Gehirntumor *m*

tumult [ˈtjuːmʌlt] N (= *uproar*) Tumult *m*; **the ~ of battle** das Schlachtgetümmel *nt* **b** (*emotional*) **his mind was in a ~** sein Inneres befand sich in Aufruhr; **a ~ of emotion/weeping** ein Gefühls-/Tränenausbruch *m*

tumultuous [tjuːˈmʌltjʊəs] ADJ *applause, day, times, relationship* stürmisch; **they gave him a ~ welcome** sie begrüßten ihn stürmisch; **a ~ sea** eine stürmische See

tumultuously [tjuːˈmʌltjʊəslɪ] ADV stürmisch

tumulus [ˈtjuːmjʊləs] N Tumulus *m*, Grabhügel *m*

tun [tʌn] N (= *cask*) Fass *nt*

tuna (fish) [ˈtjuːnə(ˈfɪʃ)] N T(h)unfisch *m*

tundra [ˈtʌndrə] N Tundra *f*

tune [tjuːn] **N** **a** (= *melody*) Melodie *f*; **sung to the ~ of ...** gesungen nach der Melodie (von) ...; **there's not much ~ to it** das ist *or* klingt nicht sehr melodisch; **give us a ~!** spiel uns was vor!; **to change one's ~** (*fig*) seine Meinung ändern; **to dance to sb's ~** (*fig*) nach jds Pfeife tanzen; **to call the ~** (*fig*) den Ton angeben; **to the ~ of £100** in Höhe von £ 100
b (= *pitch*) **to sing in ~/out of ~** richtig/falsch singen; **the piano is out of ~** das Klavier ist verstimmt; **to go out of ~** (*instrument*) sich verstimmen; (*singer*) anfangen, falsch zu singen; **the piano is not in ~ with the flute** das Klavier und die Flöte sind nicht gleich gestimmt; **to be in/out of ~ with sb/sth** (*fig*) mit jdm/etw harmonieren/nicht harmonieren, mit jdm/etw in Einklang/nicht in Einklang stehen; **he's a successful teacher because he's in ~ with young people** er ist ein erfolgreicher Lehrer, weil er auf der gleichen Wellenlänge mit den Jugendlichen ist (*inf*); **he felt out of ~ with his new environment** er fühlte sich in seiner neuen Umgebung fehl am Platze
c (*Aut*) **the carburettor is out of ~** der Vergaser ist falsch eingestellt
VT **a** (*Mus*) *instrument* stimmen
b (*Rad, TV*) einstellen; **you are ~d to the BBC World Service** Sie hören den *or* hier ist der BBC World Service
c (*Aut*) *engine, carburettor* einstellen

▶ **tune down** VT (*fig*) *enthusiasm etc* dämpfen

▶ **tune in** **VI** **a** (*Rad*) einschalten; **to tune in to Radio London** Radio London einschalten *or* hören **b** **to tune in to sth** (*to feelings etc*) sich einstellen auf etw (*acc*) **VT** *sep* **a** *radio* einschalten (*to* +*acc*); **you are tuned in to Radio 2** Sie hören *or* hier ist Radio 2 **b** **to be tuned in to sth** (*to feelings etc*) auf etw (*acc*) eingestellt sein

▶ **tune up** **VI** (*Mus*) (sein Instrument) stimmen **VT** *sep* (*Aut*) *engine* tunen

tuneful ADJ , **tunefully** ADV [ˈtjuːnfʊl, -fəlɪ] melodisch

tunefulness [ˈtjuːnfʊlnɪs] N Melodik *f*

tuneless ADJ , **tunelessly** ADV [ˈtjuːnlɪs, -lɪ] unmelodisch

tuner [ˈtjuːnə] N **a** (*Mus*) Stimmer(in) *m(f)* **b** (*Rad etc, = part of set*) Empfangsteil *nt*; (= *separate set*) Empfänger *m*, Tuner *m*

tuner-amp(lifier) [ˌtjuːnərˈæmp(lɪfaɪə)] N (*Rad etc*) Steuergerät *nt*, Receiver *m*

tune-up [ˈtjuːnʌp] N (*Aut*) **the car needs/has had a ~** das Auto muss getunt werden/ist getunt worden

tungsten [ˈtʌŋstən] N Wolfram *nt*

tungsten lamp N Wolframlampe *f*

tungsten steel N Wolframstahl *m*

tunic [ˈtjuːnɪk] N Kasack *m*, Hemdbluse *f*; (*of uniform*) Uniformrock *m*; (*of school uniform*) Kittel *m*; (*in ancient Greece*) Chiton *m*; (*in ancient Rome*) Tunika *f*

tuning [ˈtjuːnɪŋ] N **a** (*Mus*) Stimmen *nt* **b** (*Rad*) Einstellen *nt*; **it takes a lot of ~ to find the right station** man muss lange suchen, bis man den richtigen Sender gefunden hat **c** (*Aut*) Einstellen *nt*; **all the engine needed was a little ~** der Motor musste nur richtig eingestellt werden

tuning fork N (*Mus*) Stimmgabel *f*

tuning knob N (*Rad*) Stationswahlknopf *m*

Tunisia [tjuːˈnɪzɪə] N Tunesien *nt*

Tunisian [tjuːˈnɪzɪən] N Tunesier(in) m(f) ADJ tunesisch; **he is ~** er ist Tunesier

tunnel [ˈtʌnl] N Tunnel m; (under road, railway also) Unterführung f; (Min) Stollen m; **at last we can see the light at the end of the ~** (fig) endlich sehen wir wieder Licht; **that for me was always the light at the end of the ~** (fig) das war für mich immer ein Hoffnungsfunken VI (into in +acc) (through durch) einen Tunnel bauen; (rabbit) einen Bau graben; (mole) Gänge pl graben; **they ~led** (Brit) or **~ed** (US) **under the walls of the jail** sie gruben (sich dat) einen Tunnel unter den Mauern des Gefängnisses hindurch VT **they ~led** (Brit) or **~ed** (US) **a road through the mountain** sie bauten einen Straßentunnel durch den Berg; **the hillside had been ~led** (Brit) or **~ed** (US) **by rabbits** die Kaninchen hatten ihre Baue in den Hang gegraben; **to ~ one's way through sth** sich durch etw hindurchgraben

▶**tunnel out** VI sich (dat) einen Fluchttunnel graben

tunnel vision N (Med) Gesichtsfeldeinengung f; (fig) Engstirnigkeit f, beschränkter Horizont

tunny (fish) [ˈtʌnɪ(ˈfɪʃ)] N Thunfisch m

tuppence [ˈtʌpəns] N (Brit) zwei Pence; **I don't care** ~ (inf) das interessiert mich nicht für fünf Pfennig (inf), das ist mir doch so egal (inf)

tuppenny [ˈtʌpənɪ] ADJ (Brit) sweets etc für zwei Pence; **he doesn't give a ~ damn about you** (inf) er schert sich einen (feuchten) Dreck um dich (inf)

tuppenny bit, **tuppenny piece** N (Brit) Zweipencestück nt

tuppenny-ha'penny [ˈtʌpnɪˈheɪpnɪ] ADJ (Brit, inf) lächerlich

turban [ˈtɜːbən] N Turban m

turbid [ˈtɜːbɪd] ADJ **a** liquid trübe, schmutzig **b** (fig: = confused) verworren

turbidity [tɜːˈbɪdɪtɪ] N **a** (of liquid) Trübheit f, Schmutzigkeit f **b** (fig, = confusion) Verworrenheit f

turbine [ˈtɜːbaɪn] N Turbine f

turbo-charged [ˈtɜːbəʊˌtʃɑːdʒd] ADJ car, engine mit Turboaufladung f; (= exciting, powerful) gadget, person, performance rasant

turbocharger [ˈtɜːbəʊˌtʃɑːdʒə] N Turbolader m

turbojet [ˈtɜːbəʊˈdʒet] N (= engine) Turbotriebwerk nt; (= aircraft) Düsenflugzeug nt, Turbojet m

turboprop [ˈtɜːbəʊˈprɒp] N (= engine) Propellerturbine f, Turboprop f; (= aircraft) Turbo-Prop-Flugzeug nt

turbot [ˈtɜːbət] N Steinbutt m

turbulence [ˈtɜːbjʊləns] N (of person, crowd) Ungestüm nt, Wildheit f; (of emotions) Aufgewühltheit f; (of career, period) Turbulenz f; **air ~** Turbulenzen pl; **the ~ of the water** das stürmische Wasser

turbulent [ˈtɜːbjʊlənt] ADJ stürmisch; person, crowd ungestüm, wild; emotions aufgewühlt; career, period, world, politics turbulent

turd [tɜːd] N (sl) **a** Kacke f (vulg), Scheiße f no pl (vulg); (single) Haufen m (inf) **b** (pej, = person) Scheißkerl m (inf)

tureen [təˈriːn] N (Suppen)terrine f

turf [tɜːf] N pl **-s** or **turves** **a** (no pl: = lawn) Rasen m; (no pl: = squares of grass) Soden pl; (= square of grass) Sode f **b** (no pl, = peat) Torf m; (= square of peat) Torfsode f; **to cut ~** Torf(soden) stechen **c** (Sport) **the Turf** die (Pferde-) rennbahn; **all his life he was a devotee of the Turf** sein Leben galt dem Pferderennsport VT **a** he **~ed the lawn** er verlegte (Gras)soden or Fertigrasen im Garten **b** (inf) **to ~ sb down the stairs** jdn die Treppe hinunterscheuchen (inf); **to ~ sth into the corner** etw in die Ecke werfen

▶**turf out** VT sep (Brit inf) person rauswerfen, rausschmeißen (inf); plan umschmeißen (inf),

verwerfen; suggestions abtun; (= throw away) wegschmeißen (inf)

▶**turf over** VT sep **a** garden mit (Gras)soden or Fertigrasen bedecken **b** (inf, = throw over) rüberwerfen (inf) (to sb jdm)

turf accountant N (Brit) Buchmacher(in) m(f)

turfman [ˈtɜːfmən] N (esp US) Pferderennsportliebhaber m

turgid [ˈtɜːdʒɪd] ADJ (= swollen) (an)geschwollen; (fig) style schwülstig, überladen

turgidity [tɜːˈdʒɪdɪtɪ] N (lit) Schwellung f; (fig, of style) Schwülstigkeit f; **the ~ of this writer's style** der schwülstige Stil dieses Schriftstellers

Turk [tɜːk] N Türke m, Türkin f

Turkey [ˈtɜːkɪ] N die Türkei

turkey [ˈtɜːkɪ] N **a** Truthahn m/-henne f; (esp Cook) Puter m, Pute f; **it would be like ~s voting for Christmas** (esp Brit) das wäre ja, als wenn die Gänse für Weihnachten stimmten **b** **to talk ~** (dated US inf) Tacheles reden (inf) **c** (esp US inf: Film, Theat: = flop) Reinfall m (inf)

turkey: turkey buzzard N Truthahngeier m; **turkey cock** N Truthahn m; (esp Cook) Puter m; **turkey shoot** N (esp US, fig) Abschlachten nt

Turkish [ˈtɜːkɪʃ] ADJ türkisch; **she is ~** sie ist Türkin N (Ling) Türkisch nt

Turkish: Turkish bath N türkisches Bad; **Turkish coffee** N türkischer Kaffee; **Turkish delight** N Lokum nt; **Turkish towel** N Frotteehandtuch nt

Turkmenistan [ˈtɜːkmenɪsˌtɑːn] N Turkmenistan nt, Turkmenien nt

turmeric [ˈtɜːmərɪk] N Kurkuma f, Gelbwurz f

turmoil [ˈtɜːmɔɪl] N Aufruhr m; (= confusion) Durcheinander nt; **he was glad to escape from the ~ of politics** er war froh, dass er sich aus der Hektik der Politik zurückziehen konnte; **everything is in a ~** alles ist in Aufruhr; **her mind was in a ~** sie war völlig verwirrt; **her mind was in a ~ of indecision** sie wusste überhaupt nicht mehr, wie sie sich entscheiden sollte

turn [tɜːn]	
1 NOUN	3 INTRANSITIVE VERB
2 TRANSITIVE VERB	4 PHRASAL VERBS

1 – NOUN

a = movement Drehung f; **six turns of the wheel** sechs Umdrehungen des Rades; **to give sth a turn** etw drehen; **give the handle another turn** dreh den Griff noch einmal herum; **done to a turn** (Cook) genau richtig

b = change of direction (in road) Kurve f; (Sport) Wende f; **watch out for a sharp turn in the road** pass auf, wo die Straße eine scharfe Kurve macht; **take the next turn on the left** biegen Sie links ab; **"no left turn"** „Linksabbiegen verboten"; **to make a turn to the left** (driver, car) nach links abbiegen; (road also) eine Linkskurve machen; **to make a turn to port** (Naut) nach Backbord abdrehen; **the Canadian swimmer made the better turn** der kanadische Schwimmer wendete besser; **he gets his horse to make a very tight turn** er wendet sein Pferd sehr eng

♦ **on the turn** (= changing) **the leaves are on the turn** die Blätter werden gelb; **the tide is on the turn** (lit) die Ebbe/Flut setzt ein, die See ist im Stau (spec); (fig) es tritt eine Wende ein; **their fortunes may be on the turn** ihr Glück könnte sich wandeln; **the economy is on the turn** die Wirtschaft steht vor einem Umschwung

♦ **to take a turn (for)** **things took a turn for the better/worse** die Dinge wendeten sich zum Guten/zum Schlechten; **the patient took a turn for the worse/better** das Befinden des Patienten wendete sich zum Schlechteren/zum Besseren; **things took a new turn** die Dinge nahmen eine neue Wendung; **events took a tragic turn** die Dinge nahmen einen tragischen or verhängnisvollen Verlauf

♦ **turn of + noun** **at the turn of the century** um die Jahrhundertwende; **at the turn of the 18th century** an der or um die Wende des 18. Jahrhunderts; **the turn of the year** die Jahreswende, der Jahreswechsel; **turn of events** Lauf m der Ereignisse; **the latest turn of events** der neueste Lauf der Ereignisse, die neueste Wendung; **I'm very upset by the turn of events** ich bin über den Verlauf der Dinge sehr beunruhigt; **turn of phrase** Ausdrucksweise f; **turn of mind** Hang m, Neigung f; **to have a mathematical turn of mind** mathematisch begabt sein; **an optimistic/a serious turn of mind** eine optimistische/ernsthafte Einstellung; **an imaginative turn of mind** ein Hang m zur Kreativität; **to have a good turn of speed** (car) sehr schnell fahren; (horse, athlete) sehr schnell sein; **the turn of the tide** der Gezeitenwechsel; **the children were trapped on the island by the turn of the tide** die Kinder wurden durch das Einsetzen der Flut auf der Insel festgehalten; **the government just seems to be sitting back waiting for the turn of the tide** (fig) die Regierung scheint einfach nur dazusitzen und auf einen Umschwung or eine Wende zu warten

♦ **at every turn** (fig) **he has pledged to fight at every turn** er hat geschworen, mit Zähnen und Klauen or mit aller Macht zu kämpfen; **at nearly every turn, their efforts have been criticized** bei beinahe jedem Schritt wurden ihre Bemühungen kritisiert; **he was thwarted at every turn** ihm wurde auf Schritt und Tritt ein Strich durch die Rechnung gemacht

c in game, queue, series **it's your turn** du bist an der Reihe, du bist dran; **it's your turn to wash the dishes** du bist mit (dem) Abwaschen an der Reihe or dran; **now it's his turn to be jealous** jetzt ist er zur Abwechslung eifersüchtig; **whose turn is it?** wer ist an der Reihe?, wer ist dran?; **it's my turn next** ich komme als Nächste(r) an die Reihe or dran; **wait your turn** warten Sie, bis Sie an der Reihe sind; **to miss a turn** eine Runde aussetzen; **your turn will come** du kommst auch noch mal dran; **to take a turn at the wheel** (für eine Weile) das Steuer übernehmen; **to take turns to do sth** or **at doing sth** etw abwechselnd tun; **to take turns at the wheel** sich am Steuer or beim Fahren abwechseln; **to take it in turn(s) to do sth** etw abwechselnd tun; **take it in turns!** wechselt euch ab!

♦ **in turn** he told a colleague, who in turn told a reporter er sagte es einem Kollegen, der es wiederum einem Reporter erzählte; **that in turn will increase the budget deficit** dies wiederum erhöht das Defizit im Etat; **and then Anne Boleyn too, in (her) turn, ...** und dann kam die Reihe auch an Anne Boleyn ...; **they answered in turn** sie antworteten der Reihe nach; (2 people only) sie antworteten abwechselnd

♦ **by turn(s)** abwechselnd; **she was confident then depressed by turn(s)** sie war abwechselnd zuversichtlich und deprimiert

♦ **out of turn** außer der Reihe; **my secretary was speaking out of turn** es stand meiner Sekretärin nicht zu, sich darüber zu äußern; **sorry, have I spoken out of turn?** Entschuldigung, habe ich etwas Falsches gesagt?

♦ **turn and turn about** abwechselnd; **the children will just have to take turn and turn about on the swing** die Kinder werden eben abwechselnd schaukeln müssen

d = service

♦ **a good/bad turn** **to do sb a good/bad turn** jdm einen guten/schlechten Dienst erweisen; **a boy scout has to do a good turn every day** ein Pfadfinder muss jeden Tag eine gute Tat tun; **one good turn deserves another** (Prov) eine Hand wäscht die andere (prov), hilfst du mir, so helf ich dir

e = attack (Brit inf) **he had one of his (funny) turns last night** er hatte letzte Nacht wieder einen Anfall

f = shock, fright **to give sb a turn** jdm Angst or einen Schrecken einjagen; **you/it gave me**

quite a turn du hast/es hat mir einen schönen Schrecken eingejagt

g ⃞Theat etc⃞ Nummer f; **they got him to do a turn at the party** sie brachten ihn dazu, auf der Party etwas zum Besten zu geben

h ⃞= purpose⃞ **it will serve my turn** das ist für meine Zwecke gerade richtig; **we'll throw these old carpets away once they've served their turn** wir werfen diese alten Teppiche weg, wenn sie ausgedient haben

i ⃞= walk, stroll⃞ Runde f; **to take a turn in the park** eine Runde durch den Park machen

2 – TRANSITIVE VERB

a ⃞= rotate⃞ knob, key, screw, steering wheel drehen; **to turn the key in the lock** den Schlüssel im Schloss herumdrehen; **what turns the wheel?** wie wird das Rad angetrieben?; **he turned the wheel sharply** er riss das Steuer herum; **he turned his head toward(s) me** er wandte mir den Kopf zu; **he turned his back to the wall** er kehrte den Rücken zur Wand; **as soon as his back is turned** sobald er den Rücken kehrt; **to turn one's eyes toward(s) sb** jdn anblicken

b ⃞fig uses⃞ **the sight of all that food quite turned my stomach** beim Anblick des vielen Essens drehte sich mir regelrecht der Magen um; **without turning a hair** ohne mit der Wimper zu zucken; **success has turned his head** der Erfolg ist ihm zu Kopf gestiegen; **she seems to have turned his head** sie scheint ihm den Kopf verdreht zu haben; **she can still turn a few heads** die Leute schauen sich immer noch nach ihr um; **to turn one's hand to sth** sich an etw (dat) versuchen; **she turned her hand to cooking** sie versuchte sich im Kochen; **he can turn his hand to anything** er kann alles, er ist sehr geschickt → **corner**

c ⃞= turn over⃞ mattress, collar, hay wenden; soil umgraben; record umdrehen; page umblättern

d ⃞= change position of, turn round⃞ car, lorry wenden; chair, picture etc umdrehen

e ⃞= direct⃞ **to turn one's thoughts/attention to sth** seine Gedanken/Aufmerksamkeit einer Sache (dat) zuwenden; **to turn one's steps homeward** seine Schritte heimwärts lenken (liter, hum); **to turn a gun on sb** ein Gewehr auf jdn richten; **the police turned the hoses on the demonstrators** die Polizei richtete die Wasserwerfer auf die Demonstranten

f ⃞= transform, make become⃞ verwandeln (in(to) in +acc); **the shock turned his hair white overnight** durch den Schock bekam er über Nacht weiße Haare; **his success turns me green with envy** sein Erfolg lässt mich vor Neid erblassen; **the smoke turned the walls black** der Rauch schwärzte die Wände; **to turn the lights down low** das Licht herunterdrehen; **this hot weather has turned the milk (sour)** bei dieser Hitze ist die Milch sauer geworden; **to turn a boat adrift** ein Boot losmachen und treiben lassen; **his goal turned the game** sein Tor gab dem Spiel eine andere Wendung; **to turn a profit** (esp US) einen Gewinn machen, einen Profit einfahren (inf)

♦ **to turn sth into ...** the play was turned into a film das Stück wurde verfilmt; **to turn verse into prose** Lyrik in Prosa übertragen; **to turn English expressions into German** aus englischen Ausdrücken deutsche machen

♦ **to turn sb loose** jdn loslassen or laufen lassen

g ⃞= deflect⃞ abbringen; **measures to turn young people from criminal behaviour** Maßnahmen, um junge Leute or Jugendliche von kriminellem Verhalten abzubringen; **nothing will turn him from his purpose** nichts wird ihn von seinem Vorhaben ablenken or abbringen

h ⃞= shape⃞ wood drechseln; metal, pot drehen; **a well-turned sentence** ein gut formulierter Satz; **a well-turned leg** ein wohlgeformtes Bein

3 – INTRANSITIVE VERB

a ⃞= rotate, move round⃞ (key, screw, wheel) sich drehen; **the world turns on its axis** die Erde dreht sich um ihre Achse; **he turned to me and smiled** er drehte sich mir zu und lächelte;

this key won't turn dieser Schlüssel lässt sich nicht drehen; **to turn upside down** umkippen; **his stomach turned at the sight** bei dem Anblick drehte sich ihm der Magen um → **tail N a, toss VI a, turtle**

b ⃞= change direction⃞ (to one side) (person, car) abbiegen; (plane, boat) abdrehen; (= turn around) wenden; (person, on the spot) sich umdrehen; (wind) drehen; (tide) wechseln; **to turn and go left** links ab-; **to turn (to the) left** links abbiegen; **left turn!** (Mil) linksum!; **our luck turned** unser Glück wendete sich; **the game turned in the second half** das Spiel wendete sich in der zweiten Hälfte or Halbzeit

c ⃞= go⃞ **I don't know which way or where to turn for help/money** ich weiß nicht, an wen ich mich um Hilfe wenden kann/wen ich um Geld bitten kann; **I don't know which way to turn** ich weiß nicht, was ich machen soll; **to turn to sb** sich an jdn wenden; **our thoughts turn to those who ...** wir gedenken derer, die ...; **to turn to sth** sich einer Sache (dat) zuwenden; **turn to page 306** gehen or blättern Sie weiter bis Seite 306, schlagen Sie jetzt Seite 306 auf; **after her death, he turned to his books for comfort** nach ihrem Tod suchte er Trost bei seinen Büchern; **this job would make anyone turn to drink!** bei dieser Arbeit muss man ja zum Trinker werden!; **the conversation turned to the accident** das Gespräch kam auf den Unfall, man kam auf den Unfall zu sprechen

d ⃞= change⃞ (leaves) sich (ver)färben; (milk) sauer werden; (meat) schlecht werden; (weather) umschlagen; **to turn to stone** zu Stein werden; **his admiration turned to scorn** seine Bewunderung verwandelte sich in Verachtung

♦ **to turn into sth** sich in etw (acc) verwandeln; (= develop into) sich zu etw entwickeln; **their short stay turned into a three-month visit** aus ihrem Kurzaufenthalt wurde ein Aufenthalt von drei Monaten; **the prince turned into a frog** der Prinz verwandelte sich in einen Frosch; **the whole thing turned into a nightmare** die ganze Sache wurde zum Albtraum

e ⃞= become⃞ werden; **to turn traitor** zum Verräter werden; **Paul Crooks, an actor turned director, ...** der Regisseur Paul Crooks, ein ehemaliger Schauspieler, ...; **he began to turn awkward** er wurde unangenehm or ungemütlich; **to turn nasty/violent** unangenehm/gewalttätig werden; **to turn red** (leaves etc) sich rot färben; (person: = blush) rot werden; (traffic lights) auf Rot umspringen; **it has recently turned cold** es ist vor kurzem kalt geworden; **his hair is turning grey** sein Haar wird grau; **he has just turned 18** er ist gerade 18 geworden; **it has turned 2 o'clock** es ist 2 Uhr vorbei

4 – PHRASAL VERBS

▶ **turn about** (Brit) **VI** (person) sich umdrehen; (car, boat, driver etc) wenden; **we had to turn about and go home** wir mussten umkehren (und nach Hause gehen) **VT** sep car wenden; **he turned himself about** er wandte sich um

▶ **turn against VI** +prep obj sich wenden gegen **VT** sep +prep obj **they turned him against his parents** sie brachten ihn gegen seine Eltern auf; **they turned his argument against him** sie verwendeten sein Argument gegen ihn

▶ **turn around VT** sep **a** = **turn about VT b** (factory, docks) ship etc abfertigen; goods fertig stellen **c** argument umdrehen; game, fortune wenden; country, economy, company aus der Krise führen; **she has turned my life around** sie hat mein Leben in Ordnung gebracht **VI** +prep obj corner biegen um **VI** sep **the wheel turns around on its axis** das Rad dreht sich um seine Achse

▶ **turn aside VI** sich abwenden (from von) **VT** sep abwenden

▶ **turn away VI** sich abwenden **VT** sep **a** (= move) head, eyes, gun abwenden **b** (= send away) person wegschicken, abweisen; business zurückweisen, ablehnen

▶ **turn back VI a** (traveller) zurückgehen, umkehren; (plane) umkehren; (= look back) sich

umdrehen; **we can't turn back now, there's no turning back now** (fig) jetzt gibt es kein Zurück mehr

b (in book) zurückblättern (to auf +acc) **VT** sep **a** (= fold) bedclothes zurück- or aufschlagen; corner umknicken; hem umschlagen

b (= send back) person zurückschicken; **bad weather turned the plane back to Heathrow** schlechtes Wetter zwang das Flugzeug zur Rückkehr nach Heathrow; **they were turned back at the frontier** sie wurden an der Grenze zurückgewiesen

c clock zurückstellen; (fig) zurückdrehen; **to turn the clock back fifty years** (fig) die Uhr um fünfzig Jahre zurückdrehen

▶ **turn down VT** sep **a** bedclothes zurück- or aufschlagen; collar, brim herunterklappen; corner of page umknicken

b gas, heat herunterdrehen, kleiner stellen; volume, radio, television leiser stellen; lights herunterdrehen

c (= refuse) candidate, novel, offer etc ablehnen; suitor abweisen; invitation ablehnen, ausschlagen

d card verdeckt hin- or ablegen **VI** +prep obj **he turned down a side street** er bog in eine Seitenstraße ab

▶ **turn in VI a** her toes turn in when she walks sie läuft nach innen, sie läuft über den großen Onkel (inf)

b (= drive in) **the car turned in at the top of the drive** das Auto bog in die Einfahrt ein

c (inf, = go to bed) sich hinhauen (inf), in die Falle gehen (inf)

d **to turn in on oneself** sich in sich (acc) selbst zurückziehen **VT** sep **a** **she turned in her toes as she walked** sie lief nach innen, sie lief über den großen Onkel (inf); **to turn in the ends of sth** die Enden von etw umschlagen

b (inf, to police) **to turn sb in** jdn anzeigen or verpfeifen (inf); **to turn oneself in** sich (der Polizei) stellen

c (esp US inf: = give back) equipment zurückgeben or -bringen; weapons (to police) abgeben (to bei)

d (= exchange) eintauschen (for gegen)

e (Brit, inf) **turn it in!** jetzt mach aber mal einen Punkt! (inf)

▶ **turn into VTI** +prep obj = **turn 2 f 3 d**

▶ **turn off VI** abbiegen (for nach, prep obj von) **VT** sep **a** light, radio ausmachen, abschalten; gas abdrehen; tap zudrehen; TV programme abschalten; water, electricity, engine, machine abstellen **b** (inf) **to turn sb off** (= disgust) jdn anwidern; (= put off) jdm die Lust verderben or nehmen; **when they mentioned the price that turned me right off** als sie den Preis nannten, war für mich die Sache gegessen (inf)

▶ **turn on VI** (Rad, TV) **we turned on at 8 o'clock** wir haben um 8 Uhr eingeschaltet **VT** sep **a** gas, heat anstellen, anmachen; radio, television, the news einschalten; light einschalten, anmachen; tap, central heating aufdrehen; bath water einlaufen lassen; engine, machine anstellen; **to turn on the charm** seinen (ganzen) Charme spielen lassen; **he can really turn on the charm** er kann wirklich sehr charmant sein

b (sl: with drugs) antörnen (sl)

c (inf: = appeal to: music, novel etc) **sth turns sb on** jd steht auf etw (acc) (sl), jd findet etw Spitze (sl), jd fährt auf etw (acc) voll ab (sl); **whatever turns you on** wenn du das gut findest (inf); **he/it doesn't turn me on** er/das lässt mich kalt (also sexually)

d (inf: sexually) scharf machen (inf), anmachen (inf); **she really turns me on** auf sie kann ich voll abfahren (inf); **you know how to turn me on** du kannst mich wirklich auf Touren bringen (inf); **it turns me on when ...** ich werde ganz scharf, wenn ... (inf) **VI** +prep obj **a** (= turn against) sich wenden gegen; (= attack) angreifen

b (= depend on) abhängen von, ankommen auf (+acc)

▶ **turn out** VI **a** (= *appear, attend*) erscheinen, kommen

b (*firemen, police*) ausrücken; (*doctor*) einen Krankenbesuch machen

c (= *point*) **his feet turn out** er läuft nach außen

d **the car turned out of the drive** das Auto bog aus der Einfahrt

e (= *transpire*) sich herausstellen; **he turned out to be the murderer** es stellte sich heraus, dass er der Mörder war

f (= *develop, progress*) sich machen (*inf*); **how did it turn out?** (= *what happened?*) was ist daraus geworden?; (*cake etc*) wie ist er *etc* geworden?; **it all depends how things turn out** es kommt darauf an, wie sich die Dinge ergeben; **as it turned out** wie sich herausstellte; **everything will turn out all right** es wird sich schon alles ergeben; **it turned out nice in the afternoon** (*Brit*) am Nachmittag wurde es noch schön

VT *sep* **a** *light* ausmachen; *gas* abstellen

b **he turns his feet out** er läuft nach außen

c (= *produce*) produzieren; *novel etc* schreiben; **the college turns out good teachers** das College bringt gute Lehrer hervor

d (= *expel*) vertreiben (*aus*), hinauswerfen (*inf*) (*aus*); *tenant* kündigen (+*dat*), auf die Straße setzen (*inf*); **he was turned out of his job** er verlor seinen Arbeitsplatz

e (*Cook, = tip out*) *cake* stürzen; **he turned the photos out of the box** er kippte die Fotos aus der Schachtel

f (= *empty*) *pockets* (aus)leeren

g (= *clean*) *room* gründlich sauber machen

h *guard* antreten lassen

i (*usu pass:* = *dress*) **well turned-out** gut gekleidet *or* ausstaffiert; *troops* tadellos, geschniegelt und gestriegelt (*inf*)

▶ **turn over** VI **a** (*person*) sich umdrehen; (*car, plane etc*) sich überschlagen; (*boat*) umkippen, kentern; (*stomach*) sich umdrehen; **he turned over on(to) his back/stomach** er drehte sich auf den Rücken/Bauch

b **please turn over** (*with pages*) bitte wenden

c (*Aut, engine*) laufen; **with the engine turning over** mit laufendem Motor

d (*TV, Rad*) umschalten (*to* auf +*acc*)

VT *sep* **a** umdrehen; *patient* wenden; *tape, card* umdrehen, wenden; (= *turn upside down*) umkippen; *page* umblättern; *soil* umgraben; *mattress, steak* wenden; **he turned the car over** er überschlug sich (mit dem Auto); **the police turned the whole house over** (= *searched*) die Polizei durchsuchte das ganze Haus; **this doesn't make sense, I must have turned over two pages** das ergibt keinen Sinn, ich muss eine Seite überschlagen haben; **to turn an idea over in one's mind** eine Idee überdenken, sich (*dat*) eine Idee durch den Kopf gehen lassen → **leaf N a**

b (= *hand over*) übergeben (*to dat*)

c (*Comm*) *goods* umsetzen; **to turn over £500 a week** einen Umsatz von £ 500 in der Woche haben; **how much do you turn over per week?** welchen Umsatz haben Sie pro Woche?

d (*Aut*) *engine* laufen lassen

▶ **turn round** (*esp Brit*) VI **a** (= *face other way*) sich umdrehen; (= *go back*) umkehren; **to turn round and go back** umkehren; **to turn round and go back to camp** ins Lager zurückkehren; **he just turned round and hit him** er drehte sich einfach um und schlug ihn

b (*inf*) **one day she'll just turn round and leave you** eines Tages wird sie dich ganz einfach verlassen; **you can't just turn round and refuse** du kannst dich doch nicht einfach weigern

VI +*prep obj* **we turned round the corner** wir bogen um die Ecke; **the earth turns round the sun** die Erde dreht sich um die Sonne

VT *sep* **a** *head* drehen; *box* umdrehen; **turn the picture round the other way** dreh das Bild andersherum

b (= *process*) *job etc* bearbeiten

c (*factory, docks etc*) *ship* abfertigen; *goods* fertig stellen

d = **turn around VT c**

▶ **turn to** VI (= *get busy*) sich an die Arbeit machen VI +*prep obj* **a** **to turn to sb/sth** → **turn 3**

c b (= *get busy*) **after a short rest, they turned to their work again** nach einer kurzen Pause machten sie sich wieder an die Arbeit

▶ **turn up** VI **a** (= *arrive*) erscheinen, auftauchen (*inf*); **I was afraid you wouldn't turn up** ich hatte Angst, du würdest nicht kommen; **two years later he turned up in London** zwei Jahre später tauchte er in London auf (*inf*); **the queen hasn't turned up yet** (*Cards*) die Dame ist noch im Spiel

b (= *be found*) sich (an)finden, (wieder) auftauchen (*inf*); (*esp smaller things*) zum Vorschein kommen

c (= *happen*) **something is sure to turn up** irgendetwas passiert schon; **things have a habit of turning up** irgendwie findet sich alles; **it's amazing the way things turn up** es ist manchmal erstaunlich, wie sich die Dinge finden

d (= *point up*) **his nose turns up, he has a turned-up nose** er hat eine Himmelfahrts- (*inf*) *or* Stupsnase; **to turn up at the ends** sich an den Enden hochbiegen

VT *sep* **a** (= *fold*) *collar* hochklappen; *sleeve* aufrollen, aufkrempeln (*inf*); *hem* umnähen; **to turn up one's nose at sth** (*fig*) die Nase über etw (*acc*) rümpfen

b *heat, gas* aufdrehen, höher drehen; *radio* lauter drehen; *volume* aufdrehen; *light* heller machen; *pressure* verstärken, erhöhen

c (= *find*) finden, entdecken; **to turn up some information** Informationen auftreiben, an Informationen kommen

d *soil* umpflügen

e (*Brit, inf*) **turn it up!** Mensch, hör auf damit! (*inf*)

---

turnable ['tɜːnəbl] ADJ drehbar

turnaround ['tɜːnəraʊnd], **turnround** ['tɜːnraʊnd] N **a** (*also* **turnabout**: *in position, fig: in opinion etc*) Kehrtwendung *f*; **she has done a complete ~ on fiscal policy** sie hat in der Finanzpolitik eine totale Kehrtwendung gemacht *or* vollführt **b** (*also* **turnaround time**) Bearbeitungszeit *f*; (= *production time*) Fertigstellungszeit *f* **c** (*of situation, company*) Umschwung *m*, Wende *f* **d** (*of ship, aircraft*) Abfertigung *f*

turncoat ['tɜːnkəʊt] N Abtrünnige(r) *mf*, Überläufer(in) *m(f)*

turner ['tɜːnə'] N (*of metal*) Dreher(in) *m(f)*; (*of wood*) Drechsler(in) *m(f)*

turning ['tɜːnɪŋ] N **a** (*in road*) Abzweigung *f*; **take the second ~ on the left** nimm die zweite Abfahrt links; **it's a long road that has no ~** (*prov*) nichts dauert ewig **b** (*Tech, of metal*) Drehen *nt*; (*of wood*) Drechseln *nt*

turning: turning circle N (*Aut*) Wendekreis *m*; **turning lathe** N Drehbank *f*; **turning point** N Wendepunkt *m*

turnip ['tɜːnɪp] N Rübe *f*; (= *swede*) Steckrübe *f*; (*hum inf, = pocket watch*) Zwiebel *f* (*hum inf*)

turn: turnkey N (*old*) Kerkermeister *m* (*old*), Gefängniswärter(in) *m(f)*; **turnkey project** N schlüsselfertiges Projekt; **turn-off** N **a** Abzweigung *f*; (*on motorway*) Abfahrt *f*, Ausfahrt *f*; **the Birmingham ~** die Abzweigung nach Birmingham, die Abfahrt *or* Ausfahrt Birmingham **b** (*inf*) **it was a real ~** das hat einem die Lust verdorben; **hairy armpits are the ultimate ~ for me** bei Haaren unter den Achseln hörts bei mir auf (*inf*); **turn-on** N (*inf*) **that's a real ~** das macht einen an (*inf*); **she finds him/his accent a real ~** sie fährt voll auf ihn/seinen Akzent ab (*inf*)

turnout ['tɜːnaʊt] N **a** (= *attendance*) Teilnahme *f*, Beteiligung *f*; **in spite of the rain there was a good ~** (*for a match etc*) trotz des Regens war das Spiel gut besucht; (*in election*) trotz des Regens war die Wahlbeteiligung gut *or* hoch; **there was a big ~ of friends to meet us at the station** eine Menge Freunde waren gekommen, um uns am Bahnhof zu begrüßen **b** (= *clean-out*) **she gave the room a thorough ~** sie mach-

---

te den Raum gründlich sauber **c** (*Comm, = output*) Produktion *f* **d** (= *dress*) Aufmachung *f* **e** (*US*) (*in town*) Parkbucht *f*; (*in country*) Parkplatz *m*; (*big*) Rastplatz *m*

turnover ['tɜːnəʊvə'] N (= *total business*) Umsatz *m*; (*Comm, Fin: of capital*) Umlauf *m*; (*Comm, of stock*) (*Lager*)umschlag *m*; (*of staff*) Personalwechsel *m*, Fluktuation *f*

turnover tax N Umsatzsteuer *f*

turn: turnpike N (*Brit Hist*) Mautschranke *f*; (*US*) gebührenpflichtige Autobahn; **turnround** N = **turnaround**; **turnscrew** N Schraubendreher *m or* -zieher *m*; **turn signal** N (*US Aut*) Fahrtrichtungsanzeiger *m*; **turnstile** N Drehkreuz *nt*; **turntable** N Drehscheibe *f*; (*on record player*) Plattenteller *m*; **turntable ladder** N Drehleiter *f*; **turn-up** N (*Brit*) **a** (*on trousers*) Aufschlag *m* **b** (*inf, = event*) **that was a ~ for the books** das war ein (echte) Überraschung, das war (vielleicht) ein Ding (*inf*)

turpentine ['tɜːpəntaɪn] N Terpentin(öl) *nt*; **~ substitute** Terpentin(öl)ersatz *m*

turpitude ['tɜːpɪtjuːd] N Verderbtheit *f*

turps [tɜːps] N *sing* (*Brit inf*) *abbr of* **turpentine**

turquoise ['tɜːkwɔɪz] N **a** (= *gem*) Türkis *m* **b** (= *colour*) Türkis *nt* ADJ türkis(farben); **~ blue/green** türkisblau/-grün; **~ jewellery** (*Brit*) *or* **jewelry** (*US*) Türkisschmuck *m*

turret ['tʌrɪt] N (*Archit*) Mauer- *or* Eckturm *m*; (*on tank*) Turm *m*; (*on ship*) Gefechtsturm *m*

turreted ['tʌrɪtɪd] ADJ **a ~ castle** ein Schloss mit Mauer- *or* Ecktürmen

turret gun N Turmgeschütz *nt*

turtle ['tɜːtl] N (*Wasser*)schildkröte *f*; (*US also*) (*Land*)schildkröte *f*; **to turn ~** kentern → **mock turtle soup**

turtle: turtledove N (*lit, fig inf*) Turteltaube *f*; **turtleneck (pullover)** N Pullover *m* mit Stehkragen

turves [tɜːvz] PL *of* **turf**

Tuscan ['tʌskən] ADJ toskanisch N **a** Toskaner(in) *m(f)* **b** (*Ling*) Toskanisch *nt*

Tuscany ['tʌskənɪ] N die Toskana

tush [tʌʃ] INTERJ (*dated*) pah, bah

tusk [tʌsk] N (*of elephant*) Stoßzahn *m*; (*of walrus*) Eckzahn *m*; (*of boar*) Hauer *m*

tusker ['tʌskə'] N (= *elephant*) Elefant *m* mit ausgebildeten Stoßzähnen; (= *boar*) Keiler *m*

tussle ['tʌsl] N (*lit, fig*) Gerangel *nt* VI sich rangeln (*with sb for sth* mit jdm um etw)

tussock ['tʌsək] N (*Gras*)büschel *nt*

tussock grass N Rispengras *nt*

tut [tʌt] INTERJ, VTI = **tut-tut**

tutelage ['tjuːtɪlɪdʒ] N (= *teaching*) Führung *f*, Anleitung *f*; **the students made good progress under his able ~** in seinem guten Unterricht machten die Schüler große Fortschritte **b** (= *guardianship*) Vormundschaft *f*

tutelary ['tjuːtɪlərɪ] ADJ (*form, of guardian*) vormundschaftlich; **~ deity** Schutzgott *m*, Schutzgöttin *f*

tutor ['tjuːtə'] N **a** (= *private teacher*) Privat- *or* Hauslehrer(in) *m(f)* **b** (*Brit, Univ*) Tutor(in) *m(f)* VT **a** (*as private teacher*) privat unterrichten; (= *give extra lessons to*) Nachhilfe(unterricht) geben (+*dat*); **to ~ sb in Latin** jdm Privatunterricht/Nachhilfe in Latein geben **b** (*liter, = discipline*) *emotions* beherrschen

tutorial [tjuːˈtɔːrɪəl] N (*Brit, Univ*) Kolloquium *nt* ADJ Tutoren-; **the ~ system** das Tutorensystem; **the ~ staff** die Tutoren *pl*; **~ group** Seminargruppe *f*; **~ work** Arbeit *f* im Seminar

tutorship ['tjuːtəʃɪp] N (*private*) Privat- *or* Hauslehrerstelle *f*; (*Univ*) Amt *nt or* Stelle *f* eines Tutors

tutti-frutti ['tuːtɪ'fruːtɪ] N (= *ice cream*) Tuttifrutti *nt*

tut-tut ['tʌt'tʌt] INTERJ (*in disapproval*) na, na, aber, aber VI **she ~ted in disapproval** na, na!

or aber, aber!, sagte sie missbilligend **VT** *idea* missbilligen

tutu [ˈtuːtuː] N Tutu *nt*, Ballettröckchen *nt*

tu-whit tu-whoo [tʊˈwɪtːəˈwuː] INTERJ (sch)u-hu

tux [tʌks] (*inf*), **tuxedo** [tʌkˈsiːdəʊ] N (*esp US*) Smoking *m*

TV [tiːˈviː] N (*inf*) abbr of **television** Fernsehen *nt*; (= *set*) Fernseher *m* (*inf*); **on TV** im Fernsehen; **a TV programme** (*Brit*) or **program** (*US*) eine Fernsehsendung; **a TV personality** ein Fernsehstar *m* → *also* **television**

TVA abbr of **Tennessee Valley Authority**

TV dinner N Fertigmahlzeit *f*

twaddle [ˈtwɒdl] N (*inf*) Geschwätz *nt*, dummes Zeug (*inf*); **to talk** ~ dummes Zeug reden (*inf*)

twain [tweɪn] N (*old*) zwei; **in** ~ entzwei (*old*); **and ne'er the ~ shall meet** sie werden nie zueinander finden

twang [twæŋ] **N a** (*of wire, guitar string*) Doing *nt*; (*of rubber band, bowstring*) scharfer Ton **b** (*of voice*) Näseln *nt*, näselnder Tonfall; **to speak with a ~** mit näselndem Tonfall *or* mit einem Näseln sprechen **VT** zupfen; *guitar, banjo also* klimpern auf (+*dat*) **a** (*guitar, string etc*) einen scharfen Ton von sich geben; (*rubber band*) pitschen (*inf*) **b to ~ on a guitar** *etc* auf einer Gitarre *etc* herumklimpern

twangy [ˈtwæŋɪ] ADJ (+*er*) *voice* näselnd; *guitar etc* klimpernd

'twas [twɒz] (*old*) contr of **it was**

twat [twæt] **N a** (*vulg*, = *vagina*) Fotze *f* (*vulg*), Möse *f* (*vulg*) **b** (*inf*: = *fool*) Blödmann *m* (*inf*)

tweak [twiːk] **VT a** (= *pull gently*) kneifen; **she ~ed (back) the curtain** sie schob den Vorhang etwas zur Seite; **to ~ sb's ear** jdn am Ohr ziehen; **to ~ sb's nose** (*lit*) jdn an der Nase ziehen; (*fig*) jdm eins auswischen (*inf*); **to ~ sth off/out** etw abkneifen/auszupfen **b** (*inf*) *engine* hochfrisieren (*inf*) **c** (*inf*, = *alter slightly*) *system, rules, schedule, text* herumdoktern an (+*dat*) (*inf*) **N a** (= *gentle pull*) **to give sth a ~** an etw (*dat*) (herum)zupfen; **to give sb's ear/nose a ~** jdn am Ohr/an der Nase ziehen **b** (*inf*, = *slight alteration: to system, rules, schedule, text*) kleine Änderung; **to give sth a ~** (*system, rules, schedule, text*) an etw (*dat*) herumdoktern (*inf*)

twee [twiː] ADJ (+*er*) (*Brit inf*) niedlich, putzig (*inf*); *manner* geziert; *clothes* niedlich; *description* verniedlichend; *expression* gekünstelt; *words* zuckersüß; **it sounds ~** es klingt geziert

tweed [twiːd] **N a** (= *cloth*) Tweed *m* **b tweeds** PL (= *clothes*) Tweedkleidung *f*, Tweedsachen *pl*; **his old ~s** sein alter Tweedanzug, seine alten Tweedsachen **ADJ** Tweed-; **~ jacket** Tweedjacke *f*

Tweedledum [ˌtwiːdlˈdʌm] N **the twins were as alike as ~ and Tweedledee** die Zwillinge glichen sich wie ein Ei dem anderen

tweedy [ˈtwiːdɪ] ADJ (+*er*) *material* tweedartig; *clothes* aus Tweed; (*fig*) *person, shop* konservativ; **~ jacket** Tweedjacke *f*

'tween [twiːn] (*poet*) ADV, PREP = **between**

tweeny [ˈtwiːnɪ] N (*old*) Hausmagd *f*

tweet [twiːt] **N** (*of birds*) Ziepen *nt*, Piepsen *nt* *no pl*; **~ ~** ziep, ziep, pieps, pieps **VI** ziepen, piepsen

tweeter [ˈtwiːtə'] N Hochtonlautsprecher *m*

tweezers [ˈtwiːzəz] PL (*also* **pair of tweezers**) Pinzette *f*

twelfth [twelfθ] ADJ zwölfte(r, s); **a ~ part** ein Zwölftel *nt* **N** (*in series*) Zwölfte(r, s); (= *fraction*) Zwölftel *nt* → *also* **sixth**

twelfth man N (*Brit: Cricket*) Ersatzspieler *m*

Twelfth Night N Dreikönige; (= *evening*) Dreikönigsabend *m*

twelve [twelv] ADJ zwölf; **~ noon** zwölf Uhr (mittags) **N** Zwölf *f* → *also* **six**

twelve: twelve-mile limit N Zwölfmeilenzone *f*; **twelvemonth** N (*old*) zwölf Monate *pl*, ein

---

Jahr *nt*; **twelve-tone** ADJ (*Mus*) Zwölfton-; ~ **music** Zwölftonmusik *f*

twentieth [ˈtwentɪθ] ADJ zwanzigste(r, s); **a ~ part** ein Zwanzigstel *nt* **N** (*in series*) Zwanzigste(r, s); (= *fraction*) Zwanzigstel *nt* → *also* **sixth**

twenty [ˈtwentɪ] ADJ zwanzig **N** Zwanzig *f*; (= *banknote*) Zwanziger *m* → *also* **sixty**

twentyfold [ˈtwentɪfəʊld] ADJ, ADV (*old*) zwanzigfach

twenty-twenty vision [ˌtwentɪtwentɪˈvɪʒən] N 100-prozentige Sehschärfe

'twere [twɜː'] (*old*) contr of **it were**

twerp [twɜːp] N (*inf*) Einfaltspinsel *m* (*inf*), Hohlkopf *m* (*inf*)

twice [twaɪs] ADV zweimal; **~ as much/many** doppelt *or* zweimal so viel/so viele; **~ as much bread** doppelt so viel *or* zweimal so viel Brot, die doppelte Menge Brot; **~ as long as ...** doppelt *or* zweimal so lange wie ...; **at ~ the speed of sound** mit doppelter Schallgeschwindigkeit; **she is ~ your age** sie ist doppelt so alt wie du; **~ 2 is 4** zweimal 2 ist 4; **~ weekly**, **~ a week** zweimal wöchentlich, zweimal pro Woche; **a ~-weekly newspaper** eine Zeitung, die zweimal wöchentlich erscheint; **he didn't need to be asked** ~ da brauchte man ihn nicht zweimal zu fragen; **he's ~ the man John is** er steckt John in die Tasche (*inf*); **he's ~ the man he was** er ist ein ganz anderer Mensch geworden; **I'd think ~ before trusting him with it** ihm würde ich das nicht so ohne weiteres anvertrauen

twiddle [ˈtwɪdl] **VT** herumdrehen an (+*dat*); **she ~d the pencil in her fingers** ihre Finger spielten mit dem Bleistift; **to ~ one's thumbs** (*lit, fig*) Däumchen drehen **VI to ~ with a knob** an einem Knopf herumdrehen **N he gave the knob a ~** er drehte den Knopf herum

twig¹ [twɪg] N (= *thin branch*) Zweig *m*

twig² (*Brit, inf*) **VT** (= *realize*) mitkriegen (*inf*), mitbekommen; **when she saw his face, she ~ged his secret** als sie sein Gesicht sah, erriet sie sein Geheimnis (*inf*); **he's ~ged it** er hats kapiert (*inf*) **VI** schalten (*inf*), es mitkriegen (*inf*) or mitbekommen

twiggy [ˈtwɪgɪ] ADJ **a** *tree etc* voller Zweige **b** (= *very slim*) *girl* (= *gertenschlank*)

twilight [ˈtwaɪlaɪt] N (= *time*) Dämmerung *f*; (= *semi-darkness also*) Dämmer- *or* Zwielicht *nt*; **at** ~ in der Dämmerung; **the ~ of the gods** die Götterdämmerung; **the ~ of western civilization** der Herbst der westlichen Zivilisation (*liter*); **the ~ of his life, his ~ years** sein Lebensabend *m*

twilight: twilight sleep N (*Med*) Dämmerschlaf *m*; **twilight world** N Welt *f* des Zwielichts; **twilight zone** N Zwielicht *nt*

twill [twɪl] N (*Tex*) Köper *m*

'twill [twɪl] (*old*) contr of **it will**

twin [twɪn] **N** Zwilling *m*; (*of vase, object*) Gegenstück *nt*, Pendant *nt*; **her ~** (= *sister*) ihre Zwillingsschwester; (= *brother*) ihr Zwillingsbruder *m*; **where's the ~ of this sock?** wo ist die andere Socke?; **the Twins** (*Astrol*) die Zwillinge *pl* **ADJ** attr **a** Zwillings-; (*fig*) genau gleiche(r, s); ~ **boys/girls** Zwillingsjungen *pl*/-mädchen *pl*; ~ **birth** Zwillingsgeburt *f*; ~ **souls** (*fig*) verwandte Seelen *pl* **b** (= *double*) ~ **towers** Zwillingstürme *pl*; ~ **peaks** Doppelgipfel *pl* **VT** (*Brit*) *town* verschwistern; **Oxford was ~ned with Bonn** Oxford und Bonn wurden zu/waren Partnerstädten

twin: twin-bedded [ˌtwɪnˈbedɪd] ADJ Zweibett-; ~ **room** Zweibettzimmer *nt*; **twin beds** PL zwei (gleiche) Einzelbetten *pl*; **twin bill** N (*US inf*) **a** (*Sport*) zwei hintereinander gesendete Spiele *pl* **b** (*Film*) Programm *nt* mit zwei Hauptfilmen; **twin brother** N Zwillingsbruder *m*; **twin carburettors** PL Doppelvergaser *pl*; **twin-cylinder engine** N Zweizylinder(motor) *m*

twine [twaɪn] **N** Schnur *f*, Bindfaden *m* **VT** winden; **to ~ one's arms (a)round sb** seine Ar-

---

me um jdn schlingen **VI** (*around um* +*acc*) sich winden; (*plants also*) sich ranken

twin-engined [ˌtwɪnˈendʒɪnd] ADJ zweimotorig

twin engines PL zwei Motoren *pl*

twinge [twɪndʒ] N (*of pain*) Zucken *nt*, leichtes Stechen; **a ~ of pain** ein zuckender Schmerz; **my back still gives me the occasional ~** ich spüre gelegentlich noch ein Stechen im Rücken; **a ~ of rheumatism** rheumatisches Reißen; **a ~ of regret** leichtes Bedauern; **a ~ of conscience/remorse** Gewissensbisse *pl*

twining [ˈtwaɪnɪŋ] ADJ (*Bot*) rankend, Kletter-; ~ **plant** Kletterpflanze *f*

twinkle [ˈtwɪŋkl] **VI** (*stars*) funkeln, flimmern, glitzern; (*eyes*) blitzen, funkeln; **her feet ~d across the stage** sie bewegte sich leichtfüßig über die Bühne **N a** (*of stars, lights*) Funkeln *nt*, Flimmern *nt*, Glitzern *nt*; **there was a (mischievous) ~ in her eye** man sah den Schalk in ihren Augen; **no, he said with a ~ (in his eye)** nein, sagte er augenzwinkernd **b** (= *instant*) **in a ~** sofort, im Handumdrehen

twinkletoes [ˈtwɪŋklˌtəʊz] N **here comes ~!** (*iro*) da kommt ja unser Trampeltier! (*inf*)

twinkling [ˈtwɪŋklɪŋ] N **in the ~ of an eye** im Nu, im Handumdrehen

twinning [ˈtwɪnɪŋ] N (*Brit: of two towns*) Städtepartnerschaft *f*

twin: twin propellors PL Doppelschiffsschraube *f*; **twinset** N (*Brit*) Twinset *nt*; **twin sister** N Zwillingsschwester *f*; **twin-tone horn** N Zweiklanghorn *nt*; **twin town** N (*Brit*) Partnerstadt *f*; **twin-track** ADJ *approach, process, strategy* zweigleisig; **twin-tub (washing machine)** N Waschmaschine *f* mit getrennter Schleuder

twirl [twɜːl] **VT** (herum)wirbeln; *skirt* herumwirbeln; *glass* drehen; *moustache* zwirbeln; **he ~ed his partner (a)round the dance floor** er wirbelte seine Partnerin übers Parkett **VI** wirbeln; **the skater ~ed (a)round on the ice** der Eiskunstläufer wirbelte über das Eis **N** Wirbel *m*; (*in dance*) Drehung *f*; (*of moustache*) hoch stehende *or* hoch gezwirbelte Spitze; (*in writing*) Schnörkel *m*; **to give a knob a ~** einen Knopf herumdrehen; **he gave his partner a ~** er wirbelte seine Partnerin herum; **give us a ~** dreh dich doch mal

twirp [twɜːp] N (*inf*) = **twerp**

twist [twɪst] **N a** (= *action*) **to give sth a ~** etw (herum)drehen; **to give sb's arm a ~** jdm den Arm verdrehen *or* umdrehen; **to give one's ankle a ~** sich (*dat*) den Fuß vertreten; **with a quick ~ of the hand** mit einer schnellen Handbewegung **b** (= *bend*) Kurve *f*, Biegung *f*; (*fig: in story etc*) Wendung *f*; **the road is full of ~s and turns** die Straße hat viele Biegungen und Windungen; **by** *or* **in a cruel ~ of fate** durch eine grausame Laune des Schicksals **c** (= *coiled shape*) **salt in little ~s of paper** in kleine Papierstückchen eingewickeltes Salz; **~s of thread** Garnknäuel *nt*; **a ~ of French bread** ein französisches Weißbrot (*in Zopfform*) **d** (= *type of yarn*) Twist *m*, Stopfgarn *nt* **e** (*Brit, inf*) **to be/go round the ~** verrückt sein/werden; **it's/she's driving me round the ~!** das/sie macht mich wahnsinnig! **f** (= *dance*) Twist *m*; **to do the ~** Twist tanzen, twisten **g** (*on ball*) Drall *m*; (*esp Billiards*) Effet *m*; **to give a ~ to** *or* **put a ~ on a ball** einem Ball einen Drall geben **VT a** (= *wind, turn*) drehen; (= *coil*) wickeln (*into zu* +*dat*); **to ~ threads** *etc* **together** Fäden *etc* zusammendrehen *or* verflechten; **to ~ pieces of string into a rope** Bindfäden zu einem Seil drehen; **to ~ flowers into a garland** Blumen zu einer Girlande binden; **she ~ed her hair into a bun** sie drehte sich (*dat*) die Haare zu einem Knoten; **to ~ the top off a jar** den Deckel von einem Glas abdrehen; **to ~ sth (a)round sth** etw um etw (*acc*) wickeln → **finger**

b (= *bend, distort*) *rod, key* verbiegen; *part of body* verdrehen, entstellen; **to ~ sth out of shape** etw verbiegen; (*fig*) *meaning, words, truth* verdrehen, entstellen; **to ~ sb's arm** (*lit*) jdm den Arm verdrehen; **she had to ~ my arm to get me to do it** (*fig*) sie musste mich sehr überreden, bis ich es tat; **to ~ one's ankle** sich (*dat*) den Fuß vertreten; **his face was ~ed with pain** sein Gesicht war verzerrt vor Schmerz or schmerzverzerrt **c** *ball* einen Drall geben (+*dat*); **she somehow managed to ~ the red around the black** sie hat es irgendwie geschafft, die rote an der schwarzen Kugel vorbeizumanövrieren **VI a** (= *wind*) sich drehen; (*smoke*) sich kringeln or ringeln; (*plant*) sich winden or ranken; (= *wriggle: road, river, person*) sich schlängeln or winden; **the kite strings have ~ed (a)round the pole** die Drachenschnüre haben sich um den Pfahl verwickelt

     b (= *dance*) Twist tanzen, twisten **c** (*Cards*) aufnehmen und ablegen

▶ **twist about** (*Brit*) or **around VI** sich (her)umdrehen; (*road, river, = wind its way*) sich dahinschlängeln; (= *be twisty*) gewunden sein; **he twisted around in pain** er wand or krümmte sich vor Schmerzen **VT** *sep* = **twist round VT**

▶ **twist off VI** **the top twists off** der Deckel lässt sich abschrauben or ist abschraubbar **VT** *sep* abdrehen; *lid* abschrauben; *flower heads* abknipsen

▶ **twist out VI** **to twist out of sb's grasp** sich jds Griff (*dat*) entwinden **VT** *sep* herausdrehen

▶ **twist round** (*esp Brit*) **VI** sich umdrehen; (*road etc*) eine Biegung machen **VT** *sep* *head, chair* herumdrehen; **she twisted her handkerchief round in her fingers** sie drehte ihr Taschentuch zwischen den Fingern

▶ **twist up VI** (*rope etc*) sich verdrehen; (*smoke*) in Kringeln hochsteigen; (*person: with pain etc*) sich winden or krümmen **VT** *sep* *ropes, wires* verwickeln

twisted ['twɪstɪd] ADJ **a** *wires, rope* (zusammen)gedreht; (= *bent*) verbogen; (= *tangled*) *strap* verdreht; **~-pair cable** verdrilltes Kabel **b** *ankle* verrenkt **c** (*fig pej, = warped*) *mind, logic* verdreht; **bitter and ~** verbittert und verwirrt **d** (*inf, = dishonest*) unredlich **e** (= *disfigured*) *limbs* verwachsen **f** (= *sneering*) *face, smile* verzerrt

twister ['twɪstə] N **a** (*Brit, pej, = person*) Gauner(in) *m(f)*, Halunke **b** (*Brit, = question*) harte Nuss (*inf*); (= *problem*) harter Brocken (*inf*) **c** (*US, inf, = tornado*) Wirbelsturm *m*, Tornado *m* **d** (= *dancer*) Twisttänzer(in) *m(f)*

twisty ['twɪstɪ] ADJ (*+er*) *road* kurvenreich, gewunden; *story, film* kompliziert

twit [twɪt] **VT** **to ~ sb (about sth)** jdn (mit or wegen etw) aufziehen or hochnehmen **N** (*esp Brit inf, = person*) Trottel *m* (*inf*)

twitch [twɪtʃ] **N a** (= *tic*) Zucken *nt*; (= *individual spasm*) Zuckung *f*; **to give a ~** zucken **b** (= *pull*) Ruck *m* (*of an* +*dat*); **to give sth a ~** an etw (*dat*) rucken **b** (*face, muscles*) zucken; **the cat's nose ~ed when I brought in the fish** die Katze schnupperte, als ich den Fisch hereinbrachte **VT a** *tail, ears, nose, eyebrows* zucken mit **b** (= *pull*) zupfen; **he ~ed the letter from her hands** er schnappte ihr den Brief aus den Händen

twitcher ['twɪtʃə] N (*Brit, inf*) Vogelliebhaber(in) *m(f)*, Vogelnärrin *f* (*inf*)

twitch grass ['twɪtʃɡrɑːs] N Quecke *f*

twitchy ['twɪtʃɪ] ADJ **a** (*inf*) (= *physically*) *person* unruhig; *legs* zuckend **b** (= *nervous, uneasy*) *person* nervös; *market* unruhig; **to be ~ about sth** über etw (*acc*) beunruhigt sein **c** *car* wack(e)lig (*inf*)

twitter ['twɪtə] **VI** (*lit, fig*) zwitschern **VT** zwitschern **N a** (*of birds*) Zwitschern *nt*, Gezwitscher *nt* **b** (*inf*) **to be all of a ~** ganz aufgeregt or aufgelöst sein

twittery ['twɪtərɪ] ADJ *attr* zwitschernd

twittish ['twɪtɪʃ] ADJ (*Brit, inf, = stupid*) hirnlos (*inf*)

'twixt [twɪkst] PREP (*old*) = **betwixt**

two [tuː] ADJ zwei; **to break/cut sth in ~** etw in zwei Teile brechen/schneiden; **~ by ~, in ~s** zwei und zwei, zu zweit, zu zweien; **in ~s and threes** immer zwei oder drei (Leute) auf einmal; **~ minds with but a single thought** (*prov*) zwei Seelen – ein Gedanke; **to put ~ and ~ together** (*fig*) seine Schlüsse ziehen, zwei und zwei zusammenzählen; **to put ~ and ~ together and make five** einen Fehlschluss or einen falschen Schluss ziehen; **~'s company, three's a crowd** ein Dritter stört nur; **~ can play at that game** (*inf*) den Spieß kann man auch umdrehen → *also* **six** **N** Zwei *f*; **just the ~ of us/them** nur wir beide/die beiden

two: two-bit ADJ (*US, inf*) mies (*inf*); **two-by-four N** (= *wood*) Stück Holz mit den Maßen 2 x 4 Zoll **ADJ** (*esp US*) (*inf, = small*) *apartment* winzig; (= *petty*) *life, job* nullachtfünfzehn (*inf*)

twoccing ['twɒkɪŋ] N (*Brit inf*) Autodiebstahl *m*

two: two-chamber system N Zweikammersystem *nt*; **two-cycle** ADJ (*US*) = **two-stroke**; **two-cylinder** ADJ Zweizylinder-; **~ engine** Zweizylindermotor *m*; **two-dimensional** ADJ zweidimensional; (*fig, = superficial*) *performance* flach; **two-door** ADJ zweitürig; **two-edged** ADJ **a** (*lit*) zweischneidig, doppelschneidig **b** (*fig*) zweideutig; *argument* zweischneidig; **a ~ sword** or **weapon** (*fig*) ein zweischneidiges Schwert; **two-faced** ADJ (*lit*) doppelgesichtig; (*fig*) falsch; **two-fisted** ADJ **a** **a ~ boxer** ein Boxer, der mit beiden Fäusten gleich gut boxen kann **b** (*dated US, sl*) knallhart; **twofold ADJ** zweifach, doppelt; **a ~ increase** ein Anstieg um das Doppelte; **the advantages of this method are ~** diese Methode hat einen doppelten or zweifachen Vorteil **ADV** **to increase ~** um das Doppelte steigern; **two-four time** N (*Mus*) Zweivierteltakt *m*; **two-handed** ADJ *grip, blow, catch* beidhändig; **a ~ sword** ein Zweihänder *m*; **a ~ saw** eine Säge mit zwei Griffen; **a ~ backhand** eine Rückhand, bei der der Schläger mit beiden Händen gehalten wird **a ~ game** ein Spiel *nt* für zwei Spieler **ADV** zweihändig; **she caught the ball ~** sie fing den Ball mit beiden Händen; **two-hander** [,tuːˈhændə] N (*Theat*) Zweipersonenstück *nt*; **two-horse race** N (*fig*) Wettstreit, bei dem nur zwei der Teilnehmer eine Chance haben zu gewinnen; **two-income family** N Doppelverdiener *pl*; **two-legged** ADJ zweibeinig; **a ~ animal** ein Zweibeiner *m*; **two-man bobsleigh,** (*US*) **two-man bobsled** N (*Sport*) Zweierbob *m*; **two-part** ADJ **a** zweiteilig **b** (*Mus*) zweistimmig, für zwei Stimmen; **two-party system** N Zweiparteiensystem *nt*; **twopence** ['tʌpəns] N = **tuppence**; **twopence piece** [,tuːpensˈpiːs] N Zweipencestück *nt*; **twopenny** ['tʌpnɪ] ADJ = **tuppenny**; **two-phase** ADJ (*Elec*) Zweiphasen-; **~ current** Zweiphasenstrom *m*; **two-piece ADJ** zweiteilig **N a** (= *suit*) Zweiteiler *m*; (= *swimming costume*) zweiteiliger Badeanzug, Bikini *m*; **two-pin plug** N Stecker *m* mit zwei Kontakten; **two-ply** ADJ *wool* zweifädig; *wood* aus zwei Lagen or Schichten bestehend; *tissue* zweilagig; **~ sweater** aus zweifädiger Wolle gestrickter Pullover; **two-seater ADJ** zweisitzig **N** (= *car, plane*) Zweisitzer *m*; **twosome** N **a** (= *people*) Paar *nt*, Pärchen *nt*; **to go out in a ~** zu zweit ausgehen **b** (= *game*) **to have a ~ at golf** zu zweit Golf spielen; **two-star** ADJ Zweisterne-; ~ **petrol** (*Brit dated*) Normalbenzin *nt*; ~ **hotel** Zweisternehotel *nt*; ~ **general** (*US*) Zweisternegeneral(in) *m(f)*; **two-step** N Twostepp *m*; **two-storey,** (*US*) **two-story** ADJ zweistöckig; **two-stroke** (*Brit*) **ADJ** Zweitakt-; ~ **engine** Zweitaktmotor *m* **N** Zweitakter *m*; (= *fuel*) Zweitaktgemisch *nt*

twot [twɒt] N (*Brit*) = **twat**

two: two-time VT (*inf*) *boyfriend, accomplice* betrügen; **the crooks realized that he was two-timing them** die Ganoven merkten, dass er ein doppeltes Spiel spielte or trieb; **two-timer** N (*inf*) falscher Hund (*inf*); **two-timing** ADJ (*inf*)

falsch; **two-tone** ADJ (*in colour*) zweifarbig; (*in sound*) zweitönig

'twould [twʊd] (*old*) contr of **it would**

two: two-up two-down N (*Brit, inf*) kleines Reihenhäuschen; **two-way** ADJ (= *reciprocal*) *trade, exchange, relationship* wechselseitig; ~ **communications** (*Telec*) Sprechverkehr *m* in beide Richtungen; ~ **fabric** von beiden Seiten zu tragender Stoff; ~ **street** Straße *f* mit Gegenverkehr or mit Verkehr in beiden Richtungen; ~ **traffic** Gegenverkehr *m*, Verkehr *m* in beiden Richtungen; **education is a ~ process** Erziehung ist ein wechselseitiger Prozess; **two-way adaptor** N Doppelstecker *m*; **two-way mirror** N Spion(spiegel) *m*; **two-way radio** N Funksprechgerät *nt*; **two-way switch** N Wechselschalter *m*; **two-wheeler (bike)** N Zweirad *nt*, Fahrrad *nt*

tycoon [taɪˈkuːn] N Magnat(in) *m(f)*; **business/oil ~** Industrie-/Ölmagnat(in) *m(f)*

tyke [taɪk] N **a** (= *dog*) Köter *m* **b** (*inf, = child*) Lausbub *m*

tympani PL = **timpani**

tympanic [tɪmˈpænɪk] ADJ (*Anat*) ~ **bone** Mittelohrknochen *m*; ~ **membrane** Trommelfell *nt*, Tympanum *nt* (*spec*)

tympanist ['tɪmpənɪst] N Pauker(in) *m(f)*

tympanum ['tɪmpənəm] N (*Anat, = membrane*) Trommelfell *nt*, Tympanum *nt* (*spec*); (= *middle ear*) Mittelohr *nt*; (*Archit*) Tympanon *nt*

typal ['taɪpl] ADJ artspezifisch

type¹ [taɪp] **N a** (= *kind*) Art *f*; (*of produce, plant*) Sorte *f*, Art *f*; (*esp of people: = character*) Typ *m*, Typus *m*; **different ~s of aircraft** verschiedene Flugzeugtypen *pl*; **different ~s of roses** verschiedene Rosensorten or -arten *pl*; **what ~ of car is it?** was für ein Auto(typ) ist das?; **the very latest ~ of hi-fi** das allerneuste Hi-Fi-Gerät; **she has her own particular ~ of charm** sie hat ihren ganz besonderen Charme; **he has an English ~ of face** dem Gesicht nach könnte er Engländer sein; **most of the characters are recognizable ~s** die meisten Charaktere lassen sich einem bestimmten Typ zuordnen; **they're totally different ~s of person** sie sind vom Typ her völlig verschieden, sie sind völlig verschiedene Typen; **a man of this ~** ein Mann dieser Art or dieses Schlages, diese Art or Sorte (von) Mann; **that ~ of behaviour** (*Brit*) or **behavior** (*US*) ein solches Benehmen; **it's not my ~ of film** diese Art Film gefällt mir nicht; **he's not my ~** er ist nicht mein Typ; **she's my ~ of girl** sie ist mein Typ; **he's not the ~ to hit a lady** er ist nicht der Typ or Mensch, der eine Frau schlägt

     b (*inf, = man*) Typ *m*; **a strange ~** ein seltsamer Mensch, ein komischer Typ (*inf*), eine Type (*inf*) **VT** bestimmen

type² N (*Typ*) Type *f*; **large/small ~** große/kleine Schrift; **to set ~** setzen; **in ~** (= *typed*) maschinegeschrieben, getippt (*inf*); (= *set*) gesetzt, gedruckt; **to set sth up in ~** etw setzen; **printed in italic ~** kursiv gedruckt **VT** tippen, (mit der Maschine) schreiben; **a badly ~d letter** ein schlecht geschriebener or getippter Brief **VI** Maschine schreiben, tippen (*inf*)

▶ **type in** VT SEP eintippen, (*esp Comput*) eingeben; (*with typewriter*) mit Schreibmaschine ausfüllen

▶ **type out** VT *sep* **a** *letter etc* schreiben, tippen (*inf*) **b** *error* ausixen

▶ **type up** VT *sep* auf der Maschine zusammenschreiben

type: type area N (*Typ*) Satzspiegel *m*; **typecast** VT *irreg* (*Theat*) (auf eine bestimmte Rolle) festlegen; **to be ~ as a villain** auf die Rolle des Schurken festgelegt werden/sein; **typeface** N Schrift *f*; **typescript** N mit Maschine geschriebenes Manuskript, Typoskript *nt* (*geh*); **to be in ~** mit Maschine geschrieben sein; **typeset** VT setzen; **typesetter** N (Schrift)setzer(in) *m(f)*; (= *machine*) Setzmaschine *f*; **type-**

setting N Setzen *nt*, (Schrift)satz *m*; **new ~ methods** neue Satztechniken; **type size** N Schriftgröße *f*

typewrite ['taɪpraɪt] *irreg* **VI** Maschine schreiben, tippen (*inf*) **VT** (mit der Maschine) schreiben, tippen (*inf*)

typewriter ['taɪpˌraɪtə'] N Schreibmaschine *f*

typewriter ribbon N Farbband *nt*

typewriting ['taɪpˌraɪtɪŋ] N Maschinenschreiben *nt*

typewritten ['taɪpˌrɪtn] ADJ maschinegeschrieben, getippt

typhoid ['taɪfɔɪd] N (*also* **typhoid fever**) Typhus *m*; **~ injection** Impfung *f* gegen Typhus, Typhusimpfung *f*

typhoon [taɪ'fuːn] N Taifun *m*

typhus ['taɪfəs] N Fleckfieber *nt*, Flecktyphus *m*

typical ['tɪpɪkəl] ADJ typisch (*of* für); **a ~ English town** eine typisch englische Stadt; **that's ~ of him** das ist typisch für ihn; **isn't that ~!** ist das nicht wieder mal typisch!; **~ male!** typisch Mann!

typically ['tɪpɪkəlɪ] ADV typisch; **~, he did nothing but complain about the food** bezeichnenderweise hat er sich ständig über das Essen beschwert; **~, he insisted on getting there early** er wollte natürlich unbedingt früh hingehen, typisch

typify ['tɪpɪfaɪ] VT bezeichnend sein für; **he typifies the reserved Englishman** er verkörpert (genau) den Typ des zurückhaltenden Engländers

typing ['taɪpɪŋ] N Tippen *nt* (*inf*); (*with typewriter*) Maschinenschreiben *nt*; **the noise of her ~ drove me mad** ihr Tippen machte mich wahnsinnig; **his ~ isn't very good** er kann nicht besonders gut tippen

typing: typing error N Tippfehler *m*; **typing pool** N Schreibzentrale *f*; **typing speed** N Schreibgeschwindigkeit *f*

typist ['taɪpɪst] N (*professional*) Schreibkraft *f*, Stenotypist(in) *m(f)*, Tippse *f* (*pej inf*); **he couldn't find a ~ for his thesis** er konnte niemanden finden, der ihm seine Doktorarbeit tippte

typo ['taɪpəʊ] N (*Typ inf*) Druckfehler *m*; (*on typewriter, computer*) Tippfehler *m*

typographer [taɪ'pɒɡrəfə'] N Typograf(in) *m(f)*

typographic(al) [ˌtaɪpə'ɡræfɪk(əl)] ADJ typografisch; **typographical error** Druckfehler *m*

typography [taɪ'pɒɡrəfɪ] N Typografie *f*; (= *subject also*) Buchdruckerkunst *f*

typological [ˌtaɪpə'lɒdʒɪkəl] ADJ typologisch

typology [taɪ'pɒlədʒɪ] N Typologie *f*

tyrannic(al) [tɪ'rænɪk(əl), tɪ'rænɪkəlɪ] ADJ , **tyrannically** ADV tyrannisch

tyrannize ['tɪrənaɪz] VT (*lit, fig*) tyrannisieren

tyrannosaur [tɪ'rænəsɔː] N Tyrannosaurier *m*

tyrannosaurus (rex) [tɪˌrænə'sɔːrəs(reks)] N Tyrannosaurus rex *m*

tyrannous ['tɪrənəs] ADJ tyrannisch

tyranny ['tɪrənɪ] N (*lit, fig*) Tyrannei *f*, Tyrannenherrschaft *f*; **he ruled by ~** er führte eine Tyrannenherrschaft

tyrant ['taɪərənt] N (*lit, fig*) Tyrann(in) *m(f)*

tyre, (*US*) **tire** [taɪə'] N Reifen *m*; **a burst** (*Brit*) or **blown ~** ein geplatzter Reifen

tyre, (*US*) **tire**: **tyre gauge** N Reifendruckmesser *m*; **tyre lever** N Montiereisen *nt*; **tyre pressure** N Reifendruck *m*

tyro ['taɪərəʊ] N Anfänger(in) *m(f)*; **a ~ skier** *etc* ein Anfänger beim or im Skilaufen *etc*

Tyrol [tɪ'rəʊl] N **the ~** Tirol *nt*

Tyrolean ['tɪrəlɪən], **Tyrolese** [tɪrə'liːz] **ADJ** Tiroler-; **~ hat** Tirolerhut *m* **N** Tiroler(in) *m(f)*

Tyrrhenian Sea [tɪ'riːnɪən'siː] N Tyrrhenisches Meer

tzar N = tsar

tzarina N = tsarina

tzarist ADJ, N = tsarist

tzatziki [t(s)æt'siːkɪ] N (*Cook*) Tsatsiki *nt or m*, Zaziki *nt or m*

tzetze (fly) N = tsetse (fly)

U

U, u [ju:] **N a** U *nt*, u *nt* **b** (*Brit Film inf*) jugendfreier Film **ADJ** (*Brit*, = *upper class*) charakteristisch für die Gewohnheiten, Sprechweise etc der Oberschicht, vornehm

UAR *abbr of* **United Arab Republic**

UAW (*US*) *abbr of* **United Automobile Workers** *Gewerkschaft der Beschäftigten in der Kraftfahrzeugindustrie*

UB40 [ju:bi:'fɔ:tɪ] **N** (*Brit*) *Ausweis für Arbeitslose*

U-bend ['ju:bend] **N** (*in pipe*) U-Bogen *m*; (*in road*) Haarnadelkurve *f*

ubiquitous [ju:'bɪkwɪtəs] **ADJ** allgegenwärtig; **sandstone is ~ in this district** Sandstein ist in dieser Gegend überall zu finden

ubiquity [ju:'bɪkwɪtɪ] **N** Allgegenwart *f*; (= *prevalence*) weite Verbreitung

U-boat ['ju:bəʊt] **N** U-Boot *nt*

UCAS ['ju:kæs] (*Brit*) *abbr of* **Universities and Colleges Admissions Service** ≈ ZVS *f*

UCCA ['ʌkə] (*Brit, dated*) *abbr of* **Universities Central Council on Admissions** ≈ ZVS *f*

UDA *abbr of* **Ulster Defence Association**

udder ['ʌdə'] **N** Euter *nt*

UDF *abbr of* **Ulster Defence Force**

UDI *abbr of* **Unilateral Declaration of Independence**

UDP *abbr of* **Ulster Democratic Party**

UDR *abbr of* **Ulster Defence Regiment**

UEFA [ju:'eɪfə] *abbr of* **Union of European Football Associations** die UEFA

UFO ['ju:fəʊ] *abbr of* **unidentified flying object** Ufo *nt*, UFO *nt*

ufologist [ju:'fɒlədʒɪst] **N** Ufologe *m*, Ufologin *f*

ufology [ju:'fɒlədʒɪ] **N** Ufologie *f*

Uganda [ju:'gændə] **N** Uganda *nt*

Ugandan [jʊ'gændən] **ADJ** ugandisch; **he is ~** er ist Ugander **N** Ugander(in) *m(f)*

UGC (*Brit*) *abbr of* **University Grants Committee**

ugh [ɜ:h] **INTERJ** i, igitt

Ugli (fruit)® ['ʌglɪ(fru:t)] **N** *Kreuzung aus Grapefruit, Apfelsine und Mandarine*

uglify ['ʌglɪfaɪ] **VT** hässlich machen, verunstalten

ugliness ['ʌglɪnɪs] **N** Hässlichkeit *f*; (*of news*) Unerfreulichkeit *f*; (*of wound*) übler Zustand; (*of situation*) Ekelhaftigkeit *f*; (*of crime*) Gemeinheit *f*; (*of vice*) Hässlichkeit *f*, Garstigkeit *f*

ugly ['ʌglɪ] **ADJ** (+*er*) **a** (= *not pretty*) hässlich; **as ~ as sin** hässlich wie die Sünde *or* Nacht **b** (= *unpleasant, nasty*) übel; *news, wound* schlimm, übel; *rumour, scenes, crime, clouds* hässlich; *crime* übel, gemein; *vice* hässlich, übel; *situation, sky* bedrohlich; **an ~ customer** ein übler Kunde; **to cut up** *or* **grow** *or* **turn ~** (*inf*) gemein *or* fies (*inf*) werden; **censorship is an ~ word these days** Zensur ist heutzutage ein hässliches Wort

ugly duckling **N** (*fig*) hässliches Entlein

UHF *abbr of* **ultra-high frequency** UHF

uh-huh **INTERJ a** ['ʌ'hʌ] (*agreeing, understanding*) ja **b** ['ʌ,ʌ] (*disagreeing, forbidding*) nichts da (*inf*)

UHT *abbr of* **ultra heat treated** ultrahocherhitzt; **~ milk** H-Milch *f*

UK *abbr of* **United Kingdom** Vereinigtes Königreich

uke [ju:k] (*inf*), **ukelele** **N** = **ukulele**

Ukraine [ju:'kreɪn] **N the ~** die Ukraine

Ukrainian [ju:'kreɪnɪən] **ADJ** ukrainisch; **he is ~** er ist Ukrainer **N a** Ukrainer(in) *m(f)* **b** (*Ling*) Ukrainisch *nt*

ukulele, **ukelele** [ju:kə'leɪlɪ] **N** Ukulele *f*

ulcer ['ʌlsə'] **N** (*Med*) Geschwür *nt*; (= *stomach ulcer*) Magengeschwür *nt*; (*fig*) Übel *nt*

ulcerate ['ʌlsəreɪt] **VT** *stomach* ein Geschwür *nt* verursachen in (+*dat*); *skin* Geschwüre verursachen auf (+*dat*); *wound* eitern lassen **VI** (*stomach*) ein Geschwür *nt* bilden *or* bekommen; (*skin*) geschwürig werden; (*wound*) eitern

ulcerated ['ʌlsəreɪtɪd] **ADJ** geschwürig; *wound* vereitert; **an ~ stomach** ein Magengeschwür *nt*

ulceration [ʌlsə'reɪʃən] **N** (= *process*) Geschwürbildung *f*; (*of wound*) Vereiterung *f*; (= *state*) Geschwüre *pl*, Vereiterung *f*

ulcerous ['ʌlsərəs] **ADJ** geschwürig; *wound* vereitert; (= *causing ulcers*) geschwürbildend

ullage ['ʌlɪdʒ] **N** Leckage *f*, Flüssigkeitsschwund *m*

'ullo [ə'ləʊ] **INTERJ** (*Brit inf*) = **hello**

ulna ['ʌlnə] **N** *pl* **-e** *or* **-s** ['ʌlni:] (*Anat*) Elle *f*

Ulster ['ʌlstə'] **N** Ulster *nt*

ulster ['ʌlstə'] **N** (*dated*, = *coat*) Ulster *m*

Ulsterman ['ʌlstəmæn] **N** *pl* **-men** [-mən] Mann *m* aus Ulster, Einwohner *m* von Ulster

Ulsterwoman ['ʌlstəwʊmən] **N** *pl* **-women** [-wɪmɪn] Frau *f* aus Ulster, Einwohnerin *f* von Ulster

ult [ʌlt] *abbr of* **ultimo**

ulterior [ʌl'tɪərɪə'] **ADJ a** *purpose* verborgen; **~ motive** Hintergedanke *m*; **I have no ~ motive(s) for** *or* **in doing that** ich tue das ganz ohne Hintergedanken **b** (*rare*, = *lying beyond*) jenseitig

ultimata [ʌltɪ'meɪtə] *pl of* **ultimatum**

ultimate ['ʌltɪmɪt] **ADJ a** (= *final*) letzte(r, s); *destiny, solution, decision* endgültig; *control* oberste(r, s); *authority* höchste(r, s); *beneficiary* eigentlich; **~ goal** *or* **aim** Endziel *nt*; **~ result/outcome** Endergebnis *nt*; **he came to the ~ conclusion that ...** er kam schließlich zu der Einsicht, dass ...; **what is your ~ ambition in life?** was streben Sie letzten Endes *or* letztlich im Leben an?; **although they had no ~ hope of escape** obwohl letztlich *or* im Endeffekt keine Hoffnung auf Flucht bestand

b (= *that cannot be improved on*) vollendet, perfekt, ultimativ; **the ~ sports car** der Sportwagen in höchster Vollendung, der ultimative Sportwagen; **the ~ insult** der Gipfel der Beleidigung; **the ~ sin** die schlimmste Sünde; **the ~ disgrace** die größte Schande; **the ~ deterrent** (*Mil*) das endgültige Abschreckungsmittel; (*fig*) die äußerste Abschreckungsmaßnahme; **the ~ weapon** (*Mil*) die Superwaffe; (*fig*) das letzte und äußerste Mittel; **death is the ~ sacrifice** der Tod ist das allergrößte Opfer

c (= *basic*) *cause* eigentlich; *explanation* grundsätzlich; *truth* letzte(r, s); **~ principle/problem** Grundprinzip/-problem *nt*; **~ constituents** Grundbestandteile *pl*

d (= *furthest*) entfernteste(r, s); *boundary of uni-*

---

verse, frontier äußerste(r, s); *ancestors* früheste(r, s); **the ~ origins of man** die frühesten Ursprünge des Menschen

N Nonplusultra *nt*; **that is the ~ in comfort** das ist Superkomfort *or* das Höchste an Komfort

ultimately ['ʌltɪmɪtlɪ] **ADV** (= *in the end*) letztlich, letzten Endes; (= *eventually*) schließlich; (= *fundamentally*) im Grunde genommen, letztlich; **it's ~ your decision** letztlich müssen Sie das entscheiden

ultimatum [ʌltɪ'meɪtəm] **N** *pl* **-s** *or* **ultimata** (*Mil, fig*) Ultimatum *nt*; **to deliver** *or* **issue an ~ to sb** jdm ein Ultimatum stellen

ultimo ['ʌltɪməʊ] **ADV** (*dated Comm*) des letzten *or* vorigen Monats

ultra- ['ʌltrə-] **PREF** ultra-; **ultraconservative** **ADJ** erzkonservativ, ultrakonservativ; **ultrafashionable** **ADJ** ultramodern, supermodisch; **ultrahigh frequency** **N** Ultrahochfrequenz *f*; **ultra-left-wing** **ADJ** (*Pol*) ultralinke(r, s); **ultralight** **ADJ** *materials etc* ultraleicht **N** (*Aviat*) Ultraleichtflugzeug *nt*; **ultramarine** **N** Ultramarin *nt* **ADJ** ultramarin(blau); **ultramodern** **ADJ** ultra- *or* hypermodern; **ultramontane** **ADJ** (*Eccl*) ultramontan; **ultra-right-wing** **ADJ** (*Pol*) ultrarechte(r, s); **ultrashort wave** **N** Ultrakurzwelle *f*; **ultrasound** **N** Ultraschall *m*; (= *scan*) Ultraschalluntersuchung *f*; **ultrasound picture** **N** Ultraschallbild *nt* *or* -aufnahme *f*; **ultrasound scan** **N** Ultraschalluntersuchung *f*; **ultraviolet** **ADJ** ultraviolett; **~ treatment** Ultraviolettbestrahlung *f*

ululate ['ju:ljʊleɪt] **VI** (*liter, mourning women*) (weh)klagen (*liter*); (*dog etc*) heulen

ululation [ju:ljʊ'leɪʃən] **N** (*liter, of mourning women*) (Weh)klagen *nt* (*liter*); (*of dog etc*) Heulen *nt*

Ulysses [ju:'lɪsi:z] **N** Odysseus, Ulixes (*rare*), Ulysses (*rare*) *m*

um [əm] **INTERJ** äh; (*in decision, answering*) hm **VI** **to um and err** herumdrucksen; **after a lot of umming and erring** nach vielen Ähs und Öhs

umbel ['ʌmbəl] **N** Dolde *f*

umber ['ʌmbə'] **N** (= *earth*) Umbraerde *f*; (= *pigment: also* **raw umber**) Umbra *f*, Umber *m*; **burned ~** gebrannte Umbra **ADJ** umbrabraun

umbilical [ʌm'bɪlɪkəl] **ADJ** Nabel- **N** (*Space, Anat: also* **umbilical cord**) Nabelschnur *f*

umbilical cord **N** Nabelschnur *f*

umbilicus [ʌmbɪ'laɪkəs] **N** Nabel *m*

umbra ['ʌmbrə] **N** *pl* **-s** *or* **-e** ['ʌmbri:] (*Astron*, = *shadow*) Kernschatten *m*; (*in sunspot*) Umbra *f*

umbrage ['ʌmbrɪdʒ] **N** **to take ~ at sth** an etw (*dat*) Anstoß nehmen; **he took ~** er nahm daran Anstoß

umbrella [ʌm'brelə] **N** (Regen)schirm *m*; (= *sun umbrella*) (Sonnen)schirm *m*; (*Mil:* = *air umbrella, for ground troops*) Abschirmung *f*, Luftschirm *m*; (*for plane*) Jagdschutz *m*; **under the ~ of** (*fig*) unter der Kontrolle von; **to bring sth under one ~** etw zusammenfassen

umbrella: umbrella organization **N** Dachorganisation *f*; **umbrella stand** **N** Schirmständer *m*

umlaut ['ʊmlaʊt] N (= sign) Umlautpunkte pl; (= sound change) Umlaut m; **a ~** ä

ump [ʌmp] N (US inf) = umpire

umpire ['ʌmpaɪə'] **N** Schiedsrichter(in) m(f); (fig) Unparteiische(r) mf; **to act as ~** (lit) als Schiedsrichter(in) fungieren, Schiedsrichter(in) sein; (fig) schlichten **VT** (Sport) als Schiedsrichter(in) fungieren bei, Schiedsrichter(in) sein bei, schiedsrichtern bei; (fig) schlichten **VI** (in bei) Schiedsrichter(in) sein, schiedsrichtern; (fig) schlichten

umpireship ['ʌmpaɪəʃɪp] N (Jur, Sport) Schiedsrichteramt nt

umpteen ['ʌmp'tiːn] ADJ (inf) zig (inf), x (inf); **I've told you ~ times** ich habe dir zigmal or x-mal gesagt (inf)

umpteenth ['ʌmp'tiːnθ] ADJ (inf) x-te(r, s); **for the ~ time** zum x-ten Mal

UMTS (Telec) abbr of **universal mobile telecommunications system** UMTS nt

UN abbr of **United Nations** UNO f, UN pl; **UN troops** UNO-Truppen pl

'un [ən] PRON (inf) **he's a good ~** er ist 'n feiner Kerl; **a big ~** 'n großer; **the little ~s** die Kleinen pl

un- [ʌn-] PREF (before adj, adv) un-, nicht; (before n) Un-

unabashed [ʌnə'bæʃt] ADJ (= not ashamed, embarrassed) dreist, unverfroren; (= not overawed) unbeeindruckt; **he is an ~ romantic** er ist ein schamloser Romantiker

unabated [ʌnə'beɪtɪd] ADJ unvermindert; **the rain/storm continued ~** der Regen/Sturm ließ nicht nach

unabbreviated [ʌnə'briːvɪeɪtɪd] ADJ unabgekürzt, nicht abgekürzt

unable [ʌn'eɪbl] ✪ 16.3, 25.1 ADJ pred **to be ~ to do sth** etw nicht tun können, außerstande or außer Stande sein, etw zu tun; **we're still ~ to cure cancer** wir sind immer noch außerstande or außer Stande or immer noch nicht in der Lage, Krebs zu heilen

unabridged [ʌnə'brɪdʒd] ADJ ungekürzt

unacceptable [ʌnək'septəbl] ADJ plans, terms unannehmbar; excuse, offer, behaviour nicht akzeptabel; standard, unemployment level, working conditions nicht tragbar, untragbar; **it's quite ~ that we should be expected to ...** es kann doch nicht von uns verlangt werden, dass ...; **it's quite ~ for young children to ...** es kann nicht zugelassen werden, dass kleine Kinder ...; **the ~ face of capitalism** die Kehrseite des Kapitalismus; **he behaved in an ~ way** er benahm sich unmöglich

unacceptably [ʌnək'septəblɪ] ADV untragbar; high unannehmbar; poor, bad unzumutbar; **these fuels are ~ dangerous** diese Brennstoffe sind in nicht mehr tragbarem Maße gefährlich; **he suggested, quite ~, that ...** er schlug vor, was völlig unakzeptabel war, dass ...

unaccommodating [ʌnə'kɒmədeɪtɪŋ] ADJ ungefällig; attitude unnachgiebig

unaccompanied [ʌnə'kʌmpənɪd] ADJ person, child, singing ohne Begleitung; bag, suitcase (= abandoned) herrenlos; (= travelling separately) aufgegeben; **~ violin** Solovioline f

unaccomplished [ʌnə'kʌmplɪʃt] ADJ (= unfinished) unvollendet, unfertig; (fig) ungebildet; (= untalented) untalentiert

unaccountable [ʌnə'kaʊntəbl] ADJ **a** (= inexplicable) unerklärlich; phenomenon also unerklärbar **b** (= not answerable) person niemandem unterstellt; **to be ~ to sb** sich jdm gegenüber nicht verantworten müssen

unaccountably [ʌnə'kaʊntəblɪ] ADV unerklärlicherweise; disappear auf unerklärliche Weise; **an ~ long time** unerklärlich lange; **~ happy** ohne besonderen Grund glücklich

unaccounted for [ʌnə'kaʊntɪd'fɔː'] ADJ ungeklärt; **£30 is still ~** es ist noch ungeklärt, wo die £ 30 geblieben sind; **three of the passengers are still ~** drei Passagiere werden noch

vermisst, der Verbleib von drei Passagieren ist noch nicht geklärt

unaccustomed [ʌnə'kʌstəmd] ADJ **a** (= unusual) ungewohnt; **with ~ anger/zeal** mit untypischem Zorn/Eifer **b** (of person: = unused) **to be ~ to sth** etw nicht gewohnt sein, an etw (acc) nicht gewöhnt sein; **to be ~ to doing sth** es nicht gewohnt sein, etw zu tun, nicht daran gewöhnt sein, etw zu tun; **~ as I am to public speaking ...** ich bin kein großer Redner, aber ...

unachievable [ʌnə'tʃiːvəbl] ADJ task etc unausführbar; quality etc unerreichbar

unacknowledged [ʌnək'nɒlɪdʒd] ADJ letter unbeantwortet; mistake uneingestanden; champion verkannt; **to leave a letter ~** den Empfang eines Briefes nicht bestätigen; **to go ~** (person, achievement etc) nicht anerkannt werden

unacquainted [ʌnə'kweɪntɪd] ADJ pred **to be ~ with poverty** die Armut nicht kennen; **to be ~ with the facts** mit den Tatsachen nicht vertraut sein; **I'm not ~ with fame** Ruhm or Berühmtheit ist mir nicht gänzlich fremd; **they're ~ with each other** sie kennen sich nicht

unadaptable [ʌnə'dæptəbl] ADJ nicht anpassungsfähig, nicht flexibel; **to be ~ to sth** sich an etw (acc) nicht anpassen können

unadapted [ʌnə'dæptɪd] ADJ version of novel etc unadaptiert; **in the ~ version** in der Originalversion

unadopted [ʌnə'dɒptɪd] ADJ **a** (Brit) **~ road** öffentliche Straße, für deren Instandhaltung die Anlieger allein verantwortlich sind **b** child nicht adoptiert; **many children remain ~** viele Kinder werden nicht adoptiert **c** proposal nicht aufgegriffen

unadorned [ʌnə'dɔːnd] ADJ schlicht; woman's beauty natürlich; truth ungeschminkt; prose schmucklos

unadulterated [ʌnə'dʌltəreɪtɪd] ADJ **a** unverfälscht; wine rein, ungepan(t)scht; (hum) whisky unverdünnt; **~ by foreign influences** durch fremde Einflüsse nicht verfälscht **b** (fig) nonsense schier; bliss ungetrübt; **this is ~ filth** das ist der reinste Schmutz, das ist Schmutz in Reinkultur (inf)

unadventurous [ʌnəd'ventʃərəs] ADJ time, life wenig abenteuerlich, ereignislos; tastes hausbacken, bieder; style, theatrical production, football einfallslos; person wenig unternehmungslustig; **where food is concerned he is very ~** in Bezug aufs Essen ist er nicht experimentierfreudig

unadventurously [ʌnəd'ventʃərəslɪ] ADV directed einfallslos; dressed, decorated bieder, hausbacken; **rather ~ they chose Tenerife again** einfallslos or wenig abenteuerlich, wie sie sind, haben sie sich wieder für Teneriffa entschieden

unadvisable [ʌnəd'vaɪzəbl] ADJ unratsam, nicht ratsam

unaesthetic, (US) **unesthetic** [ʌniːs'θetɪk] ADJ unästhetisch

unaffected [ʌnə'fektɪd] ADJ **a** (= sincere) ungekünstelt, natürlich, unaffektiert; pleasure, gratitude echt **b** (= not damaged) nicht angegriffen (also Med), nicht in Mitleidenschaft gezogen, nicht beeinträchtigt; (= not influenced) unbeeinflusst, nicht beeinflusst; (= not involved) nicht betroffen; (= unmoved) ungerührt, unbewegt; **she remained quite ~ by his tears** sie blieb beim Anblick seiner Tränen völlig ungerührt; **our exports were ~ by the strike** unsere Exporte wurden durch den Streik nicht beeinträchtigt; **he remained quite ~ by all the noise** der Lärm berührte or störte ihn überhaupt nicht

unaffectedly [ʌnə'fektɪdlɪ] ADV (= sincerely) ungeziert, natürlich; say unaffektiert; **she was ~ pleased** ihre Freude war echt

unaffectedness [ʌnə'fektɪdnɪs] N (= sincerity) Ungeziertheit f, Natürlichkeit f, Unaffektiertheit f; (of joy etc) Aufrichtigkeit f

unafraid [ʌnə'freɪd] ADJ unerschrocken, furchtlos; **to be ~ of sb/sth** vor jdm/etw keine Angst haben; **to be ~ to do sth** keine Angst haben, etw zu tun

unaided [ʌn'eɪdɪd] **ADV** ohne fremde Hilfe; **to do sth ~** etw allein or ohne fremde Hilfe tun **ADJ** **his own ~ work** seine eigene Arbeit; **by my own ~ efforts** ganz ohne fremde Hilfe; **~ by sb** ohne jds Hilfe; **~ by sth** ohne Zuhilfenahme von etw; **with the ~ eye** mit dem bloßen Auge; **to be invisible to the ~ eye** mit dem bloßen Auge nicht sichtbar sein

unaired [ʌn'eəd] ADJ room, bed, clothes ungelüftet; argument nicht vorgebracht

unalike [ʌnə'laɪk] ADJ pred unähnlich, ungleich; **the two children are so ~** die beiden Kinder sind so verschieden or sind sich so unähnlich

unallocated [ʌn'æləkeɪtɪd] ADJ funds nicht zugewiesen or zugeteilt; **~ tickets** Karten im freien Verkauf

unalloyed [ʌnə'lɔɪd] ADJ usu attr happiness, success ungetrübt

unalterable [ʌn'ɒltərəbl] ADJ intention, decision, fact unabänderlich; laws unveränderlich

unalterably [ʌn'ɒltərəblɪ] ADV unveränderlich; **to be ~ opposed to sth** entschieden gegen etw sein

unaltered [ʌn'ɒltəd] ADJ unverändert

unambiguous ADJ , **unambiguously** ADV [ʌnæm'bɪgjʊəs, -lɪ] eindeutig, unzweideutig

unambitious [ʌnæm'bɪʃəs] ADJ person, plan nicht ehrgeizig (genug); theatrical production anspruchslos

unamenable [ʌnə'miːnəbl] ADJ unzugänglich (to +dat); **he is ~ to persuasion** er lässt sich nicht überreden; **~ to medical treatment** auf ärztliche Behandlung nicht ansprechend

un-American [ʌnə'merɪkən] ADJ unamerikanisch; **~ activities** unamerikanische Umtriebe pl

unamiable [ʌn'eɪmɪəbl] ADJ unliebenswürdig

unamused [ʌnə'mjuːzd] ADJ laugh gezwungen, unfroh; **she was ~ (by this)** sie fand es or das überhaupt nicht lustig

unanimity [juːnə'nɪmɪtɪ] N Einmütigkeit f; (of decision also) Einstimmigkeit f

unanimous [juː'nænɪməs] ADJ einmütig; decision also (Jur) einstimmig; **we were ~ in thinking ...** wir waren einmütig der Ansicht ...; **they are ~ in wanting a change** sie sind sich (darin) einig, dass sie eine Veränderung wollen; **they were ~ in their condemnation of him** sie haben ihn einmütig verdammt; **by a ~ vote** einstimmig

unanimously [juː'nænɪməslɪ] ADV einstimmig, einmütig; agree einmütig; vote einstimmig

unannounced [ʌnə'naʊnst] ADJ, ADV unangemeldet

unanswerable [ʌn'ɑːnsərəbl] ADJ question nicht zu beantworten pred, nicht zu beantwortend attr; argument, case zwingend, unwiderlegbar; **that question is ~** diese Frage lässt sich nicht beantworten

unanswered [ʌn'ɑːnsəd] ADJ unbeantwortet; **to be left ~** unbeantwortet bleiben

unapologetic [ʌnəpɒlə'dʒetɪk] ADJ unverfroren, dreist; **he was so ~ about it** es schien ihm überhaupt nicht Leid zu tun

unappealable [ʌnə'piːləbl] ADJ (Jur) nicht berufungsfähig; **the judgement is ~** gegen das Urteil kann keine Berufung eingelegt werden

unappealing [ʌnə'piːlɪŋ] ADJ nicht ansprechend, nicht reizvoll; person also unansehnlich; prospect, sight nicht verlockend; **to be ~ to sb** für jdn nicht verlockend sein

unappeased [ʌnə'piːzd] ADJ appetite, lust unbefriedigt; hunger, thirst ungestillt; person nicht besänftigt

unappetizing [ʌn'æpɪtaɪzɪŋ] ADJ unappetitlich; prospect, thought wenig verlockend

unappreciated [ʌnə'priːʃɪeɪtɪd] ADJ nicht geschätzt or gewürdigt; **she felt she was ~ by him** sie hatte den Eindruck, dass er sie nicht zu schätzen wusste; **the ~ heroines of the war** die ungewürdigten or unbeachteten Heldinnen des Krieges

unappreciative [ˌʌnəˈpriːʃɪətɪv] ADJ undankbar; *audience* verständnislos; **to be ~ of sth** etw nicht zu würdigen wissen

unapprehensive [ˌʌnæprɪˈhensɪv] ADJ **a** (= *slow*) schwerfällig; (= *slow on the uptake*) schwer von Begriff **b** (= *unconcerned*) unbekümmert, furchtlos

unapproachable [ˌʌnəˈprəʊtʃəbl] ADJ *place* unzugänglich; *person also* unnahbar

unapt [ʌnˈæpt] ADJ (= *inappropriate*) unpassend, unangebracht

unarguable [ʌnˈɑːgjʊəbl] ADJ *theory etc* nicht vertretbar

unarguably [ʌnˈɑːgjʊəblɪ] ADV unbestreitbar, zweifellos

unargued [ʌnˈɑːgjuːd] ADJ (= *without argumentation*) unbegründet; (= *undisputed*) unangefochten, unbestritten; **the point was left ~** dieser Punkt wurde nicht begründet; (= *undiscussed*) dieser Punkt wurde nicht erörtert

unarm [ʌnˈɑːm] VT = **disarm**

unarmed [ʌnˈɑːmd] ADJ unbewaffnet ADV unbewaffnet

unarmed combat N Nahkampf *m* ohne Waffe

unashamed [ˌʌnəˈʃeɪmd] ADJ schamlos; *admirer, liberal, reactionary, populist* unverhohlen; **naked but ~** nackt aber ohne Scham; **his ~ conservatism** sein unverhohlener Konservatismus; **he was quite ~ about** *or* **of it** er schämte sich dessen überhaupt nicht, er war darüber kein bisschen beschämt; **to be ~ to do sth** keine Hemmungen haben, etw zu tun

unashamedly [ˌʌnəˈʃeɪmɪdlɪ] ADV unverschämt; *say, admire* ohne Scham; *romantic* unverhohlen; *cry* hemmungslos; *in favour of, partisan* ganz offen, unverhohlen; **he's ~ proud of ...** er zeigt unverhohlen, wie stolz er auf ... ist; **they are ~ in love** sie schämen sich ihrer Liebe nicht; **this book is ~ a love story** das Buch ist ganz unverhohlen eine Liebesgeschichte

unasked [ʌnˈɑːskt] ADJ (= *unrequested*) unaufgefordert, ungefragt, ungebeten; (= *uninvited*) un(ein)geladen, ungebeten; **the question went ~** die Frage wurde nicht gestellt ADV (= *voluntarily*) unaufgefordert

unasked-for [ʌnˈɑːskfɔːʳ] ADJ ungewünscht, unwillkommen

unaspirated [ʌnˈæspɪreɪtɪd] ADJ unbehaucht

unaspiring ADJ , **unaspiringly** ADV [ˌʌnəˈspaɪərɪŋ, -lɪ] **a** (= *unambitious*) ohne Ehrgeiz **b** (= *undemanding*) anspruchslos; (= *unpretentious*) bescheiden

unassailable [ˌʌnəˈseɪləbl] ADJ unangreifbar; *fortress* uneinnehmbar, unbezwingbar; *position, reputation, record, majority* unantastbar, unanfechtbar; *conviction* unerschütterlich; *argument* unwiderlegbar, unanfechtbar, zwingend

unassisted [ˌʌnəˈsɪstɪd] ADJ, ADV = **unaided**

unassuming [ˌʌnəˈsjuːmɪŋ] ADJ bescheiden

unattached [ˌʌnəˈtætʃt] ADJ **a** (= *not fastened*) unbefestigt; *(Mil)* keinem Regiment/keiner Einheit *etc* zugeteilt; *(US) athlete* ohne Vereinszugehörigkeit; **~ vote** Wechselwähler *m* **b** (*emotionally*) ungebunden; **she's worried about still being ~** es macht ihr Sorgen, weil sie immer noch keinen Partner gefunden hat; **there aren't many ~ girls around** die meisten Mädchen hier sind nicht mehr zu haben *or* sind nicht mehr frei

unattainability [ˌʌnəˌteɪnəˈbɪlɪtɪ] N Unerreichbarkeit *f*

unattainable [ˌʌnəˈteɪnəbl] ADJ unerreichbar

unattended [ˌʌnəˈtendɪd] ADJ **a** (= *not looked after*) *children* unbeaufsichtigt; *car park, car, luggage* unbewacht; *patient* unbehandelt, nicht behandelt; *shop* ohne Bedienung; *customer* nicht bedient; *business* unerledigt; **to leave sb ~** (*leave alone, child*) jdn unbeaufsichtigt lassen; **to leave sth ~** (*car, luggage*) etw unbewacht lassen; *shop* etw unbeaufsichtigt lassen; **to leave sb/sth ~ (to)** (= *not deal with, guests, problem*) sich nicht um jdn/etw kümmern; *work* etw lie-

gen lassen, etw nicht erledigen; *patient* jdn nicht behandeln; *customer* jdn nicht bedienen; **to leave a wound ~** eine Wunde nicht versorgen; **to leave a car ~** to ein Auto nicht reparieren lassen; **to be** *or* **go ~ to** (*wound, injury*) nicht behandelt werden; (*car, fault*) nicht repariert werden; (*customer*) nicht bedient werden; (*work*) nicht erledigt sein werden/werden **b** (= *not escorted*) ohne Begleitung (*by +gen*), unbegleitet

unattested [ˌʌnəˈtestɪd] ADJ **a** (= *unconfirmed*) unbezeugt, unbestätigt **b** (*Brit: = not formally certified*) (behördlich) nicht überprüft

unattractive [ˌʌnəˈtræktɪv] ADJ *sight, place* unschön, wenig reizvoll; *offer* unattraktiv, uninteressant; *trait, scar* unschön; *character* unsympathisch; *woman* unattraktiv; **he's ~ to women** Frauen finden ihn nicht attraktiv *or* anziehend; **to be ~ to sb** (*fig, = unappealing*) für jdn nicht reizvoll sein

unattractiveness [ˌʌnəˈtræktɪvnɪs] N Unschönheit *f*; (*of woman*) geringe Attraktivität; **the ~ of the offer** das unattraktive *or* nicht verlockende Angebot

unattributed [ˌʌnəˈtrɪbjuːtɪd] ADJ *quotation* ohne Quellenangabe; *remarks* anonym; *source* ungenannt

unauthenticated [ˌʌnɔːˈθentɪkeɪtɪd] ADJ unverbürgt; *document* unbeglaubigt

unauthorized [ʌnˈɔːθəraɪzd] ADJ unbefugt, unberechtigt; **no entry for ~ persons** Zutritt für Unbefugte verboten!

unavailable [ˌʌnəˈveɪləbl] ADJ nicht erhältlich; *person* nicht zu erreichen *pred*; *library book* nicht verfügbar; **the minister was ~ for comment** der Minister lehnte eine Stellungnahme ab

unavailing [ˌʌnəˈveɪlɪŋ] ADJ vergeblich, umsonst *pred*

unavailingly [ˌʌnəˈveɪlɪŋlɪ] ADV vergeblich

unavenged [ˌʌnəˈvendʒd] ADJ ungerächt

unavoidable [ˌʌnəˈvɔɪdəbl] ADJ unvermeidlich, unvermeidbar; *conclusion, consequence* zwangsläufig, unausweichlich

unavoidably [ˌʌnəˈvɔɪdəblɪ] ADV notgedrungen; **to be ~ detained** verhindert sein; **~, war films poured out of Hollywood in 1941** es war unvermeidlich, dass 1941 Unmengen von Kriegsfilmen in Hollywood produziert wurden

unaware [ˌʌnəˈwɛəʳ] ADJ *pred* **to be ~ of sth** sich (*dat*) einer Sache (*gen*) nicht bewusst sein; **I was ~ of his presence** ich hatte ihn nicht bemerkt, dass er da war; **I was ~ that he was interested** es war mir nicht bewusst *or* ich war mir nicht bewusst, dass er interessiert war; **I was ~ that there was a meeting going on** ich wusste nicht, dass da gerade eine Besprechung stattfand; **not ~ of sth** sich (*dat*) einer Sache (*gen*) durchaus bewusst; **I was not ~ that ...** es war mir durchaus bewusst *or* klar, dass ...; **he's so ~** er weiß überhaupt nicht Bescheid; **politically ~** ohne politisches Bewusstsein

unawares [ˌʌnəˈwɛəz] ADV (= *by surprise*) unerwartet; (= *accidentally*) unbeabsichtigt, versehentlich; (= *without knowing*) unwissentlich; **to catch** *or* **take sb ~** jdn überraschen

unbalance [ʌnˈbæləns] VT (*physically, mentally*) aus dem Gleichgewicht bringen; *painting* das Gleichgewicht (*+gen*) stören; **to ~ sb's mind** jdn um den Verstand bringen

unbalanced [ʌnˈbælənst] ADJ **a** *painting, diet, economy* unausgewogen; *report, view of life* einseitig; *ship etc* nicht im Gleichgewicht; **the structure of the committee was ~** der Ausschuss war unausgewogen *or* sehr einseitig besetzt **b** *mind* unstet; (*also* **mentally unbalanced**, = *deranged, mad*) irre, verrückt; (= *slightly crazy*) nicht ganz normal **c** *account, budget* nicht saldiert *or* ausgeglichen

unban [ʌnˈbæn] VT wieder zulassen

unbandage [ʌnˈbændɪdʒ] VT den Verband abnehmen von

unbaptized [ˌʌnbæpˈtaɪzd] ADJ ungetauft

unbar [ʌnˈbɑːʳ] VT aufsperren

unbearable [ʌnˈbɛərəbl] ADJ unerträglich; **to make life ~ for sb** jdm das Leben unerträglich machen

unbearably [ʌnˈbɛərəblɪ] ADV *sad, painful, loud* unerträglich; **almost ~ beautiful** überwältigend *or* hinreißend schön, fast zu schön

unbeatable [ʌnˈbiːtəbl] ADJ unschlagbar; *army also* unbesiegbar; *record also* nicht zu überbieten *pred*, nicht zu überbietend *attr*; *offer, price also* unübertrefflich

unbeaten [ʌnˈbiːtn] ADJ ungeschlagen; *army also* unbesiegt; *record* ungebrochen, nicht überboten

unbecoming [ˌʌnbɪˈkʌmɪŋ] ADJ **a** *behaviour, language etc* unschicklich, unziemlich (*geh*); **conduct ~ to a gentleman** ein Benehmen, das sich für einen Herrn nicht schickt **b** (= *unflattering*) *clothes* unvorteilhaft; *facial hair* unschön

unbeknown(st) [ˌʌnbɪˈnəʊn(st)] ADV ohne dass es jemand wusste; **~ to me** ohne mein Wissen; **~ to his father** ohne Wissen seines Vaters

unbelief [ˌʌnbɪˈliːf] N Ungläubigkeit *f*; **in ~** ungläubig

unbelievable [ˌʌnbɪˈliːvəbl] ADJ unglaublich; (*inf, = bad*) unglaublich; (= *good*) sagenhaft (*inf*); **he has so much talent it's ~** es ist unglaublich *or* es ist nicht zu fassen, wie begabt er ist

unbelievably [ˌʌnbɪˈliːvəblɪ] ADV unglaublich; *good, pretty etc also* sagenhaft (*inf*); **they had, ~, lost both games** es war unglaublich, aber sie hatten beide Spiele verloren

unbeliever [ˌʌnbɪˈliːvəʳ] N Ungläubige(r) *mf*

unbelieving ADJ , **unbelievingly** ADV [ˌʌnbɪˈliːvɪŋ, -lɪ] ungläubig

unbend [ʌnˈbend] *pret, ptp* **unbent** VT (= *straighten*) *metal etc* gerade biegen; *arms* strecken; **~ your body** richten Sie sich auf; (*lying down*) legen Sie sich ausgestreckt hin VI (*person, = relax*) aus sich herausgehen; (= *straighten body*) sich aufrichten, sich gerade hinlegen

unbending [ʌnˈbendɪŋ] ADJ *person, attitude* unnachgiebig; *determination* unbeugsam; *commitment* unerschütterlich

unbent [ʌnˈbent] *pret, ptp of* **unbend**

unbias(s)ed [ʌnˈbaɪəst] ADJ unvoreingenommen; *opinion, report also* unparteiisch

unbidden [ʌnˈbɪdn] ADV (*form*) ungebeten; (= *not ordered also*) unaufgefordert; (= *uninvited also*) ungeladen; **to do sth ~** etw unaufgefordert tun; **the phrase came ~ into her mind** der Satz kam ihr spontan in den Sinn

unbind [ʌnˈbaɪnd] *pret, ptp* **unbound** VT (= *free*) *prisoner* losbinden, befreien; (= *untie*) *hair* lösen; (= *unbandage*) den Verband ablösen von

unbleached [ʌnˈbliːtʃt] ADJ ungebleicht

unblemished [ʌnˈblemɪʃt] ADJ *lit, fig* makellos; *reputation also* unbescholten; *skin also* tadellos; **their relationship was ~ by arguments** kein Streit hatte je ihre Beziehung getrübt

unblinking [ʌnˈblɪŋkɪŋ] ADJ *look, attention* unverwandt; *eyes* starr

unblinkingly [ʌnˈblɪŋkɪŋlɪ] ADV *stare* starr, stoisch, unverwandt

unblock [ʌnˈblɒk] VT freimachen; *sink, pipe* die Verstopfung in (*+dat*) beseitigen; *chimney* ausputzen; (*fig*) *talks* wieder in Gang bringen; *obstacles* aus dem Weg räumen

unblushing [ʌnˈblʌʃɪŋ] ADJ schamlos; *liar also* unverschämt

unblushingly [ʌnˈblʌʃɪŋlɪ] ADV ohne sich zu schämen, frech

unbolt [ʌnˈbəʊlt] VT aufriegeln; **he left the door ~ed** er verriegelte die Tür nicht

unborn [ʌnˈbɔːn] ADJ ungeboren; **generations yet ~** kommende Generationen

unbosom [ʌnˈbʊzəm] VT *feelings* offenbaren, enthüllen (*to sb* jdm); **to ~ oneself to sb** jdm sein Herz ausschütten

unbound [ʌn'baʊnd] *pret, ptp of* **unbind** ADJ **a** (= *not tied*) *hair* gelöst, nicht zusammengehalten *or* zusammengebunden; *prisoner* losgekettet, von den Fesseln befreit; (= *loose*) *wheat* ungebündelt; **Prometheus ~** der befreite Prometheus **b** *book* ungebunden

unbounded [ʌn'baʊndɪd] ADJ grenzenlos; (*fig also*) unermesslich, unendlich

unbowed [ʌn'baʊd] ADJ (*fig*) ungebrochen; *pride* ungebeugt; **he was ~ by misfortune** sein Unglück hatte ihn nicht gebrochen *or* gebeugt; **the army was defeated but ~** das Heer war besiegt, sein Mut aber ungebrochen

unbreakable [ʌn'breɪkəbl] ADJ *glass, toy* unzerbrechlich; *record* nicht zu brechen *pred*; *rule, law* unumstößlich, feststehend *attr*; *promise, silence* unverbrüchlich; **an ~ habit** eine Angewohnheit, die man nicht loswerden *or* ablegen kann; **an ~ union** eine unlösbare Verbindung

unbribable [ʌn'braɪbəbl] ADJ unbestechlich

unbridgeable [ʌn'brɪdʒəbl] ADJ unüberbrückbar

unbridled [ʌn'braɪdld] ADJ *lust, passion* ungezügelt, zügellos; *anger* hemmungslos; *tongue* lose; *capitalism* ungehemmt

un-British [ʌn'brɪtɪʃ] ADJ unbritisch

unbroken [ʌn'brəʊkən] ADJ **a** (= *intact*) unbeschädigt; *seal* nicht erbrochen; *heart, promise* nicht gebrochen
b (= *continuous*) ununterbrochen; (*Mil*) *ranks* geschlossen, nicht durchbrochen; *line of descent* direkt; **an ~ night's sleep** eine ungestörte Nacht; **a whole morning of ~ sunshine** ein ganzer Vormittag mit strahlendem Sonnenschein; **she was in government for eleven ~ years** sie regierte elf Jahre ohne Unterbrechung
c (= *unbeaten*) *record* ungebrochen, unüberboten
d *horse* nicht zugeritten
e *pride* ungebeugt; **his spirit remained ~** er war ungebrochen
f *voice* nicht gebrochen; **boys with ~ voices** Jungen vor dem Stimmbruch

unbrotherly [ʌn'brʌðəlɪ] ADJ unbrüderlich

unbuckle [ʌn'bʌkl] VT aufschnallen

unbudgeted [ʌn'bʌdʒɪtɪd] ADJ *costs, items* außerplanmäßig

unbundle [ʌn'bʌndl] VT **a** (*US*, = *itemize*) aufschlüsseln, aufgliedern **b** (*Comm*, = *asset-strip*) *finanziell gefährdete Firmen aufkaufen und anschließend deren Vermögenswerte veräußern*

unbundling [ʌn'bʌndlɪŋ] N (*Comm*) *Aufkauf finanziell gefährdeter Firmen und anschließende Veräußerung ihrer Vermögenswerte*

unburden [ʌn'bɜːdn] VT (*liter.* = *unload*) abladen; (*fig*) *conscience, heart* erleichtern; **to ~ oneself/one's heart/one's soul to sb** jdm sein Herz ausschütten; **to ~ oneself of sth** (*lit liter*) etw abladen, sich von etw befreien; (*fig*) sich (*dat*) etw von der Seele reden; *of anxiety, guilt* sich von etw befreien *or* losmachen; *of sins* etw offenbaren *or* gestehen

unbusinesslike [ʌn'bɪznɪslaɪk] ADJ wenig geschäftsmäßig; **it's very ~ to keep all your correspondence in cardboard boxes** es ist äußerst unprofessionell, die ganze Korrespondenz in Kartons aufzubewahren; **the firm handled the transaction in such an ~ way** die Firma hat die Transaktion so ungeschäftsmäßig abgewickelt; **in spite of his ~ appearance ...** obwohl er gar nicht wie ein Geschäftsmann aussieht ...

unbutton [ʌn'bʌtn] VT aufknöpfen

uncalled-for [ʌn'kɔːldfɔː] ADJ (= *unjustified*) *criticism* ungerechtfertigt; (= *unnecessary*) unnötig; (= *rude*) *remark* ungebührlich, deplatziert; **that was quite ~** das war nun wirklich nicht nötig *or* nett

uncannily [ʌn'kænɪlɪ] ADV unheimlich; **his guesses are ~ accurate** es ist unheimlich *or* nicht ganz geheuer, wie genau er alles errät; **to look ~ like sb/sth** jdm/einer Sache auf unheimliche Weise ähnlich sehen

uncanny [ʌn'kænɪ] ADJ unheimlich; **it's quite ~** das ist geradezu unheimlich; **to bear an ~ resemblance to sb** jdm auf unheimliche Weise ähnlich sehen

uncap [ʌn'kæp] VT *bottle* aufmachen, öffnen; *tax* nicht mehr kappen

uncapped [ʌn'kæpt] ADJ (*Brit Sport*) **~ player** Spieler, der/Spielerin, die noch nie in der Nationalmannschaft gespielt hat, Nationalmannschaftsneuling *m*; **he is ~** er hat noch nie in der Nationalmannschaft gespielt

uncared-for [ʌn'kɛədfɔː] ADJ *garden, hands* ungepflegt; *child* vernachlässigt, verwahrlost

uncaring [ʌn'kɛərɪŋ] ADJ gleichgültig, teilnahmslos; *parents* lieblos; **the state as an impersonal and ~ machine** der Staat als unpersönliche und gefühllose Maschine

uncarpeted [ʌn'kɑːpɪtɪd] ADJ ohne Teppich, nicht ausgelegt

uncatalogued [ʌn'kætəlɒgd] ADJ nicht katalogisiert

unceasing ADJ , **unceasingly** ADV [ʌn'siːsɪŋ, -lɪ] unaufhörlich

uncensored [ʌn'sensəd] ADJ *film, version* unzensiert; (= *unblamed*) *remark* ungetadelt, ungerügt

unceremonious [ˌʌnserɪ'məʊnɪəs] ADJ **a** (= *abrupt, rude*) *dismissal, manner* brüsk, barsch; *reply* unverbrämt, unverblümt; *behaviour* ungehobelt, ruppig; *exit, departure* überstürzt; *haste* unfein, unfeierlich; **the rather ~ treatment we got** so kurz, wie wir abgefertigt wurden **b** (= *informal, simple*) zwanglos, formlos

unceremoniously [ˌʌnserɪ'məʊnɪəslɪ] ADV **a** (= *abruptly, rudely*) ohne Umschweife, ohne viel Federlesen(s), kurzerhand **b** (= *informally, simply*) zwanglos, formlos

uncertain [ʌn'sɜːtn] ADJ **a** (= *unsure, unsteady*) unsicher; *light* undeutlich, schwach; **I was ~ as to what to do** ich war unsicher, was ich tun sollte; **to be ~ whether ...** sich (*dat*) nicht sicher sein, ob ...; **to be ~ of** *or* **about sth** sich (*dat*) einer Sache (*gen*) nicht sicher sein; **he's still ~ of the contract** er ist noch im Ungewissen über den Vertrag
b (= *unknown*) *date, result* ungewiss; *origins* unbestimmt; **a woman of ~ age** (*hum*) eine Frau von unbestimmtem Alter
c (= *unreliable*) *weather, prices* unbeständig; *temper* unberechenbar; *judgement* unverlässlich, unzuverlässig
d (= *unclear*) vage; **in no ~ terms** klar und deutlich, unzweideutig

uncertainly [ʌn'sɜːtnlɪ] ADV *say* unbestimmt; *look, move* unsicher; *smile* unsicher, zögernd

uncertainty [ʌn'sɜːtntɪ] ⦿ 16.1 N **a** (= *state*) Ungewissheit *f*; (= *indefiniteness*) Unbestimmtheit *f*; (= *doubt*) Zweifel *m*, Unsicherheit *f*; **in order to remove any ~** um alle eventuellen Unklarheiten zu beseitigen; **there is still some ~ as to whether ...** es besteht noch Ungewissheit, ob ...

uncertainty principle N (*Phys*) Unbestimmtheits- *or* Ungenauigkeits- *or* Unschärferelation *f*

unchain [ʌn'tʃeɪn] VT *dog, prisoner* losketten, losbinden; *door* die Sicherheitskette (+*gen*) lösen; (*fig also* = *free*) befreien, erlösen; *heart* freigeben

unchallengeable [ʌn'tʃælɪndʒəbl] ADJ unanfechtbar; *proof also* unwiderlegbar; *confidence* unerschütterlich

unchallenged [ʌn'tʃælɪndʒd] ADJ unbestritten, unangefochten; (*Jur*) *juryman* nicht abgelehnt; *evidence* nicht angefochten, unangefochten; **to leave sb/sth ~** (= *unopposed*) jdm/einer Sache nicht widersprechen; **to rule ~** uneingeschränkt regieren; **to go ~** (*Mil*) ohne Anruf passieren; **we passed the sentry ~** die Wache ließ uns ohne Anruf passieren; **the record was ~ for several years** der Rekord wurde jahrelang nicht überboten; **I cannot let that remark go** *or* **pass ~** diese Bemerkung kann ich nicht unwidersprochen hinnehmen

unchangeable ADJ , **unchangeably** ADV [ʌn'tʃeɪndʒəbl, -lɪ] unveränderlich

unchanged [ʌn'tʃeɪndʒd] ADJ unverändert

unchanging [ʌn'tʃeɪndʒɪŋ] ADJ unveränderlich

unchaperoned [ʌn'ʃæpərəʊnd] ADJ unbegleitet

uncharacteristic [ˌʌnkærəktə'rɪstɪk] ADJ uncharakteristisch, untypisch (*of* für); **such rudeness is ~ of him** es ist gar nicht seine Art, so unhöflich zu sein; **with ~ enthusiasm/modesty** mit (für ihn/sie *etc*) völlig untypischer Begeisterung/Bescheidenheit

uncharacteristically [ˌʌnkærəktə'rɪstɪklɪ] ADV auf uncharakteristische *or* untypische Weise; **she was ~ silent** sie war ungewöhnlich still für ihre Verhältnisse

uncharged [ʌn'tʃɑːdʒd] ADJ **a** (*Elec*) nicht (auf)geladen **b** (*Econ, Fin*) *account* unbelastet; *service etc* unberechnet

uncharitable [ʌn'tʃærɪtəbl] ADJ *remark* unfreundlich, nicht nett, lieblos; *view, person* unbarmherzig, herzlos; *criticism* schonungslos, unbarmherzig; *attitude* hartherzig; **it was most ~ of you to ...** es war wirklich nicht nett, dass Sie ...

uncharted [ʌn'tʃɑːtɪd] ADJ (= *not explored*) unerforscht, unergründet; (= *not on map*) nicht verzeichnet *or* eingezeichnet; **~ waters** *or* **territory** (*fig*) unbekanntes Terrain; **to enter ~ waters** *or* **territory** (*fig*) sich in unbekanntes Terrain begeben

unchaste [ʌn'tʃeɪst] ADJ unzüchtig; *thoughts, actions* unkeusch; *life, wife* untugendhaft

unchecked [ʌn'tʃekt] ADJ **a** (= *unrestrained*) ungehemmt, unkontrolliert; *advance* ungehindert; *anger* hemmungslos, ungezügelt; **to go ~** (*abuse*) geduldet werden; (*advance*) nicht gehindert werden; (*inflation*) nicht eingedämmt *or* aufgehalten werden; **if the epidemic goes ~** wenn der Epidemie nicht Einhalt geboten wird; **if left ~, the fungus can spread extensively** wenn der Pilzbefall nicht unter Kontrolle gebracht wird, kann er sich weit ausbreiten **b** (= *not verified*) ungeprüft, nicht überprüft

unchivalrous [ʌn'ʃɪvəlrəs] ADJ unritterlich; *remark* ungalant

unchristened [ʌn'krɪsnd] ADJ ungetauft

unchristian [ʌn'krɪstʃən] ADJ unchristlich

uncial ['ʌnsɪəl] ADJ Unzial-; **~ letter** Unzialbuchstabe *m* **N** (= *letter*) Unzialbuchstabe *m*; (= *script*) Unziale *f*, Unzialschrift *f*; (= *manuscript*) Schriftstück *or* Dokument *nt* in Unzialschrift

uncircumcised [ʌn'sɜːkəmsaɪzd] ADJ unbeschnitten

uncivil [ʌn'sɪvɪl] ADJ unhöflich

uncivilly [ʌn'sɪvɪlɪ] ADV *ask* unhöflich

uncivilized [ʌn'sɪvɪlaɪzd] ADJ *country, tribe, behaviour* unzivilisiert; (*inf*) *habit* barbarisch; **sorry to wake you at this ~ hour** (*inf*, = *early*) entschuldige, dass ich dich zu nachtschlafender *or* einer so unchristlichen Zeit wecke (*inf*)

unclad [ʌn'klæd] ADJ (*euph, hum*) bar jeglicher Kleidung

unclaimed [ʌn'kleɪmd] ADJ *prize* nicht abgeholt; *property also* herrenlos; *right, inheritance* nicht geltend gemacht; *social security etc* nicht beansprucht; **to go ~** (*prize*) nicht abgeholt werden; (*right, inheritance*) nicht geltend gemacht werden; (*social security etc*) nicht beansprucht werden

unclasp [ʌn'klɑːsp] VT *necklace* lösen; *cloak* öffnen, aufhaken; *hands* voneinander lösen; **he ~ed her hand** er löste ihre Hand

unclassified [ʌn'klæsɪfaɪd] ADJ **a** (= *not arranged*) nicht klassifiziert *or* eingeordnet **b** (= *not secret*) nicht geheim

unclassified degree N (*Brit Univ*) Hochschulabschluss *m* ohne Klassifikation

unclassified road N (*Brit*) *schlecht ausgebaute Landstraße*

uncle ['ʌŋkl] N Onkel *m*; **Uncle Sam** Uncle *or* Onkel Sam; **to say** *or* **cry ~** (*US*) aufgeben → **Dutch**

unclean [ʌnˈkliːn] ADJ unsauber (*also Bibl*); (*Rel*) *animal* unrein; *thoughts* unkeusch; (*fig*: = *contaminated*) schmutzig

unclear [ʌnˈklɪəʳ] ADJ unklar; *essay etc* undurchsichtig; **to be ~ about sth** sich (*dat*) über etw (*acc*) im Unklaren or nicht im Klaren sein; **his motives are ~ to me** mir sind seine Motive nicht klar; **it is ~ to me why ...** es ist mir unklar or nicht klar, warum ...

unclimbable [ʌnˈklaɪməbl] ADJ unbesteigbar

unclimbed [ʌnˈklaɪmd] ADJ unbestiegen, unbezwungen

unclog [ʌnˈklɒg] VT *pipe, drain* die Verstopfung in (+*dat*) beseitigen; *artery* frei machen; *wheel* befreien

unclothed [ʌnˈkləʊðd] ADJ unbekleidet

unclouded [ʌnˈklaʊdɪd] ADJ *sky* bewölkt; (*fig*) *happiness, vision, mind* ungetrübt; *mind* klar

unclubbable [ʌnˈklʌbəbl] ADJ ohne Gruppenzugehörigkeitsgefühl

uncluttered [ʌnˈklʌtəd] ADJ schlicht, einfach; *desk, room* nicht überfüllt or überladen; **a mind ~ by excess information** ein von überflüssigem Wissen freier or unbelasteter Kopf

unco [ˈʌŋkəʊ] ADV (*Scot*: = *very*) sehr

uncock [ʌnˈkɒk] VT *gun* sichern

uncoil [ʌnˈkɔɪl] VT abwickeln VIR (*snake*) sich langsam strecken; (*person*) sich ausstrecken; (*wire etc*) sich abwickeln, sich abspulen; **to ~ (oneself) from an armchair** sich im Sessel strecken und aufstehen

uncollected [ʌnkəˈlektɪd] ADJ *rubbish* nicht abgeholt; *tax* nicht eingezogen or vereinnahmt; *fare* nicht kassiert, unkassiert

uncoloured, (*US*) **uncolored** [ʌnˈkʌləd] ADJ (= *colourless*) farblos; (= *white*) weiß; (*fig*: = *unprejudiced*) nicht gefärbt; *judgement* unparteiisch

uncombed [ʌnˈkəʊmd] ADJ ungekämmt

uncomfortable [ʌnˈkʌmfətəbl] ADJ **a** unbequem; *chair, position* ungemütlich, unbequem; **I feel ~ sitting like this** es ist unbequem so zu sitzen; **if the room is too hot it'll make you feel ~** wenn das Zimmer zu heiß ist, fühlt man sich nicht wohl; **I feel ~ in this jacket** in dieser Jacke fühle ich mich nicht wohl; **it feels ~** es ist unbequem **b** (= *uneasy*) *feeling* unangenehm, ungut; *silence* (= *awkward*) peinlich; (= *nerve-racking*) beklemmend; **to feel ~** sich unbehaglich fühlen, sich nicht wohl fühlen; **I felt ~ about doing it** ich hatte ein ungutes Gefühl dabei, mir war nicht wohl dabei; **he looked ~** er sah aus, als ob er sich unbehaglich fühlte; **he was ~ in that job** er fühlte sich in dieser Stelle nicht wohl; **they make me feel ~** in ihrer Gegenwart fühle ich mich unbehaglich; **to put sb in an ~ position** jdn in eine heikle Lage bringen; **he is ~ with the idea of having no control** ihm ist nicht wohl bei der Vorstellung, die Dinge nicht unter Kontrolle zu haben **c** (= *unpleasant*) *truth, fact, time, position* unerfreulich; **we could make things ~ for you** (*euph*) wir können ungemütlich werden

uncomfortably [ʌnˈkʌmfətəblɪ] ADV **a** unbequem **b** (= *uneasily*) unbehaglich, unruhig **c** (= *unpleasantly*) unangenehm; **I became ~ aware of having insulted him** es wurde mir peinlich bewusst, dass ich ihn beleidigt hatte; **I feel ~ full** ich habe ein unangenehmes Völlegefühl

uncommissioned [ʌnkəˈmɪʃnd] ADJ (= *unauthorized*) nicht beauftragt or ermächtigt

uncommitted [ʌnkəˈmɪtɪd] ADJ **a** nicht engagiert; *party, country* neutral; **she is ~ on this issue** sie hat dazu keine Meinung; **we want to remain ~ till we get a full report** wir wollen uns nicht festlegen, bevor wir einen ausführlichen Bericht haben; **~ to** nicht festgelegt auf (+*acc*) **b** (= *half-hearted*) *attitude* gleichgültig; *performance* halbherzig

uncommon [ʌnˈkɒmən] ADJ **a** (= *unusual*) ungewöhnlich; **it is not ~ for her to be late** es ist nichts Ungewöhnliches, dass sie zu spät

kommt; **a not ~ occurrence** eine häufige Erscheinung; **a not ~ problem/sight** ein nicht ganz ungewöhnliches Problem/ungewöhnlicher Anblick **b** (= *outstanding*) außergewöhnlich

uncommonly [ʌnˈkɒmənlɪ] ADV **a** (= *unusually*) ungewöhnlich **b** (= *exceptionally*) außergewöhnlich; **that's ~ civil of you** (*dated*) das ist äußerst freundlich von Ihnen

uncommunicative [ʌnkəˈmjuːnɪkətɪv] ADJ (*by nature*) verschlossen, wortkarg; (*temporarily*) schweigsam

uncompetitive [ʌnkəmˈpetɪtɪv] ADJ *industry* nicht wettbewerbsfähig, wettbewerbsunfähig; *price* nicht konkurrenzfähig

uncomplaining [ʌnkəmˈpleɪnɪŋ] ADJ duldsam

uncomplainingly [ʌnkəmˈpleɪnɪŋlɪ] ADV geduldig, klaglos

uncompleted [ʌnkəmˈpliːtɪd] ADJ unbeendet, unvollendet

uncomplicated [ʌnˈkɒmplɪkeɪtɪd] ADJ unkompliziert; **his life was ~ by emotional problems** sein Leben wurde nicht durch emotionale Probleme kompliziert or erschwert

uncomplimentary [ʌnkɒmplɪˈmentərɪ] ADJ unschmeichelhaft; **to be ~ about sb/sth** sich nicht sehr schmeichelhaft über jdn/etw äußern

uncomprehending ADJ, **uncomprehendingly** ADV [ʌnkɒmprɪˈhendɪŋ, -lɪ] verständnislos

uncompromising [ʌnˈkɒmprəmaɪzɪŋ] ADJ kompromisslos; *dedication, honesty* rückhaltlos; *commitment* hundertprozentig; **to be ~ in sth** sich bei etw auf keinen Kompromiss einlassen

uncompromisingly [ʌnˈkɒmprəmaɪzɪŋlɪ] ADV unerbittlich; *frank* rückhaltlos, völlig; *committed* hundertprozentig; **he is ~ opposed to ...** er ist ein kompromissloser Gegner (+*gen*) ...

unconcealed [ʌnkənˈsiːld] ADJ *joy, delight etc* offen, unverhüllt; *hatred, distaste, anger, satisfaction etc* also unverhohlen

unconcern [ʌnkənˈsɜːn] N (= *lack of worry*) Unbesorgtheit *f*, Unbekümmertheit *f*; (= *indifference*) Gleichgültigkeit *f*

unconcerned [ʌnkənˈsɜːnd] ADJ **a** (= *unworried*) unbekümmert; (= *indifferent*) gleichgültig; **to be ~ about sth** sich nicht um etw kümmern; **how could he be so ~ about her safety/the problem?** wie konnte ihm ihre Sicherheit/das Problem so egal or gleichgültig sein?; **I was not ~ about your safety** ich habe mir Sorgen um deine Sicherheit gemacht; **to be ~ by sth, to be ~ at sth** von etw unberührt sein **b** (= *not involved*) unbeteiligt (*in* an +*dat*)

unconcernedly [ʌnkənˈsɜːnɪdlɪ] ADV unbekümmert; (= *indifferently*) gleichgültig

unconditional [ʌnkənˈdɪʃənl] ADJ vorbehaltlos; *surrender, love* bedingungslos; *support* vorbehaltlos, uneingeschränkt; **he was remanded on ~ bail** (*Jur*) er wurde gegen Kaution freigelassen

unconditionally [ʌnkənˈdɪʃnəlɪ] ADV *offer, agree, give* vorbehaltlos; *support* vorbehaltlos, uneingeschränkt; *surrender, withdraw, release, love* bedingungslos

unconditioned [ʌnkənˈdɪʃənd] ADJ (*Psych*) nicht konditioniert

unconfined [ʌnkənˈfaɪnd] ADJ (= *unrestricted*) unbegrenzt, unbeschränkt

unconfirmed [ʌnkənˈfɜːmd] ADJ unbestätigt

unconformable [ʌnkənˈfɔːməbl] ADJ **a** (= *incompatible*) unvereinbar (*with* mit) **b** (= *inconsistent*) nicht übereinstimmend (*to, with* mit) **c** (*Geol*) *layer, stratum* diskordant, nicht gleichstrebend or gleich gelagert **d** (*Rel, Hist*) nonkonformistisch

uncongenial [ʌnkənˈdʒiːnɪəl] ADJ *person* unliebenswürdig, nicht einnehmend; *work, surroundings* unerfreulich; **he finds this place ~** dieser Ort entspricht ihm or seinem Wesen nicht; **to be ~ to sb** sich jdm gegenüber wenig liebenswürdig verhalten

unconnected [ʌnkəˈnektɪd] ADJ **a** (= *unrelated*) nicht miteinander in Beziehung stehend *attr*; *fact* losgelöst; **several facts** unzusammenhängend; **the two events are ~** es besteht keine Beziehung zwischen den beiden Ereignissen; **the two incidents were not ~** die beiden Zwischenfälle waren nicht ohne Zusammenhang; **to be ~ with** or **to sth** zu or mit etw nicht in Beziehung stehen **b** (= *incoherent*) zusammenhanglos, unzusammenhängend **c** (*Elec*) nicht angeschlossen

unconquerable [ʌnˈkɒŋkərəbl] ADJ *army* unbesiegbar; *peak* unbezwinglich, unerreichbar; *spirit* unbezwinglich, unbezwingbar; *courage* unbezähmbar

unconquered [ʌnˈkɒŋkəd] ADJ *army* unbesiegt; *mountain* unbezwungen; *courage, spirit* ungebrochen; **large parts of Britain remained ~** weite Teile Großbritanniens wurden nicht erobert

unconscionable [ʌnˈkɒnʃnəbl] ADJ unerhört; **an ~ time** eine unerhört lange Zeit, unerhört lange

unconscious [ʌnˈkɒnʃəs] ADJ **a** (*Med*) bewusstlos; **to fall ~** bewusstlos zu Boden fallen; **the blow knocked him ~** durch den Schlag wurde er bewusstlos; **to become ~** das Bewusstsein verlieren, bewusstlos werden; **to beat sb ~** jdn bewusstlos schlagen **b** *pred* (= *unaware*) **to be ~ of sth** sich (*dat*) einer Sache (*gen*) nicht bewusst sein; **I was ~ of the fact that ...** ich war mir or es war mir nicht bewusst, dass ... **c** (= *unintentional*) *insult, allusion etc* unbewusst, unbeabsichtigt; *blunder* ungewollt, unbeabsichtigt; *humour* unfreiwillig; **she was the ~ cause of his unhappiness** ohne es zu wissen, wurde sie zur Ursache seines Unglücks; **he was the ~ tool of ...** er wurde unwissentlich zum Werkzeug (+*gen*) ... **d** (*Psych*) unbewusst; **the ~ mind** das Unbewusste; **at** or **on an ~ level** auf der Ebene des Unbewussten

N (*Psych*) **the ~** das Unbewusste; **he probed his ~** er erforschte das Unbewusste in sich (*dat*)

unconsciously [ʌnˈkɒnʃəslɪ] ADV unbewusst; **an ~ funny remark** eine ungewollt or unbeabsichtigt lustige Bemerkung; **consciously or ~** bewusst oder unbewusst

unconsciousness [ʌnˈkɒnʃəsnɪs] N **a** (*Med*) Bewusstlosigkeit *f* & (= *unawareness*) mangelndes Bewusstsein **c** (*of insult etc*) Ungewolltheit *f*; (*of humour*) Unfreiwilligkeit *f*

unconsecrated [ʌnˈkɒnsɪkreɪtɪd] ADJ (*Rel*) ungeweiht

unconsidered [ʌnkənˈsɪdəd] ADJ *fact etc* unberücksichtigt; (= *rash*) *action etc* unbedacht, unüberlegt; **he was an ~ outsider** er war ein Außenseiter, auf den niemand achtete

unconstitutional [ʌnkɒnstɪˈtjuːʃənl] ADJ nicht verfassungsgemäß, verfassungswidrig

unconstitutionally [ʌnkɒnstɪˈtjuːʃnəlɪ] ADV verfassungswidrig

unconstrained ADJ, **unconstrainedly** ADV [ʌnkənˈstreɪnd, -nɪdlɪ] ungezwungen, zwanglos

unconstructive [ʌnkənˈstrʌktɪv] ADJ nicht konstruktiv; **this is the most ~ suggestion I've ever heard** einen so wenig konstruktiven Vorschlag habe ich noch nie gehört

unconsummated [ʌnˈkɒnsjʊmetɪd] ADJ unvollzogen

uncontaminated [ʌnkənˈtæmɪneɪtɪd] ADJ nicht verseucht; *people* (*by disease*) nicht angesteckt; (*fig*) unverdorben

uncontested [ʌnkənˈtestɪd] ADJ unbestritten; *divorce* unangefochten; *election, seat* ohne Gegenkandidat; **the seat/district was ~ by the Liberals** die Liberalen stellten für das Mandat/in dem Wahlkreis keinen Kandidaten auf; **the championship went ~ for many years** der Meisterschaftstitel wurde jahrelang nicht angefochten; **the chairmanship was ~** in der Wahl für den Vorsitz gab es keinen Gegenkandidaten

uncontrollable [ˌʌnkənˈtrəʊləbl] ADJ unkontrollierbar; *child* nicht zu bändigen *attr*, nicht zu bändigen *pred*; *car, boat, aeroplane, horse, dog* nicht unter Kontrolle zu bringend *attr*, nicht unter Kontrolle zu bringen *pred*; *rage, laughter, mirth* unbezähmbar; *desire, urge* unbezwinglich, unwiderstehlich; (*physical*) unkontrollierbar; *twitch* unkontrolliert; **the epidemic is now ~** die Epidemie ist nicht mehr unter Kontrolle zu bekommen; **to become ~** außer Kontrolle geraten; **to have an ~ temper** unbeherrscht sein

uncontrollably [ˌʌnkənˈtrəʊləblɪ] ADV unkontrollierbar; *weep* hemmungslos; *laugh* unkontrolliert

uncontrolled [ˌʌnkənˈtrəʊld] ADJ ungehindert; *dogs, children* unbeaufsichtigt; *behaviour* undiszipliniert; *laughter* unkontrolliert; *weeping* hemmungslos, haltlos; **if inflation is allowed to go ~** wenn die Inflation nicht unter Kontrolle gebracht wird

uncontroversial [ˌʌnkɒntrəˈvɜːʃəl] ADJ unverfänglich

unconventional [ˌʌnkənˈvenʃənl] ADJ unkonventionell; *weapons* nicht konventionell

unconventionality [ˌʌnkənvenʃəˈnælɪtɪ] N Unkonventionalität *f*

unconventionally [ˌʌnkənˈvenʃənəlɪ] ADV unkonventionell

unconversant [ˌʌnkənˈvɜːsnt] ADJ **to be ~ with sth** mit etw nicht vertraut sein

unconvinced [ˌʌnkənˈvɪnst] ADJ nicht überzeugt (*of* von); *look* wenig überzeugt; **his arguments leave me ~** seine Argumente überzeugen mich nicht; **I remain ~** ich bin noch immer nicht überzeugt; **to be ~ by sth** von etw nicht überzeugt sein

unconvincing [ˌʌnkənˈvɪnsɪŋ] ADJ nicht überzeugend; **rather ~** wenig überzeugend; **to become ~** an Überzeugungskraft verlieren; **to look/sound ~** nicht überzeugend aussehen/klingen

unconvincingly [ˌʌnkənˈvɪnsɪŋlɪ] ADV wenig überzeugend; **somewhat ~** ohne rechte Überzeugungskraft

uncooked [ʌnˈkʊkt] ADJ ungekocht, roh

uncool [ʌnˈkuːl] ADJ (*inf*) nicht (sehr) cool (*sl*)

uncooperative [ˌʌnkəʊˈɒpərətɪv] ADJ *attitude* stur, wenig entgegenkommend; *witness, colleague* wenig hilfreich, nicht hilfsbereit; **the government office remained ~** das Regierungsamt war auch weiterhin nicht zur Kooperation bereit; **if the prisoner is still ~** wenn sich der Gefangene weiterhin weigert, mit uns zusammenzuarbeiten; **why are you being so ~?** warum helfen Sie denn nicht mit?; **you're being rather ~** Sie sind nicht sehr hilfreich; **an ~ partner** ein Partner, der nicht mitmacht; **they didn't exactly go on strike, they just became ~** sie haben nicht gerade gestreikt, sie haben nur auf stur geschaltet

uncooperatively [ˌʌnkəʊˈɒpərətɪvlɪ] ADV wenig entgegenkommend; *say* wenig hilfreich

uncoordinated [ˌʌnkəʊˈɔːdɪneɪtɪd] ADJ unkoordiniert

uncork [ʌnˈkɔːk] VT *bottle* entkorken; (*fig*) herauslassen

uncorroborated [ˌʌnkəˈrɒbəreɪtɪd] ADJ unbestätigt; *evidence* nicht bekräftigt

uncorrupted [ˌʌnkəˈrʌptɪd] ADJ unverdorben, nicht korrumpiert; *person also* rechtschaffen

uncountable [ʌnˈkaʊntəbl] ADJ (*Gram*) unzählbar

uncounted [ʌnˈkaʊntɪd] ADJ (= *innumerable*) unzählig

uncouple [ʌnˈkʌpl] VT *train, trailer* abkuppeln, abkoppeln; **to ~ sth from sth** (*fig*) etw von etw loslösen

uncourteous ADJ , **uncourteously** ADV [ʌnˈkɜːtɪəs, -lɪ] unhöflich, grob

uncouth [ʌnˈkuːθ] ADJ *person* ungehobelt, ordinär; *behaviour* unflätig, ungehobelt; *manners* ungeschliffen, ungehobelt; *expression, word* unflä-

tig, unfein; **it's very ~ to eat with your hands** es ist sehr unfein, mit den Fingern zu essen

uncover [ʌnˈkʌvə'] VT **a** (= *remove cover from*) aufdecken; *head* entblößen (*liter*); **to ~ one's face** sein Gesicht freimachen; **the men ~ed their heads** die Männer nahmen ihre Kopfbedeckung ab **b** *scandal, plot, truth, evidence etc* aufdecken; *ancient ruins, cache of weapons etc* zum Vorschein bringen

uncritical [ʌnˈkrɪtɪkəl] ADJ unkritisch (*of, about* in Bezug auf *+acc*)

uncritically [ʌnˈkrɪtɪkəlɪ] ADV unkritisch

uncross [ʌnˈkrɒs] VT **he ~ed his legs** er nahm das Bein vom Knie; **she ~ed her arms** sie löste ihre verschränkten Arme

uncrossed [ʌnˈkrɒst] ADJ *legs* nicht übereinander geschlagen or gekreuzt; **~ cheque** (*dated Brit*) Barscheck *m*

uncrowded [ʌnˈkraʊdɪd] ADJ ziemlich leer, nicht überlaufen

uncrowned [ʌnˈkraʊnd] ADJ (*lit, fig*) ungekrönt

uncrushable [ʌnˈkrʌʃəbl] ADJ *dress* knitterfrei; *carton* hart, fest; (*fig*) *belief, spirit* unerschütterlich, durch nichts kleinzukriegen (*inf*)

unction [ˈʌŋkʃən] N **a** (*Rel*, = *anointing*) Salbung *f*, Ölung *f*; **extreme ~** Letzte Ölung **b** (= *insincere fervour*) hohles or unechtes Pathos

unctuous ADJ , **unctuously** ADV [ˈʌŋktjʊəs, -lɪ] salbungsvoll

unctuousness [ˈʌŋktjʊəsnɪs] N salbungsvolle Art; (*of speech*) falsches Pathos; **the ~ of his manner** seine salbungsvolle Art

uncultivated [ʌnˈkʌltɪveɪtɪd] ADJ *land* unkultiviert, unbebaut; *person, behaviour* unkultiviert; *mind* nicht ausgebildet; *talent* brachliegend

uncultured [ʌnˈkʌltʃəd] ADJ *person, mind* ungebildet; *behaviour* unkultiviert, unzivilisiert

uncurl [ʌnˈkɜːl] **VT** auseinander rollen; **to ~ oneself** sich strecken; **she ~ed herself from the chair** sie streckte sich im Sessel und stand auf **VI** glatt werden; (*cat, snake*) sich langsam strecken; (*person*) sich ausstrecken

uncut [ʌnˈkʌt] ADJ **a** ungeschnitten; *ham, untrimmed pages* nicht aufgeschnitten; *stone, rock* unbehauen; *lawn* nicht gemäht; **~ diamond** Rohdiamant *m*; **an ~ rug** ein Schlingenteppich *m* **b** (= *unabridged*) *film, play, novel* ungekürzt; **to show a film ~** einen Film ungekürzt zeigen **c** (= *pure*) *drug* unverschnitten; **~ heroin** unverschnittenes Heroin **d** (*Med*: = *not circumcised*) nicht beschnitten

undamaged [ʌnˈdæmɪdʒd] ADJ unbeschädigt; (*fig*) *reputation* makellos; **to be ~ by sth** von etw nicht beschädigt worden sein

undated [ʌnˈdeɪtɪd] ADJ undatiert

undaunted [ʌnˈdɔːntɪd] ADJ (= *not discouraged*) nicht entmutigt, unverzagt; (= *fearless*) unerschrocken; *courage* unerschütterlich; **in spite of these failures he continued ~** trotz dieser Misserfolge machte er unverzagt weiter; **~ by these threats ...** nicht eingeschüchtert von diesen Drohungen ...

undead [ʌnˈded] N **the ~ pl** die Untoten *pl*

undeceive [ˌʌndɪˈsiːv] VT aufklären

undecided [ˌʌndɪˈsaɪdɪd] ADJ **a** *person* unentschlossen; **he is ~ as to whether he should go or not** er ist (sich) noch unschlüssig, ob er gehen soll oder nicht; **to be ~ about sth** sich (*dat*) über etw (*acc*) im Unklaren sein **b** *question* unentschieden; **what are we going to do? – I don't know, it's ~** was sollen wir tun? – ich weiß nicht, das steht noch nicht fest or ist noch nicht entschieden

undecipherable [ˌʌndɪˈsaɪfərəbl] ADJ *handwriting* unleserlich, schwer zu entziffernd *attr*; *code, signs* nicht entzifferbar

undeclared [ˌʌndɪˈkleəd] ADJ *love, candidate* heimlich, unerklärt; *war* unerklärt; *interest* uneingestanden; *supporter* heimlich; (*Customs*) *goods* nicht deklariert; **~ income** nicht angegebenes Einkommen

undefeated [ˌʌndɪˈfiːtɪd] ADJ *army, team* unbesiegt; *champion, record* ungeschlagen; *spirit* ungebrochen

undefendable [ˌʌndɪˈfendəbl] ADJ (*Mil*) *coast, frontier* schwer zu verteidigend *attr*, schwer zu verteidigen *pred*

undefended [ˌʌndɪˈfendɪd] ADJ *town, goal* unverteidigt; **the case was ~** in dem Fall wurde auf Verteidigung verzichtet

undefiled [ˌʌndɪˈfaɪld] ADJ unbefleckt

undefinable ADJ , **undefinably** ADV [ˌʌndɪˈfaɪnəbl, -lɪ] undefinierbar, unbestimmbar

undefined [ˌʌndɪˈfaɪnd] ADJ undefiniert, nicht definiert; (= *vague*) undefinierbar

undelete [ˈʌndɪˈliːt] VT (*Comput*) **to ~ sth** das Löschen von etw rückgängig machen

undeliverable [ˌʌndɪˈlɪvərəbl] ADJ *mail* unzustellbar

undemanding [ˌʌndɪˈmɑːndɪŋ] ADJ anspruchslos, keine Anforderungen or Ansprüche stellend *attr*; *task* wenig fordernd, keine großen Anforderungen stellend *attr*; **this job is so ~** dieser Job fordert mich überhaupt nicht

undemocratic [ˌʌndeməˈkrætɪk, -əlɪ] ADJ , **undemocratically** ADV undemokratisch

undemonstrative [ˌʌndɪˈmɒnstrətɪv] ADJ reserviert, zurückhaltend; **a fairly ~ race** ein Volk, das seine Gefühle wenig zeigt

undeniable [ˌʌndɪˈnaɪəbl] ADJ unbestreitbar, unleugbar; **it is ~ that ...** es lässt sich nicht bestreiten or leugnen, dass ...

undeniably [ˌʌndɪˈnaɪəblɪ] **○** 26.3 ADV zweifelsohne, zweifellos; *successful, proud* unbestreitbar

undenominational [ˌʌndɪnɒmɪˈneɪʃənl] ADJ interkonfessionell; **~ school** Gemeinschaftsschule *f*

undependable [ˌʌndɪˈpendəbl] ADJ unzuverlässig

under [ˈʌndə'] PREP **a** (= *beneath, place*) unter (*+dat*); (*direction*) unter (*+acc*); **~ it** darunter; **to come out from ~ the bed** unter dem Bett hervorkommen; **it's ~ there** es ist da drunter (*inf*); **they held his head ~ the water** sie hielten seinen Kopf unter Wasser; **~ barley** mit Gerste bebaut **b** (= *less than*) unter (*+dat*); **it took ~ an hour** es dauerte weniger als eine Stunde; **there were ~ 50 of them** es waren weniger als 50, es waren unter 50 **c** (= *subordinate to, under influence of etc*) unter (*+dat*); **he had 50 men ~ him** er hatte 50 Männer unter sich; **to study ~ sb** bei jdm studieren; **who were you ~?** (*Univ*) bei wem haben Sie studiert?; (*Mil*) unter wem haben Sie gedient?; **he was born ~ Virgo** (*Astrol*) er wurde im Zeichen der Jungfrau geboren; **he died ~ the anaesthetic** (*Brit*) or **anesthetic** (*US*) er starb in der Narkose; **you're ~ a misapprehension** Sie befinden sich im Irrtum; **~ construction** im Bau; **the matter ~ discussion** der Diskussionsgegenstand; **to be ~ treatment** (*Med*) in Behandlung sein; **to be ~ the doctor** in (ärztlicher) Behandlung sein; **which doctor are you ~?** bei welchem Arzt sind Sie?; **it's classified ~ history** es ist unter „Geschichte" eingeordnet; **you'll find the number ~ "garages"** Sie finden die Nummer unter „Werkstätten"; **~ sentence of death** zum Tode verurteilt; **~ penalty of death** unter Androhung der Todesstrafe; **~ an assumed name** unter falschem Namen; **the house is ~ threat of demolition** das Haus ist vom Abbruch bedroht **d** (= *according to*) nach (*+dat*), gemäß (*+dat*), laut (*+dat*); **~ his will** in seinem Testament; **~ the terms of the contract** nach or gemäß den Vertragsbedingungen

ADV a (= *beneath*) unten; (= *unconscious*) bewusstlos; **he came to the fence and crawled ~** er kam zum Zaun und kroch darunter durch; **to go ~** untergehen; **to get out from ~** (*fig inf*) wieder Licht sehen (*inf*) **b** (= *less*) darunter

under- PREF **a** (in rank) Unter-; **for the ~twelves/-eighteens/-forties** für Kinder unter zwölf/Jugendliche unter achtzehn/Leute unter vierzig **b** (= insufficiently) zu wenig, ungenügend

under: underachieve VI hinter den Erwartungen zurückbleiben; **underachievement** N schwache or enttäuschende Leistungen pl; **underachiever** N Johnny is an ~ Johnnys Leistungen bleiben hinter den Erwartungen zurück; **underact** VTI betont zurückhaltend spielen; (pej) schwach spielen; **underage** ADJ attr minderjährig; **underarm** ADJ **a** Unterarm-; ~ **hair** Unterarmbehaarung f; ~ **deodorant** Achselhöhlen-Deodorant nt **b** throw von unten; ~ **serve** (Tennis) Aufschlag m von unten; ADV throw, serve von unten; **underbelly** N (Zool, fig, of plane) Bauch m; **the soft ~ of Europe/democracy** die Achillesferse Europas/der Demokratie; **underbid** pret, ptp underbid VT (Comm) unterbieten VI (Cards) nicht hoch genug reizen; **underbody** N (of vehicle) Unterboden m; **underbrush** N = undergrowth; **underbuy** pret, ptp underbought VI zu wenig kaufen; **undercapitalized** ADJ (Fin) unterkapitalisiert; **undercarriage** N (Aviat) Fahrwerk nt, Fahrgestell nt; **undercharge** VI zu wenig berechnen VT **to ~ sb** jdm zu wenig berechnen; **he ~d me by 50p** er berechnete mir 50 Pence zu wenig; **underclass** N Unterklasse f; **underclothes** PL N Unterwäsche f; **underclothing** N Unterwäsche f; **undercoat** N (= paint) Grundierfarbe f; (= coat) Grundierung f; (US, Aut) Unterbodenschutz m; **undercook** VT nicht durchgaren; (accidentally also) nicht lange genug kochen; **undercover** ADJ geheim; ~ **agent** Geheimagent(in) m(f); **he did ~ work for the police** er arbeitete für die Polizei als verdeckter Ermittler **to work** ~ undercover arbeiten; (with police) als verdeckter Ermittler/verdeckte Ermittlerin arbeiten; **undercroft** N (Archit) unterirdisches Gewölbe f, Gruft f; (of church) Krypta f; **undercurrent** N (lit, fig) Unterströmung f; (in speech, attitude) Unterton m; **undercut** pret, ptp undercut VT competitor, fare (im Preis) unterbieten; (fig) efforts etc untergraben; **underdeveloped** ADJ unterentwickelt; resources ungenutzt; **underdog** N (in society) Schwächere(r) mf, Benachteiligte(r) mf, Underdog m; (in game also) sicherer Verlierer, sichere Verliererin; **underdone** ADJ nicht gar; (deliberately) steak nicht durchgebraten; **underdressed** ADJ **to be ~** (= too lightly) zu leicht angezogen sein; (= not formally enough) zu einfach angezogen sein; **underemphasize** VT nicht genügend or nicht ausreichend betonen; **I don't want to ~ her role** ich möchte ihre Rolle nicht herunterspielen; **to deliberately ~ sth** etw bewusst herunterspielen; **underemployed** ADJ nicht ausgelastet; person also unterbeschäftigt; plant, equipment also nicht voll (aus)genutzt; **underemployment** N Unterbeschäftigung f; (of person, plant also) mangelnde Auslastung; (of abilities, plant also) mangelnde Ausnutzung; **underestimate** [ʌndərˈestɪmeɪt] VT unterschätzen N [ʌndərˈestɪmɪt] Unterschätzung f; **underestimation** N Unterschätzung f; **underexpose** VT (Phot) unterbelichten; **underexposed** ADJ (Phot) unterbelichtet; **underexposure** N (Phot) Unterbelichtung f; (fig) Mangel m an Publizität; **underfed** ADJ unterernährt; **underfeed** pret, ptp underfed VT zu wenig zu essen geben (+dat); animals zu wenig füttern; **underfeeding** N (of animals) Unterernährung f; **underfelt** N Filzunterlage f; **underfinanced** ADJ unterfinanziert; **underfloor heating** N Fußbodenheizung f; **underfoot** ADV am Boden; **it is wet ~** der Boden ist nass; **to trample sb/sth ~** (lit, fig) auf jdm/etw herumtrampeln; **underfund** VT unterfinanzieren; **underfunded** ADJ unterfinanziert; **underfunding** N Unterfinanzierung f; **undergarment** N Unterkleid nt; **~s** Unterkleidung f; **undergo** pret underwent, ptp undergone VT suffering durchmachen, mitmachen; process durchmachen, durchlaufen; training mitmachen; change also erleben; test, treatment, op-

eration sich unterziehen (+dat); (machine) test unterzogen werden (+dat); **to ~ repairs** in Reparatur sein; **undergrad** (inf), **undergraduate** N Student(in) m(f) ATTR class, course für nichtgraduierte or nicht graduierte Studenten; **~uate student** Student(in) m(f)

underground [ˈʌndəɡraʊnd] ADJ **a** explosion, lake, cave, passage unterirdisch; ~ **cable** Erdkabel nt; ~ **mining** Untertagebau m; ~ **railway** (Brit) or **railroad** (US) Untergrundbahn f; ~ **line** U-Bahn-Linie f **b** (fig, = secret) Untergrund-; ~ **movement** Untergrundbewegung f; ~ **activities** Untergrundtätigkeit f **c** (= alternative) Underground-; ~ **magazine** Untergrund-Magazin nt ADV **a** unterirdisch; (Min) unter Tage; **3 m** ~ 3 m unter der Erde **b** (fig) **to go** ~ untertauchen N **a** (Brit, Rail) U-Bahn f, Untergrundbahn f **b** (= movement) Untergrundbewegung f; (= subculture) Underground m

underground (Brit Rail): **underground station** N U-Bahnhof m; **underground system** N U-Bahn-Netz nt; **underground train** N U-Bahn-Zug m

under: undergrowth N Gestrüpp nt, Gebüsch nt; (under trees) Unterholz nt; **underhand** ADJ **a** (= sly) hinterhältig **b** (Sport) = underarm; **underhanded** ADJ = underhand a; **underhandedly** ADV hinterhältigerweise; **underhung** ADJ jaw vorgeschoben; meat ungenügend or nicht genug abgehangen; **underinsured** ADJ unterversichert; **underinvestment** N mangelnde or unzureichende Investitionen pl; **industry is suffering from** ~ die Industrie leidet unter Investitionsmangel; **underlay** N (Brit) Unterlage f; **underlie** pret underlay, ptp underlain VT (lit) liegen unter (+dat); (fig, = be basis for or cause of) zugrunde or zu Grunde liegen (+dat); **underline** VT (lit, fig) unterstreichen

underling [ˈʌndəlɪŋ] N (pej) Untergebene(r) mf, Befehlsempfänger(in) m(f) (pej)

under: underlining N Unterstreichung f; **with red ~** rot unterstrichen; **why all this ~?** warum ist so viel unterstrichen?; **underlying** ADJ **a** soil, rocks tiefer liegend **b** cause eigentlich; (= deeper) tiefer; problem, message, theme zugrunde or zu Grunde liegend; honesty, strength grundlegend; tension unterschwellig; **the ~ cause of all this** was all dem zugrunde or zu Grunde liegt; **a certain ~ sense of tragedy** eine gewisse unterschwellige Tragik **c** (Econ) ~ **rate of inflation** Basis-Inflationsrate f; **undermanned** ADJ unterbesetzt; **undermanning** N Personalmangel m, Personalknappheit f; (deliberate) Unterbesetzung f; (Mil, of police force etc) Unterbemannung f; **undermentioned** ADJ unten genannt, unten erwähnt; **undermine** VT **a** (= tunnel under) unterhöhlen; (Mil) unterminieren; (= weaken) schwächen; (sea) cliffs unterspülen, unterhöhlen **b** (fig: = weaken) unterminieren, untergraben; health angreifen; **undermost** ADJ unterste(r, s)

underneath [ʌndəˈniːθ] PREP (place) unter (+dat); (direction) unter (+acc); ~ **it** darunter; **the cat came out from ~ the table** die Katze kam unter dem Tisch hervor; **from ~ the trees we could only see …** unter den Bäumen stehend/sitzend konnten wir nur … sehen ADV darunter; **the ones ~** die darunter N Unterseite f

under: undernourished ADJ unterernährt; **undernourishment** N Unterernährung f; **underoccupied** ADJ hostel, hospital etc unterbelegt; **underpaid** ADJ unterbezahlt; **underpants** PL N Unterhose(n) f(pl); **a pair of** ~ eine Unterhose, ein Paar nt Unterhosen; **underpart** N Unterteil nt; **underpass** N Unterführung f; **underpay** pret, ptp underpaid VT unterbezahlen; **underpayment** N zu geringe Bezahlung, Unterbezahlung f; **because of ~ of tax …** weil zu wenig Steuer gezahlt wurde …; **there was an ~ of £5 in your salary** Sie bekamen £ 5 zu wenig Gehalt ausbezahlt; **underpin** VT (Archit) wall, building untermauern; (fig) argument, claim untermauern; economy, market, shares etc (ab)stützen; **underpinning** N

(Archit) Untermauerung f; **underplay** VT **a** (Cards) hand nicht voll ausspielen; **to ~ one's hand** (fig) nicht alle Trümpfe ausspielen **b** (Theat) role zurückhaltend spielen **c** significance, role, extent herunterspielen; **underplot** N (of novel etc) Nebenhandlung f; **underpopulated** ADJ unterbevölkert; **underprice** VT zu billig or unter Preis anbieten; **to be ~d** zu billig gehandelt werden; **at £10 it is ~d** mit £ 10 ist es zu billig; **underpricing** N Festlegung f zu niedriger Preise; **underprivileged** ADJ unterprivilegiert **N the ~** pl die Unterprivilegierten pl; **underproduce** VI zu wenig produzieren; **underproduction** N Unterproduktion f; **underproof** ADJ spirits unterprozentig; **underqualified** ADJ unterqualifiziert; **underrate** VT (= underestimate) danger, chance, opponent, person unterschätzen; (= undervalue) qualities unterbewerten; **underrated** ADJ unterschätzt; **he is probably the most ~ songwriter in the business** er ist vielleicht der am meisten unterschätzte Songwriter der ganzen Branche; **underrepresented** ADJ unterrepräsentiert; **underripe** ADJ fruit unreif; **slightly ~** (noch) nicht ganz reif; **underscore** VT = underline; **undersea** ADJ Unterwasser-; ~ **explorer** Unterwasserforscher(in) m(f); **underseal** (Brit, Aut) N Unterbodenschutz m mit Unterbodenschutz versehen; **is it ~ed?** hat es Unterbodenschutz?; **I must have my car ~ed** ich muss Unterbodenschutz machen lassen; **underseas** ADJ Unterwasser-, untermeerisch; **undersecretary** (Brit) N **a** (also **Parliamentary Undersecretary**) (parlamentarischer) Staatssekretär **b** **Permanent Undersecretary** Ständiger Unterstaatssekretär; **undersell** pret, ptp undersold VT **a** competitor unterbieten; (= sell at lower price) goods unter Preis verkaufen, verschleudern **b** (= not publicize) nicht gut verkaufen; (as advertising technique) nicht anpreisen; **he tends to ~ himself/his ideas** er kann sich/seine Ideen normalerweise nicht verkaufen; **undersexed** ADJ **to be ~** einen unterentwickelten Geschlechtstrieb haben (form), nicht viel für Sex übrig haben; **he's not exactly ~** er ist der reinste Lustmolch (inf); **undershirt** N (US) Unterhemd nt; **undershoot** pret, ptp undershot VI (Aviat, missile) zu früh landen VT **to ~ the runway** vor der Landebahn aufsetzen; **to ~ the target** das Ziel nicht erreichen; **undershorts** PL N (US) Unterhose(n) f(pl); **underside** N Unterseite f; **undersign** VTI unterschreiben, unterzeichnen; **undersigned** ADJ (form) unterzeichnet N **we the ~** wir, die Unterzeichneten; **undersized** ADJ klein; (= less than proper size) zu klein; clothes in einer zu kleinen Größe; (pej) person also zu kurz geraten (hum); **underskirt** N Unterrock m; **undersold** pret, ptp of undersell; **underspend** pret, ptp underspent VI zu wenig ausgeben (on für); **we have underspent by £1000** wir haben £ 1000 weniger ausgegeben als geplant; **understaffed** ADJ office unterbesetzt; prison, hospital mit zu wenig Personal; **we are very ~ at the moment** wir haben momentan zu wenig Leute

understand [ʌndəˈstænd] ⊘ 12.1, 26.3 pret, ptp **understood** VT **a** language, painting, statement, speaker verstehen; action, event, person, difficulty also begreifen; **I don't ~ Russian** ich verstehe or kann kein Russisch; **that's what I can't ~** das kann ich eben nicht verstehen or begreifen; **I can't ~ his agreeing to do it** ich kann nicht verstehen or es ist mir unbegreiflich, warum er sich dazu bereit erklärt hat; **but ~ this!** aber eins sollte klar sein; **what do you ~ by "pragmatism"?** was verstehen Sie unter „Pragmatismus"?

b (= comprehend sympathetically) children, people, animals, doubts, fears verstehen; **to ~ one another** sich verstehen

c (= believe) **I ~ that you are going to Australia** ich höre, Sie gehen nach Australien; **I ~ that you've already met her** Sie haben sich, soviel ich weiß, schon kennen gelernt; **I understood (that) he was abroad/we were to have been consulted** ich dachte, er sei im Ausland/wir sollten dazu befragt werden; **am I/are we to ~ that ...?** soll das etwa heißen, dass ...?; **as I ~ it, ...** soweit ich weiß, ...; **did I ~ him to say that ...?** habe ich richtig verstanden, dass er sagte, ...?; **but I understood her to say that she agreed** aber soweit ich sie verstanden habe, hat sie zugestimmt; **to give sb to ~ that ...** jdm zu verstehen geben, dass ...; **I was given to ~ that ...** man hat mir bedeutet, dass ...; **I understood from his speech that ...** ich schloss aus seiner Rede, dass ...; **what do you ~ from his remarks?** wie verstehen Sie seine Bemerkungen?

d (*Gram:* = *supply*) word sich (*dat*) denken, (im Stillen) ergänzen → *also* **understood**

VI **a** (= *comprehend*) verstehen; **(do you) ~?** (hast du/haben Sie das) verstanden?; **you don't ~!** du verstehst mich nicht!; **but you don't ~, I must have the money now** aber verstehen Sie doch, ich brauche das Geld jetzt!; **I quite ~** ich verstehe schon

b (= *believe*) **so I ~** es scheint so; **he was, I ~, a widower** wie ich hörte, war er Witwer

understandable [ˌʌndəˈstændəbl] ADJ **a** (= *intelligible*) verständlich **b** (= *reasonable, natural*) verständlich, begreiflich

understandably [ˌʌndəˈstændəblɪ] ADV **a** (= *intelligibly*) verständlich **b** (= *reasonably, naturally*) verständlicherweise, begreiflicherweise

understanding [ˌʌndəˈstændɪŋ] **ADJ** verständnisvoll; **he asked me to be ~** er bat mich um Verständnis

N (= *intelligence*) Auffassungsgabe *f*; (= *knowledge*) Kenntnisse *pl*; (= *comprehension, sympathy*) Verständnis *nt*; **her ~ of children** ihr Verständnis *nt* für Kinder; **because of his complete lack of ~ for the problems** da ihm jedes Verständnis für die Probleme fehlte; **my ~ of the situation is that ...** ich verstehe die Situation so, dass ...; **his conduct is beyond human ~** sein Verhalten ist absolut unbegreiflich; **she's a woman of great ~** sie ist eine sehr verständnisvolle Frau; **it was my ~ that ...** ich nahm an *or* ich war der Meinung, dass ...; **he has a good ~ of the problem** er kennt sich mit dem Problem gut aus; **to promote international ~** um die internationale Verständigung zu fördern

b (= *agreement*) Abmachung *f*, Vereinbarung *f*, Verständigung *f*; **to come to** *or* **reach an ~ with sb** eine Abmachung *or* Vereinbarung mit jdm treffen; **Susie and I have an ~** Susie und ich haben unsere Abmachung; **a degree of ~** eine gewisse Übereinstimmung, ein gewisses Einvernehmen

c (= *assumption*) Voraussetzung *f*; **on the ~ that ...** unter der Voraussetzung, dass ...; **on this ~** unter dieser Voraussetzung

understandingly [ˌʌndəˈstændɪŋlɪ] ADV verständnisvoll

understate [ˌʌndəˈsteɪt] VT herunterspielen; **to ~ one's case** untertreiben

understated [ˌʌndəˈsteɪtɪd] ADJ *film etc* subtil; *picture, music, colours* gedämpft; *clothes* unaufdringlich; *performance, acting* zurückhaltend, untertrieben; *manner* zurückhaltend; *make-up* unaufdringlich

understatement [ˈʌndəˌsteɪtmənt] N Untertreibung *f*, Understatement *nt*

understeer [ˈʌndəˌstɪə] (*Aut*) **N** Untersteuerung *f* **VI** [ˌʌndəˈstɪə] untersteuern

understock [ˌʌndəˈstɒk] VTI (sich) ungenügend eindecken (*with* mit)

understood [ˌʌndəˈstʊd] *pret, ptp of* **understand** ADJ **a** (= *clear*) klar; **to make oneself ~** sich verständlich machen; **do I make myself ~?** ist das klar?; **I wish it to be ~ that ...** ich möchte klarstellen, dass ...; **(is that) ~?** (ist das) klar?; **~! gut!**

b (= *agreed*) **it was ~ between them that ...** sie hatten eine Vereinbarung, dass ...; **I thought that was ~!** ich dachte, das sei klar; **certain things always have to be ~ in a relationship** einige Dinge sollten in einer Beziehung einfach stillschweigend vorausgesetzt werden *or* immer von vornherein klar sein

c (= *believed*) angenommen, geglaubt; **he is ~ to have left** es heißt, dass er gegangen ist; **it is ~ that ...** es heißt *or* man hört, dass ...; **he let it be ~ that ...** er gab zu verstehen, dass ...

d *pred* (*Gram*) ausgelassen

understudy [ˈʌndəˌstʌdɪ] **N** (*Theat*) zweite Besetzung *f*, (*fig*) Stellvertreter(in) *m(f)* **VT** (*Theat*) zweite Besetzung sein für

undersurface **N** [ˈʌndəˌsɜːfɪs] (= *underside*) Unterseite *f* **ADJ** [ˌʌndəˈsɜːfɪs] (= *undersea(s)*) Unterwasser-; (= *subterranean*) unterirdisch

undertake [ˌʌndəˈteɪk] *pret* **undertook** [ˌʌndəˈtʊk] *ptp* **undertaken** [ˌʌndəˈteɪkn] VT **a** *job, duty, responsibility* übernehmen; *risk* eingehen, auf sich (*acc*) nehmen; *study, research, reform* durchführen; *tour* machen; **he undertook to be our guide** er übernahm es, unser Führer zu sein **b** (= *agree, promise*) sich verpflichten; (= *guarantee*) garantieren

undertaker [ˈʌndəˌteɪkə] N (Leichen)bestatter(in) *m(f)*; (= *company*) Bestattungs- *or* Beerdigungsinstitut *nt*

undertaking[1] [ˌʌndəˈteɪkɪŋ] N **a** (= *enterprise*) Vorhaben *nt*, Unternehmen *nt*; (= *project*) Projekt *nt* **b** (= *promise*) Zusicherung *f*, Wort *nt*; **I give you my solemn ~ that I will never do it again** ich verpflichte mich feierlich, es nie wieder zu tun; **I can give no such ~** das kann ich nicht versprechen **c** (= *funeral business*) Bestattungsgewerbe *nt*

undertaking[2] N (*Brit, Aut inf*) Überholen *nt* auf der Innenseite

under: undertax [ˌʌndəˈtæks] VT unterbesteuern, zu niedrig besteuern; **undertenant** [ˈʌndəˌtenənt] N Untermieter(in) *m(f)*; (*of land*) Unterpächter(in) *m(f)*; **under-the-counter** ADJ → **counter; undertone** N **a** (*of voice*) **in an ~** mit gedämpfter Stimme **b** (*fig, of criticism, discontent*) Unterton *m*; (*of colour*) Tönung *f*; **an ~ of racism** ein rassistischer Unterton; **undertook** *pret of* **undertake; undertow** N (*lit, fig*) Unterströmung *f*; **there is a lot of ~** es gibt viele Unterströmungen; **underused** ADJ *land, muscles* nicht voll genutzt; *resources, facilities also* unausgeschöpft; **underutilization** N mangelnde *or* unzureichende Nutzung; **underutilized** ADJ unzureichend *or* nicht voll genutzt; **undervalue** VT *antique, artist* unterbewerten, unterschätzen; (= *price too low*) *company, assets, shares* zu niedrig schätzen *or* veranschlagen; *person* zu wenig schätzen; **underwater** ADJ Unterwasser-; **~ photography** Unterwasserfotografie *f* **ADV** unter Wasser; **underwear** N Unterwäsche *f*; **underweight** ADJ untergewichtig; **to be (2 kg) ~** (2 kg) Untergewicht haben; **underwent** *pret of* **undergo; underwhelm** VT (*hum*) **the critics were ~ed by his second novel** sein zweiter Roman hat die Kritiker nicht gerade umgehauen (*inf*); **underworld** N (= *criminals, Myth*) Unterwelt *f*; **underwrite** *pret* **underwrote**, *ptp* **underwritten** VT (= *finance*) *company, loss, project* tragen, garantieren; (= *guarantee*) *insurance policy* garantieren, bürgen für; (= *insure*) *shipping, risk* versichern; (*St Ex*) *shares, issue* zeichnen; (*fig:* = *agree to*) *policies etc* billigen; **underwriter** N (*Insur:* = *company*) Versicherer *m*, Versicherungsgeber *m*

undeserved [ˌʌndɪˈzɜːvd] ADJ unverdient

undeservedly [ˌʌndɪˈzɜːvɪdlɪ] ADV unverdient(ermaßen)

undeserving [ˌʌndɪˈzɜːvɪŋ] ADJ *person, cause* unwürdig; **the ~ poor** die Armen, die es nicht besser verdienen; **to be ~ of sth** (*form*) einer Sache (*gen*) unwürdig sein (*form*)

undesirability [ˌʌndɪzaɪərəˈbɪlɪtɪ] N **a** (*of policy, effect*) Unerwünschtheit *f*; **because of the general ~ of the site** da der Bauplatz durchweg nur Nachteile hat **b** (*of influence, characters, area*) Übelkeit *f*

undesirable [ˌʌndɪˈzaɪərəbl] **ADJ** **a** *policy, effect* unerwünscht; **~ alien** unerwünschter Ausländer, unerwünschte Ausländerin; **an ~ person to have as a manager** kein wünschenswerter Manager; **they consider her fiancé ~** sie glau-

ben, dass ihr Verlobter keine wünschenswerte Partie ist; **it is ~ that ...** es wäre höchst unerwünscht, wenn ... **b** *influence, characters, area* übel; **~ elements** unerwünschte Elemente *pl*; **he's just generally ~** er ist ganz einfach ein übler Kerl **N** (= *person*) unerfreuliches Element; (= *foreigner*) unerwünschtes Element

undetachable [ˌʌndɪˈtætʃəbl] ADJ nicht (ab-)trennbar *or* abnehmbar

undetected [ˌʌndɪˈtektɪd] ADJ unentdeckt; **to go ~** nicht entdeckt werden; **to remain ~** unentdeckt bleiben

undetermined [ˌʌndɪˈtɜːmɪnd] ADJ (= *indefinite*) unbestimmt; (= *unsure*) *person* unentschlossen, unschlüssig; **an ~ amount (of money)** eine (Geld)summe in unbestimmter Höhe

undeterred [ˌʌndɪˈtɜːd] ADJ keineswegs entmutigt; **to continue ~** unverzagt weitermachen; **the teams were ~ by the weather** das Wetter schreckte die Mannschaften nicht ab

undeveloped [ˌʌndɪˈveləpt] ADJ unentwickelt; *land, resources* ungenutzt

undeviating [ʌnˈdiːvɪeɪtɪŋ] ADJ (= *straight*) *line* gerade; (*fig:* = *unchanging*) *route, path* direkt; *fairness, determination* unbeirrbar; *accuracy* unfehlbar

undiagnosed [ˌʌndaɪəgˈnəʊzd] ADJ *disease* unerkannt

undid [ʌnˈdɪd] *pret of* **undo**

undies [ˈʌndɪz] PL (*inf*) (Unter)wäsche *f*

undifferentiated [ˌʌndɪfəˈrenʃɪeɪtɪd] ADJ undifferenziert

undigested [ˌʌndaɪˈdʒestɪd] ADJ (*lit, fig*) unverdaut

undignified [ʌnˈdɪgnɪfaɪd] ADJ *person, behaviour* würdelos; (= *inelegant*) *way of sitting etc* unelegant; **he was never afraid of appearing ~** er hatte keine Angst, seine Würde zu verlieren

undiluted [ˌʌndaɪˈluːtɪd] ADJ unverdünnt; (*fig*) *truth, version, accent* unverfälscht; *pleasure* rein, voll; *enthusiasm, praise* unvermindert

undiminished [ˌʌndɪˈmɪnɪʃt] ADJ *enthusiasm* unvermindert; *strength, courage also* unbeeinträchtigt

undiplomatic ADJ , **undiplomatically** ADV [ˌʌndɪpləˈmætɪk, -əlɪ] undiplomatisch

undipped [ʌnˈdɪpt] ADJ (*Brit, Aut*) **~ headlights** Fernlicht *nt*

undiscerned ADJ , **undiscernedly** ADV [ˌʌndɪˈsɜːnd, -nɪdlɪ] (*form*) unbemerkt

undiscerning [ˌʌndɪˈsɜːnɪŋ] ADJ *reader, palate* anspruchslos, unkritisch; *critic* unbedarft

undischarged [ˌʌndɪsˈtʃɑːdʒd] ADJ **a** (*Fin*) *debt* unbezahlt, unbeglichen; *bankrupt* nicht entlastet **b** *cargo* nicht abgeladen; *gun* nicht abgefeuert

undisciplined [ʌnˈdɪsɪplɪnd] ADJ *mind, person* undiszipliniert; *imagination* zügellos; *hair* ungebändigt

undisclosed [ˌʌndɪsˈkləʊzd] ADJ *secret* (bisher) unaufgedeckt; *details, location, price etc also* geheim gehalten; *fee, reason, number* ungenannt, geheim gehalten; **an ~ sum** eine ungenannte *or* geheim gehaltene Summe

undiscovered [ˌʌndɪsˈkʌvəd] ADJ unentdeckt; **to lie ~** unentdeckt *or* noch nicht entdeckt sein

undiscriminating [ˌʌndɪsˈkrɪmɪneɪtɪŋ] ADJ = **undiscerning**

undisguised [ˌʌndɪsˈgaɪzd] ADJ ungetarnt; (*fig*) *truth* unverhüllt; *dislike, affection* unverhohlen; **an ~ attempt to do sth** ein unverhüllter Versuch, etw zu tun

undismayed [ˌʌndɪsˈmeɪd] ADJ ungerührt, unbeeindruckt

undisposed [ˌʌndɪsˈpəʊzd] ADJ **~ of** (*Comm*) unverkauft

undisputed [ˌʌndɪsˈpjuːtɪd] ADJ unbestritten

undistinguished [ˌʌndɪsˈtɪŋgwɪʃt] ADJ *performance* (mittel)mäßig; *appearance* durchschnittlich

undisturbed [ˌʌndɪˈstɜːbd] ADJ **a** (= *untouched*) *papers, dust* unberührt; (= *uninterrupted*) *person, sleep, quiet etc* ungestört; (= *quiet*) *village* unberührt; **to be ~ by tourism** vom Tourismus unberührt sein **b** (= *unworried*) unberührt

undivided [ˌʌndɪˈvaɪdɪd] ADJ *country, opinion, attention* ungeteilt; *support* voll; *loyalty* absolut; *love* uneingeschränkt; **we must stand firm and ~** wir müssen fest und einig sein

undo [ʌnˈduː] *pret* **undid**, *ptp* **undone** VT **a** (= *unfasten*) aufmachen; *button, dress, zip, parcel* aufmachen, öffnen; *knot* lösen; *knitting* aufziehen; *sewing* auftrennen; **will you ~ me?** (*inf*) kannst du mir den Reißverschluss/die Knöpfe *etc* aufmachen? **b** (= *reverse*) *mischief, wrong* ungeschehen machen; *work* zunichte machen, ruinieren; *decision* rückgängig machen; (*Comput*) *command* rückgängig machen; **we cannot ~ the past** wir können die Vergangenheit nicht ungeschehen machen VI aufgehen

undock [ʌnˈdɒk] (*Space*) VT entkoppeln VI sich trennen

undoing [ʌnˈduːɪŋ] N Ruin *m*, Verderben *nt*

undomesticated [ˌʌndəˈmestɪkeɪtɪd] ADJ *animal, pet* nicht ans Haus gewöhnt; *woman, husband* nicht häuslich; **men aren't as ~ as they used to be** Männer sind heute häuslicher als früher

undone [ʌnˈdʌn] *ptp of* **undo** ADJ **a** (= *unfastened*) *button, shoelace, tie, hair* offen; **to come ~** aufgehen **b** (= *neglected*) *task, work* unerledigt; **to leave sth ~** etw ungetan lassen; **we have left ~ what we ought to have done** (*Rel*) wir haben unser Tagwerk nicht getan **c** (= *cancelled out*) **she has seen her life's work ~** sie musste zusehen, wie ihr Lebenswerk zerstört wurde **d** (*obs:* = *ruined*) **I am ~!** ich bin ruiniert; **to be ~** zu Fall gebracht werden

undoubted [ʌnˈdaʊtɪd] ADJ unbestritten; *success also* unzweifelhaft

undoubtedly [ʌnˈdaʊtɪdlɪ] ✪ 15.1 ADV zweifellos, ohne Zweifel

undoubting [ʌnˈdaʊtɪŋ] ADJ unerschütterlich

undramatic [ˌʌndrəˈmætɪk] ADJ undramatisch

undreamt-of [ʌnˈdremtɒv], (*US*) **undreamed--of** [ʌnˈdriːmdɒv] ADJ ungeahnt; **in their time this was ~** zu ihrer Zeit hätte man sich das nie träumen lassen

undress [ʌnˈdres] VT ausziehen; **to get ~ed** sich ausziehen VI sich ausziehen N **in a state of ~** halb bekleidet

undressed [ʌnˈdrest] ADJ **a** *person* (*still*) (noch) nicht angezogen; (*already*) (schon) ausgezogen; **I feel ~ without my watch** ohne Uhr komme ich mir nackt vor **b** *leather* ungegerbt; *wood* unbehandelt, frisch; *stone* ungeschliffen; (*Cook*) *salad* nicht angemacht; *wound* unverbunden

undrinkable [ʌnˈdrɪŋkəbl] ADJ ungenießbar

undue [ʌnˈdjuː] ADJ (= *excessive*) übertrieben, übermäßig; (= *improper*) ungebührlich

undulant [ˈʌndjʊlənt] ADJ = **undulating**

undulate [ˈʌndjʊleɪt] VI (*sea, corn*) wogen; (*river, snake*) sich schlängeln; (*hills*) sich in sanften Wellenlinien erstrecken; (*path*) auf und ab führen; (*hair*) wallen; **her hips ~d in time to the music** ihre Hüften wiegten sich im Takt mit der Musik

undulating [ˈʌndjʊleɪtɪŋ] ADJ *movement, line* wellenförmig; *waves, sea* wogend; *hair* wallend; *countryside* hügelig; *hills* sanft; *path* auf und ab führend; *hips* wiegend

undulation [ˌʌndjʊˈleɪʃən] N (*of waves, countryside*) Auf und Ab *nt*; (*of snake, single movement*) Windung *f*, schlängelnde Bewegung; (= *curve*) Rundung *f*

undulatory [ˈʌndjʊlətrɪ] ADJ *movement* wellenförmig

unduly [ʌnˈdjuːlɪ] ADV übermäßig, übertrieben; *optimistic, pessimistic, lenient* zu; *punish* unangemessen *or* übermäßig streng; **you're worrying ~** Sie machen sich (*dat*) unnötige Sorgen

undutiful [ʌnˈdjuːtɪfʊl] ADJ pflichtvergessen; *child* ungehorsam

undying [ʌnˈdaɪɪŋ] ADJ *love* unsterblich, ewig; *fame also* unvergänglich

unearned [ʌnˈɜːnd] ADJ **a** *increment* unverdient **b** (= *undeserved*) unverdient

unearned income N Kapitalertrag *m*, arbeitsloses Einkommen

unearth [ʌnˈɜːθ] VT ausgraben; (*fig*) *book etc* aufstöbern; *information, evidence, talent* zutage *or* zu Tage bringen, ausfindig machen

unearthly [ʌnˈɜːθlɪ] ADJ (= *eerie*) *calm* gespenstisch, unheimlich; *scream* schauerlich, unheimlich; *beauty* überirdisch; (*inf:* = *awful*) *sound, noise, racket* schauerlich; **at the ~ hour of 5 o'clock** (*inf*) zu nachtschlafender Stunde um 5 Uhr

unease [ʌnˈiːz] N Unbehagen *nt*, Beklommenheit *f*

uneasily [ʌnˈiːzɪlɪ] ADV *sit* unbehaglich; *smile, listen, speak etc also* beklommen, unsicher; *sleep* unruhig; **to be ~ balanced** sehr prekär sein; **to be ~ poised** sehr wack(e)lig stehen; **to be ~ aware that ...** sich (*dat*) mit Unbehagen bewusst sein, dass ...; **to be ~ aware of sth** etw mit Unbehagen erkennen; **to sit ~ with sth** nur schlecht zu etw passen

uneasiness [ʌnˈiːzɪnɪs] N (= *anxiety: of laugh, look, = awkwardness: of silence, atmosphere*) Unbehaglichkeit *f*, Beklommenheit *f*; (*of behaviour*) Unsicherheit *f*; (*of peace, balance*) Unsicherheit *f*, Wack(e)ligkeit *f* (*inf*); (*of alliance, coalition, relationship*) Instabilität *f*, Wack(e)ligkeit *f* (*inf*); (*of person*) (= *awkwardness*) Beklommenheit *f*; (= *anxiety*) Unruhe *f*

uneasy [ʌnˈiːzɪ] ADJ (= *uncomfortable*) *sleep, night* unruhig; *conscience* schlecht; (= *worried*) *laugh, look* unbehaglich, beklommen; (= *awkward*) *silence, atmosphere* unbehaglich, beklommen; *behaviour* unsicher; *peace, balance* unsicher, prekär, wack(e)lig (*inf*); *alliance, coalition, relationship* instabil, wack(e)lig (*inf*); (= *worrying*) *suspicion, feeling* beunruhigend, beklemmend, unangenehm; **to be ~** (*person, = ill at ease*) beklommen sein; (= *worried*) beunruhigt sein; **I am** *or* **feel ~ about it** mir ist nicht wohl dabei; **to make sb ~** jdn beunruhigen, jdn unruhig machen; **I have an ~ feeling that ...** ich habe das ungute *or* unangenehme Gefühl, dass ...; **to become ~** unruhig werden; **to grow** *or* **become ~ about sth** sich über etw (*acc*) beunruhigen; **his conscience was ~** sein Gewissen plagte ihn, er hatte ein schlechtes Gewissen

uneatable [ʌnˈiːtəbl] ADJ ungenießbar

uneaten [ʌnˈiːtn] ADJ nicht gegessen; **he left the frogs' legs ~** er rührte die Froschschenkel nicht an; **the ~ food** das übrig gebliebene Essen

uneconomic [ˌʌniːkəˈnɒmɪk] ADJ unwirtschaftlich, unökonomisch

uneconomical [ˌʌniːkəˈnɒmɪkəl] ADJ unwirtschaftlich, unökonomisch; *style of running* unökonomisch; *person* verschwenderisch

unedifying [ʌnˈedɪfaɪɪŋ] ADJ unerbaulich; **rather ~** nicht gerade erbaulich

uneducated [ʌnˈedjʊkeɪtɪd] ADJ *person* ungebildet; *speech, handwriting also* unkultiviert; *style also* ungeschliffen

unemotional [ˌʌnɪˈməʊʃənl] ADJ *person, character, approach, voice* nüchtern; *reaction, description also* unbewegt; (= *without passion*) leidenschaftslos, kühl (*pej*); **try and stay ~** versuchen Sie, nüchtern und sachlich zu bleiben

unemotionally [ˌʌnɪˈməʊʃnəlɪ] ADV unbewegt, kühl (*pej*); *say, describe also* nüchtern; **state your opinion ~** bringen Sie Ihre Meinung sachlich vor

unemployable [ˌʌnɪmˈplɔɪəbl] ADJ *person* als Arbeitskraft nicht brauchbar; (*because of illness*) arbeitsunfähig

unemployed [ˌʌnɪmˈplɔɪd] ADJ *person* arbeitslos, erwerbslos; (= *unused*) *machinery* ungenutzt; (*Fin*) *capital* tot, brachliegend PL **the ~** *pl* die Arbeitslosen *pl*, die Erwerbslosen *pl*

unemployment [ˌʌnɪmˈplɔɪmənt] N Arbeitslosigkeit *f*, Erwerbslosigkeit *f*; **~ has risen this month** die Arbeitslosenziffer ist diesen Monat gestiegen

unemployment: unemployment benefit, (*US*) **unemployment compensation** N Arbeitslosenunterstützung *f*; **unemployment figures** PL Arbeitslosenziffer *f*; **unemployment insurance** N Arbeitslosenversicherung *f*; **unemployment line** N (*US*) **to be in the ~** arbeitslos sein, stempeln gehen (*inf*); **many white-collar workers find themselves in the ~s** viele Schreibtischarbeiter finden sich auf dem Arbeitsamt wieder; **unemployment rate** N Arbeitslosenquote *f*

unencumbered [ˌʌnɪnˈkʌmbəd] ADJ unbelastet; **~ property** unbelasteter Grundbesitz

unending [ʌnˈendɪŋ] ADJ (= *everlasting*) ewig, nie endend *attr*; *stream* nicht enden wollend *attr*, endlos; (= *incessant*) endlos, unaufhörlich; **it seems ~** es scheint nicht enden zu wollen

unendurable [ˌʌnɪnˈdjʊərəbl] ADJ unerträglich

unenforceable [ˌʌnɪnˈfɔːsɪbl] ADJ *law* nicht durchsetzbar; *policy* undurchführbar

un-English [ʌnˈɪŋglɪʃ] ADJ *behaviour, appearance* unenglisch

unenlightened [ˌʌnɪnˈlaɪtnd] ADJ **a** (= *uninformed*) *reader, listener* uneingeweiht; **to leave sb ~** jdn im Dunkeln lassen **b** *age, country, person* rückständig; (= *prejudiced*) intolerant

unenterprising [ʌnˈentəpraɪzɪŋ] ADJ *person, policy* ohne Unternehmungsgeist, hausbacken (*inf*); **it was very ~ of them to turn it down** dass sie abgelehnt haben beweist, wie wenig Unternehmungsgeist sie haben

unenthusiastic [ˌʌnɪnθuːzɪˈæstɪk] ADJ kühl, wenig begeistert; **he was ~ about it** er war wenig begeistert davon; **don't be so ~** zeige doch ein bisschen Begeisterung!

unenthusiastically [ˌʌnɪnθuːzɪˈæstɪkəlɪ] ADV wenig begeistert, ohne Begeisterung

unenviable [ʌnˈenvɪəbl] ADJ *position, task, record* wenig beneidenswert

unequal [ʌnˈiːkwəl] ADJ ungleich; *standard, quality* unterschiedlich, ungleichförmig; *work* unausgeglichen; **~ in length** unterschiedlich *or* verschieden *or* ungleich lang; **to be ~ to a task** einer Aufgabe (*dat*) nicht gewachsen sein; **to be ~ to doing sth** unfähig *or* nicht fähig sein, etw zu tun

unequalled, (*US*) **unequaled** [ʌnˈiːkwəld] ADJ unübertroffen; *skill, record, civilization also* unerreicht; *beauty also, stupidity, ignorance* beispiellos, ohnegleichen (*after noun*); **he is ~ by any other player** kein anderer Spieler kommt ihm gleich

unequally [ʌnˈiːkwəlɪ] ADV ungleichmäßig

unequivocal [ˌʌnɪˈkwɪvəkəl] ADJ **a** unmissverständlich, eindeutig; *answer also* unzweideutig; *evidence, proof* eindeutig, unzweifelhaft; **he was quite ~ about it** er sagte es ganz unmissverständlich *or* eindeutig *or* klar **b** (= *categorical*) *commitment, support* rückhaltlos; **to be ~ in one's support of sth** etw rückhaltlos *or* ohne Vorbehalte unterstützen

unequivocally [ˌʌnɪˈkwɪvəkəlɪ] ADV *state, answer* unmissverständlich, eindeutig; *reject* unmissverständlich, klipp und klar (*inf*); *support* rückhaltlos, ohne Vorbehalte

unerring [ʌnˈɜːrɪŋ] ADJ *judgement, eye, accuracy, ability* unfehlbar; *instinct* untrüglich; *aim, blow* treffsicher

unerringly [ʌnˈɜːrɪŋlɪ] ADV *judge* unfehlbar; *aim* treffsicher

unescapable ADJ , **unescapably** ADV [ˌʌnɪˈskeɪpəbl, -ɪ] *fate etc* unentrinnbar

UNESCO [juːˈneskəʊ] *abbr of* **United Nations Educational, Scientific and Cultural Organization** UNESCO *f*

unesthetic ADJ (*US*) = **unaesthetic**

unethical [ʌnˈeθɪkəl] ADJ unmoralisch; (*in more serious matters*) unethisch; **it's ~ for a doctor to**

do that es verstößt gegen das Berufsethos *or* die Berufsehre, wenn ein Arzt das macht

uneven [ʌnˈiːvən] ADJ **a** (= *not level*) surface uneben; (= *irregular*) line ungerade; *thickness* ungleich; *pulse, breathing, teeth* unregelmäßig; *voice* unsicher, schwankend; *pace, rate, colour, distribution* ungleichmäßig; *quality* unterschiedlich; *temper* unausgeglichen; *contest, competition* ungleich; **the engine sounds ~** der Motor läuft ungleichmäßig **b** *number* ungerade

unevenly [ʌnˈiːvənlɪ] ADV (= *irregularly*) move, spread, develop ungleichmäßig, unregelmäßig; (= *unequally*) share, distribute ungleichmäßig; **the teams were ~ matched** die Mannschaften waren sehr ungleich

unevenness [ʌnˈiːvənnɪs] N (*of surface*) Unebenheit f; (= *irregularity, of line*) Ungeradheit f; (*of thickness*) Ungleichheit f; (*of pulse, breathing, teeth*) Unregelmäßigkeit f; (*of voice*) Unsicherheit f; (*of pace, rate, colour, distribution*) Ungleichmäßigkeit f; (= *inconsistency: of quality*) Unterschiedlichkeit f; (*of contest, competition*) Ungleichheit f

uneventful [ʌnɪˈventfʊl] ADJ *day, meeting* ereignislos; *career* wenig bewegt; *life* ruhig, eintönig (*pej*)

uneventfully [ʌnɪˈventfəlɪ] ADV ereignislos

unexacting [ʌnɪgˈzæktɪŋ] ADJ *standards etc* anspruchslos, keine hohen Anforderungen stellend; *work etc* leicht, nicht anstrengend

unexampled [ʌnɪgˈzɑːmpld] ADJ beispiellos, unvergleichlich

unexceptionable [ʌnɪkˈsepʃnəbl] ADJ einwandfrei; *person* solide

unexceptional [ʌnɪkˈsepʃənl] ADJ alltäglich, durchschnittlich

unexciting [ʌnɪkˈsaɪtɪŋ] ADJ nicht besonders aufregend; (= *boring*) langweilig; **not ~** nicht gerade eintönig

unexpected [ʌnɪkˈspektɪd] ADJ unerwartet; *arrival, result, development also* unvorhergesehen; **this is an ~ pleasure** (*also iro*) welch eine Überraschung!; **their success was not ~** ihr Erfolg kam nicht unerwartet *or* überraschend; **the role of the ~ in this novel** der Überraschungseffekt in diesem Roman

unexpectedly [ʌnɪkˈspektɪdlɪ] ADV unerwartet; *arrive, happen also* plötzlich, unvorhergesehen; **but then, ~** aber dann, wie aus heiterem Himmel, ...

unexplainable [ʌnɪkˈspleɪnəbl] ADJ unerklärlich

unexplained [ʌnɪkˈspleɪnd] ADJ nicht geklärt, ungeklärt; *mystery* unaufgeklärt; *lateness, absence* unbegründet; **a few ~ technical terms** einige unerklärte Fachausdrücke; **to go ~** nicht erklärt werden; **his actions remain ~** für seine Handlungen gibt es immer noch keine Erklärung; **for some ~ reason** ohne ersichtlichen Grund, aus unerklärlichen Gründen

unexploded [ʌnɪkˈspləʊdɪd] ADJ nicht explodiert

unexploited [ʌnɪkˈsplɔɪtɪd] ADJ *resources* ungenutzt; *market* (noch) nicht erschlossen; *talent also* brachliegend *attr*; *minerals also* unausgebeutet

unexplored [ʌnɪkˈsplɔːd] ADJ *mystery* unerforscht; *territory also* unerschlossen

unexposed [ʌnɪkˈspəʊzd] ADJ **a** (= *hidden*) villain nicht entlarvt; *crime* unaufgedeckt **b** (*Phot*) *film* unbelichtet

unexpressed [ʌnɪkˈsprest] ADJ *sorrow, wish* unausgesprochen

unexpressive [ʌnɪkˈspresɪv] ADJ *style, eyes* ausdruckslos

unexpurgated [ʌnˈekspɜːgeɪtɪd] ADJ *book, version* ungekürzt, unzensiert

unfading [ʌnˈfeɪdɪŋ] ADJ (*fig*) unvergänglich, nie verblassend

unfailing [ʌnˈfeɪlɪŋ] ADJ *zeal, interest, source* unerschöpflich; *optimism, humour also* unbezwinglich; *supply also* endlos; *remedy* unfehlbar; *friend*

treu; *support, encouragement, generosity* unfehlbar; *support, encouragement* beständig; *regularity, accuracy* beständig

unfailingly [ʌnˈfeɪlɪŋlɪ] ADV immer, stets

unfair [ʌnˈfeə'] **☺** 26.3 ADJ unfair; *decision, method, remark, criticism also* ungerecht; (*Comm*) *competition also* unlauter; **to be ~ to sb** jdm gegenüber unfair sein; **to have an ~ advantage over sb/sth** einen unfairen Vorteil gegenüber jdm/ etw haben; **it is ~ to expect her to do that** es ist nicht fair, von ihr zu erwarten, dass sie das tut

unfair dismissal N ungerechtfertigte Entlassung

unfairly [ʌnˈfeəlɪ] ADV unfair; *treat, criticize etc also* ungerecht; *accuse, punish* zu Unrecht; *dismissed* ungerechterweise, zu Unrecht; **to charge ~ high prices** ungerechtfertigt hohe Preise verlangen

unfairness [ʌnˈfeənɪs] N Ungerechtigkeit f

unfaithful [ʌnˈfeɪθfʊl] ADJ **a** wife, husband, lover untreu; *friend, servant* treulos; **to be ~ to sb** jdm untreu sein **b** (= *inaccurate*) translation, description ungenau; **the translator was ~ to the original poem** der Übersetzer verfälschte das Gedicht

unfaithfulness [ʌnˈfeɪθfʊlnɪs] N **a** (*of wife, husband, lover*) Untreue f; (*of friend, servant*) Treulosigkeit f **b** (*of translation, description*) Ungenauigkeit f

unfaltering [ʌnˈfɔːltərɪŋ] ADJ *step, voice* fest; *courage* unerschütterlich

unfalteringly [ʌnˈfɔːltərɪŋlɪ] ADV *walk* mit festen Schritten; *say* mit fester Stimme

unfamiliar [ʌnfəˈmɪljə'] ADJ **a** (= *strange, unknown*) experience, taste, sight, surroundings ungewohnt; *subject, person* fremd, unbekannt; **~ territory** (*fig*) Neuland nt; **it is ~ to me** es ist ungewohnt für mich, es ist mir fremd *or* unbekannt **b** (= *unacquainted*) **to be ~ with sth** etw nicht kennen, mit etw nicht vertraut sein; *with machine etc* sich mit etw nicht auskennen; **I am not ~ with the situation** die Situation ist mir nicht gänzlich unbekannt

unfamiliarity [ʌnfəmɪlɪˈærɪtɪ] N **a** (= *strangeness, novelty, of experience, taste, sight, surroundings*) Ungewohntheit f; (*of subject, person*) Fremdheit f, Unbekanntheit f **b** (= *lack of acquaintance*) **his ~ with economics** sein Mangel *m* an ökonomischem Wissen; **because of my ~ with ...** wegen meiner mangelnden Kenntnisse (*+gen*) ... *or* Vertrautheit mit ...

unfashionable [ʌnˈfæʃnəbl] ADJ unmodern; *district* wenig gefragt; *hotel, habit, subject* nicht in Mode; *image* überholt; **science became ~** Naturwissenschaft geriet aus der Mode

unfashionably [ʌnˈfæʃnəblɪ] ADV *dressed* unmodern; *strict etc* altmodisch

unfasten [ʌnˈfɑːsn] **VT** aufmachen; *string, belt also* losmachen; (= *detach*) tag, dog, horse etc loslesbinden; *hair, bonds* lösen **VI** aufgehen; **how does this dress ~?** wie macht man das Kleid auf?

unfathomable [ʌnˈfæðəməbl] ADJ unergründlich

unfathomed [ʌnˈfæðəmd] ADJ (*lit, fig*) unergründet

unfavourable, (US) **unfavorable** [ʌnˈfeɪvərəbl] ADJ *outlook, weather, moment, result* ungünstig; *conditions, circumstances also, wind* widrig; *opinion, reaction* negativ; *reply* ablehnend, negativ; *trade balance* passiv; **conditions ~ to** *or* **for trade** ungünstige Handelsbedingungen *pl*; **on ~ terms** zu ungünstigen Bedingungen; **to be ~ to sb** ungünstig für jdn sein; **to draw** *or* **make ~ comparisons** nachteilige Vergleiche ziehen; **to show sb/sth in an ~ light** jdn/etw in einem ungünstigen Licht darstellen

unfavourably, (US) **unfavorably** [ʌnˈfeɪvərəblɪ] ADV *contrast, compare* unvorteilhaft; *react, comment* ablehnend; *respond, review* negativ; *regard* ungünstig; **to compare ~ with sth** im Vergleich mit etw schlecht abschneiden; **to look ~ on sth** einer Sache (*dat*) ablehnend gegenüberste-

hen; **to report ~ on/speak ~ of sth** etw negativ *or* ablehnend *or* ungünstig beurteilen; **to be ~ impressed by sth** einen negativen Eindruck *or* keinen guten Eindruck von etw bekommen

unfeasible [ʌnˈfiːzəbl] ADJ nicht machbar; **the weather made it ~ to be outdoors** bei dem Wetter kann man nicht draußen sein

unfeeling [ʌnˈfiːlɪŋ] ADJ gefühllos; *response, reply also* herzlos; *look* ungerührt; (= *without sensation also*) empfindungslos

unfeelingly [ʌnˈfiːlɪŋlɪ] ADV gefühllos, herzlos; *look, listen* ungerührt

unfeigned [ʌnˈfeɪnd] ADJ aufrichtig, echt, ungeheuchelt

unfeminine [ʌnˈfemɪnɪn] ADJ unweiblich

unfetter [ʌnˈfetə'] VT (*fig*) befreien (*from* von)

unfettered [ʌnˈfetəd] ADJ (*fig*) frei, unbehindert (*by* von); *right, power, freedom* uneingeschränkt

unfilial [ʌnˈfɪljəl] ADJ nicht pflichtbewusst; (= *impudent*) ungehörig, respektlos

unfilled [ʌnˈfɪld] ADJ ungefüllt; *job* offen, unbesetzt; *seat* (= *not taken*) leer; (*Pol*) unbesetzt; *order* book un(aus)gefüllt; **~ vacancies** offene Stellen *pl*

unfinished [ʌnˈfɪnɪʃt] ADJ **a** (= *incomplete*) unfertig; *work of art* unvollendet; **Schubert's Unfinished** Schuberts Unvollendete f; **~ business** unerledigte Geschäfte *pl*; **to leave sth ~** etw unvollendet lassen **b** (*Tech*) unbearbeitet; *wood* naturbelassen; **~ product** Rohprodukt *nt*

unfit [ʌnˈfɪt] **ADJ** **a** (= *unsuitable*) person, thing ungeeignet, untauglich; (= *incompetent*) unfähig; **to be ~ to do sth** (*physically*) nicht fähig sein, etw zu tun; (*mentally*) außer Stande sein, etw zu tun; **~ to drive** fahruntüchtig, nicht in der Lage zu fahren; **he is ~ to be a lawyer/for teaching** er ist als Jurist/Lehrer untauglich; **to be ~ for (human) habitation** (für Menschen) unbewohnbar sein; **this is ~ for publication** das kann nicht veröffentlicht werden; **to be ~ for (human) consumption** nicht zum Verzehr geeignet sein; **~ to eat** ungenießbar; **road ~ for lorries** für Lastkraftwagen nicht geeignete Straße; **~ to live in** unbewohnbar; **~ to plead** (*Jur*) nicht zurechnungsfähig

b (*Sport*: = *injured*) nicht fit; (*in health*) schlecht in Form, unfit; **he is very ~** er ist in sehr schlechter Form; **~ (for military service)** (dienst)untauglich; **to be ~ for work** arbeitsunfähig sein

VT (*form*) **to ~ sb for sth** jdn für etw untauglich machen; **to ~ sb to do sth** jdn untauglich machen, etw zu tun

unfitness [ʌnˈfɪtnɪs] N **a** (= *unsuitableness*) mangelnde Eignung, Untauglichkeit f; (= *incompetence*) Unfähigkeit f **b** (= *unhealthiness*) mangelnde Fitness; (*for military service*) Untauglichkeit f

unfitted [ʌnˈfɪtɪd] ADJ ungeeignet, untauglich (*for, to* für)

unfitting [ʌnˈfɪtɪŋ] ADJ *language, behaviour* unpassend, unschicklich, unziemlich

unfittingly [ʌnˈfɪtɪŋlɪ] ADV *behave* unpassend, unschicklich, unziemlich; *dressed* unpassend

unfix [ʌnˈfɪks] VT losmachen; *bayonets* abmachen; **it came ~ed** es hat sich gelöst

unflagging [ʌnˈflægɪŋ] ADJ *person, zeal, patience* unermüdlich, unentwegt; *enthusiasm* unerschöpflich; *devotion, interest* unverändert stark; **he has an ~ devotion to the cause** er stellt sich unermüdlich in den Dienst der Sache; **to be ~ in one's support of sth** etw unermüdlich unterstützen; **to be ~ in doing sth** unermüdlich darin sein, etw zu tun

unflaggingly [ʌnˈflægɪŋlɪ] ADV unentwegt, unermüdlich

unflappability [ˌʌnflæpəˈbɪlɪtɪ] N (*inf*) Unerschütterlichkeit f

unflappable [ʌnˈflæpəbl] ADJ (*inf*) unerschütterlich, nicht aus der Ruhe zu bringend *attr*; **to be ~** die Ruhe selbst sein, die Ruhe weghaben (*inf*)

unflattering [ʌn'flætərɪŋ] ADJ *portrait, comments* wenig schmeichelhaft; *dress, hairstyle, light also* unvorteilhaft; **to portray sb/sth in an ~ light** jdn/etw in einem wenig schmeichelhaften Licht erscheinen lassen

unfledged [ʌn'fledʒd] ADJ *bird* (noch) nicht flügge; *(fig)* unerfahren

unflinching [ʌn'flɪntʃɪŋ] ADJ unerschrocken; *determination, loyalty, support* unbeirrbar; *gaze* unbeirrt; **with ~ courage** unverzagt

unflinchingly [ʌn'flɪntʃɪŋlɪ] ADV unerschrocken

unflyable [ʌn'flaɪəbl] ADJ *plane* unfliegbar

unfocus(s)ed [ʌn'fəʊkəst] ADJ *eyes* unkoordiniert; *debate* weitschweifig; *campaign* zu allgemein angelegt; **to be ~** *(person)* sich nicht aufs Wesentliche konzentrieren

unfold [ʌn'fəʊld] **VT a** *paper, cloth* auseinander falten, entfalten; *(= spread out) wings* ausbreiten; *arms* lösen; *chair, table* aufklappen, auseinander klappen **b** *(fig) story* entwickeln *(to vor +dat)*; *plans, ideas* entfalten, darlegen *(to +dat)*; *secret* enthüllen, eröffnen **VI** *(story, plot)* sich abwickeln; *(truth)* an den Tag kommen, sich herausstellen; *(view, personality, flower)* sich entfalten; *(countryside)* sich ausbreiten

unforced [ʌn'fɔːst] ADJ ungezwungen, natürlich

unforeseeable [ˌʌnfɔː'siːəbl] ADJ unvorhersehbar

unforeseen [ˌʌnfɔː'siːn] ADJ unvorhergesehen, unerwartet; **due to ~ circumstances** aufgrund unvorhergesehener Umstände

unforgettable [ˌʌnfə'ɡetəbl] ADJ unvergesslich

unforgettably [ˌʌnfə'ɡetəblɪ] ADV auf unvergessliche Weise

unforgivable [ˌʌnfə'ɡɪvəbl] ✪ 18.1 ADJ unverzeihlich

unforgivably [ˌʌnfə'ɡɪvəblɪ] ADV unverzeihlich; **he said, quite ~, that ...** er sagte, und das war einfach unverzeihlich, dass ...

unforgiving [ˌʌnfə'ɡɪvɪŋ] ADJ unversöhnlich

unforgotten [ˌʌnfə'ɡɒtn] ADJ unvergessen

unformatted [ʌn'fɔːmætɪd] ADJ *(Comput) disk* unformatiert

unformed [ʌn'fɔːmd] ADJ *(= unshaped) clay, foetus* ungeformt; *(= undeveloped) character, idea* unfertig

unforthcoming [ˌʌnfɔː'θkʌmɪŋ] ADJ *person* nicht wie mitteilsam; *reply* wenig aufschlussreich; **to be ~ about sth** sich nicht zu etw äußern wollen

unfortified [ʌn'fɔːtɪfaɪd] ADJ *(Mil)* unbefestigt; *(Tech)* nicht verstärkt; *food* nicht angereichert

unfortunate [ʌn'fɔːtʃnɪt] ADJ unglücklich; *person* glücklos; *day, event, error* unglückselig; *turn of phrase* ungeschickt, unglücklich; *time* ungünstig; **to be ~** *(= person)* Pech haben; **to be ~ in life/in love** kein Glück im Leben/in der Liebe haben; **it is most ~ that ...** es ist höchst bedauerlich, dass ...; **how very ~ (for you)** welch ein Pech; **it was ~ that he hadn't been informed** ihm ist bedauerlicherweise nicht Bescheid gesagt worden; **the ~ Mr Brown** der arme or bedauernswerte Herr Brown **N** Arme(r) *mf*, Unglückliche(r) *mf*

unfortunately [ʌn'fɔːtʃnɪtlɪ] ✪ 9.3, 20.4, 26.3 ADV leider; *chosen* unglücklich; *worded* ungeschickt; **the ~-named ...** der unglücklich benannte ...; **~ for you** bedauerlicherweise für Sie; **~ not** leider nicht

unfounded [ʌn'faʊndɪd] ADJ unbegründet, nicht fundiert; *suspicion also* grundlos; *rumour also, allegations* aus der Luft gegriffen; **to prove (to be) ~** sich als unbegründet or grundlos erweisen

unframed [ʌn'freɪmd] ADJ *picture* ungerahmt

unfreeze [ʌn'friːz] *pret* **unfroze**, *ptp* **unfrozen** **VT a** *(= thaw) food etc* auftauen **b** *(Fin) wages, prices, assets* freigeben **VI** auftauen

unfrequented [ˌʌnfrɪ'kwentɪd] ADJ einsam; **the place is ~ except for ...** außer ... kommt niemand dahin

unfriendliness [ʌn'frendlɪnɪs] N Unfreundlichkeit *f*; *(of country, inhabitants also)* Feindseligkeit *f*

unfriendly [ʌn'frendlɪ] ADJ unfreundlich *(to sb* zu jdm); *(= hostile) natives, country, act* feindselig; *territory* unwirtlich; *(Fin) takeover* feindlich; *(= harmful)* schädlich

unfrock [ʌn'frɒk] VT laisieren *(spec)*, in den Laienstand zurückversetzen

unfroze [ʌn'frəʊz] *pret of* **unfreeze**

unfrozen [ʌn'frəʊzn] *ptp of* **unfreeze** ADJ **a** *lake* nicht zugefroren; *earth, food* ungefroren **b** *assets, prices* freigegeben; *(= not yet frozen)* frei

unfruitful [ʌn'fruːtfʊl] ADJ *soil, woman, discussion* unfruchtbar; *attempt* fruchtlos

unfulfilled [ˌʌnfʊl'fɪld] ADJ unerfüllt; *person, life* unausgefüllt; **their potential is ~** sie haben ihre Fähigkeiten nicht voll ausgenutzt; **to have an ~ desire** schon immer den Wunsch gehabt haben

unfunded [ʌn'fʌndɪd] ADJ *(Fin)* unfundiert

unfunny [ˌʌn'fʌnɪ] ADJ *(inf)* (gar) nicht komisch; **distinctly ~** alles andere als komisch

unfurl [ʌn'fɜːl] **VT** *flag* aufrollen; *sail* losmachen; *(peacock) tail* entfalten **VI** sich entfalten; *(flag, sails also)* sich aufrollen

unfurnished [ʌn'fɜːnɪʃt] ADJ unmöbliert

ungainly [ʌn'ɡeɪnlɪ] ADJ *animal, movement* unbeholfen; *appearance* unelegant, unansehnlich, unschön; *posture* ungraziös, unschön

ungenerous [ʌn'dʒenərəs] ADJ kleinlich

ungentlemanly [ʌn'dʒentlmənlɪ], **ungentlemanlike** [ʌn'dʒentlmənlaɪk] ADJ unfein; *(= impolite)* unhöflich; **it is ~ to do so** das gehört sich nicht für einen Gentleman; **it is ~ not to do so** ein Gentleman sollte das tun

un-get-at-able [ˌʌnɡet'ætəbl] ADJ *(inf)* unerreichbar; **he/the cottage is ~** man kommt an ihn/das Haus einfach nicht ran *(inf)*

ungifted [ʌn'ɡɪftɪd] ADJ unbegabt

ungird [ʌn'ɡɜːd] VT *sword* ablegen; *loins* entgürten

unglazed [ʌn'ɡleɪzd] ADJ *window* unverglast; *pottery* unglasiert; *photograph* nicht satiniert

ungodliness [ʌn'ɡɒdlɪnɪs] N Gottlosigkeit *f*

ungodly [ʌn'ɡɒdlɪ] **ADJ** gottlos; *(inf) noise, hour* unchristlich *(inf)*; **an ~ noise** ein Heidenlärm *m (inf)* **N the ~** *pl* die Gottlosen *pl*

ungovernable [ʌn'ɡʌvənəbl] ADJ **a** *desire, passion, rage* unbezähmbar; *temper* unbeherrscht **b** *country, people* unlenkbar, nicht zu regieren *pred*

ungraceful [ʌn'ɡreɪsfʊl] ADJ nicht anmutig; *movement, build* plump, ungelenk; *behaviour* unfein

ungracefully [ʌn'ɡreɪsfəlɪ] ADV plump; *behave* unfein; **to grow old ~** *(hum)* würdelos alt werden

ungracious [ʌn'ɡreɪʃəs] ADJ unhöflich; *(= gruff)* grunt, refusal schroff; *answer* rüde

ungraciously [ʌn'ɡreɪʃəslɪ] ADV *say* schroff; *react, respond* schroff, rüde

ungrammatical [ˌʌnɡrə'mætɪkəl] ADJ ungrammatisch, grammatikalisch falsch; **she does tend to be ~ at times** sie drückt sich manchmal grammatikalisch falsch aus

ungrammatically [ˌʌnɡrə'mætɪkəlɪ] ADV *speak, write* grammatisch falsch

ungrateful ADJ, **ungratefully** ADV [ʌn'ɡreɪtfʊl, -fəlɪ] undankbar *(to gegenüber)*

ungrounded [ʌn'ɡraʊndɪd] ADJ **a** *(= unfounded)* unfundiert; *accusations* grundlos, aus der Luft gegriffen; *fears* grundlos, unbegründet **b** *(US, Elec)* ungeerdet, ohne Erdung

ungrudging [ʌn'ɡrʌdʒɪŋ] ADJ *help, support* bereitwillig; *admiration* neidlos; *(= generous) person, contribution* großzügig; *praise, gratitude* von ganzem Herzen kommend *attr*

ungrudgingly [ʌn'ɡrʌdʒɪŋlɪ] ADV *help, support, consent, say* bereitwillig; *admire, praise* von ganzem Herzen; *give, contribute* großzügig

unguarded [ʌn'ɡɑːdɪd] ADJ **a** *(= undefended)* unbewacht **b** *(fig, = careless)* unvorsichtig, unachtsam; **to have ~ conversations** sich sorglos unterhalten; **in an ~ moment he ...** als er einen Augenblick nicht aufpasste *or* nicht vorsah, ... er ... **c** *(Tech, = unshielded) machine* ungeschützt, ohne Schutzvorrichtung

unguardedly ['ʌn'ɡɑːdɪdlɪ] ADV *(= carelessly)* unachtsam, unvorsichtig; **he spoke ~ about his job with the bank** er sprach unachtsam über seine Arbeit bei der Bank

unguent ['ʌŋɡwənt] N Salbe *f*, Unguentum *nt (spec)*

unguessable [ʌn'ɡesəbl] ADJ nicht erratbar

ungulate ['ʌŋɡjʊleɪt] **N** Huftier *nt*, Ungulat *m (spec)* **ADJ** *mammal* mit Hufen

unhair [ʌn'heə'] VT enthaaren

unhallowed [ʌn'hæləʊd] ADJ *ground* ungeweiht

unhampered [ʌn'hæmpəd] ADJ ungehindert; **~ by clothes** ohne hemmende Kleidung; **~ by regulations** ohne den Zwang von Bestimmungen

unhand [ʌn'hænd] VT *(old, hum)* freigeben, loslassen

unhandy [ʌn'hændɪ] ADJ unpraktisch

unhang [ʌn'hæŋ] VT *painting etc* ab- *or* herunternehmen

unhappily [ʌn'hæpɪlɪ] ADV *(= unfortunately)* leider, unglücklicherweise; *(= miserably)* unglücklich; **rather ~ expressed** ziemlich unglücklich ausgedrückt; **~ for you** bedauerlicherweise für Sie; **~ married** unglücklich verheiratet

unhappiness [ʌn'hæpɪnɪs] N Traurigkeit *f*; *(= discontent)* Unzufriedenheit *f (with* mit); **this is a source of much ~ to me** das macht mich ganz unglücklich

unhappy [ʌn'hæpɪ] ADJ (+er) **a** *(= sad)* unglücklich; *look, voice* traurig; *state of affairs* bedauerlich, traurig **b** *(= not pleased)* unzufrieden *(about* mit), nicht glücklich *(about* über *+acc)*; *(= uneasy)* unwohl; **to be ~ with sb/sth** mit jdm/etw unzufrieden sein; **to be ~ at work/school** unzufrieden mit der Arbeit/der Schule sein; **to be ~ about** *or* **at doing sth** nicht glücklich darüber sein, etw zu tun; **he was ~ about** *or* **at getting a decrease in his salary** er war nicht glücklich darüber, dass sein Gehalt gekürzt wurde; **if you feel ~ about it** wenn Sie darüber nicht glücklich sind; *(= worried)* wenn Ihnen dabei nicht wohl ist; **I feel ~ about letting him go** ich lasse ihn nur ungern gehen; **some were ~ to see him go** einige sahen ihn nur ungern gehen **c** *(= unfortunate) coincidence, day, match, phrasing* unglücklich; *person* glücklos; **an ~ choice/colour** *(Brit)* or **color** *(US)* **scheme** keine gute Wahl/Farbzusammenstellung

unharmed [ʌn'hɑːmd] ADJ *person* unverletzt; *thing* unbeschädigt; *reputation* ungeschädigt; *beauty* nicht beeinträchtigt; **to be ~ by sth** durch etw nicht gelitten haben

unharness [ʌn'hɑːnɪs] VT *horse* abschirren; *(from carriage)* abspannen; *(fig) energy* freisetzen

unhealthy [ʌn'helθɪ] ADJ **a** *person* nicht gesund; *climate, place, life, complexion* ungesund; *(inf) car* nicht in Ordnung; *(Econ, = weak) economy, company, finances* kränkelnd **b** *curiosity, interest* krankhaft; *influence, magazine* schädlich, schlecht; **it's an ~ relationship** das ist eine verderbliche Beziehung **c** *(inf: = dangerous)* ungesund *(inf)*, gefährlich

unheard [ʌn'hɜːd] ADJ *(fig) voice* unbeachtet; **to condemn sb ~** jdn verurteilen, ohne ihn angehört zu haben; **to go ~** *(lit)* ungehört bleiben; *(fig also)* unbeachtet bleiben

unheard-of [ʌn'hɜːdɒv] ADJ *(= unknown)* gänzlich unbekannt; *(= unprecedented)* einmalig, noch nicht da gewesen; *(= outrageous)* unerhört

unheeded [ʌn'hiːdɪd] ADJ unbeachtet; **to go ~** keine Beachtung finden, auf taube Ohren stoßen

unheedful [ʌnˈhiːdfʊl] ADJ ~ **of the danger** ohne von der Gefahr Notiz zu nehmen, ungeachtet der Gefahr (gen)

unheeding [ʌnˈhiːdɪŋ] ADJ (= not attending) unbekümmert; (= not caring also) gleichgültig, achtlos

unhelpful [ʌnˈhelpfʊl] ADJ person nicht hilfreich; advice, book nutzlos, wenig hilfreich; **that was very ~ of you** das war wirklich keine Hilfe; **you are being very ~** du bist aber wirklich keine Hilfe; **it is ~ to pretend the problem does not exist** es hilft nichts, so zu tun, als ob das Problem nicht existiert; **to be ~ to sb/sth** keine Hilfe für jdn/etw sein

unhelpfully [ʌnˈhelpfʊlɪ] ADV wenig hilfreich

unheralded [ʌnˈherəldəd] ADJ **a** (= unrecognized) unentdeckt **b** (= unexpected) unangekündigt

unhesitating [ʌnˈhezɪteɪtɪŋ] ADJ (= immediate) answer, offer prompt, unverzüglich; help also, generosity bereitwillig; (= steady) steps, progress stet; (= undoubting) answer fest; **he gave his ~ support** er half ohne zu zögern

unhesitatingly [ʌnˈhezɪteɪtɪŋlɪ] ADV ohne Zögern, ohne zu zögern; (= undoubtingly also) ohne zu zweifeln

unhindered [ʌnˈhɪndəd] ADJ (by clothes, luggage etc) unbehindert, nicht behindert; (by regulations) ungehindert, nicht gehindert; (by distraction) ungestört

unhinge [ʌnˈhɪndʒ] VT **to ~ sb/sb's mind** jdn aus der Bahn werfen, jdn völlig verstören; **he/ his mind was ~d** er hatte den Verstand verloren

unhip [ʌnˈhɪp] ADJ (inf) unmodern; **to be ~** nicht in sein (inf)

unhistorical [ʌnhɪsˈtɒrɪkəl] ADJ (= inaccurate) unhistorisch, ungeschichtlich; (= legendary) legendär

unhitch [ʌnˈhɪtʃ] VT horse (from post) losbinden; (from wagon) ausspannen; caravan, engine abkoppeln

unholy [ʌnˈhəʊlɪ] ADJ (+er) (Rel) place ungeweiht; spirits böse; (= evil, = sinful) activities übel; (inf) (= reprehensible) delight diebisch (inf); alliance übel; (= awful) mess heillos; noise, hour unchristlich (inf)

unhook [ʌnˈhʊk] **VT** latch, gate loshaken; dress aufhaken; (= take from hook) picture abhaken; (= free) losmachen; **the dress came ~ed** das Kleid ging auf **VI** sich aufhaken lassen

unhoped-for [ʌnˈhəʊptfɔːʳ] ADJ unverhofft

unhorse [ʌnˈhɔːs] VT rider abwerfen

unhurried [ʌnˈhʌrɪd] ADJ pace, person gelassen; steps, movement gemächlich; meal, journey, life gemütlich, geruhsam; **after a little ~ reflection I ...** nachdem ich mir das in Ruhe überlegt habe, ... ich ...; **we made our ~ way home** wir gingen gemächlich nach Hause

unhurriedly [ʌnˈhʌrɪdlɪ] ADV gemächlich, in aller Ruhe

unhurt [ʌnˈhɜːt] ADJ unverletzt

unhusk [ʌnˈhʌsk] VT beans enthülsen, schälen

unhygienic [ʌnhaɪˈdʒiːnɪk] ADJ unhygienisch

uni- [ˈjuːnɪ-] PREF ein-; **unicellular** einzellig

UNICEF [ˈjuːnɪsef] abbr of **United Nations International Children's Emergency Fund** UNICEF f, Weltkinderhilfswerk nt der UNO

unicolour, (US) **unicolor** [ˈjuːnɪˌkʌləʳ], **unicoloured**, (US) **unicolored** [-ˌkʌləd] ADJ einfarbig; clothes uni

unicorn [ˈjuːnɪˌkɔːn] N Einhorn nt

unicycle [ˈjuːnɪˌsaɪkl] N Einrad nt

unidentifiable [ˈʌnaɪˈdentɪˌfaɪəbl] ADJ object, smell, sound unidentifizierbar; body nicht identifizierbar; **all the bodies were ~** keine der Leichen konnte identifiziert werden

unidentified [ˈʌnaɪˈdentɪfaɪd] ADJ unbekannt; body nicht identifiziert; belongings herrenlos; ~ **flying object** unbekanntes Flugobjekt

unidiomatic [ˈʌnɪdɪəˈmætɪk] ADJ unidiomatisch

unification [ˌjuːnɪfɪˈkeɪʃən] N (of country) Einigung f; (of system) Vereinheitlichung f

uniform [ˈjuːnɪfɔːm] ADJ **a** (= unvarying) length, colour, tax einheitlich; treatment gleich, einheitlich; temperature, pace gleichmäßig, gleich bleibend; (= lacking variation) life gleichförmig, eintönig (pej); thinking gleichartig, gleichförmig, uniform (pej); scenery einförmig, eintönig (pej); **these houses are so ~** die Häuser gleichen sich alle so; ~ **in shape/size** von gleicher Form/ Größe **b** (Mil, Sch etc) Uniform-; ~ **jacket** Uniformjacke f **N** Uniform f; (fig: inf) uniformierter Polizist, uniformierte Polizistin; **in ~** in Uniform; **in full ~** in voller Uniform; **out of ~** in Zivil, ohne Uniform

uniformed [ˈjuːnɪfɔːmd] ADJ uniformiert; person also in Uniform

uniformity [ˌjuːnɪˈfɔːmɪtɪ] N (of length, colour, tax) Einheitlichkeit f; (of treatment also) Gleichheit f; (of temperature, pace) Gleichmäßigkeit f; (of life) Gleichförmigkeit f, Eintönigkeit f (pej); (of thinking) Gleichartigkeit f, Uniformität f (pej); (of scenery) Einförmigkeit f, Eintönigkeit f

uniformly [ˈjuːnɪfɔːmlɪ] ADV measure, paint, tax einheitlich; heat gleichmäßig; treat gleich; (pej) einförmig (pej); think uniform (pej)

uniform resource locator N (Comput) URL-Adresse f

unify [ˈjuːnɪfaɪ] VT einigen, einen (geh); theories, systems vereinheitlichen

unifying [ˈjuːnɪfaɪɪŋ] ADJ factor, force, purpose verbindend; **the struggle had a ~ effect on all blacks** der Kampf hatte eine einigende Wirkung auf alle Schwarzen

unilateral [ˌjuːnɪˈlætərəl] ADJ (Jur) einseitig; (Pol also) unilateral; ~ **declaration of independence** einseitige Unabhängigkeitserklärung; **to take ~ action against sb** einseitig gegen jdn vorgehen; ~ **(nuclear) disarmament** einseitige or unilaterale (atomare) Abrüstung

unilateralism [ˌjuːnɪˈlætərəlɪzəm] N einseitige Abrüstung

unilateralist [ˌjuːnɪˈlætərəlɪst] **N** Befürworter(in) m(f) einseitiger Abrüstung **ADJ** policies etc auf einseitige Abrüstung ausgerichtet

unilaterally [ˌjuːnɪˈlætərəlɪ] ADV einseitig; (Pol also) unilateral

unilingual ADJ

unilingually ADV [ˌjuːnɪˈlɪŋgwəl, -ɪ] einsprachig

unimaginable [ˌʌnɪˈmædʒɪnəbl] ADJ unvorstellbar; **this is ~ to me** das ist für mich unvorstellbar, das kann ich mir nicht vorstellen; **thrillers are ~ without violence** Thriller ohne Gewalt sind unvorstellbar or undenkbar

unimaginative [ˌʌnɪˈmædʒɪnətɪv] ADJ fantasielos, phantasielos, einfallslos; remark, book geistlos, fantasielos

unimaginatively [ˌʌnɪˈmædʒɪnətɪvlɪ] ADV fantasielos, phantasielos, einfallslos

unimpaired [ˌʌnɪmˈpeəd] ADJ quality, prestige, relationship unbeeinträchtigt; health unvermindert; eyesight, mental powers unbeeinträchtigt, unvermindert; faith, belief unerschüttert; **to be ~** nicht gelitten haben

unimpassioned [ˌʌnɪmˈpæʃənd] ADJ leidenschaftslos

unimpeachable [ˌʌnɪmˈpiːtʃəbl] ADJ reputation, conduct, character untadelig; proof, honesty, integrity unanfechtbar; source absolut zuverlässig; person über jeden Zweifel erhaben

unimpeded [ˌʌnɪmˈpiːdɪd] ADJ ungehindert

unimportant [ˌʌnɪmˈpɔːtənt] ADJ unwichtig, unbedeutend; detail also unwesentlich

unimposing [ˌʌnɪmˈpəʊzɪŋ] ADJ unscheinbar; building also wenig imponierend or beeindruckend

unimpressed [ˌʌnɪmˈprest] ADJ unbeeindruckt, nicht beeindruckt; **I was ~ by him/his story** er/ seine Geschichte hat mich überhaupt nicht beeindruckt; **I remain ~** das beeindruckt mich überhaupt nicht

unimpressive [ˌʌnɪmˈpresɪv] ADJ wenig beeindruckend; person also unscheinbar; argument, performance also, speaker wenig überzeugend

unimproved [ˌʌnɪmˈpruːvd] ADJ **a** (noch) nicht besser, unverändert schlecht; method nicht verbessert; **to leave sth ~** etw nicht verbessern **b** land unbebaut, nicht kultiviert; house nicht modernisiert or saniert

uninfluenced [ʌnˈɪnflʊənst] ADJ unbeeinflusst

uninfluential [ˌʌnɪnflʊˈenʃəl] ADJ ohne Einfluss

uninformative [ˌʌnɪnˈfɔːmətɪv] ADJ person wenig mitteilsam; document ohne Informationsgehalt

uninformed [ˌʌnɪnˈfɔːmd] ADJ (= not knowing) nicht informiert or unterrichtet (about über +acc); (= ignorant also) unwissend; criticism blindwütig; comment, rumour unfundiert; **the ~ observer** der uninformierte Beobachter; **to be ~ about sth** über etw (acc) nicht Bescheid wissen; **to keep sb ~** jdn im Dunkeln lassen **the ~** pl die schlecht Informierten pl

uninhabitable [ˌʌnɪnˈhæbɪtəbl] ADJ unbewohnbar

uninhabited [ˌʌnɪnˈhæbɪtɪd] ADJ unbewohnt

uninhibited [ˌʌnɪnˈhɪbɪtɪd] ADJ person frei von Hemmungen, ohne Hemmungen; greed, laughter hemmungslos, ungezügelt; **to be ~** keine Hemmungen haben; **to be ~ by sth** sich von etw nicht einschüchtern lassen; **to be ~ in or about doing sth** keine Hemmungen haben, etw zu tun

uninitiated [ˌʌnɪˈnɪʃɪeɪtɪd] **ADJ** nicht eingeweiht; ~ **listeners/viewers** Hörer/Zuschauer, die die näheren Zusammenhänge nicht kennen or die nicht Bescheid wissen **N the ~** pl Nichteingeweihte pl; **for the ~ that may seem strange** Nichteingeweihten mag das merkwürdig vorkommen

uninjured [ʌnˈɪndʒəd] ADJ person unverletzt; arm etc also heil

uninspired [ˌʌnɪnˈspaɪəd] ADJ teacher, performance fantasielos, phantasielos, ideenlos, einfallslos; lecture, book einfallslos; food fantasielos, phantasielos, einfallslos; **to be ~ by a subject** von einem Thema nicht begeistert werden

uninspiring [ˌʌnɪnˈspaɪərɪŋ] ADJ trocken; suggestion, idea nicht gerade aufregend

uninstall [ˌʌnɪnˈstɔːl] VT (Comput) deinstallieren

uninsured [ˌʌnɪnˈʃʊəd] ADJ nicht versichert

unintelligent [ˌʌnɪnˈtelɪdʒənt] ADJ unintelligent; approach, action unklug, ungeschickt; **not ~** eigentlich ganz intelligent

unintelligibility [ˌʌnɪnˌtelɪdʒɪˈbɪlɪtɪ] N Unverständlichkeit f

unintelligible [ˌʌnɪnˈtelɪdʒɪbl] ADJ person nicht zu verstehen; speech, writing unverständlich; (TV) image, picture nicht erkennbar; **this makes him ~** das macht es fast unmöglich, ihn zu verstehen

unintelligibly [ˌʌnɪnˈtelɪdʒɪblɪ] ADV unverständlich

unintended [ˌʌnɪnˈtendɪd], **unintentional** [ˌʌnɪnˈtenʃənl] ADJ unbeabsichtigt, unabsichtlich; joke also unfreiwillig

unintentionally [ˌʌnɪnˈtenʃnəlɪ] ADV unabsichtlich, unbeabsichtigt, ohne Absicht; funny unfreiwillig; **intentionally or ~** absichtlich oder unabsichtlich

uninterested [ʌnˈɪntrɪstɪd] ADJ desinteressiert, interesselos; **to be ~ in sth** an etw (dat) nicht interessiert sein

uninteresting [ʌnˈɪntrɪstɪŋ] ADJ uninteressant

uninterrupted [ˌʌnɪntəˈrʌptɪd] ADJ (= continuous) line ununterbrochen, kontinuierlich; noise, rain also anhaltend; (= undisturbed) rest, view ungestört; **to have an ~ view of sth** eine ungestörte Aussicht auf etw (acc) haben; **to continue ~** ungestört fortfahren; ~ **by advertisements** nicht durch Werbung unterbrochen

uninterruptedly [ˌʌnɪntəˈrʌptɪdlɪ] ADV speak, sleep, rule ununterbrochen; flow kontinuierlich

uninvited [ˌʌnɪnˈvaɪtɪd] ADJ guest ungeladen, ungebeten; criticism unerwünscht, ungebeten;

question, sexual advances unwillkommen, unerwünscht; **to arrive ~** unaufgefordert *or* uneingeladen eintreffen; **to do sth ~** etw ungebeten *or* unaufgefordert tun

uninviting [ˌʌnɪnˈvaɪtɪŋ] ADJ *appearance, atmosphere* nicht (gerade) einladend; *prospect* nicht (gerade) verlockend; *smell, food, sight* unappetitlich; **rather ~** wenig einladend/wenig verlockend/ziemlich unappetitlich

union [ˈjuːnjən] **N** **a** Vereinigung *f*, Verbindung *f*; (*Pol*) Union *f*, Vereinigung *f*; **the Union** (*US*) die Vereinigten Staaten; (*in civil war*) die Unionsstaaten *pl*; **State of the Union Address** (*US*) ≈ Bericht *m* zur Lage der Nation **b** (= *trade union*) Gewerkschaft *f* **c** (= *association*) Vereinigung *f*; (= *customs union*) Union *f*; (= *postal union*) Postverein *m*; (= *students' union*) Studentenklub *m* **d** (= *harmony*) Eintracht *f*, Harmonie *f* **e** (*form,* = *marriage*) Verbindung *f* **f** (*Tech*) Verbindung *f*; **~ joint** Anschlussstück *nt*, Verbindungsstück *nt* **g** (*Math*) Vereinigung(smenge) *f* **ADJ** *attr* (= *trade union*) Gewerkschafts-; **~ card** Gewerkschaftsausweis *m*

union bashing N (*inf*) Angriffe *pl* auf die Gewerkschaften, Herumhacken *nt* auf den Gewerkschaften

union dues PL Gewerkschaftsbeitrag *m*

unionism [ˈjuːnjənɪzəm] N **a** (= *trade unionism*) Gewerkschaftswesen *nt* **b** (*Pol*) Einigungsbewegung *f*; **Unionism** (*Brit*) Unionismus *m*, unionistische Bewegung

unionist [ˈjuːnjənɪst] **N** **a** (= *trade unionist*) Gewerkschaftler(in) *m(f)* **b** (*Pol*) Unionist(in) *m(f)*; **Ulster Unionist** Ulster Unionist *m* **ADJ** **a** (= *trade unionist*) gewerkschaftlich **b** (*Pol*) unionistisch

unionization [ˌjuːnjənaɪˈzeɪʃən] N (gewerkschaftliche) Organisierung

unionize [ˈjuːnjənaɪz] **VT** gewerkschaftlich organisieren **VI** sich gewerkschaftlich organisieren

union: Union Jack N Union Jack *m*; **Union of Soviet Socialist Republics** (*Hist*) Union *f* der Sozialistischen Sowjetrepubliken; **union rates** PL (= *wages*) Tariflohn *m*; (= *salary*) Tarifgehalt *nt*; **union shop** N gewerkschaftspflichtiger Betrieb; **union suit** N (*US*) lange Hemdhose

unique [juːˈniːk] ADJ einzig *attr*; (= *outstanding*) einzigartig, einmalig (*inf*); (*Math*) eindeutig; **you are not ~ in that** da bist du nicht der/die Einzige; **such cases are not ~ to Britain** solche Fälle sind nicht nur auf Großbritannien beschränkt; **~ among ...** einzigartig unter ... (*dat*); **~ selling point** einzigartiger Verkaufsreiz

uniquely [juːˈniːklɪ] ADV (= *solely*) einzig und allein, nur; (= *outstandingly*) einmalig (*inf*), unübertrefflich; **~ suited** außergewöhnlich geeignet; **Mary is ~ qualified for the job** Mary hat einzigartige *or* außergewöhnliche Qualifikationen für die Stellung; **~ among ...** einzigartig unter ... (+*dat*)

uniqueness [juːˈniːknɪs] N Einmaligkeit *f*, Einzigartigkeit *f*

unisex [ˈjuːnɪseks] ADJ für Männer und Frauen; (*Fashion also*) Unisex-; **~ clothing** Unisexkleidung *f*; **~ salon** Unisexsalon *m*, Salon *m* für Damen und Herren

unisexual ADJ

unisexually ADV [ˌjuːnɪˈseksjʊəl, -lɪ] eingeschlechtig; (*Bot, Zool also*) getrenntgeschlechtig

unison [ˈjuːnɪzn] N (*Mus*) Gleichklang *m*, Einklang *m* (*also fig*); **in ~** unisono (*geh*), einstimmig; **~ singing** einstimmiger Gesang; **to be in ~ (with sth)** übereinstimmen (mit etw); **to act in ~ with sb** (*fig*) in Übereinstimmung mit jdm handeln

unisonous ADJ

unisonously ADV [juːˈnɪsənəs, -lɪ] **a** (*Mus*) unisono **b** (*fig*) übereinstimmend

unit [ˈjuːnɪt] N **a** (= *entity, Mil*) Einheit *f*; (= *set of equipment*) Anlage *f*, Einheit *f*; **camera ~** Kameraeinheit *f*; **X-ray ~** Röntgenanlage *f* **b** (= *section*) Einheit *f*; (*of furniture*) Element *nt*; (*of machine*) Element *nt*, Teil *nt*; (*of organization*) Abteilung *f*; (*of course book*) Lektion *f*; **power ~** Aggregat *nt*; (*of a rocket*) Triebwerk *nt*; **where did you get those ~s in your bedroom?** wo haben Sie die Anbauelemente in Ihrem Schlafzimmer her?; **the new research ~** die neue Forschungsabteilung *or* -gruppe; **the family as the basic ~** die Familie als Grundelement **c** (= *measure*) Einheit *f*; **~ of account/length** Rechnungs-/Längeneinheit *f* **d** (*Math*) Einer *m*; **tens and ~s** Zehner und Einer *pl*

Unitarian [ˌjuːnɪˈtɛərɪən] **ADJ** unitarisch **N** Unitarier(in) *m(f)*

Unitarianism [ˌjuːnɪˈtɛərɪənɪzəm] N Unitarismus *m*

unitary [ˈjuːnɪtərɪ] ADJ (= *unified*) einheitlich; (*Pol*) *state, system* unitarisch, zentralistisch; **~ tax** einheitlicher Steuersatz

unit cost N (*Fin*) Stückkosten *pl*

unite [juːˈnaɪt] **VT** (= *join, also form:* = *marry*) vereinigen, verbinden; *party, country* (*treaty etc*) (ver)einigen, zusammenschließen; (*emotions, ties, loyalties*) (ver)einen; **the common interests which ~ us** die gemeinsamen Interessen, die uns verbinden **VI** sich zusammenschließen, sich vereinigen; **to ~ in doing sth** gemeinsam etw tun; **to ~ in grief/opposition to sth** gemeinsam trauern/gegen etw Opposition machen; **workers of the world, ~!** Proletarier aller Länder, vereinigt euch!

united [juːˈnaɪtɪd] ADJ verbunden; *group, nation, front* geschlossen; (= *unified*) *people, nation* einig; *efforts* vereint; **~ we stand, divided we fall** (*prov*) Einigkeit macht stark (*Prov*); **a ~ Ireland** ein vereintes *or* vereinigtes Irland; **to be ~ in the** *or* **one's belief that ...** einig sein in seiner Überzeugung, dass ...; **to be ~ in opposing sth** etw vereint ablehnen; **to be ~ by a common interest** durch ein gemeinsames Interesse verbunden sein; **to form/maintain/present a ~ front** eine geschlossene Front bilden/aufrechterhalten/bieten

United: United Arab Emirates PL Vereinigte Arabische Emirate *pl*; **United Arab Republic** N Vereinigte Arabische Republik; **United Kingdom** N Vereinigtes Königreich (*Großbritannien und Nordirland*); **United Nations (Organization)** N Vereinte Nationen *pl*; **United Service Organization** N Hilfsorganisation für die US-Armee, besonders für im Ausland stationierte Truppen; **United States (of America)** PL Vereinigte Staaten *pl* (von Amerika)

unit: unit furniture N Anbaumöbel *pl*; **unit-linked** ADJ (*Insur*) fondsgebunden; **unit price** N (= *price per unit*) Preis *m* pro Einheit; (= *inclusive price*) Pauschalpreis *m*; **unit trust** N (*Brit Fin*) Unit Trust *m*, Investmentgesellschaft *f*; (= *share*) Unit-Trust-Papiere *pl*, Investmentpapiere *pl*

unity [ˈjuːnɪtɪ] N **a** (= *oneness, Liter*) Einheit *f*; (= *harmony*) Einmütigkeit *f*, Einigkeit *f*; (*of a novel, painting etc*) Einheitlichkeit *f*, Geschlossenheit *f*; **national ~** (nationale) Einheit *f*; **this ~ of purpose** diese gemeinsamen Ziele; **to live in ~** in Eintracht leben; **~ is strength** Einigkeit macht stark (*Prov*) **b** (*Math*) Einheit *f*; (= *one*) Eins *f*; (*in set theory*) neutrales Element

Univ abbr of **University** Univ.

univalent [ˌjuːnɪˈveɪlənt] ADJ einwertig

univalve [ˈjuːnɪvælv] **N** Gastropod *m* **ADJ** einschalig

universal [ˌjuːnɪˈvɜːsəl] **ADJ** **a** *phenomenon, applicability, remedy* universal, universell; (= *prevailing everywhere*) *custom, game* allgemein *or* überall verbreitet; (= *applying to all*) *truth, rule* allgemein gültig, universell; (= *general*) *approval, peace* allgemein; **~ education** Allgemeinbildung *f*; **~ language** Weltsprache *f*; **~ peace** Weltfrieden *m*; **~**

remedy Allheilmittel *nt*; **to be a ~ favourite** überall beliebt sein; **to become ~** allgemein verbreitet werden **b** (*Logic*) universal, universell, allgemein **N** (*Philos*) Allgemeinbegriff *m*; (*Logic*: = *universal proposition*) Universalaussage *f*; **the ~** das Allgemeine; **the various ~s of human experience** die verschiedenen Grundelemente menschlicher Erfahrung

universal: universal coupling N = **universal joint**; **universal donor** N Universalspender(in) *m(f)*

universality [ˌjuːnɪvɜːˈsælɪtɪ] N Universalität *f*; (*of person also*) Vielseitigkeit *f*; (= *prevalence also*) allgemeine Verbreitung *f*; (= *general applicability*) Allgemeingültigkeit *f*

universal joint N Universalgelenk *nt*

universally [ˌjuːnɪˈvɜːsəlɪ] ADV allgemein; **~ applicable** allgemein gültig; **he was ~ liked** er erfreute sich allgemeiner Beliebtheit; **tips are now almost ~ included in hotel bills** Trinkgelder sind heutzutage fast immer in Hotelrechnungen inbegriffen

universal: Universal Postal Union N Weltpostverein *m*; **universal product code** N (*US*, = *bar code*) Barkode *m*; **universal suffrage** N allgemeines Wahlrecht; **universal time** N Weltzeit *f*

universe [ˈjuːnɪvɜːs] **N** **a** (= *cosmos*) (Welt)all *nt*, Universum *nt*; (= *galaxy*) Sternsystem *nt*; (= *world*) Welt *f*; **he's the funniest writer in the ~** (*inf*) er schreibt die komischsten Sachen überhaupt **b** (*Logic*) **~ of discourse** Gesamtheit *f* aller Gegenstände der Abhandlung

Universities and Colleges Admissions Service N (*Brit*) ≈ Zentralstelle *f* für die Vergabe von Studienplätzen

university [ˌjuːnɪˈvɜːsɪtɪ] **N** Universität *f*; **the ~ of life** die Schule des Lebens; **which ~ does he go to?** wo studiert er?; **to be at/go to ~** studieren; **to be at/go to London University** in London studieren **ADJ** *attr* Universitäts-; *qualifications, education* akademisch; **~ library** Universitätsbibliothek *f*; **~ teacher** Hochschullehrer(in) *m(f)*

university: university entrance (examination) N Zulassungsprüfung *f or* Aufnahmeprüfung *f* zum Studium; **university hospital** N Universitätsklinik *f*; **university man** N Akademiker *m*; **university town** N Universitätsstadt *f*

unjaundiced [ʌnˈdʒɔːndɪst] ADJ (*geh*) unvoreingenommen

unjust [ʌnˈdʒʌst] ADJ ungerecht (*to* gegen); **you're being ~** das ist ungerecht

unjustifiable [ʌnˈdʒʌstɪfaɪəbl] ADJ nicht zu rechtfertigend *attr*, nicht zu rechtfertigen *pred*; **it was ~ of them not to ...** es war ihrerseits nicht zu rechtfertigen, nicht zu ...

unjustifiably [ʌnˈdʒʌstɪfaɪəblɪ] ADV *expensive, severe, critical* ungerechtfertigt; *rude* unnötig; *criticize, dismiss, praise zu* Unrecht; *act* ungerechtfertigt; **they have been ~ wronged by the media** sie sind von den Medien zu Unrecht angegriffen worden

unjustified [ʌnˈdʒʌstɪfaɪd] ADJ **a** ungerechtfertigt **b** *text* nicht bündig; **to set sth ~** etw im Flattersatz setzen

unjustly [ʌnˈdʒʌstlɪ] ADV zu Unrecht; *judge, treat* ungerecht

unjustness [ʌnˈdʒʌstnɪs] N Ungerechtigkeit *f*

unkempt [ʌnˈkempt] ADJ *hair* ungekämmt; *appearance, garden etc* ungepflegt, vernachlässigt; *person, beard* ungepflegt

unkind [ʌnˈkaɪnd] ADJ (+*er*) **a** *person, remark, action* (= *not nice*) unfreundlich, nicht nett; (= *cruel*) lieblos, gemein; (= *harsh*) *climate, country, action* schlecht (*to* für); **don't be (so) ~!** das ist aber gar nicht nett (von dir)!; **she was ~ enough to say that...** sie hatte die Unfreundlichkeit zu sagen, dass ...; **she never has an ~ word to say about anyone** von ihr ist niemals ein unfreundliches *or* böses Wort über irgendjemanden zu hören; **to be ~ to animals** nicht gut zu Tieren sein; **~ to the skin** nicht hautfreundlich; **fate has been very ~ to him** das Schicksal hat ihn grausam behandelt; **the weather was ~ to us** das Wetter war uns nicht wohl gesonnen; **it would be ~ not to tell him the truth** es wäre gemein, ihm nicht die Wahrheit zu sagen **b** (*Sport*) *bounce* unglücklich

unkindly [ʌnˈkaɪndlɪ] ADV unfreundlich, nicht nett; (= *cruelly*) lieblos, gemein; **how ~ fate had treated her** wie grausam das Schicksal ihr mitgespielt hatte; **don't take it ~ if ...** nimm es nicht übel, wenn ...; **to take ~ to sth** etw übel nehmen

unkindness [ʌnˈkaɪndnɪs] N Unfreundlichkeit *f*; (= *cruelty*) Lieblosigkeit *f*, Gemeinheit *f*; **the ~ of the weather** das schlechte Wetter

unknot [ʌnˈnɒt] VT aufknoten, entknoten

unknowable [ʌnˈnəʊəbl] ADJ *truths* unbegreiflich, unfassbar; *person* verschlossen N **the Unknowable** das Unfassbare

unknowing [ʌnˈnəʊɪŋ] ADJ *agent* unbewusst, ohne es zu wissen; **he was the ~ cause of ...** er war unwissentlich *or* ohne es zu wissen die Ursache für ...

unknowingly [ʌnˈnəʊɪŋlɪ] ADV unwissentlich, ohne es zu wissen; **knowingly or ~** wissentlich oder unwissentlich

unknown [ʌnˈnəʊn] ADJ unbekannt; **the ~ soldier** *or* **warrior** der Unbekannte Soldat; **~ territory** (*lit, fig*) Neuland *nt*; **some ~ person** irgendein Unbekannter; **to be ~ to sb** (*feeling, territory*) jdm fremd sein; **it's ~ for him to get up for breakfast** man ist es von ihm gar nicht gewohnt, dass er zum Frühstück aufsteht; **this substance is ~ to science** diese Substanz ist der Wissenschaft nicht bekannt → **person** N (= *person*) Unbekannte(r) *mf*; (= *factor, Math*) Unbekannte *f*; (= *territory*) unerforschtes Gebiet, Neuland *nt*; **the ~** das Unbekannte; **a journey into the ~** (*lit, fig*) eine Fahrt ins Ungewisse ADV **~ to me** *etc* ohne dass *ich etc* es wusste; **~ to me, the contents of my suitcase were inspected** ohne mein Wissen *or* ohne dass ich davon wusste, wurde der Inhalt meines Koffers untersucht

unknown quantity N (= *person*) unbekannte Größe; (*Math*) Unbekannte *f*

unlabelled, (*US*) **unlabeled** [ʌnˈleɪbld] ADJ nicht etikettiert, ohne Etikett *or* Aufschrift, unbeschriftet

unlace [ʌnˈleɪs] VT aufbinden, aufschnüren

unladylike [ʌnˈleɪdɪlaɪk] ADJ undamenhaft, nicht damenhaft

unlamented [ˌʌnləˈmentɪd] ADJ *death, loss* unbeklagt, unbeweint; **he died ~** niemand trauerte um ihn

unlatch [ʌnˈlætʃ] VT entriegeln

unlawful [ʌnˈlɔːfʊl] ADJ gesetzwidrig; *means, sex, imprisonment, act* ungesetzlich, illegal; *wedding* ungültig

unlawful: unlawful assembly N (*Jur*) verbotene *or* illegale Versammlung; **unlawful entry** N (*Jur*) Einbruch *m*; **unlawful killing** N (*Jur*: = *offence*) Tötungsdelikt *nt*

unlawfully [ʌnˈlɔːfəlɪ] ADV gesetzwidrig, illegal; *married* ungültig; *imprison* ungesetzlich

unleaded [ʌnˈledɪd] ADJ *petrol* unverbleit, bleifrei N unverbleites *or* bleifreies Benzin; **I use ~** ich fahre bleifrei

unlearn [ʌnˈlɜːn] VT sich (*dat*) abgewöhnen; *habit also* ablegen

unleash [ʌnˈliːʃ] VT *dog* von der Leine lassen; (*fig, = cause*) *anger, war* entfesseln, auslösen; **to ~ a storm of criticism** einen Sturm der Kritik entfesseln; **he ~ed his fury on his wife** er ließ seine Frau seinen Zorn spüren; **to ~ a war upon the whole world** die ganze Welt in einen Krieg stürzen

unleavened [ʌnˈlevnd] ADJ *bread* ungesäuert

unless [ənˈles] CONJ es sei denn; (*at beginning of sentence*) wenn ... nicht, sofern ... nicht; **don't**

do it ~ I tell you to mach das nicht, es sei denn, ich sage es dir; **~ I tell you to, don't do it** sofern *or* wenn ich es dir nicht sage, mach das nicht; **~ I am mistaken ...** wenn *or* falls ich mich nicht irre ...; **~ otherwise stated** sofern nicht anders angezeigt *or* angegeben; **~ there is an interruption** vorausgesetzt, alles läuft ohne Unterbrechung

unlettered [ʌnˈletəd] ADJ ungebildet; (= *illiterate*) analphabetisch *attr*

unliberated [ʌnˈlɪbəreɪtɪd] ADJ *women* unemanzipiert, nicht emanzipiert; *masses, countries* nicht befreit

unlicensed [ʌnˈlaɪsənst] ADJ (= *having no licence*) *car, dog, TV* nicht angemeldet; *premises* ohne Lizenz *or* (Schank)konzession; *software* nicht lizenziert; (= *unauthorized*) unbefugt, unberechtigt; **people with ~ TV sets** Schwarzseher *pl*

unlike [ʌnˈlaɪk] ADJ unähnlich, nicht ähnlich; *poles* ungleich, gegensätzlich PREP **a** im Gegensatz zu, anders als **b** (= *uncharacteristic of*) **to be quite ~ sb** jdm (gar) nicht ähnlich sehen; (*behaviour also*) überhaupt nicht zu jdm passen; **how ~ him not to have told us** das sieht ihm gar nicht ähnlich, dass er uns nichts gesagt hat **c** (= *not resembling*) **this photograph is quite ~ her** dieses Foto sieht ihr gar nicht ähnlich; **this house is ~ their former one** dieses Haus ist ganz anders als ihr früheres

unlikeable [ʌnˈlaɪkəbl] ADJ unsympathisch

unlikelihood [ʌnˈlaɪklɪhʊd], **unlikeliness** [ʌnˈlaɪklɪnɪs] N Unwahrscheinlichkeit *f*; **despite the ~ of success** obwohl der Erfolg unwahrscheinlich war

unlikely [ʌnˈlaɪklɪ] ✪ 16.2 ADJ (+*er*) unwahrscheinlich; *explanation also* unglaubwürdig; (= *odd also*) *clothes* merkwürdig, komisch; *friendship* merkwürdig; *candidate* unpassend; **it is (most) ~/not ~ that ...** es ist (höchst) unwahrscheinlich/es kann durchaus sein, dass ...; **she is ~ to come** sie kommt höchstwahrscheinlich nicht; **it looks an ~ place for mushrooms** es sieht mir nicht nach der geeigneten Stelle für Pilze aus; **they are such an ~ couple** sie sind ein so merkwürdiges Paar; **he's an ~ choice** seine Wahl ist sehr unwahrscheinlich; **he's ~ to be chosen** es ist unwahrscheinlich, dass er gewählt wird; **in the ~ event that ...** im unwahrscheinlichen Fall, dass ...; **in the ~ event of war** im unwahrscheinlichen Fall eines Krieges

unlimited [ʌnˈlɪmɪtɪd] ADJ *wealth, time* unbegrenzt; *power also* schrankenlos; *patience* unendlich; *access, use* uneingeschränkt

unlimited company N (*Fin*) Gesellschaft *f* mit unbeschränkter Haftung

unlimited liability N (*Comm, Jur*) unbeschränkte Haftung

unlined [ʌnˈlaɪnd] ADJ *paper* unliniert; *face* faltenlos; (= *without lining*) *dress* ungefüttert

unlisted [ʌnˈlɪstɪd] ✪ 27.1 ADJ *company, items* nicht verzeichnet; *name* nicht aufgeführt; *bonds, stock* nicht notiert; **the number is ~** (*US Telec*) die Nummer steht nicht im Telefonbuch

unlisted securities market N Freiverkehr *m*

unlit [ʌnˈlɪt] ADJ *road* unbeleuchtet; *lamp* nicht angezündet; *fire, cigarette* unangezündet

unload [ʌnˈləʊd] VT **a** *ship, gun* entladen; *boot, luggage* ausladen; *car* entladen, ausladen; *cargo* löschen; *passengers* absetzen; *bomb* abwerfen **b** (*inf, = get rid of*) (*Fin*) *shares* abstoßen; *furniture, children, problem* abladen (*on(to)* bei); *job, problem* abwälzen (*on(to)* auf +*acc*) VI (*ship*) löschen; (*truck*) abladen

unlock [ʌnˈlɒk] VT *door etc* aufschließen; (*fig*) *heart, secret* offenbaren; **the door is ~ed** die Tür ist nicht abgeschlossen; **to leave a door ~ed** eine Tür nicht abschließen

unlooked-for [ʌnˈlʊktfɔː] ADJ unerwartet, unvorhergesehen; *welcome also* unverhofft

unloose [ʌnˈluːs] VT **a** (*also* **unloosen**) *knot, grasp, hair* lösen; *rope, chains* lösen, losmachen **b** *prisoner* losbinden; *dog* losmachen, loslassen

unlovable [ʌnˈlʌvəbl] ADJ wenig liebenswert *or* liebenswürdig, unsympathisch

unloved [ʌnˈlʌvd] ADJ ungeliebt

unlovely [ʌnˈlʌvlɪ] ADJ *sight* unschön; *person* (*in appearance*) abstoßend; (*in character*) garstig, unliebenswert

unloving [ʌnˈlʌvɪŋ] ADJ *person, home* lieblos, kalt

unluckily [ʌnˈlʌkɪlɪ] ADV zum Pech, zum Unglück; **~ for him** zu seinem Pech

unlucky [ʌnˈlʌkɪ] ADJ (+*er*) **a** *person* unglückselig; *defeat, loser, victim* unglücklich; **~ wretch** Unglücksrabe *m*, Pechvogel *m*; **he's always ~** er ist vom Pech verfolgt; **to be ~** Pech haben; (= *not succeed*) keinen Erfolg haben; **~ in love** unglücklich verliebt; **it was ~ for her that she was seen** Pech für sie, dass man sie gesehen hat; **how ~ for you!** was für ein Pech!, das ist wirklich dumm (für dich)!; **he was ~ enough to meet her** er hatte das Pech, sie zu treffen; **Smith was ~ not to score a second goal** Smith hatte Pech gehabt, dass er kein zweites Tor schoss **b** *object, action, place* unglückselig; *coincidence, event, choice* unglücklich; *moment* ungünstig, schlecht gewählt; **~ day** Unglückstag *m*; **to be ~** Unglück *or* Pech bringen; **London has been an ~ place for me** London hat mir nur Pech gebracht; **broken mirrors are ~** zerbrochene Spiegel bringen Unglück; **~ number** Unglückszahl *f*; **number 13:** ~ **or some** Nummer 13: für manche bedeutet das Unglück; **it's not through any fault of yours, it's just ~** es ist nicht dein Fehler, es ist nur Pech

unmade [ʌnˈmeɪd] ADJ *bed* ungemacht

unmade-up [ˌʌnmeɪdˈʌp] ADJ *face* ungeschminkt, ohne Make-up; *road* ungeteert

unmailable [ʌnˈmeɪləbl] ADJ (*esp US*) nicht postversandfähig

unman [ʌnˈmæn] VT schwach werden lassen; (= *make lose courage*) entmutigen, verzagen lassen

unmanageable [ʌnˈmænɪdʒəbl] ADJ (= *unwieldy*) *vehicle, boat* schwer zu handhaben *or* manövrieren; *parcel, size* unhandlich; *number* nicht zu bewältigen; *problem* unlösbar, (= *uncontrollable*) *animal, person, hair, child* widerspenstig, nicht zu bändigen; *situation* unkontrollierbar; **she finds the stairs ~** sie kann die Treppe nicht schaffen (*inf*) *or* bewältigen; **this company is ~** es ist unmöglich, dieses Unternehmen zu leiten; **the crowd had reached ~ proportions** die Menge hatte unkontrollierbare Ausmaße angenommen

unmanly [ʌnˈmænlɪ] ADJ *tears, behaviour* unmännlich; (= *cowardly*) feige; (= *effeminate*) weibisch

unmanned [ʌnˈmænd] ADJ (= *not requiring crew*) *lighthouse, aircraft, spacecraft, border post, level crossing* unbemannt; *vehicle* fahrerlos; (= *lacking crew*) *telephone exchange* unbesetzt, nicht besetzt

unmannerly [ʌnˈmænəlɪ] ADJ ungesittet; (*also* ungezogen; *behaviour* ungehörig; (*at table also*) unmanierlich; **it is ~ to ...** es gehört sich nicht, zu ...

unmarked [ʌnˈmɑːkt] ADJ **a** (= *unstained*) ohne Flecken *or* Spuren, fleckenlos; (= *without marking*) *face* ungezeichnet (*also fig*); *banknotes* unmarkiert; *linen* nicht gezeichnet; *boxes, crates, suitcases etc* ohne Namen *or* Adresse; *police car* nicht gekennzeichnet; (= *anonymous*) *grave* anonym; **luckily the carpet was ~ by the wine** glücklicherweise blieben keine Weinspuren auf dem Teppich zurück; **to leave sb ~** spurlos an jdm vorübergehen **b** (*Sport*) *player* ungedeckt **c** (*Sch*) *papers* unkorrigiert **d** (= *unnoticed*) unbemerkt **e** (*Ling*) unmarkiert

unmarketable [ʌnˈmɑːkɪtəbl] ADJ unverkäuflich, schlecht *or* nicht zu verkaufen

unmarriageable [ʌnˈmærɪdʒəbl] **ADJ** nicht zu verheiraten *pred*, nicht unter die Haube zu kriegen *pred* (*inf*)

unmarried [ʌnˈmærɪd] **ADJ** unverheiratet; ~ **mother** ledige Mutter

unmask [ʌnˈmɑːsk] **VT** (*lit*) demaskieren; (*fig*) entlarven **VI** die Maske abnehmen, sich demaskieren

unmasking [ʌnˈmɑːskɪŋ] **N** (*fig*) Entlarvung *f*

unmatched [ʌnˈmætʃt] **ADJ** unübertrefflich, einmalig, unübertroffen (*for* in Bezug auf +*acc*); ~ **by anyone** von niemandem übertroffen; **the scenery is ~ anywhere in the world** die Landschaft sucht (in der Welt) ihresgleichen; **to be ~ for beauty** alle anderen an Schönheit übertreffen

unmeasured **ADJ** , **unmeasuredly** **ADV** [ʌnˈmeʒəd, -lɪ] **a** *risk factors etc* nicht untersucht, unergründet **b** (*esp liter, poet*) unermesslich (*geh*), grenzenlos, unbegrenzt **c** (*fig*: = *unrestrained*) unmäßig, maßlos

unmechanical [ʌnmɪˈkænɪkəl] **ADJ** *person* technisch unbegabt

unmentionable [ʌnˈmenʃnəbl] **ADJ** tabu *pred*; *word also* unaussprechlich; **to be ~** tabu sein; **to be an ~ subject** (als Thema) tabu sein; **an ~ disease** eine Krankheit, über die man nicht spricht **PL** **the ~s** (*Brit hum dated*) die Unterwäsche *f*

unmerciful **ADJ** , **unmercifully** **ADV** [ʌnˈmɜːsɪfəl, -fəlɪ] unbarmherzig, erbarmungslos

unmerited [ʌnˈmerɪtɪd] **ADJ** unverdient

unmet [ʌnˈmet] **ADJ** *needs* unbefriedigt; *demands* unerfüllt; **to go ~** (*needs*) unbefriedigt bleiben; (*demands*) unerfüllt bleiben

unmetalled [ʌnˈmetld] **ADJ** (*Brit*) ungeteert

unmethodical [ʌnmɪˈθɒdɪkəl] **ADJ** unmethodisch

unmindful [ʌnˈmaɪndfʊl] **ADJ** **to be ~ of sth** nicht auf etw (*acc*) achten, etw nicht beachten; **I was not ~ of your needs** ich stand Ihren Bedürfnissen nicht gleichgültig gegenüber

unmingled [ʌnˈmɪŋgld] **ADJ** = **unmixed**

unmissable [ʌnˈmɪsəbl] **ADJ** (*Brit, inf*) **to be ~** ein Muss sein; **this ~ conference** diese Konferenz, die man sich nicht entgehen lassen sollte

unmistak(e)able [ʌnmɪˈsteɪkəbl] **ADJ** unverkennbar; (*visually*) nicht zu verwechseln; **to send an ~ message to sb** (*fig*) jdm eine unmissverständliche Botschaft senden

unmistak(e)ably [ʌnmɪˈsteɪkəblɪ] **ADV** zweifelsohne (*geh*), unverkennbar

unmitigated [ʌnˈmɪtɪgeɪtɪd] **ADJ** (= *not lessened*) *wrath, severity* ungemildert; (*inf*: = *complete*) *disaster* vollkommen, total; *success* total, absolut; *rubbish* komplett (*inf*); *liar, rogue* Erz- (*inf*)

unmixed [ʌnˈmɪkst] **ADJ** *blood* unvermischt; *delight, pleasure* rein, ungetrübt; **to be an ~ blessing** der reine Segen sein

unmodified [ʌnˈmɒdɪfaɪd] **ADJ** unverändert, nicht (ab)geändert

unmolested [ʌnməˈlestɪd] **ADJ** (= *unattacked*) unbelästigt; (= *undisturbed*) in Frieden, in Ruhe

unmoor [ʌnˈmuːə] **VTI** losmachen

unmotivated [ʌnˈməʊtɪveɪtɪd] **ADJ** unmotiviert; *attack* also grundlos

unmounted [ʌnˈmaʊntɪd] **ADJ** *horse* ohne Reiter; *gem* ungefasst; *gun* nicht fest montiert; *picture* (= *not on mount*) nicht aufgezogen; (= *not in album*) lose

unmourned [ʌnˈmɔːnd] **ADJ** unbeweint; *death also* unbeklagt; **an ~ tyrant** ein Tyrann *m*, dem niemand nachtrauert *or* nachweint; **they died largely ~** kaum einer trauerte um sie *or* trauerte ihnen nach ihrem Tod(e) nach

unmoved [ʌnˈmuːvd] **ADJ** *person* ungerührt; **they were ~ by his playing** sein Spiel(en) ergriff sie nicht; **it leaves me ~** das (be)rührt mich nicht; **he remained ~ by her pleas** ihr Flehen ließ ihn kalt, ihr Flehen rührte *or* erweichte ihn nicht

unmoving [ʌnˈmuːvɪŋ] **ADJ** regungslos

unmusical [ʌnˈmjuːzɪkəl] **ADJ** *person* unmusikalisch; *sound* unmelodisch

unnam(e)able [ʌnˈneɪməbl] **ADJ** unsagbar

unnamed [ʌnˈneɪmd] **ADJ** (= *nameless*) namenlos; (= *anonymous*) ungenannt

unnatural [ʌnˈnætʃrəl] **ADJ** unnatürlich; (= *abnormal also*) *relationship, crime* widernatürlich; (= *not normal*) *death* widernatürlicher Tod; **to die an ~ death** keines natürlichen Todes sterben; **it is ~ for him to be so rude** normalerweise ist er nicht so grob, es ist ungewöhnlich, dass er so grob ist; **it's not ~ to be upset** es ist nur natürlich, da bestürzt zu sein

unnaturally [ʌnˈnætʃrəlɪ] **ADV** unnatürlich; (= *extraordinarily also*) *loud, anxious* ungewöhnlich; **not ~, we were worried** es war nur normal *or* natürlich, dass wir uns Sorgen machten

unnavigable [ʌnˈnævɪgəbl] **ADJ** nicht schiffbar, nicht befahrbar

unnecessarily [ʌnˈnesəsərɪlɪ] **ADV** unnötigerweise; *strict, serious* unnötig, übertrieben

unnecessary [ʌnˈnesəsərɪ] **ADJ** unnötig; (= *superfluous also*) überflüssig; (= *not requisite*) nicht notwendig *or* nötig; **no, you needn't bother thanks, that's quite ~** nein, machen Sie sich keine Umstände, das ist wirklich nicht nötig; **it was quite ~ to be so rude** es war wirklich nicht nötig, so grob zu werden; **it was ~ for you to do that** es war nicht nötig, dass du das getan hast; **really, that was quite ~ of you!** also, das war wirklich überflüssig!

unneighbourly, (*US*) **unneighborly** [ʌnˈneɪbəlɪ] **ADJ** *behaviour* nicht gutnachbarlich; **an ~ person** ein schlechter Nachbar, eine schlechte Nachbarin; **it's ~ to do that** als guter Nachbar tut man so etwas nicht

unnerve [ʌnˈnɜːv] **VT** entnerven; (*gradually*) zermürben; (= *discourage*) *speaker* entmutigen; **~d by their reaction** durch ihre Reaktion aus der Ruhe gebracht

unnerving [ʌnˈnɜːvɪŋ] **ADJ** *experience, sincerity* entnervend; *silence also* zermürbend; (= *discouraging also*) entmutigend; **an ~ habit** eine entnervende *or* irritierende Angewohnheit

unnoticed [ʌnˈnəʊtɪst] **ADJ** unbemerkt; **to go** *or* **pass ~** unbemerkt bleiben; **to be ~ by sb** von jdm nicht bemerkt werden

unnumbered [ʌnˈnʌmbəd] **ADJ** **a** (= *countless*) unzählig, zahllos **b** (= *not numbered*) nicht nummeriert; *house* ohne Hausnummer

UNO **abbr of** United Nations Organization UNO *f*

unobjectionable [ʌnəbˈdʒekʃnəbl] **ADJ** einwandfrei; **he is a pretty ~ person** gegen ihn lässt sich kaum etwas einwenden

unobliging **ADJ** , **unobligingly** **ADV** [ʌnəˈblaɪdʒɪŋ, lɪ] ungefällig

unobservant [ʌnəbˈzɜːvənt] **ADJ** unaufmerksam; **to be ~** ein schlechter Beobachter sein; **how ~ of me** wie unaufmerksam (von mir)

unobserved [ʌnəbˈzɜːvd] **ADJ** (= *not seen*) unbemerkt; (= *not celebrated*) nicht (mehr) eingehalten *or* beachtet

unobstructed [ʌnəbˈstrʌktɪd] **ADJ** *view* ungehindert; *pipe* frei, unverstopft; *path, road* frei, unversperrt

unobtainable [ʌnəbˈteɪnəbl] ✪ 27.7 **ADJ** **a** nicht erhältlich, nicht zu bekommen; *goal* unerreichbar; **number ~** (*Brit Telec*) kein Anschluss unter dieser Nummer; **your number was ~** deine Nummer war nicht zu bekommen **b** (= *out of bounds*) *person* unantastbar

unobtrusive **ADJ** , **unobtrusively** **ADV** [ʌnəbˈtruːsɪv, -lɪ] unauffällig

unoccupied [ʌnˈɒkjʊpaɪd] **ADJ** *person* unbeschäftigt; *house* leer stehend, unbewohnt; *seat, table* frei; (*Mil*) *zone* unbesetzt

unofficial [ʌnəˈfɪʃəl] **ADJ** inoffiziell; (= *unconfirmed also*) *information* nicht amtlich; **to take ~ action** (*Ind*) inoffiziell streiken; **~ strike** inoffizieller *or* wilder Streik; **in an ~ capacity** inoffiziell

unofficially [ʌnəˈfɪʃəlɪ] **ADV** inoffiziell

unopened [ʌnˈəʊpənd] **ADJ** ungeöffnet

unopposed [ʌnəˈpəʊzd] **ADJ** **they marched on ~** sie marschierten weiter, ohne auf Widerstand zu treffen; **~ by the committee** ohne Widerspruch *or* Beanstandung seitens des Ausschusses; **to be returned ~** (*Pol*) ohne Gegenstimmen gewählt werden; **an ~ second reading** (*Parl*) eine zweite Lesung ohne Gegenstimmen

unorganized [ʌnˈɔːgənaɪzd] **ADJ** unsystematisch; *person also* unmethodisch; *life* ungeregelt; (*Ind*) nicht (gewerkschaftlich) organisiert; **he is so ~** er hat überhaupt kein System

unoriginal [ʌnəˈrɪdʒɪnəl] **ADJ** wenig originell

unorthodox [ʌnˈɔːθədɒks] **ADJ** unkonventionell, unorthodox

unpack [ʌnˈpæk] **VTI** auspacken

unpacking [ʌnˈpækɪŋ] **N** Auspacken *nt*; **to do one's ~** auspacken

unpaged [ʌnˈpeɪdʒd] **ADJ** unpaginiert, ohne Seitenzahl(en)

unpaid [ʌnˈpeɪd] **ADJ** unbezahlt **ADV** **to work ~** unbezahlt *or* ohne Bezahlung arbeiten

unpalatable [ʌnˈpælɪtəbl] **ADJ** *food, drink* ungenießbar; (*fig*) *fact, truth, mixture* unverdaulich, schwer zu verdauen; **he finds the ~ truth** die Wahrheit schmeckt ihm nicht; **to be ~ to sb** (*fig*) für jdn schwer zu akzeptieren *or* zu schlucken (*inf*) sein

unparalleled [ʌnˈpærəleld] **ADJ** einmalig, beispiellos; (= *unprecedented also*) noch nie da gewesen; **an ~ success** ein Erfolg ohnegleichen; **~ in the history of mankind** beispiellos *or* ohne Beispiel in der Geschichte der Menschheit

unpardonable [ʌnˈpɑːdnəbl] **ADJ** unverzeihlich

unparliamentary [ʌnpɑːləˈmentərɪ] **ADJ** *behaviour, language* nicht parlamentsfähig, der Würde des Parlaments nicht entsprechend *attr*; *procedure* unparlamentarisch

unpatented [ʌnˈpeɪtntɪd] **ADJ** nicht patentiert

unpatriotic [ʌnpætrɪˈɒtɪk] **ADJ** unpatriotisch

unpaved [ʌnˈpeɪvd] **ADJ** *road, courtyard* nicht gepflastert

unpeg [ʌnˈpeg] **VT** *washing* abnehmen; *prices* freigeben

unperceived [ʌnpəˈsiːvd] **ADJ** unbemerkt

unperceptive [ʌnpəˈseptɪv] **ADJ** unaufmerksam

unperfumed [ʌnˈpɜːfjuːmd] **ADJ** nicht parfümiert

unperson [ˈʌnpɜːsən] **N** (*Pol*) Unperson *f*

unperturbable [ʌnpəˈtɜːbəbl] **ADJ** nicht aus der Ruhe zu bringen *pred* or bringend *attr*

unperturbed [ʌnpəˈtɜːbd] **ADJ** nicht beunruhigt (*by* von, durch), gelassen

unphilosophical [ʌnfɪləˈsɒfɪkəl] **ADJ** unphilosophisch

unpick [ʌnˈpɪk] **VT** auftrennen; (*Brit, fig*) *plan, policy* auseinander nehmen

unpin [ʌnˈpɪn] **VT** *dress, hair* die Nadeln entfernen aus; *notice* abnehmen

unplaced [ʌnˈpleɪst] **ADJ** (*Sport*) nicht platziert; **to be ~** sich nicht platziert haben

unplanned [ʌnˈplænd] **ADJ** ungeplant, nicht geplant

unplasticized [ˈʌnˈplæstɪsaɪzd] **ADJ** **~ polyvinyl chloride** weichmacherfreies Polyvinylchlorid

unplayable [ʌnˈpleɪəbl] **ADJ** unspielbar; *pitch* unbespielbar; **the ball was in an ~ position** der Ball war nicht spielbar

unpleasant [ʌnˈpleznt] **ADJ** unangenehm; *experience, situation also* unerfreulich; *person, smile, remark* unliebenswürdig, unfreundlich; **something ~** etwas Unangenehmes *or* Unerfreuliches; **to be ~ to sb** unfreundlich zu jdm sein

unpleasantly [ʌnˈplezntlɪ] **ADV** *reply* unliebenswürdig, unfreundlich; *warm, smell* unangenehm; **he was getting ~ close to the truth** es war unangenehm, wie nah er an der Wahrheit war; **not ~ so** auf nicht unangenehme Weise

unpleasantness [ʌnˈplezntnɪs] N **a** (= *quality*) Unangenehmheit *f*; (*of experience, situation also*) Unerfreulichkeit *f*; (*of person, smile, remark*) Unfreundlichkeit *f* **b** (= *bad feeling, quarrel*) Unstimmigkeit *f*

unplug [ʌnˈplʌg] VT *radio, lamp* rausziehen; *plug* abziehen, rausziehen; ~ **it first** zieh zuerst den Stecker heraus

unplugged [ʌnˈplʌgd] ADJ (*Mus*) (rein) akustisch, unplugged *pred* (*inf*)

unplumbed [ʌnˈplʌmd] ADJ unergründet

unpoetic, unpoetical ADJ [ʌnpəʊˈetɪk, -əl], **unpoetically** [ʌnpəʊˈetɪkəlɪ] ADV unpoetisch, undichterisch

unpolished [ʌnˈpɒlɪʃt] ADJ **a** unpoliert; *stone* ungeschliffen; *shoes* ungeputzt **b** (*fig*) *person, manners* ungeschliffen, ungehobelt; *performance* unausgefeilt; *style, language* holprig, unausgefeilt

unpolitical ADJ , **unpolitically** ADV [ʌnpəˈlɪtɪkəl, -l] unpolitisch

unpolluted [ʌnpəˈluːtɪd] ADJ sauber, unverschmutzt; **to be ~ by sth** (*lit*) nicht durch etw verschmutzt *or* verunreinigt sein; (*fig*) unverdorben von etw sein

unpopular [ʌnˈpɒpjʊlə°] ADJ *person* unbeliebt (*with sb* bei jdm); *decision, move, measures, tax* unpopulär; **to make oneself ~ (with sb)** sich (bei jdm) unbeliebt machen; **I'm ~ with him just now** zur Zeit bin ich bei ihm nicht gut angeschrieben (*inf*)

unpopularity [ʌnˌpɒpjʊˈlærɪtɪ] N Unbeliebtheit *f*; (*of decision, move*) Unpopularität *f*, geringe Popularität

unpractical [ʌnˈpræktɪkəl] ADJ unpraktisch

unpractised, (*US*) **unpracticed** [ʌnˈpræktɪst] ADJ ungeübt

unprecedented [ʌnˈpresɪdəntɪd] ADJ noch nie da gewesen; *success also* beispiellos, ohnegleichen (*after noun*); *profit, step* unerhört; **this event is ~** dieses Ereignis ist bisher einmalig; **an ~ success** ein beispielloser *or* noch nie da gewesener Erfolg, ein Erfolg ohnegleichen; **on an ~ scale** in einem noch nie da gewesenen Ausmaß; **you realize it's quite ~ for a president to ...** es ist Ihnen wohl klar, dass es keinen Präzedenzfall dafür gibt, dass ein Präsident ...

unpredictable [ʌnprɪˈdɪktəbl] ADJ unvorhersehbar; *result* nicht vorherzusagen *pred*, nicht vorherzusagen *attr*; *behaviour, person, weather, nature* unberechenbar

unpredictably [ʌnprɪˈdɪktəblɪ] ADV *violent, dangerous* unberechenbar; **many children behave ~** viele Kinder verhalten sich unberechenbar

unprejudiced [ʌnˈpredʒʊdɪst] ADJ (= *impartial*) objektiv, unparteiisch; (= *not having prejudices*) vorurteilslos

unpremeditated [ʌnprɪˈmedɪteɪtɪd] ADJ unüberlegt; *crime* nicht vorsätzlich; *murder* nicht geplant

unprepared [ʌnprɪˈpeəd] ADJ nicht vorbereitet, unvorbereitet; **to be ~ for sth** für etw nicht vorbereitet sein; (= *be surprised*) auf etw (*acc*) nicht vorbereitet *or* gefasst sein; **you've caught me ~** darauf bin ich nicht vorbereitet; **to be ~ to do sth** (= *not willing*) nicht bereit sein, etw zu tun

unprepossessing [ʌnpriːpəˈzesɪŋ] ADJ wenig gewinnend, wenig einnehmend; *building, room* wenig ansprechend

unpresentable [ʌnprɪˈzentəbl] ADJ (*in appearance*) nicht präsentabel; *clothes also* unansehnlich; (*socially*) nicht gesellschaftsfähig; **most of his friends are ~** mit den meisten seiner Freunde kann man sich in der Öffentlichkeit nicht blicken lassen

unpretentious [ʌnprɪˈtenʃəs] ADJ schlicht, bescheiden; *person, manner also* natürlich; *house, meal etc also* einfach; *style, book* einfach, nicht schwülstig

unpretentiously [ʌnprɪˈtenʃəslɪ] ADV schlicht, bescheiden, einfach; *speak* natürlich; *write* in einfachen Worten

unpriced [ʌnˈpraɪst] ADJ ohne Preisschild, nicht ausgezeichnet

unprincipled [ʌnˈprɪnsɪpld] ADJ skrupellos; *person also* charakterlos

unprintable [ʌnˈprɪntəbl] ADJ nicht druckfähig; **his answer was ~** seine Antwort war nicht druckreif

unproductive [ʌnprəˈdʌktɪv] ADJ *capital* nicht gewinnbringend, keinen Gewinn bringend *attr*; *soil* unfruchtbar, ertragsarm; *discussion, meeting* unproduktiv, unergiebig; *factory, worker* unproduktiv

unprofessional [ʌnprəˈfeʃnl] ADJ unprofessionell; *work also* unfachmännisch, laienhaft, stümperhaft; *conduct* berufswidrig

unprofitable [ʌnˈprɒfɪtəbl] ADJ (*financially*) keinen Profit bringend *or* abwerfend, wenig einträglich; *mine, activities, business etc* unrentabel; (*fig*) nutzlos, sinnlos; **the company was ~** die Firma machte keinen Profit *or* warf keinen Profit ab; **we spent an ~ hour on it** wir haben eine Stunde damit verplempert; **it would be ~ to go on** es wäre sinnlos, noch weiterzumachen

unpromising [ʌnˈprɒmɪsɪŋ] ADJ nicht sehr viel versprechend; *start also* nicht sehr erfolgversprechend, wenig erfolgversprechend; **to look ~** nicht sehr hoffnungsvoll *or* gut aussehen; (*weather*) nichts Gutes versprechen

unprompted [ʌnˈprɒmptɪd] ADJ spontan, **~ by me** unaufgefordert; **his invitation was quite ~** seine Einladung kam ganz aus freien Stücken; **I'd rather he answered the questions ~** es wäre mir lieber, wenn er ohne Vorsagen antwortete

unpronounceable [ʌnprəˈnaʊnsɪbl] ADJ unaussprechbar; **that word is ~** das Wort ist nicht auszusprechen

unpropitious [ʌnprəˈpɪʃəs] ADJ *omen, moment, circumstances* ungünstig

unproportional ADJ , **unproportionally** ADV [ʌnprəˈpɔːʃənl, -ʃnəlɪ] unverhältnismäßig; (*also Math*) unproportional

unprotected [ʌnprəˈtektɪd] ADJ ohne Schutz, schutzlos; *machine, skin, eyes* ungeschützt; (*by insurance*) ohne Versicherungsschutz; (*Mil*) *building etc* ungeschützt, ohne Deckung; **~ by** nicht geschützt durch; **to be ~ from the sun** vor der Sonne geschützt sein

unprotected: unprotected intercourse N ungeschützter Geschlechtsverkehr; **unprotected sex** N ungeschützter Sex

unprovable [ʌnˈpruːvəbl] ADJ nicht beweisbar

unproven [ʌnˈpruːvən], **unproved** [ʌnˈpruːvd] ADJ **a** (= *not proved*) *allegation, charge* nicht bewiesen, unbewiesen; **the charge remains ~** die Anschuldigung bleibt unbewiesen **b** (= *not tested*) *person, technology* (noch) nicht bewährt

unprovided [ʌnprəˈvaɪdɪd] ADJ *person* unversorgt

unprovided-for [ʌnprəˈvaɪdɪdfɔː°] ADJ **a** (= *lacking*) unversorgt; **he died and left his children ~** er starb, ohne für seine Kinder gesorgt zu haben **b** (= *not anticipated*) **that eventuality was ~** auf dieses Ereignis war man nicht eingerichtet

unprovoked [ʌnprəˈvəʊkt] ADJ ohne Anlass, grundlos

unpublished [ʌnˈpʌblɪʃt] ADJ unveröffentlicht

unpunctual [ʌnˈpʌŋktjʊəl] ADJ unpünktlich

unpunctuality [ʌnprʌŋktjʊˈælɪtɪ] N Unpünktlichkeit *f*

unpunished [ʌnˈpʌnɪʃt] ADJ unbestraft; **to go ~** ohne Strafe bleiben; **if this goes ~ ...** wenn das nicht bestraft wird ...

unputdownable [ʌnpʊtˈdaʊnəbl] ADJ (*inf*) **it's absolutely ~** (*book*) es lässt einen nicht los

unqualified [ʌnˈkwɒlɪfaɪd] ADJ **a** unqualifiziert; **to be ~ (for a job)** (für eine Arbeit) nicht qualifiziert sein; **he is ~ to do that** er ist dafür nicht qualifiziert; **I was ~ to judge** ich konnte mir darüber kein Urteil erlauben **b** (= *absolute*) *delight, praise, acceptance* uneingeschränkt;

denial vollständig; *success* voll(ständig); (*inf*) *idiot, liar* ausgesprochen; **the party was an ~ disaster** die Party war eine absolute Katastrophe; **an ~ yes/no** ein uneingeschränktes Ja/Nein **c** (*Gram*) nicht bestimmt

unquenchable [ʌnˈkwentʃəbl] ADJ *fire* unlöschbar; *thirst, desire* unstillbar; *optimism* unerschütterlich; **she has an ~ spirit** sie lässt sich nicht unterkriegen (*inf*)

unquestionable [ʌnˈkwestʃənəbl] ADJ *authority* unbestritten, unanfechtbar; *evidence, fact* unbezweifelbar; *sincerity, honesty* fraglos; **a man of ~ courage** ein zweifellos *or* fraglos mutiger Mann; **one's parents' authority used to be ~** früher konnte man die Autorität seiner Eltern nicht infrage *or* in Frage stellen; **his courage is ~** sein Mut steht außer Frage

unquestionably [ʌnˈkwestʃənəblɪ] ADV fraglos, zweifellos

unquestioned [ʌnˈkwestʃənd] ADJ unbestritten; (= *unquestioning*) *belief, acceptance* bedingungslos; **I can't let that statement pass ~** ich kann diese Behauptung nicht fraglos hinnehmen; **to be ~** (*honesty etc*) außer Frage stehen; (*social order etc*) nicht infrage *or* in Frage gestellt werden

unquestioning [ʌnˈkwestʃənɪŋ] ADJ bedingungslos; *belief, faith also* blind

unquestioningly [ʌnˈkwestʃənɪŋlɪ] ADV *accept* bedingungslos; *obey* widerspruchslos, blind; **he ~ accepts everything you say** er akzeptiert alles, was Sie sagen, ohne Widerrede

unquiet [ʌnˈkwaɪət] ADJ (*liter*) unruhig; (= *restless*) ruhelos

unquote [ʌnˈkwəʊt] VI *imper only* **quote ... ~** Zitat (Anfang) ... Zitat Ende *or* Ende des Zitats → *also* quote VT a

unratified [ʌnˈrætɪfaɪd] ADJ (*Pol*) *treaty etc* nicht ratifiziert

unrationed [ʌnˈræʃnd], (*US*) [ʌnˈræʃənd] ADJ *food, petrol etc* nicht rationiert, frei erhältlich

unravel [ʌnˈrævəl] VT *knitting* aufziehen; (*lit, fig, = untangle*) entwirren; *mystery* lösen VI (*knitting*) sich aufziehen; (*fig*) sich entwirren, sich auflösen; (*mystery*) sich lösen; (*plan, system*) aufdecken

unread [ʌnˈred] ADJ *book* ungelesen; *person* wenig belesen

unreadable [ʌnˈriːdəbl] ADJ **a** *writing* unleserlich; *book* schwer zu lesen *pred*, schwer lesbar **b** (*Comput*) *data* nicht lesbar **c** (*liter, = impenetrable*) *face, eyes* undurchdringlich

unreadiness [ʌnˈredɪnɪs] N Unvorbereitetheit *f*; (*of troops*) mangelnde Bereitschaft

unready [ʌnˈredɪ] ADJ (noch) nicht fertig; **~ to do sth** nicht bereit, etw zu tun; **he was ~ for what happened next** er war nicht auf das eingestellt *or* vorbereitet, was dann kam; **he is ~ for such responsibility** er ist noch nicht reif genug, solch eine Verantwortung zu übernehmen

unreal [ʌnˈrɪəl] ADJ unwirklich; (= *fake*) unecht; **this is just ~!** (*inf: = unbelievable*) das darf doch nicht wahr sein!, das gibts doch nicht! (*inf*); **he's ~** er ist unmöglich

unrealistic [ʌnrɪəˈlɪstɪk] ADJ unrealistisch; **it is ~ to expect her to do it** es ist unrealistisch von ihr zu erwarten, dass sie es tut

unrealistically [ʌnrɪəˈlɪstɪkəlɪ] ADV *high, low* unrealistisch; *optimistic* unangemessen

unreality [ʌnrɪˈælɪtɪ] N Unwirklichkeit *f*; **there is an air of ~ about it** es hat etwas Unwirkliches an sich; **extreme exhaustion gives a feeling of ~** extreme Erschöpfung lässt alles unwirklich erscheinen; **the ~ of the characters' emotions** die Unnatürlichkeit *or* Unechtheit der Gefühle der Personen

unrealized [ʌnˈrɪəlaɪzd] ADJ unverwirklicht; (*Fin*) *assets* unverwertet; *profit* nicht realisiert

unreasonable [ʌnˈriːznəbl] ADJ *demand, price etc* unzumutbar, übertrieben; *request* unzumutbar; *expectations* übertrieben; *person* uneinsichtig; (= *showing lack of sense*) unvernünftig; **to be ~ about sth** (= *not be understanding*) kein Verständnis für etw zeigen; (= be overdemanding) in Bezug auf etw (acc) zu viel verlangen; **it is ~ to ...** es ist zu viel verlangt, zu ...; **it is ~ to blame her** es ist nicht gerechtfertigt, ihr die Schuld zu geben; **it is ~ to expect children to keep quiet** man kann doch von Kindern nicht verlangen, ruhig zu sein; **that's not ~, is it?** das ist doch nicht zu viel verlangt, oder?; **you are being very ~!** das ist wirklich zu viel verlangt!; **look, don't be ~, it is 100 miles** nun mach mal einen Punkt or nun sei mal vernünftig, es sind immerhin 100 Meilen; **an ~ length of time** übermäßig or übertrieben lange; **at this ~ hour** zu dieser unzumutbaren Zeit

unreasonableness [ʌnˈriːznəblnɪs] N (of demands etc) Unzumutbarkeit f, Übermäßigkeit f; (of person) Uneinsichtigkeit f; **I hadn't reckoned with his ~** ich hatte nicht damit gerechnet, dass er so uneinsichtig sein würde; **I commented on his ~ in expecting 20%** ich bemerkte, dass 20% wohl zu viel verlangt wären

unreasonably [ʌnˈriːznəblɪ] ADV long, slow, high, strict übermäßig, übertrieben; **he remained ~ stubborn** er blieb unnötig stur; **he argued, quite ~ I think, that we should have known** er sagte, meiner Meinung nach ungerechtfertigterweise, dass wir das hätten wissen müssen; **you must prove that your employer acted ~** Sie müssen nachweisen, dass Ihr Arbeitgeber ungerechtfertigt gehandelt hat; **not ~** nicht ohne Grund

unreasoning [ʌnˈriːznɪŋ] ADJ person kopflos, unvernünftig; action, fear, hatred blind, unsinnig

unreceptive [ʌnrɪˈsɛptɪv] ADJ unempfänglich (to für); audience also unaufgeschlossen

unrecognizable [ʌnˈrɛkəgnaɪzəbl] ADJ nicht wieder zu erkennen pred, nicht wieder zu erkennend attr; **he was ~ in his disguise** er war in seiner Verkleidung nicht zu erkennen; **they've made the old school ~** die alte Schule ist nicht wieder zu erkennen; **it was ~ as an aircraft** es war nicht als Flugzeug zu erkennen; **to be ~ to sb** für jdn nicht zu erkennen sein

unrecognized [ʌnˈrɛkəgnaɪzd] ADJ (= not noticed) person, danger, value unerkannt; (= not acknowledged) government, record nicht anerkannt; genius, talent ungewürdigt, unerkannt; **to go ~** (person, talent, achievement) nicht gewürdigt or anerkannt werden; **~ by the crowds** ohne von den Leuten erkannt zu werden

unreconciled [ʌnˈrɛkənsaɪld] ADJ unversöhnt (to, with mit)

unreconstructed [ʌnriːkənˈstrʌktɪd] ADJ (pej) system, idea, policy unverändert; **she's an ~ communist** sie ist eingefleischte Kommunistin

unrecorded [ʌnrɪˈkɔːdɪd] ADJ nicht aufgenommen; (Rad, TV) nicht aufgezeichnet; (in documents) nicht schriftlich erfasst or festgehalten; **to go ~** nicht aufgenommen/festgehalten werden

unredeemed [ʌnrɪˈdiːmd] ADJ **a** sinner, world unerlöst; **~ by** nicht ausgeglichen or wettgemacht durch **b** bill, (from pawn) pledge uneingelöst; mortgage, debt ungetilgt

unreel [ʌnˈriːl] VT abspulen, abwickeln VI sich abspulen, sich abwickeln, abrollen

unrefined [ʌnrɪˈfaɪnd] ADJ **a** petroleum, sugar, metal nicht raffiniert; food naturbelassen; cereal unbehandelt **b** person unkultiviert; manners unfein

unreflecting [ʌnrɪˈflɛktɪŋ] ADJ person gedankenlos, unbedacht; act, haste unbesonnen; emotion unreflektiert

unregarded [ʌnrɪˈgɑːdɪd] ADJ unbeachtet, nicht beachtet; **to go ~** unbeachtet bleiben; **to be ~** nicht beachtet werden

unregardful [ʌnrɪˈgɑːdfʊl] ADJ (form) ohne Rücksicht (of auf +acc), rücksichtslos (of gegen); **to be ~ of** keine Rücksicht nehmen auf +acc

unregenerate [ʌnrɪˈdʒɛnɪrɪt] ADJ (= unrepentant) reu(e)los, nicht reuig; (= unreformed) unbekehrbar; (= stubborn) reactionary hartnäckig; (= wicked) life sündig

unregistered [ʌnˈrɛdʒɪstəd] ADJ birth nicht gemeldet; car, firearm, worker nicht angemeldet; voter nicht (im Wählerverzeichnis) eingetragen; land nicht (im Grundbuch) eingetragen; trademark nicht gesetzlich geschützt; letter nicht eingeschrieben; lawyer, taxi, agent nicht zugelassen; doctor nicht approbiert

unregretted [ʌnrɪˈgrɛtɪd] ADJ absence, death nicht bedauert; person nicht vermisst; words nicht bereut

unregulated [ʌnˈrɛgjʊlɛɪtɪd] ADJ unkontrolliert

unrehearsed [ʌnrɪˈhɜːst] ADJ (Theat etc) nicht geprobt; cast schlecht eingespielt; (= spontaneous) incident spontan

unrelated [ʌnrɪˈleɪtɪd] ADJ (= unconnected) ohne Beziehung (to zu); (by family) nicht verwandt; **~ to reality** wirklichkeitsfremd; **the two events are ~/are not ~** die beiden Ereignisse stehen in keinem Zusammenhang miteinander/sind nicht gänzlich ohne Zusammenhang; **they are ~ (to each other)** (people) sie sind nicht (miteinander) verwandt

unrelenting [ʌnrɪˈlɛntɪŋ] ADJ pressure unablässig; opposition unerbittlich; violence, criticism, pain unvermindert, anhaltend; determination hartnäckig; pace, severity unvermindert; attack, struggle unerbittlich, unvermindert; rain anhaltend attr, nicht nachlassend attr; (= not merciful) person, heat unbarmherzig; **we must be ~ in our struggle** wir müssen unablässig weiterkämpfen; **they kept up an ~ attack** sie führten den Angriff mit unverminderter Stärke durch

unreliability [ˈʌnrɪˌlaɪəˈbɪlɪtɪ] N Unzuverlässigkeit f

unreliable [ʌnrɪˈlaɪəbl] ADJ unzuverlässig; **to prove (to be) ~** sich als unzuverlässig erweisen

unrelieved [ʌnrɪˈliːvd] ADJ pain, stress, gloom, anguish ungemindert; mediocrity unverändert, gleich bleibend; grey einheitlich, durch nichts aufgelockert; monotony, boredom tödlich; **a life of ~ misery** ein Leben, das ein einziges Elend ist; **to be ~ by** nicht aufgelockert sein durch or von

unremarkable [ʌnrɪˈmɑːkəbl] ADJ nicht sehr bemerkenswert, wenig bemerkenswert; **he would be ~ in a crowd** inmitten einer Menschenmenge würde ihn niemand bemerken or würde er nicht auffallen

unremarked [ʌnrɪˈmɑːkt] ADJ unbemerkt; **to go ~** unbemerkt bleiben

unremitting [ʌnrɪˈmɪtɪŋ] ADJ efforts, toil unaufhörlich, unablässig; zeal unermüdlich; hatred unversöhnlich

unremittingly [ʌnrɪˈmɪtɪŋlɪ] ADV unaufhörlich, ohne Unterlass; strive unermüdlich

unremunerative [ʌnrɪˈmjuːnərətɪv] ADJ nicht lohnend, nicht einträglich

unrepeatable [ʌnrɪˈpiːtəbl] ADJ **a** words, views nicht wiederholbar **b** offer, chance, experience einmalig

unrepentant [ʌnrɪˈpɛntənt] ADJ nicht reuig, nicht reumütig, reu(e)los; **he is ~ about it** er bereut es nicht

unreported [ʌnrɪˈpɔːtɪd] ADJ events nicht berichtet; crime nicht angezeigt; **to go ~** nicht berichtet werden; (crime) nicht angezeigt werden

unrepresentative [ʌnrɛprɪˈzɛntətɪv] ADJ minority, sample etc nicht repräsentativ; (Pol) government nicht frei gewählt; **~ of sth** nicht repräsentativ für etw; **the Party is ~ of the people** die Partei repräsentiert das Volk nicht

unrepresented [ʌnrɛprɪˈzɛntɪd] ADJ nicht vertreten; **to go ~** (Jur) nicht vertreten werden; (Parl) nicht vertreten sein

unrequited [ʌnrɪˈkwaɪtɪd] ADJ love unerwidert, unglücklich

unreserved [ʌnrɪˈzɜːvd] ADJ **a** (= frank) person nicht reserviert, offen; **he's quite ~ about his feelings** er zeigt seine Gefühle ganz offen **b** (= complete) approval, apology, support uneingeschränkt; praise, admiration uneingeschränkt, rückhaltlos **c** (= not booked) nicht reserviert

unreservedly [ʌnrɪˈzɜːvɪdlɪ] ADV speak freimütig, offen; approve, trust, recommend uneingeschränkt; sob, condemn rückhaltlos; **to apologize (to sb) ~ for sth** sich (bei jdm) uneingeschränkt für etw entschuldigen

unresisting [ʌnrɪˈzɪstɪŋ] ADJ widerstandslos, keinen Widerstand leistend attr; **I pushed open the ~ door** ich stieß die Tür auf, die ohne weiteres nachgab

unresolved [ʌnrɪˈzɒlvd] ADJ **a** difficulty, problem ungelöst **b** (= uncertain) person unschlüssig; **he is still ~ as to what to do** er ist sich (dat) noch (darüber) unschlüssig, was er tun soll

unresponsive [ʌnrɪˈspɒnsɪv] ADJ (physically) nicht reagierend attr; (emotionally, intellectually) gleichgültig, unempfänglich; **to be ~** nicht reagieren (to auf +acc); (to advances, pleas, request also) nicht empfänglich sein (to für); **an ~ audience** ein Publikum, das nicht mitgeht or nicht reagiert; **I suggested it but he was fairly ~** ich habe es vorgeschlagen, aber er ist nicht groß darauf eingegangen or er zeigte sich nicht sehr interessiert; **still heavily sedated and totally ~** unter starkem Drogeneinfluss und völlig teilnahmslos

unrest [ʌnˈrɛst] N Unruhen pl; (= discontent) Unzufriedenheit f; **there was ~ among the workers** die Arbeiter waren unzufrieden

unrested [ʌnˈrɛstɪd] ADJ unausgeruht

unresting [ʌnˈrɛstɪŋ] ADJ efforts unermüdlich

unrestrained [ʌnrɪˈstreɪnd] ADJ **a** uneingeschränkt, unkontrolliert; feelings offen, ungehemmt; joy, enthusiasm, atmosphere ungezügelt; language, behaviour ausfallend, unbeherrscht; laughter hemmungslos, unkontrolliert; violence hemmungslos, ungezügelt; **to be ~ in one's views** in seinen Ansichten nicht zurückhaltend sein **b** (physically) ungehindert

unrestrainedly [ʌnrɪˈstreɪnɪdlɪ] ADV hemmungslos, rückhaltlos; **she wept ~** sie weinte hemmungslos

unrestricted [ʌnrɪˈstrɪktɪd] ADJ **a** power, use, growth unbeschränkt, uneingeschränkt; right uneingeschränkt; travel, access ungehindert **b** (= unobstructed) view ungehindert

unreturned [ʌnrɪˈtɜːnd] ADJ **a** nicht zurückgegeben **b** love etc unerwidert, unvergolten **c** (Brit Parl) nicht gewählt (ins Parlament)

unrevealed [ʌnrɪˈviːld] ADJ facts, report nicht veröffentlicht; secret ungelüftet

unrewarded [ʌnrɪˈwɔːdɪd] ADJ unbelohnt; **to go ~** unbelohnt bleiben; (= not gain recognition) keine Anerkennung finden; **his efforts were ~ by any success** seine Bemühungen waren nicht von Erfolg gekrönt

unrewarding [ʌnrɪˈwɔːdɪŋ] ADJ work undankbar; (financially) wenig einträglich; **further study of this book would be ~** es würde sich nicht lohnen, das Buch weiterzulesen

unrhymed [ʌnˈraɪmd] ADJ ungereimt

unrhythmical [ʌnˈrɪðmɪkəl] ADJ tune, person unrhythmisch

unrig [ʌnˈrɪg] VT (Naut) abtakeln

unrighteous [ʌnˈraɪtʃəs] ADJ (Rel) sündig N **the ~** pl die Sünder pl

unripe [ʌnˈraɪp] ADJ unreif

unrivalled, (US) **unrivaled** [ʌnˈraɪvəld] ADJ unerreicht, unübertroffen; **~ in or for quality** von unübertroffener Qualität; **to be ~ in sth** in etw (dat) unerreicht or unübertroffen sein

unroadworthiness [ʌnˈrəʊdˌwɜːðɪnɪs] N mangelnde Verkehrssicherheit

unroadworthy [ʌnˈrəʊdˌwɜːðɪ] ADJ nicht verkehrssicher

unrobe [ʌnˈrəʊb] VI (form) sich entkleiden (geh); (hum) sich enthüllen (hum) VT (form) entkleiden (geh); (hum) enthüllen (hum)

unroll [ʌnˈrəʊl] VT carpet, map aufrollen, auseinander rollen; (fig) story also darlegen, schildern VI (carpet etc) sich aufrollen; (fig, plot) sich abwickeln; (landscape) sich ausbreiten

unromantic [ʌnrəˈmæntɪk] ADJ unromantisch

unroot [ʌn'ruːt] VT (esp US) = **uproot**

unrope [ʌn'rəʊp] **VT** box losbinden **VI** (Mountaineering) sich vom Seil losmachen

unrounded [ʌn'raʊndɪd] ADJ (Phon) ungerundet

unruffled [ʌn'rʌfld] ADJ person gelassen; sea ruhig, unbewegt; hair ordentlich, unzerzaust; bedclothes, sheets glatt gestrichen; calm unerschütterlich; **she was** or **remained quite ~** sie blieb ruhig und gelassen, sie bewahrte die Ruhe; **to be ~ by criticism** sich durch Kritik nicht aus der Ruhe bringen lassen

unruled [ʌn'ruːld] ADJ paper unliniert

unruliness [ʌn'ruːlɪnɪs] N Wildheit f, Ungebärdigkeit f

unruly [ʌn'ruːlɪ] ADJ (+er) child, behaviour wild, ungebärdig; employee schwer kontrollierbar, aufmüpfig (hum inf); elements, crowd, mob wild, tobend; hair widerspenstig, nicht zu bändigend attr; **~ passenger** (Aviat) randalierender Passagier

unsaddle [ʌn'sædl] VT horse absatteln; rider abwerfen

unsaddling enclosure [ʌn'sædlɪŋɪn'kləʊʒə'] N (Horse-racing) Absattelring m

unsafe [ʌn'seɪf] ADJ **a** ladder, machine, car, person nicht sicher; (= dangerous) journey, toy, wiring gefährlich; drug gesundheitsschädigend; street gefährlich, unsicher; activity gefährlich, riskant; **this is ~ to eat/drink** das ist nicht genießbar/trinkbar; **the car is ~ to drive** das Auto ist nicht verkehrssicher; **it is ~ to walk there at night** es ist gefährlich, dort nachts spazieren zu gehen; **to be ~ for human consumption** nicht zum Verzehr geeignet; **to declare a house ~ for habitation** ein Haus für unbewohnbar erklären; **to feel ~** sich nicht sicher fühlen; **he looked ~ swaying about at the top of the ladder** es sah gefährlich aus, wie er oben auf der Leiter hin und her schaukelte **b** (Jur, = unreliable) conviction, verdict ungesichert; evidence ungesichert, unzuverlässig; **~ and unsatisfactory** ungesichert und unbefriedigend

unsafe sex N ungeschützter Sex

unsaid [ʌn'sed] pret, ptp of **unsay** ADJ ungesagt, unausgesprochen; **to leave sth ~** etw unausgesprochen lassen; **it's best left ~** das bleibt besser ungesagt

unsalaried [ʌn'sælərɪd] ADJ ehrenamtlich

unsaleable, (US) **unsalable** [ʌn'seɪləbl] ADJ unverkäuflich; **to be ~** sich nicht verkaufen lassen; **bread becomes ~ after 2 days** Brot kann man nach 2 Tagen nicht mehr verkaufen

unsalted [ʌn'sɔːltɪd] ADJ ungesalzen

unsanitary [ʌn'sænɪtrɪ] ADJ unhygienisch

unsatisfactoriness [ʌnsætɪs'fæktərɪnɪs] N (of service, hotel, work) Unzulänglichkeit f; **the ~ of such a solution** eine so unbefriedigende Lösung; **because of his ~ he was not kept on** da er nicht den Erwartungen entsprach, behielt man ihn nicht

unsatisfactory [ʌnsætɪs'fæktərɪ] ADJ unbefriedigend; result also nicht zufrieden stellend; profits, figures nicht ausreichend; service, hotel unzulänglich, schlecht; (Sch) mangelhaft, ungenügend; **he was ~** er entsprach nicht den Erwartungen; **this is highly ~** das lässt sehr zu wünschen übrig

unsatisfied [ʌn'sætɪsfaɪd] ADJ person nicht zufrieden, unzufrieden; (= not fulfilled) unbefriedigt, nicht zufrieden; (= not convinced) nicht überzeugt; appetite, desire, need unbefriedigt; curiosity unbefriedigt, ungestillt; **the meal left me ~** das Essen hat mich nicht so gesättigt; **the book's ending left us ~** wir fanden den Schluss des Buches unbefriedigend; **a job that leaves him ~** eine Arbeit, die ihn nicht befriedigt; **to be ~ with sb/sth** mit jdm/etw unzufrieden sein

unsatisfying [ʌn'sætɪsfaɪɪŋ] ADJ unbefriedigend; meal unzureichend, nicht sättigend

unsaturated [ʌn'sætʃəreɪtɪd] ADJ (Chem) ungesättigt

unsavoury, (US) **unsavory** [ʌn'seɪvərɪ] ADJ **a** (= tasteless) food fade, geschmacklos **b** (= unpleasant) smell, sight widerwärtig, widerlich; appearance (= repulsive) abstoßend, widerwärtig; (= dishonest, shady etc) fragwürdig; subject, details, rumours unerfreulich; joke unfein; district übel, fragwürdig; characters zwielichtig, übel; reputation zweifelhaft, schlecht; **an ~ business** eine unfeine Geschichte

unsay [ʌn'seɪ] pret, ptp **unsaid** VT ungesagt machen

unscalable [ʌn'skeɪləbl] ADJ unbezwingbar

unscaled [ʌn'skeɪld] ADJ heights, peak unbezwungen

unscarred [ʌn'skɑːd] ADJ (fig) nicht gezeichnet

unscathed [ʌn'skeɪðd] ADJ (lit) unverletzt, unversehrt; (by war etc) unverwundet; (fig) unbeschadet; relationship heil; **to leave sb/sth ~** jdn/etw ungeschoren lassen; **to survive ~** unbeschadet or unversehrt überleben; **to emerge** or **escape ~** (lit) ohne einen Kratzer davonkommen; (fig) mit heiler Haut davonkommen, ungeschoren davonkommen

unscented [ʌn'sentɪd] ADJ ohne Duftstoffe, geruchlos

unscheduled [ʌn'ʃedjuːld] ADJ stop, flight etc außerfahrplanmäßig; meeting, visit außerplanmäßig

unscholarly [ʌn'skɒlərlɪ] ADJ work, approach unwissenschaftlich; person unakademisch; (= not learned) ungelehrt

unschooled [ʌn'skuːld] ADJ ungebildet, ohne Schulbildung; talent unausgebildet; **to be ~ in sth** nichts wissen über etw (acc)

unscientific [ʌnsaɪən'tɪfɪk] ADJ unwissenschaftlich

unscramble [ʌn'skræmbl] VT entwirren, auseinander klauben (inf); (Telec) message, signal entschlüsseln

unscratched [ʌn'skrætʃt] ADJ nicht zerkratzt; record ohne Kratzer; (= unhurt) heil, ungeschoren

unscreened [ʌn'skriːnd] ADJ **a** film nicht gezeigt, unaufgeführt; **many films remain ~** viele Filme werden nie gezeigt or bleiben unaufgeführt **b** (= not protected) door, window offen, nicht abgeschirmt **c** (= not inspected, by security) nicht überprüft; (for disease) nicht untersucht

unscrew [ʌn'skruː] **VT** (= loosen) losschrauben; plate, lid also abschrauben; **to come ~ed** sich lösen **VI** sich los- or abschrauben lassen; (= become loose) sich lösen

unscripted [ʌn'skrɪptɪd] ADJ improvisiert

unscrupulous [ʌn'skruːpjʊləs] ADJ person, behaviour skrupellos, gewissenlos; **he is ~ where money is concerned** er ist skrupellos or gewissenlos, wenn es um Geld geht

unscrupulously [ʌn'skruːpjʊləslɪ] ADV behave, exploit skrupellos

unscrupulousness [ʌn'skruːpjʊləsnɪs] N Skrupellosigkeit f, Gewissenlosigkeit f

unseal [ʌn'siːl] VT öffnen; (= remove wax seal also) entsiegeln

unsealed [ʌn'siːld] ADJ offen, unverschlossen; (= without wax seal also) unversiegelt

unseasonable [ʌn'siːznəbl] ADJ nicht der Jahreszeit entsprechend attr; **the weather is ~** das Wetter entspricht nicht der Jahreszeit

unseasonably [ʌn'siːznəblɪ] ADV (für die Jahreszeit) ungewöhnlich or außergewöhnlich; **we had an ~ warm/cold/mild winter** wir hatten einen (für die Jahreszeit) ungewöhnlich warmen/kalten/milden Winter

unseasoned [ʌn'siːznd] ADJ timber nicht abgelagert; food ungewürzt; (fig, = inexperienced) troops unerfahren, unerprobt

unseat [ʌn'siːt] VT rider abwerfen; person (from office) seines Amtes entheben

unseaworthiness [ʌn'siːˌwɜːðɪnɪs] N Seeuntüchtigkeit f

unseaworthy [ʌn'siːˌwɜːðɪ] ADJ seeuntüchtig, nicht seetüchtig

unsecured [ʌnsɪ'kjʊəd] ADJ (Fin) loan, bond ohne Sicherheit(en)

unseeded [ʌn'siːdɪd] ADJ unplatziert

unseeing [ʌn'siːɪŋ] ADJ (lit, fig) blind; gaze leer; **to stare at sb/sth with ~ eyes** jdn/etw mit leerem Blick anstarren

unseemliness [ʌn'siːmlɪnɪs] N Unschicklichkeit f, Ungebührlichkeit f

unseemly [ʌn'siːmlɪ] ADJ unschicklich, ungebührlich

unseen [ʌn'siːn] **ADJ** ungesehen; (= invisible) unsichtbar; (= unobserved) escape unbemerkt; **~ by the public** der Öffentlichkeit nicht vorgestellt; **~ translation/examination paper** (esp Brit, Sch, Univ) unvorbereitete Übersetzung/Prüfung **N** (esp Brit) unvorbereitete Herübersetzung

unselfconscious ADJ , **unselfconsciously** ADV [ʌnself'kɒnʃəs, -lɪ] unbefangen

unselfconsciousness [ʌnself'kɒnʃəsnɪs] N Unbefangenheit f

unselfish [ʌn'selfɪʃ] ADJ uneigennützig, selbstlos; (esp Ftbl) player mit selbstlosem Einsatz spielend

unselfishly [ʌn'selfɪʃlɪ] ADV uneigennützig, selbstlos; (esp Ftbl) mit selbstlosem Einsatz

unselfishness [ʌn'selfɪʃnɪs] N Uneigennützigkeit f, Selbstlosigkeit f

unsensational [ʌnsen'seɪʃənl] ADJ wenig aufregend or sensationell

unsentimental [ʌnsentɪ'mentl] ADJ unsentimental; **to be ~ about sth** von etw ungerührt sein

unserviceable [ʌn'sɜːvɪsəbl] ADJ unbrauchbar

unsettle [ʌn'setl] VT **a** (= throw off balance, confuse) aus dem Gleichgewicht bringen; (= agitate, upset) aufregen; (= disturb emotionally) verstören; person (news) beunruhigen; (defeat, failure, criticism) verunsichern; market aus dem Gleichgewicht bringen, verunsichern; faith erschüttern **b** foundations erschüttern

unsettled [ʌn'setld] ADJ **a** (= unpaid) unbezahlt, unbeglichen; (= undecided) question ungeklärt, offen; future unbestimmt, ungewiss, in der Schwebe; **to be in an ~ state of mind** mit sich selbst nicht eins sein; **he was ~ in his mind about what to do** er war sich (dat) nicht schlüssig, was er tun sollte; **the question remains ~** die Frage bleibt ungelöst **b** (= changeable) weather unbeständig, veränderlich; life, character unstet, unruhig; (Fin) market unbeständig, veränderlich; (Pol) conditions unsicher; **to be ~** durcheinander sein; (= thrown off balance) aus dem Gleis geworfen sein; (= emotionally disturbed) verstört sein; **to feel ~** sich nicht wohl fühlen **c** (= unpopulated) territory unbesiedelt **d** (= itinerant) person nomadenhaft

unsettling [ʌn'setlɪŋ] ADJ change, pace of life aufreibend; time also aufregend; defeat, knowledge verunsichernd; question, thought, news, book, film, atmosphere beunruhigend; music irritierend; **to have an ~ effect on sb** jdn aus dem Gleis werfen; (defeat, failure also) jdn verunsichern; on children also jdn verstören; **it is ~ to know he could be watching me** es beunruhigt mich zu wissen, dass er mich beobachten könnte

unsexy [ʌn'seksɪ] ADJ (inf) nicht sexy (inf)

unshackle [ʌn'ʃækl] VT prisoner befreien; (fig also) von seinen Fesseln befreien

unshaded [ʌn'ʃeɪdɪd] ADJ (from sun) schattenlos; eyes etc ungeschützt; part of drawing nicht schattiert; **~ bulb** nackte Glühbirne

unshak(e)able [ʌn'ʃeɪkəbl] ADJ unerschütterlich

unshak(e)ably [ʌn'ʃeɪkəblɪ] ADV unerschütterlich; **Anna is unshakeably honest** Anna ist grundehrlich

unshaken [ʌn'ʃeɪkən] ADJ unerschüttert; **he was ~ by the accident** der Unfall erschütterte ihn nicht; **his nerve was ~** er behielt seine Kaltblütigkeit; **to be ~ in one's belief that ...** unerschüttert in seinem Glauben sein, dass ...

unshaven [ʌnˈʃeɪvn] ADJ unrasiert; (= *bearded*) bärtig

unsheathe [ʌnˈʃiːð] VT *sword* (aus der Scheide) ziehen

unshed [ʌnˈʃed] ADJ *tears* ungeweint, unvergossen

unship [ʌnˈʃɪp] VT *cargo* löschen, ausladen, entladen; *tiller, oars* abnehmen; *mast* abbauen

unshockable [ʌnˈʃɒkəbl] ADJ durch nichts zu schockieren

unshod [ʌnˈʃɒd] ADJ *horse* unbeschlagen; *person* barfuß, ohne Schuhe; **with ~ feet** barfuß, mit nackten Füßen

unshrinkable [ʌnˈʃrɪŋkəbl] ADJ *fabric* nicht einlaufend

unshrinking [ʌnˈʃrɪŋkɪŋ] ADJ unverzagt, furchtlos, fest

unsighted [ʌnˈsaɪtɪd] ADJ **to be ~** in der or seiner Sicht behindert sein

unsightliness [ʌnˈsaɪtlɪnɪs] N Unansehnlichkeit *f*; (*stronger*) Hässlichkeit *f*

unsightly [ʌnˈsaɪtlɪ] ADJ unansehnlich; (*stronger*) hässlich

unsigned [ʌnˈsaɪnd] ADJ **a** *painting* unsigniert; *letter* nicht unterzeichnet, nicht unterschrieben; *newspaper article* anonym **b** *pop band* nicht unter Vertrag stehend *attr*; **they are still ~** sie stehen noch nicht unter Vertrag

unsinkable [ʌnˈsɪŋkəbl] ADJ unsinkbar; *battleship* unversenkbar

unsisterly [ʌnˈsɪstəlɪ] ADJ nicht schwesterlich

unskilful, (*US*) **unskillful** [ʌnˈskɪlfʊl] ADJ (= *inexpert*) ungeschickt; (= *clumsy*) unbeholfen

unskilfully, (*US*) **unskillfully** [ʌnˈskɪlfəlɪ] ADV (= *inexpertly*) ungeschickt; (= *clumsily*) unbeholfen

unskilfulness, (*US*) **unskillfulness** [ʌnˈskɪlfʊlnɪs] N (= *lack of expertise*) Ungeschicklichkeit *f*, Mangel *m* an Geschick; (= *clumsiness*) Unbeholfenheit *f*

unskilled [ʌnˈskɪld] **ADJ a** *work, worker* ungelernt; **many people remained ~** viele Menschen erlernten keinen Beruf; **to be ~ in sth** ungeübt in etw (*dat*) sein; **to be ~ in doing sth** ungeübt darin sein, etw zu tun; **~ labour** (*Brit*) or **labor** (*US*) (= *workers*) Hilfsarbeiter *pl* **b** (= *inexperienced*) ungeübt, unerfahren **N** **the ~** *pl* die ungelernten Arbeiter *pl*, die Hilfsarbeiter *pl*

unskillful *etc* (*US*) = **unskilful** *etc*

unslept-in [ʌnˈsleptɪn] ADJ unberührt

unsmilingly [ʌnˈsmaɪlɪŋlɪ] ADV ohne zu lächeln; **she stared at him ~** sie starrte ihn ohne zu lächeln an

unsnubbable [ʌnˈsnʌbəbl] ADJ (*inf*) dickfellig (*inf*)

unsociability [ʌnˌsəʊʃəˈbɪlɪtɪ] N Ungeselligkeit *f*

unsociable [ʌnˈsəʊʃəbl] ADJ ungesellig

unsocial [ʌnˈsəʊʃəl] ADJ **to work ~ hours** außerhalb der normalen Arbeitszeiten arbeiten; **at this ~ hour** zu so nachtschlafender Zeit

unsold [ʌnˈsəʊld] ADJ unverkauft; **to go** or **be left** or **remain ~** nicht verkauft werden

unsoldierly [ʌnˈsəʊldʒəlɪ] ADJ unsoldatisch

unsolicited [ʌnsəˈlɪsɪtɪd] ADJ unerbeten; *manuscript* nicht angefordert, unangefordert

unsolvable [ʌnˈsɒlvəbl] ADJ **a** (*Chem*) unauflöslich **b** (*fig*) *problem etc* unlösbar

unsolved [ʌnˈsɒlvd] ADJ *crossword, problem etc* ungelöst; *mystery also, crime* unaufgeklärt

unsophisticated [ʌnsəˈfɪstɪkeɪtɪd] **ADJ a** (= *simple*) *person* einfach; *style also* natürlich, simpel (*pej*); *tastes* schlicht; *film, machine also* unkompliziert; *technique also* simpel; (= *naïve*) naiv, simpel; (= *undiscriminating*) unkritisch **b** (= *crude*) *method* grob(schlächtig) **N** **the ~** *pl* das einfache Volk

unsought [ʌnˈsɔːt] ADJ unaufgefordert; (= *unwanted*) unerwünscht; **his help was ~** seine Hilfe kam unaufgefordert

unsound [ʌnˈsaʊnd] ADJ **a** *heart, teeth* krank; *health, gums* angegriffen; *floorboards, timber* morsch; *construction, design* unsolide; *foundations, finances* unsicher, schwach; **the ship was quite ~** das Schiff war überhaupt nicht seetüchtig; **structurally ~** (*building*) bautechnische Mängel aufweisend *attr* **b** *argument* nicht stichhaltig, anfechtbar; *advice* unvernünftig; *judgement* unzuverlässig; *doctrine* unvertretbar; *policy, move* unklug; (*Jur*) *conviction* ungesichert; **of ~ mind** (*Jur*) unzurechnungsfähig; **politically ~** (*person*) politisch unzuverlässig; *policy* politisch unklug; **ideologically/ecologically ~** ideologisch/ökologisch nicht vertretbar; **environmentally ~** umweltschädlich; **~ banking procedures** heikle Bankgeschäfte *pl*; **the company is ~** die Firma steht auf schwachen Füßen; **our financial position is ~** unsere Finanzlage ist heikel; **I'm ~ on French grammar** ich bin unsicher in französischer Grammatik; **the book is ~ on some points** das Buch weist an einigen Stellen Schwächen auf; **his views on this are ~** seine Ansichten sind nicht vertretbar

unsoundness [ʌnˈsaʊndnɪs] N **a** (*of heart etc*) Krankheit *f*; (*of health*) Angegriffenheit *f*; (*of timber*) Morschheit *f*; (*of construction, design*) unsolide Bauweise; (*of foundations, finances*) Unsicherheit *f*, Schwäche *f* **b** (*of argument*) geringe Stichhaltigkeit, Anfechtbarkeit *f*; (*of advice*) Unvernünftigkeit *f*; (*of judgement*) Unzuverlässigkeit *f*; (*of doctrine*) Unvertretbarkeit *f*; (*of policy, move*) mangelnde Klugheit *f*; (*Jur: of conviction*) Ungesichertheit *f*; **~ of mind** (*Jur*) Unzurechnungsfähigkeit *f*; **political ~** (*of person*) politische Unzuverlässigkeit; (*of policy*) politische Unklugheit

unsparing [ʌnˈspeərɪŋ] ADJ **a** (= *lavish*) großzügig, verschwenderisch, nicht kleinlich; **to be ~ with sth** mit etw nicht geizen; **to be ~ in one's efforts** keine Kosten und Mühen scheuen **b** (= *unmerciful*) *criticism* schonungslos; **the report was ~ in its criticism** der Bericht übte schonungslos Kritik

unsparingly [ʌnˈspeərɪŋlɪ] ADV **a** (= *generously*) großzügig, verschwenderisch; **to work ~ for sth** unermüdlich für etw arbeiten; **he gave ~ of his time** er opferte unendlich viel Zeit **b** (= *mercilessly*) *criticize* schonungslos

unspeakable [ʌnˈspiːkəbl] ADJ unbeschreiblich; *their* **~ trade** ihr abscheuliches Geschäft; **to do/say ~ things to sb** jdm unaussprechliche Dinge antun/sagen

unspeakably [ʌnˈspiːkəblɪ] ADV unbeschreiblich, unsagbar

unspecified [ʌnˈspesɪfaɪd] ADJ *time, amount* nicht spezifiziert or genannt, nicht genau angegeben; *location* unbestimmt; **to be imprisoned on ~ charges** ohne nähere Angabe von Gründen inhaftiert werden; **to seek/claim ~ damages** (*Jur*) Schadenersatz in unbestimmter Höhe verlangen/einklagen; **for ~ reasons** aus nicht näher ausgeführten Gründen

unspectacular [ʌnspekˈtækjʊlə] ADJ wenig eindrucksvoll; *career* wenig Aufsehen erregend

unspent [ʌnˈspent] ADJ *money* nicht ausgegeben; *energy* nicht verbraucht

unspoiled [ʌnˈspɔɪld], **unspoilt** [ʌnˈspɔɪlt] ADJ **a** *person, fruit* unverdorben; *goods* unbeschädigt; *child* nicht verwöhnt **b** (= *unchanged: by tourism, civilization*) unberührt; **to remain unspoilt** unberührt bleiben

unspoken [ʌnˈspəʊkən] ADJ *words, thoughts* unausgesprochen; *agreement, consent* stillschweigend

unsporting [ʌnˈspɔːtɪŋ], **unsportsmanlike** [ʌnˈspɔːtsmənlaɪk] ADJ *conduct, person* unsportlich, unfair

unsprung [ʌnˈsprʌŋ] ADJ *seat* ungefedert; *trap* offen, nicht zugeschnappt

unstable [ʌnˈsteɪbl] ADJ **a** *structure* nicht or wenig stabil; *foundations also, area* unsicher; *vehicle, government, country* instabil; *weather* unbeständig; *economy* unsicher, schwankend; *prices* schwankend; (*Chem, Phys*) instabil; **the patient is in an ~ condition** der Zustand des Patienten ist labil or nicht stabil **b** (*Psych, mentally*) labil; **mentally/emotionally ~** geistig/emotional labil

unstamped [ʌnˈstæmpt] ADJ *letter* unfrankiert; *document, passport* ungestempelt

unstated [ʌnˈsteɪtɪd] ADJ (= *unsaid*) *assumption, aim* unausgesprochen; *reason* nicht angegeben; **to leave something ~** etw ungesagt lassen; **for ~ reasons** aus nicht weiter angegebenen or ausgeführten Gründen

unstatesmanlike [ʌnˈsteɪtsmənlaɪk] ADJ unstaatsmännisch

unsteadily [ʌnˈstedɪlɪ] ADV *rise, walk* schwankend, unsicher; *say* mit schwankender or unsicherer Stimme

unsteadiness [ʌnˈstedɪnɪs] N (*of hand, legs, steps*) Unsicherheit *f*; (*of ladder*) Wack(e)ligkeit *f*; (*of flame*) Flackern *nt*; (*of voice, economy*) Schwanken *nt*; (*of progress*) Ungleichmäßigkeit *f*; (*of growth*) Unregelmäßigkeit *f*

unsteady [ʌnˈstedɪ] **ADJ** *hand* unsicher; *legs, steps* schwankend, unsicher; *ladder* wack(e)lig; *flame* unruhig, flackernd; *voice, economy* schwankend; (= *irregular*) *progress* schwankend, ungleichmäßig; *growth* unregelmäßig; **to be ~ on one's feet** unsicher or wackelig auf den Beinen sein; **the pound is still ~** das Pfund schwankt noch **VT** durcheinander bringen; (*stronger*) aus dem Gleichgewicht bringen

unstick [ʌnˈstɪk] *pret, ptp* **unstuck** VT lösen, losmachen → *also* **unstuck**

unstinted [ʌnˈstɪntɪd] ADJ *praise* uneingeschränkt, vorbehaltlos; *generosity, devotion, efforts* unbegrenzt

unstinting [ʌnˈstɪntɪŋ] ADJ *person* großzügig; *kindness, generosity* uneingeschränkt, unbegrenzt; *support* uneingeschränkt, vorbehaltlos; *work* unermüdlich; **to be ~ in one's efforts** keine Kosten und Mühen scheuen; **to be ~ in one's praise of sth** etw uneingeschränkt or vorbehaltlos loben; **to be ~ of one's time** unendlich viel Zeit opfern

unstintingly [ʌnˈstɪntɪŋlɪ] ADV großzügig; *generous* unendlich; *work* unermüdlich; *donate, contribute* verschwenderisch

unstitch [ʌnˈstɪtʃ] VT *seam* auftrennen; *zip* heraustrennen; **to come ~ed** aufgehen; (*fig*) nicht klappen, danebengehen

unstop [ʌnˈstɒp] VT *drain* freimachen; *bottle* öffnen, aufmachen

unstoppable [ʌnˈstɒpəbl] ADJ nicht aufzuhalten; **the Labour candidate seems ~** der Labour-Kandidat scheint unaufhaltbar zu sein

unstrap [ʌnˈstræp] VT *case etc* aufschnallen; **to ~ sb/sth from sth** jdn/etw von etw los- or abschnallen

unstreamed [ʌnˈstriːmd] ADJ (*Brit, Sch*) nicht in Leistungsgruppen eingeteilt

unstressed [ʌnˈstrest] ADJ (*Phon*) unbetont

unstring [ʌnˈstrɪŋ] *pret, ptp* **unstrung** VT *violin* die Saiten abnehmen or entfernen von; *beads* abfädeln

unstructured [ʌnˈstrʌktʃəd] ADJ unstrukturiert, nicht strukturiert

unstrung [ʌnˈstrʌŋ] *pret, ptp of* **unstring** ADJ **a** *person* demoralisiert, entnervt; *nerves* zerrüttet **b** *violin* unbesaitet

unstuck [ʌnˈstʌk] *pret, ptp of* **unstick** ADJ **to come ~** (*stamp, notice*) sich lösen; (*inf, plan*) danebengehen (*inf*), schief gehen (*inf*); (*speaker, actor*) stecken bleiben; (*pupil: in exam*) ins Schwimmen geraten; **the pay policy seems to have come ~** die Lohnpolitik scheint aus dem Gleis gekommen zu sein; **where they came ~ was ...** sie sind daran gescheitert, dass ...

unstudied [ʌnˈstʌdɪd] ADJ *grace etc* ungekünstelt, natürlich

unstylish ADJ , **unstylishly** ADV [ʌnˈstaɪlɪʃ, -lɪ] unmodisch, unelegant

unsubdued [ʌnsəbˈdjuːd] ADJ unbezwungen, unbesiegt

unsubsidized [ʌnˈsʌbsɪdaɪzd] ADJ unsubventioniert

unsubstantial [ʌnsəbˈstænʃəl] ADJ (= *flimsy*) *structure* leicht, dürftig; *meal* leicht; *evidence, proof* nicht überzeugend, nicht schlagkräftig; *claim* ungerechtfertigt

unsubstantiated [ʌnsəbˈstænʃɪeɪtɪd] ADJ *accusation, testimony, rumour* unbegründet; *gossip* unbestätigt; **these reports remain ~** diese Berichte sind weiterhin unbestätigt; **his claim was ~ by any evidence** seine Behauptung wurde durch keinerlei Indizien erhärtet

unsubtle [ʌnˈsʌtl] ADJ plump; **how ~ can you get!** plumper gehts nicht!

unsuccessful [ʌnsəkˈsesfʊl] ADJ *negotiations, venture, visit, meeting, person etc* erfolglos, ergebnislos; *writer, painter* erfolglos, ohne Erfolg; *candidate* abgewiesen; *attempt* vergeblich; *marriage, outcome* unglücklich; **to prove ~** sich als erfolglos erweisen; **I tried to persuade him but was ~** ich habe versucht, ihn zu überreden, hatte aber keinen Erfolg; **to be ~ in doing sth** keinen Erfolg damit haben, etw zu tun; **to be ~ in one's efforts to do sth** erfolglos in seinem Bemühen sein, etw zu tun; **he is ~ in everything he does** nichts gelingt ihm; **he was ~ in his exam** er hat kein Glück in seinem Examen gehabt; **he is ~ with women** er hat kein Glück *or* keinen Erfolg bei Frauen; **unfortunately, your application has been ~** wir haben uns leider nicht zur Annahme Ihrer Bewerbung entschließen können

unsuccessfully [ʌnsəkˈsesfəlɪ] ADV erfolglos; *try* vergeblich; *apply* ohne Erfolg, vergebens; **I tried ~ to grow tomatoes** ich habe ohne Erfolg versucht, Tomaten zu ziehen

unsuitability [ʌnsuːtəˈbɪlɪtɪ] N (*of moment, clothes, colour, candidate, land*) Ungeeignetsein *nt*; (*of language, attitude*) Unangebrachtheit *f*; **his ~ for the job** seine mangelnde Eignung für die Stelle; **I commented on the ~ of his clothes** ich machte eine Bemerkung über seine unpassende Kleidung; **their ~ as partners is clear** es ist klar, dass sie keine geeigneten Partner füreinander sind

unsuitable [ʌnˈsuːtəbl] ADJ unpassend; *language, attitude also* unangebracht; *moment, clothes, colour also, candidate, land, ground* ungeeignet; **it would be ~ at this moment to ...** es wäre im Augenblick unangebracht, ...; **this film is ~ for children** dieser Film ist für Kinder ungeeignet *or* nicht geeignet; **he's ~ for the position** er ist für die Stelle nicht geeignet; **she is ~ for him** sie ist nicht die Richtige für ihn; **we're ~ for each other** wir passen nicht zusammen; **she married a very ~ person** sie hat jemanden geheiratet, der gar nicht zu ihr passt

unsuitably [ʌnˈsuːtəblɪ] ADV *dressed* (*for weather conditions*) unzweckmäßig; (*for occasion*) unpassend; *designed* ungeeignet, schlecht; **they are ~ matched** sie passen nicht zusammen

unsuited [ʌnˈsuːtɪd] ADJ **to be ~ for** *or* **to sth** für etw ungeeignet *or* untauglich sein; **to be ~ to doing sth** sich nicht dazu eignen *or* nicht dazu taugen, etw zu tun; **to be ~ to sb** nicht zu jdm passen; **they are ~ (to each other)** sie passen nicht zusammen

unsullied [ʌnˈsʌlɪd] ADJ *virtue, honour etc* makellos, unbefleckt (*liter*); *snow* unberührt; **to be ~ by sth** (*by scandal, past*) von etw unberührt sein

unsung [ʌnˈsʌŋ] ADJ *heroes, deeds* unbesungen

unsupportable ADJ , **unsupportably** ADV [ʌnsəˈpɔːtəbl, -ɪ] unerträglich

unsupported [ʌnsəˈpɔːtɪd] ADJ *roof, person* ungestützt, ohne Stütze; *troops* ohne Unterstützung; *mother* allein stehend; *family* ohne Unterhalt; *claim, theory* ohne Beweise, nicht auf Fakten gestützt; *statement* unbestätigt, durch nichts gestützt; **if such families were ~ by the State**

wenn solche Familien nicht vom Staat unterstützt würden; **should the bank leave us financially ~** sollte die Bank uns finanziell nicht absichern; **the candidate/motion was ~** der Kandidat/Antrag fand keine Unterstützung; **~ by evidence** nicht durch Beweise gestützt

unsuppressed [ʌnsəˈprest] ADJ nicht unterdrückt

unsure [ʌnˈʃʊə] ADJ *person* unsicher; (= *unreliable*) *method also* unzuverlässig; **to be ~ of oneself** unsicher sein; **to be ~ (of sth)** sich (*dat*) (einer Sache *gen*) nicht sicher sein; **I'm ~ of him** ich bin mir bei ihm nicht sicher; **I am ~ of my welcome** ich bin nicht sicher, ob ich willkommen bin

unsureness [ʌnˈʃʊənɪs] N Unsicherheit *f*

unsurmountable [ʌnsəˈmaʊntəbl] ADJ unübersteigbar; (*fig*) unüberwindlich

unsurpassable [ʌnsəˈpɑːsəbl] ADJ unübertrefflich

unsurpassed [ʌnsəˈpɑːst] ADJ unübertroffen; **to be ~ by anybody** von niemandem übertroffen werden

unsurprising [ʌnsəˈpraɪzɪŋ] ADJ wenig überraschend

unsurprisingly [ʌnsəˈpraɪzɪŋlɪ] ADV wenig *or* kaum überraschend

unsuspected [ʌnsəˈspektɪd] ADJ *presence* nicht vermutet, unvermutet; *oilfields, coal deposits, causes* unvermutet; *wealth, skill, powers* ungeahnt; *consequences* unerwartet, ungeahnt; *problem* unerwartet; **to be ~** (*person*) nicht unter Verdacht stehen

unsuspecting ADJ , **unsuspectingly** ADV [ʌnsəˈspektɪŋ, -lɪ] ahnungslos, nichts ahnend

unsuspicious [ʌnsəˈspɪʃəs] ADJ (= *feeling no suspicion*) arglos; (= *causing no suspicion*) unverdächtig, harmlos

unsweetened [ʌnˈswiːtnd] ADJ ungesüßt

unswerving [ʌnˈswɜːvɪŋ] ADJ *resolve, loyalty* unerschütterlich, unbeirrbar; **the road followed its ~ course across the desert** die Straße führte schnurgerade durch die Wüste; **to be ~ in one's belief (in sth)** in seinem Glauben (an etw *acc*) unbeirrbar sein

unswervingly [ʌnˈswɜːvɪŋlɪ] ADV **to be ~ loyal to sb** jdm unerschütterlich *or* unbeirrbar treu sein; **to hold ~ to one's course** unbeirrbar seinen Weg gehen

unsymmetrical [ʌnsɪˈmetrɪkəl] ADJ unsymmetrisch

unsympathetic [ʌnsɪmpəˈθetɪk] ADJ **a** (= *unfeeling*) gefühllos, wenig mitfühlend; *reaction, attitude, response* ablehnend, abweisend; **I am not ~ to your request** ich stehe Ihrer Bitte nicht ablehnend gegenüber **b** (= *unlikeable*) unsympathisch

unsympathetically [ʌnsɪmpəˈθetɪkəlɪ] ADV ohne Mitgefühl; *say also* gefühllos, hart

unsystematic ADJ , **unsystematically** ADV [ʌnsɪstɪˈmætɪk, -əlɪ] planlos, unsystematisch, ohne System

untainted [ʌnˈteɪntɪd] ADJ einwandfrei, tadellos; *food also, person, mind* unverdorben; *reputation* tadellos, makellos

untalented [ʌnˈtælɪntɪd] ADJ unbegabt, untalentiert

untam(e)able [ʌnˈteɪməbl] ADJ *animal* unzähmbar; (*fig*) unbezähmbar, nicht zu bändigen *pred*

untamed [ʌnˈteɪmd] ADJ *animal* ungezähmt; *jungle* wild; *landscape, environment, beauty* ungezähmt, wild; *person, pride* ungebändigt; *temper* ungezügelt

untangle [ʌnˈtæŋgl] VT (*lit, fig*) entwirren

untanned [ʌnˈtænd] ADJ *hide* ungegerbt; *skin* nicht gebräunt

untapped [ʌnˈtæpt] ADJ *barrel* unangezapft; *resources also, source of wealth, talent* ungenutzt; *market* unerschlossen

untarnished [ʌnˈtɑːnɪʃt] ADJ makellos; *silver also* nicht angelaufen; (*fig*) *name* makellos, unbefleckt (*liter*)

untasted [ʌnˈteɪstɪd] ADJ (*lit, fig*) ungekostet

untaught [ʌnˈtɔːt] ADJ (= *not trained*) *person* nicht ausgebildet; *ability* angeboren; *behaviour* natürlich; **basic skills which remain ~ in our schools** Grundfähigkeiten, die in unseren Schulen weiterhin nicht vermittelt werden

untaxed [ʌnˈtækst] ADJ *goods, income* steuerfrei, unbesteuert; *car* unversteuert

unteachable [ʌnˈtiːtʃəbl] ADJ *person* unbelehrbar; *subject* nicht lehrbar; **it is ~ at this level** auf diesem Niveau kann man es nicht lehren

untearable [ʌnˈtɛərəbl] ADJ unzerreißbar

untempered [ʌnˈtempəd] ADJ *steel* ungehärtet, unvergütet; *rage* ungemildert; **justice ~ by mercy** Gerechtigkeit, die durch keinerlei Gnade gemildert wird

untenable [ʌnˈtenəbl] ADJ (*lit, fig*) unhaltbar

untenanted [ʌnˈtenəntɪd] ADJ *house* unbewohnt, leer

untended [ʌnˈtendɪd] ADJ *patient* unbehütet, unbewacht; *garden* vernachlässigt, ungepflegt

untested [ʌnˈtestɪd] ADJ *person* unerprobt; *theory, product also* ungetestet, ungeprüft; **~ players** Spieler, die sich noch nicht bewährt haben

unthankful ADJ , **unthankfully** ADV [ʌnˈθæŋkfʊl, -lɪ] undankbar

unthinkable [ʌnˈθɪŋkəbl] ADJ undenkbar, unvorstellbar; (*Philos*) undenkbar; (= *too horrible*) unvorstellbar

unthinking [ʌnˈθɪŋkɪŋ] ADJ (= *thoughtless, unintentional*) unbedacht, gedankenlos; (= *uncritical*) bedenkenlos, blind

unthinkingly [ʌnˈθɪŋkɪŋlɪ] ADV (= *thoughtlessly, unintentionally*) unbedacht, gedankenlos; *assume, suppose* ohne nachzudenken

unthoughtful ADJ , **unthoughtfully** ADV [ʌnˈθɔːtfʊl, -ɪ] gedankenlos; (= *careless*) unachtsam (*of mit*)

unthought-of [ʌnˈθɔːtɒv] ADJ (= *inconceivable*) undenkbar, unvorstellbar; **these hitherto ~ objections** diese Einwände, auf die bis dahin niemand gekommen war

unthought-out [ʌnθɔːtˈaʊt] ADJ nicht (gut) durchdacht, unausgegoren (*inf*)

unthread [ʌnˈθred] VT *needle* ausfädeln; *pearls* abfädeln

untidily [ʌnˈtaɪdɪlɪ] ADV unordentlich

untidiness [ʌnˈtaɪdɪnɪs] N (*of room*) Unordnung *f*, Unaufgeräumtheit *f*; (*of person, dress*) Unordentlichkeit *f*; **the ~ of the kitchen** die Unordnung in der Küche

untidy [ʌnˈtaɪdɪ] ADJ (+*er*) unordentlich; **to lie in an ~ heap** *or* **pile** unordentlich übereinander liegen

untie [ʌnˈtaɪ] VT *knot* lösen; *string, tie, shoelaces also* aufbinden; *shoes* aufmachen; *parcel* aufknoten; *person, animal, hands, apron* losbinden

until [ənˈtɪl] PREP **a** bis; **from morning ~ night** von morgens bis abends, vom Morgen bis zum Abend; **~ now** bis jetzt; **~ then** bis dahin

b not ~ (*in future*) nicht vor (+*dat*); (*in past*) erst; **I didn't leave him ~ the following day** ich habe ihn erst am folgenden Tag verlassen, ich bin bis zum nächsten Tag bei ihm geblieben; **the work was not begun ~ 1990** die Arbeiten wurden erst 1990 begonnen; **I had heard nothing of it ~ five minutes ago** bis vor fünf Minuten wusste ich (noch) nichts davon, ich habe erst vor fünf Minuten davon gehört

CONJ **a** bis; **wait ~ I come** warten Sie, bis ich komme

b not ~ (*in future*) nicht bevor, erst wenn; (*in past*) nicht bis, erst als; **he won't come ~ you invite him** er kommt erst, wenn Sie ihn einladen; **they did nothing ~ we came** bis wir kamen, taten sie nichts; **don't start ~ I come** fangen Sie nicht an, bevor ich da bin, fangen Sie erst an, wenn ich da bin; **they didn't start ~ we came** sie fingen erst an, als wir da waren, sie fingen nicht an, bevor wir da waren

untimeliness [ʌnˈtaɪmlɪnɪs] N (*of death*) Vorzeitigkeit *f*; (*of end also*) Verfrühtheit *f*; **because of**

the **~ of his arrival** weil er zur falschen Zeit kam

untimely [ʌnˈtaɪmlɪ] ADJ (= *premature*) *death* vorzeitig; *end also* verfrüht; (= *inopportune*) *moment* unpassend, ungelegen; *development, occurrence* unpassend, ungelegen, zur falschen Zeit; *shower, remark* zur falschen Zeit; *visit* ungelegen; **to come to** *or* **meet an ~ end** ein vorzeitiges Ende finden; **his arrival was most ~** seine Ankunft kam sehr ungelegen

untiring [ʌnˈtaɪərɪŋ] ADJ *campaigner, energy, enthusiasm, work, effort* unermüdlich; **to be ~ in one's efforts to do sth** unermüdliche Anstrengungen machen, etw zu tun

untiringly [ʌnˈtaɪərɪŋlɪ] ADV unermüdlich

untitled [ʌnˈtaɪtld] ADJ *painting* unbetitelt, ohne Titel; *person* ohne (Adels)titel

unto [ˈʌntʊ] PREP (*old, liter*) = **to**

untold [ʌnˈtəʊld] ADJ *story* nicht erzählt, nicht berichtet; *secret* unermesslich; *wealth* unermesslich; *agony, delights* unsäglich; *damage, suffering* unsäglich, unermesslich; *stars etc* ungezählt, unzählig, zahllos; *losses, varieties* unzählig; **this story is better left ~** über diese Geschichte schweigt man besser; **he died with his secret still ~** er nahm sein Geheimnis mit ins Grab; **~ thousands** unzählig viele; **to remain ~** im Dunkeln bleiben

untouchable [ʌnˈtʌtʃəbl] ADJ **a** unberührbar **b** (= *immune*) *person, rights* unantastbar **c** (= *supreme*) unantastbar N Unberührbare(r) *mf*

untouched [ʌnˈtʌtʃt] ADJ **a** (= *unhandled, unused*) unberührt, unangetastet; *bottle, box of sweets etc* unberührt, nicht angebrochen; (= *unmentioned*) nicht erwähnt; **~ by human hand** nicht von Menschenhand berührt; **he left his meal ~** er ließ sein Essen unberührt stehen **b** (= *unharmed*) heil, unversehrt; (= *unaffected*) unberührt; (= *unmoved*) ungerührt, unbewegt, unbeeindruckt; **he was ~ by her tears** ihre Tränen ließen ihn kalt **c** (= *unequalled*) unerreicht; **he is ~ by anyone** niemand kommt ihm gleich

untoward [ˌʌntəˈwɔːd] ADJ (= *unfortunate*) *event* unglücklich, bedauerlich; (= *unseemly*) unpassend, ungehörig; **nothing ~ had happened** es war kein Unheil geschehen

untraceable [ʌnˈtreɪsəbl] ADJ *person* unauffindbar; *note, bill* unbekannter Herkunft

untrained [ʌnˈtreɪnd] ADJ *person, teacher* unausgebildet; *voice, mind* ungeschult; *animal* undressiert; **to the ~ ear/eye** dem ungeschulten Ohr/Auge; **to be ~ for sth** für etw nicht ausgebildet sein; **to be ~ in sth** in etw (*dat*) nicht ausgebildet sein

untrammelled, (*US*) **untrammeled** [ʌnˈtræməld] ADJ unbeschränkt; **to be ~ by sth** nicht von etw beschränkt werden

untranslatable [ˌʌntrænzˈleɪtəbl] ADJ unübersetzbar

untravelled, (*US*) **untraveled** [ʌnˈtrævld] ADJ *road* unbefahren; *person* nicht weit gereist, nicht weit herumgekommen

untreated [ʌnˈtriːtɪd] ADJ unbehandelt; **to be ~ with sth** mit etw nicht behandelt sein

untried [ʌnˈtraɪd] ADJ **a** (= *not tested*) *person* unerprobt; *product, method* ungetestet, unerprobt; (= *not attempted*) unversucht **b** (*Jur*) *case* nicht verhandelt; *person* nicht vor Gericht gestellt; **the case is still ~** der Fall ist noch nicht verhandelt worden; **the offender can remain ~ for months** der Rechtsbrecher wird zuweilen erst nach Monaten vor Gericht gestellt

untrodden [ʌnˈtrɒdn] ADJ *path* verlassen; *snow* unberührt; **~ ground** (*fig*) neuer Boden

untroubled [ʌnˈtrʌbld] ADJ **a** (= *serene*) *appearance* unbekümmert; *sleep* ungestört; *life* sorglos; *period, ghost, person* friedlich, ruhig; *smile* unbeschwert; **to be ~ by the news** eine Nachricht gleichmütig hinnehmen; **the children seemed ~ by the heat** die Hitze schien den Kindern nichts anzuhaben *or* auszumachen; **they were ~ by thoughts of the future** der Gedanke an die Zukunft belastete sie nicht **b** (= *free from*)

to be ~ by war/injury vom Krieg/von Verletzungen verschont bleiben; **to be ~ by the authorities/police** von den Behörden/der Polizei nicht belästigt werden

untrue [ʌnˈtruː] ADJ **a** (= *false*) unwahr, falsch; (*Tech*) *reading, instrument* inkorrekt, ungenau **b** (= *unfaithful*) *person* untreu; **to be ~ to sb** jdm untreu sein; **to be ~ to one's principles/word** seinen Prinzipien/seinem Wort untreu sein

untrustworthy [ʌnˈtrʌstˌwɜːðɪ] ADJ (= *not reliable*) *source, book, person* unzuverlässig; (= *not worthy of confidence*) *person* nicht vertrauenswürdig

untruth [ʌnˈtruːθ] N Unwahrheit *f*

untruthful [ʌnˈtruːθfʊl] ADJ *statement* unwahr; *person* unaufrichtig; **you're being ~** da bist du unaufrichtig

untruthfully [ʌnˈtruːθfəlɪ] ADV fälschlich; **he said, quite ~, that ...** er sagte, und das war nicht die Wahrheit, dass ...

untruthfulness [ʌnˈtruːθfəlnɪs] N (*of statement*) Unwahrheit *f*; (*of person*) Unaufrichtigkeit *f*

untuneful [ʌnˈtjuːnfʊl] ADJ unmelodisch

unturned [ʌnˈtɜːnd] ADJ → **stone**

untutored [ʌnˈtjuːtəd] ADJ *taste, person* ungeschult; **to the ~ eye/ear** für das ungeschulte Auge/Ohr; **to be ~ in sth** in etw (*dat*) nicht unterrichtet sein

untypical [ʌnˈtɪpɪkl] ADJ untypisch (*of* für)

unusable [ʌnˈjuːzəbl] ADJ unbrauchbar; *road* unbefahrbar

unused¹ [ʌnˈjuːzd] ADJ (= *new*) unbenutzt, ungebraucht; *clothes* ungetragen; *banknote* druckfrisch; (= *not made use of*) ungenutzt; (= *no longer used*) nicht mehr benutzt *or* gebraucht; (= *left over*) *food* übrig geblieben

unused² [ʌnˈjuːst] ADJ **to be ~ to sth** nicht an etw (*acc*) gewöhnt sein, etw (*acc*) nicht gewohnt sein; **to be ~ to doing sth** nicht daran gewöhnt sein *or* es nicht gewohnt sein, etw zu tun

unusual [ʌnˈjuːʒʊəl] ADJ (= *uncommon*) ungewöhnlich; (= *exceptional*) außergewöhnlich; **it's ~ for him to be late** er kommt normalerweise nicht zu spät; **that's ~ for him** das ist sonst nicht seine Art; **that's not ~ for him** das wundert mich überhaupt nicht; **it is ~ to see this** das ist ein ungewöhnlicher Anblick; **nothing ~** nichts Außergewöhnliches; **there is something ~ about this** es hat etwas Ungewöhnliches an sich; **how ~!** (*iro*) welch Wunder!; **how do you like my new hat? – well, it's ~** wie gefällt Ihnen mein neuer Hut? – na, es ist mal was anderes

unusually [ʌnˈjuːʒʊəlɪ] ADV *large, quiet, cheerful* ungewöhnlich; **most ~, he was late** ganz gegen jede Gewohnheit kam er zu spät; **~ for her, she was late** ganz gegen ihre Gewohnheit kam sie zu spät; **~ for a big city, it has no cinema** obwohl das für eine Großstadt ungewöhnlich ist, gibt es hier/dort kein Kino

unutterable [ʌnˈʌtərəbl] ADJ *word* unaussprechlich; *joy, longing, sadness* unsäglich, unbeschreiblich; **he talks ~ rubbish** er redet völligen Unsinn

unutterably [ʌnˈʌtərəblɪ] (*liter*) ADV *sad* unbeschreiblich, unsagbar; *tired, boring* unbeschreiblich

unvaried [ʌnˈvɛərɪd] ADJ unverändert; (*pej*) eintönig

unvarnished [ʌnˈvɑːnɪʃt] ADJ *wood* ungefirnisst, unlackiert; (*fig*) *truth, language, report* ungeschminkt

unvarying [ʌnˈvɛərɪɪŋ] ADJ gleich bleibend, unveränderlich

unveil [ʌnˈveɪl] VT *statue, painting, plan* enthüllen; *results* bekannt geben; (*Comm*) *car* vorstellen; *face* entschleiern; **women mustn't go ~ed** Frauen dürfen nicht unverschleiert gehen VI sich entschleiern, den Schleier fallen lassen

unveiling [ʌnˈveɪlɪŋ] N (*lit, fig*) Enthüllung *f*; **~ ceremony** Enthüllung *f*

unventilated [ʌnˈventɪleɪtɪd] ADJ ungelüftet, nicht ventiliert

unverifiable [ʌnˈverɪfaɪəbl] ADJ nicht beweisbar, unverifizierbar (*geh*)

unverified [ʌnˈverɪfaɪd] ADJ unbewiesen

unversed [ʌnˈvɜːst] ADJ **~ in** nicht vertraut mit, unbewandert in (+*dat*)

unvisited [ʌnˈvɪzɪtɪd] ADJ nicht besucht; **we left Heidelberg with the castle ~** wir verließen Heidelberg, ohne das Schloss besucht zu haben

unvoiced [ʌnˈvɔɪst] ADJ **a** unausgesprochen **b** (*Phon*) stimmlos

unwaged [ʌnˈweɪdʒd] ADJ ohne Einkommen N **the ~** *pl* Personen *pl* ohne (festes) Einkommen

unwanted [ʌnˈwɒntɪd] ADJ **a** (= *unwelcome, unplanned*) unerwünscht; **sometimes you make me feel ~** manchmal komme ich mir (bei dir) richtig unerwünscht vor **b** (= *superfluous*) *food* überflüssig

unwarily [ʌnˈwɛərɪlɪ] ADV unvorsichtig, unbesonnen, unachtsam

unwariness [ʌnˈwɛərɪnɪs] N Unvorsichtigkeit *f*, Unbesonnenheit *f*, Unachtsamkeit *f*

unwarlike [ʌnˈwɔːlaɪk] ADJ friedliebend, friedlich

unwarrantable [ʌnˈwɒrəntəbl] ADJ nicht zu rechtfertigen *pred*, nicht zu rechtfertigend *attr*

unwarranted [ʌnˈwɒrəntɪd] ADJ ungerechtfertigt

unwary [ʌnˈwɛərɪ] ADJ unvorsichtig, unbesonnen, unachtsam

unwashed [ʌnˈwɒʃt] ADJ ungewaschen; *dishes* ungespült N **the great ~** *pl* (*hum*) der Pöbel

unwavering [ʌnˈweɪvərɪŋ] ADJ *faith, resolve* unerschütterlich; *gaze* fest, unbewegt; *course* beharrlich; *voice* fest; **to be ~ in one's opposition to sth** gegen etw beharrlich Widerstand leisten

unwaveringly [ʌnˈweɪvərɪŋlɪ] ADV *gaze, aim* fest; *support, oppose* beharrlich

unweaned [ʌnˈwiːnd] ADJ *baby* (noch) nicht entwöhnt

unwearable [ʌnˈwɛərəbl] ADJ **it's ~** das kann man nicht tragen

unwearied [ʌnˈwɪərɪd], **unwearying** [ʌnˈwɪərɪɪŋ] ADJ unermüdlich

unwed [ʌnˈwed] ADJ unverheiratet, unvermählt (*geh*)

unwelcome [ʌnˈwelkəm] ADJ *visitor* unwillkommen, unerwünscht; *news, memories* unerfreulich, unangenehm; *fact, thought, side effect, surprise* unangenehm; *reminder, change, publicity, advances* unwillkommen; **to make sb feel ~** sich jdm gegenüber abweisend verhalten; **the money was not ~** das Geld war höchst willkommen

unwelcoming [ʌnˈwelkəmɪŋ] ADJ *manner* abweisend, unfreundlich; *host also* ungastlich; *place* abweisend, ungastlich

unwell [ʌnˈwel] ADJ *pred* unwohl, nicht wohl; **to be** *or* **feel (a little) ~** sich nicht (recht) wohl fühlen; **I am afraid he's rather ~ today** es geht ihm heute leider gar nicht gut

unwholesome [ʌnˈhəʊlsəm] ADJ ungesund; *influence* ungut, verderblich; *appearance, character* schmierig; *food* minderwertig; *smell* faul; *desire, thoughts, story, jokes* schmutzig; **they are rather ~ company for her** sie sind nicht gerade ein guter Umgang für sie; **to have an ~ interest in sb/sth** ein perverses Interesse an jdm/etw haben

unwholesomeness [ʌnˈhəʊlsəmnɪs] N Ungesundheit *f*; (*of influence*) Verderblichkeit *f*; (*of appearance, character*) Schmierigkeit *f*; (*of food*) Minderwertigkeit *f*; (*of smell*) Verfaultheit *f*; (*of desire, thoughts, story, joke*) Schmutzigkeit *f*

unwieldy [ʌnˈwiːldɪ] ADJ **a** *tool* unhandlich; *object also* sperrig; (= *clumsy*) *body* schwerfällig, unbeholfen **b** (= *over-complex*) *system, bureaucracy* schwerfällig; *name* kompliziert

unwilling [ʌnˈwɪlɪŋ] ADJ *helper, admiration, pupil* widerwillig; *accomplice* unfreiwillig; **to be ~ to do sth** nicht bereit *or* gewillt *or* willens (*geh*) sein, dass jd etw tut; **to be ~ for sb to do sth** nicht wollen, dass jd etw tut

unwillingly [ʌnˈwɪlɪŋlɪ] ADV widerwillig

unwillingness [ʌnˈwɪlɪŋnɪs] N Widerwillen *nt*, Weigerung *f*; **their ~ to compromise** ihre mangelnde Kompromissbereitschaft

unwind [ʌnˈwaɪnd] *pret, ptp* **unwound** VT *thread, film, tape* abwickeln; (= *untangle*) entwirren VI **a** (*lit*) sich abwickeln; (*fig: story, plot*) sich entwickeln, sich entfalten **b** (*inf*: = *relax*) abschalten (*inf*), sich entspannen

unwise [ʌnˈwaɪz] ADJ unklug; **they were ~ enough to believe him** sie waren so töricht, ihm das zu glauben; **I thought it ~ to travel alone** ich hielt es für unklug *or* töricht, allein zu reisen

unwisely [ʌnˈwaɪzlɪ] ADV *act* unklug; **rather ~ the Government agreed** die Regierung hat unklugerweise zugestimmt

unwished-for [ʌnˈwɪʃtfɔːʳ] ADJ unerwünscht

unwitting [ʌnˈwɪtɪŋ] ADJ *accomplice* unbewusst, unwissentlich; *action also* unabsichtlich; *victim* ahnungslos; *involvement* unabsichtlich, unwissentlich; **he was the ~ cause of the argument** er war unbewusst die Ursache des Streits, er war, ohne es zu wissen, die Ursache des Streits

unwittingly [ʌnˈwɪtɪŋlɪ] ADV unbewusst; **I had agreed, albeit ~, to take part** ich hatte mich völlig ahnungslos dazu bereit erklärt, mitzumachen

unwomanly [ʌnˈwʊmənlɪ] ADJ unweiblich

unwonted [ʌnˈwəʊntɪd] ADJ ungewohnt

unwontedly [ʌnˈwəʊntɪdlɪ] ADV ungewöhnlich

unworkable [ʌnˈwɜːkəbl] ADJ *scheme, idea* undurchführbar; *law* nicht durchsetzbar; *land* nicht nutzbar; (*Min*) *mine* nicht abbaubar

unworkmanlike [ʌnˈwɜːkmənlaɪk] ADJ *job* unfachmännisch

unworldliness [ʌnˈwɜːldlɪnɪs] N Weltabgewandtheit *f*; (= *naivety*) Weltfremdheit *f*

unworldly [ʌnˈwɜːldlɪ] ADJ *life* weltabgewandt; (= *naïve*) weltfremd

unworn [ʌnˈwɔːn] ADJ (= *new*) ungetragen

unworried [ʌnˈwʌrɪd] ADJ unbekümmert, sorglos; **he was ~ by my criticism** meine Kritik (be-)kümmerte ihn nicht

unworthily [ʌnˈwɜːðɪlɪ] ADV *behave* unwürdig; **he said, rather ~, that ...** er sagte, und das war eigentlich unter seiner Würde, dass ...

unworthiness [ʌnˈwɜːðɪnɪs] N Unwürdigkeit *f*

unworthy [ʌnˈwɜːðɪ] ADJ *person* nicht wert (*of* +*gen*); *conduct also* nicht würdig, unwürdig (*of* +*gen*); **to be ~ to do sth** (es) nicht wert sein, etw zu tun; **to be ~ of an honour** (*Brit*) *or* **honor** (*US*) einer Ehre (*gen*) nicht wert sein (*geh*); **this is ~ of you** das ist unter deiner Würde; **it is ~ of our attention** das verdient unsere Aufmerksamkeit nicht, das ist unserer Aufmerksamkeit (*gen*) nicht wert; **it was ~ of you not to accept their kind offer** es war nicht anständig von dir, ihren freundlichen Vorschlag nicht anzunehmen; **it would be ~ of me not to mention also ...** es wäre nicht recht, wenn ich nicht auch ... erwähnen würde; **it is ~ of comment** es verdient keinen Kommentar

unwound [ʌnˈwaʊnd] *pret, ptp of* **unwind**

unwounded [ʌnˈwuːndɪd] ADJ nicht verwundet, unverwundet

unwrap [ʌnˈræp] VT auspacken, auswickeln

unwritten [ʌnˈrɪtn] ADJ *story, book, constitution* ungeschrieben; *agreement* stillschweigend

unwritten law N (*Jur, fig*) ungeschriebenes Gesetz

unyielding [ʌnˈjiːldɪŋ] ADJ *substance* unnachgiebig; (*fig*) *person, demand also, resistance* hart

unyoke [ʌnˈjəʊk] VT ausspannen; **he ~d his oxen from the plough** er spannte seine Ochsen aus

unzip [ʌnˈzɪp] VT **a** *zip* aufmachen; *dress, trousers, case* den Reißverschluss aufmachen an (+*dat*); **would you please ~ me?** kannst du bit-

---

te mir den Reißverschluss aufmachen? **b** *file* auspacken, entzippen VI (*zip*) aufgehen, sich öffnen; **this dress won't ~** der Reißverschluss an dem Kleid geht nicht auf *or* lässt sich nicht öffnen; **my dress must have come ~ped** der Reißverschluss an meinem Kleid muss aufgegangen sein

up [ʌp]	
✪ 16.4	
1 ADVERB	4 ADJECTIVE
2 PREPOSITION	5 TRANSITIVE VERB
3 NOUN	6 INTRANSITIVE VERB

1 – ADVERB

a indicating position (= *in high or higher position*) oben; (= *to higher position*) nach oben; **up there** dort oben, droben (*liter, S Ger*); **up here on the roof** hier oben auf dem Dach; **on your way up (to see us/them)** auf dem Weg (zu uns/ihnen) hinauf; **he climbed all the way up (to us/them)** er ist den ganzen Weg (zu uns/ihnen) hochgeklettert; **to stop halfway up** auf halber Höhe anhalten; **we were 6,000 m up when ...** wir waren 6.000 m hoch, als ...; **5 floors up** 5 Stockwerke hoch; **3 floors up from me** 3 Stockwerke über mir; **they were up above us** sie waren hoch oben; **I looked up (above)** ich schaute nach oben; **this side up** diese Seite oben!; **to go a little further up** ein bisschen weiter oben; **to go a little further up** ein bisschen höher (hinauf)gehen; **hang the picture a bit higher up** häng das Bild ein bisschen höher; **stick the notice up here** häng den Anschlag hier hin; **from up on the hill** vom Berg oben; **up on top (of the cupboard)** ganz oben (auf dem Schrank); **up in the mountains/sky** oben *or* droben (*liter, S Ger*) in den Bergen/am Himmel; **the temperature was up in the thirties** die Temperatur war über dreißig Grad; **the sun/moon is up** die Sonne/der Mond ist aufgegangen; **the tide is up** es ist Flut, die Flut ist da; **the wind is up** der Wind hat aufgefrischt; **with his collar up** mit hochgeschlagenem Kragen; **the road is up** (*Brit*) die Straße ist aufgegraben; **to be up with the leaders** vorn bei den Führenden sein; **to move up into the lead** nach vorn an die Spitze kommen; **Red Rum with Joe Smith up** Red Rum unter Joe Smith; **up and away the balloon sailed** der Ballon stieg auf und schwebte davon; **then up jumps Richard and says ...** und dann springt Richard auf und sagt ...; **the needle was up at 95** die Nadel stand auf 95; **come on, up, that's my chair!** komm, auf mit dir, das ist mein Stuhl!; **up! he shouted to his horse** spring! schrie er seinem Pferd zu; **up with the Liberals!** hoch die Liberalen!; **up with Spurs!** Spurs hoch!; **up yours!** (*inf*) du kannst mich mal (*inf*)

b = installed, built **to be up** (*building*) stehen; (*tent also*) aufgeschlagen sein; (*scaffolding*) aufgestellt sein; (*notice*) hängen, angeschlagen sein; (*picture*) hängen, aufgehängt sein; (*shutters*) zu sein; (*shelves, wallpaper, curtains, pictures*) hängen; **the new houses went up very quickly** die neuen Häuser sind sehr schnell gebaut *or* hochgezogen (*inf*) worden

♦ **to be up and running** laufen; (*committee etc*) in Gang sein

♦ **to get sth up and running** etw zum Laufen bringen; *committee etc* etw in Gang setzen; **have you got your computer up and running yet?** läuft dein Computer schon?

c = not in bed auf; **up (with you)!** auf mit dir!, raus aus dem Bett (*inf*); **to be up and about** auf sein; (*after illness also*) auf den Beinen sein; **she was up all night with him** (= *looking after him*) sie war seinetwegen die ganze Nacht auf

d = north oben; **up in Inverness** in Inverness oben, oben in Inverness; **we are going up to Aberdeen** wir fahren nach Aberdeen (hinauf); **to be/live up north** im Norden sein/wohnen; **to go up north** in den Norden fahren; **up from the country** vom Lande; **we're up for the day** wir sind (nur) für heute hier; **he was up at Susie's place** er war bei Susie zu Hause

---

e = at university (*Brit*) am Studienort; **the students are only up for half the year** die Studenten sind nur die Hälfte des Jahres am Studienort; **to go up to Cambridge** (zum Studium) nach Cambridge gehen; **he was up at Oxford in 1982** er hat 1982 in Oxford studiert

f in price, value gestiegen (*on* gegenüber); **my shares are up 70p** meine Aktien sind um 70 Pence gestiegen; **then up go prices again** und wieder steigen die Preise

g in score **to be 3 goals up** mit 3 Toren führen *or* vorn liegen (*on* gegenüber); **the score was 9 up** (*US*) es stand 9 beide; **I'll play you 100 up** ich spiele auf 100 (mit dir); **we were £100 up on the deal** wir haben bei dem Geschäft £ 100 gemacht; **to be one up on sb** jdm um einen Schritt voraus sein

h = upwards **from £10 up** von £ 10 (an) aufwärts, ab £ 10; **from the age of 13 up** ab (dem Alter von) 13 Jahren, von 13 Jahren aufwärts

i = wrong (*inf*) **what's up?** was ist los?; **what's up with him?** was ist mit dem los?, was ist los mit ihm?; **something is up** (= *wrong*) da stimmt irgendetwas nicht; (= *happening*) da ist irgendetwas im Gange; **there's something up with it** irgendetwas stimmt damit nicht *or* hier nicht

j = knowledgeable *firm*, beschlagen (*in, on* in +*dat*); **he's well up on foreign affairs** in außenpolitischen Fragen kennt er sich aus *or* ist er firm; **I'm not very up on French history** in französischer Geschichte bin ich nicht sehr beschlagen

k = finished **time's up** die Zeit ist um, die Zeit ist zu Ende; **the weekend is nearly up** das Wochenende ist fast zu Ende *or* fast vorüber; **to eat/use sth up** etw aufessen/aufbrauchen; **it's all up with him** es ist aus mit ihm (*inf*), es ist mit ihm zu Ende

l set structures

♦ **up against it** **was up against the wall** es war an die Wand gelehnt; **put it up against the wall** lehne es an die Wand; **to be up against a difficulty/an opponent** einem Problem/Gegner gegenüberstehen, es mit einem Problem/Gegner zu tun haben; **I fully realize what I'm up against** mir ist völlig klar, womit ich es hier zu tun habe; **they were really up against it** sie hatten wirklich schwer zu schaffen

♦ **up and down** auf und ab; **to walk up and down** auf und ab gehen; **to bounce up and down** hochfedern, auf und ab hüpfen; **he's been up and down all evening** (*from seat*) er hat den ganzen Abend keine Minute stillgesessen; (*on stairs*) er ist den ganzen Abend die Treppe rauf- und runtergerannt; **she's still a bit up and down** (*after illness etc*) es geht ihr immer noch mal besser, mal schlechter

♦ **up before** the matter **is up before the committee** die Sache ist vor dem Ausschuss; **the boys were up before the head teacher** die Jungen sind vor den Direktor zitiert worden; **to be up before the Court/before Judge Smith** (*case*) verhandelt werden/von Richter Smith verhandelt werden; (*person*) vor Gericht/Richter Smith stehen

♦ **up for** **to be up for sale** zu verkaufen sein; **to be up for discussion** zur Diskussion stehen; **to be up for election** (*candidate*) zur Wahl aufgestellt sein; (*candidates*) zur Wahl stehen; **to be up for trial** vor Gericht stehen

♦ **up to**

= as far as bis; **up to now/here** bis jetzt/hier; **to count up to 100** bis 100 zählen; **up to £100** bis zu £ 100; **it holds up to 8** es fasst bis zu 8; **I'm up to here in work/debt** (*inf*) ich stecke bis hier in Arbeit/Schulden; **I'm full up to here** (*inf*) ich bin bis oben (hin) voll (*inf*); **what page are you up to?** bis zu welcher Seite bist du gekommen?

= equal to **I don't feel up to it** ich fühle mich dem nicht gewachsen; (= *not well enough*) ich fühle mich nicht wohl genug dazu; **it isn't up to much** damit ist nicht viel los (*inf*); **is he up to the heavier weights?** schafft er schwerere Gewichte?; **he isn't up to running the company by himself** er hat nicht das Zeug dazu, die

Firma allein zu leiten; **it isn't up to his usual standard** das ist nicht sein sonstiges Niveau; **we're going up Ben Nevis – are you sure you're up to it?** wir wollen Ben Nevis besteigen – glaubst du, dass du das schaffst?

♦ **to be up to sb**

$\boxed{= \text{depend on}}$ **it's up to us to help him** wir sollten ihm helfen; **if it were up to me** wenn es nach mir ginge; **the success of this project is up to you now** wie erfolgreich dieses Projekt wird, hängt jetzt nur noch von Ihnen (selbst) ab, es liegt jetzt ganz an Ihnen, ob dieses Projekt ein Erfolg wird; **it's up to you whether you go or not** es liegt an or bei dir or es bleibt dir überlassen, ob du gehst oder nicht; **I'd like to accept, but it isn't up to me** ich würde gerne annehmen, aber ich habe da nicht zu bestimmen or aber das hängt nicht von mir ab; **shall I take it? – that's entirely up to you** soll ich es nehmen? – das müssen Sie selbst wissen; **what colour shall I choose? – (it's) up to you** welche Farbe soll ich nehmen? – das ist deine Entscheidung

$\boxed{= \text{be duty of}}$ **it's up to the government to put this right** es ist Sache der Regierung, das richtig zu stellen; **it's not up to the government** das ist nicht Sache der Regierung

♦ **to be up to sth** (inf) **what's he up to?** (= actually doing) was macht er da?; (= planning etc) was hat er vor?; (suspiciously) was führt er im Schilde?; **what have you been up to?** was hast du angestellt?; **what are you up to with that?** was hast du damit vor?; **he's up to no good** er führt nichts Gutes im Schilde; **I'm sure he's up to something** ich bin sicher, er hat etwas vor or (sth suspicious) er führt irgendetwas im Schilde; (child) ich bin sicher, er stellt irgendetwas an; **hey you! what do you think you're up to!** he Sie, was machen Sie eigentlich da!; **what does he think he's up to?** was soll das eigentlich?, was hat er eigentlich vor?

2 – PREPOSITION

oben auf (+dat); (with movement) hinauf (+acc); **further up the page** weiter oben auf der Seite; **to live up the hill** am Berg wohnen; **to go up the hill** den Berg hinaufgehen; **they live further up the hill/street** sie wohnen weiter oben am Berg/weiter die Straße entlang; **he lives up a dark alley** er wohnt am Ende einer dunklen Gasse; **up the road from me** (von mir) die Straße entlang; **he went off up the road** er ging (weg) die Straße hinauf; **he hid it up the chimney** er versteckte es (oben) im Kamin; **the water goes up this pipe** das Wasser geht durch dieses Rohr; **up one's sleeve** (position) im Ärmel; (motion) in den Ärmel; **as I travel up and down the country** wenn ich so durchs Land reise; **I've been up and down the stairs all night** ich bin in der Nacht immer nur die Treppe rauf- und runtergerannt; **he was up the pub** (Brit inf) er war in der Kneipe (inf); **let's go up the pub/up Johnny's place** (inf) gehen wir doch zur Kneipe/zu Johnny (inf); **to go up to sb** auf jdn zugehen

3 – NOUN

♦ **ups and downs** gute und schlechte Zeiten pl; (of life) Höhen und Tiefen pl; **after many ups and downs** nach vielen Höhen und Tiefen; **they have their ups and downs** bei ihnen gibt es auch gute und schlechte Zeiten

♦ **to be on the up and up** (inf: = improving) auf dem aufsteigenden Ast sein (inf); (sl: = honest, straight, person) keine krummen Touren machen (inf); (offer) sauber sein (inf); **he/his career is on the up and up** (inf) mit ihm/seiner Karriere geht es aufwärts

4 – ADJECTIVE

(= going up) escalator nach oben; (Rail) train, line zur nächsten größeren Stadt; **platform 14 is the up platform** auf Bahnsteig 14 fahren die Züge nach London etc

5 – TRANSITIVE VERB

(inf) price, offer hinaufsetzen; production ankurbeln; bet erhöhen (to auf +acc)

6 – INTRANSITIVE VERB

(inf) **she upped and left him** sie verließ ihn ganz plötzlich or Knall auf Fall (inf); **he upped and ran** er rannte ganz plötzlich davon

up-and-coming ['ʌpənˈkʌmɪŋ] ADJ city aufstrebend; **an ~ actor/star** ein Schauspieler/Star, der im Kommen ist

up-and-down ['ʌpənˈdaʊn] ADJ **a** (lit) ~ **movement** Auf- und Abbewegung f **b** (fig) career, fortunes, relationship, period wechselhaft

up-and-under ['ʌpənˈʌndə'] N (Rugby) hohe Selbstvorlage

up arrow N (Comput) Aufwärtspfeil m

upbeat ['ʌpbiːt] N (Mus) Auftakt m ADJ (inf) (= cheerful) fröhlich; (= optimistic) optimistisch; **to be ~ about sth** über etw (acc) optimistisch gestimmt sein

up-bow ['ʌpbəʊ] N Aufstrich m

upbraid [ʌpˈbreɪd] VT rügen; **to ~ sb for doing sth** jdn dafür rügen, dass er etw getan hat

upbringing ['ʌpbrɪŋɪŋ] N Erziehung f; (= manners also) Kinderstube f; **to have a good ~** eine gute Kinderstube haben; **we had a strict ~** wir hatten (als Kinder) eine strenge Erziehung; **he hasn't got any ~** er hat keine Kinderstube

upchuck ['ʌptʃʌk] VI (US, inf, = vomit) kotzen (sl), reihern (sl)

upcoming [ʌpˈkʌmɪŋ] ADJ (= coming soon) kommend, bevorstehend

upcountry ['ʌpˈkʌntrɪ] ADV landeinwärts ADJ town, village, person im Landesinnern; trip, tour ins Landesinnere

up-current ['ʌpkʌrənt] N (Aviat) Aufwind m, Aufströmung f

update [ʌpˈdeɪt] VT aktualisieren; file, book also, person auf den neuesten Stand bringen; **to ~ sb on sth** jdn über etw (acc) auf den neuesten Stand bringen N ['ʌpdeɪt] Aktualisierung f; (= updated version) Neufassung f; (of software package) aktualisierte Version; (= progress report) Bericht m; **can you give me an ~ on ...?** können Sie mich bezüglich ... (gen) auf den neuesten Stand bringen?

updraught, (US) **updraft** ['ʌpdrɑːft] N Zug m; (Aviat) Aufwind m, Aufströmung f

upend [ʌpˈend] VT box, sofa hochkant stellen; person, animal umdrehen

upfront ['ʌpˈfrʌnt] ADJ **a** person offen; **to be ~ about sth** sich offen über etw (acc) äußern **b** ~ **money** Vorschuss m; **an ~ commission/fee** eine Kommission/Gebühr, die im Voraus zu entrichten ist ADV **a** (= in advance) pay, charge im Voraus; **we'd like 20% ~** wir hätten gern 20% (als) Vorschuss; **we need all the cash ~** wir benötigen die ganze Summe im Voraus **b** (esp US, = openly) offen

upgrade ['ʌpˌgreɪd] N **a** (= improved version) verbesserte Version; (Comput) Upgrade nt **b** (US) Steigung f **c** (fig) **to be on the ~** sich auf dem aufsteigenden Ast befinden (inf) VT [ʌpˈgreɪd] employee befördern; job anheben; (= improve) verbessern; (= expand) computer system etc ausbauen, nachrüsten

upgrad(e)ability [ˌʌpgreɪdəˈbɪlɪtɪ] N (of computer system etc) Ausbaufähigkeit f, Nachrüstbarkeit f

upgrad(e)able [ʌpˈgreɪdəbl] ADJ computer system etc ausbaufähig (to auf +acc), nachrüstbar (to auf +acc)

upheaval [ʌpˈhiːvəl] N (Geol) Aufwölbung f, Erhebung f; (fig) Aufruhr m; **emotional ~** Aufruhr m der Gefühle; **social/political ~s** soziale/politische Umwälzungen pl

upheld [ʌpˈheld] pret, ptp of **uphold**

uphill ['ʌpˈhɪl] ADV bergauf; **to go ~** bergauf gehen, steigen; (road also) bergauf führen; (car) den Berg hinauffahren ADJ road bergauf (füh-

rend); (fig) work, struggle mühsam, mühselig; **it's ~ all the way** (lit) es geht die ganze Strecke bergauf; (fig) es ist ein harter Kampf; **an ~ struggle** or **battle** ein mühsamer or mühseliger Kampf; **~ ski** Bergski m

uphold [ʌpˈhəʊld] pret, ptp **upheld** VT (= sustain) tradition, principle, honour wahren; the law hüten; right, values schützen; (= support) person, decision, objection (unter)stützen; complaint anerkennen; (Jur) verdict, appeal bestätigen

upholder [ʌpˈhəʊldə'] N Wahrer(in) m(f); (= supporter) Verteidiger(in) m(f)

upholster [ʌpˈhəʊlstə'] VT chair etc polstern; (= cover) beziehen; **~ed furniture** Polstermöbel pl; **well-upholstered** (hum inf) gut gepolstert (hum inf)

upholsterer [ʌpˈhəʊlstərə'] N Polsterer m, Polsterin f

upholstery [ʌpˈhəʊlstərɪ] N (= padding and springs) Polsterung f; (= cover) Bezug m; (= trade) Polsterei f; (= skill) das Polstern

upkeep ['ʌpkiːp] N (= running) Unterhalt m; (= cost) Unterhaltskosten pl; (= maintenance) Instandhaltung f, Instandhaltungskosten pl; (of public gardens etc) Pflege f

upland ['ʌplənd] N (usu pl) Hochland nt no pl ADJ Hochland-; **~ area** Hochlandgebiet nt

uplift ['ʌplɪft] N (= exaltation) Erhebung f; (= moral inspiration) Erbauung f; **his sermons were full of ~** seine Predigten waren voll erbaulicher Worte; **to give sb spiritual ~** jdn erbauen; **an ~ in the economy** ein Wirtschaftsaufschwung m VT [ʌpˈlɪft] **a** spirit, heart, voice erheben; person, mind erbauen; **with ~ed arms** mit erhobenen Armen; **to feel ~ed** sich erbaut fühlen **b** (Scot, = collect) abholen

uplift bra N Stützbüstenhalter m

uplifting [ʌpˈlɪftɪŋ] ADJ experience erhebend; music, film, story erhebend, erbaulich

uplighter ['ʌplaɪtə'] N (= light) Wandfluter m

upload ['ʌpləʊd] VT (Comput) laden

up-market ['ʌpˈmɑːkɪt] ADJ customer anspruchsvoll; person vornehm; image, version, hotel exklusiv ADV sell an anspruchsvollere Kunden; **his shop has gone ~** in seinem Laden verkauft er jetzt Waren der höheren Preisklasse; **Japanese car-makers have gone ~** Japans Autohersteller produzieren jetzt für einen anspruchsvolleren Kundenkreis

upmost ['ʌpməʊst] ADJ, ADV = **uppermost**

upon [əˈpɒn] PREP = **on**

upper ['ʌpə'] ADJ **a** obere(r, s); (Anat, Geog) Ober-; **temperatures in the ~ thirties** Temperaturen hoch in den dreißig; **~ arm** Oberarm m; **~ lip** Oberlippe f; **~ body** Oberkörper m; **the ~ reaches of the Thames** der Oberlauf der Themse; **the ~ Loire** die obere Loire; **Upper Rhine** Oberrhein m

b (in importance, rank) höhere(r, s), obere(r, s); **the ~ ranks of the Civil Service** das gehobene Beamtentum; **in the ~ income bracket** in der oberen Einkommensklasse; **the ~ middle class(es)** die gehobene Mittelschicht → **hand 1 k**

N **a** **uppers** PL (of shoe) Obermaterial nt; **to be on one's ~s** (= destitute) auf den Hund gekommen sein (inf, = drug) Aufputschmittel nt, Muntermacher m (inf)

c (US, Rail) oberes Bett (im Schlafwagen)

upper: upper brain N (Anat) Großhirn nt; **upper case** N (Typ: also **upper-case letter**) Großbuchstabe m, Versal m (spec); **to set sth in ~** etw in Versalien setzen; **upper-case** ADJ groß; **an ~ T** ein großes T, ein Versal-T (spec); **upper circle** N (Brit Theat) zweiter Rang; **upper class** N obere Klasse, Oberschicht f; **the ~es** die Oberschicht; **upper-class** ADJ accent, district, person vornehm, fein; sport, expression, attitude der Oberschicht; **to be ~** (= person) der Oberschicht angehören; **upperclassman** N (US) Mitglied einer High School oder eines College; **upper crust** N (inf) obere zehntausend pl (inf); **upper-crust** ADJ (inf) (schrecklich) vornehm (*inf*); **uppercut** N Aufwärtshaken *m*, Uppercut *m*; **Upper Egypt** N Oberägypten *nt*; **upper hand** N to gain *or* get the ~ die Oberhand gewinnen (*of, over* über +*acc*), Oberwasser bekommen; **Upper House** N (*Parl*) Oberhaus *nt*

uppermost [ˈʌpəˈməʊst] ADJ oberste(r, s); (*fig*) *ambition* größte(r, s), höchste(r, s); **safety should be ~ in your minds** Sicherheit sollte für Sie an erster Stelle stehen; **it's quite obvious what is ~ in your mind** es ist ziemlich klar, wo deine Prioritäten liegen ADV **face/the blue side ~** mit dem Gesicht/der blauen Seite nach oben

upper: upper school N Oberschule *f*; **upper sixth** N (*Brit, Sch*) ≈ Oberprima *f*; **Upper Volta** [ˌʌpəˈvɒltə] N Obervolta *nt*

uppish [ˈʌpɪʃ], **uppity** [ˈʌpɪtɪ] ADJ (*inf, = arrogant*) hochnäsig (*inf*), hochmütig; *woman also* schnippisch; **to get uppity with sb** jdm gegenüber frech *or* anmaßend werden, jdm frech kommen

upraised [ʌpˈreɪzd] ADJ erhoben

upright [ˈʌpraɪt] ADJ a (*= erect*) aufrecht; (*= vertical*) *post* senkrecht; **~ chair** Stuhl *m*; **~ vacuum cleaner** Bürst(staub)sauger *m*; **~ freezer** Gefrierschrank *m* b (*fig: = honest*) *person, character* aufrecht, rechtschaffen ADV (*= erect*) aufrecht, gerade; (*vertical*) senkrecht; **to hold oneself ~** sich gerade halten; **to pull sb/oneself ~** jdn/sich aufrichten N a (*= post*) Pfosten *m* b (*= piano*) Klavier *nt*

uprightly [ˈʌpˌraɪtlɪ] ADV aufrecht, rechtschaffen

uprightness [ˈʌpˌraɪtnɪs] N Rechtschaffenheit *f*

upright piano N Klavier *nt*

uprising [ˈʌpraɪzɪŋ] N Aufstand *m*, Erhebung *f*

upriver [ˈʌpˈrɪvə] ADV flussaufwärts; **2 miles ~ from Fen Ditton** 2 Meilen flussaufwärts von Fen Ditton ADJ *place* flussaufwärts gelegen; **an ~ journey** eine Reise flussaufwärts

uproar [ˈʌprɔː] N Aufruhr *m*, Tumult *m*; **he tried to make himself heard above the ~** er versuchte, sich über den Lärm hinweg verständlich zu machen; **at this there was ~, this caused an ~** das verursachte einen (wahren) Aufruhr *or* Tumult; **the whole room/town was in ~** der ganze Saal/die ganze Stadt war in Aufruhr

uproarious [ʌpˈrɔːrɪəs] ADJ *meeting* tumultartig; *crowd* lärmend; *laughter* brüllend; *success, welcome* überwältigend, spektakulär; *personality* überschäumend; (*= very funny*) *joke* wahnsinnig komisch, zum Schreien *pred*; **in ~ spirits** in überschäumender Stimmung

uproariously [ʌpˈrɔːrɪəslɪ] ADV lärmend; *laugh* brüllend; **~ funny** wahnsinnig komisch, zum Schreien *or* Brüllen

uproot [ʌpˈruːt] VT *plant* entwurzeln; (*fig: = eradicate*) *evil* ausmerzen; **~ed by the war** durch den Krieg entwurzelt; **he ~ed his whole family (from their home) and moved to New York** er riss seine Familie aus ihrer gewohnten Umgebung und zog nach New York

upsadaisy [ˈʌpsəˌdeɪzɪ] INTERJ (*inf*) hoppla

upset [ʌpˈsɛt] *vb: pret, ptp* **upset** VT a (*= knock over*) umstoßen, umwerfen; *boat* umkippen, zum Kentern bringen; **she ~ the milk all over the new carpet** sie stieß die Milch um und alles lief auf den neuen Teppich

b (*= make sad: news, death*) bestürzen, erschüttern, mitnehmen (*inf*); (*question, insolence etc*) mitnehmen (*inf*); (*divorce, experience, accident etc*) mitnehmen (*inf*); (*= distress, excite*) *patient, parent etc* aufregen; (*= offend: unkind behaviour, words etc*) verletzen, wehtun (+*dat*); (*= annoy*) ärgern; **you shouldn't have said/done that, now you've ~ her** das hätten Sie nicht sagen/tun sollen, jetzt regt sie sich auf *or* (*offended*) jetzt ist sie beleidigt; **don't ~ yourself** regen Sie sich nicht auf; **there's no point in ~ting yourself** es hat doch keinen Zweck, dass so tragisch zu nehmen; **I don't know what's ~ him** ich weiß nicht, was er hat

c (*= disorganize*) *calculations, balance, plan, timetable etc* durcheinander bringen; **that's ~ my**

theory das hat meine Theorie umgestoßen; **to ~ the odds** die Chancen verändern; **Henman ~ the top seed** Henman hat den auf Nummer eins gesetzten Spieler überraschend geschlagen

d (*= make ill*) **the rich food ~ his stomach** das schwere Essen ist ihm nicht bekommen; **onions ~ me** von Zwiebeln bekomme ich Magenbeschwerden

VI umkippen

ADJ a (*about divorce, accident, dismissal etc*) mitgenommen (*inf*) (*about* von); (*about death, bad news etc*) bestürzt (*about* über +*acc*); (*= sad*) betrübt, geknickt (*inf*) (*about* über +*acc*); (*= distressed, worried*) aufgeregt (*about* wegen); *baby, child* durcheinander *pred*; (*= annoyed*) ärgerlich, aufgebracht (*about* über +*acc*); (*= hurt*) gekränkt, verletzt (*about* über +*acc*); **she was pretty ~ about it** das ist ihr ziemlich nahe gegangen, das hat sie ziemlich mitgenommen (*inf*); (*= distressed, worried*) sie hat sich deswegen ziemlich aufgeregt; (*= annoyed*) das hat sie ziemlich geärgert; (*= hurt*) das hat sie ziemlich gekränkt *or* verletzt; **she was ~ about something** irgendetwas hatte sie aus der Fassung gebracht; **she was ~ about the news/that he'd left her** es hat sie ziemlich mitgenommen, als sie das hörte/dass er sie verlassen hat (*inf*); **she was ~ about him leaving** sein Abschied war ihr sehr nahe gegangen; **we were very ~ to hear about her illness** wir waren sehr bestürzt, als wir von ihrer Krankheit hörten; **don't look so ~, they'll come back** guck doch nicht so traurig, sie kommen ja zurück; **would you be ~ if I decided not to go after all?** wärst du traurig *or* würdest dus tragisch nehmen, wenn ich doch nicht ginge?; **I'd be very ~ if ...** ich wäre sehr traurig *or* betrübt wenn ...; **she'd be ~ if I used a word like that** sie wäre entsetzt, wenn ich so etwas sagen würde; **the house has been broken into so of course I'm ~** bei mir ist eingebrochen worden und natürlich rege ich mich auf; **to get ~** sich aufregen (*about* über +*acc*); (*= hurt*) gekränkt *or* verletzt werden; **don't get ~ about it, you'll find another** nimm das noch nicht so tragisch, du findest bestimmt einen anderen; **to feel ~** gekränkt sein; **to sound/look ~** verstört klingen/aussehen

b [ˈʌpsɛt] *stomach* verstimmt, verdorben *attr*; **to have an ~ stomach** sich (*dat*) den Magen verdorben haben, eine Magenverstimmung haben

N [ˈʌpsɛt] a (*= disturbance*) Störung *f*; (*emotional*) Aufregung *f*; (*inf, = quarrel*) Verstimmung *f*, Ärger *m*; (*= unexpected defeat etc*) unliebsame *or* böse Überraschung; **I don't want to cause any ~s in your work** ich möchte bei Ihrer Arbeit kein Durcheinander verursachen; **children don't like ~s in their routine** Kinder mögen es nicht, wenn man ihre Routine durcheinander bringt; **it was an ~ to our plans** es hat unsere Pläne durcheinander gebracht; **it was an ~ for us** es war eine böse Überraschung für uns; **he's had a bit of an ~** er ist etwas mitgenommen (*inf*) *or* geknickt (*inf*)

b **stomach ~** Magenverstimmung *f*, verdorbener Magen

upset price N (*esp US, Comm*) Mindestpreis *m*

upsetting [ʌpˈsɛtɪŋ] ADJ (*= saddening*) traurig; (*stronger*) bestürzend; (*= disturbing*) *changes* störend; *situation* unangenehm, schwierig; (*= offending*) beleidigend, verletzend; (*= annoying*) ärgerlich; **that must have been very ~ for you** das war bestimmt nicht einfach für Sie; (*= annoying*) das muss sehr ärgerlich für Sie gewesen sein; **it is ~ (for them) to see such terrible things** es ist schlimm (für sie), so schreckliche Dinge zu sehen; **she found this experience most ~** diese Erfahrung hat sie sehr mitgenommen (*inf*), diese Erfahrung ist ihr sehr nahe gegangen; **the divorce/the change was very ~ for the child** das Kind hat unter der Scheidung/ dem Wechsel sehr gelitten; **he mustn't have any more ~ experiences** es darf nichts mehr passieren, was ihn aufregt; **it's ~ to my routine** das bringt meine Routine durcheinander

upshot [ˈʌpʃɒt] N (*= result*) Ergebnis *nt*; **the ~ of it all was that ...** es lief darauf hinaus, dass ...; **what was the ~ of your meeting?** was kam bei Ihrem Treffen heraus?; **in the ~** letzten Endes

upside down [ˈʌpsaɪdˈdaʊn] ADV verkehrt herum; **the monkey was hanging ~** der Affe hing verkehrt herum *or* mit dem Kopf nach unten; **to turn sth ~** (*lit*) etw auf den Kopf stellen; (*fig*) etw auf den Kopf stellen (*inf*); **when my daughter was born my world turned ~** als meine Tochter geboren wurde, wurde mein Leben auf den Kopf gestellt

upside-down [ˈʌpsaɪdˈdaʊn] ADJ a **in an ~ position** verkehrt herum; **to be ~** (*picture*) verkehrt herum hängen, auf dem Kopf stehen; (*world*) kopfstehen; **an ~ map of Britain** eine auf dem Kopf stehende Karte Großbritanniens; **a pineapple ~ cake** ein versunkener Ananaskuchen b (*fig, = bizarre*) **the weather is completely ~** das Wetter spielt völlig verrückt (*inf*)

upstage [ʌpˈsteɪdʒ] ADV (*Theat*) im Hintergrund der Bühne; (*with movement*) in den Bühnenhintergrund; **~ centre/left/right** im mittleren/linken/rechten Bühnenhintergrund; (*with movement*) in den mittleren/linken/rechten Bühnenhintergrund ADJ (*fig*) blasiert, hochnäsig (*with* gegenüber) VT **to ~ sb** (*Theat*) jdn zwingen, dem Publikum den Rücken zuzukehren; (*fig*) jdn ausstechen, jdm die Schau stehlen (*inf*)

upstairs [ʌpˈstɛəz] ADV oben; (*with movement*) nach oben; **the people/apartment ~** die Leute/ die Wohnung über uns; **to kick sb ~** (*fig*) jdn wegloben; **may I go ~?** (*euph*) kann ich mal aufs Örtchen?; **he hasn't got much ~** (*inf*) er ist ein bisschen schwach im Oberstübchen (*inf*) ADJ *window* im oberen Stock(werk); *room also* obere(r, s) N oberes Stockwerk

upstanding [ʌpˈstændɪŋ] ADJ a (*= strong*) kräftig; (*= honourable*) rechtschaffen b (*Jur, form*) **to be ~** stehen; **gentlemen, please be ~ for the toast** (meine Herren,) bitte erheben Sie sich zum Toast; **the court will be ~** bitte erheben Sie sich

upstart [ˈʌpstɑːt] N Emporkömmling *m* ADJ *behaviour* eines Emporkömmlings; *rival, company* emporgekommen

upstate [ˈʌpsteɪt] (*US*) ADJ im Norden (des Bundesstaates); **to live in ~ New York** im Norden des Staates New York wohnen ADV im Norden (des Bundesstaates); (*with movement*) in den Norden (des Bundesstaates)

upstream [ˈʌpstriːm] ADV flussaufwärts; **3 kms ~ from Henley** 3 km flussaufwärts von Henley ADJ *place* flussaufwärts gelegen

upstretched [ʌpˈstrɛtʃt] ADJ *arms* ausgestreckt; *neck* gereckt

upstroke [ˈʌpstrəʊk] N (*of pen*) Aufstrich *m*; (*of piston*) aufgehender Hub, Aufwärtsgang *m*

upsurge [ˈʌpsɜːdʒ] N Zunahme *f*; (*of fighting*) Eskalation *f* (*pej*); **she felt an ~ of hatred** sie fühlte Hass in sich (*dat*) aufwallen

upswept [ʌpˈswɛpt] ADJ *hair* hoch- *or* zurückgebürstet

upswing [ˈʌpswɪŋ] N (*lit, fig*) Aufschwung *m*; (*Sport*) Ausholen *nt no pl*

upsy-daisy [ˈʌpsəˌdeɪzɪ] INTERJ = upsadaisy

uptake [ˈʌpteɪk] N a (*inf*) **to be quick on the ~** schnell verstehen; **to be slow on the ~** schwer von Begriff sein (*inf*), eine lange Leitung haben (*inf*) b (*= intake*) Aufnahme *f*

up-tempo [ˈʌptɛmpəʊ] ADJ schnell

upthrust [ˈʌpθrʌst] N (*= upward movement*) Aufwärtsdruck *m*; (*Geol*) Hebung *f*

uptight [ʌpˈtaɪt] ADJ (*inf, = nervous*) nervös; (*= inhibited*) verklemmt (*inf*); (*= angry*) sauer (*inf*); *voice* gepresst; *expression* verkrampft, verkniffen; **to get ~ (about sth)** sich (wegen etw) aufregen; (*auf etw acc*) verklemmt reagieren (*inf*); (wegen etw) sauer werden (*inf*); **he's pretty ~ about these things** der sieht so was ziemlich eng (*inf*); **no need to get ~ about it!** nun krieg dich mal wieder ein (*inf*); **she's so ~ about sex** sie ist so verklemmt was Sex angeht

uptime [ˈʌptaɪm] N (of machine) Betriebszeit f

up-to-date [ˈʌptəˈdeɪt] ADJ attr, **up to date** ADJ pred auf dem neusten Stand; fashion also, book, news, information aktuell; person, method, technique also up to date pred (inf); **to keep ~ with the fashions/news** mit der Mode/den Nachrichten auf dem Laufenden bleiben; **to keep sb/sth/oneself up to date** jdn/etw/sich auf dem Laufenden halten; **would you bring me up to date on developments?** würden Sie mich über den neusten Stand der Dinge informieren?; **to be ~ with one's payments** mit seinen Zahlungen auf dem Laufenden sein; **to bring sth ~** (= modernize) etw auf den neuesten Stand bringen

up-to-the-minute [ˈʌptəðəˈmɪnɪt] ADJ news, reports allerneuste(r, s), allerletzte(r, s); style also hochmodern; **her clothes are ~** ihre Kleider sind immer der allerletzte Schrei

uptown [ˈʌptaʊn] (US) ADJ (= in Northern part of town) im Norden (der Stadt); (= in residential area) im Villenviertel; person anspruchsvoll; bar, club, theatre, store vornehm; **~ New York** der Norden von New York ADV im Norden der Stadt; im Villenviertel; (with movement) in den Norden der Stadt; ins Villenviertel N Villenviertel nt

uptrend [ˈʌptrend] N (Econ) Aufwärtstrend m; **to be in** or **on an ~** eine steigende Tendenz zeigen

upturn [ʌpˈtɜːn] VT umdrehen N [ˈʌptɜːn] (fig: = improvement) Aufschwung m

upturned [ʌpˈtɜːnd] ADJ boat, bucket, table, box etc umgedreht; face nach oben gewandt; eyes nach oben gerichtet; collar aufgeschlagen; **~ nose** Stupsnase f, Himmelfahrtsnase f (inf)

UPVC abbr of **unplasticized polyvinyl chloride** UPVC nt

upward [ˈʌpwəd] ADJ Aufwärts-, nach oben; glance nach oben; **~ movement** Aufwärtsbewegung f; **~ slope** Aufstieg m; **~ (social) mobility** (Sociol) soziale Aufstiegsmöglichkeiten pl ADV (esp US) = upwards

upwardly [ˈʌpwədlɪ] ADV aufwärts, nach oben

upwardly mobile ADJ **to be ~** ein Aufsteiger/ eine Aufsteigerin sein

upwards [ˈʌpwədz] ADV (esp Brit) a move aufwärts, nach oben; **to look ~** hochsehen, nach oben sehen; **face ~** mit dem Gesicht nach oben; **from the waist ~** von der Hüfte aufwärts; **onwards and ~** vorwärts und aufwärts b (with numbers) **prices from £4 ~** Preise von £ 4 an, Preise ab £ 4; **to be revised ~** (figures) nach oben korrigiert werden; **from childhood ~** von Kind auf or an, von Kindheit an; **and ~** und darüber; **~ of 3000** über 3000

upwind [ˈʌpwɪnd] ADJ, ADV im Aufwind; **to be/ stand ~ of sb** gegen den Wind zu jdm sein/stehen; **to sail ~** gegen den Wind segeln

Ural [ˈjʊərəl] N **the ~** (= river) der Ural; **the ~ Mountains, the ~s** das Uralgebirge, der Ural

uranium [jʊəˈreɪnɪəm] N Uran nt

Uranus [jʊəˈreɪnəs] N (Astron) Uranus m

urban [ˈɜːbən] ADJ städtisch; life also in der Stadt; **~ decay** Verfall m der Städte; **~ motorway** Stadtautobahn f; **~ America** das städtische Amerika; **~ clearway** Stadtautobahn f

urban: urban centre, (US) **urban center** N (= town) Ballungsgebiet nt; (= town centre) Stadtzentrum nt; **urban development** N Stadtentwicklung f; **urban dweller** N Stadtbewohner(in) m(f)

urbane [ɜːˈbeɪn] ADJ person, manner weltmännisch, gewandt, urban (geh); (= civil) höflich; manner, words verbindlich

urbanely [ɜːˈbeɪnlɪ] ADV say, smile weltmännisch, gewandt

urban guerilla N Stadtguerilla m

urbanity [ɜːˈbænɪtɪ] N (of person, manner) weltmännische Art, Gewandtheit f, Urbanität f (geh); (= civility) Höflichkeit f (of manner, words) Verbindlichkeit f

urbanization [ˌɜːbənaɪˈzeɪʃən] N Urbanisierung f, Verstädterung f (pej)

urbanize [ˈɜːbənaɪz] VT urbanisieren, verstädtern (pej)

urban: urban planning N Stadtplanung f; **urban renewal** N Stadterneuerung f; **urban warfare** N Stadtkampf m

urchin [ˈɜːtʃɪn] N Gassenkind nt; (mischievous) Range f

Urdu [ˈʊəduː] N Urdu nt

urea [ˈjʊərɪə] N Harnstoff m, Urea f (spec)

ureter [jʊəˈriːtə] N Harnleiter m, Ureter m (spec)

urethra [jʊəˈriːθrə] N Harnröhre f, Urethra f (spec)

urge [ɜːdʒ] N (= need) Verlangen nt, Bedürfnis nt; (= drive) Drang m no pl; (physical, sexual) Trieb m; **to feel the ~ to do sth** das Bedürfnis verspüren, etw zu tun; **I resisted the ~ (to contradict him)** ich habe mich beherrscht (und ihm nicht widersprochen); **an ~ to steal it came over me** der Drang, es zu stehlen, überkam mich; **creative ~s** Schaffensdrang m, Kreativität f; **come and stay with us if you get the ~** (inf) komm uns besuchen, wenn du Lust hast VT a (= try to persuade) sb eindringlich bitten; **to ~ sb to do sth** (= plead with) jdn eindringlich bitten, etw zu tun; (= earnestly recommend) darauf drängen, dass jd etw tut; **to ~ sb to accept/join in/come along** jdn drängen, anzunehmen/mitzumachen/mitzukommen; **he needed no urging** er ließ sich nicht lange bitten; **do it now!** he ~**d** tun Sies jetzt!, drängte er

b **to ~ sb onward/back** jdn vorwärts treiben or weitertreiben/zurücktreiben

c (= advocate) measure etc, acceptance drängen auf (+acc); **to ~ that sth should be done** darauf drängen, dass etw getan wird; **to ~ sth (up)on sb** jdm etw eindringlich nahe legen; **to ~ caution/restraint** zur Vorsicht/Zurückhaltung mahnen

d (= press) claim betonen; argument vorbringen, anführen

▶ **urge on** VT sep (lit) horse, person, troops antreiben, vorwärts treiben; (fig) team, workers antreiben (to zu); team anfeuern; **to urge sb on to do sth** jdn (dazu) antreiben, etw zu tun

urgency [ˈɜːdʒənsɪ] N Dringlichkeit f; (of tone of voice, gesture) also Eindringlichkeit f; **it's a matter of ~** das ist dringend; **to treat sth as a matter of ~** etw als dringend behandeln; **there's no ~** es eilt nicht, das hat keine Eile; **there was a note of ~ in his voice** es klang sehr dringend; **the ~ of our needs** die dringende Notwendigkeit; **his statement lacked ~** seinen Worten fehlte der Nachdruck; **das jd etw** tut; **the ~ of his step** seine eiligen Schritte; **the sense of ~ in the music** das Drängen in der Musik

urgent [ˈɜːdʒənt] ADJ a dringend; **is it ~?** (= important) ist es dringend?; (= needing speed) eilt es?; **to be in ~ need of medical attention** dringend ärztliche Hilfe benötigen; **~ letter** Eilbrief m; **the letter was marked "urgent"** der Brief trug einen Dringlichkeitsvermerk b (= insistent) tone, plea dringend, dringlich; (= hurrying) steps eilig; **he was very ~ about the need for swift action** er betonte nachdrücklich, wie notwendig schnelles Handeln sei

urgently [ˈɜːdʒəntlɪ] ADV required dringend; requested also dringlich; talk eindringlich; **he is ~ in need of help** er braucht dringend Hilfe

uric [ˈjʊərɪk] ADJ Harn-, Urin-

uric acid N Harnsäure f

urinal [ˈjʊərɪnl] N (= room) Pissoir nt; (= vessel) Urinal nt; (for patient) Urinflasche f

urinary [ˈjʊərɪnərɪ] ADJ Harn-, Urin-; infection der Harnorgane

urinary tract N Harntrakt m

urinate [ˈjʊərɪneɪt] VI Wasser lassen, urinieren (geh), harnen (spec)

urine [ˈjʊərɪn] N Urin m, Harn m

URL (Comput) abbr of **uniform resource locator** URL-Adresse f

urn [ɜːn] N a Urne f b (also **tea urn, coffee urn**) Kessel m

urogenital [ˌjʊərəʊˈdʒenɪtl] ADJ urogenital

urological [ˌjʊərəʊˈlɒdʒɪkl] ADJ urologisch

urologist [jʊəˈrɒlədʒɪst] N Urologe m, Urologin f

urology [jʊəˈrɒlədʒɪ] N Urologie f

Ursa Major [ˈɜːsəˈmeɪdʒə] N Großer Bär or Wagen

Ursa Minor [ˈɜːsəˈmaɪnə] N Kleiner Bär or Wagen

Uruguay [ˈjʊərəɡwaɪ] N Uruguay nt

Uruguayan [ˌjʊərəˈɡwaɪən] N (= person) Uruguayer(in) m(f) ADJ uruguayisch

US abbr of **United States** USA pl

US [ʌs] PERS PRON a (dir and indir obj) uns; **give it (to) us** gib es uns; **who, us?** wer, wir?; **younger than us** jünger als wir; **it's us** wir sinds; **he is one of us** er gehört zu uns, er ist einer von uns; **this table shows us the tides** auf dieser Tafel sieht man die Gezeiten; **us and them** wir und die b (inf, = me, dir obj) mich; (indir obj) mir; (pl subj) wir; **give us a look** lass mal sehen; **us English** wir Engländer; **as for us English** was uns Engländer betrifft

USA a abbr of **United States of America** USA pl b abbr of **United States Army**

usability [ˌjuːzəˈbɪlɪt] N Verwendbarkeit f; (of ideas, suggestions) Brauchbarkeit f

usable [ˈjuːzəbl] ADJ verwendbar; suggestion, ideas brauchbar; **to be no longer ~** nicht mehr zu gebrauchen sein; **in ~ condition** in brauchbarem Zustand; **to be ~ for sth** für etw verwendbar or brauchbar sein; **is this evidence ~ in court?** kann diese Aussage vor Gericht verwendet werden?

USAF abbr of **United States Air Force**

usage [ˈjuːzɪdʒ] N a (= treatment, handling) Behandlung f; **it's had some rough ~** es ist ziemlich unsanft behandelt worden b (= custom, practice) Brauch m, Sitte f, Usus m (geh); **it's common ~** es ist allgemein üblich or Sitte or Brauch c (Ling, = use, way of using) Gebrauch m no pl, Anwendung f; **words in common ~** allgemein gebräuchliche Wörter pl; **it's common in Northern ~** es ist im Norden allgemein gebräuchlich; **it's not correct ~** so darf das nicht gebraucht werden; **~ notes** (in book) Anwendungshinweise pl

USCG (US) abbr of **United States Coast Guard**

use[1] [juːz] VT a (= utilize) benutzen; dictionary, means, tools, object, materials verwenden, benutzen; sb's suggestion, idea verwenden; word, literary style gebrauchen, verwenden, benutzen; swear words gebrauchen, benutzen; brains, intelligence gebrauchen; method, system, technique, therapy, force, trickery anwenden; one's abilities, powers of persuasion, one's strength aufwenden, anwenden; tact, care walten lassen; drugs einnehmen; **~ only in emergencies** nur im Notfall gebrauchen or benutzen; **I have to ~ the toilet before I go** ich muss noch einmal zur Toilette, bevor ich gehe; **what's this ~d for?** wofür wird das benutzt or gebraucht?; **to ~ sth for sth** etw zu etw verwenden; **he ~d it as a spoon** er hat es als Löffel benutzt or verwendet; **the police ~d truncheons** die Polizei setzte Schlagstöcke ein, die Polizei benutzte or gebrauchte Schlagstöcke; **what did you ~ the money for?** wofür haben Sie das Geld benutzt or verwendet or gebraucht?; **the money is to be ~d to set up a trust** das Geld soll dazu verwendet werden, eine Stiftung einzurichten; **what toothpaste do you ~?** welche Zahnpasta benutzen or verwenden Sie?; **what sort of fuel do you ~?** welchen Treibstoff verwenden Sie?, mit welchem Treibstoff fahren Sie?; **what sort of fuel does this rocket ~?** welcher Treibstoff wird für diese Rakete verwendet?; **ointment to be ~d sparingly** Salbe nur sparsam verwenden or anwenden; **why don't you ~ a hammer?** warum nehmen Sie nicht einen Hammer dazu?, warum benutzen or verwenden Sie nicht einen Hammer dazu?; **to ~ sb's name** jds Namen verwenden *or* benutzen; (*as reference*) jds Namen angeben, sich auf jdn berufen; **~ your imagination!** zeig mal ein bisschen Fantasie *or* Phantasie!; **we can ~ the extra staff to do this** dafür können wir das übrige Personal einsetzen *or* verwenden; **I'll have to ~ some of your men** ich brauche ein paar Ihrer Leute

b (= *make use of, exploit*) *information, one's training, talents, resources, chances, opportunity* (aus-)nutzen, (aus)nützen (*S Ger*); *advantage* nutzen; *waste products* nutzen, verwerten; **not ~d to capacity** nicht voll genutzt; **you can ~ the leftovers to make a soup** Sie können die Reste zu einer Suppe verwerten; **you should ~ your free time for something creative** Sie sollten Ihre Freizeit für etwas Schöpferisches nutzen *or* gebrauchen

c (*inf*) **I could ~ a new pair of shoes** ich könnte ein neues Paar Schuhe (ge)brauchen; **I could ~ a drink** ich könnte etwas zu trinken (ge)brauchen *or* vertragen (*inf*); **it could ~ a coat of paint** das könnte ein bisschen Farbe vertragen

d (= *use up, consume*) verbrauchen; **this car ~s too much petrol** dieses Auto verbraucht zu viel Benzin; **have you ~d all the ink?** haben Sie die Tinte aufgebraucht (*inf*) *or* die ganze Tinte verbraucht?

e (*obs, liter,* = *treat*) behandeln; **she was ill ~d** ihr ist übel mitgespielt worden; **how has the world been using you?** (*not obs, liter*) wie gehts, wie stehts?

f (*pej,* = *exploit*) ausnutzen; **I feel (I've just been) ~d** ich habe das Gefühl, man hat mich ausgenutzt; (*sexually*) ich komme mir missbraucht vor

N [juːs] **a** (= *employment*) Verwendung *f*; (*of materials, tools, means, dictionary*) Benutzung *f*, Verwendung *f*; (= *operation: of machines etc*) Benutzung *f*; (= *working with: of dictionary, calculator etc*) Gebrauch *m*; (*of word, style*) Gebrauch *m*, Verwendung *f*; (*of swearwords, arms, intelligence*) Gebrauch *m*; (*of method, system, technique, force, powers of persuasion*) Anwendung *f*; (*of personnel, truncheons etc*) Verwendung *f*, Einsatz *m*; (*of drugs*) Einnahme *f*; **once you've mastered the ~ of the clutch** wenn Sie erst einmal den Gebrauch der Kupplung beherrschen; **the ~ of a calculator to solve ...** die Verwendung eines Rechners, um ... zu lösen; **directions for ~** Gebrauchsanweisung *f*; **for the ~ of** für; **for ~ in case of emergency** für Notfälle; **for external ~** äußerlich anzuwenden, zur äußerlichen Anwendung; **it's for ~ not ornament** es ist ein Gebrauchsgegenstand und nicht zur Zierde; **ready for ~** gebrauchsfertig; *machine* einsatzbereit; **to improve with ~** sich mit der Zeit bessern; **worn with ~** abgenutzt; **to make ~ of sth** von etw Gebrauch machen, etw benutzen; **can you make ~ of that?** können Sie das gebrauchen?; **in ~/out of ~** in *or* im/außer Gebrauch; *machines also* in/außer Betrieb; **to be in daily ~/no longer in ~** täglich/nicht mehr benutzt *or* verwendet *or* gebraucht werden; **to come into ~** in Gebrauch kommen; **to go** *or* **fall out of ~** nicht mehr benutzt *or* verwendet *or* gebraucht werden

b (= *exploitation, making use of*) Nutzung *f*; (*of waste products, leftovers etc*) Verwertung *f*; **to make ~ of sth** etw nutzen; **to put sth to ~** etw benutzen; **to put sth to good ~** etw gut nutzen; **to make good/bad ~ of sth** etw gut/schlecht nutzen

c (= *way of using*) Verwendung *f*; **to learn the ~ of sth** lernen, wie etw verwendet *or* benutzt *or* gebraucht wird; **it has many ~s** es ist vielseitig verwendbar; **to find a ~ for sth** für etw Verwendung finden; **to have no ~ for** (*lit, fig*) nicht gebrauchen können, keine Verwendung haben für; **to have no further ~ for sb/sth** keine Verwendung mehr haben für jdn/etw, jdn/etw nicht mehr brauchen

d (= *usefulness*) Nutzen *m*; **to be of ~ to sb** für jdn von Nutzen sein *or* nützlich sein; **this is no ~ any more** das taugt nichts mehr, das ist zu nichts mehr zu gebrauchen; **does it have a ~ in**

our society? ist es für unsere Gesellschaft von Nutzen?; **is this (of) any ~ to you?** können Sie das brauchen?, können Sie damit was anfangen?; **he/it has his/its ~s** er/das ist ganz nützlich; **you're no ~ to me if you can't spell** du nützt mir nichts, wenn du keine Rechtschreibung kannst; **he's no ~ as a goalkeeper** er taugt nicht als Torhüter, er ist als Torhüter nicht zu gebrauchen; **can I be of any ~?** kann ich irgendwie behilflich sein?; **a (fat) lot of ~ that will be to you!** (*iro inf*) da hast du aber was davon (*inf*); **this is no ~, we must start work** so hat das keinen Zweck *or* Sinn, wir müssen etwas tun; **it's no ~ you** *or* **your protesting** es hat keinen Sinn *or* es nützt nichts, wenn du protestierst; **what's the ~ of telling him?** was nützt es, wenn man es ihm sagt?; **what's the ~ in trying/going?** wozu überhaupt versuchen/gehen?; **it's no ~** es hat keinen Zweck; **ah, what's the ~!** ach, was solls!

e (= *right*) Nutznießung *f* (*Jur*); **to have the ~ of the gardens** die Gartenanlagen benutzen können; **to have the ~ of a car** ein Auto zur Verfügung haben; **to give sb the ~ of sth** jdm etw benutzen lassen; (*of car also, of money*) jdm etw zur Verfügung stellen; **to have lost the ~ of one's arm** seinen Arm nicht mehr gebrauchen *or* benutzen können; **to have the full ~ of one's faculties** im Vollbesitz seiner (geistigen und körperlichen) Kräfte sein; **have you lost the ~ of your legs?** (*hum*) hast du das Gehen verlernt?

f (= *custom*) Brauch *m*, Usus *m* (*geh*)

g (*Eccl*) Brauch *m*; **in the Roman ~** nach römisch-katholischem Brauch

▶ **use up** VT *sep food, objects, one's strength* verbrauchen; (= *finish also*) aufbrauchen; *scraps, leftovers etc* verwerten; **the butter is all used up** die Butter ist alle (*inf*) *or* aufgebraucht; **all his energy was used up** all seine Energie war verbraucht

use² [juːs] VB AUX **I didn't ~ to ...** *etc* → **used²**

use-by date ['juːzbaɪˌdeɪt] N (Mindest)haltbarkeitsdatum *nt*

used¹ [juːzd] ADJ (= *second-hand*) *clothes, car etc* gebraucht; (= *soiled*) *towel etc* benutzt; *stamp* gestempelt; **a ~-car salesman** ein Gebrauchtwagenhändler *m*; **would you buy a ~ car from this man?** (*fig hum*) würden Sie diesem Mann über den Weg trauen?

used² [juːst] VB AUX (*only in past*) **I ~ to swim every day** ich bin früher täglich geschwommen, ich pflegte täglich zu schwimmen (*geh*); **I ~ not to smoke, I didn't use to smoke** ich habe früher nicht geraucht, ich pflegte nicht zu rauchen (*geh*); **what ~ he to do** *or* **what did he use to do on Sundays?** was hat er früher *or* sonst sonntags getan?; **he ~ to play golf, didn't he?** er hat doch früher Golf gespielt, nicht wahr?; **I didn't know you smoked – I ~ not to** ich habe nicht gewusst, dass Sie rauchen – habe ich früh auch nicht; **I don't now but I ~ to** früher schon, jetzt nicht mehr!; **he ~ to be a well-known singer** er war einmal ein bekannter Sänger; **there ~ to be a field here** hier war (früher) einmal ein Feld; **things aren't what they ~ to be** es ist alles nicht mehr (so) wie früher; **life is more hectic than it ~ to be** das Leben ist hektischer als früher

used³ [juːst] ADJ **to be ~ to sb** an jdn gewöhnt sein; **to be ~ to sth** an etw (*acc*) gewöhnt sein, etw gewohnt sein; **to be ~ to doing sth** daran gewöhnt sein *or* es gewohnt sein, etw zu tun; **to be ~ to sb** *or* **sb's doing sth** daran gewöhnt sein, dass jd etw tut; **I'm not ~ to it** ich bin das nicht gewohnt; **to get ~ to sb/sth** sich an jdn/etw gewöhnen; **to get ~ to doing sth** sich daran gewöhnen, etw zu tun; **she needed to get ~ to him** *or* **his being there** sie musste sich erst an seine Anwesenheit gewöhnen; **you might as well get ~ to it!** (*inf*) daran wirst du dich gewöhnen müssen!

useful ['juːsfʊl] ADJ **a** nützlich; *person, citizen, contribution, addition* wertvoll, nützlich; (= *handy*) *tool, language* praktisch, nützlich; *size* zweck-

mäßig; *discussion* fruchtbar; *life, employment* nutzbringend; **it is ~ for him to be able to ...** das ist günstig *or* praktisch, dass er ... kann; **to make oneself ~** sich nützlich machen; **he likes to feel ~** er hat gern das Gefühl, nützlich zu sein; **he wants to be ~ to others** er möchte anderen nützen; **thank you, you've been very ~** vielen Dank, Sie haben mir/uns *etc* sehr geholfen; **is that ~ information?** nützt diese Information etwas?; **to come in ~** sich als nützlich erweisen; **we spent a ~ week in London** wir waren eine Woche in London, was sehr nützlich war; **that's ~!** (*iro*) das nützt uns was!; **he's a ~ man to know** es ist sehr nützlich ihn zu kennen; **that advice was most ~ to me** der Rat mir hat sehr genützt; **that's a ~ thing to know** es ist gut das zu wissen; **it has a ~ life of 10 years** es hat eine Nutzungsdauer von 10 Jahren; **the machine has reached the end of its ~ life** die Maschine hat das Ende ihrer Nutzungsdauer erreicht; **these drugs are ~ in treating cancer** diese Medikamente sind bei der Krebsbehandlung nützlich; **you may find it ~ to discuss the problem with your doctor** es könnte hilfreich sein, wenn Sie das Problem mit Ihrem Arzt besprechen würden; **to perform a ~ function** eine sinnvolle Funktion haben; **to prove ~** sich als nützlich erweisen; **they ought to be doing something ~ with their time** sie sollten etwas Sinnvolles mit ihrer Zeit anfangen

b (*inf*) (= *capable*) *player* brauchbar, fähig; (= *creditable*) *score* wertvoll; **to be ~ with one's hands** geschickt mit den Händen sein; **he's quite ~ with a gun/his fists** er kann ziemlich gut mit der Pistole/seinen Fäusten umgehen

usefully ['juːsfəlɪ] ADV *employed, spend time* nutzbringend; **you could ~ come along** es wäre von Nutzen, wenn Sie kämen; **is there anything I can ~ do?** kann ich irgendwie nützlich machen?; **this book can ~ be given to first-year students** dieses Buch ist für Erstsemester nützlich

usefulness ['juːsfʊlnɪs] N Nützlichkeit *f*; (*of person, contribution*) Wert *m*; (*of discussion*) Fruchtbarkeit *f* → **outlive**

useless ['juːslɪs] ADJ **a** nutzlos, (= *unusable*) unbrauchbar; *advice, suggestion* nutzlos, unnütz; *person* nutzlos, zu nichts nütze; *teacher, manager, player* untauglich, unbrauchbar; *school* untauglich; *remedy* unwirksam, wirkungslos; **to render sth ~** etw unbrauchbar machen; **to be ~ to sb** für jdn nutzlos *or* ohne Nutzen sein; **to prove ~** sich als nutzlos erweisen; (*machine, object*) sich als unbrauchbar erweisen; **to be worse than ~** völlig nutzlos sein; **it is ~ (for you) to complain** es hat keinen Sinn, sich zu beschweren; **shouting is ~** Schreien nützt nichts; **it's ~ without a handle** ohne Griff nützt es nichts *or* ist es unbrauchbar; **he's full of ~ information** er steckt voller nutzloser Informationen; **he's ~ as a goalkeeper** er ist als Torwart nicht zu gebrauchen, er taugt nichts als Torwart; **you're just ~!** du bist doch zu nichts zu gebrauchen; **to be ~ at doing sth** unfähig dazu sein, etw zu tun; **I'm ~ at languages** Sprachen kann ich überhaupt nicht; **to feel ~** sich unnütz fühlen

b (= *pointless*) zwecklos, sinnlos

uselessly ['juːslɪslɪ] ADV nutzlos

uselessness ['juːslɪsnɪs] N **a** (= *worthlessness*) Nutzlosigkeit *f*; (*of sth unusable*) Unbrauchbarkeit *f*; (*of person*) Nutzlosigkeit *f*; (*of teacher, manager, player*) Unbrauchbarkeit *f*; (*of school*) Untauglichkeit *f*; (*of remedy*) Unwirksamkeit *f*

b (= *pointlessness*) Zwecklosigkeit *f*, Sinnlosigkeit *f*

user ['juːzə'] N Benutzer(in) *m(f)*; (*of machines also*) Anwender(in) *m(f)*; **he's a ~ of heroin** *or* **a heroin ~** er nimmt Heroin; **my last boyfriend was just a ~** (*pej*) mein letzter Freund hat mich nur benutzt

user: user-definable ADJ (*Comput*) *keys* frei definierbar; **user-defined** ADJ (*Comput*) *keys* frei definiert; **user-friendliness** N Benutzer- *or* Anwenderfreundlichkeit *f*; **user-friendly** ADJ benutzer- or anwenderfreundlich; **user group** N Nutzergruppe *f*; (*Comput*) Anwendergruppe *f*; **user identification** N (*Comput*) Benutzerkode *m*; **user-interface** N (*esp Comput*) Benutzerschnittstelle *f*, Benutzeroberfläche *f*; **user language** N (*Comput*) Benutzersprache *f*; **user software** N (*Comput*) Anwendersoftware *f*; **user support** N (*esp Comput*) Benutzerunterstützung *f*

U-shaped [ˈjuːʃeɪpt] ADJ U-förmig

usher [ˈʌʃəʳ] **N** (*Theat, at wedding etc*) Platzanweiser(in) *m(f)*; (*Jur*) Gerichtsdiener(in) *m(f)* ▪ **VT** **to ~ sb into a room/to his seat** jdn in ein Zimmer/zu seinem Sitz bringen or geleiten (*geh*); **the drunk was discreetly ~ed out (of the hall)** der Betrunkene wurde unauffällig (aus dem Saal) hinauskomplimentiert

▶ **usher in** VT *sep people* hineinführen or -bringen or -geleiten (*geh*); **to usher in a new era** ein neues Zeitalter einleiten

usherette [ʌʃəˈret] N Platzanweiserin *f*

USIA (*US*) abbr of **United States Information Agency** *US-Informationsdienst, der Informationen über die amerikanische Nation, Kultur und Politik in anderen Ländern verbreitet*

USM (*US*) **a** abbr of **United States Mail** of **United States Mint b** abbr of **unlisted securities market**

USMC (*US*) abbr of **United States Marine Corps**

USN abbr of **United States Navy**

USNG abbr of **United States National Guard**

USNR abbr of **United States Naval Reserve**

USO (*US*) abbr of **United Service Organization** *Hilfsorganisation für die amerikanische Armee, besonders für im Ausland stationierte Truppen*

USP abbr of **unique selling proposition** (einzigartiges) verkaufsförderndes Merkmal

USS abbr **a** of **United States Ship b** of **United States Senate**

USSR abbr of **Union of Soviet Socialist Republics** UdSSR *f*

usual [ˈjuːʒʊəl] **ADJ** (= *customary*) üblich; (= *normal*) gewöhnlich, normal, üblich; **beer is his ~ drink** er trinkt gewöhnlich or normalerweise Bier; **when shall I come? – oh, the ~ time** wann soll ich kommen? – oh, wie üblich or oh, zur üblichen Zeit; **as is ~ on these occasions** wie (es) bei derartigen Gelegenheiten üblich (ist); **as is ~ with second-hand cars** wie gewöhnlich bei Gebrauchtwagen; **it's the ~ thing nowadays** das ist heute so üblich; **small families are the ~ thing nowadays** kleine Familien sind heutzutage die Norm; **the journey took four hours instead of or rather than the ~ two** die Reise dauerte vier Stunden statt der üblichen zwei; **the ~ stuff** (*inf*) das Übliche; **with his ~ tact** (*iro*) taktvoll wie immer, mit dem ihm eigenen Takt; **it is ~ for soldiers to wear a uniform** es ist üblich or normal für Soldaten, eine Uniform zu tragen; **it wasn't ~ for him to arrive early** es war nicht normal or typisch für ihn, zu früh da zu sein; **it's ~ to ask first** normalerweise fragt man erst; **to do sth in the ~ one's ~ way or manner** etw auf die einem übliche Art und Weise tun; **as ~, as per ~** (*inf*) wie üblich, wie gewöhnlich; **business as ~** normaler Betrieb; (*in shop*) Verkauf geht weiter; **to carry on as ~** weitermachen wie immer or wie üblich; **later/less/more than ~** später/weniger/mehr als sonst; **it's hardly ~** es ist eigentlich nicht üblich ▪ **N** (*inf*) der/die/das Übliche; **the ~ please!** (= *drink*) dasselbe wie immer, bitte!; **a pint of the ~** eine Halbe, wie immer; **what's his ~?** (= *drink*) was trinkt er gewöhnlich?; **what sort of mood was he in? – the ~** wie war er gelaunt? – wie üblich

usually [ˈjuːʒʊəlɪ] ADV gewöhnlich, normalerweise; **more than ~ careful/drunk** noch vorsich-

---

tiger/betrunkener als sonst; **do you drive to work/work overtime?** – – ~ fahren Sie mit dem Auto zur Arbeit/machen Sie Überstunden? – normalerweise or meistens; **is he ~ so rude?** ist er sonst auch so unhöflich?; **he's not ~ late** er kommt sonst or normalerweise nicht zu spät; **he's ~ early, but ...** er kommt sonst or meist or normalerweise früh, aber ...

usufruct [ˈjuːzjʊfrʌkt] N (*Jur*) Nutznießung *f*

usufructuary [juːzjʊˈfrʌktjʊərɪ] N (*Jur*) Nutznießer(in) *m(f)*

usurer [ˈjuːʒərəʳ] N Wucherer *m*, Wucherin *f*

usurious [juːˈzjʊərɪəs] ADJ wucherisch; *person* Wucher treibend *attr*; **~ price** Wucherpreis *m*

usurp [juːˈzɜːp] VT sich (*dat*) widerrechtlich aneignen, usurpieren (*geh*); *power, title, inheritance also* an sich (*acc*) reißen; *throne* sich bemächtigen (+*gen*) (*geh*); *role* sich (*dat*) anmaßen; *person* verdrängen; **he ~ed his father** er hat seinen Vater verdrängt; **she has ~ed his wife's place** sie hat seine Frau von ihrem Platz verdrängt

usurpation [juːzɜːˈpeɪʃən] N Usurpation *f* (*geh*); (*of power also*) widerrechtliche Übernahme; (*of title, inheritance*) widerrechtliche Aneignung; **~ of the throne** Thronraub *m*, Usurpation *f* des Thrones (*geh*)

usurper [juːˈzɜːpəʳ] N unrechtmäßiger Machthaber, unrechtmäßige Machthaberin, Usurpator(in) *m(f)* (*geh*); (*fig*) Eindringling *m*; **the ~ of the throne** der Thronräuber; **the ~ of his father's throne** der unrechtmäßige Nachfolger seines Vaters auf dem Thron

usury [ˈjuːʒʊrɪ] N Wucher *m*; **to practise** (*Brit*) or **practice** (*US*) ~ Wucher treiben; **32% interest is ~** 32% Zinsen sind or ist Wucher

ute [juːt] N (*Austral Mot*) Kleintransporter *m*, kleiner Lieferwagen

utensil [juːˈtensl] N Gerät *nt*, Utensil *nt*

uterine [ˈjuːtəraɪn] ADJ (*Anat*) uterin; **~ brother** Halbbruder *m* mütterlicherseits

uterus [ˈjuːtərəs] N Gebärmutter *f*, Uterus *m* (*spec*)

utilitarian [juːtɪlɪˈtɛərɪən] ADJ auf Nützlichkeit ausgerichtet; *qualities* nützlich, praktisch; (= *functional*) *object* zweckmäßig, praktisch; *building, room* zweckmäßig *f*; (*Philos*) utilitaristisch ▪ **N** (*Philos*) Utilitarist(in) *m(f)*, Utilitarier(in) *m(f)*

utilitarianism [juːtɪlɪˈtɛərɪənɪzəm] N (*Philos*) Utilitarismus *m*

utility [juːˈtɪlɪtɪ] **N a** (= *usefulness*) Nützlichkeit *f*, Nutzen *m*; **public ~** (= *company*) Versorgungsbetrieb *m*; (= *service*) Leistung *f* der Versorgungsbetriebe; **the utilities** versorgungswirtschaftliche Einrichtungen *pl* **c** (*Comput*) Utility *nt*, Hilfsprogramm *nt* ▪ **ATTR** **~ industry** Versorgungsindustrie *f*; **~ goods** Gebrauchsgüter *pl*; **~ furniture** im 2. Weltkrieg in Großbritannien hergestellte Möbel, die einfach, aber zweckmäßig waren

utility: utility company N Versorgungsbetrieb *m*; **utility man** N (*US*) Mädchen *nt* für alles (*inf*); **utility player** N (*Sport*) Spieler, der/Spielerin, die auf mehreren Positionen spielen kann; **utility program** N (*Comput*) Hilfsprogramm *nt*, Dienstprogramm *nt*; **utility room** N Allzweckraum *m*; **utility software** N (*Comput*) Hilfssoftware *f*, Utility-Software *f*; **utility vehicle** N Gebrauchsfahrzeug *nt*

utilization [juːtɪlaɪˈzeɪʃən] N Verwendung *f*; (*of situation, time*) Ausnutzung *f*; (*of opportunity, talent*) Nutzung *f*; (*of materials, resources*) Verwertung *f*

utilize [ˈjuːtɪlaɪz] VT verwenden; *situation, time* (be)nutzen; (= *take advantage of*) *opportunity, talent* nutzen; (= *make sth new*) *wastepaper, old wool etc* verwerten

utmost [ˈʌtməʊst] **ADJ a** (= *greatest*) *ease, danger* größte(r, s), höchste(r, s); *caution, candour* äußerste(r, s), größte(r, s); **they used their ~**

---

skill sie taten ihr Äußerstes; **with the ~ speed/care** so schnell/sorgfältig wie nur möglich; **matters of the ~ importance** Angelegenheiten *pl* von äußerster Wichtigkeit; **it is of the ~ importance that ...** es ist äußerst wichtig, dass ...; **I have the ~ respect for him** ich habe den allergrößten Respekt vor ihm; **a matter of (the) ~ urgency** ein Fall von äußerster Dringlichkeit; **with the ~ reluctance** mit allergrößtem Widerwillen **b** (= *furthest*) äußerste(r, s) ▪ **N** **to do/try one's ~ (to do sth)** sein Möglichstes or Bestes tun/versuchen(, um etw zu tun); **we have done our ~ to help him** wir haben unser Bestmöglichstes or Äußerstes getan, um ihm zu helfen; **that is the ~ I can do** mehr kann ich wirklich nicht tun; **to the ~ of one's ability** so gut man nur kann; **he tried my patience to the ~** er strapazierte meine Geduld aufs äußerste or Äußerste; **he trusts them to the ~** er ist vertraut ihnen voll und ganz; **one should enjoy life/oneself to the ~** man sollte das Leben in vollen Zügen genießen/sich amüsieren, so gut man nur kann; **I can give you £50 at the ~** ich kann Ihnen allerhöchstens £ 50 geben

Utopia [juːˈtəʊpɪə] N Utopia *nt*

Utopian [juːˈtəʊpɪən] **ADJ** utopisch, utopistisch (*pej*) ▪ **N** Utopist(in) *m(f)*

Utopianism [juːˈtəʊpɪənɪzəm] N Utopismus *m*

utricle [ˈjuːtrɪkl] N (*Bot*) Fangbläschen *nt*, Schlauch *m*, Utrikel *m* (*spec*); (*Anat*) Utriculus *m* (*spec*)

utter¹ [ˈʌtəʳ] ADJ total, vollkommen; *rogue, drunkard* unverbesserlich; *disgust, misery* grenzenlos; *disbelief* total; *despair* total, absolut; **a complete and ~ waste of time** eine totale Zeitverschwendung; **with ~ certainty/conviction** mit absoluter Sicherheit/Überzeugung; **an ~ stranger** ein Wildfremder *m*, eine Wildfremde; **what ~ nonsense!** so ein totaler Blödsinn! (*inf*)

utter² VT **a** (= *say*) von sich (*dat*) geben; *word* sagen; *word of complaint* äußern; *cry, sigh, threat* ausstoßen; *libel* verbreiten **b** (*form*) *forged money* in Umlauf bringen; *cheque* ausstellen

utterance [ˈʌtərəns] N **a** (= *sth said*) Äußerung *f*; **the child's first ~s** die ersten Worte des Kindes; **his last ~** seine letzten Worte; **his recent ~s in the press** seine jüngsten Presseäußerungen **b** (= *act of speaking*) Sprechen *nt*; **upon her dying father's ~ of her name** als ihr sterbender Vater ihren Namen nannte; **to give ~ to a feeling** einem Gefühl Ausdruck geben or verleihen (*geh*), ein Gefühl zum Ausdruck bringen

utterly [ˈʌtəlɪ] ADV total, völlig; *depraved also, despise* zutiefst; **~ beautiful** ausgesprochen schön; **he's ~ under her thumb** sie hat ihn vollkommen or ganz und gar unterm Pantoffel (*inf*)

uttermost [ˈʌtəməʊst] N, ADJ = **utmost**

U-turn [ˈjuːtɜːn] N (*lit, fig*) Wende *f*; **no ~s** Wenden verboten!; **to do a ~** (*fig*) seine Meinung völlig ändern; **the government has done a ~ over pensions** die Rentenpolitik der Regierung hat sich um 180 Grad gedreht

UVF abbr of **Ulster Volunteer Force**

uvula [ˈjuːvjələ] N Zäpfchen *nt*, Uvula *f* (*spec*)

uvular [ˈjuːvjələʳ] **ADJ** uvular; **the ~ R** das Zäpfchen-R ▪ **N** Zäpfchenlaut *m*, Uvular *m*

uxorious [ʌkˈsɔːrɪəs] ADJ *husband* treu ergeben

uxoriousness [ʌkˈsɔːrɪəsnɪs] N Ergebenheit *f* seiner Frau gegenüber

Uzbek [ˈʊzbek] **ADJ** usbekisch; **he is ~** er ist Usbeke ▪ **N a** Usbeke *m*, Usbekin *f* **b** (*Ling*) Usbekisch *nt*

Uzbekistan [ʌzbekɪˈstɑːn] N Usbekistan *nt*

V

V, v [viː] N V *nt*, v *nt*

V, v *abbr* **a** *of* **verse(s)** V **b** *of* **volt(s)** V **c** *of* **video** v **d** *of* **versus**

VA (*US*) *abbr of* **Veterans Administration**

Va *abbr of* **Virginia**

vac [væk] N (*Univ inf*) Semesterferien *pl*

vacancy ['veɪkənsɪ] N **a** (= *emptiness*) Leere *f*; (*of look*) Ausdruckslosigkeit *f*, Leere *f*; (*of post*) Unbesetztsein *nt*, Freisein *nt* **b** (*in boarding house*) (freies) Zimmer; **have you any vacancies for August?** haben Sie im August noch Zimmer frei?; **"no vacancies"** „belegt"; **"vacancies"** „Zimmer frei" **c** (= *job*) offene *or* freie Stelle; (*at university*) Vakanz *f*, unbesetzte Stelle; **we have a ~ in our personnel department** in unserer Personalabteilung ist eine Stelle zu vergeben; **we have a ~ for an editor** wir suchen einen Redakteur/eine Redakteurin; **to fill a ~** eine Stelle besetzen; **we are looking for somebody to fill a ~ in our personnel department** wir suchen einen Mitarbeiter für unsere Personalabteilung; **vacancies** Stellenangebote *pl*, offene Stellen *pl*

vacant ['veɪkənt] ADJ **a** *post* frei, offen; (*Univ*) unbesetzt, vakant; *WC, seat, hotel room, parking space* frei; *house, room* unbewohnt, leer stehend; *land* unbebaut; *table* frei, unbesetzt; *hospital bed* leer(stehend); **the house has been ~ for two months** das Haus steht seit zwei Monaten leer; **~ lot** unbebautes Grundstück; **with ~ possession** (*Jur*) bezugsfertig; **to become** *or* **fall ~** frei werden **b** (= *empty*) *days* unausgefüllt, lang; **the ~ future stretched before him** die Zukunft lag leer vor ihm **c** *mind, stare* leer

vacantly ['veɪkəntlɪ] ADV (= *stupidly*) blöde; (= *dreamily*) abwesend; **he gazed ~ at me** er sah mich mit leerem Blick an

vacate [vəˈkeɪt] VT *seat* freimachen; *post, throne* aufgeben; *presidency etc* niederlegen; *house, room, premises* räumen; **this post is going to be ~d** diese Stelle wird frei

vacation [vəˈkeɪʃən] N **a** (*Univ*) Semesterferien *pl*; (*Jur*) Gerichtsferien *pl* → **long vacation b** (*US*) Ferien *pl*, Urlaub *m*; **on ~** im *or* auf Urlaub; **to take a ~** Urlaub machen; **where are you going for your ~?** wohin fahren Sie in Urlaub?, wo machen Sie Urlaub?; **to go on ~** auf Urlaub *or* in die Ferien gehen; **~ trip** (Ferien-)reise *f* **c** (*of post*) Aufgabe *f*; (*of presidency etc*) Niederlegung *f*; (*of house*) Räumung *f* **VI** (*US*) Urlaub *or* Ferien machen

vacation course N (*US*) Ferienkurs *m*

vacationer [vəˈkeɪʃənəʳ], **vacationist** [vəˈkeɪʃənɪst] N (*US*) Urlauber(in) *m(f)*

vaccinate ['væksɪneɪt] VT impfen

vaccination [ˌvæksɪˈneɪʃən] N (Schutz)impfung *f*; **have you had your ~ yet?** sind Sie schon geimpft?, haben Sie sich schon impfen lassen?

vaccine ['væksiːn] N Impfstoff *m*, Vakzine *f* (*spec*)

vaccinee [ˌvæksɪˈniː] N (*US*) Impfling *m*

vacillate ['væsɪleɪt] VI (*lit, fig*) schwanken; **she ~d for a long time about accepting** sie schwankte lange, ob sie annehmen sollte oder nicht

vacillating ['væsɪleɪtɪŋ] ADJ (*fig*) schwankend, unschlüssig, unentschlossen

vacillation [ˌvæsɪˈleɪʃən] N Schwanken *nt*; (*fig also*) Unentschlossenheit *f*, Unschlüssigkeit *f*

vacua ['vækjʊə] *pl of* **vacuum**

vacuity [væˈkjuːɪtɪ] N (*liter*, = *lack of intelligence*) Geistlosigkeit *f*; (= *emptiness*) Leere *f*; **vacuities** (= *inane remarks*) Plattheiten *pl*, Plattitüden *pl*

vacuous ['vækjʊəs] ADJ *eyes, face, stare* ausdruckslos, leer; *film, play, book, remarks* nichts sagend

vacuum ['vækjʊəm] *pl* **-s** *or* **vacua** (*form*) **N a** (*Phys, fig*) (luft)leerer Raum, Vakuum *nt*; **cultural ~** kulturelles Vakuum; **this left a ~ in my life** das hinterließ eine Lücke in meinem Leben **b** (= *vacuum cleaner*) Staubsauger *m* **VT** *carpet, living room* (staub)saugen

vacuum: vacuum bottle N (*US*) = **vacuum flask**; **vacuum brake** N Unterdruckbremse *f*; **vacuum cleaner** N Staubsauger *m*; **vacuum flask** N (*Brit*) Thermosflasche *f*; **vacuum pack** N Vakuumpackung *f*; **vacuum-packed** ADJ vakuumverpackt; **vacuum pump** N Vakuum- *or* Aussaugepumpe *f*; **vacuum-sealed** ADJ vakuumdicht, vakuumversiegelt; **vacuum tube** N Vakuumröhre *f*

vade mecum ['vɑːdɪˈmeɪkʊm] N (*liter*) Vademekum *nt* (*liter*)

vagabond ['vægəbɒnd] **N** Vagabund *m*, Landstreicher(in) *m(f)* **ADJ** vagabundenhaft; *person* vagabundierend, umherziehend; *thoughts* (ab-)schweifend; **~ life** Vagabundenleben *nt*

vagary ['veɪgərɪ] N *usu pl* Laune *f*; (= *strange idea*) verrückter Einfall; **the vagaries of life** die Wechselfälle *pl* des Lebens

vagina [vəˈdʒaɪnə] N Scheide *f*, Vagina *f*

vaginal [vəˈdʒaɪnl] ADJ vaginal, Scheiden-; **~ intercourse** vaginaler Geschlechtsverkehr; **~ wall** Scheidenwand *f*

vaginismus [ˌvædʒɪˈnɪzməs] N (*Med*) Vaginismus *m*

vagrancy ['veɪgrənsɪ] N Land-/Stadtstreicherei *f* (*also Jur*)

vagrant ['veɪgrənt] **N** Landstreicher(in) *m(f)*; (*in town*) Stadtstreicher(in) *m(f)* **ADJ** *person* umherziehend; *life* unstet, nomadenhaft

vague [veɪg] ADJ (*+er*) **a** (= *not clear*) *person, plan* vage, unbestimmt; *outline, shape* verschwommen; *photograph* unscharf, verschwommen; *report, question* vage, ungenau; *murmur* dumpf, undeutlich; **I haven't the ~st idea** ich habe nicht die leiseste Ahnung; **there's a ~ resemblance** es besteht eine entfernte Ähnlichkeit; **I had a ~ idea she would come** ich hatte so eine (dunkle) Ahnung, dass sie kommen würde; **I am still very ~ on this theory** die Theorie ist mir noch nicht sehr klar; **I am very ~ on Dutch politics** von holländischer Politik habe ich nicht viel Ahnung; **he was ~ about the time of his arrival** er äußerte sich nur vage *or* unbestimmt über seine Ankunftszeit; **a ~ sense of unease** ein leichtes Unbehagen **b** (= *absent-minded*) geistesabwesend, zerstreut; **do you really understand, you look rather ~?** verstehst du das wirklich, du siehst so verwirrt aus?; **to have a ~ look in one's eyes** einen abwesenden *or* (*not having understood*) verständnislosen Gesichtsausdruck haben

vaguely ['veɪglɪ] ADV vage; *remember also* dunkel; *speak also* unbestimmt; *understand* ungefähr, in etwa; (= *uncertainly*) look flüchtig; *nod, wave* zögernd; (= *slightly*) *interested* flüchtig; *embarrassed, disappointed, surprised* leicht; **to look ~ at sb** jdn verständnislos ansehen; **to be ~ aware of sth** ein dunkles *or* vages Bewusstsein von etw haben; **to be ~ aware that ...** sich dunkel *or* vage bewusst sein, dass ...; **they're ~ similar** sie haben eine entfernte Ähnlichkeit; **it sounded ~ familiar** es kam einem irgendwie bekannt vor; **to be ~ reminiscent of sth** vage an etw erinnern; **it's only ~ like yours** es ist nur ungefähr wie deines; **it's ~ blue** es ist bläulich; **there's something ~ sinister about it** es hat so etwas Düsteres an sich; **a ~ worded agreement** eine vage formulierte Übereinkunft

vagueness ['veɪgnɪs] N **a** Unbestimmtheit *f*, Vagheit *f*; (*of outline, shape*) Verschwommenheit *f*; (*of report, question*) Vagheit *f*, Ungenauigkeit *f*; **the ~ of the resemblance** die entfernte Ähnlichkeit; **his ~ on Dutch politics** seine lückenhafte *or* wenig fundierte Kenntnis der holländischen Politik **b** (= *absent-mindedness*) Geistesabwesenheit *f*, Zerstreutheit *f*; **the ~ of her look** ihr abwesender *or* (*puzzled*) verwirrter Blick

vain [veɪn] ADJ **a** (*+er*) (*about looks*) eitel; (*about qualities*) eingebildet; **he's very ~ about his musical abilities** er bildet sich (*dat*) auf sein musikalisches Können viel ein; **he is ~ about his appearance** er ist eitel **b** (= *useless, empty*) eitel (*liter*); *attempt also* vergeblich; *pleasures, promises, words also, threat* leer; *hope also* töricht; **he had ~ hopes of getting the job** er machte sich vergeblich Hoffnung auf den Posten; **in the ~ hope that ...** in der vergeblichen Hoffnung, dass ...; **in ~** umsonst, vergeblich, vergebens; **it was all in ~** das war alles umsonst *or* vergeblich *or* vergebens; **in a ~ attempt to do sth** in einem vergeblichen Versuch, etw zu tun **c** **to take God's name in ~** den Namen Gottes missbrauchen, Gott lästern; **was someone taking my name in ~?** (*hum*) hat da wieder jemand von mir geredet? **d** (*liter*, = *worthless*) *display, ceremony* eitel (*liter*)

vainglorious [veɪnˈglɔːrɪəs] ADJ (*old*) *person* dünkelhaft; *talk* prahlerisch, ruhmredig (*old liter*); *spectacle* pompös

vainglory [veɪnˈglɔːrɪ] N (*old*) Prahlerei *f*, Selbstverherrlichung *f*; (= *characteristic*) Dünkel *m*; (*of appearance*) Pomp *m*

vainly ['veɪnlɪ] ADV **a** (= *to no effect*) vergeblich, vergebens **b** (= *conceitedly, about looks*) eitel; (*about qualities also*) eingebildet

valance ['væləns] N (*round bed frame*) Volant *m*; (*on window*) Querbehang *m*, Schabracke *f*; (*wooden*) Blende *f*; (*US*: = *pelmet*) Zierleiste *f*

vale [veɪl] N (*liter*) Tal *nt*; **this ~ of tears** dies Jammertal

valediction [ˌvælɪˈdɪkʃən] N **a** (*form*, = *act*) Abschied *m*; (= *words*) Abschiedsworte *pl*; (= *speech*) Abschiedsrede *f* **b** (*US, Sch*) Abschieds- *or* Entlassungsrede *f*

valedictorian [ˌvælɪdɪkˈtɔːrɪən] N (*US, Sch*) Abschiedsredner(in) *m(f)* (*bei der Schulentlassungsfeier*)

valedictory [ˌvælɪˈdɪktərɪ] **ADJ** (form) Abschieds-; ~ **speech** Abschiedsrede f **N** (US, Sch) = **valediction b**

valence [ˈveɪləns], **valency** [ˈveɪlənsɪ] **N** (Chem) Wertigkeit f, Valenz f; (Ling) Valenz f

valentine [ˈvæləntaɪn] **N** (= person) Freund(in), dem/der man am Valentinstag einen Gruß schickt; ~ (card) Valentinskarte f; **St Valentine's Day** Valentinstag m

valerian [vəˈlɪərɪən] **N** Baldrian m

valet [ˈvæleɪ] **N** Kammerdiener m; ~ **service** Reinigungsdienst m

valetudinarian [ˈvælɪˌtjuːdɪˈnɛərɪən] (form) **N** kränkelnde Person, (= health fiend) Gesundheitsfanatiker(in) m(f) **ADJ** (= sickly) kränklich, kränkelnd; person sehr um seine Gesundheit besorgt; habits, attitude gesundheitsbewusst

Valhalla [vælˈhælə] **N** Walhall nt, Walhalla nt or f

valiant [ˈvælɪənt] **ADJ a** (liter) soldier, deed tapfer, kühn (geh) **b he made a ~ effort to save her** er unternahm einen kühnen Versuch, sie zu retten; **she made a ~ effort to smile** sie versuchte tapfer zu lächeln; **never mind, it was a ~ attempt** machen Sie sich nichts draus, es war ein löblicher Versuch

valiantly [ˈvælɪəntlɪ] **ADV a** (liter) mutig, tapfer **b he ~ said he would help out** er sagte großzügig seine Hilfe zu

valid [ˈvælɪd] **ADJ a** ticket, passport gültig; (Jur) document, marriage (rechts)gültig; contract bindend, rechtsgültig; claim berechtigt, begründet; **no longer ~** (ticket) nicht mehr gültig; passport also abgelaufen **b** argument, reasoning, interpretation stichhaltig; excuse, reason triftig, einleuchtend; objection berechtigt, begründet; **this argument isn't ~** (in itself) dieses Argument ist nicht stichhaltig; (= not relevant) dieses Argument ist nicht zulässig or gilt nicht; **is it ~ to assume this?** ist es zulässig, das anzunehmen?; **that's a very ~ point** das ist ein sehr wertvoller Hinweis

validate [ˈvælɪdeɪt] **VT** document (= check validity) für gültig erklären; (with stamp, signature) (rechts)gültig machen; claim bestätigen; theory bestätigen, beweisen; (Jur) Rechtskraft verleihen (+dat)

validation [ˌvælɪˈdeɪʃən] **N** (of document) Gültigkeitserklärung f; (of claim) Bestätigung f; (of theory) Beweis m, Nachweis m

validity [vəˈlɪdɪtɪ] **N a** (Jur etc: of document) (Rechts)gültigkeit f; (of ticket etc) Gültigkeit f; (of claim) Berechtigung f **b** (of argument) Stichhaltigkeit f; (of excuse etc) Triftigkeit f; **the ~ of your objection** Ihr berechtigter or begründeter Einwand; **we discussed the ~ of merging these two cinematic styles** wir diskutierten, ob es zulässig ist, diese beiden Filmstile zu mischen

valise [vəˈliːz] **N** Reisetasche f

Valium® [ˈvælɪəm] **N** Valium® nt; **to be on ~** Valium® nehmen

Valkyrie [ˈvælkɪrɪ] **N** Walküre f

valley [ˈvælɪ] **N** Tal nt; (big and flat) Niederung f; **to go up/down the ~** talaufwärts/talabwärts gehen/fließen etc; **the Upper Rhine ~** die Oberrheinische Tiefebene

valor **N** (US) = **valour**

valorous [ˈvælərəs] **ADJ** (liter) heldenmütig (liter), tapfer

valour, (US) **valor** [ˈvælə] **N** (liter) Heldenmut m (liter), Tapferkeit f

valuable [ˈvæljʊəbl] **ADJ a** jewel, possessions, resources wertvoll; time, oxygen kostbar **b** (= useful) wertvoll; help, advice nützlich, wertvoll **N valuables** PL Wertsachen pl, Wertgegenstände pl

valuation [ˌvæljʊˈeɪʃən] **N** (= act) Schätzung f; (fig: of person's character) Einschätzung f; (= value decided upon) Schätzwert m, Schätzung f; (fig) Beurteilung f; **what's your ~ of him?** wie schätzen Sie ihn ein?; **to have a ~ of a painting/house done** ein Gemälde/Haus schätzen lassen; **to make a correct ~ of sth** etw genau

abschätzen; **we shouldn't take him at his own ~** wir sollten seine Selbsteinschätzung nicht einfach übernehmen

value [ˈvæljuː] **N a** Wert m; (= usefulness) Nutzen m; **to be of ~** Wert/Nutzen haben, wertvoll/nützlich sein; **her education has been of no ~ to her** ihre Ausbildung hat ihr nichts genützt; **to put a ~ on sth** etw schätzen or bewerten; on leisure etc einer Sache (dat) (hohen) Wert beimessen; **what ~ do you put on this?** was für einen Wert hat das?; (fig also) wie bewerten Sie das?; **to put too high a ~ on sth** etw zu hoch schätzen or bewerten; on leisure etc etw überbewerten; **he places a high ~ on the education of his children** er misst der Ausbildung seiner Kinder großen Wert bei; **he attaches no ~/great ~ to it** er legt keinen Wert/großen Wert darauf, ihm liegt nicht viel/sehr viel daran; **of little ~** nicht sehr wertvoll/nützlich; **of no ~** wert-/nutzlos; **of great ~** sehr wertvoll

b (in money) Wert m; **what's the ~ of your house?** wie viel ist Ihr Haus wert?; **what is its second-hand ~?** wie viel ist es gebraucht wert?; **to gain/lose (in) ~** im Wert steigen/fallen; **increase in ~** Wertzuwachs m; **loss of ~** Wertminderung f, Wertverlust m; **it's good ~** es ist preisgünstig; **in our restaurant you get ~ for money** in unserem Restaurant bekommen Sie etwas für Ihr Geld (inf); **this TV was good ~** dieser Fernseher ist sein Geld wert; **lazy employees don't give you ~ for money** faule Angestellte sind ihr Geld nicht viel/sehr viel wert; **goods to the ~ of £500** Waren im Wert von £ 500; **they put a ~ of £200 on it** sie haben es auf £ 200 geschätzt; **propaganda/shock/novelty ~** Propaganda-/Schock-/Neuigkeitswert m

c values PL (= moral standards) (sittliche) Werte pl, Wertwelt f; **he has no sense of ~s** er hat keine sittlichen Maßstäbe

d (Math) (Zahlen)wert m; (Mus) (Zeit- or Noten)wert m, Dauer f; (Phon) (Laut)wert m; (of colour) Farbwert m; **what exactly is the ~ of this word in the poem?** welchen Ausdrucks- or Stellenwert hat dieses Wort innerhalb des Gedichtes?

VT a house, jewels schätzen; **the property was ~d at £100,000** das Grundstück wurde auf £ 100.000 geschätzt

b friendship, person (wert)schätzen, (hoch) achten; opinion, advice schätzen; comforts, liberty, independence schätzen, Wert legen auf (+acc); **I ~ it/her (highly)** ich weiß es/sie (sehr) zu schätzen; **if you ~ my opinion ...** wenn Sie Wert auf meine Meinung legen ...; **if you ~ your life, you'll stay away** bleiben Sie weg, wenn Ihnen Ihr Leben lieb ist

value-added tax [ˌvæljuːˈædɪdtæks] **N** (Brit) Mehrwertsteuer f

valued [ˈvæljuːd] **ADJ** friend (hoch) geschätzt, lieb; employee (hoch) geschätzt; contribution geschätzt; **he is a ~ colleague** er ist als Kollege hoch geschätzt; **as a ~ customer** als (ein) geschätzter Kunde; **to be ~ for sth** für etw geschätzt werden

value: **value-creating activity** **N** (Econ) Wertschöpfung f; **value date** **N** (esp Brit, Fin) Verbuchungsdatum nt; (of a cheque) Eingangsdatum nt; **value-free** [ˈvæljuːˈfriː] **ADJ** wertfrei; **value judg(e)ment** **N** Werturteil nt; **valueless** **ADJ** wertlos; (= useless also) nutzlos, unnütz; judgement wertfrei

valuer [ˈvæljʊə] **N** (Brit) Schätzer(in) m(f)

value system **N** Wertsystem nt

valve [vælv] **N** (Anat) Klappe f; (Tech, on musical instrument) Ventil nt; (in pipe system) Absperrhahn m; (Rad, TV) Röhre f; **inlet/outlet ~** (Aut) Einlass-/Auslassventil nt

valvular [ˈvælvjʊlə] **ADJ** (= shaped like valve) ventilartig; (Med) Herzklappen-; ~ **inflammation** (Med) Herzklappenentzündung f

vamoose [vəˈmuːs] **VI** (US, inf) abhauen (inf), abzischen (inf)

vamp¹ [væmp] **N** (= woman) Vamp m **VT** **she's been ~ing him all the time** sie hat die ganze

Zeit ihre Reize bei ihm spielen lassen **VI** den Vamp spielen

vamp² **N a** (of shoe: = upper) Oberleder nt **b** (Mus) Improvisation f **VT a** (= repair) flicken **b** (Mus) accompaniment improvisieren, sich (dat) einfallen lassen **VI** (Mus) improvisieren, aus dem Stegreif spielen

▶ **vamp up** **VT** sep aufpolieren (inf), aufmotzen (inf)

vampire [ˈvæmpaɪə] **N** (lit, fig) Vampir(in) m(f), Blutsauger(in) m(f)

vampire bat **N** Vampir m, Blutsauger m

vampiric [væmˈpɪrɪk] **ADJ** vampiristisch; figure vampirähnlich

vampirism [ˈvæmpaɪərɪzəm] **N** Vampirismus m

van¹ [væn] **N a** (Brit Aut) Liefer- or Kastenwagen m, Transporter m **b** (Brit Rail) Wag(g)on m, Wagen m **c** (inf, = caravan) (Wohn)wagen m; **gipsy's ~** Zigeunerwagen m

van² **N** abbr of **vanguard** (lit, fig) Vorhut f; (fig also) Spitze f, Führung f; **he was in the ~ of legal reform** er stand an der Spitze der Rechtsreformer

van³ **N** abbr of **advantage** (Tennis inf) Vorteil m

vanadium [vəˈneɪdɪəm] **N** Vanadin nt, Vanadium nt

vandal [ˈvændəl] **N a** (fig) Vandale m, Vandalin f; **it was damaged by ~s** es ist mutwillig beschädigt worden **b** **Vandal** (Hist) Wandale m, Wandalin f

vandalism [ˈvændəlɪzəm] **N** Vandalismus m, blinde Zerstörungswut; (Jur) mutwillige Beschädigung (fremden Eigentums); **destroyed by an act of ~** mutwillig zerstört; **these acts of ~** dieser Vandalismus, diese mutwilligen Beschädigungen

vandalize [ˈvændəlaɪz] **VT** painting etc mutwillig beschädigen; building verwüsten; (= wreck) demolieren

vane [veɪn] **N** (also **weather vane**) Wetterfahne f, Wetterhahn m; (of windmill) Flügel m; (of propeller) Flügel m, Blatt nt; (of turbine) (Leit-) schaufel f

vanguard [ˈvænɡɑːd] **N** (Mil, Naut) Vorhut f; (fig also) Spitze f, Führung f; **in the ~ of reform** an der Spitze der Reformen

vanilla [vəˈnɪlə] **N** Vanille f **ADJ** Vanille-; ~ **ice cream** Vanilleeis nt

vanilla essence **N** Vanilleextrakt m

vanish [ˈvænɪʃ] **VI** verschwinden, entschwinden (liter); (traces also) sich verlieren; (fears) sich legen; (hopes) schwinden; (= become extinct) untergehen; **I've got to ~** (inf) ich muss weg (inf) → **thin d**

vanishing [ˈvænɪʃɪŋ]: **vanishing act** **N** = **vanishing trick**; **vanishing cream** **N** (Haut)pflegecreme f; **vanishing point** **N** (Math) Fluchtpunkt m; (fig) Nullpunkt m; **vanishing trick** **N** **to do a ~** (magician) etwas verschwinden lassen; **he did a ~ with the rabbit** er hat das Kaninchen weggezaubert; **every time he's needed he does a ~** (inf) jedes Mal, wenn man ihn braucht, verdrückt er sich (inf)

vanity [ˈvænɪtɪ] **N a** (concerning looks) Eitelkeit f; (concerning own value) Einbildung f, Eingebildetheit f; ~ **made him think he was bound to succeed** er war so eingebildet or so von sich eingenommen, dass er einen Misserfolg für ausgeschlossen hielt **b** (= worthlessness, of life, pleasures) Nichtigkeit f; (of words) Hohlheit f; (of efforts) Vergeblichkeit f; **all is ~** alles ist vergebens **c** (US, = dressing table) Frisiertisch m

vanity: **vanity case** **N** Schmink- or Kosmetikkoffer m; **Vanity Fair** **N** Jahrmarkt m der Eitelkeiten; **vanity plates** PL (US, Aut) Nummernschild mit persönlicher Note; **vanity press** **N** (esp US) Selbstkostenverlag m; **vanity publishing** **N** Veröffentlichung, für die ein Autor selbst bezahlt, da es sonst nicht zur Veröffentlichung kommen würde

---

VANITY PLATES

In Großbritannien und in den USA legen einige Kfz-Halter Wert darauf, dass die Nummernschilder ihres Wagens ihre Initialen tragen, die am besten zusätzlich noch ein Wort oder einen kurzen Satz ergeben sollten. Solche Schilder heißen **personalized number plates** (in Großbritannien) oder **vanity plates** (in den USA). Zuweilen werden erkleckliche Summen für solch ein Schild bezahlt. So könnte zum Beispiel jemand mit dem Namen James Allan Gordon sehr stolz auf folgendes Kennzeichen sein: „JAG 1".

---

vanquish ['væŋkwɪʃ] VT (*liter*) *enemy, fears* bezwingen (*geh*)

vantage ['vɑːntɪdʒ] N (*rare*) Vorteil *m*; (*Tennis*) Vorteil *m*

vantage: vantage ground N (*Mil*) günstige (Ausgangs)stellung; **vantage point** N (*Mil*) (günstiger) Aussichtspunkt; **our window is a good ~ for watching the procession** von unserem Fenster aus hat man einen guten Blick auf die Prozession; **from the ~ of the present** aus heutiger Sicht

vapid ['væpɪd] ADJ (*liter*) *conversation, remark* nichtssagend, geistlos; *person* geistlos; *book, song* nichts sagend; *smile* (= *insincere*) leer; (= *bored*) matt; *style* kraftlos; *beer, taste* schal

vapidity [væ'pɪdɪtɪ] N (*liter, of conversation, remark, person*) Geistlosigkeit *f*; (*of book, song*) Inhaltslosigkeit *f*; (*of smile*) (= *insincerity*) Ausdruckslosigkeit *f*; (*showing boredom*) Mattheit *f*; (*of style*) Kraftlosigkeit *f no pl*; (*of taste*) Schalheit *f*

vapor *etc* (*US*) = **vapour** *etc*

vaporization [ˌveɪpəraɪ'zeɪʃən] N (*by boiling etc*) Verdampfung *f*; (*natural*) Verdunstung *f*

vaporize ['veɪpəraɪz] VT (*by boiling etc*) verdampfen; (*naturally*) verdunsten lassen VI (*by boiling etc*) verdampfen; (*naturally*) verdunsten

vaporizer ['veɪpəraɪzə'] N Verdampfer *m*, Verdampfapparat *m*; (*Chem, for perfume*) Zerstäuber *m*; (*Med: for inhalation*) Inhalationsgerät *nt*

vaporous ['veɪpərəs] ADJ **a** (= *like vapour*) dampfförmig; (= *full of vapour*) dunstig; (= *of vapour*) Dunst-; **~ mists rising from the swamp** Dünste, die aus dem Sumpf aufsteigen; **~ gases round the planet** nebelartige Gase um den Planeten **b** (*liter, = fanciful*) nebulös, verblasen (*geh*)

vapour, (*US*) **vapor** ['veɪpə'] N Dunst *m*; (*Phys also*) Gas *nt*; (*steamy*) Dampf *m*; **the ~s** (*Med old*) Schwermut *f*; **thick ~s around the planet** eine dichte Dunsthülle um den Planeten

vapouring, (*US*) **vaporing** ['veɪpərɪŋ] N (*liter*) (*boastful*) Prahlerei *f*; (*empty*) Geschwafel *nt*

vapour trail, (*US*) **vapor trail** N Kondensstreifen *m*

variability [ˌvɛərɪə'bɪlɪtɪ] N (*Math*) Veränderlichkeit *f*; (*Biol*) Variabilität *f*; (*of weather, mood*) Unbeständigkeit *f*, Wechselhaftigkeit *f*; (*of costs*) Schwankung(en) *f(pl)*; (*of prices*) Unbeständigkeit *f*; (*of work*) unterschiedliche Qualität

variable ['vɛərɪəbl] ADJ **a** (= *likely to vary*) (*Math*) veränderlich, variabel; (*Biol*) variabel; *weather, mood* unbeständig, wechselhaft; **infinitely ~** (*Tech*) stufenlos; **~ winds** wechselnde Winde *pl*; **his work is very ~** er arbeitet sehr unterschiedlich **b** *speed* regulierbar; *salary level* flexibel; **the height of the seat is ~** die Höhe des Sitzes kann reguliert werden **N** (*Chem, Math, Phys, Comput*) Variable *f*; (*fig also*) veränderliche Größe; **dependent/independent ~** (*Math*) abhängige/unabhängige Variable

variable cost N variable Kosten *pl*

variable rate N (*Fin*) variabler Zinssatz; **~ mortgage** Hypothek *f* mit variablem Zinssatz

variance ['vɛərɪəns] N **a to be at ~ with sb** anderer Meinung sein als jd (*about* hinsichtlich *+gen*); **he is constantly at ~ with his parents** er hat ständig Meinungsverschiedenheiten mit seinen Eltern; **this is at ~ with what he said ear-**lier dies stimmt nicht mit dem überein, was er vorher gesagt hat **b** (= *difference*) Unterschied *m*; **a slight ~ of opinion** eine unterschiedliche Auffassung; **the predictable ~ between the two sets of figures** die vorhersehbare Abweichung der beiden Zahlenreihen (voneinander)

variant ['vɛərɪənt] **N** Variante *f*; **a spelling ~** eine Schreibvariante ADJ **a** (= *alternative*) andere(r, s); **there are two ~ spellings (of his name)** es gibt zwei verschiedene Schreibweisen *or* Schreibungen (für seinen Namen) **b** (*liter, = diverse*) verschieden, unterschiedlich

variation [ˌvɛərɪ'eɪʃən] N **a** (= *varying*) Veränderung *f*; (*Sci*) Variation *f*; (*Met*) Schwankung *f*, Wechsel *m*; (*of temperature*) Unterschiede *pl*, Schwankung(en) *f(pl)*; (*of prices*) Schwankung *f*; **an unexpected ~ in conditions** eine unerwartete Veränderung der Bedingungen; **there's been a lot of ~ in the prices recently** in letzter Zeit gab es viele Preisschwankungen; **these figures are subject to seasonal ~** diese Zahlen sind saisonbedingten Schwankungen unterworfen; **~ in opinions** unterschiedliche Ansichten *pl*; **he does it every day without ~** er macht es jeden Tag ohne Ausnahme

b (*Mus*) Variation *f*; **~s on a theme** Thema mit Variationen, Variationen zu einem *or* über ein Thema

c (= *different form*) Variation *f*, Variante *f*; (*Biol*) Variante *f*; **this is a ~ on that** das ist eine Variation *or* Abänderung dessen *or* davon; **a new ~ in the design** eine neue Variation des Musters; **regional ~s in pronunciation** regionale Aussprachevarianten *pl*; **several ~s on a basic idea** mehrere Variationsmöglichkeiten einer Grundidee

varicoloured, (*US*) **varicolored** ['vɛərɪ'kʌləd] ADJ mehrfarbig

varicose veins [ˌværɪkəʊs'veɪnz] PL Krampfadern *pl*

varied ['vɛərɪd] ADJ unterschiedlich; *career, life* bewegt; *selection* reichhaltig; *interests* vielfältig; *diet, work* abwechslungsreich; **a ~ group of people** eine gemischte Gruppe; **a ~ collection of records** eine vielseitige *or* sehr gemischte Plattensammlung

variegated ['vɛərɪgeɪtɪd] ADJ buntscheckig; (*Bot*) geflammt, panaschiert

variegation [ˌvɛərɪ'geɪʃən] N Buntscheckigkeit *f*; (*Bot*) Panaschierung *f*

variety [və'raɪətɪ] N **a** (= *diversity*) Abwechslung *f*; **to add ~ to sth** Abwechslung in etw (*acc*) bringen; **a big with a lot of ~** eine sehr abwechslungsreiche Arbeit; **~ is the spice of life** (*prov*) öfter mal was Neues (*inf*)

b (= *assortment*) Vielfalt *f*; (*Comm*) Auswahl *f* (*of an +dat*); **that's quite a ~ for one company** das ist ein ziemlich breites Spektrum für eine (einzige) Firma; **I have seen him in a ~ of different moods** ich habe ihn in einer Vielzahl unterschiedlicher Stimmungen erlebt; **in a great ~ of ways** auf die verschiedensten Arten *pl*; **in a ~ of colours** (*Brit*) *or* **colors** (*US*) in den verschiedenen Farben *pl*; **for a ~ of reasons** aus verschiedenen *or* mehreren Gründen; **for a great ~ of reasons** aus vielen verschiedenen Gründen; **a wide ~ of birds** eine große Vielfalt an Vogelarten, viele verschiedene Vogelarten; **you meet a great ~ of people at this hotel** in diesem Hotel können Sie die verschiedensten Leute treffen

c (*Biol, Bot, = species*) Art *f*, Varietät *f* (*spec*)

d (= *type*) Art *f*; (*of cigarette, potato*) Sorte *f*; (*of chair*) Modell *nt*; **a new ~ of tulip/potato** eine neue Tulpen-/Kartoffelsorte

e (*esp Brit, Theat*) Varietee *nt*, Varieté *nt*

variety: variety act N Varietee- *or* Varieténummer *f*; **variety artist** N Varietee- *or* Varietékünstler(in) *m(f)*; **variety show** N (*Theat*) Varietee- *or* Varietévorführung *f*; (*TV*) Fernsehshow *f*; (*Rad, TV*) Unterhaltungssendung *f*; **variety theatre**, (*US*) **variety theater** N Varietee- *or* Varietétheater *nt*

varifocal [vɛərɪ'fəʊkl] ADJ Gleitsicht-; **~ lenses** Gleitsichtgläser *pl* **varifocals** PL Gleitsichtbrille *f*

variform ['vɛərɪfɔːm] ADJ vielgestaltig

variola [və'raɪələ] N (*Med*) Pocken *pl*

various ['vɛərɪəs] ADJ **a** (= *different*) verschieden; **his excuses are many and ~** seine Entschuldigungen sind zahlreich und vielfältig **b** (= *several*) mehrere, verschiedene

variously ['vɛərɪəslɪ] ADV **a** unterschiedlich; **the news was ~ reported in the papers** die Nachricht wurde in den Zeitungen unterschiedlich wiedergegeben **b** verschiedentlich; **he has been ~ described as a rogue and a charmer** er wurde verschiedentlich ein Schlitzohr und Charmeur genannt

varlet ['vɑːlɪt] N (*obs, = page*) Knappe *m*; (= *rascal*) Schurke *m*, Halunke *m*

varmint ['vɑːmɪnt] N **a** (*dial: esp US*) Schurke *m*, Schurkin *f*, Halunke *m* **b** (= *animal*) Schädling *m*

varnish ['vɑːnɪʃ] **N** (*lit*) Lack *m*; (*on pottery*) Glasur *f*; (*on furniture also, on painting*) Firnis *m*; (*fig*) Politur *f* **VT** lackieren; *floorboards also* versiegeln, einlassen (*S Ger, Aus*); *painting* firnissen; *pottery* glasieren; (*fig*) *truth, facts* beschönigen

varnished ['vɑːnɪʃt] ADJ *table, chair, nails* lackiert; *floorboards also* versiegelt, eingelassen (*S Ger, Aus*)

varnisher ['vɑːnɪʃə'] N Lackierer(in) *m(f)*

varsity ['vɑːsɪtɪ] N (*Brit Univ inf*) Uni *f* (*inf*); (*US: also* **varsity team**) Schul-/Uniauswahl *f*

vary ['vɛərɪ] **VI a** (= *diverge, differ*) sich unterscheiden, abweichen (*from* von); **they ~ in price from the others** sie unterscheiden sich im Preis von den anderen; **opinions ~ on this point** in diesem Punkt gehen die Meinungen auseinander; **opinions ~ about the value** der Wert wird unterschiedlich eingeschätzt

b (= *be different*) unterschiedlich sein; **the price varies from shop to shop** der Preis ist von Geschäft zu Geschäft verschieden; **his work varies** seine Arbeit ist sehr unterschiedlich; **it varies** es ist unterschiedlich, das ist verschieden

c (= *change, fluctuate*) sich (ver)ändern; (*pressure, prices*) schwanken; **prices that ~ with the season** saisonbedingte Preise *pl*; **to ~ with the weather** sich nach dem Wetter richten

VT (= *alter*) verändern, abwandeln; (= *give variety*) abwechslungsreich(er) gestalten, variieren; **they never ~ their diet** sie essen sehr eintönig; **try to ~ your approach to the problem** Sie sollten das Problem mal von einer anderen Seite angehen

varying ['vɛərɪɪŋ] ADJ (= *changing*) veränderlich; (= *different*) unterschiedlich; **our different results were due to ~ conditions** unsere verschiedenen Resultate beruhten auf unterschiedlichen Voraussetzungen; **the ~ weather conditions here** die veränderlichen Wetterverhältnisse hier; **with ~ degrees of success** mit unterschiedlichem Erfolg; **to ~ degrees** mehr oder weniger; **in ~ degrees** mehr oder minder; **of ~ degrees of complexity** unterschiedlich komplex, von unterschiedlicher Komplexität; **of ~ sizes/abilities/ages** unterschiedlich groß/begabt/alt

vascular ['væskjʊlə'] ADJ vaskulär

vasculitis [væskjʊ'laɪtɪs] N (*Med*) Vaskulitis *f* (*spec*), Gefäßentzündung *f*

vas deferens ['væs'defərenz] N *pl* **vasa deferentia** [ˌveɪsədefə'renʃɪə] Samenleiter *m*

vase [vɑːz, (*US*) veɪz] N Vase *f*

vasectomy [væ'sektəmɪ] N Vasektomie *f* (*spec*), Sterilisation *f* (*des Mannes*)

Vaseline® ['væsɪliːn] N Vaseline *f*

vasoconstriction [ˌveɪzəʊkən'strɪkʃən] N (*Med*) Vasokonstriktion *f* (*spec*), Gefäßverengung *f*

vasoconstrictor [ˌveɪzəʊkən'strɪktə'] N (*Med*) Mittel *nt* zur Verengung der Blutgefäße

vasodilation [ˌveɪzəʊdaɪˈleɪʃən] N (Med) Vasodilatation f (spec), Gefäßerweiterung f

vasodilator [ˌveɪzəʊdaɪˈleɪtə'] N (Med) Mittel nt zur Erweiterung der Blutgefäße

vassal [ˈvæsəl] **N** (lit, fig) Vasall m **ADJ** vasallisch, Vasallen-; **~ state** Vasallenstaat m

vassalage [ˈvæsəlɪdʒ] N (Hist) (= condition) Vasallentum nt, Vasallität f; (= services due) Vasallen- or Lehenspflicht f; (= land) Lehen nt; (fig) Unterworfenheit f (geh) (to unter +acc)

vast [vɑːst] ADJ (+er) gewaltig, riesig; area also weit, ausgedehnt; bulk, difference also riesengroß; knowledge enorm; majority überwältigend; wealth, powers riesig, unermesslich; **a ~ expanse** eine weite Ebene; **the ~ expanse of the ocean** die unermessliche Weite des Ozeans; **to a ~ extent** in sehr hohem Maße; **a ~ success** ein Riesenerfolg m; **at ~ expense** zu enormen Kosten; **to be a ~ improvement on sth** eine enorme Verbesserung gegenüber etw sein

vastly [ˈvɑːstlɪ] ADV erheblich, wesentlich, bedeutend; grateful überaus, äußerst; experienced äußerst, enorm; **I was ~ amused** ich habe mich köstlich amüsiert; **it is ~ different** da besteht ein erheblicher or wesentlicher Unterschied; **~ rich** steinreich; **he is ~ superior to her** er ist ihr haushoch überlegen

vastness [ˈvɑːstnɪs] N (of size) riesiges or gewaltiges Ausmaß, riesige Größe; (of distance) ungeheures Ausmaß; (of ocean, plane, area) riesige Weite; (of sums of money) ungeheure Höhe; (of success) Ausmaß nt; (of difference) Größe f; (of knowledge, wealth) gewaltiger Umfang

VAT [ˈviːeɪˈtiː, væt] (Brit) abbr of **value-added tax** Mehrwertsteuer f, MwSt.

vat [væt] N Fass nt; (without lid) Bottich m

vatic [ˈvætɪk] ADJ (liter) prophetisch

Vatican [ˈvætɪkən] N Vatikan m; **the ~ Council** das Vatikanische Konzil; **~ roulette** (hum inf) Knaus-Ogino(-Methode) f

Vatican City N Vatikanstadt f

VAT (Brit): **VAT man** N Steuerprüfer m (für die Mehrwertsteuer); **VAT-registered** ADJ zur Mehrwertsteuer veranlagt; **VAT return** N Mehrwertsteuerausgleich m

vaudeville [ˈvəʊdəvɪl] N (US) Varietee nt, Varieté nt

vaudeville: **vaudeville show** N Varietee(-) or Varieté(vorführung f) nt; **vaudeville singer** N Varietee- or Varietésänger(in) m(f)

vault¹ [vɔːlt] **N a** (= cellar) (Keller)gewölbe nt; (= tomb) Gruft f; (in bank) Tresor(raum) m; **in the ~s** im Gewölbe etc **b** (Archit) Gewölbe nt; **the ~ of heaven** (liter) das Himmelsgewölbe (liter)

vault² **N** Sprung m; (= scissors jump) Schersprung m; (legs behind) Flanke f; (legs through arms) Hocke f; (legs apart) Grätsche f → **pole vault** **VI** springen, einen Sc5hersprung/eine Flanke/eine Grätsche machen; **to ~ into the saddle** sich in den Sattel schwingen **VT** springen über (+acc), überspringen, einen Schersprung/eine Flanke/eine Hocke/eine Grätsche machen über (+acc)

vaulted [ˈvɔːltɪd] ADJ (Archit) gewölbt

vaulting [ˈvɔːltɪŋ] N (Archit) Wölbung f

vaulting horse N (in gym) Pferd nt

vaunt [vɔːnt] **VT** rühmen, preisen (geh); **much-vaunted** viel gepriesen; **Cologne ~s a splendid cathedral** Köln kann seines herrlichen Doms rühmen **N** Loblied nt, Lobgesang m

VC abbr of **Victoria Cross** (Brit Mil) Viktoriakreuz nt (höchste britische Tapferkeitsauszeichnung)

V-chip [ˈviːtʃɪp] N V-Chip m

VCR abbr of **video cassette recorder** Videorekorder m

VD abbr of **venereal disease** Geschlechtskrankheit f; **VD clinic** Klinik für Geschlechtskrankheiten, ≈ Hautklinik f

VDT abbr of **visual display terminal**

VDU abbr of **visual display unit**

veal [viːl] N Kalbfleisch nt; **~ cutlet** Kalbschnitzel nt

veal crate [ˈviːlkreɪt] N Kälberbox f

vector [ˈvektə'] N (Math, Aviat) Vektor m; (Biol) Träger m

vector in cpds (Math) Vektor(en)-; **vector graphics** PL Vektorgrafik f

vectorial [vekˈtɔːrɪəl] ADJ vektoriell

Veda [ˈveɪdə] N Weda m

V-E DAY

In Großbritannien und in den Vereinigten Staaten ist der achte Mai der **V-E Day** (Victory in Europe Day), weil an diesem Tag der Sieg der Alliierten im Zweiten Weltkrieg 1945 in Europa gefeiert wird. Der Sieg über Japan im selben Jahr wird am 15. August begangen, am **V-J Day** (Victory over Japan Day).

---

veep [viːp] N (US, inf) = **vice president**

veer [vɪə'] **VI** (wind) (sich) drehen (im Uhrzeigersinn) (to nach); (ship) abdrehen; (car) ausscheren; (road) scharf abbiegen, abknicken; **the ship ~ed round** das Schiff drehte ab; **the road ~ed to the left** die Straße machte eine scharfe Linkskurve; **the car ~ed to the left** das Auto scherte nach links aus; **the car ~ed off the road** das Auto kam von der Straße ab; **the driver was forced to ~ sharply** der Fahrer musste plötzlich das Steuer herumreißen; **to ~ off course** vom Kurs abkommen; **it ~s from one extreme to the other** es schwankt zwischen zwei Extremen; **he ~ed round to my point of view** er ist auf meine Richtung umgeschwenkt; **he ~ed away from the subject** er kam (völlig) vom Thema ab; **the country has ~ed to the right under Thatcher** das Land ist unter Thatcher nach rechts geschwenkt
N (of wind) Drehung f; (of ship, fig: in policy) Kurswechsel m; (of car) Ausscheren nt; (of road) Knick m; **a ~ to the left politically** ein politischer Ruck nach links

veg [vedʒ] N , no pl abbr of **vegetable**
meat and two ~ Fleisch und zwei Sorten Gemüse; **he likes his meat and two ~** er liebt gutbürgerliche Kost

vegan [ˈviːgən] **N** Veganer(in) m(f) **ADJ** vegan, veganisch; **~ cheese** Käse m für Veganer; **to be ~** Veganer(in) m(f) sein

vegetable [ˈvedʒtəbl] **N a** Gemüse nt; **with fresh ~s** mit frischem Gemüse; (on menu) mit frischen Gemüsen; **what ~s do you grow in your garden?** welche Gemüsesorten hast du in deinem Garten?; **cabbage is a ~** Kohl ist eine Gemüsepflanze **b** (generic term: = plant) Pflanze f **c** (fig pej) **she's become a ~** sie ist zum körperlichen und geistigen Krüppel geworden, sie vegetiert nur noch dahin

vegetable: **vegetable dish** N (= food) Gemüsegericht nt; (= bowl) Gemüseschüssel f; **vegetable garden** N Gemüsegarten m; **vegetable kingdom** N Pflanzenreich nt; **vegetable knife** N kleines Küchenmesser; **vegetable marrow** N Gartenkürbis m; **vegetable matter** N pflanzliche Stoffe pl; **vegetable oil** N pflanzliches Öl; (Cook) Pflanzenöl nt; **vegetable salad** N Gemüsesalat m; **vegetable soup** N Gemüsesuppe f

vegetarian [ˌvedʒɪˈtɛərɪən] **N** Vegetarier(in) m(f) **ADJ** vegetarisch; **~ cheese** Käse m für Vegetarier; **to go** or **become ~** Vegetarier(in) m(f) werden

vegetarianism [ˌvedʒɪˈtɛərɪənɪzəm] N Vegetarismus m

vegetate [ˈvedʒɪteɪt] VI **a** (lit) wachsen **b** (fig) dahinvegetieren

vegetation [ˌvedʒɪˈteɪʃən] N **a** Vegetation f; **could we live on the ~ here?** könnten wir uns von dem ernähren, was hier wächst? **b** (= wasting away) (of people) Dahinvegetieren nt; (of sick people) Dahinvegetieren nt; (of mind) Verödung f, Verarmung f; **the patients just lie there in a state of ~** die Patien-

ten dämmern nur noch vor sich hin or vegetieren nur noch dahin

vegetative [ˈvedʒɪtətɪv] ADJ (Bot) vegetativ → **persistent**

veggie [ˈvedʒɪ] (inf) **N a** (= vegetarian) Vegetarier(in) m(f) **b** **~s** pl (US) = **veg** **ADJ** (= vegetarian) vegetarisch

veggieburger [ˈvedʒɪˌbɜːgə'] N Gemüseburger m

vehemence [ˈviːɪməns] N Vehemenz f (geh); (of actions, feelings also) Heftigkeit f; (of love, hatred also) Leidenschaftlichkeit f; (of protests also) Schärfe f, Heftigkeit f

vehement [ˈviːɪmənt] ADJ vehement (geh); attack also heftig, scharf; critic, opponent, opposition, protest scharf; dislike, desire heftig, stark; ally, supporter, speech leidenschaftlich; **to become** or **grow ~** heftig werden; **to be ~ in one's demands for sth** etw vehement fordern; **to be ~ in one's attack on sb/sth** jdn/etw scharf angreifen

vehemently [ˈviːɪməntlɪ] ADV vehement (geh), heftig; love, hate also leidenschaftlich; protest also heftig, mit aller Schärfe; attack scharf; deny heftig

vehicle [ˈviːɪkl] N Fahrzeug nt; (Pharm) Vehikel nt, Trägersubstanz f; (Art) Lösungsmittel nt; (fig: = medium) Mittel nt, Vehikel nt (geh); **this paper is a ~ of right-wing opinions** diese Zeitung ist ein Sprachrohr der Rechten; **language is the ~ of thought** die Sprache ist das Medium des Denkens

vehicular [vɪˈhɪkjʊlə'] ADJ Fahrzeug-; **~ traffic** Fahrzeugverkehr m; **~ accident** Verkehrsunfall m; **there is no ~ access** die Zufahrt ist nicht möglich

veil [veɪl] **N** Schleier m; **to take the ~** den Schleier nehmen, ins Kloster gehen; **the valley lay in a ~ of mist** über dem Tal lag ein Nebelschleier; **to draw** or **throw a ~ over sth** den Schleier des Vergessens über etw (acc) breiten; **under a ~ of secrecy** unter dem Mantel der Verschwiegenheit; **the ~ of secrecy over all their activities** der Schleier des Geheimnisses, der all ihre Aktivitäten umgibt
VT a (lit) person verschleiern; statue, painting verhüllen
b (fig) facts, truth verschleiern; feelings verbergen; **the clouds ~ed the moon** die Wolken verhüllten or verdeckten den Mond; **the town was ~ed by mist** die Stadt lag in Nebel gehüllt

veiled [veɪld] ADJ **a** reference, attack, criticism, threat, warning versteckt **b** (= covered) woman, face verschleiert; **to be ~ in black** schwarz verschleiert sein **c** (liter, = obscured) verborgen; mountains umhüllt

veiling [ˈveɪlɪŋ] N Schleier m; (fig: of facts, truth) Verschleierung f

vein [veɪn] N **a** (Anat, Bot, Min) Ader f; **~s and arteries** Venen und Arterien pl; **a ~ of racism** ein Hauch m von Rassismus; **there is a ~ of truth in what he says** es ist eine Spur von Wahrheit in dem, was er sagt; **a creative ~** eine künstlerische Ader; **there's a ~ of spitefulness in his character** er hat einen gehässigen Zug in seinem Charakter; **the ~ of humour** (Brit) or **humor** (US) **which runs through the book** ein humorvoller Zug, der durch das ganze Buch geht **b** (fig: = mood) Stimmung f, Laune f; **in a humorous ~** in lustiger Stimmung; **in the same ~** in derselben Art

veined [veɪnd] ADJ geädert; hand mit hervortretenden Adern; **blue-veined cheese** Blauschimmelkäse m

velar [ˈviːlə'] **ADJ** velar **N** Velar(laut) m

Velcro® [ˈvelkrəʊ] **N** Klettband nt **ADJ** **~ fastener** Klettverschluss m

veld, veldt [velt] N (in South Africa) Steppe f

vellum [ˈveləm] N Pergament nt

vellum: **vellum binding** N Pergamenteinband m; **vellum paper** N Pergamentpapier nt

velocipede [vəˈlɒsɪpiːd] N (form) Fahrrad nt, Velociped nt (old)

velocity [vəˈlɒsɪtɪ] N Geschwindigkeit f

velodrome [ˈveldrəʊm] N Velodrom nt, Radrennbahn f

velour(s) [vəˈlʊəˈ] N Velours m

velvet [ˈvelvɪt] **N** Samt m; **like ~** wie Samt, samtig **ADJ** Samt-; *skin, feel* samtweich, samten (*geh*); **~ dress** Samtkleid nt; **the ~ touch of his hand** seine sanften Hände

velveteen [ˈvelvɪtiːn] N Veloursamt m

Velvet Revolution N **the ~** die sanfte or samtene Revolution

velvety [ˈvelvɪtɪ] ADJ samtig

Ven. abbr of **Venerable**

venal [ˈviːnl] ADJ (*liter*) *person* käuflich, feil (*liter*); *practices* korrupt

venality [viːˈnælɪtɪ] N (*liter*) (*of person*) Käuflichkeit f; (*of practices*) Korruption f; **the ~ of his interests** seine eigennützigen Motive

vend [vend] VT verkaufen

vendee [venˈdiː] N (*esp Jur*) Käufer(in) m(f)

vendetta [venˈdetə] N Fehde f; (*in family*) Blutrache f; (*of gangsters*) Vendetta f; **to carry on a ~ against sb** sich mit jdm bekriegen, mit jdm in Fehde liegen; *against family member* an jdm Blutrache üben

vendible [ˈvendɪbl] ADJ (*Comm*) verkäuflich

vending: vending machine [ˈvendɪŋməˈʃiːn] N Automat m; **vending pack** [ˈvendɪŋˌpæk] N Automatenpackung f

vendition [venˈdɪʃən] N (*Econ*) Verkauf m

vendor [ˈvendɔːˈ] N (*esp Jur*) Verkäufer(in) m(f); **newspaper ~** Zeitungsverkäufer(in) m(f); **street ~** Straßenhändler(in) m(f)

vendue [venˈdjuː] N (*US, Econ*) Auktion f, Versteigerung f

veneer [vəˈnɪəˈ] **N** (*lit*) Furnier nt; (*fig*) Politur f; **it's just a ~** es ist nur Politur or schöner Schein; **he had a ~ of respectability** nach außen hin machte er einen sehr ehrbaren Eindruck; **the cities with their thin ~ of civilization** die Städte mit ihrem dünnen Lack or Putz der Zivilisation **VT** *wood* furnieren

venerable [ˈvenərəbl] ADJ ehrwürdig

venerate [ˈvenəreɪt] VT verehren, hoch achten; *sb's memory* ehren; **his name was deeply ~d** sein Andenken wurde sehr in Ehren gehalten

veneration [ˌvenəˈreɪʃən] N Bewunderung f, Verehrung f (*of für*); (*of idols*) Verehrung f; (*of traditions*) Ehrfurcht f (*of vor* +dat); **to hold sb in ~** jdn hoch achten or verehren

venereal [vɪˈnɪərɪəl] ADJ venerisch

venereal disease N Geschlechtskrankheit f, venerische Krankheit (*spec*)

Venetian [vɪˈniːʃən] **ADJ** venezianisch **N** Venezianer(in) m(f)

Venetian: Venetian blind N Jalousie f; **Venetian glass** N venezianisches Glas

Venezuela [ˌveneˈzweɪlə] N Venezuela nt

Venezuelan [ˌveneˈzweɪlən] **ADJ** venezolanisch **N** Venezolaner(in) m(f)

vengeance [ˈvendʒəns] N **a** Vergeltung f, Rache f; **to take ~ (up)on sb** Vergeltung an jdm üben **b** (*inf*) **with a ~** gewaltig (*inf*); **then the brass section comes in with a ~** dann kommt der kraftvolle or gewaltige Einsatz der Bläser; **to work with a ~** hart or mächtig (*inf*) arbeiten

vengeful [ˈvendʒfʊl] ADJ rachsüchtig

venial [ˈviːnɪəl] ADJ verzeihlich, entschuldbar; **~ sin** lässliche Sünde

veniality [ˌviːnɪˈælɪtɪ] N Entschuldbarkeit f; (*of sin*) Lässlichkeit f

Venice [ˈvenɪs] N Venedig nt

venison [ˈvenɪsən] N Reh(fleisch) nt

venom [ˈvenəm] N (*lit*) Gift nt; (*fig*) Bosheit f, Gehässigkeit f; **he spoke with real ~ in his voice** er sprach mit hasserfüllter Stimme; **a book review full of ~** ein giftiger Verriss eines Buches; **she spat her ~ at him** sie spuckte ihm wütend an; **his pen, dipped in ~** seine giftige Feder

venomous [ˈvenəməs] ADJ (*lit, fig*) giftig; *tone also* gehässig; *tongue also* scharf, böse; *attack* scharf; *sarcasm* beißend; *hatred* vernichtend, tödlich; **~ snake** Giftschlange f

venomously [ˈvenəmslɪ] ADV (*fig*) boshaft; *look, say* giftig; **~ racist** auf böse Weise rassistisch

venous [ˈviːnəs] ADJ (*form, Anat*) venös; (*Bot*) geädert

vent [vent] **N** (*for gas, liquid*) Öffnung f; (*in chimney*) Abzug m; (*in barrel*) Spundloch nt; (*in coat*) Schlitz m; (*for feelings*) Ventil nt; **jacket with a single/double ~** Jacke mit Rückenschlitz m/Seitenschlitzen pl; **to give ~ to sth** (*fig*) einer Sache (*dat*) Ausdruck verleihen; **to give ~ to one's feelings** seinen Gefühlen freien Lauf lassen; **to give ~ to one's anger** seinem Ärger Luft machen **VT** *feelings, anger* abreagieren (*on an +dat*); **to ~ one's spleen** sich (*dat*) Luft machen; **to ~ one's spleen on sb** seine Wut an jdm auslassen

ventilate [ˈventɪleɪt] VT **a** (= *control air flow*) belüften; (= *let fresh air in*) lüften **b** *blood* Sauerstoff zuführen (+*dat*), mit Sauerstoff versorgen **c** (*fig*) *grievance* vorbringen **d** (*fig*) *question, issue* erörtern; *opinion, view* äußern, kundtun

ventilated [ˈventɪleɪtɪd] ADJ *room, building* belüftet; **well/poorly ~** gut/schlecht belüftet

ventilation [ˌventɪˈleɪʃən] N **a** (= *control of air flow*) Belüftung f, Ventilation f; (= *letting fresh air in*) Lüften nt; **there's very poor ~ in here** die Belüftung dieses Raumes ist schlecht **b** (*of blood*) Sauerstoffzufuhr f **c** (*of grievance*) Vorbringen nt **d** (*of question, issue*) Erörterung f; (*of opinion, view*) Äußerung f

ventilation shaft N Luftschacht m

ventilator [ˈventɪleɪtəˈ] N **a** Ventilator m **b** (*Med*) Beatmungsgerät nt; **to be on a ~** künstlich beatmet werden

ventral [ˈventrəl] ADJ (*form*) ventral (*form*), Bauch-

ventral fin N Bauchflosse f

ventricle [ˈventrɪkəl] N Kammer f, Ventrikel m (*form*)

ventriloquism [venˈtrɪləkwɪzəm] N Bauchrednerkunst f, Bauchreden nt

ventriloquist [venˈtrɪləkwɪst] N Bauchredner(in) m(f)

ventriloquist's dummy N Bauchrednerpuppe f

ventriloquy [venˈtrɪləkwɪ] N Bauchredekunst f, Bauchreden nt

venture [ˈventʃəˈ] **N** Unternehmung f, Unternehmen nt, Unterfangen nt; **mountain-climbing is his latest ~** seit neuestem hat er sich aufs Bergsteigen verlegt; **a new ~ in publishing** ein neuer verlegerischer Versuch, ein neues verlegerisches Experiment; **this was a disastrous ~ for the company** dieses Projekt or dieser Versuch war für die Firma ein Fiasko; **his first ~ into novel-writing** sein erster Versuch, Romane zu schreiben; **he made a lot of money out of his ~s in the world of finance** er verdiente bei seinen Spekulationen in der Finanzwelt viel Geld; **his purchase of stocks was his first ~ into the world of finance** mit dem Erwerb von Aktien wagte er sich zum ersten Mal in die Finanzwelt; **his early ~s into music were successful** seine frühen musikalischen Versuche waren erfolgreich; **rowing the Atlantic alone was quite a ~** allein über den Atlantik zu rudern war ein ziemlich gewagtes Abenteuer; **the astronauts on their ~ into the unknown** die Astronauten auf ihrer abenteuerlichen Reise ins Unbekannte

VT a *life, reputation, money* aufs Spiel setzen, riskieren (*on bei*); **nothing ~d nothing gained** (*Prov*) wer nicht wagt, der nicht gewinnt (*prov*) **b** *guess, explanation, statement* wagen; *opinion* zu äußern wagen; **if I may ~ an opinion** wenn ich mir erlauben darf, meine Meinung zu sagen; **in his latest article he ~s an explanation of the phenomenon** in seinem letzten Artikel versucht er, eine Erklärung des Phänomens zu geben; **I would ~ to say that ...** ich wage sogar zu behaupten, dass ...

VI sich wagen; **no other man had dared to ~ so far** noch kein anderer Mensch hatte sich so weit vorgewagt; **to ~ out of doors** sich vor die Tür wagen; **they lost money when they ~d into book publishing** sie verloren Geld bei ihrem Versuch, Bücher zu verlegen; **the company ~d into a new field** die Firma wagte sich in ein neues Gebiet vor

▶ **venture forth** VI (*liter*) sich hinauswagen; **the soldiers ventured forth to find the enemy** die Soldaten wagten sich vor, um den Feind ausfindig zu machen; **the astronauts ventured forth into the unknown** die Astronauten wagten sich ins Unbekannte; **we ventured forth on this intellectual enterprise** wir wagten uns an dieses intellektuelle Unterfangen heran

▶ **venture on** VI +prep obj sich wagen an (+acc); **to venture on a voyage of exploration/scientific discovery** sich auf eine Entdeckungsreise/eine wissenschaftliche Forschungsreise wagen; **they ventured on a programme** (*Brit*) or **program** (*US*) **of reform** sie wagten sich an ein Reformprogramm heran

▶ **venture out** VI = **venture forth**

venture: venture capital N Beteiligungs- or Risikokapital nt; **venture capitalist** N Risikokapitalgeber(in) m(f); **~s** Kapitalbeteiligungsgesellschaft f; **Venture Scout** N (*Brit*) Rover m

venturesome [ˈventʃəsəm] ADJ *person, action* abenteuerlich

venue [ˈvenjuː] N (= *meeting place*) Treffpunkt m; (*Sport*) Austragungsort m; (*Jur*) Verhandlungsort m

Venus [ˈviːnəs] N Venus f

Venus flytrap [ˌviːnəsˈflaɪtræp] N Venusfliegenfalle f

Venusian [vəˈnjuːʃən] **N** Venusbewohner(in) m(f) **ADJ** Venus-; **~ landscape** Venuslandschaft f

veracious [vəˈreɪʃəs] ADJ *person* ehrlich, aufrichtig; *report* wahrheitsgemäß

veracity [vəˈræsɪtɪ] N (*of person*) Ehrlichkeit f, Aufrichtigkeit f; (*of report, evidence*) Wahrheit f, Richtigkeit f

veranda(h) [vəˈrændə] N Veranda f

verb [vɜːb] N Verb nt, Zeitwort nt, Verbum nt

verbal [ˈvɜːbəl] ADJ **a** (= *spoken*) *statement, agreement* mündlich; **~ abuse** Beschimpfung f; **~ attack** Verbalattacke f **b** (= *of words*) *error, skills, distinction* sprachlich; **~ memory** Wortgedächtnis nt; **a ~ reasoning test** ein Test m des logischen Denkvermögens **c** (= *literal*) *translation* wörtlich **d** (*Gram*) verbal

verbalize [ˈvɜːbəlaɪz] VT **a** (= *put into words*) ausdrücken, in Worte fassen **b** (*Gram*) verbal ausdrücken

verbally [ˈvɜːbəlɪ] ADV **a** (= *spoken*) mündlich, verbal; *threaten* verbal; **to ~ abuse sb** jdn beschimpfen; **~ abusive** ausfällig **b** (= *as a verb*) verbal

verbal noun N Verbalsubstantiv nt

verbatim [vɜːˈbeɪtɪm] **ADJ** wörtlich **ADV** wortwörtlich

verbena [vɜːˈbiːnə] N Eisenkraut nt

verbiage [ˈvɜːbɪdʒ] N Wortwust m, Wortfülle f, Blabla nt (*inf*); **you won't impress the examiners with a lot of ~** mit Geschwafel nt or Blabla nt (*inf*) kannst du die Prüfer nicht beeindrucken; **there's too much ~ in this report** dieser Bericht ist zu umständlich geschrieben

verbose [vɜːˈbəʊs] ADJ wortreich, langatmig, weitschweifig

verbosely [vɜːˈbəʊslɪ] ADV langatmig

verbosity [vɜːˈbɒsɪtɪ] N Langatmigkeit f; **it sounds impressive but it's sheer ~** es klingt beeindruckend, ist aber nichts als Geschwafel

verdant [ˈvɜːdənt] ADJ (*liter*) grün

verdict [ˈvɜːdɪkt] N **a** (*Jur*) Urteil nt; **a ~ of guilty/not guilty** ein Schuldspruch m/Freispruch *m*; **what's the ~?** wie lautet das Urteil? → **bring in**, **return b** (*of doctor, critic etc*) Urteil *nt*; (*of electors*) Entscheidung *f*, Votum *nt*; **what's your ~ on this wine?** wie beurteilst du diesen Wein?; **to give one's ~ about** *or* **on sth** sein Urteil über etw (*acc*) abgeben

verdigris ['vɜ:dɪgri:s] **N** Grünspan *m* **ADJ** *metal, copper, bronze* mit Grünspan bedeckt; *finish, effect* grünspanig

verdure ['vɜːdjʊə'] **N** (*liter*) (= *colour*) sattes Grün; (= *vegetation*) reiche Flora (*geh*)

verge [vɜːdʒ] **N a** (*Brit lit*) Rand *m*; **"keep off the ~"** „Bankette *or* Seitenstreifen nicht befahrbar" **b** (*fig*) **to be on the ~ of** *ruin/war* am Rande des Ruins/eines Krieges stehen; **to be on the ~ of a nervous breakdown** am Rande eines Nervenzusammenbruchs sein; **to be on the ~ of a discovery** kurz vor einer Entdeckung stehen; **to be on the ~ of tears** den Tränen nahe sein; **to be on the ~ of doing sth** im Begriff sein, etw zu tun; **I was on the ~ of giving away the secret** (*accidentally*) ich hätte das Geheimnis um ein Haar ausgeplaudert

▶ **verge on** **VI** +*prep obj* (*ideas, actions*) grenzen an (+*acc*); **the plot verges on the ridiculous** die Handlung grenzt ans Lächerliche; **he's verging on bankruptcy** er steht kurz vor dem Bankrott; **she is verging on fifty** sie geht auf die fünfzig zu; **she was verging on madness** sie stand am Rande des Wahnsinns

verger ['vɜːdʒə'] **N** (*Eccl*) Küster(in) *m(f)*

Vergil ['vɜːdʒɪl] **N** Virgil *m*, Vergil *m*

veridical [vəˈrɪdɪkl] **ADJ** (*form*) wahrheitsgetreu, wahrheitsgemäß

verifiability [ˌverɪfaɪə'bɪlɪtɪ] **N** Nachweisbarkeit *f*, Nachprüfbarkeit *f*, Verifizierbarkeit *f* (*geh*)

verifiable ['verɪfaɪəbl] **ADJ** nachweisbar, nachprüfbar, verifizierbar (*geh*)

verification [ˌverɪfɪˈkeɪʃən] **N** (= *check*) Überprüfung *f*; (= *confirmation*) Bestätigung *f*, Verifikation *f* (*geh*); (= *proof*) Nachweis *m*; **these claims are open to empirical ~** diese Behauptungen lassen sich empirisch nachweisen

verify ['verɪfaɪ] **VT a** (= *check up*) (über)prüfen; (= *confirm*) bestätigen, beglaubigen; *theory* beweisen, verifizieren (*geh*) **b** *suspicions, fears* bestätigen

verily ['verɪlɪ] **ADV** (*obs*) wahrlich (*obs*), fürwahr (*obs*); **~ I say unto you** wahrlich, ich sage euch

verisimilitude [ˌverɪsɪˈmɪlɪtjuːd] **N** (*form*) Wahrhaftigkeit *f* (*liter*), Echtheit *f*; (*of theory*) Plausibilität *f*, Evidenz *f* (*liter*)

veritable ['verɪtəbl] **ADJ** *genius* wahr; **a ~ disaster** die reinste Katastrophe; **a ~ miracle** das reinste Wunder

veritably ['verɪtəblɪ] **ADV** (*liter*) in der Tat, fürwahr (*obs*)

verity ['verɪtɪ] **N** (*liter*) Wahrheit *f*

vermicelli [ˌvɜːmɪˈselɪ] **N** Fadennudeln *pl*, Vermicelli *pl*

vermicide ['vɜːmɪsaɪd] **N** Wurmmittel *nt*, Vermizid *nt* (*spec*)

vermifuge ['vɜːmɪfjuːdʒ] **N** Wurmmittel *nt*, Vermifugum *nt* (*spec*)

vermilion [vəˈmɪljən] **N** Zinnoberrot *nt* **ADJ** zinnoberrot

vermin ['vɜːmɪn] **N** , *no pl* **a** (= *animal*) Schädling *m* **b** (= *insects*) Ungeziefer *nt* **c** (*pej, = people*) Pack *nt*, Ungeziefer *nt*

vermination [ˌvɜːmɪˈneɪʃən] **N** Verseuchung *f* mit Ungeziefer

verminous ['vɜːmɪnəs] **ADJ** *people, clothes* voller Ungeziefer; *place* mit Ungeziefer verseucht

vermouth ['vɜːməθ] **N** Wermut *m*

vernacular [vəˈnækjʊlə'] **N a** (= *dialect*) Mundart *f*; (= *not Latin, not official language*) Landessprache *f*; **this word has now come into the ~** dieses Wort ist jetzt in die Alltagssprache eingegangen
b (= *jargon*) Fachsprache *f or* -jargon *m*
c (*hum, = strong language*) deftige Sprache; **please excuse the ~** entschuldigen Sie bitte,

dass ich mich so drastisch ausdrücke
d (*Archit*) traditioneller Baustil
ADJ a **~ newspaper** Zeitung *f* in der regionalen Landessprache; **~ language** mundartliche Sprache; **~ poet** Mundartdichter(in) *m(f)*
b (*Archit*) traditionell
c (= *indigenous*) *style* traditionell; *crafts, furniture* einheimisch

vernal ['vɜːnl] **ADJ** Frühlings-; **~ equinox** Frühlingsäquinoktium *nt*; **~ flowers** (*liter*) Frühlingsblumen *pl*

veronica [vəˈrɒnɪkə] **N** (*Bot*) Ehrenpreis *m or nt*, Veronika *f*

verruca [veˈruːkə] **N** Warze *f*

versatile ['vɜːsətaɪl] **ADJ** vielseitig; **he has a very ~ mind** er ist geistig sehr flexibel

versatility [ˌvɜːsəˈtɪlɪtɪ] **N** Vielseitigkeit *f*; (*of sb's mind*) Flexibilität *f*

verse [vɜːs] **N a** (= *stanza*) Strophe *f*; **a ~ from "The Tempest"** ein Vers *m* aus dem „Sturm" **b** *no pl* (= *poetry*) Poesie *f*, Dichtung *f*; **in ~** in Versform; **~ drama** Versdrama *nt* **c** (*of Bible, Koran*) Vers *m*

versed [vɜːst] **ADJ** (*also* **well versed**) bewandert, beschlagen (*in* in +*dat*); **he's well ~ in the art of judo** er beherrscht die Kunst des Judos; **I'm not very well ~ in ...** ich verstehe nicht viel *or* ich habe wenig Ahnung von ...

versemonger ['vɜːsˌmʌŋgə'] **N** (*pej*) Verseschmied(in) *m(f)* (*pej*)

versification [ˌvɜːsɪfɪˈkeɪʃən] **N** (= *act*) Versbildung *f*; (= *style*) Versform *f*; (= *rules*) Verskunst *f*

versifier ['vɜːsɪfaɪə'] **N** (*pej*) Verseschmied(in) *m(f)*, Dichterling *m*

versify ['vɜːsɪfaɪ] **VT** in Versform bringen **VI** Verse schmieden (*pej*), dichten

version ['vɜːʃən] **N a** (= *account: of event, facts*) Version *f*, Darstellung *f* **b** (= *variant*) Version *f*; (*of text*) Fassung *f*; (*of car*) Modell *nt*, Typ *m* **c** (= *translation*) Übersetzung *f*

verso ['vɜːsəʊ] **N** Rückseite *f*; (*of book also*) Verso *nt* (*spec*); (*of coin also*) Revers *m* (*spec*)

versus ['vɜːsəs] **PREP** gegen (+*acc*)

vertebra ['vɜːtɪbrə] **N** *pl* **-e** ['vɜːtɪbriː] Rückenwirbel *m*

vertebral ['vɜːtɪbrəl] **ADJ** (*form*) Wirbel-

vertebral column **N** Wirbelsäule *f*

vertebrate ['vɜːtɪbrət] **N** Wirbeltier *nt*; **the ~s** die Wirbeltiere *or* Vertebraten (*spec*) **ADJ** *brain, eye etc* von Wirbeltieren

vertex ['vɜːteks] **N** *pl* **vertices** Scheitel(punkt) *m*

vertical ['vɜːtɪkəl] **ADJ a** *line, surface* senkrecht, vertikal; *pillar* senkrecht; (*Comm, Econ*) vertikal; **~ cliffs** senkrecht abfallende Klippen; **~ axis** y-Achse *f*, Ordinatenachse *f*; **~ take-off aircraft** Senkrechtstarter *m*; **~ stripes** Längsstreifen *pl*
b (= *steep*) **there is a ~ drop from the cliffs into the sea below** die Klippen fallen steil *or* senkrecht ins Meer ab **c** (*fig: = hierarchical*) vertikal **N** (= *line*) Vertikale *f*, Senkrechte *f*; **to be off the** *or* **out of the ~** nicht im Lot stehen

vertically ['vɜːtɪkəlɪ] **ADV** senkrecht, vertikal; **stand ~ or it'll fall over** stell es aufrecht hin, sonst fällt es um; **~ integrated** (*Comm*) vertikal integriert

vertices ['vɜːtɪsiːz] *pl of* **vertex**

vertiginous [vɜːˈtɪdʒɪnəs] **ADJ** (*liter*) *cliffs, descent, drop* Schwindel erregend; *heights also* schwindelnd (*geh*); *sensation* atemberaubend

vertigo ['vɜːtɪgəʊ] **N** Schwindel *m*; (*Med*) Gleichgewichtsstörung *f*; **he suffers from ~** ihm wird leicht schwindlig; (*Med*) er leidet an Gleichgewichtsstörungen *pl*

verve [vɜːv] **N** Schwung *m*; (*of person, team also*) Elan *m*; (*of play, performance also*) Ausdruckskraft *f*, Verve *f* (*geh*)

Very® ['vɪərɪ] **ADJ** (*Mil*) **~ light** Leuchtkugel *f*

very ['verɪ] **ADV a** (= *extremely*) sehr; **it's ~ well written** es ist sehr gut geschrieben; **I'm ~ sorry** es tut mir sehr Leid; **that's not ~ funny** das ist überhaupt nicht lustig; **I'm not ~ good at maths** ich bin in Mathe nicht besonders gut; **it's ~**

possible es ist durchaus *or* (sehr) gut möglich; **~ probably** höchstwahrscheinlich; **he is so ~ lazy** er ist SO faul; **how ~ odd** wie eigenartig; **Very Important Person** prominente Persönlichkeit; **~ little** sehr wenig; **~ little milk** ganz *or* sehr wenig Milch; **how well do you know her? – not ~** wie gut kennst du sie? – nicht besonders gut
b (= *absolutely*) aller-; **~ best quality** allerbeste Qualität; **~ last** allerletzte(r, s); **~ first** allererste(r, s); **she is the ~ cleverest in the class** sie ist die Klassenbeste; **at the ~ latest** allerspätestens; **this is the ~ last time I'll warn you** ich warne dich jetzt zum allerletzten Mal; **to do one's ~ best** sein Äußerstes tun; **this is the ~ best** das ist das Allerbeste; **this is the ~ most I can offer** das ist mein äußerstes Angebot; **at the ~ most** allerhöchstens; **at the ~ least** allerwenigstens; **to be in the ~ best of health** sich bester Gesundheit erfreuen; **they are the ~ best of friends** sie sind die dicksten Freunde
c **~ much** sehr; **thank you ~ much** vielen Dank; **I liked it ~ much** es hat mir sehr gut gefallen; **~ much bigger** sehr viel größer; **~ much respected** sehr angesehen; **he is ~ much the more intelligent** er ist bei weitem der Intelligentere; **he doesn't work ~ much** er arbeitet nicht sehr viel; **~ much so** sehr (sogar)
d (*for emphasis*) **he fell ill and died the ~ same day** er wurde krank und starb noch am selben Tag; **he died the ~ same day as Kennedy** er starb genau am selben Tag wie Kennedy; **the ~ same hat** genau der gleiche Hut; **we met again the ~ next day** wir trafen uns am nächsten *or* folgenden Tag schon wieder; **the ~ next day he was tragically killed** schon einen Tag später kam er unter tragischen Umständen ums Leben; **what he predicted happened the ~ next week** was er vorhersagte, trat in der Woche darauf tatsächlich ein; **my ~ own car** mein eigenes Auto; **a house of your ~ own** ein eigenes Häuschen
e **~ well, if that's what you want** nun gut, wenn du das willst; **~ good, sir** geht in Ordnung, mein Herr, sehr wohl, mein Herr (*dated*); **if you want that, ~ well, but ...** wenn du das willst, in Ordnung *or* bitte, aber ...; **I couldn't ~ well say no** ich konnte schlecht Nein sagen
ADJ a (= *precise, exact*) genau; **that ~ day/moment** genau an diesem Tag/in diesem Augenblick; **in the ~ middle of the picture** genau in der Mitte des Bildes; **this laboratory is the ~ heart of our factory** dieses Labor ist der Kern unseres Werkes; **at the ~ heart of the organization** direkt im Zentrum der Organisation; **on the ~ spot where ...** genau an der Stelle, wo ...; **those were his ~ words** genau das waren seine Worte; **before my ~ eyes** direkt vor meinen Augen; **you are the ~ person I want to speak to** mit IHNEN wollte ich sprechen; **the ~ thing/man I need** genau das, was/genau der Mann, den ich brauche; **the ~ thing!** genau das Richtige!; **to catch sb in the ~ act** jdn auf frischer Tat ertappen
b (= *extreme*) äußerste(r, s); **in the ~ beginning** ganz am Anfang; **at the ~ end** ganz am Ende; **at the ~ back/front** ganz hinten/vorn(e); **go to the ~ end of the road** gehen Sie die Straße ganz entlang *or* durch; **to the ~ end of his life** bis an sein Lebensende; **in the ~ depths of his soul** im Tiefsten seines Herzens
c (= *mere*) **the ~ thought of it** allein schon der Gedanke daran, der bloße Gedanke daran; **the ~ idea!** nein, so etwas!

very high frequency **N** Ultrakurzwelle *f*

vesicle ['vesɪkl] **N** Bläschen *nt*; (*Med also*) Vesicula *f* (*form*)

vespers ['vespəz] **PL** Vesper *f*

vessel ['vesl] **N a** (*Naut*) Schiff *nt* **b** (*form, = receptacle*) Gefäß *nt*; **drinking ~** Trinkgefäß *nt* **c** (*Anat, Bot*) Gefäß *nt*

vest¹ [vest] **N a** (*Brit*) Unterhemd *nt* **b** (*US*) Weste *f*

vest² VT (form) **to ~ sb with sth, to ~ sth in sb** jdm etw verleihen; **the rights ~ed in the Crown** die der Krone zustehenden Rechte; **Congress is ~ed with the power to declare war** der Kongress verfügt über das Recht, den Krieg zu erklären; **the authority ~ed in me** die mir verliehene Macht; **he has ~ed interests in the oil business** er ist (finanziell) am Ölgeschäft beteiligt; **the ~ed interests in the oil business** (people) die am Ölgeschäft Beteiligten pl; **he has a ~ed interest in the play** (fig) er hat ein persönliches Interesse an dem Stück

vestal ['vestl] ADJ vestalisch; **~ virgin** Vestalin f, vestalische Jungfrau N Vestalin f

vestibule ['vestɪbjuːl] N **a** (of house) Vorhalle f, Vestibül nt (dated); (of hotel) Halle f, Foyer nt; (of church) Vorhalle f **b** (Anat) Vorhof m, Vestibulum nt (spec)

vestige ['vestɪdʒ] N **a** Spur f; **the ~ of a moustache** (Brit) or **mustache** (US) der Anflug eines Schnurrbarts; **there is not a ~ of truth in what he says** es ist kein Körnchen Wahrheit an dem, was er sagt **b** (Anat) Rudiment nt

vestigial [ve'stɪdʒɪəl] ADJ spurenhaft; moustache, growth spärlich; (Anat) rudimentär; **the ~ remains of the old city walls** die Spuren or die rudimentären Reste der alten Stadtmauer; **the ~ remains of a custom** die letzten Reste eines Brauches; **the ~ remains of my interest in art** die kümmerlichen Reste meines Interesses für Kunst

vestment ['vestmənt] N **a** (of priest) Ornat m, Gewand nt **b** (= ceremonial robe) Robe f, Ornat m

vest-pocket [,vest'pɒkɪt] ADJ (US) im Westentaschenformat

vestry ['vestrɪ] N Sakristei f

Vesuvius [vɪ'suːvɪəs] N der Vesuv

vet [vet] N abbr of **veterinary surgeon** or **veterinarian** Tierarzt m/-ärztin f VT überprüfen

vetch [vetʃ] N Wicke f

veteran ['vetərən] N (Mil, fig) Veteran(in) m(f); **a ~ teacher/golfer** ein (alt)erfahrener Lehrer/Golfspieler; **a ~ actor** ein Veteran m der Schauspielkunst, ein altgedienter Schauspieler; **she's a ~ campaigner for women's rights** sie ist eine Veteranin der Frauenbewegung

veteran car N Oldtimer m, Schnauferl nt (inf)

veterinarian [,vetərɪ'neərɪən] N (US) Tierarzt m/-ärztin f

veterinary ['vetərɪnərɪ] ADJ Veterinär-; training tierärztlich; school, college für Tierärzte; **~ hospital** Tierklinik f

veterinary: veterinary medicine N Veterinärmedizin f; **veterinary practice** N Tierarztpraxis f; **veterinary surgeon** N Tierarzt m/-ärztin f

veto ['viːtəʊ] N pl **-es** Veto nt; **power of ~** Vetorecht nt; **to have a ~** das Vetorecht haben; **to use one's ~** von seinem Vetorecht Gebrauch machen VT sein Veto einlegen gegen; **if they ~ it** wenn sie ihr Veto einlegen

vetting ['vetɪŋ] N Überprüfung f

vex [veks] VT **a** (= annoy) ärgern, irritieren; animals quälen; **a problem which has been ~ing me** ein Problem, das mich quält or das mir keine Ruhe lässt **b** (= afflict) plagen, bedrücken

vexation [vek'seɪʃən] N **a** (= state) Ärger m; (= act) Verärgerung f, Ärgern nt; (of animal) Quälen nt, Quälerei f **b** (= affliction) Bedrückung f; (= cause) Plage f **c** (= thing) Ärgernis nt; **the little ~s of life** die kleinen Sorgen und Nöte des Lebens

vexatious [vek'seɪʃəs] ADJ **a** ärgerlich; regulations, headache lästig; child unausstehlich **b** (Jur) schikanös

vexed [vekst] ADJ **a** (= annoyed) verärgert; **to be ~ with sb** mit jdm böse sein, auf jdn ärgerlich sein; **to be ~ about sth** sich über etw (acc) ärgern; **to be/get ~** ärgerlich or wütend sein/ werden **b** question viel diskutiert, schwierig

vexing ['veksɪŋ] ADJ ärgerlich, irritierend; problem verzwickt

vg abbr of **very good**

VGA abbr of **video graphics array** VGA

vgc abbr of **very good condition** in sehr gutem Zustand

VHF (Rad) abbr of **very high frequency** UKW

via ['vaɪə] PREP über (+acc); (with town names also) via; **they got in ~ the window** sie kamen durchs Fenster herein

viability [,vaɪə'bɪlɪtɪ] N **a** (of life forms) Lebensfähigkeit f **b** (of plan, project) Durchführbarkeit f, Realisierbarkeit f; (of firm) Rentabilität f; **the ~ of the EC** die Lebens- or Existenzfähigkeit der EG

viable ['vaɪəbl] ADJ **a** plant, foetus lebensfähig **b** company rentabel; economy lebensfähig; suggestion, proposition brauchbar; plan, project machbar; alternative, solution gangbar; option realisierbar; **in order to secure a ~ future for the car industry** um der Autoindustrie eine Überlebenschance zu geben; **the company is not economically ~** die Firma ist unrentabel; **is this newly created state ~?** ist dieser neu entstandene Staat lebens- or existenzfähig?; **a ~ form of government** eine funktionsfähige Regierungsform

viaduct ['vaɪədʌkt] N Viadukt m

Viagra® [vaɪ'ægrə] N Viagra® nt

vial ['vaɪəl] N Fläschchen nt, Gefäß nt

via media [,vaɪə'miːdɪə, ,viː-] N (fig form) Mittelweg m

viands ['vaɪəndz] PL (form) Lebensmittel pl; (for journey) Proviant m

vibes [vaɪbz] PL (inf) **a** Vibraphon nt, Vibrafon nt **b** what sort of ~ do you get from him? wie wirkt er auf dich?; **I get good ~ from this music** diese Musik bringt mich auf Touren; **this town is giving me bad ~** diese Stadt macht mich ganz fertig (inf)

vibrancy ['vaɪbrənsɪ] N (of personality) Dynamik f; (of voice) voller Klang, Sonorität f

vibrant ['vaɪbrənt] ADJ **a** personality etc dynamisch; voice volltönend, sonor; city, community, culture lebendig, voller Leben; discussion lebhaft, angeregt; economy boomend; performance mitreißend; **the shipyard was ~ with activity** auf der Werft herrschte emsiges Treiben; **the ~ life of the city** das pulsierende Leben der Großstadt **b** (= brilliant) colour leuchtend

vibraphone ['vaɪbrəfəʊn] N Vibraphon nt, Vibrafon nt

vibrate [vaɪ'breɪt] VI (lit, fig) zittern, beben (with vor +dat); (machine, string, air) vibrieren; (notes) schwingen; **the painting ~s with life** das Bild bebt or sprüht vor Leben; **Glasgow's West End ~s with activity** im Glasgower West End pulsiert das Leben; **the town was vibrating with excitement** Aufregung hatte die Stadt ergriffen VT zum Vibrieren bringen; string zum Schwingen bringen; **they study the way the machine ~s the body** sie studieren, wie die Maschine den Körper erschüttert

vibration [vaɪ'breɪʃən] N **a** (of string, sound waves) Schwingung f; (of machine) Vibrieren nt; (of voice, ground) Beben nt **b** (inf, usu pl) = **vibes b**

vibrato [vɪ'brɑːtəʊ] N Vibrato nt ADV vibrato

vibrator [vaɪ'breɪtə'] N Vibrator m

vibratory ['vaɪbrətərɪ] ADJ vibrierend, Vibrations-

vic [vɪk] N (inf) = **victim**

vicar ['vɪkə'] N Pfarrer(in) m(f); **good evening, ~** guten Abend, Herr Pfarrer/Frau Pfarrerin

vicar apostolic N apostolischer Vikar

vicar general N Generalvikar(in) m(f)

vicarage ['vɪkərɪdʒ] N Pfarrhaus nt

vicarious [vɪ'keərɪəs] ADJ pleasure, enjoyment indirekt, mittelbar, nachempfunden; experience ersatzweise; **~ sexual thrill** Ersatzbefriedigung f; **he can't walk himself but he gets enormous pleasure from watching athletics** er kann nicht

gehen, aber das Zuschauen bei sportlichen Wettkämpfen vermittelt ihm einen großen Genuss; **to get a ~ thrill from** or **out of sth** sich an etw (dat) aufgeilen (sl); **to get ~ satisfaction (from sth)** (bei etw) eine Ersatzbefriedigung empfinden **b** authority, suffering stellvertretend **c** (form) liability, responsibility für fremdes Verschulden

vicariously [vɪ'keərɪəslɪ] ADV indirekt, mittelbar; **I can appreciate the island's beauty ~ through your writing** Ihre Beschreibung vermittelt mir die Schönheit der Insel or lässt mich die Schönheit der Insel nachempfinden

vicariousness [vɪ'keərɪəsnɪs] N Indirektheit f, Mittelbarkeit f; **the appreciation of art always involves a degree of ~** Kunstgenuss setzt immer eine bestimmte Fähigkeit des Nachempfindens voraus

vice¹ [vaɪs] N Laster nt; (of horse) Unart f, Untugend f, Mucken pl (inf); **his main ~ is laziness** sein größter Fehler ist die Faulheit; **you don't smoke or drink, don't you have any ~s?** (hum) Sie rauchen nicht, Sie trinken nicht, haben Sie denn gar kein Laster? (hum); **a life of ~** ein Lasterleben nt

vice², (US) **vise** N Schraubstock m; **to have/ hold sth in a ~-like grip** etw fest umklammern; (between legs, under arm) etw fest einklemmen

vice- PREF Vize-; **vice admiral** N Vizeadmiral(in) m(f); **vice-chairman** N stellvertretender Vorsitzender; **vice-chairmanship** N stellvertretender Vorsitz; **vice-chairwoman** N stellvertretende Vorsitzende; **vice chancellor** N (Brit Univ) = Rektor(in) m(f); **vice-consul** N Vizekonsul(in) m(f); **vice-presidency** N Vizepräsidentschaft f; **vice president** N Vizepräsident(in) m(f)

viceroy ['vaɪsrɔɪ] N Vizekönig m

vice squad N Sittenpolizei f, Sittendezernat nt, Sitte f (sl)

vice versa ['vaɪsɪ'vɜːsə] ADV umgekehrt; **economics determine politics, rather than ~** die Volkswirtschaft bestimmt die Politik und nicht umgekehrt

vicinity [vɪ'sɪnɪtɪ] N **a** Umgebung f; **in the ~** in der Nähe (of von, gen); **in the immediate ~** in unmittelbarer Umgebung; **in the ~ of £500** um die £ 500 (herum) **b** (= closeness) Nähe f

vicious ['vɪʃəs] ADJ **a** animal bösartig; dog bissig; blow, kick, gang, attack, crime, criminal brutal; murder grauenhaft, brutal; campaign bösartig, gemein; **that animal can be ~** das Tier kann heimtückisch sein; **to have a ~ temper** jähzornig sein **b** (= nasty) gemein, boshaft; remark boshaft, gehässig; look boshaft, böse; **to have a ~ tongue** eine böse or spitze Zunge haben **c** habit lasterhaft **d** (inf, = strong, nasty) headache fies (inf), gemein (inf)

vicious circle N Teufelskreis m, Circulus vitiosus m (geh); **to be caught in a ~** sich in einem Teufelskreis befinden

vicious cycle N Teufelskreis m

viciously ['vɪʃəslɪ] ADV **a** (= violently) bösartig; hit, kick brutal; murder auf grauenhafte Art; **the dog ~ attacked him** der Hund fiel wütend über ihn her **b** (= nastily) gemein, boshaft; remark gemein, gehässig; look böse; think boshaft

viciousness ['vɪʃəsnɪs] N **a** (of animal) Bösartigkeit f; (of dog) Bissigkeit f; (of blow, kick) Brutalität f; (of murder) Grauenhaftigkeit f **b** (= nastiness) Gemeinheit f; (of remark) Gemeinheit f, Gehässigkeit f; (of look) Boshaftigkeit f

vicissitude [vɪ'sɪsɪtjuːd] N usu pl Wandel m; **the ~s of life** die Launen des Schicksals, die Wechselfälle des Lebens; **the ~s of war** die Wirren des Krieges

victim ['vɪktɪm] N Opfer nt; **he was the ~ of a practical joke** ihm wurde ein Streich gespielt; **to be the ~ of sb's sarcasm** eine Zielscheibe für jds Sarkasmus sein; **the hawk flew off with its ~ in its claws** der Falke flog mit seiner Beute in den Klauen davon; **to fall (a) ~ to sth** einer Sache (dat) zum Opfer fallen; **I fell ~ to the flu** mich hatte die Grippe erwischt (inf); **to**

fall ~ **to sb's charms** jds Charme (*dat*) erliegen; **the whole of the region fell ~ to the drought** die ganze Gegend wurde ein Opfer der Dürre

victimization [ˌvɪktɪmaɪˈzeɪʃən] N ungerechte Behandlung; (= *harassment*) Schikanierung f

victimize [ˈvɪktɪmaɪz] VT ungerecht behandeln; (= *pick on*) schikanieren; **she feels ~d** sie fühlt sich ungerecht behandelt; **this ~s the public** darunter hat die Öffentlichkeit zu leiden

victimless [ˈvɪktɪmlɪs] ADJ *crime* ohne Opfer

victimology [ˌvɪktɪˈmɒlədʒɪ] N (*branch of criminology*) Viktimologie f

victor [ˈvɪktə] N Sieger(in) m(f)

Victoria Cross [vɪkˈtɔːrɪəˈkrɒs] N (*Brit*) Viktoriakreuz nt (*höchste britische Tapferkeitsauszeichnung*)

Victoria Falls [vɪkˈtɔːrɪəˈfɔːlz] PL Viktoriafälle f

Victorian [vɪkˈtɔːrɪən] N Viktorianer(in) m(f) ADJ viktorianisch; (*fig*) (sitten)streng

---

VICTORIAN

Das Adjektiv **Victorian**, viktorianisch, wird für das Großbritannien, seine Bevölkerung und Kultur unter der Regentschaft von Königin Viktoria (1837 - 1901) verwendet: „a Victorian house", „the great Victorian Prime Minister, Gladstone". Als Substantiv kann es auch auf eine Person bezogen werden, die zur damaligen Zeit lebte.

Mit **Victorian** kann man aber auch die vorherrschenden Meinungen und gesellschaftlichen Vorstellungen jener Epoche in ihrem negativen wie positiven Sinn bezeichnen. Unangenehme viktorianische Eigenschaften sind das äußerste Bedachtsein auf den gesellschaftlichen Ruf, repressiv strenge Moralvorstellungen, Humorlosigkeit, Bigotterie und Heuchelei.

Dagegen lieben es britische Politiker, die viktorianischen Tugenden hervorzuheben, wie das Streben nach Weiterbildung und gesellschaftlichem Aufstieg, Anstand, Respekt vor der Autorität und Familiensinn, Eigenschaften, die in der gegenwärtigen Gesellschaft vermisst werden.

Victoriana [vɪkˌtɔːrɪˈɑːnə] N viktorianische Antiquitäten pl

victorious [vɪkˈtɔːrɪəs] ADJ *army, allies* siegreich; *smile* triumphierend, siegesbewusst; *battle, war, campaign* erfolgreich; **to be ~ over sb/sth** jdn/ etw besiegen; **to be ~ in the struggle against ...** siegen *or* den Sieg davontragen im Kampf gegen ...; **to emerge ~ from sth** als Sieger(in) m(f) aus etw hervorgehen; **to be ~ in an election** eine Wahl gewinnen

victoriously [vɪkˈtɔːrɪəslɪ] ADV siegreich, als Sieger(in)

victory [ˈvɪktərɪ] N Sieg m; **to gain** *or* **win a ~ over sb/sth** einen Sieg über jdn/etw erringen, jdn/etw besiegen; **his final ~ over his fear** die endgültige Überwindung seiner Angst

victory roll N (*Aviat*) Siegesrolle f

victual [ˈvɪtl] (*form*) VT *army, troop* verpflegen, verproviantieren VI sich verpflegen *or* verproviantieren

victualler [ˈvɪtlə] N → **licensed**

victuals [ˈvɪtlz] PL Lebensmittel pl; (*for journey*) Proviant m, Verpflegung f

vicuña [vɪˈkuːnjə] N (= *animal, wool*) Vicunja nt

vide [ˈvaɪdeɪ] IMPER (*form, Jur*) siehe, vide (*liter*)

videlicet [vɪˈdiːlɪset] ADV (*abbr* **viz**) nämlich

video [ˈvɪdɪəʊ] N a (= *film*) Video nt b (= *recorder*) Videorekorder m c (*US*) Fernsehen nt; **on ~** im Fernsehen VT (auf Video) aufnehmen

video: **~ arcade** N Spielhalle f; **video camera** N Videokamera f; **video cassette** N Videokassette f; **video clip** N Videoclip m; **video conference** N Videokonferenz f; **video conferencing** N Videokonferenzschaltung f; **video diary** N (*TV*) Videotagebuch nt; **video disc** N Bildplatte f; **video disc play-**er N Bildplattenspieler m; **video game** N Telespiel nt; **video library** N Videothek f; **video nasty** N (*Brit*) Horrorvideo nt; **videophone** N Fernsehtelefon nt; **video recorder** N Videorekorder m; **video-recording** N Videoaufnahme f; **video rental** N Videoverleih m; **~ shop** (*esp Brit*) N Videothek f; **video screen** N Videoschirm m; **video shop** N Videothek f; **video tape** N Videoband nt; **video-tape** VT (auf Video) aufzeichnen; **video wall** N Videowand f

vidkid [ˈvɪdkɪd] N (*US inf*) fernseh- *or* videosüchtiges Kind, fernseh- *or* videosüchtiger Jugendlicher

vie [vaɪ] VI wetteifern; (*Comm*) konkurrieren; **to ~ with sb for sth** mit jdm um etw wetteifern; **to ~ with sb to do sth** mit jdm darum wetteifern, etw zu tun; **they are vying for the championship** sie kämpfen um die Meisterschaft

Vienna [vɪˈenə] N Wien nt ADJ Wiener

Viennese [ˌvɪəˈniːz] ADJ wienerisch N Wiener(in) m(f)

Vietcong [vjetˈkɒŋ] N Vietcong m

Vietnam [ˌvjetˈnæm] N Vietnam nt

Vietnamese [ˌvjetnəˈmiːz] ADJ vietnamesisch N a Vietnamese m, Vietnamesin f b (*Ling*) Vietnamesisch nt

Viet Vet [ˈviːetˈvet] N (*dated US*) Vietnam-(kriegs)veteran(in) m(f)

view [vjuː] ❂ 17.1, 26.2, 26.3 N a (= *range of vision*) Sicht f; **in full ~ of thousands of people** vor den Augen von tausenden *or* Tausenden von Menschen; **the magician placed the box in full ~ of the audience** der Zauberer stellte die Kiste so auf, dass das ganze Publikum sie sehen konnte; **the ship came into ~** das Schiff kam in Sicht; **I came into ~ of the lake** der See kam in Sicht *or* lag vor mir; **to keep sth in ~** etw im Auge behalten; **the cameraman had a job keeping the plane in ~** der Kameramann fand es schwierig, das Flugzeug zu verfolgen; **to go out of ~** außer Sicht kommen, verschwinden; **the house is within ~ of the sea** vom Haus aus ist das Meer zu sehen; **the house is exposed to ~ from passing trains** das Haus kann von vorbeifahrenden Zügen aus eingesehen werden; **hidden from ~** verborgen, versteckt; **the horses were hidden from ~ behind the trees** die Pferde waren von den Bäumen verdeckt; **she keeps the old china hidden from ~** sie bewahrt das alte Porzellan im Verborgenen auf; **the house is hidden from ~ from the main road** das Haus ist von der Hauptstraße aus nicht zu sehen; **on ~** (*for purchasing*) zur Ansicht; (*of exhibits*) ausgestellt; **the painting will be on ~ tomorrow** das Bild kann morgen besichtigt werden

b (= *prospect, sight*) Aussicht f; **there is a splendid ~ from here/from the top** von hier/ von der Spitze hat man einen herrlichen Blick *or* eine wunderschöne Aussicht; **a ~ over ...** ein Blick m über ... (*acc*); **a good ~ of the sea** ein schöner Blick aufs Meer; **a room with a ~** ein Zimmer mit schöner Aussicht; **I only got a side ~ of his head** ich habe seinen Kopf nur im Profil gesehen; **he stood up to get a better ~** er stand auf, um besser sehen zu können

c (= *photograph etc*) Ansicht f; **I want to take a ~ of the forest** ich möchte eine Aufnahme vom Wald machen; **~s of London** Ansichten pl *or* Stadtbilder pl von London; **~s of the Alps** Alpenbilder pl

d (= *opinion*) Ansicht f, Meinung f; **in my ~** meiner Ansicht *or* Meinung nach; **to have** *or* **hold ~s on sth** Ansichten über etw (*acc*) haben; **what are his ~s on this problem?** was meint er zu diesem Problem?; **do you have any special ~s on the matter?** haben Sie eine besondere Meinung zu dieser Sache?; **I have no ~s on that** ich habe keine Meinung dazu; **to take the ~ that ...** die Ansicht vertreten, dass ...; **to take a dim** (*inf*) *or* **poor ~ of sb's conduct** jds Verhalten missbilligen → **point**

e (= *mental survey*) **an idealistic ~ of the world** eine idealistische Welt(an)sicht f; **a general** *or* **o-**

verall ~ **of a problem** ein allgemeiner *or* umfassender Überblick über ein Problem; **a clear ~ of the facts** eine klare Übersicht über die Fakten; **in ~ of** wegen (+*gen*), angesichts (+*gen*); **at first ~** auf den ersten Blick; **we must not lose from ~ the fact that ...** wir dürfen die Tatsache nicht aus dem Auge verlieren, dass ...; **I'll keep it in ~** ich werde es im Auge behalten

f (= *intention, plan*) Absicht f; **to have sth in ~** etw beabsichtigen; **with a ~ to doing sth** mit der Absicht, etw zu tun; **with this in ~** im Hinblick darauf; **he has the weekend in ~ when he says ...** er denkt an das Wochenende, wenn er sagt ...

VT a (= *see*) betrachten

b (= *examine*) *house* besichtigen

c (= *consider*) *problem etc* sehen; **he ~s the prospect with dismay** er sieht dieser Sache mit Schrecken entgegen

VI (= *watch television*) fernsehen

viewable [ˈvjuːəbl] ADJ (= *visible*) zu sehen(d), sichtbar; *film etc* sehenswert; (*Comput*) lesbar

Viewdata® [ˈvjuːdeɪtə] N Bildschirmtext m, Btx m

viewer [ˈvjuːə] N a (*TV*) Zuschauer(in) m(f) b (*for slides*) Dia- *or* Bildbetrachter m

viewership [ˈvjuːəʃɪp] N Fernsehpublikum nt

viewfinder [ˈvjuːˌfaɪndə] N Sucher m

viewing [ˈvjuːɪŋ] N a (*of house, at auction etc*) Besichtigung f; **~ time** Besichtigungszeiten pl b (*TV*) Fernsehen nt; **tennis makes compulsive ~** Tennis macht die Fernsehzuschauer süchtig; **9 o'clock is peak ~ time** neun Uhr ist (die) Haupteinschaltzeit; **this programme will be given another ~ next week** dieses Programm wird nächste Woche wiederholt; **I don't do much ~** ich sehe nicht viel fern

viewing figures PL (*TV*) Zuschauerzahlen pl

viewing public N (*TV*) Zuschauer pl

viewpoint [ˈvjuːpɔɪnt] N a Standpunkt m; **from the ~ of economic growth** unter dem Gesichtspunkt des Wirtschaftswachstums; **to see sth from sb's ~** etw aus jds Sicht sehen b (*for scenic view*) Aussichtspunkt m

vigil [ˈvɪdʒɪl] N a (Nacht)wache f; **to keep ~ over sb** bei jdm wachen; **the dog kept ~ over his injured master** der Hund hielt bei seinem verletzten Herrn Wache; **her long ~s at his bedside** ihr langes Wachen an seinem Krankenbett b (*Rel*) Vigil f, Nachtwache f

vigilance [ˈvɪdʒɪləns] N Wachsamkeit f; **no move escaped their ~** keine Bewegung entging ihrem wachsamen Auge

vigilance committee N Bürgerwehr f, Selbstschutzkomitee nt

vigilant [ˈvɪdʒɪlənt] ADJ wachsam; **to be ~ about sth** auf etw (*acc*) achten; **to be ~ about over-exposing oneself to the sun** darauf achten, sich nicht zu sehr der Sonne auszusetzen; **to be ~ against sth** sich vor etw (*dat*) hüten; **to keep a ~ eye on sb/sth** ein wachsames Auge auf jdn/etw haben; **to be under sb's ~ eye** von jdm genau beobachtet werden; **the customs officers are ever ~ for drug traffickers** die Zollbeamten haben stets ein wachsames Auge auf Drogenhändler

vigilante [ˌvɪdʒɪˈlæntɪ] N Mitglied einer Selbstschutzorganisation **the ~s** die Bürgerwehr, der Selbstschutz ADJ attr Selbstschutz-; **~ group** Selbstschutzgruppe f

vigilantism [ˌvɪdʒɪˈlæntɪzəm] N Bürgerwehraktionen pl

vigilantly [ˈvɪdʒɪləntlɪ] ADV aufmerksam; *patrol* wachsam

vignette [vɪˈnjet] N Vignette f; (= *character sketch*) Skizze f, kurze und prägnante Darstellung

vigor N (*US*) = **vigour**

vigorous [ˈvɪgərəs] ADJ a (= *powerful*) kräftig; *prose, tune* kraftvoll; *protest, denial, measures, exercises, training* energisch; *walk* forsch, flott; *nod* eifrig, heftig; *match, player, activity* dynamisch; *speech* feurig; *debater* leidenschaftlich b (= *ac-*

tive) defence, campaign energisch; *opponent, advocate* engagiert

vigorously ['vɪgərəslɪ] ADV **a** (= *energetically*) *shake one's head* energisch; *shake hands* kräftig **b** (= *strongly*) *deny, protest* energisch; *defend, campaign* engagiert; *oppose* heftig

vigour, (US) **vigor** ['vɪgə'] N Kraft *f*, Energie *f*; (*of protest, denial*) Heftigkeit *f*; (*of exercises*) Energie *f*; (*of player*) Dynamik *f*; (*of speech, debater*) Leidenschaftlichkeit *f*; (*of prose*) Ausdruckskraft *f*; **sexual/youthful ~** sexuelle/jugendliche Spannkraft; **all the ~ has gone out of the undertaking** das Unternehmen hat jeglichen Schwung verloren

Viking ['vaɪkɪŋ] N Wikinger(in) *m(f)* ADJ Wikinger-; **~ ship** Wikingerschiff *nt*

vile [vaɪl] ADJ abscheulich; *mood, smell, habit also, regime, conditions* übel; *thoughts* niedrig, gemein; *language* unflätig; *weather, food* scheußlich, widerlich; **that was a ~ thing to say** es war eine Gemeinheit, so etwas zu sagen; **he was ~ to his wife** er benahm sich scheußlich gegenüber seiner Frau; **to be in a ~ temper** *or* **mood** ganz übel gelaunt sein

vilely ['vaɪllɪ] ADV abscheulich, scheußlich; (= *shamefully*) *exploit* übel

vileness ['vaɪlnɪs] N Abscheulichkeit *f*; (*of thoughts*) Niederträchtigkeit *f*; (*of smell*) Widerwärtigkeit *f*; (*of language*) Unflätigkeit *f*; (*of weather*) Scheußlichkeit *f*; **the ~ of his mood** seine Übellaunigkeit

vilification [ˌvɪlɪfɪ'keɪʃən] N Diffamierung *f*, Verleumdung *f*

vilify ['vɪlɪfaɪ] VT diffamieren, verleumden

villa ['vɪlə] N Villa *f*

village ['vɪlɪdʒ] N Dorf *nt*

village *in cpds* Dorf-; **village green** N Dorfwiese *f or* -anger *m*; **village hall** N Gemeindesaal *m*; **village idiot** N Dorftrottel *m* (*inf*)

villager ['vɪlɪdʒə'] N Dörfler(in) *m(f)*, Dorfbewohner(in) *m(f)* (*also Admin*)

villain ['vɪlən] N **a** (= *scoundrel*) Schurke *m*, Schurkin *f*; (*inf, = criminal*) Verbrecher(in) *m(f)*, Ganove *m* (*inf*) **b** (*in drama, novel*) Bösewicht *m* **c** (*inf, = rascal*) Bengel *m*; **he's the ~ of the piece** er ist der Übeltäter

villainous ['vɪlənəs] ADJ **a** böse; *deed* niederträchtig, gemein; **a ~ face** ein Verbrechergesicht *nt* **b** (*inf, = bad*) scheußlich

villainously ['vɪlənəslɪ] ADV *smile* hämisch; **he ~ murdered his brothers** in seiner Niedertracht ermordete er seine Brüder

villainy ['vɪlənɪ] N Gemeinheit *f*, Niederträchtigkeit *f*

villein ['vɪlɪn] N (*Hist*) Leibeigene(r) *mf*

vim [vɪm] N (*inf*) Schwung *m*; **he writes with great ~** er schreibt sehr schwungvoll; **full of ~ and vigour** (*Brit*) *or* **vigor** (*US*) voller Schwung und Elan

vinaigrette [ˌvɪnɪ'gret] N Vinaigrette *f* (*Cook*); (*for salad*) Salatsoße *f*

vindaloo [ˌvɪndə'luː] N *sehr scharf gewürztes indisches Currygericht*

vindicate ['vɪndɪkeɪt] VT **a** *opinion, action, decision* rechtfertigen **b** (= *exonerate*) rehabilitieren

vindication [ˌvɪndɪ'keɪʃən] N **a** (*of opinion, action, decision*) Rechtfertigung *f*; **in ~ of** zur Rechtfertigung (+*gen*) **b** (= *exoneration*) Rehabilitation *f*

vindictive [vɪn'dɪktɪv] ADJ *speech, person* rachsüchtig; *mood* nachtragend, unversöhnlich; **he is not a ~ person** er ist nicht nachtragend; **these measures are likely to make the unions feel ~** diese Maßnahmen könnten bei den Gewerkschaften auf Unwillen *or* Ressentiments stoßen; **I hope you won't feel ~ because of my rather harsh criticism** ich hoffe, Sie tragen mir meine etwas harte Kritik nicht nach *or* Sie nehmen mir meine etwas harte Kritik nicht übel; **corporal punishment can make pupils feel ~ toward(s) the teacher** die Prügelstrafe kann die Schüler gegen den Lehrer aufbringen; **to**

feel a moment's ~ pleasure einen Moment der Schadenfreude verspüren

vindictively [vɪn'dɪktɪvlɪ] ADV *say, behave* gemein

vindictiveness [vɪn'dɪktɪvnɪs] N Rachsucht *f*; (*of mood*) Unversöhnlichkeit *f*; **the ~ of his speech** seine rachsüchtige Rede

vine [vaɪn] N **a** (= *grapevine*) Rebe *f*, Weinrebe *f* **b** (= *similar plant*) Rebengewächs *nt*

vinedresser ['vaɪndresə'] N Winzer(in) *m(f)*

vinegar ['vɪnɪgə'] N Essig *m*

vinegary ['vɪnɪgərɪ] ADJ (*lit, fig*) säuerlich; **~ smell** Essiggeruch *m*

vine: vine grower N Weinbauer *m*/-bäuerin *f*; **vine-growing district** N Weingegend *f*, Weinbaugebiet *nt*; **vine harvest** N Weinlese *f*, Weinernte *f*; **vine leaf** N Rebenblatt *nt*; **vineyard** ['vɪnjəd] N Weinberg *m*

viniculture ['vɪnɪˌkʌltʃə'] N Weinbau *m*

vino ['viːnəʊ] N (*inf, = wine*) Vino *m* (*inf*)

vintage ['vɪntɪdʒ] N **a** (= *given year*) (*of wine, fig*) Jahrgang *m*; (*of car*) Baujahr *nt* **b** (= *wine of particular year*) **the 1984 ~** der Jahrgang 1984, der 84er **c** (= *harvesting, season*) Weinlese *f*, Weinernte *f* ADJ *attr* (= *old*) uralt; (= *high quality*) glänzend, hervorragend; **this typewriter is a ~ model** diese Schreibmaschine hat Museumswert; **a ~ performance from Humphrey Bogart** eine einmalige künstlerische Leistung Humphrey Bogarts

vintage: vintage car N Vorkriegsmodell *nt*, Vintage-Car *nt*; **vintage port** N Vintage-Port *m*, schwerer Port eines besonderen Jahrgangs; **vintage wine** N edler Wein; **vintage year** N **a ~ for wine** ein besonders gutes Weinjahr; **a ~ for Burgundy** ein besonders gutes Jahr für Burgunder; **it was a ~ for investment** es war ein ausgezeichnetes Jahr für Investitionen

vintner ['vɪntnə'] N Weinhändler(in) *m(f)*

vinyl ['vaɪnɪl] N Vinyl *nt*

viol ['vaɪəl] N Viola *f*

viola¹ [vɪ'əʊlə] N (*Mus*) Bratsche *f*

viola² ['vaɪələ] N (*Bot*) Veilchen *nt*

viola da gamba [vɪ'əʊlədə'gæmbə] N Gambe *f*

violate ['vaɪəleɪt] VT **a** *treaty, promise* brechen; (*partially*) verletzen; *law, rule, moral code* verstoßen gegen; *rights, airspace* verletzen; *truth* vergewaltigen **b** (= *disturb*) *holy place* entweihen, schänden; *peacefulness* stören; **to ~ sb's privacy** in jds Privatsphäre eindringen; **it's violating a person's privacy to ...** es ist ein Eingriff in jemandes Privatsphäre, wenn man ...; **the shriek of the jets now ~s that once peaceful spot** durch das Heulen der Düsenflugzeuge ist die Idylle dieses Fleckchens zerstört worden **c** (= *rape*) vergewaltigen, schänden

violation [ˌvaɪə'leɪʃən] N **a** (*of law*) Übertretung *f* (*of +gen*), Verletzung *f* (*of +gen*), Verstoß *m* (*of gegen*); (*of rule*) Verstoß *m* (*of gegen*); (*of rights*) Verletzung *f*; (*of truth*) Vergewaltigung *f*; **a ~ of a treaty** ein Vertragsbruch *m*; (*partial*) eine Vertragsverletzung; **traffic ~** Verkehrsvergehen *nt*; **he did this in ~ of the conditions agreed** er verstieß damit gegen die Vereinbarungen **b** (*of holy place*) Entweihung *f*, Schändung *f*; (*of peacefulness*) Störung *f*; (*of privacy*) Eingriff *m* (*of in +acc*) **c** (= *rape*) Vergewaltigung *f*, Schändung *f*

violator ['vaɪəleɪtə'] N (*of treaty*) Vertragsbrüchige(r) *mf*; (*of laws*) Gesetzesverletzer(in) *m(f)*; (*of holy place*) Schänder(in) *m(f)*; (*of woman*) Schänder *m*; **the ~ of these rules ...** wer gegen diese Regeln verstößt, ...

violence ['vaɪələns] N **a** (= *forcefulness, strength*) Heftigkeit *f*; (*of protest*) Schärfe *f*; (*of speech also*) Leidenschaftlichkeit *f*; **the ~ of the contrast** der krasse Gegensatz; **the ~ of his temper** sein jähzorniges Temperament, seine Jähzornigkeit **b** (= *brutality*) Gewalt *f*; (*of people*) Gewalttätigkeit *f*; (*of actions*) Brutalität *f*; **the ~ of his nature** seine gewalttätige Art; **crime of ~** Gewaltverbrechen *nt*; **act of ~** Gewalttat *f*; **robbery**

with ~ Raubüberfall *m*; **an increase in ~** eine Zunahme der Gewalttätigkeit; **to use ~ against sb** Gewalt gegen jdn anwenden; **was there any ~?** kam es zu Gewalttätigkeiten?; **outbreak of ~** Ausbruch *m* von Gewalttätigkeiten **c** (*fig*) **to do ~ to sth** etw entstellen; **it does ~ to the human spirit** das vergewaltigt den gesunden Menschenverstand

violent ['vaɪələnt] ADJ **a** (= *brutal*) *person, nature, action* brutal, gewalttätig; *crime* Gewalt-; *times, period, age* voller Gewalt; *attack, blow* heftig; *death* gewaltsam; *sport, game* brutal; *film, programme, book* gewalttätig; **to have a ~ temper** jähzornig sein; **to be in a ~ temper** toben; **to turn ~** gewalttätig werden; **to meet a ~ end** eines gewaltsamen Todes sterben; **the beginning of the second movement is rather ~** der zweite Satz beginnt sehr leidenschaftlich; **to get** *or* **become ~** gewalttätig werden; **by ~ means** (*open sth*) mit Gewalt(anwendung); *persuade* unter Gewaltanwendung **b** (= *forceful*) *demonstration, protest* heftig; *expulsion, impact* gewaltig; *wind, storm, earthquake* heftig, stark, gewaltig; **don't be so ~, open it gently** sei nicht so stürmisch, öffne es vorsichtig **c** (= *dramatic*) *contrast* krass; *change* tief greifend **d** (= *vehement*) *argument, row, opposition* heftig **e** (= *intense*) *blush* heftig, tief; *feeling, affair, speech* leidenschaftlich; *pain, dislike* heftig, stark; *colour* grell

violently ['vaɪələntlɪ] ADV **a** (= *brutally*) *kick, beat, attack, react, act* brutal; **to die ~** eines gewaltsamen Todes sterben **b** (= *forcefully*) *push, fling, hurl* kräftig; *tremble, shake, shudder* heftig; *swerve, brake* abrupt **c** (= *dramatically*) **red and pink clash ~** Rot und Rosa beißen sich; **they have quite ~ opposed temperaments** sie haben völlig unvereinbare Temperamente **d** (= *vehemently*) *speak* heftig, leidenschaftlich; *disagree* scharf; **they are ~ anti-communist** sie sind militante Antikommunisten; **to be ~ against sth** *or* **opposed to sth** ein scharfer Gegner/eine scharfe Gegnerin einer Sache (*gen*) sein; **he expresses himself rather ~** er drückt sich sehr krass aus **e** (= *intensely*) *blush* tief, heftig; *fall in love* unsterblich; **to be ~ ill** *or* **sick** sich furchtbar übergeben; **he was ~ angry** er war außer sich (*dat*) vor Wut; **to retch/cough ~** gewaltig würgen/husten

violet ['vaɪəlɪt] N (*Bot*) Veilchen *nt*; (= *colour*) Violett *nt* ADJ violett

violin [ˌvaɪə'lɪn] N Geige *f*, Violine *f*

violin case N Geigenkasten *m*

violin concerto N Violinkonzert *nt*

violinist [ˌvaɪə'lɪnɪst] N Geiger(in) *m(f)*, Violinist(in) *m(f)*

violin player N Geiger(in) *m(f)*, Geigenspieler(in) *m(f)*

violin sonata N Violinsonate *f*

violist [vɪ'əʊlɪst] N (*US*) Bratschist(in) *m(f)*

violoncello [ˌvaɪələn'tʃeləʊ] N (*form*) Violoncello *nt*

VIP N prominente Persönlichkeit, VIP *m*, Promi *m* (*hum inf*); **he got/we gave him ~ treatment** er wurde/wir haben ihn als Ehrengast behandelt; **~ lounge** Prominentensuite *f*, VIP-Lounge *f*

viper ['vaɪpə'] N (*Zool*) Viper *f*; (*fig*) Schlange *f*

viperish ['vaɪpərɪʃ] ADJ (*fig*) giftig

virago [vɪ'rɑːgəʊ] N Xanthippe *f*

viral ['vaɪərəl] ADJ Virus-; **~ infection** Virusinfektion *f*

Virgil ['vɜːdʒɪl] N Vergil(ius) *m*, Virgil *m*

virgin ['vɜːdʒɪn] N Jungfrau *f*; **the (Blessed) Virgin** (*Rel*) die (Heilige) Jungfrau Maria; **the Virgin Mary** die Jungfrau Maria; **the Black Virgin** die Schwarze Madonna; **he's still a ~** er ist noch unschuldig; **she's a political ~** sie ist in der Politik noch unbeleckt ADJ *girl, woman* jungfräulich, unberührt; (*fig*) *forest, land* unberührt; *freshness* rein; *snow* jungfräulich, unberührt; **~ olive oil** natives Olivenöl; **the Virgin Queen** *Königin Elisabeth I.* **to be ~ territory (for sb)** Neuland *nt* (für jdn) sein

virginal ['vɜːdʒɪnl] **ADJ** **a** jungfräulich; **dressed in ~ white** in jungfräuliches Weiß gekleidet **b** (*form, = unused*) jungfräulich **PL** (*Mus*) Tafelklavier *nt*

virgin birth N jungfräuliche Geburt; (*Biol*) Jungfernzeugung *f*

Virginia [vəˈdʒɪnjə] N (*= state*) Virginia *nt*; (*= tobacco*) Virginia *m*; **he smokes ~s** er raucht Virginiazigaretten

Virginia creeper N wilder Wein, Jungfernrebe *f*

Virginian [vəˈdʒɪnjən] **N** Einwohner(in) *m(f)* von Virginia, Virginier(in) *m(f)* **ADJ** von/aus Virginia

Virginia tobacco N Virginiatabak *m*

Virgin Isles N **the ~** die Jungferninseln *pl*

virginity [vəˈdʒɪnɪtɪ] N Unschuld *f*; (*of girls also*) Jungfräulichkeit *f*; **to take sb's ~** jds Unschuld rauben

Virgo ['vɜːgəʊ] N Jungfrau *f*; **he's (a) ~** er ist Jungfrau

Virgoan [vɜːˈgəʊən] (*Astrol*) **N** Jungfrau *f*; **he's a ~** er ist (eine) Jungfrau **ADJ** **he's ~** er ist (eine) Jungfrau

virgule ['vɜːgjuːl] N (*US Typ, = oblique*) Schrägstrich *m*, Virgel *f* (*spec*)

virile ['vɪraɪl] ADJ (*lit*) männlich; (*fig*) ausdrucksvoll, kraftvoll

virility [vɪˈrɪlɪtɪ] N (*lit*) Männlichkeit *f*; (*= sexual power*) Potenz *f*; (*fig*) Ausdruckskraft *f*; **political ~** politische Potenz

virologist [ˌvaɪəˈrɒlədʒɪst] N Virologe *m*, Virologin *f*, Virusforscher(in) *m(f)*

virology [ˌvaɪəˈrɒlədʒɪ] N Virologie *f*, Virusforschung *f*

virtual ['vɜːtjʊəl] ADJ *attr* **a** *certainty, impossibility* fast völlig; **it led to the ~ collapse of the economy** es führte dazu, dass die Wirtschaft so gut wie zusammenbrach; **they have a ~ monopoly** sie haben so gut wie das Monopol; **to come to a ~ halt** *or* **standstill** so gut wie zum Erliegen kommen; **she was a ~ prisoner/recluse/stranger** sie war so gut wie eine Gefangene/Einsiedlerin/Fremde; **he is the ~ leader** er ist quasi der Führer, praktisch ist er der Führer; **it was a ~ admission of guilt** es war praktisch ein Schuldgeständnis; **it was a ~ disaster** es war geradezu eine Katastrophe; **it was a ~ failure** es war praktisch ein Misserfolg *m* **b** (*Phys*) virtuell **c** (*Comput*) virtuell; **~ address** (*Comput*) virtuelle Adresse; **~ sex** virtueller Sex

virtuality [vɜːtjʊˈælɪtɪ] N Virtualität *f*

virtually ['vɜːtjʊəlɪ] ADV praktisch; *blind, lost also* fast, nahezu, mehr oder weniger; **yes, ~** ja, fast, ja so gut wie; **he is ~ the boss** er ist praktisch *or* quasi der Chef; **to be ~ certain** sich (*dat*) so gut wie sicher sein **b** (*Comput*) virtuell

virtual memory N (*Comput*) virtueller Speicher

virtual reality N (*Comput*) virtuelle Realität; **~ computer** virtueller Computer; **~ helmet** Datenhelm *m*

virtue ['vɜːtjuː] N **a** (*= moral quality*) Tugend *f*; **to make a ~ of necessity** aus der Not eine Tugend machen; **a life of ~** ein tugendhaftes Leben **b** (*= chastity*) Keuschheit *f*, Tugendhaftigkeit *f*; **a woman of easy ~** (*euph*) ein leichtes Mädchen **c** (*= advantage, point*) Vorteil *m*; **what's the ~ of that?** welchen Vorteil hat das?, wozu ist das gut?; **there is no ~ in doing that** es scheint nicht sehr zweckmäßig, das zu tun **d** (*= healing power*) Heilkraft *f*; **in** *or* **by ~ of** aufgrund *or* auf Grund (+*gen*); **in** *or* **by ~ of the authority/power** *etc* **vested in me** kraft meiner Autorität/Macht *etc* (*form*)

virtuosity [ˌvɜːtjʊˈɒsɪtɪ] N Virtuosität *f*

virtuoso [ˌvɜːtjʊˈəʊzəʊ] **N** (*esp Mus*) Virtuose *m*, Virtuosin *f* **ADJ** *performance* meisterhaft, virtuos

virtuous ['vɜːtjʊəs] ADJ **a** tugendhaft, tugendsam **b** (*pej, = self-satisfied, righteous*) *person, attitude* selbstgerecht

virtuous circle N positiver Kreislauf *m*, Circulus virtuosus *m*; **the ~ of investment and growth** die positive Auswirkung von Investitionen auf das Wachstum und umgekehrt

virtuously ['vɜːtjʊəslɪ] ADV (*pej, = righteously*) *say* selbstgerecht

virulence ['vɪrʊləns] N **a** (*Med*) Heftigkeit *f*, Bösartigkeit *f*; (*of poison*) Stärke *f* **b** (*fig*) Schärfe *f*, Virulenz *f* (*geh*)

virulent ['vɪrʊlənt] ADJ **a** (*Med*) bösartig; *poison* stark, tödlich **b** (*fig, = vicious*) *attack, speech, critic, opponent* scharf; *hatred* unversöhnlich; *colour* grell

virulently ['vɪrʊləntlɪ] ADV **a** (*Med*) virulent **b** (*fig*) scharf; **~ racist** virulent rassistisch

virus ['vaɪərəs] N **a** (*Med*) Virus *nt or m*, Erreger *m*; **polio ~** Polioerreger *m*; **the AIDS ~** das Aidsvirus; **~ disease** Viruskrankheit *f*; **she's got** *or* **caught a ~** (*inf, = flu etc*) sie hat sich (*dat*) was geholt *or* eingefangen (*inf*) **b** (*fig*) Geschwür *nt* **c** (*Comput*) Virus *nt or m*; **~-infected** virenbefallen

visa ['viːzə] **N** Visum *nt*; (*= stamp also*) Sichtvermerk *m* **VT** ein Visum ausstellen (+*dat*); **to get a passport ~ed** einen Sichtvermerk in den Pass bekommen

visage ['vɪzɪdʒ] N (*liter*) Antlitz *nt* (*liter*)

visagiste [ˌvɪzɑːˈʒiːst, ˈvɪzədʒɪst] N Visagist(in) *m(f)*

vis-à-vis ['viːzəviː] **PREP** in Anbetracht (+*gen*) **ADV** gegenüber

viscera ['vɪsərə] PL innere Organe *pl*; (*in abdomen*) Eingeweide *pl*

visceral ['vɪsərəl] ADJ viszeral (*spec*); (*of intestines also*) der Eingeweide; (*fig*) *hatred, dislike* tief sitzend; **on a ~ level** auf einer emotionalen Ebene; **a ~ feeling** (*fig liter*) ein inneres Gefühl

viscid ['vɪsɪd] ADJ (*form*) zähflüssig; (*Bot*) klebrig

viscose ['vɪskəʊs] N Viskose *f*

viscosity [vɪsˈkɒsɪtɪ] N Zähflüssigkeit *f*; (*Phys*) Viskosität *f*

viscount ['vaɪkaʊnt] N Viscount *m*

viscountcy ['vaɪkaʊntsɪ] N Rang *m* des Viscounts

viscountess ['vaɪkaʊntɪs] N Viscountess *f*

viscounty ['vaɪkaʊntɪ] N = viscountcy

viscous ['vɪskəs] ADJ (*form*) zähflüssig; (*Phys*) viskos

vise [vaɪs] N (*US*) = vice²

visibility [ˌvɪzɪˈbɪlɪtɪ] N **a** Sichtbarkeit *f* **b** (*Met*) Sichtweite *f*; **poor/good ~** schlechte/gute Sicht; **low ~** geringe Sichtweite; **~ is down to 100 metres** die Sichtweite beträgt nur 100 Meter

visible ['vɪzəbl] ADJ **a** sichtbar; **~ to the naked eye** mit dem bloßen Auge zu erkennen; **it wasn't ~ in the fog** es war im Nebel nicht zu erkennen; **the Englishman prefers his emotions not to be ~** der Engländer zeigt nicht gern seine Gefühle; **the house is ~ from the road** das Haus ist von der Straße aus zu sehen; **there is no ~ difference** man kann keinen Unterschied erkennen; **with a ~ effort** mit sichtlicher Mühe **b** (*= obvious*) sichtlich; (*= prominent*) *person* eminent, herausragend; **at management level women are becoming increasing ~** auf Führungsebene treten Frauen immer deutlicher in Erscheinung; **with no ~ means of support** (*Jur*) ohne bekannte Einkommensquellen *pl*

visible: **visible exports** PL (*Econ*) sichtbare Ausfuhr; **visible light** N (*Phys*) sichtbares Licht; **visible panty line** N (*inf*) sichtbare Slipkontur

visibly ['vɪzəblɪ] ADV sichtbar, sichtlich; *deteriorate, decay* zusehends

Visigoth ['vɪzɪgɒθ] N Westgote *m*

vision ['vɪʒən] **N** **a** (*= power of sight*) Sehvermögen *nt*; **within/beyond the range of ~** in/außer Sichtweite; **he has good ~** er sieht gut → **field g** **b** (*= foresight*) Weitblick *m*; **a man of ~** ein Mann mit Weitblick **c** (*in dream, trance*) Vision *f*, Gesicht *nt* (*liter*); **it came to me in a ~** ich hatte eine Vision **d** (*= image*) Vorstellung *f*; **Orwell's ~ of the future** Orwells Zukunftsvision *f* **e** **to have ~s of wealth** von Reichtum träumen, sich (*dat*) Reichtum vorgaukeln; **I had ~s of having to walk all the way home** (*inf*) ich sah mich im Geiste schon den ganzen Weg nach Hause laufen

visionary ['vɪʒənərɪ] **ADJ** **a** (*= impractical*) unrealistisch; (*= of visions*) vorhersehend, visionär (*geh*); (*= unreal*) eingebildet **b** (*= with a vision*) *idea, book, writer, artist* visionär **N** Visionär(in) *m(f)*, Seher(in) *m(f)* (*geh*); (*pej*) Fantast(in) *m(f)*, Phantast(in) *m(f)*

vision mixer N (*TV*) (*= person*) Bildmischer(in) *m(f)*; (*= equipment*) Bildmischpult *nt*

visit ['vɪzɪt] **N** **a** (*= call, to museum etc*) Besuch *m*; (*of doctor*) Hausbesuch *m*; (*of inspector*) Kontrolle *f*; **I felt better after a ~ to the doctor's/solicitor's** nachdem ich beim Arzt/Anwalt gewesen war, ging es mir besser; **to pay sb/sth a ~** jdm/einer Sache einen Besuch abstatten (*form*), jdn/etw besuchen; **to pay a ~** (*euph*) mal verschwinden (müssen); **to have a ~ from sb** von jdm besucht werden; **give us a ~ some time** besuchen Sie uns (doch) mal; **he went on a two-day ~ to Paris** er fuhr für zwei Tage nach Paris; **I'm going on a ~ to Glasgow next week** ich fahre nächste Woche (zu einem Besuch) nach Glasgow; **we're expecting a ~ from the police any day** wir rechnen jeden Tag mit dem Besuch der Polizei **b** (*= stay*) Aufenthalt *m*, Besuch *m*; **to be on a ~ to London** zu einem Besuch in London sein; **to be on a private/official ~** inoffiziell/offiziell da sein **VT** **a** *person, the sick, museum* besuchen; *doctor, solicitor* aufsuchen; **you never ~ us these days** Sie kommen uns ja gar nicht mehr besuchen; **the prime minister will ~ Germany next week** der Premierminister wird nächste Woche Deutschland besuchen **b** (*= go and stay with*) besuchen, aufsuchen (*geh*) **c** (*= inspect*) inspizieren, besichtigen, besuchen; **to ~ the scene of the crime** (*Jur*) den Tatort besichtigen **d** (*Bibl*) *sins* heimsuchen; **upon** an +*dat*, über +*acc*) **VI** **a** (*= call in*) einen Besuch machen; **come and ~ some time** komm mich mal besuchen; **I'm only ~ing here** ich bin nur auf Besuch hier **b** (*US, inf, = chat*) schwatzen, ein Schwätzchen halten

▶ **visit with** VI +*prep obj* (*US*) schwatzen mit

visitation [ˌvɪzɪˈteɪʃən] N **a** (*form: = visit, by official*) Besichtigung *f*, Besuch *m*; (*by ghost*) Erscheinung *f*; **after another ~ from the mother-in-law** (*hum*) nachdem uns die Schwiegermutter wieder einmal heimgesucht hatte **b** (*Rel*) **the Visitation** Mariä Heimsuchung *f* **c** (*Rel, = affliction*) Heimsuchung *f*; **a ~ for their sins** die Strafe für ihre Sünden; **the ~ of the sins of the fathers on succeeding generations** die Bestrafung der folgenden Generationen für die Sünden der ihrer Väter

visiting ['vɪzɪtɪŋ] **N** Besuche *pl* **ADJ** *scholar, expert* Gast-; *dignitary, monarch, royalty, queen* der/die zu Besuch ist

visiting: visiting card N Visitenkarte *f*; **visiting hours** PL Besuchszeiten *pl*; **visiting nurse** N (*US*) ≈ Bezirkskrankenschwester *f*; **visiting professor** N Gastprofessor(in) *m(f)*; **visiting rights** PL Besuchsrecht *nt*; **visiting team** N **the ~** die Gäste *pl*; **visiting terms** PL **I'm not on ~ with him** ich kenne ihn nicht so gut, dass ich ihn besuchen gehen würde; **visiting time** N Besuchszeit *f*

visitor ['vɪzɪtə'] N Besucher(in) *m(f)*; (*in hotel*) Gast *m*; **to have ~s/a ~** Besuch haben; **the**

great tit is a rare ~ in these parts die Kohlmeise hält sich selten in diesen Breiten auf; **~s' book** Gästebuch *nt*

visor ['vaɪzəʳ] N (on helmet) Visier *nt*; (on cap) Schirm *m*; (Aut) Blende *f*; **sun ~** Schild *m*, Schirm *m*; (Aut) Sonnenblende *f*

VISTA (US) abbr of **Volunteers in Service to America** US-Hilfsorganisation, die Freiwillige zur Hilfe Einkommensschwacher abstellt

vista ['vɪstə] N **a** (= view) Aussicht *f*, Blick *m* **b** (of past) Bild *nt*; (of future) Aussicht (of auf +acc), Perspektive (of von) *f*

visual ['vɪzjʊəl] ADJ Seh-; image, memory, impression, depiction, joke visuell; **~ cortex** Sehzentrum *nt*; **~ disorder** Sehstörung *f*; **he is a very ~ songwriter** er schreibt sehr bildliche Liedertexte **N** (grafischer) Entwurf

visual: visual aids PL Anschauungsmaterial *nt*; **visual arts** N **the ~** die darstellenden Künste *pl*; **visual display terminal** N Bildschirmterminal *nt*; **visual display unit** N Sichtgerät *nt*; **visual field** N Sehfeld *nt*, Gesichtsfeld *nt*

visualize ['vɪzjʊəlaɪz] VT **a** (= see in mind) sich (dat) vorstellen **b** (= foresee) erwarten; **we do not ~ many changes** wir rechnen nicht mit großen Veränderungen; **he ~s some changes** (= intends) er hat einige Veränderungen im Auge; **that's not how I'd ~d things** so hatte ich mir das nicht vorgestellt

visually ['vɪzjʊəlɪ] ADV visuell; **~ stunning/exciting/attractive** umwerfend/aufregend/attraktiv anzusehen; **~, the film is good entertainment** von der Aufmachung her ist der Film sehr unterhaltend; **I remember things ~** ich habe ein visuelles Gedächtnis

visually handicapped, **visually impaired** ADJ sehbehindert

vital ['vaɪtl] ADJ **a** (= of life) vital, Lebens-; (= necessary for life) lebenswichtig; **~ organs** lebenswichtige Organe *pl*; **~ spark** (fig) zündender Funke

b (= essential) unerlässlich; **of ~ importance** von größter Wichtigkeit; **this is ~** das ist unbedingt notwendig; **your support is ~ to us** wir brauchen unbedingt Ihre Unterstützung; **is it ~ for you to go?, is it ~ that you go?** müssen Sie denn unbedingt gehen?; **it's ~ that this is finished by Tuesday** das muss bis Dienstag unbedingt fertig sein; **how ~ is this?** wie wichtig ist das?; **such skills are ~** derartige Fähigkeiten sind überlebenswichtig

c (= critical) argument, issue entscheidend; error schwerwiegend, schwer wiegend; **at the ~ moment** im kritischen or entscheidenden Moment; **the ~ problem** das Kernproblem

d (= lively) person vital; artistic style lebendig **N** **the ~s** die lebenswichtigen Organe *pl*; (hum: = genitals) die edlen Teile (hum)

vital force N Lebenskraft *f*

vitality [vaɪˈtælɪtɪ] N (= energy) Energie *f*, Leben *nt*, Vitalität *f*; (of prose, language) Lebendigkeit *f*, Vitalität *f*; (of companies, new state) Dynamik *f*; (= durability) Beständigkeit *f*

vitalization [,vaɪtəlaɪˈzeɪʃən] N Belebung *f*, Aktivierung *f*

vitalize ['vaɪtəlaɪz] VT beleben

vitally ['vaɪtəlɪ] ADV **a** important äußerst, ungeheuer; necessary, needed dringend; (emph: = greatly) interested, concerned äußerst **b** (= intensely) **~ alive** quicklebendig; **~ alert** hellwach; **he writes freshly and ~** er schreibt einen frischen und lebendigen or kraftvollen Stil

vital: vital parts PL wichtige Teile *pl*; **vital signs** PL (Med) Lebenszeichen *pl*; **vital statistics** PL Bevölkerungsstatistik *f*; (inf, of woman) Maße *pl*

vitamin ['vɪtəmɪn] N Vitamin *nt*; **~ A** Vitamin A; **with added ~s** mit Vitaminen angereichert

vitamin: vitamin deficiency N Vitaminmangel *m*; **vitamin-deficiency disease** N Vitaminmangelkrankheit *f*; **vitamin pill** N Vitamintablette *f*

vitiate ['vɪʃɪeɪt] VT **a** (= spoil) air, blood verunreinigen **b** (Jur etc, = invalidate) ungültig machen; thesis widerlegen; meeting, decision, agreement aufheben

viticulture ['vɪtɪkʌltʃəʳ] N Weinbau *m*

vitreous ['vɪtrɪəs] ADJ Glas-; **~ china** Porzellanemail *nt*; **~ enamel** Glasemail *nt*

vitrifaction [,vɪtrɪˈfækʃən], **vitrification** [,vɪtrɪˈfɪˈkeɪʃən] N Verglasung *f*, Frittung *f*

vitrify ['vɪtrɪfaɪ] VT zu Glas schmelzen, verglasen VI verglasen

vitriol ['vɪtrɪəl] N (Chem) (= salt) Sulfat *nt*, Vitriol *nt*; (= acid) Schwefelsäure *f*; (fig) Bissigkeit *f*, Bosheit *f*

vitriolic [,vɪtrɪˈɒlɪk] ADJ **a** (fig) remark beißend, hasserfüllt; criticism ätzend, beißend; attack, speech hasserfüllt **b** (Chem) vitriolhaltig; (= vitriolic acid) Vitriolsäure *f*

vitro ['vi:trəʊ] ADJ, ADV → **in vitro**

vituperate [vɪˈtju:pəreɪt] VI schmähen (geh) (against +acc), verunglimpfen (against +acc)

vituperation [vɪˌtju:pəˈreɪʃən] N (form) Schmähungen *pl* (geh)

vituperative [vɪˈtju:pərətɪv] ADJ (form) language schmähend (geh); criticism, remark, attack, abuse beißend; person scharfzüngig; **~ speech** Schmährede *f*

viva ['vaɪvə] N (Brit) = **viva voce** N

vivacious [vɪˈveɪʃəs] ADJ lebhaft; character, person also temperamentvoll; colour, clothes also leuchtend bunt; smile, laugh munter, aufgeweckt

vivaciously [vɪˈveɪʃəslɪ] ADV say, laugh munter

vivaciousness [vɪˈveɪʃəsnɪs] N Lebhaftigkeit *f*; (of smile, laugh) Munterkeit *f*, Aufgeweckheit *f*

vivacity [vɪˈvæsɪtɪ] N Lebhaftigkeit *f*; (of style) Lebendigkeit *f*; (of smile, laugh) Munterkeit *f*, Aufgeweckheit *f*

vivarium [vɪˈvɛərɪəm] N Vivarium *nt*

viva voce ['vaɪvəˈvəʊtʃɪ] ADJ, ADV mündlich N (Brit) mündliche Prüfung

vivid ['vɪvɪd] ADJ **a** light hell; colour kräftig, leuchtend, lebhaft; **the ~ feathers of the bird** das bunte or auffallende Gefieder des Vogels; **a ~ blue dress** ein leuchtend blaues Kleid; **a ~ tie** eine auffällige Krawatte

b (= lively) imagination, recollection lebhaft; description, metaphor, image lebendig, anschaulich; emotions stark; **in ~ detail** in allen plastischen Einzelheiten; **the memory of that day is still quite ~** der Tag ist mir noch in lebhafter Erinnerung

c (= powerful) example, contrast deutlich; **to give a ~ demonstration of one's power** seine Macht klar und deutlich unter Beweis stellen; **to be a ~ reminder of sth** lebhaft an etw (acc) erinnern

vividly ['vɪvɪdlɪ] ADV **a** coloured lebhaft; shine hell, leuchtend; **the red stands out ~ against its background** das Rot hebt sich stark vom Hintergrund ab; **a ~ coloured** (Brit) or **colored** (US) **bird** ein bunt gefiederter or auffällig gefiederter Vogel **b** remember, recall lebhaft; describe, illustrate anschaulich, lebendig; demonstrate klar und deutlich; portray, bring to life anschaulich, plastisch

vividness ['vɪvɪdnɪs] N **a** (of colour) Lebhaftigkeit *f*; (of light) Helligkeit *f* **b** (of style) Lebendigkeit *f*; (of description, metaphor, image) Anschaulichkeit *f*; (of imagination, memory) Lebhaftigkeit *f*

vivify ['vɪvɪfaɪ] VT beleben

viviparous [vɪˈvɪpərəs] ADJ (Zool) lebend gebärend

vivisect [,vɪvɪˈsekt] VT vivisezieren

vivisection [,vɪvɪˈsekʃən] N Vivisektion *f*

vivisectionist [,vɪvɪˈsekʃənɪst] N jd, der Eingriffe am lebenden Tier vornimmt/befürwortet

vixen ['vɪksn] N (Zool) Füchsin *f*; (fig) zänkisches Weib, Drachen *m* (inf)

viz [vɪz] ADV nämlich

vizier [vɪˈzɪəʳ] N Wesir *m*

V-J Day N Tag des Sieges gegen Japan im 2. Weltkrieg

VLSI abbr of **very large scale integration** Höchst- or Größtintegration *f*, VLSI *f*

V: V-neck N V-Ausschnitt *m*; **V-necked** ADJ mit V-Ausschnitt

VoA (US) abbr of **Voice of America the ~** die Stimme Amerikas

vocabulary [vəˈkæbjʊlərɪ] N Wortschatz *m*, Vokabular *nt* (geh); (in textbook) Wörterverzeichnis *f*; **he has a limited ~** er hat einen beschränkten Wortschatz; **the ~ of the legal profession** das Vokabular der Juristen; **~ book** Vokabelheft *nt*; (printed) Vokabelbuch *nt*; **~ test** (Sch) Vokabelarbeit *f*

vocal ['vəʊkəl] ADJ **a** (= using voice) Stimm-; talent stimmlich; **~ style** Singstil *m*; **~ range/training** Stimmumfang *m*/-bildung *f*; **~ performance** gesangliche Leistung; **best male ~ performer** bester Vokalsänger; **~ music** Vokalmusik *f*; **~ group** Gesangsgruppe *f*

b communication mündlich

c (= voicing one's opinions) group, person lautstark; **to be/become ~** sich zu Wort melden; **to be ~ in sth** etw deutlich zum Ausdruck bringen; **to be ~ in demanding sth** etw laut fordern; **to become increasingly ~ in one's opposition to sth** seinen Widerstand gegen etw immer deutlicher or lauter zum Ausdruck bringen **N** (of pop song) (gesungener) Schlager; (in jazz) Vocal *nt*; **who's doing or singing the ~s for your group now?** wen habt ihr denn jetzt als Sänger?; **~s: Van Morrison** Gesang: Van Morrison; **featuring Madonna on ~s** mit Madonna als Sängerin; **backing ~s** Hintergrundgesang *m*; **lead ~s ...** Leadsänger(in) *m(f)* ...

vocal cords PL Stimmbänder *pl*

vocalic [vəʊˈkælɪk] ADJ vokalisch

vocalist ['vəʊkəlɪst] N Sänger(in) *m(f)*

vocalize ['vəʊkəlaɪz] VT **a** thoughts aussprechen, Ausdruck verleihen (+dat); feelings zum Ausdruck bringen **b** (Phon) consonant vokalisieren

vocally ['vəʊkəlɪ] ADV **a** mündlich; **the tune has now been done ~ by ...** die Melodie wurde jetzt auch gesungen von ... **b** (= outspokenly) support, oppose klar und deutlich

vocation [vəʊˈkeɪʃən] N **a** (Rel etc) Berufung *f*; (form, = profession) Beruf *m*; **to have a ~ for teaching** zum Lehrer berufen sein **b** (= aptitude) Begabung *f*, Talent *nt*

vocational [vəʊˈkeɪʃənl] ADJ Berufs-; qualifications beruflich; **~ course** Weiterbildungskurs *m*; **~ training** Berufsausbildung *f*

vocational guidance N Berufsberatung *f*

vocationally [vəʊˈkeɪʃənlɪ] ADV train beruflich; **~ oriented** berufsorientiert

vocational school N (US) ≈ Berufsschule *f*

vocative ['vɒkətɪv] N Anredeform *f*, Vokativ *m*; **~ case** Anredefall *m*, Vokativ *m*

vociferate [vəʊˈsɪfəreɪt] VT schreien; **he ~d his grievances** er machte seinem Unmut Luft VI (fig) seinem Unmut Luft machen (about über +acc)

vociferation [vəʊˌsɪfəˈreɪʃən] N Geschrei *nt*; **their ~ of their discontent** ihr lautstarker Protest

vociferous [vəʊˈsɪfərəs] ADJ class, audience laut; demands, protest, critic, minority, opponent lautstark; **to be ~ in one's opposition to sth** lautstark gegen etw opponieren; **to be ~ in demanding one's rights** lautstark seine Rechte einfordern

vociferously [vəʊˈsɪfərəslɪ] ADV lautstark

vodka ['vɒdkə] N Wodka *m*

vogue [vəʊg] N Mode *f*; **the ~ for jeans** die Jeansmode; **to be the ~ or in ~** (in) Mode or en vogue sein; **to come into ~** (clothes) in Mode kommen, modern werden; (writers) populär werden, in Mode kommen; **to go out of ~** (clothes) aus der Mode kommen, unmodern werden; (writers) aus der Mode kommen; **to en-**

joy a great ~ **with** sehr beliebt sein unter (+*dat*), große Mode sein unter (+*dat*)

vogue expression, vogue word N Modewort *nt*

voice [vɔɪs] **N** **a** (= *faculty of speech, Mus, fig*) Stimme *f*; **to lose one's ~** die Stimme verlieren; **I've lost my ~** ich habe keine Stimme mehr; **to find one's ~** sich (*dat*) Gehör verschaffen; **she hasn't got much of a ~** sie hat keine besonders gute Stimme; **to be in good/poor ~** gut/nicht gut bei Stimme sein; **in a deep ~** mit tiefer Stimme; **in a low ~** leise, mit leiser Stimme; **to like the sound of one's own ~** sich gern(e) reden hören; **his ~ has broken** er hat den Stimmbruch hinter sich; **tenor ~** Tenor *m*; **bass ~** Bass *m*; **a piece for ~ and piano** ein Gesangsstück *nt* mit Klavierbegleitung; **with one ~** einstimmig; **to give ~ to sth** etw aussprechen, einer Sache (*dat*) Ausdruck verleihen; **the Voice of America** (*Rad*) die Stimme Amerikas **b** (*fig: = say*) **we have a/no ~ in the matter** wir haben in dieser Angelegenheit ein/kein Mitspracherecht **c** (*Gram*) Aktionsart *f*, Genus (verbi) *nt*; **the active/passive ~** das Aktiv/Passiv **d** (*Phon*) Stimmhaftigkeit *f*; **plus ~** stimmhaft **VT** **a** (= *express*) *feelings, opinion* zum Ausdruck bringen **b** (*Phon*) stimmhaft aussprechen

voice box N Kehlkopf *m*

voiced [vɔɪst] ADJ (*Phon*) stimmhaft

-voiced ADJ *suf* mit ... Stimme; **soft-voiced** mit sanfter Stimme

voice: voiceless ADJ **a** stumm; **in a ~ whisper** mit lautlosem Flüstern **b** (= *having no say*) ohne Mitspracherecht **c** (*Phon*) *consonant* stimmlos; **voice mail** N Voicemail *f*, Voice-Mail *f*; **voice-operated** ADJ sprachgesteuert; **voice-over** N Filmkommentar *m*; **voice part** N **the ~s** (*Mus*) die Singstimmen *pl*; **voice production** N Stimmbildung *f*; **voice projection** N Stimmresonanz *f*; **voice range** N Stimmumfang *m*; **voice recognition** N Spracherkennung *f*; **voice synthesizer** N Sprachsynthesizer *m*

void [vɔɪd] **N** (*lit, fig*) Leere *f*; **the dead astronaut floated off into the ~** der tote Astronaut schwebte in das All **ADJ** **a** (= *empty*) leer; **~ of any sense of decency** bar jeglichen Gefühls (*geh*) *or* ohne jegliches Gefühl für Anstand; **~ of humour** (*Brit*) *or* **humor** (*US*) ohne jeglichen Humor **b** (*Jur*) ungültig, nichtig **c** (= *useless*) nichtig; **you've made all my efforts totally ~** du hast all meine Bemühungen völlig zunichte gemacht **VT** **a** (*Jur*) ungültig machen, aufheben **b** (*form, = empty*) *bowels* entleeren

voile [vɔɪl] N Voile *m*, Schleierstoff *m*

vol *abbr of* **volume** Bd; (*Measure*) V(ol.)

volatile ['vɒlətaɪl] ADJ **a** (*Chem*) flüchtig **b** *person* (*in moods*) impulsiv; (*in interests*) sprunghaft; (*Psych*: = *unpredictable*) sprunghaft; *relationship* wechselhaft; *political situation* brisant; (*St Ex*) unbeständig; **a person with a ~ temper** ein sehr unberechenbarer Mensch **c** (*Comput*) **~ memory** flüchtiger Speicher

volatile oils PL ätherische Öle *pl*

volatility [vɒlə'tɪlɪtɪ] N **a** (*Chem*) Flüchtigkeit *f* **b** (*of person, in moods*) Impulsivität *f*; (*in interests*) Sprunghaftigkeit *f*; (*of relationship*) Wechselhaftigkeit *f*; (*of political situation*) Brisanz *f*; (*of stock market*) Unbeständigkeit *f*

volatilize [vɒ'lætəlaɪz] **VT** verflüchtigen **VI** sich verflüchtigen

vol-au-vent ['vɒləʊvɑː] N (Königin)pastetchen *nt*

volcanic [vɒl'kænɪk] ADJ (*lit*) Vulkan-; *rock, dust, activity* vulkanisch; (*fig*) heftig; **~ activity** Vulkantätigkeit *f*; **~ eruption** Vulkanausbruch *m*; **~ island** Vulkaninsel *f*

volcano [vɒl'keɪnəʊ] N Vulkan *m*

volcanologist [ˌvɒlkə'nɒlədʒɪst] N Vulkanologe *m*, Vulkanologin *f*

volcanology [ˌvɒlkə'nɒlədʒɪ] N Vulkanologie *f*

vole [vəʊl] N Wühlmaus *f*; (= *common vole*) Feldmaus *f*

Volga ['vɒlgə] N Wolga *f*

volition [vɒ'lɪʃən] N Wille *m*; **simply by the exercise of your ~** mit dem Willen allein; **of one's own ~** aus freiem Willen

volitional [və'lɪʃənl] ADJ Willens-, willentlich; *control* des Willens; **~ act** Willensakt *m*

volley ['vɒlɪ] **N** **a** (*of shots*) Salve *f*; (*of arrows, stones*) Hagel *m*; (*fig of insults*) Flut *f*, Hagel *m*; (*of applause*) Sturm *m* **b** (*Tennis*) Volley *m*, Flugball *m* **VT** **to ~ a ball** (*Tennis*) einen Ball im Volley spielen, einen Volley spielen *or* schlagen **VI** **a** (*Mil*) eine Salve abfeuern; (*guns, shots*) (in einer Salve) abgefeuert werden **b** (*Tennis*) einen Volley schlagen

volleyball ['vɒlɪ,bɔːl] N Volleyball *m*

volleyer ['vɒlɪə'] N **he's a superb ~** er schlägt tolle Volleys

Vols *abbr of* **Volumes** Bde

volt [vəʊlt] N Volt *nt*

voltage ['vəʊltɪdʒ] N Spannung *f*; **what ~ is this cable?** wie viel Volt hat dieses Kabel?

voltaic [vɒl'teɪɪk] ADJ voltaisch, galvanisch; **~ cell** galvanisches Element

volte-face ['vɒlt'fɑːs] N (*fig*) Kehrtwendung *f*; **to perform a ~** sich um 180 Grad drehen

voltmeter ['vəʊltmiːtə'] N Voltmeter *nt*

volubility [ˌvɒljʊ'bɪlɪtɪ] N Redseligkeit *f*

voluble ['vɒljʊbl] ADJ *speaker* redegewandt, redselig (*pej*); *protest* wortreich

volubly ['vɒljʊblɪ] ADV wortreich; **to talk ~** sehr redselig sein

volume ['vɒljuːm] **N** **a** Band *m*; **in six ~s** in sechs Bänden; **a six-volume dictionary** ein sechsbändiges Wörterbuch; **to write ~s** ganze Bände *pl* schreiben; **that speaks ~s** (*fig*) das spricht Bände (*for* für); **it speaks ~s for him** das spricht sehr für ihn **b** (= *space occupied by sth*) Volumen *nt*, Rauminhalt *m* **c** (= *size, amount*) Umfang *m*, Ausmaß *nt* (*of* an +*dat*); **a large ~ of sales/business** ein großer Umsatz; **the ~ of traffic** das Verkehrsaufkommen; **trade has increased in ~** das Handelsvolumen hat sich vergrößert **d** (= *large amount*) **~s of smoke** Rauchschwaden *pl*; **~s of white silk** Massen *pl* von weißer Seide; **we've ~s of work to get through** wir haben noch Berge von Arbeit **e** (= *sound*) Lautstärke *f*; **is the ~ right up?** ist das volle Lautstärke?; **turn the ~ up/down** (*Rad, TV*) stell (das Gerät) lauter/leiser **ATTR** **~ discount** Mengenrabatt *m*; **~ sales** Mengenabsatz *m*

volume control N (*Rad, TV*) Lautstärkeregler *m*

volumetric [ˌvɒljʊ'metrɪk] ADJ volumetrisch

voluminous [və'luːmɪnəs] ADJ voluminös (*geh*); *figure* üppig; *writings* umfangreich; *skirts, shirt, pockets* wallend

voluntarily ['vɒləntərɪlɪ] ADV freiwillig, von sich aus; (= *unpaid*) *work* ehrenamtlich

voluntarism ['vɒləntərɪzəm] N , *no pl* Voluntarismus *m*

voluntary ['vɒləntərɪ] **ADJ** **a** (= *not obligatory*) freiwillig; **to go into ~ liquidation** in die freiwillige Liquidation gehen **b** (= *unpaid*) *help, service, work* freiwillig; **~ worker** freiwilliger Helfer, freiwillige Helferin; (*overseas*) Entwicklungshelfer(in) *m(f)*; **on a ~ basis** auf freiwilliger Basis, freiwillig **c** (= *supported by charity, charitable*) *body, agency* karitativ; **a ~ organization for social work** ein freiwilliger Wohlfahrtsverband **d** (= *having will*) *movements* willkürlich, willentlich; *crime* vorsätzlich; **man is a ~ agent** der Mensch handelt aus freiem Willen **e** (*Physiol*) **~ muscles** willkürliche Muskeln *pl* **N** (*Eccl, Mus*) Solo *nt*

voluntary: voluntary euthanasia N aktive Sterbehilfe; **voluntary manslaughter** N (*US*

Jur) vorsätzliche Tötung; **voluntary redundancy** N freiwilliges Ausscheiden; **to take ~** sich abfinden lassen

volunteer [ˌvɒlən'tɪə'] **N** (*also Mil*) Freiwillige(r) *mf*; **~ army** Freiwilligenheer *nt*; **any ~s?** wer meldet sich freiwillig?; **Volunteers in Service to America** (*US*) US-Hilfsorganisation, die Freiwillige zur Hilfe Einkommensschwacher abstellt **VT** *help, services* anbieten; *suggestion* machen; *information* geben, herausrücken mit (*inf*); **we didn't ask you to ~ any advice** wir haben Sie nicht um Rat gebeten; **he ~ed his brother** (*hum*) er hat seinen Bruder (als Freiwilligen) gemeldet **VI** **a** (= *offer one's services*) sich freiwillig melden; **to ~ for sth** sich freiwillig für etw zur Verfügung stellen; **to ~ to do sth** sich anbieten, etw zu tun; **who will ~ to clean the windows?** wer meldet sich freiwillig zum Fensterputzen? **b** (*Mil*) sich freiwillig melden (*for* zu, *for places* nach)

voluptuary [və'lʌptjʊərɪ] N Lüstling *m*

voluptuous [və'lʌptjʊəs] ADJ *a mouth, woman, movement* sinnlich; *curves* üppig; *body* verlockend; *life* ausschweifend; *kiss* hingebungsvoll; *photograph, painting* erotisch **b** (= *pleasing*) stimulierend; **~ to touch** angenehm zu berühren

voluptuously [və'lʌptjʊəslɪ] ADV *move* aufreizend, sinnlich; *kiss* hingebungsvoll; *live* ausschweifend; **her ~ curved body** ihr üppig geformter Körper; **her lips were ~ full** sie hatte einen sinnlichen Mund

voluptuousness [və'lʌptjʊəsnɪs] N (*of woman, movement*) Sinnlichkeit *f*; (*of curves*) Üppigkeit *f*; (*of body*) verlockende Formen *pl*; (*of kiss*) Hingabe *f*

volute [və'luːt] N (*Archit*) Volute *f*

voluted [və'luːtɪd] ADJ (*Archit*) mit Voluten (versehen)

vomit ['vɒmɪt] **N** Erbrochene(s) *nt*; (= *act*) Erbrechen *nt* **VT** (*lit, fig*) spucken, speien (*geh*); *food* erbrechen **VI** sich erbrechen, sich übergeben

▶**vomit out VT** *sep* (*lit*) erbrechen; (*fig*) *smoke, flames* speien; *words, secret* ausspucken (*inf*) **VI** (*fig*) **the flames were still vomiting out of the volcano** der Vulkan spie immer noch Feuer

▶**vomit up VT** *sep food* (wieder) erbrechen

voodoo ['vuːduː] N Voodoo *m*, Wodu *m*

voodooism ['vuːduːɪzəm] N Voodoo- *or* Wodukult *m*

voracious [və'reɪʃəs] ADJ *person* gefräßig; *collector* besessen; **she is a ~ reader** sie verschlingt die Bücher geradezu; **to be a ~ eater** Unmengen vertilgen; **to have a ~ appetite** einen Riesenappetit haben

voraciously [və'reɪʃəslɪ] ADV *eat* gierig; **to read ~** die Bücher nur so verschlingen

voracity [vɒ'ræsɪtɪ] N Gefräßigkeit *f*; (*fig*) Gier *f* (*for* nach)

vortex ['vɔːteks] N *pl* **-es** *or* **vortices** ['vɔːtɪsiːz] (*lit*) Wirbel *m*, Strudel *m* (*also fig*)

vorticism ['vɔːtɪˌsɪzəm] N (*Art*) Vortizismus *m*

votary ['vəʊtərɪ] N (*Rel*) Geweihte(r) *mf*; (*fig*) Jünger(in) *m(f)*

vote [vəʊt] **N** **a** (= *expression of opinion*) Stimme *f*; (= *act of voting*) Abstimmung *f*, Wahl *f*; (= *result*) Abstimmungs- *or* Wahlergebnis *nt*; **to put sth to the ~** über etw (*acc*) abstimmen lassen; **to take a ~ on sth** über etw (*acc*) abstimmen; **elected by popular ~** vom Volk gewählt; **the ~ for/against the change surprised him** dass für/gegen den Wechsel gestimmt wurde, erstaunte ihn; **the ~ was 150 to 95** das Abstimmungsergebnis war 150 zu 95; **we would like to offer a ~ of thanks to Mr Smith** wir möchten Herrn Smith unseren aufrichtigen Dank aussprechen → **censure, confidence** **b** (= *vote cast*) Stimme *f*; **to give one's ~ to a party/person** einer Partei/jdm seine Stimme geben; **single-vote majority** Mehrheit *f* von einer Stimme; **one man one ~** eine Stimme pro Wähler, ein Mann *or* Bürger, eine Stimme; **a photo of the Prime Minister casting his ~** ein Foto des Premierministers bei der Stimmabgabe; **what's your ~?** (*in panel game, competition*) wie lautet Ihr Urteil?; **he won by 22 ~s** er gewann mit einer Mehrheit von 22 Stimmen; **10% of the ~rs invalidated their ~s** 10% der Wähler machten ihren Stimmzettel ungültig

c (*Pol, collective*) **the Labour ~** die Labourstimmen *pl*; **the Labour ~ has increased** der Stimmenanteil von Labour hat sich erhöht

d (= *franchise*) Wahlrecht *nt*; **~s for women!** Wahlrecht für die Frauen!

e (= *money allotted*) Bewilligung *f*

VT a (= *elect*) wählen; **he was ~d chairman** er wurde zum Vorsitzenden gewählt; **to ~ Labour** Labour wählen

b (*inf,* = *judge*) wählen zu; **the group ~d her the best cook** die Gruppe wählte sie zur besten Köchin; **the panel ~d the record a miss** die Jury erklärte die Platte für einen Misserfolg; **I ~ we go back** ich schlage vor, dass wir umkehren

c (= *approve*) bewilligen

VI (= *cast one's vote*) wählen; **to ~ for/against sth** für/gegen etw stimmen; **~ for Clark!** wählen Sie Clark!; **to ~ with one's feet** mit den Füßen abstimmen

▶ **vote down** VT *sep proposal* niederstimmen

▶ **vote in** VT *sep law* beschließen; *person* wählen

▶ **vote on** VI +*prep obj* abstimmen über (+*acc*)

▶ **vote out** VT *sep* abwählen; *amendment* ablehnen

vote-loser ['vəʊt,luːzə'] N *unpopuläre Politik, durch die Wählerstimmen verloren gehen können*

voter ['vəʊtə'] N Wähler(in) *m(f)*

voting ['vəʊtɪŋ] N Wahl *f*; **which way is the ~ going?** welchen Verlauf nimmt die Wahl?; **a system of ~** ein Wahlsystem *nt*; **to analyze the ~** das Wahlergebnis analysieren; **~ was heavy** die Wahlbeteiligung war hoch; **light ~** geringe Wahlbeteiligung

voting: voting age N Wahlalter *nt*; **voting booth** N Wahlkabine *f*; **voting machine** N (*US*) Wahlmaschine *f*; **voting paper** N Stimmzettel *m*; **voting power** N (= *right to vote*) Stimmberechtigung *f*, Stimmrecht *nt*; (*power of a certain group*) Wahlstärke *f*; **voting precinct** N (*US Pol*) Wahlbezirk *m*; **voting right** N Stimmrecht *nt*

votive ['vəʊtɪv] ADJ Votiv-; **~ candle** Votivkerze *f*; **~ painting** Votivbild *nt*

vouch [vaʊtʃ] VI **to ~ for sb/sth** sich für jdn/etw verbürgen; (*legally*) für jdn/etw bürgen; **to ~ for the truth of sth** sich für die Richtigkeit einer Sache verbürgen

voucher ['vaʊtʃə'] N **a** (*for cash, petrol, meals etc*) Gutschein *m* → **luncheon voucher b** (= *receipt*) Beleg *m*; (*for debt*) Schuldschein *m*

vouchsafe [vaʊtʃ'seɪf] VT (*form*) gewähren (*sb* jdm); **to ~ to do sth** geruhen (*geh*) *or* die Güte haben, etw zu tun

vow [vaʊ] **N** Versprechen *nt*, Gelöbnis *nt*; (*Rel*) Gelübde *nt*; **to make a ~ to do sth** geloben, etw zu tun; **to take one's ~s** sein Gelübde ablegen; **to take a ~ of chastity** ein Keuschheitsgelübde *nt* ablegen; **to take a ~ of silence** Schweigen *nt* geloben **VT** *obedience* geloben; **to ~ vengeance on sb** jdm Rache schwören; **he is ~ed to silence** er hat Schweigen gelobt

vowel ['vaʊəl] N Vokal *m*, Selbstlaut *m*; **~ system** Vokalismus *m*; **~ sound** Vokal(laut) *m*

vox pop [vɒks'pɒp] N (*Rad, TV*) Befragungen *pl* auf der Straße

voyage ['vɔɪɪdʒ] **N a** Reise *f*, Fahrt *f*; (*esp by sea*) Seereise *f*; (*Aviat*) Flug *m*, Reise *f*; (*Space*) Flug *m*; **to make a ~** eine Reise *etc* machen; **the ~ out** die Hinreise; (*Aviat*) der Hinflug; **the ~ back** *or* **home** die Rück- *or* Heimreise; (*Aviat*) der Rückflug **b** (*fig*) **~ of discovery** Entdeckungsreise *f* **VI** eine Seereise machen; (*spaceship*) fliegen; **to ~ across an ocean** einen Ozean überqueren

voyager ['vɔɪədʒə'] N Passagier(in) *m(f)*; (*Space*) Raumfahrer(in) *m(f)*

voyeur [vwɑːˈjɜː'] N Voyeur(in) *m(f)*

voyeurism [vwɑːˈjɜːrɪzəm] N Voyeurismus *m*, Voyeurtum *nt*

voyeuristic [vwɑːjɜːˈrɪstɪk] ADJ voyeuristisch

VP *abbr of* **vice president**

VPL (*inf*) *abbr of* **visible panty line**

vroom [vruːm] INTERJ brumm

vs *abbr of* **versus**

V: V-shaped ADJ pfeilförmig, V-förmig; **V-sign** N (*Brit*) (*victory*) Victoryzeichen *nt*; (*rude*) ≈ Stinkefinger *m* (*inf*); **he gave me the ~** ≈ er zeigte mir den Stinkefinger (*inf*)

VSO (*Brit*) *abbr of* **Voluntary Service Overseas** ≈ Entwicklungsdienst *m*

VSOP *abbr of* **Very Special Old Pale** (*brandy, port*) VSOP

VTR *abbr of* **video tape recorder** Videorekorder *m*

Vulcan ['vʌlkən] N Vulcanus *m*

vulcanite ['vʌlkənaɪt] N Hartgummi *m*, Ebonit *nt*

vulcanization [ˌvʌlkənaɪˈzeɪʃən] N Vulkanisierung *f*

vulcanize ['vʌlkənaɪz] VT vulkanisieren

vulcanologist [ˌvɒlkəˈnɒlədʒɪst] N = **volcanologist**

vulcanology [ˌvɒlkəˈnɒlədʒi] N = **volcanology**

vulgar ['vʌlgə'] ADJ **a** (*pej*) (= *unrefined*) ordinär, vulgär; *clothes, joke* ordinär; (= *tasteless*) geschmacklos; **it is ~ to talk about money** es ist unfein, über Geld zu reden **b** (*old,* = *of the common people*) gemein (*old*); **~ beliefs** volks-

tümliche Auffassungen *pl*; **in the ~ tongue** in der Sprache des Volkes

Vulgar fraction N (*Math*) gemeiner Bruch

vulgarism ['vʌlgərɪzəm] N Gassenausdruck *m*, primitiver Ausdruck; (= *swearword*) vulgärer Ausdruck

vulgarity [vʌlˈgærɪti] N Vulgarität *f*; (*of gesture, joke also*) Anstößigkeit *f*; (*of colour, tie etc*) Geschmacklosigkeit *f*; **the ~ of his conduct** sein ordinäres *or* pöbelhaftes Benehmen

vulgarize ['vʌlgəraɪz] VT **a** (= *make coarse*) vulgarisieren **b** (= *popularize*) popularisieren, allgemein verständlich machen

Vulgar Latin N Vulgärlatein *nt*

vulgarly ['vʌlgəli] ADV **a** (= *coarsely*) vulgär; *dressed* geschmacklos **b** (= *commonly*) allgemein, gemeinhin; **~ called ...** gemeinhin auch genannt ...

Vulgate ['vʌlgɪt] N Vulgata *f*

vulnerability [ˌvʌlnərəˈbɪlɪti] N Verwundbarkeit *f*; (= *susceptibility*) Verletzlichkeit *f*; (*fig*) Verletzbarkeit *f*; (*of police, troops, fortress*) Ungeschütztheit *f*; **the ~ of the young fish to predators** die Wehrlosigkeit der jungen Fische gegen Raubtiere; **such is their ~ only 2% survive** sie sind so wehrlos, dass nur 2% überleben; **his emotional ~** seine Empfindsamkeit *or* Verletzbarkeit

vulnerable ['vʌlnərəbl] ADJ **a** verwundbar; (= *exposed*) verletzlich; (*fig*) verletzbar; *police, troops, fortress* ungeschützt; (*Mil*) *target, country* verwundbar; **to feel ~** sich verwundbar fühlen; **she is at a very ~ age** sie ist in einem sehr schwierigen Alter; **to be ~ to disease** anfällig für Krankheiten sein; **the skin is ~ to radiation** die Haut hat keinen Schutz gegen Radioaktivität; **the turtle on its back is completely ~** auf dem Rücken liegend ist die Schildkröte völlig wehrlos; **to be ~ to the cold** kälteanfällig sein; **to be ~ to attack** Angriffen schutzlos ausgesetzt sein; **to be ~ to temptation** für Versuchungen anfällig sein; **to be ~ to criticism** (= *exposed*) der Kritik ausgesetzt sein; (= *sensitive*) keine Kritik vertragen; **I felt extremely ~ in the discussion** ich kam mir in der Diskussion völlig wehrlos vor; **the one ~ spot in his armour** (*Brit*) *or* **armor** (*US*) die einzige ungeschützte Stelle in seiner Rüstung; **a ~ point in our argument** ein schwacher *or* wunder Punkt unseres Arguments; **economically ~** wirtschaftlich wehrlos; **hotels are acutely ~ to recession** Hotels sind äußerst rezessionsanfällig

b (*Bridge*) in Gefahr; **not ~**, **non-vulnerable** in Nichtgefahr

vulpine ['vʌlpaɪn] ADJ schlau, listig

vulture ['vʌltʃə'] N (*lit, fig*) Geier *m*

vulva ['vʌlvə] N (weibliche) Scham, Vulva *f* (*geh*)

vv *abbr of* **verses**

V wings ['viːwɪŋz] PL pfeilförmige Tragflügel *pl*

vying ['vaɪɪŋ] N (Konkurrenz)kampf *m* (*for* um)

W

W, w ['dʌblju:] N W *nt*, w *nt*

W *abbr of* **west** W

W *abbr of* **watt(s)** W

w/ *abbr of* **with** m.

WAAF *abbr of* **Women's Auxiliary Air Force**

Waaf [wæf] N (*Brit*) Mitglied *nt* der weiblichen Luftwaffe

WAC (*US*) *abbr of* **Women's Army Corps**

wack [wæk] N (*Brit inf: as address*) Kumpel *m* (*inf*)

wacko ['wækəʊ] ADJ (*inf*) durchgedreht (*inf*)

wacky ['wækɪ] ADJ (*+er*) (*inf*) verrückt (*inf*)

wacky baccy N (*hum inf*) Gras(s) *nt* (*inf*)

wad [wɒd] **N a** (= *compact mass*) Knäuel *m or nt*; (*in gun, cartridge*) Pfropfen *m*; (*of cotton wool etc*) Bausch *m*; **to use sth as a ~** etw zum Ausstopfen *or* als Polster benutzen **b** (*of papers, banknotes*) Bündel *nt*; **he's got ~s of money** (*inf*) er hat Geld wie Heu (*inf*) **VT** (= *secure, stuff*) stopfen; (= *squeeze*) zusammenknüllen; (*Sew*) wattieren

wadding ['wɒdɪŋ] N (*for packing*) Material *nt* zum Ausstopfen; (*Sew*) Wattierung *f*; (*Med, on plaster*) (Mull)tupfer *m*

waddle ['wɒdl] **N** Watscheln *nt*; **to walk with a ~** einen watschelnden Gang haben **VI** watscheln

wade [weɪd] **VT** durchwaten **VI** waten

▶ **wade in** VI **a** (*lit*) hineinwaten **b** (*fig inf*) (= *join in a fight, controversy*) sich einmischen (*inf*); (= *tackle vigorously etc*) sich voll reinstürzen *or* -werfen (*inf*), sich hineinknien (*inf*); **the new boss waded in with a few staff changes** der neue Chef hat sich gleich mächtig ins Zeug gelegt und ein paar Umbesetzungen vorgenommen (*inf*)

▶ **wade into** VI +*prep obj* (*fig inf*: = *attack*) **to wade into sb** auf jdn losgehen; **to wade into sth** etw in Angriff nehmen

▶ **wade through** VI +*prep obj* **a** (*lit*) waten durch **b** (*fig*) sich (durch)kämpfen durch

wader ['weɪdə'] N **a** (*Orn*) Watvogel *m* **b** **waders** PL (= *boots*) Watstiefel *pl*

wadi ['wɒdɪ] N Wadi *nt*

wading: wading bird ['weɪdɪŋ,bɜːd] N = **wader** a; **wading pool** ['weɪdɪŋpuːl] N (*US*) Plan(t)schbecken *nt*

wafer ['weɪfə'] N **a** (= *biscuit*) Waffel *f*; **a vanilla ~** eine Vanilleeiswaffel **b** (*Eccl*) Hostie *f* **c** (= *silicon wafer*) Wafer *f*

wafer-thin ['weɪfə'θɪn] ADJ hauchdünn

waffle¹ ['wɒfl] N (*Cook*) Waffel *f*

waffle² (*Brit, inf*) **N** Geschwafel *nt* (*inf*) **VI** (*also* **waffle on**) schwafeln (*inf*); **I managed to ~ on somehow** irgendwie habe ich was (daher)geschwafelt (*inf*)

waffle iron N Waffeleisen *nt*

waffler ['wɒflə'] N (*Brit, inf*) Schwätzer(in) *m(f)*

waft [wɑːft] **N** Hauch *m*; **a ~ of smoke** eine dünne Rauchschwade; **a ~ of cool air** ein kühler Lufthauch **VT** tragen, wehen **VI** wehen; **a delicious smell ~ed up from the kitchen** ein köstlicher Geruch zog aus der Küche herauf

wag¹ [wæg] **N** **he admonished me with a ~ of his finger** tadelnd drohte er mir mit dem Fin-

ger; **with a ~ of its tail** mit einem Schwanzwedeln **VT** *tail* wedeln mit; (*bird*) wippen mit; **to ~ one's finger at sb** jdm mit dem Finger drohen **VI** (*tail*) wedeln; (*of bird*) wippen; **as soon as he left the tongues started ~ging** (*inf*) sobald er gegangen war, fing das Gerede an; **to stop the tongues ~ging** (*inf*) um dem Gerede ein Ende zu machen; **that'll set the tongues ~ging** (*inf*) dann geht das Gerede los

wag² N (= *wit, clown*) Witzbold *m* (*inf*); **a bit of a ~** ein alter Witzbold

wage¹ [weɪdʒ] N *usu pl* Lohn *m*

wage² VT *war, campaign* führen; **to ~ war against sth** (*fig*) gegen etw einen Feldzug führen

wage *in cpds* Lohn-; **wage agreement** N Lohnabkommen *nt*, Tarifvertrag *m*; **wage bargaining** N , *no pl* Tarifverhandlung *f*, Lohnverhandlung *f*; **wage check** N (*US*) Lohnscheck *m*; **wage claim** N Lohnforderung *f*; **wage-cost inflation** N Lohnkosteninflation *f*

waged [weɪdʒd] ADJ erwerbstätig

wage: wage demand N Lohnforderung *f*; **wage determination** N Lohnfestsetzung *f*; **wage dispute** N Lohnkonflikt *m*, Lohnkampf *m*; **wage earner** N (*esp Brit*) Lohnempfänger(in) *m(f)*; **wage freeze** N Lohnstopp *m*; **wage incidentals** PL Lohnnebenkosten *pl*; **wage increase** N Lohnerhöhung *f*; **wage-intensive** ADJ lohnintensiv; **wage level** N Lohnniveau *nt*; **wage packet** N (*esp Brit*) Lohntüte *f*; **wage payment** N Lohnzahlung *f*; **wage-price spiral** N Lohn-Preis-Spirale *f*

wager ['weɪdʒə'] **N** Wette *f* (*on auf* +*acc*); **to make a ~** eine Wette eingehen *or* abschließen **VT** wetten (*on auf* +*acc*); *one's honour, life* verpfänden; **I'll ~ you £2 my horse wins** ich wette mit Ihnen um £ 2, dass mein Pferd gewinnt; **he won't do it, I ~!** (*dated*) ich wette, dass er es nicht tut! **VI** wetten (*on auf* +*acc*)

wage rates PL Lohnsatz *m*, Tarifsatz *m*

wages ['weɪdʒɪz] PL Lohn *m*; **the ~ of sin** die gerechte Strafe, der Sünde Lohn (*old*)

wages bill N (*Brit*) Lohnkosten *pl*

wage scale N Lohnskala *f*

wages clerk N (*Brit*) Lohnbuchhalter(in) *m(f)*

wage: wage settlement N Lohnabkommen *nt*, Tarifabschluss *m*; **wage slave** N (*hum inf*) Lohnsklave *m* (*hum inf*), Lohnsklavin *f* (*hum inf*); **wage slip** N Lohnstreifen *m*, Lohnzettel *m*; **wage worker** N (*US*) Lohnempfänger(in) *m(f)*

waggish ['wægɪʃ] ADJ schalkhaft, schelmisch; **he has a ~ sense of humour** ihm sitzt der Schalk im Nacken

waggishly ['wægɪʃlɪ] ADV schalkhaft

waggle ['wægl] **VT** wackeln mit; *tail* wedeln mit; (*bird*) wippen mit; **he ~d his loose tooth** er wackelte an dem lockeren Zahn **VI** wackeln; (*tail*) wedeln; (*of bird*) wippen **N with a ~ of her hips** she left the stage mit den Hüften wackelnd ging sie von der Bühne

waggly ['wæglɪ] ADJ (= *loose*) wackelig; *hips* wackelnd; *tail* wedelnd

waggon N ['wægən] (*Brit*) = **wagon**

Wagnerian [vɑːgˈnɪərɪən] **N** Wagnerianer(in) *m(f)* ADJ Wagner-; (= *like Wagner*) wagner(i)sch; **a ~ opera** eine Wagneroper

wagon ['wægən] N **a** (*horse-drawn*) Fuhrwerk *nt*, Wagen *m*; (= *covered wagon*) Planwagen *m*; (*US*: = *delivery truck*) Lieferwagen *m*; (= *child's toy cart*) Leiterwagen *m*; (= *tea wagon etc*) Wagen *m*; (*US inf*) (= *police car*) Streifenwagen *m*; (*for transporting prisoners*) grüne Minna (*inf*); (*Brit inf*) (= *car*) Karre *f* (*inf*); (= *lorry*) Laster *m* (*inf*) **b** (*Brit Rail*) Wag(g)on *m* **c** (*inf*) **I'm on the ~** ich trinke nichts; **to go on the ~** unter die Abstinenzler gehen (*inf*)

wagoner ['wægənə'] N Fuhrmann *m*

wagon: wagonload N Wagenladung *f*; **books/prisoners arrived by the ~** ganze Wagenladungen von Büchern/Gefangenen kamen an; **wagon train** N Zug *m* von Planwagen

wagtail ['wægteɪl] N (*Orn*) Bachstelze *f*

wah-wah pedal ['wɑːwɑːˌpedl] N (*Mus*) Wah-Wah-Pedal *nt*

waif [weɪf] N obdachloses *or* heimatloses Kind; (= *animal*) herrenloses Tier; **the poor little ~ ...** das arme kleine Ding, hat kein Zuhause, ...; **~s and strays** (= *children*) obdachlose *or* heimatlose Kinder *pl*; (= *animals*) herrenlose Tiere *pl*

wail [weɪl] **N** (*of baby*) Geschrei *nt*; (*of mourner, music*) Klagen *nt*; (*of sirens, wind*) Heulen *nt*; (*inf*: = *complaint*) Gejammer *nt* (*inf*); **a great ~/a ~ of protest went up** es erhob sich lautes Wehklagen/Protestgeheul **VI** (*baby, cat*) schreien; (*mourner, music*) klagen; (*siren, wind*) heulen; (*inf*: = *complain*) jammern (*over über* +*acc*)

Wailing Wall ['weɪlɪŋˈwɔːl] N Klagemauer *f*

wain [weɪn] N (*old*) Wagen *m*; **the Wain** (*Astron*) der Große Wagen

wainscot ['weɪnskət] N , *no pl* Täfelung *f*

wainscot(t)ed ['weɪnskətɪd] ADJ holzgetäfelt, paneeliert

wainscot(t)ing ['weɪnskətɪŋ] N Täfelung *f*

waist [weɪst] N Taille *f*; (*of violin*) Mittelbügel *m*; (*Naut*) Mittelteil *m*; **stripped to the ~** mit nacktem *or* bloßem Oberkörper; **too tight round the ~** zu eng in der Taille

waist: waistband N Rock-/Hosenbund *m*; **waistcoat** N (*Brit*) Weste *f*; **waist-deep** ADJ hüfthoch, bis zur Taille reichend; **the water was ~** das Wasser reichte bis zur Taille; **we stood ~ in ...** wir standen bis zur Hüfte in ...

waisted ['weɪstɪd] ADJ *clothes* tailliert

-waisted [-'weɪstɪd] ADJ *suf* mit einer ... Taille; **narrow-waisted** mit schmaler Taille

waist: waist-high ADJ hüfthoch, bis zur Taille reichend; **we picnicked in a field of ~ grass** wir picknickten in einem Feld, wo uns das Gras bis zur Hüfte reichte; **waistline** N Taille *f*

wait [weɪt] **VI a** warten (*for auf* +*acc*); **to ~ for sb to do sth** darauf warten, dass jd etw tut; **it was definitely worth ~ing for** es hat sich wirklich gelohnt, darauf zu warten; **that'll be worth ~ing for** (*iro*) da bin ich aber gespannt (*inf*); **well, what are you ~ing for?** worauf wartest du denn (noch)?; **~ for it, now he's going to get mad** warts ab, gleich wird er wild (*inf*); **this stamp is worth, ~ for it, £10,000** diese Briefmarke kostet sage und schreibe £ 10.000; **let**

him ~!, **he can ~**! lass ihn warten!, soll er warten!, der kann warten!; **can't it ~?** kann das nicht warten?, hat das nicht Zeit?; **this work will have to ~ till later** diese Arbeit muss bis später warten *or* liegen bleiben; **this work is still ~ing to be done** diese Arbeit muss noch gemacht *or* erledigt werden; **~ a minute** *or* **moment** *or* **second** (einen) Augenblick *or* Moment (mal); **(just) you ~**! warte nur ab!; *(threatening)* warte nur!; **Mummy, I can't ~** Mami, ich muss dringend mal!; **I can't ~** ich kann kaum erwarten; *(out of curiosity)* ich bin gespannt; **I can't ~ to see his face** da bin ich (aber) auf sein Gesicht gespannt; **I can't ~ to try out my new boat** ich kann es kaum noch erwarten, bis ich mein neues Boot ausprobiere; **I can hardly ~** *(usu iro)* ich kann es kaum erwarten!; **"repairs while you ~"** „Sofortreparaturen", „Reparaturschnelldienst"; **~ and see**! warten Sie (es) ab!, abwarten und Tee trinken! *(inf)*; **we'll have to ~ and see how ...** wir müssen abwarten, wie ...

b **to ~ at table** *(Brit)* servieren, bedienen; **she used to ~ at the ...** sie bediente früher im ...

VT **a** **to ~ one's turn** (ab)warten, bis man an der Reihe ist; **to ~ one's moment** *or* **chance** auf eine günstige Gelegenheit warten, eine günstige Gelegenheit abwarten; **don't ~ supper for me** warte mit dem Abendessen nicht auf mich

b *(US)* **to ~ a table** servieren, bedienen

N **a** Wartezeit *f*; **did you have a long ~?** mussten Sie lange warten?

b **to lie in ~ for sb/sth** jdm/einer Sache auflauern

c **waits** PL ≈ Sternsinger *pl*

▸**wait about** *(Brit)* *or* **around** VI warten *(for* auf +acc)

▸**wait behind** VI zurückbleiben; **to wait behind for sb** zurückbleiben und auf jdn warten

▸**wait in** VI zu Hause bleiben *(for* wegen)

▸**wait on** VI **a** *(= continue to wait)* noch (weiter) warten **VI** +prep obj **a** *(also* **wait upon**: = serve) bedienen **b** *(US)* to wait on table servieren, bei Tisch bedienen **c** *(= wait for)* warten auf (+acc); **I'm waiting on him finishing** ich warte, bis er fertig ist

▸**wait out** VT sep das Ende (+gen) abwarten; **to wait it out** abwarten

▸**wait up** VI **a** aufbleiben *(for* wegen, für) **b** *(esp US, inf)* **wait up**! langsam!

wait-and-see policy [ˌweɪtənˈsiːpɒlɪsɪ] N Politik *f* des Abwartens

waiter [ˈweɪtə] N Kellner *m*, Ober *m*; **~!** (Herr) Ober!

waiting [ˈweɪtɪŋ] N **a** Warten *nt*; **all this ~ (around)** dieses ewige Warten, diese ewige Warterei *(inf)*; **no ~** Halteverbot *nt* **b** *(= royal service)* **those in ~ at the court ...** wer bei Hof dient ... **c** *(by waiter etc)* Servieren, Bedienen *nt*

waiting: waiting game N Wartespiel *nt*; **to play a ~** ein Wartespiel spielen; **the siege/negotiations developed into a ~** die Belagerung entwickelte sich/die Verhandlungen entwickelten sich zu einer Geduldsprobe; **waiting list** N Warteliste *f*; **waiting room** N Warteraum *m*; *(at doctor's)* Wartezimmer *nt*; *(in railway station)* Wartesaal *m*

waitlist [ˈweɪtlɪst] *(US)* **N** Warteliste *f* **VT** **to be ~ed** auf der Warteliste stehen

waitress [ˈweɪtrɪs] **N** Kellnerin *f*, Serviererin *f*; **~!** Fräulein! **VI** kellnern

waitressing [ˈweɪtrɪsɪŋ] N Kellnern *nt*

wait state N *(Comput)* Wartezyklus *m*; **with zero ~s** ohne Wartezyklen

waive [weɪv] VT **a** *(= not insist on)* rights, claim, fee verzichten auf (+acc); principles, rules, age limit etc außer Acht lassen **b** *(= put aside, dismiss)* question, objection abtun

waiver [ˈweɪvə] N *(Jur)* Verzicht *m* (of auf +acc); *(= document)* Verzichterklärung *f*; *(of law, contract, clause)* Außerkraftsetzung *f*

wake¹ [weɪk] N *(Naut)* Kielwasser *nt*; **in the ~ of** *(fig)* im Gefolge (+gen); **to follow in sb's ~** in

jds Kielwasser segeln; **X follows in the ~ of Y** Y bringt X mit sich; **X brings Y in its ~** X bringt Y mit sich; **X leaves Y in its ~** X hinterlässt Y; **with ten children in her ~** *(inf)* mit zehn Kindern im Schlepptau *(inf)*

wake² N *(esp Ir: over corpse)* Totenwache *f*

wake³ pret **woke**, ptp **woken** *or* **waked** **VT** (auf-) wecken; *(fig)* wecken, erwecken *(geh)* **VI** aufwachen, erwachen *(geh)*; **he woke to find himself in prison** als er aufwachte *or* erwachte, fand er sich im Gefängnis wieder; **he woke to the sound of birds singing** als er aufwachte, sangen die Vögel; **he woke one day to find himself a rich man** als er eines Tages erwachte *or* aufwachte, war er ein reicher Mann; **they woke to their danger too late** *(fig)* sie haben die Gefahr zu spät erkannt

▸**wake up** VI *(lit, fig)* aufwachen; **to wake up to sth** *(fig)* sich *(dat)* einer Sache *(gen)* bewusst werden; **I wish he'd wake up to what's happening** ich wünschte, ihm würde endlich bewusst *or* aufgehen *or* klar, was (hier) vor sich geht; **he woke up to a new life** ein neues Leben brach für ihn an; **wake up and smell the coffee!** *(esp US inf)* wach endlich auf! **VT** sep (auf-) wecken; *(fig: = rouse from sloth)* wach- *or* aufrütteln; **to wake sb up to sth** *(fig)* jdm etw klarmachen *or* bewusst machen *or* vor Augen führen; **to wake one's ideas up** sich zusammenreißen

wakeful [ˈweɪkfʊl] ADJ *(= sleepless)* schlaflos; *(= alert)* wachsam

wakefulness [ˈweɪkfʊlnɪs] N *(= sleeplessness)* Schlaflosigkeit *f*; *(= alertness)* Wachsamkeit *f*

waken [ˈweɪkən] **VT** (auf)wecken **VI** *(liter, Scot)* erwachen *(geh)*, aufwachen; **he ~ed to see ...** beim Erwachen sah er ...; **he ~ed to another dreary day** ein neuer, trostloser Tag brach für ihn an

waker [ˈweɪkə] N **to be an early ~** früh aufwachen

wake-up call [ˈweɪkʌpˌkɔːl] N **a** *(Telec)* Weckruf *m* **b** *(esp US: = warning)* Warnsignal *nt*

wakey wakey [ˌweɪkɪˈweɪkɪ] INTERJ aufwachen!

waking [ˈweɪkɪŋ] ADJ one's **~ hours** *or* ~s Zeit *f* *(geh)*; **thoughts of her filled all his ~ hours** der Gedanke an sie beschäftigte ihn von früh bis spät; **his ~ hours were spent ...** von früh bis spät beschäftigte er sich mit ...; **~ dream** Wachtraum *m*

Wales [weɪlz] N Wales *nt*; **Prince/Princess of ~** Prinz *m*/Prinzessin *f* von Wales

walk [wɔːk] **N** **a** *(= stroll)* Spaziergang *m*; *(= hike)* Wanderung *f*; *(Sport)* Gehen *nt*; *(= competition)* Geher-Wettkampf *m*; *(= charity walk)* Marsch *m (für Wohltätigkeitszwecke)*; **a 20-mile ~ along the roads** ein 20-Meilen-Marsch die Straße entlang; **it's only 10 minutes' ~** es sind nur 10 Minuten zu Fuß; **it's a long/short ~ to the shops** zu den Läden ist es weit/nicht weit zu Fuß *or* zu gehen *or* zu laufen *(inf)*; **it's a long ~ but a short drive** zu Fuß ist es weit, aber mit dem Auto ganz nah; **that's quite a ~** das ist eine ganz schöne Strecke, das ist ganz schön weit zu Laufen *(inf)*; **he thinks nothing of a 10-mile ~** 10 Meilen zu Fuß sind für ihn gar nichts; **to go for a ~, to have** *or* **take a ~** einen Spaziergang machen, spazieren gehen; **to take sb/the dog for a ~** mit jdm/dem Hund spazieren gehen *or* einen Spaziergang machen, den Hund ausführen *or* spazieren führen; **a ~ in the park** *(fig inf: = easy)* ein Kinderspiel *nt*

b *(= gait)* Gang *m*; *(of horse)* Gangart *f*; **he went at a brisk ~** er ging schnellen Schrittes *(geh)* *or* schnell; **the horse went at a ~** das Pferd ging im Schritt; **he slowed his horse to a ~** er brachte sein Pferd in den Schritt; **he ran for a bit, then slowed to a ~** er rannte ein Stück und ging dann im Schritttempo weiter

c *(= path)* *(in garden etc)* (Park)weg *m*; *(in hills etc)* Weg *m*

d *(= route)* Weg *m*; *(signposted etc)* Wander-/Spazierweg *m*; **he knows some good ~s in the Lake District** er kennt ein paar gute Wandermöglichkeiten *or* Wanderungen im Lake Dis-

trict

e **~ of life** Milieu *nt*; **people from all ~s of life** Leute aus allen Schichten und Berufen

f *(US Baseball)* Walk *m*, Freibase *nt*

VT **a** *(= lead)* person, horse (spazieren) führen; dog ausführen; *(= ride at a walk)* im Schritt gehen lassen; **to ~ sb home/to the bus** jdn nach Hause/zum Bus bringen; **she ~ed her baby up to the table** das Kind lief, von der Mutter gehalten *or* mit Hilfe der Mutter, zum Tisch; **to ~ sb off his feet** *or* **legs** *(inf)* jdn total erschöpfen; **if we go hiking, I'll ~ the legs off you** *(inf)* wenn wir zusammen wandern gehen, dann wirst du (bald) nicht mehr mithalten können

b distance laufen, gehen; **I've ~ed this road many times** ich bin diese Straße oft gegangen

c **to ~ the streets** *(prostitute)* auf den Strich gehen *(inf)*; *(in search of sth)* durch die Straßen irren; *(aimlessly)* durch die Straßen streichen; **to ~ the boards** *(Theat)* auf den Brettern stehen; **he learned his trade by ~ing the boards before turning to films** er hat sein Handwerk auf den Brettern gelernt, bevor er zum Film ging; **to ~ the plank** mit verbundenen Augen über eine Schiffsplanke ins Wasser getrieben werden; **to ~ the wards** *(Med)* famulieren

d *(US Baseball)* einen Walk *or* ein Freibase geben *(+dat)*

VI **a** gehen, laufen; **~ a little with me** gehen Sie ein Stück mit mir; **to learn to ~** laufen lernen; **you must learn to ~ before you can run** *(prov)* man sollte den ersten Schritt vor dem zweiten tun; **to ~ in one's sleep** schlaf- *or* nachtwandeln; **to ~ with a stick** am Stock gehen

b *(= not ride)* zu Fuß gehen, laufen *(inf)*; *(= stroll)* spazieren gehen; *(= hike)* wandern; **you can ~ there in 5 minutes** da ist man in *or* bis dahin sind es 5 Minuten zu Fuß; **to ~ home** nach Hause laufen *(inf)*, zu Fuß nach Hause gehen; **we were out ~ing when the telegram arrived** wir waren gerade spazieren *or* auf einem Spaziergang, als das Telegramm kam

c *(ghost)* umgehen, spuken

d *(inf, = disappear)* Beine bekommen *(inf)*

e *(US inf, = quit one's job)* kündigen; *(= go on strike)* in den Ausstand treten

▸**walk about** *(Brit)* *or* **around** VI herumlaufen *(inf)* **VT** sep *(= lead)* person, horse auf und ab führen; *(= ride at a walk)* im Schritt gehen lassen

▸**walk away** VI weg- *or* davongehen; **he walked away from the crash unhurt** er ist bei dem Unfall ohne Verletzungen davongekommen; **you can't just walk away from ten years of marriage** du kannst doch zehn Jahre Ehe nicht einfach so abschreiben; **to walk away with a prize** etc einen Preis etc kassieren *or* einstecken *(inf)*

▸**walk in** VI hereinkommen; *(casually)* hereinspazieren *(inf)*; **"please walk in "** „bitte eintreten"

▸**walk in on** VI +prep obj hereinplatzen bei *(inf)*

▸**walk into** VI +prep obj room hereinkommen in (+acc); person anrempeln; wall laufen gegen; **to walk into sb** *(= meet unexpectedly)* jdm in die Arme laufen, jdn zufällig treffen; **to walk into a trap** in eine Falle gehen; **to walk into a job** eine Stelle ohne Schwierigkeiten bekommen; **he just walked into the first job he applied for** er hat gleich die erste Stelle bekommen, um die er sich beworben hat; **to walk right into sth** *(lit)* mit voller Wucht gegen etw rennen; **I didn't know I was going to walk into an argument** ich wusste nicht, dass ich hier mitten in einen Streit hineingeraten würde; **you walked right into that one, didn't you?** da bist du aber ganz schön reingefallen *(inf)*

▸**walk off** VT sep pounds ablaufen *(inf)*; **I'm going out to try and walk off this headache/hangover** ich gehe jetzt an die Luft, um meine Kopfschmerzen/meinen Kater loszuwerden; **we walked off our lunch with a stroll in the park** nach dem Mittagessen haben wir einen Verdauungsspaziergang im Park gemacht **VI** weggehen; **he walked off in the opposite direction** er ging in die andere Richtung davon

▶ **walk off with** VI +prep obj (inf) **a** (= take) (unintentionally) abziehen mit (inf); (intentionally) abhauen mit (inf) **b** (= win easily) prize kassieren, einstecken (inf)

▶ **walk on** VI +prep obj grass etc betreten VI **a** (= continue walking) weitergehen; **she hesitated, then walked on by** sie zögerte und ging dann weiter **b** (Theat) auftreten; (in walk-on part) auf die Bühne gehen; **to walk on(to) the stage** auf die Bühne treten, auf der Bühne erscheinen

▶ **walk out** VI **a** (= quit) gehen; **to walk out of a meeting/room** eine Versammlung/einen Saal verlassen; **to walk out on sb** jdn verlassen; (= let down) jdn im Stich lassen; (= abandon) girlfriend etc jdn sitzen lassen (inf); **to walk out on sth** aus etw aussteigen (inf) **b** (= strike) streiken, in Streik treten **c** **to walk out with sb** (dated) mit jdm gehen VT sep (dated, = court) gehen mit

▶ **walk over** VI +prep obj **a** (= defeat) in die Tasche stecken (inf) **b** **to walk all over sb** (inf) (= dominate) jdn unterbuttern (inf); (= treat harshly) jdn fertig machen (inf); **she lets her husband walk all over her** sie lässt sich von ihrem Mann herumschikanieren (inf) or völlig unterbuttern (inf)

▶ **walk through** VI +prep obj **a** (inf, = do easily) exam etc spielend schaffen (inf) **b** (Theat) part durchgehen

▶ **walk up** VI **a** (= go up, ascend) hinaufgehen; **the escalator is broken so you'll have to walk up** die Rolltreppe ist außer Betrieb, Sie müssen zu Fuß hinaufgehen **b** (= approach) zugehen (to auf +acc); **a man walked up (to me/her)** ein Mann kam auf mich zu/ging auf sie zu; **walk up!, walk up!** treten Sie näher!

walkable ['wɔːkəbl] ADJ **to be ~** sich zu Fuß machen lassen

walk: walkabout N (esp Brit: by king etc) Rundgang m; **the Queen went (on a) ~** die Königin nahm ein Bad in der Menge; **walkaway** N (US) = **walkover**

walker ['wɔːkə] N **a** (= stroller) Spaziergänger(in) m(f); (= hiker) Wanderer m, Wanderin f; (Sport) Geher(in) m(f); **to be a fast/slow ~** schnell/langsam gehen **b** (for baby, invalid) Gehhilfe f; (US: = Zimmer)® Gehwagen m

walker-on ['wɔːkər'ɒn] N Statist(in) m(f)

walkies ['wɔːkɪz] PL Gassi nt; **to go ~** (Brit inf) Gassi gehen (inf)

walkie-talkie ['wɔːkɪ'tɔːkɪ] N Sprechfunkgerät nt, Walkie-Talkie nt

walk-in ['wɔːkɪn] ADJ **a ~ cupboard** ein begehbarer Einbau- or Wandschrank N (US) (= cupboard) begehbarer Einbau- or Wandschrank; (= victory) spielender Sieg

walking ['wɔːkɪŋ] N Gehen nt; (as recreation) Spaziergehen nt; (= hiking) Wandern nt; **there's some good ~ in these hills** in diesen Bergen gibt es ein paar gute Wandermöglichkeiten; **we did a lot of ~ while we were in Wales** als wir in Wales waren, sind wir viel gewandert or gelaufen ADJ attr encyclopaedia, miracle etc lebend; **at (a) ~ pace** im Schritttempo; **the ~ wounded** die leicht Verwundeten pl, die Leichtverwundeten pl; **it's within ~ distance** dahin kann man laufen or zu Fuß gehen

walking: walking bass N (Mus) einfache Kontrabassbegleitung, Walking-Bass m; **walking boots** PL Wanderstiefel pl; **walking frame** N Gehhilfe f; **walking holiday** N (Brit) Wanderferien pl; **walking papers** N (US) **he got his ~** er ist gegangen worden; **she gave him his ~** sie hat ihm den Laufpass gegeben; **walking shoes** PL Wanderschuhe pl; **walking stick** N Spazierstock m; **walking tour** N Wanderung f

Walkman® ['wɔːkmən] N Walkman® m

walk: walk-on ADJ **~ part/role** (Theat) Statistenrolle f N Statistenrolle f; **walkout** N (= strike) Streik m; **to stage a ~** (from conference etc) de-

monstrativ den Saal verlassen; **walkover** N (Sport) Walkover m, Walk-over m; (= easy victory) spielender Sieg; (fig) Kinderspiel nt; **the government had a ~ in the debate** die Regierung hatte leichtes Spiel in der Debatte ADJ attr **~ victory** spielender Sieg; **walk-up** N (US, inf) Haus nt ohne Fahrstuhl or Lift; **walkway** N Fußweg m; **a pedestrian ~** ein Fuß(gänger)weg m

wall [wɔːl] N **a** (outside) Mauer f; (inside, of mountain) Wand f; **the Great Wall of China** die Chinesische Mauer; **the north ~ of the Eiger** die Eigernordwand; **a ~ of fire** eine Feuerwand; **a ~ of policemen/troops** eine Mauer von Polizisten/Soldaten; **~s have ears** die Wände haben Ohren; **to come up against a ~ of silence** auf eine Mauer des Schweigens stoßen; **to go up the ~** (inf) die Wände rauf- or hochgehen (inf); **I'm climbing the ~s** (inf) ich könnte die Wände hochgehen (inf); **he/his questions drive me up the ~** (inf) er/seine Fragerei bringt mich auf die Palme (inf); **this constant noise is driving me up the ~** (inf) bei diesem ständigen Lärm könnte ich die Wände rauf- or hochgehen (inf); **to go to the ~** (inf: firm etc) kaputtgehen (inf) → **brick wall, back b** (Anat) Wand f; **abdominal ~** Bauchdecke f VT mit einer Mauer umgeben

▶ **wall about** VT sep (esp Brit old, liter) ummauern

▶ **wall in** VT sep mit einer Mauer/von Mauern umgeben; **walled in on all sides by bodyguards** auf allen Seiten von Leibwächtern abgeriegelt or eingeschlossen

▶ **wall off** VT sep (= cut off) durch eine Mauer (ab)trennen; (= separate into different parts) unterteilen; **the monks walled themselves off from the outside world** die Mönche riegelten sich hinter ihren Mauern von der Welt ab

▶ **wall round** VT sep (esp Brit) ummauern

▶ **wall up** VT sep zumauern

wallaby ['wɒləbɪ] N Wallaby nt

wallah ['wɒlə] N (dated sl) Typ m (inf)

wall: wall anchor N (US) Dübel m; **wall bars** PL Sprossenwand f; **wallboard** N (US) Sperrholz nt; **wall cabinet** N Wandschrank m; **wall chart** N Plantafel f; **wall clock** N Wanduhr f; **wall covering** N Wandbekleidung f; **wall cupboard** N Wandschrank m

walled [wɔːld] ADJ von Mauern umgeben

wallet ['wɒlɪt] N Brieftasche f

wall: wallflower N (Bot) Goldlack m; (fig inf) Mauerblümchen nt; **wall hanging** N Wandbehang m, Wandteppich m; **wall lamp** N Wandleuchte f; **wall map** N Wandkarte f; **wall of death** N Todeswand f

Walloon [wɒ'luːn] N **a** Wallone m, Wallonin f **b** (dialect) Wallonisch nt ADJ wallonisch

wallop ['wɒləp] N **a** (inf: = blow) Schlag m; **he fell flat on his face with a ~** mit einem Plumps fiel er auf die Nase (inf); **to give sb/sth a ~** jdm/einer Sache einen Schlag versetzen **b** at a fair old ~ (dated inf) mit Karacho (inf) **c** (Brit, inf, = beer) Bölkstoff m (sl) VT (esp Brit inf) (= hit) schlagen; (= punish) verdreschen (inf), versohlen (inf); (= defeat) fertig machen (inf); **to ~ sb one/over the head** jdm eins reinhauen (inf)/eins überziehen (inf)

walloping ['wɒləpɪŋ] (inf) N Prügel pl (inf), Abreibung f (inf); (= defeat) Schlappe f (inf); **to give sb a ~** jdm eine Tracht Prügel geben (inf); (= defeat) jdn fertig machen (inf); **to get a ~** (= defeat) eine Schlappe erleiden (inf) ADJ (also **walloping great**) riesig; price gesalzen (inf), saftig (inf); loss, defeat gewaltig (inf); lie faustdick (inf)

wallow ['wɒləʊ] N (= act) Bad nt; (= place) Suhle f **a** (lit) (animal) sich wälzen, sich suhlen; (boat) rollen **b** (fig) **to ~ in luxury/self-pity** etc im Luxus/Selbstmitleid etc schwelgen; **to ~ in money** (inf) im Geld schwimmen (inf)

▶ **wallow about** (Brit) or **around** VI sich herumwälzen

wall: wall painting N Wandmalerei f; **wallpaper** N Tapete f VT tapezieren; **wall pass** N (Ftbl) Doppelpass m; **wall safe** N Wandsafe m; **wall socket** N Steckdose f; **Wall Street** N Wall Street f; **wall-to-wall** ADJ **~ carpeting** Teppichboden m; **his apartment is just about ~ stereo equipment** seine Wohnung ist fast eine einzige Stereoanlage; **what a bar! ~ punks** was für eine Bar! randvoll mit Punks; **the event got ~ coverage (in the media)** über das Ereignis wurde (in den Medien) umfassend berichtet

wally ['wɒlɪ] N (Brit inf: = fool) Trottel m (inf)

walnut ['wɔːlnʌt] N (= nut) Walnuss f; (= walnut tree) (Wal)nussbaum m; (= wood) Nussbaumholz nt, Nussbaum m

walrus ['wɔːlrəs] N Walross nt

walrus moustache, (US) **walrus mustache** N Walrossbart m

Walter Mitty [,wɔːl'tə'mɪtɪ] N **a ~** (character) ein Schwärmer m

waltz [wɔːls] N Walzer m VI **a** (= dance waltz) Walzer tanzen; **would you care to ~?** möchten Sie einen Walzer tanzen?; **they ~ed expertly** sie tanzten ausgezeichnet Walzer; **they ~ed across the ballroom** sie walzten durch den Ballsaal **b** (inf: = move, come etc) walzen (inf); **he came ~ing up** er kam angetanzt (inf) VT Walzer tanzen mit; **he ~ed her out onto the balcony** er walzte mit ihr auf den Balkon hinaus

▶ **waltz about** (Brit) or **around** VI (inf) herumtanzen or -tänzeln

▶ **waltz in** VI (inf) hereintanzen (inf); **to come waltzing in** angetanzt kommen (inf)

▶ **waltz off** VI (inf) abtanzen (inf)

▶ **waltz off with** VI +prep obj (inf) prizes abziehen mit

▶ **waltz through** VI +prep obj (fig inf) match, game spielend bewältigen; **she waltzed through the first round** war die erste Runde war ein Spaziergang für sie (inf)

waltzer ['wɔːlsə] N **a** (= dancer) Walzertänzer(in) m(f) **b** (at fairground) Krake f

waltz: waltz music N Walzermusik f; **waltz time** N Walzertakt m

wan [wɒn] ADJ bleich; light, smile, look matt

wand [wɒnd] N (= magic wand) Zauberstab m; (of office) Amtsstab m; (Comput, for bar codes) Lesestift m

wander ['wɒndə] N Spaziergang m; (through town, park also) Bummel m; **I'm going for a ~ (a)round the shops** ich mache einen Ladenbummel

VT hills, world durchstreifen (geh); **to ~ the streets** durch die Straßen wandern or (looking for sb/sth also) irren

VI **a** (= walk around casually) herumlaufen; (more aimlessly) umherwandern (through, about in +dat); (leisurely) schlendern; (to see the shops) bummeln; **he ~ed past me in a dream** er ging wie im Traum an mir vorbei; **he ~ed over to speak to me** er kam zu mir herüber, um mit mir zu reden; **his hands ~ed over the keys** seine Hände wanderten über die Tasten; **the bus ~ed along the lanes for a couple of hours** der Bus zuckelte ein paar Stunden durch die Sträßchen; **the river ~ed through the valley** der Fluss zog sich durch das Tal; **I enjoy just ~ing around** ich bummele gerne einfach nur herum; **if his hands start ~ing ...** (hum) wenn er seine Finger nicht bei sich (dat) behalten kann ...

b (= go off, stray) **to ~ from the path** vom Wege or Pfad abkommen; **the cattle must not be allowed to ~** das Vieh darf nicht einfach so herumlaufen; **he ~ed too near the edge of the cliff** er geriet zu nahe an den Rand des Abhangs; **I accidentally ~ed into Squire Thomas' property** ich bin aus Versehen in das Gelände von Squire Thomas geraten; **the children had ~ed out onto the street** die Kinder waren auf die Straße gelaufen; **the needle tends to ~ a bit** der Zeiger schwankt ein bisschen

c (fig: thoughts, eye) schweifen, wandern; **to let one's mind ~** seine Gedanken schweifen lassen; **during the lecture his mind ~ed a bit** während der Vorlesung wanderten seine Gedanken umher or schweiften seine Gedanken ab; **the old man's mind is beginning to ~ a bit** der alte Mann wird ein wenig wirr; **to ~ from the straight and narrow** vom Pfad der Tugend abirren or abkommen; **to ~ off a point/the subject** von einem Punkt/vom Thema abschweifen or abkommen

▶ **wander about** (Brit) or **around** VI umherziehen, umherwandern

▶ **wander back** VI (cows, strays) zurückkommen or -wandern; **shall we start wandering back to the car?** (inf) wollen wir langsam or allmählich zum Auto zurückgehen?; **after two years she wandered back to her husband** nach zwei Jahren fand or ging sie zu ihrem Mann zurück

▶ **wander in** VI ankommen (inf), anspazieren (inf); **he wandered in to see me this morning** (inf) er ist heute Morgen bei mir vorbeigekommen

▶ **wander off** VI **a** (= go off) weggehen, davonziehen (geh); **to wander off course** vom Kurs abkommen; **he wandered off into one of his fantasies** er geriet wieder ins Fantasieren or Phantasieren; **he must have wandered off somewhere** er muss (doch) irgendwohin verschwunden sein **b** (inf: = leave) allmählich or langsam gehen

wanderer ['wɒndərə'] N Wandervogel m; **the Masai are ~s** die Massai sind ein Wanderstamm m; **that child is a real ~** das Kind treibt sich überall herum

wandering ['wɒndərɪŋ] ADJ tribesman, refugees umherziehend; minstrel fahrend; thoughts (ab-)schweifend; gaze schweifend; path gewunden; **the old man's ~ mind** die wirren Gedanken des Alten; **to have ~ hands** (hum) seine Finger nicht bei sich (dat) behalten können; **the Wandering Jew** der Ewige Jude

wanderings ['wɒndərɪŋz] PL Streifzüge pl, Fahrten pl; (mental) wirre Gedanken pl; (verbal) wirres Gerede; **it's time he stopped his ~ and settled down** es wird Zeit, dass er mit dem Herumzigeunern aufhört und sesshaft wird

wanderlust ['wɒndəlʌst] N Fernweh nt

wane [weɪn] **N to be on the ~** (fig) im Schwinden sein **VI** (moon) abnehmen; (daylight) nachlassen; (fig) (influence, strength, life, power) schwinden; (reputation) verblassen

wangle ['wæŋgl] (inf) **N** Schiebung f (inf), Mauschelei f (inf); **it's a ~** das ist Schiebung; **I think we can arrange some sort of ~** ich glaube, wir können es so hinbiegen (inf) or hindern (inf) **VT** job, ticket etc organisieren (inf), verschaffen; **to ~ oneself** or **one's way in** sich hineinlavieren or -mogeln (inf); **to ~ sb in** jdn reinschleusen (inf); **he'll ~ it for you** er wird das schon für dich drehen (inf) or deichseln (inf); **to ~ money out of sb** jdm Geld abluchsen (inf); **we ~d an extra day off** wir haben noch einen zusätzlichen freien Tag rausgeschlagen (inf)

wangler ['wæŋglə'] N (inf) Schlawiner m (inf)

wangling ['wæŋglɪŋ] N (inf) Schiebung f (inf); **there's a lot of ~ goes on** da gibts ziemlich viel Schiebung (inf) or Mauschelei (inf)

wank [wæŋk] (Brit vulg) VI (also **wank off**) wichsen (sl) **VT to ~ sb (off)** jdm einen abwichsen (sl) or runterholen (inf) **N to have a ~** sich (dat) einen runterholen (inf)

wanker ['wæŋkə'] N (Brit vulg) Wichser m (sl), Arsch m (vulg); (= idiot) Schwachkopf m (inf)

wankered ['wæŋkəd] ADJ (Brit vulg: = drunk) rotzbesoffen (sl)

wanky ['wæŋkɪ] ADJ (sl) beschissen (inf)

wanly ['wɒnlɪ] ADV matt

wannabe ['wɒnəbiː] (inf) **N** Möchtegern m (inf) **ADJ** Möchtegern- (inf); **a ~ film star** ein Möchtegern-Filmstar m (inf)

wanness ['wɒnnɪs] N (= paleness) Blässe f; (of light) Mattheit f

want [wɒnt] **⊘** 8.1, 8.2, 9.5, 12.2, 18.4, 21.3 **N** **a** (= lack) Mangel m (of an +dat); **~ of judgement** mangelndes Urteilsvermögen, Mangel m an Urteilsvermögen; **for ~ of** aus Mangel an (+dat); **for ~ of anything better** mangels Besserem, in Ermangelung von etwas Besserem or eines Besseren; **for ~ of something to do I joined a sports club** weil ich nichts zu tun hatte, bin ich einem Sportverein beigetreten; **though it wasn't for ~ of trying** nicht, dass er sich/ich mich etc nicht bemüht hätte; **to feel the ~ of sth** etw vermissen **b** (= poverty) Not f; **to be in ~** Not leiden **c** (= need) Bedürfnis nt; (= wish) Wunsch m; **my ~s are few** meine Ansprüche or Bedürfnisse sind gering, meine Ansprüche sind bescheiden; **the farm supplied all their ~s** der Bauernhof versorgte sie mit allem Nötigen or Notwendigen; **to be in ~ of sth** einer Sache (gen) bedürfen (geh), etw brauchen or benötigen; **to be in ~ of help** Hilfe brauchen; **to be in ~ of repair** reparaturbedürftig sein; **to attend to sb's ~s** sich um jdn kümmern

VT **a** (= wish, desire) wollen; (more polite) mögen; **to ~ to do sth** etw tun wollen; **I ~ you to come here** ich will or möchte, dass du herkommst; **I ~ it done now** ich will or möchte das sofort erledigt haben; **I was ~ing to leave the job next month** ich hätte gerne nächsten Monat mit der Arbeit aufgehört; **what does he ~ with me?** was will er von mir?; **darling, I ~ you** Liebling, ich will dich; **I ~ my mummy** ich will meine Mami, ich will zu meiner Mami; **you don't ~ much** (iro) sonst willst du nichts? (iro); **I don't ~ strangers coming in** ich wünsche or möchte nicht, dass Fremde (hier) hereinkommen

b (= need, require) brauchen; **you ~ to see a doctor/lawyer** Sie sollten zum Arzt/Rechtsanwalt gehen; **you ~ to be careful!** (inf) du musst aufpassen; **you ~ to stop doing that** (inf) du musst damit aufhören; **he ~s to be more careful** (inf) er sollte etwas vorsichtiger sein; **that's the last thing I ~** (inf) alles, bloß das nicht (inf); **that's all we ~ed!** (iro inf) das hat uns gerade noch gefehlt!; **it only ~ed the police to turn up ...** das hätte gerade noch gefehlt, dass auch noch die Polizei anrückt ...; **does my hair ~ cutting?** muss mein Haar geschnitten werden?; **"wanted"** "gesucht"; **he's a ~ed man** er wird (polizeilich) gesucht; **to feel ~ed** das Gefühl haben, gebraucht zu werden; **you're ~ed on the phone** Sie werden am Telefon verlangt or gewünscht

c (= lack) **he ~s talent/confidence** etc es mangelt (geh) or fehlt ihm an Talent/Selbstvertrauen etc; **all the soup ~s is a little salt** das Einzige, was an der Suppe fehlt, ist etwas Salz

VI **a** (= wish, desire) wollen; (more polite) mögen; **you can go if you ~ (to)** wenn du willst or möchtest, kannst du gehen; **I don't ~** ich will or möchte nicht; **without ~ing to sound rude, ...** ich will ja nicht unhöflich sein, aber ...; **do as you ~** tu, was du willst; **he said he'd do it, but does he really ~ to?** er sagte, er würde es machen, aber will er es wirklich?

b **he does not ~ for friends** es fehlt or mangelt (geh) ihm nicht an Freunden; **they ~ for nothing** es fehlt or mangelt (geh) ihnen an nichts; **he doesn't ~ for a pound or two** er ist nicht gerade arm (inf), ihm fehlt es nicht an Kleingeld (inf)

c (liter, = live in poverty) darben (liter)

▶ **want in** VI (inf) reinwollen

▶ **want out** VI (inf) rauswollen

want ad N Kaufgesuch nt

wantage ['wɒntɪdʒ] N (US Econ) Fehlbetrag m, Defizit nt

wanted list ['wɒntɪd,lɪst] N Fahndungsliste f

wanting ['wɒntɪŋ] ADJ **a** (= lacking, missing) fehlend; **romance is ~ in the novel** diesem Roman fehlt es an Romantik; **it's a good novel, but there is something ~** der Roman ist gut, aber irgendetwas fehlt

b (= deficient, inadequate) **he is ~ in confi-**

dence/enterprise etc es fehlt or mangelt (geh) ihm an Selbstvertrauen/Unternehmungslust etc; **his courage was found ~** sein Mut war nicht groß genug; **the new engine was found ~** der neue Motor hat sich als unzulänglich erwiesen; **he was (weighed in the balance and) found ~** (liter) er wurde (gewogen und) (für) zu leicht befunden; **he was not found ~** (liter) er hat sich bewährt

c (inf, = mentally deficient) **he's a bit ~ (up top)** er ist ein bisschen unterbelichtet (inf)

wanton ['wɒntən] ADJ **a** (= licentious) life liederlich; behaviour, woman, pleasures schamlos; looks, thoughts lüstern; **Cupid, that ~ boy** (liter) Amor, dieser kleine Lüstling **b** (= wilful) cruelty, destruction mutwillig; disregard, negligence sträflich, völlig unverantwortlich; waste sträflich, kriminell (inf); **to spend money with ~ extravagance** Geld mit sträflichem Leichtsinn ausgeben; **decorated with ~ extravagance** üppig und verschwenderisch eingerichtet **c** (poet: = capricious) persons übermütig, mutwillig (poet) **N** (old: = immoral woman) Dirne f

wantonly ['wɒntənlɪ] ADV **a** (= immorally) liederlich, schamlos; look lüstern **b** (= wilfully) mutwillig; neglect, waste sträflich; **he was ~ extravagant with his wife's money** er gab das Geld seiner Frau mit sträflichem Leichtsinn aus

wantonness ['wɒntənnɪs] N **a** (= immorality) (of sb's life) Liederlichkeit f; (of behaviour, woman) Schamlosigkeit f; (of look, thought) Lüsternheit f **b** (= wilfulness) (of cruelty) Mutwilligkeit f; (of disregard, negligence) Sträflichkeit f

war [wɔː'] **N** Krieg m; **the art of ~** die Kriegskunst; **this is ~!** (fig) das bedeutet Krieg!; **the ~ against poverty/disease** der Kampf gegen die Armut/Krankheit; **~ of nerves** Nervenkrieg m; **~ of words** Wortgefecht nt; **to be at ~** sich im Krieg(szustand) befinden; **to declare ~** den Krieg erklären (on +dat); (fig also) den Kampf ansagen (on +dat); **to go to ~** (= start) (einen) Krieg anfangen (against mit); (= declare) den Krieg erklären (against +dat); (person) in den Krieg ziehen; **to make** or **wage ~** Krieg führen (on, against mit); **he/this car has been in the ~s a bit** (inf) er/dieses Auto sieht ziemlich ramponiert (inf) or mitgenommen aus; **I hear you've been in the ~s recently** (inf) ich höre, dass du zur Zeit ganz schön angeschlagen bist (inf) **VI** sich bekriegen; (fig) ringen (geh) (for um)

war baby N Kriegskind nt

warble ['wɔːbl] **N** Trällern nt **VI** trällern; **he ~d away as he stood in the shower** (inf) er trällerte fröhlich vor sich hin, während er unter der Dusche stand **VT** trällern

warbler ['wɔːblə'] N (Orn) Grasmücke f; (= wood warbler) Waldsänger m

war: war bond N Kriegsanleihe f; **war bride** N Kriegsbraut f; **war cabinet** N (Pol) Kriegskabinett nt; **war clouds** PL **the ~ are gathering** Kriegsgefahr droht; **war correspondent** N Kriegsberichterstatter(in) m(f), Kriegskorrespondent(in) m(f); **war crime** N Kriegsverbrechen nt; **war criminal** N Kriegsverbrecher(in) m(f); **war cry** N Kriegsruf m; (fig) Schlachtruf m; **the war cries of the Red Indians** das Kriegsgeheul or Kriegsgeschrei der Indianer

ward [wɔːd] **N** **a** (part of hospital) Station f; (= room) (small) (Kranken)zimmer nt; (large) (Kranken)saal m **b** (Jur: = person) Mündel nt; **~ of court** Mündel nt unter Amtsvormundschaft; **to make sb a ~ of court** jdn unter Amtsvormundschaft stellen **c** (Jur: state) **(to be) in ~** unter Vormundschaft (stehen) **d** (Admin) Stadtbezirk m; (= election ward) Wahlbezirk m **e** (of key) Einschnitt m (im Schlüsselbart); (of lock) Aussparung f, Angriff m

▶ **ward off** VT sep attack, blow, person, evil spirits abwehren; danger also, recession abwenden; depression nicht aufkommen lassen

war dance N Kriegstanz m

warden ['wɔːdn] N (of youth hostel) Herbergsvater m, Herbergsmutter f; (= game warden) Jagdaufseher(in) m(f); (= traffic warden) ≈ Verkehrspolizist m, ≈ Politesse f; (= air-raid warden) Luftschutzwart m; (= fire warden) Feuerwart(in) m(f); (of castle, museum etc) Aufseher(in) m(f); (= head warden) Kustos m; (of port) (Hafen)aufseher(in) m(f); (of mint) Münzwardein m; (Univ) Heimleiter(in) m(f); (of Oxbridge college) Rektor(in) m(f); (of prison) (Brit) Wärter(in) m(f), Aufseher(in) m(f); (US) Gefängnisdirektor(in) m(f)

War Department N (old US) Kriegsministerium nt (old)

warder ['wɔːdə'] N (Brit) Wärter(in) m(f), Aufseher(in) m(f)

war-disabled ['wɔːdɪs'eɪbld] PL the ~ die Kriegsversehrten pl

ward heeler ['wɔːdhiːlə'] N (US Pol sl) Handlanger(in) m(f) (inf)

wardress ['wɔːdrɪs] N (Brit) Wärterin f, Aufseherin f

wardrobe ['wɔːdrəʊb] N **a** (esp Brit: = cupboard) (Kleider)schrank m **b** (= clothes) Garderobe f **c** (Theat) (= clothes) Kostüme pl; (= room) Kleiderkammer f, Kostümfundus m

wardrobe: wardrobe mistress N (Theat) Gewandmeisterin f; **wardrobe trunk** N Kleiderkoffer m

ward: wardroom N (Naut) Offiziersmesse f; **ward round** N (Med) Visite f

-ward(s) [-wəd(z)] ADV suf -wärts; **southward(s)** südwärts; **town-/parkward(s)** in Richtung Stadt/Park; **in a homeward(s) direction** Richtung Heimat

wardship ['wɔːdʃɪp] N (Jur) Vormundschaft f

ward sister N (Brit Med) Stationsschwester f

ware [weə'] N **Delft/Derby ~** Delfter/Derby Porzellan nt

-ware N suf -waren pl; **glassware** Glaswaren pl; **kitchenware** Küchenutensilien pl

war effort N Kriegsanstrengungen pl

warehouse ['weəhaʊs] N Lager(haus) nt VT einlagern

warehouse club N (esp US Comm) Geschäft, in dem Waren zu Großhandelspreisen an Mitglieder verkauft werden

warehouseman ['weəhaʊsmən] N pl **-men** [-mən] Lagerarbeiter m

warehousing ['weəhaʊzɪŋ] N Lagerung f; **what sort of ~ is available?** welche Lagerungsmöglichkeiten gibt es?

wares [weəz] PL Waren pl; **to cry one's ~** (dated) seine Waren anpreisen

warfare ['wɔːfeə'] N Krieg m; (= techniques) Kriegskunst f

war: war fever N Kriegsbegeisterung f; **war game** N Kriegsspiel nt; **war grave** N Kriegsgrab nt; **warhead** N Sprengkopf m; **war hero** N Kriegsheld m; **warhorse** N (lit, fig) Schlachtross m

warily ['weərɪlɪ] ADV vorsichtig; (= suspiciously) misstrauisch, argwöhnisch; **to tread ~** (lit, fig) sich vorsehen

wariness ['weərɪnɪs] N Vorsicht f; (= mistrust) Misstrauen nt, Argwohn m; **the ~ of his reply** die Zurückhaltung, mit der er antwortete; **she had a great ~ of strangers** sie hegte starkes Misstrauen or großen Argwohn gegen Fremde

Warks (Brit) abbr of **Warwickshire**

war: warlike ADJ kriegerisch; tone, speech militant; **warlock** N Hexer m; **warlord** N Kriegsherr m

warm [wɔːm] **ADJ** (+er) **a** warm; **I am** or **feel ~** mir ist warm; **come to the fire and get ~** komm ans Feuer und wärm dich; **it's ~ work moving furniture about** beim Möbelrücken wird einem ganz schön warm; **to make things ~ for sb** (inf) es jdm ungemütlich machen (inf); **~ start** (Comput) Warmstart m
b (in party games) **am I ~?** ist es (hier) warm?; **you're getting ~** es wird schon wärmer; **you're**

very ~! heiß!
c (= hearty, warm-hearted) person, welcome, smile herzlich, warm
d (= heated) dispute, words hitzig, heftig
N we were glad to get into the ~ wir waren froh, dass wir ins Warme kamen; **come and have a ~ at the fire** komm und wärm dich am Feuer; **to give sth a ~** etw wärmen
VT wärmen; **it ~s my heart to …** mir wird (es) ganz warm ums Herz, wenn …; **his kind gesture ~ed my heart** bei seiner freundlichen Geste wurde mir ganz warm ums Herz
VI the milk was ~ing on the stove die Milch wurde auf dem Herd angewärmt; **my heart ~ed** mir wurde warm ums Herz; **I ~ed to him** er wurde mir sympathischer; **his voice ~ed as he spoke of his family** seine Stimme bekam einen warmen Ton, als er von seiner Familie sprach; **he spoke rather hesitantly at first but soon ~ed to his subject** anfangs sprach er noch sehr zögernd, doch dann fand er sich in sein Thema hinein; **to ~ to one's work** sich mit seiner Arbeit anfreunden, Gefallen an seiner Arbeit finden

▸ **warm over** VT sep (esp US) **a** food aufwärmen **b** (inf) idea (wieder) aufwärmen

▸ **warm through** VT food aufwärmen

▸ **warm up** **VI** (lit, fig) warm werden; (party, game, speaker) in Schwung kommen; (Sport) sich aufwärmen; **things are warming up** es kommt Schwung in die Sache; (= becoming dangerous) es wird allmählich brenzlig or ungemütlich (inf) **VT** sep engine warm werden lassen, warm laufen lassen; food etc aufwärmen; (fig) party in Schwung bringen; audience in Stimmung bringen

warm-blooded ['wɔːm'blʌdɪd] ADJ warmblütig; (fig) heißblütig; **~ animal** Warmblüter m

warmer ['wɔːmə'] N **foot/bottle ~** Fuß-/Flaschenwärmer m

warm-hearted ['wɔːm'hɑːtɪd] ADJ person warmherzig; action, gesture großzügig

warm-heartedness ['wɔːm'hɑːtɪdnɪs] N Warmherzigkeit f, Herzlichkeit f; (of action, gesture) Großherzigkeit f

warming pan ['wɔːmɪŋ,pæn] N Wärmepfanne f

warmish ['wɔːmɪʃ] ADJ ein bisschen warm; **~ weather** ziemlich warmes Wetter

warmly ['wɔːmlɪ] ADV warm; welcome herzlich; recommend wärmstens; **we ~ welcome it** wir begrüßen es sehr

warmness ['wɔːmnɪs] N = warmth

war: warmonger ['wɔːˌmʌŋgə'] N Kriegshetzer(in) m(f); **warmongering** ['wɔːˌmʌŋgərɪŋ] **ADJ** kriegshetzerisch **N** Kriegshetze f

warmth [wɔːmθ] N **a** (lit) Wärme f **b** (fig) (= friendliness: of voice, welcome) Wärme f, Herzlichkeit f; (= heatedness) Heftigkeit f, Hitzigkeit f

warm-up ['wɔːmʌp] N (Sport) Aufwärmen nt; (Mus) Einspielen nt; **the teams had a ~ before the game** die Mannschaften wärmten sich vor dem Spiel auf; **the audience was entertained with a ~ before the TV transmission began** das Publikum wurde vor der Fernsehübertragung in Stimmung gebracht

warm-ups ['wɔːmʌps] PL (US) Trainingsanzug m

warn [wɔːn] **VT a** (= give warning) warnen (of, about, against vor +dat); (police, judge etc) verwarnen; **to ~ sb not to do sth** jdn davor warnen, etw zu tun; **be ~ed!** sei gewarnt!, lass dich warnen!; **I'm ~ing you** ich warne dich!; **you have been ~ed!** sag nicht, ich hätte dich nicht gewarnt or es hätte dich niemand gewarnt!; **she just won't be ~ed** sie hört auf keine Warnung(en)
b (= inform) **to ~ sb that …** jdn darauf aufmerksam machen or darauf hinweisen, dass …; **her expression ~ed me that she was not enjoying the conversation** ich merkte schon an ihrem Gesichtsausdruck, dass ihr die Unterhaltung nicht gefiel; **you might have ~ed us that you were coming** du hättest uns ruhig vorher Bescheid sagen können, dass du kommst
VI warnen (of vor +dat)

▸ **warn off** VT sep warnen; **to warn sb off doing sth** jdn (davor) warnen, etw zu tun; **he warned me off** er hat mich davor gewarnt; **I warned him off my property** ich habe ihn von meinem Grundstück verwiesen; **to warn sb off a subject** jdm von einem Thema abraten; **he sat there shaking his head, obviously trying to warn me off** er saß da und schüttelte den Kopf, offensichtlich um mich davon abzubringen; **he warns everybody off who tries to get friendly with her** er lässt nicht zu, dass sich jemand um sie bemüht

warning ['wɔːnɪŋ] ✿ 2.3 **N** Warnung f; (from police, judge etc) Verwarnung f; **without ~** unerwartet, ohne Vorwarnung; **they had no ~ of the enemy attack** der Feind griff sie ohne Vorwarnung an; **he had plenty of ~** er ist oft or häufig genug gewarnt worden; (early enough) er wusste früh genug Bescheid; **to give sb a ~** jdn warnen; (police, judge etc) jdm eine Verwarnung geben; **let this be a ~ to you** lassen Sie sich (dat) das eine Warnung sein!, das soll Ihnen eine Warnung sein; **let this be a ~ to all those who …** allen denjenigen, die …, soll das eine Warnung sein; **to take ~ from sth** sich (dat) etw eine Warnung sein lassen; **the bell gives ~ or is a ~ that …** die Klingel zeigt an, dass …; **they gave us no ~ of their arrival** sie kamen unangekündigt or ohne Vorankündigung; **please give me a few days' ~** bitte sagen or geben Sie mir ein paar Tage vorher Bescheid; **to give sb due ~** (= inform) jdm rechtzeitig Bescheid sagen **ADJ** Warn-; look, tone warnend; **a ~ sign** (lit: = signboard etc) ein Warnschild nt; (fig) ein Warnzeichen nt; **to fire ~ shots** Warnschüsse abgeben

warning: warning flasher N (Aut) Warnblinkanlage f; **warning light** N Warnleuchte f

warningly ['wɔːnɪŋlɪ] ADV warnend

warning: warning shot N Warnschuss m; **warning signal** N Warnsignal nt; **warning strike** N (Econ) Warnstreik m; **warning triangle** N Warndreieck m

war: War Office N (old Brit) Kriegsministerium nt (old); **war orphan** N Kriegswaise f

warp [wɔːp] **N a** (in weaving) Kette f **b** (in wood etc) Welle f; **the ~ makes it impossible to use this wood** das Holz ist zu verzogen or wellig, als dass es noch verwenden könnte **c** (= towing cable) Schleppleine f **d** (of mind) hatred of his mother had given his mind an evil **~** der Hass, den er gegen seine Mutter hegte, hatte seinen ganzen Charakter entstellt or verbogen; **the ~ in his personality** das Abartige in seinem Wesen **VT** wood wellig werden lassen, wellen; character verbiegen, entstellen; judgement verzerren; (Aviat) verwinden **VI** (wood) sich wellen, sich verziehen, sich werfen

war: war paint N (lit, fig inf) Kriegsbemalung f; **warpath** N Kriegspfad m; **on the ~** auf dem Kriegspfad

warped [wɔːpt] ADJ **a** (lit) verzogen, wellig **b** (fig: = twisted) sense of humour, character abartig; judgement verzerrt; **he has a ~ mind** er hat eine abartige Fantasie or Phantasie

warping ['wɔːpɪŋ] N Krümmung f

warplane N Kampfflugzeug nt

warrant ['wɒrənt] **N a** (Comm) Garantie f; (Mil) Patent nt; (= search warrant) Durchsuchungsbefehl m; (= death warrant) Hinrichtungsbefehl m; **a ~ of arrest** ein Haftbefehl m; **there is a ~ out for his arrest** gegen ihn ist Haftbefehl erlassen worden (Jur), er wird steckbrieflich gesucht **b** (rare) (= justification) Berechtigung f; (= authority) Befugnis f, Ermächtigung f **VT a** (= justify) action etc rechtfertigen; **to ~ sb doing sth** jdn dazu berechtigen, etw zu tun **b** (= merit) verdienen **c** (dated inf: = assure) wetten; **I('ll) ~ (you)** ich wette **d** (= guarantee) gewährleisten; **these goods are ~ed for three months by the manufacturers** für diese Waren übernimmt der Hersteller eine Garantie von drei Monaten; **a pill ~ed to cure influenza** eine Pille, die garantiert Grippe heilt

warrant card N (*Brit, Police*) Dienstmarke *f*

warranted ['wɒrəntɪd] ADJ (= *justifiable*) *fears* berechtigt

warrantee [ˌwɒrən'tiː] N Garantieinhaber(in) *m(f)*

warrant officer N *Rang zwischen Offizier und Unteroffizier*

warrantor ['wɒrəntə'] N Garantiegeber(in) *m(f)*

warranty ['wɒrəntɪ] N (*Comm*) Garantie *f*; **it's still under ~** darauf ist noch Garantie

warren ['wɒrən] N (= *rabbit warren*) Kaninchenbau *m*; (*fig*) Labyrinth *nt*

warring ['wɔːrɪŋ] ADJ **a** (*lit*) *parties, sides* gegnerisch; *nations* Krieg führend; *interests, ideologies* gegensätzlich; *factions* sich bekriegend **b** (*fig*) *parents, couple* sich bekriegend

warrior ['wɒrɪə'] N Krieger(in) *m(f)*

Warsaw ['wɔːsɔː] N Warschau *nt*; **~ Pact** Warschauer Pakt *m*

warship ['wɔːʃɪp] N Kriegsschiff *nt*

wart [wɔːt] N Warze *f*; **~s and all** (*hum inf*) mit allen seinen/ihren *etc* Fehlern

warthog ['wɔːthɒg] N Warzenschwein *nt*

wartime ['wɔːtaɪm] **N** Kriegszeit *f*; **in ~** in Kriegszeiten **ADJ** Kriegs-; **~ atrocities** Kriegsgräuel *pl*; **in ~ England** in England im Krieg *or* während des Krieges; **~ regulations/rationing** *etc* Vorschriften *pl*/Rationierungen *pl etc* in Kriegszeiten, Kriegsvorschriften *pl*/-rationierungen *pl etc*

wartorn ['wɔːtɔːn] ADJ vom Krieg erschüttert

war: war toy N Kriegsspielzeug *nt*; **war-weary** ADJ kriegsmüde; **war widow** N Kriegswitwe *f*; **war-wounded** PL **the ~** die Kriegsversehrten *pl*

wary ['wɛərɪ] ADJ (*+er*) vorsichtig; (= *looking and planning ahead*) umsichtig, klug, wachsam; *look* misstrauisch, argwöhnisch; **to be ~ of** *or* **about sb/sth** sich vor jdm/einer Sache in Acht nehmen, vor jdm/einer Sache auf der Hut sein; **to be ~ of** *or* **about doing sth** seine Zweifel *or* Bedenken haben, ob man etw tun soll; **be ~ of talking to strangers** hüte dich davor, mit Fremden zu sprechen; **to keep a ~ eye on sb/sth** ein wachsames Auge auf jdn/etw haben

war zone N Kriegsgebiet *nt*

was [wɒz] *pret of* **be**

wash [wɒʃ] **N** **a** (= *act of washing*) **sb/sth needs a ~** jd/etw muss gewaschen werden; **to give sb/sth a (good) ~** jdn/etw (gründlich) waschen; **to give one's hands/face a ~** sich (*dat*) die Hände/das Gesicht waschen; **to have a ~** sich waschen
b (= *laundry*) Wäsche *f*; **to be in the ~** in der Wäsche sein; **it will all come out in the ~** (*fig inf*) es wird schon alles rauskommen, es wird sich schon noch alles zeigen (*inf*)
c (*of ship*) Kielwasser *nt*; (*Aviat*) Luftstrudel *m*
d (= *lapping*) (*gentle sound*) Geplätscher *nt*; (*of ocean*) sanftes Klatschen der Wellen
e (= *mouthwash*) Mundwasser *nt*; (= *liquid remains, also pej*) Spülwasser *nt*; (*for walls etc*) Tünche *f*
f (*in painting*) **a ~ of brown ink** eine leichte *or* schwache Tönung mit brauner Tünche
VT **a** *car, hair, clothes etc* waschen; *dishes* spülen, abwaschen; *floor* aufwaschen, aufwischen; *parts of body* sich (*dat*) waschen; **to ~ one's hands** sich (*dat*) die Hände waschen (*euph*); **to ~ one's hands of sb/sth** mit jdm/etw nichts mehr zu tun haben wollen; **I ~ my hands of it** ich wasche meine Hände in Unschuld; **to ~ sth clean** etw rein waschen; **the sea ~ed it clean of oil** das Öl wurde vom Meer weggewaschen; **to ~ one's dirty linen** (*Brit*) *or* **laundry** (*US*) **in public** (*fig*) seine schmutzige Wäsche in der Öffentlichkeit waschen
b (*sea etc*) umspülen; *wall, cliffs etc* schlagen gegen
c (*river, sea: = carry*) spülen; **the body was ~ed downstream** die Leiche wurde flussabwärts getrieben; **to ~ ashore** an Land spülen *or* schwemmen, anschwemmen

d **the water had ~ed a channel in the rocks** das Wasser hatte eine Rinne in die Felsen gefressen
e (= *paint*) *walls* tünchen; *paper* kolorieren
VI **a** (*have a wash*) sich waschen
b (= *do the laundry etc*) waschen; (*Brit*: = *wash up*) abwaschen
c **a material that ~es well/doesn't ~ well** ein Stoff, der sich gut wäscht/den man nicht waschen kann *or* der sich nicht waschen lässt; **that excuse won't ~** (*Brit fig inf*) diese Entschuldigung nimmt *or* kauft dir keiner ab! (*inf*)
d (*sea etc*) schlagen; **the sea ~ed over the promenade** das Meer überspülte die Strandpromenade

▶ **wash away** VT *sep* **a** (*lit*) (hin)wegspülen **b** (*fig*) **to wash away sb's sins** jdn von seinen Sünden rein waschen

▶ **wash down** VT *sep* **a** (= *clean*) *car, walls, deck* abwaschen **b** *meal, food* hinunterspülen, runterspülen (*inf*)

▶ **wash off** **VI** (*stain, dirt*) sich rauswaschen lassen; **most of the pattern has washed off** das Muster ist fast ganz verwaschen **VT** *sep* abwaschen; **wash that grease off your hands** wasch dir die Schmiere von den Händen (ab)!

▶ **wash out** **VI** sich (r)auswaschen lassen **VT** *sep* **a** (= *clean*) auswaschen; *mouth* ausspülen **b** (= *stop, cancel*) *game etc* ins Wasser fallen lassen (*inf*); **the game was washed out** das Spiel fiel buchstäblich ins Wasser (*inf*)

▶ **wash over** VI +*prep obj* **the criticism just seemed to wash over him** die Kritik schien an ihm abzuprallen; **he lets everything just wash over him** er lässt alles einfach ruhig über sich ergehen; **waves of panic washed over her** Panik überkam sie

▶ **wash up** **VI** **a** (*Brit*: = *clean dishes*) abwaschen **b** (*US*: = *have a wash*) sich waschen **VT** *sep* **a** (*Brit*) *dishes* abwaschen, (ab)spülen **b** (*sea etc*) anschwemmen, anspülen **c** **that's/we're all washed up** (*fig inf*: = *finished*) das ist gelaufen (*inf*)

washable ['wɒʃəbl] ADJ waschbar; *wallpaper* abwaschbar

wash: wash-and-wear ADJ *clothing, fabric* bügelfrei; **washbag** N (*US*) Kulturbeutel *m*; **washbasin** N Waschbecken *nt*; **washboard** N Waschbrett *nt*; **washbowl** N Waschschüssel *f*; (*in unit*) Waschbecken *nt*; **washcloth** N (*US*) Waschlappen *m*; **washday** N Waschtag *m*; **wash drawing** N Tuschezeichnung *f*

washed out ADJ *pred*, **washed-out** ADJ *attr* [ˌwɒʃt'aʊt] (*inf*) erledigt (*inf*), schlapp (*inf*); **to feel ~** wie ausgelaugt fühlen (*inf*); **to look ~** mitgenommen aussehen

washer ['wɒʃə'] N **a** (*Tech*) Dichtungsring *m* **b** (= *washing machine*) Waschmaschine *f*; (= *dishwasher*) (Geschirr)spülmaschine *f*

washerwoman ['wɒʃəˌwʊmən] N *pl* **-women** [-ˌwɪmɪn] Waschfrau *f*, Wäscherin *f*

wash: wash-hand basin N Handwaschbecken *nt*; **wash house** N Waschhaus *nt*

washing ['wɒʃɪŋ] N Waschen *nt*; (= *clothes*) Wäsche *f*; **many boys dislike ~** viele Jungen waschen sich nicht gerne; **to do the ~** Wäsche waschen; **to take in ~** (für Kunden) waschen; **if we don't get a pay increase, I'll have to take in ~!** (*hum*) wenn wir keine Gehaltserhöhung bekommen, muss ich noch putzen gehen (*inf*)

washing: washing day N = **washday**; **washing line** N Wäscheleine *f*; **washing machine** N Waschmaschine *f*; **washing powder** N Waschpulver *nt*; **washing soda** N Bleichsoda *nt*; **washing-up** N (*Brit*) Abwasch *m*; **to do the ~** spülen, den Abwasch machen; **washing-up basin**, **washing-up bowl** N (*Brit*) Spülschüssel *f*; **washing-up cloth** N (*Brit*) Spültuch *nt*, Spüllappen *m*; **washing-up liquid** N (*Brit*) Spülmittel *nt*

wash: wash leather N Waschleder *nt*; **wash load** N Waschmaschinenladung *f*; **washout** N (*inf*) Reinfall *m* (*inf*); (= *person*) Flasche *f* (*inf*), Niete *f* (*inf*); **washrag** N (*US*) = **washcloth**

washroom N Waschraum *m*; **washstand** N **a** Waschbecken *nt* **b** (*old*) Waschgestell *nt*; **washtub** N (Wasch)zuber *m*; **wash-wipe** [ˌwɒʃ'waɪp] N (*Aut*) (*on window*) Scheibenwischer *m*; (*on headlamp*) Scheinwerferwischer *m*

washy ['wɒʃɪ] ADJ wässerig → **wishy-washy**

wasn't ['wɒznt] *contr of* **was not**

WASP [wɒsp] (*US*) *abbr of* **White Anglo-Saxon Protestant** weißer angelsächsischer Protestant

wasp [wɒsp] N Wespe *f*

waspish ADJ , **waspishly** ADV ['wɒspɪʃ, -lɪ] giftig

wasp sting N Wespenstich *m*

wasp waist N Wespentaille *f*

wassail ['wɒseɪl] (*Brit, old*) **N** **a** (= *toast*) Trinkspruch *m*; **~ cup** Kelch *m* **b** (= *revelry*) Gelage *nt* **VI** **a** (= *revel*) zechen, ein Gelage abhalten **b** **to go ~ing** (= *carol-singing*) ≈ als Sternsinger gehen

wastage ['weɪstɪdʒ] N Schwund *m*; (= *action*) Verschwendung *f*; (= *amount also*) Materialverlust *m*; (*from container also*) Verlust *m*; (*unusable products etc also*) Abfall *m*; **a ~ rate of 10%** eine Verlustquote von 10% → **natural wastage**

waste [weɪst] **ADJ** (= *superfluous*) überschüssig, überflüssig; (= *left over*) ungenutzt; *land* brachliegend, ungenutzt; **~ food** Abfall *m*; **~ material/matter** Abfallstoffe *pl*; **to lay ~, to lay ~ to sth** (*liter*, = *annihilate*) etw verwüsten **N** **a** Verschwendung *f*; (= *unusable materials*) Abfall *m*; **it's a ~ of time/money** es ist Zeit-/Geldverschwendung; **it's a ~ of your time and mine** das ist nur (eine) Zeitverschwendung für uns beide; **it's a ~ of effort** das ist nicht der Mühe (*gen*) wert; **he's/it's a ~ of space** (*inf*) er/das taugt nichts; **to go to ~** (= *food*) umkommen; (*training, money, land*) ungenutzt sein/bleiben, brachliegen; (*talent etc*) verkümmern
b (= *waste material*) Abfallstoffe *pl*; (*in factory*) Schwund *m*; (= *rubbish*) Abfall *m*; **metal ~** Metallabfall *m*
c (= *land, expanse*) Wildnis *f no pl*, Einöde *f*; **the snowy ~s of Siberia** die Schneewüsten *pl* Sibiriens
VT **a** (= *use badly or wrongly*) verschwenden, vergeuden (*on an* +*acc*, für); *food* verschwenden; *life, time* vergeuden, verschwenden; *opportunity* vertun; **you're wasting your time** das ist reine Zeitverschwendung, damit vertust du nur deine Zeit; **you didn't ~ much time getting here!** (*inf*) da bist du ja schon, du hast ja nicht gerade getrödelt! (*inf*); **all our efforts were ~d** all unsere Bemühungen waren umsonst *or* vergeblich; **nothing is ~d** es wird nichts verschwendet; **your work won't be ~d** deine Arbeit ist nicht vergeblich *or* umsonst getan; **he didn't ~ any words in telling me ...** ohne viel(e) Worte zu machen *or* zu verlieren, sagte er mir ...; **to ~ oneself on sb** sich an jdn verschwenden; **I wouldn't ~ my breath talking to him** ich würde doch nicht für den meine Spucke vergeuden! (*inf*); **don't ~ your efforts on him** vergeuden Sie keine Mühe mit ihm!; **Beethoven/your joke is ~d on him** Beethoven/dein Witz ist an den verschwendet *or* vergeudet; **you're ~d in this job** Sie sind zu schade für diese Arbeit
b (= *weaken*) auszehren; *strength* aufzehren
c (= *lay waste*) verwüsten
d (*inf*: = *kill*) kaltmachen (*inf*)
VI (*food*) umkommen; (*skills*) verkümmern; (*body*) verfallen; (*strength, assets*) schwinden; **~ not, want not** (*Prov*) spare in der Zeit, so hast du in der Not (*Prov*)

▶ **waste away** VI (*physically*) dahinschwinden (*geh*), immer weniger werden

wastebasket ['weɪstbɑːskɪt], **wastebin** ['weɪstbɪn] N (*esp US*) Papierkorb *m*

wasted ['weɪstɪd] ADJ **a** **I've had a ~ journey** ich bin umsonst hingefahren; **a vote for him is a ~ vote** ihn zu wählen heißt eine Stimme verschenken **b** (= *emaciated*) *organs, muscles* geschwächt; (*inf*: = *worn out*) verbraucht, ausgelaugt (*inf*) **c** (*sl*: = *drunk, high*) dicht (*sl*), platt (*sl*), breit (*sl*)

waste: waste disposal N Müllbeseitigung *f*, Abfallentsorgung *f*; **waste disposal unit** N Müllschlucker *m*

wasteful ['weɪstful] ADJ verschwenderisch; *method, process* aufwändig, aufwendig, unwirtschaftlich; *expenditure* unnütz; **leaving all the lights on is a ~ habit** es ist Verschwendung, überall Licht brennen zu lassen; **to be ~ with sth** verschwenderisch mit etw umgehen; **it is ~ of effort** es ist unnötiger Aufwand; **this project is ~ of our resources** dieses Projekt ist eine unnütze Vergeudung unserer Ressourcen

wastefully ['weɪstfəlɪ] ADV verschwenderisch; *organized* unwirtschaftlich

wastefulness ['weɪstfʊlnɪs] N (*of person*) verschwenderische Art; (*in method, organization, of process etc*) Unwirtschaftlichkeit *f*, Aufwändigkeit *f*, Aufwendigkeit *f*; **throwing it away is sheer ~** es ist reine Verschwendung, das wegzuwerfen; **sb's ~ with sth/in doing sth** jds verschwenderische Art, mit etw umzugehen/etw zu machen; **the ~ of the government's expenditure in the field of education** die Verschwendung, die die Regierung auf dem Gebiet des Bildungswesens betreibt

waste: waste gas N (*Tech*) Abgas *nt*; **waste heat** N (*from engine etc*) Abwärme *f*; **waste heat recovery** N Abwärmerückgewinnung *f*; **wasteland** N Ödland *nt*; (*fig*) Einöde *f*; **waste management** N Abfallentsorgung *f*; **waste oil** N Altöl *nt*; **wastepaper** N Papierabfall *m*; (*fig*) Makulatur *f*; **wastepaper basket** N Papierkorb *m*; **they go straight into the ~** die wandern sofort in den Papierkorb; **wastepaper collection** N Altpapiersammlung *f*; **waste pipe** N Abflussrohr *nt*; **waste product** N Abfallprodukt *nt*

waster ['weɪstə] N **a** Verschwender(in) *m(f)*; **it's a real time-/money-waster** das ist wirklich Zeit-/Geldverschwendung; **she's a terrible ~ of electricity** sie verschwendet schrecklich viel Strom **b** (*= good-for-nothing*) Taugenichts *m*

waste: waste recovery N Abfallaufbereitung *f*, Müllaufbereitung *f*; **waste recycling** N Abfallverwertung *f*, Müllverwertung *f*; **waste reprocessing plant** N Abfallwiederaufbereitungsanlage *f*, Müllverwertungswerk *nt*; **waste separation** N Abfalltrennung *f*, Mülltrennung *f*; **waste water** N Abwasser *nt*

wasting ['weɪstɪŋ] ADJ *attr* ~ **disease** Auszehrung *f*; **this is a ~ disease** das ist eine Krankheit, bei der der Körper allmählich verfällt

wastrel ['weɪstrəl] N (*liter*) Prasser *m* (*liter*)

watch[1] [wɒtʃ] N (*Armband*)uhr *f*

watch[2] **N** **a** (*= vigilance*) Wache *f*; **to be on the ~** aufpassen; **to be on the ~ for sb/sth** nach jdm/etw Ausschau halten; **to keep ~** Wache halten; **to keep a close ~ on sb/sth** jdn/etw scharf bewachen; **to keep a close ~ on the time** genau auf die Zeit achten; **to keep ~ over sb/sth** bei jdm/etw wachen *or* Wache halten; **to set a ~ on sb/sth** jdn/etw überwachen lassen **b** (*= period of duty, people*) Wache *f*; **to be on ~** Wache haben, auf Wacht sein (*geh*); **officer of the ~** wachhabender Offizier; **in the still ~es of the night** (*old, liter*) in den stillen Stunden der Nacht **c** (*Hist, to protect public*) Wache *f* **VT** **a** (*= guard*) aufpassen auf (+*acc*); (*police etc*) überwachen **b** (*= observe*) beobachten; *match* zusehen *or* zuschauen bei; *film, play, programme on TV* sich (*dat*) ansehen; **to ~ TV** fernsehen; **to ~ sb doing sth** jdm bei etw zusehen *or* zuschauen, sich (*dat*) ansehen, wie jd etw macht; **I'll come and ~ you play** ich komme und sehe dir beim Spielen zu; **he just stood there and ~ed her drown** er stand einfach da und sah zu, wie sie ertrank; **I ~ed her coming down the street** ich habe sie beobachtet, wie *or* als sie die Straße entlang kam; **she has a habit of ~ing my mouth when I speak** sie hat die Angewohnheit, mir

auf den Mund zu sehen *or* schauen, wenn ich rede; **let's go and ~ the tennis** gehen wir uns (das) Tennis ansehen; **are you ~ing the blackboard!** du guckst *or* siehst zur Tafel!; **don't ~ the camera** sehen Sie nicht zur Kamera!; **~ this young actor, he'll be a star** beachten Sie diesen jungen Schauspieler, der wird mal ein Star; **~ the road in front of you** pass auf die Straße auf!, guck *or* achte auf die Straße!; **to ~ a case/negotiations for sb** für jdn als Beobachter bei einem Prozess/einer Verhandlung auftreten; **now ~ this closely** sehen *or* schauen Sie jetzt gut zu!, passen Sie mal genau auf!; **~ this!** pass auf!; **~ this space** warten Sies ab, demnächst mehr; **I want everyone to ~ me** ich möchte, dass mir alle zusehen *or* zuschauen!, alle mal hersehen *or* herschauen!; **just ~ me!** guck *or* schau mal, wie ich das mache!; **just ~ me go and make a mess of it!** da siehst du mal, was für einen Mist ich mache (*inf*); **we are being ~ed** wir werden beobachtet; **I can't stand being ~ed** ich kann es nicht aussstehen, wenn mir ständig einer zusieht; **a new talent to be ~ed** ein neues Talent, das man im Auge behalten muss; **it's about as exciting as ~ing grass grow** *or* **~ing paint dry** es ist sterbenslangweilig, das ist so spannend, dass einem das Gähnen kommt; **a ~ed pot never boils** (*Prov*) wenn man daneben steht, kocht das Wasser nie **c** (= *be careful of*) Acht geben *or* aufpassen auf (+*acc*); *expenses* achten auf (+*acc*); *time* achten auf (+*acc*), aufpassen auf (+*acc*); **(you'd better) ~ it!** (*inf*) pass (bloß) auf! (*inf*); **~ yourself** sieh dich vor!, sei vorsichtig!; (*well-wishing*) machs gut!; **~ your manners!** bitte benimm dich!; **~ your language!** drück dich bitte etwas gepflegter aus!; **~ him, he's crafty** sieh dich vor *or* pass auf, er ist raffiniert; **where you put your feet** pass auf, wo du hintrittst; **~ how you talk to him, he's very touchy** sei vorsichtig, wenn du mit ihm sprichst, er ist sehr empfindlich; **~ how you drive, the roads are icy** fahr vorsichtig *or* pass beim Fahren auf, die Straßen sind vereist!; **~ how you go!** machs gut!; (*on icy surface etc*) pass beim Laufen/Fahren auf! → **step** **d** *chance* abpassen, abwarten; **to ~ one's chance/time** eine günstige Gelegenheit/einen günstigen Zeitpunkt abwarten **VI** **a** (= *observe*) zusehen, zuschauen; **to ~ for sb/sth** nach jdm/etw Ausschau halten *or* ausschauen; **they ~ed for a signal from the soldiers** sie warteten auf ein Signal von den Soldaten; **to ~ for sth to happen** darauf warten, dass etw geschieht; **to be ~ing for signs of ...** nach Anzeichen von ... Ausschau halten; **you should ~ for symptoms of ...** du solltest auf ...symptome achten **b** (= *keep watch*) Wache halten; (*at sickbed*) wachen; **there are policemen ~ing all (a)round the house** das Haus wird rundherum von Polizisten bewacht

▶ **watch out** VI **a** (= *look carefully*) Ausschau halten, ausschauen; (*for sb/sth* nach jdm/etw); **a newcomer to watch out for** ein Neuling, auf den man achten sollte **b** (= *be careful*) aufpassen, Acht geben (*for* auf +*acc*); **there were hundreds of policemen watching out for trouble at the match** bei dem Spiel waren hunderte *or* Hunderte von Polizisten, die aufpassten, dass es nicht zu Zwischenfällen kam; **watch out!** Achtung!, Vorsicht!; (*threat*) pass bloß auf!, nimm dich in Acht!, sieh dich ja vor!; **watch out for him** nimm dich vor ihm in Acht

▶ **watch over** VI +*prep obj* wachen über (+*acc*)

watchable ['wɒtʃəbl] ADJ sehenswert

watch: watchband N (*US*) Uhrarmband *nt*; **watchcase** N Uhrengehäuse *nt*; **watch chain** N Uhrkette *f*; **Watch Committee** N (*Brit*) Aufsichtskommission *f*; **watchdog** N (*lit*) Wachhund *m*; (*fig*) Aufpasser *m* (*inf*), Überwachungsbeauftragte(r) *m*; **government ~** Regierungsbeauftragter *m* mit Überwachungsaufgaben; **~ body** Überwachungsgremium *nt*

watcher ['wɒtʃə] N Schaulustige(r) *mf*; (= *observer*) Beobachter(in) *m(f)*; **the ~s by the dy-**

ing man's bedside die am Bett des Sterbenden Wachenden

watchful ['wɒtʃful] ADJ wachsam; **to keep a ~ eye on sb/sth** ein wachsames Auge auf jdn/etw werfen; **to be ~ for** wachsam Ausschau halten nach

watchfully ['wɒtʃfəlɪ] ADV wachsam; **policemen sat ~ at the back of the hall** ganz hinten im Saal saßen Polizisten, die aufpassten; **the opposition waited ~ for the Government's next move** die Opposition beobachtete aufmerksam, welchen Schritt die Regierung als Nächstes unternehmen würde

watchfulness ['wɒtʃfʊlnɪs] N Wachsamkeit *f*

watch-glass ['wɒtʃglɑːs] N Uhrenglas *nt*

watching brief ['wɒtʃɪŋ'briːf] N **to hold** *or* **keep a ~** eine Kontrollfunktion ausüben; **he holds a ~ for the Government** er ist der Regierungsbeauftragte zur Überwachung der gesamten industriellen Entwicklung

watch: watchmaker N Uhrmacher(in) *m(f)*; **watchman** N (*in bank, factory etc*) Wächter(in) *m(f)*; (*also* **night watchman**) Nachtwächter(in) *m(f)*; **watch-night service** N Jahresschlussmette *f*; **watchstrap** N Uhrarmband *nt*; **watchtower** N Wachtturm *m*; **watchword** N (= *password, motto*) Parole *f*, Losung *f*

water ['wɔːtə] **N** **a** Wasser *nt*; **the field is under (two feet of) ~** das Feld steht (zwei Fuß) unter Wasser; **to take in** *or* **make ~** (*ship*) lecken; **to hold ~** wasserdicht sein; **that excuse/argument etc won't hold ~** (*inf*) diese Entschuldigung/dieses Argument *etc* ist nicht hieb- und stichfest (*inf*) **b** (*of sea, of lake etc*) **by ~** auf dem Wasserweg, zu Wasser (*geh*); **on land and ~** zu Land und zu Wasser; **we spent an afternoon on the ~** wir verbrachten einen Nachmittag auf dem Wasser; **~s** Gewässer *pl*; **the ~s** (*Bibl, liter*) die Wasser *pl*; **the ~s of the Rhine** die Wasser des Rheins (*liter*) **c** (= *urine*) Wasser *nt*; **to pass ~** Wasser lassen **d** (*at spa*) **the ~s** die Heilquelle; **to drink** *or* **take the ~s** eine Kur machen; (*drinking only*) eine Trinkkur machen **e** (*Med*) **~ on the brain** Wasserkopf *m*; **~ on the knee** Kniegelenkerguss *m*; **her ~s broke at midnight** die Fruchtblase ist um Mitternacht geplatzt **f** (= *toilet water*) **rose** *etc* ~ Rosenwasser *nt etc* **g** (*fig phrases*) **to keep one's head above ~** sich über Wasser halten; **to pour cold ~ on sth** jds Idee etw mies machen (*inf*); **to get (oneself) into deep ~(s)** ins Schwimmen kommen; **of the first ~** (*dated Brit liter*) erster Güte; **that's all ~ under the bridge now** das ist aller längst vorbei; **a lot of ~ has flowed under the bridge since then** seitdem ist so viel Wasser den Berg *or* den Bach hinuntergeflossen; **to be in/get into hot ~** (*inf*) in Schwierigkeiten *or* in (des) Teufels Küche (*inf*) sein/geraten (*over* wegen +*gen*); **he's in hot ~ with his father** (*inf*) er hat Zoff mit seinem Vater (*inf*); **to spend money like ~** (*inf*) mit dem Geld nur so um sich werfen (*inf*)

VT **a** *garden, lawn, roads* sprengen; *land, field* bewässern; *plant* (be)gießen **b** *horses, cattle* tränken **c** *wine* verwässern, verdünnen **d** **to ~ capital** (*Fin*) Aktienkapital verwässern **VI** **a** (*mouth*) wässern; (*eye*) tränen; **the smoke made his eyes ~** ihm tränten die Augen vom Rauch; **my mouth ~ed** mir lief das Wasser im Mund zusammen; **to make sb's mouth ~** jdm den Mund wässerig machen **b** (*animals*) trinken

▶ **water down** VT *sep* (*lit, fig*) verwässern; (*fig also*) abmildern, abschwächen; *liquids* (mit Wasser) verdünnen

water: water bed N Wasserbett *nt*; **water beetle** N Wasserkäfer *m*; **water bird** N Wasservogel *m*; **water biscuit** N (*Brit*) ≈ Kräcker *m*; **water blister** N Wasserblase *f*; **water boatman** N Rückenschwimmer *m*; **water**

bomb N Wasserbombe f; **waterborne** ADJ **to be ~** (ship) auf dem or im Wasser sein; **~ goods/troops** Güter/Truppen, die auf dem Wasserweg or zu Wasser befördert werden; **a ~ disease** eine Krankheit, die durch das Wasser übertragen wird; **water bottle** N Wasserflasche f; (for troops, travellers etc) Feldflasche f; **water brash** N (Med) Sodbrennen nt; **waterbuck** N Wasserbock m; **water buffalo** N Wasserbüffel m; **water butt** N Regentonne f; **water cannon** N Wasserwerfer m; **the Water Carrier** (Astrol) der Wassermann; **water cart** N Wasserwagen m; (for roads) Sprengwagen m; **water chestnut** N Wasserkastanie f; **water closet** N (abbr **WC**) (esp Brit) Wasserklosett nt; **watercolour**, (US) **watercolor** N Wasserfarbe f, Aquarellfarbe f; (= picture) Aquarell nt [ATTR] Aquarell-; **~ painter** Aquarellmaler(in) m(f); **a ~ painting** ein Aquarell nt; **watercolourist**, (US) **watercolorist** N Aquarellmaler(in) m(f); **water-cooled** ADJ wassergekühlt; **water cooler** N Trinkwasserbehälter m; **watercourse** N (= stream) Wasserlauf m; (= bed) Flussbett nt; (artificial) Kanal m; **water cracker** N (US) **water biscuit**; **watercress** N (Brunnen)kresse f; **water cure** N Wasserkur f; **water diviner** N (Wünschel)rutengänger(in) m(f); **watered-down** [ˈwɔːtədˈdaʊn] ADJ (lit, fig) verwässert; **waterfall** N Wasserfall m; **waterfast** ADJ (colour) wasserecht; **water filter** N Wasserfilter m; **waterfowl** N Wasservogel m; (pl) Wassergeflügel nt; **waterfront** N Hafenviertel nt; **we drove along the ~/down to the ~** wir fuhren am Wasser entlang/hinunter zum Wasser [ATTR] am Wasser; **a ~ restaurant** ein Restaurant direkt am Hafen or am Wasser; **they live on the Mississippi ~** sie wohnen direkt am Mississippi

Watergate [ˈwɔːtəgeɪt] N Watergate no art, die Watergate-Affäre

water: water gauge N (in tank) Wasserstandsmesser or -anzeiger m; (in rivers, lakes etc also) Pegel m; **water gun** N (esp US) = **water pistol**; **water heater** N Heißwassergerät nt; **water hole** N Wasserloch nt; **water hose** N Wasserschlauch m; **water ice** N Fruchteis nt

wateriness [ˈwɔːtərɪnɪs] N (= weakness) Wässerigkeit f, Wässrigkeit f; (of colour) Blässe f

watering [ˈwɔːtərɪŋ] N (of land, field) Bewässern nt; (of garden, lawn) Sprengen nt; (of plant) (Be-)gießen nt

watering: watering can N Gießkanne f; **watering hole** N (for animals) Wasserstelle f; (fig hum: = pub) Pinte f (inf), Kneipe f (inf); **watering place** N (= spa) Kurort m; (= seaside resort) Badeort m, Seebad nt; (for animals) Tränke f, Wasserstelle f; **watering pot** N (US) Gießkanne f

water: water jacket N Kühlmantel m, Kühlwassermantel m; **water jet** N Wasserstrahl m; **water jump** N Wassergraben m; **waterless** ADJ trocken; desert arid (spec); **a ~ planet** ein Planet m ohne Wasser; **water level** N Wasserstand m; (= measured level: of river, reservoir etc also) Pegelstand m; (= surface of water) Wasserspiegel m; **water lily** N Seerose f; **water line** N Wasserlinie f; **waterlogged** ADJ **the fields are ~** die Felder stehen unter Wasser; **the ship was completely ~** das Schiff war voll Wasser gelaufen; **to get ~** sich voll Wasser saugen; (ship) voll Wasser laufen

Waterloo [ˌwɔːtəˈluː] N **to meet one's ~** (hum) Schiffbruch erleiden; **with that woman he has finally met his ~** bei dieser Frau hat er sein Waterloo erlebt (hum)

water: water main N Haupt(wasser)leitung f; (= pipe) Hauptwasserrohr nt; **waterman** N Fährmann m; **watermark** N **a** (on wall) Wasserstandsmarke f **b** (on paper) Wasserzeichen nt; **water meadow** N (Agr) Feuchtwiese f; **watermelon** N Wassermelone f; **water meter** N Wasseruhr f; **water metering** N Berechnung f von Wasserverbrauch; **water mill** N Wassermühle f; **water nymph** N (Wasser)nixe f;

---

waterpick® N Munddusche f; **water pipe** N Wasserrohr nt; (for smoking) Wasserpfeife f; **water pistol** N Wasserpistole f; **water plant** N (Bot) Wasserpflanze f; **water pollution** N Wasserverschmutzung f; **water polo** N Wasserball m; **water power** N Wasserkraft f; **waterproof** [ADJ] (= unaffected by water) watch wasserdicht; clothes wasserundurchlässig; window (wasser)dicht; roof (wasser)dicht, wasserundurchlässig; mascara, make-up, paint wasserfest [N] **~s** (esp Brit) Regenhaut® f; **remember to put your ~s on** zieh was Wasserdichtes an [VT] wasserundurchlässig machen; material also wasserdicht machen; clothes also imprägnieren; **waterproofer** N = **waterproofing**; **waterproofing** N **a** (= process) Wasserdichtmachen nt; (of clothes) Imprägnieren nt **b** (= material) Dichtungsmittel nt; (for clothes) Imprägniermaterial nt; **water pump** N (Tech) Wasserpumpe f; **waterquake** N (Geol) Seebeben nt; **water rat** N Wasserratte f; **water rate** N (Brit) Wassergeld nt; **water-repellent** ADJ wasserabstoßend; **water-resistant** ADJ tent wasserdicht **b** (= unaffected by water) wasserbeständig; sunscreen wasserfest; **to be ~ to 50 m** bis zu 50 m wasserdicht sein; **watershed** N (Geol) Wasserscheide f; (fig) Wendepunkt m; **the 9 o'clock ~** (Brit TV) Regelung, dass vor 9 Uhr nur jugendfreie Programme gesendet werden dürfen; **waterside** N Ufer nt; (at sea) Strand m [ATTR] plant am Wasser wachsend; house, restaurant am Wasser; **water-ski** [N] Wasserski m [VI] Wasserski laufen; **water-skiing** N Wasserskilaufen nt; **water slide** N Wasserrutsche f; **water snake** N Wasserschlange f; (in lake) Seeschlange f; **water softener** N Wasserenthärter m; **water-soluble** ADJ wasserlöslich; **water spaniel** N Wasserspaniel m; **water sports** PL Wassersport m; **water spout** N **a** (Met) Wasserhose f, Trombe f **b** (= pipe) Regenrinne f; **water supply** N Wasserversorgung f; **water table** N Grundwasserspiegel m; **water tank** N Wassertank m; **watertight** ADJ (lit) wasserdicht; (fig) agreement, argument, alibi, contract also hieb- und stichfest; **water tower** N Wasserturm m; **water vapour**, (US) **water vapor** N Wasserdampf m; **waterway** N Wasserstraße f; (= channel) Fahrrinne f; **water wheel** N (Mech) Wasserrad nt; (Agr) Wasserschöpfrad nt; **water wings** PL Schwimmflügel pl, Schwimmarme pl (inf); **waterworks** N SING or PL Wasserwerk nt; **to have trouble with one's ~** (Brit hum inf) Probleme mit der Blase haben

watery [ˈwɔːtərɪ] ADJ (= weak) soup, beer, colour etc wäss(e)rig; eye tränend; (= pale) sky, sun blass; **all the sailors went to a ~ grave** alle Seeleute fanden ihr Grab in den Wellen

watt [wɒt] N Watt nt

wattage [ˈwɒtɪdʒ] N Wattleistung f; **what ~ is that bulb?** wie viel Watt hat diese Birne?

wattle [ˈwɒtl] N **a** (= material) Flechtwerk nt; **a ~ fence** ein Zaun m aus Flechtwerk **b** (Bot) australische Akazie **c** (Orn) Kehllappen m

wave [weɪv] [N] **a** (of water, Phys, Rad, in hair, fig) Welle f; (of hatred, enthusiasm) Welle f, Woge f (liter); **who rules the ~s?** wer beherrscht die Meere?; **a ~ of strikes** eine Streikwelle; **a ~ of enthusiasm** eine Welle der Begeisterung; **during the first ~ of the attack** beim ersten Ansturm or in der ersten Angriffswelle; **the attacks/attackers came in ~s** die Angriffe/Angreifer kamen in Wellen or wellenweise; **from the 5th century onwards England was attacked by ~s of invaders** vom 5. Jahrhundert an wurde England immer wieder von Eroberungswellen heimgesucht; **to make ~s** (fig inf) Unruhe stiften; **I don't want to make ~s but ...** (fig inf) ich will ja keinen Staub aufwirbeln, aber ...
b (= movement of hand) **to give sb a ~** jdm (zu)winken; **he gave us a ~ to show that he was ready** er winkte uns zu, um zu zeigen, dass er bereit war; **with a ~ he was gone** er winkte kurz und war gegangen; **with a ~ of his hand** mit einer Handbewegung
[VT] **a** (in order to give a sign or greeting) winken

---

mit (at, to sb jdm); (= to wave about) schwenken; (gesticulating, in a dangerous manner) herumfuchteln mit; **to ~ one's hand to sb** jdm winken; **he ~d a greeting to the crowd** er winkte grüßend der Menge zu; **to ~ sb goodbye, to ~ goodbye to sb** jdm zum Abschied winken; **he ~d his hat** er schwenkte seinen Hut; **he ~d the ticket under my nose** er fuchtelte mir mit der Karte vor der Nase herum; **he ~d his stick at the children who were stealing the apples** er drohte den Kindern, die die Äpfel stahlen, mit dem Stock; **he ~d his fist at the intruders** er drohte den Eindringlingen mit der Faust
b (to indicate sb should move) **he ~d the children across the road** er winkte die Kinder über die Straße; **he ~d me over to his table** er winkte mich zu sich an den Tisch; **he ~d me over** er winkte mich zu sich herüber
c hair wellen
[VI] **a** (person) winken; **to ~ at or to sb** jdm (zu)winken; **there's daddy, ~!** da ist der Papi, wink mal!; **don't just ~ at the ball, aim to hit it** nicht nur in Richtung Ball fuchteln, du sollst ihn auch treffen!
b (flag) wehen; (branches) sich hin und her bewegen; (corn) wogen
c (hair) sich wellen

▶ **wave aside** VT sep **a** (lit) person auf die Seite or zur Seite winken **b** (fig) person, objection, suggestions etc ab- or zurückweisen; help ausschlagen, zurückweisen
▶ **wave away** VT sep abwinken (+dat)
▶ **wave down** VT sep anhalten, stoppen
▶ **wave on** VT sep **the policeman waved us on** der Polizist winkte uns weiter

wave: waveband N (Rad) Wellenband nt; **wavelength** N (Rad) Wellenlänge f; **we're not on the same ~** (fig) wir haben nicht dieselbe Wellenlänge

wavelet [ˈweɪvlɪt] N (poet) kleine Welle

wave power N Wellenkraft f

waver [ˈweɪvə] VI **a** (= quiver) (light, flame, eyes) flackern; (voice) zittern **b** (= weaken) (courage, self-assurance) wanken, ins Wanken geraten; (support) nachlassen **c** (= hesitate) schwanken (between zwischen +dat); **if he begins to ~** wenn er ins Schwanken or Wanken gerät; **he's ~ing between accepting and ...** er ist sich (dat) darüber unschlüssig, ob er annehmen soll oder ...

waverer [ˈweɪvərə] N Zauderer m, Zauderin f

wavering [ˈweɪvərɪŋ] [ADJ] **a** (= shaky) voice bebend; shadow tanzend **b** (= uncertain) loyalty unsicher; courage, determination wankend; support (= hesitating) wechselhaft; (= decreasing) nachlassend [N] (= hesitation) Schwanken nt; **there will be no ~ from the course of reform** der Reformkurs wird strikt eingehalten

wavy [ˈweɪvɪ] ADJ (+er) hair, surface wellig, gewellt; **~ line** Schlangenlinie f

wax¹ [wæks] [N] Wachs nt; (= ear wax) Ohrenschmalz m; (= sealing wax) Siegellack m [ADJ] Wachs-; **~ crayon** Wachsmalstift m [VT] car, furniture wachsen; floor bohnern; moustache wichsen; legs mit Wachs behandeln

wax² VI **a** (moon) zunehmen; **to ~ and wane** (lit) ab- und zunehmen; (fig) schwanken, kommen und gehen **b** (liter, = become) werden; **to ~ enthusiastic** in Begeisterung geraten → **lyrical**

wax: wax bean N (US) Wachsbohne f; **wax candle** N Wachskerze f; **wax doll** N Wachspuppe f

waxed [wækst] ADJ gewachst; moustache gewichst; **~ cotton** gewachster Baumwollstoff; **~ paper** Wachspapier nt; **~ jacket** Wachsjacke f

waxen [ˈwæksən] ADJ **a** (old) wächsern **b** (fig: = pale) wachsbleich, wächsern

waxing [ˈwæksɪŋ] [ADJ] moon zunehmend; enthusiasm etc also wachsend [N] Zunehmen nt, Wachsen nt

wax: wax museum N (esp US) Wachsfigurenkabinett nt; **wax paper** N Wachspapier nt; **wax-**

work N Wachsfigur f; **waxworks** N sing or pl Wachsfigurenkabinett nt

waxy ['wæksɪ] ADJ (+er) wächsern

---

way [weɪ]
☉ 8.3, 16.3

1 NOUN	3 ADVERB
2 PLURAL NOUN	

1 – NOUN

a = road Weg m; **across** or **over the way** gegenüber, vis-à-vis; (motion) rüber; **Way of the Cross** Kreuzweg m; **to fall by the way** (fig) auf der Strecke bleiben

b = route Weg m; **to ask the way** nach dem Weg fragen; **you'll learn new skills along the way** Sie werden nebenbei auch neue Fertigkeiten erlernen; **to go the wrong way** sich verlaufen; (in car) sich verfahren; **to go down the wrong way** (food, drink) in die falsche Kehle kommen; **there's no way out** (fig) es gibt keinen Ausweg; **to find a way in** hineinfinden; **the way up/down** der Weg nach oben/unten; (climbing) der Auf-/Abstieg; **the way there/back** der Hin-/Rückweg; **prices are on the way up/down** die Preise steigen/fallen; **the way forward** der Weg vorwärts or in die Zukunft

♦ **by way of** (= via) über (+acc); **by way of an answer/excuse** als Antwort/Entschuldigung; **by way of illustration** zur Illustration; **he's by way of being a painter** (inf) er ist eine Art Maler (inf)

♦ **the way to the way to the station** der Weg zum Bahnhof; **can you tell me the way to the town hall, please?** können Sie mir bitte sagen, wie ich zum Rathaus komme?

♦ **on the/one's way (to) is it on the way?** (place) liegt das auf dem Weg?; (parcel etc) ist es unterwegs?; **the shop is on the/your way** der Laden liegt auf dem/deinem Weg; **to stop on the way** unterwegs anhalten; **on the (here)** auf dem Weg (hierher); **on the way to London** auf dem Weg nach London; **you pass it on your way home** du kommst auf dem Nachhauseweg or Heimweg daran vorbei; **they're on their way now** sie sind jetzt auf dem Weg or unterwegs; **to go on one's way** sich auf den Weg machen; **there's another baby on the way** da ist wieder ein Kind unterwegs; **he's on the way to becoming an alcoholic** er ist dabei or auf dem besten Weg, Alkoholiker zu werden; **she's well on the way to being a first-rate singer** sie ist auf dem besten Weg, eine erstklassige Sängerin zu werden; **I haven't finished it yet but it's on the way** ich bin noch nicht damit fertig, aber es ist im Werden (inf)

♦ **out of the/sb's way if it is out of your way** wenn es ein Umweg für Sie ist; **it took us out of our way** es war ein Umweg für uns; **to go out of one's way to do sth** (fig) sich besonders anstrengen, um etw zu tun; **please, don't go out of your way for us** (inf) machen Sie sich (dat) bitte unsertwegen keine Umstände

♦ **under way to get under way** in Gang kommen, losgehen (inf); (Naut) Fahrt aufnehmen or machen; **to be (well) under way** im Gang/in vollem Gang sein; (Naut) in (voller) Fahrt sein; (with indication of place) unterwegs sein

♦ **the/one's way in the way in** der Eingang; **on the way in** beim Hereingehen; (in car) beim Hineinfahren; **to be on the way in** (fig inf) im Kommen sein

♦ **the/one's way out the way out** der Ausgang; **please show me the way out** bitte zeigen Sie mir, wo es hinausgeht (inf) or wie ich hinauskomme; **can you find your own way out?** finden Sie selbst hinaus?; **on the way out** beim Hinausgehen; (in car) beim Hinausfahren; **to be on the way out** (fig inf) am Verschwinden or Aussterben sein → **easy**

♦ verb + **the/one's way I know my way around the town** ich finde mich in der Stadt zurecht, ich kenne mich in der Stadt aus; **she knows her way around the system** (fig inf) sie kennt sich im System aus; **can you find your way home?** finden Sie nach Hause?; **to lose/gather**

way (Naut) Fahrt verlieren/aufnehmen; **to make one's way to somewhere** sich an einen Ort or irgendwohin bewegen or begeben; **can you make your own way to the restaurant?** kannst du allein zu dem Restaurant kommen?; **to make one's way home** nach Hause gehen; (= start) sich auf den Heimweg begeben; **to make/fight/push one's way through the crowd** sich einen Weg durch die Menge bahnen, sich durch die Menge (durch)drängen/-kämpfen/-schieben; **to make one's way in the world** seinen Weg machen, sich durchsetzen; **to go one's own way** (fig) eigene Wege gehen; **they went their separate ways** (lit, fig) ihre Wege trennten sich; **to pay one's way** für sich selbst bezahlen; (company, project, machine) sich rentieren; **can the nation pay its way?** kann das Volk or Land für sich selber aufkommen?; **to prepare the way** (fig) den Weg bereiten (for sb/sth jdm/einer Sache) → **feel, lose**

c = path Weg m; **to bar** or **block the way** den Weg ab- or versperren; **to leave the way open** (fig) die Möglichkeit offen lassen, einen Weg frei lassen (for sth für etw)

♦ **in the/sb's way to be in sb's way** jdm im Weg stehen or sein; (fig also) jdn stören; **to get in the way** in den Weg kommen; (fig) stören; **her job gets in the way of her leisure interests** ihr Beruf stört sie nur bei ihren Freizeitvergnügungen; **to put difficulties in sb's way** jdm Hindernisse in den Weg stellen; **to stand in sb's way** (lit, fig) jdm im Weg stehen or sein; **don't let me stand in your way** ich will dir nicht im Weg stehen; **he lets nothing stand in his way** er lässt sich durch nichts aufhalten or beirren; **now nothing stands in our way** jetzt steht uns (dat) nichts mehr im Weg, jetzt haben wir freie Bahn; **to stand in the way of progress** den Fortschritt aufhalten or hemmen; **to put sb in the way of sth** (inf) jdm zu etw verhelfen

♦ **out of the/sb's way get out of the/my way!** (geh) aus dem Weg!, weg da!; **to get sb out of the way** (= get rid of) jdn loswerden (inf); (= remove: lit, fig) jdn aus dem Wege räumen; **to want sb out of the way** jdn aus dem Weg haben wollen; **to get sth out of the way** (work) etw hinter sich (acc) bringen; (difficulties, problems etc) etw loswerden (inf), etw aus dem Weg räumen, etw beseitigen; **to get sth out of the way of sb** jdm etw aus dem Weg räumen; **they got the children out of the way of the firemen** sie sorgten dafür, dass die Kinder den Feuerwehrleuten nicht im Weg waren; **get those people out of the way of the trucks** sich zu, dass die Leute den Lastwagen Platz machen or aus der Bahn gehen; **to keep** or **stay out of sb's/the way** (= not get in the way) jdm nicht in den Weg kommen; (jdm) aus dem Weg bleiben; (= avoid) (jdm) aus dem Weg gehen; **keep** or **stay out of the way!** weg da!, zurück!; **keep** or **stay out of my way!** komm mir nicht mehr über den Weg!; **to keep sb/sth out of the way of sb** jdn/etw nicht in jds Nähe or Reichweite (acc) kommen lassen

♦ **to make way for sb/sth** (lit, fig) für jdn/etw Platz machen; (fig also) für jdn/etw den Platz räumen; **make way!** mach Platz!, Platz machen!, Platz da!

d = direction Richtung f; **which way are you going?** in welche Richtung or wohin gehen Sie?; **down our way** (inf) bei uns (in der Nähe), in unserer Gegend or Ecke (inf); **it's out Windsor way** es ist or liegt in Richtung Windsor; **look both ways** schau nach beiden Seiten; **to look the other way** (fig) wegschauen, wegsehen; **if the chance comes your way** wenn Sie (dazu) die Gelegenheit haben; **if a good job comes my way** wenn ein guter Job für mich auftaucht; **each way** (Racing) auf Sieg und Platz; **we'll split it three/ten ways** wir werden es dritteln/in zehn Teile (auf)teilen or durch zehn teilen; **she didn't know which way to look** (fig) sie wusste nicht, wo sie hinschauen or hinsehen sollte

♦ **this way this way, please** hier(her) or hier entlang, bitte; **look this way** schau hierher!; **"this way for the lions"** „zu den Löwen"

♦ **that way he went that way** er ging dorthin or in diese Richtung

♦ **this way and that** hierhin und dorthin

♦ **every which way** ungeordnet, durcheinander; **cars parked every which way** ungeordnet or durcheinander geparkte Autos

e = side **it's the wrong way up** es steht verkehrt herum or auf dem Kopf (inf); **"this way up"** „hier oben"; **it's the other way (a)round** es ist (genau) umgekehrt; **put it the right way up/the other way (a)round** stellen Sie es richtig (herum) hin/andersherum or anders um (inf) hin

f = distance Weg m, Strecke f; **five miles? that's quite a way!** (inf) fünf Meilen? das ist eine ganz schöne Strecke! (inf); **a little/good way away** or **off** nicht/sehr weit weg or entfernt, ein kleines/ganzes or gutes Stück weit weg or entfernt; **it's only a little way to the next stop** es ist nur ein kleines Stück bis zur nächsten Haltestelle

♦ **all the way it rained all the way there** es hat auf der ganzen Strecke geregnet; **I'm behind you all the way** (fig) ich stehe voll (und ganz) hinter Ihnen; **I haven't read it all the way through yet** ich habe es noch nicht ganz gelesen

♦ **a long way that's a long way away** bis dahin ist es weit or (time) noch lange; **a long way out of town** weit von der Stadt weg; (live also) weit draußen or außerhalb; **that's a long way back** das war schon vor einer ganzen Weile; **a long way back, in 1942, when ...** vor langer Zeit, im Jahre 1942, als ...; **he's come a long way since then** (fig) er hat sich seitdem sehr gebessert; **he'll go a long way** (fig) er wird es weit bringen; **to have a long way to go** (lit, fit) weit vom Ziel entfernt sein; (with work) bei weitem nicht fertig sein; **it should go a long way toward(s) solving the problem** das sollte or müsste bei dem Problem schon ein gutes Stück weiterhelfen; **a little goes a long way** ein kleines bisschen reicht sehr lange; **a little kindness goes a long way** ein bisschen Freundlichkeit hilft viel; **that's a long way from the truth** das ist weit von der Wahrheit entfernt; **better by a long way** bei weitem or um vieles besser; **not by a long way** bei weitem nicht

g = manner Art f, Weise f; **I'd rather do it my way** ich möchte es lieber auf meine (eigene) Art or Weise machen; **that's his way of saying thank you** das ist seine Art, sich zu bedanken; **the French way of doing it** (die Art,) wie man es in Frankreich macht; **a funny way of talking** eine komische Art zu reden; **to learn the hard way** aus dem eigenen Schaden lernen; **way of thinking** Denk(ungs)art f, Denkweise f; **to my way of thinking** meiner Meinung or Auffassung or Anschauung nach; **to go on in the same old way** wie vorher weitermachen, auf die alte Tour weitermachen (inf); **in a general way this is true** ganz allgemein ist das richtig; **what a way to talk!** so etwas sagt man nicht!; **what a way to live/die!** (= unpleasant) so möchte ich nicht leben/sterben

♦ **in a big/small way in a big way** im großen Stil; (= on a large scale) in großem Ausmaß; **in a small way** in kleinem Ausmaß, im Kleinen

♦ **one way or another/the other** so oder so; **it does not matter (to me) one way or the other** es macht (mir) so oder so nichts aus, es ist mir gleich

♦ **either way** so oder so; **either way, we're bound to lose** (so oder so,) wir verlieren auf jeden Fall or auf alle Fälle

♦ **no way! (inf) no way!** nichts drin! (inf), ausgeschlossen!, is nich (inf); **there's no way I'm going to agree/you'll persuade him** auf keinen Fall werde ich zustimmen/werden Sie ihn überreden können; **there's no way that's a Porsche** ausgeschlossen, dass das ein Porsche ist; **that's no way to speak to your mother** so spricht man nicht mit seiner Mutter

♦ **have/want it both ways** you can't have it both ways du kannst nicht beides haben, beides (zugleich) geht nicht (*inf*); **he wants it both ways** er will das eine haben und das andere nicht lassen

♦ **no two ways about it this one is better, there are no two ways about it** (*inf*) dieses hier ist besser, da gibt es gar keinen Zweifel *or* das steht fest

♦ **this way** (= *like this*) so, auf diese (Art und) Weise; **do it this way** machen Sie es so *or* auf diese (Art und) Weise; **it was this way ...** es war so *or* folgendermaßen ...; **this way he need never know** auf diese Weise muss er es nie erfahren

♦ **that way** (= *like that*) in dieser Hinsicht; **I've always had a job, I've been lucky that way** ich hatte immer einen Job, in dieser Hinsicht habe ich Glück gehabt

♦ **that's the way!** ja(, so geht das)!, ja, genau!

♦ **the way (that) ...**

[= how] wie; **the way she walks/talks** (so) wie sie geht/spricht; **I don't like the way (that) he's looking at you** ich mag nicht, wie er dich ansieht, ich mag die Art nicht, wie er dich ansieht; **do you understand the way things are developing?** verstehst du, wie sich die Dinge entwickeln?; **do you remember the way it was/ we were?** erinnerst du dich noch (daran), wie es war/wie wir damals waren?; **that's not the way we do things here** so *or* auf die Art machen wir das hier nicht; **you could tell by the way he was dressed** das merkte man schon an seiner Kleidung; **it's just the way you said it** es ist die Art, wie du es gesagt hast; **do it any way you like** machen Sie es so, wie Sie wollen; **that's the way it goes!** so ist das eben, so ist das nun mal!; **the way things are** so, wie es ist *or* wie die Dinge liegen; **the way things are going**, so, wie die Dinge sich entwickeln; **that's the way the money goes** so geht das Geld weg; **it's not what you do, it's the way (that) you do it** es kommt nicht darauf an, was man macht, sondern wie man es macht

[= exactly as] so, wie; **leave everything the way it is** lass alles so, wie es ist; **it was all the way you said it would be** es war alles so, wie du (es) gesagt hattest; **do it the way I do (it)** machen Sie es so *or* auf dieselbe Art und Weise wie ich (es mache)

♦ **the way to do sth to show sb the way to do sth** jdm zeigen, wie *or* auf welche Art und Weise etw gemacht wird; **show me the way to do it** zeig mir, wie (ich es machen soll); **that's not the right way to do it** so geht das nicht, so kann man das nicht machen; **what's the best way to do it?** wie macht man das am besten?; **there is only one way to speak to him** man kann mit ihm nur auf (die) eine Art und Weise reden

♦ **ways and means** Mittel und Wege *pl*; **Ways and Means Committee** (*US*) Steuerausschuss *m*

[h] [= means] Weg *m*; **we'll find a way** wir werden (schon) einen Weg finden; **love will find a way** die Liebe überwindet jedes Hindernis *or* alle Schwierigkeiten

[i] [= method, technique] Art *f*; **he has a way of knowing what I'm thinking** er hat eine Art zu wissen, was ich denke; **we have ways of making you talk** wir haben gewisse Mittel, um Sie zum Reden zu bringen; **there are many ways of solving the problem** es gibt viele Wege *or* Möglichkeiten, das Problem zu lösen; **ha, that's one way of solving it!** ja, so kann man das auch machen!; **the best way is to put it in the freezer for ten minutes** am besten legt man es für zehn Minuten ins Gefrierfach; **he has a way with children** er versteht es, mit Kindern umzugehen, er hat eine geschickte Art (im Umgang) mit Kindern; **he has a way with him** er hat so eine (gewisse) Art

[j] [= habit] Art *f*; **it is not/only his way to ...** es ist nicht/eben seine Art, zu ...; **to get out of/into the way of doing sth** sich (*dat*) ab-/angewöhnen, etw zu tun; **the ways of the Spaniards** die spanische Lebensweise; **the ways of Providence/God** die Wege der Vorsehung/Gottes; **the way of the world** der Lauf der Welt *or* die Dinge; **that is our way with traitors** so machen

wir das mit Verrätern; **he has his little ways** er hat so seine Eigenheiten *or* Marotten (*inf*); **as is the way with ...** wie das mit ... so ist; **way of life** Lebensstil *m*; (*of nation*) Lebensart *f*

[k] [= respect] Hinsicht *f*; **in a way** in gewisser Hinsicht *or* Weise; **in no way** in keiner Weise; **in many/some ways** in vieler/gewisser Hinsicht; **in every possible way** in jeder Hinsicht; **to be better in every possible way** in jeder Hinsicht besser sein; **in more ways than one** in mehr als nur einer Hinsicht

♦ **in the way of what have you got in the way of drink/food?** was haben Sie an Getränken *or* zu trinken/an Lebensmitteln *or* zu essen?

[l] [= desire] **to get** *or* **have one's (own) way** seinen Willen durchsetzen *or* bekommen; **our team had it all their own way in the second half** in der zweiten Halbzeit ging für unsere Mannschaft alles nach Wunsch; **have it your own way!** wie du willst!

[m] [= state] Zustand *m*; **he's in a bad way** er ist in schlechter Verfassung; **things are in a bad way** die Dinge stehen schlecht

2 – ways PLURAL NOUN

(*Naut*, = *slipway*) Helling *f*, Ablaufbahn *f*

3 – ADVERB

(*inf*) **way over/up** weit drüben/oben; **it's way too big** das ist viel zu groß

♦ **way back way back when** vor langer Zeit, als; **since way back** seit Urzeiten; **that was way back** das ist schon lange her, das war schon vor langer Zeit

♦ **way out he was way out with his guess** er hatte weit daneben- *or* vorbeigeraten, er hatte weit gefehlt *or* er lag weit daneben (*inf*) mit seiner Annahme; **his guess was way out** seine Annahme war weit gefehlt; **you're way out if you think ...** da liegst du aber schief (*inf*) *or* da hast du dich aber gewaltig geirrt, wenn du glaubst, ...

way: waybill N Frachtbrief *m*; **wayfarer** ['weɪˌfɛərə] N (*liter*) Wanderer *m*, Wanderin *f*, Wandersmann *m* (*liter*); **wayfaring** ADJ (*liter*) wandernd, reisend; **~ man** Wandervogel *m*; **waylay** *pret, ptp* **waylaid** VT (= *ambush*) überfallen; (= *stop*) abfangen; **I was waylaid by the manager** der Manager hat mich abgefangen; **way-out** ADJ (*inf*) irr(e) (*dated inf*), extrem (*dated sl*); **wayside** N (*of path, track*) Wegrand *m*; (*of road*) Straßenrand *m*; **by the ~** am Weg(es)-/Straßenrand; **to fall** *or* **go by the ~** (*fig*) auf der Strecke bleiben ADJ **café, inn** am Weg/an der Straße gelegen; **~ flowers** Blumen, die am Weg-/Straßenrand blühen; **way station** N (*US*) Zwischenstation *f*, Kleinbahnhof *m*; **way train** N (*US*) Personenzug *m*

wayward ['weɪwəd] ADJ (= *self-willed*) **child, horse, disposition** eigenwillig, eigensinnig; (= *capricious*) **fancy, request, passion** abwegig; (*liter*) **stream, breeze** unberechenbar, launisch (*liter*); **their ~ son** ihr ungeratener Sohn

waywardness ['weɪwədnɪs] N (= *stubbornness: of child, horse, disposition*) Eigenwilligkeit *f*, Eigensinn *m*; (= *capriciousness: of imagination, request, passion*) Abwegigkeit *f*; (*liter, of stream, breeze*) Unberechenbarkeit *f*, Launenhaftigkeit *f* (*liter*)

WBA N *abbr of* **World Boxing Association**

WC (*esp Brit*) *abbr of* **water closet** WC *nt*

we [wiː] PRON wir; **the royal we** der Pluralis Majestatis, der Majestätsplural; **the editorial we** der Autorenplural; (*in narrative*) das Wir des Erzählers; **how are we this morning?** (*inf*) wie geht es uns (denn) heute Morgen? (*inf*)

w/e **a** *abbr of* **weekend** **b** *abbr of* **week ending**

weak [wiːk] ADJ (+*er*) schwach; **character** labil; **tea, solution** etc dünn; **stomach** empfindlich; **he was ~ from hunger** ihm war schwach vor Hunger; **to go/feel ~ at the knees** (*after illness*) sich wackelig fühlen, wackelig *or* schwach auf den Beinen sein (*inf*); (*with fear, excitement etc*) weiche Knie haben/bekommen; **the ~er sex** das schwache Geschlecht; **he must be a bit ~ in**

the head (*inf*) er ist wohl nicht ganz bei Trost (*inf*); **her maths is ~, she is ~ at** *or* **in maths** sie ist schwach in Mathe; **the dollar is ~ against the pound** der Dollar steht schwach zum Pfund; **what are his ~ points?** wo liegen seine Schwächen?; **the ~ link (in the chain)** das schwache Glied in der Kette

[N] **the ~** *pl* (= *needy, vulnerable*) die Schwachen *pl*

weaken ['wiːkən] VT (*lit, fig*) schwächen; **influence** also, **control, suspicion** etc verringern; **argument** also entkräften; **walls, foundations** angreifen; **hold** lockern; **he ~ed his grip on my arm** hielt meinen Arm nicht mehr ganz so fest VI (*lit, fig*) schwächer werden, nachlassen; (*person*) schwach *or* weich werden; (*foundations*) nachgeben; (*defence, strength*) erlahmen; (*dollar*) nachlassen; **his grip on my arm ~ed** er hielt meinen Arm nicht mehr ganz so fest

weak-kneed ['wiːk'niːd] ADJ (*after illness*) wackelig auf den Beinen (*inf*); (*with fear, excitement*) mit weichen Knien; (*fig inf*) schwach, feige

weakling ['wiːklɪŋ] N Schwächling *m*; (*of litter etc*) Schwächste(s) *nt*

weakly ['wiːklɪ] ADJ (*dated*) schwächlich ADV schwach; **he ~ gave in to their demands** schwach wie er war, ging er gleich auf ihre Forderungen ein

weak-minded ['wiːk'maɪndɪd] ADJ **a** (= *feeble-minded*) schwachsinnig **b** (= *weak-willed*) willensschwach

weakness ['wiːknɪs] ◊ 7.2 N (*all senses*) Schwäche *f*; (= *weak point*) schwacher Punkt; **the opposition criticized the ~ of the party's manifesto** die Opposition kritisierte, wie schwach das Wahlprogramm der Partei sei; **to have a ~ for sth** für etw eine Schwäche *or* Vorliebe haben

weak-willed ['wiːk'wɪld] ADJ willensschwach

weal¹ [wiːl] N (*liter*) Wohl *nt*; **the common/public ~** das allgemeine/öffentliche Wohl, das Allgemeinwohl; **~ and woe** Wohl und Wehe *nt*

weal² N (= *welt*) Striemen *m*

wealth [welθ] N **a** Reichtum *m*; (= *private fortune*) Vermögen *nt* **b** (*fig, = abundance*) Fülle *f*

wealth-creating ['welθkrɪˈeɪtɪŋ] ADJ vermögensbildend

wealthily ['welθɪlɪ] ADV wohlhabend

wealthiness ['welθɪnɪs] N Wohlhabenheit *f*

wealth tax N Vermögenssteuer *f*

wealthy ['welθɪ] ADJ (+*er*) wohlhabend, reich; (= *having a private fortune also*) vermögend [N] **the ~** *pl* die Reichen *pl*

wean [wiːn] VT **baby** entwöhnen; **to ~ sb from** *or* **off sb/sth** jdn jdm/einer Sache entwöhnen (*geh*)

weaning ['wiːnɪŋ] N (*of baby*) Entwöhnung *f*

weapon ['wepən] N (*lit, fig*) Waffe *f*; **~s of mass destruction** Massenvernichtungswaffen *pl*

weaponry ['wepənrɪ] N Waffen *pl*

weapons-grade ['wepənzˌgreɪd] ADJ **~ plutonium/uranium** waffenfähiges Plutonium/Uran

wear [wɛə] *vb: pret* **wore**, *ptp* **worn** [N] **a** (= *use*) **I've had a lot of/I haven't had much ~ out of** *or* **from this jacket** (= *worn it often/not often*) ich habe diese Jacke viel/wenig getragen; (= *it wore well/badly*) ich habe diese Jacke lange/nur kurz getragen; **he got four years' ~ out of these trousers/that carpet** diese Hose/dieser Teppich hat vier Jahre lang gehalten; **there isn't much ~/there is still a lot of ~ left in this coat/carpet** dieser Mantel/Teppich hält nicht mehr lange/hält noch lange; **this coat will stand any amount of hard ~** dieser Mantel ist sehr strapazierfähig; **for casual/evening/everyday ~** für die Freizeit/den Abend/jeden Tag

b (= *clothing*) Kleidung *f*

c (= *damage through use*) Abnutzung *f*, Verschleiß *m*; **~ and tear** Abnutzung *f*, Verschleiß *m*; **fair ~ and tear** normale Abnutzungs- *or* Verschleißerscheinungen; **to show signs of ~** (*lit*) anfangen, alt auszusehen; (*fig*) angegriffen aussehen; **to look the worse for ~** (*lit*) (*curtains, car-*

pets etc) verschlissen aussehen; (*shoes, clothes*) abgetragen aussehen; (*furniture etc*) abgenutzt aussehen; (*fig*) verbraucht aussehen; **I felt a bit the worse for ~** (*inf*) ich fühlte mich etwas angeknackst (*inf*) *or* angegriffen

VT **a** *clothing, jewellery, spectacles, beard etc* tragen; **what shall I ~?** was soll ich anziehen?; **I haven't a thing to ~!** ich habe nichts zum Anziehen *or* nichts anzuziehen; **I haven't worn that for ages** das habe ich schon seit Ewigkeiten nicht mehr angezogen *or* angehabt (*inf*) *or* getragen; **to ~ white/rags** *etc* Weiß/Lumpen *etc* tragen, in Weiß/Lumpen *etc* gehen; **he wore an air of triumph** er trug eine triumphierende Miene zur Schau; **he wore a big smile** er strahlte über das ganze Gesicht

b (= *reduce to a worn condition*) abnutzen; *clothes* abtragen; *sleeve, knee etc* durchwetzen; *velvet etc* blank wetzen; *leather articles* abwetzen; *steps* austreten; *tyres* abfahren; *engine* kaputtmachen; **to ~ holes in sth** etw durchwetzen; *in shoes* etw durchlaufen; **the carpet has been worn threadbare** der Teppich ist abgewetzt *or* ganz abgelaufen; **to ~ smooth** (*by handling*) abgreifen; (*by walking*) austreten; *pattern* angreifen; *sharp edges* glatt machen; **centuries of storms had worn the inscription smooth** die Inschrift war durch die Stürme im Laufe der Jahrhunderte verwittert; **the sea had worn the rocks smooth** die See hatte die Felsen glatt gewaschen; **you'll ~ a track in the carpet** (*hum*) du machst noch mal eine richtige Bahn *or* einen Trampelpfad (*inf*) in den Teppich → *also* **worn**

c (*Brit inf* = *accept, tolerate*) schlucken (*inf*)

VI **a** (= *last*) halten; **she has worn well** (*inf*) sie hat sich gut gehalten (*inf*); **the theory has worn well** die Theorie hat sich bewährt

b (= *become worn*) kaputtgehen; (*engine, material*) sich abnutzen; **to ~ smooth** (*by water*) glatt gewaschen sein; (*by weather*) verwittern; (*pattern*) abgegriffen sein; **the sharp edges will ~ smooth in time/with use** die scharfen Kanten werden sich mit der Zeit/im Gebrauch abschleifen (*inf*); **my patience is ~ing thin** meine Geduld ist langsam erschöpft *or* geht langsam zu Ende; **that excuse/joke is ~ing thin** diese Ausrede/dieser Witz ist (doch) schon etwas alt

c (= *proceed gradually*) **the party** *etc* **is ~ing to a close** die Party *etc* geht dem Ende zu

▶ **wear away** **VT** *sep* (= *erode*) *steps* austreten; *rock* abschleifen, abtragen; (*from underneath*) aushöhlen; *pattern, inscription* tilgen (*geh*), verwischen; (*fig*) *determination* untergraben; *sb's patience* zehren an (+*dat*) **VI** (= *disappear*) (*rocks, rough edges etc*) sich abschleifen; (*inscription*) verwittern; (*pattern*) verwischen; (*fig: patience, determination*) schwinden

▶ **wear down** **VT** *sep* **a** (= *reduce by friction*) abnutzen; *heel* ablaufen, abtreten; *tyre tread* abfahren; *lipstick* verbrauchen; *pencil* verschreiben **b** (*fig*) *opposition, strength etc* zermürben; *person* (= *make more amenable*) mürbe *or* weich machen (*inf*); (= *tire out, depress*) fix und fertig machen (*inf*) **VI** sich abnutzen; (*heels*) sich ablaufen *or* abtreten; (*tyre tread*) sich abfahren; (*lipstick etc*) sich verbrauchen; (*pencil*) sich verschreiben

▶ **wear off** **VI** **a** (= *diminish*) nachlassen, sich verlieren; **don't worry, it'll wear off!** keine Sorge, das gibt sich → **novelty** **b** (= *disappear*) (*paint*) abgehen; (*plating, gilt*) sich abwetzen

▶ **wear on** **VI** sich hinziehen, sich (da)hinschleppen; (*year*) voranschreiten; **as the evening/year** *etc* **wore on** im Laufe des Abends/Jahres *etc*

▶ **wear out** **VT** *sep* **a** (*lit*) kaputtmachen; *carpet* abtreten; *clothes, shoes* kaputtragen; *record, machinery* abnutzen **b** (*fig*: = *exhaust*) (*physically*) erschöpfen, erledigen (*inf*); (*mentally*) fertig machen (*inf*); **to be worn out** erschöpft *or* erledigt sein; (*mentally*) am Ende sein (*inf*); **to ~ oneself out** sich überanstrengen, sich kaputtmachen (*inf*) **VI** kaputtgehen; (*clothes, curtains, carpets*) verschleißen; **his patience has worn out/is rapidly wearing out** seine Geduld ist erschöpft *or* am Ende/erschöpft sich zusehends

▶ **wear through** **VT** *sep* durchwetzen; *elbows, trousers also* durchscheuern; *soles of shoes* durchlaufen **VI** sich durchwetzen; (*elbows, trousers also*) sich durchscheuern; (*soles of shoes*) sich durchlaufen; **his sweater has worn through at the elbows** sein Pullover ist an den Ellenbogen durchgewetzt

wearable ['wɛərəbl] **ADJ** (= *not worn out etc*) tragbar; **fashionable clothes which are also very ~** modische Kleidung, die sich auch gut trägt

wearer ['wɛərə] **N** Träger(in) *m(f)*; **~ of spectacles, spectacle ~** Brillenträger(in) *m(f)*

wearily ['wɪərɪlɪ] **ADV** *say* müde; *smile, gaze, nod, sigh* matt

weariness ['wɪərɪnɪs] **N** (*physical*) Müdigkeit *f*; (*mental*) Lustlosigkeit *f*; (*of smile, gaze*) Mattheit *f*; **he felt a great ~ of life** er empfand großen Lebensüberdruss *or* große Lebensmüdigkeit

wearing ['wɛərɪŋ] **ADJ** **a** **~ apparel** (*form*) (Be-)kleidung *f* **b** (= *exhausting*) anstrengend; (= *boring*) ermüdend

wearisome ['wɪərɪsəm] **ADJ** ermüdend; *climb etc* beschwerlich; (= *bothersome*) *questions* lästig; (= *tedious*) *discussion* langweilig

weary ['wɪərɪ] **ADJ** (*+er*) **a** (= *tired, dispirited*) müde; (= *fed up*) lustlos; *smile, groan* matt; **to feel** *or* **be ~** müde sein; **to be/grow ~ of sth** einer Sache leid sein/werden, einer Sache (*gen*) überdrüssig *or* müde sein/werden (*geh*) **b** (= *tiring*) *wait, routine etc* ermüdend; **for three ~ hours** drei endlose Stunden (lang); **five ~ miles** fünf lange *or* beschwerliche Meilen **VT** ermüden **VI** **to ~ of sth** einer Sache (*gen*) müde *or* überdrüssig werden (*geh*); **she wearied of being alone** sie wurde es leid *or* müde (*geh*) *or* überdrüssig (*geh*), allein zu sein

weasel ['wi:zl] **N** **a** Wiesel *nt* **b** (*inf*, = *person*) Heimtücker *m* **VI** (*esp US, inf*, = *be evasive*) schwafeln (*inf*)

▶ **weasel out** **VI** (= *wriggle out*) sich rauslavieren (*inf*) (*of* aus)

weaselly ['wi:zəlɪ] **ADJ** (*inf*) *appearance, face* fuchsartig; (= *shifty*) *character* aalglatt

weasel words **PL** (*inf*) Ausweichmanöver *pl*

weather ['wɛðə] **N** Wetter *nt*; (*in weather reports*) Wetterlage *f*; (= *climate*) Witterung *f*; **in cold/wet/this ~** bei kaltem/nassem/diesem Wetter; **what's the ~ like?** wie ist das Wetter?; **lovely ~ for ducks!** bei dem Wetter schwimmt man ja fast weg!; **in all ~s** bei jedem Wetter, bei jeder Witterung (*geh*); **to be** *or* **feel under the ~** (*inf*) angeschlagen sein (*inf*); **to make heavy ~ of sth** (*Brit inf*) sich mit etw fürchterlich anstellen (*inf*); **to keep a ~ eye open** (*inf*) Ausschau halten (*for* nach)

VT **a** (*storms, winds etc*) angreifen; *skin* gerben; **the rock had been ~ed** der Fels war verwittert **b** (= *expose to weather*) *wood* ablagern **c** (= *survive*: *also* **weather out**) *crisis, awkward situation* überstehen; **to ~ (out) the storm** (*lit, fig*) den Sturm überstehen **VI** (*rock etc*) verwittern; (*paint etc*) verblassen; (= *resist exposure to weather*) wetterfest sein; (= *become seasoned*: *wood*) ablagern

weather: weather balloon **N** (*Met*) Wetterballon *m*, Versuchsballon *m*; **weather-beaten** **ADJ** *face* vom Wetter gegerbt; *house, wood, stone* verwittert; *skin* wettergegerbt; **weatherboarding** *f*, **weatherboards** **PL** Schindeln *pl*; **weather-bound** **ADJ** *boat* aufgrund *or* auf Grund der schlechten Wetterverhältnisse manövrierunfähig; **weather bureau** **N** Wetteramt *nt*; **weathercaster** **N** (*US Rad, TV*) Wetteransager(in) *m(f)*; **weather chart** **N** Wetterkarte *f*; **weathercock** **N** Wetterhahn *m*; **weather conditions** **PL** Wetterverhältnisse *pl*, Witterungsverhältnisse *pl*

weathered ['wɛðəd] **ADJ** verwittert; *skin* wettergegerbt

weather: weather eye **N** **to keep a ~ on sth** (*fig*) etw scharf im Auge behalten; **to keep one's ~ open** (*fig*) gut aufpassen; **weather forecast** **N** Wettervorhersage *f*; **weather girl**

N Wetterfrau *f* (*inf*), Wetterfee *f* (*inf*); **weatherglass** **N** Wetterglas *nt*, Barometer *nt*

weathering ['wɛðərɪŋ] **N** (*Geol*) Verwitterung *f*

weather: weatherman **N** Wettermann *m* (*inf*); **weather map** **N** Wetterkarte *f*; **weather outlook** **N** Wetteraussichten *pl*; **weatherproof** **ADJ** wetterfest **VT** wetterfest machen; **weather report** **N** Wetterbericht *m*; **weather service** **N** Wetterdienst *m*; **weather ship** **N** Wetterschiff *nt*; **weather station** **N** Wetterwarte *f*; **weathertight** **ADJ** wetterfest; **weather vane** **N** Wetterfahne *f*; **weatherwise** **ADV** wettermäßig

weave [wi:v] **vb**: *pret* **wove**, *ptp* **woven** **N** (= *patterns of threads*) Webart *f*; (= *loosely/tightly etc woven fabric*) Gewebe *nt*; **material in a loose ~** Stoff *m* in einer lockeren Webart; **you need a tighter ~ for a skirt** für einen Rock braucht man ein festeres Gewebe

VT **a** *thread, cloth etc* weben (*into* zu); *cane, flowers, garland* flechten (*into* zu); *web* spinnen; **he wove the threads together** er verwob die Fäden miteinander

b (*fig*) *plot, story* ersinnen, erfinden; (= *add into story etc*) *details, episode* einflechten (*into* in +*acc*); **he wove a romantic tale (a)round his experiences abroad** er spann seine Erlebnisse im Ausland zu einer romantischen Geschichte aus

c *pret also* **weaved** (= *wind*) **to ~ one's way through the traffic/to the front** sich durch den Verkehr fädeln *or* schlängeln/nach vorne (durch)schlängeln; **the drunk ~d his way down the street** der Betrunkene torkelte die Straße hinunter

VI **a** (*lit*) weben

b *pret also* **weaved** (= *twist and turn*) sich schlängeln; (*drunk*) torkeln

c (*inf*) **to get weaving** sich ranhalten (*inf*); **to get weaving with sth** sich hinter etw (*acc*) klemmen (*inf*)

weaver ['wi:və] **N** Weber(in) *m(f)*

weaverbird ['wi:vɜ:d] **N** Webervogel *m*

weaving ['wi:vɪŋ] **N** Weberei *f*; (*as craft*) Webkunst *f*

web [web] **N** **a** (*lit, fig*) Netz *nt*; (*of lies*) Gewebe *nt*, Netz *nt*; **a ~ of snow-covered branches** ein Geflecht *nt* von schneebedeckten Ästen; **a ~ of little streets** ein Gewirr *nt* von kleinen Gassen **b** (*of duck etc*) Schwimmhaut *f* **c** (*Comput*) **the Web** das (World Wide) Web

webbed [webd] **ADJ** **a** *animal* mit Schwimmfüßen; **~ feet** Schwimmfüße *pl* **b** *seats* gurtbespannt

webbing ['webɪŋ] **N** Gurte *pl*; (= *material*) Gurtband *nt*

web: web browser **N** (*Comput*) Browser *m*; **webcam** **N** Webcam *f*; **web-footed** **ADJ** schwimmfüßig, mit Schwimmfüßen; **webmaster** **N** (*Comput*) Webmaster(in) *m(f)*; **web-offset** **N** Rollenrotations-Offsetdruck *m*; **web page** **N** (*Comput*) Web-Seite *f*, Homepage *f*; **website** **N** (*Comput*) Web-Site *f*; **webspace** **N** (*Comput*) Webspace *m*; **web-toed** **ADJ** webfooted; **webzine** **N** (*Comput*) Onlinemagazin *nt*, Internetmagazin *nt*

Wed *abbr of* **Wednesday** Mittw.

wed [wed] (*old*) *pret, ptp* **wed** *or* **wedded** **VI** sich vermählen (*form*), heiraten **VT** **a** (*bride, bridegroom*) ehelichen (*form*), sich vermählen mit (*form*); (*priest*) vermählen (*form*), trauen **b** (*fig*: = *combine*) paaren; **his ability ~ded to her money should make the business a success** mit seinen Fähigkeiten und ihrem Geld müsste das Geschäft eigentlich ein Erfolg werden **c** (*fig*) **to be ~ded to sth** (= *devoted*) mit etw verheiratet sein; **he's ~ded to the view that ...** er ist felsenfest der Ansicht, dass ...

we'd [wi:d] *contr of* **we would** *or* **we had**

wedded ['wedɪd] **ADJ** Ehe-; **~ bliss** Eheglück *nt*; **~ life** Eheleben *nt* → **lawful**

wedding ['wedɪŋ] **N** **a** (= *ceremony*) Trauung *f*; (= *ceremony and festivities*) Hochzeit *f*, Vermählung *f* (*form*); (= *silver, golden wedding etc*) Hochzeit f; **to have a registry office** (Brit)/**church ~** sich standesamtlich/kirchlich trauen lassen, standesamtlich/kirchlich heiraten; **when's the ~?** wann ist die Hochzeit?, wann wird geheiratet?; **to have a quiet ~** in aller Stille heiraten; **to go to a ~** zu einer or auf eine Hochzeit gehen **b** (fig) Verbindung f

wedding in cpds Hochzeits-; **wedding anniversary** N Hochzeitstag m; **wedding band** N Ehering m; **wedding breakfast** N Hochzeitsessen nt; **wedding cake** N Hochzeitskuchen m; **wedding card** N Hochzeitskarte f; **wedding day** N Hochzeitstag m; **wedding dress** N Brautkleid nt, Hochzeitskleid nt; **wedding guest** N Hochzeitsgast m; **wedding march** N Hochzeitsmarsch m; **wedding night** N Hochzeitsnacht f; **wedding present** N Hochzeitsgeschenk nt; **wedding reception** N Hochzeitsempfang m; **wedding ring** N Trauring m, Ehering m; **wedding vows** PL Ehegelübde nt, Eheversprechen nt

wedge [wedʒ] N **a** (of wood etc, fig) Keil m; **rubber ~** Gummibolzen m; **it's the thin end of the ~** so fängts immer an; **that would be the thin end of the ~** das wäre der Anfang von Ende; **she is driving a ~ between us** sie treibt einen Keil zwischen uns

b (= triangular shape) (of cake etc) Stück nt; (of cheese) Ecke f; **a ~ of land** ein keilförmiges Stück Land; **the seats were arranged in a ~** die Sitzreihen waren keilförmig angeordnet

c (= shoe) Schuh m mit Keilabsatz; (also **wedge heel**) Keilabsatz m VT **a** (= fix with a wedge) verkeilen, (mit einem Keil) festklemmen; **to ~ a door/window open/shut** eine Tür/ein Fenster festklemmen or verkeilen

b (fig: = pack tightly) **to ~ oneself/sth** sich/etw zwängen (in in +acc); **to be ~d between two things/people** zwischen zwei Dingen/Personen eingekeilt or eingezwängt sein; **the fat man sat ~d in his chair** der dicke Mann saß in seinen Stuhl gezwängt; **we were all ~d together in the back of the car** wir saßen alle zusammengepfercht or eingezwängt im Fond des Wagens; **try wedging the cracks with newspaper** versuchen Sie, die Spalten mit Zeitungspapier zuzustopfen

▸ **wedge in** VT sep (lit) post festkeilen; **to be wedged in** (car, house, person etc) eingekeilt or eingezwängt sein; **if you park there, you'll wedge me/my car in** wenn du da parkst, keilst du mich ein/wird mein Auto eingekeilt; **he wedged himself in between them** er zwängte sich zwischen sie

wedge-shaped [ˈwedʒʃeɪpt] ADJ keilförmig

wedgie [ˈwedʒɪ] N (US inf) Schuh m mit Keilabsatz

Wedgwood® [ˈwedʒwʊd] N Wedgwood nt; **~ blue** wedgwoodblau

wedlock [ˈwedlɒk] N (form) Ehe f; **to be born out of/in ~** unehelich/ehelich geboren sein

Wednesday [ˈwenzdɪ] N Mittwoch m → also **Tuesday**

Weds abbr of **Wednesday** Mittw.

wee¹ [wiː] ADJ (+er) (inf) winzig; (Scot) klein; **a ~ bit** ein kleines bisschen; **the ~ (small) hours** (Brit) die frühen Morgenstunden

wee² (Brit inf) N **to have** or **do/need a ~** Pipi machen/machen müssen (inf) VI Pipi machen (inf)

weed [wiːd] N **a** Unkraut nt no pl **b** (dated inf, = tobacco) Kraut nt (inf) **c** (inf: = marijuana) Gras(s) nt (inf) **d** (inf: = person) Schwächling m, Kümmerling m (inf) VT **a** (lit) jäten **b** (fig) = **weed out** VI jäten

▸ **weed out** VT sep **a** plant ausreißen; flowerbed Unkraut nt jäten in (+dat) **b** (fig) aussondern

▸ **weed through** VT sep durchsortieren

weeding [ˈwiːdɪŋ] N Unkrautjäten nt; **to do some ~** Unkraut nt jäten

weedkiller [ˈwiːdkɪlə] N Unkrautvernichter m, Unkrautbekämpfungsmittel nt

weeds [wiːdz] PL (= mourning clothes) Trauerkleider pl

weedy [ˈwiːdɪ] ADJ (+er) **a** ground unkrautbewachsen, voll(er) Unkraut **b** (inf) person (in appearance) schmächtig; (in character) blutarm

week [wiːk] N Woche f; **it'll be ready in a ~** in einer Woche or in acht Tagen ist es fertig; **my husband works away during the ~** mein Mann arbeitet die Woche über auswärts; **~ in, ~ out** Woche für Woche; **twice/£15 a ~** zweimal/£ 15 in der Woche or pro Woche or die Woche (inf); **a ~ today, today** or **this day ~** (Brit dial) heute in einer Woche or in acht Tagen; **a ~ tomorrow** or **on Tuesday, tomorrow/Tuesday ~** (esp Brit) morgen/Dienstag in einer Woche or in acht Tagen; **a ~ (ago) last Monday** letzten Montag vor einer Woche; **for ~s** wochenlang; **a ~'s/a two-week holiday** (Brit) or **vacation** (US) ein einwöchiger/zweiwöchiger Urlaub; **he works a 40-hour ~** er hat eine Vierzigstundenwoche or 40-Stundenwoche; **two ~s' holiday** (Brit) or **vacation** (US) zwei Wochen Ferien; **that is a ~'s work** das ist eine Woche Arbeit; **to knock sb into the middle of next ~** (inf) jdn windelweich schlagen (inf)

week: **weekday** N Wochentag m ATTR morning, afternoon eines Werktages; routine an Werktagen or Wochentagen; **weekend** N Wochenende nt; **to go/be away for the ~** übers or am Wochenende verreisen/nicht da sein; **at** (Brit) or **on** (esp US) **the ~** am Wochenende; **to take a long ~** ein langes Wochenende machen **~end-** Wochenend-; **~ trip** Wochenendreise f; **~ bag** Reisetasche f VI **he ~s in the country** er verbringt seine Wochenenden auf dem Land; **weekender** [ˌwiːkˈendə] N (= person) Wochenendler(in) m(f)

weekly [ˈwiːklɪ] ADJ Wochen-; wage, salary, income also, meeting wöchentlich; visit allwöchentlich; **~ newspaper** Wochenzeitung f **the ~ shopping expedition** der (all)wöchentliche Großeinkauf ADV wöchentlich; **twice/three times ~** zwei/drei Mal die Woche; **he is paid ~** er wird wöchentlich or pro Woche bezahlt N Wochenzeitschrift f

weeknight [ˈwiːknaɪt] N Abend nt unter der Woche; **she's not allowed out on ~s** sie darf unter der Woche abends nicht weg

weenie [ˈwiːnɪ] N (US, inf) (Wiener) Würstchen nt

weeny [ˈwiːnɪ] ADJ (+er) (inf) klitzeklein (inf), winzig

weeny-bopper [ˈwiːnɪˌbɒpə] N popbesessenes Kind, Pipimädchen nt (pej inf)

weep [wiːp] vb: pret, ptp **wept** VI **a** (person) weinen (over über +acc); **to ~ for sb/sth** (because sb/sth is missed) um jdn/etw weinen; (out of sympathy) für jdn/etw weinen; **the child was ~ing for his mother** das Kind weinte nach seiner Mutter; **to ~ with** or **for joy/with rage** vor or aus Freude/Wut weinen; **I wept to hear the news** mir kamen die Tränen, als ich die Nachricht hörte **b** (wound, cut etc) tränen, nässen VT tears weinen N **to have a good/little ~** tüchtig/ein bisschen weinen

weepie N (inf) = **weepy** N

weeping [ˈwiːpɪŋ] N Weinen nt ADJ weinend; wound nässend

weeping willow N Trauerweide f

weepy [ˈwiːpɪ] (inf) ADJ (+er) person weinerlich; (inf) film rührselig; **that was a very ~ film** (inf) der Film hat schwer auf die Tränendrüsen gedrückt (inf) N (inf: = film etc) Schmachtfetzen m (inf)

weevil [ˈwiːvl] N Rüsselkäfer m

wee-wee [ˈwiːwiː] N, VI (baby-talk) = **wee²**

weft [weft] N Einschlagfaden m, Schussfaden m

weigh [weɪ] VT **a** (lit) goods, person, oneself etc wiegen; **could you ~ these bananas/this piece of cheese for me?** könnten Sie mir diese Bananen/dieses Stück Käse abwiegen or auswiegen?

b (fig) words, problem, merits etc abwägen; **to ~**

sth in one's mind etw erwägen; **to ~ A against B** A gegen B abwägen, A und B gegeneinander abwägen

c (Naut) **to ~ anchor** den Anker lichten VI **a** (lit) wiegen; **to ~ heavy/light** (scales) zu viel/zu wenig anzeigen; (inf: material) schwer/leicht wiegen

b (fig: = be a burden) lasten (on auf +dat)

c (fig: = be important) gelten; **to ~ with sb** Gewicht bei jdm haben, jdm etwas gelten; **his age ~ed against him** sein Alter wurde gegen ihn in die Waagschale geworfen

▸ **weigh down** VT sep **a** (= bear down with weight) niederbeugen; **the heavy snow weighed the branches down** die schwere Schneelast drückte or bog die Zweige nieder; **a branch weighed down with fruit** ein Ast, der sich unter der Last des Obstes biegt; **she was weighed down with packages** sie war mit Paketen überladen; **she was weighed down with a heavy suitcase** der schwere Koffer zog sie fast zu Boden **b** (fig) niederdrücken; **to be weighed down with** or **by worry** von Sorgen niedergedrückt werden, mit Sorgen beladen sein

▸ **weigh in** VI **a** (Sport) sich (vor dem Kampf/Rennen) wiegen lassen; **he weighed in at 70 kilos** er brachte 70 Kilo auf die Waage **b** (at airport) das Gepäck (ab)wiegen lassen **c** (fig inf) (= join in) zu Hilfe kommen (with mit); (= interfere) sich einschalten VT sep luggage wiegen lassen

▸ **weigh out** VT sep abwiegen

▸ **weigh up** VT sep abwägen; person einschätzen

weigh: **weighbridge** N Brückenwaage f; **weigh-in** N (Sport) Wiegen nt

weighing machine [ˈweɪŋməˈʃiːn] N (for people) Personenwaage f; (coin-operated) Münzwaage f, Wiegeautomat m; (for goods) Waage f

weighing scales PL Waage f

weight [weɪt] N **a** (= heaviness, also Phys) Gewicht nt; (Sport, esp Boxing) Gewichtsklasse f, Gewicht nt (inf); (of cloth) Schwere f; (of blow) Wucht f, Heftigkeit f; **3 kilos in ~** 3 Kilo Gewicht, ein Gewicht von 3 Kilo; **the grocer gave me short ~** der Kaufmann hat (mir) schlecht or knapp gewogen; **a suit in a heavier ~ for winter** ein Anzug in einer schwereren Qualität für den Winter; **a blow without much ~ behind it** ein Schlag mit wenig or ohne viel Wucht or Kraft dahinter; **to feel/test the ~ of sth** sehen/probieren, wie schwer etw ist; **the branches broke under the ~ of the snow** die Zweige brachen unter der Schneelast; **to gain** or **put on ~** zunehmen; **to lose ~** abnehmen; **he carries his ~ well** man sieht ihm sein Gewicht nicht an; **I hope the chair takes my ~** ich hoffe, der Stuhl hält mein Gewicht aus; **he's/it's worth his/its ~ in gold** er/das ist Gold(es) wert

b (= metal weight, unit of weight, heavy object) Gewicht nt; **~s and measures** Maße und Gewichte (+pl vb); **to lift ~s** Gewichte heben; **will he manage to lift the 90kg ~?** wird er die 90 Kilo heben können?; **the doctor warned him not to lift heavy ~s** der Arzt warnte ihn davor, schwere Lasten zu heben; **she's quite a ~** sie ist ganz schön schwer

c (fig: = load, burden) Last f; **the ~ of evidence** die Beweislast; **they won by ~ of numbers** sie gewannen durch die zahlenmäßige Überlegenheit; **that's a ~ off my mind** mir fällt ein Stein vom Herzen

d (fig: = importance) Bedeutung f, Gewicht nt; **he/his opinion carries no ~** seine Stimme/Meinung hat kein Gewicht or fällt nicht ins Gewicht; **those arguments carry ~ with the minister/carry great ~** diesen Argumenten misst der Minister Gewicht bei/wird großes Gewicht beigemessen; **to give due ~ to an argument** einem Argument das entsprechende Gewicht geben or beimessen; **to add ~ to sth** einer Sache (dat) zusätzliches Gewicht geben or verleihen; **to pull one's ~** seinen Teil dazutun, seinen Beitrag leisten; **to put** or **throw one's full ~ behind sb/sth** sich mit seinem ganzen Gewicht or mit dem ganzen Gewicht seiner Persönlichkeit für jdn/etw einsetzen; **to throw** or **chuck** (inf) **one's ~ about** (Brit) or **around** seinen Einfluss geltend machen

VT **a** (= make heavier, put weights on) beschweren

b (fig: = bias) results verfälschen; **to ~ sth in favour** (Brit) or **favor** (US) **of/against sb** etw zu jds Gunsten/gegen jdn beeinflussen; **to ~ sth in favour** (Brit) or **favor** (US) **of/against sth** etw zugunsten or zu Gunsten einer Sache/gegen etw beeinflussen; **to be ~ed in favour** (Brit) or **favor** (US) **of sb/sth** so angelegt sein, dass es zugunsten or zu Gunsten einer Person/Sache ist; **to be ~ed against sb/sth** jdn/etw benachteiligen

▶**weight down** VT sep person (with parcels etc) überladen; corpse beschweren; (fig) belasten, niederdrücken

weighted [ˈweɪtɪd] ADJ (Econ) gewogen, gewichtet

weighted average N gewogener Durchschnitt

weightily [ˈweɪtɪlɪ] ADV gewichtig

weightiness [ˈweɪtɪnɪs] N (lit) Gewicht nt; (fig) Gewichtigkeit f; (of responsibility) Schwere f

weighting [ˈweɪtɪŋ] N (Brit: = supplement) Zulage f

weight: weightless ADJ schwerelos; **weightlessness** N Schwerelosigkeit f; **weightlifter** N Gewichtheber(in) m(f); **weightlifting** N Gewichtheben nt; **weight loss** N Gewichtsverlust m; **weight-train** [ˈweɪttreɪn] VI Krafttraining machen; **weight training** N Krafttraining nt; **weight watcher** N Figurbewusste(r) mf

weighty [ˈweɪtɪ] ADJ (+er) **a** (lit) schwer **b** (fig) gewichtig; (= influential) argument schwerwiegend, gewichtig; (= burdensome) responsibility schwerwiegend, schwer

weir [wɪə] N **a** (= barrier) Wehr nt **b** (= fish trap) Fischreuse f

weird [wɪəd] ADJ (+er) (= uncanny) unheimlich; (inf: = odd) seltsam

weirdie [ˈwɪədɪ] N (inf) verrückter Typ (inf)

weirdly [ˈwɪədlɪ] ADV (= eerily) unheimlich; (inf: = oddly) behave, dress seltsam; **~ enough** seltsamerweise, merkwürdigerweise

weirdness [ˈwɪədnɪs] N (inf: = oddness) Seltsamkeit f

weirdo [ˈwɪədəʊ] N (inf) verrückter Typ (inf)

welch VI = **welsh**

welcome [ˈwelkəm] ✪ 13, 19.3 **N** Willkommen nt; **to give sb a hearty** or **warm ~** jdm einen herzlichen Empfang bereiten; **to receive a cold/warm ~** kühl/herzlich empfangen werden, einen kühlen/herzlichen Empfang bekommen; **to bid sb ~** (form) jdm ein Willkommen entbieten (geh); **what sort of a ~ will this product get from the public?** wie wird das Produkt von der Öffentlichkeit aufgenommen werden?

ADJ **a** (= received with pleasure, pleasing) willkommen; visitor gern gesehen attr, willkommen; news angenehm, willkommen; **the money is very ~ just now** das Geld kommt gerade jetzt sehr gelegen; **to make sb ~** jdn sehr freundlich aufnehmen or empfangen; **to make sb feel ~** jdm das Gefühl geben, ein willkommener or gern gesehener Gast zu sein; **you will always be ~ here** Sie sind uns (dat) jederzeit willkommen; **I didn't feel very ~ there** ich habe mich dort nicht sehr wohl gefühlt; **a ~ addition to ...** eine willkommene Bereicherung ... (gen)

b **you're ~!** nichts zu danken!, keine Ursache!, bitte sehr!, aber gerne!; (iro) von mir aus gerne!, wenns Ihnen Spaß macht!; **you're ~ to use my room** Sie können gerne mein Zimmer benutzen; **you're ~ to try** (iro) Sie können es gerne versuchen; **you're ~ to it/her!** (iro) von mir aus herzlich gerne, das/die kannst du gerne haben!

VT (lit, fig) begrüßen, willkommen heißen (geh); **to ~ sb to one's house** jdn bei sich zu Hause or in seinem Haus begrüßen or willkommen heißen (geh); **they ~d him home with**

a big party sie veranstalteten zu seiner Heimkehr ein großes Fest

INTERJ **~ home/to Scotland/on board!** herzlich willkommen!, willkommen daheim/in Schottland/an Bord!; **~ back!** willkommen zurück!

welcome-home [ˈwelkəmˈhəʊm] ADJ attr Begrüßungs-, Willkommens-; **~ party** Begrüßungs- or Willkommensparty f; **~ present** Begrüßungs- or Willkommensgeschenk nt

welcoming [ˈwelkəmɪŋ] ADJ zur Begrüßung; smile, gesture, house, room, pub einladend; **~ ceremony** Begrüßungszeremonie f; **~ speech** Begrüßungsrede f; **to be ~ to sb** (person) jdn freundlich empfangen; **a ~ cup of tea was on the table for her** eine Tasse Tee stand zu ihrer Begrüßung auf dem Tisch; **a ~ fire blazed in the hearth when he arrived** ein warmes Feuer begrüßte ihn bei seiner Ankunft; **the crowds raised a ~ cheer for him** die Menge jubelte ihm zur Begrüßung zu

welcoming committee, welcoming party N (lit, fig) Begrüßungskomitee nt

weld [weld] **VT** **a** (Tech) schweißen; **to ~ parts together** Teile zusammenschweißen or verschweißen; **to ~ sth on** etw anschweißen (to an +acc); **~ed joint** Schweißnaht f **b** (fig: also **weld together**) zusammenschmieden (into zu) **VI** schweißen **N** Schweißnaht f, Schweißstelle f

welder [ˈweldə] N (= person) Schweißer(in) m(f); (= machine) Schweißapparat m, Schweißgerät nt

welding [ˈweldɪŋ] N Schweißen nt

welding torch N Schweißbrenner m

welfare [ˈwelfeə] N **a** (= wellbeing) Wohl nt, Wohlergehen nt **b** (= welfare work) Fürsorge f, Wohlfahrt f (dated); **child ~** Kinderfürsorge f; **social ~** soziale Fürsorge **c** (US: = social security) Sozialhilfe f; **to be on ~** Sozialhilfeempfänger(in) m(f) sein

welfare: welfare benefits PL Sozialleistungen pl; **welfare case** N Sozialfall m; **welfare check** N (US) Sozialhilfeüberweisung f; **welfare officer** N Sozialarbeiter(in) m(f), Mitarbeiter(in) m(f) des Sozialamts; **welfare recipient** N (US) Sozialhilfeempfänger(in) m(f); **welfare services** PL soziale Dienstleistungen pl; **welfare state** N Wohlfahrtsstaat m; **welfare work** N Fürsorgearbeit f, Wohlfahrtsarbeit f (dated); **welfare worker** N Fürsorger(in) m(f)

well¹ [wel] **N** **a** (= water well) Brunnen m; (= oil well) Ölquelle f; (drilled) Bohrloch nt; (fig: = source) Quelle f; **to sink a ~** einen Brunnen bohren or anlegen or graben; (for oil) ein Bohrloch nt anlegen or vorantreiben

b (= shaft) Schacht m; (for lift) Schacht m; (for stairs) Treppenschacht m; (down centre of staircase) Treppenhaus nt

c (of theatre) Parkett nt; (of auditorium) ebenerdiger Teil des Zuschauer-/Konferenz-/Versammlungsraums (Brit: of court) Teil des Gerichtssaals, in dem die Rechtsanwälte und Protokollschreiber sitzen

d (= ink well) Tintenfass nt

VI quellen; **tears ~ed in her eyes** Tränen stiegen or schossen ihr in die Augen

▶**well up** VI (water, liquid) emporsteigen, emporquellen; (fig) aufsteigen; (noise) anschwellen; **tears welled up in her eyes** Tränen stiegen or schossen ihr in die Augen

well² [wel] ✪ 11.2, 13, 23.6, 26.3 comp **better**, superl **best** **ADV** **a** (= in a good or satisfactory manner) gut; **the child speaks ~** (= is well-spoken) das Kind spricht ordentlich Deutsch/Englisch etc or gutes Deutsch/Englisch etc; **it is ~ painted** (portrait) es ist gut gemalt; (house, fence) es ist sauber or ordentlich angestrichen; **he did it as ~ as he could/as I could have done** er machte es so gut er konnte/ebenso gut, wie ich es hätte machen können; **he's doing ~ at school/in history** er ist gut or er kommt gut voran in der Schule/in Geschichte; **he did ~ in the history exam** er hat in der Geschichtsprüfung gut abgeschnitten; **for an eight-year-old he did very ~**

für einen Achtjährigen hat er seine Sache sehr gut gemacht; **his business is doing ~** sein Geschäft geht gut; **mother and child are/the patient is doing ~** Mutter und Kind/dem Patienten geht es gut, Mutter und Kind sind/der Patient ist wohlauf; **he did quite ~ at improving sales** er war recht erfolgreich in der Erhöhung des Absatzes; **if you do ~ you'll be promoted** wenn Sie sich bewähren, werden Sie befördert; **you did ~ to help** du tatest gut daran zu helfen, es war gut, dass du geholfen hast; **~ done!** gut gemacht!, bravo!, sehr gut!; **~ played!** gut gespielt!; **to do oneself ~** (inf) es sich (dat) gut gehen lassen; **to do ~ by sb** (inf) jdm gegenüber or zu jdm großzügig sein; **everything went ~/quite ~** es ging alles gut or glatt (inf)/recht or ganz gut

b (= favourably, fortunately) gut; **to speak/think ~ of sb** über jdn Gutes sagen/Positives denken, von jdm positiv sprechen/denken; **to be ~ spoken of in certain circles/by one's colleagues** einen guten Ruf in gewissen Kreisen/bei seinen Kollegen haben; **to stand ~ with sb** bei jdm angesehen sein; **to be ~ in with sb** (inf) auf gutem Fuß mit jdm stehen; **to marry ~** eine gute Partie machen; **to do ~ out of sth** etw ganz schön or ordentlich profitieren, bei etw gut wegkommen (inf); **you would do ~ to arrive early** Sie täten gut daran, früh zu kommen; **you might as ~ go** du könntest eigentlich geradeso gut or ebenso gut (auch) gehen; **are you coming? – I might as ~** kommst du? – ach, könnte ich eigentlich (auch) (inf) or ach, warum nicht

c (= thoroughly, considerably, to a great degree) gut, gründlich; **shake the bottle ~** schütteln Sie die Flasche kräftig; (on medicine) Flasche kräftig or gut schütteln; **he loved her too ~ to leave her** (liter) er liebte sie zu sehr, als dass er sie verlassen hätte; **we were ~ beaten** wir sind gründlich geschlagen worden; **he could ~ afford it** er konnte es sich (dat) sehr wohl leisten; **I'm ~ content with my lot** ich bin wohl zufrieden mit meinem Schicksal; **all** or **only too ~** nur (all)zu gut; **~ and truly** (ganz) gründlich; married, settled in ganz richtig; (iro also) fest; westernized, conditioned durch und durch; **he was ~ away** (inf) er war in Fahrt or Schwung (inf); (= drunk) er hatte einen sitzen (inf); **he sat ~ forward in his seat** er saß weit vorne auf seinem Sitz; **it was ~ worth the trouble** das hat sich wohl or sehr gelohnt; **~ out of sight** weit außer Sichtweite; **~ within ...** durchaus in ... (dat); **past midnight** lange nach Mitternacht; **it continued ~ into 1996/the night** es zog sich weit ins Jahr 1996/in die Nacht hin; **he's ~ over fifty** er ist weit über fünfzig

d (= probably, reasonably) ohne weiteres, gut, wohl; **I may ~ be late** es kann leicht or wohl or ohne weiteres sein, dass ich spät komme; **it may ~ be that ...** es ist gut or wohl or ohne weiteres möglich, dass ...; **you may ~ be right** Sie mögen wohl Recht haben; **she cried, as ~ she might** sie weinte, und das (auch) mit Grund or wozu sie auch allen Grund hatte; **you may ~ ask!** (iro) das kann man wohl fragen; **I couldn't very ~ stay** ich konnte schlecht bleiben, ich konnte wohl nicht mehr gut bleiben

e (= in addition) **as ~** auch; **if he comes as ~** wenn er auch kommt; **x as ~ as y** x sowohl als auch y, x und auch y; **she sings as ~ as dances** sie singt und tanzt auch noch

f (Brit inf: = very) **~ happy** total glücklich (inf); **~ annoyed** ganz schön verärgert (inf)

ADJ **a** (= in good health) gesund; **get ~ soon!** gute Besserung; **are you ~?** geht es Ihnen gut?; **I'm very ~, thanks** danke, es geht mir sehr gut; **he's not a ~ man** er ist gar nicht gesund; **she's not been ~ lately** ihr ging es in letzter Zeit (gesundheitlich) gar nicht gut; **I don't feel at all ~** ich fühle mich gar nicht gut or wohl

b (= satisfactory, desirable, advantageous) gut; **all is not ~ with him/in the world** mit ihm/mit or in der Welt steht es nicht zum Besten; **that's all very ~, but ...** das ist ja alles schön und gut, aber ...; **if that's the case, (all) ~ and good** wenn das der Fall ist, dann soll es mir recht sein; **it's all very ~ for you to suggest ...** Sie können leicht vorschlagen ...; **it's all very ~ for you, you don't have to ...** Sie haben gut reden or Sie können leicht reden, Sie müssen ja nicht ...; **it was ~ for him that no-one found out** es war sein Glück, dass es niemand entdeckt hat; **it would be as ~ to ask first** es wäre wohl besser or gescheiter (*inf*), sich erst mal zu erkundigen; **it's just as ~ he came** es ist (nur or schon) gut, dass er gekommen ist; **you're ~ out of that** seien Sie froh, dass Sie damit nichts mehr zu tun haben; **all's ~ that ends ~** Ende gut, alles gut

INTERJ also; (*expectantly also*) na; (*doubtfully*) na ja; **~, ~!, ~ I never (did)!** also, so was!, na so was!; **~ now** also; **~, it was like this** also, es war so or folgendermaßen; **~ there you are, that proves it!** na bitte or also bitte, das beweist es doch; **~, as I was saying** also, wie (bereits) gesagt; **~ then?** also (gut); (*in question*) na?, nun?, also?; **very ~ then!** na gut, also gut!; (*indignantly*) also bitte (sehr)!; **oh ~, never mind** nichts; **~, that's a relief!** na (also), das ist ja eine Erleichterung!

N Gute(s) *nt*; **to wish sb ~** (*in general*) jdm alles Gute wünschen; (*in an attempt, also iro*) jdm Glück wünschen (*in bei*); (*= be well-disposed to*) jdm gewogen sein; **I wish him ~, but ...** ich wünsche ihm nichts Böses, aber ...

we'll [wiːl] *contr of* **we shall** *of* **we will**

well *in cpds* gut; **well-adjusted** ADJ *attr,* **well adjusted** ADJ *pred* (*Psych*) gut angepasst; **well-advised** ADJ *attr,* **well advised** ADJ *pred plan, move* klug; **to be well advised to ...** wohl or gut beraten sein zu ..., gut daran tun, zu ...; **well-aimed** ADJ *attr,* **well aimed** ADJ *pred shot, blow, sarcasm* gut gezielt, wohl gezielt; **well-appointed** ADJ *attr,* **well appointed** ADJ *pred* gut ausgestattet; **well-argued** ADJ *attr,* **well argued** ADJ *pred* wohl begründet, gut begründet; **well-assorted** ADJ *attr,* **well assorted** ADJ *pred* gut zusammenpassend; **well-attended** ADJ *attr,* **well attended** ADJ *pred* gut besucht; **well-baby clinic** N Neugeborenenklinik *f*; **well-balanced** ADJ *pred* **a** *person, mind* ausgeglichen **b** *budget, diet* (gut) ausgewogen; **well-behaved** ADJ *attr,* **well behaved** ADJ *pred child* artig, wohlerzogen; *animal* gut erzogen; **well-being** N Wohl *nt*, Wohlergehen *nt*; **to have a sense of ~** (ein Gefühl *nt* der) Behaglichkeit or Wohligkeit empfinden; **well-born** ADJ *attr,* **well born** ADJ *pred* aus vornehmer Familie, aus vornehmem Haus; **well-bred** ADJ *attr,* **well bred** ADJ *pred* **a** (*= polite*) *person* wohlerzogen; *manners* vornehm, gepflegt; *accent* distinguiert **b** (*= of good stock*) *animal* aus guter Zucht; (*iro*) *person* aus gutem Stall; **well-built** ADJ *attr,* **well built** ADJ *pred house* gut or solide gebaut; *person* stämmig, kräftig; **well-chosen** ADJ *attr,* **well chosen** ADJ *pred remarks, words* gut or glücklich gewählt; **in a few ~ words** in wenigen wohlgesetzten Worten; **well-connected** ADJ *attr,* **well connected** ADJ *pred* **to be well connected** Beziehungen zu or in höheren Kreisen haben; **well-cooked** ADJ *attr,* **well cooked** ADJ *pred* gut zubereitet; (*= well-done*) *meat* gut durchgebraten; **well-defined** [ˌweldɪˈfaɪnd] ADJ *attr,* **well defined** ADJ *pred* **a** *problem* klar umrissen; *goals* klar **b** *eyebrows, cheekbones* markant; *muscles* ausgeprägt; **well-deserved** ADJ *attr,* **well deserved** ADJ *pred* wohlverdient; **well-developed** ADJ *attr,* **well developed** ADJ *pred muscle* gut entwickelt; *sense* (gut) ausgeprägt; *system* ausgereift; *market, industry* gut entwickelt; **well-disposed** ADJ *attr,* **well disposed** ADJ *pred* **to be well disposed toward(s) sb/sth** jdm/einer Sache gewogen sein or freundlich gesonnen sein; **well-done** ADJ *attr,* **well done** ADJ *pred steak* durchgebraten, durch *inv*; **well-dressed** ADJ *attr,* **well dressed** ADJ *pred* gut angezogen or gekleidet; **well-earned** ADJ *attr,* **well earned** ADJ *pred* wohlverdient; **well-educated** ADJ *attr,* **well educated** ADJ *pred person* gebildet; *voice* (gut) ausgebildet; **well-endowed** [ˌwel-

ɪnˈdaʊd] ADJ *attr,* **well endowed** ADJ *pred* (*euph*) **to be well endowed** von Natur aus gut or reichlich ausgestattet sein; **well-equipped** ADJ *attr,* **well equipped** ADJ *pred office, studio* gut ausgestattet; *expedition, army* gut ausgerüstet; **well-established** ADJ *attr,* **well established** ADJ *pred practice, custom* fest; *pattern* also klar; *tradition* alt; *family* alteingesessen; *reputation* gut; *company, player, writer, artist* bekannt; **it's a ~ fact that ...** es ist eine bekannte Tatsache, dass ...; **well-favoured** ADJ *attr,* **well favoured** ADJ *pred* (*old*) *girl, family* ansehnlich (*old*); **well-fed** ADJ *attr,* **well fed** ADJ *pred* wohl genährt, gut genährt; **well-founded** ADJ *attr,* **well founded** ADJ *pred* wohl begründet; **the warnings proved (to be) well founded** die Warnungen erwiesen sich als begründet; **well-groomed** ADJ *attr,* **well groomed** ADJ *pred* gepflegt; **well-grown** ADJ *attr,* **well grown** ADJ *pred animal, child* groß (gewachsen)

wellhead [ˈwelhed] N **a** (*of spring etc*) Quelle *f*; (*fig*) Ursprung *m* **b** (*= head of oil well*) Bohrturm *m*

well: well-heeled ADJ *attr,* **well heeled** ADJ *pred* (*Brit inf*) betucht (*inf*); **well-hung** ADJ *attr,* **well hung** ADJ *pred meat* abgehangen; (*inf*) *man* mit imposanter Männlichkeit, gut ausgestattet; **well-informed** ADJ *attr,* **well informed** ADJ *pred* gut informiert; *sources also* wohl unterrichtet; **to be well informed about sb/sth** über jdn/etw gut informiert or gut unterrichtet sein

wellington (boot) [ˈwelɪŋtən(ˈbuːt)] N (*Brit*) Gummistiefel *m*

well: well-intentioned ADJ *attr,* **well intentioned** ADJ *pred* wohlmeinend; **well-kept** ADJ *attr,* **well kept** ADJ *pred garden, hair etc* gepflegt; *secret* streng gehütet, gut gewahrt; **well-knit** ADJ *attr,* **well knit** ADJ *pred body* drahtig, straff; (*fig*) gut durchdacht or aufgebaut; **well-known** ADJ *attr,* **well known** ADJ *pred place, singer* bekannt; *fact also* wohl bekannt, altbekannt; **it's well known that ...** es ist allgemein bekannt, dass ...; **to be well known for sth** für etw bekannt sein; **to be well known to sb** jdm bekannt sein; **well-loved** ADJ *attr,* **well loved** ADJ *pred* viel geliebt; **well-made** ADJ *attr,* **well made** ADJ *pred* **a** *piece of furniture etc* gut gearbeitet **b** *person* gut gebaut; **well-man clinic** N Männerklinik *f*; **well-mannered** ADJ *attr,* **well mannered** ADJ *pred* mit guten Manieren; **to be well mannered** gute Manieren haben; **well-matched** ADJ *attr,* **well matched** ADJ *pred teams* gleich stark; **they're a ~ pair** sie passen gut zusammen; **well-meaning** ADJ *attr,* **well meaning** ADJ *pred* wohlmeinend; **well-meant** ADJ *attr,* **well meant** ADJ *pred action, lie* gut gemeint; **well-nigh** ADV (*form*) nahezu, beinahe, nachgerade (*geh*); **this is ~ impossible** (*not form*) das ist nahezu or beinahe unmöglich; **well-off** ADJ *attr,* **well off** ADJ *pred* (*= affluent*) reich, begütert, gut d(a)ran (*inf*); **to be well off** (*= fortunate*) gut daran sein; **you don't know when you're well off** (*inf*) du weißt (ja) nicht, wenn es dir gut geht **N the ~** *pl* die Begüterten *pl*; **well-oiled** ADJ *attr,* **well oiled** ADJ *pred* (*inf: = drunk*) beduselt (*inf*); **well-padded** ADJ *attr,* **well padded** ADJ *pred* (*inf: = not thin*) gut gepolstert (*inf*); **well-paid** ADJ *attr,* **well paid** ADJ *pred* gut bezahlt; **well-preserved** ADJ *attr,* **well preserved** ADJ *pred* gut erhalten; *person also* wohl erhalten; **well-read** ADJ *attr,* **well read** ADJ *pred* belesen; **well-respected** ADJ *attr,* **well respected** ADJ *pred* hochangesehen; **well-spent** ADJ *attr,* **well spent** ADJ *pred time* gut genützt or verbracht; *money* sinnvoll or vernünftig ausgegeben or verwendet; **well-spoken** ADJ *attr,* **well spoken** ADJ *pred* mit gutem Deutsch/Englisch etc; **to be well spoken** gutes Deutsch/Englisch etc sprechen; **well-stacked** ADJ *attr,* **well stacked** ADJ *pred* (*inf*) *woman* **to be well stacked** Holz vor der Hütte haben (*inf*); **well-stocked** ADJ *attr,* **well stocked** ADJ *pred* gut bestückt; (*Comm also*) mit gutem Sortiment; *larder, shelves also* gut gefüllt, reichlich gefüllt; *library also* reichhaltig, umfangreich;

well-thought-of ADJ angesehen; **well-timed** ADJ *attr,* **well timed** ADJ *pred* (zeitlich) gut abgepasst, zeitlich günstig; **that was a ~ interruption** die Unterbrechung kam im richtigen Augenblick; **well-to-do** ADJ wohlhabend, reich; *district also* vornehm **N the ~** *pl* die Begüterten *pl*; **well-tried** ADJ *attr,* **well tried** ADJ *pred method etc* erprobt; **well-trodden** ADJ *attr,* **well trodden** ADJ *pred* (*lit*) viel begangen; **a ~ path** (*fig*) eine beliebte Methode; **well water** N Brunnenwasser *nt*; **well-wisher** N cards from **~s** Karten von Leuten, die ihm/ihr etc alles Gute wünschen; **our cause has many ~s** unsere Sache hat viele Sympathisanten; **"from a ~"** „jemand, der es gut mit Ihnen meint"; **well-woman clinic** N Frauenklinik *f*; **well-worn** ADJ *attr,* **well worn** ADJ *pred garment* abgetragen; *carpet etc* abgelaufen; *book* abgenützt, abgegriffen; *path* ausgetreten; *saying, subject etc* abgedroschen

welly [ˈwelɪ] N (*Brit inf*) Gummistiefel *m*

Welsh [welʃ] ADJ walisisch; **the ~ National Party** *walisische Partei, die sich für die Unabhängigkeit des Landes einsetzt* **N a** (*Ling*) Walisisch *nt* **b the Welsh** PL die Waliser *pl*

welsh, welch [welʃ] VI (*inf*) sich drücken (*on sth* vor etw *dat*) (*inf*); (*bookmaker etc: = avoid payment*) die Gewinne nicht ausbezahlen (*on sb* jdm); (*by disappearing*) mit dem Geld durchgehen (*inf*)

Welsh: Welsh Assembly N the ~ die walisische Versammlung; **Welsh dresser** N (*Brit*) Anrichte *f* mit Tellerbord; **Welshman** N Waliser *m*; **Welsh Nationalism** N walisischer Nationalismus; **Welsh rabbit**, **Welsh rarebit** N überbackene Käseschnitte; **Welshwoman** N Waliserin *f*

welt [welt] N **a** (*of shoe*) Rahmen *m*; (*of pullover*) Bündchen *nt* **b** (*= weal*) Striemen *m*

welted [ˈweltɪd] ADJ *shoe* randgenäht

welter [ˈweltə] N **a** Unzahl *f*; (*of blood, cheers*) Meer *nt*; (*of emotions*) Sturm *m*, Tumult *m*; (*of verbiage*) Flut *f*

welterweight [ˈweltəweɪt] N Weltergewicht *nt*

wench [wentʃ] **N** (*old*) Maid *f* (*old*); (*= serving wench*) Magd *f*; (*hum*) Frauenzimmer *nt* **VI** sich mit Mädchen herumtreiben

wend [wend] VT **to ~ one's way home/to the bar etc** sich auf den Heimweg/zur Bar etc begeben

Wendy house [ˈwendɪhaʊs] N Spielhaus *nt*

went [went] *pret of* **go**

wept [wept] *pret, ptp of* **weep**

were [wɜː] 2nd *pers sing,* 1st, 2nd, 3rd *pers pl pret of* **be**

we're [wɪə] *contr of* **we are**

weren't [wɜːnt] *contr of* **were not**

werewolf [ˈwɪəwʊlf] N Werwolf *m*

wert [wɜːt] (*old*) 2nd *pers sing pret of* **be**

Wesleyan [ˈwezlɪən] (*Eccl*) ADJ wesleyanisch **N** Wesleyaner(in) *m(f)*

west [west] **N a the ~, the West** (*also Pol*) der Westen; **in the ~** im Westen; **to the ~** nach or gen (*liter*) Westen; **to the ~ of** westlich von, im Westen von; **he comes from the ~ (of Ireland)** er kommt aus dem Westen (von Irland); **the wind is coming from the ~** der Wind kommt von West(en) or aus (dem) Westen; **the south and ~ of the square** die Südseite und die Westseite des Platzes **b** (*= western world*) **the ~** or **West** der Westen **ADJ** West-; **the ~ coast** die Westküste; **~ wind** Westwind *m*; **Salford West** Salford West **ADV a** nach Westen, westwärts; **it faces ~** es geht nach Westen; **~ of** westlich von **b to go ~** (*fig inf*) flöten gehen (*inf*); (*= to die*) vor die Hunde gehen (*inf*)

west *in cpds* West-; **West Africa** N Westafrika *nt*; **West Bank** N (*in Middle East*) Westjordanland *nt*, West Bank *f*; **West Berlin** N Westberlin *nt*; **westbound** [ˈwestbaʊnd] ADJ *traffic, carriageway* (in) Richtung Westen; **the ~ carriageway of the M4** (*Brit*) die M4 in Richtung Westen; **to be ~** nach Westen unterwegs sein,

westwärts reisen or fahren **ADV** nach Westen, (in) Richtung Westen; **West End** N the ~ (in London) der (Londoner) Westen, das Westend; **West Ender** N Bewohner(in) m(f) des Londoner Westens or des Westend

westerly ['westəlɪ] **ADJ** westlich; **~ wind** Westwind m, Wind m aus westlicher Richtung; **in a ~ direction** in westlicher Richtung **ADV** (= wind) Westwind m, West m (poet) **ADV** nach Westen

western ['westən] **ADJ** westlich; **on the Western front** an der Westfront; **Western Europe** Westeuropa nt; **the Western Sahara** die westliche Sahara **N** Western m

Western Australia N Westaustralien nt

westerner ['westənə'] **N** **a** (Pol) Abendländer(in) m(f) **b** (US) Weststaatler(in) m(f)

Western Isles pl the ~ die Hebriden pl

westernization ['westənaɪ'zeɪʃən] **N** (= westernizing) Einführung f der westlichen Kultur or Zivilisation; (= western character) westliche Zivilisation f; (pej) Verwestlichung f

westernize ['westənaɪz] **VT** die westliche Zivilisation/Kultur einführen in (+dat); (pej) verwestlichen

westernized ['westənaɪzd] **ADJ** person, culture vom Westen beeinflusst, westlich ausgerichtet; (pej) verwestlicht

westernmost ['westənməʊst] **ADJ** westlichste(r, s), am weitesten westlich (gelegen)

Western Samoa [ˌwestənsə'məʊə] **N** Westsamoa nt

west: West Europe N (esp US) Westeuropa nt; **West European** **ADJ** westeuropäisch **N** Westeuropäer(in) m(f); **West Germany** N Westdeutschland nt, Bundesrepublik f (Deutschland); **West Indian** **ADJ** westindisch **N** Westindier(in) m(f); **West Indies** PL N Westindische Inseln pl; **west-northwest** N Westnordwest no art **ADV** nach Westnordwesten; **~ of X/the lake** westnordwestlich von X/des Sees

Westphalia [west'feɪlɪə] **N** Westfalen nt

Westphalian [west'feɪlɪən] **ADJ** westfälisch **N** Westfale m, Westfälin f

west: West Side N the ~, the Upper ~ die West Side, der Westen von Manhattan; **west-southwest** N Westsüdwest no art **ADV** nach Westsüdwesten; **~ of X/the lake** westsüdwestlich von X/des Sees

westward ['westwəd] **ADJ** direction westlich; route nach Westen, (in) Richtung Westen **ADV** (also **westwards**) westwärts, nach Westen, (in) Richtung Westen

westwardly ['westwədlɪ] **ADJ, ADV** = westward

wet [wet] vb: pret, ptp **wet** or **wetted** **ADJ** (+er) **a** nass; (= paint, varnish, ink) nass or feucht sein; **to be ~ through** nass und durch nass sein, völlig durchnässt sein; **~ with tears** tränenfeucht; **her eyes were ~ with tears** sie hatte feuchte Augen, sie hatte Tränen in den Augen; **"wet paint"** (esp Brit) "Vorsicht, frisch gestrichen"; **to get one's feet ~** nasse Füße bekommen, sich (dat) nasse Füße holen (inf); **to be ~ behind the ears** (inf) noch feucht or noch nicht trocken hinter den Ohren sein (inf) **b** (= rainy) nass, feucht; climate, country feucht; **the ~ season** die Regenzeit; **in ~ weather** bei nassem Wetter, bei Regenwetter; **it's been ~ all week** es war die ganze Woche (über) regnerisch **c** (= allowing alcohol) state, city wo kein Alkoholverbot besteht, nicht prohibitionistisch **d** (Brit inf) (= weak, spiritless) weichlich, lasch; (Pol pej) gemäßigt; **don't be so ~!** sei nicht so ein Waschlappen! (inf) **e** (with urine) child, nappy nass **f** (US, inf, = wrong) **you're all ~** da liegst du völlig falsch (inf) **g** (Brit Pol) liberal-konservativ **N** **a** (= moisture) Feuchtigkeit f **b** (= rain) Nässe f; **it's out in the ~** es ist draußen im Nassen **c** (inf: = wet season) Regenzeit f **d** (US, inf, = anti-prohibitionist) Antiprohibitionist(in) m(f)

c (Brit) (inf: = person) Waschlappen m, Weichei nt (sl); (Pol pej inf) Gemäßigte(r) mf **VT** nass machen; lips, washing befeuchten; **to ~ the baby's head** (inf) den Sohn/die Tochter begießen (inf); **to ~ one's whistle** (inf) sich (dat) die Kehle anfeuchten (inf); **to ~ the bed/one's pants/oneself** das Bett/seine Hosen/sich nass machen, ins Bett/in die Hose(n) machen; **I nearly ~ myself** (inf) ich habe mir fast in die Hose gemacht (inf)

wet: wet-and-dry N Schmirgelpapier nt **VT** (nass) schmirgeln; **wet bar** N (US) Bartresen m mit Wasseranschluss; **wet blanket** N (inf) Miesmacher(in) m(f) (inf), Spielverderber(in) m(f); **wet cell** N Nasselement nt; **wet dock** N Dock nt, Flutbecken nt; **wet dream** N feuchter Traum

wether ['weðə'] **N** Hammel m, Schöps m (dial)

wet-look ['wetlʊk] **ADJ** material (hoch)glänzend; hair (vor Gel) glänzend

wetly ['wetlɪ] **ADV** **a** nass **b** (Brit, inf) weich, lasch

wetness ['wetnɪs] **N** **a** Nässe f; (of climate, paint, ink) Feuchtigkeit f **b** (Brit, inf) Weichlichkeit f

wet: wet nurse N Amme f; **wet pack** N Kulturbeutel m; (Med) feuchte Packung, feuchter Umschlag; **wet rot** N Nassfäule f; **wet suit** N Neoprenanzug m, Taucheranzug m

wetting ['wetɪŋ] **N** unfreiwillige Dusche (inf); (= falling into water) unfreiwilliges Bad; **to get a ~** klatschnass werden, eine Dusche abbekommen (inf), ein unfreiwilliges Bad nehmen; **to give sb a ~** jdm eine Dusche/ein Bad verabreichen (inf); **~ agent** Netzmittel nt

wettish ['wetɪʃ] **ADJ** feucht

we've [wiːv] contr of **we have**

whack [wæk] **N** **a** (inf: = blow) (knallender) Schlag; **to give sb a ~** jdm einen Schlag versetzen; **to give sth a ~** auf etw (acc) schlagen **b** (esp Brit inf: = attempt) Versuch m; **to have a ~ at sth/at doing sth** etw probieren or versuchen, sich an etw (dat) versuchen; **I'll have a ~ at it** ich will mich mal (d)ranwagen **c** (esp Brit, inf: = share) (An)teil m; **we're offering £50,000, top ~** wir bieten höchstens or maximal £ 50.000; **he's earning the top ~** er bekommt das Spitzengehalt **VT** **a** (inf: = hit) schlagen, hauen (inf) **b** (inf: = defeat) (haushoch) schlagen (inf: = exhaust) erschlagen (inf)

▶ **whack off** VI (sl, = masturbate) wichsen (sl), sich (dat) einen runterholen (inf)

whacked [wækt] **ADJ** (Brit inf: = exhausted) kaputt (inf)

whacking ['wækɪŋ] **ADJ** (Brit, inf) Mords- (inf); **a ~ lie** eine Mordslüge (inf); **~ great** riesengroß; **a ~ big book** (also US) ein Monstrum nt von (einem) Buch (inf); **he earns a ~ £100,000 a year** (also US) er verdient mordsmäßige £ 100.000 pro Jahr (inf) **N** **a** (= beating) Keile f (inf); **to give sb a ~** jdm Keile or eine Tracht Prügel verpassen (inf) **b** (inf: = defeat) **we got a real ~** sie haben uns richtig in die Pfanne gehauen (inf)

whacko ['wækəʊ] **INTERJ** (dated) trefflich (dated), tipp-topp, eins a (inf)

whacky **ADJ** (+er) (inf) = **wacky**

whale [weɪl] **N** **a** Wal m **b** (inf) **a ~ of** (= exceedingly great, good etc) ein(e) riesige(r, s); **a ~ of a difference** ein himmelweiter Unterschied; **a ~ of a party** eine Wahnsinnsparty (inf); **to have a ~ of a time** sich prima amüsieren

whale: whalebone N Fischbein nt; **whale fishing** N Wal(fisch)fang m; **whale oil** N Walöl nt, Tran m

whaler ['weɪlə'] **N** (= ship) Walfänger m, Walfangschiff nt; (= person) Walfänger(in) m(f)

whaling ['weɪlɪŋ] **N** Wal(fisch)fang m; **to go ~** auf Walfang gehen; **~ ship** Walfänger m, Walfangschiff nt; **~ station** Walfangstation f

wham [wæm], **whang** [wæŋ] **INTERJ** wumm **N** (= blow) Schlag m; (= bang, thump) Knall m **VT** (= hit) schlagen; (= bang, thump) knallen **VI** knallen; **to ~ into sth** auf etw (acc) krachen (inf)

whammy ['wæmɪ] **N a double/triple ~** ein doppelter/dreifacher Schlag

wharf [wɔːf] **N** pl **-s** or **wharves** [wɔːvz] Kai m

what [wɒt] **PRON** **a** (interrog) **~ is this called?** wie heißt das?, wie nennt man das?; **~'s the weather like?** wie ist das Wetter?; **~ do 4 and 3 make?** wie viel is or macht 4 und or plus 3?; **you need a ~?** WAS brauchen Sie?; **~ is it now?**, **~ do you want now?** was ist denn?; **~?** (= pardon?) was?; **~'s that (you/he etc said)?** WAS hast du/hat er etc da gerade gesagt?, wie or was war das noch mal? (inf); **~'s that to you?** was geht dich das an?; **~ for?** wozu?, wofür?, für was? (inf); **~'s that tool for?** wofür ist das Werkzeug?; **~ are you looking at me like that for?** warum or was (inf) siehst du mich denn so an?; **~ did you do that for?** warum hast du denn das gemacht?; **~ about …?** wie wär's mit …?; **well, ~ about it? are we going?** na, wie ists, gehen wir?; **you know that restaurant? – ~ about it?** kennst du das Restaurant? – was ist damit?; **~ of or about it?** na und? (inf); **~ if …?** was ist, wenn …?; **so ~?** (inf) ja or na und?; **~ does it matter?** was macht das schon?; **you ~?** (inf) wie bitte?; **~-d'you-ma-call-him/-her/-it** (inf) wie heißt er/sie/es gleich or schnell

b (rel) was; **he knows ~ it is to suffer** er weiß, was leiden heißt or ist; **that is not ~ I asked for** danach habe ich nicht gefragt; **that's exactly ~ I want/said** genau das möchte ich/habe ich gesagt; **do you know ~ you are looking for?** weißt du, wonach du suchst?; **come ~ may** komme was wolle; **~ I'd like is a cup of tea** was ich jetzt gerne hätte, (das) wäre ein Tee; **~ with work and the new baby, life's been very hectic** die ganze Arbeit, das Baby ist da - es ist alles sehr hektisch; **~ with one thing and the other und wie es sich dann so ergab/ergibt, wie das so ist or geht; **and ~'s more** und außerdem, und noch dazu; **he knows ~'s ~** (inf) er kennt sich aus, der weiß Bescheid (inf); **(I'll) tell you ~** (inf) weißt du was?; **and ~ have you** (inf) und was sonst noch (alles), und was weiß ich; **to give sb ~ for** (inf) es jdm ordentlich geben (inf) → **whatnot**

c (with vb +prep see also there) **~ did he agree to?** wozu hat er zugestimmt?; **~ did he object to?** wogegen or gegen was hat er Einwände erhoben?; **he agreed/objected to ~ we suggested** er stimmte unseren Vorschlägen zu/lehnte unsere Vorschläge ab, er lehnte ab, was wir vorschlugen; **he didn't know ~ he was agreeing/objecting to** er wusste nicht, wozu er zustimmte/was er ablehnte; **she fell in with ~ everyone else wanted** sie schloss sich den Wünschen der Allgemeinheit an; **he didn't go into ~ he meant** er erläuterte nicht im Einzelnen, was er meinte

ADJ **a** (interrog) welche(r, s), was für (ein/eine) (inf); **~ age is he?** wie alt ist er?; **~ good would that be?** (inf) wozu sollte das gut sein?; **~ book do you want?** was für ein Buch wollen Sie?

b (rel) der/die/das; **~ little I had** das wenige, das ich hatte; **buy ~ food you like** kauf das Essen, das du willst

c (in set constructions) **~ sort of** was für ein/eine; **~ else** was noch; **~ more could a girl ask for?** was könnte sich ein Mädchen sonst noch wünschen

d (in interj, also iro) was für (ein/eine); **~ a man!** was für ein or welch ein (geh) Mann!; **~ luck!** welch(es) Glück, was für ein Glück, so ein Glück; **~ a fool I've been/I am!** ich Idiot!; **~ terrible weather** was für ein scheußliches Wetter

INTERJ was; (dated, = isn't it/he etc also) wie; **is he good-looking, or ~?** sieht der aber gut aus! (inf)

whate'er [wɒt'ɛə'] **PRON, ADJ** (poet) = **whatever**

whatever [wɒt'evə'] **PRON** **a** was (auch) (immer); (= no matter what) egal was, ganz gleich was; **~ you like** was (immer) du (auch) möchtest; **shall we go home now? – ~ you like** or **say** gehen wir jetzt nach Hause? – ganz wie du willst; **~ it's called** egal wie es heißt, soll es heißen, wie es will; **... or ~ they're called** ... oder wie sie sonst heißen; **or ~** oder sonst (so) etwas

b (*interrog*) was ... wohl; (*impatiently*) was zum Kuckuck (*inf*); **~ does he want?** was will er wohl?, was er wohl will?; (*impatiently*) was, zum Kuckuck, will er denn?; **~ do you mean?** was meinst du denn bloß?

ADJ a egal welche(r, s), welche(r, s) (auch) (*immer*); **~ book you choose** welches Buch Sie auch wählen; **~ else you do** was immer du or egal was du auch sonst machst; **for ~ reasons** aus welchen Gründen auch immer

b (*with neg*) überhaupt, absolut; **nothing ~** überhaupt or absolut gar nichts; **it's of no use ~** es hat überhaupt or absolut keinen Zweck

c (*interrog*) **good can come of it?** was kann daraus nur Gutes werden?; **~ reason can he have?** was für einen Grund kann er nur or bloß or will he do? was wird er nur or bloß or wohl noch alles machen?

whatnot ['wɒtnɒt] N (*inf*) **a and ~** (*inf*) und was sonst noch (alles), und was weiß ich **b** (= *thingummyjig*) Dingsbums nt (*inf*), Dingsda nt (*inf*)

what's [wɒts] contr of **what is** of **what has**

whatshername ['wɒtsəneɪm] N (*inf*) Soundso f

whatshername ['wɒtsɪzneɪm] N (*inf*) Soundso m

whatsit ['wɒtsɪt] N (*inf*) Dingsbums nt (*inf*), Dingsda nt (*inf*), Dingens nt (*dial inf*)

whatsitsname ['wɒtsɪtsneɪm] N (*inf*) Soundso nt

whatsoever [ˌwɒtsəʊ'evə'], **whatsoe'er** [ˌwɒtsəʊ'eə'] (*poet*) PRON, ADJ = **whatever** PRON a ADJ a, b

wheat [wi:t] N Weizen m; **to separate the ~ from the chaff** (*fig*) die Spreu vom Weizen trennen

wheaten ['wi:tn] ADJ Weizen-; **~ bread** Weizenbrot nt

wheat germ N Weizenkeim m

wheedle ['wi:dl] VT **to ~ sb into doing sth** jdn überreden or herumkriegen (*inf*), etw zu tun; **to ~ sth out of sb** jdm etw abschmeicheln

wheedler N Schmeichler(in) m(f)

wheedling ['wi:dlɪŋ] ADJ tone, voice schmeichelnd, schmeichlerisch N Schmeicheln nt

wheel [wi:l] N **a** Rad nt; (= *steering wheel*) Lenkrad nt; (*Naut*) Steuer(rad) nt; (= *roulette wheel*) Drehscheibe f; (= *paddle wheel*) Schaufelrad nt; (= *potter's wheel*) (Töpfer)scheibe f; **at the ~** (*lit*) am Steuer; (*fig also*) am Ruder; **~ (of fortune)** Glücksrad nt; **the ~s of progress** der Fortschritt; (*in history*) die Weiterentwicklung; **the ~s of government/justice** die Mühlen der Regierung or der Gerechtigkeit; **~s within ~s** gewisse Verbindungen or Beziehungen

b (*Mil*) Schwenkung f; **a ~ to the right, a right ~** eine Schwenkung nach rechts, eine Rechtsschwenkung

c **wheels** PL (*inf*, = *car*) fahrbare(r) Untersatz (*hum inf*); **do you have ~s?** bist du motorisiert? (*inf*)

VT **a** (= *push*) bicycle, pram, child schieben; (= *pull*) ziehen; (*invalid*) wheelchair fahren; **the cripple ~ed himself into the room/along** der Krüppel fuhr mit seinem Rollstuhl ins Zimmer/fuhr in seinem Rollstuhl

b (= *cause to turn*) drehen

VI (= *turn*) drehen; (*birds, planes*) kreisen; (*Mil*) schwenken; **to ~ left** nach links schwenken; **left ~!** links schwenkt!

▶**wheel (a)round** VI sich (rasch) umdrehen; (*troops*) (ab)schwenken

▶**wheel in** VT sep **a** trolley, invalid hereinrollen **b** (*inf*, = *bring into room*) vorführen (*inf*)

▶**wheel out** VT SEP **a** trolley, invalid hinausrollen, hinausschieben **b** (*fig*) hervorkramen

wheel: wheelbarrow N Schubkarre f, Schubkarren m; **wheelbarrow race** N Schubkarrenrennen nt; **wheelbase** N Rad(ab)stand m; **wheel brace** N Kreuzschlüssel m; **wheelchair** N Rollstuhl m; **he spent six months in a ~** er saß sechs Monate im Rollstuhl; **wheelchair-bound** ADJ an den Rollstuhl gefesselt or gebunden; **wheel clamp** N (*Brit*) (Park)kralle f VT krallen

wheeled [wi:ld] ADJ traffic, transport auf Rädern; vehicle mit Rädern

-wheeled ADJ suf -räd(e)rig; **four-wheeled** vierräd(e)rig

wheeler-dealer ['wi:lə'di:lə'] N (*inf*) Schlitzohr nt (*inf*), gerissener Typ (*inf*); (*in finance also*) Geschäftemacher(in) m(f)

wheelhouse ['wi:lhaʊs] N Ruderhaus nt

wheelie ['wi:lɪ] N (*inf*) **to do a ~** nur auf dem Hinterrad fahren

wheelie bin ['wi:lɪˌbɪn] N (*Brit inf*) Mülltonne f auf Rollen

wheeling and dealing ['wi:lɪŋən'di:lɪŋ] N Machenschaften pl, Gemauschel nt (*inf*); (*in business*) Geschäftemacherei f

wheelwork ['wi:lwɜ:k] N (*Tech*) Räderwerk nt

wheelwright ['wi:lraɪt] N Stellmacher(in) m(f)

wheeze [wi:z] N **a** (*of person*) pfeifender Atem no pl; (*of machine*) Fauchen nt no pl **b** (*dated inf*) Jokus m (*dated*), Scherz m; **to think up a ~** sich (*dat*) etwas einfallen lassen VT keuchen; **to ~ out a tune** eine Melodie herauspressen VI pfeifend atmen; (*machines, asthmatic*) keuchen; **if he smokes too much he starts to ~** wenn er zu stark raucht, bekommt er einen pfeifenden Atem

wheezily ['wi:zɪlɪ] ADV pfeifend, keuchend

wheeziness ['wi:zɪnɪs] N Keuchen nt; (*of breath*) Pfeifen nt

wheezy ['wi:zɪ] ADJ (+*er*) old man mit pfeifendem Atem; breath pfeifend; voice, cough keuchend; car keuchend, schnaufend; **to have a ~ chest** keuchend atmen

whelk [welk] N Wellhornschnecke f

whelp [welp] N Welpe m; (*pej*: = *boy*) Lauser m (*inf*), Lausbub m (*inf*) VI werfen, jungen

when [wen] ADV **a** (= *at what time*) wann; **since ~ have you been here?** seit wann sind Sie hier?; **... since ~ he has been here** ... und seitdem ist er hier; **say ~!** (*inf*) sag or schrei (*inf*) halt!

b (*rel*) **on the day ~** an dem Tag, an dem or als or da (*liter*) or wo (*inf*); **at the time ~** zu der Zeit, zu der or als or da (*liter*) or wo (*inf*); **he wrote last week, up till ~ I had heard nothing from him** er schrieb letzte Woche und bis dahin hatte ich nichts von ihm gehört; **in 1960, up till ~ he ...** im Jahre 1960, bis zu welchem Zeitpunkt er ...; **during the time ~ he was in Germany** während der Zeit, als or wo or die (*inf*) er in Deutschland war

CONJ **a** wenn; (*with past reference*) als; **you can go ~ I have finished** du kannst gehen, sobald or wenn ich fertig bin; **he did it ~ young** er tat es in seiner Jugend

b (+*gerund*) beim; (= *at or during which time*) wobei; **~ operating the machine** beim Benutzen or bei Benutzung der Maschine; **be careful ~ crossing the road** seien Sie beim Überqueren der Straße vorsichtig, seien Sie vorsichtig, wenn Sie über die Straße gehen; **the PM is coming here in May, ~ he will ...** der Premier kommt im Mai hierher und wird dann ...

c (= *although, whereas*) wo ... doch; **why do you do it that way – it would be much easier like this?** warum machst du es denn auf die Art, wo es doch so viel einfacher wäre?

whence [wens] ADV **a** (*old, form*) woher, von wannen (*old, liter*) **b** (*form*) **~ I conclude ...** woraus ich schließe, ...

whenever [wen'evə'] ADV **a** (= *each time*) jedes Mal wenn **b** (= *at whatever time*) wann (auch) immer, ganz egal or gleich or einerlei wann; (= *as soon as*) sobald; **I'll visit you ~ you like ich**

werde dich besuchen, wann immer du willst; **~ you like!** wann du willst!; **we'll leave ~ he's ready** wir brechen auf, sobald er fertig ist **c** (*emph*) **~ can he have done it?** wann kann er das nur or wohl getan haben?; **~ do I have the time for such things?** wann habe ich schon or je Zeit für so was?; **tomorrow, or ~** (*inf*) morgen, oder wann auch immer

where [weə'] ADV wo; **~ (to)** wohin, wo ... hin; **~ ... from** woher, wo ... her; **~ are you going (to)?** wohin gehst du?, wo gehst du hin?; **~ to, sir?** wohin (wollen Sie) bitte?; **~ are you from?** woher kommen Sie?, wo kommen Sie her?; **from ~ I'm sitting I can see the church** von meinem Platz aus kann ich die Kirche sehen; **~ should we be if ...?** was wäre nur, wenn ...?

CONJ wo; (= *in the place where*) da, wo ..., an der Stelle, wo ...; **go ~ you like** geh, wohin du willst, geh hin, wo du willst; **the bag is ~ you left it** die Tasche ist an der Stelle or da, wo sie liegen gelassen hast; **this is ~ we got out** hier sind wir ausgestiegen; **that's ~ I used to live** hier or da habe ich (früher) gewohnt; **that's ~ we differ** in diesem Punkt haben wir unterschiedliche Ansichten; **we carried on from ~ we left off** wir haben da weitergemacht, wo wir vorher aufgehört haben; **I've read up to ~ the king ...** ich habe bis dahin or bis an die Stelle gelesen, wo der König ...; **this is ~ we got to** soweit or bis hierhin or bis dahin sind wir gekommen; **~ we succeeded ~ we expected to fail** wir hatten da Erfolg, wo wir ihn nicht erwartet hatten; **you can trust him ~ money is concerned** in Geldsachen können Sie ihm trauen, Sie können ihm trauen, wo es ums Geld geht; **that's ~ da;** **that's ~ his strong point is** da liegt seine Stärke

whereabouts [ˌweərə'baʊts] ADV wo, in welcher Gegend; **I wonder ~ Martin put it** ich frage mich, wohin Martin es wohl gelegt hat N ['weərəbaʊts] sing or pl Verbleib m; (*of people also*) Aufenthaltsort m

whereafter [ˌweər'ɑ:ftə'] CONJ (*form*) woraufhin

whereas [weər'æz] ✪ 5.1, 26.3 CONJ **a** (= *whilst*) während; (= *while on the other hand*) wohingegen **b** (*esp Jur*, = *considering that*) da, in Anbetracht der Tatsache, dass ...

whereat [weər'æt] ADV (*old*) wobei

whereby [weə'baɪ] ADV (*form*) **the sign ~ you will recognize him** das Zeichen, an dem or woran Sie ihn erkennen; **the rule ~ it is not allowed** die Vorschrift, wonach es verboten ist; **a plan ~ the country can be saved** ein Plan, durch den or wodurch das Land gerettet werden kann

where'er [weər'eə'] CONJ, ADV (*poet*) contr of **wherever**

wherefore ['weəfɔ:'] ADV (*obs*) warum, weswegen CONJ (*obs*) weswegen N → **why** N

wherein [weər'ɪn] ADV (*form*) worin

whereof [weər'ɒv] ADV (*obs*) (= *about which*) worüber; (= *out of which*) woraus; (*Jur*) dessen; **in witness ~ ...** zu Urkund or Zeugnis dessen ... (*old*)

whereon [weər'ɒn] ADV (*obs*) worauf; (= *whereupon*) worauf

wheresoever [ˌweəsəʊ'evə'] ADV (*obs*), **wheresoe'er** [ˌweəsəʊ'eə'] ADV (*obs, poet*) = **wherever**

wherever [weər'evə'] CONJ **a** (= *no matter where*) egal or einerlei wo, wo (auch) immer; **~ it came from** egal or einerlei or ganz gleich, woher es kommt, woher es auch kommt **b** (= *anywhere, in or to whatever place*) wohin; **we'll go ~ you like** wir gehen, wohin Sie wollen; **he comes from Bishopbriggs, ~ that is** er kommt aus Bishopbriggs, wo auch immer das sein mag **c** (= *everywhere*) überall wo; **~ you see this sign** überall, wo Sie dieses Zeichen sehen ADV wo nur, wo bloß; **~ have I seen that before?** wo habe ich das nur or bloß schon gesehen?; **~ did you get that hat?** wo haben Sie nur or bloß diesen Hut her?; **in London or Liv-**

erpool or ~ in London oder Liverpool oder sonstwo

wherewith [wɛə'wɪθ] ADV (obs) womit, mit dem/der

wherewithal ['wɛəwɪðɔːl] N nötiges Kleingeld; (= implements) Utensilien pl

wherry ['wɛrɪ] N (= light rowing boat) Ruderkahn m; (Brit: = barge) (Fluss)kahn m; (US: = scull) Einer m, Skiff nt

whet [wɛt] VT knife, scythe wetzen; axe schleifen, schärfen; appetite, curiosity anregen

whether ['wɛðə'] ✪ 5.4, 6.3 CONJ ob; (= no matter whether) egal or ganz gleich or einerlei, ob; **I am not certain ~ they're coming or not** or **~ not they're coming** ich bin nicht sicher, ob sie kommen oder nicht; **~ they come or not, we'll go ahead** egal or ganz gleich or einerlei, ob sie kommen oder nicht (kommen), wir fangen (schon mal) an; **he's not sure ~ to go or stay** er weiß nicht, ob er gehen oder bleiben soll

whetstone ['wɛtstəʊn] N Wetzstein m

whew [hwjuː] INTERJ puh, uff

whey [weɪ] N Molke f

wheyfaced [ˌweɪ'feɪst] ADJ (liter) bleichgesichtig (geh)

which [wɪtʃ] **ADJ** **a** (interrog) welche(r, s); **~ one?** welche(r, s)?; (of people also) wer?; **I can't tell ~ key is ~** ich kann die Schlüssel nicht auseinander halten

b (rel) welche(r, s); **... by ~ time I was asleep** ... und zu dieser Zeit schlief ich (bereits); **look at it ~ way you will ...** man kann es betrachten or sehen, wie man will ...; **~ he said, ~ remark made me very angry ...** sagte er, was mich sehr ärgerte

PRON **a** (interrog) welche(r, s); **~ of the children/books** welches Kind/Buch; **~ is ~?** (of people) wer ist wer?, welche(r) ist welche(r)?; (of things) welche(r, s) ist welche(r, s)?, welche(r, s) ist der/die/das eine und welche(r, s) der/die/das andere?; **~ is for ~?** was ist wofür?

b (rel) (with n antecedent) der/die/das, welche(r, s) (geh); (with clause antecedent) was; **the bear ~ he marked ...** worauf hin er bemerkte, ...; **it rained hard, ~ upset her plans** es regnete stark, was ihre Pläne durcheinander brachte; **~ reminds me ...** dabei fällt mir ein, ...; **from ~ we deduce that ...** woraus wir ableiten, dass ...; **after ~ we went to bed** worauf or wonach wir zu Bett gingen; **the day before/after ~ he left her** an dem Tag, bevor or sie verließ/nachdem sie verlassen hatte; **the shelf on ~ I put it** das Brett, auf das or worauf ich es gelegt habe

whichever [wɪtʃ'ɛvə'] **ADJ** welche(r, s) auch immer; (= no matter which) ganz gleich or egal or einerlei welche(r, s) **PRON** welche(r, s) auch immer; **~ (of you) has the most money** wer immer (von euch) das meiste Geld hat

whichsoever [ˌwɪtʃsəʊ'ɛvə'] ADJ, PRON (form) = **whichever**

whiff [wɪf] N **a** (= puff) Zug m; (= wisp) kleine Fahne, Wolke f; (= smell) Hauch m; (pleasant) Duft m; (fig: = trace) Spur f; (of spring) Hauch m, Ahnung f; **to catch a ~ of sth** den Geruch von etw wahrnehmen **b** (= small cigar) kleiner Zigarillo

whiffle ['wɪfl] VI (wind) böig wehen; (flame) flackern; (flag etc) flattern; (fig: = be unsteady) schwanken, flatterhaft sein

whiffy ['wɪfɪ] ADJ (+er) (inf) **to be ~** streng riechen; **it's a bit ~ here** hier müffelt es etwas (inf)

Whig [wɪg] (Brit Hist) **N** frühere Bezeichnung für ein Mitglied der liberalen Partei, Whig m **ADJ** attr Whig-; **~ government** Whig-Regierung f

while [waɪl] ✪ 26.1, 26.3 **N** **a** Weile f, Weilchen nt (inf); **for a ~** (für) eine Weile, eine Zeitlang; (= a short moment) (für) einen Augenblick or Moment; **a good** or **long ~** eine ganze or lange Weile, eine ganze Zeit lang; **for/after quite a ~** ziemlich or recht lange, (für) eine ge-

raume/nach einer geraumen Weile (geh); **a little** or **short ~** ein Weilchen (inf), kurze Zeit; **it'll be ready in a short ~** es wird bald fertig sein; **a little ~ ago** vor kurzem; **a long ~ ago** vor einer ganzen Weile, vor längerer or langer Zeit; **some ~ ago** vor einiger Zeit; **all the ~** die ganze Zeit (über)

b **the ~** (liter) derweil, unterdessen

c **to be worth (one's) ~ to ...** sich (für jdn) lohnen, zu ...; **we'll make it worth your ~** es soll ihr Schaden nicht sein

CONJ **a** während; (= as long as) solange; **she fell asleep ~ reading** sie schlief beim Lesen ein; **he became famous ~ still young** er wurde berühmt, als er noch jung war; **you must not drink ~ on duty** Sie dürfen im Dienst nicht trinken

b (= although) ~ **one must admit there are difficulties ...** man muss zwar zugeben, dass es Schwierigkeiten gibt, trotzdem ...; **~ the text is not absolutely perfect, nevertheless ...** obwohl (zwar) der Text nicht einwandfrei ist, ... trotzdem; **it is difficult to be fair ~ at the same time being honest** es ist schwierig, fair und gleichzeitig auch gerecht zu sein

c (= whereas) während

▸ **while away** VT sep time sich (dat) vertreiben

whilst [waɪlst] CONJ = **while** CONJ

whim [wɪm] N Laune f; **her every ~** jede ihrer Launen; **at** or **on ~, at** or **on a ~** aus Jux und Tollerei (inf); **as the ~ takes me** etc ganz nach Lust und Laune

whimper ['wɪmpə'] **N** (of dog) Winseln nt no pl; (of person) Wimmern nt no pl; **a ~ of pain** ein schmerzliches Wimmern; **without a ~** ohne einen (Klage)laut **VI** (dog) winseln; (person) wimmern **VT** person wimmern

whimsical ['wɪmzɪkəl] ADJ wunderlich; look, remark neckisch; smile verschmitzt; idea, tale schnurrig; decision seltsam, spinnig (inf); notion grillenhaft; ornament verrückt; **to be in a ~ mood** in einer neckischen Laune sein

whimsicality [ˌwɪmzɪ'kælɪtɪ] N Wunderlichkeit f; (of behaviour) Launenhaftigkeit f, Grillenhaftigkeit f; (of decision) Seltsamkeit f; (of architecture) Verrücktheit f, Manierismus m

whimsically ['wɪmzɪkəlɪ] ADV look, say neckisch; smile verschmitzt

whimsy ['wɪmzɪ] N **a** (= caprice, fancy) Spleen m, Grille f (dated) **b** = **whimsicality**

whin [wɪn] N (esp Brit) Ginster m

whine [waɪn] **N** (of dog) Jaulen nt no pl, Heulen nt no pl, (= complaining cry) Heulen nt no pl, Gejammer nt no pl; (of child) Quengelei f no pl; (of siren, jet engine) Heulen nt no pl; (of bullet) Pfeifen nt no pl **VI** (dog) jaulen; (person: = speak, complain) jammern, klagen; (child) quengeln; (siren, jet engine) heulen; (bullet) pfeifen; **the dog was whining to be let in** der Hund jaulte, um hereingelassen zu werden; **don't come whining me about it** du brauchst nicht anzukommen und mir was vorzujammern

whiner ['waɪnə'] N (= complainer) Jammerer m

whinge [wɪndʒ] (Brit inf) **VI** (= complain) jammern, meckern (inf); (baby) plärren; **~ing Pom** (Austral) ewig meckernder Engländer (inf), ewig meckernde Engländerin (inf) **N** **to have a ~** meckern (inf), jammern

whingey ['wɪndʒɪ] ADJ (Brit inf) **to be ~** dauernd jammern or meckern (inf); (baby) dauernd plärren; **the kid's starting to get ~** das Kind fängt an zu plärren; **don't be so ~** mecker doch nicht so! (inf)

whining ['waɪnɪŋ] **N** (of dog) Gejaule nt; (= complaining) Gejammer nt **ADJ** **a** (= complaining) voice weinerlich; person jammernd, meckernd (inf) **b** sound wimmernd; (of machine) schrillend; dog jaulend

whinny ['wɪnɪ] **N** Wiehern nt no pl, Gewieher nt no pl **VI** wiehern

whip [wɪp] **N** **a** Peitsche f; (= riding whip) Reitgerte f; **to give sb a fair crack of the ~** (inf) jdm eine faire Chance geben

b (Parl) (= person) Fraktions- or Geschäftsfüh-

rer(in) m(f); (Brit: = call) Anordnung f des Fraktionsführers; **three-line ~** (Brit) Fraktionszwang m; **they have put a three-line ~ on the vote** (Brit) bei der Abstimmung besteht Fraktionszwang

c (Cook) Creme f, Speise f

VT **a** (with whip) people auspeitschen; horse peitschen; (with stick etc) schlagen; **the conductor ~ped the orchestra into a frenzy** der Dirigent brachte das Orchester in Ekstase; **to ~ sb/ sth into shape** (fig) jdn/etw zurechtschleifen

b (Cook) cream, eggs schlagen

c (= bind) seam umnähen; stick, rope umwickeln

d (inf: = defeat) vernichtend schlagen

e (fig: = move quickly) **he ~ped the book off the desk** er schnappte sich (dat) das Buch vom Schreibtisch; **he ~ped his hand out of the way** er zog blitzschnell seine Hand weg; **the thief ~ped the jewel into his pocket** der Dieb ließ den Edelstein schnell in seiner Tasche verschwinden; **to ~ sb into hospital** jdn in Windeseile ins Krankenhaus bringen; (doctor) jdn schnell ins Krankenhaus einweisen

f (inf, = steal) mitgehen lassen (inf)

VI **a** branches ~ped against the window Äste schlugen gegen das Fenster

b (= move quickly) (person) schnell (mal) laufen; **the car ~ped past** das Auto brauste or sauste or fegte (inf) vorbei

▸ **whip away** VT sep wegreißen, wegziehen (from sb jdm)

▸ **whip back** VI **a** (spring, plank) zurückschnellen, zurückfedern **b** (inf, = go back quickly) schnell (mal) zurücklaufen

▸ **whip off** VT sep clothes herunterreißen, vom Leib reißen; tablecloth wegziehen; **the wind whipped my hat off** der Wind riss mir den Hut vom Kopf; **a car whipped him off to the airport** ein Auto brachte ihn in Windeseile zum Flugplatz

▸ **whip on** VT sep **a** (= urge on) horse anpeitschen, antreiben; (fig) antreiben **b** (= put on quickly) clothes sich (dat) überwerfen; lid schnell drauftun

▸ **whip out** **VT** sep gun, pencil, camera etc zücken; **he whipped a gun/pencil** etc **out of his pocket** er zog rasch eine Pistole/einen Bleistift etc aus der Tasche; **they whipped out his tonsils** (inf) sie haben ihm schnell die Mandeln entfernt **VI** (inf: = go out quickly) schnell (mal) rausgehen (inf)

▸ **whip round** VI (esp Brit) **a** (= move quickly) **I'll just whip round to the shops** ich geh nur mal schnell einkaufen (inf); **he whipped round when he heard ...** er fuhr herum, als er hörte ...; **the car whipped round the corner** das Auto brauste or sauste or fegte (inf) um die Ecke **b** (= collect money) zusammenlegen, den Hut herumgehen lassen

▸ **whip up** VT sep **a** (= pick up) schnappen **b** (= set in motion) horses antreiben; (Cook) cream schlagen; mixture verrühren; eggs verquirlen; (inf: = prepare quickly) meal hinzaubern; (fig: = stir up) interest, feeling anheizen, entfachen; support finden, aufpeitschen (inf); audience, crowd mitreißen; **I'll just whip up something to eat** (inf) ich mach nur schnell was zu essen; **the sea, whipped up by the wind** das Meer, vom Wind aufgepeitscht

whip: whipcord N (= rope) Peitschenschnur f; (= fabric) Whipkord m; **whip hand** N **to have the ~ (over sb)** (über jdn) die Oberhand haben; **whiplash** N (Peitschen)riemen m; (Med: also **whiplash injury**) Peitschenschlagverletzung f

whipped cream [wɪpt'kriːm] N Schlagsahne f, Schlagrahm m

whipper-in [ˌwɪpər'ɪn] N Pikör(in) m(f), Vorreiter(in) m(f) (bei der Parforcejagd)

whippersnapper ['wɪpəˌsnæpə'] N (dated inf) junger Spund

whippet ['wɪpɪt] N Whippet m

whipping [ˈwɪpɪŋ] N (= beating) Tracht f Prügel; (inf, = defeat) Niederlage f; (fig: in debate etc) Pleite f; **to give sb a ~** (lit) jdm eine Tracht Prügel versetzen; (with whip) jdn auspeitschen; (fig inf) jdn in die Pfanne hauen (inf); **the government got a ~** die Regierung erlebte eine Pleite (inf)

whipping: whipping boy N Prügelknabe m; **to use sb as a ~** jdn zum Prügelknaben machen; **whipping cream** N Schlagsahne f; **whipping top** N Kreisel m

whippoorwill [ˈwɪpˌpʊəˌwɪl] N (Zool) schreiender Ziegenmelker

whippy [ˈwɪpɪ] ADJ cane, fishing rod biegsam, elastisch

whip-round [ˈwɪpraʊnd] N (esp Brit, inf) **to have a ~** den Hut herumgehen lassen

whir [wɜ:ˈ] N, VI = whirr

whirl [wɜ:l] N (= spin) Wirbeln nt no pl; (of dust, water etc, also fig) Wirbel m; (of cream etc) Tupfer m; **to give sth a ~** (lit) etw herumwirbeln; (fig inf: = try out) etw ausprobieren; **the social ~** der Trubel des gesellschaftlichen Lebens; **my head is in a ~** mir schwirrt der Kopf ◀VT◀ **a** (= make turn) wirbeln; **to ~ sb/sth round** jdn/etw herumwirbeln; **he ~ed his hat round his head** er schwenkte seinen Hut; **he ~ed the water around with his stick** er rührte mit seinem Stock im Wasser herum **b** (transport) eilends wegbringen; (person) mit sich nehmen, entführen (inf) ◀VI◀ (= spin) wirbeln; (water) strudeln; **to ~ (a)round** herumwirbeln; (water) strudeln; (person: = turn round quickly) herumfahren; **my head is ~ing** mir schwirrt der Kopf; **after a few drinks the room started ~ing** nach ein paar Gläsern fing der Raum an, sich zu drehen; **they/the countryside ~ed past us** sie wirbelten/die Landschaft flog an uns vorbei

whirligig [ˈwɜ:lɪgɪg] N (= top) Kreisel m; (= roundabout) Karussell nt, Ringelspiel nt; (fig) (ewiges) Wechselspiel nt

whirlpool [ˈwɜ:lpu:l] N Strudel m; (in health club) = Kneippbecken nt

whirlwind [ˈwɜ:lwɪnd] N Wirbelwind m; (fig) Trubel m, Wirbel m; **like a ~** wie der Wirbelwind; **to reap the ~** (prov) Sturm ernten; **he did some very stupid things, and now he's reaping the ~** er hat einige sehr große Dummheiten gemacht und jetzt muss er dafür büßen; **a ~ romance** eine stürmische Romanze

whirlybird [ˈwɜ:lɪˌbɜ:d] N (esp US, inf) Hubschrauber m

whirr, whir [wɜ:ˈ] N (of wings) Schwirren nt; (of wheels, camera, machine, quiet) Surren nt; (louder) Brummen nt, Dröhnen nt ◀VI◀ (wings) schwirren; (wheels, camera, machine, quietly) surren; (louder) brummen, dröhnen

whish [wɪʃ] N Schwirren nt, Sausen nt, Zischen nt; (of silk etc) Rascheln nt ◀VI◀ schwirren, sausen, zischen; (silk etc) rascheln

whisk [wɪsk] N **a** (= fly whisk) Wedel m; (Cook) Schneebesen m; (electric) Rührbesen m, Rührstab m, Rührgerät nt; **give the eggs a good ~** schlagen Sie die Eier gut durch **b** (= movement) Wischen nt; (of skirts) Schwingen nt; **with a ~ of its tail** mit einem Schwanzschlag ◀VT◀ **a** (Cook) schlagen; eggs verquirlen; **to ~ the eggs into the mixture** die Eier unter die Masse einrühren **b** the horse ~ed its tail das Pferd schlug mit dem Schwanz **c** (= move quickly) **she ~ed the book out of my hand** sie riss mir das Buch aus der Hand ◀VI◀ (= move quickly) fegen (inf), stieben

▶**whisk away** VT sep **a** fly, wasp etc wegscheuchen **b** (= take away suddenly) **the magician whisked away the tablecloth** der Zauberer zog das Tischtuch schnell weg; **her mother whisked the bottle away from her just in time** ihre Mutter schnappte (inf) or zog ihr die Flasche gerade noch rechtzeitig weg; **he whisked her away to the Bahamas** er entführte sie auf die Bahamas; **a big black car turned up and whisked**

him away ein großes schwarzes Auto erschien und sauste or brauste mit ihm davon

▶**whisk off** VT sep = whisk away b

▶**whisk up** VT sep eggs, mixture etc schaumig schlagen

whisker [ˈwɪskəˈ] N Schnurrhaar nt; (of person) Barthaar nt; **~s** (= moustache) Schnurrbart m; (= side whiskers) Backenbart m; (Zool) Schnurrbart m; **to win sth by a ~** etw fast gewinnen; **to miss sth by a ~** etw um Haaresbreite verpassen

whiskered [ˈwɪskəd] ADJ schnurrbärtig

whiskery [ˈwɪskərɪ] ADJ man schnurrbärtig; face bärtig, stoppelig; kiss kratzend

whisky, (US, Ir) **whiskey** [ˈwɪskɪ] N Whisky m; **~ and soda** Whisky (mit) Soda m; **two whiskies, please** zwei Whisky, bitte

whisper [ˈwɪspəˈ] N **a** (= low tone) Geflüster nt no pl, Flüstern nt no pl; (of wind, leaves) Wispern nt no pl; (mysterious) Raunen nt no pl; **to speak in a ~** im Flüsterton sprechen; **to say sth in a ~** etw im Flüsterton sagen; **they were talking in ~s** sie sprachen flüsternd or im Flüsterton **b** (= rumour) Gerücht nt; **there are ~s (going round) that ...** es geht das Gerücht or es gehen Gerüchte um, dass ...; **have you heard any ~s about who might be promoted?** haben Sie irgendwelche Andeutungen gehört or haben Sie etwas läuten hören (inf), wer befördert werden soll? ◀VT◀ **a** (= say quietly) flüstern, wispern; **to ~ sth to sb** jdm etw zuflüstern or zuwispern; (secretively) jdm etw zuraunen; **to ~ a word in(to) sb's ear** (fig) jdm einen leisen Tipp geben, jdm etw andeuten **b** (= rumour) **it's (being) ~ed that ...** es geht das Gerücht or es gehen Gerüchte um, dass ..., man munkelt or es wird gemunkelt, dass ... ◀VI◀ flüstern, wispern (also fig); (secretively) raunen; (schoolchildren) tuscheln; (poet: wind) säuseln; **to ~ to sb** jdm zuflüstern/zuwispern/zuraunen, mit jdm tuscheln; **just ~ to me** sags mir flüsternd; **stop ~ing!** hör/hört auf zu flüstern!; (schoolchildren) hört auf zu tuscheln, lasst das Getuschel!

whispering [ˈwɪspərɪŋ] N Geflüster nt no pl, Flüstern nt no pl; (poet: of wind) Säuseln nt no pl; (of schoolchildren) Tuscheln nt no pl, Getuschel nt no pl; (fig) Gemunkel nt, Getuschel nt no pl

whispering: whispering campaign N Verleumdungskampagne f; **whispering gallery** N Flüstergewölbe nt or -galerie f

whist [wɪst] N Whist nt

whist drive N Whistrunde f mit wechselnden Parteien

whistle [ˈwɪsl] N **a** (= sound) Pfiff m; (of wind) Pfeifen nt; (of kettle) Pfeifton m; **the ~ of the escaping steam** das Pfeifen des ausströmenden Dampfes; **to give a ~** einen Pfiff ausstoßen **b** (= instrument) Pfeife f; **to blow a/one's ~** pfeifen; **to blow the ~ on sb/sth** (fig inf) über jdn/ etw auspacken (inf); **to be as clean as a ~** (= clean) blitzsauber sein; (fig also) eine schneeweiße Weste haben → wet **VT** ◀VT◀ pfeifen; **to ~ (to) sb to stop** jdn durch einen Pfiff stoppen; **to ~ sb back/over** etc jdn zurück-/herüberpfeifen etc ◀VI◀ pfeifen; **the boys ~d at her** die Jungen pfiffen ihr nach; **the crowd ~d at the referee** die Menge pfiff den Schiedsrichter aus; **he ~d for a taxi** er pfiff ein Taxi heran, er pfiff nach einem Taxi; **the referee ~d for a foul** der Schiedsrichter pfiff ein Foul; **the referee ~d for play to stop** der Schiedsrichter pfiff eine Spielunterbrechung; (at the end) der Schiedsrichter pfiff das Spiel ab; **he can ~ for it** (inf) da kann er lange warten, da kann er warten, bis er schwarz wird (inf)

whistle-blowing [ˈwɪslˌbləʊɪŋ] N (fig) Verrat m

whistle-blower [ˈwɪslbləʊəˈ] N **he was the ~ in this affair** er hat über diese Affäre ausgepackt (inf)

whistle stop (US) N **a** (dated: = small town) Kleinstadt f, Nest nt (pej inf) **b** (= stop) kurzer Aufenthalt an einem kleinen Ort; (fig) Stippvisite f

whistle-stop [ˈwɪslstɒp] ATTR **~ tour** (Pol) Wahlreise f; (fig) Reise mit Kurzaufenthalten an allen Orten **VI** auf die Dörfer gehen

whistling [ˈwɪslɪŋ] N Pfeifen nt

whistling kettle [ˈwɪslɪŋˈketl] N Pfeifkessel m

whit [wɪt] N **not a** or **one ~** keine or nicht eine Spur; (of humour) kein or nicht ein Funke(n); (of truth, common sense) kein or nicht ein Gramm or Körnchen; **every ~ as good** genauso gut, (um) keinen Deut schlechter

white [waɪt] ADJ (+er) **a** weiß; (with fear, anger, exhaustion also) blass, kreidebleich; **to go** or **turn ~** (thing) weiß werden; (person also) bleich or blass werden; **as ~ as a sheet** or **ghost** leichenblass; **~r than** (lit, fig) weißer als weiß **b** (= refined: Cook) flour Weiß-; rice weiß **N** **a** (= colour) Weiß nt; (= person) Weiße(r) mf; (of egg) Eiweiß nt, Klar nt (Aus); (of eye) Weiße(s) nt; **shoot when you see the ~s of their eyes** schießt, wenn ihr das Weiße im Auge des Feinds erkennen könnt; **~s** (Brit) (household) Weißwäsche f; (Sport) weiße Kleidung; **the tennis players were wearing ~s** (Brit) die Tennisspieler trugen Weiß; **I've forgotten my ~s** ich habe mein Zeug vergessen **b** (also **white wine**) Weißwein m

white: white ant N Termite f, weiße Ameise; **whitebait** N pl **-bait** Breitling m; **whitebeam** N Mehlbeere f; **white bear** N Eisbär m; **white blood cell** N weißes Blutkörperchen m; **whiteboard** N Weißwandtafel f; **white book** N (US Pol) Weißbuch nt; **white bread** N Weißbrot nt; **whitecap** N Welle f mit Schaumkronen; **white Christmas** N a weiße Weihnacht(en); **white coal** N weiße Kohle; **white coffee** N (Brit) Kaffee m mit Milch, Milchkaffee m; **white-collar** ADJ ~ **worker** Schreibtischarbeiter(in) m(f); ~ **job** Angestelltenstelle f, Schreibtisch- or Büroposten m; ~ **criminal** Wirtschaftskriminelle(r) mf; ~ **crime** Wirtschaftskriminalität f; **a** ~ **crime** ein Wirtschaftsverbrechen nt; ~ **union** Angestelltengewerkschaft f; **white corpuscle** N weißes Blutkörperchen

whited sepulchre [ˈwaɪtɪdˈseplkəˈ] N (liter) Pharisäer m

white: white dwarf N (Astron) weißer Zwerg (-stern); **white elephant** N nutzloser Gegenstand; (= waste of money) Fehlinvestition f; **white elephant stall** N Stand m mit allerlei Krimskrams; **White Ensign** N Fahne der Royal Navy; **white feather** N weiße Feder (Zeichen der Feigheit); **to show the ~** den Schwanz einziehen; **whitefish** N Weißfisch m; **white flag** N (Mil, fig) weiße Fahne; **to raise** or **wave the ~** (lit) die weiße Fahne schwenken; (fig) sich geschlagen geben; **white fox** N Polarfuchs m; **white frost** N Raureif m; **white gold** N Weißgold nt; **white goods** PL (Comm, = electrical appliances) Haushaltsgeräte pl (Kühlschrank, Waschmaschine, Herd etc); **white-haired** ADJ **a** weißhaarig; (= blond) weißblond, semmelblond **b** (US, inf: = favourite) **the boss's ~ boy** der Liebling des Chefs; **Whitehall** N (= British government) Whitehall no art; **if ~ decides ...** wenn London beschließt ...; **white-headed** ADJ **a** = white-haired **b** gull, duck weißköpfig; **white heat** N Weißglut f; (fig) Hitze f; (with enthusiasm) Feuereifer m; **to work at ~** (under pressure) fieberhaft arbeiten; **in the ~ of his rage/passion** in seiner besinnungslosen Wut/Leidenschaft; **his rage reached ~** seine Wut erreichte den Siedepunkt; **white hope** N große or einzige Hoffnung; **white horse** N **a** Schimmel m **b** (= wave) Welle f mit einer Schaumkrone; **now there are ~s** jetzt haben die Wellen Reiter; **white-hot** ADJ weiß glühend; (fig) brennend, glühend; **White House** N **the ~** das Weiße Haus; **white knight** N (St Ex) weißer Ritter; **white lead** N Bleiweiß nt; **white lie** N kleine Unwahrheit, Notlüge f; **we all tell a ~ from time to time** wir alle sagen nicht immer ganz die Wahrheit; **white light** N weißes Licht; **white-lipped** ADJ mit bleichen Lippen, angstbleich; **white magic** N weiße Magie; **white man** N Weiße(r) m; **white man's burden** N the ~ die Bürde des weißen Mannes; **white meat** N helles Fleisch

whiten ['waɪtn] VT weiß machen ◆ VI weiß werden

whitener N (= bleach) Weißmacher m

whiteness ['waɪtnɪs] N Weiße f; (of skin) Helligkeit f; (due to illness etc) Blässe f; **the dazzling ~ of ...** das strahlende Weiß des/der ...

white night N **a** (= sleepless night) schlaflose Nacht **b** (= bright night) weiße Nacht, helle Nacht im Mittsommer

White Nile N the ~ der Weiße Nil

whitening ['waɪtnɪŋ] N weiße Farbe, Schlämmkreide f

white: **white noise** N weißes Rauschen; **White-Out®** N (US) Tipp-Ex® nt; **whiteout** N starkes Schneegestöber; **in ~ conditions** bei starkem Schneegestöber; **white paper** N (Pol) Weißbuch nt (on zu); **white pepper** N (Cook) weißer Pfeffer; **white rhino**, **white rhinoceros** N weißes Nashorn; **White Russia** N Weißrussland nt; **White Russian** N Weißrusse m, Weißrussin f; **white sale** N weiße Woche, Ausverkauf m von Haus- und Tischwäsche; **white sauce** N Mehlsoße f, helle Soße; **White Sea** N the ~ das Weiße Meer; **white settler** N weißer Siedler, weiße Siedlerin; **white shark** N weißer Hai; **white sidewall haircut** N (inf) Bürstenschnitt m (mit seitlich rasiertem oder sehr kurzen Haaren); **white slave** N weiße Sklavin; **white slaver** N Mädchenhändler(in) m(f); **white slavery**, **white slave trade** N Mädchenhandel m; **white spirit** N (Brit) Terpentinersatz m; **white stick** N Blindenstock m; **white supremacy** N Vorherrschaft f der weißen Rasse; **whitethorn** N Weißdorn m; **whitethroat** N Grasmücke f; **white tie** N (= tie) weiße Fliege; (= evening dress) Frack m; **a ~ occasion/dinner** eine Veranstaltung/ein Essen mit Frackzwang; **white trash** N (US, pej inf) weißes Pack (pej inf)

WHITE TRASH

White trash ist ein abfälliger amerikanischer Ausdruck für arme, ungebildete Weiße, vor allem für die in den Südstaaten. Sie werden als die unterste gesellschaftliche Schicht von Weißen angesehen, gelten als dumm, schmutzig und faul und haben einen ebenso schweren Stand wie ihre gleichfalls armen schwarzen, hispanischen oder indianischen Mitbürger. Der Begriff wurde bereits in der Mitte des neunzehnten Jahrhunderts von Schwarzen der Südstaaten verwendet, die damit im Elend lebende Weiße bezeichneten, die sich nichtsdestoweniger den Schwarzen immer noch aufgrund ihrer Hautfarbe überlegen fühlten.

---

white: **whitewall (tyre)** N Weißwandreifen m; **whitewash** N Tünche f; (fig) Augenwischerei f ◆ VT walls tünchen; (fig) schönfärben, beschönigen; (inf) person rein waschen; opponent zu null schlagen; **white water** N Wildwasser nt; **white-water rafting** N Rafting nt, Wildwasserfahren nt; **white wedding** N Hochzeit f in Weiß; **white whale** N Weißwal m, Beluga m; **white wine** N Weißwein m; **white witch** N weiße Hexe (die weiße Magie praktiziert); **white woman** N Weiße f; **whitewood** ADJ ~ furniture Möbel pl aus hellem Weichholz

whitey ['waɪtɪ] N (pej inf) Weiße(r) mf

whither ['wɪðə'] ADV **a** (old) wohin **b** (journalese) **~ America/socialism?** Amerika/Sozialismus, wohin? or was nun?

whiting¹ ['waɪtɪŋ] N , no pl = **whitening**

whiting² N pl - Weißling m, Weißfisch m

---

whitish ['waɪtɪʃ] ADJ colour weißlich; **~-yellow/blue** weißlich-gelb/blau

whitlow ['wɪtləʊ] N Nagelbettentzündung f, Umlauf m

Whit Monday [ˌwɪt'mʌndɪ] N (Brit) Pfingstmontag m

Whitsun ['wɪtsən] (Brit) N Pfingsten nt; (Eccl also) Pfingstfest nt ATTR Pfingst-; **~ weekend** Pfingstwochenende nt

Whit Sunday [ˌwɪt'sʌndɪ] N (Brit) Pfingstsonntag m

Whitsuntide ['wɪtsəntaɪd] N (Brit) Pfingstzeit f; **around ~** um Pfingsten (herum)

whittle ['wɪtl] VT schnitzen ◆ VI **to ~ (away) at sth** an etw (dat) (herum)schnippeln or -schnitzen or -schneiden

▶ **whittle away** VT sep **a** bark etc wegschneiden, wegschnitzen **b** (= gradually reduce) allmählich abbauen, nach und nach abbauen; rights, power etc allmählich or nach und nach beschneiden or stutzen; **the benefit/pay increase has been whittled away by inflation** der Gewinn/die Gehaltserhöhung ist durch die Inflation langsam zunichte gemacht worden

▶ **whittle down** VT sep **a** piece of wood herunterschneiden; **to whittle down to size** zurechtschneiden, zurechtstutzen **b** (= reduce) kürzen, reduzieren, stutzen (to auf +acc); gap, difference verringern

whiz(z) [wɪz] N **a** (of arrow) Schwirren nt, Sausen nt **b** (inf) Kanone f (inf); **a computer/financial ~** ein Computer-/Finanzgenie nt (inf) ◆ VI (arrow) schwirren, sausen

whiz(z) kid N (inf, in career) Senkrechtstarter(in) m(f); **financial/publishing ~** Finanz-/Verlagsgenie nt or -größe f; **a ~ like him will soon find a solution** ein solcher Intelligenzbolzen wird bald auf eine Lösung kommen (inf)

whizz [wɪz] N (sl) **a** (Brit Drugs) Speed nt **b** **to got for** (Brit) **or take a ~** (= urinate) strullern (sl), pissen gehen (vulg)

WHO abbr of **World Health Organization** WHO f, Weltgesundheitsorganisation f

who [huː] PRON **a** (interrog) wer; (acc) wen; (dat) wem; **and ~ should it be but Jeremy?** und wer wars? : natürlich Jeremy!; **~ do you think you are?** was glaubst du or bildest du dir ein, wer du bist?, für wen hältst du dich eigentlich?; **"Who's Who"** „Wer ist Wer"; **you'll soon find out ~'s ~ in the office** Sie werden bald im Büro alle kennen lernen; **~ are you looking for?** wen suchen Sie?; **~ did you stay with?** bei wem haben Sie gewohnt?

b (rel) der/die/das, welche(r, s); **any man ~ ...** jeder (Mensch), der ...; **anyone ~ wishes** or **those ~ wish to go ...** wer gehen will ...; **deny it ~ may** (form) bestreite das, wer will

whoa [wəʊ] INTERJ brr

who'd [huːd] contr of **who had** of **who would**

whodun(n)it [huːˈdʌnɪt] N (inf) Krimi m (inf, bei dem der Täter bis zum Schluss unbekannt ist)

whoever [huːˈevə'] PRON wer (auch immer); (acc) wen (auch immer); (dat) wem (auch immer); (= no matter who) einerlei or ganz gleich or egal (dat) wer/wen/wem; **~ told you that?** wer hat dir das denn (bloß) gesagt?

whole [həʊl] ADJ (= entire, unbroken, undivided) ganz; truth voll; (Bibl: = well) heil; **but the ~ purpose was to ...** aber der ganze Sinn der Sache or aber der Zweck der Übung (inf) war, dass ...; **three ~ weeks** drei volle or ganze Wochen; **the ~ lot** das Ganze; (of people) alle, der ganze Verein (inf); **a ~ lot of people** eine ganze Menge Leute; **a ~ lot better** ein ganzes Stück besser (inf), sehr viel besser (inf); **she is a ~ lot of woman** (esp US inf) sie ist eine richtige or echte Frau; **let's forget the ~ thing** vergessen wir das Ganze; **the figures don't tell the ~ story/the ~ truth** die Zahlen sagen nicht alles/nicht die ganze Wahrheit; **a ~ new wardrobe** eine völlig neue Garderobe; **out of ~ cloth** (US) von Anfang bis Ende erdichtet; **not a cup was left ~**

---

nicht eine Tasse blieb ganz or heil; **she swallowed it ~** sie schluckte es ganz or unzerkaut (hinunter); **a pig roasted ~** ein ganzes Schwein im or am Stück gebraten

◆ N Ganze(s) nt; **the ~ of the month** der ganze or gesamte Monat; **we spent the ~ of the morning at the airport** wir waren den ganzen Morgen (lang) auf dem Flughafen; **the ~ of the time** die ganze Zeit; **the ~ of his savings** seine gesamten or sämtlichen Ersparnisse; **the ~ of London** ganz London; **nearly the ~ of our production** fast unsere gesamte Produktion; **as a ~** als Ganzes; **these people, as a ~, are ...** diese Leute sind in ihrer Gesamtheit ...; **on the ~** im Großen und Ganzen, im Ganzen gesehen, alles in allem

whole: **wholefood** (esp Brit) N (also **wholefoods**) Vollwertkost f ADJ attr Vollwert(kost)-; **~ diet** Vollwert(kost)diät f; **~ shop** Bioladen m; **wholehearted** ADJ völlig, uneingeschränkt; **~ congratulations/thanks to X** X (dat) gratulieren/danken wir von ganzem Herzen; **to be ~ in one's cooperation** sich rückhaltlos mit einsetzen; **wholeheartedly** ✪ 11.1, 26.3 ADV voll und ganz; **wholeheartedness** N Rückhaltlosigkeit f; **whole hog** N **to go the ~** (inf) aufs Ganze gehen; **wholemeal** (Brit) ADJ Vollkorn-; **~ bread** Vollkornbrot nt ◆ N feiner Vollkornschrot; **whole milk** N Vollmilch f

wholeness ['həʊlnɪs] N Gesamtheit f, Ganzheit f

whole: **whole note** N (esp US Mus) ganze Note; **whole number** N ganze Zahl

wholesale ['həʊlseɪl] N Großhandel m ADJ attr **a** (Comm) Großhandels-; **~ price** Großhandelspreis m; **~ dealer** Großhändler(in) m(f), Grossist(in) m(f) **b** (fig) (= widespread) umfassend, massiv; (= indiscriminate) wild, generell; **~ redundancies** Massenentlassungen pl; **~ slaughter of the infected animals** die Abschlachtung aller infizierten Tiere ADV **a** im Großhandel **b** (fig) in Bausch und Bogen; (= in great numbers) massenweise, massenhaft; (= without modification) (so) ohne weiteres ◆ VT goods einen Großhandel betreiben mit ◆ VI (item) einen Großhandelspreis haben (at von)

wholesale business N Großhandel m

wholesale price index N Großhandelspreisindex m

wholesaler ['həʊlseɪlə'] N Großhändler(in) m(f), Grossist(in) m(f)

wholesale trade N Großhandel m

wholesaling ['həʊlseɪlɪŋ] N Großhandel m

wholesome ['həʊlsəm] ADJ **a** gesund; food gesund, bekömmlich **b** (= moral) entertainment, film erbaulich; person mustergültig

wholesomeness ['həʊlsəmnɪs] N (of food) Bekömmlichkeit f; (of appearance) Gesundheit f

whole-wheat ['həʊlwiːt] N Voll(korn)weizen m

who'll [huːl] contr of **who will** of **who shall**

wholly ['həʊlɪ] ADV völlig, gänzlich; **the project was ~ successful** das Projekt war gänzlich erfolgreich or war ein voller Erfolg; **I'm not ~ convinced that ...** ich bin nicht völlig or gänzlich überzeugt, dass ...; **this is ~ but ~ ...** das ist völlig und ganz ...

whom [huːm] PRON **a** (interrog) (acc) wen; (dat) wem **b** (rel) (acc) den/die/das; (dat) dem/der/dem; **..., all/both of ~ were drunk** ..., die alle/beide betrunken waren; **none/all of ~** von denen keine(r, s)/alle

whomp [wɒmp] (US, inf) VT (= hit) einschlagen auf (+acc); (= defeat) schlagen ◆ N Schlag m

whom(so)ever [ˌhuːm(səʊ)'evə'] PRON (form) wen/wem auch immer; (= no matter who) ganz gleich or egal wen/wem

whoop [huːp] N Ruf m, Schrei m; (= war cry also) Geschrei nt no pl, Geheul nt no pl; **with a ~ of joy** unter Freudengeschrei ◆ VT **to ~ it up** (inf) auf die Pauke hauen (inf) ◆ VI rufen, schreien; (with whooping cough) pfeifen; (with joy) jauchzen

whoop-de-doo [ˌhuːpdɪˈduː, ˌwuːp-] N (US inf) ausgelassene Fröhlichkeit, Ausgelassenheit f

whoopee [ˈwʊpiː] **N** to make ~ (dated inf) Rabatz machen (dated inf) **INTERJ** [wʊˈpiː] hurra, juchhe(i)

whooping cough [ˈhuːpɪŋˌkɒf] N Keuchhusten m

whoops [wuːps] INTERJ hoppla, huch, hups

whoosh [wuːʃ] **N** (of water) Rauschen nt; (of air) Zischen nt **VI** rauschen; (air) zischen; **a train ~ed past** ein Zug schoss or brauste vorbei

whop [wɒp] VT (inf) schlagen; **he ~ped me on the chin** er hat mir eine ans Kinn gegeben (inf)

whopper [ˈwɒpə] N (inf) (= sth big) Brocken m (inf), Apparat m (inf); (= lie) faustdicke Lüge

whopping [ˈwɒpɪŋ] ADJ (inf) Mords- (inf), Riesen-; **a ~ amount** ein Riesenbetrag m, ein Mordsbetrag m (inf); **a ~ big fish** ein mordsgroßer Fisch (inf), ein Monstrum nt von einem Fisch (inf)

whore [hɔː] **N** Hure f **VI** (also **to go whoring**) herumhuren (inf)

whore: whorehouse N (inf) Bordell nt, Freudenhaus nt; **whoremonger** N (old) Hurenbock m

whorl [wɜːl] **N** Kringel m; (of shell) (Spiral)windung f; (Bot) Quirl m, Wirtel m; (of fingerprint) Wirbel m

whortleberry [ˈwɜːtlbərɪ] N Heidelbeere f, Blaubeere f (dial)

who's [huːz] contr of **who has** or **who is**

whose [huːz] POSS PRON **a** (interrog) wessen; **~ is this?** wem gehört das?; **~ car did you go in?** in wessen Auto sind Sie gefahren? **b** (rel) dessen; (after f and pl) deren

whosoever [ˌhuːsəʊˈevə] PRON (old) = **whoever**

why [waɪ] ☉ 1.1, 17.2, 26.3 **ADV** warum, weshalb; (asking for the purpose) wozu; (= how come that ...) wieso; **~ not ask him?** warum fragst du/fragen wir ihn etc ihn nicht?; **~ wait?** warum or wozu (noch) warten?; **~ do it this way?** warum denn so?; **that's ~** darum, deshalb, deswegen; **that's exactly ~ ...** genau deshalb or deswegen ...
INTERJ ~, **of course, that's right!** ja doch or aber sicher, das stimmt so!; **are you sure? – ~ yes (of course/I think so)** sind Sie sicher? – aber ja doch; **~ that's easy!** na, das ist doch einfach!; **take the bus! ~, it's only a short walk** den Bus nehmen? ach was, das ist doch nur ein Katzensprung; **~, if it isn't Charles!** na so was, das ist doch (der) Charles!; **who did it? – it's obvious** wer das war? na or also, das ist doch klar **N** the **~s and (the) wherefores** das Warum und Weshalb

WI a abbr of **Women's Institute b** abbr of **West Indies**

wick [wɪk] N Docht m; **to get on sb's ~** (Brit inf) jdm auf den Wecker gehen (inf) or fallen (inf)

wicked [ˈwɪkɪd] ADJ **a** (= evil) person etc böse; (= immoral) schlecht, gottlos; (= indulging in vices) lasterhaft; **that was a ~ thing to do** das war aber gemein or böse or niederträchtig (von dir/ihm etc); **it's ~ to tease animals** Tiere zu quälen ist gemein; **it's ~ to tell lies/swear** Lügen/Fluchen ist hässlich
b (= vicious) böse; weapon gemein (inf), niederträchtig, heimtückisch; satire boshaft; blow, frost, wind, weather gemein (inf), böse; **he has a ~ temper** er ist unbeherrscht or aufbrausend or jähzornig; **the dog has a ~ temper** der Hund ist bösartig
c (= mischievous) smile, look, grin frech, boshaft; **you ~ girl, you** du schlimmes Mädchen or du freches Stück (inf) (du)!; **I've just had a ~ idea** mir fällt (gerade) was Tolles (inf) or (practical joke) ein guter Streich ein
d (inf, = scandalous) price etc hanebüchen (inf), unverschämt; **it's a ~ shame** es ist jammerschade; **it's ~ what they charge** es ist hanebüchen (inf) or unverschämt or nicht mehr feierlich (inf), was sie verlangen
e (sl, = very good) geil (sl)

wickedly [ˈwɪkɪdlɪ] ADV **a** (= with evil intentions) böse; (= immorally) schlecht, gottlos; (= dissolutely) lasterhaft **b** cold gemein; **a ~ accurate satire** eine scharf treffende Satire **c** (= mischievously) smile, look, grin frech **d** (inf) expensive unverschämt

wickedness [ˈwɪkɪdnɪs] N **a** (of person) Schlechtigkeit f; (= immorality) Verderbtheit f; (= indulgence in vices) Lasterhaftigkeit f **b** (= viciousness) Bösartigkeit f; (of satire) Boshaftigkeit f; (of frost, wind, weather) Gemeinheit f; **the ~ of his temper** seine aufbrausende or unbeherrschte Art **c** (= mischievousness) Boshaftigkeit f, Bosheit f **d** (inf, of prices etc) Unverschämtheit f

wicker [ˈwɪkə] **N** Korbgeflecht nt **ADJ** attr Korb-; **~ furniture** Korbmöbel pl

wicker: wicker (arm)chair N Korbsessel m; **wicker basket** N (Weiden)korb m; **wicker fence** N Weidenzaun m; **wickerwork** **N** (= activity) Korbflechten nt; (= material) Korbgeflecht nt; (= articles) Korbwaren pl **ADJ** Korb-; **~ chair** Korbsessel m; **~ basket** Weidenkorb m

wicket [ˈwɪkɪt] N **a** Gatter nt; (for selling tickets) Fenster nt **b** (Cricket) (= stumps: also **wickets**) Wicket nt, Pfostentor nt; (= pitch) Spielbahn f; **three ~s fell before lunch** es gab drei Wicketwürfe vor der Mittagspause; **we won by four ~s** wir gewannen und hatten vier Schlagmänner noch nicht in Einsatz gehabt; **to keep ~** Torwächter sein → **sticky c** (US: = croquet hoop) Tor nt

wicketkeeper [ˈwɪkɪtˈkiːpə] N (Cricket) Torwächter(in) m(f)

widdle [ˈwɪdl] (inf) **VI** pinkeln (inf) **N** to **go for a ~** (hum) pinkeln gehen (inf)

wide [waɪd] **ADJ** (+er) **a** road, smile, feet, gap breit; skirt, trousers, plain weit; eyes groß; **it is three feet ~** es ist drei Fuß breit; (material) es liegt drei Fuß breit; (room) es ist drei Fuß in der Breite; **the big ~ world** die (große) weite Welt; **her eyes were ~ with amazement** sie machte große Augen vor Erstaunen
b (= considerable, comprehensive) difference, variety groß; experience, choice reich, umfangreich; public, knowledge, range breit; interests vielfältig, breit gefächert; coverage of report umfassend; network weit verzweigt; circulation weit, groß; question weitreichend, weit reichend; **~ reading is the best education** viel zu lesen ist die beste Art der Erziehung or Bildung; **his ~ reading** seine große Belesenheit
c (missing the target) daneben pred, gefehlt; **you're a bit ~ there** da liegst du etwas daneben; **~ of the truth** nicht ganz wahrheitsgetreu; **a ~ ball** (Cricket) ein Ball, der nicht in Reichweite des Schlagmanns aufspringt; **it was ~ of the target** es verpasste das Ziel, es ging daneben
ADV a (= extending far) weit; **they are set ~ apart** sie liegen weit auseinander → **far**
b (= fully) weit; open **~!** bitte weit öffnen; **the general/writer left himself ~ open to attack** der General/Verfasser hat sich (überhaupt) nicht gegen Angriffe abgesichert; **the law is ~ open to criticism/abuse** das Gesetz bietet viele Ansatzpunkte für Kritik/öffnet dem Missbrauch Tür und Tor
c (= far from the target) daneben; **to go ~ of sth** über etw (acc) hinausgehen, an etw (dat) vorbeigehen

-wide [-waɪd] ADJ suf in dem/der gesamten ...; (country-wide etc) -weit; **Europe-wide** europaweit; **a company-wide pay increase** eine Gehaltserhöhung für die ganze Firma

wide: wide-angle (lens) N (Phot) Weitwinkel(objektiv nt) or -; **wide area network** N (Comput) Weitverkehrsnetz nt; **wide-awake** ADJ attr, **wide awake** ADJ pred (= fully awake) hellwach; (= alert) wach; **you can't fool her, she's much too wide awake** du kannst ihr nichts vormachen, dazu passt sie viel zu genau auf or dazu ist sie viel zu helle (inf); **wide-awake hat** N Schlapphut m; **wide-band** ADJ (Rad) Breitband-; **~ transmission** Breitband-

übertragung f; **wide-body aircraft** [ˈwaɪdˌbɒdɪ-] N (Aviat: inf) Großraumflugzeug nt; **wide boy** N (Brit, inf) Fuchs m (inf), Gauner m; **wide-eyed** ADJ mit großen Augen; **she gazed at him with ~ innocence** sie starrte ihn mit großen, unschuldigen Kinderaugen an; **in ~ amazement** mit großen, erstaunten Augen

widely [ˈwaɪdlɪ] ADV weit; (= by or to many people) weit und breit, überall, allgemein; (= greatly) vary stark; differing völlig; (= extensively) available fast überall; **his remarks were ~ publicized** seine Bemerkungen fanden weite Verbreitung; **the opinion is ~ held ...** es herrscht in weiten Kreisen die Ansicht ...; **it is not ~ understood why ...** es wird nicht überall or von allen verstanden, warum ...; **he became ~ known as ...** er wurde überall or in weiten Kreisen bekannt als ...; **a ~ read student** ein sehr belesener Student

widen [ˈwaɪdn] **VT** road verbreitern; passage, scope erweitern; circle of friends vergrößern; appeal erhöhen; knowledge etc erweitern **VI** breiter werden; (interests etc) sich ausweiten

▶ **widen out** VI **a** (river, valley etc) sich erweitern (into zu) **b** (interests etc) sich ausweiten

wideness [ˈwaɪdnɪs] N **a** (of road, gap) Breite f; (of skirt) Weite f **b** (of knowledge, coverage, interests) Breite f **c** (of variety, choice) Reichtum m

wide: wide-open ADJ attr, **wide open** ADJ pred **a** (= fully open) door, window ganz or weit or sperrangelweit (inf) offen; beak weit aufgerissen or aufgesperrt; eyes weit aufgerissen **b** (= not decided) match etc völlig offen; **the game is still wide open** der Spielausgang ist noch völlig offen **c** (US, inf) wo liberale Gesetze bezüglich Prostitution, Glücksspiele etc herrschen; **wide-ranging** ADJ weitreichend, weit reichend; **wide-screen** ADJ (Film) Breitwand-; **in ~ format** im Breitwandformat; **~ television set** Breitbildfernseher m; **widespread** ADJ weitverbreitet attr; **to become ~** weite Verbreitung erlangen

widgeon [ˈwɪdʒən] N Pfeifente f

widget [ˈwɪdʒɪt] N (inf) **a** (= manufactured product) Produkt nt, Ding nt (inf); **10,000 ~s per month** 10.000 Produkte or Dinger (inf) pro Monat **b** (Brit: in beer can) Widget nt, in eine Bierdose eingebaute zweite Kammer, die das Bier beim Öffnen zum Aufschäumen bringt

widish [ˈwaɪdɪʃ] ADJ ziemlich breit

widow [ˈwɪdəʊ] **N a** Witwe f; **to be left a ~** als Witwe zurückbleiben; **golf ~** (hum) Golfwitwe f → **grass widow b** (Typ) Hurenkind nt **VT** zur Witwe/zum Witwer machen; **she was twice ~ed** sie ist zweimal verwitwet

widowed [ˈwɪdəʊd] ADJ verwitwet; **a ~ mother of four** eine Witwe mit vier Kindern

widower [ˈwɪdəʊə] N Witwer m

widowhood [ˈwɪdəʊhʊd] N (of woman) (= period) Witwenschaft f; (= state also) Witwentum nt; (rare, of man) Witwerschaft f

widow's [ˈwɪdəʊz]: **widow's allowance** N (Brit) (zeitweilige) Witwenbeihilfe f; **widow's annuity** N Witwenrente f; **widow's benefits** PL (Brit) Sozialversicherungsleistungen pl an Witwen; **widow's mite** N (fig) Scherflein nt (der armen Witwe); **widow's peak** N spitzer Haaransatz; **widow's pension** N Witwenrente f

width [wɪdθ] N Breite f; (of trouser legs, skirts etc) Weite f; **six feet in ~** sechs Fuß breit; **what is the ~ of the material?** wie breit liegt dieser Stoff? **b** (= piece of material) Breite f; **three ~s of cloth** drei mal die Breite

widthways [ˈwɪdθweɪz], **widthwise** [ˈwɪdθwaɪz] ADV der Breite nach

wield [wiːld] VT pen, sword führen; axe schwingen; power, influence ausüben, haben; **~ing his sword above his head** das Schwert über seinem Haupte schwingend; **to ~ power over sth** über etw (acc) Macht ausüben

wiener [ˈwiːnə] N (US: = frankfurter) Wiener Würstchen nt

wiener dog N (US hum) Dackel m

wife [waɪf] N pl **wives** Frau f, Gattin f (form), Gemahlin f (liter, form); **the ~** (inf) die Frau; **a woman whom he would never make his ~** eine Person, die er niemals zu seiner Frau machen würde; **businessmen who take their wives with them on their trips** Geschäftsleute, die ihre (Ehe)frauen or Damen mit auf Geschäftsreise nehmen; **to take a ~** (old) sich (dat) eine Frau or ein Weib (old) nehmen; **to take sb to ~** (old) jdn zum Weibe nehmen (old)

wife-batterer ['waɪfˌbætərə], **wife-beater** ['waɪfˌbiːtə] N prügelnder Ehemann

wifeless ['waɪflɪs] ADJ man unverheiratet

wifely ['waɪflɪ] ADJ **~ duties** Pflichten pl als Ehefrau; **~ devotion** Hingabe f einer Ehefrau

wife-swapping ['waɪfˌswɒpɪŋ] N Partnertausch m; **~ party** Party f mit Partnertausch

wig [wɪɡ] N Perücke f

wigeon N = **widgeon**

wigged [wɪɡd] ADJ eine Perücke tragend; **the judges were ceremonially ~ and robed** die Richter waren zeremoniell in Roben gekleidet und trugen Perücken

wigging ['wɪɡɪŋ] N (dated inf) Standpauke f, Gardinenpredigt f; **to give sb a ~** jdm eine Standpauke or Gardinenpredigt halten, jdm die Leviten lesen (dated)

wiggle ['wɪɡl] N Wackeln nt no pl; **give it a ~ and it might come free** wackeln Sie mal daran, dann geht es vielleicht raus; **to get a ~ on** (inf) Dampf dahinter machen (inf) VT wackeln mit; eyebrows zucken mit VI wackeln; (eyebrows) zucken

wiggly ['wɪɡlɪ] ADJ wackelnd; amateur film etc wackelig, verwackelt; **~ line** Schlangenlinie f; (drawn) Wellenlinie f

wight [waɪt] N (old) Wicht m

wigmaker ['wɪɡmeɪkə] N Perückenmacher(in) m(f)

wigwam ['wɪɡwæm] N Wigwam m

wilco ['wɪlkəʊ] INTERJ (Mil etc) wird gemacht, zu Befehl

wild [waɪld] ADJ (+er) **a** (= not domesticated, not civilized) wild; people unzivilisiert; garden, wood verwildert; flowers wild wachsend; **~ animals** Tiere pl in freier Wildbahn; **the ~ animals of Northern Europe** Tiere pl Nordeuropas, die Tierwelt Nordeuropas; **a lion is a ~ animal** der Löwe lebt in freier Wildbahn; **the plant in its ~ state** die Pflanze im Naturzustand **b** (= stormy) weather, wind, sea rau, stürmisch **c** (= excited, frantic, unruly, riotous) wild (with vor +dat); (= disordered) hair wirr, unordentlich; joy, desire unbändig **d** (inf, = angry) wütend (with, at mit, auf +acc), rasend; **it drives or makes me ~** das macht mich ganz wild or rasend; **to get ~** wild werden (inf) **e** (inf, = very keen) **to be ~ about sb/sth** auf jdn/etw wild or scharf (inf) or versessen sein; **to be ~ to do sth** (esp US) wild or scharf (inf) or versessen darauf sein, etw zu tun **f** (= rash, extravagant) promise unüberlegt; exaggeration maßlos, wild; allegation wild; fluctuations stark; expectations, imagination, fancies kühn; **never in my ~est dreams** auch in meinen kühnsten Träumen nicht **g** (= wide of the mark, erratic) Fehl-; spelling unsicher; **~ throw** Fehlwurf m; **~ shot** Fehlschuss m; **it was just/he took a ~ guess** es war/er hatte nur so (wild) drauflosgeraten **h** (Cards) beliebig verwendbar **i** (inf, = fantastic, great) film, concert etc toll (inf) ADV (= in the natural state) grow wild; run frei; **to let one's imagination run ~** seiner Fantasie or Phantasie (dat) freien Lauf lassen; **the roses/the children have run ~** die Rosen/die Kinder sind verwildert; **he lets his kids run ~** (pej) er lässt seine Kinder auf der Straße aufwachsen; **in the country the kids can run ~** auf dem Land kann man die Kinder einfach laufen or herumspringen lassen **b** (= without aim) shoot ins Blaue, drauflos; (= off the mark) go, throw daneben

N Wildnis f; **in the ~** in der Wildnis, in freier Wildbahn; **the call of the ~** der Ruf der Wildnis; **the ~s** die Wildnis, out in the **~s** (hum: = not in the city) auf dem platten Lande (inf), jwd (inf); **out in the ~s of Berkshire** im hintersten Berkshire

wild: wild boar N Wildschwein nt; **wildcard** ADJ attr **~ character** Joker- or Ersatzzeichen nt; **wild card** N (Comput) Wildcard f, Jokerzeichen nt; **wildcat** N **a** (Zool) Wildkatze f **b** (inf, = woman) Wildkatze f **c** (US inf) (Comm: = risky venture) gewagte or riskante Sache; (= trial oil well) Probe- or Versuchsbohrung f ADJ attr (= risky) riskant, gewagt; **~ company** Schwindelfirma f; **wildcat strike** N wilder Streik; **wild child** N (Brit) Wildfang m; **wild duck** N Wildente f

wildebeest ['wɪldəbiːst] N Gnu nt

wilderness ['wɪldənɪs] N Wildnis f; (fig) Wüste f; **a voice crying in the ~** die Stimme eines Rufenden in der Wüste

wild: wild-eyed ADJ person wild dreinblickend attr; look wild; **wildfire** N **to spread like ~** sich wie ein Lauffeuer ausbreiten; **wildfowl** N, no pl Wildgeflügel nt; **wild goose** N Wildgans f; **wild-goose chase** N fruchtloses Unterfangen, Wolpertingerjagd f (S Ger); **to send sb out on a ~** jdn für nichts und wieder nichts losschicken; **wildlife** N die Tierwelt; **~ sanctuary** or **park** Wildschutzgebiet nt, Wildreservat nt; **wildlifer** ['waɪldlaɪfə] N Naturschützer(in) m(f)

wildly ['waɪldlɪ] ADV **a** (= violently) wild, heftig **b** (= in disorder) wirr; **his hair fell ~ over his forehead** sein Haar fiel ihm wirr in die Stirn **c** (= without aim) wild; **to hit out ~** wild um sich schlagen; **to shoot ~** wild drauflosschießen **d** (= extravagantly) guess drauflos, ins Blaue hinein; talk unausgegoren; happy rasend; exaggerated stark, maßlos; wrong, different total, völlig; **I think she is being ~ optimistic** ich denke, dass sie maßlos or übertrieben optimistisch ist **e** (= excitedly, distractedly) wild, aufgeregt **f** (= riotously) wild

wildness ['waɪldnɪs] N **a** (= rough, uncivilized state) Wildheit f **b** (of storm etc) Wildheit f, Stärke f, Heftigkeit f; **the ~ of the weather** das rauhe or stürmische Wetter **c** (= frenzy, unruliness) Wildheit f **d** (= extravagance) (of promise) Unüberlegtheit f; (of exaggeration) Maßlosigkeit f; (of fluctuations) Stärke f; (of expectations, imagination) Kühnheit f **e** (= lack of aim) Unkontrolliertheit f; (= erratic nature: of spelling) Unsicherheit f

wild: wild oat N Windhafer m → **oat**; **wild silk** N Wildseide f; **wildwater** ['waɪldˌwɔːtə] N Wildwasser nt; **Wild West** N **the ~** der Wilde Westen

wile [waɪl] N usu pl List f, Schliche pl; **she used all her ~s to persuade him** sie ließ ihren ganzen Charme spielen, um ihn zu überreden

wilful, (US) **willful** ['wɪlfʊl] ADJ **a** (= self-willed) eigensinnig, eigenwillig **b** (= deliberate) neglect, damage, waste mutwillig; murder vorsätzlich; disobedience wissentlich

wilfully, (US) **willfully** ['wɪlfʊlɪ] ADV **a** (= stubbornly) eigensinnig **b** (= deliberately) destroy, damage, waste mutwillig; ignore, neglect, disobey vorsätzlich

wilfulness, (US) **willfulness** ['wɪlfʊlnɪs] N **a** (of person) Eigensinn m, Eigenwilligkeit f **b** (of action) Mutwilligkeit f, Vorsätzlichkeit f

wiliness ['waɪlɪnɪs] N Listigkeit f, Schläue f, Hinterlist f (pej)

will¹ [wɪl] ⊕ 20.5 pret **would** MODAL AUX VB **a** (future) werden; **I'm sure that he ~ come** ich bin sicher, dass er kommt; **you ~ come to see us, won't you?** Sie kommen uns doch besuchen, ja?; **I'll be right there** komme sofort!; **I ~ have finished by Tuesday** bis Dienstag bin ich fertig; **you won't lose it, ~ you?** du wirst es doch nicht verlieren, oder?; **you won't insist on that, ~ you? – oh yes, I ~** Sie bestehen doch nicht darauf, oder? – o doch! or o ja! or doch, doch!

b (emphatic, expressing determination, compulsion etc) **I ~ not have it!** das dulde ich nicht, das kommt mir nicht infrage or in Frage nicht!; **~ you be quiet!** willst du jetzt wohl ruhig sein!, bist du or sei jetzt endlich ruhig!; **you ~ not talk to me like that!** so lasse ich nicht mit mir reden!; **he says he ~ go** er sagt, er geht und ich sage, er geht nicht

c (expressing willingness, consent etc) wollen; **he won't sign** er unterschreibt nicht, er will nicht unterschreiben; **if she won't say yes** wenn sie nicht ja sagt; **he wouldn't help me** er wollte or mochte mir nicht helfen; **wait a moment, ~ you?** warten Sie einen Moment, ja bitte?; (impatiently) jetzt warte doch mal einen Moment!; **~ she, won't she?** ob sie wohl ...?

d (in questions) **~ you have some more tea?** möchten Sie noch Tee?; **~ you accept these conditions?** akzeptieren Sie diese Bedingungen?; **won't you take a seat?** wollen or möchten Sie sich nicht setzen?; **won't you please come home?** komm doch bitte nach Hause!; **there isn't any tea, ~ coffee do?** es ist kein Tee da, darf es auch Kaffee sein? or tut es Kaffee auch? (inf)

e (insistence) **well, if he ~ drive so fast** also, wenn er (eben) unbedingt so schnell fahren muss; **well, if you won't take advice** wenn du (eben) keinen Rat annimmst, na bitte; **he ~ interrupt all the time** er muss ständig dazwischenreden

f (assumption) **he'll be there by now** jetzt ist er schon da, jetzt dürfte er schon da sein; **was that the doorbell? that ~ be for you** hats geklingelt? – das ist bestimmt für dich or das wird or dürfte für dich sein; **this ~ be our bus** das wird or dürfte unser Bus sein; **this ~ be the one you want** das dürfte (es) wohl sein, was Sie wünschen

g (tendency) **the solution ~ turn red if ...** die Lösung färbt sich rot, wenn ...; **sometimes he ~ sit in his room for hours** manchmal sitzt er auch stundenlang in seinem Zimmer

h (capability) **is the engine start now?** springt der Motor jetzt an?; **the car won't start** das Auto springt nicht an or will nicht anspringen; **the door won't open** die Tür lässt sich nicht öffnen or geht nicht auf (inf); **the cut won't heal** die Schnittwunde will nicht (ver)heilen; **the car ~ do up to 120 mph** das Auto fährt bis zu 120 Meilen pro Stunde

VI wollen; **say what you ~** du kannst sagen, was du willst; **as you ~!** wie du willst!; **it is, if you ~, a kind of mystery** das ist, wenn du so willst, eine Art Rätsel

will² ⊕ 9.3 N **a** Wille m; **to have a ~ of one's own** einen eigenen Willen haben; (hum) so seine Mucken haben (inf); **the ~ to win/live** der Wille or das Bestreben, zu gewinnen/zu leben, der Sieges-/Lebenswille; **(to go) against one's/sb's ~** gegen einen/jds Willen (handeln); **if that's your ~** wenn das dein Wunsch ist; **at ~** nach Belieben, nach Lust und Laune, beliebig; **fire at ~!** ohne Befehl schießen; **of one's own free ~** aus freien Stücken, aus freiem Willen; **with the best ~ in the world** beim or mit (dem) (aller)besten Willen; **where there is a ~ there is a way** (Prov) wo ein Wille ist, ist auch ein Weg (Prov); **to do sb's ~** (dated) jdm seinen Willen tun; **to have one's ~** (dated) seinen Kopf durchsetzen; **Thy ~ be done** Dein Wille geschehe; **to work with a ~** mit (Feuer)eifer arbeiten → **good will**, **ill** ADJ **b**

b (= testament) letzter Wille, Testament nt; **the last ~ and testament of ...** der letzte Wille or das Testament des/der ...; **to make one's ~** sein Testament machen

VT **a** (old: = ordain) wollen, bestimmen, verfügen (geh); **God has so ~ed** Gott hat es so gewollt or gefügt or bestimmt

b (= urge by willpower) (durch Willenskraft) erzwingen; **to ~ sb to do sth** jdn durch die eigene Willensanstrengung dazu bringen, dass er etw tut; **he ~ed himself to stay awake** er hat sich (dazu) gezwungen, wach zu bleiben; **she ~ed herself to get better** sie hat ihre Genesung durch ihre Willenskraft erzwungen; **he ~ed the ball into the net** er hat den Ball ins Netz hypnotisiert (*inf*)

c (*by testament*) (testamentarisch) vermachen, vererben (*sth to sb* jdm etw)

VI wollen; **if God ~s** so Gott will

will-call ['wɪlkɔ:l] **N a** (= *purchase*) Kauf, bei dem eine Anzahlung gemacht und die Ware zurückgelegt wird **b** (= *goods*) angezahlte und zurückgelegte Ware

willful etc (*US*) = **wilful** etc

William ['wɪljəm] **N** Wilhelm *m*

Williams pear ['wɪljəmz,pɛə'] **N** (*Bot*) Williams Christbirne *f*

willie ['wɪlɪ] **N** (*Brit inf*, = *penis*) Pimmel *m* (*inf*)

willies ['wɪlɪz] **PL** (*inf*) **to get the ~** Zustände kriegen (*inf*); **it/he gives me the ~** da/bei dem wird mir ganz anders (*inf*)

willing ['wɪlɪŋ] **ADJ a** (= *prepared*) **to be ~ to do sth** bereit *or* gewillt (*geh*) *or* willens (*liter*, *old*) sein, etw zu tun; **God ~** so Gott will; **he was ~ for me to take it** es war ihm recht, dass ich es nahm; **he was not ~ for us to go/for this to be done** er war nicht gewillt, uns gehen zu lassen/das geschehen zu lassen; **~ to compromise** kompromissbereit; **~ to help** hilfsbereit; **~ to make concessions** konzessionsbereit; **~ to negotiate** verhandlungsbereit; **~ to work** arbeitswillig

b (= *ready to help, cheerfully ready*) *workers, helpers* bereitwillig; **prepared to lend a ~ hand** gerne dazu bereit zu helfen

c (= *voluntary*) *sacrifice* willentlich

willingly ['wɪlɪŋlɪ] **ADV** bereitwillig, gerne; **will you help? – yes,** wollen Sie helfen? – (ja,) gerne

willingness ['wɪlɪŋnɪs] **N a** (= *readiness*) Bereitschaft *f*; **~ to compromise** Kompromissbereitschaft *f*; **~ to help** Hilfsbereitschaft *f*; **~ to make concessions** Konzessionsbereitschaft *f*; **~ to negotiate** Verhandlungsbereitschaft *f*; **~ to work** Arbeitswilligkeit *f* **b** (= *enthusiasm*) Bereitwilligkeit *f*

will-o'-the-wisp ['wɪləðə'wɪsp] **N** Irrlicht *nt*; (*fig*) Trugbild *nt*

willow ['wɪləʊ] **N** (*also* **willow tree**) Weide *f*, Weidenbaum *m*; (= *wood*) Weidenholz *nt*; (= *twigs*) Weidenruten *or* -gerten *pl*

willowherb ['wɪləʊ,hɜ:b] **N** Weidenröschen *nt*

willow pattern N chinesisches Weidenmotiv (*auf Porzellan*) **ADJ** *attr* mit chinesischem Weidenmotiv

willowy ['wɪləʊɪ] **ADJ** gertenschlank

willpower ['wɪl,paʊə'] **N** Willenskraft *f*

willy ['wɪlɪ] **N** (*Brit inf*) = **willie**

willy-nilly ['wɪlɪ'nɪlɪ] **ADV a** (= *at random*) *choose, allocate* aufs Geratewohl; *accept* wahllos, ohne weiteres **b** (= *willingly or not*) wohl oder übel, nolens volens

wilt¹ [wɪlt] (*old*) 2nd pers sing of **will¹**

wilt² **VI a** (*flowers*) welken, verwelken, welk werden **b** (*person*) matt werden; (*after physical exercise*) schlapp werden; (*enthusiasm, energy*) abflauen **VT** ausdörren

Wilts [wɪlts] *abbr of* **Wiltshire**

wily ['waɪlɪ] **ADJ** (+*er*) listig, schlau, hinterlistig (*pej*)

wimp [wɪmp] **N** (*inf*) Schwächling *m*, Waschlappen *m* (*inf*)

▶ **wimp out** **VI** (*inf*) kneifen (*inf*); **to wimp out of sth** bei etw kneifen (*inf*)

wimpish ['wɪmpɪʃ] **ADJ** (*inf*) weichlich, schlapp (*inf*)

wimpishly ['wɪmpɪʃlɪ] **ADV** (*inf*) schlapp (*inf*); **he ~ agreed to sell** Schwächling *or* Waschlappen (*inf*), der er ist, stimmte er dem Verkauf zu

wimpishness ['wɪmpɪʃnɪs] **N** (*inf*) Weichlichkeit *f*, Schlappheit *f* (*inf*)

wimple ['wɪmpl] **N** Rise *f* (*spec*), Schleier *m*; (*worn by nuns*) (Nonnen)schleier *m*

win [wɪn] *vb: pret, ptp* **won** **N** Sieg *m*; **to back a horse for a ~** auf den Sieg eines Pferdes setzen; **to have a ~** (*money*) einen Gewinn machen; (*victory*) einen Sieg erzielen; **to play for a ~** auf Sieg spielen

VT a *race, prize, battle, election, money, bet, sympathy, support, friends, glory* gewinnen; *reputation* erwerben; *scholarship, contract* bekommen; *victory* erringen; **to ~ sb's heart/love/hand** jds Herz/Liebe/Hand gewinnen; **he tried to ~ her** er versuchte, sie für sich zu gewinnen; **it won him the first prize** es brachte ihm den ersten Preis ein; **to ~ sth from** *or* **off** (*inf*) **sb** jdm etw abgewinnen

b (= *obtain, extract*) gewinnen; **the oil won from the North Sea** das aus der Nordsee gewonnene Öl; **land won from the sea** dem Meer abgewonnenes Land

c (*liter*, = *reach with effort*) *shore, summit* erreichen

VI a (*in race, election, argument etc*) gewinnen, siegen; **if ~ning becomes too important** wenn das Siegen *or* das Gewinnen zu wichtig wird; **OK, you ~, I was wrong** okay, du hast gewonnen, ich habe mich geirrt; **whatever I do, I just can't ~** egal, was ich mache, ich machs immer falsch

b (*liter*) **to ~ free** sich freikämpfen, sich befreien

▶ **win back** **VT** *sep* zurück- *or* wiedergewinnen

▶ **win out** **VI** letztlich siegen (*over sb* über jdn), sich durchsetzen (*over sb* jdm gegenüber)

▶ **win over** **VT** *sep* für sich gewinnen; **it is hard to win him over** *or* **round** es ist schwer, ihn für uns *or* für unsere Seite zu gewinnen; **his speech won over** *or* **round all the government's critics** mit seiner Rede hat er alle Kritiker der Regierung für sich gewonnen; **to win sb over to Catholicism/one's own way of thinking** jdn zum Katholizismus/zur eigenen Denkungsart bekehren; **to win sb over to a plan** jdn für einen Plan gewinnen

▶ **win round** **VT** *sep* (*esp Brit*) = **win over**

▶ **win through** **VI** (*patient*) durchkommen; **to win through to the finals** das Finale schaffen; **we'll win through in the end** wir werden es schon schaffen (*inf*)

wince [wɪns] **N** (Zusammen)zucken *nt*; **ouch,** **he said with a ~** autsch, sagte er und zuckte zusammen; **to give a ~ (of pain)** (vor Schmerz) zusammenzucken **VI** zusammenzucken

winceyette [,wɪnsɪ'et] **N** Flanellette *nt*

winch [wɪntʃ] **N** Winde *f*, Winsch *f* **VT** winschen

▶ **winch up** **VT** *sep* hochwinschen

Winchester rifle ['wɪntʃestə'raɪfl] **N** Winchesterbüchse *f*

wind¹ [wɪnd] **N a** Wind *m*; **the ~ is from the east** der Wind kommt aus dem Osten *or* von Osten; **before the ~** (*Naut*) vor dem Wind; **into the ~** (*Naut*) in den Wind; **to sail close to the ~** (*fig*) sich hart an der Grenze des Erlaubten bewegen; (*Naut*) hart am Wind segeln; **(to run) like the ~** (rennen) wie der Wind; **a ~ of change** (*fig*) ein frischer(er) Wind; **there's change in the ~** (irgend)etwas bahnt sich an *or* liegt in der Luft; **to get/have the ~ up** (*Brit inf*, = *be nervous*) Angst *or* Schiss (*sl*) kriegen/haben; **to put the ~ up sb** (*Brit inf*) jdm Angst machen, jdn ins Bockshorn jagen; **to raise the ~** (= *dated Brit inf*) das nötige Kleingeld auftreiben (*inf*); **to see which way the ~ blows** (*fig*) sehen, woher der Wind weht; **to take the ~ out of sb's sails** (*fig*) jdm den Wind aus den Segeln nehmen; **he's full of ~** (*fig*) er ist ein Schaumschläger (*inf*), er macht viel Wind (*inf*)

b (= *scent*) **to get ~ of sth** (*lit, fig*) von etw Wind bekommen

c (*compass point*) **to the four ~s** in alle (vier) Winde; **to throw caution to the ~s** Bedenken in den Wind schlagen

d (*from bowel, stomach*) Wind *m*, Blähung *f*; **to break ~** einen Wind streichen lassen; **to bring up ~** aufstoßen; (*baby also*) ein Bäuerchen machen; **to have a touch of ~** leichte Blähungen haben

e (= *breath*) Atem *m*, Luft *f* (*inf*); **to get one's ~ back** wieder Luft bekommen *or* zu Atem kommen; **to get one's second ~** den toten Punkt überwunden haben; **he's losing his ~** ihm geht der Atem aus; **sound in ~ and limb** kerngesund

VT a (*Brit*: = *knock breathless*) den Atem nehmen (+*dat*); **he was ~ed by the ball** der Ball nahm ihm den Atem

b (= *scent*) wittern

c *horses* verschnaufen lassen

d *baby* ein Bäuerchen machen lassen

wind² [waɪnd] *vb: pret, ptp* **wound** **VT a** (= *twist, wrap*) *wool, bandage* wickeln; *turban etc* winden; (*on to a reel*) spulen

b (= *turn, wind up*) *handle* kurbeln, drehen; *clock, watch, clockwork toy* aufziehen

c (= *proceed by twisting*) **to ~ one's way** sich schlängeln

VI a (*river etc*) sich winden *or* schlängeln

b **how does it ~?** (*watch*) wie herum zieht man es auf?; (*handle*) wie dreht *or* kurbelt man es?; **it won't ~** er/es lässt sich nicht aufziehen; (*handle*) er/es lässt sich nicht drehen *or* kurbeln

N a **I'll give the clock a ~** ich werde die Uhr aufziehen; **give it one more ~** zieh es noch eine Umdrehung weiter auf; (*handle*) kurbele *or* drehe es noch einmal weiter

b (= *bend*) Kehre *f*, Windung *f*

▶ **wind around** **VT** *sep* +*prep obj* wickeln um; **wind it once/twice around the post** winde *or* wickele es einmal/zweimal um den Pfosten; **to wind one's arms around sb** seine Arme um jdn schlingen *or* winden (*geh*); **to wind itself a-round sth** sich um etw schlingen **VI** (*road*) sich winden **VI** +*prep obj* (*road*) sich schlängeln durch; (*procession*) sich winden durch

▶ **wind back** **VT** *sep* *film, tape* zurückspulen

▶ **wind down** **VT** *sep* **a** *car windows etc* herunterdrehen *or* -kurbeln **b** (= *reduce*) *operations* reduzieren; *production* zurückschrauben **VI a** (= *lose speed: clock*) ablaufen **b** (*path etc*) sich hinunterwinden *or* -schlängeln **c** (*inf*: = *relax*) abspannen, entspannen

▶ **wind forward** **VT** *sep* *film* weiterspulen

▶ **wind in** **VT** *sep* *fish* einziehen *or* -holen; *rope also* aufspulen

▶ **wind on** **VT** *sep* *film* weiterspulen

▶ **wind out** **VT** *sep* *cable* abwickeln, ab- *or* runterspulen

▶ **wind round** **VTI** *sep* (*esp Brit*) = **wind around**

▶ **wind up** **VT** *sep* **a** *bucket* herauf- *or* hochholen; *car window* hinaufkurbeln *or* -drehen

b *clock, mechanism* aufziehen

c (*Brit fig inf*) *person* aufziehen; **to be wound up about sth** (*fig*) über etw (*acc*) *or* wegen einer Sache (*gen*) erregt sein

d (= *close, end*) *meeting, debate, speech* beschließen, zu Ende bringen; **he wound up the arguments for the government** er fasste die Argumente der Regierung(sseite) zusammen

e *company* auflösen; *service, series* auslaufen lassen; **to wind up one's affairs** seine Angelegenheiten abwickeln

VI a (*inf*, = *end up*) enden; **to wind up in hospital/Munich** im Krankenhaus/in München landen; **to wind up doing sth** am Ende etw tun; **to wind up with nothing** am Ende ohne etwas dastehen; **he'll wind up as director** er wird es noch bis zum Direktor bringen

b (= *conclude*) **to wind up for the government** die abschließende Rede für die Regierung halten; **we sang a song to wind up** abschließend *or* zum Schluss sangen wir noch ein Lied

c (= *proceed by twisting*) sich hinaufwinden; (*road*) sich hinaufschlängeln

wind ['wɪnd-]: **windbag N** (*inf*) Schwätzer(in) *m(f)*, Schwatzmaul (*sl*), Schwafler(in) *m(f)*; **windblown ADJ** (= *windswept*) *hair, tree, person* windzerzaust; **windborne ADJ** vom Wind getrieben; **windbreak N** Windschutz *m*; **Windbreaker®** **N** (*US*) = **windcheater**; **windburn N** Rötung *f* der Haut aufgrund *or* auf Grund von Wind; **windcheater N** (*Brit*) Windjacke *or* -bluse *f*;

wind-chill factor N Wind-Kälte-Faktor *m*; **wind cone** N (*Aviat*) Wind- or Luftsack *m*

winded ['wɪndɪd] ADJ atemlos, außer Atem

wind energy N Windenergie *f*

winder ['waɪndə'] N (*of watch*) Krone *f*, (Aufzieh)rädchen *nt*; (*of alarm clock, toy etc*) Aufziehschraube *f*

windfall ['wɪndfɔːl] N Fallobst *nt*; (*fig*) unerwartetes Geschenk, unverhoffter Glücksfall

windfall: windfall profit N (*Econ*) Marktlagengewinn *m*, Q-Gewinn *m*; **windfall tax** N (*Econ*) Spekulationssteuer *f*, Steuer *f* auf Aktiengewinne

wind: wind farm N Windfarm *f*; **wind force** N (*Met*) Windstärke *f*; **wind gauge** N Wind(stärke)messer *m*; **wind generator** N Windgenerator *m*

windiness ['wɪndɪnɪs] N Wind *m*; **because of the ~ of the area** wegen des starken Windes in dieser Gegend

winding ['waɪndɪŋ] ADJ *river, staircase* gewunden; *road also* kurvenreich N **a** (*of road, river*) Windung *f*, Kehre *f*; (*fig*) Verwicklung *f* **b** (*Elec*) (= *coil*) Wicklung *f*; (= *simple twist*) Windung *f*

winding: winding sheet N (*old*) Leichentuch *nt*; **winding staircase** N Wendeltreppe *f*; **winding-up** N (*of project*) Abschluss *m*; (*of company, society*) Auflösung *f*; **winding-up sale** N Räumungsverkauf *m*

wind instrument N Blasinstrument *nt*

windjammer ['wɪndʒæmə'] N Windjammer *m*

windlass ['wɪndləs] N (= *winch*) Winde *f*; (*Naut*) Ankerwinde *f*

windless ['wɪndlɪs] ADJ windfrei, ohne Wind, windstill

wind machine N Windmaschine *f*

windmill ['wɪndmɪl] N Windmühle *f*; (*Brit*, = *toy*) Windrädchen *nt*; **to tilt at ~s** (*fig*) gegen Windmühlen(flügel) kämpfen

window ['wɪndəʊ] N (*also Comput*) Fenster *nt*; (= *shop window*) (Schau)fenster *nt*; (*of booking office, bank*) Schalter *m*; (*Comm inf*: = *opportunity*) Gelegenheit *f*; **a ~ on the world** (*fig*) ein Fenster zur Welt; **~ of opportunity** Chance *f*, (Fenster *nt* der) Gelegenheit *f*

window: window box N Blumenkasten *m*; **windowcleaner** N Fensterputzer(in) *m(f)*; **window display** N (Schaufenster)auslage *f*; **window-dresser** N (Schaufenster)dekorateur(in) *m(f)*; **window-dressing** N Auslagen- or Schaufensterdekoration *f*; (*fig*) Mache *f*, Schau *f* (*inf*), Augen(aus)wischerei *f* (*pej*); **that's just ~** das ist alles nur Mache or alles, um nach außen hin zu wirken; **window envelope** N Fensterbriefumschlag *m*; **window frame** N Fensterrahmen *m*; **window glass** N Fensterglas *nt*

windowing ['wɪndəʊɪŋ] N (*Comput*) Fenstertechnik *f*

window: window ledge N = windowsill; **windowpane** N Fensterscheibe *f*; **window seat** N (*in house*) Fensterbank *f* or -sitz *m*; (*Rail etc*) Fensterplatz *m*; **window shade** N (*esp US*) Springrollo *nt*; **window-shopper** N jd, der einen Schaufensterbummel macht; **window-shopping** N Schaufensterbummel *m*; **to go ~** einen Schaufensterbummel machen; **windowsill** N Fensterbank *f* or -brett *nt*; (*outside also*) Fenstersims *m*

wind: windpipe N Luftröhre *f*; **wind power** N Windkraft *f*, Windenergie *f*; **wind power plant** N Windkraftanlage *f*; **windproof** ADJ luftdicht, windundurchlässig; **wind quartet** N (*Mus*) Bläserquartett *nt*; **wind rose** N (*Met*) Windrose *f*; **wind scale** N Windstärkenskala *f*; **windscreen**, (*US*) **windshield** N Windschutzscheibe *f*; **windscreen washer**, (*US*) **windshield washer** N Scheibenwaschanlage *f*; **windscreen wiper**, (*US*) **windshield wiper** N Scheibenwischer *m*; **wind section** N (*Mus*) Bläser *pl*; **wind sleeve**, **windsock** N Luft- or Windsack *m*; **windsurf** VI windsurfen; **windsurfer** N (= *person*) Windsurfer(in) *m(f)*;

(= *board*) Windsurfbrett *nt*; **windsurfing** N Windsurfen *nt*; **windswept** ADJ *beach, field* über den/die/das der Wind fegt; *person, hair* (vom Wind) zerzaust; **wind tunnel** N Windkanal *m*

wind-up ['waɪndʌp] N **a** (*US*) = winding-up **b** (*Brit inf*: = *joke*) Witz *m*

windward ['wɪndwəd] ADJ Wind-, dem Wind zugekehrt; *direction* zum Wind; **~ side** dem Wind zugekehrte Seite, Windseite *f* N Windseite *f*; **to steer to ~ of an island** auf die Windseite einer Insel zusteuern

Windward Islands PL **the Windward islands** die Inseln *pl* über dem Winde (*von Dominica bis Grenada*)

windy ['wɪndɪ] ADJ (+*er*) **a** *day, weather, place* windig **b** (*inf*: = *verbose*) *speech, style* langatmig **c** (*esp Brit inf*: = *frightened*) **to be/get ~** Angst or Schiss (*sl*) haben/bekommen

Windy City N **the ~** (*US inf*) Chicago

wine [waɪn] N Wein *m*; **cheese and ~ party** *Party, bei der Wein und Käse gereicht wird* **to put new ~ in old bottles** (*fig*) jungen Wein in alte Schläuche füllen VT **to ~ and dine sb** jdn zu einem guten Abendessen einladen; **the businessmen were ~d and dined in every city they visited** die Geschäftsleute wurden in jeder Stadt, die sie besuchten, ausgezeichnet bewirtet; **he ~d and dined her for months** er hat sie monatelang zum Abendessen ausgeführt ADJ (*colour*) burgunderrot

wine: wine bar N Weinlokal *nt*; **wine bottle** N Weinflasche *f*; **wine box** N Zapfpack *m*; **wine bucket** N Sektkühler *m*; **wine cask** N Weinfass *nt*; **wine cellar** N Weinkeller *m*; **wine cooler** N Weinkühler *m*; **wineglass** N Weinglas *nt*; **wine grower** N Winzer(in) *m(f)*, Weinbauer(in) *m(f)*; **wine growing** ADJ Wein(an)bau-; **~ region** Wein(an)baugebiet *nt* N Wein(an)bau *m*; **wine gum** N Weingummi *nt*; **wine list** N Weinkarte *f*; **wine-making** N Weinherstellung *f*; **wine merchant** N Weinhändler(in) *m(f)*; **winepress** N Weinpresse *f*, Kelter *f*; **wine rack** N Flaschenregal *nt* (für Weinflaschen)

winery ['waɪnərɪ] N (*US*) (Wein)kellerei *f*

wine: wineskin N Weinschlauch *m*; **wine taster** N Weinverkoster(in) or -prüfer(in) *m(f)*; **wine tasting** N Weinprobe *f*; **wine waiter** N (*Brit*) Weinkellner *m*, Getränkekellner *m*

wing [wɪŋ] N **a** (*of bird, plane, building, Mil, Pol, Sport*) Flügel *m*; (*of chair*) Backe *f*; (*Brit, Aut*) Kotflügel *m*; **on the ~** im Flug(e); **to take sb under one's ~** (*fig*) jdn unter seine Fittiche nehmen; **to spread one's ~s** (*fig: children*) flügge werden; **to ~** (*lit*) davonfliegen; (*project etc*) Auftrieb bekommen; **on the ~s of fantasy** (*liter*) auf den Flügeln or Schwingen der Fantasie or Phantasie; **on the ~s of song** (*liter*) auf (des) Gesanges Flügeln (*liter*); **on a ~ and a prayer** auf gut Glück; **do you expect me to grow or sprout ~s?** (*inf*) du glaubst wohl, ich kann fliegen? (*inf*); **to play on the (left/right) ~** (*Sport*) auf dem (linken/rechten) Flügel spielen **b** (*Aviat*, = *section of air force*) Geschwader *nt*; **~s** *pl* (= *pilot's badge*) Pilotenabzeichen *nt*; **to get one's ~s** (*fig*) sich (*dat*) seine Sporen verdienen **c wings** PL (*Theat*) Kulisse *f*; **to wait in the ~s** (*lit, fig*) in den Kulissen warten VT **a to ~ one's way** (= *fly*) fliegen **b** (*fig: liter*, = *give wings to*) beflügeln **c** (= *graze*) *person, bird* (mit einem Schuss) streifen; **you only ~ed it** das war nur ein Streifschuss, du hast es nur gestreift VI fliegen

wing: wingback N ['wɪŋbæk] N (*Ftbl*) (*Brit*) offensiver Außenverteidiger, offensive Außenverteidigerin; **wing** (*US*) Flügelverteidiger(in) *m(f)*; **wing beat** N Flügelschlag *m*; **wing-case** N Deckflügel *pl*, Flügeldecken *pl*; **wing chair** N Ohren- or Backensessel *m*; **wing collar** N Eckenkragen *m*; **wing commander** N (*Brit*) Oberstleutnant *m* (der Luftwaffe)

wingding ['wɪŋdɪŋ] N (*dated US, inf*) tolle Party (*inf*)

winge [wɪndʒ] VI = whinge

winged [wɪŋd] ADJ **a** (*Zool, Bot*) mit Flügeln; **the Winged Victory (of Samothrace)** die Nike von Samothrake; **the Winged Horse** (der) Pegasus **b** (*liter*) *sentiments, words* geflügelt

-winged ADJ *suf* mit ... Flügeln; *bird also* -flügelig; **red-winged** mit roten Flügeln; *bird also* rotflügelig

winger ['wɪŋə'] N (*Sport*) Flügelspieler(in) *m(f)*

wingey ['wɪndʒɪ] ADJ = whingey

wing: wing feather N Flügelfeder *f*; **wing-forward** N (*Rugby*) Flügelstürmer(in) *m(f)*; **wingless** ADJ flügellos; **wing nut** N Flügelmutter *f*; **wingspan** N Flügelspannweite *f*; **wingspread** N Spannweite *f*; **wing-three-quarter** N (*Rugby*) Dreiviertelspieler(in) *m(f)* auf dem Flügel; **wing tip** N Flügelspitze *f*

wink [wɪŋk] N **a** (*with eye*) Zwinkern *nt*, Blinzeln *nt*; **to give sb a ~** jdm zuzwinkern or zublinzeln; **to tip sb the ~** (*Brit inf*) jdm einen Wink geben (*inf*); **nod b** (= *instant*) **I didn't get a ~ of sleep, I didn't sleep a ~** (*inf*) ich habe kein Auge zugetan VT *eye* blinzeln, zwinkern mit (+*dat*) **a** (*meaningfully*) zwinkern, blinzeln; (*light, star etc*) blinken, funkeln; **to ~ at sb** jdm zuzwinkern or zublinzeln; **to ~ at sth** (*inf*) etw geflissentlich übersehen, bei etw einfach wegsehen or -schauen; **it's as easy as ~ing** (*dated inf*) das ist ein Kinderspiel; **~ing lights** (*Aut*) Blinklichter *pl*, Blinker *pl*

winker ['wɪŋkə'] N (*Brit Aut inf*) Blinker *m*

winkle ['wɪŋkl] N (*Brit*) Strandschnecke *f*

▸ **winkle out** VT *sep* (*inf*) **to winkle sth/sb out** etw herausklauben or (*behind sth*) hervorklauben (*inf*)/jdn loseisen (*inf*); **to winkle sth out of sb** etw aus jdm herauskriegen (*inf*)

winkle-pickers ['wɪŋklpɪkəz] PL (*Brit hum inf*) spitze Schuhe *pl*

winnable ['wɪnəbl] ADJ zu gewinnen *pred*

winner ['wɪnə'] N (*in race, competition*) Sieger(in) *m(f)*; (*of bet, pools etc*) Gewinner(in) *m(f)*; (= *card*) Gewinnkarte *f*; (*Tennis etc*: = *shot*) Treffer *m*; (*inf*, = *sth successful*) Renner *m* (*inf*), (Verkaufs)schlager *m* (*inf*); **to be onto a ~** (*inf*) das große Los gezogen haben (*inf*)

winning ['wɪnɪŋ] ADJ **a** (= *successful*) *person, entry* der/die gewinnt; *horse, team* siegreich; *goal* Sieges-; *point, stroke* (das Spiel) entscheidend; **the ~ time** die beste Zeit; **~ score** Spielergebnis *nt* **b** (= *charming*) *smile, ways* gewinnend, einnehmend **c winnings** PL Gewinn *m*

winningly ['wɪnɪŋlɪ] ADV *smile* gewinnend, einnehmend

winning post N Zielpfosten *m*, Zielstange *f*

winnow ['wɪnəʊ] VT *corn* worfeln, von der Spreu reinigen; (*fig liter*) sichten

winnower ['wɪnəʊə'], **winnowing machine** ['wɪnəʊɪŋməʃiːn] N Worfschaufel *f*, Worfelmaschine *f*

wino ['waɪnəʊ] N (*inf*) Penner *m* (*inf*), Saufbruder *m* (*inf*)

winsome ['wɪnsəm] ADJ *child, lass* reizend, sympathisch; *ways, smile* gewinnend, einnehmend

winter ['wɪntə'] N (*lit, fig*) Winter *m* ADJ *attr* Winter- VI überwintern, den Winter verbringen VT *cattle, horses* durch den Winter bringen

winter collection N (*Fashion*) Winterkollektion *f*

wintergreen ['wɪntəgriːn] N (= *plant*) Teebeere *f*; (= *flavouring*) Wintergrünöl *nt*

winterize ['wɪntəraɪz] VT (*US*) winterfest machen

winter jasmine N gelber Jasmin

winterly ADJ winterlich

winter: Winter Olympics PL Winterolympiade *f*; **winter quarters** PL Winterquartier *nt*; **winter resort** N Winterkurort *m*, Winterurlaubsort *m*; **winter sales** PL Winterschlussverkauf *m*; **winter solstice** N Wintersonnenwende *f*; **winter sports** PL Wintersport *m*; **winter**

term N (*Univ*) Wintersemester *nt*; **wintertime** N Winter *m*; (*for clocks*) Winterzeit *f*; **winter-weight** ADJ *clothes* Winter-; **winter wheat** N (*Agr*) Winterweizen *m*

wintery ['wɪntərɪ] ADJ winterlich; (*fig*) *look* eisig; *smile* frostig, kühl

wintriness ['wɪntrɪnɪs] N Winterlichkeit *f*

wintry ['wɪntrɪ] ADJ = **wintery**

win-win situation [,wɪn'wɪnsɪtjʊ,eɪʃən] N beidseitige Gewinnsituation, Win-Win-Situation *f*

wipe [waɪp] **N** Wischen *nt*; **to give sth a ~** etw abwischen

◆ **VT** wischen; *floor* aufwischen; *window* überwischen; *hands, feet* abwischen, abputzen (*rare*); **to ~ sb/sth dry** jdn/etw abtrocknen *or* trockenreiben; **to ~ sb/sth clean** jdn/etw sauber wischen *or* säubern; **to ~ sth with/on a cloth** etw mit/an einem Tuch abwischen; **to ~ one's brow** sich (*dat*) die Stirn abwischen; **to ~ one's eyes** sich (*dat*) die Augen wischen; **to ~ one's nose** sich (*dat*) die Nase putzen; **to ~ one's feet** sich (*dat*) die Füße oder Schuhe abstreifen *or* -wischen *or* -treten; **to ~ the tears from one's eyes** sich (*dat*) die Tränen aus den Augen wischen; **to ~ one's bottom** sich (*dat*) den Hintern abputzen, sich abputzen; **to ~ the floor with sb** (*fig inf*) jdn fertigmachen (*inf*)

▶ **wipe at** VI +*prep obj* abwischen

▶ **wipe away** VT *sep* (*lit, fig*) wegwischen; *tears also* abwischen

▶ **wipe down** VT *sep* abwaschen; (*with dry cloth*) abreiben; *window* überwischen

▶ **wipe off** **VT** *sep* **a** *mark* weg- *or* abwischen; (*from blackboard also*) ab- *or* auslöschen; **wipe that smile off your face** (*inf*) hör auf zu grinsen (*inf*); **I'll soon wipe that smile off his face** (*inf*) dem wird bald das Lachen vergehen; **to be wiped off the map** *or* **the face of the earth** von der Landkarte *or* Erdoberfläche getilgt werden **b** (*Fin*) **millions were wiped off share values yesterday** gestern kam es zu Aktienverlusten in Millionenhöhe **VI** sich weg- *or* abwischen lassen

▶ **wipe out** VT *sep* **a** (= *clean*) *bath, bowl* auswischen **b** (= *erase*) *memory, part of brain, sth on blackboard* (aus)löschen; *guilty feelings* verschwinden lassen **c** (= *cancel*) *debt* bereinigen; *gain, benefit* zunichte machen **d** (= *destroy*) *disease, village, race* ausrotten; *enemy, battalion* aufreiben

▶ **wipe up** **VT** *sep* *liquid* aufwischen, aufputzen (*Sw*); *dishes* abtrocknen **VI** abtrocknen

wipe: wipe-down N Abreibung *f*; **wipe-over** N **to give sth a ~** etw über- *or* abwischen

wiper ['waɪpə'] N (Scheiben)wischer *m*

wiper blade N (*Aut*) Wischblatt *nt*, Wischerblatt *nt*

wiping-up ['waɪpɪŋ'ʌp] N **to do the ~** abtrocknen

wire [waɪə'] **N** **a** Draht *m*; (*for electricity supply*) Leitung *f*; (= *insulated flex*) (*for home appliance etc*) Schnur *f*; (*for television*) Fernsehanschluss *m or* -kabel *nt*; (*in circus:* = *high wire*) (Hoch)seil *nt*; **to get in under the ~** (*US, inf*) etwas gerade (eben) noch rechtzeitig *or* mit Hängen und Würgen (*inf*) schaffen; **to pull ~s** (*esp US inf*) seinen Einfluss geltend machen, seine Beziehungen spielen lassen; **he's pulling your ~** (*Brit, inf*) er nimmt dich auf den Arm (*inf*); **you've got your ~s crossed there** (*inf*) Sie verwechseln da etwas; (*said to two people*) Sie reden aneinander vorbei

b (*Telec*) Telegramm *nt*, Kabel *nt* (*old*)

c (= *microphone*) Wanze *f* (*inf*)

VT **a** (= *put in wiring*) *plug* anschließen; *house* die (elektrischen) Leitungen verlegen in (+*dat*); (= *connect to electricity*) (an das Stromnetz) anschließen; **it's all ~d (up) for television** die Verkabelung für das Fernsehen ist vorhanden

b (*Telec*) telegrafieren, kabeln (*old*)

c (= *fix on wire*) *beads* auf Draht auffädeln; (= *fix with wire*) mit Draht zusammen- *or* verbinden; **to ~ the parts together** die Teile mit Draht zusammen- *or* verbinden

VI telegrafieren, drahten, kabeln (*old*)

▶ **wire up** VT *sep* *lights, battery, speakers* anschließen; *house* elektrische Leitungen *or* den Strom verlegen in (+*dat*); **we wired the room up as a recording studio** wir haben den Raum als Aufnahmestudio eingerichtet

wire: wire brush N Drahtbürste *f*; **wire cutters** PL Drahtschere *f*; **wire gauze** N Drahtgaze *f or* -netz *nt*; **wire-haired** ADJ drahthaarig, Drahthaar-; **~ terrier** Drahthaarterrier *m*

wireless ['waɪəlɪs] (*esp Brit, dated*) N **a** (*also* **wireless set**) Radio *nt*, Rundfunkgerät *nt*, Radioapparat *m* **b** (= *radio*) Rundfunk *m*; (*also* **wireless telegraphy**) drahtlose Telegrafie; (*also* **wireless telephony**) drahtlose Übertragung, drahtloses Telefon; **~ operator** (*on ship, plane*) Funker(in) *m(f)*; **to send a message by ~** eine Botschaft über Funk schicken *or* senden **VT** funken; *base etc* anfunken **VI** funken

wire: wireman N (*US, inf, for wiretapping etc*) Abhörspezialist *m*; **wire mesh** N Maschendraht *m*; **wire netting** N Maschendraht *m*; **wirephoto** N (= *method*) Bildtelegrafie *f*; (= *picture*) Bildtelegramm *nt*; **wirepuller** ['waɪə,pʊlə'] N (*esp US inf*) Drahtzieher(in) *m(f)*; **wirepulling** ['waɪə,pʊlɪŋ] N (*esp US inf*) Drahtziehen *nt*, Drahtzieherei *f*; **wire rope** N Drahtseil *nt*; **wire service** N (*US*) Nachrichtendienst *m*, Nachrichtenagentur *f*; **wiretap** ['waɪətæp] **N** (= *device*) Abhörgerät *nt*, Wanze *f*; (= *activity*) Abhören *nt*; *phone, conversation* abhören, anzapfen; *building* abhören in (+*dat*); **wiretapper** ['waɪətæpə'] N Abhörer(in) *m(f)*; **wiretapping** ['waɪətæpɪŋ] N Abhören *nt*, Anzapfen *nt* von Leitungen; **wire wheel** N Rad *nt* mit Sportfelgen; **wire wool** N Stahlwolle *f*; **wireworm** N Drahtwurm *m*

wiring ['waɪərɪŋ] N elektrische Leitungen *pl*, Stromkabel *pl*

wiring diagram N Schaltplan *m or* -schema *nt*

wiry ['waɪərɪ] ADJ (+*er*) **a** (= *coarse*) drahtig; *hair also* borstig **b** (= *thin*) *frame* drahtig

Wis N (*dated US*) abbr of **Wisconsin**

wisdom ['wɪzdəm] N Weisheit *f*; (= *prudence*) Einsicht *f*; **to show great ~** große Weisheit *or* Einsicht zeigen; **to doubt the ~ of sth** bezweifeln, ob etw klug *or* sinnvoll ist; **the conventional ~** die herkömmliche Überzeugung

wisdom tooth N Weisheitszahn *m*

wise[1] [waɪz] ADJ (+*er*) weise; (= *prudent, sensible*) *move, step etc* klug, gescheit, vernünftig; (*inf,* = *smart*) klug, schlau; **a ~ choice** eine kluge *or* gute Wahl; **the Three Wise Men** die drei Weisen; **to be ~ in the ways of the world** Lebenserfahrung haben, das Leben kennen; **to be ~ after the event** hinterher den Schlauen spielen *or* gut reden haben; **I'm none the ~r** (*inf*) ich bin nicht klüger als zuvor *or* vorher; **nobody will be any the ~r** (*inf*) niemand wird etwas (davon) merken *or* das spitzkriegen (*inf*); **you'd be ~ to ...** du tätest gut daran, ...; **it would be ~ to accept the offer** es wäre klug, das Angebot anzunehmen; **you'd better get ~** (*US, inf*) nimm endlich Vernunft an; **to get ~ to sb/sth** (*inf*) jd/etw spitzkriegen (*inf*), dahinter kommen, wie jd/etw ist; **to be ~ to sb/sth** (*inf*) jdn/etw kennen; **he fooled her twice, then she got ~ to him** zweimal hat er sie hereingelegt, dann ist sie ihm auf die Schliche gekommen; **to put sb ~ to sb/sth** (*inf*) jdn über jdn/etw aufklären (*inf*)

▶ **wise up** (*inf*) **VI** **if he doesn't wise up soon to what's going on ...** wenn er nicht bald dahinter kommt *or* wenn ihm nicht bald ein Licht aufgeht (*inf*), was da gespielt wird ...; **if he doesn't wise up soon to the need for ...** wenn er nicht bald hinter die Notwendigkeit zu ... kommt; **he's never going to wise up** der lernts nie!, der wird auch nie klüger; **wise up, man!** Mann, wach auf *or* nimm Vernunft an! **VT** *sep* aufklären (*inf*) (*to* über +*acc*)

wise[2] N , *no pl* (*old*) Weise *f*; **in this ~** auf diese Weise, so; **in no ~** in keiner Weise, keineswegs

-wise ADV *suf* -mäßig, in puncto, in Bezug auf (+*acc*); **money-wise** geldmäßig, in puncto Geld, in Bezug auf Geld

wise: wiseacre N Besserwisser(in) *m(f)*, Neunmalkluge(r) *mf*; **wisecrack** **N** Witzelei *f*; (*pej*) Stichelei *f*; **to make a ~ (about sb/sth)** witzeln (über jdn/etw) **VTI** witzeln; **wise guy** N (*inf*) Klugscheißer *m* (*inf*)

wisely ['waɪzlɪ] ADV weise; (= *sensibly*) klugerweise

wish [wɪʃ] ⊙ 8.4, 18.3, 20.6, 21.2, 23.1, 23.3, 24.2, 24.3 **N** **a** Wunsch *m* (*for* nach); **your ~ is my command** dein Wunsch ist *or* sei mir Befehl; **I have no great ~ to see him** ich habe kein Bedürfnis *or* keine große Lust, ihn zu sehen; **to make a ~** sich (*dat*) etwas wünschen; **you can make three ~es** du hast drei Wünsche; **the ~ is father to the thought** (*prov*) der Wunsch ist Vater des Gedankens (*prov*); **well, you got your ~** jetzt hast du ja, was du wolltest; **you shall have your ~** dein Wunsch soll (dir) erfüllt werden *or* soll in Erfüllung gehen

b **wishes** PL (*in greetings*) **with best ~es** mit den besten Wünschen *or* Grüßen, alles Gute; **please give him my good ~es** bitte grüßen Sie ihn (vielmals) von mir, bitte richten Sie ihm meine besten Wünsche aus; **he sends his best ~es** er lässt (vielmals) grüßen; **a message of good ~es** eine Gruß- *or* Glückwunschbotschaft; **best ~es for a speedy recovery** alles Gute für eine baldige Genesung

VT **a** (= *want*) wünschen; **I do not ~ it** ich möchte *or* wünsche (*form*) es nicht; **he ~es to be alone/to see you immediately** er möchte allein sein/dich sofort sehen; **I ~ you to be present** ich wünsche, dass Sie anwesend sind; **what do you ~ me to do?** was soll ich (bitte) tun?; **do you ~ more coffee, sir?** (*Scot, form*) hätten Sie gern *or* wünschen Sie noch Kaffee?

b (= *desire, hope, desire sth unlikely*) wünschen, wollen; **I ~ the play would begin** ich wünschte *or* wollte, das Stück finge an; **I ~ you'd be quiet** ich wünschte *or* wollte, du wärest ruhig; **how he ~ed that his wife was** *or* **were there** wie sehr er sich (*dat*) wünschte, dass seine Frau hier wäre; **~ you were here** ich wünschte *or* wollte, du wärst hier

c (= *entertain wishes towards sb*) wünschen; **to ~ sb well/ill** jdm Glück *or* alles Gute/Schlechtes *or* Böses wünschen; **I don't ~ her any harm** ich wünsche ihr nichts Böses; **to ~ sb good luck/happiness** jdm viel Glück *or* alles Gute/Glück (und Zufriedenheit) wünschen

d (= *bid, express wish*) wünschen; **to ~ sb a pleasant journey/good morning/merry Christmas** jdm eine gute Reise/guten Morgen/frohe Weihnachten wünschen; **to ~ sb goodbye** jdm Auf *or* auf Wiedersehen sagen

e **to ~ a ~** sich (*dat*) etwas wünschen; **he ~ed himself anywhere but there** er wünschte sich nur möglichst weit weg; **if I could ~ myself into the castle** wenn ich mich nur in das Schloss wünschen könnte

VI (= *make a wish*) sich (*dat*) etwas wünschen; **~ing won't solve the problem** der Wunsch allein wird das Problem nicht lösen; **to ~ upon a star** (*liter*) sich (*dat*) bei einer Sternschnuppe etwas wünschen

▶ **wish away** VT *sep* *difficulty* weg- *or* fortwünschen (*inf*)

▶ **wish for** VI +*prep obj* **to wish for sth** sich (*dat*) etw wünschen; **what more could you wish for?** etwas Besseres kann man sich doch gar nicht wünschen, was kann sich der Mensch noch mehr wünschen? (*inf*); **it was everything we had wished for** es war genauso, wie wir es uns gewünscht hatten; **she had everything she could wish for** sie hatte alles, was man sich nur wünschen kann

▶ **wish on** *or* **upon** VT *sep* +*prep obj* (*inf,* = *foist*) **to wish sb/sth on** *or* **upon sb** jdn jdm/jdm etw aufhängen (*inf*); **I would not wish that/that job on** *or* **upon my worst enemy!** das/diese Arbeit würde ich meinem ärgsten Feind nicht wünschen

wishbone [ˈwɪʃbəʊn] N Gabelbein nt

wishful [ˈwɪʃfʊl] ADJ **that's just ~ thinking** das ist reines Wunschdenken, das ist nur ein frommer Wunsch

wish fulfilment, (US) **wish fulfillment** [ˈwɪʃfʊlˈfɪlmənt] N Wunscherfüllung f

wishing well [ˈwɪʃɪŋˈwel] N Wunschbrunnen m

wishwash [ˈwɪʃwɒʃ] N (inf: drink) labb(e)riges Zeug, (fig: = talk) seichtes Geschwätz (pej)

wishy-washiness [ˈwɪʃɪˌwɒʃɪnɪs] N (of coffee, soup) Labberigkeit f, Wässrigkeit f, (of person, character) saft- und kraftlose Art, Farblosigkeit f, Laschheit f, (of colour) Verwaschenheit f, (of argument) Schwachheit f; **the ~ of this report** das allgemeine Geschwätz (inf) in diesem Bericht

wishy-washy [ˈwɪʃɪˌwɒʃɪ] ADJ coffee, soup labberig, wässrig; person, character saft- und kraftlos, farblos, lasch; colour verwaschen; argument schwach (inf); report, story ungenau, wachsweich, wischiwaschi (inf)

wisp [wɪsp] N **a** (of straw, hair etc) kleines Büschel; (of cloud) Fetzen m; (of smoke) Fahne f, Wölkchen nt **b** (= person) elfenhaftes or zartes or zerbrechliches Geschöpf **c** (= trace) zarte Spur or Andeutung; (= fragment) Hauch m

wispy [ˈwɪspɪ] ADJ (+er) grass dürr, fein; girl zerbrechlich, zart; **~ clouds** Wolkenfetzen pl; **~ hair** dünne Haarbüschel

wisteria [wɪsˈtɪərɪə] N Glyzinie f, Wistarie f

wistful [ˈwɪstfʊl] ADJ smile, thoughts, mood, eyes wehmütig; song also schwermütig

wistfully [ˈwɪstfəlɪ] ADV smile, think, look, sigh wehmütig

wistfulness [ˈwɪstfʊlnɪs] N (of smile, thoughts, look) Wehmut f, (of song) Schwermut f

wit¹ [wɪt] VI (old Jur) **to ~** nämlich, und zwar

wit² N **a** (= understanding) Verstand m; **beyond the ~ of man** über den menschlichen Verstand or Horizont hinaus; **a battle of ~s** ein geistiges Kräftemessen; **to be at one's ~s' end** am Ende seiner Weisheit sein, mit seinem Latein am Ende sein (hum inf); **I was at my ~s' end (to find a solution)** ich wusste mir keinen Rat or Ausweg mehr(, wie ich eine Lösung finden könnte); **to drive sb out of his ~s** jdn um seinen Verstand bringen; **to lose one's ~s** den or seinen Verstand verlieren; **to collect one's ~s** seine fünf Sinne (wieder) zusammennehmen; **to frighten** or **scare sb out of his ~s** jdn zu Tode erschrecken; **to be frightened** or **scared out of one's ~s** zu Tode erschreckt sein; **to have** or **keep one's ~s about one** seine (fünf) Sinne zusammen- or beisammenhaben, einen klaren Kopf haben; **to sharpen one's ~s** seinen Verstand schärfen; **to use one's ~s** seinen Verstand gebrauchen, sein Köpfchen or seinen Grips anstrengen (inf); **to live by** or **on one's ~s** sich schlau or klug durchs Leben schlagen **b** (= humour, wittiness) Geist m, Witz m; **full of ~** geistreich; **to have a ready ~** (old) schlagfertig sein; **the book is full of ~** es ist sehr viel Geistreiches in dem Buch **c** (= person) geistreicher Kopf

witch [wɪtʃ] N (lit, fig) Hexe f

witch: **witchcraft** N Hexerei f, Zauberei f; **a book on ~** ein Buch über (die) Hexenkunst; **witch doctor** N Medizinmann m

witch-elm [ˈwɪtʃelm] N Bergulme f

witchery [ˈwɪtʃərɪ] N (= witchcraft) Hexerei f, (= fascination) Zauber m

witches' [ˈwɪtʃɪz]: **witches' brew** N Zaubertrank m; (fig) Teufelszeug nt (inf); **witches' Sabbath** N Hexensabbat m

witch hazel N (Bot) Zaubernuss f; (Med) Hamelis f

witch-hunt [ˈwɪtʃhʌnt] N (lit, fig) Hexenjagd f

witching [ˈwɪtʃɪŋ] ADJ **the ~ hour** die Geisterstunde

with [wɪð, wɪθ] PREP **a** mit; **are you pleased ~ it?** bist du damit zufrieden?; **bring a book ~ you** bring ein Buch mit; **~ no ...** ohne ...; (to-

gether) **~ the Victory, it's the biggest ship of its class** neben der Victory ist es das größte Schiff in seiner Klasse; **to walk ~ a stick** am or mit einem Stock gehen; **put it ~ the rest** leg es zu den anderen; **the wind was ~ us** wir hatten den Wind im Rücken, wir fuhren etc mit dem Wind; **how are things ~ you?** wie gehts?, wie stehts? (inf) → **with it**

b (= at house of, in company of etc) bei; **I'll be ~ you in a moment** einen Augenblick bitte, ich bin gleich da; **10 years ~ the company** 10 Jahre bei or in der Firma; **the problem is still ~ us** wir haben immer noch das alte Problem

c (on person, in bag etc) bei; **I haven't got my cheque book ~ me** ich habe mein Scheckbuch nicht bei mir

d (cause) vor (+dat); **to shiver ~ cold** vor Kälte zittern; **the hills are white ~ snow** die Berge sind weiß vom Schnee; **to be ill ~ measles** die Masern haben, an Masern erkrankt sein

e (= in the case of) bei, mit; **it's always the same ~ you** es ist (doch) immer dasselbe mit dir; **the trouble ~ him is that he ...** die Schwierigkeit bei or mit ihm ist (die), dass er ...; **it's a habit ~ him** das ist bei ihm Gewohnheit; **~ God, all things are possible** bei or für Gott ist kein Ding unmöglich

f (= while sb/sth is) wo; **you can't go ~ your mother ill in bed** wo deine Mutter krank im Bett liegt, kannst du nicht gehen; **~ all this noise going on** bei diesem Lärm; **to quit ~ the job half-finished** von der halb fertigen Arbeit weglaufen; **~ the window open** bei offenem Fenster

g (= in proportion) mit; **it varies ~ the temperature** es verändert sich je nach Temperatur; **wine improves ~ age** Wein wird mit zunehmendem Alter immer besser; **it gets bigger ~ the heat** in der Wärme wird es immer größer

h (= in spite of) trotz, bei; **~ all his faults** bei allen Fehlern, trotz aller seiner Fehler

i (= in agreement, on side of) **I'm ~ you there** (inf) da stimme ich dir zu; **is he ~ us or against us?** ist er für oder gegen uns?

j (inf, expressing comprehension) **are you ~ me?** kapierst du? (inf), hast dus? (inf), kommst du mit? (inf); **I'm not ~ you** da komm ich nicht mit (inf); **are you still ~ me?** kommst du (da) noch mit? (inf), kommst du noch klar?

withdraw [wɪðˈdrɔː] pret **withdrew**, ptp **withdrawn** **VT** object, motion, charge, offer zurückziehen; troops, team also abziehen; ambassador zurückrufen or -beordern; coins, stamps einziehen, aus dem Verkehr ziehen; (from bank) money abheben; words, comment zurücknehmen, widerrufen; privileges entziehen; **the workers withdrew their labour** (Brit) or **labor** (US) die Arbeiter haben ihre Arbeit niedergelegt; **she withdrew her hand from his** sie entzog ihm ihre Hand **VI** sich zurückziehen; (Sport also) zurücktreten (from von), nicht antreten (from von/bei); (= move away) zurücktreten or -gehen; **to ~ in favour** (Brit) or **favor** (US) **of sb else** zugunsten or zu Gunsten eines anderen zurücktreten; **to ~ into oneself** sich in sich (acc) selber zurückziehen; **you can't ~ now** (from agreement) du kannst jetzt nicht zurücktreten or abspringen (inf)

withdrawal [wɪðˈdrɔːəl] N (of objects, charge) Zurückziehen nt; (of ambassador) Abziehen nt; (of coins, stamps) Einziehen nt; (of money) Abheben nt; (of words) Zurücknehmen nt, Zurücknahme f, (of troops) Rückzug m; (= withdrawing) Abziehen nt; (in sport) Abzug m; (from drugs) Entzug m; **to make a ~ from a bank** von einer Bank Geld abheben

withdrawal: **withdrawal slip** N Rückzahlungsschein m; **withdrawal symptoms** PL Entzugserscheinungen pl

withdrawn [wɪðˈdrɔːn] ptp of **withdraw** ADJ person verschlossen; manner also reserviert, zurückhaltend; life zurückgezogen

withdrew [wɪðˈdruː] pret of **withdraw**

withe [wɪθ] N (old) (dünne) Weidenrute

wither [ˈwɪðə] **VT** plants etc verdörren, austrocknen; (fig) zum Schwinden bringen; **to ~ sb with a look** jdm einen vernichtenden Blick zuwerfen **VI a** (lit) verdorren, ausdorren; (limb) verkümmern **b** (fig) welken; (religion) dahinschwinden

▶ **wither away** VI = wither VI

▶ **wither up** VI = wither VI a

withered [ˈwɪðəd] ADJ plant, grass verdorrt, vertrocknet; skin verhutzelt, hutzelig; limb verkümmert; **a ~ old man** ein verschrumpfter or hutzeliger Alter

withering [ˈwɪðərɪŋ] ADJ heat ausdörrend; criticism, look, tone vernichtend

witheringly [ˈwɪðərɪŋlɪ] ADV say, look vernichtend

withers [ˈwɪðəz] PL Widerrist m

withhold [wɪθˈhəʊld] pret, ptp **withheld** [wɪθˈheld] **VT** vorenthalten; truth also verschweigen; (= refuse) consent, help verweigern, versagen (geh); **the members threatened to ~ their payments** die Mitglieder drohten, die Zahlung der Beiträge zu verweigern; **to ~ sth from sb** jdm etw vorenthalten/verweigern; **name withheld** (in newspaper, report etc) Name der Redaktion bekannt

withholding tax [wɪθˈhəʊldɪŋtæks] (US) (vom Arbeitgeber) einbehaltene Steuer

within [wɪðˈɪn] PREP innerhalb (+gen); (temporal also) binnen (+dat or (geh) +gen), innert (+gen) (Aus, S Ger); **a voice ~ me said ...** eine Stimme in meinem Inneren or in mir sagte ...; **we were ~ 100 feet of the finish** wir waren auf den letzten 100 Fuß vor dem Ziel; **we came ~ 50 feet of the summit** wir kamen bis auf 50 Fuß an den Gipfel heran; **~ his power** in seiner Macht; **to keep ~ the law** sich im Rahmen des Gesetzes bewegen; **to live ~ one's means** or **income** im Rahmen seiner finanziellen Möglichkeiten leben

ADV (old, liter) innen; **from ~** von drinnen; (= on the inside) von innen; **let us go ~** wollen wir hineingehen; **but he's rotten ~** aber innerlich ist er verderbt

with-it [ˈwɪðɪt] ADJ attr, **with it** ADJ pred (inf) **a** (= up-to-date, trendy) up to date **b** pred (= awake, alert) **to be with it** da sein (inf)

without [wɪðˈaʊt] PREP ohne; **~ a tie/passport** ohne Krawatte/(einen) Pass; **a friend in the world** ohne einen einzigen Freund; **~ speaking** ohne zu sprechen, wortlos; **~ my noticing it** ohne dass ich es bemerkte; **times ~ number** unzählige Male pl **ADV** (old, liter) außen; **from ~** von draußen; (= on the outside) von außen **ADJ** pred ohne; **to be ~ sth** etw nicht haben, einer Sache (gen) entbehren (from); **those who are ~** (= needy) die Bedürftigen pl

without-profits [wɪðˈaʊtˌprɒfɪts] ADJ policy etc ohne Gewinnbeteiligung

with-profits [ˈwɪðˌprɒfɪts] ADJ policy etc mit Gewinnbeteiligung

withstand [wɪθˈstænd] pret, ptp **withstood** [wɪθˈstʊd] **VT** cold, scrutiny, pressure standhalten (+dat); enemy, climate, attack, temptation also trotzen (+dat); persuasion etc widerstehen (+dat); loss verkraften

withy [ˈwɪðɪ] N (= willow) Korbweide f, (= twig) Weide(nrute) f

witless [ˈwɪtlɪs] ADJ (= mentally defective) schwachsinnig; (= stupid, silly) dumm, blöd(e) (inf); (= lacking wit) prose geistlos; **to be scared ~** zu Tode erschreckt sein; **to be bored ~** sich zu Tode langweilen

witlessness [ˈwɪtlɪsnɪs] N (= stupidity) Dummheit f, Blödheit f (inf)

witness [ˈwɪtnɪs] **N a** (= person: Jur, fig) Zeuge m, Zeugin f; **~ for the defence** (Brit) or **defense** (US) Zeuge m/Zeugin f der Verteidigung; **~ for the prosecution** Zeuge m/Zeugin f der Anklage; **as God is my ~** Gott sei or ist mein Zeuge; **to call sb as a ~** jdn als Zeugen/Zeugin vorladen; **I was then ~ to a scene ...** ich wurde Zeuge einer Szene ...

b (= *evidence*) Zeugnis *nt*; **in ~ whereof** (*form*) zu Urkund *or* zum Zeugnis dessen; **to bear ~ to sth** (*lit, fig*) Zeugnis über etw (*acc*) ablegen; (*actions, events also*) von etw zeugen **VT a** (= *see*) *accident* Zeuge/Zeugin sein bei *or* (+*gen*); *scenes* (mit)erleben, mit ansehen; *changes* erleben; **the year 1945 ~ed great changes** das Jahr 1945 sah einen großen Wandel

b (= *testify*) bezeugen; **to call sb to ~ that ...** jdn zum Zeugen dafür rufen, dass ...

c (= *consider as evidence*) denken an (+*acc*), zum Beispiel nehmen; **~ the case of X** denken Sie nur an den Fall X, nehmen Sie nur den Fall X zum Beispiel

d (= *attest by signature*) *signature, will* bestätigen **VI** (= *testify*) bestätigen, bezeugen; **to ~ to sth** etw bestätigen *or* bezeugen; **to ~ against sb** gegen jdn aussagen

witness box, (*US*) **witness stand** N Zeugenbank *f*, Zeugenstand *m*

witness protection program N (*US Jur*) Zeugenschutzprogramm *nt*

witness statement N Zeugenaussage *f*

-witted ['wɪtɪd] ADJ *suf* **dull-witted** geistig träge; **quick-witted** geistig rege

witter ['wɪtə'] VI (*Brit inf: also* **witter on**) labern (*inf*)

witticism ['wɪtɪsɪzəm] N geistreiche Bemerkung

wittily ['wɪtɪlɪ] ADV (= *humorously*) witzig, geistreich

wittiness ['wɪtɪnɪs] N Witzigkeit *f*

wittingly ['wɪtɪŋlɪ] ADV bewusst, absichtlich, wissentlich (*form*); **~ or unwittingly** bewusst oder unbewusst

witty ['wɪtɪ] ADJ (+*er*) witzig, geistreich

wives [waɪvz] *pl of* **wife**

wizard ['wɪzəd] **N a** Zauberer *m*, Hexenmeister *m* **b** (*inf*) Genie *nt*, Leuchte *f* (*inf*); **a financial ~** ein Finanzgenie *nt*; **a ~ with the ball** ein Zauberer *m* am *or* mit dem Ball; **a ~ at computing** ein Computergenie *nt* (*inf*) **ADJ** (*dated Brit inf*) famos, prima (*inf*)

wizardry ['wɪzədrɪ] N (= *magic*) Hexerei *f*, Zauberei *f*; (= *great skill*) Zauberkünste *pl*; **his ~ with the ball** seine Zauberkunststücke *pl* mit dem Ball

wizened ['wɪznd] ADJ verhutzelt, verschrumpelt

wk *abbr of* **week** Wo.

wkly *abbr of* **weekly** wö.

WLTM (*inf*) *abbr of* **would like to meet**

Wm *abbr of* **William**

WMD (*Mil*) *abbr of* **weapons of mass destruction** Massenvernichtungswaffen *pl*

WNW *abbr of* **west-north-west** WNW

w/o *abbr of* **without** o.

woad [wəʊd] N (= *dye*) Waid *m*; (= *plant*) (Färber)waid *m*

wobble ['wɒbl] **N** Wackeln *nt*; **the chair has a ~** der Stuhl wackelt **VI** wackeln; (*tightrope walker, dancer also, cyclist*) schwanken; (*voice, hand, compass needle*) zittern; (*wheel*) eiern (*inf*), einen Schlag haben; (*chin, jelly etc*) schwabbeln; **he ~d about on his new bike** er wackelte auf seinem neuen Fahrrad durch die Gegend; **his massive stomach was wobbling like a jelly** (*Brit*) sein riesiger Bauch wabbelte wie ein Wackelpudding (*inf*) **VT** rütteln an (+*dat*), ruckeln an (+*dat*), wackeln an (+*dat*)

wobbly ['wɒblɪ] **ADJ** (+*er*) wackelig; *voice, notes also, hand* zitterig, zitternd; *jelly* (sch)wabbelig; *wheel* eiernd; **to be ~** (*inf, after illness*) wackelig auf den Beinen sein (*inf*); **to feel ~** sich schwach fühlen, wackelig auf den Beinen sein (*inf*) **N** (*inf, = fit of rage*) **to throw a ~** ausrasten (*inf*), einen Wutanfall bekommen

wodge [wɒdʒ] N (*Brit inf*) (*of cake, plaster etc*) Brocken *m*; (*ball of paper*) Knäuel *nt or m*; (*of cotton wool*) Bausch *m*; (*of documents, papers*) Stoß *m*

woe [wəʊ] N **a** (*liter, hum, sorrow*) Jammer *m*; **~ (is me)!** weh mir!; **~ betide him who ...!** wehe

dem, der ...!; **a tale of ~** eine Geschichte des Jammers **b** (*esp pl: = trouble, affliction*) Kummer *m*; **to pour out one's ~s to sb** sich (*dat*) seinen Kummer bei jdm von der Seele reden

woebegone ['wəʊbɪˌgɒn] ADJ kläglich, jämmerlich; *expression also* jammervoll; *voice* (weh)klagend, jammernd

woeful ['wəʊfʊl] ADJ (= *sad*) traurig; (= *deplorable*) *neglect also, ignorance, lack* bedauerlich, beklagenswert

woefully ['wəʊfəlɪ] ADV kläglich, jämmerlich; (= *very*) bedauerlich; **he is ~ ignorant of ...** es ist bestürzend, wie wenig er über ... weiß; **he discovered they were ~ ignorant of ...** er stellte zu seiner Bestürzung fest, wie wenig sie über ... wussten; **sb/sth is ~ short of** *or* **lacking in sth** jdm/einer Sache (*dat*) fehlt es bedauerlicherweise an etw (*dat*)

wog [wɒg] N (*Brit pej sl*) (= *non-white foreigner*) Bimbo *m* (*pej sl*); (= *Arab*) Ali *m* (*pej sl*)

wok [wɒk] N (*Cook*) Wok *m*

woke [wəʊk] *pret of* **wake**

woken ['wəʊkn] *ptp of* **wake**

wolf [wʊlf] **N** *pl* **wolves a** Wolf *m* **b** (*fig inf, = womanizer*) Don Juan *m* **c** (*phrases*) **a ~ in sheep's clothing** ein Wolf im Schafspelz; **to cry ~** blinden Alarm schlagen; **to keep the ~ from the door** sich über Wasser halten; **to throw sb to the wolves** jdn den Wölfen zum Fraß vorwerfen → **lone VT** (*inf: also* **wolf down**) *food* hinunterschlingen

wolf: wolf cub N (*lit*) Wolfsjunge(s) *nt*; (*Brit: = boy scout*) Wölfling *m*; **wolfhound** N Wolfshund *m*

wolfish ['wʊlfɪʃ] ADJ *grin, look* anzüglich

wolfishly ['wʊlfɪʃlɪ] ADV *grin* anzüglich

wolf pack N Rudel *nt* Wölfe; (*of submarines*) Geschwader *nt*

wolfram ['wʊlfrəm] N Wolfram *nt*

wolfsbane ['wʊlfsbeɪn] N (*Bot*) Eisenhut *m*

wolf whistle (*inf*) **N** bewundernder Pfiff; **they gave her a ~** sie pfiffen ihr nach **VI** nachpfeifen

wolverine ['wʊlvəriːn] N Vielfraß *m*

wolves [wʊlvz] *pl of* **wolf**

woman ['wʊmən] **N** *pl* **women** Frau *f*, Frauenzimmer *nt* (*pej hum*); (= *domestic help*) (Haushalts)hilfe *f*; (*inf*) (= *girlfriend*) Mädchen *nt*; (= *mistress*) Geliebte *f*, Weib *nt* (*pej*); **a ~'s work is never done** (*prov*) Frauenhände ruhen nie (*Prov*); **man that is made of ~** (*Rel*) der Mensch, vom Weib geboren; **how like a ~!** typisch Frau!; **cleaning ~** Putzfrau *f*, Reinmachefrau *f*; **~ is a mysterious creature** Frauen sind geheimnisvolle Wesen; **where's my supper, ~!** Weib, wo ist das Essen!; **the little ~** (*inf, ~ = wife*) die *or* meine Frau; **to run after women** den Frauen nachrennen; **that's ~'s work** das ist Frauenarbeit; **women's talk** Gespräche *pl* von Frau zu Frau → **old woman** **ADJ** *attr* **~ doctor** Ärztin *f*; **~ lawyer** Anwältin *f*; **~ teacher** Lehrerin *f*; **~ driver** Frau *f* am Steuer

woman: woman-hater N Frauenhasser(in) *m(f)*; **womanhood** N (= *women in general*) alle Frauen, die Frauen *pl*; **to reach ~** (zur) Frau werden

womanish ['wʊmənɪʃ] ADJ (= *womanly*) *woman* fraulich; (*pej, = effeminate*) *man* weibisch

womanize ['wʊmənaɪz] VI hinter den Frauen her sein; **this womanizing will have to stop** die Frauengeschichten müssen aufhören; **young men out for an evening's womanizing** junge Männer, die ausziehen, um sich mit Mädchen zu amüsieren

womanizer ['wʊmənaɪzə'] N Schürzenjäger *m*

womankind ['wʊmənˌkaɪnd] N das weibliche Geschlecht

womanliness ['wʊmənlɪnɪs] N Weiblichkeit *f*

womanly ['wʊmənlɪ] ADJ *figure, person* fraulich; *qualities, virtues* weiblich

womb [wuːm] N Mutterleib *m*, Gebärmutter *f* (*Med*); (*fig*) Schoß *m*; **the foetus in the ~** der

Embryo im Mutterleib; **it's just a yearning to return to the ~** das ist nur die Sehnsucht nach der Geborgenheit des Mutterschoßes

wombat ['wɒmbæt] N Wombat *m*

women ['wɪmɪn] *pl of* **woman**

womenfolk ['wɪmɪnfəʊk] PL Frauen *pl*

women's ['wɪmɪnz]: **women's lib** N (*inf*) Frauen(rechts)bewegung *f*; **women's libber** ['wɪmɪnz'lɪbə'] N (*inf*) Frauenrechtlerin *f*, Emanze *f*; **women's magazine** N Frauenzeitschrift *f*; **Women's Movement** N Frauenbewegung *f*; **women's page** N Frauenseite *f*; **women's prison** N Frauengefängnis *nt*; **women's refuge** N Frauenhaus *nt*; **women's rights** PL Frauenrechte *pl*, die Rechte *pl* der Frau; **women's room** N (*US*) Damentoilette *f*; **women's studies** PL (*Univ*) Frauenforschung *f*

won [wʌn] *pret, ptp of* **win**

wonder ['wʌndə'] **N** 16.1, 19.1, 26.1 **N a** (= *feeling*) Staunen *nt*, Verwunderung *f*; **in ~** voller Staunen; **the birth of a baby never loses its ~** eine Geburt bleibt immer etwas Wunderbares; **it fills one with a sense of ~** es erfüllt einen mit Erstaunen; **he has never lost that almost childlike sense of ~** er hat nie dieses kindliche Staunen verlernt

b (= *object or cause of wonder*) Wunder *nt*; **the ~ of electricity** das Wunder der Elektrizität; **the seven ~s of the world** die sieben Weltwunder; **the ~ of it was that ...** das Erstaunliche *or* Verblüffende daran war, dass ...; **it is a ~ that ...** es ist ein Wunder, dass ...; **it is no** *or* **little** *or* **small ~** (es) ist kein Wunder, es ist nicht zu verwundern; **no ~ (he refused)!** kein Wunder(, dass er abgelehnt hat)!; **to do** *or* **work ~s** wahre Wunder vollbringen, Wunder wirken; **~s will never cease!** es geschehen noch Zeichen und Wunder! → **nine**

VT I ~ what he'll do now ich bin gespannt, was er jetzt tun wird (*inf*); **I ~ why he did it** ich möchte (zu gern) wissen *or* ich wüsste (zu) gern, warum er das getan hat; **I ~ why!** (*iro*) ich frag mich warum?; **I was ~ing if you'd like to come too** möchten Sie nicht vielleicht auch kommen?; **I was ~ing when you'd realize that** ich habe mich (schon) gefragt, wann du das merkst; **I was ~ing if you could ...** könnten Sie nicht vielleicht ...

VI a (= *ask oneself, speculate*) **it set me ~ing** *or* **made me ~** es gab mir zu denken; **why do you ask? – oh, I was just ~ing** warum fragst du? – ach, nur so; **what will happen next, I ~?** ich frage mich *or* ich bin gespannt, was als Nächstes kommt; **what's going to happen next? – I ~!** was kommt als Nächstes? – das frage ich mich auch!; **I was ~ing about that** ich habe mir darüber schon Gedanken gemacht, ich habe mich das auch schon gefragt; **I've been ~ing about him** ich habe mir auch schon über ihn Gedanken gemacht; **I've been ~ing about him as a possibility** ich hatte ihn auch schon als eine Möglichkeit ins Auge gefasst; **I expect that will be the end of the matter – I ~!** ich denke, damit ist die Angelegenheit erledigt – da habe ich meine Zweifel *or* da bin ich gespannt; **I'm ~ing about going to the party** ich habe daran gedacht, vielleicht auf die Party zu gehen; **John, I've been ~ing, is there really any point?** John, ich frage mich, ob es wirklich (einen) Zweck hat; **could you possibly help me, I ~** könnten Sie mir vielleicht helfen

b (= *be surprised*) sich wundern; **I ~ (that) he didn't tell me** es wundert mich, dass er es mir nicht gesagt hat; **to ~ at sth** sich über etw (*acc*) wundern, über etw (*acc*) erstaunt sein; **that's hardly to be ~ed at** das ist kaum verwunderlich; **she'll be married by now, I shouldn't ~** es würde mich nicht wundern, wenn sie inzwischen verheiratet wäre

wonder *in cpds* Wunder-; **wonder boy** N Wunderknabe *m*; **wonder drug** N Wunderheilmittel *nt*

wonderful ['wʌndəfʊl] ADJ wunderbar

wonderfully ['wʌndəfəlɪ] ADV wunderbar; **he looks ~ well** er sieht wunderbar aus

wondering [ˈwʌndərɪŋ] ADJ (= astonished) tone, look verwundert, erstaunt; (= doubtful) fragend

wonderingly [ˈwʌndərɪŋlɪ] ADV (= with astonishment) verwundert, erstaunt; (= thoughtfully) nachdenklich

wonderland [ˈwʌndəˌlænd] N (= fairyland) Wunderland nt; (= wonderful place) Paradies nt; **the ~ of the Alps** die Wunderwelt der Alpen

wonderment [ˈwʌndəmənt] N = **wonder** N **a**

wonder-worker [ˈwʌndəˌwɜːkə] N Wundertäter(in) m(f)

wondrous [ˈwʌndrəs] (old, liter) ADJ wunderbar; ways also wundersam ADV wise, fair wunderbar

wondrously [ˈwʌndrəslɪ] ADV (old, liter) wunderbar; **~ beautiful** wunderschön

wonga [ˈwɒŋə] N (dated inf) Moos nt (dated sl), Knete f (dated sl)

wonk [ˈwɒŋk] N (US inf) Streber(in) m(f) (inf); **she's a policy ~** sie kennt die (Politik)richtlinien bis zum letzten Komma

wonky [ˈwɒŋkɪ] ADJ (+er) (Brit, inf) chair, marriage, grammar wackelig; machine nicht (ganz) in Ordnung; **your hat's a bit/your collar's all ~** dein Hut/dein Kragen sitzt ganz schief

wont [wəʊnt] ADJ gewohnt; **to be ~ to do sth** gewöhnlich etw tun, etw zu tun pflegen ◼ N (An)gewohnheit f; **as is/was his ~** wie er zu tun pflegt/pflegte

won't [wəʊnt] contr of **will not**

wonted [ˈwəʊntɪd] ADJ (liter) gewohnt

woo [wuː] VT **a** (dated, = court) woman den Hof machen (+dat), umwerben **b** person umwerben; (fig) stardom, sleep etc suchen; audience etc für sich zu gewinnen versuchen

▶ **woo away** VT sep employee, executive, voter, customer abwerben

wood [wʊd] ◼ N **a** (= material) Holz nt; **touch ~!** (esp Brit) **knock on ~!** (esp US) dreimal auf Holz geklopft! **b** (= small forest) Wald m; **~s** Wald m; **we're not out of the ~s yet** (fig) wir sind noch nicht über den Berg or aus dem Schneider (inf); **he can't see the ~ for the trees** (Brit, prov) er sieht den Wald vor (lauter) Bäumen nicht (prov) **c** (= cask) Holzfass nt; (Bowls) Kugel f; (Golf) Holz nt; **whisky matured in the ~** im Holzfass gereifter Whisky; **that was off the ~** (Tennis) das war Holz, das war vom Rahmen **d** (Mus) **the woods** PL die Holzblasinstrumente pl, die Holzbläser pl ◼ ADJ attr (= made of wood) Holz-; **~ floor** Holzboden m

wood: **wood alcohol** N Holzgeist m; **wood anemone** N Buschwindröschen nt

woodbine [ˈwʊdbaɪn] N (= honeysuckle) Geißblatt nt; (US: = Virginia creeper) wilder Wein, Jungfernrebe f

wood: **wood block** N (Art) Holzschnitt m; **wood carver** N (Holz)schnitzer(in) m(f); **wood carving** N (Holz)schnitzerei f; **woodchip** N (Brit, = wallpaper) Raufaser f; **woodchuck** N Waldmurmeltier nt; **woodcock** N, no pl Waldschnepfe f; **woodcraft** N **a** (= skill at living in forest) Waldläufertum nt **b** (= skill at woodwork) Geschick nt im Arbeiten mit Holz; **woodcut** N Holzschnitt m; **woodcutter** N **a** Holzfäller(in) m(f); (of logs) Holzhacker(in) m(f) **b** (Art) Holzschnitzer(in) m(f); **woodcutting** N **a** Holzfällen nt; (of logs) Holzhacken nt **b** (Art) Holzschnitzen nt **c** (= item) Holzplastik f, Holzschnitzerei f

wooded [ˈwʊdɪd] ADJ bewaldet

wooden [ˈwʊdn] ADJ **a** Holz-; **~ chair** Holzstuhl m; **the ~ horse** das hölzerne Pferd **b** (fig) expression, smile, manner, performance, acting hölzern; (pej, = dull) personality steif

woodenheaded [ˈwʊdnˈhedɪd] ADJ dumm

wooden leg N Holzbein nt

woodenly [ˈwʊdnlɪ] ADV (fig) smile, act, bow gekünstelt, steif; stand wie ein Klotz; look, stare mit unbeweglicher Miene

wooden: **wooden spoon** N (lit) Holzlöffel m, hölzerner Löffel; (fig) Trostpreis m; **woodenware** N Holzwaren pl

wood: **woodfree** ADJ paper holzfrei; **woodland** N Waldland nt, Waldung f; **woodlark** N Heidelerche f; **woodlouse** N Bohrassel f; **woodman** N = **woodsman**; **wood nymph** N Waldnymphe f; **woodpecker** N Specht m; **wood pigeon** N Ringeltaube f; **woodpile** N Holzhaufen m → **nigger**; **wood pulp** N Holzschliff m; **woodshed** N Holzschuppen m

woodsman [ˈwʊdzmən] N pl **-men** [-mən] Waldarbeiter m

wood sorrel N Waldsauerklee m

woodsy [ˈwʊdzɪ] ADJ (+er) (US, inf) waldig; **~ smell** Waldgeruch m, Geruch m von Wald

wood: **wood-turning** N Drechslerei f; **woodwind** N Holzblasinstrument nt; **the ~(s), the ~ section** die Holzbläser pl; **wood wool** N Holzwolle f; **woodwork** N **a** Holzarbeit f; (= craft) Tischlerei f; **the boys do ~ on Tuesday afternoons** dienstags nachmittags beschäftigen sich die Jungen mit Tischlern **b** (= wooden parts) Holzteile pl; **to hit the ~** (Ftbl inf) den Pfosten/die Latte treffen; **to come out of the ~** (fig) aus dem Unterholz or der Versenkung hervorkommen; **woodworking** [ˈwʊdˌwɜːkɪŋ] ◼ N Holzbearbeitung f ◼ ADJ Holz bearbeitend, Holzbearbeitungs-; **woodworm** N Holzwurm m; **it's got ~** da ist der Holzwurm drin

woody [ˈwʊdɪ] ADJ (+er) **a** (= wooded) waldig, bewaldet **b** (= like wood in texture) tissue holzig

wooer [ˈwuːə] N (dated) Werber m; (fig) Buhler(in) m(f) (of sth um etw); **a ~ of the unions** ein Buhler um die Gunst der Gewerkschaften

woof¹ [wʊf] N (Tex) Schuss m

woof² ◼ N (of dog) Wuff nt ◼ VI kläffen; **~, ~!** wau, wau!, wuff, wuff!

woofer [ˈwʊfə] N Tieftöner m

woofter [ˈwʊftə], **wooftah** [ˈwʊftə] N (Brit, sl) Warme(r) m (dated inf), Schwule(r) m (inf)

wool [wʊl] ◼ N **a** Wolle f; (= cloth) Wollstoff m; **all ~, pure ~** reine Wolle; **to pull the ~ over sb's eyes** (inf) jdm Sand in die Augen streuen (inf) **b** (= glass wool, wire wool) Wolle f ◼ ADJ Woll-; (= made of wool also) aus Wolle; **~ coat** Wollmantel m

woolen etc (US) = **woollen** etc

wool: **woolgathering** [ˈwʊlˌɡæðərɪŋ] N Träumen nt; **to be ~** vor sich (acc) hin träumen; **woolgrower** [ˈwʊlˌɡrəʊə] N Schafzüchter(in) m(f) (für Wolle)

woollen, (US) **woolen** [ˈwʊlən] ◼ ADJ Woll-; (= made of wool also) wollen, aus Wolle; **~ blanket** Wolldecke f ◼ N **woollens** PL (= garments) Wollsachen pl, Stricksachen pl; (= fabrics, blankets) Wollwaren pl

woolliness, (US) **wooliness** [ˈwʊlɪnɪs] N Wolligkeit f; (= softness also) Flauschigkeit f; (fig: of outline) Verschwommenheit f; (pej, of mind, idea) Verworrenheit f, Wirrheit f

woolly, (US) **wooly** [ˈwʊlɪ] ◼ ADJ (+er) **a** wollig, (= soft also) flauschig; **~ mammoth** (Zool) Kältesteppenmammut m **b** (fig) outline verschwommen; (pej) mind, thinking, idea verworren, wirr; **a ~ liberal** ein sentimentaler Liberaler, eine sentimentale Liberale ◼ N (inf, = sweater etc) Pulli m (inf); **winter woollies** (esp Brit: = sweaters etc) dicke Wollsachen pl (inf); (esp US: = underwear) Wollene pl (inf)

wool: **woolmark** [ˈwʊlmɑːk] N Wollsiegel nt; **woolsack** [ˈwʊlsæk] N (= seat) Wollsack m (Sitz des Lordkanzlers im britischen Oberhaus); (= office) Amt nt des Lordkanzlers

wooziness [ˈwuːzɪnɪs] N (inf) Benommenheit f

woozy [ˈwuːzɪ] ADJ (+er) (inf) benommen, duselig (inf)

wop [wɒp] N (pej sl) Spag(h)ettifresser(in) m(f) (pej sl)

Worcs abbr of **Worcestershire**

word [wɜːd] ◼ N **a** (= unit of language) Wort nt; **~s** Wörter pl; (in meaningful sequence) Worte pl; **~ division** Silbentrennung f; **foreign ~s** Fremdwörter pl; **~ for ~** (= exactly also) wortwörtlich; **cold isn't the ~ for it** kalt ist gar kein Ausdruck (dafür); **"irresponsible" would be a better ~ for it** „unverantwortlich" wäre wohl das treffendere Wort dafür; **~s cannot describe it** so etwas kann man mit Worten gar nicht beschreiben; **beyond ~s** unbeschreiblich; **too funny for ~s** unbeschreiblich komisch; **to put one's thoughts into ~s** seine Gedanken in Worte fassen or kleiden; **in a ~** mit einem Wort, kurz gesagt; **(not) in so many ~s** (nicht) direkt or ausdrücklich; **in other ~s** mit anderen Worten, anders gesagt or ausgedrückt; **in one's own ~s** mit eigenen Worten; **the last ~** (fig) der letzte Schrei (in an +dat); **he had the last ~** er hatte das letzte Wort; **I would have chosen** ich hätte es nicht so ausgedrückt; **in the ~s of Goethe** mit Goethe gesprochen, um mit Goethe zu sprechen

b (= remark) Wort nt; **~s** Worte pl; **a ~ of advice** ein Rat(schlag) m; **a ~ of encouragement/warning** eine Ermunterung/Warnung; **fine ~s** schöne Worte pl; **a man of few ~s** ein Mann, der nicht viele Worte macht; **I can't get a ~ out of him** ich kann kein Wort aus ihm herausbekommen; **by ~ of mouth** durch mündliche Überlieferung; **to say a few ~s** ein paar Worte sprechen; **to be lost** or **at a loss for ~s** nicht wissen, was man sagen soll; **to take sb at his ~** jdn beim Wort nehmen; **to have a ~ with sb (about sth)** (= talk to) mit jdm (über etw) sprechen; **to have a ~ with sb** (= reprimand, discipline) jdn ins Gebet nehmen; **John, could I have a ~?** John, kann ich dich mal sprechen?; **(could I have) a ~ in your ear?** kann ich Sie bitte allein (or unter vier Augen) sprechen?; **a ~ to the wise** ein guter Rat; **you took the ~s out of my mouth** du hast mir das Wort aus dem Mund genommen; **I wish you wouldn't put ~s into my mouth** ich wünschte, Sie würden mir nicht das Wort im Munde herumdrehen; **to put in** or **say a (good) ~ for sb** jdn ein gutes Wort einlegen; **nobody had a good ~ to say for him** niemand wusste etwas Gutes über ihn zu sagen; **without a ~** ohne ein Wort; **don't say** or **breathe a ~ about it** sag aber bitte keinen Ton or kein Sterbenswörtchen (inf) davon; **remember, not a ~ to anyone** vergiss nicht, kein Sterbenswörtchen (inf)

c **words** PL (= quarrel) **to have ~s with sb** mit jdm eine Auseinandersetzung haben

d **words** PL (= text, lyrics) Text m

e no pl (= message, news) Nachricht f; **~ went round that …** es ging die Nachricht um, dass …; **to leave ~ (with sb/for sb) that …** (bei jdm/für jdn) (die Nachricht) hinterlassen, dass …; **is there any ~ from John yet?** schon von John gehört?, schon Nachrichten von John?; **to send ~** Nachricht geben; **to send ~ to sb** jdn benachrichtigen; **to send sb ~ of sth** jdn von etw benachrichtigen; **to spread the ~** (inf) es allen sagen (inf); **what's the ~ on Charlie?** (inf) was gibts Neues von Charlie?

f (= promise, assurance) Wort nt; **~ of honour** (Brit) or **honor** (US) Ehrenwort nt; **a man of his ~** ein Mann, der zu seinem Wort steht; **to be true to** or **as good as one's ~, to keep one's ~** sein Wort halten; **I give you my ~** ich gebe dir mein (Ehren)wort; **to go back on one's ~** sein Wort nicht halten; **to break one's ~** sein Wort brechen; **I only have his ~ for it** ich habe nur sein Wort dafür; **take my ~ for it** verlass dich drauf, das kannst du mir glauben; **you don't have to take my ~ for it** du kannst das ruhig nachprüfen; **it's his ~ against mine** Aussage steht gegen Aussage; **upon my ~!** (old) **my ~!** meine Güte!

g (= order) Wort nt; (also **word of command**) Kommando nt, Befehl m; **to give the ~ (to do sth)** (Mil) das Kommando geben, etw zu tun); **just say the ~** sag nur ein Wort; **his ~ is law here** sein Wort ist hier Gesetz

h (Rel) Wort nt; **the Word of God** das Wort Gottes; **to preach the Word** das Wort Gottes or

das Evangelium verkünden
VT (in Worten) ausdrücken, formulieren, in Worte fassen (geh); letter formulieren; speech abfassen

word: word association N Wortassoziation f; **word-blind** ADJ wortblind; **word blindness** N Wortblindheit f; **wordbook** N Wörterbuch nt; (Mus) Textbuch nt, Libretto nt; **word break** ['wɜːdbreɪk] N (of a word) (Silben)trennung f; **word class** N Wortklasse f; **word-count** N (Comput) Wortzählung f; **word-crunch** VT (Comput inf) text (nach Wörtern) analysieren; **word deafness** N (Med, Psych) Worttaubheit f; **word ending** N (Ling) Wortendung f; **word formation** N Wortbildung f; **word game** N Buchstabenspiel nt

wordily ['wɜːdɪlɪ] ADV wortreich, langatmig (pej)

wordiness ['wɜːdɪnɪs] N Wortreichtum m, Langatmigkeit f (pej)

wording ['wɜːdɪŋ] N Formulierung f

word: wordless ADJ wortlos; grief stumm; **word list** N Wortliste f; **word order** N Satzstellung f, Wortstellung f; **word-perfect** ADJ sicher im Text; **to be ~** den Text perfekt beherrschen, den Text bis aufs Wort beherrschen; **word picture** N Bild nt (in Worten); **to paint a vivid ~ of sth** etw in lebhaften Farben beschreiben; **wordplay** N Wortspiel nt; **word-process** VT mit Textverarbeitung schreiben or erstellen; **word processing** N Textverarbeitung f; **word-processing** ADJ, ATTR Textverarbeitungs-; **~ software** Textverarbeitungssoftware f; **word processor** N (= machine) Text(-verarbeitungs)system nt, Textverarbeitungsanlage f; (= software) Text(verarbeitungs)programm nt; **word split** N Worttrennung f; **word square** N magisches Quadrat; **word-wrap** N (Comput) (automatischer) Zeilenumbruch

wordy ['wɜːdɪ] ADJ (+er) wortreich, langatmig (pej)

wore [wɔː'] pret of **wear**

work [wɜːk] ✪ 19.1, 19.2 **N a** (= toil, labour, task) Arbeit f; **have you got any ~ for me?** haben Sie was für mich zu tun?; (= employment) haben Sie Arbeit für mich?; **he doesn't like ~** er arbeitet nicht gern; **that's a good piece of ~** das ist gute Arbeit; **is this all your own ~?** haben Sie das alles selbst gemacht?; **closed for ~ on the roof** wegen (Reparatur)arbeiten am Dach geschlossen; **when ~ begins on the new bridge** wenn die Arbeiten an der neuen Brücke anfangen; **to be at ~ (on sth)** (an etw dat) arbeiten; **there are forces at ~ which ...** es sind Kräfte am Werk, die ...; **it's the ~ of the devil** das ist Teufelswerk or ein Machwerk des Teufels; **to do a good day's ~** ein schönes Stück Arbeit leisten; **nice** or **good ~!** gut or super (inf) gemacht!; **we've a lot of ~ before this choir can give a concert** wir haben noch viel zu tun, ehe dieser Chor ein Konzert geben kann; **you need to do some more ~ on your accent/your technique** Sie müssen noch an Ihrem Akzent/an Ihrer Technik arbeiten; **to get** or **set to ~ on sth** sich an etw (acc) machen; **I've been trying to get some ~ done** ich habe versucht zu arbeiten; **to put a lot of ~ into sth** eine Menge Arbeit in etw (acc) stecken; **it's in the ~s** (inf) es ist in der Mache (inf); **to get on with one's ~** sich (wieder) an die Arbeit machen; **to make short** or **quick ~ of sb/sth** mit jdm/etw kurzen Prozess machen; **to make ~ for sb** jdm Arbeit machen; **time/the medicine had done its ~** die Zeit/Arznei hatte ihr Werk vollbracht/ihre Wirkung getan; **the ~ of a moment** eine Angelegenheit von Sekunden; **it was hard ~ for the old car to get up the hill** das alte Auto hatte beim Anstieg schwer zu schaffen

b (= employment, job) Arbeit f; **to be (out) at ~** arbeiten sein; **to go out to ~** arbeiten gehen; **to be out of ~** arbeitslos sein; **to be in ~** eine Stelle haben; **he travels to ~ by car** er fährt mit dem Auto zur Arbeit; **do you live close to your ~?** hast du es weit zur Arbeit?; **how long does it take you to get to ~?** wie lange brauchst du, um zu deiner Arbeitsstelle zu kommen?; **at ~** an der Arbeitsstelle, am Arbeitsplatz; **what is your ~?** was tun Sie (beruflich)?; **to put** or **throw sb out of ~** jdn arbeitslos machen; **to be off ~** (am Arbeitsplatz) fehlen

c (= product) Arbeit f; (Art, Liter) Werk nt; **a ~ of art** ein Kunstwerk nt; **a ~ of reference** ein Nachschlagewerk nt; **a ~ of literature** ein literarisches Werk; **a fine piece of ~** eine schöne Arbeit; **good ~s** gute Werke pl; **a chance for artists to show their ~** eine Gelegenheit für Künstler, ihre Arbeit or Werke zu zeigen

d **works** PL (Mil) Befestigungen pl **e** **works** PL (Mech) Getriebe, Innere(s) nt; (of watch, clock) Uhrwerk nt **f** **works** SING OR PL (Brit: = factory) Betrieb m, Fabrik f; **gas/steel ~s** Gas-/Stahlwerk nt; **~s gate** Fabrik- or Werkstor nt; **~s outing** Betriebsausflug m **g** (inf) **the works** PL alles Drum und Dran; **to give sb the ~s** (= treat harshly) jdn gehörig in die Mangel nehmen (inf); (= treat generously) jdn nach allen Regeln der Kunst or nach Strich und Faden verwöhnen (inf); **to get the ~s** (= be treated harshly) gehörig in die Mangel genommen werden (inf); (= be treated generously) nach allen Regeln der Kunst or nach Strich und Faden verwöhnt werden (inf); **we had fantastic food, wine, brandy, the ~s** es gab tolles Essen, Wein, Kognak, alle Schikanen (inf); **he was giving his opponent the ~s** er machte seinen Gegner nach allen Regeln der Kunst fertig (inf)

VI a person arbeiten (at an +dat); **to ~ toward(s)/for sth** auf etw (acc) hin/für etw arbeiten; **to ~ for better conditions** etc sich für bessere Bedingungen etc einsetzen; **to ~ against a reform** gegen eine Reform kämpfen; **these factors which ~ against us/in our favour** (Brit) or **favor** (US) diese Faktoren, die gegen uns/zu unseren Gunsten arbeiten

b (= function, operate) funktionieren; (plan) funktionieren, klappen (inf); (medicine, spell) wirken; (= be successful) klappen (inf); **it won't ~** das klappt nicht; **"not ~ing"** (lift etc) „außer Betrieb"; **to get sth ~ing** etw in Gang bringen; **it ~s by** or **on electricity** es läuft auf Strom; **it ~s both ways** es trifft auch andersherum zu; **but this arrangement will have to ~ both ways** aber diese Abmachung muss für beide Seiten gelten

c (yeast) arbeiten, treiben **d** (mouth, face) zucken; (jaws) mahlen **e** (= move gradually) **to ~ loose** sich lockern; **to ~ along** sich entlangarbeiten; **to ~ round** (wind, object) sich langsam drehen (to nach); **he ~ed (a)round to asking her** er hat sich aufgerafft, sie zu fragen; **OK, I'm ~ing (a)round to it** okay, das mache ich schon noch

VT a (= make work) staff, employees, students arbeiten lassen, herannehmen (inf), schinden (pej); **to ~ oneself/sb hard** sich/jdn nicht schonen; **he ~s himself too hard** er übernimmt sich; **to ~ oneself to death** sich zu Tode arbeiten

b (= operate) machine bedienen; lever, brake betätigen; **to ~ sth by electricity/hand** etw elektrisch/mit Hand betreiben; **can we ~ that trick again?** können wir den Trick noch einmal anbringen or anwenden?

c (= bring about) change, cure bewirken, herbeiführen; **to ~ mischief** Unheil anrichten; **to ~ it (so that ...)** (inf) es so deichseln(, dass ...) (inf); **to ~ one's passage** seine Überfahrt abarbeiten; **you don't have to ~ your notice** Sie brauchen Ihre Kündigungsfrist nicht einzuhalten → **work up**

d (Sew) arbeiten; design etc sticken **e** (= shape) wood, metal bearbeiten; dough, clay also kneten, bearbeiten; **he ~ed the clay into a human shape** er formte den Ton zu einer menschlichen Gestalt; **~ the flour in gradually/the ingredients together** mischen Sie das Mehl allmählich unter/die Zutaten (zusammen)

f (= exploit) mine ausbeuten, abbauen; land bearbeiten; smallholding bewirtschaften; (salesman) area bereisen

g muscles trainieren

h (= move gradually) **to ~ one's hands free** seine Hände freibekommen; **to ~ sth loose** etw losbekommen; **to ~ one's way through a book** sich durch ein Buch arbeiten; **to ~ one's way to the top** sich nach oben arbeiten or kämpfen; **to ~ one's way up from nothing** sich von ganz unten hocharbeiten; **to ~ one's way through college** sein Studium selbst or durch eigene Arbeit finanzieren; **he ~ed his way across the rock face/through the tunnel** er überquerte die Felswand/kroch durch den Tunnel; **to ~ oneself into sb's confidence** sich in jds Vertrauen (acc) einschleichen

▶ **work away** VI vor sich hin arbeiten

▶ **work down** VI (stockings) (herunter)rutschen (inf)

▶ **work in** **VT** sep **a** (= rub in) einarbeiten; lotion einmassieren; **it had worked its way right in** es war (tief) eingedrungen **b** (= insert) bolt etc (vorsichtig) einführen **c** (in book, speech) reference einbauen, einarbeiten; jokes einbauen; **to work sth into sth** etw in etw (acc) einbauen **d** (in schedule etc) einschieben; **to work sb into a plan** jdn in einen Plan miteinbeziehen **VI a** (= fit in) passen (with in +acc); **that'll work in quite well** das passt ganz gut **b** (Ind) den Arbeitsplatz besetzen

▶ **work off** **VI** sich losmachen or lockern **VT** sep debts, fat abarbeiten; energy loswerden; feelings auslassen, abreagieren (on an +dat)

▶ **work on** **VI** weiterarbeiten
VT sep lid, washer darauf bringen
VI +prep obj **a** car, book, subject, accent arbeiten an (+dat); **who's working on this case?** wer bearbeitet diesen Fall?
b evidence, assumption ausgehen von; principle (person) ausgehen von; (machine) arbeiten nach; **there are not many clues to work on** es gibt nicht viele Hinweise, auf die man zurückgreifen könnte; **I'm working on this one lead** ich habe alles an diesem einen Anhaltspunkt aufgehängt
c **we haven't solved it yet but we're still working on it** wir haben es noch nicht gelöst, aber wir sind dabei; **if we work on him a little longer we might persuade him** wenn wir ihn noch ein Weilchen bearbeiten, können wir ihn vielleicht überreden; **obviously the other side have been working on him** ihn hat offensichtlich die Gegenseite in der Mache gehabt (inf)

▶ **work out** **VI a** (= allow solution: puzzle, sum etc) aufgehen
b (= amount to) **that works out at £105** das gibt or macht £ 105; **it works out more expensive in the end** am Ende kommt or ist es teurer; **how much does that work out at?** was macht das?
c (= succeed: plan, marriage, idea) funktionieren, klappen (inf); **things didn't work out at all well for him** es ist ihm alles schief gegangen; **how's your new job working out?** was macht die neue Arbeit?; **I hope it all works out for you** ich hoffe, dass alles klappt (inf) or dass dir alles gelingt; **things didn't work out that way** es kam ganz anders
d (in gym etc) trainieren
VT sep **a** (= solve, calculate) herausbringen; code entschlüsseln, knacken (inf); mathematical problem lösen; problem fertig werden mit; sum ausrechnen; **you can work that out for yourself** das kannst du dir (doch) selbst denken; **surely he can manage to work things out for himself** (in life) er kann doch bestimmt allein zurechtkommen; **things will always work themselves out** Probleme lösen sich stets von selbst
b (= devise) scheme (sich dat) ausdenken; (in detail) ausarbeiten
c (= understand) person schlau werden aus (+dat); **can you work out where we are on the map?** kannst du herausfinden or -bringen, wo wir auf der Karte sind?; **I can't work out why it went wrong** ich kann nicht verstehen, wieso es nicht geklappt hat
d (= complete) prison sentence absitzen; **to work out one's notice** seine Kündigungsfrist einhalten
e (= exhaust) mine ausbeuten, erschöpfen; minerals abbauen; **to work sth out of one's sys-**

tem (fig) etw überwinden, mit etw fertig werden

f (= remove) nail, tooth etc (allmählich) herausbringen

▶**work over** VT sep (inf) zusammenschlagen (inf)

▶**work through** VI +prep obj **a** (blade etc) sich arbeiten durch; (water) sickern durch **b** (= read through) sich (durch)arbeiten or (durch)ackern durch **c** (Psych) problem aufarbeiten VT SEP +prep obj **he worked the rope through the crack** er führte das Seil durch die Spalte VI (= come through: benefit, pay rise etc) durchsickern

▶**work up** VT sep **a** (= develop) business zu etwas bringen, entwickeln; enthusiasm (in oneself) aufbringen; appetite sich (dat) holen; courage sich (dat) machen; **to work one's way up (through the ranks)** von der Pike auf dienen; **to work up a sweat** richtig ins Schwitzen kommen **b** lecture, theme, notes ausarbeiten **c** (= stimulate) audience aufstacheln; **to work up feeling against sb** gegen jdn Stimmung machen; **to be worked up** aufgeregt sein; **to get worked up** sich aufregen; **to work oneself up** sich erhitzen → **frenzy** VI (skirt etc) sich hoch schieben

▶**work up to** VI +prep obj question, proposal etc zusteuern auf (+acc); **I know what you're working up to** ich weiß, worauf Sie hinauswollen; **the music works up to a tremendous climax** die Musik steigert sich zu einem gewaltigen Höhepunkt

workability [ˌwɜːkəˈbɪlɪtɪ] N **a** (Tech, of material) Bearbeitungsfähigkeit f **b** (Tech, of machine) Betriebsfähigkeit f **c** (of a plan etc) Durchführbarkeit f

workable [ˈwɜːkəbl] ADJ **a** mine abbaufähig; land bebaubar; plan, system, agreement durchführbar; solution, alternative machbar; relationship funktionierend **b** (= malleable) clay, metal formbar

workaday [ˈwɜːkədeɪ] ADJ Alltags-; ~ **life** Alltagsleben nt

workaholic [ˌwɜːkəˈhɒlɪk] N (inf) Arbeitswütige(r) mf, Arbeitssüchtige(r) mf, Arbeitstier nt

workaholism [ˈwɜːkəhɒlɪzəm] N Workaholismus m (spec), Arbeitssucht f

work: work area N Arbeitsplatz m; **work associate** N Arbeitskollege m/-kollegin f; **workbag** N (Sew) Näh- or Handarbeitsbeutel m; **work basket** N (Sew) Näh- or Handarbeitskorb m; **workbench** N Werkbank f; **workbook** N Arbeitsheft nt; **work camp** N Arbeitslager nt; **work coat** N (US) Arbeitsmantel m, Arbeitskittel m; **workday** N (esp US) Arbeitstag m; (= weekday) Werktag m

worker [ˈwɜːkə'] N Arbeiter(in) m(f); ~**s' education** Arbeiterbildung f → **fast** ¹ ADJ a **b** (also **worker ant/bee**) Arbeiterin f

worker: worker bee N Arbeiterbiene f, Arbeitsbiene f; **worker director** N Arbeitnehmer, der gleichzeitig dem Unternehmensvorstand angehört; **worker participation** N Mitbestimmung f; **worker-priest** N Arbeiterpriester m

work: work ethic N Arbeitsmoral f; **workfare** [ˈwɜːkfɛə'] N Programm, das Arbeitslose verpflichtet, eine Tätigkeit oder Ausbildung zu absolvieren, um weiterhin Zahlungen zu empfangen; **work file** N (Comput) Arbeitsdatei f; **workflow** N Arbeitsablauf m; **workflow schedule** N Arbeitsablaufplan m; **workforce** N Arbeitskräfte pl; **work glove** N Arbeitshandschuh m; **workhorse** N (lit, fig) Arbeitspferd nt; **work hour** N = **working hour**; **workhouse** N (Brit Hist) Armenhaus nt; **work-in** N Work-in nt

working [ˈwɜːkɪŋ] ADJ **a** (= engaged in work) population arbeitend, berufstätig; (Comm) partner aktiv; ~ **man** Arbeiter m; **I'm a ~ man, I need my rest** ich arbeite den ganzen Tag, ich brauche meine Ruhe; ~ **wives** berufstätige Ehefrauen pl; ~ **woman** berufstätige Frau

b (= spent in or used for working) Arbeits-; ~ **conditions** Arbeitsbedingungen pl; ~ **hours** Ar-

beitszeit f; **during ~ hours** während der Arbeitszeit; **your order will be sent within three ~ days** ihre Bestellung wird innerhalb von drei Werktagen geschickt

c (= provisional) Arbeits-; (= sufficient) majority arbeitsfähig; **to have a ~ majority** eine arbeitsfähige Mehrheit haben; ~ **hypothesis** Arbeitshypothese f; **in ~ order** funktionsfähig; **in good/perfect ~ order** voll funktionsfähig; ~ **knowledge** Grundkenntnisse pl

d farm, mill, sailing ship, steam train in Betrieb N **a** (= work) Arbeiten nt, Arbeit f **b** **workings** PL (= way sth works) Arbeitsweise f, Funktionsweise f; ~**s of fate** Wege pl des Schicksals; ~**s of the mind** Gedankengänge pl; **in order to understand the ~s of this machine/system** um zu verstehen, wie die Maschine/das System funktioniert **c** **workings** PL (Min) Schächte pl, Gänge pl; (of quarry) Grube f

working: working assets PL (Econ) Betriebsvermögen nt; **working capital** N Betriebskapital nt; **working class** N (also **working classes**) Arbeiterklasse f; **working-class** ADJ der Arbeiterklasse; (pej) ordinär, proletenhaft; **to be ~** zur Arbeiterklasse gehören; ~ **culture** Arbeiterkultur f; **working companion** N Arbeitskamerad(in) m(f); **working condition** N **a** (Tech) Betriebszustand m **b** ~**s** pl Arbeitsbedingungen pl; **working copy** N Arbeitsexemplar nt; **working dinner** N = **working lunch**; **working dog** N Arbeitshund m, Hund, der für bestimmte Aufgaben abgerichtet ist; **working expenses** PL (Econ) Betriebskosten pl; **working girl** N (euph) Prostituierte f; **working group** N Arbeitsgruppe f, Arbeitskreis m; **working holiday** N (Brit) Urlaub, in dem eine bezahlte Tätigkeit ausgeübt wird; **working hour** N Arbeitsstunde f; ~**s** pl Arbeitszeit f; **reduction in or of ~s** Arbeitszeitverkürzung f; **working life** N (of machine part) Lebensdauer f; (of animal) Nutzungsdauer f; (of person) Berufsleben nt; **working lunch** N Arbeitsessen nt; **working materials** PL Arbeitsmittel pl; **working memory** N (Comput) Arbeitsspeicher m; **working men's club** N (Brit) Arbeiterklub m; **working morale** N Arbeitsmoral f; **working-out** N (of a plan etc) Ausarbeitung f; (of a question etc) Lösung f; **working-over** N (inf) Abreibung f (inf); **to give sb a good ~** jdm eine tüchtige Abreibung verpassen (inf); **working papers** PL (Econ) Arbeitspapiere pl; **working party** N (Arbeits)ausschuss m; **working pool** N Arbeitsgemeinschaft f; **working power** N Arbeitskraft f; **working relationship** N Zusammenarbeit f; **to have a good ~ with sb** mit jdm gut zusammenarbeiten; **working title** N Arbeitstitel m; **working vacation** N (US) = **working holiday**; **working visa** N (US) Arbeitserlaubnis f; **working week** N Arbeitswoche f

work: work-in-progress N (Fin) laufende Arbeiten pl; **workless** [ˈwɜːklɪs] ADJ arbeitslos; **workload** [ˈwɜːkləʊd] N Arbeit(slast) f; **workman** N Handwerker m; **a bad ~ always blames his tools** (prov) ein schlechter Arbeiter gibt immer seinem Werkzeug die Schuld; **workmanlike** [ˈwɜːkmənlaɪk] ADJ attitude, job fachmännisch; product fachmännisch gearbeitet; **workmanship** [ˈwɜːkmənʃɪp] N Arbeit(squalität) f; **workmate** N (inf) (Arbeits)kollege m, (Arbeits)kollegin f; **workmen's comp** N (inf), **workmen's compensation** N (US, in case of occupational disease etc) Entschädigung f; **workout** N (Sport) Training nt; **to have a ~** Übungen machen; (boxer) Sparring machen; **work permit** N Arbeitserlaubnis f; **workpiece** N Werkstück nt; **workplace** N Arbeitsplatz m; **in** or **at the ~** am Arbeitsplatz; **workroom** N Arbeitszimmer nt

works [wɜːks] PL = **work** N d–g

works council, **works committee** N (esp Brit)

work: work-sharing [ˈwɜːkʃɛərɪŋ] N Arbeitsteilung f; **workshop** N Werkstatt f; **a music ~** ein Musikkurs m, ein Musik-Workshop m; **workshy** ADJ arbeitsscheu; **work space** N = **work**

area; **work station** N Arbeitsplatz m, Arbeitsbereich m; (Comput) Arbeitsplatzstation f; **work-study** [ˈwɜːkstʌdɪ] N REFA- or Arbeitsstudie f; **work surface** N Arbeitsfläche f; **worktable** N Arbeitstisch m; **work ticket** N Arbeitszettel m; **worktop** N (Brit) Arbeitsfläche f; **work-to-rule** N Dienst m nach Vorschrift; **work visa** N (US) Arbeitserlaubnis f; **workwear** [ˈwɜːkwɛə'] N Arbeitskleidung f; **workweek** [ˈwɜːkwiːk] N (esp US) Arbeitswoche f

world [wɜːld] N **a** Welt f; **in the ~** auf der Welt; **all over the ~** auf der ganzen Welt; **he jets/sails all over the ~** er jettet/segelt in der Weltgeschichte herum; **it's the same the whole ~ over** es ist (doch) überall das Gleiche; **to go (a)round the ~** eine Weltreise machen; **to sail (a)round the ~** rund um die Welt segeln; **to feel** or **be on top of the ~** munter und fidel sein; **it's not the end of the ~!** (inf) deshalb or davon geht die Welt nicht unter! (inf); **it's a small ~** wie klein doch die Welt ist; **to live in a ~ of one's own** in seiner eigenen (kleinen) Welt leben; **love makes the ~ go round** es dreht sich alles um die Liebe; **money makes the ~ go round** es dreht sich alles um das Geld, Geld regiert die Welt; **in an ideal** or **a perfect ~** in einer idealen Welt

b the **New/Old/Third World** die Neue/Alte/Dritte Welt; **the business ~** die Geschäftswelt; **the sporting ~** die Welt des Sports; **the literary ~** die literarische Welt; **the animal/vegetable ~** die Tier-/Pflanzenwelt; **in the Roman ~** zur Zeit der Römer

c (= society) Welt f; **man/woman of the ~** Mann m/Frau f von Welt; **to come** or **go down in the ~** herunterkommen; **to go up** or **to rise in the ~** es (in der Welt) zu etwas bringen; **he had the ~ at his feet** die ganze Welt lag ihm zu Füßen; **to lead the ~ in sth** in etw (dat) in der Welt führend sein; **how goes the ~ with you?** wie gehts?, wie stehts?; **all the ~ knows ...** alle Welt or jeder weiß ...; **all the ~ and his wife were there** Gott und die Welt waren da (inf); **in the eyes of the ~** vor der Welt

d (= this life) Welt f; **to come into the ~** zur Welt kommen, auf die Welt kommen; ~ **without end** (Eccl) von Ewigkeit zu Ewigkeit; **to renounce the ~** (Rel) der Welt (dat) entsagen; **to have the best of both ~s** das eine tun und das andere nicht lassen; **out of this ~** (inf) fantastisch, phantastisch; **he is not long for this ~** er steht schon mit einem Fuß im Jenseits; **to bring sb into the ~** jdn zur Welt bringen; **to bring sth into the ~** etw in die Welt setzen; **to go to a better ~** in eine bessere Welt eingehen; **to be (all) alone in the ~** allein auf der Welt sein

e (emph) Welt f; **not for (all) the ~** nicht um alles in der Welt; **nothing in the ~** nichts auf der Welt; **what/who in the ~** was/wer in aller Welt; **it did him a ~ of good** es hat ihm (unwahrscheinlich) gut getan; **a ~ of difference** ein himmelweiter Unterschied; **they're ~s apart** sie sind total verschieden; **for all the ~ like ...** beinahe wie ...; **he looked for all the ~ as if nothing had happened** er sah aus, als wäre überhaupt nichts geschehen; **to mean the ~ to sb** jdm alles bedeuten; **to think the ~ of sb** große Stücke auf jdn halten

world in cpds Welt-; **World Bank** N Weltbank f; **world-beater** N (Brit inf) **to be a ~** unschlagbar sein; **world champion** N Weltmeister(in) m(f); **world championship** N Weltmeisterschaft f; **world class** N (Sport etc) Weltklasse f; **world-class** [ˌwɜːldˈklɑːs] ADJ Weltklasse-, der Weltklasse; ~ **player** Weltklassespieler(in) m(f); **world clock** N Weltzeituhr f; **World Court** N Weltgerichtshof m; **World Cup** N Fußballweltmeisterschaft f; (= cup) Weltpokal m; **world economy** N Weltwirtschaft f; **World Fair** N Weltausstellung f; **world-famous** ADJ weltberühmt; **World Health Organization** N Weltgesundheitsorganisation f; **World Heritage Site** N Weltkulturerbe nt or -denkmal nt; **world language** N Weltsprache f *f*; **world leader** N **a** (*Pol*) **the ~s** die führenden Regierungschefs der Welt **b** (*Comm, = country, company*) weltweiter Marktführer, Weltführer *m*

worldliness [ˈwɜːldlɪnɪs] N Weltlichkeit *f*; (*of person*) weltliche Gesinnung

world literature N Weltliteratur *f*

worldly [ˈwɜːldlɪ] ADJ (+*er*) **a** (= *material*) *success, ambition, wealth* materiell; **~ things** weltliche Dinge **b** weltlich; *person* weltlich gesinnt; (= *sophisticated*) *manner* weltmännisch; **~ innocence** Weltfremdheit *f*; **~ wisdom** Weltklugheit *f*

worldly-wise [ˈwɜːldlɪˈwaɪz] ADJ weltklug

world: world market N (*Econ*) Weltmarkt *m*; **world music** N Weltmusik *f*; **world peace** N Weltfrieden *m*; **world picture** N = world-view; **world power** N Weltmacht *f*; **world rankings** PL Weltrangliste *f*; **world record** N Weltrekord *m*; **world record holder** N Weltrekordinhaber(in) *m(f)*; **world's champion** N (*US*) Weltmeister(in) *m(f)*; **World Service the ~** (*Brit Rad*) internationaler Rundfunksender der BBC; **World's Fair** N (*US*) Weltausstellung *f*; **world-shattering** ADJ welterschütternd, weltbewegend; **world's record** N (*US*) Weltrekord *m*; **world trade** N (*Econ*) Welthandel *m*; **World Trade Organization** N Welthandelsorganisation *f*; **world-view** N Weltbild *nt*; **world war** N Weltkrieg *m*; **World War One**, **World War I** N Erster Weltkrieg; **World War Two**, **World War II** N Zweiter Weltkrieg; **world-weariness** N Lebensmüdigkeit *f*; **world-weary** ADJ lebensmüde; **worldwide** ADJ, ADV weltweit; **on a ~ scale** weltweit; **World Wide Web** N World Wide Web *nt*

worm [wɜːm] N **a** (*lit, fig inf*) Wurm *m*; (= *wood worm*) Holzwurm *m*; **~s** (*Med*) Würmer *pl*; **the ~ has turned** (*prov*) das Blatt hat sich gewendet; **to get a ~'s eye view of sth** etw aus der Froschperspektive sehen; **to open a can of ~s** in ein Wespennest stechen; **this has opened a whole new can of ~s** das wirft ganz neue Probleme auf **b** (= *screw*) Schnecke *f*; (= *thread*) Schneckengewinde *nt* VT **a** (= *wriggle*) zwängen; **to ~ one's way along/through/into sth** sich an etw (*dat*) entlangdrücken/durch etw (*acc*) durchschlängeln/in etw (*acc*) hineinzwängen; **to ~ one's way forward** (= *creep*) sich nach vorne schleichen; **to ~ one's way into a position/into a group** sich in eine Stellung/eine Gruppe einschleichen; **to ~ one's way into sb's affection** sich bei jdm einschmeicheln; **to ~ one's way out of a difficulty** sich aus einer schwierigen Lage herauswinden **b** (= *extract*) **to ~ sth out of sb** jdm etw entlocken; **you have to ~ everything out of him** ihm muss man die Würmer aus der Nase ziehen **c** *dog* eine Wurmkur machen mit (+*dat*)

worm: wormcast [ˈwɜːmkɑːst] N *vom Regenwurm aufgeworfenes Erdhäufchen*; **worm-eaten** ADJ *wood* wurmstichig; (*fig inf*) wurmzerfressen; **worm gear** N Schneckengetriebe *nt*; **wormhole** N Wurmloch *nt*

worming tablet [ˈwɜːmɪŋˌtæblɪt] N Entwurmungstablette *f*

worm: worm powder N Wurmmittel *nt*; **worm wheel** N Schneckenrad *nt*; **wormwood** N Wermut *m*; (*fig*) Wermutstropfen *m*

wormy [ˈwɜːmɪ] ADJ *apple* wurmig; *wood* wurmstichig; *soil* wurmreich

worn [wɔːn] *ptp* of **wear** ADJ **a** (= *worn-out*) *coat* abgetragen; *book* zerlesen; *carpet* abgetreten; *tyre* abgefahren **b** (= *weary*) *smile* müde; *person* angegriffen; **to look ~ (with care)** verhärmt aussehen

worn-out [ˈwɔːnˌaʊt] ADJ attr, **worn out** ADJ pred **a** *coat* abgetragen; *carpet* abgetreten; (*fig*) *phrase* abgedroschen **b** (= *exhausted*) *person* erschöpft; *horse* ausgemergelt

worried [ˈwʌrɪd] ADJ besorgt (*about, by* wegen); (= *anxious also*) beunruhigt; **to be ~ sick** krank vor Sorge(n) sein (*inf*)

worriedly [ˈwʌrɪdlɪ] ADV besorgt; (= *anxiously also*) beunruhigt

worrier [ˈwʌrɪə] N **she's a great ~** sie macht sich (*dat*) immerzu Sorgen

worriment [ˈwʌrɪmənt] N (*esp US, inf*) **a** (= *vexation*) Plage *f*, Quälerei *f* **b** (= *anxiety*) Angst *f*, Sorge *f*

worrisome [ˈwʌrɪsəm] ADJ (*esp US*) beunruhigend, Besorgnis erregend; (= *annoying*) lästig

worry [ˈwʌrɪ] N Sorge *f*; **the ~ of bringing up a family** die Sorgen, die eine Familie mit sich bringt; **to be a ~ to us all** wir machen uns alle große Sorgen darüber; **I know it's a ~ for you** ich weiß, es macht dir Sorgen; **what's your main ~?** was drückt dich?; **that's the least of my worries** das macht mir noch am wenigsten Sorgen; **no worries!** (*inf*) kein Problem! VT **a** (= *cause concern*) beunruhigen, Sorgen machen (+*dat*); **it worries me** es macht mir Sorgen; **you ~ me sometimes** manchmal machst du mir wirklich Sorgen; **it's no use just ~ing, do something** es hat keinen Zweck, sich nur den Kopf zu zerbrechen, tu endlich was; **to ~ oneself sick or silly/to death** (*about or over sth*) (*inf*) sich krank machen/sich umbringen vor Sorge (um *or* wegen etw) (*inf*) **b** (= *bother*) stören; **to ~ sb with sth** jdn mit etw stören; **don't ~ me with trivialities** komm mir nicht mit Kleinigkeiten; **to ~ sb to do sth** jdn plagen, etw zu tun **c** (*dog etc*) *sheep* nachstellen (+*dat*); (= *bite*) reißen; *bone* (herum)nagen an (+*dat*) VI sich sorgen, sich (*dat*) Sorgen *or* Gedanken machen (*about, over* um, wegen); **he worries a lot** er macht sich immer so viel Sorgen; **don't ~!, not to ~!** keine Angst *or* Sorge!; **don't ~, I'll do it** lass mal, das mach ich schon; **he said not to ~** er sagte, wir sollten uns keine Sorgen machen; **don't ~ about letting me know** es macht nichts, wenn du mich nicht benachrichtigen kannst; **don't you ~ about that, I'll do it** mach dir darum keine Sorgen, das mach ich; **you should ~!** (*inf*) du hast (vielleicht) Sorgen!

worry beads PL Betperlen *pl*

worrying [ˈwʌrɪɪŋ] ADJ *problem* beunruhigend, Besorgnis erregend; **it's very ~** es macht mir große Sorge; **I know it's ~ for you** ich weiß, es macht dir Sorgen; **it is a ~ time for us** wir haben zurzeit viel Sorgen N **~ won't help** sich nur Sorgen machen, nützt nichts

worry: worry line N (*on face*) Sorgenfalte *f*; **worrywart** [ˈwʌrɪwɔːt] N (*inf*) jd, der sich ständig unnötige Sorgen macht

worse [wɜːs] ✿ 5.3, 26.2 ADJ *comp* of **bad** schlechter; (*morally, with bad consequences*) schlimmer, ärger; **it gets ~ and ~** es wird immer schlimmer; **the patient is ~ than he was yesterday** dem Patienten geht es schlechter als gestern; **the patient is getting ~** der Zustand des Patienten verschlechtert sich *or* wird schlechter; **and to make matters ~** und zu allem Übel; **his "corrections" only made it ~** er hat alles nur verschlimmbessert; **it could have been ~** es hätte schlimmer kommen können; **~ luck!** (so ein) Pech!; **it will be the ~ for you** das wird für dich unangenehme Folgen haben; **so much the ~** um so schlimmer; **to be the ~ for drink** betrunken sein; **he's none the ~ for it** er hat sich nichts dabei getan, es ist ihm nichts dabei passiert; **he'll be none the ~ for some work** etwas Arbeit wird dir nicht schaden; **I don't think any the ~ of you for it** ich halte deswegen aber nicht weniger von dir; **~ things happen at sea** (*inf*) es könnte schlimmer sein ADV *comp* of **badly** schlechter; **it hurts ~** es tut mehr weh; **to be ~ off than …** schlechter dran sein als …; **I could do a lot ~ than accept their offer** es wäre bestimmt kein Fehler, wenn ich das Angebot annähme N Schlechtere(s) *nt*; (*morally, with regard to con-*

sequences) Schlimmere(s) *nt*; **there is ~ to come** es kommt noch schlimmer; **it's changed for the ~** es hat sich zum Schlechteren gewendet

worsen [ˈwɜːsn] VT verschlechtern, schlechter machen VI sich verschlechtern, schlechter werden

worship [ˈwɜːʃɪp] N **a** (*of God, person etc*) Verehrung *f*; **public ~** Gottesdienst *m*; **place of ~** Andachtsstätte *f*; (*non-Christian*) Kultstätte *f* **b** (*Brit: in titles*) **Your Worship** (*to judge*) Euer Ehren/Gnaden; (*to mayor*) (verehrter *or* sehr geehrter) Herr Bürgermeister; **His Worship the Mayor of …** der verehrte Bürgermeister von …; **if your Worship wishes** wenn Euer Ehren *or* Gnaden wünschen VT anbeten; **he ~ped the ground she walked on** er betete den Boden unter ihren Füßen an **a** (*Rel*) den Gottesdienst abhalten; (*RC*) die Messe feiern; **the church where we used to ~** die Kirche, die wir besuchten

worshipful [ˈwɜːʃɪpfʊl] ADJ **a** *look, gaze* verehrend **b** (*Brit: in titles*) sehr verehrt *or* geehrt

worshipper [ˈwɜːʃɪpə] N Kirchgänger(in) *m(f)*; **~ of Baal** Baalsverehrer(in) *m(f)*; **sun-~** Sonnenanbeter(in) *m(f)*; **he was a lifelong ~ at this church** er ist sein Leben lang hier zur Kirche gegangen; **to be a ~ of wealth** das Geld anbeten

worst [wɜːst] ADJ *superl* of **bad** schlechteste(r, s); (*morally, with regard to consequences*) schlimmste(r, s); **the ~ possible time** die ungünstigste Zeit ADV *superl* of **badly** am schlechtesten N **the ~ is over** das Schlimmste *or* Ärgste ist vorbei; **in the ~ of the storm** im ärgsten Sturm; **when the crisis/storm was at its ~** als die Krise/der Sturm ihren/seinen Höhepunkt erreicht hatte; **at (the) ~** schlimmstenfalls; **you've never seen him at his ~** er kann noch (viel) schlimmer (sein); **the ~ of it is …** das Schlimmste daran ist, …; **if the ~ comes to the ~, if ~ comes to ~** (*US*) wenn alle Stricke reißen (*inf*); **do your ~!** (*liter*) mach zu!; **to get the ~ of it** den Kürzeren ziehen VT *enemy, opponent* besiegen, schlagen

worst case [ˈwɜːstkeɪs] N Schlimmstfall *m*, ungünstigster Fall ADJ **worst-case scenario** Schlimmstfall *m*

worsted [ˈwʊstɪd] N (= *yarn*) Kammgarn *nt*; (= *cloth also*) Kammgarnstoff *m* ADJ Kammgarn-; **~ suit** Kammgarnanzug *m*; **~ wool** Kammgarn *nt*

wort [wɜːt] N Bierwürze *f*

worth [wɜːθ] ADJ **a** wert; **it's ~ £5** es ist £ 5 wert; **it's not ~ £5** es ist keine £ 5 wert; **what's this ~?** was *or* wie viel ist das wert?; **it can't be ~ that!** so viel kann es unmöglich wert sein; **it's ~ a great deal to me** es ist mir viel wert; (*sentimentally*) es bedeutet mir sehr viel; **what's it ~ to me to do that?** (*in money*) was springt für mich dabei heraus? (*inf*); (*in advantages*) was bringt es mir, wenn ich das tue?; **will you do this for me? – what's it ~ to you?** tust du das für mich? – was ist es dir wert?; **he was ~ a million** er besaß eine Million; **he's ~ all his brothers put together** er ist so viel wert wie all seine Brüder zusammen; **for all one is ~** so sehr man nur kann; **to sing for all one is ~** aus voller Kehle *or* vollem Halse singen; **you need to exploit the idea for all it's ~** du musst aus der Idee machen, was du nur kannst; **for what it's ~, I personally don't think …** wenn mich einer fragt, ich persönlich glaube nicht, dass …; **I'll tell you this for what it's ~** ich sage dir das, ich weiß nicht, ob was dran ist; **that's my opinion for what it's ~** das ist meine bescheidene Meinung; **it's more than my life/job is ~ to tell you** ich sage es dir nicht, dazu ist mir mein Leben zu lieb/dazu liegt mir zu viel an meiner Stelle **b** (= *deserving, meriting*) wert; **to be ~ it** lohnen; **to be ~ sth** etw wert sein; **it's not ~ it** es lohnt sich nicht; **it's not ~ the trouble** es ist der Mühe nicht wert; **the museum is ~ a visit** das Museum ist einen Besuch wert; **the book**

is ~ **reading** das Buch ist lesenswert; **life isn't ~ living** das Leben ist nicht lebenswert; **is there anything ~ seeing in this town?** gibt es in dieser Stadt etwas Sehenswertes?; **it's a film ~ seeing** es lohnt sich, diesen Film anzusehen; **hardly ~ mentioning** kaum der Rede wert; **an experience ~ having** eine lohnenswerte Erfahrung; **it's not ~ having** es ist nichts; **if a thing's ~ doing, it's ~ doing well** wennschon, dennschon → **salt N a**, **while N c**

N Wert m; **hundreds of pounds' ~ of books** Bücher im Werte von hundertm von Pfund; **a man of great ~** ein sehr wertvoller Mensch; **to show one's true ~** zeigen, was man wirklich wert ist, seinen wahren Wert zeigen; **to increase in ~** im Wert steigen; **what's the current ~ of this?** wie viel ist das momentan wert? → **money**

worthily ['wɜːðɪlɪ] ADV löblich, lobenswert

worthiness ['wɜːðɪnɪs] N (of charity, cause etc) Wert m; (of person) Ehrenhaftigkeit f

worthless ['wɜːθlɪs] ADJ wertlos; person also nichtsnutzig

worthlessness ['wɜːθlɪsnɪs] N Wertlosigkeit f; (of person also) Nichtsnutzigkeit f

worthwhile ['wɜːθ'waɪl] ADJ lohnend attr; **to be ~ lohnen**; (= worth the trouble also) der Mühe (gen) wert sein; **it's a thoroughly ~ film/book** es lohnt sich wirklich, den Film zu sehen/das Buch zu lesen; **it's hardly ~ (asking him)** es lohnt sich wohl kaum(, ihn zu fragen) → also **while N c**

worthy ['wɜːðɪ] ✪ 26.3 **ADJ** (+er) **a** ehrenwert, achtbar; opponent würdig; motive, cause lobenswert, löblich; **my ~ friend** mein werter Freund **b** pred wert, würdig; **~ of remark** bemerkenswert; **~ of mention** erwähnenswert; **to be ~ of sb/sth** jds/einer Sache würdig sein (geh); **any journalist of the name** jeder Journalist, der diese Bezeichnung verdient; **this makes him ~ of (our) respect** dafür verdient er unseren Respekt; **he is ~ to be ranked among ...** er ist es wert, zu ... gezählt zu werden **N** (hum) **the local worthies** die Ortsgrößen pl (hum)

would [wʊd] ✪ 3.3, 4, 8.3, 9.1, 12.3 pret of **will** [1] MODAL AUX VB **a** (conditional) **if you asked him he ~ do it** wenn du ihn fragtest, würde er es tun; **if you had asked him he ~ have done it** wenn du ihn gefragt hättest, hätte er es getan; **I thought you ~ want to know** ich dachte, du wüsstest es gerne or du würdest es gerne wissen; **if I were you, I ~ ...** wenn ich du wäre, würde ich ...; **who ~ have thought it?** wer hätte das gedacht?; **you ~ think ...** man sollte meinen ...; **you ~ never know he was fifty** die Fünfzig sieht man ihm wirklich nicht an

b (in indirect speech) **she said she ~ come** sie sagte, sie würde kommen or sie käme; **I said I ~, so I will** ich habe gesagt, ich würde es tun und ich werde es auch tun

c (emph) **you ~ be the one to get hit** typisch, dass ausgerechnet du getroffen worden bist; **you ~ be the one to forget** typisch, dass du das vergessen hast, das sieht dir ähnlich, dass du es vergessen hast; **I ~n't know** keine Ahnung; **you ~!** das sieht dir ähnlich!; **he ~ have to come right now** ausgerechnet jetzt muss er kommen; **you ~ think of that/say that, ~n't you!** von dir kann man ja nichts anderes erwarten; **it ~ have to rain** es muss auch ausgerechnet regnen

d (insistence) **I warned him, but he ~ do it** ich habe ihn gewarnt, aber er musste es ja unbedingt or um jeden Preis tun; **he ~n't listen/behave** er wollte partout nicht zuhören/sich partout nicht benehmen; **he ~n't be told** er wollte sich (dat) einfach nichts sagen lassen

e (conjecture) **it ~ seem so** es sieht wohl so aus; **it ~ have been about 8 o'clock** es war (wohl) so ungefähr 8 Uhr; **what ~ this be?** was ist das wohl?; **you ~n't have a cigarette, ~ you?** Sie hätten nicht zufällig eine Zigarette bei sich?

f (= wish) möchten; **what ~ you have me do?** was soll ich tun?; **try as he ~** sosehr er es auch versuchte; **the place where I ~ be** (old, liter) der

Ort, an dem ich sein möchte; **~ (that) it were not so!** (old, liter) wenn das doch nur nicht wahr wäre!; **~ to God he ~ come** gebe Gott, dass er kommt; **~ to God he hadn't come** ich wünsche zu Gott, er wäre nicht gekommen **g** (in questions) **~ he come?** würde er vielleicht kommen?; **~ he have come?** wäre er gekommen?; **~ you mind closing the window?** würden Sie bitte das Fenster schließen?; **~ you care for some tea?** hätten Sie gerne etwas Tee? **h** (habit) **he ~ paint it each year** er strich es jedes Jahr, er pflegte es jedes Jahr zu streichen (geh); **50 years ago the streets ~ be empty on a Sunday** vor 50 Jahren waren sonntags die Straßen immer leer

would-be ['wʊdbiː] ADJ attr ~ **poet/politician** jemand, der gerne (ein) Dichter/(ein) Politiker würde; (pej) Möchtegerndichter(in) m(f)/-politiker(in) m(f)

wouldn't ['wʊdnt] contr of **would not**

wound[1] [wuːnd] **N** (lit) Wunde f; (fig also) Kränkung f; **my old war ~** meine alte Kriegsverletzung; **to receive** or **sustain a serious ~** schwer verwundet werden; **to open** or **re-open old ~s** (fig) alte Wunden öffnen; **to ~ to his pride** sein verletzter Stolz → **lick** **VT** (lit) verwunden, verletzen; (fig) verletzen; **~ed pride** verletzter Stolz **N** **the ~ed** pl die Verwundeten pl

wound[2] [waʊnd] pret, ptp of **wind[2]**

wounding ['wuːndɪŋ] ADJ remark, tone verletzend

wound sepsis N (Med) Wundsepsis f

wove [wəʊv] pret of **weave**

woven ['wəʊvən] ptp of **weave**

wow[1] [waʊ] **INTERJ** hui (inf), Mann (inf), Mensch (inf) **N** (inf) **it's a ~** das ist Spitze (inf) or 'ne Wucht (inf)

wow[2] N (on recording) Jaulen nt

WP N abbr of **word processor** **b** (inf) abbr of **weather permitting** bei gutem Wetter

WPC (Brit) N abbr of **Woman Police Constable** Polizistin f

wpm abbr of **words per minute** WpM, wpm

WRAC [ræk] (Brit) abbr of **Women's Royal Army Corps**

wrack[1] [ræk] N (Bot) Tang m

wrack[2] N, VT = **rack[1]**, **rack[2]**

WRAF [ræf] (Brit) abbr of **Women's Royal Air Force**

wraith [reɪθ] N Gespenst nt, Geist m

wraithlike ['reɪθlaɪk] ADJ durchgeistigt, ätherisch

wrangle ['ræŋgl] **N** Gerangel nt no pl, Hin und Her nt no pl **V** streiten, rangeln (about um); (in bargaining) feilschen

wrangler ['ræŋglə] N (US: = cowboy) Cowboy m; (Univ) Mathematikstudent in Cambridge, der mit Auszeichnung bestanden hat

wrap [ræp] **N** **a** (= garment) Umhangtuch nt; (for child) Wickeltuch nt; (= stole) Stola f; (= cape) Cape nt; (= coat) Mantel m

b **under ~s** (lit) verhüllt; car, weapon getarnt; (fig) geheim; **they took the ~s off the new project** sie haben, was das neue Projekt betrifft, die Katze aus dem Sack gelassen (inf)

c **it's a ~** (inf, = completed) das wärs **VT** **a** (lit) einwickeln; parcel, present verpacken, einwickeln; person (for warmth) einpacken (inf); **shall I ~ it for you?** soll ich es Ihnen einpacken or einwickeln?; **~ the joint in foil** den Braten in Folie einschlagen; **~ped bread** abgepacktes Brot; **to ~ sth (a)round sth** etw um etw wickeln; **he ~ped the car (a)round a lamppost** (inf) er hat das Auto um eine Laterne gewickelt (inf); **to ~ one's arms (a)round sb** jdn in die Arme schließen

b (fig) **to be ~ped in sth** in etw gehüllt sein; **she lay ~ped in his arms** sie lag in seinen Armen; **~ped in secrecy** vom Schleier des Geheimnisses umhüllt

VI (Comput) **the lines ~ automatically** der Zeilenumbruch erfolgt automatisch

► **wrap up** **VT** sep **a** (lit, fig) einpacken, einwickeln, verpacken **b** (inf, = finalize) deal festmachen, unter Dach und Fach bringen; **that just about wraps things up for today** das wärs (dann wohl) für heute **c** **to be wrapped up in sb/sth** in jdm/etw aufgehen **VI** **a** (= dress warmly) sich warm einpacken (inf) **b** (inf, = be quiet) den Mund halten (inf)

wraparound ['ræpəraʊnd], **wrapover** ['ræpəʊvə] ADJ attr Wickel-; **~ skirt** Wickelrock m

wrappage ['ræpɪdʒ] N Umschlag m, Hülle f; (= wrapping) Verpackung f

wrapper ['ræpə] N **a** Verpackung f; (of sweets) Papier(chen) nt; (of cigar) Deckblatt nt; (of book) (Schutz)umschlag m; (postal) Streifband nt **b** (= garment) leichter Morgenmantel **c** (= person: in factory etc) Packer(in) m(f)

wrapping ['ræpɪŋ] N Verpackung f (round +gen, von)

wrapping paper N Packpapier nt; (decorative) Geschenkpapier nt

wraparound ['ræpəraʊnd] ADJ attr = **wraparound**

wrath [rɒθ] N Zorn m; (liter, of storm) Wut f

wrathful ADJ , **wrathfully** ADV ['rɒθfʊl, -fəlɪ] wutentbrannt, zornentbrannt

wreak [riːk] VT destruction anrichten; chaos also stiften; (liter) vengeance üben (on an +dat); punishment auferlegen (on +dat); anger auslassen (on an +dat) → **havoc**

wreath [riːθ] N pl **-s** [riːðz] Kranz m; (of smoke etc) Kringel m

wreathe [riːð] **VT** (= encircle) (um)winden; (clouds, mist) umhüllen; (= entwine) flechten; **a garland ~d the victor's head** ein Kranz (um-) krönte das Haupt des Siegers; **his face was ~d in smiles** er strahlte über das ganze Gesicht **VI** **the smoke ~d upwards** der Rauch stieg in Kringeln auf; **to ~ round sth** (ivy etc) sich um etw ranken; (snake) sich um etw schlängeln or ringeln; (smoke) sich um etw kringeln or kräuseln; (mist) um etw wallen

wreck [rek] **N** **a** (Naut) Schiffbruch m; (= wrecked ship, car, train) Wrack nt; **lost in the ~** beim Schiffbruch verloren; **he was killed in a car ~** (US) er kam bei einem Autounfall ums Leben

b (fig inf) (= old bicycle, furniture etc) Trümmerhaufen m; (= person) Wrack nt; (of hopes, life, marriage etc) Trümmer pl, Ruinen pl; **I'm a ~, I feel a ~** ich bin ein (völliges) Wrack; (= exhausted) ich bin vollkommen fertig or erledigt; (in appearance) ich sehe verheerend or unmöglich aus → **nervous wreck**

VT **a** ship, train, plane zum Wrack machen, einen Totalschaden verursachen an (+dat); car kaputtfahren (inf), zu Schrott fahren (inf); machine, mechanism zerstören, kaputtmachen (inf); furniture, house zerstören; (person) zertrümmern, kurz und klein schlagen (inf); **to be ~ed** (Naut) Schiffbruch erleiden; (sl: = drunk) zu (inf) or dicht (sl) sein; **~ed ship** wrackes or havariertes Schiff; **~ed car** zu Schrott gefahrenes Auto

b (fig) hopes, plans, chances zunichte machen; marriage zerrütten; career, health, sb's life zerstören, ruinieren; person kaputtmachen (inf); party, holiday verderben

wreckage ['rekɪdʒ] N (lit, fig: = remains) Trümmer pl; (of ship also) Wrackteile pl; (washed ashore) Strandgut nt; (of house, town) Ruinen pl

wrecker ['rekə] N **a** (= ship wrecker) Strandräuber m (der Schiffe durch falsche Lichtsignale zum Stranden bringt) **b** (Naut, = salvager) Bergungsarbeiter(in) m(f); (= vessel) Bergungsschiff nt **c** (US = breaker, salvager) Schrotthändler(in) m(f); (for buildings) Abbrucharbeiter(in) m(f) **d** (US: = breakdown van) Abschleppwagen m

wrecking ['rekɪŋ]: **wrecking ball** N Abrissbirne f; **wrecking bar** N (US) Brechstange f; **wrecking service** N (US Aut) Abschleppdienst m

Wren [ren] N (Brit) weibliches Mitglied der britischen Marine

wren [ren] N Zaunkönig m

wrench [rentʃ] **N a** (= tug) Ruck m; (Med) Verrenkung f; **to give sth a ~** einer Sache (dat) einen Ruck geben; **he gave his shoulder a nasty ~** er hat sich (dat) die Schulter schlimm verrenkt **b** (= tool) Schraubenschlüssel m **c** (fig) **to be a ~** wehtun; **the ~ of parting** der Trennungsschmerz **VT a** (= tug) winden; **to ~ sth (away) from sb** jdm etw entwinden; **to ~ a door open** eine Tür aufzwingen; **to ~ a door off its hinges** eine Tür aus den Angeln reißen; **he ~ed the steering wheel round** er riss das Lenkrad herum; **to ~ sb's arm out of its socket** jdm den Arm ausrenken **b** (Med) **to ~ one's ankle/shoulder** sich (dat) den Fuß/die Schulter verrenken **c** (fig) reißen; **if you could ~ yourself away from the TV** wenn du dich vom Fernseher losreißen könntest

wrest [rest] VT **to ~ sth from sb/sth** jdm/einer Sache etw abringen; leadership, title jdm etw entreißen; **to ~ sth from sb's grasp** jdm etw entreißen; **to ~ oneself free** sich losreißen

wrestle [resl] **N** Ringkampf m **VT** ringen mit; (Sport also) einen Ringkampf bestreiten gegen; **he ~d the thief to the ground** er brachte or zwang den Dieb zu Boden **VI a** (lit) ringen (for sth um etw) **b** (fig: with problem, conscience etc) ringen, kämpfen (with mit); **the pilot ~d with the controls** der Pilot kämpfte mit den Instrumenten

wrestler [reslə] N Ringkämpfer m; (modern) Ringer(in) m(f)

wrestling [reslɪŋ] N Ringen nt

wrestling match N Ringkampf m

wretch [retʃ] **N a** (miserable) armer Teufel or Schlucker (inf) **b** (contemptible) Wicht m, Schuft m; (= nuisance) Blödmann m (inf); (= child) Schlingel m

wretched [retʃɪd] ADJ **a** elend; conditions, life elend, erbärmlich; clothing elend, erbärmlich; (= unhappy, depressed) (tod)unglücklich; **I feel ~** (= ill) mir geht es miserabel (inf), ich fühle mich elend; **I feel ~ about having to say no** es tut mir in der Seele weh, dass ich Nein or nein sagen muss **b** (= very bad) housing conditions, weather, novel, player erbärmlich, miserabel (inf); (inf, = damned) verflixt, elend, Mist- (all inf); **what a ~ thing to do!** so etwas Schäbiges!; **what ~ luck!** was für ein verflixtes or elendes Pech (inf)

wretchedly [retʃɪdlɪ] ADV **a** (= in misery) erbärmlich; weep, apologize, look kläglich **b** (inf, = extremely) verflixt (inf), verdammt (inf)

wretchedness [retʃɪdnɪs] N Erbärmlichkeit f; (of person: = misery) Elend nt

wrick [rɪk] **VT to ~ one's neck/shoulder** sich (dat) den Hals/die Schulter ausrenken **N to have a ~ in one's neck** sich (dat) den Hals ausgerenkt haben; **to get a ~ in one's neck** sich (dat) den Hals ausrenken

wriggle [rɪgl] **N** Schlängeln nt no pl; (of child, fish) Zappeln nt no pl; **to give a ~** (worm, snake, eel) sich schlängeln; (fish) sich winden, zappeln **VT** toes, ears wackeln mit; **to ~ one's way through sth** sich durch etw (hin)durchwinden or -schlängeln **VI** (also **wriggle about** or **around**) (worm, snake, eel) sich schlängeln; (fish) sich winden, zappeln; (person) (restlessly, excitedly) sich winden; (in embarrassment) sich winden; **to ~ along/down** sich vorwärts/nach unten schlängeln; **the fish ~d off the hook** der Fisch wand sich vom Haken; **she managed to ~ free** es gelang ihr, sich loszuwinden; **he ~d through the hole in the hedge** er wand or schlängelte sich durch das Loch in der Hecke; **do stop wriggling about** hör endlich mit dem Zappelei auf

▶**wriggle out** VI (lit) sich herauswinden (of aus); (fig also) sich herausmanövrieren (of aus); **he's wriggled (his way) out of it** er hat sich gedrückt

wriggly [rɪglɪ] ADJ (+er) sich windend attr, sich krümmend attr; fish, child zappelnd attr

wring [rɪŋ] vb: pret, ptp **wrung** VT **a** (also **wring out**) clothes, wet rag etc auswringen, auswinden; **to ~ water out of clothes** (nasse) Kleider auswringen or auswinden; **"do not ~"** (on washing instructions) nicht wringen **b** hands (in distress) ringen; **to ~ a duck's neck** einer Ente (dat) den Hals umdrehen; **I could have wrung his neck** (inf) umdrehen können; **he wrung my hand** er schüttelte mir (kräftig) die Hand; **to ~ sb's heart** jdm in der Seele wehtun **c** (= extract) **to ~ sth out of** or **from sb** etw aus jdm herausquetschen, jdm etw abringen **N to give clothes a ~** Kleider auswringen or auswinden

wringer [rɪŋə] N (Wäsche)mangel f; **to go** or **be put through the ~** (fig inf) durch die Mangel gedreht werden

wringing [rɪŋɪŋ] ADJ (also **wringing wet**) tropfnass; person also patschnass (inf)

wrinkle [rɪŋkl] **N a** (in clothes, paper) Knitter m; (on face, skin) Runzel f, Falte f; (in stocking) Falte f **b** (inf, = dodge, scheme) Kniff m (inf) **VT** fabric, paper, surface, sheet verknittern, verkrumpeln (inf); skin runzlig or faltig machen; **to ~ one's nose** die Nase rümpfen; **to ~ one's brow** die Stirne runzeln **VI** (sheet, material) (ver)knittern; (stockings) Falten schlagen; (skin etc) runzlig or faltig werden

▶**wrinkle up** VT sep nose rümpfen

wrinkled [rɪŋkld] ADJ sheet, skirt, paper zerknittert; skin runzlig, faltig; brow gerunzelt; apple, old lady schrumpelig, verschrumpelt; **~ stockings** Ziehharmonikastrümpfe pl (inf)

wrinkly [rɪŋklɪ] ADJ (+er) schrumpelig; fabric zerknittert **N** (Brit inf: = old person) Opa m (inf), Oma f (inf)

wrist [rɪst] N Handgelenk nt; **to slash one's ~s** sich (dat) die Pulsadern aufschneiden

wristband [rɪstbænd] N Armband nt; (on dress, shirt) Ärmelbündchen nt; (Sport) Schweißband nt

wristlet [rɪstlɪt] N Armband nt; **~s** pl (sl: = handcuffs) Manschetten pl (inf)

wrist: wristlock [rɪstlɒk] N Polizeigriff m; **to put a ~ on sb** jdn im Polizeigriff halten; **wrist rest** N (Comput) Handballenauflage f; **wristwatch** N Armbanduhr f

writ [rɪt] **N a** (Jur) Verfügung f; **~ of attachment** Haft- or Verhaftungsbefehl m; **~ of execution** Vollstreckungsbefehl m; **to issue a ~** eine Verfügung herausgeben; **to issue a ~ against sb** jdn vorladen (for wegen) **b the Holy Writ** (old, form) die Heilige Schrift

write [raɪt] ✪ 21.1, 21.2 pret **wrote** or (obs) **writ** [rɪt] ptp **written** or (obs) **writ** [rɪt] **VT a** (also Comput) schreiben; cheque, copy ausstellen; notes sich (dat) aufschreiben, sich (dat) machen; application form ausfüllen; **he wrote me a letter** or **schrieb mir einen Brief**; **he wrote himself a note so that he wouldn't forget** er machte sich (dat) eine Notiz, um sich zu erinnern; **he wrote five pages** er schrieb fünf Seiten voll; **print your name, don't ~ it** schreiben Sie Ihren Namen in Druckschrift, nicht in Schreibschrift; **how is that written?** wie schreibt man das?; **to ~ sth to disk** etw auf Diskette schreiben; **it is written that ...** (old) es steht geschrieben, dass ...; **writ(ten) large** (fig) verdeutlicht; (= on a larger scale) im Großen; **it was written all over his face** es stand ihm im or auf dem Gesicht geschrieben; **he had "policeman" written all over him** man sah ihm den Polizisten schon von weitem an → **shorthand** **b** (Insur) policy abschließen **VI** schreiben; **as I ~ ...** während ich dies schreibe, ...; **to ~ to sb** jdm schreiben; **we ~ to each other** wir schreiben uns; **I wrote to him to come** ich habe ihm geschrieben, er solle kommen or dass er kommen solle; **that's nothing to ~ home about** (inf) das ist nichts Weltbewegendes; **I'll ~ for it at once** ich bestelle es sofort,

ich fordere es gleich an; **he has always wanted to ~** er wollte immer (ein) Schriftsteller werden

▶**write away** VI schreiben; **to write away for sth** etw anfordern; **he wrote away asking for further information** er forderte weitere Information an, er schrieb um weitere Information

▶**write back** VI zurückschreiben, antworten; **he wrote back saying ...** er schrieb zurück, um zu sagen, ...

▶**write down** VT sep (= make a note of) aufschreiben; (= record, put in writing) niederschreiben

▶**write in VT** sep **a** word, correction etc hineinschreiben, einfügen (prep obj in +acc) **b** (US Pol) **to write sb in** seine Stimme für jdn abgeben, der nicht in der Liste aufgeführt ist **c** (= build in) condition, provision aufnehmen; **is there anything written in about that?** steht was dazu drin? **VI** schreiben (to an +acc); **someone has written in (to us) requesting this record** jemand hat uns (dat) geschrieben und um diese Platte gebeten; **to write in for sth** etw anfordern, um etw schreiben

▶**write off VI** = **write away VT** sep **a** (= write quickly) (schnell) hinschreiben; essay, poem herunterschreiben **b** debt, losses abschreiben; (fig: = regard as failure) abschreiben; **don't write him off just yet** schreib ihn noch nicht ganz ab **c** car etc (driver) zu Schrott fahren (inf); (insurance company) als Totalschaden abschreiben

▶**write out** VT sep **a** (in full) notes ausarbeiten; name etc ausschreiben **b** cheque, prescription ausstellen **c** actor, character einen Abgang schaffen (+dat); **he's been written out** ihm wurde ein Abgang aus der Serie geschaffen

▶**write up** VT sep notes ausarbeiten; report, diary schreiben; event schreiben über (+acc); (= review) play, film eine Kritik schreiben über (+acc)

write: write-in N (US) Stimmabgabe f für einen nicht in der Liste aufgeführten Kandidaten; **write-off** N **a** (= car etc) Totalschaden m; (inf, = holiday, picnic etc) Katastrophe f (inf) **b** (Comm) Abschreibung f

write-protected [raɪtprəˌtektɪd] ADJ (Comput) schreibgeschützt

write protection N (Comput) Schreibschutz m, Schreibsperre f

writer [raɪtə] N Schreiber(in) m(f); (of scenario, report etc also) Autor(in) m(f); (of TV commercials, subtitles) Texter(in) m(f); (of music) Komponist(in) m(f); (as profession) Schriftsteller(in) m(f); **the (present) ~** der Schreiber (dieser Zeilen/dieses Artikels etc); **he's a very poor ~** er schreibt sehr schlecht; (= correspondent) er ist kein großer Briefschreiber

writer's cramp [raɪtəzˈkræmp] N Schreibkrampf m

write-up [raɪtʌp] N Pressebericht m; (of play, film) Kritik f

writhe [raɪð] VI sich krümmen, sich winden (with, in vor +dat); **to ~ in ecstasy** sich vor Lust wälzen; **to make sb ~** (painfully) jdn vor Schmerzen zusammenzucken lassen; (with disgust) jdm kalte Schauer über den Rücken jagen, jdn erschauern lassen; (with embarrassment) jdn in peinliche Verlegenheit bringen

writing [raɪtɪŋ] N Schrift f; (= act, profession) Schreiben nt; (= inscription) Inschrift f; **at the time of ~** als dies geschrieben wurde; (in present) während ich dies schreibe; **in ~** schriftlich; **permission in ~** schriftliche Genehmigung; **to commit sth to ~** etw schriftlich festhalten; **this is a fantastic piece of ~** das ist fantastisch geschrieben; **his ~s** seine Werke or Schriften; **in sb's own ~** (= not typed) handgeschrieben; (= not written by sb else) in jds eigener (Hand-)schrift (dat); **he earns a bit from his ~** er verdient sich ein bisschen (Geld) mit Schreiben; **the ~ is on the wall for them** ihre Stunde hat geschlagen; **he had seen the ~ on the wall** er hat die Zeichen erkannt

writing in cpds Schreib-; **writing book** N Schreibheft nt; **writing case** N Schreibmappe *f*; **writing desk** N Schreibtisch *m*, Schreibpult *nt*; **writing materials** PL Schreibmaterial *nt*, Schreibmaterialien *pl*; **writing pad** N Schreib- or Notizblock *m*; **writing paper** N Schreibpapier *nt*; **writing stand** N Stehpult *nt*; **writing table** N Schreibtisch *m*

written ['rɪtn] *ptp of* **write** ADJ *examination, statement, evidence* schriftlich; *language* Schrift-; *word* geschrieben; *constitution* schriftlich niedergelegt

WRNS [renz] (*Brit*) *abbr of* **Women's Royal Naval Service**

wrong [rɒŋ] ✪ 12.1, 14, 18.3, 26.3 **ADJ** **a** falsch; **to be ~** nicht stimmen; (*answer also*) falsch sein; (*person*) Unrecht haben; (*watch*) falsch gehen; **it's all ~** das ist völlig verkehrt or falsch; (= *not true*) das stimmt alles nicht; **it's all ~ that I should have to …** das ist doch nicht richtig, dass ich … muss; **I was ~ about him** ich habe mich in ihm getäuscht or geirrt; **you were ~ in thinking he did it** du hast Unrecht gehabt, als du dachtest, er sei es gewesen; **how ~ can you get!** falscher gehts (wohl) nicht!; **I took a ~ turning** ich habe eine verkehrte or falsche Abzweigung genommen; **he went in the ~ direction** er ging in die verkehrte or falsche Richtung; **this is the ~ train for Bournemouth** dies ist der falsche Zug, wenn Sie nach Bournemouth wollen; **to say/do the ~ thing** das Falsche sagen/tun; **the ~ side of the fabric** die linke Seite des Stoffes; **you live in the ~ part of town** du wohnst nicht im richtigen Stadtteil; **he's got the ~ kind of friends** er hat die falschen Freunde; **you've come to the ~ man** or **person/place** da sind Sie an den Falschen/an die Falsche/an die falsche Adresse geraten; **brown is definitely the ~ colour to be wearing this season** Braun ist diese Saison absolut nicht modern; **it feels all ~ not working** es ist ganz komisch nicht zu arbeiten; **it's the ~ time for jokes** es ist nicht die richtige Zeit für Witze; **it's the ~ time and the ~ place for that** das ist weder die Zeit noch der Ort dafür; **to do sth the ~ way** etw falsch or verkehrt machen → **number** N c, **side** N e

b (*morally*) schlecht, unrecht; (= *unfair*) ungerecht, unfair; **it's ~ to steal** es ist unrecht zu stehlen, Stehlen ist Unrecht; **that was very ~ of you** das war absolut nicht richtig von dir; **you were ~ to do that** es war falsch or unrecht or nicht richtig von dir, das zu tun; **it's ~ of you to laugh** Sie sollten nicht lachen; **it's ~ that he should have to ask** es ist unrecht or falsch, dass er überhaupt fragen muss; **what's ~ with a drink now and again?** was ist schon (Schlimmes) dabei, wenn man ab und zu einen trinkt?; **what's ~ with working on Sundays?** was ist denn schon dabei, wenn man sonntags arbeitet?; **I don't see anything ~ in** or **with that** ich kann nichts Falsches daran finden, ich finde nichts daran auszusetzen

c *pred* (= *amiss*) **something is ~** (irgend)etwas stimmt nicht or ist nicht in Ordnung (**with** mit); (*suspiciously*) irgendwas stimmt da nicht or ist da faul (*inf*); **is anything** or **something ~?** ist was? (*inf*); **there's nothing ~** (es ist) alles in Ordnung; **what's ~?** was ist los?; **what's ~ with you?** was fehlt Ihnen?; **there's nothing medically ~ with her** medizinisch (gesehen) fehlt ihr nichts; **I hope there's nothing ~ at home** ich hoffe, dass zu Hause alles in Ordnung ist

ADV falsch; **you do him ~** du tust ihm unrecht; **you did ~ to do it** es war falsch or unrecht or nicht richtig von dir, das zu tun; **to get sth ~** sich mit etw vertun; **he got the answer ~** er hat die falsche Antwort gegeben; (*Math*) er hat sich verrechnet; **I think you got things a bit ~** ich glaube, Sie sehen die Sache or das nicht ganz richtig; **to get one's sums ~** sich verrechnen; **you've got him (all) ~** (= *misunderstood him*) Sie haben ihn falsch verstanden; (= *he's not like that*) Sie haben sich in ihm getäuscht; **you thought ~** Sie haben sich geirrt; **to go ~** (*on route*) falsch gehen/fahren; (*in calculation*) einen Fehler machen; (*morally*) auf Abwege geraten; (*plan etc*) schief gehen; (*affair etc*) schief laufen; **my washing machine has gone ~** meine Waschmaschine ist nicht in Ordnung; **you can't go ~** hoffentlich bleibt der Fernseher in Ordnung; **you can't go ~** du kannst gar nichts verkehrt machen; **you can't go ~ if you buy him a bottle of whisky** mit einer Flasche Whisky liegst du bei ihm immer richtig

N Unrecht *nt no pl*; (**social**) **~s** (soziale) Ungerechtigkeiten *pl*; **to be in the ~** im Unrecht sein; **two ~s don't make a right** Unrecht und Unrecht ergibt noch kein Recht; **to do sb a great ~** jdm ein großes Unrecht antun; **he can do no ~** er macht natürlich immer alles richtig; **all the little ~s he'd done her** all die kleinen Kränkungen, die er ihr zugefügt hatte

VT **to ~ sb** jdm unrecht tun; **to be ~ed** ungerecht behandelt werden

wrongdoer ['rɒŋˌduːə] N Missetäter(in) *m(f)*, Übeltäter(in) *m(f)*

wrongdoing ['rɒŋˌduːɪŋ] N Missetaten *pl*; (*single act*) Missetat *f*, Übeltat *f*

wrong-foot [ˌrɒŋ'fʊt] VT (*Sport, fig*) auf dem falschen Fuß erwischen

wrongful ['rɒŋfʊl] ADJ ungerechtfertigt

wrongfully ['rɒŋfəlɪ] ADV zu Unrecht

wrong-headed ['rɒŋ'hedɪd] ADJ querköpfig, verbohrt (*about sth* in etw *acc* or *dat*)

wrong-headedness ['rɒŋ'hedɪdnɪs] N Verbohrtheit *f*

wrongly ['rɒŋlɪ] ADV **a** (= *unjustly, improperly*) unrecht; *punished, accused* zu Unrecht **b** (= *incorrectly*) falsch, verkehrt; *maintain* zu Unrecht; *believe* fälschlicherweise

wrongness ['rɒŋnɪs] N (= *incorrectness*) Unrichtigkeit *f*; (= *unfairness*) Ungerechtigkeit *f*; **the ~ of your behaviour** dein falsches Benehmen

wrote [rəut] *pret of* **write**

wrought [rɔːt] **VT** **a** (*obs, liter*) *pret, ptp of* **work** **b** *great changes have been ~* große Veränderungen wurden errungen or herbeigeführt; **the accident ~ havoc with his plans** der Unfall durchkreuzte alle seine Pläne; **the storm ~ great destruction** der Sturm richtete große Verheerungen an **ADJ** *silver* getrieben, gehämmert

wrought: wrought iron N Schmiedeeisen *nt*; **wrought-iron** ADJ schmiedeeisern *attr*, aus Schmiedeeisen; **~ gate** schmiedeeisernes Tor; **wrought ironwork** N Kunstschmiedearbeit *f*; **wrought-up** ADJ **to be ~** aufgelöst sein, außer sich (*dat*) sein

wrung [rʌŋ] *pret, ptp of* **wring**

WRVS (*Brit*) *abbr of* **Women's Royal Voluntary Service**

wry [raɪ] ADJ (= *ironical*) ironisch; *joke, sense of humour etc* trocken; **to make** or **pull a ~ face** das Gesicht verziehen

wryly ['raɪlɪ] ADV ironisch

WSW *abbr of* **west-southwest** WSW

wt *abbr of* **weight** Gew.

wuss [wʌs] N (*esp US, inf*) Waschlappen *m* (*inf*)

WWI *abbr of* **World War One**

WWII *abbr of* **World War Two**

WWW (*Comput*) *abbr of* **World Wide Web** WWW

WX *abbr of* **women's extra-large size**

wych-elm ['wɪtʃelm] N = **witch-elm**

wych-hazel ['wɪtʃheɪzl] N = **witch hazel**

WYSIWYG ['wɪzɪwɪg] N (*Comput*) *abbr of* **what you see is what you get** WYSIWYG *nt*

X

X, x [eks] N X *nt*, x *nt* **b** (*Math, fig*) x; **Mr X**
Herr X; **X pounds** x Pfund; **X marks the spot**
die Stelle ist mit einem Kreuzchen gekennzeichnet **c** (*dated Brit*) **X-certificate film** für Jugendliche nicht geeigneter Film, für Jugendliche ab 18 Jahren freigegebener Film

x-axis ['eksæksɪs] N X-Achse *f*

X-chromosome ['ekskrəʊməsəʊm] N X-Chro-
mosom *nt*

xenophobe ['zenəfəʊb] N Fremdenhasser(in)
m(f)

xenophobia [ˌzenə'fəʊbɪə] N Fremdenfeind-
lichkeit *f*, Fremdenhass *m*, Xenophobie *f* (*geh*)

xenophobic [ˌzenə'fəʊbɪk] ADJ fremdenfeind-
lich, xenophob (*geh*)

Xerox® ['zɪərɒks] **N** (= *copy*) Xerokopie *f*; (= *process*) Xeroxverfahren *nt* **VT** xerokopieren

Xing ['eksɪŋ, 'krɒsɪŋ] N = **crossing**

XL *abbr of* **extra large**

Xmas ['eksməs, 'krɪsməs] N = **Christmas** Weihnachten *nt*

X-ray ['eks'reɪ] N Röntgenstrahl *m*; (*also* **X-ray
photograph**) Röntgenaufnahme *f or* -bild *nt*;
to take an ~ of sth etw röntgen, eine Röntgenaufnahme von etw machen; **to have an ~** ge-
röntgt werden; **she has gone for an ~** sie ist
zum Röntgen gegangen **VT** *person, heart* röntgen, durchleuchten (*dated*); *envelope, baggage*
durchleuchten

X-ray *in cpds* Röntgen-; **X-ray examination** N
Röntgenuntersuchung *f*, röntgenologische Untersuchung; **X-ray eyes** PL (*fig*) Röntgenaugen
pl

xylograph ['zaɪləgrɑːf] N Holzschnitt *m*

xylography [zaɪ'lɒgrəfɪ] N Holzschneidekunst
f, Xylografie *f*

xylophone ['zaɪləfəʊn] N Xylophon *nt*

y

Y, y [waɪ] N Y *nt*, y *nt*

yacht [jɒt] **N** Jacht *f*, Yacht *f*; **~ club** Jacht- *or* Segelklub *m*; **~ race** (Segel)regatta *f* **VI** segeln; **to go ~ing** segeln gehen; (*on cruise*) eine Segeltour *or* einen Törn machen

yachting ['jɒtɪŋ] N Segeln *nt*

yachting: yachting cap N Seglermütze *f*; **yachting circles** PL Segelkreise *pl*; **yachting cruise** N (Segel)kreuzfahrt *f*, Segelreise *f*; **yachting holiday** N (*Brit*) Segelurlaub *m*; **yachting jacket** N Segeljacke *f*

yachtsman ['jɒtsmən] N *pl* **-men** [-mən] Segler *m*

yachtsmanship ['jɒtsmənʃɪp] N Segelkunst *f*

yachtswoman ['jɒtswʊmən] N *pl* **-women** [-wɪmɪn] Seglerin *f*

yackety-yak ['jækɪtɪ'jæk] (*inf*) **VI** schnattern (*inf*), quasseln (*inf*) **N** Blabla *nt* (*pej inf*), Gequassel *nt* (*pej inf*); **listen to those two, ~** hör dir mal die beiden Schnattergänse an (*inf*); **it was ~ all evening** den ganzen Abend nichts als Gequatsche (*inf*) *or* Geschnatter (*inf*)

yah [jɑː] INTERJ (*expressing disgust*) uh, igitt(igitt); (*expressing derision*) ätsch, hähä

yahoo [jɑː'huː] N Schwein *nt* (*inf*)

yak¹ [jæk] N (*Zool*) Jak *m*, Yak *m*, Grunzochse *m*

yak² VI (*inf*) schnattern (*inf*), quasseln (*inf*)

Yakuza [jə'kuːzə] PL Yakuza *pl*, *Mitglieder einer geheimen japanischen Verbrecherorganisation*

Yale lock® ['jeɪl,lɒk] N Sicherheitsschloss *nt*

y'all [jɔːl] PRON (*US inf*) = **you-all**

yam [jæm] N **a** (= *plant*) Yamswurzel *f*, Jamswurzel *f* **b** (= *sweet potato*) Süßkartoffel *f*, Batate *f*

yammer ['jæmə'] VI (*inf*, = *moan*) jammern

Yank [jæŋk] (*inf*) **N** Ami *m* (*inf*) **ADJ** *attr* Ami- (*inf*)

yank [jæŋk] **N** Ruck *m*; **give it a good ~** zieh mal kräftig dran **VT to ~ sth** mit einem Ruck an etw (*dat*) ziehen, einer Sache (*dat*) einen Ruck geben; **he ~ed the rope free** er riss das Seil los

▶ **yank off** VT *sep* abreißen

▶ **yank out** VT *sep* ausreißen; *tooth* ziehen

Yankee ['jæŋkɪ] (*inf*) **N** Yankee *m* (*inf*); (*Hist also*) Nordstaatler(in) *m(f)* **ADJ** *attr* Yankee- (*inf*)

YANKEE

Auch wenn in Europa mit **Yankee** jeder Amerikaner bezeichnet wird, meint man in den USA damit stets einen Nordstaatler. Im Norden wiederum gelten nur die Einwohner New Englands als die wahren Yankees. Der Name entstand für das Lied „Yankee Doodle", mit dem sich ein Engländer über die Amerikaner lustig machte. Während der amerikanischen Revolution machten die Soldaten von General Washington aus diesem Spottlied ein patriotisches Kampflied, weshalb Yankee heutzutage ein durchaus positiver Begriff ist. Die Abkürzung **Yank** wird allerdings in den USA weniger benutzt, es handelt sich dabei um einen eher abfälligen Ausdruck der Briten.

---

yap [jæp] **VI** (*dog*) kläffen; (= *talk noisily*) quatschen (*inf*), labern (*inf*); **it's been ~, ~, ~ all day** von morgens bis abends nur Gequatsche (*inf*) **N** (*of dog*) Kläffen *nt*, Gekläff *nt*; (*inf, of person*) Gequatsche *nt* (*inf*), Gelaber *nt* (*inf*); **she spoke in a high-pitched ~** sie schnatterte mit schriller Stimme (*inf*)

yapping ['jæpɪŋ] **ADJ** *dog* kläffend; (*inf*) *women* quatschend (*inf*) **N** = **yap** N

yappy ['jæpɪ] ADJ (*inf*) *dog* kläffend; **a ~ little dog** ein kleiner Kläffer

yard¹ [jɑːd] **N a** (*Measure*) Yard *nt* (*0.91 m*); **he can't see a ~ in front of him** er kann keinen Meter weit sehen; **to buy cloth by the ~** ≈ Stoff meterweise *or* im Meter kaufen; **he pulled out ~s of handkerchief** (*inf*) er zog ein riesiges Taschentuch hervor (*inf*); **to have a list a ~ long of things to do** (*inf*) eine ellenlange Liste von Dingen haben, die man noch tun muss (*inf*); **his guess was ~s out** (*inf*) er lag mit seiner Schätzung völlig schief; **he wrote poetry by the ~** er produzierte Gedichte am Fließband *or* am laufenden Meter; **to go the whole nine ~s** (*US inf*) es ganz gründlich machen **b** (*Naut*) Rah *f*

yard² N **a** (*of farm, hospital, prison, school, house etc*) Hof *m*; **in the ~** auf dem Hof **b** (= *worksite*) Werksgelände *nt*; (*for storage*) Lagerplatz *m*; **builder's ~** Bauhof *m*; **shipbuilding ~** Werft *f*; **naval (dock)yard, navy ~** (*US*) Marinewerft *f*; **railway ~** (*Brit*) Rangierbahnhof *m*, Verschiebebahnhof *m*; **goods ~, freight ~** (*US*) Güterbahnhof *m* **c** (*Brit inf*) **the Yard, Scotland Yard** Scotland Yard *m* **d** (*US*: = *garden*) Garten *m*

yardage ['jɑːdɪdʒ] N Anzahl *f* von Yards, ≈ Meterzahl *f*

yardarm ['jɑːdɑːm] N (*Naut*) Nock *f*; **to hang sb from the ~** jdn am Mast aufknüpfen

Yardie ['jɑːdɪ] N (*Brit*) *Mitglied einer geheimen Verbrecherorganisation in Jamaika*

yardstick ['jɑːdstɪk] N **a** (= *measuring rod*) Elle *f* **b** (*fig*) Maßstab *m*

yarmulke ['jɑːmʊlkə] N Jarmulke *f*, Gebetskäppchen *nt*

yarn [jɑːn] **N a** (*Tex*) Garn *nt* **b** (= *tale*) Seemannsgarn *nt*; **to spin a ~** Seemannsgarn spinnen; **to spin sb a ~ about sth** jdm eine Lügengeschichte über etw (*acc*) erzählen **VI** Seemannsgarn spinnen, Geschichten erzählen

yarrow ['jærəʊ] N (*Bot*) (gemeine) Schafgarbe

yashmak ['jæʃmæk] N Schleier *m* (*von Moslemfrauen*)

yaw [jɔː] **VI** (*Naut*) gieren, vom Kurs abkommen; (*Aviat, Space*) (*off course*) vom Kurs abkommen *or* abweichen; (*about axis*) gieren; **it ~ed 20 degrees to port** es gierte um 20 Grad nach Backbord **N** Kursabweichung *f*; (*about axis*) Gieren *nt*

yawl [jɔːl] N (*Naut*) (= *rowing boat*) Beiboot *nt*; (= *sailing boat*) (Segel)jolle *f*

yawn [jɔːn] **VI a** (*person*) gähnen; **to ~ with boredom** vor Langeweile gähnen **b** (*chasm etc*) gähnen **VT** gähnen **N a** (*of person*) Gähnen *nt*; **I could tell by your ~s ...** an deinem Gähnen konnte ich sehen ...; **to give a ~** gähnen **b** (*inf,* = *bore*) **the film was a ~** der

Film war zum Gähnen (langweilig); **what a ~!** wie langweilig!; **life is just one big ~** das Leben ist vielleicht langweilig

yawning ['jɔːnɪŋ] **ADJ** *chasm etc* gähnend **N** Gähnen *nt*

yawp [jɔːp] (*US*) **N a** (*inf,* = *yelp*) Aufschrei *m*; **to give a ~** aufschreien, kreischen **b** (*inf:* = *chatter*) Geschwätz *nt*; **to have a ~** schwatzen **VI a** (*inf,* = *yelp*) aufschreien, kreischen **b** (*inf:* = *chatter*) schwatzen

yaws [jɔːz] N *sing* Frambösie *f*

y-axis ['waɪæksɪs] N Y-Achse *f*

Y-chromosome ['waɪkrəʊməsəʊm] N Y-Chromosom *nt*

yd *abbr of* **yard(s)**

ye [jiː] (*obs*) **PERS PRON** (*nominative*) Ihr (*obs*); (*objective*) Euch (*obs*); **ye gods!** (*not obs*) allmächtiger Gott! **DEF ART** = **the**

yea [jeɪ] **ADV** (*obs*) **a** (= *yes*) ja; **~ or nay** ja oder nein **b** (= *indeed*) fürwahr (*old*) **N the ~s and the nays** die Jastimmen und die Neinstimmen

yeah [jɛə] ADV (*inf*) ja

year [jɪə'] N **a** Jahr *nt*; **this/last ~** dieses/letztes Jahr; **every other ~** jedes zweite Jahr; **three times a ~** dreimal pro *or* im Jahr; **in the ~ 1989** im Jahr(e) 1989; **in the ~ of Our Lord 1997** (*form*) im Jahr(e) des Herrn 1997 (*geh*); **~ after ~** Jahr für Jahr; **~ by ~, from ~ to ~** von Jahr zu Jahr; **~ in, ~ out** jahrein, jahraus; **all (the) ~ round** das ganze Jahr über *or* hindurch; **as (the) ~s go by** mit den Jahren; **~s (and ~s) ago** vor (langen) Jahren; **to pay by the ~** jährlich zahlen; **a ~ last January** (im) Januar vor einem Jahr; **it'll be a ~ in** *or* **next January** (*duration*) es wird nächsten Januar ein Jahr sein; (*point in time*) es wird nächsten Januar ein Jahr her sein; **a ~ from now** nächstes Jahr um diese Zeit; **a hundred-year-old tree** ein hundert Jahre alter Baum, ein hundertjähriger Baum; **he is six ~s old** *or* **six ~s of age** er ist sechs Jahre (alt); **he is in his fortieth ~** er steht (*geh*) *or* ist im vierzigsten Lebensjahr; **he gets £23,000 a ~** er bekommt £ 23.000 im Jahr *or* pro Jahr im Jahr; **I haven't laughed so much in ~s** ich habe schon lange nicht mehr so gelacht; **that new hairdo has taken ~s off you** (*inf*) diese neue Frisur macht dich um Jahre jünger; **it's taken ~s off my life** es hat mich Jahre meines Lebens gekostet; **it has put ~s on me** es hat mich (um) Jahre älter gemacht

b (*Univ, Sch, of coin, stamp, wine*) Jahrgang *m*; **the 2001/02 academic ~** das akademische Jahr 2001/02; **he is bottom in his ~** (*Univ, Sch*) er ist der Schlechteste seines Jahrgangs *or* in seinem Jahrgang; **first-year student, first ~ Student(in)** *m(f)* im ersten Jahr; (= *first term student*) Student(in) *m(f)* im ersten Semester, Erstsemester *nt*; **she was in my ~ at school** sie war im selben Schuljahrgang wie ich

c from his earliest ~s von frühester Kindheit an, seit seiner frühesten Kindheit; **he looks old for his ~s** er sieht älter aus als er ist; **young for his ~s** jung für sein Alter; **well advanced** *or* **well on in ~s** im vorgerückten Alter; **to get on in ~s** in die Jahre kommen; **difference in ~s** Altersunterschied *m*

yearbook ['jɪəbʊk] N Jahrbuch *nt*

year-end [ˈjɪəˈrend] N Jahresende nt; ~ **report** Jahresbericht m, Geschäftsbericht m

yearling [ˈjɪəlɪŋ] **N** (= animal) Jährling m; (= racehorse also) Einjährige(r) mf **ADJ** einjährig

yearlong [ˈjɪəˈlɒŋ] ADJ einjährig; **she had a ~ battle against cancer** ihr Kampf gegen den Krebs dauerte ein Jahr

yearly [ˈjɪəlɪ] ADJ jährlich ADV jährlich, einmal im Jahr; (= per year) jährlich; **twice ~** zweimal jährlich or im Jahr

yearn [jɜːn] VI sich sehnen (after, for nach); **to ~ to do sth** sich danach sehnen, etw zu tun; **to ~ for home** sich nach Hause sehnen; **to ~ for sb** sich nach jdm sehnen, nach jdm verlangen

yearning [ˈjɜːnɪŋ] N Sehnsucht f, Verlangen nt (to do sth etw zu tun, for nach); **a look full of ~** ein sehnsuchtsvoller Blick; **a ~ for the past** die Sehnsucht nach der Vergangenheit ADJ desire sehnsüchtig; look also sehnsuchtsvoll, verlangend

yearningly [ˈjɜːnɪŋlɪ] ADV sehnsuchtsvoll, voller Sehnsucht; gaze also sehnsüchtig

year-round [ˈjɪəˈraʊnd] ADJ, ADV das ganze Jahr über

yeast [jiːst] N , no pl Hefe f

yeast: yeast cake N **a** (= cake) Hefekuchen m **b** (= cube) Hefewürfel m; **yeast extract** N Hefeextrakt m

yeasty [ˈjiːstɪ] ADJ taste hefig; smell nach Hefe; bread nach Hefe schmeckend; **the beer's very ~** das Bier schmeckt stark nach Hefe

yell [jel] **N** Schrei m; **to let out** or **give a ~** einen Schrei ausstoßen, schreien; **could you give me a ~ when we get there?** könnten Sie mich rufen, wenn wir da sind?; **college ~** (US) Schlachtruf m eines College
VI (also **yell out**) schreien, brüllen (with vor +dat); **he ~ed at her** er schrie or brüllte sie an; **just ~ if you need help** ruf, wenn du Hilfe brauchst; **to ~ with laughter** vor Lachen brüllen
VT (also **yell out**) schreien, brüllen; name brüllen; **he ~ed abuse at the teacher** er beschimpfte den Lehrer wüst; **she ~ed up the stairs that dinner was ready** sie rief die Treppe hinauf, dass das Essen fertig sei

yellow [ˈjeləʊ] ADJ (+er) **a** gelb; **~ hair** strohblondes or gelbblondes Haar; **to go** or **turn ~** gelb werden; (paper) vergilben **b** (inf, = cowardly) feige **c** (pej, by race) gelb **N** (= colour) Gelb nt; (of egg) Eigelb nt; (inf, = cowardice) Feigheit f
VT gelb färben; **the sunlight had ~ed the pages** die Sonne hatte die Seiten vergilben lassen; **paper ~ed with age** vor Alter vergilbtes Papier
VI gelb werden, sich gelb färben; (corn also) reifen; (pages) vergilben; **the leaves were ~ing** die Blätter färbten sich gelb

yellow: yellow-bellied ADJ (sl) feige; **yellow-belly** N (inf) Angsthase m (inf), Waschlappen m (inf); **yellow brick road** N (fig) Straße f des Erfolgs; **yellow card** N (Ftbl) gelbe Karte; **yellow fever** N Gelbfieber nt; **yellow flag** N (Naut) gelbe Flagge, Quarantäneflagge f; **yellowhammer** N (Orn) Goldammer f

yellowish [ˈjeləʊɪʃ] ADJ gelblich; **~-brown/-green** gelblich-braun/-grün

yellow: yellow jack N (Naut) gelbe Flagge, Quarantäneflagge f; **yellow jersey** N (Cycling) gelbes Trikot; **yellow journalism** N Regenbogenjournalismus m; **yellow Labrador** N Gelber Labrador; **yellow legal pad** N Notizblock m; **yellow line** N (Brit) Halteverbot nt; **double ~** absolutes Halteverbot; **to be parked on a (double) ~** im (absoluten) Halteverbot stehen; **yellow metal** N Münzmetall nt

yellowness [ˈjeləʊnɪs] N , no pl **a** Gelb nt; (of skin) gelbliche Färbung **b** (inf, = cowardice) Feigheit f

yellow: yellow ochre ADJ ockergelb; **Yellow Pages®** N SING the **~** das Branchenverzeichnis, die Gelben Seiten pl; **yellow peril** N gelbe Gefahr; **yellow press** N (dated Press) Regenbogenpresse f; **Yellow River** N Gelber

Fluss; **Yellow Sea** N Gelbes Meer; **yellow wagtail** N Gelbe Bachstelze f

yellowy [ˈjeləʊɪ] ADJ gelblich

yelp [jelp] **N** (of animal) Jaulen nt no pl; (of person) Aufschrei m; **to give a ~** (auf)jaulen; (person) aufschreien **VI** (animal) (auf)jaulen; (person) aufschreien

yelping [ˈjelpɪŋ] N (of animal) Jaulen nt; (of person) Aufschreien nt

Yemen [ˈjemən] **N the ~** der Jemen

Yemeni [ˈjemənɪ] **N** Jemenit(in) m(f) ADJ jemenitisch

yen¹ [jen] N (Fin) Yen m

yen² N (inf) Lust f (for auf +acc); **I've always had a ~ to go to Pasadena** es hat mich schon immer nach Pasadena gezogen; **I had a ~ to do that/for oysters** ich hatte plötzlich Lust, das zu machen/auf Austern

yeoman [ˈjəʊmən] N pl **-men** [-mən] **a** (Hist, = small landowner) Freibauer m; **~ farmer** (Hist) Freibauer m **b** **Yeoman of the Guard** königlicher Leibgardist; **to do ~ service** treue Dienste leisten (for sb jdm)

yeomanry [ˈjəʊmənrɪ] **N a** (Hist) Freibauernschaft f, Freibauernstand m **b** (Mil) freiwillige Kavallerietruppe

yep [jep] ADV (inf) ja; **is he sure? – ~!** ist er sicher? – klar!

yer [jɜː] PRON (sl) = your

yes [jes] **ADV** ja; (answering neg question) doch; **to say ~** Ja or ja sagen; **to say ~ to a proposal** einer Forderung (dat) nachkommen; **he said ~ to all my questions** er hat alle meine Fragen bejaht or mit Ja beantwortet; **if they say ~ to an increase** wenn sie eine Lohnerhöhung bewilligen; **I'd say ~ to 35%, no to 32%** ich würde 35% akzeptieren, 32% nicht; **she says ~ to everything** sie sagt nicht Nein or nein sagen; **~ sir!** (Mil) jawohl, Herr General/Leutnant etc; (general) jawohl, mein Herr!; **waiter! – ~ sir?** Herr Ober! – ja, bitte?; **~ indeed** o ja, allerdings; **I didn't say that – oh ~, you did** das habe ich nicht gesagt – o doch or o ja, das hast du; **~ and no** ja und nein, jein (inf); **~ ~, I know!** jaja, ich weiß doch
N Ja nt; **he just answered with ~es and noes** er hat einfach mit Ja oder Nein geantwortet

yes: yes man N Jasager m; **yes/no question** N Ja-Nein-Frage f

yesterday [ˈjestədeɪ] **N** Gestern nt; **the fashions of ~** die Mode von gestern; **all our ~s** unsere ganze Vergangenheit **ADV** (lit, fig) gestern; **~ morning/afternoon/evening** gestern Morgen/Nachmittag/Abend; **he was at home all (day)** er war gestern den ganzen Tag zu Hause; **the day before ~** vorgestern; **a week ago ~** gestern vor einer Woche → **born**

yesteryear [ˈjestəˈjɪə] **N** (poet) **of ~** vergangener Jahre (gen)

yes woman N Jasagerin f

yet [jet] ⏰ 20.5 **ADV a** (= still) noch; (= thus far) bis jetzt, bisher; **they haven't ~ returned** or **returned ~** sie sind noch nicht zurückgekommen; **this is his best book** ~ das ist bis jetzt sein bestes Buch, das ist sein bisher bestes Buch; **as ~** (with present tenses) bis jetzt, bisher; (with past) bis dahin; **no, not ~** nein, noch nicht; **I've hardly begun ~** ich habe noch gar nicht richtig angefangen; **not just ~** jetzt noch nicht; **don't come in (just) ~** komm (jetzt) noch nicht herein; **you ain't seen nothing ~** (inf) du hast noch gar nichts gesehen
b (with interrog: = so far, already) schon; **has he arrived ~?** ist er schon angekommen?, ist er schon da?; **do you have to go just ~?** müssen Sie jetzt schon gehen?
c (with affirmative: = still, remaining) noch; **they have a few days ~** sie haben noch ein paar Tage; **we've got ages ~** wir haben noch viel Zeit; **not for some time ~** noch nicht so schnell or bald; **a ~ to be decided question** eine noch unentschiedene Frage, eine Frage, die noch entschieden werden muss; **I've ~ to learn how**

to do it ich muss erst noch lernen, wie man es macht; **and they are doubtless waiting ~** und sie warten zweifellos noch immer; **he is ~ alive** er lebt noch
d (with comp: = still, even) noch; **this is ~ more difficult** dies ist (sogar) noch schwieriger; **~ more money** noch mehr Geld
e (= in addition) (and) **~ again** und wieder, und noch einmal; **and ~ again they rode off** und sie ritten wieder weg; **another arrived and ~ another** es kam noch einer und noch einer
f (with future and conditional: = before all is over) noch; **he may come ~** or **~ come** er kann noch kommen; **he could come ~** er könnte noch kommen; **I may ~ go to Italy** ich fahre vielleicht noch nach Italien; **I'll do it ~** ich schaffe es schon noch
g (liter) **nor ~** noch; **they didn't come nor ~ write** sie sind weder gekommen, noch haben sie geschrieben
CONJ doch, dennoch, trotzdem; **and ~** und doch or trotzdem or dennoch; **it's strange ~ true** es ist seltsam, aber wahr

yeti [ˈjetɪ] N Yeti m, Schneemensch m

yew [juː] N (also **yew tree**) Eibe f; (= wood) Eibe(nholz nt) f

Y-fronts® [ˈwaɪfrʌnts] PL (esp Brit) (Herren)slip m

YHA abbr of **Youth Hostels Association** ≈ DJH nt

Yid [jɪd] N (pej) Jud m (pej)

Yiddish [ˈjɪdɪʃ] **ADJ** jiddisch **N** (Ling) Jiddisch nt

yield [jiːld] **VT a** (land) fruit, crop hervorbringen; (tree) fruit tragen; (mine, oil well) bringen; (shares, money) interest, profit (ein)bringen, abwerfen; result (hervor)bringen; opportunity, clue ergeben; **the information ~ed by the poll** die Information, die die Meinungsumfrage ergeben hat; **this ~ed a weekly increase of 20%** das brachte eine wöchentliche Steigerung von 20%
b (= surrender, concede) aufgeben; **to ~ sth to sb** etw an jdn abtreten; **to ~ ground to sb** vor jdm zurückstecken; **to ~ the floor to sb** (fig) jdm das Feld überlassen; **to ~ a point to sb** jdm einen Punkt zukommen lassen; (in competition) einen Punkt an jdn abgeben; **to ~ concessions** Zugeständnisse machen; **to ~ right of way to sb** (Mot) jdm die Vorfahrt gewähren or lassen
VI a (tree, land) tragen; (mine, oil well) Ertrag bringen; (shares, money) sich verzinsen, Zinsen or Profit einbringen or abwerfen; **land that ~s well** Land, das ertragreich ist
b (= surrender, give way) **they ~ed to us** (Mil) sie haben sich uns (dat) ergeben; (general) sie haben nachgegeben; **at last she ~ed to him/to his charm** schließlich erlag sie ihm/seinem Charme doch; **to ~ to force/superior forces** (Mil) der Gewalt/Übermacht weichen or nachgeben; **to ~ to sb's threats** sich jds Drohungen (dat) beugen; **he ~ed to her requests** er gab ihren Bitten nach; **the disease ~ed to treatment** die Krankheit sprach auf die Behandlung an; **to ~ to temptation** der Versuchung erliegen; **to ~ to one's emotions** seinen Gefühlen nachgeben; **I'll have to ~ to you on that point** in diesem Punkt muss ich Ihnen Recht geben
c (= give way: branch, beam, rope, floor, ground) nachgeben; **to ~ under pressure** unter Druck nachgeben; (fig) dem Druck weichen
d (Mot) **to ~ to oncoming traffic** den Gegenverkehr vorbeilassen; **"yield"** (US, Ir) „Vorfahrt beachten"
N (of land, tree) Ertrag m; (of work also) Ergebnis nt; (of mine, well) Ausbeute f; (of industry) (= goods) Produktion f; (= profit) Gewinne pl, Erträge pl; (Fin, of shares, business) Ertrag m, Gewinn m; **~ of tax** Steueraufkommen nt

▶**yield up** VT sep rights, privileges abtreten, verzichten auf (+acc); secret enthüllen; **to yield sth up to sb** etw an jdn abtreten; **he yielded himself up to his fate** er ergab sich in sein Schicksal

yielding ['jiːldɪŋ] ADJ *person* nachgiebig; *surface, material* nachgebend; **the ground is ~** der Boden gibt nach

yike(s) [jaɪk(s)] INTERJ *(dated esp US inf)* ach du Schande *(inf)*

yip [jɪp] N, VI *(US)* = **yelp**

yipe(s) [jaɪp(s)] INTERJ *(dated esp US inf)* = **yike(s)**

yippee [jɪ'piː] INTERJ juchhu, hurra

YMCA *abbr of* **Young Men's Christian Association** CVJM *m*

yob [jɒb] N *(Brit, inf)* Halbstarke(r) *m*, Rowdy *m*

yobbish ['jɒbɪʃ] ADJ *(Brit, inf) behaviour, person* rowdyhaft; **~ mentality** Halbstarken- *or* Rowdymentalität *f*

yobbo ['jɒbəʊ] N *(Brit, inf)* Halbstarke(r) *m*, Rowdy *m*

yodel ['jəʊdl] VTI jodeln

yodeller, *(US)* **yodeler** ['jəʊdlə'] N Jodler(in) *m(f)*

yodelling, *(US)* **yodeling** ['jəʊdlɪŋ] N Jodeln *nt*

yoga ['jəʊgə] N Joga *m or nt*, Yoga *m or nt*

yoghourt, **yog(h)urt** ['jɒgət] N Jog(h)urt *m or nt*

yogi ['jəʊgɪ] N Jogi *m*, Yogi *m*

yogic flying [ˌjəʊgɪk'flaɪɪŋ] N yogisches Fliegen

yo-heave-ho ['jəʊhiːv'həʊ] INTERJ hau ruck

yoke [jəʊk] N **a** *(for oxen)* Joch *nt*; *(for carrying pails)* (Trag)joch *nt*, Schultertrage *f* **b** *pl* - (= *pair of oxen)* Joch *nt*, Gespann *nt* **c** *(fig: = oppression)* Joch *nt*; **to throw off the ~** das Joch abschütteln **d** *(on dress, blouse etc)* Passe *f* VT **a** *(also* **yoke up**) oxen (ins Joch) einspannen; **to ~ oxen to the plough** Ochsen vor den Pflug spannen **b** *pieces of machinery* zusammenschließen; **to ~ sth to sth** etw an etw *(acc)* anschließen **c** *(fig: = join together)* zusammenschließen, vereinen

yokel ['jəʊkəl] N *(pej)* Bauerntölpel *m*, Bauerntrampel *m*

yolk [jəʊk] N *(of egg)* Eigelb *nt*

yomp [jɒmp] VI *(Mil sl)* sich schleppen

yon [jɒn] ADV, ADJ *(poet, dial)* = **yonder**

yonder ['jɒndə'] *(poet, dial)* ADV *(over)* ~ dort drüben ADJ **from ~ house** von dem Haus (dort) drüben

yonks [jɒŋks] N *(Brit inf: = ages)* eine (halbe) Ewigkeit *(inf)*; **that was ~ ago** das war vor einer (halben) Ewigkeit *(inf)*; **I haven't seen her for ~** ich habe sie schon ewig nicht mehr gesehen *(inf)*

yoo-hoo [juː'huː] INTERJ huhu, hallo

yore [jɔː'] N *(obs, liter)* **in days of ~** in alten Zeiten; **men of ~** die Menschen in alten Zeiten; **in the Britain of ~** im Großbritannien längst vergangener Zeiten

Yorkshire pudding [ˌjɔːkʃə'pʊdɪŋ] N Yorkshire Pudding *m (Beilage zu Rinderbraten)*

Yorkshire terrier [ˌjɔːkʃə'terɪə'] N Yorkshireterrier *m*

you [juː] PRON **a** *(German familiar form) (sing) (nom)* du; *(acc)* dich; *(dat)* dir; *(pl) (nom)* ihr; *(acc, dat)* euch; *(German polite form: sing, pl) (nom, acc)* Sie; *(dat)* Ihnen; **all of ~** *(pl)* ihr alle/ Sie alle; **I want all of ~** *(sing)* ich will dich ganz; **if I were ~** wenn ich du/Sie wäre, an deiner/ Ihrer Stelle; **~ Germans** ihr Deutschen; **~ two/ three wait here!** ihr beide/drei wartet hier; **silly old ~** du Dussel *(inf)*, du Dumm(er)chen *(inf)*; **~ darling** du bist ein Schatz *or* Engel; **is that ~?** bist du/seid ihrs/sind Sies?; **it's ~** du bist es/ ihr seids/Sie sinds; **what's the matter? – it's ~ or ~ are** was ist los? – es liegt an dir/euch/Ihnen; **there's a fine house for ~!** das ist mal ein schönes Haus!; **now there's a woman for ~!** das ist mal eine (tolle) Frau!; **now ~ say something** sag du/sagt ihr/sagen Sie (auch) mal was; **just ~ dare!** trau dich bloß!, untersteh dich!; **sit ~ down** *(hum)* setz dich/setzt euch/setzen Sie sich; **that hat just isn't ~** *(inf)* der Hut passt ein-

fach nicht zu dir/zu Ihnen

b *(indef) (nom)* man; *(acc)* einen; *(dat)* einem; **~ never know**, **~ never can tell** man kann nie wissen, man weiß nie; **it's not good for ~** es ist nicht gut

you-all ['juːɔːl] PRON *(US, inf)* ihr

you'd [juːd] *contr of* **you would**; *of* **you had**

you'd've ['juːdəv] *contr of* **you would have**

you'll [juːl] *contr of* **you will** *of* **you shall**

young [jʌŋ] ADJ *(+er)* jung; *wine, grass also* neu; **the ~ moon** der Mond im ersten Viertel; **~ people** junge Leute *pl*; **a ~ people's magazine** eine Jugendzeitschrift; **~ people's fashions** Jugendmoden *pl*; **~ lady** junge Dame; **~ man** junger Mann; **they have a ~ family** sie haben kleine Kinder; **he is ~ at heart** er ist innerlich jung geblieben; **you are only ~ once** man ist *or* du bist nur einmal jung; **at a ~ age** in frühen Jahren; **if I were ten years ~er** wenn ich zehn Jahre jünger wäre; **I'm not getting any ~er** ich werde auch nicht jünger; **he is ~ for his age** er ist noch sehr jung; **that dress is too ~ for her** sie ist zu alt für dieses Kleid; **you ~ rascal!** *(inf)* du kleiner Schlingel!; **~ Mr Brown** der junge Herr Brown; **Pitt the Younger** Pitt der Jüngere; **the night is ~** die Nacht ist (noch) jung; **Young America** die Jugend in Amerika, die amerikanische Jugend; **he's a very ~ forty** er ist ein sehr jugendlicher *or* sehr jung gebliebener Vierziger ADV *marry, have children also* jung; **live fast, die ~** leb jetzt und stirb jung PL **a** *(= people)* **the ~** die Jugend, die jungen Leute; **~ and old** jung und alt; **books for the ~** Jugendbücher *pl*

b *(= animals)* Junge *pl*; **with ~** trächtig

Young Conservative N *(Brit Pol)* Mitglied *nt* der Jungen Konservativen; **the ~s** die Jungen Konservativen

youngest ['jʌŋgɪst] ADJ *attr superl of* **young** jüngste(r, s) N **the ~** der/die/das Jüngste; *(pl)* die Jüngsten *pl*; **the ~ of four children** das jüngste von vier Kindern; **my ~** *(= son)* mein Jüngster; *(= daughter)* meine Jüngste

youngish ['jʌŋɪʃ] ADJ ziemlich jung

young offender N jugendlicher Straftäter; **home for ~s** Jugendstrafanstalt *f*

young offenders' institution N Einrichtung *f* für jugendliche Straftäter

youngster ['jʌŋstə'] N *(= boy)* Junge *m*; *(= child)* Kind *nt*; **he's just a ~** er ist eben noch jung *or* ein Kind

your [jɔː', jə'] POSS ADJ **a** *(German familiar form) (sing)* dein/deine/dein; *(pl)* euer/eure/euer; *(German polite form: sing, pl)* Ihr/Ihre/Ihr; **~ mother and father** deine/Ihre Mutter und dein/Ihr Vater; **one of ~ friends** einer deiner/ Ihrer Freunde, einer von deinen/Ihren Freunden; **the climate here is bad for ~ health** das Klima hier ist ungesund *or* ist nicht gut für die Gesundheit → **majesty**, **worship** *etc* **b** *(= typical)* der/die/das; **~ average Englishman** der durchschnittliche Engländer

you're [jʊə', jɔː'] *contr of* **you are**

yours [jɔːz] POSS PRON *(German familiar form, sing)* deiner/deine/deins; *(pl)* eurer/eure/euers; *(German polite form: sing, pl)* Ihrer/Ihre/Ihr(e)s; **this is my book and that is ~** dies ist mein Buch und das (ist) deins/Ihres; **the idea was ~** es war deine/Ihre Idee, die Idee stammt von dir/Ihnen; **she is a cousin of ~** sie ist deine Kusine, sie ist eine Kusine von dir; **that is no business of ~** das geht dich/Sie nichts an; **that dog of ~!** dein/Ihr blöder Hund!; **you and ~** du und deine Familie/Sie und Ihre Familie, du und die deinen *or* Deinen/Sie und die Ihren *(geh)*; **~** *(in letter-writing)* mit …; **~ faithfully**, **~ truly** *(Brit: on letter)* mit freundlichem Gruß, mit freundlichen Grüßen, hochachtungsvoll *(form)*; **in reply to ~ of the 15th May** *(Comm, form)* in Antwort auf Ihr Schreiben vom 15. Mai; **what's ~?** *(to drink)* was möchtest du/was möchten Sie?, was trinkst du/was trinken Sie?; **guess who had to do all the dirty work?** **~ truly** *(inf)* und wer musste die Dreckarbeit

machen? ich natürlich; **and then ~ truly got up and said ...** und dann stand ich höchstpersönlich auf und sagte ... → **affectionately**, **ever g**

yourself [jɔː'self, jə'self] PRON *pl* **yourselves** [jɔː'selvz, jə'selvz] **a** *(reflexive) (German familiar form) (sing) (acc)* dich; *(dat)* dir; *(pl)* euch; *(German polite form: sing, pl)* sich; **have you hurt ~?** hast du dir/haben Sie sich wehgetan?; **you never speak about ~** du redest nie über dich (selbst)/Sie reden nie über sich (selbst)

b *(emph)* selbst; **you ~ told me**, **you told me ~** du hast/Sie haben mir selbst gesagt; **you are not quite ~ today** du bist heute gar nicht du selbst, du bist/Sie sind heute irgendwie verändert *or* anders; **how's ~?** *(inf)* und wie gehts dir/ Ihnen?; **you will see for ~** du wirst/Sie werden selbst sehen; **did you do it by ~?** hast du/haben Sie das allein gemacht?

yous [juːz] PRON (PL) *(dial)* ihr; *(acc, dat)* euch

youth [juːθ] N **a** *no pl* Jugend *f*; **in (the days of) my ~** in meiner Jugend(zeit); **the town of my ~** die Stadt *or* Stätte *(hum)* meiner Jugend; **in early ~** in früher Jugend; **she has kept her ~** sie ist jung geblieben **b** *pl* **-s** [juːðz] *(= young man)* junger Mann, Jugendliche(r) *m*; **when he was a ~** als er ein junger Mann war; **pimply ~** pickliger Jüngling **c** **youth** PL *(= young men and women)* Jugend *f*; **she likes working with (the) ~** sie arbeitet gerne mit Jugendlichen; **the ~ of today** die Jugend von heute; **the Hitler Youth Movement** die Hitlerjugend

youth: youth club N Jugendklub *m*; **youth custody** N *(Brit Jur)* Jugendarrest *m*; **Youth Employment Scheme** N *(Brit)* Programm *nt or* Aktionsplan *m* für jugendliche Arbeitslose

youthful ['juːθfʊl] ADJ jugendlich; **he's a ~ 65** er ist ein jugendlicher Fünfundsechziger; **a ~ mistake** eine Jugendsünde

youthfully ['juːθfʊlɪ] ADV jugendlich; **she leapt up ~** sie sprang jugendlich frisch auf

youthfulness ['juːθfʊlnɪs] N Jugendlichkeit *f*

youth: youth hostel N Jugendherberge *f*; **Youth Training Scheme** N *(Brit)* Ausbildungsprogramm *nt* für Jugendliche; **youth worker** N Jugendarbeiter(in) *m(f)*

you've [juːv] *contr of* **you have**

yowl [jaʊl] N *(of person)* Heulen *nt no pl*; *(of dog)* Jaulen *nt no pl*; *(of cat)* klägliches Miauen *no pl* VI *(person)* heulen; *(dog)* jaulen; *(cat)* kläglich miauen

yo-yo ['jəʊjəʊ] N Jo-Jo *nt*, Yo-Yo *nt*; **I've been going up- and downstairs like a ~ all morning** ich bin den ganzen Morgen wie irre die Treppe rauf- und runtergerannt *(inf)*

yr **a** *abbr of* **year(s)** **b** *abbr of* **your**

yrs **a** *abbr of* **years** **b** *abbr of* **yours**

Y-shaped ['waɪʃeɪpt] ADJ Y-förmig

YTS *(Brit)* N **a** *abbr of* **Youth Training Scheme** **b** *(= person)* Auszubildende(r) *mf*

ytterbium [ɪ'tɜːbɪəm] N *(Chem)* Ytterbium *nt*

yttrium ['ɪtrɪəm] N *(Chem)* Yttrium *nt*

yucca ['jʌkə] N Yucca *f*, Palmlilie *f*

yuck [jʌk] INTERJ *(inf)* = **yuk**

Yugoslav ['juːgəʊslɑːv] ADJ jugoslawisch N Jugoslawe *m*, Jugoslawin *f*

Yugoslavia ['juːgəʊ'slɑːvɪə] N Jugoslawien *nt*; **the former ~** das ehemalige Jugoslawien, Ex-Jugoslawien *nt (Press sl)*

Yugoslavian ['juːgəʊ'slɑːvɪən] ADJ jugoslawisch

yuk [jʌk] INTERJ *(inf)* i, igitt, igittigitt

yukky ['jʌkɪ] ADJ *(+er) (inf)* eklig, widerlich, fies *(inf)*

yule [juːl] N *(old)* Weihnachten *nt*, Julfest *nt*; **~ log** Julblock *m*

Yuletide N ['juːltaɪd] Weihnachtszeit *f*, Julzeit *f*

yummy ['jʌmɪ] *(inf)* ADJ *(+er) food* lecker; *man* toll INTERJ **~!**, **~ ~!** lecker!, jamjam! *(inf)*

yum yum ['jʌm'jʌm] INTERJ lecker, jamjam *(inf)*

yup [jʌp] ADV *(US, inf, = yes)* ja, jawoll *(inf)*

yuppie, yuppy [ˈjʌpɪ] **N** Yuppie *m* **ADJ** yuppiehaft; **~ car** Yuppieauto *nt*; **~ job** Yuppiejob *m*
yuppie flu N *krankhafter Energiemangel*

yuppiedom [ˈjʌpɪdəm] N (*inf*) **the rise of ~ in the eighties** der Aufstieg der Yuppies in den 80er Jahren

yuppy N, ADJ = **yuppie**
YWCA *abbr of* **Young Women's Christian Association** CVJF *m*

Z

Z, z [(*Brit*) zed] [(*US*) ziː] N Z *nt*, z *nt*

Zaire [zaːˈɪəˈ] N (*Hist*) Zaire *nt*

Zambesi, Zambezi [zæmˈbiːzɪ] N Sambesi *m*

Zambia [ˈzæmbɪə] N Sambia *nt*

zany [ˈzeɪnɪ] **ADJ** (+er) (= *crazy, funny*) verrückt; *person also* irrsinnig komisch **N** (*Theat Hist*) Narr *m*, Hanswurst *m*

Zanzibar [ˈzænzɪbaːˈ] N Sansibar *nt*

zap [zæp] (*inf*) **N** (= *energy, pep*) Schwung *m*, Pep *m* (*inf*) **INTERJ** zack **VT** **a** (= *hit*) **to ~ sb** jdm eine pfeffern (*inf*) *or* kleben (*inf*) **b** (*Comput, = delete*) löschen **c** (*inf*) (= *kill*) abknallen (*inf*); (= *destroy*) kaputtmachen (*inf*) **d** (*inf, = send quickly*) **he ~ped us back down to London in his Porsche** er hat uns in seinem Porsche im Düsentempo nach London zurückgebracht (*inf*) **VI** **a** (= *move fast*) düsen (*inf*) **b** (= *change channel*) umschalten; **to ~ through the channels** zappen (*inf*)

▶ **zap along** VI (*inf, = move fast*) düsen (*inf*); **the project's zapping along** das Projekt geht mit Volldampf voran (*inf*)

zapped [zæpt] ADJ (*inf, = tired, exhausted*) total geschafft (*inf*)

zapper [ˈzæpəˈ] N (*US inf: TV*) Fernbedienung *f*

zappiness [ˈzæpɪnɪs] N (*of pace, car*) Fetzigkeit *f* (*inf*); (*of prose, style*) Spritzigkeit *f*; (*of management style*) Dynamik *f*

zappy [ˈzæpɪ] ADJ *pace, car* fetzig (*inf*); (= *lively*) *prose, style* spritzig; *management style* dynamisch

zeal [ziːl] N , *no pl* Eifer *m*; **to work with great ~** mit Feuereifer arbeiten; **he is full of ~ for the cause** er ist mit Feuereifer bei der Sache

zealot [ˈzelət] N Fanatiker(in) *m(f)*; (*religious also*) (Glaubens)eiferer(in) *m(f)*; **Zealot** (*Hist*) Zelot *m*

zealotry [ˈzelətrɪ] N Fanatismus *m*, blinder Eifer

zealous [ˈzeləs] ADJ *student, worker* eifrig, emsig; *official, officer* eifrig; **~ for sth** eifrig um etw bemüht; **to be ~ to begin/help** erpicht darauf sein, anzufangen/zu helfen; **~ for the cause** für die Sache begeistert; **~ for a change** auf einen Wechsel erpicht

zealously [ˈzeləslɪ] ADV *pursue, guard, support* eifrig

zebra [ˈzebrə] N Zebra *nt*

zebra: zebra crossing N (*Brit*) Zebrastreifen *m*; **zebra finch** N (*Orn*) Zebrafink *m*

Zeitgeist [ˈzaɪtgaɪst] N Zeitgeist *m*

Zen [zen] N Zen *nt*; **~ Buddhism** Zen-Buddhismus *m*

zenith [ˈzenɪθ] N (*Astron, fig*) Zenit *m*

zephyr [ˈzefəˈ] N (*poet*) Zephir *m* (*poet*), Zephyr *m* (*poet*)

zeppelin [ˈzeplɪn] N Zeppelin *m*

zero [ˈzɪərəʊ] **N** *pl* **a** (= *figure*) Null *f*; (= *point on scale*) Nullpunkt *m*; (*Roulette*) Zero *f*; **15 degrees below ~** 15 Grad unter null; **the needle is at** *or* **on ~** der Zeiger steht auf null; **his chances were put at ~** man meinte, seine Aussichten seien gleich null; **snow reduced visibility to near ~** es schneite so stark, dass die Sicht fast gleich null war **b** (*fig: = nonentity*) Null *f* (*inf*)

ADJ **at ~ altitude** (*Aviat*) im Tiefflug; **~ altitude flying** Tiefflug *m*; **~ degrees** null Grad; **~ growth** Nullwachstum *nt*; **he's getting absolutely ~ satisfaction from it** (*inf*) das bringt ihm überhaupt nichts (*inf*); **she showed ~ interest in him** (*inf*) sie zeigte sich nicht im Geringsten an ihm interessiert

▶ **zero in** VI (*Mil*) sich einschießen (*on* auf +*acc*); **to zero in on sb/sth** (*fig, on gang leader, core of problem*) jdn/etw einkreisen; *on difficulty* sich (*dat*) etw herausgreifen; *on opportunity* sich auf etw (*acc*) stürzen

---

ZERO

Null, „0", wird je nach Kontext verschieden gesprochen. Dabei ist **zero** der gebräuchlichste Ausdruck in fast allen amerikanischen Kontexten, im britischen Englisch wird **zero** in Mathematik und Naturwissenschaften verwendet, auch bei Temperaturen und anderen Skalen.

Nought ist ein britischer Ausdruck, den man beim Aussprechen von Dezimalzahlen heranzieht: „nought point nought seven" ist 0.07. Auch bei der Benotung greift man darauf zurück, z. B. „nought out of ten". „Oh" wird „0" dagegen sowohl im britischen wie auch amerikanischen Englisch gesprochen, wenn man Zahlenreihen, wie bei einer Telefonnummer oder Kreditkarte, vorlesen muss: „oh one four one" (0141).

Nil wird häufig im britischen Sport für den Punktestand verwendet: „Liverpool won five nil/by five goals to nil". Die amerikanische Entsprechung ist **nothing**, was in Großbritannien, allerdings in der Umgangssprache, ebenfalls verwendet wird. Beim Tennis und Squash heißt es dagegen **love**: „Fifteen - love". In der amerikanischen Umgangssprache gibt es auch noch **zip**: „We won seven-zip".

---

zero: zero-emission ADJ emissionsfrei; **~ car** Null-Emissions-Auto *nt*; **zero gravity** N Schwerelosigkeit *f*; **at ~** unter Schwerelosigkeit; **zero hour** N (*Mil, fig*) die Stunde X; **zero option** N (*Pol*) Nulllösung *f*; **zero-rated** ADJ (*for VAT*) mehrwertsteuerfrei; **zero rating** N (*for VAT*) Befreiung *f* von der Mehrwertsteuer; **zero-sum game** N Nullsummenspiel *nt*; **zero tolerance** N Nulltoleranz *f*; **zero-tolerance** ADJ kompromisslos; **~ policing** Polizeiarbeit *f* nach dem Nulltoleranzprinzip

zest [zest] N **a** (= *enthusiasm*) Begeisterung *f*; **~ for life** Lebensfreude *f*; **he hasn't got much ~** er hat keinen Schwung **b** (*in style, of food etc*) Pfiff *m* (*inf*), Schwung *m*; **a story full of ~** eine Geschichte mit Schwung; **add ~ to your meals with ...!** geben Sie Ihren Gerichten Pfiff mit ...! (*inf*) **c** (= *lemon etc peel*) Zitronen-/Orangenschale *f*

zestful ADJ , **zestfully** ADV [ˈzestfʊl, -fəlɪ] schwungvoll

zesty [ˈzestɪ] ADJ *wine* pikant

zeugma [ˈzjuːgmə] N Zeugma *nt*

Zeus [zjuːs] N (*Myth*) Zeus *m*

ziggurat [ˈzɪgəræt] N Zikkur(r)at *f*

zigzag [ˈzɪgzæg] **N** Zickzack *m or nt*; **in a ~** im Zickzack; **the river cuts a ~ through the rocks** der Fluss bahnt sich im Zickzack einen Weg durch die Felsen; **we had to make a long ~ across the ice** wir mussten uns lange im Zickzack über das Eis bewegen; **a pattern of straight lines and ~s** ein Muster aus Geraden und Zickzacklinien **ADJ** Zickzack-; *road, path* zickzackförmig; **~ line** Zickzacklinie *f*; **to steer a ~ course** (*Naut*) Zickzack(kurs) fahren **ADV** zickzackförmig, im Zickzack **VI** im Zickzack laufen/fahren *etc*; (*Naut*) Zickzack(kurs) fahren; **to ~ along** im Zickzack laufen/fahren *etc*

zilch [zɪltʃ] N (*inf, = nothing*) nix (*inf*)

zillion [ˈzɪljən] (*US, inf*) **N** **~s of dollars** zig Milliarden Dollar (*inf*) **ADJ** **I've told you a ~ times ...** ich hab dir hunderttausendmal *or* zigmal gesagt ... (*inf*)

Zimbabwe [zɪmˈbaːbwɪ] N Simbabwe *nt*, Zimbabwe *nt*

Zimbabwean [zɪmˈbaːbwɪən] **ADJ** zimbabwisch, simbabwisch **N** Zimbabwer(in) *m(f)*, Simbabwer(in) *m(f)*

Zimmer® [ˈzɪmə'] N (*Brit: also* **Zimmer frame**) Gehgerät *nt*

zinc [zɪŋk] N Zink *nt*

zinc ointment N Zinksalbe *f*

zinc oxide N Zinkoxid *nt*

zine, 'zine [ziːn] (*inf*) N kleine, amateurhaft produzierte Zeitschrift, Magazin *nt*, Heftchen *nt*

zing [zɪŋ] (*inf*) **N** **a** (*noise of bullet etc*) Pfeifen *nt*, Zischen *nt* **b** (= *zest*) Pfiff *m* (*inf*) **VI** (*bullets*) pfeifen, zischen

zinger [ˈzɪŋə'] N **to be a real ~** (*inf*) wie eine Bombe einschlagen

zinnia [ˈzɪnɪə] N Zinnie *f*

Zion [ˈzaɪən] N Zion *nt*

Zionism [ˈzaɪənɪzəm] N Zionismus *m*

Zionist [ˈzaɪənɪst] **ADJ** zionistisch **N** Zionist(in) *m(f)*

ZIP [zɪp] (*US*) *abbr of* **zone improvement plan** PLZ

zip [zɪp] **N** **a** (*Brit: = fastener*) Reißverschluss *m* **b** (*sound of bullet*) Pfeifen *nt*, Zischen *nt* **c** (*inf, = energy*) Schwung *m*; **we need a bit more ~ in these translations** wir müssen etwas mehr Schwung in diese Übersetzungen kriegen (*inf*) **d** (*inf, = nothing*) nichts, nix (*inf*) **VT** **to ~ a dress/bag** den Reißverschluss eines Kleides/einer Tasche zumachen *or* zuziehen; **to ~ a file** eine Datei zippen **VI** (*inf, car*) flitzen (*inf*); (*person also*) sausen (*inf*); **to ~ past/along** *etc* vorbei-/daherflitzen *etc* (*inf*); **he ~ped through the book in no time** er hatte das Buch in null Komma nichts durch (*inf*)

▶ **zip on** **VT** *sep* **he zipped on his special gloves** er zog die Reißverschlüsse seiner Spezialhandschuhe zu **VI** **the hood zips onto the jacket** die Kapuze wird mit einem Reißverschluss an der Jacke befestigt

▶ **zip up** **VT** *sep* **to zip up a dress** den Reißverschluss eines Kleides zumachen; **will you zip me up please?** kannst du mir bitte den Reißverschluss zumachen?; **to zip up a file** eine Datei zippen **VI** **it zips up** es hat einen Reißverschluss; **it zips up at the back** der Reißverschluss ist hinten

zip: zip code N (US) Postleitzahl f; **zip fastener** N (Brit) Reißverschluss m; **zip file** N Zipdatei f; **zip gun** N (US) selbst gebastelte Pistole

---

ZIP CODE

In den USA ist die Postleitzahl ein **zip code** aus normalerweise fünf oder neun Ziffern, wobei sich die ersten drei Zahlen auf eine bestimmte Gegend des Landes beziehen, die anderen dagegen auf ein örtliches Postamt oder einen lokalen Zustellbereich: z. B. Portland, OR 97201.

---

zipped [zɪpt] ADJ mit Reißverschluss, Reißverschluss-; file gezippt

zipper ['zɪpə'] N (US) Reißverschluss m

zippy ['zɪpɪ] ADJ (+er) (inf) car flott; person also flink

zircon ['zɜːkən] N Zirkon m

zirconium [zɜːˈkəʊnɪəm] N (Chem) Zirkonium nt

zit [zɪt] N (inf, = spot) Pickel m

zither ['zɪðə'] N Zither f

zloty ['zlɒtɪ] N pl **zlotys** or **zloty** Zloty m

zodiac ['zəʊdɪæk] N Tierkreis m; **signs of the ~** Tierkreiszeichen pl

zombie ['zɒmbɪ] N **a** (lit: = revived corpse) Zombie m **b** (fig) Idiot(in) m(f) (inf), Schwachkopf m (inf); **like ~s/a ~** wie im Tran; **that new hairstyle makes her look a complete ~** mit der

neuen Frisur sieht sie total bescheuert or bekloppt aus (inf)

zonal ['zəʊnl] ADJ Zonen-, zonal; **~ boundary** Zonengrenze f

zone ['zəʊn] **N** (Geog, fig) Zone f; (US: = postal zone) Post(zustell)bezirk m; **no-parking ~** Parkverbot nt; **time ~** Zeitzone f; **~s of the body** Körperzonen pl; **to be in the ~** in einer Sache völlig aufgehen; athlete in Topform sein **VT** **a** town, area in Zonen aufteilen **b** **to ~ a district for industry** einen Bezirk zur Industriezone ernennen

zone therapy N (Med) Reflexzonenmassage f

zoning ['zəʊnɪŋ] N **a** Zoneneinteilung f **b** **the ~ of this area as ...** die Erklärung dieses Gebietes zum ...

zonked [zɒŋkt] ADJ (inf) (= drunk, high) breit (sl), zu (inf); (= exhausted) total geschafft (inf)

zoo [zuː] N Zoo m, Tierpark m, Tiergarten m

zoo keeper N Tierpfleger(in) m(f), Wärter(in) m(f)

zoological [ˌzʊəˈlɒdʒɪkəl] ADJ zoologisch; **~ gardens** zoologischer Garten

zoologist [zʊˈɒlədʒɪst] N Zoologe m, Zoologin f

zoology [zʊˈɒlədʒɪ] N Zoologie f

zoom [zuːm] **N** **a** (= sound of engine) Surren nt **b** (Aviat, = upward flight) Steilanstieg m **c** (Phot: also **zoom lens**) Zoom(objektiv) nt **VI** **a** (engine) surren **b** (inf) sausen (inf); **the car ~ed past us** der Wagen sauste an uns vorbei (inf); **we were ~ing along at 90** wir sausten mit 90 daher (inf); **he ~ed through it so quickly he can't**

possibly have read it properly er war in null Komma nichts damit fertig, er kann das unmöglich gründlich gelesen haben (inf) **c** (Aviat, plane, rocket) steil (auf)steigen; **the rocket ~ed up into the sky** die Rakete schoss in den Himmel; **prices have ~ed up to a new high** die Preise sind in unerreichte Höhen geschnellt **VT** plane steil hochziehen or hochreißen; engine auf Hochtouren laufen lassen

▶ **zoom in** VI **a** (Phot) hinzoomen, nah herangehen; **to zoom in on sth** etw heranholen; **zoom in!** näher fahren!; **he zoomed in on the problem** (inf) er kam direkt auf das Problem zu sprechen **b** (inf, = come or go in) hereinsausen (inf)

▶ **zoom out** VI **a** (Phot) wegzoomen **b** (inf, = go or come out) hinaussausen (inf)

zoomorphic [ˌzəʊəˈmɔːfɪk] ADJ zoomorph

zoot suit ['zuːtsuːt] N (US inf) Anzug mit wattierten Schultern und eng zulaufender Hose

Zoroaster [ˌzɒrəʊˈæstə'] N Zoroaster m, Zarathustra m

Zoroastrian [ˌzɒrəʊˈæstrɪən] ADJ zoroastrisch

zouk [zuːk] N (Mus) Zouk m

zucchini [zuːˈkiːnɪ] N (esp US) Zucchini pl

Zulu ['zuːluː] **ADJ** Zulu-, der Zulus; **~ chief** Zuluhäuptling m; **the ~ people** die Zulus pl **N** **a** Zulu mf **b** (Ling) Zulu nt

Zululand ['zuːluːlænd] N Zululand nt (old), Kwazulu nt

zwieback ['zwiːbæk] N (US) Zwieback m

zygote ['zaɪɡəʊt] N (Biol) Zygote f

LANGUAGE IN USE

SPRACHE AKTIV

First Edition
by
Ulrike Seeberger and Roswitha Morris

New Edition
by
Elspeth Anderson   Horst Kopleck   Christine Bahr

Language in Use

Sprache Aktiv

Contents

Inhalt

German-English

Englisch-Deutsch

Corpus Acknowledgements

We would like to acknowledge the assistance of the many hundreds of individuals and companies who have kindly given permission for copyright material to be used in the Bank of English. The written sources include many national and regional newspapers in Britain and overseas; magazine and periodical publishers in Britain, the United States and Australia. Extensive spoken data has been provided by radio and television broadcasting companies; research workers at many universities and other institutions; and numerous individual contributors. We are grateful to them all.

Korpusmaterial

Für ihre Unterstützung danken wir den vielen Einzelpersonen und Firmen, die freundlicherweise urheberrechtlich geschütztes Textmaterial zur Verwendung in unseren deutschen Korpora bereitgestellt haben. Dazu zählen eine Vielzahl von Zeitungs-, Zeitschriften- und Buchverlagen in Deutschland, Österreich und der Schweiz. Ihnen allen gilt unser Dank.

Introduction to Language in Use – New Edition

Our aim in writing Language in Use has been to help non-native speakers find fluent, natural ways of expressing themselves in the foreign language, without risk of the native-language distortion that sometimes results from literal translation. To achieve this, we have identified a number of essential language functions, such as *agreement*, *suggestions* and *apologies*, and provided a wealth of examples to show typical ways of expressing them. Users can select phrases to meet their needs using either their knowledge of the foreign language alone or by looking at the translations of the key elements.

In this revised edition of Language in Use, the authentic examples are taken from Collins vast computerized language databases of modern English and German. These databases consist of around 700 million English and German words from a variety of modern written and spoken sources: literature, magazines, newspapers, letters, radio and television. The user-friendly layout is designed to make consultation even easier. Clear headings and subdivisions enable you to find the topic of your choice at a glance. We have given guidance, where appropriate, so that you can be confident that the phrase you have chosen is as assertive, tentative, direct or indirect as you want it to be.

The linking of the main dictionary text to the Language in Use section is particularly helpful. Certain words, *suggestion*, for example, have been marked in the main dictionary to show that additional material is given in Language in Use. In these cases the Language in Use symbol ✪ appears after the relevant headword and phonetics. Numbers (**suggestion** 1.1, 1.2) tell you which Language in Use section(s) to go to – in this case, sections 1.1 and 1.2 for examples relating to *suggestion*. As all cross-referred words are underlined in the relevant Language in Use section, you will quickly be able to locate them there.

Since German forms of address corresponding to the English *you* vary according to the formality of the relationship, we have tried to reflect this in a consistent manner. As a general rule, the *Sie* form has been used, with the exception of such idioms and translations which are either spoken or by their nature demand the use of the *du* form.

Sprache aktiv – Einleitung zur Neubearbeitung

Bei der Zusammenstellung von "Sprache aktiv" ging es darum, Nichtmuttersprachlern eine Hilfestellung zur idiomatischen Ausdrucksweise in der Fremdsprache zu geben, sodass Verzerrungen, wie sie manchmal bei wörtlichen Übersetzungen auftreten, vermieden werden können.

Um dies zu erreichen, wurde eine Reihe grundlegender sprachlicher Funktionen, wie *Zustimmung*, *Ablehnung* und *Entschuldigungen*, identifiziert und eine Vielzahl von Beispielen zusammengestellt, die typische Ausdrucksweisen für die jeweilige Situation zeigen. Der Wörterbuchbenutzer hat die Möglichkeit, Wendungen auszuwählen und dabei entweder nur auf die fremdsprachlichen Muster zurückzugreifen, also seine eigenen Sprachkenntnisse anzuwenden, oder die Übersetzungen der Schlüsselelemente in den Beispielsätzen heranzuziehen.

Die vorliegende Bearbeitung von "Sprache aktiv" basiert auf authentischen Beispielen aus den von Collins unterhaltenen, umfassenden Datenbanken des heutigen Englisch und Deutsch, in der etwa 700 Millionen Wörter beider Sprachen aus einer Vielzahl von modernen schriftlichen und mündlichen Quellen gespeichert sind: Bücher, Zeitschriften, Zeitungen, Briefe, Rundfunk- und Fernsehsendungen.

Durch das sehr übersichtlich gestaltete grafische Erscheinungsbild soll die Benutzung von "Sprache aktiv" noch leichter gemacht werden. Klare Überschriften und Unterteilungen ermöglichen das schnelle Auffinden eines gesuchten Abschnitts. Wo es sich als angebracht erwies, wurden stilistische Angaben hinzugefügt, mit deren Hilfe man feststellen kann, ob die gewählte Wendung auch genauso direkt, indirekt, bestimmt oder zögernd ist wie der entsprechende Ausgangstext.

Besonders hilfreich ist die Verknüpfung von "Sprache aktiv" mit dem Wörterbuchtext. Bestimmte Wörter, zum Beispiel *Vorschlag*, wurden im Wörterbuchtext gekennzeichnet, um darauf hinzuweisen, dass "Sprache aktiv" hierzu weiteres Material enthält. Dabei folgt auf das jeweilige Stichwort und seine Lautschrift das Symbol ✪ für "Sprache aktiv". Die Ziffern zeigen, in welchem Abschnitt nachgeschlagen werden kann. Im Fall von **Vorschlag** ✪ 28.1, 28.2 zum Beispiel finden sich in den Abschnitten 28.1 und 28.2 Beispielsätze, die sich auf das Stichwort **Vorschlag** beziehen. Da alle Wörter, die so kenntlich gemacht wurden, in "Sprache aktiv" unterstrichen sind, können die Querverweise dort schnell aufgefunden werden. Bezüglich der deutschen Anrede mit *du* oder *Sie* wurde generell die *Sie*-Form verwendet, mit Ausnahme solcher Wendungen und Übersetzungen, deren situatives Umfeld und sprachliche Ebene das *Du* verlangen.

1 SUGGESTIONS

1.1 Making suggestions

Tentatively

+ **Wenn ich vielleicht einen Vorschlag machen dürfte**: Wir sollten den Altbau besser abreißen
  = if I might make a _suggestion_

+ **Wir möchten Ihnen gerne einige Vorschläge** zu Ihrer Altersversorgung **unterbreiten**
  = we would be pleased to _suggest_ a few ideas

+ **Ich würde vorschlagen**, Sie sprechen persönlich mit Ihrem Chef
  = I would _suggest_

+ **Angenommen**, Sie würden mit ihr noch einmal über alles sprechen. Vielleicht ändert sie dann ihre Meinung
  = _suppose_

+ **Sie sollten** sich für eine solche Einladung **vielleicht besser** schriftlich bedanken
  = _perhaps_ you _ought_ to

More assertively

+ **An Ihrer Stelle würde ich** dieses Angebot zurückweisen
  = if I were you, I would

+ **Ich schlage vor**, die Sitzung auf morgen zu vertagen
  = I _suggest_

+ **Ich denke**, wir sollten für heute Schluss machen
  = I _think_

+ **Am besten sollten wir** wohl einen Spezialisten zurate ziehen
  = the _best_ thing would be to

+ **Wenn Sie** nächste Woche in Bonn sind, **könnten Sie doch** mal bei uns vorbeischauen
  = if you ..., you _could_

+ **Wenn Sie meine Meinung hören wollen**: Sagen Sie zu
  = if you want my _opinion_

+ **Eigentlich brauchten Sie** Ihren Abfall **nur** ein bisschen vorzusortieren
  = you only _need_ to

+ **In diesem Falle bleibt uns wohl nichts anderes übrig, als** unser gutes Recht über das Gericht einzuklagen
  = in that case, we have no _choice_ but to

Using direct questions

+ **Was würden Sie von** einer neuen Büroausstattung **halten**?
  = how about

+ **Was würden Sie sagen, wenn** wir Ihnen weitere 10 Prozent Rabatt bieten?
  = what would you _say_ if

+ **Warum** sprechen Sie **nicht** einfach mit Ihrem Chef über diese Angelegenheit?
  = _why_ don't you

+ **Haben Sie schon einmal daran gedacht**, sich um den Posten der Kulturreferentin **zu** bewerben?
  = have you ever thought of

+ **Was hältst du von** einer kleinen Spritztour mit dem neuen Auto?
  = how about

In an impersonal way

Tentatively

+ **Vielleicht wäre es angebracht**, in dieser heiklen Angelegenheit etwas mehr Diskretion **zu** üben
  = perhaps it would be _appropriate_

+ **Vielleicht wäre es besser**, die Polizei **zu** benachrichtigen
  = it might be _better_

+ **Es wäre ja immerhin möglich, dass** wir das Programm noch einmal ändern
  = we _could_ always

+ **Wäre es nicht eine mögliche Lösung**, einerseits die Selbstbeschränkung **zu** lockern und andererseits Sozialklauseln durch**zu**setzen?
  = one possible solution might be

More assertively

+ **Es wäre eine gute Idee**, am Wochenende aufs Land **zu** fahren
  = I think it would be a _good idea_

+ **Es wäre ratsam**, eine Sicherheitskopie an**zu**legen
  = you would certainly be _advised_ to

+ **Man sollte** diesen Versuch noch einmal bei einer anderen Temperatur durchführen
  = ... _should_ be

+ **Wie wäre es mit** einer Tasse Kaffee?
  = how about

+ **Noch** ein Bier **gefällig**?
  = would you like another

1.2 Asking for suggestions

+ **Haben Sie vielleicht eine Idee, wie** wir die Außenfassade gestalten könnten?
  = do you have any _suggestions_ about how

+ **Hat vielleicht noch jemand einen besseren Vorschlag**?
  = does anyone have a _better suggestion_

+ **Was würden Sie an meiner Stelle tun**?
  = what would you do if you were me

+ **Was könnten wir** am Wochenende **unternehmen**?
  = what _could_ we do

+ **Was würden Sie vorschlagen**?
  = what would you _suggest_

2 ADVICE

2.1 Asking for advice

+ **Was würden Sie mir** in dieser Sache **raten**?
  = what would you _advise_

+ **Was würden Sie an meiner Stelle tun**?
  = what would you do if you were me

+ Welchen Zahnarzt **würden Sie mir empfehlen**?
  = would you _recommend_

+ **Meinen Sie, ich sollte lieber nicht** nach Hongkong fliegen?
  = do you think it would be better if I didn't

+ **Meinen Sie, ich sollte** mich in dieser Sache mit meinem Anwalt absprechen?
  = do you think I _should_

+ **Ich hätte** in dieser Sache **gern Ihren Rat**
  = I'd like your _advice_

+ **Ich wäre Ihnen wirklich sehr dankbar, wenn Sie mir** in dieser delikaten Angelegenheit **mit Ihrem Rat zur Seite stehen könnten**
  = I should be very _grateful_ if you would _help_ me _out_ with some advice

+ **Ich möchte mich** in diesem schwierigen Fall **von Ihnen in Ihrer Eigenschaft als** Rechtsanwalt **beraten lassen**
  = I'd like your _opinion_ as ... on

2.2 Giving advice

+ **Ich würde Ihnen raten**, so schnell wie möglich einen Arzt auf**zu**suchen
  = I would _advise_ you to

+ **Ich würde Ihnen dringend anraten**, sich in dieser Sache mit Ihrem Anwalt ab**zu**sprechen
  = I would strongly _advise_ you to

◆ **An Ihrer Stelle würde ich** mich beschweren
= *if I were you, I would*

◆ **Sie wären gut beraten**, die Kondition des Vertrages vorerst geheim **zu** halten
= *you would be well advised to*

◆ **Sie wären schlecht beraten**, jetzt klein bei**zu**geben
= *you would be ill-advised to*

◆ **Sie sollten unbedingt** die Packungsbeilage lesen
= *you really ought to*

◆ **Es liegt ganz in Ihrem Interesse**, wenn die Konkurrenz ein wenig eingeschüchtert wird
= *it is entirely in your interest*

◆ **Es empfiehlt sich nicht**, bei der Ersatzteilsuche auf ältere Fahrzeugtypen zurück**zu**greifen
= *it is inadvisable to*

> More tentatively

◆ **Wenn ich dir raten darf**, lass sie besser in Ruhe
= *can I give you some advice*

◆ **Wenn ich Ihnen einen Hinweis geben darf**: Meiden Sie lawinengefährdete Skigebiete
= *can I give you some advice*

◆ **Es scheint mir ratsam**, den Vertrag genaustens unter die Lupe **zu** nehmen
= *I think it would be advisable to*

◆ **Am besten sollten Sie vielleicht** mit der Bahn fahren
= *you might be best to*

◆ **Haben Sie schon einmal über** eine Gehaltserhöhung **nachgedacht?**
= *have you ever thought of*

◆ **Könntest du** mir das **vielleicht** selbst erklären?
= *could you maybe*

2.3 Giving warnings

◆ **Ich kann Sie nur warnen**, am langen Samstag ist in der Stadt die Hölle los
= *a word of warning*

◆ **Ich rate Ihnen dringend davon ab**, diese Vereinbarung **zu** unterschreiben
= *I strongly advise you not to*

◆ **Ich würde mich vor** übereilten Schlussfolgerungen **hüten**
= *beware of*

◆ **Sie sollten** noch einmal alle Einzelheiten überprüfen, **sonst** geht am Ende noch etwas schief
= *you'd better ..., otherwise*

◆ **Sie laufen Gefahr**, in diesen undurchsichtigen Geschäften viel Geld **zu** verlieren
= *you run the risk of*

◆ **Versuchen Sie bloß nicht**, mit ihm über seine letzten Geschäfte **zu** reden
= *do not try to*

◆ **Es wäre reiner Wahnsinn**, ausgerechnet jetzt nach Berlin **zu** fahren
= *it would be sheer madness to*

◆ **Du wirst noch in ernstliche Schwierigkeiten geraten, wenn** du den Umgang mit Geld nicht bald lernst
= *you'll get yourself into serious trouble if*

◆ **Du riskierst Kopf und Kragen, wenn** du diesen holprigen Feldweg benutzt
= *you're risking life and limb if*

◆ **Pass auf, dass** du nicht ins Wasser fällst
= *be careful (that)*

3 OFFERS

3.1 Direct offers

◆ **Wir möchten** unsere Mitarbeit in diesem Projekt **anbieten**
= *we should like to offer*

◆ **Ich könnte** Ihnen eine zuverlässige Bürokraft vermitteln, **wenn Sie das möchten**
= *I could ..., if you like*

◆ **Lassen Sie mich zumindest** die Getränke bezahlen, **bitte**
= *please allow me to*

◆ **Ich kümmere mich gerne um** die Sache, **wenn** sich sonst niemand dafür findet
= *I would be glad to take care of ... if*

◆ **Ich bin gerne bereit**, Sie zum Flughafen **zu** fahren
= *I'd be happy to*

◆ **Wenden Sie sich bitte jederzeit an mich**, wenn Sie noch zusätzliche Informationen benötigen
= *please feel free to contact me at any time*

3.2 Indirect offers

◆ **Es würde mir sehr viel Freude machen**, Ihnen die Stadt **zu** zeigen
= *it would be a great pleasure to*

◆ **Es wäre uns ein Vergnügen**, Sie in unserem Sommerhaus begrüßen **zu** können
= *we would be delighted to*

◆ **Ich würde wirklich gerne** mit Ihnen nach Weimar fahren
= *I would be more than happy to*

3.3 Using direct questions

◆ **Möchten Sie** mit uns in die Oper gehen?
= *would you like to*

◆ **Kann ich** Ihnen behilflich sein?
= *can I*

◆ **Soll ich** für Sie bei der Zimmervermittlung anrufen?
= *shall I*

◆ **Darf ich** Ihnen etwas zu trinken **anbieten?**
= *may I offer*

◆ **Was würden Sie zu** einem kleinen Wochenendausflug **sagen?**
= *what would say to*

◆ **Wie wäre es**, wenn **ich** nächste Woche mal vorbeikommen **würde?**
= *what if I were to*

◆ **Und wenn** ich dir einfach ein bisschen im Haushalt helfe?
= *what if*

4 REQUESTS

> Tentatively

◆ **Würde es Ihnen etwas ausmachen**, mir Ihr Programmheft **zu** leihen?
= *would you mind*

◆ **Mir wäre sehr geholfen, wenn** Sie mir einen Teil meiner Auslagen vorstrecken könnten
= *it would be very helpful if*

◆ **Ich wäre Ihnen sehr dankbar, wenn** Sie mein Anliegen noch in dieser Woche klären könnten
= *I would be very grateful if*

◆ **Dürfte ich Sie vielleicht bitten**, sich um die Zimmerreservierung **zu** kümmern
= *could I ask you to*

◆ **Wenn Sie vielleicht** etwas zur Seite rücken **würden?**
= *could you maybe*

◆ **Es wäre schön, wenn** Sie am Freitag Abendessen zu uns kommen würden
= *it would be nice if*

> More assertively

◆ **Ich möchte Sie bitten**, das Telefon nicht für Privatgespräche **zu** benutzen
= *I must ask you*

◆ **Könnten Sie** mir während meines Aufenthaltes einen Wagen mit Fahrer zur Verfügung stellen?
= *could you*

+ **Würden Sie bitte** in diesem Zimmer nicht rauchen?
  = _please_

+ **Wären Sie bitte so freundlich**, mir die Tür aufzuhalten?
  = _would_ you be so _kind_ as to

| More formally |

+ **Ich wäre Ihnen sehr zu Dank verpflichtet, wenn** Sie in dieser sehr persönlichen Sache äußerste Diskretion walten lassen könnten
  = I would be _obliged_ if

+ **Ich wäre Ihnen sehr verbunden, wenn** Sie mich baldmöglichst persönlich empfangen könnten
  = I would be most _obliged_ if

+ **Wir möchten Sie dringend auffordern**, die ausgeliehenen Bücher so schnell wie möglich zurückzubringen
  = you are urgently requested

+ **Wir danken im Voraus für** Ihre sofortige Antwort
  = we would be _grateful_ for

| 5 | **COMPARISONS**

| 5.1 | **Objective comparisons**

+ **Im Vergleich zu** anderen Mittelgebirgen ist die Rhön arm an Bodenschätzen
  = _compared to/with_

+ Singapur hat, **verglichen mit** ähnlich großen Städten in den USA, eine niedrige Kriminalitätsrate
  = if you _compare_ it _to/with_

+ **Wenn man** Hans **und** Paul **vergleicht**, ist Paul doch der angenehmere Charakter
  = if you _compare_ ... and

+ Der Anteil stark geschädigter Bäume ist in Nordwestdeutschland mit 16 Prozent **vergleichsweise** gering
  = _comparatively_

+ **Im Gegensatz zu** den drückenden Außentemperaturen ist es in deiner Wohnung angenehm kühl
  = in _contrast_ with

+ Es wird **immer schwieriger**, Museen zu Leihgaben zu überreden, weil die alten Kunstwerke Ortsveränderungen nicht ohne Schaden überstehen
  = increasingly _difficult_

+ Die Mitgliedsstaaten zeigen **immer weniger** Neigung, die Weltorganisation mit der Lösung neuer Konflikte zu beauftragen
  = _less and less_

+ Die neue Wohnung ist **so** groß **wie** die alte, **allerdings** etwas besser gelegen
  = _as_ ... _as_ ..., but

+ Es **sieht so aus wie** ein U-Boot, **nur** etwas kleiner
  = is _like_ ... but

+ Das Design dieser Lampe **erinnert in gewisser Weise an** die Automodelle der 50er Jahre
  = is _reminiscent_ of

+ Das neue Haus hat einen großen Garten, **während** unsere alte Wohnung nur einen kleinen Balkon hatte
  = _whereas_

+ **Was** ihn **von** vielen anderen Schriftstellern **unterscheidet**, ist sein Sprachwitz und seine positive Lebenshaltung
  = what _differentiates_ ... from

| 5.2 | **Making favourable comparisons**

+ Die Mitbewerber sind ihm aufgrund ihrer Qualifikation **weit überlegen**
  = far _superior_

+ Das Gulasch, das seine Mutter kocht, **ist eine Klasse für sich**
  = is in _a class of its own_

+ Ein Pianist **ist um mehrere Klassen besser** für den Ruf eines Restaurants in Wien **als** eine Zigeunerkapelle
  = is very much _better_ ... _than_

+ Was das Klima angeht, **ist mir** Südfrankreich natürlich **lieber als** die Bretagne
  = I _prefer_ ... to

+ Das **ist** noch **gar nichts im Vergleich zu** den Schereien, die die FDP mit ihrer Figaro-Affäre hat
  = is nothing in _comparison_ to

| 5.3 | **Making unfavourable comparisons**

+ Die Filmversion des Stoffes ist **bei weitem nicht so** interessant **wie** das Buch
  = far _less_ ... _than_

+ Die Tonqualität ist **viel schlechter als** bei einem CD-Player
  = much _worse than_

+ Die heutigen Essgewohnheiten **ähneln kaum mehr** denen vor 100 Jahren
  = _bear_ little _resemblance_ to

+ **Man kann** seinen ersten Roman **nicht mit** seinen Kurzgeschichten **vergleichen**
  = does not _compare with_

+ Seine Gedichte **können sich nicht mit** seiner Prosa **messen**
  = cannot _compare with_

+ Auf fachlichem Niveau **können** die Aushilfskräfte **nicht mit** den Facharbeitern **mithalten**
  = cannot _match_

+ Er **kann** seinem Bruder **nicht das Wasser reichen**
  = can't _hold a candle to_

+ Die Verteidigung **war** dem Ansturm der gegnerischen Mannschaft **in keiner Hinsicht gewachsen**
  = were no _match_ for

| 5.4 | **Great similarity**

+ Vieles in dem Roman **entspricht** der Wirklichkeit
  = _corresponds to_

+ Er behandelt Frauen **genauso** schlecht **wie** Männer
  = _just as_ ... _as_

+ Ich **kann keinen Unterschied zwischen** diesen beiden Methoden **feststellen**
  = I can see no _difference_ between

+ Mit seinem Sieg hat er bewiesen, **dass** sein Leistungsvermögen **an das** der Spitzenspieler **heranreicht**
  = that ... _match(es)_

+ Die Steuern dürfen nicht mehr erhöht werden, **das Gleiche gilt für** die Staatsverschuldung
  = the _same goes for_

+ Rein äußerlich **sehen sich** die beiden Herren **sehr ähnlich**
  = are very _alike_

+ **Das nimmt sich** zeitlich **nichts, ob** wir über die Autobahn oder über die Landstraße fahren
  = it makes no _difference_ ... _whether_

| 5.5 | **Great difference**

+ Sie **sind** in ihrer Lebenseinstellung **nicht miteinander zu vergleichen**
  = there is no _comparison_ between

+ Unsere Ansichten zu diesem Thema sind **grundverschieden**
  = totally _different_

+ Auf den ersten Blick **haben** die beiden **gar nichts gemein**
  = have absolutely nothing _in common_

+ Er **hat mit** dem normalen Bürger **nichts gemein**
  = has nothing _in common_ with

+ Beide haben rote Haare, **aber da hört die Ähnlichkeit auch schon auf**
  = but there the _likeness_ ends

6   OPINION

6.1   Asking for opinions

◆ **Was halten Sie (persönlich) von** einer Anhebung der Benzinpreise?
= *what do you (personally) think of*

◆ **Wie denken Sie über** eine Reform des Schulwesens?
= *what do you think about*

◆ **Wie sehen Sie** die weitere Entwicklung?
= *how do you see*

◆ **Wie schätzen Sie** den Erfolg unserer Maßnahmen **ein?**
= *how do you see*

◆ **Wie stehen Sie zu** einer möglichen Mehrwertsteuererhöhung?
= *what is your attitude to*

◆ **Mir wäre sehr an Ihrer** fachlichen **Meinung zu** diesem Problem **gelegen**
= *I would be very interested in your ... opinion on*

◆ **Es würde mich interessieren, was Ihre persönliche Meinung zu** dieser Erbschaftsangelegenheit **ist**
= *I would be interested to know your opinion on*

6.2   Expressing opinions

◆ **Ich meine**, es ist höchste Zeit für Reformen
= *I think*

◆ **Ich nehme (stark) an, dass** wir alle mehr Steuern zahlen müssen
= *I (fully) expect that*

◆ **Ich fürchte**, wir haben keine andere Wahl
= *I'm afraid*

◆ **Ich finde**, der Bundeskanzler muss in der Hauptstadt präsent sein
= *I feel*

◆ **Mir scheint**, besser und knapper kann man sich über dieses Thema gar nicht auslassen
= *it seems to me that*

◆ **Ich bin (fest) davon überzeugt, dass** der Forschungsbedarf langfristig steigen wird
= *I am convinced that*

◆ **Ich kann nicht umhin**, darin einen weiteren Beweis für die geschwächte Stellung des Staates **zu** sehen
= *I can't help*

◆ **Meiner Meinung nach** ist die Wiederverwertung von Metallen nach wie vor sinnvoll
= *in my opinion*

◆ **Ich bin der Meinung, dass** es sich hierbei um ein Missverständnis handelt
= *I'm of the opinion that*

◆ **Ich kann mir (gut) vorstellen, dass** unser Vorschlag die Zustimmung des Aufsichtsrates findet
= *I have a (good) idea that*

◆ **Wenn Sie meine Meinung hören wollen:** Ich rechne fest mit einer Umsatzsteigerung
= *if you want my opinion*

◆ **Wenn ich mich auch einmal zu diesem Problem äußern darf:** Ich halte Ihren Vorschlag für keine gute Lösung
= *if I could just say one thing about this problem*

◆ **Ich werde den Eindruck nicht los, dass** mir hier etwas angehängt werden soll
= *I can't help feeling that*

◆ **Ich habe den Eindruck, dass** der Feminismus sich vor allem auf die weibliche Opferrolle konzentriert
= *I get the impression that*

◆ **So wie ich die Sache sehe**, ist der Streit noch lange nicht beigelegt
= *as I see it*

◆ **Wenn du mich fragst**, geht es mit ihr bergab
= *if you ask me*

6.3   Avoiding expressing one's opinion

◆ **Ich habe eigentlich keine besondere Meinung zu** diesem Thema
= *I have no particular opinion about*

◆ **Ich möchte mich zu** dieser Angelegenheit **nicht äußern**
= *I would rather not comment on*

◆ **Ich möchte mir darüber besser kein Urteil erlauben**
= *I'd rather not express an opinion on that*

◆ **Es ist schwer zu sagen**, wie sich die Situation entwickeln wird
= *it is hard to say*

◆ **Es scheint mir schwierig**, die Lage objektiv **zu beurteilen**
= *I find it hard to judge*

◆ **Darüber habe ich mir ehrlich gesagt noch keine Gedanken gemacht**
= *I've honestly never thought about it*

◆ **Ich habe keine Ahnung, ob** sich der ganze Aufwand lohnt
= *I have no idea whether*

◆ **Das kommt darauf an, was Sie unter** Kunst **verstehen**
= *it depends on what you mean by*

7   LIKES, DISLIKES AND PREFERENCES

7.1   Asking what someone likes

◆ **Würden Sie gerne** zu den Salzburger Festspielen fahren?
= *would you like to*

◆ **Würde es Ihnen Freude machen**, am Sonntag mit in ein Konzert **zu** kommen?
= *how would you like to*

◆ **Hätten Sie Lust auf** eine Partie Schach?
= *do you feel like*

◆ **Was würden Sie bevorzugen** - ein neues Auto oder das Geld?
= *which would you prefer*

◆ **Was mögen Sie lieber** - Pop oder Klassik?
= *which do you prefer*

◆ **Ich wüsste gern, was Ihre Lieblings**beschäftigung **ist?**
= *I would like to know what your favourite ... is*

◆ **Was machst du** in den Ferien **am liebsten?**
= *what do you like doing best*

7.2   Saying what you like

◆ **Ich gehe gern** ins Kino
= *I like going*

◆ Die Führung durch den Dom **hat mir sehr gut gefallen**
= *I really enjoyed*

◆ Kreuzworträtsel **machen mir sehr viel Spaß**
= *I really enjoy ... a lot*

◆ **Ich schätze es sehr, wenn** Leute ihre Versprechungen halten
= *I really appreciate it when*

◆ **Es geht doch nichts über** ein gemütliches Frühstück am Sonntagmorgen
= *there's nothing like*

◆ **Nichts mag ich lieber als** eine heiße Tasse Kakao in der Dämmerung am Kamin zu trinken
= *there's nothing I like better than*

◆ **Ich habe eine Schwäche für** Schokoladenkuchen
= *I have a weakness for*

◆ Kasslerbraten **ist mein Leib- und Magengericht**
= *is my absolute favourite dish*

7.3   Saying what you dislike

◆ **Mir gefällt** seine ganze Art **nicht**
= *I don't like*

◆ **Ich mag keine** langen Abendkleider
= *I don't like*

◆ **Ich finde es schrecklich**, immer auf der Flucht sein zu müssen
= *I think it's dreadful*

◆ **Ich kann** rechthaberische Leute **nicht ausstehen**
  = I can't _stand_

◆ **Ich habe** die ewigen Tennisübertragungen **satt**
  = I'm _fed_ _up_ _with_

◆ Die Schauspielerei **ist nichts für mich**
  = isn't my cup of _tea_

◆ Die heutige Mode **ist nicht mein Fall**
  = isn't my cup of _tea_

◆ Abwaschen **ist nicht gerade meine Lieblings**beschäftigung
  = isn't exactly my _favourite_

◆ **Mir graust vor** dem eklig süßen Tee, den sie uns immer vorsetzt
  = ... makes me _sick_

◆ **Ich bin nicht gerade begeistert von** deine Kommentaren
  = I'm not wildly _enthusiastic_ about

◆ Der neueste Hormonskandal **hat mir den Appetit auf** Rindfleisch **gründlich verleidet**
  = has _put_ me _off_ ... completely

◆ **Am meisten hasse ich** seine ewigen Nörgeleien
  = the thing I _hate_ most is

◆ **Nichts hasse ich mehr als** stundenlang im Regen auf den Bus **zu** warten
  = there's nothing I _hate_ _more_ than

7.4 Saying what you prefer

◆ Die roten Vorhänge **gefallen mir besser als** die blauen
  = I _like_ ... _better_ than

◆ **Ich mag** Pfirsiche **lieber als** Aprikosen
  = I _prefer_ ... to

◆ **Ich würde lieber** ins Kino gehen, **als** zu Hause vor der Glotze **zu** hocken
  = I would _rather_ ... than

◆ **Es wäre mir lieber, wenn** ihr jetzt gehen würdet
  = I'd _rather_

◆ **Ich halte es für besser, wenn** wir vorerst Stillschweigen bewahren
  = I think it would be _better_ if

◆ Lesen **ist eine meiner Lieblings**beschäftigungen
  = is one of my _favourite_

◆ **Sie hat eine ausgeprägte Vorliebe für** Goldschmuck
  = she has a marked _preference_ for

◆ 14 Uhr **würde mir besser passen**
  = would _suit_ me _better_

7.5 Expressing indifference

◆ **Ich habe keine spezielle Vorliebe**
  = I don't have any _particular_ _preference_

◆ Diese Art von Filmen **interessiert mich überhaupt nicht**
  = doesn't _interest_ me in the slightest

◆ Die Frage, ob die Romanfiguren wirklich existiert haben, **ist** dabei **völlig belanglos**
  = of no _importance_ whatsoever

◆ Dem Kunden **ist es völlig gleichgültig**, welche Technik im Hintergrund arbeitet
  = doesn't really _care_

◆ Die Bilder blutiger Massaker **lassen ihn kalt**
  = leave him _cold_

◆ **Es ist mir egal**, was die Leute von mir denken
  = I don't _care_

◆ Ganz wie du willst, **mir ist alles recht**
  = I'm not _bothered_

◆ Wofür er sein Geld zum Fenster rausschmeißt, **ist mir doch schnuppe**
  = I _couldn't_ _care_ _less_

INTENTIONS AND DESIRES

8.1 Asking what someone intends to do

◆ **Was beabsichtigen Sie zu tun?**
  = what do you _intend_ to do

◆ **Was haben Sie** am Wochenende **vor?**
  = what _plans_ do you have for

◆ **Wie hatten Sie sich** Ihr weiteres Vorgehen in dieser Sache **vorgestellt?**
  = how had you _envisaged_

◆ **Was versprechen Sie sich von** derlei drastischen Maßnahmen?
  = what do you _expect_ to _achieve_ by

◆ **Welche Vorsätze haben Sie** für das neue Jahr?
  = what _resolutions_ have you made

◆ **Was bezwecken Sie damit?**
  = what do you _expect_ to gain by that

◆ **Ich wüsste gerne, was Sie** nächste Woche **machen wollen**
  = I would like to know what you _want_ to do

◆ **Haben Sie schon** einen bestimmten Bewerber **ins Auge gefasst?**
  = have you already got your eye on

◆ Wir wären Ihnen dankbar, wenn Sie uns bis zum Monatsende mitteilen könnten, **was Sie** in dieser Sache **zu unternehmen gedenken**
  = what you _propose_ to do

◆ **Habt ihr schon Pläne** für die Ferien **geschmiedet?**
  = have you made any _plans_

◆ **Was führst du wieder im Schilde?**
  = what are you _up to_ this time

8.2 Saying what someone intends or wants to do

Tentatively

◆ **Er spielt mit dem Gedanken**, noch dieses Jahr zurück**zu**treten
  = he's _toying_ _with_ the _idea_ of

◆ **Eines Tages kaufe ich mir doch noch** ein Ferienhaus in Südfrankreich
  = one day I'm going to buy

◆ **Sie hatte eigentlich nur vor**, kurz bei euch vorbei**zu**schauen
  = she just _wanted_ to

◆ **Ich wollte** schon vorhin mit Ihnen darüber sprechen
  = I _meant_ to

More assertively

◆ Der Aufsichtsrat **hat die Absicht**, in der Innenstadt ein neues Hotel bauen **zu** lassen
  = _intends_ to

◆ **Unsere Absicht besteht darin**, das gesamte Gewerbegebiet neu **zu** erschließen
  = it is our _intention_ to

◆ **Wir haben uns fest vorgenommen**, den Titel erfolgreich **zu** verteidigen
  = we have every _intention_ of

◆ **Sie hat den Entschluss gefasst**, das Rauchen auf**zu**geben
  = she has made up her _mind_ to

◆ **Ich habe beschlossen**, schon morgen ab**zu**reisen
  = I have _decided_ to

◆ Ich gehe **ganz bestimmt** morgen zum Zahnarzt
  = _definitely_

◆ **Ich möchte wirklich** ein paar Kilo abnehmen
  = I'd really like to

◆ **Ich plane** eine Reise nach Ungarn
  = I'm _planning_

◆ **Er ist (wild) entschlossen**, sein ganzes Leben auf den Kopf **zu** stellen
  = he is (really) _determined_ to

8.3 Saying what someone does not intend or want to do

- **Ich möchte** mich **nicht** zu diesem Thema äußern
  = I _would rather_ not

- **Ich hatte eigentlich nicht vor**, an diesem Seminar teil**zu**nehmen
  = I didn't really _intend_ to

- **Ich habe nicht die (geringste) Absicht**, den ganzen Abend Buchungsberichte durch**zu**sehen
  = I have no (not the slightest) _intention_ of

- **Ich habe nicht das Verlangen nach** neuen Abenteuern
  = I have no _desire_ for

- **Ich gedenke nicht**, mich noch einmal auf so ein Unternehmen ein**zu**lassen
  = I don't _propose_ to

- **Ich bin nicht geneigt** mit Ihnen auch noch das Hotelzimmer **zu** teilen
  = I have no _intention_ of

- **Ich bin nicht darauf erpicht**, am Ende wieder als einziger den Kopf hinhalten **zu** müssen
  = I'm not _keen_ on the _idea_ of

- **Es kommt überhaupt nicht infrage, dass** ich morgen schon wieder die Spätschicht übernehme
  = there's absolutely no _question_ of

- Spätabends noch Gruselfilme angucken wollen, **kommt gar nicht in die Tüte**
  = _no way_!

8.4 Saying what you would like to do

- **Ich hätte jetzt Lust auf** eine Partie Schach
  = I _feel like_

- **Ich möchte gerne** die Kunstsammlung besuchen
  = I would _like_ to

- **Ich hätte** ihm **gerne** selbst zu seinem Erfolg gratuliert
  = I would have _liked_ to

- **Wenn ich bloß** mehr Zeit hätte!
  = if only I

- **Es wäre wünschenswert, dass** die Bahn ihr Güterzentrum neben unserem Frachtpostamt baut
  = it is to be _hoped_ that

- **Mein innigster Wunsch ist es**, vor dem Ende meiner Tage noch einmal nach Paris **zu** fahren
  = my dearest _wish_ is to

- **Ich würde** jetzt **wahnsinnig gerne** eine Riesenportion Eis verschlingen
  = what I'd really _love_

9   PERMISSION

9.1 Asking for permission

- **Könnte ich (vielleicht)** in eine andere Arbeitsgruppe wechseln?
  = _could_ I

- **Wäre es möglich, dass** ich der Gerichtsverhandlung beiwohne?
  = _would_ it be possible to

- **Darf ich** mich zu Ihnen setzen?
  = _may_ I

- **Macht es Ihnen etwas aus, wenn** ich rauche?
  = do you _mind_ if

- **Hätten Sie etwas dagegen, wenn** ich das Fenster öffne?
  = _would_ you _mind_ if

- **Mit Ihrer Erlaubnis würde ich gern** einige Änderungen am Grundriss vornehmen
  = with your _permission_ I'd like to

- **Wenn es geht**, möchte ich morgen freinehmen
  = if _possible_

- **Ist** hier Rauchen **gestattet?**
  = is ... _permitted_

- **Sind** Ballspiele in diesem Park **erlaubt?**
  = are ... _permitted_

9.2 Giving permission

- **Ich habe nichts dagegen, wenn** mein Name unter dem Artikel erscheint
  = I don't _object_ to

- **Selbstverständlich können Sie** die Arbeitsgruppe wechseln
  = _of course_ you _can_

- **Gerne gestatten wir Ihnen** Einsicht in unsere Steuerunterlagen
  = we are _pleased_ to _allow_ you

- Rauchen **ist** hier ausdrücklich **gestattet**
  = is _permitted_

- **Sie dürfen** ihm **gerne** berichten, was wir besprochen haben
  = you _can_... if you wish

- **Ich erlaube Ihnen gerne**, morgen einen Tag frei**zu**nehmen
  = I'll happily give you _permission_ to

9.3 Refusing permission

- **Ich möchte nicht, dass** mein Foto in diesem Zusammenhang veröffentlicht wird
  = I do not want

- **Sie können** sich für dieses Seminar **nicht** mehr einschreiben
  = you _can't_

- **Sie sind nicht zu** einer Hausdurchsuchung **befugt**
  = you do not have the _authorization_ for

- **Ich untersage Ihnen (in aller Form)** die Teilnahme an dieser Verstanstaltung
  = I (absolutely) _forbid_ you to

- **Ich verbiete Ihnen**, mein Grundstück **zu** betreten
  = I _forbid_ you to

- **Leider muss ich** diesem Plan **meine Zustimmung verweigern**
  = _unfortunately_ I cannot _consent_ to

- **Ich weigere mich**, diesem waghalsigen Projekt zu**zu**stimmen
  = I _refuse_ to

- **Ich kann dir beim besten Willen nicht erlauben**, bei diesem Wetter mit dem Fahrrad in die Stadt **zu** fahren
  = with the best _will_ in the world I _can't_ _let_ you

9.4 Saying that permission has been granted

- **Wir brauchen** unseren Bericht **erst** nächste Woche ab**zu**geben
  = we don't _need_ to ... until

- **Ich bin bevollmächtigt**, während der Abwesenheit des Chefs Anweisungen **zu** erteilen
  = I am _authorized_ to

- **Ich darf** morgen freinehmen
  = I _can_

- In dieser Prüfung **ist** die Benutzung von Wörterbüchern **gestattet**
  = is _permitted_

9.5 Saying that permission has been refused

- Mein Arzt **hat mir** das Rauchen strengstens **untersagt**
  = has _forbidden_ me to

- **Ich darf** zur Zeit **nicht** arbeiten
  = I _mustn't_

- **Es ist nicht gestattet**, Gefahrenstoffe einfach in den Hausmüll **zu** geben
  = it is _forbidden_ to

- **Es ist** gesetzlich **verboten**, rassistische Äußerungen **zu** publizieren
  = ... is _prohibited_

- **Ich bin nicht berechtigt**, Ihnen Auskünfte über unsere Klienten **zu** erteilen
  = I am not _authorized_ to

- Mein Chef **ist dagegen, dass** ich nächste Woche Urlaub nehme
  = does not _want_

10   OBLIGATION

10.1   Saying what someone must do

* **Sie müssen** sie **unbedingt** um Erlaubnis fragen, ehe Sie renovieren
    = you really <u>must</u>

* **Ich bin verpflichtet**, Sie auf Ihre Rechte aus diesem Kaufvertrag hin**zu**weisen
    = it is my duty to

* **Ich kann nicht umhin**, der Behörde die Einzelheiten mit**zu**teilen
    = I cannot <u>avoid</u>

* Die Zulieferfirmen **sehen sich zu** weiterer Umstrukturierungen **gezwungen**
    = find themselves <u>forced</u> into

* Die Neuregelung der Tierschutzverordnung **ist ein unbedingtes Erfordernis**
    = is absolutely <u>essential</u>

* **Es ist gesetzlich vorgeschrieben**, alle Inhaltsstoffe auf der Verpackung an**zu**geben
    = the law <u>demands</u>

* Alle Einwohner **sind aufgefordert**, den Anweisungen der Rettungsdienste Folge **zu** leisten
    = are <u>requested</u> to

* Der Mieter hat pünktlich am 1. des Monats den fälligen Betrag **zu** überweisen
    = <u>must</u>

* **Ohne** Hits **kann man** im Musikgeschäft **nicht** überleben
    = no-one can ... without

* **Es bleibt mir wohl nichts anderes übrig, als** die unangenehme Aufgabe selbst **zu** übernehmen
    = the only thing left for me to do is

* **Ich habe keine andere Wahl, als** gute Miene zum bösen Spiel **zu** machen
    = I have no <u>choice</u> but to

10.2   Enquiring if one is obliged to do something

* **Muss ich (wirklich)** zu Hause bleiben?
    = do I (really) <u>have</u> <u>to</u>

* **Brauche ich** eine Einladung?
    = do I <u>need</u>

* **Ist es (wirklich) nötig**, noch heute Abend ab**zu**reisen?
    = do I/we really <u>have</u> to

* **Erwartet man wirklich allen Ernstes von mir, dass** ich diesen Unsinn gutheiße?
    = am I really <u>expected</u> to

10.3   Saying what someone is not obliged to do

* **Es ist nicht nötig,** vorher noch einmal an**zu**rufen
    = you don't <u>have</u> <u>to</u>

* **Es ist Ihnen freigestellt, ob** Sie den gesamten Betrag sofort oder in Raten zahlen
    = you can choose whether

* **Es zwingt Sie niemand**, an diesem Treffen teil**zu**nehmen
    = no-one is <u>forcing</u> you to

* **Ich kann Sie nicht zu** einem Geständnis **zwingen,** aber früher oder später finde ich doch die Wahrheit heraus
    = I can't <u>force</u> you into

* **Sie sind nicht verpflichtet**, den Unfall **zu** melden
    = it is not <u>compulsory</u> to

* **Sie müssen ja nicht** in der Kantine essen, **wenn** es Ihnen dort nicht schmeckt
    = you don't <u>have</u> to ... if

10.4   Saying what someone must not do

* Unbefugten betreten **verboten!**
    = <u>prohibited</u>

* **Es ist nicht gestattet**, hier **zu** parken
    = it is <u>forbidden</u> to

* **Sie können nicht einfach** die Mittagspause für private Erledigungen nutzen
    = you <u>can't</u> simply

* **Sie dürfen nicht von vornherein** mit einer Gehaltserhöhung rechnen
    = you <u>can't</u> automatically

* **Auf gar keinen Fall dürfen Sie** einer Verfassungsänderung zustimmen
    = whatever you do, don't

* **Ich verbiete Ihnen**, mein Büro je wieder **zu** betreten
    = I <u>forbid</u> you to

* **Wir können nicht zulassen, dass** die Sozialausgaben noch weiter gekürzt werden
    = we <u>cannot</u> <u>allow</u> ... to

11   AGREEMENT

11.1   Agreeing with a statement

* **Ich bin ganz Ihrer Meinung**
    = I entirely <u>agree</u>

* Das Museum ist ein Ort der Inspiration – **Ich kann Ihnen da nur beipflichten**
    = I entirely <u>agree</u> (with you)

* **Ich teile Ihre Meinung zum** Verhältniswahlrecht **uneingeschränkt**
    = I <u>agree</u> <u>wholeheartedly</u> with your <u>opinion</u> on

* **Ich schließe mich** den Worten des Vorredners **an**
    = I entirely <u>endorse</u>

* **Ich stehe voll hinter** dieser Erklärung
    = I entirely <u>agree</u> with

* **Ich muss gestehen, dass** er Recht hat
    = I must <u>admit</u> he's <u>right</u>

* **Sie haben natürlich Recht, wenn** Sie ihn einen Verbrecher nennen, aber sagen Sie das lieber nicht laut
    = you are quite <u>right</u> to

* **Wie Sie schon richtig bemerkt haben**, muss die Produktivität des neuen Standortes noch deutlich gesteigert werden
    = as you so <u>rightly</u> say

* **Im Großen und Ganzen stimme ich Ihnen zu, wenn** Sie gegen diese unseriösen Praktiken protestieren
    = broadly speaking, I <u>agree</u> with you

* **Ich neige sehr zu Ihrer Ansicht, dass** die Anklage eine unverhältnismäßig hohe Haftstrafe gefordert hat
    = I am very much inclined to <u>agree</u> with you

* Der Baum hinter dem Haus muss weg – **Meine Rede!**
    = <u>hear</u>, <u>hear</u>!

11.2   Agreeing to a proposal

* **Ich bin mit** Ihrem Vorschlag **(voll und ganz) einverstanden**
    = I am in (complete) <u>agreement</u> with

* **Ich gehe auf Ihren Vorschlag ein** und werde mich um alles Weitere kümmern
    = I <u>agree</u> with your proposal

* **Wir schließen uns** Ihrem Vorschlag **gerne an**
    = we are happy to <u>agree</u> to/with

* **Er hat** Ihrem Vorschlag **zugestimmt, ich bin auch dafür**
    = he <u>agrees</u> with ... and I am in <u>favour</u> (of it) <u>as</u> <u>well</u>

* Er ist in diesem Falle zwar nicht sachkundig, **geht** aber **mit unserer Entscheidung konform**
    = <u>agrees</u> with our decision

* **Ich werde** dieses interessante Projekt **nach Kräften unterstützen**
    = I will give my full <u>support</u> to

* **Ich gebe gern meine Einwilligung zu** den neuen Vorhaben
    = I am happy to <u>agree</u> to

◆ **Hiermit gebe ich mein Einverständnis zur** gewerblichen Nutzung der Räume im Erdgeschoss des Hauses Augustusplatz 9
= I hereby give my _consent to_

◆ Wir könnten ins Kino gehen – **Gute Idee!**
= _good idea!_

11.3 Agreeing to a request

◆ **Ich nehme** Ihre freundliche Einladung **mit großem Vergnügen an**
= I have much pleasure in _accepting_

◆ **Gerne komme ich Ihrer Bitte nach** und begleiche die offen stehenden Rechnungen noch diese Woche
= I am happy to _comply with your request_

◆ **Ich werde mich selbstverständlich an** Ihre Anweisungen **halten**
= I will, _of course, follow_

◆ **Ich werde mich bei** der Auswahl der Stoffe **ganz nach Ihren Wünschen richten**
= I will _respect_ your wishes completely in the matter of

◆ **Es wird mir ein besonderes Vergnügen sein**, Sie persönlich vom Bahnhof abzuholen
= I shall be _delighted_ to

◆ Der vorgeschlagene Termin **passt mir sehr gut**
= _suits_ me perfectly

◆ Die Verschiebung der Sitzung **kommt mir sehr gelegen**
= _suits_ me perfectly

12 DISAGREEMENT

12.1 Disagreeing with a statement

◆ **Ich bin nicht damit einverstanden, dass** wir ihm allein die Schuld geben
= I don't _agree_ that

◆ **Ich teile Ihre Meinung zu** dieser Frage **nicht**
= I don't _share_ your views on

◆ **Ich kann Ihren Standpunkt unmöglich akzeptieren**
= I really _cannot accept_ your point of view

◆ **Ich muss Ihnen widersprechen:** Sein Kunstbegriff ist sehr vage gefasst
= I _disagree_

◆ **Ich kann mich Ihrer Interpretation** von Goethes Spätwerk **nicht anschließen**
= I _cannot subscribe_ to your interpretation

◆ **Ich möchte bestreiten, dass** dies das Ende seiner Karriere ist
= I don't _agree_ that

◆ **Ihren Schlussfolgerungen kann ich nicht zustimmen**
= I _disagree_ with your conclusions

◆ **Ich verstehe nicht, wie** Sie zu dieser Schlussfolgerung kommen
= I don't _understand_ how

◆ Das mag ja Ihre Ansicht sein, **ich sehe die Sache anders**
= I _see_ things differently

◆ **Sie gehen fehl in der Annahme**, der Roman habe keinen Bezug zur Wirklichkeit
= your assumption that ... is _mistaken_

◆ **Sie liegen falsch, wenn Sie** behaupten, die Verkehrsprobleme ließen sich durch höhere Benzinpreise lösen
= you are _wrong_ to

◆ **Sie irren sich, wenn** Sie meinen, man könne diese Affäre so einfach unter den Teppich kehren
= you are _mistaken_ if

◆ **Sie täuschen sich in ihr**: Sie ist gar nicht so unschuldig, wie sie uns glauben machen will
= you are _wrong_ about her

◆ **Wie können Sie behaupten, dass** ausgerechnet die Rentner die Gewinner der Einheit sind?
= how _can_ you say that

◆ **Ich verwahre mich gegen** solche Vorwürfe
= I _object_ to

◆ **Ich bin völlig gegen** diese hinterhältigen Machenschaften
= I am completely _opposed_ to

12.2 Disagreeing with a proposal

◆ **Ich kann Ihren Vorschlag nicht gutheißen**
= I _cannot agree_ to your proposal

◆ **Ich kann** Ihren Vorschlag **nicht uneingeschränkt billigen**
= I _can't give_ ... my unqualified _support_

◆ **Ich halte nicht viel von** dieser Variante
= I don't _think much_ of

◆ **Vielen Dank für Ihr freundliches Angebot, aber** ich komme allein zurecht
= thank you very much for your kind offer, but

◆ **Es tut mir Leid aber ich kann** Ihren Vorschlag **nicht annehmen**
= I am sorry but I _cannot accept_

◆ **Sie können** Ihr Programm jetzt **wirklich nicht** mehr ändern
= you really _cannot_

◆ **Wir protestieren in aller Schärfe gegen** den geplanten Autobahnneubau
= we wish to _protest_ in the strongest possible terms against

◆ **Von** solchen Tagträumen **will ich nichts mehr hören**
= I don't _want_ to _hear_ any _more_ about

◆ **Du glaubst doch nicht im Ernst, dass** ich mich auf solchen Unsinn einlasse
= you don't _seriously_ think that

◆ **Ich weigere mich**, damit meine kostbare Zeit **zu** vertun
= I _refuse_ to

12.3 Refusing a request

◆ **Leider kann ich Ihrer Bitte nicht nachkommen**
= I am _afraid_ I _cannot_ fulfil your request

◆ **Ich kann** Ihre Wünsche **leider nicht erfüllen**
= I am _afraid_ I _cannot_ comply with

◆ **Es ist mir leider nicht möglich**, Sie am Dienstag in meinem Büro **zu** empfangen
= I am _afraid_ I will not be able to

◆ **Ich bin nicht in der Lage**, Ihnen Auskünfte **zu** erteilen
= I am not in a _position_ to

◆ **Ich kann das unmöglich** bis Freitag **schaffen**
= I _can't possibly_ manage it

◆ **Sie können unmöglich von mir verlangen, dass** ich die ganze Woche Überstunden mache
= you _cannot_ expect me to

◆ **Es kommt überhaupt nicht infrage, dass** Sie meine Sekretärin für Ihre Schreibarbeiten in Anspruch nehmen
= it is _out of the question_ for ... to

◆ **Es fällt mir nicht im Traum ein**, Ihrer Bitte um Gehaltserhöhung nach**zu**kommen
= I _wouldn't dream_ of

| In writing |

◆ Ich danke Ihnen vielmals für Ihre freundliche Einladung, **muss aber leider ablehnen**, da ich schon eine Verabredung habe
= but I am _afraid_ I must _decline_

◆ **Leider müssen wir Ihnen mitteilen, dass** die bestellten Artikel zur Zeit nicht auf Lager sind
= we _regret_ to have to _inform_ you that

13 APPROVAL

◆ **Wirklich eine gute** or **tolle Idee!**
= what a _great idea!_

◆ **Gut, dass** Sie uns so bald Bescheid gegeben haben
= (this context): thank you for

◆ **Sie haben Recht, wenn** Sie sich über diese Arbeitsbedingungen beschweren
= you are _right_ to ...

◆ **Wir sind mit Ihrer Entscheidung**, heute nicht mehr nach Paris abzureisen, **einverstanden**
= we _agree_ with your decision

◆ **Ich schätze** Ihre Offenheit in dieser Frage **sehr**
= I greatly _appreciate_

◆ **Ich finde es gut, dass Sie** sich auf die wesentlichen Punkte beschränkt haben
= I think you were _right_ to ...

◆ **Es hat mir gut gefallen, dass** die Diskussion sachlich verlaufen ist
= I _liked_ the way

◆ **Es spricht sehr für ihn, dass** er sich erst jetzt mit dieser Bitte an Sie gewandt hat
= it _says_ a lot for him that

◆ Dieser neue Vorschlag **verdient unsere Aufmerksamkeit**
= deserves our _attention_

◆ Der Entwurf des Bühnenbildes **ist** ihm **sehr gelungen**
= turned out really _well_

◆ **Ich hätte es selbst nicht besser machen können**
= I _couldn't_ have made a _better_ job of it myself

More formally

◆ **Wir stimmen im Großen und Ganzen** Ihren Vorschlägen **zu**, würden aber gern einige Details verändern
= we are in broad _agreement_ with

◆ Der Autor **betont** diesen Aspekt **(völlig) zu Recht**
= (quite) _rightly_ emphasizes

◆ **Man kann** ihren klaren Stil und ihre Eleganz **nur bewundern**
= one can only _admire_

◆ **Wir sind von** ihrer Arbeitsweise **sehr beeindruckt**
= we are very _impressed_ with

◆ **Wir begrüßen** Ihre Eigeninitiative auf diesem Gebiet
= we _welcome_

◆ **Wir sind hoch erfreut über** diese positive Entwicklung
= we are _delighted_ about

◆ Sein Vortrag **hat auf uns einen hervorragenden Eindruck gemacht**
= we were enormously _impressed_ by

◆ **Ich möchte meine Unterstützung für** diese gute Sache **betonen**
= I would like to express my complete _support_ for

◆ **Ich habe eine hohe Meinung von** seiner Forschungsarbeit
= I have a high _opinion_ of

◆ Der Vorschlag, die Gewerbesteuer abzuschaffen, **wurde mit Wohlwollen zur Kenntnis genommen**
= was given a _favourable_ _reception_

---

14   DISAPPROVAL

◆ **Ich bin mit** Ihrem Umgangston **gar nicht einverstanden**
= I really don't _approve_ of

◆ **Ich bin gar nicht glücklich über** seine Wahl zum Parteivorsitzenden
= I am far from _happy_ about

◆ **Ich halte nicht viel von** seiner Interpretation des Mephisto
= I don't _think_ much _of_

◆ **Ich bin von** den Leistungen dieses Schülers **sehr enttäuscht**
= I am very _disappointed_ with

◆ **Ich muss energisch gegen** diese Vorwürfe **protestieren**
= I must _protest_ in the strongest possible terms against

◆ Die Kunden **sind nicht gerade begeistert von** unserer neuen Marketingstrategie
= are not particularly _enthusiastic_ about

◆ **Wir sind gegen** eine totale Preiskontrolle
= we are _opposed_ _to_

◆ **Das hätte** Ihnen **wirklich nicht** passieren **dürfen**
= that really _should_ not have

◆ **Er hätte besser** die Polizei verständigt
= he would have been _wiser_ to ...

◆ **Ich finde, es war falsch**, gleich so ausfällig **zu** werden
= I think it was _wrong_ to

◆ **Es gefällt mir überhaupt nicht, dass** ausgerechnet diese Firma mit dem Bau beauftragt wurde
= I'm not at all _happy_ that

◆ **Es ist wirklich schade, dass** die Stadt diese Truppe nicht mehr finanziell unterstützt
= it is a real _shame_ that

◆ **Es ist zu bedauern, dass** dieses verantwortungslose Vorgehen wieder zu Gewaltausbrüchen geführt hat
= it is _regrettable_ that

◆ **Es passt mir gar nicht, dass** wir morgen schon wieder Besuch bekommen
= it is really _inconvenient_ that

◆ Alle Parteien **verurteilten** diesen Anschlag **einstimmig**
= were united in their _condemnation_ of

◆ **Man darf** diese undemokratischen Umtriebe **nicht tolerieren**
= we must not _tolerate_

◆ **Ich bin eine erklärte Gegnerin** jeglicher Tierversuche
= I am an avowed _opponent_ of

◆ **Was fällt dir ein**, mich so anzu**schreien**
= how _dare_ you

15.1   Expressing certainty

In an impersonal way

◆ **Es gibt nicht den geringsten Zweifel, dass** dieses Gesetz morgen verabschiedet wird
= there is absolutely no _doubt_ that

◆ **Es lässt sich kaum bestreiten, dass** die Arbeitslosenzahlen in dieser Region sehr hoch sind
= no-one can _deny_ that

◆ **Es steht völlig außer Frage, dass** die Flüchtlinge in ihre Heimat zurückgeschickt werden
= there is no _doubt_ that

◆ **Es versteht sich von selbst, dass** alle Abgeordneten zur ersten Sitzung erscheinen
= it goes without saying that

◆ **Es hat sich deutlich gezeigt, dass** man auf dem glatten Parkett der Börse auch ausrutschen kann
= it has been _clearly_ _established_ that

◆ **Es lässt sich nicht leugnen, dass** das Waldsterben weiter um sich greift
= no-one can _deny_ that

◆ **Man muss sich darüber im Klaren sein, dass** diese Friedensmission erhebliche Risiken birgt
= it _must_ be realized that

◆ **Zweifellos** wird sich die wirtschaftliche Lage noch weiter verschlechtern
= _undoubtedly_

◆ **Tatsache ist, dass** sich das ökonomische Klima deutlich verbessert hat
= _the_ _fact_ _is_ _that_

◆ Eine Neuregelung **lässt sich nicht vermeiden**
= is _inevitable_

More directly

◆ **Wir können mit Sicherheit sagen, dass** wichtige Informationen ohne unsere Zustimmung weitergegeben wurden
= we _know_ _for_ _certain_ that

◆ **Ich versichere Ihnen, dass** wir das Problem bis morgen gelöst haben
  = I can _assure_ you that

◆ **Ich bin mir sicher, dass** ich den Brief gestern abgeschickt habe
  = I am _sure_ that

◆ **Er ist davon überzeugt, dass** er die Goldmedaille gewinnen wird
  = he is _convinced_ that

◆ Sie hören von meinem Anwalt. **Verlassen Sie sich darauf!**
  = you can be _sure_ of that

15.2 Expressing probability

◆ **Höchstwahrscheinlich** ist dieses Verfahren rechtswidrig
  = it is highly _probable_ that

◆ **Wahrscheinlich** wird die Sitzung vertagt
  = _probably_

◆ **Aller Wahrscheinlichkeit nach** schlägt die Therapie an
  = in all _probability_

◆ **Anscheinend** kann er nie genug kriegen
  = it _looks as if_

◆ **Es besteht Grund zu der Annahme, dass** er von seinen Zielen abgerückt ist
  = there are _grounds for_ believing that

◆ **Es deutet alles darauf hin, dass** er zu schnell gefahren ist
  = everything _points to_ the fact that

◆ **Es sieht fast so aus, als** hätten die Spieler alles verlernt
  = it _looks as though_

◆ **Es könnte gut sein, dass** ich heute Abend kurz vorbeischaue
  = ... _might well_

◆ **Es dürfte zu spät für** eine Sanierung der maroden Finanzen **sein**
  = it _may well_ be too late for

◆ **Es muss** ihm etwas passiert sein
  = _must_ have happened

◆ Das Päckchen **müsste** morgen bei Ihnen ankommen
  = _should_

◆ **Es sollte mich nicht überraschen, wenn** er jeden Moment wie ein Unschuldslamm hier hereinspaziert kommt
  = it wouldn't _surprise_ me if

◆ **Es würde mich überhaupt nicht wundern, wenn** er wieder zu spät kommt
  = I wouldn't be at all _surprised_ if

◆ **Ich werde wohl** nächste Woche nicht da sein
  = I _probably_

◆ **Ich sehe es schon kommen, dass** ich noch einmal von ganz vorne anfangen muss
  = I can _see_ it coming

15.3 Expressing possibility

◆ **Vielleicht** ist das der neue Deutschlehrer
  = _perhaps_

◆ **Es könnte unter Umständen schon zu spät sein**, um sich noch einzuschreiben
  = it might already be too late

◆ Die Lage **kann sich** von einem Tag zum anderen schlagartig **ändern**
  = _could_ change

◆ **Es ist immerhin möglich, dass** man Ihnen nicht die Wahrheit gesagt hat
  = after all, it is _possible_ that

◆ **Es besteht die Möglichkeit, dass** uns die Konkurrenz zuvorgekommen ist
  = there is a _possibility_ that

◆ **Es sieht so aus, als könnten wir** den Bericht doch noch bis morgen fertig stellen
  = it _looks as though_ we should be able to ...

◆ Sehen Sie sich das Haus gut an: **Es käme eventuell als** Bürogebäude **für uns infrage**
  = we _might think about_ it for our

◆ **Es ist durchaus im Rahmen des Möglichen, dass** das Parlament einer Verfassungsänderung zustimmt
  = it is quite within the bounds of _possibility_ that

◆ Vier Fünftel aller Maschinenbaubetriebe sind **potenziell** bankrott
  = _potentially_

15.4 Expressing capability

◆ **Können Sie** mit einem Computer umgehen?
  = do you _know_ how

◆ **Er kann** hervorragend Gitarre spielen
  = he _can_

◆ Alle Bewerber sollten **in der Lage sein**, einfache technische Texte zu übersetzen
  = be _able_ to

◆ **Wissen Sie, wie** diese neue Maschine bedient wird?
  = do you _know_ how

---

16 DOUBT, IMPROBABILITY, IMPOSSIBILITY AND INCAPABILITY

16.1 Expressing doubt

In an impersonal way

◆ **Es ist zweifelhaft, ob** der Außenminister dem Druck der Verhandlungspartner gewachsen ist
  = it is _doubtful_ whether

◆ **Es besteht immer noch Ungewissheit über** die Zahl der Todesopfer
  = there is still some _uncertainty_ about

◆ **Es ist immer noch nicht sicher, ob** er krank ist oder nur simuliert
  = it is still not _certain_ whether

◆ **Es lässt sich noch nicht mit Sicherheit sagen, ob** das Opfer den Anschlagüberleben wird
  = it is still _impossible_ to say with any _certainty_ whether

◆ **Es gibt keinen Grund zu der Annahme, dass** diese Methode umweltfreundlicher ist
  = there is no _reason_ to assume that

◆ **Das muss nicht unbedingt bedeuten, dass** sich die wirtschaftliche Lage schlagartig verbessern wird
  = that does not _necessarily mean_ that

More directly

◆ **Ich bezweifle, dass** ich das Pensum bis heute Abend schaffe
  = I _doubt_ if

◆ **Ich glaube nicht, dass wir je** einen derart waghalsigen Plan hatten
  = I don't _think_ we ever

◆ **Ich bin nicht sicher, ob** ich Ihnen die richtige Zahl genannt habe
  = I'm not _sure_ whether

◆ **Ich bin nicht überzeugt, dass** diese Methode funktioniert
  = I'm not _sure_ whether

◆ **Ich frage mich, ob** es sich überhaupt lohnt, sich so viel Mühe zu machen
  = I _wonder_ if

◆ **Es würde mich sehr wundern, wenn** er noch einmal wiederkäme
  = I would be very _surprised_ if

◆ **Wir wissen noch immer nicht genau, wie** wir das Wohnzimmer streichen wollen
  = we still _don't know_ exactly how

◆ **Sie tappen immer noch im Dunkeln, was** das Motiv für die Tat **angeht**
  = they are still _in the dark about_

16.2 Expressing improbability

◆ Einen Sieger wird es am Sonntag **wahrscheinlich nicht** geben
  = _probably_ not

+ **Es ist höchst unwahrscheinlich, dass** die Regierung auf Atomenergie verzichtet
  = it is highly _unlikely_ that

+ **Es besteht die Gefahr, dass** Sie Ihren Pass nicht mehr rechtzeitig bekommen
  = there is a _risk_ that

+ **Es ist fraglich, ob** der Verein sich in der Bundesliga halten kann
  = it is _doubtful_ whether

+ **Es würde mich wirklich überraschen, wenn** er diese Prüfung besteht
  = I would be very _surprised_ if

+ **Allem Anschein nach ist** sie **nicht** wirklich krank
  = to _all_ _appearances_ ... is not

+ **Die Chancen**, diesen Winter ohne Grippe **zu** überstehen, **sind äußerst gering**
  = the _chances_ of ... are very slim

+ **Ich fürchte, dass es uns nicht gelingen wird**, ihn **zu** überzeugen
  = I am _afraid_ that we will not succeed in

+ **Sollte wider Erwarten doch** etwas Passendes dabei sein, gebe ich Ihnen Bescheid
  = in the _unlikely_ event that

+ Ein Umschwung der öffentlichen Meinung **steht nicht zu erwarten**
  = is not to be _expected_

16.3   Expressing impossibility

+ **Es ist unmöglich, dass** diese Schäden beim Verladen entstanden sind
  = ... _cannot possibly_

+ **Es ist ausgeschlossen, dass** wir Ihnen schon nächste Woche fertige Skizzen zeigen können
  = there is _no way we can_

+ **Es kann sich einfach nicht um** ein und dieselbe Person **handeln**
  = it _can't possibly_ be

+ **Ich kann mir unmöglich** nächste Woche schon wieder freinehmen
  = I _can't possibly_

+ **Auf gar keinen Fall** wird diese Übersetzung noch vor Weihnachten fertig
  = there is _no way that_

+ Leider **ist es mir nicht möglich**, diese Einladung an**zu**nehmen
  = I am _unable_ to

+ Eine Zusammenarbeit mit dieser Firma **kommt nicht infrage**
  = is out of the _question_

+ Der Staatsstreich **macht** jede Verhandlung fürs Erste **unmöglich**
  = has _ruled out_

+ **Es besteht nicht die geringste Möglichkeit** einer friedlichen Lösung
  = there is not the remotest _chance_ of

16.4   Expressing incapability

+ **Ich kann nicht** schwimmen
  = I _can't_

+ **Ich kann kein** Französisch
  = I don't speak

+ **Er ist nicht in der Lage** or **imstande**, selbstständig Entscheidungen **zu** fällen
  = he is totally _incapable_ of

+ **Ich weiß nicht, wie** man Topfkuchen bäckt
  = I don't _know_ how

+ **Er hat einfach kein Talent für** Sprachen
  = he has simply no _gift_ for

+ **Er ist zu** einer solchen Tat **nicht fähig**
  = he is _incapable_ of

+ **Ich bin nicht sehr gut** in Mathematik
  = I am not very _good_ at

+ **Sie waren** dieser schweren Aufgabe **nicht gewachsen**
  = they were not _up to_

---

17   EXPLANATIONS

17.1   Emphasizing the reason for something

+ **Angesichts** der schwierigen Finanzlage müssen wir das Projekt vorerst auf Eis legen
  = _in view of_

+ **In Anbetracht der Tatsache, dass** die Wahlen über die Macht entscheiden, ist es logisch, dass die Siegerparteien Einfluss auf die Medien gewinnen
  = _in view of_ the fact that

+ **Dank** steigender Auftragszahlen wird sich der Umsatz erhöhen
  = _thanks to_

+ Die U-Bahn-Station wurde **aus** Sicherheits**gründen** geschlossen
  = _for ... reasons_

+ Er wurde **aus Mangel an** Beweisen freigesprochen
  = for _lack_ of

+ Kurzsichtigkeit läßt sich **mittels** Lasertherapie behandeln
  = _by means of_

+ **Bei** solchen Windverhältnissen sollte man sich besser nicht aufs offene Meer wagen
  = _in_

+ **Durch** seine Popularität hat er einen gewissen Einfluss auf die Medien
  = _through_

+ **Aufgrund** der schlechten Sichtverhältnisse verschiebt sich der Abflug auf unbestimmte Zeit
  = _owing to_

+ **Wegen** des erhöhten Koffeingehaltes sollte dieses Produkt nur in geringen Mengen verzehrt werden
  = _because of_

+ **Infolge** des Konsums berauschender Mittel war der Angeklagte nicht zurechnungsfähig
  = _as a result of_

+ Mehrere Bauarbeiter fanden den Tod, **weil** die Gerüste nur unzureichend gesichert waren
  = _because_

+ Wir haben Ihren Roman nicht lesen können, **denn** wir sind ein Verlag und kein Lektürezirkel
  = _because_

+ Fruchtsäfte sollten nicht eiskalt getrunken werden, **da** sonst leicht eine Magenreizung entstehen kann
  = _as_

+ Er ist ohnmächtig geworden und **deswegen** erinnert er sich an nichts mehr
  = _therefore_

+ Sie hat die Angestellten **nur aus dem einen Grund** zusammengerufen, **um** mit ihnen ein Machtwort **zu** reden
  = simply (in order) to

+ Der Präsident verurteilte den Bericht **mit der Begründung**, er enthalte nicht zu rechtfertigende Schlussfolgerungen
  = _claiming_

+ **Wenn** ihm keine überzeugende Erklärung für sein Handeln einfällt, wird er sich schon bald vor dem Militärgericht wiederfinden
  = _if_

+ **Solange** keine Besserung eintritt, dürfen Sie das Haus nicht verlassen
  = _as long as_

17.2   Other useful vocabulary

+ **Die** Unfall**ursache war** überhöhte Geschwindigkeit bei schlechter Sicht
  = the ... was _caused_ by

+ **Das war so**: Ich stand auf der Leiter, als es an der Tür klingelte ...
  = it was _like_ this:

+ **Es geht um Folgendes**: Ich möchte gerne meine Wohnung renovieren
  = it's _like_ this:

◆ **Das Problem ist**, dass wir ziemlich weit weg vom Bahnhof wohnen
= *the _trouble_ is,*

◆ **Die Sache ist die**: Ich habe ihm den Kredit schon versprochen
= *the _thing_ is,*

◆ **Es lässt sich alles auf** diese Versorgungsprobleme **zurückführen**
= *it is all _due/down_ to*

◆ **Das lässt sich alles aus** seiner Weltanschauung **herleiten**
= *all _stems_ _from_*

◆ Der Börsenkrach **hat** diese Katastrophe **ausgelöst**
= *_triggered_ off*

◆ **Das lässt sich** alles **durch** die Zerstörung der Regenwälder **erklären**
= *can be _attributed_ _to_*

◆ **Woran liegt es, dass** der Neubau nicht vorankommt?
= *_why_ is it that*

◆ **Das hat** natürlich wieder **mit** dem Treibhauseffekt **zu tun**
= *is _connected_ with*

◆ **Es hat sich** dann **herausgestellt, dass** er gar kein Kapital hatte
= *it _emerged_ that*

◆ **Ich schreibe das alles** seinem krankhaften Ehrgeiz **zu**
= *I _put_ it all _down_ _to_*

◆ **Und aus genau diesem Grund** möchte ich nicht, dass Sie mir helfen
= *that is _exactly_ why*

◆ **Der Grund für** ihren kometenhaften Aufstieg ist wohl nicht nur in ihrer unbestrittenen Begabung, sondern auch in ihrem Fleiß zu suchen
= *the _reason_ for*

◆ Sein plötzliches Verschwinden **gab Anlass zu** wüsten Spekulationen
= *gave _rise_ to*

---

18   APOLOGIES

18.1   Apologizing for one's actions

◆ **Entschuldigen Sie bitte**, ich habe mich verwählt
= *I'm _sorry_*

◆ **Bitte verzeihen Sie, dass ich nicht** früher angerufen habe
= *please _forgive_ me for not*

◆ **Es tut mir schrecklich Leid, dass** ich gestern nicht kommen konnte
= *I'm terribly _sorry_ that*

◆ **Ich möchte Sie wirklich wegen** dieses Missverständnisses **um Entschuldigung bitten**
= *I really must _apologize_ for*

◆ **Können Sie mir** noch einmal **verzeihen, dass ich** die Karten nicht besorgt habe?
= *can you _forgive_ me for*

◆ **Es ist einfach unverzeihlich, dass ich** ihren Geburtstag vergessen **habe**
= *it was _unforgivable_ of me to ...*

◆ **Ich bitte tausendmal um Entschuldigung!** Ich wollte Ihnen nicht zu nahe treten
= *I really am most terribly _sorry_*

◆ **Wir möchten Sie wegen** des bedauerlichen Zwischenfalls **in aller Form um Verzeihung bitten**
= *we should like to _offer_ our most sincere _apologies_ for*

◆ **Dürfen wir Sie wegen** der gestrigen Störung **um Nachsicht bitten**
= *we hope that you will _forgive_ us for*

◆ **Ich bedaure zutiefst, dass** Sie sich durch meine Ausführungen in Ihrer persönlichen Ehre gekränkt sehen
= *I greatly _regret_ that*

18.2   Apologizing for being unable to do something

◆ **Es ist wirklich schade, aber** wir können euch nicht begleiten
= *it is a real _shame_, but*

◆ **Bedauerlicherweise** können wir Ihren Artikel in der Märzausgabe nicht mehr veröffentlichen
= *regrettably*

◆ **Zu unserem größten Bedauern** können wir Ihrer Einladung nicht nachkommen
= *much to our _regret_*

◆ **Ich bin untröstlich darüber, dass** ich Ihren Vortrag versäumen muss
= *I am deeply _sorry_ that*

◆ **Wir müssen Ihnen leider mittteilen, dass** Ihr Antrag abgelehnt wurde
= *we _regret_ to inform you that*

◆ **Ich kann es mir nicht verzeihen, dass** ich Ihnen in dieser für Sie so schweren Zeit nicht beistehen konnte
= *I cannot _forgive_ myself for*

18.3   Admitting responsibility

◆ **Es ist ganz allein meine Schuld, ich hätte** sie **nicht** allein lassen **dürfen**
= *it's entirely my _fault_: I shouldn't have*

◆ **Ich übernehme die volle Verantwortung für** diesen Irrtum
= *I take full _responsibility_ for*

◆ **Wir hatten keine andere Wahl, als** die Polizei zu informieren
= *we had no _choice_ but to*

◆ **Wir waren der irrigen Meinung, dass** wir Ihnen damit helfen würden
= *we mistakenly believed that*

◆ **Es war ein Fehler unserer Buchhaltung, dass** Sie zwei Rechnungen über den gleichen Betrag bekommen haben
= *because of an _error_ in our Accounts Department*

◆ **Das hätte ich nie** sagen sollen
= *I should _never_ have*

◆ **Ich weiß, dass es nicht richtig war**, ihm das Auto **zu** leihen, aber ...
= *I know I was _wrong_ to*

◆ **Ich gebe zu, dass** ich vielleicht nicht gut vorbereitet war, **aber** ...
= *I _admit_ that ... but*

◆ **Hätte ich doch nie** ein Sterbenswörtchen gesagt!
= *I _wish_ I had _never_*

◆ **Dummerweise** habe ich dann gleich bei ihnen angerufen
= *foolishly*

18.4   Disclaiming responsibility

◆ **Ich hoffe, dass Sie Verständnis für** diese Verzögerung **haben**, die sich ohne unsere Schuld ergeben hat
= *I hope that you will pardon*

◆ **Sicher können Sie verstehen, dass** wir in dieser Situation gar nicht anders reagieren konnten
= *I am sure that you will _appreciate_ that*

◆ **Ich habe** diese Vase **ganz bestimmt nicht mit Absicht** fallen lassen, sie ist mir aus der Hand gerutscht
= *I _certainly_ didn't ... _deliberately_*

◆ **Es war doch nur meine Absicht, Sie nicht** mit solchen Kleinigkeiten **zu belästigen**
= *I simply _wanted_ to avoid bothering you*

◆ **Ich weiß (auch) nicht, wie das passieren konnte**
= *I don't know how it happened (either)*

---

19   JOB APPLICATIONS

19.1   Opening the letter

◆ **Ich beziehe mich auf** Ihre Stellenanzeige in der heutigen Ausgabe der „Süddeutschen Zeitung" **und möchte Sie bitten, mir nähere Angaben über** die Stelle **zuzusenden**
= *in _reply_ to ... I should be grateful if you would please send me _further_ _details_ of*

◆ **Ich möchte mich um die Stelle** einer Reiseleiterin **bewerben, die Sie** im „Globus" vom Mai **ausgeschrieben haben**
= *I wish to _apply_ for the _post_ of ... which you advertised*

19 Job Applications

LEBENSLAUF

Persönliche Daten:	Müller, Dorothea Hinter dem Stausee 25 60388 Frankfurt/Main Tel.: 069/324 754 Fax: 069/324 755 geb. am 21.04.1964 in Nürnberg ledig
Schulausbildung:[1]	
1970 - 1974	Grundschule Nürnberg
1974 - 1983	Humboldt-Gymnasium Nürnberg
Hochschulausbildung:[2]	
10/1983 - 4/1989	Goethe-Universität Frankfurt/Main Studium der Psychologie Schwerpunkte: Betriebs- und Arbeitspsychologie
Praktika:	
1985	Personalabteilung Volkswagen, Wolfsburg
1987	Marketingabteilung Siemens, München
Berufspraxis:	
6/89 - 6/92	Wissenschaftliche Assistentin Lehrstuhl für Arbeitspsychologie Goethe-Universität Frankfurt/Main
7/92 - 6/94	Tutor für Organisationspsychologie Universität Birmingham/Großbritannien
seit 7/94	Referentin für Arbeitspsychologie bei der IHK Frankfurt/Main
Besondere Kenntnisse:	
EDV	Textverarbeitung (Word für Windows) Tabellenkalkulation (Excel) Präsentationsprogramme (PowerPoint)
Fremdsprachen	Englisch sehr gut Russisch Grundkenntnisse

Frankfurt/Main,
31. Juli 1999

---

[1] People with British or American etc qualifications applying for jobs in a German-speaking country might use some form of wording like "entspricht Abitur (3 A-levels)", "entspricht Staatsprüfung (MA Hons)" etc.

[2] Note that when applying for a job in Germany you must send photocopies of certificates for all qualifications gained as well as your CV.

[3] This address is appropriate when writing to a firm or institution. However, when writing to the holder of a particular post, you should put:

*An den
Personaldirektor
"Mensch und Maschine" GmbH* etc.

In this case, you should begin your letter with "Sehr geehrter Herr Personaldirektor" and end with "mit freundlichen Grüßen".

If you know the name of the person you should write:

*An Herrn
Josef Schmidthuber
Personaldirektor
"Mensch und Maschine" GmbH*

OR

*An Frau
Dr. Christine Meier
Leiterin der Personalabteilung
"Mensch und Maschine" GmbH*

Your letter should then begin "Sehr geehrter Herr Schmidthuber" or "Sehr geehrte Frau Dr. Meier".

Dorothea Müller
Hinter dem Sausee 25
60388 Frankfurt/Main
Tel.: 069/324 754
Fax: 069/324 755

Frankfurt, 31. Juli 1999

Infocomp International AG[3]
Personalabteilung
Postfach 70
40489 Düsseldorf

Ihre Anzeige vom 21.6.99 in der „Frankfurter Allgemeinen Zeitung"

Sehr geehrte Damen und Herren,

Für die von Ihnen ausgeschriebene Stelle als Personalreferentin im Bereich Personalentwicklung erfülle ich alle Voraussetzungen.

Ich bin Diplompsychologin und arbeite als Referentin bei der IHK Frankfurt. Mein Tätigkeitsbereich umfasst dabei die Konzeption, Organisation und Durchführung von Weiterbildungsseminaren für Fach- und Führungskräfte in Handel und Management sowie die psychologische Beratertätigkeit in Fragen der beruflichen Weiterbildung.

Für die Stelle bringe ich eine breite fächerübergreifende Ausbildung und eine umfassende Allgemeinbildung mit. Hinzu kommen Spezialkenntnisse der Arbeits- und Betriebspsychologie. Ich verfüge über mehrjährige Erfahrung im Umgang mit der EDV und bin selbstständiges Arbeiten gewöhnt.

Ich möchte mein Können gerne in Ihrem Unternehmen beweisen. Über eine persönliche Vorstellung würde ich mich sehr freuen.

Mit freundlichen Grüßen

Anlagen
Lebenslauf mit Foto
Zeugniskopien

◆ **Ich bewerbe mich auf Ihr Stellenangebot** in der heutigen Ausgabe der „Sächsischen Zeitung", **weil ich sicher bin**, Ihren Anforderungen an einen Betriebswirt zu entsprechen
= *I refer to your <u>advertisement</u> ... I am sure*

◆ **Auf das von Ihnen ausgeschriebene Stellenangebot bewerbe ich mich gern, weil** es meiner beruflichen Qualifikation und meinen Erwartungen entspricht
= *I have pleasure in <u>applying</u> for the advertised <u>position</u>, as*

◆ **Ich möchte sehr gern während meiner Sommersemesterferien** in Österreich **arbeiten** (möglichst im Hotelbereich) **und würde mich freuen, wenn Sie eine entsprechende Arbeit für mich hätten**
= *I am anxious to find a <u>job</u> in ... during my summer vacation from University ..., and <u>wonder</u> whether you are able to offer me <u>work</u> in any <u>capacity</u>*

19.2 | Detailing your experience and giving your reasons for applying

◆ Englisch **ist meine Muttersprache. Ich verfüge über sehr gute** Deutsch**kenntnisse** in Wort und Schrift. **Außerdem besitze ich solide Grundkenntnisse** des Russischen
= *my <u>first</u> language ... I have an <u>excellent</u> command of ... I also have a working <u>knowledge</u> of*

◆ **Ich habe** drei Jahre Büro**erfahrung**
= *I have ... <u>experience</u> of*

◆ **Ich arbeite seit** 3 Jahren in der Maschinenbaufirma Komplex in Hannover. **Meine Aufgabe besteht im** Anfertigen von technischen Zeichnungen aller Art sowie von elektronischen Schaltplänen
= *I have been <u>working</u> for ... My <u>duties</u> consist of*

◆ **Ich besitze gute Kenntnisse** im Umgang mit Tabellenkalkulationen und Textverarbeitungen
= *I am an <u>experienced</u> user of*

◆ **Ich habe zwar keine Erfahrung auf** diesem speziellen Arbeitsgebiet, **habe aber** verschiedene Ferienjobs ausgeübt
= *although I have no previous <u>experience</u> ..., I have had*

◆ **Auf Verlangen kann ich Ihnen** jederzeit **Zeugnisse** meiner früheren Arbeitgeber **vorlegen**
= *I can supply <u>references</u> from ..., if you would like them*

◆ **Zur Zeit verdiene ich** ... im Jahr **und habe einen jährlichen Anspruch auf** 25 Tage bezahlten **Urlaub**
= *my present <u>salary</u> is ..., and I have ... holiday per year*

◆ **Ich interessiere mich ganz besonders für diese Stelle, weil** ich sehr gerne im Verlagswesen arbeiten möchte
= *I am particularly interested in this <u>job</u>, as*

◆ **Ich möchte** in der Schweiz arbeiten, **um meine Sprachkenntnisse zu verbessern und Erfahrungen** in der Hotelbranche **zu sammeln**
= *I would like to ... in order to improve my languages and to gain <u>experience</u>*

19.3 | Closing the letter

◆ **Ich bin seit 5 Jahren in ungekündigter Stellung** als Leiterin der Fertigung in einem Spitzenunternehmen der Halbleiterbranche **tätig und möchte mich verändern**
= *for the past five years I have been working ... but I would <u>welcome</u> a <u>change</u>*

◆ **Ich könnte Ihnen ab** April 1998 **zur Verfügung stehen**
= *I shall be <u>available</u> from*

◆ **Die Tätigkeit könnte ich zum** frühestmöglichen Termin **aufnehmen**
= *I am <u>available</u> to commence duties at*

◆ **Ich würde mich freuen, in Ihrem Unternehmen meine Fähigkeiten beweisen zu können**
= *I would be <u>pleased</u> to use my skills for*

◆ **Über eine persönliche Vorstellung würde ich mich sehr freuen**
= *I would be happy to <u>attend</u> for <u>interview</u>*

◆ Wenn Sie an meiner Bewerbung interessiert sind, **sende ich Ihnen gerne meine vollständigen Bewerbungsunterlagen zu**
= *I shall be pleased to forward my full <u>application</u> pack*

19.4 | Asking for and giving references

◆ **Ich habe mich um eine Stelle als Privatsekretärin beworben und bin in die engere Wahl gezogen worden. Man hat mich nun gebeten, Zeugnisse meiner früheren Arbeitgeber vorzulegen. Ich wäre Ihnen sehr dankbar, wenn Sie mir so bald wie möglich ein Zeugnis über meine Tätigkeit in Ihrer Kanzlei zuschicken könnten**
= *I should be very grateful if you would send me a <u>reference</u> relating to my time in your office as soon as <u>possible</u>*

◆ **Wir wären Ihnen sehr dankbar, wenn Sie uns mitteilen könnten, ob** er Ihrer Meinung nach **für diesen Posten geeignet ist**
= *I should be grateful if you would kindly let me know whether ... is suitable for this <u>post</u>*

◆ **Ihre Antwort wird selbstverständlich streng vertraulich behandelt**
= *your <u>answer</u> will be treated in strict <u>confidence</u>*

◆ **Könnten Sie uns bitte in Ihrer Antwort mitteilen** wie lange und in welcher Eigenschaft Sie Frau Heinisch kennen und **ob Sie sie für diese Tätigkeit empfehlen können**
= *would you be kind enough to <u>mention</u> in your <u>reply</u> ... whether you can <u>recommend</u> her for this type of employment*

19.5 | Accepting and refusing

◆ **Ich komme gern** am Donnerstag, dem 24. März, um 10.30 Uhr **zu einem Vorstellungsgespräch** in Ihr Büro
= *I shall be <u>delighted</u> to <u>attend</u> for <u>interview</u>*

◆ **Ich nehme das Angebot**, in Ihrer Klinik als Krankengymnastin arbeiten zu können, **gerne an und werde den Dienst am vorgesehenen Eintrittsdatum antreten**
= *I am pleased to <u>accept</u> your <u>offer</u> of ... and will take up my <u>duties</u> on the stated date*

◆ Es hat mich sehr gefreut, dass Sie an meiner Mitarbeit interessiert sind, **ich habe mich jedoch zwischenzeitlich für ein anderes Angebot entschieden**
= *however, in the interim, I have <u>accepted</u> <u>another</u> offer*

20 | COMMERCIAL CORRESPONDENCE

20.1 | Making an enquiry

◆ **Ihrer Anzeige in der Mai-Ausgabe von** „Sport und Freizeit" **entnehmen wir, dass** Sie eine neue Sportartikelserie anbieten
= *we see from your <u>advertisement</u> in the May edition of ... that*

◆ **Wir bitten Sie, uns nähere Angaben über** das neue Sortiment **zukommen zu lassen und uns auch über** Preise, Rabatte und Lieferzeiten **zu informieren**
= *we should be <u>grateful</u> if you would <u>send</u> us full <u>details</u> of ..., including*

20.2 | Replying to an enquiry

◆ **Wir beziehen uns auf Ihre Anfrage vom** 3. März **und senden Ihnen in der Anlage Einzelheiten zu** unserem derzeitigen Warenangebot **sowie** unsere Preisliste
= *in response to your <u>enquiry</u> of ..., we <u>enclose</u> <u>details</u> of ... and*

◆ **Wir danken Ihnen für Ihre Anfrage vom** 6. Juni **und erlauben uns, Ihnen folgendes Angebot zu machen**:
= *we <u>thank</u> you for your <u>enquiry</u> of ..., and are pleased to submit the <u>following</u> <u>offer</u>:*

◆ **Dieses Angebot gilt bei** verbindlicher **Bestellung** vor dem 31. Januar des nächsten Jahres
= *this <u>offer</u> is subject to <u>acceptance</u>*

20.3 | Placing an order

◆ **Bitte senden Sie uns umgehend die folgenden Posten** in den angegebenen Größen und Stückzahlen zu: ...
= *please <u>send</u> us the <u>following</u> <u>items</u> by <u>return</u>*

20 Commercial correspondence

Architekturbüro Mittermayer & Partner
Bürogebäude, Hotels, Villen
Eschenallee 67
52078 Aachen
Tel.: 0241/453 2376   Durchwahl: 0241/453 23
Fax: 0241/453 2312   email: mittermayer@aachen.co.de

City Datenservice GmbH
Alexanderstr. 43
52062 Aachen

Ihr Zeichen	Unser Zeichen	Ihr Schreiben vom	Datum
	EDV 25/99	23. Mai 1999	31. Mai 1999

Sehr geehrte Frau Ackermann,

Bezug nehmend auf Ihr Schreiben vom 23. Mai 1999 bestätigen wir den von Ihnen vorgeschlagenen Termin für eine Vorführung Ihres Programmes „Draw Help". Für die notwendigen Absprachen wenden Sie sich bitte an Frau Dembinski (Apparat 51).

Des Weiteren möchten wir Sie bitten, uns einen Kostenvoranschlag für eine Schulung unserer Mitarbeiter an diesem System zu unterbreiten. Wir sind auch an einem Programm zur statischen Berechnung von Dachkonstruktionen interessiert und bitten um ein diesbezügliches Angebot.

Mit freundlichen Grüßen

Jürgen Schneider

Jürgen Schneider
Leiter Datenverarbeitung

Eduard Papenbrock & Sohn
Glas und Porzellan
Genthiner Str. 20
39114 Magdeburg
Tel.: 0391/857 902   Fax: 0391/857 903

Eschebach Porzellan
Verkaufsabteilung
z. Hd. Frau Klein
Erfurter Str. 105
98693 Ilmenau/Thüringen   Magdeburg, 24. Juni 1999

Sehr geehrte Frau Klein,

vielen Dank für die Zusendung Ihres neuesten Kataloges.

Hiermit bestellen wir 100 Exemplare des Speiseservice „Thüringen" sowie 75 Exemplare des Kaffeegedeckes „Junior".

Mehrere Kunden möchten von Ihrer Nachkaufgarantie Gebrauch machen. Daher bitten wir zusätzlich um die Lieferung folgender Posten:

2 Speiseteller aus der Serie „Inselberg"
1 Untertasse aus der Serie „Oberhof"
1 Sauciere aus der Serie „Schmalkalden"

Wir erwarten Ihre Lieferung fristgerecht innerhalb der nächsten 14 Tage und verbleiben

mit freundlichen Grüßen

Herbert Papenbrock

Herbert Papenbrock
Inhaber

+ **Diese Bestellung bezieht sich auf** Ihre aktuelle Preisliste, und **wir gehen von Ihrem normalen Mengenrabatt** von 10% **aus**
  = *this order is based on ..., assuming your usual discount of ... on bulk orders*

+ **Anbei unsere Bestellung Nr.** 12-566 **über** 3000 Paar feuerfeste Handschuhe
  = *please find enclosed our order No. ... for*

20.4 Replying to an order

+ **Wir danken Ihnen für Ihre Bestellung vom** 9. Mai und werden sie so bald wie möglich ausführen
  = *we thank you for your order of*

+ **Wir brauchen** etwa drei Wochen, **um Ihren Auftrag auszuführen**
  = *we shall require ... to complete this order*

+ **Leider wird sich wegen** eines Engpasses in der Versorgung mit Rohmaterialien **der Beginn der Produktion** bis zum 1. April **verzögern**
  = *unfortunately, because of ..., we cannot start manufacture*

20.5 Delivery

+ **Unsere Lieferzeit beträgt** 2 Monate, vom Eingang einer verbindlichen Bestellung aus gerechnet
  = *our delivery time is*

+ **Wir erwarten ihre Lieferanweisungen**
  = *we await your instructions with regard to delivery*

+ **Diese Waren sind am** 4. Juli per Bahn an Sie **abgegangen**
  = *these goods were sent ... on*

+ **Die bestellte Ware ist bei uns noch nicht eingegangen**
  = *we have not yet received*

+ **Sollten wir die bestellten Waren nicht bis zum Ende des Monats** erhalten, **sehen wir uns gezwungen, unsere Bestellung zu stornieren**
  = *the order will be formally cancelled*

+ **Wir bestätigen den Erhalt** der beiden von Ihnen am 3. März versandten Lieferungen
  = *we acknowledge receipt of*

20.6 Complaining and replying to a complaint

+ **Wir möchten Sie auf einen Fehler in** der hier am 3. Februar eingegangenen Lieferung **hinweisen**
  = *we wish to draw your attention to an error in*

+ **Wir bedauern sehr, dass die Lieferung nicht einwandfrei war,** und sind bereit, die entsprechenden Waren zu ersetzen
  = *we regret that the consignment was unsatisfactory*

+ **Für** diesen Schaden **können wir keine Haftung übernehmen**
  = *we cannot accept responsibility for*

20.7 Payment

+ **Anbei unsere Rechnung Nr.** 64321
  = *please find enclosed our invoice No.*

+ **Der zu zahlende Gesamtbetrag ist ...**
  = *the total amount payable is ...*

+ Wir wären Ihnen dankbar, **wenn Sie diese Rechnung umgehend begleichen könnten**
  = *if you would attend to this account immediately*

+ **In der Anlage übersenden wir Ihnen einen Scheck über ... zur Begleichung Ihrer Rechnung** Nr. 67813/31
  = *we have pleasure in enclosing our cheque for ... in settlement of your invoice*

+ **Wir müssen Sie leider auf einen Fehler in** Ihrer Rechnung Nr. 12-556 **aufmerksam machen.** Wir wären Ihnen dankbar, wenn Sie die Rechnung entsprechend berichtigen könnten
  = *we must point out an error in*

+ **In der Anlage erhalten Sie eine Gutschrift über** diesen Betrag
  = *we enclose a credit note for*

21 GENERAL CORRESPONDENCE

21.1 Starting a letter

To a friend or acquaintance

+ **Vielen Dank für deinen Brief**, der hier gestern angekommen ist
  = *thank you for your letter*

+ **Ich habe micht gefreut, wieder von dir zu hören**
  = *it was good to hear from you again*

+ **Es tut mir sehr Leid, dass ich so lange nicht geschrieben habe.** Hoffentlich bist du mir nicht böse, aber ich hatte in letzter Zeit viel zu tun und ...
  = *I am very sorry I haven't written for so long*

+ **Wir haben so lange nichts voneinander gehört.** Da dachte ich, ich muss einfach schnell ein paar Zeilen schreiben ...
  = *it's such a long time since we had any contact*

In formal correspondence

+ **Ich möchte Sie bitten, mir mitzuteilen, ob** Sie ein Buch mit dem Titel ... vorrätig haben
  = *I am writing to ask whether*

+ **Schicken Sie mir bitte ... In der Anlage sende ich** Ihnen einen Scheck über DM 129,95
  = *would you please send me ... I enclose*

+ **Ich habe** nähere Angaben über Ihre Sommerkurse **erhalten und möchte mich erkundigen, ob** Sie für ... noch Plätze frei haben
  = *I have seen the details of ... and wish to know whether*

21.2 Ending a letter (before the closing formulae)

+ **Viele herzliche Grüße an** euch alle, **auch von Peter**
  = *Peter joins me in sending very best wishes to*

+ **Viele liebe Grüße an Matthias**
  = *give my love to Matthias*

+ Barbara **lässt ganz herzlich grüßen**
  = *... sends her kindest regards (oder her love)*

+ Catherine **lässt auch grüßen**
  = *... asks me to give you ... best wishes*

+ **Bitte grüße auch** deine Mutter **von mir**. Ich hoffe, es geht ihr gut
  = *please remember me to*

+ **Ganz liebe Grüße an** Miriam und Tom, **sage ihnen, wie sehr sie mir fehlen**
  = *give my love to ... and tell them how much I miss them*

+ **Mary lässt** euch beide **recht herzlich grüßen**
  = *Mary sends her love to*

+ **Und grüße** David **schön von mir**
  = *say hello to ... for me*

+ **Ich würde mich sehr freuen, bald von Ihnen zu hören**
  = *I look forward to hearing from you soon*

+ **Ich hoffe, dass ich recht bald eine Antwort** von dir **bekomme**
  = *I hope ... will write back very soon*

+ **Schreib mal wieder, wenn** du Zeit hast
  = *do write when*

+ **Lasst** ab und zu **wieder von euch hören**
  = *send me (oder us) your news*

21.3 Enquiring about and booking accommodation

+ **Bitte schicken Sie mir nähere Informationen zu** Ihren Preisen
  = *please give me details of*

+ **Ich möchte** bei Ihnen Übernachtungen mit Frühstück **buchen**
  = *I would like to book*

+ **Ich würde gerne** ein Doppelzimmer für meine Frau und mich **sowie** ein Zweibettzimmer für unsere beiden Söhne (beide unter 12 Jahren) **reservieren**
  = *I wish to book ... and*

21   General correspondence

Hamburg, 22. Mai 1999

Liebe Thekla und Andreas,

vielen Dank für euren Brief, der schon vor einiger Zeit hier ankam. Es tut mir Leid, dass ich so lange nicht geantwortet habe, aber seit meinem Umzug hierher bleibt mir kaum ein ruhiger Augenblick, um ein paar Briefe zu beantworten. Das soll aber nicht heißen, dass ich euch vergessen habe. Im Gegenteil, ich denke oft an die gemeinsame Zeit in Berlin zurück.

Mittlerweile habe ich mich hier schon recht gut eingelebt. Meine Wohnung muss noch ein bisschen renoviert werden, aber ich hoffe, damit bald fertig zu sein. Die neue Arbeitsstelle gefällt mir sehr gut, so dass ich den Wechsel hierher keinesfalls bedaure.

Wenn ihr im Sommer etwas Zeit habt, seid ihr natürlich ganz herzlich eingeladen, ein paar Tage bei mir in Hamburg zu verbringen. Ich hoffe, es lässt sich einrichten, denn ich würde mich über ein Wiedersehen mit euch sehr freuen.

Viele liebe Grüße auch an Beate und Jens
von eurer

Christine

Elke Linke
Hertzstr. 10
13158 Berlin

Berlin, 13. Juli 1999

Edition Peters
Versandabteilung
Nürnberger Str. 35
04103 Leipzig

Sehr geehrte Damen und Herren,

einem bereits 23 Jahre alten Katalog Ihres Verlages entnahm ich, dass Sie damals verschiedene Nachdrucke der Erstausgaben von Wagners Sopranarien angeboten hatten.

Ich möchte nachfragen, ob noch Exemplare der damaligen Ausgabe der Arien in „Tannhäuser" und „Rienzi" vorhanden sind und zu welchem Preis und Versandkosten diese bei Ihnen bestellt werden können.

Ich danke Ihnen im Voraus für Ihre Bemühungen.

Mit freundlichen Grüßen

Elke Linke

Elke Linke
Kammersängerin

Standard opening and closing formulae

OPENING FORMULAE	CLOSING FORMULAE
Used when you do not know the person's name	
Sehr geehrte Damen und Herren, Sehr geehrte Herren, Sehr geehrte gnädige Frau,	Mit freundlichen Grüßen Hochachtungsvoll
Used if you know the person's name	
Sehr geehrter Herr Wagner, Sehr geehrte Frau Professor Müller,	*As above, plus:* Ich verbleibe, sehr geehrte Frau Professor, mit vorzüglicher Hochachtung Ihr/Ihre
Sehr geehrte Frau Kühn, Sehr geehrter Herr Kühn,	

To acquaintances and friends

OPENING FORMULA	CLOSING FORMULAE	
More formal		
Sehr geehrter Herr Dr. Braun,	Mit freundlichen Grüßen	*If the letter is fairly formal, "Sie" should be used*
Liebe Freunde,	Mit besten Grüßen	
Fairly informal: 'du' or 'Sie' forms could be used		
Lieber Peter,	Es grüßt Sie	
Liebe Ingrid,	Herzliche Grüße von Ihrem	
Liebe Ingrid, lieber Peter,	Viele Grüße an euch beide	

To close friends and family

OPENING FORMULAE	CLOSING FORMULAE	
	'du' and 'Ihr' are used in all these expressions	
Lieber Frank, Lieber Onkel Hans, Liebe Oma, lieber Opa, Liebe Mutti, Lieber Vati,	Liebe Grüße von Bis bald. Viele liebe Grüße Viele Grüße und Küsse von eurem Viele liebe Grüße und Küsse	

Writing to a firm or an institution (see also 20)

OPENING FORMULAE	CLOSING FORMULAE	
Sehr geehrte Damen und Herren, Sehr geehrte Herren, Sehr geehrte Damen,	Mit freundlichen Grüßen[1] or Mit besten Empfehlungen (in business letters)	[1] The first is more common and should generally be used
To someone in the same profession		
Sehr geehrter Herr Kollege, Lieber Kollege, Liebe Kollegin,	Mit freundlichen kollegialen Grüßen	

To a person in an important position

OPENING FORMULAE	CLOSING FORMULAE
Very formal	
Sehr geehrter Herr Bundesminister, Sehr geehrte Frau Präsidentin, Sehr verehrter, lieber Herr Professor,	Hochachtungsvoll

---

◆ **Bitte teilen Sie mir umgehend mit, ob** Sie für die Woche nach dem 24. Juni noch ein Einzelzimmer mit Dusche und Vollpension haben
= *please let me know by return of post if*

◆ **Ich möchte für** Frau Klein ein Einzelzimmer mit Bad für die Woche nach dem 8. Juni **buchen.** Frau Klein **bezahlt ihre Rechnung selbst**
= *I want to reserve ... in the name of ... will settle the bill herself*

◆ **Bitte senden Sie die Rechnung an** die obige Adresse
= *please send the bill to*

21.4   Confirming and cancelling a booking

◆ **Bitte betrachten Sie diese Reservierung als verbindlich** und halten Sie mir das Zimmer frei, auch wenn ich sehr spät am Abend ankommen sollte
= *please consider this a firm booking*

◆ **Wir wollen gegen Abend eintreffen, falls** nichts dazwischen kommt
= *we expect to arrive in the early evening, unless*

◆ **Leider muss ich Sie bitten,** meine Reservierung vom 24. August **auf den** 3. September **umzubuchen**
= *I am afraid I must ask you to alter my booking from ... to*

◆ **Ich muss Ihnen leider mitteilen, dass ich aufgrund** unvorhersehbarer Umstände **meine Zimmerreservierung** für die Woche ab dem 5. September **stornieren muss**
= *owing to ..., I am afraid that I must cancel my booking*

---

22   THANKS

◆ **Herzlichen Dank für** das schöne Geschenk und deinen lieben Brief
= *many thanks for*

◆ **Ich möchte Ihnen, auch im Namen meines Mannes, unseren Dank für** den schönen Abend **übermitteln**
= *I would like to thank you on behalf of my husband and myself for*

◆ **Ich weiß gar nicht, wie ich Ihnen für** Ihre Hilfe **danken soll**
= *I really don't know how to thank you for*

◆ **Als kleines Dankeschön für** deine Hilfe möchten wir dich nächste Woche einmal zum Abendessen einladen
= *as a small token of our gratitude for*

◆ **Für** die vielen Glückwünsche und Geschenke zu unserer Verlobung **möchten wir uns bei** allen Freunden und Bekannten **herzlich bedanken**
= *we would like to extend our warmest thanks to ... for*

◆ **Bitte leiten Sie unseren aufrichtigen Dank auch an** Ihre Mitarbeiterin, Frau Wagner, **weiter**
= *please pass on our sincere thanks to*

◆ **Keine Ursache. Ganz im Gegenteil: wir haben Ihnen zu danken**
= *don't mention it. On the contrary: we must thank you*

◆ **Wir sind Ihnen für** diesen Beitrag **äußerst dankbar**
= *we are very grateful to you for*

◆ Der Vorsitzende **hat mir die ehrenvolle Aufgabe übertragen, Ihnen im Namen** des Forschungskomitees **unseren herzlichen Dank für** die bereitgestellten Spendenmittel **auszusprechen**
= *I have the honour of conveying, on behalf of ..., our sincere thanks   for*

---

23   BEST WISHES

General expressions (used on special occasions only)

◆ **Mit den besten Wünschen [...] von** (+ *signature [...] will be expressions like "für Ihren Ruhestand", "für die neue Stelle", "für Glück im neuen Heim", "für eine baldige Genesung" etc*
= *with best wishes for/on ... from*

◆ **Erlauben Sie mir, dass ich Ihnen meine besten Wünsche [...] übermittle**
= *please accept my best wishes for*

◆ **Bitte richten Sie** Edgar **meine besten Wünsche aus**
= *please give ... my best wishes*

◆ **Viele herzliche Grüße und Wünsche**
= *best wishes*

- **Alle Liebe**
  = _love_
- **Unsere besten Wünsche [...]**
  = _best_ _wishes_ from both/all of us
- **Alles Gute [...]!**
  = _all_ _the_ _best_

23.2 Season's greetings

- **Fröhliche Weihnachten und ein glückliches neues Jahr** wünscht Ihnen/euch (+ signature)
  = _Merry_ _Christmas_ and a _Happy_ _New_ _Year_ from
- **Mit den besten Wünschen für ein gesegnetes Weihnachtsfest und ein glückliches und erfolgreiches neues Jahr**
  = _(often on company Christmas card sent to clients, suppliers etc.)_
- **Frohe Weihnachten und einen guten Rutsch!**
  = _(more informal, only to friends)_

23.3 Birthday greetings

- **Alles Gute zum Geburtstag!**
  = _happy_ _birthday_!
- **Herzlichen Glückwunsch zum Geburtstag** von (+ signature)
  = _many_ _happy_ _returns_ of the day from
- **Herzlichen Glückwunsch zum Namenstag** von (+ signature)
  = _best_ _wishes_ on your _saint's_ day
- **Zu Ihrem Geburtstag unsere herzlichen Glückwünsche** und alles Gute für das neue Lebensjahr
  = _(more formal)_ _many_ _happy_ _returns_ of the day and _best_ _wishes_ for the year ahead

23.4 Get well wishes

- **Gute Besserung!**
  = _(on cards)_ get well soon

23.5 Wishing someone luck

- **Ich möchte Ihnen für** Ihre Unternehmungen **viel Glück und Erfolg wünschen**
  = I wish you the _best_ of _luck_ and every _success_ in ...
- **Viel Erfolg an** Ihrer neuen Arbeitsstätte
  = I wish you every _success_ in ...
- **Wir möchten dir viel Erfolg beim** Examen **wünschen**
  = we'd like to wish you every _success_ in
- **Wir drücken dir** am Freitag alle **die Daumen**
  = we're keeping our fingers crossed
- **Viel Glück für** die Fahrprüfung!
  = _good_ _luck_ in

23.6 Congratulations

- **Herzlichen Glückwunsche zum** bestandenen Examen
  = _congratulations_ _on_
- **Zu Ihrer Beförderung möchten wir Ihnen unsere herzlichsten Glückwünsche aussprechen**
  = _(more formal)_ we would like to send you our _congratulations_ _on_
- **Ich gratuliere zur** bestandenen Fahrprüfung. **Gut gemacht!**
  = _congratulations_ _on_ ... _Well_ _done_!

24   ANNOUNCEMENTS

24.1 Announcing a birth and responding

- **Wir freuen uns über die Geburt** unserer Tochter Julia am 15. Juli. Katharina und Hans Graf, Schönberg
  = are _happy_ to _announce_ the _birth_ of

- Unsere Annika **hat ein Brüderchen bekommen. Am** 7. September **wurde** unser Sohn Christoph-Johannes **geboren. Es freuen sich** Katja und Uwe Braun
  = are _happy_ to _announce_ the _birth_ of ... on ... A brother for ...
- Karin und Rainer **haben** am 7. September **eine kleine Tochter** Sabine **bekommen. Karin geht es schon wieder ganz gut. Die beiden sind natürlich überglücklich**
  = I'm _happy_ to tell you that ... now have a little daughter ... is fully recovered. They are both _delighted_, of course
- **Herzlichen Glückwunsch zum freudigen Ereignis**
  = _congratulations_ _on_ the _happy_ event
- **Herzlichen Glückwunsch zur Geburt** Ihrer/eurer Tochter
  = _congratulations_ _on_ the _birth_ of
- Andreas und ich **freuen uns mit euch über die Geburt** eures Sohnes. **Wir gratulieren von ganzem Herzen und wünschen euch und ihm alles Gute**
  = were _delighted_ to hear of the _birth_ of ... Many _congratulations_. We wish all three of you all the best

24.2 Announcing an engagement and responding

- **Wir haben uns verlobt**. Judith Winter und Christian Schütte
  = are _engaged_
- Professor Wolfgang Schwarz und Frau Gabriele **beehren sich, die Verlobung** ihrer Tochter Erika mit Herrn Ulrich von Schlieffenberg **anzuzeigen**
  = are _happy_ to _announce_ the _engagement_ of
- **Herzlichen Glückwunsch zur Verlobung und alles Gute für** die gemeinsame Zukunft
  = _congratulations_ _on_ your _engagement_ and _best_ _wishes_ for
- **Wir freuen uns mit euch über die Verlobung** eures Sohnes und wünschen dem jungen Paar viel Glück für die Zukunft
  = we were very _happy_ to hear of the _engagement_

24.3 Announcing a marriage and responding

- **Wir heiraten am 27. April**. Heinz Müller und Jutta Müller geb. Heinisch. **Die kirkliche Trauung findet** um 10 Uhr in der Dorfkirche **statt**. Tagesadresse: Hotel Weißer Schwan, Oberammergau
  = ...are getting _married_ on 27 April. The _ceremony_ will take place
- **Mit großer Freude geben wir die Vermählung** unserer Kinder **bekannt** (+ names of both sets of parents)
  = we are _happy_ to _announce_ the wedding/_marriage_ of
- **Wir haben geheiratet**. Fred Heine und Maria Heine-Obermann
  = ... have got _married_
- **Zur Vermählung** Ihrer Tochter mit Herrn Dr Friedhelm Klöbner **möchten wir Ihnen unsere herzlichen Glückwünsche aussprechen**
  = may we offer our _congratulations_ _on_ the _marriage_ of
- **Zu eurer Hochzeit unseren herzlichen Glückwunsch** und alles Gute für eure gemeinsame Zukunft
  = _congratulations_ _on_ your _marriage_
- **Wir freuen uns mit euch über die Heirat** von Anne und Stefan **und möchten dem jungen Paar alles Gute wünschen**
  = we are _delighted_ to hear of ...'s wedding. _Best_ _wishes_ to the newly-weds
- **Für die vielen Glückwünsche und Geschenke** von Familie, Freunden und Bekannten **anlässlich unserer Hochzeit möchten wir uns herzlich bedanken**
  = we would like to thank all our ... for the many _gifts_ and _good_ _wishes_ on the occasion of our _marriage_

24.4 Announcing a death and responding

- **Plötzlich und unerwartet ist** mein geliebter Mann, unser lieber Vater, Onkel und Großvater Hans Meier **aus unserer Mitte gerissen worden. In tiefer Trauer:** Susanne Meier geb. Blume und die Kinder und Enkel
  = it is with deep _sorrow_ that I must _announce_ the sudden and unexpected departure from this life of
- **Nach schwerer Krankheit verstarb** am 15. März unsere liebe Schwester, Tante und Schwägerin Hanna Pietsch geb. Lehmann im Alter von 85 Jahren
  = after a long and painful illness

◆ **In tiefer Trauer muss ich Ihnen mitteilen, dass** mein Vater vergangene Woche nach kurzer schwerer Krankheit verstorben ist
or für immer von uns gegangen ist
= *it is with deep <u>sorrow</u> that I have to <u>inform</u> you that*

◆ **Mit tiefer Bestürzung haben wir die Nachricht vom Tod** Ihres Gatten **erhalten. Wir möchten Ihnen unser tief empfundenes Beileid aussprechen**
= *it is with <u>great</u> <u>sorrow</u> that we learnt of the <u>death</u> of ... we would like to offer our deepest <u>sympathy</u>*

◆ **Wir sind alle sehr bestürzt über den plötzlichen Tod** deines Bruders **und möchten dir unser aufrichtiges Beileid aussprechen**. Wir sind in Gedanken bei dir und wünschen dir in dieser schweren Zeit viel Kraft und Liebe
= *we are all deeply shocked to <u>hear</u> of the sudden <u>death</u> of ... and we would like to offer our deepest <u>sympathy</u>*

◆ **Für die zahlreichen Beweise und Mitgefühls** und der aufrichtigen Anteilnahme sowie für das ehrende Geleit zur letzten Ruhestätte unseres lieben Verstorbenen **danken wir allen herzlich**
= *we would like to <u>express</u> our deep <u>gratitude</u> for the numerous expressions of <u>sympathy</u>*

24.5 Announcing a change of address

◆ **Wir sind umgezogen!** *or* **Wir ziehen um!** Ab 1. April ist unsere Adresse:
= *we have moved! we're moving!*

---

25   INVITATIONS

25.1 Formal invitations

◆ **Wir würden uns freuen, Sie beim** Sektfrühstück im Anschluss an die Trauung im Hotel Goldener Schwan **als unseren Gast begrüßen zu dürfen**
= *we would be <u>delighted</u> if you would <u>join</u> us*

◆ Der Verlag „Mensch und Technik" **gibt sich die Ehre, Sie** am 12. Oktober um 11 Uhr **zu** einem Sektfrühstück an Stand 15 **einzuladen** u.A.w.g.
= *will be pleased to welcome you at*

◆ Karl und Greta Dauderstädt **geben sich die Ehre**, Herrn Günther Henrich **aus Anlass** ihrer silbernen Hochzeit am 14. Mai **zu einem festlichen Abendessen** im Hotel „Zum Goldenen Hirsch" **einzuladen**
= *<u>request</u> the pleasure of your <u>company</u> at a <u>dinner</u> to <u>celebrate</u>*

...and responding

◆ Meine Frau und ich **möchten Ihnen unseren Dank für die freundliche Einladung zum Abendessen anlässlich** Ihrer Silberhochzeit **aussprechen, die wir mit Freuden annehmen/die wir leider nicht wahrnehmen können, da ...**
= *would like to thank you for kind <u>invitation</u> to <u>dinner</u> on the occasion of ... which we have pleasure in <u>accepting</u>/but we regret that we cannot <u>attend</u>, because ...*

◆ **Ich möchte mich herzlich für Ihre Einladung zum** Abendessen am 12. Oktober **bedanken, die ich mit größtem Vergnügen annehme/der ich aber leider nicht nachkommen kann**
= *I would like to thank you very much for your <u>invitation</u> to ... which I have much pleasure in <u>accepting</u>/I am unfortunately <u>unable</u> to <u>accept</u>*

25.2 Informal invitations

◆ Unsere Verlobung **möchten wir** am 15. März um 19 Uhr im kleinen Saal des Restaurants „Stadtkrone" **mit Freunden feiern. Wir würden uns freuen, wenn ihr** zu unserem Fest **kommen könntet**
= *we are having a <u>party</u> amongst friends to <u>celebrate</u> ... and we would be very <u>glad</u> if you could come*

◆ Nächsten Sonntag **möchten wir** für Ruth und Daniel Torberg, die zur Zeit bei uns zu Gast sind, **ein kleines Abendessen geben, zu dem wir auch Sie herzlich einladen möchten**
= *we are giving a small <u>dinner</u> for ... and we would very much <u>like</u> you to come*

◆ **Hätten Sie Lust**, am Donnerstag mit mir in die Oper zu gehen?
= *would you <u>like</u>*

◆ **Könntest du dir, wenn du nächste Woche in Bonn bist, einen Abend freihalten? Wir würden dich gerne einmal zum Abendessen einladen**
= *we would very much <u>like</u> you to come to <u>dinner</u>*

◆ **Wir** wollen den ganzen Mai in unserem Ferienhaus auf Amrum verbringen und **würden uns freuen, wenn ihr uns einmal dort besuchen könntet**
= *we would be very <u>happy</u> if you could come and visit us there*

Accepting

◆ **Vielen Dank für** die freundliche Einladung. **Ich komme gerne**
= *thanks very much for ... I will be <u>pleased</u> to come*

◆ **Ich habe mich über Ihre freundliche Einladung** zur Konfirmationsfeier Ihrer Tochter **sehr gefreut und nehme gerne an**
= *thank you very much for ... I shall be <u>happy</u> to <u>accept</u>*

◆ **Ich hatte vor**, am nächsten Montag in Bonn anzukommen, und **werde mich dann telefonisch bei euch melden**
= *I was <u>planning</u> to ... and I will phone you when I <u>arrive</u>*

◆ **Wir haben uns riesig über eure Einladung** nach Amrum **gefreut und würden gerne** das Wochenende nach Himmelfahrt **kommen**
= *thank you so much for your <u>invitation</u> ... we would love to come*

◆ **Natürlich gehe ich gerne mit Ihnen** in die „Zauberflöte". **Es hat mich sehr gefreut, dass Sie an mich gedacht haben**
= *I would love to go with you to ... it was very kind of you to <u>think</u> of me*

Declining

◆ **Vielen Dank für Ihre Einladung** zum Abendessen mit den Torbergs. **Ich wäre wirklich gerne gekommen, habe ich leider schon eine andere Verabredung**, die ich nicht mehr rückgängig machen kann
= *many thanks for your <u>invitation</u> ... I would very much have liked to come, but I'm <u>afraid</u> I have a previous <u>engagement</u>*

◆ **Wir würden wirklich gern einmal** für ein Wochenende zu euch zu Besuch kommen, aber **leider passt uns keiner der vorgeschlagenen Termine**
= *we would very much like to ... but I'm <u>afraid</u> we can't make any of the dates you suggest*

◆ **Leider kann ich mich** am kommenden Dienstag **nicht freimachen. Könnten wir vielleicht** schon jetzt **etwas für** Oktober **ausmachen?**
= *I'm <u>afraid</u> I'm not free ... perhaps we can arrange something for ...*

---

26   ESSAY WRITING

26.1 The broad outline of the essay

Introductory remarks

◆ Welche Auswirkungen die neue Kommunikations- und Medientechnik auf die Zukunft des Menschen hat, **darüber wird sehr viel geschrieben und gesprochen**
= *a <u>great</u> <u>deal</u> is being written and said about*

◆ **Die Frage, ob** bakterielle Sporen auf geeigneten Himmelskörpern Fuß fassen können, **beschäftigt die Experten schon seit längerem**
= *the <u>question</u> whether ... has been preoccupying the experts for some time*

◆ **Es ist allgemein bekannt, dass** bestimmte Grundsätze sich immer durchsetzen
= *it is a well-known <u>fact</u> that*

◆ **Heute gilt allgemein als bewiesen, dass** Kernkraftwerke eine Gefahr für den Menschen darstellen. **Trotzdem fragt sich**, wie man im Falle einer Schließung die Energieversorgung sichern kann. **Das lässt sich vermuten, dass** die Lösung des Problems so einfach nicht sein kann

= it is generally *agreed* today that ... *however,* one *wonders* ... this *leads* one to *assume* that

+ **Man muss sich verstärkt fragen, ob** Fernsehen nicht eine echte Gefahr für unsere Kinder darstellt
 = one must *seriously ask* oneself whether

+ **Beinahe täglich** hört man neue Katastrophenmeldungen zum Wärmehaushalt der Erde. **Manche** Experten sagen den Hitzetod unseres Planeten voraus, **während andere** die gleichen Daten dazu benutzen, das Nahen der nächsten Eiszeit anzukündigen
 = almost every day ... some ... *while* others

+ **Man würde zu Recht** jeden auslachen, der die Aussagen der Politiker im Wahlkampf für bare Münzen nähme. Aber ...
 = one would be *justified* in

+ **Es ist wohl kaum übertrieben, wenn man sagt, dass** sich die Rolle der Gewerkschaften grundlegend gewandelt hat
 = it would hardly be an *exaggeration* to say

+ **Heutzutage kann man keine Zeitung mehr aufschlagen, ohne dass** einem alarmierende Meldungen über Mafiamethoden ins Auge springen
 = *nowadays* it is scarcely possible to open a newspaper without

+ **Es gibt in der Geschichte unzählige Beispiele für** kluge Frauen, die im Schatten ihrer berühmten Männer standen. Ein Beispiel dafür ist ...
 = history *offers* us numerous *examples* of

Explaining the aim of the essay

+ „Arbeitslose sind in Wirklichkeit nur zu faul zum Arbeiten." **Bemerkungen dieser Art hört man oft,** auch in so genannten gebildeten Kreisen. **Deshalb sollen** hier die Statistiken der Bundesanstalt für Arbeit einmal genauer **untersucht werden**
 = such remarks are *often heard* ... we will *therefore examine*

+ „Stress macht krank". Diese Feststellung veranschaulicht eines der drängendsten Probleme unserer Gesellschaft. **Es scheint deshalb angebracht, sich einmal näher mit** dem Phänomen Stress unter seinen medizinischen und sozialen Aspekten zu **befassen**
 = it *therefore* seems *appropriate* to look more closely into

+ Diese Einstellung **verdient es, genauer untersucht zu werden** und soll hier in einen größeren Gesamtzusammenhang eingeordnet werden
 = deserves closer *attention*

+ Kafka hat einmal geschrieben: „Wirkliche Realität ist immer unrealistisch". **Aus dieser Aussage ergibt sich eine grundlegende Fragestellung**: Was ist Wirklichkeit, was ist Vorstellung?
 = this *assertion* raises a *fundamental* question

+ **Heute werden wir immer wieder mit dem Problem** der zunehmenden Umweltverschmutzung **konfrontiert**
 = today we are repeatedly confronted with the problem of

Developing the argument

+ **Ich möchte mit** einer kurzen Erläuterung einiger grundlegender physikalischer Prinzipien **beginnen**
 = I *should* like to *begin* by

+ **Ich möchte zu Anfang** versuchen, die medizinische Definition von Stress einzugrenzen
 = I *should* like to *begin* by

+ **Zunächst einmal muss man darauf aufmerksam machen, dass** der Autor selber lange Jahre im Exil verbracht hat
 = the *first* thing to *point out* is that

+ **Betrachten wir zunächst** die Software als Arbeitsmittel
 = *firstly let* us look at

+ **Bevor** ich näher auf die Frage des Bewusstseins bei Primaten eingehe, **möchte ich zunächst** verschiedene Meinungen über die Hirnstruktur von Menschenaffen zusammenfassen
 = before ... I *should* like to

+ **Es wäre** an dieser Stelle **angebracht, einen Blick auf** die Familienverhältnisse des Komponisten **zu werfen**
 = it would be *appropriate* to *consider*

+ **Als Erstes sollte man sich** ein wenig **mit** der Geschichte der Gewerkschaftsbewegung **beschäftigen**
 = *let us start* by *considering*

+ **Ehe wir das** Umfrageergebnis **analysieren, müssen wir uns darüber klar werden, dass** nur Langzeitarbeitslose befragt wurden
 = before *analysing* the ... it must be made *clear* that

+ **Als ersten überzeugenden Beweis für diese Behauptung kann man anführen, dass** die Orientierungslosigkeit heute eines der größten Problem der Jugendlichen ist
 = the *first convincing argument* to support this statement is that

+ **Es stellt sich zunächst die Frage nach** dem Motiv, das die Hauptfigur des Romans bewegt, ihre Familie so plötzlich zu verlassen
 = *let us first consider*

+ **Wenn wir uns erinnern**: Im Vorjahr hatte sich Goethe gerade als Student der Rechte an der Universität von Straßburg aufgehalten
 = *let us cast our minds back:*

+ **Es ergibt sich die Frage, ob** unsere Interpretation der spätantiken Prosa in dieser Form noch haltbar ist
 = this *raises* the *question* whether

Connecting elements

+ **Wir kommen nun zur Analyse** der einzelnen Charaktere
 = *let us now analyse*

+ Nachdem wir uns eingehend mit dem Verlauf der Handlung befasst haben, **wollen wir uns nun** dem Sprachstil **zuwenden**
 = *let us now* turn to

+ **Wir** haben gesehen, dass Strahlenbelastung eine Ursache für diese Krankheit sein kann, und **wollen nun andere Faktoren untersuchen**, die für ihre Verbreitung von Bedeutung sein könnten
 = *let us now examine* other *factors*

+ **Es ist nun klar, dass** es eine Lösung im Bereich der Schulmedizin allein nicht geben kann, und **wir wollen** nun Lösungsansätze aus den sogenannten Grenzbereichen **betrachten**
 = it is now *clear* that ... let us turn our *attention* to

+ **Es wäre jetzt interessant, auch** die soziologischen Aspekte näher **zu** beleuchten
 = it would also be interesting to ...

+ **Es drängt sich hier allerdings auch ein Gegenargument auf**: nämlich wie und vor allem von wem soll diese Zensur ausgeübt werden
 = *moreover,* one *argument against* this cannot be ignored:

+ **Man kann das Problem aber auch von** der rein praktischen Seite **her betrachten**
the *problem* can *also* be looked at from

The other side of the argument

+ **Aber sind** diese traumatischen Jugenderlebnisse **wirklich der einzige Grund für** ihr Scheitern?
 = but are ... really the only *explanation* for

+ **Wären diese Argumente schon ein ausreichender Grund für** die Wiedereinführung der Todesstrafe, **oder** sprechen nicht weitaus mehr und schwergendere Argumente dagegen?
 = do these *arguments* give sufficient *grounds for* ... or

+ **Der Autor argumentiert, dass** die Form wichtiger sei als der Inhalt, **es ließe sich aber mit gleichem Recht auch das Gegenteil behaupten**
 = the author *argues* that ... but the opposite may be *equally true*

+ **Es kann freilich nicht darum gehen**, die ganze Branche zu akademisieren
 = there is *certainly* no *question* of

+ **Mit gleichem Recht lässt sich das Problem** natürlich auch dem Bereich der Psychoanalyse **zuordnen**
 = this *problem* belongs *equally* in

The balanced view

+ **Nach eingehender Betrachtung muss man zu dem Ergebnis kommen, dass** eine verantwortliche Kontrollinstanz dringend nötig wäre
  = on reflection, one is _forced_ to _conclude_ that

+ **Man sollte sich allerdings immer darüber im Klaren sein, dass** absolute Aussagen zwar eingängig, aber im Prinzip äußerst zweifelhaft sind
  = one _should_ always _remember_ that

+ **Man sollte auch** den psychologischen Aspekt einer Währungsunion **nicht außer Acht lassen**
  = ... should _also_ be taken into _consideration_

+ **Auch wenn** der Einfluss des Fernsehens auf die jugendliche Psyche unbestritten ist, **sollte man** ihn doch **nicht überschätzen**
  = _even if_ ... one must not _overestimate_

+ **Trotzdem sollte man auch einen weiteren Faktor nicht vergessen**
  = there is _however_ _another_ _factor_ which should not be ignored

+ **Schließlich müsste man sich fragen, ob** eine berufliche Karriere wirklich der einzig mögliche Lebensinhalt ist
  = _finally_, we must _ask_ ourselves whether

+ **Vielleicht sollte man noch einen Schritt weiter gehen und sich fragen, ob** Städte kategorisch für Autos gesperrt werden sollten
  = we _should_ perhaps go _further_ and _ask_ ourselves whether

In conclusion

+ **Welche Schlussfolgerungen lassen sich aus** der Analyse **ziehen**?
  = what _conclusions_ may be drawn from

+ **Die aufgeführten Argumente beweisen, dass** der naturwissenschaftliche Unterricht an unseren Schulen in vielen Punkten mangelhaft ist
  = the _arguments_ given above _prove_ that

+ **Wir sehen also, dass** dem Autor in seiner Erzählung wenig an stimmigen Handlungsabläufen und glaubhaften Personenbeschreibungen liegt. **Vielmehr** konzentriert er sich ganz auf Sprachartistik
  = we can see then, that ... _rather_

+ **Es spricht also alles dafür, dass** Frauen heute wie früher mit anderen Leistungsmaßstäben gemessen werden als Männer
  = all of this _points_ to the _fact_ that

+ **Aus all dem lässt sich nur folgern, dass** sich hinter Argumenten für die Kernkraft erhebliche wirtschaftliche Interessen verbergen
  = from this one must _conclude_ that

+ **Alles in allem** ist der Drogenmissbrauch eines der schwierigsten und wohl dringendsten Probleme unserer Zeit
  = _all_ _in_ _all_

+ **Jedenfalls** verdienen gerade die so genannten Randgruppen unserer ruppigen Leistungsgesellschaft mehr Einfühlsamkeit und Hilfe
  = _in_ _any_ _case_

+ Sein Lebenslauf **lässt den Schluss zu, dass** der Dichter durchaus in das Gemeinschaftsleben des Dorfes eingebunden war
  = _leads_ us to the _conclusion_ that

26.2 Constructing a paragraph

Assessing an idea

+ **Hier lassen sich** verschiedene Argumente **anführen**
  = at this _point_, ... may be given/cited

+ **Ehe ich** mich einer ausführlichen Stilanalyse zuwende, **möchte ich noch kurz auf** die Verwendung des Tiroler Dialektes **zu sprechen kommen**
  = before I ... I would just like to say a few words about

+ **Wie ich im Folgenden noch zeigen werde**, kann von einer genauen psychoanalytischen Bewertung hier keine Rede sein
  = _as_ I will _show_ later

+ **Und hiermit greifen wir einen Gedanken auf**, der schon einleitend erwähnt wurde
  = here we pick up an _idea_

+ **Um aber wieder auf unser Hauptthema zurückzukommen**, die Vollwertküche muss keineswegs langweilig und bieder sein
  = but to return to our main _theme_

+ **Von** dieser Reise **wird später noch ausführlich die Rede sein**, es soll hier nur kurz erwähnt werden, dass sie einen tiefen Eindruck bei ihr hinterließ
  = we will return to a more detailed discussion of ... later

+ **Zum Thema** Schwefelausstoß der Kohlekraftwerke **lässt sich sagen, dass** die neuen Filteranlagen ihn um mehr als 60% reduzieren
  = on the _subject_ of ... it must be said that

Establishing parallels

+ **Sowohl** im Inntal **als auch** in Trostberg lag die Kohlenmonoxidkonzentration bei 0,5 Milligramm
  = _both_ ... _and_

+ **In diesem Zusammenhang muss auch** die so genannte Technologiefeindlichkeit der deutschen Gesellschaft **erwähnt werden**
  = in this _context_ we should _also_ _mention_

+ **In gleicher Weise** sorgt das Programm selbstständig für die notwendigen Datei- und Satzsperren
  = _equally_

+ Die Bodenversiegelung führt **einerseits** zu Hochwasser, **andererseits** zu Grundwasserabsenkungen und damit zu Wassernotstand im Sommer
  = _on_ _(the)_ _one_ _hand_ ... and _on_ _the_ _other_ _(hand)_

+ Eine Zeitung gewinnt Glanz durch exzentrische Schreiber, leben aber tut sie von guten Redakteuren. **Erstere** kommen und gehen, **Letztere** aber sind da und halten die Maschine am Laufen
  = _the_ _former_ ... _the_ _latter_

+ Das Strafrecht untersagt es den Fernsehanstalten, Filme auszustrahlen, die bei der Jugend Aggressionsbereitschaft fördern, und **das Gleiche gilt für** Sendungen, die offensichtlich die Menschenwürde verletzen
  = and the _same_ goes for

+ **In dem Maße wie** die Privatisierung fortschreitet, werden auch immer mehr Investitions- und Finanzierungsmöglichkeiten gefunden
  = _as_

+ **Untrennbar hiermit verbunden ist die Tatsache, dass** Chopin bereits schwer erkrankt war, als er seine Schottlandreise antrat
  = this cannot be _dissociated_ from the _fact_ that

+ **Von** den Kommunisten **bis zu** den extremen rechten Gruppen sind sich **alle** in der Verurteilung des Terrorismus einig
  = _everyone_, from ... to

+ **Gleichermaßen** sollte ein Zeitungsartikel den Leser nicht wie einen unmündigen Ignoranten von oben herab belehren
  = _equally_

Adding

+ **In diesem Zusammenhang** muss man auch ein merkliches Nachlassen der schulischen Leistungen erwähnen
  = in this _context_

+ **Nebenbei bemerkt** hielt der junge Friedrich II. Luther und Calvin für recht triste Figuren
  = _incidentally_

+ **Außerdem** muss man die ökologischen Folgen bedenken
  = _furthermore_

+ **Man sollte auch nicht vergessen, dass** durch das Spülen von Mehrwegflaschen die Gewässer erheblich belastet werden
  = one must _also_ _remember_ that

+ **Hinzu kommt noch** seine liebevolle Schilderung der englischen Landschaft
  = _in_ _addition_ _to_ this there is

Detailing

- Hiervon sind verschiedene Berufsgruppen betroffen, **besonders** Berufe, die viel Bildschirmarbeit erfordern
  = in _particular_

- Es treten hier **vorzugsweise** Probleme mit den Augen, der Wirbelsäule und im Bereich des Unterarms und Handgelenks auf, **die noch** durch schlechte Sitzhaltung **verstärkt werden**
  = chiefly ... which may be made still _worse_

- **Was** nun die Bürgerinitiativen **betrifft** so sind sie ihrerseits keineswegs einer Meinung zum heißen Eisen Müllverbrennung
  = _as_ _far_ _as_ ... _are concerned_

- **Was** die Zigarettenwerbung **angeht**, ist der Zuschauer heute bedeutend kritischer
  = _as_ _far_ _as_ ... _is concerned_

Enumerating

- Zum Erfolg dieser Fernsehserie tragen verschiedene Faktoren bei. **Erstens** or **Zum Ersten** spielt die Hauptrolle ein beliebter Star, **zweitens** liegt das Thema in der Luft und **schließlich** wurde ein erstklassiger Drehbuchautor gefunden
  = _first(ly)_ ... _secondly_ ... _finally_

- Das hat drei Hauptgründe: **erstens ..., zweitens ..., drittens**
  = _first(ly)_ ... _secondly_ ... _thirdly_

- Es werden dem Kunden mehrere Möglichkeiten angeboten: er konnte **entweder** bar **oder** mit Scheck- oder Kreditkarte bezahlen **oder schließlich** ein Kundenkonto einrichten
  = _either_ ... _or_ ... _or alternatively/finally_

- Sollte man in diese Statistik alle Erkrankten aufnehmen? **Oder etwa** nur die chronisch Kranken? **Oder sollte man am Ende** sogar nach Art der Erkrankung getrennt analysieren?
  = _or else_ ... _or should one simply_

Opposing

- **Entgegen** einem landläufigen Vorurteil hatten wohl auch die schrecklichen Wikinger Angst vor anderen Völkern
  = _contrary_ _to_

- **Ungeachtet** ihrer Gräueltaten werden die Helden zu Märtyren erhoben
  = _in spite of_

- **Trotz** harter Arbeit konnten die Eltern die Kinder kaum ernähren
  = _in spite of_

- **Obwohl** es einen umfangreichen zivilen Apparat zur Verfolgung von Menschenrechtsverletzungen gibt, werden die Verantwortlichen nur selten bestraft
  = _although_

- **Wenngleich** die Schwierigkeiten des Balanceakts zwischen menschlicher Tragödie und politischem Verbrechen nicht immer zu übersehen sind, löst der Autor das Problem mit viel Mut und Geschick
  = _although_

- Schwellungen und Rötungen werden fast bei jedem Fall beobachtet, **trotzdem** stehen diese Nebenwirkungen in keinem Verhältnis zu den Folgen einer Infektion
  = _nevertheless_

Introducing one's own point of view

- **Meiner Meinung nach** ist dies sein bei weitem bestes Buch
  = in my _opinion_

- **Ich für mein(en) Teil** bedaure diese Entwicklung im Schulwesen sehr
  = I for my part

- **Was ich hier am interessantesten finde**, ist die großartige Verflechtung der verschiedenen Charaktere
  = what I find most interesting here

- **Nach meinem Dafürhalten scheint** die Autorin sich hier auf das gewagte Terrain der Vermutung zu begeben
  = it _seems_ to me that

- **Ich bin hingegen der Ansicht, dass** man Statistik nicht auf diese Weise zu seinem eigenen Zwecken umlügen darf
  = my own _point_ of _view_ is that

- Wie der Verfasser, **für meine Begriffe übrigens völlig zu Recht**, bemerkt, geht es hier um mehr als nur unsere Schulen
  = quite rightly in my _opinion_

Introducing somebody else's point of view

- **Laut Verfasser** or **Dem Verfasser zufolge** ist der Neid eine der Haupttriebfedern unseres Handelns
  = in the author's _view_

- **Nach Meinung einiger Experten** lassen sich diese Abweichungen durch unterschiedliche Ernährungsgewohnheiten erklären
  = _according_ _to_ some experts

- Die Ausgaben für den Umweltschutz bewegen sich **seiner Aussage zufolge** im Rahmen des Vertretbaren
  = in his _opinion_

- Er **glaubt/meint/erklärt dagegen**, dass dieses System unzählige Vorteile besitzt
  = _on_ _the_ _other_ hand, he _thinks/believes/declares_

- Der Autor **lenkt nun unsere Aufmerksamkeit wieder auf** die verschiedenen vorangegangenen Krisensituationen
  = once again draws our _attention_ to

- Er **weist** nun **auf** die unterschiedlichen Persönlichkeiten der Hauptakteure **hin**
  = _points_ _out_

- Sie **behauptet, dass** die Mehrheit aller Jugendlichen sich heute nicht mehr für Bücher interessiert
  = _maintains_ that

- **Die offizielle Lesart ist, dass** die Probleme für die Bevölkerung bei weitem durch die Vorteile aufgewogen werden
  = the official version is that

- Hier **möchte uns** ein so genannter Experte **glauben machen** or **davon überzeugen, dass** dieses Problem überhaupt nicht existiert
  = would have us _believe_/would like to _convince_ us that

Introducing an example, quotation or source

- **Nehmen wir zum Beispiel** or **Da wäre zum Beispiel** Gretchen im „Faust"
  = take for _example_

- **Eines der interessantesten Beispiele findet sich** gleich im ersten Kapitel des Buches
  = one of the most interesting _examples_ occurs

- **Als Beispiel braucht man nur** die problematische Lage der kleinen landwirtschaftlichen Betriebe **anzuführen**
  = to _illustrate_ this, one need only refer to

- **Die Verfasser meinen dagegen, dass** „die zentrale Bedeutung der Hehlerei für die organisierte Kriminalität lange Zeit nicht deutlich genug gesehen worden ist"
  = _however_, the authors are of the _opinion_ that

- In seinen „Xenien" **sagte/bemerkte** schon Goethe: „Amerika, du hast es besser"
  = said/_observed_

- **Was** der Minister **bereits sagte** or **gesagt hat, sei hier zitiert**: „Es hängt jetzt alles von der Einsatzbereitschaft und Toleranz unserer Mitbürger ab." **Zitat Ende**
  = _as_ ... said, and I _quote_ ... end of _quote_

- Schlegel **hat** in einem historischen Aufsatz **das Wort von** der „Revolution von oben" **geprägt, das später von** vielen kritischen Historikern **aufgenommen wurde**
  = coined the phrase ... which was later taken up by

- **Nach den Worten von** Börne fallen „Minister wie Butterbrote: gewöhnlich auf die gute Seite"
  = in the words of

- **In ihrer eindrucksvollen Studie zum** Leben der Insekten **weist** Maria Sybilla Merian bereits im 17. Jahrhundert **darauf hin, dass ...**
  = in her remarkable _study_ of ... (she) _points_ _out_ that

◆ **In einem kürzlich erschienenen Artikel in** der Zeitschrift „Der Kreis" **finden wir folgende** treffende **Bemerkung von** Hans Meier:
= *in a recent article in ... there is the <u>following</u> remark by*

◆ "Das größer gewordene Deutschland wird nicht regiert, Machterhalt ist alles." **So steht es in** der „Zeit" **aus der Feder von** Nina Grunenberg
= *writes ... in*

◆ **Zitat Raddatz**: „Ähnlich einer Steinberg-Kontur setzt dieser Künstler sich selber aus Kunststücken zusammen." **Zitat Ende**
= *to <u>quote</u> Raddatz ... end of <u>quote</u>*

26.3 The mechanics of the argument

Stating facts

◆ **Es ist richtig, dass** so manches Substitut eines Umweltgiftiges sich im Nachhinein nicht als die erhoffte ökologische Alternative entpuppt
= *it is <u>true</u> that*

◆ **Hierbei wäre zu bemerken, dass** die Experten zu diesem Thema gespaltener Auffassung sind
= *one should <u>note</u> here that*

◆ **Es handelt sich um** den Versuch, durch Fiktionen etwas Realität zu erfahren
= *this is a*

◆ Dieses Bauprogramm **zog die heftige Kritik** der Opposition **auf sich**
= *attracted strong <u>criticism</u> from*

◆ **Erinnern wir uns**: Nach jahrzehntelangen Rangeleien war endlich eine Entscheidung gefallen. Das Steuerrecht würde grundlegend reformiert werden
= *let us not <u>forget</u>:*

◆ **Beim Weiterlesen ergeben sich völlig neue Perspektiven**: ...
= *as one reads on, entirely new perspectives open up*

◆ **Es sollte erwähnt werden, dass** Tschaikowski nicht der einzige Komponist ist, der in dieser Zeit historische Ereignisse in seinen Werken umsetzt
= *<u>mention</u> should be made of the <u>fact</u> that*

Indicating a supposition

◆ **Es ist anzunehmen, dass** der wirtschaftliche Kurs sich zunehmend nach der liberalen Mitte hin einordnen wird
= *it is to be <u>expected</u> that*

◆ **Es lässt sich hier vermuten, dass** ein Teil der Befragten den Begriff „Heimat" völlig anders verstanden hat
= *one <u>may</u> <u>suppose</u> that*

◆ **Es kann gut sein, dass** Schiller dieses Gedicht im Konzept schon sehr viel früher verfasst hat
= *... <u>may</u> <u>well</u> (have ...)*

◆ **Man spricht in diesem Zusammenhang von der Möglichkeit, dass** die Visumpflicht bereits in den nächsten Monaten entfallen könnte
= *in this <u>context</u>, the <u>possibility</u> that ... has been <u>mentioned</u>*

◆ **Hierfür könnte es allerdings auch** eine andere Erklärung **geben**
= *there <u>could</u> <u>well</u> be*

◆ **Es ist durchaus möglich, dass** er mit dieser Kandidatur politisches Kapital aus seiner Beliebtheit als Schauspieler schlagen wollte
= *it is very <u>possible</u> that*

◆ **Es steht zu vermuten, dass** auch die Produktmanager in Japan in ihrem Sortiment nicht mehr so ganz durchblicken
= *it must be <u>supposed</u> that*

Expressing a certainty

◆ Die wenigen Akten, die die Regierung bisher herausgerückt hat, **lassen nur den einen Schluss zu**: Bonn hat über das kriminelle Imperium Schalk fast alles gewusst
= *leave us with only one <u>conclusion</u>*

◆ **Es steht fest, dass** Albrecht seinen späteren Mörder selbst eingelassen hat
= *it is <u>clear</u> that*

◆ Aber **es ist sicher, dass** nicht alle Sprachen, die in Europa anerkannt sind, eine Ausgabe des EU-Amtsblattes haben werden
= *it is <u>certain</u> that*

◆ Seine zweite Behauptung ist dagegen **unbestritten** or **unzweifelhaft** or **ohne Zweifel** den Argumenten seiner Gegner vorzuziehen
= *<u>indisputably/undeniably</u>*

◆ **Unbestritten ist,** dass die Bundesrepublik im internationalen Umweltschutz eine Vorreiterrolle einnimmt
= *what cannot be <u>denied</u> is that*

◆ Eine Limousine mit Chauffeur ist **zweifellos** besser gegen Diebstahl geschützt als ein Drahtesel
= *<u>doubtless</u>*

◆ **Es deutet alles darauf hin, dass** es dem SC Freiburg so ergeht wie vielen seiner Vorgänger als Aufsteiger: am Ende steht der Neuanfang in der zweiten Liga
= *all the <u>indications</u> are that*

◆ **Wie man weiß**, kann man auch in Bayern durchaus in den Genuss fiskalischer Milde gelangen
= *as everyone <u>knows</u>*

◆ **Es ist völlig klar, dass** solchen innovativen Produkten die Märkte der Zukunft gehören
= *it is very <u>clear</u> that*

◆ **Es lässt sich nicht leugnen, dass** die demographische Entwicklung das Zahlenverhältnis zwischen Beitragszahlern und Rentnern verschlechtern wird
= *it cannot be <u>denied</u> that*

Indicating doubt or uncertainty

◆ **Es scheint wohl, dass** die Liebe zu antiken Modellen der Uhrmacherkunst wieder auflebt
= *it would <u>seem</u> that*

◆ **Es könnte immerhin sein, dass** die Dauer der Studie zu kurz war
= *all the <u>same</u>, it is <u>possible</u> that*

◆ **Vielleicht wäre es besser**, wenn die Städtebauer einen Teil ihrer Großgrundstücke nachträglich wieder parzellieren
= *<u>perhaps</u> it would be better*

◆ **Es könnte sich** bei dem Streit **um** eine juristische Posse **handeln**
= *we might be <u>dealing</u> <u>with</u>*

◆ **Dies könnte unter Umständen erklären, warum** man so lange auf den zweiten Band warten musste
= *this might <u>explain</u> why*

◆ **Es fällt schwer**, in diesem Zusammenhang **an** die Objektivität der Wissenschaft **zu glauben**
= *it is <u>difficult</u> to <u>believe</u> in*

◆ Diese Ergebnisse **stellen** erneut **die allgemeine Gültigkeit** statistischer Aussagen **infrage**
= *cast <u>doubt</u> upon the general validity of*

Conceding a point

◆ In Berlin hat die Oper heute weniger Abonnenten als noch vor 10 Jahren, **trotzdem** sind sehr viele Aufführungen ausverkauft
= *<u>nonetheless</u>*

◆ **Obwohl** seine Studien sehr sorgfältig waren, muss man ihm vorwerfen, dass er die Ergebnisse der sowjetischen Gruppe außer Acht ließ
= *<u>although</u>*

◆ Ihr Stil ist sehr ausgefeilt, **allerdings** manchmal etwas langatmig
= *<u>although</u>*

◆ **Bis zu einem gewissen Punkt** muss man ihm Recht geben, wenn man sich auch nicht mit allen Rückschlüssen einverstanden erklären kann
= *up to a point*

◆ **Ich stimme mit** der Verfasserin im Prinzip **überein, möchte aber zu bedenken geben, dass** manche Folgerungen sehr extrem sind
= *I <u>agree</u> with ... but I would like to <u>raise</u> <u>the</u> point that*

◆ **Im Grunde bin ich mit** dem Autor **einer Meinung, möchte aber** einwenden, dass einige wichtige Punkte nicht berücksichtigt wurden
= *<u>basically</u>, I <u>agree</u> with ... but I would like to*

+ Fischer hält die Untersuchungen für abgeschlossen. **Es bleibt aber nach wie vor die Tatsache bestehen**, dass viele Versuche noch laufen
  = but <u>the</u> <u>fact</u> <u>remains</u> that

+ **Gewiss** hat der Regisseur Talent und Mut. **Es stellt sich trotzdem die Frage, ob** man wirklich den „Ring" an einem Abend aufführen kann
  = <u>certainly</u> ... but I would still <u>question</u> whether

+ Mit der Entwicklung des Laser-TV hat die Forschungsgruppe **zwar** Beachtliches geleistet, **ob es aber** wirklich ein Meilenstein in der Fernsehtechnik ist, bleibt umstritten
  = <u>certainly</u> ... but whether it

+ **Ohne** den ästhetischen Reiz der Darstellung **schmälern zu wollen, hätte ich es doch begrüßt**, wenn ihre Quellen offen gelegt worden wären
  = <u>without</u> <u>wishing</u> <u>to</u> <u>belittle</u> ... I would have <u>preferred</u>

+ **Man muss zwar zugeben, dass** die Verbesserung des Lebensstandards ein vorrangiges Ziel ihrer Politik ist, **muss aber gleichzeitig sagen, dass** sie noch sehr weit von diesem Ziel entfernt ist
  = one must <u>admit</u> that ... but one must <u>also</u> say that

+ **Zweifellos** ist ein hoher gesellschaftlicher Bedarf an Nervenkitzel vorhanden, **aber** das normale Leben ist keineswegs so langweilig, wie es scheint
  = <u>doubtless</u> ... but

+ **Zumindest kann man sagen, dass** das Thema durch die Untersuchung einmal ins Bewusstsein der Öffentlichkeit gekommen ist
  = <u>at</u> <u>least</u> one can say that

Emphasizing particular points

+ **Um** die Problematik **zu unterstreichen**, hat der Verfasser uns eine Reihe der häufigsten Nebenwirkungen genannt
  = in order to <u>emphasize</u>

+ Die Verfasserin **betont wiederholt, dass** sie neutrale Zurückhaltung nicht für eine angemessene Reaktion auf dieses Problem hält
  = repeatedly <u>stresses</u> that

+ **Wir müssen klarstellen, dass** wir es hier nicht mit einem Schüleraufsatz, sondern mit einem wissenschaftlichen Thesenpapier zu tun haben
  = let us make it <u>clear</u> that

+ Diese Untersuchung **wirft ein bezeichnendes Licht auf** die gegenwärtige Situation am Arbeitsmarkt
  = <u>highlights</u>

+ **Man sollte auf keinen Fall vergessen, dass** zu diesem Zeitpunkt niemand etwas von dem Unfall in Tschernobyl wusste
  = let us not <u>forget</u> that

+ **Besonders** an den Universitäten lassen sich diese politischen Strömungen erkennen
  = it is particularly ... that

+ Wenn er sich bisher noch nicht zu diesem Thema geäußert hat, **so liegt das an** politischen Erwägungen **und nicht an** mangelndem Interesse
  = it is ... and not ... that have <u>prevented</u> him

+ Er spricht sich **nicht nur** gegen die Etaterhöhung aus, **sondern** fordert **auch** strenge Sparmaßnahmen in allen Ministerien
  = <u>not</u> only ... <u>but</u> also

+ Er ist kein Dummkopf - **genau das** unterscheidet ihn von den meisten Argans der Theatergeschichte
  = that is what

+ **Er** fällt **nicht** auf die Artistik stürmischer Läufe herein, **im Gegenteil**, er konzentriert sich auf die leisen, lyrischen Passagen
  = he doesn't ..., <u>on</u> <u>the</u> <u>contrary</u>

+ Es wird wirtschaftlich weiter bergab gehen, **um so mehr, als** im Winter die Arbeitslosenzahlen ohnehin zunehmen
  = <u>all</u> <u>the</u> <u>more</u> <u>so</u> because

+ **Ich möchte sogar behaupten, dass** Albrecht Schwarz eine lästige Person ist, die vielleicht früher einmal einen Zweck erfüllt haben mochte
  = I would <u>even</u> go <u>so</u> <u>far</u> <u>as</u> <u>to</u> <u>say</u> that

+ Tritium kann die Transmutation von Thymin zu Cytosin bewirken, **und dazu kommt noch, dass** Schaden an der DNS verursacht wird
  = and, <u>furthermore</u>

+ Die Inselbewohner brauchen keine Berührungsängste zu haben, **umso weniger, als** das Fischereiabkommen weit günstiger ausgefallen ist als angenommen
  = even <u>less</u> <u>so</u> now that

Moderating a statement

+ **Ohne den Verfasser kritisieren zu wollen**, scheint es doch, dass er mit einer anderen Methode bessere Messergebnisse erzielt hätte
  = without wishing to <u>criticize</u> the author

+ **Das soll nicht heißen, dass** Exportgeschäfte groß und Menschenrechte klein geschrieben werden, **sondern vielmehr, dass** eine wertorientierte Außenpolitik der Wirtschaft den Weg ebnen muss
  = this does not <u>mean</u> that ..., but <u>rather</u> that

+ Dieses Verfahren ist **keineswegs** altruistischen Überlegungen des britischen Staates zu verdanken, **sondern vielmehr** als Instrument zur Sicherung des sozialen Friedens gedacht
  = in no way ... but <u>rather</u>

+ An sich hat die Autorin **im Großen und Ganzen** Recht, es ließe sich jedoch einwenden, dass sich inzwischen einige Details geändert haben
  = by and large

+ **Ohne Kleinigkeiten zu viel Gewicht beimessen zu wollen**, muss man doch sagen, dass ihre Zeitangaben sehr unpräzise sind
  = without laying too much emphasis on <u>details</u>

+ **Es wäre ungerecht** or **unfair**, von einem solchen Kompendium eine Art konzeptionelle Geschlossenheit zu erwarten
  = it would be <u>unfair</u> to

Indicating agreement

+ **Man muss zugeben, dass** gerade dieser Aspekt faszinierend ist
  = one must <u>admit</u> that

+ Seine Beschreibung der Situation **trifft in allen Punkten genau (zu)** or **ist bis ins Detail präzise**
  = is correct in every <u>detail</u>

+ Dieses Argument **ist völlig überzeugend** or **überzeugt völlig**
  = is completely <u>convincing</u>

+ **Wir können uns** diesen Schlussfolgerungen **nicht verschließen**
  = we cannot ignore

+ **Wie** die Verfasserin **so richtig sagt**, kommt es auch auf Details an
  = as ... so <u>rightly</u> says

+ **Es ist klar, dass** hier Geschichte geschrieben wurde
  = it is <u>clear</u> that

+ Ich **kann mich der Meinung** des Verfassers nur **uneingeschränkt anschließen**
  = <u>support</u> (his) view <u>wholeheartedly</u>

Indicating disagreement

+ Diese Sichtweise **kann man unmöglich** unwidersprochen **akzeptieren**
  = one cannot <u>possibly</u> <u>accept</u>

+ Dieses Argument **ist keiner Beachtung wert** or **verdient keine Beachtung**
  = is not <u>worthy</u> of our <u>attention</u>

+ Diesen Standpunkt **kann man** heute **nicht mehr vertreten**
  = is no longer tenable

+ Die Äußerungen des Innenministers **stehen in völligem Widerspruch zur** Haltung des Verteidigungsministers
  = completely <u>contradict</u>

+ Ich muss hier jedoch einige schwerwiegende **Bedenken gegen** diese Beweisführung **anmelden**
  = <u>express</u> <u>misgivings</u> about

+ Die Untersuchung von Professor Sommerfeld **widerlegt** klar diese Behauptung
  = <u>disproves</u>

◆ Gegen alle diese Kritikpunkte **kann man** allerdings **einwenden** or **zu bedenken geben**, dass es hier um eine neue Kunstform geht
= one can _object_/one can _argue_

◆ Diese Behauptung **scheint mir sehr zweifelhaft** or **fragwürdig**
= seems to me to be _questionable_

◆ **Der Autor irrt sich, wenn er uns zu verstehen gibt, dass** das Ergebnis schon vor Beginn der Verhandlungen feststand
= the author is _wrong_ to imply that

◆ Die Beweisführung ist bestechend, **trotzdem kann ich die Meinung** or **den Standpunkt der Verfasser nicht teilen**
= _however_ I cannot _share_ the author's view

◆ **Ich kann** seine pessimistische Weltsicht **nicht gutheißen**
= I cannot _embrace_

Indicating approval

◆ **Es ist leicht zu verstehen, dass** er mit dieser Meinung gut ankommt
= it is easy to _understand_ how

◆ **Gewiss wäre die beste Lösung**, einen lockeren Staatenbund zu bilden
= the best _solution_ would _certainly_ be

◆ Die Bundesbank **hat gut daran getan**, an der Zielvorgabe für die Geldmenge festzuhalten
= did _well_ to

◆ Der Student kritisiert **völlig zu Recht** die verbeamtete Mittelmäßigkeit der Professoren
= very _rightly_

◆ **Es war wirklich an der Zeit, dass** man sich wieder an gewisse Grundwerte der Gesellschaft erinnert
= it was high time that

◆ **Endlich einmal** ein Artikel, in dem ich mich als Lehrer wieder finden kann
= at last

◆ Dieses Buch **ist besonders willkommen, weil** alle bisherigen Biografien Clara Schumanns romantisch verklärt oder feministisch überzogen waren
= it is _especially_ welcome, _because_

Indicating disapproval

◆ **Es ist schade, dass** diese Poesie heute weitgehend verloren ist
= it is a _pity_ that

◆ **Leider** hat sich die Autorin mit der Zeichnung der Personen keine große Mühe gegeben
= _unfortunately_

◆ **Es ist schwer einzusehen**, wie das Aktionsprogramm zusätzliche Arbeitsplätze schaffen soll
= it is hard to _see_

◆ Ich möchte diese zynische Sichtweise aufs Schärfste **verurteilen**
= _condemn_

◆ Man muss seine Haltung zur Geburtenkontrolle **scharf kritisieren**
= _criticize_ ... very strongly

◆ **Man kann** dem Bürgermeister **vorwerfen, dass** er zu sehr auf die nächsten Wahlen und zu wenig auf das Wohl der Bürger bedacht war
= one may _reproach_ ... for

Making a correction

◆ Möglicherweise habe ich mich missverständlich ausgedrückt, deshalb **möchte ich** das Gesagte **an dieser Stelle richtig stellen**
= I would like to put ... right here

◆ **Tatsächlich** or **In Wirklichkeit** geht es um ganz etwas anderes
= in (_actual_) _fact_/in _reality_

◆ **Es geht** hier **nicht um** Prinzipien **sondern um** Menschenleben
= it is not a _question_ of ... but of

◆ Diese Schilderung **entspricht nicht den Tatsachen: in Wahrheit** ...
= is not in accordance with the _facts_: the truth is that

◆ Diese Befürchtungen **sind völlig grundlos**
= are completely groundless

◆ **Es wäre eine kleine Korrektur zu** dieser Behauptung **anzubringen**
= I would point out one small error in

◆ Die Äußerungen des Pressesprechers **muss ich energisch dementieren**
= I emphatically deny

Indicating the reason for something

◆ Die hohe Konzentration des Hormons **lässt sich auf** eine intravenöse Behandlung **zurückführen**
= arises from

◆ Dieses Haus ist die Mühen und Ausgaben wert, **es handelt sich nämlich um** eines der wenigen erhaltenen gotischen Privathäuser
= for you see it is/_because_ it is actually

◆ **Angesichts der Tatsache, dass** die Berechnungen nur Richtwerte geben, muss man den weiteren Ergebnissen wirklich misstrauen
= in _view_ of _the_ _fact_ _that_

◆ **Das lässt sich sicher durch** die persönliche Vergangenheit des Autors **erklären**
= the _reason_ for this _doubtless_ lies in

Setting out the consequences of something

◆ Diese Entscheidung sollte **unangenehme Folgen** haben
= unpleasant _consequences_

◆ Das Verhandlungsergebnis wird langfristig **positive Auswirkungen** für die gesamte Region haben
= beneficial _effects_

◆ Er war offensichtlich mit den angebotenen Bedingungen nicht zufrieden, **weshalb** er auch dem Ruf an die Universität Ulm nicht folgte
= which is _why_

◆ **Und deshalb** spielt die Familie in allen seinen Romanen eine herausragende Rolle
= and that is _why_

◆ Die Schließung der Fabrik **wird dazu führen, dass** ein großer Teil der Einwohner in andere Industriestädte abwandert
= will _cause_ ... to

◆ Die Flugpreise sind stark angestiegen, **was** zunächst eine rapide abnehmende Passagierzahl **zur Folge haben wird**
= and that will _cause_

◆ Bei den heutigen Lebensweise kommen die evolutionär ausgebildeten Grundfähigkeiten des Menschen zu kurz, **folglich** sind seine Krankheiten biopsychosozialer Natur
= and _consequently_

◆ Die Persönlichkeit der Anna ist **also doch** viel komplexer, als es auf den ersten Blick scheint
= _thus_/_therefore_

Contrasting or comparing

◆ **Einerseits** sollen die Produktionsmengen erhöht werden, **andererseits** jedoch wird die damit verbundene Zunahme der Abfallmenge nicht einkalkuliert
= on (_the_) _one_ _hand_ ... on _the_ _other_ (_hand_)

◆ **Einige** Kritiker **halten dies für** seine beste Inszenierung, **andere sind der Meinung, dass** er zu große Zugeständnisse an den Publikumsgeschmack gemacht hat
= some... _consider_ this ... _while_ others _believe_

◆ **Manche** Experten reden heute vom Versagen der Schule. **Andere dagegen** bejubeln den Fortschritt im Bildungswesen
= some ... _whereas_ others

◆ Die Hirnfunktionen von Alkoholikern regenerieren sich **weitaus besser als** angenommen
= _far_ _better_ than (is)

◆ **Mit** den Recherchewerkzeugen der spezialisierten Systeme **kann sich** eine einfache Textverarbeitung **nicht messen**
= is no match for

◆ **Verglichen mit** seinen früheren Werken ist dieses Buch nur ein schwacher Abglanz
= _compared_ _to_

◆ Diese beiden Inszenierungen **lassen sich einfach nicht vergleichen**
= there is simply no _comparison_ between

27   TELEFONIEREN

27.1   Getting a number

Können Sie mich bitte mit Köln 465786 verbinden?
(vier-sechs-fünf-sieben-acht-sechs)

Können Sie mich bitte mit der <u>Auskunft</u> <u>verbinden</u>?

Ich hätte gern eine <u>Nummer</u> in Köln, Firma Europost, Breite Straße 54

Ich kann die <u>Nummer</u> nicht <u>finden</u>

Das ist eine Geheim<u>nummer</u>

Wie lautet die Vorwahl von Leipzig?

Kann ich nach Peru <u>durchwählen</u>?

Wie bekomme ich den Amtston?

Wie lautet die <u>Nummer</u> der Zeitansage?

Sie müssen die <u>Nummer</u> im Telefonbuch nachschlagen

Sie können die <u>Nummer</u> bei der internationalen <u>Auskunft</u> erfragen

Wenn Sie von Deutschland nach England <u>anrufen</u>, lassen Sie die Null weg

27.2   Different types of call

Es ist ein Orts<u>gespräch</u>

Es ist ein Fern<u>gespräch</u> aus Hamburg

Ich möchte ins Ausland <u>anrufen</u>

Ich möchte ein R-<u>Gespräch</u> nach London anmelden

Ich möchte auf Kreditkarte nach Berlin <u>anrufen</u>

Ich hätte gern einen Weckruf für morgen früh 7.30 Uhr

27.3   The operator speaks

Welche <u>Nummer</u> möchten Sie?

Welche <u>Nummer</u> wünschen Sie?

Woher <u>rufen</u> Sie <u>an</u>?

Können Sie die <u>Nummer</u> bitte <u>wiederholen</u>?

Sie können <u>durchwählen</u>

<u>Legen</u> Sie <u>auf</u> und <u>wählen</u> Sie noch einmal

Ich habe Herrn Campbell mit einem R-<u>Gespräch</u> aus Canberra für Sie. <u>Nehmen</u> Sie das <u>Gespräch</u> an?

Ich <u>verbinde</u>

Ich habe keine Eintragung unter diesem Namen

Der Teilnehmer 45 77 57 84 <u>antwortet</u> nicht

Ich <u>versuche</u> es noch einmal

Bitte bleiben Sie am <u>Apparat</u>

Alle Leitungen nach Bonn sind <u>besetzt</u>, bitte <u>rufen</u> Sie später noch einmal <u>an</u>

Ich <u>versuche</u>, Sie jetzt zu <u>verbinden</u>

Wir haben ein Rufzeichen

Die Leitung ist <u>besetzt</u>

27.4   When your number answers

Können Sie mich bitte mit <u>Apparat</u> 516 <u>verbinden</u>?

Bin ich mit dem <u>Apparat</u> von Herrn Lambert <u>verbunden</u>?

Kann ich bitte mit Herrn Schmiedel <u>sprechen</u>?

27   THE TELEPHONE

27.1   Nach einer Nummer fragen

Could you get me Newhaven 465786, please?
(four-six-five-seven-eight-six)

Could you give me <u>directory</u> enquiries *(Brit)* oder <u>directory</u> assistance *(US)*, please?

Can you give me the <u>number</u> of Europost of 54 Broad Street, Newham?

It's not in the book

They're <u>ex-directory</u> *(Brit)* oder They're <u>unlisted</u> *(US)*

What is the <u>code</u> for Exeter?

Can I <u>dial</u> <u>direct</u> to Peru?

How do I make an outside <u>call</u>? *oder* What do I <u>dial</u> for an outside <u>line</u>?

What do I <u>dial</u> to get the speaking clock?

You'll have to look up the <u>number</u> in the <u>directory</u>

You should get the <u>number</u> from International <u>Directory</u> Enquiries

You omit the '0' when <u>dialling</u> England from Germany

27.2   Verschiedene Arten von Anrufen

It's a local <u>call</u>

It's a long-distance <u>call</u> from Worthing

I want to make an international <u>call</u>

I want to make a reverse charge <u>call</u> to a London number *(Brit)* oder I want to call a London number <u>collect</u> *(US)*

I'd like to make a credit card <u>call</u> to Berlin

I'd like an alarm <u>call</u> for 7.30 tomorrow morning

27.3   Vermittlung

<u>Number</u>, please

What <u>number</u> do you want? *oder* What <u>number</u> are you calling?

Where are you <u>calling</u> from?

Would you <u>repeat</u> the <u>number</u>, please?

You can <u>dial</u> the <u>number</u> direct

Replace the <u>receiver</u> and <u>dial</u> again

There's a Mr Campbell <u>calling</u> you from Canberra and wishes you to pay for the <u>call</u>. Will you <u>accept</u> it?

Go ahead, <u>caller</u>

There's no listing under that name

There's no <u>reply</u> from 45 77 57 84

I'll try to reconnect you

<u>Hold</u> the <u>line</u>, <u>caller</u>

All <u>lines</u> to Bristol are <u>engaged</u> - please try later

I'm trying it for you now

It's ringing *oder* Ringing for you now

The line is <u>engaged</u> *(Brit)* oder <u>busy</u> *(US)*

27.4   Der Teilnehmer antwortet

Could I have <u>extension</u> 516? *oder* Can you give me <u>extension</u> 516?

Is that Mr Lambert's phone?

Could I speak to Mr Swinton, please? *oder* I'd like to speak to Mr Swinton, please *oder* Is Mr Swinton there, please?

Können Sie mich bitte zu Herrn Dr. Graupner durchstellen?

Wer ist am Apparat?

Ich versuche es später noch einmal

Ich rufe in einer halben Stunde zurück

Könnte ich bitte meine Nummer hinterlassen, damit sie mich zurückrufen kann?

Ich rufe aus einer Telefonzelle an

Ich rufe aus England an

Könnten Sie ihn bitten mich zurückzurufen, wenn er wiederkommt?

Could you put me through to Dr Henderson, please?

Who's speaking?

I'll try again later

I'll call back in half an hour

Could I leave my number for her to call me back?

I'm ringing from a callbox (Brit) oder I'm calling from a pay station (US)

I'm phoning from England

Would you ask him to ring me when he gets back?

27.5 The switchboard operator speaks

Hotel Maritim, guten Tag

Wer ist am Apparat, bitte?

Wen darf ich melden?

Wissen Sie, welchen Apparat er hat?

Ich verbinde Sie

Ein Gespräch aus Tokio für Frau Böhme

Frau Fehrmann für Sie

Frau Neubert aus Paris für Sie

Herr Dr. Schwendt spricht gerade auf der anderen Leitung

Bitte bleiben Sie am Apparat

Es meldet sich niemand

Sie sind mit unserer Verkaufsabteilung verbunden

27.5 Die Zentrale antwortet

Queen's Hotel, can I help you?

Who is calling, please?

Who shall I say is calling?

Do you know his extension number?

I am connecting you now oder I'm putting you through now

I have a call from Tokyo for Mrs Thomas

I've got Miss Trotter on the line for you

Miss Paxton is calling you from Paris

Dr Craig is talking on the other line

Sorry to keep you waiting

There's no reply

You're through to our Sales Department

27.6 Answering the telephone

Hallo, Anne hier

(Kann ich mit Anne sprechen?) Am Apparat

Möchten Sie eine Nachricht hinterlassen?

Kann ich ihm etwas ausrichten?

Bitte bleiben Sie am Apparat

Legen Sie bitte auf, ich rufe Sie zurück

Hier spricht der automatische Anrufbeantworter

Bitte sprechen Sie nach dem Tonzeichen

27.6 Sich am Telefon melden

Hello, this is Anne speaking

(Is that Anne?) Speaking

Would you like to leave a message?

Can I take a message for him?

Don't hang up yet

Put the phone down and I'll call you back

This is a recorded message

Please speak after the tone

27.7 In case of difficulty

Ich komme nicht durch

Ich bekomme kein Rufzeichen

Ich bekomme immer nur „Kein Anschluss unter dieser Nummer"

Das Telefon ist gestört

Wir sind unterbrochen worden

Ich muss mich verwählt haben

Da ist noch jemand in der Leitung

Ich habe mehrmals angerufen, aber es hat sich niemand gemeldet

Sie haben mir die falsche Nummer gegeben

Ich bin mit dem falschen Apparat verbunden worden

Die Verbindung ist sehr schlecht

27.7 Bei Schwierigkeiten

I can't get through

The number is not ringing

I'm getting "number unobtainable" oder I'm getting the "number unobtainable" signal

Their phone is out of order

We were cut off

I must have dialled the wrong number

We've got a crossed line

I've called them several times with no reply

You gave me a wrong number

I got the wrong extension

This is a very bad line

28   VORSCHLÄGE

28.1 Vorschläge machen

+ **You might like to** think it over before giving me your decision
  = *vielleicht möchten Sie*

+ **If you were to** give me the negative, **I could** get copies made
  = *wenn Sie ..., könnte ich*

+ **You could** help me clear out my office, **if you don't mind**
  = *Sie könnten ..., wenn es Ihnen nichts ausmacht*

+ **We could** stop off in Venice for a day or two, **if you like**
  = *wir könnten..., wenn Sie möchten*

+ I've got an idea - **let's organize** a surprise birthday party for Hannah!
  = *lasst uns doch ... organisieren*

+ **If you've no objection(s), I'll** speak to them personally
  = *wenn Sie keine Einwände haben, werde ich*

+ **If I were you, I'd** go
  = *an Ihrer Stelle würde ich*

+ **If you ask me, you'd better** take some extra cash
  = *wenn Sie mich fragen, Sie sollten besser*

+ **I'd be very careful not to** commit myself at this stage
  = *ich würde mich hüten*

+ **I would recommend (that) you** discuss it with him before making a decision
  = *ich würde vorschlagen, (dass) Sie*

+ **It could be in your interest to** have a word with the owner first
  = *es könnte in Ihrem Interesse sein*

+ **There's a lot to be said for** living alone
  = *es spricht vieles dafür*

+ Go and see Pompeii - **it's a must!**
  = *das muss man gesehen haben*

Unschlüssiger

+ **I suggest that you** go to bed and try to sleep
  = *ich schlage vor, dass Sie*

+ **I'd like to suggest that you** seriously consider taking a long holiday
  = *ich würde vorschlagen, dass Sie*

+ **We propose that** half the fee be paid in advance, and half on completion
  = *wir schlagen vor, dass*

+ **It is very important that** you take an interest in what he is trying to do
  = *es ist sehr wichtig, dass*

+ **I am convinced that** this would be a dangerous step to take
  = *ich bin überzeugt, dass*

+ **I cannot put it too strongly: you really must** see a doctor
  = *Sie müssen wirklich*

Weniger direkt

+ **Say you were to** approach the problem from a different angle
  = *wenn Sie nun*

+ In these circumstances, **it might be better to** wait
  = *es wäre vielleicht besser*

+ **Perhaps it would be as well to** change the locks
  = *vielleicht wäre es besser*

+ **It might be a good thing** oder **a good idea to** warn her about this
  = *es wäre vielleicht gut*

+ **Perhaps you should** take up sport
  = *vielleicht sollten Sie*

+ **If I may make a suggestion**, a longer hemline might suit you better
  = *wenn ich einen Vorschlag machen dürfte*

+ **If I might be permitted to suggest something**, installing bigger windows would make the office much brighter
  = *wenn ich vielleicht einen Vorschlag machen dürfte*

+ **Might I be allowed to offer a little advice?** - talk it over with a solicitor before you go any further
  = *dürfte ich Ihnen einen Rat geben*

Als Frage

+ **How do you fancy** a holiday in Australia?
  = *was hältst du von*

+ **How would you feel about** taking calcium supplements?
  = *was halten Sie von*

+ I was thinking of going for a drink later. **How about it?**
  = *wie wäre das*

+ **What would you say to** a trip up to town next week?
  = *was würden Sie zu ... sagen*

+ **Would you like to** stay in Paris for a couple of nights?
  = *möchten Sie*

+ **Would you care to** have lunch with me?
  = *möchten Sie*

+ **What if** you try ignoring her and see if that stops her complaining?
  = *und wenn*

+ **What you need is** a change of scene. **Why not** go on a cruise?
  = *warum nicht*

+ **Suppose** oder **Supposing** you left the kids with your mother for a few days?
  = *angenommen*

+ **Have you ever thought of** starting up a magazine of your own?
  = *haben Sie schon mal daran gedacht*

28.2 Vorschläge erbitten

+ **What would you do if you were me?**
  = *was würden Sie an meiner Stelle tun*

+ **Have you any idea how I should** go about it to get the best results?
  = *haben Sie vielleicht eine Vorstellung, wie ich ... könnte*

+ I've no idea what to call our new puppy: **have you any suggestions?**
  = *haben Sie vielleicht einen Vorschlag*

+ **I wonder if you could suggest** where we might go for a few days?
  = *haben Sie vielleicht einen Vorschlag*

+ I can only afford to buy one of them: **which do you suggest?**
  = *welchen würden Sie vorschlagen*

+ **I'm a bit doubtful about** where to start
  = *ich weiß nicht genau*

29   RATSCHLÄGE

29.1 Ratschläge erbitten

+ What would you do **if you were me?**
  = *an meiner Stelle*

+ Would a pear tree grow in this spot? If not, **what would you recommend?**
  = *was würden Sie empfehlen*

+ **Do you think I ought to** tell the truth if he asks me where I've been?
  = *denken Sie, ich sollte*

+ **Would you advise me to** seek promotion within this firm or apply for another job?
  = *meinen Sie, ich sollte*

+ **What would you advise me to do** in the circumstances?
  = *was würden Sie mir raten*

+ **I'd like** oder **I'd appreciate your advice on** personal pensions
  = *ich würde Sie gern um Rat fragen*

+ **I'd be grateful if you could advise me on** how to treat this problem
  = *ich wäre Ihnen sehr dankbar wenn Sie mir raten könnten*

29.2 Rat geben

+ **It might be wise** oder **sensible to** consult a specialist
  = *es wäre vielleicht das Vernünftigste*

- **It might be a good idea to** seek professional advice
  = *es wäre vielleicht gut*
- **It might be better to** think the whole thing over before taking any decisions
  = *es wäre vielleicht besser*
- **It would certainly be advisable to** book a table
  = *es wäre sicherlich besser*
- **You'd be as well to** state your position at the outset, so there is no mistake
  = *am besten sollten Sie vielleicht*
- **You would be well-advised to** invest in a pair of sunglasses if you're going to Spain
  = *Sie wären gut beraten, wenn Sie*
- **You'd be ill-advised to** have any dealings with this firm
  = *Sie wären schlecht beraten, wenn Sie*
- **It is in your interest** oder **your best interests to** keep your dog under control if you don't want it to be reported
  = *es wäre ganz in Ihrem Interesse*
- **Do be sure to** read the small print before you sign anything
  = *auf jeden Fall sollten Sie*
- **Try to avoid** upsetting her; she'll only make your life a misery
  = *vermeiden Sie*
- **Whatever you do, don't** drink the local schnapps
  = *was auch immer Sie vorhaben, Sie sollten nie*
- **If you ask me, you'd better** take some extra cash
  = *wenn Sie mich fragen, Sie sollten besser*
- **If you want my advice, you should** steer well clear of them
  = *wenn Sie mich um Rat fragen, Sie sollten*
- **If you want my opinion, I'd** go by air to save time
  = *meiner Meinung nach sollten Sie*
- **In your shoes** oder **If I were you, I'd** be thinking about moving on
  = *an Ihrer Stelle würde ich*
- **Might I be allowed to offer a little advice?** - talk it over with a solicitor before going any further
  = *dürfte ich Ihnen einen Rat geben*
- **Take my advice** and don't rush into anything
  = *nehmen Sie meinen Ratschlag an*
- **I'd be very careful not to** commit myself at this stage
  = *ich würde mich davor hüten*
- **I think you ought to** oder **should** seek professional advice
  = *ich denke, Sie sollten*
- **My advice would be to** have nothing to do with them
  = *ich würde Ihnen raten*
- **I would advise you to** pay up promptly before they take you to court
  = *ich würde Ihnen raten*
- **I would advise against** calling in the police unless he threatens you
  = *ich würde Ihnen davon abraten, zu*
- **I would strongly advise you to** reconsider this decision
  = *ich würde Ihnen dringend anraten*
- **I would urge you to** reconsider selling the property
  = *Sie sollten unbedingt*

29.3 | Warnende Hinweise

- It's really none of my business but **I don't think you should** get involved
  = *ich denke, Sie sollten nicht*
- **A word of caution**: watch what you say to him if you want it to remain a secret
  = *ein warnender Hinweis*
- **I should warn you that** he's not an easy customer to deal with
  = *ich sollte Sie vielleicht warnen, dass*
- **Take care not to** lose the vaccination certificate
  = *achten Sie darauf, dass Sie nicht*
- **Watch you don't** trip over your shoelaces
  = *pass auf, dass du nicht*

- **Make sure that** oder **Mind that** oder **See that you don't** say anything they might find offensive
  = *auf keinen Fall sollten Sie*
- **I'd think twice about** sharing a flat with him
  = *ich würde es mir gut überlegen, ob*
- **It would be sheer madness to** attempt to drive without your glasses
  = *es wäre reiner Wahnsinn*
- **You risk** a long delay in Amsterdam **if** you come back by that route
  = *Sie riskieren ..., wenn*

30 | ANGEBOTE

- **I would be delighted to** help out, if I may
  = *ich würde sehr gerne*
- **It would give me great pleasure to** show you round the city
  = *ich würde sehr gerne*
- **We would like to offer you** the post of Sales Director
  = *wir möchten Ihnen ... anbieten*
- **I hope you will not be offended if I offer** a contribution towards your expenses
  = *ich hoffe, Sie nehmen es mir nicht übel, wenn ich*
- **Do let me know if I can** help in any way
  = *lassen Sie es mich wissen, wenn ich ... kann*
- **If we can** be of any further assistance, **please do not hesitate to** contact us
  = *falls wir ... können, zögern Sie bitte nicht*
- **Say we were to** offer you a 5% rise, **how would that sound?**
  = *und wenn wir ... wie wäre das*
- **What if I were to** call for you in the car?
  = *was halten Sie davon, wenn ich*
- **Could I** give you a hand with your luggage?
  = *kann ich vielleicht*
- **Shall I** do the photocopies for you?
  = *soll ich*
- **Would you like me to** find out more about it for you?
  = *soll ich*
- **Is there anything I can do to** help you find suitable accommodation?
  = *kann ich irgendetwas tun, um*
- **May** oder **Can I offer you** a drink?
  = *darf ich Ihnen ... anbieten*
- **Would you allow me to** pay for dinner, at least?
  = *würden Sie mir gestatten*
- **You will let me** show you around Glasgow, **won't you**?
  = *Sie werden es mir doch nicht abschlagen*

31 | BITTEN

- **Please would you** drop by on your way home and pick up the papers you left here?
  = *würden Sie bitte*
- **Could you please** try to keep the noise down while I'm studying?
  = *könnten Sie bitte*
- **Could I ask you to** watch out for anything suspicious in my absence?
  = *könnte ich Sie bitten*
- **Would you mind** looking after Hannah for a couple of hours tomorrow?
  = *würde es Ihnen etwas ausmachen*

Förmlicher

- **I should be grateful if you could** confirm whether it would be possible to increase my credit limit to £5000
  = *ich wäre Ihnen dankbar, wenn Sie ... könnten*

◆ **We would ask you not to** use the telephone for long-distance calls
  = wir möchten Sie darum _bitten_

◆ **You are requested to** park at the rear of the building
  = wir möchten Sie _bitten_

◆ **We look forward to** receiving confirmation of your order within 14 days
  = wir _freuen_ uns darauf

◆ **Kindly inform us if** you require alternative arrangements to be made
  = bitte _teilen_ Sie uns _mit_, _wenn_

Weniger direkt

◆ **I would rather you didn't** breathe a word to anyone about this
  = es wäre mir _lieber_, _wenn_ Sie nicht

◆ **I would appreciate it if you could** let me have copies of the best photos
  = es wäre schön, _wenn_ Sie ... könnten

◆ **I was hoping that you might** have time to visit your grandmother
  = ich hatte _gehofft_, du würdest vielleicht

◆ **I wonder whether you could** spare a few pounds till I get to the bank?
  = könntest du vielleicht

◆ **I hope you don't mind if I** borrow your exercise bike for half an hour
  = hoffentlich _macht_ es dir nichts _aus_, _wenn_ ich

◆ **It would be very helpful** oder **useful if you could** have everything ready beforehand
  = es wäre sehr zu _begrüßen_, _wenn_ Sie ... könnten

◆ **If it's not too much trouble, would you** pop my suit into the dry cleaner's on your way past?
  = _wenn_ es nicht zu viel _Umstände_ macht, würden Sie

◆ **You won't forget** to lock up before you leave, **will you?**
  = _vergiss_ nicht ..., ja

---

32 **VERGLEICHE**

32.1 **Objektive Vergleiche**

◆ The streets, though wide for China, are narrow **compared with** English ones
  = _verglichen_ mit

◆ The bomb used to blow the car up was small **in** oder **by comparison with** those often used nowadays
  = im _Vergleich_ zu

◆ The quality of the paintings is disappointing **beside** that of the sculpture section
  = im _Vergleich_ zu

◆ **If you compare** the facilities we have here **with** those in other towns, you soon realize how lucky we are
  = _wenn_ man ... mit ... _vergleicht_

◆ It is interesting to note **the similarities and the differences between** the two approaches
  = die Gemeinsamkeiten und _Unterschiede_ _zwischen_

◆ **In contrast to** the opulence of the Kirov, the Northern Ballet Theatre is a modest company
  = im _Gegensatz_ zu

◆ Only 30% of the females died **as opposed to** 57% of the males
  = im _Gegensatz_ zu

◆ **Unlike** other loan repayments, those to the IMF cannot simply be rescheduled
  = im _Gegensatz_ zu

◆ **Whereas** burglars often used to make off only with video recorders, they now also tend to empty the fridge
  = während

◆ **What differentiates** these wines **from** a good champagne is their price
  = was ... von ... _unterscheidet_

32.2 **Positive Vergleiche**

◆ Orwell was, indeed, **far superior to** him intellectually
  = wesentlich besser als

◆ Personally I think high-speed trains **have the edge over** both cars and aircraft for sheer convenience
  = sind ... überlegen

◆ Emma was astute beyond her years and altogether **in a class of her own**
  = einzigartig

32.3 **Negative Vergleiche**

◆ Andrew's piano playing **is not a patch on** his sister's
  = ist gar nichts _verglichen_ mit

◆ My old chair **was nowhere near as** comfortable **as** my new one
  = war in keiner _Hinsicht_ so .. wie

◆ The parliamentary opposition **is no match for** the government, which has a massive majority
  = ist .. nicht gewachsen

◆ Commercially-made ice-cream **is far inferior to** the home-made variety
  = ist viel schlechter als

◆ The sad truth was that **he was never in the same class as** his friend
  = er war einfach nicht mit ... zu _vergleichen_

◆ Ella doesn't rate anything **that doesn't measure up to** Shakespeare
  = das nicht an ... _heranreicht_

◆ Her brash charms **don't bear comparison with** Marlene's sultry sex appeal
  = _halten_ einem _Vergleich_ mit ... nicht _stand_

◆ The Australians are far bigger and stronger than us - **we can't compete with** their robot-like style of play
  = wir können mit ... nicht _mithalten_

32.4 **Vergleichbar**

◆ The new computerized system costs **much the same as** a more conventional one
  = fast dasselbe

◆ When it comes to performance, **there's not much to choose between** them
  = gibt es fast kaum _Unterschiede_ _zwischen_

◆ The impact **was equivalent to** 250 hydrogen bombs exploding
  = _entsprach_

◆ In Kleinian analysis, the psychoanalyst's role **corresponds to** that of mother
  = _entspricht_

◆ English literature written by people of the ex-colonies **is on a par with** the writings of native-born British people
  = ist genauso gut wie

◆ The immune system **can be likened to** oder **compared to** a complicated electronic network
  = kann mit ... _verglichen_ werden

◆ **There was a close resemblance between** her **and** her son
  = ... und ... waren sich sehr _ähnlich_

◆ **It's swings and roundabouts** - what you win in one round, you lose in another
  = das ist gehupft wie gesprungen

32.5 **Nicht vergleichbar**

◆ **You cannot compare** a small local library **with** a large city one
  = man kann .. nicht mit ... _vergleichen_

◆ **There's no comparison between** the sort of photos I take **and** those a professional could give you
  = ... und ... kann man einfach nicht miteinander _vergleichen_

◆ Home-made clothes **just cannot compare with** bought ones
  = sind eben nicht mit ... _vergleichbar_

◆ His books **have little in common with** those approved by the Party
  = haben wenig mit ... _gemein_

◆ We might be twins, but **we have nothing in common**
= wir haben nichts _gemein_

◆ The modern army **bears little resemblance to** the army of 1940
= hat kaum mehr Ähnlichkeit mit

33   MEINUNGEN

33.1   Meinungen erfragen

◆ **What do you think of** the new Managing Director?
= was _halten_ Sie von

◆ **What is your opinion on** women's rights?
= wie _denken_ Sie über

◆ **What are your thoughts on** the way forward?
= wie ist Ihre _Meinung_ zu

◆ **What is your attitude to** people who say there is no such thing as sexual inequality?
= wie stehen Sie zu

◆ **What are your own feelings about** the way the case was handled?
= was _halten_ Sie _persönlich_ von

◆ **How do you see** the next stage developing?
= wie sehen Sie

◆ **How do you view** an event like the Birmingham show in terms of the cultural life of the city?
= wie _schätzen_ Sie ... _ein_

◆ **I would value your opinion on** how to set this all up
= mir wäre sehr an Ihrer _Meinung_ über ... gelegen

◆ **I'd be interested to know what your reaction is to** the latest report on food additives
= ich _wüsste_ gern, was Sie von ... _halten_

33.2   Seine Meinung sagen

◆ **In my opinion**, eight years as President is quite enough for anyone
= meiner _Meinung_ nach

◆ We're prepared to prosecute the company, which **to my mind** has committed a criminal offence
= meiner _Meinung_ nach

◆ **From my point of view** activities like these should not be illegal
= aus meiner Sicht

◆ **I am of the opinion that** the rules should be looked at and refined
= ich bin der _Meinung_, dass

◆ **As I see it**, everything depended on Karlov being permitted to go to Finland
= so wie ich die _Sache_ sehe

◆ **I feel that** there is an epidemic of fear about cancer which is not helped by all the publicity about the people who die of it
= ich _persönlich_ denke, dass

◆ **Personally, I believe** the best way to change a government is through the electoral process
= _persönlich_ _glaube_ ich

◆ **It seems to me that** the successful designer leads the public
= mir _scheint_, (dass)

◆ **I am under the impression that** he is essentially a man of peace
= ich habe den _Eindruck_, dass

◆ **I have an idea that** you are going to be very successful
= ich kann mir _vorstellen_, dass

◆ **I'm convinced that** we all need a new vision of the future
= ich bin _überzeugt_, dass

◆ **I daresay** there are so many names that you get them mixed up once in a while
= ich würde sagen

◆ **As far as I'm concerned**, Barnes had it coming to him
= was mich _betrifft_

◆ It's a matter of common sense, nothing more. **That's my view of the matter**
= so sehe ich die _Sache_

◆ **It is our belief that** to be proactive is more positive than being reactive
= wir _glauben_, dass

◆ **If you ask me**, there's something a bit strange going on
= _wenn_ Sie mich _fragen_

◆ **If you want my opinion**, if you don't do it soon you'll lose the opportunity altogether
= _wenn_ Sie meine _Meinung_ hören wollen

33.3   Keine Meinung zum Ausdruck bringen

◆ Would I say she had been a help? **It depends what you mean by** help
= das _hängt_ davon _ab_, was Sie unter ... _verstehen_

◆ It could be seen as a triumph for capitalism but **it depends on your point of view**
= das _hängt_ von Ihrer _Meinung_ _ab_

◆ **It's hard** oder **difficult to say whether** she has benefited from the treatment or not
= es ist _schwer_ zu sagen, ob

◆ **I'm not in a position to comment on whether** the director's accusations are well-founded
= ich kann mich nicht dazu _äußern_, ob

◆ **I'd prefer not to comment on** operational decisions taken by the service in the past
= ich möchte mich _lieber_ nicht zu ... _äußern_

◆ **I'd rather not commit myself** at this stage
= ich möchte mich _lieber_ nicht festlegen

◆ **I don't have any strong feelings about** which of the two companies we decide to use for the job
= ich habe eigentlich keine besondere _Meinung_ über

◆ **This isn't something I've given much thought to**
= damit habe ich mich noch nicht eingehend _beschäftigt_

◆ **I know nothing about** fine wine
= ich habe keine Ahnung von

34   VORLIEBEN UND ABNEIGUNGEN

34.1   Vorlieben erfragen

◆ **Would you like to** visit the castle while you are here?
= möchten Sie

◆ **How would you feel about** Simon joining us?
= was _halten_ Sie davon, _wenn_

◆ **What do you like doing best** when you're on holiday?
= was machen Sie am liebsten

◆ **What's your favourite** film?
= was ist Ihr _Lieblings_ ...

◆ **Which of the two** proposed options **do you prefer?**
= welche der beiden ... ist Ihnen _lieber_

◆ We could either go to Rome or stay in Florence - **which would you rather do?**
= was würden Sie _lieber_ tun

34.2   Vorlieben ausdrücken

◆ **I'm very keen on** gardening
= ich ... sehr gerne

◆ **I'm very fond of** white geraniums and blue petunias
= ich _mag_ ... sehr

◆ **I really enjoy** a good game of squash after work
= ... macht mir sehr viel Spaß

◆ **There's nothing I like more than** a quiet night in with a good book
= nichts _mag_ ich _lieber_ als

◆ **I have a weakness for** rich chocolate gateaux
= ich habe eine _Schwäche_ für

◆ **I've always had a soft spot for** the Dutch
= ich habe schon immer eine _Schwäche_ für ... gehabt

34.3   Abneigung ausdrücken

◆ Acting **isn't really my thing** - I'm better at singing
= ist nichts für mich

◆ I enjoy playing golf, although this type of course **is not my cup of tea**
= *ist nicht mein <u>Fall</u>*

◆ Watching football on television **isn't exactly my favourite** pastime
= *ist nicht gerade meine <u>Lieblings</u>...*

◆ Some people might find it funny but **it's not my kind of** humour
= *ist nicht meine Art von*

◆ Sitting for hours on motorways **is not my idea of** fun
= *ist nicht gerade das, was ich mir unter ... <u>vorstelle</u>*

◆ The idea of walking home at 10 or 11 o'clock at night **doesn't appeal to me**
= *<u>gefällt</u> mir nicht*

◆ **I've gone off the idea of** cycling round Holland
= *ich habe das Interesse daran verloren*

◆ **I can't stand** oder **can't bear** the thought of seeing him
= *ich kann ... nicht <u>ertragen</u>*

◆ **I'm not enthusiastic about** shopping in large supermarkets
= *ich bin nicht gerade <u>begeistert</u> von*

◆ **I'm not keen on** seafood
= *ich <u>mag</u> ... nicht*

◆ **I dislike** laziness since I'm such an energetic person myself
= *ich <u>mag</u> ... nicht*

◆ **I don't like the fact that** he always gets away with not helping out in the kitchen
= *mir <u>gefällt</u> nicht, dass*

◆ **What I hate most is** waiting in queues for buses
= *am meisten <u>hasse</u> ich*

◆ **There's nothing I dislike more than** having to go to work in the dark
= *nichts <u>hasse</u> ich mehr als*

◆ **I have a particular aversion to** the religious indoctrination of schoolchildren
= *besonders abstoßend <u>finde</u> ich*

◆ **I find it intolerable that** people like him should have so much power
= *ich <u>finde</u> es unerträglich, dass*

34.4 Ausdrücken, was man bevorzugt

◆ **I'd prefer to** oder **I'd rather** wait until I have enough money to go by air
= *ich würde <u>lieber</u>*

◆ **I'd prefer not to** oder **I'd rather not** talk about it just now
= *ich würde <u>lieber</u> nicht*

◆ **I'd prefer you to** give oder **I'd rather you** gave me your comments in writing
= *es wäre mir <u>lieber, wenn</u> Sie*

◆ **I'd prefer you not to** oder **I'd rather you didn't** invite him
= *es wäre mir <u>lieber, wenn</u> Sie nicht*

◆ **I like** the blue curtains **better than** the red ones
= *... <u>gefallen</u> mir besser als*

◆ **I prefer** red wine **to** white wine
= *ich <u>mag lieber</u> ... als ...*

34.5 Keine Vorliebe ausdrücken

◆ **It makes no odds whether** you have a million pounds or nothing, we won't judge you on your wealth
= *es ist ganz <u>egal</u>, ob*

◆ **It doesn't matter which** method you choose to use
= *es ist <u>egal</u>, welche*

◆ **It's all the same to me whether** he comes **or** not
= *es ist mir <u>vollkommen egal</u>, ob ... oder*

◆ **I really don't care what** you tell her as long as you tell her something
= *es kümmert mich wirklich nicht, was*

◆ **I don't mind at all** - let's do whatever is easiest
= *das <u>macht</u> mir gar nichts <u>aus</u>*

◆ **I don't feel strongly about** the issue of privatization
= *ich habe keine besondere <u>Meinung</u> über*

◆ **I have no particular preference**
= *ich habe keine spezielle <u>Vorliebe</u>*

35 ABSICHTEN UND VORHABEN

35.1 Nach Absichten fragen

◆ **Will you** take the job?
= *<u>haben</u> Sie <u>vor</u>*

◆ **What do you intend to do?**
= *was <u>beabsichtigen</u> Sie zu tun*

◆ **Did you mean to** oder **intend to** tell him about it, or did it just slip out?
= *hatten Sie die <u>Absicht</u>*

◆ **What do you propose to do** with the money?
= *was <u>wollen</u> Sie ... machen*

◆ **What did you have in mind for** the rest of the programme?
= *wie hatten Sie sich ...<u>vorgestellt</u>*

◆ **Have you anyone in mind for** the job?
= *haben Sie jemanden Bestimmten für ... ins Auge gefasst*

35.2 Absichten ausdrücken

◆ **We're toying with the idea of** releasing a compilation album
= *wir spielen mit dem <u>Gedanken</u>*

◆ **I'm thinking of** retiring next year
= *ich trage mich mit dem <u>Gedanken</u>*

◆ **I'm hoping to** go and see her when I'm in Paris
= *ich <u>habe</u> eigentlich <u>vor</u>*

◆ I studied history, **with a view to** becoming a politician
= *mit der <u>Absicht</u>*

◆ We bought the land **in order to** farm it
= *um zu*

◆ We do not penetrate foreign companies **for the purpose of** collecting business information
= *um zu*

◆ **We plan to** move oder **We are planning on** moving next year
= *wir <u>planen</u>*

◆ **Our aim** oder **Our object in** buying the company **is to** provide work for the villagers
= *unsere <u>Absicht</u> bei ... <u>besteht</u> darin*

◆ **I aim to** reach Africa in three months
= *ich habe mir <u>vorgenommen</u>*

Bestimmter

◆ **I am going to** sell the car as soon as possible
= *ich <u>habe vor</u>*

◆ **I intend to** put the house on the market
= *ich <u>beabsichtige</u>*

◆ I went to Rome **with the intention of** visiting her, but she had gone away
= *mit der <u>Absicht</u>*

◆ **I have made up my mind to** oder **I have decided to** go to Japan
= *ich habe mich <u>entschieden</u>*

◆ **We have every intention of** winning a sixth successive championship
= *wir sind fest <u>entschlossen</u>*

◆ **I have set my sights on** recapturing the title
= *ich habe mir das Ziel gesteckt*

◆ **My overriding ambition is to** get into politics
= *mein allergrößter <u>Ehrgeiz</u> ist es*

◆ **I resolve to** do everything in my power to help you
= *ich habe <u>beschlossen</u>*

35.3 Ausdrücken, was man nicht beabsichtigt

+ **I don't mean to** offend you, but I think you're wrong
  = *ich möchte nicht*

+ **I don't intend to** pay unless he completes the job
  = *ich habe nicht vor*

+ **We are not thinking of** taking on more staff
  = *wir haben nicht vor*

+ **I have no intention of** accepting the post
  = *ich habe nicht die Absicht*

+ **We do not envisage** making changes at this late stage
  = *wir gedenken nicht*

35.4 Wünsche ausdrücken

+ **I'd like to** see the Sistine Chapel some day
  = *ich würde gerne*

+ **I want to** work abroad when I leave college
  = *ich möchte*

+ **We want her to** be an architect when she grows up
  = *wir möchten, dass sie*

+ **I'm keen to** develop the business
  = *ich möchte gerne*

| Enthusiastisch |

+ **I'm dying to** leave home
  = *ich kann es kaum erwarten*

+ **I long to** go to Australia but I can't afford it
  = *ich würde wahnsinnig gerne*

+ **My ambition is to** become an opera singer
  = *mein Ehrgeiz geht dahin*

+ **I insist on** speaking to the manager
  = *ich bestehe darauf*

35.5 Ausdrücken, was man nicht wünscht

+ **I would prefer not to** oder **I would rather not** have to speak to her about this
  = *ich würde lieber nicht*

+ **I wouldn't want to** have to change my plans just because of her
  = *ich möchte nicht*

+ **I don't want to** take the credit for something I didn't do
  = *ich möchte nicht*

+ **I have no wish** oder **desire to** become rich and famous
  = *ich habe nicht das Verlangen*

+ **I refuse to** be patronized by the likes of her
  = *ich lehne es ab*

36   ERLAUBNIS

36.1 Um Erlaubnis bitten

+ **Can I** oder **Could I** borrow your car this afternoon?
  = *kann ich vielleicht*

+ **Can I** use the telephone, please?
  = *könnte ich*

+ **Are we allowed to** say what we're up to or is it top secret at the moment?
  = *dürfen wir*

+ **Would it be all right if** I arrived on Monday instead of Tuesday?
  = *wäre es in Ordnung, wenn*

+ **Would it be possible for us to** leave the car in your garage for a week?
  = *wäre es möglich, dass wir*

+ We leave tomorrow. **Is that all right by you?**
  = *ist das in Ordnung*

+ **Do you mind if** I come to the meeting next week?
  = *haben Sie etwas dagegen, wenn*

+ **Would it bother you if** I invited him?
  = *würde es Sie stören, wenn*

+ **Would you let me** come into partnership with you?
  = *würden Sie mir gestatten*

+ **Would you have any objection to** sailing at once?
  = *haben Sie irgendwelche Einwände dagegen*

+ **With your permission, I'd like to** ask some questions
  = *mit Ihrer Erlaubnis würde ich gerne*

+ **Can I have the go-ahead to** order the supplies?
  = *kann ich grünes Licht bekommen*

| Zögernder |

+ **Is there any chance of** borrowing your boat while we're at the lake?
  = *wäre es vielleicht möglich*

+ **I wonder if I could possibly** use your telephone?
  = *könnte ich vielleicht*

+ **Might I be permitted to** suggest the following ideas?
  = *dürfte ich vielleicht*

+ **May I be allowed to** set the record straight?
  = *dürfte ich vielleicht*

36.2 Erlaubnis erteilen

+ **You can** have anything you want
  = *Sie können*

+ **You are allowed to** visit the museum, as long as you apply in writing to the Curator first
  = *Sie haben die Erlaubnis*

+ **You have my permission to** be absent for that week
  = *Sie haben meine Erlaubnis*

+ **It's all right by me if** you want to skip the Cathedral visit
  = *es ist mir recht, wenn*

+ **I've nothing against her** going there with us
  = *ich habe nichts dagegen, wenn sie*

+ **The Crown was agreeable to** having the case called on March 23
  = *hat zugestimmt*

+ **I do not mind if** my letter is forwarded to the lady concerned
  = *ich habe nichts dagegen, wenn*

+ **You have been authorized to** use all necessary force to protect relief supply routes
  = *Sie sind bevollmächtigt*

+ **We should be happy to allow you to** inspect the papers here
  = *gerne gestatten wir Ihnen*

+ If you need to keep your secret, **of course you must** keep it
  = *müssen Sie selbstverständlich*

+ **By all means** charge a reasonable consultation fee
  = *auf jeden Fall*

+ **I have no objection at all to your** quoting me in your article
  = *ich erhebe keinerlei Einwände dagegen, dass Sie*

+ **We would be delighted to** have you
  = *wir würden sehr gerne*

36.3 Erlaubnis verweigern

+ **You can't** oder **you mustn't** go anywhere near the research lab
  = *Sie dürfen nicht*

+ **You're not allowed to** leave the ship until relieved
  = *Sie dürfen nicht*

+ **You must not** enter the premises without the owners' authority
  = *Sie dürfen auf keinen Fall*

+ **I don't want you to** see that man again
  = *ich möchte nicht, dass Sie*

+ **I'd rather you didn't** give them my name
  = *es wäre mir lieber, wenn Sie nicht*

+ **I've been forbidden to** swim for the moment
  = *ich darf nicht*

◆ **I've been forbidden** alcohol **by** my doctor
  = ... hat mir _verboten_

◆ **I couldn't possibly allow you to** pay for all this
  = ich _kann_ Ihnen beim besten Willen nicht _erlauben_

◆ **We cannot allow** the marriage **to** take place
  = wir _können_ nicht _zulassen, dass_

Bestimmter

◆ **You are forbidden to** contact my children
  = ich _verbiete_ es Ihnen

◆ **I absolutely forbid you to** take part in any further search
  = ich _verbiete_ Ihnen _strengstens_

◆ Smoking **is strictly forbidden** at all times
  = ist _streng verboten_

◆ It **is strictly forbidden to** carry weapons in this country
  = es ist _streng verboten_

◆ **We regret that it is not possible for you to** visit the castle at the moment, owing to the building works
  = _leider_ können Sie nicht

---

37   VERPFLICHTUNG

37.1   Verpflichtung ausdrücken

◆ **You've got to** oder **You have to** be back before midnight
  = du _musst_

◆ **You must** have an address in Prague before you can apply for the job
  = Sie _müssen_

◆ **You need to** have a valid passport if you want to leave the country
  = Sie _müssen_

◆ I have no choice: this is how **I must** live and I cannot do otherwise
  = ich _muss_

◆ **He was forced to** ask his family for a loan
  = er war _gezwungen_

◆ Jews **are obliged to** accept the divine origin of the Law
  = sind _verpflichtet_

◆ A degree **is indispensable** for future entrants to the profession
  = ist _unentbehrlich_

◆ Party membership **is an essential prerequisite of** a successful career
  = ist eine _unbedingte_ Voraussetzung für

◆ **It is essential to** know what the career options are before choosing a course of study
  = man _muss unbedingt_

◆ Wearing the kilt **is compulsory** for all those taking part
  = ist _obligatorisch_

◆ One cannot admit defeat, **one is driven to** keep on trying
  = man wird dazu _gezwungen_

◆ **We have no alternative but to** fight
  = es _bleibt_ uns nichts anderes _übrig_ als zu

◆ Three passport photos **are required**
  = werden _benötigt_

◆ Club members **must not fail to** observe the regulations about proper behaviour
  = _müssen unbedingt_

◆ **You will** go directly to the headmaster's office and wait for me there
  = du _wirst_

37.2   Erfragen, ob man etwas tun muss

◆ **Do I have to** oder **Have I got to** be home by midnight?
  = _muss_ ich

◆ **Does one have to** oder **need to** book in advance?
  = _muss_ man

◆ **Is it necessary to** go into so much detail?
  = ist es _nötig_

◆ **Ought I to** tell my colleagues?
  = _sollte_ ich

◆ **Should I** call the police?
  = _soll_ ich

◆ **Am I meant to** oder **Am I expected to** oder **Am I supposed to** fill in this bit of the form?
  = _soll_ ich

37.3   Ausdrücken, was keine Verpflichtung ist

◆ **I don't have to** oder **I haven't got to** be home so early now the nights are lighter
  = ich _muss_ nicht _unbedingt_

◆ **You don't have to** oder **You needn't** go there if you don't want to
  = Sie _müssen_ nicht

◆ **You are not obliged to** oder **You are under no obligation to** invite him
  = Sie sind nicht _verpflichtet_

◆ **It is not compulsory** oder **obligatory to** have a letter of acceptance but it does help
  = es ist nicht _unbedingt_ notwendig

◆ The Council **does not expect you to** pay all of your bill at once
  = _erwartet_ nicht von Ihnen, dass

37.4   Verbote ausdrücken

◆ **On no account must you** be persuaded to give up the cause
  = auf gar keinen _Fall dürfen_ Sie

◆ **You are not allowed to** sit the exam more than three times
  = Sie _dürfen_ nicht

◆ **You mustn't** show this document to any unauthorized person
  = Sie _dürfen_ nicht

◆ **You're not supposed to** oder **meant to** use this room unless you are a club member
  = Sie _dürfen_ nicht

◆ Smoking **is not allowed** in the dining room
  = ist nicht _gestattet_

◆ These are tasks **you cannot** ignore, delegate or bungle
  = Sie _können_ nicht

◆ **I forbid you to** return there
  = ich _verbiete_ Ihnen

◆ **It is forbidden to** bring cameras into the gallery
  = es ist nicht _gestattet_

◆ **You are forbidden to** talk to anyone while the case is being heard
  = es ist Ihnen nicht _gestattet_

◆ Smoking **is prohibited** oder **is not permitted** in the dining room
  = ist nicht _gestattet_

---

38   ZUSTIMMUNG

38.1   Zustimmung zu Aussagen

◆ **I fully agree with you** oder **I totally agree with you** on this point
  = ich bin ganz Ihrer _Meinung_

◆ **We are in complete agreement** on this
  = wir sind uns völlig _einig_

◆ **I entirely take your point about** the extra vehicles needed
  = ich _akzeptiere_ Ihre Meinung _vollkommen_, was ... _betrifft_

◆ I think **we see completely eye to eye** on this issue
  = wir sind uns _einig_

◆ I talked it over with the chairman and **we are both of the same mind**
  = wir sind beide der gleichen _Meinung_

◆ **You're quite right in** pointing at distribution as the main problem
  = Sie haben _Recht, wenn_ Sie

◆ **We share your views** on the proposed expansion of the site
  = wir teilen Ihre _Ansichten_

◆ **My own experience** certainly **bears out** oder **confirms** what you say
  = *meine eigene <u>Erfahrung</u> <u>bestätigt</u>*

◆ **It's true that** you had the original idea but many other people worked on it
  = *es <u>stimmt</u>, dass*

◆ **As you have quite rightly pointed out**, this will not be easy
  = *wie Sie bereits <u>richtig</u> <u>bemerkten</u>*

◆ **I have to concede that** the results are quite eye-catching
  = *ich muss gestehen, dass*

◆ **I have no objection to** this being done
  = *ich habe keine <u>Einwände</u> gegen*

◆ **I agree in theory**, but in practice it's never quite that simple
  = *theoretisch <u>stimme</u> ich <u>zu</u>*

◆ **I agree up to a point**
  = *bis zu einem gewissen Punkt <u>stimme</u> ich <u>zu</u>*

◆ Go for a drink instead of working late? **Sounds good to me!**
  = *<u>klingt</u> gut*

◆ **That's a lovely idea**
  = *das ist eine sehr gute <u>Idee</u>*

◆ **I'm all for** encouraging a youth section in video clubs such as ours
  = *ich bin ganz dafür*

◆ **I couldn't agree with you more**
  = *ich bin <u>völlig</u> Ihrer <u>Meinung</u>*

◆ **I am delighted to wholeheartedly endorse** your campaign
  = *es ist mir eine Freude, ... von ganzem Herzen zu <u>unterstützen</u>*

◆ **Our conclusions are entirely consistent with** your findings
  = *unsere <u>Schlussfolgerungen</u> <u>entsprechen</u> <u>vollkommen</u>*

◆ Independent statistics **corroborate** those of your researcher
  = *<u>bestätigen</u>*

◆ **We applaud** the group's decision to stand firm on this point
  = *wir <u>begrüßen</u>*

38.2 Zustimmung zu Vorschlägen

◆ This certainly **seems the right way to go about it**
  = *<u>scheint</u> der richtige Verfahrensweg*

◆ **I will certainly give my backing to** such a scheme
  = *ich werde ... selbstverständlich <u>unterstützen</u>*

◆ **It makes sense to** enlist helping hands for the final stages
  = *es macht Sinn*

◆ **We certainly welcome** this development
  = *selbstverständlich <u>begrüßen</u> wir*

◆ **It's a great idea**
  = *das ist eine großartige <u>Idee</u>*

◆ Cruise control? **I like the sound of that**
  = *<u>klingt</u> wirklich gut*

◆ **I'll go along with** Ted's proposal that we open the club up to women
  = *ich <u>schließe</u> mich ... an*

Weniger direkt

◆ This solution **is most acceptable** to us
  = *ist sehr annehmbar*

◆ The proposed scheme **meets with our approval**
  = *trifft auf unsere <u>Zustimmung</u>*

◆ This is a proposal which **deserves our wholehearted support**
  = *<u>verdient</u> unsere uneingeschränkte <u>Unterstützung</u>*

38.3 Zustimmung zu Forderungen

◆ Of course **I'll be happy to** organize it for you
  = *werde ich gerne*

◆ **I'll do as you suggest** and send him the documents
  = *ich befolge Ihren <u>Rat</u>*

◆ **There's no problem about** getting tickets for him
  = *es ist kein <u>Problem</u>*

Weniger direkt

◆ Reputable builders **will not object to** this reasonable request
  = *werden ... nicht <u>ablehnen</u>*

◆ **We should be delighted to** cooperate with you in this enterprise
  = *wir würden uns <u>freuen</u>*

◆ An army statement said it **would comply with** the ceasefire
  = *sich an ... halten*

◆ **I consent to** the performance of such procedures as are considered necessary
  = *ich <u>stimme</u> ... <u>zu</u>*

39 WIDERSPRUCH

39.1 Widerspruch zu Gesagtem

◆ There must be some mistake - **it can't possibly** cost as much as that
  = *es kann auf gar keinen <u>Fall</u>*

◆ I'm afraid he **is quite wrong** if he has told you that
  = *<u>irrt</u> sich*

◆ **You're wrong in thinking that** I haven't understood
  = *Sie <u>irren</u> sich, <u>wenn</u> Sie <u>denken</u>*

◆ The article **is mistaken in** claim**ing** that debating the subject is a waste of public money
  = *geht falsch in der <u>Annahme</u>*

◆ Surveys **do not bear out** Mrs Fraser's assumption that these people will return to church at a later date
  = *<u>bestätigen</u> nicht*

◆ **I cannot agree with you** on this point
  = *ich kann Ihnen nicht <u>zustimmen</u>*

◆ **We cannot accept the view that** the lack of research and development explains the decline of Britain
  = *wir können die <u>Ansicht</u>, dass ..., nicht akzeptieren*

◆ To say we should forget about it, no, **I cannot go along with that**
  = *ich kann mich dem nicht <u>anschließen</u>*

◆ **We must agree to differ on this one**
  = *darüber sind wir wohl unterschiedlicher <u>Meinung</u>*

Bestimmter

◆ **This is most emphatically not the case**
  = *das ist auf gar keinen <u>Fall</u> so*

◆ **I entirely reject** his contentions
  = *ich lehne ... vollständig <u>ab</u>*

◆ **I totally disagree with** the previous two callers
  = *ich bin <u>völlig</u> anderer <u>Meinung</u> als*

◆ This is your view of the events: **it is certainly not mine**
  = *meine <u>Ansicht</u> ist das nicht*

◆ **I cannot support you** on this matter
  = *ich kann Sie ... nicht <u>unterstützen</u>*

◆ **Surely you can't believe that** he'd do such a thing?
  = *du kannst doch nicht wirklich <u>glauben</u>, dass*

39.2 Ablehnung von Vorschlägen

Bestimmt

◆ **I'm dead against** this idea
  = *ich bin <u>völlig</u> <u>dagegen</u>*

◆ **Right idea, wrong approach**
  = *ein guter <u>Gedanke</u>, aber er geht in die falsche Richtung*

◆ **I will not hear of** such a thing
  = *ich will von ... nichts hören*

◆ **It is not feasible to** change the schedule at this late stage
  = *es ist nicht <u>möglich</u>*

◆ This **is not a viable alternative**
  = *keine praktisch durchführbare <u>Möglichkeit</u>*

+ Trade sanctions will have an immediate effect but it **is the wrong approach**
  = ist die falsche Herangehensweise

Weniger direkt

+ **I'm not too keen on** this idea
  = ich _halte_ nicht viel von

+ **I don't think much of** this idea
  = ich _halte_ nicht viel von

+ **This doesn't seem to be the right way of** dealing with the problem
  = dies _scheint_ mir die falsche _Methode_ zu sein

+ While we are grateful for the suggestion, **we are unfortunately unable to** implement this change
  = _leider_ ist es uns _unmöglich_

+ **I regret that I am not in a position to** accept your kind offer
  = ich _bedaure_, dass ich nicht in der _Lage_ bin

39.3 Ablehnung von Forderungen

+ **I wouldn't dream of** doing a thing like that
  = es würde mir nicht im Traum _einfallen_

+ I'm sorry but **I just can't** do it
  = ich kann das einfach nicht

+ **I cannot in all conscience** leave those kids in that atmosphere
  = ich kann nicht guten Gewissens

Bestimmt

+ **This is quite out of the question** for the time being
  = das steht ja wohl außer _Frage_

+ **I won't agree to** any plan that involves your brother
  = ich werde ... nicht _zustimmen_

+ **I refuse point blank to** have anything to do with this affair
  = ich _weigere_ mich kategorisch

Weniger direkt

+ **I am afraid I must refuse**
  = es tut mir _Leid_, ich muss das _ablehnen_

+ **I cannot possibly comply with** this request
  = ich kann ... wirklich nicht _nachkommen_

+ **It is unfortunately impracticable for us to** commit ourselves at this stage
  = _leider_ ist es uns _unmöglich_

+ In view of the proposed timescale, **I must reluctantly decline to** take part
  = _muss_ ich _leider_ _ablehnen_

40   ÜBEREINSTIMMUNG

40.1 Übereinstimmung mit Gesagtem

+ **I couldn't agree** (with you) **more**
  = ich _stimme_ _vollkommen_ _zu_

+ **I couldn't have put it better myself**
  = ich hätte es selbst nicht besser sagen können

+ We must oppose terrorism, whatever its source - **Hear, hear!**
  = ganz meine _Meinung_

+ **I endorse** his feelings regarding the condition of the Simpson memorial
  = ich _befürworte_

40.2 Übereinstimmung mit Vorschlägen

+ **It's just the job!**
  = das ist _genau_ das _Richtige_

+ **This is just the sort of thing** I wanted
  = das ist _genau_ das, was ich wollte

+ **This is exactly what I had in mind**
  = das ist _genau_ das, was ich wollte

+ Thank you for sending the draft agenda: **I like the look of it very much**
  = es _gefällt_ mir sehr gut

+ **We are all very enthusiastic about** oder **very keen on** his latest set of proposals
  = wir sind alle sehr _begeistert_ von

+ **I shall certainly give it my backing**
  = ich werde es auf jeden _Fall_ _befürworten_

+ Any game which is as clearly enjoyable as this **meets with my approval**
  = _findet_ meine _Zustimmung_

+ Skinner's plan **deserves our total support** oder **our wholehearted approval**
  = _verdient_ unsere uneingeschränkte _Zustimmung_

+ **There are considerable advantages in** the alternative method you propose
  = _bietet_ entscheidende _Vorteile_

+ **We recognize the merits** of this scheme
  = wir sehen die Vorzüge

+ **We view** your proposal to extend the site **favourably**
  = wir _betrachten_ ... mit Wohlwollen

+ This project **is worthy of our attention**
  = _verdient_ unsere Aufmerksamkeit

40.3 Übereinstimmung mit einer Idee

+ **You're quite right to** wait before making such an important decision
  = Sie haben ganz _Recht_, wenn Sie

+ **I entirely approve of** the idea
  = ich _finde_ ... sehr gut

+ **I'd certainly go along with that!**
  = ich _stimme_ dem auf jeden _Fall_ _zu_

+ **I'm very much in favour of** that sort of thing
  = ich bin sehr für

+ **What an excellent idea!**
  = was für eine ausgezeichnete _Idee_

40.4 Übereinstimmung mit einer Handlung

+ **I applaud** Noble's perceptive analysis of the problems
  = ich muss ... _loben_

+ **I have a very high opinion of** their new teaching methods
  = ich habe eine sehr hohe _Meinung_ von

+ **I think very highly of** the people who have been leading thus far
  = ich habe eine sehr hohe _Meinung_ von

+ **I have a very high regard for** the work of the Crown Prosecution Service
  = ich habe großen _Respekt_ vor

+ **I certainly admire** his courage in telling her what he thought of her
  = ich bin voller _Bewunderung_ für

+ **I must congratulate you on** the professional way you handled the situation
  = ich muss Ihnen zu ... _gratulieren_

+ **I greatly appreciate** the enormous risk that they had all taken
  = ich _schätze_ ... sehr

+ **I can thoroughly recommend** the event to field sports enthusiasts
  = ich kann ... von ganzem Herzen _empfehlen_

41   ABLEHNUNG

+ **This doesn't seem to be the right way of** going about it
  = dies _scheint_ nicht der _richtige_ Weg zu sein

+ **I don't think much of** what this government has done so far
  = ich _halte_ nicht viel von

- The police **took a dim view of** her attempt to help her son break out of jail
  = _hielt_ nicht viel von
- **I can't say I'm pleased about** what has happened
  = ich bin nicht gerade _begeistert_ von
- We have a low oder **poor opinion of** opportunists like him
  = wir haben keine sehr hohe _Meinung_ von
- They **should not have refused to** give her the money
  = hätten es nicht _ablehnen_ _sollen_

[Bestimmter]

- **I'm fed up with** having to wait so long for payments to be made
  = ich habe es _satt_
- **I've had (just) about enough of** this whole supermodel thing
  = langsam _reicht_ es mir mit
- **I can't bear** oder **stand** people who smoke in restaurants
  = ich kann ... nicht ausstehen
- **How dare he** say that!
  = was _fällt_ ihm _ein_
- **He was quite wrong to** repeat what I said about her
  = es war nicht _richtig_ von ihm
- **I cannot approve of** oder **support** any sort of testing on live animals
  = ich kann ... nicht _zustimmen_
- **We are opposed to** all forms of professional malpractice
  = wir sind gegen
- **We condemn** any intervention which could damage race relations
  = wir _verurteilen_
- **I must object to** the tag "soft porn actress"
  = ich muss ... _zurückweisen_
- **I'm very unhappy about** your (idea of) going off to Turkey on your own
  = ich bin gar nicht _glücklich_ über
- **I strongly disapprove of** such behaviour
  = ich bin mit ... überhaupt nicht _einverstanden_

---

42 GEWISSHEIT, WAHRSCHEINLICHKEIT, MÖGLICHKEIT UND FÄHIGKEIT

42.1 Gewissheit

- **She was bound to** discover that you and I had talked
  = sie _musste_ einfach
- **It is inevitable that they** will get to know of our meeting
  = es lässt sich nicht _vermeiden_, dass sie
- **I'm sure** oder **certain (that)** he'll keep his word
  = ich bin _sicher_, (dass)
- **I'm positive** oder **convinced (that)** it was your mother I saw
  = ich bin _überzeugt_, (dass)
- **We now know for certain** oder **for sure that** the exam papers were seen by several students before the day of the exam
  = wir können jetzt mit _Sicherheit_ sagen, dass
- **I made sure** oder **certain that** no one was listening to our conversation
  = ich habe darauf _geachtet_, dass
- From all the evidence **it is clear that** they were planning to sell up
  = es ist _klar_, dass
- **What is indisputable is that** a diet of fruit and vegetables is healthier
  = es ist _unbestreitbar_, dass
- **It is undeniable that** racial tensions in Britain have been increasing
  = es lässt sich nicht _leugnen_, dass
- **There is no doubt that** the talks will be long and difficult
  = es steht außer _Zweifel_, dass
- **There can be no doubt about** the objective of the animal liberationists
  = ... steht außer _Zweifel_

- This crisis has demonstrated **beyond all (possible) doubt** that effective political control must be in place before the creation of such structures
  = ohne (jeglichen) _Zweifel_
- Her pedigree is **beyond dispute** oder **question**
  = steht außer _Frage_
- **You have my absolute assurance that** this is the case
  = ich _versichere_ Ihnen, dass
- **I can assure you that** I have had nothing to do with any dishonest trading
  = ich kann Ihnen _versichern_, dass
- **Make no mistake about it** - I will return when I have proof of your involvement
  = _verlassen_ Sie sich darauf

42.2 Wahrscheinlichkeit

- **It is quite likely that** you will get withdrawal symptoms at first
  = _wahrscheinlich_
- **There is a good** oder **strong chance that** they will agree to the deal
  = _höchstwahrscheinlich_
- **It seems highly likely that** it was Bert who told Peter what had happened
  = _höchstwahrscheinlich_
- You will **very probably** be met at the airport by one of our men
  = _höchstwahrscheinlich_
- **It is highly probable that** American companies will face retaliation abroad
  = _höchstwahrscheinlich_
- **The probability is that** your investment will be worth more in two years' time
  = aller _Wahrscheinlichkeit_ nach
- The child's hearing will, **in all probability**, be severely affected
  = aller _Wahrscheinlichkeit_ nach
- The person indicated is, **in all likelihood**, going to be guilty as charged
  = aller _Wahrscheinlichkeit_ nach
- **The likelihood is that** the mood of mistrust and recrimination will intensify
  = aller _Wahrscheinlichkeit_ nach
- **The chances** oder **the odds are that** he will play safe in the short term
  = es könnte sehr wohl sein, dass
- **There is reason to believe that** the books were stolen from the library
  = es _besteht_ _Grund_ zu der _Annahme_, dass
- **He must** know of the painting's existence
  = er _muss_
- The talks **could very well** spill over into tomorrow
  = können gut und gerne
- The cheque **should** reach you by Saturday
  = _müsste_
- **It wouldn't surprise me** oder **I wouldn't be surprised if** he was working for the Americans
  = es sollte mich nicht _überraschen_, wenn

42.3 Möglichkeit

- The situation **could** change from day to day
  = _kann_
- Britain **could perhaps** play a more positive role in developing policy
  = _könnte_ vielleicht
- **It may be (the case) that** they got your name from the voters' roll
  = _möglicherweise_
- **It is possible that** psychological factors play some unknown role in the healing process
  = es _könnte_ sein, dass
- **It may be that** the whole battle will have to be fought over again
  = es _könnte_ sein, dass

+ **It is conceivable that** the economy is already in recession
  = *es ist denkbar, dass*

+ **It is well within the bounds of possibility that** England could be beaten
  = *es ist durchaus im Rahmen des <u>Möglichen</u>, dass*

+ **I venture to suggest (that)** a lot of it is to do with his political ambitions
  = *ich <u>wage</u> zu <u>behaupten</u>, (dass)*

+ **There is an outside chance that** the locomotive may appear in the Gala
  = *es <u>könnte</u> eventuell <u>möglich</u> sein, dass*

+ **There is a small chance that** your body could reject the implants
  = *es <u>besteht</u> eine geringe <u>Möglichkeit</u>, dass*

42.4   Ausdruck von Fähigkeiten

+ Our Design and Print Service **can** supply envelopes and package your existing literature
  = *<u>kann</u>*

+ Applicants **must be able to** use a word processor
  = *<u>müssen</u> in der <u>Lage</u> sein*

+ He **is qualified** to teach physics
  = *ist qualifiziert*

43   ZWEIFEL, UNWAHRSCHEINLICHKEIT, UNMÖGLICHKEIT UND UNFÄHIGKEIT

43.1   Zweifel

+ **I doubt if** oder **It is doubtful whether** he knows where it came from
  = *ich <u>bezweifle</u>, dass*

+ **There is still some doubt surrounding** his exact whereabouts
  = *man <u>weiß</u> immer noch nichts <u>Genaues</u> über*

+ **I have my doubts about** replacing private donations with taxpayers' cash
  = *ich habe da so meine <u>Zweifel</u> an*

+ **It isn't known for sure** oder **It isn't certain** where she is
  = *man <u>weiß</u> nicht <u>genau</u>*

+ **No-one can say for sure** how any child will develop
  = *niemand kann mit <u>Sicherheit</u> sagen*

+ It's still all up in the air - **we won't know for certain** until next week
  = *wir werden keine <u>Gewissheit</u> haben*

+ You're asking why I should do such an extraordinary thing and **I'm not sure** oder **certain that** I really know the answer
  = *ich bin mir nicht <u>sicher</u>, dass*

+ **I'm not convinced that** you can really teach people who don't want to learn
  = *ich bin nicht <u>überzeugt</u>, dass*

+ **We are still in the dark about** where the letter came from
  = *wir tappen immer noch im Dunkeln über*

+ How long this muddle can last **is anyone's guess**
  = *<u>weiß</u> niemand so recht*

+ Sterling is going to come under further pressure. **It is touch and go whether** base rates will have to go up
  = *es steht auf des Messers Schneide, ob*

+ **I'm wondering if** I should offer to help?
  = *vielleicht <u>sollte</u> ich*

43.2   Unwahrscheinlichkeit

+ You have **probably not** yet seen the document I'm referring to
  = *<u>wahrscheinlich</u> nicht*

+ **It is highly improbable that** there will be a challenge for the party leadership in the near future
  = *es ist höchst <u>unwahrscheinlich</u>, dass*

+ **It is very doubtful whether** the expedition will reach the summit
  = *es <u>bestehen</u> starke <u>Zweifel</u>, ob*

+ **In the unlikely event that** the room was bugged, the music would drown out their conversation
  = *<u>sollte</u> ... wider <u>Erwarten</u> doch*

+ **It was hardly to be expected that** democratization would be easy
  = *es stand kaum zu <u>erwarten</u>, dass*

43.3   Unmöglichkeit

+ **There can be no** changes in the schedule
  = *... sind nicht <u>möglich</u>*

+ Nowadays Carnival **cannot** happen **without** the police telling us where to walk and what direction to walk in
  = *<u>kann</u> unmöglich ..., ohne dass*

+ People said prices would inevitably rise; **this cannot be the case**
  = *das <u>kann</u> nicht sein*

+ **I couldn't possibly** invite George and not his wife
  = *ich <u>kann</u> unmöglich*

+ The report **rules out any possibility of** exceptions, and amounts to little more than a statement of the obvious
  = *schließt jede <u>Möglichkeit</u> ... <u>aus</u>*

+ **There is no question of** us getting this finished on time
  = *es gibt keine Chance, dass*

+ A West German spokesman said **it was out of the question that** these weapons would be based in Germany
  = *es steht außer <u>Frage</u>, dass*

+ **There is not (even) the remotest chance that** oder **There is absolutely no chance that** he will succeed
  = *es <u>besteht</u> nicht die geringste <u>Möglichkeit</u>, dass*

+ The idea of trying to govern twelve nations from one centre **is unthinkable**
  = *ist <u>unvorstellbar</u>*

+ Since we had over 500 applicants, **it would be quite impossible to** interview them all
  = *wir <u>können</u> unmöglich*

43.4   Unfähigkeit

+ **I can't** drive, I'm afraid
  = *ich <u>kann</u> nicht*

+ **I don't know how to** use a word processor
  = *ich <u>weiß</u> nicht, wie*

+ The army **has been unable to** suppress the political violence in the area
  = *war nicht in der <u>Lage</u>*

+ The congress had shown itself **incapable of** real reform
  = *<u>unfähig</u> zu*

+ His fellow-directors **were not up to** running the business without him
  = *waren nicht <u>imstande</u> zu*

+ We hoped the sales team would be able to think up new marketing strategies, but they **were** unfortunately **not equal to the task**
  = *waren der Aufgabe nicht gewachsen*

+ He simply **couldn't cope with** the stresses of family life
  = *er war ... einfach nicht gewachsen*

+ I'm afraid the task **proved (to be) beyond his capabilities**
  = *<u>ging</u> über seine Kräfte*

+ I'd like to leave him but sometimes I feel that such a step **is beyond me**
  = *<u>geht</u> über meine Kräfte*

+ Far too many women accept that they are **hopeless at** oder **no good at** managing money
  = *sind <u>unfähig</u> zu*

+ **I'm not in a position to** say now how much substance there is in the reports
  = *ich bin nicht in der <u>Lage</u>*

+ **It's quite impossible for me to** describe the confusion and horror of the scene
  = *ich <u>kann</u> unmöglich*

44 ERKLÄRUNGEN

44.1 Präpositionen und Konjunktionen

- He was sacked **for the simple reason that** he just wasn't up to it any more
  = *aus dem einfachen Grunde, dass*

- **The reason that** we admire him is that he knows what he is doing
  = *der Grund dafür, dass*

- He said he could not be more specific **for** security **reasons**
  = *aus ...gründen*

- I am absolutely in favour of civil disobedience **on** moral **grounds**
  = *aus ... Gründen*

- The court had ordered his release, **on the grounds that** he had already been acquitted of most of the charges against him
  = *mit der Begründung, dass*

- The students were arrested **because of** suspected dissident activities
  = *wegen*

- Teachers in the eastern part of Germany are assailed by fears of mass unemployment **on account of** their communist past
  = *wegen*

- They are facing higher costs **owing to** rising inflation
  = *wegen*

- Parliament has prevaricated, **largely because of** the unwillingness of the main opposition party to support the changes
  = *hauptsächlich wegen*

- Morocco has announced details of the austerity package it is adopting **as a result of** pressure from the International Monetary Fund
  = *infolge*

- The full effects will be delayed **due to** factors beyond our control
  = *aufgrund*

- What also had to go was the notion that some people were born superior to others **by virtue of** their skin colour
  = *aufgrund*

- He shot to fame **on the strength of** a letter he had written to the papers
  = *aufgrund*

- **Thanks to** their generosity, the charity can afford to buy new equipment
  = *dank*

- Both companies became profitable again **by means of** severe cost-cutting
  = *mittels*

- The King and Queen's defence of old-fashioned family values has acquired a poignancy **in view of** their inability to have children
  = *in Anbetracht*

- **In the face of** this continued disagreement, the parties have asked for the polling to be postponed
  = *in Anbetracht*

- It is unclear why they initiated this week's attack, **given that** negotiations were underway
  = *in Anbetracht der Tatsache, dass*

- The police have put considerable pressure on the Government to toughen its stance **in the light of** recent events
  = *mit Blick auf*

- His soldiers had been restraining themselves **for fear of** harming civilians
  = *aus Furcht davor*

- A survey by the World Health Organization says that two out of every five people are dying prematurely **for lack of** food or health care
  = *aus Mangel an*

- Babies have died **for want of** oder **for lack of** proper medical attention
  = *aus Mangel an*

- I refused her a divorce, **out of** spite, I suppose
  = *aus*

- **Seeing that** he had a police escort, the only time he could have switched containers was on the way to the airport
  = *angesichts der Tatsache, dass*

- **As** he had been up since 4am, he was doubtless very tired
  = *da*

- International intervention was appropriate **since** tensions had reached the point where there was talk of war
  = *da*

- She could not have been deaf, **for** she started at the sound of a bell
  = *weil*

- I cannot accept this decision. **So** I confirm it is my intention to appeal to a higher authority
  = *daher*

- What the Party said was taken to be right, **therefore** anyone who disagreed must be wrong
  = *daher*

- **The thing is that** once you've retired there's no going back
  = *das Problem ist, dass*

44.2 Andere nützliche Ausdrücke

- The serious dangers to your health **caused by** oder **brought about by** cigarettes are now better understood
  = *hervorgerufen durch*

- When the picture was published recently, **it gave rise to** oder **led to** speculation that the three were still alive and being held captive
  = *gabe Anlass zu*

- The army argues that security concerns **necessitated** the demolitions
  = *erforderten*

- This lack of recognition **was at the root of** the dispute
  = *war der eigentliche Grund für*

- **I attribute** all this mismanagement **to** the fact that the General Staff in London is practically non-existent
  = *ich führe ... auf ... zurück*

- This unrest **dates from** colonial times
  = *geht zurück auf*

- The custom **goes back to** pre-Christian days
  = *geht zurück auf*

45 ENTSCHULDIGUNGEN

45.1 Entschuldigungen

- **I'm really sorry**, Steve, **but** we won't be able to come on Saturday
  = *es tut mir wirklich Leid, aber*

- **I'm sorry that** your time had been wasted
  = *es tut mir Leid, dass*

- **I am sorry to have to** say this to you but you're no good
  = *es tut mir Leid, ... zu müssen*

- **Apologies if** I wasn't very good company last nicht
  = *Entschuldigung, wenn*

- **I must apologize for** what happened. Quite unforgivable, and the man responsible has been disciplined
  = *ich muss mich für ... entschuldigen*

- **I owe you an apology**. I didn't think you knew what you were talking about
  = *ich muss mich bei Ihnen entschuldigen*

- The general back-pedalled, saying that **he had not meant to** offend the German government
  = *es lag nicht in seiner Absicht*

- **Do forgive me for** being a little abrupt
  = *verzeihen Sie mir, wenn ich*

- **Please forgive me for** behaving so badly
  = *bitte entschuldigen Sie, dass ich*

- **Please accept our apologies** if this has caused you any inconvenience
  = *bitte entschuldigen Sie vielmals*

45.2 Verantwortung eingestehen

- **I admit** I overreacted, but someone needed to speak out against her
  = ich gebe zu
- **I have no excuse for** what happened
  = ich kann keine _Entschuldigung_ für ... vorbringen
- **It is my fault that** our marriage is on the rocks
  = es ist mein _Fehler_, dass
- The Government **is not entirely to blame for** the crisis
  = trägt nicht die alleinige _Schuld_ an
- **I should never have** let him rush out of the house in anger
  = ich hätte nie ... _dürfen_
- Oh, but **if only I hadn't** lost the keys
  = _wenn_ ich nur nicht ... hätte
- I hate to admit that the old man was right, but **I made a stupid mistake**
  = ich habe einen dummen _Fehler_ gemacht
- **My mistake was in** failing to push my concerns and convictions as hard as I could have done
  = mein _Fehler_ war, dass
- **My mistake was to** arrive wearing a jacket and polo-neck jumper
  = mein _Fehler_ war
- In December and January the markets raced ahead, and I missed out on that. **That was my mistake**
  = das war mein _Fehler_

45.3 Mit Bedauern

- **I'm very upset about** her decision but I accept she needs to move on to new challenges
  = ich bin sehr mitgenommen von
- **It's a shame that** the press gives so little coverage to these events
  = _schade_, dass
- **I feel awful about** saying this but you really ought to spend more time with your children
  = es tut mir sehr _Leid_, dass
- **I'm afraid I can't** help you very much
  = ich kann _leider_ nicht
- **It's a pity that** my profession can make a lot of money out of the misfortunes of others
  = _schade_, dass
- **It is unfortunate that** the matter should have come to a head just now
  = es ist etwas _unglücklich_, dass
- David and I **very much regret that** we have been unable to reach an agreement
  = _bedauern_ sehr, dass
- The accused **bitterly regrets** this incident and it won't happen again
  = _bedauert_ zutiefst
- **We regret to inform you that** the post of Editor has now been filled
  = zu unserem _Bedauern_ müssen wir Ihnen _mitteilen_, dass

45.4 Zur Erklärung

- **I didn't do it on purpose**, it just happened
  = ich habe es nicht _absichtlich_ getan
- Sorry, Nanna. **I didn't meant to** upset you
  = ich hatte nicht die _Absicht_
- Sorry about not coming to the meeting. **I was under the impression that** it was just for managers
  = ich hatte den _Eindruck_, dass
- **We are simply trying to** protect the interests of local householders
  = wir _versuchen_ nur
- I know this hurt you but **I had no choice**. I had to put David's life above all else
  = ich hatte keine _Wahl_

- We are unhappy with 1.5%, but under the circumstances **we have no alternative but to** accept
  = wir haben keine andere _Wahl_ als
- **We were obliged to** accept their conditions
  = wir sahen uns _gezwungen_
- **I had nothing to do with** the placing of any advertisement
  = ich hatte nichts mit ... zu tun
- A spokesman for the club assured supporters that **it was a genuine error** and **there was no intention to** mislead them
  = es war ein reines _Versehen_ ... es war nicht _beabsichtigt_

---

46   BEWERBUNGEN

46.1 Nützliche Redewendungen

- **In reply to your advertisement** for a Trainee Manager in today's _Guardian_, **I would be grateful if you would send me further details of** the post
  = mit Bezug auf Ihre _Anzeige_ ... möchte ich Sie _bitten_, mir nähere _Informationen_ über ... _zuzusenden_
- **I wish to apply for the post of** bilingual correspondent, as advertised in this week's _Euronews_
  = ich möchte mich um die _Stelle_ ... _bewerben_
- **I am writing to ask if** there is any possibility of work in your company
  = ich möchte _nachfragen_, ob
- **I am writing to enquire about the possibility of joining your company on work placement** for a period of 3 months
  = ich möchte mich _erkundigen_, ob die _Möglichkeit_ _besteht_, in IhremUnternehmen ein Praktikum zu absolvieren

46.2 Berufserfahrung

- **I have** three years' **experience of** office work
  = ich _verfüge_ über ... _Erfahrung_
- **I am familiar with** word processors
  = ich bin mit ... _vertraut_
- **As well as speaking fluent** English, **I have a working knowledge of** German
  = ich _spreche_ fließend ... und habe ausreichende ..._kenntnisse_
- **As you will see from my CV**, I have worked in Belgium before
  = wie Sie meinem _Lebenslauf_ entnehmen können
- **Although I have no experience of this type of work** I have had other holiday jobs and can supply references from my employers, if you wish
  = ich habe zwar keine _Erfahrung_ auf diesem Arbeitsgebiet
- **My current salary is** ... per annum and I have four weeks' paid leave
  = zurzeit _verdiene_ ich

46.3 Motivationen ausdrücken

- **I would like to make better use of** my languages
  = ich möchte meine ..._kenntnisse_ besser einsetzen
- **I am keen to work in** public relations
  = ich möchte gerne auf dem Gebiet ... _arbeiten_

46.4 Briefschluss

- **I will be available from** the end of April
  = ich _stehe_ ab ... zur _Verfügung_
- **I am available for interview** at any time
  = über ein _Vorstellungsgespräch_ würde ich mich _freuen_
- **Please do not hesitate to contact me for further information**
  = für weitere _Informationen_ _stehe_ ich Ihnen gerne jederzeit zur _Verfügung_
- **Please do not contact** my current employers
  = ich möchte Sie _bitten_, sich nicht mit ... in _Verbindung_ zu setzen
- **I enclose** a stamped addressed envelope for your reply
  = ich lege ... bei

Garrion Orchard
Middletown
MD8 1NP

18th August 1999

The Managing Director
Messrs. J.M. Thomson Ltd,
Leeside Works
Barnton, MC45 6RB

Dear Sir or Madam,[1]

    With reference to your advertisement in today's *Guardian*, I wish to apply for the post of Human Resources Manager.

    I enclose my curriculum vitae. Please do not hesitate to contact me if you require any further details.

Yours faithfully,

[1] Diese Form der Adresse wird verwendet, wenn der Name des Empfängers nicht bekannt ist. Wenn der Name bekannt ist, wird folgende Schreibung benutzt:

Mr Eric Swanson

ODER

Mrs. Anna Carter,
Personnel Director,
Messrs. J.M. Kenyon Ltd, usw.

Als Anrede benutzen Sie „Dear Sir" bzw. „Dear Madam".

Alle Briefe, die mit dieser Anrede beginnen, werden mit der Grußformel „Yours faithfully" und Unterschrift beendet. Eine ausführliche Darstellung finden Sie auf den Seiten 1030 und 1031.

[2] Wenn Sie sich um eine Stelle im Ausland bewerben, sollten Sie auf die Entsprechungen Ihrer Qualifikationen im englischen Sprachraum hinweisen. Etwa „Abitur – German equivalent of A-levels" usw.

CURRICULUM VITAE

NAME: Andrew Iain FERRIER

ADDRESS: Garrion Orchard, Middletown

TELEPHONE: (01234) 861483

DATE OF BIRTH: 6.5.1972

MARITAL STATUS: Married (no children)

NATIONALITY: British

QUALIFICATIONS:[2]   M.A. First class Honours Degree in German with French, University of Texas, USA (June 1993)
Masters Diploma in Human Resources, Glasgow University (June 1994)
A-levels (1990): German (A), French (A), English (B)
O-levels: 9 subjects

PRESENT POST: Assistant Human Resources Manager, Abbots Art Metal Company plc., Middletown (since July 1995)

PREVIOUS EMPLOYMENT: Sept. 1994 - June 1995: Human resources trainee,
     Abbots Art Metal Company plc.
Oct. 1993 - June 1994: Student, Glasgow University

SKILLS, INTERESTS AND EXPERIENCE: fluent German & French; adequate Italian; some Russian; car owner and driver (clean licence); riding and sailing.

The following have agreed to provide references:

Ms Jocelyn Meiklejohn   Dr. Garth Tritt
Human Resources Manager   Department of German
Abbots Art Metal Company plc   University of Texas
Middletown MD1 4CU   Arizona, USA

46.5 Referenzen erbitten und erteilen

◆ In my application for the position of lecturer, I have been asked to provide the names of two referees and **I wondered whether you would mind if I gave your name** as one of them
   = *ich möchte Sie um Ihr Einverständnis <u>bitten</u>, Ihren Namen angeben zu dürfen*

◆ Ms Lee has applied for the post of Marketing Executive with our company and has given us your name as a reference. **We would be grateful if you would let us know whether you would recommend her for this position**
   = *wir wären Ihnen sehr <u>dankbar</u>, wenn Sie uns <u>mitteilen</u> könnten, ob Sie sie für diesen Posten <u>empfehlen</u> können*

◆ **Your reply will be treated in the strictest confidence**
   = *Ihre <u>Antwort</u> wird selbstverständlich <u>streng</u> vertraulich behandelt*

◆ I have known Mr Chambers for four years in his capacity as Sales Manager and **can warmly recommend him for the position**
   = *ich kann ihn für die <u>Stelle</u> wärmstens <u>empfehlen</u>*

46.6 Ein Angebot annehmen oder ablehnen

◆ Thank you for your letter of 20 March. **I will be pleased to attend for interview** at your Manchester offices on Thursday 7 April at 10am
   = *ich finde mich gern ... zu einem <u>Vorstellungsgespräch</u> ein*

◆ **I would like to confirm my acceptance of** the post of Marketing Executive
   = *ich <u>nehme</u> Ihr <u>Angebot</u> an*

◆ **I would be delighted to accept this post. However, would it be possible** to postpone my starting date until 8 May?
   = *ich würde das <u>Angebot</u> sehr gerne <u>annehmen</u>. Wäre es jedoch möglich*

◆ **I would be glad to accept your offer; however**, the salary stated is somewhat lower than what I had hoped for
   = *ich würde Ihr <u>Angebot</u> gerne <u>annehmen</u>, ich hatte jedoch*

◆ Having given your offer careful thought, **I regret that I am unable to accept**
   = *bedauerlicherweise ist es mir nicht <u>möglich</u>, Ihr <u>Angebot</u> anzunehmen*

47 GESCHÄFTSBRIEFE

47.1 Informationen erbitten

◆ **We** see from your advertisement in the Healthy Holiday Guide that you are offering cut-price holidays in Scotland, and **would be grateful if you would send us** details
   = *wir ... wären Ihnen <u>dankbar</u>, wenn Sie uns nähere <u>Informationen</u> zusenden könnten*

◆ I read about the Happy Pet Society in the NCT newsletter and would be very interested to learn more about it. **Please send me details of** membership
   = *bitte <u>senden</u> Sie mir <u>Einzelheiten</u> über ... <u>zu</u>*

... und darauf antworten

◆ **In response to your enquiry of** 8 March, **we have pleasure in enclosing** full details on our activity holidays in Cumbria, **together with** our price list, valid until May 1999
   = *wir beziehen uns auf Ihre <u>Anfrage</u> vom ... und <u>senden</u> Ihnen gerne ... sowie ... <u>zu</u>*

◆ **Thank you for enquiry about** the Society for Wildlife Protection. **I enclose** a leaflet explaining our beliefs and the issues we campaign on. **Should you wish** to join, a membership application form is also enclosed
   = *ich <u>danke</u> für Ihre <u>Anfrage</u> bezüglich ... Ich lege ... bei ... <u>Sollten</u> Sie <u>Interesse</u> an ...haben*

47.2 Bestellungen und Antwort auf Bestellungen

◆ **We would like to place an order for** the following items, in the sizes and quantities specified below
   = *wir möchten eine <u>Bestellung</u> über ... <u>aufgeben</u>*

◆ **Please find enclosed our order no.** 3011 for ...
   = *anbei unsere <u>Bestellung</u> Nr.*

◆ **The enclosed order is based on** your current price list, assuming our usual discount
   = *der beigefügten <u>Bestellung</u> liegt ... zugrunde*

◆ **I wish to order** a can of "Buzz off!" wasp repellent, as advertised in the July issue of Gardeners' Monthly, **and enclose a cheque for** £19.50
   = *ich möchte ... <u>bestellen</u>. Ich füge einen Scheck über ... bei*

◆ **Thank you for your order of** 3 May, which will be dispatched within 30 days
   = *wir <u>danken</u> Ihnen für Ihre <u>Bestellung</u> vom*

◆ **We acknowledge receipt of your order no.** 3570 and advise that the goods will be dispatched within 7 working days
   = *wir <u>bestätigen</u> den Eingang Ihrer <u>Bestellung</u> Nr.*

◆ **We regret that the goods you ordered are temporarily out of stock**
   = *leider sind die von Ihnen <u>bestellten</u> <u>Waren</u> zur Zeit nicht auf Lager*

◆ **Please allow** 28 days **for delivery**
   = *die Lieferung erfolgt innerhalb von*

47.3 Lieferungen

◆ **Our delivery time is** 60 days from receipt of order
   = *unsere Lieferzeit beträgt*

◆ **We await confirmation of your order**
   = *wir <u>erwarten</u> Ihre <u>verbindliche</u> <u>Bestellung</u>*

◆ **We confirm that the goods were dispatched on** 4 September
   = *wir <u>bestätigen</u> den Abgang der <u>Waren</u> am*

◆ **We cannot accept responsibility for** goods damaged in transit
   = *wir <u>übernehmen</u> keine <u>Haftung</u> für*

47.4 Sich beschweren

◆ **We have not yet received** the items ordered on 6 May (ref. order no. 541)
   = *... sind noch nicht bei uns eingegangen*

◆ **Unfortunately the goods were damaged** in transit
   = *leider wurden die <u>Waren</u> ... beschädigt*

◆ **The goods received differ significantly from** the description in your catalogue
   = *die eingegangenen <u>Waren</u> weichen wesentlich von ... ab*

◆ If the goods are not received by 20 October, **we shall have to cancel our order**
   = *sehen wir uns <u>leider</u> <u>gezwungen</u>, unsere <u>Bestellung</u> zu <u>stornieren</u>*

47.5 Bezahlung

◆ **The total amount outstanding is** ...
   = *der zu zahlende <u>Gesamtbetrag</u> beläuft sich auf ...*

◆ **We would be grateful if you would attend to this account** immediately
   = *wir wären Ihnen <u>dankbar</u>, wenn Sie diese <u>Rechnung</u> ... <u>begleichen</u> würden*

◆ **Please remit payment by return**
   = *bitte <u>überweisen</u> Sie den <u>Betrag</u> unverzüglich*

◆ Full payment **is due within** 14 working days from receipt of goods
   = *ist fällig innerhalb von*

◆ **We enclose** a cheque for ... **in settlement of your invoice no.** 2003L/58
   = *anbei übersenden wir Ihnen ... zur <u>Begleichung</u> Ihrer <u>Rechnung</u> Nr.*

◆ **We** must point out an error in your account and **would be grateful if you would adjust your invoice** accordingly
   = *wir ... wären Ihnen <u>dankbar</u>, wenn Sie die <u>Rechnung</u> berichtigen würden*

◆ The mistake was due to an accounting error, and **we enclose a credit note for** the sum involved
   = *in der <u>Anlage</u> erhalten Sie eine Gutschrift über*

◆ **Thank you for your cheque for** ... in settlement of our invoice
   = *wir <u>bedanken</u> uns für Ihren Scheck über ...*

◆ **We look forward to doing further business with you in the near future**
   = *wir würden uns <u>freuen</u>, schon bald wieder mit Ihnen <u>zusammenarbeiten</u> zu können*

Crosby Stills

PHOTOGRAPHIC LIBRARY

141 Academy Street
Glossop
Derby K9 4JP

22nd May 1999

Mr David Cooper
18 Crossdyke Road
Overdale
Lancs
LB3 WOD

Dear Mr Cooper,

Thank you for your recent enquiry about our limited edition photographs of classic cars. We have pleasure in enclosing our latest catalogue and current price list and would draw your attention to our free postage and packing on orders over £30. We are prepared to hold last year's prices on our range of frames and look forward to receiving your order.

Yours faithfully,

JAMES NASH
Managing Director

FABBY FABRICS LTD

**Greenknowe Industrial Estate
Barbridge, Denholm
DT4 8HF**

Our ref: WED/35/40   9th October, 1999
Your ref: HDF/JL

Moonshine Inn
3 Main Street
Newtown, NW1 4BB

For the attention of Ms H Boyle

Dear Madam,

Thank you for your letter of 21st September. We do stock a wide range of materials which are suitable for seating and would be delighted to send one of our representatives round at your earliest convenience. Please note that we also provide a made-to-measure service at very competitive prices and will be happy to supply you with a free quotation.

Yours faithfully,

Garry Scott
Sales Manager

48 ALLGEMEINE KORRESPONDENZ

48.1 Briefanfänge

An Bekannte

- **Thank you** oder **Thanks for your letter** which arrived yesterday
  = vielen _Dank_ für deinen Brief

- **It was good** oder **nice** oder **lovely to hear from you**
  = ich habe mich sehr _gefreut_, von dir zu hören

- It's such a long time since we were last in touch that **I felt I must write a few lines** just to say hello
  = und da _dachte_ ich, ich _muss_ einfach ein paar Zeilen _schreiben_

- **I'm sorry I haven't written for so long**, and hope you'll forgive me; I've had a lot of work recently and ...
  = es tut mir sehr _Leid_, dass ich solange nicht _geschrieben_ habe

An eine Firma oder Organisation

- **I am writing to ask whether** you have in stock a book entitled ...
  = ich möchte mich _erkundigen_, ob

- **Please send me** ... I enclose a cheque for ...
  = würden Sie mir bitte ... _schicken_

- When I left your hotel last week, I think I may have left a red coat in my room. **Would you be so kind as to** let me know whether it has been found?
  = würden Sie mir bitte so freundlich sein und

- I have seen the details of your summer courses, and **wish to know whether** you still have any vacancies on the Beginners' Swedish course
  = ich möchte _nachfragen_, ob

48.2 Briefschlüsse

An Bekannte

- **Gerald joins me in sending very best wishes to you all**
  = viele herzliche _Grüße_ an euch alle, auch von Gerald

- **Please remember me to** your wife - I hope she is well
  = bitte _grüßen_ Sie auch ... von mir

- **I look forward to hearing from you**
  = ich würde mich sehr _freuen_, bald von Ihnen zu hören

An Freunde

- **Say hello to Martin for me**
  = grüß Martin von mir

- **Give my love to** Daniel and Laura, and tell them how much I miss them
  = grüß ... von mir

- **Give my warmest regards to Vincent**
  = grüße bitte Vincent ganz _herzlich_ von mir

- **Do write** when you have a minute
  = _schreib_ mal wieder

- **Hoping to hear from you before too long**
  = ich _hoffe_, dass ich schon bald von dir höre

An enge Freunde

- Rhona **sends her love**/Ray **sends his love**
  = lässt herzlich _grüssen_

- Jodie and Carla **send you a big hug**
  = umarmen dich

48.3 Reiseplanung

Zimmerreservierung

- **Please send me details of** your prices
  = bitte _schicken_ Sie mir nähere _Informationen_ über ... zu

- **Please let me know by return of post if** you have one single room with bath, half board, for the week commencing 3 October
  = bitte _teilen_ Sie mir umgehend _mit_, ob

- **I would like to book** bed-and-breakfast accommodation with you
  = ich möchte ... _buchen_

Eine Buchung bestätigen oder stornieren

- **Please consider this a firm booking** and hold the room until I arrive, however late in the evening
  = bitte _betrachten_ Sie diese _Reservierung_ als _verbindlich_

- **Please confirm the following by fax**: one single room with shower for the nights of 20-23 April 1999
  = bitte _bestätigen_ Sie Folgendes per Fax

- **We expect to arrive** in the early evening, unless something unforeseen happens
  = wir werden ... eintreffen

- **I am afraid I must ask you to alter my booking from** 25 August **to** 3 September. I hope this will not cause too much inconvenience
  = leider _muss_ ich Sie _bitten_, meine _Reservierung_ vom ... auf den ... umzubuchen

- Owing to unforeseen circumstances, **I am afraid (that) I must cancel the booking** made with you for the week beginning 5 September
  = _muss_ ich meine _Reservierung_ _leider_ _stornieren_

Der Empfänger (die Empfängerin) ist Ihnen persönlich bekannt

Dear Mr Brown, Dear Mrs Hughes, Dear Mr and Mrs Boyle, Dear Miss Roberts, Dear Ms Jones, Dear Dr Armstrong,	Yours sincerely	
Dear Professor Ferrier,	With all good wishes, Yours sincerely With kindest regards, Yours sincerely	persönlicher
Dear Sir John, Dear Lady McLeod, Dear Andrew, Dear Jenny,		

Der Empfänger (die Empfängerin) ist verwandt oder befreundet

Dear Grace, My dear Andrew, Dear Aunt Hazel,	With love from Love from	
Dear Granny and Grandad, Dear Mum and Dad, My dear Caroline, Dearest Stephen, My dearest Mother,	Love to all Love from us all Yours All the best	vertrauter
My dearest Heather, My darling Garry,	With much love from Lots of love from Much love as always, All my love	herzlicher

8. South Farmway
BARCOME
BN7 2BT

9th May, 1999

Dear Jenny,

I'm so sorry that I haven't written sooner, things were pretty hectic
leading up to the wedding. I've never been so busy! Happily everything ran
like clockwork and we all had a perfect day. The house is very quiet now
with David away but I must admit I am enjoying it! Eric and I finally have
the chance to take a short break at our cottage in the Lake District. Why
don't you and James join us? There's plenty of room and I know how you
love the lakes. We will be there on Saturday of the week beginning 16th of
July for ten days. Give me a call soon if you're coming and we'll meet you
at the station. Do say you'll come!

With love,

Kerry

11 South Street
BARCOME
BN7 2BT

5th June 1999

Mr. J. Sharpe
Sharpe Knives Ltd.,
Cromwell Place
ADDENBOROUGH
AG3 9LL

Dear Mr Sharpe,

     Some years ago I bought a HANDYMAN penknife from you, and,
as you suggested, it has been invaluable to me. Unfortunately,
however, I have now lost it, and wonder if you still stock this
range? If so, I should be grateful if you would let me have
details of the various types of penknife you make, and of their
prices.

        Yours sincerely,

Thomas Thomson

In der unten stehenden Tabelle sind die üblichen Anreden und Schlussformeln für Privat- und Geschäftsbriefe aufgeführt.

Geschäftsbriefe (siehe auch 47)

Dear Sirs,[1]		[1] *Wenn Sie an eine Firma oder Behörde schreiben*
Dear Sir,[2]		[2] *Empfänger ist ein Mann*
Dear Madam,[3]	Yours faithfully	[3] *Empfänger ist eine Frau*
Dear Sir or Madam,[4]		[4] *Sie wissen nicht, ob der Empfänger ein Mann oder eine Frau ist*

An Bekannte und Freunde

Formeln, die Sie immer verwenden können		
Dear Alison, Dear Ann and Bob, Dear Uncle Alex,	Yours sincerely	
	With best wishes, Yours sincerely	
Dear Mrs Andrews,		
Dear Mr and Mrs Hope,	With kindest regards,	*persönlicher*
	Yours sincerely	
	All good wishes, Yours sincerely	
	With best wishes, Yours ever	
	Kindest regards, Best wishes	*vertrauter*
	With best wishes, As always	

49 DANKSAGUNGEN

- **Just a line to say thanks for** the lovely book which arrived today
  = *danke* für

- **I can't thank you enough for** finding my watch
  = *ich weiß gar nicht, wie ich Ihnen für ... danken kann*

- **(Would you) please thank him from me**
  = *Richten Sie ihm bitte meinen Dank aus*

- **We greatly appreciated** your support during our recent difficulties
  = *wir sind Ihnen wirklich sehr dankbar für*

- **Please accept our sincere thanks for** all your help and support
  = *wir möchten uns herzlich bei Ihnen für ... bedanken*

- **A big thank you to everyone** involved in the show this year
  = *ein herzliches Dankeschön an alle*

- **We would like to express our appreciation to** the University of Durham Research Committee for providing a grant
  = *wir möchten unserer Dankbarkeit gegenüber ... Ausdruck verleihen*

Im Namen einer Gruppe

- **Thank you on behalf of** the Manx Operatic Society **for** all your support
  = *wir danken Ihnen im Namen ... für*

- **I am instructed by** our committee **to convey our sincere thanks for** your assistance at our recent Valentine Social
  = *... hat mir die Aufgabe übertragen, unseren herzlichen Dank für ... zu übermitteln*

50 GLÜCKWÜNSCHE

50.1 Spezielle Anlässe

- **I hope you have** a lovely holiday
  = *hoffentlich hast du*

- **With love and best wishes for** your wedding anniversary
  = *mit den besten Wünschen für*

- **(Do) give my best wishes to** your mother **for** a happy and healthy retirement
  = *grüße ... von mir und wünsche ... alles Gute für*

- Len **joins me in sending you our very best wishes for** your future career
  = *... schließt sich meinen besten Wünschen für ... an*

50.2 Zu Weihnachten und Neujahr

- **Merry Christmas and a happy New Year**
  = *frohe Weihnachten und ein glückliches neues Jahr*

- **With season's greetings and very best wishes from**
  = *mit den besten Wünschen für ein gesegnetes Weihnachtsfest und ein glückliches neues Jahr*

- **May I send you all our very best wishes for** 2000
  = *ich sende euch allen die besten Wünsche für*

50.3 Zum Geburtstag

- **All our love and best wishes on your** 21st **birthday**, from Simon, Liz, Kerry and the cats
  = *alles Liebe und Gute zu deinem ... Geburtstag*

- I am writing to wish you **many happy returns (of the day)**. Hope your birthday brings you everything you wished for
  = *alles Gute zum Geburtstag*

50.4 Gute Besserung

- Sorry (to hear) you're ill - **get well soon!**
  = *gute Besserung*

- I was very sorry to learn that you were ill, and send you **my best wishes for a speedy recovery**
  = *meine besten Wünsche für eine baldige Genesung*

50.5 Erfolg wünschen

- **Good luck in** your driving test. I hope things go well for you on Friday
  = *viel Glück bei*

- Sorry to hear you didn't get the job - **better luck next time!**
  = *vielleicht klappt es beim nächsten Mal*

- **We all wish you the best of luck in** your new job
  = *wir alle wünschen dir viel Glück in*

50.6 Gratulationen

- You're expecting a baby? **Congratulations!** When is the baby due?
  = *herzlichen Glückwunsch*

- You've finished the job already? **Well done!**
  = *gut gemacht*

- **We all send you our love and congratulations on** such an excellent result
  = *wir gratulieren alle zu*

- **This is to send you our warmest congratulations and best wishes on** your engagement
  = *herzlichen Glückwunsch und die besten Wünsche anlässlich*

51 ANZEIGEN

51.1 Geburtsanzeigen

- Julia Archer **gave birth to** a 6lb 5oz **baby daughter**, Amy, last Monday. **Mother and baby are doing well**
  = *hat ... eine Tochter bekommen. Mutter und Kind sind wohlauf*

- Ian and Zoë Pitt **are delighted to announce the birth of a son**, Garry, on 9th May, 1999, at Minehead Hospital
  = *freuen sich, die Geburt ihres Sohnes ... anzuzeigen*

- At the Southern General Hospital, on 1st December, 1999, **to Paul and Diane Kelly (née Smith) a son, John Alexander**, a brother for Helen
  = *Paul and Diane Kelly, geb. Smith, freuen sich, die Geburt ihres Sohnes John Alexander ... anzuzeigen*

... und darauf antworten

- **Congratulations on the birth of** your son
  = *herzliche Glückwünsche zur Geburt*

- **We were delighted to hear about the birth of** Stephanie, and send our very best wishes to all of you
  = *wir freuen uns mit euch über die Geburt von*

51.2 Verlobungsanzeigen

- I'm sure you'll be pleased to hear that Jim and I **got engaged** yesterday
  = *haben uns verlobt*

- **It is with much pleasure that the engagement is announced between** Michael, younger son of Professor and Mrs Perkins, York, **and** Jennifer, only daugher of Dr and Mrs Campbell, Hucknall
  = *... freuen sich, die Verlobung zwischen ... und ... bekannt zu geben*

... und darauf antworten

- **Congratulations to you both on your engagement**, and very best wishes for a long and happy life together
  = *herzliche Glückwünsche anlässlich eurer Verlobung für euch beide*

- **I was delighted to hear of your engagement** and wish you both all the best for your future together
  = *ich freue mich mit euch über eure Verlobung*

51.3 Heiratsanzeigen

- **I'm getting married** in June, to a wonderful man named Lester Thompson
  = *ich werde heiraten*

◆ **At Jurby Church, on 1st June, 1999, Eve, daughter of Ian and Mary Jones, Jurby, to John, son of Ray and Myra Watt, Ayr**
= die _Vermählung_ wird _bekannt gegeben_ zwischen Eve, Tochter von Ian und Mary Jones, Jurby, und John, Sohn von Ray und Myra Watt, Ayr, am 1. Juni 1999 in der Kirche von Jurby

| ... und darauf antworten |

◆ **Congratulations on your marriage, and best wishes to you both for your future happiness**
= zu eurer _Hochzeit_ _herzliche_ _Glückwünsche_ und _alles_ Gute für eure gemeinsame Zukunft

◆ **We were delighted to hear about your daughter's marriage to** Iain, and wish them both all the best for their future life together
= mit großer Freude haben wir die _Nachricht_ von der _Vermählung_ eurer Tochter mit ... zur Kenntnis genommen

51.4 Todesanzeigen

◆ My husband **died suddenly** in March
= plötzlich und unerwartet _verstarb_

◆ **It is with great sadness that I have to tell you that** Joe's father **passed away** three weeks ago
= in tiefer _Trauer_ muss ich Ihnen _mitteilen_, dass ... für immer von uns gegangen ist

◆ **Suddenly**, at home, in Newcastle-upon-Tyne, on Saturday 3rd July, 1999, Alan, aged 77 years, **the beloved husband of** Helen and **loving father of** Matthew and Chris
= plötzlich und unerwartet _verstarb_ mein geliebter Mann, unser lieber Vater

| ... und darauf antworten |

◆ My husband and I **were greatly saddened to learn of the passing of** Dr Smith, and send (oder offer) you and your family our most sincere condolences
= mit tiefem _Bedauern_ haben wir die _Nachricht_ vom _Tode_ ... erhalten

◆ **We wish to extend our deepest sympathy for your sad loss to you and your wife**
= wir möchten Ihnen zum _Tode_ ... unser tief empfundenes _Beileid_ aussprechen

51.5 Umzugsanzeigen

◆ We are moving house next week. **Our new address** as of 4 May 1999 **will be** ...
= unsere neue Adresse ... ist

52 EINLADUNGEN

52.1 Offizielle Einladungen

◆ Mr and Mrs James Waller **request the pleasure of your company at the marriage of** their daughter Mary Elizabeth to Mr Richard Hanbury at St Mary's Church, Frampton on Saturday, 21st August, 1999 at 2 o'clock and afterwards at Moor House, Frampton
= geben sich die _Ehre_, Sie zur _Hochzeit_ ... _einzuladen_

◆ The Chairman and Governors of Hertford College, Oxford, **request the pleasure of the company of** Miss Charlotte Young and partner **at a dinner to mark** the anniversary of the founding of the College
= geben sich die _Ehre_, ... _anlässlich_ ... zu einem festlichen Abendessen _einzuladen_

| ... und darauf antworten |

◆ **We thank you for your kind invitation to** the marriage of your daughter Annabel on 20th November, **and have much pleasure in accepting**
= wir möchten uns sehr _herzlich_ für die freundliche _Einladung_ zu ... _bedanken_, die wir mit großem _Vergnügen_ _annehmen_

◆ Mr and Mrs Ian Low **thank** Dr and Mrs Green for **their kind invitation to** the marriage of their daughter Ann on 21st July **and are delighted to accept**
= möchten uns _herzlich_ bei Ihnen für die freundliche _Einladung_ zu ... _bedanken_, die wir mit großem _Vergnügen_ _annehmen_

◆ **We regret that we are unable to accept your invitation to** the marriage of your daughter on 6th May
= zu unserem _Bedauern_ können wir Ihre _Einladung_ zu ... nicht _annehmen_

52.2 Einladungen zu Feierlichkeiten

◆ **We are celebrating Rosemary's engagement to David** by holding a dinner dance at the Central Hotel on Friday 12th February, 1999, **and very much hope that you will be able to join us**
= wir würden uns sehr _freuen_, wenn wir Sie _anlässlich_ der Verlobung von Rosemary und David zu ... _begrüßen_ _dürften_

◆ **We are giving a dinner party** next Saturday, **and would be delighted if you and your wife could come**
= wir möchten ... ein Abendessen geben und _laden_ Sie und Ihre Frau _herzlich_ dazu _ein_

◆ **I'm having a party** next week for my 18th - **come along, and bring a friend**
= ich gebe eine Party ... komm doch vorbei und bring noch jemanden mit

◆ **Would you and Gordon like to come** to dinner next Saturday?
= _wollt_ Gordon und du ... kommen

◆ **Would you be free for** lunch next Tuesday?
= _können_ wir uns zum ... treffen

◆ **Perhaps we could** meet for coffee some time next week?
= vielleicht _könnten_ wir

52.3 Eine Einladung annehmen

◆ **Yes, I'd love to meet up with you** tomorrow
= ja, ich würde mich gern mit dir treffen

◆ **It was good of you to invite me**, I've been longing to do something like this for ages
= es war sehr freundlich von dir, mich _einzuladen_

◆ **Thank you for your invitation to** dinner - **I look forward to it very much**
= _herzlichen_ _Dank_ für Ihre _Einladung_ zu ... ich _freue_ mich sehr darauf

52.4 Eine Einladung ablehnen

◆ **I'd love to come, but I'm afraid** I'm already going out that night
= ich würde gern kommen, aber _leider_

◆ **I wish I could come, but unfortunately** I have something else on
= ich _wünschte_, ich könnte kommen, aber _leider_

◆ It was very kind of you to invite me to your dinner party next Saturday. **Unfortunately I will not be able to accept**
= zu meinem _Bedauern_ kann ich nicht _zusagen_

◆ **Much to our regret, we are unable to accept**
= zu unserem größten _Bedauern_ können wir nicht _zusagen_

52.5 Keine feste Zusage geben

◆ **I'm not sure** what I'm doing that night, but I'll let you know later
= ich _weiß_ nicht _genau_

◆ **It all depends on whether** I can get a sitter for Rosie at short notice
= es _hängt_ alles davon _ab_, ob

◆ **I'm afraid I can't really make any definite plans** until I know when Alex will be able to take her holidays
= _leider_ kann ich nichts Festes _planen_

53 ERÖRTERUNGEN

53.1 Beweisführung

| Ein Thema einführen |

◆ **It is often said** oder **claimed that** teenagers get pregnant in order to get council accommodation
= es wird oft _behauptet_, dass

- **It is a truism** oder **a commonplace (to say) that** American accents are infinitely more glamorous than their British counterparts
  = *es ist eine Binsenweisheit, dass*

- **It is undeniably true that** Gormley helped to turn his union members into far more sophisticated workers
  = *es steht außer <u>Zweifel</u>, dass*

- **It is a well-known fact that** in this age of technology, it is computer screens which are responsible for many illnesses
  = *es ist allgemein bekannt, dass*

- **It is sometimes forgotten that** much Christian doctrine comes from Judaism
  = *es gerät manchmal in <u>Vergessenheit</u>, dass*

- **It would be naïve to suppose that** in a radically changing world these 50-year-old arrangements can survive
  = *es wäre naiv <u>anzunehmen</u>, dass*

- **It would hardly be an exaggeration to say that** the friendship of both of them with Britten was among the most creative in the composer's life
  = *man kann ohne große Übertreibung sagen, dass*

- **It is hard to open a newspaper nowadays without reading that** electronic technology has made the written word obsolete
  = *man kann heutzutage schon keine Zeitung mehr aufschlagen, ohne zu lesen, dass*

- **First of all, it is important to try to understand** some of the systems and processes involved in order to create a healthier body
  = *<u>zunächst</u> einmal ist es <u>wichtig</u>, ... zu <u>verstehen</u>*

- **It is in the nature of** sociological theory **to** make broad generalizations about such things as the evolution of society
  = *es liegt in der Natur der ..., zu*

- **It is often the case that** early interests lead on to a career
  = *oftmals ist*

- **By way of introduction, let me** summarize the background to this question
  = *zur <u>Einführung</u> möchte ich*

- **I would like to start with** a very sweeping statement which can easily be challenged
  = *ich möchte mit ... <u>beginnen</u>*

- **Before going specifically into the issue of** criminal law, **I wish first to summarize** how Gewirth derives his principles of morality and justice
  = *bevor ich die <u>Frage</u> des ... näher <u>erörtere</u>, möchte ich <u>zunächst</u> <u>zusammenfassen</u>*

- **Let us look at** what self-respect in your job actually means
  = *<u>betrachten</u> wir*

- **We commonly think of** people **as** isolated individuals but, in fact, few of us ever spend more than an hour or two of our waking hours alone
  = *wir <u>betrachten</u> ... im Allgemeinen als*

- **What we are mainly concerned with here is** the conflict between what the hero says and what he actually does
  = *es <u>geht</u> uns hier hauptsächlich um*

- **We live in a world in which** the word "equality" is liberally bandied about
  = *in unserer Welt*

Vorstellungen und Probleme einführen

- **The concept of** controlling harmful insects by genetic means isn't new
  = *die <u>Vorstellung</u>, zu*

- **The idea of** getting rich without too much effort has universal appeal
  = *die <u>Idee</u>, zu*

- **The question of whether** Hamlet was really insane has long occupied critics
  = *die <u>Frage</u>, ob*

- **Why they were successful where their predecessors had failed is a question that has been much debated**
  = *über die <u>Frage</u> ... ist schon viel debattiert worden*

- **One of the most striking aspects of this issue is** the way (in which) it arouses strong emotions
  = *einer der interessantesten <u>Aspekte</u> dieses <u>Problems</u> ist*

- **There are a number of issues** on which China and Britain openly disagree
  = *es gibt einige <u>Fragen</u>*

Verallgemeinerungen

- **People who** work outside the home **tend to believe that** parenting is an easy option
  = *diejenigen, die ..., <u>nehmen</u> oft <u>an</u>, dass*

- **There's** always **a tendency for people** to exaggerate their place in the world
  = *der Mensch <u>neigt</u> immer dazu*

- Many gardeners **have a tendency to** treat plants like humans
  = *<u>neigen</u> dazu*

- Viewed psychologically, it would seem that **we all have the propensity for** such traits
  = *wir alle <u>neigen</u> zu*

- **For the (vast) majority of people**, literature is a subject which is studied at school but which has no relevance to life as they know it
  = *für die (aller)meisten Menschen*

- **For most of us** housework is a necessary but boring task
  = *für die meisten von uns*

- History **provides numerous examples** oder **instances of** misguided national heroes who did more harm than good in the long run
  = *<u>bietet</u> zahllose <u>Beispiele</u> für*

Genauere Angaben machen

- The impact of these theories on the social sciences, and economics **in particular**, was extremely significant
  = *im Besonderen*

- **One particular issue** raised by Butt was, suppose Hughes at the time of his conviction had been old enough to be hanged, what would have happened?
  = *eine spezielle <u>Frage</u>*

- **A more specific point** relates to using this insight as a way of challenging our hidden assumptions about reality
  = *eine <u>genauere</u> Aussage*

- **More specifically**, he accuses Western governments of continuing to supply weapons and training to the rebels
  = *<u>genauer</u> gesagt*

53.2 Die These

Einführung

- **First of all, let us consider** the advantages of urban life
  = *<u>zunächst</u> <u>sollen</u> ... <u>betrachtet</u> werden*

- **Let us begin with an examination of** the social aspects of this question
  = *<u>beginnen</u> wir mit einer <u>Untersuchung</u>*

- **The first thing that needs to be said is that** the author is presenting a one-sided view
  = *<u>zunächst</u> muss <u>erwähnt</u> werden, dass*

- **What should be established at the very outset is that** we are dealing here with a practical issue rather than a philosophical one
  = *gleich zu Anfang sollte klargestellt werden, dass*

Die Diskussion eingrenzen

- **In the next section, I will pursue the question of whether** the expansion of the Dutch prison system can be explained by Box's theory
  = *im nächsten Abschnitt werde ich auf die <u>Frage</u> <u>eingehen</u>, ob*

- **I will then deal with the question of** whether or not the requirements for practical discourse are compatible with criminal procedure
  = *danach werde ich das <u>Problem</u> ... behandeln*

- We must distinguish between the psychic and the spiritual, and **we shall see how** the subtle level of consciousness is the basis for the spiritual level
  = *wir werden sehen, wie*

- **I will confine myself to** giving an account of certain decisive facts in my militant career with Sartre
  = *ich möchte mich darauf <u>beschränken</u>*

- In this chapter, **I shall largely confine myself to** a consideration of those therapeutic methods that use visualization as a part of their procedures
  = *ich werde mich im Großen und Ganzen auf ... <u>beschränken</u>*

- **We will not concern ourselves here with** the Christian legend of St James
  = *an dieser <u>Stelle</u> soll nicht auf ... <u>eingegangen</u> werden*

- **Let us now consider** to what extent the present municipal tribunals differ from the former popular tribunals in the above-mentioned points
  = *<u>betrachten</u> wir nun*

- **Let us now look at** the ideal types of corporatism that neo-corporatist theorists developed to clarify the concept
  = *<u>betrachten</u> wir nun*

Einzelaspekte umreißen

- **The main issue under discussion is** how the party should re-define itself if it is to play any future role in Hungarian politics
  = *die Haupt<u>frage</u> ist*

- **A second, related problem is** that business ethics has mostly concerned itself with grand theorizing
  = *ein weiteres <u>Problem</u> in diesem Zusammenhang ist*

- **The basic issue at stake is this**: is research to be judged by its value in generating new ideas?
  = *das zur Debatte stehende Grund<u>problem</u> ist*

- **An important aspect of** Milton's imagery **is** the play of light and shade
  = *ein <u>wichtiger</u> <u>Aspekt</u> von ... ist*

- **It is worth mentioning here that** when this was first translated, the opening reference to Heidegger was entirely deleted
  = *an dieser <u>Stelle</u> sollte man <u>erwähnen</u>, dass*

- **Finally, there is the argument that** watching too much television may stunt a child's imagination
  = *und <u>schließlich</u> wäre da noch die <u>These</u>, dass*

Ein Argument in Frage stellen

- World leaders appear to be taking a tough stand, but **is there any real substance in** what has been agreed?
  = *hat ... Substanz*

- This is a question which **merits close(r) examination**
  = *<u>verdient</u> nähere <u>Betrachtung</u>*

- The unity of the two separate German states **has raised fundamental questions** for Germany's neighbours
  = *hat grundlegende <u>Fragen</u> ... <u>aufgeworfen</u>*

- The failure to protect our fellow Europeans in Bosnia **raises fundamental questions on** the role of the armed forces
  = *<u>wirft</u> grundlegende <u>Fragen</u> über ... <u>auf</u>*

- **This raises once again the question of** whether a government's right to secrecy should override the public's right to know
  = *dies <u>wirft</u> erneut die <u>Frage</u> ... <u>auf</u>*

- **This poses the question of** whether these measures are really helping the people they were intended to help
  = *dies <u>wirft</u> die <u>Frage</u> auf*

Analyse anbieten

- **It is interesting to consider why** this scheme has been so successful
  = *es ist interessant zu <u>betrachten</u>, warum*

- **On the question of** whether civil disobedience is likely to help end the war, Chomsky is deliberately diffident
  = *was die <u>Frage</u> nach ... <u>betrifft</u>*

- **We are often faced with the choice between** our sense of duty **and** our own personal inclinations
  = *man steht oft vor der <u>Wahl</u> zwischen ... und ...*

- **When we speak of** realism in music, **we do not at all have in mind** the illustrative bases of music
  = *wenn wir von ... <u>sprechen</u>, <u>meinen</u> wir damit ganz bestimmt nicht*

- **It is reasonable to assume that** most people living in industrialized societies are to some extent contaminated by environmental poisons
  = *es ist <u>wahrscheinlich</u> <u>anzunehmen</u>, dass*

Ein Argument unterstützen

- **An argument in support of** this approach **is that** it produces ...
  = *ein <u>Argument</u> zur <u>Bestätigung</u> ... ist, dass*

- **In support of his theory**, Dr Gold notes that most oil contains higher-than-atmospheric concentrations of helium-3
  = *um seine Theorie zu <u>bestätigen</u>*

- **This is the most telling argument in favour of** an extension of the right to vote
  = *dies ist das <u>wichtigste</u> <u>Argument</u>, dass für ... <u>spricht</u>*

- **The second reason for advocating** this course of action **is that** it benefits the community at large
  = *ein <u>weiterer</u> <u>Grund</u>, ... zu <u>unterstützen</u>, <u>besteht</u> darin, dass*

- **The third, more fundamental, reason for** looking to the future **is that** even the angriest investors realize they need a successful market
  = *ein dritter, noch <u>wichtigerer</u> <u>Grund</u> für ... ist, dass*

- Despite communism's demise, confidence in capitalism seems to be at an all-time low. **The fundamental reason for** this contradiction seems to me quite simple
  = *der wesentliche <u>Grund</u> für*

53.3 Ein Gegenargument vorstellen

Etwas kritisieren oder ablehnen

- **In actual fact, the idea of** there being a rupture between a so-called old criminology and an emergent new criminology **is somewhat misleading**
  = *tatsächlich ist die <u>Vorstellung</u> davon, dass ..., etwas irreführend*

- In order to argue this, **I will show that** Wyeth's **position is**, in actual fact, **untenable**
  = *ich werde <u>zeigen</u>, dass ... Position <u>unhaltbar</u> ist*

- **It is claimed, however**, that the strict Leboyer method is not essential for a less traumatic birth experience
  = *es wird jedoch <u>behauptet</u>*

- **This need not mean that** we are destined to suffer for ever. **Indeed, the opposite may be true**
  = *das muss nicht <u>unbedingt</u> <u>bedeuten</u>, dass ... Es könnte auch das <u>genaue</u> Gegenteil <u>zutreffen</u>*

◆ Many observers, though, **find it difficult to share his opinion that** it could mean the end of the Tamil Tigers
　= tun sich _schwer_ damit, seine _Meinung_ zu teilen, dass

◆ **On the other hand**, there are more important factors that should be taken into consideration
　= _andererseits_

◆ The judgement made **may well be true but** the evidence given to sustain it is unlikely to convince the sceptical
　= kann zwar _zutreffen_, aber

◆ Reform **is all very well, but** it is pointless if the rules are not enforced
　= ist ja schön und gut, aber

◆ The case against the use of drugs in sport rests primarily on the argument that ... . **This argument is weak**, for two reasons
　= dieses _Argument_ ist schwach

◆ According to one theory, the ancestors of vampire bats were fruit-eating bats. But **this idea does not hold water**
　= diese _Vorstellung_ ist nicht _stichhaltig_

◆ Their claim to be a separate race **does not stand up to** historical scrutiny
　= _hält_ ... nicht _stand_

◆ **This view does not stand up** if we examine the known facts about John
　= diese _Ansicht_ ist nicht _haltbar_

◆ **The trouble with this idea is not that** it is wrong, **but rather that** it is uninformative
　= das _Problem_ mit dieser _Idee_ ist nicht so sehr ..., sondern vielmehr

◆ **The difficulty with this view is that** he bases the principle on a false premise
　= die Schwierigkeit bei dieser Betrachtungsweise liegt, darin, dass

◆ **The snag with** such speculations **is that** too much turns on one man or event
　= der _Nachteil_ von ... ist, dass

◆ But removing healthy ovaries **is entirely unjustified in my opinion**
　= ist meiner _Meinung_ nach völlig ungerechtfertigt

| Eine Alternative vorschlagen |

◆ **Another approach may be to** develop substances capable of blocking the effects of the insect's immune system
　= eine andere Herangehensweise könnte sein

◆ **Another way to** reduce failure is to improve vocational education
　= ein anderer Weg, um

◆ **However, the other side of the coin is** the fact that an improved self-image really can lead to prosperity
　= die Kehrseite der Medaille ist jedoch

◆ **It is more accurate to speak of** a plurality of new criminologies rather than of a single new criminology
　= es ist präziser, von ... zu _sprechen_

◆ **Paradoxical as it may seem**, computer models of mind can be positively humanizing
　= so paradox wie es auch _erscheinen_ mag

53.4 **Die Synthese der Beweisführung**

◆ **How can we reconcile** these two apparently contradictory viewpoints?
　= wie lassen sich ... _vereinbaren_

◆ **On balance**, making money honestly is more profitable than making it dishonestly
　= _alles_ in _allem_

◆ Since such vitamins are more expensive, **one has to weigh up the pros and cons**
　= man muss das Für und Wider abwägen

◆ **We need to look at the pros and cons of** normative theory as employed by Gewirth and Phillips
　= wir müssen die _Vor-_ und _Nachteile_ der ... _betrachten_

◆ **The benefits of** partnership in a giant trading market **will** almost certainly **outweigh the disadvantages**
　= die _Vorteile_ der ... werden ... die _Nachteile_ überwiegen

◆ **The two perspectives are not mutually exclusive**
　= die beiden Betrachtungsweisen _schließen_ sich nicht gegenseitig _aus_

| Eines von mehreren Argumenten unterstützen |

◆ Dr Meaden's theory **is the most convincing explanation**
　= ist die einleuchtendste Erklärung

◆ **The truth** oder **fact of the matter is that** in a free society you can't turn every home into a fortress
　= die _Wahrheit_ ist, dass

◆ But **the truth is that** Father Christmas has a rather mixed origin
　= die _Wahrheit_ ist, dass

◆ Although this operation sounds extremely dangerous, **in actual fact** it is extremely safe
　= in _Wirklichkeit_

◆ **When all is said and done, it must be acknowledged that** a purely theoretical approach to social issues is sterile
　= letzten _Endes_ muss man erkennen, dass

| Zusammenfassen |

◆ In this chapter, **I have demonstrated** oder **shown that** the Cuban alternative has been undergoing considerable transformations
　= ich habe _nachgewiesen_, dass

◆ **This shows how**, in the final analysis, adhering to a particular theory on crime is at best a matter of reasoned choice
　= dies _beweist_, wie

◆ **The overall picture shows that** prison sentences were relatively frequent, but not particularly severe
　= der _Gesamteindruck_ _zeigt_, dass

◆ **To recap** oder **To sum up, then, (we may conclude that)** there are in effect two possible solutions to this problem
　= _zusammenfassend_ (können wir _schlussfolgern_, dass)

◆ **To sum up this chapter** I will offer two examples ...
　= um dieses Kapitel _zusammenzufassen_

◆ **To summarize**, we have seen that the old staple industries in Britain had been hit after the First World War by a deteriorating international competitive position
　= um noch einmal _zusammenzufassen_

◆ Habermas's argument, **in a nutshell**, is as follows
　= kurz gesagt

◆ But **the key to the whole argument is** a single extraordinary paragraph
　= der Schlüssel zur gesamten Beweisführung liegt in

◆ **To round off this section on** slugs, gardeners may be interested to hear that there are three species of predatory slugs in the British Isles
　= um diesen Abschnitt über ... abzurunden

| Schlussfolgerungen ziehen |

◆ **From all this, it follows that** it is impossible to extend those kinds of security measures to all potential targets of terrorism
　= aus alledem _geht_ _hervor_, dass

◆ This, of course, **leads to the logical conclusion that** those who actually produce do have a claim to the results of their efforts
　= führt zu der logischen _Schlussfolgerung_, dass

◆ **There is only one logical conclusion we can reach** which is that we ask our customers what is the Strategic Reality that they perceive in our marketing programme
= wir können hier nur zu einer logischen _Schlussfolgerung_ gelangen

◆ **The inescapable conclusion is that** the criminal justice system does not simply reflect the reality of crime; it helps create it
= die unweigerliche _Schlussfolgerung_ ist, dass

◆ **We must conclude that** there is no solution to the problem of defining crime
= wir müssen _schlussfolgern_, dass

◆ **In conclusion**, because interpersonal relationships are so complex, there can be no easy way of preventing conflict
= die _Schlussfolgerung_ ist, dass

◆ **The upshot of all this is that** treatment is unlikely to be available
= all das läuft darauf hinaus, dass

◆ **So it would appear that** butter is not significantly associated with heart disease after all
= es _scheint_ also, dass

◆ **This only goes to show that** a good man is hard to find
= all dies _zeigt_ nur, dass

◆ **The lesson to be learned** from this **is that** you cannot hope to please everyone all of the time
= aus ... kann man die Lehre ziehen, dass

◆ **At the end of the day**, the only way the drug problem will be beaten is when people are encouraged not to take them
= letzten _Endes_

◆ **Ultimately, then**, while we may have some sympathy for these young criminals, we must do our utmost to protect society from them
= letzten _Endes_

Aufbau eines Absatzes

◆ **In addition**, the author does not really empathize with his hero
= _darüber_ _hinaus_

◆ **Also**, there is the question of language
= des weiteren

◆ This award-winning writer, **in addition to** being a critic, biographer and poet, has written 26 crime novels
= ... ist nicht nur ..., sondern

◆ But this is only part of the picture. **Added to this are** fears that a major price increase would cause riots
= hinzu kommen noch

◆ **An added** complication **is that** the characters are not aware of their relationship to one another
= eine zusätzliche ... ist

◆ But, **over and above that**, each list contains fictitious names and addresses
= _darüber_ _hinaus_

◆ **Furthermore**, ozone is, like carbon dioxide, a greenhouse gas
= des weiteren

◆ **The question also arises as to** how this idea can be put into practice
= es stellt sich auch die _Frage_

◆ Politicians, **as well as** academics and educationalists, tend to feel strongly abut the way history is taught
= sowie

Vergleiche

◆ **Compared with** the heroine, Alison is an insipid character
= _verglichen_ mit

◆ **In comparison with** the Czech Republic, the culture of Bulgaria is less westernized
= im _Vergleich_ zu

◆ This is a high percentage for the English Midlands but low **by comparison with** some other parts of Britain
= im _Vergleich_ zu

◆ **On the one hand**, there is no longer a Warsaw Pact threat. **On the other (hand)**, the positive changes could have negative side-effects.
= _einerseits_ ... _andererseits_

◆ **Similarly**, a good historian is not obsessed by dates
= in _ähnlicher_ Weise

◆ There can only be one total at the bottom of a column of figures and **likewise** only one solution to any problem
= in _ähnlicher_ Weise

◆ What others say of us will translate into reality. **Equally**, what we affirm as true of ourselves will likewise come true
= _gleichermaßen_

◆ There will now be a change in the way we are regarded by our partners, and, **by the same token**, the way we regard them
= _gleichermaßen_

◆ **There is a fundamental difference between** adequate nutrient intake **and** optimum nutrient intake
= es gibt einen wesentlichen _Unterschied_ zwischen ... und

Synthese der einzelnen Elemente

◆ **First of all** oder **Firstly**, I would like to outline the benefits of the system
= _zunächst_

◆ In music we are concerned **first and foremost** with the practical application of controlled sounds relating to the human psyche
= in erster _Linie_

◆ **In order to understand** the conflict between the two nations, **it is first of all necessary to** know something of the history of the area
= um ... zu _verstehen_, ist es _zunächst_ notwendig

◆ **Secondly**, it might be simpler to develop chemical or even nuclear warheads for a large shell than for a missile
= zweitens

◆ **In the first/second/third place**, the objectives of privatization were contradictory
= erstens/zweitens/drittens

◆ **Finally**, there is the argument that watching too much television may stunt a child's imagination
= _schließlich_

Eine persönliche Meinung ausdrücken

◆ **In my opinion**, the government is underestimating the scale of the epidemic
= meiner _Meinung_ nach

◆ **My personal opinion is that** the argument lacks depth
= ich _persönlich_ bin der _Meinung_, dass

◆ This is a popular viewpoint, but **speaking personally** I cannot understand it
= _persönlich_

◆ **Personally, I think that** no one can appreciate ethnicity more than black or African people themselves
= ich _persönlich_ _glaube_, dass

◆ **My own view is that** what largely determines the use of non-national workers are economic factors rather than political ones
= ich _persönlich_ bin der _Ansicht_, dass

◆ **In my view**, it only perpetuates the very problem that it sets out to address
= meiner _Ansicht_ nach

◆ **For my part**, I cannot agree with the leadership on this question
= was mich angeht

◆ Although the author argues the case for patriotism, **I feel that** he does not do it with any great personal conviction
= ich _denke_, dass

◆ **I believe that** people do understand that there can be no quick fix
for Britain's economic problems
= ich _glaube_, dass

◆ **It seems to me that** what we have is a political problem that needs
to be solved at a political level
= es _scheint_ mir, dass

◆ **I would maintain that** we have made a significant effort to ensure
that the results are made public
= ich möchte _behaupten_, dass

Die Meinung anderer ausdrücken

◆ **He claims** oder **maintains that** intelligence is conditioned by
upbringing
= er _behauptet_, dass

◆ Bukharin **asserts that** all great revolutions are accompanied by
destructive internal conflict
= _stellt_ _fest_, dass

◆ The communiqué **states that** some form of nuclear deterrent will
continue to be needed for the foreseeable future
= _stellt_ _fest_, dass

◆ **What he is saying is that** the time of the old, highly structured
political party is over
= er will damit sagen, dass

◆ His admirers **would have us believe that** watching this film is more
like attending a church service than having a night at the pictures
= _wollen_ uns _glauben_ machen, dass

◆ **According to** the report, poverty creates a climate favourable to
violence
= laut

Beispiele geben

◆ **To take another example**: many thousands of people have been
condemned to a life of sickness and pain because ...
= um noch ein weiteres _Beispiel_ anzuführen:

◆ Let us consider, **for example** oder **for instance**, the problems faced
by immigrants arriving in a strange country
= zum _Beispiel_

◆ His meteoric rise **is the most striking example yet of** voters'
disillusionment with the record of the previous government
= ist das bisher beste _Beispiel_

◆ The case of Henry Howey Robson **serves to illustrate** the courage
exhibited by young men in the face of battle
= _veranschaulicht_

◆ Just consider, **by way of illustration**, the difference in amounts
accumulated if interest is paid gross, rather than having tax
deducted
= um dies einmal zu _veranschaulichen_

◆ **A case in point is** the decision to lift the ban on contacts with the
republic
= ein positives _Beispiel_ ist

◆ **Take the case of** the soldier returning from war
= nehmen wir zum _Beispiel_

◆ **As** the Prime Minister **remarked** recently, the Channel Tunnel will
greatly benefit the whole of the European Community
= wie ... sagte

53.6 Die Diskussion

Eine Annahme darlegen

◆ They have telephoned the president to put pressure on him. And
that could be interpreted as trying to gain an unconstitutional
political advantage
= dies könnte man als ... interpretieren

◆ Retail sales rose sharply last month. This was higher than expected
and **could be taken to mean that** inflationary pressures remain
strong
= könnte als Zeichen dafür aufgefasst werden, dass

◆ In such circumstances, **it might well be prudent** to diversify your
investments
= könnte es weise sein

◆ These substances do not remain effective for very long. **This is
possibly because** they work against the insects' natural instinct
to feed
= dies rührt _wahrscheinlich_ daher, dass

◆ His wife had become an embarrassment to him and therefore **it is not
beyond the bounds of possibility that** he may have contemplated
murdering her
= es kann nicht _ausgeschlossen_ werden, dass

◆ Mr Fraser's assertion **leads one to suppose that** he is in full
agreement with Catholic teaching as regards marriage
= lässt vermuten, dass

◆ **It is probably the case that** all long heavy ships are vulnerable
= _wahrscheinlich_

◆ After hearing nothing from the taxman for so long, most people
might reasonably assume that their tax affairs were in order
= könnten durchaus _annehmen_, dass

◆ **One could be forgiven for thinking that** because the substances
are chemicals they'd be easy to study
= man könnte fast _annehmen_, dass

◆ **I venture to suggest that** very often when people like him talk
about love, they actually mean lust
= ich _wage_ zu _behaupten_, dass

Gewissheit ausdrücken

◆ **It is clear that** any risk to the human foetus is very low
= es ist _klar_, dass

◆ Benn is **indisputably** a fine orator, one of the most compelling
speakers in politics today
= _zweifelsohne_

◆ British universities are **undeniably** good, but they are not turning out
enough top scientists
= _unbestreitbar_

◆ **There can be no doubt that** the Earth underwent a dramatic
cooling which destroyed the environment and lifestyle of these
creatures
= es lässt sich nicht bezweifeln, dass

◆ **It is undoubtedly true that** over the years there has been a much
greater emphasis on safer sex
= es ist _unbestreitbar_, dass

◆ **As we all know** adultery is far from uncommon, particularly in
springtime
= wie wir alle _wissen_

◆ **One thing is certain**: the party is far from united
= eins ist _sicher_

◆ **It is (quite) certain that** unless peace can be brought to this
troubled land no amount of aid will solve the long-term problems
of the people
= es ist _sicher_, dass

Zweifel ausdrücken

◆ **It is doubtful whether** in this present regressive climate, anyone
would be brave or foolish enough to demonstrate publicly
= es ist _fraglich_, ob

◆ **It remains to be seen whether** the security forces will try to intervene
= es bleibt _abzuwarten_, ob

◆ **I have a few reservations about** the book
= ich habe einige _Vorbehalte_ gegen

- The judges are expected to endorse the recommendation, but **it is by no means certain that** they will make up their minds today
  = es ist keineswegs _sicher, dass_

- **It is questionable whether** media coverage of terrorist organizations actually affects terrorism
  = es ist _fraglich_, ob

- **This raises the whole question of** exactly when men and women should retire
  = dies _wirft die Frage_ nach ... _auf_

- The crisis **puts a question mark against** the Prime Minister's stated commitment to intervention
  = stellt ... _infrage_

- **Both these claims are true up to a point** and they need to be made. But they are limited in their significance
  = beide _Behauptungen_ sind bis zu einem gewissen Punkt _richtig_

Zustimmung ausdrücken

- **I agree wholeheartedly with** the opinion that smacking should be outlawed
  = ich _stimme_ ... voll und ganz _zu_

- **One must acknowledge that** their history will make change more painful
  = man muss eingestehen, dass

- **It cannot be denied that** there are similarities between the two approaches
  = es lässt sich nicht _verleugnen_, dass

- Courtney - **rightly in my view** - is strongly critical of the snobbery and élitism that is all too evident in these circles
  = für meine Begriffe zu _Recht_

- Preaching was considered an important activity, **and rightly so** in a country with a high illiteracy rate
  = und das zu _Recht_

- You may dispute the Pope's right to tell people how to live their lives, **but it is hard to disagree with** his picture of modern society
  = aber man kann ... nur schwer _widersprechen_

Widerspruch ausdrücken

- **I must disagree with** Gordon's article on criminality: it is dangerous to suggest that to be a criminal one must look like a criminal
  = ich kann ... nicht _zustimmen_

- As a former teacher **I find it hard to believe that** there is no link at all between screen violence and violence on the streets
  = ich kann nur _schwer glauben_, dass

- The strength of their feelings **is scarcely credible**
  = ist kaum glaubhaft

- Her claim to have been the first to discover the phenomenon **lacks credibility**
  = ist unglaubwürdig

- Nevertheless, **I remain unconvinced by** Milton
  = ... _überzeugt_ mich nicht

- Many do not believe that water contains anything remotely dangerous. Sadly, **this is far from the truth**
  = dies _entspricht_ ganz und gar nicht der _Wahrheit_

- To say that everyone requires the same amount of a vitamin is as stupid as saying we all have blonde hair and blue eyes. **It simply isn't true**
  = es ist einfach nicht wahr

- His remarks **were** not only highly offensive to black and other ethnic minorities but **totally inaccurate**
  = waren _vollkommen_ falsch

- Stomach ulcers are often associated with good living and a fast-moving lifestyle. **(But) in reality** there is no evidence to support this theory
  = in _Wirklichkeit_ (jedoch)

- This version of a political economy **does not stand up to close scrutiny**
  = _hält_ einer _genaueren Untersuchung_ nicht _stand_

Ein Argument betonen

- **Nowadays, there is clearly** less stigma attached to unmarried mothers
  = heutzutage ist ganz offensichtlich

- Evidence shows that ..., so once again **the facts speak for themselves**
  = die Fakten _sprechen_ für sich

- **Few will argue with the principle that** such a fund should be set up
  = der _Ansicht_, dass ..., _stimmen_ im Prinzip fast alle _zu_

- Hyams **supports this claim** by looking at sentences produced by young children learning German
  = _unterstützt_ diese _Behauptung_

- **The most important thing is to** reach agreement from all sides
  = am _wichtigsten_ ist es

- Perhaps **the most important aspect of** cognition is the ability to manipulate symbols
  = der _wichtigste Aspekt_

- **It would be impossible to exaggerate the importance of** these two volumes for anyone with a serious interest in the development of black gospel music
  = man kann die Wichtigkeit ... gar nicht genug _betonen_

- The symbolic importance of Jerusalem for both Palestinians and Jews **is almost impossible to overemphasize**
  = kann gar nicht genug _betont_ werden

- **It is important to be clear that** Jesus did not identify himself with Yahweh
  = vor allem muss man sich _klar_ machen, dass

- **It is significant that** Mandalay seems to have become the central focus in this debate
  = es ist bezeichnend, dass

- **It should not be forgotten that** many of those now in exile were close to the centre of power until only one year ago
  = man _sollte_ nicht _vergessen_, dass

- **It should be stressed that** the only way pet owners could possibly contract such a condition from their pets is by eating them
  = es _sollte betont_ werden, dass

- **There is a very important point here and that is that** the accused claims that he was with Ms Martins all evening on the night of the crime
  = hierbei ist es äußerst _wichtig festzustellen_, dass

- At the beginning of the book Mr Stone **makes a telling point**. The Balkan peoples, he notes, are for the first time ...
  = gibt ein aufschlussreiches _Argument_

- Suspicion is **the chief feature of** Britain's attitude to European theatre
  = das Hauptmerkmal

- **In order to focus attention on** Hobson's distinctive contributions to macroeconomics, these wider issues are neglected here
  = um die Aufmerksamkeit auf ... zu lenken

- **These statements are interesting in that** they illustrate different views
  = diese Äußerungen sind dahin gehend interessant, dass

Language in Use

Contents

German-English

Sprache Aktiv

Inhalt

Englisch-Deutsch

WÖRTERBUCH
DEUTSCH~ENGLISCH

GERMAN~ENGLISH
DICTIONARY

A

A, a [a:] NT **-, -** or (inf) **-s, -s** A, a; **das A und (das) O** (fig) the essential thing(s), the be-all and end-all; (eines Wissensgebietes) the basics pl; **von A bis Z** (fig inf) from beginning to end, from A to Z; **sie/ihr alle, von A bis Z** them/you, the whole lot (Brit) or all of them/you; **wer A sagt, muss auch B sagen** (prov) in for a penny, in for a pound (esp Brit prov); (moralisch) if you start something, you should see it through

Ä, ä [ɛ:] NT **-, -** or (inf) **-s, -s** Ae, ae, A/a umlaut

à [a] PREP (esp Comm) at

Aa [aˈʔa] NT **-**, no pl (baby-talk) **Aa machen** to do big jobs (Brit baby-talk), to do a number two (baby-talk)

AA¹ [aːˈʔaː] NT **-s**, no pl abbr von **Auswärtiges Amt** FO (Brit), State Department (US)

AA² [aːˈʔaː] M **-s, -s** abbr von **Anonyme Alkoholiker** AA

Aal [a:l] M **-(e)s, -e** eel; **sich (drehen und) winden wie ein ~** (aus Verlegenheit) to wriggle like an eel; (aus Unaufrichtigkeit) to try and wriggle (one's way) out of it; **glatt wie ein ~** (fig) (as) slippery as an eel

aallen ['a:lən] VR (inf) to stretch out; **sich in der Sonne ~** to bask in the sun

Aal-: aallglatt (pej) ADJ slippery (as an eel), slick ADV slickly; **sich ~ herauswinden** to worm one's way out of it; **Aallsuplpe** F eel soup

a. a. O. abbr von **am angegebenen** or **angeführten Ort** loc. cit.

Aar [a:ɐ] M **-(e)s, -e** (obs liter) eagle, lord of the skies (liter)

Aarlgau ['a:ɐgaʊ] M **-s der ~** Aargau

Aas [a:s] NT **-es, -e** [-zə] **a** (= Tierleiche) carrion, rotting carcass **b** pl **Äser** [ɛːzɐ] (inf: = Luder) bugger (Brit inf), sod (Brit inf), jerk (sl), devil (inf); **kein ~** not a single bloody person (Brit inf), not a single soul

aalsen ['a:zn] VI (inf) to be wasteful; **mit etw ~** to waste sth; **mit Geld, Gütern auch** to squander sth, to be extravagant or wasteful with sth

Aas-: Aaslfliege F (Zool) carrion fly; **Aaslfreslser** M scavenger, carrion eater; **Aaslgeiler** M (lit, fig) vulture; **Aaslgeruch** M putrid or fetid stench, odour (Brit) or odor (US) of decomposition

aalsig ['a:zɪç] ADJ attr Geruch horrible, disgusting; (inf) Lächeln mean ADV (dated inf: = sehr) horribly

Aaslkälfer M burying or sexton beetle

ab [ap] ADV off, away; (Theat) exit sing, exeunt pl; **die nächste Straße rechts ab** the next street (off) to or on the right; **ab Zoologischer Garten** from Zoological Gardens; **ab Hamburg** after Hamburg; **München ab 12.20 Uhr** (Rail) leaving Munich 12.20; **ab wann?** from when?, as of when?; **ab nach Hause** go home, off you go home (Brit); **ab ins Bett mit euch!** off to bed with you or you go (Brit), time for bed; **Mützel Helm ab!** caps/hats off; **Tell ab** (Theat) exit Tell; **N und M ab** (Theat) exeunt N and M; **ab durch die Mitte** (inf) beat it! (inf), hop it! (inf); **kommt jetzt, ab durch die Mitte!** come on, let's beat

(inf) or hop (Brit inf) it!; **ab und zu** or (N Ger) **an** from time to time, now and again, now and then → **von**

PREP **+dat a** (räumlich) from; (zeitlich) from, as of, as from; **Kinder ab 14 Jahren** children from (the age of) 14 up; **alle ab Gehaltsstufe 4** everybody from grade 4 up; **ab Werk** (Comm) ex works; **ab sofort** as of now

b (Sw: in Zeitangaben) past; **Viertel ab 7** a quarter past or after (US) 7

Ablalkus ['a:bakʊs] M **-, -** abacus

abländerlbar, abländerllich ['apɛndɛlɪç] (old) ADJ alterable; Urteil revisable

ab+ändern VT sep to alter (in +acc to); (= überarbeiten auch) to revise; Gesetzentwurf to amend (in +acc to); Strafe, Urteil to revise (in +acc to)

Ablänldelrung F alteration (+gen to); (= Überarbeitung) revision; (von Strafe, Urteil) revision; (von Gesetzentwurf) amendment; **in ~** (Parl, Jur) in amendment

Ablänlderungs-: Ablänlderungslanltrag M (Parl) proposed amendment; **einen ~ einbringen** to submit an amendment; **Ablänlderungslvorlschlag** M proposed amendment; **einen ~ machen** to propose an amendment

ab+arlbeilten sep VT **a** Schuld to work off; Überfahrt to work; (= hinter sich bringen) Vertragszeit to work **b** (Comput) Programm to run; Befehl to execute VR to slave (away), to work like a slave → auch **abgearbeitet**

Ablart F variety (auch Biol); (= Variation) variation (+gen on)

ablarltig ADJ **a** abnormal, deviant, unnatural **b** (= widersinnig) perverse ADV (inf: = widerlich) abnormally; **das tut ~ weh** that hurts like hell (inf); **mir ist ~ schlecht** I feel terribly sick; **~ lang** a hell of a long time (inf)

Ablarltiglkeit F abnormality, deviancy

ab+älsen VT sep (Wild) Blätter etc to feed on; Gras to crop

Ablbau M , no pl **a** (= Förderung) (über Tage) quarrying; (unter Tage) mining **b** (lit, fig: = Demontage) dismantling **c** (Chem) decomposition; (im Körper) breakdown **d** (fig: = Verfall) decline; (der Persönlichkeit) disintegration **e** (= Verringerung) (von Personal, Produktion etc) reduction (+gen in, of), cutback (+gen in); (von überflüssigen Vorräten) gradual elimination (+gen of); (von Preisen) cut (+gen in), reduction (+gen in, of); (von Privilegien) reduction (+gen of), stripping away (+gen of); (von Vorurteilen) breaking down (+gen of); **der ~ von Beamtenstellen** the reduction in the number of civil service positions

ablbaulbar ADJ (Chem) degradable; **schwer ~e Chemikalien** chemicals that are difficult to break down; **biologisch ~** biodegradable

ab+baulen sep VT **a** (= fördern) (über Tage) quarry; (unter Tage) to mine **b** (= demontieren) System to dismantle; Maschine to strip down, to dismantle; Gerüst to take down, to dismantle; Kulissen to take down, to strike; Zelt to strike; Lager to break, to strike;

ein System allmählich ~ to phase out a system **c** (Chem) to break down, to decompose; (im Körper) to break down

d (= verringern) Produktion, Personal, Bürokratie to cut back, to reduce, to cut down on; Arbeitsplätze, Arbeitskräfte to reduce the number of; Privilegien to cut back, to strip away

VI (Sportler etc) to go downhill; (Patient) to deteriorate, to weaken; (= erlahmen) to flag, to wilt; (= abschalten) to switch off

Ablbaulproldukt NT (Chem) by-product

ab+beißen sep irreg VT to bite off; **eine Zigarre ~** to bite the end off a cigar; **sich** (dat) **die Zunge ~** to bite one's tongue off VI to take a bite; **nun beiß doch mal richtig ab!** now bite it off properly!

ab+beizen VT sep to strip

Ablbeizlmitltel NT paint stripper

ab+belkomlmen ptp **abbekommen** VT sep irreg **a** (= erhalten) to get; **etwas ~** to get some (of it); (= beschädigt werden) to get damaged; (= verletzt werden) to get hurt; (= Prügel abbekommen) to catch or cop it (Brit inf), to get yours (US inf); **das Auto/er hat dabei ganz schön was ~** (inf) the car/he really copped it (Brit inf) or got it (inf); **nichts ~** not to get any (of it); (= nicht beschädigt werden) not to get damaged; (= nicht verletzt werden) to come off unscathed; **sein(en) Teil ~** (lit, fig) to get one's fair share **b** (= abmachen können) to get off (von etw sth)

ab+belrulfen ptp **abberufen** VT sep irreg Diplomaten, Minister to recall; **(von Gott) ~ werden** (euph) to be called home (US) or to one's maker

Ablbelrulfung F recall; (euph: = Tod) departure from this life

ab+belstelllen ptp **abbestellt** VT sep to cancel; jdn auch to tell not to call or come; Telefon to have disconnected

Ablbelstelllung F cancellation; (von Telefon) disconnection

ab+betlteln VT sep jdm etw ~ to scrounge sth off or from sb (inf)

ab+belzahllen ptp **abbezahlt** sep VT Raten, Auto etc to pay off VI (auf Raten) to pay in instalments (Brit) or installments (US)

Ablbelzahllung F repayment

ab+bielgen sep irreg VT **a** Ellbogen, Knie to bend; (= abbrechen) to bend off **b** (inf: = verhindern) Thema, Verfahren to head off, to avoid; Frage to deflect; **das Gespräch ~** to change the subject; **zum Glück konnte ich das ~** luckily I managed to stop that; **diesen Vorschlag hat die Gewerkschaft abgebogen** the union put a stop to this proposal VI aux sein to turn off (in +acc into); (bei Gabelungen auch) to fork off; (Straße) to bend, to veer; **nach rechts ~** to turn (off to the) right; to fork right; to veer (to the) right

Ablbielger ['apbiːgɐ] M **-s, -**, **Ablbielgelrin** [-gərɪn] F **-, -nen** (Mot) car etc turning off

Ablbielge-: Ablbielgelspur F (Mot) filter (Brit) or turning (US) lane; **Ablbielgelverlbot** NT (Mot) turn ban; (Schild) no turning; **Ablbielgelverlkehr** M (Mot) turning traffic

Ab|bild NT (= *Nachahmung, Kopie*) copy, reproduction; (= *Spiegelbild*) reflection; (= *Wiedergabe*) picture, portrayal, representation; (*von Mensch*) image, likeness; **er ist das genaue ~ seines Vaters** he's the spitting image of his father

ab+bil|den VT *sep* (*lit, fig*) to depict, to portray, to show; *Verhältnisse etc auch* to reflect; (= *wiedergeben*) to reproduce; **auf der Titelseite ist ein Teddybär abgebildet** there's a picture of a teddy bear on the front page; **auf dem Foto ist eine Schulklasse abgebildet** there's a school class (shown) in the photo

Ab|bil|dung F **a** (= *das Abbilden*) depiction, portrayal; (= *Wiedergabe*) reproduction **b** (= *Illustration*) illustration; (= *Schaubild*) diagram; **siehe ~ S.12** see the illustration on p12; **das Buch ist mit zahlreichen ~en versehen** the book is copiously illustrated *or* has numerous illustrations

ab+bin|den *sep irreg* VT **a** (= *abmachen*) to undo, to untie; **sich** (*dat*) **die Schürze ~** to take off one's apron **b** (*Med*) *Arm, Bein etc* to ligature **c** (*Cook*) to bind VI (*Beton, Mörtel*) to set; (*Cook*) to bind

Ab|bit|te F apology; (**bei jdm wegen etw**) **~ tun** *or* **leisten** to make *or* offer one's apologies (to sb for sth), to apologize (to sb for sth)

ab+bit|ten VT *sep irreg* (*liter*) **jdm etw ~** to beg sb's pardon for sth, to make *or* offer one's apologies to sb for sth

ab+bla|sen *sep irreg* VT **a** *Staub, Schmutz* to blow off (*von etw* sth); *Tisch, Buch* to blow the dust *etc* off, to blow clean; *Gas* to release, to let off; **eine Hauswand mit Sandstrahl ~** to sandblast a house wall **b** (*Tech*) *Hochofen* to let burn down **c** (*inf*) *Veranstaltung, Feier, Streik* to call off VI (*Tech: Hochofen*) to burn down

ab+blät|tern VI *sep aux sein* (*Putz, Farbe*) to flake *or* peel (off)

ab+blei|ben VI *sep irreg aux sein* (*N Ger inf*) to get to (*inf*); **wo ist er abgeblieben?** where has he got (*Brit*) *or* gone to?; **irgendwo muss er/es abgeblieben sein** he/it must be somewhere

ab|blend|bar ADJ *Rückspiegel* antidazzle (*Brit*), antiglare (*US*)

Ab|blen|de F (*Film*) fade(-out)

ab+blen|den *sep* VT *Lampe* to shade, to screen; (*Aut*) *Scheinwerfer* to dip (*Brit*), to dim (*esp US*) VI (*Phot*) to stop down; (*Film*) to fade out; (*Aut*) to dip (*Brit*) *or* dim (*esp US*) one's headlights; **es wurde abgeblendet** the scene (was) faded out

Ab|blend|licht NT (*Aut*) dipped (*Brit*) *or* dimmed (*esp US*) headlights *pl*; **mit ~ fahren** to drive on dipped (*Brit*) *or* dimmed (*esp US*) headlights

ab+blit|zen VI *sep aux sein* (*inf*) to be sent packing (*bei* by) (*inf*); **jdn ~ lassen** to send sb packing (*inf*), to send sb off with a flea in his/her ear (*Brit inf*)

ab+blo|cken *sep* VT (*Sport, fig*) to block; *Gegner* to stall VI to stall

ab+blü|hen VI *sep aux sein* (*rare*) = **verblühen**

Ab|brand M **a** (= *Verbrennen*) combustion **b** (*Kernenergie*) burn-up

ab+brau|sen *sep* VT to give a shower; *Körperteil* to wash under the shower; **sich ~** to have *or* take a shower, to shower VI *aux sein* (*inf*) to roar off *or* away

ab+bre|chen *sep irreg* VT **a** (= *beenden*) to break off; *Raumflug, Rennstart, Experiment* to abort; (*Comput*) *Operation* to abort; *Veranstaltung, Verfahren, Verhandlung, Therapie, Start* to stop; *Streik, Suche, Mission* to call off; *Schwangerschaft* to terminate; **die diplomatischen Beziehungen ~** to break off diplomatic relations; **die Schule ~** to stop going to school → *auch* **abgebrochen b** *Ast, Außenspiegel, Antenne, Fingernagel, Spitze* to break off; *Bleistift* to break, to snap; **etw von etw ~** to break sth off sth; (**nun**) **brich dir kei-**

nen ab! (*inf*) don't make such a palaver *or* song and dance (*Brit inf*), don't make such a fuss; **sich** (*dat*) **einen ~** (*inf*) (= *Umstände machen*) to make heavy weather of it (*Brit inf*), to make a fuss about it; (= *sich sehr anstrengen*) to go to a lot of bother, to bust one's butt (*US sl*); **abgebrochen** (*Stück, Bleistiftspitze*) broken off **c** (= *abbauen*) *Zelt* to strike; *Lager* to break; (= *niederreißen*) to demolish; *Gebäude* to demolish, to pull *or* tear down → **Zelt, Brücke** VI **a** *aux sein* (*Ast, Halterung, Griff*) to break (off); (*Bleistift, Fingernagel, Lippenstift*) to break; (*Eisscholle*) to break off **b** (= *aufhören*) (*Kontakt*) to break off; (*Student*) to break off one's studies; **mitten im Satz ~** to break off in the middle of a sentence; **wir müssen jetzt leider ~** we have to stop now **c** (*Comput*) to abort **d** (= *abtreiben*) to abort; **es ist zu spät, um abzubrechen** it's too late for a termination *or* an abortion

Ab|bre|cher(in) M(F) (= *Student*) dropout

Ab|bre|cher|quo|te F dropout rate

ab+brem|sen *sep* VT *Motor* to brake; (*fig*) to curb VI to brake; **auf 30 ~** to brake down to 30

ab+bren|nen *sep irreg* VT *Wiesen* to burn off *or* away the stubble in; *Böschung* to burn off *or* away the scrub on; *Gehöft, Dorf* to burn down; *Feuerwerk, Rakete* to let off; *Kerze etc* to burn; (= *wegbrennen*) *Lack* to burn off; (*Tech: abbeizen*) to pickle, to scour; **ein Feuerwerk ~** to have fireworks, to have a firework display; **abgebrannt** (*Gebäude*) burnt down VI *aux sein* to burn down; **unser Gehöft ist abgebrannt** our farm was burned down; **wir sind abgebrannt** our house/farm *etc* was burned down; **dreimal umgezogen ist einmal abgebrannt** (*prov*) by the time you've moved house three times, you've lost as much as if the place had been burned out → *auch* **abgebrannt**

Ab|bre|vi|a|tur [abrevia'tuːɐ] F -, -en (*Typ, Mus*) abbreviation

ab+brin|gen VT *sep irreg* **a** **jdn davon ~, etw zu tun** to stop sb (from) doing sth; (= *abraten auch*) to persuade sb not to do sth, to dissuade sb from doing sth; **jdn von etw ~** to make sb change his/her mind about sth; **sich von etw ~ lassen** to allow oneself to be put off sth (*Brit*), to be dissuaded from sth; **ich lasse mich von meiner Meinung nicht ~** you won't get me to change my mind, nothing will make me change my mind; **jdn vom Thema ~** to get sb off the subject; **jdn/einen Hund von der Spur ~** to throw *or* put sb/a dog off the scent; **jdn/etw vom Kurs ~** to throw *or* put sb/sth off course **b** (*esp S Ger inf*) *Deckel etc* to get off

ab+brö|ckeln VI *sep aux sein* to crumble away; (*fig*) to fall off (*auch St Ex*), to drop off; **die Aktienkurse sind am Abbröckeln** the share prices are falling (off); **die Familie/der Ruf der Firma ist am Abbröckeln** the family's/firm's reputation is gradually declining

Ab|bruch M **a** *no pl* (= *das Niederreißen*) demolition; (*von Gebäuden*) pulling down, demolition; **auf ~ verkaufen** to sell for demolition; **auf ~ stehen** to be scheduled *or* due for demolition, to be condemned; **warmer ~** (*inf*: = *Brandstiftung*) torch job (*inf*) **b** *no pl* (= *Beendigung*) (*von Schwangerschaft*) termination; (*von Beziehungen, Verhandlungen, Reise*) breaking off; (*von Raumflug etc*) abortion, aborting; (*von Veranstaltung*) stopping; **einem Land mit ~ der diplomatischen Beziehungen drohen** to threaten to break off diplomatic relations with a country; **es kam zum ~ des Kampfes** the fight had to be stopped **c** *no pl* (= *Schaden*) harm, damage; **einer Sache** (*dat*) **~ tun** to harm *or* damage sth, to do (some) harm *or* damage to sth; **das tut der Liebe keinen ~** it doesn't harm *or* hurt their/our relationship; **das tut unseren Interessen ~** that

is detrimental to our interests **d** (= *Schwangerschaftsabbruch*) termination

Ab|bruch-: **Ab|bruch|ar|bei|ten** PL demolition work; **Ab|bruch|bir|ne** F wrecking ball; **Ab|bruch|fir|ma** F demolition firm; **Ab|bruch|haus** NT condemned building; **Ab|bruch|lis|te** F → **Abrissliste**; **ab|bruch|reif** ADJ only fit for demolition; (= *zum Abbruch freigegeben*) condemned; **Ab|bruch|rei|fe** F **das Gebäude ist bis zur ~ geschädigt** the building is so badly damaged it will have to be demolished

ab+brü|hen VT *sep* to scald; *Mandeln* to blanch → *auch* **abgebrüht**

ab+brum|men *sep* VT (*inf*) *Zeit* to do (*inf*); **eine Strafe ~** to do time (*inf*) VI *aux sein* (*inf*) to roar off *or* away

ab+bu|chen VT *sep* (*im Einzelfall*) to debit (*von* to, against); (*durch Dauerauftrag*) to pay by standing order (*von* from); (*fig*: = *abschreiben*) to write off; **für das Abbuchen erhebt die Bank Gebühren** the bank makes a charge for each debit/for a standing order

Ab|bu|chung F (*einzeln*) debit; (*durch Dauerauftrag*) (payment by) standing order; (*durch Einzugsermächtigung*) (payment by) direct debit; **etw durch ~ erledigen** to settle sth by standing order/direct debit

Ab|bu|chungs-: **Ab|bu|chungs|auf|trag** M (*Fin*) (direct) debit order; (= *Dauerauftrag*) standing order; **Ab|bu|chungs|kar|te** F (*TV*) pay-per-view card; **Ab|bu|chungs|kon|to** NT (*Fin*) debiting *or* charge (*US*) account; **Ab|bu|chungs|ver|fah|ren** NT (*Fin*) direct debiting (service), automatic payment system (*US*)

ab+bü|geln VT *sep* (*inf*: = *heruntermachen*) to pooh-pooh (*inf*)

ab+bum|meln VT *sep* (*inf*) *Stunden* to take off; **Überstunden ~** to take time off for overtime worked

ab+bürs|ten VT *sep* **a** *Staub* to brush off (*von etw* sth); *Kleid, Mantel, Jacke* to brush (down); *Schuhe* to brush **b** (*inf*: = *heruntermachen*) **jdn ~** to give sb the brushoff, to brush sb aside

ab+bus|seln VT *sep* (*Aus inf*) = **abküssen**

ab+bü|ßen VT *sep Strafe* to serve

Ab|bü|ßung F -, -en serving; **nach ~ der Strafe** after serving *or* having served the sentence

Abc [abe'tseː, aːbeː'tseː] NT -, - (*lit, fig*) ABC; **Wörter/Namen nach dem ~ ordnen** to arrange words/names in alphabetical order *or* alphabetically

ABC- *in cpds* (*Mil*) atomic, biological and chemical, Abc

ab+che|cken ['aptʃɛkn] VT *sep* to check; (= *abhaken*) to check off (*US*), to tick off (*Brit*)

Abc-Schüt|ze M , **Abc-Schüt|zin** F (*hum*) school-beginner; **dies Bild zeigt mich als ~** this picture shows me when I was starting school

ABC-Waf|fen PL atomic, biological and chemical weapons *pl*

Ab|da|chung ['apdaxʊŋ] F -, -en **a** (*Geog*) declivity, downward slope **b** (*Build*) camber, cambering

ab+däm|men VT *sep See, Fluss* to dam (up)

Ab|däm|mung F (*von Fluss etc*) dam, damming (up); (*von tief liegendem Land*) damming off; (*fig*) curb, check

Ab|dampf M exhaust steam

ab+damp|fen *sep* VT **a** *aux sein* (*Speisen*) to dry off **b** (*Chem*: = *verdunsten*) to evaporate **c** (*Zug*) to steam off; (*fig inf*: = *losgehen, -fahren*) to hit the trail (*esp Brit inf*) *or* road (*inf*), to push off (*inf*) VT (*Chem*: = *verdunsten lassen*) to evaporate

ab+dämp|fen VT *sep* = **dämpfen a**

ab+dan|ken VI *sep* to resign; (*König etc*) to abdicate; **abgedankt** (*Soldat, Offizier, Dienstbote*) discharged

---

Ab|dan|kung F -, -en **a** (= *Thronverzicht*) abdication; (= *Rücktritt*) resignation; **jdn zur ~ zwingen** to force sb to abdicate/resign **b** (*old*: = *Dienstentlassung*) retirement **c** (*Sw*: = *Trauerfeier*) funeral service

Ab|deck|cre|me F (= *Stift*) concealer, cover--up *or* blemish stick

ab+de|cken VT *sep* **a** (= *decken*) *Bedarf, Kosten, Markt* to cover **b** (= *umfassen, einschließen*) *Thema, Spektrum, Umfang, Aspekt* to cover **c** (= *zudecken*) *Fläche, Grab, Loch, Möbel* to cover (over); *Boden* to cover **d** (*Ftbl*) to mark, to cover **e** (= *freilegen*) *Dach* to take off; *Haus* to take the roof off; *Tisch* to clear **f** (*old*: = *Fell abziehen von*) *Tierkadaver* to flay, to skin

Ab|de|cker ['apdɛkɐ] M **-s**, **-**, **Ab|de|cke|rin** [-ərɪn] F **-**, **-nen** knacker (*Brit inf*), slaughterman

Ab|de|cke|rei [apdɛkə'rai] F **-**, **-en** slaughterhouse, knacker's yard (*Brit inf*)

Ab|deck-: Ab|deck|fo|lie F dust cover; (*für Möbel, Boden etc*) dustsheet; **Ab|deck|hau|be** F (dust) cover; **Ab|deck|pla|ne** F tarpaulin; **Ab|deck|stift** M (*Kosmetik*) concealer, cover--up *or* blemish stick

Ab|de|ckung F **a** cover **b** *no pl* (= *Vorgang*) covering

ab+dich|ten VT *sep* (= *isolieren*) to insulate; (= *verschließen*) *Loch, Leck, Rohr* to seal (up); *Ritzen* to fill, to stop up; **gegen Luft/Wasser ~** to make airtight/watertight; **gegen Feuchtigkeit ~** to damp-proof; **gegen Zugluft ~** to (make) draught-proof (*Brit*) *or* draft-proof (*US*); **gegen Lärm/Geräusch/Schall ~** to soundproof

Ab|dich|tung F (= *Isolierung*) insulation; (= *Verschluss, Dichtung*) seal; (= *das Verschließen*) sealing; (*von Ritzen*) filling, stopping up; **~ gegen Zugluft** draught-proofing (*Brit*), draft-proofing (*US*); (= *gegen Feuchtigkeit*) damp-proofing; **~ gegen Wasser** waterproofing; **~ gegen Lärm/Geräusch/Schall** soundproofing

ab+die|nen VT *sep* (*dated*: = *abarbeiten*) to work off; (*Mil*: = *ableisten*) to serve

Ab|di|ka|ti|on [apdika'tsio:n] F **-**, **-en** (*old*) abdication

ab|ding|bar ADJ (*Jur*) alterable subject to mutual agreement

ab+din|gen ['apdɪŋən] *pret* **dingte ab**, *ptp* **abgedungen** [ˈapɡədʊŋən] VT *sep* (*rare*) **jdm etw ~** (*Zugeständnis*) to strike a deal with sb for sth; **diese Rechte lassen wir uns nicht ~** we shall not cede these rights

ab|di|zie|ren [apdi'tsi:rən] *ptp* **abdiziert** VI *insep* (*old*) to resign; (*König etc*) to abdicate

Ab|do|men [ap'do:mən] NT **-s**, **-** *or* **Abdomina** (*Med, Zool*) abdomen

ab+don|nern VI *sep aux sein* (*inf*) to roar off, to zoom off (*inf*)

ab+dor|ren VI *sep aux sein* (*Zweig*) to dry up, to wither

ab+drän|gen VT *sep* to push away (*von* from), to push out of the way (*von* of); *Menschenmenge* to force back; (*fig*) *Verfolger etc* to shake off; **ein Auto von der Straße ~** to force a car off the road; **jdn in eine bestimmte Richtung ~** to push sb in a certain direction; **einen Spieler vom Ball ~** to push *or* barge a player off the ball; **vom Wind abgedrängt werden** to be blown off course (by the wind); **jdn an den Rand der Gesellschaft ~** to marginalize sb to the fringes of society

ab+dre|hen *sep* VT **a** *Gas, Wasser, Hahn* to turn off **b** *Film* to shoot, to film; **abgedreht** (*Szene*) completed **c** *Hals* to wring; **er drehte dem Huhn den Kopf ab** he wrung the chicken's neck; **er drehte der Blume den Kopf ab** he twisted the head off the flower → *auch* **abgedreht** VI *aux sein or haben* (= *Richtung ändern*) to change course; (*zur Seite etc*) to veer off *or* a-way; **nach Osten ~** to turn east

Ab|drift F (*Naut, Aviat*) drift

ab+drif|ten VI *sep aux sein* (*Naut, Aviat, fig*) to drift off

ab+dros|seln VT *sep Motor* to throttle back *or* (*gänzlich auch*) down; (*fig*) *Produktion* to cut back, to cut down on

Ab|dros|se|lung F, **Ab|dross|lung** ▲ F throttling back *or* (*gänzlich auch*) down; (*fig*) cutback (**+***gen* in)

Ab|druck¹ M *pl* **-drücke** imprint, impression; (= *Stempelabdruck*) stamp; (*von Schlüssel*) impression, mould (*Brit*), mold (*US*); (= *Fingerabdruck, Fußabdruck*) print; (= *Gebissabdruck*) mould (*Brit*), mold (*US*), cast, impression; (= *Gesteinsabdruck*) imprint, impression, cast; **einen ~ abnehmen** *or* **machen** (*inf*) to take *or* make an impression

Ab|druck² M *pl* **-drucke** (= *das Nachdrucken*) reprinting; (= *das Kopieren*) copying; (= *Kopie*) copy; (= *Nachdruck*) reprint; **der ~ dieses Romans wurde verboten** it was forbidden to reprint this novel; **ich habe den ~ des Interviews im "Spiegel" gelesen** I read the text *or* the printed version of the interview in "Der Spiegel"; **dieser Roman erschien auch als ~ in ...** this novel was also printed in ...

ab+dru|cken VT *sep* to print; **wieder ~** to reprint

ab+drü|cken *sep* VT **a** *Gewehr* to fire **b** (*inf*) *jdn* to squeeze, to hug **c** (= *nachbilden*) to make an impression of **d** *Vene* to constrict; **jdm fast die Finger/Hand ~** to almost squeeze sb's fingers/hand off; **jdm die Luft ~** (*inf*) (*lit*) to squeeze all the breath out of sb; (*fig*) to force sb into bankruptcy, to squeeze the life(blood) out of sb VI to pull *or* squeeze the trigger VR **sich (durch etw) ~** to show through (sth)

ab+du|cken VI *sep* (*Boxen*) to duck

ab+dun|keln VT *sep Lampe* to dim; *Zimmer auch* to darken; *Farbe* to darken, to make darker

ab+du|schen VT *sep* to give a shower; *Körperteil* to wash under the shower; **sich ~** to have *or* take a shower

ab+eb|ben ['apˌlɛbn] VI *sep aux sein* to die *or* fade away; (*Zorn, Lärm auch*) to abate

a|bend △ ['a:bnt] ADV → **Abend**

A|bend ['a:bnt] M **-s**, **-e** [-də] **a** evening; **am ~** in the evening; (= *jeden Abend*) in the evening(s); **am ~ des 4. April** on the evening *or* night of April 4th; **heute/gestern/morgen/Mittwoch ~** this/yesterday/tomorrow/Wednesday evening, tonight/last night/tomorrow night/Wednesday night; **die Vorstellung wird zweimal pro ~ gegeben** there are two performances every night *or* evening; **jeden ~** every evening *or* night; **gegen ~** toward(s) (the) evening; **~ für** *or* **um** (*geh*) every evening *or* night, night after night; **am nächsten ~, den nächsten ~** the next evening; **eines ~s** one evening; **den ganzen ~ über** the whole evening; **es wird ~** it's getting late, evening is drawing in (*Brit*); **es wurde ~** evening came; **jdm guten** *or* **Guten ~ sagen** to say good evening to sb, to bid sb good evening (*form*); **guten ~** good evening; **'n ~** (*inf*) evening (*inf*); **der ~ kommt** (*geh*) *or* **naht** (*liter*) evening is drawing nigh (*liter*) *or* on (*Brit*), it's getting late; **des ~s** (*geh*) in the evening(s), of an evening; **du kannst mich am ~ besuchen!** (*euph inf*) you can take a running jump (*Brit inf*), you can take a hike (*US inf*); **zu ~ essen** to have supper *or* dinner; **je später der ~, desto schöner** *or* **netter die Gäste** (*prov*) the best guests always come late; **es ist noch nicht aller Tage ~** it's early days still *or* yet; **man soll den Tag nicht vor dem ~ loben** (*Prov*) don't count your chickens before they're hatched (*Prov*) **b** (= *Vorabend*) eve; **am ~ vor der Schlacht** on the eve of the battle **c** (*liter*: = *Ende*) close; **am ~ des Lebens** in the twilight *or* evening of one's life (*liter*), in one's twilight years (*liter*); **am ~ des Jahrhunderts** toward(s) the close *or* end of the century

-abend M *suf* **der Mittwochabend** Wednesday evening *or* night

A|bend- *in cpds* evening; **A|bend|an|dacht** F evening service; **A|bend|an|zug** M dinner jacket *or* suit, DJ (*Brit inf*), tuxedo (*US*); **im ~ erscheinen** to come in a dinner jacket/dinner jackets *etc*; **A|bend|aus|ga|be** F evening edition; **A|bend|blatt** NT evening (news)paper; **A|bend|brot** NT supper, tea (*Scot, N Engl*); **~ essen** to have (one's) supper *or* tea; **A|bend|däm|me|rung** F dusk, twilight

a|ben|de|lang ADJ *attr* night after night; **unsere ~en Diskussionen** our discussions night after night, our nightly discussions ADV night after night

A|bend-: A|bend|es|sen NT supper, evening meal, dinner; **mit dem ~ auf jdn warten** to wait with supper *or* dinner *or* one's evening meal for sb; **A|bend|frie|de(n)** M (*liter*) still *or* quiet of the evening; **a|bend|fül|lend** ADJ taking up the whole evening; *Film, Stück* full-length; **~ sein** to take up *or* fill the whole evening; **A|bend|gar|de|ro|be** F evening dress; **A|bend|ge|bet** NT evening prayers *pl*; (= *Abendandacht*) evensong, vespers; (*baby-talk*) bedtime prayers *pl*; **A|bend|ge|sell|schaft** F soirée; **A|bend|gym|na|si|um** NT night school (*where one can study for the Abitur*); **A|bend|him|mel** M evening sky, (sky at) sunset; **A|bend|kas|se** F (*Theat*) box office; **A|bend|kleid** NT evening dress *or* gown; **A|bend|kurs** M, **A|bend|kur|sus** M evening course, evening classes *pl* (*für* in); **A|bend|land** NT , *no pl* (*geh*) West, western world, Occident (*liter*); **das christliche ~** the Christian West; **a|bend|län|disch** ['a:bntlɛndɪʃ] (*geh*) ADJ western, occidental (*liter*) ADV in a western way *or* fashion

a|bend|lich ['a:bntlɪç] ADJ *no pred* evening *attr*; **die ~e Stille** the quiet *or* still of the evening; **die ~e Kühle** the cool of the evening ADV **~ stattfindende Veranstaltungen** evening events, events taking place in the evening; **es war schon um drei Uhr ~ kühl** at three it was already as cool as (in the) evening; **~ gekleidet** dressed in evening clothes

A|bend|mahl NT **a** (*Eccl*) Communion, Lord's Supper; **das ~ nehmen** *or* **empfangen** to take *or* receive Communion, to communicate (*form*); **das ~ spenden** *or* **reichen** *or* **erteilen** to administer (Holy) Communion, to communicate (*form*); **zum ~ gehen** to go to (Holy) Communion **b** **das (Letzte)** the Last Supper

A|bend|mahls-: A|bend|mahls|got|tes|dienst M (Holy) Communion, Communion service; **A|bend|mahls|kelch** M Communion cup *or* chalice; **A|bend|mahls|wein** M Communion wine

A|bend-: A|bend|mahl|zeit F evening meal; **A|bend|nach|rich|ten** PL evening news *sing*; **A|bend|pro|gramm** NT (*Rad, TV*) evening('s) programmes *pl* (*Brit*) *or* programs *pl* (*US*); **damit ist unser heutiges ~ beendet** and that ends our programmes (*Brit*) *or* programs (*US*) for this evening; **A|bend|rot** NT , **A|bend|rö|te** F (*liter*) sunset; **die Felder lagen im ~** the fields lay bathed in the glow of the sunset *or* in the light of the setting sun

a|bends ['a:bnts] ADV in the evening, (= *jeden Abend*) in the evening(s); **spät ~** late in the evening; **~ um neun** at nine in the evening

A|bend-: A|bend|schu|le F night school; **A|bend|schü|ler(in)** M(F) night-school student; **A|bend|son|ne** F evening *or* late afternoon sun; **A|bend|spa|zier|gang** M evening walk *or* stroll; **A|bend|stern** M evening star; **A|bend|stil|le** F still *or* quiet of the evening; **A|bend|stim|mung** F evening mood *or* atmosphere, twilight mood; **A|bend|stun|de** F evening (hour); **zu dieser späten ~** at this late hour of the evening; **die frühen ~n** the early hours of the evening; **die schönen ~n** the beautiful evening hours; **sich bis in die ~n hinzie-**

hen to go on (late) into the evening; **A|bend|toi|let|te** F (= *Kleidung*) evening dress; **A|bend|ver|an|stal|tung** F evening event *or* do (*inf*); **A|bend|ver|kauf** M late-night shopping; **A|bend|vor|stel|lung** F evening performance; (*Film auch*) evening showing; **A|bend|wind** M evening breeze; **A|bend|zeit** F zur ~ in the evening; **A|bend|zei|tung** F evening paper

A|ben|teu|er ['aːbntɔyɐ] NT **-s**, **-** adventure; (= *Liebesabenteuer auch*) affair; **ein militärisches/politisches/verbrecherisches** ~ a military/political/criminal venture; **auf** ~ **ausgehen** to go out in search of adventure; **auf** ~ **aus sein** to be looking for adventure; **die** ~ **des Geistes** (*liter*) intellectual adventure

A|ben|teu|er- *in cpds* adventure; **A|ben|teu|er|buch** NT adventure story *or* book *or* novel; **A|ben|teu|er|durst** M thirst *or* longing for adventure; **A|ben|teu|er|fe|ri|en** PL adventure holiday (*esp Brit*) *or* vacation (*US*); **A|ben|teu|er|film** M adventure film, action movie (*US*); **A|ben|teu|er|geist** M adventurous spirit, spirit of adventure; **A|ben|teu|er|ge|schich|te** F adventure story

A|ben|teu|e|rin ['aːbntɔyərɪn] F **-, -nen** adventuress (*auch pej*)

a|ben|teu|er|lich ['aːbntɔyɐlɪç] ADJ **a** *Reise, Unternehmung, Politik, Mensch* adventurous; (= *erlebnishungrig*) adventuresome **b** (= *fantastisch*) bizarre; *Gestalten, Verkleidung* eccentric, bizarre; *Erzählung* fantastic; (*inf*) *Preis* outrageous; *Argument* ludicrous ADV *klingen, sich anhören* bizarre, fantastic; *gekleidet* bizarrely, fantastically, eccentrically

A|ben|teu|er|lich|keit F **-, -en** (*von Reise, Unternehmung, Politik, Mensch*) adventurousness; (= *Unwahrscheinlichkeit*) improbability, unlikeliness

A|ben|teu|er-: **A|ben|teu|er|lust** F thirst for adventure; **von der** ~ **gepackt werden** to be seized with a thirst for adventure; **a|ben|teu|er|lus|tig** ADJ adventurous, venturesome; **A|ben|teu|er|ro|man** M adventure story; **A|ben|teu|er|spiel|platz** M adventure playground; **A|ben|teu|er|ur|laub** M adventure holiday (*esp Brit*) *or* vacation (*US*)

A|ben|teu|rer ['aːbntɔyrɐ] M **-s**, **-** adventurer (*auch pej*)

A|ben|teu|rer- *in cpds* = **Abenteuer-**

A|ben|teu|re|rin ['aːbntɔyrərɪn] F **-, -nen** adventuress

A|ben|teu|rer-: **A|ben|teu|rer|le|ben** NT adventurer's life, life of an adventurer; **ein** ~ **füh|ren** to lead an adventurous life; **A|ben|teu|rer|na|tur** F adventurous person, adventurer

a|ber ['aːbɐ] CONJ **a** but; ~ **dennoch** *or* **trotzdem** but still; **es regnete,** ~ **dennoch haben wir uns köstlich amüsiert** it was raining, but we still had a great time *or* but we had a great time though *or* but we had a great time all the same; **schönes Wetter heute, was? – ja,** ~ **etwas kalt** nice weather, eh? – yes, a bit cold though *or* yes but it's a bit cold; **...,** ~ **ich wünschte, sie hätte es mir gesagt** ..., (al)though *or* but I wished she had told me; **komm doch mit!** – ~ – **ich habe keine Zeit** *or* **ich habe** ~ **keine Zeit!** come with us! – but I haven't got the time!; **da er** ~ **nicht wusste ...** but since he didn't know ..., since, however, he didn't know ..., however, since he didn't know ...; **a|ber** ~ or else **b** (*zur Verstärkung*) ~ **ja!** oh, yes!; (= *sicher*) but of course; ~ **selbstverständlich** *or* **gewiss (doch)!** but of course; ~ **nein!** oh, no!; (= *selbstverständlich nicht*) of course not!; ~ **Renate!** but Renate!; ~**,** ~**!** now, now!, tut, tut!, come, come!; ~ **ich kann nichts dafür!** but I can't help it!; ~ **das wollte ich doch gar nicht!** but I didn't want that!; **das ist** ~ **schrecklich!** but that's awful!; **das mach ich** ~ **nicht!** I will NOT do that!; **dann ist er** ~ **wütend geworden** then he really got mad, (God), did he get mad!; **das ist** ~ **heiß/schön!** that's really hot/nice; **du hast** ~ **ei|nen schönen Ball** you have *or* you've got (*Brit*)

a nice ball, haven't you?; **bist du** ~ **braun!** aren't you brown!; **das geht** ~ **zu weit!** that's just *or* really going too far!; **schreib das noch mal ab,** ~ **sauber!** write it out again, and do it neatly!

ADV (*liter*) ~ **und ~mals** again and again, time and again → *auch* **abertausend**

A|ber ['aːbɐ] NT **-s**, **-** *or* (*inf*) **-s** but; **kein ~!** no buts (about it); **die Sache hat ein** ~ there's just one problem *or* snag

A|ber|glau|be(n) M superstition; (*fig auch*) myth; **zum Aberglauben neigen** to be superstitious

a|ber|gläu|bisch ['aːbɐɡlɔybɪʃ] ADJ superstitious ADV **er hängt** ~ **an ...** he has a superstitious attachment to ...; **er fürchtet sich** ~ **vor ...** he has a superstitious fear of ...

ab+er|ken|nen ptp **aberkannt** VT *sep or (rare) insep irreg* **jdm etw** ~ to deprive *or* strip sb of sth; **jdm den Sieg** ~ (*Sport*) to disallow sb's victory

Ab|er|ken|nung F deprivation, stripping; (*von Sieg*) disallowing

a|ber-: **a|ber|ma|lig** ['aːbɐmaːlɪç] ADJ *attr* (*geh*) repeated; **a|ber|mals** ['aːbɐmaːls] ADV (*geh*) once again *or* more

ab+ern|ten VTI *sep* to harvest

Ab|er|ra|ti|on [apˈɛraˈtsioːn] F **-, -en** (*Astron*) aberration

a|ber|tau|send ▲ ADJ thousands upon thousands of; **tausend und ~, Tausend und Abertausend** thousands and *or* upon thousands; **~e** *pl*, **Abertausende** *pl* thousands upon thousands *pl*

A|ber|witz M , *no pl* (*liter*) utter *or* sheer foolishness

a|ber|wit|zig (*liter*) ADJ mad, crazy, lunatic *attr*; *Summe* crazy ADV terribly, awfully

ab+es|sen *sep irreg* VT **a** (= *herunteressen*) to eat; **sie aß nur die Erdbeeren von der Torte ab** she just ate the strawberries off the cake **b** (= *leer essen*) to eat *or* finish up; *Teller* to finish VI to eat up

A|bes|si|ni|en [abɛˈsiːniən] NT **-s** Abyssinia

A|bes|si|ni|er [abɛˈsiːniɐ] M **-s, -**, **A|bes|si|ni|e|rin** [-iərɪn] F **-, -nen** Abyssinian

a|bes|si|nisch [abɛˈsiːnɪʃ] ADJ Abyssinian

Abf. *abbr von* **Abfahrt** departure, dep.

ab+fa|ckeln VT **a** (= *verbrennen*) *Gas* to burn off; *Dschungel, Wald* to burn **b** (= *in Brand stecken*) *Gebäude, Auto* to torch

ab|fahr|be|reit ADJ ready to leave

ab+fah|ren *sep irreg aux sein* VI **a** (*Bus, Zug, Auto, Reisende*) to leave, to depart (*form*); (*Ski: = zu Tal fahren*) to ski down; **~!** (*Rail*) order given to a train driver to pull out **der Zug fährt um 8 Uhr in** *or* **von Bremen ab** the train leaves Bremen *or* departs from Bremen at 8 o'clock; **der Zug fährt in Kürze ab** the train will be leaving *or* will depart shortly; **„Ihr Zug fährt jetzt ab"** "your train is departing now"; **der Zug ist abgefahren** (*lit*) the train has left *or* gone; (*fig*) we've/you've *etc* missed the boat; **wir müssen schon um 7 Uhr** ~ we must set off *or* start (out) *or* leave at 7 o'clock

b (*inf: = abgewiesen werden*) **jdn** ~ **lassen** to tell sb to push off (*Brit inf*) *or* to get lost (*inf*); **er ist bei ihr abgefahren** she told him to push off (*Brit inf*) *or* to get lost (*inf*)

c (*inf*) **auf jdn/etw** ~ to go for sb/sth (*inf*), to be into sb/sth (*inf*); **sie fährt voll auf ihn ab** she's into him (*Brit inf*) *or* she's fallen for him in a big way (*inf*)

VT **a** (= *abholen*) *Waren* to take away, to remove, to cart off (*inf*); *Müll* to collect

b (= *abtrennen*) *Körperteil* to cut off, to sever; *Stück von Mauer etc* to knock off; **der Trecker hat ihm ein Bein abgefahren** the tractor cut off *or* severed his leg

c *aux sein or haben Strecke* (= *bereisen*) to cover, to do (*inf*); (= *überprüfen, ausprobieren*) to go over; **er hat ganz Belgien abgefahren** he trav-

elled *or* went all over Belgium; **wir mussten die ganze Strecke noch einmal ~, um ... zu suchen** we had to go over the whole stretch again to look for ...

d (= *abnutzen*) *Schienen* to wear out; *Reifen* to wear down *or* out; (= *benutzen*) *Fahrkarte* to use; (= *ausnutzen*) *Zeitkarte, Fahrkarte* to get one's money's worth; **abgefahrene Reifen/Schienen** worn tyres (*Brit*) *or* tires (*US*)/rails; **das Geld fährt du doch allemal ab** you'll certainly get your money's worth

VR (*Reifen etc*) to wear out *or* down

Ab|fahrt F **a** (*von Zug, Bus etc*) departure; **bis zur** ~ **sind es noch fünf Minuten** there's still five minutes before the train/bus *etc* leaves *or* goes; **Vorsicht bei der** ~ **des Zuges!** stand clear, the train is about to leave! **b** (*Ski*) (= *Talfahrt*) descent; (= *Abfahrtsstrecke*) (ski) run **c** (*inf: = Autobahnabfahrt*) exit; **die** ~ **Gießen** the Gießen exit, the exit for Gießen

ab|fahrt|be|reit ADJ ready to leave

Ab|fahrts-: **Ab|fahrts|lauf** M (*Ski*) downhill; **Ab|fahrts|läu|fer(in)** M(F) (*Ski*) downhill racer *or* skier, downhiller; **Ab|fahrts|ren|nen** NT (*Ski*) downhill (racing); (*einzelnes Rennen*) downhill (race); **Ab|fahrts|zeit** F departure time

Ab|fall M **a** (= *Müll*) refuse; (= *Hausabfall*) rubbish (*Brit*), garbage (*US*), trash (*US*); (= *Straßenabfall*) litter; **in den** ~ **kommen** to be thrown away *or* out, to go into the dustbin (*Brit*) *or* trash can (*US*); **Fleisch-/Stoffabfälle** scraps of meat/material

b (= *Rückstand*) waste *no pl*

c *no pl* (= *Lossagung*) break (*von* with); (*von Partei*) breaking away (*von* from); **seit ihrem** ~ **von der Kirche ...** since they broke with *or* since their break with the Church ...; **seit ihrem** ~ **von der Partei ...** since they broke away from the party ...; **seit dem** ~ **der Niederlande von Spanien** since the Netherlands broke with Spain

d *no pl* (= *Rückgang*) drop (+*gen* in), fall (+*gen* in), falling off; (= *Verschlechterung*) deterioration

Ab|fall-: **Ab|fall|be|sei|ti|gung** F refuse *or* garbage (*US*) *or* trash (*US*) disposal; **Ab|fall|ei|mer** M rubbish bin (*Brit*), waste bin, garbage can (*US*), trash can (*US*); (*auf öffentlichen Plätzen*) litter bin (*Brit*), trash can (*US*)

ab+fal|len VI *sep irreg aux sein* **a** (= *herunterfallen*) to fall *or* drop off; (*Blätter, Blüten etc*) to fall; **von etw** ~ to fall *or* drop off (from) sth

b (= *sich senken*) *Gelände* to fall *or* drop away; (= *sich vermindern*) *Druck, Temperatur* to fall, to drop; **der Weg talwärts verläuft sacht ~d** the path down to the valley slopes gently

c (= *übrig bleiben*) to be left (over); **das, was in der Küche abfällt** the kitchen leftovers; **der Stoff, der beim Schneidern abfällt** the leftover scraps of material

d (= *schlechter werden*) to fall *or* drop off, to go downhill; (*Sport: = zurückbleiben*) to drop back; **gegen etw** ~ to compare badly with sth

e (*fig: = sich lösen*) to melt away; **alle Unsicherheit/Furcht fiel von ihm ab** all his uncertainty/fear left him, all his uncertainty/fear melted away (from him) *or* dissolved

f (*von einer Partei*) to break (*von* with), to drop out (*von* of); (*Fraktion*) to break away (*von* from); **vom Glauben** ~ to break with *or* leave the faith

g (*inf: = herausspringen*) **wie viel fällt bei dem Geschäft für mich ab?** how much do I get out of the deal?; **es fällt immer ziemlich viel Trinkgeld ab** you/they *etc* always get quite a lot of tips (out of it)

Ab|fall-: **Ab|fall|er|zeug|nis** NT waste product; **Ab|fall|gru|be** F rubbish (*Brit*) *or* garbage (*US*) pit; **Ab|fall|hau|fen** M rubbish *or* refuse dump *or* tip (*Brit*), garbage dump (*US*)

ab|fäl|lig ADJ *Bemerkung, Kritik* disparaging, derisive; *Lächeln* derisive; *Urteil* adverse ADV **über jdn** ~ **reden** *or* **sprechen** to be disparaging of *or* about sb, to speak disparagingly of or about sb; **darüber wurde ~ geurteilt** a very dim view was taken of this; **über jdn/etw ~ urteilen** to be disparaging about sb/sth; **etw ~ beurteilen** to be disparaging about sth

Ạb|fäl|lig|keit F derision

Ạb|fall-: Ạb|fall|pro|dukt NT waste product; (von Forschung) by-product, spin-off; **Ạb|fall-schacht** M waste or garbage (US) disposal chute; **Ạb|fall|tou|ris|mus** M international trade in (hazardous) waste; **Ạb|fall|ver|wer-tung** F waste utilization

ab+fäl|schen VTI sep (Sport) to deflect

ab+fan|gen VT sep irreg **a** Flugzeug, Funkspruch, Brief, Ball to intercept; Menschen to catch (inf); Schlag to block **b** (= abstützen) Gebäude to prop up, to support **c** (= bremsen) Fahrzeug to bring under control; Aufprall to absorb; Trend to check

Ạb|fang|jä|ger M (Mil) interceptor

ab+fär|ben VI sep **a** (Wäsche) to run; **pass auf, die Wand färbt ab!** be careful, the paint rubs off the wall; **das rote Handtuch hat auf die wei-ßen Tischdecken abgefärbt** the colour (Brit) or color (US) has come out of the red towel onto the white tablecloths **b** (fig) **auf jdn ~** to rub off on sb

ab+fas|sen VT sep **a** (= verfassen) to write; Erst-entwurf to draft **b** (inf: = abtasten) to touch up (inf)

Ạb|fas|sung F writing; (von Erstentwurf) drafting

ab+fau|len VI sep aux sein to rot away or off

ab+fe|dern sep **VT** Sprung, Stoß to cushion; (fig) Krise, Verluste to cushion the impact of **VI** to absorb the shock; (Sport) (beim Abspringen) to push off; (beim Aufkommen) to bend at the knees; **er ist** or **hat schlecht abgefedert** he landed stiffly

ab+fe|gen VT sep Schmutz to sweep away or off; Balkon, Hof to sweep; **den Schnee vom Dach ~** to sweep the snow off the roof

ab+fei|ern VT sep (inf) **Überstunden ~** to take time off in lieu (of overtime) (Brit), to use up overtime without pay(ment) (US)

ab+fei|len VT sep to file off or (glättend) down

ab+fer|keln VI sep to have a litter

ab+fer|ti|gen sep VT **a** (= versandfertig machen) Pakete, Waren to prepare for dispatch, to make ready or get ready for dispatch, to process (form); Gepäck to check (in); (= be- und entla-den) Flugzeug to service, to make ready for takeoff; Schiff to make ready to sail; **die Schau-erleute fertigen keine Schiffe aus Chile mehr ab** the dockers won't handle any more ships from Chile

b (= bedienen) Kunden, Antragsteller, Patienten to attend to, to deal with; (inf: Sport) Gegner to deal with; **jdn kurz** or **schroff ~** (inf) to snub sb; **ich lasse mich doch nicht mit 10 Euro ~** I'm not going to be fobbed off (esp Brit) with 10 euros **c** (= kontrollieren) Waren, Reisende to clear; **beim Zoll/an der Grenze abgefertigt werden** to be cleared by customs/at the border; **die Zöllner fertigten (die Reisenden) sehr zügig ab** the cus-toms officers dealt with the travellers (Brit) or travelers (US) very quickly; **die Zollbeamten hatten den Zug fast abgefertigt, als ...** the cus-toms officials had almost finished checking the train when ...

Ạb|fer|ti|gung F **a** (zum Versand) (von Paketen, Waren) getting ready for dispatch, processing (form); (von Gepäck) checking; (von Flugzeug) servicing, getting ready for takeoff; (von Schiff) making ready to sail

b (= Bedienung) (von Kunden) service; (von An-tragstellern) dealing with; (fig: = Abweisung) re-buff, snub; **die geschickte ~ des Gegners** (Sport) the skilful (Brit) or skillful (US) way of dealing with one's opponent

c (= kontrollieren) Waren, Reisenden clearance; **die ~ an der Grenze** customs clearance; **zollamtliche ~** customs clearance

d (= Abfertigungsstelle) (für Waren) dispatch of-fice; (im Flughafen) check-in

Ạb|fer|ti|gungs-: Ạb|fer|ti|gungs|hal|le F (Aviat) terminal building; **Ạb|fer|ti|gungs-schal|ter** M dispatch counter; (von Zollamt) customs clearance; (im Flughafen) check-in desk

ab+feu|ern VT sep to fire; (Ftbl inf) to let fire with

ab+fin|den sep irreg **VT** to pay off; Gläubiger auch to settle with; (= entschädigen) to compen-sate; **er wurde von der Versicherung mit 20.000 EUR abgefunden** he was paid 20,000 EUR (in) compensation by the insurance company; **ei-nen Fürst/König mit einer Apanage ~** to endow a prince/king with an appanage; **jdn mit leeren Versprechungen ~** to fob sb off (esp Brit) with empty promises

VR **sich mit jdm/etw ~** to come to terms with sb/sth; **sich mit jdm/etw nicht ~ können** to be unable to accept sb/sth, to be unable to come to terms with sb/sth; **er konnte sich nie damit ~, dass ...** he could never accept the fact that ...; **sich mit jdm/etw schwer ~** to find it hard to accept sb/sth; **mit allem kann ich mich ~, aber nicht ...** I can put up with most things, but not ...

Ạb|fin|dung ['apfɪndʊŋ] F -, -en **a** (von Gläubi-gern) paying off; (= Entschädigung) compensa-tion **b** (= Summe) payment, (sum in) settle-ment; (= Entschädigung) compensation no pl, indemnity; (bei Entlassung) severance pay; (we-gen Rationalisierung) redundancy payment (Brit), buyout (US)

Ạb|fin|dungs|sum|me F payment, (sum in) settlement; (= Entschädigung) compensation no pl, indemnity; **eine/keine ~ für einen Unfall be-kommen** to receive an indemnity or a sum in compensation/no indemnity or no compensa-tion for an accident

ab+fi|schen VT sep to fish dry

ab+fla|chen ['apflaxn] sep **VR** (Land) to level (off), to flatten (out) **VR** (Land) to flatten out, to grow or get flatter; (fig: = sinken) to drop or fall **VI** aux sein (fig: = sinken) to drop or fall (off), to decline

Ạb|fla|chung F -, -en flattening out, (fig) drop-ping off, falling off

ab+flau|en ['apflauən] VI sep aux sein **a** (Wind) to drop, to die away or down, to abate; **nach (dem) Abflauen des Windes** when the wind had dropped or died down or abated **b** (fig) (Empörung, Erregung) to fade, to die away; (Inte-resse) to flag, to wane, to fade; (Börsenkurse) to fall, to drop; (Geschäft) to fall or drop off

ab+flie|gen sep irreg **VI** aux sein (Aviat) to take off (nach for); (Zugvögel) to migrate, to fly off or away; (inf: = sich lösen) to fly off; **sie sind ges-tern nach München/von Hamburg abgeflogen** they flew to Munich/from Hamburg yesterday **VT** Gelände to fly over; Verwundete to fly out (aus of)

ab+flie|ßen VI sep irreg aux sein (= wegfließen) to drain or run or flow away; (durch ein Leck) to leak away; (Verkehr) to flow away; **ins Ausland ~** (Geld) to flow out of the country; **der Aus-guss/die Wanne fließt nicht ab** the water isn't running or draining out of the sink/bath (at all)

Ạb|flug M takeoff; (von Zugvögeln) migration; (inf: = Abflugstelle) departure point; **~ Glasgow 8.00 Uhr** departure Glasgow 8.00 a.m.

Ạb|flug-: ạb|flug|be|reit ADJ ready for take-off; **Ạb|flug|ha|fen** M departure airport; **Ạb|flug|hal|le** F departure lounge; **Ạb|flug-schal|ter** M check-in desk

Ạb|fluss ▲ M **a** (= Abfließen) draining away; (durch ein Leck) leaking away; (fig: von Geld) draining away; **den ~ des Wassers verhindern** to prevent the water (from) draining or run-ning or flowing away; **dem ~ von Kapital ins Ausland Schranken setzen** to impose limits on the (out)flow of capital out of the country **b**

(= Abflussstelle) drain; (von Teich etc) outlet **c** (= Abflussrohr) drainpipe; (von sanitären Anlagen) waste pipe

Ạb|fluss-: Ạb|fluss|gra|ben ▲ M drainage ditch; **Ạb|fluss|hahn** ▲ M tap, drain cock; **Ạb|fluss|rei|ni|ger** ▲ M drain cleaner; **Ạb-fluss|rin|ne** ▲ F gutter; **Ạb|fluss|rohr** ▲ NT outlet; (im Gebäude) waste pipe; (außen am Ge-bäude) drainpipe; (unterirdisch) drain, sewer

ab+foh|len VI sep (Zool) to foal

Ạb|fol|ge F (geh) sequence, succession

ab+for|dern VT sep **jdm etw ~** to demand sth from sb; **jdm den Ausweis ~** to ask to see sb's papers

ab+fo|to|gra|fie|ren ptp **ạbfotografiert** VT sep to photograph

Ạb|fra|ge F (Comput) query; **eine ~ eingeben** to key in a query

ab+fra|gen VT sep **a** (Comput) Information to call up; Datenbank to query, to interrogate **b** (esp Sch) jdn or jdm etw ~ to question sb on sth; (Lehrer) to test sb orally on sth; **eine Lekti-on ~** to give an oral test on a lesson

ab+fres|sen VT sep irreg Blätter, Gras to eat; Me-tall, Schicht to eat away, to corrode; **das Aas bis auf die Knochen ~** to strip the carcass to the bones; **die Giraffe frisst die Blätter von den Bäumen ab** the giraffe strips the leaves off the trees

ab+fret|ten ['apfrɛtn] VR sep (Aus, inf) to strug-gle along

ab+frie|ren sep irreg **VI** aux sein to get frostbit-ten **VT** **sich** (dat) **etw ~** to get frostbite in sth; **ihm sind die Zehen abgefroren** he got frostbite in his toes; **abgefroren sein** (Körperteil) to be frostbitten; **sich** (dat) **einen ~** (sl) to freeze to death (inf)

ab+frot|tie|ren ptp **ạbfrottiert** VT sep to towel down or dry

Ạb|fuhr ['apfuːʁ] F -, -en **a** no pl (= Abtransport) removal **b** (inf: = Zurückweisung) snub, rebuff; **jdm eine ~ erteilen** to snub or rebuff sb, to give sb a snub or rebuff; (Sport) to thrash sb (inf), to give sb a thrashing (inf); **sich** (dat) **eine ~ holen** to meet with a snub or a rebuff, to be snubbed; **sich** (dat) (gegen jdn) **eine ~ holen** (Sport) to be given a thrashing (by sb) or to be thrashed (by sb) (inf)

ab+füh|ren sep **VT** **a** (= wegführen) to lead or take away; Gefangenen to take away; **~!** away with him/her etc, take him/her etc away!; **das führt uns vom Thema ab** that will take us away or divert us from our subject **b** (= abgeben) Be-trag to pay (an +acc to) **c** (= wegführen) **der Weg führt hier (von der Straße) ab** the path leaves the road here; **das würde vom Thema ~** that would take us off the subject **VI** **a** (= den Darm anregen) to have a laxative effect **c** (= Stuhlgang haben) to move or evacuate one's bowels, to have a bowel movement

ab+füh|rend **ADJ** **a** Mittel laxative no adv, ape-rient no adv (form) **b** Bergpfade descending; Blutgefäße leading away from the heart **ADV** **~ wirken** to have a laxative effect

Ạb|führ-: Ạb|führ|mit|tel NT laxative, aperi-ent (form); **Ạb|führ|tee** M (herbal) laxative tea

Ạb|füll-: Ạb|füll|an|la|ge F bottling plant; **Ạb|füll|be|trieb** M bottling factory; **Ạb|füll-da|tum** NT bottling date

ab+fül|len VT sep **a** (= abziehen) Wein etc to draw off (in +acc into); (in Flaschen) to bottle; Flasche to fill; **Wein in Flaschen ~** to bottle wine **b** jdn ~ (inf) to get sb sloshed (inf)

Ạb|fül|lung F filling, bottling; **aus eigener ~** (Wein etc) bottled by the grower, bottled on site; (auf Etikett) estate-bottled

ab+füt|tern¹ VT sep Vieh to feed; (hum) Men-schen to feed

ab+füt|tern² VT sep (Sew) to line

Ab|füt|te|rung F feeding no pl; (hum: = Mahlzeit) meal (inf)

Ab|ga|be F **a** no pl (= Abliefern) handing or giving in; (von Gepäck) depositing; (= Übergabe: von Brief etc) delivery, handing over; **zur ~ von etw aufgefordert werden** to be told to hand sth in **b** no pl (= Verkauf) sale; **~ von Prospekten kostenlos** leaflets given away free **c** no pl (von Wärme etc) giving off, emission **d** no pl (von Schuss, Salve) firing; **nach ~ von vier Schüssen** after firing four shots **e** (= Steuer) tax; (= soziale Abgabe) contribution **f** no pl (von Erklärung, Urteil, Meinungsäußerung etc) giving; (von Gutachten) submission, submitting; (von Stimme) casting **g** (von Abspiel) pass; **nach ~ von zwei Punkten ...** after conceding two points ...

Ab|ga|be(n)-: ab|ga|be(n)|frei ADJ (= steuerfrei, beitragsfrei) Person, Unternehmen, Einkommen not liable for tax/for social security contributions (Brit), exempt from tax/welfare contributions (US); **Ab|ga|be(n)|ord|nung** F (Jur) tax law; **Ab|ga|be(n)|pflicht** F (von Person, Unternehmen, Einkommen) liability for tax/for social security contributions (Brit) or welfare contributions (US); **ab|ga|be(n)|pflich|tig** [-pflɪçtɪç] ADJ Person, Unternehmen, Einkommen liable for tax/for social security contributions (Brit) or welfare contributions (US)

Ab|ga|be|ter|min M closing date; (für Dissertation etc) submission date

Ab|gang M pl **-gänge a** no pl (= Absendung) dispatch; **vor ~ der Post** before the post (Brit) or mail goes **b** no pl (= Abfahrt) departure **c** no pl (= Ausscheiden) (aus einem Amt) leaving, departure; (= Schulabgang) leaving; **seit seinem ~ von der Schule** since he left school; **einen ~ machen** (sl: = verschwinden) to split (sl) **d** no pl (Theat, fig) exit; **sich** (dat) **einen guten/glänzenden ~ verschaffen** to make a grand exit **e** (Sport) dismount; **einen guten/schwierigen ~ turnen** to do a good/difficult dismount from the apparatus **f** (Med: = Ausscheidung) passing; (von Eiter) discharging; (= Fehlgeburt) miscarriage, abortion (form); (= Fötus) aborted foetus (Brit) or fetus (esp US) **g** (= Person) (Sch) leaver (Brit), high school graduate (US); (Med, Mil) death **h** (sl: = Ejakulation) ejaculation **i** (Comm) waste; (Aus: = Fehlbetrag) missing amount

Ab|gän|ger ['apgɛŋɐ] M **-s, -, Ab|gän|ge|rin** [-ərɪn] F **-, -nen** (Sch) (school) leaver (Brit), graduate (US)

ab|gän|gig ADJ (Aus Admin) missing (aus from); **ein Abgängiger** a missing person

Ab|gän|gig|keits|an|zei|ge F (Aus Admin) notification to the authorities that a person is missing **~ erstatten** to report a person missing

Ab|gangs-: Ab|gangs|al|ter NT (Sch) school-leaving age; **Ab|gangs|prü|fung** F leaving examination (Brit), final examination (US); **Ab|gangs|zeug|nis** NT leaving certificate (Brit), high school diploma (US)

Ab|gas NT exhaust no pl, exhaust fumes pl, waste gas (esp Tech); **Luftverschmutzung durch ~e** exhaust gas pollution

Ab|gas-: ab|gas|arm ADJ Fahrzeug low-pollution; **das Auto ist ~** the car has a low level of exhaust emissions; **ab|gas|frei** ADJ Motor, Fahrzeug exhaust-free; **~e Produktionsverfahren** production methods which produce no waste gases **ADV ~ verbrennen** to burn without producing exhaust fumes; **Ab|gas|norm** F exhaust emission standard; **Ab|gas|rei|ni|gung** F (Aut) purification of exhaust gases; **Ab|gas|rück|füh|rung** F (Aut) exhaust gas recirculation, EGR; **Ab|gas|(son|der)|un|ter|su|chung** F (Aut) emissions test; **Ab|gas|wol|ke** F cloud of exhaust

ab+gau|nern VT sep (inf) **jdm etw ~** to con or trick sb out of sth (inf)

ABGB [a:be:ge:ˈbe:] NT **-** (Aus) abbr von **Allgemeines Bürgerliches Gesetzbuch**

ab|ge|ar|bei|tet ADJ (= verbraucht) workworn; (= erschöpft) worn out, exhausted; (Comput) Programm that has/had been run → auch **abarbeiten**

ab+ge|ben sep irreg **VT a** (= abliefern) to hand or give in; (= hinterlassen) to leave; Gepäck, Koffer to leave, to deposit; (= übergeben) to hand over, to deliver **b** (= weggeben) to give away; (= verkaufen) to sell; (an einen anderen Inhaber) to hand over; **Matratze preisgünstig abzugeben** mattress for sale at (a) bargain price **c** (= verschenken) to give away; **jdm etw ~** to give sth to sb; **jdm etwas von seinem Kuchen ~** to give sb some of one's cake **d** (= überlassen) Auftrag to hand or pass on (an +acc to); (= abtreten) Posten to relinquish, to hand over (an +acc to) **e** (Sport) Punkte, Rang to concede; (= abspielen) to pass **f** (= ausströmen) Wärme, Sauerstoff to give off, to emit **g** (= abfeuern) Schuss, Salve to fire **h** (= äußern) Erklärung to give; Gutachten to submit; Meinung to express, to give; Stimme to cast **i** (= darstellen) Rahmen, Hintergrund to give, to provide; (= liefern) Stoff, Material etc to give, to provide, to furnish; **den Vermittler ~** (inf) to act as mediator **j** (= verkörpern) to make; **er würde einen guten Schauspieler ~** he would make a good actor **VR sich mit jdm/etw ~** (= sich beschäftigen) to bother or concern oneself with sb/sth; (= sich einlassen) to associate with sb/sth **VI** (Sport) to pass

ab|ge|brannt ADJ pred (inf: = pleite) broke (inf); **völlig ~ sein** to be flat or stony (Brit) broke (inf) → auch **abbrennen**

ab|ge|bro|chen ADJ (= nicht beendet) Studium uncompleted; Worte disjointed; **mit einem ~en Studium kommt man nicht sehr weit** you don't get very far if you haven't finished university or your university course; **er ist ~er Mediziner** (inf) he broke off his medical studies → auch **abbrechen**

ab|ge|brüht ['apgəbry:t] ADJ (inf: = skrupellos) callous; (= frech) cool → auch **abbrühen**

Ab|ge|brüht|heit F **-, no pl** (inf) callousness

ab|ge|dreht ['apgədre:t] ADJ (inf: = verrückt) crazy (inf); (Aus inf: = skrupellos) unscrupulous → auch **abdrehen**

ab|ge|dro|schen ['apgədrɔʃn] ADJ (inf) hackneyed (Brit), well-worn; Witz auch corny (inf); **eine ~e Phrase** a cliché (inf); **eine ~e Redensart** a hackneyed (Brit) or trite saying

ab|ge|feimt ['apgəfaimt] ADJ cunning, wily

Ab|ge|feimt|heit F **-, -en** cunning, wiliness

ab|ge|fuckt ['apgəfakt] ADJ (sl: = heruntergekommen) Gegenstand knackered (Brit sl), clapped-out (Brit inf), on its last legs (inf); Mensch auch fucked-up (vulg)

ab|ge|grif|fen ['apgəgrɪfn] ADJ Buch (well-)worn; Leder worn; (fig) Klischees, Phrasen etc well-worn, hackneyed (Brit) → auch **abgreifen**

ab|ge|hackt ['apgəhakt] ADJ Sprechweise clipped; Schluchzen broken ADV **~ schluchzen** to sob brokenly; **~ sprechen** to speak in a clipped manner → auch **abhacken**

ab|ge|half|tert ['apgəhalftɛt] ADJ haggard; **ein ~er Politiker** a political has-been → auch **abhalftern**

ab|ge|han|gen ['apgəhaŋən] ADJ (gut) ~ (fig: = etabliert) well-established → auch **abhängen**

ab|ge|härmt ['apgəhɛrmt] ADJ careworn ADV **~ aussehen** to look careworn → auch **abhärmen**

ab|ge|här|tet ['apgəhɛrtət] ADJ tough, hardy; (fig) hardened; **gegen Erkältungen ~ sein** to be immune to colds → auch **abhärten**

ab+ge|hen sep irreg aux sein **VI a** (= abfahren) to leave, to depart (nach for); **der Zug ging in** or **von Frankfurt ab** the train left from Frankfurt; **der Zug ging in** or **von Frankfurt pünktlich ab** the train left on time **b** (Sport: = abspringen) to jump down; **er ging mit einem Doppelsalto vom Barren ab** he did a double somersault down from or off the bars **c** (Theat: = abtreten) to exit, to make one's exit; **Othello geht ab** exit Othello **d** (= ausscheiden) (von der Schule, old: aus einem Amt) to leave; **von der Schule ~** to leave school; **mit dem Tode** or **mit Tod ~** (old form) to die in office **e** (Med sl: = sterben) to die **f** (= sich lösen) to come off; (= herausgehen: Farbe etc) to come out or off; **an meiner Jacke ist ein Knopf abgegangen** a button has come off my jacket **g** (= abgesondert werden) to pass out; (Eiter etc) to be discharged; (= aborted) to be aborted; **ihm ist einer abgegangen** (sl) he shot or came off (sl) **h** (= losgehen: Schuss) to be fired, to be loosed off **i** (= abgesandt werden) to be sent or dispatched; (Funkspruch) to be sent; **etw ~ lassen** to send or dispatch sth **j** (= fehlen) **jdm geht Verständnis/Taktgefühl ab** sb lacks understanding/tact **k** (= abgezogen werden) (vom Preis) to be taken off; (von Verdienst) to be taken off, to be deducted; (vom Gewicht) to come off; **(von etw) ~** (von Preis) to be taken off (sth); (von Verdienst auch) to be deducted (from sth); (von Gewicht) to be taken off (sth); **davon gehen 5% ab** 5% is taken off that **l** (= abzweigen) to branch off; (esp bei Gabelung) to fork off **m** (= abweichen) **von einem Plan/einer Forderung ~** to give up or drop a plan/demand; **von seiner Meinung ~** to change or alter one's opinion; **von einem Thema ~** to digress (from a subject); **davon kann ich nicht ~** I must insist on that; (bei Versprechungen etc) I can't go back on that **n** (= verlaufen) to go; **gut/glatt/friedlich ~** to go well/smoothly/peacefully; **es ging nicht ohne Streit ab** there was an argument **o** (sl) **das geht gut ab** it's really great; **da geht aber was ab** it's a really happening place (inf); **gestern ging nichts ab** there was nothing doing yesterday (inf); **was geht ab?** what's doing? (inf) **VT a** (= entlanggehen) to go or walk along; (hin und zurück) to walk or go up and down; (Mil) Gebäudekomplex, Gelände to patrol; (= inspizieren) to inspect **b** (= messen) to pace out **c** (Sch inf: = verweisen) **abgegangen werden** to be thrown or chucked (inf) out

ab|ge|hend ADJ Post, Anruf, Daten outgoing; Zug, Schiff departing; **die ~en Pferde** (Sport) the starters; **die morgen ~e Post** the post (Brit) or mail which will go out tomorrow

ab|ge|hetzt ['apgəhɛtst] ADJ out of breath → auch **abhetzen**

ab|ge|ho|ben ADJ (inf: = wirklichkeitsfremd) Mensch, Politik divorced from reality, out of touch with the real world → auch **abheben**

ab|ge|kämpft ['apgəkɛmpft] ADJ exhausted, shattered (Brit inf), worn-out → auch **abkämpfen**

ab|ge|kar|tet ['apgəkartət] ADJ fixed (inf), rigged (inf); **eine ~e Sache, ein ~es Spiel** a fix (inf), a put-up job (Brit inf), a frame-up (US inf); **die Sache war von vornherein ~** the whole thing was a put-up job (Brit inf) or a frame-up (US inf) → auch **abkarten**

ab|ge|klärt ['apgəklɛ:ɐt] ADJ Mensch worldly-wise; Urteil well-considered; Sicht detached; **~**

sein to stand above things `ADV` *betrachten, beurteilen* with a certain detachment → *auch* **abklären**

Ab|ge|klärt|heit F -, *no pl* detachment

ab|ge|latscht [ˈapɡəlaːtʃt] ADJ (*sl*) *Schuhe, Teppich* worn-out

ab|ge|lebt [ˈapɡəleːpt] ADJ **a** (= *verbraucht*) *Person* decrepit; *Badeort etc* run-down **b** (= *altmodisch*) *Tradition, Vorstellung* antiquated

ab|ge|le|gen ADJ (= *entfernt*) *Dorf, Land* remote; (= *einsam*) isolated → *auch* **abliegen**

Ab|ge|le|gen|heit F remoteness; (= *Einsamkeit*) isolation

ab|ge|lei|ert [ˈapɡəlaiɐt] ADJ (*pej*) *Melodie etc* banal, trite; *Redensart etc* banal, trite, hackneyed (*Brit*); *Schallplatte* worn out, crackly

ab+gel|ten VT *sep irreg* (= *bezahlen*) *Ansprüche* to satisfy; (= *sich revanchieren für*) *Gefallen* to return; **Umweltschäden mit Geldzahlungen ~** to provide financial compensation for environmental damage; **sein Urlaub wurde durch Bezahlung abgegolten** he was given payment in lieu of holiday (*Brit*) *or* instead of vacation (*US*)

ab|ge|macht [ˈapɡəmaxt] INTERJ OK, that's settled; (*bei Kauf*) it's a deal, done ADJ **eine ~e Sache** a fix (*inf*); **das war doch schon vorher eine ~e Sache** it was all fixed up *or* arranged beforehand → *auch* **abmachen**

ab|ge|ma|gert [ˈapɡəmaːɡɐt] ADJ (= *sehr dünn*) thin; (= *ausgemergelt*) emaciated; (*fig*: = *reduziert*) scaled down → *auch* **abmagern**

ab|ge|mer|gelt [ˈapɡəmɛːɐɡlt] ADJ emaciated → *auch* **abmergeln**

ab|ge|mes|sen [ˈapɡəmɛsn] ADJ (*lit, fig*) measured `ADV` **~ gehen** to walk with measured steps; **~ sprechen** to speak in measured tones → *auch* **abmessen**

ab|ge|neigt ADJ averse *pred* (+*dat* to); **ich wäre gar nicht ~** (*inf*) actually I wouldn't mind; **einer Sache nicht ~ sein** not to be averse to sth; **jdm ~ sein** to dislike sb

Ab|ge|neigt|heit F aversion (*gegenüber* to)

ab|ge|nutzt [ˈapɡənʊtst] ADJ *Möbel, Teppich* worn, shabby; *Bürste, Besen* worn-out; *Reifen* worn-down; (*fig*) *Klischees, Phrasen* hackneyed (*Brit*), well-worn → *auch* **abnutzen**

Ab|ge|ord|ne|ten-: Ab|ge|ord|ne|ten|bank F *pl* **-bänke** bench; **Ab|ge|ord|ne|ten|haus** NT parliament; (*in Berlin*) House of Representatives

Ab|ge|ord|ne|te(r) [ˈapɡəɔrdnətə] MF *decl as adj* (elected) representative; (*von Nationalversammlung*) member of parliament; **Herr ~r!** sir; **Frau ~!** madam

ab|ge|ris|sen [ˈapɡərɪsn] ADJ **a** (= *zerlumpt*) *Kleidung, Eindruck* ragged, tattered; *Mensch* scruffy **b** (= *unzusammenhängend*) *Worte, Gedanken* disjointed, incoherent → *auch* **abreißen**

Ab|ge|sand|te(r) [ˈapɡəzantə] MF *decl as adj* envoy

Ab|ge|sang M (*Poet*) abgesang (*concluding section of the final strophe of the minnesang*); (*fig liter*) swan song, farewell

ab|ge|schabt [ˈapɡəʃaːpt] ADJ (= *abgewetzt*) *Kleider* threadbare → *auch* **abschaben**

ab|ge|schie|den [ˈapɡəʃiːdn] ADJ **a** (*geh*: = *einsam*) secluded **b** (*liter*: = *tot*) departed; **der Abgeschiedene/die Abgeschiedenen** the departed `ADV` **~ leben** to live a secluded life; **~ wohnen** to live in seclusion → *auch* **abscheiden**

Ab|ge|schie|den|heit F -, *no pl* seclusion

ab|ge|schlafft [ˈapɡəʃlaft] ADJ **a** *Muskeln* flabby **b** (*inf*: = *erschöpft*) whacked (*Brit inf*), exhausted; **~e Typen** lazy bums (*inf*) → *auch* **abschlaffen**

ab|ge|schla|gen [ˈapɡəʃlaːɡn] ADJ **a** (= *erschöpft*) washed out (*inf*), shattered (*Brit inf*) **b** (= *zurück*) *Position* badly beaten; **auf einem ~en 8. Platz** in a poor 8th place `ADV` **weit ~ liegen** to be way behind; **er lande-**

te ~ auf dem 8. Platz he finished up way down in 8th place → *auch* **abschlagen**

Ab|ge|schla|gen|heit F -, *no pl* (feeling of) exhaustion

ab|ge|schlos|sen ADJ (= *einsam*) isolated; (*attr*: = *geschlossen*) *Wohnung* self-contained; *Grundstück, Hof* enclosed `ADV` **~ leben** to live in isolation → *auch* **abschließen**

Ab|ge|schlos|sen|heit F isolation

ab|ge|schmackt [ˈapɡəʃmakt] ADJ (*pej*) *Bemerkung auch* crude; *Witz* corny, fatuous `ADV` outrageously

Ab|ge|schmackt|heit F -, **-en a** *no pl* tastelessness **b** (= *Bemerkung*) platitude; **alberne Witze und ähnliche ~en** stupid jokes and similar corny things

ab|ge|schrägt [ˈapɡəʃrɛːkt] ADJ *Brett, Wand* bevelled (*Brit*), beveled (*US*)

ab|ge|se|hen [ˈapɡəzeːən] *ptp* **es auf jdn ~ haben** to have it in for sb (*inf*); **es auf jdn/etw ~ haben** (= *interessiert sein*) to have one's eye on sb/sth; **du hast es nur darauf ~, mich zu ärgern** you're only trying to annoy me `ADV` **~ von jdm/etw** apart from sb/sth; **~ davon, dass ...** apart from the fact that ... → *auch* **absehen**

ab|ge|son|dert [ˈapɡəzɔndɐt] ADJ (= *isoliert*) isolated → *auch* **absondern**

ab|ge|spannt ADJ weary, tired → *auch* **abspannen**

Ab|ge|spannt|heit F weariness, tiredness

ab|ge|spielt [ˈapɡəʃpiːlt] ADJ (= *abgenutzt*) *Schallplatte* worn → *auch* **abspielen**

ab|ge|stan|den ADJ *Luft, Wasser* stale; *Bier, Limonade etc* flat; (*fig*) *Witz, Redensart* hackneyed (*Brit*), stale `ADV` **~ schmecken** to taste flat; (*Wasser*) to taste stale → *auch* **abstehen**

ab|ge|stor|ben ADJ *Glieder* numb; *Pflanze, Ast, Gewebe* dead; (*fig*) defunct; *Gefühle* that have/had died; **von der Kälte war mein Arm wie ~** my arm was numb with cold → *auch* **absterben**

ab|ge|straft [ˈapɡəʃtraːft] ADJ (*Aus*) = **vorbestraft**

ab|ge|stumpft [ˈapɡəʃtʊmpft] ADJ **a** (= *gefühllos*) *Mensch* insensitive; *Gefühle, Gewissen* dulled, blunted; **sie war in ihren Gefühlen so ~, dass ...** her feelings had been dulled *or* blunted so much that ... **b** (*lit*) blunt; *Kegel* truncated → *auch* **abstumpfen**

Ab|ge|stumpft|heit F -, *no pl* (*von Mensch*) insensitivity; (*von Gefühlen*) dullness

ab|ge|ta|kelt [ˈapɡətaːklt] ADJ (*pej inf*) past one's best, past it *pred* (*inf*) → *auch* **abtakeln**

ab|ge|tan ADJ *pred* (= *erledigt*) finished *or* done with; **damit ist die Sache ~** that settles the matter, that's the matter done with (*Brit*); **damit ist es (noch) nicht ~** that's not the end of the matter → *auch* **abtun**

ab|ge|tra|gen ADJ worn; **~e Kleider** old clothes → *auch* **abtragen**

ab+ge|win|nen VT *sep irreg* **a** (*lit*) **jdm etw ~** to win sth from sb **b** (*fig*) **einer Sache etwas/nichts ~ können** to be able to see some/no attraction in sth; **jdm/einer Sache keinen Reiz ~ können** to be unable to see anything attractive in sb/sth; **einer Sache** (*dat*) **Geschmack ~** to acquire a taste for sth; **jdm Achtung ~** to win respect from sb, to win sb's respect; **jdm ein Lächeln ~** to persuade sb to smile; **dem Meer Land ~** to reclaim land from the sea

ab|ge|wirt|schaf|tet [ˈapɡəvɪrtʃaftət] ADJ (*pej*) rotten; *Firma auch* run-down; **einen total ~en Eindruck machen** to be on its last legs → *auch* **abwirtschaften**

ab|ge|wo|gen ADJ *Urteil, Worte* balanced → *auch* **abwägen**

Ab|ge|wo|gen|heit F balance

ab+ge|wöh|nen VT *sep* **jdm etw ~** (*Gewohnheiten, schlechte Manieren*) to cure sb of sth; *das Rauchen, Trinken* to get sb to give up *or* stop sth;

sich (*dat*) **etw ~** to give sth up; **sich** (*dat*) **das Trinken ~** to give up *or* stop drinking; **noch eins/einen zum Abgewöhnen** (*hum*) one last one; (*Alkohol auch*) one for the road; **das/die ist ja zum Abgewöhnen** (*inf*) that/she is enough to put anyone off

ab|ge|wrackt [ˈapɡəvrakt] ADJ (*pej*) rotten; (= *abgetakelt*) *Mensch* washed-up → *auch* **abwracken**

ab|ge|zehrt [ˈapɡətseːɐt] ADJ emaciated → *auch* **abzehren**

ab+gie|ßen VT *sep irreg* **a** *Flüssigkeit* to pour off *or* away; *Kartoffeln, Gemüse* to strain; **du musst den Eimer etwas ~** you must pour some of the water *etc* out of the bucket; **er goss einen Schluck in mein Glas ab** he poured a drop into my glass **b** (*Art, Metal*) to cast

Ab|glanz M reflection (*auch fig*); **nur ein schwacher** *or* **matter ~** (*fig*) a pale reflection

Ab|gleich [ˈapɡlaiç] M **-s**, *no pl* (*von Dateien, Einträgen*) comparison

ab+glei|chen VT *sep irreg* **a** (*Build*) to level out **b** (*Elec*) to tune; (*fig*) *Termine, Vorgehensweise* to coordinate; *Dateien, Einträge* to compare

ab+glei|ten VI *sep irreg aux sein* (*geh*) **a** (= *abrutschen*) to slip; (*Gedanken*) to wander; (*Fin, Kurs*) to drop, to fall; **von etw ~** to slip off sth; **in Nebensächlichkeiten ~** to wander off *or* go off into side issues; **in Anarchie ~** to descend into anarchy; **er gleitet in Gedanken immer ab** his thoughts always wander; **von der rechten Bahn** *or* **dem rechten Weg ~** to wander *or* stray from the straight and narrow **b** (*fig*: = *abprallen*) **an** *or* **von jdm ~** to bounce off sb

ab+glit|schen VI *sep aux sein* (*inf*) to slip; **er glitschte mit den Händen ab** his hands slipped

Ab|gott M , **Ab|göt|tin** F idol; **Abgöttern dienen** to worship false gods; **jdn zum ~ machen** to idolize sb

ab|göt|tisch [ˈapɡœtɪʃ] ADJ idolatrous; **~e Liebe** blind adoration `ADV` **jdn ~ lieben** to idolize sb; *Eltern, Sohn, Tochter auch* to dote on sb; **jdn ~ verehren** to idolize sb, to worship sb (like a god)

ab+gra|ben VT *sep irreg Erdreich* to dig away; **jdm das Wasser ~** (*fig inf*) to take the bread from sb's mouth (*esp Brit*), to take away sb's livelihood

ab+gra|sen VT *sep Feld* to graze; (*fig inf*) *Ort, Geschäfte* to scour, to comb; *Gebiet, Thema* to do to death (*inf*)

ab+grät|schen VI *sep aux sein* (*Sport*) to straddle off

ab+grei|fen *sep irreg* VT **a** *Strecke, Entfernung* to measure off **b** *Buch, Heft* to wear → *auch* **abgegriffen c** (= *abtasten*) to feel; (*bei Durchsuchung*) to frisk **d** (*inf*: = *sich verschaffen*) *Geld* to get one's hands on VR to wear, to become worn

ab+gren|zen *sep* VT *Grundstück, Gelände* to fence off; (*fig*) *Rechte, Pflichten, Einflussbereich, Befugnisse, Begriff* to delimit (*gegen, von* from); **etw durch einen Zaun/ein Seil/eine Mauer/eine Hecke ~** to fence/rope/wall/hedge sth off; **diese Begriffe lassen sich nur schwer** (*gegeneinander*) **~** it is hard to distinguish (between) these two concepts VR to dis(as)sociate oneself (*gegen* from)

Ab|gren|zung F -, **-en a** *no pl* (*von Gelände*) fencing off; (*fig*) delimitation **b** (= *Distanzierung*) dis(as)sociation (*gegen* from); **Politik der ~** politics of separation **c** (= *Umzäunung, Zaun*) fencing *no pl*

Ab|grund M precipice; (= *Schlucht, fig*) abyss, chasm; **sich am Rande eines ~es befinden** (*fig*) to be on the brink (of disaster); **diese Politik bedeutet ein Wandeln am Rande des ~es** this policy is an exercise in brinkmanship; **in einen ~ von Verrat/Gemeinheit blicken** (*fig*) to stare into a bottomless pit of treason/baseness; **die menschlichen Abgründe, der ~ der menschlichen Seele** the darkest depths of the human soul

ab|grund|häss|lich ▲ ADJ loathsome, incredibly hideous

ab|grün|dig ['apgrʏndɪç] ADJ Humor, Ironie cryptic ADV lächeln cryptically

Ab|grün|dig|keit F -, no pl (von Humor etc) subtlety

ab|grund|tief ADJ Hass, Verachtung profound ADV hassen, verachten profoundly

ab+gu|cken VTI sep to copy; **jdm etw ~** to copy sth from sb; **bei jdm (etw) ~** (Sch) to copy (sth) from or off (inf) sb; **ich guck dir nichts ab!** (inf) don't worry, I've seen it all before

Ab|gunst F (old) resentment, enviousness (gegenüber of)

Ab|guss ▲ M **a** (Art, Metal) (= Vorgang) casting; (= Form) cast **b** (dial: = Ausguss) sink

ab+ha|ben VT sep irreg (inf) **a** (= abgenommen haben) Brille, Hut to have off; (= abgemacht haben) to have got off; (= abgerissen haben) to have off **b** (= abbekommen) to have; **willst du ein Stück/etwas (davon) ~?** do you want a bit/some (of it)?

ab+ha|cken VT sep to chop off, to hack off → **Rübe b** → auch abgehackt

ab+ha|ken VT sep **a** (= markieren) to tick (Brit) or check (esp US) off; (fig) to cross off **b** (= abnehmen) to unhook

ab+half|tern VT sep Pferd to take the halter off → auch abgehalftert

ab+hal|ten VT sep irreg **a** (= hindern) to stop, to prevent; **jdn von etw/vom Trinken/von der Arbeit ~** to keep sb from sth/drinking/working; **jdn davon ~, etw zu tun** to stop sb (from) doing sth, to prevent sb (from) doing sth; **lass dich nicht ~!** don't let me/us etc stop you **b** (= fern halten) Kälte, Hitze to keep off; Mücken, Fliegen to keep off or away; (= draußen halten) to keep out **c** (= veranstalten) Versammlung, Wahlen, Gottesdienst to hold **d** **ein Kind auf der Toilette/Straße ~** to hold a child over the toilet/on the street (while it goes to the toilet)

Ab|hal|tung F , no pl (= Durchführung) holding; **nach ~ der Wahlen** after the elections (were held)

ab+han|deln VT sep **a** Thema to treat, to deal with **b** (= abkaufen) **jdm etw ~** to do or strike a deal with sb for sth; **sie wollte sich** (dat) **das Armband nicht ~ lassen** she didn't want to let her bracelet go **c** (= vom Preis abhandeln) **jdm 8 Euro/etwas ~** to beat sb down 8 euros/a bit (Brit), to get sb to knock 8 euros/a bit off (the price); **er ließ sich von seinen Bedingungen nichts ~** he wouldn't give up any of his conditions

ab|han|den [ap'handn] ADV **~ kommen** to get lost; **jdm ist etw ~ gekommen** sb has lost sth

Ab|han|den|kom|men NT loss

Ab|hand|lung F **a** treatise, discourse (über +acc (up)on); **~en** (einer Akademie etc) transactions **b** (= das Abhandeln) treatment

Ab|hang M slope, incline

ab+hän|gen sep ☉ 33.3 VT **a** (= herunternehmen) Bild to take down; (= abkuppeln) Schlafwagen, Kurswagen to uncouple; Wohnwagen, Anhänger to unhitch; **(gut) abgehangen** (Fleisch) well-hung → auch abgehangen **b** (inf: = hinter sich lassen) jdn to shake off (inf) VI **a** irreg (Fleisch etc) to hang **b** irreg aux haben or (S Ger, Aus) sein **von etw ~** to depend (up)on sth, to be dependent (up)on sth; **das hängt ganz davon ab** it all depends; **davon hängt viel/zu viel ab** a lot/too much depends on it; **von jdm (finanziell) ~** to be (financially) dependent on sb **c** (inf: = Telefon auflegen) to hang up (inf)

ab|hän|gig ['aphɛŋɪç] ADJ **a** (= bedingt durch) dependent (auch Math); **etw von etw ~ machen** (= Bedingungen stellen) to make sth conditional (up)on sth **b** (= angewiesen auf, euph: = süchtig) dependent (von on); **gegenseitig** or **voneinander ~ sein** to be dependent on each other, to be mutually dependent, to be inter-

dependent; **~ Beschäftigte(r)** employee **c** (Gram) Satz subordinate; Rede indirect; Kasus oblique; **von etw ~ sein** to be governed by sth

Ab|hän|gi|ge(r) ['aphɛŋɪgə] MF decl as adj dependent, dependant → **Unzucht**

-ab|hän|gi|ge(r) MF decl as adj suf (= -süchtiger) addict; **ein Heroinabhängiger** a heroin addict

Ab|hän|gig|keit F -, -en **a** no pl (= Bedingtheit) dependency no pl (von on); (Gram: von Sätzen) subordination (von to) **b** (= Angewiesensein, euph: = Sucht) dependence (von on); **gegenseitige ~** mutual dependence, interdependence

Ab|hän|gig|keits|ver|hält|nis NT dependent relationship; (gegenseitig) interdependence; **in einem ~ mit jdm stehen** to be dependent on sb

ab+här|men VR sep to pine away (um for) → auch abgehärmt

ab+här|ten sep VT to toughen up VI **das härtet (gegen Erkältung) ab** that toughens you up (and stops you catching cold) VR to toughen oneself up; **sich gegen etw ~** to toughen oneself against sth, (fig) to harden oneself to sth → auch abgehärtet

Ab|här|tung F toughening up; (fig) hardening

ab+hau|en sep ptp **abgehauen** VI aux sein (inf) to clear out; (= verschwinden auch) to push off; (aus einem Land auch) to get away; **hau ab!** beat it! (inf), get lost! (inf) VT **a** pret **hieb** or (inf) **haute ab**, ptp **abgehauen** Kopf to chop or cut off; Baum to chop or cut down **b** pret **haute ab**, ptp **abgehauen** (= wegschlagen) Verputz, Schicht to knock off

ab+häu|ten VT sep to skin

ab+he|ben sep irreg VT **a** (= anheben) to lift (up), to raise; (= abnehmen) to take off; Telefonhörer to pick up, to lift (up); Telefon to answer; (beim Stricken) Masche to slip **b** (Cards) to take, to pick up **c** Geld to withdraw VI **a** (Flugzeug) to take off; (Rakete) to lift off **b** (= ans Telefon gehen) to answer; (beim Stricken) to slip; **lass es doch klingeln, du brauchst nicht abzuheben** let it ring, you don't have to answer (it) **c** (= Geld abheben) to withdraw money; **du kannst nicht dauernd ~!** you can't keep on withdrawing money or drawing money out; **wenn Sie ~ wollen** if you wish to make a withdrawal **d** **auf etw** (acc) **~** (form, Jur) to emphasize sth **e** (Cards) (vor Spielbeginn etc) to cut; (= Karte nehmen) to take a card **f** (inf: vor Freude) to take off → auch abgehoben VR **sich von jdm/etw ~** to stand out from sb/sth; **sich gegen jdn/etw ~** to stand out against sb/sth; **nur um sich von anderen** or **gegen andere abzuheben** just to be different (from other people), just to make oneself stand out; **sich wohltuend gegen etw ~** to make a pleasant contrast with sth, to contrast pleasantly with sth

ab+hef|ten VT sep **a** Rechnungen, Schriftverkehr to file away **b** (Sew) to tack, to baste

ab+hei|len VI sep aux sein to heal (up)

ab+hel|fen VI sep irreg +dat to remedy; einem Fehler auch to rectify, to correct; **dem ist leicht abzuhelfen** that can be or is easily remedied etc

ab+het|zen sep VT Tiere to exhaust, to tire out; **hetz mich nicht so ab!** (inf) stop rushing me like that! (inf) VR to wear or tire oneself out → auch abgehetzt

ab+heu|ern sep (Naut) VI to be paid off VT to pay off

Ab|hil|fe F , no pl remedy, cure; **~ schaffen** to take remedial action; **in einer Angelegenheit ~ schaffen** to remedy a matter

ab|hin [ap'hɪn] ADV (Sw) **vom 18.9.90 ~** from 18.9.90 onwards

Ab|hit|ze F waste heat

ab+ho|beln VT sep Holz to plane down; **wir müssen noch 2 cm ~** we need to plane another 2 cm off

ab|hold ['aphɔlt] ADJ +dat (geh) **jdm ~ sein** to be averse or ill-disposed to(wards) sb; **einer Sache** (dat) **~ sein** to be averse to sth; **jdm/einer Sache nicht ~ sein** (iro) not to be averse to sb/sth

ab+ho|len VT sep to collect (bei from); Bestelltes auch to call for (bei at); Fundsache to claim (bei from); jdn to call for; (euph: = verhaften) to take away; **jdn am Bahnhof/Flughafen ~** to collect sb from or to meet sb at the station/airport; (mit dem Auto auch) to pick sb up from the station/airport; **ich hole dich heute Abend ab** I'll call for you or I'll pick you up this evening; **er kam und wollte mich zu einem Spaziergang ~** he called and asked me to go for a walk; **etw ~ lassen** to have sth collected; **„Geldbörse gefunden, abzuholen bei ..."** "purse found, claim from ..."

Ab|ho|ler ['aphoːlɐ] M -s, -, **Ab|ho|le|rin** [-ərɪn] F -, -nen **a** **sie wartete auf ihren ~** she was waiting to be collected **b** (Comm) **~ sein** to collect one's mail from the post office/parcels from the station etc

Ab|hol|markt M warehouse (selling furniture/drinks etc)

Ab|ho|lung F -, -en collection; **zur ~ bereit** ready for or awaiting collection

ab+hol|zen VT sep Wald to clear, to deforest; Baumreihe to fell, to cut down

Ab|hol|zung F -, -en (von Wald) clearing, deforesting; (von Baumreihe) felling, cutting down

Ab|hör-: **Ab|hör|ak|ti|on** F bugging operation; **Ab|hör|an|la|ge** F bugging system

ab+hor|chen sep VT to sound, to listen to; Brust auch, Patienten to auscultate (form) VI to auscultate (form)

Ab|hör-: **Ab|hör|dienst** M monitoring service; **Ab|hör|ein|rich|tung** F bugging device; (= System) bugging system

ab+hö|ren VT sep **a** auch vi (= überwachen) Raum, Gespräch to bug; (= mithören) to listen in on; Telefon to tap; **abgehört werden** (inf) to be bugged; **der Geheimdienst darf (Telefone) ~** the Secret Service are allowed to tap telephones **b** (= zuhören) Sender, Schallplatte etc to listen to **c** (Med) to sound, to listen to; **jdm das Herz ~** to listen to or sound sb's heart **d** (Sch: = abfragen) einen or einem Schüler etw ~ to test a pupil orally on sth; **kannst du mir mal Vokabeln ~?** can you test my vocabulary?; **einen** or **einem Schüler ein Gedicht ~** to hear a pupil recite a poem

Ab|hör-: **Ab|hör|ge|rät** NT bugging device; **ab|hör|si|cher** ADJ Raum bug-proof; Telefon tap-proof; **Ab|hör|si|cher|heit** F **sich von der ~ des Zimmers/des Telefons überzeugen** to ensure the room is bug-proof/the phone is tap-proof; **hier muss absolute ~ gewährleistet sein** there must be no possibility of bugging/tapping conversations here

ab+hun|gern VT sep **er musste sich** (dat) **sein Studium ~** he had to starve himself to pay for his studies, he had to starve his way through college etc; **sich** (dat) **Gewicht/10 Kilo ~** to lose weight/10 kilos by going on a starvation diet; **abgehungerte Gestalten** emaciated figures

ab+hus|ten VI sep to have a good cough

a|bi ['abi] ADV, PREP (Aus inf) = **hinunter**

A|bi ['abi] NT -s, -s (Sch inf) abbr von **Abitur**

ab+ir|ren VI sep aux sein (geh) to lose one's way; (fig: = abschweifen) (Gedanken) to wander; **vom Weg(e) ~** to wander off the path, to stray from the path; **vom rechten Weg ~** (fig) to stray or wander or err from the straight and narrow

Ab|ir|rung F (geh) **a** (= Verirrung) lapse, aberration **b** (Astron) aberration

A|bi|tur [abi'tuːɐ] NT -s, (rare) -e school-leaving exam and university entrance qualification,

≈ A levels *pl* (*Brit*), ≈ Highers *pl* (*Scot*), ≈ high-school diploma (*US*); **(sein** *or* **das) ~ machen** to do (one's) school-leaving exam (*Brit*), ≈ to do one's A levels (*Brit*) or Highers (*Scot*), ≈ to take one's high-school diploma (*US*); **sein** *or* **das ~ ablegen** (*form*) to sit one's school-leaving exam (*Brit*), ≈ to sit one's A levels (*Brit*) or Highers (*Scot*), ≈ to take one's high-school diploma (*US*)

ABITUR

In Germany the **Abitur** examination is taken by pupils at a **Gymnasium** after thirteen years at school. The **Abitur** consists of written and oral tests in four core subjects, although the overall mark takes account of a student's performance in various courses throughout their **Kollegstufe**. The **Abitur** is also known as the **allgemeine Hochschulreife**, since it is a prerequisite for acceptance on a university course.
The Austrian equivalent is the **Matura**, taken after twelve years at school.
In Switzerland the **Maturität** is taken after twelve or thirteen years at school. Success in the examination entitles the student to be admitted to university. → Gymnasium, Kollegstufe

---

A|bi|tur|fei|er F school-leavers' (*Brit*) or graduation (*US*) party

A|bi|tu|ri|ent [abitu'riɛnt] M **-en, -en, A|bi|tu|ri|en|tin** [-'rɪɛntɪn] F **-, -nen** *person who is doing/has done the Abitur*

A|bi|tur-: A|bi|tur|klas|se F *final-year class at school which will take the Abitur*, ≈ sixth form (*Brit*), ≈ twelfth grade (*US*), **A|bi|tur|prü|fung** F school-leaving exam; **A|bi|tur|re|de** F school-leaving speech; **A|bi|tur|zei|tung** F *humorous magazine compiled by school-leavers*; **A|bi|tur|zeug|nis** NT certificate of having passed the Abitur, ≈ A level (*Brit*) or Highers (*Scot*) certificate, ≈ high-school diploma (*US*)

ab+ja|gen *sep* **jdm etw ~** to get sth off sb **VR** (*inf*) to wear oneself out

Abk. *abbr von* **Abkürzung** abbreviation, abbr

ab+kal|ben VI *sep* (*Agr*) to calve

ab+käm|men VT *sep* (*fig*) to comb, to scour

ab+kämp|fen *sep* **VT** (*geh*) **jdm etw ~** to wring sth out of sb **VR** to fight hard → *auch* **abgekämpft**

ab+kan|zeln ['apkantsln] VT *sep* (*inf*) **jdn ~** to give sb a dressing-down

Ab|kan|ze|lung F **-, -en, Ab|kanz|lung** ['apkantslʊŋ] F **-, -en** dressing-down

ab+kap|seln ['apkapsln] VR *sep* (*lit*) to become encapsulated; (*fig*) to shut or cut oneself off, to isolate oneself

Ab|kap|se|lung F **-, -en, Ab|kaps|lung** ['apkapslʊŋ] F **-, -en** (*lit*) encapsulation; (*fig*) isolation

ab+kar|ren VT *sep* to cart away; (*fig*) *Menschen* to cart off

ab+kar|ten ['apkartn] VT *sep* (*inf*) to rig (*inf*), to fix → *auch* **abgekartet**

ab+kas|sie|ren *ptp* **abkassiert** *sep* **VT** *Fahrgäste* to collect money from; *Geldsumme, Schutzgelder, Maut* to collect; (= *ausnehmen*) to clean out (*inf*) **VI** (= *großes Geld machen*) to make a killing (*inf*); **darf ich mal (bei Ihnen) ~?** could I ask you to pay now?

ab+kau|en VT *sep* *Nägel* to bite; *Bleistift* to chew; **er hat abgekaute Fingernägel** his nails are bitten right down

ab+kau|fen VT *sep* **jdm etw ~** to buy sth from or off (*inf*) sb; (*inf*: = *glauben*) to buy (*inf*); **diese Geschichte kauft uns keiner ab!** nobody will buy that story (*inf*)

Ab|kehr ['apkeːɐ] F **-, *no pl*** turning away (*von* from); (*von Glauben, von der Welt etc*) renuncia-

---

tion (*von* of); (*von der Familie*) estrangement (*von* from); **die ~ vom Materialismus** turning away from materialism, rejecting materialism

ab+keh|ren¹ VT *sep* (= *abfegen*) *Schmutz* to sweep away or off; *Hof, Dach* to sweep

ab+keh|ren² *sep* **VT** (*geh*: = *abwenden*) *Blick, Gesicht* to avert, to turn away; **sie musste den Blick (davon) ~** she had to look away (from it) **VR** (*fig*) to turn away (*von* from); (*von einer Politik*) to give up; **sich von Gott ~** to renounce God; **die von uns abgekehrte Seite des Mondes** the side of the moon away from us, the far side of the moon

ab+kip|pen *sep* **VT** (= *abladen*) *Abfälle, Baustoffe* to tip; (= *herunterklappen*) to let down **VI** *aux sein* to tilt; (*Flugzeug*) to nose-dive

ab+klä|ren *sep* **VT a** (= *sich setzen lassen*) *Flüssigkeit* to clarify **b** (= *klarstellen*) *Angelegenheit* to clear up, to clarify **VR a** (= *sich setzen*) to clarify **b** (= *sich beruhigen*) to calm down → *auch* **abgeklärt**

Ab|klä|rung F **a** (*von Flüssigkeit*) clarification, clarifying **b** (*von Angelegenheit*) clearing up

Ab|klatsch M (*Art*) cast, casting; (*fig pej*) poor imitation or copy

ab+klat|schen VT *sep* **er klatschte sie ab** he cut in on her partner; **es wird abgeklatscht** it's an excuse-me (*Brit*), you can cut in

Ab|klat|scher M (*Ftbl sl*) rebound

ab+klem|men VT *sep* *Nabelschnur, Leitung, Adern* to clamp; **er hat sich** (*dat*) **in der Maschine den Finger abgeklemmt** he lost his finger in the machine

Ab|kling|be|cken NT (*in Atomkraftwerk*) spent fuel storage bay

ab+klin|gen VI *sep irreg aux sein* **a** (= *leiser werden*) to die or fade away **b** (= *nachlassen*) to wear off, to abate; (*Erregung, Fieber*) to subside, to abate; (*radioaktives Material*) to decay

ab+klop|fen *sep* **VT a** (= *herunterklopfen*) to knock off; (= *klopfend säubern*) to brush down; *Staub etc* to brush off; *Teppich, Polstermöbel* to beat; **er klopfte die Asche von der Zigarre ab** he tapped or knocked the ash off his cigar; **sich** (*dat*) **die Schuhe ~** to knock the mud *etc* off one's shoes; **den Staub nicht abbürsten, sondern ~** do not brush the dust off, pat it off **b** (= *beklopfen*) to tap; (*Med*) to sound, to percuss (*spec*) **c** (*fig inf*: = *untersuchen*) to look into; **etw auf etw** (*acc*) **~** to trace sth (back) to sth **VI** (*Mus*) **der Dirigent klopfte ab** the conductor stopped the orchestra (*by rapping his baton*)

ab+knab|bern VT *sep* (*inf*) to nibble off; *Knochen* to gnaw at

ab+kna|cken VI *sep* (*sl*: = *schlafen*) to crash (out) (*inf*)

ab+knal|len VT *sep* (*inf*) to shoot down (*inf*)

ab+knap|pen ['apknapn], **ab+knap|sen** VT *sep* (*inf*) **sich** (*dat*) **etw ~** to scrape together sth; **sich** (*dat*) **jeden Cent ~ müssen** to have to scrimp and save; **er hat mir 20 Euro abgeknapst** he got 20 euros off me

ab+knei|fen VT *sep irreg* to nip off; (*mit Zange auch*) to clip off

ab+kni|cken *sep* **VT** (= *abbrechen*) to break or snap off; (= *einknicken*) to break **VI** *aux sein* (= *abzweigen*) to fork or branch off; **~de Vorfahrt** traffic turning left/right has priority; **in den Knien ~** to bend at the knees

ab+knip|sen VT *sep* (*inf*) **a** (*mit Zange*) *Kabel* to snip off **b** (= *fotografieren*) to take snaps of (*inf*)

ab+knöp|fen VT *sep* **a** (= *abnehmen*) to unbutton **b** (*inf*: = *ablisten*) **jdm etw ~** to get sth off sb; **jdm Geld ~** to get money out of sb

---

ab+knut|schen VT *sep* (*inf*) to canoodle (*Brit inf*) or cuddle with; **sich ~** to canoodle (*Brit inf*), to cuddle

ab+ko|chen *sep* **VT** to boil; (= *durch Kochen keimfrei machen*) to sterilize (by boiling) **VI** to cook a meal in the open air, to have a cookout (*US*)

ab+kom|man|die|ren *ptp* **abkommandiert** VT *sep* (*Mil*) (*zu anderer Einheit*) to post; (*zu bestimmtem Dienst*) to detail (*zu* for); **jdn ins Ausland ~** to post sb abroad

Ab|kom|me ['apkɔmə] M **-n, -n** (*liter: Nachkomme*) descendant

ab+kom|men VI *sep irreg aux sein* **a** *von etw ~* (= *abweichen*) to leave sth; (= *abirren*) to wander off sth, to stray from sth; **vom Kurs ~** to deviate from one's course, to leave one's course; **(vom Thema) ~** to get off the subject, to digress; **vom rechten Weg ~** (*fig*) to stray or wander from the straight and narrow

b (= *aufgeben*) **von etw ~** to drop sth, to give sth up; *von Angewohnheit* to give sth up; *von Idee, Plan* to abandon or drop sth; **von einer Meinung ~** to revise one's opinion, to change one's mind; **von diesem alten Brauch kommt man immer mehr ab** this old custom is dying out more and more

c (*Sport*: = *wegkommen*) to get away; **schlecht/gut ~** (= *wegkommen*) to get away to a bad/good start, to make a bad/good start

d (*beim Schießen*) to aim; **wie ist sie abgekommen?** how well did she shoot?, how was her shot?

Ab|kom|men ['apkɔmən] NT **-s, -** agreement (*auch Pol*)

Ab|kom|men|schaft ['apkɔmənʃaft] F **-, *no pl*** (*liter*) descendants *pl*

ab+kömm|lich ['apkœmlɪç] ADJ available; **nicht ~ sein** to be unavailable

Ab|kömm|ling ['apkœmlɪŋ] M **-s, -e a** (= *Nachkomme*) descendant; (*fig*) adherent; **er war (der) ~ einer Bankiersfamilie** he came from a banking family **b** (*Chem*) derivative **c** **Abkömmlinge** PL (*Jur*) issue *no pl*

ab+kön|nen VT *sep irreg* (*inf*) **a** (= *trinken*) **der kann ganz schön was ab** he can knock it back (*Brit inf*), he can put it away (*inf*); **er kann nicht viel ab** he can't take much (alcohol) **b** (= *vertragen*) to bear, to stand; **er kann nichts ab** he can't take it **c** (= *mögen*) **das kann ich überhaupt nicht ab** I can't stand or abide it; **ich kann ihn einfach nicht ab** I just can't stand or abide him

ab+kop|peln *sep* **VT** (*Rail*) to uncouple; *Pferd* to untie; *Degen, Pistole* to unbuckle, to take off; *Raumfähre* to undock; *Anhänger* to unhitch **VR** (*inf*: = *sich lösen*) to sever one's ties (*von* with)

Ab|kopp|lung F (*Rail*) uncoupling; (*von Raumfähre*) undocking; (*von Anhänger*) unhitching

ab+krat|zen *sep* **VT** *Schmutz etc* to scratch off; (*mit einem Werkzeug*) to scrape off; *Wand, Gegenstand* to scratch, to scrape; **die Schuhe ~** to scrape the mud/snow *etc* off one's shoes **VI** *aux sein* (*inf*: = *sterben*) to kick the bucket (*inf*), to croak (*inf*)

Ab|krat|zer M shoe scraper

ab+krie|gen VT *sep* (*inf*) = **abbekommen**

ab+ku|cken VTI = **abgucken**

ab+küh|len *sep* **VT** to cool; *Speise auch* to cool down; (*fig*) *Freundschaft, Zuneigung* to cool; *Zorn, Leidenschaft* to cool, to calm **VI** *aux sein* to cool down; (*fig*) (*Freundschaft etc*) to cool off; (*Begeisterung*) to cool **VR** to cool down or off; (*Wetter*) to become cool(er); (*fig*) to cool; (*Beziehungen*) to become cool(er), to cool

Ab|küh|lung F cooling

Ab|kunft ['apkʊnft] F **-, *no pl*** (*liter*) descent, origin; (= *Nationalität auch*) extraction; **französischer ~ sein** to be of French descent *etc*

ab+kup|fern ['apkʊpfern] VT *sep* (*inf*) to crib (*inf*), to copy

---

ạb+kup|peln VT sep = abkoppeln

ạb+kür|zen sep VT a den Weg ~ to take a short cut b (= verkürzen) to cut short; Verfahren to shorten; Aufenthalt, Urlaub to cut short, to curtail c (= verkürzt schreiben) Namen to abbreviate; (von Vortrag) shortening, cutting short; **Kilohertz wird kHz abgekürzt** kilohertz is abbreviated to kHz, kHz is the abbreviation for kilohertz VI a (= eine Abkürzung nehmen) to take a short cut; (Weg) to be a short cut b (= verkürzt schreiben) to abbreviate, to use abbreviations

Ạb|kür|zung F a (Weg) short cut; **durch die ~ haben wir eine Stunde gespart** we've saved an hour by taking the short cut, taking the short cut has saved us an hour b (von Aufenthalt) curtailment, cutting short; (von Verfahren) shortening; (von Vortrag) shortening, cutting short; **gibt es keine ~ dieses Verfahrens?** isn't there any way of shortening this process? c (von Wort) abbreviation

Ạb|kür|zungs|ver|zeich|nis NT list of abbreviations

ạb+küs|sen VT sep to smother with kisses; **sie küssten sich stundenlang ab** they kissed away for hours

ạb+la|den sep irreg VT Last, Wagen to unload; Schutt to dump; (esp Comm) Passagiere, Ware to off-load; (fig inf) Kummer, Ärger to vent (bei jdm on sb); Verantwortung to off-load, to shove (inf) (auf +acc onto); seine Kinder/Arbeit auf jdn ~ (fig inf) to unload or dump (inf) one's children/ work on sb; **sie lud ihren ganzen Kummer bei ihrem Mann ab** (inf) she unburdened herself or all her worries on her husband VI (= entladen) to unload; **bei jdm ~** (fig inf: = Sorgen loswerden) to offload on sb

Ạb|la|de|platz M unloading area; (für Schrott, Müll etc) dump, dumping ground

Ạb|la|ge F a (= Gestell) place to put sth; (zur Aufbewahrung) place to keep sth; (= Ablagekorb) filing tray; (= Gepäckablage) luggage (Brit) or baggage (US) rack; **wir brauchen eine ~ für die Akten** we need somewhere for our files, we need somewhere where we can keep our files; **der Tisch dient als ~ für ihre Bücher** her books are kept on the table; **seine ~ benutzen** (für Akten, Bücher etc) to use sth for storage; **sie haben das Bett als ~ benutzt** they put everything on the bed; **gibt es hier irgendeine ~ für Taschen und Schirme?** is there anywhere here for bags and umbrellas or where bags and umbrellas can be left? b (= Aktenordnung) filing c (Sw) = **Annahmestelle, Zweigstelle**

Ạb|la|ge|korb M filing tray

ạb+la|gern sep VT a (= anhäufen) to deposit b (= deponieren) to leave, to store VI aux sein or haben (= ausreifen) to mature; (Holz auch) to season; **~ lassen** to allow to mature; Holz auch to (allow to) season; **abgelagert** (Wein) mature; Holz, Tabak seasoned VR to be deposited; **in einem Wasserkessel lagert sich Kalk ab** a chalk deposit builds up or forms in a kettle

Ạb|la|ge|rung F (= Vorgang) depositing, deposition; (von Wein) maturing, maturation; (von Holz) maturing, seasoning; (= abgelagerter Stoff) deposit

ạb|lan|dig ['aplandɪç] ADJ (Naut) Wind offshore

Ạb|lass ▲ ['aplas] M -es, Ạblässe ['aplɛsə] a (Eccl) indulgence b no pl (= das Ablassen) letting out; (von Dampf) letting off; (= Entleerung) drainage, draining c (= Vorrichtung)

Ạb|lass|brief ▲ M (Eccl) letter of indulgence

ạb+las|sen sep irreg VT a (= herauslaufen lassen) Wasser, Luft to let out; Motoröl to drain off; Dampf to let off; (Zug, Kessel) to give or let off; **die Luft aus den Reifen ~** to let the air out of the tyres (Brit) or tires (US), to let the tyres (Brit) or tires (US) down b (= leer laufen lassen) Teich, Schwimmbecken to drain, to empty c (= verkaufen, geben) **jdm etw ~** to let sb have

sth d (= ermäßigen) to knock off (inf); **er hat mir 20 Euro (vom Preis) abgelassen** he knocked 20 euros off (the price) for me (inf), he reduced the price by 20 euros for me e (inf) (= äußern) blöde Sprüche to make; (= abreagieren) Frust, Ärger, Aggressionen to work off, to get rid of f (inf: = nicht befestigen, anziehen) to leave off VI a (= mit etw aufhören) to desist; **von einem Vorhaben** etc ~ to abandon a plan etc b (von jdm ~ (= jdn in Ruhe lassen) to leave sb alone

Ạb|lass|han|del ▲ M (Eccl) selling of indulgences

Ạb|lass|ven|til ▲ NT outlet valve

Ạb|la|tiv ['ablatiːf, 'ap-] M -s, -e [-və] ablative (case)

Ạb|lauf M a (= Abfluss) drain; (= Ablaufstelle) outlet; (= Ablaufrohr) drain(pipe); (im Haus) waste pipe; (= Rinne) drainage channel b (= Ablaufen) draining or running away c (= Verlauf) course; (von Empfang, Staatsbesuch) order of events (+gen in); (von Verbrechen) sequence of events (+gen in); (von Handlung im Buch etc) development; **er sprach mit uns den ~ der Prüfung durch** he took us through the exam; **er hat den ~ des Unglücks geschildert** he described the way the accident happened; **der ~ der Ereignisse vollzog sich wie geplant** the course of events was as planned; **nach ~ der Vorstellung ...** after the performance (was over) ...; **es gab keinerlei Störungen im ~ des Programms** the programme (Brit) or program (US) went off without any disturbances d (von Frist etc) expiry; **nach ~ der Frist** after the deadline had passed or expired e (von Zeitraum) passing; **nach ~ von 4 Stunden** after 4 hours (have/had gone by or passed); **nach ~ des Jahres/dieser Zeit** at the end of the year/this time

Ạb|lauf|brett NT (an Spüle) draining board, drain board (US)

ạb+lau|fen sep irreg VT a (= abnützen) Schuhsohlen, Schuhe to wear out; Absätze to wear down; (dat) die Beine or Hacken or Absätze or Schuhsohlen nach etw ~ (inf) to walk one's legs off looking for sth → **Horn** a b aux sein or haben (= entlanglaufen) Strecke to go or walk over; (hin und zurück) to go or walk up and down; Stadt, Straßen, Geschäfte to comb, to scour (round) VI aux sein a (= abfließen: Flüssigkeit) to drain or run away or off; (= sich leeren: Behälter) to drain (off), to empty (itself); **aus der Badewanne ~** to run or drain out of the bath; **bei ~dem Wasser** (Naut) with an outgoing tide; **an ihm läuft alles ab** (fig) he just shrugs everything off; **jede Kritik läuft an ihm ab** (fig) with him criticism is just like water off a duck's back b (= vonstatten gehen) to go off; **wie ist das bei der Prüfung abgelaufen?** how did the exam go (off)?; **zuerst sah es sehr gefährlich aus, aber dann ist die Sache doch glimpflich abgelaufen** at first things looked pretty dangerous but it was all right in the end c (= sich abwickeln: Seil, Kabel) to wind out, to unwind; (= sich abspulen: Film, Tonband) to run; (Schallplatte) to play; **einen Film ~ lassen** to run or show a film; **ein Tonband ~ lassen** to run or play a tape; **ein Programm ~ lassen** (Comput) to run a program; **abgelaufen sein** (Film etc) to have finished, to have come to an end d (= ungültig werden: Pass, Visum etc) to expire, to run out; (= enden: Frist, Vertrag etc) to run out, to expire, to be up; **die Frist ist abgelaufen** the period has run out, the period is up e (= vergehen: Zeitraum) to pass, to go by f (Sport: = starten) to start

ạb+lau|schen VT sep (geh) to learn (+dat from); **dem Leben abgelauscht** (fig liter) taken or culled (liter) from life

Ạb|laut M (Gram) ablaut

ạb+lau|ten VI sep (Gram) to undergo ablaut, to change by ablaut

Ạb|le|ben NT , no pl (form) demise (form), decease (form)

ạb+le|cken VT sep to lick; Teller, Löffel, Finger to lick (clean); Blut, Marmelade to lick off; **sich** (dat) etw von der Hand ~ to lick sth off one's hand

ạb+le|dern ['apleːdɐn] VT sep Fenster, Auto to leather (off), to polish with a leather

ạb+le|gen sep VT a (= niederlegen) to put down; Last, Waffen to lay or put down; (Zool) Eier to lay b (= abheften) Schriftwechsel, Dokumente to file (away); (Comput) Daten to store c (= ausziehen) Hut, Mantel, Kleider to take off, to take off (form) d (= nicht mehr tragen) Anzug, Kleid to discard, to cast off; Trauerkleidung, Ehering to take off; Orden, Auszeichnungen to renounce; **abgelegte Kleider** cast-off or discarded clothes e (= aufgeben) Misstrauen, Scheu, Stolz to lose, to shed, to cast off (liter); schlechte Gewohnheit to give up, to get rid of; kindische Angewohnheit to put aside; Namen to give up f (= ableisten, machen) Schwur, Eid to swear; Gelübde to make; Zeugnis to give; Bekenntnis, Beichte, Geständnis to make; Prüfung to take, to sit; (erfolgreich) to pass g (Cards) to discard, to throw down VI a (= abfahren) (Schiff) to cast off; (Space) to separate b (Schriftwechsel ablegen) to file c (Garderobe ablegen) to take one's things off; **wenn Sie ~ möchten ...** if you would like to take your things or your hats and coats off ... d (Cards) to discard VT impers (geh: = absehen) **es auf etw** (acc) ~ to be out for sth

Ạb|le|ger ['apleːgɐ] M -s, - (Bot) layer; (fig: = Zweigunternehmen) branch, subsidiary; (iro: = Sohn) son, offspring no pl; **durch ~** by layering

ạb+leh|nen sep ✪ 35.5, 38.3, 39.3, 41 VT a (= zurückweisen, nein sagen) to decline, to refuse; Antrag, Angebot, Vorschlag, Bewerber, Stelle to turn down, to reject; (Parl) Gesetzentwurf to throw out; **es ~, etw zu tun** to decline or refuse to do sth b (= missbilligen) to disapprove of; **jede Form von Gewalt ~** to be against any form of violence VI to decline, to refuse; **drei der erfolgreichen Bewerber haben abgelehnt** three of the successful applicants have declined the job offer; **eine ~de Antwort** a negative answer; **ein ~der Bescheid** a rejection; **dankend ~** to decline with thanks

Ạb|leh|nung F -, -en a (= Zurückweisung) refusal; (von Antrag, Bewerber etc) rejection; **auf ~ stoßen** to be refused/rejected, to meet with a refusal/a rejection b (= Missbilligung) disapproval; **auf ~ stoßen** to meet with disapproval

Ạb|leh|nungs-: **Ạb|leh|nungs|an|trag** M petition or motion for rejection; **Ạb|leh|nungs|be|scheid** M notice of rejection

ạb+leis|ten VT sep (form) Zeit to complete

ạb|leit|bar ADJ a (= herleitbar) derivable, deducible; Wort derivable (aus from) b (= umleitbar) Fluss able to be diverted; Rauch, Dampf, Flüssigkeit able to be drawn off or out

ạb+lei|ten sep VT a (= herleiten) to derive; (= logisch folgern) to deduce (aus from); (Math) Gleichung to differentiate b (= umleiten) Bach, Fluss to divert; (= herausleiten) Rauch, Dampf, Flüssigkeit to draw off or out; (= ablenken) Blitz to conduct VR (= sich herleiten) to be derived (aus from); (= logisch folgen) to be deduced (aus from)

Ạb|lei|tung F a no pl (= das Herleiten) derivation; (= Folgerung) deduction; (Math: von Gleichung) differentiation; (= Umleitung: von Rauch, Dampf, Flüssigkeit) drawing off or out b (= Wort, Math) derivative

Ạb|lei|tungs|sil|be F derivative affix

ab|lenk|bar ADJ leicht ~ sein to be easily distracted

ab+len|ken sep **VT** **a** (= ab-, wegleiten) to deflect (auch Phys), to turn aside or away; Wellen, Licht to refract; Schlag to parry; Katastrophe to avert

b (= zerstreuen) to distract; **er ließ sich durch nichts ~** he wouldn't let anything distract him; **wir mussten die Kinder ~** we had to find something to take the children's minds off things; **jdn von seinem Schmerz/seinen Sorgen ~** to make sb forget his/her pain/worries, to take sb's mind off his/her pain/worries

c (= abbringen) to divert; Verdacht to avert; **jdn von der Arbeit ~** to distract sb from his/her work

VI **a** (= ausweichen) (**vom Thema**) ~ to change the subject; (bei einem Gespräch auch) to turn the conversation

b (= zerstreuen) to create a distraction; **sie geht jede Woche Schwimmen, das lenkt ab** she goes swimming every week, which takes her mind off things

VR to take one's mind off things

Ab|len|kung F **a** (= Ab-, Wegleitung) deflection (auch Phys); (von Wellen, Licht) refraction **b** (= Zerstreuung) diversion, distraction; **~ brauchen** to need something to take one's mind off things; **sich** (dat) **~ verschaffen** to provide oneself with a distraction, to provide oneself with something to take one's mind off things; **zur ~ einen Spaziergang machen** to take one's mind off things by going for a walk **c** (= Störung) distraction **d** (von Plan, jds Interesse) diversion; (von Verdacht) aversion, averting

Ab|len|kungs-: **Ab|len|kungs|kam|pag|ne** F diversion campaign; **Ab|len|kungs|ma|nö|ver** NT diversionary tactic; (Ablenkung von Thema, Problem) red herring

ab|les|bar ADJ Rede, Messgerät readable; **die Erregung war von seinem Gesicht noch deutlich ~** excitement was still written all over his face; **daraus ist ohne weiteres ~, dass ...** it can be clearly seen from this that ...; **daran ist ~, ob ...** you can tell from that whether ...

Ab|les|bar|keit F -, no pl readability

ab+le|sen VT sep irreg **a** auch vi (vom Blatt) to read; **er muss alles/seine Rede ~** he has to read everything/his speech (from notes etc); **(jdm) etw von den Lippen ~** to lip-read sth (that sb says)

b auch vi (= registrieren) Messgeräte, Barometer, Strom to read; Barometerstand to take; **nächste Woche wird abgelesen** the meter(s) will be read next week

c (= herausfinden, erkennen, folgern) to see; **jdm etw vom Gesicht or von der Stirn ~** to see or tell sth from sb's face, to read sth in sb's face; **das konnte man ihr vom Gesicht ~** it was written all over her face; **aus der Reaktion der Presse war die Stimmung im Volke deutlich abzulesen** the mood of the people could be clearly gauged or read from the press reaction; **jdm jeden Wunsch an or von den Augen ~** to anticipate sb's every wish

d (= wegnehmen) Beeren, Raupen etc to pick off (von etw sth); (= leer machen) Acker, Strauch etc to pick clean

Ab|le|ser(in) M(F) meter-reader

ab+leuch|ten sep VT etw ~ to search sth with a lamp or torch or flashlight (US); Scheinwerfer to sweep

ab+leug|nen sep **VT** Schuld, Tat to deny; Glauben to renounce **VI** **er hat weiter abgeleugnet** he continued to deny it

Ab|leug|nung F denial; (von Glauben) renunciation

ab+lich|ten VT sep (form) to photocopy; (= fotografieren) to photograph

Ab|lich|tung F (form) (= Fotokopie) photocopy; (= Fotografie) photograph

ab+lie|fern VT sep (bei einer Person) to hand over (bei to); Examensarbeit auch to hand in; (bei einer Dienststelle) to hand in (bei to); (= liefern) to deliver (bei to); (inf) Kinder, Freundin to deposit (inf); (= nach Hause bringen) to take home

Ab|lie|fe|rung F (bei einer Person) handing-over no pl; (bei einer Dienststelle) handing-in no pl; (= Lieferung) delivery

Ab|lie|fe|rungs|ter|min M delivery date

ab+lie|gen VI sep irreg (= entfernt sein) to be at a distance; (fig) to be removed; **das Haus liegt weit ab** the house is a long way off or away or is quite a distance away; **das liegt sehr weit ab von unserem Thema** that is very far removed from or is a long way from the topic we are dealing with → auch abgelegen

ab+lis|ten ['aplɪstn̩] VT sep **jdm etw ~** to trick sb out of sth; **jdm die Erlaubnis ~, etw zu tun** to trick sb into giving one permission to do sth

ab+lo|cken VT sep **jdm etw ~** to get sth out of sb; **diese Äußerung lockte ihm nur ein müdes Lächeln ab** this statement only drew a tired smile from him or got a tired smile out of him; **er lockte seiner Geige süße Töne ab** he coaxed sweet sounds from his violin

ab|lös|bar ADJ **a** (= abtrennbar) removable, detachable; **die Etiketten sind nur schwer ~** the labels are difficult to remove **b** (= ersetzbar) replaceable **c** (= tilgbar) redeemable

ab+lö|schen VT sep **a** (mit dem Löschblatt) to blot **b** (Cook) to add water to

Ab|lö|se ['apløːzə] F -, -n **a** (= Abstand) key money **b** (= Ablösungssumme) transfer fee

ab+lö|sen sep **VT** **a** (= abmachen) to take off, to remove; Etikett to detach, to take off; Pflaster etc to peel off

b (Fin) (= kapitalisieren) Rente to get paid in a lump sum; (= auszahlen) to pay (off) in a lump sum; (= tilgen) Schuld, Hypothek to pay off, to redeem

c (= ersetzen) Wache to relieve; Kollegen to take over from; **drei Minister wurden abgelöst** (euph) three ministers were relieved of their duties

d (fig: = an Stelle treten von) to take the place of; Methode, System to supersede; **Regen hat jetzt das schöne Wetter abgelöst** the fine weather has now given way to rain

VR **a** (= abgehen) to come off; (Lack etc auch) to peel off; (Netzhaut) to become detached

b (auch **einander ablösen**) to take turns; (Wachen) to relieve each other; **wir lösen uns alle drei Stunden beim Babysitten ab** we each do three-hour shifts of babysitting, we take turns at babysitting, doing three hours each

c (auch **einander ablösen**) to alternate; **bei ihr lösen sich Fröhlichkeit und Trauer ständig ab** she constantly alternates between being happy and being miserable

Ab|lö|se|sum|me F (Sport) transfer fee

Ab|lö|sung F (Fin) (von Rente) lump payment; (von Hypothek, Schuld) paying off, redemption **b** (= Wachwechsel) relieving; (= Wache) relief; (= Entlassung) replacement; **wann findet die ~ der Wache statt?** when will the guard be relieved?; **er kam als ~** he came as a replacement; **bei dieser Arbeit braucht man alle zwei Stunden eine ~** you need relieving every two hours in this work **c** (= das Ablösen) removal, detachment; (= das Sichablösen) separation; (von Lack etc) peeling off; (von Netzhaut) detachment

Ab|lö|sungs|sum|me F (Sport) transfer fee

ab+lot|sen, **ab+luch|sen** VT sep (inf) **jdm etw ~** to get or wangle sth out of sb

Ab|luft F, no pl (Tech) used air

Ab|luft-: **Ab|luft|rohr** NT air outlet; **Ab|luft|schacht** M (von Brauerei etc) ventilation shaft

ab+lut|schen VT sep to lick; **das Blut/den Honig (von etw) ~** to lick the blood/honey off (sth); **sich** (dat) **die Finger ~** to lick one's fingers (clean)

ABM [aːbeːˈʔɛm] abbr **a** von **Antiballistic Missile** ABM **b** von **Arbeitsbeschaffungsmaßnahme**

> ### ABM
>
> **ABM** is an abbreviation of **Arbeitsbeschaffungsmaßnahme**. So-called **ABM-Stellen** are jobs sponsored by the employment office, which are designed to give certain groups of people the chance to work – groups such as the over-55s, the severely disabled and the long-term unemployed in areas of high unemployment. An **ABM** is normally restricted to one year and must involve work that benefits the community. It must be a genuinely new job, so that no existing posts are filled.

ab+ma|chen VT sep **a** (inf: = entfernen) to take off; Schnur, Kette etc to undo, to take off; (= herunternehmen) to take down; **er machte dem Hund die Leine ab** he took the dog's lead (Brit) or leash off **b** (= vereinbaren) to agree (on); **wir haben abgemacht, dass wir das tun werden** we've agreed to do it, we've agreed on doing it; **es ist noch nichts abgemacht worden** nothing's been agreed (on) yet → auch abgemacht **c** (= besprechen) to sort out, to settle; **etw mit sich allein ~** to sort sth out for oneself, to come to terms with sth oneself; **etw mit seinem Gewissen ~** to square sth with one's conscience

Ab|ma|chung ['apmaxʊŋ] F, -en agreement

ab+ma|gern ['apmaːgɐn] VI sep aux sein to get thinner, to lose weight; **sehr ~** to lose a lot of weight; **er war bis zum Skelett abgemagert** he was nothing but skin and bone(s), he was a walking skeleton → auch abgemagert

Ab|ma|ge|rung F -, no pl (= Auszehrung) emaciation; (= Gewichtsverlust) slimming

Ab|ma|ge|rungs|kur F diet; **eine ~ machen** to be on a diet, to be dieting; (anfangen) to go on a diet, to diet

ab+mä|hen VT sep to mow

ab+mah|nen VT sep (form) to caution

Ab|mah|nung F (form) caution

Ab|mah|nungs|schrei|ben NT (form) formal letter of caution

ab+ma|len VT sep (= abzeichnen) to paint

ab+mark|ten ['apmarktn̩] VT sep **davon lassen wir uns** (dat) **nichts ~** we will cede nothing on this point; **er ließ sich** (dat) **seine Rechte nicht ~** he would not bargain away his rights

Ab|marsch M departure; (von Soldaten auch) march-off; (von Demonstranten etc auch) moving off; **ich sah dem ~ der Bergsteiger zu** I watched the climbers setting out or off; **zum ~ antreten** (Mil) to fall in (ready) for the march-off

ab|marsch|be|reit ADJ ready to set out or off or move off; (Mil) ready to move off or march

ab+mar|schie|ren ptp **abmarschiert** VI sep aux sein to set out or off, to move off; (Mil) to march or move off

Ab|mel|de-: **Ab|mel|de|be|stä|ti|gung** F document confirming that one has cancelled one's registration with the local authorities; **Ab|mel|de|for|mu|lar** NT form to be filled in when one cancels one's registration with the local authorities

ab+mel|den sep **VT** **a** Zeitungen etc to cancel; Telefon to have disconnected; (= von einem Klub) to cancel the membership of; **sein Auto ~** to take one's car off the road; **seinen Fernsehapparat ~** to cancel one's television licence (Brit); **ein Kind von einer Schule ~** to take a child away from a school, to remove a child from a school; **seine Familie polizeilich ~** to inform or notify the police that one's family is moving away

b (inf) **abgemeldet sein** (Sport) to be outclassed; **jd/etw ist bei jdm abgemeldet** sb has lost interest in sb/sth; **er/sie ist bei mir abgemeldet** I don't want anything to do with

him/her
VR to ask for permission to be absent; (*vor Abreise*) to say one is leaving, to announce one's departure; (*im Hotel*) to check out; **sich bei jdm ~** to tell sb that one is leaving; **sich polizeilich** *or* **bei der Polizei ~** to inform *or* notify the police that one is moving away, to cancel one's registration with the police; **sich bei einem Verein ~** to cancel one's membership of a club

Ab|mel|dung F (*von Zeitungen etc*) cancellation; (*von Telefon*) disconnection; (*beim Einwohnermeldeamt*) cancellation of one's registration; (*inf: = Formular*) **form to be filled in so that one's registration with the local authorities is cancelled seit der ~ meines Autos** since I took my car off the road; **die ~ meines Fernsehapparats** the cancellation of my television licence (*Brit*); **die ~ eines Kindes von einer Schule** the removal of a child from a school; **nach seiner ~ bei dem Verein** after he had cancelled (*Brit*) *or* canceled (*US*) his membership of the club

ab+mer|geln ['apmɛrgln] VR *sep* to slave away → *auch* **abgemergelt**

ab+mes|sen VT *sep irreg* **a** (= *ausmessen*) to measure; (= *genaue Maße feststellen von*) to measure up; (= *abschätzen*) *Verlust, Schaden* to measure; **er maß seine Schritte genau ab** (*fig*) he walked with great deliberation *or* very deliberately *or* with measured tread (*liter*) → *auch* **abgemessen** **b** (= *abteilen*) to measure off

Ab|mes|sung F *usu pl* measurement; (= *Ausmaß*) dimension

ab+mil|dern VT *sep Geschmack* to tone down; *Äußerung auch* to moderate; *Aufprall* to cushion, to soften; *Schock* to lessen

ab+mi|schen VT *sep* (*TV, Rad*) to mix

ABM-Kraft [aːbeːˈɛm-] F worker employed through a job creation scheme *or* program (*US*)

ab+mon|tie|ren *ptp* **abmontiert** VT *sep Räder, Teile* to take off (*von etw* sth); *Maschine* to dismantle

ABM-Stel|le [aːbeːˈɛm-] F temporary position (through job creation scheme)

ab+mü|hen VR *sep* to struggle (away); **sich mit jdm/etw ~** to struggle *or* slave away with sb/sth

ab+murk|sen VT *sep* (*inf*) *jdn* to bump off (*inf*), to do in (*inf*); (= *schlachten*) to kill

ab+mus|tern *sep* (*Naut*) **VT** *Besatzung* to pay off **VI** to sign off, to leave the ship

ABM-Ver|trag [aːbeːˈɛm-] M (*Pol*) ABM treaty

ab+na|beln ['apnaːbln] *sep* **VT** **ein Kind ~** to cut a baby's umbilical cord **VR** to cut oneself loose, to make the break; **sich vom Elternhaus ~** to leave the parental home, to leave the nest (*inf*); **abgenabelt vom Chef** independent of the boss

Ab|na|be|lung F -, -en (*lit*) cutting the cord; (*fig*) leaving the nest, flying the coop (*inf*)

ab+na|gen VT *sep* to gnaw off; *Knochen* to gnaw; **Fleisch vom Knochen ~** to gnaw meat off a bone

ab+nä|hen VT *sep* to take in

Ab|nä|her ['apnɛːɐ] M -s, - dart

Ab|nah|me ['apnaːmə] F -, -n **a** (= *Wegnahme*) removal; (= *Herunternahme*) taking down; (= *Amputation*) amputation; **die ~ vom Kreuz(e)** the Descent from the Cross, the Deposition (*form*) **b** (= *Verringerung*) decrease (+*gen* in); (*bei Anzahl, Menge*) drop, decrease (+*gen* in); (*von Niveau, Kräften, Energie*) decline (+*gen* in); (*von Interesse, Nachfrage*) falling off, decline; (*von Aufmerksamkeit*) falling off, flagging, waning; (= *Verlust*) loss **c** (*von Prüfung*) holding; (*von Neubau, Fahrzeug etc*) inspection; (*von TÜV*) carrying out; (*von Eid*) administering; **die ~ der Parade** the taking of the parade, the review of the troops; **die ~ der Prüfung kann erst erfolgen, wenn ...** the exam can only be held if ... **d** (*Comm*) purchase; **bei ~ von 50 Kisten** if

you/we *etc* purchase *or* take 50 crates; **keine ~ finden** to find no market; **gute ~ finden** to sell well

Ab|nah|me-: Ab|nah|me|ga|ran|tie F (*Econ*) guaranteed purchase, firm order; **Ab|nah|me|pro|to|koll** NT (*Tech*) acceptance *or* test certificate

ab|nehm|bar ADJ removable, detachable

ab+neh|men *sep irreg* **VT** **a** (= *herunternehmen*) to take off, to remove; *Hörer* to lift, to pick up; *Obst* to pick; (= *lüften*) *Hut* to raise; *Vorhang, Bild, Wäsche* to take down; *Maschen* to decrease; (= *abrasieren*) *Bart* to take *or* shave off; (= *amputieren*) to amputate; (*Cards*) *Karte* to take from the pile; **das Telefon ~** to answer the telephone **b** (= *an sich nehmen*) **jdm etw ~** to take sth from sb, to relieve sb of sth (*form*); (*fig*) *Arbeit, Sorgen* to take sth off sb's shoulders, to relieve sb of sth; **darf ich Ihnen den Mantel/die Tasche ~?** can I take your coat/bag?; **kann ich dir etwas ~?** (= *tragen*) can I take something for you?; (= *helfen*) can I do anything for you?; **jdm die Beichte ~** to hear confession from sb; **jdm einen Eid ~** to administer an oath to sb; **jdm ein Versprechen ~** to make sb promise something; **jdm einen Weg ~** to save sb a journey; **jdm eine Besorgung ~** to do some shopping for sb **c** (= *wegnehmen*) to take away (*jdm* from sb); (= *rauben, abgewinnen*) to take (*jdm off* sb); (*inf: = abverlangen*) to take (*jdm off* sb); **diese Schweine haben mir alles abgenommen** (*inf*) the bastards have taken everything (I had) (*sl*) **d** (= *begutachten*) *Gebäude, Wohnung, Auto* to inspect; (= *abhalten*) *Prüfung* to hold; *TÜV* to carry out **e** (= *abkaufen*) to take (+*dat* off), to buy (+*dat* from, off) **f** *Fingerabdrücke* to take; *Totenmaske* to make (+*dat* of) **g** (*fig inf: = glauben*) to buy (*inf*); **dieses Märchen nimmt dir keiner ab!** (*inf*) nobody will buy that tale! (*inf*) **VI** **a** (= *sich verringern*) to decrease; (*Vorräte*) to go down, to decrease; (*zahlenmäßig, mengenmäßig*) to drop, to decrease; (*Unfälle, Diebstähle etc*) to decrease (in number); (*Niveau*) to go down, to decline; (*Kräfte, Energie*) to fail, to decline; (*Fieber*) to lessen, to go down; (*Interesse, Nachfrage*) to fall off, to decline; (*Aufmerksamkeit*) to fall off, to flag, to wane; (*Mond*) to wane; (*Tage*) to grow *or* get shorter; (*beim Stricken*) to decrease; **(an Gewicht) ~** to lose weight; **in letzter Zeit hast du im Gesicht abgenommen** your face has got thinner recently **b** (*Telec*) to answer; **es hat keiner abgenommen** no-one answered

Ab|neh|mer(in) M(F) (*Comm*) buyer, purchaser, customer; **keine ~ finden** not to sell; **viele/wenige ~ finden** to sell well/badly

Ab|neh|mer|kreis M buyers *pl*, customers *pl*, market

Ab|nei|gung F dislike (*gegen* of); (= *Widerstreben*) aversion (*gegen* to)

ab+nib|beln ['apnɪbln] VI *sep aux sein* (*N Ger inf*, = *sterben*) to croak (*inf*), to kick the bucket (*inf*), to snuff it (*inf*)

ab|norm [apˈnɔrm], **ab|nor|mal** ['apnɔrmaːl, apnɔrˈmaːl] ADJ abnormal ADV abnormally

Ab|nor|ma|li|tät F abnormality

Ab|nor|mi|tät [apnɔrmiˈtɛːt] F -, -en abnormality; (= *Monstrum*) freak

ab+nö|ti|gen VT *sep* (*geh*) **jdm etw ~** to wring *or* force sth from sb; **jdm Bewunderung ~** to win *or* gain sb's admiration; **jdm Respekt ~** to gain sb's respect

ab+nut|zen, (*esp S Ger, Aus, Sw*) **ab+nüt|zen** *sep* **VT** to wear out; **dieser Begriff ist schon sehr abgenutzt worden** this idea is pretty well-worn, this idea has become hackneyed (*Brit*) → *auch* **abgenutzt VR** to wear out, to get worn out

Ab|nut|zung F , (*esp S Ger, Aus, Sw*) **Ab|nüt|zung** F -, -en wear (and tear); **die jahrelange ~ der Teppiche** the years of wear (and tear) on the carpets; **die normale ~ ist im Mietpreis berücksichtigt** general wear and tear is included in the rent

Ab|nut|zungs|er|schei|nung F sign of wear (and tear)

Ab|nut|zungs|krieg M war of attrition

A|bo ['abo] NT -s, -s (*inf*) *abbr von* **Abonnement**

A|bo|kün|di|gung F (*inf*) cancellation of subscription

A|bon|ne|ment [abɔnəˈmã, (*Sw*) abɔnəˈmɛnt, abɔnˈmãː] NT -s, -s *or* **-e** **a** (*von Zeitung, Fernsehsender*) subscription; **eine Zeitung im ~ beziehen** to subscribe to a newspaper, to have a subscription for a newspaper **b** (= *Theaterabonnement*) season ticket, subscription; **ein ~ im Theater haben** to have a season ticket *or* subscription for the theatre (*Brit*) *or* theater (*US*), to have a theatre (*Brit*) *or* theater (*US*) season ticket

A|bon|ne|ment|fern|se|hen [abɔnəˈmãː-] NT subscription television, pay TV (*inf*)

A|bon|nent [abɔˈnɛnt] M -en, -en, **A|bon|nen|tin** [-ˈnɛntɪn] F -, -nen (*von Zeitung, Fernsehsender*) subscriber; (= *Theaterabonnent*) season-ticket holder

A|bon|nen|ten-Fern|se|hen NT subscription television, pay TV (*inf*)

a|bon|nie|ren [abɔˈniːrən] *ptp* **abonniert VT** *Zeitung, Fernsehsender* to subscribe to, to have a subscription to; *Konzertreihe, Theater* to have a season ticket *or* subscription for **VI** **auf eine Zeitung/einen Fernsehsender abonniert sein** to subscribe to *or* to have a subscription to a newspaper/a TV channel; **auf eine Konzertreihe abonniert sein** to have a season ticket *or* subscription for a concert series

ab+ord|nen VT *sep* to delegate; **jdn zu einer Versammlung ~** to send sb as a delegate to a meeting

Ab|ord|nung F delegation; (= *Delegation auch*) deputation

A|bort[1] [aˈbɔrt, ˈapɔrt] M -s, -e (*dated*) lavatory, toilet

A|bort[2] [aˈbɔrt] M -s, -e, **A|bor|tus** [aˈbɔrtʊs] M -, - (= *Fehlgeburt*) miscarriage, abortion (*form*); (= *Abtreibung*) abortion

A|bo|wer|bung F (*inf*) subscription promotion

ab+pa|cken VT *sep* to pack; **ein abgepacktes Brot** a wrapped loaf

ab+pas|sen VT *sep* **a** (= *abwarten*) *Gelegenheit, Zeitpunkt* to wait for; (= *ergreifen*) to seize; **den richtigen Augenblick** *or* **Zeitpunkt ~** (= *abwarten*) to bide one's time, to wait for the right time; (= *ergreifen*) to move at the right time; **ich habe den Zeitpunkt nicht richtig abgepasst** I mistimed it; **etw gut ~** to manage *or* arrange sth well; (*zeitlich auch*) to time sth well **b** (= *auf jdn warten*) to catch; (= *jdm auflauern*) to waylay

ab+pau|sen VT *sep* to trace, to make a tracing of

ab+per|len VI *sep aux sein* to drip off (*von etw* sth); (*Tautropfen*) to fall

ab+pfei|fen *sep irreg* (*Sport*) **VI** (*Schiedsrichter*) to blow one's whistle **VT** **das Spiel/die erste Halbzeit ~** to blow the whistle for the end of the game/for half-time

Ab|pfiff M (*Sport*) final whistle; **~ zur Halbzeit** half-time whistle, whistle for half-time

ab+pflü|cken VT *sep* to pick

ab+pla|cken (*inf*), **ab+pla|gen** VR *sep* to struggle (away); **sich sein ganzes Leben lang (mit etw) ~** to slave away one's whole life (at sth)

ab+plat|ten ['applatn] VT *sep* to flatten (out)

ab+prä|gen VR *sep* (*Muster*) to leave an imprint *or* mark

Ab|prall M (*von Ball*) rebound; (*von Geschoss, Kugel*) ricochet (*von* off)

ạb+prạl|len VI *sep aux sein* (*Ball*) to bounce off; (*Kugel*) to ricochet (*off*); **von** *or* **an etw** (*dat*) ~ to bounce/ricochet off sth; **an jdm** ~ (*fig*) to make no impression on sb; (*Beleidigungen*) to bounce off sb

Ạb|prall|er ['apralɐ] M -s, - (*Sport*) rebound; **er hat den** ~ **eingeköpft** he headed it in on the rebound

ạb+prẹs|sen VT *sep* **jdm etw** ~ to wring sth from sb; *Geld* to extort sth from sb; **die Angst presste ihm den Atem ab** he could scarcely breathe for fear; **die Angst presste ihm das Herz ab** fear ate into his heart

ạb+pụm|pen VT *sep Teich, Schwimmbecken* to pump dry, to pump the water out of; *Wasser, Öl* to pump off; *Muttermilch* to express

ạb+pụt|zen *sep* VT to clean; *Schmutz* to clean off *or* up; **sich** (*dat*) **die Nase/den Mund/die Hände** ~ to wipe one's nose/mouth/hands; **sich** (*dat*) **den Hintern** ~ to wipe *or* clean one's bottom; **putz dir die Schuhe ab, bevor du ins Haus kommst** wipe your feet before you come into the house VR (*S Ger, Aus, Sw*) to clean oneself

ạb+quạ̈|len *sep* VR to struggle (away); **er quält sich immer noch mit seiner Doktorarbeit ab** he's still struggling *or* sweating away over (*inf*) his PhD VT **sich** (*dat*) **ein Lächeln** ~ to force (out) a smile; **sich** (*dat*) **eine Erklärung/Antwort** ~ to finally manage to produce an explanation/answer

ạb+quạ|li|fi|zie|ren *ptp* **ạbqualifiziert** VT *sep* to dismiss, to write off

ạb+quẹt|schen VT *sep* to crush; **sich** (*dat*) **den Arm** ~ to get one's arm crushed; **sich** (*dat*) **ein paar Tränen** ~ to force *or* squeeze out a couple of tears; **sich** (*dat*) **ein Gedicht/eine Rede** ~ to deliver oneself of a poem/speech (*iro*)

ạb+rạ|ckern VR *sep* (*inf*) to struggle; **sich für jdn** ~ to slave away for sb; **warum sollen wir uns hier** ~**?** why should we break our backs here? (*inf*); **sich im Garten** ~ to sweat away in the garden (*inf*)

Ạb|ra|ham ['a:braham] M -s Abraham; **in** ~**s Schoß** in the bosom of Abraham; **sicher wie in** ~**s Schoß** safe and secure

ạb+rạh|men VT *sep Milch* to skim

Ạb|ra|ka|dạb|ra [a:braka'da:bra, 'a:braka'da:bra] NT *no pl* (*a:*) abracadabra

ạb+ra|sie|ren *ptp* **ạbrasiert** VT *sep* to shave off

ạb+rạ|ten ✿ 29.2 VTI *sep irreg* **jdm (von) etw** ~ to advise sb against sth; **jdm davon** ~, **etw zu tun** to warn *or* advise sb against doing sth

Ạb|raum M (*Min*) overburden, overlay shelf

ạb+rạ̈u|men *sep* VT *Geschirr, Frühstück* to clear up *or* away; **den Tisch** ~ to clear the table **b** (= *entfernen*) *Sitzblockierer* to remove **c** (= *abkassieren*) *Konten* to clean out; *Preise, Medaillen* to walk off with **d** (= *stehlen*) to pinch (*inf*) **e** (*esp Min*) *Flöz, Tonnen, Deich* to clear VI **a** *den Tisch abräumen* to clear up **b** (= *sich bereichern*) to clean up

Ạb|raum|hal|de F (*Min*) slag heap

ạb+rau|schen VI *sep aux sein* (*inf*) to roar away *or* off; (*Aufmerksamkeit erregend*) to sweep away; (*aus Zimmer*) to sweep out

ạb+re|a|gie|ren *ptp* **ạbreagiert** *sep* VT *Spannung, Wut* to work off, to get rid of, to abreact (*Psych*); **seinen Ärger an anderen** ~ to take it out on others VR to work it off; **er war ganz wütend, aber jetzt hat er sich abreagiert** he was furious, but he's simmered down *or* cooled down now; **sich an der Katze** ~ to take it out on the cat

ạb+rẹch|nen *sep* VI **a** (= *Kasse machen*) to cash up; **der Kellner wollte** ~ the waiter was wanting us/them to pay our/their bill; **darf ich** ~**?** would you like to settle your bill now? **b** **mit jdm** ~ to settle up with sb; (*fig*) to settle (the

score with) sb, to get even with sb VT **a** (= *abziehen*) to deduct, to take off; (= *berücksichtigen*) to allow for, to make allowance(s) for **b** **die Kasse** ~ to cash up

Ạb|rẹch|nung F **a** (= *Aufstellung*) statement (*über +acc* for); (= *Rechnung*) bill, invoice; (= *das Kassemachen*) cashing up; (*fig: = Rache*) revenge; **wie viel mussten Sie ausgeben? – ich bin gerade dabei, die** ~ **zu machen** *or* **ich bin gerade bei der** ~ how much did you have to spend? – I'm just working it out now; **bei der** ~ **der Konten** when the accounts are/were being balanced; **er muss noch die ganzen** ~**en machen** he still has to do all the accounts *or* the bookwork; **ich habe die** ~ **gemacht** I've been doing the books; **der Tag der** ~ (*fig*) the day of reckoning

b (= *Abzug*) deduction; **nach** ~ **von** after the deduction of; **in** ~ **bringen** *or* **stellen** (*form*) to deduct; **folgende Beträge kommen in** ~ (*form*) the following sums are to be deducted

Ạb|rẹch|nungs-: Ạb|rẹch|nungs|be|leg M (*Econ*) voucher; **Ạb|rẹch|nungs|kurs** M settlement price; **Ạb|rẹch|nungs|tag** M accounting date; **Ạb|rẹch|nungs|takt** M (*Telec*) billing unit; **Ạb|rẹch|nungs|ter|min** M accounting date; **Ạb|rẹch|nungs|ver|fah|ren** NT clearing procedure; **Ạb|rẹch|nungs|ver|kehr** M clearing business; **Ạb|rẹch|nungs|zeit|raum** M accounting period

Ạb|re|de F (*form*) agreement; **etw in** ~ **stellen** to deny *or* dispute sth

ạb+re|gen VR *sep* (*inf*) to calm *or* cool *or* simmer down; **reg dich ab!** relax!, cool it! (*inf*)

ạb+rei|ben VT *sep irreg Schmutz, Rost* to clean *or* rub off; (= *säubern*) *Fenster, Schuhe* to wipe; (= *trocknen*) to rub down, to give a rubdown; (*Cook*) to grate

Ạb|rei|bung F (*Med*) rubdown; (*inf: = Prügel*) hiding, beating, thrashing

ạb+rei|chern ['apraiçɐn] VT *sep* to deplete; **abgereichertes Uran** depleted uranium

Ạb|rei|se F departure (*nach* for); **bei der** *or* **meiner** ~ when I left/leave, on my departure

ạb+rei|sen VI *sep aux sein* to leave (*nach* for); **wann reisen Sie ab?** when will you be leaving?

Ạb|rei|se-: Ạb|rei|se|tag M day of departure, departure day; **Ạb|rei|se|ter|min** M departure date

ạb+rei|ßen *sep irreg* VT **a** (= *abtrennen*) to tear *or* rip off; *Tapete* to strip off; *Plakat* to tear *or* rip down; *Pflanzen* to tear out; **er hat sich** (*dat*) **den Knopf abgerissen** he's torn his button off; **den Kontakt nicht** ~ **lassen** to stay in touch; **er wird dir nicht (gleich) den Kopf** ~ (*inf*) he won't bite your head off (*inf*)

b (= *niederreißen*) *Gebäude* to pull down, to demolish; **das Abreißen von Gebäuden** the demolition of buildings; **ein abgerissenes Gebäude** a demolished building

c (*sl: = absitzen*) *Haftstrafe* to do VI *aux sein* **a** (= *sich lösen*) to tear *or* come off; (*Schnürsenkel*) to break (off); (*fig: = unterbrochen werden*) to break off; **das reißt nicht ab** (*fig*) there is no end to it → *auch* **abgerissen**

Ạb|reiß-: Ạb|reiß|block M *pl* **-blöcke** *or* **-blocks** tear-off pad; **Ạb|reiß|ka|len|der** M tear-off calendar

ạb+rei|ten *sep irreg* VI *aux sein* to ride off *or* away VT *aux sein or haben* (= *inspizieren*) *Front* to ride along; (*hin und zurück*) to ride up and down; *Strecke* to ride over; *Gelände* to patrol (on horseback)

ạb+rẹn|nen *sep irreg* (*inf*) VT **a** *aux sein or haben Stadt, Geschäfte* to scour (around), to run around (*nach looking for*) **b** **sich** (*dat*) **die Hacken** *or* **Beine (nach etw)** ~ to run one's legs off (looking for sth) VR to run oneself off one's feet

ạb+rich|ten VT *sep* **a** (= *dressieren*) *Tier, Menschen* to train; **der Hund ist nur auf Einbrecher abgerichtet** the dog is trained to go only for

burglars; **darauf abgerichtet sein, etw zu tun** to be trained to do sth **b** (*Tech*) *Werkstück, Brett* to true off *or* up

Ạb|rich|ter(in) M(F) trainer

Ạb|rich|tung F **a** (*von Tier*) training **b** (*Tech*) truing

ạb+rie|geln ['apri:gln] VT *sep* (= *verschließen*) *Tür* to bolt; (= *absperren*) *Straße, Gebiet* to seal *or* cordon *or* block off

Ạb|rie|ge|lung F -, -en, **Ạb|rieg|lung** ['apri:gl̩n] F -, -en (*von Tür*) bolting; (*von Straße, Gebiet*) sealing *or* cordoning *or* blocking off

ạb+rịn|gen VT *sep irreg* **jdm etw** ~ to wring *or* force sth from *or* out of sb, to wrest sth from sb (*liter*); **sich** (*dat*) **ein Lächeln** ~ to force a smile; **sich** (*dat*) **eine Entscheidung** ~ to force oneself into (making) a decision; **sich** (*dat*) **ein paar Worte** ~ to manage to produce a few words; **dem Meer Land** ~ (*liter*) to wrest land away from the sea (*liter*)

Ạb|riss ▲ M **a** (= *Abbruch*) demolition **b** (= *Übersicht*) outline, summary **c** (*von Eintrittskarte etc*) tear-off part

Ạb|riss-: Ạb|riss|ar|bei|ten ▲ PL demolition work; **Ạb|riss|bir|ne** ▲ F wrecking ball; **Ạb|riss|lis|te** ▲ F (*inf*) demolition list; **auf der** ~ **stehen** to be condemned; **ạbriss|reif** ▲ ADJ only fit for demolition; (= *zum Abriss freigegeben*) condemned

ạb+rọl|len *sep* VT *Papier, Stoff* to unroll; *Film, Bindfaden* to unwind, to unreel; *Kabel, Tau* to uncoil, to unwind

VI *aux sein* **a** (*Papier, Stoff*) to unroll, to come unrolled; (*Film, Bindfaden*) to unwind, to come unwound; (*Kabel, Tau*) to uncoil, to come uncoiled

b (*Sport*) to roll

c (= *abfahren*) *Züge, Waggons* to roll off *or* away; (*Flugzeug*) to taxi off

d (*inf*) (= *vonstatten gehen*) (*Programm*) to run; (*Veranstaltung*) to go off; (*Ereignisse*) to unfold; **etw rollt vor jds Augen ab** sth unfolds *or* unfurls before sb's (very) eyes; **mein ganzes Leben rollte noch einmal vor meinen Augen ab** my whole life passed before me again

VR (*Papier, Stoff*) to unroll itself, to come unrolled; (*Film, Bindfaden*) to unwind itself, to come unwound; (*Kabel, Tau*) to uncoil itself, to come uncoiled

ạb+rụb|beln ['aprʊbln] *sep* VT **a** (= *entfernen*) to rub off; *Rubbelkarte* to scratch off; **etw von etw** ~ to rub sth off sth **b** (= *frottieren*) to rub down VR to rub oneself down

ạb+rụ̈|cken *sep* VT **a** (= *wegschieben*) to move away; **etw von der Wand** ~ to move sth away from *or* out from the wall VI *aux sein* **a** (= *wegrücken*) to move away; (*fig: = sich distanzieren*) to dissociate oneself (*von* from) **b** (= *abmarschieren*) to move out

Ạb|ruf M **a** **sich auf** ~ **bereithalten** to be ready to be called (for); **Ihr Wagen steht jederzeit auf** ~ **bereit** your car will be ready at any time; **auf** ~ **zur Verfügung stehen** to be available on call **b** (*Comm*) **etw auf** ~ **bestellen/kaufen** to order/buy sth (to be delivered) on call **c** (*Comput*) retrieval; **auf** ~ **bereit** readily retrievable; **der Computer hat diese Daten auf** ~ **bereit** this data is readily retrievable *or* can readily be called up from the computer

Ạb|ruf-: ạb|ruf|bar ADJ **a** (*Comput*) *Daten* retrievable **b** (*Fin*) ready on call **c** (*fig*) accessible; **Ạb|ruf|bar|keit** F -, *no pl* retrievability; **ạb|ruf|be|reit** ADJ **a** *Mensch* ready to be called (for); (= *einsatzbereit*) ready (and waiting); (= *abholbereit*) ready to be called for **b** (*Comm, Fin*) ready on call **c** (*Comput*) *Daten* ready to be called up *or* retrieved

ạb+ru|fen VT *sep irreg* **a** (= *wegrufen*) to call away; **jdn aus dem Leben** ~ (*euph*) to gather sb to his fathers (*euph*) **b** (*Comm*) to request delivery of; (*Fin: = abheben*) to withdraw; staatliche

Zuschüsse to call **c** _Daten, Informationen_ to call up, to retrieve

ab+run|den VT _sep_ (_lit, fig_) to round off; **eine Zahl nach oben/unten ~** to round a number up/down; **wir haben die Summe abgerundet** we made it a round sum, we rounded it up/down; **EUR 13,12, also abgerundet EUR 13,10** 13 euros 12, so call it 13 euros 10; **die abgerundete, endgültige Form einer Sonate/eines Gedichts** the final polished or rounded form of a sonata/poem

Ab|run|dung F (_lit, fig_) rounding off; **zur ~ von etw** to round sth off

ab+rup|fen VT _sep Gras, Blumen_ to rip or pull up; _Laub_ to strip off; _Blätter_ to pull or strip off

ab|rupt [ap'rʊpt, a'brʊpt] ADJ abrupt ADV abruptly

Ab|rupt|heit F -, _no pl_ abruptness

ab+rüs|ten _sep_ VI **a** (_Mil, Pol_) to disarm **b** (_Build_) to take down or remove the scaffolding VT **a** (_Mil, Pol_) to disarm **b** _Gebäude_ to take down or remove the scaffolding from or on

Ab|rüs|tung F , _no pl_ **a** (_Mil, Pol_) disarmament **b** (_Build_) removal of the scaffolding

Ab|rüs|tungs-: **Ab|rüs|tungs|ab|kom|men** NT disarmament treaty; **Ab|rüs|tungs|ge|sprä|che** PL disarmament talks _pl_; **Ab|rüs|tungs|kon|fe|renz** F disarmament conference

ab+rut|schen VI _sep aux sein_ (= _abgleiten_) to slip; (_nach unten_) to slip down; (_Wagen_) to skid; (_Aviat_) to sideslip; (_fig_) (_Mannschaft, Schüler_) to drop (down) (_auf +acc_ to); (_Leistungen_) to drop off, to go downhill; (_moralisch_) to let oneself go, to go downhill

ABS [a:be:'ɛs] NT -, _no pl_ (_Aut_) _abbr von_ **Antiblockiersystem** ABS

Abs. _abbr von_ **Absatz** _von_ **Absender**

ab+sä|beln VT _sep_ (_inf_) to hack or chop off

ab+sa|cken VI _sep aux sein_ (= _sinken_) to sink; (_Boden, Gebäude auch_) to subside; (_Flugzeug, Blutdruck_) to drop, to fall; (_fig inf_: = _nachlassen_) to fall or drop off; (_Schüler_) to go down; (= _verkommen_) to go to pot (_inf_); **sie ist in ihren Leistungen sehr abgesackt** her performance has dropped off a lot

Ab|sa|ge F refusal; (_auf Einladung auch_) negative reply; **das ist eine ~ an die Demokratie** that's a denial of democracy; **jdm/einer Sache eine ~ erteilen** to reject sb/sth

ab+sa|gen _sep_ VT (= _rückgängig machen_) _Veranstaltung, Besuch_ to cancel, to call off; (= _ablehnen_) _Einladung_ to decline, to turn down, to refuse; **er hat seine Teilnahme abgesagt** he decided to withdraw his participation VI to cry off (_Brit_), to cancel; **jdm ~** to tell sb that one can't come; **wenn ich ihn einlade, sagt er jedes Mal ab** whenever I invite him he says no

ab+sä|gen VT _sep_ **a** (= _abtrennen_) to saw off **b** (_fig inf_) to chuck or sling out (_inf_); _Minister, Beamten_ to oust; _Schüler_ to make fail

Ab|sah|ne ['apza:nə] F -, _no pl_ (_inf_) bonanza

ab+sah|nen ['apza:nən] _sep_ VT _Milch_ to skim; (_fig inf_) _Geld_ to rake in; (= _sich verschaffen_) to cream off; _das Beste_ to take; **den Markt ~** to take the cream, to take the pick of the bunch VI to skim milk; (_fig inf_) to take the best; (_in Bezug auf Menschen_) to take the cream or the best; (_in Bezug auf Geld_) to clean up (_inf_)

ab+sat|teln VTI _sep_ to unsaddle

Ab|satz M **a** (= _Abschnitt_) paragraph; (_Typ_) indention; (_Jur_) section; **einen ~ machen** to start a new paragraph/to indent **b** (= _Treppenabsatz_) half landing; (= _Mauerabsatz_) overhang; (_herausragend_) ledge **c** (= _Schuhabsatz_) heel; **spitze Absätze** stilettos, stiletto heels; **sich auf dem ~ (her)umdrehen, auf dem ~ kehrtmachen** to turn on one's heel **d** (= _Verkauf_) sales _pl_; **um den/unseren ~ zu steigern** to increase sales/our sales; **~ finden** or **haben** to sell; **guten/begeis-**

Ab|satz-: **Ab|satz|chan|ce** F sales potential _no pl_; **ab|satz|fä|hig** ADJ marketable, saleable; **Ab|satz|flau|te** F slump in sales, slump in the market; **Ab|satz|för|de|rung** F sales promotion; **Ab|satz|for|schung** F sales research; **Ab|satz|ga|ran|tie** F guaranteed sales _pl_; **Ab|satz|ge|biet** NT sales area; **Ab|satz|ge|nos|sen|schaft** F marketing cooperative; **Ab|satz|kri|se** F sales crisis; **Ab|satz|la|ge** F sales situation; **Ab|satz|land** NT customer, buyer; **Ab|satz|markt** M market; **Ab|satz|pla|nung** F sales planning; **Ab|satz|rück|gang** M decline or decrease in sales; **Ab|satz|schwie|rig|kei|ten** PL sales problems _pl_; **auf ~ stoßen** to meet with sales resistance; **Ab|satz|stei|ge|rung** F increase in sales, sales increase; **Ab|satz|stra|te|gie** F sales strategy

ab|satz|wei|se ADJ in paragraphs ADV paragraph by paragraph

ab+sau|fen VI _sep irreg aux sein_ (_sl_: = _ertrinken_) to drown; (_inf_: _Motor, Min_: _Grube_) to flood; (_sl_: _Schiff etc_) to go down

ab+sau|gen VT _sep Flüssigkeit, Gas, Staub_ to suck out or off; (_mit Staubsauger_) to hoover® (_Brit_) or vacuum up; _Teppich, Sofa_ to hoover® (_Brit_), to vacuum

ABS- [a:be:'ɛs-]: **ABS-Brem|se** F ABS brakes _pl_; **ABS-Brems|sys|tem** NT ABS braking system

ab+scha|ben VT _sep_ to scrape off; (= _säubern_) to scrape (clean); _Stoff_ to wear thin → _auch_ **abgeschabt**

ab+schaf|fen _sep_ VT **a** (= _außer Kraft setzen_) _Gesetz, Regelung_ to abolish, to do away with **b** (= _nicht länger halten_) to get rid of; _Auto etc_ to give up VR (_S Ger inf_: = _sich abarbeiten_) to slave away (_inf_), to work like a slave

Ab|schaf|fung F **a** (_von Gesetz, Regelung_) abolition **b** (= _Loswerden_) getting rid of; (_von Auto etc_) giving up

ab+schä|len _sep_ VT _Haut, Rinde_ to peel off; _Baumstamm_ to strip; **die Rinde eines Baumes ~** to strip or peel the bark off a tree VR to peel off

Ab|schalt|au|to|ma|tik F automatic shutoff

ab+schal|ten _sep_ VT to switch off; _Kontakt_ to break VI (_fig_) to unwind VR to switch itself off

Ab|schal|tung F switching off; (_von Kontakt_) breaking

ab+schat|ten ['apʃatn], **ab+schat|tie|ren** _ptp_ **abschattiert** VT _sep_ (_lit_) to shade; (_fig_) to give a slight nuance to

Ab|schat|tung F -, -en, **Ab|schat|tie|rung** F (_lit_) shading; (_fig_) nuance

ab+schät|zen VT _sep_ to estimate, to assess; _Menschen, Fähigkeiten_ to assess, to appraise; **seine Lage ~** to take stock of one's position, to assess one's position; **ein ~der Blick** an appraising look; **jdn mit einer ~den Miene betrachten** to look at sb appraisingly

ab|schät|zig ['apʃɛtsɪç] ADJ disparaging; _Bemerkung auch_ derogatory ADV disparagingly; **sich über jdn äußern** to make disparaging or derogatory remarks about sb

Ab|schaum M , _no pl_ scum; **der ~ der Menschheit, der ~ der menschlichen Gesellschaft** the scum of the earth

ab+schei|den _sep irreg_ VT (= _ausscheiden_) to give off, to produce; (_Biol_) to secrete; (_Chem_) to precipitate VR (_Flüssigkeit etc_) to be given off, to be produced; (_Biol auch_) to be secreted; (_Chem_) to be precipitated VI _aux sein_ (_euph liter_: = _sterben_) to depart this life (_liter_), to pass away; **sein Abscheiden** his passing → _auch_ **abgeschieden**

Ab|schei|der ['apʃaɪdɐ] M -s, - (_für Öl, Metall_) separator

ab+sche|ren VT _sep Haare, Wolle_ to shear off; _Bart_ to shave off; _Kopf, Kinn_ to shave

Ab|scheu M -(e)s or f -, _no pl_ repugnance, repulsion, abhorrence (_vor +dat_ at); **vor jdm/etw ~ haben** or **empfinden** to loathe or detest or abhor sb/sth; **~ in jdm erregen** to repulse sb

ab+scheu|ern _sep_ VT **a** (= _reinigen_) _Fußboden, Wand_ to scrub (down) **b** (= _abschürfen_) _Haut_ to rub or scrape off **c** (= _abwetzen_) _Kleidung, Stoff_ to rub or wear thin; **ein abgescheuerter Kragen** a worn collar VR (_Stoff_) to wear thin; (_Tierfell_) to get rubbed or scraped off

ab|scheu|er|re|gend ADJ repulsive, loathsome, abhorrent

ab|scheu|lich [ap'ʃɔylɪç] ADJ abominable, atrocious, loathsome; _Verbrechen auch_ heinous; _Anblick auch_ repulsive; (_inf_) awful, terrible (_inf_); **wie ~!** how ghastly or awful or terrible! ADV _behandeln, zurichten_ atrociously, abominably; _sich anziehen_ terribly, awfully; **es ist ~ kalt** it's hideously cold; **~ riechen/schmecken** to smell/taste horrible, to be ~; **es tut ~ weh** it hurts terribly

Ab|scheu|lich|keit F -, -en **a** (= _Untat_) atrocity, abomination **b** _no pl_ heinousness; (_von Geschmack, Anblick_) repulsiveness; **die ~ des Kantinenessens** the awful or terrible food in the canteen; **ein Verbrechen von besonderer ~** a particularly heinous crime

ab+schi|cken VT _sep_ to send; _Paket, Brief_ to send off, to dispatch; (_mit der Post_) to send, to post (_Brit_), to mail (_esp US_)

Ab|schie|be|haft F (_Jur_) remand pending deportation; **jdn in ~ nehmen** to put sb on remand pending deportation

ab+schie|ben _sep irreg_ VT **a** (= _ausweisen_) _Ausländer, Häftling_ to deport **b** (_inf_: = _loswerden_) to get rid of; **jdn in eine andere Abteilung ~** to shunt sb off to another department **c** (= _wegschieben_) _Schrank etc_ to push out or away (_von_ from); (_fig_) _Verantwortung, Schuld_ to push or shift (_auf +acc_ onto); **er versucht immer, die Verantwortung auf andere abzuschieben** he always tries to pass the buck

Ab|schie|bung F (= _Ausweisung_) deportation

Ab|schied ['apʃi:t] M -(e)s, (_rare_) -e [-də] **a** (= _Trennung_) farewell, parting; **von jdm/etw ~ nehmen** to say goodbye to sb/sth, to take one's leave of sb/sth; **ein Kuss zum ~** a farewell or goodbye kiss; **zum ~ überreichte er ihr einen Blumenstrauß** on parting, he presented her with a bunch of flowers; **ein trauriger ~** a sad farewell; **es war für beide ein schwerer ~** parting was hard for both of them; **ich hasse ~e** I hate farewells or goodbyes; **es war ein ~ für immer** or **fürs Leben** it was goodbye for ever; **beim ~ meinte er, ...** as he was leaving he said ...; **beim ~ auf Bahnhöfen ...** saying goodbye at stations ...; **der ~ von der Heimat fiel ihm schwer** it was hard for him to say goodbye to the land of his birth; **ihr ~ von der Bühne/vom Film** her farewell to the stage/to films; (= _letzte Vorstellung_) her farewell performance; **ihre Heirat bedeutete für sie den ~ von der Kindheit** her marriage marked the end of her childhood; **der ~ von der Vergangenheit** breaking or the break with the past **b** (= _Rücktritt_) (_von Beamten_) resignation; (_von Offizieren_) discharge; **seinen ~ nehmen** or **einreichen** to hand in or tender one's resignation; (_Offizier_) to apply for a discharge; **seinen ~ erhalten** or **bekommen** to be dismissed; (_Offizier_) to be discharged

Ab|schieds- _in cpds_ farewell; **Ab|schieds|be|such** M farewell or goodbye visit; **Ab|schieds|brief** M letter of farewell, farewell letter; **Ab|schieds|fei|er** F farewell or going-away or leaving party; **Ab|schieds|ge|schenk** NT (_für Kollegen etc_) leaving present; (_für Freund_) going-away present; **Ab|schieds|ge|such** NT (_Pol_) letter of resignation; **sein ~ einreichen** to tender one's resignation; **Ab|schieds|gruß** M farewell; (= _Wort zum Abschied_) word of farewell; **Ab|schieds|kon|zert** NT farewell concert;

Ab|schieds|kuss ▲ M farewell or parting or goodbye kiss; **Ab|schieds|re|de** F farewell speech, valedictory (speech) (form); **Ab|schieds|schmerz** M pain of parting; **Ab|schieds|spiel** NT (Sport) testimonial (match); **Ab|schieds|stim|mung** F mood of parting or farewell; **Ab|schieds|stun|de** F time or hour of parting, time to say goodbye; **Ab|schieds|sze|ne** F farewell scene; **Ab|schieds|trä|ne** F tear at parting

Ab|schieds|vor|stel|lung F (Theat) farewell or final performance

ab+schie|ßen sep irreg **VT** **a** (= losschießen) Geschoss, Gewehr, Kanone to fire; Pfeil to shoot (off), to loose off; Rakete to launch; (auf ein Ziel) to fire; (fig) Fragen, Befehle, Bemerkung to fire (auf +acc at) **b** (= außer Gefecht setzen) Flugzeug, Pilot to shoot down; (= wegschießen) Bein etc to shoot off **c** (= totschießen) Wild to shoot; (inf) Menschen to shoot down → **Vogel** **d** (fig inf: = loswerden) to get rid of **VI** (Sport) to kick off

ab+schil|fern ['apʃɪlfɐn] VI sep aux sein to peel off

ab+schin|den VR sep irreg (inf) to knacker oneself (Brit inf), to tire oneself out; (= schwer arbeiten) to work one's fingers to the bone; **sich mit Gartenarbeit/einem schweren Koffer ~** to knacker oneself (Brit sl) or to tire oneself out gardening/carrying a heavy suitcase

Ab|schirm|dienst M (Mil) counterespionage service

ab+schir|men ['apʃɪrmən] sep **VT** to shield; (= schützen auch) to protect; (vor Licht auch) to screen; Lampe to cover; **jdn vor etw** (dat) **~** to shield or protect sb from sth; **etw gegen die Sonne ~** to screen or shield sth from the sun **VR** to shield oneself (gegen from); (= sich schützen) to protect oneself (gegen from or against); (= sich isolieren) to isolate oneself, to cut oneself off (gegen from)

Ab|schir|mung F -, -en **a** (= das Abschirmen) shielding; (= Schutz) protection; (vor Licht) screening; (von Lampe) covering **b** (fig) (= Selbstschutz, auch Pol) protection; (= Isolierung) isolation

ab+schir|ren ['apʃɪrən] VT sep to unharness; Ochsen to unyoke

ab+schlach|ten VT sep to slaughter; Menschen auch to butcher

Ab|schlach|tung F slaughter; (von Menschen auch) butchering no pl

ab+schlaf|fen ['apʃlafn] sep (inf) VI aux sein to flag → **auch abschlafft VT** to whack (inf)

Ab|schlag M **a** (= Preisnachlass) reduction; (= Abzug) deduction **b** (= Zahlung) part payment (auf +acc of) **c** (Ftbl) kickout, punt; (Hockey) bully(-off); (Golf) tee-off; (= Abschlagfläche) tee **d** (= Abholzung) felling

ab+schla|gen ✪ 30 VT sep irreg **a** (mit Hammer etc) to knock off; (mit Schwert etc) Fuß, Kopf, Hand to cut off; (mit Beil) to cut or chop off; (= herunterschlagen) to knock down **b** Gerüst etc to take down **c** (= ablehnen) to refuse; Einladung, Bitte to refuse, to turn down; **jdm etw ~** to refuse sb sth; **sie/er kann niemandem etwas ~** she/he can never refuse anybody anything **d** auch vi (Ftbl) to punt; (Hockey) to bully off; (Golf) to tee off **e** **sein Wasser ~** (dated inf) to relieve oneself → **abgeschlagen**

ab|schlä|gig ['apʃlɛːgɪç] ADJ negative; **~er Bescheid** rejection; (bei Sozialamt, Kredit etc) refusal **ADV** **jdn/etw ~ bescheiden** (form) to reject sb/sth, to turn sb/sth down

Ab|schlag(s)|zah|lung F part payment

ab|schle|cken VT sep (S Ger, Aus) = **ablecken**

ab+schlei|fen sep irreg **VT** Kanten, Ecken, Unebenheiten to grind down; Rost to polish off; Messer to grind; Holz, Holzboden to sand (down) **VR** to get worn off, to wear down; (fig) (Angewohnheit etc) to wear off; **das schleift sich (noch) ab** (fig) that'll wear off

Ab|schlepp|dienst M breakdown service, (vehicle) recovery service

ab+schlep|pen sep **VT** **a** (= wegziehen) to drag or haul off or away; Fahrzeug, Schiff to tow, to take in tow; (Behörde) to tow away **b** (inf) Menschen to drag along; (= sich aneignen) to get one's hands on (inf); (= aufgabeln) to pick up (inf) **VR** **sich mit etw ~** (inf) to struggle with sth

Ab|schlepp-: **Ab|schlepp|fahr|zeug** NT breakdown or recovery vehicle; **Ab|schlepp|kos|ten** PL recovery costs pl; **Ab|schlepp|öse** F tow loop; **Ab|schlepp|seil** NT towrope; **Ab|schlepp|stan|ge** F towbar; **Ab|schlepp|wa|gen** M breakdown truck or lorry (Brit), tow truck (US), wrecker (US)

ab|schließ|bar ADJ (= verschließbar) lockable

ab+schlie|ßen sep irreg **VT** **a** (= zuschließen) to lock; Auto, Raum, Schrank to lock (up); **etw luftdicht ~** to put an airtight seal on sth **b** (= beenden) Sitzung, Vortrag etc to conclude, to bring to a close; (mit Verzierung) to finish off; Kursus to complete; **sein Studium ~** to take one's degree, to graduate; **mit abgeschlossenem Studium** with a degree **c** (= vereinbaren) Geschäft to conclude, to transact; Versicherung to take out; Wette to place; **einen Vertrag ~** (Pol) to conclude a treaty; (Jur, Comm) to conclude a contract **d** (Comm: = abrechnen) Bücher to balance; Konto to settle, to balance; Geschäftsjahr to close; Inventur to complete; Rechnung to make up **VR** (= sich isolieren) to cut oneself off, to shut oneself away; **sich von der Außenwelt ~** to cut or shut oneself off from the outside world → **auch abgeschlossen** **VI** **a** (= zuschließen) to lock up; **sieh mal nach, ob auch abgeschlossen ist** will you see if everything's locked? **b** (= enden) to close, to come to a close, to conclude; (mit Verzierung) to be finished off **c** (Comm) (= Vertrag schließen) to conclude the deal; (= Endabrechnung machen) to do the books **d** (= Schluss machen) to finish, to end; **mit allem/dem Leben ~** to finish with everything/life; **mit der Vergangenheit ~** to break with the past

ab|schlie|ßend ADJ concluding **ADV** in conclusion, finally

Ab|schluss ▲ M **a** (= Beendigung) end; (von Untersuchung) conclusion; (inf: = Abschlussprüfung) final examination; (Univ) degree; **zum ~ von etw** at the close or end of sth; **zum ~ möchte ich ...** finally or to conclude I would like ...; **seinen ~ finden** (geh) **zum ~ kommen** to come to an end; **etw zum ~ bringen** to finish sth; **ein Wort zum ~** a final word; **kurz vor dem ~ stehen** to be in the final stages; **seinen ~ machen** (Univ) to do one's final exams; **nach ~ des Studiums/der Lehre** after finishing university/one's apprenticeship; **sie hat die Universität ohne ~ verlassen** she left the university without taking her degree → **krönen** **b** no pl (= Vereinbarung) conclusion; (von Wette) placing; (von Versicherung) taking out; **bei ~ des Vertrages** on conclusion of the contract **c** (Comm: = Geschäft) business deal; **zum ~ kommen** to make a deal **d** no pl (Comm) (der Bücher) balancing; (von Konto) settlement; (von Geschäftsjahr) close; (von Inventur) completion **e** (= Rand, abschließender Teil) border

Ab|schluss-: **Ab|schluss|ball** ▲ M (von Tanzkurs) final ball; **Ab|schluss|bi|lanz** ▲ F (Econ) final or closing balance (sheet); **Ab|schluss|fei|er** F (Sch) speech or prize-giving day; **Ab|schluss|klas|se** ▲ F (Sch) final class or year; **Ab|schluss|kom|mu|ni|kee** ▲ NT , **Ab|schluss|kom|mu|ni|qué** ▲ NT final communiqué; **Ab|schluss|prü|fung** ▲ F (Sch) final examination; (Univ) finals pl (Brit), final exam **b** (Comm) audit; **Ab|schluss|rech|nung** ▲ F final account; **Ab|schluss|zeug|nis** ▲ NT (Sch) leaving certificate (Brit), diploma (US)

ab+schmäl|zen ['apʃmɛltsn], (Aus) **ab+schmal|zen** VT sep to gratinate

ab+schmat|zen VT sep (inf) to slobber over (inf)

ab+schme|cken sep **VT** (= kosten) to taste, to sample; (= würzen) to season **VI** (= kosten) to taste; (= nachwürzen) to add some seasoning

ab+schmei|cheln VT sep **jdm etw ~** to wheedle or coax sth out of sb

ab+schmel|zen sep irreg **VT** Eis to melt; (fig: = reduzieren) Zulagen, Stellen, Kapital to reduce **VI** aux sein (Polkappe, Eis, Eisberg) to melt; (fig: Überschuss, Umsatz, Gewinne etc) to melt away

ab+schmet|tern VT sep (inf) (Sport) to smash; (fig: = zurückweisen) to throw out; **mit seinem Antrag wurde er abgeschmettert** his application was thrown or flung out; **er wurde abgeschmettert** he was shot down (inf)

ab+schmie|ren sep **VT** **a** (Tech) Auto to grease, to lubricate **b** (inf: = abschreiben) to copy, to crib (Brit inf) **VI** aux sein (Aviat) to go down

Ab|schmier|pres|se F grease gun

ab+schmin|ken sep **VT** **a** Gesicht, Haut to remove the make-up from **b** (inf: = aufgeben) **sich** (dat) **etw ~** to get sth out of one's head **VR** to take off or remove one's make-up

ab+schmir|geln VT sep to sand down

ab+schmü|cken VT sep **den Weihnachtsbaum ~** to take the decorations down from the Christmas tree

Abschn. abbr von **Abschnitt** para

ab+schna|cken VT sep (N Ger inf) **jdm etw ~** to wheedle or coax sth out of sb

ab+schnal|len sep **VT** to unfasten, to undo **VR** to unfasten one's seat belt **VI** (sl: = nicht mehr folgen können) to give up

ab+schnei|den sep irreg **VT** to cut off; Flucht auch to block off; Blumen, Scheibe to cut (off); Zigarre to cut the end off; Haar to cut; Rock, Kleid to cut the seam off; **jdm die Rede** or **das Wort ~** to cut sb short → **Scheibe b** **VI** **bei etw gut/schlecht ~** (inf) to come off well/badly in sth

ab+schnip|peln VT sep (inf) **etw von etw ~** to cut a bit off sth; (mit Schere auch) to snip sth off sth

Ab|schnitt M **a** section; (Math) segment; (Mil) sector, zone; (= Geschichtsabschnitt, Zeitabschnitt) period **b** (= Kontrollabschnitt) (von Scheck etc) counterfoil; (von Karte) section; (von Papier) slip

ab|schnitt(s)|wei|se ADV in sections; **der Lehrer nahm das Buch ~ durch** the teacher went through the book section by section **ADJ** sectionalized

ab+schnü|ren VT sep to cut off (von from); (Med) Glied to put a tourniquet on; **jdm das Blut ~** to cut off sb's circulation; **jdm die Luft ~** (lit) to stop sb breathing; (fig) to bankrupt or ruin sb; **die Angst schnürte ihr das Herz ab** (liter) she was paralyzed by fear

ab+schöp|fen VT sep to skim off; (fig) Dank, Ruhm to reap; Kaufkraft to absorb; (= für sich gewinnen) to cream off; **den Rahm** or **das Fett ~** (fig) to cream off the best part; **den Gewinn ~** to siphon off the profits

Ab|schöp|fung F (Fin: von Kaufkraft) absorption; **sparen Sie durch ~** save by automatic transfer

ab+schot|ten ['apʃɔtn] VT sep (Naut) to separate with a bulkhead, to bulkhead off; **sich gegen etw ~** (fig) to cut oneself off from sth; **etw ~** to shield or screen sth

ab+schrä|gen VT sep to slope; Holz, Brett to bevel; **ein abgeschrägtes Dach** a sloping roof; **er schrägte das Brett an den Kanten ab** he bevelled (Brit) or beveled (US) the edges of the board

Ab|schrä|gung F -, -en slope; (von Brett) bevel

ab+schrau|ben VT sep to unscrew

Deutsche Rechtschreibreform (siehe Anhang): ▲ neue Schreibung △ alte Schreibung | + trennbare Verben

ạb+schre|cken sep **VT** **a** (= fern halten) to deter, to put off; (= verjagen: Hund, Vogelscheuche) to scare off; **jdn von etw ~** to deter sb from sth, to put sb off sth; **ich lasse mich dadurch nicht ~** that won't deter me, I won't be deterred by that **b** (= abkühlen) Stahl to quench; (Cook) to rinse with cold water **VI** (Strafe) to act as a deterrent

ạb+schre|ckend ADJ **a** (= warnend) deterrent; **ein ~es Beispiel** a warning; **eine ~e Wirkung haben**, **~ wirken** to act as a deterrent **b** (= abstoßend) Hässlichkeit repulsive

Ạb|schre|ckung ['apʃrɛkʊŋ] F **-**, **-en** **a** (= das Fernhalten, Mil) deterrence; (= das Verjagen) scaring off; (= Abschreckungsmittel) deterrent **b** (= Abkühlung) (von Stahl) quenching; (Cook) rinsing with cold water

Ạb|schre|ckungs-: **Ạb|schre|ckungs|maß|nah|me** F deterrent; **Ạb|schre|ckungs|mit|tel** NT deterrent; **Ạb|schre|ckungs|po|li|tik** F (Mil) policy of deterrence; **Ạb|schre|ckungs|stra|te|gie** F (Mil) strategy of deterrence; **Ạb|schre|ckungs|theo|rie** F (Jur) theory of deterrence; **Ạb|schre|ckungs|waf|fe** F deterrent weapon

ạb+schrei|ben sep irreg **VT** **a** (= kopieren) to copy out; (Sch: = abgucken) to copy, to crib (Brit inf); (= plagiieren) to copy (bei, von from) **b** (= schreibend abnutzen) to use up → **Finger** **c** (Comm) (= absetzen, abziehen) to deduct; (= im Wert mindern) to depreciate **d** (= verloren geben) to write off; **er ist bei mir abgeschrieben** I'm through or finished with him **VI** **a** (Sch) to copy, to crib (Brit inf) **b** **jdm ~** to write to sb to tell him that one cannot come etc **VR** (Bleistift, Farbband) to get used up

Ạb|schrei|ber(in) M(F) (pej) plagiarist; (Sch) cribber (Brit inf), cheat

Ạb|schrei|bung F (= Steuerabschreibung) tax write-off; (Comm) deduction; (= Wertverminderung) depreciation

Ạb|schrei|bungs-: **Ạb|schrei|bungs|be|trag** M (Econ) depreciation (allowance); **Ạb|schrei|bungs|be|trug** M tax deduction fraud; **Ạb|schrei|bungs|fonds** M depreciation fund; **Ạb|schrei|bungs|objekt** NT tax-deductible item; **Ạb|schrei|bungs|pro|jekt** NT tax avoidance scheme

ạb+schrei|ten VT sep irreg **a** (= entlanggehen) to walk along; (hin und zurück) to walk up and down; Gelände to patrol; (= inspizieren) Front to inspect **b** (= messen) to pace out

Ạb|schrift F copy

ạb+schröp|fen VT sep jdm etw ~ (inf) to wangle sth out of sb (inf)

ạb+schrub|ben VT sep (inf) Schmutz to scrub off or away; Rücken, Kleid, Fußboden to scrub (down); **schrubbt euch richtig ab!** give yourselves a good scrub!

ạb+schuf|ten VR sep (inf) to slog one's guts out (inf)

ạb+schup|pen sep **VT** Fisch to scale **VR** to flake off

ạb+schür|fen VT sep to graze

Ạb|schür|fung F **-**, **-en** (= Wunde) graze

Ạb|schuss ▲ M **a** (= das Abfeuern) firing, shooting; (von Pfeil) shooting, loosing off; (von Rakete) launch(ing); (auf ein Ziel) firing **b** (= das Außer-Gefecht-Setzen) shooting down; (von Panzer) knocking out; **die Luftwaffe erzielte zwölf Abschüsse** the air force shot or brought down twelve planes **c** (von Wild) shooting; **Fasanen sind jetzt zum ~ freigegeben** pheasant-shooting is now permitted; **jdn zum ~ freigeben** (fig) to throw sb to the wolves; **die Zahl der Abschüsse** the number of kills; **durch ~ des Ministers** (fig inf) by getting rid of the minister **d** (Sport) (goal) kick

Ạb|schuss|ba|sis ▲ F launching base

ạb+schüs|sig ['apʃʏsɪç] ADJ sloping; **eine sehr ~e Straße** a steep road, a steeply sloping road;

auf einer ~en Bahn sein (fig) to be going rapidly downhill

Ạb|schüs|sig|keit F **-**, no pl slope

Ạb|schuss-: **Ạb|schuss|lis|te** ▲ F (inf) **er steht auf der ~** his days are numbered; **jdn auf die ~ setzen** to put sb on the hit list (inf); **auf jds ~ stehen** to be on sb's hit list (inf); **Ạb|schuss|quo|te** ▲ F (Hunt) kill quota; **Ạb|schuss|ram|pe** ▲ F launching pad

ạb+schüt|teln VT sep Staub, Schnee to shake off; Decke, Tuch to shake (out); (fig) lästige Menschen, Verfolger to shake off, to lose (inf); Gedanken, Ärger etc to get rid of; **das Joch der Knechtschaft ~** (liter) to throw off the yoke of slavery

ạb+schüt|ten VT sep Flüssigkeit, Mehl, Sand etc to pour off; (Cook) Flüssigkeit to drain off; Kartoffeln etc to drain; Eimer to empty

ạb+schwä|chen sep **VT** to weaken; Wirkung, Einfluss auch to lessen; Behauptung, Formulierung, Kontrast to tone down; Schock, Aufprall to lessen; Stoß, Eindruck to soften **VR** to drop or fall off, to diminish; (Lärm) to decrease; (Met: Hoch, Tief) to disperse; (Preisauftrieb, Andrang) to ease off; (St Ex: Kurse) to weaken

Ạb|schwä|chung F weakening; (von Behauptung, Formulierung) toning down; (von Schock, Aufprall) lessening; (von Eindruck) softening; (= Rückgang: von Lärm) decrease; (Met: von Hoch, Tief) dispersal; (von Andrang, Preisauftrieb) easing off

ạb+schwat|zen, (S Ger) **ạb+schwät|zen** VT sep (inf) **jdm etw ~** to talk sb into giving one sth; **das habe ich mir von meinem Bruder ~ lassen** I let my brother talk me into giving it to him

ạb+schwei|fen VI sep aux sein (lit, fig) to stray, to wander (off or away); (Redner auch) to digress; **er schweifte vom Thema ab** he deviated from the subject

Ạb|schwei|fung F digression; (vom Thema) deviation

ạb+schwel|len VI sep irreg aux sein (Entzündung, Fluss) to go down; (Lärm) to die or fade or ebb away; **der geschwollene Fuß ist wieder abgeschwollen** the swelling in his foot has gone down

ạb+schwem|men VT sep to wash away

ạb+schwen|ken VI sep aux sein to turn away; (Kamera) to swing round, to pan; (von der Straße) ~ to turn off (the road); **er ist nach links abgeschwenkt** (lit) he turned off to the left; (fig) he swung (over) to the left; (nach rechts) ~ (Mil) to wheel (right); **er schwenkte zur Medizin ab** he changed over to medicine

ạb+schwim|men sep irreg **VI** aux sein (= losschwimmen) to swim off or away **VT** **a** aux sein or habe Strecke to swim; Gewässer to swim along **b** (= verlieren) sich (dat) **überflüssige Pfunde ~** to swim off those extra pounds

ạb+schwin|deln VT sep jdm etw ~ to swindle sb out of sth

ạb+schwin|gen VI sep irreg (Ski) to do a downhill turn

ạb+schwir|ren VI sep aux sein to whirr off; (fig inf: = weggehen) to buzz off (inf); **die Vögel schwirrten plötzlich ab** with a flutter of wings the birds suddenly flew off

ạb+schwit|zen VT sep to sweat off; **sich** (dat) **einen ~** (sl) to sweat like mad (inf) or crazy (inf)

ạb+schwö|ren sep irreg **VI** einer Sache (dat) ~ to renounce sth; **dem Terrorismus/Glauben/Teufel ~** to renounce terrorism/one's faith/the devil; **seinen Ketzereien ~** to recant one's heresies; **dem Alkohol ~** (inf) to give up drinking **VT** (old: = ableugnen) Schuld, Mittäterschaft to deny, to repudiate; Glauben to renounce

Ạb|schwung M (Sport) dismount; (Ski) downhill turn; (Comm) downward trend, recession

ạb+se|geln sep **VI** **a** aux sein (= lossegeln) to sail off or away, to set sail; (inf: = weggehen) to

sail off; **der Schoner segelte von Bremen ab** the schooner sailed from Bremen or set sail from Bremen **b** (Sport: = die Saison beenden) to have one's last sail **VT** Strecke to sail; Küste to sail along

ạb+seg|nen VT sep (inf) Vorschlag, Plan to give one's blessing to; **von jdm abgesegnet sein** to have sb's blessing

ạb+seh|bar ADJ foreseeable; **in ~er/auf ~e Zeit** in/for the foreseeable future; **das Ende seines Studiums ist noch nicht ~** the end of his studies is not yet in sight; **die Folgen sind noch gar nicht ~** there's no telling what the consequences will be

ạb+se|hen sep irreg **VT** **a** (= abgucken) (bei) jdm etw ~ to pick sth up from sb; (= abschreiben) to copy sth from sb **b** (= voraussehen) to foresee; **es ist noch gar nicht abzusehen, wie lange die Arbeit dauern wird** there's no telling yet how long the work will take; **es ist ganz klar abzusehen, dass ...** it's easy to see that ...; **das Ende lässt sich noch nicht ~** the end is not yet in sight **VI** **von etw ~** (= verzichten) to refrain from sth; (= nicht berücksichtigen) to disregard sth, to leave sth out of account or consideration; **davon ~, etw zu tun** to dispense with doing sth, to refrain from doing sth → auch **abgesehen**

ạb+sei|fen VT sep to soap down; Gegenstand auch to wash down; **jdm den Rücken ~** to soap sb's back

ạb+sei|hen VT sep to strain

ạb+sei|len ['apzailən] sep **VT** to let or lower down on a rope **VR** to let or lower oneself down on a rope; (Bergsteiger) to abseil (down) (Brit), to rappel (US); (fig inf) to skedaddle (inf)

ạb sein ▲ VI irreg aux sein (inf) **a** (= weg sein) to be off; **die Farbe/der Knopf ist ab** the paint/button has come off **b** (= abgelegen sein) to be far away

ạb|sei|tig ['apzaitɪç] ADJ **a** (geh: = abseits liegend) remote **b** Theorie, Thema esoteric

ạb|seits ['apzaits] ADV **a** to one side; (= abgelegen) out of the way, remote; (Sport) offside; **~ liegen** to be out of the way, to be remote; **~ vom Wege** off the beaten track; **~ von der Straße** away from the road; **~ stehen** (fig) to be on the outside; (Sport) to be offside; **nicht ~** (Sport) onside, not offside; **~ bleiben** (fig) **sich ~ halten** (fig) to hold or keep to oneself PREP +gen away from; **des Weges** off the beaten track

Ạb|seits ['apzaits] NT **-**, **-** (Sport) offside; **im ~ stehen** to be offside; **ein Leben im ~ führen** (fig) **im ~ leben** (fig) to live in the shadows; **ins politische ~ geraten** to end up on the political scrapheap

Ạb|seits- (Sport): **Ạb|seits|fal|le** F offside trap; **Ạb|seits|po|si|ti|on** F offside position; **Ạb|seits|re|gel** F offside rule; **Ạb|seits|stel|lung** F offside position; **Ạb|seits|tor** NT offside goal

ạb+sen|den VT sep to send; Brief, Paket to send off, to dispatch; (mit der Post) to send, to post (Brit), to mail (esp US)

Ạb|sen|der M (= Adresse) (sender's) address

Ạb|sen|der(in) M(F) sender

Ạb|sen|der|ken|nung F sender's reference

ạb+sen|gen VT sep to singe off

ạb+sen|ken sep **VT** **a** (Build) Grundwasserstand to lower; Fundamente to sink **b** (Agr) Weinstöcke etc to layer **VR** to subside; **das Gelände senkt sich zum Seeufer ab** the terrain slopes down toward(s) the shore

Ạb|sen|ker ['apzɛŋkɐ] M **-s**, **-** (Hort: = Ableger) layer

ạb|sen|tie|ren [apzɛn'tiːrən] ptp **absentiert** VR insep (old, hum) to absent oneself

Ạb|sen|tis|mus [apzɛn'tɪsmʊs] M **-**, no pl (Ind, Sociol) absenteeism

Ab|senz [apˈzɛnts] F **-, -en** (Sch: Aus, Sw) absence

ab+ser|vie|ren ptp **abserviert** sep **VT** to clear the table **a** Geschirr, Tisch to clear **b** (inf: = entlassen, kaltstellen) jdn ~ to get rid of sb **c** (Sport sl: = besiegen) to thrash (inf)

ab|setz|bar ADJ Ware saleable; Betrag deductible; **steuerlich ~** tax-deductible

Ab|setz|bar|keit [ˈapzɛtsbaːɐkait] F (von Steuern etc) deductibility

ab+set|zen sep **VT a** (= abnehmen) Hut, Brille to take off, to remove; (= hinstellen) Gepäck, Glas to set or put down; Geigenbogen, Feder to lift; Gewehr to unshoulder **b** (= aussteigen lassen) Mitfahrer, Fahrgast to set down, to drop; Fallschirmjäger to drop; **wo kann ich dich ~?** where can I drop you? **c** (Naut) to push off **d** Theaterstück, Oper to take off; Fußballspiel, Turnier, Versammlung, Termin to cancel; **etw vom Spielplan ~** to take sth off the programme (Brit) or program (US) **e** (= entlassen) to dismiss; Minister, Vorsitzenden to dismiss, to remove from office; König, Kaiser to depose; (sl) Freund, Freundin to chuck (inf) **f** (= entwöhnen) Jungtier to wean; (Med) Medikament, Tabletten to come off, to stop taking; Behandlung to break off, to discontinue; (Mil) Ration etc to stop; **die Tabletten mussten abgesetzt werden** I/she etc had to stop taking the tablets or had to come off the tablets **g** (Comm: = verkaufen) Waren to sell; **sich gut ~ lassen** to sell well **h** (= abziehen) Betrag, Summe to deduct; **das kann man (von der Steuer) ~** that is tax-deductible **i** (= ablagern) Geröll to deposit **j** (Sew) to trim **k** (= kontrastieren) to contrast; **etw gegen etw ~** to set sth off against sth **l** (Typ) Manuskript to (type)set, to compose; **(eine Zeile) ~** to start a new line

VR a (Chem, Geol) to be deposited; (Feuchtigkeit, Staub etc) to collect **b** (inf: = weggehen) to get or clear out (aus of) (inf); (Sport: = Abstand vergrößern) to pull ahead; **sich nach Brasilien ~** to clear off to Brazil (inf) **c** **sich gegen jdn/etw ~** to stand out against sb/sth; **sich vorteilhaft gegen jdn/etw ~** to contrast favourably (Brit) or favorably (US) with sb/sth; **das macht er, nur um sich gegen die anderen abzusetzen** he only does that to be different from the others or to make himself stand out from the crowd

VI to put one's glass down; **er trank das Glas aus ohne abzusetzen** he emptied his glass in one

Ab|set|zung F **-, -en a** (= Entlassung) (von Beamten) dismissal; (von Minister, Vorsitzendem) dismissal, removal from office; (von König) deposing, deposition **b** (Fin: = Abschreibung) deduction **c** (von Theaterstück etc) withdrawal; (von Fußballspiel, Termin etc) cancellation **d** (von Jungtier) weaning; (Med) discontinuation

ab+si|chern sep **VT** to safeguard; (= garantieren) to cover; Bauplatz, Gefahrenstelle to make safe; Dach to support; (Comput) Daten to store; (= schützen) to protect; **jdn über die Landesliste ~** (Pol) ≈ to give sb a safe seat **VR** (= sich schützen) to protect oneself; (= sich versichern) to cover oneself

Ab|si|che|rung F protection; (von Gefahrenstelle) making safe; (von Ergebnissen) validation; **zur rechtlichen ~ von etw** to protect sth legally

Ab|sicht ✿ 35, 45.1, 45.4 F **-, -en** (= Vorsatz) intention; (= Zweck) purpose; (Jur) intent; **in der besten ~, in bester ~** with the best of intentions; **in der ~, etw zu tun** with the idea or object of doing sth, with a view to doing sth, with the intention of doing sth; **die ~ haben, etw zu tun** to intend to do sth; **eine ~ mit etw verfolgen** to have something in mind with sth; **etw mit/ohne ~ tun** to do/not to do sth on pur-

pose or deliberately; **ernste ~en haben** (inf) to have serious intentions; **das war nicht meine ~!** I didn't intend that; **das war doch keine ~!** (inf) it wasn't deliberate or intentional; **das ist ~** (inf) that's deliberate or intentional

ab|sicht|lich ✿ 45.4 ADJ deliberate, intentional **ADV** deliberately, intentionally

Ab|sicht|lich|keit F **-,** no pl deliberateness

Ab|sichts-: Ab|sichts|er|klä|rung F declaration of intent; **ab|sichts|los** ADJ unintentional **ADV** unintentionally; **Ab|sichts|satz** M (Gram) final clause; **ab|sichts|voll** ADJ = absichtlich

ab+sie|deln VT sep **a** (Admin) Bürger to resettle **b** (Med) Tochtergeschwulst to form

Ab|sied|lung F sep **a** (Admin) resettlement **b** (Med) metastasis

ab+sin|gen VT sep irreg **a** (vom Blatt) to sight-read **b** (bis zu Ende) to sing (right) through; **unter Absingen der Nationalhymne/Internationale** with the singing of the national anthem/the Internationale

ab+sin|ken VI sep irreg aux sein to fall, to drop; (Boden) to subside, to sink; (Temperatur, Wasserspiegel, Kurs) to fall, to go down; (Interesse, Leistungen) to fall or drop off; (fig: = moralisch absinken) to go downhill; **auf 10%/ein niedriges Niveau ~** to fall or drop to 10%/a low level

Ab|sinth [apˈzɪnt] M **-(e)s, -e** absinth(e)

ab+sit|zen sep irreg **VT a** (= verbringen) Zeit to sit out; (= verbüßen) Strafe to serve **VI** aux sein (vom Pferd) ~ to dismount (from a horse); **abgesessen!** dismount!

ab|so|lut [apzoˈluːt] ADJ (alle Bedeutungen) absolute; (= völlig auch) complete, total **ADV** absolutely; **das ist ~ unmöglich** that's quite or absolutely impossible; **~ genommen** or **betrachtet** considered in the absolute; **ich sehe ~ nicht ein, warum ...** I just don't understand why ...

Ab|so|lu|te(s) [apzoˈluːtə] NT decl as adj (Philos) Absolute, absolute

Ab|so|lut|heit F **-,** no pl absoluteness

Ab|so|lut|heits|an|spruch M claim to absolute right; **einen ~ vertreten** to claim absoluteness

Ab|so|lu|ti|on [apzoluˈtsioːn] F **-, -en** (Eccl) absolution; **jdm die ~ erteilen** to grant or give sb absolution

Ab|so|lu|tis|mus [apzoluˈtɪsmʊs] M **-,** no pl absolutism

ab|so|lu|tis|tisch [apzoluˈtɪstɪʃ] ADJ absolutist **ADV** **~ herrschen** or **regieren** to be an absolute monarch

Ab|sol|vent [apzɔlˈvɛnt] M **-en, -en, Ab|sol|ven|tin** [-ˈvɛntɪn] F **-, -nen** (Univ) graduate; **die ~en eines Lehrgangs** the students who have completed a course

ab|sol|vie|ren [apzɔlˈviːrən] ptp **absolviert** VT insep **a** (durchlaufen) Studium, Probezeit to complete; Schule to finish, to graduate from (US); Prüfung to pass; **er hat die technische Fachschule absolviert** he completed a course at technical college **b** (= ableisten) to complete **c** (Eccl) to absolve

Ab|sol|vie|rung F **-, -en** (von Studium, Probezeit) completion; (von Schule) finishing, graduation (+gen from) (US); (von Prüfung) passing

ab|son|der|lich ADJ peculiar, strange **ADV** peculiarly, strangely

Ab|son|der|lich|keit F **-, -en a** no pl strangeness **b** (= Eigenart) peculiarity

ab+son|dern sep **VT a** (= trennen) to separate; (= isolieren) to isolate **b** (= ausscheiden) to secrete **c** (inf: = von sich geben) to come out with (inf), to utter **VR a** (Mensch) to cut oneself off; **sie sondert sich immer sehr ab** she always keeps herself very much to herself → auch **abgesondert b** (= ausgeschieden werden) to be secreted

Ab|son|de|rung F **-, -en a** (= das Trennen) separation; (= Isolierung) isolation; (= Ausscheidung) secretion **b** (von Menschen) segregation **c** (= abgeschiedener Stoff) secretion

Ab|sor|ber [apˈzɔrbɐ] M **-s, -** (Tech) absorber

ab|sor|bie|ren [apzɔrˈbiːrən] ptp **absorbiert** VT insep (lit, fig) to absorb

Ab|sorp|ti|on [apzɔrpˈtsioːn] F **-, -en** absorption

ab+spal|ten VTR sep to split off; (Chem) to separate (off)

Ab|spann [ˈapʃpan] M **-s, -e** (TV, Film) final credits pl

ab+span|nen sep **VT a** (= ausspannen) Pferd, Wagen to unhitch; Ochsen to unyoke **b** (Build) to anchor **VI a** (= Pferde, Wagen abspannen) to unhitch (the) horses etc; (= Ochsen abspannen) to unyoke (the) oxen **b** (fig: = entspannen) to relax → auch **abgespannt**

Ab|span|nung F **a** (= Erschöpfung) weariness, tiredness **b** (Build) anchoring; (= Spannseil) anchor (cable)

ab+spa|ren VT sep **sich** (dat) **Geld von etw ~** to save money from sth; **sich** (dat) **ein Auto vom Lohn ~** to save up for a car from one's wages; **sich** (dat) **etw vom** or **am Munde** or **am eigenen Leib ~** to scrimp and save for sth

ab+spe|cken [ˈapʃpɛkn] sep (inf) **VT** to shed; (fig: = verkleinern) to slim down, to trim **VI** to lose weight

ab+spei|chern VT sep Daten to store (away)

ab+spei|sen VT sep **a** (= beköstigen) to feed **b** (fig inf: = abfertigen) **jdn mit etw ~** to fob sb off with sth (esp Brit)

ab|spens|tig [ˈapʃpɛnstɪç] ADJ **jdm jdn/etw ~ machen** to lure sb/sth away from sb; **jdm die Freundin ~ machen** to pinch (Brit) or steal sb's girlfriend (inf); **jdm die Kunden ~ machen** to lure or draw sb's customers away from him/her

ab+sper|ren sep **VT a** (= abriegeln) to block or close off **b** (= abdrehen) Wasser, Strom, Gas etc to turn or shut off **c** (= verschließen) to lock **VI** to lock up

Ab|sperr-: Ab|sperr|git|ter NT barrier; **Ab|sperr|hahn** M stopcock; **Ab|sperr|ket|te** F chain

Ab|sper|rung F **a** (= Abriegelung) blocking or closing off **b** (= Sperre) barrier; (= Kordon) cordon

Ab|sperr|ven|til NT stop or check or shut-off valve

Ab|spiel NT (= das Abspielen) passing; (= Schuss) pass

ab+spie|len sep **VT a** Schallplatte, Tonband to play (through); Nationalhymne to play; (vom Blatt) Musik to sight-read → auch **abgespielt b** (Sport) Ball to pass; (beim Billard) to play **VR a** (= sich ereignen) to happen; (= stattfinden) to take place; **wie mein Leben sich abspielt** what my life is like; **da spielt sich (bei mir) nichts ab!** (inf) nothing doing! (inf)

ab+split|tern sep **VI** aux sein (Farbe) to drip off; (fig: Gruppe) to break away **VR** (fig: Gruppe) to break away

Ab|split|te|rung F **-, -en** (= das Absplittern) chipping off; (von Holz auch) splintering off

Ab|spra|che F arrangement; **eine ~ treffen** to make or come to an arrangement; **ohne vorherige ~** without prior consultation

ab|spra|che|ge|mäß ADV as arranged

ab|spra|che|wid|rig ADV contrary to (previous) agreement

ab+spre|chen sep irreg **VT a** jdm etw ~ (= verweigern, Recht) to deny or refuse sb sth; (= in Abrede stellen) Begabung to deny or dispute sb's sth **b** (= verabreden) Termin to arrange; **die Zeugen hatten ihre Aussagen vorher abgesprochen** the witnesses had agreed on what to say in advance **VR** **sich mit jdm ~** to make an arrangement with sb; **die beiden hatten sich**

vorher abgesprochen they had agreed on what to do/say *etc* in advance; **ich werde mich mit ihr ~** I'll arrange *or* fix things with her

ạb+sprei|zen VT *sep* to extend; (*Build*) to brace

ạb+sprin|gen VI *sep irreg aux sein* **a** (= *herunterspringen*) to jump down (*von from*); (= *herausspringen*) to jump out (*von of*); (*Aviat*) to jump (*von from*); (*bei Gefahr*) to bale out; (*Sport*) to dismount; (= *lossspringen*) to take off; **mit dem rechten Bein ~** to take off on the right leg **b** (= *sich lösen*) to come off; (*esp Farbe, Lack*) to flake *or* peel off; (= *abprallen*) to bounce off (*von etw sth*); **c** (*fig inf*: = *sich zurückziehen*) to get out; (*von Partei, Kurs etc*) to back out; **von etw ~** to get *or* back out of sth

ạb+sprit|zen *sep* **VT** **a** *etw/jdn/sich* **~** to spray sth/sb/oneself down; *Schmutz* to spray off (*von etw* sth); (*Cook*) to sprinkle **b** (*NS euph sl*: = *töten*) to give a lethal injection to **VI** **a** *aux sein* to spray off **b** *aux haben* (*sl*: = *ejakulieren*) to spunk (*vulg*)

Ạb|sprung M jump (*auch Aviat*), leap; (*Sport*) takeoff; (= *Abgang*) dismount; **den ~ schaffen** (*fig*) to make the break (*inf*), to make it (*inf*); **er hat den ~ gewagt** (*fig*) he took the jump; **den ~ verpassen** (*fig: ins Berufsleben etc*) to miss the boat

Ạb|sprung-: Ạb|sprung|bal|ken M (*Sport*) takeoff board; **Ạb|sprung|hö|he** F (*Sport*) drop altitude; **Ạb|sprung|stel|le** F (*Sport*) jumping-off point

ạb+spu|len VT *sep Kabel, Garn* to unwind; (*inf*: = *filmen*) to shoot; (= *vorführen*) to show; (*fig*) to reel off

ạb+spü|len *sep* **VT** *Hände, Geschirr* to rinse; *Fett etc* to rinse off **VI** to wash up (*Brit*), to do the washing-up (*Brit*), to wash the dishes

ạb+stam|men VI *sep no ptp* to be descended (*von from*); (*Ling*) to be derived (*von from*)

Ạb|stam|mung F **-, -en** descent; (= *Abkunft auch*) origin, extraction; (*Ling*) origin, derivation; **ehelicher/unehelicher ~** (*Jur*) of legitimate/ illegitimate birth; **französischer ~** of French extraction *or* descent

Ạb|stam|mungs|leh|re F , **Ạb|stam|mungs|the|o|rie** F theory of evolution

Ạb|stand M **a** (= *Zwischenraum*) distance; (= *kürzerer Abstand*) gap, space; (= *Zeitabstand*) interval; (= *Punkteabstand*) gap; (*fig*) (= *Distanz*) distance; (= *Unterschied*) difference; **mit ~** by far, far and away; **~ von etw gewinnen** (*fig*) to distance oneself from sth; **in regelmäßigen Abständen/Abständen von 10 Minuten** at regular/ 10 minute intervals; **in unregelmäßigen Abständen** at irregular intervals; **~ halten** to keep one's distance; **mit großem ~ führen/gewinnen** to lead/win by a wide margin **b** (*form*: = *Verzicht*) **von etw ~ nehmen** to dispense with sth; *von Meinung, Absicht, Forderung* to abandon sth; **davon ~ nehmen, etw zu tun** to refrain from doing sth, to forbear to do sth (*old, form*) **c** (= *Abfindung*) indemnity

Ạb|stands|sum|me F (*form*) indemnity

ạb+stat|ten ['apʃtatn] VT *sep* (*form*) **jdm einen Besuch ~** to pay sb a visit; **jdm seinen Dank ~** to give thanks to sb

ạb+stau|ben VTI *sep* **a** *Möbel etc* to dust **b** (*inf*) (= *wegnehmen*) to pick up; (= *schnorren*) to cadge (*von, bei, +dat* off, from); **er will immer nur ~** he's always on the scrounge **c** (*Ftbl inf*) (**ein Tor** *or* **den Ball**) **~** to put the ball into the net, to tuck the ball away

Ạb|stau|ber¹ ['apʃtaubɐ] M **-s, -** (*Ftbl inf: auch* **Abstaubertor**) easy goal

Ạb|stau|ber², Ạb|stau|be|rin [-ərɪn] F **-, -nen** (*inf*) **a** (*Ftbl*) goal-hanger (*inf*) **b** (= *Schnorrer*) scrounger (*inf*), sponger (*inf*)

ạb+ste|chen *sep irreg* **VT** **a** **ein Tier ~** to cut an animal's throat; **jdn ~** (*inf*) to knife sb (*inf*) **b** (= *abtrennen*) *Torf* to cut; *Rasen* to trim (the

---

edges of) **c** (= *ablaufen lassen*) *Hochofen, Metall* to tap **VI** **gegen jdn/etw ~, von jdm/etw ~** to stand out against sb/sth

Ạb|ste|cher ['apʃtɛçɐ] M **-s, -** (= *Ausflug*) excursion, trip; (= *Umweg*) detour; (*fig*) sortie

ạb+ste|cken VT *sep* **a** *Gelände, Grenze, Trasse* to mark out; (*mit Pflöcken*) to peg *or* stake out; (*fig*) *Verhandlungsposition, Programm* to work out **b** *Kleid, Naht* to pin

ạb+ste|hen *sep irreg* **VI** (= *entfernt stehen*) to stand away; (= *nicht anliegen*) to stick out; **~de Ohren** ears that stick out → *auch* **abgestanden** **VT** (*inf*) **sich** (*dat*) **die Beine ~** to stand for hours and hours

ạb+stei|fen VT *sep* (*Build*) to shore up

Ạb|stei|ge F (*inf*) dosshouse (*Brit inf*), flophouse (*dated US inf*), cheap hotel

ạb+stei|gen VI *sep irreg aux sein* **a** (= *heruntersteigen*) to get off (*von etw* sth); (= *heruntersteigen*) **von einem Pferd/Rad** *etc* **~** to dismount, to get off a horse/ bicycle *etc*; **„Radfahrer ~!"** "cyclists dismount" **b** (= *abwärts gehen*) to make one's way down; (*esp Bergsteiger*) to climb down; **in ~der Linie, in der ~den Linie** in the line of descent; **auf dem ~den Ast sein** (*inf*) **sich auf dem ~den Ast befinden** (*inf*) to be going downhill, to be on the decline **c** (*dated*: = *einkehren*) to stay **d** (*Sport*: *Mannschaft*) to go down, to be relegated; **aus der ersten Liga ~** to be relegated from the first division

Ạb|stei|ge|quar|tier NT = **Absteige**

Ạb|stei|ger(in) M(F) (*Sport*) relegated team; **gesellschaftlicher ~** (*fig*) someone who has come down in the world

Ạb|stell|bahn|hof M railway yard

ạb+stel|len *sep* **VT** **a** (= *hinstellen*) to put down **b** (= *unterbringen*) to put; (*Aut*: = *parken*) to park **c** (= *abrücken, entfernt stellen*) to put away from; **das Klavier von der Wand ~** to leave the piano out from *or* away from the wall **d** (= *abkommandieren*) to order off, to detail; *Offizier* to second, to detail; (*fig*: = *abordnen*) to assign; (*Sport*) *Spieler* to release **e** (= *ausrichten auf*) **etw auf jdn/etw ~** to gear sth to sb/sth **f** (= *abdrehen*) to turn off; *Geräte, Licht* to switch *or* turn off; (= *Zufuhr unterbrechen*) *Gas, Strom* to cut off; *Telefon* to disconnect; **den Haupthahn für das Gas ~** to turn the gas off at the mains **g** (= *sich abgewöhnen*) to give up, to stop **h** (= *unterbinden*) *Mangel, Unsitte etc* to bring to an end; **das lässt sich nicht/lässt sich ~** nothing/something can be done about that; **lässt sich das nicht ~?** couldn't that be changed? **VI** **auf etw** (*acc*) **~** to be geared to sth; (= *etw berücksichtigen*) to take sth into account

Ạb|stell-: Ạb|stell|flä|che F storage surface; (*für Auto*) parking space *or* area; **Ạb|stell|gleis** NT siding; **jdn aufs ~ schieben** (*fig*) to push *or* cast sb aside; **auf dem ~ sein** *or* **stehen** (*fig*) to have been pushed *or* cast aside; **Ạb|stell|hahn** M stopcock; **Ạb|stell|he|bel** M (*Tech*) (start-)stop lever; **Ạb|stell|kam|mer** F boxroom; **Ạb|stell|platz** M **a** (*für Auto*) parking space; **ein ~ für Fahrräder** a place for leaving bicycles **b** (*fig inf*: = *beruflich ungünstiger Posten*) inferior position; **Ạb|stell|raum** M storeroom; **Ạb|stell|tisch** M (*für Speisen und Getränke*) dumb waiter; (*bei der Arbeit*) stand

ạb+stem|peln VT *sep* to stamp; *Post* to postmark; (*fig*) to stamp, to brand (*zu, als* as)

Ạb|stem|pe|lung F **-, -en, Ạb|stemp|lung** ['apʃtɛmplʊŋ] F **-, -en** stamping; (*von Post*) postmarking; (*fig*) branding

ạb+step|pen VT *sep* to stitch, to sew; *Wattiertes, Daunendecke* to quilt; *Kragen etc* to topstitch

ạb+ster|ben VI *sep irreg aux sein* (= *eingehen, auch Med*) to die; (= *gefühllos werden: Glieder*) to go *or* grow numb; (*fig*) (*Gefühle*) to die; (= *untergehen: Industriezweig, Sprachgruppe*) to die out;

---

mir sind die Zehen abgestorben my toes have gone *or* grown numb → *auch* **abgestorben**

Ạb|stich M (*von Wein*) racking; (*von Metall, Hochofen*) tapping; (= *Öffnung des Hochofens*) taphole

Ạb|stieg M (= *das Absteigen*) way down, descent; (= *Weg*) descent; (= *Niedergang*) decline; (*Sport*) relegation; **einen alten Pfad als ~ benutzen** to come down (on) an old path; **vom ~ bedroht** (*Sport*) threatened by relegation, in danger of being relegated

Ạb|stiegs-: Ạb|stiegs|ge|fahr F (*Sport*) threat of relegation; **ạb|stiegs|ge|fähr|det** ADJ (*Sport*) threatened by *or* in danger of relegation; **Ạb|stiegs|kan|di|dat(in)** M(F) (*Sport*) relegation candidate, candidate for relegation

ạb+stil|len *sep* **VT** *Kind* to wean, to stop breastfeeding **VI** to stop breastfeeding

ạb+stim|men *sep* **VI** to take a vote; **über etw** (*acc*) **~** to vote *or* take a vote on sth; **über etw** (*acc*) **~ lassen** to put sth to the vote; **geheim ~** to have a secret ballot **VT** (= *harmonisieren*) *Instrumente* to tune (*auf +acc* to); *Radio* to tune (in) (*auf +acc* to); (= *in Einklang bringen*) *Farben, Kleidung* to match (*auf +acc* with); *Termine* to coordinate (*auf +acc* with); (= *anpassen*) to suit (*auf +acc* to); (*Comm*) *Bücher* to balance; **gut auf etw** (*acc*)**/aufeinander abgestimmt sein** (*Instrumente*) to be in tune with sth/with each other; (*Farben, Speisen etc*) to go well with sth/with each other *or* together; (*Termine*) to fit in well with sth/with each other; (= *einander angepasst sein*) to be well-suited to sth/(to each other); **etw miteinander ~** (= *vereinbaren*) to settle sth amongst ourselves/ themselves etc; **abgestimmt** (= *vereinbart, Politik, Aktionen etc*) agreed; **(aufeinander) abgestimmt** (*Pläne, Strategien*) mutually agreed **VR** **sich (mit jdm/miteinander) ~** to come to an agreement (with sb/amongst ourselves/themselves etc)

Ạb|stim|mung F **a** (= *Stimmabgabe*) vote; (= *geheime Abstimmung*) ballot; (= *das Abstimmen*) voting; **eine ~ durchführen** *or* **vornehmen** to take a vote; **zur ~ bringen** (*form*) to put to the vote → **schreiten b** (*von Instrumenten*) tuning; (*von Farben, Kleidung*) matching; (*von Terminen*) coordination; (= *das Anpassen*) suiting; (*von Büchern*) balancing **c** (= *Vereinbarung*) agreement

Ạb|stim|mungs-: ạb|stim|mungs|be|rech|tigt ADJ = **stimmberechtigt; Ạb|stim|mungs|be|rech|tig|te(r)** MF *decl as adj* person entitled to vote; **Ạb|stim|mungs|er|geb|nis** NT result of the vote; **Ạb|stim|mungs|nie|der|la|ge** F **eine ~ erleiden** to be defeated in a/the vote; **Ạb|stim|mungs|sieg** M **einen ~ errin|gen** to win a/the vote

abs|ti|nẹnt [apsti'nɛnt] ADJ teetotal; (*geschlecht-lich*) abstinent, continent, not indulging in sex; (*fig*) unforthcoming; **sie sind politisch ~** they don't engage in politics ADV **~ leben** to live a life of abstinence

Abs|ti|nẹnz [apsti'nɛnts] F **-, no pl** teetotalism, abstinence; (*geschlechtlich*) abstinence

Abs|ti|nẹnz-: Abs|ti|nẹnz|er|schei|nung F (*Med*) withdrawal symptom; **Abs|ti|nẹnz|ge|bot** NT (*Eccl*) requirement of abstinence

Abs|ti|nẹnz|ler [apsti'nɛntslɐ] M **-s, -, Abs|ti|nẹnz|le|rin** [-ərɪn] F **-, -nen** teetotaller (*Brit*), teetotaler (*US*)

Abs|ti|nẹnz|tag M (*Eccl*) day of abstinence

ạb+stin|ken VI *sep irreg* (*sl*: = *einpacken*) **damit kannst du ~** you can forget it (*inf*)

ạb+stop|pen *sep* **VT** **a** *Auto, Maschine, Verkehr* to stop, to bring to a standstill *or* halt; (= *drosseln*) to halt **b** (*Sport*) *Ball* to stop; (*mit Stoppuhr*) to time; **jds Zeit ~** to time sb **VI** to stop, to come to a halt

Ạb|stoß M **a** (*Ftbl*) goal kick; (*nach Fangen des Balls*) clearance **b** **der ~ vom Ufer war so kräf-**

---

tig, dass ... the boat was pushed away from or out from the shore so forcefully that ...

ạb|sto|ßen *sep irreg* **VT a** (= *wegstoßen*) *Boot* to push off *or* away *or* out; (= *abschlagen*) *Ecken* to knock off; *Möbel* to batter; (= *abschaben*) *Ärmel* to wear thin; **sich** (*dat*) **die Ecken und Kanten ~** (*fig*) to have the rough edges knocked off one → **Horn a**
b (= *zurückstoßen*) to repel; (*Comm*) *Ware, Aktien* to get rid of, to sell off; (*Med*) *Organ* to reject; (*fig*: *anwidern*) to repulse, to repel; **dieser Stoff stößt Wasser ab** this material is water-repellent
c (*Ftbl*) **den Ball ~** to take the goal kick; (*nach Fangen*) to clear (the ball)
VR a (= *abgeschlagen werden*) to get broken; (*Möbel*) to get battered
b (*esp Sport: Mensch*) to push oneself off; **sich mit den Füßen vom Boden ~** to push oneself off
c (*Phys*) to repel; **die beiden Pole stoßen sich ab** the two poles repel each other
VI a *aux sein or haben* (= *weggestoßen werden*) to push off
b (= *anwidern*) to be repulsive; **sich von etw abgestoßen fühlen** to be repelled by sth, to find sth repulsive
c (*Ftbl*) to take a goal kick; (*nach Fangen*) to clear (the ball)

ạb|sto|ßend **ADJ** *Aussehen, Äußeres* repulsive; **sein Wesen hat etwas Abstoßendes** there's something repulsive about him **ADV** repulsively; **~ aussehen/riechen** to look/smell repulsive

Ạb|sto|ßung F -, -en (*Phys*) repulsion; (*Med:* *von Organ*) rejection

Ạb|sto|ßungs|re|ak|ti|on F (*Med*) rejection

ạb|stot|tern VT *sep* (*inf*) to pay off

ạb|stra|fen VT *sep* = **bestrafen**

abs|tra|hie|ren [apstra'hiːrən] *ptp* **abstrahiert** VTI *insep* to abstract (*aus* from)

ạb|strah|len VT *sep* **a** *Wärme, Energie, Programm etc* to emit **b** *Fassade* (*mit Sandstrahlgebläse*) to sandblast

abs|trakt [ap'strakt] **ADJ** abstract; **~e Kunst** abstract art **ADV** abstractly; **etw zu ~ ausdrücken** to express sth too abstractly *or* too much in the abstract

Abs|trakt|heit F -, (*rare*) -en abstractness

Abs|trak|ti|on [apstrak'tsioːn] F -, -en abstraction

Abs|trak|ti|ons|ver|mö|gen NT ability to abstract

Abs|trak|tum [ap'straktʊm] NT -s, **Abstrakta** [-ta] (= *Begriff*) abstract (concept); (*Ling:* = *Substantiv*) abstract noun

ạb|stram|peln VR *sep* (*inf*) to kick the bedclothes (*Brit*) *or* covers off; (*fig*) to sweat (away) (*inf*), to bust a gut (*inf*)

ạb|strei|chen *sep irreg* **VT a** (= *wegstreichen*) to wipe off *or* away; (= *säubern*) to wipe; **den Hals/die Zunge ~** (*Med*) to take a throat/tongue swab **b** (= *abziehen*) *Betrag* to knock off, to deduct; (*fig*) to discount; **davon kann** *or* **muss man die Hälfte ~** (*fig*) you have to take it with a pinch (*Brit*) *or* grain (*US*) of salt **c** (*Hunt*) *Feld* to beat; (*Mil*) *Gebiet, Himmel* to sweep **VI** *aux sein* (*Hunt*) to fly off *or* away

ạb|strei|fen VT *sep* **a** (= *abtreten*) *Schuhe, Füße* to wipe; *Schmutz* to wipe off **b** (= *abziehen*) *Kleidung, Schmuck* to take off, to remove, to slip off; (= *entfernen*) *Haut* to cast, to shed; (*fig*) *Gewohnheit, Fehler* to get rid of

ạb|strei|ten VT *sep irreg* (= *streitig machen*) to dispute; (= *leugnen*) to deny; **das kann man ihm nicht ~** you can't deny it

Ạb|strich M **a** (= *Kürzung*) cutback; **~e machen** to cut back (*an +dat* on), to make cuts (*an +dat* in); (= *weniger erwarten etc*) to lower one's sights **b** (*Med*) swab; (= *Gebärmutterabstrich*) smear; **einen ~ machen** to take a swab/

smear **c** (*Mus:* *beim Schreiben*) downstroke; **zu dicke ~e machen** to make one's downstrokes too thick

ạb|strö|men VI *sep* *aux sein* to flow away *or* off; (*Wasser auch*) to run away *or* off; (*Menschenmassen*) to stream out

abs|trus [ap'struːs] (*geh*) **ADJ** abstruse **ADV** abstrusely; **das ~ anmutende Drehbuch** the abstruse (film) script

Abs|tru|si|tät [apstruːzi'tɛːt] F -, -en (*geh*) **a** *no pl* abstruseness **b** (= *Bemerkung*) abstruse remark

ạb|stu|fen *sep* **VT** *Gelände* to terrace; *Haare* to layer; *Farben* to shade; *Gehälter, Steuern, Preise* to grade **VR** to be terraced; **der Weinberg stuft sich zum Fluss hin ab** the vineyard goes down in terraces to the river

Ạb|stu|fung F -, -en (*von Gelände*) terracing; (= *Nuancierung*) shading; (= *Nuance*) shade; (= *Staffelung*) grading; (= *Stufe*) grade

ạb|stump|fen ['apʃtʊmpfn] *sep* **VI** *aux sein* (*fig:* *Geschmack etc*) to become dulled; **wenn man ewig dasselbe machen muss, stumpft man nach und nach ab** always having to do the same thing dulls the mind; **er ist als Kritiker abgestumpft** his critical sensibilities have become blunted; **gegen etw ~** to become inured to sth **VT a** *Menschen, Sinne* to deaden; *Gerechtigkeitssinn, Gewissen, Urteilsvermögen* to dull → *auch* **abgestumpft b** (*lit*) *Ecken, Kanten* to blunt; *Messer, Schneide* to take the edge off, to blunt

Ạb|stump|fung F -, *no pl* (*von Menschen, Sinnen*) deadening; (*von Gewissen, Gerechtigkeitssinn*) dulling

Ạb|sturz M crash; (*von Börse, Unternehmen auch*) fall; (*sozial*) disaster, ruin; (*von Politiker etc*) downfall; (= *Depression*) breakdown; (*Comput*) crash; **ein Flugzeug zum ~ bringen** to bring a plane down

ạb|stür|zen VI *sep* *aux sein* **a** (*Flugzeug*) to crash; (*Bergsteiger*) to fall **b** (*inf:* *sozial*) to go to ruin **c** (*inf:* *psychisch*) to come a cropper (*Brit inf*), to fall flat on one's face **d** (*sl:* = *betrunken werden*) to go on a bender (*Brit inf*), to go on a binge (*inf*) **e** (*Comput*) to crash **f** (*sl*) **mit jdm ~** (*sich sexuell betätigen*) to have a fumble with sb (*inf*)

Ạb|sturz|stel|le F location of a/the crash; (*beim Bergsteigen*) location of a/the fall; **die Rettungsarbeiten an der ~** the rescue work at the scene of the crash

ạb|stüt|zen *sep* **VT** to support (*auch fig*), to prop up; *Haus, Mauer auch* to shore up **VR** to support oneself, to prop oneself up; (*bei Bewegung*) to support oneself

ạb|su|chen VT *sep* **a** *Unfallstelle, Gelände, Gebiet, Umgebung, Ort, Internet, Daten* to search; (*Med, Sci*) *Körper, Flüssigkeit* to scan; **jdn/etw nach etw ~** to search sb/sth for sth; **wir haben den ganzen Garten abgesucht** we searched all over the garden **b** (= *suchend absammeln*) *Raupen etc* to pick off; *Strauch etc* to pick clean

Ạb|sud ['apzuːt, ap'zuːt] M -(e)s, -e [-də] (*old*) decoction

ab|surd [ap'zʊrt] ADJ absurd, preposterous; **~es Drama** *or* **Theater** theatre (*Brit*) *or* theater (*US*) of the absurd; **das Absurde** the absurd

Ạb|sur|di|tät [apzʊrdi'tɛːt] F -, -en absurdity (*auch Philos*), preposterousness

Abs|zess ▲ [aps'tsɛs] M **-es, -e** abscess

Abs|zis|se [aps'tsɪsə] F -, -en abscissa

Abt [apt] M **-(e)s, ⁻e** ['ɛptə] abbot

Abt. *abbr von* **Abteilung** dept

ạb|ta|keln VT *sep* *Schiff* to unrig; (= *außer Dienst stellen*) to lay up → *auch* **abgetakelt**

Ạb|ta|ke|lung F -, -en, **Ạb|tak|lung** ['apta:klʊŋ] F -, -en (*von Schiff*) unrigging; (= *Außerdienststellung*) laying up

ạb|tan|zen VI *sep* (*inf*) **a** *aux haben* (= *austoben*) to really hit the dance floor (*Brit sl*), to

really cut up the floor (*US inf*) **b** *aux sein* (= *weggehen*) to push off (*inf*)

ạb|tas|ten VT *sep* to feel; (*Med auch*) to palpate; (*Elec*) to scan; (*bei Durchsuchung*) to frisk (*auf +acc* for); (*fig:* = *erproben*) jdn to sound out, to suss out (*Brit inf*); (*Sport*) to get the measure of, to size up, to suss out (*Brit inf*)

Ạb|tas|tung F -, -en (*Elec, TV*) scanning

Ạb|tau|au|to|ma|tik F (*von Kühlschrank*) auto(matic) defroster

ạb|tau|chen VI *sep* *aux sein* **a** (*U-Boot*) to dive **b** (*inf*) to go underground

ạb|tau|en *sep* **VT** to thaw out; *Kühlschrank* to defrost **VI** *aux sein* to thaw; **der Schnee ist vom Dach abgetaut** the snow has thawed from the roof

Ạb|tausch M (*Chess, Sw:* = *Tausch*) exchange

ạb|tau|schen VT *sep* (*Chess, Sw:* = *tauschen*) to exchange

Ạb|tei [ap'tai] F -, -en abbey

Ạb|tei|kir|che F abbey (church)

Ạb|teil [ap'tail, 'ap-] NT compartment; **~ erster Klasse, Erste-Klasse-Abteil** first-class compartment; **~ für Mutter und Kind, Mutter-(und-)Kind-Abteil** *compartment reserved for mothers with young children* **~ für Raucher** smoker, smoking compartment; **~ für Nichtraucher** nonsmoker, no-smoking compartment

ạb|tei|len VT *sep* **a** (= *einteilen*) to divide up; **fünf Stücke ~** to cut off five pieces **b** (= *abtrennen*) to divide off; (*mit Wand*) to divide *or* partition off

Ạb|tei|lung¹ ['aptailʊŋ] F (= *das Einteilen*) dividing up; (= *das Abschneiden*) cutting off; (= *das Abtrennen*) dividing off; (*mit Wand*) partitioning off

Ạb|tei|lung² [ap'tailʊŋ] F **a** (*in Firma, Kaufhaus, Hochschule*) department; (*in Krankenhaus, Jur*) section; (*Mil*) unit, section **b** (*old:* = *Abschnitt*) section

Ạb|tei|lungs|lei|ter(in) M(F) head of department; (*in Kaufhaus*) department manager/manageress

ạb|te|le|fo|nie|ren *ptp* **abtelefoniert** VI *sep* to telephone *or* ring *or* call to say one can't make it *or* come

ạb|teu|fen ['aptɔyfn] VT *sep* *Schacht* to sink

ạb|tip|pen VT *sep* (*inf*) to type out

Ạb|tis|sin [ɛp'tɪsɪn] F -, -nen abbess

ạb|tö|nen VT *sep* *Farbe* to tone down; **zwei Farben gegeneinander ~** to tone two colours (*Brit*) *or* colors (*US*) in with each other

Ạb|tö|nung F (*von Farbe*) toning down; (= *Farbton*) tone, shade

ạb|tö|ten VT *sep* (*lit, fig*) to destroy, to kill (off); *Nerv* to deaden; *sinnliche Begierde* to mortify; **in mir ist jedes Gefühl abgetötet** I am dead to all feeling

Ạb|tö|tung F (*lit, fig*) destruction, killing (off); (*von Nerv*) deadening; (*von Begierden*) mortification

Ạb|trag ['aptraːk] M **-(e)s** [-gəs] *no pl* (*old*) harm; **einer Sache** (*dat*) **~ tun** to harm sth

ạb|tra|gen VT *sep irreg* **a** *auch vi* (= *abräumen*) *Geschirr, Speisen* to carry away **b** (= *einebnen*) *Boden, Gelände* to level **c** (= *entfernen*) *Gebäude, Mauer* to take down; *Erdschicht, Straßenbelag* to remove; (*Wellen*) *Strand, Sand* to erode, to wear away **d** (= *abbezahlen*) *Schulden* to pay off; *Schuld* to pay; **einen Schuldenberg ~** to clear all one's debts **e** (= *abnutzen*) *Kleider, Schuhe* to wear out → *auch* **abgetragen**

ạb|träg|lich ['aptrɛːklɪç], (*Sw*) **ạb|trä|gig** ['aptrɛːgɪç] ADJ detrimental, harmful; *Bemerkung, Kritik etc* adverse, unfavourable (*Brit*), unfavorable (*US*); **einer Sache** (*dat*) **~ sein** to be detrimental *or* harmful to sth

Ạb|tra|gung F -, -en **a** (*Geol*) erosion **b** (= *Abbau*) dismantling, taking down **c** (= *Tilgung*) paying off

Ab|trans|port M transportation; (*aus Katastrophengebiet*) evacuation; **beim ~ der Gefangenen** when the prisoners were being taken away

ab+trans|por|tie|ren ptp **abtransportiert** VT sep Waren to transport; *Personen auch* to take off or away; (*aus Katastrophengebiet*) to evacuate

ab+trei|ben sep irreg **VT** **a** vom Kurs ~ (*Flugzeug*) to send or drive off course; *Boot auch, Schwimmer* to carry off course **b** (= zu Tal treiben) *Vieh* to bring down **c** *Kind, Leibesfrucht* to abort; **sie hat das Kind abgetrieben** or ~ **lassen** she had an abortion **d** (*Aus, S Ger: Cook*) to whisk **VI** **a** aux sein (**vom Kurs**) – (*Flugzeug*) to be sent or driven off course; (*Boot auch, Schwimmer*) to be carried off course **b** (= Abort vornehmen) to carry out an abortion; (*generell*) to carry out or do abortions; (= Abort vornehmen lassen) to have an abortion

Ab|trei|bung ['aptraibʊŋ] F -, -en abortion; **eine ~ vornehmen lassen** to have an abortion; **eine ~ vornehmen** to carry out an abortion

Ab|trei|bungs-: Ab|trei|bungs|be|für|wor|ter(in) M(F) pro-abortionist; **Ab|trei|bungs|geg|ner(in)** M(F) anti-abortionist, pro-lifer (*inf*); **Ab|trei|bungs|ge|setz** NT abortion law(s *pl*); **Ab|trei|bungs|kli|nik** F abortion clinic; **Ab|trei|bungs|pa|ra|graf** ▲ M abortion laws *pl*; **Ab|trei|bungs|pil|le** F abortion pill; **Ab|trei|bungs|pra|xis** F (= *Klinik*) abortion clinic; **Ab|trei|bungs|tou|ris|mus** M (*inf*) going to another country/state to have an abortion; **Ab|trei|bungs|ver|bot** NT abortion ban, ban on abortions; **Ab|trei|bungs|ver|such** M attempt at an abortion; **einen ~ vornehmen** to try to give oneself an abortion, to attempt an abortion

ab|trenn|bar ADJ (= *lostrennbar*) detachable; *Knöpfe, Besatz etc auch* removable; (= abteilbar) separable; *Verfahren* severable (*form*)

ab+tren|nen VT sep **a** (= *lostrennen*) to detach; *Knöpfe, Besatz etc* to remove, to take off; (= abschneiden) to cut off; *Bein, Finger etc (durch Unfall)* to sever, to cut off; **„hier ~"** "detach here" **b** (= abteilen) to separate off; (*mit Trennwand etc*) to divide or partition off; **diese Zeit lässt sich nicht einfach von der Geschichte des Landes ~** this period cannot simply be set aside from the history of the country

Ab|tren|nung F (= *das Abteilen*) separation; (*mit Trennwand etc*) partitioning

ab|tret|bar ADJ (*Jur*) *Ansprüche* transferable, cedable (*form*)

ab+tre|ten sep irreg **VT** **a** (= überlassen) (*jdm or an jdn to sb*) to hand over; *Gebiet, Land auch* to cede (*form*); *Rechte, Ansprüche* to transfer, to cede (*form*); *Haus, Geldsumme* to transfer, to assign (*form*)
b *Teppich* to wear; (*völlig*) to wear out; *Schnee, Schmutz* to stamp off; **sich** (*dat*) **die Füße** or **Schuhe ~** to wipe one's feet
VI aux sein (*Theat*) to go off (stage), to make one's exit; (*Mil*) to dismiss; (*inf:* = zurücktreten) (*Politiker*) to step down (*inf*), to resign; (*Monarch*) to abdicate, to step down (*inf*); (*euph:* = sterben) to make one's last exit; **~!** (*Mil*) dismiss!; **aus dem Leben ~** (*euph*) to quit this life
VR (*Teppich etc*) to wear, to get worn; (*völlig*) to wear out

Ab|tre|ter ['aptreːtɐ] M -s, - (= *Fußabtreter*) doormat

Ab|tre|tung F -, -en (*an +acc to*) transfer; (*von Rechten, Ansprüchen auch, von Gebiet*) ceding (*form*), cession (*form*); (*von Haus, Geldsumme auch*) assignment (*form*); **durch ~ aller Ansprüche an seinen Teilhaber** by transferring all rights to his partner

Ab|tre|tungs|ur|kun|de F transfer deed; (*für Grundstück*) (deed of) conveyance; (*bei Konkurs*) (deed of) assignment

Ab|trieb M **a** (= *Viehabtrieb*) **im Herbst beginnt der ~ des Viehs von den Bergweiden** in autumn (*esp Brit*) or fall (*US*) they start to bring the

---

cattle down from the mountain pastures **b** (*Tech*) output **c** (*Aus*) mixture

Ab|trift ['aptrɪft] F -, -en (*Naut, Aviat*) drift

ab+trin|ken VT sep irreg to drink; **einen Schluck ~** to have or take a sip

Ab|tritt M **a** (*Theat*) exit; (= *Rücktritt*) (*von Minister*) resignation; (*von Monarch*) abdication **b** (*old:* = Klosett) privy (*old*)

Ab|tro|cken|tuch NT *pl* **-tücher** tea towel (*Brit*), dishtowel (*US*)

ab+trock|nen sep **VT** to dry (off); *Geschirr* to dry, to wipe **VI** to dry up, to do the drying-up

ab+trop|fen VI sep aux sein to drip; (*Geschirr*) to drain; **etw ~ lassen** (*Wäsche etc*) to let sth drip; *Salat* to drain sth; (*Geschirr*) to let sth drain

ab+trot|ten VI sep aux sein (*inf*) to creep off (*inf*), to slink off (*inf*)

ab+trot|zen VT sep **jdm etw ~** (*geh*) to wring sth out of sb

ab+tru|deln VI sep aux sein **a** (*Aviat*) to go down in a spin **b** (*inf:* = weggehen) to push off (*inf*)

ab|trün|nig ['aptrʏnɪç] ADJ renegade, apostate (*form, esp Eccl*); (= *rebellisch*) rebel; **jdm/einer Gruppe** etc **~ werden** to desert sb/a group; (= *sich erheben gegen*) to rebel against sb/a group; **er ist dem Glauben ~ geworden** he has left or deserted the faith, he has apostatized (*form*)

Ab|trün|nig|keit F -, *no pl* apostasy (*form*); (= *rebellische Gesinnung*) rebelliousness; **die ~ einer der Mitverschwörer** the desertion or apostasy (*form*) of one of the plotters

ab+tun VT sep irreg **a** (*fig:* = beiseite schieben*) to dismiss; **etw mit einem Achselzucken/einem Lachen ~** to shrug/laugh sth off; **etw kurz ~** to brush sth aside → *auch* **abgetan b** (*dial:* = ablegen) to take off

ab+tup|fen VT sep *Tränen, Blut* to dab away; *Gesicht, Mundwinkel* to dab; *Wunde* to swab, to dab

ab+ur|tei|len VT sep to pass sentence or judgement on; (*fig:* = verdammen) to condemn; **Verbrecher, die noch nicht abgeurteilt worden sind** criminals upon whom sentence has not yet been passed

Ab|ur|tei|lung F -, -en sentencing; (*fig*) condemnation; **bei der ~ des Täters** when sentence was/is being passed on the accused

Ab|ver|kauf M (*Aus:* = Ausverkauf) sale

ab+ver|lan|gen ptp **abverlangt** VT sep = abfordern

ab+wä|gen VT sep irreg to weigh up; *Worte* to weigh; **er wog beide Möglichkeiten gegeneinander ab** he weighed up the two possibilities → *auch* **abgewogen**

Ab|wä|gung F -, -en weighing up; (*von Worten*) weighing

Ab|wahl F voting out; **es kam zur ~ des gesamten Vorstands** the whole committee was voted out

ab|wähl|bar ADJ **der Präsident ist nicht ~** the president cannot be voted out (of office)

ab+wäh|len VT sep to vote out (of office); (*Sch*) *Fach* to give up

ab+wäl|zen VT sep *Schuld, Verantwortung* to shift (*auf +acc onto*); *Arbeit* to unload (*auf +acc onto*); *Kosten* to pass on (*auf +acc to*); **die Schuld von sich ~** to shift the blame onto somebody else

ab|wan|del|bar ADJ *Melodie* adaptable; *Thema auch* modifiable

ab+wan|deln VT sep *Melodie* to adapt; *Thema auch* to modify

Ab|wan|de|lung F -, -en = Abwandlung

ab+wan|dern VI sep aux sein to move (away) (*aus* from); (*Bevölkerung: zu einem anderen Ort auch*) to migrate (*aus* from); (*Kapital*) to be transferred (*aus* out of); (*inf: aus einer Veranstaltung etc*) to wander away or off; **viele Spieler/Abonnenten** etc **wandern ab** a lot of players/subscribers etc are transferring

---

Ab|wan|de|rung F moving away; (*von Bevölkerung*) migration; (*von Kapital*) transference

Ab|wan|de|rungs|ver|lust M (*Sociol*) population drain

Ab|wand|lung F adaptation, variation; (*von Thema etc auch*) modification

Ab|wär|me F waste heat

Ab|wart ['apvart] M -(e)s, -e, **Ab|war|tin** [-tɪn] F -, -nen (*Sw*) concierge, caretaker

ab+war|ten sep ✪ 53.6 **VT** to wait for; **das Gewitter ~** to wait till the storm is over, to wait the storm out; **er kann es nicht mehr ~** he can't wait any longer; **das bleibt abzuwarten** that remains to be seen **VI**; **warten Sie ab!** just wait a bit!; **~ und Tee trinken** (*inf*) to wait and see; **im Moment können wir gar nichts tun, wir müssen ~** we can't do anything at the moment, we'll have to bide our time; **eine ~de Haltung einnehmen** to play a waiting game, to adopt a policy of wait-and-see

ab|wärts ['apvɛrts] ADV down; (= *nach unten auch*) downwards; **den Fluss/Berg ~** down the river/mountain; **„abwärts!"** (*im Fahrstuhl*) "going down!"; **vom Abteilungsleiter ~** from the head of department down(wards)

Ab|wärts-: Ab|wärts|ent|wick|lung F downwards or downhill trend; **Ab|wärts|fahrt** F journey down; **ab|wärts ge|hen** ▲ VI impers aux sein (*fig*) **mit ihm/dem Land geht es abwärts** he/the country is going downhill; **ab|wärts|kom|pa|ti|bel** ADJ (*Comput*) downward compatible; **Ab|wärts|trend** M downwards or downhill trend

Ab|wasch¹ ['apvaʃ] M -s, *no pl* washing-up (*Brit*), dirty dishes *pl*; **den ~ machen** to do the washing-up (*Brit*), to wash up (*Brit*), to wash the dishes; **... dann kannst du das auch machen, das ist (dann) ein ~** (*inf*) ... then you could do that as well and kill two birds with one stone

Ab|wasch² F -, -en (*Aus:* = Spülbecken) sink

ab|wasch|bar ADJ *Tapete* washable; *Kleidung* wipeable; *Tinte* non-permanent

Ab|wasch|be|cken NT sink

ab+wa|schen sep irreg **VT** *Gesicht* to wash; *Geschirr* to wash, to wash up (*Brit*); *Farbe, Schmutz* to wash off; *Pferd, Auto* to wash down; (*fig liter*) *Schande, Schmach* to wipe out; **den Schmutz (vom Gesicht) ~** to wash the dirt off (one's face) **VI** to wash up (*Brit*), to do the washing-up (*Brit*), to do the washing-up (*Brit*), to wash the dishes

Ab|wasch|lap|pen M dishcloth, washing-up cloth (*Brit*)

Ab|wasch|was|ser NT *pl* **-wässer** washing-up water (*Brit*), dishwater; (*fig inf*) dishwater (*inf*)

Ab|was|ser NT *pl* **-wässer** sewage *no pl*; **industrielle Abwässer** industrial effluents *pl* or waste *sing*

Ab|was|ser-: Ab|was|ser|auf|be|rei|tung F reprocessing of sewage; (*von Industrieabwässern*) reprocessing of effluents; **Ab|was|ser|ka|nal** M sewer; **Ab|was|ser|rei|ni|gung** F purification of sewage; (*von Industrieabwässern*) purification of effluents

ab+wech|seln VIR sep to alternate; **sich** or **ei|nander ~** to alternate; (*Menschen auch*) to take turns; **sich mit jdm ~** to take turns with sb; **(sich) miteinander ~** to alternate (with each other or one another), to take turns; **Regen und Schnee wechselten (sich) miteinander ab** it rained and snowed alternately; **ihre Launen wechseln oft blitzschnell miteinander ab** her moods often change or vary from one minute to the next

ab|wech|selnd **ADV** alternately; **wir haben ~ Klavier gespielt** we took turns playing the piano; **er war ~ fröhlich und traurig** he alternated between being happy and sad, he was by turns happy and sad **ADJ** alternate

Ab|wechs|lung ['apvɛkslʊŋ] F -, -en change; (= *Zerstreuung*) diversion; **eine angenehme/schöne**

~ a pleasant/nice change; **zur** ~ for a change; **für** ~ **sorgen** to provide entertainment; **dort ist reichlich für** ~ **gesorgt** there's quite a variety of things going on there; **hier haben wir wenig** ~ there's not much variety in life here; **da gibt es mehr** ~ there's more going on there

Ab|wechs|lungs-: ab|wechs|lungs|hal|ber ADV for a change, to make a change; **ab|wechs|lungs|los** ADJ monotonous; **ab|wechs|lungs|reich** ADJ varied ADV **den Unterricht** ~ **gestalten** to teach the class in an interesting and varied fashion; **Informationen** ~ **präsentieren** to present information in an interesting and varied way

Ab|weg ['apveːk] M (fig) mistake, error; **jdn auf** ~**e führen** to mislead sb, to lead sb astray (auch moralisch); **auf** ~**e geraten** or **kommen** to go astray; (moralisch auch) to stray from the straight and narrow

ab|we|gig ['apveːgɪç] ADJ absurd; Verdacht unfounded, groundless

Ab|we|gig|keit F -, no pl absurdity; (von Verdacht) groundlessness

Ab|wehr F , no pl **a** (Biol, Psych, Med) defence (Brit), defense (US) (+gen against); (= Schutz) protection (+gen against); **Mechanismen der** ~ **defence** (Brit) or **defense** (US) mechanisms; **der** ~ **von etw dienen** to provide or give protection against sth **b** (= Zurückweisung) repulse; (= Abweisung) rejection; (= Spionageabwehr) counterintelligence (service); **die** ~ **des Feindes** the repulsing or repelling of the enemy; **bei der** ~ **sein** to be with or in counterintelligence; **auf** ~ **stoßen** to be repulsed, to meet with a repulse **c** (Sport) defence (Brit), defense (US); (= Abwehraktion) piece of defence (Brit) or defense (US) (work); **er ist besser in der** ~ he's better in or at defence (Brit) or defense (US)

Ab|wehr-: ab|wehr|be|reit ADJ (Mil, fig) ~ **sein** to be ready to take defensive action; **Ab|wehr|be|reit|schaft** F (Mil) readiness to take defensive action; **die** ~ **des Körpers** the body's defences pl (Brit) or defenses pl (US); **Ab|wehr|dienst** M counterintelligence service

ab+weh|ren sep VT **a** Gegner to fend or ward off; Angriff, Feind to repulse, to repel (form); Flugzeug, Rakete to repel; Ball to clear; Schlag to parry, to ward off; **hervorragend, wie der Torwart den Ball abwehrte** that was a really good save the goalkeeper made (there) **b** (= fern halten) to keep away; Krankheitserreger to protect against; Gefahr, üble Folgen, Krise to avert; Inflation to fight against **c** (= abweisen) **eine** ~**de Geste** a dismissive wave of the hand VI **a** (Sport) to clear; (Torwart) to save; **mit dem Kopf** ~ to head clear; **zur Ecke** ~ to clear the ball (so that a corner is given away) **b** (= ablehnen) to refuse; **nein, wehrte sie ab** no, she said in refusal

Ab|wehr-: Ab|wehr|feh|ler M (Sport) defensive error; **Ab|wehr|hal|tung** F (Sport, Psych) (= Einstellung) defensiveness; (= Körperhaltung) defensive posture; **sich in** ~ **befinden** to be on the defensive; **Ab|wehr|hand|lung** F defence (Brit) or defense (US) reaction; **Ab|wehrkampf** M (Mil, Sport) defence (Brit), defense (US); **ein** ~ **a defensive action; Ab|wehr|kräfte** PL (Physiol) (the body's) defences pl (Brit) or defenses pl (US); **Ab|wehr|me|cha|nis|mus** M (Psych) defence (Brit) or defense (US) mechanism; **Ab|wehr|ra|ke|te** F anti-aircraft missile; **Ab|wehr|re|ak|ti|on** F (Psych) defence (Brit) or defense (US) reaction; **ab|wehr|schwach** ADJ **a** (Sport) weak in defence (Brit) or defense (US), with a poor defence (Brit) or defense (US); **das ist eine** ~**e Mannschaft** that's a team with a poor defence (Brit) or defense (US) **b** (Med) immunosuppressed; **Ab|wehr|spe|zi|a|list(in)** M(F) (in Geheimdienst) counterespionage expert; (Mil) defence (Brit) or defense (US) expert; (Sport) defensive

expert; **Ab|wehr|spiel** NT (Sport) defensive play; **Ab|wehr|spie|ler(in)** M(F) defender; **ab|wehr|stark** ADJ (Sport) strong in defence (Brit) or defense (US); **das ist eine** ~**e Mannschaft** they're a good defensive team

ab+wei|chen¹ VI sep irreg aux sein (= sich entfernen) to deviate; (= sich unterscheiden) to differ; (zwei Theorien, Auffassungen etc) to differ, to diverge; **vom Kurs** ~ to deviate or depart from one's course; **vom Thema** ~ to digress, to go off the point; **vom rechten Weg** ~ (fig) to wander or err from the straight and narrow; **ich weiche erheblich von seiner Meinung ab** I hold quite a different view from him; ~**des Verhalten** (Psych, Soziol) deviant behaviour (Brit) or behavior (US)

ab+wei|chen² VT sep Briefmarke etc to soak off

Ab|weich|ler ['apvaɪçlɐ] M -s, -, **Ab|weich|le|rin** [-ərɪn] F -, -nen deviant

ab|weich|le|risch ['apvaɪçlərɪʃ] ADJ deviant

Ab|weich|ler|tum ['apvaɪçlɐtuːm] NT -s, no pl (Pol) deviancy

Ab|wei|chung ['apvaɪçʊŋ] F -, -en (von Kurs etc) deviation; (= Unterschied) difference; (von zwei Theorien, Auffassungen etc) divergence; (von Magnetnadel) declination; ~ **von der Norm/Wahrheit** departure from the norm/truth; ~ **von der Parteilinie** failure to toe the party line, deviation from the party line; **zulässige** ~ (Tech) tolerance; (zeitlich, zahlenmäßig) allowance

ab+wei|den VT sep (rare) Wiese to graze

ab+wei|sen VT sep irreg to turn down, to reject; Bitte auch to refuse; (= wegschicken) to turn away; (Jur) Klage to dismiss; **er lässt sich nicht** ~ he won't take no for an answer

ab|wei|send ADJ Ton, Blick cold, chilly; Mensch cold ADV negatively; **er steht diesem Vorhaben nicht** ~ **gegenüber** he is not entirely opposed to the idea

Ab|wei|sung F rejection; (= das Wegschicken) turning away; (von Bitte) refusal; (von Klage) dismissal

ab+wend|bar ADJ avoidable

ab+wen|den sep reg or irreg VT **a** (= verhindern) Unheil, Folgen to avert **b** (= zur Seite wenden) to turn away; Blick to avert; Kopf to turn; **er wandte das Gesicht ab** he looked away VR to turn away

ab+wer|ben VT sep irreg to woo away (+dat from)

Ab|wer|bung F wooing away

ab+wer|fen sep irreg VT to throw off; Reiter to throw; Bomben, Flugblätter etc to drop; Ballast to jettison; Geweih to shed, to cast; Blätter, Nadeln to shed; (Cards) to discard, to throw away; (Sport) Ball, Speer to throw; Latte to knock off or down; (Comm) Gewinn to yield, to return, to show; Zinsen to bear, to yield; (fig liter) Joch, Fesseln to cast or throw off (Ftbl) to throw

ab+wer|ten sep VT **a** Währung to devalue **b** (fig) Ideale, Sprache, Kultur to debase, to cheapen; jds Leistung to devalue; **diese Tugend ist heute abgewertet** this virtue is no longer valued today; **er muss immer alles** ~ he always has to run everything down VI (Fin) to devalue

ab|wer|tend ADJ derogatory, pejorative; Blick dismissive ADV derogatorily, pejoratively

Ab|wer|tung F **a** (von Währung) devaluation; **eine** ~ **vornehmen** to devalue (the currency) **b** (fig) debasement, cheapening; **solche Ideale erfahren eine immer stärkere** ~ such ideals are valued less and less or are constantly losing their value

ab|we|send ['apveːznt] ADJ absent; (von zu Hause auch) away pred; (iro: = zerstreut auch) far away; Blick absent-minded; **die Abwesenden** the absentees

Ab|we|sen|heit ['apveːznhaɪt] F -, -en absence; (fig: = Geistesabwesenheit) abstraction; **in** ~ (Jur)

in absence, in absentia; **durch** ~ **glänzen** (iro) to be conspicuous by one's absence

Ab|wet|ter PL (Min) used air

ab+wet|zen sep VT (= abschaben) to wear smooth VT aux sein (inf) to hare off (Brit inf), to bolt (Brit inf)

ab+wi|ckeln sep VT **a** (= abspulen) to unwind; Verband to take off, to remove **b** (fig: = erledigen) to deal with; Geschäft to complete, to conclude; Kontrolle to carry out; Veranstaltung to run; (Comm: = liquidieren) to wind up; **die Versammlung wurde in aller Ruhe abgewickelt** the meeting went off peacefully VR to unwind; (= vonstatten gehen) to go or pass off

Ab|wick|lung ['apvɪklʊŋ] F -, -en **a** (= Erledigung) completion, conclusion; (von Kontrolle) carrying out; (von Veranstaltung) running; (Comm: = Liquidation) winding up; **die Polizei sorgte für eine reibungslose** ~ **der Veranstaltung** the police made sure that the event went or passed off smoothly **b** (= das Abspulen) unwinding

ab+wie|geln ['apviːgln] sep VT to appease; wütende Menge etc auch to calm down VI to calm things down; **das Abwiegeln** appeasement

ab+wie|gen VT sep irreg to weigh out

Ab|wieg|ler ['apviːglɐ] M -s, -, **Ab|wieg|le|rin** [-ərɪn] F -, -nen appeaser, conciliator

ab+wim|meln VT sep (inf) jdn to get rid of (inf); Auftrag to get out of (inf); **die Sekretärin hat mich abgewimmelt** his secretary turned me away; **lass dich nicht** ~ don't let them get rid of you (inf)

Ab|wind M (Aviat) downwash; (Met) down current

ab+win|keln ['apvɪŋkln] VT sep Arm to bend; **mit abgewinkelten Armen** (in den Hüften) with arms akimbo

ab+win|ken sep VI (inf) (abwehrend) to wave it/ him etc aside; (resignierend) to groan; (fig: = ablehnen) to say no; **als er merkte, wovon ich reden wollte, winkte er gleich ab** when he realized what I wanted to talk about he immediately put me off or stopped me; **der Chef winkt bei so einem Vorschlag bestimmt gleich ab** the boss is bound to say no to or to turn down a suggestion like that; **wenn Bonn abwinkt ...** if the (German) government turns us/them etc down or says no ... → **müde** VTI (bei Zug) to give the "go" signal; **ein Rennen** ~ to wave the chequered (Brit) or checkered (US) flag; (nach Unfall etc) to stop the race; **einen Rennfahrer** ~ to wave a driver down; **trinken/tanzen bis zum Abwinken** (inf) to drink/ dance till one drops (inf); **es gab Champagner bis zum Abwinken** (inf) there was loads and loads of champagne (inf)

ab+wirt|schaf|ten VI sep (inf) to go downhill; **abgewirtschaftet haben** to have reached rock bottom → auch **abgewirtschaftet**

ab+wi|schen VT sep Staub, Schmutz etc to wipe off or away; Hände, Nase etc to wipe; Augen, Tränen to dry; **er wischte sich** (dat) **den Schweiß von der Stirn ab** he mopped (the sweat from) his brow

ab+woh|nen VT sep **a** Möbel to wear out; Haus, Zimmer to make shabby **b** Baukostenzuschuss to pay off with the rent; **die Miete voll** ~ to stay for the time for which rent has been paid

ab+wra|cken ['apvrakn] VT sep Schiff, Auto, technische Anlage to break (up) → auch **abgewrackt**

Ab|wurf M throwing off; (von Reiter) throw; (von Bomben etc) dropping; (von Ballast) jettisoning; (von Geweih) casting; (Comm: von Zinsen, Gewinn) yield; (Sport) (der Latte) knocking down or off; (des Speers etc) throwing; **ein** ~ **vom Tor** a goal throw, a throw-out

ab+wür|gen VT sep (inf) to scotch; Motor to stall; **etw von vornherein** ~ to nip sth in the bud

ạb+zah|len VT *sep* to pay off

ạb+zäh|len *sep* **VT** to count; **er zählte zwanzig Hunderteuroscheine ab** he counted out twenty hundred-euro notes; **bitte das Fahrgeld abgezählt bereithalten** please tender exact *or* correct fare (*form*) → **Finger VI** to number off

Ạb|zähl|reim M counting-out rhyme (*such as "eeny meeny miney mo", for choosing a person*)

Ạb|zah|lung F **a** (= *Rückzahlung*) repayment, paying off **b** (= *Ratenzahlung*) hire purchase (*Brit*), HP (*Brit*), installment plan (*US*); (= *Rate*) (re)payment, instalment (*Brit*), installment (*US*); **etw auf ~ kaufen** to buy sth on HP (*Brit*) *or* on hire purchase (*Brit*) *or* on the installment plan (*US*)

Ạb|zah|lungs|ge|schäft NT hire purchase (*Brit*), HP (*Brit*), installment plan (*US*)

Ạb|zähl|vers M = **Abzählreim**

ạb+zap|fen VT *sep* to draw off; **jdm Blut ~** (*inf*) to take blood from sb; **jdm Geld ~** to get some money out of sb

ạb+zäu|men VT *sep* Pferd etc to unbridle

ạb+zäu|nen ['aptsɔynən] VT *sep* to fence off

Ạb|zäu|nung F -, -en fencing

ạb+zeh|ren *sep* (*liter*) **VT** to emaciate → *auch* **abgezehrt VR** to waste *or* pine away

Ạb|zeh|rung F emaciation

Ạb|zei|chen NT badge; (*Mil*) insignia *pl*; (= *Orden, Auszeichnung*) decoration

ạb+zeich|nen *sep* **VT a** (= *abmalen*) to draw **b** (= *signieren*) to initial **VR** (= *sichtbar sein*) to stand out; (*Unterwäsche*) to show; (*fig*) (= *deutlich werden*) to emerge, to become apparent; (= *drohend bevorstehen*) to loom (on the horizon); **sich gegen etw ~** (= *kontrastieren*) to stand out against sth

abzgl. *abbr von* **abzüglich**

Ạb|zieh|bild NT transfer

ạb+zie|hen *sep irreg* **VT a** Tier to skin; Fell, Haut to remove, to take off; grüne Bohnen to string **b** Bett to strip; Bettzeug to strip off **c** (*Sw*: = *ausziehen*) Mantel, Schürze, Ring etc to take off; Hut to raise **d** Schlüssel to take out, to remove; Abzugshahn to press, to squeeze; Pistole to fire **e** (= *zurückziehen*) Truppen, Kapital to withdraw **f** (= *subtrahieren*) Zahlen to take away, to subtract; Steuern to deduct; **EUR 20 vom Preis ~** to take EUR 20 off the price; **man hatte mir zu viel abgezogen** they'd taken off *or* deducted too much, I'd had too much deducted **g** (= *abfüllen*) Wein to bottle; **Wein auf Flaschen ~** to bottle wine **h** (*Typ*: = *vervielfältigen*) to run off; (*Phot*) Bilder to make prints of, to print; **etw zwanzigmal ~** to run off twenty copies of sth **i** (= *schleifen*) to sharpen; Rasiermesser auch to strop; Parkett to sand (down) **j** (*Cook*) Suppe, Sauce to thicken; **die Suppe mit einem Ei ~** to beat an egg into the soup → **Nummer, Schau b**
VI a aux sein (= *sich verflüchtigen*) (Rauch, Dampf) to escape, to go away; (Sturmtief etc) to move away **b** aux sein (Soldaten) to pull out (aus of), to withdraw (aus from); (*inf*: = *weggehen*) to go off *or* away; **zieh ab!** (*inf*) clear off! (*Brit inf*), beat it! (*inf*) **c** (= *abdrücken*) to pull *or* squeeze the trigger, to fire **d** (*sl*: = *schnell fahren*) **das Auto zieht ganz schön ab** that car can really move (*inf*) **VR** (*Sw*: = *sich ausziehen*) to undress, to take off one's clothes

Ạb|zie|her ['aptsiːɐ] M -s, -, **Ạb|zie|he|rin** [-ərɪn] F -, -nen (*Typ*) proof puller

Ạb|zieh|pres|se F proof press

ạb+zie|len VI *sep* **auf etw** (*acc*) **~** to aim at sth; (*in Rede*) to get at sth; (Bemerkung, Maßnahme etc) to be aimed *or* directed at sth;

---

ich merkte sofort, worauf sie mit dieser Anspielung abzielte I saw immediately what she was driving *or* getting at with that allusion

ạb+zin|sen VT *sep* (*Fin*) to discount; **abgezinste Sparbriefe** savings certificates sold at discounted interest

Ạb|zin|sung F -, -en (*Fin*) discounting

ạb+zir|keln VT *sep* (*rare*: = *mit Zirkel abmessen*) to measure (off) with compasses; (*fig*: = *vorausplanen*) to calculate very carefully; Worte, Bewegungen to measure

ạb+zi|schen VI *sep* (*inf*: = *abhauen*) to beat it (*inf*); **zisch ab!** beat it! (*inf*)

ạb+zo|cken VT *sep* (*inf*) **jdn ~** to rip sb off (*inf*); **hier wird man nur abgezockt** they just rip you off here (*inf*)

ạb+zot|teln VI *sep aux sein* (*inf*) to toddle off (*inf*)

Ạb|zug ['aptsuːk] M **a** *no pl* (= *Weggang*) departure; (*Met: von Tief*) moving away; (= *Wegnahme: von Truppen, Kapital etc*) withdrawal; **jdm freien ~ gewähren** to give *or* grant sb a safe-conduct **b** (*usu pl: vom Lohn etc*) deduction; (= *Rabatt*) discount; (= *Comm*) net terms only; **er verdient ohne Abzüge ...** before deductions *or* stoppages he earns ...; **etw in ~ bringen** (*form*) to deduct sth **c** (*Typ*) copy; (= *Korrekturfahne*) proof; (*Phot*) print **d** (= *Öffnung für Rauch, Gas*) flue; **es muss für hinreichenden ~ gesorgt werden** there must be sufficient means for the gas/smoke to escape *or* to be drawn off **e** (*am Gewehr*) trigger

ạb|züg|lich ['aptsyːklɪç] PREP +*gen* (*Comm*) minus, less

Ạb|zugs-: ạb|zugs|fä|hig ADJ (*Fin*) (tax-)deductible; **ạb|zugs|frei** ADJ (*Fin*) tax-free; **Ạb|zugs|hau|be** F extractor hood; **Ạb|zugs|rohr** NT flue (pipe)

ạb+zup|fen VT *sep* to pull *or* pluck off (*von etw* sth); (*S Ger*: = *pflücken*) to pick

ạb+zwa|cken ['aptsvakn] VT *sep* (*dial*) **a** (= *abkneifen*) to pinch off **b** = **abknapsen**

ạb+zwe|cken ['aptsvɛkn] VI *sep* **auf etw** (*acc*) **~** to be aimed at sth

Ạb|zweig M (*form*) junction; **der ~ nach Saarbrücken** the turn-off to *or* for Saarbrücken

Ạb|zweig|do|se F junction box

ạb+zwei|gen ['aptsvaign] *sep* **VI** *aux sein* to branch off **VT** (*inf*) to set *or* put on one side

Ạb|zwei|gung F -, -en junction, turn-off; (= *Nebenstrecke*) turn-off; (= *Gabelung*) fork; (*Rail*: = *Nebenlinie*) branch line; (*Elec*) junction

ạb+zwi|cken VT *sep* to pinch *or* nip off

ạb+zwin|gen VT *sep irreg* **jdm Respekt** etc **~** to gain sb's respect etc; **jdm zwang** (*dat*) **ein Lächeln ab** he forced a smile

ạb+zwit|schern VI *sep aux sein* (*inf*) to go off, to take oneself off

a cap|pel|la [a ka'pɛla] ADV (*Mus*) a cappella

Ac|ces|soires [aksɛ'soaːɐ(s)] PL accessories *pl*

A|ce|tat [atse'taːt] NT -s, -e acetate

A|ce|ton [atse'toːn] NT -s, -e acetone

A|ce|ty|len [atsety'leːn] NT -s, *no pl* acetylene

A|ce|ty|len|(sau|er|stoff)|bren|ner M oxyacetylene burner

ach [ax] **INTERJ** oh; (*poet auch*) O; (*bedauernd auch*) alas (*old, liter*); **~ nein!** oh no!; (*überrascht*) no!, really!; (*ablehnend*) no, no!; **~ nein, ausgerechnet der!** well, well, him of all people!; **~ so!** I see!, aha!; (= *ja richtig*) of course!; **~ was** *or* **wo!** of course not; **~ was** *or* **wo, das ist doch nicht so schlimm!** come on now, it's not that bad; **~ was** *or* **wo, das ist nicht nötig!** no, no that's not necessary; **~ wirklich?** oh really?, do you/does he really?; **~ je!** oh dear!, oh dear(ie) me! **ADV** (*geh*) **~ so schnell/schön** etc oh so quickly/lovely etc

---

Ach [ax] NT mit **~ und Krach** (*inf*) by the skin of one's teeth (*inf*); **eine Prüfung mit ~ und Krach bestehen** to scrape through an exam (by the skin of one's teeth); **ich habe die Behandlung überstanden, aber nur mit ~ und Weh** I had the treatment but I screamed blue murder (*Brit inf*) *or* bloody murder (*inf*)

A|chä|er [a'xɛːɐ] M -s, -, **A|chä|e|rin** [-ərɪn] F -, -nen (*Hist*) Achaean

A|chat [a'xaːt] M -(e)s, -e agate

a|cha|ten [a'xaːtn] ADJ *attr* agate

A|chill [a'xɪl] M -s, **A|chil|les** [a'xɪlɛs] M -' Achilles

A|chil|les|fer|se F Achilles heel

Ach|laut ▲ M voiceless velar fricative (*the sound "ch" in the Scottish "loch"*)

Achs- ['aks-]: **Achs|ab|stand** M wheelbase; **Achs|an|trieb** M (*Aut*) final drive; **Achs|auf|hän|gung** F (*Aut*) axle suspension; **Achs|bruch** M broken axle; **Achs|druck** M *pl* **-drücke** axle weight

Ach|se ['aksə] F -, -n **a** axis; **die ~ (Rom-Berlin)** (*Hist*) the (Rome-Berlin) Axis **b** (*Tech*) axle; (= *Propellerachse*) shaft; **auf (der) ~ sein** (*inf*) to be out (and about); (*Kraftfahrer, Vertreter etc*) to be on the road

Ach|sel ['aksl] F -, -n **a** shoulder; **die ~n** *or* **mit den ~n zucken** to shrug (one's shoulders) **b** (= *Achselhöhle*) armpit

Ach|sel-: Ach|sel|griff M underarm grip; **Ach|sel|haa|re** PL **die ~** underarm hair, the hair under one's arms; **Ach|sel|höh|le** F armpit; **Ach|sel|klap|pe** F, **Ach|sel|stück** NT (*Mil*) epaulette, epaulet (*US*); **Ach|sel|zu|cken** NT -s, *no pl* shrug; **mit einem ~** with a shrug (of one's shoulders); **ach|sel|zu|ckend ADV** with a shrug of one's shoulders; **er stand ~ da** he stood there shrugging his shoulders

Ach|sen- ['aksn-]: **Ach|sen|bruch** M broken axle; **Ach|sen|kreuz** NT (*Math*) coordinate system; **Ach|sen|mäch|te** PL (*Hist*) Axis powers *pl*

Achs-: Achs|la|ger NT axle bearing; **Achs|last** F axle weight; **Achs|schen|kel** M stub axle, steering knuckle (*US*); **Achs|stand** M wheelbase; **Achs|wel|le** F axle shaft

acht [axt] NUM eight; **für** *or* **auf ~ Tage** for a week; **in ~ Tagen** in a week's time; **heute/morgen in ~ Tagen** a week today/tomorrow, today/tomorrow week; **heute vor ~ Tagen** war ich ... a week ago today I was ...; **vor ~ Tagen werden sie wohl nicht fertig sein** they won't be ready for a week at least → *auch* **vier**

Acht¹ [axt] F -, -en eight; (*bei Fahrrad*) buckled wheel; (*beim Eislaufen etc*) figure (of) eight → *auch* **Vier**

Acht² ▲ F **sich in ~ nehmen** to be careful, to take care, to watch *or* look out; **etw außer ~ lassen** to leave sth out of consideration, to disregard sth; **etw außer aller ~ lassen** (*geh*) to pay no attention *or* heed whatsoever to sth, not to heed sth; **~ geben, ~ haben** (*geh*) to take care, to be careful (*auf +acc* of); (= *aufmerksam sein*) to pay attention (*auf +acc* to); **auf jdn/etw ~ geben** (= *beaufsichtigen*) to keep an eye on sb/sth, to look after sb/sth; **wenn man im Straßenverkehr nur einen Augenblick nicht ~ gibt, ...** if your attention wanders for just a second in traffic ...; **„O Mensch, gib ~!"** "O man, take heed"

Acht³ F -, *no pl* (*Hist*) outlawry, proscription; **jdn in ~ und Bann tun** to outlaw *or* proscribe sb; (*Eccl*) to place sb under the ban; (*fig*) to ostracize sb

acht|bar ADJ (*geh*) Gesinnung, Person worthy; Platzierung creditable, respectable

Acht|bar|keit ['axtbaːɐkaɪt] F -, *no pl* (*von Gesinnung, Person*) worthiness

Acht|eck NT octagon

acht|eckig ADJ octagonal, eight-sided

ach|tel ['axtl] ADJ eighth → *auch* **viertel**

Ach|tel ['axtl] NT **-s, -** eighth → *auch* **Viertel** ¹ **a**

Ach|tel-: Ach|tel|fi|na|le NT *round before the quarterfinal*, 2nd/3rd *etc* round; **ein Platz im ~** a place in the last sixteen; **Ach|tel|no|te** F quaver, eighth note (*US*); **Ach|tel|pau|se** F quaver rest (*Brit*), eighth note rest (*US*)

ach|ten ['axtn] ✪ 29.3, 42.1 VT **a** (= *schätzen*) to respect, to think highly of, to hold in high regard; **geachtete Leute** respected people **b** (= *respektieren*) Gesetze, Bräuche, jds Gesinnung to respect **c** (*geh*: = *betrachten*) to regard; **etw (für) gering ~** to have scant regard for sth VI **auf etw** (*acc*) **~** to pay attention to sth; **auf die Kinder ~** to keep an eye on the children; **darauf ~, dass ...** to be careful *or* to see *or* to take care that ...

äch|ten ['ɛçtn] VT (*Hist*) to outlaw, to proscribe; (*fig*) to ostracize

ach|tens ['axtns] ADV eighthly, in the eighth place

ach|tens|wert ['axtnsveːɐt] ADJ Person worthy; Motiv, Bemühungen, Handlung *auch* commendable

Ach|te(r) ['axtə] MF decl as adj eighth → *auch* **Vierte(r)**

Ach|ter ['axtə] M **-s, -** (*Rudern*) eight; (*Eislauf etc*) figure (of) eight → *auch* **Vierer**

ach|te(r, s) ['axtə] ADJ eighth → *auch* **vierte(r, s)**

Ach|ter-: Ach|ter|aus [-laus] ADV (*Naut*) astern; **Ach|ter|bahn** F big dipper (*Brit*), roller coaster, switchback; **Ach|ter|deck** M (*Naut*) afterdeck; **ach|ter|las|tig** [-lastiç] ADJ Schiff stern-heavy

ach|tern ['axtn] ADV (*Naut*) aft, astern; **nach ~ gehen** to go aft; **nach ~ abdrehen** to turn astern; **von ~** from astern

Acht- ['axt-]: **acht|fach** [-fax] ADJ eightfold; **in ~er Ausfertigung** with seven copies → *auch* **vierfach** ▲ ADV eightfold, eight times; **Acht|fü|ßer** [-fyːsɐ] M **-s, -** (*Zool*) octopod

acht+ge|ben △ VI → **Acht** ²

acht+ha|ben △ VI → **Acht** ²

Acht-: **acht|hun|dert** ['axt'hʊndɐt] NUM eight hundred; **Acht|kampf** M *a gymnastic competition with eight events*; **acht|kan|tig** ADJ (*lit*) eight-sided ▲ ADV **~ rausfliegen** (*inf*) to be flung out on one's ear (*inf*)

acht|los ADJ careless, thoughtless ▲ ADV **durchblättern** casually; **wegwerfen** thoughtlessly; **sich verhalten** carelessly; **viele gehen ~ daran vorbei** many people just pass by without noticing it

Acht|lo|sig|keit F **-,** no pl carelessness, thoughtlessness

acht|mal ['axtma:l] ADV eight times

acht|sam ['axtza:m] (*geh*) ADJ attentive; (= *sorgfältig*) careful ▲ ADV carefully; **mit etw ~ umgehen** to be careful with sth; **sich ~ benehmen** to be careful

Acht|sam|keit F **-,** no pl (*geh*) attentiveness; (= *Sorgfalt*) care

Acht-: Acht|stun|den|tag M eight-hour day; **acht|tä|gig** ADJ lasting a week, week-long; **mit ~er Verspätung** a week late; **der ~e Streik ist ...** the week-old *or* week-long strike is ...; **acht|täg|lich** ADJ weekly; **acht|tau|send** ['axt'tauznt] NUM eight thousand; **ein Achttausender** *a mountain eight thousand metres in height* → *auch* **vierfach**; **Acht|und|sech|zi|ger(in)** [axt'ʊntzɛçtsɪgɐ, -ərɪn] M(F), **68er(in)** M(F) member of the '68 generation; **die ~** the '68 generation

Ach|tung ['axtʊŋ] F **-,** no pl **a** **~!** watch *or* look out!; (*Mil*: *Befehl*) attention!; **~, ~!** (your) attention please!; **„Achtung Hochspannung!"** "danger, high voltage"; **„Achtung Lebensgefahr!"** "danger"; **„Achtung Stufe!"** "mind the step"; **~, fertig, los!** ready, steady *or* get set, go! **b** (= *Wertschätzung*) respect (*vor* +*dat* for); **die ~ vor sich selbst** one's self-respect *or* self-esteem; **bei aller ~ vor jdm/etw** with all due respect to sb/sth; **in hoher ~ bei jdm stehen** to

be held in high esteem by sb, to be highly esteemed by sb; **jdm ~ einflößen** to command *or* gain sb's respect; **~ gebietend** (*geh*) awe-inspiring; **sich** (*dat*) **~ verschaffen** to make oneself respected, to gain respect for oneself; **jdm die nötige ~ entgegenbringen** to give sb the respect due to him/her *etc*; **alle ~!** good for you/him *etc*!

Äch|tung ['ɛçtʊŋ] F **-,** -en (*Hist*) proscription, outlawing; (*fig*: *gesellschaftlich*) ostracism

ach|tung|ge|bie|tend △ ADJ → **Achtung** b

Ach|tungs-: Ach|tungs|ap|plaus M polite applause; **Ach|tungs|er|folg** M succès d'estime; **ach|tungs|voll** ADJ (*rare*) respectful

acht|zehn ['axtse:n] NUM eighteen → *auch* **vierzehn**

acht|zig ['axtsɪç] NUM eighty; **auf ~ sein** (*inf*) to be livid, to be hopping mad (*inf*); **da war er gleich auf ~** (*inf*) then he got livid → *auch* **vierzig**

Acht|zi|ger ['axtsɪgɐ] M **-s, -**, **Acht|zi|ge|rin** [-ərɪn] F **-,** -nen eighty-year-old, octogenarian → *auch* **Vierziger** ²

äch|zen ['ɛçtsn] VI to groan (*vor* +*dat* with); (*Brücke, Baum etc auch*) to creak; **~ und stöhnen** to moan and groan

Ächz|er ['ɛçtsɐ] M **-s, -** groan

Acker ['akɐ] M **-s, ≈** ['ɛkɐ] **a** (= *Feld*) field; **den ~ bestellen** to till the soil; **die Äcker bestellen** to plough (*Brit*) or plow (*US*) the fields; **einen ~ bebauen** or **bewirtschaften** to work the land; **sich vom ~ machen** (*sl*: = *verschwinden*) to split (*sl*) **b** (*old*: *Feldmaß*) ≈ acre

Acker-: Acker|bau M, *no pl* agriculture, arable farming; **~ betreiben** to farm the land; **~ treibend** farming; **~ und Viehzucht** farming; **Acker|bau|er** M *pl* -bauern, **Acker|bäu|e|rin** F farmer; **acker|bau|trei|bend** △ ADJ *attr* Ackerbau; **Acker|bür|ger** M (*Hist*) townsman who farms a smallholding; **Acker|flä|che** F area of arable land; **Acker|fur|che** F furrow; **Acker|gaul** M (*pej*) farm horse, old nag (*pej*) → **Rennpferd**; **Acker|ge|rät** NT farm *or* agricultural implement; **Acker|kru|me** F topsoil; **Acker|land** NT arable land; **Acker|mann** M *pl* -leute *or* -männer (*old, liter*) husbandman (*old, liter*)

ackern ['akɐn] VI **a** (*inf*) to slog away (*inf*) **b** (*old*) to till the soil VT (*old*: = *pflügen*) to till

Acker-: Acker|sa|lat M (*S Ger*) lamb's lettuce (*Brit*), corn salad; **Acker|schol|le** F (*liter*) soil

Ackers|mann M *pl* -leute *or* -männer (*old, liter*) husbandman (*old, liter*)

Acker-: Acker|wal|ze F (land) roller; **Acker|win|de** F (*Bot*) field bindweed

a con|to [a 'kɔnto] ADV (*Comm*) on account

Ac|ryl [a'kry:l] NT **-s,** *no pl* acrylic

Ac|ryl- in cpds acrylic; **Ac|ryl|far|be** F acrylic paint; **Ac|ryl|glas** NT acrylic glass; **Ac|ryl|plat|te** F acrylic tile

Ac|tion ['ɛkʃən] F **-,** *no pl* (*sl*) action

Ac|tion|film ['ɛkʃən-] M action film

a. D. [a:'de:] *abbr von* **außer Dienst** ret(d)

A. D. [a:'de:] *abbr von* **Anno Domini** AD

A|da|bei ['a:dabai] M **-s, -s** (*Aus, inf*) limelighter (*inf*)

ad ab|sur|dum [at ap'zʊrdʊm] ADV **~ führen** to make a nonsense of; Argument etc to reduce to absurdity *or* absurdum

ADAC [a:de:a:'tse:] *-, no pl abbr von* **Allgemeiner Deutscher Automobil-Club** ≈ AA (*Brit*), ≈ RAC (*Brit*), ≈ AAA (*US*)

ad ac|ta [at 'akta] ADV **etw ~ legen** (*fig*) to consider sth finished; Frage, Problem to consider sth closed

A|dam ['a:dam] M **-s** Adam; **seit ~s Zeiten** (*inf*) since the year dot (*inf*); **das stammt noch von ~ und Eva** (*inf*) it's out of the ark (*inf*); **bei ~ und**

Eva anfangen (*inf*) to start right from scratch (*inf*) *or* from square one (*inf*) → **Riese** ¹

A|dams|ap|fel M (*inf*) Adam's apple

A|dams|kos|tüm NT (*dated hum*) birthday suit; **im ~** in one's birthday suit, as nature made one

A|dap|ta|ti|on [adapta'tsio:n] F **-,** -en adaptation

A|dap|ter [a'daptɐ] M **-s, -** adapter, adaptor

A|dap|ter|kar|te F (*Comput*) adapter card

a|dap|tie|ren [adap'ti:rən] ptp **adaptiert** VT **a** (= *anpassen*) to adapt **b** (*Aus*: = *herrichten*) to fix up

A|dap|tie|rung F **-,** -en, **A|dap|ti|on** [adap'tsio:n] F **-,** -en adaptation

a|dap|tiv [adap'ti:f] ADJ adaptive

a|dä|quat [adɛ'kva:t, at'ɛ'kva:t] ADJ Bemühung, Belohnung, Übersetzung adequate; Stellung, Verhalten suitable; Kritik valid; **einer Sache** (*dat*) **~ sein** to be adequate to sth ADV adequately

A|dä|quat|heit F **-,** *no pl* (*geh*) adequacy; (*von Stellung, Verhalten*) suitability; (*von Kritik*) validity

ad|die|ren [a'di:rən] ptp **addiert** VT to add (up) VI to add

Ad|dier|ma|schi|ne F adding machine

Ad|dis A|be|ba ['adɪs 'a(ː)beba, - a'be:ba] NT **-, -s** Addis Ababa

Ad|di|ti|on [adi'tsio:n] F **-,** -en addition; (*fig*) agglomeration

Ad|di|ti|ons|ma|schi|ne F adding machine

Ad|di|tiv [adi'ti:f] NT **-s, -e** [-və] additive

a|de [a'de:] INTERJ (*old, S Ger*) farewell (*old, liter*), adieu (*old, liter*); **jdm ~ sagen** to bid sb farewell; **einer Sache** (*dat*) **~ sagen** to say farewell to sth

A|de|bar ['a:dəbar] M **-s, -e** (*N Ger*) stork

A|del ['a:dl] M **-s,** *no pl* **a** (= *Adelsgeschlecht, Adelsstand*) nobility; (*esp Brit*) peerage; (*esp hoher Adel*) aristocracy; **von ~ sein** to be a member of the nobility, to be of noble birth; **eine Familie von ~** an aristocratic family; **er stammt aus altem ~** he comes from an old aristocratic family; **der niedere ~** the lesser nobility, the gentry; **der hohe ~** the higher nobility, the aristocracy; **das ist verarmter ~** they are impoverished nobility; **~ verpflichtet** noblesse oblige **b** (= *Adelstitel*) title; (*esp Brit*) peerage; **erblicher ~** hereditary title/peerage **c** (*liter*: = *edle Gesinnung*) nobility; **~ der Seele/des Herzens/des Geistes** nobility of the soul/of the heart/of mind

a|de|lig ['a:dəlɪç] ADJ = **adlig**

A|de|li|ge ['a:dəlɪgə] F decl as adj = **Adlige**

A|de|li|ge(r) ['a:dəlɪgə] M = **Adlige(r)**

a|deln ['a:dln] VT to bestow a peerage on, to make a (life) peer (*Brit*), to ennoble; (= *den Titel "Sir" verleihen*) to knight; (= *niedrigen Adel verleihen*) to bestow a title on; (*fig geh*: = *auszeichnen*) to ennoble VI **etw adelt** (*geh*) sth ennobles the soul

Adels-: A|dels|be|zeich|nung F title; **A|dels|brief** M patent of nobility; **A|dels|prä|di|kat** NT mark of nobility (*in a name*); **A|dels|stand** M nobility; (*Brit auch*) peerage; (*hoher auch*) aristocracy; **in den ~ erheben** = **adeln** VT; **A|dels|stolz** M pride in one's noble birth; **A|dels|ti|tel** M title

A|de|lung ['a:dəlʊŋ] F **-,** -en raising to the peerage, ennoblement; (= *Verleihung des Titels "Sir"*) knighting; (= *Verleihung von niedrigem Adel*) bestowing a title (+*gen* on)

A|dept [a'dɛpt] M **-en, -en**, **A|dep|tin** [a'dɛptɪn] F **-,** -nen (*old*: *der Geheimwissenschaften*) initiate; (*iro geh*) disciple

A|der [a:dɐ] F **-,** -n (*Bot, Geol*) vein; (*Physiol*) blood vessel; (*Elec*: = *Leitungsdraht*) core; (*fig*: = *Veranlagung*) bent; **das spricht seine künstlerische/musikalische ~ an** that appeals to the artist/musician in him; **eine/keine ~ für etw haben** to have feeling/no feeling for sth; **eine**

poetische/musikalische ~ haben to have a poetical/musical streak; **sich** (dat) **die ~n öffnen** (geh) to slash one's wrists; **jdn zur ~ lassen** (old, fig inf) to bleed sb

Ä|der|chen ['ɛːdəçən] NT **-s, -** dim von Ader

A|der|lass ▲ [-las] M **-es, Aderlässe** [-lɛsə] (old Med) blood-letting (auch fig), bleeding; **bei jdm einen ~ machen** to bleed sb; **die Abwanderung der Akademiker ist ein ~, den sich das Land nicht länger leisten kann** the country can no longer afford the bleeding of its resources through the exodus of its academics

ä|dern ['ɛːdən] VT → **geädert**

Ä|de|rung F **-, -en** veining

Ad|hä|si|on [athɛ'zioːn] F **-, -en** (Phys) adhesion

Ad|hä|si|ons-: **Ad|hä|si|ons|kraft** F adhesive power, power of adhesion; **Ad|hä|si|ons|ver|schluss ▲** M adhesive seal

ad hoc [at 'hɔk, at 'hoːk] ADV (geh) ad hoc; **~ wurde ein Komitee gebildet** an ad hoc committee was set up

Ad-hoc- [at'hɔk-, at'hoːk-] in cpds ad hoc; **Ad-hoc-Maß|nah|me** f ad hoc measure

a|dieu [a'diøː] INTERJ (old, dial) adieu (obs), farewell (old); **jdm ~ sagen** to bid sb farewell (old), to say farewell or adieu to sb

a|di|pös [adi'pøːs] ADJ (Med: = fettleibig) obese, corpulent (liter)

Ad|jek|tiv ['atjɛktiːf] NT **-s, -e** [-və] adjective

ad|jek|ti|visch ['atjɛkti:vɪʃ, atjɛk'ti:vɪʃ] ADJ adjectival ADV adjectively

Ad|jek|ti|vum ['atjɛkti:vʊm, atjɛk'ti:vʊm] NT **-s, Adjektiva** [-va] adjective

Ad|junkt [at'jʊŋkt] M **-en, -en, Adjunk|tin** [at'jʊŋktɪn] F **-, -nen** (Aus, Sw) junior civil servant

ad|jus|tie|ren [atjʊs'ti:rən] ptp **adjustiert** VT **a** (Tech) Werkstück to adjust; Messgerät to set **b** (Aus) to issue with uniforms/a uniform

Ad|jus|tie|rung F **-, -en a** (Tech) (von Werkstück) adjustment; (von Messgerät) setting **b** (Aus: = Uniform) uniform

Ad|ju|tant [atju'tant] M **-en, -en, Ad|ju|tan|tin** [-'tantɪn] F **-, -nen** adjutant; (von General) aide-(de-camp)

Ad|la|tus [at'la:tʊs] M **-, Adlaten** or **Adlati** [-tn, -ti] (old, iro) assistant

Ad|ler ['a:dlɐ] M **-s, -** eagle

Ad|ler-: **Ad|ler|au|ge** NT (fig) eagle eye; **~n haben** to have eyes like a hawk, to be eagle-eyed; **Ad|ler|blick** M (fig) eagle eye; **Ad|ler|farn** M bracken; **Ad|ler|horst** M (eagle's) eyrie; **Ad|ler|na|se** F aquiline nose

ad|lig ['a:dlɪç] ADJ (lit, fig) noble; **~ sein** to be of noble birth

Ad|li|ge ['a:dlɪgə] F decl as adj member of the nobility, noblewoman; (Brit auch) peeress; (hohe auch) aristocrat

Ad|li|ge(r) ['a:dlɪgə] M decl as adj member of the nobility, nobleman; (Brit auch) peer; (hoher auch) aristocrat

Ad|mi|nist|ra|ti|on [atmɪnɪstra'tsioːn] F **-, -en** administration

ad|mi|nist|ra|tiv [atmɪnɪstra'ti:f] ADJ administrative ADV administratively

Ad|mi|nist|ra|tor [atmɪnɪs'tra:to:ɐ] M **-s, Administratoren** [-'to:rən], **Ad|mi|nist|ra|to|rin** [-'to:rɪn] F **-, -nen** administrator

ad|mi|nist|rie|ren [atmɪnɪs'tri:rən] ptp **administriert** VI (geh: = verwalten) to administrate

Ad|mi|ral¹ [atmi'ra:l] M **-s, -e** (Zool) red admiral

Ad|mi|ral² [atmi'ra:l] M **-s, -e** or **Admiräle** [-'rɛ:lə], **Ad|mi|ra|lin** [-'ra:lɪn] F **-, -nen** admiral

Ad|mi|ra|li|tät [atmiralɪ'tɛ:t] F **-, -en a** (= die Admirale) admirals pl **b** (= Marineleitung) admiralty

Ad|mi|rals|rang M rank of admiral

A|do|les|zenz [adoles'tsɛnts] F **-, no pl** (form) adolescence

A|do|nis [a'do:nɪs] M **-, -se** (geh) Adonis

A|do|nis|rös|chen [-rø:sçən] NT pheasant's eye

a|dop|tie|ren [adɔp'ti:rən] ptp **adoptiert** VT to adopt

A|dop|ti|on [adɔp'tsio:n] F **-, -en** adoption

A|dop|tiv- [adɔp'ti:f-]: **A|dop|tiv|el|tern** PL adoptive parents pl; **A|dop|tiv|kind** NT adopted child; **A|dop|tiv|sohn** M adopted son; **A|dop|tiv|toch|ter** F adopted daughter

Adr. abbr von **Adresse**

Ad|re|na|lin [adrena'li:n] NT **-s, no pl** adrenalin

Ad|re|na|lin-: **Ad|re|na|lin|schub** M surge of adrenalin; **Ad|re|na|lin|spie|gel** M , no pl adrenalin level; **Ad|re|na|lin|stoß** M surge of adrenalin

Ad|res|sant [adrɛ'sant] M **-en, -en, Ad|res|san|tin** [-'santɪn] F **-, -nen** (geh) sender; (Comm auch) consignor (form)

Ad|res|sat [adrɛ'sa:t] M **-en, -en, Ad|res|sa|tin** [-'sa:tɪn] F **-, -nen** (geh) addressee; (Comm auch) consignee (form); **~en** (fig) target group

Ad|res|sa|ten|grup|pe F target group

Ad|ress|buch ▲ NT directory; (privat) address book

Ad|res|se [a'drɛsə] F **-, -n a** (= Anschrift, Comput) address; **eine Warnung an jds ~** (acc) **rich|ten** (fig) to address a warning to sb; **dieser Vorwurf geht an Ihre eigene ~** this reproach is directed at or addressed to you (personally); **sich an die richtige ~ wenden** (inf) to go/come to the right place or person; **da sind Sie bei mir an der richtigen/falschen** or **verkehrten ~** (inf) you've come to the right/wrong person; **eine erste/feine ~** (inf: = Organisation) a top-class/ prominent establishment **b** (form: = Botschaft) address

Ad|res|sen-: **Ad|res|sen|än|de|rung** F change of address; **Ad|res|sen|auf|kle|ber** M address label; **Ad|res|sen|han|del** M mailing list trade or business; **Ad|res|sen|lis|te** F address list, list of addresses; (für Werbung etc) mailing list; **Ad|res|sen|ver|wal|tung** F (Comput) address filing system; **Ad|res|sen|ver|zeich|nis** NT directory of addresses

ad|res|sie|ren [adrɛ'si:rən] ptp **adressiert** VT to address (an +acc to)

Ad|res|sier|ma|schi|ne F Addressograph® (Brit), addressing machine

ad|rett [a'drɛt] (dated) ADJ smart ADV smartly

Ad|ria ['a:dria] F - Adriatic (Sea)

Ad|ri|a|ti|sches Meer [adri'a:tɪʃəs] NT (form) Adriatic Sea

Ad|strin|gens [at'strɪŋɡɛns] NT **-, Adstringen|zien** [-tsiən] astringent

Ad|van|tage [əd'va:ntɪdʒ] M **-s, -s** (Sport) advantage

Ad|vent [at'vɛnt] M **-s, -e** Advent; **im ~** in Advent; **erster/vierter ~** first/fourth Sunday in Advent

Ad|ven|tist [atvɛn'tɪst] M **-en, -en, Ad|ven|tis|tin** [-'tɪstɪn] F **-, -nen** (Rel) (Second) Adventist

Ad|vents-: **Ad|vents|ka|len|der** M Advent calendar; **Ad|vents|kranz** M Advent wreath; **Ad|vents|sonn|tag** M Sunday in Advent; **Ad|vents|zeit** F (season of) Advent

Ad|verb [at'vɛrp] NT **-s, Adverbien** [-biən] adverb

ad|ver|bi|al [atvɛr'bia:l] ADJ adverbial ADV adverbially

Ad|ver|bi|al-: **Ad|ver|bi|al|be|stim|mung** F adverbial qualification; **mit ~** qualified adverbially; **Ad|ver|bi|al|satz** M adverbial clause

ad|ver|sa|tiv [atvɛrza'ti:f] ADJ (Gram) adversative

Ad|ver|sa|tiv|satz M adversative clause

Ad|vo|ca|tus Dia|bo|li ▲ [atvo'ka:tʊs dia'bo:li] M **-, Advocati** [- -ti] (geh) devil's advocate

Ad|vo|kat [atvo'ka:t] M **-en, -en, Ad|vo|ka|tin** [-'ka:tɪn] F **-, -nen** (old Jur, fig) advocate; (Aus, Sw, auch pej) lawyer

Ad|vo|ka|tur [atvoka'tu:ɐ] F **-, -en a** legal profession **b** (= Büro) lawyer's office

Ad|vo|ka|tur|bü|ro NT (Sw), **Ad|vo|ka|turs|kanz|lei** F (Aus) lawyer's office

A|e|ro- [a'e:ro, 'ɛ:ro] in cpds aero

A|e|ro|bic [ɛ'ro:bɪk] NT **-(s)**, no pl aerobics sing

A|e|ro-: **A|e|ro|dy|na|mik** [aerody'na:mɪk] F aerodynamics sing or (bei Flugzeug etc) pl; **a|e|ro|dy|na|misch** [aerody'na:mɪʃ] ADJ aerodynamic ADV aerodynamically; **A|e|ro|gramm** [aero'gram] NT pl **-gramme** air letter, aerogram(me); **A|e|ro|nau|tik** [aero'nautɪk] F **-, no pl** aeronautics sing; **a|e|ro|nau|tisch** [aero'nautɪʃ] ADJ aeronautic(al); **A|e|ro|sol** [aero'zo:l, ɛro-] NT **-s, -e** aerosol

Af|fä|re [a'fɛ:rə] F **-, -n a** (= Angelegenheit) affair, business no pl; (= Liebesabenteuer) affair; **in eine ~ verwickelt sein** to be mixed up or involved in an affair; **sich aus der ~ ziehen** (inf) to get (oneself) out of it (inf) **b** (= Zwischenfall) incident, episode

Äff|chen ['ɛfçən] NT **-s, -** dim von Affe

Af|fe ['afə] M **-n, -n a** monkey; (= Menschenaffe) ape; **der Mensch stammt vom ~n ab** man is descended from the apes; **der nackte ~** the naked ape; **klettern wie ein ~** to climb like a monkey; **an jdm einen ~n gefressen haben** (inf) to have been really taken by sb; **du bist wohl vom (wilden) ~n gebissen!** (inf) you must be out of your tiny mind! (inf), you must be off your rocker! (inf) → **lausen, Schleifstein b** (sl: = Kerl) **ein eingebildeter ~** a conceited ass (inf) **c** (Mil inf) knapsack, backpack

Af|fekt [a'fɛkt] M **-(e)s, -e** emotion, affect (form); **im ~ begangenes Verbrechen** a crime committed under the influence of emotion, a crime committed in the heat of the moment; **im ~ handeln** to act in the heat of the moment

Af|fekt-: **af|fekt|ge|la|den** ADJ (geh) impassioned; **Af|fekt|hand|lung** F act committed under the influence of emotion

af|fek|tiert [afɛk'ti:ɐt] (pej) ADJ affected ADV affectedly; **sich ~ benehmen** to be affected, to behave affectedly

Af|fek|tiert|heit F **-, -en** affectation

af|fek|tiv [afɛk'ti:f] ADJ (Psych) affective

Af|fekt|stau M (Psych) emotional block

Af|fen-: **af|fen|ar|tig** ADJ like a monkey; (= menschenaffenartig) apelike; **mit ~er Geschwindigkeit** (inf) like greased lightning (inf), like or in a flash (inf); **~e Hitze** (inf) sweltering heat ADV **~ klettern** to climb like a monkey; **Af|fen|brot|baum** M monkey bread (tree), baobab; **af|fen|geil** (dated sl) ADJ (= super) wicked (inf), right on pred (inf); (= scharf) horny (inf) ADV really bad (inf); **Af|fen|ge|schwin|dig|keit** F (inf) ape house; **Af|fen|haus** NT ape house; **Af|fen|hit|ze** F (inf) sweltering heat (inf); **gestern war eine ~** yesterday was a scorcher (inf), yesterday it was sweltering (inf); **Af|fen|jäck|chen** NT , **Af|fen|ja|cke** F (Mil inf) monkey jacket; **Af|fen|kä|fig** M → **Affe** a monkey's/ape's cage; **Af|fen|lie|be** F blind adoration (zu of); **Af|fen|mensch** M (inf) apeman; **Af|fen|pin|scher** M griffon (terrier); **Af|fen|schan|de** F (inf) crying shame (inf); **Af|fen|schau|kel** F (inf) (Mil) fourragère; (usu pl: Frisur) looped plait (Brit) or braid (US); **Af|fen|spek|ta|kel** NT (inf) hullabaloo (Brit inf), uproar; **Af|fen|tanz** M (inf) → **Affentheater; Af|fen|tem|po** NT (inf) breakneck (Brit) or neck-breaking (US) speed (inf); **in** or **mit einem ~** at breakneck (Brit) or neck-breaking (US) speed (inf); **laufen auch** like the clappers (Brit inf); **Af|fen|thea|ter** NT (inf) to-do (inf), carry-on (inf), fuss; **ein ~ aufführen** to make a fuss; **Af|fen|weib|chen** NT → **Affe a**

female monkey/ape; **Af|fen|zahn** M (*inf*) = **Affentempo**

af|fig ['afɪç] (*inf*) ADJ (= *eitel*) stuck-up (*inf*), conceited; (= *geziert*) affected; (= *lächerlich*) ridiculous, ludicrous ADV **sich ~ anstellen** *or* **haben** to be stuck-up (*inf*)/affected/ridiculous *or* ludicrous; **~ wirken** to seem ludicrous *or* ridiculous

Af|fig|keit F -, -en (*inf*) (= *Geziertheit*) affectation; (= *Lächerlichkeit*) ridiculousness, ludicrousness

Äf|fin ['ɛfɪn] F -, -nen female monkey; (= *Menschenäffin*) female ape

Af|fi|ni|tät [afini'tɛːt] F -, -en affinity

Af|fir|ma|ti|on [afɪrma'tsioːn] F -, -en (*geh*) affirmation

af|fir|ma|tiv [afɪrma'tiːf] ADJ (*geh*) affirmative

Af|fix [a'fɪks, 'afɪks] NT -es, -e (*Ling*) affix

Af|fri|ka|ta [afri'kaːta] F -, **Affrikaten** [-tn] (*Ling*) affricate

Af|front [a'frõː] M -s, -s (*geh*) affront, insult (*gegen* to)

Af|gha|ne [af'gaːnə] M -n, -n, **Af|gha|nin** [-'gaːnɪn] F -, -nen Afghan

af|gha|nisch [af'gaːnɪʃ] ADJ Afghan; **Afghanischer Windhund** Afghan (hound)

Af|gha|nis|tan [af'gaːnɪstaːn, -tan] NT -s Afghanistan

A|fi|ci|o|na|do [afitsio'naːdo] M -s, -s aficionado

Af|ri|ka ['aːfrika, 'afrika] NT -s Africa

Af|ri|kaans [afri'kaːns] NT - Afrikaans

Af|ri|ka|ner [afri'kaːnɐ] M -s, -, **Af|ri|ka|ne|rin** [-ərɪn] F -, -nen African

af|ri|ka|nisch [afri'kaːnɪʃ] ADJ African

Af|ri|ka|nis|tik [afrika'nɪstɪk] F -, no pl African studies pl

Af|ro- ['aːfro-]: **Af|ro|ame|ri|ka|ner(in)** M(F) Afro-American; **Af|ro|asi|at(in)** M(F) Afro-Asian; **af|ro|asi|a|tisch** ADJ Afro-Asian; **Af|ro|look** M Afro-look

Af|ter ['aftɐ] M -s, - (*form*) anus

Af|ter|shave ▲ ['aːftʃeːv] NT -(s), -s aftershave

AG [aːˈgeː] F -, -s abbr von **Aktiengesellschaft** ≈ plc (*Brit*), ≈ corp. (*US*), ≈ inc. (*US*)

Ägä|is [ɛ'gɛːɪs] F - Aegean (Sea)

ä|gä|isch [ɛ'gɛːɪʃ] ADJ Aegean; **Ägäisches Meer** Aegean Sea

A|ga|ve [a'gaːvə] F -, -n agave

A|gen|da [a'gɛnda] F -, **Agenden** [-dn] a (= *Notizbuch*) notebook; (= *Terminkalender*) diary b (= *Tagesordnung*) agenda; (= *Aktionsplan*) agenda, plan of action

A|gen|de [a'gɛndə] F -, -n (*Eccl*) liturgy

A|gens ['aːgɛns] NT -, **Agenzien** [a'gɛntsiən] (*Philos, Med, Ling*) agent

A|gent [a'gɛnt] M -en, -en, **A|gen|tin** [a'gɛntɪn] F -, -nen agent; (= *Spion*) secret or foreign agent

A|gen|ten-: **A|gen|ten|aus|tausch** M spy swap; **A|gen|ten|film** M spy film or movie (*US*); **A|gen|ten|füh|rer(in)** M(F) spymaster; **A|gen|ten|netz** M spy network; **A|gen|ten|ring** M spy ring; **A|gen|ten|tä|tig|keit** F espionage; **ihre ~** her activity as a secret or foreign agent; **A|gen|ten|thril|ler** M spy thriller

A|gen|tin F -, -nen → **Agent**

A|gent pro|vo|ca|teur [a'ʒã: provoka'tøːɐ] M -, -s -s agent provocateur

A|gen|tur [agɛn'tuːɐ] F -, -en agency

A|gen|tur|be|richt M (news) agency report

Ag|glo|me|rat [aglome'raːt] NT -(e)s, -e (*Tech, Geol*) agglomerate; (*fig geh auch*) agglomeration, conglomeration

Ag|glu|ti|na|ti|on [aglutina'tsioːn] F -, -en (*Ling*) agglutination

ag|glu|ti|nie|ren [agluti'niːrən] ptp **agglutiniert** VI (*Ling*) to agglutinate; **~d** agglutinating; *Sprache auch* agglutinating

Ag|gre|gat [agre'gaːt] NT -(e)s, -e (*Geol*) aggregate; (*Tech*) unit, set of machines; (*Aut: = Motor*) engine

Ag|gre|gat|zu|stand M state; **die drei Aggregatzustände** the three states of matter

Ag|gres|si|on [agre'sioːn] F -, -en aggression (*gegen* towards); **-en gegen jdn empfinden** to feel aggressive or aggression toward(s) sb

Ag|gres|si|ons-: **ag|gres|si|ons|ge|la|den** ADJ full of aggression; **Ag|gres|si|ons|hem|mung** F , no pl inhibition of aggression; **Ag|gres|si|ons|krieg** M war of aggression; **Ag|gres|si|ons|lust** F , no pl belligerence; **ag|gres|si|ons|lüs|tern** ADJ (*pej*) belligerent, bellicose; **Ag|gres|si|ons|po|li|tik** F policy of aggression; **Ag|gres|si|ons|stau** M (*Psych*) build-up of aggression; **Ag|gres|si|ons|trieb** M (*Psych*) aggressive impulse

ag|gres|siv [agre'siːf] ADJ aggressive ADV aggressively

Ag|gres|si|vi|tät [agresivi'tɛːt] F -, -en aggressivity

ag|gres|si|vi|täts|ge|la|den ADJ full of aggression

Ag|gres|sor [a'grɛsoːɐ] M -s, **Aggressoren** [-'soːrən], **Ag|gres|so|rin** [-'soːrɪn] F -, -nen aggressor

Ägi|de [ɛ'giːdə] F -, no pl (*liter*) **unter jds ~** (*dat*) (= *Schutz*) under the aegis of sb; (= *Schirmherrschaft auch*) under sb's patronage

a|gie|ren [a'giːrən] ptp **agiert** VI to operate, to act; (*Theat*) to act; **als jd ~** (*Theat*) to act or play the part of sb

a|gil [a'giːl] ADJ (*körperlich*) agile, nimble; (**geistig**) **~** sharp, nimble-minded, mentally agile

A|gi|li|tät [agili'tɛːt] F -, no pl (*von Körper*) agility, nimbleness; (*von Geist*) sharpness

A|gio ['aːdʒo, 'aːʒio] NT -, **Agien** [a'dʒən, 'aːʒiən] (*Fin*) (*von Wertpapier*) premium; (*von Geldsorte*) agio

A|gio|pa|pie|re PL (*Fin*) securities pl redeemable at a premium

A|gi|ta|ti|on [agita'tsioːn] F -, -en (*Pol*) agitation; **~ treiben** to agitate

A|gi|ta|tor [agi'taːtoːɐ] M -s, **Agitatoren** [-'toːrən], **A|gi|ta|to|rin** [-'toːrɪn] F -, -nen (*Pol*) agitator

a|gi|ta|to|risch [agita'toːrɪʃ] (*Pol*) ADJ agitational; *Rede, Inhalt* inflammatory ADV **~ argumentieren** to argue in an inflammatory style; **sich ~ betätigen** to be an agitator

a|gi|tie|ren [agi'tiːrən] ptp **agitiert** VI to agitate

A|git|prop [agɪt'prɔp] F -, no pl agitprop

Ag|nos|ti|ker [a'gnɔstikɐ] M -s, -, **Ag|nos|ti|ke|rin** [-ərɪn] F -, -nen agnostic

ag|nos|tisch [a'gnɔstɪʃ] ADJ agnostic

Ag|nos|ti|zis|mus [agnɔsti'tsɪsmʊs] M -, no pl agnosticism

A|go|nie [ago'niː] F -, -n [-'niːən] (*lit, fig geh*) death throes pl, death pangs pl; **in (der) ~ liegen** to be in one's death throes

Ag|rar- [a'graːr] in cpds agrarian; **Ag|rar|aus|ga|ben** PL (*von EU, Staat*) agricultural spending *sing*; **Ag|rar|fab|rik** F factory farm; **Ag|rar|ge|sell|schaft** F agrarian society

Ag|ra|ri|er [a'graːriɐ] M -s, -, **Ag|ra|ri|e|rin** [-iərɪn] F -, -nen landowner

ag|ra|risch [a'graːrɪʃ] ADJ agrarian; *Rohstoffe* agricultural

Ag|rar-: **Ag|rar|kri|se** F agricultural crisis, farm or farming crisis; **Ag|rar|land** NT agrarian country; **Ag|rar|markt** M agricultural commodities market; **Ag|rar|po|li|tik** F agricultural policy; **Ag|rar|prei|se** PL farm prices pl; **Ag|rar|pro|dukt** NT agricultural or farm product; **Ag|rar|re|form** F agricultural reform; **Ag|rar|staat** M agrarian state; **Ag|rar|sub|ven|tio|nen** PL farm subsidies pl; **Ag|rar|über|schuss** M agricultural surplus; **Ag|rar|wirt|schaft** F farming; **Ag|rar|wis|sen|schaft**

F agronomy, agronomics; **Ag|rar|zoll** M import tariff (*on produce*)

Ag|ré|ment [agre'mã:] NT -s, -s (*Pol*) agrément

Ag|ri|kul|tur [agrikʊl'tuːɐ] F (*form*) agriculture

Ag|ri|kul|tur|che|mie F , **Ag|ro|che|mie** ['aːgro-] F agricultural chemistry

Ag|ro|nom [agro'noːm] M -en, -en, **Ag|ro|no|min** [-'noːmɪn] F -, -nen agronomist

Ag|ro|no|mie [agrono'miː] F -, no pl agronomy

Ag|ro|tech|nik ['aːgro-] F agricultural technology

Ägyp|ten [ɛ'gʏptn] NT -s Egypt

Ägyp|ter [ɛ'gʏptɐ] M -s, -, **Ägyp|te|rin** [-ərɪn] F -, -nen Egyptian

ägyp|tisch [ɛ'gʏptɪʃ] ADJ Egyptian; **~e Finsternis** (*liter*) Stygian darkness (*liter*)

Ägyp|to|lo|gie [ɛgʏptolo'giː] F -, no pl Egyptology

ah [aː, a] INTERJ (*genießerisch*) ooh, ah, mmm; (*überrascht, bewundernd, verstehend*) ah, oh

Ah [aː, a] NT -s, -s oh, ah

äh [ɛː] INTERJ (*beim Sprechen*) er, um; (*Ausdruck des Ekels*) ugh

a|ha [a'haː, a'ha] INTERJ aha; (*verstehend auch*) I see

A|ha- [a'haː-, a'ha-]: **A|ha-Ef|fekt** [a'haː-, a'ha-] M aha effect, now I get it effect; **A|ha-Er|leb|nis** [a'haː-, a'ha-] NT sudden insight, aha-experience (*Psych*)

Ah|le ['aːlə] F -, -n awl; (*Typ*) bodkin

Ahn [aːn] M -(e)s or -en, -en (*geh*) ancestor, forefather (*liter*); (*fig*) for(e)bear (*liter*)

ahn|den ['aːndn] VT (*liter*) *Freveltat, Verbrechen* to avenge; (*form*) *Übertretung, Verstoß* to punish

Ahn|dung F -, -en (*liter: von Freveltat, Verbrechen*) avengement; (*form: von Übertretung, Verstoß*) punishment

Ah|ne¹ ['aːnə] M -n, -n (*liter*) ancestor, forefather (*liter*); (*fig*) for(e)bear (*liter*)

Ah|ne² F -, -n (*geh*) (= *weiblicher Vorfahr*) ancestress; (*fig*) for(e)bear (*liter*)

äh|neln ['ɛːnln] VI +*dat* to be like, to be similar to, to resemble; **sich** or **einander** (*geh*) **~** to be alike, to be similar, to resemble one another; **in diesem Punkt ähnelt sie sehr ihrem Vater** she's very like her father or very similar to her father in this respect, she greatly resembles her father in this respect; **diese Erklärung ähnelt seiner früheren Aussage überhaupt nicht mehr** this explanation bears no resemblance whatsoever to his earlier statement; **die beiden Systeme ~ einander nicht sehr/~ sich wenig** the two systems are not very similar or alike/have little in common

ah|nen ['aːnən] VT (= *voraussehen*) to foresee, to know; *Gefahr, Tod etc* to have a presentiment or premonition or foreboding of; (= *vermuten*) to suspect; (= *erraten*) to guess; **das kann ich doch nicht ~!** I couldn't be expected to know that!; **nichts Böses ~** to have no sense of foreboding, to be unsuspecting; **nichts Böses ~d** unsuspectingly; **da sitzt man friedlich an seinem Schreibtisch, nichts Böses ~ d ...** (*hum*) there I was sitting peacefully at my desk minding my own business ... (*hum*); **ohne zu ~, dass ...** without dreaming or suspecting (for one minute) that ...; **ohne es zu ~** without suspecting, without having the slightest idea; **davon habe ich nichts geahnt** I didn't have the slightest inkling of it, I didn't suspect it for one moment; **so etwas habe ich doch geahnt** I did suspect something like that; **(ach,) du ahnst es nicht!** (*inf*) would you believe it! (*inf*); **du ahnst es nicht, wen ich gestern getroffen habe!** you'll never guess or believe who I met yesterday!; **die Umrisse waren nur zu ~** the contours could only be guessed at

VI (*geh*) **mir ahnt etwas Schreckliches** I have a dreadful foreboding; **mir ahnt nichts Gutes** I have a premonition that all is not well

Ah|nen-: Ah|nen|bild NT ancestral portrait; (auch **Ahnenfigur**) ancestral figure; **Ah|nen|for|schung** F genealogy; **Ah|nen|ga|le|rie** F ancestral portrait gallery; **Ah|nen|kult** M ancestor worship or cult; **Ah|nen|pass ▲** M (im Dritten Reich) proof of ancestry, pedigree; **Ah|nen|rei|he** F ancestral line; **Ah|nen|ta|fel** F genealogical tree or table, genealogy, pedigree; **Ah|nen|ver|eh|rung** F ancestor worship

Ahn-: Ahn|frau F (liter) ancestress; (= Stammmutter) progenitrix (form, liter); **Ahn|herr** M (liter) ancestor; (= Stammvater) progenitor (form, liter)

ähn|lich ['ɛːnlɪç] ✪ 32.4, 53.5 ADJ similar (+dat to); **ein dem Rokoko ~er Stil** a style similar to rococo, a similar style to rococo; **das dem Vater ~e Kind** the child that resembles his father, the child that is like his father; **~ wie er/sie** like him/her; **~ wie damals** as then; **~ wie vor 10 Jahren** as 10 years ago; **sie sind sich ~** they are similar or alike; **Ähnliches** something similar, something like it/that

ADV **ein ~ aussehender Gegenstand** a similar-looking object; **~ kompliziert/intelligent** just as complicated/intelligent; **eine ~ komplizierte Sachlage** a similarly complicated state of affairs; **ich denke ~** I feel the same way (about it); **er hat sie ~ hintergangen wie seine frühere Freundin** he cheated on her just as he did with his former girlfriend; **jdm ~ sehen** to be like sb, to resemble sb; **das sieht ihm (ganz) ~!** (inf) that's just like him!, that's him all over! (inf)

PREP +dat similar to, like

Ähn|lich|keit F -, -en (mit to) (= Vergleichbarkeit) similarity; (= ähnliches Aussehen) similarity, resemblance; **mit jdm/etw ~ haben** to resemble sb/sth, to be like sb/sth

Ah|nung ['aːnʊŋ] F -, -en a (= Vorgefühl) hunch, presentiment; (düster) foreboding, premonition

b (= Vorstellung, Wissen) idea; (= Vermutung) suspicion, hunch; **eine ~ von etw vermitteln** to give an idea of sth; **keine ~ (davon) haben, dass/wie/was** etc to have no idea that/how/ what etc; **keine ~!** (inf) no idea! (inf), I haven't a clue! (inf); **er hat keine blasse** or **nicht die geringste ~** he hasn't a clue or the foggiest (inf), he hasn't the faintest idea (inf); **hast du eine ~, wo er sein könnte?** have you any or an idea where he could be?; **hast du eine ~!** (iro inf) a (fat) lot you know (about it)! (inf), that's what YOU know (about it)!

Ah|nungs-: ah|nungs|los ADJ (= nichts ahnend) unsuspecting; (= unwissend) clueless (inf) ADV unsuspectingly, innocently; **Ah|nungs|lo|sig|keit** F -, no pl (= Unwissenheit) cluelessness (inf); **er bewies seine völlige ~ darüber, dass ...** he showed how totally unsuspecting he was of the fact that ...; **ah|nungs|voll** ADJ (geh) full of presentiment or (Böses ahnend) foreboding

a|hoi [a'hɔy] INTERJ (Naut) **Schiff ~!** ship ahoy!

A|horn ['aːhɔrn] M -s, -e maple

A|horn-: A|horn|blatt NT maple leaf; **A|horn|si|rup** M maple syrup

Äh|re ['ɛːrə] F -, -n (= Getreideähre) ear; (allgemeiner, = Grasähre) head; **~n lesen** to glean (corn)

Äh|ren-: Äh|ren|kranz M garland of corn; **Äh|ren|le|se** F gleaning; **Äh|ren|le|ser(in)** M(F) gleaner

AHV [aːhaːˈfau] (Sw) abbr von **Alters- und Hinderungsversicherung** age and disability insurance

Aide-mé|moire ['ɛːtme'moaːɐ] NT -, - aide-mémoire

Aids [eːds] NT -, no pl Aids

Aids- ['eːds] in cpds Aids; **Aids-Er|re|ger** M Aids virus; **Aids|hil|fe** F Aids support; **die Münchener ~** the Munich Aids support group; **aids|in|fi|ziert** ['---] ADJ infected with Aids; **Aids|in|fi|zier|te(r)** [-ɪnfitsiːɐtə] MF decl as adj person infected with Aids; **aids|krank**

ADJ suffering from Aids; **Aids|kran|ke(r)** MF decl as adj Aids sufferer; **Aids|test** M Aids test; **Aids|to|te(r)** MF decl as adj person/man/woman who died of Aids; **2000 ~ pro Jahr** 2000 Aids deaths or deaths from Aids per year

Ai|ki|do [ai'kiːdo] NT -(s), no pl aikido

Air [ɛːɐ] NT -(s), -s (geh) air, aura

Air- ['ɛːɐ-]: **Air|bag** ['ɛːɐbɛg] M -s, -s (Aut) airbag; **Air|bus** ['ɛːɐbʊs] M (Aviat) airbus; **Air|sur|fing** ['ɛːɐ-] NT -s, no pl air surfing

a|is, A|is ['aːɪs] NT -, - A sharp

Ai|schy|los ['aɪsçylɔs] M -' Aeschylus

AIZ [aːliˈtsɛt] F abbr von **Antiimperialistische Zelle**

Aja|tol|lah [aja'tɔla] M -(s), -s ayatollah

A|ka|de|mie [akade'miː] F -, -n [-'miːən] academy; (= Fachschule) college, school

A|ka|de|mi|ker [aka'deːmikɐ] M -s, -, **A|ka|de|mi|ke|rin** [-ərɪn] F -, -nen person with a university education; (= Student) (university) student; (= Hochschulabsolvent) (university) graduate; (= Universitätslehrkraft) academic; (rare: = Akademiemitglied) academician

a|ka|de|misch [aka'deːmɪʃ] ADJ (lit, fig) academic; **die ~e Jugend** (the) students pl; **das ~e Proletariat** (the) jobless graduates pl; **der ~e Senat** (Univ) the senate; **das ~e Viertel** (Univ) the quarter of an hour allowed between the announced start of a lecture etc and the actual start ADV **~ gebildet sein** to have (had) a university education, to be a graduate

A|ka|de|mi|sie|rung [akademi'ziːrʊŋ] F -, -en **die ~ des öffentlichen Dienstes** turning the Civil Service into a graduate profession

A|kan|thus [a'kantʊs] M -, - acanthus

A|kan|thus|blatt NT acanthus leaf

A|ka|zie [a'kaːtsiə] F -, -n acacia

A|ke|lei [akə'lai, 'a:kəlai] F -, -en aquilegia, columbine

Ak|kla|ma|ti|on [aklama'tsioːn] F -, -en (form) acclaim, acclamation; **Wahl per** or **durch ~** election by acclamation

ak|kla|mie|ren [akla'miːrən] ptp **akklamiert** (form, Aus) VI to applaud (jdm sb) VT Schauspieler, Szene to acclaim, to applaud; (= wählen) to elect by acclamation

Ak|kli|ma|ti|sa|ti|on [aklimatiza'tsioːn] F -, -en (form) acclimatization

ak|kli|ma|ti|sie|ren [aklimati'ziːrən] ptp **akklimatisiert** VR (lit, fig) (in +dat to) to become acclimatized, to acclimatize oneself VT to acclimatize

Ak|kli|ma|ti|sie|rung F -, -en acclimatization

Ak|ko|la|de [ako'laːdə] F -, -n a (Typ) brace; (Mus) accolade b (Hist) accolade

Ak|kord [a'kɔrt] M -(e)s, -e [-də] a (Mus) chord b (= Stücklohn) piece rate; **im** or **in** or **auf ~ arbeiten** to do piecework c (Jur) settlement

Ak|kord-: Ak|kord|ar|beit F piecework; **Ak|kord|ar|bei|ter(in)** M(F) pieceworker

Ak|kor|de|on [a'kɔrdeɔn] NT -s, -s accordion

Ak|kor|de|o|nist [akɔrdeo'nɪst] M -en, -en, **Ak|kor|de|o|nis|tin** [-'nɪstɪn] F -, -nen, **Ak|kor|de|on|spie|ler(in)** M(F) accordionist

Ak|kord-: Ak|kord|lohn M piece wages pl, piece rate; **Ak|kord|satz** M piece rate; **Ak|kord|zu|schlag** M piece rate bonus

ak|kre|di|tie|ren [akredi'tiːrən] ptp **akkreditiert** VT a Botschafter, Journalisten to accredit (bei to, at) b (Fin) **jdn ~** to give sb credit facilities; **akkreditiert sein** to have credit facilities; **jdn für einen Betrag ~** to credit an amount to sb or sb's account, to credit sb or sb's account with an amount

Ak|kre|di|tie|rung F -, -en a (von Botschafter, Journalist) accreditation (bei to, at) b (Fin) provision of credit facilities (+gen to); (von Betrag) crediting

Ak|kre|di|tiv [akredi'tiːf] NT -s, -e [-və] a (Pol) credentials pl b (Fin) letter of credit; **jdm ein ~ eröffnen** to open a credit in favour (Brit) or favor (US) of sb

Ak|ku ['aku] M -s, -s (inf) abbr von **Akkumulator** accumulator

Ak|ku|la|de|ge|rät ['aku-] NT battery charger

Ak|ku|mu|la|ti|on [akumula'tsioːn] F -, -en accumulation

Ak|ku|mu|la|tor [akumu'laːtoːɐ] M -s, **Akkumulatoren** [-'toːrən] accumulator

ak|ku|mu|lie|ren [akumu'liːrən] ptp **akkumuliert** VTIR to accumulate

ak|ku|rat [aku'raːt] ADJ precise; (= sorgfältig auch) meticulous ADV precisely, exactly; (= tatsächlich) naturally, of course

Ak|ku|ra|tes|se [akura'tɛsə] F -, no pl (dated) precision; (= Sorgfalt) meticulousness

Ak|ku|sa|tiv ['akuzatiːf] M -s, -e [-və] accusative; **im ~ stehen** to be in the accusative

Ak|ku|sa|tiv|ob|jekt NT accusative object

Ak|ne ['aknə] F -, -n acne

A|ko|luth [ako'luːt] M -en, -en, **A|ko|lyth** [ako'lyːt] M -en, -en (Eccl) acolyte

A|kon|to|zah|lung [a'kɔnto-] F payment on account

AKP [aːka'peː] F abbr von **Afrika, Karibik und pazifischer Raum** ACP; **die ~-Staaten** the ACP countries; **~-Bananen** bananas from the ACP countries

ak|qui|rie|ren [akvi'riːrən] ptp **akquiriert** VT a Spenden to collect; Inserate ~ to sell advertising space; **Kunden ~** to canvass for customers b (old: = erwerben) to acquire VI (Comm) to canvass for custom

Ak|qui|si|teur [akvizi'tøːɐ] M -s, -e, **Ak|qui|si|teu|rin** [-'tøːrɪn] F -, -nen agent, canvasser

Ak|qui|si|ti|on [akvizi'tsioːn] F -, -en (old) acquisition; (Comm) (customer) canvassing

Ak|ri|bie [akri'biː] F -, no pl (geh) meticulousness, (meticulous) precision

ak|ri|bisch [a'kriːbɪʃ] ADJ (geh) meticulous, precise ADV meticulously

Ak|ro|bat [akro'baːt] M -en, -en, **Ak|ro|ba|tin** [-'baːtɪn] F -, -nen acrobat

Ak|ro|ba|tik [akro'baːtɪk] F -, no pl acrobatics pl; (= Geschicklichkeit) acrobatic abilities pl or skill

ak|ro|ba|tisch [akro'baːtɪʃ] ADJ acrobatic

Ak|ro|nym [akro'nyːm] NT -s, -e acronym

Akt¹ [akt] M -(e)s, -e a (= Tat) act; (= Zeremonie) ceremony, ceremonial act b (Theat, = Zirkusakt) act c (Art: = Aktbild) nude d (= Geschlechtsakt) sexual act, coitus no art (form)

Akt² M -(e)s, -en (Aus) = Akte

Akt-: Akt|auf|nah|me F nude (photograph); **Akt|bild** NT nude (picture or portrait)

Ak|te ['aktə] F -, -n file, record; **die ~ Schmidt** the Schmidt file; **das kommt in die ~n** this goes on file or record; **etw zu den ~n legen** to file sth away, to put sth on file; (fig) Fall etc to drop sth

Ak|ten-: Ak|ten|berg M (inf) mountain of files or records (inf); **Ak|ten|de|ckel** M folder; **Ak|ten|ein|sicht** F (form) inspection of records or files; **Ak|ten|kof|fer** M attaché case, executive case; **ak|ten|kun|dig** ADJ on record; **~ werden** to be put on record; **Ak|ten|la|ge** F nach or laut ~ according to the files; **die ~ prüfen** to examine the files; **Ak|ten|map|pe** F a (= Tasche) briefcase, portfolio b (= Umschlag) folder, file; **Ak|ten|no|tiz** F memo(randum); **Ak|ten|ord|ner** M file; **Ak|ten|schrank** M filing cabinet; **Ak|ten|ta|sche** F briefcase, portfolio; **Ak|ten|ver|merk** M memo(randum); **Ak|ten|ver|nich|ter** [-fɛɐnɪçtɐ] M -s, - document (Brit) or paper shredder; **Ak|ten|wolf** M shredder, shredding machine; **Ak|ten|zei|chen** NT reference

Ak|teur [akˈtøːɐ] M **-s, -e, Ak|teu|rin** [-ˈtøːrɪn] F **-, -nen** (geh) participant, protagonist

Akt-: Akt|fo|to NT nude (photograph); **Akt|fo|to|gra|fie** F nude photography; (= Bild) nude photograph

Ak|tie [ˈaktsiə] F **-, -n** share; (= Aktienschein) share certificate; **in ~n anlegen** to invest in (stocks and) shares; **die ~n fallen/steigen** share prices are falling/rising; **die ~n stehen gut/ schlecht** (lit) share prices are looking good/ bad; (fig) things or the prospects are looking good/bad; **wie stehen die ~n?** (hum inf) how are things?; (= wie sind die Aussichten) what are the prospects?

Ak|tien-: Ak|ti|en|be|sitz M shareholdings pl, shares pl held; **Ak|ti|en|be|sit|zer(in)** M(F) shareholder, stockholder (esp US); **Ak|ti|en|bör|se** F stock exchange; **Ak|ti|en|fonds** M share or stock (US) fund; **Ak|ti|en|ge|sell|schaft** F ≈ public limited company (Brit), ≈ corporation (US); **Ak|ti|en|in|dex** M (Fin) share index; **Ak|ti|en|ka|pi|tal** NT share capital; (von Gesellschaft auch) (capital) stock; **Ak|ti|en|kurs** M share price; **Ak|ti|en|markt** M stock market; **Ak|ti|en|mehr|heit** F majority holding; **Ak|ti|en|no|tie|rung** F share or stock (US) quotation or listing; **Ak|ti|en|pa|ket** NT block of shares; **ein ~ von 20 Prozent** a shareholding of 20 per cent (Brit) or percent (US); **Ak|ti|en|spe|ku|lant(in)** M(F) stock market speculator; **Ak|ti|en|spe|ku|la|tion** F speculation on the stock market; **Ak|ti|en|tausch** M share exchange

Ak|ti|ni|um [akˈtiːniʊm] NT **-s**, no pl (abbr **Ac**) actinium

Ak|ti|on [akˈtsioːn] F **-, -en** (= Handlung) action (auch Mil); (= Kampagne) campaign; (= Werbeaktion) promotion; (= geplantes Unternehmen, Einsatz) operation (auch Mil); (Art) action painting; **in ~** in action; **sie muss ständig in ~ sein** she always has to be active or on the go (inf); **in ~ treten** to go into action

Ak|ti|o|när [aktsioˈnɛːɐ] M **-s, -e, Ak|ti|o|nä|rin** [-ˈnɛːrɪn] F **-, -nen** shareholder, stockholder (esp US)

Ak|ti|o|närs|ver|samm|lung F shareholders' or stockholders' (esp US) meeting

Ak|ti|o|nis|mus [aktsioˈnɪsmʊs] M **-**, no pl (Pol) actionism

ak|ti|o|nis|tisch [aktsioˈnɪstɪʃ] ADJ (Pol) actionist(ic)

Ak|ti|ons-: Ak|ti|ons|art F (Gram) aspect; **Ak|ti|ons|aus|schuss** ▲ M action committee; **Ak|ti|ons|ein|heit** F (Pol) unity of action, working unity; **ak|ti|ons|fä|hig** ADJ capable of action; **Ak|ti|ons|ko|mi|tee** NT action committee; **Ak|ti|ons|ma|ler(in)** M(F) action painter; **Ak|ti|ons|ma|le|rei** F action painting; **Ak|ti|ons|preis** M special-offer price; **Ak|ti|ons|pro|gramm** NT programme (Brit) or program (US) of action; **Ak|ti|ons|ra|di|us** M (Aviat, Naut) range, radius; (fig: = Wirkungsbereich) scope (for action); **ak|ti|ons|un|fä|hig** ADJ incapable of action; **Ak|ti|ons|wo|che** F (special) campaign week

ak|tiv [akˈtiːf, ˈaktiːf] ADJ active; (Econ) Bilanz positive, favourable (Brit), favorable (US); (Mil) Soldat etc on active service or duty; **~ sein** (Univ) to be a full member of a/the students' association → **Wahlrecht** ADV actively; **sich ~ an etw** (dat) **beteiligen** to take an active part in sth; **~ dienen** (Mil) to be on active duty or service

Ak|tiv[1] [ˈaktiːf] NT **-s**, (rare) **-e** [-və] (Gram) active

Ak|tiv[2] [akˈtiːf] NT **-s, -s** or **-e** [-və] (DDR) work team

Ak|ti|va [akˈtiːva] PL assets pl; **~ und Passiva** assets and liabilities

Ak|tiv-: Ak|tiv|be|stand M (Fin) assets pl; (Mil) present strength; **Ak|tiv|bi|lanz** F (Fin) credit balance

Ak|ti|ven|spre|cher(in) M(F) (Sport) participants' spokesperson

Ak|ti|ve(r) [akˈtiːvə] MF decl as adj (Sport) active participant; (Univ) full member (of a/the students' association)

Ak|tiv|fe|ri|en PL activity holiday (esp Brit) or vacation (US)

Ak|tiv|ge|schäft NT (Fin) lending business

ak|ti|vie|ren [aktiˈviːrən] ptp **aktiviert** VT (Sci) to activate; (fig) Arbeit, Kampagne to step up; Mitarbeiter to get moving; (Comm) to enter on the assets side

ak|ti|visch [akˈtiːvɪʃ, ˈaktiːvɪʃ] ADJ (Gram) active

Ak|ti|vis|mus [aktiˈvɪsmʊs] M **-**, no pl activism

Ak|ti|vist [aktiˈvɪst] M **-en, -en, Ak|ti|vis|tin** [-ˈvɪstɪn] F **-, -nen** activist

Ak|ti|vi|tät [aktiviˈtɛːt] F **-, -en** activity

Ak|tiv-: Ak|tiv|koh|le F (Chem) activated carbon; **Ak|tiv|koh|le|fil|ter** M activated carbon filter; **Ak|tiv|pos|ten** M (lit, fig) asset; **Ak|tiv|sal|do** M credit balance; **Ak|tiv|sei|te** F assets side; **Ak|tiv|ur|laub** M activity holiday (esp Brit) or vacation (US); **Ak|tiv|ver|mö|gen** NT realizable assets pl; **Ak|tiv|zin|sen** PL interest receivable sing

Akt|ma|le|rei F nude painting

Akt|mo|dell NT nude model

Ak|tri|ce [akˈtriːsə] F **-, -n** (dated) actress

Akt|stu|die F nude study

ak|tu|a|li|sie|ren [aktualiˈziːrən] ptp **aktualisiert** VT to make topical; Datei, Nachschlagewerk to update

Ak|tu|a|li|sie|rung F **-, -en** updating

Ak|tu|a|li|tät [aktualiˈtɛːt] F **-, -en** **a** relevance (to the present or current situation), topicality **b Aktualitäten** PL (geh: = neueste Ereignisse) current events pl

Ak|tu|ar [akˈtuaːɐ] M **-s, -e, Ak|tu|a|rin** [-ˈtuaːrɪn] F **-, -nen** **a** (old: = Gerichtsschreiber) clerk of the court **b** (Sw: = Schriftführer) secretary

ak|tu|ell [akˈtuɛl] ADJ relevant (to the current situation); Frage auch topical; Buch, Film auch of topical interest; Thema topical; (= gegenwärtig) Problem, Theorie, Thema current; (= modern) Mode latest attr, current; Stil latest attr, fashionable; (Econ) Bedarf, Kaufkraft actual; **von ~em Interesse** of topical interest; **von ~er Bedeutung** of relevance to the present situation; **dieses Problem ist nicht mehr ~** this is no longer a (current) problem; **das Buch ist wieder ~ geworden** the book has become relevant again, the book has regained topicality; **eine ~e Sendung** (Rad, TV) a current affairs programme (Brit) or program (US); **~e Stunde** (Parl) ≈ question time no art (Brit)

Akt|zeich|nung F nude (drawing), drawing of a nude

A|ku|pres|sur [akupreˈsuːɐ] F **-, -en** acupressure

A|ku|punk|teur [akupʊŋkˈtøːɐ] M **-s, -e, A|ku|punk|teu|rin** [-ˈtøːrɪn] F **-, -nen** acupuncturist

a|ku|punk|tie|ren [akupʊŋkˈtiːrən] ptp **akupunktiert** VT to acupuncture VI to perform acupuncture

A|ku|punk|tur [akupʊŋkˈtuːɐ] F **-, -en** acupuncture

A|kus|tik [aˈkʊstɪk] F **-**, no pl (von Gebäude etc) acoustics pl; (Phys: = Lehre) acoustics sing

A|kus|tik|kopp|ler [-ˈkɔplɐ] M **-s, -** (Comput) acoustic coupler

a|kus|tisch [aˈkʊstɪʃ] ADJ acoustic ADV acoustically; **rein ~ ist die Stereoanlage prima** the acoustics of that stereo are fantastic; **etw ~ verbessern** to improve the acoustics of sth; **ich habe dich rein ~ nicht verstanden** I simply didn't catch what you said (properly)

a|kut [aˈkuːt] ADJ (Med, fig) acute; Frage auch pressing, urgent ADV acutely; **~ auftretende Krankheiten** acute illnesses; **ihr Zustand ist ~ lebensgefährlich** her condition is listed as critical

A|kut [aˈkuːt] M **-(e)s, -e** acute (accent)

A|kut|kran|ken|haus NT acute hospital

AKW [aːkaːˈveː] NT **-s, -s** abbr von **Atomkraftwerk**

Ak|zent [akˈtsɛnt] M **-(e)s, -e** (= Zeichen, Aussprache) accent; (= Betonung auch) stress; (fig auch) emphasis, stress; **mit ~/französischem ~ sprechen** to speak with an accent/a French accent; **den ~ auf etw** (acc) **legen** (lit) to stress sth, to put the stress or accent on sth; (fig auch) to emphasize sth; **dieses Jahr liegen die (modischen) ~e bei ...** this year the accent or emphasis is on ...; **~e setzen** (fig) = Wichtiges hervorheben) to bring out or emphasize the main points or features; (= Hinweise geben) to give the main points; **dieses Jahr hat neue ~e gesetzt** this year has seen the introduction of new trends

Ak|zent-: Ak|zent|buch|sta|be M accented letter; **ak|zent|frei** ADJ, ADV without any or an accent

ak|zen|tu|ie|ren [aktsɛntuˈiːrən] ptp **akzentuiert** VT to articulate, to enunciate; (= betonen) to stress; (fig: = hervorheben) to accentuate

Ak|zent|ver|schie|bung F (Ling) stress shift; (fig) shift of emphasis

Ak|zept [akˈtsɛpt] NT **-(e)s, -e** (Comm) acceptance

ak|zep|ta|bel [aktsɛpˈtaːbl] ADJ acceptable

Ak|zep|tanz [aktsɛpˈtants] F **-**, no pl acceptance; **unsere Produkte haben keine ~ auf dem deutschen Markt** our products have not been accepted by the German market; **um die ~ unserer Produkte zu erhöhen** to make our products more acceptable

ak|zep|tier|bar ADJ acceptable

ak|zep|tie|ren [aktsɛpˈtiːrən] ✪ 38.1, 39.1 ptp **akzeptiert** VT to accept

Ak|zep|tie|rung F **-, -en** acceptance

Ak|zi|dens [ˈaktsidɛns] NT **-**, **Akzidenzien** [-ˈdɛntsiən] (Philos) accident; (Mus) accidental

ak|zi|den|tell [aktsidɛnˈtɛl], **ak|zi|den|ti|ell** [aktsidɛnˈtsiɛl] ADJ accidental

Ak|zi|denz [aktsiˈdɛnts] F **-, -en** (Typ) job; **~en** job printing

Ak|zi|denz-: Ak|zi|denz|druck M pl **-drucke** job printing; **Ak|zi|denz|dru|cke|rei** F jobbing printer's

AL [aːˈɛl] F **-, -s** abbr von **Alternative Liste**

à la [a la] ADV à la

a|laaf [aˈlaːf] INTERJ (dial) **Kölle ~!** up Cologne! (used in carnival procession)

A|la|bas|ter [alaˈbastɐ] M **-s, - a** alabaster **b** (dial: = Murmel) marble

A|larm [aˈlarm] M **-(e)s, -e** (= Warnung) alarm; (= Fliegeralarm) air-raid warning; (= Zustand) alert; **bei ~** following an alarm/air-raid warning; (während Alarm) during an alert; **~!** fire!/air raid! etc; **~ schlagen** to give or raise or sound the alarm

A|larm-: A|larm|an|la|ge F alarm system; **a|larm|be|reit** ADJ on the alert; Feuerwehr, Polizei auch standing by; **sich ~ halten** to be on the alert/standing by; **A|larm|be|reit|schaft** F alert; **erhöhte ~** high alert; **in ~ sein** or **stehen** to be on the alert; (Feuerwehr, Polizei auch) to be standing by; **in ~ versetzen** to put on the alert; **A|larm|glo|cke** F alarm bell

a|lar|mie|ren [alarˈmiːrən] ptp **alarmiert** VT Polizei etc to alert; (fig: = beunruhigen) to alarm; **~d** (fig) alarming; **aufs höchste** or **Höchste alarmiert** (fig) highly alarmed

A|larm-: A|larm|ruf M , **A|larm|schrei** M warning cry; **A|larm|sig|nal** NT alarm signal; **A|larm|stu|fe** F alert stage; **A|larm|übung** F practice exercise or drill; **A|larm|vor|rich|tung** F alarm; **A|larm|zu|stand** M alert; **im ~ sein** to be on the alert

A|las|ka [aˈlaska] NT **-s** Alaska

A|laun [aˈlaun] M **-s, -e** alum

A|laun|stein M , **A|laun|stift** M styptic pencil

Alb[1] [alp] F **-**, no pl (Geog) mountain region

Alb² ▲ M **-(e)s, -e** [-bə] (old: = Nachtmahr) demon believed to cause nightmares (fig geh: = Bedrückung) nightmare; **ihn drückte der ~** (old) he had a nightmare; **jdm wie ein ~ auf der Brust liegen** (fig geh) **wie ein ~ auf jdm lasten** (fig geh) to lie or weigh heavily (up)on sb

Alb³ M **-(e)s, -en** [-bn] (Myth) elf

Al|ba|ner [al'baːnɐ] M **-s, -**, **Al|ba|ne|rin** [-ərɪn] F **-, -nen** Albanian

Al|ba|ni|en [al'baːniən] NT **-s** Albania

al|ba|nisch [al'baːnɪʃ] ADJ Albanian

Al|bat|ros ['albatrɔs] M **-, -se** albatross

Alb|druck ▲ M pl **-drücke** (lit, fig) nightmare; **wie ein ~ auf jdm lasten** to weigh sb down

Al|be ['albə] F **-, -n** (Eccl) alb

Al|ben pl von **Alb¹** von **Albe** von **Album**

Al|be|rei [albə'rai] F **-, -en** silliness; (= das Spaßmachen) fooling about (Brit) or around; (= Bemerkung) inanity

al|bern ['albɐn] ADJ silly, stupid, foolish; (inf: = lächerlich) stupid, silly, ridiculous; **~es Zeug** (silly) nonsense ADV **klingen** silly; **sich ~ benehmen** to act silly; (= Quatsch machen) to fool about (Brit) or around; **~ fragen** to ask a silly question ⅥⅠ to fool about (Brit) or around; **ich weiß, ich bin unwiderstehlich, alberte er** I know I'm irresistible, he said jokingly

Al|bern|heit F **-, -en** a no pl (= albernes Wesen) silliness, foolishness; (= Lächerlichkeit) ridiculousness b (= Tat) silly prank; (= Bemerkung) inanity

Al|bi|nis|mus [albi'nɪsmʊs] M **-**, no pl albinism, albinoism

Al|bi|no [al'biːno] M **-s, -s** albino

Al|bi|on ['albiɔn] NT **-s** (liter) Albion (poet)

Alb|traum ▲ M (lit, fig) nightmare

alb|traum|ar|tig ▲ ADJ nightmarish

Al|bum ['albʊm] NT **-s, Alben** ['albn] album

Al|bu|min [albu'miːn] NT **-s, -e** albumen

Al|che|mie [alçe'miː] F (esp Aus), **Al|chi|mie** [alçi'miː] F **-**, no pl alchemy

Al|che|mist [alçe'mɪst] M **-en, -en**, **Al|che|mis|tin** [-'mɪstɪn] F **-, -nen** (esp Aus), **Al|chi|mist** [alçi'mɪst] M **-en, -en**, **Al|chi|mis|tin** [-'mɪstɪn] F **-, -nen** alchemist

al|che|mis|tisch [alçe'mɪstɪʃ] (esp Aus), **al|chi|mis|tisch** [alçi'mɪstɪʃ] ADJ alchemic(al)

al den|te [al 'dɛntə] ADJ al dente

A|le|man|ne [alə'manə] M **-n, -n**, **A|le|man|nin** [-'manɪn] F **-, -nen** Alemannic

a|le|man|nisch [alə'manɪʃ] ADJ Alemannic

a|lert [a'lɛrt] ADJ (geh) vivacious, lively

A|le|u|ten [ale'uːtn] PL (Geog) **die ~** the Aleutians

A|le|xan|dria [alɛ'ksandria, alɛksan'driːa] F **-**, **A|le|xand|ri|en** [alɛ'ksandriən] NT **-s** Alexandria

A|le|xand|ri|ner [alɛksan'driːnɐ] M **-s, -** (Poet) alexandrine

A|le|xand|rit [alɛksan'driːt] M **-s, -e** alexandrite

Al|ge ['algə] F **-, -n** alga

Al|geb|ra ['algebra] F **-**, no pl algebra

al|geb|ra|isch [alge'braːɪʃ] ADJ algebraic(al)

Al|gen-: Al|gen|blü|te F algae or algal bloom; **Al|gen|pest** F algae plague; **Al|gen|tep|pich** M algae slick

Al|ge|ri|en [al'geːriən] NT **-s** Algeria

Al|ge|ri|er [al'geːriɐ] M **-s, -**, **Al|ge|ri|e|rin** [-iərɪn] F **-, -nen** Algerian

al|ge|risch [al'geːrɪʃ] ADJ Algerian

Al|gier ['alʒiːɐ] NT **-s** Algiers

Al|gol [al'goːl, 'algoːl] NT **-(s)**, no pl (Comput) Algol

al|go|rith|misch [algo'rɪtmɪʃ] ADJ algorithmic

Al|go|rith|mus [algo'rɪtmʊs] M **-, Algo|rith|men** [-mən] algorithm

A|li ['aːli] M **-s, -s** (pej sl: = Araber) wog (Brit pej sl), Arab

---

a|li|as ['aːlias] ADV alias, also or otherwise known as

A|li|bi ['aːlibi] NT **-s, -s** (Jur, fig) alibi

A|li|bi-: A|li|bi|be|weis M evidence to support one's alibi; **A|li|bi|frau** F token woman; **A|li|bi|funk|ti|on** F (fig) **~ haben** to be used as an alibi

A|li|men|te [ali'mɛntə] PL maintenance sing

a|li|men|tie|ren [alimɛn'tiːrən] ptp **alimentiert** VT (geh) to maintain, to support

Alk¹ [alk] M **-(e)s, -e** (Orn) auk

Alk² [alk] M **-s**, no pl (sl: = Alkohol) booze (inf)

Al|ka|li [al'kaːli, 'alkali] NT **-s, Alkalien** [-'kaːliən] alkali; **mit ~ düngen** to fertilize with an alkali

al|ka|lisch [al'kaːlɪʃ] ADJ alkaline

Al|ka|lo|id [alkalo'iːt] NT **-(e)s, -e** [-də] alkaloid

Al|ki ['alki] M **-s, -s**, **Al|kie** M **-s, -s** (sl: = Alkoholiker) alky (inf), alkie (inf)

Al|ko|hol ['alkohoːl, alko'hoːl] M **-s, -e** alcohol; (= alkoholische Getränke auch) drink; **seinen Kummer im ~ ertränken** to drown one's sorrows; **unter ~ stehen** to be under the influence (of alcohol or drink)

Al|ko|hol-: al|ko|hol|ab|hän|gig ADJ alcohol-dependent; **~ sein** to be an alcoholic; **al|ko|hol|arm** ADJ low in alcohol (content); **~es Bier** low-alcohol beer; **Al|ko|hol|aus|schank** M sale of alcohol(ic drinks); **Al|ko|hol|ein|fluss** ▲ M , **Al|ko|hol|ein|wir|kung** F influence of alcohol or drink; **unter ~** under the influence of alcohol or drink; **Al|ko|hol|fah|ne** F (inf) smell of alcohol; **eine ~ haben** to smell of alcohol or drink; **al|ko|hol|frei** ADJ Bier alcohol-free, nonalcoholic; Getränk auch soft; Gegend, Stadt dry; **~es Bier** nonalcoholic or alcohol-free beer; **ein ~er Tag** a day without drink or alcohol; **Al|ko|hol|geg|ner(in)** M(F) opponent of alcohol; (selbst abstinent) teetotaller (Brit), teetotaler (US); (= Befürworter des Alkoholverbots) prohibitionist; **Al|ko|hol|ge|halt** M alcohol(ic) content; **Al|ko|hol|ge|nuss** ▲ M consumption of alcohol; **al|ko|hol|hal|tig** ADJ alcoholic, containing alcohol

Al|ko|ho|li|ka [alko'hoːlika] PL alcoholic drinks pl, liquor sing

Al|ko|ho|li|ker [alko'hoːlikɐ] M **-s, -**, **Al|ko|ho|li|ke|rin** [-ərɪn] F **-, -nen** alcoholic

al|ko|ho|lisch [alko'hoːlɪʃ] ADJ alcoholic

al|ko|ho|li|siert [alkoholi'ziːɐt] ADJ (= betrunken) inebriated; **in ~em Zustand** in a state of inebriation; **leicht/stark ~** slightly/extremely inebriated

Al|ko|ho|lis|mus [alkoho'lɪsmʊs] M **-**, no pl alcoholism

Al|ko|hol-: Al|ko|hol|kon|sum [-kɔnzuːm] M consumption of alcohol; **Al|ko|hol|kon|trol|le** F roadside breath test; **al|ko|hol|krank** ADJ alcoholic; **Al|ko|hol|pe|gel** M (hum), **Al|ko|hol|spie|gel** M jds or Alkoholspiegel the level of alcohol in sb's blood; **Al|ko|hol|steu|er** F duty or tax on alcohol; **Al|ko|hol|sucht** F alcohol addiction, alcoholism; **al|ko|hol|süch|tig** ADJ addicted to alcohol, suffering from alcoholism; **Al|ko|hol|süch|ti|ge(r)** MF decl as adj alcoholic; **Al|ko|hol|sün|der(in)** M(F) (inf) drunk(en) driver; **Al|ko|hol|test** M breath test; **Al|ko|hol|test|ge|rät** NT Breathalyzer®, drunkometer (US hum); **Al|ko|hol|ver|bot** NT ban on alcohol; **der Arzt hat ihm ~ verordnet** the doctor told him not to touch alcohol; **Al|ko|hol|ver|gif|tung** F alcohol(ic) poisoning

Al|ko|ven ['alkoːvn, al'koːvn] M **-s, -** alcove

all [al] INDEF PRON **~ das/mein ...** etc all the/my etc → **alle(r, s)**

All [al] NT **-s**, no pl (Sci, Space) space no art; (außerhalb unseres Sternsystems) outer space; (liter, geh) universe; **Spaziergang im ~** space walk, walk in space; **das weite ~** the immense universe

---

all-: all|abend|lich ADJ (which takes place) every evening; **der ~e Spaziergang** the regular evening walk ADV every evening; **all|be|kannt** ADJ known to all or everybody, universally known; **all|dem** [al'deːm] PRON = **alle|dem**; **all|die|weil** [aldiː'vail] (old, hum) ADV (= währenddessen) all the while CONJ (= weil) because

al|le ['alə] PRON → **alle(r, s)** ADV (inf) all gone; **die Milch ist ~** the milk's all gone, there's no milk left; **etw/jdn ~ machen** (inf) to finish sth/sb off; **ich bin ganz ~** I'm all in; **~ werden** to be finished; (Vorräte auch) to run out

al|le|dem [alə'deːm] PRON **bei/trotz** etc **~** with/in spite of etc all that; **von ~ stimmt kein Wort** there's no truth in any of that or it; **zu ~** moreover

Al|lee [a'leː] F **-, -n** [-'leːən] avenue

Al|le|go|rie [alego'riː] F **-, -n** [-'riːən] allegory

Al|le|go|rik [ale'goːrɪk] F **-**, no pl allegory; **in der griechischen ~** in Greek allegory

al|le|go|risch [ale'goːrɪʃ] ADJ allegorical ADV allegorically

Al|leg|ret|to [ale'grɛto] NT **-s, -s** or **Allegretti** [-ti] allegretto

Al|leg|ro [a'leːgro] NT **-s, -s** or **Allegri** [-gri] allegro

al|lein [a'lain] ADJ pred (esp inf: auch **alleine**) alone; Gegenstand, Wort auch by itself, on its own; (= ohne Gesellschaft, Begleitung, Hilfe auch) by oneself, on one's own; (= einsam) lonely, lonesome; **für sich ~** by oneself, on one's own, alone; **sie waren endlich ~** they were alone (together) at last, they were on their own at last; **von ~** by oneself/itself; **jdn tue es schon von ~e** I'll do that in any case; **das weiß ich von ~(e)** you don't have to tell me (that); **ganz ~** (= einsam) quite or all alone; (= ohne Begleitung, Hilfe) all by oneself, all on one's own; **jdm ganz ~ gehören** to belong to sb alone, to belong completely to sb; **auf sich** (acc) **~ angewiesen sein** to be left to cope on one's own, to be left to one's own devices
ADV (= nur) alone; **das ist ~ seine Verantwortung** that is his responsibility alone, that is exclusively or solely his responsibility; **nicht ~, ... sondern auch** not only ... but also; **~ schon der Gedanke, (schon) der Gedanke ~ ...** the very or mere thought ..., the thought alone ...; **das Porto ~ kostet ...** the postage alone costs ..., just the postage is ...; **~ erziehend** (Mutter, Vater) single, unmarried; **~ Erziehende(r)** single parent; **die ~ selig machende Kirche** the one or only true church; **der ~ selig machende Glauben** the one or only true faith; **er betrachtet seine Lehre als die ~ selig machende** he considers his doctrine to be the only true one; **~ stehend** to be on one's own, living alone; **~ Stehende(r)** single person
CONJ (old: = jedoch) however, but

Al|lein-: Al|lein|er|be M , **Al|lein|er|bin** F sole or only heir; **al|lein|er|zie|hend** △ ADJ → **allein** ADV; **Al|lein|er|zie|hen|de(r)** [-lɛtsiːəndə] MF decl as adj single parent; **Al|lein|flug** M solo flight; **im ~** solo; **Al|lein|gang** M pl **-gänge** (inf) (Sport) solo run; (von Bergsteiger) solo climb; (fig: = Tat) solo effort; **etw im ~ machen** (fig) to do sth on one's own; **die Möglichkeit eines ~s** the possibility of going it alone; **Al|lein|heit** F **-**, no pl (Philos) (universal) unity or oneness; **Al|lein|herr|schaft** F autocratic rule, absolute dictatorship; (fig) monopoly; **Al|lein|herr|scher(in)** M(F) autocrat, absolute dictator; **der ~ in der Familie sein** (fig) to reign supreme in the family

al|lei|nig [a'lainɪç] ADJ attr sole, only; (Aus, S Ger) (= allein stehend) single; (= ohne Begleitung) unaccompanied; **die ~e Führung übernehmen** to go alone into the lead

Al|lein-: Al|lein|sein NT being on one's own no def art, solitude; (= Einsamkeit) loneliness; **al|lein|se|lig|ma|chend** △ ADJ → **allein** ADV; **al|lein|ste|hend** △ ADJ → **allein** ADV; **Al|-**

lein|ste|hen|de(r) [-ʃteːəndə] MF *decl as adj* single person; **Al|lein|un|ter|hal|ter(in)** M(F) solo entertainer; **Al|lein|un|ter|mie|te** F (*Aus*) subletting (*where main tenant lives elsewhere*); **in ~ wohnen** ≈ to live in a furnished flat (*Brit*) *or* apartment; **Al|lein|ver|die|ner(in)** M(F) sole (wage) earner; **Al|lein|ver|kauf** M sole *or* exclusive right of sale (+*gen*, *von* for); **Al|lein|ver|tre|ter(in)** M(F) (*Comm*) sole agent; **Al|lein|ver|tre|tung** F (*Comm*) sole agency; (*Pol*) sole representation; **Al|lein|ver|tre|tungs|an|spruch** M (*Pol*) claim to sole representation; **Al|lein|ver|trieb** M sole *or* exclusive marketing *or* distribution rights *pl*

al|le|lu|ja [alɛˈluːja] INTERJ hallelujah(h)

al|le|mal [ˈaləˈmaːl] ADV every *or* each time; (= *ohne Schwierigkeit*) without any problem *or* trouble; **was er kann, kann ich noch ~** anything he can do I can do too; **~!** no problem *or* trouble! (*inf*) → **Mal²**

al|len|falls [ˈalənˈfals, ˈalənfals] ADV (= *nötigenfalls*) if need be, should the need arise; (= *höchstens*) at most, at the outside; (= *bestenfalls*) at best; **es waren ~ 40 Leute da** there were at most 40 people there, there were 40 people there at the outside; **das schaffen wir ~ in 3 Stunden/bis übermorgen** we'll do it in 3 hours/ by the day after tomorrow at best

al|lent|hal|ben [alɛntˈhalbn] ADV (*liter*) everywhere, on all sides

al|ler- [ˈalɛ] *in cpds with superl* (*zur Verstärkung*) by far; **das Allergrößte** by far the biggest, the biggest by far; **die Allerhübscheste** by far the prettiest, the prettiest by far

al|le(r, s) [ˈalə] ✪ 50.1, 50.3, 51.3, 53.4 INDEF PRON **a** *attr* all; (*bestimmte Menge, Anzahl*) all the; (*auf eine Person bezüglich*: = *all sein*) Geld, Liebe, Freunde, Erfahrungen all one's; **~ Kinder unter 10 Jahren** all children under 10; **~ Kinder dieser Stadt** all the children in this town; **die Eltern fuhren mit ~n Kindern weg** the parents went off with all their children; **~s Brot wird gebacken** all bread is baked; **im Geschäft war ~s Brot ausverkauft** all the bread in the shop was sold out; **meine Kinder** all (of) my children; **wir haben ~n Hass vergessen** we have forgotten all (our *or* the) hatred; **~ Anwesenden/Beteiligten/Betroffenen** all those present/ taking part/affected; **~s erforderliche Material** all the required material; **mit ~m Nachdruck** with every emphasis; **trotz ~r Mühe** in spite of every effort; **ohne ~n Grund** without any reason, with no reason at all; **mit ~r Deutlichkeit** quite distinctly; **ohne ~n Zweifel** without any doubt → *auch* **all**

b alles SING (*substantivisch*) everything; (*inf*: = *alle Menschen*) everybody, everyone; **~s, was ...** all *or* everything that ...; everybody *or* everyone who ...; **das ~s** all that; **~s Schöne** everything beautiful, all that is beautiful; **„alles für das Baby/den Heimwerker"** "everything for (the) baby/the handyman"; **(ich wünsche dir) ~s Gute** (I wish you) all the best; **~s und jedes** anything and everything; **in ~m** (= *in jeder Beziehung*) in everything; **~s in ~m** all in all; **trotz ~m** in spite of everything; **über ~s** above all else; (= *mehr als alles andere*) more than anything else; **vor ~m above all; das ist ~s, das wäre ~s** that's all, that's it (*inf*); **das ist ~s andere als ...** that's anything but ...; **er ist ~s, nur kein Vertreter** he's anything but a salesman; **das ist mir ~s gleich** it's all the same to me; **was soll das ~s?** what's all this supposed to mean?; **~s schon mal da gewesen** (*inf*) it's all been done before!; **es hat ~s keinen Sinn mehr** nothing makes sense any more, it has all become meaningless; **was habt ihr ~s gemacht?** what did you get up to?; **wer war ~s da?** who was there?; **was er (nicht) ~s weiß/kann!** the things he knows/can do!; **was es nicht ~s gibt!** well (now) I've seen everything!, well I never (*inf*)

c alle PL (*substantivisch*) all; (= *alle Menschen auch*) everybody, everyone; **sie sind ~ alt** they're all old; **die haben mir ~ nicht gefallen** I didn't like any of them; **ich habe (sie) ~ verschenkt** I've given them all away, I've given all of them away; **~ beide** both of them; **~ drei** all three of them; **~ drei/diejenigen, die ... all three/(those) who ...; **diese** ~ all (of) these; **der Kampf ~r gegen ~** the free-for-all; **~ für einen und einer für ~!** all for one and one for all; **sie kamen ~** they all came, all of them came; **sie haben ~ kein Geld mehr** none of them has any money left; **redet nicht ~ auf einmal!** don't all talk at once!

d (*mit Zeit-, Maßangaben*) *usu pl* every; **~ fünf Minuten/halbe Stunde/fünf Meilen** every five minutes/half-hour/five miles; **~ Jahre wieder** year after year

ADV → **alle**

al|ler|al|ler- [ˈalɛˈalɛ] *in cpds with superl* (*inf*: *zur Verstärkung*) far and away; **das Allerallergrößte** far and away the biggest; **die Allerallerhübscheste** far and away the prettiest

al|ler-: al|ler|art [ˈalɛˈlaːɐt] ADJ *attr inv* (*dated*) all sorts *or* kinds of; **al|ler|bes|te(r, s)** [ˈalɛˈbɛstə] ADJ very best, best of all, best ... of all; (= *exquisit*) Waren, Qualität very best; **ich wünsche Dir das Allerbeste** (I wish you) all the best; **der/die/das Allerbeste** the very best, the best of all; **es ist das ~ or am ~n, zu ...** by far the best thing would be to .../if ...; **al|ler|dings** [ˈalɛˈdɪŋs] ADV **a** (*einschränkend*) though, mind you; **ich komme mit, ich muss ~ erst zur Bank** I'm coming but I must go to the bank first though, I'm coming though I must go to the bank first; **das ist ~ wahr, aber ...** that may be true, but ..., (al)though that's true ... **b** (*bekräftigend*) certainly; **~!** (most) certainly!; **al|ler|ers|te(r, s)** [ˈalɛˈeːɐstə] ADJ very first; **al|ler|frü|hes|tens** [ˈalɛˈfryːəstns] ADV at the very earliest

Al|ler|gen [alɛrˈgeːn] NT -s, -e (*Med*) allergen

Al|ler|gie [alɛrˈgiː] F -, -n [-ˈgiːən] (*Med*) allergy; (*fig*) aversion (*gegen* to); **eine ~ gegen etw haben** to be allergic to sth (*auch fig hum*); (*fig auch*) to have an aversion to sth

Al|ler|gie-: al|ler|gie|ge|prüft, al|ler|gie|ge|tes|tet ADJ allergy-tested; **Al|ler|gie|pass ▲** M (*Med*) allergy ID; **Al|ler|gie|schock** M (*Med*) anaphylactic shock; **Al|ler|gie|test** M (*Med*) allergy test

Al|ler|gi|ker [aˈlɛrgikɐ] M -s, -, **Al|ler|gi|ke|rin** [-ərɪn] F -, -nen person suffering from an allergy

al|ler|gisch [aˈlɛrgɪʃ] ADJ (*Med, fig*) allergic (*gegen* to); **auf etw** (*acc*) **~ reagieren** to have an allergic reaction to sth; (*fig*) to react oversensitively to sth; **~ bedingt sein** to be caused by an allergy

Al|ler|go|lo|ge [alɛrgoˈloːgə] M -n, -n, **Al|ler|go|lo|gin** [-ˈloːgɪn] F -, -nen allergist

Al|ler|go|lo|gie [alɛrgoloˈgiː] F -, *no pl* (*Med*) allergology

Al|ler-: al|ler|hand [ˈalɛˈhant] ADJ *inv* (*substantivisch*) (= *allerlei*) all kinds of things; (= *ziemlich viel*) rather a lot; (*attributiv*) all kinds *or* sorts of, rather a lot of; **das ist ~!** (*zustimmend*) that's quite something!, not bad at all! (*inf*); **das ist ja** *or* **doch ~!** (*empört*) that's too much!, that's the limit!; **Al|ler|hei|li|gen** [ˈalɛˈhailɪgn] NT -s All Saints' Day, All Hallows (Day) (*Brit*); **Al|ler|hei|ligs|te(s)** [ˈalɛˈhailɪgstə] NT *decl as adj* (*Rel*: = *Raum*) inner sanctum; (*jüdisch, fig*) Holy of Holies; (*katholisch*) Blessed Sacrament

---

ALLERHEILIGEN

Allerheiligen (All Saints' Day, celebrated on November 1st) is a holiday in Catholic areas of Germany and in Austria. The following day, November 2nd, is **Allerseelen** (All Souls' Day) when the dead are commemorated. It is traditional on these days to visit cemeteries and place flowers, wreaths and lighted candles on the graves of loved ones. In Alpine regions children traditionally go from house to house asking for **Seelenwecken** (bread rolls).

In the Protestant Church **Totensonntag** falls on the last Sunday before Advent and is devoted to the remembrance of the dead.

Al|ler-: al|ler|höchs|tens [ˈalɛˈhøːçstns] ADV at the very most; **al|ler|höchs|te(r, s)** [ˈalɛˈhøːçstə] ADJ Berg etc highest of all, highest ... of all, very highest; Betrag, Belastung, Geschwindigkeit maximum; Funktionäre highest, top *attr*; Instanz, Kreise very highest; **es wird ~ Zeit, dass ...** it's really high time that ...; **al|ler|lei** [ˈalɛˈlai] ADJ *inv* (*substantivisch*) all sorts *or* kinds of things; (*attributiv*) all sorts *or* kinds of; **Al|ler|lei** [ˈalɛˈlai] NT -s, *no pl* (= *Durcheinander*) farrago, potpourri, welter; **Leipziger ~** (*Cook*) Leipzig mixed vegetables *pl*; **al|ler|letz|te(r, s)** [ˈalɛˈlɛtstə] ADJ very last; (*inf* = *allerneueste*) very latest; (*inf*: = *unmöglich*) most awful *attr* (*inf*); **in ~r Zeit** very recently; **der/die/das Allerletzte** the very last (person)/thing; **der/das ist (ja) das Allerletzte** (*inf*) he's/it's the absolute end! (*inf*); **al|ler|liebst** [ˈalɛˈliːpst] ADJ (*old*: = *reizend*) enchanting, delightful; **al|ler|liebs|te(r, s)** [ˈalɛˈliːpstə] ADJ (= *Lieblings-*) most favourite *attr* (*Brit*) *or* favorite *attr* (*US*); **sie ist mir die Allerliebste** she's my absolute favourite (*Brit*) *or* favorite (*US*); **es wäre mir das Allerliebste** *or* **am ~n, wenn ...** I would much prefer it if ...; **am ~n geh ich ins Kino** I like going to the cinema most *or* best of all; **al|ler|liebs|te(r)** [ˈalɛˈliːpstə] MF *decl as adj* (*old, hum*) beloved, love of one's life; (*Frau auch*) ladylove; **al|ler|meis|te(r, s)** [ˈalɛˈmaistə] ADJ most of all, most ... of all; (= *weitaus beste*) by far the most; **am ~n** most of all; **die Allermeisten** the vast majority; **al|ler|nächs|te(r, s)** [ˈalɛˈnɛːçstə] ADJ (*in Folge*) very next; (*räumlich*) nearest of all; Verwandte very closest; Route very shortest; **in ~r Nähe** right nearby, right close by; **in ~r Zeit** *or* **Zukunft** in the very near future; **al|ler|neu|es|te(r, s)** [ˈalɛˈnɔystə] ADJ very latest; **al|ler|neus|te(r, s)** [ˈalɛˈnɔystə] ADJ very latest; **al|ler|or|ten** [ˈalɛˈlɔrtn], **al|ler|orts** [ˈalɛˈlɔrts] ADV (*old*) everywhere; **Al|ler|see|len** [ˈalɛˈzeːlən] NT -s All Souls' Day; **al|ler|seits** [ˈalɛˈzaits] ADV on all sides, on every side; **guten Abend ~!** good evening everybody *or* everyone *or* all; **vielen Dank ~** thank you all *or* everybody *or* everyone; **al|ler|spä|tes|tens** [ˈalɛˈʃpeːtəstns] ADV at the very latest

Al|ler|welts- [ˈalɛˈvɛlts] *in cpds* (= *Durchschnitts-*) ordinary; (= *nichts sagend*) commonplace, general; **Al|ler|welts|kerl** M jack of all trades; **Al|ler|welts|the|ma** NT general subject; **Al|ler|welts|typ** M (= *Mann*) ordinary *or* average guy (*inf*); (= *Frau*) ordinary *or* average woman

Al|ler-: al|ler|we|nigs|tens [ˈalɛˈveːnɪçstns] ADV at the very least; **al|ler|we|nigs|te(r, s)** [ˈalɛˈveːnɪçstə] ADJ least of all, least ... of all; (*pl*) fewest of all, fewest ... of all; (= *äußerst wenig*) very little; (*pl*) very few; (= *geringste*) Mühe least possible; **die ~n Menschen wissen das** very (very) few people know that; **das ist noch das Allerwenigste!** that's the very least of it; **das ist doch das Allerwenigste, was man erwarten könnte** but that's the very least one could expect; **er hat von uns allen das ~** *or* **am ~n Geld** he has the least money of any of us; **sie hat von uns allen die ~n** *or* **am ~n Sorgen** she has the fewest worries of any of us; **das am ~n!** least of all that!; **Al|ler|wer|tes|te(r)** [ˈalɛˈveːɐtəstə] M *decl as adj* (*hum*) posterior (*hum*)

al|les [ˈaləs] INDEF PRON → **alle(r, s) b**

al|le|samt [ˈaləˈzamt] ADV all (of them/us *etc*), to a man; **ihr seid ~ Betrüger!** you're all cheats!, you're cheats, all of you *or* the lot of you!

Al|les-: Al|les|fres|ser M omnivore; **Al|les|kle|ber** M all-purpose adhesive *or* glue; **Al|les|schnei|der** M food-slicer; **Al|les|wis|ser** [-vɪsɐ] M -s, -, **Al|les|wis|se|rin** [-ərɪn] F -, -nen (*iro*) know-all (*Brit inf*), know-it-all (*US inf*)

al|le|we|ge [ˈaləˈveːgə] ADV (*old*) everywhere

al|le|zeit [alə'tsait] ADV (liter) = allzeit

All-: all|fäl|lig ['alfɛlıç, al'fɛlıç] (Aus, Sw) **ADJ** possible **ADV** (= eventuell) possibly; **All|ge|gen|wart** [al'ge:gnvart] F omnipresence, ubiquity; **all|ge|gen|wär|tig** [al'ge:gnvɛrtıç] ADJ DIE omnipresent, ubiquitous; **All|ge|gen|wär|tig|keit** F omnipresence, ubiquity

all|ge|mein ['algə'main] **ADJ** general; Ablehnung, Zustimmung auch common; Feiertag public; Regelungen, Wahlrecht universal; Wehrpflicht compulsory; (= öffentlich) public, general; **im Allgemeinen** in general, generally; **im ~en Interesse** in the common interest, in the public interest; **von ~em Interesse** of general interest; **~e Redensarten** (= idiomatische Ausdrücke) set expressions; (= Phrasen) commonplaces; **auf ~en Wunsch** by popular or general request; **die ~e Meinung** the general opinion, the generally held opinion, public opinion; **das ~e Wohl** the common good, (the) public welfare, the public good; **~es Aufsehen erregen** to cause or create a sensation; **die Diskussion darüber wurde ~a** general discussion developed; **wir sind ganz ~ geblieben** (inf) we stayed on a general level; **das Allgemeine und das Besondere** the general and the particular

ADV (= überall, bei allen, von allen) generally; (= ausnahmslos von allen) universally; (= generell) generally, in the main, for the most part; (= nicht spezifisch) in general terms; **seine Thesen sind so ~ abgefasst, dass ...** his theses are worded in such general terms that ...; **du kannst doch nicht so ~ behaupten, dass ...** you can't make such a generalization and say that ..., you can't generalize like that and say that ...; **es ist ~ bekannt** it's common knowledge; **~ bildend** providing (a) general or (an) all-round (Brit) education; Studium auch with general educational value; (= gültig general, universal, universally or generally applicable or valid; **es ist ~ üblich, etw zu tun** it's the general rule that we/they etc do sth, it's commonly or generally the practice to do sth; **~ verbindlich** binding; **~ verständlich** (adjektivisch) generally intelligible, intelligible to all; (adverbial) in a way intelligible to all; **etw ~ verständlich ausdrücken** to express sth in a way which everyone can understand; **~ verbreitet** widespread; **~ zugänglich** open to all, open to the general public

All|ge|mein-: All|ge|mein|arzt M , **All|ge|mein|ärz|tin** F (Med) ≈ general practitioner, ≈ GP, ≈ family practitioner (US); **All|ge|mein|be|fin|den** NT general condition, general state of being; **all|ge|mein|bil|dend** △ ADJ → **allgemein** ADV; **All|ge|mein|bil|dung** F general or all-round (Brit) education; **all|ge|mein|gül|tig** △ ADJ attr → **allgemein** ADV; **All|ge|mein|gül|tig|keit** F universal or general validity, universality; **All|ge|mein|gut** NT , no pl (fig) common property; **All|ge|mein|heit** F -, **-en** a no pl (= Öffentlichkeit) general public, public at large; (= alle) everyone, everybody **b** (= Unbestimmtheit) generality; **~en** generalities; **All|ge|mein|kran|ken|haus** NT (Med) general hospital; **All|ge|mein|me|di|zin** F general medicine; **Arzt für ~** general practitioner, GP; **All|ge|mein|me|di|zi|ner(in)** M(F) (Med) ≈ general practitioner, ≈ GP, ≈ family practitioner (US); **All|ge|mein|platz** M (pej) commonplace, platitude; **all|ge|mein|ver|bind|lich** ADJ attr △ → **allgemein** ADV; **all|ge|mein|ver|ständ|lich** ADJ → **allgemein** ADV; **All|ge|mein|ver|ständ|lich|keit** F general intelligibility; **All|ge|mein|wis|sen** NT general knowledge; **All|ge|mein|wohl** NT public good or welfare; **All|ge|mein|zu|stand** M general condition; (= Lage) general situation; (= Gesundheit) general wellbeing or health

All-: All|ge|walt ['algəvalt] F (liter) omnipotence; **all|ge|wal|tig** ['algəvaltıç] ADJ omnipotent, all-powerful; **All|heil|mit|tel** [al'hailmıtl] NT universal remedy, cure-all, panacea (esp fig); **all|hier** [al'hi:ɐ] ADV (obs, liter) here

All|li|anz [a'liants] F -, **-en** a alliance **b** (= NATO) Alliance

All|li|anz|part|ner(in) M(F) partner in the alliance; (bei NATO) partner in NATO, NATO partner

All|li|ga|tor [ali'ga:to:ɐ] M **-s,** **Alligatoren** [-'to:rən] alligator

all|li|ie|ren [ali'i:rən] ptp **alliiert** VR (geh) to form an alliance; **sich mit jdm ~** to ally (oneself) with sb

all|li|iert [ali'i:ɐt] ADJ attr allied; (im 2. Weltkrieg) Allied

All|li|ier|te(r) [ali'i:ɐtə] MF decl as adj ally; **die ~n** (im 2. Weltkrieg) the Allies

All|li|te|ra|ti|on [alıtera'tsio:n] F -, **-en** (Poet) alliteration

all|li|te|rie|rend [alıte'ri:rənt] ADJ (Poet) alliterative

allj. abbr von **alljährlich**

All-: all|jähr|lich ['al'jɛ:ɐlıç] **ADJ** annual, yearly **ADV** annually, yearly, every year; **All|macht** ['almaxt] F (esp von Gott) omnipotence; (von Konzern etc) all-pervading power; **all|mäch|tig** [al'mɛçtıç] ADJ all-powerful, omnipotent; Gott auch almighty; **All|mäch|ti|ge(r)** [al'mɛçtıgə] M decl as adj (= Gott) **der ~** Almighty God, God (the) Almighty, the Almighty; **~r!** good Lord!, heavens above!

all|mäh|lich [al'mɛ:lıç] **ADJ** attr gradual **ADV** gradually; (= schrittweise auch) bit by bit, step by step; (inf: = endlich) at last; **es wird ~ Zeit** (inf) it's about time; **~ verstand er, dass ...** it gradually dawned on him that ..., he realized gradually that ...; **ich werde (ganz) ~ müde** (inf) I'm beginning to get tired; **wir sollten ~ gehen** (inf) shall we think about going?

All|men|de [al'mɛndə] F -, **-n** common land

All-: all|mo|nat|lich ['al'mo:natlıç] **ADJ** monthly **ADV** every month, monthly; **all|mor|gend|lich** ['al'mɔrgntlıç] **ADJ** which takes place every morning; **die ~e Eile** the regular morning rush **ADV** every morning; **All|mut|ter** ['almʊtɐ] F , no pl (liter) Mother of all; **die ~ Natur** Mother Nature; **all|nächt|lich** ['al'nɛçtlıç] **ADJ** nightly **ADV** nightly, every night

All|lo|path [alo'pa:t] M **-en, -en, All|lo|pa|thin** [-tın] F -, **-nen** allopath

All|lo|pa|thie [alopa'ti:] F -, no pl allopathy

All|lo|phon [alo'fo:n] NT **-s, -e** (Ling) allophone

All|lot|ria [a'lo:tria] NT **-(s),** no pl (= Unfug) monkey business (inf) no indef art; (ausgelassen, freudig) skylarking (inf) no indef art, fooling about (Brit) or around no indef art; (= Lärm) racket (inf), din; **~ treiben** (inf) to lark about (inf), to fool about (Brit) or around

All|par|tei|en|ge|sprä|che ['alpar'taiən-] PL (Pol) all-party talks pl

All|par|tei|en|re|gie|rung F (Pol) all-party government

All|rad|an|trieb ['alra:t-] M (Aut) four-wheel drive

All|rad|len|kung F (Aut) four-wheel steering

All|round- ['ɔ:l'raund] in cpds all-round (Brit), all-around (US)

All|roun|der¹ ['ɔ:lraundɐ] M **-s, -** (= Gerät) all-rounder (Brit), versatile device

All|roun|der² ['ɔ:lraundɐ] M , **All|roun|de|rin** [-ərın] F -, **-nen** all-rounder (Brit), multi-talent (US)

All|round- ['ɔ:l'raund]: **All|round|ge|nie** NT (iro) all-round (Brit) or all-around (US) genius; **All|round|sport|ler(in)** M(F) all-rounder (Brit), multi-talent (US)

all|sei|tig ['alzaitıç] **ADJ** (= allgemein) general; (= ausnahmslos) universal; (= vielseitig) all-round attr (Brit), all-around attr (US); **zur ~en Zufriedenheit** to the satisfaction of all or everyone **ADV** **~ begabt sein** to have all-round (Brit) or all-around (US) talents, to be an all-rounder (Brit) or a multi-talent (US); **jdn ~ ausbilden** to

provide sb with a general or an all-round (Brit) education; **er wurde ~ informiert** he was informed about every (possible) area; **~ interessiert sein** to be interested in everything

all|seits ['alzaits] ADV (= überall) everywhere, on all sides; (= in jeder Beziehung) in every respect; **~ beliebt/unbeliebt** popular/unpopular with everyone, universally popular/unpopular

All|strom- ['alʃtro:m-]: **All|strom|emp|fän|ger** M (Rad) all-mains (esp Brit) or AC-DC receiver; **All|strom|ge|rät** NT (Rad) all-mains (esp Brit) or AC-DC appliance

All|tag ['alta:k] M **a** (= Werktag) weekday; **am ~, an ~en** on weekdays; **Kleidung, die man am ~ trägt** clothes for everyday wear; **mitten im ~** in the middle of the week **b** (fig) everyday life; **im ~** in everyday life; **der ~ der Ehe** the mundane side of married life

all|täg|lich ['al'tɛ:klıç, 'altɛ:klıç, al'tɛ:klıç] ADJ **a** (= tagtäglich) daily **b** (= üblich) everyday attr, ordinary, mundane (pej); Gesicht, Mensch ordinary; Bemerkung commonplace; **es ist ganz ~** it's nothing unusual, it's nothing out of the ordinary; **das ist nichts Alltägliches, dass/wenn ...** it doesn't happen every day that ..., it's not every day that ...; **was ich suche, ist nicht das Alltägliche** I'm looking for something a bit out of the ordinary

All|täg|lich|keit F -, **-en** a no pl ordinariness **b** (= Gemeinplatz) commonplace

all|tags ['alta:ks] ADV on weekdays; **etw ~ tragen** to wear sth for every day

All|tags- in cpds everyday; **All|tags|ehe** F mundane marriage; **All|tags|klei|dung** F everyday clothes pl, everday wear no pl; **All|tags|kram** M (inf) everyday or day-to-day stuff (inf); **All|tags|le|ben** NT everyday life; **danach begann wieder das ~** after that life got back to normal again; **All|tags|mensch** M ordinary person; **All|tags|rhyth|mus** M daily rhythm; **All|tags|sor|gen** PL everyday or day-to-day worries pl or cares pl; **All|tags|trott** M (inf) daily round, treadmill of everyday life

all|über|all ['alʏːbɐ'al] ADV (old, poet) everywhere

all|um|fas|send ['alʊm'fasnt] ADJ all-embracing

All|lü|ren [a'lʏːrən] PL behaviour (Brit), behavior (US); (= geziertes Verhalten) affectations pl; (eines Stars etc) airs and graces pl

All|lu|vi|um [a'lu:viʊm] NT **-s,** no pl diluvial or Holocene epoch

All-: all|wis|send ['al'vısnt] ADJ omniscient; **(Gott,) der Allwissende** God the Omniscient; **ich bin nicht ~!** I don't know everything!, I'm not omniscient!; **All|wis|sen|heit** ['al'vısnhait] F -, no pl omniscience; **all|wö|chent|lich** ['al'vœçntlıç] **ADJ** weekly **ADV** every week; **all|zeit** ['al'tsait] ADV (geh) always; **~ bereit!** be prepared!

all|zu ['altsu:] ADV all too; (+neg) too; **~ viele Fehler** far too many mistakes; **nur ~** only or all too; **~ früh** far too early; (+neg) too early; **~ gern** (mögen) only too much; (= bereitwillig) only too willingly; (+neg) all that much, too much; all that willingly, too willingly; **etw (nur) ~ gern machen** to like doing sth only too much; **etw nicht ~ gern machen** not to like doing sth all that much or too much or overmuch; **er isst Muscheln nur ~ gern** he's only too fond of mussels; **~ sehr** too much; **mögen** all too much; (+neg) too much, all that much, overmuch; sich freuen, erfreut sein only too; (+neg) too; versuchen too hard; sich ärgern, enttäuscht sein too; **sie war ~ sehr/nicht ~ sehr in ihn verliebt** she was too much in love with him/wasn't in love with him all that much; **~ viel** too much; **~ viel ist ungesund** (Prov) you can have too much of a good thing (prov)

All|zweck- ['altsvɛk] in cpds general purpose; **All|zweck|hal|le** F multipurpose hall; **All|zweck|rei|ni|ger** M all-purpose cleaner

Alm [alm] F -, -en alpine pasture

Alm|ab|trieb M *driving cattle down from the alpine pastures*

Al̦ma Ma̦ter ▲ [ˈalma ˈmaːtɐ] F - -, *no pl* alma mater

Al̦ma|nach [ˈalmanax] M -s, -e almanac

Alm-: **Alm|auf|trieb** M *driving cattle up to the alpine pastures;* **Alm|hüt|te** F alpine hut

Al̦mo|sen [ˈalmoːzn] NT -s, - **a** (geh: = Spende) alms pl (old) **b** (= geringer Lohn) pittance **c** **Almosen** PL (fig) charity

Alm|rausch M , **Alm|ro̦se** F Alpine rose or rhododendron

A̦loe [ˈaːloe] F -, -n [ˈaːloən] aloe

a̦lo|gisch [ˈaloːɡɪʃ, aˈloːɡɪʃ] ADJ (geh) illogical

Alp¹ [alp] F -, -en (= Alm) alpine pasture

Alp² △ M -(e)s, -e (old: = Nachtmahr) → **Alb²**

Al̦pa|ka [alˈpaka] NT -s, -s **a** (= Lamaart) alpaca **b** *no pl (auch* **Alpakawolle**) alpaca (wool) **c** *no pl (= Neusilber)* German or nickel silver

Alp|druck M *pl* -**drücke** (lit, fig) nightmare; **wie ein ~ auf jdm lasten** to weigh sb down

Al̦pen [ˈalpn] PL Alps *pl*

Al̦pen- *in cpds* alpine; **Al̦pen|dol̦lar** M (Hist: hum) Austrian schilling; **Al̦pen|glühen** NT -s, - alpenglow; **Al̦pen|jä̦ger(in)** M(F) (Mil) mountain infantryman/-woman **pl** mountain troops *pl* or infantry; **Al̦pen|kețte** F alpine chain; **Al̦pen|land** NT alpine country; **al̦pen|län̦disch** [-lɛndɪʃ] ADJ Literatur, Kulturgut etc of the alpine region; Mensch from the alpine region; **Al̦pen|pass** ▲ M alpine pass; **Al̦pen|re|pu̦blik** F die ~ (hum) Austria; **Al̦pen|ro̦se** F Alpine rose or rhododendron; **Al̦pen|rot** NT , *no pl* red snow; **Al̦pen|veil̦chen** NT cyclamen; **Al̦pen|vor̦land** NT foothills *pl* of the Alps

alph. *abbr von* **alphabetisch**

Al̦pha [ˈalfa] NT -(s), -s alpha

Al̦pha|bet¹ [alfaˈbeːt] NT -(e)s, -e alphabet; **nach dem ~** alphabetically, in alphabetical order; **das ~ lernen/aufsagen** to learn/say the or one's alphabet

Al̦pha|bet² [alfaˈbeːt] M -en, -en, **Al̦pha|be̦|tin** [-ˈbeːtɪn] F -, -nen literate person

al̦pha|be̦tisch [alfaˈbeːtɪʃ] ADJ alphabetical ADV alphabetically, in alphabetical order

al̦pha|be̦ti|sie̦ren [alfabetiˈziːrən] ptp **alphabetisiert** VT to make literate

Al̦pha|be̦ti|sie̦rung F -, -en ein Programm zur ~ Indiens a programme (Brit) or program (US) against illiteracy in India; **die ~ Kubas ist abgeschlossen** the population of Cuba is now largely literate

Al̦pha-: **al̦pha|nu|me̦risch** [alfanuˈmeːrɪʃ] ADJ alphanumeric ADV alphanumerically; **Al̦pha|strah̦len** PL alpha rays *pl*; **Al̦pha|teil̦chen** NT alpha particle

Alp-: **Alp|horn** NT alp(en)horn; **Alp|hüțte** F alpine hut

al̦pin [alˈpiːn] ADJ alpine (auch Ski)

Al̦pi|nișmus [alpiˈnɪsmʊs] M -, *no pl* alpinism

Al̦pi|nist [alpiˈnɪst] M -en, -en, **Al̦pi|niștin** [-ˈnɪstɪn] F -, -nen alpinist

Al̦pi|niștik [alpiˈnɪstɪk] F -, *no pl* alpinism

Älp̦ler [ˈɛlplɐ] M -s, -, **Älp̦le|rin** [-ərɪn] F -, -nen inhabitant of the Alps

älp̦le|risch [ˈɛlplərɪʃ] ADJ Kleidung, Dialekt of the alpine region

Alp-: **Alp|traum** M (lit, fig) nightmare; **alp̦|traum|ar|tig** ADJ nightmarish

Al̦raun [alˈraun] M -(e)s, -e, **Al̦rau̦ne** [alˈraunə] F -, -n mandrake

als [als] CONJ **a** (nach comp) than; **ich kam spä̦ter ~ er** I came later than he (did) or him; **Hans ist grö̦ßer ~ sein Bruder** Hans is taller than his brother; **mehr ~ arbeiten kann ich nicht** I can't do more than work **b** (bei Vergleichen) **so ... ~ ...** as ... as ...; **so viel/**

so weit ~ mö̦glich as much/far as possible; **~ wie** as; **nichts/niemand/nirgend anders ~** nothing/nobody/nowhere but; **eher** or **lieber ... ~ rather ... than; ich würde eher sterben ~ das zu tun** I would rather die than do that, I would die rather than do that; **anders sein ~** to be different from; **das machen wir anders ~ ihr** we do it differently to you; **alles andere ~** anything but **c** (in Modalsätzen) as if or though; **es sieht aus, ~ würde es bald schneien** it looks as if or though it will snow soon; **sie sah aus, ~ ob** or **wenn sie schliefe** she looked as if or though she were asleep; **~ ob ich das nicht wüsste!** as if I didn't know! → *auch* **ob** **d** (in Aufzählung) **~ (da sind) ...** that is to say ..., to wit ... (old, form) **e** (in Konsekutivsätzen) **sie ist zu alt, ~ dass sie das noch verstehen könnte** she is too old to understand that; **die Zeit war zu knapp, ~ dass wir ...** the time was too short for us to ...; **das ist umso trauriger, ~ es nicht das erste Mal war** that's all the sadder in that it wasn't the first time **f** (in Temporalsätzen) when; (= gleichzeitig) as; **gleich, ~** as soon as; **damals, ~** (in the days) when; **gerade, ~** just as **g** (= in der Eigenschaft) as; **~ Beweis** as proof; **~ Antwort/Warnung** as an answer/a warning; **sich ~ wahr/falsch erweisen** to prove to be true/ false; **~ Held/Revolutionär** as a hero/revolutionary; **~ Kind/Mädchen** etc as a child/girl etc; **~ Rentner will er ein Buch schreiben** when he retires he is going to write a book → **sowohl, insofern**

ADV (dial inf) (= immer) **etw ~ (noch mal) tun** to keep on (and on) doing sth; **gehen Sie ~ gera̦deaus** keep going straight ahead

als-: **alșbald** [alsˈbalt] ADV (old, liter) directly, straightway (old); **alșbal̦dig** [alsˈbaldɪç] ADJ (form) immediate; „**zum ~en Verbrauch be̦stimmt**" "do not keep", "for immediate use only"; **alșdann** [alsˈdan] ADV **a** (old liter: = dann) then **b** (dial) well then, well ... then

al̦so [ˈalzo] CONJ **a** (= folglich) so, therefore; **er war Künstler, ein hochsensibler Mensch ~** he was an artist, (and) therefore a highly sensitive person

b (old: = so, folgendermaßen) thus

ADV so; (nach Unterbrechung anknüpfend) well; (zusammenfassend, erklärend) that is; **~ doch** so ... after all; **du machst es ~?** so you'll do it then?; **~ wie ich schon sagte** well (then), as I said before

INTERJ (verwundert, entrüstet, auffordernd) well; (drohend) just; **~, dass du dich ordentlich be̦nimmst!** (you) just see that you behave yourself!; **~ doch!** so he/they etc did!; **na ~!** there you are!, you see?; **~, ich habs doch gewusst!** I knew it!; **~ nein!** (oh) no!; **~ nein, dass sie sich das gefallen lässt** my God, she can't put up with that!; **~ gut** or **schön** well all right then; **~ dann!** right then!; **~ so was!** well (I never)!; **~ so eine Frechheit!** what impudence!

Alșter|wașser [ˈalstɐ-] NT *pl* -**wässer** (N Ger) shandy (Brit), radler (US), beer and lemonade

alt [alt] ADJ comp **=er** [ˈɛltɐ], superl **=este(r, s)** [ˈɛltəstə] **a** old; (= sehr alt) Mythos, Sage, Aberglaube, Griechen, Geschichte ancient; Sprachen classical; **das ~e Rom** ancient Rome; **das Alte Testament** the Old Testament; **die Alte Welt** the Old World; **mein ~er Herr** (inf: = Vater) the or one's old man (inf); **~er Junge** or **Freund** old boy (dated) or fellow (dated); **Alt und Jung** (everybody) young and old; **ein drei Jahre ~es Kind** a three-year-old child, a child of three years of age; **wie ~ bist du?** how old are you?; **etw ~ kaufen** to buy sth second-hand; **man ist so ~, wie man sich fühlt** you're only as old as you feel; **~ und grau werden** to grow old and grey (Brit) or gray (US); **ich werde heute nicht ~ (werden)** (inf) I won't last long tonight (inf); **hier werde ich nicht ~** (inf) this isn't my scene (inf); **aus Alt mach Neu** (inf) make do and

mend (Prov) → **Eisen, Hase, Haus**

b (= dieselbe, gewohnt) same old; **sie ist ganz die ~e Ingrid** or **die Alte** she's the same old Ingrid, she hasn't changed a bit; **jetzt ist sie wie̦der ganz die ~e lustige Veronika** she's the old happy Veronika again; **wir bleiben die Alten, auch wenn sich alle andern verändern** we stay the same even when everybody else changes; **er ist nicht mehr der Alte** he's not what he was, he's not the man he was; **es ist nicht mehr das ~e Glasgow** it's not the (same old) Glasgow I/we etc knew; **alles bleibt beim Alten** everything stays as it was; **alles beim Alten lassen** to leave everything as it was

c (= lange bestehend) old; **in ~er Freundschaft, dein ...** yours as ever ...

d **~ aussehen** (inf: = dumm dastehen) to look stupid

Alt¹ [alt] M -s, -e (Mus) alto; (von Frau auch) contralto; (Gesamtheit der Stimmen) altos pl, contraltos pl

Alt² NT -s, - (= Bier) top-fermented German dark beer;

Al̦tan [alˈtaːn] M -(e)s, -e balcony

alt-: **alt|an|ge|se̦hen** ADJ Familie old and respected; Firma old-established; **alt|an|ge̦|seș|sen** [ˈaltˈlaŋɡəzɛsn] ADJ, **alt|an|säș|sig** ADJ old-established

Al̦tar [alˈtaːɐ] M -s, Altäre [-ˈtɛːrə] altar; **eine Frau zum ~ führen** to lead a woman to the altar

Al̦tar- *in cpds* altar; **Al̦tar|bild** NT altarpiece, reredos; **Al̦tar|ge|mäl̦de** NT altarpiece; **Al̦tar|ge|rät** NT altar furniture; **Al̦tar|raum** M chancel; **Al̦tar|schmuck** M altar decoration(s pl); **Al̦tar|stu̦fen** PL altar steps or pl; **Al̦tar|tuch** NT altar cloth, vesperal; **Al̦tar|wein** M Communion wine

Alt-: **Alt|au̦to** NT old car (ready to be scrapped or recycled); **~-Recycling** recycling of old cars; **alt|ba̦cken** [-bakn] ADJ **a** stale **b** (fig) Mensch, Kleidung old-fashioned; Ansichten outdated, old-fashioned; **Alt|bațte|rie** F used battery; **Alt|bau** M *pl* -bauten old building; **Alt|bau|mo̦der̦ni̦sie̦rung** F modernization of an old building; **Alt|bau|sa̦nie̦rung** F refurbishment (of old buildings); **Alt|bau|woh̦nung** F flat (Brit) or apartment in an old building; **alt|be|kannt** ADJ well-known; **alt|be|währt** ADJ Mittel, Methode etc well-tried; Sitte, Tradition, Freundschaft etc long-standing usu attr, of long standing; **Alt|bier** NT top-fermented German dark beer; **Alt|bun̦deș|kanz̦ler(in)** M(F) former German/Austrian Chancellor; **Alt|bun̦deș|land** NT die Altbundesländer the former West German states, the states which formed the old West Germany; **Alt|bür̦ger(in)** M(F) senior citizen; **alt|chrisțlich** ADJ early Christian; **alt|deutsch** ADJ old German; Möbel, Stil German Renaissance

Al̦te [ˈaltə] F decl as adj (= alte Frau, inf: = Ehefrau, Mutter) old woman; (inf: = Vorgesetzte) boss → *auch* **Alte(r)**

Alt-: **alt|ehr̦wür̦dig** ADJ venerable; Bräuche time-honoured (Brit), time-honored (US); **Alt|ei̦gen|tü̦mer(in)** M(F) (von Land, Gebäude) original owner; **alt|ein̦ge|führt** [ˈaltˈlaingəfyːɐt] ADJ Brauch, Firma, Arzneimittel old-established; **alt|ein̦ge̦|seșsen** [ˈaltˈlaingəzɛsn] ADJ = altangesessen; **Alt|ei̦sen** NT scrap metal; **alt|eng̦lisch** ADJ old English; **Alt|eng̦|lisch(e)** NT Old English, Anglo-Saxon

Al̦ten-: **Al̦ten|heim** NT old people's home; **Al̦ten|herr̦schaft** F gerontocracy; **Al̦ten|hil̦fe** F old people's welfare; **Al̦ten|nach̦|mit|tag** M senior citizens' afternoon or club; **Al̦ten|pfle̦ge** F care (for the elderly); **Al̦ten|pfle̦ge̦heim** NT nursing home for the elderly; **Al̦ten|pfle̦ger(in)** M(F) old people's nurse; **Al̦ten|ta̦geșstäțte** F old people's day centre (Brit) or center (US); **Al̦ten|teil** NT cottage or part of a farm reserved for the farmer when he hands the estate over to his son **sich aufs ~ setzen** or **zurückziehen** (fig) to retire or withdraw from public life; **Al|ten|treff** M senior citizens' club; **Al|ten|wohn|heim** NT sheltered housing complex (for the elderly); **sie lebt in einem ~** she lives in sheltered housing

Al|te(r) ['altə] M decl as adj (= alter Mann, inf: = Ehemann, Vater) old man; (inf: = Vorgesetzter) boss; **die ~n** (= Eltern) the folk(s) pl (inf); (= Tiereltern) the parents pl; (= ältere Generation) the old people pl or folk pl; (aus klassischer Zeit) the ancients pl; **wie die ~n sungen, so zwitschern auch die Jungen** (prov) like father like son (prov); **komischer ~r** (Theat) comic old man

äl|ter ['ɛltə] ADJ **a** comp von **alt** older; **Bruder, Tochter etc auch** elder; **werden Frauen ~ als Männer?** do women live longer than men? **b** attr (= nicht ganz jung) elderly; **die ~en Herrschaften** the older members of the party

Al|ter ['altə] NT **-s, -** age; (= letzter Lebensabschnitt, hohes Alter) old age; **im ~** in one's old age; **im ~ wird man weiser** one grows wiser with age; **in deinem ~** at your age; **er ist in deinem ~** he's your age; **im ~ von 18 Jahren** at the age of 18; **von mittlerem ~, mittleren ~s** middle-aged; **57 ist doch kein ~, um in Rente zu gehen** 57 is no age to retire; **er hat keinen Respekt vor dem ~** he has no respect for his elders; **~ schützt vor Torheit nicht** (Prov) there's no fool like an old fool (Prov)

Al|ter|chen ['altəçən] NT **-s, -** (inf) Grandad (inf)

Al|ter E|go ▲ ['altə 'eːgo, - 'ɛgo] NT **-, no pl** (esp Psych) alter ego

Äl|te|re(r) ['ɛltərə] MF decl as adj **a** (= älterer Mensch) older man/woman etc; **die ~n** the older ones **b** (bei Namen) Elder; **Holbein der ~** Holbein the Elder

al|ter|fah|ren ADJ very experienced, of long experience

al|tern ['altən] VI aux sein or (rare) haben to age; (Mensch auch) to get older; (Wein) to mature; **vorzeitig ~** to grow old before one's time; **~d** ageing VT to age; Wein to mature; Metall to age-harden

al|ter|na|tiv [alterna'tiːf] ADJ alternative; **Alternative Liste** (Pol) electoral pact of alternative political groupings ADV **~ leben** to live an alternative lifestyle; **~ vorgehen** to find an alternative; **~ eingestellt sein** to have alternative political views

Al|ter|na|tiv- in cpds alternative; **Al|ter|na|tiv|be|we|gung** F alternative or fringe movement

Al|ter|na|ti|ve [alterna'tiːvə] F **-n, -n** alternative (etw zu tun of doing sth)

Al|ter|na|tiv|ener|gie F alternative energy

Al|ter|na|ti|ve(r) [alterna'tiːvə] MF decl as adj (Pol) person with alternative views (= alternativ lebender Mensch) proponent of the alternative society; **die ~n** those who favour (Brit) or favor (US) the alternative society

Al|ter|na|tiv-: Al|ter|na|tiv|kost F biological foods pl; (= Diät) alternative diet; **Al|ter|na|tiv|kul|tur** F counter-culture, alternative culture; **al|ter|na|tiv|los** ADV **~ sein** to be the only alternative; **diese Politik ist nicht ~** there are alternatives to this policy; **Al|ter|na|tiv|me|di|zin** F alternative medicine; **Al|ter|na|tiv|pro|gramm** NT alternative programme (Brit) or program (US); **Al|ter|na|tiv|sze|ne** F **die ~** alternative society, the fringe

al|ter|nie|ren [altɛr'niːrən] ptp **alterniert** VI to alternate

al|ter|nie|rend ADJ alternate; Strom, Verse alternating; Fieber intermittent

Al|terns|for|scher(in) ['altəns-] M(F) gerontologist

Al|terns|for|schung F gerontology

al|ter|probt ['altɛrə'proːpt] ADJ well-tried

---

al|ters ['altəs] ADV (geh) **von** or **seit ~ (her)** from time immemorial; **vor ~** in olden days or times, in days of yore (old, liter)

Al|ters-: Al|ters|ab|stand M age difference; **Al|ters|ar|mut** F poverty among old people; **Al|ters|asyl** NT (Sw) old people's home; **Al|ters|auf|bau** M (Sociol) age structure; **al|ters|be|dingt** ADJ age-related; **Al|ters|be|gren|zung** F age limit; **ohne ~** without age limit; **Al|ters|be|schwer|den** PL complaints pl of old age, geriatric complaints pl; **Al|ters|durch|schnitt** M average age; **Al|ters|er|schei|nung** F sign of old age; **Al|ters|fleck** M age mark, blotch; **Al|ters|for|scher(in)** M(F) gerontologist; **Al|ters|for|schung** F gerontology; **Al|ters|für|sor|ge** F care of the elderly; **al|ters|ge|mäß** ADJ Benehmen, Entwicklung appropriate to one's/its age; **Al|ters|ge|nos|se** M , **Al|ters|ge|nos|sin** F contemporary; (Kind) child of the same age; (Psych, Sociol) peer; **wir sind ja ~n** we are the same age; **al|ters|ge|recht** ADJ suitable for one's/its age; **Al|ters|glie|de|rung** F age structure; **Al|ters|gren|ze** F age limit; (= Rentenalter) retirement age; **flexible ~** flexible retirement age; **Al|ters|grup|pe** F age group; **al|ters|hal|ber** ADV because of or on account of one's age; **Al|ters|heil|kun|de** F (Med) geriatrics sing; **Al|ters|heim** NT old people's home; **Al|ters|klas|se** F (Sport) age group; **Al|ters|krank|heit** F geriatric illness; **al|ters|lei|den** NT complaint or infirmity of old age; **al|ters|los** ADJ ageless; **Al|ters|prä|si|dent(in)** M(F) president by seniority; **Al|ters|pro|zess** ▲ M ageing process; **Al|ters|py|ra|mi|de** F age pyramid or diagram; **Al|ters|ren|te** F old age pension; **Al|ters|ru|he|geld** NT retirement benefit; **al|ters|schwach** ADJ Mensch old and infirm; Tier old and weak; Auto, Möbel etc decrepit; **Al|ters|schwä|che** F (von Mensch) infirmity (due to advancing years); (von Tier) weakness (due to old age); (hum: von Auto, Möbel etc) decrepitude; **Al|ters|schwach|sinn** M senility; **al|ters|sich|tig** [-zıçtıç] ADJ presbyopic (spec); **Al|ters|sich|tig|keit** F presbyopia (spec); **Al|ters|sitz** M **sein ~ war München** he spent his retirement in Munich; **Al|ters|so|zi|o|lo|gie** F sociology of old age; **al|ters|spe|zi|fisch** ADJ age-specific; **Al|ters|sport** M sport for the elderly; **Al|ters|starr|sinn** M senile stubbornness; **Al|ters|struk|tur** F (Sociol) age structure; **Al|ters|stu|fe** F age group; (= Lebensabschnitt) age, stage in life; **Al|ters|teil|zeit** F part-time working for people approaching retirement **in (die) ~ gehen** to switch to part-time working (when approaching retirement); **Al|ters|un|ter|schied** M age difference, difference in age; **Al|ters|ver|si|che|rung** F retirement insurance; **Al|ters|ver|sor|gung** F provision for (one's) old age; **betriebliche ~** company pension scheme; **Al|ters|vor|sor|ge** F old-age provision; **Al|ters|werk** NT later works pl; **Al|ters|weit|sich|tig|keit** F presbyopia (spec); **Al|ters|zu|la|ge** F increment for age

Al|ter|tum ['altətuːm] NT **-s, no pl** antiquity no art; **das deutsche ~** early German history

Al|ter|tü|me|lei [altəty:mə'lai] F **-, -en** antiquarianism

al|ter|tü|meln ['altəty:mln] VI to antiquarianize

Al|ter|tü|mer ['altəty:mə] PL antiquities pl

al|ter|tüm|lich ['altəty:mlıç] ADJ (= aus dem Altertum) ancient; (= veraltet) antiquated

Al|ter|tums-: Al|ter|tums|for|scher(in) M(F) archeologist; **Al|ter|tums|for|schung** F archeology, archeological research; **Al|ter|tums|kun|de** F archeology; **Al|ter|tums|wert** M **das hat schon ~** (hum) it has antique value (hum)

Al|te|rung ['altərʊŋ] F **-, no pl** (= das Altern) ageing; (von Wein) maturation; (von Metall) age hardening

Al|te|rungs|pro|zess ▲ M ageing process

Al|te(s) ['altə] NT decl as adj **das ~** (= das Gewohnte, Traditionelle) the old; (= alte Dinge) old things pl; **er hängt sehr am ~n** he clings to the past; **das ~ und das Neue** the old and the new, old and new; **sie hat Freude an allem ~n** she gets a lot of pleasure from anything old

Äl|tes|ten|rat M council of elders; (Ger Pol) parliamentary advisory committee, ≈ think-tank (Brit)

Äl|tes|te(r) ['ɛltəstə] MF decl as adj oldest; (Sohn, Tochter auch) eldest; (Eccl) elder

äl|tes|te(r, s) ['ɛltəstə] ADJ superl von **alt** oldest; Sohn, Bruder etc auch eldest

Alt-: Alt|flö|te F treble recorder; (= Querflöte) bass or alto flute; **alt|frän|kisch** ADJ quaint; Stadt etc auch olde-worlde (inf); **Alt|fran|zö|sisch(e)** NT Old French; **Alt|ge|rät** NT old appliance; **Alt|glas** NT , no pl waste glass; **Alt|glas|be|häl|ter** M , **Alt|glas|con|tai|ner** M bottle bank; **Alt|gold** NT old gold; (= Goldart) artificially darkened gold; **alt|grie|chisch** ADJ ancient Greek; (Ling auch) classical Greek; **Alt|grie|chisch(e)** NT ancient or classical Greek; **alt|her|ge|bracht, alt|her|kömm|lich** ADJ traditional; Tradition long-established; **Alt|her|ren|fuß|ball** M veterans' football; **Alt|her|ren|mann|schaft** F (Sport) team of players over thirty; **alt|hoch|deutsch** ADJ Old High German; **Alt|hoch|deutsch(e)** NT Old High German

Al|tist [al'tıst] M **-en, -en**, **Al|tis|tin** [-'tıstın] F **-, -nen** (Mus) alto

Alt|jahr(s)-: Alt|jahr(s)|abend M (dial) New Year's Eve, Hogmanay (esp Scot); **Alt|jahr(s)|tag** M (dial) New Year's Eve, Hogmanay (esp Scot)

Alt-: alt|jüng|fer|lich [alt'jʏŋfɛlıç] ADJ old-maidish, spinsterish; **Alt|kanz|ler(in)** M(F) former chancellor; **Alt|ka|tho|lik(in)** M(F) Old Catholic; **alt|ka|tho|lisch** ADJ Old Catholic; **Alt|klei|der|händ|ler(in)** M(F) second-hand clothes dealer; **Alt|klei|der|samm|lung** F collection of old clothes; **alt|klug** ADJ precocious ADV precociously; **Alt|la|ge** F (Mus) alto range; **Alt|last** F usu pl (Ökologie) dangerous waste (accumulated over the years)

alt|lich ['ɛltlıç] ADJ oldish

Alt-: Alt|ma|te|ri|al NT scrap; **Alt|meis|ter** M doyen; (Sport) ex-champion; **Alt|meis|te|rin** F doyenne; (Sport) ex-champion; **Alt|me|tall** NT scrap metal; **alt|mo|disch** ADJ old-fashioned; (= rückständig) outmoded ADV **sie kleidet sich sehr ~** the way she dresses is very old-fashioned; **ihr Haus ist ~ eingerichtet** the furnishings of her house are old-fashioned; **~ klingen** to sound old-fashioned; **sie denken ~** their ideas are old-fashioned; **Alt|neu|bau** M pre-war building; **Alt|öl** NT used oil; **Alt|pa|pier** NT wastepaper; **Alt|pa|pier|con|tai|ner** M (waste)paper bank; **Alt|pa|pier|samm|lung** F wastepaper collection; **Alt|pa|pier|ton|ne** F paper bank; **Alt|pa|pier|ver|wer|tung** F (waste)paper recycling; **Alt|par|tie** F (Mus) alto part; **Alt|phi|lo|lo|ge** M , **Alt|phi|lo|lo|gin** F classical philologist; **Alt|phi|lo|lo|gie** F classical philology; **alt|phi|lo|lo|gisch** ADJ Abteilung of classical philology; Bücher, Artikel on classical philology; **alt|re|nom|miert** ADJ old-established; **alt|ro|sa** ADJ inv old rose

Alt|ru|is|mus [altru'ısmʊs] M **-, no pl** (geh) altruism

Alt|ru|ist [altru'ıst] M **-en, -en**, **Alt|ru|is|tin** [-'ıstın] F **-, -nen** (geh) altruist

alt|ru|is|tisch [altru'ıstıʃ] (geh) ADJ altruistic ADV altruistically

Alt-: alt|säch|sisch ADJ old Saxon; **Alt|sän|ge|rin** F contralto (singer); **Alt|schlüs|sel** M (Mus) alto clef; **Alt|schnee** M old snow; **Alt|-**

sein NT being old *no art;* **Alt|sil|ber** NT old silver; (= *Silberart*) artificially darkened silver; **Alt|sprach|ler** [-ʃpraːxlɐ] M **-s,** -, **Alt|sprach|le|rin** [-ərɪn] F -, **-nen** classicist; (= *Sprachwissenschaftler*) classical philologist; **alt|sprach|lich** ADJ *Zweig, Abteilung* classics *attr;* **~es Gymnasium** ≈ grammar school (*Brit*) or high school (*US*) teaching classical languages; **Alt|stadt** F old (part of a/the) town; **die Ulmer ~** the old part of Ulm; **Alt|stadt|sa|nie|rung** F renovation of the old part of a/the town; **Alt|stein|zeit** F Palaeolithic (*Brit*) or Paleolithic (*US*) Age, Old Stone Age; **alt|stein|zeit|lich** ADJ Palaeolithic (*Brit*), Paleolithic (*US*); **Alt|stim|me** F (*Mus*) alto; (*von Frau auch*) contralto, contralto voice; (*Partie*) alto/contralto part; **Alt|stoff** M *usu pl* waste material; **~e sammeln** to collect (recyclable) waste; **gefährliche ~e** dangerous waste

Alt-Tas|te F (*Comput*) Alt key

Alt-: **alt|tes|ta|men|ta|risch**, **alt|tes|ta|ment|lich** [-tɛstamɛntlɪç] ADJ Old Testament *attr;* **alt|über|kom|men**, **alt|über|lie|fert** [ˈaltlyːbɐˈliːfɐt] ADJ traditional; **Alt|vä|ter|art** F **nach ~** in the old-fashioned way; **alt|vä|te|risch** [-fɛːtərɪʃ], **alt|vä|ter|lich** ADJ *Bräuche, Geister* ancestral; (= *altmodisch*) old-fashioned *no adv; Erscheinung etc* patriarchal; **Alt|vä|ter|sit|te** F **nach ~** in the old-fashioned way; **Alt|wäh|ler(in)** M(F) hardened voter; **Alt|wa|ren** PL second-hand goods *pl;* **Alt|wa|ren|händ|ler(in)** M(F) second-hand dealer

Alt|wei|ber- [alt'vaibɐ-] **Alt|wei|ber|ge|schwätz** NT old woman's talk; **Alt|wei|ber|som|mer** M **a** (= *Nachsommer*) Indian summer **b** (= *Spinnfäden*) gossamer

Alu¹ [ˈaːlu] NT **-s,** *no pl* (*inf: = Aluminium*) aluminium (*Brit*), aluminum (*US*)

Alu² [ˈaːlu] F -, *no pl* (*inf*) *abbr von* **Arbeitslosenunterstützung**

Alu- [ˈaːlu]: **Alu|do|se** F aluminium (*Brit*) or aluminum (*US*) can, tin can; **Alu|fel|ge** F alloy wheel, alloy (*inf*); **Alu|fo|lie** F tin or kitchen foil, aluminium (*Brit*) or aluminum (*US*) foil; **Alu|kof|fer** M aluminium (*Brit*) or aluminum (*US*) case

Alu|mi|ni|um [aluˈmiːniʊm] NT **-s,** *no pl* (*abbr* **Al**) aluminium (*Brit*), aluminum (*US*)

Alu|mi|ni|um-: **Alu|mi|ni|um|fo|lie** F tin foil, aluminium (*Brit*) or aluminum (*US*) foil; **Alu|mi|ni|um|(staub)|lun|ge** F (*Med*) aluminosis (*form*)

Al|ve|o|lar [alveoˈlaːɐ] M **-s,** -e (*Phon*) alveolar (sound)

Alz|hei|mer|kran|ke(r) [ˈaltshaimɐ-] MF *decl as adj* person/man/woman suffering from Alzheimer's (disease); (= *Patient*) Alzheimer's patient

Alz|hei|mer|krank|heit F Alzheimer's (disease)

am [am] PREP **a** *contr von* **an dem** **b** (*zur Bildung des Superlativs*) **er war am tapfersten** he was (the) bravest; **sie hat es am besten/schönsten gemalt** she painted it best/(the) most beautifully; **am besten machen wir das morgen** we'd do best to do it tomorrow, the best thing would be for us to do it tomorrow; **am seltsamsten war ...** the strangest thing was ... **c** (*als Zeitangabe*) on; **am letzten Sonntag** last Sunday; **am 8. Mai** on the eighth of May, on May (the (*Brit*)) eighth; (*geschrieben*) on May 8th; **am Morgen/Abend** in the morning/evening; **am Tag darauf/zuvor** (on) the following/previous day **d** (*als Ortsangabe*) on the; (*bei Gebirgen*) at the foot of the → *auch* **an** PREP *+dat* **a** **e** (*inf: als Verlaufsform*) **ich war gerade am Weggehen** I was just leaving **f** (*Aus: = auf dem*) on the **g** (*Comm*) **am Lager** in stock

A|mal|gam [amalˈgaːm] NT **-s,** -e amalgam

A|mal|gam|fül|lung F (*Zahnmedizin*) amalgam filling

a|mal|ga|mie|ren [amalgaˈmiːrən] *ptp* **amalgamiert** VTR (*lit, fig*) to amalgamate

A|ma|ryl|lis [amaˈrʏlɪs] F -, **Amaryllen** [-lən] amaryllis

A|ma|teur [amaˈtøːɐ] M **-s,** -e, **A|ma|teu|rin** [-ˈtøːrɪn] F -, **-nen** amateur

A|ma|teur- [amaˈtøːɐ] *in cpds* amateur; **A|ma|teur|fil|mer(in)** M(F) amateur film-maker; **A|ma|teur|funk** M amateur radio; **A|ma|teur|fun|ker(in)** M(F) radio amateur or ham (*inf*); **A|ma|teur|sport|ler(in)** M(F) amateur sportsperson, amateur sportsman/-woman; (*bestimmte Sportart*) amateur athlete/player/runner *etc*

a|ma|teur|haft [amaˈtøːɐ-] ADJ amateurish ADV amateurishly

A|ma|teu|rin [amaˈtøːrɪn] F -, **-nen** amateur

A|ma|teur|li|ga [amaˈtøːɐ-] F (*Sport*) amateur league

A|ma|zo|nas [amaˈtsoːnas] M - Amazon

A|ma|zo|ne [amaˈtsoːnə] F -, -n **a** (*Myth*) Amazon; (*fig*) amazon **b** (*Sport*) woman show-jumper

A|ma|zo|ni|en [amaˈtsoːniən] NT **-s** Amazonia

Am|ber [ˈambɐ] M **-s,** -(n) ambergris

Am|bi|en|te [amˈbiɛntə] NT -, *no pl* (*geh*) ambience

Am|bi|ti|on [ambiˈtsioːn] F -, **-en** ambition; **~en auf etw** (*acc*) **haben** to have ambitions of getting sth

am|bi|va|lent [ambivaˈlɛnt] ADJ ambivalent

Am|bi|va|lenz [ambivaˈlɛnts] F -, **-en** ambivalence

Am|boss ▲ [ˈambɔs] M **-es,** -e anvil; (*Anat auch*) incus

Am|bra [ˈambra] F -, **Ambren** [-brən] ambergris

Amb|ro|sia [amˈbroːzia] F -, *no pl* ambrosia

am|bu|lant [ambuˈlant] ADJ **a** (*Med: in Arztpraxis, Krankenhaus*) Versorgung, Behandlung, Operation outpatient *attr;* **~e Patienten** outpatients **b** (= *wandernd*) itinerant ADV **~ behandelt werden** (*Patient: in Praxis, Krankenhaus*) to receive outpatient treatment, to be treated as an outpatient; (*Fall*) to be treated in the outpatient department; **jdn ~ behandeln** to treat sb as an outpatient; **~ operieren/arbeiten** to operate on/treat outpatients

Am|bu|lanz [ambuˈlants] F -, **-en** **a** (= *Klinikstation*) outpatient department, outpatients *sing* (*inf*) **b** (= *Ambulanzwagen*) ambulance

Am|bu|lanz-: **Am|bu|lanz|kli|nik** F outpatients clinic; **Am|bu|lanz|wa|gen** M ambulance

A|mei|se [ˈaːmaizə] F -, -n ant

A|mei|sen-: **A|mei|sen|bär** M anteater; (*größer*) ant bear, great anteater; **a|mei|sen|haft** ADJ antlike; *Getriebe, Fleiß etc* beaverlike; **A|mei|sen|hau|fen** M anthill; **A|mei|sen|säu|re** F formic acid; **A|mei|sen|staat** M ant colony

a|men [ˈaːmən] INTERJ amen → **ja a**

A|men [ˈaːmən] NT **-s,** - amen; **sein ~ zu etw geben** to give one's blessing to sth; **das ist so sicher wie das ~ in der Kirche** (*prov*) you can bet your bottom dollar on that (*inf*)

A|me|ri|ci|um [ameˈriːtsiʊm] NT **-s,** *no pl* (*abbr* **Am**) americium

A|me|ri|ka|ner¹ [ameriˈkaːnɐ] M **-s,** - (*Gebäck*) flat iced cookie

A|me|ri|ka|ner² [ameriˈkaːnɐ] M **-s,** -, **A|me|ri|ka|ne|rin** [-ərɪn] F -, **-nen** American

a|me|ri|ka|nisch [ameriˈkaːnɪʃ] ADJ American

a|me|ri|ka|ni|sie|ren [amerikaniˈziːrən] *ptp* **amerikanisiert** VT to Americanize

A|me|ri|ka|ni|sie|rung F -, **-en** Americanization

A|me|ri|ka|nis|mus [amerikaˈnɪsmʊs] M **-,** **Amerikanismen** [-mən] Americanism

A|me|ri|ka|nist [amerikaˈnɪst] M **-en,** -en, **A|me|ri|ka|nis|tin** [-ˈnɪstɪn] F -, **-nen** specialist in American studies

A|me|ri|ka|nis|tik [amerikaˈnɪstɪk] F -, *no pl* American studies *pl*

A|me|thyst [ameˈtʏst] M **-s,** -e amethyst

A|mi [ˈami] M **-s,** -s (*inf*) Yank (*inf*); (= *Soldat*) GI (*inf*)

A|mi|no|säu|re [aˈmiːno-] F amino acid

Am|mann [ˈaman] M *pl* **-männer** (*Sw*) **a** mayor **b** (*Jur*) local magistrate

Am|me [ˈamə] F -, -n (*old*) foster mother; (= *Nährmutter*) wet nurse

Am|men|mär|chen NT fairy tale or story

Am|mer [ˈamɐ] F -, -n (*Orn*) bunting

Am|mo|ni|ak [amoˈniak, ˈamoniak] NT **-s,** *no pl* ammonia

Am|mo|nit [amoˈniːt] M **-en,** -en (*Geol*) ammonite

Am|mons|horn [ˈamɔns-] NT **a** (*Anat*) hippocampus major (*spec*) **b** (*Geol*) ammonite

Am|ne|sie [amneˈziː] F -, -n [-ˈziːən] (*Med*) amnesia

Am|nes|tie [amnɛsˈtiː] F -, -n [-ˈtiːən] amnesty

am|nes|tie|ren [amnɛsˈtiːrən] *ptp* **amnestiert** VT to grant an amnesty to

Am|ni|o|zen|te|se [amniotsɛnˈteːzə] F -, -n (*Med*) amniocentesis

A|mö|be [aˈmøːbə] F -, -n (*Biol*) amoeba

A|mö|ben|ruhr F (*Med*) amoebic dysentery

A|mok [ˈaːmɔk, aˈmɔk] M **~ laufen** to run amok (*esp Brit*) or amuck; **~ fahren** to drive like a madman or lunatic

A|mok-: **A|mok|fah|rer(in)** M(F) mad or lunatic driver; **A|mok|fahrt** F mad or crazy ride; **A|mok|lauf** M **einen ~ aufführen** to run amok (*esp Brit*) or amuck; **A|mok|läu|fer** M madman; **A|mok|läu|fe|rin** F madwoman; **A|mok|schüt|ze** M crazed gunman; **A|mok|schüt|zin** F crazed gunwoman

A|mor [ˈamoːɐ] M **-s** Cupid

a|mo|ra|lisch [ˈamoraːlɪʃ] ADJ amoral; (= *unmoralisch*) immoral

A|mo|ra|li|tät [amoraliˈtɛːt] F amorality; (= *Unmoral*) immorality

A|mo|ret|te [amoˈrɛtə] F -, -n little cupid, amoretto

a|morph [aˈmɔrf] ADJ (*geh*) amorphous

A|mor|ti|sa|ti|on [amɔrtizaˈtsioːn] F -, **-en** amortization

A|mor|ti|sa|ti|ons|dau|er F length of amortization period

a|mor|ti|sie|ren [amɔrtiˈziːrən] *ptp* **amortisiert** VT (*Econ*) **eine Investition ~** to ensure that an investment pays for itself VR to pay for itself

A|mou|ren [aˈmuːrən] PL (*old, hum*) amours *pl*

a|mou|rös [amuˈrøːs] ADJ (*geh*) amorous

Am|pel [ˈampl] F -, -n **a** (= *Verkehrsampel*) (traffic) lights *pl;* **er hat eine ~ umgefahren** he crashed into a traffic light and knocked it over; **halte an der nächsten ~** stop at the next (set of) (traffic) lights **b** (*geh*) (= *Hängelampe*) hanging lamp; (= *Hängeblumentopf*) hanging flowerpot

Am|pel-: **Am|pel|an|la|ge** F (set of) traffic lights *pl;* **Am|pel|ko|a|li|ti|on** F (*Pol inf*) coalition formed by SPD, FDP and Green Party; **Am|pel|kreu|zung** F (*inf*) junction controlled by traffic lights; **Am|pel|pha|se** F traffic light sequence; **die langen ~n an dieser Kreuzung** the length of time the lights take to change at this junction

Am|pere ▲ [amˈpeːɐ, amˈpɛːɐ] NT **-(s),** - amp, ampere (*form*)

Am|pere-: Am|pere|me|ter NT ammeter; **Am|pere|se|kun|de** F ampere-second; **Am|pere|stun|de** F ampere-hour

Ampf|er ['ampfɐ] M **-s, -** (*Bot*) dock; (= *Sauer-ampfer*) sorrel

Am|phe|ta|min [amfeta'mi:n] NT **-s, -e** amphetamine

Am|phi|bie [am'fi:biə] F **-, -n** (*Zool*) amphibian

Am|phi|bi|en|fahr|zeug NT amphibious vehicle

am|phi|bisch [am'fi:bɪʃ] ADJ amphibious

Am|phi|the|a|ter [am'fi:-] NT amphitheatre (*Brit*), amphitheater (*US*)

Am|pho|ra [am'fo:ra] F **-, Amphoren** [-ɐn] amphora

Am|pli|tu|de [ampli'tu:də] F **-, -n** (*Phys*) amplitude

Am|pul|le [am'pʊlə] F **-, -n a** (= *Behälter*) ampoule **b** (*Anat*) ampulla

Am|pu|ta|ti|on [amputa'tsio:n] F **-, -en** amputation

am|pu|tie|ren [ampu'ti:rən] *ptp* **amputiert** VT to amputate; **jdm den Arm ~** to amputate sb's arm; **amputiert werden** (*Mensch*) to have an amputation

am|pu|tiert ADJ *Körperteil* amputated; (*fig*) truncated

Am|pu|tier|te(r) [ampu'ti:ɐtə] MF *decl as adj* amputee

Am|sel ['amzl] F **-, -n** blackbird

Ams|ter|dam [amstɐ'dam, 'amstɐdam] NT **-s** Amsterdam

Ams|ter|da|mer[1] [amstɐ'damɐ, 'amstɐdamɐ] ADJ *attr* Amsterdam

Ams|ter|da|mer[2] [amstɐ'damɐ, 'amstɐdamɐ] M **-s, -, Ams|ter|da|me|rin** [-ərɪn] F **-, -nen** native of Amsterdam; (= *Einwohner*) inhabitant of Amsterdam

Amt [amt] NT **-(e)s, ⸚er** ['ɛmtɐ] **a** post (*Brit*), position; (*öffentlich*) office; **im ~ sein** to be in or hold office; **jdn aus einem ~ entfernen** to remove sb from office; **in ~ und Würden** in an exalted position; **von ~s wegen** (= *aufgrund von jds Beruf*) because of one's job; **kraft seines ~es** (*geh*) by virtue of one's office
b (= *Aufgabe*) duty, task; **seines ~es walten** (*geh*) to carry out or discharge (*form*) one's duties
c (= *Behörde*) (= *Fürsorgeamt*) welfare department; (= *Sozialamt*) department of social security; (= *Einwohnermeldeamt*) registration office; (= *Passamt*) passport office; (= *Finanzamt*) tax office; (= *Stadtverwaltung*) council offices *pl*; **zum zuständigen ~ gehen** to go to the relevant authority; **die Ämter der Stadt** the town authorities; **von ~s wegen** (= *auf behördliche Anordnung hin*) officially
d (= *Telefonamt*) operator; (= *Zentrale*) exchange; **geben Sie mir bitte ein ~** could you give me a line, please?

Äm|ter-: Äm|ter|häu|fung F accumulation of offices; **sie warfen ihm ~ vor** they accused him of holding too many offices at once; **Äm|ter|jagd** F position-hunting; **Äm|ter|kauf** M buying one's way into office; **Äm|ter|pat|ro|na|ge** F autocratic distribution of offices

am|tie|ren [am'ti:rən] *ptp* **amtiert** VI **a** (= *Amt innehaben*) to be in office; **~d** incumbent; **der ~de Bürgermeister** the (present) mayor; **der ~de Weltmeister** the reigning world champion; **als Minister/Bürgermeister ~** to hold the post (*Brit*) or position of minister/the office of mayor or **b** (= *Amt vorübergehend wahrnehmen*) to act; **er amtiert als Bürgermeister** he is acting mayor **c** (= *fungieren*) **als ... ~** to act as ...

amtl. *abbr von* **amtlich**

amt|lich ['amtlɪç] ADJ official; (= *wichtig*) *Miene, Gebaren* officious; (*inf*: = *sicher*) certain; **~es Kennzeichen** registration (number), license number (*US*) ADV officially; **etw ~ haben** to have official confirmation of sth

amt|li|cher|seits ['amtlɪçɐzaits] ADV officially

Amt|lich|keit F **-,** *no pl* officialdom *no pl*

Amt|mann M *pl* **-männer** or **-leute, Amt|män|nin** [-mɛnɪn] F **-, -nen a** (*Admin*) senior civil servant **b** (*Jur*) local magistrate

Amts-: Amts|adel M (*Hist*) *non-hereditary nobility who were created peers because of their office*; **Amts|an|ma|ßung** F unauthorized assumption of authority; (= *Ausübung eines Amtes*) fraudulent exercise of a public office; **Amts|an|tritt** M → **Amt a** assumption of office/one's post (*Brit*) or position; **Amts|an|walt** M , **Amts|an|wäl|tin** F prosecuting counsel in relatively minor cases; **Amts|ap|pa|rat** M official machinery; **Amts|arzt** M , **Amts|ärz|tin** F medical officer; **amts|ärzt|lich** ADJ *Zeugnis* from the medical officer; *Untersuchung* by the medical officer ADV **~ unter|sucht werden** to have an official medical examination; **sich etw ~ bescheinigen lassen** to get a medical certificate for sth; **Amts|be|fug|nis** F , **Amts|be|reich** M area of competence; **Amts|be|zirk** M area of jurisdiction; **Amts|blatt** NT gazette; **Amts|bo|te** M , **Amts|bo|tin** F official messenger; **Amts|bru|der** M (*Eccl*) fellow clergyman; **Amts|dau|er** F term of office; **Amts|deutsch(e)** NT officialese; **Amts|die|ner(in)** M(F) clerk; (= *Bote*) messenger; **Amts|eid** M oath of office; **den ~ able|gen** to be sworn in, to take the oath of office; **Amts|ein|füh|rung** F , **Amts|ein|set|zung** F installation, inauguration; **Amts|ent|he|bung** [-lɛnthe:bʊŋ] F **-, -en**, (*Sw, Aus*) **Amts|ent|set|zung** [-lɛntzɛtsʊŋ] F **-, -en** dismissal or removal from office; **Amts|er|schlei|chung** [-lɛɐʃlai-çʊŋ] F **-, -en** obtaining office by devious means; **Amts|ge|heim|nis** NT **a** (= *geheime Sache*) official secret **b** (= *Schweigepflicht*) official secrecy; **Amts|ge|richt** NT ≈ county (*Brit*) or district (*US*) court; **Amts|ge|richts|rat** M , **Amts|ge|richts|rä|tin** F ≈ county (*Brit*) or district (*US*) court judge; **Amts|ge|schäf|te** PL official duties *pl*; **Amts|ge|walt** F authority; **Amts|hal|te|tas|te** F (*am Telefon*) recall button; **amts|han|deln** VI *insep* (*Aus*) to take official action, to act officially; **Amts|hand|lung** F official duty; **seine erste ~ bestand da|rin, ...** the first thing he did in office was ...; **Amts|hil|fe** F cooperation between authorities; **Amts|kanz|lei** F (*Aus*) office; **Amts|ket|te** F chain of office; **Amts|kir|che** F church hierarchy; **Amts|klei|dung** F robes *pl* of office; **Amts|kol|le|ge** M , **Amts|kol|le|gin** F opposite number; **Amts|lei|tung** F (*Telec*) exchange line; **Amts|mie|ne** F official air; **seine ~ aufsetzen** to get or go all official (*inf*); **Amts|miss|brauch** ▲ M abuse of one's position; **Amts|nach|fol|ger(in)** M(F) successor (in office); **Amts|nie|der|le|gung** F resignation; **Amts|pe|ri|o|de** F term of office; **Amts|per|son** F official; **Amts|pflicht** F official duty; **Amts|rich|ter(in)** M(F) ≈ county (*Brit*) or district (*US*) court judge; **Amts|schim|mel** M (*hum*) officialdom; **den ~ reiten** to do everything by the book; **der ~ wiehert** officialdom rears its ugly head; **Amts|schwes|ter** F (*Eccl*) fellow clergywoman; **Amts|spra|che** F official language; **Amts|stu|be** F (*dated*) office; **Amts|stun|den** PL hours *pl* open to the public; **Amts|tracht** F robes *pl* of office; (*Eccl*) vestments *pl*; **Amts|trä|ger(in)** M(F) office bearer; **Amts|über|ga|be** F handing-over of office; **bei der ~ an seinen Nachfolger** when handing over his office to his successor; **Amts|über|nah|me** F → **Amt a** assumption of office/a post (*Brit*) or position; **Amts|ver|ge|hen** NT malfeasance (*form*); **Amts|ver|mitt|lung** F (*Telec*) connection by the operator; **Amts|vor|gän|ger(in)** M(F) , **Amts|vor|wel|ser(in)** M(F) (*old*) deputy; **Amts|vor|mund** M (*Jur*) public guardian; **Amts|vor|mund|schaft** F (*Jur*) public guardianship; **Amts|vor|stand** M ,

Amts|vor|ste|her(in) M(F) → **Amt c** head or chief of a/the department *etc*; **Amts|weg** M official channels *pl*; **den ~ beschreiten** to go through the official channels; **Amts|zei|chen** NT (*Telec*) dialling tone (*Brit*), dial tone (*US*); **Amts|zeit** F period of office; **Amts|zim|mer** NT office

A|mu|lett [amu'lɛt] NT **-(e)s, -e** amulet, charm, talisman

a|mü|sant [amy'zant] ADJ amusing; *Film, Geschichte auch* funny ADV amusingly; **er hat ~ ge|plaudert** he talked in an amusing way; **wir ha|ben ~ geplaudert** we had an amusing conversation

A|mü|se|ment [amyzə'mã:] NT **-s, -s** (*geh*) amusement, entertainment

A|mü|sier|be|trieb M (*inf*) nightclub; (= *Spielhalle etc*) amusement arcade; **der ~ in Las Vegas** the pleasure industry in Las Vegas

a|mü|sie|ren [amy'zi:rən] *ptp* **amüsiert** VT to amuse; **was amüsiert dich denn so?** what do you find so amusing or funny?; **lassen Sie sich ein bisschen ~** have some fun; **amüsiert zuschauen** to look on amused or with amusement
VR (= *sich vergnügen*) to enjoy oneself, to have a good time, to have fun; **sich mit etw ~** to amuse oneself with sth; (*iro*) to keep oneself amused with sth; **sich über etw** (*acc*) **~** to find sth funny; (= *über etw lachen*) to laugh at sth; (*unfreundlich*) to make fun of sth; **sich darüber ~, dass ...** to find it funny that ...; **sich mit jdm ~** to have a good time with sb; **amüsiert euch gut** have fun, enjoy yourselves

A|mü|sier-: [amy'zi:r-]: **A|mü|sier|lo|kal** NT nightclub; **A|mü|sier|vier|tel** NT nightclub district

a|mu|sisch ['amu:zɪʃ] ADJ unartistic

an [an] PREP **+dat a** (*räumlich: wo?*) at; (= *an etw dran*) on; **am Haus/Bahnhof** at the house/station; **an dieser Schule** at this school; **an der Wand stehen** to stand by the wall; **am Fenster sitzen** to sit at or by the window; **am Tatort** at the scene of the crime; **an der Tür/Wand** on the door/wall; **an der Donau/Autobahn/am Ufer/am Rhein** by or (*direkt an gelegen*) on the Danube/motorway/bank/Rhine; **Frankfurt an der Oder** Frankfurt on (the) Oder; **an etw hängen** (*lit*) to hang from or on sth; **zu nahe an etw stehen** to be too near to sth; **etw an etw festmachen** to fasten sth to sth; **jdn an der Hand nehmen** to take sb by the hand; **oben am Berg** up the mountain; **unten am Fluss** down by the river; **sie wohnen Tür an Tür** they live next door to one another, they are next-door neighbours (*Brit*) or neighbors (*US*); **Haus an Haus** one house after the other; **Laden an Laden** one shop after the other; **an etw vorbeigehen** to go past sth, to pass sth → **am, Bord, Land** *etc*
b (*zeitlich*) on; **an diesem Abend** (on) that evening; **am Tag zuvor** the day before, the previous day; **an dem Abend, als ich ...** the evening I ...; **an Ostern/Weihnachten** (*dial*) at Easter/Christmas → **am**
c (*fig*) *siehe auch* Substantive, Adjektive, Verben **jung an Jahren sein** to be young in years; **fünf an der Zahl** five in number; **jdn an etw erken|nen** to recognize sb by sth; **der Mangel/das Angebot an Waren** the lack/choice of goods; **an etw arbeiten/schreiben/kauen** to be working on/writing/chewing sth; **an etw sterben/leiden** to die of/suffer from sth; **was haben Sie an Wei|nen da?** what wines do you have?; **unübertrof|fen an Qualität** unsurpassed in quality; **an etw schuld sein** to be to blame for sth; **an der gan|zen Sache ist nichts** there is nothing in it; **es an der Leber** *etc* **haben** (*inf*) to have trouble with one's liver *etc*, to have liver *etc* trouble; **was findet sie an dem Mann?** what does she see in that man?; **es ist an dem** (= *es stimmt*) that's right; **sie hat etwas an sich, das ...** there is something about her that ...; **es ist an ihm, etwas zu tun** (*geh*) it's up to him to do something

---

PREP +acc **a** (*räumlich: wohin?*) to; (= *gegen*) on, against; **etw an die Wand/Tafel schreiben** to write sth on the wall/blackboard; **die Zweige reichten (bis) an den Boden/mein Fenster** the branches reached down to the ground/up to my window; **etw an etw hängen** to hang sth on sth; **er ging ans Fenster** he went (over) to the window; **An den Vorsitzenden ...** (*bei Anschrift*) The Chairman ...; **ans Telefon gehen** to answer the phone → **bis**, **Bord**, **Land**
b (*zeitlich: woran?*) **an die Zukunft/Vergangenheit denken** to think of the future/past; **bis an mein Lebensende** to the end of my days
c (*fig*) *siehe auch Substantive, Adjektive, Verben* **an die Arbeit gehen** to get down to work; **an jdn/etw glauben** to believe in sb/sth; **ich habe eine Bitte/Frage an Sie** I have a request to make of you/question to ask you; **an (und für) sich** actually; **eine (und für) sich gute Idee** actually quite a good idea, as such quite a good idea; **wie war es? – an (und für) sich ganz schön** how was it? – on the whole it was quite nice → **ab**
ADV **a** (= *ungefähr*) about; **an (die) hundert** about a hundred
b (*Ankunftszeit*) **Frankfurt an: 18.30 Uhr** arriving Frankfurt 18.30
c **von diesem Ort an** from here onwards; **von diesem Tag an** from this day on(wards); **von heute an** from today onwards
d (*inf*: = *angeschaltet, angezogen*) on; **Licht an!** lights on!; **ohne etwas an** with nothing on, without anything on → **an sein**

A|na|bap|tis|mus [anabap'tısmʊs] M -, *no pl* anabaptism

A|na|bap|tist(in) [anabap'tıst(ın)] M(F) Anabaptist

a|na|bol [ana'boːl] ADJ anabolic; **~e Steroide** anabolic steroids

A|na|bo|li|kum [ana'boːlikʊm] NT -s, **Anabolika** [-ka] anabolic steroid

A|na|chro|nis|mus [anakro'nısmʊs] M -, **Anachronismen** [-mən] (*geh*) anachronism

a|na|chro|nis|tisch [anakro'nıstıʃ] ADJ (*geh*) anachronistic

an|ae|rob [an|ae'roːp] ADJ *attr* anaerobic

A|na|gramm [ana'gram] NT *pl* **-gramme** (*Liter*) anagram

A|na|ko|luth [anako'luːt] NT **-s, -e** anacoluthon

A|na|kon|da [ana'kɔnda] F **-, -s** anaconda

a|na|kre|on|tisch [anakre'ɔntıʃ] ADJ Anacreontic

a|nal [a'naːl] **ADJ** (*Psych, Anat*) anal **ADV** *Fieber messen* anally; *einführen* into the anus; **~ untersucht werden** to undergo an anal examination; **~ fixiert sein** to have an anal fixation

A|nal-: A|nal|ero|tik F anal eroticism; **a|nal|fi|xiert** ADJ anally retentive; **A|nal|öff|nung** F (*form*) anal orifice (*form*)

a|na|log [ana'loːk] **ADJ** **a** analogous (+*dat, zu* to) **b** (*Telec*) analogue (*Brit*), analog (*US*) **c** (*Comput*) analogously **ADV** **a** analogously **b** (*Telec, Comput*) in analogue (*Brit*) or analog format

A|na|lo|gie [analo'giː] F **-, -n** [-'giːən] analogy

A|na|lo|gie-: A|na|lo|gie|bil|dung F (*Ling*) analogy; **A|na|lo|gie|schluss** ▲ M (*Philos, Jur*) argument by analogy

a|na|lo|gisch [ana'loːgıʃ] ADJ analogous

A|na|log-: A|na|log|rech|ner M analog computer; **A|na|log|uhr** F analogue (*Brit*) or analog (*US*) clock

An|al|pha|bet [an|alfa'beːt, 'an-] M **-en, -en**, **An|al|pha|be|tin** [-'beːtın] F **-, -nen** **a** illiterate (person) **b** (*pej*: = *Unwissender*) ignoramus, dunce

An|al|pha|be|ten|tum [an|alfa'beːtntuːm] NT **-s**, *no pl*, **An|al|pha|be|tis|mus** [an|alfabe'tısmʊs] M *no pl* illiteracy

an|al|pha|be|tisch [an|alfa'beːtıʃ, 'an-] ADJ illiterate

A|nal|ver|kehr M anal intercourse

A|na|ly|se [ana'lyːzə] F **-, -n** analysis (*auch Psych*)

a|na|ly|sie|ren [analy'ziːrən] *ptp* **analysiert** VT to analyze

A|na|ly|sis [a'naːlyzıs] F **-**, *no pl* (*Math*) analysis

A|na|lyst [ana'lyst] M **-en, -en**, **A|na|lys|tin** [-'lystın] F **-, -nen** (*St Ex*) investment analyst

A|na|ly|ti|ker [ana'lyːtike] M **-s, -**, **A|na|ly|ti|ke|rin** [-ərın] F **-, -nen** analyst; (= *analytisch Denkender*) analytical thinker

a|na|ly|tisch [ana'lyːtıʃ] ADJ analytical ADV analytically; **~ begabt sein** to have a talent for analytical thinking

A|nä|mie [anɛ'miː] F **-, -n** [-'miːən] anaemia (*Brit*), anemia (*US*)

a|nä|misch [a'nɛːmıʃ] ADJ anaemic (*Brit*), anemic (*US*)

A|nam|ne|se [anam'neːzə] F **-, -n** case history

A|na|nas ['ananas] F **-,** *or* **-se** pineapple

A|na|päst [ana'pɛst] M **-(e)s, -e** (*Poet*) anap(a)est

A|nar|chie [anar'çiː] F **-, -n** [-'çiːən] anarchy

a|nar|chisch [a'narçıʃ] ADJ anarchic ADV **~ leben** to live an anarchic life

A|nar|chis|mus [anar'çısmʊs] M **-**, *no pl* anarchism

A|nar|chist [anar'çıst] M **-en, -en**, **A|nar|chis|tin** [-'çıstın] F **-, -nen** anarchist

a|nar|chis|tisch [anar'çıstıʃ] ADJ anarchistic; (= *den Anarchismus vertretend auch*) anarchist *attr*

A|nar|cho [a'narço] M **-s, -s** (*pej*) anarchist

A|nar|cho- *in cpds* anarchist; **A|nar|cho|sze|ne** F anarchist scene

An|äs|the|sie [anɛste'ziː] F **-, -n** [-'ziːən] anaesthesia (*Brit*), anesthesia (*US*)

an|äs|the|sie|ren [anɛste'ziːrən] *ptp* **anästhesiert** VT to anaesthetize (*Brit*), to anesthetize (*US*)

An|äs|the|sist [anɛste'zıst] M **-en, -en**, **An|äs|the|sis|tin** [-'zıstın] F **-, -nen** anaesthetist (*Brit*), anesthesiologist (*US*)

An|äs|the|ti|kum [anɛs'teːtikʊm] NT **-s, Anästhetika** [-ka] anaesthetic (*Brit*), anesthetic (*US*)

an|äs|the|tisch [anɛs'teːtıʃ] ADJ anaesthetic (*Brit*), anesthetic (*US*)

A|na|to|li|en [ana'toːliən] NT **-s** Anatolia

A|na|to|li|er [ana'toːlie] M **-s, -**, **A|na|to|li|e|rin** [-ərın] F **-, -nen** Anatolian

a|na|to|lisch [ana'toːlıʃ] ADJ Anatolian

A|na|tom [ana'toːm] M **-en, -en**, **A|na|to|min** [-'toːmın] F **-, -nen** anatomist

A|na|to|mie [anato'miː] F **-, -n** [-'miːən] **a** (= *Wissenschaft, Körperbau*) anatomy **b** (= *Institut*) anatomical institute

A|na|to|mie|saal M anatomical *or* anatomy lecture theatre (*Brit*) *or* theater (*US*)

a|na|to|misch [ana'toːmıʃ] **ADJ** anatomical **ADV** anatomically; **~ begründet sein** to have anatomical causes

an|ba|cken *sep* VT (*Cook*) to start baking VI *aux sein* **a** (= *kurz gebacken werden*) to bake for a short time **b** (= *sich festsetzen*) to bake on (*an* +*dat* -to); (*dial: Lehm, Schnee etc*) to stick (*an* +*dat* to)

an|bag|gern VT *sep* (*inf*) to chat up (*inf*)

an|bah|nen *sep* VT to initiate VR (= *sich andeuten*) to be in the offing; (*Unangenehmes*) to be looming; (*Möglichkeiten, Zukunft etc*) to be opening up; **zwischen den beiden bahnt sich etwas an** (*Liebesverhältnis*) there is something going on between those two

An|bah|nung ['anbaːnʊŋ] F **-, -en** initiation (*von*, +*gen* of)

an|ban|deln ['anbandln] (*S Ger, Aus*), **an|bän|deln** ['anbɛndln] VI *sep* **a** (= *Bekanntschaft schließen*) to take up (*mit* with) **b** (= *Streit anfangen*) to start an argument (*mit* with)

An|bau¹ M **-**, *no pl* **a** (= *Anpflanzung*) cultivation, growing **b** (*von Gebäuden*) building; **den ~ einer Garage planen** to plan to build on a garage

An|bau² M *pl* **-bauten** (= *Nebengebäude*) extension; (*frei stehend*) annexe; (= *Stallungen etc*) outhouse, outbuilding

an+bau|en *sep* VT **a** *Kartoffeln, Weizen, Hanf etc* to cultivate, to grow; (= *anpflanzen*) to plant; (= *säen*) to sow **b** (*Build*) to add, to build on; **etw ans Haus ~** to build sth onto the house VI to build an extension; **Möbel zum Anbauen** unit furniture

An|bau-: an|bau|fä|hig ADJ **a** *Boden* cultivable; *Gemüse* growable **b** (*Build*) extendible; **An|bau|flä|che** F (area of) cultivable land; (= *bebaute Ackerfläche*) area under cultivation; **An|bau|ge|biet** NT cultivable area, area of cultivation; **ein gutes ~ für etw** a good area for cultivating sth; **An|bau|gren|ze** F limit of cultivation; **An|bau|mö|bel** PL unit furniture; **An|bau|schrank** M cupboard unit; **An|bau|tech|nik** F, **An|bau|ver|fah|ren** NT (*Agr*) growing methods *pl*

an+be|feh|len *ptp* **anbefohlen** VT *sep irreg* (*liter*) **a** (= *befehlen*) to urge (*jdm etw* sth on sb) **b** (= *anvertrauen*) to commend (*jdm etw* sth to sb)

An|be|ginn M (*geh*) beginning; **von ~ (an)** from the (very) beginning; **seit ~ der Welt** since the world began

an+be|hal|ten *ptp* **anbehalten** VT *sep irreg* to keep on

an|bei [an'bai, 'anbai] ADV (*form*) enclosed; **~ schicken wir Ihnen ...** please find enclosed ...

an+bei|ßen *sep irreg* VI (*Fisch*) to bite; (*fig*) to take the bait VT *Apfel etc* to bite into; **ein angebissener Apfel** a half-eaten apple; **sie sieht zum Anbeißen aus** (*inf*) she looks good enough to eat

an+be|kom|men *ptp* **anbekommen** VT *sep irreg* (*inf*) to (manage to) get on; *Feuer* to (manage to) get going

an+be|lan|gen *ptp* **anbelangt** VT *sep* to concern; **was das/mich anbelangt ...** as far as that is/I am concerned ...

an+bel|len VT *sep* to bark at

an+be|que|men *ptp* **anbequemt** VR *sep* (*geh*) **sich einer Sache** (*dat*) **~** to adapt (oneself) to sth

an+be|rau|men ['anbəraumən] *ptp* **anberaumt** VT *sep or* (*rare*) *insep* (*form*) to arrange, to fix; *Termin, Tag auch* to set; *Treffen auch* to call

an+be|ten VT *sep* to worship; *Menschen auch* to adore → **Angebetete(r)**

An|be|ter ['anbeːte] M **-s, -**, **An|be|te|rin** [-ərın] F **-, -nen** (= *Verehrer*) admirer

An|be|tracht ⊘ 44.1 M **in ~** (+*gen*) in consideration *or* view of; **in ~ dessen, dass ...** in consideration *or* view of the fact that ...

an+be|tref|fen *ptp* **anbetroffen** VT *sep irreg* to concern; **was das/mich anbetrifft ...** as far as that is/I am concerned ...

an+bet|teln VT *sep* to beg from sb; **jdn um etw ~** to beg sth from sb

An|be|tung ['anbeːtʊŋ] F **-**, (*rare*) **-en** worship; (*von Menschen auch*) adoration

an+be|tungs|wür|dig ADJ admirable; *Schönheit* adorable

an+be|zah|len *ptp* **anbezahlt** VT *sep* = **anzahlen**

an+bie|dern ['anbiːdɐn] VR *sep* (*pej*) **sich (bei jdm) ~** to try to get pally (with sb) (*inf*)

An|bie|de|rung F **-, -en** currying favour (*Brit*) *or* favor (*US*) (+*gen* with)

An|bie|de|rungs|ver|such M **einen ~ bei jdm unternehmen** to attempt to curry favour (*Brit*) *or* favor (*US*) with sb

an+bie|ten *sep irreg* ⊘ 30 VT to offer (*jdm etw* sb sth); (*Comm*) *Waren* to offer for sale; *seinen Rücktritt* to tender; **haben wir etwas zum Anbieten da?** have we anything to offer our guests?;

---

jdm das Du ~ to suggest sb uses the familiar form of address
VR a (*Mensch*) to offer one's services; (*Ftbl*) to be in position; **sich für die Arbeit ~**, **sich ~, die Arbeit zu tun** to go about the work; **sich zur Unzucht ~** to solicit; **der Ort bietet sich für die Konferenz an** that is the obvious place for the conference; **das Fahrrad bietet sich geradezu zum Mitnehmen an** that bicycle is just asking to be taken
b (= *in Betracht kommen: Gelegenheit*) to present itself; **das bietet sich als Lösung an** that would provide a solution; **es bieten sich mehrere Lösungsmöglichkeiten an** there are several possible solutions, several possible solutions present themselves; **es bietet sich an, das Museum zu besuchen** the thing to do would be to visit the museum

An|bie|ter(in) M(F) supplier

an+bin|den VT *sep irreg* (*an +acc or dat to*) **a** (= *festbinden*) to tie (up); *Pferd* to tie up, to tether; *Boot* to tie up, to moor; **jdn ~** (*fig*) to tie sb down → *auch* **angebunden b** (= *verbinden*) to connect; (= *verketten*) to link

An|bin|dung F (= *Verbindung*) connection; (= *Verkettung*) linkage, linking

an+blaf|fen VT *sep* (*inf*) (*lit, fig*) to bark at

an+bla|sen VT *sep irreg* **a** (= *blasen gegen*) to blow at; (= *anfachen*) to blow on; **jdm mit Rauch ~** to blow smoke at sb **b** (*Mus*) *Instrument* to blow; *Ton* to sound **c** (= *durch Blassignal ankündigen*) **die Jagd ~** to sound the horn for the start of the hunt

an+ble|cken VT *sep* (*lit, fig*) to bare one's teeth at

an+blen|den VT *sep* to flash at; (*fig: = kurz erwähnen*) to touch on

An|blick M sight; **beim ersten ~** at first sight; **beim ~ des Hundes** when he *etc* saw the dog; **in den ~ von etw versunken sein** to be absorbed in looking at sth

an+bli|cken VT *sep* to look at; **jdn lange/feindselig ~** to gaze/glare at sb

an+blin|ken VT *sep* **jdn ~** (*Fahrer, Fahrzeug*) to flash (at) sb; (*Lampe*) to flash in sb's eyes; (*Gold*) to shine before sb's very eyes

an+blin|zeln VT *sep* **a** (= *blinzelnd ansehen*) to squint at **b** (= *zublinzeln*) to wink at

an+boh|ren VT *sep* **a** (= *teilweise durchbohren*) to bore into; (*mit Bohrmaschine*) to drill into **b** (= *zugänglich machen*) *Quellen etc* to open up (by boring/drilling)

an+bor|gen VT *sep* (*dated*) **jdn (um etw) ~** to borrow (sth) from sb

An|bot ['anboːt] NT **-(e)s, -e** (*Aus*) = **Angebot**

an+bran|den VI *sep aux sein* to surge

an+bra|ten VT *sep irreg* (*Steak etc*) to sear; **etw zu scharf ~** to brown sth too much

an+brau|chen VT *sep* to start using; **eine angebrauchte Schachtel/Flasche** an opened box/bottle; **das ist schon angebraucht** that has already been used/opened

an+bräu|nen VT *sep* (*Cook*) to brown (lightly)

an+brau|sen VI *sep aux sein* to roar up; **angebraust kommen** to come roaring up

an+bre|chen *sep irreg* **VT a** *Packung, Flasche etc* to open; *Vorrat* to broach; *Ersparnisse, Geldsumme, Geldschein* to break into **b** (= *teilweise brechen*) *Brett, Gefäß, Knochen etc* to crack; **angebrochen sein** to be cracked → *auch* **angebrochen VI** *aux sein* (*Epoche etc*) to dawn; (*Tag auch*) to break; (*Nacht*) to fall; (*Jahreszeit*) to begin; (*Winter*) to close in

an+brem|sen VTI *sep* **(den Wagen) ~** to brake, to apply the brakes

an+bren|nen *sep irreg* **VI** *aux sein* to start burning, to catch fire; (*Holz, Kohle etc*) to catch light; (*Essen*) to burn, to get burned; (*Stoff*) to scorch, to get scorched; **mir ist das Essen angebrannt** I burned the food, I let the food get burned; **nichts ~ lassen** (*inf: = keine Zeit verschwenden*) to

be quick, to be quick off the mark (*Brit inf*); (= *sich nichts entgehen lassen*) not to miss out on anything → *auch* **angebrannt VT** to light

an+brin|gen VT *sep irreg* **a** (= *befestigen*) to fix, to fasten (*an +dat* (on)to); (= *aufstellen, aufhängen*) to put up; *Telefon, Feuermelder etc* to put in, to install; *Stiel an Besen* to put on; *Beschläge, Hufeisen* to mount; *Komma* to insert **b** (= *äußern*) *Bemerkung, Bitte, Gesuch, Beschwerde* to make (*bei* to); *Kenntnisse, Wissen* to display; *Argument* to use; **er konnte seine Kritik nicht mehr ~** he couldn't get his criticism in → *auch* **angebracht c** (= *hierher bringen*) to bring (with one); (*nach Hause*) to bring home (with one) **d** (*inf: = loswerden*) *Ware* to get rid of (*inf*) **e** (*inf: = ankommen*) to (manage to) get on; *Feuer* to (manage to) get going

An|brin|gung F -, *no pl* (= *das Befestigen*) fixing, fastening; (= *das Aufstellen, Aufhängen*) putting up; (*von Telefon, Feuermelder etc*) putting in, installing

An|bruch M , *no pl* **a** (*geh: = Anfang*) beginning; (*von Zeitalter, Epoche*) dawn(ing); **bei ~ des Tages** *or* **Morgens** at daybreak, at break of day; **bei ~ der Nacht** *or* **Dunkelheit** at nightfall **b** (*Min*) seam **c** (*Hunt*) rotting game **d** (*Forest*) decayed *or* rotten wood

an+brül|len *sep* **VT** (*Löwe etc*) to roar at; (*Kuh, Stier*) to bellow at; (*inf: Mensch*) to shout *or* bellow at **VI gegen etw ~** to shout above (the noise of) sth

an+brum|men *sep* **VT** to growl at; (*fig*) to grumble at **VI** *aux sein* **angebrummt kommen** to come roaring along *or* (*auf einen zu*) up

an+brü|ten VT *sep* to begin to sit on

An|chor|man ['ɛŋkɔrmən] M **-s,** Anchormen ['ɛŋkɔrmɛn] (*TV*) anchorman

An|cho|vis [an'ʃoːvɪs, an'ʃoːvɪs] F **-, -** anchovy

An|dacht ['andaxt] F **-, -en a** *no pl* (= *das Beten*) (silent) prayer *or* worship; **~ halten** to be at one's devotions; **in tiefer ~ versunken sein** to be sunk in deep devotion **b** (= *Gottesdienst*) prayers *pl* **c** (= *Versenkung*) rapt interest; (= *Ehrfurcht*) reverence; **in tiefe(r) ~ versunken sein** to be completely absorbed; **er trank den Wein mit ~** (*hum*) he drank the wine reverently; **etw voller ~ tun** to do sth reverently

an|däch|tig ['andɛçtɪç] **ADJ a** (= *im Gebet versunken*) in prayer; **die ~en Gläubigen** the worshippers at their devotions *or* prayers **b** (= *versunken*) rapt; (= *ehrfürchtig*) reverent **ADV a** (= *inbrünstig*) raptly **b** (*hum: = ehrfürchtig*) reverently

An|dachts-: An|dachts|bild NT devotional picture; **an|dachts|voll** ADJ, ADV = **andächtig b**

An|da|lu|si|en [anda'luːziən] NT **-s** Andalusia

An|da|lu|si|er [anda'luːziɐ] M **-s, -, An|da|lu|si|e|rin** [-iərɪn] F **-, -nen** Andalusian

an+dau|en VT *sep* to begin to digest; **angedaute Speisen** partially digested food

An|dau|er F , *no pl* **bei langer ~ des Fiebers** if the fever continues for a long time

an+dau|ern VI *sep* to continue; (= *anhalten*) to last; **das dauert noch an** that is still going on, that is continuing; **der Regen dauert noch an** the rain hasn't stopped; **das schöne Wetter wird nicht ~** the fine weather won't last; **die bis in die frühen Morgen ~den Verhandlungen** the negotiations which went on *or* continued till early morning

an|dau|ernd ADJ (= *ständig*) continuous; (= *anhaltend*) continual **ADV** constantly, continuously, continually; **wenn du mich ~ unterbrichst ...** if you keep on interrupting me ...

An|den ['andn] PL Andes *pl*

an+den|ken VT *sep irreg* **etw ~** to give a little thought to sth; **das sollten wir zumindest mal ~** we should at least start thinking about it

An|den|ken ['andɛŋkn] NT **-s, -** **a** *no pl* memory; **das ~ von etw feiern** to commemorate sth; **jdn in freundlichem ~ behalten** to have fond memories of sb; **im ~ an jdn/etw** in memory of sb/sth; **zum ~ an jdn** (*an Verstorbenen etc*) in memory *or* remembrance of sb; **zum ~ an etw** (*an Urlaub etc*) to remind you/us *etc* of sth **b** (= *Reiseandenken*) souvenir (*an +acc* of); (= *Erinnerungsstück*) memento, keepsake (*an +acc* from)

än|der|bar ADJ alterable, changeable; **eine nicht mehr ~e Entscheidung** a decision which can no longer be changed; **der Entwurf ist jederzeit ~** the draft can be altered *or* changed at any time

Än|der|bar|keit ['ɛndɐbaːɐkait] F **-,** *no pl* **die ~ von Vertragsbestimmungen** (the fact) that a contract's terms can be altered *or* changed

an|de|ren-: an|de|ren|falls ADV otherwise; **an|de|ren|orts** ADV (*geh*) elsewhere; **an|de|ren|tags** ADV (*geh*) (on) the next *or* following day; **an|de|ren|teils** ADV (*geh*) = **andererseits**

an|de|re(r, s) ['andərə] **INDEF PRON** (*adjektivisch*) **a** different; (= *weiterer*) other; **ein ~r Mann/~s Auto** a different man/car; (= *ein weiterer etc*) another man/car; **eine ~ Frau** a different woman; (= *eine weitere*) another woman; **jede ~ Frau hätte ...** any other woman would have ...; **haben Sie noch ~ Fragen?** do you have any more questions?; **ich habe eine ~ Auffassung als sie** my view is different from hers, I take a different view from her; **das machen wir ein ~s Mal** we'll do that another time; **das ~ Geschlecht** the other sex; **er ist ein ~r Mensch geworden** he is a changed *or* different man; **~ Länder, ~ Sitten** (*prov*) different countries have different customs
b (= *folgend*) next, following; **am ~n Tag, ~n Tags** (*liter*) (on) the next *or* following day
INDEF PRON (*substantivisch*) **a** (= *Ding*) **ein ~r** a different one; (= *noch einer*) another one; **etwas ~s** something *or* (*jedes, in Fragen*) anything else; **alle ~n** all the others; **er hat noch drei ~** he has three others *or* (*von demselben*) more; **ja, das ist etwas ~s** yes, that's a different matter; **das ist etwas ganz ~s** that's something quite different; **hast du etwas ~s gedacht?** did you think otherwise?; **ich muss mir etwas ~s anziehen** I must put on something else *or* different; **einen Tag um den ~n** every single day; **ein Mal ums ~** every single time; **ich habe ~s gehört** I heard differently; **nichts ~s** nothing else; **nichts ~s als ...** nothing but ...; **es blieb mir nichts ~s übrig, als selbst hinzugehen** I had no alternative but to go myself; **und ~s mehr** and more besides; **und vieles ~ mehr** and much more besides; **alles ~** (= *alle anderen Dinge*) everything else; **alles ~ als zufrieden** anything but pleased, far from pleased; **bist du müde? – nein, alles ~ als das** are you tired? – no, far from it *or* anything but; **unter ~m** among other things; **es kam eins zum ~n** one thing led to another; **... man kann doch eines tun, ohne das ~ zu lassen** ... but you can have the best of both worlds; **sie hat sich eines ~n besonnen** she changed her mind; **von einem Tag zum ~n** overnight; **von etwas ~m sprechen** to change the subject; **eines besser als das ~** each one better than the next
b (= *Person*) **ein ~r/eine ~** a different person; (= *noch einer*) another person; **er/sie und ~** he/she and others; **jeder ~/kein ~r** anyone/no-one else; **es war kein ~r als ...** it was none other than ...; **niemand ~s** no-one else; **jemand ~s** somebody else; **das haben mir ~ auch schon gesagt** other people *or* others have told me that too; **die ~n** the others; **alle ~n** all the others, everyone else; **jemand ~s** *or* (*S Ger*) **~r** somebody else; (*jeder, in Fragen*) anybody else; **wer ~s?** who else?; **wir/ihr ~** the rest of us/you; **sie hat einen ~n** she has someone else; **der eine oder der ~ von unseren Kollegen** one or other of our colleagues; **es gibt immer den**

einen oder den ~n, der faulenzt there is always someone who is lazy; **der eine ..., der ~ ...** this person ..., that person...; **einer nach dem ~n** one after the other; **eine schöner als die ~** each one more beautiful than the next; **der eine kommt, der ~ geht** as one person comes another goes; (= *man geht ein und aus*) people are coming and going; **das kannst du ~n erzählen!** (*inf*) who are you kidding! (*inf*)

ạn|de|rer|seits ✪ 53.3, 53.5 ADV on the other hand

Ạn|der|kon|to ['andɐ-] NT (*Fin*) nominee account

ạn|der|lei ['andɐlai] ADJ *inv* (*geh*) other

ạn|der|mal ['andɐˈmaːl] ADV **ein ~** some other time

ạn|dern- *in cpds* = **anderen-**

ạ̈n|dern ['ɛndɐn] **VT** (= *anders werden*) to change, to alter; *Meinung, Richtung* to change; *Kleidungsstück* to alter; **das ändert die Sache** that changes things, that puts a different complexion on things; **ich kann es nicht ~** I can't do anything about it; **das ist nicht zu ~,** nothing can be done about it; **das lässt sich nicht (mehr) ~** nothing can be done about it; **das ändert nichts an der Tatsache, dass ...** that doesn't alter the fact that ... **VR a** to change, to alter; (*Meinung, Richtung*) to change; **hier ändert sich das Wetter oft** the weather here is very changeable; **es hat sich nichts/viel geändert** nothing/a lot has changed **b** (*Mensch*) to change; (= *sich bessern*) to change for the better; **wenn sich das nicht ändert ...** if things don't improve ...

ạn|ders ['andɐs] ADV **a** (= *sonst*) else; **jemand/niemand ~** somebody *or* anybody/nobody else; **wer/wo ~?** who/where else?; **irgendwo ~** somewhere else; **wie ~ hätte ich es machen sollen?** how else should I have done it? **b** (= *verschieden, besser, schöner*) differently; (= *andersartig*) *sein, aussehen, klingen, schmecken* different (*als* to); **~ als jd denken/reagieren** to think/react differently from sb; **~ denkend** dissident, dissenting, of a different opinion; **~ Denkende(r)** dissident, dissenter; **~ als jd aussehen** to look different from sb; **~ als jd** (*geh*: = *im Gegensatz zu*) unlike sb; **es** *or* **die Sache verhält sich ganz ~** things *or* matters are quite different; **~ geartet sein als jd** to be different from *or* to sb; **~ gesinnt** of a different opinion; **~ gesinnt sein** to have a different opinion, to disagree (*in +dat* on); **~ ausgedrückt** to put it another way, in other words; **das machen wir so und nicht ~** we'll do it this way and no other; **das hat sie nicht ~ erwartet** she expected nothing else; **wie nicht ~ zu erwarten** as was to be expected; **sie ist ~ geworden** she has changed; **wie könnte es ~ sein?** how could it be otherwise?; **es geht nicht ~** there's no other way; **ich kann nicht ~** (= *kann es nicht lassen*) I can't help it; (= *muss leider*) I have no choice; **~ lautend** (*form*) contrary; **~ lautende Berichte** contrary reports, reports to the contrary; **entgegen ~ lautenden Berichten** despite reports to the contrary; **es sich** (*dat*) **~ überlegen** to change one's mind; **da wird mir ganz ~** I start to feel funny *or* (*übel auch*) peculiar; **ich kann auch ~** (*inf*) you'd/he'd *etc* better watch it (*inf*); **das klingt schon ~** (*inf*) now that's more like it **c** (*inf*: = *anderenfalls*) otherwise, *or* else

Ạn|ders-: **ạn|ders|ar|tig** ADJ *no comp* different; **Ạn|ders|ar|tig|keit** F, *no pl* (*des Lebens*) different quality; **jdn wegen seiner ~ nicht verstehen** not to understand sb because he/she is different; **ạn|ders|den|kend** △ ADJ *attr* → **anders b**; **Ạn|ders|den|ken|de(r)** [-dɛŋkndɐ] MF *decl as adj* person of a different opinion; (= *Dissident*) dissident, dissenter; **die Freiheit des ~n** the freedom to have one's own opinion

ạn|der|seits ['andɐˈzaits] ADV = **andererseits**

Ạn|ders-: **ạn|ders|far|big** ADJ of a different colour (*Brit*) *or* color (*US*); **ạn|ders|ge|ar|tet** △ ADJ → **anders b**; **ạn|ders|ge|schlecht|lich** ADJ of the other *or* opposite sex; **ạn|ders|ge-**

sinnt △ ADJ → **anders b**; **Ạn|ders|ge|sinn|te(r)** [-gəzɪntə] MF *decl as adj* person of a different opinion; **ạn|ders|gläu|big** ADJ of a different faith *or* religion *or* creed; **~ sein** to be of *or* have a different faith *etc*; **Ạn|ders|gläu|bi|ge(r)** MF *decl as adj* person of a different faith *or* religion *or* creed; **ạn|ders|he|rum** ADV the other way (a)round; **~ gehen** to go the other way (a)round; **dreh die Schraube mal ~** turn the screw the other way ADJ (*inf*: = *homosexuell*) **~ sein** to be bent (*inf*); **ạn|ders|lau|tend** △ ADJ *attr* → **anders b**; **ạn|ders|rum** (*inf*) ADJ ADJ = **andersherum**; **ạn|ders|spra|chig** ADJ *Literatur* foreign(-language); **die ~e Minderheit** the minority who speak a different language; **ạn|ders|wie** ADV (= *auf andere Weise*) some other way; (= *unterschiedlich*) differently; **ạn|ders|wo** ADV elsewhere; **das gibt es nicht ~** you don't get that anywhere else; **ạn|ders|wo|her** ADV from elsewhere; **ạn|ders|wo|hin** ADV elsewhere; **ich gehe nicht gerne ~** I don't like going anywhere else

ạn|dert|halb ['andɐt'halp] NUM one and a half; **~ Pfund Kaffee** a pound and a half of coffee; **~ Stunden** an hour and a half; **das Kind ist ~ Jahre alt** the child is eighteen months old, the child is one and a half

ạn|dert|halb-: **ạn|dert|halb|fach** ADJ one and a half times; **nimm die ~e Menge/das Anderthalbfache** use half as much again → *auch* **vierfach**; **ạn|dert|halb|mal** ADV one and a half times; **~ so viel/so viele** half as much/many again

Ạ̈n|de|rung ['ɛndərʊŋ] F -, -en change, alteration (*an +dat, gen* in, to); (*in jdm*) change (*in +dat* in); (*an Kleidungsstück, Gebäude*) alteration (*an +dat* to); (*der Gesellschaft, der Politik etc*) change (*+gen* in)

Ạ̈n|de|rungs-: **Ạ̈n|de|rungs|an|trag** M (*Parl*) amendment; **Ạ̈n|de|rungs|kün|di|gung** F (*Econ, Jur*) notification of a change (in the terms of employment); **Ạ̈n|de|rungs|schnei|der(in)** M(F) tailor (who does alterations); **Ạ̈n|de|rungs|vor|schlag** M suggested change *or* alteration; **einen ~ machen** to suggest a change *or* an alteration; **Ạ̈n|de|rungs|wunsch** M wish to make changes *or* alterations; **haben Sie Änderungswünsche?** are there any changes *or* alterations you would like to have made?

ạn|der-: **ạn|der|wär|tig** ['andɐˈvɛrtɪç] ADJ *attr* (*geh*) = **anderweitig** ADJ; **ạn|der|wärts** ['andɐˈvɛrts] ADV elsewhere, somewhere else; **ạn|der|weit** ['andɐ'vait] ADV (*geh*) = **anderweitig** ADV; **ạn|der|wei|tig** ['andɐ'vaitɪç] ADJ *attr* (= *andere, weitere*) other; **~e Ölvorkommen** (= *an anderer Stelle*) other oil strikes, oil strikes elsewhere ADV (= *anders*) otherwise; (= *an anderer Stelle*) elsewhere; **~ vergeben/besetzt werden** to be given to/filled by someone else; **etw ~ verwenden** to use sth for a different purpose

ạn+deu|ten *sep* **VT** (= *zu verstehen geben*) to hint, to intimate (*jdm etw* sth to sb); (= *kurz erwähnen*) *Problem* to mention briefly; (*Art, Mus*) to suggest; (= *erkennen lassen*) to indicate; **der Wald war nur mit ein paar Strichen angedeutet** a few strokes gave a suggestion of the wood **VR** to be indicated; (*Melodie etc*) to be suggested; (*Gewitter*) to be in the offing

Ạn|deu|tung F (= *Anspielung, Anzeichen*) hint; (= *flüchtiger Hinweis*) brief *or* brief mention; (*Art, Mus*) suggestion *no pl*; (= *Spur*) sign, trace; (= *Anflug eines Lächelns etc*) faint suggestion, hint; **eine ~ machen** to drop a hint (*über +acc* about); **versteckte ~en machen** to drop veiled hints; **eine Besserung zeichnet sich in ~en ab** there are vague signs of an improvement

ạn|deu|tungs|wei|se ADV (= *als Anspielung, Anzeichen*) by way of a hint; (= *als flüchtiger Hinweis*) in passing; **jdm ~ zu verstehen geben, dass ...** to hint to sb that ...; **man kann die Mauern noch ~ erkennen** you can still see traces of the walls ADJ *attr* (*rare*) faint

ạn+dich|ten VT *sep* **a** jdm etw ~ (*inf*) to impute sth to sb; *Fähigkeiten* to credit sb with sth; **alles kann man ihm ~, aber ...** you can say what you like about him but ... **b** jdn ~ to write a poem/poems to sb; **jdn in Sonetten ~** to write sonnets to sb

ạn+di|cken ['andɪkn] VT *sep Suppe, Soße* to thicken

ạn+die|nen *sep* (*pej*) **VT** jdm etw ~ to press sth on sb; **man diente ihm einen hohen Posten im Ausland an, um ihn loszuwerden** they tried to get rid of him by palming him off with a high position abroad **VR** sich jdm ~ to offer sb one's services (*als* as)

Ạn|die|nungs|stra|ße F (*Mot*) service road

ạn+dis|ku|tie|ren *ptp* **andiskutiert** VT *sep* to discuss briefly, to touch on

ạn+do|cken *sep* **VI a** (*Schiff*) to dock (*an +dat* at); (*Raumfähre*) to dock (*an +dat* with) **b** (*Physiol, Chem*) to link up (*an +dat* to) **VT a** *Raumfähre* to dock (*an +dat or acc* at) **b** (*Comput*) to connect up (*an +dat or acc* to)

Ạn|dor|ra [an'dɔra] NT -s Andorra

Ạn|dor|ra|ner [andɔ'raːnɐ] M -s, -, **Ạn|dor|ra|ne|rin** [-ərɪn] F -, -nen Andorran

ạn|dor|ra|nisch [andɔ'raːnɪʃ] ADJ Andorran

Ạn|drang M, *no pl* **a** (= *Zustrom, Gedränge*) crowd, crush; **es herrschte großer ~** there was a great crowd *or* crush **b** (*von Blut*) rush; (*von Wassermassen*) onrush

ạn+drän|gen VI *sep aux sein* to push forward; (*Menschenmenge auch*) to surge forward; (*Wassermassen*) to surge; **die ~de Menschenmenge** the surging crowd

Ạnd|re|as [an'dreːas] M -' Andrew

Ạnd|re|as|kreuz NT diagonal cross; (*Rel*) St Andrew's cross

ạn+dre|hen VT *sep* **a** (= *anstellen*) to turn on **b** (= *festdrehen*) to screw on **c** jdm etw ~ (*inf*) to palm sth off on sb

ạn|dren- ['andrən] *in cpds* = **anderen-**

ạn|dre(r, s) ['andrə] ADJ = **andere(r, s)**

ạn|drer|seits ['andrɐzaits] ADV = **andererseits**

ạn+drin|gen VI *sep irreg aux sein* (*geh*) (*Menschen etc*) to push forward, to press (*gegen* towards); (*Wasser*) to press, to push (*gegen* against)

Ạnd|ro|gen [andro'geːn] NT -s, -e androgen

ạn|dro|gyn [andro'gyːn] ADJ androgynous

Ạnd|ro|gy|ne [andro'gyːn] M -s, -e androgyne

Ạnd|ro|gy|ni|tät [androgyniˈtɛːt] F -, *no pl* androgyny

ạn+dro|hen VT *sep* to threaten (*jdm etw* sb with sth)

Ạn|dro|hung F threat; **unter ~ der** *or* **von Gewalt** with the threat of violence; **unter der ~, etw zu tun** with the threat of doing sth; **unter ~** (*Jur*) under penalty (*von, +gen* of)

Ạnd|ro|id [andro'iːt] M -en, -en [-dn], **Ạnd|ro|i|de** [andro'iːdə] M -n, -n android

Ạn|druck M *pl* -drucke **a** (*Typ*) proof **b** *no pl* (*Space*) G-force, gravitational force

ạn+dru|cken *sep* (*Typ*) **VT** to pull a proof of **VI** to pull proofs; (= *mit dem Druck beginnen*) to start *or* begin printing

ạn+drü|cken VT *sep* **a** *Pflaster* to press on (*an +acc* to); **als ich kräftiger andrückte** when I pressed *or* pushed harder **b** (= *beschädigen*) *Obst etc* to bruise **c** (= *durch Druck einschalten*) *Licht etc* to switch on (by pressing a button)

Ạn|druck|exem|plar NT (*Typ*) proof copy

ạn+du|deln VT *sep* sich (*dat*) einen ~ (*dated inf*) to get merry *or* tipsy (*inf*)

ạn+düns|ten VT *sep* (*Cook*) to braise lightly

Ạ̈ne|as [ɛ'neːas] M -' Aeneas

ạn+ecken ['anɛkn] VI *sep aux sein* (*inf*) (**bei jdm/allen**) ~ to rub sb/everyone up the wrong way; **mit seinen** *or* **wegen seiner Bemerkungen ist er schon oft angeeckt** his remarks have often rubbed people up the wrong way

ạn+ei̯fern VT *sep* (*S Ger, Aus*) = **anspornen**

ạn+ei̯gnen VT *sep* **sich** (*dat*) **etw ~** (= *etw erwerben*) to acquire sth; (= *etw wegnehmen*) to appropriate sth; (= *sich mit etw vertraut machen*) to learn sth; (= *sich etw angewöhnen*) to pick sth up

Ạnei̯gnung F (= *Erwerb*) acquisition; (= *Wegnahme*) appropriation; (= *Lernen*) learning; **wi̱derrechtliche ~** (*Jur*) misappropriation

anei̯nander [anai̯ˈnandə] ADV **a** (= *gegenseitig, an sich*) **~ denken** to think of each other; **sich ~ gewöhnen** to get used to each other; **sich ~ halten** to hold on to each other; **sich ~ stoßen** (*lit*) to knock into each other; **Freude ~ haben** to enjoy each other's company **b** (*mit Richtungsangabe*) **~ vorübergehen** or **vorbeigehen** to go past each other; **~ vorbeireden** to talk *or* be at cross-purposes **c** (= *einer am anderen, zusammen*) *befestigen* together; **die Häuser stehen zu dicht ~** the houses are built too close together

anei̯nander: anei̯nander bau̱en ▲ VT to build together; **die Häuser waren ganz dicht aneinander gebaut** the houses were built very close together; **anei̯nander fü̱gen** ▲ **a** **VT** to put together **VR** to join together; **anei̯nander gera̱ten** ▲ VI *irreg aux sein* to come to blows (*mit* with); (= *streiten*) to have words (*mit* with); **anei̯nander grenzen** ▲ VI to border on each other; **in Istanbul grenzen Orient und Okzident aneinander** in Istanbul East and West meet; **anei̯nander ha̱lten** ▲ VT *irreg* to hold against each other; **anei̯nander hä̱ngen** ▲ *irreg* **VI a** (= *zusammenhängen*) to be linked (together) **b** (*fig: Menschen*) to be attached to each other **VT** to link together; **anei̯nander kle̱ben** ▲ **VT** to stick together **VI** to be stuck together (*inf*: = *unzertrennlich sein*) to be glued together (*inf*); **anei̯nander ko̱ppeln** ▲ VT to couple; *Raumschiffe* to link up; **anei̯nander le̱hnen** ▲ VR to lean on *or* against each other; **anei̯nander lie̱gen** ▲ VI *irreg* to be adjacent (to each other), to be next to each other; **anei̯nander pra̱llen** ▲ VI *aux sein* to collide; (*fig*) to clash; **anei̯nander rei̱hen** ▲ **VT** to string together **VR** to be strung together; (*zeitlich: Tage etc*) to run together

Anei̯nanderrei̱hung F **-, -en** stringing together

anei̯nander: anei̯nander schmie̱gen ▲ VR to snuggle up; **anei̯nander se̱tzen** ▲ VT to put together; **anei̯nander ste̱llen** ▲ VT to put together; **anei̯nander sto̱ßen** ▲ *irreg* **VT** to bang together **VI** *aux sein* to collide; (*Fahrzeuge, Köpfe auch, Menschen*) to bump into each other; (= *aneinander grenzen*) to meet

Ä̱nei̯s [ɛˈneːɪs] F - Aeneid

Ạnekdö̱tchen [anɛkˈdøːtçən] NT **-s, -** (*hum*) little story *or* anecdote

Ạnekdo̱te [anɛkˈdoːtə] F **-, -n** anecdote

ạnekdo̱tenhaft ADJ anecdotal

ạnekdo̱tisch [anɛkˈdoːtɪʃ] (*Liter*) ADJ anecdotic ADV **sein Vortrag war ~ aufgelockert** his lecture was lightened by anecdotes; **er erzählte ~ aus seinem Leben** he told anecdotes about his life; **~ über etw** (*acc*) **reden** to talk about sth in anecdotes; **~ überliefert** retold in the form of an anecdote

ạn+ekeln VT *sep* **a** (= *anwidern*) to disgust, to nauseate; **die beiden ekeln sich nur noch an** they just find each other nauseating, they just make each other sick → *auch* **angeekelt b** (*inf*: = *beleidigen*) to be offensive to; **..., ekelte er mich an** ..., he spat at me

Ane̱mo̱ne [aneˈmoːnə] F **-, -n** anemone

ạn+empfe̱hlen ptp **anempfohlen** VT *sep or insep irreg* (*geh*) to recommend

ạnempfu̱nden [ˈanʔɛmpfʊndn̩] ADJ (*geh*) artificial, spurious, false; **nicht echt, sondern nur ~** not genuine

Ạnerbe M (*old*) heir to a/the farm

ạn+erbie̱ten ptp **anerboten** VR *sep irreg* (*geh*) to offer one's services; **sich ~, etw zu tun** to offer to do sth

Ạnerbie̱ten [ˈanʔɛrbiːtn̩] NT **-s, -** (*geh*) offer

Ạnerbin F (*old*) heiress to a/the farm

ạnerka̱nnt [ˈanʔɛrkant] ADJ recognized; *Tatsache auch* established; *Werk* standard; *Bedeutung* accepted; *Experte* acknowledged → *auch* **anerkennen**

ạnerka̱nntermaßen [ˈanʔɛrkantɐˈmaːsn̩] ADV **diese Mannschaft ist ~ besser** it is generally recognized *or* accepted *or* acknowledged that this team is better, this team is generally recognized *etc* to be better

ạn+erke̱nnen ptp **anerkannt** VT *sep or insep irreg* *Staat, König, Rekord* to recognize; *Forderung auch, Rechnung* to accept; *Vaterschaft* to accept, to acknowledge; (= *würdigen*) *Leistung, Bemühung* to appreciate; *Meinung* to respect; (= *loben*) to praise; **..., das muss man ~** (= *zugeben*) admittedly, ...; (= *würdigen*) ..., one has to appreciate that; **als gleichwertiger Partner anerkannt sein** to be accepted as an equal partner; **ihr ~der Blick** her appreciative look → *auch* **anerkannt**

ạnerke̱nnenswert ADJ commendable

Ạnerke̱nntnis NT (*Jur*) acknowledgement

Ạnerke̱nnung F recognition; (*von Forderung auch, von Rechnung*) acceptance; (*von Vaterschaft*) acknowledgement; (= *Würdigung*) appreciation; (*von Meinung*) respect; (= *Lob*) praise

Ạnerke̱nnungsschreiben NT letter of appreciation *or* commendation

ạnerzie̱hen ptp **anerzogen** VT *insep irreg* **jdm etw ~** (*Kindern*) to instil (*Brit*) *or* instill (*US*) sth into sb; *neuem Angestellten etc auch* to drum sth into sb; **sich** (*dat*) **etw ~** to train oneself to do sth

ạnerzo̱gen [ˈanʔɛrtsoːgn̩] ADJ *Eigenschaft, Verhalten* acquired; **das ist alles ~** he/she *etc* has been trained to be like that

Anf. *abbr von* **Anfang**

ạn+fa̱chen [ˈanfaxn̩] VT *sep* (*geh*) **a** *Glut, Feuer* to fan **b** (*fig*) to arouse; *Leidenschaft* to inflame, to arouse

ạn+fa̱hren *sep irreg* **VI** *aux sein* **a** (= *losfahren*) to start (up); **angefahren kommen** (= *herbeifahren*) (*Wagen, Fahrer*) to drive up; (*Fahrrad*) to ride up; (*Zug*) to pull up; (= *ankommen*) to arrive; **beim Anfahren** when starting (up); **das Anfahren am Berg üben** to practise (*Brit*) *or* practice (*US*) a hill start

b (*inf*) **lass mal noch eine Runde ~** let's have another round

VT a (= *liefern*) to deliver **b** (*inf*: = *spendieren*) to lay on **c** (= *ansteuern*) *Ort, Hafen* to stop *or* call at; (*Aut*) *Kurve* to approach; **die Insel wird zweimal wöchentlich von der Fähre angefahren** the ferry calls twice a week at the island **d** (= *anstoßen*) *Passanten, Baum etc* to run into, to hit; (*fig: ausschelten*) to shout at **e** (= *in Betrieb setzen*) *Reaktor, Anlage* to start up

Ạnfahrt F (= *Anfahrtsweg, Anfahrtszeit*) journey; (= *Zufahrt*) approach; (= *Einfahrt*) drive; **„nur ~ zum Krankenhaus"** "access to hospital only"

Ạnfall M **a** attack; (= *Wutanfall, epileptischer Anfall*) fit; **einen ~ haben/bekommen** (*lit*) to have an attack *or* fit; (*fig inf*) to have *or* throw a fit (*inf*); **da könnte man Anfälle kriegen** (*inf*) it's enough to send *or* drive you round (*Brit*) *or* around (*US*) the bend (*inf*); **in einem ~ von** (*fig*) in a fit of **b** (= *Ertrag, Nebenprodukte*) yield (*an +dat* of); (*von Zinsen*) accrual, yield (*von Reparaturen, Kosten*) amount (*an +dat* of); (*form*: = *Anhäufung*) accumulation; **bei ~ von Reparaturen** if repairs are necessary

ạn+fa̱llen *sep irreg* **VT a** (= *überfallen*) to attack; (*Sittenstrolch etc*) to assault **b** (*liter*) *Heimweh/Sehnsucht fiel ihn an* he was assailed by homesickness/filled with longing **VI** *aux sein* (= *sich ergeben*) to arise; (*Zinsen*) to accrue; (*Nebenprodukte*) to be obtained; (= *sich anhäufen*) to ac-

cumulate; **die ~den Kosten/Reparaturen/Probleme** the costs/repairs/problems incurred; **die ~de Arbeit** the work which comes up

ạnfä̱llig ADJ (= *nicht widerstandsfähig*) delicate; *Motor, Maschine* temperamental; **für etw ~ sein** to be susceptible to sth; **für eine Krankheit ~ sein** to be prone to an illness

Ạnfä̱lligkeit F delicate health; (*von Motor, Maschine etc*) temperamental nature

Ạnfang [ˈanfaŋ] M **-(e)s, Anfänge** [-fɛŋə] (= *Beginn*) beginning, start; (= *erster Teil*) beginning; (= *Ursprung*) beginnings *pl*, origin; **zu** *or* **am ~** to start with; (= *anfänglich*) at first; **gleich zu ~ darauf hinweisen, dass ...** to mention right at the beginning *or* outset that ...; **am ~ schuf Gott Himmel und Erde** (*Bibl*) in the beginning God created the heaven(s) and the earth; **im ~ war das Wort** (*Bibl*) in the beginning was the Word; **~ fünfzig** in one's early fifties; **~ Juni/1998** *etc* at the beginning of June/1998 *etc*; **von ~ an** (right) from the beginning *or* start; **von ~ bis Ende** from start to finish; **den ~ machen** to start *or* begin; (= *den ersten Schritt tun*) to make the first move; **wer macht den ~?** (*bei Spiel etc*) who's going to start?; **einen neuen ~ machen** to make a new start; (*im Leben*) to turn over a new leaf; **ein ~ ist gemacht** it's a start; **seinen ~ nehmen** (*geh*) to commence; **aller ~ ist schwer** (*Prov*) the first step is always the most difficult; **aus kleinen/bescheidenen Anfängen** from small/humble beginnings; **der ~ vom Ende** the beginning of the end

ạn+fa̱ngen *sep irreg* **VT a** (= *beginnen*) *Arbeit, Brief, Gespräch* to start, to begin; (*inf*: = *anbrauchen*) *neue Tube etc* to start, to begin; *Streit, Verhältnis, Fabrik* to start

b (= *anstellen, machen*) to do; **das musst du anders ~** you'll have to go about it differently; **was soll ich damit ~?** what am I supposed to do with that?; (= *was nützt mir das?*) what's the use of that?; **damit kann ich nichts ~** (= *nützt mir nichts*) that's no good to me; (= *verstehe nicht*) it doesn't mean a thing to me; **nichts mit sich/jdm anzufangen wissen** not to know what to do with oneself/sb; **mit dir ist heute (aber) gar nichts anzufangen!** you're no fun at all today!

VI to begin, to start; **wer fängt an?** who's going to start *or* begin?; **fang (du) an!** (you) begin *or* start!; **ich habe schon angefangen** I've already started; **du hast angefangen!** you started!; (*bei Streit*) you started it!; **es fing zu regnen an** *or* **an zu regnen** it started raining *or* to rain; **das fängt ja schön** *or* **heiter an!** (*iro*) that's a good start!; **jetzt fängt das Leben erst an** life is only just beginning; **fang nicht wieder davon** *or* **damit an!** don't start all that again!, don't bring all that up again!; **mit etw ~** to start sth; **klein/unten ~** to start small/at the bottom; **er hat als kleiner Handwerker angefangen** he started out as a small-time tradesman; **bei einer Firma ~** to start with a firm, to start working for a firm

Ạnfä̱nger(in) M(F) beginner; (= *Neuling*) novice; (*Aut*) learner; (*inf*: = *Nichtskönner*) amateur (*pej*); **du ~!** (*inf*) you amateur; **sie ist keine ~in mehr** (*hum*) she's certainly no beginner

Ạnfä̱nger-: Ạnfä̱ngerkurs M , **Ạnfä̱ngerkursus** M beginners' course; **Ạnfä̱ngerübung** F (*Univ*) introductory course

ạnfä̱nglich [ˈanfɛŋlɪç] ADJ *attr* initial ADV at first, initially

ạnfangs [ˈanfaŋs] ADV at first, initially; **wie ich schon ~ erwähnte** as I mentioned at the beginning; **gleich ~ auf etw** (*acc*) **hinweisen** to mention sth right at the beginning *or* outset PREP *+gen* **~ der zwanziger Jahre** *or* **Zwanzigerjahre** in the early twenties; **~ des Monats** at the beginning of the month

Ạnfangs- *in cpds* initial; **Ạnfangsbuchstabe** M first letter; **kleine/große ~n** small/large *or* capital initials; **Ạnfangsgehalt** NT initial *or* starting salary; **Ạnfangsgeschwindigkeit** F starting speed; (*esp Phys*) initial velocity;

An|fangs|grün|de PL rudiments *pl*, elements *pl*; **An|fangs|ka|pi|tal** NT starting capital; **An|fangs|kurs** M *(Fin)* opening price; **An|fangs|sil|be** F first *or* initial syllable; **An|fangs|sta|di|um** NT initial stage; **im ~ dieser Krankheit/dieses Projekts** in the initial stages of this illness/project; **meine Versuche sind schon im ~ stecken geblieben** my attempts never really got off the ground; **An|fangs|un|ter|richt** M first lessons *pl*; **An|fangs|zeit** F starting time

an+fas|sen *sep* [VT] [a] *(= berühren)* to touch; **fass mal meinen Kopf an** just feel my head [b] *(= bei der Hand nehmen)* **jdn ~** to take sb's hand, to take sb by the hand; **sich** *or* **einander** *(geh)* **~** to take each other by the hand; **fasst euch an!** hold hands!; **angefasst gehen** to walk holding hands [c] *(fig)* *(= anpacken)* *Problem* to tackle, to go a-bout; *(= behandeln)* *Menschen* to treat [d] *(geh: = befallen)* to seize [VI] [a] *(= berühren)* to feel; **nicht ~!** don't touch! [b] *(= mithelfen)* **mit ~** to give a hand [c] *(fig)* **zum Anfassen** *(Sache)* accessible; *Mensch auch* approachable; **Politik zum Anfassen** grassroots politics [VR] *(= sich anfühlen)* to feel; **es fasst sich weich an** it feels *or* is soft (to the touch)

an+fau|chen VT *sep* *(Katze)* to spit at; *(fig inf)* to snap at

an+fau|len VI *sep aux sein* to begin to go bad; *(Holz)* to start rotting; **angefault** half-rotten

An|fecht|bar|keit ['anfɛçtbaːɐkait] F -, *no pl* **wegen der ~ seiner Argumentation/des Urteils** because his argument/the judgement is/was contestable

an+fech|ten VT *sep irreg* [a] *(= nicht anerkennen)* to contest; *Meinung, Aussage* to challenge, to contest; *Urteil, Entscheidung* to appeal against; *Vertrag* to dispute; *Ehe* to contest the validity of [b] *(= beunruhigen)* to trouble; *(= in Versuchung bringen)* to tempt, to lead into temptation; **das ficht mich gar nicht an** that doesn't concern me in the slightest [c] *(obs: = einfallen, überkommen)* **was ficht/focht dich an, das zu tun?** what possessed you to do that?

An|fech|tung ['anfɛçtʊŋ] F -, -en [a] *(= das Nichtanerkennen)* contesting; *(von Meinung, Aussage)* challenging; *(von Urteil, Entscheidung)* appeal *(+gen* against); *(von Vertrag)* disputing; *(von Ehe)* action for nullification *or* annulment [b] *(= Versuchung)* temptation; *(= Selbstzweifel)* doubt

An|fech|tungs|kla|ge F *(Jur)* *(zu Ehescheidung)* action for nullification *or* annulment; *(zu Testament)* action to set aside a/the will; *(zu Patent)* opposition proceedings *pl*

an+fe|gen VI *sep aux sein* *(inf)* **angefegt kommen** to come belting *(Brit)* *or* racing along *or* *(auf einen zu)* up *(inf)*

an+fein|den ['anfaindn] VT *sep* to treat with hostility

An|fein|dung F -, -en hostility; **trotz aller ~en** although he/she *etc* had aroused so much animosity

an+fer|ti|gen VT *sep* to make; *Arznei* to make up; *Schriftstück* to draw up; *Hausaufgaben, Protokoll* to do; **jdm etw ~** to make sth for sb; **sich** *(dat)* **einen Anzug** *etc* **~ lassen** to have a suit *etc* made

An|fer|ti|gung F making; *(von Arznei)* making up; *(von Schriftstück)* drawing up; *(von Protokoll, Hausaufgaben)* doing; **die ~ dieser Übersetzung/der Arznei hat eine halbe Stunde gedauert** it took half an hour to do the translation/to make up the prescription

an+feuch|ten ['anfɔyçtn] VT *sep* to moisten; *Schwamm, Lippen auch* to wet; *Bügelwäsche auch* to dampen

an+feu|ern VT *sep Ofen* to light; *(Ind)* to fire; *(fig: = ermutigen)* to spur on

An|feu|e|rung F *(fig)* spurring on

An|feu|e|rungs|ruf M cheer; *(esp Pol)* chant; *(= Anfeuerungswort)* shout of encouragement

an+fin|den VR *sep irreg* to be found, to turn up (again)

an+fi|xen VT *sep* *(sl)* **jdn ~** to give sb his/her first fix *(inf)*; *(= abhängig machen)* to get sb hooked (on drugs) *(inf)*

an+flach|sen ['anflaksn] VT *sep* *(inf, = veralbern)* **jdn ~** to make fun of sb, to tease sb, to take the piss out of sb *(Brit inf)*

an+flan|schen ['anflanʃn] VT *sep* *(Tech)* to fix on with a flange *(an +dat* to); *(fig, inf: = verbinden)* to link up *(an +dat* with)

an+flat|tern VI *sep aux sein Schmetterling, Vogel* to flutter along, to come fluttering up *or* along

an+fle|geln VT *sep* *(inf)* to speak rudely to; **ich lasse mich doch nicht von dir ~!** I'm not prepared to have you swearing at me!

an+fle|hen VT *sep* to beseech, to implore *(um* for); **ich flehe dich an, tu das nicht!** I beg you, don't!

an+flet|schen VT *sep* to bare one's teeth at

an+flie|gen *sep irreg* [VI] *aux sein* *(auch* **angeflogen kommen** *(Flugzeug)* to come in to land; *(Vogel, Geschoss, fig geh: Pferd, Fuhrwerk, Reiter)* to come flying up [VT] [a] *(Flugzeug)* *Flughafen, Piste* to approach; *(Mil)* *Stellung* to approach; *(= landen)* to land *(an +dat* in, *auf +dat* on); **diese Fluggesellschaft fliegt Bali an** this airline flies to Bali *or* operates a service to Bali [b] *(geh: = befallen)* to overcome

an+flit|zen VI *sep aux sein* *(inf)* **angeflitzt kommen** to come racing along *or* *(auf einen zu)* up *(inf)*

An|flug M [a] *(= Flugweg)* flight; *(= das Heranfliegen)* approach; **wir befinden uns im ~ auf Paris** we are now approaching Paris [b] *(= Spur)* trace; *(fig: = Hauch)* hint, trace

An|flug-: An|flug|hö|he F approach altitude; **An|flug|weg** M landing path; **An|flug|zeit** F *(= Zeitraum)* descent; *(= Zeitpunkt)* time of starting a/the descent

an+flun|kern VT *sep* *(inf)* to tell fibs/a fib to

an+for|dern VT *sep* to request, to ask for

An|for|de|rung F [a] *(= Anspruch)* requirement; *(= Belastung)* demand; **große ~en an jdn/etw stellen** to make great demands on sb/sth; **ho-he/zu hohe ~en stellen** to demand a lot/too much *(an +acc* of); **den ~en im Beruf/in der Schule gewachsen sein** to be able to meet the demands of one's job/of school [b] **Anforderungen** PL *(= Niveau)* standards *pl* [c] *no pl* *(= das Anfordern)* request *(+gen, von* for); **auf ~** on request; **bei der ~ von Ersatzteilen** when requesting spare parts

An|for|de|rungs|pro|fil NT *(für Personen)* job description; *(für Software etc)* product profile; **dem ~ entsprechen** to fit the job description/product profile

An|fra|ge ☉ 47.1 F *(auch Comput)* inquiry; *(Parl)* question; **kleine ~** Parliamentary question dealt with in writing **große ~** Parliamentary question dealt with at a meeting of the Lower House

an+fra|gen VI *sep* to inquire *(bei jdm* of sb), to ask *(bei jdm* sb); **um Erlaubnis/Genehmigung ~** to ask for permission/approval

an+fres|sen VT *sep irreg* [a] *(Maus)* to nibble at; *(Vogel)* to peck (at); **sich** *(dat)* **einen Bauch ~** *(inf)* to get a potbelly through overeating [b] *(= zersetzen)* to eat away, to erode

an+freun|den ['anfrɔyndn] VR *sep* to make *or* become friends; **sich mit etw ~** *(fig)* to get to like sth; **mit Popmusik etc** to acquire a taste for sth

an+frie|ren VI *sep irreg aux sein* *(= leicht gefrieren)* to start to freeze; *(Pflanze)* to get a touch of frost; *(= haften bleiben)* to freeze on *(an +acc* -to); *(fig: Mensch)* to freeze stiff

an+fü|gen VT *sep* to add

An|fü|gung F addition; *(zu einem Buch)* addendum

an+füh|len *sep* [VT] to feel [VR] to feel; **sich glatt/weich** *etc* **~** to feel smooth/soft *etc*, to be smooth/soft *etc* to the touch

An|fuhr ['anfuːɐ] F -, -en transport(ation)

an+führ|bar ADJ quotable

an+füh|ren VT *sep* [a] *(= vorangehen, befehligen)* to lead [b] *(= zitieren)* to quote, to cite; *Tatsachen, Beispiel* to quote, to cite, to give; *Einzelheiten* to give; *Umstand* to cite, to refer to; *Grund, Beweis* to give, to offer; *(= benennen)* **jdn** to name, to cite [c] *(Typ)* to indicate *or* mark with quotation marks *or* inverted commas [d] **jdn ~** *(inf)* to have sb on *(inf)*, to take sb for a ride *(inf)*; **der lässt sich leicht ~** he's easily taken in

An|füh|rer(in) M(F) *(= Führer)* leader; *(pej: = Anstifter)* ringleader

An|füh|rung F [a] *(= das Vorangehen)* leadership; *(= Befehligung)* command; **unter ~ von ...** under the leadership of ..., led by ... [b] *(= das Zitieren)* quotation; *(von Tatsachen, Beispiel)* citation; *(von Umstand)* citing, referring to; *(von Grund, Beweis)* giving, offering; *(= Benennung)* naming, citing; *(= Zitat)* quotation; **die ~ von Zitaten/Einzelheiten** giving quotations/details

An|füh|rungs|strich M , **An|füh|rungs|zei|chen** NT quotation mark, inverted comma; **in ~en** *or* **Anführungszeichen** in inverted commas, in quotation marks, in quotes; **das habe ich in Anführungszeichen gesagt** I was saying that in inverted commas; **einfache/doppelte Anführungszeichen** *(pl)* *or* **~e** *(pl)* single/double quotation marks *pl* *or* quotes *pl*; **Anführungszeichen Anfang/Ende** *(beim Diktieren)* quote/unquote; *(beim Zitieren)* (I) quote/end of quote

an+fül|len VT *sep* to fill (up); **mit etw angefüllt sein** to be full of sth, to be filled with sth

an+fun|keln VT *sep* to flash at

an+fun|ken VT *sep* to radio

an+fut|tern VT *sep* *(inf)* **sich** *(dat)* **einen Bauch ~** to acquire *or* develop a potbelly

An|ga|be ['anga-] F [a] *usu pl* *(= Aussage)* statement; *(= Anweisung)* instruction; *(= Zahl, Detail)* detail; **~n über etw** *(acc)* **machen** to give details about sth; **laut ~n** *(+gen)* according to; **nach Ihren eigenen ~n** by your own account; **nach ~n des Zeugen** according to *(the testimony of)* the witness; **~n zur Person** *(form)* personal details *or* particulars; **~n zur Sache machen** *(Jur)* to give details of the case [b] *(= Nennung)* giving; **wir bitten um ~ der Einzelheiten/Preise** please give *or* quote details/prices; **er ist ohne ~ seiner neuen Adresse verzogen** he moved without informing anyone of his new address *or* without telling anyone his new address; **ohne ~ von Gründen** without giving any reasons; **vergessen Sie nicht die ~ des Datums auf dem Brief** don't forget to give *or* put the date on the letter [c] *no pl* *(inf: = Prahlerei)* showing off; *(esp durch Reden)* bragging, boasting [d] *(Sport: = Aufschlag)* service, serve; **wer hat ~?** whose service *or* serve is it?, whose turn is it to serve?

an+gaf|fen ['anga-] VT *sep* *(pej)* to gape at

an+gäh|nen ['angɛ:-] VT *sep* to yawn at

an+ga|lop|pie|ren ['anga-] *ptp* **angaloppiert** VI *sep aux sein* to gallop up; **angaloppiert kommen** to come galloping up

an|gän|gig ['angɛ-] ADJ *(form)* *(= erlaubt)* permissible; *(= möglich)* feasible

an+ge|ben ['angɛ:-] *sep irreg* [VT] [a] *(= nennen)* to give; *(als Zeugen)* to name, to cite; *(schriftlich)* to indicate; *(= erklären)* to explain; *(beim Zoll)* to declare; *(= anzeigen)* *Preis, Temperatur etc* to indicate; *(= aussagen)* to state; *(= behaupten)* to maintain → *auch* **angegeben** [b] *(= bestimmen)* *Tempo, Kurs* to set; *(Mus)* *Tempo, Note* to give; **den Takt** *(= klopfen)* to beat time → **Ton** [2] **a** [c]

(*dated*: = *anzeigen*) to report (*bei* to) **VI** **a** (= *prahlen*) to show off, to pose (*inf*); (*esp durch Reden*) to boast, to brag (*mit* about) **b** (*Tennis etc*) to serve **c** (*Cards*) to deal

An|ge|ber(in) ['ange:-] M(F) (= *Prahler*) show--off, poser (*inf*); (*esp durch Reden*) boaster

An|ge|be|rei [ange:bə'rai] F -, -en (*inf*) **a** no pl (= *Prahlerei*) showing off, posing (*inf*) (*mit* about); (*esp verbal*) boasting, bragging (*mit* about) **b** usu pl (= *Äußerung*) boast

an|ge|be|risch ['ange:-bərɪʃ] **ADJ** *Reden* boastful; *Aussehen, Benehmen, Tonfall* pretentious, posy (*inf*) **ADV** pretentiously; **sich ~ benehmen** to be pretentious

An|ge|ber|tum ['ange:bətu:m] NT -s, no pl (*in äußerer Erscheinung*) ostentation; (*durch Reden*) boastfulness; (*in Benehmen*) pretension

An|ge|be|te|te(r) ['ange:bə:tətə] MF *decl as adj* (*hum, geh*) (= *verehrter Mensch*) idol; (= *Geliebte(r)*) beloved

An|ge|bin|de ['ange:-] NT (*dated geh*) gift, present

an|geb|lich ['ange:-plɪç] **ADJ** *attr* so-called, alleged **ADV** supposedly, allegedly; **er ist ~ Musiker** he says he's a musician

an|ge|bo|ren ['angə-] ADJ innate, inherent; (*Med, fig inf*) congenital (*bei* to); **an seine Faulheit musst du dich gewöhnen, die ist ~** (*inf*) you'll have to get used to his laziness, he was born that way

An|ge|bot ['angə-] ✪ 46.6 NT **a** (= *Anerbieten, angebotener Preis*) offer; (*bei Auktion*) bid; (*Comm:* = *Offerte*) offer, tender (*über* +acc, *für* for); (*Comm:* = *Kostenvoranschlag*) offer, quote; **im ~** (*preisgünstig*) on special offer **b** no pl (*Comm, Fin*) supply (*an* +dat, *von* of); (*inf:* = *Sonderangebot*) special offer; **~ und Nachfrage** supply and demand

An|ge|bots-: An|ge|bots|la|ge F supply situation; **An|ge|bots|lü|cke** F gap in the market; **An|ge|bots|preis** M asking price; **An|ge|bots|über|hang** M surplus supply

an|ge|bracht ['angəbraxt] ADJ appropriate; (= *sinnvoll*) reasonable; **schlecht ~** uncalled-for → *auch* **anbringen**

an|ge|brannt ['angə-] **ADJ** burned **ADV** **~ riechen/schmecken** to smell/taste burned; **es riecht hier so ~** there's a smell of burning here → *auch* **anbrennen**

an|ge|bro|chen ['angə-] ADJ **a** *Packung, Flasche* open(ed); **wie viel ist von den ~en hundert Euro übrig?** how much is left from the 100 euros we'd started using?; **ein ~er Abend/Nachmittag/Urlaub** (*hum*) the rest of an evening/ afternoon/a holiday (*esp Brit*) or vacation (*US*); **er wusste mit dem ~en Tag nichts anzufangen** he didn't know what to do for the rest of the day; **das Parken kostet für jede ~e Stunde einen Euro** parking costs one euro for every hour or part of an hour **b** *Knochen* cracked → *auch* **anbrechen**

an|ge|bun|den ['angə-] ADJ (= *beschäftigt*) tied (down); **kurz ~ sein** (*inf*) to be abrupt or curt or brusque → *auch* **anbinden**

an+ge|dei|hen ['angə-] *ptp* **angediehen** VT *sep irreg* **jdm etw ~ lassen** (*geh*) to provide sb with sth

An|ge|den|ken ['angə-] NT , no pl (*geh*) remembrance; **mein Großvater seligen ~s** my late lamented grandfather

an|ge|du|selt ['angədu:zlt] ADJ (*inf*) tipsy, merry (*Brit inf*)

an|ge|ekelt ['angəe:klt] **ADV** in disgust **ADJ** disgusted → *auch* **anekeln**

an|ge|gam|melt ['angəgamlt] ADJ (*inf*) **~e Lebensmittel** food that is going off (*Brit*) or bad

an|ge|gan|gen ['angəgaŋən] ADJ **~ sein** to have gone off (*Brit*) or bad; **~e Lebensmittel** food which has gone off (*Brit*) or bad → *auch* **angehen**

an|ge|ge|ben ['angəge:bn] ADJ *Ziel* declared, stated; *Zeitraum* given, stated; **die ~e Telefonnummer** the phone number given; **am ~en Ort** loco citato → *auch* **angeben**

an|ge|gilbt ['angəgɪlpt] ADJ yellowed

an|ge|gos|sen ['angəgɔsn] ADV **wie ~ sitzen** or **passen** to fit like a glove

an|ge|graut ['angəgraut] ADJ grey (*Brit*), gray (*US*); *Schläfen, Haar auch* greying (*Brit*), graying (*US*)

an|ge|grif|fen ['angəgrɪfn] ADJ *Gesundheit* weakened; *Mensch, Aussehen* frail; (= *erschöpft*) exhausted; (*nervlich*) strained; **sie ist nervlich immer noch ~** her nerves are still strained; **sie ist gesundheitlich immer noch ~** she is still weak or frail → *auch* **angreifen**

an|ge|hal|ten ['angəhaltn] ADJ **~ sein, etw zu tun** to be required or obliged to do sth; **~ sein, etw zu unterlassen** to be required or obliged to refrain from doing sth; **zu Pünktlichkeit ~ sein** to be required to be punctual → *auch* **Atem, anhalten**

an|ge|haucht ['angəhauxt] ADJ **links/rechts ~ sein** to have or show left-wing/right-wing tendencies or leanings → *auch* **anhauchen**

an|ge|hei|ra|tet ['angəhairatət] ADJ related by marriage; **ein ~er Cousin** a cousin by marriage

an|ge|hei|tert ['angəhaitɛt] ADJ tipsy, merry (*Brit inf*)

an+ge|hen ['ange:-] *sep irreg* **VI** *aux sein* **a** (*inf:* = *beginnen*) (*Schule, Theater etc*) to start; (*Feuer*) to start burning, to catch; (*Radio*) to come on; (*Licht*) to come or go on
b (= *entgegentreten*) **gegen jdn ~** to fight sb, to tackle sb; **gegen etw ~** to fight sth; *gegen Flammen, Hochwasser* to fight sth back, to combat sth; *gegen Missstände, Zustände* to take measures against sth; **dagegen muss man ~** something must be done about it
c → **angegangen**
VT **a** *aux haben or (S Ger) sein* (= *anpacken*) *Aufgabe, Schwierigkeiten, Hindernis* to tackle; *Gegner* to attack; *Kurve* to take
b *aux haben or (S Ger) sein* (= *bitten*) to ask (*jdn um etw* sb for sth)
c *aux sein* (= *betreffen*) to concern; **was mich angeht** for my part; **was geht das ihn an?** (*inf*) what's that got to do with him?; **das geht ihn gar nichts** or **einen Dreck** or **einen feuchten Staub an** (*inf*) that's none of his business, that's got nothing or damn all (*inf*) to do with him
VI *impers aux sein* **das geht nicht/keinesfalls an** that won't do, that's not on, that's quite out of the question

an|ge|hend ADJ *Musiker, Künstler, Manager etc* budding; *Lehrer, Ehemann, Vater* prospective; **mit 16 ist sie jetzt schon eine ~e junge Dame** at 16 she's rapidly becoming or is almost a young lady; **er ist ein ~er Sechziger** he's approaching sixty

an+ge|hö|ren ['angə-] *ptp* **angehört** VI *sep* +dat to belong to; (*einer Partei, einer Familie auch*) to be a member of; **jdm/einander ~** (*liter*) to belong to sb/one another or each other

an|ge|hö|rig ['angə-] ADJ *form* belonging (+*dat* to); **keiner Partei ~e Bürger** citizens who do not belong to any party

An|ge|hö|ri|ge(r) ['angəhø:rɪgə] MF *decl as adj* **a** (= *Mitglied*) member **b** (= *Familienangehörige*) relative, relation; **der nächste ~** the next of kin

An|ge|hö|rig|keit F (*zu einer Partei etc*) membership (*zu* of)

an|ge|jahrt ['angəja:ɐt] ADJ (*inf*) *Mensch* ageing; **dieser Film ist reichlich ~** this film is really dated

An|ge|klag|te(r) ['angəkla:ktə] MF *decl as adj* accused, defendant

an|ge|knackst ['angəknakst] ADJ *Wirbel, Bandscheibe* damaged; (*inf*) *Mensch* (*seelisch*) uptight (*inf*); *Selbstvertrauen, Selbstbewusstsein* weakened; *Mythos* tarnished; **er/seine Gesundheit ist ~** he is in bad shape or a bad way; **sie ist noch im-**

mer etwas ~ she still hasn't got over it yet; **der Aufwärtstrend scheint ~ zu sein** the upward trend seems to be slowing → *auch* **anknacksen**

an|ge|krän|kelt ['angəkreŋklt] ADJ (*geh*) sickly, frail, ailing; **von keinem Zweifel ~ sein** not to have the slightest doubt; **von des Gedankens Blässe ~** (*liter*) plagued by or with misgivings

an|ge|kratzt ['angəkratst] ADJ (*inf*) *Person* the worse for wear; *Image, Mythos* dented → *auch* **ankratzen**

An|gel ['aŋl] F -, -n **a** (= *Türangel, Fensterangel*) hinge; **etw aus den ~n heben** (*lit*) to lift sth off its hinges; (*fig*) to revolutionize sth completely; **die Welt aus den ~n heben** (*fig*) to turn the world upside down **b** (= *Fischfanggerät*) (*fishing*) rod and line (*Brit*), fishing pole (*US*); (*zum Schwimmenlernen*) swimming harness; **die ~ auswerfen** to cast (the line); **jdm an die ~ gehen** (*fig*) to fall for or swallow sb's line

an|ge|le|gen ['angə-] ADJ **sich** (*dat*) **etw ~ sein lassen** (*form*) to concern oneself with sth

An|ge|le|gen|heit ['angə-] F matter; (*politisch, persönlich*) affair; (= *Aufgabe*) concern; **das ist meine/nicht meine ~** that's my/not my concern or business; **sich um seine eigenen ~en kümmern** to mind one's own business; **in einer dienstlichen ~** on official business; **in eigener ~** on a private or personal matter

an|ge|le|gent|lich ['angə-] (*geh*) **ADJ** *Bitte, Frage* pressing, insistent; (= *dringend*) pressing, urgent; *Bemühung* enthusiastic; *Empfehlung* warm, eager **ADV** in particular; **sich ~ nach jdm erkundigen** to ask particularly about sb

an|ge|legt ['angəle:kt] ADJ **a** (= *gerichtet*) calculated (*auf* +acc for); **b** **künstlich ~** (*Hügel, Landschaft*) artificial, man-made; **breit ~** (*Wissenschaft, Strategie*) wide-ranging → *auch* **anlegen**

an|ge|lernt ['angə-] ADJ **a** *Arbeiter* semiskilled; **der Lohn für Angelernte** the wage for semiskilled workers **b** *Verhalten* acquired; *Wissen* superficially acquired → *auch* **anlernen**

An|gel- ['aŋl-]: **An|gel|fi|sche|rei** F angling; **An|gel|ge|rät** NT fishing tackle *no pl*; **An|gel|ha|ken** M fish-hook; **An|gel|kar|te** F fishing or angler's licence (*Brit*) or license (*US*); **An|gel|lei|ne** F fishing line

an|geln ['aŋln] **VI** **a** (= *fischen*) to angle (*esp Brit*), to fish; **~ gehen** to go angling (*esp Brit*) or fishing; **nach etw** or **auf** (*form*) **etw** (*acc*) **~** (*lit*) to fish for sth; **nach Komplimenten/Lob** *etc* **~** to fish or angle (*esp Brit*) for compliments/praise *etc* **b** (= *zu greifen versuchen, hervorziehen*) to fish; **nach etw ~** to fish (around) for sth **VT** *Fisch* to fish for; (= *fangen*) to catch; **sich** (*dat*) **einen Mann ~** (*inf*) to catch (oneself) a man; **den werde ich mir ~** (*inf:* = *vornehmen*) I'll give him a piece of my mind

An|geln ['aŋln] PL (*Hist*) Angles *pl*

an+ge|lo|ben ['angə-] *ptp* **angelobt** VT *sep* **a** (*liter*) **jdm etw ~** to swear sth to sb **b** (*Aus:* = *vereidigen*) to swear in

An|gel-: An|gel|platz M fishing ground; **An|gel|punkt** M crucial or central point; (= *Frage*) key or central issue; **An|gel|ru|te** F fishing rod

An|gel|sach|se ['aŋl-] M , **An|gel|säch|sin** F Anglo-Saxon

an|gel|säch|sisch ADJ Anglo-Saxon

An|gel-: An|gel|schein M fishing permit; **An|gel|schnur** F fishing line; **An|gel|sport** M angling (*esp Brit*), fishing; **an|gel|weit** ADV **~ sperrangelweit**

an|ge|mes|sen ['angə-] **ADJ** (= *passend, entsprechend*) appropriate (+*dat* to, for); (= *adäquat*) adequate (+*dat* for); *Preis* reasonable, fair; **eine der Leistung ~e Bezahlung** payment commensurate with performance **ADV** appropriately; **jds Einsatz ~ würdigen** to give sb enough credit for their efforts

An|mes|sen|heit F appropriateness; (= *Adäquatheit*) adequacy; (*von Preis*) fairness, reasonableness

an|ge|nehm ['angə-] ADJ pleasant, agreeable; **das wäre mir sehr ~** I should be very or most grateful, I should greatly appreciate it; **es ist mir gar nicht ~, wenn ich früh aufstehen muss** I don't like getting up early; **es ist mir gar nicht ~, dass er mich besuchen will** I don't like the idea of him wanting to visit me; **ist es Ihnen so ~?** is that all right for you?, is it all right like that for you?; **wenn Ihnen das ~er ist** if you prefer; **~e Ruhe/Reise!** etc have a good or pleasant rest/journey etc; **(sehr) ~!** (form) delighted (to meet you); **das Angenehme mit dem Nützlichen verbinden** to combine business with pleasure
　ADV pleasantly, agreeably

an|ge|nom|men ['angənɔmən] ✪ 28.1 ADJ assumed; (*Name auch, Kind*) adopted CONJ assuming → *auch* **annehmen**

an|ge|passt ▲ ['angəpast] ADJ *Mensch* conformist; (= *modifiziert*) *Version* adapted (*dat* to); **gesellschaftlich ~** conformist ADV **sich ~ verhalten** to conform, to fit in; **sich ~ zeigen** to try to conform or to fit in → *auch* **anpassen**

An|ge|passt|heit ▲ F -, no pl (*von Mensch*) conformism

An|ger ['aŋɐ] M **-s**, **-** (*dial*) **a** (= *Dorfanger*) village green; (*old:* = *Wiese*) pasture, meadow **b** (= *Schindanger*) knacker's yard (*Brit*), slaughterhouse

An|ger|dorf NT village built around a village green

an|ge|regt ['angəre:kt] ADJ lively, animated ADV **sie diskutierten ~** their discussion was lively or animated; **sie unterhielten sich ~** they had a lively or animated conversation → *auch* **anregen**

An|ge|regt|heit F -, no pl liveliness, animation

an|ge|säu|selt ['angəzɔyzlt] ADJ (*inf*) tipsy, merry (*Brit inf*) → *auch* **ansäuseln**

an|ge|schla|gen ['angəʃla:gn] ADJ (*inf*) *Mensch, Aussehen, Nerven* shattered (*inf*); *Gesundheit* poor (*inf*); *Ruf* tarnished; *Ehe, Unternehmen, Volkswirtschaft* failing, on the rocks *pred* (*inf*); (= *betrunken*) sloshed (*inf*); **von etw ~ sein** to be shattered by sth (*inf*) → *auch* **anschlagen**

an|ge|schmiert ['angəʃmi:ɐt] ADJ *pred* (*inf*) in trouble, in dead shtuck (*Brit inf*); **mit dem/der Waschmaschine bist du ganz schön ~** he/the washing machine is not all he/it is cracked up to be (*inf*); **der/die Angeschmierte sein** to have been had (*inf*) → *auch* **anschmieren**

an|ge|schmutzt ['angəʃmʊtst] ADJ soiled; (*Comm*) shopsoiled (*Brit*), damaged

an|ge|schrie|ben ['angəʃri:bn] ADJ (*inf*) **bei jdm gut/schlecht ~ sein** to be in sb's good/bad books, to be well in/not very well in with sb (*inf*) → *auch* **anschreiben**

An|ge|schul|dig|te(r) ['angəʃʊldɪçtə] MF *decl as adj* suspect

an|ge|se|hen ['angəze:ən] ADJ respected → *auch* **ansehen**

an|ge|ses|sen ['angəzɛsn] ADJ = **eingesessen**

An|ge|sicht ['angə-] NT **-(e)s**, **-er** *or* Aus **-e** (*geh*) face, countenance (*liter*); **von ~ zu ~** face to face; **jdm von ~ sehen** to see sb face to face; **jdn von ~ kennen** to know sb by sight; **im ~** +*gen* (*fig*) in the face of

an|ge|sichts ['angəzɪçts] PREP +*gen* in the face of; (= *im Hinblick auf*) in view of; **~ des Todes** in the face of death; **des Sternenhimmels kommt sich der Mensch winzig und nichtig vor** in contrast to the starry sky man seems minute and insignificant

an|ge|spannt ['angəʃpant] ADJ **a** (= *angestrengt*) *Nerven* tense, strained; *Aufmerksamkeit* close, keen; **aufs höchste** *or* **Höchste ~ sein** to be very or highly tense **b** (= *bedrohlich*) *politische Lage* tense, strained; (*Comm*) *Markt, Lage*

---

tight, overstretched ADV *dasitzen, verfolgen* tensely; *zuhören* attentively, closely; **~ wirken** to seem tense → *auch* **anspannen**

An|ge|spannt|heit F **a** (*von Nerven*) tenseness **b** (= *Bedrohlichkeit: von Lage*) tension; (*Comm: von Marktlage*) tightness

Angest. *abbr von* **Angestellte(r)**

an|ge|stammt ['angəʃtamt] ADJ (= *überkommen*) traditional; (= *ererbt*) *Rechte* hereditary, ancestral; *Besitz* inherited

an|ge|stellt ['angəʃtɛlt] ADJ *pred* **~ sein** to be an employee (*bei* of), to be on the staff (*bei* of); **er ist bei Collins ~** he works for Collins; **fest ~ sein** to be on the permanent staff; **ich bin nicht beamtet, sondern nur ~** I don't have permanent tenure in my job → *auch* **anstellen**

An|ge|stell|ten-: An|ge|stell|ten|ge|werk|schaft F white-collar union; **An|ge|stell|ten|ver|hält|nis** NT employment (without permanent tenure); **im ~** in non-tenured employment; **An|ge|stell|ten|ver|si|che|rung** F (salaried) employees' insurance

An|ge|stell|te(r) ['angəʃtɛltə] MF *decl as adj* (salaried) employee; (= *Büroangestellte*) office worker, white-collar worker; (= *Behördenangestellte*) public employee (without tenure)

an|ge|sto|chen ['angəʃtɔxn] ADJ (*inf*) **wie ~ like a stuck pig** (*inf*) → *auch* **anstechen**

an|ge|strengt ['angəʃtrɛŋt] ADJ *Gesicht* strained; *Arbeiten, Denken* hard ADV *diskutieren, nachdenken* carefully → *auch* **anstrengen**

an|ge|tan ['angəta:n] ADJ *pred* **a von jdm/etw ~ sein** to be taken with sb/sth; **es jdm ~ haben** to have made quite an impression on sb; **das Mädchen hat es ihm ~** he has fallen for that girl **b** *danach or dazu* **~ sein, etw zu tun** (*geh*) to be suitable for doing sth; (*Wesen, Atmosphäre, Benehmen etc*) to be apt or calculated to do sth **c** (= *bekleidet*) **mit etw ~ sein** to be dressed in sth → *auch* **antun**

An|ge|trau|te(r) ['angətrautə] MF *decl as adj* (*hum*) spouse, better half (*hum*)

an|ge|trun|ken ['angətrʊŋkn] ADJ *Mensch, Zustand* inebriated, intoxicated; **in ~em Zustand Auto fahren** to drive under the influence (of alcohol) → *auch* **antrinken**

an|ge|wandt ['angə-] ADJ *attr Wissenschaft etc* applied → *auch* **anwenden**

an|ge|wie|sen ['angəvi:zn] ADJ **auf jdn/etw ~ sein** to have to rely on sb/sth, to be dependent on sb/sth; **auf sich selbst ~ sein** to have to fend for oneself; (*Kind*) to be left to one's own devices; **in dieser Arbeit war er auf sich selbst und sein eigenes Wissen ~** in this work he had to rely on himself and his own knowledge; **darauf bin ich nicht ~** I can get along without it, I don't need it; **ich bin selbst auf jeden Euro ~** I need every euro myself → *auch* **anweisen**

an+ge|wöh|nen ['angə-] *ptp* **angewöhnt** VT *sep* **jdm etw ~** to get sb used to sth, to accustom sb to sth; **sich** (*dat*) **etw ~** to get into the habit of sth; **es sich** (*dat*) **~, etw zu tun** to get into the habit of doing sth

An|ge|wohn|heit ['angə-] F habit

an|ge|zeigt ['angətsaikt] ADJ (*form*) advisable; (= *angebracht*) appropriate; **etw für ~ halten** to consider sth advisable/appropriate → *auch* **anzeigen**

an+gif|ten ['angɪ-] VT *sep* (*pej inf*) to snap at, to let fly at

An|gi|na [aŋ'gi:na] F -, **Anginen** [-nən] (*Med*) angina; **~ pectoris** angina (pectoris)

An|gi|o|gra|fie ▲ [aŋgiogra'fi:] F -, **-n** [-'fi:ən] (*Med*) angiography

An|gi|o|plas|tie [aŋgioplas'ti:] F -, no pl (*Med*) angioplasty

an+glei|chen ['angl-] *sep irreg* VT to bring into line, to align (+*dat, an* +*acc* with) VR (*gegenseitig: Kulturen, Geschlechter, Methoden*) to grow closer together; **sich jdm/einer Sache ~** (*einseitig*) to become like sb/sth; **die beiden haben**

---

sich (aneinander) angeglichen the two of them have become more alike

An|glei|chung F **a** (= *das Angleichen*) alignment (*an* +*acc* with) **b** (= *das Gleicherwerden*) **die zunehmende ~ der Kulturen** the increasing similarity between the cultures; **die ~ Deutschlands an Amerika** Germany's growing similarity with America

Ang|ler ['aŋlɐ] M **-s**, **-**, **Ang|le|rin** [-ərɪn] F **-, -nen** angler (*esp Brit*), fisherman

an+glie|dern ['angl-] VT *sep Verein, Partei* to affiliate (+*dat, an* +*acc* to (*Brit*) or with (*US*)); *Land* to annexe (*Brit*) or annex (*US*) (+*dat, an* +*acc* to)

An|glie|de|rung F affiliation; (*von Land*) annexation

ang|li|ka|nisch [aŋgli'ka:nɪʃ] ADJ Anglican; **die ~e Kirche** the Anglican Church, the Church of England

Ang|li|ka|nis|mus [aŋglika'nɪsmʊs] M -, no pl Anglicanism

ang|li|sie|ren [aŋgli'zi:rən] *ptp* **anglisiert** VT to anglicize

Ang|li|sie|rung F -, no pl anglicizing

Ang|list [aŋ'glɪst] M **-en, -en**, **Ang|lis|tin** [-'glɪstɪn] F **-, -nen** English specialist, Anglicist; (= *Student*) student of English

Ang|lis|tik [aŋ'glɪstɪk] F -, no pl English (language) and literature

Ang|li|zis|mus [aŋgli'tsɪsmʊs] M -, **Anglizismen** [-mən] anglicism

Ang|lo- ['aŋglo] *in cpds* Anglo; **Ang|lo|ame|ri|ka|ner(in)** M(F) (= *aus England stammender Amerikaner*) Anglo-American; **die ~** (= *Briten und Amerikaner*) the Anglo-Saxons; **ang|lo|phil** [aŋglo'fi:l] ADJ anglophile; **ang|lo|phob** [aŋglo'fo:p] ADJ anglophobe, anglophobic

an+glot|zen ['angl-] VT *sep* (*inf*) to gawp or gape at (*inf*)

an+glü|hen ['angl-] VT *sep* (*lit*) to heat red-hot; (*fig*) to glow at

An|go|la [aŋ'go:la] NT **-s** Angola

An|go|la|ner [aŋgo'la:nɐ] M **-s**, **-**, **An|go|la|ne|rin** [-ərɪn] F **-, -nen** Angolan

an|go|la|nisch [aŋgo'la:nɪʃ] ADJ Angolan

An|go|ra- [aŋ'go:ra] *in cpds* Angora; **An|go|ra|ka|nin|chen** NT Angora rabbit; **An|go|ra|kat|ze** F Angora cat; **An|go|ra|wol|le** F Angora (wool); **An|go|ra|zie|ge** F Angora goat

An|gos|tu|ra [aŋgɔs'tu:ra] M **-s**, **-s** Angostura (bitters® *pl*)

an|greif|bar ADJ *Behauptung, Politiker* open to attack

an+grei|fen ['angr-] *sep irreg* VT **a** (= *überfallen, kritisieren, Sport*) to attack **b** (= *schwächen*) *Organismus, Organ, Nerven* to weaken; *Gesundheit, Pflanzen* to affect; (= *ermüden, anstrengen*) to strain; (= *schädlich sein für, zersetzen*) *Lack, Farbe* to attack; **seine Krankheit hat ihn sehr angegriffen** his illness weakened him greatly; **das hat ihn sehr angegriffen** that affected him greatly → *auch* **angegriffen** **c** (= *anbrechen*) *Vorräte, Geld* to break into, to draw on **d** (*dial:* = *anfassen*) to touch **e** (*fig:* = *unternehmen, anpacken*) to attack, to tackle VI **a** (*Mil, Sport, fig*) to attack **b** (*geh:* = *ansetzen*) to proceed, to start (*an* +*dat* from) **c** (*dial:* = *anfassen*) to touch VR (*dial:* = *sich anfühlen*) to feel

An|grei|fer ['angraifɐ] M **-s**, **-**, **An|grei|fe|rin** [-ərɪn] F **-, -nen** attacker (*auch Sport, fig*)

an+gren|zen ['angr-] VI *sep* **an etw** (*acc*) **~** to border on sth, to adjoin sth

an|gren|zend ADJ *attr* adjacent (*an* +*acc* to), adjoining (*an etw acc* sth)

An|griff ['angr-] M (*Mil, Sport, fig*) attack (*gegen, auf* +*acc* on); (= *Luftangriff*) (air) raid; **~ ist die**

beste Verteidigung (*prov*) attack is the best means of defence (*Brit*) *or* defense (*US*); **zum ~ übergehen** to go over to the attack, to take the offensive; **zum ~ blasen** (*Mil, fig*) to sound the charge; **etw in ~ nehmen** to tackle sth, to set about sth

an|grif|fig ['angr-] ADJ (*Sw*) aggressive

An|griffs-: An|griffs|flä|che F target; **jdm/einer Sache eine ~ bieten** (*lit, fig*) to provide sb/ sth with a target; **eine ~ bieten** to present a target; **An|griffs|fuß|ball** M attacking football; **An|griffs|krieg** M war of aggression; **An|griffs|li|nie** F (*Ballspiel*) attack line; **An|griffs|lust** F aggressiveness; **an|griffs|lus|tig** ADJ aggressive; **An|griffs|punkt** M target; **An|griffs|rei|he** F (*Sport*) forwards *pl*; **An|griffs|spiel** NT (*Sport*) aggressive *or* attacking game; **An|griffs|spie|ler(in)** M(F) (*Sport*) attacking player; (*Ftbl*) forward; **An|griffs|spit|ze** F (*Mil*) spearhead; **An|griffs|tak|tik** F attacking tactics *pl*; **An|griffs|waf|fe** F offensive weapon

an+grin|sen ['angr-] VT *sep* to grin at

angst [aŋst] ADJ *pred* afraid; **ihr wurde ~ (und bange)** she became worried *or* anxious; **mir ist um deine Gesundheit ~** I'm worried about your health → *auch* **Angst**

Angst [aŋst] F -, ⸚e ['ɛŋstə] (= *innere Unruhe, Psych*) anxiety (*um* about); (= *Sorge*) worry (*um* about); (= *Befürchtung*) fear (*um* for, *vor +dat* of); (*stärker:* = *Furcht, Grauen*) fear, dread (*vor +dat* of); (= *Existenzangst*) angst; **~ haben** to be afraid *or* scared; **~ vor Spinnen/vorm Fliegen haben** to be afraid *or* scared of spiders/flying; **um jdn/etw haben** to be anxious *or* worried about sb/sth; **~ bekommen** *or* **kriegen** to get *or* become afraid *or* scared; (= *erschrecken*) to take fright; **das machte ihm ~ (und Bange)** that worried him, that made him anxious; **aus ~, etw zu tun** for fear of doing sth; **keine ~!** don't be afraid; **keine ~, ich sage es ihm schon** don't you worry, I'll tell him; **jdm ~ machen** to scare sb; **jdm ~ einflößen** *or* **einjagen** to frighten sb; **jdn in ~ und Schrecken versetzen** to terrify sb; **in tausend Ängsten schweben** to be terribly worried *or* anxious

Angst-: angst|er|füllt [-ləɐfvlt] ADJ *Gesicht, Stimme* frightened ADV fearfully, with fear; **angst|frei** ADJ free from fear, anxiety-free ADV without fear; **Angst|ge|fühl** NT feeling of anxiety; **Angst|geg|ner(in)** M(F) most feared opponent; **Bayern München ist unser ~** Bayern Munich is the team we fear (the) most; **Angst|ha|se** M (*inf*) scaredy-cat (*inf*)

ängs|ti|gen ['ɛŋstɪgn] VT to frighten; (= *unruhig machen*) to worry VR to be afraid; (= *sich sorgen*) to worry; **sich vor etw** (*dat*) **~** to be afraid of sth; **sich wegen etw ~** to worry about sth

Angst-: Angst|kauf M panic buying *no pl*; **Angst|laut** M alarm cry

ängst|lich ['ɛŋstlɪç] ADJ **a** (= *verängstigt*) anxious, apprehensive; (= *schüchtern*) timid, timorous **b** (= *übertrieben genau*) fastidious ADV **~ darauf bedacht sein, etw zu tun** to be at pains to do sth; **ein ~ gehütetes Geheimnis** a closely guarded secret; **etw ~ verbergen** to conceal sth scrupulously

Angst|lich|keit F -, *no pl* (= *das Verängstigtsein*) anxiety, apprehension; (= *Schüchternheit*) timidity, timorousness

Angst-: Angst|lust F (*Psych*) enjoyment and excitement combined with fear; **Angst|ma|che** F , *no pl* (*inf*) scaremongering *no pl* (*Brit*), inciting *no pl* fear; **Angst|ma|cher(in)** M(F) (*inf*) scaremonger (*Brit*), sb who incites fear; **Angst|neu|ro|se** F anxiety neurosis; **Angst|neu|ro|ti|ker(in)** M(F) neurotic; **Angst|pa|ro|le** F (*inf*) scaremongering *no pl* (*Brit*), inciting *no pl* fear; **~n verbreiten** to incite fear, to scaremonger (*Brit*); **Angst|par|tie** F (*inf*) nerve-racking affair; **Angst|psy|cho|se** F anxiety psychosis

Angst|röm ['aŋstrøːm, 'ɔŋstrøːm] NT -(s), - (*Phys*) angstrom

Angst-: angst|schlot|ternd [-ʃlɔtɐnd] ADJ (*inf*) trembling *or* shaking with fear; **Angst|schrei** M cry of fear; **Angst|schweiß** M cold sweat; **mir brach der ~ aus** I broke out in a cold sweat; **Angst|traum** M nightmare; **angst|ver|zerrt** [-fɛɐtsɛrt] ADJ *Gesicht* petrified, terror-struck; **angst|voll** ADJ *Stille, Schweigen* apprehensive; *Hast* fearful; **Angst|zu|stand** M state of panic; **Angstzustände bekommen** to get into a state of panic

an+gu|cken ['angʊ-] VT *sep* (*inf*) to look at

an+gur|ten ['angʊrtn] VT *sep* = **anschnallen** VT **b**

an+ha|ben VT *sep irreg* **a** (= *angezogen haben*) to have on, to wear **b** (= *zuleide tun*) to do harm; **jdm etwas ~ wollen** to want to harm sb; **die Kälte kann mir nichts ~** the cold doesn't worry *or* bother me **c** (= *am Zeuge flicken*) **Sie können/die Polizei kann mir nichts ~!** (*inf*) you/ the police can't touch me

an+haf|ten VI *sep* **a** (*lit*) to stick (*an +dat* to), to cling (*an +dat* to); **~de Farbreste** bits of paint left sticking on **b** (*fig*) *+dat* to stick to, to stay with; (= *zugehören: Risiko etc*) to be attached to

An|halt M (= *Hinweis*) clue (*für* about); (*für Verdacht*) grounds *pl* (*für* for); (= *Hilfe*) hint, indication (*für* of, about)

an+hal|ten *sep irreg* VI **a** (= *stehen bleiben*) to stop; **mit dem Sprechen ~** to stop talking **b** (= *fortdauern*) to last **c** (= *werben*) (**bei jdm**) **um ein Mädchen** *or* **um die Hand eines Mädchens ~** to ask (sb) for a girl's hand in marriage VT **a** (= *stoppen*) to stop → **Atem a, Luft b b** (= *anlegen*) *Lineal* to use; **sie hielt mir/sich das Kleid an** she held the dress up against me/herself **c** (= *anleiten*) to urge, to encourage → *auch* **angehalten**

an|hal|tend ADJ continuous, incessant ADV continuously, constantly

An|hal|ter(in) M(F) hitchhiker, hitcher (*esp Brit inf*); **per ~ fahren** to hitchhike, to hitch (*esp Brit inf*)

An|halts|punkt M (= *Vermutung*) clue (*für* about); (*für Verdacht*) grounds *pl* (*für* for); **ich habe keinerlei ~e** I haven't a clue (*inf*), I have no idea

an|hand [an'hant], **an Hand** PREP *+gen* **~ eines Beispiels** with an example; **~ dieses Berichts/ dieser Unterlagen** from this report/these documents

An|hang M **a** (= *Nachtrag*) appendix; (*von Testament*) codicil **b** *no pl* (= *Gefolgschaft*) following; (= *Angehörige*) family; **Witwe, 62, ohne ~** widow, 62, no family; **an ~ gewinnen/verlieren** to gain/lose support

an+hän|gen *sep* VT **a** (= *ankuppeln*) to attach (*an +acc* to); (*Rail*) to couple on (*an +acc* -to); *Anhänger* to hitch up (*an +acc* to); (*fig:* = *anfügen*) to add (*+dat, an +acc* to) **b** (*inf*) **jdm etw ~** (= *verkaufen*) to palm sth off on sb; (= *andrehen*) to foist sth on sb; *Krankheit* to pass sth on to sb; (= *nachsagen, anlasten*) to blame sb for sth, to blame sth on sb; *schlechten Ruf, Spitznamen* to give sb sth; *Verdacht, Schuld* to pin sth on sb; **ich weiß nicht, warum er mir unbedingt etwas ~ will** I don't know why he always wants to give me a bad name
VR (*lit*) to hang on (*+dat, an +acc* to); (*fig*) to tag along (*+dat, an +acc* with); (= *jdm hinterherfahren*) to follow (*+dat, an +acc* sth)
VI *irreg* (*fig*) **a** (= *anhaften*) **jdm ~** to stay with sb; (*schlechter Ruf, Gefängnisstrafe auch*) to stick with sb **b** (= *sich zugehörig fühlen*) *+dat* to adhere to, to subscribe to

An|hän|ger M **a** (= *Wagen*) trailer; (= *Straßenbahnanhänger*) second car; **die Straßenbahn hatte zwei ~** the tram (*esp Brit*) *or* streetcar (*US*) had two extra cars **b** (= *Schmuckstück*) pendant **c** (= *Kofferanhänger etc*) tag, label

An|hän|ger(in) M(F) supporter; (*von Sportart auch*) fan; (*von Partei auch*) follower; (*von Verein*) member

An|hän|ger|kupp|lung F (*Aut*) trailer coupling

An|hän|ger|schaft ['anhɛŋɐʃaft] F -, *no pl* → **Anhänger(in)** supporters *pl*; fans *pl*; following, followers *pl*; membership, members *pl*

An|hän|ger|zahl F → **Anhänger(in)** number of supporters/fans/followers/members

An|hän|ge-: An|hän|ge|schild NT *pl* **-schilder** tag, label; **An|hän|ge|vor|rich|tung** F coupling device; (*an Auto etc*) towbar

an|hän|gig ['anhɛŋɪç] ADJ (*Jur*) sub judice; *Zivilverfahren* pending; **etw ~ machen** to start legal proceedings over sth

an|häng|lich ['anhɛŋlɪç] ADJ **mein Sohn/Hund ist sehr ~** my son/dog is very attached to me

An|häng|lich|keit F -, *no pl* **die ~ an etw** (*acc*) one's attachment to sth; **die ~ meiner Nichte/ Katze** my niece's/cat's fondness for me *or* attachment to me; **aus ~** out of attachment to it/him *etc*

An|häng|sel ['anhɛŋzl] NT -s, - **a** (= *Überflüssiges, Mensch*) appendage (*an +dat* to); (*von Gruppe, Partei*) hanger-on; **das ist ein ~ am Wort** that is added onto the word **b** (= *Schildchen*) tag; (*rare:* = *Schmuckstück*) pendant; (*an Armband*) charm; (*an Uhrenkette*) fob; **die ~ am Weihnachtsbaum** the things hanging on the Christmas tree **c** (= *Zusatz*) addition; (= *Nachtrag*) appendix

An|hauch M (*geh*) aura; (*in Stimme*) trace, tinge

an+hau|chen VT *sep* to breathe on → *auch* **angehaucht**

an+hau|en VT *sep* **a** (*inf:* = *ansprechen*) to accost (*um* for); **jdn um etw ~** to be on the scrounge for sth from sb (*inf*); *um Geld auch* to touch sb for sth (*Brit inf*), to hit sb up for sth (*US inf*) **b** (*auch irreg*) *Baum* to cut a notch in

an+häu|fen *sep* VT to accumulate, to amass; *Vorräte, Geld* to hoard VR to pile up, to accumulate; (*Zinsen*) to accumulate, to accrue

An|häu|fung F accumulation, amassing; (*von Geld*) hoarding

an+he|ben¹ *sep irreg* VT **a** (= *hochheben*) to lift (up); *Glas* to raise **b** (= *erhöhen*) to raise VI to lift

an+he|ben² *pret* **hob** *or* (*obs*) **hub an**, *ptp* **angehoben** VI *sep irreg* (*old*) to commence, to begin; **zu singen ~** to begin singing; **..., hub er an** (*obs*) ..., quoth he (*old*)

An|he|bung F increase (*+gen, von* in); (= *das Anheben auch*) raising (*+gen, von* of); (*von Betrag, Größe auch*) rise (*+gen, von* in); **eine ~ der Gehälter um 5%** an increase *or* a rise (*Brit*) *or* raise (*US*) of 5% in salaries

an+hef|ten VT *sep* (*an +acc or dat* to) to fasten (on), to attach; **jdm einen Orden ~** to pin a medal on sb; **etw mit Reißzwecken/Heftklammern/Büroklammern/Stichen ~** to pin/staple/paperclip/tack sth on (*an +acc or dat* to)

an+hei|len VI *sep aux sein* to heal (up); (*Knochen*) to set, to mend

an|hei|melnd ['anhaimlnt] ADJ (*geh*) homely; *Klänge* familiar

an|heim [an'haim]: **an|heim fal|len** ▲ VI *irreg aux sein +dat* (*liter*) to pass *or* fall to; *einer Krankheit* to fall prey to; *einem Betrug* to fall victim to; **der Vergessenheit ~** to sink into oblivion; **an|heim ge|ben** ▲ VT *irreg +dat* (*liter*) to commit *or* entrust to; **etw den Flammen ~** to consign sth to the flames; **etw der Entscheidung eines anderen ~** to entrust the decision about sth to somebody else; **an|heim stel|len** ▲ VT *+dat* (*geh*) **jdm etw ~** to leave sth to sb's discretion

an|hei|schig [an'haiʃɪç] ADV (*form*) **sich ~ machen, etw zu tun** to take it upon oneself to do sth

---

an+hei|zen VT *sep* **a** *Ofen* to light **b** *(fig inf)* (= *ankurbeln*) *Wirtschaft, Wachstum* to stimulate; (= *verschlimmern*) *Krise* to aggravate; *Inflation* to fuel

an+herr|schen VT *sep* to bark at

an+het|zen VI *sep aux sein* **angehetzt kommen** to come rushing along *or (auf einen zu)* up

an+heu|ern VTI *sep (Naut, fig)* to sign on *or* up

An|hieb M **auf (den ersten) ~** *(inf)* straight *or* right away, straight off *(inf)*, first go *(inf)*; **das kann ich nicht auf ~ sagen** I can't say offhand

An|him|me|lei [anhɪmə'laɪ] F **-, -en** *(inf)* adulation, idolization; (= *schwärmerische Blicke*) adoring gaze

an+him|meln [ˈanhɪmln] VT *sep (inf)* to idolize, to worship; (= *schwärmerisch ansehen*) to gaze adoringly at

an|hin [ˈanhɪn] ADV **bis ~** *(Sw: = bisher)* until now

An|hö|he F hill

an+hö|ren *sep* **VT** **a** (= *Gehör schenken*) to hear; *Schallplatten, Konzert* to listen to; **jdn ganz ~** to hear sb out; **sich** *(dat)* **etw ~** to listen to sth; **das höre ich mir nicht mehr länger mit an** I'm not going to listen to that any longer; **können Sie sich mal einen Moment ~, was ich zu sagen habe?** can you just listen for a moment to what I have to say? **b** (= *zufällig mithören*) to overhear; **ich kann das nicht mehr mit ~** I can't listen to that any longer **c** (= *anmerken*) **man konnte ihr** *or* **ihrer Stimme die Verzweiflung ~** one could hear the despair in her voice; **das hört man ihm aber nicht an!** you can't tell that from his accent *or* from hearing him speak; **man hört ihm sofort den Ausländer an** you can hear at once that he's a foreigner **VR** (= *klingen*) to sound; **das hört sich ja gut an** *(inf)* that sounds good

An|hör|ter|min M date for a hearing

An|hö|rung [ˈanhøːrʊŋ] F **-, -en** hearing

An|hö|rungs|ver|fah|ren NT hearing

an+hu|pen VT *sep* to hoot at, to sound one's horn at

an+hus|ten VT *sep* to cough at; **jdn ~** to cough in sb's face

Ä|nig|ma [ɛˈnɪgma] NT **-s, -ta** *or* **Änigmen** [-ta, -mən] *(liter)* enigma

A|ni|lin [aniˈliːn] NT **-s,** *no pl* aniline

A|ni|lin|far|be F aniline dye

A|ni|ma [ˈanima] F **-, -s** *(Psych)* anima

a|ni|ma|lisch [aniˈmaːlɪʃ] ADJ animal; *(pej auch)* bestial, brutish

A|ni|ma|teur [animaˈtøːɐ] M **-s, -e** host, entertainment officer

A|ni|ma|teu|rin [animaˈtøːrɪn] F **-, -nen** hostess, entertainment officer

A|ni|ma|ti|on [animaˈtsioːn] F **-, -en** *(Film)* animation

A|ni|ma|ti|ons|film M (animated) cartoon (film)

A|ni|ma|tor [aniˈmaːtoːɐ] M **-s, Animatoren** [-ˈtoːrən], **A|ni|ma|to|rin** [-ˈtoːrɪn] F **-, -nen** *(Film)* animator

A|ni|mier|da|me F nightclub *or* bar hostess

a|ni|mie|ren [aniˈmiːrən] *ptp* **animiert** VT **a** (= *anregen*) to encourage; **jdn zu einem Streich ~** to put sb up to a trick; **sich animiert fühlen, etw zu tun** to feel prompted to do sth; **durch das schöne Wetter animiert** encouraged *or* prompted by the good weather **b** *(Film)* to animate

a|ni|mie|rend *(geh)* **ADJ** stimulating **ADV** **~ wirken** to have a stimulating effect

A|ni|mier-: **A|ni|mier|lo|kal** NT hostess bar, clip joint *(pej)*; **A|ni|mier|mäd|chen** NT nightclub *or* bar hostess

A|ni|mo [ˈaːnimo] NT **-s,** *no pl (Aus)* **a** (= *Vorliebe*) liking **b** (= *Schwung*) **mit ~ mitmachen** to join in with gusto

A|ni|mo|si|tät [animoziˈtɛːt] F **-, -en** *(geh)* (= *gegen towards*) (= *Feindseligkeit*) animosity, hostility; (= *Abneigung*) hostility; (= *Äußerung*) hostile remark

A|ni|mus [ˈaːnimʊs] M **-,** *no pl* **a** *(Psych)* animus **b** *(inf)* hunch *(inf)*, feeling

An|i|on [ˈanioːn] NT *(Chem)* anion

A|nis [aˈniːs, *(S Ger, Aus)* ˈaːnɪs] M **-(es), -e** (= *Gewürz*) aniseed; (= *Schnaps*) aniseed brandy; (= *Pflanze*) anise

A|ni|sett [aniˈzɛt] M **-s, -s, A|nis|li|kör** M anisette, aniseed liqueur

A|nis-: **A|nis|plätz|chen** NT aniseed biscuit *(Brit)* or cookie *(US)*; **A|nis|schnaps** M aniseed brandy

Ank. *abbr von* **Ankunft** arr.

an+kämp|fen VI *sep (fig)* **gegen etw ~** (*gegen die Elemente, Strömung*) to battle with sth; *gegen Gefühle, Neigungen, Versuchungen, Müdigkeit* to fight sth; *gegen Inflation, Missbrauch, Korruption, Ideen* to fight (against) sth; **gegen jdn ~** to fight (against) sb, to (do) battle with sb; **~ gegen die Tränen ~** to fight back one's tears

an+kar|ren [ˈanka-] VT *sep (inf)* to cart along

An|kauf [ˈankauf] M purchase, purchasing; **durch den ~ einer Sache** *(gen)* through the purchase of sth, by purchasing sth; **An- und Verkauf von ...** we buy and sell ...; **An- und Verkauf(s-Geschäft)** ≈ second-hand shop

an+kau|fen [ˈankau-] *sep* **VTI** to purchase, to buy **VR** **sich (an einem Ort) ~** to buy oneself a place (somewhere)

An|käu|fer(in) [ˈankɔy-] M(F) purchaser, buyer

An|kaufs|recht NT *(Jur)* option, right of purchase

an+kei|fen [ˈankai-] VT *sep (inf)* to scream *or* holler *(inf)* at

An|ker [ˈaŋkɐ] M **-s, -** *(Naut, Archit, fig)* anchor; *(Elec)* armature; *(von Uhr)* anchor; **~ werfen** to drop anchor; **vor ~ gehen** to drop anchor; *(fig)* *(hum: = heiraten)* to settle down *(bei* with); *(inf: = Rast machen)* to stop over; **sich vor ~ legen** to drop anchor; **vor ~ liegen** *or* **treiben** to lie or ride *or* be at anchor; **ein Schiff vor ~ legen** to bring a ship to anchor; **den/die ~ hieven** *or* **lichten** to weigh anchor

An|ker-: **An|ker|bo|je** F anchor buoy; **An|ker|grund** M anchorage; **An|ker|ket|te** F anchor cable; **An|ker|klü|se** F *(Naut)* hawsehole; **An|ker|mann** M *pl* **-männer** *(TV)* anchorman

an|kern [ˈaŋkɛn] VI (= *Anker werfen*) to anchor; (= *vor Anker liegen*) to be anchored

An|ker-: **An|ker|platz** M anchorage; **An|ker|tau** NT anchor hawser *or* rope; **An|ker|win|de** F capstan

an+ket|ten [ˈankɛ-] VT *sep* to chain up *(an +acc or dat* to); **angekettet sein** *(fig)* to be tied up

an+keu|chen [ˈankɔy-] VI *sep aux sein (inf)* **angekeucht kommen** to come panting along *or (auf einen zu)* up

an+kie|ken [ˈanki-] VT *sep (N Ger inf)* to look at

an+kit|ten [ˈankɪ-] VT *sep* to stick on (with putty) *(an +acc* -to)

an+kläf|fen [ˈankl-] VT *sep (pej)* to bark at; *(kleiner Hund)* to yap at

An|kla|ge [ˈankl-] F **a** *(Jur)* charge; (= *Anklagevertretung*) prosecution; **gegen jdn ~ erheben** to bring *or* prefer charges against sb; **jdn unter ~ stellen** to charge sb *(wegen* with); **(wegen etw) unter ~ stehen** to have been charged (with sth); **als Vertreter der ~ fragte Herr Stein ...** acting for the prosecution Mr Stein asked ..., Mr Stein, prosecuting *or* for the prosecution, asked ... **b** *(fig)* (= *Verurteilung*) condemnation *(gegen +gen* of); (= *Beschuldigung*) accusation; (=

Anprangerung) indictment *(an +acc* of); **ihr Blick war voller ~** her eyes were full of reproach

An|kla|ge-: **An|kla|ge|bank** F *pl* **-bänke** dock; **auf der ~ (sitzen)** *(lit, fig)* (to be) in the dock; **jdn auf die ~ bringen** to put sb in the dock; **An|kla|ge|be|hör|de** F prosecution; **An|kla|ge|er|he|bung** F preferral of charges

an+kla|gen [ˈankl-] *sep* **VT** **a** *(Jur)* to charge, to accuse; **jdn einer Sache** *(gen)* **or wegen etw ~** to charge sb with sth, to accuse sb of sth **b** *(fig)* (= *verurteilen*) to condemn; *(Buch, Rede)* to be a condemnation of; (= *anprangern*) to be an indictment of; **jdn einer Sache** *(gen)* **~** (= *beschuldigen*) to accuse sb of sth; **jdn ~, etw getan zu haben** to accuse sb of having done sth **VI** to cry out in protest *or* accusation; *(Buch, Bilder etc)* to cry out in condemnation

an|kla|gend **ADJ** *Ton* accusing, accusatory; *Blick* reproachful; *Buch, Bild* that cries out in condemnation **ADV** reproachfully

An|kla|ge|punkt M charge

An|klä|ger(in) [ˈankl-] M(F) *(Jur)* prosecutor

an|klä|ge|risch [ˈanklɛːgərɪʃ] ADJ = **anklagend**

An|kla|ge-: **An|kla|ge|schrift** F indictment; **An|kla|ge|ver|le|sung** F arraignment; **An|kla|ge|ver|tre|ter(in)** M(F) (public) prosecutor, counsel for the prosecution

an+klam|mern [ˈankl-] *sep* **VT** *(mit Büroklammer)* to clip *(an +acc or dat* (on)to); *(mit Heftmaschine)* to staple *(an +acc or dat* on(to), to); *Wäsche* to peg *(an +acc or dat* on) **VR** **sich an etw** *(acc or dat)* **~** to cling (on)to sth, to hang onto sth

An|klang [ˈankl-] M **a** *no pl* (= *Beifall*) approval; **~ (bei jdm) finden** to meet with (sb's) approval, to be well received (by sb); **großen/wenig/keinen ~ finden** to be very well/poorly/badly received **b** (= *Reminiszenz*) **Anklänge an etw** *(acc)* **enthalten** to be reminiscent of sth; **die Anklänge an Mozart sind unverkennbar** the echoes of Mozart are unmistakable; **ich konnte in seinem Buch einen deutlichen ~ an Thomas Mann erkennen** I found his book (to be) distinctly reminiscent of Thomas Mann

an|klat|schen [ˈankl-] *sep (inf)* **VT** *Plakat etc* to slap *or* bung up *(inf)* **VI** *aux sein* **seine Kleider klatschen an** *or* **sind angeklatscht** his clothes are clinging to him; **seine Haare klatschen an** *or* **sind angeklatscht** his hair is plastered down

an+kle|ben [ˈankl-] *sep* **VT** to stick up *(an +acc or dat* on) **VI** *aux sein* to stick

an+kle|ckern [ˈankl-] VI *sep aux sein (inf)* **angekleckert kommen** to come drifting along *or (auf einen zu)* up; (= *nach und nach eintreffen*) to come in dribs and drabs *(inf)*

An|klei|de|ka|bi|ne F changing cubicle

an+klei|den [ˈankl-] VTR *sep (geh)* to dress

An|klei|de|pup|pe F (= *Schaufensterpuppe*) display dummy, mannequin *(dated)*; (= *Anziehpuppe*) dress-up doll

An|klei|der [ˈanklaidɐ] M **-s, -, An|klei|de|rin** [-ərɪn] F **-, -nen** *(Theat)* dresser

An|klei|de|raum M **, An|klei|de|zim|mer** NT dressing room; *(im Schwimmbad, Geschäft)* changing room

an+kli|cken [ˈankl-] VT *(Comput)* to click on

an+klin|geln [ˈankl-] VTI *sep (inf)* to ring *or* phone (up) *(esp Brit)*, to call (up) *(esp US)*; **jdn** *or* **bei jdm ~** to give sb a ring *(esp Brit)* or a buzz *(inf)*, to ring *or* phone sb (up) *(esp Brit)*, to call sb (up) *(esp US)*

an+klin|gen [ˈankl-] VI *sep aux sein* (= *erinnern*) to be reminiscent *(an +acc* of); (= *angeschnitten werden*) to be touched (on); (= *spürbar werden*) to be discernible; **in diesem Lied klingt etwas von Sehnsucht an** there is a suggestion *or* hint *or* note of longing (discernible) in this song

an+klop|fen [ˈankl-] VI *sep* to knock *(an +acc or dat* at on); **bei jdm wegen etw ~** *(fig inf)* to go knocking on sb's door for sth; **Anklopfen** (*Telec*) call waiting (service)

an+knab|bern ['ankn-] VT *sep* (*inf*) (= *annagen*) to gnaw *or* nibble (at); (*fig*) *Ersparnisse etc* to gnaw away at, to nibble away at; **zum Anknabbern (aussehen)** (*fig*) (to look) good enough to eat

an+knack|sen ['anknaksn] VT *sep* (*inf*) **a** *Knochen* to crack; *Fuß, Gelenk etc* to crack a bone in **b** (*fig*) *Gesundheit* to affect; *Stolz* to injure, to deal a blow to; **sein Selbstvertrauen/Stolz wurde dadurch angeknackst** that was a blow to his self-confidence/pride → *auch* **angeknackst**

an+knat|tern ['ankn-] VI *sep aux sein* (*inf*) **angeknattert kommen** to come roaring along *or* (*auf einen zu*) up

an+knip|sen ['ankn-] VT *sep* to switch *or* put on; **ein Lächeln ~** (*inf*) to put on a smile

an+knöp|fen ['ankn-] VT *sep* to button on (*an +acc or dat* -to)

an+kno|ten ['ankn-] VT *sep* to tie on (*an +acc or dat* -to)

an+knüp|fen ['ankn-] *sep* **VT** to tie on (*an +acc or dat* -to); *Beziehungen* to establish; *Verhältnis* to form, to start up; *Gespräch* to start up, to enter into **VI** **an etw** (*acc*) **~** to take sth up

An|knüp|fung F -, -en (*von Beziehungen*) establishing; (*von Verhältnis*) forming, starting up; (*von Gespräch*) starting up; **in ~ an etw** (*acc*) following on from sth

An|knüp|fungs|punkt M link

an+knur|ren ['ankn-] VT *sep* (*lit, fig*) to growl at

an+ko|chen VT *sep* (= *kurz kochen*) to parboil; (= *blanchieren*) *Gemüse* to blanch

An|koch|stu|fe F (*bei Kochplatte*) full heat *or* high (setting)

an+koh|len ['anko-] VT *sep* **a** (= *ansengen*) *Baum, Einrichtung* to char **b** (*inf:* = *belügen*) to have on (*inf*)

an+kom|men ['anko-] *sep irreg aux sein* **VI** **a** (= *eintreffen*) to arrive; (*Zug, Bus etc*) to get in, to arrive; **bist du gut angekommen?** did you arrive safely?, did you get there all right?; **bei etw angekommen sein** to have reached sth, to have got to sth; **wir sind schon beim Dessert angekommen** we've already reached the dessert stage; **das Kind soll in 6 Wochen ~** the baby is due (to arrive) in 6 weeks **b** (= *Anklang, Resonanz finden*) (*bei* with) to go down well; (*Mode, Neuerungen*) to catch on; **dieser Witz kam gut an** the joke went down very well; **mit deinem dummen Gerede kommst du bei ihm nicht an!** you won't get anywhere with him with your stupid talk!; **ein Lehrer, der bei seinen Schülern ausgezeichnet ankommt** a teacher who is a great success with his pupils, a teacher who hits it off marvellously (*Brit*) *or* marvelously (*US*) with his pupils **c** (*inf*) (= *auftreten, erscheinen*) to come along; (= *wiederholt erwähnen*) to come up (*mit* with); **jdm mit etw ~** to come to sb with sth; **komm mir nachher nicht an und verlange, dass ich ...** don't come running to me afterwards wanting me to ...; **komm mir nur nicht wieder damit an, dass du Astronaut werden willst** don't start up again with this business about (your) wanting to be an astronaut **d** (= *sich durchsetzen*) **gegen etw ~** (*gegen Gewohnheit, Sucht etc*) to be able to fight sth; **gegen jdn ~** to be able to cope with sb; **gegen diese Konkurrenz kommen wir nicht an** we can't fight this competition; **er ist zu stark, ich komme gegen ihn nicht an** he's too strong, I'm no match for him

VI *impers* **a** (= *wichtig sein*) **es kommt auf etw** (*acc*) **an** sth matters; **darauf kommt es (uns) an** that is what matters (to us); **es kommt darauf an, dass wir ...** what matters is that we ...; **auf eine halbe Stunde kommt es jetzt nicht mehr an** it doesn't matter about the odd half-hour, an extra half-hour is neither here nor there (*inf*); **darauf soll es mir nicht ~** that's not the

problem **b** (= *abhängig sein*) to depend (*auf +acc* on); **es kommt darauf an** it (all) depends; **es käme auf einen Versuch an** we'd have to give it a try; **es kommt (ganz) darauf an, in welcher Laune er ist** it (all) depends (on) what mood he's in **c** (*inf*) **es darauf ~ lassen** to take a chance, to chance it; **lass es nicht drauf ~!** don't push your luck! (*inf*); **lassen wirs darauf ~** let's chance it; **er ließ es in der Prüfung darauf ~** he took a chance in the exam; **er ließ es auf einen Streit/einen Versuch ~** he was prepared to argue about it/to give it a try; **lass es doch nicht deswegen auf einen Prozess ~** for goodness' sake don't let it get as far as the courts

VT (= *sein, erscheinen*) **etw kommt jdn schwer/hart an** sth is difficult/hard for sb; **das Rauchen aufzugeben, kommt ihn sauer an** he's finding it difficult to give up smoking

an+kop|peln ['ankɔ-] VT *sep* to hitch up (*an +acc* to) *or* on (*an +acc* -to); (*Rail*) to couple up (*an +acc* to) *or* on (*an +acc* -to); (*Space*) to link up (*an +acc*, with to)

an+kot|zen ['ankɔ-] VT *sep* (*sl:* = *anwidern*) to make sick (*inf*)

an+kral|len ['ankr-] VR *sep* to clutch (*an +dat* at)

an+krat|zen ['ankr-] VT *sep* to scratch; (*fig*) *jds Ruf etc* to damage → *auch* **angekratzt**

an+krau|sen ['ankr-] VT *sep* (*Sew*) to gather

an+krei|den ['ankraidn] VT *sep* **a** (*obs:* = *Schulden aufschreiben*) to chalk up **b** (*fig*) **jdm etw (dick** *or* **übel) ~** to hold sth against sb; **jdm sein Benehmen als Frechheit/Schwäche ~** to regard sb's behaviour (*Brit*) *or* behavior (*US*) as an impertinence/as weakness

An|kreis ['ankr-] M (*Math*) escribed circle

an+kreu|zen ['ankr-] *sep* **VT** *Stelle, Fehler, Antwort* to mark with a cross, to put a cross beside **VI** *aux sein or haben* (*Naut*) **gegen den Wind ~** to sail against *or* into the wind

an+kün|den ['ankʏ-] VTR *sep* (*old*) = **ankündigen**

an+kün|di|gen ['ankʏ-] *sep* **VT** **a** (= *ansagen, anmelden*) to announce; (*auf Plakat, in Zeitung etc*) to advertise; **heute kam endlich der angekündigte Brief** today the letter I/we had been expecting finally arrived **b** (= *auf etw hindeuten*) to be a sign of **VR** (*fig*) to be heralded (*durch* by); **der Frühling kündigt sich an** spring is in the air; **diese Krankheit kündigt sich durch ... an** this illness is preceded by ...; **er besucht uns nie, ohne (sich) (nicht) vorher anzukündigen** he never visits us without letting us know in advance *or* without giving us advance notice

An|kün|di|gung F announcement; (= *vorherige Benachrichtigung*) advance notice; **Preisänderungen nur nach vorheriger ~** price changes will be announced in advance, advance notice will be given of price changes

An|kunft ['ankʊnft] F -, **Ankünfte** [-kʏnftə] arrival; **bei** *or* **nach ~** on arrival

An|kunfts-: **An|kunfts|bahn|steig** M (*Rail*) arrival platform (*esp Brit*) *or* track (*US*); **An|kunfts|flug|ha|fen** M arrival *or* destination airport; **An|kunfts|hal|le** F arrivals lounge; **An|kunfts|ort** M *pl* -orte place of arrival; **An|kunfts|ta|fel** F arrivals (indicator) board; **An|kunfts|zeit** F time of arrival

an+kup|peln ['ankʊ-] VT *sep* = **ankoppeln**

an+kur|beln ['ankʊ-] VT *sep* *Maschine* to wind up; (*Aut*) to crank; (*fig*) *Wirtschaft, Konjunktur* to boost, to reflate

An|kur|be|lung F -, -en (*fig*) reflation

an+ku|scheln ['ankʊ-] VR *sep* **sich bei jdm** *or* **an jdn ~** to snuggle up to sb

Anl. *abbr von* **Anlage** encl.

an+la|bern VT *sep* (*sl*) to speak to; (*aufreißen wollen*) *Mädchen* to chat up (*Brit inf*), to put the moves on (*US inf*)

an+lä|cheln VT *sep* to smile at; (*fig: Schicksal, Glück etc*) to smile (up)on; **jdn ~** to smile at sb, to give sb a smile; **der Kuchen lächelte mich förmlich an** (*hum*) the cake sat there just asking to be eaten

an+la|chen VT *sep* to smile at; (*fig: Himmel, Sonne*) to smile (up)on; **sich** (*dat*) **jdn ~** (*inf*) to pick sb up (*inf*)

An|la|ge ☼ 47.5 F **a** (= *Fabrikanlage*) plant **b** (= *Grünanlage, Parkanlage*) (public) park; (*um ein Gebäude herum*) grounds *pl* **c** (= *Einrichtung*) (*Mil, Elec*) installation(s *pl*); (= *sanitäre Anlagen*) bathroom *or* sanitary (*form*) installations *pl*; (= *Sportanlage etc*) facilities *pl* **d** (*inf:* = *Stereoanlage*) (stereo) system *or* equipment; (= *EDV-Anlage*) system **e** (= *Plan, Grundidee*) conception; (*eines Dramas etc*) structure **f** *usu pl* (= *Veranlagung*) aptitude, gift, talent (*zu* for); (= *Neigung*) predisposition, tendency (*zu* to) **g** (= *das Anlegen*) (*von Park*) laying out; (*von Stausee etc*) construction, building; **die ~ einer Kartei veranlassen** to start a file; **die Stadt hat die ~ von weiteren Grünflächen beschlossen** the town has decided to provide more parks **h** (= *Kapitalanlage*) investment **i** (= *Beilage zu einem Schreiben*) enclosure; **als ~** *or* **in der ~ erhalten Sie ...** please find enclosed ...

an|la|ge|be|dingt ADJ inherent; **Krampfadern sind ~** some people have an inherent tendency *or* a predisposition to varicose veins

An|la|ge-: **An|la|ge|be|ra|ter(in)** M(F) investment advisor; **An|la|ge|be|ra|tung** F investment management *or* counselling (*Brit*) *or* counseling (*US*), investment consultancy, portfolio management; **An|la|ge|be|trag** M amount *or* sum (to be) invested; **An|la|ge|dauer** F investment period; **An|la|ge|ka|pi|tal** NT investment capital; **An|la|ge|mög|lich|keit** F investment opportunity; **An|la|ge|pa|pier** NT long-term investment bond

an+la|gern *sep* **VT** to take up **VR** (*Chem*) to be taken up (*an +acc* by)

An|la|ge|ver|mö|gen NT fixed assets *pl*

an+lan|den *sep* **VT** **a** *aux sein* (*Naut*) to land **b** *aux sein or haben* (*Geol*) to accrete **VT** to land

an+lan|gen *sep* **VI** *aux sein* (*an einem Ort*) to arrive; **in der Stadt/am Gipfel angelangt sein** to have reached the town/summit, to have arrived in *or* at the town/at the summit **VT** **a** (= *betreffen*) to concern **b** (*S Ger:* = *anfassen*) to touch

An|lass ▲ ['anlas] ☼ 44.2 M -es, **Anlässe** [-lɛsə] **a** (= *Veranlassung*) (immediate) cause (*zu* for); **zum ~ von etw werden** to bring sth about, to trigger sth off; **das war zwar nicht der Grund aber der ~** that wasn't the real reason but that's what finally brought it about *or* triggered it off; **welchen ~ hatte er, das zu tun?** what prompted him to do that?; **er hat keinen ~ zur Freude** he has no cause *or* reason *or* grounds for rejoicing; **es besteht kein ~ ...** there is no reason ...; **es besteht ~ zur Hoffnung** there is reason for hope; **das ist kein ~ zu feiern** that's no reason to celebrate; **etw zum ~ nehmen, zu ...** to use sth as an opportunity to ...; **beim geringsten ~** for the slightest reason; **bei jedem ~** at every opportunity; **jdm ~ zu Beschwerden geben, jdm ~ geben, sich zu beschweren** to give sb reason *or* cause *or* grounds for complaint *or* for complaining **b** (= *Gelegenheit*) occasion; **aus ~** (+*gen*) on the occasion of; **aus gegebenem ~** in view of the occasion; **aus diesem ~** on this occasion; **dem ~ entsprechend** as befits the occasion, as is befitting the occasion **c** (*Sw:* = *Lustbarkeit*) social

An|lass|bat|te|rie ▲ F (*Aut*) starter battery

an•las•sen sep irreg **VT a** (= in Gang setzen) Motor, Wagen to start (up) **b** (inf) Schuhe, Mantel to keep on **c** (inf) Wasserhahn, Motor to leave running or on; Licht, Radio to leave on; Kerze to leave burning; Feuer to leave in or burning **VR** **sich gut/schlecht ~** to get off to a good/bad start; (Lehrling, Student, Geschäft etc auch) to make a good/bad start or beginning; **das Wetter lässt sich gut an** the weather looks promising; **wie lässt er sich in der Sache denn an?** what sort of start has he made on it?

An•las•ser ['anlasɐ] M **-s, -** (Aut) starter

an•läss•lich ['anleslɪç] **▲** ☼ 50.6, 51.2, 52.1, 52.2 PREP +gen on the occasion of

an•las•ten VT sep **a** jdm etw ~ to blame sb for sth, to lay the blame for sth on sb; **jdm die Schuld für etw ~** to lay the blame for sth at sb's door or on sb; **jdm etw als Schwäche ~** to regard or see sth as a weakness on sb's part **b** (dated) Kosten to charge (jdm to sb)

an•lat•schen VI sep aux sein **angelatscht kommen** (inf) to come slouching along or (auf einen zu) up

An•lauf M **a** (Sport) run-up; (Ski) approach run; (Mil: = Ansturm) onset, attack; **mit ~** with a run-up; **ohne ~** from standing; **Sprung mit/ohne ~** running/standing jump; **~ nehmen** to take a run-up; **~ zu etw nehmen** (fig) to pluck up courage to do sth **b** (fig: = Versuch) attempt, try; **beim ersten/zweiten ~** at the first/second attempt, first/second go (inf); **noch einen ~ nehmen** or **machen** to have another go (inf) or try, to make another attempt **c** (= Beginn) start

an•lau•fen sep irreg aux sein **a** (= beginnen) to begin, to start; (Film) to open; (Motor) to start **b** **angelaufen kommen** to come running along or (auf einen zu) up **c** (= beschlagen) (Brille, Spiegel etc) to steam or mist up; (Metall) to tarnish; **rot/blau** ~ to turn or go red/blue **d** (Sport) (= zu laufen beginnen) to start off; (= Anlauf nehmen) to take a run-up **e** **gegen etw ~** (fig) to stand up to sth; **er kann kaum gegen so einen starken Wind ~** he can hardly walk against such a strong wind **VT** (Naut) Hafen etc to put into, to call at

An•lauf-: An•lauf•ha•fen M (Naut) port of call; **An•lauf•kos•ten** PL (Econ) initial or start-up cost(s pl); **An•lauf•pha•se** F initial stage; **in der ~** in the initial stages; **An•lauf•stel•le** F shelter, refuge; **An•lauf•zeit** F (Aut) warming-up time or period; (fig) time to get going or started; (Film, Theat) (time of the) first few performances pl; **ein paar Wochen ~** a few weeks to get going or started

An•laut M (Phon) initial sound; **im ~ stehen** to be in initial position

an•lau•ten VI sep to begin

an•läu•ten VTI sep (dial: = anrufen) jdn or **bei jdm ~** to ring or phone sb (up) (esp Brit), to call sb

an•lau•tend ADJ attr Vokal initial

an•le•cken VT sep to lick

An•le•ge•brü•cke F landing stage, jetty

an•le•gen sep **VT a** Leiter to put up (an +acc against); Brett, Karte, Dominostein to lay (down) (an +acc next to, beside); Holz, Kohle to put or lay on; Lineal to position, to set; **das Gewehr ~** to raise the gun to one's shoulder; **das Gewehr auf jdn/etw ~** to aim the gun at sb/sth; **den Säugling ~** to put the baby to one's breast; **strengere Maßstäbe ~** to lay down or impose stricter standards (bei in)
b (geh: = anziehen) to don (form)
c (= anbringen) jdm etw ~ to put sth on sb → **Zügel**
d Kartei, Akte to start; Vorräte to lay in; Garten, Gelände, Aufsatz, Bericht, Schaubild to lay out; Liste, Plan, Statistiken to draw up; Roman, Drama to structure
e (= investieren) Geld, Kapital to invest; (= ausgeben) to spend (für on)
f **es darauf ~, dass ...** to be determined that

...; **du legst es wohl auf einen Streit mit mir an** you're determined to have a fight with me, aren't you? → auch **angelegt**
VI a (Naut) to berth, to dock
b (Cards) to lay down cards/a card (bei jdm on sb's hand)
c (= Gewehr anlegen) to aim (auf +acc at)
VR **sich mit jdm ~** to pick an argument or a quarrel or a fight with sb

An•le•ge•platz M berth

An•le•ger ['anle:gɐ] M **-s, -**, **An•le•ge•rin** [-ərɪn] F **-, -nen** (Fin) investor

An•le•ge-: An•le•ge•steg M jetty, landing stage; **An•le•ge•stel•le** F mooring

an•leh•nen sep **VT** to lean or rest (an +acc against); Tür, Fenster to leave ajar, to leave slightly open; **angelehnt sein** (Tür, Fenster) to be ajar, to be slightly open **VR** (lit) to lean (an +acc against); **sich an etw** (acc) ~ (fig) to follow sth

An•leh•nung F **-, -en a** (= Stütze) support (an +acc of); (= Anschluss) dependence (an +acc on); **~ an jdn suchen** to seek sb's support **b** (= Imitation) following (an jdn/etw sb/sth); **in ~ an jdn/etw** following sb/sth

An•leh•nungs-: An•leh•nungs•be•dürf•nis NT need of loving care; **an•leh•nungs•be•dürf•tig** ADJ in need of loving care

an•lei•ern VT sep (inf: = in die Wege leiten) to get going

An•lei•he F , (Sw) **An•lei•hen** ['anlaɪən] NT **-s, - a** (Fin) (= Geldaufnahme) loan; (= Wertpapier) bond; **eine ~ aufnehmen** to take out a loan; **bei jdm eine ~ machen** to borrow (money) from sb **b** (von geistigem Eigentum) borrowing; **bei jdm eine ~ machen** (hum inf) to borrow from sb

An•lei•he-: An•lei•he•ka•pi•tal NT (Fin) loan capital; **An•lei•he•pa•pier** NT (Fin) bond; **An•lei•he•schuld** F (Fin) bonded debt

an•lei•men VT sep to stick on (an +acc or dat -to); **jdn ~** (inf: = foppen) to pull sb's leg; (= betrügen) to do sb (inf)

an•lei•nen ['anlaɪnən] VT sep (= festmachen) to tie up; (fig) to keep tied to one's apron strings; **den Hund ~** to put the dog's lead (esp Brit) or leash on, to put the dog on the lead (esp Brit) or leash; **den Hund an etw** (acc or dat) ~ to tie the dog to sth

an•lei•ten VT sep **a** (= unterweisen) to show, to teach, to instruct; **jdn bei einer Arbeit ~** to teach sb a job, to show sb how to do a job **b** (= erziehen) jdn zu etw ~ to teach sb sth; **jdn zu selbstständigem Denken ~** to teach sb to think for himself/herself

An•lei•tung F (= Erklärung, Hilfe) instructions pl; **unter der ~ seines Vaters** under his father's guidance or direction

An•lern•be•ruf M semiskilled job

an•ler•nen VT sep **a** (= ausbilden) to train **b** (= oberflächlich lernen) **sich** (dat) **etw ~** to learn sth up → auch **angelernt**

An•lern•ling ['anlɛrnlɪŋ] M **-s, -e** trainee

an•le•sen VT sep irreg **a** Buch, Aufsatz to begin or start reading; **das angelesene Buch** the book I have/she has etc started reading **b** (= aneignen) **sich** (dat) **etw ~** to learn sth by reading; **angelesenes Wissen** knowledge which comes straight out of books

an•leuch•ten VT sep jdn ~ to shine a light/lamp etc at sb; **jdn mit etw ~** to shine sth at sb

an•lie•fern VT sep to deliver

An•lie•fe•rung F delivery

an•lie•gen VI sep irreg **a** (= anstehen, vorliegen) to be on **b** (Kleidung) to fit closely or tightly (an etw (dat) sth); (Haar) to lie flat (an +dat against, on) **c** (Naut) **den richtigen Kurs ~** to be (headed) on the right course

An•lie•gen ['anli:gn] NT **-s, - a** (= Bitte) request **b** (= wichtige Angelegenheit) matter of concern

an•lie•gend ADJ **a** Ohren flat; (eng) ~ (Kleidung) tight-fitting, close-fitting **b** (in Briefen) enclosed **c** Grundstück adjacent

An•lie•ger ['anli:gɐ] M **-s, -**, **An•lie•ge•rin** [-ərɪn] F **-, -nen** neighbour (Brit), neighbor (US); (= Anwohner) (local) resident; **die ~ der Nordsee** the countries bordering (on) the North Sea; **~ frei, frei für ~** residents only

An•lie•ger-: An•lie•ger•staat M **die ~en des Schwarzen Meers** the countries bordering (on) the Black Sea; **An•lie•ger•ver•kehr** M (local) residents' vehicles pl; „Anliegerverkehr frei" "residents only"

an•lin•sen ['anlɪnzn] VT sep (inf) to take a sly look at; **jdn aus den Augenwinkeln ~** to look at sb out of the corner of one's eye

an•lo•cken VT sep Touristen to attract; Vögel, Tiere auch to lure

An•lo•ckung F attraction

an•lö•ten VT sep to solder on (an +acc or dat -to)

an•lü•gen VT sep irreg to lie to, to tell lies to

an•lu•ven VT sep (Naut) to luff

Anm. abbr von **Anmerkung**

An•ma•che F (sl) chatting-up (inf); (= Spruch) chat-up line (inf); **sexuelle ~** advances pl

an•ma•chen VT sep **a** (inf: = befestigen) to put up (an +acc or dat on) **b** (= zubereiten) to mix; Salat to dress **c** (= anstellen) Radio, Licht, Heizung etc to put or turn on; Feuer to light **d** (inf) (= ansprechen) to chat up (Brit inf), to put the moves on (US inf); (= scharf machen) to turn on (inf); (sl: = belästigen) to harass; **mach mich nicht an** leave me alone (sl: sexuell) to turn on (inf); **der Typ macht mich total an** that guy really turns me on (inf) **f** (sl: = kritisieren) to slam (inf)

an•mah•nen VT sep to send a reminder about

An•mah•nung F (Econ) notice, reminder

an•mai•len ['anme:ln] VT sep to e-mail

an•ma•len sep **VT a** (= bemalen) Wand, Gegenstand to paint; (= ausmalen) to colour (Brit) or color (US) **b** (= anstreichen) to paint (an +acc on) **c** (= schminken) **sich** (dat) **die Lippen/Lider** etc ~ to paint one's lips/eyelids etc; **sich** (dat) **einen Schnurrbart/Sommersprossen** ~ to paint a moustache (Brit) or mustache (US)/freckles on one's face or on oneself **VR** (pej: = schminken) to paint one's face or oneself

An•marsch M , no pl (= Weg) walk (there); (Mil) advance; **im ~ sein** to be advancing (auf +acc on); (hum inf) to be on the way

an•mar•schie•ren ptp **anmarschiert** VI sep aux sein (Mil) to advance; **anmarschiert kommen** to come marching along or (auf einen zu) up

An•marsch•weg M walk

an•ma•ßen ['anma:sn] VT sep **sich** (dat) **etw ~** (Befugnis, Recht) to claim sth (for oneself); Kritik to take sth upon oneself; Titel, Macht, Autorität to assume sth; **sich** (dat) **ein Urteil/eine Meinung über etw** (acc) ~ to presume to pass judgement on/have an opinion about sth; **sich** (dat) **~, etw zu tun** to presume to do sth

an•ma•ßend ADJ presumptuous

An•ma•ßung F **-, -en** presumption, presumptuousness; **mit seinen ständigen ~en machte er sich viele Feinde** his presumptuousness made him many enemies; **es ist eine ~ zu meinen, ...** it is presumptuous to maintain that ...

an•me•ckern VT sep (inf) to keep on at (inf)

An•mel•de-: An•mel•de•be•schei•ni•gung F , **An•mel•de•be•stä•ti•gung** F (resident's) registration document; **An•mel•de•for•mu•lar** NT application form; **An•mel•de•frist** F registration period; **An•mel•de•ge•bühr** F registration fee

an•mel•den sep **VT a** (= ankündigen) Besuch to announce; **einen Freund bei jdm ~** to let sb know that a friend is coming to visit **b** (bei Schule, Kurs etc) to enrol (Brit), to enroll

(*US*) (*bei* at, *zu* for)

c (= *eintragen lassen*) *Patent* to apply for; *neuen Wohnsitz, Auto, Untermieter* to register (*bei* at); *Fernseher* to get a licence (*Brit*) or license (*US*) for; *Waffe* to register; **Konkurs ~** to declare oneself bankrupt

d (= *vormerken lassen*) to make an appointment for

e (*Telec*) **ein Gespräch nach Deutschland ~** to book a call to Germany

f (= *geltend machen*) *Recht, Ansprüche* to declare; (*zu Steuerzwecken, bei Zoll*) to declare; *Bedenken, Zweifel, Protest* to register; *Wünsche, Bedürfnisse* to make known; **ich melde starke Bedenken an** I have serious doubts about that, I'm very doubtful *or* dubious about that

VR a (= *ankündigen*) (*Besucher*) to announce one's arrival; (*im Hotel*) to book (in); (*fig*) (*Baby*) to be on the way; (*Probleme, Zweifel etc*) to appear on the horizon; **sich bei jdm ~** to tell sb one is coming

b (*an Schule, zu Kurs etc*) to enrol (*Brit*) or enroll (*US*) (oneself) (*an +dat* at, *zu* for); **sich polizeilich ~** to register with the police

c (= *sich einen Termin geben lassen*) to make an appointment; **sich beim Arzt** *etc* **~** to make an appointment at the doctor's *etc* or with the doctor *etc*

Ạn|mel|de-: Ạn|mel|de|pflicht F (*für Fernsehgerät, Hund*) compulsory licensing; (*für Auto, Untermieter, Ausländer, Waffe*) compulsory registration; (*für Einfuhr*) compulsory notification; **ạn|mel|de|pflich|tig** [-pflɪçtɪç] ADJ **~ sein** (*Fernsehgerät, Hund*) to have to be licensed; (*Auto, Untermieter, Ausländer, Waffe*) to have to be registered; (*Einfuhr*) to be notifiable; **Ạn|mel|de|schein** M registration form; **Ạn|mel|de|schluss** ▲ M deadline *or* closing date for registration(s); **Ạn|mel|de|stel|le** F registration office; **Ạn|mel|de|ter|min** M deadline for registration(s); **Ạn|mel|de|ver|fah|ren** NT registration procedure

Ạn|mel|dung F **a** (*von Besuch*) announcement; (*im Hotel*) booking; (*an Schule, zu Kurs etc*) enrolment (*Brit*), enrollment (*US*) (*an +dat* at, *zu* for); (*bei Polizei*) registration; (*beim Arzt etc*) making an appointment; **die ~ eines Gespräches** booking a call; **nur nach vorheriger ~** by appointment only **b** (*von Patent*) application (*von, +gen* for); (*von Auto*) registration; (*von Fernseher*) licensing **c** (= *Anmelderaum*) reception

Ạn|mel|dungs|for|mu|lar NT , **Ạn|mel|dungs|vor|druck** M registration form

ạn+mer|ken VT *sep* (= *sagen*) to say; (= *anstreichen*) to mark; (*als Fußnote*) to note; **sich** (*dat*) **etw ~** to make a note of sth, to note sth down; **jdm seine Verlegenheit** *etc* **~** to notice sb's embarrassment *etc* or that sb is embarrassed *etc*; **sich** (*dat*) **etw ~ lassen** to let sb show; **man merkt ihm nicht an, dass ...** you wouldn't know *or* you can't tell that he ...

Ạn|mer|kung ['anmɛrkʊŋ] F **-, -en** (= *Erläuterung*) note; (= *Fußnote*) (foot)note; (*iro:* = *Kommentar*) remark, comment

ạn+mes|sen VT *sep irreg* **jdm etw ~** (*geh*) to measure sb for sth

ạn+mie|ten VT *sep* to rent; *Auto etc auch* to hire

ạn|mit ['anmɪt] ADV (*Sw*) herewith

ạn+mon|tie|ren *ptp* **ạnmontiert** VT *sep* to fix on (*an +acc or dat* -to)

ạn+mo|sern VT *sep* (*inf*) to have a (real) go at (*esp Brit inf*), to tear *or* lay into

ạn+mot|zen VT *sep* (*inf*) to have a (real) go at (*esp Brit inf*), to tear *or* lay into, to yell at

ạn+mus|tern VTI (*Naut*) to sign on

Ạn|mut ['anmuːt] F **-,** *no pl* grace; (= *Grazie auch*) gracefulness; (= *Schönheit*) beauty, loveliness; (*von Landschaft, Gegenständen*) charm, beauty

ạn+mu|ten *sep* **VT** (*geh*) to appear, to seem (*jdn* to sb); **jdn seltsam ~** to appear *or* seem odd to sb; **es mutete ihn wie ein Traum an** it seemed like a dream to him **VI es mutet son-**

---

derbar an it is *or* seems curious; **eine eigenartig ~de Geschichte** a story that strikes one as odd

ạn|mu|tig ADJ (*geh*) (= *geschmeidig, behende*) Bewegung graceful; (= *hübsch anzusehen*) lovely, charming

ạn|mut(s)- (*geh*): **ạn|mut(s)|los** ADJ graceless, lacking grace; (= *nicht hübsch*) lacking charm; **ạn|mut(s)|voll** ADJ *Lächeln* lovely, charming; (= *geschmeidig, behände*) graceful

ạn+na|geln VT *sep* to nail on (*an +acc or dat* -to); **er stand wie angenagelt da** he stood there rooted to the spot

ạn+na|gen VT *sep* to gnaw (at); (*fig*) *Ersparnisse etc* to gnaw away at, to nibble away at

ạn+nä|hen VT *sep* to sew on (*an +acc or dat* -to)

ạn+nä|hern *sep* **VT** to bring closer (*+dat, an +acc* to); (= *in größere Übereinstimmung bringen auch*) to bring more into line (*+dat, an +acc* with); **zwei Standpunkte so weit als möglich ~** to bring two points of view as much into line (with each other) as possible **VR a** (*lit, fig:* = *sich nähern*) to approach (*einer Sache* (*dat*) sth) **b** (= *sich angleichen, näher kommen*) to come closer (*+dat, an +acc* to)

ạn|nä|hernd ADJ (= *ungefähr*) approximate, rough ADV (= *etwa*) roughly; (= *fast*) almost; **können Sie mir den Betrag ~ nennen?** can you give me an approximate *or* a rough idea of the amount?; **nicht ~** not nearly, nothing like; **nicht ~ so viel** not nearly as much, nothing like as much

Ạn|nä|he|rung F (*lit:* = *das Näherkommen*, *fig:* = *Angleichung*) approach (*an +acc* towards); (*von Standpunkten*) convergence (*+dat, an +acc* with); **eine ~ an die Wirklichkeit** an approximation of reality; **die ~ zwischen Ost und West** the rapprochement of East and West; **die ~ von zwei Menschen** two people coming closer together; **die ~ an den Partner** coming closer to one's partner

Ạn|nä|he|rungs-: Ạn|nä|he|rungs|po|li|tik F policy of rapprochement; **Ạn|nä|he|rungs|ver|such** M overtures *pl* → **plump**; **ạn|nä|he|rungs|wei|se** ADV approximately; **Ạn|nä|he|rungs|wert** M (*Math*) approximate value

Ạn|nah|me ['anaːmə] ❂ **39.1, 42.2** F **-, -n a** (= *Vermutung, Voraussetzung*) assumption; **in der ~, dass ...** on the assumption that ...; **gehe ich recht in der ~, dass ...?** am I right in assuming *or* in the assumption that ...?; **der ~ sein, dass ...** to assume that ...; **von einer ~ ausgehen** to work on *or* from an assumption

b (= *das Annehmen*) acceptance; (*von Geld*) acceptance, taking; (*von Rat, Telegramm, Gespräch, Reparaturen*) taking; (*von Arbeit, Auftrag, Bewerber*) acceptance, taking on; (*von Herausforderung, Angebot*) taking up; (= *Billigung*) approval; (*von Gesetz*) passing; (*von Resolution, Staatsangehörigkeit*) adoption; (*von Antrag*) acceptance; (*von Gewohnheit*) picking up; (*von Akzent, Tonfall*) acquisition; (*von Gestalt, Name*) assuming; **~ an Kindes statt** (child) adoption

c = **Annahmestelle**

Ạn|nah|me-: Ạn|nah|me|be|stä|ti|gung F acknowledgement of receipt; **Ạn|nah|me|er|klä|rung** F (*Econ*) notice *or* declaration of acceptance; **Ạn|nah|me|frist** F **~ bis zum 17. Juli** closing date 17th July; **die ~ für die Bewerbung ist schon vorbei** applications can no longer be accepted; **Ạn|nah|me|schluss** ▲ M closing date; **Ạn|nah|me|stel|le** F (*für Pakete, Telegramme*) counter; (*für Wetten, Lotto, Toto etc*) place where bets *etc* are accepted; (*für Reparaturen*) reception; (*für Material*) delivery point; **die ~ für Autobatterien ist ...** please bring your old car batteries to ..., old car batteries will be taken at ...; **Ạn|nah|me|ver|wei|ge|rung** F refusal; **bei ~** when delivery is refused

Ạn|na|len [a'naːlən] PL annals *pl*; **in die ~ eingehen** (*fig*) to go down in the annals *or* in history

---

ạn|nehm|bar ADJ acceptable; (= *nicht schlecht*) reasonable, not bad; **sein altes Auto hat noch einen ~en Preis erzielt** he didn't get a bad price *or* he got a reasonable price for his old car ADV reasonably well

Ạn|nehm|bar|keit ['anneːmbaːɐ̯kait] F **-, -en** acceptability

ạn+neh|men *sep irreg* ❂ **27.3, 29.2, 46.6, 52.1, 53.1, 53.2, 53.6 VT a** (= *entgegennehmen, akzeptieren*) to accept; *Geld* to accept, to take; *Nahrung, einen Rat, Telegramm, Gespräch, Telefonat, Lottoschein, Reparaturen* to take; *Arbeit, Auftrag* to accept, to take on; *Herausforderung, Angebot* to take up, to accept → **Vernunft**

b (= *billigen*) to approve; *Gesetz* to pass; *Resolution* to adopt; *Antrag* to accept

c (= *sich aneignen*) *Sitte, Gewohnheit etc* to pick up, to adopt; *Staatsangehörigkeit* to take on, to adopt; *Akzent, Tonfall* to acquire, to take on; *Gestalt, Namen* to assume, to take on; **ein angenommener Name** an assumed name

d (= *zulassen*) *Patienten, Bewerber* to accept, to take on

e (= *adoptieren*) to adopt; **jdn an Kindes statt ~** to adopt sb

f (= *aufnehmen*) *Farbe* to take; **dieser Stoff/das Gefieder nimmt kein Wasser an** this material is/the feathers are water-repellent

g (= *vermuten*) to presume, to assume; **von jdm etw ~** (= *erwarten*) to expect sth of sb; (= *glauben*) to believe sth of sb; **er ist nicht so dumm, wie man es von ihm ~ könnte** he's not as stupid as you might think *or* suppose

h (= *voraussetzen*) to assume; **wir wollen ~, dass ...** let us assume that ...; **etw als gegeben** *or* **Tatsache ~** to take sth as read *or* for granted; **das kann man wohl ~** you can take that as read → *auch* **angenommen**

i (*Sport*) to take

VR sich jds ~ to look after sb; **sich einer Sache** (*gen*) **~** to see to *or* look after a matter

ạn|nehm|lich ['anneːmlɪç] ADJ agreeable; *Bedingungen* acceptable

Ạn|nehm|lich|keit F **-, -en a** (= *Bequemlichkeit*) convenience; (= *Vorteil*) advantage **b** **Annehmlichkeiten** PL comforts *pl*

an|nek|tie|ren [anɛk'tiːrən] *ptp* **annektiert** VT to annex

An|nek|tie|rung F **-, -en** annexation

Ạn|nex [a'nɛks] M **-es, -e** (*Archit*) annexe (*Brit*), annex (*US*); (*Jur*) annex, appendix

An|ne|xi|on [anɛ'ksioːn] F **-, -en** annexation

ạn+nie|sen VT *sep* to sneeze over *or* on

ạn+nie|ten VT *sep* to rivet on (*an +acc or dat* -to)

ạn|no ['ano] ADV in (the year); **der härteste Winter seit ~ zwölf** the coldest winter since 1912; **ein harter Winter, wie ~ 81** a cold winter, like the winter of '81; **von ~ dazumal** *or* **dunnemals** *or* **Tobak** (*all inf*) from the year dot (*Brit inf*), forever; **das war im Deutschland von ~ dazumal so üblich** that was the custom in Germany in olden days; **ein Überbleibsel von ~ dazumal** *or* **dunnemals** *or* **Tobak** (*all inf*) a hangover from the olden days; **~ dazumal** *or* **dunnemals war alles viel billiger** in those days everything was much cheaper

Ạn|no Do|mi|ni ['ano 'doːmini] ADV in the year of Our Lord

An|non|ce [a'nõːsə] F **-, -n** advertisement, advert (*Brit inf*), ad (*inf*)

An|non|cen|teil [a'nõːsn-] M classified (advertisement) section

an|non|cie|ren [anõ'siːrən, anɔn'siːrən] *ptp* **annonciert** VI to advertise VT to advertise; (*geh:* = *ankündigen*) *Veröffentlichung, Heirat etc* to announce

an|nul|lie|ren [anʊ'liːrən] *ptp* **annulliert** VT (*Jur*) to annul

An|nul|lie|rung F **-, -en** annulment

A|no|de [a'noːdə] F **-, -n** anode

an+öden ['anløːdn] VT sep (inf: = langweilen) to bore stiff (inf) or to tears (inf)

a|no|mal [ano'maːl, 'anomaːl] ADJ (= regelwidrig) unusual, abnormal; (= nicht normal) strange, odd

A|no|ma|lie [anoma'liː] F -, -n [-'liːən] anomaly; (Med: = Missbildung) abnormality

a|no|nym [ano'nyːm] ADJ anonymous; **Anonyme Alkoholiker** Alcoholics Anonymous ADV anonymously; **~ angerufen werden** to get anonymous phone calls

a|no|ny|mi|sie|ren [anonymi'ziːrən] ptp **anonymisiert** VT (Admin) Daten, Fragebögen to make anonymous

A|no|ny|mi|sie|rung F -, -en (Admin) **die ~ der Daten ist erforderlich** data must be made anonymous

A|no|ny|mi|tät [anonymi'tɛːt] F -, no pl anonymity; **er wollte die ~ wahren** he wanted to preserve his anonymity

A|no|ny|mus [a'noːnymʊs] M -, **Anonymi** or **Anonymen** [-mi, -mən] anonym (rare), anonymous artist/author etc

A|no|rak ['anorak] M -s, -s anorak

an+ord|nen VT sep **a** (= befehlen, festsetzen) to order **b** (= nach Plan ordnen, aufstellen) to arrange; (systematisch) to order

An|ord|nung F **a** (= Befehl) order; **laut (polizeilicher) ~** by order (of the police); **auf ~ des Arztes** on doctor's orders; **~en treffen** to give orders **b** (= Aufstellung) arrangement; (= systematische Anordnung) order; (= Formation) formation; **in welcher ~ wollen Sie die Tische für die Konferenz?** how do you want the tables arranged for the conference?

A|no|re|xie [anore'ksiː] F -, -n [-'ksiːən] anorexia (nervosa)

an|or|ga|nisch ['anɔrɡaːnɪʃ, anɔr'ɡaːnɪʃ] ADJ **a** (Chem) inorganic **b** (rare) haphazard; Wachstum random attr ADV **die Stadt ist ~ gewachsen** the town has grown in a haphazard way

a|nor|mal ['anɔrmaːl] ADJ (inf) = anomal

an+pa|cken sep (inf) VT **a** (= anfassen) to take hold of, to grab **b** (= handhaben, beginnen) Problem, Thema to tackle, to set about **c** (= umgehen mit jdn) to treat VI (= helfen: auch **mit anpacken**) to lend a hand

an+pap|pen sep (inf) VT **to stick on** (an +dat -to) VI aux sein to stick (an +dat to)

an+pas|sen sep VT **a** Kleidung to fit (+dat on); Bauelemente to fit (+dat to) **b** (= abstimmen) **etw einer Sache** (dat) **~** to suit sth to sth **c** (= angleichen) **etw einer Sache** (dat) **~** to bring sth into line with sth VR to adapt (oneself) (+dat to); (gesellschaftlich) to conform; **Kinder passen sich leichter an als Erwachsene** children adapt (themselves) more easily or are more adaptable than adults; **wir mussten uns ihren Wünschen ~** we had to fit in with their wishes or with them → auch **angepasst**

An|pas|sung F -, -en (an +acc to) adaptation; (von Gehalt etc) adjustment; (an Gesellschaft, Normen etc) conformity

An|pas|sungs-: **an|pas|sungs|fä|hig** ADJ adaptable; **An|pas|sungs|fä|hig|keit** F adaptability; **An|pas|sungs|me|cha|nis|mus** M (Sociol) adaptation mechanism; **An|pas|sungs|schwie|rig|kei|ten** PL difficulties pl in adapting; **An|pas|sungs|ver|mö|gen** NT (Sociol) adaptability

an+pei|len VT sep (= ansteuern) to steer or head for; (mit Radar, Funk etc) to take a bearing on; **etw ~** (fig inf) to set or have one's sights on sth; **jdn ~** (inf) to eye sb

an+peit|schen VT sep to push (hard); **von der Menge angepeitscht** driven or pushed on by the crowd

An|peit|scher ['anpaitʃɐ] M -s, -, **An|peit|sche|rin** [-ərɪn] F -, -nen slave-driver; (fig) rabble-rouser

an+pe|sen VI sep aux sein (inf) **angepest kommen** to come belting along or (auf einen zu) up (inf)

an+pfei|fen sep irreg **VI** (Sport) to blow the whistle **VT a** (Sport) **das Spiel ~** to start the game (by blowing one's whistle) **b** (inf) to bawl out (inf)

An|pfiff M **a** (Sport) (starting) whistle; (= Spielbeginn) (Ftbl) kickoff; (Eishockey) face-off **b** (inf) bawling out (inf)

an+pflan|zen VT sep (= bepflanzen) to plant; (= anbauen) to grow

An|pflan|zung F **a** no pl (= das Bepflanzen) planting; (= Anbau) growing **b** (Fläche) cultivated area; **eine ~ anlegen** to lay out an area for cultivation

an+pflau|men ['anpflaumən] VT sep (inf) to poke fun at; (aggressiv) to have a go at (inf)

an+pflo|cken ['anpflɔkn] VT sep to tie up; Tier auch to tether

an+piep|sen VT sep (Telec inf) to page, to bleep (Brit), to beep (US)

an+pin|keln VT sep (inf) to pee on (inf); (fig: = kritisieren) to put down

an+pin|nen ['anpɪnən] VT sep (N Ger inf) to pin up (an +acc or dat on)

an+pin|seln VT sep to paint; Parolen etc to paint (up)

an+pir|schen sep **VT** to stalk **VR** to creep up (an +acc on)

An|pö|be|lei F (inf) rudeness no pl

an+pö|beln VT sep (inf) to be rude to

an+po|chen VI sep to knock (an +acc on, at); **bei jdm ~, ob ...** (inf) to sound sb out (as to) whether ...

An|prall M impact; **beim ~ gegen** on impact with

an+pral|len VI sep aux sein to crash (an or gegen jdn/etw into sb/against sth)

an+pran|gern ['anpraŋɐn] VT sep to denounce; **jdn als Betrüger/etw als Korruption ~** to denounce sb as a fraud/sth as corrupt

An|pran|ge|rung F -, -en denunciation

an+prei|sen VT sep irreg to extol (jdm etw sth to sb); **sich (als etw) ~** to sell oneself (as sth)

an+pre|schen VI sep aux sein **angeprescht kommen** to come hurrying along or (auf einen zu) up

an+pres|sen VT sep to press on (an +acc -to); **das Ohr an die Tür ~** to press or put one's ear to the door

An|pro|be F **a** fitting **b** (= Raum) (im Kaufhaus) changing room; (beim Schneider) fitting room

an+pro|bie|ren ptp **anprobiert** sep **VT** to try on; **jdm etw ~** (inf) to try sth on sb **VI** (beim Schneider) to have a fitting; **kann ich mal ~?** can I try this/it etc on?; **ich muss noch ~** I'll have to try it on

an+pum|pen VT sep (inf) to borrow from; **jdn um 50 Euro ~** to touch sb for 50 euros (Brit inf), to hit sb up for 50 euros (US inf), to borrow 50 euros from sb

an+pus|ten VT sep (inf) to blow at; Feuer to blow on

an+quas|seln VT sep (inf) to speak to

an+quat|schen ['ankvatʃn] VT sep (inf) to speak to; Mädchen to chat up (Brit inf), to put the moves on (US inf)

An|rai|ner ['anrainɐ] M -s, -, **An|rai|ne|rin** [-ərɪn] F -, -nen **a** neighbour (Brit), neighbor (US); **die ~ der Nordsee** the countries bordering (on) the North Sea **b** (esp Aus: = Anwohner) (local) resident

An|rai|ner-: **An|rai|ner|grund|stück** NT neighbouring (Brit) or neighboring (US) property; **An|rai|ner|staat** M **die ~en des Mittelmeers/der Donau** the countries bordering (on) the Mediterranean/the Danube

an+ran|zen ['anrantsn] VT sep (inf) to bawl out (inf)

An|ran|zer ['anrantsɐ] M -s, - (inf) bawling out (inf)

an+ra|sen VI sep aux sein **angerast kommen** to come tearing or rushing along or (auf einen zu) up

an+ra|ten ○ 29.2 VT sep irreg **jdm etw ~** to recommend sth to sb; **auf Anraten des Arztes** etc on the doctor's etc advice or recommendation

an+rat|tern VI sep aux sein **angerattert kommen** to come clattering or rattling along or (auf einen zu) up

an+rau|chen VT sep Zigarre etc to light (up); **eine angerauchte Zigarette** a partly or half-smoked cigarette

an+räu|chern VT sep to smoke lightly

an+rau|en ▲, **an+rau|hen** △ VT sep to roughen; **angeraut sein** to be rough

an+raun|zen VT sep (inf) to tell off, to tick off (Brit inf)

An|raun|zer ['anrauntsɐ] M -s, - (inf) telling off, ticking off (Brit inf)

an+rau|schen VI sep aux sein **angerauscht kommen** to come rushing or hurrying along or (auf einen zu) up

an|re|chen|bar ADJ countable; **auf etw** (acc) **~ sein** to count toward(s) sth

an+rech|nen VT sep **a** (= in Rechnung stellen) to charge for (jdm sb); **das wird Ihnen später angerechnet** you'll be charged for that later, that will be charged to you later **b** (= gutschreiben) to count, to take into account (jdm for sb); **das alte Auto rechnen wir (Ihnen) mit EUR 500 an** we'll allow (you) EUR 500 for the old car; **den alten Fernseher ~** to allow something on the old television **c** (= bewerten) **dem Schüler wird die schlechte Arbeit nicht angerechnet** the pupil's bad piece of work is not being taken into account; **jdm etw hoch ~** to think highly of sb for sth; **jdm etw als Fehler ~** (Lehrer) to count sth as a mistake for sb; (fig) to consider sth as a fault on sb's part; **ich rechne es ihm als Verdienst an, dass ...** I think it is greatly to his credit that ..., I think it says a lot for him that ...; **ich rechne es mir zur Ehre an** (form) I consider it an honour (Brit) or an honor (US), I consider myself honoured (Brit) or honored (US)

An|rech|nung F allowance; (fig: = Berücksichtigung) counting, taking into account (auf +acc towards); **jdm etw in ~ bringen** or **stellen** (form) to charge sb for sth

an|rech|nungs|fä|hig ADJ = anrechenbar

An|recht NT **a** (= Anspruch) right, entitlement (auf +acc to); **ein ~ auf etw** (acc) **haben** or **besitzen** (auf Respekt, Ruhe etc) to be entitled to sth; auf Geld, Land etc auch to have a right to sth; **sein ~ (auf etw) geltend machen** to enforce one's right (to sth) **b** (= Abonnement) subscription

An|re|de F form of address; (= Briefanrede auch) salutation (form)

An|re|de|fall M , **An|re|de|ka|sus** M (Gram) vocative (case)

an+re|den sep **VT** to address; **jdn mit „du" ~** to address sb as "du", to use the "du" form (of address) to sb; **jdn mit seinem Titel ~** to address sb by his title **VI gegen jdn ~** to argue against sb; **gegen etw ~** to make oneself heard against sth

an+re|gen VT sep **a** (= ermuntern) to prompt (zu to); **jdn zum Denken ~** to make sb think **b** (geh: = vorschlagen) Verbesserung to propose, to suggest **c** (= beleben) to stimulate; Appetit to whet, to sharpen; **Kaffee** etc **regt an** coffee etc is a stimulant, coffee etc has a stimulating effect → auch **angeregt d** (Phys) to activate

an|re|gend ADJ stimulating; **ein ~es Mittel** a stimulant; **die Verdauung/den Kreislauf ~e Mit-**

tel stimulants to the digestion/circulation **ADV** ~ **wirken** to have a stimulating effect

An|re|gung F **a** (= *Antrieb, Impuls*) stimulus; **jdm eine ~ zum Denken geben** to make sb think **b** (= *Vorschlag*) idea; **auf ~ von** or *+gen* at or on the suggestion of **c** (= *Belebung*) stimulation

An|re|gungs|mit|tel NT stimulant

an+rei|chen VT *sep* to pass, to hand

an+rei|chern ['anraiçɐn] *sep* **VT** (= *gehaltvoller machen*) to enrich; (= *vergrößern*) *Sammlung* to enlarge, to increase; **hoch/niedrig** or **schwach angereichertes Uran** high/low enriched uranium; **das Gemisch mit Sauerstoff ~** (= *zufügen*) to add oxygen to the mixture; **angereichert werden** (*Chem*: = *gespeichert werden*) to be accumulated; **mit Rauch angereicherte Luft** smoky air **VR** (*Chem*) to accumulate

An|rei|che|rung F **-, -en** (= *Bereicherung*) enrichment; (= *Vergrößerung*) enlargement; (= *Speicherung*) accumulation; (*von Uran*) enriching

an+rei|hen *sep* **VT** **a** (= *einer Reihe anfügen*) to add (*an +acc* to) **b** (= *anheften*) to tack on; *Saum* to tack (up) **VR** to follow (*einer Sache* (*dat*) sth); **reihen Sie sich bitte hinten an!** join the end of the queue (*Brit*) or line (*US*), please

An|rei|se F **a** (= *Anfahrt*) journey there/here; **die ~ zu diesem abgelegenen Ort ist sehr mühsam** it is very difficult to get to this remote place **b** (= *Ankunft*) arrival; **Tag der ~ war Sonntag** the day of arrival was Sunday

an+rei|sen VI *sep aux sein* **a** (= *ein Ziel anfahren*) to make a/the journey or trip (there/here); **über welche Strecke wollen Sie ~?** which route do you want to take (there/here)? **b** (= *eintreffen: auch* **angereist kommen**) to come

An|rei|se|tag M day of arrival

an+rei|ßen VT *sep irreg* **a** (= *einreißen*) to tear, to rip **b** (*inf*: = *anbrechen*) to start, to open **c** *Außenbordmotor etc* to start (up) **d** (*Tech*) to mark (out) **e** (= *kurz zur Sprache bringen*) to touch on **f** (*pej inf*) *Kunden* to draw, to attract **g** *Streichholz* to strike

An|rei|ßer¹ ['anraisɐ] M **-s, -** bait

An|rei|ßer² ['anraisɐ] M **-s, -, An|rei|ße|rin** [-ərın] F **-, -nen** (*pej inf*: = *Kundenfänger*) tout

an|rei|ße|risch ADJ (*pej inf*) attention-grabbing *attr*

An|reiß|schab|lo|ne F (*Tech*) template

an+rei|ten *sep irreg* **VI** *aux sein* **angeritten kommen** to come riding along or (*auf einen zu*) up **VT** **a** *Ziel etc* to ride toward(s) **b** **gegen etw ~** (*Mil*) to charge sth

An|reiz M incentive; **ein ~ zum Lernen** *etc* an incentive to learn *etc* or for learning *etc*; **jdm den ~ nehmen, etw zu tun** to take away sb's incentive for doing sth

an+rei|zen *sep* **VT** **a** (= *anspornen*) to encourage; **jdn zum Kauf ~** to encourage sb to buy; **jdn zu großen Leistungen ~** to encourage sb to perform great feats **b** (= *erregen*) to stimulate, to excite **VI** to act as an incentive (*zu* to); **dazu ~, dass jd etw tut** to act as an incentive for sb to do sth

an+rem|peln VT *sep* **a** (= *anstoßen*) to bump into; (*absichtlich*) *Menschen* to jostle **b** (*fig*: = *beschimpfen*) to insult

an+ren|nen VI *sep irreg aux sein* **a** **gegen etw ~** (*gegen Wind etc*) to run against sth; (*Mil*) to storm sth; (*Sport*) to attack sth; (= *sich stoßen*) to run into sth; (*fig*: = *bekämpfen*) to fight against sth **b** **angerannt kommen** (*inf*) to come running

An|rich|te ['anrıçtə] F **-, -n** **a** (= *Schrank*) dresser; (= *Büfett*) sideboard **b** (= *Raum*) pantry

an+rich|ten VT *sep* **a** (= *zubereiten*) *Speisen* to prepare; (= *servieren*) to serve; *Salat* to dress; **es ist angerichtet** (*form*) dinner *etc* is served (*form*) **b** (*fig*: = *verursachen*) *Schaden, Unheil* to cause, to bring about; **etwas ~** (*inf*: = *anstellen*) to get up to something (*inf*); **da hast du aber**

etwas angerichtet! (*inf*) (= *verursachen*) you've started something there all right; (= *anstellen*) you've really made a mess there

an+rie|chen VT *sep irreg* to sniff at; **jdm/einer Sache etw ~** to be able to tell sth by smelling sb/sth; **ich rieche dir doch an, dass du geraucht hast** I can smell that you've been smoking

An|riss ▲ M (*Tech*) scribing, marking

An|ritt M (*old*) approach (on horseback) (*auf +acc* towards); (= *Angriff*) charge (*gegen* on, against)

an+rit|zen VT *sep* to slit (slightly)

an+rol|len *sep* **VI** *aux sein* (= *zu rollen beginnen*) to start to roll; (= *heranrollen*) to roll up; (*Aviat*) to taxi; **gegen etw/jdn ~** (*fig: in feindlicher Absicht*) to move against sth/sb; **angerollt kommen** to roll along or (*auf einen zu*) up **VT** to roll; (= *heranrollen*) to roll up

an+ros|ten VI *sep aux sein* to get (a bit) rusty

an+rös|ten VT *sep* to brown lightly

an|rü|chig ['anrʏçıç] ADJ **a** (= *von üblem Ruf*) *Geschäfte* disreputable; (= *berüchtigt*) *Lokal etc* notorious, disreputable **b** (= *anstößig*) offensive; (= *unanständig*) indecent

An|rü|chig|keit F **-,** *no pl* (*von Lokal etc*) notoriety; (= *Anstößigkeit*) offensiveness; (= *Unanständigkeit*) indecency; **einer Sache** (*dat*) **die ~ nehmen** to give sth an air of greater respectability; **dieser Branche haftet eine gewisse ~ an** this line of business is considered somewhat disreputable

an+rü|cken *sep* **VI** *aux sein* **a** (*Truppen*) to advance; (*Polizei etc*) to move in; (*hum: Essen, Besuch*) to turn up; **die Verwandten kamen angerückt** the relations turned up **b** (= *weiter heranrücken*) to move up or closer **VT** to move up; **etw an etw** (*acc*) **~** to push sth against sth

An|ruf M **a** (*Telec*) call **b** (*Mil: eines Wachtpostens*) challenge; **etw auf ~ tun** to do sth when called; **ohne ~ schießen** to shoot without warning

An|ruf|be|ant|wor|ter [-bəˈantvɔrtɐ] ✪ 27.6 M **-s, -** (telephone) answering machine, answerphone

an+ru|fen *sep irreg* ✪ 27 **VT** **a** (= *zurufen*) to shout to; (*Telec*) to ring (*esp Brit*), to phone, to call; (*Mil: Posten*) to challenge; **darf ich dich ~?** can I give you a ring? (*esp Brit*), can I call you?; **kann man Sie ~?** (= *haben Sie Telefon?*) are you on the phone? **b** (*fig*: = *appellieren an*) (*um* for) to appeal to; *Gott* to call on **VI** (*inf*: = *telefonieren*) to phone, to make a (phone) call/ phone calls; **bei jdm ~** to phone sb; **kann man hier bei Ihnen ~?** can I make a (phone) call from here?; **ins Ausland/nach Amerika ~** to phone abroad/America

An|ru|fer(in) M(F) caller

An|ruf|um|lei|tung F (*Telec*) call diversion

An|ru|fung F **-, -en** (*Gottes, der Heiligen etc*) invocation; (*Jur*) appeal (*+gen* to); **nach ~ des Gerichts** after an appeal to the court

an+rüh|ren VT *sep* **a** (= *berühren, sich befassen mit*) to touch; (*fig*) *Thema* to touch upon; **er rührt kein Fleisch/keinen Alkohol an** he doesn't touch meat/alcohol **b** (*fig liter*: = *rühren*) to move, to touch **c** (= *mischen*) *Farben* to mix; *Sauce* to blend; (= *verrühren*) to stir

an|rüh|rend ADJ touching

an+ru|ßen VT *sep* to blacken

ans [ans] *contr von* **an das sich ~ Arbeiten machen** or (*geh*) **begeben** to set to work; **wenn es ~ Sterben geht** when it comes to dying

an+sä|en VT *sep* to sow

An|sa|ge F announcement; (= *Diktat*) dictation; (*Cards*) bid; **er übernimmt bei diesem Programm die ~** he is doing the announcements for this programme (*Brit*) or program (*US*); **einen Brief nach ~ schreiben** to take a letter down (on dictation); **er hat die ~** (*Cards*) it's his bid

an+sa|gen *sep* **VT** **a** (= *ankündigen*) to announce; **jdm den Kampf ~** to declare war on sb → **Bankrott**

b (*Cards*) (*Bridge*) to bid; (*Skat*) to declare **c** (*inf*) **angesagt sein** (= *modisch sein*) to be in; (= *erforderlich sein*) to be called for; (= *auf dem Programm stehen*) to be the order of the day; **Spannung ist angesagt** we are in for a bit of excitement **VR** (= *Besuch ankündigen*) to say that one is coming; (= *Termin vereinbaren*) to make an appointment; (*Zeit, Frühling*) to announce itself (*liter*)

VI **a** (*old, liter*) **sag an, Fremdling ...** pray tell, stranger (*old, liter*) ... **b** **sie sagt im Radio an** she's an announcer on the radio

an+sä|gen VT *sep* to saw into

An|sa|ger ['anzaːɡɐ] M **-s, -, An|sa|ge|rin** [-ərın] F **-, -nen** (*Rad etc*) announcer; (*im Kabarett*) compère (*Brit*), emcee (*US*)

an+sam|meln *sep* **VT** **a** (= *anhäufen*) to accumulate; *Reichtümer, Erfahrung* to amass; *Vorräte* to build up; *Zinsen* to build up, to accrue (*form*) **b** (= *zusammenkommen lassen*) to gather together **VR** **a** (= *sich versammeln*) to gather, to collect **b** (= *aufspeichern, aufhäufen*) to accumulate; (*Staub*) to collect, to accumulate; (*Flüssigkeit, Schadstoffe, Fragen*) to collect; (*fig: Wut, Frust, Misstrauen*) to build up; (*Zinsen*) to build up, to accrue (*form*)

An|samm|lung F **a** (= *Anhäufung*) accumulation; (= *Sammlung*) collection; (*von Druck, Stau, Wut*) build-up; (= *Haufen*) pile **b** (= *Auflauf*) gathering, crowd; (*von Truppen*) concentration

an|säs|sig ['anzɛsıç] ADJ (*form*) resident; **eine in München ~e Firma** a firm based in Munich; **sich in London ~ machen** to settle or to take up residence (*form*) in London; **alle in diesem Ort Ansässigen** all local residents

An|satz M **a** (*von Hals, Arm, Henkel etc*) base; (*an Stirn*) hairline; (= *Haarwurzeln*) roots *pl* **b** (*Tech*) (= *Zusatzstück*) attachment; (*zur Verlängerung*) extension; (= *Naht*) join **c** (= *das Ansetzen: von Rost, Kalk etc*) formation, deposition; (= *Schicht*) coating, layer **d** (= *erstes Anzeichen, Beginn*) first sign(s *pl*), beginning(s *pl*); (= *Versuch*) attempt (*zu etw* at sth); (= *Ausgangspunkt*) starting point; **den ~ zu etw zeigen** to show the first signs or the beginnings of sth; **einen neuen ~ zu etw machen** to make a fresh attempt at sth; **Ansätze zeigen, etw zu tun** to show signs of doing sth; **sie zeigte Ansätze von Senilität** she showed signs of senility; **die ersten Ansätze** the initial stages; **im ~** basically **e** (*esp Philos, Liter etc*) approach **f** (*Sport*) takeoff; (= *Anlauf*) run-up **g** (*Math*) formulation **h** (*Mus*) intonation; (= *Lippenstellung*) embouchure **i** (*Econ form*) estimate; (= *Fonds für Sonderzwecke*) appropriation; **außer ~ bleiben** to be excluded, to be left out of account; **etw für etw in ~ bringen** to appropriate sth for sth

An|satz-: An|satz|punkt M starting point; **An|satz|stück** NT (*Tech*) attachment; (*zur Verlängerung*) extension; **an|satz|wei|se** ADV ~ **zeigen/enthalten** to show/to have the beginnings of

an+säu|ern *sep* **VT** to make sour; *Brotteig* to leaven; (*Chem*) to acidify **VI** *aux sein* to start to go sour

an+sau|fen VT *sep irreg* (*inf*) **sich** (*dat*) **einen (Rausch) ~** to get plastered or sloshed (*inf*); **sich** (*dat*) **einen Bauch ~** to get a beer belly

an+sau|gen *sep* **VT** to suck or draw in; (= *anfangen zu saugen*) to start to suck **VR** to attach itself (*by suction*)

An|saug-: An|saug|ge|blä|se NT (*Tech*) suction fan; **An|saug|lei|tung** F (*Chem*) inlet; **An|saug|rohr** NT induction pipe; (*Auto*) intake pipe

an+säu|seln VT *sep* **sich** (*dat*) **einen ~** (*hum inf*) to have a tipple (*inf*) → *auch* **angesäuselt**

an+schaf|fen *sep* **VT** **(sich** *dat*) **etw ~** to get oneself sth; (= *kaufen*) to buy sth; **sich** (*dat*) **Kinder ~** (*inf*) to have children **VI** **a** (*Aus, S Ger*) to give orders; **jdm ~** to order sb about, to give sb orders **b** (*sl: durch Prostitution*) **~ gehen** to be on the game (*inf*); **für jdn ~ gehen** to go on the game for sb (*inf*); **jdn ~** or **zum Anschaffen schicken** to send sb out on the game (*inf*)

An|schaf|fung F **a** *no pl* acquisition; **ich habe mich zur ~ eines Autos entschlossen** I have decided to get or buy a new car **b** (= *Gegenstand*) acquisition; (*gekauft*) purchase, buy; **~en machen** to acquire things; (= *kaufen*) to make purchases

An|schaf|fungs-: **An|schaf|fungs|kos|ten** PL cost *sing* of purchase; **An|schaf|fungs|kre|dit** [-kredi:t] M loan; **An|schaf|fungs|preis** M purchase price; **An|schaf|fungs|wert** M value at the time of purchase

an+schal|ten VT *sep* to switch on

an+schau|en VT *sep* (*esp dial*) to look at; (*prüfend*) to examine; **sich** (*dat*) **etw ~** to have a look at sth; (**da**) **schau einer an!** (*inf*) well I never! (*inf*)

an|schau|lich ['anʃaulıç] ADJ clear; (= *lebendig, bildhaft*) *Beschreibung* vivid; *Beispiel* concrete; **etw ~ machen** to illustrate sth; **den Unterricht sehr ~ machen** to make teaching come alive ADV clearly; (= *lebendig*) vividly

An|schau|lich|keit F -, *no pl* clearness; (= *Bildhaftigkeit*) vividness; (*von Beschreibung*) graphicness

An|schau|ung ['anʃauʊŋ] F -, -en (= *Ansicht, Auffassung*) view; (= *Meinung*) opinion; (= *Vorstellung*) idea, notion; (= *innere Versenkung*) contemplation; (= *Anschauungsvermögen*) ability to visualize things; **nach neuerer ~** according to the current way of thinking; **in ~** +*gen* (*geh*) in view of; **aus eigener ~** from one's own experience

An|schau|ungs-: **An|schau|ungs|ma|te|ri|al** NT illustrative material, visual aids *pl*; **An|schau|ungs|un|ter|richt** M visual instruction; **An|schau|ungs|ver|mö|gen** NT ability to visualize things; **An|schau|ungs|wei|se** F (*geh*) view

An|schein M appearance; (= *Eindruck*) impression; **dem ~ nach** apparently; **allem ~ nach** to all appearances, apparently; **den ~ erwecken, als ...** to give the impression that ...; **sich** (*dat*) **den ~ geben, als ob man informiert sei** to pretend to be informed; **es hat den ~, als ob ...** it appears that ..., it seems as if ...

an+schei|nen VT *sep irreg* to shine (up)on

an|schei|nend ADV apparently ADJ apparent

an+schei|ßen VT *sep irreg* **a** (*inf: = beschimpfen*) **jdn ~** to give sb a bollocking (*Brit sl*), to kick sb's ass (*US sl*) **b** (*sl: = anöden*) to piss off (*sl*)

an+sche|sen VI *sep aux sein* **angeschest kommen** (*N Ger inf*) to come tearing along or (*auf einen zu*) up (*inf*)

an+schi|cken VR *sep* **sich ~, etw zu tun** (*geh*) (= *sich bereit machen*) to get ready to do sth, to prepare to do sth; (= *im Begriff sein*) to be on the point of doing sth, to be about to do sth

an+schie|ben VT *sep irreg* **a** *Fahrzeug* to push; **können Sie mich mal ~?** can you give me a push? **b** (*fig*) *Wirtschaft, Konjunktur* to kick-start

an+schie|ßen *sep irreg* **VT** **a** (= *verletzen*) to shoot (and wound); *Vogel* (*in Flügel*) to wing; **angeschossen** (*Mensch, Tier*) shot and wounded; **wie ein Angeschossener** (*inf*) like a scalded cat (*inf*) **b** (*Sport*) *Rennen* to start **c** *Tor* to shoot at; *Spieler* to hit; (= *treffen*) *Schiff, Billardkugel* to hit **d** (*inf: = kritisieren*) to hit out at (*inf*) **VI** *aux sein* (= *heranrasen*) to shoot up; **angeschossen kommen** to come shooting along or (*auf einen zu*) up

an+schim|meln VI *sep aux sein* to (start to) go mouldy (*Brit*) or moldy (*US*)

an+schir|ren ['anʃırən] VT *sep* to harness

An|schiss ▲ M -es, -e (*inf*) bollocking (*Brit sl*), ass-kicking (*US sl*)

An|schlag M **a** (= *Plakat*) poster, bill, placard; (= *Bekanntmachung*) notice; **einen ~ machen** to put up a poster/notice
  b (= *Überfall*) attack (*auf* +*acc* on); (= *Attentat*) attempt on sb's life; (= *Verschwörung*) plot (*auf* +*acc* against); **einen ~ auf jdn verüben** to make an attempt on sb's life; **einem ~ zum Opfer fallen** to be assassinated; **einen ~ auf jdn vorhaben** (*hum: = etwas von jdm wollen*) to have a favour (*Brit*) or favor (*US*) to ask of sb
  c (= *Kostenanschlag*) estimate; **etw in ~ bringen** (*form*) to take sth into account; **eine Summe in ~ bringen** (*form*) to calculate an amount
  d (= *Aufprall*) impact
  e (*Sport*) (*beim Schwimmen*) touch; (*beim Versteckspiel*) home
  f (*von Klavier(spieler), Schreibmaschine*) touch; **200 Anschläge in der Minute** ≈ 40 words per minute
  g (*in Strickanleitung*) **~ von 20 Maschen** cast on 20 stitches
  h (*von Hund*) bark
  i (*bei Hebel, Knopf etc*) stop; **etw bis zum ~ durchdrücken** to push sth right down; **etw bis zum ~ drehen** to turn sth as far as it will go
  j (*Mil*) aiming or firing position; **ein Gewehr im ~ haben** to have a rifle at the ready

An|schlag|brett NT notice board (*esp Brit*), bulletin board (*US*)

an+schla|gen *sep irreg* **VT** **a** (= *befestigen*) to fix on (*an* +*acc* to); (*mit Nägeln*) to nail on (*an* +*acc* to); (= *aushängen*) *Plakat* to put up, to post (*an* +*acc* on)
  b *Stunde, Taste, Akkord* to strike; (= *anstimmen*) *Melodie* to strike up; (*Mus*) to play; **eine schnellere Gangart ~** (*fig*) to strike up a faster pace, to speed up; **ein anderes Thema/einen anderen Ton ~** (*fig*) to change the subject/one's tune; **einen weinerlichen/frechen Ton ~** to adopt a tearful tone/cheeky (*Brit*) or fresh (*US*) attitude
  c (= *beschädigen, verletzen*) *Geschirr* to chip; **sich** (*dat*) **den Kopf etc ~** to knock one's head etc → *auch* **angeschlagen**
  d (*Sport*) *Ball* to hit; **den Ball seitlich ~** to chip the ball
  e (*Aus: = anzapfen*) *Fass* to tap
  f (= *vormarkieren*) *Baum* to mark (for felling)
  g (= *aufnehmen*) *Maschen* to cast on
  h (*Naut*) to fasten; *Segel, Tau* to bend
  i (*geh*) *Kosten etc* to estimate
  VI **a** (*Welle*) to beat (*an* +*acc* against); **mit etw gegen/an etw** (*acc*) **~** to strike or knock sth against/on sth
  b (*Sport*) (*Tennis etc*) to serve; (*beim Schwimmen*) to touch
  c (*Glocke*) to ring
  d (= *Taste betätigen*) to strike the keys
  e (= *Laut geben*) (*Hund*) to give a bark; (*Vogel*) to give a screech
  f (= *wirken: Arznei etc*) to work, to take effect
  g (*inf: = dick machen*) **bei jdm ~** to make sb put on weight

An|schlag-: **an|schlag|frei** ADJ *Drucker* non-impact; **An|schlag|säu|le** F advertising pillar; **An|schlag|ta|fel** F notice board (*esp Brit*), bulletin board (*US*); **An|schlag|zet|tel** M notice

an+schlei|chen *sep irreg* **VI** *aux sein* to creep along or (*auf einen zu*) up; **angeschlichen kommen** (*inf*) to come creeping along/up **VR** **sich an jdn/etw ~** to creep up on sb/sth; (= *sich anpirschen*) to stalk sb/sth

an+schlei|fen VT *sep* (*inf: = herbeischleppen*) to drag along; **was schleifst du denn da für einen Plunder an?** what's that junk you're carting up? (*inf*)

an+schlen|dern VI *sep aux sein* to stroll or saunter along or (*auf einen zu*) up

an+schlep|pen VT *sep* **a** *Auto* to tow-start **b** (*inf*) (= *unerwünscht mitbringen*) to bring along; (*nach Hause*) to bring home; (= *mühsam herbeibringen*) to drag along (*inf*); (*hum: = hervorholen, anbieten*) to bring out

an+schlie|ßen *sep irreg* ◑ 38.2, 39.1, 50.1 **VT**
  a (*an* +*acc* to) (*Tech, Elec, Telec etc: = verbinden*) to connect; (*in Steckdose*) to plug in; **angeschlossen** connected(-up)
  b (*an* +*acc* to) to lock; (*mit Schnappschloss*) to padlock; (= *anketten*) to chain (up)
  c (*fig: = hinzufügen*) to add; **angeschlossen** (*Organisation etc*) affiliated (*dat* to or (*US*) with), associated (*dat* with)
  VR **sich jdm** or **an jdn ~** (= *folgen*) to follow sb; (= *zugesellen*) to join sb; (= *beipflichten*) to side with sb; **sich einer Sache** (*dat*) or **an etw** (*acc*) **~** (= *folgen*) to follow sth; (= *beitreten, sich beteiligen*) to join sth; (= *beipflichten*) to endorse sth; (= *angrenzen*) to adjoin sth; **dem Vortrag** or **an den Vortrag schloss sich ein Film an** the lecture was followed by a film
  VI **an etw** (*acc*) **~** to follow sth

an|schlie|ßend ADV afterwards ADJ following; *Ereignis, Diskussion auch* ensuing; **Essen mit ~em Tanz** dinner dance; **an einen Kurs ~e Prüfung** exam at the end of a course

An|schluss ▲ ◐ 27.7 M **a** (= *Verbindung*) connection; (= *Beitritt*) entry (*an* +*acc* into); (*an Klub*) joining (*an* +*acc* of); (*Hist euph*) Anschluss; **~ haben nach** (*Rail*) to have a connection to; **den ~ verpassen** (*Rail etc*) to miss one's connection; (*fig*) to miss the boat or bus; (*alte Jungfer*) to be left on the shelf (*inf*); **ihm gelang der ~ an die Spitze** (*Sport*) he managed to catch up with the leaders
  b (*Telec, Comput*) connection; (= *Anlage*) telephone (connection); (= *weiterer Apparat*) extension; (= *Wasseranschluss*) supply point; (*für Waschmaschine*) point; **elektrischer ~** power point; **einen ~ beantragen** (*Telec*) to apply for a telephone to be connected; **~ bekommen** (*Telec*) to get through; **der ~ ist besetzt** (*Telec*) the line is engaged (*Brit*) or busy (*esp US*); **kein ~ unter dieser Nummer** (*Telec*) number unobtainable (*Brit*), this number is not in service (*US*)
  c **im ~ an** (+*acc*) (= *nach*) subsequent to, following; (= *mit Bezug auf*) in connection with, further to; (= *in Anlehnung an*) following, after
  d (*fig*) (= *Kontakt*) contact (*an* +*acc* with); (= *Bekanntschaft*) friendship, companionship; (= *Aufnahme*) integration; **~ finden** to make friends (*an* +*acc* with); **er sucht ~** he wants to make friends

An|schluss-: **An|schluss|do|se** ▲ F **a** (*Elec*) junction box; (= *Steckdose*) socket **b** (*Telec*) connection box; **an|schluss|fer|tig** ▲ ADJ fully wired; **An|schluss|fi|nan|zie|rung** ▲ F follow-up financing; **An|schluss|flug** ▲ M connecting flight; **An|schluss|num|mer** ▲ F extension; **An|schluss|rohr** ▲ NT connecting pipe; **An|schluss|schnur** ▲ F extension lead; **An|schluss|stel|le** ▲ F (*Mot*) junction; **An|schluss|zug** ▲ M (*Rail*) connecting train, connection

an+schmach|ten VT *sep* **jdn ~** to gaze lovingly at sb

an+schmei|ßen VT *sep irreg* (*inf: = in Gang setzen*) to turn on

an+schmie|den VT *sep* to forge on (*an* +*acc* -to); (= *anketten*) to chain (*an* +*acc* to); (*fig inf: = fesseln*) to rivet (*an* +*acc* to)

an+schmie|gen *sep* **VT** to nestle (*an* +*acc* against) **VR** **sich an jdn/etw ~** (*Kind, Hund*) to snuggle or nestle up to sb/sth; (*Kleidung*) to cling to sb/sth; (*geh: Dorf an Berg etc*) to nestle against sth

an|schmieg|sam ['anʃmi:kza:m] ADJ *Wesen* affectionate; *Material* smooth

an+schmie|ren *sep* **VT** **a** (= *bemalen*) to smear **b** *jdn/sich mit etw ~* (*inf*) (= *beschmutzen*) to get sth all over sb/oneself; (*pej: = schminken*) to smear sth over sb's/one's lips/face etc **c** (*inf*)

(= *betrügen*) to con (*inf*), to take for a ride (*inf*); (= *Streiche spielen*) to play tricks on → *auch* **angeschmiert** VR **sich bei jdm ~** (*inf*) to make up to sb (*Brit inf*), to be all over sb (*inf*)

an+schmo|ren VT *sep* (*Cook*) to braise lightly

an+schnal|len *sep* VR to fasten one's seat belt; **bitte ~!** fasten your seat belts, please!; **hast du dich angeschnallt?, bist du angeschnallt?** have you fastened your seat belt?, are you strapped in? ▶ VT a *Skier* to clip on b *Person, Kind* to strap up; (*in etw*) to strap in; **jdn ~** (*Aviat, Aut*) to fasten sb's seat belt

An|schnall-: An|schnall|gurt M (*Aviat, Mot*) seatbelt; **An|schnall|pflicht** F , *no pl* mandatory wearing of seat belts; **für Kinder besteht ~** children must wear seat belts

an+schnau|ben *sep* VT to snort at; (*fig inf*: = *anschnauzen*) to bawl out (*inf*) VI *aux sein* **angeschnaubt kommen** (*inf*) to come along huffing and puffing

an+schnau|fen VI *sep aux sein* **angeschnauft kommen** to come panting along or (*auf einen zu*) up

an+schnau|zen VT *sep* (*inf*) to yell at

An|schnau|zer M (*inf*) **sich** (*dat*) **einen ~ holen, einen ~ kriegen** to get yelled at (*inf*)

an+schnei|den VT *sep irreg* a *Brot etc* to (start to) cut b (*fig*) *Frage, Thema* to touch on c (*Aut*) *Kurve* to cut; (*Sport*) *Ball* to cut d (*Archeol*) to come across

An|schnitt M (= *Schnittfläche*) cut part; (= *erstes Stück*) first slice; (= *Ende*) cut end

an+schnor|ren VT *sep* (*pej inf*) to (try to) tap (*Brit inf*) or bum (*US inf*); **jdn um etw ~** to cadge sth from sb (*Brit*), to tap sb for sth (*Brit inf*), to bum sth from sb (*US inf*)

An|scho|vis [anˈʃoːvɪs] F -, - anchovy

an+schrau|ben VT *sep* to screw on (*an +acc* -to); (= *festschrauben*) to screw tight or up

an+schrei|ben *sep irreg* VT a *Behörde, Versandhaus etc* to write to; **es antworteten nur 20% der Angeschriebenen** only 20% of the people written to replied b (= *aufschreiben*) to write up (*an +acc* on); **etw mit Kreide ~** to chalk sth up; **angeschrieben stehen** to be written up → *auch* **angeschrieben** c (*inf*: = *in Rechnung stellen*) to chalk up (*inf*) VI (*inf*) **unser Kaufmann schreibt nicht an** our grocer doesn't give anything on tick (*Brit inf*) or on credit; **sie lässt immer ~** she always buys on tick (*Brit inf*) or on credit

An|schrei|ben NT -s, - (= *Brief*) cover note, covering letter

An|schrei|be|ta|fel F scoreboard; (*Billard*) billiard marker

an+schrei|en VT *sep irreg* to shout or yell at

An|schrift F address; **ein Brief ohne ~** an unaddressed letter

An|schub|fi|nan|zie|rung [ˈanʃuːp-] F (*Econ*) start-up funds *pl*

an+schul|di|gen [ˈanʃʊldɪgn] VT *sep* to accuse (*+gen* of)

An|schul|di|gung F -, -en accusation

an+schwär|men *sep* VT (*inf*: = *verehren*) to idolize, to have a crush on (*inf*) VI *aux sein* (*auch* **angeschwärmt kommen**) to come in swarms

an+schwär|zen VT *sep* a (*fig inf*) **jdn ~** to blacken sb's name (*bei* with); (= *denunzieren*) to run sb down (*bei* to) b (*lit*) to blacken; (= *beschmutzen*) to get dirty

an+schwe|ben VI *sep aux sein* a (*Aviat*) to come in to land b (*fig*) **sie kam angeschwebt** she came floating along or (*auf einen zu*) up

an+schwei|gen VT *sep irreg* to say nothing to; (*demonstrativ*) to refuse to speak to; **sich gegenseitig ~** to say nothing to each other

an+schwei|ßen VT *sep* a (*Tech*) to weld on (*an +acc* -to) b (*Hunt*) to wound, to draw blood from

an+schwel|len VI *sep irreg aux sein* to swell (up); (*Wasser auch, Lärm*) to rise; **dick angeschwollen** very swollen

an+schwem|men *sep* VT to wash up or ashore; **angeschwemmtes Land** alluvial land VI *aux sein* to be washed up or ashore

An|schwem|mung F -, -en (*in Fluss, Hafen*) silting up

an+schwim|men *sep irreg* VT *Ziel* to swim toward(s) VI a *aux sein* **angeschwommen kommen** (*Schwimmer, Wasservogel*) to come swimming along or (*auf einen zu*) up; (*Leiche, Brett*) to come drifting along or (*auf einen zu*) up; (*Flasche*) to come floating along or (*auf einen zu*) up b *aux sein* **gegen etw ~** to swim against sth

an+schwin|deln VT *sep* (*inf*) **jdn ~** to tell sb fibs (*inf*)

an+se|geln *sep* VT (= *zusegeln auf*) to sail for or toward(s), to make for; (= *anlegen in*) *Hafen* to put into VI *aux sein* **angesegelt kommen** (*inf*: *lit, fig*) to come sailing along or (*auf einen zu*) up

an+se|hen VT *sep irreg* a (= *betrachten*) to look at; **er sah mich ganz verwundert an** he looked at me with great surprise; **er sah mich ganz groß an** he stared at me; **er sah mich ganz böse an** he gave me an angry look; **hübsch/schrecklich** etc **anzusehen** pretty/terrible etc to look at; **jdn nicht mehr ~** (*fig inf*) not to want to know sb any more; **sieh mal einer an!** (*inf*) well, I never! (*inf*) b (*fig*) to regard, to look upon (*als, für* as); **ich sehe es als meine Pflicht an** I consider it to be my duty; **sie sieht ihn nicht für voll an** she doesn't take him seriously → *auch* **angesehen** c (*sich* (*dat*)) **etw ~** (= *besichtigen*) to (have a) look at sth; *Fernsehsendung* to watch sth; *Film, Stück, Sportveranstaltung* to see sth; **sich** (*dat*) **jdn/etw gründlich ~** (*lit, fig*) to take a close look at sb/sth; **sich** (*dat*) **die Welt ~** to see something of the world d **das sieht man ihm an** he looks it; **das sieht man ihm nicht an** he doesn't look it; **das sieht man ihm an der Gesichtsfarbe an** you can tell (that) by the colour (*Brit*) or color (*US*) of his face; **man kann ihm die Strapazen der letzten Woche ~** he's showing the strain of the last week; **man sieht ihm sein Alter nicht an** he doesn't look his age; **jdm etw** (**an den Augen** or **an der Nasenspitze** (*hum*)) **~** to tell or guess sth by looking at sb; **jeder konnte ihm sein Glück ~** everyone could see that he was happy e **etw** (**mit**) **~** to watch sth, to see sth happening; **das kann man doch nicht mit ~** you can't stand by and watch that; **ich kann das nicht länger mit ~** I can't stand it any more; **das habe ich** (**mir**) **lange genug** (**mit**) **angesehen!** I've had enough of that!

An|se|hen NT -s, *no pl* a (= *guter Ruf*) (good) reputation, standing; (= *Prestige*) prestige; **jdn zu ~ bringen** to bring sb standing, to bring sb a good reputation; **großes ~ genießen** to enjoy a good reputation, to have a lot of standing; **zu ~ kommen** to acquire standing, to acquire a good reputation; (**bei jdm**) **in hohem ~ stehen** to be held in high regard or esteem (*by sb*); **an ~ verlieren** to lose credit or standing b (= *Aussehen*) appearance; **ein anderes ~ gewinnen** to take on a different appearance or (*fig*) aspect; **jdn vom ~ kennen** to know sb by sight c (*Jur*) **ohne ~ der Person** without respect of person

an|sehn|lich [ˈanzeːnlɪç] ADJ a (= *beträchtlich*) considerable; *Leistung* impressive; **ein ~es Sümmchen** (*hum*) a pretty or tidy little sum; **ein ~er Bauch** (*hum*) quite a stomach b (*dated*: = *gut aussehend, stattlich*) handsome

An|sehn|lich|keit F -, *no pl* a (*von Leistung*) impressiveness; **die ~ seines Bankkontos** his considerable bank balance b (*dated*: = *respektables Äußeres*) handsome appearance

An|se|hung [ˈanzeːʊŋ] F **in ~** +*gen* (*form*) in view of

an+sei|len [ˈanzailən] VT *sep* **jdn/sich ~** to rope sb/oneself up; **etw ~ und herunterlassen** to fasten sth with a rope and let it down

an sein ▲ VI *irreg aux sein* (*inf*) to be on

an+sen|gen VT *sep* to singe; **es riecht angesengt** there's a smell of singeing

an+set|zen *sep* VT a (= *anfügen*) to attach (*an +acc* to), to add (*an +acc* to), to put on (*an +acc* -to); (= *annähen*) to sew on b (= *in Ausgangsstellung bringen*) to place in position; **eine Leiter an etw** (*acc*) **~** to put a ladder up against sth; **den Bleistift/die Feder ~** to put pencil/pen to paper; **die Flöte/Trompete** etc **~** to raise the flute/trumpet to one's mouth; **das Glas ~** to raise the glass to one's lips; **an welcher Stelle muss man den Wagenheber ~?** where should the jack be put or placed? c (*mit, auf +acc* at) (= *festlegen*) *Kosten, Termin* to fix; (= *veranschlagen*) *Kosten, Zeitspanne* to estimate, to calculate d (= *einsetzen*) **jdn auf jdn/etw ~** to put sb on (-to) sb/sth; **Hunde (auf jdn/jds Spur) ~** to put dogs on sb/sb's trail e (= *entstehen lassen*) *Blätter etc* to put out; *Frucht* to form, to produce; **Fett ~** (*Mensch*) to put on weight; (*Tier*) to get fatter; **Rost ~** to get rusty f (*Cook*) (= *vorbereiten*) to prepare; *Bowle* to start; (= *auf den Herd setzen*) to put on g (*Math*) to formulate VR (*Rost*) to form; (*Kalk etc*) to be deposited; (*Gekochtes*) to stick VI a (= *beginnen*) to start, to begin; **zur Landung ~** (*Aviat*) to come in to land; **zum Sprung/Start ~** to get ready or prepare to jump/start; **er setzte immer wieder an, aber ...** (*zum Sprechen*) he kept opening his mouth to say something but ... b (= *hervorkommen*) (*Knospen*) to come forth; (*Früchte*) to set; (*Bäume*) to sprout c (*Cook*: = *sich festsetzen*) to stick

An|sicht ✿ 38.1, 39.1, 53.3, 53.5, 53.6 F -, -en a (= *Blick*) view; **von hinten/vorn** rear/front view; **von oben/unten** view from above/below, top/bottom view (*Tech*) b (= *das Betrachten, Prüfen*) inspection; **bei ~** (**von unten** etc) on inspection (from below etc); **zur ~** (*Comm*) for (your/our etc) inspection; **jdm Waren zur ~ schicken** (*Comm*) to send sb goods on approval c (= *Meinung*) opinion, view; **nach ~** +*gen* in the opinion of; **meiner ~ nach** in my opinion or view; **ich bin der ~, dass ...** I am of the opinion that ...; **anderer/gleicher ~ sein** to be of a different/the same opinion, to disagree/agree; **über etw** (*acc*) **anderer ~ sein** to take a different view of sth, to have a different opinion about sth; **ich bin ganz Ihrer ~** I entirely agree with you; **die ~en sind geteilt** or **verschieden** opinions differ, opinion is divided

an|sich|tig [ˈanzɪçtɪç] ADJ **jds/einer Sache ~ werden** (*dated, geh*) to set eyes on sb/sth

An|sichts-: An|sichts|e|xem|plar NT specimen or inspection copy; **An|sichts(post)|kar|te** F picture postcard; **An|sichts|sa|che** F **das ist ~** that is a matter of opinion; **An|sichts|sen|dung** F article(s *pl*) sent on approval; **jdm eine ~ schicken** to send sb articles/an article on approval

an+sie|deln *sep* VT to settle; *Tierart* to introduce; *Vogelkolonie, Industrie* to establish; **dieser Begriff ist in der Literaturkritik angesiedelt** this term belongs to the field of literary criticism VR to settle; (*Industrie etc*) to get established; (*Bakterien etc*) to establish themselves

An|sied|ler(in) M(F) settler

An|sied|lung F a settlement b (= *das Ansiedeln*) settling; (= *Kolonisierung von Tieren*) colonizing; (= *von Betrieben*) establishing

An|sin|nen [ˈanzɪnən] NT -s, - (*dated, geh*) (= *Gedanke*) notion, idea; (= *Vorschlag*) suggestion;

ein seltsames ~ an jdn stellen to make an unreasonable suggestion to sb

An|sitz M **a** (*Hunt*) raised hide **b** (*Aus*) residence; **„Ansitz Claudia"** "Claudia House"

an|sonsten [anˈzɔnstn̩] ADV (= *im anderen Fall, inf: = im Übrigen*) otherwise; **~ gibts nichts Neues** (*inf*) there's nothing new apart from that; **~ hast du nichts auszusetzen?** (*iro*) have you any more complaints?

an+span|nen sep **VT** **a** (= *straffer spannen*) to tauten, to tighten; *Muskeln* to tense **b** (= *anstrengen*) to strain, to tax; **jdn zu sehr ~** to overtax sb; **alle seine Kräfte ~** to strain every nerve, to exert all one's energy → *auch* **angespannt** **c** *Wagen* to hitch up; *Pferd* to harness; *Ochsen* to yoke up (*zu* for); **jdn (zu einer Arbeit) ~** (*inf*) to get sb to do a job **VI** (= *Pferde/Wagen anspannen*) to hitch up; **~ lassen** to get a/the carriage ready; **es ist angespannt!** the carriage is ready

An|span|nung F (*fig*) strain; (= *körperliche Anstrengung auch*) effort; **unter ~ aller Kräfte** by exerting all one's energies

an+spa|ren VT sep to save

An|spar|pha|se F (*bei Bausparvertrag*) saving period

an+spa|zie|ren ptp **anspaziert** VI sep aux sein **anspaziert kommen** to come strolling along or (*auf einen zu*) up

an+spei|en VT sep irreg to spit at

An|spiel NT (*Sport*) start of play; (*Cards*) lead; (*Chess*) first move

an+spie|len sep **VT** **a** (*Sport*) to play the ball etc to; *Spieler* to pass to **b** (*Mus*) *Stück* to play part of; *Instrument* to try out (for the first time); **ein paar Takte ~** to play a few bars **VI** **a** (= *Spiel beginnen*) to start; (*Ftbl*) to kick off; (*Cards*) to lead, to open; (*Chess*) to open **b** **auf jdn/etw ~** to allude to sb/sth; **worauf wollen Sie ~?** what are you driving at?, what are you insinuating?; **spielst du damit auf mich an?** are you getting at me?

An|spie|lung [ˈanʃpiːlʊŋ] F **-, -en** allusion (*auf +acc* to); (*böse*) insinuation (*auf +acc* regarding)

an+spin|nen sep irreg **VT** *Faden* to join; (*fig*) *Verhältnis, Thema* to develop, to enter into **VR** (*fig*) to develop, to start up; **da spinnt sich doch etwas an!** (*inf*) something is going on there!

an+spit|zen VT sep **a** *Bleistift etc* to sharpen **b** (*inf*: = *antreiben*) to have a go at; **jdn ~, dass er etw tut** to have a go at sb to do sth

An|sporn M , no pl incentive; **ihm fehlt der innere ~** he has no motivation

an+spor|nen VT sep *Pferd* to spur (on); (*fig auch*) to encourage (*zu* to); *Mannschaft* to cheer on; **Kinder zum Lernen ~** to encourage children to learn

An|spra|che F **a** (= *Rede*) address, speech; **eine ~ halten** to give an address, to make a speech **b** (= *Beachtung*) attention

an+sprech|bar ADJ (= *bereit, jdn anzuhören*) approachable; (= *gut gelaunt*) amenable; *Patient* responsive; **er ist beschäftigt/wütend und zurzeit nicht ~** he's so busy/angry that no-one can talk to him just now; **er ist jederzeit für seine Studenten ~** his students can speak to him at any time; **auf etw** (*acc*) **~ sein** to respond to sth

an+spre|chen sep irreg **VT** **a** (= *anreden*) to speak to; (= *das Wort an jdn richten, mit Titel, Vornamen etc*) to address; (*belästigend*) to accost; **jdn auf etw** (*acc*)/**um etw ~** to ask or approach sb about/for sth; **es kommt darauf an, wie man die Leute anspricht** it depends on how you talk to people; **damit sind Sie alle angesprochen** this is directed at all of you **b** (= *gefallen*) to appeal to; (= *Eindruck machen auf*) to make an impression on **c** (*fig geh*) **etw als ... ~** (= *ansehen*) to declare

sth to be ...; (= *beschreiben*) to describe sth as ... **d** (= *erwähnen*) to mention **VI** **a** (*auf +acc* to) (= *reagieren*) (*Patient, Gaspedal etc*) to respond; (*Messgerät*) to react, to respond; **diese Tabletten sprechen bei ihr nicht an** these tablets don't have any effect on her; **leicht ~de Bremsen** very responsive brakes **b** (= *Anklang finden*) to go down well, to meet with a good response

an|spre|chend ADJ (= *reizvoll*) *Äußeres, Verpackung etc* attractive, appealing; (= *angenehm*) *Umgebung etc* pleasant ADV attractively; **~ wirken** to be attractive

An|sprech-: **An|sprech|part|ner(in)** M(F) (*form*) contact; **An|sprech|zeit** F (*Aut, Tech*) response or operating time

an+sprin|gen sep irreg **VT** **a** (= *anfallen*) to jump; (*Raubtier*) to pounce (up)on; (*Hund*: = *hochspringen*) to jump up at **b** (*Sport*) *Gerät, Latte* to jump at; *Rolle, Überschlag* to dive into **VI** **a** (*Motor*) to start; (*fig*: = *in Gang kommen*) to get going **b** **angesprungen kommen** to come bounding along or (*auf einen zu*) up; **auf etw** (*acc*) **~ (fig inf)** to jump at sth (*inf*); **gegen etw ~** to jump against sth **c** (*Sport*) to jump

an|sprit|zen sep **VT** (= *bespritzen*) to splash; (*mit Spritzpistole, -düse etc*) to spray **VI** aux sein **angespritzt kommen** (*inf*) to come tearing (*inf*) along or (*auf einen zu*) up

An|spruch M **a** (*esp Jur*) claim; (= *Recht*) right (*auf +acc* on); **~ auf etw** (*acc*) **haben** to be entitled to sth, to have a right to sth; **~ auf Schadenersatz erheben** to make a claim for damages; **~ auf Schadenersatz haben** to be entitled to damages **b** (= *Anforderung*) demand; (= *Standard*) standard, requirement; **an jdn dauernd Ansprüche stellen** to make constant demands on sb; **große** *or* **hohe Ansprüche stellen** to be very demanding; (= *hohes Niveau verlangen*) to demand high standards; **den erforderlichen Ansprüchen gerecht werden** to meet the necessary requirements **c** (= *Behauptung*) claim, pretension; **diese Theorie erhebt keinen ~ auf Unwiderlegbarkeit** this theory does not claim to be irrefutable, this theory lays no claim to irrefutability **d** **etw in ~ nehmen** (*Recht*) to claim sth; *jds Hilfe, Dienste* to enlist sth; *Möglichkeiten, Kantine etc* to take advantage of sth; *Zeit, Aufmerksamkeit, Kräfte* to take up sth; **jdn völlig in ~ nehmen** to take up all of sb's time; (*jds Aufmerksamkeit, Gedanken*) to engross or preoccupy sb completely; **sehr in ~ genommen** very busy/preoccupied; **darf ich Ihre Aufmerksamkeit in ~ nehmen?** may I have your attention?

An|spruchs-: **an|spruchs|be|rech|tigt** ADJ **~ sein** to be entitled to claim; **An|spruchs|be|rech|tig|te(r)** [-bərɛçtɪçtə] MF *decl as adj* person entitled to claim; **alle ~n** all those entitled to claim; **An|spruchs|den|ken** NT high expectations *pl* (of one's entitlements); **an|spruchs|los** ADJ (= *ohne große Ansprüche*) undemanding; (= *geistig nicht hoch stehend*) lowbrow; (= *minderwertig*) *Produkte* down-market; (= *wenig Pflege, Geschick etc erfordernd*) undemanding ADV simply; **~ leben** to lead a modest life; **An|spruchs|lo|sig|keit** F **-**, no pl (= *anspruchslose Art*) undemanding nature; (*geistig*) lowbrow nature; (*wenig Pflege, Geschick etc erfordernd*) undemanding nature; **die stilistische ~ dieser Technokraten** the lack of stylistic sophistication of these technocrats; **er lehrte Disziplin und ~** he taught discipline and modesty in one's demands; **an|spruchs|voll** ADJ (= *viel verlangend*) demanding; (= *übertrieben anspruchsvoll*) hard to please, fastidious; (= *wählerisch*) discriminating; (= *kritisch*) critical; (= *hohe Ansprüche stellend*) *Stil, Buch* ambitious; *Geschmack, Musik* highbrow; (= *kultiviert*) sophisticated; (= *hochwertig*) high-quality, superior, up-market; **eine Zeitung für Anspruchsvolle** a newspaper for the discriminating reader; **der Füllhalter für Anspruchsvolle** the pen for people who are

hard to please ADV (= *kultiviert*) in a sophisticated manner

an+spu|cken VT sep to spit at or on

an+spü|len VT sep to wash up or ashore

an+sta|cheln VT sep to spur (on); (= *antreiben*) to drive or goad on

An|stalt [ˈanʃtalt] F **-, -en** **a** institution (*auch euph*); (= *Institut*) institute; **eine ~ öffentlichen Rechts** a public institution **b** **Anstalten** PL (= *Maßnahmen*) measures *pl*; (= *Vorbereitungen*) preparations *pl*; **für** *or* **zu etw ~ treffen** to take measures/make preparations for sth; **~en/keine ~en machen, etw zu tun** to make a/no move to do sth

An|stalts-: **An|stalts|arzt** M , **An|stalts|ärz|tin** F resident physician; **An|stalts|geist|li|che(r)** MF *decl as adj* resident chaplain; **An|stalts|klei|dung** F institutional clothing; (*in Gefängnis*) prison clothing; **An|stalts|lei|ter(in)** M(F) director of an/the institution; **An|stalts|zög|ling** M (*in Erziehungsanstalt*) child from an institution; (*in Internat*) boarding school pupil; (*in Fürsorgeheim*) child from a home

An|stand¹ M **a** no pl (= *Schicklichkeit*) decency, propriety; (= *Manieren*) (good) manners *pl*; **keinen ~ haben** to have no sense of decency/no manners; **den ~ verletzen** to offend against decency; **das kann man mit ~ tun** it's quite in order to do that; **das kann man nicht mit ~ tun** you can't in all decency do that; **sich mit ~ zurückziehen** to withdraw with good grace **b** (*geh*: = *Einwand*) **ohne ~** without demur (*form*) or hesitation; **~/keinen ~ an etw** (*dat*) **nehmen** to object/not to object to sth, to demur/not to demur at sth (*form*); **keinen ~ nehmen, etw zu tun** not to hesitate to do sth **c** (*esp S Ger*: = *Ärger*) trouble no *pl*

An|stand² M (*Hunt*) raised hide; **auf den ~ gehen** to sit in the raised hide

an|stän|dig ADJ decent; *Witz auch* clean; (= *ehrbar*) respectable; (*inf*: = *beträchtlich*) sizeable, large; **das war nicht ~ von ihm** that was pretty bad of him; **bleib ~!** behave yourself!; **eine ~e Tracht Prügel** (*inf*) a good hiding ADV decently; **sich ~ benehmen** to behave oneself; **sich ~ hinsetzen** to sit properly; **jdn ~ bezahlen** (*inf*) to pay sb well; **~ essen/ausschlafen** (*inf*) to have a decent meal/sleep; **es regnet ganz ~** (*inf*) it's raining pretty hard; **sie hat sich ~ gestoßen** (*inf*) she really took a knock (*inf*)

an|stän|di|ger|wei|se ADV out of decency; **du könntest ihm die zerbrochene Vase ~ bezahlen** you could in all decency pay him for the broken vase

An|stän|dig|keit F **-**, no pl decency; (= *Ehrbarkeit*) respectability

An|stands-: **An|stands|be|such** M formal call; (*aus Pflichtgefühl*) duty visit; **An|stands|da|me** F chaperon(e); **An|stands|for|men** PL manners *pl*; **an|stands|hal|ber** ADV out of politeness; **An|stands|hap|pen** M (*inf*) **einen ~ übrig lassen** to leave something out of good manners; **an|stands|los** ADV without difficulty; **An|stands|un|ter|richt** M lessons *pl* in deportment; **An|stands|wau|wau** M (*hum inf*) chaperon(e); **den ~ spielen** to play gooseberry (*Brit*), to be the third wheel (*US*)

an+star|ren VT sep to stare at

an|statt [anˈʃtat] PREP +gen instead of CONJ **~ zu arbeiten** instead of working; **~, dass er das tut, ...** instead of doing that, he ...

an+stau|ben VI sep aux sein to become or get dusty

an+stau|en sep **VT** *Wasser* to dam up; *Gefühle* to bottle up **VR** to accumulate; (*Blut in Adern etc*) to congest; (*fig*: *Gefühle*) to build up, to accumulate; **angestaute Wut** pent-up rage

an+stau|nen VT sep to gaze or stare at in wonder, to marvel at; (= *bewundern*) to admire; **was staunst du mich so an?** what are you staring at me like that for?, why are you staring at me like that?

An|stau|ung F (von Wasser) accumulation; (von Blut) congestion; (fig: von Gefühlen) build-up

an+ste|chen VT sep irreg to make a hole in, to pierce; Kartoffeln, Fleisch to prick; Reifen to puncture; Blase to lance, to pierce; Fass to tap, to broach; (Archeol) to open up → auch **angestochen**

an|ste|cken sep **VT a** (= befestigen) to pin on; Ring to put or slip on **b** (= anzünden) to light; (= in Brand stecken) to set fire to, to set alight **c** (Med, fig) to infect; **ich will dich nicht ~** I don't want to give it to you **VR sich (mit etw) ~** to catch sth (bei from) **VI** (Med, fig) to be infectious or catching; (durch Berührung, fig) to be contagious

an|ste|ckend ADJ (Med, fig) infectious, catching pred (inf); (durch Berührung, fig) contagious

An|ste|cker M (= Button) badge; (= Schmuck) small brooch

An|steck|na|del F (= Button) badge; (= Schmuck) small brooch

An|ste|ckung [ˈanʃtɛkʊŋ] F -, -en (Med) infection; (durch Berührung) contagion

An|ste|ckungs-: **An|ste|ckungs|ge|fahr** F risk of infection; **An|ste|ckungs|herd** M centre (Brit) or center (US) of infection

an+ste|hen VI sep irreg aux haben or (S Ger, Aus, Sw also) sein **a** (in Schlange) to queue (up) (Brit), to stand in line (nach for) **b** (= auf Erledigung warten) to be due to be dealt with; (Verhandlungspunkt) to be on the agenda; **~de Probleme** problems facing us/them etc; **etw ~ lassen** to put off or delay or defer sth; **eine Schuld ~ lassen** to put off paying a debt, to defer payment of a debt (form) **c** (Jur: Termin etc) to be fixed or set (für for) **d** (geh: = zögern) **nicht ~, etw zu tun** not to hesitate to do sth **e** (geh: = geziemen) **jdm ~** to become or befit sb (form, old); **das steht ihm schlecht an** that ill becomes or befits him (form, old) **f** (Geol) to be exposed, to crop out (Geol); **~des Gestein** outcrop

an+stei|gen VI sep irreg aux sein to rise; (Weg auch, Mensch) to ascend; (Temperatur, Preis, Zahl auch) to go up, to increase

an|stel|le [anˈʃtɛlə] PREP +gen instead of, in place of

an+stel|len sep **VT a** (= daneben stellen) to place; (= anlehnen) to lean (an +acc against) **b** (= dazustellen) to add (an +acc to) **c** (= beschäftigen) to employ, to take on; **jdn zu etw ~** (inf) to get sb to do sth → auch **angestellt** **d** (= anmachen, andrehen) to turn on; (= in Gang setzen) to start **e** Betrachtung, Vermutung etc to make; Vergleich to draw, to make; Experiment to conduct; **(neue) Überlegungen ~(, wie ...)** to (re)consider (how ...) **f** (= machen, unternehmen) to do; (= fertig bringen) to manage; **ich weiß nicht, wie ich es ~ soll** or **kann** I don't know how to do or manage it **g** (inf: = Unfug treiben) to get up to, to do; **etwas ~** to get up to mischief; **was hast du da wieder angestellt?** what have you done now?, what have you been up to now? **VR a** (= Schlange stehen) to queue (up) (Brit), to stand in line **b** (inf: = sich verhalten) to act, to behave; **sich dumm/ungeschickt ~** to act stupid/clumsily, to be stupid/clumsy; **sich geschickt ~** to go about sth well **c** (inf: = sich zieren) to make a fuss, to act up (inf); **stell dich nicht so an!** don't make such a fuss!; (= sich dumm anstellen) don't act so stupid!

An|stel|le|rei [anʃtɛləˈraɪ] F -, -en (inf) **a** (= Ziererei) fuss; **lass diese ~!** don't make such a fuss!

b (= Schlangestehen) queueing (Brit), standing in line

an|stel|lig [ˈanʃtɛlɪç] ADJ (dated) clever, quick to learn

An|stel|lung F employment; (= Stelle) position, employment

An|stel|lungs-: **An|stel|lungs|ver|hält|nis** NT contractual relationship between employer and employee; (= Vertrag) contract; **im** or **mit ~** under or with a contract (of employment); **im ~ sein** to have a contract, to be under contract; **An|stel|lungs|ver|trag** M employment contract

an|steu|ern VT sep to make or steer or head (auch hum) for; (lit, fig) Kurs to head on to, to follow; (fig) Thema to steer onwards

An|stich M (von Fass) tapping, broaching; (= erstes Glas) first draught (Brit) or draft (US); (= erster Spatenstich) digging the first sod; (Archeol) opening

an+stie|feln VI sep aux sein **angestiefelt kommen** (inf) to come marching along or (auf einen zu) up

An|stieg M **a** (= Aufstieg) climb, ascent; (= Weg) ascent **b** (von Straße) incline; (von Temperatur, Kosten, Preisen etc) rise, increase (+gen in)

an+stie|ren VT sep (pej) to stare at

an+stif|ten VT sep (= anzetteln) to instigate; (= verursachen) to bring about, to cause; **jdn zu etw ~** to incite sb to (do) sth, to put sb up to sth (inf); **jdn zu einem Verbrechen ~** to incite sb to commit a crime

An|stif|ter(in) M(F) instigator (+gen, zu of); (= Anführer) ringleader

An|stif|tung F (von Mensch) incitement (zu to); (von Tat) instigation

an+stim|men sep **VT a** (singen) to begin singing; (Chorleiter) Grundton to give; (spielen) to start playing; (Kapelle) to strike up, to start playing **b** (fig) **ein Geheul/Geschrei/Proteste** etc **~** to start whining/crying/protesting etc; **ein Gelächter ~** to burst out laughing **VI** to give the keynote

an+stin|ken sep irreg (fig inf) **VT das stinkt mich an** I'm sick of that **VI dagegen/gegen ihn kannst du nicht ~** you can't do anything about it/him

an+stol|zie|ren ptp **anstolziert** VI sep aux sein **anstolziert kommen** to come strutting or swaggering along or (auf einen zu) up; (Pfau etc) to come strutting along/up

An|stoß M **a den (ersten) ~ zu etw geben** to initiate sth, to get sth going; **den ~ zu weiteren Forschungen geben** to give the impetus to further research, to stimulate further research; **jdm den ~ geben, etw zu tun** to give sb the inducement to do sth, to induce sb to do sth; **der ~ zu diesem Plan/der ~ ging von ihr aus** she originally got this plan/things going; **den ~ zu etw bekommen, den ~ bekommen, etw zu tun** to be prompted or encouraged to do sth; **es bedurfte eines neuen ~es** new impetus or a new impulse was needed **b** (Sport) kickoff; (Hockey) bully-off **c** (= Ärgernis) annoyance (für to); **~ erregen** to cause offence (Brit) or offense (US) (bei to); **ein Stein des ~es** (= umstrittene Sache) a bone of contention; **die ungenaue Formulierung des Vertrags war ein ständiger Stein des ~es** the inexact formulation of the contract was a constant obstacle or a constant stumbling block; **das ist mir ein Stein des ~es** or **ein Stein des ~s für mich** that really annoys me **d** (= Hindernis) difficulty; **ohne jeden ~** without a hitch, without any difficulty

an+sto|ßen sep irreg **VI a** aux sein **an etw** (acc) **~** to bump into sth; **pass auf, dass du nicht anstößt** take care that you don't bump into anything; **mit dem Kopf an etw** (acc) **~** to bump or knock one's head on sth; **mit der Zunge ~** to lisp **b** (mit den Gläsern) **~** to touch or clink glasses; **auf jdn/etw ~** to drink to sb/sth

c (Sport) to kick off; (Hockey) to bully off **d** aux sein (= Anstoß erregen) to cause offence (Brit) or offense (US); **bei jdm ~** to offend sb **e** (= angrenzen) **an etw** (acc) **~** to adjoin sth; (Land auch) to border on sth **VT** jdn to knock (into); (mit dem Fuß) to kick; (= in Bewegung setzen) to give a push; Kugel, Ball to hit; **sich** (dat) **den Kopf/Fuß** etc **~** to bang or knock one's head/foot

an|sto|ßend ADJ **a** (= aneckend) offensive **b** = angrenzend

An|stö|ßer [ˈanʃtøːsɐ] M -s, -, **An|stö|ße|rin** [-ərɪn] F -, -nen (Sw: = Anwohner) (local) resident

an|stö|ßig [ˈanʃtøːsɪç] ADJ offensive; Kleidung indecent ADV offensively; gekleidet, aufgemacht shockingly

An|stö|ßig|keit F -, -en **a** no pl offensiveness; (von Kleidung) indecency **b** (= Bemerkung) offensive remark; (= Stelle) offensive passage

an+strah|len VT sep to floodlight; (im Theater) to spotlight; (= strahlend ansehen) to beam at; **das Gebäude wird rot/von Scheinwerfern angestrahlt** the building is lit with a red light/is floodlit; **sie strahlte** or **ihre Augen strahlten mich an** she beamed at me

an+stre|ben VT sep to strive for

an|stre|bens|wert ADJ worth striving for

an+strei|chen VT sep irreg **a** (mit Farbe etc) to paint **b** (= markieren) to mark; (jdm) **etw als Fehler ~** to mark sth wrong (for sb); **er hat das angestrichen** (als Fehler) he marked it wrong; **er hat nichts angestrichen** he didn't mark anything wrong

An|strei|cher [ˈanʃtraɪçɐ] M -s, -, **An|strei|che|rin** [-ərɪn] F -, -nen (house) painter

an+stren|gen [ˈanʃtrɛŋən] sep **VT a** Augen to strain; Muskel, Gehirn, Geist to exert; (= strapazieren) jdn to tire out; esp Patienten to fatigue; **das viele Lesen strengt meine Augen/mich an** all this reading is or puts a strain on my eyes/is a strain (for me); **alle Kräfte ~** to use all one's strength or (geistig) faculties; **sein Gedächtnis ~** to rack one's brains; **streng doch mal deinen Verstand ein bisschen an** think hard → auch **angestrengt** **b** (Jur) **eine Klage/einen Prozess ~** to initiate or institute proceedings (gegen against) **VR** to make an effort; (körperlich auch) to exert oneself; **sich mehr/sehr ~** to make more of an effort/a big effort; **sich übermäßig ~** to make too much of an effort; (körperlich auch) to over-exert oneself; **sich ~, etw zu tun** to make an effort to do sth, to try hard to do sth; **unsere Gastgeberin hatte sich sehr angestrengt** our hostess had gone to or had taken a lot of trouble

an|stren|gend ADJ (körperlich) strenuous; (geistig) demanding, taxing; Zeit taxing, exhausting; (= erschöpfend) exhausting, tiring; **das ist ~ für die Augen** it's a strain on the eyes

An|stren|gung F -, -en effort; (= Strapaze) strain; **große ~en machen** to make every effort; **~en machen, etw zu tun** to make an effort to do sth; **mit äußerster/letzter ~** with very great/one last effort

An|strich M **a** (= das Anmalen, Tünchen) painting; (= Farbüberzug) paint; (fig) (= Anflug) touch; (von Wissenschaftlichkeit etc) veneer; (= Anschein) air; **ein zweiter ~** a second coat of paint **b** (Mus) first touch **c** (beim Schreiben) upstroke

an+stri|cken VT sep to knit on (an +acc -to); Strumpf to knit a piece onto

an+strö|men VI sep aux sein (Menschenmassen) to stream along; (Wasser) to flow in; **angeströmt kommen** to come streaming or rushing along or (auf einen zu) up; **~de Kaltluft** a stream of cold air

an+stü|ckeln, an+stü|cken VT sep Stück to attach (an +acc to); **etw (an etw** acc) **~** to add sth (onto sth)

An|sturm M onslaught; (= *Andrang*) (*auf Kaufhaus etc*) rush; (*auf Bank*) run; (= *Menschenmenge*) crowd

an+stür|men VI *sep aux sein* **gegen etw ~** (*Mil*) to attack or storm sth; (*Wellen, Wind*) to pound sth; (*fig: = ankämpfen*) to attack sth; **angestürmt kommen** to come storming along or (*auf einen zu*) up

an+stür|zen VI *sep aux sein* **angestürzt kommen** to charge along or (*auf einen zu*) up

an+su|chen VI *sep (dated, Aus)* **bei jdm um etw ~** (= *bitten um*) to ask sb for sth; (= *beantragen*) to apply to sb for sth

An|su|chen ['anzuːxn] NT **-s, -** (*dated, Aus*) request; (= *Gesuch*) application; **auf jds ~** (*acc*) at sb's request

An|ta|go|nis|mus [antagoˈnɪsmʊs] M **-, Antagonismen** [-mən] antagonism

An|ta|go|nist [antagoˈnɪst] M **-en, -en, An|ta|go|nis|tin** [-ˈnɪstɪn] F **-, -nen** antagonist

an|ta|go|nis|tisch [antagoˈnɪstɪʃ] ADJ antagonistic

an+tan|zen VI *sep aux sein* **a** (*fig inf*) to turn or show up (*inf*); **er kommt jeden Tag angetanzt** (*inf*) he turns up here every day **b** (*lit*) to come dancing along

Ant|ark|ti|ka [antˈʔarktika] F **-**, *no pl* Antarctica

Ant|ark|tis [antˈʔarktɪs] F **, *no pl*** Antarctic

ant|ark|tisch [antˈʔarktɪʃ] ADJ antarctic

an+tas|ten VT *sep* **a** (= *verletzen*) Ehre, Würde to offend; Rechte to infringe, to encroach upon; (= *anbrechen*) Vorräte, Ersparnisse etc to break into **b** (= *berühren*) to touch; (*fig*) Thema, Frage to touch on, to mention

an+tau|en VTI *sep* (*vi: aux sein*) to begin to defrost

an+täu|schen VI *sep* to feint; (*Ftbl etc auch*) to dummy; (*Tennis*) to disguise one's shot; **links ~** to feint/dummy to the left

An|teil M **a** share; (*Fin*) share, interest; **er hat bei dem Unternehmen ~e von 30%** he has a 30% interest or share in the company **b** (= *Beteiligung*) **~ an etw** (*dat*) **haben** (= *beitragen*) to contribute to sth, to make a contribution to sth; (= *teilnehmen*) to take part in sth; **an dieser Sache will ich keinen ~ haben** I want no part in this **c** (= *Teilnahme: an Leid etc*) sympathy (*an +dat* with); **an etw** (*dat*) **~ nehmen** (*an Leid etc*) to be deeply sympathetic over sth; **an Freude etc** to share in sth; **sie nahmen alle an dem Tod seiner Frau ~** they all felt deeply for him when his wife died; **sie nahmen alle an seinem Leid ~** they all felt for him in his sorrow **d** (= *Interesse*) interest (*an +dat* in), concern (*an +dat* about); **regen ~ an etw** (*dat*) **nehmen/zeigen** or **bekunden** (*geh*) to take/show a lively interest in sth

an|tei|lig, an|teil|mä|ßig ADJ proportionate, proportional ADV proportionately, proportionally

An|teil|nah|me [-naːmə] F **-**, *no pl* **a** (= *Beileid*) sympathy (*an +dat* with); **mit ~ zuhören** to listen sympathetically (= *Beteiligung*) participation (*an +dat* in)

An|teil|schein M (*Fin*: = *Aktie*) share certificate

An|teils|eig|ner(in) M(F) (*Fin*: = *Aktionär*) shareholder, stockholder (*esp US*)

an|teils|mä|ßig ADJ, ADV = **anteilig**

an+te|le|fo|nie|ren *ptp* **antelefoniert** VTI *sep* (*inf*) to phone; **jdn** or **bei jdm ~** to phone sb up

An|ten|ne [anˈtɛnə] F **-, -n** (*Rad*) aerial, antenna (*esp US*); (*Zool*) feeler, antenna; **eine/keine ~ für etw haben** (*fig inf*) to have a/no feeling for sth

An|ten|nen-: An|ten|nen|ka|bel NT aerial or antenna (*esp US*) cable or lead; **An|ten|nen|mast** M radio mast; **An|ten|nen|steck|do|se** F aerial or antenna (*esp US*) socket; **An|**

ten|nen|ste|cker M aerial or antenna (*esp US*) plug or jack; **An|ten|nen|wald** M forest of aerials or antennas (*esp US*)

An|tho|lo|gie [antoloˈgiː] F **-, -n** [-ˈgiːən] anthology

Anth|rax ['antraks] NT **-, *no pl*** (*Biol*) anthrax

Anth|rax-: Anth|rax|brief M anthrax(-laced) letter; **Anth|rax|pul|ver** NT anthrax powder, powdered anthrax

Anth|ra|zit [antraˈtsiːt] M **-s**, (*rare*) **-e** anthracite

anth|ra|zit|(far|ben) [antraˈtsiːt(farbn)], **anth|ra|zit|far|big** ADJ charcoal-grey (*Brit*), charcoal-gray (*US*), charcoal

Anth|ro|po|lo|ge [antropoˈloːgə] M **-n, -n, Anth|ro|po|lo|gin** [-ˈloːgɪn] F **-, -nen** anthropologist

Anth|ro|po|lo|gie [antropoloˈgiː] F **-, *no pl*** anthropology

anth|ro|po|lo|gisch [antropoˈloːgɪʃ] ADJ anthropological ADV anthropologically

anth|ro|po|morph [antropoˈmɔrf] ADJ anthropomorphous

Anth|ro|po|soph [antropoˈzoːf] M **-en, -en, Anth|ro|po|so|phin** [-ˈzoːfɪn] F **-, -nen** anthroposophist

Anth|ro|po|so|phie [antropozoˈfiː] F **-, *no pl*** anthroposophy

anth|ro|po|so|phisch [antropoˈzoːfɪʃ] ADJ anthroposophic ADV **jdn ~ erziehen** to raise sb according to anthroposophic ideals; **~ angehaucht** influenced by anthroposophy

anth|ro|po|zent|risch [antropoˈtsɛntrɪʃ] ADJ anthropocentric

An|ti- [anti] PREF anti; **An|ti|al|ko|ho|li|ker(in)** M(F) teetota(l)ler; **An|ti|ame|ri|ka|nis|mus** M , *no pl* anti-Americanism; **an|ti|au|to|ri|tär** ADJ anti-authoritarian ADV **~ eingestellt sein** to be anti-authoritarian; **jdn ~ erziehen** to raise sb using anti-authoritarian methods or principles; **An|ti|ba|by|pil|le** F (*inf*) contraceptive pill; **an|ti|bak|te|ri|ell** ADJ antibacterial ADV antibacterially; **~ wirken** to work as an antibacterial agent; **An|ti|be|schlag|tuch** NT *pl* **-tücher** (*Aut*) anti-mist cloth; **An|ti|bio|ti|kum** NT **-s**, **Antibiotika** [-ka] antibiotic; **An|ti|blo|ckier-(brems)|sys|tem** [antiblɔˈkiːɐ-] NT (*Aut*) anti-lock braking system

an|ti|chamb|rie|ren [antiʃamˈbriːrən] *ptp* **antichambriert** VI (*pej*) **(bei jdm) ~** to bow and scrape (to sb), to kowtow (to sb)

Anti-: An|ti|christ¹ ['anti-] M **-(s)** Antichrist; **An|ti|christ²** M **-en, -en, An|ti|chris|tin** F **-, -en** opponent of Christianity, Antichristian; **an|ti|christ|lich** ADJ Antichristian ADV **~ eingestellt sein** to be Antichristian; **an|ti|de|mo|kra|tisch** ADJ antidemocratic; **An|ti|de|pres|si|vum** [antidepreˈsiːvʊm] NT **-s, Antidepressiva** [-va] antidepressant

An|ti|fa¹ ['antifa] F *abbr von* **Antifaschismus** antifascism

An|ti|fa² F **-, *no pl*** (*inf*: = *autonome Bewegung*) antifascist movement; **~-Gruppe** antifascist group

---

ANTIFA

Antifa is an abbreviation of **Antifaschismus**. It became a slogan of the Communists and the New Left, who broadened the term to encompass the "struggle against Western colonialism and imperialism". Antifa demonstrations are organized to protest against the violence of right-wing extremist groups.

An|ti-: An|ti|fa|schis|mus M antifascism; **An|ti|fa|schist(in)** M(F) antifascist; **an|ti|fa|schis|tisch** ADJ antifascist ADV **~ erzogen werden** to be raised to be antifascist; **~ orientiert sein** to be antifascist; **sich ~ geben** to pose as an antifascist

An|ti|gen [antiˈgeːn] NT **-s, -e** (*Med, Biol*) antigen

An|ti-: An|ti|haft|be|schich|tung F nonstick surface or coating; **mit ~** (*Pfanne, Topf*) nonstick *attr*; **An|ti|held** M antihero; **An|ti|hel|din** F antiheroine; **An|ti|his|ta|min** NT antihistamine; **an|ti|im|pe|ria|lis|tisch** ADJ anti-imperialistic

an|tik [anˈtiːk] ADJ **a** (*Hist*) ancient; **der ~e Mensch** man in the ancient world **b** (*Comm, inf*) antique

An|ti|ke [anˈtiːkə] F **-, -** **a** *no pl* antiquity; **die Kunst der ~** the art of the ancient world **b** (= *Kunstwerk*) antiquity

An|ti|kern|kraft|be|we|gung F antinuclear movement

an|ti|kisch ADJ in the ancient style

Anti-: an|ti|kle|ri|kal ADJ anticlerical ADV **~ eingestellt sein** or **gesinnt sein** to be anticlerical; **An|ti|kle|ri|ka|lis|mus** M anticlericalism; **An|ti|klopf|mit|tel** [antiˈklɔpf-] NT (*Tech*) antiknock (mixture); **An|ti|kom|mu|nis|mus** M anti-Communism; **An|ti|kom|mu|nist(in)** M(F) anti-Communist; **an|ti|kom|mu|nis|tisch** ADJ anti-Communist ADV **~ eingestellt** or **gesinnt sein** to be anti-Communist; **An|ti|kör|per** M (*Med*) antibody

An|ti|lo|pe [antiˈloːpə] F **-, -n** antelope

An|ti-: An|ti-Ma|fia-Ge|setz NT anti-Mafia law; **An|ti|ma|te|rie** F (*Phys*) antimatter; **An|ti|mi|li|ta|ris|mus** M antimilitarism; **An|ti|mi|li|ta|rist(in)** M antimilitarist; **an|ti|mi|li|ta|ris|tisch** ADJ antimilitaristic

An|ti|mon [antiˈmoːn] NT **-s**, *no pl* (*abbr* **Sb**) antimony

An|ti-: an|ti|mo|nar|chisch ADJ antimonarchist; **An|ti|o|xi|dans** NT [antiˈɔksidans] NT **-, Antioxidanzien** [-ɔksiˈdantsiən], **An|ti|o|xi|da|ti|ons|mit|tel** NT (*Chem*) antioxidant; **An|ti|pa|thie** [antipaˈtiː] F **-, -n** [-ˈtiːən] antipathy (*gegen* to); **An|ti|per|so|nen|mi|ne** F antipersonnel mine

An|ti|po|de [antiˈpoːdə] M **-n, -n** (*lit*) antipodean; (*fig*) adversary; **die Engländer sind die ~n Australiens** the English live on the opposite side of the world from Australia

an+tip|pen VT *sep* to tap; Pedal, Bremse to touch; (*fig*) Thema to touch on; **jdn ~** to tab sb on the shoulder/arm etc; **bei jdm ~(, ob ...)** (*inf*) to sound sb out (as to whether ...)

An|ti|qua [anˈtiːkva] F **-, *no pl*** (*Typ*) roman (type)

An|ti|quar [antiˈkvaːɐ] M **-s, -e, An|ti|qua|rin** [-ˈkvaːrɪn] F **-, -nen** antiquarian or (*von moderneren Büchern*) second-hand bookseller

An|ti|qua|ri|at [antikvaˈriaːt] NT **-(e)s, -e** (= *Laden*) antiquarian or (*modernerer Bücher*) second-hand bookshop; (= *Abteilung*) antiquarian/second-hand department; (= *Handel*) antiquarian/second-hand book trade; **modernes ~** remainder bookshop/department

an|ti|qua|risch [antiˈkvaːrɪʃ] ADJ antiquarian; (*von moderneren Büchern*) second-hand ADV second-hand; **ein Buch ~ kaufen** to buy a book second-hand

an|ti|quiert [antiˈkviːɐt] ADJ (*pej*) antiquated

An|ti|qui|tät [antikviˈtɛːt] F **-, -en** *usu pl* antique

An|ti|qui|tä|ten-: An|ti|qui|tä|ten|ge|schäft NT antique shop; **An|ti|qui|tä|ten|han|del** M antique business or trade; **An|ti|qui|tä|ten|händ|ler(in)** M(F) antique dealer; **An|ti|qui|tä|ten|la|den** M antique shop; **An|ti|qui|tä|ten|samm|ler(in)** M(F) antique collector

An|ti-: An|ti|ra|ke|te F , **An|ti|ra|ke|ten|ra|ke|te** F anti(missile) missile; **An|ti|sa|tel|li|ten|waf|fe** F antisatellite weapon; **An|ti|se|mit(in)** M(F) antisemite; **an|ti|se|mi|tisch** ADJ anti-Semitic ADV anti-Semitically; **~ eingestellt sein** to be anti-Semitic; **sich ~ äußern** to make anti-Semitic remarks; **An|ti|se|mi|tis|mus** [antizemiˈtɪsmʊs] M **-, *no pl*** antisemitism; **An|ti|sep|ti|kum** NT **-s, Antiseptika** (Med, Pharm) antiseptic; **an|ti|sep|tisch** ADJ antiseptic ADV antiseptically; **An|ti|sta|tik|tuch** NT antistatic cloth; **an|ti|sta|tisch** ADJ antistatic ADV **etw ~ behandeln** to treat sth with an antistatic agent; **An|ti|teil|chen** NT (Phys) antiparticle

An|ti|ter|ror- in cpds antiterrorist; **An|ti|ter|ror|ein|heit** F antiterrorist unit; **An|ti|ter|ror|kampf** M fight or struggle against terrorism, fighting terrorism

An|ti|the|se F antithesis

an|ti|the|tisch [-'te:tɪʃ] ADJ antithetical

An|ti-: An|ti|trans|pi|rant [-transpi'rant] NT **-s, -e** or **-s** (form) antiperspirant; **An|ti|typ** M **ein ~ zu jdm sein, jds ~ sein** to be the complete opposite of sb; **An|ti|vi|ren|pro|gramm** [anti-'vi:rən-] NT (Comput) anti-virus program, virus checker; **An|ti-Vi|ren-Soft|ware** [anti'vi:rən-] F (Comput) anti-virus software

An|ti|zi|pa|ti|on [antitsipa'tsio:n] F **-, -en** (geh) anticipation no pl

an|ti|zi|pie|ren [antitsi'pi:rən] ptp **antizipiert** VT insep (geh) to anticipate

an|ti|zyk|lisch ADJ anticyclical ADV **~ verlaufen** to be anticyclical

Ant|litz ['antlɪts] NT **-es, -e** (poet) countenance (liter), face

an+to|ben VI sep **a gegen jdn/etw ~** to rail at sb/sth **b angetobt kommen** to come storming along or (auf einen zu) up

An|to|nym [anto'ny:m] NT **-s, -e** antonym

an+tör|nen ['antœrnən] sep (sl) VT (Drogen, Musik) to turn on (inf) VI **das törnt an** it turns you on (inf)

an+tra|ben VI sep aux sein to start trotting, to go into a trot; **angetrabt kommen** to come trotting along or (auf einen zu) up

An|trag ['antra:k] M **-(e)s, Anträge** [-trɛːgə] **a** (auf +acc for) application; (= Gesuch) request; (= Formular) application form; **einen ~ auf etw** (acc) **stellen** to make an application for sth; **auf ~ +gen** at the request of **b** (Jur) petition; (= Forderung bei Gericht) claim; **einen ~ auf etw** (acc) **stellen** to file a petition/claim for sth **c** (Parl) motion; **einen ~ auf etw** (acc) **stellen** to propose a motion for sth **d** (dated: = Angebot) proposal; **jdm unzüchtige Anträge machen** to make improper suggestions to sb **e** (= Heiratsantrag) proposal; **jdm einen ~ machen** to propose (marriage) to sb

an+tra|gen VT sep irreg (geh) to offer (jdm etw sb sth)

An|trags-: An|trags|for|mu|lar NT application form; **An|trags|frist** F application period

An|trag|stel|ler [-ʃtɛlɐ] M **-s, -, An|trag|stel|le|rin** [-ərɪn] F **-, -nen** claimant; (für Kredit etc) applicant

an+trai|nie|ren ptp **antrainiert** VT sep **jdm/sich schnelle Reaktion/Tricks/gute Manieren ~** to train sb/oneself to have fast reactions/to do tricks/to be well-mannered

an+trau|en VT sep (old) **jdn jdm ~** to marry sb to sb; **mein angetrauter Ehemann** my lawful wedded husband

an+tref|fen VT sep irreg to find; Situation auch to meet; (zufällig auch) to come across; **er ist schwer anzutreffen** it's difficult to catch him in; **ich habe ihn in guter Laune angetroffen** I found him in a good mood

an+trei|ben sep irreg VT **a** (= vorwärts treiben) Tiere, Gefangene, Kolonne to drive; (fig) to urge; (= veranlassen: Neugier, Liebe, Wunsch etc) to drive on; **jdn zur Eile/Arbeit ~** to urge sb to hurry up/to work; **jdn zu größerer Leistung ~** to urge sb to achieve more; **ich lasse mich nicht ~** I won't be pushed **b** (= bewegen) Rad, Fahrzeug etc to drive; (mit Motor) to power, to drive **c** (= anschwemmen) to wash up; (an Strand) to wash up or ashore; **etw ans Ufer ~** to wash sth (up)

on to the bank VI aux sein to wash up; (an Strand auch) to wash ashore

An|trei|ber(in) M(F) (pej) slave-driver (pej)

an+tre|ten sep irreg VT **a** Reise, Strafe to begin; Stellung to take up; Amt to take up, to assume; Erbe, Erbschaft to come into; **den Beweis ~** to offer proof; **den Beweis ~, dass ...** to prove that ...; **seine Lehrzeit ~** to start one's apprenticeship; **seine Amtszeit ~** to take office; **die Regierung ~** to come to power **b** Motorrad to kick-start **c** (= festtreten) Erde to press or tread down firmly VI aux sein **a** (= sich aufstellen) to line up; (Mil) to fall in **b** (= erscheinen) to assemble; (bei einer Stellung) to start; (zum Dienst) to report **c** (zum Wettkampf) to compete; (= spurten) to put on a spurt; (Radfahrer) to sprint

An|trieb M **a** impetus no pl; (innerer) drive; **jdm ~/neuen ~ geben, etw zu tun** to give sb the impetus/a new impetus to do sth; **aus eigenem ~** on one's own initiative, off one's own bat (Brit inf) **b** (= Triebkraft) drive; **Auto mit elektrischem ~** electrically driven or powered car; **welchen ~ hat das Auto?** how is the car driven or powered?

An|triebs-: An|triebs|ach|se F (Aut) propeller shaft; **An|triebs|ag|gre|gat** NT (Tech) drive unit; **an|triebs|arm** ADJ **= antriebsschwach; An|triebs|kraft** F (Tech) power; **An|triebs|leis|tung** F drive or driving power; **an|triebs|los** ADJ (= träge) (completely) lacking in drive or motivation; **An|triebs|ma|schi|ne** F (Tech) engine; **An|triebs|rad** NT drive wheel; **An|triebs|rie|men** M drive belt; **An|triebs|schei|be** F drive or driving pulley; **an|triebs|schwach** ADJ (Psych) lacking in drive; **An|triebs|schwä|che** F (Med) lack of drive or motivation; **an|triebs|stark** ADJ (Psych) full of drive; **An|triebs|stu|fe** F (von Rakete) propulsion stage; **An|triebs|wel|le** F drive shaft, half-shaft

An|tritt M , no pl **a** (= Beginn) beginning, commencement (form); **bei ~ der Reise** when beginning one's journey; **nach ~ der Stellung/des Amtes/der Erbschaft/der Regierung** after taking up the position/taking up or assuming office/coming into the inheritance/coming to power **b** (Sport: = Spurt) acceleration no indef art

An|tritts-: An|tritts|be|such M (esp Pol) (formal) first visit; **An|tritts|re|de** F inaugural speech; (Parl) maiden speech; **An|tritts|vor|le|sung** F inaugural lecture

an+trock|nen VI sep aux sein to dry on (an, in +dat -to); (= trocken werden) to begin or start to dry

an+tu|ckern VI sep aux sein (inf) **angetuckert kommen** to chug along or (auf einen zu) up

an+tun VT sep irreg **a** (= erweisen) **jdm etw ~** to do sth for sb; **jdm etwas Gutes ~** to do sb a good turn; **tun Sie mir die Ehre an, und speisen Sie mit mir** (geh) do me the honour (Brit) or honor (US) of dining with me **b** (= zufügen) **jdm etw ~** to do sth to sb; **das könnte ihr nicht ~** I couldn't do that to her; **sich** (dat) **etwas ~** (euph) to do away with oneself; **jdm Schaden/Unrecht ~** to do sb an injury/injustice; **tu mir keine Schande an!** don't bring shame upon me; **tu mir das nicht an!** don't do this to me!; **tun Sie sich** (dat) **keinen Zwang an!** (inf) don't stand on ceremony; **darf ich rauchen?** – **tu dir keinen Zwang an!** may I smoke? – feel free or please yourself **c** (= Sympathie erregen) **es jdm ~** to appeal to

sb

d (Aus) **sich** (dat) **etwas ~** (= sich aufregen) to get het up (esp Brit inf) or excited; (= sich Mühe geben) to take a lot of trouble **e** Kleid etc to put on → auch angetan

an+tur|nen[1] ['antʊrnən] VI sep (Sport) to open the season with a gymnastic event

an+tur|nen[2] △ ['antœrnən] sep **= antörnen**

Antw. abbr von **Antwort**

Ant|wort ['antvɔrt] ✪ 46.5 F **-, -en a** answer, reply; (= Lösung, bei Examen, auf Fragebogen) answer; **sie gab mir keine ~** she didn't reply (to me), she didn't answer (me); **sie gab mir keine ~ auf die Frage** she didn't reply to or answer my question; **das ist doch keine ~** that's no answer; **in ~ auf etw** (acc) (form) in reply to sth; **etw zur ~ bekommen** to receive sth as a response; **jdm etw zur ~ geben** to give sb sth as a response; **um umgehende ~ wird gebeten** please reply by return; **um ~ wird gebeten** (auf Einladungen) RSVP; **keine ~ ist auch eine ~** (Prov) your silence is answer enough → **Rede** **b** (= Reaktion) response; **als ~ auf etw** (acc) in response to sth; **die deutsche ~ auf Hollywood** (= Entsprechung) Germany's answer to Hollywood

Ant|wort|brief M reply, answer

ant|wor|ten ['antvɔrtn] ✪ 27.3 VI **a** (= Antwort geben) to answer, to reply; **jdm ~** to answer sb, to reply to sb; **auf etw** (acc) **~** to answer sth, to reply to sth; **was soll ich ihm ~?** what answer should I give him?, what should I tell him?; **jdm auf eine Frage ~** to reply to or answer sb's question; **mit Ja/Nein ~** to answer yes/no, to answer in the affirmative/negative **b** (= reagieren) to respond (auf +acc, mit with)

Ant|wort-: Ant|wort|kar|te F reply card; **Ant|wort|schein** M (international) reply coupon; **Ant|wort|schrei|ben** NT reply, answer

an+ver|trau|en ptp **anvertraut** sep VT **a** (= übergeben, anheim stellen) **jdm etw ~** to entrust sth to sb or sb with sth **b** (= vertraulich erzählen) **jdm etw ~** to confide sth to sb; **etw seinem Tagebuch ~** to confide sth to one's diary VR **sich jdm ~** (= sich mitteilen) to confide in sb; (= sich in jds Schutz begeben) to entrust oneself to sb; **sich jds Führung** (dat)**/Schutz** (dat) **~** to entrust oneself to sb's leadership/protection

an|ver|wandt ADJ (geh) related

An|ver|wand|te(r) MF decl as adj (geh) relative, relation

an+vi|sie|ren ptp **anvisiert** VT sep (lit) to sight; (fig) to set one's sights on; Entwicklung, Zukunft etc to envisage

an+wach|sen VI sep irreg aux sein **a** (= festwachsen) to grow on; (Haut) to take; (Nagel) to grow; (Pflanze etc) to take root; **auf etw** (dat) **~** to grow onto sth; **bei ihr sind die Ohrläppchen angewachsen** her ear lobes are attached to the side of her head **b** (= zunehmen) to increase (auf +acc to)

An|wach|sen NT **-s,** no pl **a** (= das Festwachsen) growing on; (von Haut) taking; (von Nagel) growing; (von Pflanze) taking root **b** (= Zunahme) increase; (von Lärm) growth; **im ~ (begriffen) sein** to be on the increase, to be growing

an+wa|ckeln VI sep aux sein **angewackelt kommen** to come waddling along or (auf einen zu) up; (fig inf) to come wandering up

an+wäh|len VT sep to dial; jdn to call; (Comput) Funktion, Befehl to call up

An|walt ['anvalt] M **-(e)s, Anwälte** [-vɛltə], **An|wäl|tin** [-vɛltɪn] F **-, -nen a** → **Rechtsanwalt** **b** (fig: = Fürsprecher) advocate

An|walts|bü|ro NT **a** lawyer's office **b** (= Firma) firm of solicitors (Brit) or lawyers

An|walt|schaft ['anvaltʃaft] F **-, -en a** (= Vertretung) case or brief; (= Übernahme) the taking over a case; **die ~ für jdn übernehmen** to accept sb's brief, to take over sb's case **b** (= Gesamtheit der An-

wälte) solicitors *pl* (*Brit*), lawyers *pl*, legal profession

An|walts-: An|walts|ge|bühr F lawyer's fees *pl*; **An|walts|kam|mer** F *professional association of lawyers*, ≈ Law Society (*Brit*); **An|walts|kanz|lei** F (*S Ger*) → Anwaltsbüro; **An|walts|kos|ten** PL legal expenses *pl*; **An|walts|pra|xis** F legal practice; (= *Räume*) lawyer's office; **An|walts|zwang** M *obligation to be represented in court*

an+wal|zen VI *sep aux sein* **angewalzt kommen** to come rolling along *or* (*auf einen zu*) up

an+wan|deln VT *sep* (*geh*) to come over; **jdn wandelt die Lust an, etw zu tun** sb feels the desire to do sth

An|wand|lung F (*von Furcht etc*) feeling; (= *Laune*) mood; (= *Drang*) impulse; **aus einer ~ heraus** on (an) impulse; **in einer ~ von Freigebigkeit** *etc* in a fit of generosity *etc*; **dann bekam er wieder seine ~en** (*inf*) then he had one of his fits again

an+wär|men VT *sep* to warm up

An|wär|ter(in) M(F) (= *Kandidat*) candidate (*auf +acc* for); (*Sport*) contender (*auf +acc* for); (= *Thronanwärter*) heir (*auf +acc* to); **der ~ auf den Thron** the pretender *or* (= *Thronerbe*) heir to the throne

An|wart|schaft ['anvart∫aft] F -, *no pl* candidature; (*Sport*) contention; **seine ~ auf die Titel anmelden** to say one is in contention for the title; **~ auf den Thron** claim to the throne

An|warts|schafts|zeit F (*Admin*) *minimum period between registering as unemployed and receiving unemployment benefit*, waiting days *pl*

an+wat|scheln VI *sep aux sein* (*inf*) **angewatschelt kommen** to come waddling along *or* (*auf einen zu*) up

an+we|hen *sep* VT Sand to blow; *Schnee* to drift; *jdn* (*fig geh: Gefühl*) to come over; **warme Luft wehte ihm/sein Gesicht an** warm air blew over his/his face VI *aux sein* to drift

an+wei|sen VT *sep irreg* a (= *anleiten*) *Schüler, Lehrling etc* to instruct; (= *beauftragen, befehlen*) to order, to instruct b (= *zuweisen*) (*jdm etw* sb sth) to allocate; *Zimmer auch* to give; **jdm einen Platz ~** to show sb to a seat c *Geld* to transfer → *auch* **angewiesen**

An|wei|sung F a (*Fin*) payment; (*auf Konto etc*) transfer; (= *Formular*) payment slip; (= *Postanweisung*) postal order b (= *Anordnung*) instruction, order; **eine ~ befolgen** to follow an instruction, to obey an order; **~ haben, etw zu tun** to have instructions to do sth; **auf ~ der Schulbehörde** on the instructions of *or* on instruction from the school authorities c (= *Zuweisung*) allocation d (= *Anleitung*) instructions *pl*

an|wend|bar ADJ *Produkt* usable; *Theorie, Regel* applicable (*auf +acc* to); **die Methode ist auch hier ~** the method can also be applied *or* used here; **das ist in der Praxis nicht ~** that is not practicable

An|wend|bar|keit ['anvɛntba:ɐkait] F -, -en (*von Theorie, Regel*) applicability (*auf +acc* to)

an+wen|den VT *sep auch irreg* a (= *gebrauchen*) *Methode, Mittel, Technik, Gewalt* to use (*auf +acc* on); *Sorgfalt, Mühe* to take (*auf +acc* over); **etw gut** *or* **nützlich ~** to make good use of sth b *Theorie, Prinzipien, Regel* to apply (*auf +acc* to); *Erfahrung, Einfluss* to use (*auf +acc* on), to bring to bear (*auf +acc* on); **sich auf etw** (*acc*) **lassen** to be applicable to sth → *auch* **angewandt**

An|wen|der ['anvɛndɐ] M -s, -, **An|wen|de|rin** [-ərɪn] F -, -nen (*Comput*) user

An|wen|der-: An|wen|der|pro|gramm NT user *or* application program; **An|wen|der|soft|ware** F user *or* applications software

An|wen|dung F a (= *Gebrauch*) use (*auf +acc* on); (*von Sorgfalt, Mühe*) taking; **etw in ~** (*acc*) *or* **zur ~ bringen** (*form*) to apply sth; **zur ~ gelangen** *or* **kommen** (*form*) ~ **finden** (*form*) to be ap-

plied b (*von Theorie, Prinzipien, Regel*) application (*auf +acc* to); (*von Erfahrung, Einfluss*) bringing to bear (*auf +acc* on) c (*Comput*) application

An|wen|dungs-: An|wen|dungs|bei|spiel NT example of use, usage example; **An|wen|dungs|be|reich** M , **An|wen|dungs|ge|biet** NT area of application; **An|wen|dungs|mög|lich|keit** F possible application; **An|wen|dungs|vor|schrift** F instructions *pl* for use

an+wer|ben VT *sep irreg* to recruit (*für* to); (*Mil auch*) to enlist (*für* in); **sich ~ lassen** to enlist

An|wer|bung F recruitment (*für* to); (*Mil auch*) enlistment (*für* in)

an+wer|fen *sep irreg* VT (*Tech*) to start up; *Propeller* to swing; (*inf*) *Gerät* to switch on VI (*Sport*) to take the first throw

An|we|sen NT (*geh*) estate

an|we|send ['anve:znt] ADJ present; **die nicht ~en Mitglieder** the members who are not present; **~ sein** to be present (*bei, auf +dat* at); **ich war nicht ganz ~** (*hum inf*) my thoughts were elsewhere, I was thinking of something else

An|we|sen|de(r) ['anve:zndə] MF *decl as adj* person present; **die ~n** those present; **jeder ~** everyone present; **alle ~n** all those present; **~ ausgenommen** present company excepted

An|we|sen|heit ['anve:znhait] F -, *no pl* presence; **in ~** +*gen or* **von** in the presence of

An|we|sen|heits-: An|we|sen|heits|kon|trol|le F roll call; **An|we|sen|heits|lis|te** F attendance list; **An|we|sen|heits|pflicht** F obligation to attend

an+wi|dern ['anvi:dɐn] VT *sep* **jdn ~** (*Essen, Anblick*) to make sb feel sick; **es/er widert mich an** I can't stand it/him, I detest it/him; **er wandte sich angewidert ab** he turned away in disgust

an+win|keln ['anvɪŋkln] VT *sep* to bend

An|woh|ner ['anvo:nɐ] M -s, -, **An|woh|ne|rin** [-ərɪn] F -, -nen resident; **die ~ des Rheins** the people who live on the Rhine

An|woh|ner|schaft ['anvo:nɐʃaft] F -, *no pl* residents *pl*

An|wurf M a (*Sport*) first throw b (*dated Build*) roughcast

an+wur|zeln VI *sep aux sein* to take root; **wie angewurzelt dastehen/stehen bleiben** to stand rooted to the spot

An|zahl F , *no pl* number; **die Parteien waren in ungleicher ~ vertreten** the parties were not represented in equal numbers; **eine ganze ~** quite a number

an+zah|len VT *sep Ware* to pay a deposit on, to make a down payment on; **einen Betrag/100 Euro ~** to pay an amount/100 euros as a deposit

an+zäh|len VT *sep* (*Sport*) **jdn ~** to start giving sb the count

An|zah|lung F deposit, down payment (*für, auf +acc* on); (= *erste Rate*) first instalment (*Brit*) *or* installment (*US*); **eine ~ machen** *or* **leisten** (*form*) to pay a deposit

an+zap|fen VT *sep Fass* to broach; *Fluss* to breach; *Baum, Telefon, elektrische Leitung* to tap; **jdn (um Geld) ~** (*inf*) to touch sb (*Brit*) *or* hit sb up (*US*) (for money); **jdn ~** (*inf*) (= *ausfragen*) to pump sb; (*Telec*) to tap sb's phone

An|zei|chen NT sign; (*Med auch*) symptom; **alle ~ deuten darauf hin, dass ...** all the signs are that ...; **wenn nicht alle ~ trügen** if all the signs are to be believed

an+zeich|nen VT *sep* to mark; (= *zeichnen*) to draw (*an +acc* on)

An|zei|ge ['antsaigə] ✪ 46.1 F -, -n a (*bei Behörde*) report (*wegen* of); (*bei Gericht*) legal proceedings *pl*; **gegen jdn ~ erstatten** to report sb to the authorities; **wegen etw (eine) ~ bei der Polizei erstatten** *or* **machen** to report sth to the police; **wegen etw (eine) ~ bei Gericht erstatten** *or* **machen** to institute legal proceedings o-

ver sth; **jdn/etw zur ~ bringen** (*form*) (*bei Polizei*) to report sb/sth to the police; (*bei Gericht*) to take sb/bring sth to court b (= *Bekanntgabe*) (*auf Karte, Brief*) announcement; (*in Zeitung*) notice; (= *Inserat, Reklame*) advertisement c (= *das Anzeigen: von Temperatur, Geschwindigkeit etc*) indication; (= *Messwerte*) reading; (*auf Informationstafel*) information; **auf die ~ des Spielstands warten** to wait for the score to be shown *or* indicated d (= *Anzeigetafel, Comput*) display e (= *Instrument*) indicator, gauge

an+zei|gen *sep* ✪ 51.1 VT a (= *angeben*) *Spielstand, Temperatur, Zeit, Wetterlage, Geschwindigkeit, Messwert* to show, to indicate; *Datum* to show; (*fig: deuten auf*) to indicate, to show b (= *bekannt geben*) *Heirat, Verlobung etc* to announce; (= *Reklame machen für*) to advertise c (= *mitteilen*) to announce; *Richtung* to indicate; **jdm etw ~** (*durch Zeichen*) to signal sth to sb d (*Comput*) to display e **jdn ~** (*bei der Polizei*) to report sb (to the police); (*bei Gericht*) to institute legal proceedings against sb; **sich selbst ~** to give oneself up f → **angezeigt** VI (*Zeiger, Kompassnadel etc*) to register; (*Messgerät, Instrument*) to show, to indicate

An|zei|gen-: An|zei|gen|ab|tei|lung F advertising department; **An|zei|gen|an|nah|me** F a *no pl* (= *das Annehmen*) acceptance *or* taking of advertisements *or* ads (*inf*) b (= *Anzeigenstelle*) advertising office; **An|zei|gen|blatt** NT advertiser, freesheet; **An|zei|gen|kam|pag|ne** F advertising campaign; **An|zei|gen|kun|de** M , **An|zei|gen|kun|din** F advertiser, advertising customer; **An|zei|gen|lei|ter(in)** M(F) (*bei Zeitung, Verlag*) head of advertising; **An|zei|gen|prei|se** PL advertising rates *pl*; **An|zei|gen|schluss** ▲ M deadline (for advertisements); (*Tag*) closing date (for advertisements); **An|zei|gen|teil** M advertisement section; **An|zei|gen|wer|bung** F newspaper and magazine advertising

An|zei|ge|pflicht F , *no pl obligation to notify or report an event, illness etc* **der ~ unter|liegen** (*form: Krankheit*) to be notifiable

an|zei|ge|pflich|tig [-pflɪçtɪç] ADJ notifiable

An|zei|ger M a (*Tech*) indicator b (= *Zeitung*) advertiser, gazette

An|zei|ger(in) M(F) (*bei Polizei*) *person reporting crime etc to the police*

An|zei|ge|ta|fel F indicator board; (*Sport*) scoreboard

an+zet|teln ['antsetln] VT *sep* to instigate; *Unsinn* to cause

an+zie|hen *sep irreg* VT a *Kleidung* to put on; **sich** (*dat*) **etw ~** to put sth on; (*fig inf*) to take sth personally; **angezogen** dressed b (= *straffen*) to pull (tight); *Bremse* (= *betätigen*) to apply, to put on; (= *härter einstellen*) to adjust; *Zügel* to pull; *Saite, Schraube* to tighten; (*dial*) *Tür* to pull to c (= *an den Körper ziehen*) to draw up d (*lit*) *Geruch, Feuchtigkeit* to absorb; (*Magnet, fig*) to attract; *Besucher* to attract, to draw; **sich von etw angezogen fühlen** to feel attracted to *or* drawn by sth e (*obs*: = *zitieren*) to quote, to cite VI a (= *sich in Bewegung setzen*) (*Pferde*) to start pulling *or* moving; (*Zug, Auto*) to start moving; (= *beschleunigen*) to accelerate b (*Chess etc*) to make the first move c (*Fin: Preise, Aktien*) to rise d *aux sein* (= *heranziehen*) to approach; **aus vielen Ländern angezogen kommen** to come from far and near VR a (= *sich kleiden*) to get dressed b (*fig*) (*Menschen*) to be attracted to each other; (*Gegensätze*) to attract

an|zie|hend ADJ (= *ansprechend*) attractive; (= *sympathisch*) pleasant

---

An|zieh|pup|pe F dress-up doll

An|zie|hung F , *no pl* attraction; **die Stadt hat eine große ~ für sie** she is very attracted to the town

An|zie|hungs|kraft F (*Phys*) force of attraction; (*fig*) attraction, appeal; **eine große ~ auf jdn ausüben** to attract sb strongly

an+zi|schen *sep* **VT** (*lit, fig inf*) to hiss at **VI** *aux sein* **angezischt kommen** to come whizzing along or (*auf einen zu*) up

An|zug **a** (= *Herrenanzug*) suit; **aus dem ~ kippen** (*inf*) to be bowled over (*inf*), to be flabbergasted (*inf*); (= *ohnmächtig werden*) to pass out → **hauen VT e b** (*Sw:* = *Bezug*) cover **c** (= *das Heranrücken*) approach; **im ~ sein** to be coming; (*Mil*) to be advancing; (*fig*) (*Gewitter, Gefahr*) to be in the offing; (*Krankheit*) to be coming on **d** (*Chess etc*) opening move; **Weiß ist als erster im ~** white has first move **e** (*von Auto etc*) acceleration

an|züg|lich ['antsyːklɪç] ADJ suggestive; **~ werden** to start making suggestive remarks; **er ist mir gegenüber immer so ~** he always makes suggestive remarks to me **ADV** suggestively

An|züg|lich|keit F -, -en suggestiveness; **~en** suggestive remarks

An|zugs|kraft F , **An|zugs|ver|mö|gen** NT acceleration

an+zün|den VT *sep* Feuer to light; **das Haus** etc **~** to set fire to the house etc, to set the house etc on fire

An|zün|der M lighter

an+zwei|feln VT *sep* to question, to doubt

an+zwin|kern VT *sep* to wink at

an+zwit|schern *sep* (*inf*) **VT** sich (*dat*) **einen ~** to get tipsy **VI** *aux sein* **angezwitschert kommen** to come strolling along or (*auf einen zu*) up

AOK [aːoˈkaː] F -, -s *abbr von* **Allgemeine Ortskrankenkasse**

AOK

The AOK – short for **Allgemeine Ortskrankenkasse** – is the largest state health insurance scheme in Germany. Almost half of all employees are insured by it. In every large town there is an independently run **AOK** office. Foreign nationals may also receive help from these offices if they fall ill while in Germany.

Äols|har|fe ['ɛːɔls-] F aeolian harp

Äon [ɛˈɔːn, ɛˈɔn] M -s, -en *usu pl* (*geh*) aeon (*Brit*), eon (*US*)

A|or|ta [aˈɔrta] F -, **Aorten** [-tn] aorta

A|pal|li|ker [aˈpalɪkɐ] M -s, -, **A|pal|li|ke|rin** [-ərɪn] F -, -nen (*Med*) person suffering from PVS

A|pa|na|ge [apaˈnaːʒə] F -, -n appanage (*obs*), (large) allowance (*auch fig*)

a|part [aˈpart] ADJ distinctive, unusual; *Mensch, Aussehen, Kleidungsstück auch* striking **ADV a** (= *schick*) chicly **b** (*old:* = *separat*) separately, individually

A|part|heid [aˈpaːɐthait] F -, *no pl* apartheid

A|part|heid|po|li|tik F policy of apartheid, apartheid policy

A|part|ment [aˈpartmənt] NT -s, -s flat (*Brit*), apartment

A|part|ment-: A|part|ment|haus NT block of flats (*Brit*), apartment house (*esp US*), condominium (*US*), condo (*US inf*); **A|part|ment|wohnung** F flat (*Brit*), apartment

A|pa|thie [apaˈtiː] F -, -n [-ˈtiːən] apathy; (*von Patienten*) listlessness

a|pa|thisch [aˈpaːtɪʃ] ADJ apathetic; *Patient* listless **ADV** apathetically; (= *matt*) listlessly

a|per ['aːpɐ] ADJ (*Sw, Aus, S Ger*) snowless

A|per|çu [apɛrˈsyː] NT -s, -s (*geh*) witty remark, bon mot

A|pe|ri|tif [aperiˈtiːf] M -s, -s or -e aperitif

a|pern ['aːpɐn] VI (*Sw, Aus, S Ger*) **es apert** the snow is going; **die Hänge ~** the snow on the slopes is going

A|pex ['aːpɛks] M -, **Apizes** ['aːpitseːs] **a** (*Astron*) apex **b** (*Phon*) (= *Längezeichen*) length mark; (= *Akzentzeichen*) stress mark

Ap|fel ['apfl] M -s, **¨** ['ɛpfl] apple; **in den sauren ~ beißen** (*fig inf*) to bite the bullet, to swallow the bitter pill; **etw für einen ~ und ein Ei kaufen** (*inf*) to buy sth dirt cheap (*inf*), to buy sth for a song (*inf*); **der ~ fällt nicht weit vom Stamm** (*Prov*) it's in the blood, an apple doesn't fall far from the tree (*US*), like father like son (*prov*)

Ap|fel- *in cpds* apple; **Ap|fel|aus|ste|cher** [-lausʃtɛçɐ] M -s, - (*Gerät*) apple corer; **Ap|fel|baum** M apple tree; **Ap|fel|blü|te** F **a** apple blossom **b** (= *das Blühen*) blossoming of the apple trees; **zur Zeit der ~ geboren** born when the apple trees were in blossom

Äp|fel|chen ['ɛpflçən] NT -s, - *dim von* **Apfel**

Ap|fel-: Ap|fel|es|sig M apple cider vinegar; **Ap|fel|ge|lee** M OR NT apple jelly; **Ap|fel|griebs** [-griːps] M -(es), -e (*dial*) apple core; **ap|fel|grün** ADJ apple green *attr*, apple green *pred*; **Ap|fel|kern** M (apple) pip, appleseed (*US*); **Ap|fel|kla|re(r)** M *decl as adj* clear apple schnapps; **Ap|fel|kom|pott** NT stewed apple, apple compote; **Ap|fel|ku|chen** M apple cake; **Ap|fel|küch|le** NT -s, - (*S Ger*) ≈ apple fritter; **Ap|fel|most** M apple juice; **Ap|fel|mus** NT apple purée or (*als Beilage*) sauce; **jdn zu ~ hauen** (*inf*) to beat sb to a pulp; **Ap|fel|saft** M apple juice; **Ap|fel|saft|schor|le** F apple juice and sparkling mineral water; **Ap|fel|säu|re** F malic acid; **Ap|fel|scha|le** F apple skin or peel; **Ap|fel|schim|mel** M dapple-grey (*Brit*) or dapple-gray (*US*) (horse); **Ap|fel|schor|le** F = Apfelsaftschorle

Ap|fel|si|ne [apflˈziːnə] F -, -n **a** orange **b** (= *Baum*) orange tree

Ap|fel-: Ap|fel|stru|del M apple strudel; **Ap|fel|ta|sche** F apple turnover; **Ap|fel|wein** M cider; **Ap|fel|wick|ler** [-vɪklɐ] M -s, - (*Zool*) codlin moth

A|pha|sie [afaˈziː] F -, -n [-ˈziːən] (*Psych*) aphasia

A|pho|ris|mus [afoˈrɪsmʊs] M -, **Aphorismen** [-mən] aphorism

a|pho|ris|tisch [afoˈrɪstɪʃ] ADJ aphoristic

Aph|ro|di|si|a|kum [afrodiˈziːakʊm] NT -s, **Aphrodisiaka** [-ka] aphrodisiac

A|plomb [aˈplõː] M -s, *no pl* (*geh*) **mit ~** with aplomb (*form*)

A|po, APO ['aːpo] F -, *no pl abbr von* **außerparlamentarische Opposition**

a|po|dik|tisch [apoˈdɪktɪʃ] (*geh*) ADJ apodictic **ADV** apodictically

A|po|ka|lyp|se [apokaˈlypsə] F -, -n apocalypse

a|po|ka|lyp|tisch [apokaˈlyptɪʃ] ADJ apocalyptic; **die ~en Reiter** the Four Horsemen of the Apocalypse

a|po|li|tisch ['apoliːtɪʃ, apoˈliːtɪʃ] ADJ nonpolitical, apolitical

A|poll [aˈpɔl] M -s, (*rare*) -s **a** (*Myth*) Apollo **b** (*fig geh:* = *schöner Mann*) **er ist nicht gerade ein ~** he's not exactly look like a Greek god

a|pol|li|nisch [apɔˈliːnɪʃ] ADJ (*geh*) Apollonian

A|pol|lo [aˈpɔlo] M -s Apollo

A|po|lo|get [apoloˈgeːt] M -en, -en, **A|po|lo|ge|tin** [-ˈgeːtɪn] F -, -nen (*geh*) apologist

A|po|lo|ge|tik [apoloˈgeːtɪk] F -, -en (*geh*) **a** (= *Apologie*) apologia **b** (*Theologie*) apologetics *sing*

A|po|lo|gie [apoloˈgiː] F -, -n [-ˈgiːən] apologia

A|po|rie [apoˈriː] F -, -n [-ˈriːən] (*geh*) aporia (*rare*), problem

A|pos|tel [aˈpɔstl] M -s, - apostle

A|pos|tel-: A|pos|tel|brief M epistle; **A|pos|tel|ge|schich|te** F Acts of the Apostles *pl*

a|pos|te|ri|o|risch [apɔsteˈrioːrɪʃ] ADJ (*Philos*) a posteriori

a|pos|to|lisch [apɔsˈtoːlɪʃ] ADJ apostolic; **der Apostolische Stuhl** the Holy See; **das Apostolische Glaubensbekenntnis** the Apostles' Creed; **Apostolischer Nuntius** Apostolic Nuncio

A|po|stroph [apoˈstroːf] M -s, -e apostrophe

a|po|stro|phie|ren [apostroˈfiːrən] *ptp* **apostrophiert** VT **a** (*Gram*) to apostrophize **b** (= *bezeichnen*) **jdn als etw** (*acc*) **~** to call sb sth, to refer to sb as sth

A|po|the|ke [apoˈteːkə] F -, -n **a** (dispensing) chemist's (*Brit*), pharmacy **b** (= *Hausapotheke*) medicine chest or cupboard; (= *Reiseapotheke, Autoapotheke*) first-aid box

A|po|the|ken|hel|fer(in) M(F) chemist's (*Brit*) or pharmacist's assistant, assistant pharmacist

a|po|the|ken|pflich|tig [-pflɪçtɪç] ADJ available only at a chemist's shop (*Brit*) or pharmacy

A|po|the|ker [apoˈteːkɐ] M -s, -, **A|po|the|ke|rin** [-ərɪn] F -, -nen pharmacist, (dispensing) chemist (*Brit*)

A|po|the|ker|ge|wicht NT apothecaries' weight

A|po|the|ker|waa|ge F (set of) precision scales *pl*

A|po|the|o|se [apoteˈoːzə] F -, -n apotheosis

Ap|pa|la|chen [apaˈlaxn] PL (*Geog*) Appalachian Mountains *pl*, Appalachians *pl*

Ap|pa|rat [apaˈraːt] ⚙ 27 M -(e)s, -e **a** apparatus *no pl*, appliance; (= *esp kleineres, technisches, mechanisches Gerät*) gadget; (= *Röntgenapparat etc*) machine **b** (= *Radio*) radio; (= *Fernseher*) set; (= *Rasierapparat*) razor; (= *Fotoapparat*) camera **c** (= *Telefon*) (tele)phone; (= *Anschluss*) extension; **am ~** on the phone; (*als Antwort*) speaking; **wer war am ~?** who did you speak to?; **jdn am ~ verlangen** to ask to speak to sb; **bleiben Sie am ~!** hold the line **d** (*inf*) (= *unbestimmter Gegenstand*) thing; (= *großer Gegenstand*) whopper (*inf*) **e** (*sl:* = *Penis*) tool (*inf*); **einen geilen ~ haben** to be hung like a horse (*inf*), to be well-hung (*inf*) **f** (= *Personen und Hilfsmittel*) setup; (= *Verwaltungsapparat, Parteiapparat*) machinery, apparatus; (*technischer etc*) equipment, apparatus **g** (= *Zusammenstellung von Büchern*) collection of books to be used in conjunction with a particular course **h** (*Liter*) (**text**)**kritischer ~** critical apparatus

Ap|pa|ra|te-: Ap|pa|ra|te|bau M , *no pl* instrument-making, machine-making; **Ap|pa|ra|te|me|di|zin** F (*pej*) hi-tech medicine

ap|pa|ra|tiv [aparaˈtiːf] ADJ **~e Einrichtungen** (technical) appliances or equipment; **~e Neuerungen** new ideas in technical equipment; **~er Aufwand** expenditure on equipment; **~e Untersuchung** examination using technical equipment; **~er Versuch** experiment using technical equipment; **~e Lernhilfen** technical teaching aids

Ap|pa|rat|schik [apaˈratʃɪk] M -s, -s (*pej*) apparatchik

Ap|pa|ra|tur [aparaˈtuːɐ] F -, -en **a** equipment *no pl*, apparatus *no pl*; **~en** pieces of equipment; **eine ~** a piece of equipment **b** (*fig Pol*) machinery, apparatus

Ap|pa|ril|lo [apaˈrɪlo] M -s, -s (*hum inf*) contraption

Ap|par|te|ment [apartəˈmãː] NT -s, -s **a** (= *Wohnung*) flat (*Brit*), apartment **b** (= *Zimmerflucht*) suite

Ap|pel ['apl] M -s, **¨** ['ɛpl] (*N Ger:* = *Apfel*) apple; **für 'n und 'n Ei** (*inf*) for peanuts (*inf*)

Ap|pell [aˈpɛl] M -s, -e **a** (= *Aufruf*) appeal (*an* +*acc* to, *zu* for); **einen ~ an jdn richten** to (make an) appeal to sb **b** (*Mil*) roll call; **zum ~ antreten** to line up for roll call

---

Ap|pel|la|ti|on [apɛlaˈtsioːn] F -, -en (*Jur: obs, Sw*) appeal

Ap|pel|la|tiv [ˈapɛlatiːf] NT -s, -a [-va], **Ap|pel|la|ti|vum** [apɛlaˈtiːvʊm] NT -s, **Appellativa** [-va] (*Ling*) appellative

ap|pel|lie|ren [apɛˈliːrən] *ptp* **appelliert** VI to appeal (*an +acc* to)

Ap|pen|dix [aˈpɛndɪks] M -, **Appendizes** [-ditseːs] appendix; (*fig: = Anhängsel*) appendage

Ap|pen|zell [apnˈtsɛl, ˈapntsɛl] NT -s Appenzell

Ap|pe|tit [apeˈtiːt] M -(e)s, *no pl* (*lit, fig*) appetite; **~ auf etw** (*acc*) **haben** (*lit, fig*) to feel like sth; **jdm ~ auf etw** (*acc*) **machen** to whet sb's appetite for sth; **das kann man mit ~ essen** that's something you can really tuck into (*inf*) or enjoy; **guten ~!** enjoy your meal; **den ~ anregen** to sharpen the appetite; **jdm den ~ verderben** to spoil sb's appetite; (*inf: Witz etc*) to make sb feel sick; **jdm den ~ an etw** (*dat*) **verderben** (*fig*) to put sb off sth; **der ~ kommt beim** or **mit dem Essen** (*prov*) appetite grows with the eating (*prov*)

Ap|pe|tit-: **ap|pe|tit|an|re|gend** ADJ *Speise etc* appetizing; **~es Mittel** appetite stimulant ADV **~ wirken** to stimulate the appetite; **Ap|pe|tit|bis|sen** M , **Ap|pe|tit|hap|pen** M canapé; **ap|pe|tit|hem|mend** ADJ appetite-suppressing; **~es Mittel** appetite suppressant ADV **~ wirken** to curb the appetite; **Ap|pe|tit|hem|mer** [-hɛmɐ] M -s, - appetite suppressant; **ap|pe|tit|lich** [apeˈtiːtlɪç] ADJ (*= lecker*) appetizing; (*= verlockend aussehend, riechend*) tempting; (*= hygienisch*) hygienic, savoury (*Brit*), savory (*US*); (*fig*) *Mädchen, Anblick* attractive ADV appetizingly; **ap|pe|tit|los** ADJ without any appetite; **~ sein** to have lost one's appetite; **Ap|pe|tit|lo|sig|keit** F -, *no pl* lack of appetite; **Ap|pe|tit|züg|ler** [-tsyːglɐ] M -s, - appetite suppressant

Ap|pe|ti|zer [ˈɛpitaizɐ] M -s, -s (*Pharm*) appetite stimulant

ap|plau|die|ren [aplauˈdiːrən] *ptp* **applaudiert** VTI to applaud; **jdm/einer Sache ~** to applaud sb/sth

Ap|plaus [aˈplaus] M -es [-zəs] *no pl* applause

Ap|plet [ˈɛplet] NT -s, -s (*Comput*) applet

ap|pli|ka|bel [apliˈkaːbl̩] ADJ (*geh*) applicable

Ap|pli|ka|ti|on [aplikaˈtsioːn] F -, -en a (*Comput*) application b (*geh, Med*) (*= Anwendung*) application; (*von Heilmethode*) administering c (*Sew*) appliqué

Ap|pli|ka|tor [apliˈkaːtoːɐ] M -s, **Applikatoren** [-ˈtoːrən] (*für Salbe, Makeup*) applicator

ap|pli|zie|ren [apliˈtsiːrən] *ptp* **appliziert** VT a (*geh: = anwenden*) to apply; (*Med*) *Heilmethode* to administer b (*Sew*) (*= aufbügeln*) to apply; (*= aufnähen*) to appliqué

ap|port [aˈpɔrt] INTERJ (*Hunt*) fetch

Ap|port [aˈpɔrt] M -s, -e a (*Hunt*) retrieving, fetching b (*Parapsychologie*) apport

ap|por|tie|ren [apɔrˈtiːrən] *ptp* **apportiert** VTI to retrieve, to fetch

Ap|por|tier|hund M retriever

Ap|po|si|ti|on [apoziˈtsioːn] F apposition

ap|pre|tie|ren [apreˈtiːrən] *ptp* **appretiert** VT (*Tex*) to starch; (*= imprägnieren*) to waterproof; *Holz* to dress, to finish; *Papier* to glaze

Ap|pre|tur [apreˈtuːɐ] F -, -en (*= Mittel*) finish; (*Tex*) starch; (*= Wasserundurchlässigkeit*) waterproofing; (*für Papier*) glaze, finish

Ap|pro|ba|ti|on [aprobaˈtsioːn] F -, -en (*von Arzt, Apotheker etc zu praktizieren*) certificate (*enabling a doctor etc to practise*); **einem Arzt die ~ entziehen** to take away a doctor's licence to practise (*Brit*) or license to practice (*US*), to strike a doctor off (*the register*) (*Brit*)

ap|pro|bie|ren [aproˈbiːrən] *ptp* **approbiert** VT (*old: = genehmigen*) to approve

ap|pro|biert [aproˈbiːɐt] ADJ *Arzt, Apotheker* registered, certified

Ap|pro|xi|ma|ti|on [aprɔksimaˈtsioːn] F -, -en (*Math*) approximation, approximate value

Ap|rès-Ski [apreˈʃiː] NT -, -s après-ski; (*= Kleidung*) après-ski clothes *pl*

Ap|ri|ko|se [apriˈkoːzə] F -, -n apricot; **Wangen wie ~n** soft rosy cheeks

Ap|ri|ko|sen-: **Ap|ri|ko|sen|li|kör** M apricot brandy; **Ap|ri|ko|sen|mar|me|la|de** F apricot jam

Ap|ril [aˈprɪl] M -(s), -e April; **~, ~!** April fool!; **jdn in den ~ schicken** to make an April fool of sb → *auch* **März**

Ap|ril-: **Ap|ril|scherz** M April fool's trick; **das ist doch wohl ein ~** (*fig*) you/they *etc* must be joking; **Ap|ril|wet|ter** NT April weather

a pri|o|ri [a priˈoːri] ADV (*Philos, geh*) a priori

a|pri|o|risch [apriˈoːrɪʃ] ADJ (*Philos*) a priori

ap|ro|pos [aproˈpo] ADV by the way, that reminds me; **~ Afrika** talking about Africa

Ap|si|de [aˈpsiːdə] F -, -n (*Astron*) apsis

Ap|sis [ˈapsɪs] F -, **Apsiden** [aˈpsiːdn̩] a (*Archit*) apse b (*von Zelt*) bell

A|qua|drom [akvaˈdroːm] NT -s, -e aquadrome

A|quä|dukt [akvɛˈdʊkt] NT -(e)s, -e aqueduct

A|qua-: **A|qua|ma|rin** [akvamaˈriːn] NT -s, -e aquamarine; **a|qua|ma|rin|blau** ADJ aquamarine; **A|qua|naut** [akvaˈnaut] M -en, -en, **A|qua|nau|tin** [-ˈnautɪn] F -, -nen aquanaut; **A|qua|pla|ning** [akvaˈplaːnɪŋ] NT -s, *no pl* (*Aut*) aquaplaning

A|qua|rell [akvaˈrɛl] NT -s, -e watercolour (*Brit*) or watercolor (*US*) (painting); **~ malen** to paint in watercolours (*Brit*) or watercolors (*US*)

A|qua|rell-: **A|qua|rell|far|be** F watercolour (*Brit*), watercolor (*US*); **A|qua|rell|ma|ler(in)** M(F) watercolourist (*Brit*), watercolorist (*US*); **A|qua|rell|ma|le|rei** F a (*Bild*) watercolour (*Brit*) or watercolor (*US*) (painting) b (*= Vorgang*) painting in watercolours (*Brit*) or watercolors (*US*), watercolour (*Brit*) or watercolor (*US*) painting

A|qua|ri|en- [aˈkvaːriən] *in cpds* aquarium; **A|qua|ri|en|fisch** M aquarium fish

A|qua|ri|um [aˈkvaːriʊm] NT -s, **Aquarien** [-riən] aquarium

A|qua|tin|ta [akvaˈtɪnta] F -, **Aquatinten** [-tn] aquatint

Ä|qua|tor [ɛˈkvaːtoːɐ] M -s, *no pl* equator

ä|qua|to|ri|al [ɛkvatoˈriaːl] ADJ equatorial

Ä|qua|tor|tau|fe F (*Naut*) crossing-the-line ceremony

A|qua|vit [akvaˈviːt] M -s, -e aquavit

Ä|qui|lib|rist [ɛkviliˈbrɪst] M -en, -en, **Ä|qui|lib|ris|tin** [-ˈbrɪstɪn] F -, -nen juggler; (*= Seiltänzer*) tightrope walker

Ä|qui|nok|ti|um [ɛkviˈnɔktsiʊm] NT -s, **Äquinoktien** [-tsiən] equinox

A|qui|ta|ni|en [akviˈtaːniən] NT -s Aquitaine

ä|qui|va|lent [ɛkvivaˈlɛnt] ADJ equivalent

Ä|qui|va|lent [ɛkvivaˈlɛnt] NT -s, -e equivalent; (*= Ausgleich*) compensation

Ä|qui|va|lenz [ɛkvivaˈlɛnts] F equivalence

Ar [aːɐ] NT OR M -s, -e (*Measure*) are (*100 m²*)

Ä|ra [ˈɛːra] F -, **Ären** [ˈɛːrən] era; **die ~ Adenauer** the Adenauer era

A|ra|ber¹ [ˈarabɐ, ˈaːrabɐ, aˈraːbɐ] M -s, - (*= Pferd*) Arab

A|ra|ber² [ˈarabɐ, ˈaːrabɐ, aˈraːbɐ] M -s, -, **A|ra|be|rin** [-ərɪn] F -, -nen Arab

A|ra|bes|ke [araˈbɛskə] F -, -n arabesque; (*= Verzierung*) flourish

A|ra|bi|en [aˈraːbiən] NT -s Arabia

a|ra|bisch [aˈraːbɪʃ] ADJ Arab; *Ziffer, Sprache, Schrift etc* Arabic; **die Arabische Halbinsel** (*Geog*) the Arabian Peninsula, Arabia

A|ra|bisch(e) [aˈraːbɪʃ] NT Arabic → *auch* **Deutsch(e)**

A|ra|bist [araˈbɪst] M -en, -en, **A|ra|bis|tin** [-ˈbɪstɪn] F -, -nen specialist in Arabic studies

A|ra|bis|tik [araˈbɪstɪk] F -, *no pl* Arabic studies *pl*

A|ra|gón [araˈɡɔn] NT -s, **A|ra|go|ni|en** [araˈɡoːniən] NT -s Aragon

a|ra|go|nisch [araˈɡoːnɪʃ] ADJ Aragonese

A|ral|see [ˈaːra(ː)l-] M Aral Sea, Lake Aral

a|ra|mä|isch [araˈmɛːɪʃ] ADJ Aramaic

A|ra|mid|fa|ser [araˈmiːt-] F aramid fibre (*Brit*) or fiber (*US*)

Ar|beit [ˈarbait] F -, -en a (*= Tätigkeit, Phys, Sport*) work; (*Pol, Econ*) labour (*Brit*), labor (*US*); **~ und Kapital** capital and labour (*Brit*) or labor (*US*); **Tag der ~** Labour (*Brit*) or Labor (*US*) Day; **die ~en am Stadium** the work on the stadium; **es kann mit den ~en begonnen werden** work can begin; **bei der ~ mit Kindern** when working with children; **~ sparend** labour-saving (*Brit*), labor-saving (*US*); **viel ~ machen** to be a lot of work (*für* for sb); **das ist/kostet viel ~** it's a lot of work, it's a big job; **an** or **bei der ~ sein** to be working; **sich an die ~ machen, an die ~ gehen** to get down to work, to start working; **an die ~!** let's get to work!; **jdm bei der ~ zusehen** to watch sb working; **etw ist in ~** work on sth has started, work on sth is in progress; **Ihr Bier ist in ~** (*inf*) your beer is on its way; **etw in ~ haben** to be working on sth; **etw in ~ nehmen** to undertake to do or (*manuelle Arbeit*) make sth; **etw in ~ geben** to have sth done/made; **jdm etw in ~ geben** to get sb to do/make sth; **die ~ läuft dir nicht davon** (*hum*) the work will still be there when you get back; **erst die ~, dann das Vergnügen** (*prov*) business before pleasure (*prov*); **~ schändet nicht** (*Prov*) work is no disgrace

b *no pl* (*= Ausführung*) work; **gute** or **ganze** or **gründliche ~ leisten** (*lit, fig iro*) to do a good job

c *no pl* (*= Mühe*) trouble, bother; **jdm ~ machen** to put sb to trouble; **machen Sie sich keine ~** I don't go to any trouble or bother; **das war vielleicht eine ~!** what hard work that was!, what a job that was!; **die ~ zahlt sich aus** it's worth the trouble or effort

d (*= Berufstätigkeit, = Arbeitsplatz, Arbeitsstelle, Arbeitszeit*) work *no indef art*; (*= Arbeitsverhältnis*) employment; (*= Position*) job; **eine ~ als etw** work or a job as sth; **(eine) ~ suchen/finden** to look for/find work or a job; **~ suchend** looking for work or a job, seeking employment; **~ Suchende(r)** person/man/woman looking for a job; **einer (geregelten) ~ nachgehen** to have a (steady) job; **ohne ~ sein** to be out of work, to be unemployed; **zur** or **auf** (*inf*) **~ gehen** to go to work; **auf ~ sein** (*inf*) to be at work; **von der ~ kommen** to come back from work

e (*= Aufgabe*) job; **seine ~ besteht darin, zu …** his job is to …

f (*= Produkt*) work; (*handwerkliche*) piece of work; (*Prüfungsarbeit*) (examination) paper; (*wissenschaftliche*) paper; (*= Buch, Kunstwerk*) work

g (*Sch*) test; **~en korrigieren** to mark test papers; **eine ~ schreiben/schreiben lassen** to do/set a test

ar|bei|ten [ˈarbaitn̩] ⊕ 46.3 VI a (*= sich betätigen*) to work (*an +dat* on); **der Sänger hat viel an sich** (*dat*) **gearbeitet** the singer has worked hard or has done a lot of work; **~ wie ein Pferd/Wilder** (*inf*) to work like a Trojan or horse/like mad (*inf*); **die Zeit arbeitet für uns** we have time on our side, time is on our side; **die Zeit arbeitet gegen uns** time is against us; **er arbeitet für zwei** (*inf*) he does the work of two, he does enough work for two; **er arbeitet über Schiller** he's working on Schiller; **er arbeitet mit Ölfarben** he works in or uses oils

b (*= funktionieren*) (*Organ, Maschine*) to function, to work; **die Anlage arbeitet automatisch** the plant is automatic; **die Anlage arbeitet**

elektrisch/mit Kohle the plant runs or operates on electricity/coal

c (= *berufstätig sein*) to work; **~ gehen** (= *zur Arbeit gehen*) to go to work; (= *einen Arbeitsplatz haben*) to have a job; **seine Frau arbeitet auch** his wife works too, his wife goes out to work too; **für eine** or **bei einer Firma/Zeitung ~** to work for a firm/newspaper; **die ~de Bevölkerung** the working population

d (= *in Bewegung sein*) to work; (*Most etc*) to ferment; (*Holz*) to warp; **in meinem Magen arbeitet es** my stomach's rumbling; **in seinem Kopf arbeitet es** his mind is at work; **in ihm begann es zu ~** he started to react, it began to work on him

VR **a** **sich krank/müde ~** to make oneself ill/tire oneself out with work; **sich krüpplig ~** (*inf*) to work oneself silly (*inf*); **sich zu Tode ~** to work oneself to death; **sich** (*dat*) **die Hände wund ~** to work one's fingers to the bone

b (= *sich fortbewegen*) to work oneself (*in +acc* into, *durch* through, *zu* to); **sich in die Höhe** or **nach oben/an die Spitze ~** (*fig*) to work one's way up/(up) to the top

c *impers* **es arbeitet sich gut/schlecht** you can/can't work well; **es arbeitet sich hier auch nicht besser** it's no better working here either; **mit ihr arbeitet es sich angenehm** it's nice working with her

VT **a** (= *herstellen*) to make; **bei jdm ~ lassen** (= *schneidern*) to have or get one's clothes made by sb

b (= *tun*) to do; **was arbeitest du dort?** what are you doing there?; (*beruflich*) what do you do there?; **ich habe heute noch nichts gearbeitet** I haven't done any work or anything today; **du kannst auch ruhig mal was ~!** (*inf*) it wouldn't hurt you to do some work either!

Ạr|bei|ter ['arbaɪtɐ] M **-s, -, Ạr|bei|te|rin** [-ərɪn] F **-, -nen** worker; (*im Gegensatz zum Angestellten*) blue-collar worker; (*auf Bau, Bauernhof*) labourer (*Brit*), laborer (*US*); (*bei Straßenbau, im Haus*) workman; **der 22-jährige ~ Horst Kuhn** the 22-year-old factory worker/labourer (*Brit*) or laborer (*US*)/workman Horst Kuhn; **die ~** (= *Proletariat, Arbeitskräfte*) the workers; **~ und ~innen** male and female workers; **er ist ein guter/langsamer ~** he is a good/slow worker

Ạr|bei|ter-: Ạr|bei|ter|amei|se F worker (ant); **Ạr|bei|ter|auf|stand** M workers' revolt; **Ạr|bei|ter|be|we|gung** F labour (*Brit*) or labor (*US*) movement; **Ạr|bei|ter|bie|ne** F worker (bee); **Ạr|bei|ter|de|monst|ra|ti|on** F workers' demonstration; **Ạr|bei|ter|denk|mal** NT (*lit*) monument erected to the labouring (*Brit*) or laboring (*US*) or working classes **b** (*hum*) monument to inactivity (*hum*); **Ạr|bei|ter|dich|ter(in)** M(F) poet of the working class; **Ạr|bei|ter|dich|tung** F working-class literature; **Ạr|bei|ter|fa|mi|lie** F working-class family; **ạr|bei|ter|feind|lich** ADJ anti-working-class; **ạr|bei|ter|freund|lich** ADJ pro-working-class; **Ạr|bei|ter|füh|rer(in)** M(F) (*Pol*) leader of the working classes; **Ạr|bei|ter|ge|werk|schaft** F blue-collar (trade) union, labor union (*US*)

Ạr|bei|te|rin F **-, -nen** **a** → Arbeiter **b** (*Zool*) worker

Ạr|bei|ter-: Ạr|bei|ter|ju|gend F young workers *pl*; **Ạr|bei|ter|kam|mer** F (*Aus*) ≈ workers' and employees' professional association; **Ạr|bei|ter|kampf|gruß** M clenched-fist salute; **Ạr|bei|ter|kampf|lied** NT socialist workers' song; **Ạr|bei|ter|kind** NT child from a working-class family or background; **Ạr|bei|ter|klas|se** F working class(es *pl*); **Ạr|bei|ter|knei|pe** F workers' pub (*Brit*), bar frequented by workers; **Ạr|bei|ter|lied** NT workers' song; **Ạr|bei|ter|li|te|ra|tur** F working-class literature; **Ạr|bei|ter|mas|sen** PL working masses *pl*; **Ạr|bei|ter|mi|li|eu** NT working-class environment; **im ~** in a working-class environment; **Ạr|bei|ter|or|ga|ni|sa|ti|on** F association of workers, labour (*Brit*) or

labor (*US*) organization; **Ạr|bei|ter|par|tei** F workers' party; **Ạr|bei|ter|pries|ter** M worker-priest; **Ạr|bei|ter|rat** M workers' council; **Ạr|bei|ter|schaft** ['arbaɪtɐʃaft] F **-, -en** workforce; **Ạr|bei|ter|schrift|stel|ler(in)** M(F) working-class writer; **Ạr|bei|ter|selbst|ver|wal|tung** F workers' control; **Ạr|bei|ter|sied|lung** F workers' housing estate (*Brit*) or development (*US*); **Ạr|bei|ter|sohn** M son of a working-class family; **Ạr|bei|ter|stadt** F working-class town; **Ạr|bei|ter|toch|ter** F daughter of a working-class family; **Ạr|bei|ter-und-Bau|ern-Staat** M (*DDR Hist*) workers' and peasants' state; **Ạr|bei|ter-und-Sol|da|ten-Rat** M (*Hist*) workers' and soldiers' council; **Ạr|bei|ter|un|ru|hen** PL worker unrest, unrest among the workers; **Ạr|bei|ter|vier|tel** NT working-class area; **Ạr|bei|ter|wohl|fahrt** F workers' welfare association; **Ạr|bei|ter|zei|tung** F paper of the labour (*Brit*) or labor (*US*) movement

Ạr|beit|ge|ber(in) M(F) employer

Ạr|beit|ge|ber-: Ạr|beit|ge|ber|an|teil M employer's contribution; **Ạr|beit|ge|ber|sei|te** F employers' side; **Ạr|beit|ge|ber|ver|band** M employers' federation

Ạr|beit|neh|mer(in) M(F) employee

Ạr|beit|neh|mer-: Ạr|beit|neh|mer|an|teil M employee's contribution; **Ạr|beit|neh|mer|frei|be|trag** M , **Ạr|beit|neh|mer|pau|scha|le** F (*Fin*) personal or income tax allowance; **Ạr|beit|neh|mer|schaft** ['arbaɪtneːmɐ-ʃaft] F **-, -en** employees *pl*; **Ạr|beit|neh|mer|sei|te** F employees' side; **Ạr|beit|neh|mer|ver|tre|tung** F (= *Organ*) employee representation; (= *Vertreter*) employee representatives *pl*

Ạr|beits|ab|lauf M work routine; (*von Fabrik*) production *no art*

ạr|beit|sam ['arbaɪtzaːm] ADJ industrious, hard-working

Ạr|beits|amei|se F worker (ant)

Ạr|beit|sam|keit F **-, *no pl*** industriousness

Ạr|beits-: Ạr|beits|amt NT employment exchange (*Brit old*), job centre (*Brit*), unemployment office (*US*); **Ạr|beits|an|fall** M workload; **Ạr|beits|an|ge|bot** NT (job) vacancies *pl*; **Ạr|beits|an|lei|tung** F instructions *pl*; **Ạr|beits|an|tritt** M commencement of work (*form*); **beim ~** when starting work; **Ạr|beits|an|wei|sung** F working instructions *pl*; **Ạr|beits|an|zug** M working suit; **Ạr|beits|at|mos|phä|re** F work(ing) atmosphere, work climate; **Ạr|beits|auf|fas|sung** F attitude to work; **Ạr|beits|auf|trag** M job order, commission; **Ạr|beits|auf|wand** M labour (*Brit*), labor (*US*); **mit geringem/großem ~** with little/a lot of work; **ạr|beits|auf|wän|dig** ▲ ADJ labour-intensive (*Brit*), labor-intensive (*US*); **~/nicht sehr ~ sein** to involve a lot of/not much work; **Ạr|beits|aus|fall** M loss of working hours; **Ạr|beits|aus|schuss** ▲ M working party; **Ạr|beits|be|din|gun|gen** PL working conditions *pl*; **Ạr|beits|be|ginn** M start of work; **bei ~** when one starts work; **Ạr|beits|be|las|tung** F workload; **Ạr|beits|be|reich** M (= *Arbeitsgebiet*) field of work; (= *Aufgabenbereich*) area of work; **das gehört nicht in meinen ~** that's not my job **b** (= *Umkreis*) field of operations; (*von Kran etc*) operating radius; **Ạr|beits|be|richt** M work report; **Ạr|beits|be|schaf|fung** F **a** (= *Arbeitsplatzbeschaffung*) job creation **b** (= *Auftragsbeschaffung*) getting or bringing work in *no art*; **Ạr|beits|be|schaf|fungs|maß|nah|me** F (*Admin*) job creation scheme; **Ạr|beits|be|schaf|fungs|pro|gramm** NT job creation scheme or program (*US*); **Ạr|beits|be|schei|ni|gung** F certificate of employment; **Ạr|beits|be|such** M working visit; **Ạr|beits|bie|ne** F worker (bee); (*fig*) busy bee; **Ạr|beits|blatt** NT (*Comput*) worksheet, spreadsheet; **Ạr|beits|dienst** M (*NS*) labour (*Brit*) or labor (*US*) service; **Ạr|beits|di|rek|tor(in)**

M(F) personnel manager; **Ạr|beits|dis|zip|lin** F discipline at work *no art*; **Ạr|beits|ei|fer** M enthusiasm for one's work; **Ạr|beits|ein|heit** F **a** (*Ind*) work group **b** (*Phys*) unit of work **c** (*Comput*) work unit (*DDR*: = Maßeinheit) unit of work; **Ạr|beits|ein|kom|men** NT earned income; **Ạr|beits|ein|stel|lung** F **a** (= *Arbeitsauffassung*) attitude to work **b** (= *Arbeitsniederlegung*) walkout; **die Belegschaft reagierte mit ~** the workforce reacted by downing tools or by walking out; **Ạr|beits|emig|rant(in)** M(F) immigrant worker; **Ạr|beits|en|de** NT = Arbeitsschluss; **Ạr|beits|ent|gelt** NT remuneration; **einmalig gezahltes ~** one-off payment; **Ạr|beits|er|laub|nis** F (= *Recht*) permission to work; (= *Bescheinigung*) work permit; **Ạr|beits|er|leich|te|rung** F **das bedeutet eine große ~** that makes the work much easier; **Ạr|beits|er|spar|nis** F labour-saving *no pl* (*Brit*), labor-saving *no pl* (*US*); **die neuen Maschinen bedeuten eine große ~** the new machines are very labour-saving (*Brit*) or labor-saving (*US*); **Ạr|beits|es|sen** NT (*mittags*) working lunch; (*abends*) working dinner; **Ạr|beits|ethos** NT work ethic; **Ạr|beits|exem|plar** NT desk copy; **ạr|beits|fä|hig** ADJ *Person* able to work; (= *gesund*) fit for or to work; *Regierung etc* viable; **im ~en Alter sein** to be of working age; **Ạr|beits|fä|hig|keit** F (*von Person*) ability to work; (= *Gesundheit*) fitness for work; (*von Regierung*) viability; **Ạr|beits|feld** NT (*geh*) field of work; **Ạr|beits|fie|ber** NT work mania; **Ạr|beits|flä|che** F work surface, worktop; **Ạr|beits|för|de|rung** F job creation or promotion; **Ạr|beits|för|de|rungs|ge|setz** NT *law for the promotion of employment measures*; **ạr|beits|frei** ADJ **~er Tag** day off; (*Feiertag*) public or legal (*US*) holiday; **~er Vormittag/Nachmittag** morning/afternoon off; **Ạr|beits|freu|de** F willingness to work; **ạr|beits|freu|dig** ADJ keen to work, willing to work; (*bei der Arbeit*) enthusiastic about work; **Ạr|beits|frie|de(n)** M peaceful labour (*Brit*) or labor (*US*) relations *pl, no art*; **Ạr|beits|gang** M *pl* **-gänge** **a** (= *Abschnitt*) operation **b** (= *Arbeitsablauf*) work routine; (*von Fabrik*) production *no art*; **Ạr|beits|ge|biet** NT field of work; **Ạr|beits|ge|mein|schaft** F team; (*Sch, Univ*) study group; (*in Namen*) association; **Ạr|beits|ge|neh|mi|gung** F (= *Recht*) permission to work; (= *Bescheinigung*) work permit; **Ạr|beits|ge|rät** NT **a** tool **b** *no pl* tools *pl*, equipment *no pl*; **Ạr|beits|ge|richt** NT industrial tribunal (*Brit*), labor court (*US*); **Ạr|beits|ge|setz** NT labour (*Brit*) or labor (*US*) law; **Ạr|beits|ge|spräch** NT discussion about work; **Ạr|beits|grup|pe** F team; **Ạr|beits|hal|tung** F attitude to work; **Ạr|beits|haus** NT (*old*) workhouse; **Ạr|beits|heft** NT (*Sch*) workbook; **Ạr|beits|hil|fe** F aid; **Ạr|beits|hy|gie|ne** F work hygiene; **Ạr|beits|hy|po|the|se** F working hypothesis; **Ạr|beits|in|spek|ti|on** F (*Aus, Sw*) factory supervision; **ạr|beits|in|ten|siv** ADJ labour-intensive (*Brit*), labor-intensive (*US*); **Ạr|beits|kampf** M industrial action; **Ạr|beits|kampf|maß|nah|men** PL industrial action *sing*; **Ạr|beits|kit|tel** M overall (*Brit*), overalls *pl* (*US*); **Ạr|beits|klei|dung** F working clothes *pl*; **Ạr|beits|kli|ma** NT work climate, work(ing) atmosphere; **Ạr|beits|kol|le|ge** M , **Ạr|beits|kol|le|gin** F (*bei Angestellten etc*) colleague; (*bei Arbeitern auch*) workmate; **Ạr|beits|kol|lek|tiv** NT (*DDR*) team; **Ạr|beits|kon|flikt** M industrial dispute; **Ạr|beits|kos|ten** PL labour (*Brit*) or labor (*US*) costs *pl*

Ạr|beits|kraft F **a** *no pl* capacity for work; **die menschliche ~ ersetzen** to replace human labour (*Brit*) or labor (*US*); **seine ~ verkaufen** to sell one's labour (*Brit*) or labor (*US*) **b** (= *Arbeiter*) worker

Ạr|beits|kräf|te PL workforce

Ar|beits|kräf|te-: **Ar|beits|kräf|te|ab|bau** M reduction *or* cuts *pl* in manpower, downsizing; **Ar|beits|kräf|te|man|gel** M labour (*Brit*) *or* labor (*US*) shortage; **Ar|beits|kräf|te|über|hang** M labour (*Brit*) *or* labor (*US*) surplus

Ar|beits-: **Ar|beits|kreis** M team; (*Sch, Univ*) study group; (*in Namen*) association; **Ar|beits|la|ger** NT labour (*Brit*) *or* labor (*US*) camp, work camp; **Ar|beits|lärm** M industrial noise; **Ar|beits|last** F burden of work; **Ar|beits|le|ben** NT working life; **Ar|beits|leis|tung** F (*quantitativ*) output, performance; (*qualitativ*) performance; **Ar|beits|lohn** M wages *pl*, earnings *pl*

ar|beits|los ADJ **a** *Mensch* unemployed, out of work **b** *Einkommen* unearned

Ar|beits|lo|sen-: **Ar|beits|lo|sen|geld** NT earnings-related unemployment benefit, job-seeker's allowance (*Brit*); **Ar|beits|lo|sen|heer** NT army of unemployed; **Ar|beits|lo|sen|hil|fe** F unemployment benefit; **Ar|beits|lo|sen|quo|te** F rate of unemployment; **Ar|beits|lo|sen|un|ter|stüt|zung** F (*dated*) unemployment benefit, dole (money) (*Brit inf*); **Ar|beits|lo|sen|ver|si|che|rung** F ≈ National Insurance (*Brit*), ≈ social insurance (*US*) **b** (*Amt*) ≈ Department of Social Security (*Brit*), ≈ social insurance office (*US*); **Ar|beits|lo|sen|zah|len** PL , **Ar|beits|lo|sen|zif|fer** F unemployment figures *pl*

ARBEITSLOSENVERSICHERUNG

Every German employee is compulsorily insured under **Arbeitslosenversicherung** – that is, a certain proportion of their gross monthly salary must be paid to the **Bundesanstalt für Arbeit**, which is responsible for among other things for running the employment offices. In return, if the employee becomes unemployed they can claim **Arbeitslosengeld** or **Arbeitslosenhilfe**. **Arbeitslosengeld** is paid at about two-thirds of previous net earnings, usually for one year. If, after a year, you still have not found a job, the payment is reduced (and called **Arbeitslosenhilfe**) and the amount determined by whether your spouse or even your parents or children have an income. People who are unemployed must report every three months to the employment office, where they must also prove that they are actively seeking work.

Ar|beits|lo|se(r) [ˈarbaitsloːzə] MF *decl as adj* unemployed person/man/woman *etc*; **die ~n** the unemployed; **die Zahl der ~n** the number of unemployed, the number of people out of work

Ar|beits|lo|sig|keit F -, *no pl* unemployment

Ar|beits-: **Ar|beits|lust** F enthusiasm for work; **Ar|beits|man|gel** M lack of work; **Ar|beits|markt** M labour (*Brit*) *or* labor (*US*) market; **ar|beits|mä|ßig** ADJ with respect to work ADV professionally; **er ist ~ stark engagiert** he's very involved in his work; **~ ist der Job okay** the work I do is okay; **Ar|beits|ma|te|ri|al** NT material for one's work; (*Sch*) teaching aids *pl*; **Ar|beits|me|di|zin** F industrial medicine; **Ar|beits|me|di|zi|ner(in)** M(F) occupational health specialist *or* practitioner; **Ar|beits|mensch** M (hard) worker; **Ar|beits|merk|ma|le** PL job characteristics *pl*; **Ar|beits|me|tho|de** F method of working; **Ar|beits|mi|nis|ter(in)** M(F) Employment Secretary (*Brit*), Secretary of Labor (*US*); **Ar|beits|mit|tel** NT material for one's work; (*Sch*) teaching aid; **Ar|beits|mo|dell** NT working model; **Ar|beits|mög|lich|keit** F **a** (= *Gelegenheit*) job opportunity **b** (= *freie Stelle*) vacancy; **Ar|beits|mo|ral** F work ethic; **Ar|beits|mo|ti|va|ti|on** F motivation *or* incentive to work, work incentive; **Ar|beits|nach|weis** M **a** employment agency; (*amtlich*) employment exchange (*Brit old*) **b** (= *Bescheinigung*)

certificate of employment; **Ar|beits|nie|der|le|gung** F walkout; **Ar|beits|norm** F average work rate; **Ar|beits|ord|nung** F work regulations *pl*, work rules *pl* (*US*); **Ar|beits|or|ga|ni|sa|ti|on** F organization of the/one's work; **Ar|beits|ort** M *pl* -orte place of work; **Ar|beits|pa|pier** NT **a** working paper **b** **Ar|beitspapiere** PL cards *pl*, employment papers *pl* (*form*)

ar|beit|spa|rend ADJ △ → Arbeit a

Ar|beits-: **Ar|beits|pau|se** F break; **Ar|beits|pen|sum** NT quota of work; **Ar|beits|pferd** NT (*lit*) workhorse; (*fig*) slogger (*Brit inf*), hard worker; **Ar|beits|pflicht** F requirement to work; **Ar|beits|plan** M work schedule; (*in Fabrik*) production schedule; **Ar|beits|plat|te** F worktop

Ar|beits|platz M **a** (= *Arbeitsstätte*) place of work, workplace; **am ~** at work; (*in Büro auch*) in the office; (*in Fabrik auch*) on the shop floor; **Demokratie am ~** industrial democracy **b** (*in Fabrik*) work station; (*in Büro*) workspace; **die Bibliothek hat 75 Arbeitsplätze** the library has room for 75 people to work *or* has working space for 75 people **c** (= *Stelle*) job; **freie Arbeitsplätze** vacancies

Ar|beits|platz-: **Ar|beits|platz|ab|bau** M job cuts *pl*; **Ar|beits|platz|an|ge|bot** NT job offer; (*mehrere*) job vacancies *pl*; **Ar|beits|platz|be|schaf|fung** F job creation; **Ar|beits|platz|be|schrei|bung** F job description; **Ar|beits|platz|com|pu|ter** M personal computer; **Ar|beits|platz|ga|ran|tie** F guaranteed job; **eine ~ aussprechen** to offer guaranteed employment, to offer a job guarantee; **Ar|beits|platz|ge|stal|tung** F workplace design; **Ar|beits|platz|rech|ner** M (*Comput*) workstation; **Ar|beits|platz|si|che|rung** F safeguarding of jobs; **Ar|beits|platz|stu|die** F workplace study; **Ar|beits|platz|tei|lung** F job sharing; **Ar|beits|platz|ver|lust** M loss of a job; (*insgesamt*) job losses *pl*; **Ar|beits|platz|ver|nich|tung** F destruction of jobs *or* workplaces; **Ar|beits|platz|wech|sel** M change of jobs *or* employment (*form*)

Ar|beits-: **Ar|beits|pro|be** F sample of one's work; **Ar|beits|pro|duk|ti|vi|tät** F productivity per man-hour worked; **Ar|beits|pro|gramm** NT work programme (*Brit*) *or* program (*US*); **Ar|beits|pro|zess** ▲ M work process; **Ar|beits|psy|cho|lo|gie** F industrial psychology; **Ar|beits|raum** M workroom; (*für geistige Arbeit*) study; **Ar|beits|recht** NT industrial law; **Ar|beits|recht|ler** M -s, - *pl*, **Ar|beits|recht|le|rin** [-ərɪn] F -, -nen industrial *or* labor (*US*) lawyer; **ar|beits|recht|lich** ADJ *Streitfall, Angelegenheit* concerning industrial law; *Verbot* in accordance with industrial law; **~e Konsequenzen/Literatur** consequences in terms of/literature in industrial law; **ar|beits|reich** ADJ *Leben, Wochen etc* full of work, filled with work, busy; **es ist ~, das zu tun** it requires a lot of work to do that; **Ar|beits|re|ser|ven** PL labour (*Brit*) *or* labor (*US*) reserves *pl*; **Ar|beits|rhyth|mus** M work rhythm; **Ar|beits|rich|ter(in)** M(F) judge in an industrial tribunal; **Ar|beits|ru|he** F (*kurze Zeit*) break from work; **gestern herrschte ~** the factories and offices were closed yesterday; **Ar|beits|sa|chen** PL (*inf*) working clothes *pl* or things *pl* (*inf*); **ar|beits|scheu** ADJ workshy; **Ar|beits|scheu** F workshyness; **Ar|beits|scheue(r)** MF *decl as adj* workshy person; **Ar|beits|schicht** F (work)shift; **Ar|beits|schluss** ▲ M end of work; **~ ist um 17.00 Uhr** work finishes at 5 pm; **nach ~** after work

Ar|beits|schutz M maintenance of industrial health and safety standards

Ar|beits|schutz-: **Ar|beits|schutz|be|stim|mung** F health and safety regulation; **Ar|beits|schutz|ge|setz|ge|bung** F legislation concerning health and safety at work; **Ar|**

beits|schutz|vor|schrif|ten PL health and safety regulations *pl*

Ar|beits-: **Ar|beits|sit|zung** F working session; **Ar|beits|skla|ve** M , **Ar|beits|skla|vin** F slave labourer (*Brit*) *or* laborer (*US*); **~n** *pl* slave labour (*Brit*) *or* labor (*US*) *sing*; **Ar|beits|so|zio|lo|gie** F industrial sociology; **ar|beits|spa|rend** ADJ labour-saving; **Ar|beits|spei|cher** M (*Comput*) main memory; **Ar|beits|spra|che** F (*bei Konferenz etc*) working language; **Ar|beits|stab** M planning staff; **Ar|beits|stät|te** F place of work; **Goethes ~** the place where Goethe worked; **Ar|beits|stel|le** F **a** place of work **b** (= *Stellung*) job **c** (= *Abteilung*) section; **Ar|beits|stil** M work style, style of working; **Ar|beits|stim|mung** F **in der richtigen ~ sein** to be in the (right) mood for work; **Ar|beits|stu|die** F time and motion study; **Ar|beits|stun|de** F man-hour; **~n werden extra berechnet** labour (*Brit*) *or* labor (*US*) will be charged separately; **Ar|beits|su|che** F search for work *or* employment *or* a job; **auf ~ sein** to be looking for a job, to be job hunting; **Ar|beits|su|chen|de(r)** MF *decl as adj* job-seeker; **Ar|beits|sucht** F addiction to work, workaholism (*inf*); **ar|beits|süch|tig** ADJ addicted to work(ing), workaholic (*inf*); **~ sein/werden** to be/become a workaholic (*inf*); **Ar|beits|tag** M working day; **ein harter ~** a hard day; **Ar|beits|ta|gung** F conference, symposium; **Ar|beits|takt** M (*Tech*) **a** (*von Motor*) power stroke **b** (*bei Fließbandarbeit*) time for an/the operation, phase time; **Ar|beits|tä|tig|keit** F work; **Ar|beits|team** NT team; **Ar|beits|tech|nik** F technique of working; **ar|beits|tei|lig** ADJ based on the division of labour (*Brit*) *or* labor (*US*) ADV on the principle of the division of labour (*Brit*) *or* labor (*US*); **Ar|beits|tei|lung** F division of labour (*Brit*) *or* labor (*US*); **Ar|beits|tem|po** NT rate of work; **Ar|beits|the|ra|pie** F work therapy; **Ar|beits|tier** NT **a** (*lit*) working animal **b** (*fig inf*) workaholic (*inf*); **Ar|beits|tisch** M worktable; (*für geistige Arbeit*) desk; (*für handwerkliche Arbeit*) workbench; **Ar|beits|ti|tel** M provisional *or* draft title; **Ar|beits|über|las|tung** F (*von Mensch*) overworking; (*von Maschine*) overloading; **wegen ~ ist es uns nicht möglich, ...** pressure of work makes it impossible for us to ...

Ar|beit-: **Ar|beit|su|che** F = Arbeitssuche; **ar|beit|su|chend** △ ADJ *attr* → Arbeit d; **Ar|beit|su|chen|de(r)** [-zuːxndə] MF *decl as adj* person/man/woman looking for work

Ar|beits-: **Ar|beits|un|fä|hig** ADJ unable to work; (= *krank*) unfit for *or* to work; *Regierung etc* non-viable; **Ar|beits|un|fä|hig|keit** F inability to work; (*wegen Krankheit*) unfitness for work; (*von Regierung etc*) non-viability; **dauernde ~** permanent disability; **Ar|beits|un|fä|hig|keits|be|schei|ni|gung** F certificate of unfitness for work; **Ar|beits|un|fall** M industrial accident, accident at work; **Ar|beits|un|lust** F disinclination to work; **Ar|beits|un|ter|la|ge** F work paper; (*Buch etc*) source for one's work; **ar|beits|un|wil|lig** ADJ reluctant *or* unwilling to work; **Ar|beits|un|wil|li|ge(r)** MF *decl as adj* person/man/woman reluctant *or* unwilling to work; **Ar|beits|ur|laub** M working holiday, combined business trip and vacation (*US*); (*Mil*) leave from the forces to carry on one's usual employment; **Ar|beits|ver|bot** NT prohibition from employment; **er wurde mit ~ belegt** he has been banned from working; **Ar|beits|ver|dienst** M earned income; **Ar|beits|ver|ein|fa|chung** F simplification of the/one's work; **Ar|beits|ver|fah|ren** NT process; **Ar|beits|ver|hält|nis** NT **a** employee-employer relationship; **ein ~ eingehen** to enter employment **b** **Arbeitsverhältnisse** PL working conditions *pl*; **Ar|beits|ver|lust** M loss of working hours; **Ar|beits|ver|mitt|lung** F **a** (= *Vorgang*) arranging employment **b** (= *Amt*) employment exchange;

(privat) employment agency; **Ar|beits|ver|trag** M contract of employment; **Ar|beits|ver|wei|ge|rung** F refusal to work; **Ar|beits|vor|be|rei|tung** F **a** preparation for the/one's work **b** (Ind) production planning; **Ar|beits|vor|gang** M work process; **Ar|beits|vor|ha|ben** NT project; **Ar|beits|vor|la|ge** F sketch or (= Modell) model to work from; (= Schablone) template; **Ar|beits|weg** M way to (one's) work; (von Pendler) commute; **Ar|beits|wei|se** F (= Praxis) way or method of working, working method; (von Maschine) mode of operation; **die ~ dieser Maschine** the way this machine works; **Ar|beits|welt** F working world; **die industrielle ~** the world of industry; **Ar|beits|wil|le** M **ihm fehlt der ~** he has no desire to work; **ar|beits|wil|lig** ADJ willing to work; **Ar|beits|wil|li|ge(r)** [-vɪlɪgə] MF decl as adj person/man/woman etc willing to work; **Ar|beits|wis|sen|schaft** F industrial science, manpower studies sing (US); **Ar|beits|wo|che** F working week; **Ar|beits|wut** F work mania; **ihn hat die ~ gepackt** he's turned into a workaholic (inf); **ar|beits|wü|tig** ADJ work-happy (inf)

Ar|beits|zeit F **a** working hours pl; **während der ~** in or during working hours; **eine wöchentliche ~ von 35 Stunden** a working week of 35 hours **b** (= benötigte Zeit) **die ~ für etw** the time spent on sth; (in Fabrik) the production time for sth; **er ließ sich die ~ bezahlen** he wanted to be paid for his time

Ar|beits|zeit-: **Ar|beits|zeit|kon|to** NT record of hours worked; **Überstunden auf dem ~ gutschreiben** to record hours worked as overtime; **Ar|beits|zeit|mo|dell** NT working hours model or scheme; **Ar|beits|zeit|ord|nung** F working-time regulations pl; **Ar|beits|zeit|re|ge|lung** F (= Regulierung) regulation of working hours; (= Vorschrift) regulation on working hours; **Ar|beits|zeit|ver|kür|zung** F reduction in working hours

Ar|beits-: **Ar|beits|zeug** NT pl -zeuge (inf) **a** (= Arbeitskleidung) working clothes pl **b** (= Werkzeug) tools pl; **Ar|beits|zeug|nis** NT reference from one's employer; **Ar|beits|zim|mer** NT study; **Ar|beits|zwang** M requirement to work

Ar|bit|ra|ge [arbi'traːʒə] F -, -n (St Ex) arbitrage no art; (= Arbitragegeschäft) arbitrage business

ar|bit|rär [arbi'trɛːɐ] ADJ (geh) arbitrary

Ar|bo|re|tum [arbo'reːtʊm] NT -s, Arboreten [-tn] arboretum

Ar|cha|i|kum [ar'çaːikʊm] NT -s, no pl, **Ar|chä|i|kum** [ar'çɛːikʊm] NT -s, no pl (Geol) Archaean (Brit) or Archean (US) period

ar|cha|isch [ar'çaːɪʃ] ADJ archaic

Ar|cha|is|mus [arça'ɪsmʊs] M -, Archaismen [-mən] archaism

Ar|chä|o|lo|ge [arçeo'loːgə] M -n, -n, **Ar|chä|o|lo|gin** [-'loːgɪn] F -, -nen archaeologist (Brit), archeologist (US)

Ar|chä|o|lo|gie [arçeolo'giː] F -, no pl archaeology (Brit), archeology (US)

ar|chä|o|lo|gisch [arçeo'loːgɪʃ] ADJ archaeological (Brit), archeological (US) ADV archaeologically (Brit), archeologically (US); **~ interessiert** interested in archaeology (Brit) or archeology (US); **~ vorgebildet sein** to have a basic background in archaeology (Brit) or archeology (US)

Ar|che ['arçə] F -, -n **die ~ Noah** Noah's Ark

Ar|che|typ [arçe'tyːp, 'arçe-] M archetype

ar|che|ty|pisch [arçe'tyːpɪʃ] ADJ archetypal

Ar|che|ty|pus [arçe'tyːpʊs] M archetype

Ar|chi|me|des [arçi'meːdɛs] M -' Archimedes

ar|chi|me|disch [arçi'meːdɪʃ] ADJ Archimedean; **~es Axiom** (Math) Archimedes' theorem; **~e Schraube** (Tech) Archimedes' screw; **~er Punkt** (fig) crucial or central point

Ar|chi|pel [arçi'peːl] M -s, -e archipelago

Ar|chi|tekt [arçi'tɛkt] M -en, -en, **Ar|chi|tek|tin** [-'tɛktɪn] F -, -nen (lit, fig) architect

Ar|chi|tek|ten-: **Ar|chi|tek|ten|bü|ro** NT architect's office; **Ar|chi|tek|ten|kol|lek|tiv** NT team of architects

Ar|chi|tek|to|nik [arçitɛk'toːnɪk] F -, -en architecture; (geh: = Aufbau von Kunstwerk) structure, architectonics sing (form)

ar|chi|tek|to|nisch [arçitɛk'toːnɪʃ] ADJ architectural; (geh: = Aufbau von Kunstwerk) structural, architectonic (form) ADV architecturally

Ar|chi|tek|tur [arçitɛk'tuːɐ] F -, -en architecture (auch Comput); (= Bau) piece of architecture

Ar|chi|tek|tur|bü|ro NT architect's or architects office

Ar|chit|rav [arçi'traːf] M -s, -e [-və] architrave

Ar|chiv [ar'çiːf] NT -s, -e [-və] archives pl

Ar|chi|va|li|en [arçi'vaːliən] PL records pl

Ar|chi|var [arçi'vaːɐ] M -s, -e, **Ar|chi|va|rin** [-'vaːrɪn] F -, -nen archivist

Ar|chiv-: **Ar|chiv|bild** NT library photo, photo from the archives; **Ar|chiv|exemp|lar** NT file copy

ar|chi|vie|ren [arçi'viːrən] ptp **archiviert** VT to archive (auch Comput)

Ar|chi|vie|rung F -, -en archiving (auch Comput)

Ar|chiv|ma|te|ri|al NT records pl

Ar|cus ['arkʊs] M -, ['arkuːs] (Math) arc

ARD [aːɛr'deː] F -, no pl abbr von **Arbeitsgemeinschaft der öffentlich-rechtlichen Rundfunkanstalten der Bundesrepublik Deutschland**

ARD

ARD is an amalgamation of the broadcasting stations of the Länder. Since 1954 it has run the **Erstes Deutsches Fernsehen**, the first German national TV channel. The individual stations produce programmes for the network and for the regional channels, which concentrate on local interest and educational programming. They also control up to five regional radio stations each. **ARD** is financed through licence fees and strictly controlled advertising. It concentrates on information, news and educational programmes.

A|re ['aːrə] F -, -n (Sw: = Ar) are (100 m²)

A|re|al [are'aːl] NT -s, -e area

a|re|li|gi|ös ['aːreligiøːs] ADJ areligious

Ä|ren pl von **Ära**

A|re|na [a're:na] F -, Arenen [-nən] (lit, fig) arena; (= Zirkusarena, Stierkampfarena) ring

A|re|o|pag [areo'paːk] M -s, no pl (Hist) Areopagus

arg [ark] ADJ comp **²er** ['ɛrgə], superl **²ste(r, s)** ['ɛrkstə] (esp S Ger) **a** (old: = böse) evil, wicked; **~ denken** to think evil thoughts **b** (= schlimm) bad; Gestank, Katastrophe, Verlust, Blamage, Verlegenheit, Schicksal terrible; Enttäuschung, Feind bitter; Säufer, Raucher confirmed, inveterate; **sein ärgster Feind** his worst enemy; **etw noch ärger machen** to make sth worse; **das Ärgste befürchten** to fear the worst; **ich habe an nichts Arges gedacht** I didn't think anything of it; **etw liegt im Argen** sth is at sixes and sevens; **das ist mir ~** (dial) I'm very sorry about that **c** attr (= stark, groß) terrible; (dial) Freude, Liebenswürdigkeit etc tremendous ADV comp **²er**, superl **am ²sten** (= schlimm) badly; (dial inf: = sehr) terribly (inf); **es geht ihr ~ schlecht** (inf) she's in a really bad way; **er hat sich ~ vertan** (inf) he's made a bad mistake; **sie ist ~ verliebt** (inf) she is very much in love, she is terribly in love; **es zu ~ treiben** to go too far, to take things too far

Arg [ark] NT -s, no pl (old) malice

Ar|gen|ti|ni|en [argɛn'tiːniən] NT -s Argentina, the Argentine

Ar|gen|ti|ni|er [argɛn'tiːniɐ] M -s, -, **Ar|gen|ti|ni|e|rin** [-iərɪn] F -, -nen Argentine, Argentinian

ar|gen|ti|nisch [argɛn'tiːnɪʃ] ADJ Argentine, Argentinian

Ar|ge(r) ['argə] M decl as adj no pl (old) **der ~** Satan, the devil

är|ger comp von **arg**

Är|ger ['ɛrgɐ] M -s, no pl **a** annoyance; (stärker) anger; **wenn ihn der ~ packt** when he gets annoyed/angry; **~ über etw** (acc) **empfinden** to feel annoyed about sth; **zu jds ~, jdm zum ~** to sb's annoyance **b** (= Unannehmlichkeiten, Streitigkeiten) trouble; (= ärgerliche Erlebnisse) bother, trouble; (= Sorgen) worry; **jdm ~ machen** or **bereiten** to cause sb a lot of trouble or bother; **der tägliche ~ im Büro** the hassle in the office every day (inf); **~ bekommen** or **kriegen** (inf) to get into trouble; **~ mit jdm haben** to be having trouble with sb; **mach keinen ~!** (inf) don't make or cause any trouble!, cool it! (inf); **mach mir keinen ~** (inf) don't make any trouble for me; **so ein ~!** (inf) how annoying!, what a nuisance!; **es gibt ~** (inf) there'll be trouble

är|ger|lich ['ɛrgɐlɪç] ADJ **a** (= verärgert) annoyed, cross; Tonfall, Handbewegung angry; **~ über** or **auf jdn/über etw sein** to be annoyed or cross with sb/about sth, to be angry or infuriated with sb/about sth, to be mad at sb/about sth (inf) **b** (= unangenehm) annoying; (stärker) maddening, infuriating; **eine ~e Tatsache** an unpleasant fact ADV crossly; (= böse) angrily; **~ klingen** to sound cross/angry; **jdn ~ ansehen** to give sb an angry look

Är|ger|lich|keit F -, -en **a** no pl (= das Verärgertsein) annoyance, crossness; **die ~ seines Tons** the annoyance in his voice **b** (= ärgerlicher Vorfall) nuisance, annoyance

är|gern ['ɛrgɐn] VT **a** (= ärgerlich machen) to annoy, to irritate; (stärker) to make angry; **jdn krank** or **zu Tode ~** to drive sb mad; **das ärgert einen doch!** but it's so annoying! **b** (= necken) to torment VR (= ärgerlich sein/werden) to be/ get annoyed; (stärker) to be/get angry or infuriated (über jdn/etw with sb/about sth); **sich krank** or **zu Tode ~** to drive oneself to distraction; **über so etwas könnte ich mich krank** or **zu Tode ~** that sort of thing drives me mad (inf); **du darfst dich darüber nicht so ~** you shouldn't let it annoy you so much; **nicht ~, nur wundern!** (inf) that's life

Är|ger|nis ['ɛrgɐnɪs] NT -ses, -se **a** no pl (= Anstoß) offence (Brit), offense (US), outrage; **~ erregen** to cause offence (Brit) or offense (US); **~ an etw** (dat) **nehmen** (old) to be offended by sth; **bei jdm ~ erregen** to offend sb; **wegen Erregung öffentlichen ~ses angeklagt werden** to be charged with offending public decency **b** (= etwas Anstößiges) outrage; (= etwas Ärgerliches) terrible nuisance; **es ist ein ~ für sie, wenn ...** it annoys her (terribly) when ...; **um ~se zu vermeiden** to avoid upsetting anybody **c** (= Ärgerlichkeit, Unannehmlichkeit) trouble no pl

Arg|list ['arklɪst] F -, no pl (= Hinterlist) cunning, guile, craftiness; (= Boshaftigkeit) malice; (Jur) fraud

arg|lis|tig ['arklɪstɪç] ADJ cunning, crafty; (= böswillig) malicious; **~e Täuschung** fraud ADV cunningly, craftily; (= böswillig) maliciously

Arg|lis|tig|keit F -, no pl cunning, craftiness; (= Böswilligkeit) maliciousness

arg|los ['arkloːs] ADJ innocent; (= ohne Täuschungsabsicht) guileless ADV innocently

Arg|lo|sig|keit F -, no pl innocence

Ar|gon ['argɔn] NT -s, no pl (abbr **Ar**) argon

Ar|go|naut [argo'naʊt] M -en, -en (Myth) Argonaut

Ar|got [ar'goː] M OR NT -s, -s argot

ärgs|te(r, s) superl von **arg**

Ar|gu|ment [arguˈmɛnt] ✪ 53.2, 53.3, 53.6 NT -(e)s, -e argument; **das ist kein ~** that's no argument; (= *wäre unsinnig*) that's no way to go about things; (= *keine Entschuldigung*) that's no excuse

Ar|gu|men|ta|ti|on [argumɛntaˈtsioːn] F -, -en **a** argument; (= *Darlegung*) argumentation *no pl* **b** (*Sch*: = *Aufsatz*) critical analysis

Ar|gu|men|ta|ti|ons|hil|fe F (*form*) advice on how to present one's case

ar|gu|men|ta|tiv [argumɛntaˈtiːf] (*geh*), **ar|gu|men|ta|to|risch** [argumɛntaˈtoːrɪʃ] (*rare*) **ADJ** **~e Werbung betreiben** to use persuasive advertising; **einen ~en Wahlkampf führen** to run an election campaign that concentrates on issues; **~e Funktion** (*Ling*) argumentative function **ADV** **die Beweisführung war ~ überzeugend/schwach** the arguments presented were very convincing/weak; **eine Aussage ~ widerlegen** to refute an argument; **~ ist er sehr schwach** his argumentation is very weak; **etw ~ erreichen** to achieve sth by (force of) argument; **etw ~ bekämpfen** to fight sth with arguments

ar|gu|men|tie|ren [argumɛnˈtiːrən] *ptp* **argumentiert** VI to argue; **mit etw ~** to use sth as an argument

Ar|gus [ˈargʊs] M -, -se Argus

Ar|gus|au|ge NT (*geh*) Argus eye; **mit ~n** Argus-eyed

Arg|wohn [ˈarkvoːn] M -s, *no pl* suspicion; **jds ~ erregen/zerstreuen** to arouse/allay sb's suspicions; **~ gegen jdn hegen/schöpfen** (*geh*) to have/form doubts about sb, to be/become suspicious of sb; **mit** *or* **voller ~** suspiciously

arg|wöh|nen [ˈarkvøːnən] VT *insep* (*geh*) to suspect

arg|wöh|nisch [ˈarkvøːnɪʃ] **ADJ** suspicious **ADV** suspiciously

a|rid [aˈriːt] ADJ (*Geog*) arid

A|ri|di|tät [aridiˈtɛːt] F -, *no pl* (*Geog*) aridity

A|rie [ˈaːriə] F -, -n (*Mus*) aria

A|ri|er [ˈaːriɐ] M -s, -, **A|ri|e|rin** [-iərɪn] F -, -nen Aryan

A|ri|er|pa|ra|graf ▲ M (*NS*) *law precluding non-Aryans from becoming public servants*

A|ri|es [ˈaːriɛs] M - (*Astron*) Aries

a|risch [ˈaːrɪʃ] ADJ **a** (*Ling*) Indo-European, Indo-Germanic **b** (*NS*) Aryan

a|ri|sie|ren [ariˈziːrən] *ptp* **arisiert** VT (*NS sl*) to Aryanize

A|ris|to|krat [arɪstoˈkraːt] M -en, -en, **A|ris|to|kra|tin** [-ˈkraːtɪn] F -, -nen aristocrat

A|ris|to|kra|tie [arɪstokraˈtiː] F -, -n [-ˈtiːən] aristocracy

a|ris|to|kra|tisch [arɪstoˈkraːtɪʃ] ADJ aristocratic

A|ris|to|te|les [arɪsˈtoːteləs] M -' Aristotle

A|ris|to|te|li|ker [arɪstoˈteːlikɐ] M -s, -, **A|ris|to|te|li|ke|rin** [-ərɪn] F -, -nen Aristotelian

a|ris|to|te|lisch [arɪstoˈteːlɪʃ] ADJ Aristotelian

A|rith|me|tik [arɪtˈmeːtɪk] F -, *no pl* arithmetic

A|rith|me|ti|ker [arɪtˈmeːtikɐ] M -s, -, **A|rith|me|ti|ke|rin** [-ərɪn] F -, -nen arithmetician

a|rith|me|tisch [arɪtˈmeːtɪʃ] ADJ arithmetic(al); (*Comput*) arithmetic

Ar|ka|de [arˈkaːdə] F -, -n **a** (= *Bogen*) arch (-way) **b** **Arkaden** PL (= *Bogengang*) arcade

Ar|ka|di|en [arˈkaːdiən] NT -s Arcadia

ar|ka|disch [arˈkaːdɪʃ] ADJ (*geh*) Arcadian

Ark|tis [ˈarktɪs] F -, *no pl* Arctic

ark|tisch [ˈarktɪʃ] **ADJ** arctic **ADV** **~ kalt** cold as the arctic

Ar|kus [ˈarkʊs] M -, - [ˈarkuːs] (*Math*) arc

arm [arm] **ADJ** *comp* **~er** [ˈɛrmɐ], *superl* **~ste(r, s)** [ˈɛrmstə] (*lit, fig*) poor; (= *gering*) *Vegetation, Wachstum* sparse; **Arm und Reich** rich and poor; **die Armen** the poor; **du machst mich noch mal ~** (*inf*) you'll ruin me yet; **an etw** (*dat*) **~ sein** to be somewhat lacking in sth; **der Boden ist ~ an Nährstoffen** the soil is poor in nutri-

ents; **~ an Vitaminen** low in vitamins; **um jdn/etw ärmer werden** to lose sb/sth; **um jdn/etw ärmer sein** to have lost sb/sth; **um 55 Euro ärmer sein** to be 55 euros poorer *or* worse off; **ach, du/Sie Armer!** (*auch iro*) you poor thing!, poor you!; **ich Armer!** poor me!, woe is me! (*poet*); **~e Seelen** (*Rel*) holy souls; **~es Schwein** (*inf*) poor so-and-so (*inf*); **~er Irrer** (*inf*) mad fool (*inf*); (= *bedauernswert*) poor fool

ADV *comp* **~er**, *superl* **am ~sten jdn ~ plündern** to take everything sb has; **jdn ~ rauben** to rob sb of everything they have; **du isst mich noch mal ~!** (*inf*) you'll eat me out of house and home!; **~ dran sein** (*inf*) to have a hard time of it

Arm [arm] M -(e)s, -e (*Anat, Tech, fig*) arm; (*von Fluss, Baum*) branch; (*von Waage*) beam; (= *Ärmel*) sleeve; **~ in ~** arm in arm; **über/unter den ~ o-ver/under one's arm; ~ voll** armful; **zwei ~ voll Holz** two armfuls of wood; **die ~e voll haben** to have one's arms full; **jds ~ nehmen** to take sb's arm, to take sb by the arm; **jdm den ~ bieten** (*geh*) *or* **reichen** to offer sb one's arm; **jdn im ~** *or* **in den ~en halten** to hold sb in one's arms; **jdn am ~ führen** to lead sb by the arm; **jdn in den ~ nehmen** to take sb in one's arms; **jdn in die ~e schließen** to take *or* clasp sb in an embrace; **sich in den ~en liegen** to lie in each other's arms; **jdm/sich in die ~e fallen** *or* **sinken** to fall into sb's/each other's arms; **sich aus jds ~en lösen** (*geh*) to free oneself from sb's embrace; **jdn auf den ~ nehmen** to take sb onto one's arm; (*fig inf*) to pull sb's leg (*inf*); **jdm unter die ~e greifen** (*fig*) to help sb out; **jdm in die ~e laufen** (*fig inf*) to run *or* bump (*inf*) into sb; **jdn mit offenen ~en empfangen** (*fig*) to welcome sb with open arms; **jdm in den ~ fallen** (*fig*) to put a spoke in sb's wheel (*Brit*), to spike sb's guns (*Brit*), to throw sb a curve ball (*US*); **sich jdm/einer Sache in die ~e werfen** (*fig*) to throw oneself at sb/into sth; **jdn/einer Sache in die ~e treiben** (*fig*) to drive sb into sb's arms/to sth; **jdn am steifen ~ verhungern lassen** (*lit hum*) to get sb in an armlock; (*fig*) to put the screws on sb (*inf*); **der ~ des Gesetzes** (*fig*) justice; **einen langen/den längeren ~ haben** (*fig*) to have a lot of/more pull (*inf*) or influence; **jds verlängerter ~** an extension of sb

Ar|ma|da [arˈmaːda] F -, -s *or* **Armaden** [-dn] (*lit, fig*) armada

Ar|ma|ged|don [armaˈɡɛdɔn] NT -(s) Armageddon

Arm- *in cpds* arm; **arm|am|pu|tiert** [-amputiːet] ADJ with an arm amputated; **~ sein** to have had an arm amputated; **Arm|ar|beit** F (*Boxen*) fist work

Ar|ma|tur [armaˈtuːɐ] F -, -en *usu pl* (*Tech*) *Hahn, Leitung etc*) fitting; (= *Instrument*) instrument

Ar|ma|tu|ren-: **Ar|ma|tu|ren|be|leuch|tung** F (*Aut*) dash light; **Ar|ma|tu|ren|brett** NT instrument panel; (*Aut*) dashboard

Arm-: **Arm|band** [-bant] NT *pl* **-bänder** bracelet; (*von Uhr*) (watch)strap; **Arm|band|uhr** F wristwatch; **Arm|beu|ge** F **a** inside of one's elbow **b** (*Sport*) arm bend; **Arm|bin|de** F armband; (*Med*) sling; **Arm|bruch** M (*Med*) broken *or* fractured arm; **Arm|brust** F crossbow

Ärm|chen [ˈɛrmçən] NT -s, - *dim von* **Arm**

arm|dick ADJ as thick as one's arm

Ar|mee [arˈmeː] F -, -n [-ˈmeːən] (*Mil, fig*) army; (= *Gesamtheit der Streitkräfte*) (armed) forces *pl*; **bei der ~** in the army/forces

Ar|mee- *in cpds* army; **Ar|mee|be|fehl** M army order

Är|mel [ˈɛrml] M -s, - sleeve; **sich** (*dat*) **die ~ hochkrempeln** *or* **aufkrempeln** (*lit, fig*) to roll up one's sleeves; **etw aus dem ~ schütteln** to produce sth just like that

Är|mel|auf|schlag M cuff

Är|mel|leu|te- [armɛˈlɔytə-]: **Är|mel|leu|te|es|sen** NT poor man's food; **Är|mel|leu|te|ge|ruch** M smell of poverty

Är|mel|hal|ter M sleeve band

-är|me|lig [ɛrmǝlɪç] ADJ *suf* -sleeved; **kurzärme|lig** short-sleeved

Är|mel|ka|nal M (English) Channel

är|mel|los ADJ sleeveless

Är|mel|scho|ner M oversleeve

Ar|men|haus NT (*old, fig*) poorhouse

Ar|me|ni|en [arˈmeːniən] NT -s Armenia

Ar|me|ni|er [arˈmeːniɐ] M -s, -, **Ar|me|ni|e|rin** [-iərɪn] F -, -nen Armenian

ar|me|nisch [arˈmeːnɪʃ] ADJ Armenian

Ar|men-: **Ar|men|kas|se** F (*Hist*) poor box; **Ar|men|kü|che** F soup kitchen; **Ar|men|recht** NT (*dated Jur*) legal aid

Ar|men|sün|der- [armɛnˈzʏndɐ] *in cpds* (*Aus*) = Armsünder-

Ar|men|vier|tel NT poor district *or* quarter

är|mer *comp von* **arm**

Ar|mes|län|ge F arm's length; **um zwei ~n** by two arms' length

Ar|me|sün|der [armǝˈzʏndɐ] M Armensünders, Armensünder (*obs*) condemned man

Ar|me|sün|der- *in cpds* = Armsünder-

Arm-: **Arm|flor** M black armband; **Arm|ge|lenk** NT elbow joint; **Arm|he|bel** M (*Sport*) arm lever

ar|mie|ren [arˈmiːrən] *ptp* **armiert** VT **a** (*old Mil*) to arm **b** (*Tech*) *Kabel* to sheathe; *Beton* to reinforce

-ar|mig [armɪç] ADJ *suf* -armed; **einarmig** one-armed; **ein siebenarmiger Leuchter** a seven-branched candelabra

Arm-: **arm|lang** ADJ arm-length; **Arm|län|ge** F arm length; **Arm|leh|ne** F armrest; (*von Stuhl etc auch*) arm; **Arm|leuch|ter** M **a** chandelier **b** (*pej inf*: = *Mensch*) twit (*inf*), fool, twerp (*inf*)

ärm|lich [ˈɛrmlɪç] **ADJ** (*lit, fig*) poor; *Kleidung, Wohnung* shabby; *Essen* meagre (*Brit*), meager (*US*); *Verhältnisse* humble; **einen ~en Eindruck machen** to look poor/shabby; **aus ~en Verhältnissen** from a poor family **ADV** poorly, shabbily; **~ leben** to live in poor conditions

Ärm|lich|keit F -, *no pl* (*von Kleidung, Wohnung*) shabbiness; (*von Essen*) meagreness (*Brit*), meagerness (*US*); **die ~ der Verhältnisse** the poor conditions

-ärm|lig [ɛrmlɪç] ADJ *suf* = -ärmelig

Ärm|ling [ˈɛrmlɪŋ] M -s, -e oversleeve

Arm-: **Arm|loch** NT **a** armhole **b** (*euph*: = *Arschloch*) bum (*inf*); **Arm|mus|kel** M biceps; **Arm|pols|ter** NT **a** (*an Kleidung*) shoulder padding **b** (= *Armlehne*) padded armrest; **Arm|pro|the|se** F artificial arm; **Arm|reif** M, **Arm|rei|fen** M bangle; **Arm|schlüs|sel** M (*Sport*) armlock, hammerlock (*US*); **Arm|schutz** M (*Sport*) arm guard

arm|se|lig ADJ (= *dürftig*) miserable; (= *jämmerlich*) pathetic, pitiful, piteous; *Lügner* miserable, wretched; *Summe, Ausrede* paltry; **für ~e zwei Euro** for a paltry two euros, for two paltry euros; **das ist wirklich ~!** it's really pathetic!

Arm|se|lig|keit F (= *Jämmerlichkeit*) piteousness; (*von Feigling*) wretchedness; **die ~ ihrer Hütten** the miserable condition of their huts; **die ~ dieser Männer!** these pathetic men!; **die ~ dieser Ausrede** this paltry excuse; **die ~ dieses Lügners** such a wretched liar

Arm|ses|sel M, **Arm|stuhl** (*old*) M armchair

ärms|te(r, s) *superl von* **arm**

Arm-: Arm|stum|mel M (inf), **Arm|stumpf** M stump of one's arm; **Arm|stüt|ze** F armrest

Arm|sün|der- [arm'zʏndɐ-]: **Arm|sün|der|bank** F pl **-bänke, Arm|sün|der|bänk|chen** NT (hum) (beim Essen) small table at which children sit (bei Prüfung, Quiz etc) hot seat; **dasitzen wie auf dem Armsünderbänkchen** to be sitting there looking as though the world were about to end; **Arm|sün|der|glo|cke** F knell tolled during an execution; **Arm|sün|der|mie|ne** F (hum) hangdog expression

Ar|mut ['armuːt] F -, no pl (lit, fig) poverty; **charakterliche ~** lack of character; **geistige ~** intellectual poverty; (von Mensch) lack of intellect; **neue ~** new poverty

-ar|mut F suf in cpds lack of

Ar|muts-: Ar|muts|gren|ze F , no pl poverty line; **Ar|muts|zeug|nis** NT (fig) **jdm/sich (selbst) ein ~ ausstellen** to show or prove sb's/one's (own) shortcomings; **das ist ein ~ für ihn** that shows him up

Arm|voll △ M -, - → **Arm**

Ar|ni|ka ['arnika] F -, -s arnica

A|rom [a'roːm] NT -s, -e (poet) fragrance, scent

A|ro|ma [a'roːma] NT -s, **Aromen** or -s or (dated) **-ta** **a** (= Geruch) aroma **b** (= Geschmack) flavour (Brit), flavor (US), taste **c** no pl flavouring (Brit), flavoring (US)

A|ro|ma|the|ra|pie F (Med) aromatherapy

a|ro|ma|tisch [aro'maːtɪʃ] **ADJ** **a** (= wohlriechend) aromatic **b** (= wohlschmeckend) savoury (Brit), savory (US) **c** (Chem) aromatic **ADV** **~ riechen** to smell fragrant or aromatic; **~ schmecken** to taste aromatic

a|ro|ma|ti|sie|ren [aromati'ziːrən] ptp **aromatisiert** VT to give aroma to; **aromatisiert** aromatic; **zu stark aromatisiert sein** to have too strong an aroma

A|rons|stab ['aːrɔns-] M arum

Ar|rak ['arak] M -s, -s or -e arrack

Ar|ran|ge|ment [arãʒə'mãː] NT -s, -s (alle Bedeutungen) arrangement

Ar|ran|geur [arã'ʒøːɐ] M -s, -e, **Ar|ran|geu|rin** [-'ʒøːrɪn] F -, -nen (geh) organizer; (Mus) arranger; **er war der ~ dieses Abkommens** he arranged this agreement

ar|ran|gie|ren [arã'ʒiːrən] ptp **arrangiert** VTI (alle Bedeutungen) to arrange (jdm for sb) VR **sich mit jdm ~** to come to an arrangement with sb; **sich mit etw ~** to come to terms with sth

Ar|rest [a'rɛst] M -(e)s, -s **a** (Sch, Mil, Jur: = Jugendarrest) detention; **seine Eltern bestraften ihn mit ~** his parents punished him by grounding him **b** (Econ, Jur) (auch persönlicher Arrest) attachment; (auch dinglicher Arrest) distress (form), distraint; **~ in jds Vermögen** distress (form) upon sb's property

Ar|res|tant [arɛs'tant] M -en, -en, **Ar|res|tan|tin** [-'tantɪn] F -, -nen (dated Jur) detainee

Ar|rest-: Ar|rest|lo|kal NT (dated) detention room; (Mil) guardroom; **Ar|rest|zel|le** F detention cell

ar|re|tie|ren [are'tiːrən] ptp **arretiert** VT **a** (dated) jdn to take into custody **b** (Tech) to lock (in place)

Ar|re|tie|rung F -, -en **a** (dated: = Verhaftung) taking into custody **b** (Tech) locking; (= Vorrichtung) locking mechanism

Ar|rhyth|mie [arʏt'miː] F -, -n [-'miːən] (Med) arrhythmia

ar|ri|vie|ren [ari'viːrən] **arriviert** VI aux sein to make it (inf), to become a success; **zu etw ~** to rise to become sth

ar|ri|viert [ari'viːɐt] ADJ successful; (pej) upstart; **er ist jetzt ~** he has arrived, he has made it (inf)

Ar|ri|vier|te(r) [ari'viːɐtə] MF decl as adj arrivé, parvenu (pej)

ar|ro|gant [aro'gant] **ADJ** arrogant **ADV** arrogantly

Ar|ro|ganz [aro'gants] F -, no pl arrogance

ar|ron|die|ren [arɔn'diːrən, arõ-] ptp **arrondiert** VT (geh) **a** Grenze to realign, to adjust; Grundstück to realign or adjust the boundaries of **b** Kanten etc to round off

Arsch [arʃ, a:ɐʃ] M -(e)s, ⸚e ['ɛrʃə, 'ɛːɐʃə] **a** (vulg) arse (Brit sl), ass (US sl), bum (Brit inf), fanny (US sl), butt (US inf); **jdm** or **jdn in den ~ treten** to give sb a kick up the arse (Brit sl) or ass (US sl); **den ~ voll kriegen** to get a bloody good hiding (Brit inf), to get an ass-kicking (US sl); **leck mich am ~!** (= lass mich in Ruhe) get stuffed! (inf), fuck off! (vulg); (= verdammt noch mal) bugger! (Brit sl), fuck it! (vulg); (sl: überrascht) bugger me! (Brit sl), fuck me! (vulg); **er kann mich (mal) am ~ lecken** he can get stuffed (Brit inf), he can fuck off (vulg); **ich könnte mich** or **mir in den ~ beißen** (sl) I could kick myself; **jdm in den ~ kriechen** (inf) to lick sb's arse (Brit sl) or ass (US sl); **du hast wohl den ~ offen!** (sl) you're out of your tiny mind (inf); **er kriegt wieder den ~ nicht hoch** (inf) he won't get his arse (Brit) or ass (US) in gear (sl); **~ mit Ohren** (dated sl) silly bugger (Brit sl); **am ~ der Welt** (inf) in the back of beyond; **im** or **am ~ sein** (sl) to be fucked up (vulg); **fürn ~ sein** (sl) to be crap (inf); **einen kalten ~ kriegen** (sl: = Angst kriegen) to shit oneself (sl); **den ~ zukneifen** (sl) to kick the bucket (inf); **jdm den ~ aufreißen** (sl, esp Mil) to work the shit out of sb (sl); **sich (dat) den ~ aufreißen** (sl) to bust a gut (inf); **ihm geht der ~ mit** or **auf Grundeis** (dated sl) he's scared shitless (sl), he's shit-scared (Brit sl); **das geht mir am ~ vorbei** (sl: = ist mir egal) I don't give a shit (about it) (sl); **Schütze ~** (Mil) simple private; **sich auf den** or **seinen ~ setzen** (lit) to park one's arse (Brit sl) or ass (US sl); (fig dated sl: = sich Mühe geben) to get one's arse (Brit) or ass (US) in gear (sl), to get one's finger out (inf); **sich (dat) den ~ abfrieren** (sl) to freeze one's arse (Brit) or ass (US) off (sl); **seinen ~ in Bewegung setzen** (sl) to get one's arse (Brit) or ass (US) in gear (sl); **schwing deinen ~ weg** (sl) move your fat arse (Brit sl) or ass (US sl)
b (sl: = Mensch) bastard (sl), bugger (Brit sl), sod (sl); (= Dummkopf) stupid bastard etc (sl); **kein ~ war da** nobody fucking turned up (vulg)

Arsch-: Arsch|ba|cke F (sl) buttock, cheek; **Arsch|fi|cker** [-fɪkɐ] M -s, - **a** (lit vulg) bumfucker (Brit vulg), butt-fucker (US inf) **b** (fig vulg) slimy bastard (sl); **Arsch|gei|ge** F (dated sl) = **Arsch** b; **arsch|kalt** ADJ (inf) bloody (Brit inf) or damn (inf) cold; **Arsch-krie|che(in)** M(F) (sl) ass-kisser (sl); **Arsch-krie|che|rei** F (sl) ass-kissing (sl)

ärsch|lings ['ɛrʃlɪŋs, 'ɛːɐʃ-] ADV (old) backwards, arse (Brit) or ass (US) first (sl)

Arsch-: Arsch|loch NT (vulg) **a** (lit) arsehole (Brit sl), asshole (US sl) **b** = **Arsch** b; **Arsch-tritt** M (sl) kick up the arse (Brit sl) or ass (US sl); **Arsch-und-Tit|ten-Pres|se** F (sl) tit-and-bum press (Brit inf), tit-and-ass media pl (US inf)

Ar|sen [ar'zeːn] NT -s, no pl (abbr **As**) arsenic

Ar|se|nal [arze'naːl] NT -s, -e (lit, fig) arsenal

ar|sen|hal|tig ADJ containing arsenic

Ar|se|nik [ar'zeːnɪk] NT -s, no pl arsenic, arsenic trioxide (form)

Ar|sen|ver|gif|tung F arsenic poisoning

Art [aːɐt] F -, -en **a** kind, sort, type; **diese ~ Leute/Buch** people/books like that, that kind or sort of person/book; **jede ~ (von) Buch/Terror** any kind etc of book/terrorism, a book of any kind etc/terrorism in any form; **alle möglichen ~en von Büchern, Bücher aller ~** all kinds or sorts of books, books of all kinds or sorts; **einzig in seiner ~ sein** to be the only one of its kind, to be unique; **aus der ~ schlagen** not to take after anyone in the family **b** (Biol) species **c** (= Methode) way; **auf die ~** in that way or manner; **auf die ~ geht es am schnellsten** that is the quickest way; **auf merkwürdige/grausame**

---

etc **~** in a strange/cruel etc way; **die einfachste ~, etw zu tun** the simplest way to do sth or of doing sth; **auf diese ~ und Weise** in this way **d** (= Wesen) nature; (= übliche Verhaltensweise) way; **es entspricht nicht meiner ~** it's not my nature; **das ist eigentlich nicht seine ~** it's not like him; **von lebhafter ~ sein** to have a lively nature; **eine ~ haben** to have a lively way (with one) **e** (= Stil) style; **nach bayrischer ~** Bavarian style; **Schnitzel nach ~ des Hauses** schnitzel à la maison **f** (= Benehmen) behaviour (Brit), behavior (US); **das ist doch keine ~!** that's no way to behave!; **was ist das (denn) für eine ~?** what sort of a way to behave is that?; **ist das vielleicht** or **etwa eine ~!** that's no way to behave!

Art. abbr von **Artikel**

Art-: Art|an|ga|be F (Gram) adverb of manner; (= Adverbialbestimmung) adverbial phrase of manner; **Art|bil|dung** F speciation (form)

Ar|te|fakt [arte'fakt] NT -(e)s, -e artefact

art|ei|gen ADJ species-specific

ar|ten ['aːrtn] VI aux sein (geh) **nach jdm ~** to take after sb → auch **geartet**

Ar|ten-: ar|ten|reich ADJ Lebensraum, Wald etc species-rich; **diese Tierklasse ist sehr ~** this class of animal contains a large number of species; **Ar|ten|reich|tum** M (Biol) diversity of species; **Ar|ten|schutz** M protection of species

Ar|ten|schutz-: Ar|ten|schutz|ab|kom|men NT agreement on the protection of endangered species, biodiversity treaty; **Ar|ten|schutz-kon|fe|renz** F conference on the protection of endangered species

Ar|ten|schwund M extinction of species

Ar|ten|ster|ben NT extinction of species

Ar|ten|tod M extinction as a species; **vom ~ bedroht sein** to be threatened with extinction as a species; **den ~ sterben** to become extinct or die out as a species

Art-: art|er|hal|tend **ADJ** survival attr **ADV** **das wirkte sich ~ aus** that contributed to the survival of the species; **Art|er|hal|tung** F survival of the species

Ar|te|rie [ar'teːriə] F -, -n artery

ar|te|ri|ell [arte'riɛl] ADJ arterial

Ar|te|ri|en|ver|kal|kung F (inf) hardening of the arteries; **~ haben** (fig) to be senile

Ar|te|ri|o|skle|ro|se [arterioskle'roːzə] F arteriosclerosis

ar|te|sisch [ar'teːzɪʃ] ADJ **-er Brunnen** artesian well

Art-: art|fremd ADJ (Biol) foreign (to the species); **Art|ge|nos|se** M , **Art|ge|nos|sin** F (= Tier/Pflanze) animal/plant of the same species; (= Mensch) person of the same type; **art|ge|recht** ADJ appropriate to the species; **eine ~e Tierhaltung** livestock farming methods which are appropriate for each species; **art|gleich** ADJ (Biol) of the same species; Mensch of the same type

Arth|ri|tis [ar'triːtɪs] F -, **Arthritiden** [artri'tiːdn] arthritis

arth|ri|tisch [ar'triːtɪʃ] ADJ arthritic

Arth|ro|se [ar'troːzə] F -, -n arthrosis

ar|ti|fi|zi|ell [artifi'tsiɛl] ADJ (geh) artificial

ar|tig ['aːrtɪç] ADJ **a** Kind, Hund etc good, well-behaved no adv; **sei schön ~** be a good boy/dog etc!, be good! **b** (old: = galant) courteous **c** (old: = anmutig) charming

-ar|tig ADJ suf -like; **gummiartig** rubberlike, rubbery

Ar|tig|keit F -, -en **a** (= Wohlerzogenheit) good behaviour (Brit) or behavior (US); (old) (= Galanterie) courtesy, courteousness; (= Anmut) charm **b** (= Kompliment) compliment; (= höfliche Bemerkung) pleasantry; **jdm einige ~en sagen** to make a few courteous remarks to sb

---

Ar|ti|kel [ar'tiːkl, -'tɪkl] M **-s, -** (alle Bedeutungen) article; (= Lexikonartikel auch) entry; (Comm auch) item

Ar|ti|kel-: Ar|ti|kel|rei|he F , **Ar|ti|kel|se|rie** F series of articles; **Ar|ti|kel|über|schrift** F (= Schlagzeile) headline

Ar|ti|ku|la|ti|on [artikula'tsioːn] F **-, -en** articulation; (= deutliche Aussprache auch) enunciation; (Mus) phrasing

Ar|ti|ku|la|ti|ons-: ar|ti|ku|la|ti|ons|fähig ADJ articulate; (Phon) able to articulate; **Ar|ti|ku|la|ti|ons|fähig|keit** F articulateness; (Phon) ability to articulate; **Ar|ti|ku|la|ti|ons|or|ga|ne** PL organs pl of speech; **Ar|ti|ku|la|ti|ons|ver|mö|gen** NT = Artikulationsfähigkeit

ar|ti|ku|la|to|risch [artikula'toːrɪʃ] ADJ (Phon) articulatory

ar|ti|ku|lie|ren [artiku'liːrən] ptp **artikuliert** VTI to articulate; (= deutlich aussprechen auch) to enunciate; (Mus) to phrase; **sich artikuliert aus|drücken** to be articulate VR (fig geh) to express oneself

Ar|ti|ku|lie|rung F **-, -en** articulation; (= deutliche Aussprache auch) enunciation; (Mus) phrasing

Ar|til|le|rie ['artɪləri, artɪlə'riː] F **-, -n** [-'riːən] artillery

Ar|til|le|rie- in cpds artillery; **Ar|til|le|rie|be|schuss** ▲ M artillery fire; **Ar|til|le|rie|ge|fecht** NT artillery fighting or engagement

Ar|til|le|rist ['artɪlərɪst, artɪlə'rɪst] M **-en, -en** artilleryman

Ar|ti|scho|cke [arti'ʃɔkə] F **-, -n** (globe) artichoke

Ar|ti|scho|cken|bo|den M usu pl artichoke bottom

Ar|ti|scho|cken|herz NT artichoke heart

Ar|tist [ar'tɪst] M **-en, -en, Ar|tis|tin** [-'tɪstɪn] F **-, -nen** a (circus or (im Varietee) variety) artiste or performer b (obs, geh: = Meister) artist (+gen at) c (inf: = spielerisch handelnder Mensch) joker (inf)

Ar|tis|ten|fa|kul|tät F (Hist) Faculty of Arts

Ar|tis|tik [ar'tɪstɪk] F **-,** no pl artistry; (= Zirkus/ Varieteekunst) circus/variety performing

ar|tis|tisch [ar'tɪstɪʃ] ADJ a **sein ~es Können** his ability as a performer; **eine ~e Glanzleis|tung/~ einmalige Leistung** (in Zirkus/Varietee) a miraculous/unique feat of circus/variety artistry; **eine ~e Sensation** a sensational performance b (= geschickt) masterly no adv c (= formalkünstlerisch) artistic

Ar|to|thek [arto'teːk] F **-, -en** picture (lending) library

Ar|tur ['artʊr] M **-s** Arthur

Ar|tus ['artʊs] M **-'** (Hist, Myth) (King) Arthur

Art-: art|ver|schie|den ADJ of different species; **art|ver|wandt** ADJ of the same type; (Biol) species-related; **Art|ver|wandt|schaft** F (Biol) species relationship; **Art|wort** NT pl **-wörter** (Gram) adjective

Arz|nei [aːɐts'nai, arts'nai] F **-, -en** (lit, fig) medicine; **das war für ihn eine bittere/heilsame ~** (fig) that was a painful/useful lesson for him

Arz|nei-: Arz|nei|buch NT pharmacopoeia; **Arz|nei|fläsch|chen** NT medicine bottle; **Arz|nei|kun|de** F , **Arz|nei|leh|re** F pharmacology

Arz|nei|mit|tel NT drug

Arz|nei|mit|tel-: Arz|nei|mit|tel|for|schung F pharmacological research; **Arz|nei|mit|tel|ge|setz** NT law governing the manufacture and prescription of drugs; **Arz|nei|mit|tel|her|stel|ler(in)** M(F) drug manufacturer or company; **Arz|nei|mit|tel|leh|re** F pharmacology; **Arz|nei|mit|tel|miss|brauch** ▲ M drug abuse; **Arz|nei|mit|tel|sucht** F addiction to medicines, dependency on medication,

pharmacomania (spec); **Arz|nei|mit|tel|ver|sor|gung** F provision of drugs (+gen to)

Arz|nei-: Arz|nei|pflan|ze F medicinal plant; **Arz|nei|schränk|chen** NT medicine cupboard

Arzt [aːɐtst, artst] M **-es, ⸚e** ['ɛːɐtstə, 'ɛrtstə], **Ärz|tin** ['ɛːɐtstɪn, 'ɛrtstɪn] F **-, -nen** doctor, physician (old, form), medical practitioner (form); (= Facharzt) specialist; (= Chirurg) surgeon; **praktischer ~, praktische Ärztin** general practitioner, GP; **eine Ärztin** a (woman or female) doctor

Arzt|be|ruf M medical profession

Ärz|te-: Ärz|te|be|steck NT set of surgical instruments; **Ärz|te|kam|mer** F ≈ General Medical Council (Brit); ≈ State Medical Board of Registration (US); **Ärz|te|kol|le|gi|um** NT , **Ärz|te|kom|mis|si|on** F medical advisory board; **Ärz|te|kon|gress** ▲ M medical or doctors' congress; **Ärz|te|man|gel** M shortage of doctors

Ärz|te|schaft ['ɛːɐtstəʃaft, 'ɛrtstə-] F **-, -en** medical profession

Ärz|te|ver|tre|ter(in) M(F) (von Arzneimittelfirma) medical representative

Arzt-: Arzt|frau F doctor's wife; **Arzt|hel|fer(in)** M(F) , **Arzt|hil|fe** F (doctor's) receptionist

Ärz|tin F → Arzt

Arzt-: Arzt|kit|tel M (doctor's) white coat; **Arzt|kos|ten** PL doctor's or medical fees pl

ärzt|lich ['ɛːɐtstlɪç, 'ɛrtst-] ADJ medical ADV beraten, untersuchen medically; **er ließ sich ~ behandeln** he went to a doctor for treatment; **~ empfohlen** recommended by doctors; **bei uns sind Sie bestens ~ aufgehoben** you get the best medical treatment here

Arzt-: Arzt|pra|xis F doctor's practice; **Arzt|rech|nung** F doctor's bill; **Arzt|ro|man** M hospital romance; **Arzt|wahl** F choice of doctor

As¹ △ [as] NT **-es, -e** → Ass

As² NT **-, -** (Mus) A flat

As|best [as'bɛst] NT **-(e)s,** no pl asbestos

As|best- in cpds asbestos; **As|best|be|ton** M asbestos cement; **as|best|frei** ADJ free from or of asbestos, asbestos-free; **as|best|hal|tig** ADJ containing asbestos pred, asbestos-containing attr

As|bes|to|se [asbɛs'toːzə] F **-, -n** asbestosis

As|best-: As|best|plat|te F (für Topf) asbestos mat; (für Bügeleisen) asbestos stand; **As|best|sa|nie|rung** F asbestos abatement; **As|best|staub** M asbestos particles pl, asbestos dust; **as|best|ver|seucht** ADJ contaminated with asbestos pred

A|schan|ti|nuss ▲ [a'ʃanti-] F (Aus) peanut, groundnut

Asch- [aʃ-]: **Asch|be|cher** M ashtray; **asch|blond** ADJ ash blond

A|sche ['aʃə] F **-, -n** ash(es pl); (von Zigarette, Vulkan) ash; (fig) (= sterbliche Überreste) ashes pl; (= Trümmer) ruins pl; (nach Feuer) ashes pl; **zu ~ werden** to turn to dust; **sich** (dat) **~ aufs Haupt streuen** (fig geh) to wear sackcloth and ashes

Ä|sche ['ɛʃə] F **-, -n** grayling

Asch|ei|mer ['aʃ-] M (dial) ash can (esp US), ash bin

A|schen-: A|schen|bahn F cinder track; **A|schen|be|cher** M ashtray; **A|schen|brö|del** [-brøːdl] NT **-s, -** (Liter, fig) Cinderella, Cinders (Brit inf); **A|schen|brö|del|da|sein** NT Cinderella existence; **A|schen|ei|mer** M ash can (esp US), ash bin; **A|schen|kas|ten** M ash pan; **A|schen|platz** M (Ftbl) cinder pitch; (Tennis) clay court; **A|schen|put|tel** [-pʊtl] NT **-s, -** (Liter, fig) Cinderella, Cinders (Brit inf); **A|schen|re|gen** M shower of ash

A|scher ['aʃɐ] M **-s, -** (inf) ashtray

A|sche|re|gen M ashfall, shower of ash

A|scher|mitt|woch [aʃɐ'mɪtvɔx] M Ash Wednesday

ASCHERMITTWOCH

Aschermittwoch (Ash Wednesday) is the day following **Karneval** and the first day of Lent. On this day devout Catholics go to church and have a cross of ashes smeared on their foreheads as a reminder of the transience of human life.

In Bavaria there is also **politischer Aschermittwoch**. Each political party holds a mass rally at which it reviews its own policies and more especially those of the other parties. The speakers are not only local politicians but also often the national party leaders. For this reason **politischer Aschermittwoch** is a focus of attention for the whole of Germany. → **Karneval**

Asch-: asch|fahl ADJ ashen; **asch|far|ben** [-farbn], **asch|far|big** ADJ ash-coloured (Brit), ash-colored (US); **asch|grau** ADJ ash-grey (Brit), ash-gray (US); **Asch|kas|ten** M ash pan

Asch|ram ['aʃram] M **-s, -s** ashram

ASCII- ['aski-] (Comput): **ASCII-Da|tei** F ASCII file; **ASCII-Kode** M ASCII code

As|cor|bin|säu|re [askɔr'biːn-] F ascorbic acid

ASEAN ['eːsiən] F OR M - abbr von **Association of South East Asian Nations** ASEAN; **~-Staat** ASEAN country or state

A-Sei|te ['aː-] F (von Schallplatte) A-side

A|sen ['aːzn] PL (Myth) Aesir pl

ä|sen ['ɛːzn] (Hunt) VIR to graze, to browse VT to graze on

a|sep|tisch [a'zɛptɪʃ] ADJ aseptic ADV aseptically

Ä|ser¹ ['ɛːzɐ] M **-s, -** (Hunt) mouth

Ä|ser² pl von Aas

A|ser|baid|schan [azɛrbai'dʒaːn] NT **-s** Azerbaijan

A|ser|baid|scha|ner [azɛrbai'dʒaːnɐ] M **-s, -**, **A|ser|baid|scha|ne|rin** [-ərɪn] F **-, -nen** Azerbaijani

a|ser|baid|scha|nisch [azɛrbai'dʒaːnɪʃ] ADJ Azerbaijani

A|ser|baid|schan etc [azɛrbai'dʒaːn] NT = **Aserbaidschan** etc

a|se|xu|ell ['azɛksuɛl, azɛ'ksuɛl] ADJ asexual

Ash|ram ['aʃram] M **-s, -s** ashram

A|si|at [a'ziaːt] M **-en, -en, A|si|a|tin** [a'ziaːtɪn] F **-, -nen** Asian

A|si|a|ti|ka [a'ziaːtika] PL Orientalia pl

a|si|a|tisch [a'ziaːtɪʃ] ADJ Asian, Asiatic; **~e Grippe** Asian or Asiatic (US) flu; **der ~-pazifi|sche Raum** the Pacific Rim

A|si|en ['aːziən] NT **-s** Asia

As|ke|se [as'keːzə] F **-,** no pl asceticism

As|ket [as'keːt] M **-en, -en, As|ke|tin** [-'keːtɪn] F **-, -nen** ascetic

as|ke|tisch [as'keːtɪʃ] ADJ ascetic ADV ascetically

As|kor|bin|säu|re [askɔr'biːn-] F ascorbic acid

Äs|ku|lap- [ɛsku'laːp-]: **Äs|ku|lap|schlan|ge** F snake of Aesculapius; **Äs|ku|lap|stab** M staff of Aesculapius

Ä|sop [ɛ'zoːp] M **-s** Aesop

ä|so|pisch [ɛ'zoːpɪʃ] ADJ Aesopic; **eine ~e Fabel** one of Aesop's Fables

a|so|zi|al ['azotsiaːl, azo'tsiaːl] ADJ asocial ADV asocially

A|so|zi|a|le(r) ['azotsiaːlə] MF decl as adj (pej) antisocial person/man/woman etc; **~ pl** antisocial elements

A|so|zi|a|li|tät [azotsiali'tɛːt] F **-,** no pl (von Mensch) antisocial nature; (= Verhalten) antisocial behaviour (Brit) or behavior (US)

As|par|tam® [aspar'ta:m] NT **-s, -e** aspartame

As|pekt [as'pɛkt] M **-(e)s, -e** aspect; **unter diesem ~ betrachtet** looking at it from this aspect or from this point of view; **einen neuen ~ bekommen** to take on a different complexion

As|phalt [as'falt, 'asfalt] M **-(e)s, -e** asphalt

As|phalt-: As|phalt|be|ton M asphalt; **As|phalt|blatt** NT (pej inf) scandal sheet; (= Boulevardzeitung) tabloid (newspaper); **As|phalt|de|cke** F asphalt surface; **As|phalt|dschun|gel** M (pej inf: = Großstadt) asphalt jungle

as|phal|tie|ren [asfal'ti:rən] ptp **asphaltiert** VT to asphalt, to tarmac

as|phal|tiert [asfal'ti:ɛt] ADJ asphalt

As|phalt-: As|phalt|ma|le|rei F pavement (Brit) or sidewalk (US) art; **As|phalt|stra|ße** F asphalt road

As|pik [as'pi:k, as'pɪk] M OR (AUS) NT **-s, -e** aspic

As|pi|rant [aspi'rant] M **-en, -en, As|pi|ran|tin** [-'rantɪn] F **-, -nen -a** (geh) candidate (für, auf +acc for) **-b** (DDR Univ) research assistant

As|pi|ran|tur [aspiran'tu:ɐ] F **-, -en** (DDR) research assistantship

As|pi|ra|ta [aspi'ra:ta] F **-, Aspiraten** [-tn] (Phon) aspirate

As|pi|ra|ti|on [aspira'tsio:n] F **-, -en -a** usu pl (geh) aspiration; **~en auf etw** (acc) or **nach etw haben** to have aspirations toward(s) sth, to aspire to sth **-b** (Phon) aspiration

as|pi|rie|ren [aspi'ri:rən] ptp **aspiriert** VI (geh) to aspire (auf +acc to); (Aus) to apply (auf +acc for) VT (Phon) to aspirate

aß pret von **essen**

Ass ▲ [as] NT **-es, -e** (lit, fig) ace; **alle vier ~e** (lit) all the aces

As|se|ku|ranz [aseku'rants] F **-, -en** (old) assurance; (= Gesellschaft) assurance company

As|sel [asl] F **-, -n** isopod (spec); (= Rollassel, Kellerassel, Landassel auch) woodlouse

As|sem|bler [ə'sɛmblɐ] M **-s, -** (Comput) assembler

As|sem|bler|spra|che F (Comput) assembly language

As|ser|vat [asɛr'va:t] NT **-(e)s, -e** (court) exhibit

As|ser|va|ten|kam|mer F , **As|ser|va|ten|raum** M room where court exhibits are kept

As|ses|sor [a'sɛso:ɐ] M **-s, Assessoren** [-'so:rən], **As|ses|so|rin** [-'so:rɪn] F **-, -nen** graduate civil servant who has completed his/her traineeship

As|si|mi|la|ti|on [asimila'tsio:n] F **-, -en** assimilation; (= Anpassung) adjustment (an +acc to)

as|si|mi|la|to|risch [asimila'to:rɪʃ] ADJ assimilatory, assimilative

as|si|mi|lie|ren [asimi'li:rən] ptp **assimiliert** VT/I to assimilate VR to become assimilated; **sich an etw** (acc) **~** (Mensch) to adjust to sth

As|sis|tent [asɪs'tɛnt] M **-en, -en, As|sis|ten|tin** [-'tɛntɪn] F **-, -nen** assistant

As|sis|tenz [asɪs'tɛnts] F **-, (rare) -en** assistance; **unter ~ von ...** with the assistance of ...

As|sis|tenz-: As|sis|tenz|arzt M , **As|sis|tenz|ärz|tin** F junior doctor (Brit), intern (US); **As|sis|tenz|pro|fes|sor(in)** M(F) assistant professor

as|sis|tie|ren [asɪs'ti:rən] ptp **assistiert** VI to assist (jdm sb)

As|so|nanz [aso'nants] F **-, -en** (Poet) assonance

As|so|zi|a|ti|on [asotsia'tsio:n] F **-, -en** association

As|so|zi|a|ti|ons-: As|so|zi|a|ti|ons|frei|heit F freedom of association; **As|so|zi|a|ti|ons|ket|te** F chain of associations; **As|so|zi|a|ti|ons|test** M (Psych) (free) association test

as|so|zi|a|tiv [asotsia'ti:f] (Psych, geh) ADJ associative ADV verbunden through association; **Erinnerungen ~ hervorrufen** to evoke memories

through association; **etw ~ mit etw verbinden** to associate sth with sth

as|so|zi|ie|ren [asotsi'i:rən] ptp **assoziiert** (geh) VT to associate; **mit etw assoziiert werden** to be associated with sth; **mit Grün assoziiere ich Ruhe** I associate green with peace; **die Musik assoziierte bei mir Unangenehmes** the music suggested something unpleasant to me VT to make associations; **frei ~** to make free associations VR **-a** (Vorstellungen etc) to have associations (in +dat, bei for); **beim Anblick des Hauses ~ sich in** or **bei mir Kindheitserinnerungen** when I see the house I think of my childhood **-b** (= an-, zusammenschließen) **sich mit jdm ~** to join with sb; **sich an jdn/etw ~** to become associated to sb/sth

as|so|zi|iert [asotsi'i:ɛt] ADJ associated; **Mitgliedschaft** associate; **mit der EU ~ sein** to be an associate member of the EU

As|su|an(stau)|damm [a'sua:n-] M Aswan (High) Dam

As|sy|rer [a'sy:rɐ] M **-s, -, As|sy|re|rin** [-ərɪn] F **-, -nen** Assyrian

As|sy|ri|en [a'sy:riən] NT **-s** Assyria

As|sy|ri|er [a'sy:riɐ] M **-s, -, As|sy|ri|e|rin** [-iərɪn] F **-, -nen** Assyrian

as|sy|risch [a'sy:rɪʃ] ADJ Assyrian

Ast [ast] M **-(e)s, ⸚e** ['ɛstə] **-a** branch, bough; (fig: von Nerv) branch; **sich in Äste teilen** to branch; (= absägen, **auf dem man sitzt** (fig) to dig one's own grave; **einen ~ durchsägen** (hum) to snore like a grampus (inf), to saw wood (US inf) → **absteigen b -b** (im Holz) knot **-c** (inf) (= Rücken) back; (= Buckel) hump(back), hunchback; **sich** (dat) **einen ~ lachen** (inf) to double up (with laughter)

AStA ['asta] M **-s, Asten** ['astn] (Univ) abbr von **Allgemeiner Studentenausschuss**

As|tat [a'sta:t, as'ta:t] NT **-s, no pl, As|ta|tin** [asta'ti:n] NT **-s, no pl** (abbr **At**) astatine

Äst|chen ['ɛstçən] NT **-s, -** dim von **Ast**

as|ten ['astn] (inf) VI **-a** (= sich anstrengen) to slog (inf); (= büffeln) to swot (Brit); to cram **-c** aux sein (= sich fortbewegen) to drag oneself VT to hump (inf), to lug (Brit inf)

As|ter ['astɐ] F **-, -n** aster, Michaelmas daisy

As|te|ro|id [astero'i:t] M **-en, -en** [-dn] (Astron) asteroid

Ast|ga|bel F fork (of a branch); **eine ~** a fork of a branch

As|the|ni|ker [a'ste:nikɐ, as'te:-] M **-s, -, As|the|ni|ke|rin** [-ərɪn] F **-, -nen** asthenic

Äs|thet [ɛs'te:t] M **-en, -en, Äs|the|tin** [-'te:tɪn] F **-, -nen** aesthete

Äs|the|tik [ɛs'te:tɪk] F **-, no pl -a** (= Wissenschaft) aesthetics sing **-b** (= Schönheit) aesthetics pl **-c** (= Schönheitssinn) aesthetic sense

Äs|the|ti|ker [ɛs'te:tikɐ] M **-s, -, Äs|the|ti|ke|rin** [-ərɪn] F **-, -nen** aesthetician

äs|the|tisch [ɛs'te:tɪʃ] ADJ aesthetic

äs|the|ti|sie|ren [ɛsteti'zi:rən] ptp **ästhetisiert** (geh: usu pej) VT to aestheticize VI to talk about aesthetics

Äs|the|ti|zis|mus [ɛsteti'tsɪsmʊs] M **-, no pl** (pej geh) aestheticism

Äs|the|ti|zist [ɛsteti'tsɪst] M **-en, -en, Äs|the|ti|zis|tin** [-'tsɪstɪn] F **-, -nen** aestheticist

Asth|ma ['astma] NT **-s, no pl** asthma

Asth|ma-: Asth|ma|an|fall M asthma attack; **asth|ma|krank** ADJ asthmatic, suffering from asthma pred

Asth|ma|ti|ker [ast'ma:tikɐ] M **-s, -, Asth|ma|ti|ke|rin** [-ərɪn] F **-, -nen** asthmatic

asth|ma|tisch [ast'ma:tɪʃ] ADJ asthmatic

as|tig ['astɪç] ADJ Holz knotty, gnarled

As|tig|ma|tis|mus [astɪgma'tɪsmʊs] M **-, no pl** (Med) astigmatism, astigmia

Ast|loch NT knothole

as|tral [as'tra:l] ADJ astral

Ast|ral-: Ast|ral|kör|per M , **Ast|ral|leib** M (Philos) astral body; (iro inf) beautiful or heavenly body; **Ast|ral|rei|se** F astral journey

ast|rein ADJ **-a** Holz, Brett free of knots **-b** (fig inf: = moralisch einwandfrei) straight (inf), above board, on the level (inf) **-c** (fig inf: = echt) genuine **-d** (dated sl: = prima) fantastic ADV (dated sl: = prima) fantastically

Astro-: Ast|ro|lo|ge [astro'lo:gə] M **-n, -n, Ast|ro|lo|gin** [-'lo:gɪn] F **-, -nen** astrologer; **Ast|ro|lo|gie** [astrolo'gi:] F **-, no pl** astrology; **ast|ro|lo|gisch** [astro'lo:gɪʃ] ADJ astrological ADV **~ interessiert sein** to be interested in astrology; **Ast|ro|me|di|zin** F astro-medicine; **Ast|ro|naut** [astro'naut] M **-en, -en, Ast|ro|nau|tin** [-'nautɪn] F **-, -nen** astronaut; **Ast|ro|nau|tik** [astro'nautɪk] F astronautics sing; **ast|ro|nau|tisch** [astro'nautɪʃ] ADJ astronautic(al); **Ast|ro|nom** [astro'no:m] M **-en, -en, Ast|ro|no|min** [-'no:mɪn] F **-, -nen** astronomer; **Ast|ro|no|mie** [astrono'mi:] F **-, no pl** astronomy; **ast|ro|no|misch** [astro'no:mɪʃ] ADJ (lit) astronomical; (fig auch) astronomic; **~e Navigation** astronavigation

ast|ro|phisch ['astro-fɪʃ, a'stro:-] ADJ (Poet) not divided into strophes

Ast|ro-: [astro-]: Ast|ro|phy|sik F astrophysics sing; **ast|ro|phy|si|ka|lisch** ADJ astrophysical; **Ast|ro|phy|si|ker(in)** M(F) astrophysicist

Ast|werk NT branches pl

ASU ['a:zu] F **-, no pl** abbr von **Abgassonderuntersuchung**

Äsung ['ɛ:zʊŋ] F **-, -en** (Hunt) grazing

ASW [a:ɛs've:] no art **-, no pl** abbr von **außersinnliche Wahrnehmung** ESP

Asyl [a'zy:l] NT **-s, -e -a** (= Schutz) sanctuary no art (liter); (= politisches Asyl) (political) asylum no art; **jdm ~ gewähren** to grant sb sanctuary (liter)/(political) asylum; **um ~ bitten** or **nachsuchen** (form) to ask or apply (form) for (political) asylum **-b** (old: = Heim) home, asylum

Asy|lant [azy'lant] M **-en, -en, Asy|lan|tin** [-'lantɪn] F **-, -nen** asylum seeker

Asy|lan|ten|wohn|heim NT hostel for asylum seekers

Asyl-: Asy|lan|trag M application for (political) asylum; **asyl|be|rech|tigt** ADJ entitled to (political) asylum; **Asyl|be|wer|ber(in)** M(F) asylum seeker; **Asyl|recht** NT (Pol) right of (political) asylum; **Asyl|su|chen|de(r)** [-zu:xndə] MF decl as adj asylum seeker; **Asyl|ver|fah|ren** NT court hearing to determine a person's right to political asylum; **Asyl|wer|ber(in)** M(F) (Aus) asylum seeker

Asym|met|rie [azyme'tri:] F lack of symmetry, asymmetry

a|sym|met|risch ['azyme:trɪʃ, az'ymetrɪʃ] ADJ a-symmetric(al); (Comput) asymmetric; (fig) Gespräch one-sided ADV asymmetrically

Asymp|to|te [azymp'to:tə] F **-, -n** asymptote

a|symp|to|tisch [azym'pto:tɪʃ] ADJ asymptotic

a|syn|chron ['azynkro:n, azyn'kro:n] ADJ asynchronous (form, Comput), out of synchronism ADV (Comput) out of synchronism

A|syn|chron|mo|tor [azyn'kro:n-] M (Tech) asynchronous motor

a|syn|de|tisch ['azynde:tɪʃ, azyn'de:tɪʃ] ADJ (Ling) asyndetic

A|syn|de|ton [a'zyndetɔn] NT **-s, Asyndeta** [-ta] (Ling) parataxis

As|zen|dent [astsɛn'dɛnt] M **-en, -en -a** (Astrol) ascendant **-b** (= Vorfahr) ancestor, ascendant (form)

as|zen|die|ren [astsɛn'di:rən] ptp **aszendiert** VI **-a** aux sein (Astrol) to be in the ascendant **-b** aux sein or haben (obs) to be promoted (zu to)

As|ze|se [as'tse:zə] F **-, no pl** asceticism

at [a:t] abbr von **Atmosphäre** (Phys)

A. T. abbr von **Altes Testament** OT

a̲|ta [ˈata] ADV *(baby-talk)* ~ (~) **gehen** to go walkies *(baby-talk)*

a|ta̲k|tisch [aˈtaktɪʃ, ˈataktɪʃ] ADJ uncoordinated

A|ta|vis̲|mus [ataˈvɪsmʊs] M **-,** **Atavismen** [-mən] atavism

a|ta|vis̲|tisch [ataˈvɪstɪʃ] ADJ atavistic **ADV** atavistically

A|te|li̲er [ateˈlieː, atəˈlieː] NT **-s, -s** studio; **das Filmprojekt ging letzte Woche ins ~** shooting (on the film) started last week

A|te|li̲er- [ateˈlieː-, atəˈlieː-]: **A|te|li̲er|auf|nah|me** F **a** *(= Produkt)* studio shot **b** *usu pl (= Vorgang)* studio work *no pl*; **A|te|li̲er|fens|ter** NT studio window; **A|te|li̲er|fest** NT studio party; **A|te|li̲er|woh|nung** F studio apartment

A̲|tem [ˈaːtəm] M **-s,** *no pl* **a** *(= das Atmen)* breathing; **den ~ anhalten** *(lit, fig)* to hold one's breath; **mit angehaltenem ~** *(lit)* holding one's breath; *(fig)* with bated breath; **einen kurzen ~ haben** to be short-winded; **außer ~ sein** to be out of breath; **wieder zu ~ kommen** to get one's breath back; **einen langen/den längeren ~ haben** *(fig)* to have a lot of/more staying power; **jdn in ~ halten** to keep sb in suspense *or* on tenterhooks; **das verschlug mir den ~** that took my breath away → **ausgehen VI j** **b** *(lit, fig:* = *Atemluft)* breath; **~ holen** *or* **schöpfen** *(lit)* to take *or* draw a breath; *(fig)* to get one's breath back **c** *(fig geh:* = *Augenblick)* **in einem/im selben ~** in one/the same breath

A̲|tem-: A̲|tem|be|klem|mung F difficulty in breathing; **a̲|tem|be|rau|bend ADJ** breathtaking **ADV** breathtakingly; **A̲|tem|be|schwer|den** PL trouble *sing* in breathing; **A̲|tem|ge|rät** NT breathing apparatus; *(Med)* respirator; **A̲|tem|ge|räusch** NT respiratory sounds *pl*; **A̲|tem|gift** NT respiratory poison; **A̲|tem|gym|nas|tik** F breathing exercises *pl*; **A̲|tem|ho|len** NT **-s,** *no pl* breathing; **man kommt nicht mehr zum ~** *(fig)* you hardly have time to breathe; **zum ~ auftauchen** to come up for air; **A̲|tem|läh|mung** F respiratory paralysis; **a̲|tem|los ADJ** *(lit, fig)* breathless **ADV** breathlessly; **A̲|tem|lo|sig|keit** F **-,** *no pl* breathlessness; **A̲|tem|luft** F **unsere ~** the air we breathe; **A̲|tem|mas|ke** F breathing mask; **A̲|tem|not** F difficulty in breathing; **A̲|tem|pau|se** F *(fig)* breathing time *no art*, breathing space; **eine ~ einlegen/brauchen** to take/need a breather; **A̲|tem|schutz|ge|rät** NT breathing apparatus; **A̲|tem|schutz|mas|ke** F breathing mask; **A̲|tem|still|stand** M respiratory standstill, apnoea *(Brit)*, apnea *(US)*; **A̲|tem|tech|nik** F breathing technique; **A̲|tem|übung** F *(Med)* breathing exercise; **A̲|tem|we|ge** PL *(Anat)* respiratory tracts *pl*; **A̲|tem|wegs|er|kran|kung** F respiratory disease; **A̲|tem|zent|rum** NT *(Anat)* respiratory centre *(Brit)* or center *(US)*; **A̲|tem|zug** M breath; **in einem/im selben ~** *(fig)* in one/the same breath

a te̲r|go [a ˈtɛrɡo] ADV on top

A|the̲|is|mus [ateˈɪsmʊs] M **-,** *no pl* atheism

A|the̲|ist [ateˈɪst] M **-en, -en,** **A|the̲|is|tin** [-ˈɪstɪn] F **-, -nen** atheist

a|the̲|is|tisch [ateˈɪstɪʃ] ADJ atheist(ic)

A̲|then [aˈteːn] NT **-s** Athens

A|the̲|ner¹ [aˈteːnɐ] ADJ Athenian

A|the̲|ner² [aˈteːnɐ] M **-s, -,** **A|the̲|ne|rin** [-ərɪn] F **-, -nen** Athenian

a|the̲|nisch [aˈteːnɪʃ] ADJ Athenian

Ä̲|ther [ˈɛːtɐ] M **-s,** *no pl* **a** ether **b** *(poet)* (a)ether *(poet)*; **etw in den ~ schicken** to put sth on the air; **über den ~** over the air

ä|the̲|risch [ɛˈteːrɪʃ] ADJ *(Liter)* ethereal; *(Chem)* essential

ä|the|ri|si̲e|ren [ɛteriˈziːrən] *ptp* **ätherisi̲ert** VT to etherize

Ä̲|ther-: Ä̲|ther|nar|ko|se F etherization; **Ä̲|ther|wel|len** PL *(Rad)* radio waves *pl*

Ä|thi̲|o|pi|en [ɛˈtioːpiən] NT **-s** Ethiopia

Ä|thi̲|o|pi|er [ɛˈtioːpiɐ] M **-s, -,** **Ä|thi̲|o|pi|e|rin** [-iərɪn] F **-, -nen** Ethiopian

ä|thi̲|o|pisch [ɛˈtioːpɪʃ] ADJ Ethiopian

Ath|le̲t [atˈleːt] M **-en, -en,** **Ath|le̲|tin** [-ˈleːtɪn] F **-, -nen** athlete

Ath|le̲|tik [atˈleːtɪk] F **-,** *no pl* athletics *sing*

Ath|le̲|ti|ker [atˈleːtikɐ] M **-s, -,** **Ath|le̲|ti|ke|rin** [-ərɪn] F **-, -nen** athletic type

ath|le̲|tisch [atˈleːtɪʃ] ADJ athletic **ADV** athletically; **~ aussehen** to look athletic

Ä̲|thyl|al|ko|hol [ɛˈtyːl-] M ethyl alcohol

Ä̲|thyl|äther M ethyl ether

At̲|lant [atˈlant] M **-en, -en** atlas

At̲|lan|ten *pl von* **Atlas** *von* **Atlant**

At|lan̲|tik [atˈlantɪk] M **-s** Atlantic

At|lan̲|tik|wall M *(Mil Hist)* Atlantic Wall

at|lan̲|tisch [atˈlantɪʃ] ADJ Atlantic; **ein ~es Hoch** a high-pressure area over the Atlantic; *(vom Atlantik kommend)* a high-pressure area from the Atlantic; **der Atlantische Ozean** the Atlantic Ocean; **das Atlantische Bündnis** the Atlantic Alliance

At̲|las¹ [ˈatlas] M **-** *or* **-ses, -se** *or* **Atlanten** [atˈlantn] atlas

At̲|las² M **-',** *no pl (Myth)* Atlas

At̲|las³ M **-ses, -se** *(= Seidenatlas)* satin; *(mit Baumwolle)* sateen

At̲|las⁴ M **-** *(Geog)* Atlas Mountains *pl*

At̲|las|sei|de F satin

at̲|men [ˈaːtmən] **VT** *(lit, fig geh)* to breathe **VI** to breathe, to respire *(form)*; **frei ~** *(fig)* to breathe freely

At|mo|sphä̲|re [atmoˈsfɛːrə] F *(Phys, fig)* atmosphere

At|mo|sphä̲|ren-: At|mo|sphä̲|ren|druck M *pl* **-drücke** atmospheric pressure; *(= Maßeinheit)* atmosphere; **At|mo|sphä̲|ren|über|druck** M **a** atmospheric excess pressure **b** *(= Maßeinheit)* atmosphere *(of pressure)* above atmospheric pressure

at|mo|sphä̲|risch [atmoˈsfɛːrɪʃ] ADJ atmospheric; **~e Störungen** atmospherics *pl* **ADV** **~ dichte Musik** very atmospheric music; **ein ~ reiches Bild/Bühnenbild** a picture/scene full of atmosphere; **die Beziehungen zwischen den beiden Ländern haben sich ~ verbessert** the atmosphere between the two countries has improved

At̲|mung [ˈaːtmʊŋ] F **-,** *no pl* breathing; *(Eccl, Med)* respiration

At̲|mungs-: at̲|mungs|ak|tiv ADJ *Material, Stoff* breathable; **At̲|mungs|ap|pa|rat** M breathing apparatus; *(Med)* respirator; **At̲|mungs|or|ga|ne** PL respiratory organs *pl*; **At̲|mungs|zent|rum** NT respiratory centre *(Brit)* or center *(US)*

A̲|toll [aˈtɔl] NT **-s, -e** atoll

A̲|tom [aˈtoːm] M **-s, -e** atom

A̲|tom- *in cpds* atomic → *auch* **Kern-; A̲|tom|ab|fall** M nuclear *or* radioactive *or* atomic waste; **A̲|tom|an|griff** M nuclear attack; **A̲|tom|an|la|ge** F nuclear plant; **A̲|tom|an|trieb** M nuclear *or* atomic propulsion; **ein U-Boot mit ~** a nuclear-powered submarine

a|to̲|mar [atoˈmaːɐ] **ADJ** atomic, nuclear; *Struktur* atomic; *Drohung* nuclear **ADV** *bedrohen, vernichten* with a nuclear attack; **~ bestückt** armed with nuclear warheads; **~ angetrieben** nuclear-powered

A̲|tom-: A̲|tom|aus|stieg M , *no pl* abandonment of nuclear energy; **A̲|tom|ba|sis** F nuclear base; **A̲|tom|be|hör|de** F Atomic Energy Authority *(Brit)* or Commission *(US)*; **a̲|tom|be|trie|ben** [-bətriːbn] ADJ nuclear-powered; **A̲|tom|bom|be** F atomic *or* atom *(esp Brit)* bomb; **A̲|tom|bom|ben|ex|plo|si|on** F atomic *or* nuclear explosion; **a̲|tom|bom|ben|si|cher** ADJ atomic *or* nuclear blast-proof **ADV** **~ gebaut** capable of withstanding a nuclear attack; **~ untergebracht** protected against

---

nuclear attack; **A̲|tom|bom|ben|ver|such** M atomic *or* nuclear test; **A̲|tom|bom|ber** M nuclear bomber; **A̲|tom|bun|ker** M atomic *or* nuclear blast-proof bunker; **A̲|tom|bu|sen** M *(dated inf)* big bust *or* boobs *pl (inf)*; **A̲|tom|ener|gie** F nuclear energy; **A̲|tom|ener|gie|be|hör|de** F **die (Internationale) ~** the (International) Atomic Energy Agency; **A̲|tom|ex|plo|si|on** F atomic *or* nuclear explosion; **A̲|tom|for|scher(in)** M(F) nuclear scientist; **A̲|tom|for|schung** F atomic *or* nuclear research; **A̲|tom|for|schungs|zent|rum** NT atomic *or* nuclear research centre *(Brit)* or center *(US)*; **A̲|tom|geg|ner(in)** M(F) **~ sein** to be antinuclear; **aktiver ~** antinuclear activist; **A̲|tom|ge|mein|de** F pronuclear lobby; **a̲|tom|ge|trie|ben** [-ɡətriːbn] ADJ nuclear-powered; **A̲|tom|ge|wicht** NT atomic weight; **A̲|tom|in|dust|rie** F nuclear industry

a|to̲|misch [aˈtoːmɪʃ] ADJ *(Sw)* = **atomar**

a|to|mi|si̲e|ren [atomiˈziːrən] *ptp* **atomisi̲ert** VT to atomize; *(fig)* to smash to pieces *or* smithereens

A|to|mis̲|mus [atoˈmɪsmʊs] M **-,** *no pl* atomism

A̲|tom-: A̲|tom|ka|ta|stro|phe F nuclear disaster; **A̲|tom|kern** M atomic nucleus; **A̲|tom|klub** M *(Press sl)* nuclear club; **A̲|tom|kraft** F atomic *or* nuclear power *or* energy; **A̲|tom|kraft|geg|ner(in)** M(F) anti-nuclear (power) protester; **A̲|tom|kraft|werk** NT atomic *or* nuclear power station; **A̲|tom|krieg** M atomic *or* nuclear war; **A̲|tom|lob|by** F nuclear power lobby; **A̲|tom|macht** F nuclear power; **A̲|tom|mas|se** F *(Chem, Phys)* atomic mass; **A̲|tom|me|di|zin** F *no pl* nuclear medicine; **A̲|tom|mei|ler** M nuclear reactor; **A̲|tom|mo|dell** NT model of the atom

A̲|tom|müll M atomic *or* nuclear *or* radioactive waste

A̲|tom|müll-: A̲|tom|müll|de|po|nie F nuclear waste disposal site; **A̲|tom|müll|end|la|ger** NT (final) disposal *or* dumping *(pej)* site for nuclear *or* radioactive waste; **A̲|tom|müll|trans|port** M transport of nuclear *or* radioactive waste

A̲|tom-: A̲|tom|phy|sik F atomic *or* nuclear physics *sing*; **A̲|tom|phy|si|ker(in)** M(F) nuclear physicist; **A̲|tom|pilz** M mushroom cloud; **A̲|tom|po|li|tik** F nuclear policy; **A̲|tom|ra|ke|te** F nuclear-powered rocket; *(= Waffe)* nuclear missile; **A̲|tom|re|ak|tor** M nuclear reactor; **A̲|tom|rüs|tung** F nuclear armament; **A̲|tom|schwel|le** F nuclear threshold; **A̲|tom|spal|tung** F nuclear fission; **die erste ~** the first splitting of the atom; **A̲|tom|sperr|ver|trag** M nuclear *or* atomic weapons nonproliferation treaty; **A̲|tom|spreng|kopf** M atomic *or* nuclear warhead; **A̲|tom|spreng|kör|per** M nuclear explosive; **A̲|tom|staat** M nuclear power; **A̲|tom|stopp** M nuclear ban; **A̲|tom|strah|lung** F nuclear radiation; **A̲|tom|streit|macht** F nuclear capability; **A̲|tom|strom** M *(inf)* electricity generated by nuclear power; **A̲|tom|tech|nik** F nuclear technology, nucleonics *sing*

A̲|tom|test M nuclear test

A̲|tom|test-: A̲|tom|test|stopp M nuclear test ban; **A̲|tom|test|stopp|ab|kom|men** NT nuclear test ban treaty

A̲|tom-: A̲|tom|tod M *(Press sl)* nuclear death; **A̲|tom|trieb|werk** NT nuclear engine; **A̲|tom-U-Boot** NT nuclear submarine; **A̲|tom|uhr** F atomic clock; **A̲|tom|ver|such** M nuclear test; **A̲|tom|ver|suchs|stopp** M nuclear test ban

A̲|tom|waf|fe F nuclear *or* atomic weapon

A̲|tom|waf|fen-: a̲|tom|waf|fen|frei ADJ nuclear-free; **A̲|tom|waf|fen|sperr|ver|trag** M nuclear *or* atomic weapons nonproliferation treaty; **A̲|tom|waf|fen|test** M , **A̲|tom|waf|fen|ver|such** M nuclear test

---

A|tom-: A|tom|wirt|schaft F nuclear industry; **A|tom|wis|sen|schaft** F nuclear or atomic science; **A|tom|wis|sen|schaft|ler(in)** M(F) nuclear or atomic scientist; **A|tom|zeit** F nuclear time; **A|tom|zeit|al|ter** NT atomic or nuclear age; **A|tom|zer|fall** M atomic disintegration or decay; **A|tom|zer|trüm|me|rung** F splitting of the atom

a|to|nal [atona:l, ato'na:l] ADJ atonal

A|to|na|li|tät [atonali'tɛ:t] F -, no pl atonality

A|to|pi|ker [a'to:pikɐ] M -s, -, **A|to|pi|ke|rin** [-ərɪn] F -, -nen (Med) atopy sufferer

a|to|pisch [a'to:pɪʃ] ADJ (Med) atopic

a|to|xisch ['a:tɔksɪʃ, a'tɔksɪʃ] ADJ (form) nontoxic

At|ra|zin [atra'tsi:n] NT -s, no pl (Chem) atrazine

At|ri|um ['a:triʊm] NT -s, **Atrien** [-riən] (Archit, Anat) atrium

At|ri|um|haus NT house built around an open court or atrium

A|tro|phie [atro'fi:] F -, -n [-'fi:ən] (Med) atrophy

a|tro|phisch [a'tro:fɪʃ] ADJ atrophied

ätsch [ɛ:tʃ] INTERJ (inf) ha-ha

At|ta|ché [ata'ʃe:] M -s, -s attaché

At|ta|cke [a'takə] F -, -n (= Angriff) attack; (Mil Hist) (cavalry) charge; **eine ~ gegen jdn/etw rei|ten** (lit) to charge sb/sth; (fig) to attack sb/sth

at|ta|ckie|ren [ata'ki:rən] ptp **attackiert** VT (= angreifen) to attack; (Mil Hist) to charge

At|ten|tat ['atnta:t, atɛn'ta:t] NT -(e)s, -e assassination; (= Attentatsversuch) assassination attempt; **ein ~ auf jdn verüben** to assassinate sb; (bei gescheitertem Versuch) to make an attempt on sb's life; **ich habe ein ~ auf dich vor** (hum) listen, I've got a great idea

At|ten|tä|ter(in) M(F) assassin; (bei gescheitertem Versuch) would-be assassin

At|ten|tis|mus [atɛn'tɪsmʊs] M -, no pl (pej) wait-and-see policy

At|test [a'tɛst] NT -(e)s, -e certificate

at|tes|tie|ren [atɛs'ti:rən] ptp **attestiert** VT (form) to certify; **jdm seine Dienstuntauglichkeit etc** ~ to certify sb as unfit for duty etc

At|ti|ka ['atika] NT -s (Geog) Attica

At|ti|ka|woh|nung F (Sw) penthouse (flat (Brit) or apartment)

at|tisch ['atɪʃ] ADJ Attic

At|ti|tü|de [ati'ty:də] F -, -n (geh) **a** attitude **b** (= Geste) gesture

At|trak|ti|on [atrak'tsio:n] F -, -en attraction

at|trak|tiv [atrak'ti:f] ADJ attractive

At|trak|ti|vi|tät [atraktivi'tɛ:t] F -, no pl attractiveness

At|trap|pe [a'trapə] F -, -n dummy; (fig: = Schein) sham; **die ~ eines ...** a dummy ...; **bei ihr ist alles ~** everything about her is false

At|tri|but [atri'bu:t] NT -(e)s, -e (geh, Gram) attribute

At|tri|but|satz M (Gram) relative clause

a|tü [a'ty:] abbr von **Atmosphärenüberdruck**

a|ty|pisch ['a:typɪʃ, a'ty:pɪʃ] ADJ (geh) atypical

ät|zen ['atsn] VT (Hunt) to feed

ät|zen ['ɛtsn] VTI **a** (auf Platte) to etch **b** (Säure) to corrode **c** (Med) to cauterize

ät|zend ADJ **a** (lit) Säure corrosive; (Med) caustic **b** Geruch pungent; Rauch choking; Spott, Kritik caustic **c** (inf: = furchtbar) lousy (inf); **der Typ ist echt ~** that guy really grates on you (inf)

Ätz- ['ɛts-]: **Ätz|mit|tel** NT (Chem) corrosive; (Med) cautery, caustic; **Ätz|nat|ron** NT caustic soda; **Ätz|stift** M (Med) cautery; (bei Friseur) styptic pencil

Ät|zung ['atsʊŋ] F -, -en (Hunt, hum) (= Vorgang) feeding; (= Futter) food, fodder; **wann gibt es ~?** (hum) when is it feeding time?

Ät|zung ['ɛtsʊŋ] F -, -en etching; (mit Säure) corrosion; (Med) cauterization, cautery

au [au] INTERJ **a** ow, ouch; **au, das war knapp!** oh or God, that was close! **b** (Ausdruck der Begeisterung) oh

AU [a:'ʔu:] F -, no pl abbr von **Abgasuntersuchung**

Au [au] F -, -en (S Ger, Aus) meadow, pasture

aua ['aua] INTERJ ow, ouch

au|ber|gi|ne [ober'ʒi:nə] ADJ pred, **au|ber|gi|ne|far|ben** [-farbn] ADJ aubergine

Au|ber|gi|ne [ober'ʒi:nə] F -, -n aubergine, eggplant (esp US)

auch [aux] ADV **a** (= zusätzlich, gleichfalls) also, too, as well; **die Engländer müssen ~ zugeben, dass ...** the English must admit too or as well that ..., the English must also admit that ...; ~ **die Engländer müssen ...** the English too must ...; **das kann ich ~** I can do that too or as well; **das ist ~ möglich** that's possible too or as well, that's also possible; **ja, das ~** yes, that too; ~ **gut** that's OK too; **du ~?** you too?, you as well?; ~ **nicht** not ... either; **das ist ~ nicht rich|tig** that's not right either; **er kommt – ich –** he's coming – so am I or me too; **ich will eins – ich ~** I want one – so do I or me too; **er kommt nicht – ich ~ nicht** he's not coming – nor or neither am I, he's not coming – I'm not either or me neither; ~ **das noch!** that's all I needed! **b** (= tatsächlich) too, as well; **und das tue/meine ich –** and I'll do it/I mean it too or as well; **wenn sie sagt, sie geht, dann geht sie ~** if she says she's going then she'll go; **Frechheit! – ja, das stimmt ~** what impudence! – you can say that again; **du siehst müde aus – das bin ich ~** you look tired – (so) I am; **das ist er ja ~** (and so) he is; **so ist es ~** (so) it is **c** (= sogar) even; ~ **wenn du Vorfahrt hast** even if you (do) have right of way; **ohne ~ nur zu fragen** without even asking **d** (emph) **den Teufel ~!** damn it (all)! (inf); **zum Donnerwetter ~!** blast it! (inf); **so ein Dummkopf ~!** what an absolute blockhead! (inf); **so was Ärgerliches aber ~!** it's really too annoying!; **wozu ~?** what on earth for? (inf), whatever for? **e** (= auch immer) **wie dem ~ sei** be that as it may; **was er ~ sagen mag** whatever he might say; **und mag er ~ noch so klug sein, wenn er ~ noch so klug ist** however clever he may be; **so schnell er ~ laufen mag** however fast he runs or he may run, no matter how fast he runs → **immer**

Au|di|enz [au'diɛnts] F -, -en (bei Papst, König etc) audience

Au|di|enz|saal M audience chamber

Au|di|max [audi'maks, 'audimaks] NT -, no pl (Univ sl) main lecture hall

au|dio-: au|dio|phil [audio'fi:l] ADJ audiophile; **Au|dio|phi|le(r)** [audio'fi:lə] MF decl as adj audiophile; **au|dio|vi|su|ell** [audiovi'zuɛl] ADJ audiovisual ADV audiovisually; gestalten using audiovisual aids; werben using audiovisual media

Au|dit ['au:dit] M OR NT -s, -s (esp Sw) audit

au|di|tiv [audi'ti:f] ADJ auditory

Au|di|to|ri|um [audi'to:riʊm] NT -s, **Auditorien** [-riən] **a** (= Hörsaal) lecture hall; ~ **maximum** (Univ) main lecture hall **b** (geh: = Zuhörerschaft) audience

Aue ['auə] F -, -n **a** (dial, poet) meadow, pasture, lea (poet), mead (poet) **b** (dial: = Insel) island

Au|en-: Au|en|land|schaft F pasture landscape, pastureland; **Au|en|wald** M riverside wood(s pl) or forest

Au|er|bach|sprung ['auɐbax-] M (Sport) backward or reverse somersault

Au|er|hahn ['auɐ-] M pl **Auerhähne** or (Hunt) -en capercaillie

Au|er|hen|ne F, **Au|er|huhn** NT capercaillie (hen)

Au|er|och|se M aurochs

---

auf [auf]	
1 PRÄPOSITION (+dat)	3 ADVERB
2 PRÄPOSITION (+acc)	4 BINDEWORT

In Verbindung mit Substantiven, Verben etc siehe auch dort.

1 – PRÄPOSITION (+dat)

a ❘Ort❘ on; **das Buch lag auf dem Tisch** the book was lying on the table; **auf einem Stuhl sitzen** to sit on a chair; **auf (der Insel) Kos** on (the island of) Kos; **auf den Orkneyinseln** on or in the Orkney Islands; **auf See** at sea; **auf der Bank/Post/dem Rathaus** at the bank/post office/town hall; **mein Geld ist auf der Bank** my money is in the bank; **auf meinem Zimmer** in my room; **auf der Straße** on or in the street; **Greenwich liegt auf 0 Grad** Greenwich lies at 0 degrees; **die Tachonadel steht auf 105** the speedometer is at or on 105

b ❘andere Wendungen❘ **auf der Fahrt/dem Weg** on the journey/way; **auf der Geige spielen** to play the violin; **etw auf dem Klavier spielen** to play sth on the piano; **auf einem Ohr taub sein** to be deaf in one ear; **das hat nichts auf sich, damit hat es nichts auf sich** it doesn't mean anything; **was hat es damit auf sich?** what does it mean?

2 – PRÄPOSITION (+acc)

a ❘Ort❘ on; **etw auf einen Zettel schreiben** to write sth on a piece of paper; **etw auf etw stellen** to put sth on(to) sth; **etw auf etw heben** to lift sth onto sth; **sich auf etw setzen/legen** to sit/lie (down) on sth; **sich auf die Straße setzen** to sit down in the road; **das Wrack ist auf den Meeresgrund gesunken** the wreck sank to the bottom of the sea; **er ist auf die Orkneyinseln gefahren** he has gone to the Orkney Islands; **er segelt auf das Meer hinaus** he is sailing out to sea; **man konnte nicht weiter als auf zehn Fuß herankommen** you couldn't get any nearer than ten feet; **geh mal auf die Seite** move aside; **Geld auf die Bank bringen** to take money to the bank; (= einzahlen) to put money in the bank; **auf sein Zimmer/die Post/die Polizei gehen** to go to one's room/the post office/the police; **aufs Gymnasium gehen** ≈ to go to grammar school (Brit), ≈ to go to high school (US); **auf eine Party/eine Hochzeit gehen** to go to a party/wedding

b ❘Zeit❘ **die Uhr auf 10 stellen** to put or set the clock to 10; **Heiligabend fällt auf einen Dienstag** Christmas Eve falls on a Tuesday; **die Sitzung auf morgen verschieben** to postpone the meeting until tomorrow; **die Dauer auf ein Jahr reduzieren** to reduce the duration to one year; **auf drei Tage** for three days; **die Nacht (von Montag) auf Dienstag** Monday night; **auf morgen/bald!** see you tomorrow/soon!; **zwanzig auf sieben** (dial) twenty to seven

c ❘Häufig❘ **Niederlage auf Niederlage** defeat after or upon defeat; **Beleidigung auf Beleidigung** insult upon or after insult; **einer auf den anderen** one after another

d = **für** **auf 10 km** for 10 km; **auf eine Tasse Kaffee/eine Zigarette** or **Zigarettenlänge** for a cup of coffee/a smoke; **ein Manuskript auf Fehler prüfen** to check a manuscript for errors

e = **pro** **auf einen Polizisten kommen 1.000 Bürger** there is one policeman for or to every 1,000 citizens; **auf jeden kamen zwei Flaschen Bier** there were two bottles of beer (for) each

f ❘andere Wendungen❘ **auf ihn!** get him!; **auf unseren lieben Onkel Egon/ein glückliches Gelingen!** here's to dear Uncle Egon/a great success!; **auf deine Gesundheit!** (your very) good health!; **auf das** or **aufs schändlichste/liebenswürdigste** or **Schändlichste/Liebenswürdigste** (geh) most shamefully/kindly; **auf die elegante/ehrliche Art** elegantly/honestly; **auf die billige Tour** on the cheap

♦ **auf etw** (acc) **hin** (als Reaktion) at; **auf seinen Vorschlag/seine Bitte (hin)** at his suggestion/request; **auf meinen Brief hin** on receiving my letter

♦ **auf jdn/etw zu** er kam auf mich zu und sagte ... he came up to me and said ...; **während er auf mich zukam** as he was coming toward(s) me; **es geht auf Weihnachten zu** Christmas is approaching → *auch* **gehen 1 c**

3 – ADVERB

a = offen | open; **die Tür/das Fenster ist auf** the door's/window's open; **ist das Fenster auf oder zu?** is the window open or shut?; **Mund/Fenster auf!** open your mouth/the window! → **auf sein**

b andere Wendungen | **Helm auf!** helmets on!; **Handschuhe an, Mütze auf, so wird er sich nicht erkälten** with his gloves and hat on he won't catch cold; **nachmittags Unterricht, und dann noch so viel auf!** (*inf*) school in the afternoon, and all that homework too!; **auf, an die Arbeit!** right, let's get down to work!; **auf nach Chicago!** let's go to Chicago; **auf gehts!** let's go!; **auf und ab** up and down; **auf und nieder** (*geh*) up and down; **sie ist auf und davon** she has disappeared; **ihr Mann verließ sie und ging auf und davon** her husband just walked out and left her; **Sprung auf! marsch, marsch!** (*Mil*) jump to it!, at (*Brit*) or on (*US*) the double!; **die Jagd ist auf** the hunt is on

4 – BINDEWORT

♦ **auf dass** (*liter*) that (*old, liter*); **richtet nicht, auf dass ihr nicht gerichtet werdet** (*Bibl*) judge not, that ye be not judged (*Bibl*); **auf dass wir niemals vergessen mögen** lest we forget

Auf [auf] NT *inv* das ~ und Ab *or* **Nieder** the up and down; (*fig*) the ups and downs; **das ~ und Ab des Kolbens** the up(ward) and down(ward) movement of the piston

auf+ad|die|ren *ptp* **aufaddiert** VTR *sep* to add up

auf+ar|bei|ten VT *sep* **a** (= *erneuern*) to refurbish, to do up; *Möbel etc* to recondition **b** (= *auswerten*) *Literatur etc* to incorporate critically; *Vergangenheit* to reappraise **c** (= *erledigen*) *Korrespondenz, Liegengebliebenes* to catch up with *or* on, to clear **d** (*Phys*) *Brennelemente* to reprocess

Auf|ar|bei|tung F -, -en **a** (= *Erneuerung*) refurbishing; (*von Möbeln*) reconditioning **b** (= *Auswertung*) (*von Literatur*) critical incorporation; (*von Vergangenheit*) reappraisal **c** (= *Erledigung*: *von Korrespondenz etc*) catching up; **die ~ des Liegengebliebenen dauerte einige Zeit** it took some time to catch up with *or* clear the backlog **d** (*Phys: von Brennelementen*) reprocessing

auf+at|men VI *sep* (*lit, fig*) to breathe *or* heave a sigh of relief; **ein Aufatmen** a sigh of relief

auf+ba|cken VT *sep* to warm *or* crisp up

auf+bah|ren ['aufbaːrən] VT *sep Sarg* to lay on the bier; *Leiche* to lay out; **einen Toten feierlich ~** to put a person's body to lie in state

Auf|bah|rung F -, -en laying out; (*feierlich*) lying in state

Auf|bau M *pl* **-bauten a** *no pl* (= *das Aufbauen*) construction, building; (*von neuem Staat*) building; (*von Netzwerk, System*) setting up; (= *das Wiederaufbauen*) reconstruction; **der wirtschaftliche ~** the building up of the economy; **der ~ Ost** the rebuilding of East Germany **b** (= *Aufgebautes, Aufgesetztes*) top; (*von Auto, LKW*) coachwork *no pl*, body → **Aufbauten c** *no pl* (= *Struktur*) structure

AUFBAU OST

Aufbau Ost is a colloquial term for the **Wirtschaftsförderung Ost**, by means of which the economic system of the former East Germany is being brought into line with the demands of the social market economy. Partly by using funds from the **Solidaritätszuschlag**, the Federal Government is seeking to subsi-

---

dize investment within the East, to develop the infrastructure and to support research, environmental conservation and the creation of new businesses. → **SOLIDARITÄTSZUSCHLAG**

Auf|bau|ar|beit F construction (work); (= *Wiederaufbau*) reconstruction (work)

auf+bau|en *sep* VT **a** (= *errichten*) to put up; *Verbindung, Netzwerk, System* to set up; (= *hinstellen*) *Ausstellungsstücke, kaltes Büfett, Brettspiel etc* to set *or* lay out; (*inf*) *Posten, Ordnungspersonal etc* to post; (= *zusammenbauen*) *elektrische Schaltung etc* to put together, to assemble

b (= *darauf bauen*) *Stockwerk* to add (on), to build on; *Karosserie* to mount

c (*fig:* = *gestalten*) *Organisation, Land, Armee, Geschäft, Angriff, Druck, Spannung, Verbindung* to build up; *Zerstörtes* to rebuild; *Theorie, Plan, System* to construct; **sich** (*dat*) **eine (neue) Existenz** *or* **ein Leben ~** to build (up) a new life for oneself

d (*fig:* = *fördern, weiterentwickeln*) *Gesundheit, Kraft* to build up; *Star, Politiker* to promote; *Beziehung* to build; **jdn/etw zu etw ~** to build sb/sth up into sth

e (*fig:* = *gründen*) *etw auf etw* (*dat or acc*) **~** to base *or* found sth on sth

f (= *strukturieren, konstruieren*) to construct; *Aufsatz, Rede, Organisation* to structure

VI a (= *sich gründen*) to be based *or* founded (*auf* +*dat or acc* on)

b **wir wollen ~ und nicht zerstören** we want to build and not destroy

VR a (*inf:* = *sich postieren*) to take up position; **sie bauten sich in einer Reihe auf** they formed (themselves) up into a line; **er baute sich vor dem Feldwebel/Lehrer auf und ...** he stood up in front of the sergeant/teacher and ...; **sich vor jdm drohend ~** to plant oneself in front of sb (*inf*)

b (= *sich bilden*: *Wolken, Hochdruckgebiet*) to build up

c (= *bestehen aus*) **sich aus etw ~** to be built up *or* composed of sth

d (= *sich gründen*) **sich auf etw** (*dat or acc*) **~** to be based *or* founded on sth

Auf|bau-: Auf|bau|hil|fe F development(al) aid *or* assistance; **Auf|bau|kurs** M continuation course

auf+bäu|men ['aufbɔymən] VR *sep* (*Tier*) to rear; **sich gegen jdn/etw ~** (*fig*) to rebel *or* revolt against sb/sth; **sich vor Schmerz ~** to writhe with pain

Auf|bau-: Auf|bau|pha|se F development(al) phase; **Auf|bau|prä|pa|rat** NT regenerative product; **Auf|bau|prin|zip** NT structural principle; **die Motoren sind alle nach demselben ~ konstruiert** the engines are all constructed on the same principle

auf+bau|schen *sep* **VT** to blow out; *Segel auch* to (make) billow out, to belly out; (*fig*) to blow up, to exaggerate **VR** to blow out; (*Segel auch*) to billow (out), to belly (out); (*fig*) to blow up (*zu* into)

Auf|bau-: Auf|bau|stu|di|um NT (*Univ*) course of further study; **Auf|bau|stu|fe** F (*Sch*) school class leading to university entrance, ≈ sixth form (*Brit*), ≈ twelfth grade (*US*)

Auf|bau|ten PL (*Naut*) superstructure

Auf|bau|trai|ning NT (*Sport*) stamina training

auf+be|geh|ren *ptp* **aufbegehrt** VI *sep* (*geh*) to rebel, to revolt (*gegen* against)

auf+be|hal|ten *ptp* **aufbehalten** VT *sep irreg* *Hut, Brille etc* to keep on; *Tür, Schrank etc* to leave *or* keep open; *Knopf* to leave *or* keep undone

auf+bei|ßen VT *sep irreg* *Verpackung etc* to bite open; *Nuss etc* to crack with one's teeth; **sich** (*dat*) **die Lippe ~** to bite one's lip (and make it bleed)

auf+be|kom|men *ptp* **aufbekommen** VT *sep irreg* (*inf*) **a** (= *öffnen*) to get open **b** *Aufgabe* to get as homework; **habt ihr keine Hausarbeiten**

~? didn't you get any homework? **c** *Essen* to (manage to) eat up; **ich habe nur die halbe Portion ~** I could only manage (to eat) half a portion

auf+be|rei|ten *ptp* **aufbereitet** VT *sep* to process; *Trinkwasser auch* to purify; *Erze* to prepare, to dress; *Daten* to edit; *Text etc* to work up; **etw literarisch ~** to turn sth into literature; **etw dramaturgisch ~** to adapt sth for the theatre (*Brit*) or theater (*US*)

Auf|be|rei|tung F processing; (*von Trinkwasser auch*) purification; (*von Erz, Kohle*) preparation, dressing; (*von Daten*) editing; (*von Texten*) working up; (*fürs Theater*) adaptation

Auf|be|rei|tungs|an|la|ge F processing plant

auf+bes|sern VT *sep* to improve; *Gehalt etc auch* to increase

Auf|bes|se|rung F , **Auf|bess|rung** ['aufbɛsrʊŋ] ▲ F -, -en improvement; (*von Gehalt auch*) increase

auf+be|wah|ren *ptp* **aufbewahrt** VT *sep* to keep; *Lebensmittel auch* to store; (= *behalten*) *alte Zeitungen etc auch* to save; *Wertsachen etc* to look after; **ein Dokument gut ~** to keep a document in a safe place; **Medikamente kühl ~** to keep medicines in a cool place; **jds Dokumente ~** to be looking after sb's documents, to have sb's documents in one's keeping; **kann ich hier meinen Koffer ~ lassen?** can I leave my suitcase here?

Auf|be|wah|rung F **a** (= *das Aufbewahren*) keeping; (*von Lebensmitteln*) storage; **jdm etw zur ~ übergeben** to give sth to sb for safekeeping, to put sth in(to) sb's safekeeping; **einen Koffer in ~ geben** to deposit a suitcase (at the left-luggage (*Brit*) or checkroom (*US*)) **b** (= *Stelle*) left-luggage (office) (*Brit*), checkroom (*US*)

Auf|be|wah|rungs|ort M *pl* **-orte** place where something is to be kept **etw an einen sicheren ~ bringen** to put sth in a safe place; **das ist kein geeigneter ~ für Medikamente** that is not the right place to keep medicines; **einen ~ für etw finden** to find a place to keep sth, to find a home for sth (*inf*)

Auf|be|wah|rungs|schein M left-luggage receipt or ticket (*Brit*), checkroom ticket (*US*)

auf+bie|gen *sep irreg* **VT** to bend open **VR** (*Ring etc*) to bend open

auf+bie|ten VT *sep irreg* **a** *Menschen, Mittel* to muster; *Kräfte, Einfluss* to summon (up); *Militär, Polizei* to call in; (*old*) *Soldaten* to levy (*old*) **b** *Brautpaar* to call the banns of **c** (*bei Auktionen*) to put up

Auf|bie|tung F -, *no pl* (*von Menschen, Mitteln*) mustering; (*von Kräften, Fähigkeiten*) summoning (up); (*von Polizei, Militär*) calling in; **unter** or **bei ~ aller Kräfte ...** summoning (up) all his/her *etc* strength ...

auf+bin|den VT *sep irreg* **a** (= *öffnen*) *Schuh etc* to undo, to untie **b** (= *hochbinden*) *Haare etc* to put *or* tie up; *Pflanzen, Zweige etc* to tie (up) straight **c** (= *befestigen*) to tie on; **etw auf etw** (*acc*) **~** to tie sth on(to) sth **d** **lass dir doch so etwas nicht ~** (*fig*) don't fall for that; **jdm eine Lüge ~** to take sb in, to tell sb a lie **e** (*Typ*) *Buch* to bind

auf+blä|hen *sep* **VT** to blow out; *Segel auch* to fill, to billow out, to belly out; (*Med*) to distend, to swell; (*fig*) to inflate **VR** to blow out; (*Segel auch*) to billow *or* belly out; (*Med*) to become distended *or* swollen; (*fig pej*) to puff oneself up

Auf|blä|hung F (*Med*) distension

auf+blas|bar ADJ inflatable

auf+bla|sen *sep irreg* **VT a** *Ballon* to blow up; *Reifen etc* to inflate, to blow up; *Backen* to puff out, to blow out **b** (= *hochblasen*) to blow up **VR** (*fig pej*) to puff oneself up → *auch* **aufgeblasen**

auf+blät|tern *sep* VT *Buch etc* to open (up)

auf+blei|ben VI *sep irreg aux sein* **a** (= *nicht schlafen gehen*) to stay up; **wegen jdm ~** to wait up *or* to stay up for sb **b** (= *geöffnet bleiben*) to stay open

Auf|blen|de F (*Film*) fade-in

auf+blen|den *sep* **VI** (*Phot*) to open up the lens, to increase the aperture; (*Film*) to fade in; (*Aut*) to turn the headlights on full (beam); **er fährt aufgeblendet** he drives on full beam **VT** (*Aut*) *Scheinwerfer* to turn on full (beam); (*Film*) *Einstellung* to fade in

auf+bli|cken VI *sep* to look up; **zu jdm/etw ~** (*lit, fig*) to look up to sb/sth

auf+blin|ken VI *sep* (*lit, fig*) to flash; (*Aut inf*: = *kurz aufblenden*) to flash (one's headlights)

auf+blit|zen VI *sep* **a** (*Licht, Strahl, Blitz, Augen*) to flash **b** *aux sein* (*fig*) (*Emotion, Hass etc*) to flare up; (*Gedanke, Erinnerung*) to flash through one's mind

auf+blü|hen VI *sep aux sein* **a** (*Knospe*) to blossom (out); (*Blume*) to bloom **b** (*fig*) (*Mensch*) to blossom out; (*Wissenschaft, Kultur*) to (begin to) flourish; **das ließ sie/die Stadt ~** it allowed her/the town to flourish

auf+bo|cken VT *sep Auto* to jack up; *Motorrad* to put on its stand

auf+boh|ren VT *sep* to bore *or* drill a hole in; *Zahn auch* to drill

auf+bran|den VI *sep aux sein* (*geh*) to surge; (*fig: Beifall*) to burst forth; **Beifall brandete immer wieder auf** there was wave upon wave of applause

auf+bra|ten VT *sep irreg Essen* to warm up; (*in der Pfanne auch*) to fry up

auf+brau|chen *sep* **VT** to use up; **seine Geduld ist aufgebraucht** his patience is exhausted **VR** (= *sich verbrauchen*) to get used up; (*Reifen*: = *sich abnutzen*) to get worn out, to wear out

auf+brau|sen VI *sep aux sein* **a** (*Brandung etc*) to surge; (*Brausetablette, Brause etc*) to fizz up; (*fig: Beifall, Jubel*) to break out, to burst forth **b** (*fig: Mensch*) to flare up, to fly off the handle (*inf*)

auf|brau|send ADJ *Temperament* irascible; *Mensch auch* quick-tempered, liable to flare up

auf+bre|chen *sep irreg* **VT** to break *or* force open; *Tresor, Auto* to break into; *Deckel* to prise off; *Boden, Asphalt, Oberfläche* to break up; (*geh*) *Brief* to break open; (*fig*) *System, soziale Struktur etc* to break down **VI** *aux sein* **a** (= *sich öffnen*) (*Straßenbelag etc*) to break up; (*Knospen*) to (burst) open; (*Wunde*) to open **b** (*fig: Konflikte, Hass etc*) to break out **c** (= *sich auf den Weg machen*) to start out *or* off, to set out *or* off

auf+bren|nen *sep irreg* **VT** **a einem Tier ein Zeichen ~** to brand an animal; **jdm eins ~** (*inf*) (= *schlagen*) to wallop *or* clout (*Brit*) sb (one) (*inf*); (= *anschießen*) to shoot sb, to put a slug into sb (*inf*); **sie brannte dem Hund eins auf** (*inf*: = *schlug*) she hit the dog **b** (= *verbrennen*) *Kerze, Kohlen etc* to burn up **VI** *aux sein* (*Feuer, Leidenschaft*) to flare up

auf+brin|gen VT *sep irreg* **a** (= *beschaffen*) to find; *Geld* to raise, to find; *Kraft, Mut, Energie* to find, to summon up **b** (= *erzürnen*) to make angry, to irritate; **jdn gegen jdn/etw ~** to set sb against sb/sth → *auch* **aufgebracht c** (= *ins Leben rufen*) to start **d** (*Naut*) *Schiff* to seize; (= *in Hafen zwingen*) to bring in **e** (= *auftragen*) *Farbe etc* to put on, to apply; **etw auf etw** (*acc*) **~** to put sth on sth, to apply sth to sth **f** (*dial*: = *aufbekommen*) *Tür etc* to get open

Auf|bruch M **a** *no pl* (= *Abreise, das Losgehen*) departure; **das Zeichen zum ~ geben** to give the signal to set out *or* off; **der ~ ins 21. Jahrhundert** the emergence into the 21st century; **eine Zeit des ~s** a time of new departures **b** (= *aufgebrochene Stelle*) crack

Auf|bruchs-: auf|bruchs|be|reit ADJ ready to set off *or* go *or* depart; **Auf|bruchs|sig|nal** NT signal to set off; **hast du das ~ gehört?** did

---

you hear the off?; **Auf|bruch(s)|stim|mung** F **a hier herrscht schon ~** (*bei Party etc*) it's all breaking up; (*in Gastwirtschaft*) they're packing up; **es herrschte allgemeine ~ (unter den Gästen)** the party was breaking up; **bist du schon in ~?** are you wanting *or* ready to go already? **b** (= *Euphorie*) euphoric mood; **es herrscht ~** there is a spirit of optimism

auf+brü|hen VT *sep* to brew up

auf+brül|len VI *sep* to shout *or* yell out; (*Tier*) to bellow

auf+brum|men *sep* **VT** (*inf*) **jdm etw ~** to give sb sth; **jdm die Kosten ~** to land sb with the costs (*inf*) **VI a** (*Motor*) to roar out **b** *aux sein* (*Aut inf*) to bang, to prang (*Brit inf*) (*auf +acc* into); (*Naut sl*) to run aground, to hit the bottom

auf+bü|geln VT *sep* **a** *Kleidungsstück* to iron out; (*fig inf*) to vamp up (*inf*) **b** *Flicken, Bild etc* to iron on; **Flicken zum Aufbügeln** iron-on patches

auf+bum|sen VI *sep* (*inf*) *aux sein* to bang; **etw auf etw** (*dat*) **~ lassen** to plump *or* plonk (*esp Brit inf*) sth down on sth; **mit dem Hinterkopf ~** to bump *or* bang the back of one's head

auf+bür|den VT *sep* (*geh*) **jdm etw ~** (*lit*) to load sth onto sb; (*fig*) to encumber sb with sth; **jdm die Schuld für etw ~** to put the blame for sth on sb

auf+bürs|ten VT *sep etw ~* to give sth a brush, to brush sth

auf dass ▲ CONJ → **auf 4**

auf+de|cken *sep* **VT a** *jdn* to uncover; *Bett(decke*) to turn down; *Gefäß* to open; *Spielkarten* to show **b** (*fig*) *Wahrheit, Verschwörung, Zusammenhänge* to discover, to uncover; *Verbrechen* to expose, to uncover; *Schwäche* to lay bare; *Geheimnis, Rätsel* to solve; *wahren Charakter* to disclose, to lay bare, to expose **c** (= *auf den Esstisch stellen*) to put on the table; **das Geschirr ~** (*Brit*) *or* set the table **VI** to lay (*Brit*) *or* set the table

Auf|de|ckung F (*fig*) (*von Wahrheit, Verschwörung, Zusammenhängen*) uncovering; (*von Verbrechen*) exposing, exposure; (*von Schwäche*) laying bare; (*von Geheimnis, Rätsel*) solving; (*von wahrem Charakter*) disclosing, disclosure

auf+don|nern VR *sep* (*pej inf*) to tart oneself up (*Brit pej inf*), to get dolled up (*Brit inf*), to get tarted up (*Brit pej inf*), to deck oneself out (*US inf*) → *auch* **aufgedonnert**

auf+drän|gen *sep* **VT jdm etw ~** to impose *or* force *or* push sth on sb **VR** to impose; **sich jdm ~** (*Mensch*) to impose oneself *or* one's company on sb; (*fig: Erinnerung*) to come involuntarily to sb's mind; **dieser Gedanke/Verdacht drängte sich mir auf** I couldn't help thinking/suspecting that

auf+dre|hen *sep* **VT a** *Wasserhahn, Wasser etc* to turn on; *Ventil* to open; *Schraubverschluss* to unscrew; *Schraube* to loosen, to unscrew; *Lautstärke* to turn up; (*Aus*: = *einschalten*) *Licht, Radio etc* to turn *or* switch on **b** (= *aufrollen*) *Haar* to put in rollers; *Schnurrbart* to turn *or* twist up **VI** (= *beschleunigen*) to put one's foot down hard, to open up; (*fig*) to get going, to start going like the clappers (*Brit inf*); (*fig*: = *ausgelassen werden*) to get going, to let it all hang out (*inf*) → *auch* **aufgedreht**

auf+drin|gen VTR *sep irreg* = **aufdrängen**

auf|dring|lich ADJ *Mensch, Benehmen* pushing, pushy (*inf*); *Farbe* loud, garish; *Geruch, Parfüm* overpowering; **die ~e Art meines Mitreisenden** the way my fellow passenger forced himself *or* his company upon me; **dieser ~e Kerl kam einfach auf mich zu** this guy just forced himself *or* his company on me (*inf*); **beim Tanzen wurde er ~** when we/they were dancing he kept trying to get fresh (*esp US inf*)

Auf|dring|lich|keit F (*von Mensch*) pushiness; **die ~ meiner Nachbarin** the way my neighbour (*Brit*) *or* neighbor (*US*) forces herself *or* her

---

company on you; **die ~ ihres Parfüms** her overpowering perfume; **die ~ der Tapete** the loud *or* garish wallpaper

auf+drö|seln [ˈaufdrøːzln] VT *sep* (*lit, fig*) to unravel; *Strickarbeit* to undo

Auf|druck M *pl* -**drucke** **a** (= *Aufgedrucktes*) imprint; (*auf Briefmarke*) overprint **b** (*Phys*) upward pressure

auf+dru|cken VT *sep* **etw auf etw** (*acc*) **~** to print sth on sth; **Postwertstempel auf Briefe ~** to stamp letters

auf+drü|cken *sep* **VT a** **etw (auf etw** *acc*) **~** to press sth on (sth); **den Bleistift nicht so fest ~!** don't press (on) your pencil so hard **b** (= *aufdrucken*) **etw auf etw** (*acc*) **~** to stamp sth on sth; **ein Siegel auf einen Brief ~** to impress a seal on a letter; **jdm einen ~** (*inf*) to give sb a kiss *or* a quick peck (*inf*) → **Stempel b c** (= *öffnen*) *Tür etc* to push open; *Pickel etc* to squeeze **d** (*inf*: = *durch Knopfdruck öffnen*) *Tür* to open (*by pressing the button*); **er drückte die Tür auf** he pressed *or* pushed the button and the door opened **VI a** (= *drücken*) to press **b** (*inf*: = *die Tür elektrisch öffnen*) to open the door (*by pressing a button*) **VR** to leave an impression (*auf +acc* on)

auf|ei|nan|der [aufʔaiˈnandɐ] ADV **a** on (top of) each other *or* one another **b ~ folgend** (*zeitlich*) successive; **drei schnell ~ folgende Tore** three goals in quick succession; **sich ~ verlassen können** to be able to rely on each other *or* one another; **~ zufahren** to drive toward(s) each other

auf|ei|nan|der: auf|ei|nan|der bei|ßen ▲ VT *irreg Zähne* to clench, to bite together; **auf|ei|nan|der drü|cken** ▲ VT to press together; **auf|ei|nan|der fah|ren** ▲ VI *irreg aux sein* to drive *or* crash into each other

Auf|ei|nan|der|fol|ge F , *no pl* sequence; (*zeitlich auch*) succession; **in schneller ~** in quick succession

auf|ei|nan|der fol|gen ▲ VI *sep aux sein* to follow each other *or* one another, to come after each other *or* one another; **die beiden Termine folgten unmittelbar aufeinander** the two appointments followed *or* came one immediately after the other, one appointment came immediately after the other

auf|ei|nan|der|fol|gend △ ADJ → **aufeinander b**

auf|ei|nan|der: auf|ei|nan|der hän|gen ▲ VI *irreg* **a** (*inf: Leute*) to hang around together (*inf*); **die beiden Autos hängen zu nah aufeinander** the two cars are sticking too close (together); **in einer kleinen Wohnung hängt man immer zu eng aufeinander** in a small flat (*Brit*) *or* apartment you're always too much on top of each other (*inf*) **b** (= *übereinander hängen*) to hang one over the other **VT** to hang on top of each other; **auf|ei|nan|der het|zen** ▲ VT to set on *or* at each other; **auf|ei|nan|der ho|cken** ▲ VI (*inf*) = aufeinander hängen VI a; **auf|ei|nan|der knal|len** ▲ (*inf*) **VI** *aux sein* (*lit, fig*) to collide; to bang together; **auf|ei|nan|der le|gen** ▲ **VT** to lay on top of each other, to lay one on top of the other **VR** to lie on top of each other; **auf|ei|nan|der lie|gen** ▲ **VI** *irreg aux sein or haben* to lie on top of each other; **auf|ei|nan|der pas|sen** ▲ VI to fit on top of each other; **auf|ei|nan|der pral|len** ▲ VI *aux sein* (*Autos etc*) to collide; (*Truppen etc, Meinungen*) to clash; **auf|ei|nan|der pres|sen** ▲ VT to press together; **auf|ei|nan|der ra|sen** ▲ VI *aux sein* to hurtle into each other; **auf|ei|nan|der schich|ten** ▲ VT to put in layers one on top of the other; **auf|ei|nan|der schla|gen** ▲ *irreg* **VI** *aux sein* to knock *or* strike against each other **VT** to knock *or* strike together; **auf|ei|nan|der set|zen** ▲ **VT** to put on top of each other **VR** (*Gegenstände*) to be placed one on top of the other *or* on top of

---

each other; (*Bienen etc*) to settle on each other; **auf|ei|nan|der sit|zen** ▲ VI *irreg aux sein or haben* **a** (*Gegenstände*) to lie on top of each other **b** (*inf*) **die Autos sitzen zu dicht aufeinander** the cars are too close together **c** (*inf: Menschen*) to sit on top of each other (*inf*); (= *eng wohnen*) to live on top of each other (*inf*); **auf|ei|nan|der stel|len** ▲ VT to put or place on top of each other VR to get on top of each other; **auf|ei|nan|der sto|ßen** ▲ VI *irreg aux sein* to bump into each other, to collide; (*fig: Meinungen, Farben*) to clash; **auf|ei|nan|der tref|fen** ▲ VI *irreg aux sein* (*Mannschaften, Gruppen etc*) to meet; (*Meinungen*) to clash, to come into conflict; (*Kugeln, Gegenstände etc*) to hit each other; **auf|ei|nan|der tür|men** ▲ VT to pile on top of each other

Auf|ent|halt ['aufʔɛnthalt] M **a** (= *das Sichaufhalten*) stay; (= *das Wohnen*) residence; **der ~ im Aktionsbereich des Krans ist verboten** do not stand within the radius of the crane, keep well clear of the crane **b** (= *Aufenthaltszeit*) stay, sojourn (*liter*) etc **c** (*esp Rail*) stop; (*bei Anschluss*) wait; **der Zug hat 20 Minuten ~** the train stops for 20 minutes; **wie lange haben wir ~?** how long do we stop for?; (*bei Anschluss*) how long do we have to wait? **d** (*geh* = *Verzögerung*) delay, wait **e** (*geh* = *Aufenthaltsort*) abode (*form*), domicile, place of residence; **~ nehmen** to take up residence

Auf|ent|hal|ter(in) M(F) (*Sw*) foreign resident, resident alien (*form*)

Auf|ent|halts-: **Auf|ent|halts|be|rech|ti|gung** F right of residence; **Auf|ent|halts|be|schrän|kung** F restriction on residence, limitation of (period of) residence; **Auf|ent|halts|be|wil|li|gung** F residence permit; **Auf|ent|halts|dau|er** F length or duration of stay; **Auf|ent|halts|er|laub|nis** F, **Auf|ent|halts|ge|neh|mi|gung** F residence permit; **Auf|ent|halts|ort** M *pl* -**orte** whereabouts *sing or pl*; (*Jur*) abode, residence; **man weiß nicht, was sein augenblicklicher ~ ist** his present whereabouts is or are not known; **Auf|ent|halts|raum** M day room; (*in Betrieb*) recreation room; (*auf Flughafen*) lounge; **Auf|ent|halts|ver|bot** NT **jdm ~ erteilen** to ban sb from staying (in a country etc); **er hat ~** he is not allowed to stay (in the country etc), he is banned

auf+er|le|gen *ptp* **auferlegt** VT *sep or insep* (*geh*) to impose (*jdm* on sb); *Strafe auch* to inflict (*jdm* on sb)

Auf|er|stan|de|ne(r) ['aufʔɛrʃtandnə] M *decl as adj* (*Rel*) der ~ Christ

auf+er|ste|hen *ptp* **auferstanden** VI *sep or insep irreg aux sein* to rise from the dead, to rise again (*esp Rel*); **Christus ist auferstanden** Christ is (a)risen

Auf|er|ste|hung ['aufʔɛrʃteːʊŋ] F -, -**en** resurrection; (*fröhliche*) ~ **feiern** (*hum*) to have been resurrected

Auf|er|ste|hungs|fest NT (*geh*) Feast of the Resurrection

auf+er|we|cken *ptp* **auferweckt** VT *sep or insep* (*geh*) to raise from the dead; (*fig*) to reawaken

Auf|er|we|ckung F raising from the dead

auf+es|sen *sep irreg* VT to eat up VI to eat (everything) up

auf+fä|chern *sep* VT (*fig*) to arrange or order neatly VR to fan out

auf+fä|deln VT *sep* to thread or string (together)

auf+fah|ren *sep irreg* VI *aux sein* **a** (= *aufprallen*) **auf jdn/etw ~** to run or drive into sb/sth; **auf eine Sandbank ~** to run onto a sandbank, to run aground on a sandbank
b (= *näher heranfahren*) to drive up, to move up; **zu dicht ~** to drive too close behind (the car in front); **mein Hintermann fährt dauernd so dicht auf** the car behind me is right on my tail all the time

c (= *nach oben fahren*) (*Bergleute*) to go up; (*Rel*) to ascend
d (= *hinauffahren*) **auf etw** (*acc*) ~ to drive onto sth; (*auf Autobahn*) to enter sth
e (= *aufschrecken*) to start; **aus dem Schlaf ~** to awake with a start
f (= *aufbrausen*) to flare up, to fly into a rage
VT **a** (= *herbeischaffen*) *Truppen etc* to bring up; *Sand, Erde, Torf etc* to put down; (*inf*) *Getränke etc* to serve up; *Speisen, Argumente* to dish (*inf*) or serve up; **lass mal eine Runde ~** (*inf*) how about buying us a round? (*inf*)
b (= *aufwühlen*) to churn or dig up

auf|fah|rend ADJ *Temperament* irascible, hasty; *Mensch auch* quick-tempered

Auf|fahrt F **a** (= *das Hinauffahren*) climb, ascent **b** (= *Zufahrt*) approach (road); (*bei Haus etc*) drive; (= *Rampe*) ramp **c** (*von Fahrzeugen*) driving up **d** (*Sw*) = **Himmelfahrt**

Auf|fahr|un|fall M (*von zwei Autos*) collision; (*von mehreren Autos*) pile-up

auf+fal|len *sep irreg* VI *aux sein* **a** (= *sich abheben*) to stand out; (= *unangenehm auffallen*) to attract attention; (= *sich hervortun*) to be remarkable (*durch* for); **er fällt durch seine roten Haare auf** his red hair makes him stand out; **er ist schon früher als unzuverlässig/Extremist aufgefallen** it has been noticed before that he is unreliable/an extremist; **angenehm/unangenehm ~** to make a good/bad impression; **man soll möglichst nicht ~** you should try to be as inconspicuous as possible, you should keep a low profile, you should try to avoid being noticed; **nur nicht ~!** just don't be conspicuous, just don't get yourself noticed
b (= *bemerkt werden*) **jdm fällt etw auf** sb notices sth, sth strikes sb; **so etwas fällt doch sofort auf** that will be noticed immediately; **so etwas fällt doch nicht auf** that will never be noticed; **der Fehler fällt nicht besonders auf** the mistake is not all that noticeable, the mistake does not show all that much; **fällt es/der Fleck auf?** does it/the stain show?, is it/the stain noticeable?; **das muss dir doch aufgefallen sein!** surely you must have noticed (it)!
c (= *auftreffen*) *Regen, Licht etc* **auf etw** (*acc*) ~ to fall onto sth, to strike sth; **er fiel mit dem Knie (auf einen Stein) auf** he fell and hurt his knee (on a stone)
d *aux haben* (*rare*: = *verletzen*) **sich** (*dat*) **etw ~** to fall and hurt sth, to fall on sth

auf|fal|lend ADJ conspicuous, noticeable; *Schönheit, Ähnlichkeit, Farbe, Kleider* striking; **das Auffallendste an ihr sind die roten Haare** her most striking feature is her red hair, the most striking thing about her is her red hair ADV conspicuously, noticeably; (= *besonders*) *schön, nett* remarkably, strikingly; **er ist ~ intelligent** he is strikingly or remarkably intelligent; **stimmt ~!** (*hum*) too true!, how right you are!

auf|fäl|lig ADJ conspicuous; *Farbe, Kleidung* striking; **~ werden** (*Mensch*) to get oneself noticed; **~ ist, dass/wie ...** it's striking or quite amazing that/how ...; **~ ist seine Vorliebe für ...** his preference for ... is very marked, he has a very marked preference for ... ADV conspicuously; (= *besonders*) *lang, kurz* amazingly; **sich ~ verhalten** to get oneself noticed; **er hat sich ~ genau erkundigt** he made a point of inquiring precisely; **er hat ~ wenig mit ihr geredet** it was conspicuous how little he talked with her; **~er gehts nicht mehr** they/he *etc* couldn't make it more obvious or conspicuous if they/he *etc* tried

Auf|fäl|lig|keit F **a** (= *etw Auffälliges*) striking feature **b** *no pl* (= *das Auffälligsein*) **die ~ ihrer Kleidung** her striking clothes

auf+fal|ten *sep* VT to unfold; *Fallschirm* to open VR to unfold; (*Fallschirm*) to open; (*Geol*) to fold upward

Auf|fang|be|cken NT collecting tank; (*fig*) gathering place; (*für Flüchtlinge*) focal point

auf+fan|gen VT *sep irreg* **a** *Ball, Gesprächsfetzen* to catch; *Wagen, Flugzeug* to get or bring under control; *Flugzeug* to pull out; (*Telec*) *Nachricht* to pick up; **jds Blick ~** to catch sb's eye **b** (= *abfangen*) *Aufprall etc* to cushion, to absorb; *Faustschlag* to block; (*fig*) *Preissteigerung, Verluste* to offset, to counterbalance; **jdn ~** (*fig: nach Niederlage, Schicksalsschlag*) to support sb, to be there for sb **c** (= *sammeln*) *Regenwasser etc* to collect, to catch; (*fig*) *Flüchtlinge etc* to assemble

Auf|fang-: **Auf|fang|ge|sell|schaft** F (*Fin*) rescue company; **Auf|fang|la|ger** NT reception camp, reception centre (*Brit*) or center (*US*)

auf+fas|sen *sep* VT **a** (= *interpretieren*) to interpret, to understand; **etw als etw** (*acc*) ~ to take sth as sth; **die Planeten als Götter ~** to conceive of the planets as gods; **das Herz als (eine Art) Pumpe ~** to think or conceive of the heart as a (kind of) pump; **etw falsch/richtig ~** to take sth the wrong way/in the right way **b** (= *geistig aufnehmen*) to take in, to grasp VI to understand

Auf|fas|sung F **a** (= *Meinung, Verständnis*) opinion, view; (= *Begriff*) conception, view; **nach meiner ~** in my opinion, to my mind; **nach christlicher ~** according to Christian belief **b** (= *Auffassungsgabe*) perception

Auf|fas|sungs-: **auf|fas|sungs|fä|hig** ADJ intelligent; **Auf|fas|sungs|fä|hig|keit** F, **Auf|fas|sungs|ga|be** F **er hat eine große ~** he has a tremendous grasp of things; **Auf|fas|sungs|kraft** F intellectual or mental powers *pl*; **Auf|fas|sungs|sa|che** F (*inf*) question of interpretation; (= *Ansichtssache*) matter of opinion; **Auf|fas|sungs|ver|mö|gen** NT = **Auffassungsfähigkeit**; **Auf|fas|sungs|wei|se** F interpretation; **es hängt von der ~ ab** it depends (on) how you interpret it

auf+fe|gen *sep* VT to sweep up VI to sweep (up)

auf|fi ['aufi] ADV (*Aus*) = **herauf, hinauf**

auf|find|bar ADJ **es ist nicht/ist ~** it isn't/is to be found, it can't/can be found; **es ist schwer ~** it's hard to find

auf+fin|den VT *sep irreg* to find, to discover

auf+fi|schen VT *sep* **a** *Gegenstand* to fish up; (*inf*) *Schiffbrüchige* to fish out **b** (*fig inf*) *Menschen* to find, to dig up (*inf*)

auf+fla|ckern VI *sep aux sein* (*lit, fig*) to flare up

auf+flam|men VI *sep aux sein* (*lit, fig: Feuer, Unruhen etc*) to flare up; **in seinen Augen flammte Empörung auf** his eyes flashed in indignation

auf+flat|tern VI *sep aux sein* (*Vogel*) to flutter up; (*Buch*) to rustle

auf+flie|gen VI *sep irreg aux sein* **a** (= *hochfliegen*) to fly up **b** (= *sich öffnen*) to fly open **c** (*fig inf:* = *jäh enden*) (*Konferenz etc*) to break up; (*Rauschgiftring, Verbrecher etc*) to be busted (*inf*); **einen Schmugglerring ~ lassen** to bust a ring of smugglers (*inf*); **eine Konferenz ~ lassen** to bust up or break up a meeting

auf+for|dern VT *sep* **a** (= *ersuchen*) to ask; **wir fordern Sie auf, ...** you are required to ... **b** (= *bitten*) to ask, to invite; (*zum Wettkampf etc*) to challenge **c** (= *zum Tanz bitten*) to ask to dance

auf|for|dernd ADJ inviting

Auf|for|de|rung F request; (*nachdrücklicher*) demand; (= *Einladung*) invitation; (*Jur*) incitement; **eine ~ zum Tanz** (*fig*) a challenge

Auf|for|de|rungs-: **Auf|for|de|rungs|cha|rak|ter** M (*Psych*) stimulative nature; **den ~ einer Äußerung nachweisen** (*Jur*) to prove that a statement constitutes incitement; **Auf|for|de|rungs|satz** M (*Gram*) (*als Hauptsatz*) imperative sentence, command (sentence); (*als Teilsatz*) imperative clause

auf+fors|ten *sep* VT *Gebiet* to reafforest; *Wald* to retimber, to restock VI **man ist dabei aufzu-**

---

forsten they are doing some reafforesting/re-timbering

Auf|fors|tung ['auffɔrstʊŋ] F -, -en (von Gebiet) reafforestation; (von Wald) retimbering, restocking

auf+fres|sen sep irreg **VT** (lit, fig) to eat up; **ich könnte dich ~** (inf) I could eat you; **er wird dich deswegen nicht gleich ~** (inf) he's not going to eat you (inf) **VI** (Tier) to eat all its food up; (inf: = aufessen) to finish eating

auf+fri|schen sep **VT** to freshen (up); Anstrich, Farbe auch to brighten up; Möbel etc to renovate, to refurbish; (= ergänzen) Vorräte to replenish; (fig) Erinnerungen to refresh; Kenntnisse to polish up; Sprachkenntnisse to brush up; persönliche Beziehungen to renew; Impfung to boost **VI** aux sein or haben (Wind) to freshen **VI** impers aux sein to get fresher or cooler

Auf|fri|schung ['auffrɪʃʊŋ] F -, -en freshening (up); (von Farbe, Anstrich auch) brightening up; (von Möbeln) renovation, refurbishment; (= Ergänzung: von Vorräten) replenishment; (von Erinnerungen) refreshing; (von Kenntnissen) polishing up; (von Sprachkenntnissen) brushing up; (von Beziehungen) renewal; (von Impfung) boosting

Auf|fri|schungs-: Auf|fri|schungs|imp|fung F booster; **eine ~ vornehmen lassen** to have a booster; **Auf|fri|schungs|kurs** M refresher course

auf+fri|sie|ren VT sep **a** Haar to touch up, to titivate **b** (fig) Tisch, Auto etc to do up; Motor to soup up (inf)

auf|führ|bar ADJ (Mus) performable; (Theat auch) stageable; **Faust II ist praktisch gar nicht ~** it is practically impossible to perform or stage Faust II

auf+füh|ren sep **VT** **a** Theaterstück, Ballett to put on; Drama, Oper to stage, to perform, to put on; Musikwerk, Komponist to perform; **ein Theater ~** (fig) to make a scene **b** (= auflisten) to list; (= nennen) Beispiel to quote, to cite; **einzeln ~** to itemize **VR** to behave; **sich wie ein Betrunkener ~** to act like a drunkard; **wie er sich wieder aufgeführt hat!** what a performance!

Auf|füh|rung F **a** (Theat) putting on; (von Drama, Oper) staging, performance; (= Vorstellung) performance; **etw zur ~ bringen** (form) to perform sth; **zur ~ kommen** or **gelangen** (form) to be performed **b** (= Auflistung) listing; (= Liste) list; **einzelne ~** itemization

Auf|füh|rungs-: Auf|füh|rungs|recht NT performing rights pl; **auf|füh|rungs|reif** ADJ ready to be performed

auf+fül|len VT sep **a** (= vollständig füllen) to fill up; (= nachfüllen) to top up; Mulde etc to fill in or up; **darf ich Ihr Glas ~?** can I top you up? **b** (= ergänzen) Flüssigkeit to dilute; Vorräte to replenish; Öl to top up (Brit) or off (US), Benzin ~ to tank up, to fill up with petrol (Brit) or gas (US) **c** Suppe, Essen to serve

auf+fut|tern VT sep (inf) to eat up, to polish off

Auf|ga|be F **a** (= Arbeit, Pflicht) job, task; **es ist deine ~, ...** it is your job or task or responsibility to ...; **es ist nicht ~ der Regierung, ...** it is not the job or task or responsibility of the government to ...; **sich (dat) etw zur ~ machen** to make sth one's job or business **b** (= Zweck, Funktion) purpose, job **c** (esp Sch) (= Problem) question; (zur Übung) exercise; (usu pl: = Hausaufgabe) homework no pl **d** (= Abgabe, Übergabe) (von Koffer, Gepäck) registering, registration; (Aviat) checking (in); (von Brief, Postsendung) handing in; (von Anzeige) placing no pl, insertion **e** (= Verzicht auf weiteren Kampf, weitere Anstrengungen) (Sport) retirement; (Mil etc) surrender; **er hat das Spiel durch ~ verloren** he lost the game by retiring; **die Polizei forderte die Geiselnehmer zur ~ auf** the police appealed to the kidnappers to give themselves up or to surrender

f (von Gewohnheit, Geschäft) giving up; (von Plänen, Forderungen) dropping, giving up; (von Hoffnung, Studium) abandoning, abandonment; **unter ~ all ihrer Habe** abandoning all their property; **er riet ihm zur ~ seines Studiums** he advised him to give up or abandon or drop his studies

g (= das Verlorengeben) giving up for lost **h** (Volleyball, Tennis etc) service, serve

auf+ga|beln VT sep Heu, Mist etc to fork up; (fig inf) jdn to pick up (inf); **wo hat er denn die aufgegabelt?** (inf) where did he dig her up? (inf)

Auf|ga|ben-: Auf|ga|ben|be|reich M , **Auf|ga|ben|ge|biet** NT area of responsibility; **Auf|ga|ben|heft** NT (Sch) homework book; **Auf|ga|ben|kreis** M (geh) area of responsibility; **Auf|ga|ben|samm|lung** F set of exercises or problems; (von Mathematikaufgaben) maths (Brit) or math (US) question book; **Auf|ga|ben|stel|lung** F **a** (= Formulierung) formulation **b** (= Aufgabe) type of problem; **Auf|ga|ben|ver|tei|lung** F allocation of responsibilities or tasks

Auf|ga|be-: Auf|ga|be|ort M pl -orte place where a letter etc was posted (Brit) or mailed (esp US); **Auf|ga|be|stem|pel** M postmark

Auf|gang M pl -gänge **a** (von Sonne, Mond, Stern) rising; (fig: von Stern) appearance, emergence **b** (= Treppenaufgang) stairs pl, staircase; **im ~** on the stairs or staircase **c** (= Aufstieg) ascent **d** (Sport) opening, beginning, start

Auf|gangs|punkt M (Astron) **der ~ eines Sterns** the point at which a star rises

auf+ge|ben sep irreg ♦ 47.2 **VT** **a** Hausaufgaben to give, to set; schwierige Frage, Problem to pose (jdm for sb); **jdm viel/nichts ~** (Sch) to give or set sb a lot of/no homework **b** (= übergeben, abgeben) Koffer, Gepäck to register, to check in; Fluggepäck to check in; Brief, Paket to post (Brit), to mail (esp US); Anzeige to put in, to place; Bestellung to place **c** Kampf, Hoffnung, Arbeitsstelle, Freund etc to give up; **gibs auf!** why don't you give up? **d** (= verloren geben) Patienten to give up; (fig) Sohn, Schüler to give up (with or on) **e** (inf) Essen to serve; **jdm etw ~** to give sb sth **VI** **a** (= sich geschlagen geben) to give up or in; (Mil) to surrender **b** (inf: bei Tisch) to serve (jdm sb); **kann ich dir noch mal ~?** can I give you some more?

auf|ge|bla|sen ['aufgəbla:zn] ADJ (fig) puffed-up, self-important → auch **aufblasen**

Auf|ge|bla|sen|heit F -, no pl (fig) self-importance

Auf|ge|bot NT **a** (Jur) public notice **b** (zur Eheschließung) notice of intended marriage; (Eccl) banns pl; **das ~ bestellen** to give notice of one's intended marriage; (Eccl) to put up or post the banns; **das ~ veröffentlichen** to publish the announcement of one's intended marriage; (Eccl) to call the banns **c** (= Ansammlung) (von Menschen) contingent; (von Material etc) array **d** (= Aufbietung) **mit dem ~ unter ~ aller Kräfte** ... summoning all his/her etc strength ...

auf|ge|bracht ['aufgəbraxt] ADJ outraged, incensed → auch **aufbringen**

auf|ge|don|nert ['aufgədɔnɛt] ADJ (pej inf) tarted-up (Brit pej inf), decked-out (US inf) → auch **aufdonnern**

auf|ge|dreht ['aufgədre:t] ADJ (inf) in high spirits → auch **aufdrehen**

auf|ge|dun|sen ADJ swollen, bloated; Gesicht auch puffy

auf+ge|hen VI sep irreg aux sein **a** (Sonne, Mond, Sterne) to come up, to rise **b** (= sich öffnen) to open; (Theat: Vorhang) to go up; (Knopf, Knoten, Reißverschluss, Jacke etc) to come undone **c** (= aufkeimen, Med: Pocken) to come up **d** (Cook) to rise **e** (= klar werden) **jdm geht etw auf** sb realizes sth, sth dawns on sb, sth becomes apparent to

sb

f (Math: Rechnung etc) to work out, to come out; (fig) to come off, to work (out); **wenn man 20 durch 6 teilt, geht das nicht auf** 20 divided by 6 doesn't go; **im Kriminalroman muss alles sauber ~** in a detective story everything has to work out or to be resolved neatly

g (= seine Erfüllung finden) **in etw (dat) ~** to be wrapped up in sth, to be taken up with sth; **er geht ganz in der Familie auf** his whole life revolves around his family

h (= sich auflösen) **in Flammen etc ~** to go up in flames etc; **in der Masse ~** to disappear or merge into the crowd

i (Hunt: Jagdzeit) to begin

auf|ge|ho|ben ['aufgəho:bn] ADJ **(bei jdm) gut/schlecht ~ sein** to be/not to be in good hands (with sb) → auch **aufheben**

auf+gei|len VR sep (sl) **er geilt sich an diesen Fotos auf** he gets off on these photos (inf)

auf|ge|klärt ['aufgəkle:ɐt] ADJ **a** enlightened (auch Philos); **der ~e Absolutismus** (Hist) Benevolent Despotism **b** (sexualkundlich) **~ sein** to know the facts of life → auch **aufklären**

Auf|ge|klärt|heit F -, no pl enlightenment; (sexualkundlich) knowledge of the facts of life

auf|ge|knöpft ['aufgəknœpft] ADJ (inf: = mitteilsam) chatty (inf) → auch **aufknöpfen**

auf|ge|kratzt ['aufgəkratst] ADJ (inf) in high spirits, full of beans (Brit inf), boisterous → auch **aufkratzen**

Auf|ge|kratzt|heit F -, no pl high spirits pl, boisterousness

Auf|geld NT (dial: = Zuschlag) extra charge; (old: = Anzahlung) deposit, earnest (money) (old)

auf|ge|legt ['aufgəle:kt] ADJ **gut/schlecht** etc ~ in a good/bad etc mood; **(dazu) ~ sein, etw zu tun** to feel like doing sth; **zum Musikhören ~ sein** to be in the mood for listening to music, to feel like listening to music → auch **auflegen**

auf|ge|löst ['aufgəlø:st] ADJ **a** (= außer sich) beside oneself (vor +dat with), distraught; (= bestürzt) upset; **in Tränen ~** in tears **b** (= erschöpft) exhausted, drained, shattered (inf) → auch **auflösen**

auf|ge|räumt ['aufgərɔymt] ADJ (geh: = gut gelaunt) jovial, light-hearted → auch **aufräumen**

auf|ge|regt ['aufgəre:kt] ADJ (= erregt) excited; (= nervös) nervous; (= durcheinander) flustered **ADV** excitedly → auch **aufregen**

Auf|ge|regt|heit F -, no pl (= Erregtheit) excitement; (= Nervosität) nervousness; (= Durcheinandersein) flustered state

auf|ge|schlos|sen ['aufgəʃlɔsn] ADJ (= nicht engstirnig) open-minded (für, gegenüber as regards, about); (= empfänglich) receptive, open (für, gegenüber to); **ich bin Vorschlägen gegenüber** or **für Vorschläge jederzeit ~** I'm always open to suggestion(s); **einer Sache (dat) ~ gegenüberstehen** to be open-minded as regards or about sth → auch **aufschließen**

Auf|ge|schlos|sen|heit F -, no pl open-mindedness (für, gegenüber as regards, about); (= Empfänglichkeit) receptiveness, openness (für, gegenüber to)

auf|ge|schmis|sen ['aufgəʃmɪsn] ADJ pred (inf) in a fix (inf), stuck (inf) → auch **aufschmeißen**

auf|ge|schos|sen ['aufgəʃɔsn] ADJ **(hoch** or **lang) ~** (Mensch) who has shot up or grown; **ein lang ~er Junge** a tall lanky lad (esp Brit) or boy → auch **aufschießen**

auf|ge|schwemmt ['aufgəʃvɛmt] ADJ bloated, swollen; Mensch auch → auch **aufschwemmen**

auf|ge|setzt ADJ **a** **sie tötete sich mit einem ~en Kopfschuss** she killed herself by shooting herself in the head **b** (= geheuchelt) Sprüche hypocritical, insincere; Laune, Mimik put on; **~ wirken** (= unecht) to seem false or put on → auch **aufsetzen**

auf|ge|stellt ADJ (*Sw*: = *frohsinnig, gute Laune verbreitend*) convivial → *auch* **aufstellen**

auf|ge|ta|kelt ['aʊfgətaːklt] ADJ (*pej*) dressed (up) to the nines (*inf*) → *auch* **auftakeln**

auf|ge|weckt ['aʊfgəvɛkt] ADJ bright, quick, sharp → *auch* **aufwecken**

Auf|ge|weckt|heit F -, *no pl* mental quickness, sharpness

auf|ge|wühlt ['aʊfgəvyːlt] ADJ (*geh*) agitated, in a turmoil *pred*; *Gefühle auch* turbulent; *Wasser, Meer* churning, turbulent; **völlig ~** (*fig*) in a complete turmoil → *auch* **aufwühlen**

auf|gie|ßen VT *sep irreg* **a** *etw* (**auf etw** *acc*) **~** to pour sth on (sth); **das angebräunte Mehl mit Brühe ~** to pour stock on(to) the browned flour **b** *Kaffee* to make; *Tee* to make, to brew

auf+glän|zen VI *sep aux sein* (*lit, fig*) to light up; (*Mond, Sonne, Sterne*) to come out; (*Strahlen reflektierend*) to (begin to) gleam

auf+glie|dern *sep* VT **a** (*in* +*acc*) into) to split up, to (sub)divide; (= *analysieren auch*) to break down, to analyse (*Brit*), to analyze (*US*); (*in Kategorien auch*) to categorize, to break down VR (*in* +*acc* into) to (sub)divide, to break down

Auf|glie|de|rung F division; (= *Analyse auch*) breakdown, analysis; (*in Kategorien*) categorization, breakdown

auf+glim|men VI *sep irreg aux sein* to light up, to begin to glow; (*fig*) to glimmer

auf+glü|hen VI *sep aux sein or haben* to light up, to begin to glow; (*fig*) (*Gesicht*) to light up, to glow; (*Hass, Neid*) to (begin to) gleam; (*Leidenschaft, Liebe*) to awaken

auf+gra|ben VT *sep irreg* to dig up

auf+grät|schen VI *sep aux sein or haben* (*Sport*) **auf etw** (*acc*) **~** to straddle sth

auf+grei|fen VT *sep irreg* **a** (= *festnehmen*) to pick up, to apprehend (*form*) **b** (= *weiterverfolgen*) *Thema, Gedanken* to take up, to pick up; (= *fortsetzen*) *Gespräch* to continue, to take up again

auf|grund ['aʊfgrʊnt], **auf Grund** ✪ 44.1 PREP +*gen* on the basis of; **~ von Zeugenaussagen** on the basis or strength of the witnesses' testimonies; **~ einer Verwechslung/seiner Eifersucht** owing to or because of a mistake/his jealousy

auf+gu|cken VI *sep* (*inf*) to look up (*von* from)

Auf|guss ▲ M brew, infusion (*auch Sci*); (*in Sauna*) pouring of water onto hot coals (*fig pej*) rehash

Auf|guss|beu|tel ▲ M sachet (containing coffee/herbs etc) for brewing; (= *Teebeutel*) tea bag

auf+ha|ben *sep irreg* VT **a** *Hut, Brille* to have on, to wear; **sie hat ihre Brille nicht aufgehabt** she didn't have her glasses on, she wasn't wearing her glasses **b** *Tür, Augen, Laden, Jacke* to have open **c** (*Sch*: *als Hausaufgabe*) **etw ~** to have sth (to do); **ich habe heute viel auf** I've got a lot of homework today **d** (*inf*: = *aufgemacht haben*) to have got or gotten (*US*) open **c** (*inf.* = *aufgegessen haben*) to have eaten up VI (*Laden etc*) to be open

auf+ha|cken VT *sep Straße* to break up; (*Vogel*) to break or peck open

auf+hal|sen ['aʊfhalzn] VT *sep* (*inf*) **jdm/sich etw ~** to saddle or land sb/oneself with sth (*inf*), to land sth on sb/oneself (*inf*); **sich** (*dat*) **etw ~ lassen** to get oneself saddled or landed with sth (*inf*)

auf+hal|ten *sep irreg* VT **a** (= *zum Halten bringen*) *Fahrzeug, Entwicklung* to stop, to halt; *Inflation etc* to check; (= *verlangsamen*) to hold up, to delay; (= *abhalten, stören*) (*bei* from) to hold back, to keep back; **ich will dich nicht länger ~** I don't want to keep or hold you back any longer **b** (*inf*: = *offen halten*) to keep open; **die Hand ~** to hold one's hand out VR **a** (= *an einem Ort bleiben*) to stay **b** (= *sich verzögern*) to stay on, to linger; (*bei*

der Arbeit etc) to take a long time (*bei* over) **c** (= *sich befassen*) **sich bei etw ~** to dwell on sth, to linger over sth; **sich mit jdm/etw ~** to spend time dealing with sb/sth **d** (= *sich entrüsten*) **sich über etw** (*acc*) **~** to rail against sth

auf+hän|gen *sep* VT **a** *Kleidung, Bild* to hang up; (*Aut*) *Rad* to suspend **b** (= *töten*) to hang (*an* +*dat* from) **c** (*inf*) **jdm etw ~** (= *aufschwatzen*) to palm sth off on sb; (= *glauben machen*) to talk sb into believing sth; (= *aufbürden*) to land or saddle sb with sth (*inf*) **d** *etw an einer Frage/einem Thema ~* (*fig*: = *entwickeln*) to use a question/subject as a peg to hang sth on VR (= *sich töten*) to hang oneself (*an* +*dat* from); (*hum*: = *seine Kleider aufhängen*) to hang one's things up

Auf|hän|ger M tag, loop; **ein ~ für etw** (*fig inf*) a peg to hang sth on (*fig*)

Auf|hän|ge|vor|rich|tung F hanger, suspender; (*Tech*) suspension device

Auf|hän|gung ['aʊfhɛŋʊŋ] F -, -en (*Tech*) suspension

auf+har|ken VT *sep* to rake up

auf+hau|en *sep* VT *reg or* (*geh*) *irreg* (= *öffnen*) to knock open, to hew open (*liter*); *Eis* to open up, to hew open (*liter*); **sich** (*dat*) **den Kopf** *etc* **~** to gash one's head *etc* open VI *aux sein* (*lit*: = *auftreffen*) **mit dem Kopf** *etc* **auf etw** (*acc or dat*) **~** to bash (*inf*) or bump one's head *etc* against or on sth

auf+häu|fen *sep* VT to pile up, to accumulate; (*fig auch*) to amass VR to accumulate, to pile up

auf|heb|bar ADJ *Gesetz, Regelung* revocable

auf+he|beln ['aʊfheːbln] VT *sep* (*inf, mit Brecheisen*) *Tür, Kiste* to force or break open

auf+he|ben *sep irreg* VT **a** (*vom Boden*) to pick up; *größeren Gegenstand* to lift up; (= *in die Höhe heben*) to raise, to lift (up); *Deckel* to lift off **b** (= *nicht wegwerfen*) to keep; **jdm etw ~** to put sth aside for sb, to keep sth (back) for sb → *auch* **aufgehoben c** (= *ungültig machen*) to abolish, to do away with; *Gesetz* to repeal, to abolish, to rescind; *Vertrag* to cancel, to annul, to revoke; *Urteil* to reverse, to quash; *Verlobung* to break off; **dieses Gesetz hebt das andere auf** this law supersedes the other **d** (= *beenden*) *Blockade, Belagerung* to raise, to lift; *Beschränkung* to remove, to lift; *Sitzung* to close; *Parlament* to dissolve → **Tafel c** **e** (= *ausgleichen*) to offset, to make up for; *Widerspruch* to resolve; *Schwerkraft* to neutralize, to cancel out **f** (*obs*: = *festnehmen*) to capture, to come to seize VR **a** (*old*: = *aufstehen*) to rise (*old, form*) **b** (= *sich ausgleichen*) to cancel each other out, to offset each other; (*Math*) to cancel (each other) out

Auf|he|ben NT -s, *no pl* fuss; **viel ~(s) (von** *or* **um etw) machen** to make a lot of fuss (about or over sth); **viel ~(s) von jdm** *or* **um jdn machen** to make a lot of fuss about sb; **ohne (jedes) ~** without any fuss; **ohne viel** *or* **großes ~** without much or a big fuss

Auf|he|bung F **a** (= *Abschaffung*) abolition; (*von Gesetz auch*) repeal, rescinding; (*von Vertrag*) cancellation, annulment, revocation; (*von Urteil*) reversal, quashing; (*von Verlobung*) breaking off **b** (= *Beendigung*) (*von Blockade etc*) raising, lifting; (*von Beschränkung*) removal; (*von Sitzung*) closing; (*von Parlament*) dissolving **c** (*von Widerspruch*) resolving, resolution; (*von Schwerkraft*) neutralization, cancelling out **d** (*obs*: = *Festnahme*) capture, seizure

Auf|he|bungs|ver|trag M termination agreement

auf+hei|tern ['aʊfhaitɐn] *sep* VT *jdn* to cheer up; *Rede, Leben* to brighten up (*jdm* for sb) VR (*Himmel*) to clear, to brighten (up); (*Wetter*) to clear up, to brighten up

auf+hei|ternd ADJ **a** (*Met*) becoming brighter, brightening up **b** *Buch etc* cheerful

Auf|hei|te|rung F -, -en (= *Erheiterung*) cheering up; (*von Rede, Leben*) brightening up; (*Met*) brighter period; **zunehmende ~** gradually brightening up

auf+hei|zen *sep* VT to heat (up); (*fig*) *Zuhörer* to inflame, to stir up; **die Stimmung ~** to whip or stir up feelings VR to heat up; (*fig*) to hot up (*inf*), to intensify, to build up

auf+hel|fen *sep irreg* VT (*lit*: *beim Aufstehen*) to help up (*jdm* sb); **einer Sache** (*dat*) **~** (= *aufbessern*) to help sth (to) improve; (*stärker*) to help strengthen sth

auf+hel|len ['aʊfhɛlən] *sep* VT to brighten (up); *Haare* to lighten; (*fig*: = *klären*) to throw or shed light upon VR (*Himmel, Wetter, fig: Miene*) to brighten (up); (*fig: Sinn*) to become clear

Auf|hel|ler ['aʊfhɛlɐ] M -s, - (*in Reinigungsmitteln*) colour (*Brit*) or color (*US*) brightener; (*für Haare*) lightener

Auf|hel|lung F -, -en brightening; (*von Haaren*) lightening; (*fig*: = *Klärung*) clarification; **es kam zu zeitweisen ~en** from time to time the weather brightened up

auf+het|zen VT *sep* to stir up, to incite; **jdn gegen jdn/etw ~** to stir up sb's animosity against sb/sth; **jdn zu etw ~** to incite sb to (do) sth

Auf|het|ze|rei F (*inf*) agitation; (*esp durch Reden*) rabble-rousing

auf|het|ze|risch ADJ inflammatory, rabble-rousing

Auf|het|zung F -, -en incitement, agitation

auf+heu|len VI *sep* to give a howl (*vor* of), to howl (*vor* with); (*Sirene*) to (start to) wail; (*Motor, Menge*) to (give a) roar; (= *weinen*) to start to howl

auf+ho|cken VI *sep aux sein or haben* **a** (*Sport*) to crouch-jump (*auf* +*acc* on to) **b** (*dial*) **auf etw** (*acc*) **~** to sit on sth

auf+ho|len *sep* VT **a** *Zeit, Verspätung, Vorsprung* to make up; *Lernstoff* to catch up on; *Strecke* to make up, to catch up; **Versäumtes ~** to make up for lost time **b** (*Naut*) to haul up, to raise VI (*Wanderer, Mannschaft, Schüler, Arbeiter*) to catch up; (*Läufer, Rennfahrer etc auch*) to make up ground; (*Zug etc*) to make up time; (= *Versäumnisse aufholen*) to make up for lost time

Auf|hol|jagd F (*Sport*) pursuit race; (*fig*) race to catch up

auf+hor|chen VI *sep* to prick up one's ears, to sit up (and take notice); **das ließ ~** that made people sit up (and take notice)

auf+hö|ren VI *sep* to stop; (*Musik, Lärm, Straße auch, Freundschaft, Korrespondenz*) to (come to an) end; (*bei Arbeitsstelle*) to finish; **nicht ~/~, etw zu tun** to keep on/stop doing sth; **hör doch endlich auf!** (will you) stop it!; **mit etw ~** to stop sth; **da hört sich doch alles auf!** (*inf*) that's the (absolute) limit!; **da hört bei ihm der Spaß auf** (*inf*) he's not amused by that

auf+hüp|fen VI *sep aux sein* (*Mensch*) to jump or leap up; (*Vogel*) to hop; (*Ball etc*) to bounce; **vor Angst/Freude ~** to jump with fear/for joy

auf+ja|gen VT *sep* (*lit*) to disturb; (*fig*) to chase away

auf+jauch|zen VI *sep* to shout (out) (*vor* with)

auf+jau|len VI *sep* to give a howl (*vor* of), to howl (*vor* with)

auf+ju|beln VI *sep* to shout (out) with joy, to cheer

auf+juch|zen VI *sep* to whoop with joy, to give a whoop of joy

Auf|kauf M buying up

auf|kau|fen VT *sep* to buy up

Auf|käu|fer(in) M(F) buyer

auf+keh|ren VTI *sep* (*esp S Ger*) to sweep up

auf+kei|men VI *sep aux sein* to germinate, to sprout; (*fig*) (*Hoffnung, Liebe, Sympathie*) to bud, to burgeon (*liter*); (*Zweifel*) to (begin to) take root; **~d** (*fig*) budding, burgeoning (*liter*), nascent (*liter*); *Zweifel* growing, nascent (*liter*)

auf+klaf|fen VI *sep aux sein or haben* to gape; (*Abgrund auch*) to yawn; **~d** (*lit, fig*) gaping

auf|klapp|bar ADJ *Fenster, Tafel* hinged; *Truhe, Schreibpult* with a hinged lid; *Klappe* which lets down; *Verdeck* which folds back, fold-back

Auf|klapp|buch NT pop-up book

auf+klap|pen *sep* VT to open up; *Klappe* to lift up; *Verdeck* to fold back; *Messer* to unclasp; *Fensterläden, Buch, Landkarte* to open ◼ *aux sein* to open

auf+kla|ren ['aufklaːrən] *sep* (*Met*) VI *impers* to clear (up), to brighten (up) (*auch fig*) VI (*Wetter*) to clear or brighten (up); (*Himmel*) to clear, to brighten (up)

auf+klä|ren *sep* VT **a** *Missverständnis, Irrtum* to clear up, to resolve; *Verbrechen, Rätsel* to solve, to clear up; *Ereignis, Vorgang* to throw or shed light upon, to elucidate

  b *jdn* to enlighten; **Kinder ~** (*sexualkundlich*) to explain the facts of life to children, to tell children the facts of life; (*in der Schule*) to give children sex education; **jdn über etw** (*acc*) **~** to inform sb about sth; **klär mich mal auf, wie ...** (*inf*) (can you) enlighten me as to how ... → *auch* **aufgeklärt**

  c (*Mil*) to reconnoitre (*Brit*), to reconnoiter (*US*)

  VR (*Irrtum, Geheimnis etc*) to resolve itself, to be cleared up; (*Himmel*) to clear, to brighten (up); (*fig: Miene, Gesicht*) to brighten (up)

Auf|klä|rer¹ ['aufklɛːrə] M **-s, -** (*Mil*) reconnaissance plane; (*klein*) scout (plane)

Auf|klä|rer² ['aufklɛːrə] M **-s, -**, **Auf|klä|re|rin** [-ərɪn] F **-, -nen** (*Philos*) philosopher of the Enlightenment

auf|klä|re|risch ['aufklɛːrərɪʃ] ADJ (*Philos*) (of the) Enlightenment; (= *freigeistig*) progressive, striving to enlighten the people; (= *erzieherisch, unterrichtend*) informative; (*Pol*) educational

Auf|kla|rung ['aufklaːrʊŋ] F (*des Wetters*) clearing up; (*des Himmels*) clearing

Auf|klä|rung F (*Philos*) **die ~** the Enlightenment **b** (*von Missverständnis*) clearing up, resolution; (*von Verbrechen, Rätsel*) solution; (*von Ereignis, Vorgang*) elucidation **c** (= *Information*) enlightenment; (*von offizieller Stelle*) information (*über +acc* about); (*Pol*) instruction **d** (**sexuelle**) **~** (*in Schulen*) sex education; **die ~ von Kindern** explaining the facts of life to children **e** (*Mil*) reconnaissance

Auf|klä|rungs-: **Auf|klä|rungs|ar|beit** F instructional or educational work; **Auf|klä|rungs|bro|schü|re** F informative pamphlet; (*sexualkundlich*) sex education pamphlet; **Auf|klä|rungs|buch** NT sex education book; **Auf|klä|rungs|film** M sex education film; **Auf|klä|rungs|flug** M (*Mil*) reconnaissance flight or mission; **Auf|klä|rungs|flug|zeug** NT reconnaissance plane; (*klein*) scout (plane); **Auf|klä|rungs|kam|pag|ne** F information campaign; **Auf|klä|rungs|li|te|ra|tur** F informative literature; (*Pol*) educational literature; (*sexualkundlich*) sex education literature; (*Philos*) literature of the Enlightenment; **Auf|klä|rungs|ma|te|ri|al** NT informational material; **Auf|klä|rungs|pflicht** F (*Jur*) judge's duty to ensure that all the relevant facts of a case are clearly presented (*Med*) duty to inform the patient of the possible dangers of an operation/a course of treatment etc; **Auf|klä|rungs|quo|te** F (*in Kriminalstatistik*) success rate (in solving cases), percentage of cases solved; **Auf|klä|rungs|sa|tel|lit** M spy satellite; **Auf|klä|rungs|schiff** NT (*Mil*) reconnaissance ship; **Auf|klä|rungs|schrift** F information pamphlet; (*Pol*) educational pamphlet; (*sexualkundlich*) sex education pamphlet; **Auf|klä|rungs|trup|pe** F (*Mil*) armoured reconnaissance troop(s *pl*); **Auf|klä|rungs|un|ter|richt** M (*Sch*) sex education (classes *pl*); **Auf|klä|rungs|zeit** F , **Auf|klä|rungs|zeit|al|ter** NT

Age of Enlightenment; **Auf|klä|rungs|ziel** NT (*Mil*) reconnaissance object, object of reconnaissance

auf+klat|schen VI *sep aux sein* (*auf +acc* on) to land with a smack; (*auf Wasser auch*) to land with a splash

auf+klau|ben VT *sep* (*dial: lit, fig*) to pick up

Auf|kle|be|ad|res|se F (gummed or adhesive) address label

auf+kle|ben VT *sep* (*auf +acc* to) to stick on; (*mit Leim, Klebstoff auch*) to glue on; (*mit Kleister*) to paste on; *Briefmarke* to put or stick on, to affix (*form*) (*auf +acc* to)

Auf|kle|ber M sticker

auf+klin|gen VI *sep irreg aux sein* to ring out; (*fig*) to echo

auf+klin|ken ['aufklɪŋkn] VT *sep Tür* to open, to unlatch

auf+klop|fen VT *sep* (= *öffnen*) *Nuss* to crack open

auf+knab|bern VT *sep* (*inf*) to nibble up; **sie hat alle Chips aufgeknabbert** she gobbled up all the crisps (*Brit*) or potato chips (*US, inf*)

auf+kna|cken VT *sep Nüsse etc* to crack (open); (*inf*) *Tresor* to break into, to break open, to crack (*inf*); *Auto* to break into

auf+knal|len *sep* (*inf*) VI *aux sein* (*Auto*) to crash; (*Gegenstand, Mensch*) to crash down; **auf etw** (*acc*) **~** (= *gegen etw knallen*) to crash into sth; (= *auf etw fallen*) to crash (down) onto sth; **mit dem Kopf (auf etw** *acc*) **~** to bang or hit one's head on sth VT (*als Strafe*) to give

auf+knöp|fen VT *sep* (= *öffnen*) to unbutton, to undo; **aufgeknöpft** (*Hemd*) unbuttoned; **etw auf etw** (*acc*) **~** to button sth to sth → *auch* **aufgeknöpft**

auf+kno|ten VT *sep* to untie, to undo

auf+knüp|fen *sep* VT **a** (= *aufhängen*) to hang (*an +dat* from), to string up (*inf*) (*an +dat* on)   **b** (= *aufknoten*) to untie, to undo VR to hang oneself (*an +dat* from)

auf+ko|chen *sep* VT **a** (= *zum Kochen bringen*) to bring to the (*Brit*) or a (*US*) boil **b** (= *erneut kochen lassen*) to boil up again VI **a** *aux sein* to come to the (*Brit*) or a (*US*) boil; (*fig*) to begin to boil or seethe; **etw ~ lassen** to bring sth to the (*Brit*) or a (*US*) boil; **das Pulver in die ~de Milch schütten** sprinkle the powder in the milk as it comes to the (*Brit*) or a (*US*) boil **b** (*Aus*) to prepare a fine spread

auf+kom|men VI *sep irreg aux sein* **a** (*lit, fig:* = *entstehen*) to arise; (*Nebel*) to come down; (*Wind*) to spring or get up; (= *auftreten: Mode etc*) to appear (on the scene), to arise; **etw ~ lassen** (*fig, Zweifel, Kritik*) to give rise to sth; **üble Stimmung** to allow sth to develop

  b **~ für** (= *Kosten tragen*) to bear the costs of, to pay for; (= *Verantwortung tragen*) to carry the responsibility for, to be responsible for; (= *Haftung tragen*) to be liable for; **für die Kinder ~** (*finanziell*) to pay for the children's upkeep; **für die Kosten ~** to bear or defray (*form*) the costs; **für den Schaden ~** to make good the damage, to pay for the damage

  c **gegen jdn/etw ~** to prevail against sb/sth; **gegen jdn nicht ~ können** to be no match for sb

  d **er lässt niemanden neben sich** (*dat*) **~** he won't allow anyone to rival him

  e (= *aufsetzen, auftreffen*) to land (*auf +dat* on)

  f (*dated*) (= *sich erheben*) to rise, to get up; (= *sich erholen*) to recover

  g (*Naut:* = *herankommen*) to come up; (*Sport:* = *Rückstand aufholen*) (*bei Match*) to come back; (*bei Wettlauf, -rennen*) to catch up, to make up ground

  h (*dial: Schwindel, Diebstahl etc*) to come out, to be discovered

Auf|kom|men NT **-s, -** **a** *no pl* (= *das Auftreten*) appearance; (*von Methode, Mode etc*) advent, emergence; **~ frischer Winde gegen Abend** fresh winds will get up toward(s) evening **b**

(*Fin*) (= *Summe, Menge*) amount; (*von Steuern*) revenue (*aus, +gen* from) **c** *no pl* (*von Flugzeug*) landing; **beim ~** on touchdown

auf+kor|ken ['aufkɔrkn] VT *sep* to uncork

auf+krat|zen *sep* VT (= *zerkratzen*) to scratch; (= *öffnen*) *Wunde* to scratch open → *auch* **aufgekratzt** VR to scratch oneself sore

auf+krei|schen VI *sep* (*Mensch*) to scream, to shriek, to give a scream or shriek; (*Bremsen, Maschine*) to (give a) screech

auf+krem|peln VT *sep* (**jdm/sich**) **die Ärmel/Hose ~** to roll up sb's/one's sleeves/trousers

auf+kreu|zen VI *sep* **a** *aux sein* (*inf:* = *erscheinen*) to turn or show up (*inf*) **b** *aux sein or haben* **gegen den Wind ~** (*Naut*) to tack

auf+krie|gen VT *sep* (*inf*) = **aufbekommen**

auf+kün|den (*geh*), **auf+kün|di|gen** VT *sep Vertrag etc* to revoke, to terminate; **jdm den Dienst ~** to hand in one's notice to sb, to give notice to sb that one is leaving (one's employment); **jdm die Freundschaft ~** (*geh*) to terminate one's friendship with sb; **jdm den Gehorsam ~** to refuse obedience to sb

Auf|kün|di|gung F termination, revocation; (*von Freundschaft*) termination

Aufl. *abbr von* **Auflage**

auf|la|chen VI *sep* to (give a) laugh; (*schallend*) to burst out laughing

auf|lad|bar ADJ chargeable; (= *neu aufladbar*) rechargeable; **~e Geldkarte** electronic cash card

auf+la|den *sep irreg* VT **a** *etw* (**auf etw** *acc*) **~** to load sth on(to) sth; **jdm/sich etw ~** to load sb/oneself down with sth, to burden sb/oneself with sth; (*fig*) to saddle sb/oneself with sth **b** (*elektrisch*) to charge; (= *neu aufladen*) to recharge; *Geldkarte* to reload; **emotional aufgeladen** (*fig*) emotionally charged **c** (*Aut*) *Motor* to supercharge, to boost VR (*Batterie etc*) to be charged; (*neu*) to be recharged; (= *elektrisch/elektrostatisch geladen werden*) to become charged

Auf|la|dung F (*Elec*) (= *das Aufladen*) charging; (= *Ladung*) charge

Auf|la|ge F **a** (= *Ausgabe*) edition; (= *Druck*) impression; (= *Auflagenhöhe*) number of copies; (*von Zeitung*) circulation; **das Buch hat hohe ~n erreicht** a large number of copies of this book have been published; **die Zeitung hat hohe ~n erreicht** this paper has attained a large circulation

  b (*Ind:* = *Fertigungsmenge*) production; **limitierte ~** limited edition

  c (= *Bedingung*) condition; **jdm etw zur ~ machen** to impose sth on sb as a condition; **jdm zur ~ machen, zu tun** to make it a condition for sb to do sth, to impose a condition on sb that he do sth; **er bekam die Genehmigung nur mit der ~, das zu tun** he obtained permission only on condition that he do that; **die ~ haben, etw zu tun** to be obliged to do sth

  d (= *Stütze*) support, rest

  e (= *Überzug*) coating; (= *Polsterung*) pad, padding *no pl*; **eine ~ aus Silber** silver plating or coating

Auf|la|ge-: **Auf|la|ge|flä|che** F supporting surface; **Auf|la|ge|hö|he** F (*von Buch*) number of copies published; (*von Zeitung*) circulation; **das Buch hatte eine ~ von 12.000** 12,000 copies of the book were published; **die Zeitung hatte eine ~ von ...** the paper had a circulation of ...

Auf|la|gen- = **Auflage-**

Auf|la|ge-: **Auf|la|ge|punkt** M point of support; **auf|la|ge|schwach** ADJ low-circulation *attr*; **auf|la|ge|stark** ADJ high-circulation *attr*; **Auf|la|ge|zif|fer** F circulation (figures *pl*); (*von Buch*) number of copies published

auf|lan|dig ['auflandıç] ADJ (*Naut*) landward, coastward; *Wind auch* onshore *attr*

auf+las|sen VT *sep irreg* **a** (*inf:* = *offen lassen*) to leave open; (= *aufbehalten*) *Hut* to keep or leave on; **das Kind länger ~** to let the child stay up (longer) **b** (= *schließen*) (*Min*) Grube to close *or* shut down; (*Aus, S Ger*) Betrieb to close *or* shut down; **eine aufgelassene Grube** a closed-down *or* an abandoned mine **c** (*Jur*) Grundstück to convey (*form*), to transfer, to make over (*form*)

Auf|las|sung F -, -en **a** (*Min, Aus, S Ger*: von Geschäft) closing down, shutdown **b** (*Jur*) conveyancing (*form*), conveyance (*form*), transference

Auf|las|sungs|vor|mer|kung F (*Jur*) deed of conveyance

auf+las|ten VT sep = **aufbürden**

auf+lau|ern VI sep +dat to lie in wait for; (*und angreifen, ansprechen*) to waylay

Auf|lauf M **a** (= *Menschenauflauf*) crowd **b** (*Cook*) (baked) pudding (*sweet or savoury*)

auf+lau|fen VI sep irreg aux sein **a** (= *auf Grund laufen*: Schiff) to run aground (*auf +acc or dat* on); (*fig*) to run into trouble; **jdn ~ lassen** to drop sb in it (*inf*) **b** (= *aufprallen*) **auf jdn/etw ~** to run into sb/sth, to collide with sb/sth; **jdn ~ lassen** (*Ftbl*) to bodycheck sb **c** (= *sich ansammeln*) to accumulate, to mount up; (*Zinsen*) to accrue **d** (*Wasser.* = *ansteigen*) to rise; **~des Wasser** flood tide, rising tide **e** (*dial*: = *anschwellen*) to swell (up)

Auf|lauf|form F (*Cook*) ovenproof dish

auf+le|ben VI sep aux sein to revive; (= *munter, lebendig werden*) to liven up, to come to life again; (= *neuen Lebensmut bekommen*) to find a new lease of life; **Erinnerungen wieder ~ lassen** to revive memories

auf+le|cken VT sep to lick up

auf+le|gen sep ⊙ 27.3, 27.6 **VT a** Tischdecke, Schallplatte etc to put on; Gedeck to set; Kompresse to apply, to put on; Hörer to put down, to replace; **jdm die Hand ~** (*Rel*) to lay hands on sb **b** (= *herausgeben*) Buch to bring out, to publish; **ein Buch neu ~** to reprint a book; (*neu bearbeitet*) to bring out a new edition of a book **c** (*zur Einsichtnahme*) to display, to put up **d** (*Econ*) Serie to launch **e** (*Fin*) Aktien to issue, to float; Fonds to set up **f** (*Naut*) Schiff to lay up **g** (*rare*: = *auferlegen*) **sich** (*dat*) **Entbehrungen** etc ~ to impose sacrifices etc on oneself, to suffer self-imposed privations etc **h** → **aufgelegt** **VI a** (= *Telefonhörer auflegen*) to hang up, to ring off (*Brit*) **b** (*Feuerholz/Kohle etc auflegen*) to put on more firewood/coal etc

auf+leh|nen sep **VR** sich gegen jdn/etw ~ to revolt *or* rebel against sb/sth **VT** (*dial*) **den Arm ~** to lean on one's arm; **die Arme auf etw** (*acc or dat*) ~ to lean one's arms on sth

Auf|leh|nung F -, -en revolt, rebellion

auf+lei|men VT sep to glue on (*auf +acc* -to)

auf+le|sen VT sep irreg (*lit, fig inf*) to pick up; **jdn/etw von der Straße ~** to pick sb/sth up off the street

auf+leuch|ten VI sep aux sein or haben (*lit, fig*) to light up

auf+lich|ten sep **VT a** (= *aufhellen*) Bild, Raum to brighten up; (*fig*) Hintergründe, Geheimnis to clear up, to get to the bottom of **VR** (*Himmel*) to clear; (*fig: Hintergründe*) to be cleared up, to become clear

Auf|lich|tung F (= *Aufhellung*) brightening up; (*fig: von Hintergründen, Geheimnis*) clearing up

Auf|lie|fe|rer M -s, -, **Auf|lie|fe|rin** F -, -nen (*form*) sender; (*von Fracht*) consignor

auf+lie|fern VT sep (*form*) to dispatch; Fracht to consign (*for delivery*)

auf+lie|gen sep irreg **VI a** (= *auf etw sein*) to lie or rest on top; (*Schallplatte*) to be on the turntable; (*Hörer*) to be on; (*Tischdecke*) to be on (the table); **auf etw** (*dat*) ~ to lie or rest on sth, to be on sth **b** (= *ausliegen*) (*zur Ansicht*) to be displayed; (*zur Benutzung*) to be available **c** (= *er-*

schienen sein: Buch) to be published **d** (*Naut*) to be laid up **VR** (*inf: Patient*) to get bedsores **VT** (*inf*) **sich** (*dat*) **den Rücken** etc ~ to get bedsores on one's back etc

Auf|lie|ger ['aufliːgɐ] M -s, - (*von Lkw*) trailer

auf+lis|ten ['auflistn] VT sep to list

Auf|lis|tung F -, -en (*auch Comput*) listing; (= *Liste*) list

auf+lo|ckern sep **VT a** Boden to break up, to loosen (up) **b die Muskeln ~** to loosen up (one's muscles); (*durch Bewegung auch*) to limber up **c** (= *abwechslungsreicher machen*) Unterricht, Stoff, Vortrag to make less monotonous, to give relief to (*durch with*); (= *weniger streng machen*) to make less severe; Frisur, Muster to soften, to make less severe **d** (= *entspannen, zwangloser machen*) to make more relaxed; Verhältnis, Atmosphäre to ease; **in aufgelockerter Stimmung** in a relaxed mood **VR a** (*Sport*) to limber or loosen up **b** (*Bewölkung*) to break up, to disperse

Auf|lo|cke|rung F **a** (*von Boden*) breaking up, loosening (up); (*von Muskeln*) loosening up; **... trägt zur ~ des Stoffes/des strengen Musters bei** ... helps to make the material less monotonous/the pattern less severe; **ihm gelang die ~ einer gespannten Atmosphäre** he succeeded in easing a tense atmosphere **b** (*Sport*) limbering or loosening up **c** (*von Bewölkung*) breaking up, dispersal, dispersing

Auf|lo|cke|rungs|ü|bung F (*Sport*) limbering-up exercise

auf+lo|dern VI sep aux sein (*Flammen*) to flare up; (= *in Flammen aufgehen*) to go up in flames; (= *lodernd brennen*) to blaze; (*fig: Kämpfe, Hass, Leidenschaft*) to flare up

auf|lös|bar ADJ soluble; Gleichung auch solvable; Ehe dissoluble; Verlobung that can be broken off; Vertrag revocable, able to be cancelled (*Brit*) or canceled (*US*)

Auf|lös|bar|keit ['aufløːsbaːɐkait] F -, no pl solubility; (*von Gleichung*) solvability; (*von Ehe*) dissolubility; (*von Vertrag*) revocability

auf+lö|sen sep **VT a** (*in Flüssigkeit*) to dissolve; (= *in Bestandteile zerlegen, Phot*) to resolve (*in +acc* into); (*Math*) Klammern to eliminate; Gleichung to (re)solve; (*Mus*) Vorzeichen to cancel; Dissonanz to resolve (*in +acc* into) → *auch* **aufgelöst b** (= *aufklären*) Widerspruch, Missverständnis to clear up, to resolve; Rätsel to solve **c** (= *zerstreuen*) Wolken, Versammlung to disperse, to break up **d** (= *aufheben*) to dissolve (*auch Parl*); Einheit, Gruppe to disband; Firma to wind up; Verlobung to break off; Vertrag to cancel; Konto to close; Haushalt to break up **e** (*geh*) Haar to let down; geflochtenes Haar to let loose; **mit aufgelösten Haaren** with one's hair loose **VR a** (*in Flüssigkeit*) to dissolve; (= *sich zersetzen*: Zellen, Reich, Ordnung) to disintegrate; (*Zweifel, Probleme*) to disappear; **all ihre Probleme haben sich in nichts aufgelöst** all her problems have dissolved into thin air or have disappeared **b** (= *sich zerstreuen*) to disperse; (*Wolken*) to break up, to disperse; (*Nebel*) to lift, to disperse **c** (= *auseinander gehen*) (*Verband*) to disband; (*Firma*) to cease trading; (= *sich formell auflösen*: esp Parl) to dissolve **d** (= *sich aufklären*) (*Missverständnis, Problem*) to resolve itself, to be resolved; (*Rätsel*) to be resolved or solved **e sich in etw** (*acc*) ~ (= *verwandeln*) to turn into sth; (= *undeutlich werden*) to dissolve into sth **f** (*geh: Schleife, Haar*) to become undone **g** (*Phot*) to be resolved

Auf|lö|sung F **a** (= *das Auflösen*) (*in Flüssigkeit*) dissolving; (*in Bestandteile*) resolution; (*von Widerspruch, Missverständnis*) clearing up, resolving; (*von Rätsel*) solving; (*von Wolken, Versammlung*) dispersal; (*von Einheit, Gruppe*) disbanding; (*von*

Firma) winding up; (*von Verlobung*) breaking off; (*von Vertrag*) cancellation; (*von Konto*) closing; (*von Haushalt*) breaking up; (*von Reich, Ordnung, Zellen*) disintegration; (*von Parlament*) dissolution; (*Math*) (*von Klammern*) elimination; (*von Gleichung*) (re)solving; (*Mus: von Vorzeichen*) cancellation **b** (= *Lösung*) (*von Problem etc*) resolution; (*von Rätsel*) solution (+*gen*, *von* to) **c** (*Phot, Comput, von Bildschirm*) resolution **d** (= *Verstörtheit*) distraction

Auf|lö|sungs-: Auf|lö|sungs|er|schei|nung F sign of breaking up; **Auf|lö|sungs|pro|zess** ▲ M process of disintegration; **Auf|lö|sungs|ver|trag** M (*Econ, Jur*) cancellation or termination contract; **Auf|lö|sungs|zei|chen** NT (*Mus*) natural

auf+ma|chen sep **VT a** (= *öffnen*) to open; (= *lösen, aufknöpfen, aufschnallen*) to undo; Haar to loosen; (*inf*: = *operieren*) to open up (*inf*), to cut open (*inf*) **b** (= *eröffnen, gründen*) Geschäft, Unternehmen to open (up) **c** (= *gestalten*) Buch, Zeitung to make or get up; (= *zurechtmachen*) jdn to dress, to get up (*inf*); (*in Presse*) Ereignis, Prozess etc to feature; **der Prozess wurde groß aufgemacht** the trial was given a big spread or was played up (in the press) **d** (*dial*: = *anbringen*) Plakat, Vorhänge to put up, to hang (up) **VI** (= *Tür öffnen*) to open up, to open the door; (= *Geschäft (er)öffnen*) to open (up) **VR a** (= *sich zurechtmachen*) to get oneself up (*inf*) **b** (= *sich anschicken*) to get ready, to make preparations; (= *aufbrechen*) to set out, to start (out); **sich zu einem Spaziergang ~** to set out on a walk

Auf|ma|cher M (*Press*) lead

Auf|ma|chung ['aufmaxʊŋ] F -, -en **a** (= *Kleidung*) turnout, rig-out (*inf*); **in großer ~ erscheinen** to turn up in full dress **b** (= *Gestaltung*) presentation, style; (*von Buch*) presentation, make-up; (*von Seite, Zeitschrift*) layout; **der Artikel erschien in großer ~** the article was given a big spread, the article was featured prominently **c** (*Press*: = *Artikel etc auf Titelseite*) lead feature

auf+ma|len VT sep to paint on (*auf etw acc* sth); (*inf*) to scrawl (*auf +acc* on)

Auf|marsch M **a** (*Mil*) (= *das Aufmarschieren*) marching up; (*in Stellung, Kampflinie*) deployment; (= *Parade*) march past **b** (*Sw*) attendance

Auf|marsch|ge|biet NT deployment zone

auf+mar|schie|ren ptp **aufmarschiert** VI sep aux sein (= *heranmarschieren*) to march up; (= *vorbeimarschieren*) to march past; (*Mil*: = *in Stellung gehen*) to deploy; **~ lassen** (*Mil: an Kampflinie etc*) to deploy; (*fig hum*) to have march up/past

Auf|maß NT (*Build*) dimension

auf+mei|ßeln VT sep (*Med*) to trephine

auf+mer|ken VI sep (= *aufhorchen*) to sit up and take notice; (*geh*: = *Acht geben*) to pay heed or attention (*auf +acc* to)

auf|merk|sam ['aufmɛrkzaːm] **ADJ a** Zuhörer, Beobachter, Schüler attentive; Augen keen; (= *scharf beobachtend*) observant; **jdn auf etw** (*acc*) **~ machen** to draw sb's attention to sth; **jdn darauf ~ machen, dass ...** to draw sb's attention to the fact that ...; **auf jdn/etw ~ werden** to become aware of sb/sth; **~ werden** to sit up and take notice **b** (= *zuvorkommend*) attentive; (**das ist**) **sehr ~ von Ihnen** (that's) most kind of you **ADV** zusehen carefully; zuhören attentively; **Felix beteiligt sich ~ am Unterrichtsgeschehen** Felix pays attention in class

Auf|merk|sam|keit F -, -en **a** no pl attention, attentiveness; **das ist meiner ~ entgangen** I failed to notice that, that escaped my notice or attention **b** no pl (= *Zuvorkommenheit*) attentiveness **c** (= *Geschenk*) token (gift); (**nur) eine**

kleine ~ (just) a little something or gift; **kleine ~en** little gifts

auf|mi|schen VT sep (inf) (= in Unruhe versetzen) to stir up; (= verprügeln) to beat up, to lay into (inf)

auf+mö|beln ['aufmøːbln] VT sep (inf) Gegenstand to do up (inf); Kenntnisse to polish up (inf); jdn (= beleben) to buck up (inf), to pep up (inf); (= aufmuntern) to buck up (inf), to cheer up

auf+mon|tie|ren ptp **aufmontiert** VT sep to mount, to fit (on); **etw auf etw** (acc) **~** to mount sth on sth, to fit sth on or to sth

auf+mot|zen sep (inf) **VT** to zap up (inf); Theaterstück auch to revamp (inf) **VI** to get cheeky (Brit) or fresh (US)

auf+mu|cken, auf+muck|sen VI sep (inf) to protest (gegen at, against)

auf+mun|tern ['aufmʊntɐn] VT sep (= aufheitern) to cheer up; (= beleben) to liven up, to ginger up (inf); (= ermutigen) to encourage; **jdn zu etw ~** to encourage sb to do sth; **ein ~des Lächeln** an encouraging smile

Auf|mun|te|rung F -, -en a no pl cheering up; (= Belebung) livening up, gingering up (inf) b (= Ermutigung) encouragement

auf|müp|fig ['aufmʏpfɪç] ADJ (inf) rebellious

Auf|müp|fig|keit F -, -en (inf) rebelliousness

auf+na|geln VT sep to nail on (auf +acc -to)

auf+nä|hen VT sep to sew on (auf +acc -to)

Auf|nä|her ['aufnɛːɐ] M -s, - (auf Jacke) (sew-on) badge (Brit) or patch (US)

Auf|nah|me ['aufnaːmə] F -, -n a (= Empfang, fig: = Reaktion) reception; (= Empfangsraum) reception (area); **bei jdm freundliche ~ finden** (lit, fig) to meet with a warm reception from sb; **jdm eine freundliche ~ bereiten** to give sb a warm reception; **die ~ in ein Krankenhaus** admission (in +acc to) to hospital; **wie war die ~ beim Publikum?** how did the audience receive it or react? b (in Verein, Orden etc) admission (in +acc to); (= Aufgenommener) recruit c no pl (lit, fig: = Absorption) absorption; (= Nahrungsaufnahme) taking, ingestion (form) d no pl (= Einbeziehung) inclusion, incorporation; (in Liste, Bibliografie) inclusion e no pl (von Geldern, Kapital, Hypothek) raising f no pl (= Aufzeichnung) (von Protokoll, Diktat) taking down; (von Personalien) taking (down); (von Telegramm) taking; **die ~ eines Unfalls** taking down details of an accident g no pl (= Beginn) (von Gespräch etc) start, commencement; (von Tätigkeit) taking up; (von Beziehung, Verbindung) establishment h no pl (= das Fotografieren) taking, photographing; (= das Filmen) filming, shooting; **Achtung, ~!** action! i (= Fotografie) photo(graph), shot (inf); (= Schnappschuss, Amateuraufnahme) snap (inf); **eine ~ machen** to take a photo(graph) etc j (auf Tonband) recording

Auf|nah|me-: Auf|nah|me|an|trag M application for membership or admission; **Auf|nah|me|be|din|gung** F condition of admission; **auf|nah|me|be|reit** ADJ Boden ready for planting; Kamera ready to shoot; (fig) receptive, open (für to); **Auf|nah|me|be|reit|schaft** F (fig) receptiveness, receptivity; **auf|nah|me|fä|hig** ADJ a für etw **~ sein** to be able to take sth in; **ich bin nicht mehr ~** I can't take anything else in b Markt receptive; **Auf|nah|me|fä|hig|keit** F a ability to take things in b (von Markt) receptiveness; **Auf|nah|me|for|ma|li|tä|ten** PL admission formalities pl; **Auf|nah|me|ge|bühr** F enrolment (Brit) or enrollment (US) fee; (in Verein) admission fee; **Auf|nah|me|ge|rät** NT (Film) (film) camera; (= Tonbandgerät) recorder; **Auf|nah|me|la|ger** NT reception camp; **Auf|nah|me|land** NT host country (für to); **Auf|nah|me|lei|ter(in)** M(F) (Film) production manager; (Rad, TV) pro-

ducer; **Auf|nah|me|prü|fung** F entrance examination; **Auf|nah|me|stopp** M (für Flüchtlinge etc) ban on immigration; **Auf|nah|me|stu|dio** NT (film) studio; (für Tonaufnahmen) (recording) studio; **Auf|nah|me|tech|nik** F (Tonaufnahmen) recording method; (Phot, Film) shooting or filming technique; **Auf|nah|me|ver|fah|ren** NT (für Schule, Verein etc) admission(s) procedure; (für Tonaufnahmen) recording technique; **Auf|nah|me|ver|mö|gen** NT a (= Aufnahmefähigkeit) receptiveness, receptivity (für to) b (= Fassungsvermögen) capacity; **Auf|nah|me|wa|gen** M (Rad) recording van; **auf|nah|me|wür|dig** ADJ (für Verein) worthy of admittance; (für Wörterbuch etc) worth including

Auf|nahms|prü|fung F (Aus) entrance examination

auf+neh|men VT sep irreg a (vom Boden) to pick up; (= heben) to lift up b (lit: = empfangen, fig: = reagieren auf) to receive c (= unterbringen) to take (in); (= fassen) to take, to hold; Arbeitskräfte, Einwanderer to absorb d (in Verein, Orden, Schule etc) to admit (in +acc to); (Aus: = anstellen) to take on e (= absorbieren) to absorb, to take up; (= im Körper aufnehmen) to take; (fig) (= eindringen lassen) Eindrücke to take in; (= begreifen) to grasp, to take in; **etw in sich** (dat) **~** to take sth in; **er nimmt (alles) schnell auf** he takes things in quickly, he grasps things quickly, he's quick on the uptake f (= mit einbeziehen) to include, to incorporate; (in Liste, Bibliografie) to include; (fig: = aufgreifen) to take up g (esp Ftbl) Ball to take, to receive h (dial) (= aufwischen) to wipe up i (= beginnen) to begin, to commence; Tätigkeit, Studium to take up, to begin; Verbindung, Beziehung to establish; **Kontakt** or **Fühlung mit jdm ~** to contact sb → Kampf j Kapital to borrow; Kredit, Hypothek to take out k (= niederschreiben) Protokoll, Diktat to take down; Personalien to take (down); Telegramm to take l (= fotografieren) to take (a photograph or picture of), to photograph; (= filmen) to film, to shoot (inf) m (auf Tonband) to record, to tape n (beim Stricken) Maschen to cast on; (zusätzliche) to increase, to make o **es mit jdm/etw ~ können** to be a match for sb/sth, to be able to match sb/sth; **es mit jdm/ etw nicht ~ können** to be no match for sb/sth; **an Naivität kann es keiner mit ihm ~** where naivety is concerned there's no-one to beat him

auf+neh|mens|wert ADJ = aufnahmewürdig

Auf|neh|mer M (dial) a (N Ger: = Scheuertuch) cloth b (= Müllschaufel) shovel

äuf|nen ['ɔyfnən] VT (Sw) Geld etc to accumulate

auf+nes|teln VT sep (inf) Knoten, Schnur to undo; Bluse, Haken auch to unfasten

auf+no|tie|ren ptp **aufnotiert** VT sep (sich dat) etw **~** to note sth down, to make a note of sth

auf+nö|ti|gen VT sep jdm etw **~** (Geld, Essen) to force or press sth on sb; Entscheidung, Meinung to force or impose sth on sb; **die Lage nötigt (uns) Vorsicht auf** the situation requires or demands that we be cautious, the situation requires caution (on our part)

auf+okt|roy|ie|ren ptp **aufoktroyiert** VT sep jdm etw **~** to impose or force sth on sb

auf+op|fern sep **VR** to sacrifice oneself **VT** to sacrifice, to give up

auf|op|fernd **ADJ** Mensch self-sacrificing; Liebe, Tätigkeit, Arbeit devoted; **ein ~es Leben** a life of self-sacrifice **ADV** selflessly, self-sacrificing

Auf|op|fe|rung F a (= Aufgabe) sacrifice; **durch ~ einer Sache** (gen) by sacrificing sth; **un|ter ~ einer Sache** (gen) at the cost of sth b (= Selbstaufopferung) self-sacrifice; **mit ~** with devotion

Auf|op|fe|rungs-: auf|op|fe|rungs|be|reit ADJ self-sacrificing; **Auf|op|fe|rungs|be|reit|schaft** F self-sacrifice; **auf|op|fe|rungs|voll** **ADJ** self-sacrificing **ADV** selflessly, self-sacrificingly

auf+pa|cken VT sep jdm/einem Tier etw **~** to load sth onto sb/an animal, to load sb/an animal with sth; **jdm etw ~** (fig) to burden or saddle (inf) sb with sth; **er packte sich** (dat) **den Rucksack auf** he put on his rucksack

auf+päp|peln VT sep (inf) (mit Nahrung) to feed up; (durch Pflege) to nurse back to health

auf+pas|sen ✪ 29.3 VI sep a (= beaufsichtigen) **auf jdn/etw ~** to watch sb/sth, to keep an eye on sb/sth; (= hüten) to look after or to mind sb/sth; (= Aufsicht führen) to supervise sb/sth; (bei Examen) to invigilate sb b (= aufmerksam sein, Acht geben) to pay attention; **pass auf!, aufgepasst!** look, watch; (= sei aufmerksam) pay attention; (= Vorsicht) watch out, mind (out)

Auf|pas|ser ['aufpasɐ] M -s, -, **Auf|pas|se|rin** [-ərɪn] F -, -nen (pej) (= Aufseher, Spitzel) spy (pej), watchdog (inf); (für VIP etc) minder; (= Beobachter) supervisor; (bei Examen) invigilator; (= Wächter) guard

auf+peit|schen VT sep Meer, Wellen to whip up; (fig) Sinne to inflame, to fire; Menschen to inflame, to work up; (stärker) to whip up into a frenzy; **eine ~de Rede** a rabble-rousing (pej) or inflammatory speech

auf+pep|pen ['aufpɛpn] VT sep (inf) to jazz up (inf)

auf+pflan|zen sep **VT** to plant; (Mil) Bajonett to fix **VR** **sich vor jdm ~** to plant oneself in front of sb

auf+pfrop|fen VT sep (lit) to graft on (+dat -to); (fig) to superimpose (+dat on)

auf+pi|cken VT sep a (Vogel) to peck up; (fig) to glean, to pick up b (= öffnen) to peck open

auf+pin|seln VT sep (inf: = hinschreiben) to scrawl (auf +acc on)

auf+plat|zen VI sep aux sein to burst open; (Lack) to crack; (Wunde) to open up, to rupture

auf+plus|tern sep **VT** Federn to ruffle up; (fig) Vorfall, Ereignis to blow up, to exaggerate **VR** (Vogel) to ruffle (up) its feathers, to puff itself up; (Mensch) to puff oneself up

auf+po|lie|ren ptp **aufpoliert** VT sep (lit, fig) to polish up

auf+prä|gen VT sep to emboss, to stamp; **einen Stempel auf etw** (acc) **~** to emboss sth with a stamp

Auf|prall M impact

auf+pral|len VI sep aux sein **auf etw** (acc) **~** to strike or hit sth; (Fahrzeug auch) to collide with sth, to run into sth

Auf|preis M extra or additional charge; **gegen ~** for an extra or additional charge

auf+pres|sen VT sep to press on (auf +acc -to); (= öffnen) to press open

auf+pro|bie|ren ptp **aufprobiert** VT sep to try (on)

auf+pum|pen VT sep Reifen, Ballon to pump up, to inflate; Fahrrad to pump up or inflate the tyres (Brit) or tires (US) of

auf+pus|ten VT sep (inf) = aufblasen VT a

auf+put|schen sep **VT** a (= aufwiegeln) to rouse; Gefühle, öffentliche Meinung to stir up (gegen against); **jdn zu etw ~** to incite sb to (do) sth b (durch Reizmittel) to stimulate; **~de Mittel** stimulants **VR** to pep oneself up (inf), to dope oneself (Sport inf)

Auf|putsch|mit|tel NT stimulant

Auf|putz M get-up (inf), rig-out (inf); (festlich geschmückt) finery (iro), attire (iro)

auf+put|zen VT sep a (= schönmachen) jdn to dress up, to deck out; (fig: = aufpolieren) Gegenstand to do up; Image to polish or brush up b (dial: = aufwischen) Boden to clean (up); Flüssigkeit to mop or wipe up

auf+quel|len VI *sep irreg aux sein* **a** (= *anschwellen*) to swell (up); **aufgequollen** swollen; *Gesicht auch* puffy, bloated; *Mensch* bloated (-looking); **etw ~ lassen** to soak sth (to allow it to swell up) **b** (*geh: = aufsteigen*) (*Rauch*) to rise

auf+raf|fen *sep* VR to pull oneself up; (*vom Boden auch*) to pick oneself up; **sich ~, etw zu tun** (*inf*) **sich ~** ~ (*inf*) to rouse oneself to do sth VT *Rock, Papiere, Eigentum* to gather up; (= *schnell aufheben*) to snatch up

auf+ra|gen VI *sep aux sein* (= *in die Höhe aufragen*) to rise; (*sehr hoch, groß auch*) to tower (up) (*über +dat* above, over); **die hoch ~den Türme** the soaring towers; **die hoch ~den Fabrikkamine/Tannen** the towering factory chimneys/fir trees

auf+rap|peln VR *sep* (*inf*) **a** = **aufraffen** VR **b** (= *wieder zu Kräften kommen*) to recover, to get over it; **er hat sich nach seiner Krankheit endlich wieder aufgerappelt** he at last recovered from or got over his illness

auf+rau|chen VT *sep* (= *zu Ende rauchen*) to finish (smoking); (= *aufbrauchen*) to smoke, to get through

auf+rau|en ▲ VT *sep* to roughen (up); (*Tex*) *Stoff* to nap; *Haut, Hände* to roughen, to make rough

auf+räu|men *sep* VT to tidy or clear up; (= *wegräumen auch*) to clear or put away; **aufgeräumt** (*Zimmer*) tidy → *auch* **aufgeräumt** VI **a** **mit etw ~** to do away with sth **b** (*pej: = dezimieren*) **unter der Bevölkerung (gründlich) ~** (*Seuche etc*) to decimate the population, to wreak havoc among the population; (*Tyrann etc*) to slaughter the population wholesale

Auf|räu|mungs|ar|bei|ten PL clear(ing)-up operations *pl*

auf+rech|nen VT *sep* **a** **jdm etw ~** to charge sth to or to sb's account; (*fig: = vorwerfen*) to throw sth in sb's face **b** **etw gegen etw ~** to set sth off against sth, to offset sth against sth

auf|recht ['aufrɛçt] ADJ (*lit, fig*) upright; *Körperhaltung, Gangart auch* erect; **in** or **mit ~em Gang** (*fig*) with one's head held high ADV **~ gehen/stehen** to walk/stand upright or erect; **~ sitzen** to sit up(right); **etw ~ hinstellen** to place sth upright, to place sth in an upright position; **halte dich ~!** stand up straight!

auf|recht+er|hal|ten *ptp* **aufrechterhalten** VT *sep irreg* to maintain; *Kontakt, Bräuche auch* to keep up; *Behauptung auch* to stick to; *Entschluss, Glauben auch* to keep or adhere to, to uphold; *Verein* to keep going; (= *moralisch stützen*) *jdn* to keep going, to sustain

Auf|recht|er|hal|tung F maintenance, maintaining; (*von Kontakten, Bräuchen auch*) keeping up

auf+re|den VT *sep* = **aufschwatzen**

auf+re|gen *sep* VT (= *ärgerlich machen*) to irritate, to annoy; (= *nervös machen*) to make nervous or edgy (*inf*); (= *beunruhigen*) to agitate, to disturb; (= *bestürzen*) to upset; (= *erregen*) to excite; **du regst mich auf!** you're getting on my nerves; **er regt mich auf** he drives me mad (*inf*) VR to get worked up (*inf*) or excited (*über +acc* about) → *auch* **aufgeregt**

auf|re|gend ADJ exciting

Auf|re|gung F excitement *no pl*; (= *Beunruhigung*) agitation *no pl*; **nur keine ~!** don't get excited, don't get worked up (*inf*) or in a state (*inf*)!; **die Nachricht hat das ganze Land in ~ versetzt** the news caused a great stir throughout the country; **jdn in ~ versetzen** to put sb in a flurry, to get sb in a state (*inf*); **alles war in heller ~** everything was in utter confusion, there was complete bedlam

auf+rei|ben *sep irreg* VT **a** (= *wund reiben*) *Haut etc* to chafe, to rub sore; **sich** (*dat*) **die Hände/Haut ~** to chafe one's hands/oneself, to rub one's hands/oneself sore **b** (*fig: = zermürben*) to wear down or out **c** (*Mil: = völlig vernichten*) to wipe out, to annihilate VR (*durch Sorgen*

etc) to wear oneself out; (*durch Arbeit auch*) to work oneself into the ground

auf|rei|bend ADJ (*fig*) wearing, trying; (*stärker*) stressful; **nervlich ~** stressful

auf+rei|hen *sep* VT (*in Linie*) to line up, to put in a line/lines or a row/rows; *Perlen* to string; (*fig: = aufzählen*) to list, to enumerate VR to line up, to get in a line/lines or a row/rows

auf+rei|ßen[1] *sep irreg* VT **a** (= *durch Reißen öffnen, aufbrechen*) to tear or rip open; *Straße* to tear or rip up **b** *Tür, Fenster* to fling open; *Augen, Mund* to open wide **c** (= *beschädigen*) *Kleidung* to tear, to rip; *Haut* to gash **d** (*Sport inf*) *Deckung, Abwehr* to open up **e** (= *in groben Zügen darstellen*) *Thema* to outline **f** (*inf*) *Mädchen* to pick up (*inf*) VI *aux sein* (*Naht*) to split, to burst; (*Hose*) to tear, to rip; (*Wunde*) to tear open; (*Wolkendecke*) to break up

auf+rei|ßen[2] VT *sep irreg* (*Tech*) to draw the/an elevation of

auf+rei|zen VT *sep* **a** (= *herausfordern*) to provoke; (= *aufwiegeln*) to incite **b** (= *erregen*) to excite; (*stärker*) to inflame

auf|rei|zend ADJ provocative ADV provocatively

auf+rib|beln ['aufrɪbln] VT *sep* (*inf*) to unpick

Auf|rich|te ['aufrɪçtə] F -, -n (*Sw: = Richtfest*) topping-out ceremony

auf+rich|ten *sep* VT **a** (= *in aufrechte Lage bringen*) *Gegenstand* to put or set upright; *jdn* to help up; *Oberkörper* to raise (up), to straighten (up) **b** (= *aufstellen*) to erect, to put up; (*fig*) to set up **c** (*fig: moralisch*) to put new heart into, to give fresh heart to, to lift VR (= *gerade stehen*) to stand up (straight); (= *gerade sitzen*) to sit up (straight); (*aus gebückter Haltung*) to straighten up; (*fig: moralisch*) to pick oneself up, to get back on one's feet; **sich im Bett ~** to sit up in bed; **sich an jdm ~** (*fig*) to find new strength in sb, to take heart from sb

auf|rich|tig ADJ sincere (*zu, gegen* towards); (= *ehrlich auch*) honest ADV sincerely, honestly; *hassen, verabscheuen* truly

Auf|rich|tig|keit F sincerity (*zu, gegen* towards); (= *Ehrlichkeit auch*) honesty

auf+rie|geln ['aufri:gln] VT *sep* to unbolt

Auf|riss ▲ M **a** (*Tech*) elevation; **etw im ~ zeichnen** to draw the side/front elevation of sth **b** (*fig: = Abriss*) outline, sketch

Auf|riss|zeich|nung ▲ F (*Tech, Archit*) elevation

auf+rit|zen VT *sep* (= *öffnen*) to slit open; (= *verletzen*) to cut (open)

auf+rol|len *sep* VT **a** (= *zusammenrollen*) *Teppich, Ärmel* to roll up; *Kabel* to coil or wind up; (*auf Rolle*) to roll **b** (= *entrollen*) to unroll; *Fahne* to unfurl; *Kabel* to uncoil, to unwind; (*von Rolle*) to unwind, to reel off **c** (*fig*) *Problem* to go into; **einen Fall/Prozess wieder ~** to reopen a case/trial **d** (*Mil, Comm: = angreifen*) *Stellung, Markt* to penetrate VR (= *sich zusammenrollen*) to roll up

auf+rü|cken VI *sep aux sein* **a** (= *weiterrücken, aufschließen*) to move up or along **b** (= *befördert werden*) to move up, to be promoted; (*Schüler*) to move or go up; **zum Geschäftsleiter ~** to be promoted to manager

Auf|ruf M **a** **appeal** (*an +acc* to); **einen ~ an jdn richten** to appeal to sb; **~ zum Streik/Handeln** call for a strike/for negotiations **b** (*von Namen*) **seinen ~ abwarten** to wait for one's name to be called, to wait to be called; **nach ~** on being called, when called; **letzter ~ für Flug LH 1615** last call for flight LH 1615 **c** (*Comput*) call **d** (*Fin: von Banknoten*) calling in

auf+ru|fen *sep irreg* VT **a** *Namen* to call; *Wartenden* to call (the name of); **Sie werden aufgerufen** your name or you will be called; **einen Schüler ~** to ask a pupil (to answer) a question **b** (= *auffordern*) **jdn zu etw ~** (*zu Mithilfe, Unterstützung etc*) to appeal to or call upon sb for

sth; **jdn ~, etw zu tun** to appeal to or call upon sb to do sth; **Arbeiter zum Streik/zu einer Demonstration ~** to call upon workers to strike/to attend a demonstration **c** (*Jur*) *Zeugen* to summon **d** (*Comput*) to call up **e** (*Fin: = einziehen*) *Banknoten* to call in VI **zum Widerstand/Streik** *etc* **~** to call for resistance/a strike *etc*, to call upon people to resist/strike *etc*

Auf|ruhr ['aufru:ɐ] M -(e)s, -e **a** (= *Auflehnung*) revolt, rebellion, uprising **b** (= *Bewegtheit, fig: = Erregung*) tumult, turmoil; **ihr innerlicher ~** the tumult or turmoil within her; **in ~ sein** to be in a tumult or turmoil; **in ~ geraten** to get into a state of turmoil; **jdn in ~ versetzen** to throw sb into a turmoil

auf+rüh|ren VT *sep* to stir up; (*fig auch*) *Gefühle* to rouse; **alte Geschichten wieder ~** to rake or stir up old stories

Auf|rüh|rer ['aufry:rɐ] M -s, -, **Auf|rüh|re|rin** [-ərɪn] F -, -nen rabble-rouser

auf|rüh|re|risch ['aufry:rərɪʃ] ADJ **a** (= *aufwiegelnd*) *Rede, Pamphlet* rabble-rousing, inflammatory **b** *attr* (= *in Aufruhr*) rebellious; (= *meuternd*) mutinous ADV *fragen, sagen* provocatively

auf+run|den VT *sep* *Betrag, Zahl etc* to round up (*auf +acc* to)

auf+rüs|ten VT *sep* **a** *auch vi* (*Mil*) to arm; **ein Land atomar ~** to give a country nuclear arms; **wieder ~** to rearm **b** (*Tech*) *Gerät, Computer* to upgrade **c** (*fig*) **jdn moralisch ~** to boost sb's morale

Auf|rüs|tung F **a** (*Mil*) arming; **atomare ~** acquiring nuclear armaments **b** (*Tech, von Gerät, Computer*) upgrading

auf+rüt|teln VT *sep* to rouse (*aus* from); (*aus Lethargie etc auch*) to shake up (*aus* out of); **jdn/jds Gewissen ~** to stir sb/sb's conscience; **jdn zum Handeln ~** to rouse sb to action

Auf|rüt|te|lung F -, -en, **Auf|rütt|lung** ['aufrʏtlʊŋ] F -, -en (*fig*) (= *das Aufrütteln*) rousing; (*aus Lethargie etc auch*) shaking up; (*Zustand*) excitement

aufs [aufs] *contr von* **auf das**

auf+sa|gen VT *sep* **a** *Gedicht etc* to recite, to say **b** (*geh: = für beendet erklären*) **jdm die Freundschaft ~** to break off one's friendship with sb; **jdm den Dienst/Gehorsam ~** to refuse to serve/obey sb

auf+sam|meln VT *sep* (*lit, fig*) to pick up

auf|säs|sig ['aufzɛsɪç] ADJ rebellious; *esp Kind auch* recalcitrant, obstreperous

Auf|säs|sig|keit F -, *no pl* rebelliousness; (*esp von Kind auch*) recalcitrance, obstreperousness

auf+sat|teln VT *sep* *Pferd* to saddle (up)

Auf|satz M **a** (= *Abhandlung*) essay; (*Sch*) essay, composition **b** (= *oberer Teil*) top or upper part; (*zur Verzierung*) bit on top; (*von Kamera etc*) attachment; **ein Schrank mit abnehmbarem ~** a cupboard with a removable top part or section **c** (*Mil: von Geschütz*) (gun) sight

Auf|satz-: Auf|satz|heft NT essay or composition book; **Auf|satz|samm|lung** F collection of essays; **Auf|satz|the|ma** NT essay subject

auf+sau|gen VT *sep irreg* *Flüssigkeit* to soak up; (*Sonne auch*) to absorb; (*fig*) to absorb; **etw mit dem Staubsauger ~** to vacuum sth up; **etw in sich** (*dat*) **~** (*Mensch*) to absorb sth, to soak sth up

auf+schau|en VI *sep* (*dial*) = **aufblicken**

auf+schau|feln VT *sep* **a** (= *aufhäufen*) to pile up **b** (= *aufgraben*) to dig up

auf+schau|keln VR *sep* (*fig: Hass, Emotionen*) to build up

auf+schäu|men *sep* VI *aux sein* (*Meer*) to foam; (*Getränke*) to foam or froth up; **vor Zorn ~** to boil with anger VT *Kunststoff* to foam

auf+**schei**|**nen** VI *sep irreg aux sein* **a** (*geh*: = *aufleuchten*) to light up; (*Licht*) to appear; (*fig liter*) to shine out **b** (*Aus*: = *erscheinen*) to appear

auf+**scheu**|**chen** VT *sep* to startle; (*inf*) *Öffentlichkeit* to startle, to shock; **jdn aus etw ~** to jolt sb out of sth; **jdn von seiner Arbeit/Lektüre ~** to disturb sb when he is working/reading

auf+**scheu**|**ern** *sep* VT *Fuß etc* to rub sore; *Haut* to chafe; **sich** (*dat*) **die Hände/Füße ~** to take the skin off one's hands/feet VR to rub oneself sore

auf+**schich**|**ten** VT *sep* to stack, to pile up; *Stapel* to build up

Auf|**schich**|**tung** F stacking, piling up; (*von Stapel*) building

auf+**schie**|**ben** VT *sep irreg Fenster, Tür* to slide open; *Riegel* to push or slide back; (*fig*: = *verschieben*) to put off; **aufgeschoben ist nicht aufgehoben** (*prov*) putting something off doesn't mean it won't happen

auf+**schie**|**ßen** *sep irreg* VI *aux sein* **a** (*Saat, Jugendlicher*) to shoot up; (*Flammen, Fontäne etc*) to leap or shoot up; **wie Pilze ~** (*Hochhäuser etc*) to mushroom → *auch* **aufgeschossen** **b** (= *emporschnellen, hochfahren*) to shoot or leap up VT (*Naut*) *Tau* to coil

auf+**schim**|**mern** VI *sep aux sein or haben* (*geh*) to flash; **in etw** (*dat*) **~** (*fig*) to illuminate sth

Auf|**schlag** M **a** (= *das Aufschlagen*) impact; (= *Geräusch*) crash **b** (*Tennis etc*) service, serve; **wer hat ~?** whose service or serve is it?; **sie hat ~** she's serving, it's her service or serve **c** (= *Preisaufschlag*) surcharge, extra charge **d** (= *Ärmelaufschlag*) cuff; (= *Hosenaufschlag*) turn-up (*Brit*), cuff (*US*); (= *Mantelaufschlag etc*) lapel

Auf|**schlag**|**ball** M (*Tennis*) service, serve

auf+**schla**|**gen** *sep irreg* VI **a** *aux sein* (= *auftreffen*) **auf etw** (*dat*) **~** to hit sth; **das Flugzeug schlug in einem Waldstück auf** the plane crashed into a wood; **mit dem Kopf etc auf etw** (*acc or dat*) **~** to hit one's head etc on sth; **dumpf ~** to thud (*auf +acc* onto); **sie fühlte, wie ihr Kopf hart aufschlug** she felt the hard crack on her head **b** *aux sein* (= *sich öffnen*) to open **c** *aux sein* (*Flammen*) to leap or blaze up (*aus* out of) **d** *aux haben or* (*rare*) *sein* (*Waren, Preise*) to rise, to go up (*um* by) **e** (*Tennis etc*) to serve; **du musst ~** it's your service or serve VT **a** (= *durch Schlagen öffnen*) to crack (open); *Nuss* to crack (open); *Eis* to crack a hole in; **jdm/sich den Kopf ~** to crack or cut open sb's/one's head; **jdm/sich die Augenbraue ~** to cut open sb's/one's eyebrow **b** (= *aufklappen*) to open; (= *zurückschlagen*) *Bett, Bettdecke* to turn back; (= *hochschlagen*) *Kragen etc* to turn up; *Schleier* to lift up, to raise; **schlagt Seite 111 auf** open your books at page 111 **c** *Augen* to open **d** (= *aufbauen*) *Bett, Liegestuhl* to put up; *Zelt* to pitch, to put up; (*Nacht*)*lager* to set up, to pitch; **er hat seinen Wohnsitz in Wien/einem alten Bauernhaus aufgeschlagen** he has taken up residence in Vienna/an old farmhouse **e** (*Comm*) *Preise* to put up, to raise; **10% auf etw** (*acc*) **~** to put 10% on sth

Auf|**schlä**|**ger(in)** M(F) (*Tennis etc*) server

Auf|**schlag-:** **Auf**|**schlag**|**feh**|**ler** M service fault; **Auf**|**schlag**|**spiel** NT service game; **Auf**|**schlag**|**zün**|**der** M (*Mil*) percussion fuse

auf+**schle**|**cken** VT *sep* (*S Ger*) to lick up

auf+**schlie**|**ßen** *sep irreg* VT **a** (= *öffnen*) to unlock; (*geh*: = *erklären*) to elucidate (*jdm* to sb); **jdm die Tür** *etc* **~** to unlock the door *etc* for sb **b** (*geh*: = *offenbaren*) **jdm sein Herz ~** to open one's heart to sb; **jdm sein Innerstes ~** to tell sb one's innermost thoughts **c** (*Chem, Biol*) to break down **d** *Rohstoffvorkommen, Bauland* to develop VR (*geh*) **sich leicht ~** to find it easy

to be open or frank; **sich jdm ~** to be open or frank with sb VR **a** (= *öffnen*) (**jdm**) **~** to unlock the door (for sb) **b** (= *heranrücken*) to close up; (*Sport*) to catch up (*zu* with) → *auch* **aufgeschlossen**

auf+**schlit**|**zen** VT *sep* to rip (open); (*mit Messer auch*) to slit (open); *Gesicht* to slash; *Bauch* to slash open

Auf|**schluss** ▲ M **a** (= *Aufklärung*) information *no pl*; (**jdm**) **~ über etw** (*acc*) **geben** to give (sb) information about sth; **~ über etw** (*acc*) **verlangen** to demand an explanation of sth **b** (*Chem, Biol*) breaking down **c** (*Min*: = *Erschließung*) development

auf+**schlüs**|**seln** [ˈaʊfʃlʏsln] VT *sep* to break down (*nach* into); (= *klassifizieren*) to classify (*nach* according to)

Auf|**schlüs**|**se**|**lung** F -, -en, **Auf**|**schlüss**|**lung** ▲ [ˈaʊfʃlʏsloŋ] (*rare*) F -, -en breakdown (*nach* into); (= *Klassifikation*) classification (*nach* according to)

auf|**schluss**|**reich** ▲ ADJ informative, instructive

auf+**schmei**|**ßen** VT *sep irreg* **a** (*Aus inf*) *jdn* to send up (*inf*) **b** → **aufgeschmissen**

auf+**schmie**|**ren** VT *sep* (*inf*) to spread on; *Farbe* to smear on

auf+**schnal**|**len** VT *sep* **a** (= *befestigen*) to buckle or strap on (*auf etw acc* -to) sth) **b** (= *losschnallen*) to unbuckle, to unstrap

auf+**schnap**|**pen** *sep* VT to catch; (*inf*) *Wort etc* to pick up VI *aux sein* to snap or spring open

auf+**schnei**|**den** *sep irreg* VT **a** (= *öffnen*) to cut open; (= *tranchieren*) *Braten* to carve; *Buch* to cut; (*Med*) *Geschwür* to lance → **Pulsader b** (= *in Scheiben schneiden*) to slice VI (*inf*: = *prahlen*) to brag, to boast

Auf|**schnei**|**der(in)** M(F) (*inf*) boaster, braggart

Auf|**schnei**|**de**|**rei** F -, -en (*inf*) bragging *no pl*, boasting *no pl*

auf|**schnei**|**de**|**risch** [ˈaʊfʃnaɪdərɪʃ] ADJ (*inf*) boastful

auf+**schnel**|**len** VI *sep aux sein* (= *hochschnellen*) to leap or jump up

Auf|**schnitt** M , *no pl* (assorted) sliced cold meat, cold cuts *pl* (*US*); (= *Käse*) (assorted) sliced cheeses *pl*; **kalter ~** (assorted) sliced cold meat, cold cuts *pl* (*US*)

auf+**schnü**|**ren** VT *sep* **a** (= *lösen*) to untie, to undo **b** (*rare*: = *befestigen*) to tie on (*auf +acc* -to)

auf+**schram**|**men** VT *sep* = **aufschürfen**

auf+**schrau**|**ben** VT *sep* **a** *Schraube etc* to unscrew; *Flasche etc* to take the top off **b** (= *festschrauben*) to screw on (*auf +acc* -to)

auf+**schre**|**cken** *sep pret* **schreckte auf**, *ptp* **aufgeschreckt** VT to startle; (*aus Gleichgültigkeit*) to rouse (*aus* from), to jolt (*aus* out of); **jdn aus dem Schlaf ~** to rouse sb from sleep VI *pret auch* **schrak auf** *aux sein* to start (up), to be startled; **aus dem Schlaf ~** to wake up with a start; **aus Gedanken ~** to start

Auf|**schrei** M yell; (*schriller Aufschrei*) scream, shriek; **ein ~ der Empörung/Entrüstung** (*fig*) an outcry

auf+**schrei**|**ben** VT *sep irreg* **a** (= *niederschreiben*) **etw ~** to write or note sth down **b** (= *notieren*) **sich** (*dat*) **etw ~** to make a note of sth **c** (= *als Schulden anschreiben*) to put on the slate (*inf*), to chalk up (*inf*) **d** (*inf*: = *verordnen*) to prescribe **e** (*inf*: = *polizeilich aufschreiben*) **jdn ~** to take sb's particulars; **das Auto ~** to take the car's number

auf+**schrei**|**en** VI *sep irreg* to yell out; (*schrill*) to scream or shriek out

Auf|**schrift** F (= *Beschriftung*) inscription; (= *Etikett*) label; **eine Flasche mit der ~ „Vorsicht**

Gift" versehen to label a bottle "Danger - Poison"

Auf|**schub** M (= *Verzögerung*) delay; (= *Vertagung*) postponement; **die Sache duldet** or **leidet** (*old*) **keinen ~** (*geh*) the matter brooks no delay (*liter*); **jdm ~ gewähren** (= *Zahlungsaufschub*) to give sb an extension of the payment deadline, to allow sb grace

auf+**schür**|**fen** VT *sep* **sich** (*dat*) **die Haut/das Knie ~** to graze or scrape oneself/one's knee

auf+**schüt**|**teln** VT *sep Kissen etc* to shake or plump up

auf+**schüt**|**ten** VT *sep* **a** *Flüssigkeit* to pour on; **Wasser auf etw** (*acc*) **~** to pour water on or over sth; **Kaffee ~** to make coffee **b** (= *nachfüllen*) *Kohle* to put on (the fire) **c** *Stroh, Steine* to spread; *Damm, Deich* to throw up; *Straße* to raise **d** (*Geol*) to deposit

Auf|**schüt**|**tung** F -, -en **a** (= *Damm*) bank of earth **b** (*Geol*) deposit

auf+**schwat**|**zen**, **auf**+**schwät**|**zen** (*dial*) VT *sep* (*inf*) **jdm etw ~** to talk sb into taking sth; **sie hat ihr ihren Sohn aufgeschwatzt** she talked her into marrying her son

auf+**schwei**|**ßen** VT *sep* to cut open (with an oxyacetylene torch)

auf+**schwel**|**len** *sep* VI *irreg aux sein* to swell (up)

auf+**schwem**|**men** VT *sep* **jdn ~** to make sb bloated; **jds Gesicht ~** to make sb's face bloated or puffy → *auch* **aufgeschwemmt**

auf+**schwin**|**gen** VR *sep irreg* to swing oneself up; (*Vogel*) to soar (up); (*fig*: *Gedanken*) to rise to higher realms; **sich zu etw ~** (= *sich aufraffen*) to bring oneself to do sth; (= *sich aufwerfen*) to set oneself up to be sth; (= *sich hocharbeiten*) to work one's way up to be(come) sth; (*hum*: = *etw kaufen*) to bring oneself to get sth

Auf|**schwung** M **a** (= *Antrieb*) lift; (*der Fantasie*) upswing; (*der Seele*) uplift; (*der Wirtschaft etc*) upturn, upswing (*+gen* in); **das gab ihr (einen) neuen ~** that gave her a lift; **der ~ Ost** the economic upturn in Eastern Germany **b** (*Turnen*) swing-up

auf+**se**|**hen** VI *sep irreg* to look up; **zu jdm/etw ~** (*lit*) to look up at sb/sth; (*fig*) to look up to sb/sth

Auf|**se**|**hen** NT -s, *no pl* sensation; **~ erregend** sensational; **~ erregen** to cause a sensation or stir; **um etw viel ~ machen** to make a lot of fuss about sth; **ohne großes ~** without any to-do (*inf*) or fuss; **ich möchte jedes ~ vermeiden** I want to avoid any fuss; **bitte kein ~, meine Herren** no fuss please, gentlemen

auf|**se**|**hen**|**er**|**re**|**gend** △ ADJ = **Aufsehen**

Auf|**se**|**her(in)** M(F) (*allgemein*) supervisor; (*bei Prüfung*) invigilator; (= *Sklavenaufseher*) overseer; (= *Gefängnisaufseher*) warder (*Brit*), guard (*US*); (= *Parkaufseher, Museumsaufseher etc*) attendant

auf sein ▲ VI *irreg aux sein* **a** (= *aufgestanden sein*) to be up **b** (= *geöffnet sein*) to be open

auf|**sei**|**ten** [aʊfˈzaɪtn], **auf Sei**|**ten** PREP *+gen* on the part of

auf+**set**|**zen** *sep* VT **a** (= *auf etw setzen*) *Brille, Hut, Topf, Essen, Flicken* to put on; *Kegel* to set up; *Steine* to lay; *Tonarm* to lower; *Fuß* to put on the ground, to put down; (*fig*) *Lächeln, Miene etc* to put on; **ich kann den Fuß nicht richtig ~** I can't put any weight on my foot; **sich** (*dat*) **den Hut ~** to put on one's hat → *auch* **aufgesetzt**, **Dämpfer**, **Horn a b** *Flugzeug* to land, to bring down; *Boot* to pull up, to beach; (*unabsichtlich*) to ground, to run aground **c** (= *aufrichten*) *Kranken etc* to sit up **d** (= *verfassen*) to draft VR to sit up VI (*Flugzeug*) to touch down, to land; (*Tonarm*) to come down

Auf|**set**|**zer** [ˈaʊfzɛtsɐ] M -s, - (*Sport*) bouncing ball

auf+**seuf**|**zen** VI *sep* (**tief/laut**) **~** to heave a (deep/loud) sigh

Auf|sicht [ˈaufzɪçt] F **-, -en** a *no pl* (= *Überwachung*) supervision (*über +acc* of); (= *Obhut*) charge; **unter jds ~** (*dat*) under the supervision of sb, in the charge of sb; **unter polizeilicher/ärztlicher ~** under police/medical supervision; **~ über jdn/etw führen** to be in charge of sb/sth; **bei einer Prüfung ~ führen** to invigilate an exam; **im Pausenhof ~ führen** to be on duty during break; **jdn ohne ~ lassen** to leave sb unsupervised *or* without supervision; **der Kranke darf niemals ohne ~ sein** the patient must be kept under constant supervision; **jdm obliegt die ~ über etw** (*acc*) (*form*) sb is in charge of *or* responsible for sth
b (= *Aufsicht Führender*) person in charge; (= *Aufseher*) supervisor; **~ führend** supervisory; *Beamter* supervising; *Lehrer* on duty *pred*; (*bei Prüfung*) invigilating; **~ Führende(r)** person in charge; (= *Aufseher*) supervisor; (= *Lehrer*) teacher on duty; (*in Examen*) invigilator
c (*Math*: = *Draufsicht*) top view

Auf|sicht-: auf|sicht|füh|rend △ ADJ *attr* → **Aufsicht b**; **Auf|sicht|füh|ren|de(r)** [-fy:rəndə] MF *decl as adj* person in charge; (= *Aufseher*) supervisor

Auf|sichts-: Auf|sichts|amt NT board of control, inspectorate; **Auf|sichts|be|am|te(r)** M *decl as adj*, **Auf|sichts|be|am|tin** F (*in Museum, Zoo etc*) attendant; (*bei Gericht, Polizei*) warder (*Brit*), guard (*US*); **Auf|sichts|be|hör|de** F supervisory authority *or* body; **Auf|sichts|per|son** F person in charge; **Auf|sichts|per|so|nal** NT supervisory staff; **Auf|sichts|pflicht** F (*Jur*) legal responsibility to care for sb *esp* a child **die elterliche ~, die ~ der Eltern** (legal) parental responsibility; **Auf|sichts|rat¹** M (supervisory) board; **im ~ einer Firma sitzen** to be *or* sit on the board of a firm; **Auf|sichts|rat²** , **Auf|sichts|rä|tin** F member of the board; **Auf|sichts|rats|vor|sit|zen|de(r)** MF *decl as adj* chairman/chairwoman of the board

auf+sit|zen VI *sep irreg* a (= *aufgerichtet sitzen, aufbleiben*) to sit up b *aux sein* (*auf Reittier*) to mount; (*auf Fahrzeug*) to get on; **aufs Pferd ~** to mount the horse; **aufgesessen!** (*Mil*) mount! c (= *ruhen auf*) to sit on (*auf +dat*) sth d (*Naut*) to run aground (*auf +dat* on) e *aux sein* (*inf*: = *hereinfallen*) **jdm/einer Sache ~** to be taken in by sb/sth f *aux sein* (*inf*) **jdn ~ lassen** (= *im Stich lassen*) to leave sb in the lurch (*inf*), to let sb down; (= *Verabredung nicht einhalten*) to stand sb up (*inf*)

auf+spal|ten VTR *sep* to split up; (*fig auch*) to split up; **eine Klasse in drei Gruppen ~** to split up *or* divide up a class into three groups

Auf|spal|tung F splitting; (*fig auch*) splitting up; **seit der ~ der Partei** since the party split up

auf+span|nen VT *sep* a *Netz, Sprungtuch* to stretch *or* spread out; *Schirm* to put up, to open b (= *aufziehen*) *Leinwand* to stretch (*auf +acc* onto); *Saite* to put on (*auf etw* (*acc*) sth)

auf+spa|ren VT *sep* to save (up), to keep; **sich** (*dat*) **eine Bemerkung bis zum Ende ~** to save *or* keep a remark until the end

auf+spei|chern VT *sep* to store (up); *Energie auch* to accumulate; (*fig*) *Zorn etc* to build up

Auf|spei|che|rung F storage; (*von Energie auch*) accumulation

auf+sper|ren VT *sep* a (*inf*: = *aufreißen*) *Tür, Schnabel* to open wide; **die Ohren ~** to prick up one's ears b (*S Ger, Aus*: = *aufschließen*) *Tür etc* to unlock

auf+spie|len *sep* VI (*dated*) to play; (= *anfangen*) to strike up; **die Mannschaft spielte glänzend auf** the team played brilliantly VR (*inf*) a (*inf*: *sich wichtig tun*) to give oneself airs b (= *sich ausgeben als*) **sich als etw ~** to set oneself up as sth; **sich als Boss ~** to play the boss

auf+spie|ßen VT *sep* to spear; (= *durchbohren*) to run through; (*mit Hörnern*) to gore; *Schmetter-*

linge to pin; *Fleisch* (*mit Spieß*) to skewer; (*mit Gabel*) to prong

auf+split|ten [ˈaufʃplɪtn, ˈaufsp-] VT *sep* (*fig inf*: = *spalten*) *Unternehmen, Einnahmen* to divide *or* split up

auf+split|tern *sep* VT to split (up) VR (*Gruppe etc*) to split (up)

auf+spren|gen VT *sep* to force open; (*mit Sprengstoff*) to blow open

auf+sprie|ßen VI *sep irreg aux sein* (*geh*) to burst forth, to sprout

auf+sprin|gen VI *sep irreg aux sein* a (= *hochspringen*) to jump *or* leap to one's feet, to jump *or* leap up; **auf etw** (*acc*) **~** to jump onto sth b (= *auftreffen*) (*Ski*) to land c (= *sich öffnen*: *Tür*) to burst *or* fly open; (= *platzen*) to burst; (*Rinde, Lack*) to crack; (*Haut, Lippen etc*) to crack, to chap; (*liter*: *Knospen*) to burst open

auf+sprit|zen *sep* VT **etw (auf etw** *acc*) **~** to spray sth on (sth) VI *aux sein* to spurt (up)

auf+spru|deln VI *sep aux sein* to bubble up

auf+sprü|hen *sep* VT **etw (auf etw** *acc*) **~** to spray sth on (sth) VI *aux sein* to spray up

Auf|sprung M (*Sport*) landing; (*von Ball*) bounce

auf+spu|len VT *sep* to wind on a spool; *Angelschnur, Garn auch* to wind on a reel

auf+spü|len VT *sep* a (= *anspülen*) *Sand, Schlick etc* to wash up b (= *aufwirbeln*) *Sand, Schlamm etc* to whirl up

auf+spü|ren VT *sep* (*lit, fig*) to track down

auf+sta|cheln VT *sep* to spur (on); (= *antreiben*) to goad on; **jdn ~, etw zu tun** (= *aufwiegeln*) to goad sb on to do sth *or* into doing sth

auf+stamp|fen VI *sep* to stamp; **mit dem Fuß ~** to stamp one's foot

Auf|stand M rebellion, revolt; **im ~** in rebellion *or* revolt; **den ~ proben** (*fig*) to flex one's muscles

auf|stän|disch ADJ rebellious, insurgent

Auf|stän|di|sche(r) [ˈaufʃtɛndɪʃə] MF *decl as adj* rebel, insurgent

auf+sta|peln VT *sep* to stack *or* pile up

auf+stau|en *sep* VT *Wasser* to dam; **etw in sich** (*dat*) **~** (*fig*) to bottle sth up inside (oneself) VR to accumulate, to collect; (*fig*: *Ärger*) to become bottled up

auf+ste|chen VT *sep irreg* (*Med*) to puncture; to lance, to pierce; (*dial*: = *aufdecken*) to bring into the open

auf+ste|cken *sep* VT a (= *auf etw stecken*) to put on (*auf +acc* -to); *Fahne* to put up (*auf +acc* on); (*Comput*) *Modul, Karte* to plug in; **sich** (*dat*) **einen Ring ~** to put on a ring; **jdm einen Ring ~** to put a ring on sb's finger; **Kerzen auf einen Leuchter/den Baum ~** to put candles in a candlestick/on the tree b (*mit Nadeln*) to pin up; *Haar* to put up c (*inf*: = *aufgeben*) to pack in (*inf*) VI (*inf*: = *aufgeben*) to pack it in (*inf*); (*bei Rennen etc auch*) to retire

auf+ste|hen VI *sep irreg aux sein* a (= *sich erheben*) to get *or* stand up; (*morgens aus dem Bett*) to get up; (*fig*: *Persönlichkeit*) to arise; **aus dem Sessel ~** to get up out of the chair; **aus dem Bett ~** to get out of bed; **vor jdm/für jdn ~** to stand up for sb; **~ dürfen** (*Kranker*) to be allowed (to) get up; **er steht nicht mehr auf** he's a goner (*inf*); **da musst du früher *or* eher ~!** (*fig inf*) you'll have to do better than that!
b (*inf*: = *offen sein*) to be open
c (= *sich auflehnen*) to rise (in arms)
d *aux haben* (= *auf dem Boden etc stehen*) to stand (*auf +dat* on); **der Tisch steht nur mit drei Beinen/nicht richtig auf** the table is only standing on three legs/is not standing firmly

auf+stei|gen VI *sep irreg aux sein* a (*auf Berg, Leiter*) to climb (up); (*Vogel, Drachen*) to soar (up); (*Flugzeug*) to climb; (*Stern, Sonne, Nebel*) to rise; (*Gewitter, Wolken*) to gather; (*Gefühl*) to rise;

(*geh*: = *aufragen*) to tower, to rise up; (*drohend*) to loom; **zum Gipfel ~** to climb (up) to the summit; **einen Ballon ~ lassen** to release a balloon; (*in einem Ballon*) **~** to go up in a balloon; **an die Oberfläche ~** to rise to the surface; **~de Linie** ascending line; **in jdm ~** (*Hass, Verdacht, Erinnerung etc*) to well up in sb
b **auf ein Fahrrad/Motorrad ~** to get on(to) a bicycle/motorbike; **auf ein Pferd ~** to mount a horse, to get on(to) a horse
c (*fig*: *im Rang etc*) to rise (*zu* to); (*esp beruflich*) to be promoted; (*Sport*) to go up, to be promoted (*in +acc* to); **zum Abteilungsleiter ~** to rise to be head of department; **das ~de Bürgertum** the rising middle classes

Auf|stei|ger(in) M(F) a (*Sport*) league climber; (*in höhere Liga*) promoted team b (*sozialer*) **~** social climber

auf+stel|len *sep* VT a (= *aufrichten, aufbauen*) to put up (*auf +dat* on); *etw Liegendes* to stand up; *Zelt* to pitch, to put up; *Schild, Mast, Denkmal* to erect, to put up; *Kegel* to set up; *Maschine* to put in, to install; *Falle* to set; (*Mil*) to deploy; (= *postieren*) *Wachposten* to post, to station; *Wagen* to line up; (= *hochstellen*) *Kragen* to turn up; (= *aufrichten*) *Ohren, Stacheln* to prick up
b *Essen etc* (*auf Herd*) to put on
c (*fig*: = *zusammenstellen*) *Truppe* to raise; (*Sport*) *Spieler* to select, to pick; *Mannschaft* to draw up
d (= *benennen*) *Kandidaten* to nominate
e (= *erzielen*) *Rekord* to set (up)
f *Forderung, Behauptung, Vermutung* to put forward; *System* to establish; *Programm, Satzungen, Rechnung* to draw up; *Liste* to make, to draw up
g (*Sw*) → **aufgestellt**
VR a (= *sich postieren*) to stand; (*hintereinander*) to line up; (*Soldaten*) to fall into line; **sich im Karree/Kreis** *etc* **~** to form a square/circle *etc*
b (*Ohren etc*) to prick up

Auf|stel|lung F a *no pl* (= *das Aufstellen*) putting up; (*von Zelt*) pitching; (*von Schild, Mast, Denkmal*) erection, putting up; (*von Verkehrsampel*) installation; (*von Maschine*) putting in, installation; (*von Falle*) setting; (*Mil*) deployment; (*von Wachposten*) posting, stationing; (*von Wagen*) lining up; **~ nehmen** (*Mil*) to take up position
b *no pl* (= *das Zusammenstellen*) (*von Truppen*) raising; (*von Spielern*) selecting, picking; (*von Mannschaft*) drawing up
c *no pl* (*von Kandidaten*) nominating; (*von Rekord*) setting
d *no pl* (*von Forderung, Behauptung, Vermutung*) putting forward; (*von System*) establishing; (*von Programm, Satzung, Rechnung, Liste*) drawing up
e (= *Liste*) list; (= *Tabelle*) table; (= *Inventar*) inventory
f (= *Mannschaft*) line-up (*inf*), team

auf+stem|men VT *sep* to force *or* pry open (with a chisel *etc*); (*mit der Schulter*) to force open

auf+stem|peln VT *sep* to stamp on; **etw auf etw** (*acc*) **~** to stamp sth on sth

auf+step|pen VT *sep* to sew *or* stitch on (*auf etw* (*acc*) -to sth)

auf+stie|ben VI *sep irreg aux sein* to fly up

Auf|stieg M a *no pl* (*auf Berg*) climb, ascent; (*von Flugzeug, Rakete*) climb; (*von Ballon*) ascent b (*fig*: = *Aufschwung*) rise; (*beruflich, politisch, sozial*) advancement; (*Sport*: *von Mannschaft*) climb, rise; (*in höhere Liga*) promotion (*in +acc* to); **den ~ zu etw schaffen** to rise to (become) sth; **den ~ ins Management schaffen** to work one's way up into the management c (= *Weg*) way up (*auf etw* (*acc*) sth), ascent (*auf +acc* of)

Auf|stiegs-: Auf|stiegs|chan|ce F , **Auf|stiegs|mög|lich|keit** F prospect of promotion; **Auf|stiegs|run|de** F (*Sport*) round deciding promotion; **Auf|stiegs|spiel** NT (*Sport*) match deciding promotion

auf+stö|bern VT *sep* *Wild* to start, to flush; *Rebhühner etc auch* to put up; (*fig*: = *stören*) to disturb; (*inf*: = *entdecken*) to dig up (*inf*)

auf+sto|cken sep **VT a** Haus to build another storey (Brit) or story (US) onto **b** Kapital, Kredit, Armee to increase (um by); Vorräte to build or stock up **VI** to build another storey (Brit) or story (US)

Auf|sto|ckung F (Archit) storey (Brit) or story (US) extension; (Econ) accumulation of capital

auf+stöh|nen VI sep to groan loudly, to give a loud groan; **erleichtert ~** to give a loud sigh of relief

auf+stö|ren VT sep to disturb; Wild to start; **jdn aus dem** or **im Schlaf ~** to disturb sb while he/she is sleeping

auf+sto|ßen sep irreg **VT a** (= öffnen) to push open; (mit dem Fuß) to kick open **b** (rare) etw auf etw (acc) ~ to strike sth on sth, to hit sth against sth; **er stieß den Stock (auf den Boden) auf** he tapped his stick on the ground **c** (= verletzen) **sich** (dat) **das Knie ~** to graze one's knee **VI a** aux sein auf etw (acc) ~ to hit (on or against) sth; **ich bin mit dem Ellbogen auf die Tischkante aufgestoßen** I hit my elbow on or against the edge of the table **b** aux haben (= rülpsen) to burp **c** aux sein or haben (Speisen) to repeat; **Radieschen stoßen mir auf** radishes repeat on me; **das könnte dir noch sauer** or **übel ~** (fig inf) you might have to pay for that; **das ist mir sauer aufgestoßen** (fig inf) it left a nasty taste in my mouth **d** aux sein (fig: = auffallen) to strike (jdm sb) **VR** to graze oneself

Auf|sto|ßen NT -s, no pl burping, flatulence (form)

auf+stre|ben VI sep aux sein (geh: = aufragen) to soar, to tower; **hoch ~de Türme/Berge** high soaring towers/mountains

auf|stre|bend ADJ (fig) Land, Volk striving for progress, aspiring; Stadt up-and-coming, striving; Persönlichkeit ambitious; Bürgertum, Volkswirtschaft rising

auf+strei|chen VT sep irreg to put on (auf etw (acc) sth); Butter etc to spread (auf +acc on)

auf+streu|en VT sep to sprinkle on; etw auf etw (acc) ~ to sprinkle sth on(to) or over sth; **Split/Salz auf die Straßen ~** to grit/salt the roads

Auf|strich M **a** (auf Brot) spread; **was möchten Sie als ~?** what would you like on your bread/toast etc? **b** (Mus) up-bow **c** (beim Schreiben) upstroke

auf+stül|pen VT sep (= draufstülpen) to put on; (fig: = aufzwingen) to force on; etw auf etw (acc) ~ to put sth on sth; **sich** (dat) **den Hut/eine Perücke ~** to put on one's hat/a wig

auf+stüt|zen sep **VT** Kranken etc to prop up; Ellbogen, Arme to rest (auf +acc or dat on); **den Kopf ~** to rest one's head on one's hand **VR** to support oneself; (im Bett, beim Essen) to prop oneself up; **sich auf die** or **der Hand ~** to support oneself with one's hand

auf+su|chen VT sep **a** Bekannten to call on; Arzt, Ort, Toilette to go to; **das Bett ~** (geh) to retire to bed **b** (= aufsammeln) to pick up; (auf Landkarte, in Buch) to find

auf+sum|men, auf+sum|mie|ren ptp **aufsummiert** VTR sep to add up

auf+ta|feln VTI sep to serve (up)

auf+ta|keln VT sep (Naut) to rig up; **sich ~** (pej inf) to tart oneself up (Brit pej inf), to do (esp US) or make oneself up (inf) → auch **aufgetakelt**

Auf|takt M **a** (= Beginn) start; (= Vorbereitung) prelude; **den ~ von** or **zu etw bilden** to mark the beginning or start of sth/to form a prelude to sth **b** (Mus) upbeat; (Poet) arsis (form)

auf+tan|ken VTI sep to fill up; (Aviat) to refuel; **500 Liter** to refuel with; **10 Liter** to take on;

put in; **Benzin ~** to fill up with petrol (Brit) or gas (US)

auf+tau|chen VI sep aux sein **a** (aus dem Wasser) to surface, to come up **b** (fig) (= sichtbar werden) to appear; (aus Nebel etc) to emerge, to appear; (Zweifel, Problem) to arise **c** (= gefunden werden, sich zeigen, kommen) to turn up

auf+tau|en sep **VI** aux sein to thaw; (fig auch) to unbend **VT** Eis to thaw; Tiefkühlkost, Wasserleitung to thaw (out)

Auf|tau|stu|fe F (von Mikrowellengerät) defrost setting

auf+tei|len VT sep **a** (= aufgliedern) to divide or split up (in +acc into) **b** (= verteilen) to share out (an +acc between)

Auf|tei|lung F (= Aufgliederung) division (in +acc into); (= Verteilung) sharing out (an +acc between)

auf+tip|pen VI sep aux sein to bounce

auf+ti|schen ['auftɪʃn] VT sep to serve up; (fig inf) to come up with; **jdm etw ~** (lit) to give sb sth, to serve sb (with) sth; **jdm Lügen** etc ~ (inf) to give or tell sb a lot of lies etc

Auf|trag ['auftraːk] M -(e)s, **Aufträge** [-trɛːɡə] **a** no pl (= Anweisung) orders pl, instructions pl; (= zugeteilte Arbeit) job, task; (Jur) brief; **jdm den ~ geben, etw zu tun** to give sb the job of doing sth, to instruct sb to do sth; **einen ~ ausführen** to carry out an order; **ich habe den ~, Ihnen mitzuteilen ...** I have been instructed to tell you ...; **in jds ~** (dat) (= für jdn) on sb's behalf; (= auf jds Anweisung) on sb's instructions; **die Oper wurde im ~ des Königs komponiert** the opera was commissioned by the king; **i. A.** or **im ~ G. W. Kurz** pp G. W. Kurz **b** (Comm) order (über +acc for); (bei Künstlern, Freischaffenden etc) commission (über +acc for); **etw in ~ geben** to order/commission sth (bei from); **im ~ und auf Rechnung von** by order and for account of **c** no pl (geh: = Mission, Aufgabe) task **d** (von Farbe etc) application

auf+tra|gen sep irreg **VT a** (= servieren) to serve; **es ist aufgetragen!** (geh) lunch/dinner etc is served! **b** Farbe, Salbe, Schminke to apply, to put on; etw auf etw (acc) ~ to apply sth to sth, to put sth on sth **c** jdm etw ~ (form) to instruct sb to do sth; **er hat mir Grüße an Sie aufgetragen** he has asked me to give you his regards **d** Kleider to wear out **VI a** (Kleider) to make sb look fat; **die Jacke trägt auf** the jacket is not very flattering to your/her/his figure **b** (= übertreiben) **dick** or **stark ~** (inf) to lay it on thick (inf), to lay it on with a trowel (Brit inf)

Auf|trag-: **Auf|trag|ge|ber(in)** M(F) client; (von Firma, Freischaffenden) customer; **Auf|trag|neh|mer(in)** M(F) (Comm) firm accepting the order; (Build) contractor

Auf|trags-: **Auf|trags|ab|wick|lung** F order processing; **Auf|trags|ar|beit** F commissioned work; **Auf|trags|be|stän|de** [-bəʃtɛndə] PL backlog sing of orders; **Auf|trags|be|stä|ti|gung** F confirmation of order; **Auf|trags|buch** NT usu pl order book; **Auf|trags|dienst** M (Telec) (= telephone) answering service; **Auf|trags|ein|bruch** M dramatic reduction or slump in orders; **Auf|trags|ein|gang** M **bei ~** on receipt of order; **hohe Auftragseingänge** a high number of orders; **Auf|trags|er|tei|lung** F placing of orders; (bei einer Ausschreibung) award; **Auf|trags|for|mu|lar** NT order form; **auf|trags|ge|mäß** ADJ, ADV as instructed; (Comm) as per order; **Auf|trags|la|ge** F order situation, situation concerning orders; **Auf|trags|pols|ter** NT **wir haben ein dickes ~** our order books are well-filled; **Auf|trags|rück|gang** M drop in orders; **Auf|trags|ver|ga|be** F, no pl placing of orders; (bei Ausschreibungen) award of contract; **Auf|trags|vo|lu|men** NT volume of orders; **Auf|trags|wal|ze** F (Typ) inking roller; **Auf|trags|werk** NT commissioned work or piece

auf+tref|fen VI sep irreg aux sein **auf etw** (dat or acc) ~ to hit or strike sth; (Rakete) to land on sth; **er traf mit dem Kopf auf der Kante auf** he hit his head on the edge; **~de Strahlen** incident rays

auf+trei|ben VT sep irreg **a** (inf) (= beschaffen) Geld, Heroin, Geräte to get hold of; (= ausfindig machen) Wohnung, Geschenk, Sponsor, Mieter, Täter to find **b** Leib to distend, to bloat; **sein aufgetriebener Bauch** his swollen or distended stomach **c** Vieh (zum Verkauf) to drive to market; (auf die Alm) to drive up to the (Alpine) pastures

auf+tren|nen VT sep to undo

auf+tre|ten sep irreg **VI** aux sein **a** (lit) to tread; **der Fuß tut so weh, dass ich (mit ihm) nicht mehr ~ kann** my foot hurts so much that I can't walk on it or put my weight on it **b** (= erscheinen) to appear; **als Zeuge/Kläger ~** to appear as a witness/as plaintiff; **zum ersten Mal (im Theater) ~** to make one's début or (appearance), to make one's first (stage) appearance; **er tritt zum ersten Mal in Köln auf** he is appearing in Cologne for the first time; **gegen jdn/etw ~** to stand up or speak out against sb/sth; **geschlossen ~** to put up a united front **c** (fig: = eintreten) to occur; (Schwierigkeiten etc) to arise **d** (= sich benehmen) to behave; **bescheiden/arrogant ~** to have a modest/arrogant manner; **vorsichtig ~** to tread warily **e** (= handeln) to act; **als Vermittler/Friedensstifter** etc ~ to act as (an) intermediary/(a) peacemaker etc **VT** Tür etc to kick open

Auf|tre|ten NT -s, no pl **a** (= Erscheinen) appearance **b** (= Benehmen) manner **c** (= Vorkommen) occurrence; **bei ~ von Schwellungen ...** in case swelling occurs ..., in the event of swelling ...

Auf|trieb M **a** no pl (Phys) buoyancy (force); (Aviat) lift **b** no pl (fig) (= Aufschwung) impetus; (= Preisauftrieb) upward trend (+gen in); (= Ermunterung) lift; **das wird ihm ~ geben** that will give him a lift **c** (von Alpenvieh) **der ~ findet Anfang Mai statt** the cattle are driven up to the (Alpine) pastures at the beginning of May **d** (von Marktvieh) **der ~ an Vieh/Kälbern** the number of cattle/calves (at the market)

Auf|triebs|kraft F buoyancy force; (Aviat) lift

Auf|tritt M **a** (= Erscheinen) entrance; **ich habe meinen ~ erst im zweiten Akt** I don't go or come on until the second act **b** (Theat: = Szene) scene **c** (= Streit) row

Auf|tritts|ver|bot NT stage ban; **~ bekommen/haben** to be banned from making a public appearance; **~ über jdn verhängen** (inf) to ban sb from appearing

auf+trump|fen VI sep to be full of oneself (inf); (= sich schadenfroh äußern) to crow; (= seine Leistungsstärke zeigen) to show how good one is; **~d sagte er ...** ..., he crowed

auf+tun sep irreg **VT a** (inf: = ausfindig machen) to find **b** (= öffnen) Tür, Tor to open; **er hat den Mund nicht aufgetan** he didn't open his mouth **c** (inf: = servieren) **jdm/sich etw ~** to put sth on sb's/one's plate, to help sb/oneself to sth **d** (dial: = aufsetzen) to put on **VR a** (= sich öffnen) to open up **b** (= sich ergeben) (Kluft) to open up; (Differenz, Möglichkeiten, Probleme, Widersprüche) to arise **VI** (= öffnen) **jdm ~** to open the door to sb

auf+tür|men sep **VT** to pile or stack up; (Geol) to build up (in layers) **VR** (Gebirge etc) to tower or loom up; (Schwierigkeiten) to pile or mount up; **hoch aufgetürmte Felsen** towering cliffs

auf+wa|chen VI sep aux sein (lit, fig) to wake up; **aus seiner Lethargie ~** to snap out of one's lethargy; **aus einer Narkose ~** to come out of an anaesthetic (Brit) or anesthetic (US)

Auf|wach|raum M (Med, nach Operation) recovery room

auf+**wach|sen** VI *sep irreg aux sein* to grow up

auf+**wal|len** VI *sep aux sein* to bubble up; (*Cook*) to boil up; (*Leidenschaft etc*) to surge up; **die So-ße einmal ~ lassen** bring the sauce to the (*Brit*) *or a* (*US*) boil; **seine ~de Wut** his seething rage; **seine ~de Leidenschaft** the passion surging up in him

Auf|wal|lung F (*fig*) (*von Leidenschaft*) surge; (*von Wut*) outburst, fit (of rage)

Auf|wand ['aufvant] M **-(e)s** [-dəs] *no pl* **a** (*von Geld*) expenditure (*an* +*dat* of); **das erfordert einen ~ von 10 Millionen Euro** that will cost *or* take 10 million euros; **das erfordert einen gro-ßen ~** (**an Zeit/Energie/Geld**) that requires a lot of time/energy/money; **der dazu nötige ~ an Konzentration/Zeit** the concentration/time needed **b** (= *Luxus, Prunk*) extravagance; (**gro-ßen**) **~ treiben** to be (very) extravagant; **was da für ~ getrieben wurde!** the extravagance!

auf|wän|dig ▲ ['aufvɛndɪç] **ADJ** (= *teuer*) costly; (= *üppig*) lavish **ADV** extravagantly

Auf|wands|ent|schä|di|gung F expense allowance

auf+**wär|men** *sep* **VT** to heat *or* warm up; (*inf*: = *wieder erwähnen*) to bring up, to drag up (*inf*) **VR** to warm oneself up; (*Sport*) to warm *or* lim-ber up

Auf|wärm-: **Auf|wärm|pha|se** F (*Sport*) warm-up phase; **Auf|wärm|ü|bun|gen** PL warm-up *or* warming-up *or* limbering-up exercises *pl*

Auf|war|te|frau F char(woman) (*Brit*), cleaner

auf+**war|ten** VI *sep* **a** (*geh*: = *bedienen*) to serve (*jdm* sb); (**bei Tisch**) **~** to wait at table (*Brit*), to wait a table (*US*); **uns wurde mit Sekt aufgewar-tet** we were served champagne **b** (= *zu bieten haben*) **mit etw ~** to offer sth; **er hat viel Geld, damit kann ich nicht ~** he's very rich, I can't compete with that **c** (*dated*: = *besuchen*) **jdm ~** to wait (up)on sb (*old*), to visit sb

auf|wärts ['aufverts] **ADV** up, upward(s); (= *bergauf*) uphill; **die Ecken haben sich ~ gebo-gen** the corners have curled up; **den Fluss ~** upstream; **von einer Million ~** from a million up(wards); **vom Feldwebel ~** from sergeant up → **aufwärts gehen**

Auf|wärts-: **Auf|wärts|be|we|gung** F upward movement; (*Tech*) upstroke; **Auf|wärts|ent-wick|lung** F upward trend (+*gen* in); **auf|-wärts ge|hen** ▲ VI *impers irreg aux sein* **mit dem Staat/der Firma geht es aufwärts** things are looking up *or* getting better *or* improving for the country/firm; **mit ihm geht es aufwärts** (*fi-nanziell, beruflich*) things are looking up for him; (*in der Schule, gesundheitlich*) he's doing *or* getting better; **mit seinen Leistungen geht es aufwärts** he's doing better; **Auf|wärts|ha|ken** M (*Bo-xen*) uppercut; **auf|wärts|kom|pa|ti|bel** ADJ (*Comput*) upward compatible; **Auf|wärts|-trend** M upward trend

Auf|war|tung F **a** *no pl* (*dated*) (= *Bedienung*) waiting at table (*Brit*), waiting a table (*US*); (= *Reinemachen*) cleaning **b** (*geh*: = *Besuch*) **jdm seine ~ machen** to wait on sb (*old*), to visit sb **c** (*dial*: = *Aufwartefrau etc*) char(woman) (*Brit*), cleaner

Auf|wasch ['aufvaʃ] M **-(e)s**, *no pl* (*dial*) = **Ab-wasch**[1]

auf+**wa|schen** *sep irreg* (*dial*) **VT** *Geschirr* to wash, to wash up (*Brit*) **VI** to wash up (*Brit*), to do the washing-up (*Brit*), to wash the dishes

auf+**we|cken** VT *sep* to wake (up), to waken (*fig*) to rouse → *auch* **aufgeweckt**

auf+**we|hen** *sep* **VT** **a** (= *in die Höhe wehen*) to blow up; (= *auftürmen*) to pile up; **der Wind hat Dünen aufgeweht** the wind has blown the sand into dunes **b** (= *öffnen*) to blow open **VI** *aux sein* to blow up

auf+**wei|chen** *sep* **VT** to make soft; *Weg, Boden* to make sodden; *Brot* to soak; (*durch Wärme*) to soften; (*fig*: = *lockern*) to weaken; *Doktrin, Gesetz* to water down; *Gegner* to soften up **VI** *aux sein*

to become *or* get soft; (*Weg, Boden*) to become *or* get sodden; (*fig*) (= *sich lockern*) to be weak-ened; (*Doktrin, Gesetz*) to become *or* get watered down

auf+**wei|sen** VT *sep irreg* to show; **die Leiche wies keinerlei Verletzungen auf** the body showed no signs of injury; **das Buch weist eini-ge Fehler auf** the book contains some mistakes *or* has some mistakes in it; **etw aufzuweisen ha-ben** to have sth to show for oneself; **man muss schon einiges an Veröffentlichungen aufzuwei-sen haben** you have to have something to show in the way of publications

auf+**wen|den** VT *sep irreg* to use; *Zeit, Energie* to expend; *Mühe* to take; *Geld* to spend; **viel Mü-he/Zeit ~, etw zu tun** to take a lot of trouble/spend a lot of time doing sth; **das wäre unnütz aufgewandte Zeit/Energie** that would be a waste of time/energy

auf|wen|dig ADJ, ADV = **aufwändig**

Auf|wen|dung F **a** *no pl* using; (*von Zeit, Ener-gie*) expenditure; (*von Mühe*) taking; (*von Geld*) spending; **unter ~ von ...** by using/expending/taking/spending ... **b** **Aufwendungen** PL expenditure

auf+**wer|fen** *sep irreg* ✪ 53.2, 53.6 **VT** **a** (= *nach oben werfen*) to throw up; (= *aufhäufen*) to pile up; *Damm etc* to build (up) **b** *Kopf* to toss; *Lippen* to purse **c** *Tür* to throw open **d** (= *zur Sprache bringen*) *Frage, Probleme, Thema* to raise, to bring up; *Verdacht* to raise **VR** **sich zu etw ~** to set oneself up as sth; **sich zum Richter ~** to set oneself up as judge

auf+**wer|ten** VT *sep* **a** *auch vi Währung* to reval-ue **b** (*fig*) to increase the value of; *Menschen, Ideal* to enhance the status of

Auf|wer|tung F (*von Währung*) revaluation; (*fig*) increase in value; **das kommt einer ~ des Terrorismus gleich** that is tantamount to en-hancing the status of terrorism

auf+**wi|ckeln** VT *sep* (= *aufrollen*) to roll up; (*inf*) *Haar* to put in curlers

auf Wie|der|se|hen [auf 'vi:dɐzeːən], **auf Wie|der|schau|en** [auf 'vi:dɐʃauən] (*geh, S Ger, Aus, Sw*) INTERJ goodbye

Auf|wie|ge|lei [aufvi:gə'lai] F **-, -en** incitement *no pl*

auf+**wie|geln** ['aufvi:gln] VT *sep* to stir up; **jdn zum Streik/Widerstand ~** to incite sb to strike/resist

Auf|wie|ge|lung ['aufvi:gəlʊŋ] F **-, -en** incite-ment *no pl*

auf+**wie|gen** VT *sep irreg* (*fig*) to offset; **das ist nicht mit Geld aufzuwiegen** that can't be meas-ured in terms of money

Auf|wieg|ler ['aufvi:glɐ] M **-s, -**, **Auf|wieg|le-rin** [-ərɪn] F **-, -nen** agitator; (= *Anstifter*) instiga-tor

auf|wieg|le|risch ['aufvi:glərɪʃ] ADJ seditious; *Rede, Artikel auch* inflammatory

Auf|wind M (*Aviat*) upcurrent; (*Met*) upwind; **guter ~** good upcurrents *pl*; (**durch etw**) **neuen ~ bekommen** (*fig*) to get new impetus (from sth); **einer Sache** (*dat*) **~ geben** (*fig*) to give sth impetus; **sich im ~ fühlen** to feel one is on the way up *or* in the ascendant

auf+**wir|beln** *sep* **VI** *aux sein* (*Staub, Schnee*) to swirl *or* whirl up **VT** to swirl *or* whirl up; *Staub auch* to raise; (**viel**) **Staub ~** (*fig*) to cause a (big) stir

auf+**wi|schen** *sep* **VT** *Wasser etc* to wipe *or* mop up; *Fußboden* to wipe; **die Küche (feucht) ~** to wash the kitchen floor; **das Bier vom Boden ~** to mop the beer up off the floor **VI** to wipe the floor(s); **feucht ~** to wash the floor(s)

Auf|wisch|lap|pen M , **Auf|wisch|tuch** NT cleaning rag, floorcloth

auf+**wo|gen** VI *sep aux sein* (*liter*) to heave

auf+**wöl|ben** VR *sep* to swell, to buckle; (*Archit*) to arch

auf+**wüh|len** VT *sep* **a** (*lit*) *Erde, Meer* to churn (up) **b** (*geh*) to stir; (*schmerzhaft*) to churn up; *Leidenschaften* to rouse; **das hat seine Seele zu-tiefst aufgewühlt** that stirred him to the depths of his soul; **~d** stirring → *auch* **aufgewühlt**

auf+**zah|len** VT *sep* (*S Ger, Aus*) **50 Euro/einen Zuschlag ~** to pay an additional 50 euros/a surcharge (on top)

auf+**zäh|len** VT *sep* to list; *Beispiele, Details, Na-men auch, Liste* to give; **er hat mir alle meine Fehler aufgezählt** he told me all my faults, he listed all my faults; **man kann die Fälle an den Fingern einer Hand ~** the instances can be counted on the fingers of one hand

Auf|zah|lung F (*S Ger, Aus*) additional charge

Auf|zäh|lung F list; (*von Gründen, Fehlern etc auch*) enumeration

auf+**zäu|men** VT *sep* to bridle; **etw verkehrt ~** to go about sth the wrong way

auf+**zeh|ren** *sep* **VT** to exhaust; (*fig*) to sap **VR** to burn oneself out

Auf|zeh|rung F exhaustion; (*fig*) sapping

auf+**zeich|nen** VT *sep* **a** *Plan etc* to draw, to sketch **b** (= *notieren, Rad, TV*) to record

Auf|zeich|nung F **a** (= *Zeichnung*) sketch **b** *usu pl* (= *Notiz*) note; (= *Niederschrift*) record **c** (= *Magnetbandaufzeichnung, Filmaufzeichnung*) recording

auf+**zei|gen** *sep* **VT** to show; (= *nachweisen auch*) to demonstrate **VI** (*dated Sch*: = *sich mel-den*) to put one's hand up

auf+**zie|hen** *sep irreg* **VT** **a** (= *hochziehen*) to pull *or* draw up; (*mit Flaschenzug etc*) to hoist up; *Schlagbaum, Zugbrücke* to raise; *Flagge, Segel* to hoist; *Jalousien* to let up; (*Med*) *Spritze* to fill; *Flüssigkeit* to draw up

b (= *öffnen*) *Reißverschluss* to undo; *Schleife etc* to untie, to undo; *Schublade* to (pull) open; *Gar-dinen* to draw (back)

c (= *aufspannen*) *Foto etc* to mount; *Leinwand, Stickerei* to stretch; *Landkarte etc* to pull up; *Saite, Reifen* to fit, to put on; **Saiten/neue Saiten auf ein Instrument ~** to string/restring an instru-ment → **Saite b**

d (= *spannen*) *Feder, Uhr etc* to wind up

e (= *großziehen*) *Kind* to bring up, to raise; *Tier* to raise, to rear

f (*inf*) (= *veranstalten*) to set up; *Fest* to arrange; (= *gründen*) *Unternehmen* to start up

g (= *verspotten*) **jdn ~** (*inf*) to make fun of sb, to tease sb (*mit* about)

VI *aux sein* (*dunkle Wolke*) to come up; (*Gewitter, Wolken auch*) to gather; (= *aufmarschieren*) to march up; **die Wache zog vor der Kaserne auf** the soldiers mounted guard in front of the bar-racks

VR to wind; **sich von selbst ~** to be self-wind-ing

Auf|zin|sung ['auftsɪnzʊŋ] F **-, -en** (*Fin*) accu-mulation

Auf|zucht F **a** *no pl* (= *das Großziehen*) rearing, raising **b** (= *Nachwuchs*) young family

Auf|zug M **a** (= *Fahrstuhl*) lift (*Brit*), elevator (*US*) **b** (*Phot*) wind-on **c** (= *Marsch, Festzug*) parade; **der ~ der Wache** the mounting of the guard **d** (*von Gewitter etc*) gathering **e** (*Turnen*) pull-up **f** (*Theat*) act **g** *no pl* (*pej inf*: = *Klei-dung*) get-up (*inf*)

Auf|zug- *in cpds* lift (*Brit*), elevator (*US*); **Auf|-zug|füh|rer(in)** M(F) lift (*Brit*) *or* elevator (*US*) operator; **Auf|zug(s)|schacht** M lift (*Brit*) *or* elevator (*US*) shaft

auf+**zwi|cken** VT *sep* (*Aus inf*) **sich** (*dat*) **jdn ~** to chat sb up (*Brit inf*), to put the moves on sb (*US inf*)

auf+**zwin|gen** *sep irreg* **VT** **jdm etw ~** to force sth on sb; **jdm seinen Willen ~** to impose one's will on sb **VR** to force itself on one; **sich jdm ~** to force itself on sb; (*Gedanke*) to strike sb for-cibly; **das zwingt sich einem doch förmlich auf** the conclusion is unavoidable

auf·zwir·beln VT *sep Bart* to twirl up, to twist up; *Garn* to twist up, to roll between one's fingers

Aug·ap·fel M eyeball; **jdn/etw wie seinen ~ hüten** to cherish sb/sth like life itself

Au·ge ['augǝ] -s, -n

SUBSTANTIV (NT)

a ⌐= Sehorgan⌐ eye; **Auge um Auge, Zahn um Zahn** (*Bibl*) an eye for an eye and a tooth for a tooth; **wieder einmal waren meine Augen größer als der Bauch** as usual my eyes were bigger than my stomach; **ganz Auge und Ohr sein** to be all ears; **Augen zu und durch!** (*inf*) grit your teeth and get on with it!; **Augen rechts/links!** (*Mil*) eyes right/left!; **das Auge des Gesetzes** the eye of the law

♦ **Auge(n) + haben gute/schlechte Augen haben** to have good/bad eyesight; **ein sicheres Auge für etw haben** to have a good eye for sth; **da muss man seine Augen überall** or **hinten und vorn** (*inf*) **haben** you need eyes in the back of your head; **ich kann doch meine Augen nicht überall haben** I don't have eyes in the back of my head; **haben Sie keine Augen im Kopf?** (*inf*) haven't you got eyes in your head?, use your eyes!; **die Augen offen haben** to keep one's eyes open; **ich hab doch hinten keine Augen!** I don't have eyes in the back of my head!; **er hatte nur Augen für sie** he only had eyes for her; **ein Auge auf jdn/etw haben** (= *aufpassen*) to keep an eye on sb/sth; **ein Auge auf jdn/etw (geworfen) haben** to have one's eye on sb/sth

♦ **Auge(n) + andere Verben die Augen aufmachen** or **aufsperren** (*inf*) or **auftun** (*inf*) to open one's eyes; **sich** (*dat*) **die Augen ausweinen** to cry one's eyes out; **da blieb kein Auge trocken** (*hum*) there wasn't a dry eye in the house; (*vor Lachen*) everyone laughed till they cried; **dem fallen bald die Augen raus** (*sl*) his eyes will pop out of his head in a minute (*inf*); **er guckte** (*inf*) **sich** (*dat*) **die Augen aus dem Kopf** his eyes were popping out of his head (*inf*); **die Augen offen halten** to keep one's eyes open; **er lässt kein Auge von ihr** he doesn't let her out of his sight; **große Augen machen** to be wide-eyed; **jdm schöne** or **verliebte Augen machen** to make eyes at sb; **die Augen öffnen** to open one's eyes; **jdm die Augen öffnen** (*fig*) to open sb's eyes; **so weit das Auge reicht** as far as the eye can see; **ein Auge riskieren** (*hum*) to have a peep (*inf*); **die Augen schließen** (*lit*) to close one's eyes; (*euph*) to fall asleep; **die Augen vor etw** (*dat*) **verschließen** to close one's eyes to sth; **sich** (*dat*) **die Augen aus dem Kopf weinen** (*inf*) to cry one's eyes out; **ein Auge** or **beide Augen zudrücken** (*inf*) to turn a blind eye; **ich habe kein Auge zugetan** I didn't sleep a wink → **blau a, Luchs, vier b**

b ⌐mit Präposition⌐

♦ **aufs Auge jdm etw aufs Auge drücken** (*inf*) to force sth on sb

♦ **aus + Augen aus den Augen, aus dem Sinn** (*Prov*) out of sight, out of mind (*Prov*); **ich konnte kaum aus den Augen sehen** or **gucken** I could hardly see straight; **geh mir aus den Augen!** get out of my sight!; **sie ließen ihn nicht aus den Augen** they didn't let him out of their sight; **jdn/etw aus den Augen verlieren** to lose sight of sb/sth; (*fig*) to lose touch with sb/sth

♦ **fürs Auge etwas fürs Auge sein** (*Gegenstand*) to be nice to look at, to look nice; (*Mensch*) to be nice-looking; **nur fürs Auge** just nice to look at

♦ **im Auge etw im Auge haben** (*lit*) to have sth in one's eye; (*fig*) to have one's eye on sth; **jdn im Auge behalten** (= *beobachten*) to keep an eye on sb; (= *vormerken*) to keep or bear sb in mind; **etw im Auge behalten** to keep or bear

sth in mind; **sein Ziel im Auge behalten** to keep one's objective in view

♦ **ins Auge dem Tod ins Auge sehen** to look death in the eye; **etw ins Auge fassen** to contemplate sth; **das springt** or **fällt einem gleich ins Auge** it strikes one immediately; **ins Auge stechen** (*fig*) to catch the eye; **das kann leicht ins Auge gehen** (*fig inf*) it might easily go wrong

♦ **in + Auge(n) in den Augen der Leute/Öffentlichkeit** in the eyes of most people/the public; **in meinen Augen** in my opinion or view; **jdm in die Augen sehen** to look sb in the eye(s); **ich schau dir in die Augen, Kleines** here's looking at you, kid; **Auge in Auge** face to face

♦ **mit + Auge(n) mit den Augen zwinkern** to wink; **mit den Augen blinzeln** to blink; **jdn/etw mit den Augen verschlingen** to devour sb/sth with one's eyes; **jdn/etw mit anderen Augen (an)sehen** to see sb/sth with different eyes; **etw mit eigenen Augen gesehen haben** to have seen sth with one's own eyes; **mit bloßem** or **nacktem Auge** with the naked eye; **du brauchst mich gar nicht mit großen Augen anzusehen** you needn't look at me with those big eyes; **mit offenen Augen schlafen** to daydream; **mit verbundenen Augen** (*lit, fig*) blindfold; **mit einem lachenden und einem weinenden Auge** with mixed feelings

♦ **unter + Augen unter jds Augen** before sb's very eyes; **komm mir nicht mehr unter die Augen!** keep out of my sight!; **wenn du mir noch einmal unter die Augen kommst, ...** if you let me see you again ...

♦ **vor + Auge(n) jdm etw vor Augen führen** (*fig*) to make sb aware of sth; **das muss man sich** (*dat*) **mal vor Augen führen!** just imagine it!; **es führt sich offenbar niemand richtig vor Augen, dass ...** it obviously isn't clear to everyone that ...; **etw noch genau** or **lebhaft vor Augen haben** to remember sth clearly or vividly; **etw steht** or **schwebt jdm vor Augen** sb has sth in mind; **etw/den Tod vor Augen sehen** to face sth/death; **vor aller Augen** in front of everybody; **vor meinem geistigen** or **inneren Auge** in my mind's eye

c ⌐= Knospenansatz⌐ *bei Kartoffel* eye; (*bei Zweig*) axil

d ⌐= Fettauge⌐ little globule of fat

e ⌐bei Spielen⌐ **wie viele Augen hat der König?** what is the king worth?; **wer zuerst sechs Augen würfelt** the person who first throws a six

f ⌐in technischen Zusammenhängen⌐ (*von Hurrikan*) eye; **magisches Auge** (*Rad*) magic eye

äu·gen ['ɔygn] VI to look

Augen-: Au·gen·ab·stand M interocular distance (*form*), distance between the eyes; **Au·gen·arzt** M , **Au·gen·ärz·tin** F eye specialist, eye doctor, ophthalmologist; **au·gen·ärzt·lich** ADJ *attr Gutachten etc* ophthalmological; *Behandlung* eye *attr*, ophthalmic ADV *untersucht werden by* an ophthalmologist or eye doctor; **ein ~ interessanter Fall** an interesting ophthalmological case; **Au·gen·auf·schlag** M look; **Au·gen·aus·wi·sche·rei** [-ausvɪʃǝ'raɪ] F -, -en (*fig inf*) eyewash; **Au·gen·bad** NT eyebath; **ein ~ nehmen** to bathe one's eye(s); **Au·gen·bank** F *pl* -banken eyebank; **Au·gen·bin·de** F eye bandage; (= *Augenklappe*) eye patch

Au·gen·blick M moment; **alle ~e** constantly, all the time; **jeden ~** any time or minute or moment; **einen ~, bitte** one moment please!; **~ mal!** (*inf*) just a minute or second!, just a sec! (*inf*); **im ~** at the moment; **in diesem** or **im selben ~...** at that moment ...; **im letzten/richtigen** *etc* **~** at the last/right *etc* moment; **im ersten ~** for a moment; **im nächsten ~** the (very) next moment; **er ist gerade im ~ gegangen** he just left this very moment; **es geschah in einem ~** it happened in an instant; **er zögerte keinen ~** he didn't hesitate for a moment

au·gen·blick·lich ['augnblɪklɪç, augn'blɪklɪç] ADJ **a** (= *sofort*) immediate **b** (= *gegenwärtig*)

present, current; **die ~e Lage** the present or current situation, the situation at the moment **c** (= *vorübergehend*) temporary; (= *einen Augenblick dauernd*) momentary ADV **a** (= *sofort*) at once, immediately, instantly **b** (= *zur Zeit*) at the moment, presently

au·gen·blicks [-blɪks] ADV at once, immediately, instantly

Augenblicks-: Au·gen·blicks·auf·nah·me F (*Phot*) snapshot; **Au·gen·blicks·er·folg** M short-lived success; **Au·gen·blicks·idee** F idea thought up on the spur of the moment; **Au·gen·blicks·mensch** M spontaneous or spur-of-the-moment person or type; **Au·gen·blicks·sa·che** F quick job; **das ist nur eine ~** it'll just take a moment; **das war eine ~** it was over in a flash; **Au·gen·blicks·stim·mung** F **aus einer ~ heraus** on the spur of the moment

Augen-: Au·gen·blin·zeln NT -s, *no pl* wink; **Au·gen·braue** F eyebrow; **Au·gen·brau·en·stift** M eyebrow pencil; **Au·gen·bren·nen** NT stinging eyes *pl*, stinging of or in the eyes; **Au·gen·de·ckel** M eyelid; **Au·gen·ent·zün·dung** F inflammation of the eyes; **au·gen·fäl·lig** ADJ conspicuous; (= *offensichtlich*) obvious; **Au·gen·far·be** F colour (*Brit*) or color (*US*) of eyes; **Menschen mit einer dunklen ~** people with dark eyes; **Au·gen·feh·ler** M eye defect; **Au·gen·flim·mern** NT -s, *no pl* flickering before the eyes; **au·gen·freund·lich** ADJ *Bildschirm, Größe der Buchstaben etc* easy on the eyes; **Au·gen·glas** NT (*dated*) monocle; **Au·gen·glä·ser** PL (*esp Aus*) glasses *pl*, spectacles *pl*; **Au·gen·gym·nas·tik** F eye exercises *pl*; **Au·gen·heil·kun·de** F ophthalmology; **Au·gen·hö·he** F **in ~** at eye level; **Au·gen·höh·le** F eye socket, orbit (*form*); **Au·gen·klap·pe** F **a** eye patch **b** (*für Pferde*) blinker, blinder (*US*); **Au·gen·kli·nik** F eye clinic or hospital; **Au·gen·krank·heit** F eye disease; **Au·gen·lei·den** NT eye complaint; **Au·gen·licht** NT , *no pl* (eye)sight; **Au·gen·lid** NT eyelid; **Au·gen·maß** NT , *no pl* eye; (*für Entfernungen*) eye for distance(s); (*fig*) perceptiveness; **nach ~** by eye; **~ haben** (*lit*) to have a good eye (for distance(s)); (*fig*) to be able to assess or gauge things or situations; **ein gutes/schlechtes ~ haben** to have a good eye/no eye (for distance(s)); **ein ~ für etw haben** (*fig*) to have an eye for sth; **Au·gen·mensch** M (*inf*) visual(ly oriented) person; **Au·gen·merk** [-mɛrk] NT -s, *no pl* (= *Aufmerksamkeit*) attention; **jds/sein ~ auf etw** (*acc*) **lenken** or **richten** to direct sb's/one's attention to sth; **einer Sache** (*dat*) **sein ~ zu·wenden** to turn one's attention to a matter; **Au·gen·mit·tel** NT (*Med*) eye medication, ophthalmic agent (*spec*); **Au·gen·nerv** M optic nerve; **Au·gen·ope·ra·ti·on** F eye operation; **Au·gen·op·ti·ker(in)** M(F) optician; **Au·gen·paar** NT pair of eyes; **Au·gen·par·tie** F eye area; **Au·gen·pro·the·se** F artificial eye; **Au·gen·pul·ver** NT (*fig inf*: = *Schrift, Buch etc*) tiny or microscopic print; **das ist ja das reinste ~** you'd strain your eyes trying to read that; **Au·gen·rän·der** PL rims *pl* of the/one's eyes; **er hatte rote ~, seine ~ waren gerötet** the rims of his eyes were red; **Au·gen·rei·zung** F (*Med*) eye irritation; **Au·gen·rin·ge** PL rings *pl* round or under the/one's eyes; **Au·gen·sal·be** F eye ointment; **Au·gen·schat·ten** PL shadows *pl* under the/one's eyes; **Au·gen·schein** M , *no pl* **a** (= *Anschein*) appearance; **dem nach** by all appearances, to judge by appearances; **der ~ trügt** appearances are deceptive; **nach dem ~ urteilen** to judge by appearances **b** **jdn/etw in ~ nehmen** to look closely at sb/sth, to have a close look at sb/sth; **au·gen·schein·lich** ['augnʃaɪnlɪç, augn'ʃaɪnlɪç] ADJ obvious, evident ADV obviously; **die beiden sind ~ zerstritten** the two have obviously or clearly had a quarrel; **Au·gen·schmaus** M (*hum*) feast for the eyes; **Au·gen·schutz** M visor, eye visor; **Au·gen·spie·gel** M ophthalmoscope; **Au·gen·spie·ge·lung** F ophthalmoscopy;

Au|gen|stern M **a** (*Liter:* = *Pupille*) pupil, orb (*poet*) **b** (*dated:* = *Liebstes*) apple of one's eye, darling; **Au|gen|trop|fen** PL eye drops *pl*; **Au|gen|ver|let|zung** F eye injury *or* damage; **Au|gen|wei|de** F , *no pl* feast *or* treat for the eyes; **nicht gerade eine ~** (*iro*) a bit of an eyesore; **Au|gen|wim|per** F eyelash; **Au|gen|win|kel** F corner of the/one's eye; **Au|gen|wi|sche|rei** [-vɪʃə'raɪ] F **-,** *-en* (*fig*) eyewash; **Au|gen|zahl** F (*Cards etc*) number of points; **Au|gen|zahn** M eyetooth; **Au|gen|zeu|ge** M , **Au|gen|zeu|gin** F eyewitness (*bei* to); **ich war** ~ **dieses Unfalls** *or* **bei diesem Unfall** I was an eyewitness to this accident; **Au|gen|zeu|gen|be|richt** M eyewitness account; **Au|gen|zwin|kern** NT **-s,** *no pl* winking; **Au|gen|zwin|kernd** ADJ winking *attr*; (*fig*) sly ADV with a wink; **er grinste mich** ~ **an** he grinned at me, winking; **sie sahen sich** ~ **an** they winked at each other; **jdm etw** ~ **zu verstehen geben** to let sb know sth with a wink

Au|gi|as|stall [au'gi:as-, 'augias-] M (*fig geh*) dunghill, Augean stables *pl* (*liter*)

-äu|gig [ɔygɪç] ADJ *suf* -eyed; **braunäugig** brown-eyed

Au|gur ['augur] M **-s** *or* **-en,** *-en* [au'gu:rən] (*Hist, fig geh*) augur

Au|gu|ren|lä|cheln NT (*pej geh*) knowing smile

Au|gust[1] [au'gʊst] M **-(e)s** *or* **-, -e** August → *auch* **März**

Au|gust[2] ['august] M **-s** Augustus; **der dumme** ~ (*inf*) the clown; **den dummen** ~ **spielen** to play *or* act the clown *or* fool

Au|gust|ap|fel M Laxton

Au|gust|fei|er F (*Sw*) August public holiday

Au|gus|ti|ner|(mönch) [augus'ti:nɐ-] M **-s, -** Augustinian (monk)

Auk|ti|on [auk'tsio:n] F **-, -en** auction

Auk|ti|o|na|tor [auktsio'na:to:ɐ] M **-s,** Auktionatoren [-'to:rən], **Auk|ti|o|na|to|rin** [-'to:rɪn] F **-, -nen** auctioneer

auk|ti|o|nie|ren [auktsio'ni:rən] ptp **auktioniert** VT to auction

Auk|ti|ons-: **Auk|ti|ons|hal|le** F auction room; **Auk|ti|ons|haus** NT auction house *or* company, auctioneers *pl*

Au|la ['aula] F **-,** Aulen [-lən] (*Sch, Univ etc*) (assembly) hall; (= *Atrium*) atrium

Au-pair- [o'pɛ:ɐ-]: **Au-pair-Jun|ge** M , **Au-pair|jun|ge** ▲ M (male) au pair; **Au-pair-Mäd|chen** NT , **Au|pair|mäd|chen** ▲ NT au pair (girl); **als** ~ **arbeiten** to work (as an) au pair; **Au-pair-Stel|le** F , **Au|pair|stel|le** ▲ F au pair job

Au|ra ['aura] F **-,** *no pl* (*Med, geh*) aura

Au|re|o|le [aure'o:lə] F **-, -n** (*Art*) aureole, halo; (*Met*) corona, aureole; (*fig: rare*) aura

Au|ri|kel [au'ri:kl] F **-, -n** (*Bot*) auricula

Au|ro|ra [au'ro:ra] F **-s** (*Myth, liter*) Aurora

aus [aus] PREP **+dat a** (*räumlich*) from; (= *aus dem Inneren von*) out of; ~ **dem Fenster/der Tür** out of the window/door; ~ **unserer Mitte** from our midst; ~ **der Flasche trinken** to drink from the bottle, to drink out of the bottle; **jdm** ~ **einer Verlegenheit helfen** to help sb out of a difficulty

b (*Herkunft, Quelle bezeichnend*) from; ~ **dem Deutschen** from (the) German; ~ **ganz Frankreich** from all over France; ~ **guter Familie** from *or* of a good family; **ein Wort** ~ **dem Zusammenhang herausgreifen** to take a word out of (its) context

c (*auf Ursache deutend*) out of; ~ **Hass/Gehorsam/Mitleid** out of hatred/obedience/sympathy; ~ **Erfahrung** from experience; ~ **Furcht vor/Liebe zu** for fear/love of; ~ **dem Grunde, dass ...** for the reason that ...; ~ **einer Laune heraus** on (an) impulse; ~ **Spaß** for fun, for a laugh (*inf*); ~ **Unachtsamkeit** due to carelessness; ~ **Versehen** by mistake; ~ **sich heraus** of one's

own accord, off one's own bat (*Brit inf*); **ein Mord** ~ **Berechnung** a calculated murder; **ein Mord** *or* **ein Verbrechen** ~ **Leidenschaft** a crime of passion

d (*zeitlich*) from; ~ **dem Barock** from the Baroque period

e (= *beschaffen aus*) (made out) of; **ein Herz** ~ **Stein** a heart of stone

f (*Herstellungsart*) out of, from; (*fig: Ausgangspunkt*) out of; **kann man** ~ **diesem Stoff noch etwas machen?** can something still be made out of *or* from this material?; **einen Soldaten/Pfarrer** ~ **jdm machen** to make a soldier/minister (out) of sb; **einen anständigen Menschen** ~ **jdm machen** to make sb into a decent person; **was ist** ~ **ihm/dieser Sache geworden?** what has become of him/this?; ~ **der Sache ist nichts geworden** nothing came of it; ~ **ihm wird einmal ein guter Arzt** he'll make a good doctor one day; ~ **mir ist nichts geworden** I never got anywhere (in life)

g ~ **dem Gleichgewicht** out of balance; *Mensch, Gegenstand* off balance; ~ **der Mode** out of fashion

h (*Aus:* = *in*) in; **eine Prüfung** ~ **Geschichte** an examination in *or* on history

i (*Typ*) **gesetzt** ~ **...** set in ...

ADV → *auch* **aus sein a** (*Sport*) out; (*Ftbl, Rugby*) out (of play), in touch **b** (*inf:* = *vorbei, zu Ende*) over; ~ **jetzt!** that's enough!, that'll do now! (*inf*); ~ **und vorbei** over and done with **c** (= *gelöscht*) out; (*an Geräten*) off; **Licht ~!** lights out! **d** (*in Verbindung mit von*) **vom Fenster** ~ from the window; **von München** ~ from Munich; **von sich** (*dat*) ~ off one's own bat (*Brit inf*), of one's own accord; **von ihm** ~ as far as he's concerned; **ok, von mir** ~ OK, if you like → **ein**

Aus [aus] NT **-, -** **a** *no pl* (*Ftbl, Rugby*) touch *no art*; **ins** ~ **gehen** to go out of play; (*seitlich*) to go into touch; **ins politische** ~ **geraten** to end up in the political wilderness **b** *no pl* (= *Ausscheiden*) exit (*für* of) **c** (= *Ende*) end; **das** ~ **für die Firma ist unabwendbar** the company is doomed to close down

aus+ar|bei|ten *sep* VT to work out; (= *errichten, entwerfen auch*) *System, Gedankengebäude* to elaborate, to draw up; (= *vorbereiten*) to prepare; (= *formulieren*) to formulate, to compose VR (*Sport*) to have a work-out

Aus|ar|bei|tung F **-, -en** working out; (= *Vorbereitung*) preparation; (= *Formulierung*) formulation, composition

aus+ar|ten VI *sep aus sein* **a** (*Party etc*) to get out of control; ~ **in** (+*acc*) *or* **zu** to degenerate into **b** (= *ungezogen etc werden*) to get out of hand, to become unruly; (= *pöbelhaft, ordinär etc werden*) to misbehave; (= *fluchen*) to use bad language

aus+at|men VTI *sep* to breathe out, to exhale

aus+ba|cken VT *sep irreg* **a** (= *in Fett backen*) to fry **b** (= *zu Ende backen*) to bake (for) long enough; (= *durchbacken*) to bake (right) through

aus+ba|den VT *sep* (*fig inf*) to carry the can for (*Brit inf*), to take the rap for (*inf*), to pay for; **ich muss jetzt alles** ~ I have to carry the can (*Brit inf*), I have to take the rap (*inf*)

aus+bag|gern VT *sep* Graben to excavate; *Fahrrinne, Schlamm* to dredge (out)

aus+ba|lan|cie|ren ptp **ausbalanciert** *sep* (*lit, fig*) VT to balance (out) VR to balance (each other out)

aus+bal|do|wern ptp **ausbaldowert** VT *sep* (*inf*) to scout out (*inf*); ~**, ob ...** to scout *or* nose around to find out whether ... (*inf*)

Aus|ball M (*Sport*) **bei** ~ when the ball goes out of play

Aus|bau M *pl* **-bauten a** *no pl* (= *das Ausbauen*) removal; (*lit, fig:* = *Erweiterung*) extension (*zu* into); (*von Befestigungsanlagen*) reinforcement; (= *Umbau*) conversion (*zu* (in)to); (*von Beziehungen, Freundschaft*) building up, cultivation; (= *Festi-*

gung: *von Position, Vorsprung*) consolidation, strengthening **b** (*am Haus*) extension **c** (= *Einzelgehöft*) (small) farmstead (*separated from main settlement*)

Aus|bau|ar|bei|ten PL extension *or* conversion work *sing*

aus+bau|en VT *sep* **a** (= *herausmontieren*) to remove (*aus* from) **b** (*lit, fig:* = *erweitern, vergrößern*) to extend (*zu* into); *Befestigungsanlagen* to reinforce; (= *umbauen*) to convert (*zu* (in)to); (= *innen ausbauen*) to fit out; *Beziehungen, Freundschaft* to build up, to cultivate; *Plan* to elaborate; (= *festigen*) *Position, Vorsprung* to consolidate, to strengthen; **ausgebaut** (= *umgebaut*) converted; (= *erweitert*) *Schul-, Verkehrssystem etc* fully developed; **ein ausgebautes Dachgeschoss** a loft conversion; **gut/nicht gut ausgebaut** well/badly planned

aus|bau|fä|hig ADJ *Position* with good prospects; *Geschäft, Produktion, Markt, Computer* expandable; *Beziehungen* that can be built up; *Machtstellung* that can be consolidated *or* strengthened; (*inf*) *Schüler, Mitarbeiter* promising

Aus|bau|fä|hig|keit F development potential; (*von Computer*) expandability

Aus|bau-: **Aus|bau|plan** M development plan; **Aus|bau|stre|cke** F (*Mot*) section of improved road **„Ende der ~"** ≈ "road narrows"; **Aus|bau|stu|fe** F (*von Kraftwerk, Flughafen etc*) development stage; **Aus|bau|woh|nung** F extension flat (*esp Brit*), granny annexe (*Brit inf*), in-law apartment (*US*)

aus+be|din|gen ptp **ausbedungen** VT *sep irreg* **sich** (*dat*) **etw** ~ to insist on sth, to make sth a condition; **sich** (*dat*) ~**, dass ...** to stipulate that ..., to make it a condition that ...; **ich bin dazu bereit, aber ich bedinge mir aus, ...** I'm prepared to do it but (only) on condition that ...; **sich** (*dat*) **das Recht ~, etw zu tun** to reserve the right to do sth

aus+bei|ßen VT *sep irreg* **sich** (*dat*) **einen Zahn** ~ to break *or* lose a tooth (*when biting into sth*); **sich** (*dat*) **die Zähne an etw** (*dat*) ~ (*fig*) to have a tough time of it with sth

aus+be|kom|men ptp **ausbekommen** VT *sep irreg* (*inf*) to get off

aus+bes|sern VT *sep* to repair; *Gegenstand, Wäsche etc auch* to mend; *Roststelle etc* to remove; *Gemälde etc* to restore; *Fehler* to correct

Aus|bes|se|rung F repair; (= *das Flicken*) mending; (*von Gemälde*) restoration; (*von Fehler*) correction

Aus|bes|se|rungs-: **Aus|bes|se|rungs|ar|bei|ten** PL repair work *sing*; **aus|bes|se|rungs|be|dürf|tig** ADJ in need of repair *etc*; **Aus|bes|se|rungs|werk** NT (*Rail*) repair shop

aus+be|to|nie|ren ptp **ausbetoniert** VT *sep* to concrete

aus+beu|len *sep* VT **a** *Kleidung* to make baggy; *Hut* to make floppy; **ausgebeult** (*Kleidung*) baggy; *Hut* battered **b** (= *Beule entfernen*) to remove a dent/dents in; (*Tech: durch Hämmern*) to beat out VR (*Hose*) to go baggy; (*Hut*) to go floppy

Aus|beu|te F (= *Gewinn*) profit, gain; (*Ertrag einer Grube etc*) yield (*an* +*dat* in); (*fig*) result(s) *pl*; (= *Einnahmen*) proceeds *pl*; **die ~ an verwertbaren Erkenntnissen war gering** the useful results (gleaned) were minimal

aus+beu|ten ['ausbɔytn] VT *sep* (*lit, fig*) to exploit; (*Min*) *eine Grube auch* to work; (*Agr*) *Boden* to overwork, to deplete

Aus|beu|ter ['ausbɔytɐ] M **-s, -,** **Aus|beu|te|rin** [-ərɪn] F **-, -nen** exploiter; ~ **und Ausgebeutete** the exploiters and the exploited

Aus|beu|ter|be|trieb M (*pej*) sweatshop

Aus|beu|te|rei [ausbɔytə'raɪ] F **-, -en** (*pej*) exploitation

Aus|beu|ter|ge|sell|schaft F society based on exploitation

aus|beu|te|risch [ˈausbɔytərɪʃ] **ADJ** exploitative **ADV** die Arbeiter ~ zu Überstunden antreiben to exploit the workers by forcing them to work overtime

Aus|beu|tung F -, -en (lit, fig) exploitation; (Min, von Grube auch) working

aus+be|zah|len ptp **ausbezahlt** VT sep Geld to pay out; Arbeitnehmer to pay off; (= abfinden) Erben etc to buy out, to pay off; **in bar ausbezahlt** paid in cash; **wie viel kriegst du pro Woche ausbezahlt?** what is your weekly take-home pay?

Aus|be|zah|lung F payment; (von Erben etc) buying out, paying off

aus+bie|ten VT sep irreg to put on offer, to offer (for sale); **ausgeboten werden** to be on offer; (bei Versteigerung auch) to be up for auction

aus+bil|den sep **VT** **a** (beruflich, Sport, Mil) to train; (= unterrichten) to instruct, to train; (akademisch) to educate; **sich in etw** (dat)/**als** or **zu etw ~ lassen** (esp Arbeiter, Lehrling) to train in sth/as sth; (= studieren) to study sth/to study to be sth; (= Qualifikation erwerben) to qualify in sth/as sth; **sich am Klavier** etc **~ lassen** to have piano etc tuition (Brit), to have private piano etc lessons; **jdn als Sänger ~ lassen** to have sb trained as a singer; **ein ausgebildeter Übersetzer** a trained/qualified translator **b** Fähigkeiten to develop, to cultivate; (Mus) Stimme to train **c** (= formen) to form; (= gestalten) to shape; (= entwickeln) to develop; **etw oval ~** to give sth an oval shape; (Designer etc) to design sth with an oval shape **VR** **a** (= sich entwickeln) to develop; (= sich bilden) to form **b** (= sich schulen) **sich in etw** (dat) **~** (esp Arbeiter, Lehrling) to train in sth; (= studieren) to study sth; (= Qualifikation erwerben) to qualify in sth

Aus|bil|der [ˈausbɪldɐ] M -s, -, **Aus|bil|de|rin** [-ərɪn] F -, -nen instructor; (Frau auch) instructress

Aus|bild|ner [ˈausbɪldnɐ] M -s, -, **Aus|bild|ne|rin** [-ərɪn] F -, -nen (Aus Mil) instructor; (Frau auch) instructress

Aus|bil|dung F **a** (beruflich, Sport, Mil) training; (akademisch) education; **er ist noch in der ~** he hasn't yet finished his education **b** (= das Herausbilden: von Fähigkeiten) development, cultivation; (= Formung) formation; (= Gestaltung) shaping; (= Entwicklung) development

Aus|bil|dungs-: **Aus|bil|dungs|bei|hil|fe** F (für Schüler) (education) grant; (für Lehrling) training allowance; **Aus|bil|dungs|be|ruf** M occupation that requires training; **Aus|bil|dungs|be|trieb** M company that takes on trainees; **Aus|bil|dungs|dau|er** F training or qualification period; **die ~ für einen Ingenieur beträgt sechs Jahre** it takes six years to become an engineer; **Aus|bil|dungs|för|de|rung** F promotion of training; (akademisch) promotion of education; (= Stipendium) grant; **Aus|bil|dungs|gang** M pl -gänge training; **Aus|bil|dungs|jahr** NT year of training; **Aus|bil|dungs|kom|pa|nie** F training unit (for weapons training); **Aus|bil|dungs|kos|ten** PL cost sing of training or of a traineeship; (für Studium) cost sing of studying; **Aus|bil|dungs|kurs** M , **Aus|bil|dungs|kur|sus** M , **Aus|bil|dungs|lehr|gang** M training course; **Aus|bil|dungs|la|ger** NT training camp; **Aus|bil|dungs|lei|ter(in)** M(F) chief or head instructor, head trainer; **Aus|bil|dungs|me|tho|de** F training method, method of training; **Aus|bil|dungs|mög|lich|kei|ten** PL training opportunities; (Studium) opportunities for studying; **Aus|bil|dungs|mu|ni|ti|on** F blank ammunition (used in training); **Aus|bil|dungs|of|fi|zier(in)** M(F) training officer; **Aus|bil|dungs|ord|nung** F training regulations pl; **Aus|bil|dungs|platz** M place to train; (= Stelle) training vacancy; **Aus|bil|dungs|stand** M level of training; **Aus|bil-**

dungs|stät|te F place of training; **Aus|bil|dungs|ver|gü|tung** F payment made during training; **Aus|bil|dungs|ver|hält|nis** NT **sie steht noch im ~** she's still a trainee, she's still in training; **Aus|bil|dungs|ver|si|che|rung** F education insurance; **Aus|bil|dungs|ver|trag** M articles pl of apprenticeship; **Aus|bil|dungs|zeit** F period of training; **nach zweijähriger ~** after a two-year period of training or training period; **Aus|bil|dungs|ziel** NT aims pl of education; **die ~e der Schule** the aims of school education or education at school

aus+bit|ten VT sep irreg **sich** (dat) **(von jdm) etw ~** (geh) to ask (sb) for sth, to request sth (from sb) (form); **das möchte ich mir (auch) ausgebeten haben!** I should think so too!; **ich bitte mir Ruhe aus!** I must or will have silence!

aus+bla|sen VT sep irreg to blow out; Hochofen to shut down, to extinguish; Ei to blow

aus+blei|ben VI sep irreg aux sein (= fortbleiben) to stay out; (= nicht erscheinen: Gäste, Schüler, Schneefall) to fail to appear; (= nicht eintreten: Erwartung, Befürchtung) to fail to materialize; (= überfällig sein) to be overdue; (= aufhören: Puls, Atmung etc) to stop; **die Strafe/ein Krieg wird nicht ~** punishment/a war is inevitable; **das blieb nicht lange aus** that wasn't long in coming; **es konnte nicht ~, dass ...** it was inevitable that ...; **bei manchen Patienten bleiben diese Symptome aus** in some patients these symptoms are absent or do not appear

Aus|blei|ben NT -s, no pl (= Fehlen) absence; (= das Nichterscheinen) nonappearance; **bei ~ von ...** in the absence of ...; **bei ~ der Periode** if your period doesn't come

aus+blei|chen VTI sep irreg (vi: aux sein) to fade, to bleach

aus+blen|den sep **VTI** (TV etc) to fade out; (plötzlich) to cut out **VR** **sich (aus einer Übertragung) ~** to leave a transmission

Aus|blen|dung F (TV etc) fade-out; (plötzlich) cutting out, cut

Aus|blick M **a** view (auf +acc of), outlook (auf +acc over, onto); **ein Zimmer mit ~ auf die Straße/aufs Meer** a room overlooking the street/with a view of the sea or overlooking the sea **b** (fig) prospect, outlook (auf +acc, in +acc for); **einen ~ auf etw** (acc) **geben** to give the prospects for sth

aus+bli|cken VI sep (geh) **nach jdm ~** to look for sb

aus+blu|ten sep **VI** aux sein (= verbluten) to bleed to death; (fig) to be bled white; **ein Schwein ~ lassen** to bleed a pig dry **VT** (fig) to bleed white

aus+boh|ren VT sep to bore; (mit Bohrgerät, Med) to drill; (= herausbohren) to bore/drill out

aus+bom|ben VT sep to bomb out; **die Ausgebombten** people who have been bombed out (of their homes)

aus+boo|ten [ˈausboːtn] sep **VT** **a** (inf) jdn to kick or boot out (inf) **b** (Naut) to disembark (in boats); (= abladen) to unload **VI** (Naut) to disembark (in boats)

aus+bor|gen VT sep (inf) **sich** (dat) **etw (von jdm) ~** to borrow sth (from sb); **jdm etw ~** to lend sb sth, to lend sth (out) to sb

aus+bra|ten sep irreg **VT** (= auslassen) Speck to fry the fat out of **VI** aux sein (Fett) to run out (aus of); **ausgebratenes Fett** melted bacon etc fat

aus+bre|chen sep irreg **VI** **a** (= beginnen, Krieg, Seuche, Feuer) to break out; (Konflikt, Gewalt, Hysterie, Unruhen) to break out, to erupt; (Jubel, Zorn, Frust) to erupt, to explode; (Zeitalter) to arrive, to begin; **in Gelächter/Tränen** or **Weinen ~** to burst into laughter/tears, to burst out laughing/crying; **in Jubel ~** to erupt with jubilation; **in Beifall ~** to break into applause; **in den Ruf "...." ~** to burst out with the cry "...”; **in Schweiß ~** to break out in a sweat; **bei dir ist wohl der Wohlstand ausgebrochen** (fig inf) have

you struck it rich? (inf) **b** (aus Gefangenschaft) to break out (aus of); (Tier) to escape (aus from); (fig: = sich befreien) to get out (aus of), to escape (aus from); **aus dem Gefängnis ~** to escape from prison **c** (Vulkan) to erupt **VT** Zahn to break; Steine to break off; **sich** (dat) **einen Zahn ~** to break a tooth

Aus|bre|cher[1] [ˈausbrɛçɐ] M -s, - (inf: = Tier) escaped animal, runaway **b** (= Pferd) horse that swerves round jumps

Aus|bre|cher[2] [ˈausbrɛçɐ] M -s, -, **Aus|bre|che|rin** [-ərɪn] F -, -nen (inf: = Gefangener) escaped prisoner, escapee; (= notorischer Ausbrecher) jailbreaker (inf)

aus+brei|ten sep **VT** Landkarte, Handtuch to spread (out); Flügel, Äste to spread (out), to extend; Arme to stretch out, to extend; (= ausstellen, fig: = zeigen) to display; Licht, Wärme to spread; **einen Plan vor jdm ~** to unfold a plan to sb; **sein Leben vor jdm ~** to lay one's whole life before sb **VR** **a** (= sich verbreiten) to spread **b** (= sich erstrecken) to extend, to stretch (out), to spread out **c** (inf: = sich breit machen) to spread oneself out **d** **sich über etw** (acc) **~** (fig) to dwell on sth; **sich in Einzelheiten ~** to go into great detail; **darüber will ich mich jetzt nicht ~** I'd rather not go into that now

Aus|brei|tung [ˈausbraitʊŋ] F -, -en (= das Sichausbreiten) spread; (= das Ausbreiten) spreading

aus+brem|sen VT sep **a** (Aut) **den Hintermann ~** to brake, forcing the person behind to slow down **b** (fig inf: = stoppen) Widersacher etc to thwart

aus+bren|nen sep irreg **VI** aux sein **a** (= zu Ende brennen) to burn out; (Vulkan) to become extinct **b** (= völlig verbrennen) to be burned out, to be gutted; **ausgebrannt** burned-out; Gebäude auch gutted; Brennstab spent → auch **ausgebrannt** **VT** to burn out; (Sonne: = ausdörren) to scorch; (Med) to cauterize

aus+brin|gen VT sep irreg **a** Trinkspruch to propose **b** (Naut) Boot, Anker to lower **c** (Typ) Zeile to space out

Aus|bruch M **a** (aus from) (aus Gefängnis) break-out (auch Mil), escape (auch fig) **b** (= Beginn) outbreak; (von Vulkan) eruption; **zum ~ kommen** to break out **c** (fig) (= Gefühlsausbruch, Zornausbruch) outburst; (stärker) eruption, explosion; **zum ~ kommen** to erupt, to explode

Aus|bruchs-: **Aus|bruchs|herd** M (Geol) focus (of an earthquake); **Aus|bruchs|ver|such** M (aus from) attempted break-out (auch Mil) or escape, break-out or escape attempt; (fig) attempt at escape

aus+brü|ten VT sep to hatch; (esp in Brutkasten) to incubate; (fig inf) Plan etc to cook up (inf), to hatch (up); **eine Erkältung ~** to be coming down with a cold

aus+bu|chen VT sep → **ausgebucht**

aus+büch|sen [ˈausbʏksn] VI sep (N Ger: = ausreißen) to break out, to run away

aus+buch|ten [ˈausbʊxtn] sep **VT** Ufer to hollow out; Straße to make a curve in the side of; Wand to round out **VR** to bulge or curve out

Aus|buch|tung F -, -en bulge; (von Strand) (small) cove

aus+bu|deln VT sep (inf) to dig up (auch fig inf)

aus+bü|geln VT sep to iron out; (inf) Fehler, Verlust, Mängel to make good; Missverständnis, Angelegenheit to iron out (inf)

aus+bu|hen VT sep (inf) to boo

Aus|bund M , no pl (von Tugend, Schönheit) paragon, model, epitome; **ein ~ von Tugend** a paragon or model of virtue, the epitome of virtue; **er ist ein ~ an** or **von Gemeinheit/Frechheit** he is baseness/impudence itself or personified

aus+bür|gern ['ausbʏrgən] VT *sep* **jdn ~** to expatriate sb

Aus|bür|ge|rung ['ausbʏrgərʊŋ] F **-, -en** expatriation

aus+bürs|ten VT *sep* to brush out (*aus of*); *Anzug* to brush

aus+bü|xen ['ausbʏksn] VI *sep aux sein* (*hum inf*) to run off, to scarper (*inf*); **jdm ~** to run away from sb

aus+che|cken ['austʃɛkn] VI *sep* (*Flug, Hotel etc*) to check out (*aus of*); **hast du schon (dein Gepäck) ausgecheckt?** have you picked up your luggage (*Brit*) or baggage yet?

Ausch|witz ['auʃvɪts] NT **-'** Auschwitz

Ausch|witz-Lüge F holocaust denial

Aus|dau|er F , *no pl* staying power, stamina; (*im Ertragen*) endurance; (= *Beharrlichkeit*) perseverance, persistence, tenacity; (= *Hartnäckigkeit*) persistence; **beim Lernen/Lesen keine ~ haben** to have no staying power when it comes to learning/reading

aus|dau|ernd ADJ **a** *Mensch* with staying power, with stamina; (*im Ertragen*) with endurance; (= *beharrlich*) persevering, tenacious; (= *hartnäckig*) persistent; *Bemühungen, Anstrengungen* untiring **b** (*Bot*) *Pflanze* perennial ADV diligently; **~ lernen** to apply oneself to learning, to study diligently

Aus|dau|er|trai|ning NT stamina training

aus+deh|nen *sep* VT **a** (= *vergrößern*) to expand, (= *dehnen*) to stretch, to extend; (= *länger machen*) to elongate, to stretch **b** (*fig*) to extend; (*zeitlich*) to prolong (*auf +acc* to) VR **a** (= *größer werden*) to expand; (*durch Dehnen*) to stretch; (= *sich erstrecken*) to extend, to stretch (*bis* as far as); **die Seuche/der Krieg dehnte sich über das ganze Land aus** the epidemic/the war spread over the whole country **b** (*fig*) to extend (*über +acc* over, *bis* as far as, to); (*zeitlich*) to go on (*bis* until), to extend (*bis* until) → *auch* **ausgedehnt**

Aus|deh|nung F **a** (= *das Vergrößern*) expansion; (= *das Dehnen*) stretching, extension; (*fig, zeitlich*) extension **b** (= *Umfang*) expanse; (*Math: von Raum*) extension; **eine ~ von 10.000 Quadratmetern haben** to cover an area of 10,000 square metres (*Brit*) or meters (*US*)

Aus|deh|nungs-: **aus|deh|nungs|fä|hig** ADJ (*esp Phys*) capable of expansion, expansile, expansible; **Aus|deh|nungs|fä|hig|keit** F ability to expand; **Aus|deh|nungs|ver|mö|gen** NT (*esp Phys*) capacity to expand, expansibility

aus+den|ken VT *sep irreg* **sich** (*dat*) **etw ~** (= *erfinden*) to think sth up; *Idee, Plan auch* to devise sth; (*in Einzelheiten*) to think sth out, to devise sth; *Wunsch* to think of sth; *Entschuldigung* to contrive sth, to think sth up; *Überraschung* to plan sth; *Geschichte* to make or think sth up; (= *sich vorstellen*) to imagine sth; (= *durchdenken*) to think sth through; **eine ausgedachte Geschichte** a made-up story; **das ist nicht auszudenken** (= *unvorstellbar*) it's inconceivable; (= *zu schrecklich etc*) it doesn't bear thinking about; **da musst du dir schon etwas anderes ~!** (*inf*) you'll have to think of something better than that!

aus+deu|ten VT *sep* to interpret; *Äußerung, Wort auch* to construe; **falsch ~** to misinterpret, to misconstrue

aus+deut|schen ['ausdɔʏtʃn] VT *sep* (*Aus inf*) **jdm etw ~** to explain sth to sb in words of one syllable, to explain sth to sb in plain English

Aus|deu|tung F interpretation

aus+die|nen VI *sep* **ausgedient haben** (*Mil old*) to have finished one's military service; (= *im Ruhestand sein*) to have been discharged; (*fig inf*) to have had its day; (*Kugelschreiber etc*) to be used up, to be finished; **ein ausgedienter Sol-**

dat (*dated*) a veteran, an ex-serviceman → *auch* **ausgedient**

aus+dis|ku|tie|ren *ptp* **ausdiskutiert** *sep* VT *Thema* to discuss fully VI (= *zu Ende diskutieren*) to finish discussing or talking

aus+dor|ren VI *sep aux sein* = **ausdörren** VI

aus+dör|ren *sep* VT to dry up; *Kehle* to parch; *Pflanzen* to shrivel VI *aux sein* to dry up; (*Boden auch*) to become parched; (*Pflanze auch*) to shrivel up → *auch* **ausgedörrt**

aus+dre|hen VT *sep* (= *ausschalten*) to turn or switch off; *Licht auch* to turn out

aus+dre|schen *sep irreg* VT to thresh (fully) VI (*das Dreschen beenden*) to finish (the) threshing

Aus|druck[1] M *pl* **-drücke** **a** *no pl* (= *Gesichtsausdruck*) expression; **der ~ ihrer Gesichter** the expression(s) on their faces **b** *no pl* **als ~ meiner Dankbarkeit** as an expression of my gratitude; **mit dem ~ des Bedauerns** (*form*) expressing regret, with an expression of regret; **ohne jeden ~ singen/spielen** to sing/play without any expression; **etw zum ~ bringen, einer Sache** (*dat*) **~ geben** or **verleihen** (*form*) to express sth, to give expression to sth; **in seinen Worten/seinem Verhalten kam Mitleid zum ~** his words expressed/his behaviour (*Brit*) or behavior (*US*) showed his sympathy **c** (= *Wort*) expression; (= *Fachausdruck, Math*) term; **das ist gar kein ~!** that's not the word for it; **sich im ~ vergreifen** to use the wrong word

Aus|druck[2] M *pl* **-drucke** (*von Computer etc*) print-out; (*Typ*) end of printing

aus+dru|cken *sep* VT **a** (*Comput*) to print out **b** (*Typ*) (= *fertig drucken*) to finish printing; (= *ungekürzt drucken*) to print in full; **ausgedruckte Exemplare** fully printed copies VI (*Buchstaben etc*) to come out

aus+drü|cken *sep* VT **a** (= *zum Ausdruck bringen*) to express (*jdm* to sb); (*Verhalten, Gesicht*) *Trauer etc* to reveal, to express; **um es anders/gelinde auszudrücken** to put it another way/mildly; **anders ausgedrückt** in other words; **einfach ausgedrückt** put simply, in simple terms, in words of one syllable **b** *Frucht* to press out, to squeeze out; *Tube, Pickel* to squeeze; *Schwamm, Lappen* to squeeze out; (= *ausmachen*) to put out; *Zigarette* to stub out; **den Saft einer Zitrone ~** to press or squeeze juice out of a lemon, to squeeze a lemon VR (*Mensch*) to express oneself; (*Emotion*) to be expressed or revealed; **in ihrem Gesicht/Verhalten drückte sich Verzweiflung aus** her face/behaviour (*Brit*) or behavior (*US*) showed her despair; **er kann sich gewandt ~** he is very articulate

aus+drück|lich ['ausdrʏklɪç, aus'drʏklɪç] ADJ *attr* *Wunsch, Genehmigung* express ADV expressly; (= *besonders*) particularly; **etw ~ betonen** to emphasize sth particularly or specifically

Aus|drück|lich|keit F **-,** *no pl* **in aller ~** expressly

Aus|drucks-: **Aus|drucks|be|dürf|nis** NT need to express oneself; **aus|drucks|fä|hig** ADJ expressive; (= *gewandt*) articulate; **Aus|drucks|fä|hig|keit** F expressiveness; (= *Gewandtheit*) articulateness; **Aus|drucks|form** F form of expression; **Aus|drucks|kraft** F , *no pl* expressiveness; (*von Schriftsteller*) articulateness, word power; **aus|drucks|leer** ADJ expressionless; **Aus|drucks|lee|re** F expressionlessness; **aus|drucks|los** ADJ inexpressive; *Gesicht, Blick auch* expressionless; **Aus|drucks|lo|sig|keit** F **-,** *no pl* inexpressiveness; (*von Gesicht, Blick*) expressionlessness; **Aus|drucks|mit|tel** NT means of expression; **Aus|drucks|mög|lich|keit** F mode of expression; **aus|drucks|schwach** ADJ inexpressive; **Aus|drucks|stark** ADJ expressive; **Aus|drucks|stär|ke** F expressiveness; **Aus|drucks|tanz** M free dance; **aus|drucks|voll** ADJ expressive; **Aus|drucks|wei|se** F way of expressing oneself, mode of expression; **was ist**

denn das für eine ~! what sort of language is that to use!

aus+dün|nen ['ausdʏnən] *sep* VT **a** *Pflanzen, Haare* to thin out **b** *Verkehr, Kapital* to reduce VR (*Kursus*) to thin out

aus+düns|ten *sep* VT *Geruch* to give off; (*Med, Bot auch*) to transpire VI (= *Dunst/Geruch absondern*) to give off vapour (*Brit*) or vapor (*US*)/a smell; (*Bot, Med*) to transpire

Aus|düns|tung F **-, -en** **a** (= *das Ausdünsten*) evaporation; (*von Körper, Pflanze*) transpiration **b** (= *Dampf*) vapour (*Brit*), vapor (*US*); (= *Geruch*) fume, smell; (*von Tier*) scent; (*von Mensch*) smell; (*fig*) emanation

aus|ei|nan|der [ausai'nandɐ] ADV **a** (= *voneinander entfernt, getrennt*) apart; **weit ~** far apart; *Augen, Beine etc* wide apart; *Zähne* widely spaced; *Meinungen* very different; **die Ereignisse liegen (um) zwei Tage ~** the events are separated by two days or are two days apart; **etw ~ schreiben** to write sth as two words; **zwei Kinder ~ setzen** to separate two children; **sich ~ setzen (im Alter)** to sit apart; **die beiden sind (im Alter) ein Jahr ~** there is a year between the two of them; **~ sein** (*inf: Paar*) to have broken or split up; **die Verlobung ist ~** (*inf*) the engagement is off **b** (= *jedes aus dem anderen*) from one another, one from another or the other; **diese Begriffe kann man nur ~ erklären** one can only explain these concepts in relation to one another

aus|ei|nan|der: **aus|ei|nan|der be|kom|men** ▲ VT *irreg* to be able to get apart; **aus|ei|nan|der bie|gen** ▲ VT *irreg* to bend apart; **aus|ei|nan|der bre|chen** ▲ *irreg* VT to break in two VI *aux sein* (*lit, fig*) to break up; **aus|ei|nan|der brei|ten** ▲ VT to unfold; **aus|ei|nan|der brin|gen** ▲ VT *irreg* (*inf*) to manage or be able to get apart (*auch fig*); **aus|ei|nan|der di|vi|die|ren** ▲ VT to divide; **eine Gruppe ~** to create divisions within a group; **aus|ei|nan|der drif|ten** ▲ VI to drift apart; **aus|ei|nan|der ent|wi|ckeln** ▲ VR to grow apart (from each other); (*Partner*) to drift apart; **aus|ei|nan|der fal|len** ▲ VI *irreg aux sein* **a** (= *zerfallen*) to fall apart; (= *zusammenfallen*) to collapse, to fall apart **b** (*fig: sich gliedern*) to divide up (*in +acc* into); **aus|ei|nan|der fal|ten** ▲ VT to unfold; **aus|ei|nan|der flie|gen** ▲ VI *irreg aux sein* to fly apart; (*nach allen Seiten*) to fly in all directions; **aus|ei|nan|der flie|ßen** ▲ VI *irreg aux sein* (*nach allen Seiten*) to flow in all directions; (= *zerfließen*) to run; **aus|ei|nan|der ge|hen** ▲ VI *irreg aux sein* **a** (*lit, fig: = sich trennen*) (*Menschen, Vorhang*) to part, to separate; (*Menge*) to disperse; (*Versammlung, Ehe etc*) to break up; (= *auseinander fallen: Schrank etc*) to fall apart **b** (= *sich verzweigen: Weg etc*) to divide, to branch, to fork; (*zwei Wege*) to diverge; (*fig: Ansichten etc*) to diverge, to differ **c** (*inf: = dick werden*) to get fat → **Hefeteig**; **aus|ei|nan|der hal|ten** ▲ VT *irreg* to keep apart; (= *unterscheiden*) *Begriffe* to distinguish between; *esp Zwillinge etc* to tell apart; **aus|ei|nan|der ja|gen** ▲ VT to scatter; **aus|ei|nan|der ken|nen** ▲ VT *irreg* (*inf*) to tell apart; **aus|ei|nan|der klaf|fen** ▲ VI *aux sein* to gape open; (*fig: Meinungen*) to be far apart, to diverge (wildly); **aus|ei|nan|der kla|mü|sern** ▲ VT (*dial, hum*) to sort out; **jdm etw ~** to spell sth out for sb; **aus|ei|nan|der klau|ben** ▲ VT (*esp S Ger, Aus, Sw*) to sort out; **aus|ei|nan|der krie|gen** ▲ VT (*inf*) to be able to get apart; **aus|ei|nan|der lau|fen** ▲ VI *irreg aux sein* **a** (= *zerlaufen*) to melt; (*Farbe*) to run; (= *sich ausbreiten*) to spread **b** (*inf: = sich trennen*) to break up; (*Menge*) to disperse; (= *sich auseinander entwickeln*) to go their separate ways **c** (*Wege*) to divide, to fork, to diverge; **aus|ei|nan|der le|ben** ▲ VR to drift apart (*mit* from); **aus|ei|nan|der ma|chen** ▲ VT (*inf*) **a** (= *auseinander nehmen*) to take apart **b** (= *auseinander falten*) to unfold **c** (= *spreizen*) *Arme, Beine* to spread (apart), to open; **aus|ei|nan|der neh-**

men ▲ VT irreg to take apart; Maschine etc auch to dismantle; (kritisch) to tear apart or to pieces; **aus|ei|nan|der pflü|cken** ▲ VT (lit, fig) to pick to pieces; **aus|ei|nan|der rei|ßen** ▲ VT irreg to tear or rip apart; (fig) Familie to tear apart; **aus|ei|nan|der schrau|ben** ▲ VT to unscrew; **aus|ei|nan|der set|zen** ▲ [VT] (fig) (jdm to sb) to explain; (schriftlich auch) to set out [VR] **sich mit etw ~** (= sich befassen) to have a good look at sth; **sich kritisch mit etw ~** to have a critical look at sth; **sich damit ~, was/ weshalb ...** to tackle the problem of what/why ...; **sich mit jdm ~** to talk or (sich streiten) to argue with sb; **sich mit jdm gerichtlich ~** to take sb to court

Aus|ei|nan|der|set|zung [aus|ai'nandɛzɛtsʊŋ] F -, -en a (= Diskussion) discussion, debate (über +acc about, on); (= Streit) argument; (= feindlicher Zusammenstoß) clash (wegen over) b (= das Befassen) examination (mit of); (kritisch) analysis (mit of)

aus|ei|nan|der: aus|ei|nan|der sprei|zen ▲ VT to open, to spread apart; **aus|ei|nan|der sprin|gen** ▲ VI irreg aux sein to shatter; **aus|ei|nan|der stie|ben** ▲ VI irreg aux sein to scatter; **aus|ei|nan|der stre|ben** ▲ VI aux sein (geh fig: Meinungen, Tendenzen) to diverge; **aus|ei|nan|der trei|ben** ▲ irreg [VT] (= trennen) to drive apart; (= auseinander jagen) to scatter; Demonstranten to disperse [VI] aux sein to drift apart; **aus|ei|nan|der zie|hen** ▲ irreg [VT] a (= dehnen) to stretch b (= trennen) to pull apart; Gardinen auch to pull open [VI] aux sein (= gemeinsame Wohnung aufgeben) to separate (and live apart) [VR] to spread out; (Kolonne auch) to string out

aus+er|kie|sen ptp **auserkoren** VT sep irreg (liter) to choose; (Gott) to ordain (liter); **zu etw auserkoren (worden) sein** to be chosen or selected for sth

aus|er|ko|ren ['aus|ɛɛko:rən] ADJ (liter) chosen, selected; **jds Auserkorene(r)** (hum) sb's intended (inf)

aus|er|le|sen [ADJ] (= ausgesucht) select; Speisen, Weine auch choice attr [PTP] **zu etw ~ (worden) sein** to be chosen or selected for sth [ADV] (verstärkend) particularly, especially

aus+er|se|hen ptp **ausersehen** VT sep irreg (geh) to choose; (für Amt auch) to designate (zu as); **dazu ~ sein, etw zu tun** to be chosen to do sth

aus+er|wäh|len ptp **auserwählt** VT sep (geh) to choose

aus|er|wählt ADJ (geh) chosen; (= ausgesucht) select; **das ~e Volk** the Chosen People

Aus|er|wähl|te(r) ['aus|ɛvɛ:ltə] MF decl as adj (geh) chosen one; **die ~n** the elect, the chosen (ones); **seine ~** (hum) his intended (Brit inf), the woman of his choice (US inf); **ihr ~r** (hum) her intended (Brit inf), the man of her choice (US inf)

aus+es|sen sep irreg [VT] Speise to eat up, to finish (eating); Schüssel to empty, to clear; Pampelmuse to eat [VI] to finish eating

aus+fä|deln VR sep sich ~ aus (Aut) to slip out of or from

aus|fahr|bar ADJ extensible, extendable; Antenne, Fahrgestell, Klinge retractable

aus+fah|ren sep irreg [VT] a jdn (im Kinderwagen) to take for a walk (in the pushchair (Brit) or stroller (US)); (im Rollstuhl) to take for a walk (in his/her wheelchair); (im Auto) to take for a drive or ride b (= ausliefern) Waren to deliver c (= abnutzen) Weg to rut, to wear out; **sich in ausgefahrenen Bahnen bewegen** (fig) to keep to well-trodden paths d (Aut) Kurve to (drive) round; (mit aux sein) Rennstrecke to drive round e (= austragen) Rennen to hold f **ein Auto etc (voll) ~** to drive a car etc flat out (esp Brit) or at full speed g (Tech) to extend; Fahrgestell etc to lower

[VI] aux sein a (= spazieren fahren) to go for a ride or (im Auto auch) drive; **mit dem Baby ~** to take the baby out in the pushchair (Brit) or stroller (US) b (abfahren) (Zug) to pull out (aus of), to leave; (Schiff) to put to sea, to sail; **aus dem Hafen ~** to sail out of the harbour (Brit) or harbor (US), to leave harbour (Brit) or harbor (US) c (Min: aus dem Schacht) to come up d (= Straße verlassen) to turn off, to leave a road/motorway (Brit) or highway (US) e (Tech: Fahrgestell, Gangway) to come out f (= eine heftige Bewegung machen) to gesture; **mit ~den Bewegungen** with expansive gestures g (böser Geist) to come out (aus of)

Aus|fah|rer(in) M(F) (Aus, S Ger) delivery man/woman

Aus|fahrt F a no pl (= Abfahrt) departure; (Min: aus Schacht) ascent (aus from); **der Zug hat keine ~** the train has not been cleared for departure b (= Spazierfahrt) drive, ride; **eine ~ machen** to go for a ride or (im Auto auch) drive c (= Ausgang, Autobahnausfahrt) exit; **~ Gütersloh** Gütersloh exit, exit for Gütersloh; **„Ausfahrt freihalten"** "keep clear"

Aus|fahrt(s)-: **Aus|fahrt(s)|schild** NT pl -schilder exit sign; **Aus|fahrt(s)|sig|nal** NT (Rail) departure signal; **Aus|fahrt(s)|stra|ße** F exit road

Aus|fall M a (= Verlust, Fehlbetrag, Mil) loss; (= das Versagen) (Tech, Med) failure; (von Motor) breakdown; (= Produktionsstörung) stoppage; **bei ~ des Stroms ...** in case of a power failure ... b no pl (= das Herausfallen) loss c no pl (von Sitzung, Unterricht etc) cancellation; **wir hatten einen hohen ~ an or von Schulstunden** a lot of school lessons were cancelled (Brit) or canceled (US) d no pl (= das Ausscheiden) dropping out; (im Rennen) retirement; (= Abwesenheit) absence e (Ling) dropping, omission f (Mil: = Ausbruch) sortie, sally g (Sport) (Fechten) thrust, lunge; (Gewichtheben) jerk h (fig: Angriff) attack

Aus|fall|bürg|schaft F (Fin: = Haftungssumme) security

aus+fal|len VI sep irreg aux sein a (= herausfallen) to fall out; (Chem) to be precipitated; (Ling) to be dropped or omitted; **mir fallen die Haare aus** my hair is falling out b (= nicht stattfinden) to be cancelled (Brit) or canceled (US); **etw ~ lassen** to cancel sth; **die Schule/die erste Stunde fällt morgen aus** there's no school/first lesson tomorrow c (= nicht funktionieren) to fail; (Motor) to break down d (= wegfallen: Verdienst) to be lost e (= ausscheiden) to drop out; (= fernbleiben) to be absent f **gut/schlecht etc ~** to turn out well/badly etc; **die Rede ist zu lang ausgefallen** the speech was too long, the speech turned out to be too long; **die Bluse fällt zu eng aus** the blouse is too tight g (Mil) to fall, to be lost (bei in); (old: = einen Ausfall machen) to make a sortie h (Fechten) to thrust, to lunge i **~ ausgefallen**

aus+fäl|len VT sep (Chem) to precipitate

aus|fal|lend, aus|fäl|lig ADJ abusive; **~ werden** to become abusive [ADV] abusively

Aus|fall|stra|ße F arterial road

Aus|fall(s)|win|kel M (Phys) angle of reflection

Aus|fall|zeit F (Insur) time which counts toward(s) pension although no payments were made

aus+fa|sern VI sep aux sein or haben to fray, to become frayed

aus+fech|ten VT sep irreg (fig) to fight (out)

aus+fe|gen VT sep Schmutz to sweep up; Zimmer to sweep out

aus+fei|len VT sep to file (out); (= glätten) to file down; (fig) to polish → auch ausgefeilt

aus+fer|ti|gen VT sep (form) a Dokument to draw up; Rechnung, Lieferschein to make out; Pass b (= unterzeichnen) to sign

Aus|fer|ti|gung F (form) a no pl (von Dokument) drawing up; (von Rechnung, Lieferschein) making out; (von Pass) issuing b (= Abschrift) copy; **die erste ~** the top copy; **ein Dokument in einfacher ~** one copy or a single copy of a document; **in doppelter/dreifacher ~** in duplicate/triplicate; **Zeugnisse in vierfacher etc ~** four etc copies of references

Aus|fer|ti|gungs|da|tum NT (von Pass, Urkunde) date of issue

aus+fin|dig ADJ **~ machen** to find, to discover; (= Aufenthaltsort feststellen) to locate, to trace

aus+fi|schen VT sep Karpfen etc to catch; Teich to fish dry or out

aus+flag|gen VT sep a Schiff (= schmücken) to dress; (= unter Billigflagge fahren lassen) to allow to sail under a flag of convenience b Weg, Piste to mark out (with flags)

aus+flen|nen VR sep (inf) = ausheulen VR

aus+flie|gen sep irreg [VI] aux sein (= wegfliegen) to fly away or off; (aus Gebiet etc) to fly out (aus of); (= flügge werden) to leave the nest; (fig inf: weggehen) to go out; **ausgeflogen sein** (fig inf) to be out, to have gone out; **der Vogel ist ausgeflogen** (fig inf) the bird has or is flown [VT] (Aviat) a Verwundete etc to evacuate (by air), to fly out (aus from) b Flugzeug to fly full out

aus+flie|sen VT sep to tile

aus+flie|ßen VI sep irreg aux sein (= herausfließen) to flow out (aus of); (Eiter etc) to be discharged; (= auslaufen: Öl etc, Fass) to leak (aus out of)

aus+flip|pen ['ausflipn] VI sep aux sein (inf) to freak out (inf) → auch ausgeflippt

aus+flo|cken ['ausflɔkn] VTI sep (vi: aux sein) (Chem) to precipitate

Aus|flucht ['ausflʊxt] F -, Ausflüchte [-flʏçtə] excuse; (geh: = Flucht) escape (in +acc into); **Ausflüchte machen** to make excuses; **keine Ausflüchte! (I want) no excuses!**

Aus|flug M trip, outing; (esp mit Reisebüro) excursion; (= Betriebsausflug, Schulausflug) outing; (= Wanderung) walk, hike; (fig) excursion; **einen ~ machen** to go on or for a trip etc; **einen ~ in die Politik machen** to make an excursion into politics b (von Vögeln etc) flight; (von Bienen) swarming c (am Bienenstock) hive exit

Aus|flüg|ler ['ausfly:glɐ] M -s, -, **Aus|flüg|le|rin** [-ərɪn] F -, -nen tripper; **Fahrkarte für ~** excursion ticket

Aus|flug|schnei|se F (Aviat) takeoff path

Aus|flugs-: **Aus|flugs|damp|fer** M pleasure steamer; **Aus|flugs|fahrt** F pleasure trip, excursion; **Aus|flugs|lo|kal** NT tourist café; (am Meer) seaside café; **Aus|flugs|ort** M -(e)s -orte place to go for an outing; **Aus|flugs|ver|kehr** M (an Feiertagen) holiday (esp Brit) or vacation (US) traffic; (am Wochenende) weekend holiday (esp Brit) or vacation (US) traffic; **Aus|flugs|ziel** NT destination (of one's outing)

Aus|fluss ▲ M a (= das Herausfließen) outflow; (= das Auslaufen) leaking b (= Ausflussstelle) outlet c (Med) discharge d (fig geh) product, result

aus+fol|gen VT sep (Aus form) to hand over (jdm to sb)

aus+for|men sep [VT] to mould (Brit), to mold (US), to shape (zu into); Manuskript etc to polish, to refine [VR] to take shape, to be formed

aus+for|mu|lie|ren ptp **ausformuliert** VT sep to formulate; Rede to tidy up

Aus|for|mung F **a** (= *das Formen*) moulding (*Brit*), molding (*US*), shaping; (*von Manuskript etc*) polishing, refining **b** (= *Form*) shape, form

aus+for|schen VT *sep* **a** *Sache* to find out; (= *erforschen*) to investigate **b** (*Aus*) *Täter* to apprehend

Aus|for|schung F **a** (= *Erforschung*) investigating **b** (= *Befragung*) questioning **c** (*Aus: von Täter*) apprehension

aus+fra|gen VT *sep* to question, to quiz (*inf*) (*nach* about); (*strenger*) to interrogate; **so fragt man die Leute aus** (*inf*) that would be telling (*inf*)

aus+fran|sen *sep* VIR (*vi: aux sein*) to fray, to become frayed VT to fray

aus+frat|scheln ['ausfraːtʃln] VT *sep* (*Aus inf*) to quiz (*inf*)

aus+fres|sen VT *sep irreg* **a** (= *auffressen*) to eat up **b** (= *ausspülen: Wasser, Fluss*) to erode, to eat away **c** (*inf: = anstellen*) **etwas ~** to do something wrong; **was hat er denn wieder ausgefressen?** what's he (gone and) done now? (*inf*)

Aus|fuhr ['ausfuːɐ] F **-, -en a** *no pl* (= *das Ausführen*) export; (= *Ausfuhrhandel*) exports *pl*
Ausfuhren PL (= *Ausfuhrgüter*) exports *pl*

Aus|fuhr- *in cpds* auch **Export-** export; **Aus|fuhr|ar|ti|kel** M export

aus|führ|bar ADJ **a** *Plan* feasible, practicable, workable; (*Comput*) *Programm* executable; **schwer ~** difficult to carry out **b** (*Comm*) exportable

Aus|führ|bar|keit ['ausfyːɐbaːɐkait] F **-,** *no pl* feasibility, practicability

Aus|fuhr-: Aus|fuhr|be|schrän|kung F export restriction; **Aus|fuhr|be|stim|mun|gen** PL export regulations *pl*; **Aus|fuhr|be|wil|li|gung** F export licence (*Brit*) or license (*US*) or permit

aus+füh|ren VT *sep* **a** (*zu Spaziergang, ins Theater etc*) to take out; *Hund* to take for a walk; (*hum*) *Kleid* to parade
b (= *durchführen*) *Anweisung* to carry out; *Aufgabe* to perform, to carry out; *Auftrag, Plan, Befehl, Bewegung* to execute, to carry out; *Operation* (*Mil*) to execute, to carry out; (*Med*) to perform, to carry out; *Gesetz* to implement; *Bauarbeiten* to undertake; (*Sport*) *Freistoß etc* to take; (*Comput*) *Programm* to execute **c** (= *gestalten*) *Plan, Entwurf, Bild etc* to execute **d** (= *erklären*) to explain; (= *darlegen*) to set out; (*argumentierend*) to argue; (= *sagen*) to say **e** (*Comm*) *Waren* to export

aus|füh|rend ADJ *Künstler* performing; *Organe* executive; **die ~e Baufirma** the firm carrying out the building work; **die ~e Gewalt** (*Pol*) the executive

Aus|füh|ren|de(r) ['ausfyːrəndə] MF *decl as adj*
a (= *Künstler*) performer **b** (= *Handelnder*) executive

Aus|fuhr-: Aus|fuhr|ge|neh|mi|gung F export licence (*Brit*) or license (*US*) or permit; **Aus|fuhr|gü|ter** PL export goods *pl*, exports *pl*; **Aus|fuhr|ha|fen** M port of exportation; **Aus|fuhr|han|del** M export trade; **Aus|fuhr|land** NT **a** (= *Land, das ausführt*) exporting country; **ein ~ für Jute** a jute-exporting country **b** (= *Land, in das ausgeführt wird*) export market

aus|führ|lich ['ausfyː(ɐ)lɪç, (*Aus*) aus'fyːɐlɪç] ADJ detailed; *Informationen, Gespräche, Katalog* auch full ADV in detail, in full; **sehr ~** in great detail; **~er** in more or greater detail

Aus|führ|lich|keit F **-,** *no pl* detail; **in aller ~** in (great) detail

Aus|fuhr-: Aus|fuhr|lis|te F export list; **Aus|fuhr|prä|mie** F export premium; **Aus|fuhr|quo|te** F export quota; **Aus|fuhr|sper|re** F export ban or embargo; **Aus|fuhr|über|schuss**
▲ M export surplus

Aus|füh|rung F **a** *no pl* (= *Durchführung*) carrying out; (*von Operation, Aufgabe*) performance, carrying out; (*von Auftrag, Plan, Befehl, Bewegung*)

execution, carrying out; (*von Gesetz*) implementation; (*von Freistoß*) taking; **zur ~ gelangen** or **kommen** to be carried out **b** (= *Gestaltung: von Plan, Entwurf, Bild*) execution **c** (= *Erklärung*) explanation; (*von Thema etc*) exposition; (= *Bemerkung*) remark; (*usu pl*: = *Bericht*) report **d** (*von Waren*) design; (*Tech*: = *äußere Ausführung*) finish; (= *Qualität*) quality; (= *Modell*) model

Aus|fuhr-: Aus|fuhr|ver|bot NT ban on exports, export embargo; **Aus|fuhr|vo|lu|men** NT volume of exports; **Aus|fuhr|wa|ren** PL exports *pl*, export goods *pl*; **Aus|fuhr|zoll** M export duty

aus+fül|len VT *sep* to fill; *Loch* to fill (up or out); *Ritze* to fill in; *Platz* to take up; *Formular* to fill in (*Brit*) or out; *Posten* to fill; **jdn (voll** or **ganz) ~** (= *befriedigen*) to give sb (complete) fulfilment (*Brit*) or fulfillment (*US*), to satisfy sb (completely); (= *Zeit in Anspruch nehmen*) to take (all) sb's time; **er füllt den Posten nicht/gut aus** he is not fitted/well-fitted for the position; **der Gedanke an dich füllt mich ganz aus** the thought of you occupies my every minute; **seine Zeit mit etw ~** to pass one's time doing sth, to fill up one's time with sth; **ein ausgefülltes Leben** a full life

aus+füt|tern VT *sep* (*Sew*) to line

Aus|ga|be F **a** *no pl* (= *Austeilung*) (*von Proviant, Decken etc*) distribution, giving out; (*von Befehl, Fahrkarten, Dokumenten etc*) issuing; (*von Essen*) serving **b** (= *Schalter*) issuing counter; (*in Bibliothek*) issue desk; (*in Kantine*) serving counter; (= *Stelle, Büro*) issuing office **c** (*von Buch, Zeitung, Sendung*) edition; (*von Zeitschrift*) edition, issue; (*von Aktien*) issue **d** (= *Ausführung*) version **e** (= *Geldaufwand*) expense, expenditure *no pl* / **Ausgaben** PL (= *Geldverbrauch*) expenditure *sing* (*für* on); (= *Kosten*) expenses *pl*, costs *pl* **f** (*Comput*) *= Ausdruck*) print-out; (*am Bildschirm*) output

Aus|ga|be-: Aus|ga|be|da|tei F (*Comput*) output file; **Aus|ga|be|da|ten** PL (*Comput*) output data; **Aus|ga|be|ge|rät** NT (*Comput*) output device; **Aus|ga|be|kurs** M (*Fin*) rate of issue

Aus|ga|ben-: Aus|ga|ben|be|gren|zung F limit on expenditure; **Aus|ga|ben|be|leg** M receipt for expenditure; **Aus|ga|ben|buch** NT cash-book; **Aus|ga|ben|kür|zung** F expenditure cut, cut in expenditure; **Aus|ga|ben|po|li|tik** F expenditure policy; **Aus|ga|ben|sei|te** F expenditure column

Aus|ga|be-: Aus|ga|be|schal|ter M issuing counter; (*in Bibliothek etc*) issue desk; **Aus|ga|be|ter|min** M date of issue

Aus|gang M *pl -gänge* **a** (= *Auslass, Weg nach draußen*) exit, way out (+*gen*, *von* from); (= *Dorfausgang*) end; (*von Wald*) edge; (*Med, von Organ*) opening (+*gen* out of); (*Aviat*) gate **b** (= *Erlaubnis zum Ausgehen*) permission to go out; (*Mil*) pass; **~ haben** to have the day off or (*am Abend*) the evening off; (*Mil*) to have a pass; **bis 10 Uhr ~ haben** to be allowed out/to have a pass till 10 o'clock **c** (= *Spaziergang*) walk (*under supervision*) **d** *no pl* (= *Ende*) end; (*esp von Epoche*) close; (*von Roman, Film*) ending, end; (= *Ergebnis*) outcome, result; **ein Unfall mit tödlichem ~** a fatal accident; **ein Ausflug mit tragischem ~** an excursion with a tragic outcome **e** *no pl* (= *Ausgangspunkt*) starting point; (*von Reise auch*) point of departure; (= *Anfang*) beginning; **von hier nahm diese weltweite Bewegung ihren ~** this was where this worldwide movement started **f** *no pl* (= *Abschicken von Post*) mailing, sending off **g Ausgänge** PL (*Post*) outgoing mail *sing*; (*Waren*) outgoing goods *pl*

aus|gangs ['ausgaŋs] PREP +*gen* at the end of; (*der Schlusskurve etc*) coming out of; **eine Frau ~ der Siebziger** a woman in her late seventies

ADV **~ (von) Hamburg** on the outskirts of Hamburg, just outside Hamburg

Aus|gangs-: Aus|gangs|ba|sis F starting point, basis; **Aus|gangs|fra|ge** F initial question; **Aus|gangs|la|ge** F initial or starting position; **Aus|gangs|ma|te|ri|al** NT source material; **Aus|gangs|po|si|ti|on** F initial or starting position; **Aus|gangs|punkt** M starting point; (*von Reise auch*) point of departure; **Aus|gangs|si|tu|a|ti|on** F starting or initial situation, point of departure; **Aus|gangs|sper|re** F ban on going out; (*esp bei Belagerungszustand*) curfew; (*für Soldaten*) confinement to barracks; **~ haben** (*Soldat*) to be confined to barracks; (*Schüler*) to be banned from going out, to be gated (*Brit*); **Aus|gangs|spra|che** F source language; **Aus|gangs|stel|lung** F (*Sport*) starting position; (*Mil*) initial position; **Aus|gangs|text** M (*einer Übersetzung*) source text; **Aus|gangs|tür** F exit (door); **Aus|gangs|ver|bot** NT = Ausgangssperre; **Aus|gangs|zei|le** F (*Typ*) club line, widow; **Aus|gangs|zu|stand** M initial or original condition; (= *Lage*) initial or original position; (*esp Pol*) status quo

aus+ge|ben *sep irreg* VT **a** (= *austeilen*) *Proviant, Decken etc* to distribute, to give out; (= *aushändigen*) *Dokumente, Fahrkarten, Aktien etc* to issue; *Befehl* to issue, to give; *Essen* to serve; (*Cards*) to deal; (= *ausdrucken*) *Text* to print out
b *Geld* to spend (*für* on); **eine Runde ~** to stand a round (*inf*); **ich gebe heute Abend einen aus** (*inf*) it's my treat this evening; **unser Chef hat einen ausgegeben** our boss treated us; **darf ich dir einen/einen Whisky ~?** may I buy you a drink/a whisky?; **er gibt nicht gern einen aus** he doesn't like buying people drinks **c jdn/etw als** or **für jdn/etw ~** to pass sb/sth off as sb/sth; **sich als jd/etw ~** to pose as sb/sth, to pass oneself off as sb/sth
VR (= *sein Geld ganz ausgeben*) to exhaust oneself; (= *sein Geld ganz ausgeben*) to spend all one's money

Aus|ge|beu|te|te(r) ['ausgəbɔytətə] MF *decl as adj* **die ~n** the exploited *pl*

aus|ge|brannt ADJ (*fig*) burned-out (*inf*); **geistig ~** mentally exhausted; **er ist ~** he's burned out (*inf*) → *auch* **ausbrennen**

aus|ge|bucht ['ausgəbuːxt] ADJ *Reise etc* booked up; (*inf*) *Person* booked up

Aus|ge|burt F (*pej*) (*der Fantasie etc*) monstrous product or invention; (= *Geschöpf, Kreatur, Institution*) monster; **der die Hölle** a fiend from hell, a fiendish monster; **sie ist eine ~ von Eitelkeit und Dummheit** she is a monstrous combination of vanity and stupidity

aus|ge|dehnt ['ausgədeːnt] ADJ *Gummiband* (over)stretched; (= *breit, groß, fig*: = *weitreichend*) extensive; (*zeitlich*) lengthy, extended; *Spaziergang* long, extended → *auch* **ausdehnen**

aus|ge|dient ADJ (*inf*: = *unbrauchbar*) *Auto, Maschine* clapped-out (*Brit inf*), worn-out (*inf*); **meine ~en Sachen/Bücher** *etc* the things/books *etc* I don't have any further use for → *auch* **ausdienen**

aus|ge|dörrt ['ausgədœrt] ADJ dried up; *Boden, Kehle* parched; *Pflanzen* shrivelled (*Brit*), shriveled (*US*); *Land, Gebiet* arid; (*fig*) *Hirn* ossified, dull; **mein Hirn ist völlig ~** (*fig*) I can't think straight any more → *auch* **ausdörren**

aus|ge|fal|len ['ausgəfalən] ADJ **a** *Unterrichtsstunde etc* cancelled (*Brit*), canceled (*US*) **b** (= *ungewöhnlich*) unusual; (= *übertrieben*) extravagant; *Mensch* eccentric; (= *überspannt*) odd, weird → *auch* **ausfallen**

Aus|ge|fal|len|heit F **-, -en a** (= *Ungewöhnlichkeit*) unusualness **b** (= *Übertriebenheit*) extravagance; (*von Mensch*) eccentricity; (= *Überspanntheit*) oddness, weirdness

aus|ge|feilt ['ausgəfailt] ADJ (*fig*) polished; *Schrift* stylized → *auch* **ausfeilen**

Aus|ge|feilt|heit F **-,** *no pl* (*von Stil*) polished nature, polish

aus|ge|flippt ['ausgəflɪpt] ADJ (inf) freaky (inf), freaked-out (inf), flipped-out (inf); (aus der Gesellschaft) dropout (inf); **er ist ein richtig ~er Typ** he's really freaky (inf), he's a real dropout (inf) → auch **ausflippen**

Aus|ge|flipp|te(r) ['ausgəflɪptə] MF decl as adj (inf) freak (inf); (aus der Gesellschaft) dropout (inf)

aus|ge|fuchst ['ausgəfʊkst] ADJ (inf) clever; (= listig) crafty (inf); Kartenspieler cunning

aus|ge|gli|chen ['ausgəglɪçn] ADJ balanced; Spiel, Klima even; Torverhältnis equal; (= gleich bleibend) consistent → auch **ausgleichen**

Aus|ge|gli|chen|heit F -, no pl balance; (von Spiel, Klima) evenness; **ihre ~** her even nature

aus|ge|go|ren ['ausgəgo:rən] ADJ Most fully fermented; (fig inf) Pläne worked out; **wenig ~** half-baked (inf)

aus+ge|hen sep irreg aux sein **VI** **a** (= weggehen, zum Vergnügen) to go out; (= spazieren gehen) to go out (for a walk); **er geht selten aus** he doesn't go out much; **wir gehen heute Abend ganz groß aus** we're going out for a big celebration tonight
b (= ausfallen: Haare, Federn, Zähne) to fall out; (Farbe) to run; (dial: Stoff) to fade; **ihm gehen die Haare aus** his hair is falling out; **ihm gehen die Zähne aus** he is losing his teeth
c (= seinen Ausgang nehmen) to start (von at); (= herrühren: Idee, Anregung etc) to come (von from); **von dem Platz gehen vier Straßen aus** four streets lead or go off (from) the square; **etw geht von jdm/etw aus** (= wird ausgestrahlt) sb/sth radiates sth; **von der Rede des Ministers ging eine große Wirkung aus** the minister's speech had a great effect
d (= abgeschickt werden: Post) to be sent off; **die ~de Post** the outgoing mail
e (= zugrunde legen) to start out (von from); **gehen wir einmal davon aus, dass ...** let us assume that ..., let us start from the assumption that ...; **wovon gehst du bei dieser Behauptung aus?** on what are you basing your statement?; **davon kann man nicht ~** you can't go by that
f auf etw (acc) ~ to be intent on sth; **auf Gewinn ~** to be intent on making a profit; **auf Eroberungen ~** (hum inf) to be out to make a few conquests
g (= einen bestimmten Ausgang haben: esp Sport) to end; (= ausfallen) to turn out; **gut/schlecht ~** to turn out well/badly; (Film etc) to end happily/unhappily; (Abend, Spiel) to end well/badly
h (Ling: = enden) to end
i **straffrei** or **straflos ~** to receive no punishment, to get off scot-free (inf); **leer ~** (inf) to come away empty-handed
j (= zu Ende sein: Vorräte etc) to run out; (dial: Vorstellung, Schule etc) to finish; **mir ging die Geduld aus** I lost (my) patience; **mir ging das Geld aus** I ran out of money; **ihm ist die Luft** or **die Puste** or **der Atem ausgegangen** (inf) (lit) he ran out of breath or puff (Brit inf); (fig) he ran out of steam (inf); (finanziell) he ran out of funds
k (= aufhören zu brennen) to go out
l (inf: = sich ausziehen lassen) to come off; **die nassen Sachen gehen so schwer aus** these wet things are so hard to take off
VR (Aus) **es geht sich aus** it works out all right; (Vorräte, Geld etc) there is enough

aus|ge|hend ADJ attr **im ~en Mittelalter** toward(s) the end of the Middle Ages; **das ~e 20. Jahrhundert** the end or close of the 20th century

Aus|geh|er|laub|nis F permission to go out; (Mil) pass

aus|ge|hun|gert ['ausgəhʊŋɐt] ADJ starved; (= abgezehrt) Mensch etc emaciated; **wie ~e Wölfe** like starving wolves; **nach etw ~ sein** (fig) to be starved of sth → auch **aushungern**

Aus|geh-: Aus|geh|uni|form F walking-out uniform; **Aus|geh|ver|bot** NT jdm ~ **erteilen** to forbid sb to go out; (Mil) to confine sb to

---

barracks; **~ haben/bekommen** to be forbidden to go out; (Mil) to be confined to barracks

aus|ge|klü|gelt ['ausgəkly:glt] ADJ (inf) System cleverly thought-out; (= genial) ingenious → auch **ausklügeln**

aus|ge|kocht ['ausgəkɔxt] ADJ (pej inf) (= durchtrieben) cunning; **er ist ein ~er Bursche** he's a thoroughly bad character → auch **auskochen**

aus|ge|las|sen ['ausgəlasn] ADJ (= heiter) lively; Stimmung happy; (= wild) Kinder boisterous; Stimmung, Party mad **ADV** wildly, boisterously; **dort geht es ~ zu** things are wild there → auch **auslassen**

Aus|ge|las|sen|heit F (= Heiterkeit) liveliness; (= Wildheit: von Kindern) boisterousness

aus|ge|las|tet ['ausgəlastət] ADJ Mensch fully occupied; Maschine, Anlage working to capacity; **mit dem Job ist er nicht (voll)** ~ he is not fully stretched in that job (esp Brit), he is not working at his full capacity in that job; **mit den vier Kindern ist sie voll ~** her four children keep her fully occupied, she has her hands full with her four children; **unsere Kapazitäten sind voll ~** we're working at full capacity → auch **auslasten**

aus|ge|latscht ['ausgəla:tʃt] ADJ (inf) Schuhe worn; **meine Schuhe sind völlig ~** my shoes have gone completely out of shape

aus|ge|lei|ert ['ausgəlaiɐt] ADJ Gummiband, Gewinde, Feder worn; Hosen, Pullover baggy; Redensart hackneyed (Brit), trite → auch **ausleiern**

aus|ge|lernt ['ausgəlɛrnt] ADJ (inf) qualified → auch **auslernen**

aus|ge|le|sen ['ausgəle:zn] ADJ (fig geh) Ware select, choice → auch **auslesen**

Aus|ge|lie|fert|sein ['ausgəli:fɐtzain] NT subjection (an +acc to); **unser ~ an die Gesellschaft** the fact that we are at the mercy of society

aus|ge|lutscht ['ausgəlʊtʃt] ADJ (lit, fig inf: = alt, verbraucht) Kaugummi, Floskel stale; Technik, Witz old hat pred (inf); Thema, Streit stale → auch **auslutschen**

aus|ge|macht ADJ **a** (= abgemacht) agreed; **es ist eine ~e Sache, dass ...** it is agreed that ...
b attr (inf: = vollkommen) complete, utter → auch **ausmachen**

aus|ge|mer|gelt ['ausgəmɛrglt] ADJ Körper, Gesicht, Tier emaciated → auch **ausmergeln**

aus|ge|nom|men ['ausgənɔmən] CONJ except, apart from; **niemand/alle, ~ du** or **dich ~** no-one/everyone except (for) you or apart from yourself or save yourself; **täglich ~ sonntags** daily except for or excluding Sundays; **~ wenn/dass ...** except when/that ... → auch **ausnehmen**

aus|ge|picht ['ausgəpɪçt] ADJ (inf) (= raffiniert) Mensch, Plan cunning; (= verfeinert) Geschmack refined

aus|ge|po|wert ['ausgəpauɐt] ADJ (inf) Mensch washed-out (inf), done in (inf) → auch **auspowern²**

aus|ge|prägt ['ausgəprɛ:kt] ADJ Gesicht distinctive; Eigenschaft, Charakter auch distinct; Interesse marked, pronounced; **ein (stark) ~er Sinn für alles Schöne** a well-developed sense for everything beautiful → auch **ausprägen**

Aus|ge|prägt|heit F -, no pl distinctiveness

aus|ge|pumpt ['ausgəpʊmpt] ADJ (inf) whacked (Brit inf), worn-out (inf) → auch **auspumpen**

aus|ge|rech|net ['ausgərɛçnət] ADV **~ du/er** etc you/he etc of all people; **~ mir muss das passieren** why does it have to happen to me (of all people)?; **~ heute/gestern** today/yesterday of all days; **muss das ~ heute sein?** does it have to be today (of all days)?; **~ jetzt kommt er** he would have to come just now; **~ dann kam er** he would have to come just at that moment; **~, als wir spazieren gehen wollten, ...** just when

---

we wanted to go for a walk ... → auch **ausrechnen**

aus|ge|schamt ['ausgəʃa:mt] ADJ (dial) = **unverschämt**

aus|ge|schlos|sen ADJ pred (= unmöglich) impossible; (= nicht infrage kommend) out of the question; **es ist nicht ~, dass ...** it's just possible that ...; **diese Möglichkeit ist nicht ~** it's not impossible; **jeder Irrtum ist ~** there is no possibility of a mistake → auch **ausschließen**

aus|ge|schnit|ten ['ausgəʃnɪtn] ADJ Bluse, Kleid low-cut; **sie geht heute tief ~** (inf) she's wearing a very low-cut dress/blouse etc today; **ein weit** or **tief ~es Kleid** a dress with a plunging neckline → auch **ausschneiden**

aus|ge|spielt ['ausgəʃpi:lt] ADJ **~ haben** to be finished; **er hat bei mir ~** (inf) he's had it as far as I am concerned (inf), I'm finished or through with him → auch **ausspielen**

aus|ge|spro|chen ['ausgəʃprɔxn] **ADJ** (= besonders) Schönheit, Qualität, Vorliebe definite; (= ausgeprägt) Trinkernase etc pronounced; Begabung particular; Ähnlichkeit marked; Geiz, Großzügigkeit extreme; (= groß) Pech, Freundlichkeit, Hilfsbereitschaft etc real; **eine ~e Frohnatur** a very sunny person; **ein ~er Chauvi** (inf) an out-and-out male chauvinist; **~es Pech haben** to have really bad luck, to be really unlucky **ADV** really; schön, begabt, groß, hilfsbereit etc auch extremely; geizig, frech etc auch terribly → auch **aussprechen**

aus|ge|spro|che|ner|ma|ßen ['ausgəʃprɔxnə'ma:sn] ADV = **ausgesprochen ADV**

aus+ge|stal|ten ptp **ausgestaltet** VT sep (künstlerisch, musikalisch) to arrange; (= planend gestalten) to organize; (= dekorieren, einrichten) to decorate; (= ausbauen) Theorie, Begriff, Methode to build up; **Bücher künstlerisch ~** to do the art work for books

Aus|ge|stal|tung F **a** (künstlerisch, musikalisch) arranging; (= Planung) organizing; (= Einrichtung, Dekoration) decorating; (von Theorie, Begriff, Methode) building up **b** (= Gestalt, Form) form

aus|ge|stellt ADJ Rock etc flared → auch **ausstellen**

aus|ge|stor|ben ['ausgəʃtɔrbn] ADJ Tierart extinct; (fig) deserted; **der Park war wie ~** the park was deserted → auch **aussterben**

Aus|ge|sto|ße|ne(r) ['ausgəʃto:snə] MF decl as adj outcast

aus|ge|sucht **ADJ** **a** (= besonders groß) extreme, exceptional **b** (= erlesen) Wein, Aktien choice, select; Gesellschaft select; Worte well-chosen **ADV** (= überaus, sehr) extremely, exceptionally → auch **aussuchen**

aus|ge|tre|ten ['ausgətre:tn] ADJ Schuhe well-worn; Pfad well-trodden; Stufe worn down; **~e Wege gehen** (fig) to tread a beaten track → auch **austreten**

aus|ge|wach|sen ADJ fully grown; (inf) Blödsinn utter, complete; Skandal huge → auch **auswachsen**

aus|ge|wählt ADJ select; Satz etc well-chosen; Werke selected → auch **auswählen**

Aus|ge|wan|der|te(r) ['ausgəvandɐtə] MF decl as adj emigrant

aus|ge|wie|sen ['ausgəvi:zn] ADJ **a** (= namhaft) well-known, renowned **b** (Sw: = nachgewiesen) identified; Fachmann qualified → auch **ausweisen**

Aus|ge|wie|se|ne(r) ['ausgəvi:znə] MF decl as adj expellee

aus|ge|wo|gen ['ausgəvo:gn] ADJ balanced; Maß equal; **ein ~es Kräfteverhältnis** a balance of powers → auch **ausweisen**

Aus|ge|wo|gen|heit F balance

aus|ge|zeich|net **ADJ** excellent **ADV** excellently; **sie kann ~ schwimmen/tanzen** she is an excellent swimmer/dancer; **es geht mir ~** I'm feeling marvellous (Brit) or marvelous (US) → auch **auszeichnen**

---

aus|gie|big [ˈausgiːbɪç] **ADJ** *Mahlzeit etc* substantial, large; *Mittagsschlaf, Gespräch* (good) long; *Gebrauch* extensive; **~en Gebrauch von etw machen** to make full *or* good use of sth **ADV** **~ frühstücken** to have a substantial breakfast; **~ schlafen/schwimmen** to have a (good) long sleep/swim; **~ einkaufen** to buy a lot of things; **etw ~ gebrauchen** to use sth extensively

Aus|gie|big|keit F **-**, *no pl* **in aller ~ frühstücken** to have a substantial breakfast; **in aller ~ schlafen/baden** to have a (good) long sleep/bath; **in aller ~ die Zeitung lesen** to take one's time reading the newspaper

aus|gie|ßen VT *sep irreg* **a** *(aus einem Behälter)* to pour out; (= *weggießen*) to pour away; *Behälter* to empty; (= *verschütten*) to spill; (= *über jdn/etw gießen*) to pour *(über +acc* over); **seinen Spott über jdn ~** (*geh*) to pour scorn on sb (*esp Brit*); **seinen Hohn über jdn ~** (*geh*) to mock sb **b** (= *füllen*) *Gussform* to fill; *Ritzen, Fugen* to fill in

Aus|gleich [ˈausglaɪç] M **-(e)s**, *(rare)* **-e a** (= *Gleichgewicht*) balance; *(von Konto)* balancing; *(von Schulden)* settling; *(von Verlust, Fehler, Mangel)* compensation; *(von Abweichung, Unterschieden)* balancing out; *(von Meinungsverschiedenheiten, Konflikten)* evening out; **zum** *or* **als ~ für etw** in order to compensate for sth; **er treibt zum ~ Sport** he does sport for exercise; **Tennisspielen ist für mich ein guter ~** I like playing tennis, it gives me a change; **wenn er ins Ausland geht, bekommt sie zum ~ ein Auto** when he goes abroad, she gets a car to even things out; **dieses Jahr fährt es zum ~ ans Meer** this year he's going to the seaside for a change; **zum ~ Ihres Kontos** to balance your account **b** *no pl (Ballspiele)* equalizer *(Brit)*, tie; *(Tennis)* deuce

aus|glei|chen *sep irreg* **VT** *Ungleichheit, Unterschiede* to even out; *Unebenheit* to level out; *Konto* to balance; *Schulden* to settle; *Verlust, Fehler* to make good; *Mangel* to compensate for; *Meinungsverschiedenheiten, Konflikte* to reconcile; **etw durch etw ~** to compensate for sth with sth/by doing sth; **~de Gerechtigkeit** poetic justice → *auch* **ausgeglichen** **VI a** *(Sport)* to equalize; **zum 1:1 ~** to equalize the score at 1 all *(Brit)*, to even up the score to 1 all *(US)* **b** (= *vermitteln*) to act as a mediator; **~des Wesen** conciliatory manner **VR** to balance out; *(Einnahmen und Ausgaben)* to balance; **das gleicht sich wieder aus** it balances itself out; **das gleicht sich dadurch aus, dass ...** it's balanced out by the fact that ...

Ausgleichs-: **Aus|gleichs|ab|ga|be** F *(Jur)* countervailing duty *or* charge; **Aus|gleichs|fonds** [-fõː] M *(Econ)* equalization fund; **Aus|gleichs|for|de|rung** F equalization claim; **Aus|gleichs|ge|trie|be** NT *(Tech)* differential gear; **Aus|gleichs|gym|nas|tik** F exercises *pl*; **Aus|gleichs|leis|tung** F *(Jur)* compensatory payment; **Aus|gleichs|sport** M keep-fit activity; **als ~** to keep fit; **Aus|gleichs|tor** NT, **Aus|gleichs|tref|fer** M equalizer *(Brit)*, equalizing *(Brit)* *or* tying *(US)* goal; **Aus|gleichs|zah|lung** F compensation

aus|glei|ten VI *sep irreg aux sein* **a** (= *ausrutschen*) to slip *(auf +dat* on); **es ist ihm ausgeglitten** it slipped from his hands *or* grasp **b** *(Boot, Skifahrer)* to coast in

aus|glie|dern VT *sep* to exclude

Aus|glie|de|rung F exclusion; *(Econ: einer Firma)* spin-off, hiving off *(Brit)*

aus|glit|schen VI *sep aux sein* (= *ausrutschen*) to slip *(auf +dat* on)

aus|glü|hen VT *sep (Tech) Metall* to anneal; *(Med)* to sterilize *(by heating)*

aus|gra|ben VT *sep irreg* to dig up; *Grube, Loch* to dig out; *Altertümer* to excavate; *(fig)* to dig up; (= *hervorholen*) *alte Geschichten* to bring up

Aus|gra|bung F (= *das Ausgraben*) excavation; *(Ort)* excavation site; (= *Fund*) (archaeological *(Brit)* *or* archeological *(US)*) find

Aus|gra|bungs-

Aus|gra|bungs|fund M archaeological *(Brit)* *or* archeological *(US)* find

Aus|gra|bungs|ort M , **Aus|gra|bungs|stät|te** F excavation site, (archaeological *(Brit)* *or* archeological *(US)*) dig

aus+grä|ten [ˈausgrɛːtn] VT *sep Fisch* to fillet, to bone

aus+grei|fen VI *sep irreg (Pferd)* to lengthen its stride; *(beim Gehen)* to stride out; *(fig: Redner)* to go far afield; **weit ~d** *(Schritte)* long, lengthy; *Bewegung* striding

aus+gren|zen VT *sep* to exclude

Aus|gren|zung F **-**, **-en** exclusion

aus|grün|den VT *sep (Econ)* to establish

Aus|guck [ˈausgʊk] M **-(e)s**, **-e** lookout; **~ halten** to keep a lookout

aus+gu|cken *sep (inf)* **VI a** (= *Ausschau halten*) to look out *(nach* for) **b** (= *auskundschaften*) to have a look **VI** *(suchend)* **sich** *(dat)* **die Augen nach jdm ~** to look everywhere for sb **b** (= *aussuchen, entdecken*) **sich** *(dat)* **jdn ~** to set one's sights on sb, to pick sb out

Aus|guss ▲ M **a** (= *Becken*) sink; (= *Abfluss*) drain; *(dial: = ausgegossene Flüssigkeit)* waste *(water etc)*; (= *Tülle*) spout **b** *(Tech)* tap hole

Aus|guss|be|cken ▲ NT sink

aus+ha|ben *sep irreg (inf)* **VT** (= *fertig sein mit*) *Buch, Essen etc* to have finished; (= *ausgezogen haben*) to have taken off **VI** *(Arbeit, Schule etc:* = *beendet haben)* to finish

aus+ha|cken VT *sep* **a** *Unkraut* to hoe; *Rüben etc* to hoe out **b** *(Vogel) Augen* to peck out; *Federn* to tear out → **Krähe**

aus+ha|ken *sep* **a** *Fensterladen, Kette* to unhook; *Reißverschluss* to undo **VI** *(inf)* **es hat bei ihm ausgehakt** (= *nicht begreifen*) he gave up *(inf)*; (= *wild werden*) something in him snapped *(inf)* **VR** *(Reißverschluss)* to come undone

aus+hal|ten *sep irreg* **VT a** (= *ertragen können*) to bear, to stand, to endure; (= *standhalten*) *Gewicht etc* to bear; *Druck* to stand, to withstand; *jds Blick* to return; **den Vergleich mit etw ~** to bear comparison with sth; **es lässt sich ~** it's bearable; **hier lässt es sich ~** this is not a bad place; **das ist nicht auszuhalten** *or* **zum Aushalten** it's unbearable; **ich halte es vor Hitze/zu Hause nicht mehr aus** I can't stand the heat/being at home any longer; **er hält es in keiner Stellung lange aus** he never stays in one job for long; **wie kann man es bei der Firma bloß ~?** how can anyone stand working for that firm?; **es bis zum Ende ~** *(auf Party etc)* to stay until the end; **hältst du es nicht bis zur nächsten Tankstelle aus?** *(inf)* can you hold out till the next garage?; **er hält viel aus** he can take a lot; **er hält nicht viel aus** he can't take much; **ein Stoff, der viel ~ muss** a material which has to take a lot of wear (and tear) **b** *Ton* to hold **c** *(inf: = unterhalten)* to keep; **sich von jdm ~ lassen** to be kept by sb **VI a** (= *durchhalten*) to hold out; **hältst du noch aus?** can you hold out (any longer)? **b** **auf einem Ton ~** to hold a note

aus+häm|mern VT *sep Beule* to hammer out; *Gefäß* to beat out

aus+han|deln VT *sep Vertrag, Lösung* to negotiate; *bessere Bedingungen, höhere Löhne* to negotiate for; *(erfolgreich)* to negotiate

aus+hän|di|gen [ˈaushɛndɪgn] VT *sep* **jdm etw ~** to hand sth over to sb; **jdm einen Preis ~** to give sb a prize; **wann können Sie mir die Ware ~?** when can you deliver (the goods)?

Aus|hän|di|gung F **-**, **-en** handing over; *(von Gütern etc)* delivery; **nach ~ seiner Papiere** after his papers had been handed over to him; **die ~**

der Preise nimmt der Direktor vor the headmaster will be giving out the prizes

Aus|hang M (= *Bekanntmachung*) notice, announcement; (= *das Aushängen*) posting; **etw durch ~ bekannt geben** to put up a notice about sth; **etw im ~ lesen** to read a notice of *or* about sth

Aus|hän|ge|kas|ten M (glass-fronted) notice *(Brit)* *or* bulletin *(US)* board

aus+hän|gen *sep* **VT a** (= *bekannt machen*) *Nachricht etc* to put up; *Plakat* to post, to put up; (= *ausstellen*) to show **b** (= *herausheben*) *Tür* to unhinge; *Haken* to unhook **VI** *irreg (Anzeige, Aufgebot)* to have been put up; *(inf: Brautleute)* to have the banns up *(Brit)*, to have the official wedding notice up *(US)*; **am schwarzen Brett ~** to be on the notice *(Brit)* *or* bulletin *(US)* board **VR** (= *sich glätten: Falten, Locken*) to drop out; **das Kleid wird sich ~** the creases will drop *or* hang out of the dress

Aus|hän|ger M *(von Buch)* folded section

Aus|hän|ge|schild NT *pl* **-schilder** *(lit: = Reklametafel)* sign; *(fig: = Reklame)* advertisement

aus+har|ren VI *sep (geh)* to wait; **auf seinem Posten ~** to stand by one's post *(Brit)*, to stay at one's post *(US)*

aus+hau|chen VT *sep (geh) Luft, Atem, Rauch* to exhale; *(fig) Worte, Seufzer* to breathe; (= *ausströmen*) *Geruch, Dünste* to emit; **sein Leben ~** to breathe one's last (breath)

aus+hau|en VT *sep irreg* **a** *Loch, Stufen* to cut out; *Weg, Durchgang* to hew out **b** (= *roden*) *Wald, Weinberg* to clear; (= *einzelne Bäume fällen*) to cut down; (= *Zweige entfernen*) to prune

aus|häu|sig [ˈaushɔyzɪç] ADJ (= *außer Haus*) outside the home; (= *unterwegs*) away from home; **du warst doch letzte Woche wieder ~?** you were out gallivanting again last week, weren't you?

aus+he|beln [ˈausheːbln] VT *sep (form)* to annul, to cancel

aus+he|ben VT *sep irreg* **a** *Tür etc* to take off its hinges; **sich** *(dat)* **die Schulter ~** *(dial inf)* to put out one's shoulder *(inf)* **b** *Erde* to dig out; *Graben, Grab* to dig **c** *Vogelnest* to rob; *Vogeleier, Vogeljunge* to steal; *(fig) Diebesnest* to raid; *Bande* to make a raid on; *(Aus: = leeren) Briefkasten* to empty **d** *(old) Truppen* to levy *(old)*

Aus|he|bung F *(old: von Truppen)* levying

aus+he|cken [ˈaushɛkn] VT *sep (inf) Plan* to cook up *(inf)*, to hatch; **neue Streiche ~** to think up new tricks

aus+hei|len *sep* **VT** *Krankheit* to cure; *Organ, Wunde* to heal **VI** *aux sein (Krankheit)* to be cured; *(Organ, Wunde)* to heal **VR** to recover

Aus|hei|lung F *(von Organ, Wunde)* healing; **nach völliger ~ der Krankheit** after a complete recovery from the illness; **nach völliger ~ der Wunde** after the wound is completely healed

aus+hel|fen VI *sep irreg* to help out *(jdm* sb)

aus+heu|len *sep (inf)* **VI** (= *aufhören*) to stop crying; *(Sirene)* to stop sounding **VR** to have a good cry; **sich bei jdm ~** to have a good cry on sb's shoulder

Aus|hil|fe F **a** help, aid; (= *Notbehelf*) temporary *or* makeshift substitute; **jdn zur ~ haben** to have sb to help out; **Stenotypistin zur ~ gesucht** shorthand typist wanted for temporary work **b** *(Mensch)* temporary worker; *(esp im Büro)* temp *(inf)*; **als ~ arbeiten** to help out; *(im Büro auch)* to temp *(inf)*

Aushilfs-: **Aus|hilfs|ar|beit** F temporary work, temporary jobs *pl*; **Aus|hilfs|job** M temporary job; *(im Büro)* temping job; **Aus|hilfs|kell|ner** M stand-in waiter; **Aus|hilfs|kell|ne|rin** F stand-in waitress; **Aus|hilfs|koch** M , **Aus|hilfs|kö|chin** F stand-in cook; **Aus|hilfs|kraft** F temporary worker; *(esp im Büro)* temp *(inf)*; **Aus|hilfs|leh|rer(in)** M(F) supply *(Brit)* *or* substitute *(US)* teacher; **Aus|hilfs|per|so|nal** NT temporary staff;

Aus|hilfs|tä|tig|keit F temporary job; **aus|hilfs|wei|se** ADV on a temporary basis; (= vorübergehend) temporarily; **sie kocht ab und zu ~** she sometimes cooks to help out

aus+höh|len ['aushø:lən] VT sep to hollow out; Ufer, Steilküste to erode; (fig) (= untergraben) to undermine; (= erschöpfen) to weaken

Aus|höh|lung F **a** (= ausgehöhlte Stelle) hollow **b** no pl (= das Aushöhlen) hollowing out; (von Ufer, Steilküste) erosion; (fig: = Untergrabung) undermining

aus+ho|len VI sep **a** (zum Schlag) to raise one's hand/arm etc; (zum Wurf) to reach back; (mit Schläger, Boxer) to take a swing; **weit ~** (zum Schlag, beim Tennis) to take a big swing; (zum Wurf) to reach back a long way; (fig: Redner) to go far afield; **bei einer Erzählung weit ~** to go a long way back in a story; **mit dem Arm/Hand zum Wurf/Schlag ~** to raise one's arm/hand ready to throw/strike; **zum Gegenschlag ~** (lit, fig) to prepare for a counterattack **b** (= ausgreifen) to stride out; **er ging mit weit ~den Schritten** he walked with long strides

aus+hor|chen VT sep (inf) jdn to sound out

aus+hül|sen ['aushʏlzn] VT sep Erbsen to shell, to pod

aus+hun|gern VT sep to starve out → auch **ausgehungert**

aus+hus|ten sep VT to cough up VI (= zu Ende husten) to finish coughing; (Schleim/Blut aushusten) to cough up phlegm/blood VR to finish coughing; **er hustete sich aus, bis ...** he coughed and coughed until ...

aus+ixen ['aus|ɪksn] VT sep (inf) to cross or ex out

aus+jam|mern VR sep to have a good moan, to gripe (inf)

aus+jä|ten VT sep Blumenbeet to weed; **im Garten Unkraut ~** to weed the garden

aus+käm|men VT sep **a** (= entfernen) Staub, Haare to comb out **b** (= frisieren) to comb out **c** (fig: = durchsuchen) to comb

aus+ke|geln sep VT **den Pokal ~** to bowl for the cup VI to finish bowling

aus+keh|ren sep VT Schmutz to sweep away; Zimmer to sweep out VI to do the sweeping

aus+kei|len VI sep **a** (= ausschlagen) to kick out **b** (= keilförmig auslaufen) to taper off

aus+kei|men VI sep aux sein (Getreide) to germinate; (Kartoffeln) to sprout

aus+ken|nen VR sep irreg (an einem Ort) to know one's way around; (auf einem Gebiet) to know a lot (auf or in +dat about); **sich in der Stadt ~** to know one's way around the town; **sich bei Männern/Frauen (gut) ~** to know (a lot) about men/women; **man kennt sich bei ihm nie aus** you never know where you are with him

aus+ker|nen ['auskɛrnən] VT sep Obst to stone (Brit), to remove the pit of (US)

aus+kip|pen VT sep (inf) to empty (out); Flüssigkeit to pour out

aus+klam|mern VT sep Problem to leave aside, to ignore; (Math) Zahl to put outside the brackets

aus+kla|mü|sern ptp **ausklamüsert** VT sep (inf) to work out

Aus|klang M (geh) conclusion, end; (esp Mus) finale; **zum ~ des Abends ...** to conclude the evening ...

aus|klapp|bar ADJ folding; Blatt fold-out; **dieser Tisch ist ~** this table can be opened out; **diese Fußstütze ist ~** this footrest can be pulled out

aus+klap|pen VT sep to open out; Fußstütze etc to pull out

aus+klau|ben VT sep (dial) to pick out, to sort out; Erz to select

aus+klei|den sep VT **a** (geh: = entkleiden) to undress **b** (= beziehen) to line VR (geh) to get undressed

Aus|klei|dung F lining

aus+klin|gen VI sep irreg **a** (Glocken) to finish ringing **b** aux sein (Lied) to finish; (Abend, Feier etc) to end (in +dat with); **die Verhandlungen klangen in die hoffnungsvolle Note aus, dass ...** the negotiations ended on the hopeful note that ...; **das ~de Jahrhundert** (geh) the close of the century

aus+klin|ken ['ausklɪŋkn] sep VT Scanner, Bombe, Seil to release VI (= innerlich abschalten) to switch off VR (= sich zurückziehen, nicht mehr mitmachen) to withdraw; **sich aus etw ~** to withdraw from sth; aus dem Alltag, dem Beruf to get away from sth; aus dem Solidaritätsprinzip to reject sth; **sich aus seiner Zeit ~** to reject modern technology

aus+klop|fen VT sep Teppich to beat; Pfeife to knock out; Kleider to beat the dust out of

Aus|klop|fer M carpet beater

aus+klü|geln VT sep to work out → auch **ausgeklügelt**

aus+knei|fen VI sep irreg aux sein (inf) to run away (+dat, von from)

aus+knip|sen VT sep (inf) Licht, Lampe to turn out or off, to switch off; Gerät to turn or switch off

aus+kno|beln VT sep **a** (inf) Plan to figure (inf) or work out **b** (= durch Knobeln entscheiden) ≈ to toss for

aus+kno|cken ['ausnɔkn] VT sep (Boxen, fig) to knock out

aus|knöpf|bar ADJ Futter detachable

aus+ko|chen VT sep **a** (Cook) Knochen to boil; (dial) Fett, Speck to melt **b** Wäsche to boil; (Med) Instrumente to sterilize (in boiling water); (fig inf: = sich ausdenken) to cook up (inf) → auch **ausgekocht**

aus+kom|men VI sep irreg aux sein **a** (= genügend haben, zurechtkommen) to get by (mit on), to manage (mit on, with); **das Auto kommt mit sieben Litern auf 100 km aus** the car only uses seven litres (Brit) or liters (US) every 100 kilometres (Brit) or kilometers (US); **ohne jdn/etw ~** to manage or do without sb/sth **b** **mit jdm (gut) ~** to get on or along (well) with sb; **mit ihm ist nicht auszukommen** he's impossible to get on or along with

Aus|kom|men NT -s, no pl (= Einkommen) livelihood; **sein ~ haben/finden** to get by; **mit ihr ist kein ~** she's impossible to get on or along with

aus|kömm|lich ['auskœmlɪç] ADJ Gehalt adequate; Verhältnisse comfortable ADV **~ leben** to live comfortably

aus+kos|ten VT sep **a** (= genießen) to make the most of; Leben to enjoy to the full **b** (geh: = erleiden) etw **~ müssen** to have to suffer sth

aus+kot|zen sep (vulg) VT to throw up (inf); (fig inf) Wissen to spew out (inf) VR to throw up (inf); (fig inf: = sich aussprechen) to have a bloody good moan (Brit inf) or a really good gripe (inf)

aus+kra|men VT sep (inf: = hervorholen) Gegenstand to dig out, to unearth; (fig) alte Geschichten etc to bring up; Schulkenntnisse to dig up

aus+krat|zen VT sep to scrape out; (Med) Gebärmutter to scrape; Patientin to give a scrape; **jdm die Augen ~** to scratch sb's eyes out

Aus|krat|zung F -, -en (Med) scrape

aus+krie|chen VI sep irreg aux sein to hatch out

aus+krie|gen VT sep (inf) Buch to finish; Flasche etc to empty

Aus|kris|tal|li|sa|ti|on F crystallization

aus+kris|tal|li|sie|ren ptp **auskristallisiert** VTIR sep (vi: aux sein) to crystallize

Aus|kuck ['auskʊk] M -(e)s, -e (N Ger) = **Ausguck**

aus+ku|cken VTI sep (N Ger) = **ausgucken**

aus+ku|geln VT sep **sich** (dat) **den Arm/die Schulter ~** to dislocate one's arm/shoulder

aus+küh|len sep VT Speise to cool; Ofen etc to cool down; Körper, Menschen to chill through VI aux sein (= abkühlen) to cool down; (Körper, Menschen) to chill through; **etw ~ lassen** to leave sth to cool

Aus|küh|lung F cooling; (von Mensch) loss of body heat

aus+kund|schaf|ten sep VT Weg, Lage to find out; Versteck to spy out; Geheimnis to ferret out; (esp Mil) to reconnoitre (Brit), to reconnoiter (US), to scout VI to find out; **jdn zum Auskundschaften vorschicken** to send sb ahead to reconnoitre (Brit) or reconnoiter (US)

Aus|kunft ['auskʊnft] ✪ 27.1 F -, Auskünfte [-kʏnftə] **a** (= Mitteilung) information no pl (über +acc about); **nähere ~** more information, further details; **jdm eine ~ erteilen** or **geben** to give sb some information; **wo bekomme ich ~?** where can I get some information?; **eine ~** or **Auskünfte einholen** or **einziehen** to make (some) inquiries (über +acc about) **b** (= Informationsstelle) information office; (= Schalter) information desk; (am Bahnhof) inquiry office/desk; (Telec) directory inquiries no art **c** (inf: = Auskunftsperson) information man/woman (inf)

Aus|kunf|tei [auskʊnf'tai] F -, -en credit inquiry agency

Aus|kunfts-: **Aus|kunfts|be|am|te(r)** M decl as adj, **Aus|kunfts|be|am|tin** F information officer; (am Bahnhof) information clerk; **Aus|kunfts|bü|ro** NT enquiry office, information office; **Aus|kunfts|dienst** M information service; **aus|kunfts|freu|dig** ADJ informative; **Aus|kunfts|per|son** F informer; (= Beamter) information clerk; **Aus|kunfts|pflicht** F (Jur) obligation to give information; **die Bank hat gegenüber der Polizei ~** the bank has a duty or is obliged to inform the police authorities; **die ~ des Arbeitgebers gegenüber der Polizei** the employer's duty to inform the police; **aus|kunfts|pflich|tig** [-pflɪçtɪç] ADJ (Jur) required to give information; **Aus|kunfts|schal|ter** M information desk; (am Bahnhof) inquiry desk; **Aus|kunfts|stel|le** F information office

aus+kun|geln VT sep (inf) etw **~** to work sth out on the q.t. (inf)

aus+kup|peln VI sep to disengage the clutch

aus+ku|rie|ren ptp **auskuriert** sep (inf) VT to cure; Krankheit auch to get rid of (inf) VR to get better

aus+la|chen sep VT jdn to laugh at; **lass dich nicht ~** don't make a fool of yourself VR to have a good laugh VI to stop laughing

aus+la|den sep irreg VT Ware, Ladung to unload; (Naut) to discharge, to unload **b** (inf) jdn **~** to tell sb not to come, to uninvite sb (hum) VI (Äste) to spread; (Dach, Balkon) to protrude, to jut out

aus|la|dend ADJ Kinn etc protruding; Gebäudekomplex auch projecting; Dach overhanging, projecting; Kleid wide; Gebärden, Bewegung, Ansprüche sweeping

Aus|la|ge F **a** (von Waren) display; (= Schaufenster) (shop) window; (= Schaukasten) showcase **b** (Sport) basic stance; (Fechten) on guard position **c** usu pl expense; **seine ~n für Verpflegung** his outlay for food

aus+la|gern VT sep to evacuate; (= aus dem Lager bringen) to take out of store

Aus|land NT , no pl foreign countries pl; (fig: = die Ausländer) foreigners pl; **ins/im ~** abroad; **aus dem** or **vom ~** from abroad; **wie hat das ~ darauf reagiert?** what was the reaction abroad?; **Handel mit dem ~** foreign trade, trade with other countries; **das feindliche/nichtkapitalistische** or **nicht kapitalistische ~** enemy/noncapitalist countries; **im benachbarten/europäischen ~** in neighbouring (Brit) or neighboring (US) other European countries; **im ~ lebende Deutsche** expatriate Germans, Germans living abroad

Aus|län|der ['auslɛndɐ] M **-s, -, Aus|län|de|rin** [-ərɪn] F **-, -nen** foreigner; (*Admin, Jur*) alien

Aus|län|der-: Aus|län|der|amt NT foreigners' registration office; **Aus|län|der|an|teil** M proportion *or* percentage of foreigners/foreign workers *etc*; **Aus|län|der|be|auf|trag|te(r)** MF *decl as adj* official looking after foreign immigrants; **Aus|län|der|be|hör|de** F ≈ immigration authority; **aus|län|der|feind|lich** ADJ hostile to foreigners, xenophobic; *Anschlag* on foreigners ADV ~ **motivierte Straftaten** crimes with a racist motive; **Aus|län|der|feind|lich|keit** F hostility toward(s) foreigners, xenophobia; **aus|län|der|freund|lich** ADJ *Land, Politik* friendly to foreigners; **Aus|län|der|ge|setz** NT (*Jur*) law on immigrants; **Aus|län|der|hass** ▲ M xenophobia

Aus|län|de|rin F → **Ausländer**

Aus|län|der-: Aus|län|der|kind NT child of immigrants *or* from an immigrant family; **Aus|län|der|po|li|tik** F policy on immigrants; **Aus|län|der|wahl|recht** NT allgemeines/kommunales ~ aliens' right to vote in general/local elections; **Aus|län|der|wohn|heim** NT immigrant hostel

aus|län|disch ['auslɛndɪʃ] ADJ **a** *attr* foreign; (*Bot*) exotic **b** (*fig: = fremdländisch*) exotic

Aus|lands- *in cpds* foreign; **Aus|lands|ab|tei|lung** F (*Econ*) export *or* foreign sales department; **Aus|lands|amt** NT (*an Universität etc*) international students' office; **Aus|lands|an|lei|he** F foreign loan; **Aus|lands|auf|ent|halt** M stay abroad; **Aus|lands|be|tei|li|gung** F (*Econ*) foreign investment; **Aus|lands|be|zie|hun|gen** PL foreign relations *pl*; **Aus|lands|brief** M overseas (*Brit*) *or* foreign letter; (*ins Ausland auch*) letter going abroad; (*aus dem Ausland auch*) letter from abroad; **Aus|lands|deut|sche(r)** MF *decl as adj* expatriate German, German national (living abroad); **Aus|lands|dienst** M foreign service; **Aus|lands|ein|satz** M (*von Soldaten, Journalisten etc*) deployment abroad; (*für mehrere Monate/Jahre*) foreign posting; **Aus|lands|flug** M international flight; **Aus|lands|ge|schäft** NT foreign business *or* trade; **Aus|lands|ge|spräch** NT international call; **Aus|lands|in|ves|ti|ti|on** F foreign investment; **Aus|lands|ka|pi|tal** NT (*Econ*) foreign capital; **Aus|lands|kon|to** NT (*Econ*) foreign account, account abroad *or* overseas (*US*); **Aus|lands|kor|res|pon|dent(in)** M(F) foreign correspondent; **Aus|lands|kran|ken|schein** M (*Med*) certificate of entitlement to benefits in kind (*during a stay abroad*); **Aus|lands|rei|se** F journey *or* trip abroad; **Aus|lands|schul|den** PL foreign exchange debts *pl*; **Aus|lands|schu|le** F British/German *etc* school (abroad); **die ~n in Brüssel** the foreign schools in Brussels; **Aus|lands|schutz|brief** M international travel cover; (*= Dokument*) certificate of entitlement for international travel cover; **Aus|lands|stu|di|um** NT (course of) studies *pl* abroad; **ein ~ machen** to study abroad; **Aus|lands|ver|tre|tung** F agency abroad; (*von Firma*) foreign branch; **Aus|lands|zu|la|ge** F (*auf Gehalt*) overseas *or* expatriation allowance, foreign allowance (*US*)

aus+las|sen *sep irreg* VT **a** (*= weglassen, aussparen, übergehen*) to leave *or* miss out; (*= versäumen*) *Chance, Gelegenheit* to miss; **er lässt kein Geschäft aus** he doesn't miss a chance to make a deal **b** (*= abreagieren*) to vent (*an +dat* on); **seine Gefühle ~** to vent one's feelings, to let off steam (*inf*) **c** *Butter, Fett* to melt; *Speck* to render (down) **d** *Kleider etc* to let out; *Gefäß* to leave down **e** (*inf*) *Radio, Motor, Ofen etc* to leave off; *Licht* to leave off, to leave out; (*= nicht anziehen*) *Kleidung* to leave off **f** (*Aus*) (*= los-, freilassen*) to let go; (*= in Ruhe lassen*) to leave alone **g** → **ausgelassen**

VR to talk (*über +acc* about); **sich über jdn/etw ~** (*pej*) to go on about sb/sth (*pej*); **er hat sich nicht näher darüber ausgelassen** he didn't say any more about it

VI a (*Aus: = loslassen*) to let go **b** (*= versagen*) to fail

Aus|las|sung F **-, -en a** (*= Weglassen*) omission **b Auslassungen** PL (*pej: = Äußerungen*) remarks *pl*

Aus|las|sungs-: Aus|las|sungs|punk|te PL suspension points *pl*, ellipsis *sing*; **Aus|las|sungs|zei|chen** NT apostrophe

aus+las|ten VT *sep* **a** *Fahrzeug* to make full use of; *Maschine auch* to use to capacity **b** *jdn* to occupy fully → *auch* **ausgelastet**

Aus|las|tung F **-, -en** (*von Maschine*) full *or* capacity utilization

aus+lat|schen VT *sep* (*inf*) to wear *or* stretch out of shape; **latsch deine Schuhe nicht so aus** don't walk on your shoes like that → *auch* **ausgelatscht**

Aus|lauf M **a** *no pl* (*= Bewegungsfreiheit*) exercise; (*für Kinder*) room to run about **b** (*Gelände*) run **c** (*Sport*) (*Leichtathletik*) slowing down; (*Ski: = Strecke*) out-run **d** *no pl* (*= das Auslaufen*) discharge; (*= das Lecken*) leakage **e** (*Stelle*) outlet

aus+lau|fen *sep irreg* VI *aux sein* **a** (*Flüssigkeit*) to run out (*aus* of); (*Behälter*) to empty; (*= undicht sein*) to leak; (*Wasserbett, Blase, Auge*) to drain; (*Eiter*) to drain, to discharge **b** (*Naut: Schiff, Besatzung*) to sail **c** (*= nicht fortgeführt werden: Modell, Serie*) to be discontinued; (*= ausgehen: Vorräte, Lager*) to run out; **etw ~ lassen** (*Produkt etc*) to phase sth out **d** (*= aufhören: Straße, Vertrag etc*) to run out **e** (*= ein bestimmtes Ende nehmen*) to turn out **f** (*= zum Stillstand kommen*) (*Motor, Förderband*) to come to a stop; (*Sport*) (*Läufer*) to ease off, to slow down; (*Skifahrer*) to coast to a stop **g** (*= übergehen in*) to run; (*fig: Streit etc*) to turn (*in +acc* into); **die Berge laufen in die Ebene/spitz aus** the mountains run into the plain/come to a point; **in eine Bucht ~** to open out into a bay **h** (*Farbe, Stoff*) to run

VR to have some exercise; **sich ~ können** (*Kinder*) to have room to run about

aus|lau|fend ADJ *Vertrag, Frist* expiring; **im ~en Jahr** in the year about to end; **~es Modell** = **Auslaufmodell**

Aus|läu|fer M **a** (*Bot*) runner **b** (*Met*) (*von Hoch*) ridge; (*von Tief*) trough **c** (*= Vorberge*) foothill *usu pl* **d** (*von Stadt*) suburb **e** (*Sw: = Bote*) delivery boy/man

Aus|läu|fe|rin F (*Sw: = Botin*) delivery girl/woman

Aus|lauf|mo|dell NT **a** (*lit*) discontinued model **b** (*fig, inf: Person*) old model (*hum inf*); **ein ~ sein** (*fig inf: Konzept, Idee*) to be old hat (*inf*)

aus|lauf|si|cher ADJ leak-proof

aus+lau|gen ['auslaugn] VT *sep* (*lit*) *Boden* to exhaust; (*Regen*) to wash the goodness out of; *Haut* to dry out; (*fig*) to exhaust, to wear out

Aus|laut M (*Ling*) final position

aus+lau|ten VI *sep* to end (*auf +dat* in); **~der Konsonant** final consonant

aus+läu|ten *sep* VT to ring out; *Gottesdienst* to ring out the end of VI to finish *or* cease ringing

aus+le|ben *sep* VR (*Mensch*) to live it up; (*Fantasie etc*) to run free VT (*geh*) to realize

aus+le|cken VT *sep* to lick out

aus+lee|ren VT *sep Flüssigkeit* to pour out, to empty; *Gefäß* to empty

aus+le|gen *sep* VT **a** (*= ausbreiten*) to lay out; *Waren etc* to display; *Köder* to put down; *Reusen* to drop; *Kabel, Minen* to lay; *Saatgut* to sow; *Kartoffeln* to plant **b** (*= bedecken*) to cover; (*= auskleiden*) to line; (*mit Einlegearbeit*) to inlay; **den Boden/das Zim-**

mer (mit Teppichen) ~ to carpet the floor/room **c** (*= erklären*) to explain; (*= deuten*) to interpret; **etw richtig ~** to interpret sth correctly; **etw falsch ~** to interpret sth wrongly, to misinterpret sth; **jds Scherz/Tat übel ~** to take sb's joke/action badly **d** *Geld* to lend (*jdm etw* sb sth); **sie hat die 5 Euro für mich ausgelegt** she paid the 5 euros for me **e** (*Tech*) to design (*auf +acc, für* for); **straff ausgelegt sein** (*Federung*) to be tightly set VI (*dial inf: = dicklich werden*) to put (it) on a bit (*inf*) VR (*Fechten*) to adopt the on guard position

Aus|le|ger¹ ['auslegɐ] M **-s, -** **a** (*von Kran etc*) jib, boom **b** (*an Ruderboot*) rowlock; (*= Kufe gegen Kentern*) outrigger

Aus|le|ger² ['auslegɐ] M **-s, -, Aus|le|ge|rin** [-ərɪn] F **-, -nen** (*= Deuter*) interpreter

Aus|le|ge|wa|re F floor covering; (*= Teppiche*) carpeting

Aus|le|gung ['auslegʊŋ] F **-, -en** (*= Deutung*) interpretation; (*= Erklärung*) explanation (*zu* of); **falsche ~** misinterpretation

Aus|le|gungs-: Aus|le|gungs|fra|ge F question *or* matter of interpretation; **Aus|le|gungs|me|tho|de** F method of interpretation; **Aus|le|gungs|sa|che** F matter of interpretation

Aus|leg|wa|re F = **Auslegeware**

aus+lei|den VI *sep irreg* **sie hat ausgelitten** her suffering is at an end

aus+lei|ern *sep* VT (*inf*) *etw* ~ (*Gummiband, Gewinde, Feder*) to wear sth out; *Hosen, Pullover* to make sth go baggy VI *aux sein* to wear out; (*Pullover*) to go baggy → *auch* **ausgeleiert**

Aus|leih|bi|blio|thek F, **Aus|leih|bü|che|rei** F lending library

Aus|lei|he F (*= das Ausleihen*) lending; (*= Schalter*) issue desk; **eine ~ ist nicht möglich** it is not possible to lend out anything

aus+lei|hen VT *sep irreg* (*= verleihen*) to lend (*jdm, an jdn* to sb); (*= von jdm leihen*) to borrow; **sich** (*dat*) **etw ~** to borrow sth (*bei, von* from)

aus+ler|nen VI *sep* (*Lehrling*) to finish one's apprenticeship; (*inf: Schüler, Student etc*) to finish school/college *etc*; **man lernt nie aus** (*prov*) you live and learn (*prov*) → *auch* **ausgelernt**

Aus|le|se F **a** *no pl* (*= Auswahl*) selection; (*Liter: verschiedener Autoren*) anthology; **natürliche ~** natural selection; **eine ~ treffen** *or* **vornehmen** to make a selection **b** (*= Elite*) **die ~** the élite **c** (*= Wein*) high-quality wine made from selected grapes

aus+le|sen *sep irreg* VT **a** (*= auswählen*) to select; (*= aussondern*) *Schlechtes* to pick out; *Erbsen, Linsen etc* to pick over → *auch* **ausgelesen** **b** *Buch etc* to finish reading; **er legte das ausgelesene Buch beiseite** he put away the book he had finished reading VI (*= zu Ende lesen*) to finish reading; **hast du bald ausgelesen?** will you finish (reading) it soon?

Aus|le|se-: Aus|le|se|pro|zess ▲ M selection process; **Aus|le|se|ver|fah|ren** NT selection procedure

aus+leuch|ten VT *sep* to illuminate; (*fig*) to throw light on

Aus|leuch|tung F **-, -en** illumination

aus+lich|ten VT *sep* to thin out

aus+lie|fern VT *sep* **a** *Waren* to deliver **b** *jdn* to hand over (*an +acc* to); (*fig: = preisgeben*) to leave (*jdm* in the hands of); **sich der Polizei/Justiz ~** to give oneself up *or* surrender oneself to the police/to justice; **jdm/einer Sache ausgeliefert sein** to be at sb's mercy/the mercy of sth

Aus|lie|fe|rung F **a** (*von Ware*) delivery **b** (*von Menschen*) handing over; (*von Gefangenen*) extradition

Aus|lie|fe|rungs-: Aus|lie|fe|rungs|ab|kom|men NT (*Pol*) extradition treaty; **Aus|lie|fe|rungs|an|trag** M (*Jur*) application for extradition; **Aus|lie|fe|rungs|be|geh|ren** NT (*Jur*) extradition request; **ein ~ stellen** to make an extradition request; **Aus|lie|fe|rungs|haft** F (*Jur*) extradition custody; **Aus|lie|fe|rungs|la|ger** NT (*Comm*) distribution centre (*Brit*) or center (*US*); **Aus|lie|fe|rungs|ver|fah|ren** NT (*Jur*) extradition proceedings *pl*; **Aus|lie|fe|rungs|ver|trag** M (*Jur*) extradition treaty

aus+lie|gen VI *sep irreg* (*Waren*) to be displayed; (*Zeitschriften, Liste etc*) to be available (to the public); (*Schlinge, Netz etc*) to be down

Aus|li|nie F (*Sport*) (*Ftbl*) touchline; (*bei Tennis, Hockey etc*) sideline; **die ~n** (*Tennis*) the tramlines *pl*

aus+lo|ben VT *sep* (*form*) (= *als Belohnung aussetzen*) *Geldbetrag* to offer as a reward; (= *als Preis aussetzen*) to offer as a prize

Aus|lo|bung F -, -en (= *Belohnung*) reward

aus+löf|feln VT *sep Suppe etc* to eat up completely; *Teller* to empty; **etw ~ müssen** (*inf*) to have to take the consequences of sth; **~ müssen, was man sich eingebrockt hat** (*inf*) to have to take the consequences

aus|log|gen ['auslɔgn] VR (*Comput*) to log out or off; **sich aus dem System ~** to log out of the system

aus+lö|schen VT *sep* **a** *Feuer* to put out, to extinguish; *Kerze auch* to snuff out; (*geh*) *Licht* to extinguish **b** (= *auswischen*) *Spuren* to obliterate; (*mit Schwamm etc*) to wipe out; *Schrift* to erase (*mit +dat* from); *Erinnerung, Schmach* to blot out; **ein Menschenleben ~** (*geh*) to destroy or blot out a human life

aus+lo|sen VT *sep* to draw lots for; *Preis, Gewinner* to draw; **es wurde ausgelost, wer beginnt** lots were drawn to see who would start

aus+lö|sen VT *sep* **a** *Mechanismus, Alarm, Reaktion* to set or trigger off, to trigger; *Kameraverschluss, Bombe* to release; (*fig*) *Wirkung* to produce; *Begeisterung, Mitgefühl, Überraschung* to arouse; *Aufstand, Beifall* to trigger off **b** (*dated*: = *einlösen*) *Gefangene* to release; (*durch Geld*) to ransom; *Wechsel, Pfand* to redeem **c** (*dial*) *Knochen etc* to take out

Aus|lö|ser ['auslø:zɐ] M -s, - **a** trigger; (*für Bombe*) release button; (*Phot*) shutter release **b** (= *Anlass*) cause; **der ~ für etw sein** to trigger sth off **c** (*Psych*) trigger mechanism

Aus|lo|sung F draw

Aus|lö|sung F **a** (*von Gefangenen*) release; (*von Wechsel, Pfand*) redemption; (= *Lösegeld*) ransom **b** (= *Entschädigung*) travel allowance

aus+lo|ten VT *sep* (*Naut*) *Fahrrinne* to sound the depth of; *Tiefe* to sound; (*Tech*) *Mauer* to plumb; (*fig geh*) to plumb; *jds Wesen, Charakter* to plumb the depths of; **die Sache muss ich doch mal ~** (*fig inf*) I'll have to try to get to the bottom of the matter, I'll have to try to fathom it out

aus+lüf|ten VTI *sep* to air; **lüfte dein Gehirn ein bisschen aus** (*inf*) get your thoughts or ideas straightened out

aus+lut|schen VT *sep* (*inf*) *Orange, Zitrone etc* to suck; *Saft* to suck out; (*fig*) to suck dry → *auch* **ausgelutscht**

aus+ma|chen ✪ 28.1, 31, 34.5 VT *sep* **a** *Feuer, Kerze, Zigarette* to put out; *elektrisches Licht, Radio, Gas* to turn off

b (= *ermitteln, sichten*) to make out; (= *ausfindig machen*) to locate; (= *feststellen*) to determine; **es lässt sich nicht mehr ~, warum ...** it can no longer be determined why ...

c (= *vereinbaren*) to agree; *Streitigkeiten* to settle; **einen Termin ~** to agree (on) a time; **wir müssen nur noch ~, wann wir uns treffen** we only have to arrange when we should meet; **etw mit sich selbst ~ (müssen)** to (have to) sort sth out for oneself → *auch* **ausgemacht**

d (= *bewirken, darstellen*) (to go) to make up; **alles, was das Leben ausmacht** everything that is a part of life; **all der Luxus, der ein angenehmes Leben ausmacht** all the luxuries which (go to) make up a pleasant life; **ihm fehlt alles, was**

einen Musiker ausmacht he has none of the qualities which (go to) make up a musician; **der Hintergrund macht den Reiz an diesem Bild aus** the background makes this picture attractive

e (= *betragen*) *Summe, Unterschied* to come to; (*zeitlich*) to make up

f (= *bedeuten*) **viel ~** to make a big difference; **wenig** or **nicht viel ~** not to make much difference; **das macht nichts aus** that doesn't matter; (= *ist egal auch*) that doesn't make any difference

g (= *stören*) to matter (*jdm* to); **macht es Ihnen etwas aus, wenn ...?** would you mind if ...?; **es macht mir nichts aus, den Platz zu wechseln** I don't mind changing places

h (*dial*) *Kartoffeln, Rüben* to dig up

aus+mah|len VT *sep* to grind (down)

aus+ma|len VT *sep* **sich** (*dat*) **etw ~** to imagine sth; **sich** (*dat*) **sein Leben ~** to picture one's life

aus+ma|növ|rie|ren *ptp* **ausmanövriert** VT *sep* to outmanoeuvre (*Brit*), to outmaneuver (*US*)

aus+mä|ren ['ausmɛːrən] VR *sep* (*dial inf*) (= *langsam arbeiten*) to dawdle (*inf*); (= *viel erzählen*) to rattle on (*über +acc* about) (*inf*); **mär dich endlich aus!** stop dawdling! (*inf*)

Aus|marsch M departure

aus+mar|schie|ren *ptp* **ausmarschiert** VI *sep aux sein* to march out

Aus|maß NT **a** (= *Größe: von Gegenstand, Fläche*) size; (*Umfang: von Katastrophe*) extent; (*Grad*) degree, extent; (*von Liebe etc*) extent; (= *Größenordnung: von Änderungen, Verlust etc*) scale; **ein Verlust in diesem ~** a loss on this scale; **das Feuer war nur von geringem ~** the fire was only on a small scale **b** **Ausmaße** PL proportions *pl*; **erschreckende -e annehmen** to assume alarming proportions

aus+mer|geln ['ausmɛrgln] VT *sep Gesicht, Körper etc* to emaciate; *Boden* to exhaust → *auch* **ausgemergelt**

aus+mer|zen ['ausmɛrtsn] VT *sep* (= *ausrotten*) *Ungeziefer, Unkraut* to eradicate; (= *aussondern*) *schwache Tiere* to cull; (*fig*) *schwache Teilnehmer* to sort or weed out; *Fehler, Missstände* to eradicate; *Erinnerungen* to obliterate

aus+mes|sen VT *sep irreg Raum, Fläche etc* to measure (out); **das Zimmer ~** (*fig*) to pace up and down the room

Aus|mes|sung F **a** (= *das Messen*) measuring (out) **b** (= *Maße*) dimensions *pl*

aus+mis|ten *sep* **VT** *Stall* to muck out (*Brit*), to clear (*US*); (*fig inf*) *Schrank etc* to tidy (*esp Brit*) or clean out; *Zimmer* to clean out **VI** (*lit*) to muck out (*Brit*), to clear of dung (*US*); (*fig*) to have a clean-out

aus+mon|tie|ren *ptp* **ausmontiert** VT *sep* to take out

aus+mus|tern VT *sep Maschine, Fahrzeug etc* to take out of service; (*Mil*: = *entlassen*) to invalid out (*Brit*), to discharge

Aus|nah|me ['ausna:mə] F -, -n exception; **mit ~ von** or **+gen** with the exception of; **mit ~ von ihm** with the exception of him, except (for) him; **ohne ~** without exception; **~n bestätigen die Regel** (*prov*) keine Regel ohne **~** (*prov*) the exception proves the rule (*prov*)

Ausnahme-: **Aus|nah|me|be|stim|mung** F special regulation; **Aus|nah|me|er|schei|nung** F exception; **Aus|nah|me|fall** M exception, exceptional case; **Aus|nah|me|ge|neh|mi|gung** F special (case) authorization; **Aus|nah|me|si|tu|a|ti|on** F special or exceptional situation; **Aus|nah|me|stel|lung** F special position; **Aus|nah|me|zu|stand** M (*Pol*) state of emergency; **den ~ verhängen** to declare a state of emergency

aus|nahms|los ADV without exception ADJ *Bewilligung, Zustimmung* unanimous; **das ~e Erscheinen der ganzen Belegschaft** the appearance of all the staff without exception

aus|nahms|wei|se ADV **darf ich das machen? – ~** **~** may I do that? – just this once; **wenn er ~ auch mal einen Fehler macht** when he makes a mistake too just for once; **sie hat es mir ~ einmal erlaubt** she let me do it once as a special exception; **er darf heute ~ früher von der Arbeit weggehen** as an exception he may leave work earlier today

aus+neh|men *sep irreg* **VT** **a** (*fig*) *Verbrecherbande, Diebesnest etc* to raid; (*Mil*) *Stellung* to take out; **das Nest ~** to remove the eggs from the nest **b** *Fisch, Kaninchen* to gut, to dress; *Geflügel* to draw; *Hammel, Rind etc* to dress; *Eingeweide, Herz etc* to take out, to remove **c** (= *ausschließen*) *jdn* to make an exception of; (= *befreien*) to exempt; **ich nehme keinen aus** I'll make no exceptions → *auch* **ausgenommen** **d** (*inf: finanziell*) *jdn* to fleece (*inf*); (*beim Kartenspiel*) to clean out (*inf*) **e** (*Aus*: = *erkennen*) to make out **VR** (*geh*: = *wirken*) **sich schön** or **gut/schlecht ~** to look good/bad

aus|neh|mend ADJ (*geh*) exceptional ADV exceptionally; **das gefällt mir ~ gut** I like that very much indeed

aus+nüch|tern ['ausnʏçtɐn] VTIR *sep* to sober up

Aus|nüch|te|rung F -, -en sobering up

Aus|nüch|te|rungs|zel|le F drying-out cell

aus+nut|zen (*esp S Ger, Aus, Sw*) **aus+nüt|zen** VT *sep* to use, to make use of; *jdn* to use; (= *ausbeuten*) to exploit; *Gelegenheit* to make the most of; *jds Gutmütigkeit, Leichtgläubigkeit etc* to take advantage of

Aus|nut|zung F -, *no pl* (*esp S Ger, Aus, Sw*) **Aus|nüt|zung** F -, *no pl* use; (= *Ausbeutung*) exploitation

aus+pa|cken *sep* **VT** *Koffer* to unpack; *Geschenk* to unwrap **VI** (*inf*) (= *alles sagen*) to talk (*inf*); (= *seine Meinung sagen*) to speak one's mind

aus+par|ken *sep* VI to get out of a/the parking space

aus+peit|schen VT *sep* to whip

aus+pel|len *sep* (*inf*) **VT** to peel; *Nuss, Erbsen* to shell **VR** to strip off

Aus|pend|ler(in) M(F) commuter

aus+pen|nen VIR *sep* (*inf*) to have a (good) kip (*Brit inf*) or nap

aus+pfei|fen VT *sep irreg* to boo or hiss at; *Stück, Schauspieler* to boo off the stage

aus+pflan|zen VT *sep* (*Hort*) to plant out

Aus|pi|zi|um [aus'pi:tsiɔm] NT -s, **Auspizien** [-tsiən] *usu pl* (*geh*) auspice

aus+plap|pern VT *sep* (*inf*) to blurt out (*inf*)

aus+plau|dern *sep* **VT** to let out **VR** (*dial*) to have a good chat

aus+plün|dern VT *sep Dorf etc* to plunder, to pillage; *Kasse, Laden* to raid; (*hum*) *Speisekammer etc* to raid; *jdn* to plunder (*inf*), to clean out (*inf*)

aus+pols|tern VT *sep Mantel etc* to pad (out); *Kiste, Raum etc* to line, to pad

aus+po|sau|nen *ptp* **ausposaunt** VT *sep* (*inf*) to broadcast (*inf*)

aus+po|wern[1] ['auspo:vɐn] VT *sep* (= *verarmen*) to impoverish; (= *ausbeuten*) *Massen, Boden* to exploit; **ein wirtschaftlich ausgepowertes Land** an impoverished country

aus+po|wern[2] ['auspauən] VR (*inf, in Fitness-Studio etc*) to have a good work-out

Aus|po|we|rung F -, -en impoverishment; (= *Ausbeutung*) exploitation

aus+prä|gen *sep* **VT** *Münzen etc* to mint; **Metall zu Münzen ~** to stamp coins out of metal **VR** (*Begabung, Charaktereigenschaft etc*) to reveal or show itself; **die Erziehung prägt sich im Charakter/Verhalten aus** one's upbringing leaves its stamp on one's character/behaviour (*Brit*) or behavior (*US*) → *auch* **ausgeprägt**

Aus|prä|gung F **a** *no pl* (*von Charakter*) shaping, moulding (*Brit*), molding (*US*) **b** *no pl* (=

das Ausgeprägtsein) markedness; **in einer derart starken ~ ist mir diese Krankheit noch nicht untergekommen** I have never come across this illness to such a marked degree **c** (= *Ausdruck*) expression

aus+prei|sen VT *sep* Waren to price

aus+pres|sen VT *sep* **a** (= *herauspressen*) Saft, Schwamm etc to squeeze out; *Zitrone etc* to squeeze **b** (*fig*: = *ausbeuten*) to squeeze dry, to bleed white **c** (*fig*: = *ausfragen*) to press; **jdn wie eine Zitrone ~** to squeeze sb like a lemon (for information)

aus+pro|bie|ren *ptp* **ausprobiert** VT *sep* to try out; *Auto auch* to test-drive

Aus|puff M *pl* **-puffe** exhaust

Aus|puff-: Aus|puff|ga|se PL exhaust fumes *pl;* **Aus|puff|krüm|mer** [-kʀʏmɐ] M **-s, -** (*Aut*) exhaust manifold; **Aus|puff|rohr** NT exhaust pipe; **Aus|puff|topf** M silencer (*Brit*), muffler (*US*)

aus+pum|pen VT *sep* **a** (= *leeren*) to pump out **b** (*inf*: = *erschöpfen*) to drain → *auch* **ausgepumpt**

aus+punk|ten [ˈauspʊŋktn] VT *sep* (*Boxen*) to outpoint, to beat on points

aus+pus|ten VT *sep* (*inf*) to blow out; **die Luft kräftig ~** to blow out hard; **jdm das Lebenslicht ~** to snuff out sb's life

aus+put|zen VT *sep* **a** (*esp S Ger, Aus*: = *reinigen*) to clean out; *Kleider* to clean; *Flecken* to get out **b** (*Ftbl*) *Ball* to clear **c** (*dial*: = *ausnutzen*) to use VI (*Ftbl*) to clear (the ball); (= *Ausputzer sein*) to act as or be the sweeper

Aus|put|zer [ˈauspʊtsɐ] M **-s, -, Aus|put|ze|rin** [-əʀɪn] F **-, -nen** (*Ftbl*) sweeper; (*fig inf*) troubleshooter

aus+quar|tie|ren [ˈauskvaʀtiːʀən] *ptp* **ausquartiert** VT *sep* to move out; (*Mil*) to billet out

Aus|quar|tie|rung F **-, -en** moving out; (*Mil*) billeting out

aus+quat|schen [ˈauskvatʃn] VR *sep* (*inf*) to have a heart-to-heart (*bei jdm* with sb), to get a load off one's chest

aus+quet|schen VT *sep* Saft etc to squeeze out; *Zitrone* to squeeze; (*inf*: = *ausfragen*) (*Polizei etc*) to grill (*inf*); (*aus Neugier*) to pump (*inf*)

aus+ra|die|ren *ptp* **ausradiert** VT *sep* to rub out, to erase; (*fig*: = *vernichten*) to wipe out; **etw aus dem Gedächtnis ~** to erase sth from one's mind or memory

aus+ran|gie|ren *ptp* **ausrangiert** VT *sep* (*inf*) Kleider to throw out; *Maschine, Auto* to scrap; **ein altes ausrangiertes Auto** an old disused car

aus+ra|sie|ren *ptp* **ausrasiert** VT *sep* to shave; *Koteletten* to trim; **jdm/sich die Haare im Nacken ~** to shave sb's/one's neck

aus+ras|ten *sep* VI *aux sein* **a** (*Tech*) to come out **b** (*hum inf*: = *zornig werden*) to blow one's top (*inf*), to do one's nut (*Brit inf*) VR (*Aus, S Ger*: = *ausruhen*) to have a rest VI *impers* (*inf*) **es rastet bei jdm aus** something snaps in sb (*inf*)

aus+rau|ben VT *sep* to rob

aus+räu|bern VT *sep* (*auch hum*) to plunder, to raid; **jdn ~** to clean sb out (*inf*)

aus+rau|chen *sep* VT *Zigarette etc* to finish (smoking) VI **a** (= *zu Ende rauchen*) to finish smoking **b** *aux sein* (*Aus*) (= *verdunsten*) to evaporate; (= *Geschmack verlieren*) to lose its taste

aus+räu|chern VT *sep* Zimmer to fumigate; *Tiere, Schlupfwinkel, Bande* to smoke out

aus+rau|fen VT *sep* to tear or pull out; **ich könnte mir die Haare ~** I could kick myself

aus+räu|men VT *sep* to clear out; *Möbel* to move out; *Magen, Darm* to purge; (*fig*) *Missverständnisse, Konflikt* to clear up; *Vorurteile, Bedenken* to dispel; (*inf*: = *ausrauben*) to clean out (*inf*)

aus+rech|nen VT *sep* to work out; (= *ermitteln*) Gewicht, Länge etc to calculate; **sich** (*dat*) **etw ~**

können (*fig*) to be able to work sth out (for oneself); **sich** (*dat*) **große Chancen/einen Vorteil ~** to reckon or fancy that one has a good chance/an advantage → *auch* **ausgerechnet**

Aus|rech|nung F working out; (*von Gewicht, Länge etc*) calculation

aus+re|cken VT *sep* to stretch (out); **sich** (*dat*) **den Hals ~** to crane one's neck

Aus|re|de F excuse

aus+re|den *sep* VI to finish speaking; **er hat mich gar nicht erst ~ lassen** he didn't even let me finish (speaking) VT **jdm etw ~** to talk sb out of sth VR (*esp Aus*) (= *sich aussprechen*) to have a heart-to-heart (talk); (= *Ausflüchte machen*) to make excuses; **er versucht sich immer auf irgendwas auszureden** he is always trying to make some excuse

aus+reg|nen VIR *impers sep* to stop raining

aus+rei|ben VT *sep irreg* Fleck etc to rub out; *Topf etc* to scour; *Gläser* to wipe out; **sich** (*dat*) **die Augen ~** to rub one's eyes

aus+rei|chen VI *sep* to be sufficient or enough; **die Zeit reicht nicht aus** there is not sufficient time; **mit etw ~** (*dial*) to manage on sth

aus+rei|chend ADJ sufficient, enough; (*Sch*) satisfactory ADV sufficiently

aus+rei|fen VI *sep aux sein* to ripen; (*fig*) to mature

Aus|rei|se F **bei der ~** on leaving the country; (= *Grenzübertritt*) on crossing the border; **jdm die ~ verweigern** to prohibit sb from leaving the country

Aus|rei|se-: Aus|rei|se|an|trag M application for an exit visa; **Aus|rei|se|er|laub|nis** F, **Aus|rei|se|ge|neh|mi|gung** F exit permit

aus+rei|sen VI *sep aux sein* to leave (the country); **ins Ausland/nach Frankreich ~** to go abroad/to France

Aus|rei|se-: Aus|rei|se|sper|re F ban on leaving the country; **Aus|rei|se|ver|bot** NT ban on leaving a/the country; **Aus|rei|se|ver|kehr** M traffic leaving the country; **Aus|rei|se|vi|sum** NT exit visa; **Aus|rei|se|wel|le** F wave of departures, emigration wave; **Aus|rei|se|wil|li|ge(r)** [ˈausʀaɪzəvɪlɪɡə] MF *decl as adj* prospective emigrant

aus+reiß|bar ADJ Ärmel, Jackenfutter detachable

aus+rei|ßen *sep irreg* VT Haare, Blatt to tear out; *Unkraut, Blumen, Zahn* to pull out; **einem Käfer die Flügel/Beine ~** to pull a beetle's wings/legs off; **er hat sich** (*dat*) **kein Bein ausgerissen** (*inf*) he didn't exactly overstrain himself, he didn't exactly bust a gut (*inf*); **ich könnte Bäume ~** (*inf*) I feel full of beans (*inf*) VI *aux sein* **a** (= *sich lösen*) (*Ärmel etc*) to come away; (= *einreißen*) (*Naht*) to come out; (*Knopfloch*) to tear **b** (+*dat* from) (*inf*: = *davonlaufen*) to run away; (*Sport*) to break away

Aus|rei|ßer[1] [ˈausʀaɪsɐ] M **-s, -** (*Mil*) stray bullet **b** (= *Ausnahme*) anomaly, aberration; **ein statistischer ~** a statistical anomaly

Aus|rei|ßer[2] [ˈausʀaɪsɐ] M **-s, -, Aus|rei|ße|rin** [-əʀɪn] F **-, -nen** (*inf*) runaway; (*Sport*) runner who breaks away; (*Radfahrer*) cyclist who breaks away

aus+rei|ten *sep irreg* VI *aux sein* to ride out, to go riding, to go for a ride VT *Pferd* to take out, to exercise; **ein Pferd voll ~** to ride a horse to its limit

aus+rei|zen VT *sep* Karten to bid up to strength; *Kontrahenten* to outbid; (*fig*: = *ausschöpfen*) Möglichkeiten, Potenzial, Thema to exhaust; *Mittel* to exploit, to exhaust

aus+ren|ken [ˈausʀɛŋkn] VT *sep* to dislocate; **sich/jdm den Arm ~** to dislocate one's/sb's arm; **sich** (*dat*) **(fast) den Hals ~** (*inf*) to crane one's neck

aus+rich|ten *sep* ☼ 27.6, 49 VT **a** (= *aufstellen*) to line up; **jdn/etw auf etw** (*acc*) **~** (= *einstellen*) to orientate sb/sth to sth, to align sb/sth with sth; (= *abstellen*) to gear sb/sth to sth

b (= *veranstalten*) to organize; *Hochzeit, Fest* to arrange, to organize

c (= *erreichen*) to achieve; **ich konnte bei ihr nichts ~** I couldn't get anywhere with her **d** (= *übermitteln*) to tell; *Nachricht* to pass on; **jdm ~, dass ...** to tell sb (that) ...; **jdm etwas ~** to give sb a message; **kann ich etwas ~?** can I give him/her etc a message?; **bitte richten Sie ihm einen Gruß aus** please give him my regards **e** (*Aus*: *schlecht machen*) to run down VR to line up in a straight row; (*Mil*) to dress ranks; **sich nach dem Nebenmann/Vordermann/Hintermann ~** to line up (exactly) with the person next to/in front of/behind one; **ausgerichtet in einer Reihe stehen** to stand next to one another in a straight line; **sich an etw** (*dat*) **~** (*fig*) to orientate oneself to sth

Aus|rich|tung F **a** (*fig*) (*auf Ideologie etc*) orientation (*auf +acc* towards), alignment (*auf +acc* with); (*auf Bedürfnisse etc*) gearing (*auf +acc* to); (*an einer Ideologie*) orientation (*an +dat* to) **b** (*von Veranstaltung*) organization; (*von Hochzeit, Fest*) arrangement, organization **c** (= *Aufstellung*) lining up; (= *Einstellung*) alignment (*auf +acc* with)

aus+rin|gen VT *sep irreg* (*dial*: = *auswringen*) to wring out

Aus|ritt M ride (out); (= *das Ausreiten*) riding out

aus+rol|len *sep* VT Teig, Teppich to roll out; *Kabel* to run out VI *aux sein* (*Flugzeug*) to taxi to a standstill or stop; (*Fahrzeug*) to coast to a stop

aus+rot|ten [ˈausʀɔtn] VT *sep* to wipe out; *Wanzen etc* to destroy; *Religion, Ideen* to stamp out, to eradicate

Aus|rot|tung F **-, -en** wiping out; (*von Wanzen etc*) destruction; (*von Religion, Ideen*) stamping out, eradication

aus+rü|cken *sep* VI *aux sein* **a** (*Mil*) to move or set out; (*Polizei, Feuerwehr*) to turn out **b** (*inf*: = *ausreißen*) to make off; (*von zu Hause*) to run away; (*aus Gefängnis*) to run away, to get out VT **a** (*Tech*) to disengage, to release **b** (*Typ*) Zeilen etc to reverse-indent (*spec*), to move out

Aus|ruf M **a** (= *Ruf*) cry, shout **b** (= *Bekanntmachung*) proclamation; **etw durch ~ bekannt machen** to proclaim sth

aus+ru|fen VT *sep irreg* to exclaim; *Schlagzeilen* to cry out; *Waren* to cry; (*auf Auktion*) to start; (= *verkünden*) to call out; *Haltestellen, Streik* to call; **die Stunden ~** (*Hist*) to call the hours; **jdn zum or als König ~** to proclaim sb king; **jdn or jds Namen ~ (lassen)** (*über Lautsprecher etc*) to put out a call for sb; (*im Hotel*) to page sb

Aus|ru|fer [ˈausʀuːfɐ] M **-s, -, Aus|ru|fe|rin** [-əʀɪn] F **-, -nen** (*Hist*) (town) crier; (*von Waren*) crier

Aus|ru|fe-: Aus|ru|fe|satz M exclamation; **Aus|ru|fe|wort** NT *pl* **-wörter** exclamation, interjection; **Aus|ru|fe|zei|chen** NT exclamation mark (*Brit*), exclamation point (*US*)

Aus|ru|fung F **-, -en** proclamation; **die ~ eines Streiks** a strike call

Aus|ru|fungs|zei|chen NT exclamation mark (*Brit*), exclamation point (*US*)

aus+ru|hen VTIR *sep* to rest; (*Mensch*) to take or have a rest; **ausgeruht** (well) rested; **meine Augen müssen (sich) ein wenig ~** I shall have to rest my eyes a little; **seine Augen ~ (lassen)** to rest one's eyes → **Lorbeer b**

aus+rup|fen VT *sep* to pull out; *Federn* to pluck out

aus+rüs|ten VT *sep* (*lit, fig*) to equip; *Fahrzeug, Schiff* to fit out; *Tuch* to treat; **ein Fahrzeug mit etw ~** to fit a car with sth

Aus|rüs|ter [ˈausʀʏstɐ] M **-s, -, Aus|rüs|te|rin** [-əʀɪn] F **-, -nen** (*Sport*: = *Sponsor*) sponsor

Aus|rüs|tung F **a** *no pl* (= *das Ausrüsten*) equipping; (*von Fahrzeug, Schiff*) fitting out; (*von Tuch*) treating **b** (= *Ausrüstungsgegenstände*) equipment; (= *esp Kleidung*) outfit

---

Aus|rüs|tungs|ge|gen|stand M , **Aus|rüs|tungs|stück** NT piece of equipment

aus+rut|schen VI *sep aux sein* to slip; *(fig inf)* (= *sich schlecht benehmen*) to drop a clanger *(Brit inf)*, to put one's foot in it; (= *straffällig werden*) to get into trouble; **das Messer/die Hand ist mir ausgerutscht** my knife/my hand slipped

Aus|rut|scher M *(inf)* *(lit, fig)* slip; (= *schlechte Leistung*) slip-up

Aus|saat F **a** *no pl* (= *das Säen*) sowing **b** (= *Saat*) seed

aus+sä|en VT *sep (lit, fig)* to sow

Aus|sa|ge F statement; (= *Behauptung*) opinion; (= *Bericht*) report; *(Jur)* *(eines Beschuldigten, Angeklagten)* statement; (= *Zeugenaussage*) evidence *no pl*, testimony; *(fig: von Roman etc)* message; **eine eidliche/schriftliche ~** a sworn/written statement; **hier steht ~ gegen ~** it's one person's word against another's; **der Angeklagte verweigerte die ~** the accused refused to make a statement; **der Zeuge verweigerte die ~** the witness refused to give evidence *or* testify; **eine ~ machen** to make a statement, to give evidence; **nach ~ seines Chefs** according to his boss

Aus|sa|ge-: Aus|sa|ge|kraft F , *no pl* meaningfulness; **aus|sa|ge|kräf|tig** ADJ meaningful

aus+sa|gen *sep* VT to say (*über +acc* about); (= *behaupten*) to state; *(unter Eid)* to testify; **was will der Roman ~?** what message does this novel try to convey?; **etw über jdn ~** *(Jur)* to give sth in evidence about sb VI *(Jur)* *(Zeuge)* to give evidence; *(Angeklagter, schriftlich)* to make a statement; *(unter Eid)* to testify; **eidlich** *or* **unter Eid ~** to give evidence under oath; **für/gegen jdn ~** to give evidence *or* to testify for/against sb; **schriftlich ~** to make a written statement

aus+sä|gen VT *sep* to saw out

Aus|sa|ge-: Aus|sa|ge|satz M statement; **aus|sa|ge|stark** ADJ powerful; *Bewerbung* strong; **Aus|sa|ge|ver|wei|ge|rung** F *(Jur)* refusal to give evidence *or* to testify; **ein Recht auf ~ haben** to have a right to refuse to give evidence *or* to testify

Aus|satz M , *no pl (Med)* leprosy; *(fig)* pestilence

aus|sät|zig ADJ *(Med)* leprous

Aus|sät|zi|ge(r) [ˈauszɛtsɪgə] MF *decl as adj (lit, fig)* leper

aus+sau|fen *sep irreg* VT *(Tier)* *Wasser* to drink up; *Napf* to empty

aus+sau|gen VT *sep Saft etc* to suck out; *Frucht* to suck (dry); *Wunde* to suck the poison out of; *(fig: = ausbeuten)* to drain dry; **jdn bis aufs Blut** *or* **Mark ~** to bleed sb white

aus+scha|ben VT *sep* to scrape out; *(Med)* to curette

Aus|scha|bung F -, -en *(Med)* curettage, scrape

aus+schach|ten [ˈausʃaxtn] VT *sep* to dig, to excavate; *Brunnen* to sink

Aus|schach|tung F -, -en **a** *no pl* (= *das Ausschachten*) digging, excavation; *(von Erde)* digging up **b** (= *Grube etc*) excavation

Aus|schach|tungs|ar|bei|ten PL excavation work

aus+schaf|fen VT *sep (Sw, form: = abschieben)* to deport

Aus|schaf|fung F *(Sw, form: = Abschiebung)* deportation

aus+scha|len [ˈausʃaːlən] VT *sep (Build)* = **verschalen**

Aus|schalt|au|to|ma|tik F auto *or* automatic stop

aus+schal|ten VT *sep* **a** (= *abstellen*) to switch off, to turn off; **sich (automatisch) ~** to switch *or* turn (itself) off (automatically) **b** *(fig)* to eliminate

Aus|schal|tung F **a** (= *das Abstellen*) switching off, turning off **b** *(fig)* elimination

Aus|schank¹ M -(e)s, **Ausschänke** [-ˈʃɛŋkə] **a** (= *Schankraum*) bar, pub *(Brit)*; (= *Schanktisch*) bar, counter **b** *(no pl: = Getränkeausgabe)* serving of drinks; **„Ausschank von 9.00 Uhr bis 14.00 Uhr"** "open from 9.00 to 14.00"; **~ über die Straße** ≈ off-sales *pl (Brit)*, selling of drinks for consumption off the premises **„kein ~ an Jugendliche unter 16 Jahren"** "drinks not sold to persons under the age of 16"

Aus|schank² F -, **Ausschänke** *(Aus)* = **Ausschank¹** a

Aus|schank|er|laub|nis F licence *(Brit)*, license *(US)*

Aus|schau F , *no pl* **~ halten** to look out, to be on the lookout

aus+schau|en VI *sep* **a** *(geh)* *(nach* for*)* to look out, to be on the lookout, to keep a lookout **b** *(dial)* = **aussehen a wie schauts aus?** *(inf)* how's things? *(esp Brit inf)*, how are things going?

aus+schau|feln VT *sep Grube, Grab* to dig; *Erde* to dig out; *Leiche* to dig up

aus+schäu|men VT *sep (Tech)* to foam

aus+schei|den *sep irreg* VT (= *aussondern*) to take out; *esp Menschen* to remove; *(Physiol)* to excrete VI *aux sein* **a** (= *aus einem Amt*) to retire *(aus* from); *(aus Club, Firma)* to leave *(aus etw* sth); *(Sport)* to be eliminated; *(in Wettkampf)* to drop out; **wer unfair kämpft, muss ~** whoever cheats will be disqualified **b** (= *nicht in Betracht kommen: Plan, Möglichkeit etc*) to be ruled out; **das/er scheidet aus** that/he has to be ruled out

Aus|schei|dung F **a** *no pl* (= *das Aussondern*) removal; *(Physiol)* excretion **b Ausscheidungen** PL *(Med)* excretions *pl* **c** *(Sport)* elimination; (= *Vorkampf*) qualifying contest *(Brit)*, preliminary (round)

Aus|schei|dungs- in cpds *(Physiol)* excretory; *(Sport)* qualifying *(Brit)*, preliminary; **Aus|schei|dungs|kampf** M *(Sport)* qualifying contest *(Brit)*, preliminary (round); *(Leichtathletik, Schwimmen)* heat; **Aus|schei|dungs|or|gan** NT excretory organ; **Aus|schei|dungs|pro|dukt** NT excretory product; **Aus|schei|dungs|run|de** F *(Sport)* qualifying round; **Aus|schei|dungs|spiel** NT qualifying match *or* game; **Aus|schei|dungs|wett|kampf** M *(Sport)* qualifying contest, qualifier; *(bei Leichtathletik)* (qualifying) heat

aus+schei|ßen VR *sep (vulg)* to have a good shit *(sl)*

aus+schel|ten VT *sep irreg (geh)* to scold

aus+schen|ken VTI *sep* to pour (out); *(am Ausschank)* to serve

aus+sche|ren VI *sep aux sein (aus Kolonne) (Soldat)* to break rank; *(Fahrzeug, Schiff)* to leave the line *or* convoy; *(Flugzeug)* to break formation, to peel off; *(zum Überholen)* to pull out; (= *ausschwenken, von gerader Linie abweichen)* to swing out; *(fig)* to step out of line; **aus der Parteilinie ~** to deviate from the party line

aus+schi|cken VT *sep* to send out

aus+schie|ßen *sep irreg* VT **a jdm ein Auge ~** to shoot out sb's eye **b** *(in Wettbewerb)* to shoot for **c** *(old: = aussondern)* to reject, to throw out **d** *(Typ)* to impose VI *aux sein* **a** *(Pflanzen)* to shoot up **b** *(S Ger, Aus: = verbleichen)* to fade

aus+schif|fen *sep* VT to disembark; *Ladung, Waren* to unload, to discharge VR to disembark

Aus|schif|fung F -, -en disembarkation; *(von Ladung)* unloading, discharging

aus+schil|dern VT *sep* to signpost

aus+schimp|fen VT *sep* to tell off

aus+schir|ren [ˈausʃɪrən] VT *sep Pferd* to unharness; *Ochsen* to unyoke

ausschl. *abbr von* **ausschließlich** excl.

aus+schlach|ten VT *sep* **a** *Tier, Beute* to gut, to dress **b** *(fig) Fahrzeuge, Maschinen etc* to can-

nibalize **c** *(fig inf: = ausnutzen) Skandal, Ereignis* to exploit; *Buch, Werk etc* to get everything out of

aus+schla|fen *sep irreg* VT *Rausch etc* to sleep off VIR to have a good sleep

Aus|schlag M **a** *(Med)* rash; **(einen) ~ bekommen** to come out in *or* get a rash **b** *(von Zeiger etc)* swing; *(von Kompassnadel)* deflection **c** *(fig)* decisive factor; **den ~ geben** *(fig)* to be the decisive factor; **die Stimme des Vorsitzenden gibt den ~** the chairman has the casting vote

aus+schla|gen *sep irreg* VT **a** (= *herausschlagen*) to knock out; *(dial: = ausschütteln) Staubtuch etc* to shake out; **jdm die Zähne ~** to knock sb's teeth out **b** *Feuer* to beat out **c** (= *verkleiden*) to line; *(mit Kacheln, Tapete)* to cover **d** (= *ablehnen*) to turn down; *Erbschaft* to waive; **jdm etw ~** to refuse sb sth VI **a** *aux sein or haben (Baum, Strauch)* to come out, to start to bud, to burgeon (out) *(liter)* **b** (= *los-, zuschlagen)* to hit *or* lash out; *(Pferd)* to kick **c** *aux sein or haben (Zeiger, Nadel, Pendel)* to swing; *(Kompassnadel)* to be deflected; *(Wünschelrute etc)* to dip; **nach oben/unten ~** *(Börsenkurse etc)* to go up/down **d** *ausgeschlagen haben (Turmuhr)* to have finished striking; *(liter: Herz)* to have beat its last *(liter)* **e** *aux sein* **günstig/nachteilig ~** to turn out well *or* favourably *(Brit)* *or* favorably *(US)*/badly; **zu jds Schaden ~** to turn out badly for sb; **zum Guten ~** to turn out all right

aus|schlag|ge|bend ADJ decisive; *Stimme auch* deciding; **~ sein** to be the decisive factor; **das ist von ~er Bedeutung** that is of prime importance

aus+schle|cken VT *sep (S Ger)* to lick out

aus+schlei|fen VT *sep irreg (Tech)* to grind out

aus+schlie|ßen ✪ 43.3, 53.4, 53.6 VT *sep irreg* **a** (= *aussperren*) to lock out **b** (= *entfernen*) to exclude; *(aus Gemeinschaft)* to expel; *(vorübergehend)* to suspend; *(Sport)* to disqualify; *(Typ)* to justify; *Panne, Fehler, Möglichkeit etc* to rule out; **das eine schließt das andere nicht aus** the one does not exclude the other; **ich will nicht ~, dass er ein Dieb ist, aber …** I don't want to rule out the possibility that he's a thief but …; **die Öffentlichkeit ~** *(Jur)* to exclude the public → *auch* **ausgeschlossen**

aus|schließ|lich [ˈausʃliːslɪç, ˌausʃl-, ausˈʃl-] ADJ *attr* exclusive; *Rechte* exclusive, sole ADV exclusively PREP +*gen* exclusive of, excluding

Aus|schließ|lich|keit F -, *no pl* exclusiveness

Aus|schließ|lich|keits|an|spruch M claim to sole rights

Aus|schlie|ßung F = **Ausschluss**

aus+schlüp|fen VI *sep aux sein* to slip out; *(aus Ei, Puppe)* to hatch out

Aus|schluss ▲ M (= *Entfernung*) exclusion; *(aus Gemeinschaft)* expulsion; *(vorübergehend)* suspension; *(Sport)* disqualification; *(Typ)* spacing material; **mit ~ von** *(dated)* with the exception of; **unter ~ der Öffentlichkeit stattfinden** to be closed to the public → **Rechtsweg**

Aus|schluss-: Aus|schluss|frist ▲ F time limit; **Aus|schluss|ver|fah|ren** ▲ NT disqualification system *or* procedure

aus+schmü|cken VT *sep* to decorate; *(fig) Erzählung* to embroider, to embellish; **~de Details** embellishments

Aus|schmü|ckung F -, -en decorating, decoration; *(fig: von Erzählung)* embroidery, embellishment

Aus|schnei|de|bo|gen M cutout sheet

aus+schnei|den VT *sep irreg* **a** (= *herausschneiden*) to cut out; *Zweige etc* to cut away **b** *Baum etc* to prune → *auch* **ausgeschnitten**

Aus|schnitt M **a** (= *Zeitungsausschnitt*) cutting, clipping **b** (*Math*) sector **c** (= *Kleidausschnitt*) neck; **ein tiefer ~** a low neckline; **er versuchte, ihr in den ~ zu schauen** he was trying to look down her dress **d** (*fig: = Teil*) part; (*aus einem Bild*) detail; (*aus einem Roman*) excerpt, extract; (*aus einem Film*) clip; **ich kenne das Buch/den Film nur in ~en** I only know parts of the book/ film

aus|schnitt|wei|se ADJ partial; *Veröffentlichung* in extracts; **bei ~m Lesen** by reading sections ADV *wahrnehmen, vermitteln, erfassen* partially; **etw ~ sehen/hören/zitieren** to see/hear/quote parts of sth

aus+schnit|zen VT *sep* to carve out

aus+schnüf|feln VT *sep* (*inf*) to ferret *or* nose out (*Brit inf*), to sniff out

aus+schöp|fen VT *sep* **a** (= *herausschöpfen*) *Wasser etc* to ladle out (*aus* of); (*aus Boot*) to bale out (*aus* of) **b** (= *leeren*) *Fass etc* to drain, to empty; *Boot* to bale out; (*fig*) to exhaust; **die Kompetenzen voll ~** to do everything within one's power

aus+schrei|ben VT *sep irreg* **a** (*in Buchstaben*) *Zahlen* to write out; (= *ungekürzt schreiben*) *Namen, Abkürzung* to write (out) in full **b** (= *ausstellen*) *Rechnung* to make out; *Rezept, Überweisung* to write out **c** (= *bekannt machen*) to announce; *Versammlung, Wahlen* to call; *Stellen* to advertise; *Projekt, Auftrag* to invite tenders for; *Grundstück* (*zum Verkauf*) to advertise; **etw öffentlich/europaweit ~** (*Stelle*) to advertise sth to the general public/throughout Europe; **jdn zur Fahndung/Festnahme ~** to put sb on the wanted list; **einen Haftbefehl auf jdn ~** to make out a warrant for sb's arrest

Aus|schrei|bung F **a** (= *Bekanntmachung*) announcement; (*von Versammlung, Wahlen*) calling; (*von Projekt*) invitation of tenders (+*gen* for); (*von Stellen*) advertising **b** (= *Ausstellung*) (*von Rechnung*) making out

aus+schrei|en *sep irreg* VT **a** = *ausrufen* **b** (= *schreien*) **sich** (*dat*) **die Kehle** *or* **Lunge ~** (*inf*) to shout one's head off (*inf*) **c** (= *ausbuhen*) to shout down VR (*inf: = zu Ende schreien*) to finish shouting VI to finish shouting

aus+schrei|ten *sep irreg* VI *aux sein* (*geh*) to stride out, to step out VT to pace

Aus|schrei|tung F **-, -en** *usu pl* (= *Aufruhr*) riot, rioting *no pl*; (*dated: = Ausschweifung*) excess

aus+schu|len *sep* VT **ausgeschult werden** to leave school VI *aux sein* (*Aus*) to leave school

Aus|schuss ▲ M **a** *no pl* (*Comm*) rejects *pl*; (*fig inf*) trash **b** (= *Komitee*) committee **c** (*eines Geschosses*) exit point; (= *Wunde*) exit wound

Aus|schuss-: **Aus|schuss|mit|glied** ▲ NT committee member; **Aus|schuss|öff|nung** ▲ F point of exit, exit point; (= *Wunde*) exit wound; **Aus|schuss|sit|zung** ▲ F committee meeting; **Aus|schuss|wa|re** F ▲ (*Comm*) rejects *pl*

aus+schüt|teln VT *sep* to shake out

aus+schüt|ten *sep* VT **a** (= *auskippen*) to tip out; *Eimer, Glas, Füllhorn* to empty; **jdm sein Herz ~** (*fig*) to pour out one's heart to sb → **Kind b** (= *verschütten*) to spill **c** (*Fin*) *Dividende etc* to distribute VR **sich (vor Lachen) ~** (*inf*) to split one's sides laughing

Aus|schüt|tung F **-, -en a** (*Fin*) distribution; (*von Dividende*) dividend **b** (*Phys*) fallout

aus+schwär|men VI *sep aux sein* (*Bienen, Menschen*) to swarm out; (*Mil*) to fan out

aus+schwe|feln VT *sep* to sulphur (*Brit*), to sulfur (*US*), to fumigate (with sulphur (*Brit*) or sulfur (*US*))

aus+schwei|fen *sep* VI *aux sein* (*Redner*) to digress; (*Fantasie*) to run riot; (*in Lebensweise*) to lead a dissipated life VT *Möbelstück* to curve

aus|schwei|fend ADJ *Leben* dissipated; *Fantasie* wild

Aus|schwei|fung F (= *Maßlosigkeit*) excess; (*in Lebensweise*) dissipation

aus+schwei|gen VR *sep irreg* to remain silent (*über* +*acc*, *zu* about); **sich eisern ~** to maintain a stony silence

aus+schwem|men VT *sep* to wash out; *Giftstoffe* to flush out (*aus* of); (= *aushöhlen*) to hollow out

aus+schwen|ken *sep* VT (= *ausspülen*) to rinse out VI *aux sein* **a** (*Mil*) to wheel; **nach links/ rechts ~** to wheel left/right **b** (*Kran, Boot*) to swing out

aus+schwit|zen *sep* VT to sweat out; (*Wände*) to sweat VI *aux sein* to sweat

aus+seg|nen VT *sep* (*Eccl*) *Toten* to give the last blessing to

Aus|seg|nungs|hal|le F chapel of rest

aus+se|hen VI *sep irreg* **a** to look; **gut ~** to look good; (*hübsch*) to be good looking; (*gesund*) to look well; **gesund/elend ~** to look healthy/wretched; **zum Fürchten ~** to look frightening; **es sieht nach Regen aus** it looks like rain, it looks as if it's going to rain; **wie jd/ etw ~** to look like sb/sth; **weißt du, wie ein Gnu aussieht?** do you know what a gnu looks like?; **wie siehts aus?** (*inf:* = *wie stehts*) how's things?; (*esp Brit inf*), how are things going?; **wie siehst du denn (bloß) aus?** what DO you look like?, just look at you!; **ich habe (vielleicht) ausgesehen!** you should have seen me!; **er sieht nach nichts aus** he doesn't look (like) anything special; **es soll nicht etwas ~** it's got to look good; **es sieht danach** *or* **so aus, als ob ...** it looks as if ...; **ihr seht mir danach aus** (*iro*) I bet!; **seh ich so** *or* **danach aus?** (*inf*) what do you take me for?; **so siehst du (gerade) aus!** (*inf*) that's what you think!; **er sieht ganz so** *or* **danach aus** he looks it; **es sieht nicht gut mit ihm aus** things don't look good for him; **bei mir sieht es gut aus** I'm doing fine **b** (*geh:* = *Ausschau halten*) to look out (*nach* for)

Aus|se|hen NT **-s**, *no pl* appearance; **dem ~ nach** to go by appearances, by the looks of it; **etw dem ~ nach beurteilen** to judge sth by appearances

aus sein ▲ *irreg aux sein* VI (*inf*) **a** (= *zu Ende sein*) (*Schule*) to be out, to have finished; (*Krieg, Stück*) to have ended; (= *nicht an sein*) (*Feuer, Ofen*) to be out; (*Radio, Fernseher etc*) to be off; (*Sport*) (= *außerhalb sein*: *Ball*) to be out (of play); (= *ausgeschieden sein*: *Spieler*) to be out **b auf etw** (*acc*) **~** to be (only) after sth *or* interested in sth *or* out for sth; **auf jdn ~** to be after sb (*inf*); **nur auf Männer/auf eins ~** to be interested only in men/one thing **c** (= *ausgehen*) **ich war gestern Abend (mit ihr) aus** I went out (with her) last night VI *impers* **es ist aus (und vorbei) zwischen uns** it's (all) over between us; **es ist aus mit ihm** he is finished, he has had it (*inf*); **es ist aus (und vorbei) mit dem bequemen Leben** the life of leisure is (all) over; **daraus ist nichts geworden, damit ist es aus** nothing came of it, it's finished *or* all over

au|ßen ['aʊsn] ADV **a die Tasse ist ~ bemalt** the cup is painted on the outside; **~ an der Windschutzscheibe** on the outside of the windscreen (*Brit*) *or* windshield (*US*); **von ~ sieht es gut aus** outwardly *or* on the outside it looks good; **er läuft ~** he's running on the outside; **er spielt ~** he's playing on the wing; **das Fenster geht nach ~ auf** the window opens outwards; **nach ~ hin** (*fig*) outwardly; **~ stehend** (*Beobachter etc*) outside *attr* **b ~ vor sein** to be left out; **etw ~ vor lassen** (= *etw ausschließen*) to leave sth out, to exclude sth **c** (*Aus*) = **draußen**

Au|ßen[1] ['aʊsn] M **-, -** (*Sport*) wing; **~ spielen** to play on the wing

Au|ßen[2] NT **-**, *no pl* outside

Au|ßen-: **Au|ßen|ab|mes|sung** F external dimensions *pl*; **Au|ßen|an|sicht** F exterior,

view of the outside; **Au|ßen|an|ten|ne** F outdoor aerial (*Brit*) or antenna (*esp US*); **Au|ßen|ar|bei|ten** PL work on the exterior; **Au|ßen|auf|nah|me** F outdoor shot, exterior; **Au|ßen|bahn** F outside lane; **Au|ßen|be|leuch|tung** F exterior lighting; **Au|ßen|be|zirk** M outlying district; **Au|ßen|bor|der** ['aʊsnbɔrdɐ] M **-s, -** (*inf*) outboard; **Au|ßen|bord|mo|tor** M outboard motor; **au|ßen|bords** ['aʊsnbɔrts] ADV (*Naut*) outboard; **Au|ßen|deich** M outside dyke

aus+sen|den VT *sep irreg* to send out

Au|ßen|dienst M external duty; **im ~ sein** to work outside the office; **~ machen** or **haben** to work outside the office

Au|ßen|dienst|mit|ar|bei|ter(in) M(F) sales representative

Au|ßen-: Au|ßen|flä|che F outside, outside *or* exterior surface; (= *Flächeninhalt*) external surface area; **Au|ßen|ha|fen** M outer harbour (*Brit*) *or* harbor (*US*); (= *Hafenstadt*) port

Au|ßen|han|del M foreign trade

Au|ßen|han|dels-: **Au|ßen|han|dels|be|zie|hun|gen** PL foreign trade relations *pl*; **Au|ßen|han|dels|bi|lanz** F balance of trade; **Au|ßen|han|dels|po|li|tik** F foreign trade policy

Au|ßen-: **Au|ßen|haut** F outer skin; **Au|ßen|kur|ve** F outside bend; **Au|ßen|li|nie** F (*Sport*) boundary (line); **Au|ßen|mi|nis|ter(in)** M(F) foreign minister, foreign secretary (*Brit*), secretary of state (*US*); **Au|ßen|mi|nis|te|ri|um** NT foreign ministry, Foreign Office (*Brit*), State Department (*US*); **Au|ßen|netz** NT (*Ftbl*) side netting; **Au|ßen|po|li|tik** F (*Gebiet*) foreign politics *sing*; (*bestimmte*) foreign policy; **Au|ßen|po|li|ti|ker(in)** M(F) foreign affairs politician; **au|ßen|po|li|tisch** ADJ *Debatte, Einfluss, Sprecher* on foreign affairs; *Schaden* to foreign affairs; *Fehler* as regards foreign affairs; *Berichterstattung* of foreign affairs; *Schulung, Erfahrung* in foreign affairs; **~e Angelegenheiten** foreign affairs; **aus ~er Sicht** from the point of view of foreign affairs; **ein Experte auf ~em Gebiet** an expert on foreign affairs ADV in terms of foreign policy; **sinnvoll sein** to be sensible foreign policy; **~ gesehen** from the point of view of foreign affairs; **Au|ßen|sei|te** F outside; **die vordere ~ des Hauses** the front of the house

Au|ßen|sei|ter ['aʊsnzaitɐ] M **-s, -**, **Au|ßen|sei|te|rin** [-ərɪn] F **-, -nen** (*Sport, fig*) outsider

Au|ßen|sei|ter-: **Au|ßen|sei|ter|rol|le** F role as an outsider; **eine ~ spielen** to play the role of an outsider; **Au|ßen|sei|ter|tum** ['aʊsnzaitɛtuːm] NT **-s**, *no pl* being an outsider; **das ~ als literarisches Thema** the outsider as a literary theme

Au|ßen-: **Au|ßen|spie|gel** M (*Aut*) outside mirror; **Au|ßen|stän|de** PL (*esp Comm*) outstanding debts *pl*, arrears *pl*; **wir haben noch 2.000 Euro ~** we still have *or* there are still 2,000 euros outstanding; **au|ßen|ste|hend** ADJ → **außen** a; **Au|ßen|ste|hen|de(r)** ['aʊsnʃteːəndə] MF *decl as adj* outsider; **Au|ßen|stel|le** F branch; **Au|ßen|stür|mer(in)** M(F) (*Ftbl*) wing; **Au|ßen|ta|sche** F outside pocket; **Au|ßen|tem|pe|ra|tur** F outside temperature; (*außerhalb Gebäude*) outdoor temperature; **wir haben 20° ~** the temperature outdoors is 20°; **Au|ßen|tem|pe|ra|tur|an|zei|ge** F (*Aut*) external temperature gauge; **Au|ßen|toi|let|te** F outside toilet; (*auf dem Flur*) shared toilet; **Au|ßen|trep|pe** F outside staircase; **Au|ßen|wand** F outer wall; **Au|ßen|welt** F outside world; **Au|ßen|wer|bung** F outdoor advertising; **Au|ßen|win|kel** M (*Math*) exterior or angle; **Au|ßen|wirt|schaft** F foreign trade; **Au|ßen|zoll** M external tariff

au|ßer ['aʊsɐ] PREP +*dat or* (*rare*) *gen* **a** (*räumlich*) out of; **~ Sicht/Gefecht/Kurs** *etc* out of sight/action/circulation *etc*; **~ sich** (*acc*) **geraten** to go wild; **~ sich** (*dat*) **sein** to be beside oneself; **~ Haus** or **Hauses sein/essen** to be/eat out; **~ Atem** out of breath → **Acht²**, **Betrieb b**, **Land c b** (= *ausgenommen*) except (for); (= *abgesehen von*) apart from, aside from (*esp US*); **~ ihm habe ich keine Verwandten mehr** I have no relatives left apart from him or left but him **c** (= *zusätzlich zu*) in addition to **CONJ** except; **~ dass ...** except that ...; **~ wenn ...** except when...; **~ sonntags** except Sundays

Au|ßer-: Au|ßer|acht|las|sung [ausɐ'ʔaxtlasʊŋ] F -, *no pl* disregard; **unter ~ der Regeln** in total disregard of the rules, with total disregard for the rules; **au|ßer|amt|lich** ADJ unofficial; **au|ßer|be|trieb|lich** ADJ Veranstaltung, Regelung private; Tätigkeiten, Arbeitsplätze outside; Berufsbildungsstätte external ADV veranstalten, regeln privately; ausbilden externally; **sie treffen sich auch ~** they also meet outside work

au|ßer|dem ['ausɐde:m, ausɐ'de:m] ADV besides; (= *dazu*) in addition, as well; (= *überdies*) anyway; **ich kann ihn nicht leiden, (und) ~ lügt er immer** I can't stand him and besides or anyway he always tells lies; **er ist Professor und ~ noch Gutachter** he's a professor and a consultant besides or as well

au|ßer|dienst|lich ADJ (= *nicht dienstlich*) Telefonat, Angelegenheit private; (= *außerhalb der Arbeitszeit*) social ADV **ich bin heute ~ unterwegs** I'm not on business today; **dürfte ich Sie mal ~ sprechen?** could I speak to you privately?

au|ßer|ehe|lich ADJ extramarital; Kind illegitimate ADV outside marriage; **das Kind war ~ gezeugt worden** the child had been conceived out of wedlock

äu|ße|re(r, s) ['ɔysərə] ADJ (= *außerhalb gelegen*, Geog) outer; Durchmesser, Verletzung external; (= *außenpolitisch*) external; Schein, Eindruck outward

Äu|ße|re(s) ['ɔysərə] NT decl as adj exterior; (fig: = *Aussehen auch*) outward appearance; **das ~ täuscht oft** appearances are often deceptive; **Minister ~n** (form) foreign minister, foreign secretary (Brit), secretary of state (US)

Au|ßer-: außer|eu|ro|pä|isch ADJ attr non-European; Raum outside Europe; **au|ßer|fahr|plan|mä|ßig** ADJ nonscheduled ADV **dieser Zug verkehrt ~** this train is running outside of the normal timetable; **au|ßer|ge|richt|lich** ADJ, ADV out of court; **au|ßer|ge|setz|lich** ADJ extralegal; (= *gesetzbrecherisch*) illegal; **au|ßer|ge|wöhn|lich** ADJ unusual, out of the ordinary; (= *sehr groß*) remarkable; **Außergewöhnliches leisten** to do some remarkable things ADV (= *sehr*) extremely

au|ßer|halb ['ausɐhalp] PREP +gen outside; **~ der Stadt** outside the town, out of town; **~ der Dienststunden** out of or outside office hours; **~ der Legalität** outside the law ADV (= *außen*) outside; (= *außerhalb der Stadt*) out of town; **~ wohnen/arbeiten** to live/work out of town; **nach ~** outside; (der Stadt) out of town; **von ~** from outside/out of town; **~ stehen** (fig) to be on the outside

Au|ßer-: außer|ir|disch ADJ extraterrestrial; **Au|ßer|ir|di|sche(r)** ['ausɐʔɪrdɪʃə] MF decl as adj extraterrestrial; **au|ßer|kirch|lich** ADJ nonecclesiastic(al); Trauung civil; **Au|ßer|kraft|set|zung** [ausɐ'kraftzɛtsʊŋ] F -, -en repeal; **Au|ßer|kurs|set|zung** [ausɐ'kʊrszɛtsʊŋ] F -, -en (von Währung) withdrawal (from circulation); (fig) rejection

äu|ßer|lich ['ɔysɐlɪç] ADJ **a** external; **„nur ~!“**, **„nur ~ zur Anwendung!“** for external use only **b** (fig: = *oberflächlich*) superficial; (= *scheinbar*) outward; (esp Philos) Wahrnehmung external; **einer Sache** (dat) **~ sein** (geh) to be extrinsic to sth ADV **a** externally; **~ schien er unverletzt** he seemed to have no external injuries **b** (fig) (= *oberflächlich*) outwardly, superficially; **sie wirkt ~ jung** in terms of appearance she seems young; **rein ~** externally on the face of it

Äu|ßer|lich|keit F -, -en **a** (fig) triviality; (= *Oberflächlichkeit*) superficiality; (= *Formalität*) for-

mality **b** (lit) external characteristic; **~en** pl (outward) appearances

äu|ßerln ['ɔysɐln] VTI infin only (Aus) **einen Hund ~ (führen)** to take a dog for a walk

äu|ßern ['ɔysɐn] ✪ 33.3 **VT** (= *sagen*) to say; Wunsch etc to express; Worte to utter; Kritik to voice; **seine Meinung ~** to give one's opinion or views **VR** (Mensch) to speak; (Krankheit, Symptom) to show or manifest itself; **sich dahin gehend ~, dass ...** to make a comment to the effect that ...; **ich will mich dazu nicht ~** I don't want to say anything about that

Au|ßer-: außer|or|dent|lich ADJ extraordinary; (= *ungewöhnlich*) exceptional; (= *bemerkenswert*) remarkable, exceptional; Professor associate; **~e Hauptversammlung** extraordinary general meeting; **Außerordentliches leisten** to achieve some remarkable things ADV (= *sehr*) exceptionally, extremely, extraordinarily; **au|ßer|orts** ['ausɐʔɔrts] ADV (Sw, Aus) out of town; **au|ßer|par|la|men|ta|risch** ADJ extraparliamentary; **au|ßer|plan|mä|ßig** ADJ Besuch, Treffen, Sitzung unscheduled; Mahlzeit additional; Ausgaben unbudgeted; Defizit unplanned ADV **sie trafen sich ~** they had an unscheduled meeting; **dieser Bus verkehrt ~** this bus is running outside of the normal timetable; **au|ßer|schu|lisch** ADJ Aktivitäten, Interessen extracurricular; **au|ßer|sinn|lich** ADJ extrasensory; **~e Wahrnehmung** extrasensory perception

äu|ßerst ['ɔysɛst] ADV extremely, exceedingly

au|ßer|stan|de [ausɐ'ʃtandə, 'ausɐʃtandə] ADV (= *unfähig*) incapable; (= *nicht in der Lage*) unable; **~ sein, etw zu tun** to be incapable of doing sth, to be unable to do sth

äu|ßers|ten|falls ADV at most

äu|ßers|te(r, s) ['ɔysɛstə] ADJ superl von **äußere(r, s)** (räumlich) furthest; Planet, Schicht outermost; Norden etc extreme; (zeitlich) latest possible; (fig) utmost, extreme; **der ~ Preis** the last price; **mein ~s Angebot** my final offer; **im ~n Falle** if the worst comes to the worst, if worst comes to worst (US); **mit ~r Kraft** with all one's strength; **von ~r Dringlichkeit/Wichtigkeit** of (the) utmost urgency/importance

Äu|ßers|te(s) ['ɔysɛstə] NT decl as adj **bis zum ~n gehen** to go to extremes; **er geht bis zum ~n** he would go to any extreme; **er hat sein ~s gegeben** he gave his all; **das ~ wagen** to risk everything; **ich bin auf das ~ gefasst** I'm prepared for the worst

au|ßer-: au|ßer|ta|rif|lich ADJ Regelung nonunion; Zuschlag supplementary to agreed union rates ADV **~ bezahlt werden** to be paid nonunion rates; **au|ßer|tour|lich** [-tuːɐlɪç] (Aus, S Ger) ADJ additional; **ein ~er Bus** a special ADV in addition; **und ich mache ~ noch Überstunden** and I do overtime as well or on top

Äu|ße|rung ['ɔysərʊŋ] F -, -en (= *Bemerkung*) remark, comment; (Ling, = *Behauptung*) statement; (= *Zeichen*) expression; **Tränen als ~ der Trauer** tears as an expression of mourning

Äu|ße|rungs|form F manifestation

aus+set|zen sep **VT a** Kind, Haustier to abandon; Wild, Fische to release; Pflanzen to plant out; (Naut) Passagiere to maroon; Boot to lower **b** (= *preisgeben*) **jdn/etw einer Sache** (dat) **~ to** expose sb/sth to sth; **jdm/einer Sache ausgesetzt sein** (= *ausgeliefert*) to be at the mercy of sb/sth; **jdn dem Gelächter ~** to expose sb to ridicule **c** (= *festsetzen*) Belohnung, Preis to offer; (in Testament) to bequeath, to leave; **auf jds Kopf** (acc) **1000 Dollar ~** to put 1,000 dollars on sb's head; **für Hinweise, die zur Ergreifung der Täter führen, sind 5.000 Euro Belohnung ausgesetzt** a reward of 5,000 euros is being offered for information leading to the arrest of the suspects **d** (= *unterbrechen*) to interrupt; Debatte, Prozess to adjourn; Zahlung to break off

e (= *vertagen*) Strafvollstreckung, Verfahren to suspend; Urteilsverkündung to defer; **eine Strafe zur Bewährung ~** to give a suspended sentence **f** an jdm/etw etwas auszusetzen haben to find fault with sb/sth; **daran ist nichts auszusetzen** there is nothing wrong with it; **daran habe ich nur eines auszusetzen** I've only one objection to make to that; **was haben Sie daran auszusetzen?** what don't you like about it? **g** Billardkugel to place **h** (Eccl) to expose **VI** (= *aufhören*) to stop; (Mensch) to break off, to stop; (bei Spiel) to sit out; (Herz) to stop (beating); (Motor) to fail, to stop; (= *versagen*) to give out; **mit etw ~** to stop sth; **mit der Pille ~** to stop taking the pill; **mit der Behandlung ~** to interrupt the treatment; **zwei Wochen mit der Arbeit ~** to interrupt one's work for two weeks; **ich setze besser mal aus** I'd better have a break; (bei Spiel) I'd better sit this one out; **einen Tag ~** to take a day off; **ohne auszusetzen** without a break

Aus|set|zung F -, -en **a** (von Kind, Tier) abandonment; (von Fischen, Wild) release; (von Pflanzen) planting out; (Naut) (von Passagieren) marooning; (von Boot) lowering **b** (= *Festsetzung*) (von Belohnung) offer; (in Testament) bequest; **durch ~ einer Belohnung** by offering a reward, by the offer of a reward **c** (= *Unterbrechung*) interruption; (von Debatte, Prozess) adjournment; (von Zahlung) breaking off **d** (Jur) (von Vollstreckung, Verfahren) suspension; (von Urteilsverkündung) deferment; **die ~ der Strafe zur Bewährung war in diesem Falle nicht möglich** it was impossible to give a suspended sentence in this case **e** (Eccl: des Allerheiligsten) exposition

Aus|sicht F -, -en **a** (= *Blick*) view (auf +acc of); **ein Zimmer mit ~ auf den Park** a room overlooking the park; **jdm die ~ nehmen/verbauen** to block or obstruct sb's view **b** (fig) prospect (auf +acc of); **die ~, dass etw geschieht** the chances of sth happening; **gute ~en haben** to have good prospects; **unser Plan hat große ~en auf Erfolg** our plan has every prospect or chance of succeeding; **keine ~** no prospect or chance; **nicht die geringste ~** not the slightest prospect or chance; **etw in ~ haben** to have good prospects of sth; **jdn/etw in ~ nehmen** (form) to take sb/sth into consideration; **jdm etw in ~ stellen** to promise sb sth; **in ~ stehen** to be in prospect; **das sind ja schöne ~en!** (iro inf) what a prospect!

Aus|sichts-: aus|sichts|los ADJ hopeless; (= *zwecklos*) pointless; **eine ~e Sache** a lost cause; **Aus|sichts|lo|sig|keit** F -, no pl hopelessness; (= *Zwecklosigkeit*) pointlessness; **Aus|sichts|platt|form** F viewing or observation platform or deck; **Aus|sichts|punkt** M viewpoint; (fig) vantage point; **aus|sichts|reich** ADJ promising; Stellung with good prospects; **Aus|sichts|turm** M observation or lookout tower; **aus|sichts|voll** ADJ promising; **Aus|sichts|wa|gen** M (Rail) observation car

aus+sie|ben VT sep (lit, fig) to sift out

aus+sie|deln VT sep to resettle; (= *evakuieren*) to evacuate

Aus|sied|ler(in) M(F) (= *Auswanderer*) emigrant; (= *Evakuierter*) evacuee where they are by the setting-up of local schemes to help with housing, jobs and German-language education.

Aus|sied|lung F resettlement; (= *Evakuierung*) evacuation

aus+sit|zen VT *sep irreg* Problem to sit out

aus+söh|nen ['aʊszøːnən] *sep* **VT** jdn mit jdm/ etw ~ to reconcile sb with sb/to sth; jdn ~ to appease sb **VR** sich mit jdm/etw ~ to become reconciled with sb/to sth; **wir haben uns wieder ausgesöhnt** we have made it up again **VI** mit etw ~ to compensate for sth

Aus|söh|nung F -, -en reconciliation (*mit jdm* with sb, *mit etw* with sth)

aus+son|dern VT *sep* **a** (= *auslesen*) to select; *Schlechtes* to pick out; (*euph*) *Menschen* to single out; **die ausgesonderte Ware wird billig abgegeben** the reject goods are sold cheaply **b** (*Physiol*) to secrete

Aus|son|de|rung F -, -en **a** selection; (*von Schlechtem*) picking out; (*euph*: *von Menschen*) singling out **b** (*Physiol*) secretion

aus+sor|gen VI *sep* **ausgesorgt haben** to have no more money worries, to be set up for life

aus+sor|tie|ren *ptp* **aussortiert** VT *sep* to sort out

aus+spä|hen *sep* **VI** nach jdm/etw ~ to look out for sb/sth **VT** to spy out; (*Mil*) to reconnoitre

aus+span|nen *sep* **VT** **a** *Tuch, Netz* to spread out; *Schnur, Leine* to put up **b** (= *ausschirren*) to unharness, to unhitch; *Ochsen* to unyoke; (*aus Schreibmaschine*) *Bogen* to take out **c** (*fig inf*) **jdm etw ~** to do sb out of sth (*inf*); **jdm die Freundin** *etc* ~ to pinch (*Brit inf*) or steal sb's girlfriend *etc* **VI** **a** (= *sich erholen*) to have a break **b** (*Pferde ausspannen*) to unharness the horses; (*Ochsen ausspannen*) to unyoke the oxen

Aus|span|nung F , *no pl* (*fig*) relaxation; **zur ~** for relaxation

aus+spa|ren VT *sep* *Fläche* to leave blank; (*fig*) to omit

Aus|spa|rung F -, -en (= *Lücke*) gap; (*= unbeschriebene Stelle*) blank space

aus+spei|en *sep irreg* **VT** (= *ausspucken*) to spit out; (= *erbrechen*) to bring up, to disgorge (*form*); (*fig*: = *herausschleudern*) to spew out or forth **VI** to spit out; **das Ausspeien** spitting

aus+sper|ren VT *sep* to lock out

Aus|sper|rung F (*Ind*) lockout; **mit ~ drohen** to threaten (the workers with) a lockout; **die ~ sollte illegal sein** lockouts should be made illegal

aus+spie|len *sep* **VT** **a** *Karte* to play; (*am Spielanfang*) to lead with; **einen Trumpf ~** (*lit*) to play a trump (card); (*fig*) to play a or one's trump card; **seinen letzten Trumpf ~** (*fig*) to play one's last card
b *Rolle, Szene* to act out; **er hat (seine Rolle) ausgespielt** (*fig*) he's finished or through (*inf*), he's played out (*inf*)
c (= *zu Ende spielen*) to finish playing
d (*fig*: = *einsetzen*) *Überlegenheit etc* to display
e (*fig*) **jdn/etw gegen jdn/etw ~** to play sb/sth off against sb/sth
f (*Sport*) *Pokal, Meisterschaft* to play for; *Gegner* to outplay
g *Gewinne* to give as a prize/as prizes
VI **a** (*Cards*) to play a card; (*als erster*) to lead; **wer spielt aus?** whose lead is it?, who has the lead?
b (= *zu Ende spielen*) to finish playing → *auch* **ausgespielt**

Aus|spie|lung F -, -en (*im Lotto*) payout

aus+spin|nen VT *sep irreg* to spin out; (= *sich ausdenken*) to think up

aus+spi|o|nie|ren *ptp* **ausspioniert** VT *sep* Pläne *etc* to spy out; *Person* to spy (up)on

aus+spot|ten VT *sep* (*S Ger, Sw, Aus*) = **verspotten**

Aus|spra|che F **a** pronunciation; (= *Art des Artikulierens*) articulation; (= *Akzent*) accent **b** (= *Meinungsaustausch*) discussion; (= *Gespräch*) talk; **es kam zu einer offenen ~ zwischen den beiden** they talked things out; **eine ~ herbeiführen** to bring things out into the open

Aus|spra|che-: Aus|spra|che|an|ga|be F , **Aus|spra|che|be|zeich|nung** F (*Ling*) phonetic transcription; **Aus|spra|che|wör|ter|buch** NT dictionary of pronunciation, pronouncing dictionary

aus|sprech|bar ADJ pronounceable; **leicht/ schwer ~** easy/difficult to pronounce; **nicht ~** unpronounceable

aus+spre|chen *sep irreg* **VT** *Wort, Urteil etc* to pronounce; *Scheidung* to grant; (= *zu Ende sprechen*) *Satz* to finish; (= *äußern*) to express (*jdm* to sb); *Verdächtigung* to voice; *Warnung* to give, to deliver; **jdm ein Lob ~** to give sb a word of praise; **der Regierung sein Vertrauen ~** to pass a vote of confidence in the government
VR **a** (*Partner*) to talk things out; (= *sein Herz ausschütten, seine Meinung sagen*) to say what's on one's mind; **sich mit jdm (über etw acc) ~** to have a talk with sb (about sth); (= *jdm sein Herz ausschütten*) to have a heart-to-heart (talk) with sb (about sth); **sich für/gegen etw ~** to declare or pronounce oneself in favour (*Brit*) or favor (*US*) of/against sth, to come out in favour (*Brit*) or favor (*US*) of/against sth; **sich lobend über jdn/etw ~** to speak highly of sb/sth
b (*Wort*) to be pronounced; **dieses Wort spricht sich leicht/schwer aus** this word is easy/difficult to pronounce
VI (= *zu Ende sprechen*) to finish (speaking) → *auch* **ausgesprochen**

aus+spren|gen VT *sep* (*mit Sprengstoff*) to blast out

aus+sprit|zen VT *sep* **a** *Flüssigkeit* to squirt out; (*sprühend*) to spray out **b** *Bottich* to flush (out); (*Med*) *Zahn etc* to rinse out; *Ohr* to syringe **c** *Feuer* to put out

Aus|spruch M remark; (= *geflügeltes Wort*) saying

aus+spu|cken *sep* **VT** to spit out; (*fig*) *Produkte* to pour or spew out; (*hum inf*) *Geld* to cough up (*inf*); *Gelerntes* to regurgitate; **sie hat das ganze Essen wieder ausgespuckt** (*inf*: = *erbrochen*) she vomited or spewed (*inf*) the whole meal back up again **VI** to spit; **vor jdm ~** to spit at sb's feet; (*fig*) to spit upon sb

aus+spü|len VT *sep* to rinse (out); (*kräftiger*) to flush (out); (*Med, Geol*) to wash out; **sich** (*dat*) **den Mund ~** to rinse one's mouth (out)

Aus|spü|lung F (*Med*) irrigation; (*Geol*) erosion

aus+staf|fie|ren ['aʊsʃtafiːrən] *ptp* **ausstaffiert** VT *sep* (*inf*) to equip, to fit out; *jdn* to rig or kit (*Brit*) out; (= *herausputzen*) to dress up; **sein Roman ist mit sämtlichen Klischees ausstaffiert** his novel is peppered with clichés

Aus|staf|fie|rung F -, -en (*inf*) equipment, fittings *pl*; (= *Kleidung*) rig(-out) (*inf*), outfit

Aus|stand M **a** (= *Streik*) strike, industrial action (*Brit*); **im ~ sein** to be on strike; **in den ~ treten** (go on) strike, to take industrial action (*Brit*) **b** *usu pl* (*Comm*) outstanding debt **c** **seinen ~ geben** to throw a leaving party

aus|stän|dig ADJ (*esp Aus*) outstanding

aus+stan|zen VT *sep* *Metallteil* to stamp out; *Loch* to punch (out)

aus+stat|ten ['aʊsʃtatn] VT *sep* to equip; (= *versorgen*) to provide, to furnish; (*mit Rechten*) to vest (*esp Jur*); (= *möblieren*) to furnish; *Buch* to produce; **mit Intelligenz etc ausgestattet sein** to be endowed with intelligence *etc*; **ein Zimmer neu ~** to refurbish a room

Aus|stat|ter ['aʊsʃtatɐ] M -, -, **Aus|stat|te|rin** [-ərɪn] F -, -nen **a** (= *Herrenausstatter*) gentleman's outfitter, haberdasher (*US*) **b** (= *Raumausstatter*) interior decorator; (*Firma*) (firm of) interior decorators *pl*, interior decorating

company **c** (*Film, Theat etc*) set designer; (*Kostüme*) wardrobe designer

Aus|stat|tung F -, -en **a** (= *Ausrüstung*) equipment; (*Tech auch*) fittings *pl*; (= *Kapital*) provisions *pl*; (*von Zimmer etc*) furnishings *pl*; (*Theat*) décor and costumes *pl*; (= *Mitgift*) dowry; (*von Buch*) presentation **b** (= *das Ausstatten*) equipping; (= *Versorgung*) provision; (*mit Rechten*) vesting; (= *das Möblieren*) furnishing; (*von Buch*) production

Aus|stat|tungs-: Aus|stat|tungs|film M spectacular (film); **Aus|stat|tungs|stück** NT **a** (*Theat*) spectacular (show) **b** (= *Möbelstück*) piece of furniture

aus+ste|chen VT *sep irreg* **a** *Pflanzen, Unkraut* to dig up; *Torf, Plätzchen* to cut out; *Apfel* to core; *Graben* to dig (out) **b** *Augen* (*esp als Strafe*) to gouge out, to put out **c** (*fig*) *jdn* (= *verdrängen*) to push out; (= *übertreffen*) to outdo; **jdn bei einem Mädchen ~** to take sb's place in a girl's affections; **jdn beim Chef ~** to push sb out of favour (*Brit*) or favor (*US*) with the boss

Aus|stech|form F , **Aus|stech|förm|chen** NT (*Cook*) cutter

aus+ste|hen *sep irreg* **VT** (= *ertragen*) to endure; (= *erdulden auch*) to put up with; *Sorge, Angst* to go through, to suffer; **ich kann ihn/so etwas nicht ~** I can't bear or stand him/anything like that; **jetzt ist es ausgestanden** now it's all over; **mit jdm viel auszustehen haben** to have to go through a lot with sb, to have to put up with a lot from sb
VI **a** (= *fällig sein*) to be due; (*Antwort*) to be still to come; (*Buch*) to be still to appear; (*Entscheidung*) to be still to be taken; (*Lösung*) to be still to be found; (= *noch zu erwarten sein*) to be still expected
b (*Schulden, Zahlung*) to be outstanding; **Geld ~ haben** to have money owing; **~de Forderungen** outstanding demands

aus+stei|gen VI *sep irreg aux sein* **a** (*aus Fahrzeug*) to get out (*aus* of); (*aus Bus, Zug etc auch*) to get off (*aus etw* sth), to alight (*aus* from) (*form*); (*Aviat sl*) to bale or bail out (*aus* of); (*fig: aus Gesellschaft*) to opt out; **alles ~!** everybody out!; (*von Schaffner*) all change!; **das Aussteigen während der Fahrt ist verboten** do not alight while train etc is in motion (*form*) **b** (*Sport:* = *aufgeben*) to give up, to retire (*aus* from); (*bei Wettrennen auch*) to drop out (*aus* of); **einen Gegenspieler ~ lassen** (*esp Ftbl*) to outplay an opponent **c** (*inf: aus Geschäft etc*) to get out (*aus* of)

Aus|stei|ger(in) M(F) (*aus Gesellschaft*) person who opts out, dropout (*esp pej*); (*aus Terroristenszene, Sekte, Prostitution*) dropout

aus+stel|len *sep* **a** (= *zur Schau stellen*) to display; (*auf Messe, in Museum etc*) to exhibit **b** (= *ausschreiben*) to make out (*jdm* to sb), to write (out) (*jdm* sb); (= *behördlich ausgeben*) to issue (*jdm etw* sb with sth, sth to sb); **einen Scheck auf jdn ~** to make out a cheque (*Brit*) or check (*US*) to sb, to make a cheque (*Brit*) or check (*US*) payable to sb; **eine Rechnung über EUR 500 ~** to make out a bill for EUR 500 **c** (= *ausschalten*) *Gerät* to turn or switch off **d** → **ausgestellt VI** to exhibit

Aus|stel|ler ['aʊsʃtɛlɐ] M -s, -, **Aus|stel|le|rin** [-ərɪn] F -, -nen **a** (*auf Messe*) exhibitor **b** (*von Dokument*) issuer; (*von Scheck*) drawer

Aus|stell|fens|ter NT (*Aut*) quarterlight (*Brit*), vent (window) (*US*)

Aus|stel|lung F **a** (= *Kunstausstellung, Messe*) exhibition; (= *Blumenausstellung, Hundeausstellung etc*) show **b** *no pl* (*von Scheck, Rezept, Rechnung etc*) making out; (*behördlich*) issuing

Aus|stel|lungs-: Aus|stel|lungs|be|su|cher(in) M(F) visitor (*to an/the exhibition*); **Aus|stel|lungs|da|tum** NT date of issue; **Aus|stel|lungs|flä|che** F exhibition area; **Aus|stel|lungs|ge|län|de** NT exhibition site or area; **Aus|stel|lungs|hal|le** F exhibition hall; **Aus|stel|lungs|ka|ta|log** M exhibition catalogue (*Brit*) *or* catalog (*US*); **Aus|stel|lungs|stand** M exhibition stand; **Aus|stel|lungs|stück** NT (*in Ausstellung*) exhibit; (*in Schaufenster etc*) display item; **Aus|stel|lungs|tag** M day of issue

aus+stem|peln VI *sep* (*bei Arbeitsende*) to clock out *or* off

Aus|ster|be|etat M (*hum*) **auf dem ~ stehen** *or* **sein** to be being phased out; **etw auf den ~ setzen** to phase sth out

aus+ster|ben VI *sep irreg aux sein* to die out; (*esp Spezies, Geschlecht auch*) to become extinct; **die Dummen sterben nie aus** there's one born every minute → *auch* **ausgestorben**

Aus|ster|ben NT extinction; **im ~ begriffen** dying out, becoming extinct; **vom ~ bedroht sein** to be threatened by extinction

Aus|steu|er F dowry

aus+steu|ern VT *sep* **a** (*Insur*) to disqualify **b** *Gerät, Sound* to balance; **schlecht ausgesteuerte Musik** music with poor sound balance

Aus|steu|e|rung F (*Insur*) disqualification

Aus|steu|e|rungs|au|to|ma|tik F automatic tuning

Aus|steu|er|ver|si|che|rung F endowment insurance (*for one's daughter's wedding etc*)

Aus|stieg M **a** *no pl* (= *das Aussteigen*) climbing out (*aus of*); (*aus Bus, Zug etc*) getting out *or* off, alighting (*aus from*) (*form*); (*fig: aus Gesellschaft*) opting out (*aus of*); **der ~ aus der Kernenergie** abandoning nuclear energy; **der ~ aus einer Organisation** withdrawal from an organization **b** (= *Ausgang*) exit **c** (*auch* **Ausstieggluke**) exit *or* escape hatch

Aus|stiegs|lu|ke F (*Tech: aus Raumfahrzeug etc*) exit hatch; (*für Notfall*) escape hatch

aus+stop|fen VT *sep Kissen etc, Tiere* to stuff; *Ritzen* to fill; **sich** (*dat*) **den Bauch ~** to pad one's stomach

aus+stöp|seln VT *sep* (*Elec*) to unplug

Aus|stoß M **a** (*esp Phys, Tech: = das Ausstoßen*) expulsion, ejection, discharge; (*von Torpedo, Geschoss*) firing **b** (= *Ausschluss: aus Verein etc*) expulsion **c** (= *Produktion*) output, production

aus+sto|ßen VT *sep irreg* **a** (= *äußern*) to utter; *Schrei* to give; *Seufzer* to heave
b (= *ausschließen: aus Verein, Armee etc*) to expel (*aus from*); (= *verbannen*) to banish (*aus from*); **jdn aus der Gesellschaft ~** to banish sb from society, to cast sb out from society → **Ausgestoßene(r)**
c (= *herausstoßen*) to eject, to discharge; *Atem, Plazenta* to expel; *Gas etc* to give off, to emit; (*Naut*) *Torpedo* to fire; (= *herstellen*) *Teile, Stückzahl* to put *or* turn out, to produce
d sich (*dat*) **ein Auge/einen Zahn ~** to lose an eye/a tooth; **jdm ein Auge ~** to put sb's eye out; **jdm einen Zahn ~** to knock sb's tooth out
e (*Ling*) *Laut* to drop

Aus|stoß|rohr NT (*Naut*) torpedo tube

Aus|sto|ßung ['ausʃtoːsʊŋ] F -, -en **a** (*aus from*) (= *Ausschließung*) expulsion; (*aus der Gesellschaft*) banishment; (*aus einer Gemeinschaft*) exclusion **b** (*Ling: eines Lautes*) dropping

aus+strah|len *sep* **VT** to radiate (*auch fig*); *esp Licht, Wärme auch* to give off; (*Rad, TV*) to transmit, to broadcast **VI** *aux sein* to radiate; (*esp Licht, Wärme auch*) to be given off; (*Schmerz*) to extend, to spread (*bis in +acc* as far as); **seine Freude strahlte auf die Zuhörer aus** his joy was communicated to the listeners

Aus|strah|lung F radiation; (*Rad, TV*) transmission, broadcast(ing); (*fig: von Ort*) aura; (*von Mensch*) charisma

aus+stre|cken *sep* **VT** to extend (*nach towards*); *Fühler auch* to put out; *Hand auch, Beine etc* to stretch out; *Zunge* to stick out (*nach at*); **mit ausgestreckten Armen** with arms extended **VR** to stretch (oneself) out

aus+strei|chen VT *sep irreg* **a** *Geschriebenes* to cross *or* strike (*Brit*) out, to delete; (*fig*) to ob-

literate; **jds Namen auf einer Liste ~** to cross *or* strike (*Brit*) sb's name off a list, to delete sb's name from a list **b** (= *glätten*) *Falten* to smooth out **c** *Backform* (*mit Fett*) to grease

aus+streu|en VT *sep* to scatter, to spread; (*fig*) *Gerücht* to spread, to put about; **die Garage mit Holzspänen ~** to cover the garage floor with wood shavings

aus+strö|men *sep* **VI** *aux sein* **a** (= *herausfließen*) to stream *or* pour out (*aus of*); (= *entweichen*) to escape (*aus from*) **b** (= *ausstrahlen*) **die Hitze, die vom Ofen ausströmt** the heat which is radiated from the stove; **etw strömt etw/etw aus** (*fig*) sb/sth radiates sth **VT** *Duft, Gas* to give off; (= *ausstrahlen*) *Wärme, Ruhe etc* to radiate

aus+stu|die|ren *ptp* **ausstudiert** VI *sep* (*inf*) to finish studying

aus+su|chen VT *sep* **a** (= *auswählen*) to choose; (*esp iro*) to pick; **such dir was aus!** choose *or* pick what you want, take your pick → *auch* **ausgesucht** **b** (*old: = durchsuchen*) to search

aus+tä|feln VT *sep* to panel

aus+ta|pe|zie|ren *ptp* **austapeziert** VT *sep* to paper

aus+ta|rie|ren *ptp* **austariert** VT *sep* **a** (= *ins Gleichgewicht bringen*) to balance **b** (*Aus: = Leergewicht feststellen*) to determine the tare weight of

Aus|tausch M exchange; (= *Ersatz*) replacement; (*Sport*) substitution; **im ~ für** *or* **gegen** in exchange for

aus|tausch|bar ADJ exchangeable; (= *untereinander austauschbar*) interchangeable; (= *ersetzbar*) replaceable

Aus|tausch|bar|keit ['austauʃbaːɐkait] F -, *no pl* interchangeability; (= *Ersetzbarkeit*) replaceability

Aus|tausch|do|zent(in) M(F) exchange lecturer, visiting faculty member (*US*)

aus+tau|schen VT *sep* (*lit, fig*) to exchange (*gegen for*); (= *untereinander austauschen*) to interchange; (= *ersetzen*) to replace (*gegen* with); **er ist wie ausgetauscht** (*fig*) he's (become) a different person, he's completely changed

Aus|tausch-: **Aus|tausch|leh|rer(in)** M(F) exchange teacher; **Aus|tausch|mo|tor** M replacement engine; **Aus|tausch|pro|fes|sor(in)** M(F) exchange (*Brit*) *or* visiting (*US*) professor; **Aus|tausch|pro|gramm** NT (*für Schüler-, Studentenaustausch*) exchange programme (*Brit*) *or* program (*US*); **Aus|tausch|schü|ler(in)** M(F) exchange student *or* pupil; **Aus|tausch|stu|dent(in)** M(F) exchange student; **aus|tausch|wei|se** ADV as part of an exchange; (*bei Studenten etc*) on an exchange basis

aus+tei|len VT *sep* to distribute (*unter +dat, an +acc* among); (= *aushändigen auch*) to hand out (*unter +dat, an +acc* to); *Spielkarten* to deal (out); *Essen* to serve; *Sakrament* to administer, to dispense; *Befehle* to give, to issue; *Prügel* to hand out, to administer

Aus|tei|lung F distribution; (= *Aushändigung auch*) handing out; (*von Essen etc*) serving; (*von Sakrament*) administration, dispensation

Aus|ter ['austɐ] F -, -n oyster

Aus|tern-: **Aus|tern|bank** F *pl* **-bänke** oyster bed *or* bank; **Aus|tern|fi|scher** M (*Orn*) oystercatcher; **Aus|tern|fi|sche|rei** F oyster fishing; **Aus|tern|park** M oyster farm *or* park; **Aus|tern|pilz** M oyster mushroom; **Aus|tern|scha|le** F oyster shell; **Aus|tern|zucht** F oyster farm; (= *Austernzüchtung*) oyster farming

aus+tes|ten ['austɛstn] VT *sep* to test; (*Comput*) *Programm etc* to debug

Aus|til|gung F eradication; (*von Schädlingen auch, von Menschen*) extermination; (*von Erinnerung*) obliteration

aus+to|ben *sep* **VT** to work off (*an +dat* on) **VR** **a** (*Mensch*) to let off steam; (= *sich müde machen*) to tire oneself out; (= *ein wildes Leben führen*) to have one's fling; **ein Garten, wo sich die Kinder ~ können** a garden where the children can romp about; **hat sie sich jetzt ausgetobt?** has she cooled down now? **b** (= *abebben: Leidenschaft, Sturm, Fieber etc*) to die down

aus+tol|len VR *sep* (= *umherspringen etc*) to have a good romp; (= *Energie loswerden*) to let off steam; (= *sich amüsieren*) to let one's hair down

Aus|trag ['austraːk] M -(e)s [-gəs] *no pl* settlement, resolution; **zum ~ kommen** to be up for settlement; **zum ~ gelangen** to be settled *or* decided

aus+tra|gen *sep irreg* **VT** **a** *Problem, Frage* to deal with; *Duell, Wettkampf etc* to hold; **einen Streit mit jdm ~** to have it out with sb **b** *Waren, Post etc* to deliver **c** **ein Kind ~** to carry a child (through) to full term; (= *nicht abtreiben*) to have a child **d** (= *abmelden*) to sign out; (= *löschen*) *Zahlen, Daten* to take out; (*aus Liste, bei Buchung*) *jdn* to cancel sb's name **VR** to sign out

Aus|trä|ger M delivery man/boy; (*von Zeitungen*) newspaper man/boy; **wir suchen Studenten als ~** we are looking for students to deliver newspapers

Aus|trä|ge|rin F delivery woman/girl; (*von Zeitungen*) newspaper woman/girl → *auch* **Austräger**

Aus|trag(s)|haus NT (*S Ger, Aus*) ≈ small house for farmers in retirement

Aus|tra|gung ['austraːgʊŋ] F -, -en (*Sport*) holding

Aus|tra|gungs|ort M *pl* **-orte** (*Sport*) venue

aus|trai|niert ['austrɛniːɐt, 'austrɛniːɐt] ADJ (*Sport*) well-prepared

Aust|ra|li|de(r) [austraˈliːdə] MF *decl as adj* Australoid

Aust|ra|li|en [ausˈtraːliən] NT -s Australia; **~ und Ozeanien** Australasia

Aust|ra|li|er [ausˈtraːliɐ] M -s, -, **Aust|ra|li|e|rin** [-iərɪn] F -, -nen Australian

aust|ra|lisch [ausˈtraːlɪʃ] ADJ Australian; **Australischer Bund** the Commonwealth of Australia

Aust|ral|ne|ger(in) [ausˈtraːl-] M(F) (*dated*) Australoid

aus+träu|men VT *sep* to finish dreaming; **sein Traum von Reichtümern ist ausgeträumt** (*fig*) his dream of riches is over

aus+trei|ben *sep irreg* **VT** **a** (= *vertreiben*) to drive out; *Teufel etc* to exorcise, to drive out; **..., dass es mir den Schweiß austrieb** ... until the sweat was pouring off me; **jdm etw ~** to cure sb of sth; (*esp durch Schläge*) to knock sth out of sb **b** (*Typ*) *Zeilen* to space out **c** *Vieh* to drive *or* turn out **VI** (= *sprießen*) to sprout

Aus|trei|bung ['austraibʊŋ] F -, -en expulsion; (*von Teufel etc*) exorcism, driving out, casting out (*esp old, liter*)

aus+tre|ten *sep irreg* **VI** *aux sein* **a** (= *herauskommen*) to come out (*aus of*); (*esp Blut*) to issue (*aus from*); (= *entweichen: Gas etc*) to escape (*aus from, through*) **b** (*Med: bei Bruch*) to protrude **c** (= *zur Toilette gehen*) to go to the toilet; (*Sch*) to be excused (*euph*) **d** (= *ausscheiden*) to leave (*aus etw* sth); (*formell*) to resign (*aus from*); (*aus politischer Gemeinschaft*) to withdraw (*aus from*) **e** (*Hunt*) to come out (into the open); **aus der Deckung ~** to break cover **VT** *Spur, Feuer etc* to tread out; *Schuhe* to wear out of shape → *auch* **ausgetreten**

Aust|ri|a|zis|mus [austriaˈtsɪsmʊs] M -, **Austriazismen** [-ˈtsɪsmən] (*Ling*) Austriacism

aus+trick|sen VT *sep* (*inf: Sport, fig*) to trick

aus+trin|ken VTI *sep irreg* to finish; **trink (deine Milch) aus!** drink (your milk) up

Aus|tritt M *no pl* (= *das Heraustreten*) (*von Flüssigkeit*) outflow; (= *das Entweichen*) escape; (*von Kugel*) exit; (*esp von Eiter*) discharge; (*von*

Blut) issue; (*Med: von Bruch*) protrusion **b** (= *das Ausscheiden*) leaving *no art* (*aus etc* sth); (*formell*) resignation (*aus* from); (*aus politischer Gemeinschaft*) withdrawal (*aus* from); **die ~e aus der Kirche häufen sich** there are more and more people leaving the church

Aus|tritts|er|klä|rung F (notice of) resignation

aust|ro-, Aust|ro- [ˈaustro] *in cpds* Austro-; **aust|ro|ame|ri|ka|nisch** ADJ Austro-American

aus+trock|nen *sep* **VI** *aux sein* to dry out; (*Fluss etc*) to dry up; (*Kehle*) to become parched **VT** to dry out; *Fluss etc* to dry up; *Kehle* to make parched; (= *trockenlegen*) *Sumpf* to drain

Aus|trock|nung F -n, -en *usu sing* drying up; (*Med*) dehydration

aus+trom|meln VT *sep* (*Hist*) to announce on the drum; (*fig*) to shout from the rooftops

aus+trom|pe|ten *ptp* **austrompetet** VT *sep* (*inf*) to broadcast (*inf*)

aus+tüf|teln VT *sep* (*inf*) to work out; (= *ersinnen*) to think up

aus+üben VT *sep* **a** *Beruf, Kunst* to practise (*Brit*), to practice (*US*); *Aufgabe, Funktion, Amt* to perform; (= *innehaben*) *Amt* to hold **b** *Druck, Einfluss* to exert (*auf +acc* on); *Macht, Recht* to exercise; *Wirkung* to have (*auf +acc* on); **einen Reiz auf jdn ~** to have *or* hold an attraction for sb

aus|übend ADJ *Arzt, Rechtsanwalt, Künstler* practising (*Brit*), practicing (*US*); *Gewalt* executive

Aus|übung F *von Beruf, Kunst*) practice; (*von Aufgabe, Funktion, Amt*) performance; (= *das Innehaben: von Amt*) holding; **in ~ seines Dienstes/ seiner Pflicht** (*form*) in the execution of his duty; **in ~ seines Berufs** (*form*) in pursuance of one's profession (*form*) **b** (*von Druck*) exertion; (*von Macht*) exercising

aus+ufern [ˈausˌuːfɐn] VI *sep aux sein* (*Fluss*) to burst *or* break its banks; (*fig*) to get out of hand; (*Konflikt etc*) to escalate (*zu* into)

Aus|ver|kauf M (clearance) sale; (*wegen Geschäftsaufgabe*) closing-down sale; (*fig: = Verrat*) sellout; **etw im ~ kaufen** to buy sth at the sale(s)

aus+ver|kau|fen *ptp* **ausverkauft** VT *sep* to sell off, to clear

Aus|ver|kaufs|wa|re F sale goods *pl*, sale merchandise (*US*)

aus|ver|kauft [ˈausfɛɐkauft] ADJ sold out; **vor ~em Haus spielen** to play to a full house

aus|ver|schämt ADJ, ADV (*dial*) = **unverschämt**

aus+wach|sen *sep irreg* **VR** **a** (= *verschwinden*) to disappear **b** (= *sich entwickeln*) **aus etw ~** (*fig: Streit etc*) to turn into sth **VI** *aux sein* **a** **das ist (ja) zum Auswachsen** (*inf*) it's enough to drive you mad (*Brit inf*) *or* crazy, it's enough to drive you round the bend (*Brit inf*) *or* up a tree (*US inf*); **zum Auswachsen langweilig** (*inf*) incredibly boring → *auch* **ausgewachsen b** (= *herauswachsen: gefärbte Haare*) to grow out

Aus|wahl F selection (*an +dat* of); (= *Angebot auch*) range; (= *Wahl*) choice; (= *die Besten*) pick; (= *Vielfalt*) variety; (*Sport*) representative team; **ohne ~** indiscriminately; **viel/eine reiche ~** a large/wide selection *or* range; **hier gibt es keine ~** there is no choice; **viele Sachen zur ~ haben** to have many things to choose from; **drei Bewerber stehen zur ~** there are three applicants to choose from, there is a choice of three applicants; **jdm drei Sachen zur ~ vorlegen** to offer sb a choice of three things; **eine ~ treffen** (= *eines auswählen*) to make a choice; (= *einige auswählen*) to make a selection

Aus|wahl-: Aus|wahl|ant|wort F answer (to a/the multiple choice question); **Aus|wahl|band** [-bant] M *pl* **-bände** selection

aus+wäh|len VT *sep* to select, to choose (*unter +dat* from among); **sich** (*dat*) **etw ~** to select *or* choose sth (for oneself) → *auch* **ausgewählt**

Aus|wahl-: Aus|wahl|kri|te|ri|um F selection criterion; **Aus|wahl|mann|schaft** F representative team; **Aus|wahl|mög|lich|keit** F choice; **Aus|wahl|prin|zip** NT selection principle, criterion; **Aus|wahl|spie|le(r)(in)** M(F) (selection of) samples; **Aus|wahl|spie|ler(in)** M(F) representative player; **Aus|wahl|ver|fah|ren** NT selection procedure

aus|wal|zen VT *sep* **a** *Metall* to roll out **b** (*fig*) to go to town on; *Thema auch* to drag out

Aus|wan|de|rer M , **Aus|wan|de|rin** F emigrant

Aus|wan|de|rer-: Aus|wan|de|rer|schiff NT emigrant ship; **Aus|wan|de|rer|vi|sum** NT emigration visa

aus+wan|dern VI *sep aux sein* to emigrate (*nach, in +acc* to); (*Volk*) to migrate

Aus|wan|de|rung F emigration; (= *Massenauswanderung*) migration

aus|wär|tig [ˈausvɛrtɪç] ADJ *attr* **a** (= *nicht ansässig*) nonlocal; *Schüler, Mitglied* from out of town **b** (*Pol*) foreign; **der ~e Dienst** the foreign service; **das Auswärtige Amt** the Foreign Ministry, the Foreign Office (*Brit*), the State Department (*US*); **der Minister des Auswärtigen** (*form*) the foreign minister, the foreign secretary (*Brit*), the secretary of state (*US*)

Aus|wär|ti|ge(r) [ˈausvɛrtɪgə] MF *decl as adj* non-local (person), stranger

aus|wärts [ˈausvɛrts] ADV **a** (= *nach außen*) outwards **b** (= *außerhalb des Hauses*) away from home; (= *außerhalb der Stadt*) out of town; (*Sport*) away; **von ~ anrufen** to call long distance; **~ essen** to eat out; **~ sprechen** (*hum inf*) to speak foreign (*hum inf*)

Aus|wärts-: Aus|wärts|nie|der|la|ge F (*Sport*) away defeat; **Aus|wärts|sieg** M (*Sport*) away win *or* victory; **Aus|wärts|spiel** NT (*Sport*) away (match *or* game)

aus+wa|schen *sep irreg* **VT** to wash out; (= *spülen*) to rinse (out); (*Geol*) to erode **VR** (*Farbe*) to wash out

aus|wech|sel|bar ADJ (ex)changeable; (= *untereinander auswechselbar*) interchangeable; (= *ersetzbar*) replaceable

aus+wech|seln *sep* **VT** to change; (*esp gegenseitig*) to exchange; (= *ersetzen*) to replace; (*Sport*) to substitute (*gegen* for); **er ist wie ausgewechselt** (*fig*) he's a changed *or* different person **VI** (*Sport*) to bring on a substitute, to make a substitution

Aus|wech|sel|spie|ler(in) M(F) substitute

Aus|wech|se|lung [ˈausvɛksəluŋ] F -, -en, **Aus|wechs|lung** [ˈausvɛkslʊŋ] F -, -en exchange; (= *Ersatz*) replacement; (*Sport*) substitution

Aus|weg M way out; (*fig: = Lösung auch*) solution; **der letzte ~** a last resort; **er sieht** *or* **weiß keinen anderen ~ als ...** he can see no other way out but ...; **sich** (*dat*) **einen ~ offen lassen** *or* **offen halten** to leave oneself an escape route *or* a way out

Aus|weg-: aus|weg|los ADJ (*fig*) hopeless; **Aus|weg|lo|sig|keit** F -, *no pl* (*fig*) hopelessness

aus+wei|chen VI *sep irreg aux sein* **a** (= *Hindernis, Gefahr umgehen*) to get out of the way (+*dat* of); (= *Platz machen*) to make way (+*dat* for); **nach rechts ~** to get out of the way/to make way by going to the right **b** (= *zu entgehen versuchen*) (*lit*) to get out of the way; (*fig*) to evade the issue; **einer Sache** (*dat*) **~** (*lit*) to avoid sth; (*fig*) to evade *or* dodge (*inf*) sth; **jdm/einer Begegnung ~** to avoid sb/a meeting; **dem Feind ~** to avoid (contact with) the enemy; **eine ~de Antwort** an evasive answer **c** **auf etw** (*acc*) **~** (*fig*) to switch to sth

Aus|weich-: Aus|weich|flug|ha|fen M alternative airport; **Aus|weich|gleis** NT (*Rail*) siding; **Aus|weich|la|ger** NT reserve depot *or* store; **Aus|weich|ma|nö|ver** NT evasive ac-

tion *or* manoeuvre (*Brit*) *or* maneuver (*US*); **Aus|weich|mög|lich|keit** F (*fig*) alternative; (*auf Straße*) possibility of getting out of the way; **Aus|weich|stel|le** F (*auf Straßen*) passing place; **Aus|weich|quar|tier** NT alternative accommodation

aus+wei|den VT *sep* (*Hunt*) to break up; *Opfertier etc* to disembowel

aus+wei|nen *sep* **VR** to have a (good) cry; (= *zu Ende weinen*) to finish crying; **sich bei jdm ~** to have a cry on sb's shoulder **VI** to finish crying **VT** **seinen Kummer** *etc* **~** to weep (*bei jdm* on sb's shoulder); **sich** (*dat*) **die Augen ~** to cry one's eyes *or* heart out (*und mehr*)

Aus|weis [ˈausvais] M **-es, -e** [-zə] **a** (= *Mitglieds-/Leser-/Studentenausweis etc*) (membership/library/student *etc*) card; (= *Personalausweis*) identity card; (= *Berechtigungsnachweis*) pass; **~, bitte** your papers please **b** (= *Beleg*) proof; (*von Identität*) proof of identity, identification; **nach ~** +*gen* (*form*) according to **c** (= *Bankausweis*) bank return **d** (*dated Aus Sch*: = *Zeugnis*) report

aus+wei|sen *sep irreg* **VT** **a** (*aus dem Lande*) to expel, to deport → **Ausgewiesene(r) b** (= *Identität nachweisen*) to identify **c** (= *zeigen*) to reveal **d** (= *für bestimmten Zweck vorsehen*) *Gebiet, Fläche* to designate; **ein Gebiet als Naturschutzgebiet/zur gewerblichen Nutzung ~** to designate an area as a nature reserve/for commercial purposes **VR** **a** (*mit Ausweis, Pass*) to identify oneself; **können Sie sich ~?** do you have any means of identification? **b** (= *sich erweisen*) **sich als etw ~** to prove oneself to be sth → *auch* **ausgewiesen**

Aus|weis-: Aus|weis|kar|te F = **Ausweis** a; **Aus|weis|kon|trol|le** F identity check

aus|weis|lich [ˈausvaislɪç] PREP +*gen* (*geh*) according to

Aus|weis-: Aus|weis|pa|pie|re PL identity papers *pl*; **Aus|weis|pflicht** F obligation to carry an identity card

Aus|wei|sung F expulsion, deportation

Aus|wei|sungs|be|fehl M , **Aus|wei|sungs|ver|fü|gung** F (*form*) expulsion *or* deportation order

aus+wei|ten *sep* **VT** to widen; *esp Dehnbares* to stretch; (*fig*) to expand (*zu* into) **VR** to widen; (*esp Dehnbares*) to stretch; (*fig*) (*Thema, Bewegung*) to expand (*zu* into); (= *sich verbreiten*) to spread

Aus|wei|tung F -, -en widening; (= *Ausdehnung*) stretching; (*fig*) expansion; (*von Konflikt etc*) widening; (= *Verbreitung*) spreading

aus|wen|dig ADV by heart, from memory; **etw ~ können/lernen** to know/learn sth (off) by heart; **das kann ich schon ~** (*fig inf*) I know it backwards (*inf*) *or* by heart; **ein Musikstück ~ spielen** to play a piece (of music) from memory → **inwendig**

Aus|wen|dig|ler|nen NT -s, *no pl* (*von Geschichtszahlen, Fakten*) learning by heart, memorizing; **ein Gedicht zum ~** a poem to learn by heart

aus+wer|fen VT *sep irreg* **a** *Anker, Netz, Leine* to cast **b** (= *hinausschleudern*) *Lava, Asche* to throw out, to eject; *Geschosshülsen* to eject **c** (= *ausspucken*) *Schleim, Blut* to cough up **d** (= *herausschaufeln*) to shovel out; *Graben* to dig out **e** (= *verteilen*) *Dividende* to pay out; (= *zuteilen*) *Mittel, Summen* to allocate **f** (= *produzieren*) to produce, to put *or* turn out **g** **jdm ein Auge ~** to put out sb's eye

aus+wer|ten VT *sep* **a** (= *bewerten*) to evaluate; (= *analysieren*) to analyse **b** (= *nutzbar machen*) to utilize

Aus|wer|tung F **a** (= *Bewertung*) evaluation; (= *Analyse*) analysis **b** (= *Nutzbarmachung*) utiliza-

aus+wet|zen VT *sep* to grind out

aus+**wi**|**ckeln** VT *sep Paket, Bonbon etc* to unwrap; **ein Kind ~** to take a child out of its blankets *etc*; (*Hist:* = *Windeln entfernen*) to unswaddle a child

aus+**wie**|**gen** VT *sep irreg* to weigh (out) → *auch* **ausgewogen**

aus+**wil**|**dern** VT *sep Tiere* to release *or* to set free into the wild

aus+**wir**|**ken** VR *sep* to have an effect (*auf* +*acc* on); **sich günstig/negativ ~** to have a favourable (*Brit*) *or* favorable (*US*)/negative effect; **sich in etw** (*dat*) **~** to result in sth; **sich zu jds Vorteil ~** to work *or* turn out to sb's advantage

Aus|**wir**|**kung** F (= *Folge*) consequence; (= *Wirkung*) effect; (= *Rückwirkung*) repercussion

aus+**wi**|**schen** VT *sep* to wipe out; *Glas etc, Wunde* to wipe clean; *Schrift etc* to rub *or* wipe out; **sich** (*dat*) **die Augen ~** to rub *or* wipe one's eyes; **jdm eins ~** (*inf*) to get (*Brit*) *or* pull (*esp US*) one over on sb (*inf*); (*aus Rache*) to get one's own back on sb (*esp Brit*), to get back at sb

aus+**wrin**|**gen** VT *sep irreg* to wring out

Aus|**wuchs** ['ausvuːks] M **-es, Auswüchse** [-vyːksə] **a** (out)growth; (*Med, Bot auch*) excrescence (*form*); (= *Missbildung*) deformity **b** (*fig*) (= *Erzeugnis*) product; (= *Missstand, Übersteigerung*) excess

aus+**wuch**|**ten** VT *sep Räder* to balance

Aus|**wurf** M , *no pl* **a** (*von Lava etc*) ejection, eruption; (= *ausgeworfene Lava etc auch*) ejecta *pl* (*Geol*) **b** (*Med*) sputum; **~ haben** to bring up phlegm; **blutigen ~ haben** to be coughing up blood **c** (*pej*) (= *Abschaum*) scum; (= *Schund*) trashy product; **der ~ der Menschheit** the dregs *pl or* scum of humanity

aus+**wür**|**feln** *sep* **VI** to throw dice; (= *das Glück entscheiden lassen*) to draw lots **VT** to throw (*Brit*) *or* roll (*US*) dice for

aus+**za**|**cken** VT *sep* to serrate

aus+**zah**|**len** *sep* **VT** *Geld etc* to pay out; *Arbeiter, Gläubiger* to pay off; *Kompagnon, Miterben* to buy out; **er bekommt EUR 500 die Woche ausgezahlt** his net pay is 500 euros a week **VR** *sich lohnen* to pay (off)

aus+**zäh**|**len** *sep* **VT** *Stimmen* to count (up); (= *durch Zählen wählen*) *Person* to choose *or* select (by counting); *Boxer* to count out **VI** (*bei Kinderspielen*) to count out

Aus|**zähl**|**reim** M = **Abzählreim**

Aus|**zah**|**lung** F (*von Geld*) paying out; (*von Arbeiter, Gläubiger*) paying off; (*von Kompagnon*) buying out; **zur ~ kommen** (*form*) *or* **gelangen** (*form*) to be paid out

Aus|**zäh**|**lung** F (*von Stimmen etc*) counting (up), count

Aus|**zah**|**lungs-: Aus**|**zah**|**lungs**|**an**|**wei**|**sung** F order to pay; **Aus**|**zah**|**lungs**|**stel**|**le** F payments (*Brit*) *or* payment (*US*) office

Aus|**zähl**|**vers** M = **Abzählreim**

aus+**zah**|**nen** VT *sep* (*Tech*) to tooth

aus+**zan**|**ken** VI *sep* (= *zu Ende zanken*) to finish quarrelling

aus+**zeh**|**ren** VT *sep* to drain, to exhaust; *Land* to drain; **~de Krankheit** wasting disease

Aus|**zeh**|**rung** F **a** (= *Kräfteverfall*) emaciation; **unter personeller ~ leiden** (*fig*) to be short--staffed **b** (*obs Med*) consumption (*old*)

aus+**zeich**|**nen** *sep* **VT** **a** (= *mit Zeichen versehen*) to mark; *Waren* to label; (*Typ*) *Manuskript* to mark up; **etw mit einem Preis(schild) ~** to price sth

b (= *ehren*) to honour (*Brit*), to honor (*US*); **jdn mit einem Orden ~** to decorate sb (with a medal); **jdn mit einem Preis/Titel ~** to award a prize/title to sb

c (= *hervorheben*) to distinguish (from all others); (= *kennzeichnen*) to be a feature of **VR** to stand out (*durch* due to), to distinguish oneself (*durch* by) (*auch iro*); **dieser Wagen zeichnet sich durch gute Straßenlage aus** one

of the remarkable features of this car is its good roadholding, what makes this car stand out is its good roadholding → *auch* **ausgezeichnet**

Aus|**zeich**|**nung** F **a** (*no pl:* = *das Auszeichnen*) (*von Baum etc*) marking; (*von Waren*) labelling (*Brit*), labeling (*US*); (*mit Preisschild*) pricing; (*Typ: von Manuskript*) mark up **b** (*no pl:* = *das Ehren*) honouring (*Brit*), honoring (*US*); (*mit Orden*) decoration; **seine ~ mit einem Preis** his being awarded a prize **c** (= *Markierung*) marking (+*gen, an* +*dat* on); (*an Ware*) ticket; (*Typ: auf Manuskript*) mark up **d** (= *Ehrung*) honour (*Brit*), honor (*US*), distinction; (= *Orden*) decoration; (= *Preis*) award, prize; **mit ~ bestehen** to pass with distinction

Aus|**zeit** F (*Sport*) time out

aus|**zieh**|**bar** ADJ extendible, extensible; *Antenne* telescopic; **ein ~er Tisch** a pull-out table

aus+**zie**|**hen** *sep irreg* **VT** **a** *Kleider, Schuhe, Handschuhe* to take off, to remove; *jdn* to undress; **jdm die Jacke** *etc* **~** to take off sb's jacket *etc*; **sich** (*dat*) **etw ~** to take off sth; **die Uniform ~** (*fig*) to retire from the services; **das zieht einem ja die Schuhe** *or* **Socken** *or* **Stiefel aus!** (*dated sl*) it's enough to make you cringe!

b (= *herausziehen*) to pull out; (= *verlängern auch*) to extend; *Metall* (*zu Draht*) to draw out (*zu* into)

c *Wirkstoffe* (*aus Kräutern*) to extract

d (= *ausbleichen*) *Farbe* to bleach (out), to take out

e (= *nachzeichnen*) *Linie* to trace (*mit Tusche in* ink)

VR (= *sich entkleiden*) to undress, to take off one's clothes; **sich nackt ~** to take off one's clothes; (*bei Leibesvisitation*) to strip naked

VI *aux sein* (= *aufbrechen, abreisen*) to set out; (*demonstrativ*) to walk out; (*aus einer Wohnung*) to move (*aus* out of); **auf Abenteuer ~** to set off *or* out in search of adventure; **auf Raub ~** to set off *or* out to rob and steal; **zur Jagd ~** to set off for the hunt; **zum Kampf ~** to set off to battle

Aus|**zieh-: Aus**|**zieh**|**fe**|**der** F drawing pen; **Aus**|**zieh**|**lei**|**ter** F extension ladder; **Aus**|**zieh**|**plat**|**te** F (*von Tisch*) leaf; **Aus**|**zieh**|**tisch** M extending *or* pull-out table; **Aus**|**zieh**|**tu**|**sche** F drawing ink

aus+**zi**|**schen** VT *sep* (*Theat*) to hiss (off)

Aus|**zu**|**bil**|**den**|**de(r)** ['austsubɪldndə] MF *decl as adj* trainee

Aus|**zug** M **a** (= *das Weggehen*) departure; (*demonstrativ*) walkout; (*zeremoniell*) procession; (*aus der Wohnung*) move; **der ~ der Kinder Israel** (*Bibl*) the Exodus (of the Children of Israel) **b** (= *Ausschnitt, Exzerpt*) excerpt; (*aus Buch*) extract, excerpt; (= *Zusammenfassung*) abstract, summary; (= *Kontoauszug*) statement; (*Chem*) extract; (*Mus*) arrangement; **etw in Auszügen drucken** to print extracts of sth **c** (= *ausziehbarer Teil*) extension

Aus|**zugs-: Aus**|**zugs**|**mehl** NT superfine flour; **aus**|**zugs**|**wei**|**se** ADV in extracts, in excerpts; (= *gekürzt*) in an/the abridged version; **~ aus etw lesen** to read extracts from sth

au|**tark** [au'tark] ADJ self-sufficient (*auch fig*), autarkic (*Econ*)

Au|**tar**|**kie** [autar'kiː] F -, -n [-'kiːən] self-sufficiency (*auch fig*), autarky (*Econ*)

au|**then**|**tisch** [au'tɛntɪʃ] ADJ authentic; (*Mus*) *Kadenz* perfect

Au|**then**|**ti**|**zi**|**tät** [autɛntitsi'tɛːt] F -, *no pl* authenticity

Au|**tis**|**mus** [au'tɪsmʊs] M -, *no pl* autism

Au|**tist** [au'tɪst] M -en, -en, **Au**|**tis**|**tin** [au'tɪstɪn] F -, -nen autistic child/person, autistic (*form*)

au|**tis**|**tisch** [au'tɪstɪʃ] ADJ autistic ADV autistically

Au|**to** ['auto] NT -s, -s car, automobile (*esp US, dated*); **~ fahren** (*selbst*) to drive (a car); (*als Mitfahrer*) to go by car; **mit dem ~ fahren** to go by car; **er guckt wie ein ~** (*inf*) his eyes are popping out of his head (*inf*)

Au|**to-: Au**|**to**|**ab**|**ga**|**se** PL (*Mot*) car exhaust fumes *pl*, car emissions *pl*; **Au**|**to**|**apo**|**the**|**ke** F first-aid kit (for the car); **Au**|**to**|**at**|**las** M road atlas; **Au**|**to**|**auf**|**kle**|**ber** M bumper sticker

Au|**to**|**bahn** F motorway (*Brit*), interstate (highway *or* freeway) (*US*); (*esp in Deutschland*) autobahn; (*gebührenpflichtig*) turnpike (*US*)

AUTOBAHN

There is no general speed limit on German **Autobahnen** (motorways), although there is a recommended limit of 130kph (80mph). In actual fact there are very few sections of road that are not subject to speed restrictions, introduced for reasons of safety and reduced exhaust emissions. No special charge is made for using the **Autobahnen** in Germany. However, in Austria and Switzerland one must purchase a **Vignette**. An additional toll, a **Maut**, is payable on some sections → VIGNETTE

Au|**to**|**bahn-** *in cpds* motorway (*Brit*), interstate (highway *or* freeway) (*US*); **Au**|**to**|**bahn**|**auf**|**fahrt** F motorway *etc* access road, slip road, freeway on-ramp (*US*); **Au**|**to**|**bahn**|**aus**|**fahrt** F motorway *etc* exit, freeway off-ramp (*US*); **Au**|**to**|**bahn**|**drei**|**eck** NT motorway *etc* merging point; **Au**|**to**|**bahn**|**ge**|**bühr** F toll; **Au**|**to**|**bahn**|**kreuz** NT motorway *etc* intersection; **Au**|**to**|**bahn**|**meis**|**te**|**rei** F -, -en motorway *etc* maintenance authority; **Au**|**to**|**bahn**|**po**|**li**|**zei** F motorway *etc* police; **Au**|**to**|**bahn**|**po**|**li**|**zist(in)** M(F) motorway *etc* policeman/-woman; **Au**|**to**|**bahn**|**rast**|**hof** M , **Au**|**to**|**bahn**|**rast**|**stät**|**te** F motorway service area (*Brit*), motorway services *pl* (*Brit*), rest area (*US*); **Au**|**to**|**bahn**|**ring** M motorway *etc* ring road; **Au**|**to**|**bahn**|**vig**|**net**|**te** F motorway *etc* toll disc *or* badge, tollway smart card (*US*); **Au**|**to**|**bahn**|**zu**|**brin**|**ger** M motorway approach road (*Brit*), motorway feeder (*Brit*), highway *or* freeway approach (*US*)

Au|**to-: Au**|**to**|**bat**|**te**|**rie** F car battery; **Au**|**to**|**bi**|**o**|**graf(in)** ▲ M(F) autobiographer; **Au**|**to**|**bi**|**o**|**gra**|**fie** ▲ F autobiography; **au**|**to**|**bi**|**o**|**gra**|**fisch** ▲ ADJ autobiographical ADV autobiographically; **Au**|**to**|**bom**|**be** F car bomb

Au|**to**|**bus** M bus; (= *Reiseomnibus*) coach (*Brit*), bus; **einstöckiger/zweistöckiger ~** single-decker/double-decker (bus)

Au|**to**|**cam**|**ping** NT driving and camping

Au|**to**|**car** M (*Sw*) coach (*Brit*), bus

au|**toch**|**thon** [autɔx'toːn] ADJ (*geh*) autochthonous (*form*)

Au|**to-: Au**|**to-Cross** ['autokrɔs] NT -, -, **Au**|**to**|**cross** ▲ NT -, - autocross; **Au**|**to**|**da**|**fé** [autoda'feː] NT -s, -s (*geh*) auto-da-fé; **Au**|**to**|**deck** NT (*auf Fähren*) car deck; **Au**|**to**|**di**|**dakt** [autodi'dakt] M -en, -en, **Au**|**to**|**di**|**dak**|**tin** [-'daktɪn] F -, -nen autodidact (*form*), self-educated person; **Au**|**to**|**di**|**dak**|**ten**|**tum** [autodi'daktntuːm] NT -s, *no pl* autodidacticism (*form*); **au**|**to**|**di**|**dak**|**tisch** [autodi'daktɪʃ] ADJ autodidactic (*form*), self-taught *no adv* ADV **sich ~ bilden** to educate oneself; **Au**|**to**|**dieb(in)** M(F) car thief; **Au**|**to**|**dieb**|**stahl** M car theft; **Au**|**to**|**drom** [auto'droːm] NT -s, -s **a** motor-racing circuit **b** (*Aus*) Dodgems® *pl*, bumper cars *pl*; **Au**|**to**|**drosch**|**ke** F (*dated*) taxicab; **Au**|**to**|**elek**|**trik** F (*car*) electrics *pl*; **Au**|**to**|**ero**|**tik** F autoeroticism; **Au**|**to**|**fab**|**rik** F car factory *or* plant; **Au**|**to**|**fäh**|**re** F car ferry; **Au**|**to**|**fah**|**ren** NT -s, *no pl* driving (a car); (*als Mitfahrer*) driving in a car; **Au**|**to**|**fah**|**rer(in)** M(F) (car) driver; **Au**|**to**|**fah**|**rer**|**gruß** M (*iro inf*) **jdm den ~ bieten** ≈ to give sb a V sign (*Brit*) *or* the finger (*US*); **Au**|**to**|**fahrt** F drive; **Au**|**to**|**fal**|**le** F (*bei Überfällen*) road trap; (= *Radarkontrolle*) speed *or* radar trap; **Au**|**to**|**fo**|**kus**-**ka**|**me**|**ra** F ['autofoːkʊs-] autofocus camera; **au**|**to**|**frei** ADJ *Innenstadt, Urlaubsort, Sonntag* car-free; **Au**|**to**|**fried**|**hof** M (*inf*) car dump; **Au**|**to**|**gas** NT liquefied petroleum gas

au|to|gen [auto'ge:n] ADJ autogenous; **~es Training** (*Psych*) relaxation through self-hypnosis

Au|to|gen|schwei|ßen NT **-s**, *no pl* autogenous welding

au|to|ge|recht ADJ (*speziell für Autos gebaut*) Straßen etc car-friendly

Au|to|graf ▲ [auto'gra:f] NT **-s, -en** autograph

Au|to|gramm [auto'gram] NT *pl* **-gramme** autograph

Au|to|gramm-: Au|to|gramm|jä|ger(in) M(F) autograph hunter; **Au|to|gramm|stun|de** F autograph(ing) session

Au|to-: Au|to|graph NT = **Autograf**; **Au|to|händ|ler(in)** M(F) car *or* automobile (*US*) dealer; **Au|to|hyp|no|se** F autohypnosis; **Au|to|im|mun|er|kran|kung** F , **Au|to|im|mun|krank|heit** F (*Med*) autoimmune disease; **Au|to|in|dus|trie** F car industry; **Au|to|kar|te** F road map; **Au|to|ki|no** NT drive-in cinema (*Brit*), drive-in movie theater (*US*); **Au|to|knacker(in)** M(F) (*inf*) car thief; **Au|to|ko|lon|ne** F line of cars; **Au|to|krat** [auto'kra:t] M **-en, -en**, **Au|to|kra|tin** [-'kra:tɪn] F **-, -nen** autocrat; **Au|to|kra|tie** [autokra'ti:] F **-, -n** [-'ti:ən] autocracy; **au|to|kra|tisch** [auto'kra:tɪʃ] ADJ autocratic ADV autocratically; **Au|to|kun|de** M , **Au|to|kun|din** F customer with a car; **Au|to|len|ker(in)** M(F) (*Sw*) (car) driver; **Au|to|mar|der** M **a** (= *Tier*) marten (*that chews brake pipes etc*) **b** (*inf*: = *Autoknacker*) car thief; **Au|to|mar|ke** F make (of car)

Au|to|mat [auto'ma:t] M **-en, -en** (*auch fig*: = *Mensch*) machine; (= *Verkaufsautomat*) vending machine; (= *Roboter*) automaton, robot; (= *Musikautomat*) jukebox; (= *Spielautomat*) slot machine; (= *Rechenautomat*) calculator; (*rare*: = *Telefonautomat*) payphone; (*Elec*: = *selbsttätige Sicherung*) cutout

Au|to|ma|ten-: Au|to|ma|ten|buf|fet NT (*esp Aus*) automat; **Au|to|ma|ten|knacker(in)** M(F) (*inf*) vandal (*who breaks into vending machines*); **Au|to|ma|ten|pa|ckung** F vending-machine pack; **Au|to|ma|ten|res|tau|rant** NT automat; **Au|to|ma|ten|stra|ße** F vending machines *pl*

Au|to|ma|tik¹ [auto'ma:tɪk] M **-s, -s** (*Aut*) automatic

Au|to|ma|tik² F **-, -en** **a** automatic mechanism (*auch fig*) **b** (= *Gesamtanlage*) automatic system; (*Rad*) automatic frequency control, AFC; (*Aut*) automatic transmission

Au|to|ma|tik-: Au|to|ma|tik|ge|trie|be NT (*Aut*) automatic transmission; **Au|to|ma|tik|gurt** NT inertia(-reel) seat belt; **Au|to|ma|tik|schal|tung** F automatic transmission; **Au|to|ma|tik|wa|gen** M automatic

Au|to|ma|ti|on [automa'tsio:n] F **-**, *no pl* automation

au|to|ma|tisch [auto'ma:tɪʃ] ADJ automatic ADV automatically

au|to|ma|ti|sie|ren [automati'zi:rən] *ptp* **automatisiert** VT to automate

au|to|ma|ti|siert [automati'zi:ɐt] ADJ automated

Au|to|ma|ti|sie|rung F **-, -en** automation

Au|to|ma|tis|mus [automa'tɪsmʊs] M **-, Automatismen** [-mən] automatism

Au|to-: Au|to|me|cha|ni|ker(in) M(F) car *or* motor mechanic; **Au|to|mi|nu|te** F minute by car, minute's drive

Au|to|mo|bil [automo'bi:l] NT **-s, -e** (*dated, geh*) motorcar, automobile (*esp US, dated*)

Au|to|mo|bil-: Au|to|mo|bil|aus|stel|lung F motor show; (= *ständige Automobilausstellung*) car exhibition; **Au|to|mo|bil|bau** M , *no pl* car *or* automobile (*US*) manufacture

Au|to|mo|bi|list [automobi'lɪst] M **-en, -en**, **Au|to|mo|bi|lis|tin** [-'lɪstɪn] F **-, -nen** (*Sw, geh*) (car) driver

Au|to|mo|bil-: Au|to|mo|bil|klub M automobile association; **Au|to|mo|bil|sa|lon** M motor show

Au|to-: Au|to|mo|dell NT (car) model; (= *Miniaturauto*) model car; **au|to|nom** [auto'no:m] ADJ autonomous (*auch fig*); *Nervensystem* autonomic; **Au|to|no|me(r)** [auto'no:mə] MF *decl as adj* (*Pol*) independent; **Au|to|no|mie** [autono'mi:] F **-, -n** [-'mi:ən] autonomy (*auch fig*); **Au|to|no|mist** [autono'mɪst] M **-en, -en**, **Au|to|no|mis|tin** [-'mɪstɪn] F **-, -nen** autonomist; **Au|to|num|mer** F (car) number; **Au|to|öl** NT motor oil; **Au|to|pi|lot** M (*Aviat*) autopilot; **vom ~en gesteuert werden** to be on autopilot

Au|top|sie [autɔ'psi:] F **-, -n** [-'psi:ən] (*Med*) autopsy

Au|tor ['auto:ɐ] M **-s, Autoren** [au'to:rən] author

Au|to-: Au|to|ra|dio NT car radio; **Au|to|rei|fen** M car tyre (*Brit*) *or* tire (*US*); **Au|to|rei|se|zug** M train carrying holidaymakers' cars, ≈ motorail train (*Brit*); **mit dem ~ fahren** to go by motorail (*Brit*)

Au|to|ren-: Au|to|ren|film M ≈ film written and directed by the same person; **Au|to|ren|kol|lek|tiv** NT team of authors

Au|to-: Au|to|renn|bahn F motor-racing circuit; **Au|to|ren|nen** NT (motor) race; (*Rennsport*) motor racing; **Au|to|renn|sport** M motor racing

Au|to|ren|re|gis|ter NT index of authors

Au|to|re|pa|ra|tur|werk|statt F garage, car repair shop (*US*)

Au|to|re|verse-Funk|ti|on ['autorivøɐs-, 'au-torivœrs-] F auto-reverse (function)

Au|to|rin [au'to:rɪn] F **-, -nen** author, authoress

Au|to|ri|sa|ti|on [autoriza'tsio:n] F **-, -en** (*geh*) authorization

au|to|ri|sie|ren [autori'zi:rən] *ptp* **autorisiert** VT to authorize

au|to|ri|tär [autori'tɛ:ɐ] ADJ authoritarian ADV in an authoritarian manner; **ein ~ geführtes Land** a country ruled by an authoritarian government

Au|to|ri|tät [autori'tɛ:t] F **-, -en** (*alle Bedeutungen*) authority

au|to|ri|ta|tiv [autorita'ti:f] ADJ (*geh*) authoritative

Au|to|ri|täts-: au|to|ri|täts|gläu|big ADJ trusting in authority; **Au|to|ri|täts|gläu|big|keit** F trust in authority; **au|to|ri|täts|hö|rig** ADJ slavishly following authority; **~ sein** to be a slave to authority

Au|tor|kor|rek|tur F (= *Korrekturfahne*) author's proof; (= *Änderung*) author's correction

Au|tor|schaft ['auto:ɐʃaft] F **-, -en** authorship

Au|to-: Au|to|sa|lon ['autozalɔŋ, (*esp S Ger, Aus*) -zalo:n, (*esp Sw*) -salõ:] M motor show, auto(-mobile) show (*US*); **Au|to|schal|ter** M drive-in counter; **Au|to|schlan|ge** F queue (*Brit*) *or* line of cars; **Au|to|schlos|ser(in)** M(F) panel beater; **Au|to|schlos|se|rei** F body shop; **Au|to|schlüs|sel** M car key; **Au|to|skoo|ter** ['autosku:tɐ] M **-s, -** Dodgem® (*Brit*) *or* bumper car; **Au|to|speng|ler(in)** M(F) (*S Ger, Aus, Sw*) panel beater; **Au|to|speng|le|rei** F (*S Ger, Aus, Sw*) body shop; **Au|to|sport** M motor sport; **Au|to|stell|platz** M (car) parking space; **Au|to|stopp** M hitchhiking, hitching (*esp Brit inf*); **~ machen, per ~ fahren** to hitchhike; **Au|to|stra|ße** F main road, highway (*esp US*); **Au|to|strich** M (*inf*) prostitution to car drivers (= *Gegend*) kerb-crawling (*Brit*) *or* curb-crawling (*US*) area (*inf*); **Au|to|stun|de** F hour's drive; **Au|to|sug|ges|ti|on** F autosuggestion; **Au|to|te|le|fon** NT car phone; **Au|to|ty|pie** [autoty'pi:] F **-, -n** [-'pi:ən] autotypy; **Au|to|un|fall** M car accident; **Au|to|ver|kehr** M (motor) traffic; **Au|to|ver|leih** M , **Au|to|ver|mie|tung** F car hire *or* rental (*Firma*) car hire *or* rental firm; **Au|to|ver|si|che|rung** F car *or* motor insurance; **Au|to|wasch|an|la|ge** F car wash; **Au|to|werk|statt** F garage, car repair shop (*US*); **Au|to|wrack** NT

(car) wreck, wrecked car; **Au|to|zoom** NT (*Phot*) automatic zoom (lens); **Au|to|zu|be|hör** NT car *or* motor accessories *pl*; **Au|to|zug** M train carrying holidaymakers' cars, ≈ motorail train (*Brit*); **mit dem ~ fahren** to go by motorail (*Brit*)

autsch [autʃ] INTERJ (*inf*) ouch, ow

Au|wald M riverside wood(s *pl*) *or* forest

au|weh [au've:], **au|wei(a)** [au'vai(a)] INTERJ oh dear

A|van|ce [a'vã:sə] F **-, -n** **jdm ~n machen** (*geh*) to make approaches to sb

a|van|cie|ren [avã'si:rən] *ptp* **avanciert** VI *aux sein* (*dated, geh*) to advance (*zu* to)

A|vant-: A|vant|gar|de [a'vã:gardə, avã'gardə] F (*geh*) (*Art*) avant-garde; (*Pol*) vanguard; **A|vant|gar|dis|mus** [avãgar'dɪsmʊs, avant-] M **-**, *no pl* avant-gardism; **A|vant|gar|dist** [avãgar'dɪst, avant-] M **-en, -en**, **A|vant|gar|dis|tin** [-'dɪstɪn] F **-, -nen** member of the avant-garde, avant-gardist; **a|vant|gar|dis|tisch** [avãgar'dɪstɪʃ, avant-] ADJ avant-garde

AvD [a:fau'de:] *abbr von* **Automobilclub von Deutschland**

A|ve-Ma|ria ['a:vema'ri:a] NT **-(s), -(s)** Ave Maria; (*Gebet auch*) Hail Mary

A|vers [a'vɛrs] M **-es, -e** face, obverse

A|ver|si|on [avɛr'zio:n] F **-, -en** aversion (*gegen* to)

A|vi|a|ri|um [avi'a:rium] NT **-s, Aviarien** [-riən] NT aviary

A|vis [a'vi:] M OR NT **-, -**, **A|vis** [a'vi:s] M OR NT **-es, -e** (*Comm*) advice; (*schriftlich*) advice note

a|vi|sie|ren [avi'zi:rən] *ptp* **avisiert** VT to send notification of, to advise of

A|vi|so [a'vi:zo] NT **-s, -s** (*Aus Comm*) advice; (*schriftlich*) advice note

A|vi|ta|mi|no|se [avitami'no:zə] F **-, -n** (*Med*) a-vitaminosis

A|vo|ca|do [avo'ka:do] F **-, -s**, **A|vo|ca|to** [avo-'ka:to] F **-, -s** avocado

A-Waf|fe ['a:-] F *abbr von* **atomare Waffe**

A|xel ['aksl] M **-s, -** (*Sport*) axel

a|xi|al [a'ksia:l] ADJ axial

Axi|al|la|ger NT (*Tech*) axial *or* thrust bearing

A|xi|om [a'ksio:m] NT **-s, -e** axiom

A|xi|o|ma|tik [aksio'ma:tɪk] F **-**, *no pl* axiomatics *sing*

a|xi|o|ma|tisch [aksio'ma:tɪʃ] ADJ axiomatic

Axt [akst] F **-, ⸚e** ['ɛkstə] axe (*Brit*), ax (*US*); **sich wie eine *or* im Wald benehmen** (*fig inf*) to behave like a peasant *or* boor; **die ~ im Haus erspart den Zimmermann** (*Prov*) self-help is the best help; **die ~ an etw** (*acc*) *or* **an die Wurzel einer Sache** (*gen*) **legen** (*fig*) to tear up the very roots of sth

Axt|hieb M blow of the/an axe (*Brit*) *or* ax (*US*)

A|ya|tol|lah [aja'tɔla] M **-s, -s** ayatollah

A|za|lee [atsa'le:ə] F **-, -n**, **A|za|lie** [a'tsa:liə] F **-, -n** (*Bot*) azalea

A|ze|tat [atse'ta:t] NT **-s, -e** acetate

A|ze|tat|sei|de F acetate silk

A|ze|ton [atse'to:n] NT **-s**, *no pl* (*Chem*) acetone

A|ze|ty|len [atsety'le:n] NT **-s**, *no pl* (*Chem*) acetylene

A|zi|mut [atsi'mu:t] NT **-s, -e** (*Astron*) azimuth

A|zo|ren [a'tso:rən] PL (*Geog*) Azores *pl*

A|zo|ren|hoch NT (*Met*) high over the Azores

Az|te|ke [ats'te:kə] M **-n, -n**, **Az|te|kin** [-'te:kɪn] F **-, -nen** Aztec

Az|te|ken|reich NT Aztec empire

az|te|kisch [ats'te:kɪʃ] ADJ Aztec

A|zu|bi [a'tsu:bi:, (a(:)'tsubi] M **-s, -s** *or* f **-, -s** *abbr von* **Auszubildende(r)**

A|zur [a'tsu:ɐ] M **-s**, *no pl* (*poet*) azure sky; (= *Farbe*) azure

a|zur|blau [a'tsu:ɐ-], **a|zurn** [a'tsu:ɐn] (*poet*) ADJ azure (blue)

a|zyk|lisch ['atsy:klɪʃ, a'tsy:klɪʃ] ADJ acyclic

B

B, b [be:] NT **-, -** B, b; (*Mus*) (= *Ton*) B flat; (= *Versetzungszeichen*) flat; **B-Dur** (the key of) B flat major; **b-Moll** (the key of) B flat minor

Baas [ba:s] M **-es, -e** ['ba:zə] (*Naut*) boss

bạb|beln ['babln] VI (*inf*) to babble; (*Schwätzer auch*) to chatter

Bạ|bel ['ba:bl] NT **-s** (*Bibl*) Babel; (*fig*) (= *Sündenbabel*) sink of iniquity; (*von Sprachen*) melting pot

Ba|by ['be:bi] NT **-s, -s** baby

Ba|by- ['be:bi] *in cpds* baby; **Ba|by|aus|stat|tung** F layette; **Ba|by|boom** M baby boom; **Ba|by|doll** ['be:bidɔl, be:bi'dɔl] NT **-(s), -s** baby-dolls *pl*, baby-doll pyjamas *pl*; **Ba|by|jahr** NT (*für Mutter nach Geburt*) maternity leave (*for one year*); (*Insur*) year of pension contributions credited to women for each child; **Ba|by|korb** M bassinet; **Ba|by|kost** F baby food

Ba|by|lon ['ba:bylɔn] NT **-s** Babylon

ba|by|lo|nisch [baby'lo:nɪʃ] ADJ Babylonian; **eine ~e Sprachverwirrung** a Babel of languages; **der Babylonische Turm** the Tower of Babel; **die Babylonische Gefangenschaft** the Babylonian captivity

Ba|by- ['be:bi-]: **Ba|by|nah|rung** F baby food; **Ba|by|pau|se** F (*der Mutter*) maternity leave; (*des Vaters*) paternity leave; **eine ~ einlegen** to have or take or go on maternity or paternity leave; **sie will eine zweijährige ~ einlegen** she wants to take a two-year break to have a baby; **ba|by|sit|ten** ['be:bizɪtn] VI *insep* to babysit; **Ba|by|sit|ter** ['be:bizɪtɐ] M **-s, -,** **Ba|by|sit|te|rin** [-ərɪn] F **-, -nen** babysitter; **Ba|by|speck** M (*inf*) puppy fat (*Brit*), baby fat (*US*); **Ba|by|spra|che** F baby talk; **Ba|by|strich** M child prostitution *no art*; (= *Gegend*) pick-up place for child prostitutes; **Ba|by|tra|ge|ta|sche** F carrycot (*Brit*), traveling baby bed (*US*); **Ba|by|waa|ge** F scales *pl* for weighing babies; **Ba|by|wip|pe** F bouncy chair; **Ba|by|zel|le** F (*Elec* = *Kleinstbatterie*) round cell

Bạc|ca|ra ['bakara] NT **-s,** *no pl* (*Cards*) baccarat

Bac|cha|nal [baxa'na:l] NT **-s, -e** or **-ien** [-liən] **a** (*der Antike*) Bacchanalia **b** (*geh:* = *Gelage*) bacchanal, drunken orgy

Bac|chant [ba'xant] M **-en, -en,** **Bac|chan|tin** [-'xantɪn] F **-, -nen** bacchant

bac|chan|tisch [ba'xantɪʃ] ADJ bacchanalian

bac|chisch ['baxɪʃ] ADJ (*Myth*) Bacchic

Bac|chus ['baxus] M **-'** (*Myth*) Bacchus; **dem ~ huldigen** (*geh*) to imbibe (*form*)

Bach [bax] M **-(e)s, ⸚e** ['bɛçə] stream (*auch fig*), brook; (*Naut, Aviat: sl:* = *Gewässer*) drink (*inf*); **den ~ heruntergehen** (*inf: Firma etc*) to go down the tubes (*inf*)

bach|ạb [bax'|ap] ADV (*Sw*) downstream; **etw ~ schicken** (*fig inf*) to throw sth away; **~ gehen** (*fig inf*) to go up the creek (*inf*) or spout (*inf*)

Bach|bett NT stream bed

Bach|blü|ten PL (*Med*) Bach flower extracts *pl*

Bach|blü|ten|the|ra|pie F (*Med*) Bach or Bach's flower remedy (therapy); **eine ~ machen** to take Bach's flower remedy or remedies

Bạ|che ['baxə] F **-, -n** (wild) sow

Bä|chel|chen ['bɛçlçən] NT **-s, -** *dim von* **Bach**

Bach|fo|rel|le F brown trout

Bäch|lein ['bɛçlain] NT **-s, -** *dim von* **Bach** (small) stream, brooklet; **ein ~ machen** (*baby-talk*) to do a wee-wee (*baby-talk*)

Bach|stel|ze F wagtail

bạck [bak] ADV (*Naut*) back

Bạck [bak] F **-, -en** (*Naut*) **a** (= *Deck*) forecastle, fo'c'sle **b** (= *Schüssel*) dixie, mess tin, mess kit (*US*); (= *Tafel*) mess table; (= *Besatzung*) mess

Bạck|blech NT baking tray (*Brit*), baking pan (*US*)

Bạck|bord NT, *no pl* (*Naut*) port (side); **von ~ nach Steuerbord** from port to starboard; **über ~** over the port side

bạck|bord(s) ['bakbɔrt(s)] ADV (*Naut*) on the port side; **(nach) ~** to port

Bạck|brett NT baking board

Bäck|chen ['bɛkçən] NT **-s, -** (little) cheek

Bạ|cke ['bakə] F **-, -n** **a** (= *Wange*) cheek; **mit vollen ~n kauen** to chew or eat with bulging cheeks; (*mit Genuss*) to eat heartily; **au ~!** (*dated inf*) oh dear! **b** (*inf:* = *Hinterbacke*) buttock, cheek; **auf einer ~** (*inf:* = *mit Leichtigkeit*) easily, no problem (*inf*) **c** (*von Schraubstock*) jaw; (= *Bremsbacke*) (*bei Auto*) shoe; (*bei Fahrrad*) block; (*von Skibindung*) toe-piece; (*von Gewehr*) cheek-piece

bạ|cken¹ ['bakn] *pret* **bạckte** or (*old*) **buk** ['bakтə, bu:k], *ptp* **gebạcken** [gə'bakn] VT to bake; *Brot, Kuchen* to make, to bake; (*dial:* = *braten*) *Fisch, Eier etc* to fry; (*dial:* = *dörren*) *Obst* to dry; **frisch/knusprig gebackenes Brot** fresh/crusty bread; **wir ~ alles selbst** we do all our own baking; **gebackener Fisch** fried fish; (*im Ofen*) baked fish VI (*Brot, Kuchen*) to bake; (*dial:* = *braten*) to fry; (*dial:* = *dörren*) to dry; **der Kuchen muss noch 20 Minuten ~** the cake will have to be in the oven or will take another 20 minutes; **sie bäckt gern** she enjoys baking

bạ|cken² (*dial inf*) VI (= *kleben: Schnee etc*) to stick (*an +dat* to), to cake (*an +dat* on, onto) VT **etw an etw** (*acc*) **~** to stick sth onto sth

Bạ|cken-: **Bạ|cken|bart** M sideboards *pl* (*Brit*), sideburns *pl*, (side) whiskers *pl*; **Bạ|cken|brem|se** F (*bei Auto*) shoe brake; (*bei Fahrrad*) block brake; **Bạ|cken|kno|chen** M cheekbone; **Bạ|cken|ta|sche** F (*Zool*) cheek pouch; **Bạ|cken|zahn** M molar

Bạ|cker ['bɛkɐ] M **-s, -,** **Bạ|cke|rin** [-ərɪn] F **-, -nen** baker; **~ lernen** to learn the baker's trade, to be an apprentice baker; **~ werden** to be or become a baker; **beim ~** at the baker's; **zum ~ gehen** to go to the baker's

Bạck|erb|sen PL (*S Ger, Aus*) ≈ small pasta balls put into soups

Bạ|cke|rei [bɛkə'rai] F **-, -en** **a** (= *Bäckerladen*) baker's (shop); (= *Backstube*) bakery **b** (= *Gewerbe*) bakery, baking trade **c** (*Aus* = *Gebäck*) pastries *pl*; (= *Kekse*) biscuits *pl* (*Brit*), cookies *pl* (*US*)

Bạ|cker|ge|sel|le M, **Bạ|cker|ge|sel|lin** F (trained) baker

Bạ|cke|rin F → **Bäcker**

Bạ|cker-: **Bạ|cker|jun|ge** M baker's boy; (= *Lehrling*) baker's apprentice; **Bạ|cker|la|den** M baker's (shop); **Bạ|cker|meis|ter(in)** M(F) master baker

Bạ|ckers|frau F baker's wife

Bạck|fei|ge F (*dial*) = **Ohrfeige**

Bạck-: **bạck|fer|tig** ADJ oven-ready; **Bạck|fett** NT cooking fat; **Bạck|fisch** M **a** fried fish **b** (*dated*) teenager, teenage girl; **Bạck|form** F baking tin (*Brit*) or pan (*US*); (*für Kuchen*) cake tin (*Brit*) or pan (*US*)

Bạck|gam|mon [bɛk'gɛmən] NT **-(s),** *no pl* backgammon

Bạck|ground ['bɛkgraunt] M **-s, -s** background

Bạck-: **Bạck|hähn|chen** NT, **Bạck|hendl** NT (*S Ger, Aus*), **Bạck|huhn** NT, **Bạck|hühn|chen** NT roast chicken; **Bạck|mi|schung** F cake mix; **Bạck|mul|de** F kneading or dough trough, dough tray, hutch; **Bạck|obst** NT dried fruit; **Bạck|ofen** M oven; **es ist heiß wie in einem ~** it's like an oven; **bạck|ofen|fest** ADJ ovenproof; **Bạck|pa|pier** NT baking parchment, grease-proof paper; **Bạck|pfei|fe** F (*dial*) slap on or round (*inf*) the face; **Bạck|pflau|me** F prune; **Bạck|pul|ver** NT baking powder; **Bạck|röh|re** F, (*Aus*) **Bạck|rohr** NT oven

Bạck|slash ['bɛkslɛʃ] M **-s, -s** (*Typ:* = *umgekehrter Schrägstrich*) backslash

Bạck|space|tas|te ['bɛkspe:s-] F, **Bạck|space-Tas|te** F (*Comput*) backspace key

Bạck|stein M brick

Bạck|stein-: **Bạck|stein|bau** M *pl* **-bauten** brick building; **Bạck|stein|bau|wei|se** F brick (building) style; **ein Haus in ~** a brick (-built) house; **Bạck|stein|go|tik** F Gothic architecture built in brick

Bạck|stu|be F bakery

bạckt [bɛkt] 3. PERS SING *pres von* **backen¹**

Bạck|trog M kneading or dough trough, dough tray, hutch

Back-up ['bɛkap] NT **-s, -s** (*Comput*) backup

Back-up-Pro|gramm NT (*Comput*) backup program

Bạck-: **Bạck|vor|schrift** F baking instructions *pl*; **Bạck|wa|ren** PL bread, cakes and pastries *pl*; **Bạck|werk** NT (*old*) cakes and pastries *pl*; **Bạck|zeit** F baking time

Bad [ba:t] NT **-(e)s, ⸚er** ['bɛ:dɐ] **a** (= *Wannenbad, Badewanne, Phot*) bath; (= *das Baden*) bathing; **ein ~ nehmen** to have or take a bath; (**sich** *dat*) **ein ~ einlaufen lassen** to run (oneself) a bath; **jdm Bäder verschreiben** (*Med*) to prescribe sb a course of (therapeutic) baths; **~ in der Menge** (*fig*) walkabout; **ein ~ in der Menge nehmen** to go (on a) walkabout **b** (*im Meer etc*) bathe, swim; (= *das Baden*) bathing, swimming **c** (= *Badezimmer*) bathroom; **Zimmer mit ~** room with (private) bath **d** (= *Schwimmbad*) (swimming) pool or bath(s); **die städtischen Bäder** the public baths (*Brit*) or pools (*US*); **türkisches ~** Turkish or Russian bath

---

e (= *Heilbad*) spa; (= *Seebad*) (seaside) resort; ~ **Doberan** Bad Doberan

Ba|de-: Ba|de|an|stalt F (public) swimming baths (*Brit*) or pools (*US*) *pl*; **Ba|de|an|zug** M swimsuit, bathing suit (*esp US*); **Ba|de|arzt** M , **Ba|de|ärz|tin** F spa doctor; **Ba|de|gast** M **a** (*im Kurort*) spa visitor **b** (*im Schwimmbad*) bather, swimmer; **kannst du hier baden gehen? kann man da baden? gibt es dort eine ~?** can you swim there?; **Ba|de|hand|tuch** NT bath towel; **Ba|de|hau|be** F (*dated*) swimming cap or hat, bathing cap; **Ba|de|ho|se** F (swimming or bathing) trunks *pl*; **eine ~** a pair of (swimming or bathing) trunks; **Ba|de|ka|bi|ne** F changing cubicle; **Ba|de|kap|pe** F swimming cap or hat, bathing cap; **Ba|de|kos|tüm** NT (*geh*) swimming or bathing costume (*Brit*), bathing suit (*esp US*); **Ba|de|la|ken** NT bath sheet; **Ba|de|lus|ti|ge(r)** MF *decl as adj; usu pl* bather, swimmer; **Ba|de|man|tel** M beach robe; (= *Morgenmantel*) bathrobe, dressing gown (*Brit*); **Ba|de|mat|te** F bath mat; **Ba|de|meis|ter(in)** M(F) (*im Schwimmbad*) (pool) attendant; **Ba|de|mo|de** F swimwear, beachwear; **Ba|de|müt|ze** F swimming cap or hat, bathing cap

ba|den ['baːdn] **VI a** (*in der Badewanne*) to have a bath, to bath (*Brit*), to bathe (*US*); **hast du schon gebadet?** have you had your bath already?; **warm/kalt ~** to have a hot/cold bath **b** (*im Meer, Schwimmbad etc*) to swim, to bathe; **sie hat im Meer gebadet** she swam or bathed in the sea, she had a swim in the sea; **die Badenden** the bathers; **~ gehen** to go swimming; (*einmal*) to go for a swim **c** (*inf*) **~ gehen** to come a cropper (*inf*); **wenn das passiert, gehe ich ~** I'll be (in) for it if that happens (*inf*)

VT a *Kind etc* to bath (*Brit*), to bathe (*US*); **er ist als Kind zu heiß gebadet worden** (*hum*) he was dropped on the head as a child (*hum*); **in Schweiß gebadet** bathed or drenched in sweat **b** *Augen, Wunde etc* to bathe

VR to bathe, to have a bath

Ba|den ['baːdn] NT **-s** (*Geog*) Baden

Ba|de|ner ['baːdənɐ] M **-s**, **-**, **Ba|de|ne|rin** [-ərɪn] F **-**, **-nen** person or man/woman from Baden; **er ist ~** he comes from Baden

Ba|de|ni|xe F (*hum*) bathing beauty or belle (*dated*)

Ba|den|ser [baːˈdɛnzɐ] M **-s**, **-**, **Ba|den|se|rin** [-ərɪn] F **-**, **-nen** (*inf*) = **Badener**

Ba|den-Würt|tem|berg ['baːdnˈvʏrtəmbɛrk] NT **-s** Baden-Württemberg

Ba|de-: Ba|de|ofen M boiler; **Ba|de|ort** M *pl* **-orte** (= *Kurort*) spa; (= *Seebad*) (seaside) resort; **Ba|de|platz** M place for bathing

Ba|der ['baːdɐ] M **-s**, **-** (*old*) barber (*old*); (*dial*: = *Arzt*) village quack (*hum*)

Bä|der|be|hand|lung F *medical treatment using therapeutic baths*

Ba|de|rei|se F (*dated*) trip to a spa

Bä|der-: Bä|der|kun|de F balneology; **Bä|der|kur** F *medical treatment using therapeutic baths*

Ba|de-: Ba|de|sa|chen PL swimming gear, swimming or bathing things *pl*; **Ba|de|sai|son** F swimming season; (*in Kurort*) spa season; **Ba|de|salz** NT bath salts *pl*; **Ba|de|schaum** M bubble bath; **Ba|de|schuh** M sandal; (= *Latschen*) flip flop; **Ba|de|schwamm** M sponge; **Ba|de|see** M (bathing) lake; **Ba|de|strand** M (bathing) beach; **Ba|de|stu|be** F (*N Ger*) bathroom; **Ba|de|tuch** NT *pl* **-tücher** bath towel; **Ba|de|ur|laub** M holiday at the seaside, beach or seaside holiday, vacation by the sea (*US*); **~ machen** to go to the seaside for one's holiday (*Brit*) or vacation (*US*); **Ba|de|ver|bot** NT ban on bathing; **Ba|de|wan|ne** F bath(tub); **Ba|de|was|ser** NT bath water; **Ba|de|wet|ter** NT weather warm enough for bathing or swimming; **Ba|de|zeit** F bathing or swimming season; **Ba|de|zeug** NT , no

pl swimming gear, swimming or bathing things *pl*; **Ba|de|zim|mer** NT bathroom; **Ba|de|zu|satz** M *bath salts, bubble bath etc*

ba|disch ['baːdɪʃ] ADJ Baden *attr*; *Wein etc auch* from Baden; *Dialekt auch* of Baden; *Landschaft auch* around Baden; **das Dorf ist ~** or **im Badischen** the village is in Baden

Bad|min|ton ['bɛtmɪntən] NT **-**, *no pl* badminton

baff [baf] ADJ *pred* (*inf*) **~ sein** to be flabbergasted

BA|föG ['baːføk] NT **-**, *no pl*, **Ba|fög** NT **-**, *no pl abbr von* **Bundesausbildungsförderungsgesetz er kriegt ~** he gets a grant

BA|föG-Emp|fän|ger(in) ['baːføk-] M(F) recipient of a (state) grant

Ba|ga|ge [baˈgaːʒə] F **-**, *no pl* **a** (*old, Sw:* = *Gepäck*) luggage, baggage **b** (*dated inf*) (= *Gesindel*) crowd, crew (*inf*), gang (*inf*); (= *Familie*) pack (*inf*); **die ganze ~** the whole bloody lot (*Brit inf*), the whole darn group (*US*)

Ba|ga|tell [bagaˈtɛl] F **-**, **-en** (*Aus inf*) trifle, bagatelle

Ba|ga|tell|de|likt NT (*Jur*) petty or minor offence (*Brit*) or offense (*US*)

Ba|ga|tel|le [bagaˈtɛlə] F **-**, **-n** trifle, bagatelle; (*Mus*) bagatelle

Ba|ga|tell|fall M (*Jur*) petty lawsuit

ba|ga|tel|li|sie|ren [bagatɛliˈziːrən] *ptp* **bagatellisiert** VT to trivialize, to minimize VI to trivialize

Ba|ga|tell-: Ba|ga|tell|sa|che F (*Jur*) petty or minor case; **Ba|ga|tell|scha|den** M minor or superficial damage; **Ba|ga|tell|ver|let|zung** F minor or superficial injury

Bag|dad ['bakdat, bakˈdaːt] NT **-s** Baghdad

Bag|ger ['bagɐ] M **-s**, **-** excavator; (*für Schlamm*) dredger

Bag|ger|füh|rer(in) M(F) → **Bagger** driver of an/the excavator, driver of a/the dredger

bag|gern ['bagɐn] VT *Graben* to excavate, to dig; *Fahrrinne* to dredge VI (*sl:* = *Mädchen/Jungen anmachen*) to pull (*Brit inf*), to pick up (*inf*)

Bag|ger-: Bag|ger|schau|fel F excavator shovel; **Bag|ger|see** M *artificial lake in quarry etc*

Ba|guette [baˈgɛt] NT OR F **-s**, **-s** baguette

bah [baː], **bäh** [bɛː] INTERJ **a** (*aus Schadenfreude*) hee-hee (*inf*); (*vor Ekel*) ugh **b** ~ **machen** (*baby-talk: Schaf*) to baa, to go baa

Ba|ha|ma|in|seln [baˈhaːma-] PL , **Ba|ha|mas** [baˈhaːmas] PL Bahamas *pl*

Bäh|lamm ['bɛːlam] NT (*baby-talk*) baa-lamb (*baby-talk*)

Bahn [baːn] F **-**, **-en a** (= *Weg*) path, track; (*von Fluss*) course; (*fig*) path; (= *Fahrbahn*) carriageway; **~ frei!** make way!, (get) out of the way!; **jdm/einer Sache die ~ ebnen/freimachen** (*fig*) to pave/clear the way for sb/sth; **die ~ ist frei** (*fig*) the way is clear; **sich** (*dat*) **~ brechen** (*lit*) to force one's way; (*fig*) to make headway; (*Mensch*) to forge ahead; **einer Sache** (*dat*) **~ brechen** to blaze the trail for sth; **sich auf neuen ~en bewegen** to break new or fresh ground; **in gewohnten ~en verlaufen** (*fig*) to go on in the same old way, to continue as before; **von der rechten ~ abkommen** (*geh*) to stray from the straight and narrow; **jdn auf die rechte ~ bringen** (*fig*) to put sb on the straight and narrow; **etw in die richtige ~** or **die richtigen ~en lenken** (*fig*) to channel sth properly; **jdn aus der ~ werfen** or **schleudern** (*fig*) to throw sb off the track → **schief**
b (= *Eisenbahn*) railway (*Brit*), railroad (*US*); (= *Straßenbahn*) tram (*esp Brit*), streetcar (*US*); (= *Zug*) (*der Eisenbahn, U-Bahn*) train; (*der Straßenbahn*) tram (*esp Brit*), streetcar (*US*); (= *Bahnhof*) station; (*Verkehrsnetz, Verwaltung*) railway *usu pl* (*Brit*), railroad (*US*); **mit der** or **per ~** by train or rail/tram (*esp Brit*) or streetcar (*US*); **frei ~** (*Comm*) free on rail; **er ist** or **arbeitet bei der ~** he's with the railways (*Brit*) or railroad (*US*), he works for or on the railways (*Brit*)
c (*Sport*) track; (*für Pferderennen auch*) course; (*in Schwimmbecken*) pool; (= *Kegelbahn*) (bowling) alley; (*für einzelne Teilnehmer*) lane; (= *Schlittenbahn, Bobbahn*) run
d (*Phys, Astron*) orbit, path; (= *Raketenbahn, Geschossbahn*) (flight) path, trajectory
e (= *Stoffbahn, Tapetenbahn*) length, strip
f (*Tech: von Werkzeug*) face

Bahn-: bahn|amt|lich ADJ *Tarife etc* official railway (*Brit*) or railroad (*US*) *attr*; **Bahn|an|schluss** ▲ M railway (*Brit*) or railroad (*US*) connection or link; **~ haben** to be connected or linked to the railway (*Brit*) or railroad (*US*) (system); **Bahn|ar|bei|ter(in)** M(F) rail worker, railroader (*US*); **Bahn|be|am|te(r)** M *decl as adj*, **Bahn|be|am|tin** F railway (*Brit*) or railroad (*US*) official; **Bahn|be|triebs|werk** NT railway (*Brit*) or railroad (*US*) depot; **bahn|bre|chend** ▲ ADJ pioneering; **Bahnbrechendes leisten** to pioneer new developments; **~ sein** to be pioneering; (*Erfinder etc*) to be a pioneer **ADV** **~ wirken** to be pioneering; (*Erfinder etc*) to be a pioneer; **Bahn|bre|cher(in)** M(F) pioneer; **Bahn|bus** M bus run by railway company; **BahnCard®** [-kaːɛd] F **-**, **-s** ≈ railcard, *entitling the holder to reduced fares*

Bähn|chen ['bɛːnçən] NT **-s**, **-** *dim von* **Bahn**

Bahn|damm M (railway) embankment

bah|nen ['baːnən] VT *Pfad* to clear; *Flussbett* to carve or channel out; **jdm/einer Sache den/einen Weg ~** to clear the/a way for sb/sth; (*fig*) to pave or prepare the way for sb/sth; **sich** (*dat*) **einen Weg ~** to fight one's way

bah|nen|wei|se ADV in lengths or strips

Bah|ner ['baːnɐ] M **-s**, **-**, **Bah|ne|rin** [-ərɪn] F **-**, **-nen** (*inf*) railway (*Brit*) or railroad (*US*) employee

Bahn-: Bahn|fahrt F rail journey; **Bahn|fracht** F rail freight; **bahn|frei** ADJ, ADV (*Comm*) free on rail; **Bahn|ge|län|de** NT railway (*Brit*) or railroad (*US*) area; **Bahn|gleis** NT railway (*Brit*) or railroad (*US*) line; (*von Straßenbahn*) tram (*esp Brit*) or streetcar (*US*) line

Bahn|hof M (railway (*Brit*) or railroad (*US*)) station; (= *Busbahnhof*) bus station; (*dated:* =

Straßenbahndepot) tram (*esp Brit*) or streetcar (*US*) depot; **am** or **auf dem ~** at the station; **~ Schöneberg** Schöneberg station; **ich verstehe nur ~** (*hum inf*) it's as clear as mud (to me) (*Brit inf*), it's all Greek to me (*inf*); **er wurde mit großem ~ empfangen** he was given the red carpet treatment, they rolled the red carpet out for him; **es wurde auf einen großen ~ verzichtet** they didn't bother with the red carpet treatment

Bahn|hof- *in cpds* (*esp Sw*) = **Bahnhofs-: Bahn|hof|buf|fet** NT (*Sw*) station buffet

Bahn|hofs- *in cpds* station; **Bahn|hofs|buch|hand|lung** F (railway (*Brit*) or railroad (*US*)) station bookshop; **Bahn|hofs|buf|fet** NT (*esp Aus*) station buffet; **Bahn|hofs|gast|stät|te** F station restaurant; **Bahn|hofs|hal|le** F (station) concourse; **in der ~** in the station; **Bahn|hofs|mis|si|on** F *charitable organization for helping needy passengers*, traveller's (*Brit*) or traveler's (*US*) aid

---

BAHNHOFSMISSION

Founded in 1897 by the Protestant and Catholic Churches, the **Bahnhofsmission** is a charitable organization found in every sizeable railway station. Its role is to provide assistance to passengers in difficulty and to others, such as the homeless, who may require help. Many of those working in the **Bahnhofsmission** are volunteers.

Bahn|hofs-: Bahn|hofs|platz M station square; **Bahn|hofs|uhr** F station clock; **Bahn|hofs|vier|tel** NT (seedy) area around the main station; **sich auf dem ~ versammeln** to meet in front of the station; **Bahn|hofs|vor|platz** M station forecourt; **Bahn|hofs|vor|stand** M (*Aus*), **Bahn|hofs|vor|ste|her(in)** M(F) stationmaster; **Bahn|hofs|wirt|schaft** F station bar; (= *Bahnhofsrestaurant*) station restaurant

Bahn-: Bahn|ki|lo|me|ter M kilometre (*Brit*) or kilometer (*US*) travelled (*Brit*) or traveled (*US*) by rail, ≈ passenger mile; **Bahn|kör|per** M track; **bahn|la|gernd** ADJ, ADV (*Comm*) to be collected from (*esp Brit*) or picked up at the station; **etw ~ schicken** to send sth to be collected from (*esp Brit*) or picked up at the station

Bähn|ler ['bɛːnlɐ] M -s, -, **Bähn|le|rin** [-ərɪn] F -, -nen (*Sw*) railway (*Brit*) or railroad (*US*) employee

Bahn-: Bahn|li|nie F (railway (*Brit*) or railroad (*US*)) line or track; **Bahn|meis|te|rei** [-maistə'rai] F -, -en railway (*Brit*) or railroad (*US*) board; **Bahn|netz** NT rail(way) (*Brit*) or railroad (*US*) network; **Bahn|po|li|zei** F railway (*Brit*) or railroad (*US*) police; **Bahn|rei|sen|de(r)** MF *decl as adj* rail traveller (*Brit*) or traveler (*US*), rail passenger; **Bahn|schran|ke** F , (*Aus*) **Bahn|schran|ken** M level (*Brit*) or grade (*US*) crossing barrier or gate; **Bahn|steig** M platform; **Bahn|steig|kar|te** F platform ticket; **Bahn|stre|cke** F railway (*Brit*) or railroad (*US*) route or line; **Bahn|sur|fen** NT , **Bahn-|Sur|fen** NT train surfing; **Bahn|trans|port** M rail transport; (= *Güter*) consignment sent by rail; **Bahn|über|füh|rung** F railway (*Brit*) or railroad (*US*) footbridge; **Bahn|über|gang** M level (*Brit*) or grade (*US*) crossing; **beschrankter ~** level (*Brit*) or grade (*US*) crossing with gates; **unbeschrankter ~** unguarded level (*Brit*) or grade (*US*) crossing; **Bahn|un|ter|füh|rung** F railway (*Brit*) or railroad (*US*) underpass; **Bahn|ver|bin|dung** F train service; **nach einer ~ fragen** to inquire about a train connection; **Bahn|wär|ter(in)** M(F) (*an Bahnübergängen*) gatekeeper, (level (*Brit*) or grade (*US*) crossing) attendant; (= *Streckenwärter*) platelayer (*Brit*), trackman (*US*)

Bah|re ['baːrə] F -, -n (= *Krankenbahre*) stretcher; (= *Totenbahre*) bier

---

Bah|rein [ba'rain, bax'rain] NT -s Bahrain

Bahr|tuch NT *pl* **-tücher** pall

Bai [bai] F -, -en bay

bai|risch ['bairɪʃ] ADJ (*Hist, Ling*) Bavarian

Bai|ser [bɛ'zeː] NT -s, -s meringue

Bais|se ['bɛːs(ə)] F -, -n (*St Ex*) fall; (*plötzliche*) slump; **auf (die) ~ spekulieren** to bear

Bais|se|spe|ku|lant(in) ['bɛːs(ə)-] M(F) , **Bais|sier** [bɛ'sieː] M -s, -s (*St Ex*) bear

Ba|ja|dere [baja'deːrə] F -, -n bayadere

Ba|jaz|zo [ba'jatso] M -s, -s clown

Ba|jo|nett [bajo'nɛt] NT -(e)s, -e bayonet → **fäl|len**

Ba|jo|nett-: Ba|jo|nett|fas|sung F (*Elec*) bayonet fitting; **Ba|jo|nett|ver|schluss** ▲ M (*Elec*) bayonet socket

Ba|ju|wa|re [baju'vaːrə] M -n, -n, **Ba|ju|wa|rin** [-'vaːrɪn] F -, -nen (*old, hum*) Bavarian

ba|ju|wa|risch [baju'vaːrɪʃ] ADJ (*old, hum*) Bavarian

Ba|ke ['baːkə] F -, -n (*Naut*) marker buoy; (*Aviat*) beacon; (= *Verkehrszeichen*) distance warning signal; (*Surv*) marker pole

Ba|ke|lit® [bakə'liːt] NT -(e)s, *no pl* Bakelite®

Bak|ka|rat ['bakara(t), baka'ra] NT -s, *no pl* (*Cards*) baccarat

Bak|schisch ['bakʃɪʃ] NT -s, -e *or* -s baksheesh; (= *Bestechungsgeld*) bribe, backhander (*inf*); **~ geben** to give baksheesh/a bribe or backhander (*inf*)

Bak|te|rie [bak'teːriə] F -, -n *usu pl* germ, bacterium (*spec*); **~n** *pl* germs *pl*, bacteria *pl*

bak|te|ri|ell [baktə'riɛl] ADJ bacterial ADV bacterially; **~ verursacht** caused by germs or bacteria

Bak|te|rien- *in cpds* bacteria; **Bak|te|ri|en|kul|tur** F bacteria culture; **Bak|te|ri|en|stamm** M strain of bacteria; **Bak|te|ri|en|trä|ger(in)** M(F) carrier; **Bak|te|ri|en|züch|tung** F growing or culturing of bacteria

Bak|te|ri|o|lo|ge [bakterio'loːgə] M -n, -n, **Bak|te|ri|o|lo|gin** [-'loːgɪn] F -, -nen bacteriologist

Bak|te|ri|o|lo|gie [bakteriolo'giː] F -, *no pl* bacteriology

bak|te|ri|o|lo|gisch [bakterio'loːgɪʃ] ADJ *Forschung, Test* bacteriological; *Krieg* biological

Bak|te|ri|um [bak'teːriʊm] NT -s, **Bakterien** [-'teːriən] (*form*) = **Bakterie**

bak|te|ri|zid [bakteri'tsiːt] ADJ germicidal, bactericidal

Bak|te|ri|zid [bakteri'tsiːt] NT -s, -e [-də] germicide, bactericide

Ba|la|lai|ka [bala'laika] F -, -s *or* **Balalaiken** [-'laikn] balalaika

Ba|lan|ce [ba'lãːs(ə)] F -, -n balance, equilibrium; **die ~ halten/verlieren** to keep/lose one's balance

Ba|lan|ce- [ba'lãːs(ə)-]: **Ba|lan|ce|akt** [ba-'lãːs(ə)-] M (*lit*) balancing or tightrope or high-wire act; (*fig*) balancing act; **Ba|lan|ce|reg|ler** [ba'lãːs(ə)-] M (*Tech*) balance control

ba|lan|cie|ren [balã'siːrən] *ptp* **balanciert** VI *aux sein* to balance; (*fig*) to achieve a balance (*zwischen +dat* between); **über etw** (*acc*) **~** to balance one's way across sth VT to balance

Ba|lan|cier|stan|ge F (balancing) pole

bal|bie|ren [bal'biːrən] *ptp* **balbiert** VT (*inf*) **jdn über den Löffel ~** to pull the wool over sb's eyes, to lead sb by the nose (*inf*)

bald [balt] ADV *comp* **eher** *or* **≠er** ['bɛldɐ] (*old, dial*) *superl* **am ehesten** [a] (= *schnell, in Kürze*) soon; **er kommt ~** he'll be coming soon; **~ ist Weihnachten/Winter** it will soon be Christmas/winter; **~ darauf** soon afterwards, a little later; **(all)zu ~** (all) too soon; **so ~ wie** or **als möglich, möglichst ~** as soon as possible; **das gibt es so ~ nicht noch einmal** you won't find one of those again in a hurry; (*besonderes Ereignis*) that

---

won't happen again in a hurry; **wirst du wohl ~ ruhig sein?** will you just be quiet!; **wirds ~?** get a move on; **bis ~!** see you soon

[b] (= *fast*) almost, nearly; **das ist ~ nicht mehr schön** that is really beyond a joke (*Brit*), that's going too far

CONJ (*geh*) **~ ..., ~ ...** one moment ..., the next ..., now ..., now ...; **~ hier, ~ da** now here, now there; **~ so, ~ so** now this way, now that

Bal|da|chin ['baldaxin, balda'xiːn] M -s, -e canopy, baldachin; (*Archit*) baldachin, baldaquin

Bäl|de ['bɛldə] F **in ~** in the near future

bal|dig ['baldɪç] ADJ *attr no comp* quick, speedy; *Antwort, Wiedersehen* early; **wir hoffen auf Ihr ~es Kommen** we hope you will come soon; **auf ~es Wiedersehen!** (hope to) see you soon!

bal|digst ['baldɪçst] ADV *superl von* **baldig** (*form*) as soon as possible, without delay

bald|mög|lichst ADV as soon as possible

bal|do|wern [bal'doːvɐn] *ptp* **baldowert** VT (*inf*) = **ausbaldowern**

Bald|ri|an ['baldriaːn] M -s, -e valerian

Bald|ri|an|trop|fen PL valerian (drops *pl*)

Bal|dur ['baldʊr] M -s (*Myth*) Balder

Ba|le|a|ren [bale'aːrən] PL **die ~** the Balearic Islands *pl*

Balg¹ [balk] M -(e)s, **≠e** ['bɛlgə] [a] (= *Tierhaut*) pelt, skin; (*von Vogel*) skin; (*inf*: = *Bauch*) belly (*Brit inf*), stomach; (*einer Puppe*) body; **einem Tier den ~ abziehen** to skin an animal; **sich** (*dat*) **den ~ voll schlagen** or **voll stopfen** (*inf*) to stuff oneself (*inf*); **ich habe eine Wut im ~** (*inf*) I'm mad or livid **~ rücken** VI [b] (= *Blasebalg, Phot, Rail*) bellows *pl*; **die Bälge treten** to work the bellows

Balg² [balk] M OR NT -(e)s, **≠er** ['bɛlgɐ] (*pej inf*: = *Kind*) brat (*pej inf*)

bal|gen ['balgn] VR to scrap (*um* over)

Bal|gen ['balgn] M -s, - (*Phot*) bellows *pl*

Bal|ge|rei [balgə'rai] F -, -en scrap, tussle; **hört jetzt auf mit der ~!** stop scrapping!

Bal|kan ['balkaːn] M -s [a] (= *Balkanhalbinsel, Balkanländer*) **der ~** the Balkans *pl*; **auf dem ~** in the Balkans; **vom ~** from the Balkans; **dort herrschen Zustände wie auf dem ~** (*fig inf*) things are in a terrible state there **~** (= *Balkangebirge*) Balkan Mountains *pl*

Bal|kan|halb|in|sel F Balkan Peninsula

bal|ka|nisch [bal'kaːnɪʃ] ADJ Balkan

bal|ka|ni|sie|ren [balkani'ziːrən] *ptp* **balkanisiert** VT to Balkanize

Bal|ka|ni|sie|rung F -, -en Balkanization

Bal|kan-: Bal|kan|län|der PL Balkan States; **Bal|kan|staat** M Balkan state

Bälk|chen ['bɛlkçən] NT -s, - *dim von* **Balken**

Bal|ken ['balkn] M -s, - [a] (= *Holzbalken, Schwebebalken*) beam; (= *Stützbalken*) prop, shore; (= *Querbalken*) joist, crossbeam; (*Sport: bei Hürdenlauf*) rail; **der ~ im eigenen Auge** (*Bibl*) the beam in one's own eye; **lügen, dass sich die ~ biegen** (*inf*) to lie through one's teeth, to tell a pack of lies; **Wasser hat keine ~** (*Prov*) not everyone can walk on water **~** (= *Strich*) bar; (*Her*) fess(e); (= *Uniformstreifen*) stripe **c** (*an Waage*) beam

Bal|ken-: Bal|ken|brü|cke F girder bridge; **Bal|ken|code** M = **Balkenkode**; **Bal|ken|de|cke** F ceiling with wooden beams; **Bal|ken|di|a|gramm** NT bar chart; **Bal|ken|holz** NT (piece of) (squared) timber; (= *Balkengerüst*) timbers *pl*, beams *pl*; **Bal|ken|kode** M barcode (*Brit*), universal product code (*US*); **Bal|ken|kon|struk|ti|on** F timber frame construction; **Bal|ken|über|schrift** F (*Press*) banner headline; **Bal|ken|waa|ge** F (beam) balance; **Bal|ken|werk** NT timbering, timbers *pl*, beams *pl*

Bal|kon [bal'kɔŋ, bal'koːn] M -s, -s *or* (*bei dt. Aussprache*) **-e** balcony; (*Theat*) (dress) circle (*esp Brit*), balcony; **~ sitzen** (*Theat*) to have seats in the (dress) circle (*esp Brit*) or balcony

---

Balkon- [balˈkɔn-, balˈkoːn-]: **Balkonblume** F balcony plant; **Balkonmöbel** PL garden furniture *sing*; **Balkonpflanze** F balcony plant; **Balkontür** F French window(s *pl*); **Balkonzimmer** NT room with a balcony

Ball¹ [bal] M -(e)s, ⸚e [ˈbɛlə] ball; ~ **spielen** to play (with a) ball; **am ~ sein** (*lit*) to have the ball, to be in possession of the ball; **immer am ~ sein** (*fig*) to be on the ball; **am ~ bleiben** (*lit*) to keep (possession of) the ball; (*fig: = auf dem neuesten Stand bleiben*) to stay on the ball; **bei jdm am ~ bleiben** (*fig*) to keep in with sb; **er bemüht sich, bei ihr am ~ zu bleiben** he is trying to keep in the running with her; **hart am ~ bleiben** to stick at it; **jdm den ~ zuspielen** (*lit*) to pass (the ball) to sb; **jdm/sich gegenseitig die Bälle zuspielen** *or* **zuwerfen** (*fig*) to feed sb/ each other lines; **den ~ aufgreifen** *or* **aufnehmen** (*fig*) to take up the theme; **einen ~ machen** (*Billard*) to pocket a ball; **der glutrote ~ der Sonne** (*poet*) the sun's fiery orb (*poet*)

Ball² M -(e)s, ⸚e [ˈbɛlə] (= *Tanzfest*) ball; **auf dem ~** at the ball

ballaballa [balaˈbala] ADJ *pred* (*dated inf*) mad, crazy (*inf*), nuts (*inf*)

Ballabgabe F (*Sport*) pass; **bei der ~** when the ball was played, when he/she *etc* played the ball

Ballade [baˈlaːdə] F -, -n ballad

balladenhaft ADJ balladic, ballad-like ADV in a balladic *or* ballad-like way *or* manner

Balladensänger(in) M(F) balladeer, ballad singer

balladesk [balaˈdɛsk] ADJ, ADV = **balladenhaft**

Ballannahme F (*Sport*) stopping and controlling the ball; (*aus der Luft*) bringing down the ball

Ballast [ˈbalast, baˈlast] M -(e)s, (*rare*) -e (*Naut, Aviat*) ballast; (*fig*) burden, encumbrance; (*in Büchern*) padding; **~ abwerfen** *or* **über Bord werfen** (*lit*) to discharge *or* shed ballast; (*fig*) to get rid of a burden *or* an encumbrance; **mit ~ beladen** *or* **beschweren** to ballast, to load with ballast; **jdn/etw als ~ empfinden** to find sb/sth (to be) a burden *or* an encumbrance

Ballaststoffe PL (*Med*) roughage *sing*, dietary fibre (*Brit*) *or* fiber (*US*)

ballaststoffreich ADJ high-fibre (*Brit*) *or* -fiber (*US*); **~e Nahrung** *or* **Ernährung** high-fibre (*Brit*) *or* -fiber (*US*) food(s *pl*) *or* diet

Ball-: Ballbeherrschung F (*Sport*) ball control; **Ballbesitz** M (*Sport*) **im ~ sein** to have possession (of the ball), to be in possession of the ball

Bällchen NT -s, - *dim von* **Ball¹**

ballen [ˈbalən] VT **Faust** to clench; *Papier* to crumple (into a ball); *Lehm etc* to press (into a ball) → *auch* **geballt**, **Faust** VR (*Menschenmenge*) to crowd; (*Wolken*) to gather, to build up; (*Verkehr*) to build up; (*Faust*) to clench

Ballen [ˈbalən] M -s, - **a** bale; (= *Kaffeeballen*) sack; **in ~ verpacken** to bale **b** (*Anat: an Daumen, Zehen*) ball; (*an Pfote*) pad **c** (*Med: am Fußknochen*) bunion

ballenweise ADV in bales

Ballerei [baləˈrai] F -, -en (*inf*) shoot-out (*inf*), shoot-up (*inf*)

Ballerina¹ [baləˈriːna] F -, **Ballerinen** [-ˈriːnən] ballerina, ballet dancer

Ballerina² M -s, -s (= *Schuh*) pump

Ballermann [ˈbaləman] M *pl* **-männer** (*dated sl*) iron (*inf*), gun

ballern [ˈbalən] VI (*inf*) to shoot, to fire; (*Schuss*) to ring out; **gegen die Tür ~** to hammer *or* beat on the door VT *Stein etc* to hurl; *Tür etc* to slam

Ballett [baˈlɛt] NT -(e)s, -e ballet; **beim ~ sein** (*inf*) to be (a dancer) with the ballet, to be a ballet dancer; **zum ~ gehen** to become a ballet dancer

Balletttänzer(in) △ M(F) → **Balletttänzer**

Balletteuse [balɛˈtøːzə] F -, -n (*usu pej*) ballet dancer

Ballett- *in cpds* ballet; **Ballettmeister(in)** M(F) ballet master/mistress; **Ballettratte** F (*inf*) ballet pupil; **Ballettröckchen** NT tutu; **Ballettschuh** M ballet shoe; **Balletttänzer(in)** ▲ M(F) ballet dancer; **Balletttruppe** F ballet (company)

Ball-: ballförmig ADJ ball-shaped, round; **Ballführung** F (*Sport*) ball control; **Ballgefühl** NT (*Sport*) feel for the ball

Ballistik [baˈlɪstɪk] F -, *no pl* ballistics *sing*

ballistisch [baˈlɪstɪʃ] ADJ ballistic

Ball-: Balljunge M (*Tennis*) ball boy; **Ballkleid** NT ball dress *or* gown; **Ballkönigin** F belle of the ball; **Ballkünstler(in)** M(F) (*Ftbl*) artist with the ball; **Ballmädchen** NT (*Tennis*) ball girl

Ballon [baˈlɔŋ, baˈloːn, baˈloː] M -s, -s *or* (*bei deutscher Aussprache*) -e **a** balloon **b** (*Chem*) carboy, demijohn

Ballon- [baˈlɔŋ-, baˈloːn-, baˈloː-]: **Ballondilatation** F -, -en (*Med*) balloon dilatation; **Ballonfahrer(in)** M(F) balloonist; **Ballonfahrt** F balloon ride *or* trip; **eine ~ machen** to go up in a/one's balloon; **Ballonmütze** F baker's boy cap; **Ballonreifen** M balloon tyre (*Brit*) *or* tire (*US*)

Ball-: Ballsaal M ballroom; **Ballschani** [ˈbalʃaːni] M -s, - (*Aus inf*) ball boy; **Ballschuh** M evening *or* dancing shoe; **Ballspiel** NT ball game; **Ballspielen** NT -s, *no pl* playing ball; **„Ballspielen verboten"** "no ball games"; **Balltechnik** F (*Sport*) technique with the ball; **Balltreter(in)** M(F) (*inf*) footballer (*Brit*), soccer player (*US*)

Ballung [ˈbaluŋ] F -, -en concentration; (*von Truppen auch*) massing

Ballungs-: Ballungsgebiet NT , **Ballungsraum** M conurbation; **Ballungszentrum** NT centre (*Brit*) *or* center (*US*, *of population, industry etc*)

ballverliebt ADJ (*Sport*) *Fußballspieler* selfish; **~ sein** to hold onto the ball, to refuse to let go of the ball; **M. ist einfach zu ~** M. won't pass the ball

Ballwechsel M (*Sport*) rally

Balneologie [balneoloˈgiː] F -, *no pl* balneology

Balparadox [ˈbal paraˈdɔks] M -, -s - *ball at which women ask men to dance*

Balparé [ˈbal paˈreː] M -, -s -s grand ball

Balsaholz [ˈbalza-] NT balsa wood

Balsam [ˈbalzaːm] M -s, -e balsam, balm (*liter*); (*fig*) balm; **~ in jds Wunden** (*acc*) **träufeln** (*liter*) to pour balm on sb's wounds; **die Zeit ist ein heilender ~** (*liter*) time is a great healer

Balsamessig M balsamic vinegar

balsamieren [balzaˈmiːrən] *ptp* **balsamiert** VT to embalm

balsamisch [balˈzaːmɪʃ] ADJ (*liter*) **a** (= *duftend*) balmy (*liter*), fragrant **b** (= *lindernd*) soothing

Balte [ˈbaltə] M -n, -n, **Baltin** F -, -nen person *or* man/woman from the Baltic; **er ist ~** he comes from the Baltic

Baltenrepublik F Baltic republic

Baltenstaat M Baltic state

Baltikum [ˈbaltikum] NT -s *das* ~ the Baltic States *pl*

Baltin F → **Balte**

baltisch [ˈbaltɪʃ] ADJ Baltic *attr*

Balustrade [balʊsˈtraːdə] F -, -n balustrade

Balz [balts] F -, -en **a** (= *Paarungsspiel*) courtship display **b** (= *Paarungszeit*) mating season

balzen [ˈbaltsən] VI to perform the courtship display; (*pej: Sänger*) to croon

Balz-: Balzruf M mating call *or* cry; **Balzverhalten** NT mating *or* courtship display *or* behaviour (*Brit*) *or* behavior (*US*); **Balzzeit** F mating season

Bambi¹ [ˈbambi] NT -s, -s (*inf: = Rehkitz*) young deer

Bambi² M -s, -s Bambi (*German film award*)

Bambule [bamˈbuːlə] F -, -n (*sl*) ructions *pl* (*inf*); **~ machen** to go on the rampage

Bambus [ˈbambus] M -ses *or* -, -se bamboo

Bambus- *in cpds* bamboo; **Bambusrohr** NT bamboo cane; **Bambussprossen** PL bamboo shoots *pl*; **Bambusstab** M (*Sport*) bamboo (vaulting) pole; **Bambusvorhang** M (*Pol*) bamboo curtain

Bammel [ˈbaml] M -s, *no pl* (*inf*) **(einen) ~ vor jdm/etw haben** to be nervous *or* (*stärker*) scared of sb/sth

bammeln [ˈbamln] VI (*inf*) to swing, to dangle (*an +dat, from*)

banal [baˈnaːl] ADJ banal, trite ADV banally, tritely; **~ klingen**, **sich ~ anhören** to sound banal *or* trite

banalisieren [banaliˈziːrən] *ptp* **banalisiert** VT to trivialize

Banalität [banaliˈtɛːt] F -, -en **a** *no pl* banality, triteness **b** *usu pl* (*Äußerung*) platitude; **-en äußern** to utter platitudes

Banane [baˈnaːnə] F -, -n banana

Bananen-: Bananendampfer M banana boat; **Bananenflanke** F (*Ftbl inf*) curving cross; **Bananenrepublik** F (*Pol pej*) banana republic; **Bananenschale** F banana skin; **Bananenstaude** F banana tree; **Bananenstecker** M jack plug

Banause [baˈnauzə] M -n, -n, **Banausin** F [-ˈnauzɪn] F -, -nen (*pej*) peasant (*inf*), (= *Kulturbanause auch*) Philistine

Banausen-: banausenhaft ADJ Philistine ADV **sich äußern**, **sich benehmen** like a Philistine; **Banausentum** [baˈnauzntuːm] NT -s, *no pl* (*pej*) Philistinism

band *pret von* **binden**

Band¹ [bant] NT -(e)s, ⸚er [ˈbɛndɐ] **a** (= *Seidenband etc*) ribbon; (= *Isolierband, Maßband, Zielband*) tape; (= *Haarband, Hutband*) band; (= *Schürzenband*) string; (*Tech: zur Verpackung*) (metal) band; (= *Fassband*) hoop; (*Art: = Ornament*) band; **das Blaue ~** the Blue Riband; **das silberne ~ des Nils** (*liter*) the silver ribbon of the Nile **b** (= *Tonband*) (recording) tape; **etw auf ~ aufnehmen** to tape *or* (*tape-*)record sth; **etw auf ~ sprechen** to record sth on tape; **etw auf ~ diktieren** to dictate sth onto tape **c** (= *Fließband*) conveyor belt; (*als Einrichtung*) production line; (= *Montageband*) assembly line; (*in Autowerk*) track (*inf*); **am ~ arbeiten** *or* **stehen** to work on the production line *etc*; **vom ~ laufen** to come off the conveyor belt *etc*; **ein neues Auto auf ~ legen** (*Ind inf*) to put a new car into production; **durchs ~ (weg)** (*Sw*) every single one (without exception); **am laufenden ~** (*fig*) nonstop, continuously; **es gab Ärger am laufenden ~** there was nonstop *or* continuous trouble; **etw am laufenden ~ tun** to keep on doing sth **d** (*Rad*) wavelength, frequency band; **auf dem 44m-Band senden** to broadcast on the 44m band **e** (*Anat*) *usu pl* ligament **f** (= *Baubeschlag*) hinge

Band² NT -(e)s, -e [-də] (*liter*) **a** **das ~ der Freundschaft/Liebe** *etc* the bonds *or* ties of friendship/love *etc*; **familiäre ~e** family ties; **mit jdm freundschaftliche ~e anknüpfen** to become *or* make friends with sb; **zarte ~e knüpfen sich an** Cupid is at work; **zarte ~e knüpfen** to start a romance **b Bande** PL (= *Fesseln*) bonds *pl*, fetters *pl*; (*fig auch*) shackles *pl*; **jdn in ~e schlagen** to clap *or* put sb in irons

Band³ M -(e)s, ⸚e (= *Buchband*) volume; **ein gewaltiger ~** a mighty tome; **darüber könnte man Bände schreiben** or **erzählen** you could write volumes or a book about that; **mit etw Bände füllen** to write volumes about sth; **das spricht Bände** that speaks volumes

Band⁴ [bɛnt] F -, -s (*Mus*) band; (= *Beatband auch*) group

Ban|da|ge [banˈdaːʒə] F -, -n bandage; **mit harten ~ kämpfen** (*fig inf*) to fight with no holds barred

ban|da|gie|ren [bandaˈʒiːrən] *ptp* **bandagiert** VT to bandage (up)

Band-: **Band|auf|nah|me** F tape recording; **Band|auf|nah|me|ge|rät** NT tape recorder; **Band|brei|te** F **a** (*Rad*) waveband, frequency range **b** (*fig*) range **c** (*Fin*) (range of) fluctuation or variation

Bänd|chen [ˈbɛntçən] NT -s, - *dim von* **Band ¹ a** *von* **Band ³**

Ban|de¹ [ˈbandə] F -, -n gang; (= *Schmugglerbande*) band; (*inf*: = *Gruppe*) bunch (*inf*), crew (*inf*)

Ban|de² F -, -n (*Sport*) (*von Eisbahn, Reitbahn*) barrier; (*Billard*) cushion; (*von Kegelbahn*) edge; **die Kugel an die ~ spielen** to play the ball off the cushion/edge

Band|ei|sen NT metal hoop

Bän|del ▲ [ˈbɛndl] M OR NT -s, - (*dial*) ribbon; (= *Schnürsenkel*) shoelace; **jdn am ~ haben** or **führen** (*dated inf*) to be able to twist sb round one's little finger (*inf*)

Ban|den-: **Ban|den|be|kämp|fung** F (*Mil sl*) guerilla warfare; **Ban|den|chef**(in) M(F) (*inf*) gang leader; **Ban|den|dieb|stahl** M (*Jur*) gang robbery; **Ban|den|füh|rer**(in) M(F) gang leader; **Ban|den|krieg** M gang war; **Ban|den|kri|mi|na|li|tät** F gang crime; **Ban|den|mit|glied** NT member of a/the gang, gang member, gangbanger (*sl*); **Ban|den|wer|bung** F pitch-perimeter advertising; **Ban|den|we|sen** NT gangsterism

Ban|de|rol|le [bandəˈroːlə] F -, -n tax or revenue seal

Bän|der- (*Med*): **Bän|der|riss** ▲ M torn ligament; **Bän|der|zer|rung** F pulled ligament

Band-: **Band|fil|ter** M OR NT (*Rad*) band-pass filter; **Band|för|de|rer** M conveyor belt

-bän|dig [bɛndiç] ADJ *suf* -volume; **eine dreibändige Ausgabe** a three-volume edition, an edition in three volumes

bän|di|gen [ˈbɛndiɡn] VT (= *zähmen*) to tame; (= *niederhalten*) *Menschen, Tobenden etc* to (bring under) control, to subdue; (= *zügeln*) *Leidenschaften etc* to (bring under) control, to master; *Wut* to control; *Naturgewalten* to harness; *Kinder* to (bring under) control; **du musst lernen, dich zu ~** you must learn to control yourself

Bän|di|ger [ˈbɛndiɡɐ] M -s, -, **Bän|di|ge|rin** [-ərɪn] F -, -nen (*animal*) tamer

Bän|di|gung F -, -en (= *Zähmung*) taming; (*von Menschen*) subduing; (*von Leidenschaften*) mastering; (*von Naturgewalten*) harnessing

Ban|dit [banˈdiːt] M -en, -en, **Ban|di|tin** [-ˈdiːtɪn] F -, -nen bandit, brigand; (*fig pej*) brigand; **einarmiger ~** one-armed bandit

Ban|di|ten|tum [banˈdiːtntuːm] NT -s, *no pl*, **Ban|di|ten(un)we|sen** NT banditry

Band|ke|ra|mik F (*Archeol*) ribbon ware, band ceramics *pl*

Bändl [ˈbɛndl] NT -s, - = **Bändel**

Band|lauf|werk NT (*Comput*) tape streamer

Band|lea|der [ˈbɛntliːdɐ] M -s, -, **Band|lea|de|rin** [-ərɪn] F -, -nen band leader

Band-: **Band|maß** NT tape measure; **Band|nu|deln** PL ribbon noodles *pl*

Ban|dog [ˈbɛndɔk] M -s, -s bandog

Ban|do|ne|on [banˈdoːneɔn] NT -s, -s, **Ban|do|ni|on** [banˈdoːniɔn] M -s, -s bandoneon, bandonion

---

Band-: **Band|sä|ge** F band saw; **Band|sa|lat** M (*inf*) **dann bekommen Sie ~** then your tape gets tangled up, then your tape gets into a tangle; **Band|schei|be** F (*Anat*) (intervertebral) disc; **er hats an** or **mit der ~** (*inf*) he has slipped a disc, he has a slipped disc; **Band|schei|ben|scha|den** M , **Band|schei|ben|vor|fall** M slipped disc; **Band|stahl** M strip or band steel; **Band|werk** NT (*Art*) interlace; **Band|wurm** M tapeworm; **ein ~ von einem Satz** (*hum*) an endless or never-ending sentence; **Band|wurm|satz** M (*inf*) long or lengthy sentence

bang [baŋ] ADJ *comp* **-er** or **⸚er** [ˈbɛŋə], *superl* **-ste(r, s)** or **⸚ste(r, s)** [ˈbɛŋstə] **a** *attr* (= *ängstlich*) scared, frightened; **mir ist ~ vor ihm** I'm scared or frightened or afraid of him; **mir ist ~ vor der Prüfung** I'm scared or frightened of the exam; **das wird schon klappen, da ist mir gar nicht ~** it will be all right, I am quite sure of it → **angst**, **Angst**

b (*geh*: = *beklommen*) uneasy; *Augenblicke, Stunden auch* anxious, worried (*um* about); **es wurde ihr ~ ums Herz** her heart sank, she got a sinking feeling; **ihr wurde ~ und bänger** she became more and more afraid; **eine ~e Ahnung** a sense of foreboding

c (*S Ger*) **ihr war ~ nach dem Kinde** she longed or yearned (*liter*) for the child, she longed or yearned (*liter*) to be with the child

Bang|büx [ˈbaŋbʏks] F -, -en (*N Ger inf*) scaredy-cat (*inf*)

ban|ge [ˈbaŋə] ADJ *comp* **-r** or **⸚r** [ˈbɛŋə], *superl* **bangste(r, s)** or **bängste(r, s)** [ˈbɛŋstə] = **bang**

Ban|ge [ˈbaŋə] F -, *no pl* (*esp N Ger*) **~ haben** to be scared or frightened (*vor* +*dat* of); **jdm ~ machen** to scare or frighten sb; **~ machen gilt nicht** (*inf*) you can't scare me, you won't put the wind up me (*Brit inf*); **nur keine ~!** (*inf*) don't worry

Ban|ge-: **Ban|ge|ma|chen** NT -s, *no pl* scaremongering (*esp Brit*); **~ gilt nicht** (*inf*) you can't scare me, you won't put the wind up me (*Brit inf*); **Ban|ge|ma|cher(in)** M(F) scaremonger (*esp Brit*), alarmist

ban|gen [ˈbaŋən] (*geh*) **VI** **a** (= *Angst haben*) to be afraid (*vor* +*dat* of); **es bangt mir vor ihm, mir bangt vor ihm** I'm afraid or frightened of him, I fear him **b** (= *sich sorgen*) to worry, to be worried (*um* about); **um jds Leben ~** to fear for sb's life **c** (*dial, liter*) **nach jdm/etw ~** to long or yearn (*liter*) for sb/sth **VR** to be worried or anxious (*um* about)

Ban|gig|keit [ˈbaŋɪçkait] F -, *no pl* (= *Furcht*) nervousness; (= *Sorge*) anxiety; (= *Beklemmung*) apprehension

Bang|la|desch [baŋlaˈdɛʃ] NT -s Bangladesh

Bang|la|de|scher [baŋlaˈdɛʃɐ] M -s, -, **Bang|la|de|sche|rin** [-ərɪn] F -, -nen Bangladeshi

Bang|la|desh [baŋlaˈdɛʃ] NT -s, - Bangladesh

Bang|la|de|shi [baŋlaˈdɛʃi] MF -, - Bangladeshi

bäng|lich [ˈbɛŋlɪç] ADJ (*geh*) nervous

Ban|jo [ˈbanjo, ˈbɛndʒo, ˈbɛndʒo] NT -s, -s banjo

Bank¹ [baŋk] F -, ⸚e [ˈbɛŋkə] **a** bench; (*mit Lehne*) seat; (= *Kirchenbank*) pew; (= *Parlamentsbank*) bench; (= *Anklagebank*) dock; **auf** or **in der ersten/letzten ~** on the front/back bench *etc*; **er predigte vor leeren Bänken** he preached to an empty church; **die Debatte fand vor leeren Bänken statt** the debate took place in an empty house; **(alle) durch die ~ (weg)** (*inf*) every single or last one, the whole lot (of them) (*inf*); **etw auf die lange ~ schieben** (*inf*) to put sth off **b** (= *Arbeitstisch*) (work)bench; (= *Drehbank*) lathe **c** (= *Sandbank*) sandbank, sandbar; (= *Nebelbank, Wolkenbank*) bank; (= *Austernbank*) bed; (= *Korallenbank*) reef; (*Geol*) layer, bed **d** (*Ringen*) crouch (position)

Bank² F -, -en (*Fin, Comm*) bank; **Geld auf der ~ liegen haben** to have money in the bank;

---

bei der ~ at the bank; **ein Konto bei einer ~ eröffnen** to open an account with a bank; **bei der ~ arbeiten** or **sein** (*inf*) to work for the bank, to be with the bank **b** (*bei Glücksspielen*) bank; **(die) ~ halten** to hold or be the bank, to be banker; **die ~ sprengen** to break the bank

Bank-: **Bank|an|ge|stell|te(r)** MF *decl as adj* bank employee; **Bank|an|wei|sung** F banker's order; **Bank|auf|sicht** F = **Bankenaufsicht**; **Bank|auf|sichts|be|hör|de** F = **Bankenaufsichtsbehörde**; **Bank|au|to|mat** M cash dispenser (*Brit*), money machine (*US*), ATM; **Bank|be|am|te(r)** M *decl as adj* (*dated*), **Bank|be|am|tin** F (*dated*) bank employee; **Bank|bürg|schaft** F (*Fin*) bank guarantee

Bänk|chen [ˈbɛŋkçən] NT -s, - *dim von* **Bank ¹ a**

Bank-: **Bank|di|rek|tor(in)** M(F) director of a/the bank; **Bank|ein|bruch** M bank raid; **Bank|ein|la|ge** F (*Comm*) bank deposit; **Bank|ein|zug** M (*Comm*) direct debit, automatic payment (*US*) or draft (*US*); **per ~ zahlen** to pay by direct debit or automatic draft (*US*); **Bank|ein|zugs|ver|fah|ren** NT (*Comm*) direct debiting, automatic payment transfer (*US*)

Bän|kel- [ˈbɛŋkl-]: **Bän|kel|lied** NT street ballad; **Bän|kel|sang** M -(e)s, *no pl* ballad; **Bän|kel|sän|ger** M ballad singer, minstrel

Ban|ken-: **Ban|ken|auf|sicht** F (*Fin*) **a** (*Behörde*) banking regulatory authority **b** (*Kontrolle*) banking regulation; **Ban|ken|auf|sichts|be|hör|de** F banking regulatory authority; **Ban|ken|kon|sor|ti|um** NT banking syndicate or group; **Ban|ken|platz** M banking or financial centre (*Brit*) or center (*US*); **Ban|ken|vier|tel** NT banking area

Ban|ker [ˈbɛŋkɐ] M -s, -, **Ban|ke|rin** [-ərɪn] F -, -nen (*inf*) banker

Ban|kert [ˈbaŋkɐt] M -s, -e (*old pej*) bastard

Ban|kett¹ [banˈkɛt] NT -(e)s, -e (= *Festessen*) banquet

Ban|kett² NT -(e)s, -e, **Ban|ket|te** [banˈkɛtə] F -, -n (*an Straßen*) verge (*Brit*), shoulder (*US*); (*an Autobahnen*) (hard) shoulder; **„Bankette nicht befahrbar"**, **„weiche ~e"** "soft verges (*Brit*) or shoulder (*US*)" **b** (*Build*) footing

Bank-: **Bank|fach** NT **a** (= *Beruf*) banking, banking profession; **im ~ in** banking, in the banking profession **b** (= *Schließfach*) safety-deposit box; **Bank|fi|li|a|le** F branch of a bank; **Bank|ge|bäu|de** NT bank; **Bank|ge|bühr** F bank charge; **Bank|ge|heim|nis** NT confidentiality in banking; **Bank|ge|schäft** NT **a** banking transaction **b** *no pl* (= *Bankwesen*) banking world; **Bank|ge|wer|be** NT banking industry; **Bank|gut|ha|ben** NT bank balance; **Bank|hal|ter(in)** M(F) (*bei Glücksspielen*) bank, banker; **Bank|haus** NT **~ Grün & Co** Grün & Co, Bankers

Ban|ki|er [baŋˈkie:] M -s, -s banker

Ban|king [ˈbɛŋkɪŋ] NT -s, *no pl* (*Fin*) banking

Bank-: **Bank|kar|te** F bank card; **Bank|kauf|frau** F , **Bank|kauf|mann** M (qualified) bank clerk; **Bank|kon|to** NT bank account; **Bank|kre|dit** [-kredi:t] M bank loan; **Bank|krei|se** [-kraizə] PL banking circles *pl*, the banking community *sing*; **Bank|leh|re** F training as a bank clerk; **eine ~ machen** to train as a bank clerk; **Bank|leit|zahl** F bank code number, (bank) sort code (*Brit*); **Bank|nach|bar(in)** M(F) (*Sch*) **sie ist meine ~in** I sit next to her (at school); **Bank|no|te** F banknote, bill (*US*)

Ban|ko|mat [baŋkoˈmaːt] M -en, -en cash dispenser, hole-in-the-wall (*inf*), ATM (*US*)

Ban|ko|mat|kar|te F cash card, ATM card (*US*)

Bank-: **Bank|platz** M = **Bankenplatz**; **Bank|pro|vi|si|on** F (*Fin*) bank commission; **Bank|ra|te** M official discount rate; **Bank|raub** M bank robbery; **Bank|räu|ber(in)** M(F) bank robber

---

bank|rott [baŋ'krɔt] ADJ bankrupt; *Mensch, Politik* discredited; *Kultur* debased; *(moralisch)* bankrupt; **jdn ~ machen** to make sb (go) bankrupt, to bankrupt sb; **er ist politisch/innerlich ~** he is a politically discredited/a broken man

Bank|rott [baŋ'krɔt] M **-(e)s, -e** bankruptcy; *(fig)* breakdown, collapse; *(moralisch)* bankruptcy; **~ gehen** or **machen** to become or go bankrupt; **den ~ anmelden** or **ansagen** or **erklären** to declare oneself bankrupt

Bank|rott|er|klä|rung F declaration of bankruptcy; *(fig)* sellout *(inf)*

Bank|rot|teur [baŋkrɔ'tøːɐ] M **-s, -e**, **Bank|rot|teu|rin** [-'tøːrɪn] F **-, -nen** *(lit, fig)* bankrupt; *(fig)* moral bankrupt

Bank-: **Bank|schal|ter** M bank counter or window; **Bank|scheck** M cheque *(Brit)*, check *(US)*; **Bank|schließ|fach** NT safety-deposit box *(in bank)*; **Bank|schuld|ver|schrei|bung** F *(Fin)* (bank) bond; **Bank|spe|sen** PL bank (-ing) charges *pl*; **Bank|über|fall** M bank raid; **Bank|über|wei|sung** F bank transfer; **bank|üb|lich** ADJ **es ist ~** it is normal banking practice; **Bank|ver|bin|dung** F banking arrangements *pl*; **geben Sie bitte Ihre ~ an** please give your account details; **Bank|ver|kehr** M bank transactions *pl*; **Bank|we|sen** NT **das ~** banking

Bann [ban] M **-(e)s, -e** a *no pl (geh: = magische Gewalt)* spell; **im ~ eines Menschen/einer Sache stehen** or **sein** to be under sb's spell/the spell of sth; **jdn in seinen ~ schlagen** to captivate sb; **sie zog** or **zwang ihn in ihren ~** she cast her spell over him **b** *(Hist: = Kirchenbann)* excommunication; **jdn in den ~ tun**, **jdn mit dem ~ belegen**, **den ~ über jdn aussprechen** to excommunicate sb; **jdn vom ~ lösen** to absolve sb

Bann|brief M , **Bann|bul|le** F *(Hist)* letter of excommunication

ban|nen ['banən] VT **a** *(geh: = bezaubern)* to bewitch, to captivate, to entrance; **jdn/etw auf die Platte** *(inf)*/**die Leinwand ~** *(geh)* to capture sb/sth on film/canvas → *auch* **gebannt b** *(= vertreiben)* böse Geister, Teufel to exorcize; *(= abwenden)* Gefahr to avert, to ward off **c** *(Hist)* to excommunicate

Ban|ner ['banɐ] NT **-s, -** *(geh)* banner; *(fig auch)* flag; *(Internet)* banner; **das ~ des Sozialismus hochhalten** to fly the flag of socialism, to wave the banner of socialism

Banner-: **Ban|ner|trä|ger(in)** M(F) *(geh)* standard-bearer; *(fig)* vanguard *no pl*; **Banner|wer|bung** F *(Internet) (= Anzeige)* banner ad; *(das Werben)* banner advertising

Bann|fluch M excommunication

ban|nig ['banɪç] ADV *(N Ger inf)* terribly, really; **das hat ~ Spaß gemacht** that was great fun

Bann-: **Bann|kreis** M *(fig)* **in jds ~** *(dat)* **stehen** to be under sb's influence; **Bann|mei|le** F inviolable precincts *pl (of city, Parliament etc)*; **Bann|spruch** M excommunication; **Bann|strahl** M *(liter)* excommunication; **Bann|wald** M *(Aus, Sw)* protected forest that acts as a shield against avalanches etc; **Bann|wart** M **-(e)s, -e**, **Bann|war|tin** [-tɪn] F **-, -nen** *(Sw)* forester

Ban|tam ['bantam] NT **-s, -s** bantam

Bantam-: **Ban|tam|ge|wicht** NT bantamweight; **Ban|tam|ge|wicht|ler** [-gəvɪçtlɐ] M **-s, -**, **Ban|tam|ge|wicht|le|rin** [-ərɪn] F **-, -nen** bantamweight; **Ban|tam|huhn** NT bantam

Ban|tu ['bantu] M **-(s), -(s)** Bantu

Bantu-: **Ban|tu|frau** F Bantu woman; **Ban|tu|ne|ger(in)** M(F) Bantu; **Ban|tu|spra|che** F Bantu language

Bap|tist [bap'tɪst] M **-en, -en**, **Bap|tis|tin** [-'tɪs-tɪn] F **-, -nen** Baptist

Bap|tis|te|ri|um [baptɪs'teːriʊm] NT **-s, Baptisterien** [-riən] *(Eccl)* baptistry; *(= Taufbecken)* font

---

bar [baːɐ] ADJ *no comp* **a** cash; **~es Geld** cash; **(in) ~ bezahlen** to pay (in) cash; **~ auf die Hand** cash on the nail; **(Verkauf) nur gegen ~** cash (sales) only; **etw für ~e Münze nehmen** *(fig)* to take sth at face value **b** *attr (= rein)* Zufall pure; *Unsinn auch* utter, absolute **c** *pred +gen (liter)* devoid of, utterly or completely without; **~ aller Hoffnung, aller Hoffnung ~** devoid of hope, completely or utterly without hope **d** *(liter: = bloß)* bare; **~en Hauptes** bareheaded

Bar¹ [baːɐ] F **-, -s a** *(= Nachtlokal)* nightclub, bar **b** *(= Theke)* bar

Bar² NT **-s, -s** *(Met)* bar

Bär [bεːɐ] M **-en, -en a** bear; **stark wie ein ~** *(inf)* (as) strong as an ox or a horse; **der Große/Kleine ~** *(Astron)* the Great/Little Bear *(Brit)*, Ursa Major/Minor, the Big/Little Dipper; **jdm einen ~en aufbinden** *(inf)* to have *(Brit)* or put *(US)* sb on *(inf)* → **schlafen** VI **b** *(Tech) (= Schlagbär)* hammer; *(= Rammbär)* rammer

Ba|ra|ber [ba'raːbɐ] M **-s, -**, **Ba|ra|be|rin** [-ərɪn] F **-, -nen** *(Aus inf)* labourer *(Brit)*, laborer *(US)*; *(= Straßenarbeiter)* navvy *(inf)*

ba|ra|bern [ba'raːbɐn] *ptp* **barabert** VI *(Aus inf)* to labour *(Brit)*, to labor *(US)*

Bar|ab|he|bung F cash withdrawal

Ba|ra|cke [ba'rakə] F **-, -n** hut, shack

Ba|ra|cken|la|ger NT , **Ba|ra|cken|sied|lung** F camp (made of huts); *(für Flüchtlinge)* refugee camp

Bar-: **Bar|aus|schüt|tung** F *(Fin)* cash distribution; **Bar|aus|zah|lung** F cash payment

Bar|bar [bar'baːɐ] M **-en, -en**, **Bar|ba|rin** [-'baː-rɪn] F **-, -nen a** *(pej)* barbarian; *(= Rohling auch)* brute **b** *(Hist)* Barbarian

Bar|ba|ra|zweig ['barbara-] M *usu pl* sprig cut on St. Barbara's Day (4 Dec.) to flower for Christmas

Bar|ba|rei [barba'rai] F **-, -en** *(pej)* **a** *(= Unmenschlichkeit)* barbarity **b** *(no pl: = Kulturlosigkeit)* barbarism

bar|ba|risch [bar'baːrɪʃ] ADJ **a** *(pej) (= unmenschlich)* Grausamkeit, Folter, Sitten barbarous, savage, brutal; *(= ungebildet)* Benehmen, Mensch barbaric, uncivilized **b** *(Hist)* Volk, Stamm barbarian ADV **a** *misshandeln, quälen* brutally, savagely **b** *(= entsetzlich)* heiß, kalt terribly, horribly

Bar|ba|ris|mus [barba'rɪsmʊs] M **-, Barbarismen** [-mən] *(Liter)* barbarism

Bar|be ['barbə] F **-, -n** *(Zool)* barbel

Bar|be|cue ['baːbikjuː] NT **-(s), -s** barbecue

bär|bei|ßig ['bεːɐbaisç] ADJ *(inf)* Gesicht, Miene, Mensch grouchy *(inf)*, grumpy; Antwort etc gruff, grumpy; Manieren surly

Bar-: **Bar|be|stand** M *(Comm)* cash; *(Buchführung)* cash in hand; **Bar|be|trag** M cash sum or amount

Bar|bie® ['barbi] F **-, -s** Barbie®

Bar|bie-Pup|pe® F , **Bar|bie|pup|pe®** F Barbie® doll

Bar|bier [bar'biːɐ] M **-s, -e** *(old, hum)* barber

bar|bie|ren [bar'biːrən] *ptp* **barbiert** VT *(old, hum)* **jdn ~** to shave sb; *(= Bart beschneiden)* to trim sb's beard; *(= die Haare schneiden)* to cut sb's hair; **sich ~ lassen** to go to the barber's → **balbieren**

Bar|bi|tu|rat [barbitu'raːt] NT **-s, -e** barbiturate

Bar|bi|tur|säu|re [barbi'tuːɐ-] F barbituric acid

bar|brüs|tig [-brʏstç], **bar|bu|sig** [-buːzɪç] ADJ topless ADV *auftreten, bedienen, tanzen* topless

Bar|code ['baːkoːt] M barcode

Bar|da|me F barmaid; *(euph: = Prostituierte)* hostess *(euph)*

Bar|de ['bardə] M **-n, -n** *(Liter)* bard; *(iro)* minstrel

---

Bar-: **Bar|ein|gän|ge** [-aingεŋə] PL *(Fin)* cash receipts *pl*; **Bar|ein|la|ge** [-ainlaːgə] F *(Fin)* cash deposit

Bä|ren-: **Bä|ren|dienst** M **jdm/einer Sache einen ~ erweisen** to do sb/sth a bad turn, to do sb/sth a disservice; **Bä|ren|dreck** M *(S Ger, Aus, Sw: inf)* liquorice; **Bä|ren|fang** M *(= Likör)* ≈ mead; **Bä|ren|fell** NT bearskin; **Bä|ren|fell|müt|ze** F bearskin (hat); *(hohe Mütze)* bearskin (cap), busby *(Brit Mil)*; **Bä|ren|füh|rer(in)** M(F) bear trainer; *(hum)* (tourist) guide; **Bä|ren|hatz** F bear hunt; **Bä|ren|haut** F **auf der ~ liegen**, **sich auf die ~ legen** *(dated)* to laze or loaf about; **Bä|ren|hun|ger** M *(inf)* **einen ~ haben** to be famished *(inf)* or ravenous *(inf)*; **Bä|ren|jagd** F bear hunt; **Bä|ren|jun|ge(s)** NT *decl as adj (Zool)* (bear) cub; **Bä|ren|klau** F **-, -** or m **-s, -** *(Bot) (= Heracleum)* hogweed; *(= Akanthus)* bear's-breech; **Bä|ren|kräf|te** PL the strength *sing* of an ox; **Bä|ren|markt** M *(St Ex)* bear market; **Bä|ren|müt|ze** F bearskin, busby; **Bä|ren|na|tur** F **eine ~ haben** *(inf)* to be (physically) tough; **bä|ren|stark** **a** strapping, strong as an ox **b** *(inf)* terrific; **ein ~es Buch** an amazing book; **Bä|ren|tat|ze** F bear's paw

Ba|rents|see ['baːrənts-] F *(Geog)* Barents Sea

Bä|ren|zwin|ger M bear cage

Ba|rett [ba'rεt] NT **-(e)s, -e** or **-s** cap; *(für Geistliche, Richter etc)* biretta; *(Univ)* mortarboard; *(= Baskenmütze)* beret

Bar|frau F barmaid

bar|fuß ['baːɐfuːs] ADJ *pred* barefoot(ed); **~ gehen** to go/walk barefoot(ed); **ich bin ~** I've got nothing on my feet, I am barefoot(ed)

bar|fü|ßig ADJ barefooted

barg *pret von* **bergen**

Bar-: **Bar|geld** NT cash; **bar|geld|los** ADJ cashless, without cash; **~er Zahlungsverkehr** payment by money transfer ADV without using cash; **Bar|gut|ha|ben** NT cash balance, ready money; **bar|haupt** ['baːɐhaupt] ADJ *pred (liter)*, **bar|häup|tig** ['baːɐhɔyptɪç] ADJ *(geh)* bareheaded; **Bar|ho|cker** M (bar) stool

bä|rig ['bεːrɪç] *(Aus inf)* ADJ tremendous, fantastic ADV tremendously, fantastically

Bä|rin ['bεːrɪn] F **-, -nen** (she-)bear

Ba|ri|ton ['baːrɪtɔn] M **-s, -e** [-toːnə] baritone

Ba|ri|um ['baːriʊm] NT **-s**, *no pl (abbr* **Ba**) barium

Bark [bark] F **-, -en** *(Naut)* barque

Bar|ka|ro|le [barka'roːlə] F **-, -n** *(Mus)* barcarol(l)e

Bar|kas|se [bar'kasə] F **-, -n** launch; *(= Beiboot auch)* longboat

Bar|kauf M cash purchase; **~ ist billiger** it is cheaper to pay (in) cash

Bar|ke ['barkə] F **-, -n** *(Naut)* skiff; *(liter)* barque *(liter)*

Bar|kee|per ['baːɐkiːpɐ] M **-s, -** barman, bartender

Bar-: **Bar|kode** ['baːɐkoːt] M barcode; **Bar|kre|dit** [-kreːdiːt] M cash loan

Bär|lapp ['bεːɐlap] M **-s, -e** *(Bot)* lycopod(ium)

Bär|lauch ['bεːɐlaux] M **-s, -e** *usu sing (Bot, Cook)* bear's garlic

Bar|mann M *pl* **-männer** barman

bar|men ['barmən] VI *(dial)* to moan, to grumble *(über +acc* about) VT *(liter)* **er barmt mich** I feel pity for him

barm|her|zig [barm'hεrtsç] ADJ *(liter, Rel)* merciful; *(= mitfühlend)* compassionate; **~er Himmel!** *(old, dial)* good heavens above!; **der ~e Samariter** *(Bibl, fig)* the good Samaritan; **Barmherzige Schwestern** Sisters of Charity

Barm|her|zig|keit F **-**, *no pl (liter, Rel)* mercy, mercifulness; *(= Mitgefühl)* compassion; **~ (an jdm) üben** to show mercy (to sb)/compassion (towards sb); **Herr, übe ~ an mir!** Lord, have mercy on me! → **Gnade**

Bar|mit|tel PL cash (reserves *pl*)

Bar|mi|xer M barman

Bar|mi|xe|rin F barmaid

ba|rock [ba'rɔk] ADJ baroque; *(fig)* (= *überladen auch, verschnörkelt*) ornate; *Sprache* florid; (= *seltsam*) *Einfälle* bizarre, eccentric; **sie hat eine sehr ~e Figur** *(hum)* she has a very ample figure *(esp Brit)*

Ba|rock [ba'rɔk] NT OR M **-(s)**, *no pl* baroque; **das Zeitalter des ~** the baroque age

Ba|rock- *in cpds* baroque; **Ba|rock|bau** M *pl* **-bauten** baroque building; **Ba|rock|stil** M *(Archit)* baroque (style); **eine Kirche im ~** a baroque church; **Ba|rock|zeit** F baroque style

Ba|ro|me|ter [baro'meːtɐ] NT **-s**, **-** *(lit, fig)* barometer; **das ~ steht auf Sturm** the barometer is on stormy; *(fig)* things look stormy

Ba|ro|me|ter|stand M barometer reading

ba|ro|met|risch [baro'meːtrɪʃ] ADJ *attr* barometric

Ba|ron [ba'roːn] M **-s**, **-e** **a** baron; **~ (von) Schnapf** Baron *or* Lord Schnapf; **Herr ~** my lord **b** *(fig: = Industriebaron etc)* baron, magnate

Ba|ro|ness ▲ [baro'nɛs] F **-**, **-en** *(dated)*, **Ba|ro|nes|se** [baro'nɛsə] F **-**, **-n** daughter of a baron; **Fräulein ~** my lady

Ba|ro|nin [ba'roːnɪn] F **-**, **-nen** baroness; **Frau ~** my lady

Bar|ras ['baras] M **-**, *no pl (dated sl)* army; **beim ~** in the army; **zum ~ gehen** to join up *(inf)*, to join the army; **er muss nächstes Jahr zum ~** he's got to do his military service next year, he'll be drafted next year *(US)*

Bar|rel ['bɛrəl] NT **-s**, **-s** *or* **-** barrel

Bar|ren ['barən] M **-s**, **-** **a** (= *Metallbarren*) bar; (= *esp Goldbarren*) ingot **b** *(Sport)* parallel bars *pl* **c** *(S Ger, Aus: = Futtertrog)* trough

Bar|ren|gold NT gold bullion

Bar|re|ser|ven PL cash reserves *pl*

Bar|ri|e|re [ba'rieːrə] F **-**, **-n** *(lit, fig)* barrier

Bar|ri|ka|de [bari'kaːdə] F **-**, **-n** barricade; **auf die ~n gehen** *(lit, fig)* to go to the barricades

Bar|ri|ka|den-: Bar|ri|ka|den|kampf M street battle; (= *das Kämpfen*) street fighting *no pl*; **Bar|ri|ka|den|stür|mer(in)** M(F) *(fig)* revolutionary

bar|ri|ka|die|ren [barika'diːrən] *ptp* **barrikadiert** VT to barricade

barsch [barʃ] ADJ brusque, curt; **jdm eine ~e Abfuhr erteilen** to give sb short shrift ADV brusquely, curtly; **jdn ~ anfahren** to snap at sb

Barsch [barʃ] M **-(e)s**, **-e** bass; (= *Flussbarsch*) perch

Bar|schaft ['baːɐ̯ʃaft] F **-**, *(rare)* **-en** cash; **meine ganze ~ bestand aus 10 Euro** all I had on me was 10 euros

Bar|scheck M open *or* uncrossed cheque *(Brit)*, open check *(US)*

Barsch|heit F **-**, **-en** brusqueness, curtness; *(von Befehl auch)* peremptoriness

Bar|soi [bar'zɔy] M **-s**, **-s** borzoi

Bar|sor|ti|ment NT book wholesaler's

barst *pret von* **bersten**

Bart [baːɐ̯t] M **-(e)s**, **-e** ['bɛːɐ̯tə] **a** *(von Mensch, Ziege, Vogel, Getreide)* beard; *(von Katze, Maus, Robbe etc)* whiskers *pl*; **sich** *(dat)* **einen ~ wachsen** *or* **stehen lassen** to grow a beard; **ein drei Tage alter ~** three days' growth (on one's chin) **b** *(fig inf)* **(sich** *dat)* **etwas in den ~ murmeln** *or* **brumme(l)n** to murmur *or* mutter sth in one's boots *or* beard *(inf)*; **jdm um den ~ gehen**, **jdm Honig um den ~ schmieren** *or* **streichen** to butter sb up *(inf)*, to soft-soap sb *(inf)*; **der Witz hat einen ~** that's a real oldie *(inf)*, that's an old chestnut *(inf)*; **der ~ ist ab** that's that!, that's the end of it *or* that **c** (= *Schlüsselbart*) bit

Bart|bin|de F *device for keeping a moustache in shape*

Bärt|chen ['bɛːɐ̯tçən] NT **-s**, **-** (= *Kinnbärtchen*) (small) beard; (= *Oberlippenbärtchen*) toothbrush moustache *(Brit)* or mustache *(US)*; (= *Menjoubärtchen*) pencil moustache *(Brit)* or mustache *(US)*

Bar|teln ['bartln] PL *(Zool)* barbels *pl*

Bar|ten|wal ['bartn-] M whalebone *or* baleen whale

Bart-: Bart|fä|den PL *(Zool)* barbels *pl*; **Bart|flech|te** F **a** *(Med)* sycosis, barber's itch **b** *(Bot)* beard lichen *or* moss; **Bart|haar** NT facial hair; (= *Bart auch*) beard

Bar|thel ['bartl] M **wissen, wo (der) ~ den Most holt** *(inf)* to know what's what *(inf)*

Bar|tho|lo|mä|us [bartolo'mɛːʊs] M **-'** Bartholomew

Bar|tho|lo|mä|us|nacht F *(Hist)* Massacre of St. Bartholomew

bär|tig ['bɛːɐ̯tɪç] ADJ bearded

Bär|ti|ge(r) M *decl as adj* bearded man, man with a beard

Bart-: bart|los ADJ beardless; (= *glatt rasiert*) clean-shaven; **Bart|nel|ke** F sweet william; **Bart|stop|pel** F piece of stubble; **Bart|stop|peln** PL stubble *sing*; **Bart|tas|se** F moustache cup; **Bart|tracht** F beard style; **Bart|wisch** M **-(e)s**, **-e** *(S Ger, Aus)* hand brush; **Bart|wuchs** M beard; *(esp weiblicher)* facial hair *no indef art*; **er hat starken ~** he has a strong *or* heavy growth of beard; **Bart|zot|teln** PL wispy beard *sing*

Bar-: Bar|über|wei|sung F *(Fin)* cash transfer; **Bar|ver|kauf** M cash sales *pl*; **ein ~** a cash sale; **Bar|ver|mö|gen** NT cash *or* liquid assets *pl*; **Bar|wert** M *(Fin)* (actual) cash value; **Bar|zah|lung** F payment by or in cash; *(Verkauf)* **nur gegen ~** cash (sales) only; **bei ~ 3% Skonto** 3% discount for cash; **Bar|zah|lungs|ra|batt** M *(Comm)* cash discount

Ba|salt [ba'zalt] M **-(e)s**, **-e** basalt

ba|sal|ten [ba'zaltn], **ba|sal|tig** [ba'zaltɪç] ADJ basaltic

Ba|sar [ba'zaːɐ̯] M **-s**, **-e** **a** (= *orientalischer Markt*) bazaar; **auf dem ~** in the bazaar **b** (= *Wohltätigkeitsbasar*) bazaar

Bäs|chen ['bɛːsçən] NT **-s**, **-** *dim von* **Base** ¹

Ba|se¹ ['baːzə] F **-**, **-n** *(old, dial)* cousin; (= *Tante*) aunt

Ba|se² F **-**, **-n** *(Chem)* base

Base|ball ['beːsbɔːl] M **-s**, *no pl* baseball

Baseball-: Base|ball|müt|ze ['beːsbɔːl-] F baseball cap; **Base|ball|schlä|ger** ['beːsbɔːl-] M baseball bat

Ba|se|dow ['baːzədo] M **-s**, *no pl (inf)*, **Ba|se|dow|krank|heit** F **-**, **-e** , **ba|se|dow|sche Krank|heit** ['baːzədoʃə] F (exophthalmic) goitre *(Brit)* or goiter *(US)*

Ba|sel ['baːzl] NT **-s** Basle, Basel

Ba|se|ler ['baːzlɐ] ADJ *attr* = **Basler**

Ba|sen *pl von* **Basis** *von* **Base**

ba|sie|ren [ba'ziːrən] *ptp* **basiert** VI *(auf +dat* on) to be based, to rest VT to base *(auf +acc* or *(rare) +dat* on)

Ba|si|li|ka [ba'ziːlika] F **-**, **Basiliken** [-kn] basilica

Ba|si|li|kum [ba'ziːlikʊm] NT **-s**, *no pl* basil

Ba|si|lisk [bazi'lɪsk] M **-en**, **-en** basilisk

Ba|si|lis|ken|blick M *(liter)* baleful glare

Ba|sis ['baːzɪs] F **-**, **Basen** [ba'zn] basis; *(Archit, Mil, Math)* base; **auf breiter ~** on a broad basis; **auf einer festen** *or* **soliden ~ ruhen** to be firmly established; **sich auf gleicher ~ treffen** to meet on an equal footing, to meet on equal terms; **~ und Überbau** *(Pol, Socio)* foundation and superstructure; **die ~** *(inf)* the grass roots (level); (= *die Leute*) (those at) the grass roots

Basis-: Ba|sis|ar|beit F *(Pol)* groundwork; **Ba|sis|camp** NT base camp

ba|sisch ['baːzɪʃ] *(Chem)* ADJ basic ADV **~ rea|gie|ren** to show a basic reaction

Ba|sis-: Ba|sis|de|mo|kra|tie F grass-roots democracy; **ba|sis|de|mo|kra|tisch** ADJ grass-roots *attr* ADV **der ~ gewählte Kandidat** the candidate elected by the grass roots; **~ organi|sierter Verein** grass-roots organization; **Ba|sis|grup|pe** F action group; **Ba|sis|la|ger** NT base camp; **Ba|sis|preis** M *(Fin: von Kaufoption)* call exercise price; **Ba|sis|wis|sen** NT basic knowledge; **Ba|sis|zins** M *(Fin)* base (interest) rate

Bas|ke ['baskə] M **-n**, **-n**, **Bas|kin** ['baskɪn] F **-**, **-nen** Basque

Bas|ken-: Bas|ken|land NT Basque region; **Bas|ken|müt|ze** F beret

Bas|ket|ball ['baːskət-, 'baskət-] M **-s**, *no pl* basketball

Bas|kin F **-**, **-nen** Basque

bas|kisch ['baskɪʃ] ADJ Basque

Bas|kisch(e) ['baskɪʃ] NT Basque → *auch* **Deutsch(e)**

Bas|ler¹ ['baːzlɐ] ADJ *attr* Basle *attr*

Bas|ler² ['baːzlɐ] M **-s**, **-**, **Bas|le|rin** [-ərɪn] F **-**, **-nen** native of Basle; (= *Einwohner*) inhabitant of Basle

Bas|re|li|ef ['barelief, bare'lief] NT *(Archit, Art)* bas-relief

bass ▲ [bas] ADV *(old, hum)* **~ erstaunt** much *or* uncommonly *(old)* amazed

Bass ▲ [bas] M **-es**, **-e** ['bɛsə] **a** (= *Stimme, Sänger*) bass; **hoher/tiefer** *or* **schwarzer ~** basso cantante/profundo; **einen hohen/tiefen ~ haben** to be a basso cantante/profundo **b** (= *Instrument*) double bass; *(im Jazz auch)* bass **c** (= *Basspartie*) bass (part)

Bass|ba|ri|ton ▲ M bass baritone

Bas|sett|horn ['basɛt-] NT basset horn

Bass-: Bass|gei|ge ▲ F *(inf)* (double) bass; **Bass|gi|tar|re** ▲ F bass guitar

Bas|sin [ba'sɛ̃ː] NT **-s**, **-s** (= *Schwimmbassin*) pool; (= *Gartenbassin*) pond

Bas|sist¹ [ba'sɪst] M **-en**, **-en** (= *Sänger*) bass (singer)

Bas|sist² [ba'sɪst] M **-en**, **-en**, **Bas|sis|tin** [-'sɪstɪn] F **-**, **-nen** *(im Orchester etc)* (double) bass player; **~ sein** to be a (double) bass player, to play the (double) bass

Bass-: Bass|kla|ri|net|te ▲ F bass clarinet; **Bass|par|tie** ▲ F bass part; **Bass|sän|ger** ▲ M bass (singer); **Bass|schlüs|sel** ▲ M bass clef; **Bass|stim|me** ▲ F bass (voice); (= *Partie*) bass (part)

Bast [bast] M **-(e)s**, *(rare)* **-e** **a** *(zum Binden, Flechten)* raffia; *(Bot)* bast, phloem **b** *(an Geweih)* velvet

bas|ta ['basta] INTERJ **(und damit) ~!** (and) that's that

Bas|tard ['bastart] M **-(e)s**, **-e** [-də] **a** *(Hist: uneheliches Kind)* bastard **b** *(Biol: = Kreuzung)* (= *Pflanze*) hybrid; (= *Tier*) crossbreed, cross; (= *Mensch*) half-caste, half-breed

Bas|tei [bas'tai] F **-**, **-en** bastion

Bas|tel-: Bas|tel|ar|beit F piece of handcraft, handicraft; (= *das Basteln*) (doing) handcraft *or* handicrafts; **etw in langer ~ bauen** to spend a long time making *or* building sth; **sich viel mit ~en beschäftigen** to do a lot of handcraft *or* handicrafts; **Bas|tel|e|cke** F *(in Zimmer)* handicraft corner; *(in Zeitschrift)* hobbies corner *or* page

Bas|te|lei [bastə'lai] F **-**, **-en** *(inf)* handcraft, handicraft; (= *Stümperei*) botched job *(inf)*

bas|teln ['bastln] VI **a** *(als Hobby)* to make things with one's hands; (= *Handwerksarbeiten herstellen*) to do handcraft *or* handicrafts; **sie kann gut ~** she is good with her hands **b** **an etw** *(dat)* **~** to make sth, to work on sth; *an Modellflugzeug etc* to build *or* make sth; (= *an etw herumbasteln*) to mess around with sth, to tinker with sth **VT** to make; *Geräte etc auch* to build

Bas|teln NT -s, *no pl* handicraft, handicrafts *pl*

Bas|tel|raum M workroom

Bast|fa|ser F bast fibre (*Brit*) *or* fiber (*US*)

Bas|til|le [basˈtiːjə, -ˈtɪljə] F - (*Hist*) **der Sturm auf die** ~ the storming of the Bastille

Bas|ti|on [basˈtioːn] F -, -en bastion, ramparts *pl*; (*fig*) bastion, bulwark

Bast|ler [ˈbastlɐ] M -s, -, **Bast|le|rin** [-ərɪn] F -, -nen (*von Modellen etc*) modeller (*Brit*), modeler (*US*); (*von Möbeln etc*) do-it-yourselfer; **ein guter ~ sein** to be good *or* clever with one's hands, to be good at making things

Bas|to|na|de [bastoˈnaːdə] F -, -n bastinado

Bast|sei|de F wild silk, shantung (*silk*)

bat *pret von* **bitten**

BAT [beːʔaːˈteː] *abbr von* **Bundesangestelltentarif**

> **BAT**
>
> BAT is an abbreviation of **Bundesangestelltentarif** and refers to the salary scale for public service employees. Private firms also use these rates as a guide: wording such as **Bezahlung nach BAT** can often be seen in job advertisements. Lists of the relevant salary scales are obtainable from the **ÖTV**, the trade union for public service workers.

Ba|tail|le [baˈtaːjə, baˈtaljə] F -, -n (*old*) battle

Ba|tail|lon [batalˈjoːn] NT -s, -e (*Mil, fig*) battalion

Ba|tail|lons|füh|rer(in) M(F), **Ba|tail|lons|kom|man|deur(in)** M(F) battalion commander

Ba|ta|te [baˈtaːtə] F -, -n sweet potato, yam (*esp US*), batata

Ba|tik [ˈbaːtɪk] F -, -en *or m* -s, -en batik

ba|ti|ken [ˈbaːtɪkn] **VI** to do batik **VT** to decorate with batik; **eine gebatikte Bluse** a batik blouse

Ba|tist [baˈtɪst] M -(e)s, -e batiste, cambric

Bat|te|rie [batəˈriː] F -, -n [-ˈriːən] (*Elec, Mil, = Legebatterie*) battery; (*= Mischbatterie etc*) regulator; (*= Reihe: von Flaschen etc*) row, battery

Bat|te|rie-: Bat|te|rie|an|zei|ger M battery display *or* meter; **Bat|te|rie|be|trieb** M **das Radio ist für ~ eingerichtet** the radio takes batteries, the radio can be battery-powered; **bat|te|rie|be|trie|ben** [-bətriːbn] ADJ battery-powered; **Bat|te|rie|fach** NT battery compartment; **Bat|te|rie|ge|rät** NT battery-powered radio *etc*; **Bat|te|rie|huhn** NT battery hen *or* chicken; **Bat|te|rie|la|de|ge|rät** NT battery charger; **Bat|te|rie|zün|dung** F battery ignition (system)

Bat|zen [ˈbatsn] M -s, - **a** (*dated: = Klumpen*) clod, lump **b** (*obs: = Münze*) batz (*silver coin*); **ein (schöner) ~ Geld** (*inf*) a tidy sum (*inf*), a pretty penny (*inf*)

Bau [bau] M **a** -(e)s, *no pl* (*= das Bauen*) building, construction; **im** *or* **in ~** under construction; **sich im ~ befinden** to be under construction; **das im ~ befindliche Kraftwerk** the power station which is under construction; **der ~ des Hauses dauerte ein Jahr** it took a year to build the house; **mit dem ~ beginnen, an den ~ gehen** to begin building *or* construction; **den ~ beenden, mit dem ~ fertig sein** to finish building, to complete construction

b -(e)s, *no pl* (*= Aufbau*) structure; (*von Satz, Maschine, Apparat auch*) construction; (*= Körperbau*) **von kräftigem/schwächlichem ~ sein** to be powerfully/slenderly built, to have a powerful/ slender build *or* physique

c -s, *no pl* (*= Baustelle*) building site; **auf dem ~ arbeiten, beim ~ sein** to be a building worker, to work on a building site; **vom ~ sein** (*fig inf*) to know the ropes (*inf*)

d -(e)s, -ten [-tn] (*= Gebäude*) building; (*= Bau-*

werk) construction; **~ten** (*Film*) sets

e -(e)s, -e (*= Erdhöhle*) burrow, hole; (*= Biberbau*) lodge; (*= Fuchsbau*) den; (*= Dachsbau*) set(t); **heute gehe ich nicht aus dem ~** (*inf*) I'm not sticking my nose out of doors today (*inf*); **zu ~ gehen** (*Hunt*) to go to earth

f -(e)s, -e (*Min*) workings *pl*; **im ~ sein** to be down the pit *or* mine

g -(e)s, *no pl* (*Mil sl*) guardhouse; **4 Tage ~** 4 days in the guardhouse

h -(e)s, -e (*inf: = Gefängnis*) **in den ~ wandern** to end up in the slammer (*inf*)

Bau-: Bau|ab|nah|me F building inspection; **Bau|ab|schnitt** M stage *or* phase of construction; **Bau|amt** NT planning department and building control office (*Brit*), Board of Works (*US*); **Bau|an|lei|tung** F construction manual; **Bau|ar|bei|ten** PL building *or* construction work *sing*; (*= Straßenbau*) roadworks *pl* (*Brit*), road construction (*US*); **Bau|ar|bei|ter(in)** M(F) building *or* construction worker, building labourer (*Brit*) *or* laborer (*US*); **Bau|art** F construction, design; (*= Stil*) style; **Bau|auf|sicht** F supervision of building *or* construction; **die ~ liegt bei der Flughafenverwaltung** the airport authority is supervising the construction; **Bau|aus|füh|rung** F construction, building; **~ Firma Meyer** builders *or* constructors Meyer and Co; **Bau|be|ginn** M start of construction (work); **Bau|be|hör|de** F planning department and building control office (*Brit*), Board of Works (*US*); **Bau|be|wil|li|gung** F planning permission; **Bau|bio|lo|ge** M , **Bau|bio|lo|gin** F building biologist; **Bau|bio|lo|gie** F building biology; **bau|bio|lo|gisch** ADJ *attr* building biology ADV **~ unbedenkliche Wohnungen** *apartments built safely according to the principles of building biology*; **Bau|block** M *pl* **-blocks** block; **Bau|bu|de** F building workers' hut

Bauch [baux] M -(e)s, **Bäuche** [ˈbɔʏçə] **a** (*von Mensch*) stomach, tummy (*inf*); (*Anat*) abdomen; (*von Tier*) stomach, belly; (*= Fettbauch*) paunch, potbelly (*inf*); **ihm tat der ~ weh** he had stomach ache *or* tummy ache (*inf*); **sich** (*dat*) **den ~ voll schlagen** (*inf*) to stuff oneself (*inf*); **ein voller ~ studiert nicht gern** (*Prov*) you can't study on a full stomach; **sich** (*dat*) (**vor Lachen**) **den ~ halten** (*inf*) to split one's sides (laughing) (*inf*); **einen dicken ~ haben** (*sl: = schwanger sein*) to have a bun in the oven (*inf*); **vor jdm auf dem ~ rutschen** (*inf*) *or* **kriechen** (*inf*) to grovel *or* kowtow to sb (*inf*), to lick sb's boots (*inf*); **etw aus dem ~ heraus entscheiden** to decide sth according to (a gut) instinct; **mit etw auf den ~ fallen** (*inf*) to come a cropper with sth (*Brit inf*), to fall flat on one's face with sth (*inf*) → **Wut a**, **Loch**, **Bein**

b (*= Wölbung, Hohlraum*) belly; (*= Innerstes: von Schiff auch, von Erde*) bowels *pl*

Bauch-: Bauch|an|satz M beginning(s) of a paunch; **Bauch|bin|de** F **a** (*für Frack*) cummerbund; (*Med*) abdominal bandage *or* support **b** (*um Zigarre, Buch*) band; **Bauch|de|cke** F abdominal wall; **Bauch|fell** NT **a** (*Anat*) peritoneum **b** (*= Fell am Bauch*) stomach *or* belly fur; **Bauch|fell|ent|zün|dung** F peritonitis; **Bauch|fleck** M (*Aus inf*) belly flop (*inf*); **Bauch|flos|se** F ventral fin; **Bauch|ge|gend** F abdominal region; **Bauch|grim|men** NT -s, *no pl* (*inf*) stomach ache, tummy ache (*inf*); **Bauch|höh|le** F abdominal cavity, abdomen; **Bauch|höh|len|schwan|ger|schaft** F ectopic pregnancy

bau|chig [ˈbauxɪç] ADJ *Gefäß* bulbous; *Schrift* rounded

Bauch-: Bauch|klat|scher M (*inf*) belly flop (*inf*); **Bauch|la|den** M sales tray (*carried round the neck*); **Bauch|lan|dung** F (*inf*) (*Aviat*) belly landing; (*bei Sprung ins Wasser*) belly flop (*inf*); **mit dem neuen Stück/mit der neuen Firma haben wir eine ~ gemacht** (*fig*) the new play/the new company was a flop

Bäuch|lein [ˈbɔʏçlain] NT -s, - tummy (*inf*); (*hum: = Fettbäuchlein*) bit of a stomach *or* tummy (*inf*)

bäuch|lings [ˈbɔʏçlɪŋs] ADV on one's front, face down

Bauch-: Bauch|mus|kel M stomach *or* abdominal muscle; **Bauch|mus|ku|la|tur** F stomach *or* abdominal muscles *pl*; **Bauch|na|bel** M navel, bellybutton (*inf*); **bauch|pin|seln** VT (*inf*) → **gebauchpinselt**; **bauch+re|den** VI *sep usu infin* to ventriloquize; **Bauch|red|ner(in)** M(F) ventriloquist; **Bauch|schmer|zen** PL stomach ache, tummy ache (*inf*); (*fig*) discomfort, anguish; **jdm ~ bereiten** (*fig*) to cause sb major problems; **wegen etw ~ haben** (*fig*) to feel uncomfortable because of sth; **Bauch|schuss** ▲ M shot in the stomach; (*= Verletzung*) stomach wound; **einen ~ abbekommen** to be shot in the stomach; **Bauch|speck** M (*Cook*) belly of pork; (*hum*) spare tyre (*Brit inf*) *or* tire (*US inf*); **Bauch|spei|chel|drü|se** F pancreas; **Bauch|tanz** M belly dancing; (*einzelner Tanz*) belly dance; **bauch+tan|zen** VI *sep usu infin* to belly-dance; **Bauch|tän|ze|rin** F belly dancer; **Bauch|um|fang** M stomach girth, wasteline

Bau|chung [ˈbauxʊŋ] F -, -en bulge

Bauch-: Bauch|wand F stomach *or* abdominal wall; **Bauch|weh** NT stomach ache, tummy ache (*inf*); **Bauch|wel|le** F (*Sport*) circle on the beam

Bau|con|tai|ner M Portakabin®, prefabricated hut

Baud [baut, bɔːt] NT -(s), - (*Comput*) baud

Bau-: Bau|dar|le|hen NT building loan; **Bau|denk|mal** NT historical monument

Baud-Ra|te [ˈbaut-, ˈbɔːt-] F (*Comput*) baud rate

Bau|ele|ment NT component part

bau|en [ˈbauən] **VT a** (*= erbauen*) to build, to construct; (*= anfertigen auch*) *Satz* to construct; *Höhle* to dig, to make; **sich** (*dat*) **ein Haus ~** to build oneself a house; **sich** (*dat*) **ein Nest ~** to make *or* build oneself a nest (*auch fig*); **seine Hoffnung auf jdn/etw ~** to build one's hopes on sb/sth; **die Betten ~** (*esp Mil*) to make the beds → *auch* **gebaut**

b (*inf: = verursachen*) *Unfall* to cause; **da hast du Scheiße gebaut** (*inf*) you really messed (*inf*) *or* cocked (*Brit inf*) that up; **bleib ruhig, bau keine Scheiße** (*inf*) cool it, don't make trouble (*inf*)

c (*inf: = machen, ablegen*) *Prüfung etc* to pass; **den Führerschein ~** to pass one's driving test; **seinen Doktor ~** to get one's doctorate

VI a (*= Gebäude errichten*) to build; **wir haben neu/auf Sylt gebaut** we built a new house/a house on Sylt; **nächstes Jahr wollen wir ~** we're going to build *or* to start building next year; **an etw** (*dat*) **~** to be working on sth, to be building sth (*auch fig*); **hier wird viel gebaut** there is a lot of building *or* development going on round (*Brit*) *or* around here; **hoch ~** to build high-rise buildings

b (*= vertrauen*) to rely, to count (*auf +acc* on)

Bau|ent|wurf M building plans *pl*

Bau|er[1] [ˈbauɐ] M -n *or* (*rare*) -s, -n **a** (*= Landwirt*) farmer; (*als Vertreter einer Klasse*) peasant; (*pej: = ungehobelter Mensch*) (country) bumpkin, yokel; **die dümmsten ~n haben die größten** *or* **dicksten Kartoffeln** (*prov inf*) fortune favours (*Brit*) *or* favors (*US*) fools (*prov*); **was der ~ nicht kennt, das frisst er nicht** (*prov inf*) some people won't try anything new **b** (*Chess*) pawn; (*Cards*) jack, knave

Bau|er[2] [ˈbauɐ] M -s, -, **Bau|e|rin** [-ərɪn] F -, -nen (*= Erbauer*) builder; (*fig auch*) architect

Bau|er[3] NT OR M -s, - (*= Käfig*) (bird)cage

Bäu|er|chen [ˈbɔʏɐçən] NT -s, - **a** *dim von* **Bauer**[1] **b** (*baby-talk*) burp; (**ein**) **~ machen** to (do a) burp

Bäu|e|rin [ˈbɔyərɪn] F -, -nen **a** (= Frau des Bauern) farmer's wife **b** (= Landwirtin) farmer; (als Vertreterin einer Klasse) peasant (woman)

bäu|e|risch [ˈbɔyərɪʃ] ADJ = bäurisch

Bäu|er|lein [ˈbɔyɛlaɪn] NT -s, - (liter, hum) farmer

bäu|er|lich [ˈbɔyɛlɪç] ADJ rural; (= ländlich) Fest, Bräuche, Sitten rustic, country attr; **~e Klein- und Großbetriebe** small and large farms ADV **~ geprägt sein** to be rural; **~ eingerichtet** rustically furnished

Bäu|er|lich|keit F -, no pl rurality

Bauern-: Bau|ern|auf|stand M peasants' revolt or uprising; **Bau|ern|brot** NT coarse rye bread; **Bau|ern|dorf** NT farming or country village; **Bau|ern|fang** M auf ~ ausgehen (inf) to play con tricks (inf); **Bau|ern|fän|ger** M (inf) con man (inf), swindler; **Bau|ern|fän|ge|rei** [-fɛŋəˈraɪ] F -, -en (inf) con (inf), swindle; **Bau|ern|fän|ge|rin** F (inf) swindler, con woman (inf); **Bau|ern|frau** F farmer's wife; **Bau|ern|früh|stück** NT bacon and potato omelette; **Bau|ern|gut** NT farm(stead); **Bau|ern|haus** NT farmhouse; **Bau|ern|hoch|zeit** F country wedding; **Bau|ern|hof** M farm; **Bau|ern|jun|ge** M country boy, country lad (esp Brit inf); **Bau|ern|ka|len|der** M country almanac; **Bau|ern|krieg** M (Hist) Peasant War(s); **Bau|ern|le|gen** NT -s, no pl (Hist, Pol pej) expropriation of peasants' land; **Bau|ern|mäd|chen** NT country girl, country lass (esp Brit inf); **Bau|ern|magd** F farmer's maid; **Bau|ern|mö|bel** PL farmhouse furniture sing; **Bau|ern|op|fer** NT (fig) (= Mensch) fall guy; (= Sache) necessary sacrifice; **Bau|ern|par|tei** F (Pol) country party; **Bau|ern|re|gel** F country saying; **Bau|ern|schä|del** M (large) head; (pej) thick skull (inf); **Bau|ern|schaft** [ˈbauɐnʃaft] F -, no pl farming community; (ärmlich) peasantry; **Bau|ern|schläue** F native or low cunning, craftiness, shrewdness; **Bau|ern|schrank** M farmhouse cupboard, cupboard in rustic style; **Bau|ern|stand** M farming community, farmers pl; **Bau|ern|stu|be** F farmhouse parlour (Brit) or parlor (US); (in Gasthaus) country-style dining room; **Bau|ern|the|a|ter** NT rural folk theatre (Brit) or theater (US); **Bau|ern|töl|pel** M (pej) country bumpkin, yokel; **Bau|ern|tum** [ˈbauɐntu:m] NT -s, no pl (= Bauernstand) farming community, farmers pl; **er ist stolz auf sein ~** he is proud of coming from farming stock; **Bau|ern|ver|band** M farmers' organization

Bauers-: Bau|ers|frau F farmer's wife; **Bau|ers|leu|te** PL farm(ing) folk, farmers pl; **Bau|ers|mann** M pl -leute (old, liter) farmer

Bau-: Bau|er|war|tungs|land NT (Admin) development area; **Bau|fach** NT construction industry; **bau|fäl|lig** ADJ dilapidated; Decke, Gewölbe unsound, unsafe; **Bau|fäl|lig|keit** F dilapidation; **wegen ~ gesperrt** closed because building unsafe; **Bau|fi|nan|zie|rung** F construction or mortgage financing, construction or building finance; **Bau|fir|ma** F building contractor or firm; **Bau|flucht** F line; **Bau|form** F form or shape (of a building); **Bau|ge|län|de** NT land for building; (= Baustelle) building site; **Bau|geld** NT building capital; **Bau|ge|neh|mi|gung** F planning and building permission; **Bau|ge|nos|sen|schaft** F housing association; **Bau|ge|rüst** NT scaffolding; **Bau|ge|schäft** NT building firm; **Bau|ge|sell|schaft** F property company; **Bau|ge|wer|be** NT building and construction trade; **bau|gleich** ADJ Modell, Ausführung structurally identical; **Bau|glied** NT (Archit) part of a building; **Bau|gru|be** F excavation; **Bau|grund** M (= Gelände) building land, development site; (= Grundstück) site, (building) plot; **Bau|grund|stück** NT (building) plot, plot of land for building; **Bau|hand|werk** NT building trade; **Bau|hand|wer|ker(in)** M(F) (trained) building worker; **Bau|haus** NT (Archit, Art) Bauhaus; **Bau|herr(in)** M(F) client

(for whom sth is being built); **seitdem er ~ ist ...** since he has been having a house built ...; **~in ist die Stadt** the clients are the town authorities; **~ Ministerium des Innern** under construction for the Ministry (Brit) or Department (US) of the Interior; **Bau|her|ren|mo|dell** NT scheme by which tax relief is obtained on investment in building projects; **Bau|holz** NT building timber; **Bau|hüt|te** F **a** (= Baubude) building workers' hut **b** (Hist, Archit) church masons' guild; **Bau|in|dust|rie** F building and construction industry; **Bau|in|ge|ni|eur(in)** M(F) civil engineer

Bauj. abbr von Baujahr

Bau-: Bau|jahr NT year of construction; (von Gebäude auch) year of building; (von Auto) year of manufacture; **VW ~ 98** 1998 VW; **welches ~?** what year?; **Bau|kas|ten** M building or construction kit; (mit Holzklötzchen) box of bricks; (= Chemiebaukasten) set; **Bau|kas|ten|prin|zip** NT building-block principle; **Bau|kas|ten|sys|tem** NT (Tech) modular or unit construction system; **Bau|klotz** M (building) brick or block; **Bauklötze(r) staunen** (inf) to gape (in astonishment); **Bau|klötz|chen** NT (building) block; **Bau|ko|lon|ne** F gang of building workers; (bei Straßenbau) gang of navvies (Brit inf), construction unit (US); **Bau|kos|ten** PL building or construction costs pl; **Bau|kos|ten|zu|schuss** ▲ M building subsidy or grant; **Bau|kran** M construction or builder's crane; **Bau|kunst** F (geh) architecture; **Bau|land** NT building land; (für Stadtplanung) development area; **einen Acker als ~ verkaufen** to sell a field for building; **Bau|lei|ter(in)** M(F) (building) site manager; **Bau|lei|tung** F **a** (= Aufsicht) (building) site supervision; (= Büro) site office **b** (= die Bauleiter) (building) site supervisory staff; **bau|lich** [ˈbaulɪç] ADJ structural; **in gutem/schlechtem ~em Zustand** structurally sound/unsound ADV structurally; **das Gebäude ist in einem ~ schlechten Zustand** structurally, the building is in bad condition; **Bau|lö|we** M building speculator; **Bau|lü|cke** F empty site, gap site

Baum [baum] M -(e)s, Bäume [ˈbɔymə] tree; **auf dem ~ in the tree; der ~ der Erkenntnis** (Bibl) the tree of knowledge; **er ist stark wie ein ~** he's as strong as an ox; **zwischen ~ und Borke stecken** or **stehen** to be in two minds; **die Bäume wachsen nicht in den Himmel** (prov) all good things come to an end; **einen alten ~ or alte Bäume soll man nicht verpflanzen** (prov) you can't teach an old dog new tricks (prov); **ein Kerl wie ein ~** (inf) a tall, athletic guy (inf) → **ausreißen** VT, **Wald**

Bau-: Bau|man|gel M usu pl construction defect; (strukturell) structural defect; **Bau|markt** M property market; (= Geschäft für Heimwerker) DIY superstore; **Bau|ma|schi|ne** F piece of building machinery; **Bau|ma|schi|nen** PL building machinery or plant sing; **Bau|maß|nah|men** PL building operations pl; **Bau|ma|te|ri|al** NT building material

Baum-: Baum|be|stand M tree population no pl, stock of trees; **Baum|blü|te** F blossom

Bäum|chen [ˈbɔymçən] NT -s, - small tree; (= junger Baum auch) sapling; **~, wechsle dich spielen** to play tag; (hum: = Partnertausch) to swap partners

Baum|chi|rurg(in) M(F) tree surgeon

Baum|meis|ter(in) M(F) **a** master builder; (= Bauunternehmer) building contractor; (= Architekt) architect **b** (= Erbauer) builder

bau|meln [ˈbaumln] VI to dangle (an +dat from); **die Haarsträhnen baumelten ihm ins Gesicht** the strands of hair hung in his face; **jdn ~ lassen** (sl) to let sb swing (inf)

Baum-: Baum|farn M tree fern; **Baum|fäu|le** F (in Holz) dry rot; (in Baum) rot in a/the living tree; **Baum|fre|vel** M (form) malicious damage to trees; **Baum|gren|ze** F tree or timber line; **Baum|grup|pe** F coppice, cluster of

trees; **Baum|haus** NT tree house; **baum|hoch** ADJ tree-high; **Baum|kro|ne** F treetop; **Baum|ku|chen** M (Cook) ≈ cylindrical cake built up from horizontal layers baked successively; **baum|lang** ADJ **ein ~er Kerl** (inf) a beanpole (inf); **Baum|läu|fer** M tree creeper; **baum|los** ADJ treeless; **baum|reich** ADJ wooded; **Baum|rie|se** M (liter) giant tree; **Baum|rin|de** F tree bark; **Baum|sche|re** F (tree) pruning shears pl, secateurs pl; **Baum|schu|le** F tree nursery; **Baum|stamm** M tree trunk; **baum|stark** ADJ Arme, Beine massive; Mann beefy (inf), hefty; **Baum|step|pe** F scrub; **Baum|ster|ben** NT tree death; **Baum|struk|tur** F (Comput) tree structure; **Baum|strunk** M , **Baum|stumpf** M tree stump; **Baum|wip|fel** M treetop

Baum|woll- in cpds cotton

Baum|wol|le F cotton; **ein Hemd aus ~** a cotton shirt

baum|wol|len ADJ attr cotton

Baum|woll-: Baum|woll|hemd NT (100%) cotton shirt; **Baum|woll|spin|ne|rei** F cotton mill; **Baum|woll|strauch** M cotton plant

Baum|wuchs M tree growth

Bau-: Bau|ord|nung F building regulations pl; **Bau|plan** M building plan; (= Vorhaben auch) building project; (Biol: genetischer, biologischer etc) blueprint; **Bau|pla|nung** F planning (of a building); **Bau|plas|tik** F architectural sculpture; **Bau|platz** M site (for building); **Bau|po|li|zei** F building control department (Brit), Board of Works (US); **bau|po|li|zei|lich** ADJ building control attr (Brit) ADV **~ genehmigt** covered by a building permit; **Bau|preis** M building price; **Bau|rat** M , **Bau|rä|tin** F head of the planning department and building control office (Brit), head of the Board of Works (US); **Bau|recht** NT planning and building laws and regulations; **bau|reif** ADJ Grundstück available for building; **Bau|rei|he** F (von Auto) model range; (von Flugzeug, Computer) series

bäu|risch [ˈbɔyrɪʃ] ADJ (pej) boorish, rough

Bau-: Bau|ru|i|ne F (inf) unfinished building; **Bau|sach|ver|stän|di|ge(r)** MF decl as adj quantity surveyor; **Bau|satz** M kit

Bausch [bauʃ] M -es, Bäusche or -e **a** (= Wattebausch) ball; (Med auch) swab **b** (= Krause) (an Vorhang) pleat; (an Kleid) bustle; (an Ärmel) puff **c** in ~ und Bogen lock, stock and barrel

Bäusch|chen [ˈbɔyʃçən] NT -s, - dim von Bausch

bau|schen [ˈbauʃn] VR **a** (= sich aufblähen) to billow (out) **b** (Kleidungsstück) to puff out; (ungewollt) to bunch (up) VT **a** Segel, Vorhänge to fill, to swell **b** (= raffen) to gather; **gebauschte Ärmel** puffed sleeves VI (Kleidungsstück) to bunch (up), to become bunched

Bau|schen [ˈbauʃn] M -s, - (S Ger, Aus: = Wattebausch) ball; (Med auch) swab

bau|schig [ˈbauʃɪç] ADJ Wolken billowing; Rock, Vorhänge full; Watte fluffy

Bau-: Bau|schlos|ser(in) M(F) fitter on a building site; **Bau|schutt** M building rubble; **Bau|schutt|mul|de** F skip; **Bau|sek|tor** M building or construction sector

Bau|spar|dar|le|hen [ˈbauʃpaːɐ-] M building society loan (Brit), loan from a/one's building and loan association (US)

bau+spa|ren VI sep usu infin to save with a building society (Brit) or building and loan association (US)

Bau|spa|rer(in) M(F) saver with a building society (Brit) or building and loan association (US)

Bau|spar-: Bau|spar|kas|se F building society (Brit), building and loan association (US); **Bau|spar|ver|trag** M savings contract with a building society (Brit) or building and loan association (US)

Bau-: Bau|stahl M mild or structured steel; **Bau|stein** M stone (for building); (Spielzeug) brick; (= *elektronischer Baustein*) chip; (*fig:* = *Bestandteil*) building block; (*Tech*) module; **Bau**|**stel**|**le** F building *or* construction site; (*bei Straßenbau*) roadworks *pl* (*Brit*), road construction (*US*); (*bei Gleisbau*) railway (*Brit*) *or* railroad (*US*) construction site; „**Achtung, ~!**" "danger, roadworks (*Brit*) *or* road construction (*US*)"; „**Betreten der ~ verboten**" "unauthorized entry prohibited", "trespassers will be prosecuted"; **die Strecke ist wegen einer ~ gesperrt** the road is closed because of roadworks (*Brit*) *or* road construction (*US*); (*Bahnstrecke*) the line is closed because of (railway (*Brit*) *or* railroad (*US*)) construction work; **Bau**|**stel**|**len**|**ver**|**kehr** M heavy traffic (from a building site); „**Achtung, ~!**" "construction traffic"; **Bau**|**stil** M architectural style; **Bau**|**stoff** M building material; **Bau**|**stopp** M **einen ~ verordnen** to impose a halt on building (projects); **Bau**|**stu**|**fe** F construction stage *or* phase, stage *pr* phase of construction; **Bau**|**sub**|**stanz** F fabric, structure; **die ~ ist gut** the house is structurally sound; **Bau**|**sum**|**me** F total building cost; **Bau**|**tä**|**tig**|**keit** F building; **eine rege ~** a lot of building; **Bau**|**tech**|**ni**|**ker(in)** M(F) site engineer; **bau**|**tech**|**nisch** ADJ structural; **eine ~e Glanzleistung** a superb feat of structural engineering; **Bau**|**teil**[1] M (= *Gebäudeteil*) part (of a building); **Bau**|**teil**[2] NT (= *Bauelement*) component

Bau|**ten** *pl von* **Bau** d
Bau-: Bau|**tisch**|**ler(in)** M(F) joiner; **Bau**|**trä**|**ger(in)** M(F) builder, building contractor; **Bau**|**un**|**ter**|**neh**|**men** NT **a** (= *Firma*) building contractor **b** (= *Bauvorhaben*) building project *or* scheme; **Bau**|**un**|**ter**|**neh**|**mer(in)** M(F) building contractor, builder; **Bau**|**vo**|**lu**|**men** NT volume of building; **Bau**|**vor**|**ha**|**ben** NT building project *or* scheme; **Bau**|**wei**|**se** F type *or* method of construction; (= *Stil*) style; **in konventioneller ~** built in the conventional way/style; **offene ~** detached houses; **geschlossene ~** terraced (*Brit*) *or* row (*US*) houses; **Bau**|**werk** NT construction; (= *Gebäude auch*) edifice, building; **Bau**|**we**|**sen** NT *, no pl* building and construction industry; **ein Ausdruck aus dem ~** a building term; **Bau**|**wich** [ˈbaʊvɪç] M -(e)s, -e (*Archit*) space between two neighbouring (*Brit*) *or* neighboring (*US*) buildings; **Bau**|**wirt**|**schaft** F building and construction industry; **Bau**|**wut** F building frenzy *or* craze

Bau|**xit** [baʊˈksiːt] M -s, -e bauxite
bauz [baʊts] INTERJ wham, crash, bang; **~ machen** (*baby-talk*) to go (crash bang) wallop
Bau-: Bau|**zaun** M hoarding, fence; **Bau**|**zeich**|**nung** F building plan *usu pl*; **Bau**|**zeit** F time taken for building *or* construction; **die ~ betrug drei Jahre** it took three years to build
b. a. w. *abbr von* **bis auf weiteres** until further notice
Bay|**er** [ˈbaɪɐ] M -n, -n, **Ba**|**ye**|**rin** [ˈbaɪərɪn] F -, -nen Bavarian
bay|**e**|**risch** [ˈbaɪərɪʃ] ADJ Bavarian; **der Bayerische Wald** the Bavarian Forest
Bay|**e**|**risch(e)** [ˈbaɪərɪʃ] NT Bavarian (dialect) → *auch* **Deutsch(e)**
Bay|**ern** [ˈbaɪɐn] NT -s Bavaria
bay|**risch** [ˈbaɪrɪʃ] ADJ = **bayerisch**
Bay|**risch(e)** [ˈbaɪrɪʃ] NT = **Bayerisch(e)**
Ba|**zar** [baˈzaːɐ] M -s, -e = **Basar**
Ba|**zi** [ˈbaːtsi] M -, - (*Aus inf*) blighter (*Brit inf*), scoundrel
Ba|**zil**|**le** [baˈtsɪlə] F -, -n **a** (*inf*: = *Bazillus*) bacillus; (= *Krankheitserreger*) germ **b** **linke ~** (*sl*: = *übler Typ*) sly git (*sl*)
Ba|**zil**|**len-: Ba**|**zil**|**len**|**furcht** F germ phobia; **Ba**|**zil**|**len**|**trä**|**ger(in)** M(F) carrier
Ba|**zil**|**lus** [baˈtsɪlʊs] M -, Bazillen [-ˈtsɪlən] **a** bacillus; (= *Krankheitserreger*) germ **b** (*fig*) cancer, growth
Ba|**zoo**|**ka** [baˈzuːka] F -, -s bazooka

Bd. *abbr von* **Band**[3]
BDA [beːdeːˈʔaː] F - **a** *abbr von* **Bundesvereinigung der Arbeitgeberverbände** employers' association, ≈ CBI (*Brit*) **b** *abbr von* **Bund deutscher Architekten**
Bde. *abbr von* **Bände** → **Band**[3]
BDI [beːdeːˈʔiː] M -, *no pl abbr von* **Bundesverband der Deutschen Industrie** manufacturing industries' association, ≈ CBI (*Brit*)
BDM [beːdeːˈʔɛm] M -, *no pl* (*NS*) *abbr von* **Bund Deutscher Mädel**
BE *abbr von* **Broteinheit**
be|**ab**|**sich**|**ti**|**gen** [bəˈʔapzɪçtɪgn] ✪ 35.1, 35.2, 45.4 *ptp* **beabsichtigt** VT to intend; **eine Reise/ Steuererhöhung ~** (*form*) to intend to go on a journey/to increase taxes; **das hatte ich nicht beabsichtigt** I didn't mean it to happen, I didn't intend that to happen; **das war beabsichtigt** that was deliberate *or* intentional; **die beabsichtigte Wirkung** the desired *or* intended effect
be|**ach**|**ten** *ptp* **beachtet** VT **a** (= *befolgen*) to heed; *Ratschlag auch* to follow; *Vorschrift, Verbot, Verkehrszeichen* to observe, to comply with; *Regel* to observe, to follow; *Gebrauchsanweisung* to follow; **etw besser ~** to pay more attention to sth → **Vorfahrt**
b (= *berücksichtigen*) to take into consideration *or* account; **es ist zu ~, dass ...** it should be taken into consideration *or* account that ...
c (= *Aufmerksamkeit schenken*) jdn to notice, to pay attention to; *(bei Erklärungen, Reiseführung etc)* to observe; **jdn nicht ~** to ignore sb, to take no notice of sb; **von der Öffentlichkeit kaum beachtet** scarcely noticed by the public; **das Ereignis wurde in der Öffentlichkeit kaum/stark beachtet** the incident aroused little/considerable public attention
be|**ach**|**tens**|**wert** [bəˈʔaxtnsveːɐt] ADJ noteworthy, remarkable
be|**acht**|**lich** [bəˈʔaxtlɪç] ADJ **a** (= *beträchtlich*) considerable; *Verbesserung, Zu- or Abnahme* marked; *Erfolg* notable; *Talent* remarkable **b** (= *bedeutend*) *Ereignis* significant; (= *lobenswert*) *Leistung* considerable, excellent; (= *zu berücksichtigend*) relevant; **~!** (*dated*) well done; **er hat im Leben/Beruf Beachtliches geleistet** he has achieved a considerable amount in life/his job **ADV** (= *sehr*) significantly, considerably
Be|**ach**|**tung** F **a** (= *das Befolgen*) heeding; *(von Ratschlag, Gebrauchsanweisung)* following; *(von Vorschrift, Regel, Verbot, Verkehrszeichen)* observance, compliance (+*gen* with); **die ~ der Vorschriften** observance of *or* compliance with the regulations; **unter ~ der Vorschriften** in accordance with the regulations
b (= *Berücksichtigung*) consideration; **unter ~ aller Umstände** taking into consideration *or* considering all the circumstances
c (= *das Beachten*) notice, attention (+*gen* to); „**zur ~**" please note; **~ finden/verdienen** to receive/deserve attention; **jdm/einer Sache ~ schenken** to pay attention to sb/sth, to take notice of sb/sth; **jdm keine ~ schenken** to ignore sb, to take no notice of sb
Beach|**vol**|**ley**|**ball** [ˈbiːtʃvɔli-] M beach volleyball
be|**ackern** *ptp* **beackert** VT **a** *Feld* to till, to work **b** (*inf*) *Thema, Wissensgebiet* to go into, to examine
Bea|**gle** [ˈbiːgl] M -s, -(s) beagle
bea|**men** [ˈbiːmən] VT to beam VR to beam oneself
Bea|**mer** [ˈbiːmɐ] M -s, - (*Tech, Opt*) digital projector, LCD projector
Be|**am**|**te** M = **Beamte(r)**
Be|**am**|**ten-: Be**|**am**|**ten**|**an**|**wär**|**ter(in)** M(F) civil service trainee; **Be**|**am**|**ten**|**ap**|**pa**|**rat** M bureaucracy; **Be**|**am**|**ten**|**be**|**lei**|**di**|**gung** F insulting an official; **Be**|**am**|**ten**|**be**|**ste**|**chung** F bribing an official; **Be**|**am**|**ten**|**da**|**sein** NT (*usu pej*) life of *or* as a minor official *or* civil servant; **ein eintöniges ~ führen** to lead the

routine-bound life of a minor official; **Be**|**am**|**ten**|**deutsch** NT officialese; **Be**|**am**|**ten**|**lauf**|**bahn** F career in the civil service; **die ~ einschlagen** to enter *or* join the civil service; **Be**|**am**|**ten**|**men**|**ta**|**li**|**tät** F bureaucratic mentality; **Be**|**am**|**ten**|**recht** NT civil service law; **Be**|**am**|**ten**|**schaft** [bəˈʔamtnʃaft] F -, *no pl* civil servants *pl*, civil service; **Be**|**am**|**ten**|**see**|**le** F (*pej*) petty official; **Be**|**am**|**ten**|**stand** M (*dated*) civil service; **Be**|**am**|**ten**|**sta**|**tus** M civil servant status; **Be**|**am**|**ten**|**tum** [bəˈʔamtntuːm] NT -s, *no pl* **a** civil service; (= *Beamtenschaft auch*) civil servants *pl* **b** (*Wesen*) **sein ~** the civil servant in him; **es ist Kennzeichen des ~s, dass ...** it is the mark of civil servants that ...; **Be**|**am**|**ten**|**ver**|**hält**|**nis** NT **im ~ stehen** to be a civil servant; **ins ~ übernommen werden** to become a civil servant; **Be**|**am**|**ten**|**will**|**kür** F arbitrariness of officials; **das war ~** that was an arbitrary bureaucratic decision
Be|**am**|**te(r)** [bəˈʔamtə] M *decl as adj*, **Be**|**am**|**tin** [bəˈʔamtɪn] F -, -nen official; (= *Staatsbeamte*) civil servant; (= *Zollbeamte*) official, officer; (= *Polizeibeamte*) officer; (*dated:* = *Bürobeamte, Schalterbeamte*) clerk; **politischer ~r** politically-appointed civil servant; **er ist ~r** (*bei Land, Bund*) he is a civil servant, he is in the civil service; **~r auf Widerruf** (*Ger*) civil servant employed by the state for a probationary period **~r auf Zeit** civil servant on a temporary contract **~r auf Lebenszeit** civil servant on a life-term contract, person retaining civil service status for life **er ist ein typischer ~r** (*pej*) he is a typical petty official *or* bureaucrat; **ein kleiner ~r** a minor *or* (*esp pej*) petty official
be|**am**|**tet** [bəˈʔamtət] ADJ (*form*) established, appointed on a permanent basis (*by the state*)
be|**ängs**|**ti**|**gen** *ptp* **beängstigt** VT (*geh*) to alarm, to frighten, to scare
be|**ängs**|**ti**|**gend** ADJ alarming, frightening; **sein Zustand ist ~** his condition is giving cause for concern ADV alarmingly, frighteningly
Be|**ängs**|**ti**|**gung** [bəˈʔɛŋstɪgʊŋ] F -, -en alarm, fear; **in großer ~** in (a state of) great alarm
be|**an**|**spru**|**chen** [bəˈʔanʃprʊxn] *ptp* **beansprucht** VT **a** (= *fordern*) to claim; *Gebiet auch* to lay claim to; **etw ~ können** to be entitled to sth
b (= *erfordern*) to take; *Zeit auch* to take up; *Platz auch* to take up, to occupy; *Kräfte auch, Aufmerksamkeit* to demand; (= *benötigen*) to need
c (= *ausnützen*) to use; *jds Gastfreundschaft* to take advantage of; *jds Geduld* to demand; *jds Hilfe* to ask for; **ich möchte Ihre Geduld nicht zu sehr ~** I don't want to try your patience
d (= *strapazieren*) *Maschine etc* to use; jdn to occupy, to keep busy; **jdn stark ~** to keep sb very busy *or* occupied; **eine höchst beanspruchte Maschine** a heavily used machine; **ihr Beruf beansprucht sie ganz** her job is very demanding, her job takes up all her time and energy
Be|**an**|**spru**|**chung** F -, -en **a** (= *Forderung*) claim (+*gen* to); (= *Anforderung*) demand **b** (= *Ausnutzung: von jds Geduld, Hilfe etc*) demand (*von* on) **c** (= *Belastung, Abnutzung*) use; (*beruflich*) demands *pl*
be|**an**|**stan**|**den** [bəˈʔanʃtandn] *ptp* **beanstandet** VT to query, to complain about; **das ist beanstandet worden** there has been a query *or* complaint about that; **er hat an allem etwas zu ~** he has complaints about everything; **die beanstandete Ware** the goods complained about *or* queried
Be|**an**|**stan**|**dung** F -, -en complaint (+*gen* about); **zu ~en Anlass geben** (*form*) to give cause for complaint; **er hat jahrelang ohne jede ~ seine Pflicht getan** for years he did his duty without giving any cause for complaint
be|**an**|**tra**|**gen** [bəˈʔantraːgn] *ptp* **beantragt** VT to apply for (*bei* to); (*Jur*) *Strafe* to demand, to ask for; (= *vorschlagen: in Debatte etc*) to move, to propose; **er beantragte, versetzt zu werden**

he applied for a transfer, he applied to be transferred; **etw bei der Behörde ~** to apply to the authorities for sth

Be|an|tra|gung F -, -en application (+gen for); (von Strafe) demand (+gen for); (= Vorschlag) proposal

be|ant|wort|bar ADJ answerable; **das ist nicht so einfach ~** there's no easy answer to that (question)

be|ant|wor|ten ptp **beantwortet** VT to answer; Anfrage, Brief auch to reply to; Gruß, Beleidigung, Herausforderung auch to respond to; **jdm eine Frage ~** to answer sb's question; **eine Frage mit Nein ~** to answer a question in the negative; **leicht zu ~** easily answered

Be|ant|wor|tung [bə'antvɔrtʊŋ] F -, -en (+gen to) answer; (von Anfrage, Brief auch) reply; (von Gruß, Beleidigung, Herausforderung auch) response

be|ar|bei|ten ptp **bearbeitet** VT **a** (= behandeln) to work on; Stein, Holz to work, to dress; (inf: mit Chemikalien) to treat; **etw mit dem Hammer/Meißel ~** to hammer/chisel sth **b** (= sich befassen mit) to deal with; Fall to handle, to deal with; Bestellungen etc to process **c** (= redigieren) to edit; (= neu bearbeiten) to revise; (= umändern) Roman etc to adapt; Musikstück to arrange; **etw für die Drucklegung ~** to prepare sth for press **d** (inf: = einschlagen auf) Klavier, Trommel etc to hammer or bash away at; Geige to saw away at; **jdn mit Fußtritten ~** to kick sb about (inf); **jdn mit Fäusten ~** to thump sb **e** (inf: = einreden auf) jdn to work on **f** Land to cultivate

Be|ar|bei|ter(in) M(F) **a** (von Angelegenheit) person dealing with sth; (von Fall auch) person handling sth; (von Bestellung) person processing sth; **wer war der ~ der Akte?** who dealt with the file? **b** (= Redakteur) editor; (von Neubearbeitung) reviser; (von Umänderung) adapter; (von Musik) arranger

Be|ar|bei|tung [bə'arbaitʊŋ] F -, -en **a** (= Behandlung) working (on); (von Stein, Holz) dressing; (mit Chemikalien) treating; **die ~ von Granit ist schwierig** it is difficult to work or dress granite **b** (von Angelegenheit, Antrag etc) dealing with; (von Fall) handling; (von Bestellung) processing; **die ~ meines Antrags hat lange gedauert** it took a long time to deal with my claim **c** (= Redigieren) editing; (= Neubearbeitung) revising; (= Umänderung) adapting; (von Musik) arrangement; (= bearbeitete Ausgabe etc) edition; revision; revised edition; arrangement; **neue ~** (von Film etc) new version; **die deutsche ~** the German version; **ein polnisches Volkslied in der ~ von Chopin** a Polish folk song as arranged by Chopin

Be|ar|bei|tungs-: Be|ar|bei|tungs|ge|bühr F handling charge; **Be|ar|bei|tungs|zeit** F (Admin) (time for) processing; **die ~ beträgt zwei Wochen** processing will take two weeks

be|arg|wöh|nen ptp **beargwöhnt** VT to be suspicious of

Beat [biːt] M -(s), no pl **a** (= Musik) beat or pop music **b** (= Rhythmus) beat

Beat|band ['biːtbɛnt] F pl **-bands** beat or pop group

Beat|ge|ne|ra|ti|on F beat generation

Be|a|ti|fi|ka|ti|on [beatifika'tsioːn] F -, -en (Eccl) beatification

be|a|ti|fi|zie|ren [beatifi'tsiːrən] ptp **beatifiziert** VT to beatify

be|at|men ptp **beatmet** VT Ertrunkenen to give artificial respiration to; Gewässer to oxygenate; **jdn künstlich ~** to keep sb breathing artificially

Be|at|mung F -, -en artificial respiration; (von Gewässer) oxygenation

Be|at|mungs|ge|rät NT respirator, ventilator

Beat|mu|sik ['biːt-] F beat or pop music

Beat|nik ['biːtnɪk] M -s, -s beatnik

Beat|schup|pen ['biːt-] M (inf) beat club

Beau [boː] M -, -s good-looker (inf)

Beau|fort|ska|la, Beau|fort-Ska|la [bo'foːɐ-skaːla, 'boːfɐt-] F (Met) Beaufort scale

be|auf|sich|ti|gen [bə'aufzɪçtɪgn] ptp **beaufsichtigt** VT Arbeit, Bau to supervise; Klasse, Schüler, Häftlinge auch to keep under supervision; Kind to mind (Brit), to look after; Prüfung to invigilate at; **jdn bei einer Arbeit/beim Arbeiten ~** to supervise sb's work/sb working; **staatlich beaufsichtigt** state-controlled, under state control

Be|auf|sich|ti|gung F -, -en supervision, supervising; (von Kind) minding (Brit), supervision; (bei Prüfung) invigilation; **die ~ von drei Kindern unter 10 Jahren ist nicht leicht** looking after three children under 10 is not easy

be|auf|tra|gen [bə'auftraːgn] ptp **beauftragt** VT **a** (= heranziehen) to engage; Firma auch to hire; Architekten, Künstler etc, Forschungsinstitut to commission; Ausschuss etc to appoint, to set up; **jdn mit etw ~** to engage etc sb to do sth **b** (= anweisen) Untergebenen etc to instruct; **wir sind beauftragt, das zu tun** we have been instructed to do that

Be|auf|trag|te(r) [bə'auftraːktə] MF decl as adj representative

be|aug|ap|feln [bə'aukˌapfln] ptp **beaugapfelt** VT (hum) to eye

be|äu|geln [bə'ɔygln] ptp **beäugelt** VT (hum) to make eyes at (inf), to ogle

be|äu|gen [bə'ɔygn] ptp **beäugt** VT (inf) to gaze or look at

Beau|té [boː'teː] F -, -s (geh), **Beau|ty** ['bjuːti] F -, -s (Press sl) stunner (inf), beauty

Beau|ty-Case ['bjuːtikeːs] NT OR M -, -s make-up case or bag; (zum Reisen) vanity case

Beau|ty|farm ['bjuːtifarm] F beauty farm

be|bän|dern [bə'bɛndən] ptp **bebändert** VT usu ptp to decorate with ribbons, to beribbon (liter)

be|bar|tet [bə'baːɐtət] ADJ (usu hum) bearded

be|bau|bar ADJ **a** Boden cultiv(at)able **b** Grundstück suitable for building; (= zum Bau freigegeben) available for building

Be|bau|bar|keit [bə'baubaːɐkait] F -, no pl (von Grundstück) suitability for building

be|bau|en ptp **bebaut** VT **a** Grundstück to build on, to develop; **das Grundstück ist jetzt mit einer Schule bebaut** the piece of land has had a school built on it; **das Viertel war dicht bebaut** the area was heavily built-up; **ein Gelände mit etw ~** to build sth on a piece of land **b** (Agr) to cultivate; Land to farm

Be|bau|ung [bə'bauʊŋ] F -, -en **a** (= Vorgang) building (+gen on); (von Gelände) development; (= Bauten) buildings pl; **Viertel mit dichter ~** densely built-up area **b** (Agr) cultivation; (von Land) farming

Be|bau|ungs-: Be|bau|ungs|dich|te F density of building or development; **für geringere ~ sorgen** to ensure development is less dense; **Be|bau|ungs|plan** M development plan or scheme

Bé|bé [be'beː] NT -s, -s (Sw) baby

be|ben ['beːbn] VI to shake, to tremble; (Stimme auch) to quiver (vor +dat with); **am ganzen Leib** or **an allen Gliedern ~** to tremble or shake all over; **vor jdn ~** (liter) to be in fear and trembling of sb; **um jdn ~** (liter) to tremble for sb

Be|ben ['beːbn] NT -s, - (= Zittern) shaking, trembling; (von Stimme auch) quivering (= Erdbeben) earthquake

be|bil|dern [bə'bɪldən] ptp **bebildert** VT Buch, Vortrag to illustrate

Be|bil|de|rung F -, -en illustrations pl (+gen in)

be|brillt [bə'brɪlt] ADJ (hum inf) bespectacled

be|brü|ten ptp **bebrütet** VT Eier to incubate; **die Lage ~** (fig inf) to brood over the situation

Bé|cha|mel|so|ße [beʃa'mɛl-] F (Cook) béchamel (sauce)

Be|cher ['bɛçɐ] M -s, - **a** cup; (old: = Kelch) goblet; (= Glasbecher) glass, tumbler; (= esp aus Porzellan, Ton, mit Henkel) mug; (Joghurtbecher etc) carton, tub; (= Eisbecher) (aus Pappe) tub; (aus Metall) sundae dish; **ein ~ Eis** a tub of ice cream/an ice-cream sundae **b** (Bot: = Eichelbecher) cup, cupule (spec)

Be|cher-: be|cher|för|mig ADJ cup-shaped; **Be|cher|glas** NT **a** (= Trinkglas) glass, tumbler **b** (Chem) glass, beaker

be|chern ['bɛçɐn] VI (hum inf) to have a few (inf)

be|cir|cen [bə'tsɪrtsn] ptp **becirct** VT = bezirzen

Be|cken ['bɛkn] NT -s, - **a** (= Brunnenbecken, Hafenbecken, Waschbecken, Geol) basin; (= Abwaschbecken) sink; (= Toilettenbecken) bowl, pan; (= Schwimmbecken) pool; (= Staubecken) reservoir; (= Fischbecken) pond; (= Taufbecken) font **b** (Anat) pelvis, pelvic girdle; **ein breites ~** broad hips **c** (Mus) cymbal

Be|cken- (Anat, Med): **Be|cken|bruch** M fractured pelvis, pelvic fracture; **Be|cken|end|la|ge** F breech position or presentation; **Be|cken|kno|chen** M hipbone; **Be|cken|rand** M (von Schwimmbecken) edge of the pool

Beck|mes|ser ['bɛkmɛsɐ] M -s, - (pej) caviller, carper

Beck|mes|se|rei [bɛkmɛsə'rai] F -, -en (pej) cavilling (Brit), caviling (US), carping

beck|mes|se|risch ['bɛkmɛsərɪʃ] ADJ (pej) carping, cavilling (Brit), caviling (US)

beck|mes|sern ['bɛkmɛsɐn] VI (pej) to cavil, to carp

Bec|que|rel [bɛkə'rɛl] NT -(s), - becquerel

be|da|chen [bə'daxn] ptp **bedacht** VT to roof

be|dacht [bə'daxt] ADJ **a** (= überlegt) prudent, careful, cautious **b** **auf etw** (acc) **~ sein** to be concerned about sth; **er ist nur auf sich ~** he only thinks about himself; **darauf ~ sein, etw zu tun** to be concerned about doing sth, to be concerned to do sth → auch **bedachen, bedenken**

Be|dacht [bə'daxt] M -s, no pl (geh) **mit ~** (= vorsichtig) prudently, carefully, with care; (= absichtlich) deliberately; **voll ~** very prudently or carefully, with great care; **ohne ~** without thinking, imprudently; **etw mit (gutem) ~ tun** to do sth (quite) deliberately

Be|dach|te(r) [bə'daxtə] MF decl as adj (Jur) beneficiary

be|däch|tig [bə'dɛçtɪç] ADJ (= gemessen) Schritt, Sprache measured no adv, deliberate; Wesen deliberate, steady; (= besonnen) thoughtful, reflective; **mit ~en Schritten** or **~en Schrittes** (liter) **gehen** to walk with measured or deliberate steps ADV gehen with measured or deliberate steps; **langsam und ~ sprechen** to speak in slow, measured tones

Be|däch|tig|keit F -, no pl (= Gemessenheit) (von Schritten, Sprache) measuredness, deliberateness; (= Besonnenheit) thoughtfulness, reflectiveness; **etw mit großer ~ tun** to do sth very thoughtfully or reflectively

be|dacht|sam [bə'daxtzaːm] (geh) ADJ careful, deliberate ADV carefully, deliberately

Be|dacht|sam|keit F -, no pl (geh) care, deliberation

Be|da|chung F -, -en roofing; (= Dach auch) roof

be|dan|ken ☾ 47.5, 49, 52.1 ptp **bedankt** VR **a** to say thank you, to express one's thanks (form); **sich bei jdm (für etw) ~** to thank sb (for sth), to say thank you to sb (for sth); **ich bedanke mich herzlich** thank you very much, (very) many thanks; **dafür können Sie sich bei Herrn Weitz ~** (iro) you've got Mr Weitz to thank for that (iro), you can thank Mr Weitz for that (iro) **b** (iro inf) **ich bedanke mich, dafür bedanke**

ich mich (bestens) no thank you (very much); **dafür** or **für dergleichen wird er sich ~** he'll just love that (iro)

VT (form) **seien Sie (herzlich) bedankt!** please accept my/our (grateful or deepest) thanks (form)

Be|darf [bə'darf] M **-(e)s, -e,** no pl **a** (= Bedürfnis) need (an +dat for); (= Bedarfsmenge) requirements pl, requisites pl; **bei ~** as or when required; **bei dringendem ~** in cases of urgent need; **der Bus hält hier nur bei ~** the bus stops here only on request; **Dinge des täglichen ~s** basic or everyday necessities; **alles für den häuslichen ~** all household requirements or requisites; **seinen ~ an Wein/Lebensmitteln** etc **einkaufen** to buy one's supply of wine/food etc, to buy the wine/food etc one needs; **einem ~ abhelfen** to meet a need; **an etw** (dat) **~ haben** to need sth, to be in need of sth; **danke, kein ~** (iro inf) no thank you, not on your life (inf) → **decken** VT **e**

b (Comm: = Nachfrage) demand (an +dat for); (je) nach **~** according to demand; **den ~ übersteigen** to exceed demand; **über ~ in** excess of demand

Be|darfs-: Be|darfs|ampel F traffic lights pl operated by pedestrians, pelican crossing (Brit); **Be|darfs|ana|ly|se** F (Comm etc) demand analysis; **Be|darfs|ar|ti|kel** M requisite; **Be|darfs|be|frie|di|gung** F , **Be|darfs|de|ckung** F satisfaction of the/sb's needs; **Be|darfs|fall** M (form) need; **im ~** if necessary; (= wenn gebraucht) as necessary or required; **für den ~ vorsorgen** to provide for a time of need; **wir wissen nicht, wann der ~ eintritt** we don't know when the need will arise; **be|darfs|ge|recht** ADJ Politik designed to meet people's needs; **ein ~es Warenangebot** a range of goods which meets consumer demands **ADV** as needed; **~ produzieren** to match production to demand; **Be|darfs|gü|ter** PL consumer goods pl; **Be|darfs|hal|te|stel|le** F request (bus) stop; **Be|darfs|len|kung** F (Comm etc) demand management, consumption control; **Be|darfs|trä|ger(in)** M(F) (Comm) consumer; **Be|darfs|we|ckung** F **-,** no pl stimulation of demand

be|dau|er|lich [bə'dauɐlɪç] ADJ regrettable, unfortunate; **~!** how unfortunate

be|dau|er|li|cher|wei|se ADV regrettably, unfortunately

be|dau|ern [bə'dauɐn] ✪ 39.2, 45.3 ptp **bedauert** VT **a** etw to regret; **einen Irrtum ~** to regret one's mistake, to regret having made a mistake; **wir ~, Ihnen mitteilen zu müssen, ...** we regret to have to inform you ...; **er hat sehr bedauert, dass ...** he was very sorry that ...; **er schüttelte ~d den Kopf** he shook his head regretfully; **(ich) bedau(e)re!** I am sorry

b (= bemitleiden) jdn to feel or be sorry for; **sich selbst ~** to feel sorry for oneself; **er ist zu ~** he is to be pitied, one or you should feel sorry for him; **er lässt sich gerne ~, er will immer bedauert sein** he always wants people to feel sorry for him

Be|dau|ern ✪ 45.3, 51.4, 52.1, 52.4 [bə'dauɐn] NT **-s,** no pl regret; **(sehr) zu meinem ~** (much) to my regret; **zu meinem ~ kann ich nicht kommen** I regret that I will not be able to come, to my regret I will not be able to come; **zu meinem größten ~ muss ich Ihnen mitteilen ...** it is with the deepest regret that I must inform you ...; **mit ~ habe ich ...** it is with regret that I ...

be|dau|erns|wert, be|dau|erns|wür|dig (geh) ADJ Mensch pitiful; Zustand deplorable

be|de|cken ptp bedeckt **VT** **a** (= zudecken) to cover; **von etw bedeckt sein** to be covered in sth; **mit einem Tuch/mit Papieren/Pickeln/Staub bedeckt sein** to be covered with a cloth/with or in papers/spots/dust; **sie hat ihre Familie mit Schande bedeckt** (liter) she brought shame upon her family **b** (Astron) Stern to eclipse, to occult (spec) **VR** **a** (= sich zudecken) to cover

oneself **b** (Himmel) to become overcast, to cloud over; **der Himmel bedeckte sich mit Wolken** it or the sky clouded over or became overcast → auch **bedeckt**

be|deckt [bə'dɛkt] ADJ **a** (= zugedeckt) covered; **~en Hauptes** (old) with one's head covered **b** (= bewölkt) overcast, cloudy; **bei ~em Himmel** when the sky or it is overcast or cloudy **c** sich **~ halten** (fig) to keep a low profile → auch **bedecken**

Be|deckt|sa|mer [bə'dɛktza:mɐ] M , **Be|deckt|sa|mi|ge** [-za:mɪɡə] PL decl as adj (Bot) Angiospermae pl

Be|de|ckung F **-, -en** **a** (= das Bedecken) covering **b** (= Deckendes) cover, covering **c** (Mil) (= Geleitschutz) guard, escort; (= Leibwache) guard; **der Konvoi hatte drei Fregatten zur ~** the convoy was escorted by three frigates, the convoy had an escort of three frigates **d** (Astron: von Stern) eclipse, occultation (spec)

be|den|ken ptp bedacht [bə'daxt] irreg **VT** **a** (= überlegen) Sache, Lage, Maßnahme etc to consider, to think about; **das will wohl bedacht sein** (geh) that calls for careful consideration; **wenn man es recht bedenkt, ...** if you think about it properly ...

b (= in Betracht ziehen) Umstand, Folgen etc to consider, to take into consideration; **man muss ~, dass ...** one must take into consideration the fact that ...; **das hättest du früher** or **vorher ~ sollen** you should have thought about that sooner or earlier; **ich gebe zu ~, dass ...** I would ask you to consider that ...; **bedenke, dass du sterben musst** remember you are mortal

c (in Testament) to remember; **jdn mit einem Geschenk ~** (geh) to give sb a present; **jdn reich ~** (geh) to be generous to sb; **ich wurde auch diesmal reich bedacht** (geh) I did very well this time; **mit etw bedacht werden** to receive sth; **auch ich wurde bedacht** I was not forgotten (either), there was something for me too → **Bedachte(r)**

VR (geh) to think (about it), to reflect; **bedenke dich gut, ehe du ...** think well before you ...; **ohne sich lange zu ~** without stopping to think or reflect → auch **bedacht**

Be|den|ken [bə'dɛŋkn] NT **-s, -** **a** usu pl (= Zweifel, Einwand) doubt, reservation, misgiving; **moralische ~** moral scruples; **~ haben** or **tragen** (geh) to have one's doubts (bei about); **ihm kommen ~** he is having second thoughts; **ohne ~ vorgehen** to act relentlessly or unrelentingly **b** no pl (= das Überlegen) consideration (+gen of), reflection (+gen (up)on); **nach langem ~** after much thought; **ohne ~** without thinking

be|den|ken|los ADJ **a** (= ohne Zögern) Zustimmung unhesitating, prompt **b** (= skrupellos) heedless of others; (= unüberlegt) thoughtless **ADV** **a** (= ohne Zögern) unhesitatingly, with no reservations; **ich würde ~ hingehen** I would not hesitate to go, I would have no reservations about going; **~ zustimmen** to agree with no reservations **b** (= skrupellos) unscrupulously; **etw ~ tun** (= unüberlegt) to do sth without thinking

Be|den|ken|lo|sig|keit F **-,** no pl **a** (= Bereitwilligkeit) readiness, promptness **b** (= Skrupellosigkeit) unscrupulousness, lack of scruples; (= Unüberlegtheit) thoughtlessness, lack of thought

be|den|kens|wert ADJ worth thinking about or considering

Be|den|ken|trä|ger M die **~** all those who object

be|denk|lich [bə'dɛŋklɪç] **ADJ** **a** (= zweifelhaft) Geschäfte, Mittel etc dubious, questionable **b** (= Besorgnis erregend) Lage, Verschlimmerung etc serious, disturbing, alarming; Gesundheitszustand serious; **der Zustand des Kranken ist ~** the patient's condition is giving cause for concern; **der Himmel sah ~ aus** the sky looked ominous

c (= besorgt) apprehensive, anxious; **ein ~es Gesicht machen** to look apprehensive

ADV **a** (= zweifelhaft) **sie handelten ~** their behaviour (Brit) or behavior (US) was questionable or dubious

b (= Besorgnis erregend) seriously, disturbingly, alarmingly; **~ hohe Schulden** alarmingly high debts; **~ zunehmen** to rise alarmingly; **der Termin rückt ~ nahe** the date is getting alarmingly close

c (= besorgt) apprehensively, anxiously; **~ mit dem Kopf schütteln** to shake one's head apprehensively; **jdn ~ stimmen** to make sb (feel) apprehensive

Be|denk|lich|keit F **-,** no pl **a** (= Zweifelhaftigkeit) dubiousness **b** (= Besorgnis erregende Natur) seriousness; (= Besorgtheit) apprehension, anxiety

Be|denk|zeit F jdm zwei Tage/bis Freitag **~ geben** or **einräumen** to give sb two days/until Friday to think about it; **sich** (dat) **(eine) ~ ausbitten** or **erbitten, um ~ bitten** to ask for time to think about it

be|dep|pert [bə'dɛpɐt] ADJ (inf) **a** (= ratlos) dazed, stunned **b** (= trottelig) dopey (inf), gormless (Brit inf)

be|deu|ten ✪ 53.3 ptp **bedeutet** VT **a** (= gleichzusetzen sein mit, heißen, bezeichnen) to mean; (Math, Ling) to stand for, to denote; (= versinnbildlichen) to signify, to symbolize; **was bedeutet dieses Wort?** what does this word mean?, what's the meaning of this word?; **was soll das ~?** what does that mean?; **was soll denn das ~?** what's the meaning of that?; **das hat nichts zu ~** it doesn't mean anything; (= macht nichts aus) it doesn't matter

b (= ankündigen, zur Folge haben) to mean; **diese Wolken ~ schlechtes Wetter** these clouds mean or spell bad weather; **das bedeutet nichts Gutes** that spells trouble, that bodes ill (form)

c (= gelten) to mean (+dat, für to); **Geld bedeutet mir nichts** money doesn't mean anything or means nothing to me; **sein Name bedeutet etwas in der Medizin** his name means something in the field of medicine, he is a name in the field of medicine

d (geh: = einen Hinweis geben) to indicate, to intimate; (mit Geste) to indicate, to gesture; Abneigung, Zustimmung to indicate; **ich bedeutete ihm, das zu tun** I indicated or intimated that he should do that; **man bedeutete mir, dass ...** I was given to understand that ...

be|deu|tend **ADJ** **a** (= wichtig, bemerkenswert) Persönlichkeit important, distinguished, eminent; Leistung, Rolle, Kunstwerk significant, important; **etwas Bedeutendes leisten** to achieve something important or significant **b** (= groß) Summe, Erfolg considerable, significant **ADV** (= beträchtlich) considerably

be|deut|sam [bə'dɔytza:m] **ADJ** **a** (= wichtig) Gespräch, Fortschritt etc important; (= folgenschwer) significant (für for) **b** (= viel sagend) meaningful, significant; Rede eloquent; Blick meaningful **ADV** meaningfully; **jdm ~ zulächeln** to smile meaningfully at sb

Be|deut|sam|keit F **-,** no pl **a** (= Wichtigkeit) importance; (= Folgenschwere) significance **b** (geh) (= Bedeutung) meaningfulness, significance; (von Rede, Blick) eloquence

Be|deu|tung F **a** (= Sinn, Wortsinn) meaning; **in wörtlicher/übertragener ~** in the literal/figurative sense **b** (= Wichtigkeit) importance, significance; (= Tragweite) significance; **von ~ sein** to be important or significant, to be of significance; **von (großer** or **tieferer/geringer) ~ sein** to be of (great/little) importance, to be (very/not very) important; **ein Mann von ~** an important figure; **nichts von ~** nothing of any importance; **ohne ~** of no importance; **große ~ besitzen** to be of great importance; **an ~ gewinnen/verlieren** to gain/lose in importance

Be|deu|tungs-: Be|deu|tungs|er|wei|te|rung F (Ling) extension of meaning; **Be|deu|tungs|ge|halt** M meaning; **be|deu|tungs-**

gleich ADJ synonymous, identical in meaning; **Be|deu|tungs|leh|re** F (*Ling*) semantics *sing*, science of meaning (*old*); **be|deu|tungs|los** ADJ **a** (= *unwichtig*) insignificant, unimportant **b** (= *nichts besagend*) meaningless; **Be|deu|tungs|lo|sig|keit** F -, *no pl* insignificance, unimportance; **zur ~ verurteilt sein** to be condemned to insignificance; **be|deu|tungs|schwan|ger** ADJ (*geh*) pregnant with meaning; **be|deu|tungs|schwer** ADJ (*geh*) meaningful, laden *or* pregnant with meaning; (= *folgenschwer*) momentous; **Be|deu|tungs|un|ter|schied** M difference in meaning; **Be|deu|tungs|ver|en|gung** F (*Ling*) narrowing of meaning; **Be|deu|tungs|ver|schie|bung** F (*Ling*) shift of meaning, sense *or* semantic shift; **be|deu|tungs|ver|wandt** ADJ (*Ling*) semantically related; **be|deu|tungs|voll** ADJ, ADV = **bedeutsam**; **Be|deu|tungs|wan|del** M (*Ling*) change in meaning, semantic change; **Be|deu|tungs|wör|ter|buch** NT (defining) dictionary

be|dien|bar ADJ **leicht/schwer ~** easy/hard to use; **elektrisch ~** electrically operated

Be|dien|bar|keit [bə'diːnbaːɐkait] F -, *no pl* usability; **leichte ~** ease of use

be|die|nen ptp **bedient** [VT] **a** (*Verkäufer*) to serve, to attend to; (*Kellner, Diener etc*) to wait on, to serve; **werden Sie schon bedient?** are you being attended to *or* served?; **hier wird man gut bedient** the service is good here; **er lässt sich gern ~** he likes to be waited on; **mit diesem Ratschlag war ich schlecht bedient** I was ill-served by that advice; **mit dieser Ware/damit sind Sie sehr gut bedient** these goods/that should serve you very well; **ich bin bedient!** (*inf*) I've had enough, I've had all I can take; (*Aus sl*) I'm pissed (*Brit inf*) *or* smashed (*inf*)

b (*Verkehrsmittel*) to serve; **diese Flugroute wird von X bedient** X operate (on) this route **c** (= *handhaben*) *Maschine, Geschütz etc* to operate; *Telefon* to answer **d** (*Fin*) *Schulden* to service **e** (*Sport*) to pass *or* feed (the ball) to **f** (*Cards*) **(eine) Farbe ~** to follow suit; **Karo ~** to follow suit in diamonds

[VI] **a** (*in Geschäft, bei Tisch*) to serve; (*Kellner auch*) to wait (at table (*Brit*) *or* a table (*US*)); (*als Beruf*) to wait, to be a waiter/waitress **b** (*Cards*) **du musst ~** you must follow suit; **falsch ~** to revoke, to fail to follow suit

[VR] **a** (*bei Tisch*) to help *or* serve oneself (*mit* to); **bitte ~ Sie sich** please help *or* serve yourself **b** (*geh*: = *gebrauchen*) **sich jds/einer Sache ~** to use sb/sth

Be|die|ner M -s, -, **Be|die|ne|rin** F -, -nen (*Comput*) operator

Be|die|ner-: be|die|ner|freund|lich ADJ user-friendly; **Be|die|ner|füh|rung** F , *no pl* (*Comput*) context-sensitive help

Be|die|ne|rin F **a** (*Comput*) operator **b** (*Aus*: = *Aufwartefrau*) charwoman (*Brit*), cleaner

Be|die|ner|ober|flä|che F (*Comput*) user interface

be|diens|tet [bə'diːnstət] ADJ **bei jdm ~ sein** to be in service with sb; **~ sein** (*Aus*: *im öffentlichen Dienst*) to be in the civil service

Be|diens|te|te(r) [bə'diːnstətə] MF *decl as adj* **a** (*im öffentlichen Dienst*) public employee **b** (*old*: = *Diener*) servant

Be|die|nung [bə'diːnʊŋ] F -, -en **a** *no pl* (*in Restaurant etc*) service; (*von Maschinen*) operation; **die ~ der Kunden** serving the customers; **eine Tankstelle mit ~** a petrol station with forecourt service; **ein Restaurant mit ~** a restaurant with waiter service; **zur freien** *or* **gefälligen** (*old*) **~** please take one, please help yourself; **die ~ des Geräts erlernen** to learn how to operate the machine **b** (*Fin*: *von Schulden*) servicing **c** (= *Bedienungsgeld*) service (charge)

---

d (= *Bedienungspersonal*) staff; (= *Kellner etc*) waiter; (*weiblich*) waitress; **kommt denn hier keine ~?** isn't anyone serving here?; **hallo, ~!, ~ bitte!** waiter/waitress! **e** (*Mil*: = *Bedienungsmannschaft*) crew

Be|die|nungs-: Be|die|nungs|an|lei|tung F , **Be|die|nungs|an|wei|sung** F operating instructions *pl or* directions *pl*; **Be|die|nungs|auf|schlag** M , **Be|die|nungs|geld** NT service charge; **Be|die|nungs|feh|ler** M mistake in operating a/the machine; **be|die|nungs|freund|lich** ADJ user-friendly; **Be|die|nungs|he|bel** M operating lever; **Be|die|nungs|kom|fort** M (*Comput, Tech*) ease of operation; **Be|die|nungs|mann|schaft** F (*Mil*) crew; **Be|die|nungs|vor|schrift** F operating instructions *pl*; **Be|die|nungs|zu|schlag** M service charge

be|din|gen ptp **bedingt** VT **a** (= *bewirken*) to cause; (= *notwendig machen*) to necessitate; (*Psych, Physiol*) to condition; (= *logisch voraussetzen*) to presuppose; **sich gegenseitig ~** to be mutually dependent; **~de Konjunktion** conditional conjunction → *auch* **bedingt b** (= *voraussetzen, verlangen*) to call for, to demand

be|dingt [bə'dɪŋt] ADJ **a** (= *eingeschränkt*) limited; *Lob auch* qualified **b** (= *an Bedingung geknüpft*) *Annahme, Straferlass, Strafaussetzung* conditional **c** (*Physiol*) *Reflex* conditioned **a** (= *eingeschränkt*) partly, partially; **~ tauglich** (*Mil*) fit for limited duties; **gefällt es Ihnen hier? – ~!** do you like it here? – with some reservations; **(nur) ~ richtig** (only) partly *or* partially valid; **(nur) ~ gelten** to be (only) partly *or* partially valid → *auch* **bedingen b** (*Sw, Aus*) conditionally

Be|din|gung [bə'dɪŋʊŋ] F -, -en **a** (= *Voraussetzung*) condition; (= *Erfordernis*) requirement; **die erste ~ für etw** the basic requirement for sth; **mit** *or* **unter der ~, dass ...** on condition that ..., with the proviso that ...; **unter keiner ~** in *or* under no circumstances, on no condition; **(nur) unter einer ~** (only) on one condition; **unter jeder anderen ~** in any other circumstances; **von einer ~ abhängen** *or* **abhängig sein** to be conditional on one thing; **~ (für meine Zustimmung) ist, dass ...** it is a condition (of my consent) that ...; **etw zur ~ machen** to make sth a condition; **es zur ~ machen, dass ...** to stipulate that ...; **~en (für etw) stellen** to place conditions (on sth)

b (= *Forderung*) term, condition; **zu günstigen ~en** (*Comm*) on favourable (*Brit*) *or* favorable (*US*) terms **c** **Bedingungen** PL (= *Umstände*) conditions *pl*; **unter guten/harten ~en arbeiten** to work in good/under *or* in difficult conditions

Be|din|gungs-: Be|din|gungs|form F (*Gram*) conditional (form); **be|din|gungs|los** ADJ *Kapitulation* unconditional; *Hingabe, Gehorsam, Gefolgschaft* unquestioning **ADV** unconditionally; **~ für etw eintreten** to support sth without reservation; **Be|din|gungs|lo|sig|keit** F -, *no pl* (*von Hingabe, Gehorsam, Gefolgschaft*) unquestioning nature; **Be|din|gungs|satz** M conditional clause

be|drän|gen ptp **bedrängt** VT *Feind* to attack; *gegnerische Mannschaft* to put pressure on, to pressurize; (= *belästigen*) to plague, to badger; *Schuldner* to press (for payment); *Passanten, Mädchen* to pester; (= *bedrücken: Sorgen*) to beset; (= *heimsuchen*) to haunt; **ein bedrängtes Herz** (*liter*) a troubled heart; **sich in einer bedrängten Lage/in bedrängten Verhältnissen finden** to be in dire *or* desperate straits; **die Bedrängten und Verzweifelten** people in distress and despair

Be|dräng|nis [bə'drɛŋnɪs] F -ses, -se (*geh*) (= *seelische Bedrängnis*) distress, torment; **in arger** *or* **großer ~, in einer argen** *or* **großen ~** in dire *or* desperate straits; **jdn/etw in ~ bringen** to get sb/sth into trouble; **in ~ geraten** to get into difficulties

---

Be|drän|gung [bə'drɛŋʊŋ] F -, -en **a** (= *das Bedrängen*) attacking; (*der gegnerischen Mannschaft*) pressurizing; (= *Belästigung*) plaguing, badgering; (*von Schuldner*) pressing; (*von Passanten, Mädchen*) pestering; (*durch Sorgen*) distress **b** = **Bedrängnis**

be|dripst [bə'drɪpst] ADJ (*N Ger*) stunned, dazed

be|dro|hen ptp **bedroht** VT to threaten; (= *gefährden*) to endanger; **den Frieden ~** to be a threat to peace; **vom Tode bedroht** in mortal danger; **von Überschwemmung bedroht** in danger of being flooded; **vom Aussterben bedroht** threatened with extinction, in danger of becoming extinct

be|droh|lich [bə'droːlɪç] ADJ (= *gefährlich*) alarming; (= *Unheil verkündend*) menacing, threatening; **in ~e Nähe rücken** *or* **kommen** to get dangerously *or* perilously close; **Aids ist eine ~e Krankheit** AIDS is a dangerous illness **ADV** dangerously, alarmingly; **sich ~ verschlechtern** to deteriorate alarmingly; **der Himmel war ~ schwarz** the sky was an ominous *or* a menacing black

Be|droh|lich|keit F -, *no pl* (= *Gefährlichkeit*) dangerousness; **seine ~ verlieren** to become less of a threat

Be|dro|hung F threat (+*gen* to); (= *das Bedrohen auch*) threatening (+*gen* of); **in ständiger ~ leben** to live under a constant threat

Be|dro|hungs|ana|ly|se F (*Mil*) threat analysis

be|dröp|pelt [bə'drœplt] ADJ (*N Ger inf*) **~ dastehen** *or* **dreinschauen** (= *niedergeschlagen*) to look crestfallen; (= *verlegen*) to look sheepish

be|dru|cken ptp **bedruckt** VT to print on; **ein bedrucktes Kleid** a print dress; **bedruckter Stoff** print, printed fabric; **etw mit einem Muster ~** to print a pattern on sth

be|drü|cken ptp **bedrückt** VT **a** (= *belasten*) to depress; **jdn ~** to depress sb, to make sb feel depressed; **was bedrückt dich?** what is (weighing) on your mind?; **Sorgen bedrückten ihn** cares were weighing upon him → *auch* **bedrückt b** (*old*: = *unterdrücken*) to oppress

be|drü|ckend ADJ *Anblick, Nachrichten, Vorstellung* depressing; (= *lastend*) oppressive; *Sorge, Not* pressing

Be|drü|cker [bə'drʏkɐ] M -s, -, **Be|drü|cke|rin** [-ərɪn] F -, -nen (*old*) oppressor

be|drückt [bə'drʏkt] ADJ (= *niedergeschlagen*) depressed, dejected; *Schweigen* oppressive → *auch* **bedrücken**

Be|drü|ckung [bə'drʏkʊŋ] F -, -en **a** (= *Niedergeschlagenheit*) depression, dejection **b** (*old*: = *Unterdrückung*) oppression

Be|du|i|ne [bedu'iːnə] M -n, -n, **Be|du|i|nin** [-'iːnɪn] F -, -nen Bedouin

be|dür|fen ptp **bedurft** VI *irreg* +*gen* (*geh*) to need, to require; (= *erfordern*) to require, to call for; **das bedarf keiner weiteren Erklärung** there's no need for any further explanation; **es hätte nur eines Wortes bedurft, um ...** it would only have taken a word to ...; **es bedarf nur eines Wortes von Ihnen** you only have to *or* need to say the word; **es bedarf einiger Mühe** some effort is called for *or* required; **ohne dass es eines Hinweises bedurft hätte, ...** without having to be asked ...

Be|dürf|nis [bə'dʏrfnɪs] NT -ses, -se **a** (= *Notwendigkeit*) need; (*no pl*: = *Bedarf auch*) necessity; **die ~se des täglichen Lebens** everyday needs; **dafür liegt kein ~ vor, dafür besteht kein ~** there is no need *or* necessity for that

b *no pl* (= *Verlangen*) need; (*form*: = *Anliegen*) wish, desire; **es war ihm ein ~, ...** it was his wish *or* desire to ..., he wished *or* desired to ...; **es ist mir ein wirkliches ~** it is my sincere wish/desire; **ich hatte das ~/das dringende ~, das zu tun** I felt the need/an urgent need to do that; **das ~ nach Schlaf haben** *or* **fühlen** to be *or* feel in need of sleep

---

c (old: = Notdurft) call of nature; **(s)ein ~ verrichten** to relieve oneself

Be|dürf|nis-: Be|dürf|nis|an|stalt F (dated form, hum) **öffentliche ~** public convenience or restroom (US); **Be|dürf|nis|be|frie|di|gung** F satisfaction of one's/sb's needs; **be|dürf|nis|los** ADJ Mensch etc modest in one's needs; **ein ~es Leben** a modest lifestyle; **Be|dürf|nis|lo|sig|keit** F , no pl (von Mensch) modest lifestyle; **die ~ eines mönchischen Lebens** a monk's modest lifestyle

be|dürf|tig [bə'dʏrftɪç] ADJ **a** (= hilfsbedürftig) needy, in need; **die Bedürftigen** the needy pl, those in need **b** **einer Sache** (gen) **~ sein** (geh) to be or stand in need of sth, to have need of sth

Be|dürf|tig|keit F -, no pl need; **jds ~ (amtlich) feststellen** to give sb a means test

be|du|seln [bə'du:zln] ptp **beduselt** VR (inf) to get sozzled (Brit inf) or tipsy (inf)

be|du|selt [bə'du:zlt] ADJ (inf) (= angetrunken) sozzled (Brit inf), tipsy (inf); (= benommen) bemused, befuddled

Beef|bur|ger ['bi:fbøːɐgɐ] M (beef)burger

Beef|steak ['bi:fste:k] NT steak; **deutsches ~** hamburger, beefburger

be|eh|ren ptp **beehrt** VT (geh) to honour (Brit), to honor (US); **wann ~ Sie uns (mit einem Besuch)?** when will you hono(u)r us with a visit?; **bitte ~ Sie uns bald wieder** (Kellner etc) I hope you'll do us the hono(u)r of coming again soon VR **sich ~, etw zu tun** (form) to have the hono(u)r or privilege of doing sth (form)

be|ei|den [bə'aidn] ptp **beeidet** VT (= beschwören) Sache, Aussage to swear to; (= vereidigen) Dolmetscher, Experten to swear in

be|ei|di|gen [bə'aidɪgn] ptp **beeidigt** VT **a** (= beeiden) to swear to **b** (Jur.: = vereidigen) to swear in; **jdn auf etw** (acc) **~** to have or make sb swear on sth; **beeidigte Dolmetscherin** sworn interpreter

be|ei|len ptp **beeilt** VR to hurry (up), to get a move on (inf); **sich sehr** or **mächtig** (inf) **~** to get a real move on (inf); **er beeilte sich hinzuzufügen ...** (form) he hastened to add ...

Be|ei|lung [bə'ailʊŋ] INTERJ (inf) get a move on! (inf), step on it! (inf)

be|ein|dru|cken [bə'aindrʊkn] ptp **beeindruckt** VT to impress; (= Eindruck hinterlassen auch) to make an impression on; **davon lasse ich mich nicht ~** I won't be impressed by that

be|ein|dru|ckend ADJ impressive ADV impressively

be|ein|fluss|bar ▲ ADJ Mensch impressionable, suggestible; **er ist nur schwer ~** he is hard to influence or sway; **diese Vorgänge sind nicht ~** these events cannot be influenced or changed

be|ein|flus|sen [bə'ainflʊsn] ptp **beeinflusst** VT jdn to influence; Urteil, Meinung, Aussage auch to sway; Ereignisse, Vorgänge auch to affect; **jdn günstig/nachhaltig ~** to have a favourable (Brit) or favorable (US) or good/lasting influence on sb; **er ist leicht/schwer zu ~** he is easily influenced/hard to influence; **kannst du deinen Freund nicht ~?** can't you persuade your friend?; **durch etw beeinflusst sein** to be or to have been influenced or affected by sth

Be|ein|flus|sung F -, -en (= das Beeinflussen) influencing; (= Einfluss) influence (durch of); **~ der Rechtspflege** (Jur) prejudicing the outcome of a trial

be|ein|träch|ti|gen [bə'aintrɛçtɪgn] ptp **beeinträchtigt** VT **a** (= stören) to spoil; Vergnügen, Genuss auch to detract from, to spoil; Rundfunkempfang to interfere with, to impair; **sich gegenseitig ~** (Empfangsgeräte) to interfere with one another **b** (= schädigen) jds Ruf to damage, to harm; (= vermindern) Gesundheit, Sehvermögen etc to impair; Appetit, Energie, Qualität, Absatz, Wert to re-

duce; **dadurch wird der Wert erheblich beeinträchtigt** that reduces the value considerably; **den Wettbewerb ~** to restrict competition; **sich gegenseitig ~** (Entwicklungen, Interessen) to have an adverse effect on one another; **das beeinträchtigt schottische Interessen/die Interessen unserer Firma** this is detrimental to Scottish interests/to our firm's interests

c (= hemmen) Entscheidung to interfere with; (= einschränken) Freiheit, Entschlusskraft to restrict, to interfere with, to curb; **jdn in seiner Freiheit** or **jds Freiheit ~** to restrict or interfere with or curb sb's freedom; **jdn in seinen Rechten ~** (Jur) to infringe sb's rights

Be|ein|träch|ti|gung F -, -en **a** (= Stören) spoiling; (von Genuss, Vergnügen) detracting (+gen from), spoiling (+gen of); (von Konzentration) disturbance; (von Rundfunkempfang) interference (+gen with) **b** (= Schädigen: von Ruf) damage, harm (+gen to); (= Verminderung: von Appetit, Energie, Qualität) reduction (+gen of, in); (von Gesundheit, Sehvermögen, Leistung, Reaktion) impairment **c** (= Einschränken: von Freizeit, Entschlusskraft) restriction, curbing (+gen of); **ohne ~ von jds Rechten** (Jur) without detriment to sb's rights

be|e|len|den [bə'e:lɛndn] ptp **beelendet** VT (Sw) to upset, to distress

Beel|ze|bub [be'ɛltsəbuːp, 'be:ltsə-] M -s (Bibl) Beelzebub → **Teufel a**

be|en|den ptp **beendet, be|en|di|gen** ptp **beendigt** VT to end; Arbeit, Aufgabe etc to finish, to complete; Vortrag, Brief, Schulstunde, Versammlung to end, to bring to an end, to conclude; Streik, Streit, Krieg, Verhältnis to end, to bring to an end; Studium to complete; **der Abend wurde mit einer Diskussion beendet** the evening ended with or finished with a discussion; **etw vorzeitig ~** to cut sth short; **sein Leben ~** (geh) to end one's days; (durch Selbstmord) to take one's life; **damit ist unser Konzert/unser heutiges Programm beendet** that brings to an end or concludes our concert/our programmes (Brit) or programs (US) for today

Be|en|di|gung [bə'ɛndɪgʊŋ] F -, no pl, **Be|en|dung** F , no pl ending; (= Ende) end; (= Fertigstellung) completion; (= Schluss) conclusion; **zur ~ dieser Arbeit ...** to finish this piece of work ...; **zur ~ des heutigen Abends ...** to round off this evening ...; **nach ~ des Unterrichts** after school (ends)

be|en|gen [bə'ɛŋən] ptp **beengt** VT (lit) Bewegung to restrict, to cramp; (Möbel etc) Zimmer to make cramped; (fig) to stifle, to inhibit; **das Zimmer beengt mich** the room is too cramped for me; **das Kleid beengt mich** the dress is too tight for me; **~de Kleidung** tight or restricting clothing

be|engt [bə'ɛŋt] ADJ cramped, confined; (fig auch) stifled; **sich ~ fühlen** to feel confined etc; **~e Verhältnisse** (fig) restricted circumstances ADV **~ wohnen** to live in cramped conditions

Be|engt|heit F -, no pl confinement; (von Räumen) cramped conditions pl; **ein Gefühl der ~ haben** to feel restricted or confined; (fig auch) to feel stifled

be|er|ben ptp **beerbt** VT jdn **~** to inherit sb's estate, to be heir to sb; (inf: bezüglich Stelle, Posten) to succeed sb

be|er|di|gen [bə'e:ɐdɪgn] ptp **beerdigt** VT to bury; **jdn kirchlich ~** to give sb a Christian burial

Be|er|di|gung F -, -en burial; (= Beerdigungsfeier) funeral

Be|er|di|gungs- in cpds → auch **Bestattungs-** funeral; **Be|er|di|gungs|fei|er** F funeral service; **Be|er|di|gungs|ins|ti|tut** NT undertaker's, funeral director's (form), funeral home (US); (Schild) Undertakers, Funeral Directors; **Be|er|di|gungs|kos|ten** PL funeral expenses pl

Bee|re ['be:rə] F -, -n berry; (= Weinbeere) grape; **~n tragen** to bear fruit; **~n sammeln, in die ~n**

gehen (dial) to go berry-picking; (Brombeeren) to go blackberrying (Brit), to go blackberry-picking (US)

Bee|ren-: Bee|ren|aus|le|se F (= Wein) wine made from specially selected grapes; **Bee|ren|frucht** F berry; **Bee|ren|le|se** F fruit picking; **Bee|ren|obst** NT soft fruit

Beet [be:t] NT -(e)s, -e (= Blumenbeet, Spargelbeet) bed; (= Gemüsebeet) patch; (= Rabatte) border (mit of)

Bee|te ['be:tə] F -, -n = **Bete**

be|fä|hi|gen [bə'fɛ:ɪgn] ptp **befähigt** VT to enable; (Ausbildung) to qualify, to equip; **jdn zu etw ~** to enable sb to do sth; to qualify or equip sb to do sth

be|fä|higt [bə'fɛ:ɪçt] ADJ capable, competent; (durch Ausbildung) qualified; **sie ist zum Richteramt ~** she is qualified to be or become a judge; **zu etw ~ sein** to be capable of doing sth, to be competent to do sth

Be|fä|hi|gung F -, no pl **a** (durch Ausbildung, Voraussetzung) qualifications pl; **die ~ zum Richteramt** the qualifications to be or become a judge **b** (= Können, Eignung) capability, ability; **er hat nicht die ~ dazu** he does not have the ability to do that; **~ zu etw zeigen** to show talent or a gift for sth

Be|fä|hi|gungs|nach|weis M certificate of qualifications

be|fahl pret von **befehlen**

be|fahr|bar ADJ Straße, Weg passable; Seeweg, Fluss navigable; **~ sein** (Straße) to be open to traffic; **nicht ~ sein** (Straße, Weg) to be closed (to traffic); (wegen Schnee etc auch) to be impassable; (Seeweg, Fluss) to be unnavigable → **Bankette, Seitenstreifen**

Be|fahr|bar|keit [bə'fa:ɐˌba:ɐkait] F -, no pl (von Seeweg, Fluss) navigability; **die ~ der Straße ist beeinträchtigt** the road is only passable with care

be|fah|ren¹ [bə'fa:rən] ptp **befahren** VT irreg **a** Straße, Weg to use, to drive on or along; Passstraße to drive over; Gegend, Land to drive or travel through; Kreuzung, Seitenstreifen to drive onto; Eisenbahnstrecke to travel on; **der Pass kann nur im Sommer ~ werden** the pass is only open to traffic or passable in summer; **die Straße darf nur in einer Richtung ~ werden** this road is only open in one direction; **dieser Weg kann nur mit dem Fahrrad ~ werden** you can only use a bicycle on this path; **die Straße darf nicht ~ werden** the road is closed; **die Straße wird von Panzern ~** tanks use this road; **diese Straße wird stark/wenig ~** this road is used a lot/isn't used much, there is a lot of/not much traffic on this road

b (Schiff, Seemann) to sail; Fluss to sail up/down; Seeweg to navigate; Küste to sail along; **der See wird von vielen Booten ~** many boats sail on this lake, many boats use this lake; **diese Route wird nicht mehr von Schiffen ~** ships no longer sail this route

c (Min) Schacht to go down; **die Grube wird nicht mehr ~** the mine is not worked any more **d** (= abladen auf) to spread; **ein Feld mit Dung ~** to spread manure on a field

be|fah|ren² ADJ **a** Straße, Seeweg, Kanal used; **eine viel** or **stark ~e Straße** etc a much/little used road etc **b** (Naut: = erprobt) seasoned attr, experienced; **(ein) ~es Volk** seasoned or experienced sailors pl or seamen pl **c** (Hunt: = bewohnt) inhabited

Be|fah|ren NT -s, no pl use (+gen of); (= Vorgang) using; **beim ~ der Brücke** when using the bridge; **„Befahren verboten"** "road closed", **„Befahren der Brücke verboten"** "bridge closed"

Be|fall M , no pl attack; (mit Schädlingen) infestation; **es kam zum ~ aller Organe** all organs were affected; **der ~ (des Kohls) mit Raupen** the blight of caterpillars on the cabbage

be|fal|len¹ [bə'falən] ptp **befallen** VT irreg **a** (geh: = überkommen) to overcome; (Angst) to grip, to overcome; (*Durst, Hunger*) to grip, to seize; (*Fieber, Krankheit, Seuche*) to attack, to strike; (*Missgeschick, Schicksal etc*) to befall, to affect; **eine Schwäche befiel sie** she felt faint; **eine Ohnmacht befiel sie** she fainted **b** (= *angreifen, infizieren*) to affect; (*Schädlinge, Ungeziefer*) to infest

be|fal|len² ADJ affected (*von* by); (*von Schädlingen*) infested (*von* with)

be|fan|gen ADJ **a** *Mensch, Lächeln* diffident; *Schweigen, Stille* awkward

b (*esp Jur*: = *voreingenommen*) prejudiced, bias(s)ed; **als ~ gelten** to be considered (to be) prejudiced or bias(s)ed; (*Jur*) to be considered (to be) an interested party; **sich für ~ erklären** (*Jur*) to declare oneself disqualified due to a conflict of interests; **jdn als ~ erklären** to claim that sb is not qualified due to a conflict of interests; **jdn als ~ ablehnen** (*Jur*) to object to sb on grounds of suspected bias

c (*geh*: = *verstrickt*) **in der Vorstellung ~ sein, dass ...** or **... zu ...** to have the impression that ...; **er ist in seinen eigenen Anschauungen ~** he can only see his own point of view; **in einem Irrtum ~ sein** to labour (*Brit*) or labor (*US*) under a misapprehension

Be|fan|gen|heit F -, no pl **a** (= *Verlegenheit*) (*von Mensch, Lächeln*) diffidence; (*von Schweigen, Stille*) awkwardness **b** (= *Voreingenommenheit*) bias, prejudice; (*Jur*) interest; **jdn wegen (Besorgnis der) ~ ablehnen** (*Jur*) to object to sb on grounds of suspected bias

be|fas|sen *ptp* **befasst** VR **a** (= *sich beschäftigen*) **sich mit etw ~** to deal with sth; *mit Problem, Frage auch* to look into sth; *mit Fall, Angelegenheit auch* to attend to sth; *mit Arbeit auch, mit Forschungsbereich etc* to work on sth; **sich mit jds Vorleben ~** to look into sb's past; **damit haben wir uns jetzt lange genug befasst** we have spent long enough on or over that; **er hat sich lange damit befasst, alle Einzelheiten auszuarbeiten** he spent a long time working out all the details; **mit solchen Kleinigkeiten hat er sich nie befasst** he has never bothered with or concerned himself with such trivialities

b (= *sich annehmen*) **sich mit jdm ~** to deal with sb, to attend to sb; *mit Kindern auch* to see to sb; **sich mit jdm sehr ~** to give sb a lot of attention

VT **a** (*dial*: = *anfassen*) to touch

b (*form*) **jdn mit etw ~** to get sb to deal with sth; **mit etw befasst sein** to be dealing with sth; **die mit diesem Fall befassten Richter** the judges engaged on this case

be|feh|den [bəˈfeːdn] *ptp* **befehdet** VT (*Hist*) to be feuding with; (*fig*) to attack VR to be feuding; **sich mit Worten ~** to attack each other verbally

Be|fehl [bəˈfeːl] M -(e)s, -e **a** (= *Anordnung*) order, command (*an* +*acc* to, *von* from); (*Comput, Physiol*) command; **einen ~ verweigern** to refuse to obey an order *etc*; **er gab (uns) den ~, ...** he ordered us to ...; **wir hatten den ~, ...** we had orders to ..., we were ordered to ...; **wir haben ~, Sie festzunehmen** we have orders or have been ordered to arrest you; **auf seinen ~ (hin)** on his orders, at his command; **auf ~** to order; (= *sofort*) at the drop of a hat (*inf*); **auf ~ handeln** to act under or according to orders; **auf höheren ~** on orders from above; **zu ~, Herr Hauptmann** (*Mil*) yes, sir; (*nach erhaltenem Befehl auch*) very good, sir; **zu ~, Herr Kapitän** aye aye, sir; **~ ausgeführt!** mission accomplished; **~ ist ~** orders are orders; **von oben** orders from above; **~ vom Chef!** boss's orders; **dein Wunsch ist mir ~** (*hum*) your wish is my command

b (= *Befehlsgewalt*) command; **den ~ haben** or **führen** to have command, to be in command (*über* +*acc* of); **den ~ übernehmen** to take or assume command

be|feh|len [bəˈfeːlən] *pret* **befahl** [bəˈfaːl], *ptp* **befohlen** [bəˈfoːlən] VT **a** (= *anordnen*) to order; **er befahl Stillschweigen** or **zu schweigen** he or-

dered them/us *etc* to be silent; **sie befahl ihm Stillschweigen** or **zu schweigen** she ordered him to be silent; **er befahl, den Mann zu erschießen, er befahl die Erschießung des Mannes** he ordered the man to be shot; **sie befahl, dass ...** she ordered or gave orders that ...; **du hast mir gar nichts zu ~, von dir lasse ich mir nichts ~** I won't take orders from you; **gnädige Frau ~?** (*old form*) was ~ **gnädige Frau?** (*old form*) yes, Madam?, what can I do for you, Madam? **b** (= *beordern*) (*an die Front etc*) to order, to send; (*= zitieren*) to summon

c (*liter.*: = *anvertrauen*) to entrust, to commend (*liter*); **seine Seele Gott/in die Hände Gottes ~** to commend or entrust one's soul to God/into God's hands

VI **a** (= *Befehle erteilen*) to give orders; **schweigen Sie, befahl er** be quiet, he ordered; **er befiehlt gern** he likes giving orders; **hier habe nur ich zu ~** I give the orders around here; **wie Sie ~** as you wish; **wer ~ will, muss erst gehorchen lernen** (*prov*) if you wish to command you must first learn to obey

b (*Mil*: = *den Befehl haben*) to be in command, to have command (*über* +*acc* of); **über Leben und Tod ~** to be in absolute command

be|feh|le|risch [bəˈfeːlərɪʃ] ADJ *Ton, Wesen* imperious, dictatorial

be|feh|li|gen [bəˈfeːlɪgn] *ptp* **befehligt** VT (*Mil*) to command, to be in command of, to have command of or over

Be|fehls-: Be|fehls|aus|ga|be F (*Mil*) issuing of orders; **um 15 Uhr ist ~** orders will be issued at 1500 hours; **Be|fehls|be|reich** M (*Mil*) (area of) command; **Be|fehls|code** M = **Befehlskode; Be|fehls|emp|fän|ger(in)** M(F) recipient of an order; **~ sein** to follow orders (+*gen* from); **jdn zum ~ degradieren** (*fig*) to lower sb to the level of just following orders; **Be|fehls|fol|ge** F (*Comput*) command sequence; **Be|fehls|form** F (*Gram*) imperative; **be|fehls|ge|mäß** ADJ, ADV as ordered, in accordance with (sb's) orders; **er muss sich ~ um 9 Uhr dort einfinden** his orders are to report there at 9 o'clock; **Be|fehls|ge|walt** F (*Mil*) command; **~ haben** to be in or to have command (*über* +*acc* over); **jds ~** (*dat*) **unterstehen** to be under sb's command; **Be|fehls|ha|ber** [-haːbɐ] M -s, -, **Be|fehls|ha|be|rin** [-ərɪn] F -, -nen commander; **be|fehls|ha|be|risch** [-haːbərɪʃ] ADJ dictatorial; **Be|fehls|kode** M (*Comput*) command code; **Be|fehls|not|stand** M (*Jur*) compulsion or necessity to obey orders; **unter ~ handeln** to be acting under orders; **Be|fehls|satz** M (*Gram*) imperative, command; **Be|fehls|spra|che** F (*Comput*) command language; **Be|fehls|ton** M , no pl peremptory tone; **Be|fehls|ver|wei|ge|rung** F (*Mil*) refusal to obey orders; **be|fehls|wid|rig** ADJ, ADV contrary to orders, against orders; **Be|fehls|zei|le** F (*Comput*) command line

be|fein|den [bəˈfaɪndn] *ptp* **befeindet** VT (*geh*) *Land* to be hostile towards; *Ideologie, Schriften, Schriftsteller* to attack VR to be hostile (towards each other)

be|fes|ti|gen *ptp* **befestigt** VT **a** (*an* +*dat* to) (= *anbringen*) to fasten; *Boot* to tie up; **etw durch Nähen/Kleben** *etc* **~** to sew/glue *etc* sth; **etw an der Wand/Tür ~** to attach or fix sth to the wall/door; **die beiden Enden/Teile werden (aneinander) befestigt** the two ends/parts are fastened together; **die Wäsche mit Klammern an der Leine ~** to peg the washing on the line; **ein loses Brett ~** to fasten down or secure a loose board **b** (= *fest, haltbar machen*) *Böschung, Deich* to reinforce; *Fahrbahn, Straße* to make up; **eine Straße gut ~** to make up a road with good foundations

c (*Mil*: = *mit Festungsanlagen versehen*) to fortify VR (*Fin*) *Preis, Börsenkurs* to stabilize

Be|fes|ti|gung F **a** (= *das Befestigen*) fastening; (*von Boot*) tying up; **zur ~ des Plakats ...** in order to attach the poster ... **b** (= *Vorrichtung zum Befestigen*) fastening, catch **c** (= *das Halt-*

barmachen*) reinforcement; (*fig*: = *Stärkung*) consolidation; **zur ~ der Macht des ...** in order to consolidate the power of ... **d** (*Mil*) fortification

Be|fes|ti|gungs|an|la|ge F , **Be|fes|ti|gungs|bau** M pl -**bauten, Be|fes|ti|gungs|werk** NT fortification, defence (*Brit*), defense (*US*)

be|feuch|ten [bəˈfɔʏçtn] *ptp* **befeuchtet** VT to moisten; *Finger auch* to wet; *Wäsche* to damp (-en); **das vom Tau befeuchtete Gras** the grass moistened by the dew

be|feu|ern *ptp* **befeuert** VT **a** (= *beheizen*) to fuel **b** (*Naut, Aviat*) *Wasserstraße, Untiefen* to light or mark with beacons; *Start- und Landebahn* to light, to mark with lights **c** (*lit, fig: mit Geschossen*) to bombard **d** (*geh*: = *anspornen*) to fire with enthusiasm

Be|feu|e|rung F (*Aviat, Naut*) lights pl, beacons pl

Beff|chen [ˈbɛfçən] NT -s, - Geneva band

be|fie|dert [bəˈfiːdɐt] ADJ feathered

be|fiehlt [bəˈfiːlt] 3. PERS SING pres von **befehlen**

be|fin|den *ptp* **befunden** [bəˈfʊndn] *irreg* VR **a** (= *sein*) to be; (= *liegen auch*) to be situated; (*in Maschine, Körper etc*) to be (situated or located); **sich auf Reisen ~** to be away; **unter ihnen befanden sich einige, die ...** there were some amongst them who ...; **die Abbildung befindet sich in diesem Buch** the illustration can be found or is in this book; **sich in Verwirrung/guter Laune/im Irrtum ~** to be confused/in a good mood/mistaken; **sich auf dem Weg der Besserung ~** to be on the road to recovery; **wenn man sich in schlechter Gesellschaft befindet ...** if you find yourself in bad company ...

b (*form*: = *sich fühlen*) to feel; **wie ~ Sie sich heute?** how are you (feeling) today?, how do you feel today?

VT (*form*: = *erachten*) to deem (*form*), to find; **etw für nötig/angemessen/für** or **als gut ~** to deem or find sth (to be) necessary/appropriate/good; **Ihre Papiere wurden in Ordnung befunden** your papers were found to be in order; **jdn für schuldig ~** to find sb guilty → **wiegen²**

VI (*geh*: = *entscheiden*) to come to or make a decision, to decide (*über* +*acc* about, *in* +*dat* on); **darüber hat der Arzt zu ~** that is for the doctor to decide; **darüber habe ich nicht zu ~** that is not for me to decide; **über jdn/etw ~** to pass judgement on sb/sth, to reach a verdict on sb/sth

Be|fin|den [bəˈfɪndn] NT -s, no pl **a** (*form*: = *Gesundheitszustand*) (state of) health; (*eines Kranken*) condition; **seelisches ~** mental state or condition; **wie ist das (werte)** or **Ihr (wertes) ~?** (*form*) how are you (feeling)? **b** (*geh*: = *das Dafürhalten*) view, opinion; **nach meinem ~** in my view or opinion; **nach eigenem ~ entscheiden** to decide according to one's own judgement

be|find|lich [bəˈfɪntlɪç] ADJ usu attr (*form*) **a** (*an einem Ort*) *Gebäude, Park* situated, located; (*in Behälter*) contained; **der hinter dem Hause ~e Garten** the garden (situated) behind the house; **alle in der Bibliothek ~en Bücher** all the books in the library **b** (*in einem Zustand*) **das im Umbau ~e Hotel** the hotel which is being renovated; **das im Umlauf ~e Geld** the money in circulation; **die in Kraft ~e Verordnung** the regulation which is in force

Be|find|lich|keit F -, -en sensitivities pl; **nationale ~en** national sensitivities

be|fin|gern [bəˈfɪŋɐn] *ptp* **befingert** VT (*inf*) (= *betasten*) to finger

be|fi|schen [bəˈfɪʃn] *ptp* **befischt** VT *Gewässer, Meer* to fish

be|flag|gen *ptp* **beflaggt** VT *Häuser* to (be)deck or decorate with flags; *Schiff* to dress; **die beflaggten Straßen** the flag-decked streets, the streets (be)decked or decorated with flags; **anlässlich seines Todes wurden alle öffentlichen**

Gebäude beflaggt flags were flown on all public buildings to mark his death

Be|flag|gung [bə'flagʊŋ] F -, -en **a** (= *das Beflaggen*) (*von Gebäuden*) decoration with flags; (*von Schiffen*) dressing **b** (= *Fahnenschmuck*) flags *pl*

be|fle|cken [bə'flɛkn] *ptp* **befleckt** VT **a** (*lit*) to stain; **er hat seinen Anzug mit Farbe befleckt** he got paint on his suit; **er hat sich** *or* **seine Hände mit Blut befleckt** (*fig*) he has blood on his hands **b** (*fig geh*) *Ruf, Ehre* to cast a slur on, to besmirch, to sully; *Heiligtum* to defile, to desecrate

be|fleckt [bə'flɛkt] ADJ **a** stained; **sein mit Blut ~er Anzug** his bloodstained suit **b** *Ruf, Ehre* sullied, besmirched

Be|fle|ckung F -, -en **a** (= *Beschmutzen*) staining **b** (*von Ruf, Ehre*) besmirching, sullying; (*von Heiligtum*) defilement, desecration

be|flei|ßen [bə'flaisn] *pret* **befliss** [bə'flɪs], *ptp* **beflissen** [bə'flɪsn] VR (*old*) = **befleißigen**

be|flei|ßi|gen [bə'flaisɪgn] *ptp* **befleißigt** VR (*geh*) **sich einer Sache** (*gen*) ~ to cultivate sth; **sich ~, etw zu tun** to make a great effort to do sth; **sich größter** *or* **der größten Höflichkeit ~** to go out of one's way to be polite

be|flie|gen *ptp* **beflogen** [bə'floːgn] VT *irreg* (*Aviat*) *Strecke* to fly, to operate (on); *Gegend* to fly over; *Raum* to fly through *or* in; **eine viel beflogene Strecke** a heavily used route

be|fliss ▲ *pret von* **befließen**

be|flis|sen [bə'flɪsn] *ptp von* **befleißen** ADJ (*geh*: = *bemüht*) *Mensch* zealous; (*pej*: = *unterwürfig*) obsequious; **um etw ~ sein** to be concerned for sth; **er war sehr um die Zufriedenheit seiner Gäste ~** he was very anxious *or* concerned to please his guests; **~ sein, etw zu tun** to be concerned to do sth; **ängstlich ~** anxious ADV zealously; (*pej*) obsequiously

Be|flis|sen|heit F -, *no pl* (= *Bemühtheit*) zeal; (= *Unterwürfigkeit*) obsequiousness

be|flis|sent|lich [bə'flɪsntlɪç] ADV = **geflissentlich**

be|flü|geln [bə'flyːgln] *ptp* **beflügelt** VT (*geh*) to inspire, to fire; **die Angst beflügelte seine Schritte** (*liter*) fear winged his steps (*liter*); **der Gedanke an Erfolg beflügelte ihn** the thought of success spurred him on

be|foh|len *ptp von* **befehlen**

be|fol|gen *ptp* **befolgt** VT *Vorschrift, Befehl etc* to obey, to comply with; *grammatische Regel* to follow, to obey; *Ratschlag* to follow, to take

Be|fol|gung [bə'fɔlgʊŋ] F -, *no pl* obeying, compliance (+*gen* with); (*von grammatischer Regel*) following, obeying; (*von Ratschlag*) following, taking; **~ der Vorschriften** obeying the rules, compliance with the rules

Be|för|de|rer M , **Be|för|de|rin** F (*form*) carrier

be|för|dern *ptp* **befördert** VT **a** *Waren, Gepäck* to transport, to carry; *Personen* to carry; *Post* to handle; **etw mit der Post/per Luftpost/Bahn/Schiff ~** to send sth by mail/airmail/rail/ship; **to ship sth; jdn/etw von A nach B ~** to transport *or* convey sb/sth from A to B; **jdn an die (frische) Luft** *or* **zur Tür hinaus** *or* **ins Freie ~** (*fig*) to fling *or* chuck sb out (*inf*); **jdn ins Jenseits ~** (*inf*) to bump sb off (*inf*), to do sb in (*inf*) **b** (= *dienstlich aufrücken lassen*) to promote; **er wurde zum Major befördert** he was promoted to (the rank of) major

Be|för|de|rung F **a** (= *Transport*) transportation, carriage; (*von Personen*) carriage; (*von Post*) handling; **die ~ der Post/eines Briefes dauert drei Tage** the post/a letter takes three days (to arrive); **für von 35 Personen zugelassen** permitted to carry 35 persons; **für die ~ der Kursteilnehmer wird gesorgt** transport will be arranged for course participants; **~ zu Lande/zur Luft/per Bahn** land/air/rail transportation **b** (*beruflich*) promotion

Be|för|de|rungs-: Be|för|de|rungs|aus|sich|ten PL (= *Aufstiegschancen*) promotion prospects *pl*, chances *pl* or prospects *pl* of promotion; **Be|för|de|rungs|be|din|gun|gen** PL terms *pl* or conditions *pl* of carriage; **Be|för|de|rungs|dau|er** F delivery time; **Be|för|de|rungs|kos|ten** PL transport costs *pl*; **Be|för|de|rungs|lis|te** F promotion list; **Be|för|de|rungs|mit|tel** NT means of transport; **Be|för|de|rungs|pflicht** F obligation of taxis, buses etc to accept passengers; **Be|för|de|rungs|stau** M (*im Beruf*) promotion bottleneck; **Be|för|de|rungs|steu|er** F transport tax; **Be|för|de|rungs|stopp** ▲ M (*im Beruf*) promotion moratorium, moratorium on promotion(s); **Be|för|de|rungs|ta|rif** M transportation *or* (*bei Postbeförderung*) postage charge

be|frach|ten [bə'fraxtn] *ptp* **befrachtet** VT *Fahrzeug, Schiff* to load; (*fig geh auch*) to burden; **ein schwer befrachtetes Schiff** a heavily laden ship; **seine übermäßig mit Emotionen befrachtete Rede** his speech, overladen with emotion

Be|frach|ter [bə'fraxte] M -s, -, **Be|frach|te|rin** [-ərɪn] F -, -nen shipper, freighter

Be|frach|tung F -, -en loading

be|frackt [bə'frakt] ADJ in tails, tail-coated (*Brit*), in tail coat (*US*)

be|fra|gen *ptp* **befragt** VT **a** (*über +acc, zu, nach* about) to question; *Zeugen auch* to examine; **jdn im Kreuzverhör ~** to cross-question *or* (*esp Jur*) to cross-examine sb; **auf Befragen** when questioned **b** (= *um Stellungnahme bitten*) to consult (*über +acc, nach* about); **jdn um Rat/nach seiner Meinung ~** to ask sb for advice/his opinion, to ask sb's advice/opinion; **jdn in einer Angelegenheit ~** to consult sb about *or* on a matter **c** (*dated*) to consult; (= *sich erkundigen*) to make inquiries; **sich bei jdm/etw ~** to consult sb/sth

Be|frag|te(r) [bə'fraːktə] MF *decl as adj* person asked; (*in Umfrage auch*) interviewee; **alle ~n** all those asked

Be|fra|gung [bə'fraːgʊŋ] F -, -en **a** (= *das Befragen*) questioning; (*von Zeugen auch*) examining, examination **b** (*von Fachmann*) consultation (+*gen* with) **c** (= *Umfrage*) survey

be|franst [bə'franst] ADJ fringed, with a fringe

be|frei|en *ptp* **befreit** VT **a** (= *frei machen*) to free, to release; *Volk, Land* to liberate, to free; (= *freilassen*) *Gefangenen, Tier, Vogel* to set free, to free; **jdn aus einer schwierigen Lage ~** to rescue sb from a tricky situation, to get sb out of a tricky situation

b (= *freistellen*) (*von* from) to excuse; (*von Militärdienst, Steuern*) to exempt; (*von Eid etc*) to absolve; (*von Pflicht*) to release; **sich vom Religionsunterricht ~ lassen** to be excused religious instruction

c (= *erlösen*: *von Schmerz etc*) to release, to free; **jdn von einer Last ~** to take a weight off sb's mind; **ein ~des Lachen** a healthy *or* an unrepressed laugh → *auch* **befreit**

d (= *reinigen*) (*von* of) (*von Ungeziefer etc*) to rid; (*von Schnee, Eis*) to free; **seine Schuhe von Schmutz ~** to remove the dirt from one's shoes VR **a** (*Volk, Land*) to free oneself; (= *entkommen*) to escape (*von, aus* from); **sich aus einer schwierigen Lage ~** to get oneself out of a difficult situation

b (= *erleichtern*) to rid oneself (*von* of), to free oneself (*von* from)

Be|frei|er [bə'fraiɐ] M -s, -, **Be|frei|e|rin** [-ərɪn] F -, -nen liberator

be|freit [bə'frait] ADJ (= *erleichtert*) relieved ADV *lächeln* with relief; **~ aufatmen/aufseufzen** to heave (*Brit*) or breathe a sigh of relief; **die Bevölkerung kann endlich ~ aufatmen** the people can finally breathe easy again → *auch* **befreien**

Be|frei|ung [bə'fraiʊŋ] F -, -en **a** (= *das Befreien*) freeing, releasing; (*von Volk, Land*) liberation, freeing; (*von Gefangenen, Tieren*) setting free, freeing **b** (= *Freistellung*) excusing; (*von Militär-*

dienst, Steuern) exemption; (*von Eid*) absolving; (*von Pflichten*) releasing; **um ~ von etw bitten** to ask to be excused/exempted from sth **c** (*von Schmerz*) releasing **d** (*von Ungeziefer*) ridding; (*von Schnee, Eis*) freeing

Be|frei|ungs-: Be|frei|ungs|ak|ti|on F liberation campaign; **Be|frei|ungs|be|we|gung** F liberation movement; **Be|frei|ungs|front** F liberation front; **Be|frei|ungs|kampf** M struggle for liberation; **Be|frei|ungs|krieg** M war of liberation; **Be|frei|ungs|or|ga|ni|sa|ti|on** F liberation organization; **Be|frei|ungs|schlag** M (*Eishockey, Ftbl*) clearance; (*fig*) coup; **Be|frei|ungs|theo|lo|ge** M liberation theologian; **Be|frei|ungs|theo|lo|gie** F liberation theology; **Be|frei|ungs|theo|lo|gin** F liberation theologian; **Be|frei|ungs|ver|such** M escape attempt

be|frem|den [bə'frɛmdn] *ptp* **befremdet** VT to disconcert; **es befremdet mich, dass ...** I'm rather taken aback that ...; **das befremdet mich an ihr** that (side of her) disconcerts me → *auch* **befremdet** VT to cause disconcertment

Be|frem|den [bə'frɛmdn] NT -s, *no pl* disconcertment; **nicht ohne ~ ...** it is with some disconcertment that ...

be|frem|dend ADJ disconcerting

be|frem|det [bə'frɛmdət] ADJ disconcerted, taken aback → *auch* **befremden**

be|fremd|lich [bə'frɛmtlɪç] ADJ (*geh*) = **befremdend**

Be|frem|dung F -, *no pl* = **Befremden**

be|freun|den [bə'frɔyndn] *ptp* **befreundet** VR **a** (= *sich anfreunden*) to make *or* become friends; **ich habe mich schnell mit ihm befreundet** I quickly made friends with him, he and I quickly became friends; **die beiden haben sich (miteinander) befreundet** the pair made *or* became friends **b** (*fig*) (*mit Gedanken etc*) **sich mit etw ~** to get used to sth, to get *or* grow accustomed to sth

be|freun|det [bə'frɔyndət] ADJ **wir/sie sind schon lange (miteinander) ~** we/they have been friends *or* friendly for a long time; **gut** *or* **eng ~ sein** to be good *or* close friends; **alle ~en Familien** all the families we *etc* are friendly with; **ein uns ~er Staat** a friendly nation; **das ~e Ausland** friendly (foreign) countries; **ein uns ~er Arzt** a doctor (who is a) friend of ours; **~e Zahlen** (*Math*) amicable numbers

be|frie|den [bə'friːdn] *ptp* **befriedet** VT (*geh*) to pacify

be|frie|di|gen [bə'friːdɪgn] *ptp* **befriedigt** VT to satisfy; *Gläubiger auch* to pay; *Gelüste auch* to gratify; *Ansprüche, Forderungen, Verlangen auch* to meet; **jdn (sexuell) ~** to satisfy sb (sexually); **er ist leicht/schwer zu ~** he's easily/not easily satisfied, he's easy/hard to satisfy → *auch* **befriedigt** VT to be satisfactory; **Ihre Leistung hat nicht befriedigt** your performance was unsatisfactory VR **sich (selbst) ~** to masturbate

be|frie|di|gend ADJ satisfactory; *Verhältnisse, Leistung, Arbeit, Antwort auch* adequate; *Lösung auch* acceptable; *Gefühl* satisfying; (*als Schulnote*) fair; **nicht ~ sein** to be unsatisfactory/inadequate/unacceptable ADV satisfactorily

be|frie|digt [bə'friːdɪçt] ADJ satisfied, contented; **bist du nun endlich ~?** are you satisfied at last? ADV with satisfaction; **er lächelte ~** he smiled with satisfaction → *auch* **befriedigen**

Be|frie|di|gung F -, -en **a** (= *das Befriedigen*) satisfaction, satisfying; **sexuelle ~** sexual satisfaction; **zur ~ deiner Neugier ...** to satisfy your curiosity ... **b** (= *Genugtuung*) satisfaction; **seine ~ in etw** (*dat*) **suchen** to look for *or* seek satisfaction in sth

Be|frie|dung F -, -en (*geh*) pacification

be|fris|ten [bə'frɪstn] *ptp* **befristet** VT to limit, to restrict (*auf +acc* to); *Aufgabe, Projekt* to put a time limit on

be|fris|tet [bə'frɪstət] ADJ *Genehmigung, Visum* restricted, limited (*auf +acc* to); *Arbeitsverhältnis,*

Anstellung temporary; **~ sein** (*Pass etc*) to be valid for a limited time; **auf zwei Jahre ~ sein** (*Visum etc*) to be valid for two years; **mein Arbeitsverhältnis ist auf zwei Jahre ~** my appointment is limited *or* restricted to two years

Be|fris|tung F -, -en limitation, restriction (*auf +acc* to)

be|fruch|ten *ptp* **befruchtet** VT **a** (*lit*) *Eizelle* to fertilize; *Blüte* to pollinate; **künstlich ~** to inseminate artificially **b** (*fig: = fruchtbar machen*) to make fertile **c** (*fig: = geistig anregen*) to stimulate, to have a stimulating effect on

be|fruch|tend [bəˈfrʊxtnt] ADJ (*fig*) fruitful, stimulating ADV **~ wirken** to have a stimulating effect (*auf +acc* on) → *auch* **befruchten**

Be|fruch|tung [bəˈfrʊxtʊŋ] F -, -en fertilization; (*von Blüte*) pollination; **künstliche ~** artificial insemination

be|fu|gen [bəˈfuːgn] *ptp* **befugt** VT (*form*) to authorize; **wer hat Sie dazu befugt?** who authorized you to do that?

Be|fug|nis [bəˈfuːknɪs] F -, -se (*form*) authority *no pl*; (*= Erlaubnis*) authorization *no pl*; **eine ~ erhalten/erteilen** to receive/give authorization *or* authority; **besondere ~se erhalten** to receive *or* be given special authority; **Zutritt ohne ~ nicht gestattet** no entry to unauthorized persons

be|fugt [bəˈfuːkt] ADJ (*form*) **~ sein(, etw zu tun**) to have the authority *or* (*= ermächtigt worden sein*) be authorized (to do sth)

be|füh|len *ptp* **befühlt** VT to feel; (*= hinstreichen über auch*) to run one's hands over

be|fum|meln *ptp* **befummelt** VT (*inf: = betasten*) to paw (*inf*)

Be|fund M results *pl*, findings *pl*; **der ~ war positiv/negativ** (*Med*) the results were positive/negative; **ohne ~** (*Med*) (results) negative

be|fürch|ten *ptp* **befürchtet** VT to fear, to be afraid of; **ich befürchte das Schlimmste** I fear the worst; **es ist** *or* **steht zu ~, dass …** it is (to be) feared that …; **dabei sind Komplikationen zu ~** it is feared there may be complications; **dabei ist gar nichts zu ~** there's nothing to fear with that

Be|fürch|tung [bəˈfʏrçtʊŋ] F -, -en fear *usu pl*; **~en** *or* **die ~ haben, dass …** to fear *or* be afraid that …; **die schlimmsten ~en haben** *or* **hegen** (*geh*) to fear the worst

be|für|wor|ten [bəˈfyːɐvɔrtn] ✪ 40.1, 40.2 *ptp* **befürwortet** VT to approve

Be|für|wor|ter [bəˈfyːɐvɔrtɐ] M -s, -, **Be|für|wor|te|rin** [-ərɪn] F -, -nen supporter; (*von Idee auch*) advocate

Be|für|wor|tung F -, -en approval, support

be|ga|ben [bəˈgaːbn] *ptp* **begabt** VT *usu pass* (*liter*) to endow; **mit etw begabt sein** to be endowed with sth

be|gabt [bəˈgaːpt] ADJ talented; (*esp geistig, musisch auch*) gifted; **für etw ~ sein** to be talented at sth; **für Musik, Kunst etc auch** to have a gift for sth

Be|gab|ten-: Be|gab|ten|aus|le|se F selection of the most gifted *or* talented people; **Be|gab|ten|för|de|rung** F (educational) grant

Be|gab|te(r) [bəˈgaːptə] MF *decl as adj* talented *or* gifted person/man/woman *etc*

Be|ga|bung [bəˈgaːbʊŋ] F -, -en **a** (*= Anlage*) talent; (*geistig, musisch*) gift, talent; **er hat eine ~ dafür, immer das Falsche zu sagen** he has a gift for *or* a knack of always saying the wrong thing; **er hat ~ zum Lehrer** he has a gift for teaching; **mangelnde ~** a lack of talent, insufficient talent **b** (*= begabter Mensch*) talented person; **sie ist eine musikalische ~** she has a talent for music

be|gaf|fen *ptp* **begafft** VT (*pej inf*) to gape *or* goggle at (*inf*)

be|gann *pret von* **beginnen**

be|ga|sen *ptp* **begast** VT (*Agr*) to gas

be|gat|ten [bəˈgatn] *ptp* **begattet** (*esp Zool*) VT to mate *or* copulate with; (*geh, hum*) to copulate with VR to mate, to copulate; (*geh, hum*) to copulate

Be|gat|tung F -, -en (*esp Zool*) mating, copulation; (*geh, hum*) copulation

Be|gat|tungs|or|ga|ne PL reproductive organs *pl*

be|gau|nern [bəˈgaunɐn] *ptp* **begaunert** VT to swindle, to cheat

be|geb|bar [bəˈgeːpbaːɐ] ADJ (*Fin*) *Wertpapiere* (*= übertragbar*) transferable; (*= verkäuflich*) negotiable

be|ge|ben *ptp* **begeben** *irreg* VR **a** (*geh: = gehen*) to betake oneself (*liter*), to go; **sich nach Hause ~, sich auf den Heimweg ~** to wend (*liter*) *or* make one's way home; **sich auf eine Reise ~** to undertake a journey; **sich zu Bett ~** to retire to one's bed (*liter*); **sich zur Ruhe ~** to retire; **sich an seinen Platz ~** to take one's place; **sich in ärztliche Behandlung ~** to undergo medical treatment; **sich an die Arbeit ~** to commence work

b (*= sich einer Sache aussetzen*) **sich in Gefahr ~** to expose oneself to danger, to put oneself in danger; **sich in jds Schutz** (*acc*) **~** to place oneself under sb's protection → **Gefahr a**

c (*old liter: = geschehen*) to come to pass (*old liter*); **es begab sich aber zu der Zeit, dass …** (*Bibl*) and it came to pass at that time that …; **es hatte sich vieles ~** many things had happened

d (*geh: = aufgeben*) +*gen* to relinquish, to renounce

VT (*Fin*) to issue

Be|ge|ben|heit [bəˈgeːbnhait] F -, -en (*geh*), **Be|geb|nis** [bəˈgeːpnɪs] NT -ses, -se (*old*) occurrence, event

be|geg|nen [bəˈgeːgnən] *ptp* **begegnet** VI *aux sein +dat* **a** (*= treffen*) to meet; **sich** *or* **einander** (*geh*) **~** to meet; **ihre Augen** *or* **Blicke begegneten sich** their eyes met; **unsere Wünsche ~ sich** (*liter*) our wishes coincide (*form*)

b (*= stoßen auf*) **einer Sache** (*dat*) **~** to encounter sth; *Schwierigkeiten* to encounter sth, to run into sth; **dieses Wort wird uns später noch einmal ~** we will encounter this word again later

c (*= widerfahren*) **jdm ist etw begegnet** sth has happened to sb; **es war mir schon einmal begegnet, dass …** it had happened to me once before that …

d (*geh: = behandeln*) to treat; **man begegnete mir nur mit Spott** I only met with derision

e (*geh*) (*= entgegentreten*) *einer Krankheit, Seuche, der Not* to combat; *einem Übel, Angriff, Unrecht auch* to oppose, to resist; (*= überwinden*) *einer Gefahr, Schwierigkeiten, dem Schicksal* to confront, to meet, to face; (*= reagieren auf*) *einem Wunsch, Vorschlag, einer Ansicht* to meet, to respond to; **man begegnete seinen Vorschlägen mit Zurückhaltung** his suggestions met with reserve

f (*geh: = einwenden gegen*) *Behauptungen etc* to counter

Be|geg|nung F -, -en **a** (*= Treffen*) meeting, encounter; (*fig: mit Idee etc*) encounter; **bei der ersten/letzten ~ der beiden** at the first/last meeting between the two; **ein Ort internationaler ~** an international meeting place **b** (*Sport*) encounter, match; **die ~ Spanien-Italien findet nächsten Monat statt** Spain and Italy meet next month

Be|geg|nungs|stät|te F meeting place

be|geh|bar ADJ (*lit*) *Weg* passable; *Schrank, Skulptur* walk-in *attr* **b** (*fig*) *Weg, Pfad* practical

be|ge|hen *ptp* **begangen** VT *irreg* **a** (*= verüben*) *Selbstmord, Ehebruch, Sünde* to commit; *Verbrechen* to commit, to perpetrate (*form*); *Fehler* to make; **eine Indiskretion (gegenüber jdm) ~** to be indiscreet (about sb); **einen Mord an jdm ~** to murder sb; **eine Dummheit/Taktlosigkeit/Unvorsichtigkeit ~** to do something stupid/tactless/careless; **die Dummheit/Taktlosigkeit/Unvorsichtigkeit ~, …** to be so stupid/tactless/

careless as to …; **an jdm ein Unrecht ~** to wrong sb, to be unjust to sb; **Verrat an jdm/etw ~** to betray sb/sth; **ein oft begangener Fehler** a frequent mistake

b (*= entlanggehen*) *Weg* to use; **der Weg wird viel begangen** the path is used a lot, it is a much-used path; **„Begehen der Brücke auf eigene Gefahr“** "persons using this bridge do so at their own risk", "cross bridge at own risk"

c (*= abschreiten*) *Bahnstrecke, Felder, Baustelle* to inspect (on foot)

d (*geh: = feiern*) to celebrate

Be|gehr [bəˈgeːɐ] M OR NT -s, *no pl* (*old*) wish, desire; **er fragte nach meinem ~** he inquired after my wishes

be|geh|ren [bəˈgeːrən] *ptp* **begehrt** VT **a** (*geh: = Verlangen haben nach*) to desire, to crave; *Frau* to desire; *Gegenstände, Besitz eines andern* to covet; **ein Mädchen zur Frau ~** (*liter*) to desire a girl's hand in marriage; **sie bekam die von ihr so begehrte Rolle** she was given the role she desired so much; **du sollst nicht ~ …** (*Bibl*) thou shalt not covet … (*Bibl*) → *auch* **begehrt b** (*old: = wollen*) to desire

Be|geh|ren [bəˈgeːrən] NT -s, (*rare*) - **a** (*geh: = Verlangen*) desire (*nach* for); **das ~ fühlen** *or* **haben, etw zu tun** to feel the *or* a desire to do sth; **heißes ~** burning desire **b** (*old: = Wunsch, Forderung*) wish; **nach jds ~ fragen** to inquire after sb's wishes, to ask what sb wants; **auf mein ~ (hin**) at my request

be|geh|rens|wert ADJ desirable, attractive; *Frau* desirable

be|gehr|lich [bəˈgeːɐlɪç] (*geh*) ADJ covetous ADV longingly, yearningly

Be|gehr|lich|keit F -, -en (*geh*) **a** *no pl* covetousness **b** (*= Verlangen*) desire (*nach* for)

be|gehrt [bəˈgeːɐt] ADJ much *or* very sought-after; *Posten auch* desirable; *Partner etc auch, Ferienziel* popular; *Junggeselle* eligible → *auch* **begehren**

Be|ge|hung [bəˈgeːʊŋ] F -, -en **a** (*form*) (*einer Sünde*) committing; (*eines Verbrechens*) committing, perpetrating (*form*); **nach ~ des Verbrechens** after committing *etc* the crime **b** (*= das Abschreiten*) inspection (on foot)

be|gei|fern *ptp* **begeifert** VT (*fig pej*) to run down, to slam (*inf*); (*lit*) to dribble on

be|geis|tern *ptp* **begeistert** VT *jdn* to fill with enthusiasm; (*= inspirieren*) to inspire; **er begeistert alle durch sein** *or* **mit seinem Talent** everybody is enthusiastic about his talent; **er ist für nichts zu ~** he's never enthusiastic about anything VR to be *or* feel enthusiastic (*an +dat, für* about) → *auch* **begeistert**

be|geis|ternd ADJ inspiring; *Rede auch* stirring ADV inspiringly; **~ wirken** to be inspiring

be|geis|tert [bəˈgaistɐt] ✪ 34.3, 40.2, 41 ADJ enthusiastic (*von* about) ADV enthusiastically → *auch* **begeistern**

Be|geis|te|rung [bəˈgaistərʊŋ] F -, *no pl* enthusiasm (*über +acc* about, *für* for); **etw mit ~ tun** to do sth enthusiastically *or* with enthusiasm; **in ~ geraten** to become enthusiastic, to be filled with enthusiasm; **sich in ~ reden** to get carried away with what one is saying

Be|geis|te|rungs-: be|geis|te|rungs|fä|hig ADJ able to get enthusiastic; *Publikum etc* quick to show one's enthusiasm; **sie ist zwar ~, aber …** her enthusiasm is easily aroused but …; **Be|geis|te|rungs|fä|hig|keit** F capacity for enthusiasm; **ein Pessimist, dem jegliche ~ abgeht** a pessimist who never shows enthusiasm for anything; **Be|geis|te|rungs|sturm** M storm of enthusiasm; **Be|geis|te|rungs|tau|mel** M frenzy of enthusiasm

Be|gier [bəˈgiːɐ] F -, *no pl* (*liter*), **Be|gier|de** [bəˈgiːɐdə] F -, -n (*geh*) desire (*nach* for); (*= Sehnsucht*) longing, yearning; **vor ~ brennen, etw zu tun** to be longing *or* burning to do sth

be|gie|rig [bəˈgiːrɪç] ADJ (*= voll Verlangen*) hungry, greedy; (*= gespannt*) eager, keen; *Leser* avid;

auf etw (acc) **~ sein** to be eager for sth; **~ (darauf) sein, etw zu tun** to be eager or keen to do sth `ADV` (= verlangend) greedily; (= gespannt) eagerly

be|gie|ßen ptp **begossen** [bəˈgɔsn] VT irreg **a** (mit Wasser) to pour water on; Blumen, Beet to water; (mit Fett) Braten etc to baste → auch **begossen b** (fig inf) freudiges Ereignis, Vereinbarung to celebrate; **das muss begossen werden!** that calls for a drink!

Be|ginn [bəˈgɪn] M -(e)s, no pl beginning, start; **am** or **bei** or **zu ~** at the beginning; **mit ~ der Verhandlungen** at the beginning or start of the negotiations; **gleich zu ~** right at the beginning or start, at the very beginning or start

be|gin|nen [bəˈgɪnən] ✪ 53.1, 53.2 pret **begann** [bəˈgan], ptp **begonnen** [bəˈgɔnən] VI to start, to begin, to commence (form); (in Beruf etc auch) to start off; **mit einer Arbeit ~** to start or begin (to do) a job; **mit der Arbeit ~** to start or begin work; **es beginnt zu regnen** it's starting or beginning to rain; **er hat als Lehrling/mit nichts begonnen** he started (off) or began as an apprentice/with nothing
VT **a** (= anfangen) to start, to begin; Gespräch, Verhandlungen, Rede auch to open; **~, etw zu tun** to start or begin to do sth, to start doing sth **b** (= anpacken) Aufgabe etc to tackle, to go or set about **c** (geh: = unternehmen) to do; **ich wusste nicht, was ich ~ sollte** I didn't know what to do

Be|gin|nen [bəˈgɪnən] NT -s, no pl (geh: = Vorhaben) enterprise, plan, scheme

be|gin|nend ADJ attr incipient (form); **eine ~e Erkältung** the beginnings of a cold; **bei ~er Dämmerung/Nacht** at dusk/nightfall; **im ~en 19. Jahrhundert** in the early 19th century

be|glän|zen ptp **beglänzt** VT (poet) to light up, to illumine (poet)

be|glau|bi|gen [bəˈglaʊbɪgn] ptp **beglaubigt** VT **a** Testament, Unterschrift to witness; Zeugnisabschrift to authenticate; Echtheit to attest (to); **etw behördlich/notariell ~ lassen** to have sth witnessed etc officially/by a notary **b** Gesandten, Botschafter to accredit (bei to)

be|glau|bigt [bəˈglaʊbɪçt] ADJ certified; **~e Abschrift** certified copy; (als Vermerk) true copy → auch **beglaubigen**

Be|glau|bi|gung F -, -en **a** (von Testament, Unterschrift) witnessing; (von Zeugnisabschrift) authentication; (von Echtheit) attestation **b** (von Gesandtem, Botschafter) accrediting, accreditation (form)

Be|glau|bi|gungs|schrei|ben NT credentials pl

be|glei|chen ✪ 47.5 ptp **beglichen** [bəˈglɪçn] VT irreg (lit: = bezahlen) Rechnung, Zeche to settle, to pay; Schulden auch to discharge (form); (fig) Schuld to pay (off), to discharge; **mit Ihnen habe ich noch eine Rechnung zu ~** (fig) I've a score to settle with you

Be|glei|chung ✪ 47.5 F (von Rechnung, Zeche) settlement, payment; (von Schulden auch) discharging; **vollständige ~** payment in full; **teilweise ~** part (Brit) or partial (US) payment

be|gleit-: Be|gleit|ad|res|se F dispatch note; **Be|gleit|brief** M covering letter (Brit), cover letter (US); **Be|gleit|do|ku|men|te** PL accompanying documents pl

be|glei|ten ptp **begleitet** VT **a** (= mitgehen, mitfahren mit) to accompany; (zu Veranstaltung auch) to go/come with; (zum Schutz auch) to escort, to convoy; **esp Mil** auch to escort, to convoy; **er wurde stets von seinem Hund begleitet** his dog always went everywhere with him; **ein paar ~de Worte** a few accompanying words; **meine Wünsche ~ Sie** my best wishes go with you; **die Umstände** attendant or accompanying circumstances (form) **b** (Mus) to accompany (an or auf +dat on)

Be|glei|ter [bəˈglaɪtɐ] M -s, -, **Be|glei|te|rin** [-ərɪn] F -, -nen **a** companion (zum Schutz) es-

cort; (von Reisenden) courier; **ständiger ~** constant companion **b** (Mus) accompanist

Be|gleit-: Be|gleit|er|schei|nung F concomitant (form); (Med) side effect; **ist Jugendkriminalität eine ~ der Wohlstandsgesellschaft?** does juvenile delinquency go hand in hand with an affluent society?; **Be|gleit|fahr|zeug** NT escort vehicle; **Be|gleit|flug|zeug** NT escort plane; **Be|gleit|in|stru|ment** NT accompanying instrument; **Be|gleit|ma|te|ri|al** NT backup or accompanying material(s pl); **Be|gleit|mu|sik** F accompaniment; (in Film etc) incidental music; **Be|gleit|pa|pie|re** PL (Comm) accompanying documents pl; **Be|gleit|per|son** F escort; **die ~ eines Jugendlichen** the person accompanying a minor; **Be|gleit|per|so|nal** NT escort; **Be|gleit|schein** M dispatch note; **Be|gleit|schiff** NT (Mil) escort (ship); **Be|gleit|schrei|ben** NT covering letter (Brit), cover letter (US); (für Waren auch) advice note; **Be|gleit|schutz** M escort; **Be|gleit|text** M (accompanying) text; **Be|gleit|um|stän|de** PL attendant circumstances pl

Be|glei|tung [bəˈglaɪtʊŋ] F -, -en **a** no pl company; **er bot ihr seine ~ an** he offered to accompany or (zum Schutz auch) escort her; **in ~ seines Vaters** accompanied by his father; **in Peters ~** accompanied by Peter; **ich bin in ~ hier** I'm with someone **b** (= Begleiter) companion; (zum Schutz) escort; (= Gefolge) entourage, retinue; **ohne ~** unaccompanied **c** (Mus) (= Begleitmusik) accompaniment; (= das Begleiten auch) accompanying; (= Begleitstimme) harmony; **ohne ~ spielen** to play unaccompanied

be|glot|zen ptp **beglotzt** VT (inf) to goggle or gape at (inf), to gawp (Brit) or gawk at (inf)

be|glü|cken ptp **beglückt** VT jdn ~ to make sb happy; **er hat uns gestern mit seinem Besuch beglückt** (iro) he honoured (Brit) or honored (US) us with a visit yesterday; **Casanova hat tausende** or **Tausende von Frauen beglückt** (hum) Casanova bestowed his favours (Brit) or favors (US) upon thousands of women; **ein ~des Gefühl/Erlebnis** a cheering feeling/experience; **er ist sehr beglückt darüber** he's very happy or pleased about it; **beglückt lächeln** to smile happily

Be|glü|cker [bəˈglʏkɐ] M -s, - (liter, iro) benefactor; **er fühlt sich als ~ aller Frauen** (hum) he thinks he's God's gift (to women)

Be|glü|cke|rin [bəˈglʏkərɪn] F -, -nen (liter, iro) benefactress

be|glück|wün|schen [bəˈglʏkvʏnʃn] ptp **beglückwünscht** VT to congratulate, to offer one's congratulations (form) (zu on); **lass dich ~!** congratulations!

be|gna|den [bəˈgnaːdn] ptp **begnadet** VT (liter) to bless (liter), to endow; **ein begnadeter Künstler/Musiker** a gifted artist/musician

be|gna|di|gen [bəˈgnaːdɪgn] ptp **begnadigt** VT to reprieve, (= Strafe erlassen) to pardon

Be|gna|di|gung F -, -en reprieve; (= Straferlass) pardon; **um jds ~ ersuchen** to seek a reprieve (for sb)

Be|gna|di|gungs-: Be|gna|di|gungs|ge|such NT plea for (a) reprieve; **Be|gna|di|gungs|recht** NT right of reprieve

be|gnü|gen [bəˈgnyːgn] ptp **begnügt** VR **sich mit etw ~** to be content or satisfied with sth, to content oneself with sth; **sich damit ~, etw zu tun** to be content or satisfied with doing sth or to do sth, to content oneself with doing sth; **damit begnüge ich mich nicht** that doesn't satisfy me, I'm not satisfied with that

Be|go|nie [beˈgoːniə] F -, -n begonia

be|gon|nen ptp von **beginnen**

be|gos|sen ADJ **er stand da wie ein ~er Pudel** (inf) he looked that small, he looked so sheepish → auch **begießen**

be|gra|ben ptp **begraben** VT irreg **a** (= beerdigen) to bury; **dort möchte ich nicht ~ sein** (inf) I wouldn't like to be stuck in that hole (inf);

der kann sich ~ lassen (inf) he is worse than useless → **Hund a b** (= verschütten) to bury; **beim Einsturz begrub das Gebäude alle Bewohner unter sich** when the building collapsed all the residents were buried **c** (= aufgeben) Hoffnung, Wunsch to abandon, to relinquish; (= beenden) Streit, Angelegenheit, Feindschaft to end; **ein längst ~er Wunsch** a long-abandoned wish; **diese Angelegenheit ist längst ~** this matter was over (and done with) long ago

Be|gräb|nis [bəˈgrɛːpnɪs] NT -ses, -se burial; (= Begräbnisfeier) funeral

Be|gräb|nis-: Be|gräb|nis|fei|er F funeral (ceremony), obsequies pl (form); **Be|gräb|nis|kos|ten** PL funeral costs pl; **Be|gräb|nis|stät|te** F (geh) burial place

be|grab|schen VT (inf) to grope (inf)

be|gra|di|gen [bəˈgraːdɪgn] ptp **begradigt** VT to straighten

Be|gra|di|gung F -, -en straightening

be|grap|schen VT (inf) to grope (inf)

be|grast [bəˈgraːst] ADJ grassy, grass-covered

be|greif|bar ADJ conceivable

Be|greif|bar|keit [bəˈgraɪfbaːɐkaɪt] F -, no pl conceivability

be|grei|fen ptp **begriffen** [bəˈgrɪfn] irreg VT **a** (= verstehen) to understand; Aufgabe, Problemstellung, Zusammenhang to understand, to grasp, to comprehend; jdn, jds Handlung or Haltung to understand, to comprehend; Sinn, Notwendigkeit, (Schwierigkeit einer) Lage auch to see, to appreciate; **~, dass ...** (= einsehen) to realize that ...; **er begriff nicht, worum es ging** he didn't understand or comprehend what it was about; **hast du mich begriffen?** did you understand what I said?; **es ist kaum zu ~** it's almost incomprehensible; **es lässt sich leicht ~, dass ...** it's easy to understand that ...; **wie kann man Gott/die Unendlichkeit ~?** how can one comprehend God/infinity?; **ich begreife mich selbst nicht** I don't understand myself
b (= auffassen, interpretieren) to view, to see **c** (geh: = einschließen) **etw in sich** (dat) **~** to encompass or include sth **d** (dial: = anfassen) to touch
VI to understand, to comprehend; **leicht** or **schnell ~** to be quick on the uptake; **schwer** or **langsam ~** to be slow on the uptake
VR to be understandable; **eine solche Tat lässt sich nicht leicht ~** such an action cannot be easily understood → auch **begriffen**

be|greif|lich [bəˈgraɪflɪç] ADJ understandable; **es wird mir allmählich ~, warum ...** I'm beginning to understand why ...; **ich kann mich ihm nicht ~ machen** I can't make myself clear to him; **ich habe ihm das ~ gemacht** I've made it clear to him

be|greif|li|cher|wei|se ADV understandably

be|gren|zen ptp **begrenzt** VT **a** (= Grenze sein von) to mark or form the boundary of no pass; Horizont to mark; Straße etc to line; **das Gebiet wird durch einen** or **von einem Wald begrenzt** a forest marks or forms the boundary of the area **b** (= beschränken) to restrict, to limit (auf +acc to)

be|grenzt [bəˈgrɛntst] ADJ (= beschränkt) restricted, limited; (= geistig beschränkt) limited; **meine Aufenthaltsdauer ist nicht zeitlich ~** there's no time limit on (the length of) my stay; **eine genau ~e Aufgabe** a clearly defined task `ADV` (zeitlich) for a limited time; **sich nur ~ bewegen können** to be restricted in one's movements; **~ Einfluss nehmen** to exert limited influence

Be|grenzt|heit F -, no pl (von Menschen) limitations pl; **die ~ der Mittel/des Einkommens** the limited means/income; **die ~ ihres Talents** her limited talents

Be|gren|zung [bəˈgrɛntsʊŋ] F -, -en **a** (= das Begrenzen) (von Gebiet, Straße etc) demarcation; (von Horizont) marking; (von Geschwindigkeit, Redezeit) restriction **b** (= Grenze) boundary

Be|griff M **a** (*objektiv*) (= *Bedeutungsgehalt*) concept; (= *Terminus*) term; **etw in ~e fassen** to put sth into words; **in neuen ~en denken** to think in new terms; **sein Name ist mir ein/kein ~** his name means something/doesn't mean anything to me; **sein Name ist in aller Welt ein ~** his name is known all over the world; **ein ~ für Qualität!** a byword for quality

b (*subjektiv*: = *Vorstellung, Eindruck*) idea; **sein ~ von** or **der Freiheit** his idea or conception of freedom; **falsche ~e von etw haben** to have the wrong ideas about sth; **sich** (*dat*) **einen ~ von etw machen** to imagine sth; **du machst dir keinen ~ (davon)** (*inf*) you've no idea (about it) (*inf*); **das geht über meine ~e** that's beyond me; **es war über alle ~e schön** it was incredibly beautiful; **nach unseren heutigen ~en** by today's standards; **nach menschlichen ~en** in human terms; **für meine ~e** in my opinion

c **im ~ sein** or **stehen** (*form*), **etw zu tun** to be on the point of doing sth, to be about to do sth

d **schwer** or **langsam/schnell von ~ sein** (*inf*) to be slow/quick on the uptake; **sei doch nicht so schwer von ~!** (*inf*) don't be so dense (*inf*)

be|grif|fen ADJ **in etw** (*dat*) **~ sein** (*form*) to be in the process of doing sth; **ein noch in der Entwicklung ~er Plan** a plan still in the process of being developed → *auch* **begreifen**

be|griff|lich [bəˈɡrɪflɪç] ADJ **a** *attr* (= *bedeutungsmäßig*) conceptual; **~e Klärung** clarification of one's terms **b** (= *gedanklich, abstrakt*) abstract ADV **a** (= *bedeutungsmäßig*) conceptually; **~ bestimmen** to define (in clear terms); **~ ordnen** to arrange according to conceptual groups; **das Wort ist mir ~ unklar** the meaning of that word is not clear to me; **mit dem Wort kann ich ~ nichts anfangen** I have no idea what that word means **b** (= *gedanklich*) abstractly; **etw ~ erfassen** to understand sth in the abstract

Be|griff|lich|keit F -, -en **~en** (abstract) concepts

Be|griffs-: **Be|griffs|be|stim|mung** F definition; **Be|griffs|bil|dung** F formation of a concept/concepts; **Be|griffs|in|halt** M meaning; (*in der Logik*) connotation; **be|griffs|mä|ßig** ADJ conceptual; **be|griffs|stut|zig**, (*Aus*) **be|griffs|stüt|zig** [-ʃtʏtsɪç] ADJ ~ *attr* thick (*inf*); **Be|griffs|stut|zig|keit** F, *no pl* (*inf*) **von einer unglaublichen ~** unbelievably thick (*inf*); **~ mi|men** to act dumb (*inf*); **ich kann mir nur über deine ~ wundern** I can't believe how thick you are! (*inf*); **Be|griffs|sys|tem** NT system of concepts; **Be|griffs|ver|mö|gen** NT understanding; **das ging über ihr ~** that was beyond her grasp or understanding; **Be|griffs|ver|wir|rung** F confusion of concepts; (*von Termini*) confusion of terms; **Be|griffs|welt** F (*einer Person*) conceptual range

be|grün|den *ptp* **begründet** VT **a** (= *Gründe anführen für*) to give reasons for; (*rechtfertigend*) *Forderung, Meinung, Ansicht* to justify; *Verhalten* to account for; *Verdacht, Behauptung* to substantiate; **wie** or **womit begründete er seine Ablehnung?** how did he account for or justify his refusal?, what reason(s) did he give for his refusal?; **etw eingehend/näher ~** to give detailed/specific reasons for sth; **ein ~der Satz** (*Gram*) a causal clause → **begründet b** (= *beginnen, gründen*) to establish

Be|grün|der(in) M(F) founder

be|grün|det [bəˈɡrʏndət] ADJ well-founded; (= *berechtigt*) justified; (= *bewiesen*) *Tatsache etc* proven; **es besteht ~e/keine ~e Hoffnung, dass ...** there is reason/no reason to hope that ...; **das halte ich für nicht ~** I think that's unfounded/unjustified; **sachlich ~** founded on fact; **etw liegt** or **ist in etw** (*dat*) **~** sth has its roots in sth

Be|grün|det|heit F, *no pl* well-foundedness

Be|grün|dung ✪ 44.1 F **a** reason (*für*, +*gen* for), grounds *pl* (*für*, +*gen* for); (*von Anklage, Behauptung etc*) grounds *pl* (+*gen* for); **etwas zur**

or **als ~ sagen** to say something in explanation **b** (= *Gründung*) establishment; (*von Schule, Verein, Geschäft auch*) foundation; (*von Hausstand*) setting up

Be|grün|dungs|satz M (*Gram*) causal clause

be|grü|nen *ptp* **begrünt** VT *Hinterhöfe, Plätze* to cover with greenery, to landscape

be|grünt [bəˈɡryːnt] *ptp von* **begrünen** ADJ green; (= *bepflanzt*) planted with grass or trees, bushes *etc*; **~e Flächen** *pl* green areas *pl* or spaces *pl* → *auch* **begrünen**

Be|grü|nung [bəˈɡryːnʊŋ] F -, -en planting with trees and grass, landscaping

be|grü|ßen ✪ 31, 38.1, 38.2, 52.2 *ptp* **begrüßt** VT **a** *jdn* to greet; (*als Gastgeber*) to greet, to welcome; **jdn herzlich ~** to greet sb heartily, to give sb a hearty welcome; **es ist mir eine große Ehre, Sie bei mir ~ zu dürfen** (*form*) it's a great honour (*Brit*) or honor (*US*) to (be able to) welcome you here; **wir würden uns freuen, Sie bei uns ~ zu dürfen** (*form*) we would be delighted to have the pleasure of your company (*form*)

b (= *gut finden*) *Kritik, Entschluss etc* to welcome; (*esp iro, form*) to appreciate; **es ist zu ~, dass ...** it's a good thing that ...

c (*Sw*: = *um Erlaubnis fragen*) to ask (*um* for, *wegen* about)

be|grü|ßens|wert ADJ welcome; **es wäre ~, wenn ...** it would be desirable if ...

Be|grü|ßung [bəˈɡryːsʊŋ] F -, -en greeting; (*der Gäste*) (= *das Begrüßen*) welcoming; (= *Zeremonie*) welcome; **er nickte zur ~ mit dem Kopf** he nodded his head in greeting; **jdm einen Blumenstrauß zur ~ überreichen** to welcome sb with a bouquet of flowers; **jdm die Hand zur ~ reichen** to hold out one's hand to sb in welcome

Be|grü|ßungs-: **Be|grü|ßungs|an|spra|che** F welcoming speech; **Be|grü|ßungs|for|mel** F welcoming words *pl*, words *pl* of welcome; (*Anrede*) salutation; **Be|grü|ßungs|kuss** ▲ M welcoming kiss; **Be|grü|ßungs|trank** M welcoming drink; **Be|grü|ßungs|worte** PL welcoming words *pl*, words *pl* of welcome

be|gu|cken *ptp* **beguckt** VT (*inf*) to look at; **lass dich mal ~** let's (have or take a) look at you!

be|güns|ti|gen [bəˈɡʏnstɪɡn] *ptp* **begünstigt** VT **a** (= *förderlich sein für*) to favour (*Brit*), to favor (*US*); *Wachstum, Handel* to encourage; *Pläne, Beziehungen* to further; (*Jur*) to aid and abet; **vom Schicksal begünstigt** smiled upon by fate; **durch die Dunkelheit begünstigt** assisted by the darkness **b** (= *bevorzugen*) *jdn* ~ to favour (*Brit*) or favor (*US*) sb; **von jdm begünstigt werden** to be favo(u)red by sb, to be shown favo(u)r by sb

Be|güns|tig|te(r) [bəˈɡʏnstɪçtə] MF *decl as adj* (*Jur*) beneficiary

Be|güns|ti|gung F -, -en **a** (*Jur*) aiding and abetting; **persönliche ~** aiding and abetting; **sachliche ~** (acting as an) accessory; **im Amt** connivance **b** (= *Bevorzugung*) preferential treatment; (= *Vorteil*) advantage **c** (= *Förderung*) favouring (*Brit*), favoring (*US*); (*von Wachstum, Handel*) encouragement; (*von Plänen, Beziehungen*) furthering

be|gut|ach|ten *ptp* **begutachtet** VT (= *beurteilen, Gutachten abgeben*) to give expert advice about; *Kunstwerk, Stipendiaten* to examine; *Projekte, Leistung* to judge; *Gelände, Haus* to survey; (*inf*: = *ansehen*) to have or take a look at; **etw ~ lassen** to get or obtain expert advice about sth

Be|gut|ach|ter(in) M(F) expert; (*von Haus, Gelände*) surveyor

Be|gut|ach|tung [bəˈɡuːtʔaxtʊŋ] F -, -en (expert) assessment; (*von Haus, Gelände*) survey; (= *das Begutachten*) surveying; **psychologische/grafologische** *etc* **~** (expert) psychological/graphological *etc* assessment

be|gü|tert [bəˈɡyːtɐt] ADJ **a** (*dated*: = *Landgüter besitzend*) landed *attr*, propertied **b** (= *reich*) wealthy, affluent; **die ~e Klasse/Schicht** the rich *pl*

be|gü|ti|gen [bəˈɡyːtɪɡn] *ptp* **begütigt** VT to pacify, to placate, to appease

be|gü|ti|gend ADJ *Worte etc* soothing ADV soothingly; **~ auf jdn einreden** to calm sb down

be|haart [bəˈhaːɐt] ADJ hairy, hirsute; **stark ~** very hairy; **dicht ~** (thickly) covered with hair; **schwarz ~** covered with black hair

Be|haa|rung [bəˈhaːrʊŋ] F -, -en covering of hair, hairs *pl* (+*gen, an* +*dat* on)

be|hä|big [bəˈhɛːbɪç] ADJ **a** *Mensch* portly; (= *phlegmatisch, geruhsam*) stolid; (*fig*) *Leben, Möbel, Auto* comfortable; *Architektur* solid; *Sprache, Ton* complacent **b** (*old liter, Sw*: = *wohlhabend*) well-to-do, affluent ADV **a** (*breit und*) **~ herumsitzen** to sit on one's fat backside (*inf*)

Be|hä|big|keit F -, *no pl* (*von Mensch*) portliness; (= *Geruhsamkeit*) stolidity; (*von Architektur*) solidness; (*von Sprache, Ton*) complacency

be|haf|tet [bəˈhaftət] ADJ **mit etw ~ sein** (*mit Krankheit etc*) to be afflicted with sth; *mit Fehlern, Vorurteilen etc* to be full of sth; *mit einer schweren Last, mit Sorgen, Schulden etc* to be encumbered with sth; *mit Makel* to be tainted with sth

be|ha|gen [bəˈhaːɡn] *ptp* **behagt** VI **etw behagt jdm** sth pleases sb, sb likes sth; **etw behagt jdm nicht** (*nicht gefallen*) sth doesn't please sb, sb doesn't like sth; (= *beunruhigen*) sb feels uneasy about sth; **er behagt ihr nicht** she doesn't like him

Be|ha|gen [bəˈhaːɡn] NT -s, *no pl* contentment; **mit sichtlichem ~** with visible or obvious pleasure; **mit ~ essen** to eat with relish or pleasure

be|hag|lich [bəˈhaːklɪç] ADJ cosy; (= *heimelig auch*) snug, homely; (= *bequem*) comfortable; (= *zufrieden*) contented ADV (= *gemütlich*) comfortably; (= *genussvoll*) contentedly; **~ warm** comfortably warm; **es sich** (*dat*) **~ machen** to make oneself comfortable; **~ in der Sonne sitzen** to sit comfortably in the sun; **die Katze streckte sich ~** the cat stretched contentedly

Be|hag|lich|keit F -, *no pl* cosiness; (= *Heimeligkeit auch*) snugness, homeliness; (= *Bequemlichkeit*) comfort; (= *Zufriedenheit*) contentment

be|hal|ten *ptp* **behalten** VT *irreg* **a** (= *nicht weggeben, nicht zurückgeben*) to keep **b** (= *lassen, wo es ist*) to keep; **~ Sie (doch) Platz!** please don't get up!; **den Hut auf dem Kopf ~** to keep one's hat on; **jdn an der Hand ~** to keep hold of sb's hand; **der Kranke kann nichts bei sich ~** the patient can't keep anything down → **Auge a**

c (= *nicht verlieren*) to keep; *Wert auch* to retain; **die Ruhe ~** to keep one's cool (*inf*); **die Nerven ~** to keep one's nerve (*Brit*), to keep one's nerves under control (*US*); **wenn wir solches Wetter ~** if this weather lasts → **Fassung c, Kopf d, Zügel** *etc*

d (= *nicht vergessen*) to remember; **im Gedächtnis/im Kopf ~** to remember, to keep in one's head; **er behielt die Melodie im Ohr** he kept the tune in his head; **ich habe die Zahl/seine Adresse nicht ~** I've forgotten the number/his address

e (= *nicht weitersagen*) **etw für sich ~** to keep sth to oneself

f (= *nicht weggehen lassen*) to keep; *Mitarbeiter* to keep on; **jdn bei sich ~** to keep sb with one; **einen Gast zum Abendbrot bei sich ~** to invite a guest to stay to (*esp Brit*) or for supper

g (= *nicht aufgeben*) *Stellung, Namen, Staatsangehörigkeit* to keep; **sie muss immer ihren Willen ~** she always has to have her own way

h (= *aufbewahren, versorgen*) *Kinder, Katze, Gegenstand* to look after; (= *nicht wegwerfen*) *Briefe etc* to keep; **jdn/etw in guter/schlechter Erinnerung ~** to have happy/unhappy memories of sb/sth → **Andenken a**

i (= *zurückbehalten, nicht loswerden*) to be left

with; *Schock, Schaden* to suffer; **vom Unfall hat er ein steifes Knie ~** after the accident he was left with a stiff knee

Be|häl|ter [bə'hɛltɐ] M **-s, -** **a** container, receptacle (*form*) **b** (= *Container*) container

Be|häl|ter|schiff NT container ship

be|häm|mern *ptp* **behämmert** VT (*lit, fig*) to hammer

be|häm|mert [bə'hɛmɐt] ADJ (*inf*) screwy (*inf*)

be|händ [bə'hɛnt] ▲, **be|hän|de** ▲ [bə'hɛndə] (*geh*) ADV (= *flink*) swiftly, quickly; (= *gewandt*) nimbly, agilely ADJ (= *flink*) swift, quick; (= *gewandt*) nimble, agile

be|han|deln *ptp* **behandelt** VT **a** *Material, Stoff, Materie* to treat **b** *Thema, Frage, Problem, Antrag* to deal with **c** (= *in bestimmter Weise umgehen mit*) to treat; (= *verfahren mit*) to handle; **jdn/etw gut/schlecht ~** to treat sb/sth well/badly; **er weiß, wie man Kinder/die Maschine ~ muss** he knows how to handle children/the machine; **eine Angelegenheit diskret ~** to treat or handle a matter with discretion; **jdn/etw ungeschickt ~** to handle sb/sth clumsily **d** (*ärztlich*) *Patienten, Krankheit* to treat; *Zähne* to attend to; **jdn/etw operativ ~** to operate on sb/sth; **der ~de Arzt** the doctor in attendance

be|hän|di|gen [bə'hɛndɪɡn] *ptp* **behändigt** VT (*Sw: = an sich nehmen*) to take; (= *stehlen auch*) to steal

Be|hän|dig|keit ▲ [bə'hɛndɪçkait] F **-**, *no pl* (*geh*, = *Flinkheit*) swiftness, quickness; (= *Gewandtheit*) nimbleness, agility

Be|hand|lung F **a** (*von Material*) treatment **b** (*von Frage, Problem*) treatment; **wir sind jetzt bei der ~ dieses Themas** we are now dealing with this subject; **um schnelle ~ des Antrags wird gebeten** please deal with the application as quickly as possible **c** (= *Umgang mit Menschen*) treatment; (*von Angelegenheit*) handling; **die schlechte ~ seiner Frau und Kinder** the ill-treatment or maltreatment of his wife and children **d** (*ärztlich*) treatment; (*von Zähnen*) attention (+*gen* to); **waren Sie deswegen schon früher in ~?** have you had treatment or been treated for this before?; **bei wem sind Sie in ~?** who's treating you?

Be|hand|lungs-: Be|hand|lungs|art F type of treatment; **be|hand|lungs|be|dürf|tig** ADJ in need of treatment; **Be|hand|lungs|form** F form of treatment; **Be|hand|lungs|kos|ten** PL cost *sing* of treatment; **Be|hand|lungs|me|tho|de** F (method of) treatment; **Be|hand|lungs|raum** M treatment room; **Be|hand|lungs|schein** M (= *Krankenschein*) health insurance certificate; (= *Überweisungsschein*) referral (note); **Be|hand|lungs|stuhl** M doctor's chair; (*von Zahnarzt*) dentist's chair; **Be|hand|lungs|ver|fah|ren** NT therapy; **Be|hand|lungs|wei|se** F treatment; **Be|hand|lungs|zim|mer** NT consulting room, surgery (*Brit*), (doctor's) office (*US*)

be|hand|schuht [bə'hantʃuːt] ADJ gloved

Be|hang M **a** curtain; (= *Wandbehang*) hanging; (= *Schmuck*) decorations *pl*; **der Birnbaum hat einen guten ~** the pear tree promises a good crop **b** (*Hunt: von Hund*) lop-ears *pl*

be|hän|gen *ptp* **behängt** or **behangen** VT to decorate; *Wände auch* to hang VR (*pej*) to deck oneself out (**mit** in or with)

be|har|ken *ptp* **beharkt** VT (*inf*) to set about (*inf*), to have a go at (*inf*) VR to have a go at each other (*inf*)

be|har|ren [bə'harən] *ptp* **beharrt** VI **a** (= *hartnäckig sein*) to insist (**auf** +*dat* on); (= *nicht aufgeben*) to persist, to persevere (**bei** in) **b** (= *bleiben*) **in etw** (*dat*) **~** (*in Zustand*) to persist in sth; (*an Ort*) to remain in sth

Be|har|ren NT **-s**, *no pl* **a** (*auf Meinung, Anrecht etc*) insistence (**auf** on); (= *Ausdauer*) persistence, perseverance (**bei** in) **b** (= *das Bleiben*) (*in* +*dat* in) (*in Zustand*) persistence, perseverance; (*an Ort*) remaining

be|harr|lich [bə'harlıç] ADJ (= *hartnäckig*) insistent; (= *ausdauernd*) persistent; *Glaube, Liebe* steadfast, unwavering; **~er Fleiß** perseverance ADV (= *hartnäckig*) insistently; (= *ausdauernd*) persistently; *glauben* steadfastly; **~ fortfahren, etw zu tun** to persist in doing sth

Be|harr|lich|keit F **-**, *no pl* (= *Hartnäckigkeit*) insistence; (= *Ausdauer*) persistence; (*von Glaube, Liebe*) steadfastness

Be|har|rung F **-**, *no pl* (*Phys*) inertia

Be|har|rungs|ver|mö|gen NT (*Phys*) inertia

be|hau|chen *ptp* **behaucht** VT to breathe on; (*Ling*) to aspirate; **behauchte Laute** (*Ling*) aspirates

be|hau|en *ptp* **behauen** VT *irreg Holz* to hew; *Stein* to cut; (*mit dem Meißel*) to carve

be|haup|ten [bə'hauptn] ✪ 42.3, 53 *ptp* **behauptet** VT **a** (= *sagen*) to claim; (= *bestimmte Aussage aufstellen*) to maintain; **steif und fest ~** to insist; **von jdm ~, dass ...** to say of sb that ...; **es wird behauptet, dass ...** it is said or claimed that ... **b** (= *erfolgreich verteidigen*) *Stellung, Recht* to maintain; *Meinung* to assert; *Markt* to keep one's share of → **Feld e** VR to assert oneself; (*bei Diskussion*) to hold one's own or one's ground (**gegenüber, gegen** against); **sich auf dem Markt ~** to maintain one's hold on the market

Be|haup|tung ✪ 53.6 F **-, -en** **a** claim; (= *esp unerwiesene Behauptung*) assertion **b** (= *Aufrechterhaltung*) assertion; (*von Stellung*) successful defence (*Brit*) or defense (*US*) **c** (= *das Sichbehaupten*) assertion; **die ~ der Firma auf dem Markt** the firm's ability to maintain its hold on the market

Be|hau|sung [bə'hauzʊŋ] F **-, -en** **a** *no pl* (*liter*: = *das Behausen*) accommodation, housing **b** (*geh, hum*: = *Wohnung*) dwelling

Be|ha|vi|o|ris|mus [biheviaˈrɪsmʊs] M **-**, *no pl* behaviourism (*Brit*), behaviorism (*US*)

Be|ha|vi|o|rist [biheviaˈrɪst] M **-en, -en**, **Be|ha|vi|o|ris|tin** [-ˈrɪstɪn] F **-, -nen** behaviourist (*Brit*), behaviorist (*US*)

be|ha|vi|o|ris|tisch [biheviaˈrɪstɪʃ] ADJ behaviouristic (*Brit*), behavioristic (*US*)

be|he|ben *ptp* **behoben** [bə'hoːbn] VT *irreg* **a** (= *beseitigen*) to remove; *Mängel, Missstände* to rectify, to remedy; *Schaden* to repair, to put right; *Störung* to clear **b** (*Aus: = abheben*) *Geld* to withdraw

Be|he|bung F **-**, *no pl* **a** (= *Beseitigung*) removal; (*von Mangel, Missstand*) rectification, remedying; (*von Schaden*) repairing, putting right; (*von Störung*) clearing **b** (*Aus: von Geld*) withdrawal

be|hei|ma|ten [bə'haimatn] *ptp* **beheimatet** VT to find a home for

be|hei|ma|tet [bə'haimatət] ADJ (= *ansässig*) resident (*in* +*dat* in); (= *heimisch*) *Pflanze, Tier, Volk* indigenous, native (*in* +*dat* to); **wo sind Sie ~?** where is your home?; **eine in Schottland ~e Pflanze** a plant (that is) indigenous to Scotland

be|heiz|bar ADJ heatable; *Heckscheibe, Außenspiegel* heated

be|hei|zen *ptp* **beheizt** VT to heat

Be|hei|zung F **-**, *no pl* heating

Be|helf [bə'hɛlf] M **-(e)s, -e** **a** (= *Ersatz*) substitute; (= *Notlösung*) makeshift; **als ~ dienen** to serve or act as a substitute/makeshift **b** (*Jur*: = *Rechtsbehelf*) (legal) remedy

be|hel|fen *ptp* **beholfen** [bə'hɔlfn] VR *irreg* **a** (= *Ersatz verwenden*) to manage, to make do; **sich mit Ausreden ~** to resort to excuses; **sich mit Ausflüchten ~** to be evasive **b** (= *auskommen*) to manage, to get by; **er weiß sich allein**

nicht zu ~ he can't manage alone, he can't get by alone

Be|helfs- *in cpds* temporary; **Be|helfs|aus|fahrt** F (*auf Autobahn*) temporary exit; **Be|helfs|bau** F **-s, -bauten** temporary building; (*improvisiert*) makeshift building; **Be|helfs|heim** NT temporary accommodation; **be|helfs|mä|ßig** ADJ makeshift; (*zeitlich begrenzt*) *Straßenbelag, Ausweis* temporary ADV temporarily; **etw ~ reparieren** to make makeshift repairs to sth; **Be|helfs|maß|nah|men** PL stopgap or temporary or emergency measures *pl*; **Be|helfs|un|ter|kunft** F temporary accommodation *no pl*; (*für Notfall auch*) emergency accommodation *no pl*; **be|helfs|wei|se** ADV temporarily; **er hat sich ~ eingerichtet** his furnishings are only makeshift

be|hel|li|gen [bə'hɛlɪɡn] *ptp* **behelligt** VT to bother

Be|hel|li|gung F **-, -en** bother *no pl*; **jds ~ mit Fragen** (= *das Behelligen*) bothering sb with questions; (= *das Behelligtwerden*) sb being bothered with questions

be|helmt [bə'hɛlmt] ADJ helmeted

be|hend △ [bə'hɛnt], **be|hen|de** △ [bə'hɛndə] → **behänd**

Be|hen|dig|keit △ [bə'hɛndɪçkait] F **-**, *no pl* → **Behändigkeit**

be|her|ber|gen [bə'hɛrbɛrɡn] *ptp* **beherbergt** VT (*lit, fig*) to house; *Gäste* to accommodate

Be|her|ber|gung F **-, -en** housing; (= *Unterkunft*) accommodation

Be|her|ber|gungs|ge|wer|be NT hotel trade, (tourist) accommodation industry

be|herr|schen *ptp* **beherrscht** VT **a** (= *herrschen über*) to rule, to govern; (*fig: Gefühle, Vorstellungen haben*) to dominate **b** (*fig: = das Übergewicht haben*) *Stadtbild, Landschaft, Ebene, Markt* to dominate → **Feld d, Szene a c** (= *zügeln*) to control; *Zunge* to curb **d** (= *gut können*) *Handwerk, Sprache, Instrument, Tricks, Spielregeln* to master **e** (= *bewältigen*) *Situation* to have control of VR to control oneself; **ich kann mich ~!** (*iro inf*) not likely! (*inf*) → *auch* **beherrscht**

be|herr|schend [bə'hɛrʃənt] ADJ (*fig: = vorherrschend*) dominating; **~es Thema der Verhandlungen war ...** topic number one or the leading topic of the talks was ... → *auch* **beherrschen**

Be|herr|scher(in) M(F) (*liter*) ruler

be|herrscht [bə'hɛrʃt] ADJ (*fig*) self-controlled ADV with self-control → *auch* **beherrschen**

Be|herrscht|heit F **-**, *no pl* (*fig*) self-control

Be|herr|schung [bə'hɛrʃʊŋ] F **-**, *no pl* control; (= *Selbstbeherrschung*) self-control; (*des Markts*) domination; (*eines Fachs*) mastery; **die ~ verlieren** to lose one's temper

be|her|zi|gen [bə'hɛrtsɪɡn] *ptp* **beherzigt** VT to take to heart, to heed

Be|her|zi|gung F **-**, *no pl* heeding; **dies zur ~!** (*old*) heed this!, take heed!

be|herzt [bə'hɛrtst] (*geh*) ADJ courageous, brave ADV courageously, bravely

Be|herzt|heit F **-**, *no pl* (*geh*) courage, bravery

be|he|xen *ptp* **behext** VT to bewitch

be|hielt *pret von* **behalten**

be|hilf|lich [bə'hɪlflɪç] ADJ helpful; **jdm (bei etw) ~ sein** to help sb (with sth)

be|hin|dern *ptp* **behindert** VT to hinder; *Sicht* to impede; (*bei Sport, im Verkehr*) to obstruct; **jdn bei etw ~** to hinder sb in sth

be|hin|dert ADJ (*mit einer Behinderung*) disabled; **geistig/körperlich ~** mentally/physically handicapped **b** (*sl*: = *blöd*) stupid; **~es Auto** shitheap (*sl*); **ein ~er Typ** a tosser (*sl*)

Be|hin|der|ten-: Be|hin|der|ten|ar|beit F work with the disabled; **Be|hin|der|ten|aus|weis** M *disabled person card or ID*; **be|hin|der|ten|ge|recht** ADJ adapted to the needs of the disabled; **etw ~ umbauen/gestalten** to alter/design sth to fit the needs of the disabled; **Be|hin|der|ten|olym|pi|a|de** F Paralympics pl; **Be|hin|der|ten|sport** M disabled sport; **Be|hin|der|ten|toi|let|te** F disabled or handicapped toilet, toilet for the disabled or handicapped; **Be|hin|der|ten|werk|statt** F sheltered workshop

Be|hin|der|te(r) [bəˈhɪndətə] MF decl as adj disabled or handicapped person/man/woman; **die ~n** the handicapped pl or disabled pl

Be|hin|de|rung F hindrance; (im Sport, Verkehr) obstruction; (körperlich, = Nachteil) handicap; **mit ~en muss gerechnet werden** delays or hold-ups are likely to occur

Be|hör|de [bəˈhøːɐdə] F -, -n authority usu pl; (= Amtsgebäude) office usu pl; **die ~n** the authorities; **die zuständige ~** the appropriate or proper authorities

Be|hör|den-: Be|hör|den|ap|pa|rat M (pej) administrative machinery, bureaucratic machine, bureaucracy; **Be|hör|den|deutsch** NT (pej) (German) officialese (pej); **Be|hör|den|gang** M visit to the authorities; **Be|hör|den|spra|che** F bureaucratic language; **Be|hör|den|un|we|sen** NT sprawling bureaucracy; **Be|hör|den|ver|tre|ter(in)** M(F) official; **Be|hör|den|weg** M administrative procedure; **auf dem ~** following the proper administrative channels; **Be|hör|den|we|sen** NT bureaucracy; **Be|hör|den|will|kür** F **die deutsche ~** the arbitrary nature of German authorities

be|hörd|lich [bəˈhøːɐtlɪç] ADJ official ADV officially

be|hörd|li|cher|seits [bəˈhøːɐtlɪçɐzaits] ADV (form) by the authorities; (= auf behördlicher Seite) on the part of the authorities

Be|huf [bəˈhuːf] M (old form) **zu diesem ~** to this end, for this purpose

be|huft [bəˈhuːft] ADJ hoofed

be|hü|ten ptp **behütet** VT (= beschützen, bewachen) to look after; (esp Engel etc) to watch over; **jdn vor etw** (dat) ~ to save or protect sb from sth; **(Gott) behüte!** (inf) God or Heaven forbid!; **behüt dich Gott!** (old, S Ger) (may) God be with you! → auch **behütet**

Be|hü|ter [bəˈhyːtɐ] M -s, -, **Be|hü|te|rin** [-ərɪn] F -, -nen (geh) protector, (Frau auch) protectress

be|hü|tet [bəˈhyːtət] ADJ Mädchen carefully brought up; Jugend, Alltag sheltered ADV ~ **aufwachsen** to have a sheltered upbringing → auch **behüten**

be|hut|sam [bəˈhuːtzaːm] ADJ cautious, careful; (= zart auch) gentle ADV carefully; streicheln gently; **man muss es ihr ~ beibringen** it will have to be broken to her gently

Be|hut|sam|keit F -, no pl care(fulness), cautiousness; (= Zartheit auch) gentleness; (= Feingefühl) delicacy

bei [bai]

PRÄPOSITION (+dat)

a ⟨Nähe⟩ near; **sie wohnt beim Rathaus** she lives near the town hall; **wir treffen uns beim Leuchtturm/bei der Kirche** we'll meet by the lighthouse/the church; **dicht bei dem Ort, wo ...** very near the place where ...; **die Völkerschlacht bei Leipzig** the Battle of the Nations near Leipzig; **Altdorf bei Nürnberg** Altdorf near Nuremberg; **ich stand/saß bei ihm** I stood/sat beside him or next to him; **er bot sich an, beim Gepäck zu bleiben** he offered to stay by the luggage; **ich bleibe bei den Kindern, dann kannst du einkaufen** I'll stay with the children so you can go shopping; **bei X schneiden sich die beiden Geraden** the two lines bisect at X; **der Wert liegt bei tausend Euro** the value is around a thousand euros; **nicht bei sich sein** (inf) to be out of one's mind (inf)

b ⟨Aufenthalt⟩ at; **ich war bei meiner Tante** I was at my aunt's; **ich bin bei Gabriele zum Kaffee eingeladen** I'm invited to Gabriele's for coffee;

er wohnt bei seinen Eltern he lives with his parents; **bei jdm übernachten** to spend the night at sb's; **bei Müller** (auf Briefen) care of or c/o Müller; **bei uns zu Hause** (im Haus) at our house; (im Land, in Familie) at home, back home (US); **bei uns in Deutschland** in Germany; **bei uns fängt man um 8 Uhr zu arbeiten an** (here) we start work at 8 o'clock; **bei uns ist um 12.30 Uhr Mittagspause** we have our lunch break at 12.30; **bei jdm arbeiten** to work for sb; **bei Siemens angestellt sein** to work at Siemens; **er ist or arbeitet bei der Post** he works for the post office; **beim Film/Fernsehen sein** to be in films/TV; **beim Fleischer/Friseur** at the butcher's/hairdresser's; **beim Militär** in the army; **ein Konto bei der Bank** an account at the bank; **bei Collins erschienen** published by Collins; **bei jdm Unterricht haben** to have lessons with sb; **bei Shakespeare liest man ...** Shakespeare says ...; **ich habe keine Taschentücher bei mir** I haven't got a hanky; **hast du Geld bei dir?** have you any money with or on you?; **bei Tisch** at table

c ⟨Berührung⟩ by; **er nahm mich bei der Hand** he took me by the hand; **jdn beim Arm/bei den Schultern packen** to grab sb by the arm/shoulder

d = zusammen mit among; **bei den Briefen lag auch das Schreiben mit meiner Kündigung** among the letters was one giving me notice; **bei meiner Post sind immer mehr Rechnungen als Privatbriefe** there are always more bills than letters in my mail

e ⟨Teilnahme⟩ at; **bei einer Hochzeit sein** to be at a wedding; **bei einer Aufführung anwesend sein** to be present at a performance; **bei einer Ausstellungseröffnung eine Rede halten** to give a speech at the opening of an exhibition; **machst du bei der Demonstration mit?** are you taking part in the demonstration?; **ich habe bei der Party mitgeholfen** I helped with the party; **er hat bei der Aufführung der Elektra mitgewirkt** he took part in the performance of Elektra

f = betreffend **bei ihm ist es 8 Uhr** he makes it or he has (US) 8 o'clock; **bei mir ist Schluss für heute** I've had enough for today; **das war bei ihm der Fall** that was the case with him; **man weiß nicht, woran man bei ihm ist** (inf) you never know where you are with him; **bei mir hast du damit kein Glück** you won't get anywhere with me; **bei Kühen findet man Maul- und Klauenseuche** you get foot-and-mouth in cows; **bei Franzosen isst man die Schnecken mit Knoblauchbutter** the French eat snails with garlic butter → **weit 2 f, Wort g, Name**

g ⟨Zeit⟩ **beim letzten Ton des Zeitzeichens ...** at the last pip ...; **beim letzten Gewitter** during the last storm; **bei meiner Ankunft** on my arrival; **Vorsicht bei der Abfahrt** (des Zuges)! stand clear, the train is about to leave!; **beim Erwachen** on waking; **beim Erscheinen der Königin** when the queen appeared; **bei Beginn und Ende der Vorstellung** at the beginning and end of the performance; **bei Nacht** by night; **bei Tag** by day; **bei Tag und Nacht** day and night

h ⟨Umstand⟩ **bei dieser Schlacht** in or during this battle; **bei dem Zugunglück starben viele Menschen** a lot of people died in the train crash; **ich habe ihm beim Arbeiten or bei der Arbeit geholfen** I helped him with the work; **bei der Arbeit solltest du keine Musik hören** you shouldn't listen to music while you're working; **beim Fernsehen stricken** to knit while watching television; **er verliert beim Kartenspiel immer** he always loses at cards; **ich gehe gerne bei Regen spazieren** I love walking in the rain; **bei Kerzenlicht essen** to eat by candlelight; **bei offenem Fenster schlafen** to sleep with the window open; **etw bei einer Flasche Wein bereden** to discuss sth over a bottle of wine; **bei zehn Grad unter null** when it's ten degrees below zero; **das Schönste bei der Sa-**

che the best thing about it; **bei guter Gesundheit sein** to be in good health → **Bewusstsein b, Kraft a, Verstand** etc

i ⟨Bedingung⟩ in case of; **bei Feuer Scheibe einschlagen** in case of fire break glass; **bei Gefahr Notbremse ziehen** in case of emergency pull the communication cord; **bei Nebel und Glatteis muss man vorsichtig fahren** when there is fog and ice you have to drive carefully; **bei Regen findet die Veranstaltung im Saale statt** if it rains the event will take place in the hall; **bei einer Erkältung sollte man sich warm halten** when you've got a cold you should keep warm

j ⟨Grund⟩ with; **bei seinem Talent** with his talent; **bei dieser Sturheit/so vielen Schwierigkeiten** with this stubbornness/so many difficulties; **bei reiflicher Überlegung** upon mature reflection; **bei solcher Hitze braucht man sich nicht zu wundern, dass niemand auf der Straße ist** when it's as hot as this it's no wonder there's nobody in the streets

k ⟨Einschränkung⟩ in spite of, despite; **bei aller Vorsicht** in spite of or despite all one's caution; **bei all seinen Bemühungen hat er es trotzdem nicht geschafft** despite all his efforts he still didn't manage it; **es geht beim besten Willen nicht** with the best will in the world, it's not possible

l ⟨in Schwurformeln⟩ by; **bei Gott** by God; **bei meiner Ehre** (up)on my honour (Brit) or honor (US); **beim Zeus!** by Jove!

bei+be|hal|ten ptp **beibehalten** VT sep irreg to keep; Bräuche, Regelung auch to retain; Leitsatz, Richtung to keep to; Gewohnheit to keep up

Bei|be|hal|tung F , no pl keeping; (von Bräuchen, Regelung auch) retention; (von Leitsatz, Richtung) keeping to; (von Gewohnheit) keeping up

bei+bie|gen VT sep irreg **jdm etw ~** (inf) to get sth through to sb (inf)

Beibl. abbr von **Beiblatt**

Bei|blatt NT (Press) insert, supplement

Bei|boot NT (Naut) dinghy

bei+brin|gen VT sep irreg **a** **jdm etw ~** (= mitteilen) to break sth to sb; (= zu verstehen geben) to get sth across to sb, to get sb to understand sth **b** (= unterweisen in) to teach (jdm etw sb sth) **c** (= zufügen) Verluste, Wunde, Niederlage, Schläge to inflict (jdm etw sth on sb) **d** (= herbeischaffen) to produce; Dokumente, Beweis, Geld etc to furnish, to supply

Bei|brin|gung [ˈbaibrɪŋʊŋ] F -, no pl (von Verlusten, Wunde, Niederlage) infliction; (= das Herbeischaffen) production; (von Dokumenten, Beweis, Geld) furnishing, supplying

Beich|te [ˈbaiçtə] F -, -n confession; **zur ~ gehen** to go to confession; **(bei jdm) die ~ ablegen** to make one's confession (to sb); **eine ~ ablegen** (fig) to make a confession; **jdm die ~ abnehmen** to hear sb's confession; **~ hören** or **sitzen** (inf) to hear or take confession

beich|ten [ˈbaiçtn̩] (lit, fig) VT to confess (jdm etw sth to sb) VI to confess; **~ gehen** to go to confession

Beicht-: Beicht|for|mel F form of words used at confession; **Beicht|ge|heim|nis** NT seal of confession or of the confessional; **das ~ wahren** to observe the seal of confession or of the confessional; **beicht+hö|ren** VI sep (inf, Aus) to hear confession; **Beicht|sie|gel** NT = **Beichtgeheimnis; Beicht|stuhl** M confessional; **Beicht|va|ter** M father confessor; **Beicht|zet|tel** M (= Aufstellung) list of sins; (= Bescheinigung) absolution

beid-: beid|ar|mig ADJ with both arms; Lähmung of or in both arms ADV **ein ~ gelähmter Mann** a man paralyzed in both arms; **er war ~ amputiert** he had had both arms amputated; **beid|bei|nig** ADJ with both legs; Lähmung of or in both legs; Absprung double-footed ADV **~ abspringen** to take off with both feet; **ein ~ ge-**

lähmter Mann a man paralyzed in both legs; **er war ~ amputiert** he had had both legs amputated

bei|de ['baidə] PRON **a** (adjektivisch) (ohne Artikel) both; (mit Artikel) two; **alle ~n Teller** both plates; **seine ~n Brüder** both his brothers, his two brothers; **~ Mal** both times **b** (als Apposition) both; **ihr ~(n)** the two of you; **euch ~** the two of you; **euch ~n herzlichen Dank** many thanks to both of you; **wer von uns ~n?** which of us (two); **wie wärs denn mit uns ~n?** (inf) how about it? (inf) **c** (substantivisch) (ohne Artikel) both (of them); (mit Artikel) two (of them); **alle ~** both (of them); **alle ~ wollten gleichzeitig Geld haben** both of them or they both wanted money at the same time; **keiner/keines** etc **von ~n** neither of them; **ich habe ~ nicht gesehen** I haven't seen either of them, I've seen neither of them **d** **~s** (substantivisch: zwei verschiedene Dinge) both; **(alles) ~s ist erlaubt** both are permitted

bei|de|mal △ ['baidəmaːl] ADV → beide a

bei|der-: bei|der|lei ['baidəlai] ADJ attr inv both; **bei|der|sei|tig** ['baidəzaitıç] ADJ (= auf beiden Seiten) on both sides; (= gegenseitig) Abkommen, Vertrag etc bilateral; Versicherungen, Einverständnis etc mutual; **bei|der|seits** ['baidə-zaits] ADV on both sides; **sie haben ~ versichert ...** they have given mutual assurances or assurances on both sides ... PREP +gen on both sides of

Bei|der|wand ['baidəvant] F OR NT -(e)s [-dəs] no pl (Tex) linsey-woolsey

Beid-: beid|fü|ßig ADJ two-footed; Absprung double-footed ADV **~ abspringen** to take off with both feet; **Beid|hän|der¹** ['baithɛndɐ] M -s, - (= Schwert) two-handed sword; **Beid|hän|der²** ['baithɛndɐ] M -s, -, **Beid|hän|de|rin** [-ərɪn] F -, -nen ambidextrous person; **beid|hän|dig** ADJ (= mit beiden Händen gleich geschickt) ambidextrous; (= mit beiden Händen zugleich) two-handed ADV **~ schießen/schreiben können** to be able to shoot/write with either hand or both hands

bei+dre|hen VI sep (Naut) to heave to

beid-: beid|sei|tig ['baitzaitıç] ADJ (= auf beiden Seiten) on both sides; (= gegenseitig) mutual; **~e Zufriedenheit** satisfaction on both sides; mutual satisfaction ADV on both sides; **beid|seits** ['baitzaits] PREP +gen (Sw, S Ger) on both sides of

bei|ei|nan|der [bai.ai'nandɐ] ADV together

bei|ei|nan|der: bei|ei|nan|der ha|ben ▲ VT irreg (inf) to have together; **du hast sie nicht richtig** or **alle beieinander** you can't be all there (inf); **bei|ei|nan|der hal|ten** ▲ VT irreg to keep together; **bei|ei|nan|der sein** ▲ VI irreg aux sein (inf) (gesundheitlich) to be in good shape (inf); (geistig) to be all there (inf); **gut ~** to be in good shape; to be all there; (S Ger: = dick sein) to be a bit chubby (inf); **Bei|ei|nan|der-sein** NT being together no art; (von Gruppe) get-together

Bei|fah|rer(in) M(F) (Aut) (front-seat) passenger; (bei einem Motorrad) im Beiwagen) sidecar passenger; (auf dem Soziussitz) pillion rider or passenger; (= berufsmäßiger Mitfahrer, Sport) co-driver

Bei|fah|rer-: Bei|fah|rer|air|bag M (Aut) passenger airbag; **Bei|fah|rer|platz** M passenger seat; **Bei|fah|rer|sitz** M passenger seat; (auf Motorrad) pillion

Bei|fall M , no pl (= Zustimmung) approval; (= das Händeklatschen) applause; (= Zuruf) cheering, cheers pl; **~ finden** to meet with approval; **~ heischend** looking for approval; (= Applaus wollend) looking for applause; **~ spenden/klatschen/klopfen** etc to applaud; **~ spendend** applauding

bei|fall|hei|schend △ ADJ → Beifall

bei|fäl|lig ADJ approving; **~e Worte/Laute** words/noises of approval ADV approvingly; **er**

---

nickte **~ mit dem Kopf** he nodded his head approvingly or in approval; **dieser Vorschlag wurde ~ aufgenommen** this suggestion was favourably (Brit) or favorably (US) received, this suggestion met with approval

Bei|falls-: Bei|falls|äu|ße|rung F expression of (one's) approval; **Bei|falls|be|kun|dung** F show or demonstration of (one's) approval; **Bei|falls|be|zei|gung** [-bətsaigʊŋ] F -, -en, **Bei|falls|kund|ge|bung** F applause no pl

bei|fall|spen|dend △ ADJ → Beifall

Bei|falls-: Bei|falls|ruf M cheer; **Bei|falls-sturm** M storm of applause

Bei|fang M , no pl (Fishing) unwanted catch

Bei|fang|quo|te F (Fishing) quota of unwanted catch

Bei|film M supporting film

bei|fü|gen VT sep (= mitschicken) to enclose (+dat with); (= beiläufig sagen) to add

Bei|fü|gung F a no pl (form) enclosure; **unter ~ eines Fotos** enclosing a photo **b** (Gram) attribute

Bei|fü|gungs|satz M (Gram) attributive clause

Bei|fuß M , no pl (Bot) mugwort

Bei|fut|ter NT supplementary fodder

Bei|ga|be F **a** (= das Beigeben) addition; **eine ~ von etw empfehlen** to recommend adding sth, to recommend the addition of sth; **unter ~ eines Löffels Senf** adding a spoonful of mustard **b** (= Beigefügtes, Begleiterscheinung) addition; (= Beilage: Gemüse, Salat etc) side dish; (Comm: = Zugabe) free gift; (= Grabbeigabe) burial gift

beige [beːʃ, 'beːʒə, 'bɛːʒə] ADJ (geh: inv) beige

Beige¹ [beːʃ, 'beːʒə, 'bɛːʒə] NT -, - or (inf) -s beige

Beige² ['baigə] F -, -n (S Ger, Aus, Sw) pile

bei+ge|ben sep irreg VT (= zufügen) to add (+dat to); (= mitgeben) jdn to assign (jdm to sb) VI **klein ~** (inf) to give in

bei|ge|bun|den ['baigəbʊndn] ADJ (Typ) bound in

beige|far|ben ['baigəfarbn-, 'beːʒə-, 'bɛːʒə-] ADJ beige(-coloured) (Brit), beige(-colored) (US)

bei+ge|hen VI sep irreg aux sein (dial) to start

bei|ge|ord|net ADJ (Gram) Nebensatz coordinate → auch beiordnen

Bei|ge|ord|ne|te(r) ['baigəʔɔrdnətə] MF decl as adj (town) councillor (Brit), councilor (US)

Bei|ge|schmack M aftertaste; (fig: von Worten) flavour (Brit), flavor (US); **es hat einen unangenehmen ~** (lit, fig) it has a nasty or an unpleasant taste (to it)

bei+ge|sel|len ptp beigesellt sep (geh) VT **ihr wurde ein Beschützer beigesellt** she was provided with an escort VR **sich jdm ~** to join sb

Beig|net [bɛn'jeː] M -s, -s (Cook) fritter

Bei|heft NT supplement; (= Lösungsheft) answer book

bei+hef|ten VT sep to append, to attach

Bei|hil|fe F **a** (= finanzielle Unterstützung) financial assistance no indef art; (= Zuschuss, Kleidungsbeihilfe) allowance; (für Arztkosten) contribution; (= Studienbeihilfe) grant; (= Subvention) subsidy **b** (Jur) abetment; **wegen ~ zum Mord** because of being an or acting as an accessory to the murder

bei|hil|fe|fä|hig ADJ (form) → Beihilfe eligible for financial assistance/a contribution/contributions etc

bei+ho|len VT sep (Naut) to take in (the sail)

Bei|jing [beɪ'dʒɪŋ] NT -s Beijing, Peking

Bei|klang M (lit) (accompanying) sound; (fig) overtone usu pl

bei+kom|men VI sep irreg aux sein **a jdm ~** (= zu nahe bekommen) to get hold of sb; (= fertig werden mit) to get the better of sb; **einer Sache** (dat) **~** (= bewältigen) to deal with sth **b** (old inf: = einfallen) **jdm ~** to occur to sb; **lass dir das**

---

ja nicht ~! don't even think of it! **c** (dial: = herkommen) to come **d** (dial: = heranreichen) **ich komme da nicht bei** I can't reach it

Bei|kost F supplementary diet

Beil [bail] NT -(e)s, -e axe (Brit), ax (US); (kleiner) hatchet; (= Fleischerbeil) cleaver; (zum Hinrichten) axe (Brit), ax (US); (= Fallbeil) blade (of a/the guillotine)

beil. abbr von beiliegend

bei+la|den VT sep irreg **a** Ladung to add (+dat to) **b** (Jur) to call in

Bei|la|dung F **a** (= das Beiladen) additional loading; (= zusätzliche Ladung) extra or additional load **b** (Jur) calling in; **notwendige ~** subpoena

Bei|la|ge F **a** (= Gedrucktes) insert; (= Beiheft) supplement **b** (= das Beilegen) enclosure; (in Buch) insertion; (Aus: = Anlage zu Brief) enclosure **c** (Cook) side dish; (= Gemüsebeilage) vegetables pl; (= Salatbeilage) side salad; **Erbsen und Kartoffeln als ~ zum Hähnchen** chicken with peas and potatoes

Bei|la|ger NT (Hist) consummation; (obs: = Beischlaf) sexual relations pl

bei|läu|fig ADJ **a** casual; Bemerkung, Erwähnung casual, passing attr **b** (Aus: = ungefähr) approximate ADV **a** (= nebenbei) erwähnen, bemerken casually, in passing **b** (Aus) approximately, about

Bei|läu|fig|keit F -, -en **a** (in Benehmen etc) casualness; (= Nebensächlichkeit) triviality; **mit einer erstaunlichen ~** amazingly casually **b** Beiläufigkeiten PL trivia pl

bei+le|gen VT sep **a** (= hinzulegen) to insert (+dat in); (einem Brief, Paket) to enclose (+dat with, in) **b** (= beimessen) to attribute, to ascribe (+dat to); **einer Sache** (dat) **Bedeutung** or **Gewicht/Wert ~** to attach importance/value to sth **c** (= schlichten) to settle **d** (Naut: = anlegen) to moor

Bei|le|gung ['bailegʊŋ] F -, -en (= Schlichtung) settlement

bei|lei|be [bai'laibə] ADV **~ nicht!** certainly not; **das darf ~ nicht passieren** that mustn't happen under any circumstances; **~ kein ...** by no means a ..., certainly no ...

Bei|leid ♦ 51.4 NT condolence(s), sympathy; **jdm sein ~ aussprechen** or **ausdrücken** or **bezeigen** to offer sb one's condolences, to express one's sympathy with sb; **mein ~!** (iro) you have my sympathy!

Bei|leids- in cpds of condolence or sympathy; **Bei|leids|be|kun|dung** F expression of sympathy; **Bei|leids|be|such** M visit of condolence; **Bei|leids|be|zei|gung** [-bətsaigʊŋ] F -, -en, **Bei|leids|be|zeu|gung** F expression of sympathy; (Brief, Telegramm etc) condolence(s); **Bei|leids|kar|te** F sympathy or condolence card; **Bei|leids|schrei|ben** NT letter of condolence

Bei|hieb M blow with or from an axe (Brit) or ax (US)

bei+lie|gen VI sep irreg **a** (= beigefügt sein) to be enclosed (+dat with, in); (einer Zeitschrift etc) to be inserted (+dat in) **b** (Naut) to lie to **c** (obs) **jdm ~** to lie with sb (obs)

bei|lie|gend ADJ enclosed ADV enclosed; **~ senden wir Ihnen ...** please find enclosed ...

beim [baim] contr von bei dem

bei+ma|chen VR sep (dial) to get down to it

bei+men|gen VT sep to add (+dat to)

bei+mes|sen VT sep irreg **jdm/einer Sache Bedeutung** or **Gewicht/Wert ~** to attach importance/value to sb/sth

bei+mi|schen VT sep to add (+dat to); **unserer Freude war eine leichte Traurigkeit beigemischt** our joy was tinged with sadness

Bei|mi|schung F addition; **eine leichte ~ von ...** (fig) a touch of ...

Bein [bain] NT **-(e)s, -e** [a] leg; **mit übereinander geschlagenen ~en** cross-legged; **von einem ~ aufs andere treten** to shift from one leg or foot to the other; **sich kaum auf den ~en halten können** to be hardly able to stay or stand on one's feet; **er ist noch gut auf den ~en** he's still sprightly; **schwach auf den ~en sein** to be a bit shaky; **jdm ein ~ stellen** (lit, fig) to trip sb up; **jdm wieder auf die ~e helfen** (lit, fig) to help sb back on his feet; **auf den ~en sein** (= nicht krank, in Bewegung) to be on one's feet; (= unterwegs sein) to be out and about; **sich auf die ~e machen** (inf) to make tracks (inf); **jdm ~e machen** (inf) (= antreiben) to make sb get a move on (inf); (= wegjagen) to make sb clear off (inf); **die ~ unter dem Arm** or **in die Hand nehmen** (inf) to take to one's heels; **meine Tasche hat ~e bekommen** (fig) my bag has vanished into thin air, my bag seems to have grown legs and walked; **sich** (dat) **die ~e in den Bauch** or **Leib stehen** (inf) to stand around until one is fit to drop (inf); **mit beiden ~en im Leben** or **auf der Erde stehen** (fig) to have both feet (firmly) on the ground; **mit einem ~ im Grab stehen** (fig) to have one foot in the grave; **mit einem ~ im Gefängnis stehen** (fig) to be likely to end up in jail; **das steht auf schwachen ~en** (fig) that isn't very sound; **auf eigenen ~en stehen** (fig) to be able to stand on one's own two feet; **auf einem ~ kann man nicht stehen!** (fig inf) you can't stop at one!; **er fällt immer wieder auf die ~e** (fig) he always falls on his feet; **wieder auf die ~e kommen** (fig) to get back on one's feet again; **jdn wieder auf die ~e bringen** or **stellen** (fig) to get sb back on his/her feet again; **etw auf die ~e stellen** (fig) to get sth off the ground; Geld etc **to raise sth; die ~e breit machen** (sl: zum Geschlechtsverkehr) to spread one's legs (sl); **sich** (dat) **etw ans ~ binden** (fig) to saddle oneself with sth; **jdn/etw am ~ haben** (fig inf) to have sb/sth (a)round one's neck (inf) → **ausreißen** VT, **Knüppel, Lüge, Klotz**
[b] (= Knochen) bone; **der Schreck ist ihm in die ~e gefahren** the shock went right through him; **Fleisch am ~** (old) meat on the bone → **Stein c, Mark** [1]
[c] (= Elfenbein) ivory
[d] (dial: = Fuß) foot

bei|nah [ˈbaina:, ˈbaiˈna:], **bei|na|he** [ˈbaina:ə, ˈbaiˈna:ə, bainaˈ] ADV almost, nearly; **~(e) in allen Fällen, in ~(e) allen Fällen** in almost or nearly every case; **das kommt ~(e) auf dasselbe heraus** that comes to almost or nearly the same thing

Bei|na|he|ka|ta|stro|phe F near disaster or catastrophe

Bei|na|he|zu|sam|men|stoß M (Aviat) near miss

Bei|na|me M epithet; (= Spitzname) nickname

Bein-: Bein|am|pu|ta|ti|on F leg amputation; **bein|am|pu|tiert** [-lamputi:ɐt] ADJ with an amputated leg/amputated legs; **~ sein** to have had a leg/both legs amputated; **Bein|am|pu|tier|te** [-lamputi:ɐtə](r) MF decl as adj leg amputee; **Bein|ar|beit** F (Sport) footwork; (beim Schwimmen) legwork; **Bein|bruch** M fracture of the leg; **das ist kein ~** (fig inf) it could be worse (inf) → **Hals- und Beinbruch**

bei|nern [ˈbainen] ADJ (= aus Knochen) made of bone; (= aus Elfenbein) ivory

Bein|frei|heit F , no pl legroom

be|in|hal|ten [bəˈɪnhaltn] ptp **beinhaltet** VT insep (form) to comprise

bein|hart ADJ Mensch hard as nails; Erde, Piste, Kuchen rock-hard; Wettstreit, Kampf fierce; Geschäft very hard; Druck, Stress intense; Argument, Bemerkung scathing ADV verhandeln, spielen fiercely; **die Gewerkschaft ging den Minister ~ an** the union gave the minister a rough ride; **~ gegen Schuldner vorgehen** to give debtors a rough time or ride; **die Vertragsbedingungen sind ~ formuliert** the terms of the contract are really harsh

Bein|haus NT charnel house

-bei|nig [bainɪç] ADJ suf -legged; **zweibeinig** two-legged

Bein-: Bein|kleid NT usu pl (old, hum) breeches pl (old); **Bein|ling** [ˈbainlɪŋ] M **-s, -e** leg; **Bein|pro|the|se** F artificial leg; **Bein|raum** M leg room; **Bein|schie|ne** F (Hist) greave; (Sport) shin pad; (bei Cricket) (leg) pad; (Med) splint; **Bein|schüt|zer** [-ʃʏtsɐ] M (Sport) shin pad; **Bein|stumpf** M stump

bei+ord|nen VT sep [a] (Gram) to coordinate → auch **beigeordnet** [b] (= beigeben) **jdm/einer Sache beigeordnet sein** to be assigned to sb/appointed to sth; **bei einer Prüfung beigeordnet sein** to sit in on an examination

Bei|pack M additional consignment or order; (= Frachtgut) part load (zu with)

bei+pa|cken VT sep to enclose; Frachtgut to add (+dat to)

Bei|pack|zet|tel M instruction leaflet; (= Inhaltsverzeichnis) list (Brit) or table of contents

bei+pflich|ten VI sep **jdm/einer Sache in etw** (dat) **~** to agree with sb/sth on sth

Bei|pro|gramm NT supporting programme (Brit) or program (US)

Bei|rat[1] M (= Körperschaft) advisory council or committee or body

Bei|rat[2] M , **Bei|rä|tin** F adviser

Bei|rat|schaft F [ˈbaira:tʃaft] F **-, -en** (Sw Jur) (legal) care and protection

Bei|ried [ˈbairi:t] NT **-s**, no pl (Aus: Cook) piece of beef loin

be|ir|ren [bəˈɪrən] ptp **beirrt** VT (= verwirren) to disconcert; **sich nicht in etw** (dat) **~ lassen** to not let oneself be shaken or swayed in sth; **sich (durch etw) ~/nicht ~ lassen** to let/not to let oneself be put off (by sth); **er lässt sich nicht ~** he won't be put off; **nichts konnte ihn (in seinem Vorhaben) ~** nothing could shake him (in his intentions)

bei|sam|men [baiˈzamən] ADV together

bei|sam|men- PREF together; **bei|sam|men+blei|ben** VI sep irreg aux sein (inf) Gruppe, Leute etc to stay or remain together; **bei|sam|men+ha|ben** VT sep irreg (inf) Geld, Leute to have got together; **seine Gedanken ~** to have one's wits about one; **seinen Verstand** or **seine fünf Sinne ~** to have all one's wits about one; **(sie) nicht alle ~** not to be all there; **Bei|sam|men|le|ben** NT , no pl living together; **bei|sam|men sein** ▲ VI irreg aux sein (fig) (körperlich) to be in good shape; (geistig) to be all there; **gut ~** to be in good shape; (= kräftig gebaut sein) to be well built; **Bei|sam|men|sein** NT get-together

Bei|sas|se [ˈbaizasə] M **-n, -n** (Hist) citizen without full civic rights

Bei|satz M (Gram) appositive

bei+schaf|fen VT sep (dial) to bring

bei+schie|ßen VT sep irreg (inf) to chip in with (inf)

Bei|schlaf M (Jur) sexual intercourse or relations pl

bei+schla|fen VI sep irreg (form) to have sexual intercourse or relations (+dat with)

bei+schlie|ßen VT sep irreg (Aus) to enclose (+dat with)

Bei|schluss ▲ M (Aus) enclosure; **unter ~ von ... enclosing ...**

Bei|se|gel NT studdingsail

Bei|sein NT presence; **in jds ~** in sb's presence; **ohne jds ~** without sb being present

bei|sei|te [baiˈzaitə] ADV aside (auch Theat); treten, gehen, stehen auch to one side; **legen lassen** auch on one side; **Spaß** or **Scherz ~!** joking aside or apart!; **jdn/etw ~ schaffen** or **bringen** to get rid of sb/hide sth away

Bei|sei|te|schaf|fung F removal

Bei|sel [ˈbaizl] NT **-s, -n** (Aus inf) pub (Brit), bar

bei+set|zen VT sep [a] (= beerdigen) to inter (form), to bury; Urne to install (in its resting place) [b] (Naut) Segel to set, to spread [c] (old) = zusetzen

Bei|set|zung [ˈbaizɛtsʊŋ] F **-, -en** funeral; (von Urne) installing in its resting place

Bei|set|zungs|fei|er|lich|kei|ten PL funeral ceremony sing, obsequies pl (form)

bei+sit|zen VI sep irreg (in Versammlung) to attend; (einem Ausschuss) to have a seat (+dat on), to sit (+dat on); (bei Prüfung) to sit in (bei on)

Bei|sit|zer [ˈbaizɪtsɐ] M **-s, -**, **Bei|sit|ze|rin** [-ərɪn] F **-, -nen** [a] (Jur) assessor [b] (= Ausschussmitglied) committee member; (bei Prüfung) observer

Bei|sl [ˈbaizl] NT **-s, -n** (Aus inf) pub (Brit), bar

Bei|spiel ✪ 53.1, 53.5 NT example; **zum ~ for** example or instance; **wie zum ~** such as; **jdm als ~ dienen** to be an example to sb; **jdm ein ~ geben** to set sb an example; **sich** (dat) **ein ~ an jdm nehmen** to take a leaf out of sb's book; **sich** (dat) **ein ~ an etw** (dat) **nehmen** to take sth as an example; **mit gutem ~ vorangehen** to set a good example

Bei|spiel-: bei|spiel|ge|bend ADJ exemplary; **~ für etw sein** to serve as an example for sth; **bei|spiel|haft** ADJ exemplary ADV exemplarily; **bei|spiel|hal|ber** ADV (= als Beispiel) by way of example; (= zum Beispiel) for example, for instance; **bei|spiel|los** ADJ unprecedented; (= unerhört) outrageous; **Bei|spiel|satz** M example

bei|spiels|hal|ber ADV (= als Beispiel) by way of example; (= zum Beispiel) for example, for instance

bei|spiels|wei|se ADV for example or instance

bei+sprin|gen VI sep irreg aux sein **jdm ~** to rush to sb's aid; (mit Geldbeträgen) to help sb out

bei|ßen [ˈbaisn] pret **biss** [bɪs], ptp **gebissen** [gəˈbɪsn] VTI to bite; (= brennen: Geschmack, Geruch, Schmerzen) to sting; (= kauen) to chew; **in den Apfel ~** to bite into the apple, to take a bite out of the apple; **ich kann dieses Brot nicht ~** this bread is too hard for me; **der Hund hat mich** or **mir ins Bein gebissen** the dog has bitten my leg or me in the leg; **der Rauch/Wind beißt in den Augen/mich in die Augen** (inf) the smoke/wind makes one's/my eyes sting; **er wird dich schon nicht ~** (fig) he won't eat or bite you; **etwas/nichts zu ~** (inf: = essen) something/nothing to eat; **an etw** (dat) **zu ~ haben** (fig) to have sth to chew over (Brit) or on → **Gras**

VR (Farben) to clash; **sich** (acc or dat) **auf die Zunge/Lippen ~** to bite one's tongue/lips; **sich in den Arsch ~** (vulg) or **Hintern** (sl) ~ to kick oneself (inf)

bei|ßend ADJ (lit, fig) biting; Wind auch, Bemerkung cutting; Geschmack, Geruch pungent, sharp; Schmerz gnawing; Ironie, Hohn, Spott bitter

Bei|ßer|chen [ˈbaisɐçən] PL (baby-talk) toothy-pegs pl (baby-talk)

Beiß-: Beiß|korb M (für Hunde) muzzle; **Beiß|ring** M teething ring; **Beiß|zan|ge** [ˈbais-] F (pair of) pincers pl or pliers pl; (pej inf) shrew; **das würde ich nicht mit der ~ anfassen** or **anpacken** (inf) I wouldn't touch that with a barge pole (Brit inf) or a 10-foot pole (US inf)

Bei|stand M [a] no pl (= Hilfe) help, assistance; (= Unterstützung) support; (von Priester) attendance, presence; **jdm ~ leisten** to give sb help or assistance; to give or lend sb one's support; to attend sb [b] (Jur) legal adviser or representative; (in Duell) aid, representative, second; **einen ~ stellen** (Jur) to appoint a legal adviser or representative

Beistands-: Bei|stands|ab|kom|men NT , **Bei|stands|pakt** M mutual assistance pact;

Bei|stands|ver|trag M treaty of mutual assistance

bei+ste|hen VI sep irreg jdm ~ to stand by sb

bei+stel|len VT sep **a** (= daneben stellen) to put or place beside **b** (Aus: = zur Verfügung stellen) (+dat for) to make available, to provide **c** (Rail: = bereitstellen) to put on

Bei|stell-: Bei|stell|herd M auxiliary cooker (Brit) or kitchen range **b** (US); **Bei|stell|mö|bel** PL occasional (Brit) or extra (US) furniture sing; **Bei|stell|tisch** M occasional table

bei+steu|ern VT sep to contribute

bei+stim|men VI sep = **zustimmen**

Bei|strich M (esp Aus) comma

Bei|tel ['baitl] M -s, - chisel

Bei|trag ['baitraːk] M -(e)s, ⁻e [-treːɡə] **a** (= Anteil) contribution; (= Aufsatz auch) article; **einen ~ zu etw leisten** to make a contribution to sth, to contribute to sth **b** (= Betrag) contribution; (= Versicherungsbeitrag) premium; (= Mitgliedsbeitrag) fee (Brit), dues pl

bei+tra|gen VTI sep irreg to contribute (zu to); (= mithelfen auch) to help (zu to); **das trägt nur dazu bei, die Lage zu verschlimmern** that only helps to make the position worse

Bei|trags-: Bei|trags|be|mes|sungs|gren|ze F (Insur) income threshold (for insurance contributions); **Bei|trags|er|hö|hung** F increase in contributions, premium increase, increased contributions pl or premiums pl; **bei|trags|frei** ADJ noncontributory; Person not liable to pay contributions; **Bei|trags|frei|heit** F non--liability to pay contributions; **Bei|trags|grup|pe** F, **Bei|trags|klas|se** F insurance group; (bei Verein etc) class of membership; **Bei|trags|mar|ke** F stamp; **Bei|trags|pflicht** F liability to pay contributions; **bei|trags|pflich|tig** [-pflɪçtɪç] ADJ Arbeitsentgelt contributory; ~ **sein** (Mensch) to have to pay contributions; **Bei|trags|rück|er|stat|tung** F contribution or premium refund; **Bei|trags|rück|stand** M arrears pl; **Bei|trags|satz** M membership rate; **Bei|trags|schlüs|sel** M, **Bei|trags|sys|tem** NT contributory system; **Bei|trags|zah|len|de(r)** [-tsaːləndə] MF decl as adj, **Bei|trags|zah|ler(in)** M(F) contributor; **Bei|trags|zah|lung** F premium or contribution payment, payment of the contribution or of contributions

bei+trei|ben VT sep irreg Steuern to collect; Schulden auch to recover; (esp Jur) to enforce (the) payment of

Bei|trei|bung ['baitraibʊŋ] F -, -en (Jur) collection

bei+tre|ten VI sep irreg aux sein +dat to join; einem Pakt, Abkommen to enter into; einem Vertrag to accede to

Bei|tritt M joining (zu etw sth); (zu einem Pakt, Abkommen) agreement (zu to); (zu einem Vertrag) accession (zu to); **seinen ~ erklären** to become a member

Bei|tritts-: Bei|tritts|er|klä|rung F confirmation of membership; **Bei|tritts|ge|such** NT application for membership; **Bei|tritts|ver|hand|lun|gen** PL membership talks pl or negotiations pl

Bei|wa|gen M **a** (beim Motorrad) sidecar **b** (dated: = Anhänger) carriage

Bei|wa|gen|ma|schi|ne F (inf: = Motorrad mit Beiwagen) (motorcycle) sidecar combination

Bei|werk NT additions pl; (bei Aufsatz etc) details pl; (modisch) accessories pl

bei+wil|li|gen ['baivɪlɪgn] VI sep (Sw) = **zustimmen**

bei+woh|nen VI sep +dat (geh) **a** (= dabei sein) to be present at **b** (dated euph) to have sexual relations with

Bei|woh|nung F **a** (form: = Anwesenheit) presence **b** (Jur) intimacy no art

Bei|wort NT pl -wörter **a** (= Adjektiv) adjective **b** (= beschreibendes Wort) epithet

Beiz [baits] F -, -en (Sw, S Ger: inf) pub (Brit), bar

Bei|ze¹ ['baitsə] F -, -n **a** (= Beizmittel) corrosive fluid; (= Metallbeize) pickling solution, pickle; (= Holzbeize) stain; (zum Gerben) lye; (= Tabakbeize) sauce; (Agr) disinfectant; (= Färbemittel, Typ) mordant; (Cook) marinade **b** (= das Beizen) steeping in a/the corrosive fluid etc **c** (Hunt) hawking

Bei|ze² F -, -n (dial) pub (Brit), bar

bei|zei|ten [bai'tsaitn] ADV in good time

bei|zen ['baitsn] VT **a** Holz to stain; Häute to bate, to master; Tabak to steep in sauce; Saatgut to disinfect, to treat; Kupfer to etch; Metal to pickle; (Cook) to marinate **b** (Hunt) to hawk

bei+zie|hen ['baitsiːən] VT sep irreg (esp S Ger, Aus, Sw) Experten etc to call in; Bücher, Unterlagen to consult

Bei|zie|hung ['baitsiːʊŋ] F -, -en usu sing (von Experten etc) consultation, consulting (+gen a/an)

Beiz-: Beiz|jagd F hawking, falconry; **Beiz|mit|tel** NT = Beize¹ a; **Beiz|vo|gel** M falcon, hawk

be|ja|gen VT (Hunt) Wild to hunt; Gebiet to hunt in

be|ja|hen [bə'jaːən] ptp **bejaht** **VT** to answer in the affirmative; (= gutheißen) to approve of; **das Leben ~** to have a positive attitude toward(s) life **VI** to answer in the affirmative

be|ja|hend ADJ positive, affirmative; Einstellung positive **ADV** affirmatively; **etw ~ beantworten** (form) to answer sth in the affirmative

be|jahrt [bə'jaːɐt] ADJ elderly, advanced in years

Be|ja|hung F -, -en affirmative answer (+gen to); (= Gutheißung) approval

Be|ja|hungs|fall M (form) im ~**e** in the event of an affirmative answer

be|jam|mern ptp **bejammert** VT to lament; Schicksal, Los auch to bewail (liter); jdn to lament for

be|jam|merns|wert, **be|jam|merns|wür|dig** (rare) ADJ deplorable, lamentable; Mensch pitiable; Schicksal pitiable, dreadful

be|ju|beln ptp **bejubelt** VT to cheer; Ereignis to rejoice at; **sie wurden als Befreier bejubelt** they were acclaimed as liberators

be|ka|keln [bə'kaːkln] ptp **bekakelt** VT (N Ger inf) to talk over, to discuss

be|kal|men [bə'kalmən] ptp **bekalmt** VT (Naut) to becalm

be|kam pret von **bekommen**

be|kämp|fen ptp **bekämpft** VT to fight; (fig auch) to combat; Ungeziefer to control; **sich gegenseitig ~** to fight one another

Be|kämp|fung [bə'kɛmpfʊŋ] F -, (rare) -en fight, battle (von, -gen against); (von Ungeziefer) controlling; **zur ~ der Terroristen** to fight or combat the terrorists

Be|kämp|fungs|mit|tel NT (= Insektenbekämpfungsmittel) pesticide, insecticide; (= Unkrautbekämpfungsmittel) weedkiller

be|kannt [bə'kant] ADJ **a** (= allgemein gekannt, gewusst) well-known (wegen for); Mensch auch famous; **die ~eren Spieler** the better-known or more famous players; **die ~esten Spieler** the best-known or most famous players; **wie ist er ~ geworden?** how did he become famous?; **sie ist in Wien ~** she is (well-)known in Vienna; **er ist ~ dafür, dass er seine Schulden nicht bezahlt** he is well-known for not paying his debts; **das ist mir ~** I know about that; **sie ist mir ~** I know her, she is known to me; **es ist allgemein/durchaus ~, dass ...** it is common knowledge/a known fact that ...; **ich darf diese Tatsachen als ~ voraussetzen** I assume that these facts are known **b** (= nicht fremd) familiar; **jdn mit etw ~ machen** (mit Aufgabe etc) to show sb how to do sth; mit Gebiet, Fach etc to introduce sb to sth; mit Problem to familiarize sb with sth; **sich mit etw ~ machen** to familiarize or acquaint oneself with sth; **jdn/sich (mit jdm) ~ machen** to introduce sb/oneself (to sb); **wir sind miteinander ~** we already know each other, we have already met → auch **bekennen**

Be|kann|ten|kreis M circle of acquaintances

Be|kann|te(r) [bə'kantə] MF decl as adj friend; (= entfernter Bekannter) acquaintance

be|kann|ter|ma|ßen [bə'kantɐ'maːsn] ADV (form) as is known

Be|kannt|ga|be F announcement; (in Zeitung etc) publication

be|kannt ge|ben ▲ ✿ 51.2, 51.3 VT irreg to announce; (in Zeitung etc) to publish; **ihre Verlobung geben bekannt ...** the engagement is announced between ...

Be|kannt|heit F -, no pl fame; (von Fakten) knowledge; **aufgrund der ~ dieser Tatsachen** because these facts are known

Be|kannt|heits|grad M **einen hohen/niedrigen ~ haben** to be well-known/little-known

be|kannt|lich [bə'kantlɪç] ADV ~ **gibt es ...** it is known that there are ...; **er hat ~ eine Schwäche für Frauen** he is known to have a weakness for women; **London ist ~ die Hauptstadt Englands** London is known to be the capital of England

be|kannt ma|chen ▲ VT to announce; (= der Allgemeinheit mitteilen) to publicize → auch **bekannt b**

Be|kannt|ma|chung [bə'kantmaxʊŋ] F -, -en **a** (= das Bekanntmachen) announcement; (= Veröffentlichung) publicizing **b** (= Anschlag etc) announcement, notice

Be|kannt|schaft [bə'kantʃaft] F -, -en **a** (= das Bekanntwerden) acquaintance; (mit Materie, Gebiet) knowledge (mit of); **jds ~ machen** to make sb's acquaintance; **mit etw ~ machen** to come into contact with sth; **bei näherer ~** on closer acquaintance **b** (inf: = Bekannte) acquaintance; **meine ganze ~** all my acquaintances; **ich habe gestern eine nette ~ gemacht** I met a nice person yesterday

Be|kannt|schafts|an|zei|ge F personal ad; ~**n** pl (Zeitungsrubrik) personal ads pl or column sing, lonely hearts column sing (inf)

be|kannt wer|den ▲ VI irreg aux sein to become known; (Geheimnis) to leak out

be|keh|ren ptp **bekehrt** **VT** to convert (zu to); **VR** to be(come) converted (zu to); **er hat sich endlich bekehrt** (fig) he has finally turned over a new leaf, he has finally mended his ways

Be|keh|rer [bə'keːrɐ] M -s, -, **Be|keh|re|rin** [-ərɪn] F -, -nen apostle (+gen to); (= Missionar) missionary (+gen to); (fig) proselytizer

Be|kehr|te(r) [bə'keːrtə] MF decl as adj convert, proselyte

Be|keh|rung [bə'keːrʊŋ] F -, -en conversion

be|ken|nen ptp **bekannt** [bə'kant] irreg **VT** to confess, to admit; Sünde to confess; Wahrheit to admit; (Rel) Glauben to bear witness to **VR** **sich (als or für) schuldig ~** to admit or confess one's guilt; **sich zum Christentum/zu einem Glauben/zu Jesus ~** to profess Christianity/a faith/one's faith in Jesus; **sich zu jdm/etw ~** to declare one's support for sb/sth; **sich nicht zu jdm ~** to deny sb; **die Bekennende Kirche** the (German) Confessional Church

be|ken|nend ADJ Katholik, Homosexueller professed

Be|ken|ner(in) M(F) confessor

Be|ken|ner-: Be|ken|ner|an|ruf M call claiming responsibility; **Be|ken|ner|brief** M (nach Anschlag, Attentat etc) letter claiming responsibility, written responsibility claim; **Be|ken|ner|geist** M, **Be|ken|ner|mut** **M** courage of one's convictions

Be|ken|ne|rin F confessor

Be|ken|ner|schrei|ben NT (*nach Anschlag, Attentat etc*) letter claiming responsibility, written responsibility claim

Be|kennt|nis [bə'kɛntnɪs] NT **-ses, -se** **a** (= *Geständnis*) confession (*zu* of); (*zum religiösen Glauben auch*) profession (*zu* to); **ein ~ zu den Menschenrechten** a declaration of belief in human rights; **sein ~ zum Sozialismus** his declared belief in socialism; **ein ~ zur Demokratie ablegen** to declare one's belief in democracy; **ein ~ zum Christentum ablegen** to profess one's Christianity **b** (*Rel*: = *Konfession*) denomination

Be|kennt|nis-: Be|kennt|nis|christ(in) M(F) member of the Confessional Church; **Be|kennt|nis|frei|heit** F freedom of religious belief; **be|kennt|nis|freu|dig** ADJ eager to make confessions; **Be|kennt|nis|kir|che** F (German) Confessional Church; **be|kennt|nis|los** ADJ uncommitted to any religious denomination; **Be|kennt|nis|schu|le** F denominational school

be|kie|ken ptp **bekiekt** (*N Ger, inf*) **VT** to look at **VR** to (have a) look at oneself; (*gegenseitig*) to look at each other

be|kiest [bə'kiːst] ADJ gravelled (*Brit*), graveled (*US*), gravel *attr*

be|kif|fen ptp **bekifft** VR (*inf*) to get stoned (*inf*); **bekifft sein** to be stoned (*inf*)

be|kin|dert [bə'kɪndɐt] ADJ (*form*) with children

be|kla|gen ptp **beklagt** **VT** **a** to lament; *Los* to bewail; *Tod, Verlust* to mourn; **Menschenleben sind nicht zu ~** there are no casualties **b** → **beklagt** **VR** to complain (*über* +*acc, wegen* about); **sich bei jdm über etw** (*acc*) **~** to complain or make a complaint to sb about sth; **ich kann mich nicht ~** I can't complain, I've nothing to complain about

be|kla|gens|wert, be|kla|gens|wür|dig (*geh*) ADJ *Mensch* pitiful; *Zustand* lamentable, deplorable; *Misserfolg, Vorfall, Scheitern* regrettable, unfortunate; *Unfall* terrible

be|klagt [bə'klaːkt] ADJ (*Jur*) **die ~e Partei** the defendant; (*bei Scheidung*) the respondent; **der ~e Ehegatte** the respondent → *auch* **beklagen**

Be|klag|te(r) [bə'klaːktə] MF *decl as adj* (*Jur*) defendant; (*bei Scheidung*) respondent

be|klat|schen ptp **beklatscht** VT **a** (= *applaudieren*) to clap, to applaud **b** (*inf*: = *Klatsch verbreiten über*) to gossip about

be|klau|en ptp **beklaut** VT (*inf*) jdn to rob

be|kle|ben ptp **beklebt** VT etw **(mit Papier/Plakaten etc) ~** to stick paper/posters etc on(to) sth; **etw mit Etiketten ~** to stick labels on(to) sth, to label sth

be|kle|ckern ptp **bekleckert** (*inf*) **VT** to stain; **ich habe mir das Kleid bekleckert** I've made a mess on my dress **VR** **sich (mit Saft etc) ~** to spill juice etc all down or over oneself; **er hat sich nicht gerade mit Ruhm bekleckert** (*inf*) he didn't exactly cover himself with glory

be|kleck|sen ptp **bekleckst** **VT** (*inf*) to splatter (*mit* with); **etw (mit Tinte/Farbe) ~** to splatter ink/paint on sth; **du bist ja von oben bis unten bekleckst!** (*inf*) you're covered in ink/paint etc! **VR** to splatter oneself with ink/paint etc

be|klei|den ptp **bekleidet** **VT** **a** (= *anziehen*) to dress (*mit* in); (= *Kleidung geben*) to clothe; **er war nur mit einer Hose bekleidet** he was only wearing a pair of trousers; **etw mit etw ~** (*geh*) to cover sth in sth **b** (= *innehaben*) *Amt etc* to occupy, to hold; **jdn mit einem Amt/einer Würde ~** to bestow an office/a title on sb **VR** to get dressed

be|klei|det [bə'klaɪdət] ADJ dressed, clad (*mit* in); **sie war nur leicht ~** she was only lightly or (*spärlich*) scantily dressed or clad; **nur mit einer Hose ~ sein** to be clad in or wearing only a pair of trousers

Be|klei|dung F **a** (= *Kleider*) clothes *pl*, clothing; (= *Aufmachung*) dress, attire; **ohne ~** with-

out any clothes on **b** (*form*: *eines Amtes*) tenure; (*rare*: *mit einem Amt*) honouring (*Brit*), honoring (*US*)

Be|klei|dungs-: Be|klei|dungs|amt NT (*Mil*) quartermaster's store; **Be|klei|dungs|ar|ti|kel** M , **Be|klei|dungs|ge|gen|stand** M garment, article of clothing; **Be|klei|dungs|ge|wer|be** NT clothing or garment (*esp US*) trade; **Be|klei|dungs|in|dust|rie** F clothing or garment industry, rag trade (*inf*); **Be|klei|dungs|stück** NT garment, article of clothing; **Be|klei|dungs|vor|schrif|ten** PL clothing regulations *pl*; (*bezüglich Uniform*) uniform regulations *pl*

be|kleis|tern ptp **bekleistert** VT **a** *Tapete etc* to paste **b** (= *bekleben*) **eine Wand (mit Plakaten) ~** to stick posters all over a wall

be|klem|men ptp **beklemmt** VT (*fig*) to oppress; (*Schuld auch*) to weigh upon

be|klem|mend ADJ (= *beengend*) oppressive, constricting; (= *beängstigend*) tormenting, oppressive **ADV** oppressively; **der Raum war ~ eng** the room was so small it was oppressive; **~ wirken** to be oppressive

Be|klemm|nis [bə'klɛmnɪs] F **-, -se** feeling of oppressiveness; (= *Gefühl der Angst*) feeling of apprehension or trepidation

Be|klem|mung [bə'klɛmʊŋ] F **-, -en** *usu pl* feeling of oppressiveness; (= *Gefühl der Angst*) feeling of apprehension or trepidation; **~en haben** to feel oppressed; to be full of apprehension or trepidation; (*bei enger Kleidung*) to feel restricted

be|klom|men [bə'klɔmən] **ADJ** apprehensive, anxious; *Mensch auch* full of trepidation; *Schweigen* uneasy **ADV** apprehensively; **sie saß da und schwieg ~** she sat there in uneasy silence; **~ klingen** to sound troubled

Be|klom|men|heit F **-,** *no pl* trepidation, apprehensiveness

be|klö|nen ptp **beklönt** VT (*N Ger inf*) to talk over

be|klop|fen ptp **beklopft** VT to tap; *Brust auch* to sound

be|kloppt [bə'klɔpt] ADJ (*inf*) *Mensch* loony, crazy, mad (*all inf*); *Sache* lousy, stupid, crappy (*all inf*)

be|knackt [bə'knakt] (*sl*) **ADJ** *Mensch, Frage, Idee* daft (*Brit inf*), stupid; *Spruch, Frage* idiotic **ADV** *sich verhalten, sich anstellen* like a total idiot (*inf*); **~ fragen** to ask daft (*Brit inf*) or stupid questions

be|knien ptp **bekniet** VT (*inf*) jdn to beg

be|ko|chen ptp **bekocht** VT (*inf*) to cook for

be|kö|dern ptp **beködert** VT to bait

be|kom|men ptp **bekommen** irreg **VT** **a** (= *erhalten*) to get; *Genehmigung, Stimmen, Nachricht* to get, to obtain; *Geschenk, Brief, Lob, Belohnung* to get, to receive; *Zug, Bus, Krankheit* to get, to catch; *Schlaganfall, Junges, ein Kind, Besuch* to have; *Spritze, Tadel* to be given; **ein Jahr Gefängnis ~** to be given one year in prison; **wir ~ Kälte/anderes Wetter** the weather is turning cold/ is changing; **wir ~ Regen/Schnee** we're going to have rain/snow; **einen Stein/Ball** etc **an den Kopf ~** to be hit on the head by a stone/ball etc; **kann ich das schriftlich ~?** can I have that in writing?; **wir haben das große Bett nicht nach oben ~** we couldn't get the big bed upstairs; **jdn ins/aus dem Bett ~** to get sb into/out of bed; **was ~ Sie(, bitte)?** what will you have, sir/madam?; **ich bekomme bitte ein Glas Wein** I'll have a glass of wine, please; **was ~ Sie dafür?** how much is that?; **was ~ Sie von mir?** how much do I owe you?; **jdn dazu ~, etw zu tun** to get sb to do sth; **er bekam es einfach nicht über sich, ...** he just could not bring himself to ...; **ich bekomme den Deckel nicht abgeschraubt** (*inf*) I can't unscrew the lid

b (= *entwickeln*) *Fieber, Schmerzen, Vorliebe, Komplexe* to get, to develop; *Zähne* to get, to cut; *Übung, neue Hoffnung* to gain; **Rost/Risse ~** to

get or become rusty/cracked, to develop rust/ cracks; **Heimweh ~** to get or become homesick; **Sehnsucht ~** to develop a longing (*nach* for); **graue Haare/eine Glatze ~** to go grey (*Brit*) or gray (*US*)/bald; **Hunger/Durst ~** to get or become hungry/thirsty; **Angst ~** to get or become afraid; **einen roten Kopf ~** to go red

c (*mit Infinitivkonstruktion*) to get; **etw zu essen ~** to get sth to eat; **etw zu sehen/hören ~** to get to see/hear sth; **was muss ich denn da zu hören ~?** what's all this I've been hearing?; **es mit jdm zu tun ~** to get into trouble with sb; **etw zu fassen ~** to catch hold of sth; **wenn ich ihn zu fassen bekomme ...** if I get my hands on him ...

d (*mit ptp oder adj siehe auch dort*) **etw gemacht ~** to get or have sth done; **seine Arbeit fertig** or **gemacht** (*inf*) **~** to get one's work finished or done; **etw geschenkt ~** to be given sth (as a present); **ich habe das Buch geliehen ~** I have been lent the book; **etw bezahlt ~** to get paid for sth; **einen Wunsch erfüllt ~** to have a wish fulfilled; **das Haus sauber ~** to get the house clean; **etw satt ~** to have enough of sth

e (*in Verbindung mit n siehe auch dort*) **Lust ~, etw zu tun** to feel like doing sth; **es mit der Angst/Wut ~** to become afraid/angry; **Ärger ~** to get into trouble; **eine Ohrfeige** or **eine** (*inf*) **~** to catch (*Brit*) or get it (*inf*); **Prügel** or **sie** (*inf*) or **es** (*inf*) **~** to be given or to get a hiding

VI **a** *aux sein* +*dat* (= *zuträglich sein*) **jdm (gut) ~** to do sb good; (*Essen*) to agree with sb; **jdm nicht** or **schlecht ~** not to do sb any good; (*Essen*) to disagree with sb, not to agree with sb; **wie ist Ihnen das Bad ~?** how was your bath?; **wie bekommt ihm die Ehe?** how is he enjoying married life?; **es ist ihm schlecht ~, dass er nicht gearbeitet hat** not working did him no good; **wohl bekomms!** your health!

b (= *bedient werden*) **~ Sie schon?** are you being attended to or served?

be|kömm|lich [bə'kœmlɪç] ADJ *Mahlzeit, Speisen* (easily) digestible; *Luft, Klima* beneficial; **leicht ~ sein** to be easily digestible; **schwer/besser ~ sein** to be difficult/easier to digest

Be|kömm|lich|keit F **-,** *no pl* (*von Mahlzeit, Speisen*) digestibility; (*von Luft, Klima*) beneficial qualities *pl*

be|kös|ti|gen [bə'kœstɪɡn] ptp **beköstigt** VT to cater for

Be|kös|ti|gung F **-, -en** (= *das Beköstigen*) catering (+*gen* for); (= *Kost*) food

be|kräf|ti|gen ptp **bekräftigt** VT to confirm; *Vorschlag* to support, to back up; **etw nochmals ~** to reaffirm sth; **seine Aussage mit einem Eid ~** to reinforce one's evidence by swearing an oath; **eine Vereinbarung mit einem Handschlag ~** to seal an agreement by shaking hands; **er nickte ~d** he nodded in support

Be|kräf|ti|gung F confirmation; (= *Versicherung*) assurance; **zur ~ seiner Worte** to reinforce his words

be|krän|zen ptp **bekränzt** VT to crown with a wreath; (*mit Blumen*) to garland

be|kreu|zen ptp **bekreuzt** **VT** (*Eccl*) to bless (with the sign of the cross) **VR** to cross oneself

be|kreu|zi|gen ptp **bekreuzigt** VR to cross oneself

be|krie|gen ptp **bekriegt** VT to wage war on; (*fig*) to fight; **sie ~ sich (gegenseitig) schon seit Jahren** they have been at war with one another for years; **bekriegt werden** to be attacked

be|krit|teln ptp **bekrittelt** VT to criticize; *Arbeit auch* to find fault with

be|krit|zeln ptp **bekritzelt** VT to scribble over; **das Buch mit Bemerkungen ~** to scribble comments all over the book

be|krö|nen ptp **bekrönt** VT to crown (*auch fig*); (*Archit*) to surmount

be|ku|cken ptp **bekuckt** VT (*N Ger*) = **begucken**

be|küm|mern ptp **bekümmert** `VT` to worry; **das braucht dich nicht zu ~** there is no need for you to worry about that `VR` **sich über etw** (acc) **~** to worry about sth; **sich um etw ~** to concern oneself with sth → auch **bekümmert**

Be|küm|mer|nis F (geh) distress

be|küm|mert [bə'kʏmɐt] ADJ worried (über +acc about) → auch **bekümmern**

be|kun|den [bə'kʊndn] ptp **bekundet** `VT` to show, to express; (in Worten auch) to state; (Jur: = bezeugen) to testify to; **~, dass ...** (Jur) to testify that ... `VR` (geh) to manifest itself

Be|kun|dung F -, -en expression, manifestation; (in Worten auch) statement; (Jur) testimony

be|la|bern ptp **belabert** VT (inf) **jdn ~** to keep on at sb; **er hat mich belabert** (= überreden) he talked me into it

be|lä|cheln ptp **belächelt** VT to smile at

be|la|chen ptp **belacht** VT to laugh at

be|la|den[1] [bə'la:dn] ptp **beladen** irreg `VT` Schiff, Zug to load (up); (fig: mit Sorgen etc) jdn to burden; **etw mit Holz** etc **~** to load sth with wood etc, to load wood etc onto sth; **ein Tier mit einer schweren Last ~** to put a heavy load on an animal `VR` (mit Gepäck etc) to load oneself up; **sich mit Verantwortung/Sorgen ~** to take on responsibilities/worries; **sich mit Schuld ~** to incur guilt

be|la|den[2] [bə'la:dn] ADJ loaded; Mensch laden; (mit Schuld) laden, burdened; **mit etw ~ sein** to be loaded with sth; (Mensch) to be loaded down or laden with sth; (mit Schuld etc) to be weighed down or laden or burdened with sth

Be|la|dung [bə'la:dʊŋ] F -, -en usu sing loading (up)

Be|lag [bə'la:k] M -(e)s, ⸚e [-'lɛ:gə] coating; (= Schicht) layer; (= Ölfilm etc) film; (auf Pizza, Brot) topping; (auf Tortenboden, zwischen zwei Brotscheiben) filling; (auf Zahn) film; (= Zungenbelag) fur; (= Bremsbelag) lining; (= Fußbodenbelag) covering; (= Straßenbelag) surface

Be|la|ge|rer [bə'la:gərɐ] M -s, -, **Be|la|ge|rin** [-ərɪn] F -, -nen besieger

be|la|gern ptp **belagert** VT (Mil) to besiege (auch fig), to lay siege to

Be|la|ge|rung F siege

Be|la|ge|rungs-: **Be|la|ge|rungs|krieg** M siege warfare; **Be|la|ge|rungs|ma|schi|ne** F siege engine; **Be|la|ge|rungs|zu|stand** M state of siege; **den ~ ausrufen** to declare a state of siege

Bel|ami [bɛla'miː] M -(s), -s (dated) lady-killer (inf)

be|läm|mert ▲ [bə'lɛmɐt] ADJ (= betreten) sheepish; (= niedergeschlagen) miserable; (= scheußlich) Wetter, Angelegenheit lousy (inf) ADV (= dumm) like an idiot

Be|lang [bə'laŋ] M -(e)s, -e a (no pl: = Wichtigkeit) importance, significance; **von/ohne ~ (für jdn/etw) sein** to be of importance/of no importance (to sb/for or to sth) b **Belange** PL interests c (form: = Sache) matter; **in diesem ~** as regards this matter

be|lan|gen ptp **belangt** VT a (Jur) to prosecute (wegen for); (wegen Beleidigung, Verleumdung) to sue; **dafür kann man belangt werden** you could be prosecuted for that b (dated: = betreffen) **was mich belangt** as far as I am concerned

be|lang|los ADJ inconsequential, trivial; **das ist für das Ergebnis ~** that is irrelevant to the result

Be|lang|lo|sig|keit F -, -en triviality

Be|lang|sen|dung F (Aus: TV, Rad) party political broadcast

be|lan|gung F -, -en prosecution; (wegen Beleidigung, Verleumdung) suing

be|lang|voll ADJ relevant (für to)

be|las|sen ptp **belassen** VT irreg to leave; **wir wollen es dabei ~** let's leave it at that; **jdn in dem Glauben ~, dass ...** to allow sb to go on

believing that ...; **jdn in seinem Amt ~** to allow sb to remain in office; **etw an seinem Ort ~** to leave sth in its place; **das muss ihm ~ bleiben** that must be left up to him

be|last|bar ADJ a (mit Last, Gewicht) **bis zu 50 Tonnen ~ sein** to have a maximum load of or load-bearing capacity of 50 tons; **wie hoch ist diese Brücke ~?** what is the maximum load of this bridge? b (fig) **daran habe ich bemerkt, wie ~ ein Mensch ist** that made me see how much a person can take; **das Gedächtnis ist nur bis zu einem gewissen Grad ~** the memory can only absorb a certain amount; **weiter waren seine Nerven nicht ~** his nerves could take no more, his nerves were at breaking point c (= beanspruchbar) (Med) Mensch, Körper, Organe, Kreislauf resilient; **der Steuerzahler ist nicht weiter ~** the tax payer cannot be burdened any more; **die Atmosphäre ist nicht unbegrenzt (durch Schadstoffe) ~** the atmosphere cannot stand an unlimited degree of contamination; **da wird sich zeigen, wie ~ das Stromnetz/unser Wasserhaushalt ist** that will show how much pressure our electricity/water supply will take d **wie hoch ist mein Konto ~?** what is the limit on my account?; **der Etat ist nicht unbegrenzt ~** the budget is not unlimited

Be|last|bar|keit [bə'lastba:ɐkait] F -, -en a (von Brücke, Aufzug) load-bearing capacity b (von Menschen, Nerven) ability to cope with stress; (von Gedächtnis) capacity c (von Stromnetz etc) maximum capacity; (von Mensch, Organ) maximum resilience; **die höhere physische ~ eines Sportlers** an athlete's higher degree of physical resilience d (von Haushalt) (maximum) limit (+gen of, on)

be|las|ten ptp **belastet** `VT` a (lit) (mit Gewicht) Brücke, Balken, Träger, Ski to put weight on; (mit Last) Fahrzeug, Fahrstuhl to load; **etw mit 50 Tonnen ~** to put a 50 ton load on sth, to put a weight of 50 tons on sth; **den Träger gleichmäßig ~** to distribute weight evenly over the girder; **das darf nur mit maximal 5 Personen/Tonnen belastet werden** its maximum load is 5 people/ tons; **die Brücke zu sehr ~** to put too much weight on the bridge; **das Fahrzeug zu sehr ~** to overload the vehicle b (fig) **jdn mit etw ~** (mit Arbeit) to load sb with sth; mit Verantwortung, Sorgen, Wissen to burden sb with sth; **das Gedächtnis mit unnützem Wissen ~** to clutter up one's memory with useless knowledge; **jdn ~** (mit Arbeit, Verantwortung, Sorgen) to burden sb; (= nervlich, körperlich anstrengen) to put a strain on sb; **jdn mit zu viel Arbeit ~** to overload sb with work; **jdn mit zu viel Verantwortung** etc **~** to overburden sb with responsibility etc; **~d sein** to be a strain → **erblich** c (fig: = bedrücken) **jdn/jds Gewissen/Seele mit etw ~** (Mensch) to burden sb/sb's conscience/ soul with sth; **jdn ~** (Schuld etc) to weigh on sb or sb's mind; **jds Gewissen ~** to weigh on sb's conscience; **das belastet ihn sehr** it weighs heavily on his mind; **mit einer Schuld belastet sein** to be weighed down or burdened by guilt; **von Sorgen belastet** weighed down with cares d (= beanspruchen) Wasserhaushalt, Stromnetz, Leitung to put pressure on, to stretch; Atmosphäre to pollute; (Med) Kreislauf, Magen, Organe, Körper, Mensch to put a strain on, to strain; Nerven to strain, to tax; Steuerzahler to burden; **jdn/etw zu sehr** or **stark ~** to overstrain sb/sth; Wasserhaushalt etc to put too much pressure on sth, to overstretch sth e (Jur) Angeklagten to incriminate; **~des Material** incriminating evidence f (Fin) Konto to charge; Etat to be a burden on; (steuerlich) jdn to burden; **etw mit einer Hypothek ~** to mortgage sth; **das Konto mit einem Betrag ~** to debit the account with a sum, to debit a sum to the account; **jdn mit den Kosten ~** to charge the costs to sb; **dafür werden wir Sie mit 50 Euro ~** we will charge you 50 euros

for that `VR` a **sich mit etw ~** (mit Arbeit) to take sth on; mit Verantwortung to take sth upon oneself; **mit Sorgen** to burden oneself with sth; **sich mit Schuld ~** to incur guilt; **damit belaste ich mich nicht** (mit Arbeit, Verantwortung) I don't want to take that on; **ich will mich nicht ~** (mit Wissen) I don't want to know (about it) b (Jur) to incriminate oneself

be|läs|ti|gen [bə'lɛstɪgn] ptp **belästigt** VT (= zur Last fallen) to bother; (= zudringlich werden) to pester; (körperlich) to molest; (Licht, Geräusch, Geruch) to irritate

be|läs|ti|gend ADJ annoying, aggravating; Licht, Geruch etc irritating

Be|läs|ti|gung F -, -en annoyance; (durch Lärm etc) irritation; (= Zudringlichkeit) pestering; **etw als eine ~ empfinden** to feel sth as a nuisance; **sie beklagte sich über die ~en durch ihren Chef** she complained about being harassed by her boss; **sexuelle ~** sexual harassment

Be|las|tung [bə'lastʊŋ] F -, -en a (= das Belasten) putting weight on; (von Fahrzeug, Fahrstuhl) loading; (= Last, Gewicht) weight; (in Fahrzeug, Fahrstuhl etc) load; **die erhöhte ~ der Brücke** the increased weight put on the bridge; **maximale ~ der Brücke** weight limit of the bridge; **maximale ~ des Fahrstuhls** maximum load of the lift b (= das Belasten) (mit Arbeit) loading; (mit Verantwortung etc) burdening; (= Anstrengung) strain; (= Last, Bürde) burden c (= Bedrückung) burden (+gen on) d (= Beeinträchtigung) pressure (+gen on); (von Atmosphäre) pollution (+gen of); (von Kreislauf, Magen) strain (+gen on) e (Jur) incrimination f (Fin) (von Konto) charge (+gen on); (von Etat, steuerlich) burden (+gen on); (mit Hypothek) mortgage (+gen on)

Be|las|tungs-: **Be|las|tungs|elek|tro|kar|di|o|gramm** NT, **Be|las|tungs-EKG** NT (Med) exercise electrocardiogram or ECG; **be|las|tungs|fä|hig** ADJ = belastbar; **Be|las|tungs|fä|hig|keit** F -, no pl a (von Brücke, Aufzug) load-bearing capacity b (von Menschen, Nerven) ability to cope with stress; (von Gedächtnis) capacity c (von Stromnetz etc) maximum capacity; (von Mensch, Organ) maximum resilience; **die höhere physische ~ eines Sportlers** an athlete's higher greater physical resilience d (von Haushalt) (maximum) limit (+gen of, on); **Be|las|tungs|gren|ze** F (von Brücke, Balken etc) weight limit; (von Fahrzeug) maximum load; (von Atmosphäre, Wasserhaushalt) maximum capacity; (seelisch, physisch) limit; (Elec) level of peak load; **ich habe meine ~ erreicht** I've reached my limit, I've had enough; **ich habe meine ~ überschritten** I've overdone it; **Be|las|tungs|ma|te|ri|al** NT (Jur) incriminating evidence; **Be|las|tungs|pro|be** F endurance test; **Be|las|tungs|spit|ze** F (Elec) peak load; **Be|las|tungs|zeu|ge** M, **Be|las|tungs|zeu|gin** F (Jur) witness for the prosecution

be|lat|schern [bə'la:tʃɐn] ptp **belatschert** VT (dial inf) to talk round (Brit), to persuade

be|lau|ben [bə'laubn] ptp **belaubt** VR to come into leaf; **spärlich/dicht belaubt sein** to have sparse/thick foliage

Be|lau|bung F -, no pl (= Laub) leaves pl, foliage; (= das Sichbelauben) coming into leaf

be|lau|ern ptp **belauert** `VT` to watch (secretly); **jdn misstrauisch ~** to eye sb suspiciously `VR` to eye each other or one another

be|lau|fen ptp **belaufen** irreg `VR` **sich auf etw** (acc) **~** to come or amount to sth `VT` (rare: = begehen) to walk; **ein viel ~er Weg** a well-trodden path `VI` aux sein (dial) = **beschlagen**[2]

be|lau|schen ptp **belauscht** VT to eavesdrop on; (= genau beobachten) to observe

be|le|ben ptp **belebt** `VT` a (= anregen) to liven up; (= neu beleben) Natur to revive; (= aufmuntern) to brighten up, to liven up; Absatz, Konjunktur, jds Hoffnungen to stimulate; **eine kalte**

Dusche wird dich neu ~ a cold shower will refresh you **b** (= *lebendiger gestalten*) to brighten up; *Unterhaltung auch* to animate **c** (= *zum Leben erwecken*) to bring to life **VR** (*Konjunktur*) to be stimulated; (*Augen, Gesicht*) to light up; (*Natur, Stadt*) to come to life; (= *geschäftiger werden*) to liven up → *auch* belebt **VI** das belebt that livens you up

be|le|bend **ADJ** invigorating; **ein ~es Element in etw** (*acc*) **einbringen** to liven sth up **ADV ~ wirken** to have a stimulating effect

be|lebt [bə'le:pt] **ADJ** **a** *Straße, Stadt etc* busy **b** (= *lebendig*) living; **die ~e Natur** the living world; **~er Schlamm** activated sludge → *auch* beleben

Be|lebt|heit F -, *no pl* (*von Straße, Stadt etc*) bustle

Be|le|bung [bə'le:buŋ] F -, **-en** revival; (*der Wirtschaft, Konjunktur*) stimulation; **zur ~ trank er einen starken Kaffee** he drank a cup of strong coffee to revive himself

Be|le|bungs|ver|such M (*Med*) resuscitation attempt

be|le|cken *ptp* beleckt **VT** to lick

Be|leg [bə'le:k] M -(e)s, -e [-gə] **a** (= *Beweis*) instance, piece of evidence; (= *Quellennachweis*) reference; **~e für den Gebrauch eines Wortes** instances of the use of a word **b** (= *Quittung*) receipt

Be|leg|arzt M , Be|leg|ärz|tin F *general practitioner who also looks after a certain number of patients in a hospital*

be|leg|bar **ADJ** verifiable

Be|leg|bett NT *hospital bed at the disposal of a general practitioner*, GP bed

be|le|gen *ptp* belegt **VT** **a** (= *bedecken*) to cover; *Brote, Tortenboden* to fill; **etw mit Fliesen/Teppich ~** to tile/carpet sth; **mit Beschuss ~** to bombard; **mit Bomben ~** to bomb, to bombard → *auch* belegt **b** (= *besetzen*) *Wohnung, Hotelbett, Sitzplatz* to occupy; (= *reservieren*) to reserve, to book; (*Univ*) *Fach* to take; *Seminar, Vorlesung* to enrol (*Brit*) or enroll (*US*) for; **den fünften Platz ~** to take fifth place, to come fifth **c** (= *beweisen*) to verify **d** (= *auferlegen*) **jdn mit etw ~** to impose sth on sb; **jdn mit dem Bann ~** to proscribe sb; (*Eccl*) to excommunicate sb; **etw mit einem Namen ~** to give sth a name

Be|leg-: Be|leg|exem|plar NT specimen copy; Be|leg|frist F (*Univ*) enrolment (*Brit*) or enrollment (*US*) period; Be|leg|kran|kenhaus NT ≈ hospital providing wards for non-resident doctors, general practitioners' hospital (*Brit*); Be|leg|le|ser M OCR reader; Be|leg|ma|te|ri|al NT documentation

Be|leg|schaft [bə'le:kʃaft] F -, **-en** **a** (= *Beschäftigte*) staff; (*esp in Fabriken etc*) workforce **b** (*inf*: = *die Anwesenden*) **die ganze ~** the whole mob (*inf*) or gang (*inf*)

Be|leg|schafts-: Be|leg|schafts|ak|ti|en PL employees' shares; Be|leg|schafts|mit|glied NT employee; Be|leg|schafts|ra|batt M staff discount; Be|leg|schafts|ver|samm|lung F meeting of employees

Be|leg-: Be|leg|stel|le F reference; Be|leg|stück NT piece of evidence

be|legt [bə'le:kt] **ADJ** *Zunge* furred; *Stimme* hoarse; *Zimmer, Bett, Wohnung* occupied; **~e Brote** open (*Brit*) or open-faced (*US*) sandwiches → *auch* belegen

be|leh|nen *ptp* belehnt **VT** **a** (*Hist*) to enfeoff **b** (*Sw*) *Haus* to mortgage

be|lehr|bar **ADJ** teachable

be|leh|ren *ptp* belehrt **VT** (= *unterweisen*) to teach, to instruct; (= *aufklären*) to inform, to advise (*form*) (*über* +*acc* of); **jdn eines anderen ~** to teach sb otherwise; **sich eines anderen ~ lassen** to learn or be taught otherwise; **da musste ich mich ~ lassen** I realized I was wrong; **er ist**

nicht zu ~, er lässt sich nicht ~ he won't be told; ich bin belehrt! I've learned my lesson → besser ADJ a

be|leh|rend **ADJ** didactic; der ~e Zeigefinger (*fig*) a lecturing or moralizing tone **ADV auf jdn ~ einreden** to give sb a lecture; **~ sprechen** to lecture

Be|leh|rung [bə'le:ruŋ] F -, **-en** explanation, lecture (*inf*); (= *Anweisung*) instruction (*über* +*acc* about); (*von Zeugen, Angeklagten*) caution; **deine ~en kannst du dir sparen** there's no need to lecture me

be|leibt [bə'laipt] **ADJ** stout, corpulent, portly

Be|leibt|heit F -, *no pl* corpulence, stoutness

be|lei|di|gen [bə'laidɪgn] *ptp* beleidigt **VT** *jdn* to insult; (*Verhalten, Anblick, Geruch etc*) to offend; (*Jur*) (*mündlich*) to slander; (*schriftlich*) to libel

be|lei|digt [bə'laidɪçt] **ADJ** insulted; (= *gekränkt*) offended; *Gesicht, Miene* hurt; **er fühlt sich in seiner Ehre ~** he feels his honour (*Brit*) or honor (*US*) has been insulted; **die ~e Leberwurst spielen** (*inf*) to be in a huff (*inf*); **bist du jetzt ~?** have I offended you?; **jetzt ist er ~** now he's in a huff (*inf*) **ADV** in a huff (*inf*), offended; **~ weggehen** to go off in a huff (*inf*)

Be|lei|di|gung F -, **-en** insult; (*Jur*) (*mündliche*) slander; (*schriftliche*) libel; **eine ~ für den Geschmack** an insult to one's taste; **eine ~ für das Auge** an eyesore; **etw als ~ auffassen** to take sth as an insult, to take offence (*Brit*) or offense (*US*) at sth

Be|lei|di|gungs-: Be|lei|di|gungs|kla|ge F → Beleidigung (*Jur*) slander/libel action, action for slander/libel; Be|lei|di|gungs|pro|zess ▲ M (*Jur*) → Beleidigung slander/libel trial

be|leih|bar [bə'laiba:ɐ] **ADJ** (*Fin*) eligible as collateral; *Sicherheit* pledgeable; *Immobilie* mortgageable

be|lei|hen *ptp* beliehen [bə'li:ən] **VT** *irreg* **a** (*Comm*) to lend money on; *Haus, Grundstück* to give a mortgage on **b** (*Hist*: belehnen) to enfeoff

Be|lei|hung [bə'laiʊŋ] F -, **-en** (*Fin*) raising of a loan or mortgage (+*gen* on)

Be|lei|hungs|gren|ze F (*Fin*) lending limit

be|lem|mert △ [bə'lɛmɐt] **ADJ, ADV** → belämmert

be|le|sen [bə'le:zn] **ADJ** well-read

Be|le|sen|heit F -, *no pl* **eine gewisse ~** wide reading

Bel|eta|ge [bɛle'ta:ʒə] F (*old*) first floor (*Brit*), second floor (*US*)

be|leuch|ten *ptp* beleuchtet **VT** (= *Licht werfen auf*) to light up, to illuminate; (= *mit Licht versehen*) *Straße, Bühne etc* to light; (*fig*: = *betrachten*) to examine

Be|leuch|ter(in) M(F) lighting technician

Be|leuch|ter|brü|cke F lighting bridge

be|leuch|tet [bə'lɔyçtət] **PTP** *von* beleuchten **ADJ** lit up, illuminated; **gut/schlecht ~** well-lit/badly lit *attr*, well/badly lit *pred*

Be|leuch|tung [bə'lɔyçtʊŋ] F -, **-en** **a** (= *das Beleuchten*) lighting; (= *das Bestrahlen*) illumination; (*fig*) examination, investigation **b** (= *Licht*) light; (= *das Beleuchtetsein*) lighting; (= *Lichter*) lights *pl*; **die ~ der Straßen** street lighting; **die ~ der Fahrzeuge** lights *pl* on vehicles

Be|leuch|tungs-: Be|leuch|tungs|an|la|ge F lighting (installation); Be|leuch|tungs|kör|per M lighting appliance; Be|leuch|tungs|stär|ke F intensity of light; Be|leuch|tungs|tech|nik F lighting engineering

be|leum|det [bə'lɔymdət], be|leu|mun|det [bə'lɔymʊndət] **ADJ gut/schlecht ~ sein** to have a good/bad reputation; **ein schlecht ~es Etablissement** an establishment with a bad reputation

bel|fern ['bɛlfɐn] **VI** to bark; (*Kanone*) to boom

Bel|gi|en ['bɛlgiən] NT -s Belgium

Bel|gi|er ['bɛlgiɐ] M -s, -, Bel|gi|e|rin [-iərɪn] F -, **-nen** Belgian

bel|gisch ['bɛlgɪʃ] **ADJ** Belgian

Bel|grad ['bɛlgraːt] NT -s Belgrade

Bel|gra|der[1] ['bɛlgraːdɐ] **ADJ** *attr* Belgrade

Bel|gra|der[2] ['bɛlgraːdɐ] M -s, -, Bel|gra|de|rin [-ərɪn] F -, **-nen** native of Belgrade; (= *Einwohner*) inhabitant of Belgrade

be|lich|ten *ptp* belichtet **VT** (*Phot*) to expose; **wie lange muss ich das Bild ~?** what exposure should I give the shot?

Be|lich|tung F (*Phot*) exposure

Be|lich|tungs-: Be|lich|tungs|au|to|ma|tik F automatic exposure; Be|lich|tungs|dau|er F exposure (time); Be|lich|tungs|mes|ser M -s, - light meter; Be|lich|tungs|ta|bel|le F exposure chart or table; Be|lich|tungs|zeit F exposure (time)

be|lie|ben *ptp* beliebt **VI** *impers* (*geh*) **wie es Ihnen beliebt** as you like or wish; **was beliebt?** (*old*: = *wird gewünscht*) what can I do for you? **VT** (*old, iro*) **es beliebt jdm, etw zu tun** (= *jd hat Lust*) sb feels like doing sth; (*iro*) sb deigns or condescends to do sth; **jd beliebt, etw zu tun** (= *jd neigt dazu*) sb likes doing sth; **er beliebt zu scherzen** (*iro*) he must be joking

Be|lie|ben NT -s, *no pl* **nach ~** just as you/they *etc* like, any way you *etc* want (to); **das steht** or **liegt in Ihrem ~** that is up to you, that is left to your discretion

be|lie|big [bə'li:bɪç] **ADJ** any; **(irgend)eine/jede ~e Zahl** any number at all or whatever or you like; **nicht jede ~e Zahl** not every number; **jeder Beliebige** anyone at all; **eine ganz ~e Reihe von Beispielen** a quite arbitrary series of examples; **in ~er Reihenfolge** in any order whatever; **alles Beliebige** anything whatever; **die Auswahl ist ~** the choice is open or free **ADV** as you *etc* like; **Sie können ~ lange bleiben** you can stay as long as you like; **die Zahlen können ~ ausgewählt werden** you can choose any number you like

be|liebt [bə'li:pt] **ADJ** popular (*bei* with); **sich bei jdm ~ machen** to make oneself popular with sb

Be|liebt|heit F -, *no pl* popularity

Be|liebt|heits|ska|la F -, **-skalen** *usu sing* popularity scale

be|lie|fern *ptp* beliefert **VT** to supply; **jdn (mit etw) ~** to supply sb (with sth)

Be|lie|fe|rung F supplying; **die ~ einer Firma einstellen** to stop supplying a firm

Bel|la|don|na [bɛla'dɔna] F -, Belladonnen [-'dɔnən] (= *Extrakt*) belladonna

bel|len ['bɛlən] **VI** to bark; **etw ins Telefon/Mikrofon ~** to yell or shout sth into the telephone/microphone **VT** to bark; **Befehle ~** to bark out

bel|lend **ADJ** *Husten* hacking; *Stimme* gruff

Bel|let|ris|tik [bɛle'trɪstɪk] F -, *no pl* fiction and poetry, belles lettres *pl*

bel|let|ris|tisch [bɛle'trɪstɪʃ] **ADJ** *Zeitschrift, Neigung* literary; **~e Literatur** fiction and poetry; **~e Bücher** books of fiction and poetry; **~e Abteilung** department for fiction and poetry

be|lo|bi|gen [bə'lo:bɪgn] *ptp* belobigt **VT** to commend, to praise

Be|lo|bi|gung F -, **-en** (*form*) commendation

Be|lo|bi|gungs|schrei|ben NT commendation

be|loh|nen *ptp* belohnt, (*Sw*) be|löh|nen *ptp* belöhnt **VT** to reward; **starker Beifall belohnte den Schauspieler** the actor received hearty applause

Be|loh|nung [bə'lo:nʊŋ] F -, **-en** (*Sw*), Be|löh|nung [bə'lø:nʊŋ] F -, **-en** reward; (= *das Belohnen*) rewarding; **zur** or **als ~ (für)** as a reward (for); **eine ~ aussetzen** to offer a reward; **zur ~ der Kinder für ihr gutes Benehmen** in order to reward the children for their good behaviour (*Brit*) *or* behavior (*US*)

Belt [bɛlt] M **-s, -e der Große/Kleine ~** the Great/Little Belt

be|lüf|ten *ptp* **belüftet** VT to ventilate

Be|lüf|tung F **a** (= *das Belüften*) ventilating, airing **b** (*inf*: = *ganze Anlage*) ventilation

Be|lüf|tungs-: Be|lüf|tungs|an|la|ge F ventilation (system); **Be|lüf|tungs|ven|til** NT (*Tech*) ventilation valve

Be|lu|ga [beˈluːɡa] M **-s, -s** (*Zool*) beluga (whale)

be|lü|gen *ptp* **belogen** [bəˈloːɡn] VT *irreg* to lie *or* tell lies/a lie to; **sich selbst ~** to deceive oneself

be|lus|ti|gen [bəˈlʊstɪɡn] *ptp* **belustigt** **VT** to amuse **VR** (*geh*) **sich über jdn/etw ~** to make fun of sb/sth; **sich an etw** (*dat*) **~** to laugh at sth; **sich mit etw ~** to amuse oneself by (doing) sth

be|lus|tigt [bəˈlʊstɪçt] **ADJ** *Gesichtsausdruck, Ton, Stimme* amused **ADV** in amusement

Be|lus|ti|gung F **-, -en** (*geh*: = *Veranstaltung*) entertainment; (= *das Belustigtsein*) amusement

Bel|ze|bub [ˈbɛltsəbuːp] M **-s** (*Bibl*) Beelzebub → **Teufel**

be|ma|chen *ptp* **bemacht** VR (*inf*) **a** (= *sich beschmutzen*) to make oneself dirty *or* filthy **b** (= *sich aufregen*) to get het up (*Brit inf*) *or* worked up

be|mäch|ti|gen [bəˈmɛçtɪɡn] *ptp* **bemächtigt** VR (*geh*) **a** (= *in seine Gewalt bringen*) **sich eines Menschen/einer Sache ~** to take *or* seize hold of sb/sth; **sich des Thrones ~** to seize *or* take the throne; (*durch Intrige*) to usurp the throne **b** (*Gefühl, Gedanke*) **sich jds ~** to come over sb

be|mähnt [bəˈmɛːnt] **ADJ** *Tier* maned; (*hum*) *Jugendliche* shaggy-haired

be|mä|keln *ptp* **bemäkelt** VT to find fault with, to pick holes in

be|ma|len *ptp* **bemalt** **VT** to paint; (= *verzieren auch*) to decorate; **etw mit Blumen ~** to paint flowers on sth; **bemalt sein** (*pej*) to be heavily made up **VR** to paint oneself; (*pej*: = *schminken*) to put on one's war paint (*inf*)

Be|ma|lung [bəˈmaːlʊŋ] F **-, -en** (= *das Bemalen, Farbschicht*) painting; (*zur Verzierung auch*) decoration

be|män|geln *ptp* **bemängelt** VT to find fault with, to fault; **was die Kritiker an dem Buch ~, ist ...** the fault the critics find with the book is ...

Be|män|ge|lung F **-, -en** finding fault (+*gen* with), faulting (+*gen* of)

be|man|nen [bəˈmanən] *ptp* **bemannt** VT *U-Boot, Raumschiff* to man; **sie ist seit neuestem wieder bemannt** (*inf*) she has just recently got herself a man again *or* a new boyfriend

Be|man|nung F **-, -en** manning; (*rare*: = *Mannschaft*) crew

be|män|teln [bəˈmɛntln] *ptp* **bemäntelt** VT to cover up

Be|män|te|lung F **-, -en** covering up

Bem|bel [ˈbɛmbl] M **-s, -** (*dial*) pitcher

be|merk|bar ADJ noticeable, perceptible; **sich ~ machen** (= *sich zeigen*) to make itself felt, to become noticeable; (= *auf sich aufmerksam machen*) to draw attention to oneself, to attract attention; **mach dich ~, wenn du etwas brauchst** let me know if you need anything

be|mer|ken ❍ 38.1 *ptp* **bemerkt** VT **a** (= *wahrnehmen*) to notice; *Schmerzen auch* to feel; **er bemerkte rechtzeitig/zu spät, dass ...** he realized in time/too late that ... **b** (= *äußern*) to remark, to comment (*zu* on); **ganz richtig, bemerkte sie** quite right, she said; **nebenbei bemerkt** by the way; **ich möchte dazu ~, dass ... I** would like to say *or* add, that ...; **er hatte eini-**

ges zu **~** he had quite a few comments *or* remarks to make

Be|mer|ken [bəˈmɛrkn] NT (*form*) **mit dem ~** with the observation

be|mer|kens|wert **ADJ** remarkable **ADV** remarkably

Be|mer|kung [bəˈmɛrkʊŋ] F **-, -en a** remark, comment (*zu* on) **b** (*old*: = *Wahrnehmung*) observation

be|mes|sen *ptp* **bemessen** *irreg* **VT** (= *zuteilen*) to allocate; (= *einteilen*) to calculate; **der Raum ist für eine kleine Gruppe ~** the room is designed for a small group of people; **reichlich ~** generous; **knapp ~** not very generous; **meine Zeit ist kurz** *or* **knapp ~** my time is limited *or* restricted **VR** (*form*) to be proportionate (*nach* to)

Be|mes|sung F **a** (= *Zuteilung*) allocation; (= *Einteilung*) calculation **b** (*Build*) building specification

Be|mes|sungs-: Be|mes|sungs|grund|la|ge F (*Fin*) basis of assessment; **Be|mes|sungs|-zeit|raum** M (*Fin, von Steuern*) assessment period

be|mit|lei|den [bəˈmɪtlaidn] *ptp* **bemitleidet** VT to pity, to feel pity for, to feel sorry for; **er ist zu ~** he is to be pitied; **sich selbst ~** to feel sorry for oneself

be|mit|lei|dens|wert [bəˈmɪtlaidnsveːɐt] ADJ pitiable, pitiful

be|mit|telt [bəˈmɪtlt] ADJ well-to-do, well-off

Bem|me [ˈbɛmə] F **-, -n** (*dial*) slice of buttered bread; (*zusammengeklappt*) sandwich

be|mo|geln *ptp* **bemogelt** VT (*inf*) to cheat

be|moo|sen [bəˈmoːzn] *ptp* **bemoost** VR to become overgrown with moss

be|moost [bəˈmoːst] ADJ mossy, moss-covered; **~es Haupt** (*inf*) old fogey (*inf*); (= *Student*) perpetual student

be|mü|hen [bəˈmyːən] *ptp* **bemüht** **VT** to trouble, to bother; *Rechtsanwalt etc* to engage; **jdn zu sich ~** to call in sb, to call upon the services of sb; **die Bibel** *or* **Bibelstellen ~** to quote from the Bible **VR a** (= *sich Mühe geben*) to try hard, to endeavour (*Brit*), to endeavor (*US*); **sich um gute Beziehungen/eine Stelle ~** to try to establish good relations/get a job; **sich um jds Wohl ~** to take trouble over sb's wellbeing; **sich um jds Vertrauen ~** to try to win sb's trust; **sich um jds Gunst ~** to court sb's favour (*Brit*) *or* favor (*US*); **sich um eine Verbesserung der Lage ~** to try to improve the situation; **sich um jdn ~** (*für eine Stelle*) to try to get sb; (*um Kranken etc*) to look after sb; (*um jds Gunst*) to court sb; **bitte ~ Sie sich nicht** please don't trouble yourself *or* put yourself out; **sich redlich ~** to make a genuine effort → *auch* **bemüht**
b (*geh*: = *gehen*) to go, to proceed (*form*); **sich ins Nebenzimmer ~** to proceed to the next room (*form*); **sich zu jdm ~** to go to sb; **sich auf die Polizei ~** to go to the police

Be|mü|hen [bəˈmyːən] NT **-s**, *no pl* (*geh*) efforts *pl*, endeavours (*Brit*) *or* endeavors (*US*) *pl* (*um* for)

be|müht [bəˈmyːt] ADJ **~ sein, etw zu tun** to try hard to do sth, to endeavour (*Brit*) *or* endeavor (*US*) to do sth; **um etw ~ sein, darum ~ sein, etw zu tun** to be at pains to do sth, to endeavour (*Brit*) *or* endeavor (*US*) to do sth → *auch* **bemühen**

Be|mü|hung F **-, -en** effort, endeavour (*Brit*), endeavor (*US*); **vielen Dank für Ihre (freundlichen) ~en** (*form*) thank you for your efforts *or* trouble

be|mü|ßi|gen [bəˈmyːsɪɡn] *ptp* **bemüßigt** VR (*geh*) **sich einer Sache** (*gen*) **~** to avail oneself of sth

be|mü|ßigt [bəˈmyːsɪçt] ADJ **sich ~ fühlen/sehen/finden** (*geh, usu iro*) to feel called upon *or* obliged

be|mut|tern [bəˈmʊtɐn] *ptp* **bemuttert** VT to mother

Be|mut|te|rung F **-, -en** *usu sing* mothering; **ihre ständige ~ geht mir auf die Nerven I** hate the way she keeps nannying *or* people

be|mützt [bəˈmʏtst] ADJ wearing a cap; **weiß ~e Bergkuppen** snowcapped mountains

be|nach|bart [bəˈnaxbaːɐt] ADJ neighbouring *attr* (*Brit*), neighboring *attr* (*US*); *Haus, Familie auch* next door; *Staat auch* adjoining; **die Häuser sind ~** the houses are next (door) to one another

be|nach|rich|ti|gen [bəˈnaːxrɪçtɪɡn] *ptp* **benachrichtigt** VT to inform (*von* of); (*amtlich auch*) to notify (*von* of)

Be|nach|rich|ti|gung F **-, -en** (= *Nachricht*) notification; (*Comm*) advice note; **die ~ der Eltern ist in solchen Fällen vorgeschrieben** the parents must be notified in such cases

Be|nach|rich|ti|gungs|schrei|ben NT letter of notification

be|nach|tei|li|gen [bəˈnaːxtailɪɡn] *ptp* **benachteiligt** VT to put at a disadvantage; (*wegen Geschlecht, Klasse, Rasse, Glauben etc*) to discriminate against; **benachteiligt sein** to be at a disadvantage; to be discriminated against

Be|nach|tei|lig|te(r) [bəˈnaːxtailɪçtə] MF *decl as adj* **der/die ~ sein** to be at a disadvantage

Be|nach|tei|li|gung F **-, -en** (= *das Benachteiligen*) disadvantaging; (*wegen Geschlecht, Rasse, Glauben*) discrimination (+*gen* against); (*Zustand*) disadvantage; discrimination *no pl*

be|na|geln *ptp* **benagelt** VT **eine Wand/das Dach** *etc* **mit etw ~** to nail sth onto a wall/the roof *etc*

be|na|gen *ptp* **benagt** VT to gnaw at

be|nä|hen *ptp* **benäht** VT **das Kleid** *etc* **mit etw ~** to sew sth onto the dress

be|näs|sen *ptp* **benässt** VT (*geh*) to moisten

Bench|mark [ˈbɛntʃmaːk] F **-, -s** (*Econ etc*) benchmark

Ben|del △ [ˈbɛndl] M OR NT **-s, -** → **Bändel**

be|ne|beln [bəˈneːbln] *ptp* **benebelt** VT (*inf*) **jdn** *or* **jds Sinne** *or* **jds Kopf ~** to make sb's head swim *or* reel; (*Narkose, Sturz*) to daze sb, to make sb feel dazed; **benebelt sein** to be feeling dazed *or* (*von Alkohol*) woozy (*inf*)

be|ne|dei|en [bene'daiən] VT (*Eccl*) to bless; *Gott* to glorify

Be|ne|dik|ti|ner¹ [benedɪk'tiːnɐ] M **-s, -** (= *Likör*) Benedictine

Be|ne|dik|ti|ner² M **-s, -** (*Eccl*) Benedictine (friar/monk)

Be|ne|dik|ti|ne|rin [benedɪk'tiːnərɪn] F **-, -nen** (*Eccl*) Benedictine (nun)

Be|ne|dik|ti|ner- *in cpds* Benedictine; **Be|ne|dik|ti|ner|klos|ter** NT Benedictine monastery

Be|ne|dik|tus [bene'dɪktʊs] NT **-, -** (*Eccl*) Benedictus

Be|ne|fiz [bene'fiːts] NT **-es, -e** benefit

Be|ne|fi|zi|um [bene'fiːtsi̯ʊm] NT **-s, Benefizien** [-tsi̯ən] **a** benefice **b** (*Hist*) fee, feoff

Be|ne|fiz-: Be|ne|fiz|kon|zert NT charity *or* benefit concert; **Be|ne|fiz|spiel** NT benefit match; **Be|ne|fiz|vor|stel|lung** F charity performance

be|neh|men *ptp* **benommen** [bəˈnɔmən] *irreg* **VR** to behave; (*in Bezug auf Umgangsformen auch*) to behave oneself; **benimm dich!** behave yourself!; **sich gut ~** to behave oneself, to behave well; **sich schlecht ~** to behave (oneself) badly, to misbehave **VT** (*geh*) **a** (= *rauben*) to take away; **jdm den Atem ~** to take sb's breath away **b** (*rare*: = *die Sinne trüben*) **jdm die Sinne** *or* **den Kopf** *or* **jdn ~** to make sb feel dazed → *auch* **benommen**

Be|neh|men [bəˈneːmən] NT **-s**, *no pl* **a** behaviour (*Brit*), behavior (*US*); **kein ~ haben** to have no manners, to be bad-mannered **b**

(form: = Einvernehmen) **sich mit jdm ins ~ setzen** to get in touch with sb; **im ~ mit jdm** in conjunction with sb

be|nei|den [bɛˈnaɪdn] VT to envy; **jdn um etw ~** to envy sb sth; **er ist nicht zu ~** I don't envy him

be|nei|dens|wert [bəˈnaɪdnsveːɐt] ADJ enviable **ADV** wonderfully; **reich** enviably; **~ naïv** (iro) amazingly naïve

Be|ne|lux [ˈbeːnəlʊks, beneˈlʊks] abbr von **Belgien, Niederlande, Luxemburg**

Be|ne|lux|län|der [ˈbeːnəlʊks-, beneˈlʊks-] PL, **Be|ne|lux|staa|ten** PL Benelux countries pl

be|nen|nen ptp **benannt** [bəˈnant] VT irreg to name; **jdn auch** to call; **jdn/etw nach jdm ~** to name or call sb/sth after or for (US) sb

Be|nen|nung F (= das Benennen) naming; (von Mensch auch) calling; (= Bezeichnung) name, designation (form)

be|net|zen ptp **benetzt** VT (geh) to moisten; (Tau, Tränen auch) to cover

Ben|ga|le [bɛŋˈgaːlə] M -n, -n, **Ben|ga|lin** [-ˈgaːlɪn] F -, -nen Bengalese, Bengali

Ben|ga|len [bɛŋˈgaːlən] NT -s Bengal

ben|ga|lisch [bɛŋˈgaːlɪʃ] ADJ **a** Bengalese; Mensch, Sprache auch Bengali **b** -es Feuer Bengal light; **-es Hölzchen** Bengal match; **-e Beleuchtung** subdued multicoloured (Brit) or multicolored (US) lighting

Ben|gel [ˈbɛŋl] M -s, -(s) **a** boy, lad (Brit inf); (= frecher Junge) rascal; **ein süßer ~** (inf) a dear little boy **b** (dial: = Knüppel) stick; **den ~ wegwerfen** (dial) to lose courage

Be|nimm [bəˈnɪm] M -s, no pl (inf) manners pl

Be|nimm|re|gel F usu pl etiquette sing; **eine ~** a rule of etiquette

Be|nin [beˈniːn] M -s Benin

Ben|ja|min [ˈbɛnjamiːn] M -s, -e Benjamin; **er ist der ~** he is the baby of the family

be|nom|men [bəˈnɔmən] ADJ dazed; (von Ereignissen auch) bemused → auch **benehmen**

Be|nom|men|heit F -, no pl daze, dazed state

be|no|ten [bəˈnoːtn] ptp **benotet** VT to mark (Brit), to grade (esp US); **etw mit „gut" ~** to mark (Brit) or grade (esp US) sth "good"

be|nö|ti|gen ✪ 37.1 ptp **benötigt** VT to need, to require; **das benötigte Geld** etc the necessary money etc, the money etc needed

Be|no|tung F -, -en mark (Brit), grade (esp US); (= das Benoten) marking (Brit), grading (esp US)

be|nutz|bar ADJ usable; Weg passable

Be|nutz|bar|keit [bəˈnʊtsbaːɐkaɪt] F -, no pl usability

be|nut|zen ptp **benutzt**, (esp S Ger, Aus, Sw) **be|nüt|zen** ptp **benützt** VT (= verwenden) to use; Gelegenheit auch to make use of, to take advantage of; Literatur to consult; **etw als Schlafzimmer/Vorwand ~** to use sth as a bedroom/an excuse; **das benutzte Geschirr** the dirty dishes

Be|nut|zer M -s, -, **Be|nut|ze|rin** F -, -nen user; (von Leihbücherei) borrower

Be|nüt|zer [bəˈnʏtsɐ] M -s, -, **Be|nüt|ze|rin** F -, -nen (esp S Ger, Aus, Sw) user; (von Leihbücherei) borrower

Be|nut|zer-: be|nut|zer|freund|lich ADJ Computer, Telefonsystem user-friendly **ADV etw ~ gestalten** to make sth user-friendly; **~ konzipiert/designt sein** to be conceived/designed to be user-friendly; **Be|nut|zer|freund|lich|keit** F user-friendliness; **Be|nut|zer|hand|buch** NT user's guide, user handbook

Be|nut|ze|rin F, **Be|nüt|ze|rin** F → **Benutzer**, **Benützer**

Be|nut|zer-: Be|nut|zer|kreis M users pl; **Be|nut|zer|ober|flä|che** F (Comput) user or system interface; **Be|nut|zer|schnitt|stel|le** F (Comput) user interface; **Be|nut|zer|spra|che** F (Comput) user language

Be|nut|zung F, (esp S Ger, Aus, Sw) **Be|nüt|zung** [bəˈnʏtsʊŋ] F -, -en use; **etw in ~ haben/nehmen** to be/start using sth; **jdm etw zur ~ überlassen** to put sth at sb's disposal; **etw zur ~ freigeben** or **bereitstellen** to open sth

Be|nut|zungs|ge|bühr F charge; (= Leihgebühr) hire charge

ben|zen [ˈbɛntsn] VI (Aus inf) **a** (= betteln) to beg **b** (= klagen) to complain

Ben|zin [bɛnˈtsiːn] NT -s, -e (für Auto) petrol (Brit), gasoline (US), gas (US); (= Reinigungsbenzin) benzine; (= Feuerzeugbenzin) lighter fuel

Ben|zin-: Ben|zin|ab|schei|der [-lapʃaɪdɐ] M -s, - petrol (Brit) or gasoline (US) separator; **Ben|zin|ein|sprit|zung** F fuel injection

Ben|zi|ner [bɛnˈtsiːnɐ] M -s, - (inf) car which runs on petrol (Brit) or gasoline (US)

Ben|zin-: Ben|zin|feu|er|zeug NT petrol lighter (Brit), gasoline lighter (US); **Ben|zin|fres|ser** M (inf) petrol or fuel guzzler (Brit), gas guzzler (US); **Ben|zin|gut|schein** M petrol coupon (Brit), gasoline coupon (US); **Ben|zin|hahn** M fuel cock; **den ~ zudrehen** (fig) to stop the supply of petrol (Brit) or gasoline (US); **Ben|zin|ka|nis|ter** M petrol can (Brit), gasoline can (US); **Ben|zin|kos|ten** PL fuel costs pl, petrol (Brit) or gas (US) costs pl; **Ben|zin|kos|ten|be|tei|li|gung** F (gegen) (in Annonce) share petrol (Brit) or gas (US) costs; **Ben|zin|lei|tung** F fuel pipe, petrol pipe (Brit), gasoline pipe (US); **Ben|zin|mo|tor** M petrol engine (Brit), gasoline engine (US); **Ben|zin|preis** M cost of petrol (Brit) or gas(oline) (US), petrol (Brit) or gas (US) prices pl, cost or price of fuel; **Ben|zin|pum|pe** F (Aut) fuel pump; (an Tankstellen) petrol pump (Brit), gasoline pump (US); **Ben|zin|tank** M petrol (Brit) or gas (US) tank, fuel tank; **Ben|zin|uhr** F fuel gauge; **Ben|zin|ver|brauch** M fuel consumption, petrol consumption (Brit), gasoline consumption (US)

Ben|zoe [ˈbɛntsoe] F -, no pl benzoin

Ben|zo|e|säu|re F benzoic acid

Ben|zol [bɛnˈtsoːl] NT -s, -e benzol(e)

be|obacht|bar ADJ observable

be|obach|ten [bəˈoːbaxtn] ptp **beobachtet** VT to observe; (= bemerken auch) to notice, to see; (= genau verfolgen, betrachten auch) to watch; **etw an jdm ~** to notice sth in sb; **jdn ~ lassen** (Polizei etc) to put sb under surveillance; **er wird von der Polizei beobachtet** he's under police surveillance; **sich beobachtet fühlen** to feel (as if) one is being watched

Be|obach|ter [bəˈoːbaxtɐ] M -s, -, **Be|obach|te|rin** [-ərɪn] F -, -nen observer

Be|obach|ter-: Be|obach|ter|sta|tus M (form) observer status; **bei einer Konferenz** etc **~ haben** to take part in a conference etc as an observer; **Be|obach|ter|trup|pen** PL (Mil) observer force sing

Be|obach|tung F -, -en observation; (polizeilich) surveillance; **die ~ habe ich oft gemacht** I've often noticed that; **bei der ~ der Vorgänge ...** as I etc observed or watched these developments ...

Be|obach|tungs-: Be|obach|tungs|bal|lon M observation balloon; **Be|obach|tungs|ga|be** F talent for observation; **er hat eine gute ~** he has a very observant eye; **Be|obach|tungs|pos|ten** M (Mil) observation post; (= Mensch) lookout; **auf ~ sein** to be on lookout duty; **Be|obach|tungs|sa|tel|lit** M (Mil) observation satellite; **Be|obach|tungs|sta|ti|on** F **a** (Med) observation ward; (nach Operation) postoperative ward **b** (Met) weather station; **Be|obach|tungs|zeit|raum** M period of observation

be|or|dern ptp **beordert** VT to order; (= kommen lassen) to summon, to send for; (an andern Ort) to instruct or order to go; **jdn zu sich ~** to send for sb

be|pa|cken ptp **bepackt** VT to load (up); **jdn/etw mit etw ~** to load sb/sth up with sth VR to load oneself up

be|pflan|zen ptp **bepflanzt** VT to plant; **das Blumenbeet mit etw ~** to plant sth in the flower bed

Be|pflan|zung F **a** (= das Bepflanzen) planting **b** (= Gesamtheit der Pflanzen) plants pl (+gen in)

be|pflas|tern ptp **bepflastert** VT Straße to pave; (fig: = behängen) to plaster

be|pin|keln ptp **bepinkelt** (inf) VT to pee on (inf) VR to wet oneself (inf)

be|pin|seln ptp **bepinselt** VT to paint (auch fig); (Cook, Med) to brush; Zahnfleisch to paint; Wand to brush down; (= voll schreiben) to scribble on

be|pis|sen ptp **bepisst** VT (vulg) to piss on (sl) VR **a** (vulg: = urinieren) to piss (Brit sl) or wet oneself **b** (sl: = sich amüsieren) to piss oneself (laughing) (sl)

Be|plan|kung [bəˈplaŋkʊŋ] F -, -en (Tech) planking

be|pu|dern ptp **bepudert** VT to powder (auch fig)

be|quas|seln ptp **bequasselt** VT (inf) to talk over

be|quat|schen [bəˈkvatʃn] ptp **bequatscht** VT (inf) **a** etw to talk over **b** (= überreden) jdn to persuade; **wir haben sie bequatscht, dass sie kommt** we talked her into coming

be|quem [bəˈkveːm] ADJ (= angenehm) comfortable; Gast, Schüler etc easy; (= leicht, mühelos) Weg, Methode easy; Ausrede convenient; (= träge) Mensch idle; **es ~ haben** to have an easy time of it; **es sich** (dat) **~ machen** to make oneself comfortable; **machen Sie es sich ~** make yourself at home **ADV** (= leicht) easily; (= angenehm) comfortably; **sich ~ tragen** to be comfortable to wear; **auf dem Stuhl sitzt es sich ~** this chair is comfortable to sit in

be|que|men [bəˈkveːmən] ptp **bequemt** VR **sich zu etw ~, sich (dazu) ~, etw zu tun** to bring oneself to do sth; **endlich bequemten sie sich nach Hause** they finally forced themselves to go home

be|quem|lich [bəˈkveːmlɪç] ADJ (dated) = **bequem**

Be|quem|lich|keit F -, -en **a** no pl (= Behaglichkeit) comfort; (= Trägheit) laziness; **aus (reiner) ~** out of (sheer) laziness **b** (Einrichtung) convenience

be|rap|pen [bəˈrapn] ptp **berappt** VTI (inf) to fork or shell out (inf); **er musste schwer ~** he had to fork out a lot (inf)

be|ra|ten ✪ 29.2 ptp **beraten** irreg VT **a** jdn to advise sb, to give sb advice; **gut/schlecht ~ sein** to be well-advised/ill-advised; **jdn gut/schlecht ~** to give sb good/bad advice; **sich von jdm ~ lassen(, wie ...)** to ask sb's advice (on how ...), to consult sb (about how ...) **b** (= besprechen) to discuss VI to discuss; **mit jdm über etw** (acc) **~** to discuss sth with sb; **sie ~ noch** they are still in discussion, they are still discussing it VR (= gegenseitig Rat spenden) to give each other advice; (= sich besprechen) to discuss; **sich mit jdm ~** to consult (with) sb (über +acc about); **das Kabinett tritt heute zusammen, um sich zu ~** the cabinet meets today for talks

be|ra|tend ADJ advisory, consultative; Ingenieur consultant; **~es Gespräch** consultation; **er hat nur eine ~e Stimme** he is only in an advisory capacity **ADV** in an advisory capacity; **jdm ~ zur Seite stehen** to act in an advisory capacity to sb; **~ an einer Konferenz teilnehmen** to attend a conference in a consultative or an advisory capacity

Be|ra|ter [bəˈraːtɐ] M -s, -, **Be|ra|te|rin** [-ərɪn] F -, -nen adviser

Be|ra|ter-: Be|ra|ter|fir|ma F consulting *or* consultancy firm, firm of consultants; **Be|ra|ter|funk|ti|on** F advisory function; **Be|ra|ter|stab** M team of advisers, think tank (*inf*); **Be|ra|ter|tä|tig|keit** F consultancy work; **Be|ra|ter|ver|trag** M consultancy contract

be|rat|schla|gen ptp **beratschlagt** VTI insep to discuss

Be|rat|schla|gung F -, -en discussion

Be|ra|tung [bəˈraːtʊŋ] F -, -en a (= *das Beraten*) advice; (*bei Rechtsanwalt, Arzt etc*) consultation b (= *Besprechung*) discussion; **eine ~ haben** *or* **abhalten** to have *or* hold talks *or* discussions

Be|ra|tungs-: Be|ra|tungs|dienst M advice *or* advisory service; (*esp Comm, Fin auch*) consultancy; **Be|ra|tungs|ge|bühr** F consultancy fee; **Be|ra|tungs|ge|spräch** NT consultation; **Be|ra|tungs|stel|le** F advice centre (*Brit*) *or* center (*US*); **Be|ra|tungs|zim|mer** NT consultation room

be|rau|ben ptp **beraubt** VT to rob; **jdn einer Sache** (*gen*) **~** to rob sb of sth; **seiner Freiheit, seines Rechtes** ~ to deprive sb of sth; **aller Hoffnung beraubt** having lost all hope

be|rau|schen ptp **berauscht** VT (= *trunken machen*) to intoxicate; (*Alkohol etc auch*) to inebriate; (*Droge auch*) to make euphoric; (= *in Verzückung versetzen*) to intoxicate, to enrapture (*liter*); (*Geschwindigkeit*) to exhilarate; (*Blut, Gräueltat etc*) to put in a frenzy; **der Erfolg hat ihn völlig berauscht** he was carried away *or* drunk with success; **von Glück/Leidenschaft berauscht ...** in transports of happiness/passion ...; **berauscht von dem Wein** intoxicated by the wine; **berauscht von der Poesie/den Klängen** intoxicated *or* enraptured by the poetry/the sounds VR **sich an etw** (*dat*) **~** (*an Wein, Drogen*) to become intoxicated with sth; **an Geschwindigkeit** to be exhilarated by sth; **an Blut, Gräueltat etc** to be in a frenzy over sth

be|rau|schend ADJ *Getränke, Drogen* intoxicating; **das war nicht sehr ~** (*iro*) that wasn't very enthralling *or* exciting

Ber|ber¹ [ˈbɛrbə] M -s, - (*auch* **Berberteppich**) Berber carpet

Ber|ber² [ˈbɛrbə] M -s, -, **Ber|be|rin** [-ərɪn] F -, -nen (*in Nordafrika*) Berber b (*sl: = Penner*) tramp, bum (*esp US inf*), hobo (*US*)

Ber|be|rit|ze [bɛrbəˈrɪtsə] F -, -n (*Bot*) berberis

Ber|ber|tep|pich M Berber carpet

be|re|chen|bar ADJ *Kosten* calculable; *Verhalten etc* predictable

Be|re|chen|bar|keit [bəˈrɛçnbaːrkait] F -, no pl (*von Kosten*) calculability; (*von Verhalten etc*) predictability

be|rech|nen ptp **berechnet** VT a (= *ausrechnen*) to calculate; (= *schätzen*) to estimate; *Worte, Gesten* to calculate the effect of; **alles, was sie tut, ist berechnet** everything she does is calculated b (= *in Rechnung stellen*) to charge; **das ~ wir Ihnen nicht** we will not charge you for it; **das hat er mir mit 75 Euro berechnet** he charged me 75 euros for it c (= *vorsehen*) to intend, to mean; **alle Rezepte sind für 4 Personen berechnet** all the recipes are (calculated) for 4 persons; **auf eine bestimmte Wirkung berechnet sein** to be intended *or* calculated to have a particular effect

be|rech|nend ADJ (*pej*) *Mensch* calculating

Be|rech|nung F a (= *das Berechnen*) calculation; (= *Schätzung*) estimation; **meiner ~ nach, nach meiner ~** according to my calculations, by my reckoning b (*Comm: = Aufführen auf Rechnung*) charge; **ohne ~** without any charge c (*pej: = Eigennutz*) **aus ~ handeln** to act in a calculating manner, to act calculatingly; **mit kühler ~ vorgehen** to act in a cool and calculating manner; **es war alles genaue ~** it was all calculated exactly; **er ist nur aus ~ so freundlich** (= *weil er etwas will*) he's only being so friendly because he wants something; **sie hat**

mir viel geholfen, aber nur aus ~ she helped me a lot, but only because she wanted something

Be|rech|nungs|grund|la|ge F basis of calculation; (*von Steuer*) basis of assessment

be|rech|ti|gen [bəˈrɛçtɪɡn] ptp **berechtigt** VTI to entitle; **(jdn) zu etw ~** to entitle sb to sth; **diese Karte berechtigt nicht zum Eintritt** this ticket does not entitle the bearer to admittance; **er/seine Begabung berechtigt zu den größten Hoffnungen** he/his talent gives grounds for the greatest hopes; **das berechtigt zu der Annahme, dass ...** this justifies the assumption that ...

be|rech|tigt [bəˈrɛçtɪçt] ADJ justifiable; *Vorwurf auch* just; *Forderung, Einwand auch* justified; *Frage, Hoffnung* legitimate; *Anspruch* legitimate, rightful; **~ sein, etw zu tun** to be entitled to do sth; **einen ~en Anspruch auf etw** (*acc*) **haben** to have a legitimate *or* rightful claim to sth, to be fully entitled to sth

be|rech|tig|ter|wei|se [bəˈrɛçtɪçtɐˈvaizə] ADV legitimately; (= *verständlicherweise*) justifiably

Be|rech|ti|gung F -, -en a (= *Befugnis*) entitlement; (= *Recht*) right; **die ~/keine ~ haben, etw zu tun** to be entitled/not to be entitled to do sth b (= *Rechtmäßigkeit*) legitimacy; (= *Verständlichkeit*) justifiability

Be|rech|ti|gungs|schein M authorization

be|re|den ptp **beredet** VT a (= *besprechen*) to discuss, to talk over b (= *überreden*) **jdn zu etw ~** to talk sb into sth; **jdn dazu ~, etw zu tun** to talk sb into doing sth c (*inf: = beklatschen*) to gossip about VR **sich mit jdm über etw** (*acc*) **~** to talk sth over with sb, to discuss sth with sb; **die beiden haben sich miteinander beredet** the two of them talked it over

be|red|sam [bəˈreːtzaːm] ADJ (*geh*) eloquent; (*iro: = redselig*) talkative; **ein ~es Stück Geschichte** a telling period of history

Be|red|sam|keit F -, no pl (*geh*) eloquence

be|redt [bəˈreːt] (*geh*) ADJ eloquent; **mit ~en Worten** eloquently ADV eloquently; **~ Zeugnis von etw ablegen** to bear eloquent witness to sth

Be|redt|heit F -, no pl (*geh*) eloquence

be|reg|nen ptp **beregnet** VT to water, to sprinkle; (*vom Flugzeug aus*) to spray (with water); **beregnet werden** to be watered *etc*; (*natürlich*) to get rain

Be|reg|nung [bəˈreːɡnʊŋ] F -, -en watering, sprinkling; (*vom Flugzeug aus*) spraying (with water); (*natürliche*) rain(fall)

Be|reg|nungs|an|la|ge F sprinkler

Be|reich [bəˈraiç] M -(e)s, -e a area; **in nördlicheren ~en** in more northerly regions; **im ~ der Kaserne** inside the barracks; **im ~ des Domes** in the precincts of the cathedral; **im ~ der Innenstadt** in the city centre (*Brit*) *or* center (*US*) (area) b (= *Einflussbereich, Aufgabenbereich*) sphere; (= *Sachbereich*) area, sphere, field; (= *Sektor*) sector; **im ~ des Möglichen liegen** to be within the realms *or* bounds of possibility; **Musik aus dem ~ der Oper** music from the realm of opera; **in jds ~** (*acc*) **fallen** to be within sb's province

be|rei|chern [bəˈraiçɐn] ptp **bereichert** VT (*lit, fig*) to enrich; (= *vergrößern*) to enlarge; **das Gespräch hat mich sehr bereichert** I gained a great deal from the conversation VR to make a lot of money (*an +dat* out of); **sich auf Kosten anderer ~** to feather one's nest at the expense of other people

Be|rei|che|rung F -, -en a (= *das Bereichern*) enrichment; (= *Vergrößerung*) enlargement; **persönliche ~** (*Jur*) personal gain; **~ im Amt** (*Jur*) exploiting one's position for personal gain b (= *das Reichwerden*) moneymaking; **seine eigene ~** making money for oneself c (= *Gewinn*) boon; **das Gespräch mit Ihnen war mir eine ~** I gained a lot from my conversation with you;

das ist eine wertvolle ~ that is a valuable addition

be|rei|fen ptp **bereift** VT (*Aut*) *Wagen* to put tyres (*Brit*) *or* tires (*US*) on; *Rad* to put a tyre (*Brit*) *or* tire (*US*) on; *Fass* to hoop; **gut/richtig bereift sein** (*Auto*) to have good/the right tyres (*Brit*) *or* tires (*US*)

Be|rei|fung [bəˈraifʊŋ] F -, -en (*Aut*) set of tyres (*Brit*) *or* tires (*US*); **eine neue ~** new tyres (*Brit*) *or* tires (*US*), a new set of tyres (*Brit*) *or* tires (*US*); **die ~ bei diesem Auto** the tyres (*Brit*) *or* tires (*US*) on this car

be|rei|ni|gen ptp **bereinigt** VT to clear up, to resolve; *Meinungsverschiedenheiten auch* to settle; **ich habe mit ihr noch etwas zu ~** I have something to clear up with her; **die Sache hat sich von selbst bereinigt** the matter resolved itself, the matter cleared itself up; **den Markt ~** (*Comm euph*) to remove the competition from the market

be|rei|nigt [bəˈrainɪçt] ADJ (= *korrigiert*) *Statistik, Quote* adjusted

Be|rei|ni|gung F clearing up, resolving; (*von Meinungsverschiedenheit*) settling

be|rei|sen ptp **bereist** VT *ein Land* to travel around; (*Comm*) *Gebiet* to travel, to cover; **die Welt/fremde Länder ~** to travel the world/in foreign countries

be|reit [bəˈrait] ADJ *usu pred* a (= *fertig*) ready; (= *vorbereitet auch*) prepared; **es ist alles zum Essen ~** the meal is all ready *or* prepared; **es ist alles zum Aufbruch ~** we're all ready to go; **zum Einsatz ~e Truppen** troops ready *or* prepared to go into action → **bereithaben, bereithalten VR** b (= *willens*) willing, prepared; **zu Zugeständnissen/Verhandlungen ~ sein** to be prepared to make concessions/to negotiate; **~ sein, etw zu tun** to be willing *or* prepared to do sth; **sich ~ zeigen, etw zu tun** to show oneself willing *or* prepared *or* ready to do sth; **sich ~ erklären, etw zu tun** to agree to do sth; **sich zu etw ~ finden** to be willing *or* prepared to do sth → **Schandtat**

be|rei|ten¹ [bəˈraitn] ptp **bereitet** VT a (= *zubereiten*) (+*dat* for) to prepare; *Arznei* to make up; *Bett* to make (up) b (= *verursachen*) to cause; *Überraschung, Empfang, Freude, Kopfschmerzen* to give; **jdm Kummer/Ärger ~** to cause sb grief/trouble; **er hat mir Schwierigkeiten bereitet** he made difficulties for me; **das bereitet mir Schwierigkeiten** it causes me difficulties; **einer Sache** (*dat*) **ein Ende ~** to put an end to sth; **es bereitet mir (viel *or* ein großes) Vergnügen** (*form*) it gives me (the greatest) pleasure VR **sich zu etw ~** (*geh*) to prepare oneself for sth

be|rei|ten² ptp **beritten** [bəˈrɪtn] VT irreg *Gebiet* to ride over

be|reit-: be|reit+ha|ben ▲ VT sep irreg **eine Antwort/Ausrede ~** to have an answer/excuse ready, to have a ready answer/excuse; **be|reit+hal|ten** sep irreg VT *Fahrkarten etc* to have ready; (*für den Notfall*) to keep ready; *Überraschung* to have in store; **wer weiß, was das Schicksal für uns bereithält?** who knows what fate has in store for us? ▲ VR **sich ~** to be ready *or* prepared; **be|reit+le|gen** VT sep to lay out ready; **be|reit+lie|gen** VI sep irreg to be ready; **be|reit+ma|chen** VT sep to get ready

be|reits [bəˈraits] ADV already; **~ vor drei Wochen/vor 100 Jahren** even three weeks/100 years ago; **~ damals/damals, als ...** even then/when ...; **das haben wir ~ gestern *or* gestern ~ gemacht** we did that yesterday; **er ist ~ vor zwei Stunden angekommen** he arrived two hours ago; **ich warte ~ seit einer Stunde** I've (already) been waiting for an hour; **der Bus ist ~ abgefahren** the bus has already left; **das hat man mir ~ gesagt** I've been told that already; **~ am nächsten Tage** on the very next day

Be|reit|schaft [bəˈraitʃaft] F -, -en a no pl readiness; (= *Bereitwilligkeit auch*) willingness, preparedness; **in ~ sein** to be ready; (*Polizei, Feuerwehr, Soldaten etc*) to be on stand-by; (*Arzt*) to be on call or (*im Krankenhaus*) on duty; **etw in ~ haben** to have sth ready or in readiness **b** *no pl* (= *Bereitschaftsdienst*) ~ **haben** (*Arzt etc*) to be on call or (*im Krankenhaus*) on duty; (*Apotheke*) to provide emergency or after-hours service; (*Polizei etc*) to be on stand-by **c** (= *Mannschaft*) squad

Be|reit|schafts-: Be|reit|schafts|arzt M , **Be|reit|schafts|ärz|tin** F doctor on call; (*im Krankenhaus*) duty doctor; **Be|reit|schafts|-dienst** M emergency service; **~ haben → Bereitschaft b**; **Be|reit|schafts|po|li|zei** F riot police

Be|reit-: be|reit+ste|hen VI *sep irreg* to be ready; (*Flugzeug auch, Truppen*) to stand by; **die Truppen stehen bereit** the troops are standing by; **etw ~ haben** to have sth ready; **Ihr Wagen steht bereit** your car is waiting; **zur Abfahrt ~** to be ready to depart; **be|reit+stel|len** VT *sep* to get ready; *Material, Fahrzeug, Mittel* to provide, to supply; (*Rail*) to make available; *Truppen* to put on stand-by; **Be|reit|stel|lung** F preparation; (*von Auto, Material, Mitteln*) provision, supply; (*von Truppen*) putting on stand-by

Be|rei|tung [bəˈraitʊŋ] F -, -en preparation

Be|reit-: be|reit|wil|lig ADJ (= *entgegenkommend*) willing; (= *eifrig*) eager; **~e Auskunft erteilen** to give information willingly **ADV** willingly, annehmen, Auskunft erteilen gladly; **Be|reit|wil|lig|keit** F (= *Entgegenkommen*) willingness; (= *Eifer*) eagerness

be|ren|nen *ptp* **berannt** VT *irreg* (*Mil*) to charge, to assault; (*Sport*) to rush, to storm

be|ren|ten [bəˈrɛntn] *ptp* **berentet** VT (*Admin sl*) **berentet werden** to retire and receive a pension; **sich ~ lassen** to retire with a pension

Bé|ret [beˈrɛ] NT -s, -s, **Be|ret** NT -s, -s (*Sw*) beret

be|reu|en *ptp* **bereut** **VT** to regret; *Schuld, Sünden* to repent of; **~, etw getan zu haben** to regret having done sth; **das wirst du noch ~!** you will be sorry (for that)! **VI** to repent

Berg [bɛrk] M -(e)s, -e [-gə] **a** hill; (*größer*) mountain; **wenn der ~ nicht zum Propheten kommt, muss der Prophet zum ~ kommen** (*Prov*) if the mountain won't come to Mahomet, then Mahomet must go to the mountain (*Prov*); **~e versetzen (können)** to (be able to) move mountains; **~e versetzend** (*Glaube*) colossal; **mit etw hinterm ~ halten** (*fig*) to keep sth to oneself, to keep quiet about sth; **mit seinem Alter** to be cagey about sth; **in die ~e fahren** to go to the hills *etc*; **über ~ und Tal** up hill and down dale; **über den ~ sein** (*inf*) to be out of the woods; **über alle ~e sein** (*inf*) to be long gone, to be miles away (*inf*); **jdm goldene ~e versprechen** to promise sb the moon; **die Haare standen ihm zu ~e** his hair stood on end; **da stehen einem ja die Haare zu ~e** it's enough to make your hair stand on end; **am ~ sein** (*Sw fig* = *ratlos*) to be in the dark → **kreißen, Ochs a b** (= *große Menge*) heap, pile; (*von Sorgen*) mass; (*von Papieren*) mountain, heap, pile **c** (*inf:* = *Bergwerk*) pit; **im ~ arbeiten** to work down the pit

Berg- *in cpds* mountain; (= *Bergbau-*) mining; **berg|ab** [bɛrkˈlap] ADV downhill; **es geht mit ihm ~** (*fig*) he is going downhill; **Berg|ab|hang** M side of a mountain, mountainside; **Berg|ab|satz** M ledge; **Berg|ab|sturz** M drop; **berg|ab|wärts** [bɛrkˈlapvɛrts] ADV downhill; **Berg|ahorn** M sycamore (tree); **Berg|aka|de|mie** F mining college

Ber|ga|mot|te [bɛrgaˈmɔtə] F -, -n bergamot

Berg-: Berg|amt NT mining authority; **berg|an** [bɛrkˈlan] ADV = **bergauf**; **Berg|ar|bei|ter(in)** M(F) miner; **berg|auf(|wärts)** [bɛrkˈlauf(vɛrts)] ADV uphill; **es geht wieder bergauf** (*fig*) things are getting better or looking up; **es geht mit seinem Geschäft/seiner Gesundheit wieder bergauf** his business/health is looking up;

Berg|bahn F mountain railway; (= *Seilbahn*) funicular or cable railway; **Berg|bau** M , *no pl* mining; **Berg|bau|er** M mountain farmer; **Berg|bäu|e|rin** F (female) mountain farmer; **Berg|be|woh|ner(in)** M(F) mountain dweller; **Berg|dorf** NT mountain village

Ber|ge-: ber|ge|hoch ADJ, ADV = **berghoch**; **Ber|ge|lohn** M (*Naut*) salvage (money)

ber|gen [ˈbɛrgn] *pret* **barg** [bark], *ptp* **geborgen** [gəˈbɔrgn] VT **a** (= *retten*) *Menschen* to save, to rescue; *Leichen* to recover; *Ladung, Schiff, Fahrzeug* to salvage; *Ernte* to get or gather (in); (*Naut*) *Segel* to furl; **aus dem Wasser tot/lebend geborgen werden** to be brought out of the water dead/alive; **25 Passagiere konnten lebend geborgen werden** (*nach Flugzeugabsturz*) 25 passengers were brought out alive **b** (*geh:* = *enthalten*) to hold; *Schätze auch* to hide; **das birgt viele Gefahren in sich** that holds many dangers; **diese Möglichkeit birgt die Gefahr/das Risiko in sich, dass ...** this possibility involves the danger/risk that ... **c** (*liter:* = *verbergen*) *Gesicht* to hide; *Verfolgten etc* to shelter; **sie barg ihren Kopf an seiner Schulter** she buried her face in his shoulder → *auch* **geborgen**

ber|ge-: ber|ge|ver|set|zend △ ADJ → **Berg a**; **ber|ge|weise** ADV by the ton

Berg-: Berg|fach NT mining; **Berg|fahrt** F **a** mountaineering or climbing expedition; **auf ~ gehen** to go mountaineering *etc* or on a mountaineering *etc* expedition **b** (*auf Fluss*) upstream passage; (*von Seilbahn*) uphill or upward journey; **Berg|fex** M (*inf*) mountaineering enthusiast or freak (*inf*); **Berg|fried** [ˈbɛrkfriːt] M -(e)s, -e [-də] keep; **Berg|füh|rer(in)** M(F) mountain guide; **Berg|geist** M mountain troll; **Berg|gip|fel** M mountain top; **Berg|grat** M mountain ridge; **Berg|hang** M mountain slope; **berg|hoch** ADJ *Wellen, Haufen* mountainous; **berghoher Müll** mountains of rubbish **ADV** **die Wellen stiegen ~** the waves reached mountainous heights; **der Müll türmt sich ~** mountains of rubbish are piling up; **die Akten stapeln sich schon ~** the files are already piling up a mile high; **Berg|hüt|te** F mountain hut or refuge, bothy (*Scot*)

ber|gig [ˈbɛrgɪç] ADJ hilly; (= *mit hohen Bergen*) mountainous

Berg-: Berg|in|ge|ni|eur(in) M(F) mining engineer; **Berg|kamm** M mountain crest; **Berg|kes|sel** M cirque, corrie; **Berg|ket|te** F mountain range or chain, range or chain of mountains; **berg|krank** ADJ affected by mountain sickness; **Berg|krank|heit** F mountain sickness; **Berg|krax|ler** [-kraksle] M -s, -, **Berg|krax|le|rin** [-ərɪn] F -, -nen (*inf*) mountaineer; **Berg|kris|tall** M rock crystal; **Berg|kup|pe** F (round) mountain top; **Berg|land** NT hilly or (= *Gebirgsland*) mountainous country; (= *Gegend*) hilly/mountainous region; (= *Landschaft*) hilly/mountainous scenery; **Berg|luft** F mountain air

Berg|mann M *pl* **-leute** miner

berg|män|nisch [-mɛnɪʃ] ADJ miner's *attr*

Berg|manns-: Berg|manns|gruß M miner's greeting; **Berg|manns|spra|che** F mining terminology

Berg-: Berg|not F **in ~ sein/geraten** to be in/get into difficulties while climbing; **jdn aus ~ retten** to rescue sb who was in difficulties while climbing; **Berg|pfad** M mountain path; **Berg|pla|teau** NT mountain plateau; **Berg|pre|digt** F (*Bibl*) Sermon on the Mount; **berg|reich** ADJ mountainous; **Berg|ren|nen** NT (*Sport*) hill climbing; **ein ~** a hill climb; **Berg|ret|tungs|dienst** M mountain rescue service; **Berg|rie|se** M gigantic mountain; **Berg|rü|cken** M mountain ridge or crest; **Berg|rutsch** M landslide (*auch fig*), landslip; **Berg|sat|tel** M (mountain) saddle, col; **Berg|schrund** M bergschrund (*spec*); **Berg|schuh** M climbing boot; **berg|seits** [ˈbɛrkzaits],

berg|sei|tig ADV on the mountain side; **Berg|spit|ze** F mountain peak; **Berg|sport** M mountaineering, mountain climbing; **Berg|sta|ti|on** F top station, summit station; **berg+steigen** VI *sep irreg aux sein or haben, infin and ptp only* to go mountain climbing or mountaineering, to mountaineer; **~ gehen** to go mountain climbing or mountaineering; **(das) Bergsteigen** mountaineering, mountain climbing; **Berg|stei|ger(in)** M(F) mountaineer, mountain climber; **Berg|stei|ge|rei** [bɛrkʃtaigəˈrai] F -, -en (*inf*) mountaineering, mountain climbing; **Berg|stei|ge|risch** [ˈbɛrkʃtaigərɪʃ] **ADJ** mountaineering, mountain-climbing **ADV** from a mountaineering point of view; **Berg|stock** M **a** (= *Wanderstock*) alpenstock **b** (*Geol*) massif; **Berg|stra|ße** F mountain road; **die ~** (*Geog*) *wine-producing area north of Heidelberg*

Berg-: Berg|sturz M landslide, landslip; **Berg|tour** F trip round the mountains; (= *Bergbesteigung*) (mountain) climb; **Berg-und-Tal-Bahn** F roller coaster, big dipper (*Brit*), switchback (*Brit*); **Berg-und-Tal-Fahrt** F ride on the roller coaster *etc*; **das war die reinste ~** (*fig*) it was like being on a roller coaster

Ber|gung F -, -en **a** (*von Menschen*) saving, rescue; (*von Leiche*) recovery; (*von Ladung, Schiff, Fahrzeug*) salvage, salvaging; (*von Ernte*) gathering (in) **b** (*liter. von Verfolgten*) sheltering

Ber|gungs-: Ber|gungs|ak|ti|on F rescue operation; (*bei Schiffen etc*) salvage operation; **Ber|gungs|ar|bei|ten** PL rescue work *sing*; (*bei Schiffen etc*) salvage work *sing or operation sing*; **Ber|gungs|damp|fer** M salvage vessel; **Ber|gungs|fahr|zeug** NT rescue vehicle; (*bei Flugzeugabsturz auch*) crash vehicle; (*Naut*) salvage vessel; **Ber|gungs|hub|schrau|ber** M rescue helicopter; **Ber|gungs|kom|man|do** NT (*esp Mil*) **Ber|gungs|mann|schaft** **F** rescue team

Ber|gungs|schiff NT salvage vessel, **Ber|gungs|trupp** M rescue team

Berg-: Berg|volk NT **a** mountain race **b** (*rare:* = *Bergleute*) miners **c** (*= Bergbesteigung*) (mountain) ledge; **Berg|vor|sprung** M (mountain) ledge; **Berg|wacht** F mountain rescue service; **Berg|wald** M mountain forest or wood(s *pl*); **Berg|wand** F mountain face; **Berg|wan|dern** NT mountain hiking; **Berg|wan|de|rung** F walk or hike in the mountains; **berg|wärts** [ˈbɛrkvɛrts] ADV uphill; **Berg|welt** F mountains *pl*; **Berg|werk** NT mine; **im ~ arbeiten** to work down the mine; **Berg|wie|se** F mountain pasture; **Berg|zin|ne** F (*geh*) mountain pinnacle

Be|ri|be|ri [beriˈbeːri] F -, *no pl* (*Med*) beriberi

Be|richt [bəˈrɪçt] M -(e)s, -e report (*von* on, *über +acc* about, on); (= *Erzählung auch*) account; (= *Zeitungsbericht auch*) story; (*Sch:* = *Aufsatzform*) commentary; **der ~ eines Augenzeugen** an eyewitness account; **~e zum Tagesgeschehen** news reports; **eigener ~** from our correspondent; (*über etw acc*) **~ erstatten** to report (on sth), to give a report (on sth); **jdm über etw** (*acc*) **~ erstatten** to give sb a report on sth

be|rich|ten *ptp* **berichtet** VTI to report; (= *erzählen*) to tell; **jdm über etw** (*acc*) **~** to report to sb about sth; (= *erzählen*) to tell sb about sth; **mir ist (darüber) berichtet worden, dass ...** I have received reports that ..., I have been told that ...; **uns wird soeben berichtet, dass ...** (*Rad, TV*) news is just coming in that ...; **wie unser Korrespondent** according to our correspondent; **wie soeben berichtet wird, sind die Verhandlungen abgebrochen worden** we are just receiving reports that negotiations have been broken off; **gibt es Neues zu ~?** has anything new happened?; **sie berichtete, dass ...** she said *or* reported that ...; **sie hat bestimmt viel(es) zu ~** she is sure to have a lot to tell us

Be|richt-: Be|richt|er|stat|ter [bə'rıçt|ɛɐʃtatɐ] M -s, -, **Be|richt|er|stat|te|rin** [-ərın] F -, -nen reporter; (= *Korrespondent*) correspondent; **~ ist ...** (*bei Jahresversammlung etc*) the report will be given by ...; **Be|richt|er|stat|tung** F reporting; **eine objektive ~** objective reporting; **~ durch Presse/Rundfunk** press/radio reporting; **die ~ über diese Vorgänge in der Presse** press coverage of these events; **zur ~ zurückgerufen werden** to be called back to report *or* to make a report

be|rich|ti|gen [bə'rıçtıgn] ✪ 47.5 *ptp* **berichtigt** VT to correct; *Fehler auch* to rectify; (*Jur*) to rectify; *Text, Aussage auch* to amend

Be|rich|ti|gung F -, -en correction; (*von Fehler auch, Jur*) rectification; (*von Text, Aussage auch*) amendment

Be|rich|ti|gungs|ak|tie F (*St Ex*) bonus share

Be|richts-: Be|richts|heft NT apprentice's record book; **Be|richts|jahr** NT (*Comm*) year under review *or* report; **Be|richts|zeug|nis** NT (*Sch*) (school) report (*giving a written assessment of the pupil's work rather than grades*), report card (*US, Scot*)

be|rie|chen *ptp* **berochen** [bə'rɔxn] VT *irreg* to sniff at, to smell; **sich (gegenseitig) ~** (*fig inf*) to size each other up

be|rie|seln *ptp* **berieselt** VT **a** (*mit Flüssigkeit*) to spray with water *etc*; (*durch Sprinkleranlage*) to sprinkle **b** (*fig inf*) **von etw berieselt werden** (*fig*) to be exposed to a constant stream of sth; **sich von Musik ~ lassen** to have a (constant stream of) music going on in the background

Be|rie|se|lung [bə'ri:zəluŋ] F -, -en watering; **die ständige ~ der Kunden mit Musik/Werbung** exposing the customers to a constant stream of music/advertisements; **die ~ mit** *or* **durch etw** (*fig*) the constant stream of sth

be|rin|gen *ptp* **beringt** VT to put a ring on; *Vogel auch* to ring; **mit Diamanten beringte Finger** fingers ringed with diamonds

Be|ring|meer ['be:rıŋ-] NT Bering Sea

Be|ring|stra|ße ['be:rıŋ-] F Bering Strait(s *pl*)

Be|rin|gung [bə'rıŋʊŋ] F -, -en putting a ring on; (*von Vogel auch*) ringing; (= *Ring*) ring

be|rit|ten [bə'rıtn] ADJ mounted, on horseback; **~e Polizei** mounted police

Ber|ke|li|um [bɛr'ke:liʊm] NT -s, *no pl* (*abbr* **Bk**) berkelium

Ber|lin [bɛr'li:n] NT -s Berlin

Ber|li|ner¹ [bɛr'li:nɐ] ADJ *attr* Berlin; **~ Weiße (mit Schuss)** light, fizzy beer (*with fruit juice added*)

Ber|li|ner² [bɛr'li:nɐ] M -s, - (*auch* **Berliner Pfannkuchen**) doughnut (*Brit*), donut (*US*)

Ber|li|ner³ [bɛr'li:nɐ] M -s, -, **Ber|li|ne|rin** [-ərın] F -, -nen Berliner

ber|li|ne|risch [bɛr'li:nərıʃ] ADJ (*inf*) Dialekt Berlin *attr*; **er spricht Berlinerisch** he speaks the Berlin dialect

ber|li|nern [bɛr'li:nɐn] *ptp* **berlinert** VI (*inf*) to speak in the Berlin dialect

ber|li|nisch [bɛr'li:nıʃ] ADJ Berlin *attr*

Ber|mu|da|drei|eck [bɛr'mu:da-] NT Bermuda triangle

Ber|mu|da|in|seln [bɛr'mu:da-] PL , **Ber|mu|das¹** [bɛr'mu:das] PL Bermuda *sing, no def art*; **auf den ~** in Bermuda, in the Bermudas

Ber|mu|das² [bɛr'mu:das] PL , **Ber|mu|da|shorts** [bɛr'mu:da-] PL Bermuda shorts *pl*, Bermudas *pl*

Bern [bɛrn] NT -s Bern(e)

Ber|ner¹ ['bɛrnɐ] ADJ *attr* Berne(se)

Ber|ner² ['bɛrnɐ] M -s, -, **Ber|ne|rin** [-ərın] F -, -nen Bernese

Bern|har|di|ner [bɛrnhar'di:nɐ] M -s, - Saint Bernard (dog)

Bern|stein ['bɛrnʃtain] M , *no pl* amber

bern|stein|far|ben [-farbn], **bern|stein|gelb** ADJ amber(-coloured) (*Brit*), amber(-colored) (*US*)

be|rockt [bə'rɔkt] ADJ (*hum*) (dressed) in a skirt

Ber|ser|ker [bɛr'zɛrkɐ, 'bɛrzɛrkɐ] M -s, - (*Hist*) berserker; **wie ein ~ arbeiten/kämpfen** to work/fight like mad (*inf*) *or* fury; **wie ein ~ toben** to go berserk; **auf jdn einschlagen wie ein ~** to go berserk and attack sb

bers|ten ['bɛrstn] *pret* **barst** [barst], *ptp* **geborsten** [gə'bɔrstn] VI *aux sein* (*geh*) to crack; (= *aufbersten, zerbrechen*) to break; (= *zerplatzen*) to burst; (*fig: vor Wut etc*) to burst (*vor* with); **als wollte ihm das Herz in der Seele ~** as if his heart would burst; **die Erde barst** the earth broke asunder (*liter*); **vor Ungeduld/Neugier/Zorn** *etc* **~** to be bursting with impatience/curiosity/anger *etc*; **zum Bersten voll** (*auch inf*) full to bursting

Berst|schutz M (*im Kernreaktor*) safety containment

be|rüch|tigt [bə'rʏçtıçt] ADJ notorious, infamous

be|rü|cken *ptp* **berückt** VT (*geh*) to charm, to enchant

be|rü|ckend ADJ charming, enchanting; **das ist nicht gerade ~** (*iro inf*) it's not exactly stunning

be|rück|sich|ti|gen [bə'rʏkzıçtıgn] *ptp* **berücksichtigt** VT (= *beachten, bedenken*) to take into account *or* consideration; *Mangel, Alter, geringe Erfahrung, körperliches Leiden* to make allowances for; (= *in Betracht ziehen*) *Antrag, Bewerbung, Bewerber* to consider; **das ist zu ~** that must be taken into account *or* consideration; **meine Vorschläge wurden nicht berücksichtigt** my suggestions were disregarded

Be|rück|sich|ti|gung F -, -en consideration; **in** *or* **unter ~ der Umstände/der Tatsache, dass ...** in view of the circumstances/the fact that ...; **eine ~ Ihres Antrags ist zurzeit nicht möglich** it is impossible for us to consider your application at present

Be|ruf [bə'ru:f] M (= *Tätigkeit*) occupation; (*akademischer auch*) profession; (*handwerklicher*) trade; (= *Stellung*) job; **freie ~e** independent professions; **was sind Sie von ~?** what is your occupation *etc*?, what do you do for a living?; **von ~ Arzt/Bäcker/Hausfrau sein** to be a doctor by profession/a baker by *or* to (*Brit*) trade/a housewife by occupation; **ihr stehen viele ~e offen** many careers are open to her; **seinen ~ verfehlt haben** to have missed one's vocation; **im ~ stehen** to be working; **von ~s wegen** on account of one's job

be|ru|fen¹ [bə'ru:fn] *ptp* **berufen** *irreg* VT **a** (= *ernennen, einsetzen*) to appoint; **jdn auf einen Lehrstuhl/zu einem Amt ~** to appoint sb to a chair/an office **b** (*old: = kommen lassen*) **jdn zu sich/an einen Ort ~** to call *or* summon sb to one/to a place; **Gott hat ihn zu sich ~** he has been called to his Maker **c** (*inf: = beschwören*) **ich will/wir wollen** *etc* **es nicht ~** touch wood (*Brit inf*), knock on wood (*US inf*); **ich will es nicht ~, aber ...** I don't want to tempt fate, but ... **d** (*dial: = ermahnen*) to tell off, to reproach VR **sich auf jdn/etw ~** to refer to sb/sth VI (*Aus Jur: = Berufung einlegen*) to appeal

be|ru|fen² [bə'ru:fn] ADJ **a** (= *befähigt*) Kritiker competent, capable; **von ~er Seite, aus ~em Mund** from an authoritative source; **zu etw ~ sein, ~ sein, etw zu tun** to be competent to do sth **b** (= *ausersehen*) **zu etw ~ sein** to have a vocation for sth; (*esp Rel*) to be called to sth; **viele sind ~** (*Bibl*) many are called; **sich zu etw ~ fühlen** to feel one has a mission to be/do sth

be|ruf|lich [bə'ru:flıç] ADJ (*esp auf akademische Berufe bezüglich*) professional; *Weiterbildung auch* job- *or* career-orientated; **sein ~er Werdegang** his career; **im ~en Leben** in my *etc* working life, in my *etc* career; **meine ~en Probleme** my problems at work *or* in my job; **was das Berufliche betrifft, bin ich zufrieden** as far as my job is concerned I am satisfied ADV professionally, jobwise; **~ ist sie sehr erfolgreich** she is very successful in her career; **sich ~ weiterbilden** to undertake further job- *or* career-orientated *or* professional training; **er ist ~ viel unterwegs** he is away a lot on business; **sich ~ verbessern** to get a better job; **was machen Sie ~?** what do you do for a living?; **er ist ~ Elektriker** he's an electrician by *or* to (*Brit*) trade

Be|rufs- *in cpds* professional; **Berufs|all|tag** M (everyday) working life; **Be|rufs|an|fän|ger(in)** M(F) **sie ist ~in** she has just entered the job market; **wir suchen Lexikografen, keine ~** vacancies for lexicographers, experience necessary; **Be|rufs|auf|bau|schu|le** F vocational school preparing adult learners for technical college; **Be|rufs|aus|bil|dung** F training (*for an occupation*); (*für Handwerk*) vocational training; **Be|rufs|aus|bil|dungs|bei|hil|fe** F supplementary allowance for people on vocational training courses; **Be|rufs|aus|sich|ten** PL job prospects *pl*; **Be|rufs|aus|ü|bung** F pursuit of one's career; **jdm die ~ untersagen** not to allow sb to pursue his or her career, to exclude sb from his or her profession; **Be|rufs|be|am|ten|tum** NT civil service with tenure; **Be|rufs|be|am|te(r)** M *decl as adj*, **Be|rufs|be|am|tin** F civil servant with tenure; **be|rufs|be|dingt** ADJ occupational, caused by one's occupation; **be|rufs|be|glei|tend** ADJ in tandem with work; **ein ~es Studium absolvieren** to complete a course of study while working; **Be|rufs|be|ra|ter(in)** M(F) careers adviser; **Be|rufs|be|ra|tung** F careers guidance; **Be|rufs|be|zeich|nung** F job title; **be|rufs|be|zo|gen** [-bətso:gn] ADJ relevant to one's job; *Unterricht* vocationally orientated ADV practically orientated; **Be|rufs|bild** NT job outline; **be|rufs|bil|dend** ADJ **~e Schulen** vocational schools; **Be|rufs|boxen** NT professional boxing; **Be|rufs|chan|cen** [-ʃã:sn] PL job *or* career prospects *pl*; **be|rufs|er|fah|ren** ADJ (professionally) experienced; **Be|rufs|er|fah|rung** F (professional) experience; **Be|rufs|ethos** NT professional ethics *pl*; **Be|rufs|fach|schu|le** F training college (*attended full-time*); **Be|rufs|feu|er|wehr** F fire service; **Be|rufs|frei|heit** F freedom to choose and carry out one's career; **be|rufs|fremd** ADJ *Tätigkeit* unconnected with one's occupation; *Mensch* from outside the/a profession/trade; **ei|ne ~e Tätigkeit** a job outside one's profession; (*handwerklich*) a job outside one's trade; **Be|rufs|frem|de(r)** MF *decl as adj* person from outside the/a profession/trade; **Be|rufs|fuß|ball** M professional football (*Brit*) or soccer (*US*); **Be|rufs|ge|heim|nis** NT professional secret; (= *Schweigepflicht*) professional secrecy, confidentiality; **das ~ wahren** to observe professional secrecy *or* confidentiality; **Be|rufs|ge|nos|sen|schaft** F → **Beruf** professional/trade association; **Be|rufs|grup|pe** F occupational group; **Be|rufs|heer** NT professional or regular army; **Be|rufs|klei|dung** F working clothes pl; **Be|rufs|krank|heit** F occupational disease; **Be|rufs|kri|mi|na|li|tät** F professional crime; **Be|rufs|le|ben** NT working or professional life; **im ~ stehen** to be working, to be in employment; **be|rufs|los** ADJ without a profession/trade; **be|rufs|mä|ßig** ADJ professional **ADV** professionally; **etw ~ betreiben** to do sth professionally, to do sth on a professional basis; **Be|rufs|of|fi|zier(in)** M(F) regular officer; **Be|rufs|pflicht** F professional duty; **Be|rufs|po|li|ti|ker(in)** M(F) professional or career politician; **Be|rufs|prak|ti|kum** NT (practical) work experience; (von Arzt, Lehrer etc) (practical (Brit)); **Be|rufs|re|vo|lu|tio|när(in)** M(F) (esp pej) professional revolutionary; **Be|rufs|ri|si|ko** NT occupational hazard or risk; **Be|rufs|schu|le** F vocational school, ≈ technical college (Brit); **Be|rufs|schü|ler(in)** M(F) student at a vocational school, ≈ student at a technical college (Brit); **Be|rufs|sol|dat(in)** M(F) regular or professional soldier; **Be|rufs|spie|ler(in)** M(F) professional player; **Be|rufs|sport** M professional sport; **Be|rufs|sport|ler(in)** M(F) professional sportsman/ -woman; **Be|rufs|stand** M profession, professional group; (= Gewerbe) trade; **Be|rufs|start** M **ein erfolgreicher ~** a successful start to his/ her etc career; **be|rufs|tä|tig** ADJ working; **~ sein** to be working, to work; **halbtags ~ sein** to work part-time; **ich bin auch ~** I go out to work too; **nicht mehr ~ sein** to have stopped work; **Be|rufs|tä|ti|ge(r)** [-tɛːtɪgə] MF decl as adj working person; **Be|rufs|tä|tig|keit** F (= Ausübung eines Berufs) occupation; **während meiner ~** during my working life; **Frauen** (dat) **die ~ ermöglichen** to enable women to go out to work; **Bewerber sollten eine dreijährige ~ nachweisen können** applicants should be able to provide proof of three years' work experience; **be|rufs|un|fä|hig** ADJ occupationally disabled; **Be|rufs|un|fä|hig|keit** F inability to practise one's profession; **Be|rufs|un|fä|hig|keits|ren|te** F disability pension (Brit), disability (US); **Be|rufs|un|fall** M occupational accident; **Be|rufs|ver|band** M → Beruf professional/trade organization or association; **Be|rufs|ver|bot** NT exclusion from a civil service profession by government ruling **jdm ~ erteilen** to ban sb from a profession; **unter das ~ fallen** to be banned from a profession; **Be|rufs|ver|bre|cher(in)** M(F) professional criminal; **Be|rufs|ver|kehr** M commuter traffic; **Be|rufs|vor|be|rei|tungs|jahr** NT year in which students gain practical skills in preparation for entry into the job market; **Be|rufs|wahl** F → Beruf choice of occupation/profession/trade; **Be|rufs|wech|sel** M change of occupation/ profession/trade; **Be|rufs|wunsch** M preferred choice of job or career; **Be|rufs|ziel** NT occupation/profession/trade one is aiming for; **Be|rufs|zweig** M → Beruf branch of an occupation/profession/trade; (= Berufsgruppe) occupation/profession/trade

Be|ru|fung [bəˈruːfʊŋ] F -, -en **a** (= das Berufen) appeal; (Jur) appeal; **in die ~ gehen**, **~ einlegen** to appeal (bei to) **b** (in ein Amt etc) appointment (auf or an +acc to) **c** (= innerer Auftrag) vocation; (Rel) mission, vocation, calling; **die ~ zu etw in sich** (dat) **fühlen** to feel one has a vocation etc to be sth **d** (form) **die ~ auf jdn/etw** reference to sb/sth; **unter ~ auf etw** (acc) with reference to sth

Be|ru|fungs-: Be|ru|fungs|an|trag M petition for appeal; **einen ~ stellen** to file a petition for appeal; **Be|ru|fungs|aus|schuss** ▲ M appeal tribunal; **Be|ru|fungs|frist** F period in which an appeal must be submitted; **Be|ru|fungs|ge|richt** NT appeal court, court of appeal; **Be|ru|fungs|in|stanz** F court of appeal; **Be|ru|fungs|kla|ge** F appeal; **Be|ru|fungs|klä|ger(in)** M(F) appellant; **Be|ru|fungs|ver|fah|ren** NT appeal proceedings pl

be|ru|hen ptp **beruht** VI to be based or founded (auf +dat on); **das beruht auf Gegenseitigkeit** (inf) the feeling is mutual; **etw auf sich ~ lassen** to let sth rest

be|ru|hi|gen [bəˈruːɪgn] ptp **beruhigt** **VT** to calm (down); Baby to quieten (Brit), to quiet (US); (= trösten) to soothe, to comfort; (= versichern) to reassure; Magen to settle; Nerven to soothe, to calm; Verkehr to calm; Gewissen to soothe, to ease; Schmerzen to ease, to relieve; **na, dann bin ich ja beruhigt** well I must say I'm quite relieved; **dann kann ich ja beruhigt schlafen/nach Hause gehen** then I can go to sleep/ go home with my mind at rest; **~d** (körperlich, = beschwichtigend) soothing; (= tröstlich) reassuring; **es ist ~d zu wissen, dass ...** it is reassuring to know that ... **VR** to calm down; (Krise auch) to ease off, to lessen; (Gewissen) to be eased; (Andrang, Verkehr, Kämpfe) to subside, to lessen; (Börse, Preise, Magen) to settle down; (Krämpfe, Schmerzen) to lessen, to ease; (Meer) to become calm; (Sturm) to die down, to abate; **sie konnte sich gar nicht darüber ~, dass ...** she could not get over the fact that ...; **beruhige dich doch!** calm down!

Be|ru|hi|gung F -, no pl **a** (= das Beruhigen) calming (down); (von Baby) quietening (Brit), quieting (US); (= das Trösten) soothing, comforting; (= das Versichern) reassuring; (von Magen) settling; (von Nerven) soothing; (von Verkehr) calming; (von Gewissen) soothing, easing; (von Schmerzen) easing, relieving; **zu Ihrer ~ kann ich sagen ...** you'll be reassured to know that ... **b** (= das Sichberuhigen) calming down; (von Krise auch) easing off, lessening; (von Andrang, Verkehr, Kämpfen) subsiding, lessening; (von Börse, Preisen, Magen) settling down; (von Meer) calming; (von Sturm) abatement; **ein Gefühl der ~** a reassuring feeling

Be|ru|hi|gungs-: Be|ru|hi|gungs|mit|tel NT sedative, tranquillizer (Brit), tranquilizer (US); **Be|ru|hi|gungs|pil|le** F, **Be|ru|hi|gungs|tab|let|te** F sedative (pill), tranquillizer (Brit), tranquilizer (US), downer (inf); **Be|ru|hi|gungs|sprit|ze** F sedative (injection)

be|rühmt [bəˈryːmt] ADJ famous, **wegen** or **für etw ~ sein** to be famous or renowned for sth; **das war nicht ~** (inf) it was nothing to write home about (inf)

be|rühmt-be|rüch|tigt ADJ infamous, notorious

Be|rühmt|heit F -, -en **a** fame; **~ erlangen** to become famous; **zu trauriger ~ gelangen** to become notorious or infamous **b** (= Mensch) celebrity

be|rüh|ren ptp **berührt** **VT** **a** (= anfassen, streifen, Math) to touch; (= grenzen an) to border on; (= auf Reise streifen) Länder to touch; Hafen to stop at; (= erwähnen) Thema, Punkt to touch on; **Berühren verboten** do not touch **b** (= seelisch bewegen) to move; (= auf jdn wirken) to affect; (= betreffen) to affect, to concern; **das berührt mich gar nicht!** that's nothing to do with me; **von etw peinlich/schmerzlich berührt sein** to be embarrassed/pained by sth; **es berührt mich angenehm/seltsam, dass ...** I am pleased/surprised that ... **VR** to touch; (Menschen auch) to touch each other; (Drähte etc) to be in contact, to touch; (Ideen, Vorstellungen, Interessen) to coincide

Be|rüh|rung F -, -en touch; (zwischen Drähten etc, = menschlicher Kontakt) contact; (= Erwähnung) mention; **mit jdm/etw in ~ kommen** to come into contact with sb/sth; **jdn mit jdm/etw in ~ bringen** to bring sb into contact with sb/ sth; **körperliche ~** physical or bodily contact; **die ~ der Instrumente ist zu vermeiden** avoid touching the instruments; **bei ~ Lebensgefahr!** danger – do not touch!; **Ansteckung durch ~** contagion, infection by contact

Be|rüh|rungs-: Be|rüh|rungs|angst F usu pl reservation (mit about); **die Berührungsängste vor diesem Thema sind noch groß** there is still

great reluctance to deal with this subject; **Be|rüh|rungs|bild|schirm** M touch screen; **Be|rüh|rungs|gift** NT contact poison; **Be|rüh|rungs|punkt** M point of contact; (Math auch) tangential point

Be|ryl|li|um [beˈrylɪʊm] NT -s, no pl (abbr **Be**) beryllium

bes. abbr von **besonders**

be|sab|bern ptp **besabbert** (inf) **VT** to slobber all over or on **VR** to slobber all over oneself

be|sä|en ptp **besät** VT (lit) to sow → auch **besät**

be|sa|gen ptp **besagt** VT to say; (= bedeuten) to mean, to imply; **das besagt nichts** that does not mean anything; **das besagt viel** that means a lot; **das besagt nicht, dass ...** that does not mean (to say) that ...

be|sagt [bəˈzaːkt] ADJ attr (form) said (form), aforementioned (form)

be|sai|ten [bəˈzaitn] ptp **besaitet** VT to string; **etw neu ~** to restring sth → **zart**

be|sa|men [bəˈzaːmən] ptp **besamt** VT to fertilize; (künstlich) to inseminate; (Bot) to pollinate

be|sam|meln ptp **besammelt** VR (esp Sw) to assemble, to gather

Be|samm|lung F (esp Sw) assembly

Be|sa|mung F -, -en fertilization; (künstlich) insemination; (Bot) pollination

Be|san [beˈzaːn, ˈbeːzaːn] M -s, -e (Naut) mizzen; (= Segel auch) mizzen sail; (= Mast auch) mizzenmast

be|sänf|ti|gen [bəˈzɛnftɪgn] ptp **besänftigt** **VT** to calm down, to soothe; Menge auch to pacify; jds Zorn, Erregung, Gemüt to soothe; **er war nicht zu ~** it was impossible to calm him down **VR** (Mensch) to calm down; (Meer, Elemente) to become calm

Be|sänf|ti|gung F -, -en calming (down), soothing; (von Menge auch) pacifying; (von Zorn, Erregung, Gemüt) soothing

Be|san|mast M (Naut) mizzenmast

be|sät [bəˈzɛːt] ADJ covered; (mit Blättern etc) strewn; (iro: mit Orden) studded; **der mit Sternen ~e Himmel** the star-spangled sky (liter) → auch **besäen**

Be|satz M **a** edging, trimming; (an Tischtuch auch) border; **einen ~ aus etw haben** to be trimmed with sth **b** (= Bestand) stock

Be|sat|zer [bəˈzatsə] M -s, - (pej inf) occupying forces pl

Be|sat|zung F **a** (= Mannschaft) crew; (= Verteidigungstruppe) garrison **b** (= Besatzungsarmee) occupying army or forces pl

Be|sat|zungs-: Be|sat|zungs|ar|mee F occupying army, army of occupation; **Be|sat|zungs|kind** NT illegitimate child of member of the occupying forces; **Be|sat|zungs|macht** F occupying power; **Be|sat|zungs|sol|dat(in)** M(F) soldier in/of the occupying army or forces; **Be|sat|zungs|sta|tut** NT statute of occupation; **Be|sat|zungs|streit|kräf|te** PL, **Be|sat|zungs|trup|pen** PL occupying forces pl; **Be|sat|zungs|zo|ne** F occupation zone; **die amerikanische ~** the American(-occupied) zone

be|sau|fen ptp **besoffen** [bəˈzɔfn] VR irreg (inf) to get plastered (inf) or pissed (Brit inf) → auch **besoffen**

Be|säuf|nis [bəˈzɔyfnɪs] NT -ses, -se (inf) booze-up (inf), chug-a-lug (US inf)

be|säu|seln ptp **besäuselt** VR (inf) to get merry (Brit inf) or tipsy; **besäuselt** tipsy, merry (Brit inf)

be|schä|di|gen ptp **beschädigt** VT to damage; **beschädigt** damaged; Schiff auch disabled

Be|schä|dig|te(r) [bəˈʃɛːdɪçtə] MF decl as adj disabled person/man/woman

Be|schä|di|gung F damage (von to); **das Auto hat mehrere ~en** the car is damaged in several places

be|schaf|fen[1] ptp **beschafft** VT to procure (form), to get (hold of), to obtain; **jdm**

etw ~ to get (hold of) *or* obtain sth for sb; **jdm/ sich eine Stelle ~** to get sb/oneself a job; **das ist schwer zu ~** that is difficult to get (hold of)

be|schaf|fen² ADJ *(form)* **wie ist es mit seiner Gesundheit ~?** what about his health?; **mit jdm/damit ist es gut/schlecht ~** sb/it is in a good/bad way; **so ~ sein wie ...** to be the same as ...; **das ist so ~, dass ...** that is such that ...

Be|schaf|fen|heit F -, *no pl* composition; *(von Mensch) (körperlich)* constitution; *(seelisch)* nature, qualities *pl*; **die glatte ~ des Steins** the smoothness of the stone; **er hat für diesen Beruf nicht die seelische/körperliche ~** he doesn't have the right sort of psychological make-up/ physique for this job; **je nach ~ der Lage** according to the situation

Be|schaf|fung F *no pl* procuring, obtaining

Be|schaf|fungs-: **Be|schaf|fungs|kos|ten** PL procurement costs *pl*, cost *sing* of acquisition; **Be|schaf|fungs|kri|mi|na|li|tät** F drug-related crime; **Be|schaf|fungs|pros|ti|tu|ti|on** F drug-related prostitution

be|schäf|ti|gen [bəˈʃɛftɪgn] ✪ 33.3 *ptp* **beschäftigt** VR **sich mit etw ~** to occupy oneself with sth; (= *sich befassen, abhandeln*) to deal with sth; **sich mit dem Tod ~** to think about death; **sich mit Literatur ~** to study literature; **sich mit der Frage ~, ob ...** to consider the question of whether ...; **sich mit jdm ~** to devote one's attention to sb; **sie beschäftigt sich viel mit den Kindern** she devotes a lot of her time to the children; **sie beschäftigt sich gerade mit den Kindern** she is busy with the children just now

VT **a** (= *innerlich beschäftigen*) **jdn ~** to be on sb's mind; **die Frage beschäftigt sie sehr** she is very preoccupied with that question, that question has been on her mind a lot

b (= *anstellen*) to employ

c (= *eine Tätigkeit geben*) to occupy, to keep occupied; **jdn mit etw ~** to give sb sth to do

be|schäf|tigt [bəˈʃɛftɪçt] ADJ **a** busy; **mit dem Nähen/jdm ~ sein** to be busy sewing/with sb; **mit sich selbst/seinen Problemen ~ sein** to be preoccupied with oneself/one's problems **b** (= *angestellt*) employed *(bei* by, at)

Be|schäf|tig|te(r) [bəˈʃɛftɪçtə] MF *decl as adj* employee

Be|schäf|ti|gung F -, -en **a** (= *berufliche Arbeit*) work *no indef art*, job; (= *Anstellung, Angestelltsein*) employment; **eine ~ suchen** to be looking for work *or* a job, to seek employment *(form)*; **einer ~ nachgehen** *(form)* to be employed; **ohne ~ sein** to be unemployed, to be out of work

b (= *Tätigkeit*) activity, occupation; **jdm eine ~ geben** to give sb something to do; **~ haben** to have something to do

c (= *geistige Beschäftigung*) preoccupation; *(mit Frage)* consideration; *(mit Thema)* treatment *(mit* of); *(mit Literatur)* study *(mit* of); *(mit sich, seinen Problemen)* preoccupation

d (= *von Kindern, Patienten etc*) occupying, keeping occupied; **die ~ der Patienten** keeping the patients occupied

Be|schäf|ti|gungs-: **Be|schäf|ti|gungs|la|ge** F employment situation; **be|schäf|ti|gungs|los** ADJ unoccupied; (= *arbeitslos*) unemployed, out-of-work; **Be|schäf|ti|gungs|nach|weis** M proof of employment; **Be|schäf|ti|gungs|of|fen|si|ve** F job creation campaign; **Be|schäf|ti|gungs|pro|gramm** NT job creation scheme; **Be|schäf|ti|gungs|the|ra|peut(in)** M(F) occupational therapist; **Be|schäf|ti|gungs|the|ra|pie** F occupational therapy; **Be|schäf|ti|gungs|ver|hält|nis** NT *(form)* employment, employment status; **in was für einem ~ stehen Sie?** what type of employment are you in?

be|schä|len *ptp* **beschält** VT *(form)* to cover, to serve

Be|schä|ler [bəˈʃɛːlɐ] M -s, - *(form)* stallion, stud

be|schal|len [bəˈʃalən] *ptp* **beschallt** VT **a** *(mit Lautsprechern)* to fill with sound **b** *(Med, Tech,*

mit Ultraschall) **jdn ~** *(zur Behandlung)* to treat sb with ultrasound; *(zur Diagnose)* to give sb an ultrasound scan

Be|schal|lung [bəˈʃɛːlʊŋ] F -, -en *(form)* covering, service

be|schä|men *ptp* **beschämt** VT to shame; *(jds Großzügigkeit)* to embarrass; **es beschämt mich, zu sagen ...** I feel ashamed to have to say ...; **beschämt** ashamed, abashed; **ich fühle mich durch deine Großzügigkeit beschämt** I am embarrassed by your generosity

be|schä|mend ADJ **a** (= *schändlich*) shameful; **es war ~ für seine ganze Familie** it brought shame on *or* to his whole family **b** (= *vorbildlich*) shaming; *Großzügigkeit* embarrassing **c** (= *demütigend*) humiliating, shaming ADV (= *schändlich*) disgracefully, shamefully

Be|schä|mung [bəˈʃɛːmʊŋ] F -, *(rare)* -en shame; (= *Verlegenheit*) embarrassment; **zu meiner ~** to my shame; **in tiefer ~ ging er nach Hause** he went home feeling very ashamed

be|schat|ten [bəˈʃatn] *ptp* **beschattet** VT **a** *(geh)* *(Schatten geben)* to shade; *(fig: = trüben)* to overshadow **b** (= *überwachen*) to shadow, to tail; **jdn ~ lassen** to have sb shadowed *or* tailed **c** *(Sport)* to mark closely

Be|schat|ter [bəˈʃatɐ] M -s, -, **Be|schat|te|rin** [-ərɪn] F -, -nen **a** (= *Polizist etc*) tail **b** *(Sport)* marker

Be|schat|tung F -, -en **a** (= *Überwachung*) shadowing, tailing **b** *(Sport)* marking

Be|schau F -, *no pl* inspection

be|schau|en *ptp* **beschaut** VT **a** *Fleisch etc* to inspect **b** *(dial: = betrachten)* to look at; **sich (dat) etw ~** to look at sth

Be|schau|er [bəˈʃauɐ] M -s, -, **Be|schau|e|rin** [-ərɪn] F -, -nen **a** inspector **b** (= *Betrachter*) spectator; *(von Bild)* viewer

be|schau|lich [bəˈʃaulɪç] ADJ **a** (= *geruhsam*) *Leben, Abend* quiet, tranquil; *Charakter, Mensch* pensive, contemplative **b** *(Rel)* contemplative ADV (= *geruhsam*) quietly, tranquilly; **~ dasitzen** to sit contemplating; **~ leben** to lead a simple life

Be|schau|lich|keit F -, *no pl* (= *Geruhsamkeit*) *(von Leben, Abend)* tranquillity; *(von Charakter, Mensch)* pensiveness

Be|schau|ung [bəˈʃauʊŋ] F -, -en inspection

Be|scheid [bəˈʃait] M -(e)s, -e [-də] **a** (= *Auskunft*) information; (= *Nachricht*) notification; (= *Entscheidung auf Antrag etc*) decision; **wir erwarten Ihren ~** we look forward to hearing from you; **ich warte noch auf ~** I am still waiting to hear, I still have not heard anything; **jdm (über etw acc or von etw) ~ sagen or geben** to let sb know (about sth), to tell sb (about sth); **jdm ordentlich ~ sagen, jdm gründlich ~ stoßen** *(inf)* to tell sb where to get off *(inf)*; **~ hinterlassen** to leave word

b *(über etw acc or in etw dat)* **~ wissen** to know (about sth); **weißt du ~ wegen Samstagabend?** do you know about Saturday evening?; **weißt du ~ mit den Maschinen?** do you know how to deal with these machines?, do you know about these machines?; **ich weiß hier nicht ~** I don't know about things around here; **er weiß gut ~** he is well informed; **auf dem Gebiet weiß ich nicht ~** I don't know much about that sort of thing; **weißt du schon ~?** do you know?, have you heard?; **sag ihr, Egon habe angerufen, dann weiß sie schon ~** if you tell her Egon phoned she'll understand

be|schei|den¹ [bəˈʃaidn] *pret* **beschied** [bəˈʃiːt], *ptp* **beschieden** [bəˈʃiːdn] VT **a** *(form: = bestellen)* to summon *(form)* *(zu jdm* to sb)

b (= *form: = entscheiden*) *Gesuch, Antrag* to decide upon; **etw abschlägig ~** to turn sth down

c *(form: = informieren)* **jdn dahin gehend ~, dass ...** to inform *or* notify sb that ...

d *(geh: = zuteil werden lassen)* **jdm etw ~** to grant sb sth; **es war ihr nicht beschieden, den Erfolg zu genießen** she was not granted the

opportunity to enjoy the success, it was not given to her to enjoy the success *(liter)*

VR *(geh)* to be content; **sich mit wenigem ~** to be content *or* to content oneself with little

be|schei|den² [bəˈʃaidn] ADJ **a** modest; *Mensch, Verhalten* modest, unassuming; **in ~en Verhältnissen leben** to live modestly; **eine ~e Frage** one small question; **aus ~en Anfängen** from humble beginnings **b** *(euph: = beschissen)* awful, terrible; *(inf: = mäßig)* mediocre ADV **a** *leben* modestly; **darf ich mal ~ fragen, ob ...** may I venture to ask whether ... **b** *(euph) sich fühlen* terrible; *spielen* terribly; **ich habe in der Englischarbeit ~ abgeschnitten** I got a terrible mark *(Brit)* or grade *(esp US)* in English

Be|schei|den|heit F -, *no pl* modesty; **nur keine falsche ~** no false modesty now; **~ ist eine Zier, doch weiter kommt man ohne ihr** *(hum inf)* modesty is fine but it doesn't get you very far

be|schei|nen *ptp* **beschienen** [bəˈʃiːnən] VT *irreg* to shine on; *(Feuer)* to light up; **vom Mond beschienen** moonlit; **von der Sonne beschienen** sunlit

be|schei|ni|gen [bəˈʃainɪgn] *ptp* **bescheinigt** VT to certify; *Gesundheit, Tauglichkeit* to confirm in writing; *Empfang* to confirm, to acknowledge; *(durch Quittung)* to sign for, to give a receipt for; *(inf: = mündlich bestätigen)* to confirm; **sich (dat) die Arbeit/Überstunden ~ lassen** to get written confirmation of having done the work/overtime; **können Sie mir ~, dass ...** can you confirm in writing that ..., can you give me written confirmation that ...; **hiermit wird bescheinigt, dass ...** this is to certify that ...; **jdm äußerste Kompetenz ~** to confirm sb's extreme competence

Be|schei|ni|gung F -, -en (= *das Bescheinigen*) certification; *(der Gesundheit, Tauglichkeit)* confirmation; *(= Schriftstück)* certificate; written confirmation; (= *Quittung*) receipt

be|schei|ßen *ptp* **beschissen** [bəˈʃisn] *irreg (inf)* VT **jdn** to swindle, to cheat, to do *(um out of)* → *auch* **beschissen** VI to cheat

be|schen|ken *ptp* **beschenkt** VT **jdn** to give presents/a present to; **jdn mit etw ~** to give sb sth (as a present); **sich (gegenseitig) ~** to give each other presents; **jdn reich ~** to shower sb with presents; **damit bin ich reich beschenkt** that's very generous

be|sche|ren *ptp* **beschert** VTI **a jdn ~** to give sb a Christmas present/presents; **jdn mit etw ~** to give sb sth for Christmas; **um 5 Uhr wird beschert** the Christmas presents will be given out at 5 o'clock; **jdm eine Überraschung ~** to give sb a nice surprise **b** (= *zuteil werden lassen*) **jdm etw ~** to grant sb sth, to bestow sth upon sb; *(Gott)* to bless sb with sth

Be|sche|rung [bəˈʃeːrʊŋ] F -, -en **a** (= *Feier*) giving out of Christmas presents **b** *(iro inf)* **das ist ja eine schöne ~!** this is a nice mess; **die (ganze) ~** the (whole) mess; **da haben wir die ~!** I told you so!, what did I tell you!

be|scheu|ert [bəˈʃɔyɐt] *(inf)* ADJ stupid; *Mensch auch* dumb *(inf)* ADV **sich ~ anstellen** to act stupidly; **wie ~ putzen** to clean like crazy *(inf)*; **~ aussehen** to look idiotic *or* ridiculous; **~ fragen** to ask idiotic *or* stupid questions

be|schich|ten *ptp* **beschichtet** VT *(Tech)* to coat, to cover; **mit Kunststoff beschichtet** laminated; **PVC-beschichtet** PVC-coated

Be|schich|tung [bəˈʃɪçtʊŋ] F -, -en **a** *(Schicht)* coat(ing) **b** *(Tech: = das Beschichten)* coating

be|schi|cken *ptp* **beschickt** VT **a** (= *Vertreter schicken auf*) to send representatives to; (= *Exemplare schicken auf*) to send exhibits to; **eine Ausstellung mit jdm/etw ~** to send sb/sth to an exhibition; **die Firma hat die Messe beschickt** the firm exhibited at the fair; **der Kongress wurde von den meisten Ländern beschickt** most countries sent representatives to the congress **b** (*Tech*) *Hochofen* to charge; *Kessel* to fire

be|schi|ckert [bəˈʃɪkɐt] ADJ (*inf*) tipsy

Be|schi|ckung F -, -en (*Tech*) (*von Hochofen*) charging; (*von Kessel*) firing; (= *Ladung*) load

be|schied *pret von* **bescheiden**[1]

be|schie|den *ptp von* **bescheiden**[1]

be|schie|ßen *ptp* **beschossen** [bəˈʃɔsn] VT *irreg* **a** *Gebäude, Stadt, Menschen* to shoot at, to fire on *or* at; (*mit Geschützen, fig: mit Fragen, Vorwürfen, Argumenten*) to bombard **b** (*Phys*) *Atomkern* to bombard

Be|schie|ßung [bəˈʃiːsʊŋ] F -, -en **a** shooting (+*gen* at), firing (+*gen* on, at); (*mit Geschützen*) bombardment (+*gen* of) **b** (*Phys: von Atomkern*) bombarding

be|schil|dern *ptp* **beschildert** VT to put a sign or notice/signs or notices on; (*mit Schildchen*) *Ausstellungsgegenstand, Käfig etc* to label; (*mit Verkehrsschildern*) to signpost

Be|schil|de|rung F -, -en (*mit Schildchen*) labelling (*Brit*), labeling (*US*); (*mit Verkehrsschildern*) signposting; (= *Schilder*) signs *pl*; (= *Schildchen*) labels *pl*; (= *Verkehrsschilder*) signposts *pl*

be|schimp|fen *ptp* **beschimpft** VT *jdn* to swear at, to abuse; **jdn als Nazi ~** to accuse sb of being a Nazi

Be|schimp|fung [bəˈʃɪmpfʊŋ] F -, -en **a** (= *das Beschimpfen*) abusing, swearing (+*gen* at); (*Jur*) slander (+*gen* on) **b** (= *Schimpfwort*) insult

be|schir|men *ptp* **beschirmt** VT **a** (*geh*: = *beschützen*) to shield, to protect **b** (*geh*: = *sich breiten über*) to shade **c** (= *mit Schirm versehen*) **ich werde dich ~** (*hum inf*) I'll let you share my umbrella

Be|schiss [bəˈʃɪs] ▲ M -es, -e (*inf*) swindle, rip off (*inf*); **das ist ~** it's a swindle or swizz (*Brit inf*)

be|schis|sen [bəˈʃɪsn] (*inf*) ADJ bloody awful (*Brit inf*), lousy (*inf*), shitty (*inf*) ADV **das schmeckt ~** that tastes lousy (*inf*); **mir gehts ~** I feel bloody awful (*Brit inf*) or shitty (*sl*); **sich ~ verhalten** to behave like a louse (*inf*); **jdn ~ behandeln** to treat sb like (a piece of) shit (*sl*); **wir werden ~ bezahlt** our pay is bloody awful (*Brit*), our pay is lousy or shitty (*inf*); **ich komme mir echt ~ vor** I feel really shitty (*inf*) → *auch* **bescheißen**

be|schla|fen *ptp* **beschlafen** VT *irreg* (*inf*) **a** *Sache* to sleep on **b** *Mädchen* to sleep with

Be|schlag M **a** (*an Koffer, Truhe, Buch*) (ornamental) fitting; (*an Tür, Fenster, Möbelstück, Sattel*) (ornamental) mounting; (= *Scharnier/Schließe*) ornamental hinge/clasp; (*von Pferd*) shoes *pl* **b** (= *das Beschlagen: von Pferd*) shoeing **c** (*auf Metall*) tarnish; (*auf Speisen*) layer of mould (*Brit*) or mold (*US*); (*auf Glas, Spiegel etc*) condensation; **der Löffel hat einen ~** the spoon is tarnished **d** *jdn/etw mit ~ belegen, jdn/etw in ~ nehmen* to monopolize sb/sth; **mit ~ belegt sein** to be being used; (*Mensch*) to be occupied

be|schla|gen[1] *ptp* **beschlagen** *irreg* VT **a** (= *mit Beschlägen versehen*) *Truhe, Möbel, Tür* to put (metal) fittings on; *Schuhe, Schuhe* to put metal tips on; (*mit Ziernägeln*) to stud; **ein Fass mit Reifen ~** to put hoops on a barrel, to hoop a barrel; **ist das Pferd ~?** is the horse shod?

b (*Hunt*) *Wild* to cover, to serve
c (*Sw*: = *betreffen*) to concern
VIR (*vi: aux sein*) (*Brille, Glas, Fenster*) to steam up, to get steamed up, to mist up or over; (*Wand*) to get covered in condensation, to get steamed up; (*Silber etc*) to tarnish; **würden Sie bitte die ~en Scheiben abwischen?** the windows are getting steamed up *etc*, could you give them a wipe?

be|schla|gen[2] ADJ (= *erfahren*) well-versed; **in etw** (*dat*) (**gut**) **~ sein** to be well-versed in sth; **auf einem Gebiet ~ sein** to be well-versed in a subject

---

Be|schla|gen|heit F -, *no pl* sound knowledge (*in* +*dat* of)

Be|schlag|nah|me [bəˈʃlaːknaːmə] F -, -n = **Beschlagnahmung**

be|schlag|nah|men [bəˈʃlaːknaːmən] *ptp* **beschlagnahmt** VT *insep* **a** (= *konfiszieren*) to confiscate; *Vermögen, Grundbesitz, Drogen* to seize; *Kraftfahrzeug, Boot* to impound **b** (*inf*: = *in Anspruch nehmen*) (*Mensch*) to monopolize, to hog (*inf*); (*Arbeit*) *Zeit* to take up

Be|schlag|nah|mung F -, -en (*von Eigentum, Pass*) confiscation; (*von Vermögen, Grundbesitz, Drogen*) seizure; (*von Kraftfahrzeug, Boot*) impounding

be|schlei|chen *ptp* **beschlichen** [bəˈʃlɪçn] VT *irreg* to creep or steal up to or up on; *Wild* to stalk; (*fig*) to creep over

be|schleu|ni|gen [bəˈʃlɔynɪɡn] *ptp* **beschleunigt** VT to accelerate, to speed up; *Arbeit, Lieferung etc auch* to expedite; *Tempo auch* to increase; *Atem, Puls auch* to quicken; *Verfall, wirtschaftlichen Zusammenbruch etc* to precipitate, to hasten, to accelerate; **die Angst beschleunigte ihre Schritte** fear quickened or hastened her steps → *auch* **beschleunigt** VR to accelerate, to speed up; (*Tempo auch*) to increase; (*Atem, Puls auch*) to quicken; (*Verfall, Zusammenbruch*) to be precipitated or hastened VI (*Fahrzeug, Fahrer*) to accelerate

Be|schleu|ni|ger [bəˈʃlɔynɪɡɐ] M -s, - (*Phys, Chem*) accelerator

be|schleu|nigt [bəˈʃlɔynɪçt] ADJ faster; **~es Verfahren** (*Jur*) summary proceedings *pl* ADV **~ ge-stiegene Preise** an accelerated increase in prices; **eine sich ~ fortsetzende Entwicklung** a continuously accelerating development → *auch* **beschleunigen**

Be|schleu|ni|gung F -, -en **a** acceleration (*auch Aut, Phys*), speeding up; (*von Tempo auch*) increase; (*von Atem, Puls auch*) quickening; (*von Verfall etc*) precipitation, hastening; **wir tun alles, was zur ~ der Arbeit führen könnte** we are doing everything we can toward(s) speeding up or in order to speed up the work **b** (= *Eile*) speed

Be|schleu|ni|gungs-: Be|schleu|ni|gungs|an|la|ge F , **Be|schleu|ni|gungs|ma|schi|ne** F accelerator; **Be|schleu|ni|gungs|ver|mö|gen** NT accelerating power, acceleration; **Be|schleu|ni|gungs|wert** M (*Aut*) acceleration ratio

be|schlie|ßen ✪ 35.2 *ptp* **beschlossen** [bəˈʃlɔsn] *irreg* VT **a** (= *Entschluss fassen*) to decide on; *Gesetz* to pass; *Statuten* to establish; **~, etw zu tun** to decide or resolve to do sth **b** (= *beenden*) to end; *Brief, Abend, Programm* to end, to conclude, to wind up VI **über etw** (*acc*) **~** to decide on sth → *auch* **beschlossen**

be|schlos|sen [bəˈʃlɔsn] ADJ (= *entschieden*) decided, agreed; **das ist ~e Sache** that's settled → *auch* **beschließen**

Be|schluss ▲ M **a** (= *Entschluss*) decision, resolution; **einen ~ fassen** to pass a resolution; **auf ~ des Gerichts** by order of the court; **wie lautete der ~ des Gerichts?** what was the court's decision? **b** (*obs*: = *Schluss*) conclusion, end

Be|schluss-: be|schluss|fä|hig ▲ ADJ **a** **~ sein** to have a quorum; **~e Anzahl** quorum **b** *Dokument* ready for a decision; **Be|schluss|fä|hig|keit** ▲ F , *no pl* quorum; **Be|schluss|fas|sung** ▲ F (passing of a) resolution; **Be|schluss|la|ge** F (*esp Pol*) policy position; **Be|schluss|recht** ▲ NT competence (to pass or make a resolution); **be|schluss|reif** ▲ ADJ *Gesetz* ready to be voted on, ready for the vote; **Be|schluss|rei|fe** ▲ F readiness for the vote; **~ haben** to be ready for the vote or to be voted on; **be|schluss|un|fä|hig** ▲ ADJ **~ sein** not to have a quorum; **Be|schluss|un|fä|hig|keit** ▲ F lack of a quorum

---

be|schmei|ßen *ptp* **beschmissen** [bəˈʃmɪsn] VT *irreg* (*inf*) to pelt, to bombard

be|schmie|ren *ptp* **beschmiert** VT **a** (= *bestreichen*) *Brot* to spread; *Körperteil, Maschinenteil* to smear, to cover; **Brot mit Butter ~** to butter bread; **Brot mit Käse ~** to spread cheese on bread **b** *Kleidung* to (be)smear; *Wand* to smear, to bedaub; *Tafel* to scribble or scrawl all over; **ein Buch mit Bemerkungen ~** to scrawl comments all over a book VR to get (all) dirty, to get oneself in a mess; **sich von oben bis unten mit etw ~** to get sth all over oneself, to cover oneself with sth

be|schmun|zeln *ptp* **beschmunzelt** VT to smile (quietly) at; **der alte Scherz wird immer noch beschmunzelt** the old joke still raises (*Brit*) or gets a smile

be|schmut|zen *ptp* **beschmutzt** VT to (make or get) dirty, to soil; (*fig*) *Ruf, Namen* to besmirch, to sully; *Ehre* to stain → **Nest c** VR to make or get oneself dirty

Be|schmut|zung [bəˈʃmʊtsʊŋ] F -, -en dirtying, soiling; (*von Namen, Ruf*) besmirching, sullying; (*von Ehre*) staining

be|schna|cken *ptp* **beschnackt** VT (*esp N Ger, inf*) **a** (= *besprechen*) to talk over, to discuss **b** (= *überreden*) to talk round, to persuade; **jdn ~, etw zu tun** to talk sb into doing sth

be|schnei|den *ptp* **beschnitten** [bəˈʃnɪtn] VT *irreg* **a** (= *zurechtschneiden, stutzen*) to trim; *Sträucher, Reben* to prune; *Bäume* to prune, to trim, to lop; *Flügel* to clip **b** (*Med, Rel*) to circumcise **c** (*fig*: = *beschränken*) *Rechte, Ansprüche* to cut back, to curtail

Be|schnei|dung [bəˈʃnaidʊŋ] F -, -en **a** (*Med, Rel*) circumcision **b** (*von Sträuchern, Reben*) pruning; (*von Bäumen*) pruning, lopping; (*von Flügeln*) clipping **c** (*von Finanzen*) cutback; (*von Rechten*) curtailing, curtailment

be|schnei|en *ptp* **beschneit** VT to cover with artificial snow

be|schneit [bəˈʃnait] ADJ snow-covered; *Berge auch* snowcapped

Be|schnei|ungs|an|la|ge [bəˈʃnaiʊŋs-] F artificial snowblower

be|schnüf|feln *ptp* **beschnüffelt** VT to sniff at; (*fig*: = *vorsichtig untersuchen*) to sniff out, to suss out (*inf*); *jdn* to size up; (= *bespitzeln*) to spy out VR (*Hunde*) to have a sniff at each other, to sniff each other; (*fig*) to size each other up

be|schnup|pern *ptp* **beschnuppert** VTR = **beschnüffeln**

be|schö|ni|gen [bəˈʃøːnɪɡn] *ptp* **beschönigt** VT to gloss over; **~der Ausdruck** euphemism; **... sagte er ~d** ... he said, trying to make things seem better

Be|schö|ni|gung F -, -en glossing over; **was er zur ~ angeführt hat, ...** what he said to make things seem better ...

be|schot|tern *ptp* **beschottert** VT *Straße* to macadamize, to metal; (*Rail*) to ballast

be|schrän|ken [bəˈʃrɛŋkn] ✪ 53.2 *ptp* **beschränkt** VT (*auf* +*acc* to) to limit, to restrict; *Anzahl, Ausgaben, Bedeutung eines Wortes etc auch* to confine VR (*auf* +*acc* to) to limit, to restrict; (*esp Jur, Rede, Aufsatz etc auch*) to confine oneself; (= *sich einschränken*) to restrict oneself; **das Wort beschränkt sich auf regionalen Gebrauch** the word is limited or restricted or confined to regional usage

be|schrankt [bəˈʃraŋkt] ADJ *Bahnübergang* with gates

be|schränkt [bəˈʃrɛŋkt] ADJ **a** (= *eingeschränkt, knapp*) limited; *Gebrauch* limited, restricted; **wir sind räumlich/zeitlich/finanziell ~** we have only a limited amount of space/time/money; **~e Haftung** limited liability; **Gesellschaft mit ~er Haftung** limited company (*Brit*), corporation (*US*) **b** (*pej*) (*geistig*) *Mensch, Intelligenz* limited; (= *engstirnig auch*) narrow; **wie kann man nur so ~ sein?** how can anyone be so dim (*inf*) or stu-

---

pid? **ADV a** (= *knapp*) ~ **leben** to live on a limited income; ~ **wohnen** to live in cramped conditions; **jdn ~ unterstützen** to give sb limited support **b** (*pej*) like an idiot

Be|schränkt|heit F -, *no pl* **a** (= *Knappheit*) **die ~ der Plätze/unserer Mittel** the limited (number of) places/our limited means **b** (*geistig, von Mensch*) limited intelligence; (= *Engstirnigkeit*) narrowness; **er konnte in seiner ~ nicht begreifen, dass ...** his simple mind could not grasp that ...

Be|schrän|kung F -, -en **a** (= *das Beschränken*) limitation, restriction; (*von Anzahl, Ausgabe, Bedeutung auch*) confinement; **eine ~ der Teilnehmerzahl scheint unvermeidbar zu sein** it seems unavoidable that the number of participants will have to be limited or restricted **b** (= *das Sichbeschränken*) (*auf +acc* to) limitation, restriction; (*esp Jur: von Rede, Aufsatz*) confinement; **c** (*Maßnahme*) restriction, limitation; **jdm ~en auferlegen** to impose restrictions on sb

be|schrei|ben *ptp* **beschrieben** [bəˈʃriːbn] VT *irreg* **a** (= *darstellen*) to describe, to give a description of; **sein Glück/Schmerz war nicht zu ~** his happiness/pain was indescribable or was beyond (all) description; **ich kann dir nicht ~, wie erleichtert ich war** I can't tell you how relieved I was; **~de Psychologie/Grammatik** descriptive psychology/grammar **b** (= *voll schreiben*) to write on **c** *Kreis, Bahn* to describe

Be|schrei|bung F **a** description **b** (= *Gebrauchsanweisung*) instructions *pl*

be|schrei|en *ptp* **beschrie(e)n** VT *irreg* (*inf*) = **berufen** VT **c**

be|schrei|ten *ptp* **beschritten** [bəˈʃrɪtn] VT *irreg* (*lit geh*) *Pfad* to walk or step along; *Brücke* to walk or step across; (*fig*) *neue Wege* to follow, to pursue; *neue Methode* to follow, to pursue

be|schrif|ten [bəˈʃrɪftn] *ptp* **beschriftet** VT to write on; *Grabstein, Sockel etc* to inscribe; (*mit Aufschrift*) to label; *Umschlag* to address; *Karikatur* to give a caption (to); **etw mit seinem Namen ~** to write one's name on sth; **die Funde waren mit Tusche beschriftet** the finds were marked with ink

Be|schrif|tung F -, -en **a** (= *das Beschriften*) inscribing; (*mit Etikett*) labelling (*Brit*), labeling (*US*); (*von Umschlag*) addressing; (*von Karikatur*) giving a caption to; (*von Funden*) marking; **bei der ~ der Etiketten** while filling in the labels **b** (= *Aufschrift*) writing; (*auf Grabstein, Sockel*) inscription; (*von Karikatur*) caption; (= *Etikett*) label

be|schu|hen [bəˈʃuːən] *ptp* **beschuht** VT to shoe; (*Tech*) *Pfahl, Spitze etc* to tip with metal

be|schuht [bəˈʃuːt] ADJ wearing shoes, shod

be|schul|di|gen [bəˈʃʊldɪgn] *ptp* **beschuldigt** VT to accuse; (*esp Jur*) to accuse, to charge; (*liter*) to charge; **jdn einer Sache** (*gen*) ~ to accuse sb of sth, to charge sb with sth

Be|schul|dig|te(r) [bəˈʃʊldɪçtə] MF *decl as adj* accused

Be|schul|di|gung F -, -en accusation; (*esp Jur auch, liter*) charge

Be|schu|lung F , *no pl* provision of school(ing) facilities (+*gen* for)

be|schum|meln *ptp* **beschummelt**, **be|schup|pen** *ptp* **beschuppt** VTI (*inf*) to cheat; **jdn um etw ~** to cheat or diddle (*inf*) sb out of sth

be|schuppt [bəˈʃʊpt] ADJ scaly; **dick ~** thick-scaled, with thick scales

be|schup|sen *ptp* **beschupst** VTI (*inf*) = **beschummeln**

Be|schuss ▲ M -es, *no pl* (*Mil*) fire; (*mit Granaten auch*) shelling, bombardment; (*Phys*) bombardment, bombarding; **jdn/etw unter ~ nehmen** (*Mil*) to (start to) bombard or shell sb/sth; *Stellung* to fire on; (*fig*) to attack sb/sth, to launch an attack on sb/sth; **unter ~ stehen** or **liegen** (*Mil*) to be under fire; **unter ~ geraten** (*Mil, fig*) to come under fire

be|schüt|ten *ptp* **beschüttet** VT (*mit Sand etc*) to cover; **jdn/etw (mit Wasser etc) ~** to pour water etc on or over sb/sth; **die Straße mit Sand ~** to throw or put sand on the road; **ein Feld mit Jauche ~** to put liquid manure on a field

be|schüt|zen *ptp* **beschützt** VT to protect, to shield, to shelter (*vor +dat* from); **~d** protective

Be|schüt|zer [bəˈʃʏtsɐ] M -s, -, **Be|schüt|ze|rin** [-ərɪn] F -, -nen protector; (*Frau auch*) protectress

be|schwat|zen *ptp* **beschwatzt**, (*esp S Ger*) **be|schwät|zen** *ptp* **beschwätzt** VT (*inf*) **a** (= *überreden*) to talk over; **jdn zu etw ~** to talk sb into sth; **sich zu etw ~ lassen** to get talked into sth **b** (= *bereden*) to chat about, to have a chat about

Be|schwer [bəˈʃveːɐ] F - or NT -s, *no pl* (*obs*) hardship

Be|schwer|de [bəˈʃveːɐdə] F -, -n **a** (= *Klage*) complaint; (*Jur*) appeal; **eine ~ gegen jdn** a complaint about sb; **wenn Sie eine ~ haben** if you have a complaint or grievance; **~ führen** or **einlegen** or **erheben** (*form*) to lodge a complaint; **jdm Grund zur ~ geben** to give sb grounds or cause for complaint **b Beschwerden** PL (= *Leiden*) trouble; **das macht mir immer noch ~n** it's still causing or giving me trouble; **mit etw ~n haben** to have trouble with sth; **wenn Sie wieder ganz ohne ~n sind** when the trouble's cleared up completely **c** (= *Mühe*) hardship

Be|schwer|de-: **Be|schwer|de|brief** M letter of complaint, written complaint; **Be|schwer|de|buch** NT complaints book; **be|schwer|de|frei** ADJ (*Med*) fit and healthy; **er war nie wieder ganz ~** the symptoms never completely disappeared; **Be|schwer|de|frist** F (*Jur*) *period of time during which an appeal may be lodged or filed*; **die ~e Partei** (*Jur*) the appealing party, the appellant; **Be|schwer|de|füh|ren|de(r)** [-fyːrəndə] MF *decl as adj*, **Be|schwer|de|füh|rer(in)** M(F) (*form*) person who lodges a complaint; (*Jur*) appellant; **Be|schwer|de|schrift** F written or formal complaint, petition; **Be|schwer|de|weg** M (= *Möglichkeit of lodging a complaint with sb (in authority)*) **auf dem ~** by (means of) lodging or making a complaint; **den ~ beschreiten** to lodge a complaint

be|schwe|ren [bəˈʃveːrən] *ptp* **beschwert** VT (*mit Gewicht*) to weigh(t) down; (*fig: = belasten*) *Problem, Kummer* to weigh on; **von Kummer beschwert** weighed down with sorrow VR **a** (= *sich beklagen*) to complain **b** (= *sich belasten*) (*lit*) to weigh oneself down; (*fig*) to encumber oneself

be|schwer|lich [bəˈʃveːɐlɪç] ADJ laborious, arduous; *Reise* arduous; **jdm ~ fallen/werden** (*old*) to be/become a burden to sb; **das Gehen/Atmen ist für ihn ~** he finds walking/breathing hard work

Be|schwer|lich|keit F -, -en arduousness *no pl*; **die ~en des Alters** the heavy weight of years; **die ~en des Lebens** life's burdens; **die ~en der Reise** the difficulties of the journey

Be|schwer|nis [bəˈʃveːɐnɪs] F -, -se or *nt* -ses, -se (*geh*: = *Mühsal*) hardship

Be|schwe|rung F -, -en **a** (= *das Beschweren*) weigh(t)ing down **b** (*Gegenstand*) weight

be|schwich|ti|gen [bəˈʃvɪçtɪgn] *ptp* **beschwichtigt** VT *jdn* to appease, to pacify; *Kinder* to calm down, to soothe; *jds Zorn, Gewissen* to soothe, to appease, to calm

Be|schwich|ti|gung F -, -en appeasement, pacification; (*von Kindern*) calming down, soothing; (*von Gewissen, Zorn*) soothing, appeasement, calming; (= *beschwichtigende Worte*) calming or soothing words *pl*

Be|schwich|ti|gungs-: **Be|schwich|ti|gungs|for|mel** F reassuring words *pl*, words *pl* of reassurance; **diplomatische ~n** diplomatic

words of reassurance; **Be|schwich|ti|gungs|po|li|tik** F policy of appeasement

be|schwin|deln *ptp* **beschwindelt** VT (*inf*) **a** (= *belügen*) **jdn ~** to tell sb a lie or a fib (*inf*) **b** (= *betrügen*) to cheat, to swindle, to do (*inf*)

be|schwin|gen *ptp* **beschwingt** VT to exhilarate, to elate

be|schwingt [bəˈʃvɪŋt] ADJ elated, exhilarated; *Musik, Mensch* vibrant; **sich ~ fühlen** to walk on air; **ein ~es Gefühl** a feeling of elation or exhilaration; **~en Schrittes** (*geh*) or **Fußes** (*liter*) with a spring or bounce in one's step, lightly tripping (*liter*)

Be|schwingt|heit F -, *no pl* elation, exhilaration; (*von Mensch, Musik*) vibrancy

be|schwip|sen [bəˈʃvɪpsn] *ptp* **beschwipst** (*inf*) VT to make tipsy, to go to sb's head VR to get tipsy

be|schwipst [bəˈʃvɪpst] ADJ (*inf*) tipsy

be|schwö|ren *ptp* **beschworen** [bəˈʃvoːrən] VT *irreg* **a** (= *beeiden*) to swear to; (*Jur auch*) to swear on oath **b** (= *anflehen*) to implore, to beseech; **sie hob ~d die Hände** she raised her hands imploringly or beseechingly **c** (= *erscheinen lassen*) to conjure up; *Verstorbene* to raise, to call up; *Schlangen* to charm **d** (*geh*: = *hervorrufen*) *Erinnerung etc* to conjure up; **das beschwor Erinnerungen in mir** that conjured up memories

Be|schwö|rung [bəˈʃvøːrʊŋ] F -, -en **a** (= *das Flehen*) entreaty **b** (= *das Heraufbeschwören*) conjuring up, conjuration; (*von Verstorbenen*) raising, calling up; (*von Schlangen*) charming **c** (*auch* **Beschwörungsformel**) incantation

be|see|len [bəˈzeːlən] *ptp* **beseelt** VT **a** (*lit*: = *mit Seele versehen*) to give a soul to; *Natur, Kunstwerk* to breathe life into; **das beseelte Spiel des Pianisten** (*geh*) the pianist's inspired playing **b** (= *erfüllen*) to fill; **neuer Mut beseelte ihn** he was filled or imbued with fresh courage; **ein neuer Geist beseelt unser Jahrhundert** a new spirit pervades or informs (*liter*) our century

be|se|hen *ptp* **besehen** *irreg* VT (*auch* **sich** *dat* **besehen**) to take a look at, to look at VR to (take a) look at oneself

be|sei|beln [bəˈzaibln] *ptp* **beseibelt**, **be|sei|bern** [bəˈzaibɐn] *ptp* **beseibert** VT (*dial*) to dribble all over, to slobber all over

be|sei|ti|gen [bəˈzaitɪgn] *ptp* **beseitigt** VT **a** (= *entfernen*) to remove, to get rid of; *Abfall, Schnee* to clear (away); *Atommüll* to dispose of; *Schwierigkeiten* to sort or smooth out; *Fehler* to eliminate; *Missstände* to get rid of, to do away with **b** (*euph*: = *umbringen*) to get rid of, to eliminate

Be|sei|ti|gung F -, *no pl* **a** (= *das Entfernen*) removal, getting rid of; (*von Abfall, Schnee*) clearing (away); (*von Atommüll*) disposal; (*von Schwierigkeiten*) sorting or smoothing out; (*von Fehlern*) elimination; (*von Missständen*) doing away with **b** (*euph: von Menschen*) getting rid of, elimination

be|se|li|gen [bəˈzeːlɪgn] *ptp* **beseligt** VT to make blissfully happy; **~d/beseligt** blissful

Be|sen [ˈbeːzn] M -s, - **a** (= *Kehrbesen*) broom; (= *Reisigbesen*) besom; (*zum Rühren*) whisk; (*von Hexe*) broomstick; **ich fresse einen ~, wenn das stimmt** (*inf*) if that's right, I'll eat my hat (*inf*); **neue ~ kehren gut** (*Prov*) a new broom sweeps clean (*Prov*) **b** (*pej inf*: = *Frau*) old bag (*inf*), old boot (*Brit inf*), besom (*dial pej inf*)

Be|sen-: **Be|sen|bin|der(in)** M(F) broom-maker; **Be|sen|kam|mer** F broom cupboard; **Be|sen|ma|cher(in)** M(F) broom-maker; **be|sen|rein** ADJ well-swept; **ADV eine Wohnung ~ verlassen** to leave an apartment in a clean and tidy condition (for the next tenant); **Be|sen|schrank** M broom cupboard; **Be|sen|stiel** M broomstick, broom handle; **steif wie ein ~** as stiff as a poker; **er sitzt da als hätte er einen ~ verschluckt** (*inf*) he's sitting there as stiff as a board

---

BESENWIRTSCHAFT

Besenwirtschaften are found in Germany's wine regions. They are private bars opened by wine-growers as soon as the new wine (known as **Federweißer**) has fermented and is ready to drink. A broom is placed in front of the door - or in some regions a bunch of flowers is hung over the door, giving rise to the name **Straußwirtschaft** - as a sign that the **Besenwirtschaft** is open. As well as home-produced wine, substantial cold snacks are also normally available. In Austria such places are called **Buschenschenken**.

---

be|ses|sen [bəˈzɛsn] ADJ (*von bösen Geistern*) possessed (*von* by); (*von einer Idee, Leidenschaft etc*) obsessed (*von* with); **wie ~** like a thing possessed, like one possessed → *auch* **besitzen**

Be|ses|se|ne(r) MF *decl as adj* one possessed *no art*; **die ~n** the possessed; **wie ein ~r** like one possessed

Be|ses|sen|heit F -, *no pl* (*mit bösen Geistern*) possession; (*mit Idee, Leidenschaft etc*) obsession

be|set|zen *ptp* **besetzt** VT **a** (= *belegen*) to occupy; (= *reservieren*) to reserve; (= *füllen*) *Plätze, Stühle* to fill; **ist hier** *or* **dieser Platz besetzt?** is this place taken?; **irgendjemand hat die (Telefon)leitung stundenlang besetzt** somebody was on the line for hours, somebody was keeping the line busy for hours → *auch* **besetzt b** (*mit Person*) *Stelle, Amt, Posten* to fill; (*Theat*) *Rolle* to cast; (*mit Tieren*) to stock; **eine Stelle neu ~** to find a new person to fill a job **c** (*esp Mil*: = *eingenommen haben*) to occupy; (*Hausbesetzer*) to squat in **d** (= *dekorieren*) to trim; (*mit Edelsteinen*) to stud

Be|set|zer(in) M(F) (= *Hausbesetzer*) squatter

be|setzt [bəˈzɛtst] ⊘ 27.3 ADJ (= *belegt*) *Telefon, Nummer, Leitung* engaged (*Brit*), busy (*esp US*); (= *in Gebrauch*) *Spielautomat etc* being used, taken, busy; *WC* occupied, engaged; *Abteil, Tisch* taken; *Hörsaal* being used; *Gebiet* occupied; (= *vorgebucht*) booked; (*voll*) *Bus, Wagen, Abteil etc* full (up); (= *anderweitig beschäftigt, verplant*) *Mensch* busy; **Freitag ist schon ~** Friday I'm/he's *etc* busy, Friday's out; **eine international ~e Jury** an international jury; **ein negativ ~es Thema** a very negative subject → *auch* **besetzen**

Be|setzt|ton M *pl* **-töne**, **Be|setzt|zei|chen** NT (*Telec*) engaged (*Brit*) *or* busy (*esp US*) tone

Be|set|zung [bəˈzɛtsʊŋ] F -, **-en a** (= *das Besetzen, von Stelle*) filling; (*von Rolle*) casting; (*mit Tieren*) stocking; (*Theat*: = *Schauspieler*) cast; (*Mus*: = *Arrangement*) arrangement; (*Sport*: = *Mannschaft*) team, side; **die Nationalelf in der neuen ~** the new line-up for the international team; **das Stück in der neuen ~** the play with the new cast; **zweite ~** (*Theat*) understudy **b** (*Mil, von Gebäude, durch Hausbesetzer*) occupation

Be|set|zungs|couch F (*hum inf*) casting couch

Be|set|zungs|lis|te F (*Theat, Film*) cast list

be|sich|ti|gen [bəˈzɪçtɪɡn] *ptp* **besichtigt** VT (= *ansehen*) *Kirche, Sehenswürdigkeit* to have a look at, to visit; *Stadt* to visit; *Betrieb* to tour, to have a look over *or* (a)round; (*zur Prüfung*) *Haus* to view, to have a look at, to look over; *Ware* to have a look at, to inspect; *Schule* to inspect; (= *inspizieren*) *Truppen* to inspect, to review; (*hum*) *Baby, zukünftiger Schwiegersohn etc* to inspect

Be|sich|ti|gung F -, **-en** (*von Sehenswürdigkeiten*) sightseeing tour; (*von Museum, Kirche, Betrieb*) tour; (*zur Prüfung*) (*von Haus*) viewing; (*von Waren, Schule, Baby*) inspection; (*von Truppen*) inspection, review; **nach einer kurzen ~ der Kirche/des Museums/Betriebs** *etc* after a short look (a)round the church/museum/factory *etc*; **die Waren liegen zur ~ aus** the goods are on display

Be|sich|ti|gungs-: Be|sich|ti|gungs|rei|se F, **Be|sich|ti|gungs|tour** F (*zum Vergnügen*) sightseeing tour *or* trip; (*zur Überprüfung*) tour of inspection; **Be|sich|ti|gungs|zei|ten** PL hours *pl* of opening

be|sie|deln *ptp* **besiedelt** VT (= *ansiedeln*) to populate, to settle (*mit* with); (= *sich niederlassen in*) to settle; (= *kolonisieren*) to colonize; (*Tiere*) to populate, to inhabit; (*Pflanzen*) to be found in, to inhabit; **dicht/dünn/schwach besiedelt** densely/thinly/sparsely populated

Be|sie|de|lung [bəˈziːdəluŋ] F -, **-en**, **Be|sied|lung** F -, **-en** settlement; (= *Kolonisierung*) colonization; **dichte/dünne/schwache ~** dense/thin/sparse population

Be|sied|lungs|dich|te F population density

be|sie|geln *ptp* **besiegelt** VT to seal

Be|sie|ge|lung [bəˈziːɡəluŋ] F -, **-en** sealing

be|sie|gen *ptp* **besiegt** VT (= *schlagen*) to defeat, to beat; *Feind auch* to conquer, to vanquish (*liter*); (= *überwinden*) to overcome, to conquer

Be|sieg|te(r) [bəˈziːktə] MF *decl as adj* **die ~n** the conquered

Be|sie|gung [bəˈziːɡʊŋ] F -, *no pl* defeat; (*von Feind auch*) conquest, vanquishing; (= *Überwindung*) overcoming

be|sin|gen *ptp* **besungen** [bəˈzʊŋən] VT *irreg* **a** (= *rühmen*) to sing of, to sing (*poet*); **jdn/etw ~** to sing the praises of sb/sth **b** *Schallplatte, Tonband* to record

be|sin|nen *ptp* **besonnen** [bəˈzɔnən] *irreg* **VR** (= *überlegen*) to reflect, to think; (= *erinnern*) to remember (*auf jdn/etw* sb/sth); (= *es sich anders überlegen*) to have second thoughts; **besinne dich, mein Kind!** take thought, my child; **sich anders** *or* **eines anderen ~** to change one's mind; **sich eines Besseren ~** to think better of it; **er hat sich besonnen** he has seen the light; **ohne sich (viel) zu ~, ohne langes Besinnen** without a moment's thought *or* hesitation; **wenn ich mich recht besinne** if I remember correctly → *auch* **besonnen VT** (*geh*: = *bedenken*) to reflect on, to ponder, to consider

be|sinn|lich ADJ contemplative; *Texte, Worte* reflective; **eine ~e Zeit** a time of contemplation; **~ werden** to become thoughtful *or* pensive

Be|sinn|lich|keit F reflection

Be|sin|nung [bəˈzɪnʊŋ] F -, *no pl* **a** (= *Bewusstsein*) consciousness; **bei/ohne ~ sein** to be conscious/unconscious; **die ~ verlieren** to lose consciousness; (*fig*) to lose one's head; **wieder zur ~ kommen** to regain consciousness, to come to; (*fig*) to come to one's senses; **jdn zur ~ bringen** to bring sb round (*Brit*) *or* around (*US*); (*fig*) to bring sb to his senses **b** (= *das Sichbesinnen*) contemplation (*auf +acc* of), reflection (*auf +acc* upon) **c** (= *das Nachdenken*) reflection; **ich brauche Zeit, zur ~ zu kommen** I need time to reflect *or* for reflection

Be|sin|nungs-: Be|sin|nungs|auf|satz M discursive essay; **be|sin|nungs|los** ADJ unconscious, insensible; (*fig*) blind; *Wut* blind, insensate; **~ werden** to lose consciousness; **Be|sin|nungs|lo|sig|keit** F -, *no pl* (*lit*) unconsciousness

Be|sitz [bəˈzɪts] M , *no pl* **a** (= *das Besitzen*) possession; **im ~ von etw sein** to be in possession of sth; **ich bin im ~ Ihres Schreibens** I am in receipt of your letter; **etw in ~ nehmen** to take possession of sth; **von etw ~ ergreifen** to seize possession of sth; **von jdm ~ ergreifen** to take *or* seize hold of sb; (*Zweifel, Wahnsinn etc*) to take possession of sb's mind; **in privatem ~** in private ownership **b** (= *Eigentum*) property; (= *Landgut*) estate; **in jds ~ übergehen** to become sb's property

Be|sitz|an|spruch M claim of ownership; (*Jur*) title; **einen ~ auf etw** (*acc*) **haben** to have a claim to sth; **seine Besitzansprüche (auf etw** *acc*) **anmelden** to make one's claims (to sth), to lay claim to sth

be|sitz|an|zei|gend ADJ (*Gram*) possessive

Be|sitz|bür|ger|tum NT middle-class property owners *pl*, property-owning bourgeoisie

be|sit|zen *ptp* **besessen** [bəˈzɛsn] VT *irreg* to have, to possess; *käufliche Güter* to have, to own; *Vermögen* to possess, to own; *Wertpapiere* to have, to possess, to hold; *Narbe, grüne Augen* to have; *Rechte, jds Zuneigung etc* to enjoy, to have, to possess; **große Schönheit/Fähigkeiten** *etc* **~** to be possessed of great beauty/abilities *etc*; **die ~den Klassen** the propertied classes → *auch* **besessen**

Be|sit|zer(in) M(F) owner; (*von Wertpapieren auch, von Führerschein etc*) holder; (= *Inhaber auch*) proprietor; **den ~ wechseln** to change hands

Be|sit|zer|grei|fung [-ˈɛɡraɪfʊŋ] F -, (*rare*) **-en** seizure

Be|sit|zer-: Be|sit|zer|stolz M pride of possession; **voller ~** proudly; **Be|sit|zer|wech|sel** M change of ownership

Be|sitz-: Be|sitz|ge|mein|schaft F (= *Gütergemeinschaft*) community of property; **Be|sitz|gier** F (acquisitive) greed, acquisitiveness; **be|sitz|los** ADJ without possessions; **Be|sitz|lo|se(r)** [-loːzə] MF *decl as adj* unpropertied person; (*entwurzelt*) dispossessed person; **Be|sitz|lo|sig|keit** F -, *no pl* lack of possessions; **Be|sitz|nah|me** [-naːmə] F -, *no pl* seizure; **Be|sitz|stand** M (*form*) assets *pl*; (*fig*) vested rights *pl*; **Be|sitz|stands|wah|rung** F (*fig*) protection of vested rights

Be|sitz|tum [bəˈzɪtstuːm] NT **-s, -tümer** [-tyːmɐ] (= *Eigentum*) possession, property *no pl*; (= *Grundbesitz*) estate(s *pl*), property

Be|sit|zung F possession; (= *privater Land- und Grundbesitz*) estate(s *pl*)

Be|sitz-: Be|sitz|ver|hält|nis|se PL property situation *or* conditions *pl*; **Be|sitz|ver|tei|lung** F distribution of property

be|sof|fen [bəˈzɔfn] ADJ (*inf*: = *betrunken*) pissed (*Brit sl*), smashed (*inf*) → *auch* **besaufen**

Be|sof|fe|ne(r) [bəˈzɔfnə] MF *decl as adj* (*inf*) drunk

be|soh|len *ptp* **besohlt** VT to sole; (= *neu besohlen*) to resole

Be|soh|lung [bəˈzoːluŋ] F -, **-en** soling *no pl*; (= *Neubesohlung*) resoling

be|sol|den [bəˈzɔldn] *ptp* **besoldet** VT to pay

Be|sol|dung F -, **-en** pay

Be|sol|dungs-: Be|sol|dungs|grup|pe F pay *or* salary group; **Be|sol|dungs|ord|nung** F pay *or* salary regulations *pl*

be|son|de|re(r, s) [bəˈzɔndərə] ADJ **a** (= *ungewöhnlich, eine Ausnahme bildend*) special; (= *hervorragend*) *Qualität, Schönheit etc* exceptional; **er ist ein ganz ~r Freund** he is a very special friend; **es ist eine ~ Freude** it is a special *or* particular pleasure; **das sind ~ Umstände** those are special circumstances; **das ist ein ganz ~s Gemälde** that is a very unusual painting **b** (= *speziell*) special, particular; (= *bestimmt*) particular; **unser ~s Interesse gilt ...** we are particularly *or* (e)specially interested in ...; **wir legen ~n Wert auf ...** we place particular *or* special emphasis on ...; **ohne ~ Begeisterung** without any particular enthusiasm; **er hat sich mit ~m Eifer darangemacht** he set about it with particular enthusiasm; **es ist mein ganz ~r Wunsch, dass ...** it is my very special wish that ..., I particularly wish that ...; **in diesem ~n Fall** in this particular case; **keine ~n Vorlieben** no special *or* particular preferences; **das ist von ~r Bedeutung** it is of special *or* particular importance **c** (= *zusätzlich, separat, gesondert*) special, separate

Be|son|de|re(s) [bəˈzɔndərə] NT *decl as adj* **a** **das ~ und das Allgemeine** the particular and the general; **im ~n** (= *im Einzelnen*) in particular cases; (= *vor allem*) in particular **b** **etwas/nichts**

~s something/nothing special; **er möchte etwas ~s sein** he thinks he's something special; **das ist doch nichts ~s** that's nothing special, that's nothing out of the ordinary, what's special about that?; **das ~ daran** the special thing about it

Be|son|der|heit [bə'zɔndɐhait] F **-, -en** unusual quality or feature; (= besondere Eigenschaft) peculiarity

be|son|ders [bə'zɔndɐs] ADV gut, hübsch, teuer etc particularly, (e)specially; (= ausdrücklich, vor allem) particularly, in particular, (e)specially; (= gesondert) separately, individually; (= speziell) anfertigen etc specially; **du müsstest das wissen** you particularly or in particular or especially should know that; **nicht ~ (lustig/kalt)** not particularly or not (e)specially (funny/cold); **nicht ~ viel Geld** not a particularly or not an especially large amount of money; **ich habe nicht ~ wenig Geld** I'm not particularly badly off; **das Essen/der Film war nicht ~** (inf) the food/film was nothing special, the food/film was nothing to write home about (inf); **wie gehts dir? – nicht ~** (inf) how are you? – not too hot (inf); **~ wenig Fehler** an exceptionally or a particularly low number of mistakes; **er hat ~ viel/wenig gearbeitet** he did a particularly large/small amount of work; **er hat ~ viel gegessen** he ate a particularly large amount of food; **er hat ~ wenig gegessen** he ate particularly little

be|son|nen [bə'zɔnən] **ADJ** level-headed; Politik, Urteil considered; **ihre ruhige, ~e Art** her calm and collected way **ADV** (= mit vorsichtiger Bedachtsamkeit) in a careful and thoughtful manner; **die Polizei ist ~ vorgegangen** the police proceeded in a careful and thoughtful way → auch **besinnen**

Be|son|nen|heit F **-,** no pl level-headedness; **durch seine ~ hat er eine Katastrophe verhindert** by staying calm and collected he avoided a disaster; **zur ~ aufrufen/mahnen** to call for/urge calm; **jdn zur ~ mahnen** to urge sb to stay calm

be|sonnt [bə'zɔnt] **ADJ** sunny; **vom Glück ~** blessed with luck

be|sor|gen ptp **besorgt** VT **a** (= kaufen, beschaffen etc) to get; (euph inf: = stehlen) to acquire (euph inf); **jdm/sich etw ~** to get sth for sb/oneself, to get sb/oneself sth; **jdm eine Stelle ~** to get or find a job for sb, to fix sb up with a job **b** (= erledigen) to attend or see to; **was du heute kannst ~, das verschiebe nicht auf morgen** (Prov) never put off until tomorrow what you can do today **c** (= versorgen) to take care of, to look after **d** (inf) **es jdm ~** to sort sb out (inf), to fix sb (inf) **e** (sl: sexuell) **es jdm ~** to have it off with sb (inf), to give sb one (inf); **es sich** (dat) **selber ~** to bring oneself off (sl)

Be|sorg|nis [bə'zɔrknɪs] F **-, -se** anxiety, worry, apprehension; **~ erregend** (adjektivisch) alarming, disquieting; (adverbial) alarmingly

be|sorg|nis|er|re|gend △ **ADJ, ADV** → **Besorgnis**

be|sorgt [bə'zɔrkt] **ADJ a** (= voller Sorge) anxious, worried (wegen about) **b um jdn/etw ~ sein** to be concerned about sb/sth **ADV** anxiously

Be|sorgt|heit F **-,** no pl concern, solicitude (form)

Be|sor|gung [bə'zɔrguŋ] F **-, -en a** (= das Kaufen) purchase; **er wurde mit der ~ von ... beauftragt** he was asked to get ... **b** (= Erledigung) **jdn mit der ~ seiner Geschäfte betrauen** to entrust sb with looking after one's affairs **c** (= Einkauf) errand; **~en** shopping; **~en machen** to do some shopping

be|span|nen ptp **bespannt** VT **a** (= überziehen) (mit Material) to cover; (mit Saiten, Fäden etc) to string **b** (mit Zugtieren) Wagen to harness up;

den Wagen mit zwei Pferden ~ to harness two horses to the cart

Be|span|nung F **a** no pl (= das Bespannen) covering; (mit Saiten etc) stringing; (mit Pferden) harnessing **b** (= Material) covering; (= Saiten, Fäden etc) strings pl

be|spei|en ptp **bespie(e)n** [bə'ʃpiː(ə)n] VT irreg (geh) to spit at or (up)on

be|spi|cken ptp **bespickt** VT (mit Fett) to lard; (mit Nägeln) to stud, to spike; (fig: = dicht bestecken) to cover; **seine mit Orden bespickte Brust** his chest bristling with medals

be|spie|geln ptp **bespiegelt** VR (lit: im Spiegel) to look at oneself in a/the mirror; (fig: = Selbstbetrachtung anstellen) to contemplate oneself, to contemplate one's own navel (hum) VT (geh) das eigene Ich to contemplate; (= darstellen, verarbeiten) Vergangenheit, Gefühle, Nöte to portray, to give a picture of

be|spiel|bar ADJ Rasen etc playable; Kassette capable of being recorded on

be|spie|len ptp **bespielt** VT **a** Schallplatte, Tonband to record on, to make a recording on; **das Band ist mit klassischer Musik bespielt** the tape has a recording of classical music on it **b** (Theat) Ort to play **c** (Sport) to play on

be|spit|zeln ptp **bespitzelt** VT to spy on

Be|spit|ze|lung [bə'ʃpɪtsəluŋ] F **-, -en**, **Be|spitz|lung** [bə'ʃpɪtsluŋ] F **-, -en** spying

be|spöt|teln ptp **bespöttelt** VT to mock (at), to scoff at, to ridicule

be|spre|chen ptp **besprochen** [bə'ʃprɔxn] irreg VT **a** (= über etw sprechen) to discuss, to talk about; **wie besprochen** as arranged **b** (= rezensieren) to review **c** Schallplatte, Tonband to make a recording on; **ein besprochenes Band** a tape of sb's voice or of sb talking **d** (= beschwören) to (attempt a) cure by magic or incantation VR **sich mit jdm ~** to confer with sb, to consult (with) sb (über +acc about); **sich über etw** (acc) **~** to discuss sth

Be|spre|chung [bə'ʃprɛçuŋ] F **-, -en a** (= Unterredung) discussion, talk; (= Konferenz) meeting; **nach ~ mit ...** after discussion with ..., after talking with ...; **er ist bei einer ~, er hat eine ~** he's in a meeting **b** (= Rezension) review, notice **c** (von Tonbändern, Schallplatten) recording **d** (= Beschwörung) conjuring away

Be|spre|chungs-: Be|spre|chungs|exem|plar NT review copy; **Be|spre|chungs|zim|mer** NT meeting room

be|spren|gen ptp **besprengt** VT to sprinkle

be|spren|keln ptp **besprenkelt** VT (mit Farbe, Schmutz) to speckle; (fig: = übersäen) to stud

be|sprin|gen ptp **besprungen** [bə'ʃpruŋən] VT irreg (Tier) to mount, to cover

be|sprit|zen ptp **bespritzt** VT to spray; (= beschmutzen) to (be)spatter, to splash VR to spray oneself; (= sich beschmutzen) to (be)spatter oneself, to splash oneself

be|sprü|hen ptp **besprüht** VT to spray VR to spray oneself

be|spu|cken ptp **bespuckt** VT to spit at or (up)on

bes|ser ['bɛsɐ] ✪ 28.1, 29.2 **ADJ** comp von **gut a** better; **~e Kreise/Gegend** better circles/area; **~e Leute** better class of people; **er hat ~e Tage or Zeiten gesehen** (iro) he has seen better days; **du willst wohl etwas Besseres sein!** (inf) I suppose you think you're better than other people, I suppose you think yourself superior; **soll es etwas Besseres sein?** did you have something of rather better quality in mind?; **~ werden** to improve, to get better; **das ist auch ~ so** it's better that way; **das wäre noch ~** (iro) no way; **Besseres zu tun haben** (inf) to have better things to do; **eine Wendung zum Besseren nehmen** to take a turn for the better; **jdn eines Besseren belehren** to teach sb otherwise or better → **besinnen**

b das Essen war nur ein ~er Imbiss the meal

was just a glorified snack

ADV comp von **gut, wohl a** better; **~ ist** (it is) better to be on the safe side; **umso ~!** (inf) so much the better!; **~ (gesagt)** or rather, or better; **~ gestellt** better-off; **sie will immer alles ~ wissen** she always thinks she knows better; **das macht nichts ~** that doesn't improve matters, that doesn't make things any (the) better; **es kommt noch ~** (iro) there's worse or more to come or follow; **es ~ haben** to have a better life **b** (= lieber) **lass das ~ bleiben** you had better leave well alone; **das solltest du ~ nicht tun** you had better not do that; **du tätest ~ daran ...** you would do better to ..., you had better ...; **dann geh ich ~** then I'd better go

bes|ser ge|hen ▲ VI impers irreg aux sein **es geht jdm besser** sb is feeling better; **jetzt gehts der Firma wieder besser** the firm is doing better again now, things are going better again for the firm now

bes|ser|ge|stellt △ ADJ → **besser** ADV a

Bes|ser|ge|stell|te(r) [-gəʃtɛltə] MF decl as adj **die ~n** pl those who are better off, the better-off (people), the well-to-do

bes|sern ['bɛsɐn] VT **a** (= besser machen) to improve, to (make) better; Verbrecher etc to reform **b** (old) (= ausbessern) to mend; (= verbessern) to improve VR (moralisch, im Benehmen) to mend one's ways; **bessere dich** (hum inf) mend your ways!

bes|ser: bes|ser ste|hen ▲ VR irreg (inf) to be better off; **bes|ser stel|len ▲** VT jdn **~** to improve sb's financial position VR to be better off

Bes|ser|stel|lung F **-, -n** (financial/social etc) betterment

Bes|se|rung ['bɛsəruŋ] ✪ 50.4 F **-,** no pl improvement; (von Verbrecher etc) reformation; (= Genesung) recovery; **(ich wünsche dir) gute ~!** I wish you a speedy recovery, I hope you get better soon; **auf dem Wege der ~ sein** to be getting better, to be improving; (Patient auch) to be on the road to recovery

Bes|se|rungs-: Bes|se|rungs|an|stalt F (dated) reformatory (dated), approved (Brit dated) or reform school; **bes|se|rungs|fä|hig** ADJ improvable; Verbrecher capable of being reformed, reformable; **Bes|se|rungs|maß|nah|me** F (Jur) corrective measure; **bes|se|rungs|wil|lig** ADJ willing to reform (oneself)

Bes|ser-: Bes|ser|ver|die|nen|de(r) [-vɛɐdiːnəndə] MF decl as adj **die ~n** pl those earning more, those on higher incomes, the upper income bracket(s pl); **Bes|ser|wes|si** ['bɛsɐvɛsi] M **-s, -s** (pej inf) West German know-all or know-it-all (US); **Bes|ser|wis|ser** [bɛsɐvɪsɐ] M **-s, -,** **Bes|ser|wis|se|rin** [-ərɪn] F **-, -nen** (inf) know-all (Brit inf), know-it-all (US inf), smart aleck (inf), smart-ass (esp US inf); **Bes|ser|wis|se|rei** [bɛsɐvɪsə'rai] F **-,** no pl (inf) know-all etc manner; **bes|ser|wis|se|risch** ['bɛsɐvɪsərɪʃ] (inf) **ADJ** Einstellung, Art, Beifahrer etc know(-it)-all attr **ADV** in a superior or know(-it)-all manner

best- [bɛst] in cpds mit adj best

be|stal|len [bə'ʃtalən] ptp **bestallt** VT (form) to install, to appoint (zu as)

Be|stal|lung F **-, -en** (form) installation, appointment

Be|stal|lungs|ur|kun|de F certificate of appointment

Be|stand M **a** (= Fortdauer) continued existence, continuance; **von ~ sein, ~ haben** to be permanent, to endure; **das Gesetz hat noch immer ~** the law still continues to exist; **zum 100-jährigen ~ des Vereins** (Aus) on the (occasion of the) 100th anniversary of the society **b** (= vorhandene Menge, Tiere) stock (an +dat of); (= Forstbestand) forest or timber (US) stand; **~ auf|nehmen** to take stock **c** (Aus: = Pacht) lease, tenure; **in ~ geben** to let (out) or put out on lease

be|stan|den [bəˈʃtandn] ADJ **a** (= *bewachsen*) covered with trees; *Allee* lined with trees; **mit Bäumen ~** (*Allee*) tree-lined; *Abhang* tree-covered; **der Wald ist gut ~** the forest is well stocked **b** **nach ~er Prüfung** after passing the/an exam; **bei nicht ~er Prüfung** if you *etc* don't pass the exam; **sie feiert die ~e Prüfung** she's celebrating passing her exam **c** (*Sw: = alt*) advanced (in years) → *auch* **bestehen**

be|stän|dig [bəˈʃtɛndɪç] ADJ **a** *no pred* (= *dauernd*) constant, continual **b** (= *gleich bleibend*) constant; *Mitarbeiter* steady; *Wetter* settled **c** (= *widerstandsfähig*) resistant (*gegen* to); *Farbe* fast; (= *dauerhaft*) *Freundschaft, Beziehung* lasting, durable ADV **a** (= *dauernd*) constantly, continually; **ich mache mir ~ Sorgen** I am constantly *or* continually worried **b** (= *gleich bleibend*) consistently, steadily

-be|stän|dig ADJ *suf* -resistant; **hitzebeständig** heat-resistant

Be|stän|dig|keit F -, *no pl* **a** (= *gleich bleibende Qualität*) constant standard; (*von Mitarbeiter*) steadiness; (*von Liebhaber*) constancy; (*von Wetter*) settledness **b** (= *Widerstandsfähigkeit*) resistance; (*von Farbe*) fastness; (= *Dauerhaftigkeit: von Freundschaft*) durability

Be|stands-: Be|stands|auf|nah|me F stocktaking; **Be|stands|ka|ta|log** M (*in Bibliothek etc*) catalogue (*Brit*) *or* catalog (*US*) of holdings; **Be|stands|lis|te** F inventory, stock list

Be|stand|teil M component, part, element; (*fig*) essential *or* integral part; **sich in seine ~e auflösen** to fall to pieces, to come apart; **etw in seine ~e zerlegen** to take sth apart *or* to pieces

be|stär|ken [bəˈʃtɛrkn] *ptp* **bestärkt** VT to confirm; *Verdacht auch* to reinforce; **jdn in seinem Vorsatz/Wunsch ~** to confirm sb in his intention/desire, to make sb's intention/desire firmer *or* stronger; **das hat mich nur darin bestärkt, es zu tun** that merely made me all the more determined to do it

Be|stär|kung F confirmation; (*von Verdacht auch*) reinforcement

be|stä|ti|gen [bəˈʃtɛːtɪɡn] ✪ 38.1, 39.1, 47.2, 47.3, 48.3, 53.2 *ptp* **bestätigt** VT **a** *Aussage, Verdacht, jdn* to confirm; *Theorie, Alibi etc* to bear out, to corroborate; (*Jur*) *Urteil* to uphold; **sich in etw** (*dat*) **bestätigt finden** to be confirmed in sth; **ich hatte angenommen, dass ... und fand mich darin bestätigt** I had assumed that ... and my assumption was confirmed *or* borne out; **~d** confirmatory, confirmatory; **ein ~des Kopfnicken** a nod of confirmation; **... sagte er ~d ...** he said in confirmation **b** (*Comm*) *Empfang, Brief* to acknowledge (receipt of) **c** (= *beurkunden*) to confirm, to certify, to attest; **hiermit wird bestätigt, dass ...** this is to confirm *or* certify that ...; **jdn (im Amt) ~** to confirm sb's appointment **d** (= *anerkennen*) to acknowledge, to recognize VR to be confirmed, to prove true, to be proved true; **das tut er nur, um sich selbst zu ~** he only does it to boost his ego

Be|stä|ti|gung ✪ 53.2 F -, -en **a** confirmation (*auch Dokument*); (*von Theorie, Alibi*) bearing out, corroboration; (*Jur: von Urteil*) upholding **b** (= *Empfangsbestätigung*) acknowledgement (of receipt) **c** (= *Beurkundung*) confirmation, certification, attestation; (*im Amt*) confirmation of appointment **d** (= *Anerkennung*) recognition

Be|stä|ti|gungs|schrei|ben NT letter of confirmation

be|stat|ten [bəˈʃtatn] *ptp* **bestattet** VT to bury; **bestattet liegen** to be *or* lie buried (*in +dat* in); **wann wird er bestattet?** when is the funeral (service)?

Be|stat|ter [bəˈʃtatɐ] M -s, -, **Be|stat|te|rin** [-ərɪn] F -, -nen undertaker, mortician (*US*)

Be|stat|tung F -, -en burial; (= *Feuerbestattung*) cremation; (= *Feier*) funeral; **kirchliche/weltliche ~** Christian/secular burial

Be|stat|tungs-: Be|stat|tungs|in|sti|tut NT , **Be|stat|tungs|un|ter|neh|men** NT undertaker's, mortician's (*US*); **Be|stat|tungs|kos|ten** PL funeral expenses *pl*; **Be|stat|tungs-un|ter|neh|mer(in)** M(F) undertaker, funeral director, mortician (*US*)

be|stäu|ben *ptp* **bestäubt** VT to dust (*auch Cook*), to sprinkle; (*Bot*) to pollinate; (*Agr*) to dust, to spray

Be|stäu|bung [bəˈʃtɔybʊŋ] F -, -en dusting, sprinkling; (*Bot*) pollination; (*Agr*) dusting, spraying

be|stau|nen *ptp* **bestaunt** VT to marvel at, to gaze at in wonder *or* admiration; (*verblüfft*) to gape at, to stare at in astonishment; **lass dich ~** let's have a good look at you; **sie wurde von allen bestaunt** they all gazed at her in admiration/gaped at her

best- [ˈbɛst]: **best|be|mit|telt** ADJ (*Aus*) extremely well-off; **best|be|währt** ADJ *attr* well-proven; **best|be|zahlt** ADJ *attr* best-paid

bes|te → **beste(r, s)**

be|ste|chen *ptp* **bestochen** [bəˈʃtɔxn] *irreg* VT **a** (*mit Geld, Geschenken etc*) to bribe; *Beamte* to bribe, to corrupt; **ich lasse mich nicht ~** I'm not open to bribery; (*mit Geld etc auch*) I don't take bribes **b** (= *beeindrucken*) to captivate VI (= *Eindruck machen*) to be impressive (*durch* because of); **ein Mädchen, das durch Schönheit besticht** a girl of captivating beauty

be|ste|chend ADJ *Schönheit, Eindruck* captivating; *Angebot* tempting, enticing; *Klarheit* irresistible; *Geist, Kondition* winning ADV (= *beeindruckend*) *einfach, elegant, klar* impressively; *schön, logisch* incredibly

be|stech|lich [bəˈʃtɛçlɪç] ADJ bribable, corruptible, venal

Be|stech|lich|keit F -, *no pl* corruptibility, venality

Be|ste|chung [bəˈʃtɛçʊŋ] F -, -en bribery; (*von Beamten etc auch*) corruption; **aktive ~** (*Jur*) offering of bribes/a bribe (to an official); **passive ~** (*Jur*) taking of bribes/a bribe (by an official)

Be|ste|chungs-: Be|ste|chungs|af|fä|re F corruption *or* bribery scandal; **Be|ste|chungs|geld** NT *usu pl* bribe; **Be|ste|chungs|skan|dal** M corruption *or* bribery scandal; **Be|ste|chungs|sum|me** F bribe; **Be|ste|chungs|ver|such** M attempted bribery

Be|steck [bəˈʃtɛk] NT -(e)s, -e **a** (= *Essbesteck*) knives and forks *pl*, cutlery *sing* (*Brit*), flatware *sing* (*US*); (= *Set, für ein Gedeck*) set of cutlery (*Brit*) *or* flatware (*US*); **ein silbernes ~** a set of silver cutlery (*Brit*) *or* flatware (*US*); **Herr Ober, ich habe kein ~** waiter, I haven't any cutlery (*Brit*) *or* flatware (*US*) **b** (= *Instrumentensatz*) set of instruments; (= *Raucherbesteck*) pipe-cleaning implements *pl*, smoker's set; (= *Drogenbesteck*) needles; **chirurgisches ~** (set of) surgical instruments **c** (*Naut*) reckoning, ship's position

be|ste|cken *ptp* **besteckt** VT to decorate

Be|steck-: Be|steck|kas|ten M cutlery (*Brit*) *or* flatware (*US*) tray; (*mit Deckel*) cutlery canteen, flatware chest (*US*); **Be|steck|(schub)-fach** NT cutlery (*Brit*) *or* flatware (*US*) drawer

be|ste|hen ✪ 35.2, 35.4, 42.2, 42.3, 43.2, 43.3, 46.1, 53.2 *ptp* **bestanden** [bəˈʃtandn] *irreg* VT **a** *Examen, Probe* to pass; **eine Prüfung mit Auszeichnung/„sehr gut" ~** to get a distinction/"very good" (in an exam), to pass an exam with distinction/"very good" → *auch* **bestanden b** (= *durchstehen*) *Schicksalsschläge* to withstand; *schwere Zeit* to come through, to pull through; *Gefahr* to overcome; *Kampf* to win VI **a** (= *existieren*) to exist, to be in existence; (*Brauch auch*) to be extant; (*Zweifel, Hoffnung, Aussicht, Gefahr, Probleme etc*) to exist; **~ bleiben** (*Frage, Hoffnung etc*) to remain; **die Universität/**

Firma besteht seit hundert Jahren the university/firm has been in existence *or* has existed for a hundred years; **es besteht die Aussicht/der Verdacht/die Hoffnung, dass ...** there is a prospect/a suspicion/a hope that ... **b** (= *Bestand haben*) to continue to exist; (*Zweifel, Problem etc*) to continue to exist, to persist **c** (= *sich zusammensetzen*) to consist (*aus* of); **in etw** (*dat*) **~** to consist in sth; (*Aufgabe*) to involve sth; **seine einzige Chance besteht darin, ...** his only chance is to ...; **die Schwierigkeit/das Problem besteht darin, dass ...** the difficulty/problem consists *or* lies in the fact that ..., the difficulty/problem is that ...; **das Problem besteht darin, zu zeigen ...** the problem consists in showing ... **d** (= *standhalten, sich bewähren*) to hold one's own (*in +dat* in); **vor etw** (*dat*) **~** to stand up to *or* against sth **e** (= *durchkommen*) to pass; (**in einer Prüfung**) **mit „sehr gut" ~** to get a "very good" (in an exam) **f** **auf etw** (*dat*) **~** to insist on sth; **ich bestehe darauf** I insist

Be|ste|hen NT -s, *no pl* **a** (= *Vorhandensein, Dauer*) existence; **seit ~ der Firma/des Staates** ever since the firm/state has existed *or* came into existence; **das 100-jährige ~ von etw feiern** to celebrate the hundredth anniversary *or* first hundred years of (the existence of) sth **b** (= *Beharren*) insistence (*auf +dat* on) **c** (*von Prüfung*) passing; (*von Schicksalsschlägen*) withstanding; (*von schwerer Zeit*) coming *or* pulling through; (*von Gefahr*) overcoming; **bei ~ der Prüfung** on passing the exam

be|ste|hen blei|ben ▲ VI *irreg aux sein* to last, to endure; (*Hoffnung*) to remain; (*Versprechen, Vereinbarungen*) to hold good

be|ste|hend ADJ existing; *Gesetze auch* present, current; *Umstände, Verhältnisse auch* prevailing; *Preise* current; **die seit 1887 ~en Gesetze** the laws which have existed since 1887

be|ste|hen las|sen ▲ *ptp* **bestehen lassen** VT *irreg* to keep, to retain

be|steh|len *ptp* **bestohlen** [bəˈʃtoːlən] VT *irreg* to rob; **jdn (um etw) ~** (*lit, fig*) to rob sb of sth

be|stei|gen *ptp* **bestiegen** [bəˈʃtiːɡn] VT *irreg* **a** *Berg, Turm, Leiter* to climb (up), to ascend (*literl*); *Fahrrad, Pferd* to mount, to get *or* climb on(to); *Bus, Flugzeug* to get on, to enter; *Auto, Segelflugzeug, Hubschrauber* to get into; *Schiff* to go on *or* aboard; *Thron* to ascend **b** (= *bespringen*) to mount, to cover; (*sl: Mensch*) to mount (*inf*)

Be|stei|gung F (*von Berg*) climbing, ascent; (*von Thron*) accession (*+gen* to)

Be|stell-: Be|stell|block M *pl* -blöcke *or* -blocks order pad, pad of order forms; **Be|stell|buch** NT order book

be|stel|len ✪ 47.2 *ptp* **bestellt** VT **a** (= *anfordern, in Restaurant*) to order; (= *abonnieren auch*) to subscribe to; **sich** (*dat*) **etw ~** to order sth; **das Material ist bestellt** the material has been ordered, the material is on order; **wie bestellt und nicht abgeholt** (*hum inf*) like orphan Annie (*inf*) **b** (= *reservieren*) to book, to reserve **c** (= *ausrichten*) **bestell ihm (von mir), dass ...** tell him (from me) that ...; **soll ich irgendetwas ~?** can I take a message?, can I give him/her a message?; **~ Sie ihm schöne Grüße von mir** give him my regards; **er hat nicht viel/nichts zu ~** he doesn't have much/any say here **d** (= *kommen lassen*) *jdn* to send for, to summon; **jdn zu jdm/an einen Ort ~** to summon sb to sb/a place, to ask sb to come to sb/a place; **ich bin um** *or* **für 10 Uhr bestellt** I have an appointment for *or* at 10 o'clock **e** (= *einsetzen, ernennen*) to nominate, to appoint **f** (= *bearbeiten*) *Land* to till **g** (*fig*) **es ist schlecht um ihn/mit seinen Finanzen bestellt** he is/his finances are in a bad

way; **damit ist es schlecht bestellt** that's rather difficult
VI (= *anfordern: in Restaurant*) to order

Be|stel|ler [bəˈʃtɛlɐ] M **-s, -**, **Be|stel|le|rin** [-ərɪn] F **-, -nen** customer; (= *Abonnent*) subscriber; **Hinweise für den ~** ordering instructions, instructions on how to order

Be|stell|geld NT price including postage and packing; (*für Zeitungen etc*) subscription rate *or* charge

Bestellliste △ F → **Bestellliste**

Be|stell-: **Be|stell|kar|te** F order form; **Be|stell|lis|te** ▲ F order list; **Be|stell|men|ge** F order quantity; **Be|stell|num|mer** F order number *or* code; **Be|stell|pra|xis** F (*Med*) appointments-only surgery (*Brit*), surgery (*Brit*) *or* doctor's office (*US*) with an appointments system; **Be|stell|schein** M order form *or* slip

Be|stel|lung ✿ 47.2, 47.3, 47.4 F **a** (= *Anforderung, das Angeforderte*) order; (= *das Bestellen*) ordering **b** (= *das Reservieren*) booking, reservation **c** (= *Nachricht*) message **d** (= *Ernennung*) nomination, appointment **e** (*von Acker, Land*) tilling

Be|stell|zet|tel M order form *or* slip

bes|ten ADV am **~** → **beste(r, s)** ADV

bes|ten|falls [ˈbɛstn̩fals] ADV at best

bes|tens [ˈbɛstns] ADV (= *sehr gut*) very well; (= *herzlich*) danken very warmly; **sie lässt ~ grüßen** she sends her best regards

bes|te(r, s) [ˈbɛstə] ✿ 29.2 ADJ superl von **gut** **a** *attr* best; **im ~n Fall** at (the) best; **im ~n Alter, in den ~n Jahren** in the prime of (one's) life; **mit (den) ~n Grüßen/Wünschen** with best wishes; **in ~n Händen** in the best of hands; **aus ~m Hause sein** to come from the very best of homes; **das kommt in den ~n Familien vor** (*hum*) that can happen in the best of families; **jds ~s Stück, jds ~r Freund** (*hum sl: = Penis*) sb's John Thomas (*Brit hum inf*), sb's Johnnie (*US hum sl*) **b** **der/die/das Beste** the best; **der/die Beste sein** to be the best; (*in der Klasse auch*) to be top (of the class); **meine Beste!** (*dated inf*) (my) dear lady; **mein Bester!** (*dated inf*) (my) dear fellow; **zu deinem Besten** for your good; **ich will nur dein Bestes** I've your best interests at heart; **sein Bestes tun** to do one's best; **sein Bestes geben** to give of one's best; **wir wollen das Beste hoffen** let's hope for the best; **der/die/das erste** *or* **nächste Beste** the first (person/job *etc*) that comes along; the first (hotel/cinema *etc*) one comes to; **ich hielte es für das Beste, wenn ...** I thought it (would be) best if ...; **das Beste wäre, wir ...** the best thing would be for us to ..., it would be best for us to ...; **aufs** *or* **auf das Beste** very well; **zum Besten** for the best; **es steht nicht zum Besten** it does not look too promising *or* good *or* hopeful; **jdn zum Besten haben** *or* **halten** to pull sb's leg, to have sb on (*Brit inf*); **etw zum Besten geben** (= *erzählen*) to tell sth; **jdm eine Geschichte/ein Liedchen zum Besten geben** to entertain sb with a story/song

ADV am **~n** best; **ich hielt es für am ~n, wenn ...** I thought it (would be) best if ...; **am ~n würden wir gleich gehen** we'd be best to go immediately; **am ~n gehe ich jetzt** I'd *or* I had best go *or* be going now

be|sternt [bəˈʃtɛrnt] ADJ (*geh*) star-studded, starry

Bes|te(s) [ˈbɛstə] NT → **beste(r, s)** ADJ **b**

be|steu|ern ptp **besteuert** VT to tax; **Luxusartikel sind sehr hoch besteuert** there is a high tax on luxury goods, luxury goods are heavily taxed

Be|steu|e|rung F taxation; (= *Steuersatz*) tax

Best-: **Best|form** F (*esp Sport*) top *or* best form; **in ~ sein** to be in top form, to be on one's best form; **best|ge|hasst** ▲ [-gəhast] ADJ *attr* (*iro*) most hated; **best|ge|klei|det** [-gəklaidət] ADJ *attr* best-dressed

bes|ti|a|lisch [bɛsˈtiaːlɪʃ] ADJ bestial; (*inf*) awful, beastly (*inf*) ADV (*inf*) terribly, incredibly; *stinken, zurichten* dreadfully; *wehtun* like hell (*inf*); *zurichten* brutally; **~ kalt** incredibly cold; **~ stinken** to stink to high heaven (*inf*)

Bes|ti|a|li|tät [bɛstialiˈtɛːt] F **-, -en** bestiality

be|sti|cken ptp **bestickt** VT to embroider

Bes|tie [ˈbɛstiə] F **-, -n** beast; (*fig*) animal

be|stimm|bar ADJ determinable; **schwer ~ sein** to be difficult to determine

be|stim|men ptp **bestimmt** **VI a** (= *festsetzen*) to determine; *Grenze, Ort, Zeit etc auch* to fix, to set; (= *entscheiden auch*) to decide; **sie will immer alles ~** she always wants to decide the way things are to be done → *auch* **bestimmt**
b (= *prägen*) Stadtbild, Landschaft to characterize; (= *beeinflussen*) Preis, Anzahl to determine; Entwicklung, Werk, Stil etc to have a determining influence on; (*Gram*) Kasus, Tempus to determine; **näher ~** (*Gram*) to qualify
c (= *wissenschaftlich feststellen*) Alter, Standort to determine, to ascertain; Pflanze, Tier, Funde to classify; (= *definieren*) Wort, Bedeutung to define **d** (= *vorsehen*) to intend, to mean (*für* for); **jdn zu etw ~** to choose *or* designate sb as sth; **er ist zu Höherem bestimmt** he is destined for higher things; **wir waren füreinander bestimmt** we were meant for each other
VI a (= *entscheiden*) to decide (*über +acc* on); **du hast hier nicht zu ~** you don't make the decisions here
b (= *verfügen*) **er kann über sein Geld allein ~** it is up to him what he does with his money; **du kannst nicht über ihn/seine Zeit ~** it's not up to you to decide what he's going to do/ how his time is to be spent
VR sich nach etw ~ to be determined by sth

be|stim|mend ADJ (= *entscheidend*) Faktor, Einfluss determining, decisive, determinant; **die ~e Figur innerhalb der Partei** the most influential figure within the party; **für etw ~ sein** to be characteristic of sth; (= *entscheidend*) to have a determining influence on sth; **an etw** (*dat*) **~ mitwirken** to play a determining *or* decisive part in sth

be|stimmt [bəˈʃtɪmt] ADJ **a** (= *gewiss, nicht genau genannt*) Leute, Dinge, Vorstellungen, Aussagen etc certain; (= *speziell, genau genannt*) particular, definite; (= *festgesetzt*) Preis, Tag set, fixed; (= *klar, deutlich*) Angaben, Ausdruck definite, precise; (*Gram*) Artikel, Zahlwort definite; **suchen Sie etwas Bestimmtes?** are you looking for anything in particular?; **den ganz ~en Eindruck gewinnen, dass ...** to get *or* have a definite *or* the distinct impression that ... → *auch* **bestimmen**
b (= *entschieden*) Auftreten, Ton, Mensch firm, resolute, decisive; **höflich, aber ~** polite but firm
ADV a (= *sicher*) definitely, certainly; **ich weiß ganz ~, dass ...** I know for sure *or* for certain that ...; **kommst du? – ja – ~?** are you coming? – yes – definitely?; **ich schaffe es ~** I'll manage it all right; **er schafft es ~ nicht** he definitely won't manage it
b (= *wahrscheinlich*) no doubt; **das hat er ~ verloren** he's bound to have lost it; **er kommt ~ wieder zu spät** he's bound to be late again

Be|stimmt|heit F **-, no pl a** (= *Sicherheit*) certainty; **ich kann mit ~ sagen, dass ...** I can say definitely *or* with certainty that ...; **ich weiß aber mit ~, dass ...** but I know for sure *or* for certain that ... **b** (= *Entschiedenheit*) firmness; **in** *or* **mit aller ~** quite categorically

Be|stim|mung F **a** (= *Vorschrift*) regulation; **gesetzliche ~en** legal requirements
b *no pl* (= *Zweck*) purpose; **eine Brücke/Straße/ Anlage ihrer ~ übergeben** to open a new bridge/road/plant officially
c (= *Schicksal*) destiny
d (*old*: = *Ort*) destination
e (*Gram*) modifier; **adverbiale ~** adverbial modifier
f (= *das Bestimmen*) determination, determin-

ing; (*von Grenze, Zeit etc*) fixing, setting; (*Gram, von Preis, Anzahl*) determining, determination; (*von Alter, Standort*) determining, determination, ascertaining, ascertainment; (*von Pflanze, Tier, Funden*) classification; (= *Definition*) definition; **seine ~ zu dieser Aufgabe** choosing him for this task; **nähere ~** (*durch Adverb*) qualifying, qualification

Be|stim|mungs-: **Be|stim|mungs|bahn|hof** M (station of) destination; **be|stim|mungs|gemäß** ADJ, ADV in accordance with the requirements; **Be|stim|mungs|glei|chung** F (*Math*) conditional equation; **Be|stim|mungs|grö|ße** F (*Math, Phys*) defining quantity; **Be|stim|mungs|ha|fen** M (port of) destination; **Be|stim|mungs|land** NT (country of) destination; **Be|stim|mungs|ort** M *pl* **-orte** (place of) destination; **Be|stim|mungs|wort** NT *pl* **-wör-ter** (*Gram*) modifier

Best-: **best|in|for|miert** ADJ *attr* best-informed; **Best|leis|tung** F (*esp Sport*) best performance; **seine persönliche ~** his personal best; **Best|mar|ke** F record; **best|mög|lich** ADJ *no pred* best possible; **wir haben unser Bestmögliches getan** we did our (level (*Brit*)) best **ADV** in the best way possible

Best. Nr. *abbr von* **Bestellnummer**

be|sto|cken ptp **bestockt** VT to stock; **der Wald ist gut bestockt** the forest is well timbered

Be|sto|ckung F (= *das Bestocken*) stocking; (= *Bestand*) stock

be|stra|fen ptp **bestraft** VT to punish; (*Jur*) jdn to sentence (*mit* to); (*Sport*) Spieler, Foul to penalize; **der Schiedsrichter bestrafte das Foul mit einem Elfmeter** the referee awarded *or* gave a penalty for the foul

Be|stra|fung F **-, -en** punishment; (*Jur*) sentencing; (*Sport*) penalization; **wir fordern eine strengere ~ von ...** we demand more severe punishments *or* (*Jur auch*) sentences for ...

be|strah|len ptp **bestrahlt** VT to shine on; (= *beleuchten*) Gebäude, Bühne to light up, to illuminate; (*Med*) to give radiotherapy *or* ray *or* radiation treatment to; Lebensmittel to irradiate; **er ließ sich von der Sonne ~** he was soaking up the sun

Be|strah|lung F illumination; (*Med*) radiotherapy, ray *or* radiation treatment; (= *von Lebensmitteln*) irradiation; **Pflanzen der direkten ~ der Sonne aussetzen** to expose plants to direct sunlight, to expose plants directly to the sun's rays; **15 ~en verordnen** to prescribe (a course of) 15 doses of radiotherapy

Be|strah|lungs|ka|no|ne F (*Med*) radiation gun

Be|strah|lungs|lam|pe F radiation *or* ray lamp

Be|stre|ben NT endeavour (*Brit*), endeavor (*US*); **im** *or* **in seinem ~, dem Fußgänger auszuweichen** in his efforts *or* attempts *or* endeavo(u)rs to avoid the pedestrian

be|strebt [bəˈʃtreːpt] ADJ **~ sein, etw zu tun** to endeavour (*Brit*) *or* endeavor (*US*) to do sth; **wir waren immer ~, ...** we have always endeavo(u)red ..., it has always been our endeavo(u)r ...

Be|stre|bung F *usu pl* endeavour (*Brit*), endeavor (*US*), attempt, effort

be|strei|chen ptp **bestrichen** [bəˈʃtrɪçn̩] VT *irreg* **a** (*mit Salbe, Flüssigkeit*) to spread; (*mit Butter*) to spread, to butter; (*Cook, mit Milch etc*) to coat; (*mit Farbe*) to paint; **etw mit Butter/Fett/Öl ~** to butter/grease/oil sth; **etw mit Butter/Salbe/ Klebstoff ~** to spread butter/ointment/glue on sth; **etw mit Farbe ~** to put a coat of paint on sth **b** (*Mil*) to rake, to sweep **c** (*Scheinwerfer, Strahl*) to sweep (over); (*in der Elektronik*: = *abtasten*) to scan

be|strei|ken ptp **bestreikt** VT to black (*Brit*), to boycott; **bestreikt** strikebound; **die Fabrik wird zurzeit bestreikt** there's a strike on in the factory at the moment; **„dieser Betrieb wird bestreikt"** "please do not cross the picket line"

Be|strei|kung [bəˈʃtraɪkʊŋ] F **-, -en** blacking (*Brit*), boycotting; **die ~ einer Fabrik beschließen** to decide to take strike action against a factory, to decide to black (*Brit*) or boycott a factory

be|streit|bar ADJ disputable, contestable

be|strei|ten ptp **bestritten** [bəˈʃtrɪtn] VT irreg **a** (= *abstreiten*) to dispute, to contest, to challenge; (= *leugnen*) to deny; **jdm das Recht auf ... ~** to dispute etc sb's right to ...; **das möchte ich nicht ~** I'm not disputing or denying it **b** (= *finanzieren*) to pay for, to finance; **Kosten** to carry, to defray (*form*) **c** (= *tragen, gestalten*) to provide for, to carry; **er hat das ganze Gespräch allein bestritten** he did all the talking

Be|strei|tung [bəˈʃtraɪtʊŋ] F **-, -en a** (= *das Leugnen*) denial **b** (= *Finanzierung*) financing; (*von Kosten*) carrying, defrayal (*form*)

best|re|nom|miert [ˈbɛst-] ADJ attr most renowned

be|streu|en ptp **bestreut** VT to cover (*mit* with); (*Cook*) to sprinkle

be|stri|cken ptp **bestrickt** VT **a** (*fig*) to charm, to captivate; **~der Charme** alluring charms **b** (*hum inf*) to knit things for

be|strumpft [bəˈʃtrʊmpft] ADJ in stockings; *Beine* stockinged

Best|sel|ler [ˈbɛstzɛlɐ] M **-s, -** bestseller

Best|sel|ler-: Best|sel|ler|au|tor(in) M(F) bestselling author, bestseller; **Best|sel|ler|lis|te** F bestseller list; (*von Schallplatten*) charts pl

best|si|tu|iert [ˈbɛst-] ADJ attr (esp Aus) well-to-do, well-off

be|stü|cken [bəˈʃtʏkn] ptp **bestückt** VT to fit, to equip; (*Mil*) to arm; *Lager* to stock; **sie ist gut bestückt** (*hum inf*) she's pretty well-stacked (*inf*)

Be|stü|ckung F **-, -en a** (= *das Bestücken*) fitting, equipping; (*Mil*) arming; (*von Lager*) stocking **b** (= *Ausstattung*) equipment; (= *Geschütze*) guns pl, armaments pl

Be|stuh|lung [bəˈʃtuːlʊŋ] F **-, -en** seating no indef art

be|stür|men ptp **bestürmt** VT to storm; (*mit Fragen, Bitten*) to bombard; (*mit Anfragen, Briefen, Anrufen*) to inundate

Be|stür|mung [bəˈʃtʏrmʊŋ] F **-, -en** storming; (*mit Fragen, Bitten*) bombardment; (*mit Anfragen, Briefen, Anrufen*) inundation

be|stür|zen ptp **bestürzt** VT to shake, to fill with consternation → *auch* **bestürzt**

be|stür|zend ADJ alarming; **ich finde es ~, wie wenig die Schüler wissen** it fills me with consternation or it dismays me to see how little the children know ADV *hoch, niedrig* alarmingly

be|stürzt [bəˈʃtʏrtst] ADJ filled with consternation; **sie machte ein ~es Gesicht** a look of consternation came over her face ADV in consternation; **er sah mich ~ an** he looked at me in consternation → *auch* **bestürzen**

Be|stürzt|heit F **-,** no pl consternation

Be|stür|zung [bəˈʃtʏrtsʊŋ] F **-,** no pl consternation

be|stusst ▲ [bəˈʃtʊst] ADJ (*inf*) *Kerl, Ausrede, Behauptung* crazy

Best-: Best|wert M (*Fin*) top value; (*Tech, Sport*) best performance; **Best|zeit** F (*esp Sport*) best time; **Best|zu|stand** M perfect condition

Be|such [bəˈzuːx] M **-(e)s, -e a** (= *das Besuchen*) visit (*des Museums etc* to the museum etc); (*von Schule, Veranstaltung*) attendance (+*gen* at); **ein ~ (von) meiner Tante** a visit from my aunt; **zu seinen Aufgaben gehört auch der ~ der Klienten** his jobs include visiting clients; **bei jdm auf** or **zu ~ sein** to be visiting sb; **(von jdm) ~ erhalten** or **bekommen** to have or get a visit (from sb); **jdm einen ~ abstatten, einen ~ bei**

jdm machen to pay sb a visit **b** (= *Besucher*) visitor; visitors pl; **ist dein ~ wieder abgefahren?** have your visitors/has your visitor gone?; **er hat ~** he has company or visitors/a visitor; **er bekommt viel ~** he has a lot of visitors, he often has visitors

be|su|chen ptp **besucht** VT *jdn* to visit, to pay a visit to; (*Arzt*) *Patienten* to visit; *Vortrag, Schule, Seminar, Gottesdienst* to attend, to go to; *Kino, Theater, Lokal* to go to; *Bordell, Museum* to go to, to visit; **du kannst mich mal am Abend** or **im Mondschein ~** (*euph inf*) you know what you can do (*inf*) → *auch* **besucht**

Be|su|cher(in) M(F) visitor; (*von Kino, Theater*) patron (*form*); **etwa 1.000 ~ waren zu der Veranstaltung/dem Vortrag/der Ausstellung gekommen** about 1,000 people attended or went to the function/lecture/visited the exhibition; **ein regelmäßiger ~ der Oper** a regular opera-goer, an habitué of the opera

Be|su|cher-: Be|su|cher|re|kord M record number of visitors; (*Sport*) record attendance; **die Ausstellung verzeichnete einen ~** the exhibition broke all attendance records; **Be|su|cher|rit|ze** F (*hum inf*) crack between the two mattresses of twin beds; **Be|su|cher|schar** F crowd of visitors; **Be|su|cher|ter|ras|se** F (*von Flughafen etc*) observation terrace; **Be|su|cher|zahl** F attendance figures pl; (*bei Schloss, Museum, Ausstellung etc*) number of visitors

Be|suchs-: Be|suchs|er|laub|nis F visitor's card; (*für Land*) visitor's visa; **~ haben** to be allowed to receive visitors; **~ bekommen** to obtain permission to visit sb; **Be|suchs|recht** NT (*Jur, nach Scheidung*) (right of) access; **das ~ bei ihrem Sohn** the right to visit her son; **Be|suchs|tag** M visiting day; **be|suchs|wei|se** ADV on a visit; **Be|suchs|zeit** F visiting time; **jetzt ist keine ~** it's not visiting time; **Be|suchs|zim|mer** NT visitor's room

be|sucht [bəˈzuːxt] ADJ **gut/schlecht/schwach ~ sein** to be well/badly/poorly attended; (*Schloss etc*) to get a lot of/not many/only a handful of visitors → *auch* **besuchen**

be|su|deln ptp **besudelt** (*geh*) VT *Wände* to besmear; *Kleidung, Hände* to soil; (*fig*) *Andenken, Namen, Ehre* to besmirch, to sully VR **sich mit Blut ~** (*fig*) to get blood on one's hands

Be|ta [ˈbeːta] NT **-(s), -s** beta

Be|ta|blo|cker M (*Med*) beta-blocker

be|tagt [bəˈtaːkt] ADJ (*geh*) aged, well advanced in years

Be|tagt|heit F **-,** no pl (*geh*) advancing years pl

be|ta|keln ptp **betakelt** VT (*Aus* = *betrügen*) to swindle

be|tan|ken ptp **betankt** VT *Fahrzeug* to fill up; *Flugzeug* to refuel

Be|tan|kung F **-, -en** (*von Fahrzeug*) filling-up (*Brit*), refueling (*US*); (*von Flugzeug, Rennwagen*) refuelling (*Brit*), refueling (*US*)

be|tas|ten ptp **betastet** VT to feel; (*Med auch*) to palpate (*form*)

Be|ta-: Be|ta|strah|len PL beta rays pl; **Be|ta|strah|lung** F beta radiation; **Be|ta|teil|chen** NT beta particle

be|tä|ti|gen ptp **betätigt** VT **a** *Muskeln, Gehirn, Darm, Auslöser* to activate; *Bremse* to apply, to put on; *Mechanismus* to operate, to work, to activate, to actuate (*form*); *Taste, Knopf* to press; (= *drehen*) to turn; *Schalter, Blinker* to turn on; *Hebel* to move, to operate; *Sirene* to operate, to sound **b** (*liter*. = *bewirken*) to bring about, to effect **c** (*liter*. = *einsetzen*) to put into effect VR to busy oneself; (*körperlich*) to get some exercise; **sich politisch ~** to be active in politics; **sich als etw ~** (*beruflich*) **sich wissenschaftlich/literarisch ~** to do (some) scientific work/some writing; **sich künstlerisch ~** to do (some) painting/sculpture etc; **sich sportlich ~** to do sport; **sich geistig und körperlich ~** to stay active in

body and mind; **wenn man sich längere Zeit nicht geistig betätigt hat** if you haven't used your mind for months

Be|tä|ti|gung F **a** (= *Tätigkeit*) activity; **an ~ fehlt es mir nicht** I've no lack of things to do **b** (= *Aktivierung*) operation; (*von Muskel, Gehirn, Darm*) activation; (*von Bremsen*) applying, application; (*von Mechanismus*) operation, activation, actuation (*form*); (*von Knopf*) pressing; (*durch Drehen*) turning; (*von Schalter*) turning on; (*von Hebel*) moving; (*von Sirene*) sounding; **etw zur ~ der Muskeln tun** to do sth to exercise one's muscles; **die ~ des Mechanismus erfolgt durch Knopfdruck** pressing the button activates the mechanism or sets the mechanism in motion

Be|tä|ti|gungs-: Be|tä|ti|gungs|drang M need for activity; **Be|tä|ti|gungs|feld** NT sphere or field of activity

Be|tat|ron [ˈbeːtatrɔːn] NT **-s, -e** betatron

be|tat|schen ptp **betatscht** VT (*inf*) to paw (*inf*)

be|täu|ben [bəˈtɔybn] ptp **betäubt** VT (= *unempfindlich machen*) *Körperteil* to (be)numb, to deaden; *Nerv* to deaden; *Schmerzen* to kill, to deaden; (*durch Narkose*) to anaesthetize; (*mit einem Schlag*) to stun, to daze; (*fig*) *Kummer, Gewissen* to ease; (*fig:* = *benommen machen*) to stun; **er versuchte, seinen Kummer mit Alkohol zu ~** he tried to drown his sorrows with alcohol; **~der Lärm** deafening noise; **ein ~der Duft** an overpowering smell; **der Duft betäubte mich fast** I was almost overcome by the smell

Be|täu|bung F **-, -en a** (= *das Betäuben*) (be)numbing, deadening; (*von Nerv, Schmerz*) deadening; (*von Schmerzen*) killing; (*durch Narkose*) anaesthetization; (*durch Schlag*) stunning, dazing; (*von Gewissen, Kummer*) easing **b** (= *Narkose*) anaesthetic; **örtliche** or **lokale ~** local anaesthetic

Be|täu|bungs|mit|tel NT anaesthetic; (= *Droge*) narcotic

Be|täu|bungs|mit|tel|ge|setz NT *law concerning drug abuse*, narcotics law (*US*)

be|taut [bəˈtaut] ADJ dewy, bedewed

Bet- [ˈbeːt-]: **Bet|bank** F pl **-bänke** kneeler; **Bet|bru|der** M (*pej inf*) churchy type, Holy Joe (*Brit pej inf*) or Roller (*US pej inf*)

Be|te [ˈbeːtə] F **-, (*rare*) -n** beet; **Rote ~** beetroot

be|tei|len ptp **beteilt** VT (*Aus*) to give presents to; *Flüchtlinge etc* to give gifts to; **jdn mit etw ~** to give sb sth

be|tei|li|gen [bəˈtaɪlɪgn] ptp **beteiligt** VT **jdn an etw** (*dat*) **~** to let sb take part in sth, to involve sb in sth; (*finanziell*) to give sb a share in sth VR to take part, to participate (*an* +*dat* in); (*finanziell*) to have a share (*an* +*dat* in); **sich an den Unkosten ~** to contribute to the expenses; **ich möchte mich bei** or **an dem Geschenk ~** I would like to put something toward(s) the present

be|tei|ligt [bəˈtaɪlɪçt] ADJ **an etw** (*dat*) **~ sein/werden** to be involved in sth, to have a part in sth; (*finanziell*) to have a share in sth; **am Gewinn ~** to have a slice of sth or a share in sth; **an einem Unfall/einer Schlägerei ~ sein** to be involved in an accident/a fight; **an einer Tat/Sache ~ sein** to be party to a deed/cause; **er war an dem Gelingen der Aktion maßgeblich ~** he made a major contribution to the success of the campaign; **er ist an dem Geschäft (mit 250.000 Euro) ~** he has a (250,000-euro) share in the business

Be|tei|lig|te(r) [bəˈtaɪlɪçtə] MF decl as adj person involved; (= *Teilhaber*) partner; (*Jur*) party; **die an der Diskussion ~n** those taking part in or involved in the discussion; **die am Unfall ~n** those involved in the accident; **an alle ~n** to all concerned

Be|tei|li|gung F **-, -en a** (= *Teilnahme*) (*an* +*dat* in) participation; (*finanziell*) share; (*an Unfall*) involvement **b** (= *das Beteiligen*) involvement

---

(*an +dat* in); **die ~ der Arbeiter am Gewinn** giving the workers a share in the profits

Be|tei|li|gungs|ge|sell|schaft F (*Fin, Comm*) holding company

Be|tei|lung F (*Aus*) giving; **die ~ der Armen mit ...** the giving of ... to the poor

Be|tel ['be:tl] M **-s,** *no pl* betel

Be|tel|nuss ▲ F betel nut

be|ten ['be:tn] **VI** to pray (*um, für, zu* to), to say one's prayers; (*bei Tisch*) to say grace **VT** to say

be|teu|ern [bə'tɔyɐn] *ptp* **beteuert** VT to declare, to aver, to asseverate (*liter*); *Unschuld auch* to protest, to affirm; **er beteuerte mir seine Liebe** he declared his love to me, he professed his love for me

Be|teu|e|rung F declaration, averment, asseveration (*liter*); (*von Unschuld auch*) protestation

be|tex|ten *ptp* **betextet** VT *Bild* to write a caption for; *Lied* to write the words *or* lyric(s) for

Bet-: Bet|glo|cke F church bell; **Bet|haus** NT temple

be|ti|teln *ptp* **betitelt** VT to entitle; (= *anreden*) *jdn* to address as, to call; (= *beschimpfen*) to call; **die Sendung ist betitelt ...** the broadcast is entitled ...; **wie ist das Buch betitelt?** what is the book called?, what's the book's title?; **er betitelte seinen Artikel ...** he called his article ..., he gave his article the title ..., he entitled his article ...

Be|ti|te|lung [bə'ti:təlʊŋ] F **-, -en** **a** *no pl* (= *das Betiteln*) **eine andere ~ des Films wäre besser** it would be better to call the film something else, it would be better to find a different title for the film **b** (= *Titel*) title; (= *Anrede*) form of address; (= *Benennung*) name; **ich verbitte mir eine solche ~** I refuse to be called names like that

Be|ton [be'tɔŋ, be'tõ:, (*esp Aus*) be'to:n] M **-s,** (*rare*) **-s** concrete

Be|ton- [be'tɔŋ-, be'tõ:-, (*esp Aus*) be'to:n-] *in cpds* concrete; **Be|ton|bau** M **a** *pl* **-bauten** concrete building *or* structure **b** *no pl* (= *Bauweise*) concrete construction; **Be|ton|bau|er(in)** M(F) *pl* **-bauer(innen)** builder; **Be|ton|bau|wei|se** F concrete construction; **ein Gebäude in ~ errichten** to erect a building as a concrete construction; **Be|ton|bun|ker** M **a** (*lit*) concrete bunker; (= *Luftschutzbunker*) concrete air-raid shelter **b** (*fig pej*: = *Betonhochhaus*) concrete block (*pej*); **Be|ton|burg** F (*pej*) pile of concrete; **Be|ton|de|cke** F concrete ceiling; (*von Straße*) concrete surface

be|to|nen ✪ 53.6 *ptp* **betont** VT **a** (= *hervorheben*) to emphasize; *Hüften, Augen auch* to accentuate; (= *Gewicht legen auf auch*) to stress; **ich möchte noch einmal ~, dass ...** I want to stress *or* emphasize once again that ... → *auch* **betont** **b** (*Ling, Mus*: = *einen Akzent legen auf*) to stress; (= *Tonfall gebrauchen*) to intonate (*form*); **ein Wort falsch ~** to give a word the wrong stress, to stress a word wrongly; **du musst den Satz anders ~** you must stress the sentence differently; (*mit Tonfall*) you must say the sentence with a different intonation

Be|ton|frak|ti|on [be'tɔŋ-, be'tõ:-, (*esp Aus*) be'to:n-] F (*Pol inf*) hardline faction

be|to|nie|ren [beto'ni:rən] *ptp* **betoniert** **VT** **a** (*lit*) to concrete; **betoniert** concrete **b** (*fig*: = *festlegen*) to firm up **VI** **a** (*lit*) to concrete **b** (*Sport sl*) to block the goal (area)

Be|to|nie|rung F **-, -en** (= *das Betonieren*) concreting; (*von Straße auch*) concrete surface

Be|ton- [be'tɔŋ-, be'tõ:-, (*esp Aus*) be'to:n-]: **Be|ton|klotz** M (*lit*) block of concrete, concrete block; (*fig pej*) concrete block; **Be|ton|kopf** M (*pej inf*) reactionary die-hard; **Be|ton|mi|scher** M ; **Be|ton|misch|ma|schi|ne** F cement mixer; **Be|ton|pfei|ler** M concrete pillar; **Be|ton|plat|te** F concrete slab; **Be|ton|rie|ge** F (*Pol inf*) hardline faction; **Be|ton|si|lo** M (*pej inf*) high-rise block (*pej*)

be|tont [bə'to:nt] **ADJ** *Höflichkeit* emphatic, deliberate; *Kühle, Sachlichkeit* pointed; *Eleganz* pronounced **ADV** *knapp, kühl* deliberately, pointedly, emphatically; **~ sparsam leben** to live a markedly modest life; **sich ~ einfach kleiden** to dress with marked *or* pronounced simplicity → *auch* **betonen**

Be|to|nung F **-, -en** **a** *no pl* (= *das Betonen*) emphasis; (*von Hüften, Augen*) accentuation; (= *Unterstreichung*) stressing **b** (= *Akzent*) stress; (*fig*: = *Gewicht*) emphasis, stress, accent; **die ~ liegt auf der ersten Silbe** the stress is on the first syllable

Be|to|nungs|zei|chen NT stress mark

Be|ton|wüs|te F (*pej*) concrete jungle

be|tö|ren [bə'tø:rən] *ptp* **betört** VT to bewitch, to beguile

be|tö|rend ADJ bewitching; *Worte auch* beguiling; (*stärker*) seductive

Be|tö|rer [bə'tø:rɐ] M **-s, -, Be|tö|re|rin** [-ərɪn] F **-, -nen** (*geh*) bewitcher, beguiler

Be|tö|rung F **-, -en** bewitchment

Bet|pult NT prie-dieu, kneeler

betr. *abbr von* **betreffend** *von* **betrifft** *von* **betreffs**

Betr. *abbr von* **Betreff** *von* **betrifft**

Be|tracht [bə'traxt] M **-(e)s,** *no pl* **a** **außer ~ bleiben** to be left out of consideration, to be disregarded; **etw außer ~ lassen** to leave sth out of consideration, to disregard sth; **in ~ kommen** to be considered; **nicht in ~ kommen** to be out of the question; **jdn in ~ ziehen** to take sb into consideration, to consider sb; **etw in ~ ziehen** to take sth into account *or* consideration **b** (*dated*: = *Hinsicht*) **in diesem ~** in this respect; **in gewissem ~** in certain respects

be|trach|ten ✪ 40.2, 48.3, 53.1, 53.2, 53.4 *ptp* **betrachtet** VT **a** (= *sehen, beurteilen*) to look at; *Verhältnisse, Situation etc* to look at, to view; **sich** (*dat*) **etw ~** to have a look at sth; **bei näherem Betrachten** on closer examination **b** (= *halten für*) **als jd** *or* **jdn/etw ~** to look upon *or* regard *or* consider as sb/sth; **ich betrachte ihn als Freund** I regard *etc* him as a friend

Be|trach|ter [bə'traxtɐ] M **-s, -, Be|trach|te|rin** [-ərɪn] F **-, -nen** (*von Anblick*) observer, beholder (*liter*); (*von Situation*) observer; **der aufmerksame ~ wird bei diesem Bild festgestellt haben ...** to the alert eye it will have become apparent that in this picture ...

be|trächt|lich [bə'trɛçtlɪç] **ADJ** considerable; **um ein ~es** considerably **ADV** (= *in starkem Maße*) *höher, niedriger* considerably

Be|trach|tung [bə'traxtʊŋ] ✪ 53.2 F **-, -en** **a** (= *das Betrachten*) contemplation; **bei näherer ~** on closer examination, when you look more closely; **eine neuartige ~ des Problems** a new way of looking at the problem **b** (= *Überlegung, Untersuchung*) reflection; **über etw** (*acc*) **~en anstellen** to reflect on sth, to contemplate sth; **in ~en versunken** lost in thought *or* meditation

Be|trach|tungs|wei|se F **verschiedene ~n der Lage** different ways of looking at the situation; **er hat eine völlig andere ~** he has a completely different way of looking at things

Be|trag [bə'tra:k] ✪ 47.5 M **-(e)s, ~e** [-'trɛ:gə] amount, sum; **der gesamte ~** the total (amount); **~ dankend erhalten** (*payment*) received with thanks

be|tra|gen *ptp* **betragen** *irreg* **VT** to be; (*Kosten, Rechnung auch*) to come to, to amount to; **die Entfernung 25 km** the distance was 25 km; **der Unterschied beträgt 100 Euro** the difference amounts to *or* is 100 euros **VR** to behave (oneself); **sich gut/schlecht ~** to behave (oneself) well/badly; **sich unhöflich ~** to behave impolitely

Be|tra|gen NT **-s,** *no pl* behaviour (*Brit*), behavior (*US*); (*esp im Zeugnis*) conduct

be|trau|en *ptp* **betraut** VT **jdn mit etw ~** to entrust sb with sth; **jdn damit ~, etw zu tun** to

give sb the task of doing sth; **jdn mit einem öffentlichen Amt ~** to appoint sb to public office

be|trau|ern *ptp* **betrauert** VT to mourn; *jdn auch* to mourn for

be|träu|feln *ptp* **beträufelt** VT **den Fisch mit Zitrone ~** to sprinkle lemon juice over the fish; **die Wunde mit der Lösung ~** to put drops of the solution on the wound

Be|trau|ung F entrustment, entrusting

Be|treff [bə'trɛf] M **-(e)s, -e** (*form*) **~: Ihr Schreiben vom ...** re your letter of ...; **den ~ angeben** to state the reference *or* subject matter; **in ~ dieser Frage** with respect *or* regard to this question; **in diesem ~** (*old*) in this regard (*old*) *or* respect

be|tref|fen ✪ 33.2, 38.1, 53.2 *ptp* **betroffen** [bə'trɔfn] VT *irreg* **a** (= *angehen*) to concern; **das betrifft dich** it concerns you; **von dieser Regelung werde ich nicht betroffen** this rule does not concern *or* affect me; **was mich betrifft ...** as far as I'm concerned; **was das betrifft ...** as far as that goes *or* is concerned ...; **betrifft** re → *auch* **betreffend, betroffen** **b** (*geh*: = *widerfahren*) to befall **c** (*geh*: = *seelisch treffen*) to affect, to touch; **jdn schwer ~** to affect sb deeply

be|tref|fend ADJ *attr* (= *erwähnt*) in question; (= *zuständig, für etw relevant*) relevant; **das ~e Wort richtig einsetzen** to insert the appropriate word in the right place; **alle (mein Fach) ~en Artikel** all the articles relevant to my subject, all the relevant articles

Be|tref|fen|de(r) [bə'trɛfndə] MF *decl as adj* person concerned; **die ~n** those concerned

be|treffs [bə'trɛfs] PREP +*gen* (*form*) concerning, re (*esp Comm*)

be|trei|ben *ptp* **betrieben** [bə'tri:bn] VT *irreg* **a** (= *vorantreiben*) to push ahead *or* forward; **auf jds Betreiben** (*acc*) **hin** at sb's instigation **b** (= *ausüben*) *Gewerbe, Handwerk* to carry on; *Geschäft* to conduct; *Handel auch, Sport* to do; *Studium, Politik* to pursue **c** (*Tech*) to operate **d** (*Sw*) to obtain a writ of account against

Be|trei|ber(in) M(F) operating authority

Be|trei|bung [bə'traibʊŋ] F **-, -en** (= *Ausübung*) carrying on; (*von Geschäft*) conduct; **bei der ~ einer Klage** in the pursuit of a legal action

be|tresst ▲ [bə'trɛst] ADJ braided

be|tre|ten¹ [bə'tre:tn] *ptp* **betreten** VT *irreg* (= *hineingehen in*) to enter, to go/come into; (= *auf etw treten*) *Rasen, Spielfeld etc* to walk on; *frischen Zementboden* to step or walk on; *Bühne, Brücke* to walk or step onto; *Podium* to step (up) onto; **wir ~ damit ein noch unerforschtes Gebiet** we are here entering unknown *or* unexplored territory; „**Betreten (des Rasens) verboten!**" "keep off (the grass) "; „**Betreten für Unbefugte verboten**" "no entry to unauthorized persons"

be|tre|ten² **ADJ** embarrassed **ADV** with embarrassment; **er sah ~ zu Boden** he looked at the floor, embarrassed

Be|tre|ten|heit F **-,** *no pl* embarrassment

be|treu|en [bə'trɔyən] *ptp* **betreut** VT to look after; *Reisegruppe, Abteilung auch* to be in charge of; **betreutes Wohnen** assisted living

Be|treu|er [bə'trɔyɐ] M **-s, -, Be|treu|e|rin** [-ərɪn] F **-, -nen** person who is in charge of *or* looking after sb; (= *Kinderbetreuer*) child minder (*Brit*), babysitter (*US*); (*von alten Leuten, Kranken*) nurse; **wir suchen noch ~ für ...** we are still looking for people to look after *or* take charge of ...; **der medizinische ~ der Nationalelf** the doctor who looks after the international team

Be|treu|ung F **-, -en** looking after; (*von Patienten, Tieren etc*) care; **er wurde mit der ~ der Gruppe beauftragt** he was put in charge of the group, the group was put in his care

Be|trieb M **a** (= *Firma*) business, company, concern; (= *Fabrik*) factory, works *sing or pl*; (= *Arbeitsstelle*) place of work; **wir kommen um 5**

Uhr aus dem ~ we leave work at 5 o'clock; **der Direktor ist heute nicht im ~** the director isn't at work *or* in (the office) today

b (= *Tätigkeit*) work; (*von Maschine, Fabrik*) working, operation; (*von Eisenbahn*) running; (*von Bergwerk*) working; **den ~ stören** to be disruptive, to cause disruption; **er hält den ganzen ~ auf** he's holding everything up; **der ganze ~ stand still** everything stopped *or* came to a stop; **außer ~** out of order; **die Maschinen sind in ~** the machines are running; **eine Maschine in ~ setzen** to start a machine up; **eine Maschine außer ~ setzen** to stop a machine; **eine Fabrik außer ~ setzen** to put a factory out of operation; **eine Maschine/Fabrik in ~ nehmen** to put a machine/factory into operation, to start operating a machine/in a factory; **einen Bus in ~ nehmen** to put a bus into service; **etw dem ~ übergeben** to open sth

c (= *Betriebsamkeit*) bustle; **in den Geschäften herrscht großer ~** the shops are very busy; **auf den Straßen ist noch kein ~** there is nobody about in the streets yet; **bei dem ~ soll sich ein Mensch konzentrieren können!** how can anybody concentrate with all that (bustle) going on?

d (*inf*) **ich habe den ganzen ~ satt!** I'm fed up with the whole business! (*inf*); **ich schmeiß den ganzen ~ hin!** I'm going to chuck it all up! (*Brit inf*), I'm going to chuck the whole business in (*inf*)

be|trieb|lich [bəˈtriːplɪç] ADJ *attr* company *attr*; *Nutzungsdauer etc* operational ADV **eine Sache ~ regeln** to settle a matter within the company; **~ bedingte Entlassungen/Rationalisierungen** redundancies/rationalization measures caused by company restructuring

Be|triebs- *in cpds* (= *Fabrik-*) factory, works; (= *Firmen-*) company

be|trieb|sam [bəˈtriːpzaːm] ADJ busy, bustling *no adv* ADV **seine Assistenten huschten ~ herum** his assistants bustled around

Be|trieb|sam|keit F -, *no pl* bustle; (*von Mensch*) active nature; **wegen der ständigen ~ meiner Mutter ...** because my mother is a very busy *or* active person ...

Be|triebs-: **Be|triebs|an|ge|hö|ri|ge(r)** MF *decl as adj* employee; **Be|triebs|an|lei|tung** F , **Be|triebs|an|wei|sung** F operating instructions *pl*, operating *or* user's manual; **Be|triebs|art** F operating mode; **Be|triebs|arzt** M ; **Be|triebs|ärz|tin** F company doctor; **Be|triebs|aus|flug** M (annual) works (*Brit*) *or* company (*esp US*) outing; **be|triebs|be|dingt** ADJ **es gab 50 ~e Kündigungen** 50 people were made redundant because of restructuring; **Be|triebs|be|ge|hung** F round of inspection; **Be|triebs|be|ra|tung** F management consultancy; **be|triebs|be|reit** ADJ operational; **Be|triebs|be|reit|schaft** F operational readiness; **Be|triebs|be|sich|ti|gung** F tour of a/the factory *or* firm; **be|triebs|blind** ADJ blind to the shortcomings of one's (own) company; **Be|triebs|blind|heit** F blindness to the shortcomings of one's (own) company; **Be|triebs|da|ten** PL operational data *sing*; **be|triebs|ei|gen** ADJ company *attr*; **Be|triebs|er|geb|nis** NT (*Fin*) trading result; **Be|triebs|er|laub|nis** F operating licence (*Brit*) *or* license (*US*); **be|triebs|fä|hig** ADJ in working condition, operational; **Be|triebs|fä|hig|keit** F operational capability; **Be|triebs|fe|ri|en** PL (annual) holiday (*esp Brit*), vacation close-down (*US*); **wegen ~ geschlossen** closed for holidays (*esp Brit*) *or* vacation (*US*); **be|triebs|fremd** ADJ outside; **~e Personen** people visiting a/the company; **Be|triebs|frie|den** M industrial peace; **Be|triebs|füh|rung** F management; **Be|triebs|ge|heim|nis** NT trade secret; **Be|triebs|ge|mein|schaft** F staff and management *pl*; **Be|triebs|ge|neh|mi|gung** F operating licence (*Brit*) *or* license (*US*); **Be|triebs|in|ge|ni|eur(in)** M(F) production engineer; **be|triebs|in|tern** ADJ internal

company *attr*; *Ausbildung, Kenntnisse* in-house *attr* ADV **etw ~ regeln** to settle sth within the company; **Be|triebs|ka|pi|tal** NT (= *laufendes Kapital*) working capital; (= *Anfangskapital*) initial capital; **Be|triebs|kin|der|gar|ten** M company kindergarten *or* daycare (center) (*US*); **Be|triebs|kli|ma** NT atmosphere at work, working atmosphere; **Be|triebs|kos|ten** PL (*von Firma etc*) overheads *pl*, overhead expenses *pl*; (*von Maschine*) running costs *pl*; **Be|triebs|kran|ken|kas|se** F company health insurance scheme; **Be|triebs|lei|ter(in)** M(F) (works *or* factory) manager; **Be|triebs|lei|tung** F management; **Be|triebs|mit|tel** NT means of production *pl*; **Be|triebs|nu|del** F (*inf*) live wire (*inf*); (= *Witzbold*) office/club *etc* clown; **Be|triebs|prak|ti|kum** NT work placement (*Brit*), internship (*US*); **ein ~ absolvieren** to go on *or* to do a work placement (*Brit*) *or* internship (*US*); **Be|triebs|prü|fung** F (government) audit; **Be|triebs|psy|cho|lo|gie** F industrial psychology; **Be|triebs|rat¹** M (= *Gremium*) works *or* factory committee, employee organization (*US*); **Be|triebs|rat²** M , **Be|triebs|rä|tin** F works *or* factory committee member, employee representative (*US*); **Be|triebs|rats|vor|sit|zen|de(r)** MF *decl as adj* chair of works *or* factory committee; **Be|triebs|rats|wahl** F works committee (*Brit*) *or* employee organization (*US*) elections *pl*; **Be|triebs|ren|te** F company pension; **Be|triebs|ru|he** F shutdown; **Be|triebs|schlie|ßung** F (complete) shutdown (of a/the factory), (factory) closure; **Be|triebs|schluss** ▲ M (*von Firma*) end of business hours; (*von Fabrik*) end of factory hours; **nach ~** after business/factory hours; **was macht der Durchschnittsbürger nach ~?** what does the average citizen do after work?; **Be|triebs|schutz** M (*von Anlagen*) factory *or* works security; (= *Arbeitsschutz*) industrial safety; **be|triebs|si|cher** ADJ safe (to operate); **Be|triebs|si|cher|heit** F **a** (operational) safety **b** (*von Betrieb*) factory *or* works security; **Be|triebs|so|zio|lo|gie** F industrial sociology; **Be|triebs|still|le|gung** ▲ F (complete) shutdown (of a/the factory), (factory) closure; **es gab viele ~en** many factories had to close down; **Be|triebs|sto|ckung** F hold-up (in production); **Be|triebs|stoff** M **a** (= *Treibstoff etc*) fuel **b** (= *Rohstoff*) raw *or* working materials *pl*; **Be|triebs|stö|rung** F breakdown; **Be|triebs|sys|tem** NT (*Comput*) operating system; **Be|triebs|treue** F faithful service to the company; **Be|triebs|un|fall** M industrial accident; (*hum inf*) accident; **Be|triebs|ur|laub** M company holiday *or* vacation (*US*); **Be|triebs|ver|ein|ba|rung** F internal agreement; **Be|triebs|ver|fas|sung** F regulations governing industrial relations within a company; **Be|triebs|ver|fas|sungs|ge|setz** NT law governing industrial relations within a company; **Be|triebs|ver|samm|lung** F company meeting; **Be|triebs|wirt(in)** M(F) management expert, graduate in business management *or* administration; (*Student*) student of business management *or* administration; **Be|triebs|wirt|schaft** F , *no pl* business management *or* administration; **Be|triebs|wirt|schaft|ler(in)** M(F) management expert, graduate in business management *or* administration; (*Student*) student of business management *or* administration; **Be|triebs|wirt|schaft|lich** ADJ business management *or* administration *attr* ADV in terms of business management *or* administration; **Be|triebs|wirt|schafts|leh|re** F business management *or* administration; **Be|triebs|zu|ge|hö|rig|keit** F nach zehnjähriger ~ after ten years of employment with the company

be|trin|ken *ptp* **betrunken** [bəˈtrʊŋkn] VR *irreg* to get drunk → *auch* **betrunken**

be|trof|fen [bəˈtrɔfn] ADJ **a** affected (*von* by) **b** (= *bestürzt*) sad; *Schweigen* embarrassed, awkward ADV (= *bestürzt*) in consternation; (=

betrübt) sadly, in dismay; **jdn ~ ansehen** to look at sb in consternation → *auch* **betreffen**

Be|trof|fe|ne(r) [bəˈtrɔfnə] MF *decl as adj* person affected; **schließlich sind wir die ~n** after all we are the ones who are affected *or* who are on the receiving end (*inf*)

Be|trof|fen|heit F -, *no pl* sadness; **stumme ~** embarrassed *or* awkward silence

be|trog *pret von* **betrügen**

be|tro|gen *ptp von* **betrügen**

be|trü|ben *ptp* **betrübt** VT to sadden, to distress; **es betrübt mich sehr ...** it grieves *or* saddens me greatly ... → **betrübt** VR (*dated, hum*) **die Lage ...** to grieve (*über +acc* over)

be|trüb|lich [bəˈtryːplɪç] ADJ sad, distressing; *Zustände, Unwissenheit, Unfähigkeit* deplorable ADV **die Lage sieht ~ aus** things look bad

be|trüb|li|cher|wei|se [bəˈtryːplɪçɐˈvaɪzə] ADV lamentably

Be|trüb|nis [bəˈtryːpnɪs] F -, -se (*geh*) grief, sadness *no pl*, distress *no pl*; **-se** sorrows

be|trübt [bəˈtryːpt] ADJ saddened, distressed

Be|trübt|heit F -, *no pl* sadness, distress, grief

Be|trug M deceit, deception; (*Jur*) fraud; **das ist ja (alles) ~** it's (all) a cheat (*Brit*) *or* fraud; **das ist ja ~, du hast geguckt!** that's cheating, you looked! → **fromm d**

be|trü|gen [bəˈtryːgn] *pret* **betrog** [bəˈtroːk], *ptp* **betrogen** [bəˈtroːgn] VT to deceive; (*geschäftlich auch*) to cheat; *Freund, Ehepartner* to be unfaithful to, to cheat (on); (*Jur*) to defraud; **jdn um etw ~** to cheat *or* swindle sb out of sth, to defraud sb of sth; **sie betrügt mich mit meinem besten Freund** she is having an affair with my best friend; **ich fühle mich betrogen** I feel betrayed; **sich um etw betrogen sehen** to feel deprived of sth, to feel done out of sth (*Brit*); **ich sah mich in ihm betrogen** he disappointed me, he let me down, I was deceived in him; **sich in seinen Hoffnungen betrogen sehen** to be disappointed in one's hopes; **sich in seinem Vertrauen zu jdm betrogen sehen** to be proved wrong in trusting sb VR to deceive oneself

Be|trü|ger [bəˈtryːgɐ] M -s, -, **Be|trü|ge|rin** [-ərɪn] F -, -nen (*beim Spiel*) cheat; (*geschäftlich*) swindler; (*Jur*) defrauder; (= *Hochstapler*) confidence trickster (*esp Brit*), con man/woman

Be|trü|ge|rei [bətryːgəˈraɪ] F -, -en deceit; (*geschäftlich*) cheating *no pl*, swindling *no pl*; (*von Ehepartner*) deceiving *no pl*; (*Jur*) fraud; **seine Frau ist nie hinter seine ~en gekommen** (*inf*) his wife never found out that he was deceiving her *or* being unfaithful to her

be|trü|ge|risch [bəˈtryːgərɪʃ] ADJ deceitful; (*Jur*) fraudulent; **in ~er Absicht** with intent to defraud

be|trun|ken [bəˈtrʊŋkn] ADJ drunk *no adv*, drunken *attr*; **er torkelte ~ nach Hause** he staggered home drunk, he staggered drunkenly home; **Fahren in ~em Zustand** driving while under the influence of drink (*Brit*) *or* alcohol (*form*), drunk driving → *auch* **betrinken**

Be|trun|ke|ne(r) [bəˈtrʊŋknə] MF *decl as adj* drunk

Be|trun|ken|heit F -, *no pl* drunkenness

Bet-: **Bet|sche|mel** M kneeler; **Bet|schwes|ter** F (*pej*) churchy type, Holy Roller (*US pej inf*); **Bet|stuhl** M prie-dieu, kneeler; **Bet|stun|de** F prayer meeting

Bett [bɛt] NT -(e)s, -en (*alle Bedeutungen*) bed; (= *Federbett*) (continental) quilt, duvet; **das ~ machen** to make the bed; **~en bauen** (*esp Mil*) to make the beds; **Frühstück ans ~** breakfast in bed; **an jds ~ sitzen** to sit at sb's bedside, to sit by sb's bed; **im ~** in bed; **ins** *or* **zu ~ gehen** to go to bed; **jdn ins** *or* **zu ~ bringen** to put sb to bed; **mit jdm ins ~ gehen/steigen** (*euph*) to go to/jump into bed with sb; **mit jdm das ~ teilen** to share sb's bed; **er hat sich ins ge-**

machte ~ **gelegt** (*fig*) he had everything handed to him on a plate → **französisch**

Bet|tag ['beːttaːk] M → **Buß- und Bettag**

Bett-: Bett|an|zug M (*Sw*) duvet *or* (continental) quilt cover; **Bett|bank** F *pl* -bänke (*Aus*) bed settee (*Brit*), pullout couch (*US*); **Bett-be|zug** M duvet *or* (continental) quilt cover; **Bett|couch** F bed settee (*Brit*), pullout couch (*US*); **Bett|de|cke** F blanket; (*gesteppt*) (continental) quilt, duvet; **sich unter der ~ verstecken** to hide under the bedclothes (*Brit*) *or* bedcovers (*US*)

Bet|tel ['bɛtl] M -s, *no pl* **a** (*obs*: = das Betteln) begging **b** (*dial*: = Gerümpel) rubbish, lumber, junk; **den (ganzen) ~ hinschmeißen** (*inf*) to chuck the whole thing *or* business (*inf*)

Bet|tel-: bet|tel|arm ADJ destitute; **Bet|tel-brief** M begging letter; **Bet|tel|bru|der** M **a** (= Bettelmönch) mendicant *or* begging friar **b** (*pej*: = Bettler) beggar, panhandler (*US inf*)

Bet|te|lei [bɛtəˈlai] F -, **-en** begging

Bet|tel-: Bet|tel|geld NT (*pej*) pittance; **Bet|tel|kram** M = **Bettel b**; **Bet|tel|lohn** M (*pej*) pittance; **Bet|tel|mönch** M mendicant *or* begging monk; **Bet|tel|mu|si|kant(in)** M(F) (*dated*) street musician

bet|teln ['bɛtln] VI to beg; **um ein Almosen ~** to beg (for) alms; **„Betteln verboten"** "no begging"; (**bei jdm**) **um etw ~** to beg (sb) for sth

Bet|tel-: Bet|tel|or|den M mendicant order; **Bet|tel|sack** M beggar's sack; **Bet|tel-schwes|ter** F (*pej*: = Bettlerin) beggar, panhandler (*US inf*); **Bet|tel|stab** M **an den ~ kommen** to be reduced to beggary; **jdn an den ~ bringen** to reduce sb to beggary; **Bet|tel|weib** NT (*old*) beggar woman (*dated*)

bet|ten ['bɛtn] VT **a** (= legen) to make a bed for, to bed down (*Brit*); *Unfallopfer* to lay *or* bed (*Brit*) down; *Kopf* to lay; **jdn weich ~** to put sb on a soft bed; **jdn flach ~** to lay sb down flat; **die Patienten werden zweimal am Tag gebettet** the patients have their beds made up twice a day; **das Dorf liegt ins** *or* **im Tal gebettet** (*liter*) the village nestles *or* lies nestling in the valley → **Rose a**
VR to make a bed for oneself, to bed oneself down (*Brit*); **wie man sich bettet, so liegt man** (*Prov*) as you make your bed so you must lie on it (*Brit Prov*), you make the bed you lie in (*US Prov*); **sich weich ~** to sleep on a soft mattress; **er hat sich schön weich gebettet** (*mit Heirat*) he's feathered his nest very nicely; (*in Stellung*) he's got a nice cushy little number for himself (*inf*)

Bet|ten-: Bet|ten|burg F (*pej inf*) (= riesiges Hotel) large concrete hotel; (= Urlaubsort) large concrete tourist development; **Bet|ten|man|gel** M (a) shortage of beds

Bett-: Bett|fe|der F bedspring; **Bett|fe|dern** PL (= Daunen) bed feathers *pl*; **Bett|fla|sche** F hot-water bottle; **Bett|ge|flüs|ter** NT pillow talk; **Bett|ge|nos|se** M , **Bett|ge|nos|sin** F (*dated, iro*) bedfellow; **~n** bedroom antics; **Bett|ge|schich|te** F (*love*) affair; **Bett|ge|stell** NT bedstead; **Bett|hä|schen** [-hɛːsçən] NT , **Bett|ha|se** M (*inf*) sexy piece (*Brit inf*) *or* thing (*inf*); **Bett|him|mel** M canopy; **Bett-hup|ferl** [-hʊpfl] NT -s, - (*S Ger*) bedtime sweets; **Bett|ja|cke** F bed jacket; **Bett|kan|te** F edge of the bed; **Bett|kas|ten** M linen drawer; **Bett|la|de** F (*S Ger, Aus*) bedstead; **bett|lä|ge|rig** [-lɛːgərɪç] ADJ bedridden, confined to bed; **Bett|lä|ge|rig|keit** F -, *no pl* confinement to bed; **Bett|la|ken** NT sheet; **Bett|lek|tü|re** F bedtime reading

Bett|ler ['bɛtlɐ] M -s, -, **Bett|le|rin** [-ərɪn] F -, **-nen** beggar, mendicant (*form*)

Bett-: Bett|nach|bar(in) M(F) neighbour (*Brit*), neighbor (*US*), person in the next bed; **Bett|näs|sen** NT -s, *no pl* bed-wetting; **Bett-näs|ser** ['bɛtnɛsɐ] M -s, -, **Bett|näs|se|rin** [-ərɪn] F -, **-nen** bed-wetter; (*sl*: Schimpfwort)

tosser (*sl*); **Bett|pfan|ne** F bedpan; **Bett-pfos|ten** M bedpost; **Bett|platz** M (*Rail*) sleeping berth; **Bett|rand** M edge of the bed; **bett|reif** ADJ ready for bed; **Bett|rost** M (bed) base; **Bett|ru|he** F confinement to bed, bed rest; **der Arzt hat eine Woche ~ verordnet** the doctor ordered him *etc* to stay in bed for one week; **Bett|schüs|sel** F bedpan; **Bett-schwe|re** F (*inf*) **die nötige ~ haben/bekommen** to be/get tired enough to sleep; **Bett-statt** F *pl* -stätten *or* (*Sw*) -statten, **Bett|stel-le** F bed; **Bett|sze|ne** F bedroom scene; **Bett|tuch** ▲ NT (*U*) -tücher sheet; **Bett-wurf** M bedspread, counterpane; **Bett|über|zug** M duvet *or* (continental) quilt cover

Bett|tuch △ NT → **Betttuch**

Bett|um|ran|dung F bed surround

Bet|tung ['bɛtʊŋ] F -, **-en** (*Tech*) bed(ding); (*Rail*) ballast; (*Mil*: = Geschützbettung) platform

Bett-: Bett|vor|la|ge F (*dial*), **Bett|vor|le|ger** M bedside rug; **Bett|wan|ze** F bedbug; **Bett-wär|me** F warmth of one's bed; **Bett|wä|sche** F bed linen; **Bett|zeug** NT , *no pl* bedding; **Bett|zip|fel** M corner of the bed cover; **nach dem ~ schielen** (*hum*) to be longing for one's bed

be|tucht [bəˈtuːxt] ADJ (*inf*) well-to-do

be|tu|lich [bəˈtuːlɪç] ADJ **a** (= übertrieben besorgt) fussing *attr*; *Redeweise* old-womanish; **sei doch nicht so ~** don't be such an old mother hen (*inf*) **b** (= beschaulich) leisurely *no adv*
ADV **a** (= überbesorgt) fussily; *reden* like an old woman, **tu nicht so ~** don't be such an old woman **b** (= gemächlich) in a calm, unhurried fashion

Be|tu|lich|keit F -, *no pl* **a** (= übertriebene Besorgtheit) fussing; **er redet mit einer schrecklichen ~** he talks in such a dreadfully old-womanish way **b** (= Gemächlichkeit) leisureliness; (= Biederkeit) staidness

be|tun *ptp* **betan** [bəˈtaːn] VR *irreg* (*inf*) **a** (= sich zieren) to make a song and dance (*inf*) **b** (= übertrieben besorgt sein) to make a fuss, to fuss about

be|tup|fen *ptp* **betupft** VT to dab; (*Med*) to swab

be|tup|pen [bəˈtʊpn] *ptp* **betuppt** VT (*dial inf*) to cheat, to trick

be|tüt|tern [bəˈtyːtɐn] *ptp* **betütert** (*N Ger, inf*)
VT to mollycoddle (*esp Brit*), to pamper VR to get tipsy

be|tü|tert [bəˈtyːtɐt] ADJ (*N Ger inf*, = betrunken) tipsy; (= verwirrt) dazed

beug|bar ADJ (*Gram*) *Substantiv, Adjektiv etc* declinable; *Verb* conjugable

Beu|ge ['bɔygə] F -, **-n** bend; (*von Arm auch*) crook; (= Rumpfbeuge) forward bend; (*seitlich*) sideways bend; (= Kniebeuge) knee bend; **in die ~ gehen** to bend

Beu|ge|haft F (*Jur*) coercive detention

Beu|gel ['bɔygl] M -s, - (*Aus*) croissant

Beu|ge|mus|kel M flexor

beu|gen ['bɔygn] VT **a** (= krümmen) to bend; (*Phys*) *Wellen* to diffract; *Strahlen, Licht* to deflect; (*fig*) *Stolz, Starrsinn* to break; **das Recht ~** to pervert the course of justice; **vom Alter gebeugt** bent *or* bowed by age; **von der Last gebeugt** bowed down with the weight; **von Kummer/Gram gebeugt** bowed down with grief/sorrow → *auch* **gebeugt**
b (*Gram*) *Substantiv, Adjektiv etc* to decline; *Verb* to conjugate
VR to bend; (*fig*) to submit, to bow (+*dat* to); **sich nach vorn ~** to bend *or* lean forward; **sich aus dem Fenster ~** to lean out of the window; **er beugte sich zu mir herüber** he leaned across to me; **über seine Bücher/seinen Teller gebeugt** hunched over his books/his plate; **sich der Mehrheit ~** to bow *or* submit to the will of the majority

Beu|ger ['bɔygɐ] M -s, - (*Anat*) flexor

Beu|ge|stel|lung F bent position

Beu|gung F -, **-en a** (= Krümmung) bending; (*Phys*) (*von Wellen*) diffraction; (*von Strahlen, Licht*) deflection; (*von Stolz, Starrsinn*) breaking; **eine ~ des Rechts** a perversion of (the course of) justice **b** (*Gram*) declension; (*von Verb*) conjugation

Beu|le ['bɔylə] F -, **-n** (*von Stoß etc*) bump; (*eiternd*) boil; (= Delle) dent

beu|len ['bɔylən] VI to bag

Beu|len|pest F bubonic plague

be|un|ru|hi|gen [bəˈʔʊnruːɪgn] *ptp* **beunruhigt** VT to worry; (*Nachricht etc auch*) to disquiet, to disturb; (*Mil*) to harass; **über etw** (*acc*) **beunruhigt sein** to be worried *or* disturbed about sth; **es ist ~d** it's worrying *or* disturbing, it gives cause for concern VR to worry (oneself) (*über +acc, um, wegen* about)

Be|un|ru|hi|gung F -, **-en** concern, disquiet; (*Mil*) harassment

be|ur|kun|den [bəˈʔuːʁkʊndn] *ptp* **beurkundet** VT **a** (= mit Urkunde bestätigen) to certify; *Vertrag* to record; *Geschäft* to document **b** (*old*: = bezeugen) *Gefühle, Gesinnung, Haltung* to give evidence of

Be|ur|kun|dung F -, **-en a** (= das Beurkunden) certification; (*von Vertrag*) recording; (*von Geschäft*) documentation **b** (= Dokument) documentary proof *or* evidence *no indef art, no pl*

be|ur|lau|ben *ptp* **beurlaubt** VT **a** to give *or* grant leave (of absence); (*Univ*) *Studenten* to give time off; *Lehrpersonal* to give *or* grant sabbatical leave; (= von Pflichten befreien) to excuse (*von* from); **beurlaubt sein** to be on leave, to have leave of absence; to have time off; to be on sabbatical leave; (= suspendiert sein) to have been relieved of one's duties; **sich ~ lassen** to take leave (of absence)/time off/sabbatical leave (*dated*: = sich zurückziehen) to excuse oneself

Be|ur|lau|bung F -, **-en** (+*gen* to) granting of leave (of absence); (*von Studenten*) giving time off; (*von Lehrpersonal*) granting of sabbatical leave; (= das Beurlaubtsein) leave (of absence); (*von Studenten*) time off; (*von Lehrpersonal*) sabbatical leave; **seine ~ vom Dienst** (= Befreiung) his being excused (from) his duties; (= Suspendierung) his being relieved of his duties

be|ur|tei|len *ptp* **beurteilt** VT to judge (*nach* by, from); *Buch, Bild etc* to give an opinion of; *Leistung, Wert* to assess; **etw richtig ~** to judge sth correctly; **etw falsch ~** to misjudge sth; **du kannst das doch gar nicht ~** you are not in a position to judge

Be|ur|tei|ler(in) M(F) judge

Be|ur|tei|lung F (= das Beurteilen) judging, judgement; (*von Leistung, Wert*) assessing, assessment; (= Urteil) assessment; (= Kritik: von Stück etc) review

Be|ur|tei|lungs-: Be|ur|tei|lungs|ge|spräch NT appraisal interview; **Be|ur|tei|lungs|maß|stab** M criterion

Beu|schel ['bɔyʃl] NT -s, - (*Aus*) **a** dish made of offal **b** (*sl*) lungs *pl*; (= Eingeweide) entrails *pl*

Beu|te¹ ['bɔytə] F -, *no pl* **a** (= Kriegsbeute, auch fig hum) spoils *pl*, booty, loot *no indef art*; (= Diebesbeute) haul, loot (*inf*); (*von Raubtieren etc*) prey; (*getötete*) kill; (= Jagdbeute) bag; (*beim Fischen*) catch; **reiche** *or* **fette ~ machen** to capture a lot of booty/make a good haul/a good kill/get a good bag/a good catch; **ohne ~** (*Hunt, fig*) empty-handed **b** (*liter*: = Opfer) prey; **eine leichte ~** easy prey; **jdm/einer Sache zur ~ fallen** (*liter*) to fall (a) prey to sb/sth

Beu|te² F -, **-n** (= Bienenkasten) (bee)hive

beu|te|gie|rig ADJ *Tier* eager for the kill, ravening *attr*; (*fig*) eager for booty *or* a haul

Beu|te|kunst F , *no pl* works of art taken by the occupying forces during a war

Beu|tel ['bɔytl] M **-s, -** **a** (= Behälter) bag; (= Tasche) (drawstring) bag or purse; (= Tragetasche) carrier bag; (= Tabaksbeutel, Zool) pouch; (dial) (= Tüte) paper bag; (= Päckchen) packet **b** (inf: = Geldbeutel) (von Frau) purse; (von Mann) wallet; **tief in den ~ greifen** to put one's hand in one's pocket, to dig deep into one's pocket(s); **jds ~ ist leer** sb has no money, sb is broke (inf); (von Staat etc) sb's coffers are empty; **das geht an den ~** that costs money!; **die Hand auf dem ~ haben** (dated) **den ~ zuhalten** (dated) to be tightfisted → **Loch**

beu|teln ['bɔytln] VT (dial) to shake; (fig) to shake about; **mich hats gebeutelt!** (= bin gefallen) I fell, I came a cropper (Brit inf); (= bin krank geworden) I've come down with it/ with flu etc

Beu|tel-: Beu|tel|rat|te F opossum; **Beu|tel-schnei|der(in)** M(F) (obs: = Gauner) cutpurse (obs), pickpocket; (dated geh: = Wucherer) swindler; **Beu|tel|schnei|de|rei** F (obs) theft, thievery (old); (geh: = Nepp) swindling; **Beu-tel|tier** NT marsupial

Beu|te-: Beu|te|recht NT right of plunder; **Beu|te|stück** NT booty; **Beu|te|tier** NT prey, quarry; **Beu|te|zug** M raid (auch fig); **auf ~ durch die Geschäfte gehen** (fig) to go on a foray of the shops

Beut|ler ['bɔytlɐ] M **-s, -** (Zool) marsupial

be|völ|kern [bə'fœlkɐn] ptp **bevölkert** **VT** **a** (= bewohnen) to inhabit; (= beleben) to crowd, to fill; **schwach/stark** or **dicht bevölkert** thinly or sparsely/densely or thickly populated; **tausende** or **Tausende bevölkerten den Marktplatz** the marketplace was crowded with thousands of people **b** (= besiedeln) to populate **VR** to become inhabited; (fig) to fill up

Be|völ|ke|rung F **-, -en** **a** (= die Bewohner) population **b** no pl (= das Bevölkern) peopling, populating

Be|völ|ke|rungs-: Be|völ|ke|rungs|ab|nah-me F fall or decrease in population; **Be|völ-ke|rungs|be|we|gung** F population movement; **Be|völ|ke|rungs|dich|te** F density of population, population density; **Be|völ|ke-rungs|ex|plo|si|on** F population explosion; **Be|völ|ke|rungs|grup|pe** F section of the population; **Be|völ|ke|rungs|po|li|tik** F population policy; **Be|völ|ke|rungs|py|ra|mi|de** F population pyramid; **Be|völ|ke|rungs|rück-gang** M fall or decline in population; **Be|völ-ke|rungs|schicht** F class of society, social stratum or class; **Be|völ|ke|rungs|sta|tis|tik** F population statistics pl; **Be|völ|ke|rungs-struk|tur** F population structure; **Be|völ|ke-rungs|wachs|tum** NT population growth, rise or increase in population; **Be|völ|ke|rungs-zahl** F (total) population; **Be|völ|ke|rungs-zu|nah|me** F rise or increase in population

be|voll|mäch|ti|gen [bə'fɔlmɛçtɪɡn] ⊙ 36.2 ptp **bevollmächtigt** VT to authorize (zu etw to do sth)

Be|voll|mäch|tig|te(r) [bə'fɔlmɛçtɪçtə] MF decl as adj authorized representative; (Pol) plenipotentiary

Be|voll|mäch|ti|gung F **-, -en** authorization (durch from)

be|vor [bə'foːɐ] CONJ before; **~ Sie (nicht) die Rechnung bezahlt haben** until you pay or you have paid the bill

be|vor|mun|den ptp **bevormundet** VT to treat like a child; **jdn ~** to make sb's decisions (for him/her), to make up sb's mind for him/her; **ich lasse mich von niemandem ~** I shan't (esp Brit) or won't let anyone make my decisions (for me) or make up my mind for me

Be|vor|mun|dung F **-, -en** seine Schüler/Untergebene etc **wehren sich ge-gen die ständige ~** his pupils/subordinates etc object to his constantly making up their minds for them; **unsere ~ durch den Staat** the State's making up our minds for us

be|vor|ra|ten [bə'foːˌraːtn] ptp **bevorratet** VT insep (form) to stock up

Be|vor|ra|tung [bə'foːˌraːtʊŋ] F **-, -en** usu sing (form) stockingup, stockpiling

be|vor|rech|tigt [bə'foːˌrɛçtɪçt] ADJ (= privilegiert) privileged; (= wichtig) high-priority; (Fin) Gläubiger, Verbindlichkeiten preferential

Be|vor|rech|ti|gung [bə'foːˌrɛçtɪɡʊŋ] F **-, -en** preferential treatment no pl

be|vor|schussen [bə'foːˌʃʊsn] ptp **bevorschusst** VT insep (rare) to make an advance to

be|vor+ste|hen VI sep irreg to be imminent; (Winter etc) to be near, to approach; **jdm ~** to be in store for sb; **ihm steht eine Überraschung bevor** there's a surprise in store for him; **das Schlimmste steht uns noch bevor** the worst is yet or still to come; **die Prüfung stand ihm noch bevor** the exam was yet or still to come, the exam still lay ahead

be|vor|ste|hend ADJ forthcoming; Gefahr, Krise imminent; Winter approaching

be|vor|zu|gen [bə'foːˌtsuːɡn] ptp **bevorzugt** VT to prefer; (= begünstigen) to favour (Brit), to favor (US), to give preference to, to give preferential treatment to; **keines unserer Kinder wird bevorzugt** we don't give preference to any of our children; **hier wird niemand bevorzugt** there's no favouritism (Brit) or favoritism (US) here

be|vor|zugt [bə'foːˌtsuːkt] **ADJ** preferred; Behandlung preferential; (= privilegiert) privileged; **die von mir ~en Bücher** the books I prefer **ADV** **jdn ~ abfertigen/bedienen** etc to give sb preferential treatment; **etw ~ abfertigen/bedienen** etc to give sth priority

Be|vor|zu|gung F **-, -en** preference (+gen for); (= vorrangige Behandlung) preferential treatment (bei in)

be|wa|chen ptp **bewacht** VT to guard; (Sport) Tor to guard; Spieler to mark

Be|wa|cher [bə'vaxɐ] M **-s, -**, **Be|wa|che|rin** [-ərɪn] F **-, -nen** guard; (Sport: von Spieler) marker

be|wach|sen¹ [bə'vaksn] ptp **bewachsen** VT irreg to grow over, to cover

be|wach|sen² [bə'vaksn] ADJ overgrown, covered (mit in, with)

Be|wa|chung [bə'vaxʊŋ] F **-, -en** guarding; (= Wachmannschaft) guard; (Sport) marking; **jdn unter ~ halten/stellen** to keep/put sb under guard

be|waff|nen ptp **bewaffnet** **VT** to arm **VR** (lit, fig) to arm oneself

be|waff|net [bə'vafnət] ADJ armed; **bis an die Zähne ~** armed to the teeth

Be|waff|ne|te(r) [bə'vafnətə] MF decl as adj armed man/woman/person

Be|waff|nung F **-, -en** **a** no pl (= das Bewaffnen) arming; **man hat die ~ der Poli-zei beschlossen** it was decided to arm the police **b** (= Waffen) weapons pl

be|wah|ren ptp **bewahrt** VT **a** (= beschützen) to protect (vor +dat from); **jdn vor etw ~** to protect or save or preserve sb from sth; **(i** or **Gott) bewahre!** (inf) heaven or God forbid!, heaven or saints preserve us! **b** (geh: = aufbewahren) to keep; **jdn/etw in guter Erinnerung ~** to have happy memories of sb/sth **c** (= beibehalten) to keep, to retain, to preserve; Denkmal to conserve; **sich** (dat) **etw ~** to keep or retain or preserve sth

be|wäh|ren ptp **bewährt** VR (Mensch) to prove oneself, to prove one's worth; (Gerät etc) to prove itself, to prove its worth; (Methode, Plan, Investition, Sparsamkeit, Fleiß) to pay off, to prove (to be) worthwhile; (Auto) to prove (to be) a good investment; **sich im Leben ~** to make something of one's life; **wenn sich der Straftä-ter bewährt** if the offender proves he has reformed; **die Methode hat sich gut/schlecht be-währt** the method proved/didn't prove (to be) very worthwhile; **das Gerät hat sich gut/**

schlecht bewährt the appliance proved/didn't prove (to be) a very good investment; **es be-währt sich immer, das zu tun** it's always worthwhile doing that; **ihre Freundschaft hat sich be-währt** their friendship stood the test of time → **auch bewähren**

Be|wah|rer [bə'vaːrɐ] M **-s, -**, **Be|wah|re|rin** [-ərɪn] F **-, -nen** (rare) guardian, custodian, keeper

be|wahr|hei|ten [bə'vaːɐhaitn] ptp **bewahrhei-tet** VR (Befürchtung, Hoffnung, Gerücht) to prove (to be) well-founded; (Prophezeiung) to come true

be|währt [bə'vɛːɐt] ADJ proven, tried and tested, reliable; Geldanlage worthwhile; Rezept tried and tested; **vielfach ~** tried and tested; **seit lan-gem ~** well-established → auch **bewähren**

Be|währt|heit F **-,** no pl reliability

Be|wah|rung F **a** (= das Beschützen) protection (vor +dat from) **b** (= das Aufbewahren) keeping **c** (= Wahrung) keeping

Be|wäh|rung F **a** (von Menschen) proving oneself or one's worth; (von Gerät) proving itself or its worth; (von Methode, Plan, Investition) proving itself worthwhile; **bei ~ der Methode ...** if the method proves (to be) worthwhile ... **b** (Jur) probation; **eine Strafe zur ~ aussetzen** to impose a suspended sentence; **ein Jahr Ge-fängnis mit ~** a suspended sentence of one year; **10 Monate Freiheitsstrafe ohne ~** a 10--month prison sentence without probation; **er hat noch ~** he is still on probation; **er ist nur auf ~ auf freiem Fuß** he is only out on probation **c** (Bewährungsfrist) (period of) probation, probation(ary) period

Be|wäh|rungs-: Be|wäh|rungs|auf|la|ge F (Jur) probation order; **Be|wäh|rungs|frist** F (Jur) probation(ary) period, (period of) proba-tion; **Be|wäh|rungs|heim** NT home for young offenders; **Be|wäh|rungs|hel|fer(in)** M(F) probation officer; **Be|wäh|rungs|hil|fe** F probation service; **Be|wäh|rungs|pro|be** F test; **etw einer ~** (dat) **unterziehen** to put sth to the test; **Be|wäh|rungs|stra|fe** F (Jur) suspended sentence, (period of) probation; **Be|wäh-rungs|zeit** F time spent on probation

be|wal|den [bə'valdn] ptp **bewaldet** **VT** to plant with trees, to afforest (form) **VR** allmählich be-waldet **sich das Gebiet** trees are gradually beginning to grow in the area

be|wal|det [bə'valdət] ADJ wooded

Be|wal|dung F **-, -en** (= das Bewalden) planting with trees, afforestation (form); (= Baumbestand) trees pl, woodlands pl; **spärliche ~** few trees; **dichte ~** dense woodlands

be|wäl|ti|gen [bə'vɛltɪɡn] ptp **bewältigt** VT (= meistern) Schwierigkeiten, Problem to cope with; Arbeit, Aufgabe auch, Strecke to manage; (= überwinden) Vergangenheit, Erlebnis etc to get over; Schüchternheit to overcome, to get over; (= erledigen, beenden) to deal with; (= aufessen) to manage

Be|wäl|ti|gung F **-,** no pl die **~ der Schwierig-keiten** coping with the difficulties; **die ~ der Arbeit** managing the work; **die ~ eines Erleb-nisses** getting over an experience

be|wan|dert [bə'vandɐt] ADJ experienced; **in etw** (dat) **~ sein** to be familiar with or well-versed in sth; **auf einem Gebiet ~ sein** to be experienced or well-versed in a field

be|wandt [bə'vant] ADJ (old) **es ist so ~, dass ...** the situation or position is such that ...; **wie ist es damit ~?** how does the matter lie?

Be|wandt|nis [bə'vantnɪs] F **-, -se** reason, explanation; **damit hat es** or **das hat eine andere ~** there's another reason or explanation for that; **damit hat es** or **das hat seine eigene ~** that's a long story; **damit hat es** or **das hat fol-gende ~** the fact of the matter is this/the facts of the matter are these be|wäs|sern ptp bewässert VT to irrigate; (mit Sprühanlage) to water

Be|wäs|se|rung [bəˈvɛsərʊŋ] F , no pl irrigation; (mit Berieselungsanlage) watering

Be|wäs|se|rungs-: Be|wäs|se|rungs|an|la|ge F irrigation plant; Be|wäs|se|rungs|gra|ben M irrigation channel, feeder; Be|wäs|se|rungs|ka|nal M irrigation canal; Be|wäs|se|rungs|sys|tem NT irrigation system

be|weg|bar ADJ = beweglich a

be|we|gen¹ [bəˈveːgn] ptp bewegt VT a (= Lage verändern, regen) to move; Erdmassen, Möbelstück to move, to shift; Hund, Pferd to exercise

b (= innerlich bewegen) to move; (= beschäftigen, angehen) to concern; dieser Gedanke bewegt mich seit langem this has been on my mind a long time; ~d moving → bewegt

c (= bewirken, ändern) to change

VR a (= in Bewegung sein) to move; beide Reden bewegten sich in der gleichen Richtung both speeches were along the same lines

b (= Bewegung haben: Mensch) to get some exercise; (inf: = spazieren gehen) to stretch one's legs, to get some exercise

c (fig: = variieren, schwanken) to vary, to range (zwischen between); der Preis bewegt sich um die 50 Euro the price is about 50 euros; die Verluste ~ sich in den tausenden or Tausenden losses are in the thousands

d (= sich ändern, Fortschritte machen) to change; es bewegt sich etwas things are beginning to happen

e (= auftreten, sich benehmen) to behave, to act → auch bewegt

be|we|gen² pret bewog [bəˈvoːk], ptp bewogen [bəˈvoːgn] VT jdn zu etw ~ to induce or persuade sb to do sth; was hat dich dazu bewogen? what induced you to do that?; sich dazu ~ lassen, etw zu tun to allow oneself to be persuaded to do sth

Be|weg|grund M motive

be|weg|lich [bəˈveːklɪç] ADJ a (= bewegbar) movable; Hebel, Griff movable, mobile; Truppe mobile b (= wendig) agile; Fahrzeug manoeuvrable (Brit), maneuverable (US); (= geistig beweglich) agile-minded, nimble-minded; (fig) Geist nimble; mit einem Kleinwagen ist man in der Stadt ~er you're more mobile in town with a small car

Be|weg|lich|keit F -, no pl a (von Hebel, Griff etc) mobility b (= Wendigkeit) agility; (von Fahrzeug) manoeuvrability (Brit), maneuverability (US); (geistig) mental agility; (körperlich) agility; (von Gliedmaßen) flexibility; die neue ~ the new mobility of the population

be|wegt [bəˈveːkt] ADJ a (= unruhig) Wasser, See choppy; Zeiten, Vergangenheit, Leben eventful; Jugend eventful, turbulent; die See war stark ~/kaum ~ the sea was rough/fairly calm b (= gerührt) Stimme, Worte, Stille emotional; ~ sein to be moved → auch bewegen

Be|wegt|heit F -, no pl emotion

Be|we|gung [bəˈveːgʊŋ] F -, -en a movement; (= Handbewegung auch) gesture; (Sci, Tech) movement, motion; eine falsche ~! one false move!; keine ~! freeze! (inf), don't move!; in ~ sein (Fahrzeug) to be moving, to be in motion; (Menge) to mill around; sich in ~ setzen to start moving, to begin to move; etw in ~ setzen or bringen to set sth in motion, to start sth moving; jdn in ~ bringen to get sb moving; Himmel und Hölle or alle Hebel in ~ setzen to move heaven and earth; jdn in ~ halten to keep sb moving, to keep sb on the go (inf)

b (= körperliche Bewegung) exercise; sich (dat) ~ verschaffen or machen to get (some) exercise

c (= Unruhe) agitation; in ~ geraten to get into a state of agitation; diese Nachricht ließ die ganze Stadt in ~ geraten this news threw the whole town into a state of agitation; plötzlich kam ~ in die Menschenmenge the crowd suddenly became agitated

d (= Entwicklung) progress; etw kommt in ~ sth

gets moving; endlich kam ~ in die Verhandlungen at last there was some progress in the negotiations

e (= Ergriffenheit) emotion

f (Pol, Art etc) movement

Be|we|gungs-: Be|we|gungs|ap|pa|rat M , no pl (Anat) locomotor system; Be|we|gungs|ar|mut F , no pl lack of exercise; Be|we|gungs|bild NT (Admin) record of (sb's) movements; Be|we|gungs|drang M urge or impulse to be active; Be|we|gungs|ener|gie F kinetic energy; be|we|gungs|fä|hig ADJ mobile; Be|we|gungs|fä|hig|keit F mobility; Be|we|gungs|frei|heit F freedom of movement; (fig) freedom of action; Be|we|gungs|krieg M mobile warfare; be|we|gungs|los ADJ motionless, immobile ADV without moving; liegen, sitzen, stehen motionless; Be|we|gungs|lo|sig|keit F -, no pl motionlessness, immobility; Be|we|gungs|man|gel M , no pl lack of exercise; Be|we|gungs|mel|der M sensor (which registers movement); Be|we|gungs|nerv M motor nerve; Be|we|gungs|spiel NT (Sport) active game; Be|we|gungs|stö|rung F (Med) motor disturbance, akinesia (spec); Be|we|gungs|stu|die F a (Ind) time and motion study b (Art) study in movement; Be|we|gungs|the|ra|pie F (aktiv) therapeutic exercise; (passiv) manipulation; Be|we|gungs|trieb M urge or impulse to be active; be|we|gungs|un|fä|hig ADJ unable to move; (= gehunfähig) unable to move about, unable to get about; Be|we|gungs|un|fä|hig|keit F inability to move; (= Gehunfähigkeit) inability to move about or get about; Be|we|gungs|un|schär|fe F (Phot) camera shake; Be|we|gungs|zu|stand M state of motion

be|weh|ren ptp bewehrt (old) VT to fortify; (= bewaffnen) to arm VR (auch iro) to arm oneself

Be|weh|rung [bəˈveːrʊŋ] F -, -en (old) a (= Befestigung) fortifying; (= Bewaffnung) arming b (= Wehranlagen) fortifications pl; (= Waffen) arms pl

be|wei|ben [bəˈvaibn] ptp beweibt VR (dated) to take a wife (dated), to wed (dated)

be|wei|den ptp beweidet VT (Agr) Land to pasture; (Kühe) to graze on

be|weih|räu|chern [bəˈvairɔyçɐn] ptp beweihräuchert VT to (in)cense; (fig) to heap praise on; sich (selbst) ~ to indulge in self-adulation

be|wei|nen ptp beweint VT to mourn (for), to weep for

be|wei|nens|wert [bəˈvainənsveːɐt] ADJ (geh) lamentable

Be|wei|nung [bəˈvainʊŋ] F -, (rare) -en mourning; die ~ Christi (Art) the Mourning of Christ

Be|weis [bəˈvais] M -es, -e [-zə] proof (für of); (= Zeugnis) evidence no pl; als or zum ~ as proof or evidence; das ist kein ~ für das, was du behauptest that doesn't prove or that's no proof of what you have been claiming; ein eindeutiger ~ seines Schuldgefühls his silence is proof or evidence of his feeling of guilt; etw unter ~ stellen to prove sth; den ~ antreten, einen/den ~ führen to offer evidence or proof; den ~ für seiner Unschuld erbringen to produce or supply evidence or proof of sth/of one's innocence; ~ erheben (Jur) to hear or take evidence; jdm einen ~ seiner Hochachtung geben to give sb a token of one's respect

Be|weis-: Be|weis|an|trag M (Jur) motion to take or hear evidence; Be|weis|auf|nah|me F (Jur) taking or hearing of evidence; be|weis|bar ADJ provable, demonstrable, capable of being proved; Be|weis|bar|keit [bəˈvaisbaːɐkait] F -, no pl demonstrability

be|wei|sen ⊙ 53.4 ptp bewiesen [bəˈviːzn] irreg VT a (= nachweisen) to prove; was zu ~ war QED, quod erat demonstrandum; was noch zu ~ wäre that remains to be seen b (= erkennen lassen, dated: = erweisen) to show VR to prove oneself/itself

Be|weis-: be|weis|er|heb|lich ADJ (Jur) evidentiary (spec); Be|weis|er|he|bung F (Jur) taking (or) hearing of evidence; Be|weis|füh|rung F (Jur) presentation of one's case; (Math) proof; (= Argumentation) (line of) argumentation or reasoning (Brit), line of argument; Be|weis|gang M pl -gänge argumentation (in proving sth); Be|weis|ge|gen|stand M (esp Jur) point at issue; Be|weis|grund M argument; Be|weis|ket|te F chain of proof; (Jur auch) chain of evidence; Be|weis|kraft F evidential (Brit) or evidentiary (US) value, value as evidence; be|weis|kräf|tig ADJ evidential (Brit), evidentiary (US), probative (form); Be|weis|la|ge F (Jur) body of evidence; Be|weis|last F (Jur) onus, burden of proof; Be|weis|ma|te|ri|al NT (body of) evidence; Be|weis|mit|tel NT evidence no pl; Be|weis|not F (Jur) lack of evidence; in ~ sein to be lacking evidence; Be|weis|pflicht F (Jur) onus, burden of proof; Be|weis|stück NT exhibit; Be|weis|wür|di|gung F (Jur) assessment of the evidence

be|wen|den VT impers es bei or mit etw ~ lassen to be content with sth; wir wollen es dabei ~ lassen let's leave it at that

Be|wen|den NT damit hatte es sein/die Angelegenheit ihr ~ the matter rested there, that was the end of the matter

Be|werb [bəˈvɛrp] M -(e)s, -e [-bə] (Aus Sport) = Wettbewerb

be|wer|ben ⊙ 46.1 ptp beworben [bəˈvɔrbn] irreg VR to apply (um for, als for the position or job of); sich bei einer Firma ~ to apply to a firm (for a job); sich um jdn ~ (dated) to ask for sb's hand in marriage VT Produkte, Firmen to promote

Be|wer|ber(in) M(F) applicant; (dated: = Freier) suitor (dated)

Be|wer|bung F application; (dated: um Mädchen) wooing (dated), courting (dated)

Be|wer|bungs-: Be|wer|bungs|bo|gen M , Be|wer|bungs|for|mu|lar NT application form; Be|wer|bungs|ge|spräch NT (job) interview; Be|wer|bungs|schrei|ben NT (letter of) application; Be|wer|bungs|un|ter|la|gen PL application documents pl; Be|wer|bungs|ver|fah|ren NT application procedure

be|wer|fen ptp beworfen [bəˈvɔrfn] VT irreg a jdn/etw mit etw ~ to throw sth at sb/sth; mit Steinen, Eiern auch to pelt sb with sth; (fig) to hurl sth at sb/sth; jdn/jds guten Namen mit Schmutz or Dreck ~ to throw or sling mud at sb/sb's good name b (Build) to face, to cover; (mit Rauputz) to roughcast; mit Kies beworfen pebble-dashed

be|werk|stel|li|gen [bəˈvɛrkʃtɛlɪgn] ptp bewerkstelligt VT to manage; Geschäft to effect, to bring off; es ~, dass jd etw tut to manage or contrive to get sb to do sth

Be|werk|stel|li|gung F -, no pl managing

be|wer|ten ptp bewertet VT jdn to judge; Leistung auch, Schularbeit to assess; Gegenstand to value, to put a value on; etw zu hoch/niedrig ~ to overvalue/undervalue sth; jdn/etw nach einem Maßstab ~ to judge sb/measure sth against a yardstick; etw mit der Note 5 ~ to give sth a mark (Brit) or grade (US) of 5; eine Arbeit mit (der Note) „gut" ~ to mark (Brit) or grade (US) a piece of work "good"

Be|wer|tung F judgement; (von Leistung auch, von Schularbeit) assessment; (von Gegenstand) valuation

Be|wer|tungs-: Be|wer|tungs|kri|te|ri|um NT criterion; Be|wer|tungs|maß|stab M set of criteria; Be|wer|tungs|ska|la F scale of assessment or valuation

be|wie|sen ADJ (= nachgewiesen) proven → auch beweisen

be|wie|se|ner|ma|ßen [bəˈviːznɐˈmaːsn] ADV was er sagt, ist ~ unwahr it has been proved that what he is saying is untrue, there is evidence to show that what he is saying is untrue;

er ist ~ ein Betrüger he has been proved to be a fraud

be|wil|li|gen ptp **bewilligt** VT to allow; *Mittel, Geld, Darlehen etc* auch to grant; *Planstelle auch, Etat, Steuererhöhung etc* to approve; *Stipendium* to award; **jdm etw ~** to allow/grant/award sb sth

Be|wil|li|gung [bə'vɪlɪɡʊŋ] F -, -en allowing; *(von Planstelle auch, von Etat, Steuererhöhung)* approving, approval; *(von Geldern auch)* granting; *(von Stipendium)* awarding; *(= Genehmigung)* approval; **dafür brauchen Sie eine ~** you need approval for that; **die ~ für einen Kredit bekommen** to be allowed *or* granted credit

Be|wil|li|gungs-: **Be|wil|li|gungs|be|scheid** M approval; **be|wil|li|gungs|pflich|tig** [-pflɪçtɪç] ADJ subject to approval

be|will|komm|nen [bə'vɪlkɔmnən] ptp **bewillkommnet** VT insep (geh) to welcome

Be|will|komm|nung F -, -en (rare) welcoming no pl, reception

be|wim|pert [bə'vɪmpɐt] ADJ *Auge* lashed; *(Zool)* ciliate(d) (spec)

be|wir|ken ptp **bewirkt** VT **a** *(= verursachen)* to cause, to bring about, to produce; **~, dass etw passiert** to cause sth to happen **b** *(= erreichen)* to achieve; **mit so einem Auftreten kannst du bei ihm nichts ~** you won't get anywhere *or* achieve anything with him if you behave like that; **damit bewirkst du bei ihm nur das Gegenteil** that way you'll only achieve the opposite effect

be|wir|ten [bə'vɪrtn̩] ptp **bewirtet** VT **jdn ~** to feed sb; *(bei offiziellem Besuch etc)* to entertain sb *(by giving them a meal)*; **wir wurden während der ganzen Zeit köstlich bewirtet** we were very well fed all the time, we were given excellent food all the time; **jdn mit Kaffee und Kuchen ~** to entertain sb to coffee and cakes; **wenn man so viele Leute zu ~ hat** if you have so many people to cater for *or* to feed

be|wirt|schaf|ten ptp **bewirtschaftet** VT **a** *Betrieb etc* to manage, to run; **die Berghütte wird im Winter nicht/wird von Herrn und Frau X bewirtschaftet** the mountain hut is not serviced in the winter/is managed *or* run by Mr and Mrs X **b** *Land* to farm, to cultivate, to work **c** *(= staatlich kontrollieren) Waren* to ration; *Devisen, Wohnraum* to control

Be|wirt|schaf|tung [bə'vɪrtʃaftʊŋ] F -, -en **a** *(von Betrieb)* management, running **b** *(von Land)* farming, cultivation, working **c** *(= staatliche Kontrolle)* rationing; *(von Devisen, Wohnraum)* control

Be|wir|tung F -, -en *(= das Bewirten)* hospitality; *(im Hotel)* (food and) service; *(rare: = Essen und Getränke)* food (and drink); **die ~ so vieler Gäste** catering for *or* feeding so many guests

Be|wir|tungs|kos|ten PL entertainment expenses pl

be|wit|zeln ptp **bewitzelt** VT to make fun of

be|wog pret von **bewegen** [2]

be|wo|gen ptp von **bewegen** [2]

be|wohn|bar ADJ *Gegend, Land etc* habitable **b** *Haus, Wohnung etc* habitable, fit to live in; *(= beziehbar)* habitable, ready to live in

be|woh|nen ptp **bewohnt** VT to live in; *Haus, Zimmer, Bau, Nest auch* to occupy; *(Volk)* to inhabit; **das Zimmer/das Haus war jahrelang nicht bewohnt** the room was unoccupied/the house was uninhabited *or* unoccupied for years → auch **bewohnt**

Be|woh|ner [bə'voːnɐ] M -s, -, **Be|woh|ne|rin** [-ərɪn] F -, -nen *(von Land, Gebiet)* inhabitant; *(von Haus etc)* occupier; **dieser Vogel ist ein ~ der Wälder** this bird is a forest dweller, this bird is a denizen of the forest (liter)

Be|woh|ner|schaft [bə'voːnɐʃaft] F -, -en occupants pl

be|wohnt [bə'voːnt] ADJ *Land, Gebiet, Planet* inhabited; *Haus etc auch* occupied → auch **bewohnen**

---

be|wöl|ken [bə'vœlkn̩] ptp **bewölkt** VR (lit, fig) to cloud over, to darken

be|wölkt [bə'vœlkt] ADJ cloudy; **~ bis bedeckt** (Met) cloudy, perhaps overcast

Be|wöl|kung F -, -en *(= das Bewölken)* clouding over, darkening; **wechselnde bis zunehmende ~** (Met) variable amounts of cloud, becoming cloudier

Be|wöl|kungs-: **Be|wöl|kungs|auf|lo|cke|rung** F break-up of the cloud; **Be|wöl|kungs|zu|nah|me** F increase in cloud

be|wu|chern ptp **bewuchert** VT to grow over, to cover

Be|wuchs M , no pl vegetation

Be|wun|de|rer [bə'vʊndərɐ] M -s, -, **Be|wun|de|rin** [bə'vʊndərɪn] F -, -nen admirer

be|wun|dern ptp **bewundert** VT to admire (wegen for); **~d** admiring; **ein überall bewunderter Künstler** a universally admired artist

be|wun|derns|wert, **be|wun|derns|wür|dig** ADJ admirable ADV admirably

Be|wun|de|rung [bə'vʊndərʊŋ] ✪ 40.4 F -, (rare) -en admiration

be|wun|de|rungs|wert, **be|wun|de|rungs|wür|dig** ADJ admirable ADV admirably

Be|wund|re|r [bə'vʊndrɐ] M -s, -, **Be|wund|re|rin** [-ərɪn] F -, -nen admirer

Be|wurf M **a** (Build) facing, covering; *(= Rauputz)* roughcast; *(= Kiesbewurf)* pebble dash **b** *(= das Bewerfen)* **der ~ der Feinde/Mauern mit Steinen** throwing stones at the enemy/walls, pelting the enemy/walls with stones

be|wur|zeln ptp **bewurzelt** VR to root, to grow roots

be|wusst ▲ [bə'vʊst] ADJ **a** usu attr (Philos, Psych) conscious

b attr *(= überlegt)* conscious; *Mensch* self-aware; **er führte ein sehr ~es Leben** he lived a life of total awareness

c pred **sich** (dat) **einer Sache** (gen) **~ sein/werden** to be/become aware *or* conscious of sth, to realize sth; **etw ist jdm ~** sb is aware *or* conscious of sth; **es wurde ihm allmählich ~, dass ...** he gradually realized (that) ..., it gradually dawned on him (that) ...

d attr *(= willentlich)* deliberate, intentional; *Lüge* deliberate

e attr *(= überzeugt)* convinced; **er ist ein ~er Kommunist** he is a convinced communist

f attr *(= bekannt, besagt)* in question; *Zeit* agreed; **die ~e Kreuzung** the crossroads in question

ADV **a** consciously; **leben** in total awareness **b** *(= willentlich)* deliberately, intentionally

Be|wusst|heit ▲ F -, no pl awareness; *(= Absichtlichkeit)* deliberateness

Be|wusst-: **be|wusst|los** ▲ ADJ unconscious, senseless; **~ werden** to lose consciousness, to become unconscious; **in ~em Zorn** in a blind rage ADV **jdn ~ prügeln/schlagen** to beat sb unconscious *or* senseless; **~ zusammenbrechen** to fall senseless, to collapse unconscious; **Be|wusst|lo|se(r)** ▲ [bə'vʊstloːzə] MF decl as adj unconscious man/woman/person etc; **die ~n** the unconscious; **Be|wusst|lo|sig|keit** ▲ F -, no pl unconsciousness; **bis zur ~** (inf) ad nauseam; **be|wusst ma|chen** ▲ VT **jdm etw ~** to make sb aware *or* conscious of sth, to make sb realize sth; **sich** (dat) **etw ~** to realize sth

Be|wusst|sein ▲ NT **a** *(= Wissen)* awareness, consciousness; **etw kommt jdm zu(m) ~** sb becomes aware *or* conscious of sth, sb realizes sth; **jdm etw zu ~ bringen**, **jdm etw ins ~ rufen** to make sb (fully) conscious *or* aware of sth; **etw tritt in jds ~** (acc) sth occurs to sb; **jdm etw ins ~ rücken** to make sb aware of sth; **das allgemeine ~** general awareness; **im ~** (+gen)/, **dass ...** in the knowledge of/that ...

b (Philos, Psych, Med) consciousness; **das ~ verlieren/wiedererlangen** to lose/regain consciousness; **bei ~ sein** to be conscious; **zu(m) ~ kommen** to regain consciousness; **bei vollem ~** fully

---

conscious; **jdm schwindet das ~** (geh) sb faints or swoons (liter)

c **er tat es mit (vollem/ohne ~** he was (fully) aware/he was not aware of what he was doing **d** *(= Anschauungen)* convictions pl

Be|wusst|seins-: **Be|wusst|seins|bil|dung** ▲ F (Pol) shaping of political ideas; **Be|wusst|seins|e|be|ne** ▲ F plane of consciousness; **be|wusst|seins|er|wei|ternd** ▲ ADJ ~e Drogen mind-expanding drugs; **Be|wusst|seins|er|wei|te|rung** ▲ F heightening of (one's) awareness; **Be|wusst|seins|in|halt** ▲ M usu pl (Philos) content of consciousness; **Be|wusst|seins|kunst** ▲ F (Liter) stream-of-consciousness technique; **Be|wusst|seins|la|ge** ▲ F (Pol) state of political awareness; **Be|wusst|seins|len|kung** ▲ F (Sociol) manipulation of consciousness; **Be|wusst|seins|schwel|le** ▲ F (Psych) threshold of consciousness; **Be|wusst|seins|spal|tung** ▲ F (Med, Psych) splitting of the consciousness; **Be|wusst|seins|stö|rung** ▲ F (Psych) disturbance of consciousness; **Be|wusst|seins|strom** ▲ M (Liter) stream of consciousness; **Be|wusst|seins|trü|bung** ▲ F (Psych) dimming of consciousness; **be|wusst|seins|ver|än|dernd** ▲ ADJ (Psych) ~e Drogen drugs which alter one's (state of) awareness; **~e Erfahrungen** experiences which alter one's outlook; **Be|wusst|seins|ver|än|de|rung** ▲ F change in the state of mind; *(durch Erfahrungen)* change in outlook; **(politische)** ~ change in political outlook

Be|wusst|wer|dung ▲ [-veːɐdʊŋ] F -, no pl dawning of consciousness

bez. abbr **a** von **bezahlt** paid **b** von **bezüglich** with reference to, re

Bez. abbr von **Bezirk**

be|zahl|bar ADJ payable; **das ist zwar recht teuer, aber für die meisten doch durchaus ~** although it's quite expensive most people can certainly afford it

be|zah|len ptp **bezahlt** VT **a** *Menschen, Betrag* to pay; *Rechnung, Schuld* to pay (off), to settle; **jdm 10 Euro ~** to pay sb 10 euros; **etw an jdn ~** to pay sb sth

b *Sache, Leistung, Schaden* to pay for; *Zeche* to pay, to foot (inf); **etw bezahlt bekommen** *or* **kriegen** (inf) to get paid for sth; **für etw nichts bezahlt bekommen** *or* **kriegen** (inf) not to get paid for sth; **jdm etw ~** *(= für jdn kaufen)* to pay for sth for sb; *(= Geld geben für)* to pay sb for sth; **lass mal, ich bezahl das** it's OK, I'll pay for that *or* I'll get that; **er hat seinen Fehler mit dem Leben bezahlt** he paid for his mistake with his life; **... als ob er es bezahlt bekäme** (inf) like mad *or* crazy (inf), like hell (inf); **Liebe ist nicht mit Geld zu ~** money can't buy love, love cannot be bought

VI to pay; **Herr Ober, ~ bitte!** waiter, the bill (Brit) *or* check (US) please!

Be|zahl|fern|se|hen NT , no pl pay TV

be|zahlt [bə'tsaːlt] ADJ paid; **sich ~ machen** to be worth it, to pay off

Be|zah|lung F **a** *(= das Bezahlen)* payment; *(von Rechnung, Schulden)* paying off, settlement; *(von Leistung, Schaden)* paying for *(einer Sache* (gen) sth) **b** *(= Lohn, Gehalt)* pay; *(für Dienste)* payment; **ohne/gegen** *or* **für ~** without/for payment

be|zäh|men ptp **bezähmt** VT **a** *(fig geh) Begierden, Leidenschaften* to master, to control, to curb **b** *(lit obs: = zähmen)* to tame VR to control *or* restrain oneself

be|zau|bern ptp **bezaubert** VT **a** (fig) to charm, to captivate VI to be bewitching *or* captivating

be|zau|bernd ADJ enchanting, charming

Be|zau|be|rung [bə'tsaubərʊŋ] F -, -en bewitchment, captivation; *(= Entzücken)* enchantment, delight

be|ze|chen ptp **bezecht** VR (inf) to get drunk

be|zecht [bə'tsɛçt] (inf) ADJ drunk; **völlig ~** dead (Brit) *or* completely drunk (inf)

---

be|zeich|nen ptp **bezeichnet** VT **a** (= kennzeichnen) (durch, mit by) to mark; Takt, Tonart to indicate **b** (= genau beschreiben) to describe; **er bezeichnete uns den Weg** he described the way to us **c** (= benennen) to call, to describe; **ich weiß nicht, wie man das bezeichnet** I don't know what that's called; **das würde ich schlicht als eine Unverschämtheit ~** I would describe that as sheer effrontery or impudence, I would call that sheer effrontery or impudence; **so kann man es natürlich auch ~** of course, you can call it that or describe it that way too; **jd/etw wird mit dem Wort ... bezeichnet** sb/sth is described by the word ..., the word ... describes sb/sth; **er bezeichnet sich gern als Künstler** he likes to call himself an artist **d** (= bedeuten) to mean, to denote **e** (geh: = typisch sein für) to epitomize

be|zeich|nend ADJ (für of) characteristic, typical; **es ist ~ für ihre Unfähigkeit, dass ...** (= ist ein Beweis für) it's indicative of her incompetence that ...

be|zeich|nen|der|wei|se [bəˈtsaiçnəndɐˈvaizə] ADV **die Regierung hat ~ die Wahlversprechen wieder nicht eingehalten** typically (enough), the government hasn't kept its election promises again

Be|zeich|nung F **a** (= Kennzeichnung) marking; (von Tonart, Takt) indication; (= Beschreibung, Benennung) description **b** (= Ausdruck) expression, term

Be|zeich|nungs|leh|re F (Ling) onomastics sing

be|zeu|gen ptp **bezeugt** VT **a** (Sache) to attest; (Person auch) to testify to; **~, dass ...** to attest the fact that ...; to testify that ... **b** (geh) **jdm etw ~** to show sb sth

Be|zeu|gung F attestation; **urkundliche ~** documentary proof or evidence

be|zich|ti|gen [bəˈtsɪçtɪgn] ptp **bezichtigt** VT to accuse; **jdn einer Sache** (gen) **~** to accuse sb of sth, to charge sb with sth; **jdn ~, etw getan zu haben** to accuse sb of having done sth

Be|zich|ti|gung F -, -en accusation, charge

be|zieh|bar ADJ **a** (= bezugsfertig) Wohnung etc ready to move into **b** (= erhältlich) Waren etc obtainable **c** relatable, referable; **das ist auf einen Vorfall in seiner Jugend ~** that can be related to an incident in his youth

be|zie|hen ptp **bezogen** [bəˈtso:gn] irreg VT **a** (= überziehen) Polster, Regenschirm to (re)cover; Bettdecke, Kissen to put a cover on; (mit Saiten) Geige etc to string; **die Betten frisch ~** to put clean sheets on the beds, to change the beds **b** (= einziehen in) Wohnung to move into **c** (esp Mil: = einnehmen) Posten, Position, Stellung to take up; (old) Universität to enter, to go up to; (fig) Standpunkt to take up, to adopt; **ein Lager ~** to encamp; **Wache ~** to mount guard, to go on guard **d** (= sich beschaffen) to get, to obtain; Zeitungen etc to take, to get **e** (= erhalten) to get, to receive; Einkommen, Rente etc to draw; Prügel etc to get **f** (= in Beziehung setzen) **etw auf jdn/etw ~** to apply sth to sb/sth; **warum bezieht er (bloß) immer alles auf sich?** why does he always take everything personally?; **auf jdn/etw bezogen** referring to sb/sth **g** (Sw: = einfordern) Steuern to collect **VR a** (= sich bedecken: Himmel) to cloud over, to darken **b** (= betreffen) **sich auf jdn/etw ~** to refer to sb/sth; **diese Bemerkung bezog sich nicht auf dich** this remark wasn't meant to refer to you or wasn't intended for you **c** (= sich berufen) **sich ~ auf** (+acc) to refer to

Be|zie|her [bəˈtsi:ɐ] M -s, -, **Be|zie|he|rin** [-ərɪn] F -, -nen (von Zeitung) regular reader; (= Abonnent, von Aktien) subscriber; (von Waren) purchaser; (von Einkommen, Rente) drawer

Be|zie|hung F **a** (= Verhältnis) relationship; (Philos, Math) relation **b** usu pl (= Kontakt) relations pl; **diplomatische ~en aufnehmen/abbrechen** to establish/break off diplomatic relations; **intime ~en zu jdm haben** to have intimate relations with sb; **menschliche ~en** human relations or intercourse **c** (= Zusammenhang) connection (zu with), relation; **etw zu etw in ~ setzen** to relate sth to sth; **zwischen den beiden Dingen besteht keinerlei ~** there is absolutely no connection between the two (things), the two (things) are totally unconnected or unrelated; **in keiner ~ zueinander stehen** to have no connection (with each other); **etw hat keine ~ zu etw** sth has no bearing on sth, sth has no relationship to sth; **jd verliert die ~ zur Wirklichkeit** sb feels cut off from reality **d** usu pl (= Verbindung) connections pl (zu with); **er hat die Stelle durch ~en bekommen** he got the position through his connections or through knowing the right people; **seine ~en spielen lassen** to pull strings; **~en haben** to have connections, to know the right people; **~en muss/müsste man haben** you need to know the right people, you need to be able to pull strings **e** (= Sympathie) (zu etw) feeling (zu for); (zu jdm) affinity (zu for), rapport (zu with); **ich habe keine ~ zu abstrakter Malerei** I have no feeling for abstract art, abstract painting doesn't do anything for me; **er hat überhaupt keine ~ zu seinen Kindern** he just doesn't relate to his children, he has no affinity for his children **f** = Bezug g **g** (= Hinsicht) **in einer/keiner ~** in one/no respect or way; **in jeder ~** in every respect, in all respects; **in mancher ~** in some or certain respects; **in dieser ~** in this respect

Be|zie|hungs-: **Be|zie|hungs|ge|flecht** NT network of connections; **Be|zie|hungs|kis|te** F (inf) relationship; **be|zie|hungs|los** ADJ **a** unrelated, unconnected **b** (= ohne menschliche Beziehungen) devoid of relationships; **Be|zie|hungs|lo|sig|keit** F -, no pl **a** unrelatedness, unconnectedness **b** (= Mangel an menschlichen Beziehungen) lack of relationships; **be|zie|hungs|reich** ADJ rich in associations; **be|zie|hungs|voll** ADJ suggestive; **Be|zie|hungs|wahn** M (Psych) paranoia

Be|zie|hungs|wei|se CONJ **a** (= oder aber) or **b** (= im anderen Fall) and ... respectively; **zwei Briefmarken, die 25 ~ 55 Cent kosten** two stamps costing 25 and 55 cents respectively; **geben Sie in Ihrer Bestellung rot ~ blau als gewünschte Farbe an** state your choice of colour (Brit) or color (US) in your order: red or blue **c** (= genauer gesagt) or rather, or that is to say

Be|zie|hungs|wort NT pl -wörter (Gram) antecedent

be|zif|fer|bar [bəˈtsɪfeba:ɐ] ADJ quantifiable; **nicht ~** unquantifiable

be|zif|fern [bəˈtsɪfɐn] ptp **beziffert** VT **a** (= mit Ziffern versehen) to number; Bass to figure **b** (= angeben) to estimate (auf +acc, mit at); **man bezifferte den Schaden auf 500.000 Euro** the damage was estimated at or was put at 500,000 euros VR **sich ~ auf** (+acc) (Verluste, Schaden, Gewinn) to amount to, to come to; (Teilnehmer, Besucher) to number

be|zif|fert [bəˈtsɪfɐt] ADJ (Mus) Bass figured; **ein Zuschuss in nicht ~er Höhe** a subsidy of an unspecified amount

Be|zif|fe|rung F -, -en **a** (= das Beziffern) numbering; (Mus) figuring **b** (= Zahlen) numbers pl, figures pl

Be|zirk [bəˈtsɪrk] M -(e)s, -e **a** (= Gebiet) district; (fig: = Bereich) sphere, realm **b** (= Verwaltungseinheit) (von Stadt) ≈ district; (von Land) ≈ region

Be|zirks-: **Be|zirks|arzt** M , **Be|zirks|ärz|tin** F district medical officer; **Be|zirks|beam|te(r)** M decl as adj, **Be|zirks|beam|tin** F local government officer; **Be|zirks|ge|richt** NT (Aus, Sw) district court; **Be|zirks|haupt|mann** M (Aus) head official of local government; **Be|zirks|klas|se** F (Sport) regional division; **Be|zirks|kran|ken|haus** NT regional hospital; (= psychiatrische Klinik) psychiatric clinic or hospital, mental hospital; **Be|zirks|li|ga** F (Sport) regional league; **Be|zirks|re|gie|rung** F regional administration; **Be|zirks|rich|ter(in)** M(F) (Aus, Sw) district court judge; **Be|zirks|spi|tal** NT (esp Sw) district hospital; **Be|zirks|stadt** F ≈ county town

be|zir|zen [bəˈtsɪrtsn] ptp **bezirzt** VT (inf) to bewitch

Be|zo|ge|ne(r) [bəˈtso:gnə] MF decl as adj (Fin) (von Scheck) drawee; (von Wechsel) acceptor

be|zug △ → Bezug h

Be|zug M **a** (= Überzug) (für Kissen, Polster etc) cover; (für Kopfkissen) pillowcase, pillowslip **b** (= Bespannung) strings pl **c** (= Erwerb) (von Waren etc) buying, purchase; (von Zeitung) taking; **der ~ der diversen Magazine kostet uns ...** the various magazines we subscribe to cost (us) ... **d** (= Erhalt: von Einkommen, Rente etc) drawing **e** **Bezüge** PL (= Einkünfte) income, earnings pl; **Bezüge aus Nebenerwerb** income or earnings from secondary sources **f** (= Zusammenhang) = Beziehung c **g** (form: = Berufung) reference; **~ nehmen auf** (+acc) to refer to, to make reference to; **~ nehmend auf** (+acc) referring to, with reference to; **mit** or **unter ~ auf** (+acc) with reference to **h** (= Hinsicht) **in ~ auf** (+acc) regarding, with regard to, concerning; **in ~ darauf** regarding that

Be|zü|ger [bəˈtsy:gɐ] M -s, -, **Be|zü|ge|rin** [-ərɪn] F -, -nen (Sw) **a** = Bezieher **b** (von Steuern) collector

be|züg|lich [bəˈtsy:klɪç] **PREP** +gen (form) regarding, with regard to, concerning, re (Comm) **ADJ** (= sich beziehend) **das ~e Fürwort** (Gram) the relative pronoun; **auf etw** (acc) **~** relating to sth; **alle darauf ~en Fragen** all questions relating to that

Be|zug|nah|me [-na:mə] F -, -n (form) reference; **unter ~ auf** (+acc) with reference to

Be|zugs-: **Be|zugs|be|din|gun|gen** PL (von Zeitschriften) terms pl of delivery or subscription; (bei Katalogbestellungen etc) conditions pl of purchase; **be|zugs|be|rech|tigt** ADJ entitled to draw; **Be|zugs|be|rech|tig|te(r)** [-bərɛçtɪçtə] MF decl as adj (von Rente etc) authorized drawer; (von Versicherung) beneficiary; **be|zugs|be|reit**, **be|zugs|fer|tig** ADJ Haus etc ready to move into, ready for occupation; **Be|zugs|grö|ße** F standard for comparison

Be|zug|schein M = Bezugsschein

Be|zugs-: **Be|zugs|per|son** F **die wichtigste ~ des Kleinkindes** the person to whom the small child relates most closely; **Be|zugs|preis** M (von Zeitungsabonnement etc) subscription charge (Brit) or price (US); **Be|zugs|punkt** M (lit, fig) point of reference; **Be|zugs|quel|le** F source of supply; **Be|zugs|rah|men** M terms pl of reference; **Be|zugs|recht** NT (Fin) option (on a new share issue), subscription right; **Be|zugs|satz** M (Gram) relative clause; **Be|zugs|schein** M (ration) coupon; **etw auf** or **durch ~ bekommen** to get sth on coupons; **be|zugs|schein|pflich|tig** [-pflɪçtɪç] ADJ rationed, available only on coupons; **Be|zugs|sys|tem** NT frame of reference; (Statistik) reference system; **Be|zugs|(wort)|satz** M relative clause

be|zu|schus|sen [bəˈtsu:ʃʊsn] ptp **bezuschusst** VT to subsidize

Be|zu|schus|sung F -, -en subsidizing; (= Betrag) subsidy

be|zwe|cken [bə'tsvɛkn] *ptp* **bezweckt** VT to aim at; *(Regelung, Maßnahme auch)* to have as its object; **etw mit etw ~** *(Mensch)* to intend sth by sth; **das bezweckt doch gar nichts** that doesn't get you anywhere (at all); **was soll das ~?** what's the point of that?

be|zwei|feln ✪ 43.1 *ptp* **bezweifelt** VT to doubt, to question, to have one's doubts about; **das ist nicht zu ~** that's unquestionable, that's beyond question; **~, dass ...** to doubt that ..., to question whether ...

be|zwing|bar ADJ conquerable; *Feind auch* defeatable; *(Sport auch)* beatable

be|zwin|gen *ptp* **bezwungen** [bə'tsvʊŋən] *irreg* **VT** to conquer; *Feind auch* to defeat, to overcome, to vanquish *(liter)*; *(Sport)* to beat, to defeat; *Festung* to capture; *Zorn, Gefühle* to master, to overcome; *Berg* to conquer, to vanquish *(liter)*; *Strecke* to do **VR** *(= seine Gefühle/Wünsche etc beherrschen)* to overcome *or* master one's emotions/desires *etc*

be|zwin|gend ADJ compelling; *Charme, Ausstrahlung* captivating, irresistible

Be|zwin|ger [bə'tsvɪŋɐ] M **-s**, **-**, **Be|zwin|ge|rin** [-ərɪn] F **-**, **-nen** *(von Berg, Feind)* conqueror, vanquisher *(liter)*; *(Sport)* winner (+*gen* over); *(von Festung, Burg)* captor

Be|zwin|gung [bə'tsvɪŋʊŋ] F **-**, **-en** conquering, conquest; *(von Feind auch)* defeat(ing), overcoming, vanquishing *(liter)*; *(Sport)* beating, defeat (-ing); *(von Festung)* capture, capturing; *(von Zorn, Gefühlen)* mastering, overcoming; *(von Berg)* conquering, vanquishing *(liter)*

Bf. *abbr von* **Bahnhof** *von* **Brief**

BfA [be:|ɛf'|a:] F - *abbr von* **Bundesversicherungsanstalt für Angestellte** *federal pensions office for salaried employees*

BGB [be:ge:'be:] NT **-**, *no pl abbr von* **Bürgerliches Gesetzbuch**

BGBl [be:ge:be:'|ɛl] NT **-**, *no pl abbr von* **Bundesgesetzblatt**

BGH [be:ge:'ha:] M **-s** *abbr von* **Bundesgerichtshof**

BGS [be:ge:'|ɛs] M - *abbr von* **Bundesgrenzschutz**

BH [be:'ha:] M **-(s)**, **-(s)** *abbr von* **Büstenhalter** bra

Bhagwan ['bagvan] M **-s**, *no pl* Bhagwan

Bhf. *abbr von* **Bahnhof**

bi [bi:] ADJ *pred (inf)* ac/dc *(inf)*, bi *(inf)*

bi- [bi:], **Bi-** PREF bi-; **bidirektional** *(Comput)* bidirectional

Bi|ath|let(in) M(F) biathlete

Bi|ath|lon ['bi:atlɔn] NT **-s**, **-s** *(Sport)* biathlon

bib|bern ['bɪbɐn] VI *(inf) (vor Angst)* to tremble, to shake; *(vor Kälte)* to shiver; **um jdn/etw ~** to fear for sb/sth

Bi|bel ['bi:bl] F **-**, **-n** *(lit)* Bible; *(fig)* bible

Bi|bel|aus|le|gung F interpretation of the Bible

Bi|be|les|käs ['bɪbələs-] M , **Bi|be|les|kä|se** M *(dial: = Quark)* quark

Bibel- : bi|bel|fest ADJ well versed in the Bible; **Bi|bel|fes|tig|keit** F thorough knowledge of the Bible; **Bi|bel|for|scher(in)** M(F) *(dated)* Jehovah's witness; **Bi|bel|kom|men|tar** M Bible commentary; **Bi|bel|spra|che** F biblical language; **Bi|bel|spruch** M biblical saying, quotation from the Bible; **Bi|bel|stel|le** F passage *or* text from the Bible; **Bi|bel|stun|de** F Bible study *no pl*; **Bi|bel|text** M text of the Bible; *(= Auszug)* text *or* passage from the Bible; **Bi|bel|über|set|zung** F translation of the Bible, Bible translation; **Bi|bel|vers** M verse from the Bible; **Bi|bel|wort** NT *pl* **-worte** biblical saying

Bi|ber ['bi:bɐ] M **-s**, **-** *(= Tier, Pelz, Tuch)* beaver **b** *auch* NT *(= Tuch)* flannelette sheet *(esp Brit)* **c** *(inf) (= Vollbart)* full beard; *(= Mensch)* man with a beard, bearded man

Biber- : Bi|ber|bau M *pl* **-baue** beaver's lodge; **Bi|ber|bett|tuch** ▲ NT flannelette sheet *(esp*

Brit); **Bi|ber|burg** F beaver's lodge; **Bi|ber|geil** [-gail] NT **-(e)s**, *no pl* castor(eum); **Bi|ber|pelz** M beaver (fur); **Bi|ber|schwanz** M **a** beaver's tail **b** *(Build: = Dachziegel)* flat tile, plain tile; **Bi|ber|tuch** NT , *no pl* flannelette sheet *(esp Brit)*

Bib|li|o|graf ▲ [biblio'gra:f] M **-en**, **-en**, **Bib|li|o|gra|fin** ▲ [-'gra:fɪn] F **-**, **-nen** bibliographer

Bib|li|o|gra|fie ▲ [bibliogra'fi:] F **-**, **-n** [-'fi:ən] bibliography

bib|li|o|gra|fie|ren ▲ [bibliogra'fi:rən] *ptp* **bibliografiert** *insep* **VT a** *(= verzeichnen)* to record in a/the bibliography **b** *(= einordnen)* to take (the) bibliographical details of **VT** to take bibliographical details

bib|li|o|gra|fisch ▲ [biblio'gra:fɪʃ] ADJ bibliographic(al) ADV bibliographically

Bib|li|o|ma|ne [biblio'ma:nə] M **-n**, **-n**, **Bib|li|o|ma|nin** [-'ma:nɪn] F **-**, **-nen** bibliomaniac

Bib|li|o|ma|nie [biblioma'ni:] F bibliomania

bib|li|o|ma|nisch [biblio'ma:nɪʃ] ADJ bibliomaniac(al) *(form)*

bib|li|o|phil [biblio'fi:l] ADJ *Mensch* bibliophilic *(form)*, bibliophil(e) *(form)*, book-loving *attr*; *Ausgabe* for bibliophil(e)s, for book-lovers ADV *ausgestattet* for collectors of books, for book-lovers

Bib|li|o|phi|le(r) [biblio'fi:lə] MF *decl as adj* book-lover, bibliophil(e)

Bib|li|o|phi|lie [bibliofi'li:] F **-**, *no pl* love of books, bibliophily *(form)*

Bib|li|o|thek [biblio'te:k] F **-**, **-en** library

Bib|li|o|the|kar [bibliote'ka:ɐ] M **-s**, **-e**, **Bib|li|o|the|ka|rin** F **-**, **-nen** librarian

bib|li|o|the|ka|risch [bibliote'ka:rɪʃ] ADJ library *attr*; **~e Ausbildung** training in librarianship, training as a librarian ADV **~ ausgebildet sein** to be a trained/qualified librarian

Bibliotheks- : Bib|li|o|theks|ka|ta|log M library catalogue *(Brit)* or catalog *(US)*; **Bib|li|o|theks|kun|de** F librarianship; **bib|li|o|theks|kund|lich** [-kʊntlɪç] ADJ library *attr*; **Bib|li|o|theks|leh|re** F (practical aspects of) librarianship; **Bib|li|o|theks|saal** M (library) reading room; **Bib|li|o|theks|we|sen** NT , *no pl* libraries *pl*; *(als Fach)* librarianship; **Bib|li|o|theks|wis|sen|schaft** F librarianship

bib|lisch ['bi:blɪʃ] ADJ biblical; **ein ~es Alter** a great age, a ripe old age

Bick|bee|re ['bɪk-] F *(N Ger)* bilberry, blueberry *(esp US)*

Bi|det [bi'de:] NT **-s**, **-s** bidet

bie|der ['bi:dɐ] ADJ **a** *(= rechtschaffen)* honest; *Mensch, Leben auch* upright **b** *(pej)* conventional, conservative; *Miene* worthy *(iro)* ADV *(pej)* conventionally, conservatively

Bie|der|keit F **-**, *no pl* **a** *(= Rechtschaffenheit)* honesty; *(von Mensch, Leben auch)* uprightness **b** *(pej)* conventionality, conservatism; *(von Miene)* worthiness

Bieder- : Bie|der|mann M *pl* **-männer a** *(dated, iro)* honest man **b** *(pej geh)* petty bourgeois; **bie|der|män|nisch** [-mɛnɪʃ] ADJ **a** *(dated)* honest **b** *(pej geh)* petty bourgeois; *Geschmack, Gesinnung auch* Philistine

Bie|der|mei|er ['bi:dɐmaiɐ] NT **-s**, *no pl* Biedermeier period

Biedermei|er- *in cpds* Biedermeier; **Bie|der|mei|er|stil** M *no pl* Biedermeier style; **Bie|der|mei|er|sträuß|chen** NT posy (with paper frill); **Bie|der|mei|er|zeit** F , *no pl* Biedermeier period

Bieder- : Bie|der|mie|ne F *(geh)* worthy air; **Bie|der|sinn** M , *no pl (geh)* **a** *(dated)* honest mentality **b** *(pej)* middle-class *or* petty-bourgeois mentality

bieg|bar ADJ flexible; *Material auch* pliable

Bie|ge ['bi:gə] F **-**, **-n** *(dial)* bend, curve; **eine ~ drehen/fahren/fliegen** *(inf)* to go for a walk/a

short ride *or* a spin *(inf)*/a short flight *or* a spin *(inf)*; **die ~ machen** *(inf)* to disappear

Bie|ge|fes|tig|keit F *(Tech)* bending strength

bie|gen ['bi:gn] *pret* **bog** [bo:k], *ptp* **gebogen** [gə'bo:gn] **VT a** *Draht, Rohr etc* to bend; *Glieder* to bend, to flex; *(fig: = manipulieren)* to wangle *(inf)*; **das Recht ~** *(fig dated)* to bend the law; **auf Biegen und** *or* **oder Brechen** *(inf)* by hook or by crook *(inf)*, come hell or high water *(inf)* → *auch* **gebogen**

b *(Aus Gram: = flektieren)* to inflect

VI *aux sein (Mensch, Wagen)* to turn; *(Weg, Straße auch)* to curve

VR to bend; *(= sich verziehen) (Schallplatte, Holz)* to warp; *(Metall)* to buckle; **seine Nase biegt sich leicht nach oben** his nose turns up slightly, his nose is slightly turned-up; **sich vor Lachen ~** *(fig)* to double up *or* crease up *(inf)* with laughter

bieg|sam ['bi:kza:m] ADJ flexible; *Material auch* pliable; *Glieder, Körper* supple, lithe; *(fig)* pliable, pliant

Bieg|sam|keit F **-**, *no pl* flexibility; *(von Material auch)* pliability; *(von Gliedern, Körper)* suppleness, litheness

Bie|gung F **-**, **-en a** bend; *(von Weg, Fluss)* bend, curve (+*gen* in); *(von Wirbelsäule)* curve (+*gen* in); **die ~en der Straße** the (twists and) turns *or* the curves in the road; **der Fluss/die Straße macht eine ~** the river/road curves *or* bends **b** *(Aus Gram)* inflection

Bie|ne ['bi:nə] F **-**, **-n a** bee **b** *(inf: = Mädchen)* bird *(Brit inf)*, chick *(esp US inf)*

Bienen- : bie|nen|ar|tig ADJ *Insekt* bee-like; *(fig)* bustling *attr*; **Bie|nen|fleiß** M bustling industriousness; **bie|nen|flei|ßig** ADJ industrious; **bie|nen|fleiß|ig** ADJ industrious; **Bie|nen|gift** NT bee poison; **Bie|nen|hal|tung** F beekeeping; **Bie|nen|hau|be** F bee veil(s); **Bie|nen|haus** NT apiary; **Bie|nen|honig** M real *or* natural honey; **Bie|nen|kas|ten** M (bee)hive; **Bie|nen|kö|ni|gin** F queen bee; **Bie|nen|korb** M (bee)hive; **Bie|nen|schwarm** M swarm (of bees); **Bie|nen|spra|che** F language of bees; **Bie|nen|staat** M bee colony; **Bie|nen|stich** M **a** bee sting **b** *(Cook)* cake coated with sugar and almonds and filled with custard *or* cream; **Bie|nen|stock** M (bee)hive; **Bie|nen|volk** NT bee colony, colony of bees; **Bie|nen|wa|be** F honeycomb; **Bie|nen|wachs** NT beeswax; **Bie|nen|zucht** F beekeeping, apiculture; **Bie|nen|züch|ter(in)** M(F) beekeeper, apiarist

Bi|en|na|le [biɛ'na:lə] F **-**, **-n** biennial film/art festival

Bier [bi:ɐ] NT **-(e)s**, **-e** beer; **zwei ~, bitte!** two beers, please; **zwanzig verschiedene ~e** twenty different kinds of beer, twenty different beers; **dunkles/helles ~** dark/light beer; **~ vom Fass** draught *(Brit)* or draft *(US)* beer; **das ist mein etc ~** *(fig inf)* that's my *etc* business

BIER

Beer has a particularly long tradition in Germany and is of two main types: top-fermented beers (**Weizenbier**, made from wheat and barley) and bottom-fermented beers (lager beers that are stored in the barrel for four to six weeks). These are further divided into light, medium and dark. Some beers, such as **Kölsch** or **Berliner Weiße**, are drunk mainly in the region in which they are produced, but **Pilsener** or **Pils** – a light beer with a strong bitter taste, served in traditional tulip glasses – is found everywhere. Light beers such as **Dortmunder**, which is also called **Helles** or **Export** depending on the region and the brewing method, have a slightly bitter taste. Medium beers include **Märzen** and **Wiener Bier**. Dark beers taste more strongly of malt and are therefore somewhat sweet.

Bier- *in cpds* beer; **Bier|bass** ▲ M *(inf)* deep bass voice; **Bier|bauch** M *(inf)* beer gut *(inf)*, beer belly (inf), potbelly; **Bier|brau|e|rei** F (= das Brauen) (beer-)brewing; (= Betrieb) brewery

Bier|chen ['biːɐçən] NT -s, - (glass of) beer

Bier-: Bier|de|ckel M beer mat (Brit) or coaster (US); **Bier|do|se** F beer can; **Bier|durst** M (inf) **~ haben** to feel like a beer; **Bier|ei|fer** M , **Bier|ernst** M (inf) deadly (Brit) or complete seriousness; **bier|ernst** (inf) **ADJ** deadly (Brit) or completely serious, solemn **ADV** solemnly; **Bier|fass** ▲ NT keg; **Bier|filz** M beer mat; **Bier|fah|ne** F beery or beery breath; **eine ~ ha-ben** to smell of beer; **Bier|fla|sche** F beer bottle; **Bier|gar|ten** M beer garden

---

BIERGARTEN

Biergärten are unpretentious open-air bars that serve mainly beer and simple food. Most of them are located in the gardens and back-yards of pubs. However, some bars operate exclusively as Biergärten and these are closed in the winter. Biergärten are original-ly a Bavarian institution but can now be found all over Germany.

Bier-: Bier|glas NT beer glass; **Bier|hal|le** F (auf Volksfest etc) beer hall; **Bier|kas|ten** M beer crate; **Bier|kel|ler** M (= Lager) beer cellar; (= Gaststätte auch) bierkeller; **Bier|krug** M tankard (esp Brit), beer mug; (aus Steingut) (beer) stein; **Bier|krü|gel** NT (A) half-litre (Brit) or half-liter (US) beer mug; **Bier|kut|scher** M **a** brewer's drayman **b** (inf) beer-lorry (Brit) or beer-truck (US) driver; **Bier|lau|ne** F (inf) **in einer ~, aus einer ~ heraus** after a few beers; **Bier|lei|che** F (inf) drunk; **es lagen noch einige ~n herum** there were still a few drunks lying around dead to the world; **Bier|rei|se** F (hum) pub-crawl; **Bier|ru|he** F (inf) cool (inf); **Bier|schin|ken** M ham sausage; **Bier|sei|del** NT tankard (esp Brit), beer mug; **bier|se|lig** ADJ Mensch boozed up (inf); **er kam in einer ~en Stimmung nach Hause** he came home pretty merry (Brit inf) or a bit drunk; **Bier|ulk** M (inf) drunken prank; **Bier|ver|lag** M , **Bier|ver|trieb** M beer wholesaler's; **Bier|wär|mer** [-vɛrmɐ] M -s, - beer-warmer; **Bier|wurst** F ham sausage; **Bier|zei|tung** F (inf) comic newspaper; **Bier|zelt** NT beer tent

Bie|se ['biːzə] F -, -n **a** (an Hose) braid **b** (Sew) tuck; (an Schuh) decorative seam

Biest [biːst] NT -(e)s, -er ['biːstɐ] (pej inf) **a** (= Tier) creature; (= Insekt) bug **b** (= Mensch) (little) wretch; (= Frau) bitch (sl), cow (inf); **sie ist ein süßes ~** she looks like a sweet little thing but she can be a bitch at times (sl) **c** (= Sache) beast (of a thing) (inf)

Bies|te|rei [biːstə'raɪ] F -, -en (inf) **a** (= Gemeinheit) horrible thing **b** (= Anstößendes) obscenity **c** (= Schinderei) beast of a job (inf)

bies|tig ['biːstɪç] ADJ (inf) beastly (inf), horrible; (= schlechter Laune) ratty (Brit inf), grumpy

Biet [biːt] NT -(e)s, -e (Sw) area

bie|ten ['biːtn] ✪ 40.2, 53.1 pret **bot** [boːt], ptp **geboten** [gə'boːtn] **VT** **a** (= anbieten) to offer (jdm etw sb sth, sth to sb); (bei Auktion) to bid (auf +acc for); Möglichkeit, Gelegenheit to offer, to give (jdm etw sb sth, sth to sb); **jdm die Hand ~** to hold out one's hand to sb, to offer sb one's hand; (fig auch) to make a conciliatory gesture to sb; **jdm die Hand zur Versöhnung ~** (fig) to hold out the olive branch to sb; **jdm den Arm ~** to offer sb one's arm; **wer bietet mehr?** will anyone offer me etc more?; (bei Auktion) any more bids?; **mehr bietet dir niemand** no-one will give or offer you more, no-one will make you a higher offer; **diese Stadt/dieser Mann hat nichts zu ~** this town/man has nothing to offer

b (= geben) to give (jdm etw sb sth); Gewähr, Sicherheit, Anlass etc auch to provide (etw sth, jdm etw sb with sth); Asyl to grant (jdm etw sb sth)

c (= haben, aufweisen) to have; Problem, Schwie-

---

rigkeit to present; **das Hochhaus bietet Wohnun-gen für fünfzig Familien** the tower block (Brit) or apartment building (US) provides accommo-dation for fifty families

d (= zeigen, darbieten) Anblick, Bild to present; Film to show; Leistung to give; **die Mannschaft bot den Zuschauern ein hervorragendes Spiel** the team put on an excellent game for the spectators → Blöße c, Stirn, Trotz

e (= zumuten) **sich** (dat) **etw ~ lassen** to stand for sth; **so etwas könnte man mir nicht ~** I wouldn't stand for that sort of thing; **ist dir so etwas schon einmal geboten worden?** have you ever known the like (inf) or anything like it?

f (geh: = sagen) **jdm einen Gruß ~** to greet sb; **jdm einen guten Morgen ~** to bid sb good morning (old, liter) → **Paroli, geboten**

VI (Cards) to bid; (bei Auktion auch) to make a bid (auf +acc for)

VR (Gelegenheit, Lösung, Anblick etc) to present itself (jdm to sb); **ein grauenhaftes Schauspiel bot sich unseren Augen** a terrible scene met our eyes

Bie|ter ['biːtɐ] M -s, -, **Bie|te|rin** [-ərɪn] F -, -nen bidder

bi|fo|kal [bifo'kaːl] ADJ bifocal

Bi|fo|kal|bril|le [bifo'kaːl-] F bifocals pl

Bi|ga|mie [biga'miː] F -, -n [-'miːən] bigamy

Bi|ga|mist [biga'mɪst] M -en, -en, **Bi|ga|mis|tin** [-'mɪstɪn] F -, -nen bigamist

bi|ga|mis|tisch [biga'mɪstɪʃ] **ADJ** bigamous **ADV** leben bigamously

Big Bang ['bɪg 'bɛŋ] M -, -, - -s (Astron, Fin, fig) big bang

bi|gott [bi'gɔt] ADJ overly pious

Bi|got|te|rie [bigɔtə'riː] F -, -n [-'riːən] (pej) **a** no pl excessive piousness **b** (= Handlung) over-ly pious behaviour (Brit) or behavior (US) no pl; (= Bemerkung) overly pious remark

Bi|jou|te|rie [biʒutə'riː] F -, -n [-'riːən] **a** (= Schmuck) jewellery (Brit), jewelry (US) **b** (Sw, obs: = Geschäft) jeweller's shop

Bi|kar|bo|nat ['biːkarbonaːt, bikarbo'naːt] NT bicarbonate

Bi|ker ['baikɐ] M -s, -, **Bi|ke|rin** ['baikərɪn] F -, -nen (inf: = Motorradfahrer) biker

Bi|ki|ni [bi'kiːni] M -s, -s bikini

bi|kon|kav [bikɔn'kaːf, bikɔŋ'kaːf] ADJ bicon-cave

bi|kon|vex [bikɔn'vɛks] ADJ biconvex

bi|la|bi|al [bilabi'aːl] ADJ (Ling) bilabial

Bi|lanz [bi'lants] F -, -en **a** (Econ, Comm) (= Lage) balance; (= Abrechnung) balance sheet; **eine ~ aufstellen** to draw up a balance sheet; **~ ma-chen** (fig) to check one's finances **b** (fig: = Ergebnis) end result; **(die) ~ ziehen** to take stock (aus of)

Bi|lanz-: Bi|lanz|buch|hal|ter(in) M(F) company accountant (who balances end-of--year accounts); **Bi|lanz|fäl|schung** F accounting fraud, window dressing of ac-counts (inf), cooking the books (inf)

bi|lan|zie|ren [bilan'tsiːrən] ptp **bilanziert** VTI **a** to balance; (fig) to assess

Bi|lanz-: Bi|lanz|prü|fer(in) M(F) auditor; **Bi|lanz|sum|me** F balance

bi|la|te|ral ['biːlateraːl, bilate'raːl] ADJ bilateral

Bild [bɪlt] NT -(e)s, -er ['bɪldɐ] **a** (lit, fig) picture; (= Fotografie) photo, picture; (Film) frame; (Art) (= Zeichnung) drawing; (= Gemälde) painting; (Cards) court or face (US) card, picture card (inf); **~ oder Wappen** heads or tails; **ein ~ ma-chen** to take a photo or picture; **etw im ~ fest-halten** to photograph/paint/draw sth as a per-manent record; **sie ist ein ~ von einer Frau** she's a fine specimen of a woman; **ein ~ des Elends** a picture of misery; **~: Hans Schwarz** (TV, Film) camera: Hans Schwarz → **schwach**

b (= Abbild) image; (= Spiegelbild auch) reflec-tion; **Gott schuf den Menschen ihm zum ~e** (Bibl) God created man in His own image

---

c (= Anblick, Ansicht) sight; **das äußere ~ der Stadt** the appearance of the town

d (Opt) image

e (Theat: = Szene) scene → **lebend**

f (= Metapher) metaphor, image; **um mit einem or im ~ zu sprechen ...** to use a metaphor ...; **etw mit einem ~ sagen** to say or express sth metaphorically; **im ~ bleiben** to use the same metaphor

g (= Erscheinungsbild) character; **sie gehören zum ~ dieser Stadt** they are part of the scene in this town

h (fig: = Vorstellung) image, picture; **im ~e sein** to be in the picture (über +acc about); **jdn ins ~ setzen** to put sb in the picture (über +acc a-bout); **sich** (dat) **von jdm/etw ein ~ machen** to get an idea of sb/sth; **du machst dir kein ~ da-von, wie schwer das war** you've no idea or con-ception how hard it was; **das ~ des Deutschen/Amerikaners** the image of the German/Ameri-can

Bild-: Bild|ab|tas|tung F (Tech) scanning; **Bild|ar|chiv** NT picture library; **Bild|at|las** M pictorial atlas; **Bild|auf|lö|sung** F (TV, Com-put) resolution; **Bild|aus|fall** M (TV) loss of vision; **Bild|aus|schnitt** M detail; **Bild|au|tor(in)** M(F) photographer; **Bild|band** [-bant] M pl -**bände** illustrated book, coffee-table book

bild|bar ADJ (lit, fig) malleable; **der Charakter des Kindes ist noch ~** the child's character can still be shaped

Bild-: Bild|bei|la|ge F colour (Brit) or color (US) supplement; **Bild|be|richt** M photo-graphic report; **Bild|be|schrei|bung** F (Sch) description of a picture; **Bild|be|trach|tung** F art appreciation

Bild|chen ['bɪltçən] NT -s, - dim von **Bild**

Bild-: Bild|do|ku|ment NT → **Bild a** a photo-graph/drawing/painting of documentary value; **Bild|ebe|ne** F (Phot) focal plane; **Bild|emp|fän|ger** M (Tech) picture receiver

bil|den ['bɪldn] **VT** **a** (= formen) to form; Figuren etc auch to fashion; (fig) Charakter auch to shape, to mould (Brit), to mold (US); Körper, Figur to shape; **sich** (dat) **ein Urteil/eine Meinung ~** to form a judgement/an opinion

b (= hervorbringen, Gram) to form; **der Magen hat ein Geschwür gebildet** an ulcer formed in the stomach, the stomach developed an ulcer

c (= einrichten) Fonds, Institution etc to set up

d (= zusammenstellen) Kabinett, Regierung to form; Ausschuss, Gruppe auch to set up; Vermögen to acquire

e (= ausmachen) Höhepunkt, Regel, Ausnahme, Problem, Gefahr etc to constitute; Dreieck, Kreis etc to form; **die Teile ~ ein Ganzes** the parts make up or form a whole; **die drei ~ ein hervorragen-des Team** the three of them make (up) an ex-cellent team

f (= erziehen) to educate

VR **a** (= entstehen) to form, to develop; **damit sich keine Vorurteile ~ ...** so that no prejudices are allowed to form ...

b (= lernen) to educate oneself; (durch Lesen etc) to improve one's mind; (durch Reisen etc) to broaden one's mind → auch **gebildet**

VI (= der Bildung dienen) to be educational; (Le-sen) to improve the or one's mind; (Reisen) to broaden the or one's mind

bil|dend ADJ **die ~e Kunst** art; **die ~en Künste** the fine arts; **~er Künstler** artist

Bil|der|bo|gen M illustrated broadsheet

Bil|der|buch NT **a** picture book; **eine Land-schaft wie im ~** a picturesque landscape **b** (rare: = Bildband) illustrated book, coffee-table book

Bil|der|buch- in cpds (lit) picture-book; (fig) per-fect; **Bil|der|buch|lan|dung** F **eine ~** a per-fect or textbook landing; **Bil|der|buch|ver|lag** M publisher of picture books

Bil|der-: Bil|der|ge|schich|te F **a** picture story **b** (in Comic, Zeitung) strip cartoon; (lustig auch) comic strip; **Bil|der|kult** M (Rel) image

---

worship, iconolatry (form); **Bil|der|rah|men** M picture frame; **Bil|der|rät|sel** NT picture puzzle; **bil|der|reich** ADJ Buch etc full of pictures; (fig) Sprache rich in imagery ADV **~ spre-chen** to use a lot of images; **Bil|der|reich|tum** M wealth of pictures; (fig) richness of imagery; **Bil|der|schrift** F pictographic writing system; **Bil|der|spra|che** F metaphorical language; **Bil|der|streit** M (Eccl Hist) controversy over image worship, iconographic controversy; **Bil|der|sturm** M (Eccl Hist) iconoclasm; **Bil|der|stür|mer(in)** M(F) (lit, fig) iconoclast; **bil|der|stür|me|risch** [-∫tyrmərɪ∫] ADJ (lit, fig) iconoclastic; **Bil|der|ver|eh|rung** F (Rel) image worship, iconolatry (form)

Bild-: Bild|fern|spre|cher M videophone; **Bild|flä|che** F **a** (= Leinwand) projection surface; (von Fotoapparat) film plane **b** (fig inf) **auf der ~ erscheinen** to appear on the scene; **von der ~ verschwinden** to disappear (from the scene); **Bild|fol|ge** F sequence of pictures; (Film) sequence of shots; **Bild|for|mat** NT picture size; (Quer-/Längsformat) picture or image format; (Film) frame size; **Bild|fre|quenz** F picture or image frequency; (Kameraeinstellung auch) filming speed; **Bild|funk** M radio photography; **Bild|ge|schich|te** F strip cartoon; **bild|haft** ADJ pictorial; Beschreibung, Vorstellung, Sprache vivid ADV vividly; **Bild|haf|tig-keit** ['bɪlthaftɪçkaɪt] F -, no pl pictorial nature; (von Beschreibung, Vorstellung, Sprache) vividness; **Bild|hau|er(in)** M(F) sculptor; **Bild|hau|e|rei** [bɪlthauə'raɪ] F -, no pl sculpture; **bild|hau|e|risch** ['bɪlthauərɪ∫] ADJ sculptural; **Bild|hau|er|kunst** F sculpture; **Bild|hau|er|werk|statt** F sculptor's workshop or studio; **bild|hau|ern** ['bɪlthauən] VTI insep (inf) to sculpt; **bild|hübsch** ADJ Mädchen (as) pretty as a picture; Kleid, Garten etc really lovely; **Bild|jour|na|list(in)** M(F) photojournalist; **Bild|kar|te** F court or face (US) card, picture card (inf); **Bild|kon|ser|ve** F film recording

bild|lich ['bɪltlɪç] ADJ pictorial; Ausdruck etc metaphorical, figurative ADV pictorially, vividly; meinen, gebrauchen, verwenden metaphorically, figuratively; **sich** (dat) **etw ~ vorstellen** to picture sth in one's mind's eye; **stell dir das mal ~ vor!** just picture it

Bild|lich|keit F -, no pl (von Beschreibung) graphicness; **die große ~ seiner Sprache** his highly figurative language

Bild-: Bild|ma|te|ri|al NT pictures pl; (für Vortrag) visual material, photographic and film material; (für Buch) pictorial material; (Sch) visual aids pl; **Bild|mi|scher** [-mɪ∫e] M -s, -, **Bild|mi|sche|rin** [-ərɪn] F -, -nen (TV) vision mixer; **Bild|nach|weis** M (Typ: für Abbildungen in Medien) photo credits pl

Bild|ner ['bɪltne] M -s, -, **Bild|ne|rin** [-ərɪn] F -, -nen (geh: = Schöpfer) creator

bild|ne|risch ['bɪltnərɪ∫] ADJ Begabung, Fähigkeit, Wille, Werk artistic; Element, Mittel, Gestaltung visual

Bild|nis ['bɪltnɪs] NT -ses, -se (liter) portrait

Bild-: Bild|plat|te F video disc; **Bild|plat-ten|spie|ler** M video disc player; **Bild|punkt** M pixel; **Bild|qua|li|tät** F (TV, Film) picture quality; (Phot) print quality; **Bild|re|dak-teur(in)** M(F) picture editor; **Bild|re|porta-ge** F (in Zeitschrift etc) picture story; (TV, Film) film documentary; **Bild|röh|re** F (TV) picture tube; **Bild|schär|fe** F definition no indef art

Bild|schirm M (TV, Comput) screen

Bild|schirm-: Bild|schirm|ab|strah|lung F , no pl screen radiation; **Bild|schirm|ar|bei-ter(in)** M(F) VDU operator; **Bild|schirm|ar-beits|platz** M work station; **Bild|schirm-fens|ter** NT (Comput) window; **Bild|schirm-fil|ter** M (Comput) screen filter; **Bild|schirm-ge|rät** NT visual display unit, VDU; **Bild-schirm|scho|ner** M (Comput) screen saver; **Bild|schirm|sei|te** F (TV: Teletext; Internet)

screen page; **Bild|schirm|text** M Viewdata® sing, Prestel®

Bild-: Bild|schnit|zer(in) M(F) woodcarver; **Bild|schnit|ze|rei** F (wood) carving; **bild-schön** ADJ beautiful; **Bild|sei|te** F **a** face, obverse (form) **b** (von Buch) picture page; **Bild|stel|le** F educational film hire service; **Bild|stock** M **a** wayside shrine **b** (Typ) block; **Bild|stö|rung** F (TV) interference (on vision or on the picture); **Bild|such|lauf** M picture search; **Bild|sym|bol** NT pictogram; (Comput) icon; **bild|syn|chron** ADJ (Film, TV) synchronized (with the picture); **Bild|ta|fel** F plate; **Bild|te|le|fon** NT videophone; **Bild-te|le|gramm** NT phototelegram; **Bild|text** M caption

Bil|dung ['bɪldʊŋ] F -, -en **a** (= Erziehung) education; (= Kultur) culture; **zu seiner ~ macht er Abendkurse** he does evening classes to try and educate himself; **zu seiner ~ liest er viel** he reads to improve his mind; **die allgemeine ~** general education; (eines Menschen) one's general education; **höhere ~** higher education; **~ ha-ben** to be educated
  b no pl (= das Formen) formation, forming; (von Figuren etc) fashioning; (fig: von Charakter etc) shaping; **zur ~ des Passivs** to form the passive
  c (= Form: von Baum, Hand etc, Ling: = Wort etc) form
  d no pl (= Entstehung: von Rost etc) formation
  e no pl (= Einrichtung) setting up
  f no pl (= Zusammenstellung) (von Kabinett, Regierung) formation, forming; (von Ausschuss, Gruppe) setting up, forming; (von Vermögen) acquisi-tion

Bil|dungs-: Bil|dungs|ab|schluss ▲ M (educational) qualifications pl; **Bil|dungs|an-stalt** F (form) educational establishment; **Bil-dungs|ar|beit** F work in the field of education; **bil|dungs|be|flis|sen** ADJ eager to improve one's mind; **Bil|dungs|be|flis|sen|heit** F eagerness to improve one's mind; **Bil-dungs|bür|ger(in)** M(F) member of the educated classes; **Bil|dungs|bür|ger|tum** NT educated classes pl; **Bil|dungs|chan|cen** PL educational opportunities pl; **Bil|dungs|drang** M desire for education; **Bil|dungs|dün|kel** M intellectual snobbery; **Bil|dungs|ei|fer** M desire to be educated; **bil|dungs|ei|frig** ADJ eager to be educated; **Bil|dungs|ein|rich|tung** F educational institution; (= Kulturstätte) cultural institution; **Bil|dungs|fab|rik** F (pej) educational mill, diploma mill (US); **bil|dungs-fä|hig** ADJ educable; **bil|dungs|feind|lich** ADJ anti-education; **Bil|dungs|gang** M pl -gänge school (and university) career; **Bil-dungs|grad** M level of education; **Bil-dungs|gut** NT , no pl established part of one's general education; **das gehört zum deutschen ~** that is part of the German cultural heritage; **Bil|dungs|hun|ger** M thirst for education; **bil|dungs|hung|rig** ADJ thirsting for education; **der ~e Student** the eager student; **Bil-dungs|ide|al** NT educational ideal; **Bil-dungs|in|sti|tut** NT educational institution; (= Kulturstätte) cultural institution; **Bil|dungs-lü|cke** F gap in one's education; **Bil|dungs-mi|se|re** F die ~ the sad state of education; **Bil|dungs|mo|no|pol** NT monopoly on education; **Bil|dungs|ni|veau** NT standard or level of education; **Bil|dungs|not|stand** M chronic shortage of educational facilities; **Bil-dungs|pla|nung** F education(al) planning no indef art; **Bil|dungs|po|li|tik** F education policy; **Bil|dungs|po|li|ti|ker(in)** M(F) politician with a special interest in or responsibility for education; **bil|dungs|po|li|tisch** ADJ Maßnahmen, Fehlentscheidung with regard to educational policy; Sprecher on educational policy ADV in terms of educational policy; **Bil-dungs|re|form** F educational reform; **Bil-dungs|rei|se** F educational trip or journey; **Bil|dungs|ro|man** M (Liter) Bildungsroman (form), novel concerned with the intellectual

or spiritual development of the main character; **Bil|dungs|stand** M level of education, educational level; **Bil|dungs|stät|te** F (geh) place or seat of learning; **Bil|dungs|stre|ben** NT striving after education; **Bil|dungs|stu|fe** F level of education; **eine hohe/niedrige ~ ha-ben** to be highly/not very educated; **Bil-dungs|ur|laub** M educational holiday (esp Brit) or vacation (US); (in Firma) study leave; **Bil|dungs|weg** M jds ~ the course of sb's education; **auf dem zweiten ~** through night school; **einen anderen ~ einschlagen** to opt for a different type of education

---

ZWEITER BILDUNGSWEG

The school system in Germany is strictly regulated and relatively inflexible. Pupils who decide after leaving school that the certificate they gained does not reflect their true abilities or allow them to pursue their desired career in the way they would wish can correct this by following the **zweiter Bildungs-weg**. The courses on offer range from the **mittlere Reife** and **Abitur** – in evening and half-day classes held by means of distance teaching – to short courses and courses for gaining extra qualifications → MITTLERE REIFE, ABITUR

Bil|dungs|we|sen NT education system

Bild-: Bild|un|ter|schrift F caption; **Bild|vor-la|ge** F (für Gemälde, Zeichnung) subject for a/the picture; **Bild|wand** F projection wall; **Bild|wer|fer** M projector; **Bild|wie|der|hol-fre|quenz** F , **Bild|wie|der|hol|ra|te** F (TV, Comput) refresh or scan rate; **Bild|win|kel** M (Opt, Phot) angle of view; **Bild|wör|ter|buch** NT pictorial or picture dictionary; **Bild|zei|le** F (TV etc) (scanning) line; **Bild|zu|schrift** F reply enclosing photograph

Bil|ge ['bɪlgə] F -, -n (Naut) bilge

Bil|har|zi|o|se [bɪlhar'tsio:zə] F -, -n (Med) bilharzia

bi|lin|gu|al [bilɪŋ'gua:l], **bi|lin|guisch** [bi'lɪŋ-guɪ∫] (form) ADJ bilingual ADV **an der Uni Biel wird ~ unterrichtet** at the University of Biel courses are taught in two languages; **sie er-zieht ihre Kinder ~** she is bringing her children up to be bilingual

Bi|li|ru|bin [biliru'bi:n] NT -s, no pl bilirubin

Bil|lard ['bɪljart] NT -s, -e [-də] or (Aus) -s **a** (= Spiel) billiards sing **b** (inf: = Spieltisch) billiard table

Bil|lard- in cpds billiard; **Bil|lard|ball** M , **Bil-lard|ku|gel** F billiard ball; **Bil|lard|queue** NT OR (AUS INF) M , **Bil|lard|stock** M billiard cue; **Bil|lard|tisch** M billiard table

Bil|le|teur [bɪljɛ'tø:ɐ] M -s, -e **a** (Aus: = Platzan-weiser) usher **b** (Sw: = Schaffner) conductor

Bil|le|teu|rin [bɪljɛ'tø:rɪn] F -, -nen (Aus: Platzan-weiserin) usherette

Bil|le|teu|se [bɪljɛ'tø:zə] F -, -n (Sw: = Schaffne-rin) conductress

Bil|lett [bɪl'jɛt] NT -(e)s, -e or -s **a** (Sw, dated: = Fahrbillett, Eintrittskarte) ticket **b** (Aus, obs: = Schreiben) note; (= Briefkarte) letter (Brit) or correspondence (US) card

Bil|lett|steu|er F (Sw) entertainment tax

Bil|li|ar|de [bɪl'jardə] F -, -n million billion (Brit), thousand trillion (US)

bil|lig ['bɪlɪç] ADJ **a** (= preisgünstig) cheap; Preis low; (= minderwertig) cheap, cheapo (inf); **~ ab-zugeben** going cheap; **~es Geld** (inf: = leicht ver-dient) easy money; **etw für ~es Geld kaufen** to buy sth cheap; **~ davonkommen** (inf) to get off lightly **b** (pej: = primitiv) cheap; Trick, Masche cheap, shabby; Ausrede feeble; **ein ~er Trost** cold comfort **c** (old) (= angemessen) proper, meet (old); (= gerecht, berechtigt) just, fair → recht

Bil|lig- in cpds cheap; **Bil|lig|an|bie|ter(in)** M(F) supplier of cheap goods; **Bil|lig|an|ge|bot** NT cut-price offer

bil|li|gen ['bɪlɪgn] VT to approve; **etw stillschweigend ~** to condone sth; **~, dass jd etw tut** to approve of sb's doing sth

bil|li|ger|ma|ßen ['bɪlɪgə'ma:sn], **bil|li|ger|wei|se** ADV (old) (= mit Recht) rightly; (= gerechterweise) by rights

Bil|lig-: Bil|lig|flag|ge F (Naut) flag of convenience; **unter ~ fahren** to sail under a flag of convenience; **Bil|lig|flug** M cheap or bargain flight; **Billigflüge** pl cheap or cut-price air travel

Bil|lig|keit F -, no pl a (= Preisgünstigkeit) cheapness; (von Preis) lowness b (pej: = Primitivität) cheapness; (von Ausrede) feebleness; **die ~ dieser Masche** this cheap trick; **die ~ der Aufmachung** the cheap presentation c (old) (= Angemessenheit) properness, meetness (old); (= Gerechtigkeit, Berechtigung, Jur) justness, fairness

Bil|lig-: Bil|lig|land NT country with low production costs; **Bil|lig|lohn|land** NT low-wage country; **Bil|lig|preis** M low price; **Bil|ligpreis|land** NT low-cost country; **Bil|lig|rei|se** F cheap holiday (Brit) or vacation (US); **~ pl** (Firmenangebote) cut-price or bargain travel; **Bil|lig|ta|rif** M (Telec etc) cheap rate; **zum ~ reisen/telefonieren** to travel cut-price/to make cheap-rate phone calls; **Reisen zum ~** (Angebot) cut-price or bargain travel (offers pl)

Bil|li|gung F -, -en approval; **jds ~ finden** to meet with sb's approval

Bil|li|on [bɪ'lio:n] F -, -en thousand billion (Brit), trillion (US)

bim [bɪm] INTERJ ding

bim|bam ['bɪm'bam] INTERJ ding-dong

Bim|bam ['bɪm'bam] M **ach, du heiliger ~!** (inf) hell's bells! (inf)

Bim|bim ['bɪm'bɪm] F -, -s (baby-talk) tram (esp Brit), streetcar (US)

Bim|bo ['bɪmbo] M -s, -s (pej sl: = Schwarzer) wog (Brit pej sl), nigger (pej sl)

Bi|me|tall ['bi:-] NT (= Material) bimetal; (= Bimetallstreifen) bimetal strip

Bim|mel ['bɪml] F -, -n (inf) bell

Bim|mel|bahn F (inf) small train with a warning bell

Bim|me|lei [bɪmə'laɪ] F -, no pl (pej) ringing

bim|meln ['bɪmln] VI (inf) to ring

Bims [bɪms] M -es, -e a pumice stone b (Build) breeze block

Bim|se ['bɪmzə] F -, no pl (inf) **~ kriegen** to get a walloping (esp Brit inf) or a beating

bim|sen ['bɪmzn] VT (inf) a (= drillen) to drill b (= einüben) Vokabeln etc to swot (Brit inf), to cram (inf); Griffe etc to practise (Brit), to practice (US)

Bims|stein M a pumice stone b (Build) breeze block

bin [bɪn] 1. pers sing pres von **sein**

bi|när [bi'nɛ:ə], **bi|nar** [bi'na:ə], **bi|na|risch** [bi'na:rɪʃ] ADJ binary

Bi|när-: Bi|när|kode M binary code; **Bi|närzahl** F binary number

Bin|de ['bɪndə] F -, -n a (Med) bandage; (= Schlinge) sling b (= Band) strip of material; (= Schnur) cord; (= Armbinde) armband; (= Augenbinde) blindfold c (= Monatsbinde) (sanitary) towel or (esp US) napkin d (dated: = Krawatte) tie; **sich** (dat) **einen hinter die ~ gießen** or **kippen** (inf) to put a few drinks away

Bin|de-: Bin|de|ge|we|be NT (Anat) usu sing connective tissue; **Bin|de|ge|webs|schwäche** F , no pl (Med) connective tissue weakness; **Bin|de|glied** NT connecting link; **Binde|haut** F (Anat) conjunctiva; **Bin|de|hautent|zün|dung** F conjunctivitis; **Bin|de|mittel** NT binder

bin|den ['bɪndn] pret **band** [bant], ptp **gebunden** [gə'bʊndn] VT a (= zusammenbinden) to tie; (=

festbinden) to bind; (fig geh) to bind, to unite; **etw zu etw** or **in etw** (acc) **~** to tie or bind sth into sth

b (= durch Binden herstellen) to bind; Strauß, Kranz to make up; Knoten etc to tie; Fass to hoop

c (= zubinden) Schal to tie; Krawatte to knot; **sich** (dat) **die Schuhe ~** to tie (up) one's shoelaces

d (= fesseln, befestigen) (an +acc) to tie (up); Ziege, Pferd auch to tether; Boot to moor; (fig) Menschen to bind, to tie; (an einen Ort) to tie; Geldmittel to tie up; (Versprechen, Vertrag, Eid etc) to bind; **jdn an Händen und Füßen ~** to tie or bind sb hand and foot; **jdm die Hände auf den Rücken ~** to tie sb's hands behind his back; **mir sind die Hände gebunden** (fig) my hands are tied; **nichts bindet mich an Glasgow** I have no special ties to keep me in Glasgow; **sie versuchte, ihn an sich zu ~** she tried to tie him to her → auch **gebunden, Nase** a

e (= festhalten) Staub, Erdreich to bind; (Chem) (= aufnehmen) to absorb; (= sich verbinden mit) to combine with

f (= zusammenhalten, auch Cook) Farbe, Soße to bind

g (= verbinden) (Poet) to bind; (fig geh auch) to unite; (Mus) Töne to slur; gleiche Note to tie; **was Gott gebunden hat, soll der Mensch nicht trennen** what God has joined together let no man put asunder

VI (Mehl, Zement, Soße etc) to bind; (Klebstoff) to bond; (fig) to be tying, to tie one down; (Erlebnisse) to create a bond

VR (= sich verpflichten) to commit oneself (an +acc to); **ich will mich nicht ~** I don't want to get involved

bin|dend ADJ binding (für on); Zusage definite

Bin|der¹ ['bɪndə] M -s, - a (= Krawatte) tie b (Agr) (= Bindemaschine) binder; (= Mähbinder) reaper (Brit) or grain (US) binder c (Build) (= Stein) header; (= Balken) truss beam d (= Bindemittel) binder

Bin|der² ['bɪndə] M -s, -, **Bin|de|rin** [-ərɪn] F -, -nen (S Ger, Aus: = Böttcher) cooper

Bin|de|rei [bɪndə'raɪ] F -, -en (= Buchbinderei) bindery; (= Blumenbinderei) wreath and bouquet department

Bin|de-: Bin|de|strich M hyphen; **Bin|destrich|frau** F (hum, pej) woman with hyphenated surname made up of her husband's name and her own; **Bin|de|vo|kal** M thematic vowel; **Bin|de|wort** NT pl **-wörter** (Gram) conjunction

Bind|fa|den M string; **ein (Stück) ~** a piece of string; **es regnet Bindfäden** (inf) it's sheeting down (Brit inf), it's coming down in buckets (US inf)

-bin|dig [bɪndɪç] ADJ suf (Chem) **dieses Element ist vierbindig** this element has a valency of four

Bin|dig|keit F -, no pl (Chem) valency

Bin|dung ['bɪndʊŋ] F -, -en a (= Beziehung zu einem Partner) relationship (an +acc with); (= Verbundenheit mit einem Menschen, Ort) tie, bond (an +acc with); (= Verpflichtung: an Beruf etc, durch Vertrag) commitment (an +acc to); **seine enge ~ an die Heimat** his close ties with his home country b (= Skibindung) binding c (Chem) bond d (Tex) weave

Bin|dungs-: Bin|dungs|angst F usu pl (Psych) fear of commitment no pl; **bin|dungs|fä|hig** ADJ capable of commitment; **nicht ~ sein** to be incapable of having a (personal) relationship

bin|go ['bɪŋgo] INTERJ (inf) (= ok) OK; (= aha) bingo

Bin|go ['bɪŋgo] NT -(s), no pl bingo

Bin|kel ['bɪŋkl] M -s, -(n) (Aus inf) a = **Bündel** b (= Dummkopf) twit (inf) c = **Beule**

bin|nen ['bɪnən] PREP +dat or (geh) +gen (form) within; **~ kurzem** shortly

Bin|nen-: bin|nen|bords [-bɔrts] ADV (Naut) inboard; **Bin|nen|deich** M inner dyke (Brit) or dike (esp US); **bin|nen|deutsch** ADJ Ausdruck, Wort used in Germany; Sprache, Dialekt spoken in Germany; **Bin|nen|deut|sche(r)** MF decl as adj German living in Germany; **Binnen|fi|sche|rei** F freshwater fishing; **Binnen|ge|wäs|ser** NT inland water; **Bin|nengren|ze** F internal border; **Bin|nen|ha|fen** M river port; **Bin|nen|han|del** M domestic trade; **Bin|nen|land** NT a (= Landesinneres) interior b (N Ger: = eingedeichtes Gebiet) dyked (Brit) or diked (esp US) land; **Bin|nen|län|der** [-lɛndə] M -s, -, **Bin|nen|län|de|rin** [-ərɪn] F -, -nen inlander; **bin|nen|län|disch** [-lɛndɪʃ] ADJ inland; **Bin|nen|markt** M home market; **der europäische ~** the European Single Market; **Bin|nen|meer** NT a inland sea b (= Binnensee) lake, continental lake (form); **Bin|nenreim** M (Poet) internal rhyme; **Bin|nenschif|fer(in)** M(F) sailor on inland waterways; (auf Schleppkahn) bargeman/-woman; **Bin|nenschiff|fahrt ▲** F inland navigation; **Bin|nensee** M lake, continental lake (form); **Binnen|staat** M landlocked country or state; **Bin|nen|ver|kehr** M inland traffic; **Bin|nenwäh|rung** F internal currency; **Bin|nen|wasser|stra|ße** F inland waterway; **Bin|nenwirt|schaft** F domestic economy; **Bin|nenzoll** M internal duty

Bi|nom [bi'no:m] NT -s, -e binomial

bi|no|misch [bi'no:mɪʃ] ADJ binomial

Bin|se ['bɪnzə] F -, -n usu pl rush; **in die ~n gehen** (fig inf) (= misslingen) to be a washout (inf); (= verloren gehen) to go west (inf), to go for a burton (Brit inf); (= kaputtgehen) to give out (inf)

Bin|sen|wahr|heit F , **Bin|sen|weis|heit** F truism

bio ['bi:o] ADJ (inf) Nahrungsmittel, Anbau etc organic; **das ist alles ~** it's all organic food

Bio ['bi:o] F -, no pl (Sch inf) biol (inf), bio (esp US inf), bilge (hum sl)

bio- [bio, 'bi:o], **Bio-** in cpds bio-; **Bi|o|ab|fall** M biological waste; **bi|o|ak|tiv** [biolak'ti:f, 'bi:o-] ADJ Waschmittel biological; **Bi|o|bau|er** M , **Bi|o|bäu|e|rin** F organic farmer; **Gemüse vom ~n** organic vegetables pl; **Bi|o|che|mie** [bioçe'mi:] F biochemistry; **bi|o|che|misch** ADJ biochemical ADV biochemically; **Bi|o|diesel** ['bi:o-] M biodiesel; **bi|o|dy|na|misch** [biody'na:mɪʃ] ADJ biodynamically; **Gemüse ~ anbauen** to grow vegetables biodynamically; **Bi|o|ener|ge|tik** [biolener'ge:tɪk] F , no pl bioenergetics sing; **Bi|o|ethik** ['bi:ole:tɪk] F , no pl bioethics sing or pl; **Bi|oethi|ker(in)** ['bi:ole:tɪkə, -ərɪn] M(F) bioethicist; **Bi|o|gas** ['bi:o-] NT methane gas; **Bi|oge|ne|se** [bioge'ne:zə] F biogenesis; **bi|o|gene|tisch** [bioge'ne:tɪʃ] ADJ biogenetic

Bi|o|graf ▲ [bio'gra:f] M -en, -en, **Bi|o|gra|fin ▲** [-'gra:fɪn] F -, -nen biographer

Bi|o|gra|fie ▲ [biogra'fi:] F -, -n [-'fi:ən] biography

bi|o|gra|fisch ▲ [bio'gra:fɪʃ] ADJ biographical ADV biographically

Bi|o-: Bi|o|kost F , no pl organic food; **Bi|o|laden** ['bi:o-] M wholefood or health-food shop

---

BIOLADEN

A **Bioladen** is a shop that mainly sells organic food. You can also buy environmentally-friendly goods such as recycled-paper products and bleach-free detergents. Vegetarians are well catered for by **Biolädens**, which stock food guaranteed to be of purely vegetable origin.

Bi|o|lo|ge [bio'lo:gə] M -n, -n, **Bi|o|lo|gin** [-'lo:gɪn] F -, -nen biologist

Bi|o|lo|gie [biolo'gi:] F -, no pl biology

bi|o|lo|gisch [bio'lo:gɪʃ] **ADJ** biological; *Anbau* organic; **~-technische Assistentin, ~-technischer Assistent** laboratory technician **ADV** biologically; **anbauen** organically

Bi|o-: Bi|o|mas|se ['bi:o-] F , *no pl* (*Chem*) organic substances *pl*; **Bi|o|met|rie** [biome'tri:] F -, *no pl*, **Bi|o|met|rik** [bio'me:trɪk] F -, *no pl* biometrics *sing*, **bi|o|met|risch** [bio'me:trɪʃ] **ADJ** biometric; **Bi|o|müll** ['bi:o-] M organic waste

Bi|o|nik [bi'o:nɪk] F -, *no pl* bionics *sing*

Bi|o|phy|sik [biofy'zi:k, 'bi:o-] F biophysics *sing*

bi|o|phy|si|ka|lisch [biofyzi'ka:lɪʃ] **ADJ** biophysical

Bi|op|sie [biɔ'psi:] F -, **-n** [-'psi:ən] (*Med*) biopsy

Bi|o-: Bi|o|re|ak|tor ['bi:o-] M bioreactor; **Bi|o|rhyth|mus** ['bi:o-] M biorhythm; **das verlangt mein ~** my internal clock tells me it's necessary; **Bi|o|sphä|re** ['bi:o-] F -, *no pl* biosphere; **Bi|o|sphä|ren|re|ser|vat** NT biosphere reserve; **Bi|o|tech|nik** [bio'teçnɪk, 'bi:o-] F biotechnology; **Bi|o|tech|ni|ker(in)** [bio'teçnɪkɐ, 'bi:o-, -ərɪn] M(F) bioengineer; **bi|o|tech|nisch** [bio'teçnɪʃ, 'bi:o-] **ADJ** biotechnological; **Bi|o|tech|no|lo|gie** [bioteçnolo'gi:, 'bi:o-] F **a** *no pl* (*Wissenschaft*) biotechnology **b** (*Verfahren*) biotechnological method *or* process; **Bi|o|ton|ne** ['bi:o-] F organic waste bin; **Bi|o|top** [bio'to:p] NT **-s**, **-e** biotope; **Bi|o|wasch|mit|tel** ['bi:o-] NT biological detergent; **Bi|o|wis|sen|schaft** ['bi:o-] F biological science; **Bi|o|wis|sen|schaft|ler(in)** M(F) bioscientist

BIP [be:li:'pe:] NT - *abbr von* **Bruttoinlandsprodukt** GDP

bi|quad|ra|tisch [bikva'dra:tɪʃ, 'bi:-] **ADJ** biquadratic

Bir|cher|mües|li ['bɪrçɐ-] NT (*Sw*), **Bir|cher|müs|li** NT muesli (*with fresh fruit*)

birgt [bɪrkt] 3. PERS SING *pres von* **bergen**

Bir|ke ['bɪrkə] F -, **-n** birch; (= *Baum auch*) birch tree

Bir|ken-: Bir|ken|pilz M boletus (scaber); **Bir|ken|wald** M birch wood *or* forest; **Bir|ken|was|ser** NT *pl* **-wässer** hair lotion (*made from birch sap*)

Birk- ['bɪrk-]: **Birk|hahn** M black cock; **Birk|huhn** NT black grouse

Bir|ma ['bɪrma] NT **-s** Burma

Bir|ma|ne [bɪr'ma:nə] M **-n**, **-n**, **Bir|ma|nin** [-'ma:nɪn] F -, **-nen** Burmese

bir|ma|nisch [bɪr'ma:nɪʃ] **ADJ** Burmese

Birn|baum M (*Baum*) pear tree; (*Holz*) pear wood

Bir|ne ['bɪrnə] F -, **-n a** pear **b** (= *Glühlampe*) (light) bulb **c** (*inf*: = *Kopf*) nut (*inf*)

Bir|nen-: Bir|nen|fas|sung F (= *Lampenfassung*) light-bulb socket; **bir|nen|för|mig** **ADJ** pear-shaped; **Bir|nen|was|ser** NT (= *Birnenschnaps*) pear brandy

birst 3. PERS SING *pres von* **bersten**

bis[1] [bɪs] **ADV** (*Mus*) bis, twice

bis[2] [bɪs]

1 PRÄPOSITION	2 BINDEWORT

1 – PRÄPOSITION (+acc)

a zeitlich until; (= *bis spätestens*) by

> Im Sinne von **bis spätestens** wird **bis** meist mit **by** übersetzt.

bis 5 Uhr mache ich Hausaufgaben, und dann ... I do my homework until 5 o'clock, and then ...; **das muss bis Ende Mai warten** that will have to wait until *or* till the end of May; **ich kann nur (noch) bis nächste Woche warten** I can only wait until next week, no longer; **er ist bis gegen 5 Uhr noch da** he'll be there (up) until *or* till about 5 o'clock; **bis zum Schluss war unklar, wie der Prozess ausgehen würde** the outcome of the trial was in doubt right up

to the end; **es dauert mindestens/höchstens bis nächste Woche** it will take until next week at the very least/most; **bis jetzt hat er nichts gesagt** up to now *or* so far he has said nothing; **bis spätestens Montag darfst du es behalten** you can keep it until Monday, no longer; **die Wäsche ist frühestens bis nächsten Montag fertig** the laundry won't be ready until *or* before next Monday at the earliest; **bis zu diesem Zeitpunkt** up to this time; **dieser Brauch hat sich bis ins 19. Jahrhundert gehalten** this custom continued into the 19th century; **bis in den Sommer/die Nacht hinein** into the summer/night; **bis 5 Uhr kann ich das unmöglich machen/gemacht haben** I can't possibly do it/ get it done by 5 o'clock; **bis Ende Mai bin ich wieder in Berlin** I'll be in Berlin again by the end of May; **das sollte bis zum nächsten Sommer fertig sein** it should be finished by next summer; **das hätte eigentlich bis jetzt fertig sein müssen** that should really have been finished by now; **bis spätestens Montag brauche ich das Geld** I need the money by Monday at the latest; **bis gegen 5 Uhr ist das fertig** it'll be ready by about 5 o'clock; **Montag bis Freitag** Monday to *or* through (*US*) Friday; **bis einschließlich 5. Mai** up to and including 5th May; **bis ausschließlich 5. Mai** up to but not including 5th May; **bis bald/später/morgen!** see you soon/later/tomorrow!; **bis wann gilt der Fahrplan?** when is the timetable valid till?; **bis wann bleibt ihr hier?** how long are you staying here?; **bis wann ist das fertig?** when will that be finished?; **bis wann können Sie das machen?** when can you do it by?; **bis dato** (*form*) to date; **bis anhin** (*Sw*) hitherto; **bis auf weiteres** until further notice; **bis auf weiteres halten wir die Regelung so** until further notice we'll make this the arrangement; **sie geht bis auf weiteres auf die Schule in der Kantstraße** for the time being, she'll continue going to the school on Kantstraße

♦ **bis dahin** *or* **dann bis dahin** *or* **dann muss die Arbeit fertig sein** the work must be finished by then; **bis dahin hatte sie noch nie etwas von Schröder gehört** up to then she hadn't heard anything about Schröder; **bis dahin ist noch viel Zeit** that's still a long time off; **bis dahin bin ich alt und grau** I'll be old and grey (*Brit*) *or* gray (*US*) by then; **bis dahin ist er längst weg** he will have gone long before then; **bis dann!** see you then!

♦ **von ... bis ...** from ... to *or* till *or* through (*US*) ...; (*mit Uhrzeiten*) from ... till *or* to ...; **vom 10. Mai bis 12. Oktober** from 10th May until 12th October; **vom 10. Mai bis einschließlich 12. Oktober** from 10th May until 12th October inclusive; **von 10 Uhr bis 17 Uhr** from 10am till 5pm

b räumlich to; (*in Buch, Film, Erzählung*) up to; **bis durch/über/unter** right through/over/under; **ich fahre nur bis München** I'm only going to Munich *or* as far as Munich; **ich habe nur bis Seite 35 gelesen** I've only read up to *or* as far as page 35; **bis an unsere Mauer** up to *or* right to our wall; **bis vor den Baum** (up) to the tree; **bis hinter den Baum** (up) to the tree; **es sind noch 10 km bis nach Schlüchtern** it's another 10 km to Schlüchtern; **bis ins Letzte** *or* **Kleinste** down to the smallest detail; **bis auf alles bis ins Kleinste ausgearbeitet** he's worked everything out down to the smallest detail; **bis wo/wohin?** how far?; **bis wohin ist Ihnen der Mann gefolgt?** how far did the man follow you?; **bis dort** *or* **dorthin** *or* **dahin** (to) there; **wie weit ist es zum nächsten Supermarkt? – bis dorthin sind es nur 5 km** how far is the nearest supermarket? – it's only 5 km (away); **bis hierher** this far; **bis hierher hast du ja Recht gehabt** so *or* this far you've been right; **bis hierher und nicht weiter** (*lit, fig*) this far and no further; **ich gehe bis hierher, aber nicht weiter** I'll go as far as that, but no further; **höchstens bis Carlisle** to Carlisle at the furthest; **bis mindestens Carlisle** at least as far as Carlisle; **bis einschließ-**

lich up to and including; **bis einschließlich Kapitel 3** up to the end of chapter 3; **bis ausschließlich** up to but not including

c mit Maßangaben up to; **Kinder bis sechs Jahre, bis sechs Jahre alte Kinder** children up to the age of six; **für Wagen bis sechs Tonnen** for vehicles up to six tons; **bieten Sie bis 100 Euro** offer up to 100 euros

d andere Wendungen

♦ **bis zu** (= *bis zu einer oberen Grenze von*) up to; (= *bis zu einer unteren Grenze von*) (down) to; **Totschlag wird mit Gefängnis bis zu 8 Jahren bestraft** manslaughter is punishable by up to 8 years imprisonment; **er ist genau bis zur Haarspalterei** he is exact to the point of hair-splitting

♦ **bis auf** (+*acc*) (= *außer*) except (for); (= *einschließlich*) (right) down to; **es sind alle gekommen, bis auf Sandra** they all came, except Sandra; **das Schiff ging unter und sie ertranken alle, bis auf den letzten Mann** the ship sank and every single one of them drowned

2 – BINDEWORT

a beiordnend to; **zehn bis zwanzig Stück** ten to twenty; **bewölkt bis bedeckt** cloudy to overcast

b unterordnend zeitlich until, till; (= *nicht später als*) by the time; **ich warte noch, bis es dunkel wird** I'll wait until *or* till it gets dark; **bis es dunkel wird, möchte ich zu Hause sein** I want to get home before it gets dark; **das muss gemacht sein, bis ich nach Hause komme** it must be done by the time I come home; **bis das einer merkt!** it'll be ages before anyone realizes (*inf*); **du gehst hier nicht weg, bis das (nicht) gemacht ist** you're not leaving until *or* before it's done; **bis dass der Tod euch scheide(t)** (*form*) until *or* till death you do part (*form*)

c = sobald (*Aus inf*) when; **gleich bis er kommt** the moment he comes (*inf*), as soon as he comes

Bi|sam ['bi:zam] M **-s**, **-e** *or* **-s a** (= *Pelz*) musquash **b** *no pl* (= *Moschus*) musk

Bi|sam|rat|te F muskrat (beaver)

Bi|schof ['bɪʃɔf, 'bɪʃo:f] M **-s**, **-e** ['bɪʃœfə, 'bɪʃø:fə], **Bi|schö|fin** ['bɪʃœfɪn, 'bɪʃø:fɪn] F -, **-nen** bishop

bi|schöf|lich ['bɪʃœflɪç, 'bɪʃø:flɪç] **ADJ** episcopal

Bi|schofs-: Bi|schofs|amt NT episcopate; **Bi|schofs|müt|ze** F **a** (bishop's) mitre (*Brit*) *or* miter (*US*) **b** (= *Kaktus*) bishop's mitre (*Brit*) *or* miter (*US*); **Bi|schofs|sitz** M diocesan town; **Bi|schofs|stab** M crosier, (bishop's) crook; **Bi|schofs|stuhl** M cathedra, bishop's seat

Bi|se|xu|a|li|tät [bizɛksuali'tɛːt, 'bi:-] F bisexuality, bisexualism

bi|se|xu|ell [bizɛ'ksu̯ɛl, 'bi:-] **ADJ** bisexual

bis|her [bɪs'he:ɐ] **ADV** until *or* till now, hitherto; (= *und immer noch*) up to now; **~ nicht** not until *or* till now, not before; (= *und immer noch nicht*) not as yet; **das wusste ich ~ nicht** I didn't know that before; **~ habe ich es ihm nicht gesagt** I haven't told him as yet; **ein ~ unbekannter Stern** a hitherto *or* previously unknown star, a star unknown until *or* till now; **alle ~ bekannten Sterne** all the known stars

bis|he|rig [bɪs'he:rɪç] **ADJ** attr (= *vorherig*) previous; (= *momentan*) present, up to now; **der ~e Stellvertreter ist jetzt Vorsitzender** the previous deputy is now chairman; **der ~e Stellvertreter wird jetzt Vorsitzender** the present deputy will become chairman; **wegen unserer ~en Arbeitsweise war das unmöglich** because of our previous way of working *or* because of the way we worked before that wasn't possible; **wegen unserer ~en Arbeitsweise ist das unmöglich** because of our present way of working *or* because of the way we have worked up to now that isn't possible; **wir müssen unsere ~en Anschauungen revidieren** we will have to revise our present views; **das ist mir in meiner ~en Karriere noch nicht vorgekommen** I've never known that in my career up to now; **die ~en Bestimmungen gelten seit letzter Woche nicht mehr** the regulations previously in force ceased to be valid last week; **die ~en Bestimmungen gelten ab nächster Woche nicht mehr** the regulations presently in force cease to be valid next week

Bis|ka|ya [bɪs'kaːja] F - **die ~** (the) Biscay; **Golf von ~** Bay of Biscay

Bis|kuit [bɪs'kviːt, bɪs'kuiːt] NT OR M -(e)s, -s or -e (fatless) sponge

Bis|kuit-: Bis|kuit|ge|bäck NT sponge cake/ cakes; **Bis|kuit|rol|le** F Swiss roll; **Bis|kuit|teig** M sponge mixture

bis|lang [bɪs'laŋ] ADV = **bisher**

Bis|marck|he|ring [ˈbɪsmark-] M Bismarck herring, filleted pickled herring

Bi|son [ˈbiːzɔn] M -s, -s bison

biss ▲ pret von **beißen**

Biss ▲ [bɪs] M -es, -e bite; (Zahnmedizin auch) occlusion; (fig) vigour (Brit), vigor (US), spirit; **mit einem ~ war das Törtchen verschwunden** the tart disappeared in one mouthful; **Spag(h)etti/Bohnen mit ~** spaghetti/beans al dente; **~ haben** (dated inf) to have punch; **einer Sache den ~ nehmen** to take the sting out of sth

biss|chen ▲ [ˈbɪsçən] ADJ inv **ein ~ Geld/Liebe/ Wärme** a bit of or a little money/love/warmth; **ein ~ Milch/Wasser** a drop or bit of milk/water, a little milk/water; **ein klein ~ ...** a little bit/ drop of ...; **kein ~ ...** not one (little) bit/not a drop of ...; **das ~ Geld/Whisky** that little bit of money/drop of whisky; **ich habe kein ~ Hunger** I'm not a bit hungry

ADV **ein ~** a bit, a little; **ein klein ~** a little bit; **ein ~ wenig** not very much; **ein ~ mehr/viel/teuer** etc a bit more/much/expensive etc; **ein ~ zu wenig** not quite enough; **ein ~ sehr** (inf) a little bit too much; **ein ~ sehr teuer** etc (inf) a (little) bit too expensive etc

NT inv **ein ~** a bit, a little; (von Flüssigkeit) a drop, a little; **ein ganz ~** (inf) just a tiny bit/ drop → **lieb**

bis|sel [ˈbɪsl] (dial) = **bisschen**

Bis|sen [ˈbɪsn] M -s, - mouthful; (= Imbiss) bite (to eat); **er will keinen ~ anrühren** he won't eat a thing; **einen ~ zu sich nehmen** to have a bite to eat; **sich** (dat) **jeden ~ vom** or **am Munde absparen** to watch every penny one spends

bis|sen|wei|se ADV mouthful by mouthful; (fig) bit by bit

bis|serl [ˈbɪsɛl] (dial) = **bisschen**

bis|sig [ˈbɪsɪç] ADJ a (lit, fig) vicious; **~ sein** to bite; **„Vorsicht, ~er Hund"** "beware of the dog"; b (= übellaunig) waspish; **du brauchst nicht gleich ~ zu werden** there's no need to bite my etc head off

Bis|sig|keit F -, -en a (lit, fig) viciousness; (Bemerkung) vicious remark b (= Übellaunigkeit) waspishness; (Bemerkung) waspish remark

bissl [ˈbɪsl] ADJ, ADV, NT inv (dial) = **bisschen**

Biss|wun|de ▲ F bite

bist [bɪst] 2. pers sing pres von **sein**

bis|te [ˈbɪstə] (dial inf) contr von **bist du**

Bist|ro [ˈbɪstro, bɪsˈtroː] NT -s, -s bistro

Bis|tum [ˈbɪstuːm] NT -s, ̈-er [-tyːmɐ] diocese, bishopric

bis|wei|len [bɪsˈvailən] ADV (geh) from time to time, now and then

Bit [bɪt] NT -(s), -(s) (Comput) bit

Bit-: Bit|dich|te F (Comput) bit density; **Bit|ra|te** F (Comput) bit rate

Bitt|brief M petition

bit|te [ˈbɪtə] INTERJ a (bittend, auffordernd) please; **~ schön** please; **nun hör mir doch mal ~ zu** listen to me please; **sei so gut und ruf mich an** would you phone me, please?, would you please phone me?; **wo ist ~ das nächste Telefon?** could you please tell me where the nearest telephone is?; **~ nicht!** no, please!,

please don't!; **ja ~!**, **~ ja!** yes please; **~ ~ machen** (inf) (Kind) ≈ to say pretty please; (Hund) to (sit up and) beg; **~ zahlen, zahlen ~!** (could I/we have) the bill (Brit) or check (US), please; **~ nach Ihnen!** after you

b (bei höflicher Frage, Aufforderung; meist nicht übersetzt) **~ schön?**, **~(, was darf es sein?)** (in Geschäft) can I help you?; (in Gaststätte) what would you like?; **~(, Sie wünschen?)** what can I do for you?; **~ (schön** or **sehr)(, Ihr Bier/Kaffee)!** your beer/coffee, here you are (inf); **ja ~?** yes?; **~(, treten Sie ein)!** come in!, come!; **~ (, nehmen Sie doch Platz)!** (form) please or do sit down; **~ hier, hier ~!** (over) here, please; **Entschuldigung! – ~!** I'm sorry! – that's all right; **~, mit (dem größten) Vergnügen!** (form) with pleasure; **aber ~!** sure (inf), go (right) ahead (inf); **~, nur zu!** help yourself; **na ~!** there you are!

c (sarkastisch: = nun gut) all right; **~, wie du willst** (all right,) just as you like; **~, soll er doch kommen, mir ist das egal** (all right,) let him come, it's all the same to me

d (Dank erwidernd) you're welcome, not at all (Brit), sure (US inf); **~ sehr** or **schön** you're welcome, not at all (Brit); **~(, gern geschehen)** (not at all,) my pleasure; **~, keine Ursache** it was nothing; **~, nichts zu danken** don't mention it; **aber ~!** there's no need to thank me

e (nachfragend) **(wie) ~?** (I beg your) pardon? (auch iro), sorry(, what did you say?)

Bit|te [ˈbɪtə] F -, -n request; (inständig) plea; **auf jds ~** (acc) at sb's request; **auf seine ~ hin** at his request; **ich habe eine große ~ an dich** I have a (great) favour (Brit) or favor (US) to ask you; **sich mit einer ~ an jdn wenden** to make a request to sb; **er kann ihr keine ~ ausschlagen** or **abschlagen** he can't refuse her anything; **er gab den ~n der Kinder nach** he gave in to the children's pleas

bit|ten [ˈbɪtn] ✪ 31, 46.1, 46.5, 46.6, 48.3 pret **bat** [baːt], ptp **gebeten** [gəˈbeːtn] VT a jdn ~ to ask; (inständig) to beg; (Eccl) to beseech; **jdn um etw ~** to ask/beg/beseech sb for sth; **jdn (darum) ~, etw zu tun** or **dass er etw tut** to ask etc sb to do sth; **jdn um etw ~** (acc) ~ (dated) to ask sth of sb; **darf ich Sie um Ihren Namen ~?** might I ask your name?; **um Ruhe wird gebeten** silence is requested; (auf Schild) silence please; **darf ich Sie um den nächsten Tanz ~?** may I have the pleasure of the next dance?; **wir ~ dich, erhöre uns!** (Eccl) we beseech Thee to hear us; (katholisch, anglikanisch) Lord hear us; **ich bitte dich um alles in der Welt** I beg or implore you; **er lässt sich gerne ~** he likes people to keep asking him; **er lässt sich nicht (lange) ~** you don't have to ask him twice; **aber ich bitte dich!** not at all; **ich bitte dich, wie kann man nur so dumm sein?** I ask you, how can anyone be so stupid?; **wenn ich ~ darf** (form) if you please, if you wouldn't mind; **ich bitte darum** (form) I'd be glad if you would, if you wouldn't mind; **(keineswegs,) ich bitte sogar darum** (form) (not at all,) I should be glad; **darum möchte ich doch sehr gebeten haben!** (form) I should hope so indeed; **ich muss doch (sehr) ~!** well I must say!

b (= einladen) to ask, to invite; **jdn auf ein Glas Wein ~** to invite sb to have a glass of wine; **jdn zum Abendessen (zu sich) ~** to ask or invite sb to dinner; **jdn zu Tisch ~** to ask sb to come to table; **jdn ins Zimmer ~** to ask or invite sb to come in

c (= bestellen) **jdn an einen Ort ~** to ask sb (to come) somewhere; **jdn zu sich ~** to ask sb to come and see one

VI a (= eine Bitte äußern) to ask; (inständig) to plead, to beg; **um etw ~** to ask (for) or request sth; (inständig) to plead or beg for sth; **bei jdm um etw ~** to ask sb for sth; **~ und betteln** to beg and plead

b (= einladen) **der Herr Professor lässt ~** the Professor will see you now; **ich lasse ~** he/she can come in now, would you ask him/her to

come in now?; **darf ich zu Tisch ~?** lunch/dinner is served; **darf ich (um den nächsten Tanz) ~?** may I have the pleasure (of the next dance)?

Bit|ten NT -s, no pl pleading; **sich aufs ~ verlegen** to resort to pleas or pleading; **auf ~ von** at the request of

bit|tend ADJ pleading; **mit ~en Augen** with a look of pleading ADV pleadingly

bit|ter [ˈbɪtɐ] ADJ a bitter; Schokolade plain; (fig) Geschmack nasty → **Pille** b (fig) Enttäuschung, Erfahrung, Ironie bitter; Wahrheit, Lehre, Verlust hard, painful; Zeit, Schicksal hard; Ernst, Feind deadly; Hohn, Spott cruel; **ein ~es Gefühl** a feeling of bitterness; **bis zum ~en Ende** to the bitter end c (fig: = verbittert) bitter; **jdn ~ machen** to embitter sb, to make sb bitter; **~e Klagen führen** to complain bitterly d (= stark) Kälte, Frost, Reue, Tränen bitter; Not, Notwendigkeit dire; Leid, Unrecht grievous ADV a **~ schmecken** to taste bitter b (= sehr) bereuen bitterly; bezahlen, büßen dearly; **jdn/etw ~ entbehren/vermissen** to miss sb/ sth terribly; **etw ~ nötig haben** to be in dire need of sth; **~ wenig Geld haben** to be desperately short of money; **solche Fehler rächen sich ~** one pays dearly for mistakes like that

Bit|ter [ˈbɪtɐ] M -s, - bitters pl

bit|ter|bö|se ADJ furious ADV furiously

Bit|te|re(r) [ˈbɪtərə] M decl as adj bitters pl

Bit|ter-: bit|ter|ernst ADJ Situation etc extremely serious; Mensch deadly (Brit) or very serious; **damit ist es mir ~** I am deadly (Brit) or very serious, I am in deadly (Brit) or complete earnest; **bit|ter|kalt** ADJ attr bitterly cold, bitter; **Bit|ter|keit** F -, no pl (lit, fig) bitterness; **bit|ter|lich** [ˈbɪtɐlɪç] ADJ bitter ADV bitterly; **Bit|ter|man|del** F bitter almond

Bit|ter|nis [ˈbɪtɐnɪs] F -, -se (geh) bitterness no pl; (fig: von Mensch auch) embitterment no pl; (= Leiden) adversity, hardship

Bit|ter-: Bit|ter|oran|ge F Seville or bitter orange; **Bit|ter|salz** NT Epsom salts pl; **Bit|ter|scho|ko|la|de** F plain chocolate; **Bit|ter|stoff** F usu pl bitter constituent; **bit|ter|süß** ADJ (lit, fig) bittersweet

Bit|te|schön [ˈbɪtəʃøːn] NT -s, -s (bittend, auffordernd) please; (Dank erwidernd) not at all; (anbietend) (von Verkäufer) can I help you?; (von Kellner) what would you like?

Bitt-: Bitt|gang M pl -gänge a (geh) einen ~ zu jdm machen to go to sb with a request; **das war ein schwerer ~** it was hard (for him etc) to ask that b (Eccl) pilgrimage; (= Bittprozession) rogation procession; **Bitt|ge|bet** NT (prayer of) supplication; **Bitt|ge|such** NT petition; **Bitt|got|tes|dienst** M rogation service

bitt|schön [ˈbɪtʃøːn] INTERJ = **bitte schön** → **bitte a, b, d**

Bitt-: Bitt|schrift F (dated) petition; **Bitt|stel|ler** [ˈbɪtʃtɛlɐ] M -s, -, **Bitt|stel|le|rin** [-ərɪn] F -, -nen petitioner, supplicant

Bi|tu|men [biˈtuːmən] NT -s, - or **Bitu|mina** [-ˈtuː-mina] bitumen

bi|va|lent [bivaˈlɛnt] ADJ bivalent

Bi|wak [ˈbiːvak] NT -s, -s or -e bivouac

bi|wa|kie|ren [bivaˈkiːrən] ptp **biwakiert** VI to bivouac

bi|zarr [biˈtsar] ADJ bizarre; Form, Gestalt etc auch fantastic ADV geformt, gestaltet bizarrely, fantastically

Bi|zar|re|rie [bitsarəˈriː] F -, -n [-ˈriːən] (geh) a no pl bizarreness b (= Gedanke) bizarre idea; (= Verhalten) bizarre behaviour (Brit) or behavior (US) no pl; (= Bemerkung) bizarre comment

Bi|zeps [ˈbiːtsɛps] M -(es), -e biceps

Bj. abbr von **Baujahr**

BK [beːˈkaː] F -, no pl abbr von **bildende Kunst** (Sch inf) art

BKA [beːkaːˈʔaː] NT - *abbr von* **Bundeskriminalamt**

BKB [beːkaːˈbeː] F - *abbr (in Annoncen) von* **Benzinkostenbeteiligung**

bla|bla [blaˈblaː] INTERJ (*inf*) blah blah blah (*inf*)

Bla|bla [blaˈblaː] NT -s, *no pl* (*inf*) waffle (*inf*)

Bla|che [ˈblaxə] F -, -n (*esp Sw*) = **Plane**

Black|box ▲ [ˈblɛkbɔks] F -, -es, **Black Box** F -, -es (*Aviat, Telec, Comput*) black box

Black-out ▲ [blɛkˈaut] NT OR M -(s), -s, **Black|out** NT OR M -(s), -s blackout

blaf|fen [ˈblafn], **bläf|fen** [ˈblɛfn] VI to yelp; (= *schimpfen*) to snap

Blag [blaːk] NT -s, -en [-gn], **Bla|ge** [ˈblaːgə] F -, -n (*pej inf*) brat

blä|hen [ˈblɛːən] VT to swell; *Segel auch* to belly (out), to fill; *Anorak, Gardine, Windsack* to fill; *Nasenflügel, Nüstern* to flare; **voller Stolz blähte er seine Brust** his chest swelled with pride VR to swell; (*Segel auch*) to belly out, to billow; (*Anorak, Gardine*) to billow; (*Nasenflügel, Nüstern*) to flare; (*fig: Mensch*) to puff oneself up (*inf*) VI to cause flatulence *or* wind *or* (*US*) gas

blä|hend ADJ (*Med*) flatulent (*form*)

Blä|hung F -, -en *usu pl* (*Med*) wind *no pl*, flatulence *no pl*; **eine ~ abgehen lassen** to break wind

bla|kig [ˈblaːkɪç] ADJ (= *verrußt*) sooty; (= *rußend*) smoky

bla|ma|bel [blaˈmaːbl] ADJ shameful

Bla|ma|ge [blaˈmaːʒə] F -, -n disgrace

bla|mie|ren [blaˈmiːrən] *ptp* **blamiert** VT to disgrace → **Innung** VR to make a fool of oneself; (*durch Benehmen*) to disgrace oneself

blan|chie|ren [blãˈʃiːrən] *ptp* **blanchiert** VT (*Cook*) to blanch

blank [blaŋk] ADJ **a** (= *glänzend, sauber*) shiny, shining; (= *abgescheuert*) *Hosenboden etc* shiny; **etw scheuern/polieren, bis es ~ wird** to clean/polish sth till it shines; **der ~e Hans** (*poet*) the wild North Sea

b (*poet*: = *strahlend*) *Licht* bright; *Augen* bright, shining; **der ~e Tag** broad daylight

c (= *nackt*) bare; *Schwert etc auch* naked; (*Aus*: = *ohne Mantel*) coatless; (*inf*: = *ohne Geld*) broke; (*Cards*: = *einzeln*) single

d (= *rein*) pure, sheer; *Hohn* utter

ADV **a** (= *glänzend*) *scheuern, polieren* till it shines; **~ gewetzt** (worn) shiny; **~ poliert** brightly polished

b **eine Karte ~ haben** to have only one card of a suit; **die Herzzehn habe ich ~** the ten of hearts is the only heart I have

Blan|kett [blaŋˈkɛt] NT -s, -e (*Fin*) blank form

blank|ge|wetzt △ [-gəvɛtst] ADJ *attr* → **blank** ADV **a**

blan|ko [ˈblaŋko] ADJ *pred* **a** *Papier* plain **b** *Scheck etc* blank

Blan|ko- *in cpds* blank; **Blan|ko|ak|zept** NT (*Fin*) blank acceptance; **Blan|ko|kre|dit** [-kreːdiːt] M open *or* blank credit; **Blan|ko|scheck** M blank cheque (*Brit*) *or* check (*US*); **jdm einen ~ ausstellen** (*fig*) to give sb carte blanche *or* (*US*) a blank check; **Blan|ko|un|ter|schrift** F blank signature; **Blan|ko|voll|macht** F carte blanche, unlimited power(s)

blank|po|liert △ [-poliːɐt] ADJ *attr* → **blank** ADV **a**

Blank|vers M blank verse

Bläs|chen [ˈblɛːsçən] NT -s, - *dim von* **Blase b** (*Med*) vesicle (*form*), small blister

Bläs|chen|aus|schlag M herpes *sing*, blistery rash (*inf*)

Bla|se [ˈblaːzə] F -, -n **a** (= *Seifenblase, Luftblase*) bubble; (= *Sprechblase*) balloon; **~n werfen** *or* **ziehen** (*Farbe*) to blister; (*Teig*) to become light and frothy **b** (*Med*) blister; (= *Fieberblase auch*) vesicle (*form*); **sich** (*dat*) **~n laufen** to get blisters from walking *etc* **c** (*Anat*) bladder; **sich**

(*dat*) **die ~ erkälten** to get a chill on the bladder **d** (*pej inf*: = *Clique*) gang (*inf*), mob (*inf*)

Bla|se|balg M (pair of) bellows

bla|sen [ˈblaːzn] *pret* **blies** [bliːs], *ptp* **geblasen** [gəˈblaːzn] VI to blow; (*Posaunenbläser etc*) to play; (*auf Essen*) to blow on it; (*auf Wunde etc*) ≈ to kiss it better; **zum Rückzug ~** (*lit, fig*) to sound the retreat; **zum Aufbruch ~** (*lit*) to sound the departure; (*fig*) to say it's time to go; **es bläst** (*inf*) it's blowy (*inf*) *or* windy, there's a wind blowing → **tuten, Horn b**

VT **a** to blow

b *Melodie, Posaune etc* to play

c (*inf*) **dir/ihm werd ich was ~!** I'll give you/him a piece of my mind → **Marsch** [1] **b, Trübsal**

d (*inf*: = *mitteilen*) to tell; **jdm etw ins Ohr ~** to whisper sth in sb's ear

e (*sl*: = *fellieren*) **jdm einen ~** to give sb a blow job (*sl*)

Bla|sen-: Bla|sen|bil|dung F formation of bubbles; (*bei Anstrich, an Fuß etc*) blistering; **Bla|sen|ent|zün|dung** F, **Bla|sen|ka|tarr(h)** M cystitis (*spec*); **Bla|sen|lei|den** NT bladder trouble *no art*; **Bla|sen|spie|ge|lung** F (*Med*) cystoscopy (*spec*); **Bla|sen|stein** M bladder stone; **Bla|sen|tee** M herb tea beneficial in cases of bladder trouble

Blä|ser [ˈblɛːzɐ] M -s, -, **Blä|se|rin** [-ərɪn] F -, -nen (*Mus*) wind player; **die ~** the wind (section)

Blä|ser|quar|tett NT wind quartet

bla|siert [blaˈziːɐt] ADJ (*pej geh*) blasé

Bla|siert|heit F -, -en (*pej geh*) blasé attitude

bla|sig [ˈblaːzɪç] ADJ full of bubbles; *Flüssigkeit etc* aerated; *Teig* light and frothy; (*Med*) blistered

Blas-: Blas|in|stru|ment NT wind instrument; **Blas|ka|pel|le** F brass band; **Blas|mu|sik** F brass band music

Blas|phe|mie [blasfeˈmiː] F -, -n [-ˈmiːən] blasphemy

blas|phe|misch [blasˈfeːmɪʃ] ADJ blasphemous

Blas|rohr NT **a** (= *Waffe*) blowpipe **b** (*Tech*) blast pipe

blass ▲ [blas] ADJ **a** *Gesicht, Haut etc* pale; **~ werden** (*Brit*) *or* grow pale, to pale; (*vor Schreck auch*) to blanch; **~ wie der Tod** (*geh*) deathly pale; **~ wie Kreide** white as chalk (*Brit*) *or* a sheet; **~ vor Neid werden** to go green with envy; **etw macht jdn ~** sth makes sb look pale

b *Farbe, Schrift etc* pale

c (*geh*) *Licht, Mond* pale, wan

d (*fig*) faint; *Ahnung, Vorstellung auch* vague; *Erinnerung auch* dim, vague; *Ausdruck, Sprache, Schilderung* colourless (*Brit*), colorless (*US*); **ich habe keinen ~en Schimmer** *or* **Dunst (davon)** (*inf*) I haven't a clue *or* the faintest (idea) (about it) (*inf*)

e (*rare*: = *pur*) sheer, pure

blass-: blass- ▲ *in cpds* pale; **blass|blau** ▲ ADJ pale blue

Bläs|se [ˈblɛsə] F -, -n paleness; (*von Haut, Gesicht etc*) pallor; (*von Licht*) paleness, wanness; (*fig: von Ausdruck, Schilderung etc*) colourlessness (*Brit*), colorlessness (*US*)

blass|grün ▲ ADJ pale green

Bläss|huhn ▲ [ˈblɛs-] NT coot

bläss|lich ▲ [ˈblɛslɪç] ADJ palish, rather pale

blass|ro|sa ▲ ADJ pale pink

bläst [blɛːst] 3. PERS SING *pres von* **blasen**

Blatt [blat] NT -(e)s, =er [ˈblɛtə] **a** (*Bot*) leaf; **kein ~ vor den Mund nehmen** not to mince one's words

b (*Papier etc*) sheet; **ein ~ Papier** a sheet of paper; **(noch) ein unbeschriebenes ~ sein** (= *unerfahren*) to be inexperienced; (= *ohne Image*) to be an unknown quantity; **er ist kein unbeschriebenes ~** he's been around (*inf*); (*Krimineller*) he's got a record → **fliegend**

c (= *Seite*) page; **das steht auf einem anderen ~** (*fig*) that's another story; **ein neues ~ in der**

Geschichte *or* **im Buch der Geschichte** a new chapter of history

d (= *Notenblatt*) sheet; **vom ~ singen/spielen** to sight-read

e (= *Kunstblatt*) print; (= *Reproduktion*) reproduction

f (*bei Landkartenserien*) sheet

g (= *Zeitung*) paper

h (*von Messer, Ruder, Propeller*) blade

i (*Cards*) hand; (= *Einzelkarte*) card; **das ~ hat sich gewendet** (*fig*) the tables have been turned

j (*Hunt, Cook*) shoulder

Blatt|ader F (*Bot*) leaf vein

Blätt|chen [ˈblɛtçən] NT -s, - *dim von* **Blatt** (*pej*: = *Zeitung*) rag (*inf*)

Blat|ter [ˈblatə] F -, -n **a** (*dated Med*: = *Pocke*) pock, pustule **b Blattern** PL (= *Krankheit*) smallpox

blätt|rig [ˈblɛtərɪç] ADJ *Teig* flaky; *Farbe etc* flaking; **~ werden** (*Farbe etc*) to start flaking

-blätt|rig ADJ *suf* -leaved; **ein vierblättriges Kleeblatt** a four-leaved clover

Blät|ter|ma|gen M (*Zool*) omasum (*spec*)

blät|tern [ˈblɛtɐn] VI **a** (*in Buch*) to leaf *or* (*schnell*) flick through it/them; (*Comput*) to scroll; **in etw** (*dat*) **~** to leaf *or* flick through sth **b** *aux sein* (*rare*) (= *in Schichten zerfallen*) to flake; (= *abblättern*) to flake off VT *Geldscheine, Spielkarten* to put down one by one; **er blätterte mir die 100 Euro auf den Tisch** he put the 100 euros down note by note (*Brit*) *or* bill by bill (*US*) on the table for me

Blat|ter-: Blat|ter|nar|be F (*dated*) pockmark; **blat|ter|nar|big** ADJ (*dated*) pockmarked

Blät|ter-: Blät|ter|pilz M agaric; **Blät|ter|schmuck** M (*poet*) beautiful foliage; **Blät|ter|teig** M puff pastry *or* paste (*US*); **Blät|ter|teig|ge|bäck** NT puff pastry; (= *Backwaren*) puff pastries *pl*; **Blät|ter|teig|pas|te|te** F vol-au-vent; **Blät|ter|wald** M (*Press hum*) press; **es rauscht im deutschen ~** there are murmurings in the German press; **Blät|ter|werk** NT, *no pl* foliage

Blatt-: Blatt|fe|der F (*Tech*) leaf spring; **Blatt|form** F (*Bot*) leaf shape; **blatt|för|mig** ADJ leaf-shaped, foliar (*form*); **Blatt|ge|mü|se** NT greens *pl*, green *or* leaf (*form*) vegetables *pl*; **ein ~** a leaf vegetable; **Blatt|ge|wächs** NT foliate plant; **Blatt|gold** NT gold leaf; **Blatt|grün** NT chlorophyll; **Blatt|knos|pe** F leaf bud; **Blatt|laus** F greenfly, aphid; **blatt|los** ADJ leafless; **Blatt|pflan|ze** F foliate plant

blätt|rig [ˈblɛtrɪç] ADJ = **blätterig**

-blätt|rig ADJ *suf* = -blätterig

Blatt-: Blatt|rip|pe F (*Bot*) (leaf) rib *or* vein; **Blatt|sä|ge** F pad saw; **Blatt|sa|lat** M green salad; **Blatt|schuss** ▲ M (*Hunt*) shot through the shoulder to the heart; **Blatt|sil|ber** NT silver leaf; **Blatt|spi|nat** M leaf spinach; **Blatt|stän|gel** ▲ M petiole, leafstalk; **Blatt|stel|lung** F leaf arrangement; **Blatt|stiel** M petiole, leafstalk; **Blatt|trieb** M leaf shoot; **Blatt|ver|gol|dung** F gilding; **blatt|wei|se** ADV leaf by leaf; (*bei Papier*) sheet by sheet; **Blatt|werk** NT, *no pl* foliage

Blätz [blɛts] M -, - (*Sw*) cloth

Blätz|li [ˈblɛtsli] NT -(s), -(s) (*Sw*) cutlet

blau [blau] ADJ **a** blue; **Forelle** *etc* **~** (*Cook*) trout *etc* au bleu; **~er Anton** (*inf*) boiler suit (*Brit*), workman's overalls; **ein ~es Auge** (*inf*) a black eye; **ich tu das nicht wegen deiner schönen ~en Augen** (*fig*) I'm not doing it for the sake of your bonny blue eyes; **mit einem ~en Auge davonkommen** (*fig*) to get off lightly; **die ~e Blume** (*Liter*) the Blue Flower; **~es Blut in den Adern haben** to have blue blood in one's veins; **ein ~er Fleck** a bruise; **~e Flecken haben** to be bruised; **die ~en Jungs** (*inf*) the boys in blue (*inf*), the navy; **der Blaue Nil** the Blue Nile; **der Blaue Planet** the blue planet; **der Blaue Reiter** (*Art*) the Blaue Reiter; **die ~e Stunde** (*poet*) the twilight hour; **er wird sein ~es**

Wunder erleben (inf) he won't know what's hit him (inf) → **Dunst**

b usu pred (inf: = betrunken) drunk, tight (inf), canned (inf) → **Veilchen**

c (inf: = geschwänzt) **einen ~en Montag machen** to skip work on Monday (inf); **der letzte Freitag war für mich ~** I skipped work last Friday (inf)

d **ein ~er Brief** (Sch) letter informing parents that their child must repeat a year (von Hauswirt) notice to quit; (von der Firma) one's cards

---

BLAUER BRIEF

A **blauer Brief** is a letter from a school telling parents that their child is in danger of having to repeat a year. Until the mid-1970s it was actually delivered in a blue envelope. **Blauer Brief** is also a colloquial term for the dismissal notice issued by a firm. This derives from the time when officers learned of their discharge from the army by means of a letter in a blue envelope.

Blau [blau] NT **-s, -** or (inf) **-s** blue

Blau-: Blau|al|gen PL blue-green algae pl; **blau|äu|gig** ADJ blue-eyed; (fig) naïve; **Blau|äu|gig|keit** F **-**, no pl (lit) blue eyes pl; (fig) naïvety; **Blau|bart** M (geh) Bluebeard; **Blau|bee|re** F bilberry, blueberry (esp US); **blau|blü|tig** ADJ blue-blooded; **Blau|blü|tig|keit** F **-**, no pl blue blood

Blaue ['blauə] M = **Blaue(r)**, **Blaue(s)**

Bläue ['blɔyə] F **-**, no pl blueness; (des Himmels auch) blue

blau|en ['blauən] VI (liter: Himmel) to turn blue

bläu|en ['blɔyən] VT **a** (= blau färben) to dye blue; Lackmuspapier etc to turn blue **b** Wäsche to blue **c** ▲ (= schlagen) to beat

Blaue(r) ['blauə] M decl as adj **a** (inf: = Polizist) cop (inf), copper (inf) **b** (sl Hist: = Hundertmarkschein) hundred-mark note (Brit) or bill (US)

Blaue(s) ['blauə] NT decl as adj **a** **das ~** (= Farbe) the blue; **es spielt ins ~** it has a touch of blue in it; **das ~ vom Himmel (herunter)lügen** (inf) to tell a pack of lies; **das ~ vom Himmel (herunter) reden** (inf) to talk one's head off (inf), to prattle away nineteen to the dozen (Brit inf), to talk a mile a minute (US inf); **jdm das ~ vom Himmel (herunter)versprechen** (inf) to promise sb the moon **b** (ohne Ziel) **ins ~ hinein** (inf) at random; arbeiten with no particular goal; **wir wollen ins ~ fahren** we'll just set off and see where we end up; **eine Fahrt ins ~** a trip to nowhere in particular; (= Veranstaltung) a mystery tour

Blau-: Blau|fel|chen M whitefish, powan (spec); **Blau|fil|ter** M OR NT (Phot) blue filter; **Blau|fuchs** M arctic fox; **blau|grau** ADJ blue-grey (Brit), blue-gray (US), bluish or bluey grey (Brit) or gray (US); **blau|grün** ADJ blue-green, bluish or bluey green; **Blau|helm** M (Press sl) UN soldier, blue helmet; **Blau|hemd** NT (DDR) **a** blue shirt (worn by members of the Free German Youth) **b** (inf: = Mensch) member of the Free German Youth; **Blau|ja|cke** M (inf) bluejacket (inf), sailor; **Blau|kohl** M (dial), **Blau|kraut** M (S Ger, Aus) red cabbage; **Blau|kreuz|ler** [-krɔytslə] M **-s, -**, **Blau|kreuz|le|rin** [-ərɪn] F **-, -nen** member of the Blue Cross Temperance League

bläu|lich ['blɔylɪç] ADJ bluish, bluey

Blau-: Blau|licht NT (von Polizei etc) flashing blue light; (= Lampe) blue light; **mit ~** with its blue light flashing; **blau|ma|chen** sep (inf) VI to skip work VT **den Freitag/zwei Tage ~** to skip work on Friday/for two days; **Blau|mann** M pl **-männer** (inf) boiler suit (Brit), workman's overalls; **Blau|mei|se** F bluetit; **Blau|pau|se** F blueprint; **Blau|pa|pier** NT carbon paper; **blau|rot** ADJ purple; **Blau|säu|re** F prussic or hydrocyanic acid; **Blau|schim|mel** M blue

mould (Brit) or mold (US); **Blau|schim|mel|kä|se** M blue cheese; **blau|schwarz** ADJ blue-black, bluey black; **Blau|stich** M (Phot) blue cast; **blau|sti|chig** [-ʃtɪçɪç] ADJ (Phot) with a blue cast; **Blau|stift** M blue pencil; (zum Malen) blue crayon; **Blau|strumpf** M bluestocking; **blau|strümp|fig** [-ʃtrʏmpfɪç] ADJ bluestocking attr; **Blau|sucht** F **,** no pl (Med) cyanosis; **Blau|tan|ne** F blue or Colorado spruce; **blau|vio|lett** ADJ (dark) bluish or bluey purple; **Blau|wal** M blue whale

Bla|zer ['bleːzɐ] M **-s, -**, **Bla|zer|ja|cke** F blazer

Blech [blɛç] NT **-(e)s, -e** **a** no pl (sheet) metal; (von Auto) body; **eine Dose aus ~** a tin (Brit), a metal container; **das ist doch nur ~** it's just ordinary metal **b** (= Blechstück) metal plate **c** (= Backblech) (baking) tray (Brit), baking sheet **d** no pl (= Blechinstrumente) brass **e** no pl (pej inf: = Orden etc) gongs pl (inf), fruit salad (US inf) **f** no pl (inf: = Unsinn) rubbish no art (inf), trash no art (inf); **red kein ~** don't talk crap (inf)

Blech-: Blech|blä|ser(in) M(F) brass player; **die ~** the brass (section); **Blech|blas|in|stru|ment** NT brass instrument; **Blech|büch|se** F tin (Brit), can; **Blech|do|se** F tin container; (esp für Konserven) tin (Brit), can

ble|chen ['blɛçn] VTI (inf) to cough or pay up (inf), to fork out (inf)

ble|chern ['blɛçɐn] ADJ **a** attr metal **b** Geräusch, Stimme etc tinny; (fig: = hohl) hollow, empty ADV tinnily; klingen, tönen, scheppern tinny; **das klingt ~** that sounds tinny

Blech-: Blech|ge|schirr NT metal pots and pans pl, metal utensils pl (form); **Blech|in|stru|ment** NT brass instrument; **Blech|ka|nis|ter** M metal can; **Blech|kis|te** F (pej inf) (old) crate (inf); **Blech|la|wi|ne** F (pej inf) vast column of cars; **Blech|leh|re** F metal gauge; **Blech|mu|sik** F (usu pej) brass (band) music; **Blech|napf** M metal bowl; **Blech|scha|den** M damage to the bodywork; **Blech|sche|re** F (pair of) metal shears; (= Maschine) metal shearer; **Blech|trom|mel** F tin drum; **Blech|walz|werk** NT sheet (rolling) mill

ble|cken ['blɛkn] VT **die Zähne ~** to bare or show one's teeth

Blei [blai] NT **-(e)s, -e** **a** no pl (abbr **Pb**) lead; **jdm wie ~ in den Gliedern** or **Knochen liegen** (Schreck) to paralyze sb; (Depression) to weigh sb down; **die Müdigkeit/Anstrengung lag ihm wie ~ in den Gliedern** or **Knochen** his whole body ached with tiredness/the exertion → **Magen** **b** (= Lot) plumb, plumb (plumb) bob **c** (= Munition) lead; (Typ) hot metal

Blei- in cpds lead; **Blei|ader** F lead vein

Blei|be ['blaibə] F **-, -n** **a** (= Unterkunft) place to stay; **eine/keine ~ haben** to have somewhere/nowhere to stay **b** (= Institution) home

blei|ben ['blaibn] pret **blieb** [bliːp], ptp **geblieben** [gə'bliːbn] VI aux sein **a** (= sich nicht verändern) to stay, to remain; **unbelohnt/unbestraft ~** to go unrewarded/unpunished; **unbeachtet ~** to go unnoticed, to escape notice; **unbeantwortet ~** to be left or to remain unanswered; **unvergessen ~** to continue to be remembered; **an Samstagen bleibt unser Geschäft geschlossen** this shop is closed on Saturdays; **in Verbindung ~** to keep or stay or remain in touch; **in Übung/Form ~** to keep in practice/form; **jdm in** or **jds Erinnerung ~** to stay or remain in sb's mind; **ruhig/still ~** to keep calm/quiet; **wach ~** to stay or keep awake; **Freunde ~** to stay or remain friends, to go on being friends

b (= sich nicht bewegen, zu Besuch bleiben) to stay; (= nicht weggehen, nicht zurückkommen) to stay, to remain; **sitzen/stehen ~** to stay sitting down/standing up, to remain seated/standing; **bitte, ~ Sie doch sitzen** please don't get up; **jdn zum Bleiben einladen** or **auffordern** to invite sb to stay; **von etw ~** to stay or keep away from sth; **wo bleibst du so lange?** (inf) what's keeping you (all this time)?; **wo bleibt er so**

lange? (inf) where has he got to?; **wo sind denn all die alten Häuser geblieben?** what (has) happened to all the old houses?, where have all the old houses gone (to)?; **hier ist meines Bleibens nicht (mehr** or **länger)** (geh) I cannot remain here (any longer) → **Ball ¹, Land c, Apparat c**

c (fig) **bei etw ~** to keep or stick (inf) to sth; **das bleibt unter uns** that's (just) between ourselves; **wir möchten für** or **unter uns ~** we want to keep ourselves to ourselves → **dabei g, Sache e**

d (= übrig bleiben) to be left, to remain; **es blieb mir keine andere Wahl/Möglichkeit** I had no other choice/possibility; **es blieb keine andere Wahl/Möglichkeit** there was no other choice/possibility; **es blieb mir keine Hoffnung** I lost all hope

e (= sein) **es bleibt abzuwarten** it remains to be seen; **es bleibt zu hoffen** or **wünschen, dass ...** I/we can only hope that ...

f (inf: = versorgt werden) **sie können (selber) sehen, wo sie ~** they'll just have to look out for themselves (inf); **und wo bleibe ich?** and what about me?; **sieh zu, wo du bleibst!** you're on your own! (inf), you'd better look out for yourself! (inf)

g (euph: = umkommen) **er ist auf See geblieben** he died at sea; **er ist im Krieg geblieben** he didn't come back from the war

blei|bend ADJ Wert, Erinnerung etc lasting; Schaden, Zähne permanent

blei|ben las|sen ▲ ptp **bleiben lassen** VT irreg (inf) **a** (= unterlassen) **etw ~** to give sth a miss (inf); **das werde ich/wirst du ganz schön ~** I'll/you'll do nothing of the sort! **b** (= aufgeben) to give up; **das Rauchen/Nägelkauen ~** to give up or to stop smoking/biting one's nails

Blei|be|recht NT **,** no pl right of residence

bleich [blaiç] ADJ pale; (fig) Grauen, Entsetzen sheer; **~ wie der Tod** deathly pale, pale as death

Blei|che ['blaiçə] F **-, -n** **a** no pl paleness; (von Mensch auch) pallor **b** (= Bleichplatz) bleachery (obs), green where sheets etc were laid out to be bleached by the sun

blei|chen ['blaiçn] VT to bleach VI pret **bleichte** or (old) **blich** ['blaiçtə, blɪç], ptp **gebleicht** or (old) **geblichen** to be or become bleached; **in der Sonne ~** to be bleached by the sun

Bleich-: Bleich|ge|sicht NT **a** (inf: = blasser Mensch) pasty-face (inf), pale-faced person **b** (= Weißer) paleface; **bleich|ge|sich|tig** [-gəzɪçtɪç] ADJ (inf) pale-faced, pasty-faced; **Bleich|mit|tel** NT bleach, bleaching agent; **Bleich|sucht** F (old Med) anaemia; **bleich|süch|tig** (old Med) anaemic

blei|ern ['blaiɐn] ADJ **a** attr (= aus Blei) lead; (fig) Farbe, Himmel leaden; **wie eine ~e Ente schwimmen** (hum) to swim like a brick **b** (fig) leaden; Beine like lead; Müdigkeit heavy; Verantwortung onerous ADV (fig) heavily; **die Verantwortung lastete ~ auf ihm/seiner Seele** the responsibility weighed heavily upon him/his mind; **es lag ihr ~ in den Gliedern** her limbs were like lead → **Magen**

Blei-: Blei|erz NT lead ore; **Blei|far|be** F lead paint; **blei|far|big, blei|far|ben** [-farbn] ADJ lead-coloured (Brit), lead-colored (US), lead-grey (Brit), lead-gray (US); Himmel leaden; **blei|frei** ADJ Benzin etc lead-free, unleaded ADV **~ fahren** to use lead-free or unleaded petrol (Brit) or gas (US); **mein Auto fährt ~** my car runs on lead-free or unleaded petrol (Brit) or gas (US); **Blei|frei** NT **-s,** no pl (= bleifreies Benzin) lead-free; **Blei|fuß** M **mit ~ fahren** (inf) to keep one's foot down, to drive with or to have a lead foot (US); **Blei|ge|halt** M lead content; **Blei|ge|wicht** NT lead weight; (Angeln) sinker; **Blei|gie|ßen** NT **-s,** no pl New Year's Eve custom of telling fortunes by the shapes made by molten lead dropped into cold wa-

---

ter; **Blei|glanz** M galena, galenite; **blei|grau** ADJ lead-grey (*Brit*), lead-gray (*US*); **blei|hal|tig** ADJ containing lead; *Erz, Gestein* plumbiferous (*spec*); *Benzin etc* leaded; **~/zu ~ sein** to contain lead/too much lead; **Blei|hüt|te** F lead works *pl*; **Blei|kris|tall** NT lead crystal; **Blei|ku|gel** F lead bullet, lead ball; **Blei|lot** NT plumb line; **Blei|men|ni|ge** F minium, red lead; **Blei|oxid** NT , **Blei|oxyd** NT lead oxide; **gelbes ~** lead monoxide; **rotes ~** red lead; **Blei|satz** M (*Typ*) hot-metal setting; **Blei|schür|ze** F lead apron; **blei|schwer** ADJ, **~ bleiern** ADJ b ADV; **Blei|sol|dat** M ≈ tin soldier

Blei|stift M pencil; (*zum Malen*) crayon; **mit/in ~** with a/in pencil

Blei|stift- *in cpds* pencil; **Blei|stift|ab|satz** M stiletto heel; **Blei|stift|spit|zer** M pencil sharpener

Blei-: **Blei|ver|gif|tung** F lead poisoning; **blei|ver|glast** ADJ leaded; **Blei|ver|gla|sung** F lead glazing; **Fenster mit ~** leaded windows; **blei|ver|seucht** [-fɛɛzɔʏçt] ADJ lead-polluted; **Blei|weiß** NT white lead

Blen|de ['blɛndə] F **-, -n** a (= *Lichtschutz*) shade, screen; (*Aut*) (sun) visor; (*an Fenster*) blind b (*Opt*) filter c (*Phot*) (= *Öffnung*) aperture; (= *Einstellungsposition*) f-stop; (= *Vorrichtung*) diaphragm; **die ~ schließen** to stop down; **bei** *or* **mit ~ 2.8** at (an aperture setting of) f/2.8 d (*Film, TV, Tontechnik: = Aufblende, Abblende*) fade e (*Naut*) deadlight f (*Archit*) (= *Fenster*) blind window; (= *Bogen*) blind arch g (*Sew*) trim h (= *Verkleidung*) cover i (*Geol*) blende

blen|den ['blɛndn] **VT** a (*lit, fig: = bezaubern*) to dazzle; (*fig geh: = täuschen auch*) to blind, to hoodwink b (= *blind machen*) to blind **VI** a (*Licht, Scheinwerfer*) to be dazzling; **~d weiß** (**sein**) (to be) shining *or* dazzling white b (*fig: = täuschen*) to dazzle

Blen|den|au|to|ma|tik F (*Phot*) automatic diaphragm

blen|dend *prp von* **blenden** ADJ splendid; *Pianist, Schüler etc* brilliant; *Laune, Stimmung* sparkling ADV splendidly; **es geht mir ~** I feel wonderful; **sich ~ amüsieren** to have a splendid *or* wonderful time

blen|dend|weiß △ ADJ *attr* → **blenden VI a**

Blen|den- (*Phot*): **Blen|den|ein|stel|lung** F aperture (setting); (= *Vorrichtung*) aperture control; **Blen|den|öff|nung** F aperture; **Blen|den|vor|wahl** F aperture priority

Blen|der ['blɛndɐ] M **-s, -**, **Blen|de|rin** [-ərɪn] F **-, -nen** phoney (*Brit inf*), phony (*US inf*)

Blend-: **blend|frei** ADJ dazzle-free; *Glas, Fernsehschirm* nonreflective; **Blend|gra|na|te** F (*Mil*) stun grenade; **Blend|la|ter|ne** F signalling (*Brit*) *or* signaling (*US*) lantern; **Blend|rah|men** M a (*Art*) canvas-stretcher b (*Build*) frame; **Blend|schutz** M a protection against dazzle (*Brit*) *or* glare (*US*) b (= *Vorrichtung*) antidazzle (*Brit*) *or* antiglare (*US*) device; **Blend|schutz|git|ter** NT , **Blend|schutz|zaun** M antidazzle (*Brit*) *or* antiglare (*US*) barrier

Blen|dung F **-, -en** a (= *das Blindmachen, Täuschen*) blinding b (= *das Geblendetsein*) blindness

Blend-: **Blend|werk** NT (*liter*) illusion; (= *Vortäuschung*) deception; **hinter einem ~ schöner Worte** *or* **aus schönen Worten** behind a screen of pretty words; **ein ~ des Teufels** *or* **der Hölle** a trap set by the devil; **Blend|zaun** M antidazzle (*Brit*) *or* antiglare (*US*) barrier

Bles|se ['blɛsə] F **-, -n** a (= *Fleck*) blaze b (= *Tier*) horse with a blaze

Bless|huhn ▲ ['blɛs-] NT coot → *auch* **Blässhuhn**

bles|sie|ren [blɛ'siːrən] *ptp* **blessiert** VT (*old: = verwunden*) to wound

Bles|sur [blɛ'suːɐ] F **-, -en** (*old*) wound

bleu [bløː] ADJ *inv* (*Fashion*) light blue

bleu|en △ ['blɔʏən] VT → **bläuen c**

---

blich (*old*) *pret von* **bleichen VI**

Blick [blɪk] ☼ 44.1 M **-(e)s, -e** a (= *das Blicken*) look; (= *flüchtiger Blick*) glance; **auf den ersten ~** at first glance; **Liebe auf den ersten ~** love at first sight; **auf den zweiten ~** when one looks (at it) again, the second time one looks (at it); **mit einem ~, auf einen ~** at a glance; **jds ~** (*dat*) **ausweichen** to avoid sb's eye; **jds ~ erwidern** to return sb's gaze; **~e miteinander wechseln** to exchange glances; **jdn mit (seinen) ~en verschlingen** to devour sb with one's eyes; **er folgte ihr mit ~en** *or* **mit dem ~** his eyes followed her; **sie zog alle ~e auf sich** everybody's eyes were drawn to her; **einen ~ auf etw** (*acc*) **tun** *or* **werfen** to throw a glance at sth; **einen ~ hinter die Kulissen tun** *or* **werfen** (*fig*) to take a look behind the scenes; **sie würdigte ihn keines ~es** she did not deign to look at him; **jdm einen ~ schenken** to look at sb; **jdm keinen ~ schenken** to not to spare sb a glance; **wenn ~e tö|ten könnten!** if looks could kill! → **durchbohren** [1]

b (= *Blickrichtung*) eyes *pl*; **mein ~ fiel auf sein leeres Glas** my eye fell on his empty glass; **von hier aus fällt der ~ auf den Dom** from here one can see the cathedral; **den ~ heben** to raise one's eyes, to look up; **den ~ senken** to look down

c (= *Augenausdruck*) expression *or* look in one's eyes; **den bösen ~ haben** to have the evil eye; **in ihrem ~ lag Verzweiflung** there was a look of despair in her eyes; **er musterte sie mit durchdringendem/finsterem ~** he looked at her penetratingly/darkly

d (= *Ausblick*) view; **ein Zimmer mit ~ auf den Park** a room with a view of the park, a room overlooking the park; **dem ~ entschwinden** (*geh*) to disappear from view *or* sight, to go out of sight; **etw aus dem ~ verlieren** to lose sight of sth; **mit ~ auf, im ~ auf** (*hinsichtlich*) in view of

e (= *Verständnis*) **seinen ~ für etw schärfen** to increase one's awareness of sth; **einen klaren ~ haben** to see things clearly; **einen (guten) ~ für etw haben** to have an eye *or* a good eye for sth; **er hat keinen ~ dafür** he doesn't see *or* notice that sort of thing; **etw in den ~ nehmen** (= *berücksichtigen*) to take account of sth

blick|dicht ADJ *Strümpfe* opaque

bli|cken ['blɪkn] **VI** (*auf +acc* at) to look; (= *flüchtig blicken*) to glance; (*fig: = hervorsehen*) to peep; **sich ~ lassen** to put in an appearance; **lass dich hier ja nicht mehr ~!** don't let me see you here again!, don't show your face here again!; **lass dich doch mal wieder ~!** why don't you drop in some time?; **danach hat er sich nie wieder ~ lassen** after that he was never seen again; **das lässt tief ~** that's very revealing **VT** (*inf: = verstehen*) to get

Blick-: **Blick|fang** M eye-catcher; **als ~** to catch the eye; **Blick|feld** NT field of vision; **ein enges ~ haben** (*fig*) to have narrow horizons; **ins ~** (*der Öffentlichkeit*) **rücken** to become the focus of (public) attention; **Blick|kon|takt** M eye contact; **Blick|punkt** M a (= *Zentrum der Aufmerksamkeit*) centre (*Brit*) *or* center (*US*) of one's field of vision; **im ~ der Öffentlichkeit stehen** to be in the public eye b (*fig: = Standpunkt*) viewpoint, point of view; **Blick|rich|tung** F line of vision *or* sight; (*fig*) outlook; **in ~ (nach) links** looking to the left; **Blick|wech|sel** M exchange of glances; (*fig*) change in one's viewpoint; **Blick|win|kel** M angle of vision; (*fig*) viewpoint

blind [blɪnt] ADJ a (*lit, fig*) blind (*für* to); *Zufall* pure, sheer; *Alarm* false; **~ für etw sein, ~ in Be|zug auf etw** (*acc*) **sein** (*fig*) to be blind to sth; **ich bin doch nicht ~!** (*fig*) I'm not blind; **~ ge|boren** blind from birth; **jdn ~ machen** (*lit, fig*) to blind sb, to make sb blind; **ein ~es Huhn findet auch mal ein Korn** (*Prov*) anyone can be lucky now and again; **~er Fleck** (*Anat*) blind spot; **in ~er Liebe** blinded with love; **ihr Blick war von** *or* **vor Tränen** ~ she was blinded with tears; **~e**

Gewalt brute force; **~er Eifer** blind enthusiasm; **~er Eifer schadet nur** (*Prov*) it's not a good thing to be overenthusiastic; **ein ~er Schuss** (= *nicht scharf*) a shot with a blank cartridge; (= *nicht gezielt*) a blind shot

b (= *getrübt*) dull; *Spiegel, Glasscheibe* clouded; *Fleck* blind

c (= *verdeckt*) *Naht etc* invisible; (= *vorgetäuscht, Archit*) false; *Fenster, Tür* blind, false; **ein ~er Passa|gier** a stowaway

d (*sl: = betrunken*) pissed (*Brit inf*), plastered (*inf*)

ADV a (= *wahllos*) at random, indiscriminately; **etw ~ herausgreifen** to take *or* pick sth at random; **~ in etw** (*acc*) **hineingreifen** to put one's hand in sth without looking

b (= *ohne zu überlegen*) folgen, vertrauen, glauben blindly; **jdm ~ gehorchen** to obey sb blindly

c (= *ohne zu sehen*) without being able to see; **~ landen** (*Aviat*) to make a blind landing, to land blind; **~ (Schach) spielen** to play (chess) blind; **der Nebel war so dicht, dass ich ~ fahren musste** the fog was so thick that I had to drive without being able to see anything

Blind-: **Blind|band** [-bant] M *pl* **-bände** (*Typ*) dummy; **Blind|be|wer|bung** F speculative (*Brit*) *or* unsolicited *or* cold (*US inf*) application; **Blind|bo|den** M (*Archit*) subfloor

Blind|darm M (*Anat*) caecum (*Brit*), cecum (*US*); (*inf: = Wurmfortsatz*) appendix

Blind|darm-: **Blind|darm|ent|zün|dung** F appendicitis; **Blind|darm|ope|ra|ti|on** F append(ic)ectomy; **Blind|darm|rei|zung** F grumbling appendix

Blin|de|kuh *no art* (= *Spiel*) blind man's buff

Blin|den-: **Blin|den|an|stalt** F home for the blind; **Blin|den|füh|rer(in)** M(F) blind person's guide; **Blin|den|hund** M guide dog; **Blin|den|schrift** F braille; **Blin|den|schu|le** F school for the blind; **Blin|den|sen|dung** F (*Post*) mail *no pl* for the blind

Blin|de(r) ['blɪndə] MF *decl as adj* blind person/ man/woman *etc*; **die ~n** the blind; **die ~n und die Lahmen** (*Bibl*) the lame and the blind; **das sieht doch ein ~r (mit dem Krückstock)** (*hum inf*) any fool can see that; **unter den ~n ist der Einäugige König** (*Prov*) in the country of the blind the one-eyed man is king (*prov*); **der ~ verlacht den Lahmen** (*Prov*) the pot calling the kettle black; **von etw reden, wie der ~ von der Farbe** (*prov*) to talk about sth when one knows nothing about it

Blind-: **Blind|fens|ter** NT false window; **blind flie|gen** ▲ *irreg aux sein* to fly blind; **Blind|flug** M blind flight; (= *das Blindfliegen*) blind flying; **das kann ich im ~ machen** (*fig inf*) I can do that in my sleep (*fig*); **Blind|gän|ger** [1] [-ɡɛŋɐ] M **-s, -** (*Mil*) dud (shot); **Blind|gän|ger** [2] [-ɡɛŋɐ] M **-s, -**, **Blind|gän|ge|rin** [-ərɪn] F **-, -nen** (*inf: = Versager*) dud (*inf*), dead loss (*inf*); **blind|ge|bo|ren** △ ADJ *attr* → **blind** ADJ a; **Blind|ge|bo|re|ne(r)** [-ɡəbo:rənə] MF *decl as adj* person blind from birth; **blind|gläu|big** ADJ credulous ADV folgen, vertrauen blindly; **Blind|heit** F *no pl* (*lit, fig*) blindness; **jdn mit ~ schlagen** (*Bibl, liter*) to strike sb blind; **wie mit ~ geschlagen** (*fig*) as though blind; **mit ~ geschlagen sein** (*fig*) to be blind; **Blind|lan|dung** F blind *or* instrument landing; **blind|lings** ['blɪntlɪŋs] ADV blindly; **Blind|ma|te|ri|al** NT (*Typ*) leads *pl*; **Blind|schlei|che** [-ʃlaɪçə] F **-, -n** slowworm; **blind schrei|ben** ▲ VTI *irreg* to touch-type; **Blind|schreib|ver|fah|ren** NT touch-typing; **Blind|spiel** NT (*Chess*) blind game; **blind spie|len** ▲ VI to play blind; **Blind|start** M (*Aviat*) blind takeoff; **Blind|ver|such** M (*Med, Psych*) blind test; **blind|wü|tig** ADJ *Mensch* in a blind rage; *Angriff* furious ADV in a blind rage, furiously

blin|ken ['blɪŋkn] **VI** a (= *funkeln*) to gleam b (= *Blinkzeichen geben*) (*Boje, Leuchtturm*) to flash; (*Aut*) to indicate **VT** *Signal* to flash; **SOS ~** to flash an SOS (signal); **rechts/links ~** to indicate right/left; **er hat mir geblinkt, dass ich überholen kann** he signalled for me to overtake (*Brit*), he signaled for me to pass (*US*)

Blin|ker ['blɪŋkɐ] M **-s, -** **a** (*Aut*) indicator (*esp Brit*), winker (*Brit inf*), turn signal (*US*), blinker (*US inf*) **b** (*Angeln*) spinner

blin|kern ['blɪŋkn] VI **a** (*inf:* = *blinken*) to flash; **er blinkerte mit den Augen** he blinked **b** (*Angeln*) to use a spinner

Blink-: Blink|feu|er NT flashing light; **Blink|leuch|te** F indicator (*esp Brit*), turn signal (*US*), **Blink|licht** NT flashing light; (*inf:* = *Blinkleuchte*) indicator (*esp Brit*), winker (*Brit inf*), turn signal (*US*), blinker (*US inf*) **Blink|licht|an|la|ge** F warning light system; **Blink|zei|chen** NT signal

blin|zeln ['blɪntsln], **blin|zen** ['blɪntsn] (*dated*) VI to blink; (= *zwinkern*) to wink; (*geblendet*) to squint

Blitz [blɪts] M **-es, -e** **a** (= *das Blitzen*) lightning *no pl, no indef art*; (= *Blitzstrahl*) flash of lightning; (= *Lichtstrahl*) flash (of light); **vom ~ getroffen/erschlagen werden** to be struck by lightning; **wie vom ~ getroffen** (*fig*) thunderstruck; **aus ihren Augen schossen** or **sprühten ~e** her eyes flashed; **einschlagen wie ein ~** (*fig*) to be a bombshell; **die Nachricht schlug überall wie ein ~ ein** the news came as a bombshell to everyone; **wie ein ~ aus heiterem Himmel** (*fig*) like a bolt from the blue; **wie der ~** (*inf*) like lightning; **laufen wie ein geölter ~** (*inf*) to run like greased lightning; **die Antwort kam wie ein geölter ~** (*inf*) the answer came in a flash **b** (*Phot inf*) flash; (= *Blitzlichtgerät*) flash(gun)

Blitz- *in cpds* (*esp Mil:* = *schnell*) lightning; **Blitz|ab|lei|ter** M lightning conductor; **jdn als ~ benutzen** or **missbrauchen** to vent one's anger on sb; **Blitz|ak|ti|on** F lightning operation; **Blitz|an|griff** M (*Mil*) lightning attack; **der ~ auf London** the London Blitz; **blitz|ar|tig** ADJ lightning *attr* ADV (= *schnell*) reagieren like lightning; (= *plötzlich*) verschwinden in a flash; **Blitz|be|such** M (*inf*) flying or lightning visit

blitz|e|blank ['blɪtsə'blaŋk], **blitz|blank** ['blɪts'blaŋk] (*inf*) ADJ spick and span ADV *putzen, polieren* until it shines

Blitz|ein|bruch M (*inf:* = *Verbrechen*) ram raid

blit|zen ['blɪtsn] VI *impers* **es blitzt** there is lightning; (*mehrmals auch*) there are flashes of lightning; **es blitzt und donnert** there is thunder and lightning; **hat es eben geblitzt?** was that (a flash of) lightning?; **es fing an zu ~** lightning began; **bei dir blitzt es** (*hum inf*) your slip is showing, Charlie's dead (*Brit inf*); **gleich blitzt es!** there'll be trouble VI **a** (= *strahlen*) to flash; (*Gold, Zähne*) to sparkle; **vor Sauberkeit ~** to be sparkling clean; **Zorn blitzte aus seinen Augen** his eyes flashed with anger **b** (*inf:* = *unbekleidet flitzen*) to streak **c** (*Phot inf*) to use (a) flash VI **a** (*Phot inf*) to take a flash photograph of; (*inf: in Radarfalle*) to flash

Blit|zer ['blɪtsɐ] M **-s, -**, **Blit|ze|rin** F **-, -nen** (*inf*) streaker

Blit|zes|schnel|le F lightning speed; **mit ~** at lightning speed; **in ~** in a flash

Blitz-: Blitz|ge|rät NT (*Phot*) flash(gun); **blitz|ge|scheit** ADJ (*inf*) brilliant; **Blitz|ge|spräch** NT special priority telephone call; **Blitz|kaf|fee** M (*Sw*) instant coffee; **Blitz|kar|ri|e|re** F rapid rise; **eine ~ machen** to rise rapidly; **Blitz|krieg** M blitzkrieg

Blitz|licht NT (*Phot*) flash(light)

Blitzlicht-: Blitz|licht|auf|nah|me F flash shot; **Blitz|licht|bir|ne** F flashbulb; **Blitz|licht|ge|wit|ter** NT popping of flashbulbs; **Blitz|licht|wür|fel** M flashcube

Blitz-: Blitz|mer|ker [-mɛrkɐ] M **-s, -**, **Blitz|mer|ke|rin** [-ərɪn] F **-, -nen** (*inf: usu iro*) bright spark (*inf*); **Blitz|rei|se** F flying visit; **blitz|sau|ber** ADJ spick and span ADV *putzen, polie-*

ren until it shines; **Blitz|scha|den** M damage caused by lightning; **Blitz|schlag** M flash of lightning; **vom ~ getroffen** struck by lightning; **blitz|schnell** ADJ lightning *attr* ADV like lightning; (= *plötzlich*) verschwinden in a flash; **Blitz|schutz|an|la|ge** F lightning protection equipment; **Blitz|sieg** M lightning victory; **Blitz|start** M lightning or jump start; **Blitz|strahl** M flash of lightning; **Blitz|um|fra|ge** F quick poll; **Blitz|wür|fel** M (*Phot*) flashcube

Bliz|zard ['blɪzɐt] M **-s, -s** blizzard

Bloch [blɔx] M OR NT **-(e)s, -e** or **=er** ['blœçə] (*S Ger, Aus*) log

Block [blɔk] M **-(e)s, -s** or **=e** ['blœkə] **a** block (*von, aus of*); (*von Seife, Schokolade*) bar **b** *pl auch* **-s** (= *Häuserblock, Haus, Reaktorblock*) block **c** *pl auch* **-s** (= *Papierblock*) pad; (= *Briefmarkenblock*) block; (*von Fahrkarten*) book **d** *pl* **-s** (*Rail*) block **e** (= *Zusammengefasstes*) block; **etw im ~ kaufen** to buy sth in bulk **f** *pl auch* **-s** (*Pol*) = *Staatenblock*) bloc; (= *Fraktion*) faction **g** (*NS*) smallest organizational unit of Nazi party based on a block of houses **h** (*Sport*) wall *pl auch* **-s** (*inf:* = *Blockierung*) (mental) block **k** (*Comput*) block **i** (= *Folterblock*) stocks *pl* **k** (*Comput*) block

Blo|cka|de [blɔ'kaːdə] F **-, -n** (= *Absperrung*) blockade; **eine ~ brechen** to run or break a blockade

Blo|cka|de|bre|cher(in) M(F) blockade runner

Block-: Block|bau M **a** *pl* **-bauten** (= *Gebäude*) log cabin **b** *no pl* (*auch* **Blockbauweise**) method of building houses from logs; **Block|bil|dung** F (*Pol*) formation of blocs; (= *Fraktionsbildung*) formation of factions; **Block|buch|sta|be** M block letter or capital; **Block|di|a|gramm** NT block diagram

blo|cken ['blɔkn] VTI **a** (*Rail*) to block **b** (*Hunt*) to perch **c** (= *abfangen*) to block, to stop; (= *verhindern*) to block, to stall **d** (*Sport:* = *sperren*) to block **e** (*dial:* = *bohnern*) to polish **f** (*Comput*) to block

Blo|cker ['blɔkɐ] M **-s, -** (*S Ger:* = *Bohner*) floor--polishing brush

Block-: Block|flö|te F recorder; (*Pol sl:* = *Person*) fellow traveller (*Brit*) or traveler (*US*), comrade; **block|frei** ADJ nonaligned; **Block|frei|heit** F nonalignment; **Block|haus** NT log cabin; **Block|heiz|kraft|werk** NT block heating and generating plant; **Block|hüt|te** F log cabin

blo|ckie|ren [blɔ'kiːrən] *ptp* **blockiert** VT **a** (= *sperren, hemmen*) to block; *Verkehr, Verhandlung* to obstruct; *Flugverkehr* to halt; *Gesetz* to block the passage of; *Rad, Lenkung* to lock **b** (= *mit Blockade belegen*) to blockade VI to jam; (*Bremsen, Rad etc*) to lock

Blo|ckie|rung F **-, -en** blocking; (*von Verkehr, Verhandlung*) obstruction; (*von Rad, Lenkung*) locking; (= *Blockade*) blockade

Block-: Block|lei|ter(in) M(F) (*NS*) block leader; **Block|malz** NT type of cough drop; **Block|par|tei** F (*esp DDR*) party in a faction; **Block|po|li|tik** F joint policy; **Block|satz** M (*Typ*) justification; **Block|scho|ko|la|de** F , *no pl* cooking chocolate; **Block|schrift** F block capitals *pl* or letters *pl*; **Block|staat** M aligned state; **Block|sta|ti|on** F , **Block|stel|le** F (*Rail*) block signal; **Block|stun|de** F (*Sch*) double period; **Block|sys|tem** NT **a** (*Rail*) block system **b** (*Pol*) system of factions; **Block|un|ter|richt** M (*Sch*) teaching by topics; **Block|wart** [-vart] M **-(e)s, -e**, **Block|war|tin** [-vartɪn] F **-, -nen** (*NS*) block leader; **Block|werk** NT (*Rail*) block signal

blöd [bløːt], **blö|de** ['bløːdə] (*inf*) ADJ **a** (= *dumm*) silly, stupid, idiotic; *Wetter* terrible; *Gefühl* funny; **das Blöde daran ist, dass ...** the silly *etc* thing about it is that ... **b** (*Med:* = *schwachsinnig*) imbecilic **c** (*Sw:* = *schüchtern*) shy **d** (*S Ger:* = *abgescheuert*) worn ADV (= *dumm*) stu-

pidly, idiotically; **~ fragen** to ask stupid questions

Blö|del ['bløːdl] M **-s, -** (*inf*) stupid fool (*inf*) or idiot (*inf*); (= *ungeschickter Mensch*) clumsy fool (*inf*) or idiot (*inf*)

Blö|de|lei F **-, -en** (*inf*) (= *Albernheit*) messing (*inf*) or fooling around; (= *Witz*) joke; (= *dumme Streiche*) pranks *pl*; **lass die ~** stop messing (*inf*) or fooling around

blö|deln ['bløːdln] VI (*inf*) to mess (*inf*) or fool around; (= *Witze machen*) to make jokes; **mit jdm ~** to have fun with sb

blö|der|wei|se ['bløːdɐˈvaizə] ADV (*inf*) stupidly

Blöd|heit F **-, -en** **a** (= *Dummheit*) stupidity **b** (= *blödes Verhalten*) stupid thing; (= *alberne Bemerkung*) silly or stupid remark; **es ist eine ~, das zu machen** it's stupid to do that **c** (*Med:* = *Schwachsinnigkeit*) imbecility **d** (*Sw:* = *Schüchternheit*) shyness

Blö|di|an ['bløːdiaːn] M **-(e)s, -e** (*inf*) idiot

Blöd|mann M *pl* **-männer** (*inf*) stupid fool (*inf*)

Blöd|sinn M , *no pl* **a** (= *Unsinn*) nonsense, rubbish; (= *Unfug*) stupid tricks *pl*; **so ein ~** what nonsense or rubbish/how stupid; **das ist doch ~** that's nonsense or rubbish/stupid; **~ machen** to fool or mess around; **wer hat diesen ~ hier gemacht?** what fool did this?; **mach keinen ~** don't fool or mess around **b** (= *Schwachsinn*) imbecility

blöd|sin|nig ADJ **a** stupid, idiotic **b** (*Med*) imbecilic

Blöd|sin|nig|keit F **-, -en** (*inf*) **a** (= *Eigenschaft*) stupidity, idiocy **b** (= *Verhalten*) stupid thing; **lass diese ~en** stop being stupid

blö|ken ['bløːkn] VI (*Schaf*) to bleat; (*geh: Rinder*) to low

blond [blɔnt] ADJ **a** (= *blondhaarig*) *Frau* blonde, fair(-haired); *Mann, Menschenrasse* blond, fair-haired; **~es Gift** (*hum inf*) blonde bombshell (*inf*) **b** (*hum inf:* = *hellfarbig*) light--coloured (*Brit*), light-colored (*US*); *Bier* light, pale ADV **~ gefärbt** dyed blond; (*bei Frauen auch*) dyed blonde; **sich** (*dat*) **die Haare ~ färben** to dye one's hair blond or (*Frau auch*) blonde; **~ gelockt** with fair curly hair; *Haar* fair curly *attr*; **~ gelockt sein** to have fair curly hair

Blond [blɔnt] NT **-s**, *no pl* blonde, blond

Blon|de(s) ['blɔndə] NT *decl as adj* (*inf:* = *Bier*) ≈ lager

Blond-: blond|ge|färbt △ ADJ *attr* → **blond** ADV; **blond|ge|lockt** △ ADJ → **blond** ADV; **blond|haa|rig** ADJ fair-haired; *Frau auch* blonde; *Mann, Rasse auch* blond

blon|die|ren [blɔnˈdiːrən] *ptp* **blondiert** VT to bleach; **blondiert** (*Haare*) bleached

Blon|die|rung F **-, -en** **a** (= *Vorgang*) bleaching **b** (= *Zustand*) bleachedness

Blon|di|ne [blɔnˈdiːnə] F **-, -n** blonde

Blond-: Blond|kopf M **a** (*von Frau*) fair or blonde hair or head; (*von Mann*) fair or blond hair or head **b** (*Frau/Mädchen*) fair-haired or blonde woman/girl; (*Mann/Junge*) fair-haired or blond man/boy; **blond|lo|ckig** ADJ *Frau* with fair or blonde curly hair; *Mann* with fair or blond curly hair; **Blond|schopf** M = **Blondkopf**

bloß [bloːs] ADJ **a** (= *unbedeckt*) bare; **etw auf der ~en Haut tragen** to wear sth without anything on underneath; **mit ~en Füßen** barefooted, barefoot; **mit der ~en Hand** with one's bare hand → **Oberkörper** **b** *attr* (= *alleinig*) mere; *Neid, Dummheit* sheer; (= *allein schon*) *Gedanke, Anblick* very, mere; **er kam mit dem ~en Schrecken davon** he got off with no more than a fright ADV only; **ich möchte es schon machen, ~ weiß ich nicht wie** I'd like to but or only I don't know how; **wie kann so etwas ~ geschehen?** how on earth can something like that happen?; **was er ~ hat?** what on earth or whatever is wrong with him?; **tu das ~ nicht wieder!** don't you dare do that again; **geh mir ~ aus dem Weg** just get out of my way; **nicht ~ ...,** **sondern auch ...** not only ... but also ...

Blö|ße ['blø:sə] F **-, -n a** (geh) (= Unbedecktheit) bareness; (= Nacktheit) nakedness **b** (im Wald) clearing **c** (Sport) opening; **jdm eine ~ bieten** (lit) to drop one's guard with sb; (fig) to show sb one's ignorance; **sich** (dat) **eine ~ geben** (fig) to reveal or show one's ignorance

Bloß-: **bloß+le|gen** VT sep to uncover; (= ausgraben auch, Med) to expose; (fig) Geheimnis to reveal; Hintergründe to bring to light; **bloß+lie|gen** VI sep irreg aux sein to be or lie uncovered; (Ausgegrabenes auch, Med) to be exposed; (fig geh, Geheimnis) to be revealed; **bloß+stel|len** sep VT jdn to show up; Lügner, Betrüger to unmask, to expose VR to show oneself up, to expose oneself; **Bloß|stel|lung** F showing up; (von Lügner, Betrüger) unmasking; **bloß+stram|peln** VR sep to kick one's covers off

Blou|son [blu'zõ:] M OR NT **-(s), -s** blouson (Brit), bomber jacket

Blow-out ▲ ['bloaut] M **-s, -s, Blow|out** M **-s, -s** (von Bohrinsel etc) blowout

blub|bern ['blʊbɐn] VI (inf) to bubble; (dial: = undeutlich sprechen) to gabble; (= Blödsinn reden) to waffle (inf)

Blü|cher ['bly:çɐ] M **er geht ran wie ~** (inf) he doesn't hang about (inf)

Blue|jeans ▲ ['blu:dʒi:ns] PL **, Blue Jeans** PL (pair of) (blue) jeans or denims

Blues [blu:s] M **-, -** blues sing or pl; **(einen) ~ tanzen** to smooch (inf)

Bluff [blʊf, (dated) blœf] M **-(e)s, -s** bluff

bluf|fen ['blʊfn, (dated) 'blœfn] VTI to bluff

blü|hen ['bly:ən] VI **a** (Blume) to be in flower or bloom, to bloom, to flower; (Bäume) to be in blossom, to blossom; (Garten, Wiese) to be full of flowers; (fig: = gedeihen) to flourish, to thrive; **weiß ~** to have or bear white flowers **b** (inf: = bevorstehen) to be in store (jdm for sb); **... dann blüht dir aber was** ... then you'll be in for it (inf); **das kann mir auch noch ~** that may happen to me too VI impers **es blüht** there are flowers

blü|hend ADJ Baum blossoming; Blume, Pflanze auch blooming; Garten, Wiese, Feld full of flowers; (fig) Aussehen radiant; Geschäft, Handel, Industrie, Kultur, Stadt flourishing, thriving; Fantasie vivid, lively; Unsinn absolute; Zukunft glowing; **~e Landschaften** green pastures; **ein wirtschaftlich ~es Land** a country with a thriving economy; **wie das ~e Leben aussehen, ~ aussehen** to look the very picture of health

Blüm|chen ['bly:mçən] NT **-s, -** dim von **Blume**

Blüm|chen-: **Blüm|chen|kaf|fee** M (hum) weak coffee; **Blüm|chen|mus|ter** NT (small) floral pattern

Blu|me ['blu:mə] F **-, -n a** (= Blüte, Pflanze) flower; (= Topfblume) pot plant; (poet: = Frau) pearl; **vielen Dank für die ~** (iro) thanks for nothing, thank you very much (iro); **jdm etw durch die ~ sagen/zu verstehen geben** to say/put sth in a roundabout way to sb; **die blaue ~ der Romantik** the blue flower (symbol of German Romanticism) **b** (von Wein, Weinbrand) bouquet; (von Bier) head **c** (Hunt) (von Kaninchen, Hasen) scut; (von Fuchs) tag

Blu|men- in cpds flower; **Blu|men|bank** F pl **-bänke** (am Fenster) windowsill; (= Blumenständer) flower stand; **Blu|men|beet** NT flowerbed; **Blu|men|bin|der(in)** M(F) florist; **Blu|men|blatt** NT petal; **Blu|men|bu|kett** NT (old) bouquet (of flowers); **Blu|men|draht** M florist's wire; **Blu|men|dün|ger** M plant feed; **Blu|men|er|de** F potting compost; **Blu|men|fens|ter** NT window full of flowers; (Archit) window for keeping and displaying flowers and pot plants; **Blu|men|flor** M (liter) abundance of flowers; **Blu|men|frau** F flower

woman; **Blu|men|ge|schäft** NT flower shop; (Brit auch) florist('s); (US auch) florist; **blu|men|ge|schmückt** [-gəʃmʏkt] ADJ adorned with flowers; **Blu|men|gruß** M jdm einen ~ übermitteln to send sb flowers; **Blu|men|händ|ler(in)** M(F) florist; **Blu|men|igel** M pinholder; **Blu|men|kas|ten** M window box; **Blu|men|kind** NT (inf) flower child, hippie; **~er** flower children or people, hippies; **Blu|men|kohl** M , no pl cauliflower; **Blu|men|kohl|ohr** NT (inf) cauliflower ear; **Blu|men|kor|so** M flower carnival; **Blu|men|kranz** M floral wreath; **Blu|men|kü|bel** M flower tub; **Blu|men|la|den** M flower shop, florist('s) (esp Brit), florist (esp US); **Blu|men|mäd|chen** NT flower girl; **Blu|men|meer** NT sea of flowers; **Blu|men|mus|ter** NT floral pattern; **Blu|men|pracht** F brilliant display of flowers; **Blu|men|ra|bat|te** F herbaceous border; **blu|men|reich** ADJ full of flowers, flowery; (fig) Stil, Sprache etc flowery, ornate ADV (fig) sprechen in a flowery way; schreiben in a flowery style; **Blu|men|schmuck** M flower arrangement(s pl), floral decoration(s pl); **Blu|men|spra|che** F language of flowers; **Blu|men|stän|der** M flower stand; **Blu|men|stock** M flowering plant; **Blu|men|strauß** M pl **-sträu|ße** bouquet or bunch of flowers; **Blu|men|stück** NT (Art) flower painting; **Blu|men|tep|pich** M carpet of flowers; **Blu|men|topf** M flowerpot; (= Pflanze) flowering plant; **damit ist kein ~ zu gewinnen** (inf) there's nothing to write home about (inf); **Blu|men|topf|er|de** F potting compost; **Blu|men|va|se** F (flower) vase; **Blu|men|zucht** F growing of flowers, floriculture (form); **Blu|men|züch|ter(in)** M(F) flower grower, floriculturist (form); **Blu|men|zwie|bel** F bulb

blü|me|rant [blymə'rant] ADJ Gefühl strange; **jdm wird es ~** sb feels strange

blu|mig ['blu:mɪç] ADJ Parfüm flowery; Wein auch with a flowery bouquet; (fig) Stil, Sprache ornate, flowery

Blu|mig|keit F **-,** no pl floweriness; (fig auch) ornateness

Blüs|chen ['bly:sçən] NT **-s, -** dim von **Bluse**

Blu|se ['blu:zə] F **-, -n** blouse

Blü|se ['bly:zə] F **-, -n** (Naut) flare

blu|sig ['blu:zɪç] ADJ bloused, blouse attr

Blut [blu:t] NT **-(e)s,** no pl (lit, fig) blood; **~ bildend** haematinic (Brit spec), hematinic (US spec); Nahrung für alle to feed; **jdm ~ abnehmen** to take blood from sb; **er lag in seinem ~** he lay in a pool of blood; **es ist viel ~ vergossen worden** or **geflossen** there was a lot of bloodshed; **nach ~ lechzen** or **dürsten** to thirst for blood; **er kann kein ~ sehen** he can't stand the sight of blood; **~ lecken** (lit: Hund) to taste blood; (fig) to develop a taste or liking for it; **etw mit seinem ~ besiegeln** to lay down one's life for sth; **böses ~ machen** or **schaffen** or **geben** to cause bad blood or ill feeling; **jdm steigt das ~ in den Kopf** the blood rushes to sb's head; **ihnen gefror** or **stockte** or **gerann das ~ in den Adern** their blood froze; **ihm kocht das ~ in den Adern** his blood is boiling; **vor Scham/Zorn schoss ihr das ~ ins Gesicht** she blushed with shame/went red with anger; **alles ~ wich aus ihrem Gesicht** she went deathly pale; **blaues ~ haben** (= adelig sein) to have blue blood; **heißes** or **feuriges ~ haben** to be hot-blooded; **etw im ~ haben** to have sth in one's blood; **das liegt mir im ~** it's in my blood; **kaltes ~ bewahren** to remain unmoved; **kalten ~es** cold-bloodedly; **(nur) ruhig ~** keep your shirt on (inf); **jdn bis aufs ~ hassen** to loathe (and detest) sb; **jdn/sich bis aufs ~ bekämpfen** to fight sb/fight bitterly; **jdn bis aufs ~ reizen** (inf) to make sb's blood boil; **ein junges ~** (liter) a young blood (dated) or (Mädchen) thing; **frisches ~** (fig) new blood; **~ und Eisen** blood and iron; **~ und Boden** (NS) blood and soil, idea that political stability and power depend on unification of

race and territory **~ und Wasser schwitzen** (inf) to sweat blood; **die Stimme des ~es** the call of the blood; **es geht (einem) ins ~** it gets into your blood

Blut-: **Blut|acker** M (Bibl) field of blood; **Blut|ader** F vein; **Blut|al|gen** PL red algae pl; **Blut|al|ko|hol** M , **Blut|al|ko|hol|ge|halt** M ; **Blut|al|ko|hol|spie|gel** M blood alcohol level or content; **Blut|ana|ly|se** F (Med) blood analysis; **Blut|an|drang** M congestion; **Blut|ap|fel|si|ne** F blood orange; **blut|arm** ADJ **a** ['blu:t|arm] (Med) anaemic (Brit), anemic (US); (fig auch) colourless (Brit), colorless (US) **b** [blu:t'arm] (liter) very poor, penniless; **Blut|ar|mut** F (Med) anaemia (Brit), anemia (US); **Blut|auf|fri|schung** F blood replacement; **Blut|aus|tausch** M (Med) exchange transfusion; **Blut|bad** NT bloodbath; **Blut|bahn** F bloodstream; **Blut|bank** F pl **-banken** blood bank; **Blut|bann** M power over life and death; **blut|be|fleckt** ADJ (lit, fig) bloodstained; **blut|be|schmiert** [-bəʃmi:ɐt] ADJ smeared with blood; **blut|be|spritzt** [-bəʃprɪtst] ADJ blood-spattered; **Blut|beu|tel** M blood bag; **Blut|bild** NT blood count; **blut|bil|dend** ADJ △ → **Blut**; **Blut|bil|dung** F formation of blood, blood formation; **Blut|bla|se** F blood blister; **Blut|bu|che** F copper beech

Blut|druck M , no pl blood pressure

Blut|druck-: **blut|druck|er|hö|hend** ADJ, ADV = bludrucksteigernd; **Blut|druck|mes|ser** M **-s, -, Blut|druck|mess|ge|rät** ▲ NT (Med) blood pressure gauge; **Blut|druck|mes|sung** F blood pressure reading; **eine stündliche ~ wäre ratsam** taking an hourly blood pressure reading would be advisable; **blut|druck|sen|kend** ADJ hypotensive; Mittel antihypertensive ADV **~ sein** or **wirken** to reduce high blood pressure; **blut|druck|stei|gernd** ADJ hypertensive; Mittel antihypotensive ADV **~ sein** or **wirken** to increase low blood pressure

Blut-: **Blut|durst** M (geh) blood lust; **blut|dürs|tig** [-dʏrstɪç] ADJ (geh) bloodthirsty

Blü|te ['bly:tə] F **-, -n a** (Bot: = Pflanzenteil) (von Blume) flower, bloom; (von Baum) blossom; **~n treiben** to be in flower or bloom, to be flowering or blooming; (Baum) to be blossoming or in blossom; **seltsame ~n treiben** to produce strange effects; (Fantasie, Angst) to produce strange ideas; **eine ~ seiner Fantasie** a figment of his imagination **b** (= das Blühen, Blütezeit) **zur ~ des Klees** when the clover is in flower or bloom; **zur ~ der Kirschbäume** when the cherry trees are blossoming or in blossom; **die ~ beginnt** the flowers are coming into bloom; (bei Bäumen) the trees are coming into blossom; **die ~ der Apfelbäume ist vorüber** the apple trees are no longer blossoming or in blossom; **in (voller) ~ stehen** to be in (full) flower (esp Brit) or blossom; (Bäume) to be in (full) blossom; (Kultur, Geschäft) to be flourishing; **sich zur vollen ~ entfalten** to come into full flower; (Mädchen, Kultur) to blossom; **seine ~ erreichen** or **erleben** (Kultur etc) to reach its peak; **ein Zeitalter kultureller ~** an age of cultural ascendency; **in der ~ seiner Jahre** in his prime, in the prime of his life; **eine neue ~ erleben** to undergo a revival **c** (Med: = Ausschlag) rash, efflorescence (spec) **d** (inf: = gefälschte Note) dud (inf)

Blut|egel M leech

blu|ten ['blu:tn] VI to bleed (an +dat, aus from); **mir blutet das Herz** my heart bleeds; **~den Herzens** with heavy heart; **für etw (schwer) ~** (inf) to cough up a lot of money for sth (inf)

Blüt-: **Blü|ten|blatt** NT petal; **Blü|ten|ho|nig** M honey (made from flowers); **Blü|ten|kelch** M calyx; **Blü|ten|knos|pe** F flower bud; **blü|ten|los** ADJ nonflowering; **Blü|ten|meer** NT sea of blossom(s); **Blü|ten|pflan|ze** F flowering plant; **Blü|ten|ran|ke** F blossom tendril; **Blü|ten|stand** M inflorescence; **Blü|ten|staub** M pollen

Blut|ent|nah|me F taking of a blood sample

Blü|ten|zweig M flowering twig

Blu|ter ['bluːtɐ] M **-s, -** (Med) haemophiliac (Brit), hemophiliac (US)

Blut|er|guss ▲ ['bluːtɐˌgʊs] M haematoma (Brit spec), hematoma (US spec); (= blauer Fleck) bruise

Blu|ter|krank|heit ['bluːtɐ-] F haemophilia (Brit), hemophilia (US)

Blü|te|zeit F **a** die ~ der Obstbäume ist vorbei the fruit trees are no longer in blossom **b** (fig) heyday; (von Mensch) prime

Blut-: Blut|farb|stoff M haemoglobin (Brit), hemoglobin (US); **Blut|fa|ser|stoff** M fibrin; **Blut|feh|de** F blood feud; **Blut|fett** NT blood fat, blood lipids pl; **Blut|fett|wer|te** PL (Physiol) blood lipid level(s pl); **Blut|fett|sen|ker** M **-s, -** (Pharm) blood-fat-lowering agent; **Blut|fett|spie|gel** M (Med) blood-fat level; **Blut|fleck** M bloodstain; **Blut|flüs|sig|keit** F blood plasma; **Blut|ge|fäß** NT blood vessel; **Blut|geld** NT blood money; **Blut|ge|rinn|sel** NT blood clot; **Blut|ge|rin|nung** F clotting of the blood; **Blut|ge|rin|nungs|fak|tor** M (Med) blood clotting factor; **Blut|ge|rüst** NT (liter) scaffold; **blut|ge|tränkt** [-gətrɛŋkt] ADJ blood-soaked, soaked in blood; **Blut|gier** F blood lust; **blut|gie|rig** ADJ bloodthirsty

Blut|grup|pe F blood group; **die ~ 0 haben** to be blood group 0; **jds ~ bestimmen** to type or group sb's blood

Blut|grup|pen-: Blut|grup|pen|be|stim|mung F blood-typing; **Blut|grup|pen|un|ter|su|chung** F (Jur) blood test (to determine paternity)

Blut-: Blut|hoch|druck M high blood pressure; **Blut|hoch|zeit** F (Hist) Massacre of St. Bartholomew; **Blut|hund** M (lit, fig) bloodhound; **Blut|hus|ten** M haemoptysis (Brit spec), hemoptysis (US spec); **er hat ~** he is coughing (up) blood

blu|tig ['bluːtɪç] ADJ **a** (lit, fig) bloody; **sich ~ machen** to get blood on oneself; **~e Tränen weinen** (liter) to shed bitter tears **b** (inf) Anfänger absolute; Ernst unrelenting **ADV** bloodily; **er wurde ~ geschlagen/gepeitscht** he was beaten/ whipped until he bled

-blü|tig [blyːtɪç] ADJ suf **a** Tier, Mensch -blooded; **kaltblütig** cold-blooded **b** Pflanze **eine rotblütige Tulpe** a red tulip

Blut-: blut|jung ADJ very young; **Blut|kon|ser|ve** F unit or pint of stored blood; **Blut|kon|takt** M contact through blood; **Blut|kör|per|chen** [-kœrpɐçən] NT **-s, -** blood corpuscle; **Blut|krank|heit** F blood disease; **Blut|krebs** M leukaemia (Brit), leukemia (US); **Blut|kreis|lauf** M blood circulation; **Blut|la|che** [-laxə, -laːxə] F pool of blood; **blut|leer** ADJ bloodless; **Blut|lee|re** F, no pl lack of blood; **blut|los** ADJ bloodless; (fig) Stil colourless (Brit), colorless (US), anaemic (Brit), anemic (US); **Blut|op|fer** NT **a** (= Opferung) blood sacrifice **b** (= Geopferter) victim; (fig) casualty; **Blut|oran|ge** F blood orange; **Blut|pass** ▲ M card giving blood group etc; **Blut|pfropf** M clot of blood; **Blut|plas|ma** NT blood plasma; **Blut|plätt|chen** NT platelet; **Blut|pro|be** F blood test; (= entnommene Blutmenge) blood sample; **Blut|ra|che** F blood feud; **Blut|rausch** M frenzy; **blut|rei|ni|gend** ADJ blood-cleansing, depurative (spec) **ADV** **~ sein** or **wirken** to cleanse the blood; **Blut|rei|ni|gung** F cleansing of the blood; **Blut|rei|ni|gungs|tee** M blood-cleansing tea; **blut|rot** (liter) ADJ blood-red **ADV** **~ gefärbt** blood-red; **blut|rüns|tig** [-rynstɪç] ADJ bloodthirsty; **Blut|sau|ger(in)** M(F) (lit, fig) bloodsucker; (= Vampir) vampire

Bluts-: Bluts|ban|de PL (geh) bonds pl or ties pl of blood; **Bluts|bru|der** M blood brother; **Bluts|brü|der|schaft** F blood brotherhood

Blut-: Blut|schan|de F incest; **Blut|schuld** F (liter) blood guilt; **eine ~ auf sich** (acc) **laden** to sully one's hands with blood (liter); **Blut|schwamm** M (Med) strawberry mark; **Blut|sen|kung** F (Med) sedimentation of the blood; **eine ~ machen** to test the sedimentation rate of the blood; **Blut|se|rum** NT , no pl blood serum; **Blut|spen|de** F unit or pint of blood (given by a donor); **Blut|spen|den** NT **-s,** no pl giving blood no art; **zum ~ aufrufen** to appeal for blood donors; **Blut|spen|de|pass** ▲ M blood donor card; **Blut|spen|der(in)** M(F) blood donor; **Blut|spur** F trail of blood; **~en traces of blood; **Blut|stau|ung** F congestion; **Blut|stein** M haematite (Brit), hematite (US); **blut|stil|lend** ADJ styptic **ADV** **~ wirken** to have a styptic effect; **Blut|strahl** M stream of blood; **Blut|strom** M bloodstream; (aus Wunde) stream of blood

Bluts|trop|fen M drop of blood

Blut-: Blut|stuhl M , no pl (Med) blood in the faeces (Brit) or feces (US); **Blut|sturz** M haemorrhage (Brit) or hemorrhage (US)

Bluts-: bluts|ver|wandt ADJ related by blood; **Bluts|ver|wand|te(r)** MF decl as adj blood relation or relative; **Bluts|ver|wandt|schaft** F blood relationship

blutt [blʊt] ADJ (Sw: = nackt) bare

Blut-: Blut|tat F bloody deed; **Blut|test** M blood test; **Blut|trans|fu|si|on** F blood transfusion; **blut|trie|fend** ADJ attr bloody, dripping with blood; **blut|über|strömt** [-ˈyːbɐʃtrøːmt] ADJ streaming with blood; **Blut|über|tra|gung** F blood transfusion

Blu|tung ['bluːtʊŋ] F **-, -en** bleeding no pl; (starke) haemorrhage (Brit), hemorrhage (US); (monatliche) period; **eine/die ~ stillen** to stop the bleeding

Blut-: blut|un|ter|lau|fen ADJ suffused with blood; Augen bloodshot; **Blut|un|ter|su|chung** F blood test; **Blut|ver|dün|nungs|mit|tel** NT anticoagulant (spec); **Blut|ver|gie|ßen** NT **-s,** no pl bloodshed no indef art; **Blut|ver|gif|tung** F blood poisoning no indef art; **Blut|ver|lust** M loss of blood; **blut|ver|schmiert** ADJ bloody, smeared with blood; **blut|voll** ADJ vivid, lively; **Blut|wal|lung** F congestion; (bei Frau) hot flush (Brit) or (US) flash; **Blut|wä|sche** F (Med) detoxification of the blood; **Blut|was|ser** NT , no pl blood serum; **Blut|wurst** F blutwurst (US), blood sausage; (zum Warmmachen) black (Brit) or blood (US) pudding; **Blut|zel|le** F blood corpuscle or cell; **Blut|zeu|ge** M , **Blut|zeu|gin** F (old) martyr; **Blut|zir|ku|la|ti|on** F blood circulation; **Blut|zoll** M (geh) toll (of lives); **Blut|zu|cker** M blood sugar; **Blut|zu|cker|spie|gel** M blood sugar level; **Blut|zu|fuhr** F blood supply

BLZ [beːʔɛlˈtsɛt] F **-, -s** abbr von **Bankleitzahl**

BMX-Rad [beːʔɛmˈʔɪks-] NT BMX bike

BND [beːʔɛnˈdeː] M **-(s)** abbr von **Bundesnachrichtendienst**

Bö [bøː] F **-, -en** ['bøːən] gust (of wind); (stärker, mit Regen) squall

Boa ['boːa] F **-, -s** (= Schlange, Schal) boa

Board|mar|ker ['bɔːrdmaːˌrkɐ] M **-s, -** (= Faserschreiber für Weißwandtafeln) whiteboard pen

Bob [bɔp] M **-s, -s** bob(sleigh) (Brit), bobsled

Bob-: Bob|bahn F bob(sleigh) (Brit) or bobsled run; **Bob|fah|rer(in)** M(F) bobber (inf); **Bob|schlit|ten** M bobsleigh, bobsled

Boc|cia ['bɔtʃa] NT **-(s)** or F **-,** no pl bowls sing

Bock¹ [bɔk] M **-(e)s, ¨e** ['bœkə] **a** (= Rehbock, Kaninchenbock) buck; (= Schafsbock) ram; (= Ziegenbock) he-goat, billy goat; **alter ~** (inf) old goat (inf); **sturer ~** (inf) stubborn old devil (inf); **geiler ~** (inf) randy (Brit) or horny old goat (inf); **wie ein ~ stinken** to smell like a pig (inf),

to stink to high heaven (inf); **die Böcke von den Schafen scheiden** or **trennen** (fig) to separate the sheep from the goats; **den ~ zum Gärtner machen** (fig) to be asking for trouble; **einen ~ schießen** (fig inf) to make a boob (Brit inf) or blunder (inf); (= Fauxpas) to drop a clanger (Brit inf), to make a blunder (inf) **b** (inf: = Trotz) stubbornness; **(s)einen ~ haben** to be awkward (esp Brit) or difficult, to play up (inf) **c** (= Gestell) stand; (= Stützgerät) support; (für Auto) ramp; (aus Holzbalken, mit Beinen) trestle; (= Sägebock) sawhorse **d** (Sport) vaulting horse, **den** or **einen ~ machen** to bend over (for someone to vault over) **e** (= Schemel) (high) stool **f** (= Kutschbock) box (seat) **g** (= Ramme) (battering) ram **h** (sl: = Lust, Spaß) **null ~!** couldn't be buggered! (Brit sl), I don't feel like it; **Böcke** or **~ auf etw** (acc) **haben** to fancy sth (inf), to be bent on sth; **Böcke** or **~ haben, etw zu tun** to fancy doing sth (inf), to be bent on doing sth; **ich hab keinen** or **null ~, das zu tun** I can't be buggered doing that (Brit sl), I just don't feel like doing that; **null ~ auf nichts** pissed off with everything (inf)

Bock² NT OR M **-s, -** bock (beer) (type of strong beer)

Bock-: bock|bei|nig ADJ (inf) contrary, awkward; **Bock|bier** NT bock (beer) (type of strong beer)

bo|cken ['bɔkn] VI **a** (Zugtier etc) to refuse to move; (= nicht springen wollen: Pferd) to refuse; (fig inf: Auto, Motor etc) (= nicht anspringen) to refuse to start; (= nicht richtig funktionieren) to refuse to go properly; **vor einer Hürde ~** to refuse a jump **b** (inf: = trotzen) to play or act up (inf) **c** (sl: = Spaß machen) **das bockt** that's the business (sl)

bo|ckig ['bɔkɪç] ADJ (inf) stubborn, awkward

Bo|ckig|keit F **-, -en** stubbornness, awkwardness; **noch so ein paar ~en und ...** any more of your stubbornness and ...

Bock-: Bock|lei|ter F stepladder; **Bock|mist** M (inf) (= dummes Gerede) bullshit (sl); **~ machen** to make a balls-up (Brit inf), to make a big blunder (inf)

Bocks- ['bɔks-]: **Bocks|beu|tel** M wide, rounded bottle containing Franconian wine; **Bocks|horn** NT **jdn ins ~ jagen** to put the wind up sb (Brit inf); **sich von jdm ins ~ jagen lassen** to let sb upset one; **sie ließ sich nicht ins ~ jagen** she didn't let herself get into a state

Bock-: Bock|sprin|gen NT **-s,** no pl leapfrog; (Sport) vaulting; **~ machen** to play leapfrog; **Bock|sprung** M **a** (= Sprung über Menschen) leapfrog; (Sport) vault **b** (= ungeschickter Sprung) leap, bound; **Bock|wurst** F bockwurst (type of sausage)

Bod|den ['bɔdn] M **-s, -** (Geol) ≈ shallow bay

Bo|den ['boːdn] M **-s, ¨** ['bøːdn] **a** (= Erde, Grundfläche) ground; (= Erdreich auch) soil; (= Fußboden) floor; (= Grundbesitz) land; (no pl: = Terrain) soil; **auf spanischem ~** on Spanish soil; **zu ~ fallen** to fall to the ground; **jdn zu ~ schlagen** or **strecken** to knock sb down, to floor sb; **festen ~ unter den Füßen haben, auf festem ~ sein** to be or stand on firm ground, to be on terra firma; (fig = finanziell abgesichert) to be secure; (= fundierte Argumente haben) to be on firm ground; **den ~ unter den Füßen verlieren** (lit) to lose one's footing; **keinen Fuß auf den ~ bekommen** (fig) to be unable to find one's feet; (fig: in Diskussion) to get out of one's depth; **der ~ brannte ihm unter den Füßen** (fig) ihm wurde **der ~ (unter den Füßen) zu heiß** (fig) things were getting too hot for him; **jdm den ~ unter den Füßen wegziehen** (fig) to cut the ground from under sb's feet (Brit), to pull the carpet out from under sb's feet; **ich hätte (vor Scham) im ~ versinken können** (fig) I was so ashamed that I wished the ground would (open and) swallow me up; **am ~ zerstört sein** (inf) to be shattered (Brit fig inf) or devastated; **(an) ~ gewinnen/verlieren** (fig) to gain/lose ground; **~ gutmachen** or **wettmachen** (fig) to make up ground, to catch up; **etw aus dem ~ stampfen** (fig) to conjure sth up out of nothing; **Häuser auch** to build overnight; **er stand wie aus dem ~ gewachsen vor mir** he appeared in front of me as if by magic; **auf fruchtbaren ~ fallen** (fig) to fall on fertile ground; **jdm/einer Sache den ~ bereiten** (fig) to prepare the ground for sb/sth; **durch alle Böden (hindurch)** (Sw: = um jeden Preis) at any price → **Fass, Grund a, schießen VI b**

b (= unterste Fläche) (von Behälter) bottom; (von Meer auch) seabed; (von Hose) seat; (= Tortenboden) base → **doppelt** ADJ

c (Raum) (= Dachboden, Heuboden) loft; (= Trockenboden) (für Getreide) drying floor; (für Wäsche) drying room

d (fig = Grundlage) **auf dem ~ der Wissenschaft/Tatsachen/Wirklichkeit stehen** to base oneself on scientific fact/on fact/on reality; (Behauptung) to be based or founded on scientific fact/on fact/on reality; **sie wurde hart auf den ~ der Wirklichkeit zurückgeholt** she was brought down to earth with a bump; **auf dem ~ der Tatsachen bleiben** to stick to the facts; **den ~ der Tatsachen verlassen** to go into the realm of fantasy; **sich auf unsicherem ~ bewegen** to be on shaky ground; **er steht auf dem ~ des Gesetzes** (= nicht ungesetzlich) he is within the law; (= hat Gesetz hinter sich) he has the backing of the law; **einem Gerücht den ~ entziehen** to show a rumour (Brit) or rumor (US) to be unfounded

Bo|den-: Bo|den|ab|stand M (Mot) (ground) clearance; **Bo|den|ab|wehr** F ground defence (Brit) or defense (US); **Bo|den|be|ar|bei|tung** F cultivation of the land or soil, tillage; **Bo|den|be|lag** M floor covering; **Bo|den|be|schaf|fen|heit** F condition of the ground; (von Acker etc) condition of the soil; **Bo|den|brü|ter** M (Orn) ground nester, ground-nesting bird; **Bo|den|de|cker** [-dɛkɐ] M **-s, -** (Bot) ground-cover plant; **Bo|den|er|he|bung** F elevation; **Bo|den|ero|si|on** F soil erosion; **Bo|den|er|trag** M (Agr) crop yield; **Bo|den|feuch|te** F, **Bo|den|feuch|tig|keit** F (Hort, Agr) soil or ground humidity; (im Haus) rising damp; **Bo|den|flä|che** F (Agr) area of land; (von Zimmer) floor space or area; **Bo|den|frost** M ground frost; **bo|den|ge|stützt** [-ɡəʃtʏtst] ADJ Flugkörper ground-launched; **Bo|den|grup|pe** F (Aut) substructure, floorpan; **Bo|den|haf|tung** F (Aut) road holding or grip; **Bo|den|hal|tung** F (Agr, von Hühnern etc) keeping (of hens etc) in free-range conditions „aus ~" "free-range"; **Bo|den|hei|zung** F underfloor (central) heating; **Bo|den|kam|mer** F attic; **Bo|den|kon|trol|le** F (Space) ground control; **Bo|den|le|ger** [-le:ɡɐ] M **-s, -**, **Bo|den|le|ge|rin** [-ərɪn] F **-, -nen** floor layer; **bo|den|los** ADJ bottomless; (inf: = unerhört) indescribable, incredible; **ins Bodenlose fallen** to fall into an abyss ADV (inf) frech, unverschämt, gemein unbelievably, incredibly; **Bo|den|ne|bel** M ground mist; **Bo|den|nut|zung** F land utilization; **Bo|den|or|ga|ni|sa|ti|on** F (Aviat) ground organization; **Bo|den|per|so|nal** NT (Aviat) ground personnel pl or staff pl; **Bo|den|plat|te** F (Build) floor slab; (Tech) base plate; **Bo|den|pro|be** F soil sample or specimen; **Bo|den|re|form** F land or agrarian reform; **Bo|den|satz** M sediment; (von Kaffee) grounds pl, dregs pl; (fig: Menschen) dregs; (fig: von Gefühlen) hidden reservoir; **Bo|den|schät|ze** PL mineral resources pl; **Bo|den|schicht** F layer of soil; (Geol) stratum; **Bo|den|schwel|le** F speed bump or ramp; **Bo|den|see** M der ~ Lake Constance; **Bo|den|sen|ke** F depression, hollow; **Bo|den|sicht** F (Aviat) ground visibility; **Bo|den|spe|ku|la|ti|on** F land speculation; **bo|den|stän|dig** ADJ

(= lang ansässig) long-established; (fig: = unkompliziert) down-to-earth; **Bo|den|sta|ti|on** F (Space) ground station; **Bo|den|streit|kräf|te** PL ground forces pl; **Bo|den|struk|tur** F soil structure; **Bo|den|tur|nen** NT floor exercises pl; **Bo|den|übung** F (Sport) floor exercise; **Bo|den|va|se** F floor vase; **Bo|den|ver|bes|se|rung** F (Agr, Hort) soil improvement; **Bo|den|wel|le** F **a** bump **b** (Rad) ground wave

Bod|me|rei [bo:dmə'raɪ] F **-, -en** (Naut) bottomry

Bo|dy ['bɔdɪ] M **-s, -s** body

Bo|dy-: Bo|dy|buil|der ['bɔdɪbɪldɐ] M **-s, -**, **Bo|dy|buil|de|rin** [-ərɪn] F **-, -nen** bodybuilder; **Bo|dy|buil|ding** ['bɔdɪbɪldɪŋ] NT **-s**, no pl bodybuilding; **~ machen** to do bodybuilding exercises; **Bo|dy|check** ['bɔdɪtʃɛk] M **-s, -s** (Sport) bodycheck; **Bo|dy|guard** ['bɔdɪgaːɐt] M **-s, -s** (= Leibwächter) bodyguard; **Bo|dy|lo|ti|on** ['bɔdɪloːʃn] F body lotion; **Bo|dy|suit** ['bɔdɪsuːt] M **-(s), -s** body stocking or suit

Böe ['bøːə] F **-, -n** gust (of wind); (stärker, mit Regen) squall

bog pret von **biegen**

Bo|gen ['boːgn] M **-s, -** or **¨** ['bøːgn] **a** (= gekrümmte Linie) curve; (= Kurve) bend; (= Umweg) detour; (Math) arc; (Mus) (zwischen zwei Noten gleicher Höhe) tie; (zur Bindung von verschiedenen Noten) slur (mark); (Ski) turn; **einen ~ fahren** (Ski) to do or execute a turn; **den ~ heraushaben** (inf) to have got the hang of it (inf); **den ~ heraushaben, wie ...** (inf) to have got the hang of how ... (inf); **einen ~ machen** (Fluss etc) to curve, to describe a curve (form); (= einen Umweg machen) to make a detour; **einen großen ~ um jdn/etw machen** (= meiden) to keep well clear of sb/sth, to give sb/sth a wide berth; **jdn in hohem ~ hinauswerfen** (inf) to send sb flying out; **der Ball flog in hohem ~ ins Tor** the ball flew into the net

b (Archit) arch

c (= Waffe, Mus: = Geigenbogen etc) bow; **den ~ überspannen** (fig) to overstep the mark, to go too far

d (= Papierbogen) sheet (of paper)

Bo|gen-: Bo|gen|fens|ter NT bow window; **bo|gen|för|mig** ADJ arched ADV in the shape of an arch; **Bo|gen|füh|rung** F (Mus) bowing; **Bo|gen|gang** M pl **-gänge a** (Archit) arcade **b** (Anat: von Ohr) semicircular canal; **Bo|gen|lam|pe** F arc lamp or light; **Bo|gen|maß** NT (Math) radian or circular measure; **Bo|gen|mi|nu|te** F (Math) arc minute; **Bo|gen|pfei|ler** M pillar, column (supporting an arch); **Bo|gen|schie|ßen** NT **-s**, no pl archery; **Bo|gen|schüt|ze** M , **Bo|gen|schüt|zin** F archer; **Bo|gen|seh|ne** F bowstring; **Bo|gen|se|kun|de** F (Math) arc second; **Bo|gen|strich** M (Mus) bowing

Bo|heme [bo'eːm, bɔ'eːm] F **-**, no pl Bohemian world

Bo|he|mi|en [boe'miɛ̃:, bohe'miɛ̃:] M **-s, -s**, **Bo|he|mi|enne** [boemi'ɛn, bohemi'ɛn] F **-, -s** Bohemian

Boh|le ['boːlə] F **-, -n** (thick) board; (Rail) sleeper

böh|ma|keln ['bøːmakln] VI (Aus inf) to speak with a dreadful accent

Böh|me ['bøːmə] M **-n, -n**, **Böh|min** ['bøːmɪn] F **-, -nen** Bohemian (inhabitant of Bohemia)

Böh|men ['bøːmən] NT **-s** Bohemia

Böh|mer|wald ['bøːmɐ-] M Bohemian Forest

böh|misch ['bøːmɪʃ] ADJ Bohemian; **die Böhmischen Brüder** (Rel) the Bohemian Brethren; **das sind für mich ~e Dörfer** (inf) that's all Greek to me (inf); **~ einkaufen** (Aus inf) to shoplift

Böhn|chen ['bøːnçən] NT **-s**, dim von **Bohne**

Boh|ne ['boːnə] F **-, -n** bean; (inf: = Kot des Kaninchens, Rehs) droppings pl; **dicke/grüne/weiße ~n** broad/green or French or runner/haricot (Brit) or string or navy (US) beans; **rote ~n** kidney beans; **blaue ~** (dated Mil sl) bullet; **nicht die ~**

(inf) not a scrap (inf), not one little bit; **das kümmert mich nicht die ~** I don't care a fig about that (Brit inf), I don't give a hoot about that; **du hast wohl ~n in den Ohren** (inf) are you deaf?

Boh|nen-: Boh|nen|ein|topf M bean stew; **Boh|nen|kaf|fee** M real coffee; **gemahlener ~** ground coffee; **Boh|nen|kraut** NT savo(u)ry; **Boh|nen|ran|ke** F tendril; **Boh|nen|sa|lat** M (Cook) (French) bean salad; **Boh|nen|stan|ge** F bean support; (fig inf) beanpole (inf); **Boh|nen|stroh** NT **dumm wie ~** (inf) (as) thick as two (short) planks (inf); **Boh|nen|sup|pe** F bean soup

Boh|ner ['boːnɐ] M **-s, -**, **Boh|ner|be|sen** M , **Boh|ner|bürs|te** F floor-polishing brush

boh|nern ['boːnɐn] VTI to polish

Boh|ner|wachs NT floor polish or wax

Bohr|ar|bei|ten PL drillings pl

boh|ren ['boːrən] VT to bore; (mit Bohrer, Bohrmaschine auch) to drill; Brunnen to sink; (= hineindrücken) Stange, Pfahl, Schwert etc to sink (in +acc into); **ein Schiff in den Grund ~** to send a ship to the bottom of the sea

VI **a** (mit Bohrer) to bore (in +dat into), to drill (nach for); **in einem Zahn ~** to drill a tooth; **in der Nase ~** to pick one's nose

b (fig) (= drängen) to keep on; (= peinigen: Schmerz, Zweifel etc) to gnaw; **er bohrte und bohrte, bekam aber keine Antwort** he kept on and on but got no reply; **der Schmerz bohrte ihm im Magen** he had a gnawing pain in his stomach

VR **sich in/durch etw** (acc) **~** to bore its way into/through sth; **ein grelles Licht bohrte sich durchs Dunkel** a glaring light pierced the darkness

boh|rend ADJ (fig) Blick piercing; Schmerz, Zweifel, Hunger, Reue gnawing; Frage probing

Boh|rer¹ ['boːrɐ] M **-s, -** (elektrisch, = Drillbohrer) drill; (= Handbohrer) gimlet, auger

Boh|rer² ['boːrɐ] M **-s, -**, **Boh|re|rin** [-ərɪn] F **-, -nen** driller

Bohr-: Bohr|feld NT oil/gas field; **Bohr|fut|ter|schlüs|sel** M chuck key; **Bohr|in|sel** F drilling rig; (für Öl auch) oil rig; **Bohr|kopf** M drilling or boring head, bit; **Bohr|loch** NT borehole; (in Holz, Metall etc) drill hole; **Bohr|ma|schi|ne** F drill; **Bohr|mei|ßel** M boring tool, drill bit, cutter; **Bohr|pro|be** F drilling; **Bohr|stan|ge** F drill rod; **Bohr|turm** M derrick

Bohr|ung F **-, -en a** (= das Bohren) boring; (mit Bohrer, Bohrmaschine auch) drilling; (von Brunnen) sinking **b** (= Loch) bore(hole); (in Holz, Metall etc) drill hole

bö|ig ['bøːɪç] ADJ gusty; (stärker, mit Regen) squally

Boi|ler ['bɔylɐ] M **-s, -** (hot-water) tank; **den ~ anstellen** to put the water heater on

Bo|je ['boːjə] F **-, -n** buoy

Bo|le|ro [bo'leːro] M **-s, -s** (= Tanz, Jäckchen) bolero

Bo|li|de [bo'liːdə] M **-n, -n a** (Aut: = Rennwagen) (high-performance) racing car **b** (Comput) high-performance computer; (= Superrechner) supercomputer

Bo|li|via|ner [bolivi'aːnɐ] M **-s, -**, **Bo|li|via|ne|rin** [-ərɪn] F **-, -nen** Bolivian

bo|li|vi|a|nisch [bolivi'aːnɪʃ] ADJ Bolivian

Bo|li|vi|en [bo'liːviən] NT **-s** Bolivia

Bölk|stoff ['bœlk-] M (sl: = Bier) wallop (Brit sl)

Böl|ler ['bœlɐ] M **-s, -** (small) cannon (for ceremonial use)

bol|lern ['bɔlɐn] VI **a** aux sein (dial: = poltern) to thud **b** (Ftbl sl) to fire the ball blindly at the goal

böl|lern ['bœlɐn] VI to fire; **es böllert** there is firing

Böl|ler|schuss ▲ M gun salute; **5 Böller-schüsse** 5 shots from the cannon

Bol|ler|wa|gen ['bɔlɐ-] M handcart

Boll|werk ['bɔl-] NT (lit, fig) bulwark (usu fig), bastion, stronghold; (= Kai) bulwark

Bol|sche|wik [bɔlʃe'vɪk] M **-en, -en** or **-i**, **Bol|sche|wi|kin** [-'vɪkɪn] F **-, -nen** Bolshevik

Bol|sche|wis|mus [bɔlʃe'vɪsmʊs] M **-, no pl** Bolshevism

Bol|sche|wist [bɔlʃe'vɪst] M **-en, -en**, **Bol|sche|wis|tin** [-'vɪstɪn] F **-, -nen** Bolshevist

bol|sche|wis|tisch [bɔlʃe'vɪstɪʃ] ADJ Bolshevist, Bolshevik attr

bol|zen ['bɔltsn] (inf) **VI** to kick about; **es wurde mehr gebolzt als gespielt** they just kicked (the ball) about instead of playing football (Brit) or soccer (US) **VT** Ball to slam

Bol|zen ['bɔltsn] M **-s, -** **a** (Tech) pin; (esp mit Gewinde) bolt **b** (= Geschoss) bolt

Bol|zen-: bol|zen|ge|ra|de ADJ (as) straight as a poker; (vertikal) bolt upright

Bol|zen|schnei|der M bolt cutters pl

Bol|zen|schuss|ap|pa|rat ▲ M (für Schlachtung) bolt apparatus, humane killer (inf)

Bolz|platz M piece of ground where children play football

Bom|bar|de|ment [bɔmbardə'mãː, (Aus) bɔm-bard'mãː] NT **-s, -s** bombardment; (mit Bomben) bombing; **ein ~ von** (fig) a deluge or shower of

bom|bar|die|ren [bɔmbar'diːrən] ptp **bombardiert** VT (= mit Bomben belegen) to bomb; (= mit Granaten beschießen, fig) to bombard

Bom|bar|die|rung F **-, -en** (mit Bomben) bombing; (mit Granaten, fig) bombardment

Bom|bast [bɔm'bast] M **-(e)s, no pl** bombast

bom|bas|tisch [bɔm'bastɪʃ] ADJ Sprache bombastic; Architektur, Hauseinrichtung overdone pred; Aufwand ostentatious **a** (= schwülstig) bombastically; (= pompös) eingerichtet, gebaut ostentatiously

Bom|bay ['bɔmbe] NT **-s** Bombay

Bom|be ['bɔmbə] F **-, -n** bomb; (dated: = Könner) ace (in +dat at); (Sport inf: = Schuss) cracker (inf); **mit ~n belegen** to bomb; **wie eine ~ einschlagen** to come as a (real) bombshell; **eine/die ~ platzen lassen** (fig) to drop a/the bombshell

bom|ben ['bɔmbn] VT (Sport inf) Ball to smash (inf), to slam (inf)

Bom|ben- in cpds (Mil) bomb; (inf: = hervorragend) fantastic (inf), great (inf); **Bom|ben|alarm** M bomb scare; **Bom|ben|an|griff** M bomb attack or raid; **Bom|ben|an|schlag** M bomb attack; **Bom|ben|at|ten|tat** NT bomb attempt; **Bom|ben|be|set|zung** F (inf) fantastic or great cast (inf); **Bom|ben|dro|hung** F bomb threat or scare; **Bom|ben|er|folg** M (inf) smash hit (inf); **bom|ben|fest** **ADJ** **a** (Mil) bombproof **b** (inf) Klebestelle, Naht absolutely secure; Entschluss unshakeable **ADV** (inf) etw ~ zusammenkleben to stick sth securely together; **Bom|ben|flug|zeug** NT bomber; **Bom|ben|form** F (Sport; inf) **in ~ sein** to be in great shape; **Bom|ben|ge|schä|dig|te(r)** MF decl as adj bomb victim; **Bom|ben|ge|schäft** NT (inf) **ein ~ sein** to be a gold mine (fig inf); **ein ~ machen** to do a roaring trade (inf) (mit in); **Bom|ben|ge|schwa|der** NT bomber squadron; **Bom|ben|hit|ze** F (inf) sweltering heat no indef art; **Bom|ben|kra|ter** M bomb crater; **Bom|ben|le|ger** [-le:gɐ] M **-s, -**, **Bom|ben|le|ge|rin** [-ərɪn] F **-, -nen** bomber; **Bom|ben|nacht** F night of bombing; **Bom|ben|schacht** M (Mil: in Flugzeug) bomb bay; **Bom|ben|scha|den** M bomb damage; **Bom|ben|schuss** ▲ M (inf) unstoppable shot; **bom|ben|si|cher** **ADJ** **a** (Mil) bombproof **b** (inf) dead certain (inf); Landung absolutely safe; **eine ~e Geschäftsidee** an absolute winner of a business idea **ADV** **a** (Mil) lagern, unterbringen in a bombproof place **b**

(inf) **das steht ~ fest** that's absolutely certain; **Bom|ben|split|ter** M bomb fragment; **Bom|ben|stel|lung** F (inf) job in a million (inf), fantastic job (inf); **Bom|ben|stim|mung** F , no pl (inf) terrific or tremendous atmosphere; **sie waren in ~** they were or felt on top of the world (inf); **Bom|ben|tep|pich** M **einen ~ legen** to blanket-bomb an/the area; **Bom|ben|ter|ror** M terror bombing; **Bom|ben|trich|ter** M bomb crater

Bom|ber¹ ['bɔmbɐ] M **-s, -** (= Bombenflugzeug) bomber

Bom|ber² ['bɔmbɐ] M **-s, -**, **Bom|be|rin** [-ərɪn] F **-, -nen** **a** (= Attentäter) bomber **b** (Ftbl inf) powerful striker

Bom|ber|ja|cke F bomber jacket

Bom|mel ['bɔml] F **-, -n** bobble

Bon [bɔŋ, bõː] M **-s, -s** voucher, coupon; (= Kassenzettel) receipt, (sales) slip

Bon|bon [bɔŋ'bɔŋ, bõbõː] NT OR M **-s, -s** sweet (Brit), candy (US); (fig) treat

bon|bon|far|ben [bɔŋ'bɔŋfarbn, bõbõː-], **bon|bon|far|big** ADJ candy-coloured (Brit), candy-colored (US)

Bon|bon|nie|re [bɔŋbɔ'nie:rə, bõ-] F **-, -n** box of chocolates

Bon|bon|pa|pier [bɔŋ'bɔŋpa-, bõbõː-] NT sweet (Brit) or candy (US) wrapper

Bond [bɔnt] M **-s, -s** (Fin) bond; **festverzinsliche ~s** pl fixed-income bonds pl

bon|gen ['bɔŋən] VT (inf) Betrag etc to ring up; **das ist gebongt** (inf) okey-doke, righto (inf)

Bon|go ['bɔŋɡo] **NT** **-(s), -s** **F** **-, -s**, **Bon|go|trom|mel** F bongo (drum)

Bo|ni|fi|ka|ti|on [bonifika'tsio:n] F **-, -en** (Fin) (= Bonus) bonus; (= Provision) commission

bo|ni|fi|zie|ren [bonifi'tsi:rən] ptp **bonifiziert** VTI (Comm) to reimburse, to remunerate

Bo|ni|tät [boni'tɛːt] F **-, -en** (Fin) financial standing, creditworthiness

Bo|ni|täts|prü|fung F (Fin) credit investigation

Bon|mot [bõ'moː] NT **-s, -s** bon mot

Bonn [bɔn] NT **-s** Bonn

Bon|ner¹ ['bɔnɐ] ADJ attr Bonn

Bon|ner² ['bɔnɐ] M **-s, -**, **Bon|ne|rin** [-ərɪn] F **-, -nen** native of Bonn; (= Einwohner) inhabitant of Bonn

Bon|sai ['bɔnzai] NT **-s, -s** bonsai

Bo|nus ['bo:nʊs] M **- or -ses, - or -se** (Comm, fig) bonus; (Univ, Sport: = Punktvorteil) bonus points pl

Bo|nus|mei|le F air mile (Brit), bonus mile (US)

Bo|nus|sys|tem NT bonus system

Bon|vi|vant [bõvi'vãː] M **-s, -s** (= Lebemann) bon vivant; (Theat) rake, roué

Bon|ze ['bɔntsə] M **-n, -n** **a** (Rel) bonze **b** (pej) bigwig (inf), big shot (inf)

Boo|gie(-Woo|gie) ['buːɡi('vʊɡi)] M **-(s), -s** boogie-woogie

Boom [buːm] M **-s, -s** boom

boo|men ['buːmən] VI to boom

Boos|ter ['buːstɐ] M **-s, -** (an Triebwerk) booster rocket; (Elec) booster; (Med) booster (injection)

Boot [boːt] NT **-(e)s, -e** boat; **~ fahren** to go out in a boat; (zum Vergnügen) to go boating; **wir sitzen alle in einem** or **im selben** or **im gleichen ~** (fig) we're all in the same boat

boo|ten ['buːtn] VTI (Comput) to boot (up)

Boots-: Boots|an|hän|ger M boat trailer; **Boots|bau|er(in)** M(F) pl **-bauer(innen)** boatbuilder; **Boots|deck** NT boat deck; **Boots|fahrt** F boat trip; **Boots|flücht|lin|ge** PL boat people; **Boots|haus** NT boathouse; **Boots|län|ge** F (Sport) (boat's) length; **Boots|mann** M pl **-leute** (Naut) bo'sun, boatswain; (= Dienstgrad) petty officer; **Boots|ren|nen** NT boat race; **Boots|schup|pen** M

boatshed; **Boots|steg** M landing stage; **Boots|ver|leih** M boat hire (business); **Boots|ver|lei|her(in)** M(F) boat hirer

Bor ['boːɐ] NT **-s, no pl** (abbr **B**) boron

Bo|rax ['bo:raks] M **-(es), no pl** borax

Bord¹ [bɔrt] M **-(e)s** [-dəs] no pl **an ~ (eines Schiffes/der „Bremen")** on board (a ship/the "Bremen"); **alle Mann an ~!** all aboard!; **frei an ~** (Comm) free on board, f.o.b.; **an ~ gehen** to board or to go aboard (the ship/plane), to go on board; **Mann über ~!** man overboard!; **über ~ gehen** to go overboard; (fig) to go by the board; **über ~ werfen** (lit, fig) to throw overboard, to jettison; **die Vorsicht über ~ werfen** to throw caution to the winds; **von ~ gehen** to leave (the) ship/the plane; (esp Passagiere am Ziel) to disembark

Bord² NT **-(e)s, -e** (= Wandbrett) shelf

Bord³ NT **-(e)s, -e** (Sw) (= Rand) ledge, raised edge; (= Böschung) embankment, bank

Bord-: Bord|buch NT log(book); **Bord|case** [-keɪs] NT OR M **-, -s** [-keɪsɪz] flight or carry-on case; **Bord|com|pu|ter** M on-board computer; **Bord|ei|gen** ADJ ship's/plane's etc; **Bord|e|lek|tro|nik** F (Aviat) avionics pl, on-board electronics pl

Bor|dell [bɔr'dɛl] NT **-s, -e** brothel

Bor|dell|ier [bɔrdə'lie:] M **-s, -** brothel keeper

Bor|dell-: Bor|dell|vier|tel NT red-light district; **Bor|dell|wir|tin** F brothel keeper, madam

Bord-: Bord|funk M (Naut) (ship's) radio; (Aviat) (aircraft) radio equipment; **Bord|fun|ker(in)** M(F) (Naut, Aviat) radio operator; **Bord|ge|päck** NT (Aviat) hand luggage or baggage (esp US), carry-on baggage (esp US)

bor|die|ren [bɔr'di:rən] ptp **bordiert** VT (Sew) to edge, to border

Bord-: Bord|in|ge|ni|eur(in) M(F) (Aviat) flight engineer; (Naut) ship's engineer; **Bord|ka|me|ra** F (Mil) on-board camera; **Bord|ka|no|ne** F (Mil) (an Flugzeug) aircraft cannon; (an Panzer) gun; **Bord|kan|te** F kerb (Brit), curb (US); **Bord|kar|te** F boarding pass or card; **Bord|me|cha|ni|ker(in)** M(F) ship's/aircraft mechanic; **Bord|mit|tel** PL **mit ~n** (lit) with our/their etc on-board equipment; (fig) with the means we have or had at our disposal/they etc have or had at their etc disposal; **Bord|stein** M kerb (Brit), curb (US); **den ~ mitnehmen** (inf) to hit the kerb (Brit) or curb (US); **Bord|stein|kan|te** F , **Bord|stein|rand** M kerb (Brit), curb (US)

Bor|dü|re [bɔr'dy:rə] F **-, -n** edging, border

Bord-: Bord|waf|fen PL (Mil) (von Flugzeug) aircraft armaments pl; (von Panzer) tank armaments pl; (von Schiff) ship armaments pl; **Bord|wand** F (Naut) ship's side; (Aviat) side of the aircraft

bo|re|al [bore'aːl] ADJ Nadelwald etc boreal

bor|gen ['bɔrɡn] VTI **a** (= erhalten) to borrow (von from) **b** (= geben) to lend, to loan (jdm etw sb sth, sth to sb)

Bor|ke ['bɔrkə] F **-, -n** bark

Bor|ken-: Bor|ken|flech|te F (Med) ringworm; **Bor|ken|kä|fer** M bark beetle; **Bor|ken|krepp** M (Tex) crepe

Born [bɔrn] M **-(e)s, -e** (old, liter) (= Brunnen) well; (= Quelle) spring; (fig) fountain, fount (liter)

bor|niert [bɔr'niːɐt] ADJ bigoted

Bor|niert|heit F -, no pl bigotry

Bor|re|li|o|se [bɔre'lio:zə] F **-, -n** usu sing (Med) borreliosis (spec), Lyme disease

Bor|retsch ['bɔrɛtʃ] M **-(e)s, no pl** borage

Bor|sal|be F boric acid ointment

Bor|sa|li|no [bɔrza'li:no] M **-s, -s** fedora

Bör|se ['bœrzə, 'bɶrzə] F **-, -n** **a** (= Geldbörse) (für Frauen) purse; (für Männer) wallet (Brit), billfold (US) **b** (= Wertpapierhandel) stock market;

(*Ort*) stock exchange; **an die ~ gehen** to be floated on the stock market *or* stock exchange

Börsen- (*St Ex*): **Börsenaufsicht** F **a** (*Behörde*) stock market regulator, ≈ Securities and Investments Board (*Brit*), ≈ Securities and Exchange Commission (*US*) **b** *no pl* (*Kontrolle*) regulation of the stock market; **Börsenaufsichtsbehörde** F = Börsenaufsicht a; **Börsenbarometer** NT (*inf fig*) (stock) market barometer; **Börsenbeginn** M opening of the stock market; **bei ~** when the stock market opens; **Börsenbericht** M stock market report; **Börsencrash** M (*inf*) stock market crash; **Börseneinführung** F flotation on the stock exchange; **börsenfähig** ADJ negotiable on the stock exchange; **Börsenfähigkeit** F negotiability on the stock exchange; **Börsengang** M stock market flotation; **Börsengeschäft** NT (= *Wertpapierhandel*) stockbroking; (= *Transaktion*) stock market transaction; **Börsenhandel** M stock exchange trading; **Börsenindex** M stock exchange index; **Börsenjobber(in)** M(F) (*inf*) (stock) jobber; **Börsenkrach** M stock market crash; **Börsenkrise** F crisis on the stock market; **Börsenkurs** M stock market price; **Börsenmakler(in)** M(F) stockbroker; **Börsennachrichten** PL financial news *sing or* report *sing*; **börsennotiert** [-notiːt] ADJ *Firma* listed; **Börsennotierung** F quotation (on the stock exchange); **Börsenordnung** F stock exchange rules *pl*; **Börsenplatz** M stock exchange; **Börsenprospekt** M (stock exchange) prospectus; **Börsenschluss** ▲ M , *no pl* close of the stock market; **Börsenschwankungen** PL fluctuations on the stock market; **Börsenschwindel** M stock market swindle *or* fiddle (*inf*); **Börsenspekulant(in)** M(F) speculator on the stock market; **Börsenspekulation** F speculation on the stock market; **Börsenspiel** NT (= *Wettbewerb mit fiktiven Börsengeschäften*) stock market simulation game; **Börsensturz** M collapse of the market; **Börsentendenz** F market trend; **Börsentipp** M market tip; **Börsenumsatzsteuer** F stock exchange tax; **Börsenverkehr** M stock market dealings *pl or* transactions *pl*; **Börsenwesen** NT stock market

Börsianer [bœrziaːnɐ] M -s, -, **Börsianerin** [-ərɪn] -, **-nen** (*inf*) (= *Makler*) broker; (= *Spekulant*) speculator

Borste [ˈbɔrstə] F -, **-n** bristle

Borsten-: **Borstentier** NT pig, swine; **Borstenvieh** NT pigs *pl*, swine *pl*

borstig [ˈbɔrstɪç] ADJ bristly; (*fig*) snappish

Borte [ˈbɔrtə] F -, **-n** braid trimming

Borwasser NT , *no pl* boric acid lotion

bös [bøːs] ADJ, ADV = **böse**

bösartig ADJ *Mensch, Wesen* malicious, nasty; *Tier* vicious; (*Med*) *Geschwür* malignant

Bösartigkeit F -, **-en** maliciousness, nastiness; (*von Tier, stärker: von Mensch, Wesen*) viciousness; (*Med: von Geschwür*) malignancy

Böschung [ˈbœʃʊŋ] F -, **-en** (*von Straße*) bank, embankment; (*von Bahndamm*) embankment; (*von Fluss*) bank

Böschungswinkel M gradient

böse [ˈbøːzə] ADJ **a** (= *sittlich schlecht*) bad; (*stärker*) evil, wicked; (*inf*: = *unartig*) naughty, bad; **die ~ Fee/Stiefmutter** the Wicked Fairy/Stepmother; **ein ~r Geist** an evil spirit; **das war keine ~ Absicht** there was no harm intended; **eine ~ Zunge haben, ein ~s Mundwerk haben** to have a malicious *or* wicked tongue → **Blick b** *no pred* (= *unangenehm, übel*) *Traum, Angelegenheit, Krankheit* bad; *Überraschung, Streich, Geschichte* nasty; **ein ~s Erwachen** a rude awakening; **~ Folgen** dire consequences; **~ Zeiten** bad times → **Blut, Ende ² c** (= *verärgert*) angry, cross (+*dat, auf +acc, mit* with); **ein ~s Gesicht machen** to scowl

d (*inf*) (= *schmerzend, entzündet*) bad *attr*, sore; (= *krank, schlimm*) bad; *Wunde, Husten* nasty, bad **e** (*inf*: *verstärkend*) real (*inf*); *Enttäuschung, Gewitter, Sturz* bad, terrible

ADV **a** (= *übel gesinnt*) nastily; (*stärker*) evilly; **das war nicht ~ gemeint** I/he *etc* didn't mean it nastily

b (= *schlimm*) nastily; *verprügeln* badly; **er ist ~ dran** life's not easy for him; (*gesundheitlich*) he's in a bad way; **das/es sieht ~ aus** things look/it looks bad

c (*inf*: = *sehr*) badly, terribly; **er hat ~ geschimpft** he didn't half curse (*Brit inf*), he cursed like hell (*inf*)

Böse(r) [ˈbøːzə] MF *decl as adj* wicked *or* evil person; (*Film, Theat*) villain, baddy (*inf*); **die ~n** the wicked; **der ~** (= *Teufel*) the Evil One

Böse(s) [ˈbøːzə] NT *decl as adj* evil; (= *Schaden, Leid*) harm; **jdm ~s antun** to do sb harm; **ich will dir doch nichts ~s** I don't mean you any harm; **im ~n auseinandergehen** to part on bad terms; **mir schwant ~s** it sounds/looks ominous (to me); **ich dachte an gar nichts ~s, als ...** I was quite unsuspecting when ...; **ich habe mir gar nichts ~s dabei gedacht, als ich das sagte** I didn't mean any harm when I said that; **und erlöse uns von dem ~n** (*Eccl*) and deliver us from evil → **ahnen** VT

Bösewicht [ˈbøːzəvɪçt] M -(e)s, **-e** *or* **-er** (*old, hum*) villain

boshaft [ˈboːshaft] ADJ malicious, nasty ADV *grinsen, lächeln* maliciously, spitefully, nastily

Boshaftigkeit [ˈboːshaftɪçkaɪt] F -, **-en** **a** *no pl* maliciousness, nastiness **b** (*Bemerkung*) malicious *or* nasty remark

Bosheit F -, **-en** malice; (*Bemerkung*) malicious remark; (*Handlung*) malicious thing to do; **er hat es mit konstanter ~ getan** maliciously he kept on doing it; **aus lauter ~** from pure malice

Boskop [ˈbɔskɔp] M -s, - ≈ russet

Bosnien [ˈbɔsniən] NT **-s** Bosnia

Bosnien-Herzegowina [ˈbɔsniənhɛrtseˈgoːvina, -hɛrtsegoˈviːna] NT **-s** Bosnia-Herzegovina

Bosnier [ˈbɔsniɐ] M -s, -, **Bosnierin** [-ərɪn] F -, **-nen** Bosnian

bosnisch [ˈbɔsnɪʃ] ADJ Bosnian

Bosporus [ˈbɔspɔrʊs] M - der - the Bosporus

Boss ▲ [bɔs] M -es, **-e** (*inf*) boss (*inf*)

Bossa Nova [ˈbɔsa ˈnoːva] M - -, - -s bossa nova

bosseln [ˈbɔsln] (*inf*) VI to tinker *or* fiddle about (*inf*) (**an** +*dat* with) VT (= *zusammenbasteln*) to rig up (*inf*) (**jdm** for sb)

böswillig ADJ malicious; (*Jur auch*) wilful; **in ~er Absicht** with malicious intent ADV (= *mit böser Absicht*) maliciously; (*Jur auch*) wilfully

Böswilligkeit F -, *no pl* malice

bot *pret von* **bieten**

Botanik [boˈtaːnɪk] F -, *no pl* botany

Botaniker [boˈtaːnikɐ] M -s, -, **Botanikerin** [-ərɪn] F -, **-nen** botanist

botanisch [boˈtaːnɪʃ] ADJ botanic

botanisieren [botaniˈziːrən] *ptp* **botanisiert** VI to collect and study plants, to botanize (*rare*)

Botanisiertrommel F (botanist's) specimen container

Bötchen [ˈbøːtçən] NT -s, - *dim von* **Boot** little boat

Bote [ˈboːtə] M -n, **-n** **a** (*usu mit Nachricht*) messenger; (= *Kurier*) courier; (= *Postbote*) postman (*esp Brit*), mailman (*US*); (= *Zeitungsbote*) paperboy; (= *Laufbursche*) errand boy; (= *Gerichtsbote*) messenger-at-arms **b** (*fig*: = *Anzeichen*) herald, harbinger (*liter*)

Boten-: **Botenbericht** M (*Liter*) report by messenger; **Botendienst** M errand; (= *Einrichtung*) messenger service; **Botengang** M *pl*

-gänge errand; **einen ~ machen** to run an errand; **Botenlohn** M delivery fee; (= *Bezahlung des Boten*) messenger's fee; (*von Laufbursche*) errand boy's fee; **Botenstoff** M (*Med*) neurotransmitter

Botin [ˈboːtɪn] F -, **-nen** messenger; (= *Kurierin*) courier; (= *Postbotin*) postwoman (*esp Brit*), mailwoman (*US*); (= *Zeitungsbotin*) papergirl; (*für Botengänge*) errand girl; (= *Gerichtsbotin*) messenger-at-arms

botmäßig ADJ (*old, geh*) (= *untertänig*) compliant, submissive; (= *gehorsam*) obedient; **jdm ~ sein** to be at sb's command

Botmäßigkeit F , *no pl* (*old, geh*) **a** (= *Herrschaft*) dominion, rule **b** (= *Untertänigkeit*) compliance, submissiveness; (= *Gehorsamkeit*) obedience

Botschaft [ˈboːtʃaft] F -, **-en** **a** (= *Mitteilung*) message; (*esp amtlich*) communication; (= *Neuigkeit*) piece of news, news *no indef art, no pl*; (= *Aussage*) message; **eine freudige ~** good news, glad tidings *pl* (*liter, hum*); **die ~ in ihren Protestliedern** the message in her protest songs → **froh b b** (*Pol*: = *Vertretung*) embassy

Botschafter [ˈboːtʃaftɐ] M -s, -, **Botschafterin** [-ərɪn] F -, **-nen** ambassador

Botschafterebene F **auf ~** at ambassadorial level

Botschafts-: **Botschaftsbesetzung** F occupation of an/the embassy; **Botschaftssekretär(in)** M(F) secretary (*in the diplomatic service*)

Bott [bɔt] NT -(e)s, **-e** (*Sw*) general meeting

Böttcher [ˈbœtçɐ] M -s, -, **Böttcherin** [-ərɪn] F -, **-nen** cooper

Böttcherei [bœtçəˈraɪ] F -, **-en** **a** *no pl* (= *Gewerbe*) cooper's trade, cooperage **b** (= *Werkstatt*) cooper's (work)shop, cooperage

Bottich [ˈbɔtɪç] M -(e)s, **-e** tub

Bottleparty ▲ [ˈbɔtl-] F , **Bottle-Party** F bottle party

Botulismus [botuˈlɪsmʊs] M -, *no pl* (*Med*: = *Lebensmittelvergiftung*) botulism (*spec*)

Bouclé [buˈkleː] NT -s, **-s** bouclé (yarn)

Boudoir [buˈdoaːɐ] NT -s, **-s** (*dated geh*) boudoir

Bougainvillea [bugɛ̃ˈvɪlea] F -, **Bougainvilleen** [-leən] (*Bot*) bougainvillea

Bouillon [bʊlˈjɔŋ, bʊlˈjõː, (*Aus*) buˈjõː] F -, **-s** stock, bouillon; (*auf Speisekarte*) bouillon, consommé

Bouillonwürfel M stock *or* bouillon cube

Boule [buːl] NT -(s), *no pl* boules *sing*

Boulevard [buləˈvaːɐ, bulˈvaːɐ] M -s, **-s** boulevard

Boulevard-: **Boulevardblatt** NT (*inf*) popular daily, tabloid (*auch pej*); **Boulevardpresse** F (*inf*) popular press; **Boulevardstück** NT (*Theat*) light comedy; **Boulevardtheater** NT light theatre (*Brit*) *or* theater (*US*); **Boulevardzeitung** F popular daily (*Brit*), tabloid (*auch pej*)

Bouquet [buˈkeː] NT -s, **-s** **a** (= *Strauß*) bouquet **b** (*von Wein*) bouquet, nose

bourgeois [bʊrˈʒoa] ADJ (*geh*) bourgeois, middle-class

Bourgeois [bʊrˈʒoa] M -, - (*geh*) bourgeois

Bourgeoisie [bʊrʒoaˈziː] F -, **-n** [-ˈziːən] (*geh*) bourgeoisie

Boutique [buˈtiːk] F -, **-n** boutique

Bovist [ˈboːvɪst, boˈvɪst] M -s, **-e** (*Bot*) puffball, bovista (*spec*)

Bowle [ˈboːlə] F -, **-n** **a** (= *Getränk*) punch; **eine ~ ansetzen** to prepare (some) punch **b** (= *Gefäß, Schüssel*) punchbowl; (= *Garnitur*) punch set (*punchbowl and cups*)

Bowlen-: **Bowlenschüssel** F punchbowl; **Bowlenservice** [-zɛrviːs] NT punch set (*punchbowl and cups*)

Bow|ling [ˈboːlɪŋ] NT **-s, -s** (= *Spiel*) (tenpin) bowling; (= *Ort*) bowling alley; **~ spielen gehen** to go bowling

Bowling- [ˈboːlɪŋ]: **Bow|ling|bahn** F bowling alley; **Bow|ling|ku|gel** F bowl

Box [bɔks] F **-, -en a** (= *abgeteilter Raum*) compartment; (*für Pferde*) box; (*in Großgarage*) (partitioned-off) parking place; (*für Rennwagen*) pit; (*bei Ausstellungen*) stand **b** (= *Kamera*) box camera **c** (= *Behälter*) box **d** (= *Lautsprecherbox*) speaker (unit)

bo|xen [ˈbɔksn] VI (*Sport*) to box; (*zur Übung*) to spar; (= *mit Fäusten zuschlagen*) to hit out, to punch; **um einen Titel ~** to fight for a title; **gegen jdn ~** to fight sb VT **a** (= *schlagen*) jdn to punch, to hit **b** (*Sport sl:* = *antreten gegen*) to fight **c** (*mit der Faust*) *Ball* to punch, to thump **d** (*fig:* = *durchsetzen*) to force; **ein Produkt auf den Markt ~** to push a product VR **a** (*inf:* = *sich schlagen*) to have a punch-up (*Brit inf*) or a fight **b** (= *sich einen Weg bahnen*) to fight one's way; **sich durchs Leben/nach oben ~** (*fig inf*) to fight one's way through life/up

Bo|xen NT **-s,** *no pl* (*Sport*) boxing

Bo|xen|stopp M pit stop

Bo|xer¹ [ˈbɔksɐ] M **-s, -** (= *Hund*) boxer

Bo|xer² [ˈbɔksɐ] M **-s, -**, **Bo|xe|rin** [-ərɪn] F **-, -nen** (= *Sportler*) boxer

Boxer-: Bo|xer|auf|stand M (*Hist*) Boxer Rebellion; **Bo|xer|mo|tor** M (*Tech*) opposed cylinder engine (*Brit*), boxer engine (*US*); **Bo|xer|na|se** F boxer's nose, broken nose; **Bo|xer|shorts** PL boxer shorts *pl*; **Bo|xer|stel|lung** F boxer's stance

Box-: Box|hand|schuh M boxing glove; **Box|kalf** [ˈbɔkskalf] NT **-s,** *no pl* box calf; **Box|ka|me|ra** F box camera; **Box|kampf** M (= *Disziplin*) boxing *no art*; (= *Einzelkampf*) fight, bout, (boxing) match; **Box|ring** M boxing ring; **Box|sport** M (sport of) boxing

Boy [bɔy] M **-s, -s** pageboy (*Brit*), bellhop (*esp US*)

Boy|kott [bɔyˈkɔt] M **-(e)s, -e** or **-s** boycott

Boy|kott|dro|hung [bɔyˈkɔt-] F threat of a boycott

boy|kot|tie|ren [bɔykɔˈtiːrən] *ptp* **boykottiert** VT to boycott

BP [beːˈpeː] *abbr* **von Bundespost**

brab|beln [ˈbrabln] VI (*inf*) to mumble, to mutter; (*Baby*) to babble

brach¹ *pret von* **brechen**

brach² [braːx] ADJ *attr* (*old*) fallow

Bra|che [ˈbraːxə] F **-, -n** (*old*) (= *Land*) fallow (land); (= *Zeit*) fallow period

Brach|feld NT fallow field

Bra|che|jahr NT (*Agr*) fallow year; (*nach EU-Regelung*) set-aside

bra|chi|al [braˈxiaːl] ADJ *Mittel, Methode* primitive; **mit ~er Gewalt** by brute force

Bra|chi|al|ge|walt F brute force

Brach-: Brach|land NT fallow (land); **brach+le|gen** VT *sep* to leave fallow; **brach+lie|gen** VI *sep irreg* to lie fallow; (*fig*) to be left unexploited; **~de Kenntnisse/Kräfte** unexploited knowledge/powers; **Brach|mo|nat** M , **Brach|mond** (*obs*) M June

brach|te *pret von* **bringen**

Brach|vo|gel M curlew

Brack [brak] NT **-s, -s** brackish water

bra|ckig [ˈbrakɪç] ADJ brackish

Brack|was|ser NT *pl* **-wasser** brackish water

Brah|man [braˈman] NT **-s,** *no pl* Brahma

Brah|ma|ne [braˈmaːnə] M **-n, -n**, **Brah|ma|nin** [-ˈmaːnɪn] F **-, -nen** Brahman, Brahmin

brah|ma|nisch [braˈmaːnɪʃ] ADJ Brahminical, Brahman *attr*

Brah|ma|nis|mus [bramaˈnɪsmʊs] M **-,** *no pl* Brahmanism

Braille|schrift [braj-] F , *no pl* Braille, braille

Brain|drain ▲ [ˈbreːndreːn] M **-s,** *no pl*, **Brain--Drain** M **-s,** *no pl* brain drain (*inf*)

Brain|stor|ming [ˈbreːnstɔːmɪŋ] NT **-s, -s** brainstorming session

Brain|trust ▲ [ˈbreːntrast] M **-(s), -s**, **Brain--Trust** M **-(s), -s** brains (*Brit*) or brain (*US*) trust

bra|mar|ba|sie|ren [bramarbaˈziːrən] *ptp* **bramarbasiert** VI (*geh*) to brag (*von* about), to boast (*von* about), to swagger

Bram- [braːm-]: **Bram|se|gel** NT topgallant sail; **Bram|sten|ge** [-ʃtɛŋə] F **-, -n** topgallant stay

Bran|che [ˈbrãːʃə] F **-, -n** (= *Fach*) field, department; (= *Gewerbe*) trade; (= *Geschäftszweig*) area of business, trade; (= *Wirtschaftszweig*) (branch of) industry; **das gehört in seine ~** that's in his line or field

Branchen- [ˈbrãːʃn-]: **Bran|chen|ad|ress|buch** ▲ NT , **Bran|chen|buch** NT (*Telec*) classified directory, Yellow Pages®; **bran|chen|fremd** ADJ → **Branche** *Waren* foreign to the trade/industry; *Kollege* not familiar with the trade; **Bran|chen|füh|rer(in)** M(F) market leader; **Bran|chen|ken|ner(in)** M(F) → **Branche er ist ~** he knows the trade/industry, he has a good knowledge of the trade/industry; **Bran|chen|kennt|nis** F → **Branche** knowledge of the trade/industry; **bran|chen|kun|dig** ADJ → **Branche** experienced or well-versed in the trade/industry; **Bran|chen|lea|der** [-liːdɐ] M **-s, -**, **Bran|chen|lea|de|rin** [-ərɪn] F **-, -nen** market leader; **bran|chen|üb|lich** ADJ → **Branche** usual in the trade/industry; **bran|chen|un|üb|lich** ADJ → **Branche** not usual in the trade/industry; **Bran|chen|ver|zeich|nis** NT (*Telec*) classified directory, Yellow Pages®

Brand [brant] M **-(e)s, ⸚e** [ˈbrɛndə] **a** (= *Feuer*) fire; (*lodernd*) blaze, conflagration (*liter*); **in ~ geraten** to catch fire; (*in Flammen aufgehen*) to burst into flames; **in ~ stehen** to be on fire, to be ablaze; **etw in ~ setzen** or **stecken** to set fire to sth, to set sth alight or on fire; **einen ~ legen** to set a fire **b** *usu pl* (= *brennendes Holz etc*) firebrand **c** (*fig geh, der Liebe, des Hasses*) burning passion **d** (= *das Brennen, von Porzellan etc*) firing **e** (*fig inf:* = *großer Durst*) raging thirst **f** (*dial inf*) (= *Brennstoff*) fuel; (= *Holz auch*) firewood **g** (*Med*) gangrene *no art* **h** (*Pflanzenkrankheit*) blight

Brand-: brand|ak|tu|ell ADJ (*inf*) *Thema, Frage* red-hot (*inf*); *Buch* hot from the presses; *Platte etc* the latest thing (*inf*); **Brand|an|schlag** M arson attack; **Brand|be|kämp|fung** F firefighting; **Brand|bin|de** F bandage for burns; **Brand|bla|se** F (burn) blister; **Brand|bom|be** F firebomb, incendiary bomb or device; **Brand|brief** M (*inf*) (= *Bettelbrief*) begging letter; (= *Mahnbrief*) urgent reminder; **Brand|di|rek|tor(in)** M(F) ≈ fire chief; **brand|ei|lig** ADJ (*inf*) extremely urgent; **brand|heiß** ADJ (*inf*) = **brandaktuell**

bran|den [ˈbrandn] VI to surge (*auch fig*); **an** or **gegen etw** (*acc*) **~** to break against sth; **~der Beifall** thunderous applause

Bran|den|burg [ˈbrandnbʊrk] NT **-s** Brandenburg

Brand-: Brand|fa|ckel F firebrand; **Brand|fleck** M burn; **Brand|gans** F shelduck; **Brand|ge|fahr** F danger of fire; **bei ~** when there is danger of fire; **Brand|ge|ruch** M smell of burning; **Brand|herd** M source of the fire or blaze; (*fig*) source

bran|dig [ˈbrandɪç] ADJ **a** (*Bot*) suffering from blight; (*Med*) gangrenous **b** **~ riechen** to smell of burning; (*bei ausgegangenem Brand*) to have a burnt smell

Brand-: Brand|in|spek|tor(in) M(F) fire inspector; **Brand|kas|se** F fire insurance company; **Brand|ka|ta|stro|phe** F fire disaster; **Brand|le|ger** [-leːɡɐ] M **-s, -**, **Brand|le|-**

---

ge|rin [-ərɪn] F **-, -nen** (*esp Aus*) fire raiser (*esp Brit*), arsonist (*esp Jur*), incendiary (*Jur*); **Brand|loch** NT burn hole; **Brand|mal** NT *pl* **-male** brand; (*fig*) stigma; **Brand|ma|le|rei** F (*Art*) **a** *no pl* (= *Kunstrichtung*) pyrography, pokerwork (*Brit*) **b** (= *eingebranntes Bild*) (piece of) pyrography or pokerwork (*Brit*); **brand|mar|ken** [ˈbrantmarkn] VT *insep* to brand; (*fig*) to denounce; **jdn als etw ~** (*fig*) to brand sb (as) sth; **Brand|mau|er** F (fireproof) wall; **Brand|meis|ter(in)** M(F) fire chief; **brand|neu** ADJ (*inf*) brand-new, spanking new (*inf*); **Brand|op|fer** NT **a** (*Rel*) burnt offering **b** (= *Mensch*) fire victim; **Brand|re|de** F harangue; **Brand|ro|dung** F slash-and-burn; **Brand|sal|be** F ointment for burns; **Brand|satz** M incendiary compound; **Brand|scha|den** M fire damage; **brand|schat|zen** [ˈbrantʃatsn] VT *insep* to sack, to lay waste to; **die ~den Horden** the pillaging mob; **Brand|schat|zung** F **-, -en** sack, pillage; **Brand|schutz** M protection against fire; **Brand|sohle** F insole; **Brand|stel|le** F (= *Ort des Brandes*) fire, blaze; (= *verbrannte Stelle*) burned patch; **Brand|stif|ter(in)** M(F) fire raiser (*esp Brit*), arsonist (*esp Jur*), incendiary (*Jur*); **Brand|stif|tung** F arson (*auch Jur*), fire raising (*esp Brit*); **Brand|teig** M choux pastry

Bran|dung [ˈbrandʊŋ] F **-, -en** surf, breakers *pl*; (*fig geh*) surge

Bran|dungs|wel|le F breaker

Brand-: Brand|ur|sa|che F cause of a/the fire or blaze; **Brand|wa|che** F **a** (= *Überwachung der Brandstelle*) firewatch **b** (= *Personen*) firewatch team; **Brand|wun|de** F burn; (*durch Flüssigkeit*) scald; **Brand|zei|chen** NT brand

brann|te *pret von* **brennen**

Brannt|wein M spirits *pl*, (hard) liquor (*esp US*), schnap(p)s; **jede Art von ~** all types or every type of spirit(s) or (*esp US*) liquor; **Whisky ist ein ~** whisky is a (type of) spirit or (*esp US*) liquor

Branntwein-: Brannt|wein|bren|ner(in) M(F) distiller; **Brannt|wein|bren|ne|rei** F distillery; (= *Branntweinbrennen*) distilling or distillation of spirits or (*esp US*) liquor; **Brannt|wein|schank** [-ʃaŋk] F **-, -en** (*Aus*) ≈ public house (*Brit*), ≈ bar; **Brannt|wein|steu|er** F tax on spirits or (*esp US*) liquor

brä|sig [ˈbrɛːzɪç] ADJ (*esp N Ger:* = *behäbig, untätig*) complacent; **faul ~ herumsitzen** to sit around on one's backside (*inf*)

Bra|sil¹ [braˈziːl] F **-, -(s)** Brazil cigar

Bra|sil² M **-s, -e** or **-s** (= *Tabak*) Brazil(ian) tobacco

Bra|sil|holz NT brazil wood

Bra|si|li|a|ner [braziˈliaːnɐ] M **-s, -**, **Bra|si|li|a|ne|rin** [-ərɪn] F **-, -nen** Brazilian

bra|si|li|a|nisch [braziˈliaːnɪʃ] ADJ Brazilian

Bra|si|li|en [braˈziːliən] NT **-s** Brazil

Bras|se [ˈbrasə] F **-, -n a** (*Naut*) brace **b** (= *Fisch*) bream

bras|sen [ˈbrasn] VT (*Naut*) to brace

brät [brɛːt] 3. PERS SING *pres von* **braten**

Brät [brɛːt] NT **-s,** *no pl* sausage meat

Brat|ap|fel M baked apple

bra|ten [ˈbraːtn] *pret* **briet** [briːt], *ptp* **gebraten** [ɡəˈbraːtn] VTI (*am Spieß, im Ofen: mit Fett*) to roast; (*im Ofen: ohne Fett*) to bake; (*in der Pfanne*) to fry; **etw braun ~** to roast/fry sth until it is brown; **etw knusprig ~** to roast/fry sth until it is crispy VI (*inf: in der Sonne*) to roast (*inf*); **sich ~ lassen** to roast oneself (*inf*)

Bra|ten [ˈbraːtn] M **-s, -** ≈ pot roast meat *no indef art, no pl*; (*im Ofen gebraten*) joint (*Brit*), roast, roast meat *no indef art, no pl*; **kalter ~** cold meat; **ein fetter ~** (*fig*) a prize catch; **den ~ riechen** or **schmecken** (*inf*) to smell a rat (*inf*), to get wind of it/something; **einen ~ in der Röhre haben** (*inf*) to have a bun in the oven (*inf*)

Bra|ten-: Bra|ten|fett NT meat fat and juices *pl*, drippings (*esp US*); **Bra|ten|fleisch** NT meat for roasting, roasting meat; (*für die Pfanne*) meat for frying, frying meat; **Bra|ten|rock** M frock coat, Prince Albert (coat) (*US*); **Bra|ten|-saft** M meat juices *pl*, meat drippings *pl* (*esp US*), juices *pl* or drippings *pl* (*esp US*) from the meat; **Bra|ten|so|ße** F gravy; **Bra|ten|wen|der** [-vɛndɐ] M -s, - fish slice

Brat-: brat|fer|tig ADJ oven-ready; **Brat|fett** NT fat for roasting; (*für die Pfanne*) fat for frying; **Brat|fisch** M fried fish; **Brat|hähn|chen** NT , (*Aus, S Ger*) **Brat|hendl** NT roast chicken; **Brat|he|ring** M fried herring (*sold cold*); **Brat|huhn** NT , **Brat|hühn|chen** NT roast chicken; (= *Huhn zum Braten*) roasting chicken; **Brat|kar|tof|feln** PL fried or sauté potatoes; **Brat|kar|tof|fel|ver|hält|nis** NT (*hum*) **er hat ein ~ mit ihr** he only sees her because she feeds and waters him (*hum*); **er sucht ein ~** he's looking for a meal ticket

Brat|ling ['braːtlɪŋ] M **-s, -e** (*Cook*) veggieburger, Vegeburger®, vegetarian rissole

Brat-: Brat|ofen M oven; **Brat|pfan|ne** F frying pan; **Brat|röh|re** F oven; **Brat|rost** M grill; (*bei offenem Feuer auch*) gridiron

Brat|sche ['braːtʃə] F -, -n viola

Brat|scher ['braːtʃɐ] M **-s, -**, **Brat|sche|rin** [-ərɪn] F -, -nen, **Brat|schist** [braˈtʃɪst] M **-en, -en**, **Brat|schis|tin** [-ˈtʃɪstɪn] F -, -nen violist, viola player

Brat-: Brat|spieß M skewer; (= *Teil des Grills*) spit; (= *Gericht*) kebab; **Brat|wurst** F , **Brat|würst|chen** NT (*zum Braten*) (frying) sausage; (*gebraten*) (fried) sausage

Bräu [brɔy] NT **-(e)s, -e** (*esp S Ger*) (= *Biersorte*) brew, beer; (= *Brauerei*) brewery; (*rare: = Schenke*) inn (*old*), pub (*Brit*)

Brauch [braux] M **-(e)s, Bräuche** ['brɔyçə] custom, tradition; **nach altem ~** according to (established) custom or tradition; **etw ist ~** sth is traditional, sth is the custom; **so ist es ~, so will es der ~** that's the tradition or custom; **das ist bei uns so ~** (*inf*) that's traditional with us

brauch|bar ADJ **a** (= *benutzbar*) useable; *Plan* workable; (= *nützlich*) useful **b** (= *ordentlich*) *Schüler, Idee* decent, reasonable; *Arbeit, Arbeiter etc auch* attr (*inf*)

Brauch|bar|keit ['brauxbaːɐkait] F -, *no pl* usefulness; (*von Plan*) workability

brau|chen ['brauxn] VT **a** (= *nötig haben*) to need, to require (*form*) (*für, zu* for) **b** (*bei Zeitangaben*) *Zeit/zwei Minuten etc* ~ to need time/two minutes *etc*; **normalerweise brauche ich zwei Stunden dafür** I normally take two hours to do it; **wenn 5 Männer 3 Stunden ~,** ... if 5 men take 3 hours ...; **es braucht alles seine Zeit** everything takes time; **das braucht seine Zeit** that takes time; **wie lange braucht man, um ...?** how long does it take to ...?; **er hat zwei Tage dafür gebraucht** he took two days over it (*Brit*), he needed two days to do it **c** (*dated, geh: = bedürfen*) **es braucht einer Sache** sth is necessary **d** (*inf: = nützlich finden*) **das könnte ich ~** I could do with that, I could use that; **wir können das/ihn nicht ~** we could or can do without that/him, we don't need that/him; **das kann ich gerade ~!** (*iro*) that's all I need!; **kannst du die Sachen ~?** have you any use for the things?, are the things of any use to you?; **er ist zu allem zu ~** (*inf*) he's a really useful type (to have around) (*inf*); **heute bin ich zu nichts zu ~** I'm useless today (*inf*) **e** (= *benutzen*) *Waffe, Verstand, Gerät* to use → *auch* **gebraucht** **f** (*inf: = verbrauchen*) to use (up); *Strom etc* to use

▸ V AUX to need; **du brauchst das nicht tun** you needn't do that, you've no need to do that, you don't have or need to do that; **du brauchst es ihm nicht (zu) sagen** you needn't tell him that, you don't need to tell him that; (= *er weiß* ...

... *das schon*) you don't need to tell him that; **du hättest das nicht (zu) tun ~** you needn't have done that, you didn't need to do that, you had no need to do that; **du brauchst nur an(zu)rufen** you only have or need to call, you need only call; **du brauchst nicht besonders betont zu werden, dass ...** there's no need to stress the fact that ...; **es hätte nicht sein ~** there was no need for that; (= *das hätte nicht geschehen müssen*) that needn't have happened

Brauch|tum ['brauxtuːm] NT **-s**, (*rare*) **-tümer** [-tyːmɐ] customs *pl*, traditions *pl*; **zum ~ in diesem Land gehört ...** one of the customs in this country is ...

Brauch|was|ser NT process water

Braue ['brauə] F -, -n (eye)brow

brau|en ['brauən] VT *Bier* to brew; (*inf: = zubereiten*) *Tee* to brew up; *Kaffee* to make; *Zaubertrank, Punsch etc* to concoct ▸ VI **a** (= *Bier brauen*) to brew **b** (*old liter, Nebel*) to build up

Brau|er ['brauɐ] M **-s, -**, **Brau|e|rin** [-ərɪn] F -, -nen brewer

Brau|e|rei [brauəˈrai] F -, -en **a** brewery **b** *no pl* (= *das Brauen*) brewing

Brau|e|rei|we|sen NT brewing trade or industry

Brau-: Brau|haus NT brewery; **Brau|meis|ter(in)** M(F) master brewer

braun [braun] ADJ brown; (*von Sonne auch*) *Mensch, Haut* (sun)tanned; (*inf: = braunhaarig*) brown-haired; (*pej: = Nazibraun*) Nazi; ~ **werden** (*Mensch*) to get a (sun)tan, to go (*Brit*) or get brown, to tan; (*Brit*) to get brown, to tan; **~ gebrannt** (sun)tanned, bronzed, brown; **von der Sonne ~ gebrannt sein** to be tanned (by the sun); **die Braunen** (*old: = Pferde*) the brown or bay horses; (= *Nazis*) the Brownshirts

Braun [braun] NT **-s, -** brown

Braun-: braun|äu|gig ADJ brown-eyed; **Braun|bär** M brown bear

Brau|ne(r) ['braunə] M *decl as adj* **a** (= *Pferd*) bay (horse) **b** (*Aus: = Kaffee*) **ein großer/kleiner ~r** a large/small white coffee, a large/small coffee with milk

Bräu|ne ['brɔynə] F -, *no pl* (= *braune Färbung*) brown(ness); (*von Sonne*) (sun)tan

bräu|nen ['brɔynən] VT (*Cook*) to brown; (*Sonne etc*) to tan → *auch* **gebräunt** ▸ VI (*Cook*) to go or turn brown; (*Mensch*) to tan, to go brown (*Brit*); (*Sonne*) to tan; **sich in der Sonne ~ lassen** to get a (sun)tan (*Brit*) or to get or (*Brit*) go brown; (*Mensch auch*) to tan

Braun-: Braun|fäu|le F (*Bot, Agr*) blight; **braun|ge|brannt** △ ADJ *attr* → **braun**; **braun|haa|rig** ADJ brown-haired; *Frau auch* brunette; **Braun|hemd** NT *usu pl* (*Hist: = Nazi*) (Nazi) brownshirt or Brownshirt; **Braun|kohl** M (*dial*) (curly) kale; **Braun|koh|le** F brown coal

bräun|lich ['brɔynlɪç] ADJ brownish, browny

braun|rot ADJ reddish brown

Braun|sche Röh|re ['braunʃə-] F (*Tech*) cathode-ray tube

Braun|schweig ['braunʃvaik] NT **-s** Brunswick

Bräu|nung F -, -en browning; (*von Haut*) bronzing; **eine tiefe ~ der Haut** a deep (sun)tan

Bräu|nungs|creme F (quick-)tanning lotion

Bräu|nungs|stu|dio NT tanning studio

Braus [braus] M → **Saus**

Brau|se ['brauzə] F -, -n **a** (= *Dusche, Duschvorrichtung*) shower; **sich unter die ~ stellen** to have a shower **b** (= *Brauseaufsatz*) shower attachment; (*an Schlauch, Gießkanne*) rose, spray (attachment) **c** (= *Getränk*) pop; (= *Limonade*) (fizzy) lemonade; (= *Brausepulver*) lemonade powder

Brau|se-: Brau|se|bad NT shower (bath); **Brau|se|kopf** M (*dated*) hothead

brau|sen ['brauzn] VI **a** (= *tosen*) to roar; (*Orgel, Beifall*) to thunder; (*Jubel*) to ring out; (*Ohren*) to ring, to buzz; (= *sprudeln*) (*Wasser, Bran-*

... *dung*) to foam; (*geh, Blut*) to pound; **es brauste mir in den Ohren, es brauste in meinen Ohren** my ears were ringing or buzzing; **~der Beifall** thunderous applause **b** *aux sein* (= *rasen, rennen, schnell fahren*) to race **c** *auch* vr (= *duschen*) to (have a) shower **d** VT (= *abspülen*) *Gegenstände* to rinse (off); (= *abduschen*) *Körperteil, Kinder* to put under the shower

Brau|se-: Brau|se|pul|ver NT sherbet; **Brau|se|tab|let|te** F effervescent tablet; **Brau|se|wür|fel** M tablet of lemonade powder

Braut [braut] F **-, Bräute** ['brɔytə] **a** (*bei Hochzeit*) bride; (*dated*) (= *Verlobte*) fiancée, betrothed (*old*), bride-to-be; (= *Freundin*) girl(friend); ~ **Christi** bride of Christ **b** (*sl: = Frau, Mädchen*) bird (*esp Brit inf*), chick (*esp US inf*)

Braut-: Braut|bett NT nuptial or marital bed; **Braut|füh|rer** M ≈ person who gives away the bride; **Braut|ge|mach** NT (*Hist*) nuptial chamber

Bräu|ti|gam ['brɔytɪɡam, 'brɔytɪɡaːm] M **-s, -e** (bride)groom; (*dated*) (= *Verlobter*) fiancé, betrothed (*old*), husband-to-be

Braut-: Braut|jung|fer F bridesmaid; **Braut|kleid** NT wedding dress; **Braut|kranz** M *headdress of myrtle leaves traditionally worn by a bride*; **Braut|leu|te** PL = **Brautpaar**; **Braut|mut|ter** F *pl* **-mütter** bride's mother; **Braut|paar** NT bride and (bride)groom, bridal pair or couple; (*dated*: = *Verlobte*) engaged couple; **Braut|schau** F **auf die** ~ **gehen** to go looking for a bride or wife; **auf ~ sein** to be looking for a bride or wife; (*hum sl*) to be out to make a kill (*inf*); **Braut|schlei|er** M wedding or bridal veil; **Braut|schmuck** M wedding jewellery (*esp Brit*) or jewelry (*esp US*); **Braut|staat** M wedding finery; **Braut|stand** M , *no pl* (*dated*) engagement; **Braut|su|che** F = **Brautschau**; **Braut|un|ter|richt** M *in RC church, religious instruction of engaged couple prior to marriage*; **Braut|va|ter** M bride's father; **Braut|wer|bung** F courtship, wooing; **Braut|zeit** F last few weeks before the wedding

Brau|we|sen NT , *no pl* brewing (industry)

brav [braːf] ADJ **a** (= *gehorsam*) *Kind* good, well-behaved; **sei schön ~!** be a good boy/girl **b** (= *rechtschaffen*) upright, worthy; (= *bieder*) *Frisur, Kleid* plain **c** (*dated: = tapfer*) brave ▸ ADV **a** (= *artig*) ~ **(gemacht)!** (*zu Tier*) good boy!, well done; **iss das ~ leer** eat it up like a good boy/girl and eat it up, eat it up like a good boy/girl **b** (= *ganz ordentlich*) ~ **seine Pflicht tun** to do one's duty without complaining; **etw zu ~ spielen** (*pej*) to give an uninspired rendition of sth

Brav|heit F -, *no pl* **a** (= *Gehorsamkeit: von Kind*) good behaviour (*Brit*) or behavior (*US*) **b** (= *Rechtschaffenheit*) uprightness, worthiness; (= *Biederkeit: von Frisur, Kleid*) plainness **c** (*dated: = Tapferkeit*) bravery

bra|vo ['braːvo] INTERJ well done; (*für Künstler*) bravo

Bra|vo|ruf M cheer

Bra|vour [braˈvuːɐ] F -, *no pl* (*geh*) bravura; (*old: = Kühnheit*) bravery, daring; **mit ~** with style

Bra|vour|leis|tung [braˈvuːɐ-] F (*geh*) brilliant performance

bra|vou|rös [bravuˈrøːs] (*geh*) ADJ **a** (= *meisterhaft*) brilliant **b** (= *forsch*) with **~em Tempo** with verve ▸ ADV **a** (= *meisterhaft*) brilliantly **b** (= *kühn*) boldly; **etw ~ in Angriff nehmen** to attack or tackle sth with verve or gusto

Bra|vour|stück [braˈvuːɐ-] NT (*geh*) brilliant coup; (*Mus*) bravura

Bra|vur [braˈvuːɐ] F (*etc*) → **Bravour** *etc*

BRD [beːɛrˈdeː] F - *abbr von* **Bundesrepublik Deutschland** FRG

Germany (**DDR**). Since re-unification on October 3rd 1990 the **BRD** has consisted of 16 **Länder**, whose powers are subordinate to those of the Federal Government. The constitution of the **BRD** is set by the Grundgesetz.

Break [breːk] NT OR M **-s, -s** (*Tennis*) break

Break-even-Point [breːkˈiːvnpɔɪnt] M **-s, -s** (*Econ*) breakeven point

Brẹch-: brẹch|bar ADJ (*lit, fig*) breakable; **Brẹch|boh|nen** PL French beans *pl* (*Brit*), green *or* wax beans (*US*); **Brẹch|durch|fall** M diarrhoea (*Brit*) *or* diarrhea (*US*) and sickness; **Brẹch|ei|sen** NT crowbar; (*von Dieb*) jemmy, jimmy (*US*)

brẹ|chen [ˈbrɛçn̩] *pret* **brach** [braːx], *ptp* **gebrochen** [gəˈbrɔxn̩] VT a (= *zerbrechen, herausbrechen*) to break; *Schiefer, Stein, Marmor* to cut; *Widerstand* to overcome, to break; *Licht* to refract; (*geh*: = *pflücken*) *Blumen* to pluck, to pick; **sich/jdm den Arm ~** to break one's/sb's arm; **einer Flasche den Hals ~** to crack (open) a bottle; **das wird ihm das Genick** *or* **den Hals ~** (*fig*) that will bring about his downfall; **jdm die Treue ~** to break trust with sb; (*Liebhaber etc*) to be unfaithful to sb → *auch* **gebrochen, Bahn a, Eis a, Ehe**
b (= *erbrechen*) to vomit (up), to throw up VI a *aux sein* to break; **seine Augen brachen** (*old, liter*) he passed away; **mir bricht das Herz** it breaks my heart; **zum Brechen** *or* **~d voll sein** to be full to bursting
b **mit jdm/etw ~** to break with sb/sth
c (= *sich erbrechen*) to be sick, to throw up
VR (*Wellen*) to break; (*Lichtstrahl*) to be refracted; (*Schall*) to rebound (*an* +*dat* off)

Brẹ|cher [ˈbrɛçɐ] M **-s, -** a (= *Welle*) breaker b (*Tech*) crusher

Brẹch-: Brẹch|mit|tel NT emetic; **er/das ist das reinste ~ (für mich)** he/it makes me feel ill *or* sick; **Brẹch|reiz** M nausea; **ein leichter ~ a** slight touch of nausea; **Brẹch|stan|ge** F crowbar; **mit der ~** (*fig*) using the sledgehammer approach

Brẹ|chung [ˈbrɛçʊŋ] F **-, -en** a (*der Wellen*) breaking; (*des Lichts*) refraction; (*des Schalls*) rebounding b (*Ling*) mutation

Brẹ|chungs|win|kel M angle of refraction

Brẹ|douil|le [breˈdʊljə] F **-**, *no pl* **in der ~ sein** *or* **sitzen** to be in a scrape (*inf*); **in die ~ geraten** *or* **kommen** to get into a scrape (*inf*)

Brei [braɪ] M **-(e)s, -e** mush, paste, goo (*inf*); (*für Kinder, Kranke*) mash (*Brit*), mush (*esp US*), semi-solid food; (= *Haferbrei*) porridge; (= *Grießbrei*) semolina; (= *Reisbrei*) rice pudding; (= *Papierbrei*) pulp; **verrühren Sie die Zutaten zu einem dünnen ~** mix the ingredients to a thin paste; **die Lava fließt wie ein zäher ~** the lava flows like a sluggish pulp; **jdn zu ~ schlagen** (*inf*) to beat sb to a pulp (*inf*); **um den heißen herumreden** (*inf*) to beat about (*Brit*) *or* around the bush (*inf*); **jdm ~ um den Mund** *or* **ums Maul schmieren** (*inf*) to soft-soap sb (*inf*) → **Katze, Koch**

brei|ig [ˈbraɪɪç] ADJ mushy; **eine ~e Masse** a paste, a paste-like substance

breit [braɪt] ADJ a broad; (*esp bei Maßangabe*) wide; *Bekanntenkreis, Publikum* wide; *Interessen* broad, wide; *Schrift* broadly spaced, sprawling; **etw ~er machen** to broaden *or* widen sth; **~es Lachen** guffaw; **er hat ein ~es Lachen** the guffaws; **die ~e Masse** the masses *pl*, the broad mass of the population; **die ~e Öffentlichkeit** the public at large; **ein ~es Angebot** a broad *or* wide selection; **~e Streuung des Eigentums** widespread distribution of property, distribution of property on a broad basis; **er hat einen ~en Rücken** *or* **Buckel** (*fig inf*) he has a broad back, his shoulders are broad
b (*sl*: = *betrunken, unter Drogen*) high
ADV **den Stoff ~ nehmen** to take the material widthways; **~ lachen** to guffaw; **~ sprechen** to speak with a broad accent; **~ gebaut** sturdily

built; **~ gefächert** (*Firmengruppe, Messe, Kritik*) wide-ranging; **ein ~ gefächertes Angebot** a wide range; **die Schuhe ~ treten** to wear one's shoes out of shape; **der Stoff liegt doppelt ~** the material is double width; **sich ~ hinsetzen** to sit down squarely; **setz dich doch nicht so ~ hin** don't take up so much room

Breit|band- [-bant-]: **Breit|band|an|ti|bio|ti|kum** NT (*Pharm*) broad-spectrum antibiotic; **Breit|band|ka|bel** NT broadband cable; **Breit|band|(kom|mu|ni|ka|ti|ons)|netz** NT (*Telec*) broadband (communications) network; **Breit|band|laut|spre|cher** M (*Tech*) full--range loudspeaker; **Breit|band|ver|tei|ler** M broadband distributor

breit-: breit|bei|nig ADJ **in ~er Stellung** with one's legs apart; **~er Gang** rolling gait ADV **with one's legs apart; Breit|cord** M **-(e)s, -e** *or* **-s = Breitkord; breit drü|cken** ▲ VT to press flat

Brei|te [ˈbraɪtə] F **-, -n** a breadth; (*von Dialekt, Aussprache*) broadness; (*esp bei Maßangaben*) width; (*von Angebot*) breadth; (*von Interessen*) breadth, wide range; **der ~ nach** widthways; **etw in aller ~ erklären** to explain sth in great detail; **in voller ~ vor jdm** smack in front of sb (*inf*); **in die ~ gehen** to go into detail; (*inf*: = *dick werden*) to put on weight, to put it on a bit (*inf*)
b (*Geog*) latitude; (= *Gebiet*) part of the world; **in südlichere ~n fahren** (*inf*) to travel to more southerly climes *or* parts; **es liegt (auf) 20° nördlicher/südlicher ~** it lies 20° north/south; **in unseren ~n** in our area

brei|ten [ˈbraɪtn̩] VTR to spread; **jdm etw über die Beine** *etc* ~ to spread sth across sb's legs *etc*; **sich über das Tal/jds Gesicht ~** to spread across the valley/across *or* over sb's face

Breiten-: Brei|ten|ar|beit F , *no pl* broader *or* more general work; **Brei|ten|grad** M (degree of) latitude; **Brei|ten|kreis** M parallel; **Brei|ten|sport** M popular sport; **Brei|ten|wir|kung** F (*von Roman etc*) large *or* widespread impact

Breit-: breit|flä|chig ADJ *Gesicht* wide; *Ausbreitung* over a wide area ADV over a wide area; **~ malen** to paint with broad strokes; **breit|ge|fä|chert** △ [-gəfɛçɐt] ADJ → **breit** ADV; **Breit|kord** [-kɔrt] M **-(e)s, -s** *or* **-e** [-də] (*Tex*) jumbo cord; **breit|krem|pig** [-krɛmpɪç] ADJ broad--brimmed; **breit ma|chen** ▲ VR (*inf, Mensch*) to make oneself at home; (*Gefühl, Angst, Skepsis, Befürchtung*) to spread; **wenn er sich auf dem Sofa breit macht …** when he plants himself on the sofa …; **mach dich doch nicht so breit!** don't take up so much room; **die Touristen haben sich im Hotel breit gemacht** the tourists in the hotel are behaving as if they owned the place → **Bein a; breit|na|sig** ADJ *Mensch* broad-nosed, flat-nosed; **breit|ran|dig** ADJ *Hut* broad-brimmed; *Schwimmbecken, Gefäß, Brille* broad-rimmed; **Breit|rei|fen** M (*Mot*) wide tyre (*Brit*) *or* tire (*US*); **breit+schla|gen** VT *sep irreg* (*inf*) **jdn (zu etw) ~** to talk sb round (*Brit*) *or* around (*US*) to sth); **sich ~ lassen** to let oneself be talked round (*Brit*) *or* around (*US*); **breit|schul|te|rig, breit|schult|rig** ADJ broad-shouldered; **Breit|schwanz** M , *no pl* caracul; **Breit|sei|te** F (*Naut, auch fig*) broadside; (*von Tisch*) short end; **eine ~ abge|ben** to fire a broadside (*auch fig*); **Breit|spur|bahn** F broad-gauge railway; **breit|spu|rig** [-ʃpuːrɪç] ADJ *Bahn* broad-gauge *attr*; *Straße* wide-laned ADV (*fig*) flashily, showily; **~ re|den/auftreten** to speak/behave in a showy manner; **breit+tre|ten** VT *sep irreg* (*inf*) to go on about (*inf*); *Thema, Witz* to flog to death (*inf*); **Breit|wand** F wide screen; **etw in ~ dre|hen** to film sth for the wide screen; **Breit|wand|film** M film for the wide screen

Bre|men [ˈbreːmən] NT **-s** Bremen

Bre|mer[1] [ˈbreːmɐ] ADJ *attr* Bremen

Bre|mer[2] [ˈbreːmɐ] M **-s, -**, **Bre|me|rin** [-ərɪn] F **-, -nen** native of Bremen; (= *Einwohner*) inhabitant of Bremen

bre|misch [ˈbreːmɪʃ] ADJ Bremen *attr*

Brems-: Brems|ab|stand M (*Mot*) braking distance; **Brems|an|la|ge** F braking system; **Brems|ba|cke** F brake block; **Brems|be|lag** M brake lining

Brem|se[1] [ˈbrɛmzə] F **-, -n** (*bei Fahrzeugen*) brake; **auf die ~(n) treten/steigen** (*inf*) to put on *or* apply/slam on (*inf*) the brake(s)

Brem|se[2] F **-, -n** (= *Insekt*) horsefly

brem|sen [ˈbrɛmzn̩] VI (*Fahrer, Auto*) to brake; (*Vorrichtung*) to function as a brake; **der Dynamo bremst** the dynamo acts as a brake; **der Wind bremst** the wind slows you *etc* down
b (*inf*: = *zurückstecken*) to ease off, to put on the brakes (*inf*); **mit etw ~** to cut down (on) sth; **jetzt sollten wir mit den Ausgaben ~** it's time to apply the (financial) brakes
VT a *Fahrzeug* to brake
b (*fig*) to restrict, to limit; *Entwicklung* to slow down; *Begeisterung* to dampen; (*inf*) *jdn* to check; **er ist nicht zu ~** (*inf*) there's no stopping him
VR (*inf*) **sich in seiner Ausdrucksweise ~** to moderate one's language; **ich kann** *or* **werd mich ~** not likely!, no fear!

Brem|sen|stich M horsefly bite

Brem|ser [ˈbrɛmzɐ] M **-s, -** (*Rail, Sport*) brakeman

Brem|se|rin [ˈbrɛmzərɪn] F **-, -nen** (*Rail, Sport*) brakewoman

Brems-: Brems|fall|schirm M brake parachute; **Brems|flüs|sig|keit** F brake fluid; **Brems|griff** M brake lever; **Brems|he|bel** M brake lever; **Brems|klap|pe** F (*Aviat*) brake flap; **Brems|klotz** M (*Aut*) brake pad; **Brems|kraft** F braking power; **Brems|kraft|ver|stär|ker** M servo brake; **Brems|leis|tung** F braking efficiency; **Brems|leuch|te** F , **Brems|licht** NT brake light; **Brems|pe|dal** NT brake pedal; **Brems|pro|be** F brake test; **eine ~ machen** to test one's brakes; **Brems|prüf|stand** M brake test stand; **Brems|ra|ke|te** F retrorocket; **Brems|schlauch** M brake hose; **Brems|schuh** M brake shoe; **Brems|seil** NT brake cable; **Brems|spur** F skid mark *usu pl*; **Brems|stre|cke** F braking *or* stopping distance

Brems|sung F **-, -en** braking

Brems-: Brems|vor|rich|tung F brake mechanism; **Brems|weg** M braking *or* stoppng distance

Brenn-: brenn|bar ADJ combustible, inflammable, flammable; **leicht ~** highly combustible *or* inflammable; **Brenn|bar|keit** F [ˈbrɛnbaˑɐkait] , *no pl* combustibility, inflammability, flammability; **Brenn|dau|er** F (*von Glühbirnen*) life; **Brenn|ele|ment** NT fuel element

bren|nen [ˈbrɛnən] *pret* **brannte** [ˈbrantə], *ptp* **ge|brannt** [gəˈbrant] VI to burn; (*Haus, Wald auch*) to be on fire; (*elektrisches Gerät, Glühbirne etc*) to be on; (*Zigarette, Sparflamme*) to be alight; (*Stich*) to sting; (*Füße*) to hurt, to be sore; **das Streichholz/Feuerzeug brennt nicht** the match/lighter won't light; **auf der Haut/in den Augen ~** to burn *or* sting the skin/eyes; **das Licht ~ lassen** to leave the light on; **im Zimmer brennt noch Licht** the light is still on in the room; **es brennt!** fire, fire!; (*fig*) it's urgent; **wo brennts denn?** (*inf*) what's the panic?; **darauf ~, etw zu tun** to be dying to do sth; **das brennt mir auf der Seele** that is preying on my mind; **es brennt mir unter den Nägeln, zu erfahren, ob …** I am itching (*inf*) *or* dying to know if … → **Boden a**
VT to burn; *Branntwein* to distil (*Brit*), to distill (*US*); *Mandeln, Kaffee* to roast; *Porzellan, Ton, Ziegel* to fire, to bake
VR (*lit*) to burn oneself (*an* +*dat* on); (*inf*: = *sich täuschen*) to be very much mistaken

bren|nend `ADJ` *(lit, fig)* burning; *Zigarette* lighted; *Durst* raging; *Hass* consuming `ADV` *(inf: = sehr)* terribly; **sich ~ für etw interessieren** to be really *or* incredibly interested in sth; **ich wüsste ja ~ gern …** I'm dying *or* itching *(inf)* to know …

Brẹn|ner¹ ['brɛnɐ] M -s, - *(Tech)* burner

Brẹn|ner² ['brɛnɐ] M -s, -, **Brẹn|ne|rin** [-ərɪn] F -, -nen *(= Branntweinbrenner)* distiller; *(= Kaffeebrenner)* coffee roaster; *(= Ziegelbrenner)* brick-firer

Brẹn|ne|rei [brɛnə'raɪ] F -, -en distillery; *(= Kaffeebrennerei)* coffee-roasting plant; *(= Ziegelbrennerei)* brickworks *sing or pl*

Brẹnnessel △ F = **Brennnessel**

Brẹnn-: Brẹnn|glas NT burning glass; **Brẹnn|holz** NT firewood; **Brẹnn|kam|mer** F combustion chamber; **Brẹnn|ma|te|ri|al** NT fuel (for heating); **Brẹnn|nes|sel** ▲ F stinging nettle; **Brẹnn|ofen** M kiln; **Brẹnn|punkt** M *(Math, Opt)* focus; **im ~ des Interesses stehen** to be the focal point *or* the focus of attention; **etw in den ~ rücken** *(fig)* to focus attention on sth; **Brẹnn|sche|re** F curling tongs *pl (Brit)*, curling iron *(US)*; **Brẹnn|schluss** M *(von Rakete)* burnout; **Brẹnn|spie|gel** M burning glass; **Brẹnn|spi|ri|tus** M [-ʃpiːritʊs] methylated spirits *sing or pl*; **Brẹnn|stab** M fuel rod; **Brẹnn|stoff** M fuel; **Brẹnn|stoff|kreis|lauf** M *(in Atomkraftwerk)* (nuclear) fuel cycle; **Brẹnn|wei|te** F *(Opt)* focal length; **Brẹnn|wert** M *(Tech, Physiol)* calorific value

brẹnz|lig ['brɛntslɪç] `ADJ` **a** ein ~er Geruch a smell of burning **b** *(inf) Situation, Angelegenheit* precarious, dicey *(Brit inf)*; **die Sache/die Lage wurde ihm zu ~** things got too hot for him `ADV` **~ riechen** to smell of burning

Brẹ|sche ['brɛʃə] F -, -n breach, gap; **in etw** *(acc)* **eine ~ schießen** to breach sth; **in die ~ springen** *(fig)* to step into *or* fill the breach; **für jdn/etw eine ~ schlagen** *(fig)* to stand up for sb/sth

Bre|tag|ne [bre'tanjə] F **die ~** Brittany

Bre|to|ne [bre'toːnə] M -n, -n, **Bre|to|nin** [-'toːnɪn] F -, -nen Breton

bre|to|nisch [bre'toːnɪʃ] ADJ Breton

Brẹtt [brɛt] NT -(e)s, -er ['brɛtə] **a** *(= Holzplatte)* board; *(länger und dicker)* plank; *(= Spielbrett, Sprungbrett)* board; *(= Bücherbrett, Gewürzbrett)* shelf; *(inf: = Tablett)* tray; *(= Frühstücksbrett)* platter, wooden plate; **schwarzes ~** notice board *(Brit)*, bulletin board *(US)*; **etw mit ~ern vernageln** to board sth up; **hier ist die Welt mit ~ern vernagelt** this is a parochial little place; **ich habe heute ein ~ vor dem Kopf** *(inf)* I can't think straight today → **Stein a** **b Bretter** PL *(fig)* (= Bühne) stage, boards *pl*, planks *pl (inf)*; *(= Boden des Boxrings)* floor, canvas; *(= Skier)* planks *pl (sl)*; **über die ~er gehen** *(Theat)* to be put on; **die ~er, die die Welt bedeuten** the stage; **auf den ~ern stehen** to be on the stage; *(auf Skiern)* to ski; **jdn auf die ~er schicken** *(Sport)* to send sb to the canvas, to floor sb, to knock sb down

Brẹtt|chen ['brɛtçən] NT -s, - *(inf)* platter, wooden plate; *(zum Schneiden)* board

Brẹtt|ter-: Brẹtt|ter|bo|den M wooden floor *(made from floorboards)*; **Brẹtt|ter|bu|de** F booth; *(pej)* shack

brẹtt|tern ['brɛtɐn] VI *(inf, Fahrzeug, Fahrer)* to race (along); **über die Autobahn ~** to tear along the motorway *(Brit)* or freeway *(US)*

Brẹtt|ter-: Brẹtt|ter|wand F wooden wall; *(= Trennwand)* wooden partition; *(= Zaun, für Reklame)* hoarding; **Brẹtt|ter|ver|schlag** M *(= Schuppen)* (wooden) shed; *(angebaut)* (wooden) lean-to; *(= Trennwand)* wooden partition; **Brẹtt|ter|zaun** M wooden fence; *(an Baustellen auch)* hoarding

Brẹtt|spiel NT board game

Brẹt|zel F -, -n *(Sw)* pretzel

Bre|vier [bre'viːɐ] NT -s, -e **a** *(Eccl)* breviary **b** *(= Auswahl von Texten)* extracts *pl*; *(= Leitfaden)* guide *(+gen* to)

Bre|ze ['breːtsə] F -, -n *(S Ger)* pretzel

Bre|zel ['breːtsl] F -, -n pretzel; **das geht wies ~ backen** it's no trouble at all

brich [brɪç] IMPER *sing von* **brechen**

Bridge [brɪtʃ] NT -, *no pl (Cards)* bridge

Brief [briːf] M -(e)s, -e **a** letter; *(Bibl)* epistle; **aus seinen ~en** from his letters *or* correspondence; **etw als ~ schicken** to send sth (by) letter post *(esp Brit)*; **jdm ~ und Siegel auf etw** *(acc)* **geben** to give sb one's word **b** *(St Ex: = Briefkurs)* selling rate, offer price

Brief- *in cpds* letter; **Brief|ab|la|ge** F letter file; **Brief|adel** M title conferred by letters patent; *(= Leute)* nonhereditary nobility; **Brief|be|schwe|rer** [-bəˈveːrɐ] M -s, - paperweight; **Brief|block** M *pl* -blöcke *or* -blocks writing *or* letter pad; **Brief|bo|gen** M (sheet of) writing *or* letter *or* note paper; **Brief|bom|be** F letter bomb

Brief|chen ['briːfçən] NT -s, - **a** note **b** *(für Shampoo, Creme, Pulver)* sachet; *(für Streichhölzer)* book; *(für Nadeln)* packet, paper; *(für Rauschgift)* small packet *(containing drugs)*

Brief-: Brief|druck|sa|che F circular; **Brief|ein|wurf** M *(in Tür)* letter box *(Brit)*, mailbox *(US)*; *(in Postamt etc)* postbox *(Brit)*, mailbox *(US)*

brie|fen [briːfn] VT *(= informieren, einweisen)* to brief

Brief-: Brief|fach NT pigeonhole; **Brief|form** F **in ~** in letter form; *(= mittels Brief)* by letter; **Brief|freund(in)** M(F) pen friend, pen pal *(inf)*; **Brief|freund|schaft** F correspondence with a pen friend; **eine ~ mit jdm haben** to be pen friends with sb; **Brief|ge|heim|nis** NT privacy of the post *(Brit)* or mail

Brie|fing ['briːfɪŋ] NT -s, -s briefing

Brief|kar|te F correspondence card

Brief|kas|ten M *(am Haus)* letter box *(Brit)*, mailbox *(US)*; *(der Post)* postbox *(Brit)*, pillar box *(dated Brit)*, mailbox *(US)*; *(in Zeitungen)* problem column, agony column; **elektronischer ~** *(Comput)* electronic mailbox → **tot b**

Brief|kas|ten-: Brief|kas|ten|fir|ma F das ist nur eine ~ that firm is just an accommodation address; **Brief|kas|ten|on|kel** M *(inf)* agony columnist *or* uncle *(inf)*; **Brief|kas|ten|tan|te** F *(inf)* agony columnist *or* aunt *(inf)*

Brief-: Brief|kon|takt M written contact; **in ~ stehen** to correspond with; **sie stehen in ~** they correspond (with each other), they write to each other; **Brief|kopf** M letterhead; *(handgeschrieben)* heading; **Brief|kurs** M *(St Ex)* selling rate, offer price; **Brief|ku|vert** NT envelope

brief|lich ['briːflɪç] `ADJ` by letter; **wir bitten um ~e Mitteilung** please inform us by letter; **~er Verkehr** correspondence `ADV` by letter; **mit jdm ~ verkehren** to correspond with sb

Brief|mar|ke F stamp

Brief|mar|ken- *in cpds* stamp; **Brief|mar|ken|al|bum** NT stamp album; **Brief|mar|ken|au|to|mat** M stamp machine; **Brief|mar|ken|bo|gen** M sheet of stamps; **Brief|mar|ken|kun|de** F philately; **Brief|mar|ken|samm|ler(in)** M(F) stamp collector, philatelist; **Brief|mar|ken|samm|lung** F stamp collection

Brief-: Brief|öff|ner M letter opener, paper knife; **Brief|pa|pier** NT letter *or* writing *or* note paper; **Brief|por|to** NT postage; *(= Gebühr)* postage rate for letters, letter post; **Brief|post** F letter post *(esp Brit)*; **Brief|qua|li|tät** F *(Comput)* letter quality; **Brief|ro|man** M epistolary novel, novel in letter form; **Brief|sen|dung** F letter, item sent by letter post *(esp Brit)*; **Brief|ta|sche** F wallet, billfold *(US)*; **Brief|tau|be** F carrier pigeon; **Brief|trä|ger** M postman *(Brit)*, mailman *(US)*; **Brief|trä|ge|rin** F postwoman *(Brit)*, mail-

---

woman *(US)*; **Brief|um|schlag** M envelope; **Brief|ver|kehr** M correspondence; **Brief|waa|ge** F letter scales *pl*; **Brief|wahl** F postal vote; **seine Stimme durch ~ abgeben** to use the postal vote, to vote by post *(Brit)*; **Brief|wäh|ler(in)** M(F) postal voter; **Brief|wech|sel** M correspondence; **im ~ mit jdm stehen, einen ~ mit jdm führen** to be in correspondence with sb, to be corresponding with sb; **Brief|zu|stel|ler** M *(form)* postman *(Brit)*, mailman *(US)*; **Brief|zu|stel|le|rin** F *(form)* postwoman *(Brit)*, mailwoman *(US)*

Brie|kä|se ['briː-] M brie

Bries [briːs] NT -es, -e [-zə] *(Physiol)* thymus; *(Cook)* sweetbread

briet *pret von* **braten**

Bri|ga|de [bri'gaːdə] F -, -n **a** *(Mil)* brigade **b** *(DDR)* (work) team *or* group

Bri|ga|de|ge|ne|ral(in) M(F) brigadier *(Brit)*, brigadier general *(US)*; *(in Luftwaffe)* air commodore *(Brit)*, brigadier general *(US)*

Bri|ga|dier [briga'diːɐ] M -s, -e *(DDR)* (work) team leader

Brigg [brɪk] F -, -s *(Naut: = Schiff)* brig

Bri|kett [bri'kɛt] NT -s, -s *or (rare)* -e briquette

Bri|kett|zan|ge F fire tongs *pl*

bril|lant [brɪl'jant] `ADJ` brilliant `ADV` brilliantly; **~ aussehen** to look beautiful

Bril|lant [brɪl'jant] M -en, -en brilliant, diamond ▲

Bril|lant- *in cpds* diamond; **Bril|lant|feu|er|werk** NT cascade; **Bril|lant|kol|li|er** NT diamond necklace; **Bril|lant|ring** M diamond ring; **Bril|lant|schmuck** M diamonds *pl*

Bril|lanz [brɪl'jants] F -, *no pl* brilliance

Bril|le ['brɪlə] F -, -n **a** *(Opt)* glasses *pl*, spectacles *pl*, specs *(inf) pl*; *(= Schutzbrille)* goggles *pl*; *(= Sonnenbrille)* glasses *pl*; **eine ~** a pair of glasses *or* spectacles; **eine ~ tragen** to wear glasses **→ rosa b** *(= Klosettbrille)* (toilet) seat

Bril|len-: Bril|len|etui N, **Bril|len|fut|te|ral** NT glasses *or* spectacle case; **Bril|len|fas|sung** F, **Bril|len|ge|stell** NT spectacle frames *pl*; **Bril|len|glas** NT lens; **Bril|len|schlan|ge** F *(pej)* four-eyes *(pej inf)*, woman who wears glasses; **Bril|len|trä|ger(in)** M(F) person who wears glasses; **er ist ~** he wears glasses

Bril|li ['brɪli] M -s, -s *(inf)* diamond, rock *(inf)*

bril|lie|ren [brɪl'jiːrən] *ptp* **brilliert** VI *(geh)* to be brilliant; **sie brillierte mit ihrem Gesang** her singing was brilliant

Brim|bo|ri|um [brɪm'boːriʊm] NT -s, *no pl (inf)* fuss

---

brin|gen ['brɪŋən]
pret **brachte** ['braxtə], *ptp* **gebracht** [gə'braxt]

TRANSITIVES VERB

> Im Sinne von **herbringen** wird **bringen** im Englischen mit **to bring** übersetzt, im Sinne von **woanders hinbringen** mit **to take**.

a = herbringen to bring; *(= holen)* to bring, to get *(jdm* for sb); **bring mir bitte meine Schuhe** please bring me my shoes; **der Besuch hat mir Blumen gebracht** my visitors brought me flowers; **was für Nachricht bringen Sie?** what news have you got?; **sich** *(dat)* **etw bringen lassen** to have sth brought to one; **der letzte Sommer brachte uns viel Regen** last summer brought us a lot of rain; **Schäfchenwolken bringen schönes Wetter** fleecy clouds bring fine weather; **jdn/etw unter** *or* **in seine Gewalt bringen** to gain control over *or* of sb/sth; **er bringt es nicht übers Herz** *or* **über sich** he can't bring himself to do it; **etw an sich** *(acc)* **bringen** to acquire sth

♦ **etw mit sich bringen der Frühling bringt viele prächtige Blüten mit sich** spring brings lots of wonderful flowers; **seine Vergesslichkeit bringt viele Probleme mit sich** his forgetfulness causes a lot of problems; **die Liebe**

---

bringt es mit sich, dass man alles durch eine rosarote Brille sieht love means you see everything through rose-coloured spectacles (*Brit*) or rose-colored glasses (*US*)

b = woanders hinbringen to take; **jdn ins Krankenhaus/zum Bahnhof/nach Hause bringen** to take sb to hospital/to the station/home; **kannst du mich zum Bahnhof bringen?** can you give me a lift to the station?; **bring das Auto in die Garage** put the car in the garage; **die Kinder zu** or **ins Bett bringen** to put the children to bed; **das Essen auf den Tisch bringen** to serve the food; **jdm eine Nachricht bringen** to give sb some news; **etw hinter sich** (*acc*) **bringen** to get sth over and done with

c = einbringen *Geld, Gewinn* to bring in, to make; (*Boden, Mine etc*) to produce; *Ärger* to cause; *Vorteile* to bring; **das Bild brachte 500 Euro** the picture went for 500 euros; **Freude bringen** to bring joy; **Vergnügen bringen** to give pleasure; **(jdm) Glück/Unglück bringen** to bring (sb) luck/bad luck; **Unglück über jdn bringen** to bring sb unhappiness; **das bringt nichts** (*inf*) it's pointless

d = lenken, versetzen **in die richtige Form bringen** to get or put in the right form; **jdn/sich in Gefahr bringen** to put sb/oneself in danger; **das bringt dich vors Gericht/ins Gefängnis** you'll end up in court/prison if you do that; **das Gespräch/die Rede auf etw** (*acc*) **bringen** to bring the conversation/talk round to sth; **jdn auf die schiefe Bahn bringen** to lead sb astray; **jdn wieder auf den rechten Weg bringen** (*fig*) to get sb back on the straight and narrow; **jdn außer sich** (*acc*) **bringen** to upset sb; **zum Stillstand bringen** (*Verkehr, Verhandlungen*) to bring to a standstill; *Fahrzeug* to bring to a halt; **jdn zum Lachen/Weinen bringen** to make sb laugh/cry; **jdn zur Verzweiflung bringen** to drive sb to despair; **jdn dazu bringen, etw zu tun** to get sb to do sth

♦ **so weit bringen, dass sie bringt ihn mit ihrer Nörgelei noch so weit, dass er kündigt** her nagging will make him hand in his notice; **wir bringen ihn mit ständigen Ermunterungen noch so weit, dass er sich als Kandidat aufstellen lässt** if we keep on encouraging him we'll get him to put himself forward as a candidate; **du wirst es noch so weit bringen, dass man dich hinauswirft** you will make them throw you out

e = veröffentlichen (*Verlag*) to publish; (*Zeitung*) to print; (= *senden*) *Bericht etc* to broadcast; **etw in die Zeitung bringen** to publish sth in the paper; *Verlobung, Angebot* to announce sth in the paper; **die Zeitung/das Fernsehen brachte nichts darüber** there was nothing in the paper/on television about it; **die Zeitung brachte einen Artikel darüber** there was an article in the paper about it; **alle Zeitungen brachten es auf der ersten Seite** all the papers had it on the front page; **wir bringen einen Sonderbericht aus Kuba** we now have a special report from Cuba; **wir bringen Nachrichten** here is the news; **um zehn Uhr bringen wir Nachrichten** at ten o'clock we have the news; **die nächsten Nachrichten bringen wir um 10 Uhr** the next news will be at 10 o'clock; **was bringt das Fernsehen/Radio heute Abend?** what's on television/the radio tonight?

f = aufführen *Stück* to do; **welche Lieder bringt sie auf ihrer Tournee?** what songs is she doing on her tour?

g = schaffen, leisten (*sl*) **ich bringe diese Übung nicht** I can't do this exercise; **das bringt er nicht** he's not up to it; **hat er das tatsächlich gebracht?** did he really do it?; **er bringts** he's got what it takes; **das Auto bringt 180 km/h** (*inf*) the car can do 180 km/h; **der Motor bringts nicht mehr** the engine has had it (*inf*); **ihr Typ bringts nicht mehr** her boyfriend can't stand the pace any more (*inf*); **das kannst du doch nicht bringen** that's not on (*inf*)

h andere Wendungen

♦ **es bringen** (= *erreichen*) **es auf 80 Jahre bringen** to reach the age of 80; **der Motor hat es**

auf 180.000 km gebracht the engine has done 180,000 km; **das Auto hat es auf 180.000 km gebracht** the car has clocked up 180,000 km; **er hat es auf 25 Punkte gebracht** he got 25 points; **es zu etwas/nichts bringen** to get somewhere/nowhere; **es (im Leben) weit bringen** to do very well; **es zu Ehren bringen** to win honours (*Brit*) or honors (*US*); **er hat es bis zum Hauptmann/Direktor gebracht** he made it to captain/director, he got to be captain/director → *auch* **g**

♦ **jdn um etw bringen** to do sb out of sth; **das bringt mich noch um den Verstand** it's driving me mad (*Brit*) or crazy; **der Lärm hat mich um den Schlaf gebracht** the noise stopped me getting any sleep; **jdn/sich ums Leben bringen** to kill sb/oneself

---

Bring|schuld F (*Jur*) obligation to be performed at creditor's habitual residence (*fig*) obligation to fulfil (*Brit*) or fulfill (*US*)

bri|sant [bri'zant] ADJ (*lit, fig*) explosive

Bri|sanz [bri'zants] F -, -en explosive force; (*fig*) explosive nature; **ein Thema von äußerster ~** an extremely explosive subject

Bri|se ['briːzə] F -, -n breeze

Bri|tan|ni|en [bri'tanion] NT -s (*Hist*) Britain, Britannia (*Hist*); (*Press*: = *Großbritannien*) Britain

bri|tan|nisch [bri'taniʃ] ADJ (*Hist*) Britannic

Bri|te ['brɪtə, 'briːtə] M -n, -n, **Bri|tin** ['brɪtɪn, 'briːtɪn] F -, -nen Briton, Brit (*inf*); **er ist ~** he is British; **die ~n** the British

bri|tisch ['brɪtɪʃ, 'briːtɪʃ] ADJ British; **die Britischen Inseln** the British Isles

Bröck|chen ['brœkçən] NT -s, - *dim von* **Brocken**

bröck|e|lig ['brœkəlɪç] ADJ crumbly; *Mauer, Putz* crumbling; **~ werden** to (start to) crumble

bröck|eln ['brœkln] VI *aux sein* **a** (*Haus, Fassade*) to crumble; (*Gestein auch*) to crumble away; (*Preise, Kurse*) to tumble; (*Streikfront*) to crumble; (*Argwohn, Vertrauen etc*) to disintegrate **b** (*sl*: = *sich übergeben*) to puke (*inf*)

bro|cken ['brɔkn] VT *Brot* to break

Bro|cken ['brɔkn] M -s, - lump, chunk; (*fig*: = *Bruchstück*) scrap; (*Hunt*) bait; (*inf*: *Person*) lump (*inf*); **das Baby ist ein richtiger ~** the baby's a regular little dumpling (*Brit inf*), the baby's as plump as a dumpling (*US inf*); **ein paar ~ Spanisch** a smattering of Spanish; **er schnappte den anderen die besten ~ weg** he snapped up all the best titbits (*Brit*) or tidbits (*US*); **ein harter ~** (= *Person*) a tough/hard nut (*inf*), a tough cookie (*inf*); **das ist ein harter** or **dicker ~** that's a tough nut to chuck (*inf*); **die ~ hinschmeißen** (*inf*) to chuck it all in (*inf*)

brocken|wei|se ADV bit by bit

bro|deln ['broːdln] VI (*Wasser, Suppe*) to bubble; (*in Krater auch*) to seethe; (*Dämpfe, liter: Nebel*) to swirl, to seethe; **es brodelt** (*fig*) there is seething unrest

Bro|dem ['broːdəm] M -s, - (*liter*) foul-smelling vapour (*Brit*) or vapor (*US*)

Broi|ler ['brɔylɐ] M -s, - (*dial*) roast chicken

Bro|kat [bro'kaːt] M -(e)s, -e brocade

Bro|ker ['broːkɐ] M -s, -, **Bro|ke|rin** [-ərɪn] F -, -nen (*St Ex*) (stock)broker; (*Comm*) broker

Bro|ker|fir|ma F (*St Ex*) brokerage firm

Bro|ker|haus NT (*St Ex*) brokerage house

Brok|ko|li ['brɔkoli] PL broccoli *sing*

Brom [broːm] NT -s, *no pl* (*abbr* **Br**) bromine

Brom|bee|re ['brɔm-] F blackberry, bramble

Brom|beer|strauch M blackberry or bramble bush

Brom|sil|ber ['broːm-] NT silver bromide

bron|chi|al [brɔn'çiaːl] ADJ bronchial

Bron|chi|al-: **Bron|chi|al|asth|ma** NT bronchial asthma; **Bron|chi|al|ka|tarr(h)** M bronchial catarrh; **Bron|chi|al|tee** M bronchial tea

Bron|chie ['brɔnçiə] F -, -n *usu pl* bronchial tube, bronchus (*form*)

Bron|chi|tis [brɔn'çiːtɪs] F -, **Bronchitiden** [-çi'tiːdn] bronchitis

Bronn [brɔn] M -s, -en, **Bron|nen** ['brɔnən] M -s, - (*obs, liter*) fount (*liter*)

Bron|to|sau|rus [brɔnto'zaurʊs] M -, -se, **Bron|to|sau|ri|er** M brontosaurus

Bron|ze ['brõːsə] F -, -n bronze

Bron|ze- ['brõːsə-]: **Bron|ze|me|dail|le** ['brõːsə-] F bronze medal; **bron|ze|far|ben** ['brõːsə-farbn] ADJ bronze, bronze-coloured (*Brit*) or -colored (*US*)

bron|zen ['brõːsn] ADJ bronze ADV **~ schimmern** to glint like bronze

Bron|ze- ['brõːsə-]: **Bron|ze|plas|tik** ['brõːsə-] F (*Art*) bronze sculpture, bronze; **Bron|ze|zeit** ['brõːsə-] F , *no pl* Bronze Age

Bro|sa|me ['broːzaːmə] F -, -n (*liter*) crumb

Bro|sche ['brɔʃə] F -, -n brooch

bro|schiert [brɔ'ʃiːrt] ADJ *Ausgabe* paperback; (= *geheftet*) sewn; (= *geklammert*) wire-stitched; **jetzt auch ~ erhältlich** now also available in paperback; **~es Heftchen** booklet

Bro|schur [brɔ'ʃuːɐ] F -, -en (*Typ*) cut flush binding

Bro|schur|ar|beit F (*Typ*) cut flush work

Bro|schü|re [brɔ'ʃyːrə] F -, -n brochure

Bro|schur|ein|band M (*Typ*) cut flush binding

Brö|sel ['brøːzl] M -s, - crumb

brö|se|lig ['brøːzəlɪç] ADJ crumbly; **~ werden** to (start to) crumble

brö|seln ['brøːzln] VI (*Kuchen, Stein*) to crumble; (*Mensch*) to make crumbs

brös|lig ['brøːzlɪç] ADJ = **bröselig**

Brot [broːt] NT -(e)s, -e bread; (= *Laib*) loaf (of bread); (= *Scheibe*) slice (of bread); (= *Butterbrot*) bread and butter *no art, no pl*, slice or piece of bread and butter; (= *Stulle*) sandwich; (*fig*: = *Unterhalt*) daily bread (*hum*), living; **ein ~ mit Käse** a slice of bread and cheese; **belegte ~** open (*Brit*) or open-face (*US*) sandwiches; **das ist ein hartes** or **schweres ~** (*fig*) that's a hard way to earn one's living; **wes ~ ich ess, des Lied ich sing** (*Prov*) he who pays the piper calls the tune (*Prov*); **der Mensch lebt nicht vom allein** (*Prov*) man does not live by bread alone → **täglich** ADJ

BROT

Bread plays an important nutritional role in German-speaking countries – at least one meal a day is based around bread or rolls – and consequently there are many different varieties of bread. There are two basic sorts: pale bread made exclusively or mainly from wheat flour, and darker bread made principally from rye flour. **Vollkornbrot** is produced using wholemeal flour and is coarse-textured. A particular speciality is **Laugengebäck**: pretzels, rolls and crescent shapes that are made from a special wheat dough and dipped in caustic soda before baking, thus acquiring their typical brown crust and distinctive taste.

Brot-: **Brot|auf|strich** M spread (*for bread*); **Brot|be|lag** M topping (*for bread*); **Brot|be|ruf** M bread and butter job; **Brot|beu|tel** M haversack

Bröt|chen ['brøːtçən] NT -s, - roll; (**sich** *dat*) **seine ~ verdienen** (*inf*) to earn one's living, to earn one's daily bread (*hum*); **kleine ~ backen** (*inf*) to set one's sights lower

Bröt|chen|ge|ber(in) M(F) (*inf*) employer, provider (*hum*)

Brot-: **Brot|ein|heit** F carbohydrate exchange (*Brit*), bread unit (*US*); **Brot|er|werb** M (way of earning one's) living; **etw zum ~ betreiben**

to do sth for a living; **Brot|ge|ber(in)** M(F) (hum), **Brot|herr(in)** M(F) (obs) employer, provider (hum); **Brot|ge|trei|de** NT bread grain, bread cereals pl; **Brot|kas|ten** M bread bin; **Brot|korb** M bread basket; **jdm den ~ höher hängen** (fig) to keep sb short; **Brot|kru|me** F breadcrumb; **Brot|krus|te** F crust; **brot|los** ADJ unemployed, out of work; **jdn ~ machen** to put sb out of work → **Kunst d**; **Brot|ma|schi|ne** F bread slicer; **Brot|mes|ser** NT bread knife; **Brot|neid** M envy of other people's incomes; (in Bezug auf Arbeitsplatz) envy of other people's jobs; **das ist der reine ~** he etc is just jealous of your etc salary/job; **Brot|rin|de** F crust; **Brot|schnei|de|ma|schi|ne** F bread slicer; **Brot|schnit|te** F slice of bread; **Brot|sup|pe** F soup made from bread, stock etc; **Brot|teig** M bread dough; **Brot|ver|die|ner(in)** M(F) breadwinner; **Brot|ver|meh|rung** F **die wunderbare ~** (Bibl) the miracle of the loaves and fishes; **Brot|zeit** F a (S Ger. = Pause) tea break (Brit), snack break (US) b (= Essen) sandwiches pl

Brow|ser ['brauzɐ] M -s, - (Comput) browser

Brow|ser-Soft|ware ['brauzɐ-] F , **Brow|ser-soft|ware** F (Comput) browser software

brr [br] INTERJ (Befehl an Zugtiere) whoa; (Zeichen des Ekels) ugh, yuck; (bei Kälte) brr

Bruch¹ [brʊx] M -(e)s, ⁼e ['brʏçə] a (= Bruchstelle) break; (in Porzellan etc) crack; (in Damm) breach; (= das Brechen) breaking; (von Fels) breaking off; (von Damm) breaching; **das führte zu einem ~ an der Achse** it caused the axle to break; **zu ~ gehen** to get broken; **zu ~ fahren** to smash; **~ machen** (inf) (mit Flugzeug, Auto) to crash (mit etw sth); (beim Abwaschen) to break something
b (fig) (von Vertrag, Eid etc) breaking; (von Gesetz, Abkommen) violation, infringement, breaking; (mit Vergangenheit, Partei, in einer Entwicklung) break; (des Vertrauens) breach; (von Freundschaft) break-up; (von Verlöbnis) breaking off; (im Stil) discontinuity, break; **in die Brüche gehen** (Ehe, Freundschaft) to break up; **es kam zum ~ zwischen ihnen** they broke up
c (= zerbrochene Ware) broken biscuits/chocolate etc; (= Porzellan) breakage
d (Med) (= Knochenbruch) fracture, break; (= Eingeweidebruch) hernia, rupture; **sich (dat) einen ~ heben** to rupture oneself (by lifting something), to give oneself a hernia
e (= Steinbruch) quarry
f (Geol) fault
g (= Knick) fold
h (Math) fraction
i (sl: = Einbruch) break-in; **(einen) ~ in einem Geschäft machen** to break into a shop; **einen ~ machen** to do a break-in

Bruch² [brʊx, bruːx] M OR NT -(e)s, ⁼e ['brʏçə, 'bryːçə] marsh(land), bog

Bruch-: Bruch|band [-bant] NT pl -bänder truss; **Bruch|bu|de** F (pej) hovel; **bruch|fest** ADJ unbreakable; **Bruch|fes|tig|keit** F robustness; (von Knochen) strength; **Bruch|flä|che** F surface of the break; **die ~n zusammendrücken** press the two broken edges together

brü|chig ['brʏçɪç] ADJ Material, Knochen brittle, fragile; Gestein, Mauerwerk crumbling; Leder cracked, split; Fingernägel brittle; (fig) Stimme cracked, rough; Verhältnisse, Ehe unstable, crumbling; Moral crumbling; Frieden fragile; Annahme shaky; **~ werden** (Gestein, Macht etc) to (begin to) crumble; (Ehe, Verhältnisse auch) to (begin to) break up; (Leder) to crack, to split

Brü|chig|keit F -, no pl (von Material, Knochen) brittleness, fragility; (von Gestein etc) crumbliness; (fig) (von Stimme) roughness; (von Ehe, Verhältnissen) instability

Bruch-: Bruch|kan|te F edge (of break); **Bruch|lan|dung** F crash-landing; **eine ~ machen** to crash-land; **bruch|rech|nen** VI infin only to do fractions; **Bruch|rech|nen** NT fractions sing or pl; **Bruch|rech|nung** F fractions

sing or pl; (= Aufgabe) sum with fractions; **Bruch|schrift** F Gothic script; **Bruch|stein** M rough, undressed stone; **Bruch|stel|le** F break; (von Knochen auch) fracture; **Bruch|strich** M (Math) line (of a fraction), fraction line or bar; **Bruch|stück** NT fragment; (von Lied, Rede etc auch) snatch; **bruch|stück|haft** ADJ fragmentary ADV in a fragmentary way; **ich kenne die Geschichte nur ~** I only know parts or fragments of the story; **Bruch|teil** M fraction; **im ~ einer Sekunde** in a split second; **Bruch|zahl** F (Math) fraction; **Bruch|zo|ne** F (Geol) fault or rift zone

Brü|cke ['brʏkə] F -, -n a (lit, fig) bridge; **alle ~n hinter sich (dat) abbrechen** (fig) to burn one's boats (Brit) or bridges; **jdm eine ~ bauen** (fig) to give sb a helping hand; **jdm goldene ~n bauen** (liter) to build or throw (liter) a bridge (über +acc across); **~n schlagen** (fig) to forge links b (Turnen) crab; (Ringen) bridge c (Anat) pons (Varolii) d (Naut) bridge; (= Landungsbrücke) gangway, gangplank e (= Zahnbrücke) bridge f (Elec) bridge g (= Teppich) rug

Brücken-: Brücken|bau M a no pl bridge-building b pl -bauten (= Brücke) bridge; **Brü|cken|bo|gen** M arch (of a/the bridge); **Brü|cken|ge|bühr** F toll; **Brücken|ge|län|der** NT parapet; **Brücken|kopf** M (Mil, fig) bridgehead; **Brü|cken|pfei|ler** M pier (of a/the bridge); **Brü|cken|schlag** M (fig) das war der erste ~ that forged the first link; **Brü|cken|tag** M extra day off (taken between two public holidays or a public holiday and a weekend); **Brü|cken|waa|ge** F platform scale; **Brü|cken|zoll** M bridge toll

Bru|der ['bruːdɐ] M -s, ⁼ ['bryːdɐ] a brother; **Brüder** pl (Rel) brothers pl, brethren pl; **der gro|ße ~** (fig) Big Brother; **die Brüder Müller** the Müller brothers; **die Brüder Grimm** the Brothers Grimm; **unter Brüdern** (inf) between friends; **Brüder im Geiste** (geh) spiritual brothers; **und willst du nicht mein ~ sein, so schlag ich dir den Schädel ein** (prov) if you're not prepared to agree with me, then you'd better watch out! b (= Mönch) friar, brother; (= Diakon) deacon; **~ Franziskus** (als Anrede) Brother Francis; **die Brüder** pl the brothers pl, the brethren pl c (inf: = Mann) guy (inf), bloke (Brit inf); **ein warmer ~** (dated inf) a poof (Brit inf), a pansy (inf); **ein zwielichtiger ~** a shady character or customer (inf); **das sind alles ganz windige Brü|der** (pej) they're a shady lot (Brit) or crew (Brit inf) or bunch (inf); **euch Brüder kenn ich** (pej) I know YOU lot (Brit) or bunch (inf)

Bru|der|bund M pl -bünde (geh) (link of) comradeship, fraternal or brotherly link

Brü|der|chen ['bryːdɐçən] NT -s, - little brother, baby brother

Bru|der-: Bru|der|hand F (liter) hand of brotherhood; **Bru|der|hass** ▲ M fraternal hatred, hatred between brothers; **Bru|der|herz** NT (hum) dear brother; **na ~, wie gehts?** well, brother dear or dear brother, how are you?; **Bru|der|krieg** M war between brothers, fratricidal war; **Bru|der|kuss** ▲ M (fig) fraternal or brotherly kiss; **Bru|der|land** NT (sozialistisch) brother nation

Brü|der|lein ['bryːdəlaɪn] NT -s, - little brother

brü|der|lich ['bryːdəlɪç] ADJ fraternal, brotherly no adv ADV like brothers; **ich bin ihm ~ verbunden** he's like a brother to me; **~ teilen** to share and share alike; **mit jdm ~ teilen** to share generously with sb

Brü|der|lich|keit F -, no pl brotherliness → **Freiheit**

Bru|der-: Bru|der|lie|be F brotherly love; **Bru|der|mord** M fratricide; **Bru|der|mör|der(in)** M(F) fratricide; **Bru|der|par|tei** F (sozialistisch) brother party

Brü|der|schaft ['bryːdɐʃaft] F -, -en, **Bru|der|schaft** F -, -en (esp Eccl) a (Eccl)

brotherhood b (= Freundschaft) close or intimate friendship (in which the familiar "du" is used); **mit jdm ~ trinken** to agree over a drink to use the familiar "du"

Bru|der-: Bru|der|volk NT (geh) sister nation; **unser ~ in Kuba** our Cuban brothers; **Bru|der|zwist** M (liter) fraternal feud

Brüg|ge ['brʏɡə] NT -s Bruges

Brü|he ['bryːə] F -, -n (= Suppe) (clear) soup; (als Suppengrundlage) stock; (dial: von Gemüse) vegetable water; (pej) (= schmutzige Flüssigkeit) sludge; (= Getränk) dishwater (inf), muck (inf)

brü|hen ['bryːən] VT a (= mit heißem Wasser begießen) to blanch, to pour boiling water over b Tee to brew; Kaffee to make in the jug or pot

Brüh-: brüh|heiß ADJ scalding (hot), boiling hot; **Brüh|kar|tof|feln** PL potatoes pl boiled in meat stock; **brüh|warm** (inf) ADJ hot from the press (inf) ADV **er hat das sofort ~ weitererzählt** he promptly went straight off and spread it around; **Brüh|wür|fel** M stock cube; **Brüh|wurst** F sausage (to be heated in water)

Brüll|af|fe M howling monkey, howler; (inf: = Mensch) loudmouth (inf)

brül|len ['brʏlən] VI to shout, to roar; (pej: = laut weinen) to yell, to bawl; (Stier) to bellow; (Elefant) to trumpet; **brüll doch nicht so!** don't shout!; **er brüllte vor Schmerzen** he screamed with pain; **vor Lachen ~** to roar or howl or scream with laughter; **~des Gelächter** roars or howls or screams of laughter (all pl); **~ wie am Spieß** to cry or scream blue (Brit) or bloody murder (inf); **das ist zum Brüllen** (inf) it's a scream (inf) VT to shout, to roar; **jdm seine Wut ins Gesicht ~** to shout furiously at sb

Brumm-: Brumm|bär M (inf) a (baby-talk) teddy bear (baby-talk); b (= brummiger Mann) crosspatch (Brit inf), grouch (inf); **Brumm|bart** M (inf) crosspatch (Brit inf), grouch (inf); **Brumm|bass** ▲ M (inf: = Bassgeige) (double) bass; (= Bassstimme) deep bass (voice)

brum|meln ['brʊmln] VTI (inf) to mumble, to mutter

brum|men ['brʊmən] VI a (Insekt) to buzz; (Bär) to growl; (Motor, Bass) to drone; (Kreisel etc) to hum; **mir brummt der Kopf** or **Schädel** my head is throbbing b (beim Singen) to drone c (= murren) to grumble, to grouch (inf), to grouse (inf) d (= brummeln) to mumble, to mutter e (inf = in Haft sein) to be locked up (inf); (Sch: = nachsitzen) to be kept in; **vier Monate ~** to do four months (inf) f (Wirtschaft, Geschäft) to boom, to flourish VT a (= brummeln) to mumble, to mutter b (beim Singen) to drone

Brum|mer M -s, - a (= Schmeißfliege) bluebottle; (hum inf: = Sänger) droner b (inf) (= etwas Großes) whopper (inf); (= Lastwagen) juggernaut (Brit), semi (US)

Brum|mi ['brʊmi] M -s, -s (inf: = Lastwagen) lorry (Brit), truck

brum|mig ['brʊmɪç] ADJ grumpy, grouchy (inf), sour-tempered

Brumm-: Brumm|krei|sel M (inf) humming top; **Brumm|schä|del** M (inf) thick head (inf); **Brumm|ton** M low(-pitched) hum, humming sound or noise

Brunch [brantʃ, branʃ] M -(e)s, -(e)s or -e brunch

brü|nett [bry'nɛt] ADJ dark(-haired); **~es Mädchen** dark-haired girl, brunette; **sie ist ~** she is (a) brunette

Brü|net|te [bry'nɛtə] F -, -n brunette

Brunft [brʊnft] F -, ⁼e ['brʏnftə] (Hunt) rut; (= Brunftzeit auch) rutting season; **in der ~ sein** to be rutting

brunf|ten ['brʊnftn] VI (Hunt) to rut

brunf|tig ['brʊnftɪç] ADJ (Hunt) rutting

Brunft-: Brunft|platz M rutting ground; **Brunft|schrei** M bell, mating or rutting call (auch fig); **Brunft|zeit** F rutting season, rut

Brun|nen [ˈbrʊnən] M **-s, -** [a] well; (fig liter) fountain, fount (liter); **den ~ erst zudecken, wenn das Kind hineingefallen ist** to lock the stable door after the horse has bolted (prov); **erst, wenn das Kind in den ~ gefallen ist** but not until things had gone wrong [b] (= Springbrunnen) fountain [c] (= Heilquelle) spring; **~ trinken** to take the waters

Brun|nen-: **Brun|nen|bau|er(in)** M(F) pl **-bauer(innen)** well digger, well borer; **Brun|nen|be|cken** NT basin (of a well); (von Springbrunnen) basin (of a fountain); **Brun|nen|fi|gur** F (decorative) sculpture on a fountain; **Brun|nen|haus** NT pump room; **Brun|nen|kres|se** F watercress; **Brun|nen|kur** F (course of) spa treatment, cure; **Brun|nen|schacht** M well shaft; **Brun|nen|ver|gif|ter** M **-s, -**, **Brun|nen|ver|gif|te|rin** F [-ərɪn] **-nen** [a] well poisoner [b] (fig pej) (political) troublemaker; **Brun|nen|ver|gif|tung** F well poisoning; **politische** ~ political calumny; **Brun|nen|was|ser** NT pl **-wässer** well water

Brünn|lein [ˈbrʏnlaɪn] NT **-s, -** dim von **Brunnen**

Brunst [brʊnst] F **-, ⁼e** [ˈbrʏnstə] (von männlichen Tieren) rut; (von weiblichen Tieren) heat; (= Brunstzeit) rutting season; heat; (hum: von Mensch) lust, sexual appetite; **in der ~** rutting; on (Brit) or in (esp US) heat

brüns|tig [ˈbrʏnstɪç] ADJ [a] (von männlichen Tieren) rutting; (von weiblichen Tieren) on (Brit) or in (esp US) heat; (hum: von Mensch) (feeling) sexy (hum) [b] (liter: = inbrünstig) ardent, fervent

Brunst-: **Brunst|schrei** M mating call; **Brunst|zeit** F rutting season

brun|zen [ˈbrʊntsn] VI (S Ger inf) to (have a) piss (sl) or slash (Brit inf)

brüsk [brʏsk] ADJ brusque, abrupt, curt ADV brusquely, abruptly, curtly; **sich ~ abwenden** to turn away abruptly or brusquely

brüs|kie|ren [brʏsˈkiːrən] ptp **brüskiert** VT to snub

Brüs|kie|rung F **-, -en** snub

Brüs|sel [ˈbrʏsl] NT **-s** Brussels

Brüs|se|ler¹ [ˈbrʏsələ], **Brüss|ler** ▲ [ˈbrʏslə] ADJ attr Brussels; **~ Spitzen** Brussels lace; **~ Salat** (Sw: = Chicorée) chicory

Brüs|se|ler² [ˈbrʏsələ] M **-s, -**, **Brüs|se|le|rin** [-ərɪn] F **-, -nen**, **Brüss|ler** ▲ [-ərɪn] F **-, -nen** inhabitant or (gebürtiger) native of Brussels; **er ist ~** he lives in Brussels; (dort geboren) he comes from Brussels

Brust [brʊst] F **-, ⁼e** [ˈbrʏstə] [a] (= Körperteil) chest; (fig: = Inneres) breast, heart; **einen zur ~ nehmen** (inf) to have a quick drink or a quick one or a quickie (inf); **~ (he)raus!** chest out!; **~ an ~** face to face; **sich an jds ~ (dat) ausweinen** to cry on sb's shoulder; **sich (dat) an die ~ schlagen** (fig) to beat one's breast; **sich in die ~ werfen** (fig) to puff oneself up; **sich (dat) jdn zur ~ nehmen** to have a word with sb; **sich (dat) etw zur ~ nehmen** to criticize sth harshly; **mit geschwellter ~** (fig) as proud as Punch or a peacock; **schwach auf der ~ sein** (inf) to have a weak chest; (hum: = an Geldmangel leiden) to be a bit short (inf) [b] (= weibliche Brust) breast; **einem Kind die ~ geben, ein Kind an die ~ legen** to feed a baby (at the breast), to nurse a baby [c] (Cook) breast [d] (= Brustschwimmen) breaststroke

Brust-: **Brust|am|pu|ta|ti|on** F (Med) mastectomy (spec); **Brust|bein** NT (Anat) breastbone, sternum; **Brust|beu|tel** M money bag (worn around the neck); **Brust|bild** NT half-length portrait; **Brust|brei|te** F **um ~** by a whisker

Brüst|chen [ˈbrʏstçən] NT **-s, -** dim von **Brust**

Brüst|drü|se F mammary gland

brüs|ten [ˈbrʏstn] VR to boast, to brag (mit about)

Brust-: **Brust|fell** NT (Anat) pleura; **Brust|fell|ent|zün|dung** F pleurisy; **Brust|flos|se** F pectoral fin; **Brust|ge|gend** F thoracic region; **Brust|haar** NT hair on the chest, chest hair; **Brust|har|nisch** M breastplate; **brust|hoch** ADJ chest-high; **Brust|höh|le** F chest high; **Brust|höh|le** F thoracic cavity; **Brust|kas|ten** M (inf, Anat) thorax; **Brust|kind** NT breastfed baby; **Brust|korb** M (Anat) thorax; **Brust|krebs** M breast cancer, cancer of the breast; **Brust|kreuz** NT (Eccl) pectoral cross; **Brust|la|ge** F prone position; **in ~ schwimmen** to swim in the prone position; **Brust|mus|kel** M pectoral muscle; **Brust|o|pe|ra|ti|on** F (Med) breast operation; (= Schönheitsoperation) breast enhancement, boob job (inf); **Brust|pan|zer** M breastplate; **Brust|plas|tik** F cosmetic breast surgery; **Brust|schutz** M (esp Fechten) breast or chest protector, plastron; **brust|schwim|men** VI infin only to swim or do the breaststroke; **Brust|schwim|men** NT breaststroke; **Brust|schwim|mer(in)** M(F) breaststroke swimmer; **Brust|stim|me** F chest voice; **Brust|stück** NT (Cook) breast; **Brust|ta|sche** F breast pocket; (= Innentasche) inside (breast) pocket; **Brust|tee** M herbal tea (for infections of the respiratory tract); **brust|tief** ADJ chest-deep, up to one's chest; **Brust|ton** M pl **-töne** (Mus) chest note; **im ~ der Überzeugung, (dass ...)** in a tone of utter conviction (that ...); **Brust|um|fang** M chest measurement; (von Frau) bust measurement

Brüs|tung [ˈbrʏstʊŋ] F **-, -en** parapet; (= Balkonbrüstung etc auch) balustrade; (= Fensterbrüstung) breast

Brust-: **Brust|wand** F (Anat) thoracic or chest wall; **Brust|war|ze** F nipple; **Brust|wehr** F (Mil) breastwork; (Hist) parapet; **Brust|wei|te** F chest measurement; (von Frau) bust measurement; **Brust|wi|ckel** M chest compress; **Brust|wir|bel** M thoracic or dorsal vertebra

Brut [bruːt] F **-, -en** [a] no pl (= das Brüten) brooding, sitting, incubating [b] (= die Jungen) brood; (pej) lot, mob (inf) [c] (bei Pflanzen) offset, offshoot

bru|tal [bruˈtaːl] ADJ brutal; (= gewalttätig auch) violent ADV [a] **zuschlagen** brutally; **behandeln** cruelly; **jdm etw ganz ~ sagen** to be brutally or cruelly frank to sb about sth, to tell sb sth quite brutally [b] (inf: = sehr) incredibly; **das tut ~ weh** (inf) that hurts like hell (inf)

bru|ta|li|sie|ren [brutaliˈziːrən] ptp **brutalisiert** VT to brutalize

Bru|ta|li|sie|rung F **-, -en** brutalization

Bru|ta|li|tät [brutaliˈtɛːt] F **-, -en** [a] no pl brutality; (= Gewalttätigkeit auch) violence [b] (= Gewalttat) act of violence or brutality; **~en** pl brutalities, acts of violence or brutality

Bru|ta|lo [bruˈtaːlo] M **-s, -s** (inf) bruiser (inf), thug

Brut|ap|pa|rat M incubator

brü|ten [ˈbryːtn] VI to brood, to sit, to incubate; (fig) to ponder (über +dat over); **~de Hitze** oppressive or stifling heat; **~d heiß** sweltering, boiling (hot) (inf) VT [a] (künstlich) to incubate; (Tech) to breed [b] (geh) Rache, Verrat to plot

brü|tend|heiß △ ADJ attr → **brüten** VI

Brü|ter [ˈbryːtə] M **-s, -** (Tech) breeder (reactor); **schneller ~** fast-breeder (reactor)

Brut-: **Brut|hen|ne** F sitting hen; **Brut|hit|ze** F (inf) stifling or sweltering heat; **Brut|kas|ten** M (Med) incubator; **hier ist eine Hitze wie in einem ~** (inf) it's like an oven or a furnace in here (inf); **Brut|ofen** M (fig) furnace; **Brut|pfle|ge** F care of the brood; **Brut|platz** M breeding ground; **Brut|re|ak|tor** M breeder (reactor); **Brut|schrank** M (Med, Agr etc) incubator; **Brut|stät|te** F breeding ground (+gen for); (fig auch) hotbed (+gen of); **Brut|teich** M spawning pond

brut|to [ˈbrʊto] ADV gross; **~ EUR 1000, EUR 1000 ~** EUR 1000 gross

Brut|to-: **Brut|to|be|trag** M gross amount; **Brut|to|ein|kom|men** NT gross or before-tax income; **Brut|to|er|trag** M gross or before-tax profit; **Brut|to|ge|halt** NT gross salary; **Brut|to|ge|wicht** NT gross weight; **Brut|to|ge|winn** M gross or before-tax profit; **Brut|to|in|lands|pro|dukt** NT gross domestic product, GDP; **Brut|to|lohn** M gross or before-tax wage(s); **Brut|to|na|ti|o|nal|pro|dukt** NT (Aus Econ) gross national product, GNP; **Brut|to|preis** M gross price; **Brut|to|re|gis|ter|ton|ne** F register ton; **Brut|to|so|zi|al|pro|dukt** NT gross national product, GNP; **Brut|to|ver|dienst** M gross or before-tax earnings pl

Brut|zeit F incubation (period)

brut|zeln [ˈbrʊtsln] (inf) VI to sizzle (away) VT to fry (up)

Bru|yère¹ [bryˈjɛːr] NT **-s**, no pl, **Bru|yère|holz** [bryˈjɛːr-] NT briar or brier (wood)

Bru|yère² [bryˈjɛːr] F **-, -s**, **Bru|yère|pfei|fe** [bryˈjɛːr-] F briar or brier (pipe)

BSE [beːˈɛsˈeː] abbr von **Bovine Spongiforme Enzephalopathie** BSE

BSE- [beːˈɛsˈeː] in cpds BSE; **BSE-Er|re|ger** M BSE virus; **BSE-frei** ADJ Betrieb, Fleisch, Tiere free from BSE

B-Sei|te [ˈbeː-] F (von Schallplatte) B-side

BSE- [beːˈɛsˈeː] **BSE-Kri|se** F BSE crisis; **BSE-Seu|che** F BSE epidemic; **BSE-ver|seucht** [beːˈɛsˈeː-] ADJ Fleisch BSE-contaminated, contaminated with BSE pred

BTA [beːteːˈaː] M **-s, -s** F **-, -s** abbr von **biologisch-technische Assistentin, von biologisch-technischer Assistent**

Btx [beːteːˈɪks] M **-**, no pl abbr von **Bildschirmtext**

Bub [buːp] M **-en, -en** [-bn] (S Ger, Aus, Sw) boy, lad (Brit)

Büb|chen [ˈbyːpçən] NT **-s, -** dim von **Bub**

Bu|be [ˈbuːbə] M **-n, -n** [a] (old) rogue, knave (old) [b] (Cards) jack, knave

bu|ben|haft [-haft] ADJ boyish ADV boyishly

Bu|ben|streich M , **Bu|ben|stück** NT , **Bü|be|rei** [byːbəˈraɪ] F **-, -en** [a] (old) piece of knavery (old) or villainy, knavish trick (old) [b] (= Streich) silly or foolish or childish prank

Bu|bi [ˈbuːbi] M **-s, -s** (inf) little boy or lad (Brit), laddie (Brit inf); (pej inf) (school)boy; (als Anrede) laddie (Brit inf), (little) boy

Bu|bi-: **Bu|bi|kopf** M bobbed hair no pl, bob; **sich (dat) einen ~ machen lassen** to have one's hair bobbed, to have one's hair cut in a bob; **Bu|bi|kra|gen** M Peter Pan collar

bü|bisch [ˈbyːbɪʃ] ADJ [a] (old: = schurkenhaft) villainous, knavish (old) [b] (= verschmitzt) roguish, mischievous ADV (= verschmitzt) grinsen, lächeln, sagen roguishly, mischievously

Bu|bi|strich M , **Bu|bi-Strich** M (= Prostitution) prostitution by rent boys; (= Gebiet) red-light district for rent boys, rent-boy area

Buch [buːx] NT **-(e)s, ⁼er** [ˈbyːçɐ] [a] book (auch Bibl); (= Band) volume; (= Drehbuch) script; **über den Büchern sitzen** to pore over one's books; **er redet wie ein ~** (inf) he never stops talking; **ein Gentleman, wie er im ~ steht** a perfect example of a gentleman; **ein Tor, wie es im ~ steht** a textbook or copybook goal; **das erste ~ Mose** (Bibl) Genesis; **das Goldene ~ der Stadt** the VIP visitor's book; **ein ~ mit sieben Siegeln** (fig) a closed book; **er ist für mich ein offenes** or **aufgeschlagenes ~** I can read him like a book; **sich ins ~ der Geschichte eintragen** (geh) to enter one's name in the annals or book of history; **~ machen** (Pferderennen) to make a book [b] usu pl (Comm: = Geschäftsbuch) books pl, accounts pl; **über etw (acc) ~ führen** to keep a record of sth; **jdm die Bücher führen** to keep sb's accounts *or* books; **zu ~ (e) schlagen** to make a (significant) difference; **das schlägt mit 1000 Euro zu ~(e)** that gives you 1000 euros; **zu ~ stehen mit** to be valued at

Buch-: Buch|be|spre|chung F book review; **Buch|bin|der(in)** M(F) bookbinder; **Buch|bin|de|rei** F (= *Betrieb*) bookbindery; (= *Handwerk*) bookbinding; **Buch|block** M *pl* **-blocks** book block; **Buch|deckel** M book cover; **Buch|druck** M , *no pl* letterpress (printing); **Buch|drucker(in)** M(F) printer; **Buch|dru|cke|rei** F (= *Betrieb*) printing works *sing or pl*; (= *Handwerk*) printing; **Buch|dru|cker|kunst** F art of printing

Bu|che ['buːxə] F **-, -n** (= *Baum*) beech (tree); (= *Holz*) beech(wood)

Buch|ecker ['buːxˌɛkɐ] F **-, -n** beechnut

Buch|ein|band M binding, (book) cover

bu|chen¹ ['buːxn] ◊ 48.3 VT **a** (*Comm*) to enter, to post (*spec*); (*Kasse*) to register; (*fig*: = *registrieren*) to register, to record; **einen Erfolg für sich ~** to chalk up (*inf*) or mark up a success (for oneself); **etw als Erfolg ~** to put sth down as a success **b** (= *vorbestellen*) to book, to reserve

bu|chen² ADJ (*rare*) (made) of beech(wood), beech

Buchen-: Bu|chen|holz NT beechwood; **Bu|chen|wald** M beech wood

Bü|cher-: Bü|cher|ba|sar M book sale; **Bü|cher|bord** NT , **Bü|cher|brett** NT bookshelf; **Bü|cher|bus** M mobile library

Bü|che|rei [byːçəˈraɪ] F **-, -en** (lending) library

Bü|cher-: Bü|cher|freund(in) M(F) book-lover, bibliophile; **Bü|cher|ge|stell** NT bookcase; **Bü|cher|gut|schein** M book token; **Bü|cher|markt** M book market; **Bü|cher|nar|rin** F book-fan, book freak (*inf*); **er ist ein richtiger ~** he's book mad (*inf*), he's crazy about books, he's a real book freak (*inf*); **Bü|cher|reff** NT case for transporting books; **Bü|cher|re|gal** NT bookshelf; **Bü|cher|re|vi|si|on** F audit; **Bü|cher|schrank** M bookcase; **Bü|cher|sen|dung** F consignment of books; (*im Postwesen*) books (sent) at printed paper rate; **Bü|cher|stu|be** F bookshop; **Bü|cher|stüt|ze** F book end; **Bü|cher|ver|bot** NT ban on books; **Bü|cher|ver|bren|nung** F burning of books; **Bü|cher|ver|zeich|nis** NT bibliography; **Bü|cher|wand** F wall of book shelves; (*als Möbelstück*) (large) set of book shelves; **Bü|cher|weis|heit** F book learning; **Bü|cher|wurm** M (*lit, fig hum*) bookworm

Buch|fink M chaffinch

Buch-: Buch|form F **in ~** in book form; **Buch|for|mat** NT format for a book; **Buch|füh|rung** F book-keeping, accounting; **einfache/doppelte ~** single/double entry book-keeping; **Buch|geld** NT (*Fin*) bank deposit money; **Buch|ge|lehr|sam|keit** F book-learning; **Buch|ge|mein|schaft** F book club; **Buch|ge|winn** M (*St Ex, Fin*) paper profit(s *pl*), profit(s *pl*) on paper; **Buch|hal|ter(in)** M(F) book-keeper; **buch|hal|te|risch** [-haltərɪʃ] ADJ book-keeping **ADV sich ~ ausbilden lassen** to be trained in book-keeping *or* as a book-keeper; **ein Problem ~ sehen** to see something as a book-keeping problem, to view a problem in terms of book-keeping; **Ihre Abrechnung ist ~ korrekt** your book-keeping is correct; **sie ist ~ versiert** she is good at book-keeping; **~ kompliziert** complicated in terms of book-keeping; **Buch|hal|tung** F **a** book-keeping, accounting **b** (*Abteilung einer Firma*) accounts department; **Buch|han|del** M book trade; **im ~ erhältlich** available *or* on sale in bookshops; **Buch|händ|ler(in)** M(F) bookseller; **buch|händ|le|risch** [-hɛndlərɪʃ] **ADV** of *or* connected with the book trade; **eine -e Ausbildung haben** to be a trained bookseller **ADV ~ tätig sein** to be a bookseller; **Buch|hand|lung** F bookshop, bookstore (*US*); **Buch|hül|le** F dust jacket *or* cover; **Buch|klub** M book club;

Buch|kri|tik F **a** (= *das Rezensieren*) book reviewing; (= *Rezension*) book review **b** *no pl* (= *die Rezensenten*) book reviewers *pl* or critics *pl*; **Buch|la|den** M bookshop, bookstore (*US*); **Buch|ma|cher(in)** M(F) bookmaker, bookie (*inf*); **Buch|ma|le|rei** F illumination; **Buch|mes|se** F book fair; **Buch|prü|fer(in)** M(F) auditor; **Buch|prü|fung** F audit; **Buch|rü|cken** M spine

Buchs ['buːks] M **-es, -e**, **Buchs|baum** M box (tree)

Büchs|chen ['byːksçən] NT **-s, -** *dim von* Büchse

Buch|se ['buːksə] F **-, -n** (*Elec*) socket; (*Tech*) (*von Zylinder*) liner; (*von Lager*) bush

Büch|se ['byːksə] F **-, -n a** tin; (= *Konservenbüchse*) can, tin (*Brit*); (= *Sammelbüchse*) collecting box; **die ~ der Pandora** (*Myth, liter*) Pandora's box **b** (= *Gewehr*) rifle, (shot)gun

Büch|sen-: Büch|sen|fleisch NT canned *or* tinned (*Brit*) meat; **Büch|sen|ma|cher(in)** M(F) gunsmith; **Büch|sen|milch** F tinned (*Brit*) *or* evaporated milk; **Büch|sen|öff|ner** M can-opener, tin-opener (*Brit*)

Buch|sta|be ['buːxʃtaːbə] M **-n(s), -n** letter; (= *esp Druckbuchstabe*) character; **kleiner ~** small letter; **großer ~** capital (letter); **ein fetter ~** a bold character, a character in bold (face); **in fetten -n** in bold (face); **Betrag in -n** amount in words; **dem ~n nach** (*fig*) literally; **auf den ~n genau** (*fig*) exactly; **auf den letzten ~n** (*fig*) to the letter; **nach dem -n des Gesetzes ist das verboten, aber ...** according to the letter of the law that's illegal but ... → **vier b**

Buch|sta|ben-: Buch|sta|ben|fol|ge F (*alphabetisch*) alphabetical order; (= *Aneinanderreihung von Buchstaben*) sequence of letters; **buch|sta|ben|ge|treu** **ADJ** literal **ADV etw ~ befolgen** to follow sth to the letter; **Buch|sta|ben|glau|be** M literalism; **buch|sta|ben|gläu|big** ADJ literalist(ic); **Buch|sta|ben|kom|bi|na|ti|on** F combination (of letters); **Buch|sta|ben|rät|sel** NT word puzzle, anagram; **Buch|sta|ben|schrift** F alphabetic script; **Buch|sta|ben|treue** F adherence to the letter

buch|sta|bie|ren [buːxʃtaˈbiːrən] *ptp* **buchstabiert** VT **a** *Wort, Namen* to spell **b** (= *mühsam lesen*) to spell out

Buch|sta|bier-: Buch|sta|bier|me|tho|de F alphabetical method; **Buch|sta|bier|ta|fel** F word spelling alphabet

buch|stäb|lich ['buːxʃtɛːplɪç] **ADJ** literal **ADV** literally

Buch|stüt|ze F book-end

Bucht [buːxt] F **-, -en a** (*im Meer*) bay; (*kleiner*) cove **b** (*für Schweine etc*) stall

Buch|teln ['buːxtln] PL (*Aus Cook*) sweet bread roll with jam filling

buch|ten|reich, **buch|tig** ['buːxtɪç] ADJ *Küste* indented

Buch-: Buch|ti|tel M (book) title; **Buch|um|schlag** M dust jacket *or* cover

Bu|chung ['buːxʊŋ] F **-, -en** (*Comm*) entry; (= *Reservierung*) booking, reservation

Bu|chungs-: Bu|chungs|be|leg M (*Econ, Fin*) accounting record, (bookkeeping) voucher; (*für Reisebuchung*) booking receipt; **Bu|chungs|com|pu|ter** M computerized booking system; **ich kann Sie im ~ nicht finden** I can't find your booking on the computer; **Bu|chungs|kar|te** F charge card; **Bu|chungs|ma|schi|ne** F accounting machine; **Bu|chungs|num|mer** F (*Econ, Fin*) entry number; (*für Reisebuchung*) booking number; **Bu|chungs|sys|tem** NT booking system

Buch|ver|lag M (book) publisher(s *pl*), (book) publisher's

Buch|wei|zen M buckwheat

Buch-: Buch|wert M (*Comm*) book value; **Buch|wis|sen** NT (*pej*) book learning

Bu|ckel ['bʊkl] M **-s, - a** hump(back), hunchback; (*inf*: = *Rücken*) back; **einen ~ machen** (*Katze*) to arch its back; **steh gerade, mach nicht so einen ~!** stand up (straight), don't hunch your back *or* shoulders like that!; **einen krummen ~ machen** (*fig inf*) to bow and scrape, to kowtow; **den ~ voll kriegen** (*inf*) to get a good hiding, to get a belting (*inf*); **er kann mir den ~ (he)runterrutschen** (*inf*) he can (go and) take a running jump, he can get lost *or* knotted (*all inf*); **viel/genug auf dem ~ haben** (*inf*) to have a lot/enough on one's plate (*inf*); **den ~ voll Schulden haben** (*inf*) to be up to one's neck *or* eyes in debt (*inf*); **den ~ hinhalten** (*fig inf*) to carry the can (*inf*); **seine 80 Jahre auf dem ~ haben** (*inf*) to be 80 (years old), to have seen 80 summers → **jucken VTI, breit ADJ** **b** (*inf*: = *Hügel*) hummock, hillock **c** (*inf*: = *Auswölbung*) bulge, hump **d** (*von Schild*) boss

bu|cke|lig ['bʊkəlɪç] ADJ hunchbacked, humpbacked; (*inf*) *Straße* bumpy; *Landschaft* undulating, hilly

Bu|cke|li|ge(r) ['bʊkəlɪgə] MF *decl as adj* hunchback, humpback

bu|ckeln ['bʊkln] VI (*pej*) to bow and scrape, to kowtow; **nach oben ~ und nach unten treten** to bow to superiors and tread inferiors underfoot

Bu|ckel-: Bu|ckel|pis|te F (*Ski*) mogul piste; **Bu|ckel|rind** NT zebu; **Bu|ckel|wal** M humpback whale

bü|cken ['bʊkn] VR to bend (down), to stoop; **sich nach etw ~** to bend down *or* to stoop to pick sth up → *auch* **gebückt**

Bu|ckerl ['bʊkɐl] NT **-s, -(n)** (*Aus inf*) bow

buck|lig ['bʊklɪç] ADJ *etc* = **buckelig**

Buck|li|ge(r) ['bʊklɪgə] MF *decl as adj* hunchback, humpback

Bück|ling ['bʏklɪŋ] M **-s, -e a** (*Cook*) smoked herring **b** (*hum inf*: = *Verbeugung*) bow

Bu|da|pest ['buːdapɛst] NT **-s** Budapest

Büd|chen ['byːtçən] NT **-s, -** *dim von* Bude **a**

Bud|del ['bʊdl] F **-, -n** (*N Ger inf*) bottle

Bud|de|lei [bʊdəˈlaɪ] F **-, -en** (*im Sand*) digging; (*inf*: = *Tiefbauarbeiten*) constant digging (up) (*of road etc*)

Bud|del|kas|ten M (*dial*) sandbox

bud|deln ['bʊdln] **VI** (*inf*) to dig; **in der Straße wird dauernd gebuddelt** they're always digging up the road **VT** (*dial*) (= *ausgraben*) *Kartoffeln* to dig up; *Loch* to dig

Bud|dha ['bʊda] M **-s, -s** Buddha

Bud|dhis|mus [bʊˈdɪsmʊs] M **-**, *no pl* Buddhism

Bud|dhist [bʊˈdɪst] M **-en, -en**, **Bud|dhis|tin** [-ˈdɪstɪn] F **-, -nen** Buddhist

bud|dhis|tisch [bʊˈdɪstɪʃ] **ADJ** Buddhist(ic) **ADV jdn ~ erziehen** to bring sb up (as) a Buddhist; **~ beeinflusst** influenced by Buddhism; **~ heiraten** to marry in a Buddhist ceremony

Bu|de ['buːdə] F **-, -n a** (= *Bretterbau*) hut; (= *Baubude*) (workmen's) hut; (= *Marktbude, Verkaufsbude*) stall, stand, booth; (= *Zeitungsbude*) kiosk **b** (*pej inf*: = *Laden, Lokal etc*) dump (*inf*); **c** (*inf*) (= *Zimmer*) room; (= *Wohnung*) pad (*inf*); **Leben in die ~ bringen** to liven *or* brighten up the place; **jdm die ~ einrennen** *or* **einlaufen** to pester *or* badger sb; **jdm auf die ~ rücken** (*als Besucher*) to drop in on sb, to land on sb (*inf*); (*aus einem bestimmten Grund*) to pay sb a visit, to go/come round to sb's place (*inf*); **jdm die ~ auf den Kopf stellen** to turn sb's place upside down (*inf*)

Bu|del ['buːdl] F **-, -n** (*Aus inf*) (shop) counter

Bu|den-: Bu|den|be|sit|zer(in) M(F) (market) stallholder; **Bu|den|zau|ber** M (*dated inf*) knees-up (*dated sl*), jamboree (*dated inf*)

Bud|get [bʏˈdʒeː] NT **-s, -s** budget

bud|ge|tär [bʏdʒeˈtɛːɐ] ADJ budgetary

Bud|get- [bʏ'dʒe:-] (*Pol*): **Bud|get|be|ra|tung** F budget debate; **Bud|get|ent|wurf** M draft budget

bud|ge|tie|ren [bʏdʒe'ti:rən] *ptp* **budgetiert** [bʏdʒe'ti:rt] VTI (*Pol, Comm, Fin*) to budget

Bud|get|vor|la|ge [bʏ'dʒe:-] F presentation of the budget

Bu|di|ke [bu'di:kə] F -, -n (*dial*) bar, pub (*Brit*), saloon (*US*)

Bu|di|ker [bu'di:kɐ] M -s, -, **Bu|di|ke|rin** [-ərɪn] F -, -nen (*dial*) bar keeper, landlord/landlady (*Brit*)

Bu|e|nos Ai|res ['bue:nɔs 'aires] NT - - Buenos Aires

Bü|fett [bʏ'fɛt] NT -(e)s, -e *or* -s **a** (= *Geschirr-schrank*) sideboard **b** (= *Schanktisch*) bar; (= *Verkaufstisch*) counter **c** **kaltes ~** cold buffet **d** (*Sw*: = *Bahnhofsgaststätte*) (station) buffet

Bü|fett|da|me F , **Bü|fett|fräu|lein** NT , **Bü|fett|mam|sell** F (*dated*) (*in Gastwirtschaft*) bar-maid; (*in Konditorei*) (counter) assistant

Bü|fett|tier [bʏ'fe:tie:] M -s, -s barman

Büf|fel [bʏfl] M -s, - buffalo

Büf|fe|lei [bʏfə'lai] F -, -en (*inf*) swotting (*Brit inf*), cramming (*inf*)

Büf|fel-: **Büf|fel|her|de** F herd of buffalo; **Büf|fel|le|der** NT buff (leather), buffalo skin

büf|feln ['bʏfln] (*inf*) VI to swot (*Brit inf*), to cram (*inf*) VT *Lernstoff* to swot up (*Brit inf*), to bone up on (*US inf*)

Buf|fet [bʏ'fe:] NT -s, -s , **Büf|fet** [bʏ'fe:] NT -s, -s (*esp Aus*) = **Büfett**

Buf|fo ['bʊfo] M -s, -s *or* **Buffi** ['bʊfi] buffo

Bug [bu:k] M -(e)s, ⁼e *or* -e ['by:gə, 'bu:gə] **a** (= *Schiffsbug*) bow *usu pl*; (= *Flugzeugbug*) nose; **jdm eins vor den ~ knallen** (*inf*) to sock sb one (*inf*) **b** (*Cook*: = *Schultergegend*) shoulder **c** (*Tech*) brace, strut

Bü|gel ['by:gl] M -s, - **a** (= *Kleiderbügel*) (coat) hanger **b** (= *Steigbügel*) stirrup **c** (= *Stromabnehmer*) bow (collector) **d** (*von Säge, Handtasche*) frame; (= *Brillenbügel*) side piece, earpiece, bow; (*von Gewehr*) trigger guard; (*für Einweckgläser*) clip, clamp; (*am Lift*) T-bar

Bü|gel-: **Bü|gel|au|to|mat** M rotary iron; **Bü|gel-BH** M underwired bra; **Bü|gel|brett** NT ironing board; **bü|gel|echt** ADJ ironable; **Bü|gel|ei|sen** NT iron; **Bü|gel|fal|te** F crease in one's trousers (*esp Brit*) *or* pants (*esp US*); **bü|gel|fer|tig** ADJ ready for ironing; **Bü|gel|fla|sche** F flip-top bottle; **bü|gel|frei** ADJ noniron; **Bü|gel|ma|schi|ne** F rotary iron

bü|geln ['by:gln] VT *Wäsche* to iron; *Hose* to press → **gebügelt** VI to iron

Bü|gel-: **Bü|gel|sä|ge** F hacksaw; **Bü|gel|tisch** F ironing table; **Bü|gel|wä|sche** F ironing

Bug|gy ['bagi] M -s, -s buggy

Büg|ler ['by:glɐ] M -s, -, **Büg|le|rin** F -, -nen ironer

Bug-: **Bug|mann** M *pl* **-männer** *or* **-leute** (*Rudern*) bow(man); **Bug|frau** F (*Rudern*) bow; **Bug|rad** NT (*Aviat*) nose wheel; **Bug|see** F (*Naut*) bow wave

Bug|sier|damp|fer M , **Bug|sier|schlep|per** M (*Naut*) tug(boat)

bug|sie|ren [bʊ'ksi:rən] *ptp* **bugsiert** VT **a** (*Naut*) to tow **b** (*inf*) *Möbelstück etc* to manoeuvre (*Brit*), to maneuver (*US*), to edge; **jdn aus dem Zimmer ~** to steer *or* hustle sb out of the room **c** (*inf*: = *lancieren*) **jdn in einen Posten ~** to wangle *or* fiddle *or* finagle (*US*) a job for sb (*inf*) VI (*Naut*) to tow; **Schlepper, die im Hafen ~** tugs that do the towing in the port

Bug|sie|rer [bʊ'ksi:rɐ] M -s, - (*Naut*) tug(boat)

Bug|sier|tau NT , **Bug|sier|tros|se** F (*Naut*) towline, towrope

Bug- (*Naut*): **Bug|spriet** NT bowsprit; **Bug|wel|le** F bow wave

buh [bu:] INTERJ boo

Buh [bu:] NT -s, -s (*inf*) boo

Bü|hel ['by:əl] M -s, -, **Bühl** [by:l] M -s, - (*S Ger, Aus, Sw*) hill

bu|hen ['bu:ən] VI (*inf*) to boo

Buh|frau F -, -en bogeywoman (*inf*)

Buh|le¹ ['bu:lə] M -n, -n (*old liter*) paramour (*obs, liter*), lover

Buh|le² F -, -n (*old liter*) paramour (*obs, liter*), mistress

buh|len ['bu:lən] VI **a** (*pej*: = *werben*) **um jdn/Anerkennung ~** to woo sb/recognition; **um jds Gunst ~** to woo *or* court sb's favour (*Brit*) *or* favor (*US*) **b** (*obs*) **mit jdm ~** to have a love affair with sb

Buh|ler ['bu:lɐ] M -s, -, **Buh|le|rin** [-ərɪn] F -, -nen **a** (*old liter*) paramour (*obs, liter*); (*Mann auch*) lover, (*Frau auch*) mistress **b** (*pej*: = *Werbender*) wooer

Buh|le|rei [bu:lə'rai] F -, no pl (*pej*) wooing (*um jdn/etw* of sb/sth)

Buh|mann ['bu:man] M *pl* **-männer** (*inf*) bogeyman (*inf*)

Buh|ne ['bu:nə] F -, -n groyne, breakwater

Büh|ne ['by:nə] F -, -n **a** (*lit, fig*) stage; (*von Konzertsaal, Aula etc*) stage, platform; **über die ~ gehen** (*fig inf*) to go or pass off; **etw über die ~ bringen** (*fig inf*) to stage sth; **wie haben Sie Ihren ersten Elternabend/Ihre Antrittsvorlesung über die ~ gebracht?** how did you manage your first parents' evening/your inaugural lecture?; **hinter der ~** (*lit, fig*) behind the scenes; **von der ~ abtreten** *or* **verschwinden** (*inf*) **die ~ verlassen** to make one's exit, to leave the scene **b** (= *Theater*) theatre (*Brit*), theater (*US*); **Städtische ~n** Municipal Theatres (*Brit*) *or* Theaters (*US*); **zur ~ gehen** to go on the stage, to go into the theatre (*Brit*) *or* theater (*US*); **an** *or* **bei der ~ sein** to be on the stage, to be in the theatre (*Brit*) *or* theater (*US*); **sie steht seit zwanzig Jahren auf der ~** she has been on the stage *or* in the theatre (*Brit*) *or* theater (*US*) for twenty years; **das Stück ging über alle ~n** the play was put on *or* staged everywhere *or* in all the theatres (*Brit*) *or* theaters (*US*) **c** (*dial*: = *Dachboden*) loft **d** (*Tech*: = *Hebebühne*) ramp

Büh|nen-: **Büh|nen|an|wei|sung** F stage direction; **Büh|nen|ar|bei|ter(in)** M(F) stage hand; **Büh|nen|aus|bil|dung** F dramatic training; **Büh|nen|aus|spra|che** F standard *or* received pronunciation; **Büh|nen|aus|stat|tung** F stage property *or* props *pl*; **Büh|nen|au|tor(in)** M(F) playwright, dramatist; **Büh|nen|be|ar|bei|tung** F stage adaptation; **Büh|nen|be|leuch|ter(in)** M(F) lighting man/woman; **Büh|nen|be|leuch|tung** F stage lighting; **Büh|nen|bild** M (stage) set; **Büh|nen|bild|ner(in)** M(F) set designer; **Büh|nen|dich|ter(in)** M(F) playwright, dramatist; **Büh|nen|dich|tung** F dramatic verse; **Büh|nen|ef|fekt** M stage effect; **Büh|nen|er|fah|rung** F stage experience; **Büh|nen|er|folg** M success; (= *Stück auch*) (stage) hit; **Büh|nen|fas|sung** F stage adaptation; **büh|nen|ge|recht** ADJ suitable for the stage ADV **etw ~ bearbeiten** to adapt sth for the stage; **Büh|nen|ge|stalt** F (dramatic) character; **Büh|nen|haus** NT stage hero; **Büh|nen|held** M stage hero; **Büh|nen|hel|din** F stage heroine; **Büh|nen|him|mel** M cyclorama; **Büh|nen|ma|ler(in)** M(F) scene painter; **Büh|nen|ma|le|rei** F scene painting; **Büh|nen|ma|nu|skript** NT script; **Büh|nen|meis|ter(in)** M(F) stage manager; **Büh|nen|mu|sik** F incidental music; **Büh|nen|per|so|nal** NT theatre (*Brit*) *or* theater (*US*) staff; **Büh|nen|prä|senz** F stage presence; **Büh|nen|raum** M stage and backstage area; **büh|nen|reif** ADJ ready for the stage; **Büh|nen|schaf|fen|de(r)** [-ʃafndə] MF *decl as adj* (*geh*) dramatic artist; **Büh|nen|spra|che** F standard *or* received pronunciation; **Büh|nen|stück** NT (stage) play; **Büh|nen|tech|nik** F stage technique; **Büh|nen-**

tech|ni|ker(in) M(F) stage technician; **Büh|nen|werk** NT stage entertainment, dramatic work; **büh|nen|wirk|sam** ADJ effective on the stage ADV *bearbeiten, umgestalten* effectively for the stage; **lässt sich dieser Stoff ~ gestalten?** would this material be effective on the stage?; **Büh|nen|wirk|sam|keit** F effectiveness on the stage; **Büh|nen|wir|kung** F dramatic effect

Buh-: **Buh|ruf** M boo, catcall; **Buh|ru|fer(in)** M(F) **der Redner wurde von ~n empfangen** the speaker was booed, the speaker was greeted by boos *or* booing; **die ~ wurden aus dem Saal entfernt** those who had booed were removed from the auditorium

buk (*old*) *pret von* **backen**

Bu|ka|rest ['bu:karɛst] NT -s Bucharest

Bu|kett [bu'kɛt] NT -s, -s *or* -e (*geh*) **a** (= *Blumenbukett*) bouquet **b** (*von Wein*) bouquet, nose

Buk|lee ▲ [bu'kle:] NT -s, -s bouclé (yarn)

Bu|ko|lik [bu'ko:lɪk] F -, no pl (*Liter*) bucolic *or* pastoral poetry

bu|ko|lisch [bu'ko:lɪʃ] ADJ (*Liter*) bucolic, pastoral

Bu|let|te [bu'lɛtə] F -, -n (*dial*) meat ball; **ran an die ~** (*inf*) go right ahead!

Bul|ga|re [bʊl'ga:rə] M -n, -n, **Bul|ga|rin** [-'ga:rɪn] F -, -nen Bulgarian

Bul|ga|ri|en [bʊl'ga:riən] NT -s Bulgaria

bul|ga|risch [bʊl'ga:rɪʃ] ADJ Bulgarian

Bul|ga|risch(e) [bʊl'ga:rɪʃ] NT Bulgarian → *auch* **Deutsch(e)**

Bu|li|mie [buli'mi:] F -, no pl (*Med*) bulimia

Bulk|la|dung ['bʊlk-] F (*Naut*) bulk cargo

Bull|au|ge ['bʊl-] NT (*Naut*) porthole

Bull|dog|ge ['bʊl-] F bulldog

Bull|do|zer ['bʊldo:zɐ] M -s, - bulldozer

Bul|le¹ ['bʊlə] M -n, -n **a** bull **b** (*inf*: = *starker Mann*) great ox of a man **c** (*pej sl*: = *Polizist*) cop (*inf*); **die ~n** the fuzz (*pej sl*), the cops (*inf*)

Bul|le² F -, -n (*Hist, Eccl*) bull

Bul|len-: **Bul|len|bei|ßer¹** [-baisɐ] M -s, - (= *Hund*) bulldog; **Bul|len|bei|ßer²** [-baisɐ] M -s, -, **Bul|len|bei|ße|rin** [-ərɪn] F -, -nen (*pej*) cantankerous *or* sour-tempered (*esp Brit*) character; **Bul|len|hit|ze** F (*inf*) sweltering *or* boiling (*inf*) heat; **Bul|len|markt** M (*St Ex inf*) bull market (*inf*); **bul|len|stark** ADJ (*inf*) beefy (*inf*), brawny, strong as an ox

Bul|le|rei [bʊlə'rai] F -, no pl (*sl*) cop-shop (*Brit inf*), police station

bul|le|rig ['bʊlərɪç] ADJ (*dial*) sour-tempered (*esp Brit*), cantankerous

bul|lern ['bʊlɐn] VI (*inf*) **a** (= *poltern*) to thud, to rumble; (*Wasser, Flüssigkeit*) to bubble; (*Ofen*) to roar **b** (*dial*: = *schimpfen*) to bellyache (*inf*), to moan and groan (*inf*)

Bul|le|tin [bʏl'tɛ̃:] NT -s, -s bulletin

Bul|le|tin|board ['bʊlətɪn'bɔ:ed] NT -s, -s, **Bulle|tin-Board** NT -s, -s (*Comput*) bulletin board

bul|lig ['bʊlɪç] ADJ (*inf*) **a** brawny, beefy (*inf*) **b** *Hitze* sweltering, boiling (*inf*)

Bul|lig|keit F -, no pl brawniness, beefiness (*inf*)

bul|rig ['bʊlrɪç] ADJ = **bullerig**

Bull|ter|ri|er ['bʊl-] M bull terrier

bum [bʊm] INTERJ bang; (*tiefer*) boom

Bu|me|rang ['bu:məraŋ, 'bʊməraŋ] M -s, -s *or* -e (*lit, fig*) boomerang

Bu|me|rang|ef|fekt M boomerang effect

Bum|mel ['bʊml] M -s, - stroll; (*durch Lokale*) wander (*durch* around), tour (*durch* of); **einen ~ machen, auf einen ~ gehen** to go *or* take a stroll; **einen ~ durch die Stadt machen** to go for *or* take a stroll (a)round (the) town, to (go for a) wander (a)round (the) town; **einen ~**

durch die **Nachtlokale machen** to take in a few nightclubs

Bum|me|lant [bʊmə'lant] M **-en, -en, Bum|me|lan|tin** [-'lantɪn] F **-, -nen** (inf) **a** (= Trödler) slowcoach (Brit inf), slowpoke (US inf), dawdler **b** (= Faulenzer) loafer (inf), idler

Bum|mel|ten|tum [bʊmə'lantntuːm] NT **-s**, no pl (pej) absenteeism

Bum|me|lei [bʊmə'lai] F **-, -en** (inf) (= Trödelei) dawdling; (= Faulenzerei) loafing about (inf), i-dling

Bum|mel|frit|ze M (inf) loafer (inf), idler

bum|me|lig ['bʊməlɪç] ADJ (= trödelnd) slow; (= faul) idle

Bum|mel|le|ben NT (inf) life of idleness

bum|meln ['bʊmln] VI **a** aux sein (= spazieren gehen) to stroll; (= Lokale besuchen) to go (a)round the pubs/bars etc; (= ausgehen) to go out on the town; **im Park ~ gehen** to go for or take a stroll in the park **b** (= trödeln) to dawdle, to hang about (inf) **c** (= faulenzen) to idle or fritter one's time away, to take it easy

Bum|mel-: Bum|mel|streik M go-slow; **Bum|mel|zug** M (inf) slow or stopping train

Bum|merl ['bʊmɐl] NT **-s, -(n)** (Aus inf) point a-gainst

bum|mern ['bʊmɐn] VI (dial) to hammer, to bang

Bumm|ler ['bʊmlɐ] M **-s, -, Bumm|le|rin** [-ərɪn] F **-, -nen** **a** (= Spaziergänger) stroller **b** (= Trödler) slowcoach (Brit inf), slowpoke (US inf), dawdler

bumm|lig ['bʊmlɪç] ADJ (inf) = bummelig

bums [bʊms] INTERJ thump, thud; **~, da fiel der Kleine hin** bang! down went the little one

Bums [bʊms] M **-es, -e** (inf, = Schlag) bang, thump

Bums|bom|ber M (sl) plane carrying sex tourists

bum|sen ['bʊmzn] VI impers (inf: = dröhnen) ..., **dass es bumste** ... with a bang; **er schlug gegen die Tür, dass es bumste** he hammered or thumped on the door; **es bumste, als ...** there was a thump or thud when ...; **es hat gebumst** (von Fahrzeugen) there's been a smash-up (esp Brit inf) or crash VI **a** (= schlagen) to thump, to hammer; (Ftbl sl) to kick **b** aux sein (= prallen, stoßen) to bump, to bang, to clout (inf); (= fallen) to fall with a bang or bump; **mit dem Kopf gegen etw ~** to bump or bang or clout (inf) one's head on sth **c** (inf: = koitieren) to have it off (Brit inf), to have sex or nookie (hum inf) VT (inf) **jdn ~** to lay sb (sl), to have it off with sb (Brit inf), to have sex or a bit of nookie (hum inf) with sb; **gebumst werden** to get laid (sl)

Bum|se|rei [bʊmzə'rai] F **-, -en** (inf) screwing (sl)

Bums-: Bums|knei|pe F (pej inf), **Bums|lo|kal** NT (pej inf) (low) dive; **Bums|mu|sik** F (inf) loud (vulgar) music; **bums|voll** ADJ (inf) full to bursting

Bund¹ [bʊnt] M **-(e)s, ⸚e** ['bʏndə] **a** (= Vereinigung, Gemeinschaft) bond; (= Bündnis) alliance; **der Alte/Neue ~** (Bibl) the Old/New Testament or Covenant; **mit jdm im ~e stehen** or **sein** to be in league with sb; **sich** (dat) **die Hand zum ~e reichen** (geh) to enter into a bond of friendship; **den ~ der Ehe eingehen** to enter (into) the bond of marriage; **ein ~ der Freundschaft** a bond of friendship; **den ~ fürs Leben schließen** to take the marriage vows → **australisch** **b** (= Organisation) association, (con)federation; (= Staatenbund) league, alliance **c** (Pol: = Bundesstaat) Federal Government; **~ und Länder** the Federal Government and the/its Länder **d** (inf: = Bundeswehr) **der ~** the army, the services pl

e (an Kleidern) waistband **f** (Mus: bei Saiteninstrumenten) fret

Bund² NT **-(e)s, -e** ['bʊndə] (von Stroh, Flachs, Reisig etc) bundle; (von Radieschen, Spargel etc) bunch

BUND [bʊnt] **-**, no pl abbr von **Bund für Umwelt und Naturschutz Deutschland** ≈ German union for environmental and nature concerns

Bünd|chen ['bʏntçən] NT **-s, -** (am Hals) neckband; (am Ärmel) sleeve band

Bün|del ['bʏndl] NT **-s, -** bundle, sheaf; (= Strohbündel) sheaf; (von Banknoten) wad, bundle; (von Karotten, Radieschen etc) bunch; (Opt: = Strahlenbündel) pencil; (Math) sheaf; (fig) (von Fragen, Problemen etc) cluster; (von Vorschlägen etc) set; **ein hilfloses/schreiendes ~** a helpless/howling (little) bundle; **sein ~ schnüren** or **packen** (dated) to pack one's bags; **jeder hat sein ~ zu tragen** everybody has his cross to bear

Bün|del|funk M (Telec) trunking (Brit)

bün|deln ['bʏndln] VT Zeitungen etc to bundle up, to tie into bundles/a bundle; Garben, Stroh to sheave; Karotten etc to tie into bunches/a bunch; (Opt) Strahlen to focus, to concentrate; (fig) Widerstand, Aktionen to consolidate → auch **gebündelt**

bün|del|wei|se ADV by the bundle, in bundles; **er holte ~ Banknoten aus der Tasche** he pulled wads of banknotes out of his pocket

Bün|den ['bʏndn] NT **-s** (= Graubünden) the Grisons

Bun|des- in cpds federal; **Bun|des|amt** NT Federal Office; **Bun|des|an|ge|stell|ten|ta|rif** M (Ger) statutory salary scale; **Bun|des|an|lei|he** F (Ger) government bond; **Bun|des|an|stalt** F (Ger) Federal Institute; **~ für Arbeit** Federal Institute of Labour (Brit) or Labor (US); **Bun|des|an|walt** M , **Bun|des|an|wäl|tin** F **a** (Ger) attorney of the Federal Supreme Court **b** (Sw) ≈ Public Prosecutor; **Bun|des|an|walt|schaft** F (Ger) Federal Prosecutor's Office; (= Gesamtheit der Anwälte) Federal bar; **Bun|des|an|zei|ger** M (Ger) Federal legal gazette; **Bun|des|ärz|te|kam|mer** F (Ger) professional organization of German doctors, ≈ General Medical Council (Brit), ≈ State Medical Board of Registration (US); **Bun|des|auf|sicht** F (Ger) Government supervision; **Bun|des|auf|sichts|amt** NT Federal Regulator; **Bun|des|aus|bil|dungs|för|de|rungs|ge|setz** NT law regarding grants for higher education; **Bun|des|au|to|bahn** F (Ger, Aus) Federal autobahn (maintained by the Federal Government); **Bun|des|bahn** F (Ger, Aus, Sw) Federal Railway(s pl); **Bun|des|bank** F , no pl (Ger) Federal bank; **Deutsche ~** Federal Bank of Germany; **Bun|des|be|auf|trag|te(r)** MF decl as adj Federal representative or official; **~r für Datenschutz** federal commissioner for data protection; **Bun|des|be|hör|de** F Federal authority; **Bun|des|blatt** NT (Sw) Federal Law Gazette; **Bun|des|bru|der** M (Univ) fellow member of a/the student fraternity); **Bun|des|bür|ger(in)** M(F) (Ger) German, citizen of Germany; **bun|des|deutsch** ADJ German; (Hist: = westdeutsch) West German; **Bun|des|deut|sche(r)** MF decl as adj German; (Hist: = Westdeutsche(r)) West German; **Bun|des|ebe|ne** F auf ~ at a national level; **bun|des|ei|gen** ADJ (federal-owned), national; **Bun|des|ein|heit|lich** ADJ Federal, national ADV nationally; **etw ~ regeln** to regulate sth at national level

Bun|des-: Bun|des|fern|stra|ße F (Ger) trunk (Brit) or main road (maintained by the Federal Government); **Bun|des|fi|nanz|hof** M (Ger) Federal Fiscal Court; **Bun|des|ge|biet** NT (Ger) Federal territory; **Bun|des|ge|nos|se** M , **Bun|des|ge|nos|sin** F ally, confederate; **Bun|des|ge|richt** NT **a** (Ger, Aus) Federal Court **b** (Sw) Federal Appeal Court; **Bun|des|ge|richts|hof** M , no pl (Ger) Federal Supreme Court; **Bun|des|ge|schäfts|füh|rer(in)** M(F) (von Partei, Verein) general secretary; **Bun|des|ge|setz|blatt** NT (Ger, Aus) Federal Law Gazette; **Bun|des|grenz|schutz** M (Ger) Federal Border Guard; **Bun|des|haupt|stadt** F Federal capital; **Bun|des|haus** NT (Ger, Sw) Federal Houses of Parliament; **Bun|des|haus|halt** M Federal budget; **Bun|des|heer** NT (Aus) services pl, army, (federal) armed forces; **Bun|des|ka|bi|nett** NT (Ger) Federal cabinet; **Bun|des|kanz|lei** F (Sw) Federal Chancellery; **Bun|des|kanz|ler(in)** M(F) **a** (Ger, Aus) Chancellor **b** (Sw) Head of the Federal Chancellery; **Bun|des|kanz|ler|amt** NT (Ger, Aus) Federal Chancellery

Bun|des-: Bun|des|kri|mi|nal|amt NT (Ger) Federal Criminal Police Office; **Bun|des|la|de** F (Bibl) Ark of the Covenant; **Bun|des|land** NT state; (Ger auch) Land of the Federal Republic of Germany; **die neuen Bundesländer** the former East German states; **die alten Bundesländer** the former West German states; **Bun|des|li|ga** F (Ger Sport) national league; **Bun|des|li|gist** [-lɪgɪst] M **-en, -en** (Ger Sport) national league team; **Bun|des|mi|nis|ter(in)** M(F) (Ger, Aus) Federal Minister; **Bun|des|mi|nis|te|ri|um** NT (Ger, Aus) Federal Ministry; **Bun|des|mit|tel** PL Federal funds pl; **Bun|des|nach|rich|ten|dienst** M (Ger) Federal Intelligence Service; **Bun|des|post** F (Ger) **die (Deutsche) ~** the (German) Federal Post (Office); **Bun|des|prä|si|dent(in)** M(F) (Ger, Aus) (Federal) President; (Sw) President of the Federal Council

präsident is also the head of state, but he is elected by the people. His term of office is six years and he too can be re-elected only once. He can dissolve the **Nationalrat** and appoints and dismisses the **Bundeskanzler**. In Switzerland the **Bundespräsident** is the chairman of the **Bundesrat** and is in office for a period of one year only. He is not actually head of state, but he represents the country abroad → Bundeskanzler, Bundesrat, Bundesversammlung, Nationalrat

Bun|des-: **Bun|des|pres|se|amt** NT *(Ger)* Federal Government's Press and Information Office; **Bun|des|rat**[1] M *(Ger)* Bundesrat, *upper house of the German Parliament (Sw)* Council of Ministers; **Bun|des|rat**[2] M , **Bun|des|rä|tin** F *(Sw)* Minister of State

---

BUNDESRAT

The **Bundesrat** is the second chamber of the Federal Republic of German, representing the **Länder**. It has 69 members, who are not elected but delegated by the 16 **Land** governments. The most important of the **Bundesrat**'s duties concerns legislation: Federal laws that impinge upon the responsibilities of the **Länder** require its approval. The **Bundesrat** may also object to other laws, although the **Bundestag** can overrule the objection. As a result, Federal policy can be influenced by parties who are in opposition in the **Bundestag** if these parties hold a majority in most of the **Land** parliaments.

In Austria the **Bundesrat** has 63 members. Apart from being able to introduce its own proposals for legislation, the **Bundesrat** has certain rights of veto and approval with regard to laws passed by the **Nationalrat**.

In Switzerland, however, the **Bundesrat** is the executive body, i.e. the government. The **Bundesversammlung** appoints seven **Bundesräte** (ministers), who must come from different cantons, for a period of four years. Each of these ministers is then placed in charge of a **Departement** → Bundestag, Bundesversammlung, Nationalrat

---

Bun|des-: **Bun|des|rech|nungs|hof** M , *no pl* *(Ger)* Federal Audit Office, Federal Accounting Office; **Bun|des|recht** NT Federal law; **Bun|des|re|gie|rung** F *(Ger, Aus)* Federal Government; **Bun|des|re|pub|lik** F Federal Republic; ~ **Deutschland** Federal Republic of Germany; **Bun|des|re|pub|li|ka|ner(in)** M(F) *(Ger)* citizen of the Federal Republic of Germany; **bun|des|re|pub|li|ka|nisch** ADJ *(Ger)* German; **Bun|des|schatz|brief** M *(Ger Fin)* Federal treasury bill; **Bun|des|schul|den|ver|wal|tung** F *(Fin)* Federal Debt Administration; **Bun|des|staat** M (= *Staatenbund, Gliedstaat*) federal state; **bun|des|staat|lich** ADJ federal ADV **die USA sind ~ organisiert** the US is divided into federal states; **Bun|des|stra|ße** F *(Ger)* Federal road (*maintained by the Federal Government*)

Bun|des|tag M , *no pl (Ger)* Bundestag, *lower house of the German Parliament* (Hist) Diet of the German Confederation

---

BUNDESTAG

The German **Bundestag** is the representative body of the Federal Republic of Germany and is elected by the people every four years. There are at least 656 elected representatives, of whom half are directly elected (**Erststimme**) and half taken from the parties' **Landeslisten** (**Zweitstimme**). The **Bundestag** passes Federal laws, elects the **Bundeskanzler**, exercises parliamentary control over the Federal government and sets the Federal budget. Although the General Assembly is its public face, the **Bundestag** carries out most

---

of its work in committees, composition of which reflects that of the **Bundestag**.
At the **Land** level there is usually a similar body, the **Landtag** → Bundeskanzler, Erststimme/Zweitstimme

Bun|des|tags- *(Ger)*: **Bun|des|tags|ab|ge|ord|ne|te(r)** MF *decl as adj* German member of Parliament, member of the Bundestag; **Bun|des|tags|frak|ti|on** F group *or* faction in the Bundestag; **Bun|des|tags|mit|glied** NT member of the Bundestag, member of (the German) parliament; **Bun|des|tags|prä|si|dent(in)** M(F) President of the Bundestag *or* German Parliament; **Bun|des|tags|wahl** F (federal) parliamentary elections *pl*

Bun|des-: **Bun|des|trai|ner(in)** M(F) *(Ger Sport)* national coach; **Bun|des|ver|band** M (= *bundesweite Vereinigung*) federal association; **Bun|des|ver|dienst|kreuz** NT *(Ger)* order of the Federal Republic of Germany, ≈ OBE *(Brit)*; **Bun|des|ver|fas|sung** F Federal constitution; **Bun|des|ver|fas|sungs|ge|richt** NT *(Ger)* Federal Constitutional Court; **Bun|des|ver|samm|lung** F **a** *(Ger, Aus)* Federal Convention **b** *(Sw)* Federal Assembly

---

BUNDESVERSAMMLUNG

In Germany the **Bundesversammlung** is the body that elects the **Bundespräsident**. Half of the **Bundesversammlung** is made up of members of the **Bundestag** and half of delegates from the **Landtage**.

In Austria the **Bundesversammlung** is the joint body of the **Nationalrat** and **Bundesrat**. Its most important function is the swearing-in of the **Bundespräsident**.

The Swiss **Bundesversammlung** is a two-chamber parliament (**Nationalrat** and **Ständerat**) responsible for legislation. It also elects the **Bundesrat**, the **Bundeskanzler** and, every year, the **Bundespräsident**. The two chambers discuss the various bills independently of one another → Bundeskanzler, Bundespräsident, Bundesrat, Bundestag, Nationalrat, Ständerat

---

Bun|des-: **Bun|des|ver|si|che|rungs|an|stalt** F ~ **für Angestellte** federal pensions office for salaried employees; **Bun|des|ver|wal|tungs|ge|richt** NT *(Ger)* Supreme Administrative Court; **Bun|des|wehr** F , *no pl (Ger)* services *pl*, army, *(German)* Federal Armed Forces *pl*; **bun|des|weit** ADJ nationwide ADV nationwide, nationally; **sie bewarb sich ~ bei verschiedenen Firmen** she applied to different companies all over the country; **Bun|des|zent|ral|re|gis|ter** NT central criminal register

---

BUNDESWEHR

The **Bundeswehr** is the name for the German armed forces. It came into being in 1955, originally as a volunteer army. However, since 1956 every male between the ages of 18 and 30 has been liable for **Wehrdienst** (military service). The Defence Minister has control over the **Bundeswehr**, although in the event of war this would pass to the **Bundeskanzler**. Currently the **Bundeswehr** is composed of men performing their military service, soldiers serving voluntarily for a set period of between 2 and 15 years, and professional soldiers → Bundeskanzler, Wehrdienst

---

Bund-: **Bund|fal|te** F pleat; **Hose mit ~** pleated trousers *pl*; **Bund|fal|ten|ho|se** F pleated trousers *pl* *(esp Brit)* or pants *pl* *(esp US)*; **Bund|ho|se** F knee breeches *pl*

bün|dig [ˈbʏndɪç] ADJ **a** (= *schlüssig*) conclusive; (= *kurz, bestimmt*) concise, succinct **b** (=

---

in gleicher Ebene) flush *pred*, level ADV *fassen, formulieren* concisely, succinctly → **kurz**

Bün|dig|keit F -, *no pl* (= *Schlüssigkeit*) conclusiveness; (= *Kürze, Bestimmtheit*) conciseness, succinctness

bün|disch [ˈbʏndɪʃ] ADJ **die ~e Jugend** *(Hist)* members of the "free youth movement"

Bünd|nis [ˈbʏntnɪs] NT **-ses, -se** alliance; (= *Nato*) (NATO) Alliance; ~ **90** political alliance of civil rights campaigners from the former GDR ~ **für Arbeit** informal alliance between employers and unions to help create jobs

---

BÜNDNIS 90/DIE GRÜNEN

In 1993 the West German party **Die Grünen** joined forces with the East German grouping **Bündnis 90**, which had emerged from civil rights groups of the former **DDR**. The present party **Bündnis 90/Die Grünen** sees itself as a party of ecological reform. In addition to its environmental concerns, the party aims to increase social justice through a restructuring of the tax, social security and pension systems. It also demands an equitable sharing of burdens and interests between West and East Germany.

Bünd|nis-: **Bünd|nis|block** M *pl* **-blöcke** allied bloc; **Bünd|nis|grü|ne(r)** MF *(Pol)* member of Bündnis 90/Die Grünen; **Bünd|nis|part|ner** M *(Pol)* ally; **Bünd|nis|po|li|tik** F policy vis-à-vis one's allies; **Bünd|nis|sys|tem** NT system of alliances; **Bünd|nis|treue** F loyalty to the alliance; **die ~ der Ruritanier** the loyalty of the Ruritanians to the *or* their alliance; **Bünd|nis|ver|pflich|tung** F commitment to one's allies; **Bünd|nis|ver|trag** M pact of alliance

Bund-: **Bund|wei|te** F waist measurement; **Bund|zei|chen** NT jointing mark

Bun|ga|low [ˈbʊŋgalo] M **-s, -s** bungalow

Bun|gee-Sprin|gen [ˈbandʒi-] NT , **Bun|gee-sprin|gen** NT bungee jumping

Bun|ker [ˈbʊŋkɐ] M **-s, -** **a** *(Mil)* bunker; (= *Luftschutzbunker*) air-raid shelter **b** (= *Sammelbehälter*) bin; (= *Kohlenbunker*) bunker; (= *Getreidebunker*) silo **c** *(Golf)* bunker **d** *(Mil sl:* = *Gefängnis)* clink *(inf)*, jankers *(Brit Mil sl)*

bun|kern [ˈbʊŋkɐn] VTI **a** *Kohle* to bunker; *Öl* to refuel **b** *(sl:* = *anhäufen, verwahren)* to stash (away) *(inf)*

Bun|ker|öl NT bunker oil *or* fuel

Bun|sen|bren|ner [ˈbʊnzn-] M Bunsen burner

bunt [bʊnt] ADJ **a** (= *farbig*) coloured *(Brit)*, colored *(US)*; (= *mehrfarbig*) colo(u)rful; (= *vielfarbig*) multicolo(u)red, many-colo(u)red; (= *gefleckt*) mottled, spotted; **zu ~e Kleidung** loud *or* gaudy clothing; **~e Farben** bright *or* gay colo(u)rs; **~es Glas** stained glass; **Abzüge in Bunt** *(Phot)* **~e Abzüge** *(Phot)* colo(u)r prints; **ich sehe lieber Filme in Bunt** I prefer seeing films in colo(u)r → **Hund**
b (*fig:* = *abwechslungsreich*) varied; **eine ~e Menge** an assorted *or* a motley crowd; **ein ~es Bild** a colourful *(Brit)* or colorful *(US)* picture; **in ~er Reihenfolge** in a varied sequence; **ein ~er Teller** a plate of cakes and sweets *(Brit)* or candy *(US)*; **ein ~er Abend** a social; *(Rad, TV)* a variety programme *(Brit)* or program *(US)*
c *(fig:* = *wirr)* confused, higgledy-piggledy
ADV **a** (= *farbig*) *anstreichen, anmalen* colourfully *(Brit)*, colorfully *(US)*; *gekleidet* brightly, colo(u)rfully; *bemalt, bemalen* brightly, gaily, in bright colo(u)rs; **etw ~ bekleben** to stick colo(u)red paper on sth; **~ fotografieren** *(inf)* to photograph in colo(u)r; **~ geblümt** *(Stoff, Kleid)* with a colo(u)rful flower design or pattern; **~ gefärbt** multicolo(u)red, many-colo(u)red; **~ gefiedert** with multi-colo(u)red or bright feathers or plumage; **~ gefleckt** *(Tier)* spotted, mottled; **~ gemischt** *(Programm)* varied; *Truppe, Team* diverse; **~ kariert** with a colo(u)red check

---

(pattern); ~ **gestreift** with colo(u)red stripes; ~ **schillernd** iridescent; (= *farbig, fig*) colo(u)rful; *Vergangenheit auch* chequered (*Brit*), checkered (*US*)

b (= *ungeordnet*) ~ **durcheinander** (= *unordentlich*) higgledy-piggledy; **es geht ~ durcheinander** it's all a complete mess

c (*inf*. = *wild*) **jetzt wird es mir zu ~** I've had enough of this; **jetzt wirds mir aber zu ~!** that's going too far!, I've had enough!; **es geht hier ~ zu** it's lively here, this is some sort of madhouse (*pej inf*); **es zu ~ treiben** to carry things too far, to overstep the mark

Bunt-: bunt|be|malt △ [-bəma:lt] ADJ *attr →* **bunt** ADJ a; **Bunt|druck** M *pl* **-drucke** colour (*Brit*) *or* color (*US*) print; **bunt|far|big** ADJ colourful (*Brit*), colorful (*US*), brightly coloured (*Brit*) *or* colored (*US*); **Bunt|film** M (*inf*) colour (*Brit*) *or* color (*US*) film; **bunt|ge|blümt** △ ADJ *attr →* **bunt** ADV a; **bunt|ge|färbt** △ ADJ *attr →* **bunt** ADV a; **bunt|ge|fiedert** △ ADJ *attr →* **bunt** ADV a; **bunt|ge|fleckt** △ ADJ *attr →* **bunt** ADV a; **bunt|ge|mischt** △ ADJ *attr →* **bunt** ADV a; **bunt|ge|streift** △ ADJ *attr →* **bunt** ADV a; **Bunt|heit** F -, *no pl* colourfulness (*Brit*), colorfulness (*US*), gay *or* bright colours (*Brit*) *or* colors (*US*) *pl*; **bunt|ka|riert** △ ADJ *attr →* **bunt** ADV a; **Bunt|me|tall** NT nonferrous metal; **Bunt|pa|pier** NT coloured (*Brit*) *or* colored (*US*) paper; **Bunt|sand|stein** M new red sandstone; **bunt|sche|ckig** ADJ spotted; *Pferd* dappled; (*fig*) motley; **bunt|schil|lernd** △ ADJ *attr →* **bunt** ADV a; **Bunt|specht** M spotted woodpecker; **Bunt|stift** M coloured (*Brit*) *or* colored (*US*) pencil; **Bunt|wä|sche** F coloureds *pl* (*Brit*), coloreds *pl* (*US*)

Bür|de ['byrdə] F -, **-n** (*geh*) load, weight; (*fig*) burden; **jdm eine ~ aufladen** (*fig*) to impose a burden on sb

bür|den ['byrdn] VT (*dated geh*) **etw auf jdn ~** (*lit, fig*) to load sth upon sb

Bu|re ['bu:rə] M -**n**, -**n**, **Bu|rin** ['bu:rɪn] F -, **-nen** Boer

Bu|ren|krieg M Boer War

Burg [bʊrk] F -, **-en** [-gn] **a** castle; (= *Strandburg*) wall of sand (*built on beach by holidaymaker to demarcate his chosen spot*) **b** (= *Biberbau*) (beaver's) lodge

Burg-: Burg|an|la|ge F castle buildings *pl or* complex; **Burg|berg** M castle hill *or* mound

Bür|ge¹ ['byrgə] M -**n**, -**n** (*für* sb) guarantee (*für* a)

Bür|ge² ['byrgə] M -**n**, -**n**, **Bür|gin** ['byrgɪn] F -, **-nen** guarantor; **für jdn ~ sein** to be sb's guarantor, to stand surety for sb; **einen ~n stellen** (*Fin*) to offer surety

bür|gen ['byrgn] VI **für etw ~** to guarantee sth, to vouch for sth; (*fig*) to guarantee sth, to be a guarantee of sth; **für jdn ~** (*Fin*) to stand surety for sb; (*fig*) to vouch for sb; **Sie ~ mir persönlich dafür, dass ...** you are personally responsible *or* answerable to me that ...

Bür|ger ['byrgə] M -**s**, -, **Bür|ge|rin** [-ərɪn] F -, **-nen** (*von Staat, Gemeinde*) citizen, burgher (*Hist*); (*Sociol, pej*) bourgeois; **die ~ von Ulm** the townsfolk of Ulm

Bür|ger-: Bür|ger|ak|ti|on F citizens' initiative, citizens' action group; **Bür|ger|be|auf|trag|te(r)** MF *decl as adj* ombudsman/-woman; **Bür|ger|be|geh|ren** NT (*Ger*) public petition; **Bür|ger|be|ra|tungs|stel|le** F citizens' advice bureau; **Bür|ger|block** M *pl* **-blöcke** conservative alliance; **Bür|ger|brief** M patent (*Brit*) *or* certificate (*US*) of citizenship; **Bür|ger|eid** M civic oath; **Bür|ger|ent|scheid** M (*Ger*) citizens' *or* public decision; **Bür|ger|fa|mi|lie** F merchant family; **bür|ger|fern** ADJ nonpopulist; **Bür|ger|fo|rum** NT open *or* public debate; **Bür|ger|haus** NT **a** town house *or* residence **b** (*dated*: = *Bürgerfamilie*) merchant family

Bür|ge|rin F → **Bürger**

Bür|ger-: Bür|ger|ini|ti|a|ti|ve F citizens' initiative *or* action group; **Bür|ger|ko|mi|tee** NT citizens' committee; **Bür|ger|krieg** M civil war; **bür|ger|kriegs|ähn|lich** ADJ civil warlike *attr*; **~e Zustände** civil war conditions

bür|ger|lich ['byrgəlɪç] ADJ **a** *attr* Ehe, Recht etc civil; *Pflicht* civic; **Bürgerliches Gesetzbuch** Civil Code **b** (= *dem Bürgerstand angehörend*) middle-class (*auch pej*), bourgeois (*esp pej*); (*Hist*) bourgeois; **aus guter ~er Familie** from a good respectable *or* middle-class family; **~es Essen/Küche** good plain food/cooking; **~es Trauerspiel** (*Liter*) domestic tragedy **ADV diese Stadt ist ~ geprägt** this town is very middle-class; **ein ~ orientierter Politiker** a politician who aims for the middle-class vote; **~ essen** to eat good plain food

Bür|ger|li|che(r) ['byrgəlɪçə] MF *decl as adj* commoner

Bür|ger|lich|keit F -, *no pl* (*von Lebensstil*) middle-class way of life; (*von Denkweise*) middle-class mentality

Bür|ger-: Bür|ger|meis|ter M mayor; **Bür|ger|meis|ter|amt** NT **a** (= *Aufgabe*) office of mayor **b** (= *Behörde, Gebäude*) town hall; **Bür|ger|meis|te|rei** [-maɪstəˈraɪ] F -, **-en** (*old*) **a** district council; (= *Gebäude*) district council offices *pl* **b** (*dial*: = *Bürgermeisteramt*) town hall; **Bür|ger|meis|te|rin** F mayor(ess); (= *Frau eines Bürgermeisters*) mayoress; **bür|ger|nah** ADJ populist; **Bür|ger|nä|he** F populism; **Bür|ger|pflicht** F civic duty; **Ruhe ist die erste ~** law and order is the citizen's first duty, the first duty of the citizen is law and order; **Bür|ger|recht** NT *usu pl* civil rights *pl*; **jdm die ~e aberkennen** *or* **entziehen** to strip sb of his civil rights; **Bür|ger|recht|ler** [-rɛçtlɐ] M -**s**, -, **Bür|ger|recht|le|rin** [-ərɪn] F -, **-nen** civil rights campaigner

Bür|ger|rechts-: Bür|ger|rechts|be|we|gung F civil rights movement; **Bür|ger|rechts|kämp|fer(in)** M(F) civil rights campaigner

Bür|ger|schaft ['byrgəʃaft] F -, **-en** (= *Vertretung*) City Parliament

Bür|ger|schafts|wahl F metropolitan council election (*in Hamburg and Bremen*)

Bür|ger|schreck M bog(e)y of the middle classes

Bür|gers|frau ['byrgəs-] F (*old*) middle-class woman, bourgeoise (*Hist*)

Bür|gers|mann ['byrgəs-] M *pl* **-leute** (*old*) citizen, bourgeois (*Hist*)

Bür|ger(s)|sohn M (*usu iro*) son of the middle classes

Bür|ger|stand M (*old*) middle class(es), bourgeoisie (*Hist*)

Bür|ger|steig M pavement (*Brit*), sidewalk (*US*); **die ~e hochklappen** (*inf*) to shut up *or* down (for the night)

Bür|gers|toch|ter ['byrgəs-] F (*usu iro*) daughter of the middle classes

Bür|ger|tum ['byrgətu:m] NT -**s**, *no pl* (*Hist*) bourgeoisie (*Hist*)

Bür|ger|ver|samm|lung F town *or* citizens' meeting

Bür|ger|wehr F (*Hist*) militia

Burg-: Burg|fräu|lein NT damsel of the/a castle (*old*); **Burg|fried** [-fri:t] M -(**e**)**s**, -**e** [-də] keep; **Burg|frie|de(n)** M -**s**, -(*fig*) truce **b** (*Hist*) castle precincts *pl*, castellany; **Burg|herr** M lord of the/a castle; **Burg|her|rin** F lady of the/a castle

Bür|gin F → **Bürge²**

Burg|ru|i|ne F ruined castle, castle ruins *pl*

Bürg|schaft ['byrkʃaft] F -, **-en** (*Jur*) (*gegenüber Gläubigern*) security, surety; (= *Haftungssumme*) penalty; (*old liter*) pledge (*old liter*); **~ für jdn leisten** to stand surety for sb, to act as guarantor for sb; (*fig*) to vouch for sb; **er verlangte eine ~** he demanded (a) security *or* surety

Bürg|schafts-: Bürg|schafts|er|klä|rung F declaration of suretyship; **Bürg|schafts|neh|mer(in)** M(F) creditor

Bur|gund [bʊrˈgʊnt] NT -**s** Burgundy

Bur|gun|der¹ [bʊrˈgʊndɐ] M -**s**, - (*auch* **Burgunderwein**) Burgundy

Bur|gun|der² [bʊrˈgʊndɐ] M -**s**, -, **Bur|gun|de|rin** [-ərɪn] F -, **-nen** Burgundian

bur|gun|der|far|ben [-farbn], **bur|gun|der|rot** ADJ burgundy (red)

bur|gun|disch [bʊrˈgʊndɪʃ] ADJ Burgundian; **die Burgundische Pforte** the Belfort Gap

Burg|ver|lies NT (castle) dungeon

Bu|rin F -, **-nen** Boer

Bur|ka ['bʊrka] F -, -**s** chador

Bur|ki|na Fa|so [bʊrˈki:na ˈfa:zo] NT -**s** Burkina-Faso

bur|lesk [bʊrˈlɛsk] ADJ burlesque *no adv*

Bur|les|ke [bʊrˈlɛskə] F -, -**n** burlesque

Bur|ma ['bʊrma] NT -**s** Burma

Bur|me|se [bʊrˈme:zə] M -**n**, -**n**, **Bur|me|sin** [-ˈme:zɪn] F -, **-nen** Burmese

bur|me|sisch [bʊrˈme:zɪʃ] ADJ Burmese

Burn|out ['bœrnaut, 'bøːɛnaut] M -**s**, *no pl*, **Burn-out** M -**s**, *no pl* (*Med*) burnout

Burn|out-Syn|drom ['bœrnaut-, 'bøːɛnaut-] NT (*Med*) burnout syndrome

Bur|nus ['bʊrnʊs] M - *or* -**ses**, -**se** burnous(e)

Bü|ro [byˈro:] NT -**s**, -**s** office

Bü|ro- *in cpds* office; **Bü|ro|an|ge|stell|te(r)** MF *decl as adj* office worker; **Bü|ro|ar|beit** F office work; **Bü|ro|ar|ti|kel** M item of office equipment; (*pl*) office supplies *pl or* equipment; **Bü|ro|au|to|ma|ti|on** F office automation; **Bü|ro|be|darf** M office supplies *pl or* equipment; **Bü|ro|dreh|stuhl** M swivel (desk) chair; **Bü|ro|ein|rich|tung** F office equipment *or* setup; **Bü|ro|flä|che** F office space *no pl*; **Bü|ro|ge|bäu|de** NT office building; **Bü|ro|ge|hil|fe** M, **Bü|ro|ge|hil|fin** F (office) junior; **Bü|ro|haus** NT office block; **Bü|ro|hengst** M (*pej inf*) office worker; **all die ~e** all the office crowd; **Bü|ro|hoch|haus** NT multistorey (*Brit*) *or* multistory (*US*) *or* high-rise office block; **Bü|ro|kauf|frau** F, **Bü|ro|kauf|mann** M office administrator; **Bü|ro|klam|mer** F paper clip; **Bü|ro|kom|mu|ni|ka|ti|on** F, *no pl* office communication; **Bü|ro|kraft** F (office) clerk; **Bü|ro|kram** M (*inf pej*) odd bits *pl* of paperwork

Bü|ro|krat [byroˈkra:t] M -**en**, -**en**, **Bü|ro|kra|tin** [-ˈkra:tɪn] F -, **-nen** bureaucrat

Bü|ro|kra|tie [byrokraˈti:] F, *no pl* bureaucracy

bü|ro|kra|tisch [byroˈkra:tɪʃ] (*usu pej*) ADJ bureaucratic **ADV** bureaucratically

bü|ro|kra|ti|sie|ren [byrokratiˈzi:rən] *ptp* **büro|kratisiert** VT to bureaucratize

Bü|ro|kra|tis|mus [byrokraˈtɪsmʊs] M -, *no pl* bureaucracy

Bü|ro-: Bü|ro|land|schaft F office environment *no pl*; **Bü|ro|lei|ter(in)** M(F) office manager; **Bü|ro|ma|schi|ne** F office machine; **Bü|ro|ma|te|ri|al** NT office supplies *pl*; (= *Schreibwaren*) stationery *no pl*; **Bü|ro|mensch** M (*inf*) office worker, pen pusher (*pej inf*); **Bü|ro|mö|bel** PL office furniture *sing*; **Bü|ro|schluss** ▲ M office closing time; **nach ~** after office hours; **Bü|ro|stun|den** PL office hours *pl*; **Bü|ro|tä|tig|keit** F office work; **Bü|ro|tech|nik** F office technology; **Bü|ro|turm** M office block; **Bü|ro|vor|ste|her(in)** M(F) (*dated*) senior *or* chief *or* head clerk; **Bü|ro|zeit** F office hours *pl*

Bürsch|chen ['byrʃçən] NT -**s**, - *dim von* **Bursche** little lad (*Brit*) *or* fellow; **freches ~** cheeky (*Brit*) *or* fresh (*US*) little devil; **mein ~!** laddie! (*Brit*), young man!

Bur|sche ['bʊrʃə] M -**n**, -**n** **a** (*old, dial*) boy (*Brit*); **ein toller ~** quite a lad (*Brit*) *or* young man **b** (*inf*: = *Kerl*) fellow, guy (*inf*), so-and-so (*pej inf*); **ein übler ~** a bad lot (*Brit*), a shady character (*US*) **c** (*Univ* = *Verbindungsmitglied*) member of a student fraternity **d** (= *Laufbursche*) boy **e** (*old Mil*) batman (*Brit*), orderly **f** (*inf*: = *großes Exemplar*) **das ist vielleicht ein ~** what a whopper! (*inf*); **da haben wir den ~n** that's got it *or* him! (*inf*)

Bur|schen-: Bur|schen|herr|lich|keit F good old student days; **Bur|schen|schaft** [ˈbʊrʃn-ʃaft] F -, -en student fraternity; **Bur|schen-schaf|ter** [-ʃaftɐ] M -s, -, **Bur|schen|schaft-ler** [-ʃaftlɐ] M -s, - member of a student fraternity; **bur|schen|schaft|lich** [-ʃaftlɪç] ADJ *attr* of a/the (student) fraternity; **~e Verbindung** student fraternity

BURSCHENSCHAFT

Burschenschaften are student organizations similar to the American fraternities. They continue a tradition going back to the early 19th century, when they were politically very active and influential. Prior to the 1980s they were either banned or – during times of student unrest – marginalized, being regarded as deeply conservative and nationalist. Typical **Burschenschaftler** are recognizable by their bright sashes and peaked caps and are most often seen in university cities such as Heidelberg or Tübingen. Even when they have completed their studies, former students tend to remain loyal to their **Burschenschaft** and to offer it their support. In so-called **schlagende Verbindungen**, the Mensur, a fencing bout, is compulsory.

bur|schi|kos [bʊrʃiˈkoːs] ADJ **a** (= *jungenhaft*) (tom)boyish **b** (= *unbekümmert*) casual ADV (tom)boyishly; **benimm dich doch nicht so ~** stop behaving like a tomboy

Bur|schi|ko|si|tät [bʊrʃikoziˈtɛːt] F -, -en **a** (= *Jungenhaftigkeit*) (tom)boyishness **b** (= *Unbekümmertheit*) casualness

Bur|se [ˈbʊrzə] F -, -n hostel

Bürs|te [ˈbʏrstə] F -, -n brush; (*inf* = *Bürstenfrisur*) crew cut

bürs|ten [ˈbʏrstn] VT to brush; (*vulg* = *koitieren*) to screw (*sl*)

Bürs|ten-: Bürs|ten|bin|der(in) M(F) brushmaker; **wie ein ~** (*inf*) like mad (*inf*) → **saufen**; **Bürs|ten|fri|sur** F , **Bürs|ten|haar|schnitt** M crew cut; **Bürs|ten|ma|cher(in)** M(F) brushmaker; **Bürs|ten|mas|sa|ge** F brush massage; **Bürs|ten|schnitt** M crew cut

Bu|run|di [buˈrʊndi] NT -s Burundi

Bu|run|di|er [buˈrʊndiɐ] M -s, -, **Bu|run|di|e-rin** [-iərɪn] F -, -nen Burundian

bu|run|disch [buˈrʊndiʃ] ADJ Burundian

Bür|zel [ˈbʏrtsl] M -s - **a** (*Orn*) rump **b** (*Hunt*) tail **c** (*Cook*) parson's nose

Bus¹ [bʊs] M -ses, -se bus; (= *Privat- und Überlandbus*) bus, coach (*Brit*)

Bus² M -, -se (*Comput*) bus

Bus|bahn|hof M → **Bus¹** bus/coach (*Brit*) station

Busch [bʊʃ] M -(e)s, ¨e [ˈbʏʃə] **a** (= *Strauch*) bush, shrub; **etwas ist im ~** (*inf*) there's something up; **mit etw hinter dem ~ halten** (*inf*) to keep sth quiet *or* to oneself; **auf den ~ klopfen** (*inf*) to fish (about) for information (*inf*); **bei jdm auf den ~ klopfen** (*inf*) to sound sb out; **sich (seitwärts) in die Büsche schlagen** (*inf*) to slip away; (= *euph hum*) to go behind a tree (*euph hum*) **b** (*Geog*: *in den Tropen*) bush; (*inf*: = *Wildnis*) jungle **c** (= *Strauß*) bunch; (*rare*: = *Büschel*) tuft

Busch|boh|ne F dwarf bean

Bü|schel [ˈbʏʃl] NT -s, - (*von Gras, Haaren*) tuft; (*von Heu, Stroh*) bundle; (*von Blumen, Rettichen*) bunch; **in ~n wachsen** to grow in tufts; (*Blumen*) to grow in clumps

bü|sche|lig [ˈbʏʃəlɪç] ADJ in tufts; *Blüten in clusters*

bü|scheln [ˈbʏʃln] VT (*S Ger, Sw*) to tie into bunches

bü|schel|wei|se ADV (*von Gras, Haaren*) in tufts; (*von Heu, Stroh*) in bundles; (*von Blumen, Rettichen*) in bunches; (*von Blumenpflanzen*) in clumps

Bu|schen [ˈbʊʃn] M -s, - (*dial*) bunch of leaves *etc*

Bu|schen|schän|ke ▲ F , **Bu|schen|schen-ke** F (*Aus*) ≈ inn

Busch|feu|er NT (*lit*) bush fire; **sich wie ein ~ ausbreiten** to spread like wildfire

Bu|schi [ˈbʊʃi] M -s, -s (*Sw*) baby

bu|schig [ˈbʊʃɪç] ADJ bushy

büsch|lig [ˈbʏʃlɪç] ADJ = büschelig

Busch-: Busch|mann M *pl* **-männer** *or* **-leute** bushman; **Busch|mann|frau** F bushwoman; **Busch|mes|ser** NT machete; **Busch|ne-ger(in)** M(F) maroon; **Busch|werk** NT bushes *pl*; **Busch|wind|rös|chen** [-rø:sçən] NT (wood) anemone

Bu|sen [ˈbuːzn] M -s, - (*von Frau*) bust, bosom; (*old*: = *Oberteil des Kleides*) bodice; (*liter*: *von Mann*) breast (*liter*); (*fig geh*: = *Innerstes, von Natur*) bosom (*liter*); **ein Geheimnis in seinem ~ wahren** to keep a secret deep in one's heart (*liter*)

Bu|sen-: bu|sen|frei ADJ topless ADV **sich ~ sonnen** to sunbathe topless; **Bu|sen|freund(in)** M(F) (*iro*) bosom friend; **Bu|sen|grab|scher** M -s, -, **Bu|sen|grap|scher** M -, - (*inf*) groper (*inf*); **Bu|sen|star** M (*inf*) busty film star (*inf*)

Bus-: Bus|fah|rer(in) M(F) → **Bus¹** bus/coach (*Brit*) driver; **Bus|fahr|plan** M bus timetable (*Brit*) *or* schedule (*US*); **Bus|fahrt** F → **Bus¹** bus/coach (*Brit*) ride; **Bus|hal|te|stel|le** F bus stop

Bu|si|ness|class [ˈbɪznɪsklaːs] F -, *no pl*, **Bu|si-ness|klas|se** ▲ [ˈbɪznɪs-] F -, *no pl* business class

Bus|li|nie F bus route; **welche ~ fährt zum Bahnhof?** which bus goes to the station?

Bus|sard [ˈbʊsart] M -s, -e [-də] buzzard

Bu|ße [ˈbuːsə] F -, -n **a** (*Rel*) (= *Reue*) repentance, penitence; (= *Bußauflage*) penance; (= *tätige Buße*) atonement; **~ tun** to do penance; **zur ~ as a penance; **zur ~ bereit sein** to be ready to do penance *or* to atone; **das Sakrament der ~** the sacrament of penance **b** (*Jur*) (= *Schadenersatz*) damages *pl*; (= *Geldstrafe*) fine; **eine ~ von 100 Euro** a 100 euro fine; **jdn zu einer ~ verurteilen** to make sb pay (the) damages; to fine sb, to impose a fine on sb

Bus|sel [ˈbʊsl] NT -s, -(n) (*Aus*) kiss

bus|seln [ˈbʊsln], **bus|sen** [ˈbʊsn] VTI (*S Ger, Aus*) to kiss

bü|ßen [ˈbyːsn] VT to pay for; *Sünden* to atone for, to expiate; **das wirst** *or* **sollst du mir ~** I'll make you pay for that, you'll pay for that VI **für etw ~** (*auch Rel*) to atone for sth; (= *wieder gutmachen*) to make amends for sth; **für Leichtsinn** *etc* to pay for sth; **schwer (für etw) ~ müssen** to have to pay dearly (for sth)

Bü|ßer [ˈbyːsɐ] M -s, -, **Bü|ße|rin** [-ərɪn] F -, -nen penitent

Bü|ßer|ge|wand NT , **Bü|ßer|hemd** NT penitential robe, hair shirt

Bus|se(r)l [ˈbʊsɐl] NT -s, -(n) (*S Ger, Aus*) kiss

bus|se(r)ln [ˈbʊsɐln] VTI (*S Ger, Aus*) to kiss

Bü|ßer|schnee M (*spec*) penitent snow (*spec*)

Buß- [ˈbuːs-]: **buß|fer|tig** ADJ repentant, contrite; (*Rel auch*) penitent; **Buß|fer|tig|keit** F repentance, contrition; **Buß|gang** M *pl* **-gänge** penitential pilgrimage; **einen ~ antreten** (*fig*) to don sackcloth and ashes; **Buß|ge|bet** NT prayer of repentance

Buß|geld NT fine

Buß|geld-: Buß|geld|be|scheid M notice of payment due (*for traffic violation etc*); **Buß-geld|ka|ta|log** M list of offences punishable by fines; **Buß|geld|stel|le** F fine payment office (*for traffic offenders*); **Buß|geld|ver|fah-ren** NT fining system

Buß|ge|sang [ˈbuːs-] M , **Buß|lied** NT penitential hymn

Bus|si [ˈbusi] NT -s, -s (*S Ger*) kiss

Bus|so|le [bʊˈsoːlə] F -, -n compass; (*Elec*) galvanometer

Buß-: Buß|pre|di|ger(in) M(F) preacher of repentance; **Buß|pre|digt** F sermon calling to repentance

Bus|spur F bus lane

Buß-: Buß|sa|kra|ment NT sacrament of penance; **Buß|tag** M **a** day of repentance **b** = **Buß- und Bettag**; **Buß|übung** F act of penance; **Buß- und Bet|tag** M day of prayer and repentance

Büs|te [ˈbʏstə] F -, -n bust; (= *Schneiderbüste*) tailor's dummy; (*weibliche*) dressmaker's dummy

Büs|ten|hal|ter M bra, brassière (*dated*)

Bus|ti|er [bʏsˈtie:] NT -s, -s (*ohne Träger*) bustier, boob tube (*Brit inf*); (*mit Trägern*) bra top

Bu|su|ki [buˈzuːki] F -, -s bouzouki

Bus|ver|bin|dung F → **Bus¹** bus/coach connection

Bu|tan [buˈtaːn] NT -s, -e, **Bu|tan|gas** NT butane (gas)

Butt [bʊt] M -(e)s, -e flounder, butt; **die ~e** the bothidae (*form*), flounders

Bütt [bʏt] F -, -en (*dial*) speaker's platform; **in die ~ steigen** to mount the platform

Büt|te [ˈbʏtə] F -, -n **a** (= *Bütte*) vat; (= *Wanne*) tub **b** (*für Trauben*) grape container

Büt|te [ˈbʏta] F -, -n vat; (*dial*: = *Wanne*) tub

Büt|tel [ˈbʏtl] M -s, -, (*old*) bailiff; (*pej*) henchman (*pej*); (= *Polizist*) cop(per) (*inf*); **die ~** the law (*inf*), the cops *pl* (*inf*); **ich bin doch nicht dein ~** (*inf*) I'm not going to do your dirty work (*pej inf*), I'm not your henchman

Büt|tel|dienst M dirty work (*pej inf*)

Büt|ten|(pa|pier) [ˈbʏtn-] NT -s, *no pl* handmade paper (*with deckle edge*)

Büt|ten-: Büt|ten|rand M deckle edge; **Büt-ten|re|de** F carnival speech; **Büt|ten|red-ner(in)** M(F) *speaker on the platform at carnival*

But|ter [ˈbʊtɐ] F -, *no pl* butter; **braune ~** browned (melted) butter; **echte ~** real butter; **es schmolz wie ~ in der Sonne** (*fig*) it vanished into thin air; **alles (ist) in ~** (*inf*) everything is fine or OK or hunky-dory (*inf*); **sein Herz ist weich wie ~** his heart is as soft as butter; **jdm die ~ auf dem Brot nicht gönnen** (*fig inf*) to begrudge sb the very air he/she breathes; **wir lassen uns** (*dat*) **nicht die ~ vom Brot nehmen** (*inf*) we're not going to let somebody put one over on us (*inf*), we're going to stick up for our rights

But|ter- *in cpds* butter; **But|ter|bem|me** F (*dial*) bread and butter *no art, no pl*, slice or piece of bread and butter; (*inf*: = *Sandwich*) sandwich; **But|ter|berg** M butter mountain; **But|ter|blu|me** F buttercup; **But|ter-brot** NT bread and butter *no art, no pl*, slice or piece of bread and butter; (*inf*: = *Sandwich*) sandwich; **für ein ~** (*inf*) for next to nothing; *kaufen, verkaufen auch* for a song; **das musst du mir nicht ständig aufs ~ streichen** *or* **schmieren** there's no need to keep rubbing it in; **But|ter-brot|pa|pier** NT greaseproof paper; **But|ter-creme** F butter cream; **But|ter|creme|tor|te** F cream cake; **But|ter|damp|fer** M (*dated inf*) **a** *ferry sailing to another country to allow purchase of cheap goods* **b** *boat which sells duty-free goods once outside a country's territorial waters*; **But|ter|do|se** F butter dish; **But|ter|fahrt** F (*pej*) boat/bus trip to buy *cheap or duty-free goods*; **Bu̱t|ter|fass** ▲ NT butter churn; **Bu̱t|ter|fett** NT butterfat; **Bu̱t|ter|flöck|chen** NT　(*Cook*) (small knob of) butter

Bu̱t|ter|fly|(stil) ['batɐflai-] M **-s**, *no pl* butterfly (stroke)

Bu̱t|ter|fly|mes|ser ['batɐflai-] NT butterfly knife

Bu̱t|ter-: bu̱t|ter|gelb ADJ butter yellow; **Bu̱t|ter|gelb** NT　**a** (= *Farbe*) butter yellow　**b** (= *Farbstoff*) butter colour (*Brit*) or color (*US*)

bu̱t|te|rig ['bʊtərɪç] ADJ buttery

Bu̱t|ter-: Bu̱t|ter|kä|se M (full fat) hard cheese; **Bu̱t|ter|keks** M ≈ rich tea biscuit (*Brit*), ≈ butter cookie (*US*); **Bu̱t|ter|krem** F butter cream; **Bu̱t|ter|mes|ser** NT butter knife; **Bu̱t|ter|milch** F buttermilk

bu̱t|tern ['bʊtɐn] **VT**　**a** *Brot* to butter　**b** *Milch* to make into butter　**c** (*inf*: = *investieren*) to put (*in +acc* into)　**VI** to make butter

Bu̱t|ter-: Bu̱t|ter|pilz M boletus luteus (*form*); **Bu̱t|ter|säu|re** F butyric acid; **Bu̱t|ter|schmalz** NT clarified butter; **Bu̱t|ter-** (*lit*) buttered side; **auf die ~ fallen** (*fig inf*) to fall on one's feet (*inf*); **bu̱t|ter|weich** ADJ *Frucht, Landung* beautifully soft; (*Sport inf*) *Abgabe, Pass, Aufschlag* gentle ADV *landen, aufkommen* softly, gently; **~ formulierte Regelungen** vaguely worded regulations

Bu̱t|je(r) ['bʊtjə] M **-s**, **-s** (*N Ger*) kid (*inf*), child

Bütt|ner ['bytnɐ] M **-s**, **-**, **Bütt|ne|rin** [-ərɪn] F **-**, **-nen** (*dial*) cooper

But|ton ['batn] M **-s**, **-s** badge

But|ton-down-Kra|gen [batn'daun-] M button-down collar

bu̱tt|rig ['bʊtrɪç] ADJ = **butterig**

Bu̱tz¹ [bʊts] M **-en**, **-en** (*dial*) (= *Zwerg*) hobgoblin; (= *Schreckgestalt*) bog(e)y(man)

Bu̱tz² M **-en**, **-en** (*dial*) (apple) core

Bu̱t|ze|mann ['bʊtsə-] M *pl* **-männer** (= *Zwerg*) hobgoblin; (= *Schreckgestalt*) bog(e)yman

Bu̱t|zen ['bʊtsn] M **-s**, **-** (*dial*)　**a** (= *Kerngehäuse*) (apple) core　**b** (*in Butzenscheibe*) bulge (*in a bull's-eye pane*)

bü̱t|zen ['bʊtsn] VTI　(*dial*) to kiss

Bu̱t|zen|schei|be ['bʊtsn-] F bulls'-eye (window) pane

Büx [bʏks] F **-**, **-en**, **Bu̱|xe** ['bʊksə] F **-**, **-n** (*N Ger*) trousers *pl* (*esp Brit*), pants *pl* (*esp US*); **fünf ~en** five pairs of trousers (*esp Brit*) or pants (*esp US*)

Bux|te|hu|de [bʊkstə'huːdə] NT **-s**　**a** Buxtehude (*town near Hamburg*)　**b** (*inf*) **aus/nach ~** from/to the back of beyond (*inf*); **in ~ leben** to live in the back of beyond (*inf*); **das macht man vielleicht noch in ~** perhaps they still do that in the provincial backwaters

Buy-out ▲ ['baiaut] M **-s**, **-s**, **Buy|out** M **-s**, **-s** buyout

BVG [beːfauˈgeː] NT **-** *abbr von* **Bundesverfassungsgericht**

Bw *abbr von* **Bundeswehr**

b. w. *abbr von* **bitte wenden** pto

B-Waf|fe ['beː-] F *von* **biologische Waffe**

BWL [beːveːˈɛl] F **-** *abbr von* **Betriebswirtschaftslehre**

BWV [beːveːˈfau] NT **-(s)** *abbr von* **Bachwerkeverzeichnis** ≈ list of J. S. Bach's works

By|pass ['baipas] M **-(es)**, **-es** or **Bypässe** [-pɛsə] (*Med*) bypass; **dreifacher/vierfacher ~** triple/quadruple bypass

By|pass-Ope|ra|ti|on ['baipas-] F bypass operation

Byte ['bait] NT **-s**, **-s** byte

By|zan|ti|ner [bytsanˈtiːnɐ] M **-s**, **-**, **By|zan|ti|ne|rin** [-ərɪn] F **-**, **-nen** Byzantine

by|zan|ti|nisch [bytsanˈtiːnɪʃ] ADJ　**a** Byzantine　**b** (= *üppig*) extravagant

By|zan|ti|nist [bytsantiˈnɪst] M **-en**, **-en**, **By|zan|ti|nis|tin** [-ˈnɪstɪn] F **-**, **-nen** Byzantine scholar

By|zan|ti|nis|tik [bytsantiˈnɪstɪk] F **-**, *no pl* Byzantine studies *pl*

By|zanz [byˈtsants] NT **-'** Byzantium

B-Zel|le ['beː-] F (*Med*) B-cell, B-lymphocyte

bzgl. *abbr von* **bezüglich**

bzw. *abbr von* **beziehungsweise**

C

C, c [tse:] NT **-,** - C, c

C abbr von **Celsius**

ca. abbr von **circa** approx

Ca|brio ['ka:brio] NT **-s, -s** (Aut inf) convertible

Ca|bri|o|let [kabrio'le:] NT **-s, -s** (Aut) convertible

Cache [kɛʃ] M **-, -s** (Comput) cache; **externer ~** secondary or external cache; **interner ~** primary or internal cache

Cache-Spei|cher ['kɛʃ-] M (Comput) cache memory → auch **Cache**

Ca|chou [ka'ʃu:] NT **-s, -s, Ca|chou|bon|bon** [ka'ʃu:-] NT cachou

CAD [tse:a:'de:] NT **-s,** no pl abbr von **computer aided design** CAD

Cad|die ['kɛdi] M **-s, -s** (Golf) caddie, caddy; (= Einkaufswagen) trolley, caddy (US)

Cad|mi|um ['katmiʊm] NT **-s,** no pl (abbr **Cd**) cadmium

Cae|sar ['tse:zar] M **-s** Caesar

Ca|fé [ka'fe:] NT **-s, -s** café

Ca|fe|te|ria [kafetə'ri:a] F **-, -s** cafeteria

Ca|fe|tier [kafe'tie:] M **-s, -s, Ca|fe|tie|re** [kafe-'tie:rə] F **-, -n** (old, Aus) coffee-house proprietor

cal abbr von **(Gramm)kalorie** (gram) calorie

Ca|lais [ka'le:] NT **-'** Calais; **die Straße von ~** the Straits of Dover

Cal|ci|um ['kaltsiʊm] NT **-s,** no pl calcium

Ca|li|for|ni|um [kali'fɔrniʊm] NT **-s,** no pl (abbr **Cf**) californium

Call- ['kɔ:l-]: **Call|box** ['kɔ:l-] F (Telec) voicemail no art; **Call|boy** ['kɔ:l-] M male prostitute; **Call|cen|ter** ['kɔ:l-] NT (Comm) call centre (Brit) or center (US); **Call|girl** ['kɔ:l-] NT call girl

Cal|va|dos [kalva'do:s] M **-,** - Calvados

cal|vi|nisch ADJ ETC = **kalvinisch**

Ca|lyp|so [ka'lɪpso] M **-(s), -s** calypso

CAM [tse:a:'ɛm] NT **-s,** no pl abbr von **computer--aided manufacture** CAM

Cam|cor|der ['kamkɔrdɐ] M **-s,** - camcorder

Ca|mem|bert ['kamɑmbe:ɐ, kamɑ'be:ɐ] M **-s, -s** Camembert

Ca|mi|on ['kamiõ:] M **-s, -s** (Sw) lorry (Brit), truck

Ca|mor|ra [ka'mɔra] F **-,** no pl Camorra

Ca|mouf|la|ge [kamu'fla:ʒə] F **-, -n** (dated, geh) camouflage

Camp [kɛmp] NT **-s, -s** camp; (= Gefangenenlager auch) compound

cam|pen ['kɛmpn] VI to camp

Cam|per¹ ['kɛmpɐ] M **-s,** -, **Cam|pe|rin** ['kɛmpə-rɪn] F **-, -nen** camper

Cam|per² ['kɛmpɐ] M **-s,** - (Wohnmobil) camper van (Brit), camper (US); (größer) motorhome

cam|pie|ren [kam'pi:rən] ptp **campiert** VI **a** = **kampieren b** (Aus, Sw. = campen) to camp

Cam|ping ['kɛmpɪŋ] NT **-s,** no pl camping no art; **zum ~ fahren** to go camping

Cam|ping- ['kɛmpɪŋ] in cpds camping; **Cam|ping|an|hän|ger** M (für Fahrzeug) camping

---

trailer, travel trailer (US); **Cam|ping|ar|ti|kel** M piece or item of camping equipment; (pl) camping equipment sing; **Cam|ping|bus** M Dormobile® (Brit), camper (esp US); **Cam|ping|füh|rer** M camping or camper's guide(-book); **Cam|ping|gas** NT camping gas; **Cam|ping|ko|cher** M camping stove; **Cam|ping|platz** M camp site; **Cam|ping|ur|laub** M camping holiday or trip (Brit), camping vacation (US); **~ machen** to go on a camping holiday (Brit) or trip (Brit) or vacation (US), to go camping; **Cam|ping|zu|be|hör** NT camping equipment

Cam|pus ['kampʊs] M **-,** no pl (Univ) campus; **auf dem ~** on (the) campus

Ca|nas|ta [ka'nasta] NT **-s,** no pl canasta

Can|can [kã'kã:] M **-s, -s** cancan

cand. abbr von **candidatus** → **Kandidat ~ phil./ med** etc final year arts/medical etc student

Can|na|bis ['kanabɪs] M **-,** no pl cannabis

Can|nel|lo|ni [kanɛ'lo:ni] PL cannelloni sing or pl

Ca|ñon ['kanjɔn] M **-s, -s** canyon

Ca|nos|sa [ka'nɔsa] NT **-s** (fig) humiliation; **nun muss er nach ~ gehen** he now has to eat humble pie → **Gang¹ b**

Can|to ['kanto] M **-s, -s** (Liter) canto

Cape [ke:p] NT **-s, -s** cape

Cap|puc|ci|no [kapu'tʃi:no] M **-s, -s** cappuccino

Cap|ric|cio [ka'prɪtʃo] NT **-s, -s** (Mus) caprice, capriccio

Car [ka:ɐ] M **-s, -s** (Sw) abbr von **Autocar**

Ca|ra|van ['ka(:)ravan, kara'va:n] M **-s, -s a** (= Kombiwagen) estate car (Brit), station wagon **b** (= Wohnwagen) caravan (Brit), trailer (US)

Ca|ra|va|ning ['ka(:)rava:nɪŋ] NT **-s,** no pl caravanning (Brit), trailer camping (US)

CARE-Pa|ket ['kɛ:ɐ-], **Care|pa|ket** ['kɛ:ə-] NT CARE packet or parcel or package (esp US)

Car|pool ['ka:ɐpu:l] M car pool

Car|port ['ka:ɐpɔrt] M **-s, -s** carport

car|ra|risch [ka'ra:rɪʃ] ADJ Marmor Carrara

Car|rier ['kɛriɐ] M **-s, -s** (Aviat, Comm, Telec) carrier

Car-Sha|ring ['ka:ɐʃɛ:rɪŋ] NT **-s,** no pl, **Car|sha|ring** NT **-s,** no pl car sharing

car|te|si|a|nisch [karte'zia:nɪʃ] ADJ ETC = **kartesianisch**

Car|toon [kar'tu:n] M OR NT **-(s), -s** cartoon; (= Bildergeschichte auch) strip cartoon

Car|too|nist [kartu'nɪst] M **-en, -en, Car|too|nis|tin** [-'nɪstɪn] F **-, -nen** cartoonist

Car|ving ['ka:ɐvɪŋ] NT **-s,** no pl (Ski) carving

Car|ving|ski [-ka:ɐvɪŋʃi:] M (Ski) carver (ski)

Ca|sa|no|va [kaza'no:va] M **-s, -s** (fig) Casanova

Cä|sar¹ ['tse:zar] M **-s** Caesar

Cä|sar² ['tse:zar] M **-en, -en** [tse'za:rən] (= Titel) Caesar

Cä|sa|ren- [tse'za:rən-]: **Cä|sa|ren|herr|schaft** F autocratic rule, dictatorship; **Cä|sa|ren|wahn|(sinn)** M megalomania

---

Cä|sa|ris|mus [tseza'rɪsmʊs] M **-,** no pl Caesarism, autocracy

cash [kɛʃ] ADV (inf) cash; **~ zahlen** to pay in cash

Cash [kɛʃ] NT **-,** no pl (inf) cash

Ca|shew|nuss ▲ ['kɛʃu-] F cashew (nut)

Cash-Flow ['kɛʃflo:] M **-s,** no pl, **Cash|flow** ▲ M **-s,** no pl cash flow

Ca|si|no [ka'zi:no] NT **-s, -s** = **Kasino**

Cä|si|um ['tse:ziʊm] NT **-s,** no pl (abbr **Cs**) caesium (Brit), cesium (US)

Cas|set|te [ka'sɛtə] F **-, -n** (etc) → **Kassette**

Cas|ting ['ka:stɪŋ] NT **-s, -s** (für Filmrolle etc) casting session

Cas|tor® ['kasto:ɐ] M **-s,** -, **Cas|tor-Be|häl|ter** M spent fuel rod container

Cas|tor|trans|port ['kasto:ɐ-] M **-s, -e** Castor transport, spent fuel rod transport

---

CASTOR

CASTOR containers are special containers for the transport and temporary storage of radioactive waste or fuel elements. The term itself is an abbreviation of the English "cask for storage and transport of radioactive material". Since nuclear energy is extremely controversial in Germany, demonstrations against the transport of **CASTOR** containers to temporary storage sites are a regular occurrence.

Ca|sus Bel|li ▲ ['ka:zʊs 'bɛli] M **- -, - -** ['ka:zu:s] (geh) casus belli (form)

Catch-as-catch-can ['kɛtʃəz'kɛtʃ'kɛn] NT **-,** no pl (lit) catch-as-catch-can, all-in wrestling (esp Brit); (fig) free-for-all

cat|chen ['kɛtʃn] VI to do catch(-as-catch-can) wrestling, to do all-in wrestling (esp Brit); **er catcht gegen X** he has an all-in (esp Brit) or catch bout against X; **er catcht gut** he's a good all-in (esp Brit) or catch wrestler

Cat|cher ['kɛtʃɐ] M **-s,** -, **Cat|che|rin** ['kɛtʃərɪn] F **-, -nen** catch(-as-catch-can) wrestler, all-in wrestler (esp Brit)

Ca|te|ring ['ke:tərɪŋ] NT **-(s),** no pl catering

Ca|te|ring-Ser|vice ['ke:tərɪŋzø:ɐvɪs, -zœrvɪs] M, **Ca|te|ring|ser|vice** M catering service

Ca|tull [ka'tʊl] M **-s** Catullus

Cause cé|lèb|re [koz se'lɛbr] F **- -, -s -s** (geh) cause célèbre

Ca|yenne|pfef|fer [ka'jɛn-] M cayenne (pepper)

CB-Funk [tse:'be:-] M, no pl Citizens' Band, CB (radio)

CB-Fun|ker(in) [tse:'be:-] M(F) CB (radio) user

cbm abbr von **Kubikmeter** cubic metre (Brit) or meter (US)

ccm abbr von **Kubikzentimeter** cc, cubic centimetre (Brit) or centimeter (US)

CD [tse:'de:] F **-, -s** abbr von **Compact Disc** CD

CD- [tse:'de:] in cpds CD; **CD-Bren|ner** M CD writer or burner; **CD-Ge|rät** NT CD player; **CD-I** [tse:de:'li:] F abbr von **Compact Disc - Interactive** (Comput) CD-I; **CD-Lauf|werk** NT

CD drive; **CD-Play|er** [-ple:ɐ] NT CD player; **CD-Re|kor|der** M CD recorder; **CD-Roh|ling** M blank CD, recordable CD; **CD-ROM** [tse:-de:'rɔm] F -, -s CD-ROM; **CD-ROM-Lauf|werk** [tse:de:'rɔm-] NT CD-ROM drive; **CD-Spie|ler** M CD player; **CD-Stän|der** M CD rack; (Turm auch) CD tower

CDU [tse:de:'|u:] F - abbr von **Christlich-Demokratische Union** Christian Democratic Union

---

CDU

The **CDU** (**Christlich-Demokratische Union Deutschlands**) is a popular political party in Germany standing for Christian, conservative values and a social market economy. Founded in 1945, it contests elections in all Länder except Bavaria, where its sister party, the CSU, represents conservative voters → CSU

CD- [tse:'de:-]: **CD-Vi|deo** F video disc; **CD-Vi|de|o|ge|rät** NT video disc player, CD video; **CD-Wechs|ler** M CD changer

Ce|dil|le [se'di:j(ə)] F -, -n cedilla

Ce|les|ta [tʃe'lesta] F -, -s or **Ce|les|ten** [-'lɛstn] celeste, celesta

Cel|list [tʃe'lɪst] M -en, -en, **Cel|lis|tin** [-'lɪstɪn] F -, -nen cellist

Cel|lo ['tʃelo] NT -s, -s or **Cel|li** ['tʃeli] cello

Cel|lo|phan® [tsɛlo'fa:n] NT -s, no pl, **Cel|lo|phan|pa|pier** NT (inf) cellophane (paper)

Cel|lu|li|te [tsɛlu'li:tə] F -, no pl, **Cel|lu|li|tis** [tsɛlu'li:tɪs] F -, no pl (Med) cellulite → auch Zellulitis

Cel|lu|loid [tsɛlu'lɔyt, tsɛlu'lɔi:t] NT -s, no pl celluloid → auch Zelluloid

Cel|si|us ['tsɛlziʊs] no art inv Celsius, centigrade

Cel|si|us|ska|la F centigrade scale

Cem|ba|lo ['tʃembalo] NT -s, -s cembalo, harpsichord

Cent [(t)sɛnt] M -(s), -(s) cent; **30** ~ 30 cents; **mit dem** or **jedem** ~ **rechnen müssen** (fig) to have to watch or count every penny (Brit) or cent (US); **jeden** ~ **(dreimal) umdrehen** (fig inf) to think twice about every penny (Brit) or cent (US) one spends

Cent|be|trag M es war nur ein ~ it was only a matter of pennies (Brit) or cents (US)

Cen|ter¹ ['sɛntɐ] NT -s, - (= Einkaufscenter) shopping centre (Brit) or center (US)

Cen|ter² ['sɛntɐ] M -s, -(s), **Cen|te|rin** [-ərɪn] F -, -nen (Sw Sport: = Mittelstürmer) centre (Brit) or center (US) forward

Cent-: Cent|stück NT cent (piece); **cent|wei|se** ADV cent by cent, one cent at a time

Cer [tse:ɐ] NT -s, no pl (abbr Ce) cerium

ce|ri|se [sə'ri:z] ADJ inv (Fashion) cerise, cherry

Cer|ve|lat [tservə'la:t] M -s, -s (Sw) cervelat, German salami

ces [tsɛs] NT -, -, **Ces** NT -, - (Mus) C flat

Cey|lon ['tsailɔn] NT -s Ceylon

Cey|lo|ne|se [tsailo'ne:zə] M -n, -n, **Cey|lo|ne|sin** [-'ne:zɪn] F -, -nen Ceylonese, Sin(g)halese

cey|lo|ne|sisch [tsailo'ne:zɪʃ] ADJ Ceylonese, Sin(g)halese

Cha-Cha-Cha ['tʃa'tʃa'tʃa] M -(s), -s cha-cha (-cha)

Chag|rin|le|der [ʃa'grɛ̃-] NT shagreen

Chai|se ['ʃɛ:zə] F -, -n a (old) (= Kutsche) (post) chaise (old); (= Stuhl) chair b (inf) jalopy (inf), banger (Brit inf)

Chai|se|longue [ʃɛzə'lɔŋ] F -, -s chaise longue

Cha|let ['ʃale:] NT -s, -s chalet

Cha|mä|le|on [ka'mɛ:leɔn] NT -s, -s (lit, fig) chameleon

cha|mä|le|on|ar|tig ADJ (lit, fig) chameleon--like ADV like a chameleon

Chamb|re sé|pa|rée ['ʃɑ̃:brəsepa're] NT -, -s -s (dated) private room

Cha|mois [ʃa'moa] NT -, no pl a (= Farbe) buff (colour (Brit) or color (US)), (light) tan (colour (Brit) or color (US)) b (auch **Chamoisleder**) chamois (leather)

Champ [tʃɛmp] M -s, -s (inf: Sport, fig) champ

Cham|pag|ner [ʃam'panjɐ] M -s, - champagne

cham|pag|ner|far|ben [ʃam'panjɐfarbn] ADJ champagne, champagne-coloured (Brit), champagne-colored (US)

Cham|pig|non ['ʃampɪnjɔŋ, 'ʃɑ̃:pɪnjõ:] M -s, -s mushroom

Cham|pig|non- ['ʃampɪnjɔŋ-, 'ʃɑ̃:pɪnjõ:-]: **Cham|pig|non|kul|tur** F mushroom culture; **Cham|pig|non|zucht** F mushroom cultivation or growing

Cham|pi|on ['tʃɛmpiən] M -s, -s champion; (= Mannschaft) champions pl

Chan|ce ['ʃɑ̃:sə, (Aus) ʃɑ̃:s] F -, -n a chance; (bei Wetten) odds pl; **keine** ~ **haben** not to have or stand a chance; **nicht die geringste** ~ **haben** not to have an earthly (chance) (inf); **ich sehe keine** ~, **das noch rechtzeitig zu schaffen** I don't see any chance of being able to do it in time; **die** ~, **von einem Auto überfahren zu werden** the chances of being run over by a car; **jdm eine letzte** ~ **geben** to give sb one last chance; **die** ~ **steht nicht schlecht, dass...** there's a good chance that...; **wie sieht es mit deiner Beförderung aus? – na ja, die** ~**n stehen nicht schlecht** what about your promotion? – well, I'm in with a good chance (Brit) or well, the odds are in my favor (US); **die** ~**n stehen 100:1** the odds are a hundred to one; **die** ~**n verringern sich/steigen** the odds are lengthening/shortening; (fig auch) the chances are getting worse/improving b **Chancen** PL (= Aussichten) prospects pl; **im Beruf** ~**n haben** to have good career prospects; **(bei jdm)** ~**n haben** (inf) to stand a chance (with sb) (inf)

Chan|cen- ['ʃɑ̃:sn-]: **chan|cen|gleich** ADJ Aufstiegsmöglichkeiten equal; **sie waren** ~ they had equal opportunities; **Chan|cen|gleich|heit** F equal opportunities pl; **chan|cen|los** ADJ Spieler, Partei bound to lose; Plan, Produkt bound to fail; **Chan|cen|lo|sig|keit** F -, no pl lack of prospects for success

chan|gie|ren [ʃa'ʒi:rən, ʃaŋ'ʒi:rən] ptp **changiert** VI a (= schillern) to be iridescent; ~**de Seide** shot silk b (Pferd) to change step

Chan|son [ʃa'sõ:] NT -s, -s (political/satirical) song

Chan|so|net|te [ʃãso'nɛta] F -, -n, **Chan|son|net|te** [ʃãsɔ'nɛta] F -, -n singer of political/satirical songs

Chan|son|ni|er [ʃãsɔ'nie:] M -s, -s singer of political/satirical songs; (= Dichter) political/satirical songwriter

Cha|os ['ka:ɔs] NT -, no pl chaos; **einem** ~ **gleichen, einem** ~ **sein** to be in utter chaos

Cha|os- ['ka:ɔs]: **Cha|os|for|schung** ['ka:ɔs-] F research into the chaos theory; **Cha|os|ta|ge** ['ka:ɔs-] PL (inf) a chaos days pl, chaotic period b (Pol sl) meeting of the lunatic fringe; **Cha|os|the|o|rie** ['ka:ɔs-] F (Math, Phys) chaos theory

Cha|ot [ka'o:t] M -en, -en, **Cha|o|tin** [ka'o:tɪn] F -, -nen (Pol pej) anarchist (pej); (= unordentlicher Mensch) scatterbrain (inf); **er ist ein richtiger** ~ he's completely chaotic

cha|o|tisch [ka'o:tɪʃ] ADJ chaotic; ~**e Zustände** a state of (utter) chaos ADV chaotically; **es geht** ~ there is utter chaos; **in deinem Zimmer sieht es** ~ **aus** your room looks chaotic

Cha|peau claque [ʃapo 'klak] M -, -x -s opera hat

Cha|rak|ter [ka'raktɐ] M -s, -e [-'te:rə] a (= Wesen, Eigenart) character; **er ist ein Mann von** ~ he is a man of character; **etw prägt den** ~ sth

is character-forming; **keinen** ~ **haben** (ohne Prägung) to have no character, to lack character; (nicht ehrenhaft auch) to have no principles; **die Party bekam immer mehr den** ~ **einer Orgie** the party became more and more like an orgy; **seine Warnung hatte mehr den** ~ **einer Drohung** his warning was more like a threat; **der vertrauliche** ~ **dieses Gespräches** the confidential nature of this conversation b (= Person) character, personality; (Liter, Theat) character; **sie sind ganz gegensätzliche** ~**e** their characters are entirely different, they have entirely different personalities c (dated Typ) character

Cha|rak|ter-: Cha|rak|ter|an|la|ge F characteristic, trait; **angeborene** ~**n** innate characteristics; **jds gute** ~**n fördern** to encourage sb's good qualities or (character) traits; **Cha|rak|ter|bild** NT character (image); (= Charakterschilderung) character study; **cha|rak|ter|bil|dend** ADJ character-forming; **Cha|rak|ter|bil|dung** F character formation; **Cha|rak|ter|dar|stel|ler(in)** M(F) character actor/actress; **Cha|rak|ter|ei|gen|schaft** F character trait; **Cha|rak|ter|feh|ler** M character defect; **cha|rak|ter|fest** ADJ strong-minded, of firm or strong character; **ein** ~**er Mann** a man of firm or strong character; **Cha|rak|ter|fes|tig|keit** F strength of character, strong-mindedness

cha|rak|te|ri|sie|ren [karakteri'zi:rən] ptp **charakterisiert** VT to characterize; **jdn als etw** ~ to portray or characterize sb as sth

Cha|rak|te|ri|sie|rung F -, -en characterization

Cha|rak|te|ris|tik [karakte'rɪstɪk] F -, -en a description; (= typische Eigenschaften) characteristics pl b (Tech) characteristic curve

Cha|rak|te|ris|ti|kum [karakte'rɪstɪkʊm] NT -s, **Charakteristika** [-ka] (geh) characteristic (feature)

cha|rak|te|ris|tisch [karakte'rɪstɪʃ] ADJ characteristic (für of)

cha|rak|te|ris|ti|scher|wei|se ADV characteristically

Ch|arak|ter-: Cha|rak|ter|kopf M (= Kopf) distinctive or striking features pl; **cha|rak|ter|lich** [ka'raktɐlɪç] ADJ strength of character; ~**e Stärke** strength of character; ~**e Mängel** character defects; ~**e Qualitäten** personal qualities; ~**e Anforderungen stellen** to make demands on one's character ADV in character; **sie hat sich** ~ **sehr verändert** her character has changed a lot; **jdn** ~ **stark prägen** to have a strong influence on sb's character; **cha|rak|ter|los** ADJ a (= niederträchtig) Mensch, Verhalten etc unprincipled b (= ohne Prägung) characterless; Spiel, Vortrag colourless (Brit), colorless (US) ADV in an unprincipled way; **Cha|rak|ter|lo|sig|keit** F -, -en a (= Niederträchtigkeit) lack of principles; (Handlung) unprincipled behaviour (Brit) or behavior (US) no pl b no pl (= Prägungslosigkeit) characterlessness; (von Spiel, Vortrag) colourlessness (Brit), colorlessness (US); **Cha|rak|ter|merk|mal** NT characteristic

Cha|rak|te|ro|lo|ge [karaktero'lo:gə] M -n, -n, **Cha|rak|te|ro|lo|gin** [-'lo:gɪn] F -, -nen characterologist

Cha|rak|te|ro|lo|gie [karakterolo'gi:] F -, no pl characterology

cha|rak|te|ro|lo|gisch [karaktero'lo:gɪʃ] ADJ characterological

Cha|rak|ter-: Cha|rak|ter|rol|le F character part or role; **Cha|rak|ter|sa|che** F (inf) das ist ~ it's a matter of character; **Cha|rak|ter|schau|spie|ler(in)** M(F) character actor/actress; **cha|rak|ter|schwach** ADJ weak, of weak character; **Cha|rak|ter|schwä|che** F weakness of character; **Cha|rak|ter|schwein** NT (inf) unprincipled character; **cha|rak|ter|stark** ADJ strong, of strong character; **Cha|rak|ter|stär|ke** F strength of character; **Cha|rak|ter|stück** NT (Mus) mood piece; **Cha|rak|ter|stu|die** F character study; **cha|rak|-**

ter|voll ADJ **a** (= *anständig*) *Verhalten* which shows character; **dazu ist er zu ~** he has too much character for that **b** (= *ausgeprägt*) full of character; **eine ~e Stadt** a town (full) of character; **Cha|rak|ter|zug** M characteristic; (*von Menschen auch*) (character) trait; **es ist kein sehr schöner ~ von ihm, ...** it is not very nice of him ...

Char|ge ['ʃarʒə] F -, -n **a** (*Mil, fig*: = *Dienstgrad, Person*) rank; **die unteren ~n** the lower ranks or echelons **b** (*Theat*) minor character part

char|gie|ren [ʃarˈʒiːrən] ptp **chargiert** VI (*Theat*) (= *übertreiben*) to overact, to ham (*inf*); (= *eine Charge spielen*) to play a minor character part

Cha|ris|ma ['çaːrɪsma, 'çarɪsma, kaˈrɪsma] NT -s, **Charismen** or **Charismata** [-mən, -mata] (*Rel, fig*) charisma

Cha|ris|ma|ti|ker [çarɪsˈmaːtɪkɐ] M -s, -, **Cha|ris|ma|ti|ke|rin** [-ərɪn] F -, -nen (*Rel*) member of the charismatic movement; (*fig*) charismatic person

cha|ris|ma|tisch [çarɪsˈmaːtɪʃ] ADJ charismatic **ADV** charismatically

Charles|ton ['tʃarlstn] M -, -s charleston

Char|lot|ten|bur|ger ['ʃarlɔtnbʊrɡɐ] M -s, - **ei|nen ~ machen** (*dial sl*) to blow out snot using one's fingers and flick it away

char|mant [ʃarˈmant] **ADJ** charming **ADV** *lächeln, sich verhalten* charmingly

Charme [ʃarm] M -s, *no pl* charm

Char|meur [ʃarˈmøːɐ] M -s, -e charmer; (= *Schmeichler*) flatterer; **du alter ~!** you old smoothy! (*inf*)

Char|meuse [ʃarˈmøːz] F -, *no pl* (*Tex*) Charmeuse®

Chart [tʃart] M OR NT -, -s **a** (*Comput*) chart; (= *grafische Darstellung*) chart, graph **b** **die ~s** (= *Hitparade*) the charts

Char|ta ['karta] F -, -s charter; **Magna ~** Magna Carta

Char|ter ['tʃartɐ] M -s, -s charter

Char|ter-: **Char|ter|flug** M charter flight; **Char|ter(flug)|ge|sell|schaft** F charter (flight) company; **Char|ter|ma|schi|ne** F charter plane

char|tern ['tʃartɐn] VT *Schiff, Flugzeug* to charter; (*fig inf*) *Taxi, Arbeitskräfte etc* to hire

Char|ter|ver|kehr M charter flights *pl*

Chas|sis [ʃaˈsiː] NT -, - [-iːs], -iːs] (*Aut, Rad, TV*) chassis

chat|ten ['tʃɛtn] VI (*Comput inf*) to chat

Chauf|feur [ʃɔˈføːɐ] M -s, -e, **Chauf|feu|rin** [-ˈføːrɪn] F -, -nen chauffeur

chauf|fie|ren [ʃɔˈfiːrən] ptp **chauffiert** VTI (*dated*) to chauffeur, to drive

Chaus|see [ʃɔˈseː] F -, -n [-ˈseːən] (*dated*) high road; (*in Straßennamen*) Avenue

Chaus|see-: **Chaus|see|baum** M (*dated*) roadside tree; **Chaus|see|gra|ben** M (*dated*) ditch

Chau|vi ['ʃoːvi] M -s, -s (*inf*) male chauvinist pig (*pej inf*), MCP (*Brit pej inf*)

Chau|vi|nis|mus [ʃoviˈnɪsmʊs] M -, **Chauvinismen** [-mən] (*männlicher*) chauvinism; (= *männlicher Chauvinismus*) male chauvinism; (= *Benehmen/Äußerung*) chauvinist(ic) action/remark

Chau|vi|nist [ʃoviˈnɪst] M -en, -en, **Chau|vi|nis|tin** [-ˈnɪstɪn] F -, -nen (*Pol*) chauvinist; (= *männlicher Chauvinist*) male chauvinist (pig)

chau|vi|nis|tisch [ʃoviˈnɪstɪʃ] **ADJ a** (*Pol*) chauvinist(ic); **er ist sehr ~** he is a real chauvinist **b** (= *männlich-chauvinistisch*) male chauvinist(ic) **ADV a** (*Pol*) chauvinistically; **~ klingende Wahlpropaganda** chauvinistic election propaganda; **~ angehauchte Politiker** politicians with chauvinistic tendencies **b** (= *männlich-chauvinistisch*) in a male chauvinist way; **sich ~ verhalten** to behave like a male chauvinist

che|cken ['tʃɛkn] **VT a** (= *überprüfen*) to check **b** (*inf*: = *verstehen*) to get (*inf*) **c** (*inf*: = *merken*)

to cotton (*Brit*) or catch on to (*inf*), to wise up to (*inf*); **er hat das nicht gecheckt** he didn't cotton (*Brit*) or catch on (*inf*), he didn't wise up to it (*inf*) **VTI** (*Eishockey*) to block; (= *anrempeln*) to barge

Check- ['tʃɛk-]: **Check|lis|te** F check list; **Check|point** [-pɔynt] M -s, -s checkpoint; **Check-up** [tʃɛkap] M OR NT -(s), -s (*Med*) checkup

Chef [ʃɛf, (*Aus*) ʃeːf] M -s, -s boss; (*von Bande, Delegation etc*) leader; (*von Organisation, inf*: = *Schuldirektor*) head; (*der Polizei*) chief; (*Mil: von Kompanie*) commander; **~ des Stabes** Chief of Staff; **er ist der ~ vom Ganzen** he's in charge or the boss here; **hallo ~!** (*inf*) hey, gov(ernor) or chief or squire (*all Brit inf*) or mac (*US inf*)

Chef-: **Chef|an|klä|ger(in)** M(F) (*Jur*) chief prosecutor; **Chef|arzt** M , **Chef|ärz|tin** F senior consultant; **Chef|eta|ge** F management or executive floor; (*fig*: = *Unternehmensleitung*) management; **Chef|ideo|lo|ge** M , **Chef|ideo|lo|gin** F (*inf*) chief ideologist

Che|fin ['ʃefɪn, (*Aus*) 'ʃeːfɪn] F -, -nen **a** boss; (*Sch*) head; (*von Delegation etc*) head **b** (*inf*: = *Frau des Chefs*) boss's wife; **Frau ~!** ma'am (*US*), ≈ excuse me

Chef-: **Chef|koch** M , **Chef|kö|chin** F chef, head cook; **Chef|re|dak|teur(in)** M(F) editor in chief; (*einer Zeitung*) editor; **Chef|re|dak|ti|on** F **a** (= *Aufgabe*) (chief) editorship **b** (= *Büro*) main editorial office **c** (= *Personal*) main editorial staff; **Chef|sa|che** F **etw zur ~ erklären** to make sth a matter for decision at the top level; **das ist ~** it's a matter for the boss; **Chef|sek|re|tär(in)** M(F) personal assistant; **Chef|ses|sel** M (*inf, fig*) boss's job; **auf dem ~ sitzen** to be the boss; **es auf den ~ abgesehen haben** to have one's eye on the boss's job; **Chef|un|ter|händ|ler(in)** M(F) chief negotiator; **Chef|vi|si|te** F (*Med*) consultant's round

chem. *abbr von* **chemisch**

Che|mie [çeˈmiː, (*esp S Ger*) keˈmiː] F -, *no pl* (*lit, fig*) chemistry; (*inf*: = *Chemikalien*) chemicals *pl*; **was die so essen, ist alles ~** they just eat synthetic food

Che|mie-: **Che|mie|ar|bei|ter(in)** M(F) chemical worker; **Che|mie|be|ruf** M job in industrial chemistry; **Che|mie|fa|ser** F synthetic or man-made fibre (*Brit*) or fiber (*US*); **Che|mie|klo** NT (*inf*) chemical toilet; **Che|mie|kon|zern** M chemicals group; **Che|mie|toi|let|te** F chemical toilet; **Che|mie|un|fall** M chemical accident; **Che|mie|un|ter|richt** M chemistry; **Che|mie|waf|fe** F *usu pl* chemical weapon; **che|mie|waf|fen|frei** ADJ free of chemical weapons; **~e Zone** chemical-weapon-free zone

Che|mi|kal [çemiˈkaːl, (*esp S Ger*) ke-] NT -s, -ien [-liən], **Che|mi|ka|lie** [çemiˈkaːliə, (*esp S Ger*) ke-] F -, -n *usu pl* chemical

Che|mi|ker ['çeːmikɐ, (*esp S Ger*) 'keː-] M -s, -, **Che|mi|ke|rin** [-ərɪn] F -, -nen chemist

Che|mi|née ['ʃmɪne] NT -s, -s (*Sw*) fireplace

che|misch ['çeːmɪʃ, (*esp S Ger*) 'keː-] **ADJ** chemical → **Reinigung** **ADV** *behandeln, untersuchen* chemically; **~ reinigen** to dry-clean sth

Che|mo- [çemo-, (*esp S Ger*) ke-]: **Che|mo|tech|nik** F chemical engineering, technochemistry; **Che|mo|tech|ni|ker(in)** M(F) chemical engineer; **Che|mo|the|ra|peu|ti|kum** [-təraˈpɔytikʊm] NT -s, **-therapeutika** [-ka] (*Pharm*) chemotherapeutic drug; **che|mo|the|ra|peu|tisch** **ADJ** chemotherapeutic **ADV** *jdn ~ behandeln* to give sb chemotherapy; **Che|mo|the|ra|pie** F chemotherapy

-chen [çən] NT *suf dim* little; **Hündchen** little dog; **ein Löffelchen** a small spoon

Che|rub ['çeːrʊp] M -s, -im ['çeːrubiːm] or **-inen** [çeruˈbiːnən] cherub

che|va|le|resk [ʃəvaləˈrɛsk] ADJ (*geh*) chivalrous

Chi|as|mus ['çiasmʊs] M -, **Chiasmen** [-mən] (*Ling*) chiasmus

Chic [ʃik] M = **Schick**

chic [ʃik] ADJ, ADV = **schick**

Chi|ca|na [tʃiˈkaːna] F -, -s chicana

Chi|ca|no [tʃiˈkaːno] M -s, -s chicano

Chi|co|rée ['ʃikore, ʃikoˈreː] F - *or* m -s, *no pl* chicory

Chif|fon ['ʃifɔ̃, ʃiˈfõː] M -s, -s chiffon

Chiff|re ['ʃifrə, 'ʃifrɐ] F -, -n **a** cipher **b** (*in Zeitung*) box number

Chiff|re-: **Chiff|re|an|zei|ge** F advertisement with a box number; **Chiff|re|num|mer** F (*für Zeitungsannonce*) box number; **Chiff|re|schrift** F cipher, code

chiff|rie|ren [ʃiˈfriːrən] ptp **chiffriert** VTI to encipher, to code; **chiffriert** coded

Chi|le ['tʃiːle, 'çiːlə] NT -s Chile

Chi|le|ne [tʃiˈleːnə, çiˈleːnə] M -n, -n, **Chi|le|nin** [-ˈleːnɪn] F -, -nen Chilean

chi|le|nisch [tʃiˈleːnɪʃ, çiˈleːnɪʃ] ADJ Chilean

Chi|le|sal|pe|ter M chile saltpetre (*Brit*) or saltpeter (*US*), sodium nitrate

Chi|li [tʃiːli] M -s, *no pl* chil(l)i (pepper)

Chi|li- ['tʃiːli]: **Chi|li|pul|ver** ['tʃiːli-] NT *usu sing* chil(l)i powder; **Chi|li|so|ße** ['tʃiːli-] F chil(l)i sauce

Chi|mä|re [çiˈmɛːrə] F -, -n **a** (*Zool, Biol*) chimaera **b** (*Myth*) = **Schimäre**

Chi|na ['çiːna, (*esp S Ger*) 'kiːna] NT -s China

Chi|na-: **Chi|na|cra|cker** M banger (*Brit*), firecracker (*US*); **Chi|na|kohl** M Chinese cabbage; **Chi|na|kra|cher** M banger (*Brit*), firecracker (*US*); **Chi|na|krepp** M crêpe de Chine; **Chi|na|res|tau|rant** NT Chinese restaurant

Chin|chil|la¹ [tʃɪnˈtʃila] F -, -s (= *Tier*) chinchilla

Chin|chil|la² NT -s, -s **a** (= *Pelz*) chinchilla **b** (*auch* **Chinchillakaninchen**) chinchilla rabbit

Chi|ne|se [çiˈneːzə, (*esp S Ger*) ki-] M -n, -n Chinese (man); **zum ~n gehen** to go to a/the Chinese restaurant

Chi|ne|sen|vier|tel [çiˈneːzn-, (*esp S Ger*) ki-] NT (= *Wohngebiet*) Chinatown

Chi|ne|sin [çiˈneːzɪn, (*esp S Ger*) ki-] F -, -nen Chinese (woman)

chi|ne|sisch [çiˈneːzɪʃ, (*esp S Ger*) ki-] ADJ Chinese; **die Chinesische Mauer** the Great Wall of China

Chi|ne|sisch(e) [çiˈneːzɪʃ, (*esp S Ger*) ki-] NT (*Ling*) Chinese; **das ist ~ für mich** (*inf*) that's all Greek or Chinese to me (*inf*) → *auch* **Deutsch(e)**

Chi|nin [çiˈniːn] NT -s, *no pl* quinine

Chi|noi|se|rie [ʃinoazəˈriː] F -, -n [-ˈriːən] chinoiserie

Chip [tʃɪp] M -s, -s **a** (= *Spielchip*) chip **b** (*usu pl*: = *Kartoffelchip*) (potato) crisp (*Brit*), potato chip (*US*) **c** (*Comput*) chip

Chip|kar|te F smart card

Chi|ro|mant [çiroˈmant] M -en, -en, **Chi|ro|man|tin** [-ˈmantɪn] F -, -nen chiromancer

Chi|ro|man|tie [çiromanˈtiː] F -, *no pl* chiromancy

Chi|ro- [çiro-]: **Chi|ro|prak|tik** F , *no pl* chiropractic; **Chi|ro|prak|ti|ker(in)** M(F) chiropractor; **Chi|ro|the|ra|peut(in)** M(F) chiropractor

Chi|rurg [çiˈrʊrk] M -en, -en [-gn], **Chi|rur|gin** [çiˈrʊrgɪn] F -, -nen surgeon

Chi|rur|gie [çirʊrˈgiː] F -, -n [-ˈgiːən] surgery; **er liegt in der ~** he's in surgery

chi|rur|gisch [çiˈrʊrgɪʃ] **ADJ** surgical; **ein ~er Eingriff** surgery **ADV** surgically; **tätig sein** to be a surgeon, to do surgical work

Chi|tin [çiˈtiːn] NT -s, *no pl* chitin

Chlor [kloːɐ] NT -s, *no pl* (*abbr* **Cl**) chlorine

Chlor|ak|ne F chloracne

chlo|ren ['kloːrən], **chlo|rie|ren** [kloˈriːrən] ptp **chloriert** VT to chlorinate

chlor-: chlor|frei ADJ *Papier, Kunststoff* chlorine-free ADV **~ gebleichtes Papier** paper bleached without the use of chlorine; **chlor|-hal|tig** [-haltɪç] ADJ *Wasser* chlorinated

Chlo|rid [klo'ri:t] NT **-s, -e** [-də] chloride

chlo|rig ['klo:rɪç] (*Chem*) ADJ chlorous ADV **~ riechen** to smell of chlorine

Chlor|koh|len|was|ser|stoff M (*Chem*) chlorinated hydrocarbon

Chlo|ro- [kloro-]: **Chlo|ro|form** [-'fɔrm] NT **-s,** *no pl* chloroform; **chlo|ro|for|mie|ren** [-fɔr'mi:rən] *ptp* **chloroformiert** VT to chloroform; **Chlo|ro|phyll** [-'fyl] NT **-s,** *no pl* chlorophyll

Chlor|was|ser NT , *no pl* a (*Chem*) chlorine water b (*im Hallenbad*) chlorinated water

Choke [tʃoːk] M **-s, -s, Cho|ker** ['tʃoːkɐ] M **-s,** - choke

Cho|le|ra ['koːlera] F **-,** *no pl* cholera

Cho|le|ri|ker [ko'leːrikɐ] M **-s, -, Cho|le|ri|ke|rin** [-ərɪn] F **-, -nen** choleric person; (*fig*) irascible *or* hot-tempered person

cho|le|risch [ko'leːrɪʃ] ADJ choleric

Cho|les|te|rin [çolestə'riːn, ko-] NT **-s,** *no pl* cholesterol

Cho|les|te|rin-: Cho|les|te|rin|ge|halt M cholesterol content; **Cho|les|te|rin|spie|gel** M cholesterol level

Chor¹ [koːɐ] M **-(e)s, -ᴇe** ['køːrə] a (= *Sängerchor*) choir; (= *Bläserchor etc*) section; **im ~ singen** to sing in the choir; (= *zusammen singen*) to sing in chorus, to chorus; **im ~ sprechen/rufen** to speak/shout in chorus; **ja** *or* **Ja, riefen sie im ~** yes, they chorused b (*Theat*) chorus c (= *Komposition*) choral work *or* composition d (*bei Orgel*) rank e (*bei Klavier, Laute etc*) group of strings tuned in unison *or* to the same pitch

Chor² [koːɐ] M OR (RARE) NT **-(e)s, -e** *or* **-ᴇe** ['køːrə] (*Archit*) a (= *Altarraum*) chancel, choir b (= *Chorempore*) loft, gallery

Cho|ral [ko'raːl] M **-s, Chorä|le** [-'rɛːlə] (*Mus*) a (*Gregorianischer*) chant, plainsong b (= *Kirchenlied*) hymn

Cho|reo- [koreo-]: **Cho|re|o|graf** ▲ [-'graːf] M **-en, -en, Cho|re|o|gra|fin** ▲ [-'graːfɪn] F **-, -nen** choreographer; **Cho|re|o|gra|fie** ▲ [-gra'fiː] F **-, -n** [-'fiːən] choreography; **cho|re|o|gra|fie|ren** ▲ [-gra'fiːrən] *ptp* **choreografiert** VT to choreograph, to write *or* do the choreography for VI to write *or* do (the) choreography; **cho|re|o|gra|fisch** ▲ [-'graːfɪʃ] ADJ choreographic(al)

Chor-: Chor|frau F (*Eccl*) canoness; **Chor|ge|bet** NT Divine Office; **Chor|ge|sang** M (= *Lied*) choral music; (= *das Singen*) choral singing; **Chor|ge|stühl** NT choir stalls *pl*; **Chor|herr** M (*Eccl*) canon

cho|risch ['koːrɪʃ] ADJ choral

Cho|rist [ko'rɪst] M **-en, -en, Cho|ris|tin** [-'rɪstɪn] F **-, -nen** = **Chorsänger(in)**

Chor-: Chor|kna|be M choirboy; **Chor|lei|ter** M choirmaster; **Chor|lei|te|rin** F choirmistress; **Chor|sän|ger(in)** M(F) member of a choir; (*im Kirchenchor*) chorister; (*im Opernchor etc*) member of the chorus; **Chor|schran|ke** F choir *or* rood screen; **Chor|stuhl** M choir stall

Cho|rus ['koːrʊs] M **-, -se** a (*obs* = *Altarraum*) chancel, choir b (*Jazz* = *Variationsthema*) theme

Cho|se ['ʃoːzə] F **-, -n** (*inf*) a (= *Angelegenheit*) business, thing b (= *Zeug*) stuff; **die ganze ~** the whole lot

Chow-Chow [tʃau'tʃau] M **-s, -s** chow

Chr. *abbr von* **Christus**

Christ¹ [krɪst] M **-s** (*old, geh* = *Christus*) Christ

Christ² [krɪst] M **-en, -en, Chris|tin** ['krɪstɪn] F **-, -nen** Christian

Christ|baum ['krɪst-] M Christmas tree; (*Mil inf*) flares *pl*

Christ|baum- *in cpds* → *auch* **Weihnachtsbaum**: **Christ|baum|ku|gel** F Christmas tree ball;

Christ|baum|schmuck M a Christmas tree decorations *pl* b (*iro:* = *Orden*) gongs *pl* (*Brit inf*), fruit salad (*US inf*)

Christ-: Christ|de|mo|krat(in) M(F) Christian Democrat; **christ|de|mo|kra|tisch** ADJ Christian Democratic ADV **eine ~ geführte Regierung** a Christian Democrat-led government; **~ wählen** to vote Christian Democrat

Chris|ten- ['krɪstn-]: **Chris|ten|ge|mein|de** F Christian community; **Chris|ten|glau|be(n)** M Christian faith; **Chris|ten|heit** F **-,** *no pl* Christendom; **Chris|ten|pflicht** F (one's) duty as a Christian, (one's) Christian duty; **Chris|ten|tum** ['krɪstntuːm] NT **-s,** *no pl* Christianity; **Chris|ten|ver|fol|gung** F persecution of the Christians

Christ|fest NT (*dated, dial*) Christmas

Chris|ti *gen von* **Christus**

chris|ti|a|ni|sie|ren [krɪstiani'ziːrən] *ptp* **christianisiert** VT to convert to Christianity, to Christianize VI to convert people to Christianity

Chris|ti|a|ni|sie|rung F **-, -en** conversion to Christianity, Christianization

Chris|tin F Christian

Christ-: Christ|kind(chen) NT , *no pl* baby *or* infant Jesus, Christ Child; (= *Sinnbild für Weihnachten*) Christmas; (*das Geschenke bringt*) ≈ Father Christmas; (*fig inf* = *Dummerchen*) little innocent; **Christ|kindl** NT , **Christ|kind|chen** (*dial*) a = **Christkind(chen)** b (*dial:* = *Geschenk*) Christmas present; **zum ~** as a Christmas present, for Christmas

Christ|kindles|markt ['krɪstkɪndləs-] M (*Fränkisch*) Christmas market

Christ|kindl|markt M (*S Ger, Aus*) Christmas market

christ|lich ['krɪstlɪç] ADJ Christian; **er ist bei der ~n Seefahrt** (*hum*) he is a seafaring man; **Christlicher Verein Junger Männer** Young Men's Christian Association ADV **like** *or* **as a Christian**; **~ leben** to live a Christian life; **~ handeln** to act like a Christian; **~ aufwachsen** to grow up as a Christian; **jdn ~ erziehen** to bring sb up as a Christian; **eine ~ orientierte Moral** a Christian(-orientated) morality; **etw ~ teilen** to let the other person have the larger share of sth

Christ|lich|keit F **-,** *no pl* Christianity

Christ-: Christ|mes|se F Midnight Mass; **Christ|met|te** F (*katholisch*) Midnight Mass; (*evangelisch*) Midnight Service

Chris|toph ['krɪstɔf] M **-s** Christopher

Chris|to|pho|rus [krɪs'to:forʊs] M **-'** Saint Christopher

Christ|ro|se F Christmas rose

Christ|so|zi|a|le(r) [-zotsia:lə] MF *decl as adj* member of the CSU

Christ|stol|len M (*Cook*) (Christmas) stollen, fruit loaf

Chris|tus ['krɪstʊs] M *gen* **Christi** ['krɪsti], *dat* - *or* (*form*) **Christo** ['krɪsto], *acc* - *or* (*form*) **Chris|tum** ['krɪstʊm] Christ; (= *Christfigur auch*) figure of Christ; **vor Christi Geburt, vor Christo** (*form*) *or* **~ before Christ, BC; nach Christi Geburt, nach Christo** (*form*) *or* **~ AD,** Anno Domini, in the year of our Lord (*liter*); **Christi Himmelfahrt** the Ascension of Christ; (= *Himmelfahrtstag*) Ascension Day

Chrom [kroːm] NT **-s,** *no pl* chrome; (*Chem: abbr* **Cr**) chromium

Chro|ma|tik [kro'maːtɪk] F **-,** *no pl* a (*Mus*) chromaticism b (*Opt*) chromatics *sing*

chro|ma|tisch [kro'maːtɪʃ] ADJ (*Mus, Opt*) chromatic

chrom|blit|zend ADJ gleaming with chrome

Chro|mo|som [kromo'zoːm] NT **-s, -en** chromosome

Chro|mo|so|men-: Chro|mo|so|men|paar NT pair of chromosomes; **Chro|mo|so|men-**

satz M set of chromosomes; **Chro|mo|so|men|zahl** F chromosome count, number of chromosomes

Chro|nik ['kroːnɪk] F **-, -en** chronicle; **etw in einer ~ aufzeichnen** to chronicle sth, to record sth in a chronicle

chro|nisch ['kroːnɪʃ] ADJ (*Med, fig*) chronic ADV chronically; **~ krank sein** to be chronically ill; **ein ~ defizitäres Unternehmen** a company which is chronically in deficit

Chro|nist [kro'nɪst] M **-en, -en, Chro|nis|tin** [-'nɪstɪn] F **-, -nen** chronicler

Chro|no|lo|gie [kronolo'giː] F **-, -n** [-'giːən] chronology

chro|no|lo|gisch [krono'loːgɪʃ] ADJ chronological ADV chronologically

Chro|no|me|ter [krono'meːtɐ] NT **-s, -** chronometer

Chry|san|the|me [kryzan'teːmə] F **-, -n** chrysanthemum

chtho|nisch ['çtoːnɪʃ] ADJ (*liter*) chthonian (*liter*), chthonic (*liter*)

Chuz|pe ['xʊtspə] F **-,** *no pl* (*inf*) chutzpa(h) (*sl*), audacity

CIA ['siːaiʔeː] F **-** *or* m **-s** CIA

Ci|ce|ro¹ ['tsiːtsero] M **-s** Cicero

Ci|ce|ro² F OR M **-,** *no pl* (*Typ*) twelve-point type, pica

Ci|ce|ro|ne [tʃitʃe'roːnə] M **-(s), -s** *or* (*geh*) **Cice|roni** [-ni] a (= *Mensch*) cicerone (*form*), guide b (= *Buch*) (travel) guide(book)

Cie. *abbr von* **Kompanie**

Cinch|buch|se ['sɪntʃbʊksə] F (*Tech*) cinch socket

Cinch|ste|cker ['sɪntʃ-] M (*Tech*) cinch connector *or* jack *or* plug

Ci|ne|ast [sine'ast] M **-en, -en, Ci|ne|as|tin** [-'astɪn] F **-, -nen** cineaste

Ci|ne|ma|thek [sinema'teːk] F **-, -en** film library *or* archive

cir|ca ['tsɪrka] ADV **= zirka**

Cir|ce ['tsɪrtsə] F **-, -n** (*Myth*) Circe; (*fig geh*) femme fatale

cir|cen|sisch [tsɪr'tsɛnzɪʃ] ADJ **= zirzensisch**

Cir|cu|lus vi|ti|o|sus ['tsɪrkulus viˈtsioːzʊs] M **-, Circuli vitiosi** ['tsɪrkuli viˈtsioːzi] (*geh*) (= *Teufelskreis*) vicious circle; (= *Zirkelschluss auch*) circular argument, petitio principii (*form*)

cis [tsɪs] NT , **Cis** NT **-, -** (*Mus*) C sharp

Ci|ty ['sɪti] F **-, -s** city centre (*Brit*) *or* center (*US*)

Ci|ty- ['sɪti]: **Ci|ty-Bahn** F , **Ci|ty|bahn** F express commuter train; **Ci|ty-La|ge** F , **Ci|ty|la|ge** F central location; **in Citylage** central, (situated) in the town *or* city centre (*Brit*) *or* center (*US*), downtown (*US*); **ci|ty|nah** ADJ close to the town *or* city centre (*Brit*) *or* center (*US*), central; **Ci|ty-Nä|he** F , **Ci|ty|nä|he** F central location; **in Citynähe** central(ly), close to the town *or* city centre (*Brit*) *or* center (*US*)

CJK [tseːjɔt'kaː] *abbr von* **Creuzfeldt-Jakob-Krankheit** CJD

Claim [kleːm] NT **-(s), -s** (*lit, fig*) claim; **seine ~s abstecken** to stake one's claim

Clair-obs|cur [klɛrɔpsˈkyːɐ] NT **-,** *no pl* (*Art*) chiaroscuro

Clan [klaːn] M **-s, -s** *or* (*rare*) **-e** (*lit, fig*) clan

Cla|queur [kla'køːɐ] M **-s, -e, Cla|queu|rin** [-'køːrɪn] F **-, -nen** hired applauder, claqueur

Cla|vi|cem|ba|lo [klaviˈtʃɛmbalo] NT **-s, -s** *or* **Clavicembali** [-li] clavicembalo, harpsichord

clean [kliːn] ADJ *pred* (*inf*) clean (*inf*), off drugs; **~ werden** to kick the habit (*inf*), to get clean (*inf*)

Clea|ring ['kliːrɪŋ] NT **-s, -s** (*Econ*) clearing

Clea|ring|stel|le ['kliːrɪŋ-] F (*Fin*) clearing house

Cle|ma|tis [kleˈmaːtɪs, ˈkleːmatɪs] F **-, -** (*Bot*) clematis

Cle|men|ti|ne [klemɛn'tiːnə] F -, -n clementine

cle|ver ['klɛvɐ] **ADJ** clever; (= *raffiniert*) sharp, shrewd; (= *gerissen*) crafty, cunning **ADV** (= *raffiniert*) sharply; (= *gerissen*) craftily; **sich ~ verhalten** to be crafty

Cle|ver|ness ▲ ['klɛvɐnɛs] F -, no pl cleverness; (= *Raffiniertheit*) sharpness, shrewdness; (= *Gerissenheit*) craftiness, cunning

Cliff|han|ger ['klɪfhɛŋɐ] M -s, -, **Cliff|hän|ger** M (*inf*) cliffhanger

Clinch [klɪntʃ] M -(e)s, no pl (*Boxen, fig*) clinch; **in den ~ gehen** (*lit, fig*) to go into a clinch; (*fig: Verhandlungspartner*) to get stuck into each other (*inf*); **jdn in den ~ nehmen** (*lit*) to go into a clinch with sb; (*fig*) to get stuck into sb (*inf*); **sich aus dem ~ lösen, den ~ lösen** to break the clinch; **mit jdm im ~ liegen** (*fig*) to be at loggerheads with sb

clin|chen ['klɪntʃn] VI to clinch

Clip [klɪp] M -s, -s (= *Haarclip, am Füller etc*) clip; (= *Brosche*) clip-on brooch; (= *Ohrclip*) (clip-on) earring

Clip|board ['klɪpbɔːɐd] NT -s, -s (*Comput*) clipboard

Clips [klɪps] M -, -e (clip-on) earring

Cli|que ['klɪkə] F -, -n **a** (= *Freundeskreis*) group, set; **wir fahren mit der ganzen ~ weg** the whole gang *or* crowd of us are going away together; **Thomas und seine ~** Thomas and his set **b** (*pej*) clique

Cli|quen-: Cli|quen|bil|dung F forming of cliques; **da kam es natürlich zur ~** then of course it started getting cliquey (*inf*), then of course people started forming cliques; **Cli|quen|(un)we|sen** NT (*pej*) cliquishness; **Cli|quen|wirt|schaft** F (*pej inf*) cliquey setup (*inf*)

Clo|chard [klɔ'ʃaːr] M -s, -s tramp

Clou [kluː] M -s, -s (*von Geschichte*) (whole) point; (*von Show*) highlight, high spot; (*von Begebenheit*) show stopper; (= *Witz*) real laugh (*inf*); **und jetzt kommt der ~ der Geschichte** and now, wait for it, ...; **das ist doch gerade der ~** but that's just it, but that's the whole point; **das wäre der ~** that'd be a real laugh (*inf*)

Clown [klaʊn] M -s, -s (*lit, fig*) clown; **den ~ spielen** to clown around, to play the fool; **sich/ jdn zum ~ machen** to make a clown of oneself/ sb

Clow|ne|rie [klaʊnə'riː] F -, -n [-'riːən] clowning (around) no pl

clow|nesk [klaʊ'nɛsk] ADJ clownish

Clow|nin ['klaʊnɪn] F -, -nen (*lit, fig*) clown

Club [klʊb] M -s, -s club

cm abbr von **Zentimeter** cm

C-Netz ['tseː-] NT (*Telec*) cellular (analogue) network

Co-, co- ['koː] in cpds co-

Co. abbr von **Kompagnon** von **Kompanie** Co

Coach [koːtʃ] M -(s), -s (*Sport*) coach

coa|chen ['koːtʃn] VTI (*Sport*) to coach

Co|au|tor(in) ['koː-] M(F) coauthor

Co|ca ['koːka] F -, -s (*inf*) Coke® (*inf*)

Co|cker|spa|ni|el ['kɔkɐ-] M cocker spaniel

Cock|pit ['kɔkpɪt] NT -s, -s cockpit

Cock|tail ['kɔkteːl] M -s, -s **a** (= *Getränk, fig*) cocktail **b** (= *Empfang*) reception **c** (= *Cocktailparty*) cocktail party; **jdn zum ~ einladen** to invite sb for cocktails, to invite sb to a cocktail party

Cock|tail-: Cock|tail|kleid NT cocktail dress; **Cock|tail|par|ty** F cocktail party; **Cock|tail|to|ma|te** F cherry tomato

Co|com ['koːkɔm] NT - Cocom

Code [koːt] M -s, -s code

Co|de|in [kode'iːn] NT -s, no pl codeine

Co|dex ['koːdɛks] M -es or -, -e or **Codizes** ['koːditseːs] = **Kodex**

Cog|nac® ['kɔnjak] M -s, -s cognac → auch **Kognak**

Coif|feur [koa'føːr] M -s, -e, **Coif|feu|se** [-'føːzə] F -, -n (*Sw*) hairdresser; (*geh*) hair stylist

Coif|fure [koa'fyːr] F -, -n **a** (*geh*) hairstyling **b** (*Sw*) hairdressing salon

Co|la ['koːla] F -, -s (*inf*) Coke® (*inf*)

Co|la|do|se F Coke® can

Co|la|nuss ▲ F cola nut

Col|la|ge [kɔ'laːʒə] F -, -n (*Art, fig*) collage; (*Mus*) medley

Col|lege ['kɔlɪtʃ, -ɪdʒ] NT -(s), -es [-ɪz] (*Univ*) college

Col|lie ['kɔli] M -s, -s collie

Col|li|er [kɔ'lieː] NT -s, -s necklet, necklace → auch **Kollier**

Col|lo|qui|um [kɔ'lɔkviʊm] NT -s, **Colloquien** [-kviən] colloquium; (*Aus Univ: = Prüfung*) examination → auch **Kolloquium**

Co|lo|nia-: [ko'loːnia-]: **Co|lo|nia|kü|bel** M (*Aus*) dustbin (*Brit*), trash *or* garbage can (*US*); **Co|lo|nia|wa|gen** M (*Aus*) refuse lorry (*Brit*) or truck

co|lor ['koːloːr, ko'loːr] ADV (*inf*) in colour (*Brit*) or color (*US*)

Co|lor ['koːloːr, ko'loːr] NT in ~ in colour (*Brit*) or color (*US*)

Co|lor- ['koːloːr, ko'loːr] in cpds colour (*Brit*), color (*US*); **Co|lor|film** M colour (*Brit*) or color (*US*) film

Colt® [kɔlt] M -s, -s Colt®

Com|bo ['kɔmbo] F -, -s combo

Come-back ▲ [kam'bek] NT -(s), -s, **Come|-back** NT -(s), -s comeback

Co|me|con ['kɔmekɔn] M OR NT , **COMECON** M OR NT - (*Hist*) Comecon

Co|me|dy-Se|rie, Co|me|dy|se|rie ['kɔmədi-] F (*TV*) (television) comedy series; (*mit Situationskomödie*) sitcom (*inf*)

Co|mic ['kɔmɪk] M -s, -s comic strip

Co|mic-: Co|mic|fi|gur F cartoon character; **Co|mic|heft** NT comic, comic book (*US*)

Co|ming-out ['kamɪŋaʊt] NT -s, no pl (*inf, als Homosexueller*) coming out; **er erlebte sein ~ als Schlagersänger** he emerged as a pop singer

Com|mu|ni|qué [kɔmyni'keː] NT -s, -s communiqué

Com|pact|disc [kɔm'pakt 'dɪsk] F -, -s, **Com|pact Disc** F -, -s, **Com|pact Plat|te** F compact disc

Com|pi|ler [kɔm'paɪlɐ] M -s, - (*Comput*) compiler

Com|pu|ter [kɔm'pjuːtɐ] M -s, - computer; **auf ~** on computer; **per ~** by computer

Com|pu|ter- in cpds computer-; **Com|pu|ter|a|ni|ma|ti|on** F computer animation; **com|pu|ter|a|ni|miert** ADJ computer-animated; **Com|pu|ter|ar|beits|platz** M computer work station; **Com|pu|ter|blitz** M (*Phot*) electronic flash; **Com|pu|ter|di|ag|nos|tik** F (*Med*) computer diagnosis; **Com|pu|ter|fach|frau** F, **Com|pu|ter|fach|mann** M computer *or* IT consultant *or* expert; **Com|pu|ter|freak** M computer freak; **Com|pu|ter|ge|ne|ra|ti|on** F computer generation; **com|pu|ter|ge|recht ADJ** computer-compatible **ADV** übertragen in computer-compatible form; **com|pu|ter|ge|steu|ert** [-gəʃtɔyɐt] ADJ controlled by computer, computer-controlled; **com|pu|ter|ge|stützt** [-gəʃtʏtst] ADJ computer-based; **-es De-sign** computer-aided *or* -assisted design; **Com|pu|ter|gra|fik** F computer graphics pl; **Com|pu|ter|her|stel|ler** M computer manufacturer(s pl)

com|pu|te|ri|sie|ren [kɔmpjutəri'ziːrən] ptp **computerisiert** VT to computerize

Com|pu|te|ri|sie|rung [kɔmpjutəri'ziːrʊŋ] F -, no pl computerization

Com|pu|ter-: Com|pu|ter|kas|se F computer cash register; **Com|pu|ter|kri|mi|na|li|tät** F computer crime; **com|pu|ter|les|bar** ADJ machine-readable; **Com|pu|ter|lin|gu|is|tik** F computational linguistics sing; **Com|pu|ter|mes|se** F computer fair; **Com|pu|ter|sa|bo|ta|ge** F computer sabotage; **Com|pu|ter|satz** M computer typesetting; **Com|pu|ter|si|cher|heit** F computer security; **Com|pu|ter|si|mu|la|ti|on** F computer simulation; **Com|pu|ter|spiel** NT computer game; **Com|pu|ter|spra|che** F computer language; **Com|pu|ter|to|mo|graf** M computer tomograph; **Com|pu|ter|to|mo|gra|fie** ▲ F computer tomography; **Com|pu|ter|to|mo|gramm** NT computer tomogram; **com|pu|ter|un|ter|stützt** [-ʊn-təʃtʏtst] ADJ computer-aided; **Com|pu|ter-Vi|rus, Com|pu|ter|vi|rus** NT OR M computer virus; **Com|pu|ter|wis|sen|schaft** F computer science

Com|tes|se [kɔm'tɛsə] F -, -n countess

Con|di|tio si|ne qua non [kɔn'diːtsio 'ziːnə 'kva: 'noːn] F - - - -, no pl (*geh*) sine qua non

Con|do|me|rie [kɔndomə'riː] F -, -n [-'riːən] (*inf*) = **Kondomerie**

Con|fé|ren|ci|er [kõferã'sieː] M -s, -s compère, MC

Con|fi|se|rie [kɔnfizə'riː] F -, -n [-'riːən] (*Sw*) **a** (= *Konfekt*) confectionery **b** (= *Konditorei*) cake shop; (*mit Café*) café

Con|nais|seur [kɔnɛ'søːr] M -s, -e, **Con|nais|seu|rin** [-'søːrɪn] F -, -nen (*geh*) connoisseur

Con|sen|sus [kɔn'zɛnzʊs] M -, [-zuːs] (*geh*) agreement, assent, consent

Con|tai|ner [kɔn'teːnɐ] M -s, - container; (= *Blumentrog*) plant box; (= *Bauschuttcontainer*) skip; (= *Müllcontainer*) waste container; (= *Transportcontainer*) container; (= *Wohncontainer*) prefabricated hut, Portakabin®

Con|tai|ner- [kɔn'teːnɐ] in cpds container; **Con|tai|ner|bahn|hof** M container depot; **Con|tai|ner|dorf** NT village of prefabricated huts; **Con|tai|ner|ha|fen** M container port; **Con|tai|ner|schiff** NT container ship; **Con|tai|ner|ter|mi|nal** M OR NT container terminal; **Con|tai|ner|ver|kehr** M container traffic; **auf ~ umstellen** to containerize

Con|tain|ment [kɔn'teːnmənt] NT -s, -s containment

Con|te|nance [kõtə'nãːs(ə)] F -, no pl (*geh*) composure

Con|ter|gan® [kɔntɐr'gaːn] NT -s thalidomide

Con|ter|gan|kind NT (*inf*) thalidomide child

Con|tra ['kɔntra] M -s, -s (*Pol*) Contra

Con|trol|ler¹ [kɔn'troːlɐ] M -s, - (*Comput*) controller

Con|trol|ler² [kɔn'troːlɐ] M -s, -, **Con|trol|le|rin** [-ərɪn] F -, -nen (*Fin: = Finanzbuchhalter*) cost controller

Con|trol|ling [kɔn'troːlɪŋ] NT -s, no pl (*Fin*) cost control

cool ['kuːl] ADJ **a** (*inf: = gefasst*) cool (*inf*), laid-back (*inf*); **du musst ~ bleiben** you must keep your cool (*inf*), you must stay cool (*inf*) **b** (*sl: = angenehm*) cool (*inf*); **die Party war ~** the party was (real) cool (*inf*)

Cool|ness ['kuːlnɛs] F -, no pl (*inf*) coolness

Co|pi|lot(in) ['koː-] M(F) copilot

Co|py|right ['kɔpirait] NT -s, -s copyright

Co|py|shop ['kɔpiʃɔp] M -s, -s copy shop

co|ram pu|bli|co ['koːram 'puːbliko] ADV (*geh*) publicly

Cord [kɔrt] M -s, -e [-də] *or* -s (*Tex*) cord, corduroy

Cord- in cpds cord, corduroy → auch **Kord** etc; **Cord|ho|se** F cord trousers pl (*esp Brit*) or pants pl (*esp US*), cords pl; **Cord|jeans** PL cords pl

Cor|don bleu [kɔrdõ'bløː] NT -, -s -s (*Cook*) veal cordon bleu

Cor|ner ['kɔːɐnɐ] M **-s, -** (Aus Sport) corner

Corn|flakes® ['kɔːɐnfleːks] PL , **Corn Fla-kes®** PL cornflakes pl

Cor|ni|chon [kɔrni'ʃõː] NT **-s, -s** gherkin

Cor|po|ra De|lic|ti ▲ pl von **Corpus delicti**

Cor|po|rate I|den|ti|ty ['kɔːpɐrit ai'dɛntəti] F **-, - -s** corporate identity

Corps [koːɐ] NT **-, -** (Mil) corps; (Univ) (duelling (Brit) or dueling (US)) corps

Cor|pus ['kɔrpʊs] NT **-, Corpora** ['kɔrpora] (Ling) corpus

Cor|pus De|lic|ti ▲ ['kɔrpʊs de'lɪkti] NT **- -, Corpora -** ['kɔrpora] corpus delicti; (hum) culprit (inf)

cos abbr von **Kosinus** cos

Co|sa Nost|ra ['koːza 'nɔstra] F **- -,** no pl Cosa Nostra

Cos|ta Ri|ca ['kɔsta 'riːka] NT **-s** Costa Rica

Cos|ta-Ri|ca|ner ▲ [kɔstari'kaːnɐ] M **-s, -, Cos|ta-Ri|ca|ne|rin** ▲ [-ərɪn] F **-, -nen** Costa Rican

cos|ta-ri|ca|nisch ▲ [kɔstari'kaːnɪʃ] ADJ Costa Rican

Couch [kautʃ] F **-, -s** or **-en** or (Sw) m **-s, -(e)s** couch

Couch- ['kautʃ-]: **Couch|gar|ni|tur** F three--piece suite; **Couch|po|ta|to** [-poteːto] F **-, -es** (inf) couch potato (inf); **Couch|tisch** M coffee table

Cou|leur [ku'løːɐ] F **-, -s** a (geh) kind, sort; **Fa-schisten/Sozialisten jeder ~** fascists/socialists of every shade b (Univ) colours pl (Brit), colors pl (US); **~ tragen** to wear the colours of one's student society (Brit), to wear the colors of one's fraternity (US)

Count-down ▲ ['kaunt'daun] M OR NT **-s, -s, Count|down** M OR NT **-s, -s** (Space, fig) count-down

Coup [kuː] M **-s, -s** coup; **einen ~ (gegen jdn/ etw) landen** to bring or pull (inf) off a coup (a-gainst sb/sth)

Cou|pé [ku'pe:] NT **-s, -s** coupé

Coup|let [ku'ple:] NT **-s, -s** cabaret song

Cou|pon [ku'põ:] M **-s, -s** a (= Zettel) coupon b (Fin) (interest) coupon c (= Stoffcoupon) length (of material) → auch **Kupon**

Cour [kuːɐ] F (dated) **einem Mädchen die ~ ma-chen** or **schneiden** to court a young lady (da-ted)

Cou|ra|ge [ku'raːʒə] F **-,** no pl (geh) courage, pluck

cou|ra|giert [kura'ʒiːɐt] (geh) ADJ courageous ADV courageously

Cour|ta|ge [kʊr'taːʒə] F **-, -n** (Fin) commission

Cous|cous ['kʊskʊs] M OR NT **-, -** (Cook) cous-cous

Cous|in [ku'zɛ̃ː] M **-s, -s, Cou|si|ne** [ku'ziːnə] F **-, -n** cousin

Cou|vert [ku've:ɐ, ku'veːɐ] NT **-s, -s** a (= Brief-umschlag) envelope b (= Gedeck) cover

Co|ver ['kavɐ] NT **-s, -s** cover

Co|ver- ['kavɐ]: **Cover|girl** ['kavɐ-] NT cover girl; **Cover|ver|si|on** ['kavɐ-] F (Mus) cover (ver-sion)

Cow|boy ['kaubɔy] M cowboy

Cow|boy|stie|fel ['kaubɔy-] M cowboy boot

Cox O|ran|ge ['kɔks o'rãːʒə] M OR F **- -, - -** or **- -n** Cox's (Orange) Pippin, Cox

C-Par|tei ['tseː-] F (Pol inf) **die ~en** the CDU and CSU

Crack¹ [krɛk] M **-s, -s** (= Sportler) ace

Crack² NT **-,** no pl (= Droge) crack

cra|cken ['krɛkn] VT (Chem) = **kracken**

Cra|cker ['krɛkɐ] M **-s, -(s)** a (= Keks) cracker b (= Feuerwerkskörper) banger (Brit), firecracker (US)

Cra|que|lé [krakə'le:] NT **-s, -s** crackle

Crash [krɛʃ] M **-s, -s** (inf: = Unfall, St Ex, Comput) crash

Crash- ['krɛʃ-]: **Crash|kid** NT **-s, -s** (inf) joyrider; **Crash|kurs** M crash course; **Crash|pro-gramm** M (Comput) crash program; **Crash|test** M (Aut) crash test

Cre|do ['kreːdo] NT **-s, -s** (lit, fig) creed, credo

creme [kreːm, krɛːm] ADJ pred (Fashion) cream

Creme [kreːm, krɛːm] F **-, -s** (= Hautcreme, Cook, fig) cream; **die ~ der Gesellschaft** the cream of society, the crème de la crème (liter); **die ~ de la ~** the crème de la crème

creme-: creme|ar|tig ADJ cream-like; **creme|-far|ben** [-farbn] ADJ cream-coloured (Brit), cream-colored (US)

Crème fraîche [krɛm 'frɛʃ] F **-,** no pl (Cook) crème fraîche

Creme|tor|te F cream gateau

cre|mig ['kreːmɪç] ADJ creamy ADV like cream; **rühren** until creamy

Crêpe [krɛp] F **-, -s** (Cook) crêpe

Crêpe de Chine [krɛp də 'ʃin] M **- - -, -s - -** crêpe de Chine

Cre|scen|do [kre'ʃɛndo] NT **-s, -s** or **Crescendi** [-di] a (Mus) crescendo b (Sport) final spurt

Creutz|feldt-Ja|kob-Krank|heit [krɔytsfɛlt-'jakɔp-] F Creutzfeldt-Jakob disease

Creutz|feldt-Ja|kob-Syn|drom NT Creutz-feldt-Jakob syndrome

Crew [kruː] F **-, -s** crew; (= Kadettenjahrgang) ca-dets pl of the same year/age

Crois|sant [kroa'sã:] NT **-s, -s** croissant

Cro|mar|gan® [kromar'ga:n] NT **-s,** no pl stain-less steel

Cross [krɔs] M **-,** no pl, **Cross-Count|ry** [krɔs'-kantri] NT **-,** no pl (Sport) cross-country; (= Mo-torradrennen) motocross

Cross|(ball) ['krɔs-] M **-,** - (Tennis) cross-court shot

Crou|pier [kru'pie:] M **-s, -s** croupier

Crou|ton|we|cken [kru'tõ:-] M (Aus) French bread; (= Laib) French loaf

Cruise|mis|sile ▲ [kruːz'mɪsaɪl, -'mɪsl] NT **-s, -s** (Mil) cruise missile

Crux [krʊks] F **-,** no pl a (= Last) nuisance b (= Schwierigkeit) trouble, problem; **die ~ bei der Sache ist, ...** the trouble or problem (with that) is ...

C-Schlüs|sel ['tseː-] M alto or C clef

CSFR [tʃeː|ɛs|ɛf'ɛr] F - (Hist) = **Tschechoslowakei**

CS-Gas ['tseː-|ɛs-] NT CS gas

CSSR [tʃeː|ɛs|ɛs'ɛr] F - (Hist) = **Tschechoslowakei**

CSU [tseː|ɛs'uː] F - abbr von **Christlich-Soziale Union** Christian Social Union

---

CSU

The **CSU** (Christlich-Soziale Union) is the sis-ter party of the **CDU** and contests elections only in Bavaria. Founded in 1945, it empha-sizes Christian, conservative values and a so-cial market economy. It also champions the sovereignty of the **Länder**, especially Bavaria. The **CSU** frequently receives an absolute ma-jority in **Landtag** elections and so can rely on a broad basis of support → CDU

---

c. t. [tseː'te:] abbr von **cum tempore** ADV within fifteen minutes of the time stated; **18.30 ~** 6.30 for 6.45

cum gra|no sa|lis [kʊm 'graːno 'zaːlɪs] ADV (geh) with a pinch of salt

cum lau|de [kʊm 'laudə] ADV (Univ) cum laude (form), with distinction

Cun|ni|lin|gus [kʊni'lɪŋɡʊs] M **-, Cunnilingi** [-gi] cunnilingus, cunnilinctus

Cup [kap] M **-s, -s** (Sport) cup

Cu|pi|do [ku'piːdo] M **-s** Cupid

Cu|rie [ky'riː] NT **-, -** (abbr **Ci**) Curie

Cu|ri|um ['kuːriʊm] NT **-s,** no pl (abbr **Cu**) cu-rium

Cur|ling ['kœːɐlɪŋ, 'kœrlɪŋ] NT **-s,** no pl curling

Cur|ri|cu|la (geh) pl von **Curriculum**

cur|ri|cu|lar [kʊriku'laːɐ] ADJ attr (geh) curricu-lar

Cur|ri|cu|lum [kʊ'riːkulʊm] NT **-s, Curricula** [-la] (geh) curriculum

Cur|ri|cu|lum|for|schung F curriculum devel-opment

Cur|ry ['kari] M OR NT **-s, -s** curry

Cur|ry|wurst ['kari-] F curried sausage

Cur|sor ['kœːɐsɐ, 'kœrsɐ] M **-s, -s** (Comput) cursor

Cur|sor|steu|e|rung ['kœːɐsɐ-, 'kœrsɐ-] F (Com-put) cursor control; (Taste) cursor control key

Cut [kœt, kat] M **-s, -s, Cu|ta|way** ['kœtəve, 'kat-] M **-s, -s** (dated) cutaway

cut|ten ['katn] VTI (Film, Rad, TV) to cut, to edit

Cut|ter ['katɐ] M **-s, -, Cut|te|rin** ['katərɪn] F **-, -nen** (Film, Rad, TV) editor

CVJF [tseː'faujɔt'ɛf] M **-s** abbr von **Christlicher Ver-ein Junger Frauen** YWCA

CVJM [tseː'faujɔt'ɛm] M **-s** abbr von **Christlicher Verein Junger Männer** YMCA

C-Waf|fe ['tseː-] F abbr von **chemische Waffe**

Cy|an [tsy'aːn] NT **-s,** no pl cyan

Cy|a|nid [tsya'niːt] NT **-s, -e** [-də] cyanide

Cy|ber- ['saibɐ] in cpds cyber-; **Cy|ber|ca|fé** ['saibɐkafe:] NT (Comput) cybercafé, Internet café; **Cy|ber|naut** ['saibɛnɔːt] M **-en, -en, Cy|ber|nau|tin** [-nɔːtɪn] F **-, -nen** cybernaut; **Cy|ber|space** ['saibɐspeːs] M **-,** no pl (Comput) cy-berspace; **Cy|ber|welt** ['saibɛ-] F (Comput) cy-berspace

Cyc|la|mat® [tsykla'maːt] NT **-s, -e** cyclamate

Cy|pern ['tsyːpɐn] NT **-s** = **Zypern**

cys|tisch ['tsystɪʃ] ADJ = **zystisch**

D

D, d [deː] NT -, - D, d

da [daː] ⊛ 44.1 **ADV a** (*örtlich*) (= *dort*) there; (= *hier*) here; **es liegt da draußen/drinnen/drüben/vorn** it's out there/in there/over there/there in front; **das liegt etwa da herum** it's somewhere round about there, it's somewhere thereabouts; **geh da herum** go round there; **da und da** what's-its-name (*inf*); **hier und da, da und dort** here and there; **wer da?** who goes there?; **he, Sie da!** hey, you there!; **die Frau da** that woman (over) there; **da bin ich/sind wir** here I am/we are; **da bist du ja!** there you are!; **da kommt er ja** here he comes; **wir sind gleich da** we'll soon be there, we're almost there; **da, wo ...** where ...; **wo die Straße über den Fluss geht, da fängt Schottland an** Scotland begins where the road crosses the river, where the road crosses the river, that's where Scotland begins; **ach, da war der Brief!** so that's where the letter was; **da möchte ich auch einmal hinfahren** (*inf*) I'd like to go there one day; **geben Sie mir ein halbes Pfund von dem da** give me half a pound of that one (there); **da haben wirs** or **den Salat** (*inf*) that had to happen; **da hast du deinen Kram/dein Geld!** (there you are,) there's your stuff/money; **da, nimm schon!** here, take it! → **als**

b (*zeitlich*: = *dann, damals*) then; **ich ging gerade aus dem Haus, da schlug es zwei** I was just going out of the house when the clock struck two; **vor vielen, vielen Jahren, da lebte ein König** (*liter*) long, long ago there lived a king or there once was a king; **da werden wir uns den Schaden mal ansehen** (*inf*) let's have a look at the damage; **da kommen Sie mal mit** (*inf*) you just come along with me; **da siehst du, was du angerichtet hast** now see what you've done

c (= *daraufhin*) sagen to that; *lachen* at that; **sie weinte, da ließ er sich erweichen** when she started to cry he softened, she started to cry, whereupon he softened (*liter*); **als er das Elend der Leute sah, da nahm er sich vor ...** when he saw the people's suffering he decided ...

d (= *folglich*) so; (= *dann*) then; **es war niemand im Zimmer, da hatte ich** ... there was nobody in the room, so I ...; **wenn ich schon gehen muss, da gehe ich lieber gleich** if I have to go, (then) I'd rather go straight away

e (*inf*: = *in diesem Fall*) there; **da haben wir aber Glück gehabt!** we were lucky there!; **da muss man vorsichtig sein** you've got to be careful there; **was gibts denn da zu lachen?** what's funny about that?; **was gibts denn da zu fragen?** what is there to ask?; **da kann man nichts mehr machen** there's nothing more to be done (there or about it); **da kann man** or **lässt sich nichts machen** nothing can be done about it; **da könnte man aus der Haut fahren** it would drive you mad (*esp Brit*) or crazy (*inf*); **da kann man nur lachen/sich nur fragen, warum** you can't help laughing/asking yourself why; **da kann man sich nur wundern** you can't help being amazed; **da kann man nur noch still sein** you can't say anything; **und da fragst du noch?** and you still have to ask?; **und da soll einer** or **ein Mensch wissen, warum!** and you're meant to know why!; **da fragt man sich (doch), ob der Mann noch normal ist** it makes you wonder if

the man's normal; **da hat doch jemand gelacht/alle Kirschen gegessen** somebody laughed/has eaten all the cherries

f (*zur Hervorhebung*) **wir haben da eine neue Mitschülerin/Ausführung des Artikels** we've got this new girl in our school/this new model; **da fällt mir gerade ein ...** it's just occurred to me ...

g (*N Ger*) → **dabei, dafür** *etc*

CONJ a (= *weil*) as, since, seeing that

b (*liter*: = *als*) when; **die Stunde, da du ...** the hour when you ...; **nun** or **jetzt, da** now that

d. Ä. *abbr von* **der Ältere** sen

DAAD [deːaːaːˈdeː] M - *abbr von* **Deutscher Akademischer Austauschdienst** German Academic Exchange Service

da+be|hal|ten *ptp* **dabehalten** VT *sep irreg* to keep (here/there); (*in Haft auch*) to detain (there); *Schüler* to keep behind

da|bei [daˈbai, (*emph*) ˈdaːbai] ADV **a** (*örtlich*) with it; (*bei Gruppe von Menschen, Dingen*) there; **ein Häuschen mit einem Garten ~** a little house with a garden (attached to it or attached); **ist die Lösung ~?** is the solution given (there)?; **nahe ~** nearby

b (*zeitlich*) (= *gleichzeitig*) at the same time; (= *währenddessen, wodurch*) in the course of this; **er aß weiter und blätterte ~ in dem Buch** he went on eating, leafing through the book as he did so or at the same time; **warum arbeiten Sie im Stehen? Sie können doch auch ~ sitzen** why are you working standing up? you can sit down while you're doing it; **nach der Explosion entstand eine Panik; ~ wurden drei Kinder verletzt** there was a general panic after the explosion, in the course of which or during which three children were injured; **... orkanartige Winde; ~ kam es zu schweren Schäden** ... gale-force winds, which have resulted in serious damage

c (= *außerdem*) as well, into the bargain (*inf*), with it (*inf*); **sie ist schön und ~ auch noch klug** she's pretty, and clever as well

d (*wenn, während man etw tut*) in the process; *ertappen, erwischen* at it; **er wollte helfen und wurde ~ selbst verletzt** he wanted to help and got injured in the process or (in) doing so or while he was about it (*inf*); **du warst bei einem Jugendtreffen? hast du denn ~ etwas gelernt?** you were at a youth meeting? did you learn anything there or from it?; **~ darf man nicht vergessen, dass ...** it shouldn't be forgotten that ...; (*Einschränkung eines Arguments*) it should not be forgotten here that ...; **die ~ entstehenden Kosten** the expenses arising from this/that; **als er das tat, hat er ~ ...** when he did that he ...; **wenn man das tut, muss man ~ ...** when you do that you have to ...; **wir haben ihn ~ ertappt, wie er über den Zaun stieg** we caught him in the act of climbing over the fence

e (= *in dieser Angelegenheit*) **das Schwierigste ~** the most difficult part of it; **wichtig ~ ist ...** the important thing here or about it is ...; **mir ist nicht ganz wohl ~** I don't really feel happy about it; **~ kann man viel Geld verdienen** there's a lot of money in that; **er hat ~ einen Fehler**

gemacht he's made a mistake; **sie hat sich ~ sehr dumm benommen** she behaved very stupidly; **es kommt doch nichts ~ heraus** nothing will come of it

f (*einräumend*: = *doch*) (and) yet; **er hat mich geschlagen, ~ hatte ich gar nichts gemacht** he hit me and I hadn't even done anything or and yet I hadn't done anything; **ich habe fünf Stück gegessen, ~ hatte ich gar keinen Hunger** I've eaten five pieces, and I wasn't even hungry

g **du gehst sofort nach Hause, und ~ bleibt es!** you're going straight home and that's that or that's the end of it!; **es bleibt ~, dass ihr morgen alle mitkommt** we'll stick to that or keep it like that, you're all coming tomorrow; **ich bleibe ~** I'm not changing my mind; **er bleibt ~, dass er es nicht gewesen ist** he still insists that he didn't do it, he's still sticking to his guns that he didn't do it; **aber ~ sollte es nicht bleiben** but it shouldn't stop there or at that; **lassen wir es ~** let's leave it at that!; **was ist schon ~?** so what? (*inf*), what of it? (*inf*); **was ist schon ~, wenn man das tut?** what harm is there in doing that?; **ich finde gar nichts ~** I don't see any harm in it; **es ist nichts ~, wenn man das tut** (= *schadet nichts*) there's no harm in doing that; (= *will nichts bedeuten*) doing that doesn't mean anything; **nimm meine Bemerkung nicht so ernst, ich habe mir nichts ~ gedacht** don't take my remark so seriously, I didn't mean anything by it; **ich habe mir nichts ~ gedacht, als ich den Mann aus der Bank kommen sah** I didn't think anything of it when I saw the man coming out of the bank; **was hast du dir denn ~ gedacht?** what were you thinking of?; **~ kann er sich nicht viel gedacht haben** he can't have thought about it much

da|bei+blei|ben VI *sep irreg aux sein* to stay or stick (*inf*) with it; (*bei Firma, Stelle, Armee etc*) to stay on → *auch* **dabei g**

da|bei+ha|ben VT *sep irreg* (*inf*) to have with one; *Geld, Pass, Schirm etc auch* to have on one

da|bei sein ▲ VI *irreg aux sein* **a** (= *anwesend sein*) to be there (*bei* at); (= *mitmachen*) to be involved (*bei* in); **ich bin dabei!** count me in!; **er war bei der Flugzeugentführung dabei** he was there when the plane was hijacked, he was there at the hijacking; **ein wenig Furcht ist immer dabei** I'm/you're *etc* always a bit scared; **er will überall ~** he wants to be in on everything

b (= *im Begriff sein*) **~, etw zu tun** to be just doing sth; **ich bin (gerade) dabei** I'm just doing it

Da|bei sein NT **~ ist alles** it's all about taking part

da|bei+sit|zen VI *sep irreg aux haben or (S Ger, Aus, Sw) sein* to sit there; **bei einer Besprechung ~** to sit in on a discussion

da|bei+ste|hen VI *sep irreg aux haben or (S Ger, Aus, Sw) sein* to stand there

da+blei|ben VI *sep irreg aux sein* to stay (on); (= *nachsitzen*) to stay behind; **(jetzt wird) dageblieben!** (you just) stay right there!

da ca|po [da ˈkaːpo] ADV da capo; **~ rufen** to call for an encore

Dach [dax] NT -(e)s, ⸚er [ˈdɛçɐ] **a** roof; **das ~ der Welt** the roof of the world; **ein/kein ~ über**

dem **Kopf haben** (*inf*) to have a/no roof over one's head; **mit jdm unter einem ~ wohnen** to live under the same roof as sb; **jdm das ~ überm Kopf anzünden** to burn down sb's house; **unterm ~ juchhe** (*inf*) right under the eaves; **unterm ~ wohnen** (*inf*) to live in an attic room/flat (*Brit*) or apartment; (*im obersten Stock*) to live right on the top floor; **unter einem ~ unter one roof**; **unter – und Fach sein** (= *abgeschlossen*) to be all wrapped up, to be all in the bag (*inf*); (*Vertrag, Geschäft auch*) to be signed and sealed; (= *in Sicherheit*) to be safely under cover; (*Ernte*) to be safely in; **etw unter – und Fach bringen** to get sth all wrapped up/ signed and sealed/safely under cover

b (*fig inf*) **jdm eins aufs ~ geben** (= *schlagen*) to smash sb on the head (*inf*); (= *ausschimpfen*) to give sb a (good) talking-to; **eins aufs ~ bekommen** *or* **kriegen** (= *geschlagen werden*) to get hit on the head; (= *ausgeschimpft werden*) to be given a (good) talking-to; **jdm aufs ~ steigen** (*inf*) to get onto sb (*inf*); **unter dem ~** +*gen* under the umbrella of

Dach- *in cpds* roof; **Dach|an|ten|ne** F roof aerial *or* antenna; **Dach|bal|ken** M roof joist *or* beam; **Dach|be|de|ckung** F , **Dach|be|lag** M roofing; **Dach|bo|den** M attic, loft; (*von Scheune*) loft; **auf dem ~** in the attic; **Dach|de|cker** [-dɛkə] M -s, -, **Dach|de|cke|rin** [-ərɪn] F -, -nen roofer; (*mit Ziegeln*) tiler; (*mit Schiefer*) slater; (*mit Stroh*) thatcher; **das kannst du halten wie ein ~** (*fig inf*) it doesn't matter two ha'pence (*Brit inf*) *or* one jot (*esp Brit inf*); **Dach|de|cker|ar|bei|ten** PL roofing; tiling; slating; thatching

da|chen ['daxn] VT (*obs*) to roof

Dach-: **Dach|er|ker** M dormer window; **Dach|fens|ter** NT skylight; (*ausgestellt*) dormer window; **Dach|first** M ridge of the roof; **dach|för|mig** ADJ rooflike; **Dach|gar|ten** M roof garden; **Dach|ge|bälk** NT roof timbers *pl*; **Dach|ge|päck|trä|ger** M (*Aut*) roof rack; **Dach|ge|schoss** ▲ NT , **Dach|ge|schoß** (*Aus, S Ger*) NT attic (storey (*Brit*) *or* story (*US*)); (= *oberster Stock*) top floor *or* storey (*Brit*) *or* story (*US*); **Dach|ge|sell|schaft** F parent company; **Dach|ge|sims** NT (roof) cornice; **Dach|ge|stühl** NT roof truss; **Dach|gie|bel** M gable; **Dach|glei|che** [-ɡlaɪça] F *decl as adj*, **Dach|glei|chen|fei|er** F (*Aus*) topping-out ceremony; **Dach|ha|se** M (*hum*) cat; **Dach|kam|mer** F attic room, garret (*dated*); **Dach|lat|te** F tile *or* roof batten *or* lath; **Dach|la|wi|ne** F snowfall from a/the roof; **Dach|lu|ke** F skylight; **Dach|nei|gung** F slope of the roof; **Dach|or|ga|ni|sa|ti|on** F umbrella *or* (*Comm*) parent organization; **Dach|pap|pe** F roofing felt (*Brit*) *or* paper; **Dach|pfan|ne** F (roof) tile; **Dach|rei|ter** M (*Archit*) roof *or* ridge turret; **Dach|rin|ne** F gutter

Dachs [daks] M -es, -e **a** (*Zool*) badger; **schlafen wie ein ~** (*inf*) to sleep like a log (*inf*) **b** (*inf*: = *Mensch*) **ein frecher ~!** a cheeky devil! (*Brit*), a smart-alec!; **ein junger ~** a young whippersnapper (*dated inf*)

Dachs|bau M *pl* -baue badger's sett

Dach-: **Dach|scha|den** M **a** (*lit*) damage to the roof **b** (*inf*) **einen (kleinen) ~ haben** to have a slate loose (*inf*); **Dach|schie|fer** M roofing slate; **Dach|schin|del** F (roof) shingle

Dachs|hund M dachshund

Dach|sil|hou|et|te F outline of the roof

Däch|sin ['dɛksɪn] F -, -nen female badger

Dach-: **Dach|spar|ren** M rafter; **Dach|stein** M (cement) roofing slab; **Dach|stroh** NT thatch; **Dach|stu|be** F , **Dach|stüb|chen** NT attic room, garret (*dated*); **Dach|stuhl** M roof truss; **Dach|stuhl|brand** M roof fire

dach|te *pret von* **denken**

Dach-: **Dach|ter|ras|se** F roof terrace; **Dach|trä|ger** M (*Aut*) roof rack; **Dach|trau|fe** F rain spout; (*dial* = *Dachrinne*) gutter; **Dach|ver|band** M umbrella organization; **Dach|wohl**

---

nung F attic flat (*Brit*) *or* apartment; **Dach|zie|gel** M roofing tile; **Dach|zim|mer** NT attic room, garret (*dated*)

Da|ckel ['dakl] M -s, - dachshund, sausage dog (*inf*); (*inf*: = *Person*) silly clot (*Brit inf*), ninny (*US inf*)

Da|ckel|bei|ne PL (*inf*) short stumpy legs *pl*

Da|da|is|mus [dada'ɪsmʊs] M -, *no pl* Dadaism, Dada

Da|da|ist [dada'ɪst] M -en, -en, **Da|da|is|tin** [-'ɪstɪn] F -, -en Dadaist; **die –en** the Dada group, the Dadaists

da|da|is|tisch [dada'ɪstɪʃ] ADJ Dadaist

Dad|del|au|to|mat ['dadl-] M (*inf*) fruit machine

Dad|del|hal|le F (*inf*) amusement arcade

dad|deln ['dadln] VI (*inf*) to play the fruit machines

da|durch [da'dʊrç, (*emph*) 'da:dʊrç] ADV **a** (*örtlich*) through there; (*wenn Bezugsobjekt vorher erwähnt*) through it; (*geh: in Relativsatz*) through which

b (*kausal*) thereby (*form*); (= *mithilfe von, aus diesem Grund auch*) because of this/that, through this/that; (= *durch diesen Umstand, diese Tat etc auch*) by *or* with that; (= *auf diese Weise*) in this/that way; **was willst du ~ gewinnen?** what do you hope to gain by *or* from that?; **meinst du, ~ wird alles wieder gut?** do you think that will make everything all right again?; **~ kam es, dass er nicht dabei sein konnte** that was why he couldn't be there

c **~, dass er das tat, hat er ...** (= *durch diesen Umstand, diese Tat*) by doing that he ...; (= *deswegen, weil*) because he did that he ...; **~, dass ich das tat, hat er ...** by my doing that he ..., because I did that he ...; **~, dass er den zweiten Satz gewonnen hat, sind seine Chancen wieder gestiegen** his chances improved again with him *or* his winning the second set; **~, dass das Haus isoliert ist, ist es viel wärmer** the house is much warmer because it's insulated *or* for being insulated

Daff|ke ['dafkə] **aus ~** (*dial inf*) (= *aus Trotz*) out of spite; (= *aus Spaß*) for fun, for the fun of it

da|für [da'fy:ɐ, (*emph*) 'da:fy:ɐ] ADV **a** (= *für das, diese Tat etc*) for that/it; **wir haben kein Geld ~** we've no money for that; **~ haben wir kein Geld** we've no money for that sort of thing; **der Grund ~ ist, dass ...** the reason for that is (that) ...; **warum ist er so böse? er hat doch keinen Grund ~** why is he so angry? there's no reason for it *or* he has no reason to be; **~ war er nicht zu haben** it wasn't his scene (*inf*); (= *erlaubte es nicht*) he wouldn't have it; **~ ist er immer zu haben** he never says no to that; **ich bin nicht ~ verantwortlich, was mein Bruder macht** I'm not responsible for what my brother does; **~ bin ich ja hier** that's what I'm here for, that's why I'm here; **er ist ~ bestraft worden, dass er frech zum Lehrer war** he was punished for being cheeky to (*Brit*) *or* sassy with (*US*) the teacher

b (*Zustimmung*) for that/it, in favour (*Brit*) *or* favor (*US*) (of that/it); **ich bin ganz ~** I'm all for it (*inf*), I'm all in favo(u)r; **~ sein (ganz ~), dass wir sie das machen** I'm (all) for *or* in favo(u)r of doing that/them doing that; **~ stimmen** to vote for it; **ich bin nicht ~, dass das so gemacht wird** I don't think it should be done like that, I'm not in favo(u)r of it being done that way

c (*als Ersatz*) instead, in its place; (*als Bezahlung*) for that/it; (*bei Tausch*) in exchange; (*als Gegenleistung*) in return; **... ich mache dir ~ deine Hausaufgaben ...** and I'll do your homework in return

d (*zum Ausgleich*) but ... to make up; **in Physik ist er schlecht, ~ kann er gut Golf spielen** he's very bad at physics but he makes up for it at golf *or* but he's good at golf to make up; **ich hatte diesmal immer nur Kurzferien, ~ habe ich umso mehr gesehen** I've only had short holi-

---

days (*Brit*) *or* a short vacation (*US*) this time but I've seen a lot more for all that

e (= *im Hinblick darauf*) **der Junge ist erst drei Jahre, ~ ist er sehr klug** the boy is only three, (so) considering that he's very clever; **~, dass er erst drei Jahre ist, ist er sehr klug** seeing *or* considering that he's only three he's very clever

f (*in Verbindung mit n, vb etc siehe auch dort*) **er interessiert sich nicht ~** he's not interested in that/it; **~ interessiert er sich nicht** he's not interested in that sort of thing; **er gibt sein ganzes Geld ~ aus** he spends all his money on that/it; **ein Beispiel ~ wäre ...** an example of that would be ...; **ich kann mich nicht ~ begeistern** I can't get enthusiastic about it, I can't rouse any enthusiasm for it; **sie ist dreißig/sehr intelligent – ~ hätte ich sie nicht gehalten** she's thirty/very intelligent – I would never have thought it *or* thought she was; **~ werde ich schon sorgen** I'll see to that, I'll take care of that; **ich werde ~ sorgen, dass ...** I'll see to it ...

da|für-: **da|für|hal|ten** VI *sep irreg* (*geh*) to be of the opinion; **ich halte dafür, dass wir zu Hause bleiben** I am of the opinion that we should stay at home; **nach meinem Dafürhalten** in my opinion; **da|für kön|nen** ▲ VT *irreg* **er kann nichts dafür** he can't help it, it's not his fault; **er kann nichts dafür, dass er dumm ist** he can't help being stupid, it's not his fault that he's stupid; **er kann nichts dafür, dass es kaputtgegangen ist** it's not his fault that it broke, he couldn't help it breaking; **er kann etwas dafür, dass es kaputtgegangen ist** it was his fault that it broke; **was kann ich dafür, dass es heute regnet?** it's not my fault (that) *or* I can't help that it's raining today; **als ob ich was dafür könnte!** as if I could help it!, as if it were my fault!; **da|für|ste|hen** VIR *sep irreg* (*Aus*) to be worth it, to be worthwhile

DAG [de:ʔaː'ge:] F - *abbr von* **Deutsche Angestellten-Gewerkschaft** Trade Union of German Employees

da|ge|gen [da'ge:gn, (*emph*) 'da:ge:gn] ✪ 36.1, 36.2, 39.2 ADV **a** (*örtlich*) against it; **es stand ein Baum im Weg und der Vogel/Wagen prallte ~** there was a tree in the way and the bird/car crashed into it; **die Tür war verschlossen, also pochte er ~** the door was locked, so he hammered on it; **mache das Licht an und halte das Dia ~** put the light on and hold the slide up to it *or* against it

b (*als Einwand, Ablehnung*) against that/it; **~ sein** to be against it, to be opposed (to it); **etwas ~ haben** to object; **nichts ~ haben** not to object; **ich habe etwas ~** I object to that; **was hat er ~, dass wir früher anfangen?** what has he got against us starting earlier?, why does he object to us *or* our starting earlier?; **haben Sie was ~, wenn ich rauche?** do you mind if I smoke?, would you mind *or* object if I smoked?; **sollen wir ins Kino gehen? – ich hätte nichts ~ (einzuwenden)** shall we go to the cinema? – that's okay by me (*inf*); **ich hätte nichts ~, wenn er nicht kommen würde** I wouldn't mind at all if he didn't come; **ich werde ~ protestieren** I will protest against that/it; **ich werde ~ protestieren, dass das gemacht wird** I will protest against that being done

c (*als Gegenmaßnahme*) **tun, unternehmen** about it; **Medikamente einnehmen etc** for it; **~ lässt sich nichts machen** nothing can be done about it; **bei mir regnet es herein, aber ich kann nichts ~ machen** the rain comes in, but I can't do anything to stop it *or* about it

d (= *verglichen damit*) compared with that/it/ them, in comparison; **die Stürme letztes Jahr waren furchtbar, ~ sind die jetzigen nicht so schlimm** the gales last year were terrible, compared with them *or* those, these aren't so bad *or* these aren't so bad in comparison

e (*als Ersatz, Gegenwert*) for that/it/them

CONJ (= *im Gegensatz dazu*) on the other hand,

---

however; **er sprach fließend Französisch, ~ konnte er kein Deutsch** he spoke French fluently, but (on the other hand) he could not speak any German

da|ge|gen-: da|ge|gen+hal|ten VT *sep irreg* **a** (= *vergleichen*) to compare it/them with; **wenn wir das Original ...** if we compare the original with it ... **b** (= *einwenden*) = **dagegensetzen; da|ge|gen+set|zen** VT *sep* (*fig*) **seine eigene Meinung ~** to put forward one's own opinion in opposition; **das Einzige, was Sie ~ könnten, wäre ...** the only objection you could put forward would be ...; **er setzte dagegen, dass ...** he put forward the objection that ...; **da|ge|gen+spre|chen** VI *sep irreg* to be against it; **was spricht dagegen?** what is there against it?; **was spricht dagegen, dass wir es so machen?** what is there against us doing it that way?, why shouldn't we do it that way?; **es spricht nichts dagegen, es so zu machen** there's no reason not to do it that way; **da|ge|gen+stel|len** VR *sep* to oppose it; **warum musst du dich immer ~?** why must you always oppose everything?; **da|ge|gen+stem|men** VR *sep* to fight it, to oppose it bitterly; **da|ge|gen+wir|ken** VI *sep* to act against it

da|ha|ben VT *sep irreg* **a** (= *vorrätig haben*) to have here/there; (*in Geschäft etc*) to have in stock **b** (= *zu Besuch haben*) to have here/there; (*zum Essen etc*) to have in

da|heim [daˈhaɪm] ADV (*esp S Ger, Aus, Sw*) at home; (*nach prep*) home; **bei uns ~** back home (where I/we come from); **das Buch liegt bei mir ~** or **~ bei mir** I've got the book at home; **wir haben bei mir ~** or **~ bei mir gefeiert** we had a celebration at my place; **~ sein** (*lit, fig*) to be at home; (*nach Reise*) to be home; **wo bist du ~?** where's your home?; **ich bin für niemanden ~** I'm not at home to anybody; **~ ist ~** (*Prov*) east, west, home's best (*prov*), there's no place like home (*prov*)

Da|heim NT *, no pl* (*esp S Ger, Aus, Sw*) home

Da|heim-: Da|heim|ge|blie|be|ne(r) [-ɡəbliːbnə] MF *decl as adj* **die/alle ~n** those/all those at home; **Da|heim|sein** NT **das ~ ist auch schön** being (at) home is nice too, it's nice being (at) home

da|her [daˈheːɐ, (*emph*) ˈdaːheːɐ] ✪ 44.1 ADV **a** (= *von dort*) from there; **von ~** from there; **~ habe ich das** that's where I got it from **b** (*dial*: = *hierher*) here **c** (*aufgrund dieses Umstand*) that is why; **~ weiß ich das** that's how or why I know that; **~ die große Eile/all der Lärm** that's why there's all this hurry/noise, that's the reason for all this hurry/noise; **~ der Name X** that's why it's/he's *etc* called X; **~ kommt es, dass ...** that is (the reason) why ...; **ich bin überzeugt, dass seine Krankheit ~ kommt** that's why he's ill; **das kommt** or **rührt ~, dass ...** that is because ... CONJ (= *deshalb*) that is why; **~ die Verspätung** that's what is causing the delay, hence the delay

da|her-: da|her+brin|gen VT *sep irreg* (*Aus*) to produce, to bring along; **da|her+flie|gen** VI *sep irreg aux sein* to fly along; **da|her|ge|lau|fen** ADJ **jeder Dahergelaufene**, **jeder ~e Kerl** any Tom, Dick or Harry, any guy who comes/came along; **diese ~en Kerle in der Politik** these self-important nobodies in politics; **sie hat so einen ~en Kerl geheiratet** she married some fellow who just happened along (*inf*) → *auch* **daherlaufen; da|her+kom|men** VI *sep irreg aux sein* to come along; **da kommt so einer daher ...** he comes along ... (*inf*); **wie kann man nur so geschminkt/schlampig ~?** (*inf*) how can anybody go around with make-up like that/looking so scruffy?; **da|her+lau|fen** VI *sep irreg aux sein (gehen)* to walk up; (*laufen*) to run up; **dahergelaufen kommen** to come running up → *auch* **dahergelaufen; da|her+re|den** *sep* VI to talk away; **red doch nicht so (dumm) daher!** don't talk such rubbish (*Brit inf*) or

nonsense! VT to say without thinking; **was er alles/für ein blödes Zeug daherredet** the things/the rubbish (*inf*) or nonsense he comes out with! (*inf*); **das war nur so dahergeredet** I/he *etc* just said that; **da|her+sa|gen** VT *sep* to say without thinking

da|he|rum [ˈdaːherʊm] ADV (a)round there

da|hin [daˈhɪn, (*emph*) ˈdaːhɪn] ADV **a** (*räumlich*) there; (= *hierhin*) here; **kommst du auch ~?** are you coming too?; **~ und dorthin blicken** to look here and there; **~ gehe ich nie wieder, da gehe ich nie wieder hin** (*inf*) I'm never going there again; **bis ~** as far as there, up to that point; **ist es noch weit bis ~?** is it still a long way?; **bis ~ dauert es noch zwei Stunden** it'll take us another two hours to get there; **es steht mir bis ~** I've had it up to here (*inf*) **b** (*fig*: = *so weit*) **~ kommen** to come to that, to reach such a pass; **es ist ~ gekommen, dass ...** things have got to the stage where ..., things have reached such a pass that ...; **du wirst es ~ bringen, dass ...** you'll bring things to such a pass that ... **c** (= *in dem Sinne, in die Richtung*) **er äußerte sich ~ gehend, dass ...** he said something to the effect that ...; **eine ~ gehende Aussage/Änderung** *etc* a statement/change *etc* to that effect; **ein ~ gehender Befehl, dass ...** an order to the effect that ...; **wir sind ~ gehend verblieben, dass ...** we agreed that ...; **er hat den Bericht ~ (gehend) interpretiert, dass ...** he interpreted the report as saying ...; **wir haben uns ~ geeinigt/abgesprochen, dass ...** we have agreed that ...; **alle meine Hoffnungen/Bemühungen gehen ~, dass ich dieses Ziel bald erreiche** all my hopes/efforts are directed toward(s) (my) reaching this goal soon; **seine Meinung geht ~, dass ...** he tends to feel that ..., he tends to the opinion that ... **d** (*zeitlich*) then → **bis**²

ADJ *pred* **~ sein** to have gone; **sein Leben** or **er ist ~** (*geh*) his life is over; **das Auto ist ~** (*hum inf*) the car has had it (*inf*)

da-: da|hi|nab [dahɪˈnap] ADV = **dorthinab; da|hi|nauf** [dahɪˈnauf] ADV = **dorthinauf; da|hi|naus** [dahɪˈnaus] ADV there; *transportieren, bringen* out that way; **muss der Dieb entkommen sein** that must be where the thief escaped; **~ will er also!** (*fig*) so that's what he's getting at!

da|hin-: da|hin+be|we|gen *ptp* **dahinbewegt** VR *sep* to move on one's way; (*Fluss*) to flow on its way; **da|hin+däm|mern** VI *sep aux sein* to lie/sit there in a stupor; **da|hin+ei|len** VI *sep aux sein (liter)* to hurry along; (*Zeit*) to pass swiftly

da|hi|nein [dahɪˈnain] ADV = **dorthinein**

da|hin-: da|hin+fah|ren VI *sep irreg aux sein* (*liter*: = *sterben*) to pass away or over; **da|hin+flie|gen** VI *sep irreg aux sein* (*liter*) (= *wegfliegen*) to fly off; (*fig*: = *schnell fahren, vergehen*) to fly along or past; **da|hin+ge|ben** VT *sep irreg* (*liter*) *Leben, Gut, Besitz* to give up; **Da|hin|ge|gan|ge|ne(r)** [-ɡəɡaŋənə] MF *decl as adj* (*liter*) departed

da|hin|ge|gen [dahɪnˈɡeːɡn] ADV on the other hand

da|hin-: da|hin+ge|hen VI *sep irreg aux sein* (*geh*) **a** (= *vergehen: Zeit, Jahre*) to pass (*jdm for sb*) **b** (= *vorbeigehen, entlanggehen*) to pass **c** (= *sterben*) to pass away or on; **Da|hin|ge|schie|de|ne(r)** [-ɡəʃiːdənə] MF *decl as adj* (*liter*) departed

da|hin|ge|stellt ADJ **~ sein lassen, ob ...** to leave it open whether ...; **es bleibt** or **sei ~, ob ...** it is an open question whether ...

da|hin+le|ben VI *sep* to exist, to vegetate (*pej*)

da|hin+raf|fen VT *sep* (*liter*) to carry off

da|hin+re|den VI *sep* to say the first thing that comes into one's head

da|hin+sa|gen VT *sep* to say without (really) thinking; **das war nur so dahingesagt** I/he *etc* just said that (without thinking)

da|hin+schei|den VI *sep irreg aux sein (geh)* to pass away

da|hin+schlep|pen VR *sep* (*lit*: = *sich fortbewegen*) to drag oneself along; (*fig*: *Verhandlungen, Zeit*) to drag on

da|hin+schwin|den VI *sep irreg aux sein (geh)* (*Vorräte, Geld, Kraft*) to dwindle (away); (*Interesse, Gefühle etc*) to dwindle; (= *vergehen: Zeit*) to go past

da|hin+sie|chen VI *sep aux sein (geh)* to waste away; **vor Kummer ~** to pine away; **jahrelang siechte er in einem dunklen Keller dahin** for years he languished in a dark cellar

da|hin+ste|hen VI *sep irreg* to be debatable

da|hin|ten [daˈhɪntn, (*emph*) ˈdaːhɪntn] ADV over there; (*hinter Sprecher*) back there; **ganz weit ~** right or way (*inf*) over there

da|hin|ter [daˈhɪntɐ, (*emph*) ˈdaːhɪntɐ] ADV **a** (*räumlich*) behind (it/that/him *etc*); **was sich wohl ~ verbirgt?** (*lit, fig*) I wonder what's behind that?; **da ist schon etwas ~** (*fig*) there's something in that; **da ist nichts ~** (*fig*) there's nothing behind it **b** (= *danach*) beyond

da|hin|ter|her [dahɪntɐˈheːɐ] ADJ **~ sein** (*inf*) to push (*dass* to see that); **die Polizei ist ~, die Jugendkriminalität einzudämmen** the police are pretty hot on keeping juvenile delinquency under control (*inf*)

da|hin|ter: da|hin|ter klem|men ▲, **da|hin|ter knien** ▲ VR (*inf*) to put one's back into it, to get or pull one's finger out (*inf*); **klemm** or **knie dich mal ein bisschen dahinter** make a bit of an effort; **da|hin|ter kom|men** ▲ VI *irreg aux sein* (*inf*) to find out; (= *langsam verstehen*) to get it (*inf*); **da|hin|ter set|zen** ▲ VR = **dahinter klemmen; da|hin|ter ste|cken** ▲ VI (*inf*) to be behind it/that; **da steckt doch etwas dahinter** there's something behind it; **da steckt doch etwas dahinter, dass er jetzt gehen will** there's something behind his or him wanting to go now; **da werden die Eltern ~, dass er nicht mehr kommen will** his parents must be behind his or him not wanting to come any more; **er redet viel, es steckt aber nichts dahinter** he talks a lot but there's nothing behind it; **da|hin|ter ste|hen** ▲ VI **a** (= *unterstützen*) to back it/that, to be behind it/that **b** (= *zugrunde liegen*) to underlie it/that

da|hi|nun|ter [dahɪˈnʊntɐ, (*emph*) ˈdaːhɪnʊntɐ] ADV = **dorthinunter**

da|hin+ve|ge|tie|ren *ptp* **dahinvegetiert** VI *sep* to vegetate

Dah|lie [ˈdaːliə] F *-, -n* dahlia

DAK [deːʔaːˈkaː] F *- abbr von* **Deutsche Angestellten-Krankenkasse** German Employees' Health Insurance

Da|ka|po [daˈkaːpo] NT *-s, -s* encore

Da|ka|po|ruf M call for an encore

dak|ty|lisch [dakˈtyːlɪʃ] ADJ (*Poet*) dactylic

Dak|ty|lo- [daktylo-]: **Dak|ty|lo|gra|fie** ▲ [-ɡraˈfiː] F *-, -n* [-ˈfiːən] (*Sw*) typing; **Dak|ty|lo|gramm** [-ˈɡram] NT *pl* **-gramme** (*von einem Finger*) fingerprint; (*von ganzer Hand*) fingerprints *pl*; **Dak|ty|lo|sko|pie** [-skoˈpiː] F *-, -n* [-ˈpiːən] fingerprinting

Dak|ty|lus [ˈdaktylʊs] M *-, Daktylen* [-lən] (*Poet*) dactyl

Da|lai-La|ma [ˈdaːlaiˈlaːma] M *-(s), -s* (*Rel*) Dalai Lama

da-: da|las|sen VT *sep irreg* to leave (here/there); **da+lie|gen** VI *sep irreg* to lie there; **... sonst liegst du nachher da mit einer schweren Grippe** (*inf*) ... otherwise you'll be in bed with a bad dose of (the) flu

Dalk [dalk] M *-(e)s, -e* (*Aus inf*) (= *Dummkopf*) fathead (*Brit inf*), blockhead (*inf*); (= *ungeschickter Mensch*) clumsy oaf (*inf*)

dal|ke(r)t ['dalkət, 'dalkɛt] ADJ *(Aus inf)* daft *(inf)*

dal|li ['dali] ADV *(inf)* ~, ~! on the double! *(inf)*, look smart! *(inf)*; **mach ein bisschen ~!** get a move on! *(inf)*; **verzieh dich, aber ~!** beat it, go on, quick!

Dal|ma|ti|en [dal'ma:tsiən] NT **-s** Dalmatia

Dal|ma|ti|ner [dalma'ti:nɐ] M **-s, -** *(Hund)* dalmatian

da|ma|lig ['da:ma:lɪç] ADJ *attr* at that *or* the time; *Inhaber eines Amtes auch* then *attr*; *Sitten auch* in those days

da|mals ['da:ma:ls] ADV at that time, then; **seit ~** since then, since that time; **von ~** of that time; **~, als ...** at the time when ...; **wenn ich daran denke, was ~ war** when I think of that time, when I think of what things were like then

Da|mas|kus [da'maskʊs] NT **-** Damascus

Da|mast [da'mast] M **-(e)s, -e** damask

da|mas|ten [da'mastn] ADJ *attr (liter)* damask

Da|mas|ze|ner|klin|ge [damas'tse:nɐ-] F damascene sword

Dam|bock ['dam-] M fallow deer

Däm|chen ['dɛ:mçən] NT **-s, -** *(pej)* precocious young madam; *(= Dirne)* tart *(Brit inf)*, floozy *(inf)*

Da|me ['da:mə] F **-, -n** **a** lady; **sehr verehrte** *(form) or* **meine ~n und Herren!** ladies and gentlemen!; **guten Abend, die ~n** *(old, hum)* good evening, ladies; **„Damen"** *(= Toilette)* "Ladies"; **die ~ wünscht?** *(old)* can I be of assistance, madam? *(form)*; **ganz ~ sein** to be the perfect lady, to be every inch a lady
b *(allgemein gesehen: = Tanzpartnerin, Begleiterin)* lady; *(auf einen bestimmten Herrn bezogen)* partner; *(bei Cocktailparty, Theaterbesuch etc)* (lady) companion; **seine ~ ist eben mit einem anderen weggegangen** the lady he came with has just left with someone else; **bringen Sie ruhig Ihre ~n mit** do by all means bring your wives and girlfriends
c *(Sport)* woman, lady; **Hundert-Meter-Staffel der ~n** women's *or* ladies' hundred metre *(Brit) or* meter *(US)* relay
d *(Spiel)* draughts *sing (Brit)*, checkers *sing (US)*; *(= Doppelstein)* king

Da|me|brett NT draughtboard *(Brit)*, checkerboard *(US)*

Da|men- *in cpds* ladies'; **Da|men|bart** M facial hair; **Da|men|be|glei|tung** F ~ **erwünscht** please bring a lady *or (bei Ball)* partner; **in ~** in the company of a lady; **Da|men|be|kannt|-schaft** F female acquaintance *(inf)*; **eine ~ machen** to make the acquaintance of a lady; **Da|men|be|such** M lady visitor/visitors; **Da|men|bin|de** F sanitary towel *or* napkin *(US)*; **Da|men|dop|pel** NT *(Tennis etc)* ladies' doubles *sing*; **Da|men|ein|zel** NT *(Tennis etc)* ladies' singles *sing*; **Da|men|fahr|rad** NT ladies' bicycle *or* bike *(inf)*; **Da|men|fri|seur** M, **Da|men|fri|seu|rin** F ladies' hairdresser; *(= Geschäft)* ladies' hairdresser's, beauty salon *(US)*; **Da|men|fuß|ball** M women's football *(esp Brit) or* soccer; **Da|men|ge|sell|schaft** F **a** *no pl (= Begleitung von Dame)* company of ladies /a lady **b** *(= gesellige Runde)* ladies' gathering; **Da|men|grö|ße** F *(= Konfektionsgröße)* ladies' size; **da|men|haft** ADJ ladylike *no adv* ADV *sich benehmen, sich kleiden* in a ladylike way; **Da|men|kon|fek|ti|on** F ladies' wear (department); **Da|men|man|gel** M shortage of ladies; **Da|men|ober|be|klei|dung** F ladies' wear; **Da|men|rad** NT ladies' bicycle *or* bike *(inf)*; **Da|men|sat|tel** M side-saddle; **im ~ reiten** to ride side-saddle; **Da|men|schnei|der(in)** M(F) dressmaker; **Da|men|schnei|de|rei** F **a** dressmaking **b** *(= Werkstatt)* dressmaker's; **Da|men|sitz** M side-saddle style of riding; **im ~** side-saddle; **Da|men|toi|let|te** F **a** *(= WC)* ladies, ladies' toilet *or* restroom *(US)* **b** *(= Kleidung)* ladies' toilette; **Da|men|un|ter|wä|sche**

F ladies' underwear, lingerie; **Da|men|wahl** F ladies' choice; **Da|men|welt** F *, no pl (dated hum)* ladies *pl*; **in *or* bei der ~ beliebt** popular with the ladies

Da|me-: Da|me|spiel NT draughts *sing (Brit)*, checkers *sing (US)*; **Da|me|stein** M draughtsman *(Brit)*, checker *(US)*

Dam|hirsch ['dam-] M fallow deer

da|misch ['da:mɪʃ] *(S Ger, Aus)* ADJ **a** *(= dämlich)* daft *(inf)* **b** *(pred: = schwindelig)* dizzy, giddy ADV *(= sehr)* terribly *(inf)*

da|mit [da'mɪt, *emph* 'da:mɪt] ADV → *auch* **mit**, *vbs* +**mit** **a** *(= mit diesem Gegenstand, dieser Tätigkeit, mit Hilfe davon)* with it/that; **sie hatte zwei Koffer und stand ~ am Bahnhof** she had two (suit)cases and was standing there with them in the station; **sie hat Ärger mit der Waschmaschine – ~ habe ich auch Probleme** she's having trouble with her washing machine – I've got problems with mine too; **was will er ~?** what does he want that for?, what does he want with that?; **was soll ich ~?** what am I meant to do with that?; **ist Ihre Frage ~ beantwortet?** does that answer your question?; **~ kann er mich ärgern** I get really annoyed when he does that
b *(= mit, in dieser Angelegenheit)* **meint er mich ~?** does he mean me?; **weißt du, was er ~ meint?** do you know what he means by that?; **was ist ~?** what about it?; **wie wäre es ~?** how about it?; **er konnte mir nicht sagen, was es ~ auf sich hat** he couldn't tell me what it was all about; **wie sieht es ~ aus?** what's happening about *or* with *(esp US)* it?; **muss er denn immer wieder ~ ankommen?** *(= davon reden)* must he keep on about it?; *(mit Bitten, Forderungen etc)* must he keep coming back about it?; **das/er hat gar nichts ~ zu tun** that/he has nothing to do with it; **~ ist nichts** *(inf)* it's no go *(inf)*; **hör auf ~!** *(inf)* lay off! *(inf)*; **~ hat es noch Zeit** there's no hurry for that
c *(bei Verben)* → *vb* +**mit** **was willst du ~ sagen?** what's that supposed *or* meant to mean?; **~ will ich nicht sagen, dass ...** I don't mean to say that ...; **sind Sie ~ einverstanden?** do you agree to that?; **er hatte nicht ~ gerechnet** he hadn't reckoned on *or* with that; **~, dass du dich jetzt aufregst, machst du den Schaden auch nicht wieder gut** you're not making anything better by getting excited; **sie fangen schon ~ an** they're already starting on it; **sie fangen schon ~ an, das Haus abzureißen** they're already starting to pull down the house; **~ fing der Streit an** the argument started with that; **der Streit fing ~ an, dass er behauptete ...** the argument started when he said ...; **er fing ~ an, dass er ... sagte** he began by saying that ...
d *(bei Befehlen)* **with it; weg/heraus ~!** away/out with it!; **her ~!** give it here! *(inf)*; **Schluss *or* genug ~!** that's enough (of that)!
e *(begründend)* therefore; **er verlor den zweiten Satz und ~ das Spiel** he lost the second set and therefore the match; **~ ist es klar, dass es war** from that it's clear that it was he *(form) or* him
f *(= daraufhin, dann, jetzt)* with that; **schließe ich für heute** I'll close with that for today; **~ kommen wir zum Ende des Programms** that brings us to the end of our programmes *(Brit) or* programs *(US)*
CONJ so that; **~ er nicht fällt** so that he does not fall, lest he (should) fall *(old)*

däm|lich ['dɛ:mlɪç] *(inf)* ADJ stupid, dumb *(inf)* ADV stupidly; **guck nicht so ~** don't give me that dumb look *(inf)*; **komm mir nicht so ~!** don't give me that! *(inf)*, don't come that with me! *(Brit inf)*; **er ist mir vielleicht ~ gekommen** he acted really dumb *(inf) or* stupid; **fragen** to ask stupid *or* dumb *(inf)* questions/a stupid *or* dumb *(inf)* question

Däm|lich|keit F **-, -en** **a** *no pl* stupidity, dumbness *(inf)* **b** *(= dumme Handlung)* stupid *or* dumb *(inf)* thing

Damm [dam] M **-(e)s, ⸚e** ['dɛmə] **a** *(= Deich)* dyke *(Brit)*, dike *(esp US)*; *(= Staudamm)* dam; *(= Hafendamm)* wall; *(= Uferdamm)* embankment, levee *(esp US)*; *(= Verkehrsverbindung zu Insel)* causeway; *(fig)* barrier; **einen ~ gegen etw aufbauen** *(fig)* einer Sache *(dat)* einen ~ **(entgegen)setzen** *(fig)* to check sth; **wenn wir das kleinste bisschen nachgeben, werden alle Dämme brechen** if we give way at all, the floodgates will open
b *(= Bahndamm, Straßendamm)* embankment
c *(dial: = Fahrdamm)* road
d *(Anat)* perineum
e *(fig inf)* **wieder auf dem ~ sein** to be back to normal; **geistig auf dem ~ sein** to be with it *(inf)*; **nicht recht auf dem ~ sein** not to be up to the mark *(inf)*

Damm|bruch M breach in a/the dyke *(Brit) or* dike *(esp US) etc*

däm|men ['dɛmən] VT **a** *(Tech) Wärme* to keep in; *Schall* to absorb **b** *(fig: = eindämmen) Abfallflut, Überfluss* to contain

Däm|mer ['dɛmɐ] M **-s, *no pl* a** *(poet)* = **Dämmerung b** *(fig geh)* nebulousness

däm|me|rungs|ak|tiv ADJ *(Zool)* twilight-active, active at twilight *pred*

däm|mer|haft ADJ *(liter)* hazy, nebulous

däm|me|rig ['dɛmərɪç] ADJ *Licht* dim, faint; *Zimmer* gloomy; *Stunden* twilight *attr*; **es wird ~** *(abends)* dusk is falling; *(morgens)* dawn is breaking

Däm|mer|licht NT twilight; *(abends auch)* dusk; *(= Halbdunkel)* half-light, gloom

däm|mern ['dɛmɐn] VI **a** *(Tag, Morgen)* to dawn; *(Abend)* to fall; **als der Tag *or* Morgen/Abend dämmerte ...** as dawn was breaking/dusk was falling ...; **die Erkenntnis *or* es dämmerte ihm, dass ...** *(inf)* he began to realize that ... **b** *(= im Halbschlaf sein)* to doze; *(Kranker)* to be dopey; **vor sich hin ~** *(= im Halbschlaf sein)* to doze; *(= nicht bei klarem Verstand sein)* to be dopey VI *impers* **es dämmert** *(morgens)* dawn is breaking; *(abends)* dusk is falling; **jetzt dämmerts (bei) mir!** *(inf)* now it's dawning (on me)!

Däm|mer-: Däm|mer|schein M *(liter)* glow; **Däm|mer|schlaf** M doze; **ich war nur im ~** I was only dozing; **Däm|mer|schop|pen** M early evening drink; **Däm|mer|stun|de** F twilight, dusk

Däm|me|rung ['dɛmərʊŋ] F **-, -en** twilight; *(= Abenddämmerung auch)* dusk; *(= Morgendämmerung auch)* dawn; *(= Halbdunkel)* half-light; **bei *or* mit Anbruch der ~** when dusk began/begins to fall; **when dawn began/begins to break; **in der ~** at dusk/dawn

Däm|mer|zu|stand M *(= Halbschlaf)* dozy state; *(= Bewusstseinstrübung)* dopey state

Dämm-: Dämm|ma|te|ri|al NT *(Build, Tech)* insulating *or* insulation material; **Dämm|plat|te** F *(Build, Tech)* insulating board, softboard

dämm|rig ['dɛmrɪç] ADJ = **dämmerig**

Damm-: Damm|riss ▲ M *(Med)* tear of the perineum; **Damm|rutsch** M landslide which destroys a dyke *etc*; **Damm|schnitt** M *(Med)* episiotomy

Dämm|stof|fe PL insulating materials *pl*

Dämm|mung ['dɛmʊŋ] F **-, -en** insulation

Damm|weg M causeway

Dam|num ['damnʊm] NT **-s, Damna** [-na] *(Fin)* debt discount

Da|mok|les|schwert ['da:mɔklɛs-] NT *(lit, fig)* sword of Damocles

Dä|mon ['dɛ:mɔn] M **-s, Dämonen** [dɛ'mo:nən] demon; **ein böser ~** an evil spirit, a demon

Dä|mo|nie [dɛmo'ni:] F **-, -n** [-'ni:ən] demonic nature

dä|mo|nisch [dɛ'mo:nɪʃ] ADJ demonic ADV demonically

dä|mo|ni|sie|ren [dɛmoni'zi:rən] *ptp* **dämonisiert** VT to demonize

Dä|mo|nis|mus [dɛmoˈnɪsmʊs] M **-**, *no pl* (*Rel*) demonism

Dampf [dampf] M **-(e)s, ∸e** [ˈdɛmpfə] **a** vapour (*Brit*), vapor (*US*); (= *Wasserdampf*) steam; **~ ablassen** or **abblasen** (*lit, fig*) to let off steam; **unter ~ sein** or **stehen** to have (its) steam up; **aus dem Schornstein quoll der ~ in weißen Wolken** clouds of white smoke poured from the chimney **b** (*inf:* = *Wucht, Schwung*) force; **jdm ~ machen** (*inf*) to make sb get a move on (*inf*); **~ dahinter machen** or **setzen** to get a move on (*inf*); **mit ~** (*inf*) at full tilt; **vorm Chef hat sie unheimlich ~** the boss really puts the wind up her (*inf*); **~ drauf haben** (*dated inf*) to be going at full steam

Dampf- *in cpds* steam; **Dampf|an|trieb** M steam drive; **Maschine mit ~** steam-driven engine; **Dampf|bad** NT steam bath; **Dampf|boot** NT steamboat; **Dampf|bü|gel|ei|sen** NT steam iron; **Dampf|druck** M *pl* **-drücke** steam pressure

damp|fen [ˈdampfn] VI **a** (= *Dampf abgeben*) to steam; (*Badezimmer etc*) to be full of steam; (*Pferd*) to be in a lather; **ein ~des Bad/Essen** a steaming hot bath/meal **b** *aux sein* (*Zug, Schiff*) to steam **c** *aux sein* (*inf*) (= *mit Dampfer fahren*) to sail, to steam; (= *mit Zug fahren*) to go by (steam) train

dämp|fen [ˈdɛmpfn] VT **a** (= *abschwächen*) to muffle; *Geräusch, Lärm, Schall auch* to deaden, to dampen; *Geige, Trompete, Farbe* to mute; *Licht, Stimme* to lower; *Wut* to calm; *Freude, Begeisterung, Stimmung* to dampen; *Aufprall* to deaden; (*fig*) *jdn* to subdue; *Konjunktur* to depress → *auch* **gedämpft** **b** (*Cook*) to steam **c** (= *bügeln*) to press with a damp cloth; (*mit Dampfbügeleisen*) to press with a steam iron

Damp|fer [ˈdampfɐ] M **-s, -** steamer, steamship; **auf dem falschen ~ sein** or **sitzen** (*fig inf*) to have got the wrong idea

Dämp|fer [ˈdɛmpfɐ] M **-s, -** **a** (*Mus: bei Klavier*) damper; (*bei Geige, Trompete*) mute; **dadurch hat er/sein Optimismus einen ~ bekommen** that dampened his spirits/optimism; **jdm einen ~ aufsetzen** to dampen sb's spirits; **einer Sache** (*dat*) **einen ~ aufsetzen** (*inf*) to put a damper on sth (*inf*) **b** (*Cook:* = *Dampfkochtopf*) steamer

Dampf|er-: **Dampf|fer|an|le|ge|stel|le** F steamer jetty; **Dampf|fer|fahrt** F boat trip; **Dampf|fer|li|nie** F steamship line

Dampf-: **dampf|för|mig** ADJ vaporous; **Dampf|ham|mer** M steam hammer; **Dampf|hei|zung** F steam heating

damp|fig [ˈdampfɪç] ADJ steamy

dämp|fig [ˈdɛmpfɪç] ADJ **a** (*Vet*) broken-winded **b** (*dial:* = *schwül*) muggy

Dampf-: **Dampf|kes|sel** M (*Tech*) steam-boiler; (*Cook*) steamer; **Dampf|ko|cher** M , **Dampf|koch|topf** M pressure cooker; **Dampf|kraft** F steam power; **Dampf|kraft|werk** NT steam power station; **Dampf|lo|ko|mo|ti|ve** F , **Dampf|lok** F (*inf*) steam engine or locomotive; **Dampf|ma|schi|ne** F steam (-driven) engine; **Dampf|nu|del** F (*Cook*) *sweet yeast dumpling cooked in milk and sugar* **aufgehen wie eine ~** (*fig inf*) to blow up like a balloon (*inf*); **Dampf|pfei|fe** F steam whistle; (*von Schiff*) siren; **Dampf|ram|me** F steam-operated pile driver; **Dampf|rei|ni|ger** M (*für Teppiche etc*) steam cleaner; **Dampf|schiff** NT steamship, steamer; **Dampf|schiff|fahrt** ▲ F steam navigation; **Dampf|schiff|fahrt|ge|sell|schaft** ▲ F steamship company; **Dampf|strahl|rei|ni|ger** M (*für Steinböden, Fliesen etc*) steam cleaner; **Dampf|tur|bi|ne** F steam turbine

Dämp|fung [ˈdɛmpfʊŋ] F **-, -en** (*Mus*) damping; (*Phys, Rad, TV*) attenuation

Dampf|wal|ze F steamroller

Dam|wild [ˈdam-] NT fallow deer

da|nach [daˈnaːx, (*emph*) ˈdaːnaːx] ADV **a** (*zeitlich*) after that/it; (= *nachher auch*) afterwards,

after (*inf*); **ich habe einen Whisky getrunken, ~ fühlte ich mich schon besser** I had a whisky and after that or afterwards felt better, I had a whisky and felt better after that or afterwards or after (*inf*); **ich las das Buch zu Ende, erst ~ konnte ich einschlafen** only when I had finished reading the book could I get to sleep; **zehn Minuten ~ war sie schon wieder da** ten minutes later she was back; **um die Zwanziger ~** around the twenties and after **b** (*in der Reihenfolge*) (*örtlich*) behind that/it/him/them *etc*; (*zeitlich*) after that/it/him/them *etc*; **als erster ging der Engländer durchs Ziel und gleich ~ der Russe** The Englishman finished first, immediately followed by the Russian or and the Russian immediately after him; **bei ihm kommt als erstes die Arbeit, ~ lange nichts und dann das Privatleben** work comes first with him, and then, a long, long way behind, his private life **c** (= *dementsprechend*) accordingly; (= *laut diesem*) according to that; (= *im Einklang damit*) in accordance with that/it; **wir haben hier einen Bericht, ~ war die Stimmung damals ganz anders** we have a report here, according to which the atmosphere at the time was quite different; **~ sein** (*Wetter, Bedingungen, Stimmung etc*) to be right; **sie hat den Aufsatz in zehn Minuten geschrieben – ~ ist er auch** (*inf*) she wrote the essay in ten minutes – it looks like it too; **sie sieht auch/nicht ~ aus** she looks/doesn't look it; (= *als ob sie so was getan hätte*) she looks/doesn't look the type; **~ siehst du gerade aus** (*iro*) I can just see that (*iro*); **lesen Sie Paragraph 218;** ~ **ist es verboten** read paragraph 218, under that it is illegal; **~ zu urteilen** judging by or from that; **mir war nicht ~** (*inf*) or **zumute** or **zu Mute** I didn't feel like it; **mir steht der Sinn nicht ~** (*geh*) I don't feel inclined to **d** (*in bestimmte Richtung*) toward(s) it; **er griff schnell ~** he grabbed at it, he made a grab for it; **hinter ihm war etwas, aber er hat sich nicht ~ umgesehen** there was something behind him, but he didn't look round (*Brit*) or around to see what it was **e** (*in Verbindung mit n, vb etc siehe auch dort*) **sie sehnte sich ~** she longed for that/it; **sie sehnte sich ~, ihren Sohn wiederzusehen** she longed to see her son again; **er hatte großes Verlangen ~** he felt a great desire for it; **er hatte großes Verlangen ~, wieder einmal die Heimat zu sehen** he felt a great desire to see his home again; **~ kann man nicht gehen** you can't go by that; **wenn es ~ ginge, was ich sage/was mir Spaß macht, dann ...** if it were a matter of what I say/enjoy then ...; **sich ~ erkundigen, ob ...** to inquire whether ...

Da|na|er|ge|schenk [ˈdaːnaɐ-] NT (*fig*) two--edged gift

Dan|dy [ˈdɛndi] M **-s, -s** dandy

dan|dy|haft [ˈdɛndihaft] ADJ (*pej*) dandyish

Dä|ne [ˈdɛːnə] M **-n, -n** Dane, Danish man/boy

da|ne|ben [daˈneːbn, (*emph*) ˈdaːneːbn] ADV **a** (*räumlich*) (= *in unmittelbarer Nähe von jdm/etw*) next to him/her/that/it *etc*; (*zum Vergleich*) beside him/her/that/it *etc*; **links/rechts ~** (*neben Sache*) to the left/right of it; (*neben Mensch*) to his/her *etc* left/right; **ich stand direkt ~, als die Bombe losging** the bomb went off right next to me; **wir wohnen im Haus ~** we live in the house next door **b** (= *verglichen damit*) compared with that/it/him/them *etc*, in comparison **c** (= *außerdem*) besides that, as well as that, in addition (to that); (= *gleichzeitig*) at the same time

da|ne|ben-: **da|ne|ben+be|neh|men** *ptp* **danebenbenommen** VR *sep irreg* (*inf*) to make an exhibition of oneself; **da|ne|ben+fal|len** VI *sep irreg aux sein* to miss (it or one's mark); **da|ne|ben+ge|hen** VI *sep irreg aux sein* **a** (= *verfehlen: Schuss etc*) to miss **b** (*inf:* = *scheitern*) to go wrong; (*Witz*) to fall flat; **da|ne|ben+ge|ra|ten** *ptp* **danebengeraten** VI *sep irreg aux sein* to go

wrong; (*Übersetzung*) not to hit the mark; **da|ne|ben+grei|fen** VI *sep irreg* **a** (= *verfehlen*) (*auf dem Klavier etc*) to play a wrong note/ some wrong notes; (*beim Fangen*) to miss (the mark), to be wide of the mark **b** (*fig inf, mit Schätzung, Prognose etc*) to be wide of the mark, to be way out (*inf*); **im Ton ~** to strike the wrong note; **im Ausdruck ~** to put things the wrong way; **mit seiner Bemerkung hat er aber ganz schön danebengegriffen** he really put his foot in it with that remark (*inf*); **da|ne|ben+hal|ten** *sep irreg* VT jdn/etw ~ to compare him/her/it *etc* with sb/sth VI (= *danebenzielen*) to aim to miss; **da|ne|ben+hau|en** VI *sep irreg* **a** (*beim Schlagen*) to miss; (*beim Klavierspielen*) to play a wrong note/some wrong notes **b** (*inf:* = *sich irren*) to miss the mark, to be wide of the mark; (*beim Berechnen, Raten, Schätzen auch*) to be way out (*inf*); **da|ne|ben+lie|gen** VI *sep irreg* (*inf:* = *sich irren*) to be quite wrong, to be way out (*inf*); **da|ne|ben+ra|ten** VI *sep irreg* (*inf*) to guess wrong; **da|ne|ben+schie|ßen** VI *sep irreg* **a** (= *verfehlen*) to miss **b** (= *absichtlich vorbeischießen*) to shoot to miss; **da|ne|ben+schla|gen** VI *sep irreg* to miss; **da|ne|ben sein** ▲ VI *irreg aux sein* (*inf*) **a** (= *verwirrt sein*) to be completely confused; (= *sich nicht wohl fühlen*) not to feel up to it (*inf*) **b** (= *unangebracht sein*) to be out of order (*inf*); **da|ne|ben+tip|pen** VI *sep* (*inf*) to guess wrong; **da|ne|ben+tref|fen** VI *sep irreg* to miss; **da|ne|ben+zie|len** VI *sep* to aim to miss

Dä|ne|mark [ˈdɛːnəmark] NT **-s** Denmark

da|nie|den [daˈniːdn] ADV (*obs*) down below; **~ auf Erden** on earth below

da|nie|der+lie|gen VI *sep irreg* **a** (*old liter.:* = *krank sein*) to be laid low (*Brit*) or up (*inf*), to be ill **b** (*fig geh:* = *schwach sein*) to be depressed

Dä|nin [ˈdɛːnɪn] F **-, -nen** Dane, Danish woman/girl

dä|nisch [ˈdɛːnɪʃ] ADJ Danish

Dä|nisch(e) [ˈdɛːnɪʃ] NT Danish → *auch* **Deutsch(e)**

dank [daŋk] PREP *+gen* or *dat* thanks to

Dank [daŋk] ✪ 48.1, 49, 52.3 M **-(e)s**, *no pl* (*ausgedrückt*) thanks *pl*; (= *Gefühl der Dankbarkeit*) gratitude; **besten** or **herzlichen** or **schönen** or **vielen ~** many thanks, thank you very much, thanks a lot (*inf*); **tausend** or **herzlichen/tausend ~!** many/very many thanks!, thanks a million! (*inf*); **~ sei dem Herrn** (*Eccl*) thanks be to God; **haben Sie/hab ~!** (*geh*) thank you!; (*für Hilfe auch*) I'm much obliged to you; **jdm für etw ~ sagen** (*liter*) to express one's or give (*esp Eccl*) thanks to sb for sth; **~ sagen** (*Aus*) to express one's thanks; (*Eccl*) to give thanks; **jdm ~ schulden** (*form*) to owe sb a debt of gratitude; **jdm für etw ~ wissen** (*form*) to be indebted to sb for sth; **etw mit ~ annehmen** to accept sth with thanks; **mit bestem ~ zurück!** many thanks for lending it/them to me; (*iro:* = *Retourkutsche*) thank you, the same to you!; **das war ein schlechter ~** that was poor thanks; **das ist der (ganze) ~ dafür** that's all the thanks one gets; **als ~ für seine Dienste** in grateful recognition of his service; **zum ~ (dafür)** as a way of saying thank you; **das ist der ~ des Vaterlandes!** (*iro*) that's all the thanks one gets!; **der ~ des Vaterlandes ist dir gewiss** (*iro*) you'll get a medal for that

Dank|ad|res|se F official letter of thanks

dank|bar ✪ 29.1, 31, 46.5, 47.1, 47.5, 49 ADJ **a** (= *dankerfüllt*) grateful; (= *erleichtert, froh*) thankful; *Publikum, Zuhörer* appreciative; **jdm ~ sein** to be grateful to sb (*für* for); **sich ~ erweisen** or **zeigen** to show one's gratitude (*gegenüber* to); **ich wäre dir ~, wenn du ...** I would be grateful if you ..., I would appreciate it if you ... **b** (= *lohnend*) *Arbeit, Aufgabe, Rolle* rewarding; *Stoff* easy-care *attr*; (= *haltbar*) hard-wearing; *Opfer* worthwhile; **eine ~e Pflanze** a plant which doesn't need much attention **ADV** (= *voller Dank*) gratefully

Dank|bar|keit ['daŋkbaːɛkait] **۞** 49 F -, *no pl* gratitude (*gegen, gegenüber* to); (= *Gefühl der Erleichterung*) thankfulness

Dank|brief M thank-you letter

dan|ke ['daŋkə] **INTERJ** **a** thank you, thanks (*inf*), ta (*Brit inf*); (*ablehnend*) no thank you; **~ ja, ja, ~** yes please, yes, thank you; **~ nein, nein, ~** no thank you; **~ schön** *or* **sehr** thank you *or* thanks (*inf*) very much; **(zu jdm) (schön) sagen** to say thank you (to sb); **ich soll dir von meiner Schwester ~ schön sagen** my sister sends (you) her thanks; **~ vielmals** many thanks; (*iro*) thanks a million (*inf*); **~ der Nachfrage** (*form*) thank you for your concern; **wie gehts? – ~, ich kann nicht klagen** how's it going? – (I) can't complain; **soll ich helfen? – ~, ich glaube, ich komme allein zurecht** can I help? – thanks (all the same), but I think I can manage → *auch* **danken**

b (*inf*) **mir gehts ~** I'm OK (*inf*); **sonst gehts dir (wohl) ~!** (*iro*) are you feeling all right?

dan|ken ['daŋkn] **۞** 47.1, 47.2, 49 **VI** **a** (= *Dankbarkeit zeigen*) to express one's thanks; **jdm ~ to** thank sb (*für* for); **mit überschwänglichen Worten ~** to be effusive in one's thanks; **mit einem Strauß Blumen ~** to express one's thanks with a bunch of flowers; **ich danke dir für das Geschenk/die Gastfreundschaft** *etc* thank you for your *or* the present/your hospitality *etc*; **wir ~ für die Einladung** thank you for your *or* the invitation; **(ich) danke!** yes please; (*ablehnend*) no thank you, no thanks (*inf*); **(ich) danke bestens** (*iro*) thanks a million (*inf*), thanks for nothing (*inf*); **man dankt** (*inf*) thanks (*inf*), ta (*Brit inf*); **ich danke Ihnen (dafür), dass Sie mir den Betrag überwiesen haben** thank you for transferring the money (to me); **jdm ~ lassen** to send sb one's thanks; **bestellen Sie bitte Ihrem Vater, ich lasse herzlich ~** please give your father my thanks; **nichts zu ~** don't mention it, not at all (*Brit*), you're welcome; **dafür danke ich, für so was danke ich** (*iro*) not on your life!, not a chance! (*inf*); **na, ich danke** (*iro*) no thank you; **etw ~d annehmen/ablehnen** to accept/decline sth with thanks

b (= *ablehnen*) to decline

c (= *Gruß erwidern*) to return a/the greeting

VT **a** (*geh*: = *verdanken*) **jdm/einer Sache etw ~** to owe sth to sb/sth; **ihm danke ich es, dass ...** I owe it to him that ...; **nur dem rechtzeitigen Erscheinen der Polizei ist es zu ~, dass ...** it was only thanks to the prompt turnout of the police that ...

b **jdm etw ~** (= *jdm dankbar sein für*) to thank sb for sth; (= *jdm etw lohnen*) to repay sb for sth; **man wird es dir nicht ~** you won't be thanked for it; **man wird es nicht zu ~ wissen** it won't be appreciated; **sie werden es mir später einmal ~, dass ich das getan habe** they'll thank me for doing that one day; **all meine Hilfe wurde mir mit keinem Wort gedankt** I didn't get a single word of thanks for all my help; **man hat es mir schlecht gedankt, dass ich das getan habe** I got small thanks for doing it, I didn't get a lot of thanks for doing it; **wie kann ich Ihnen das jemals ~?** how can I ever thank you?

dan|kens|wert **ADJ** *Bemühung*, *Hingabe* commendable; *Hilfe* kind; (= *lohnenswert*) *Aufgabe*, *Arbeit* rewarding; **in ~er Weise** (= *löblich*) (most) commendably; (= *freundlicherweise*) very kindly

dan|kens|wer|ter|wei|se ['daŋknsvɛːɐtɐˈvaizə] **ADV** thankfully; **Herr Kopleck hat uns ~ informiert** Mr Kopleck was kind enough to inform us

dank|er|füllt [-ʔəfʏlt] **ADJ** (*liter*) grateful

Dan|kes- ['daŋkəs]: **Dan|kes|be|zei|gung** [-bətsaigʊŋ] F -, -en demonstration of one's gratitude *or* thanks; **Dan|kes|brief** M thank-you letter, letter of thanks

Dan|ke|schön **۞** 49 **NT** -s, *no pl* thank you

Dan|kes- ['daŋkəs]: **Dan|kes|re|de** F speech of thanks, words *pl* of thanks; **Dan|kes|wor|te** PL words *pl* of thanks; (*von Redner*) vote *sing* of thanks

Dank-: **Dank|ge|bet** NT prayer of thanksgiving; **Dank|got|tes|dienst** M service of thanksgiving; **Dank|op|fer** NT thanks offering; **dank|sa|gen** *pret* danksagte, *ptp* dankgesagt, *infin auch* danzusagen VI (*geh*) to express one's thanks (*jdm* to sb); (*Eccl*) to give thanks (*jdm* to sb); **Dank|sa|gung** ['daŋkzaːgʊŋ] F -, -en **a** (*Eccl*) thanksgiving **b** (= *Brief*) note of thanks; **Dank|schrei|ben** NT letter of thanks

dann [dan] **ADV** **a** (*Reihenfolge ausdrückend*, = *später*) then; **~ und ~** (a)round about then; **von ~ bis ~** for some time (a)round then; **~ und wann** now and then; **gerade ~, wenn ...** just when ...; **wenn das gemacht ist, ~ kannst du gehen** when that's done you can go; **noch eine Woche, ~ ist Weihnachten** another week till Christmas, another week and (then) it's Christmas → **bis²**

b (= *unter diesen Umständen*) then; **wenn ..., ~** if ..., (then); **wenn du was brauchst, ~ sagst dus mir, nicht?** just tell me if you need anything, if you need anything (then) just tell me; **ja, selbst ~** yes, even then; **nein, selbst ~ nicht** no, not even then; **selbst ~/selbst ~ nicht, wenn ...** even/not even if ...; **erst ~, wenn ...** only when ...; **ja, ~!** (oh) well then!; **ich habe keine Lust mehr – ~ hör doch auf!** I'm not in the mood any more – well stop then!; **und wie es ~ so geht** *or* **ist, kommt natürlich Besuch** and as was bound to happen, I got visitors, but you know how it is, I got visitors; **wenn er seine Gedichte selbst nicht versteht, wer ~?** if he can't understand his own poems, who else could (understand them)?; **wenn man nicht einmal in Schottland echten Whisky bekommt, wo ~?** if you can't get real whisky in Scotland, where *can* you expect to find it?; **wenn ich nicht einmal das Einmaleins bei euch voraussetzen kann, was ~?** if I can't even assume you know your (multiplication) tables, what can I assume you know?; **~ eben nicht** well, in that case (there's no more to be said); **~ erst recht nicht!** in that case no way (*inf*) *or* not a chance! (*inf*); **~ ist ja alles in Ordnung** (oh well,) everything's all right then, in that case everything's all right; **~ will ich lieber gehen** well, I'd better be getting along (then); **ja ~, auf Wiedersehen** well then, goodbye; **also ~ bis morgen** right then, see you tomorrow, see you tomorrow then

c (= *außerdem*) **~ ... noch** on top of that; **strohdumm und ~ auch noch frech** as thick as they come and cheeky into the bargain (*Brit*), as dumb as they come and a smart alec too (*esp US*); **kommandier mich herum und meint ~ auch noch ...** orders me around and then on top of that thinks ...

dan|nen ['danən] **ADV von ~** (*obs*: = *von woher*) thence (*old*), from thence (*Eccl*); (*liter*: = *weg*) away

dan|tesk [dan'tɛsk] **ADJ** Dantesque

dan|tisch ['dantɪʃ] **ADJ** Dantean

da|ran [da'ran, (*emph*) 'da:ran] **ADV** **a** (*räumlich*: = *an dieser Stelle, diesem Ort, Gegenstand*) on it/that; *schieben, lehnen, stellen* against it/that; *legen* next to it/that; *kleben, befestigen, machen, gehen* to it/that; *sich setzen* at it/that; **nahe** *or* **dicht ~** right up against it, up close against it; **nahe ~ sein** (*fig*) to be on the point of it, to be just about to; **nahe ~ sein, etw zu tun** to be on the point of doing sth, to be just about to do sth; **zu nahe ~** too close (to it); **~ vorbei** past it; **er hat dicht ~ vorbeigeschossen** his shot just missed it; **~ kommen** *or* **fassen/riechen/schlagen** to touch/smell/hit it/that; **er hielt seine Hand ~** he touched it with his hand; **die Kinder sind wieder ~ gewesen** (*inf*) the children have been at it again

b (*zeitlich*: = *danach anschließend*) **im Anschluss**

~, ~ anschließend following that/this; **im Anschluss ~ findet eine Diskussion statt** it/this/that will be followed by a discussion; **erst fand ein Vortrag statt, ~ schloss sich eine Diskussion** first there was a lecture which was followed by a discussion *or* and after that a discussion

c (*inf*) **er ist schlecht ~** (*gesundheitlich, finanziell*) he's in a bad way (*inf*); **er ist gut ~** (*gesundheitlich, finanziell*) he's OK (*inf*); **ich weiß nie, wie ich (bei ihm) ~ bin** I never know where I am with him; **sie sind sehr arm ~** (= *haben wenig Geld*) they're not at all well-off; (= *sind bedauernswert*) they are poor creatures

d (*in Verbindung mit* n, adj, vb *siehe auch dort*) arbeiten on it/that; *sterben, erinnern, Bedarf, Mangel* of it/that; *interessieren, sich beteiligen, arm, reich* in it/that; *sich klammern* to it/that; **sticken/bauen** to embroider/build it/that; **was macht der Aufsatz? – ich bin zur Zeit ~** how's the essay doing? – I'm (working) on it now; **er war ~ interessiert** he was interested in it; **er war ~ interessiert, es zu tun** he was interested in doing it; **ich zweifle nicht ~** I don't doubt it; **ich zweifle nicht ~, dass ...** I don't doubt that ...; **erinnere mich ~** remind me about *or* of that; **erinnere mich ~, dass ich das machen soll** remind me to do that, remind me that I must do that; **~ wird er zugrunde** *or* **zu Grunde gehen** that will be the ruin of him; **wir haben großen Anteil ~ genommen** we sympathized deeply; **wird sich etwas ~ ändern?** will that change at all?; **wir können nichts ~ machen** we can't do anything about it; **~ sieht man, wie ...** there you (can) see how ...; **Sie würden gut ~ tun, dieses Angebot anzunehmen** you would do well *or* would be well-advised to accept this offer; **das Beste/Schönste/Schlimmste** *etc* **~** the best/nicest/worst *etc* thing about it; **es ist kein wahres Wort ~** there isn't a word of truth in it, not a word of it is true; **es ist nichts ~** (= *ist nicht fundiert*) there's nothing in it; (= *ist nichts Besonderes*) it's nothing special → *auch* **dran**

da|ran-: **da|ran+ge|ben** VT *sep irreg* (*geh*) to sacrifice; **da|ran+ge|hen** VI *sep irreg aux sein* to set about it; **~ etw zu tun** to set about doing sth; **da|ran+ma|chen** VR *sep* (*inf*) to set about it; (= *endlich in Angriff nehmen*) to get down to it; **sich ~, etw zu tun** to set about doing sth; to get down to doing sth; **da|ran+set|zen** *sep* **VT** (= *einsetzen*) to exert; (= *aufs Spiel setzen*) to stake, to risk; **seine ganzen Kräfte ~, etw zu tun** to spare no effort to do sth; **sich ~** **VR** to sit down to it; **da|ran+wen|den** VT *sep irreg* (*geh*) to exert; **seine ganzen Kräfte ~, etw zu tun** to spare no effort to do sth

da|rauf [da'rauf, (*emph*) 'da:rauf] **ADV** **a** (*räumlich*: on it/that/them *etc*; (*in Richtung*) toward(s) it/that/them *etc*; *schießen, zielen, losfahren* at it/that/them *etc*; (*fig*) *fußen, basieren, aufbauen* on it/that; *zurückführen, beziehen* to it/that; **da er es nicht wagte herunterzuklettern, musste er ~ sitzen bleiben** since he didn't dare climb down he just had to sit (up) there; **er hielt den Nagel fest und schlug mit dem Hammer ~** he held the nail in place and hit it with the hammer; **seine Behauptungen stützen sich ~, dass der Mensch von Natur aus gut ist** his claims are based on the supposition that man is naturally good

b (*Reihenfolge: zeitlich, örtlich*) after that; **die Tage, die ~ folgten** the days which followed; **~ folgte ...** that was followed by ..., after that came ...; **~ folgend** after him/it/that *etc*; *Tag etc* following; *Wagen etc* behind *pred*; **zuerst kam der Wagen des Premiers, ~ folgten Polizisten** the prime minister's car came first, followed by policemen; **am Tag/Abend/Jahr ~** the next day/evening/year, the day/evening/year after (that)

c (= *infolgedessen*) because of that; **er hat gestohlen und wurde ~ von der Schule verwiesen** he was caught stealing and because of that was expelled

d (*als Reaktion*) *sagen, reagieren* to that; **~ antworten** to answer that; **eine Antwort ~** an answer to that; **er hat ein Gedicht ~ geschrieben**

that prompted him to write a poem; **~ wurde er ganz beschämt** that made him feel quite ashamed; **~ haben sich viele Interessenten gemeldet** a lot of people have shown an interest in it/that; **nimm die Marke, ~ bekommst du ein Essen in der Kantine** take this token, you'll get a meal in the canteen for or with it; **~ steht die Todesstrafe/stehen mindestens fünf Jahre Gefängnis** that carries the death penalty/a minimum sentence of five years' imprisonment **c** (in Verbindung mit n, adj, vb siehe auch dort) bestehen, verlassen, wetten, Zeit/Mühe verschwenden, Einfluss on that/it; hoffen, warten, sich vorbereiten, gefasst sein, reinfallen for that/it; trinken to that/it; stolz sein of that/it; **ich bin stolz ~, dass sie gewonnen hat** I'm proud that she won, I'm proud of her winning; **ich bestehe ~, dass du kommst** I insist that you come, I insist on your coming; **wir müssen ~ Rücksicht nehmen/Rücksicht ~ nehmen, dass ...** we must take that into consideration/take into consideration that ...; **ich möchte ~ hinweisen, dass ...** I would like to point out that ...; **gib mir die Hand ~** shake on it; **~ freuen wir uns schon** we're looking forward to it already; **~ kommen** (= auffinden) to come (up)on that/it; (= sich erinnern) to think of that/it; **wir kamen auch ~ zu sprechen** we talked about that too; **wie kommst du ~?** what makes you think that?, how do you work that out? (inf); **~ willst du hinaus!** that's what you're getting at!; **er war nur ~ aus** he was only after that, he was only interested in that; **er war nur ~ aus, möglichst viel Geld zu verdienen** he was only interested in earning as much money as possible

da|rauf|fol|gend △ ADJ attr → darauf b

da|rauf|hin [darauf'hɪn, (emph) 'da:raufhɪn] ADV **a** (= aus diesem Anlass, deshalb) as a result (of that/this); (= danach) after that, thereupon **b** (= im Hinblick darauf) with regard to that/this; **wir müssen es ~ prüfen, ob es für unsere Zwecke geeignet ist** we must test it with a view to whether it is suitable for our purposes

da|raus [da'raus, (emph) 'da:raus] ADV **a** (räumlich) out of that/it/them; **~ kann man nicht trinken!** you can't drink out of that/it! **b** (= aus diesem Material etc) from or out of that/it/them; **~ kann man Wein herstellen** you can make wine from that **c** (= aus dieser Sache, Angelegenheit) from that/it/them; **~ ergibt sich/folgt, dass ...** it follows from that that ...; **~ sieht man ...** from this it can be seen ...

da|ben ['darbn] VI (geh) (= entbehren) to live in want; (= hungern) to starve

dar+bie|ten ['da:ɐ-] sep irreg (geh) ▮**VT**▮ **a** (= vorführen) Tänze, Schauspiel to perform; (= vortragen) Lehrstoff to present **b** (= anbieten) to offer; Speisen to serve; (= reichen) Hand, Geschenk etc to offer, to proffer (form) ▮**VR**▮ to present itself; (Gelegenheit, Möglichkeit auch) to offer itself; **dort bot sich (ihnen) ein schauerlicher Anblick dar** a horrible sight met their eyes, they were faced with a horrible sight

Dar|bie|tung ['da:ɐbi:tʊŋ] F -, -en (= das Darbieten) performance; (= das Dargebotene) act

dar+brin|gen ['da:ɐ-] VT sep irreg (geh) Opfer to offer

Dar|da|nel|len [darda'nɛlən] PL **die ~** the Dardanelles pl

da|rein [da'rain, (emph) 'da:rain] ADV **a** (räumlich: = hinein) in there; (wenn Bezugsobjekt vorher erwähnt) in it/them; **hierein? – nein, ~!** in here? – no, in there **b** (old: = in diese Lage) einwilligen, sich ergeben to that; **wir müssen uns ~ fügen** we must accept that, we must bow to that

da|rein- PREF → auch **drein-**: **da|rein+fin|den** VR sep irreg (geh) to come to terms with it, to learn to accept it; **sich ~, etw zu tun** to come to terms with doing sth, to learn to accept doing sth; **da|rein+mischen** sich ~ etw (fig geh) = **dareinsetzen**; **da|rein+re|den** VI sep (in Angelegenheiten) to interfere (jdm in sb's affairs); **da|rein+set|zen** VT sep (fig geh) Energie to put in-

to it, to devote to it; **seine ganze Energie ~, etw zu tun** to put all one's energy into doing sth, to devote all one's energy to doing sth; **er setzte seinen ganzen Stolz darein** it was a matter of pride with him

darf [darf] 3. PERS SING pres von **dürfen**

da|rin [da'rɪn, (emph) 'da:rɪn] ADV **a** (räumlich) in there; (wenn Bezugsobjekt vorher erwähnt) in it/them; (fig) in that/it; **~ liegt ein Widerspruch** there is a contradiction in that **b** (= in dieser Beziehung) in that respect; **~ ist er ganz groß** (inf) he's very good at that; **~ unterscheiden sich die beiden** the two of them differ in that (respect); **die beiden unterscheiden sich ~, dass ...** the two of them differ in that ...; **~ liegt der Unterschied** that is the difference, that is where the difference is; **der Unterschied liegt ~, dass ...** the difference is that ...; **wir stimmen ~ überein, dass ...** we agree that ... **c** (old: = worin) in which

da|rin|nen [da'rɪnən] ADV (old) therein (old)

Dark|room ['darkru:m] M **-s, -s** darkened room for anonymous sex

dar+le|gen ['da:ɐ-] VT sep to explain (jdm to sb); Theorie, Plan, Ansichten auch to expound (jdm to sb)

Dar|le|gung ['da:ɐle:gʊŋ] F -, -en explanation

Dar|le|hen ['da:ɐle:ən] NT **-s, -** loan; **als ~** as a loan

Dar|le|hens-: Dar|le|hens|bank F pl -banken lending or credit bank; **Dar|le|hens|ge|ber(in)** M(F) lender; **Dar|le|hens|kas|se** F credit bank; **Dar|le|hens|kon|to** NT loan account; **Dar|le|hens|neh|mer(in)** M(F) borrower; **Dar|le|hens|schuld** F loan; **Dar|le|hens|um|me** F **die ~** the amount of the/a loan; **eine ~** a loan; **Dar|le|hens|zin|sen** PL interest sing on loans, lending rate(s pl)

Dar|lehn ['da:ɐle:n] NT **-s, -** loan; **als ~** as a loan

Darm [darm] M **-(e)s, ⸚e** [ˈdɛrmə] intestine(s pl), bowel(s pl), gut(s pl); (für Wurst) (sausage) skin or case; (= Material: für Saiten, Schläger etc) gut; **Wurst in echtem/künstlichem ~** sausage in real/synthetic skin

Darm- in cpds intestinal; **Darm|aus|gang** M anus; **Darm|bak|te|rie** F usu pl (Physiol) intestinal or gut bacterium; **die ~n** pl the intestinal flora sing; **Darm|be|we|gung** F peristalsis no art, no pl, peristaltic movement; **Darm|ent|lee|rung** F evacuation of the bowels; **Darm|flo|ra** F (Physiol) intestinal flora; **Darm|grip|pe** F gastric influenza or 'flu; **Darm|ka|tarr(h)** M enteritis; **Darm|krebs** M cancer of the intestine; **Darm|lei|den** NT intestinal trouble no art; **Darm|sai|te** F gut string; **Darm|spie|ge|lung** F enteroscopy (spec); (des Dickdarms) colonoscopy (spec); **Darm|spü|lung** F enema; **Darm|tä|tig|keit** F peristalsis no art; **die ~ fördern/regulieren** to stimulate/regulate the movement of the bowels; **Darm|träg|heit** F underactivity of the intestines; **Darm|ver|schlin|gung** F volvulus (form), twisting of the intestine; **Darm|ver|schluss** ▲ M obstruction of the bowels or intestines

dar|nach [dar'nax, 'darna:x] ADV (old) = **danach**

dar|ne|ben [dar'ne:bn] ADV (old) = **daneben**

da|rob [da'rɔp, (emph) 'da:rɔp] ADV (old) **a** = **darüber b** (= deswegen) **er war ~ sehr erstaunt** he was very surprised by that; **er wurde ~ sehr bewundert** he was much admired for that or on that account

Dar|re ['darə] F **-, -n** drying kiln or oven; (= Hopfendarre, Malzdarre) oast

dar+rei|chen ['da:ɐ-] VT sep (liter) (= anbieten) to offer (jdm etw sb sth, sth to sb); (= reichen auch) to proffer (form) (jdm etw sth to sb)

Dar|rei|chungs|form ['da:rraiçʊŋs-] F presentation; (von Medikamenten) (form of) administration

dar|ren ['darən] VT to (kiln-)dry; Malz, Hopfen to (oast-)dry

Darr|ofen M drying kiln or oven; (für Hopfen, Malz) oast

dar|stell|bar ['da:ɐ-] ADJ (in Literaturwerk etc) portrayable; (in Bild etc auch) depictable; (durch Diagramm etc) representable; (= beschreibbar) describable; **schwer/leicht ~** hard/easy to portray/depict/show/describe; **dieses Phänomen ist grafisch ~** this phenomenon can be shown on a graph; **das ist auf dem Bildschirm nicht ~** this can't be displayed or shown on screen

dar+stel|len ['da:ɐ-] sep ▮**VT**▮ **a** (= abbilden) to show; (= ein Bild entwerfen von) to portray, to depict; (Theat) to portray; Rolle to play; (= beschreiben) to describe; (auf Bildschirm) to display, to show; **etw in einem möglichst günstigen Licht ~** to show sth in the best possible light; **etw kurz** or **knapp ~** to give a short description of sth; **was sollen diese verworrenen Striche ~?** what are these confused lines supposed to show or (in Zeichnung) be?; **die -den Künste** (= Theater) the dramatic or performing arts; (= Malerei, Plastik) the visual arts; **er stellt etwas/nichts dar** (fig) he has a certain air/doesn't have much of an air about him **b** (Math) Funktion to plot; (Chem) to produce; **~de Geometrie** projective geometry **c** (= bedeuten) to constitute, to represent ▮**VR**▮ (= Eindruck vermitteln) to appear (jdm to sb); (= sich erweisen) to show oneself; **die Sache stellte sich (als) sehr fragwürdig dar** the matter appeared (to be) very dubious; **bei dem Talentwettbewerb stellte er sich als begabter Sänger dar** at the talent competition he showed himself to be a gifted singer

Dar|stel|ler ['da:ɐʃtelɐ] M **-s, -** (Theat) actor; **der ~ des Hamlet** the actor playing Hamlet; **ein hervorragender ~ tragischer Rollen** an excellent actor in tragic roles

Dar|stel|le|rin ['da:ɐʃtelərɪn] F **-, -nen** (Theat) actress → auch **Darsteller**

dar|stel|le|risch ['da:ɐʃtelərɪʃ] ADJ dramatic; **eine ~e Höchstleistung** a magnificent piece of acting ADV (= in darstellerischer Hinsicht) in terms of acting; **~ war die Weber der Klein weit überlegen** as an actress Weber was much superior to Klein

Dar|stel|lung ['da:ɐ-] F **a** portrayal; (in Buch, Bild auch) depiction; (durch Diagramm etc) representation; (= Beschreibung) description; (= Bericht) account; **an den Wänden fand man ~en der Heldentaten des Königs** on the walls one could see the King's heroic deeds depicted; **eine falsche ~ der Fakten** a misrepresentation of the facts; **er gab eine großartige ~ des Hamlet** his performance as Hamlet was superb; **der Stoff war in** or **durch ~en von Wanderbühnen bekannt geworden** the material became known through being performed by travelling theatre (Brit) or traveling theater (US) groups **b** (Math) **grafische ~** graph **c** (Chem) preparation

Dar|stel|lungs-: Dar|stel|lungs|form F form of expression; (Theat) dramatic art form; **Dar|stel|lungs|kunst** F skills pl of portrayal; (von Schauspieler) acting technique; **Dar|stel|lungs|mit|tel** NT technique (of representation)

Darts [da:ts] NT **-,** no pl darts sing

dar+tun ['da:ɐ-] VT sep irreg (geh) to set forth; Überlegenheit to demonstrate

da|rü|ber [da'ry:bɐ, (emph) 'da:ry:bɐ] ✪ 53.3 ADV **a** (räumlich) over that/it/them; (= quer darüber) across or over there; (wenn Bezugsobjekt vorher erwähnt) across or over it/them; (= höher als etw) above (there/it/them); (= direkt auf etw) on top (of it/them); **geh ~, nicht hierüber!** go across or over there, not here!; **die Aufgabe war sehr schwer, ich habe lange ~ gesessen** the exercise was very difficult, I sat over it for a long time; **~ hinweg sein** (fig) to have got over it; **~ hinaus** apart from this/that, in addition; **~ hinaus kann ich nichts sagen** over and above that I can't say anything; **~ hinaus log sie mich auch noch an** on top of that she also lied to me; **jetzt ist er ~ hinaus** (fig) he is past that now

b (= *deswegen, in dieser Beziehung*) about that/it; **sich ~ beschweren/beklagen** etc to complain/moan etc about it; **sich ~ beschweren/beklagen** etc**, dass ...** to complain/moan etc that ...; **wir wollen nicht ~ streiten, ob ...** we don't want to argue or disagree about whether ...

c (= *davon*) about that/it; **Rechenschaft ~ ablegen** to account for it; **sie führt eine Liste ~** she keeps a list of it

d (= *währenddessen*) in the meantime; **Wochen gingen ~ hin** meanwhile or in the meantime weeks went past

e (= *mehr, höher*) above or over that; **21 Jahre/4 Euro und ~** 21 years/4 euros and above or over; **kein Cent ~** not a penny over (that) or more; **~ hinaus** over and above that; **es geht nichts ~** there is nothing to beat it

da|rü̱|ber: da|rü̱|ber fah|ren ▲ VI *irreg aux sein* (fig) to run over it; **wenn du mit der Hand darüber fährst, ...** if you run your hand over it ...; **da|rü̱|ber lie|gen ▲** VI *irreg* (fig) to be higher; **da|rü̱|ber schrei|ben ▲** VT *irreg* to write above it; **da|rü̱|ber ste|hen ▲** VI *irreg* (fig) to be above such things

da|ru̱m [da:ˈrʊm, (emph) ˈda:rʊm] ADV **a** (*räumlich*) (a)round that/it/him/her/them; **~ herum** (a)round about or (it/him/her/them); **~, wo ...** (a)round where ...

b (= *um diese Angelegenheit*) (*in Verbindung mit n, vb siehe auch dort*) **es geht ~, dass ...** the thing is that ...; **~ geht es gar nicht** that isn't the point; **~ geht es** that is what it is about, that's it; **~ geht es mir** that's my point; **~ geht es mir nicht** that's not the point for me; **es geht mir ~, Ihnen das klarzumachen** I'm trying to make it clear to you; **wir kommen leider nicht ~ herum, die Preise heraufzusetzen** unfortunately we cannot avoid raising prices; **wir wollen nicht lange ~ herumreden** we don't want to spend a long time talking around the subject; **ich gäbe viel ~, die Wahrheit zu erfahren** I would give a lot to learn the truth; **ich habe ihn schon ein paar Mal ~ gebeten, aber ...** I've asked him a few times (for it/to do it), but ...; **könntest du ihn ~ bitten, zu mir zu kommen?** could you ask him to come to see me?; **sie haben sich ~ gestritten** they argued over it; **sie haben sich ~ gestritten, wer ...** they argued over who ...

c (*liter.* = *darüber, davon*) about that/it; **nur wenige wissen ~, wie ...** (geh) few people know how ...

d (= *deshalb*) that's why, because ...; **~, dass** or **weil ...** because ...; **eben ~** that is exactly why; **ach ~!** so that's why!; **~?** because of that?; **warum willst du nicht mitkommen? – ~!** (inf) why don't you want to come? – (just) 'cos! (inf); **er ist faul, aber ~ nicht dumm** he's lazy but that doesn't mean he's stupid → *auch* **drum**

da|ru̱m-: da|ru̱m+kom|men VI *sep irreg aux sein* to lose it/them; **~, etw zu tun** to lose the opportunity of doing sth; **da|ru̱m+le|gen** VT *sep* to put around it/them; **da|ru̱m+ste|hen** VI *sep irreg aux haben or sein* to stand around; **da|ru̱m+wi|ckeln** VT *sep* to wrap round (*Brit*) or around (*US*) it/them

da|ru̱n|ter [da:ˈrʊntɐ, (emph) ˈda:rʊntɐ] ADV **a** (*räumlich*) under that/it/them, underneath or beneath (that/it/them); (= *niedriger als etw*) below or under(neath) (that/it/them); **hervorkommen** to appear from underneath; **als weitere Belastung kam der Tod seiner Mutter, ~ ist er dann zusammengebrochen** his mother's death was an added burden and he broke down under this strain

b (= *weniger*) under that; **Leute im Alter von 35 Jahren und ~** people aged 35 and under; **der Preis beträgt 50 Euro, ~ kann ich die Ware nicht abgeben** the price is 50 euros, I can't sell for less; **kein Cent ~** not a penny under that or less; **~ macht sies nicht** (inf) she won't do it for less

c (= *dabei*) among them; **~ waren viele Ausländer** there were a lot of foreigners among them

d (= *unter dieser Angelegenheit*) (*in Verbindung mit n, vb siehe auch dort*) **was verstehen Sie ~?** what do you understand by that/it?; **~ kann ich mir nichts vorstellen** that doesn't mean anything to me → *auch* **drunter**

da|ru̱n|ter: da|ru̱n|ter blei|ben ▲ VI *irreg aux sein* (fig) to be lower; **Sie kennen die Anforderungen, wenn Sie mit** or **in Ihrer Leistung ~, werden Sie entlassen** you are aware of the requirements, if you fail to meet them you will be dismissed; **da|ru̱n|ter fal|len ▲** VI *irreg aux sein* (fig) (= *dazugerechnet werden*) to be included; (= *davon betroffen werden*) to come or fall under it/them; **da|ru̱n|ter ge|hen ▲** VI *irreg aux sein* (= *darunter passen*) to fit underneath; **da|ru̱n|ter lie|gen ▲** VI *irreg* **a** *aux haben or sein* (lit) to lie underneath **b** (fig) = **darunter bleiben**; **da|ru̱n|ter mi|schen ▲** VT *Mehl etc* to mix in VR (*Mensch*) to mingle with them; **da|ru̱n|ter schrei|ben ▲** VT *irreg* to write underneath; *Namen auch* to sign at the bottom; **da|ru̱n|ter set|zen ▲** VT *Unterschrift* to put to it

da̱s [das] → **der²**

da̱ sein ▲ [das] VI *irreg aux sein* (lit, fig inf) to be there; **noch ~** to be still there; (= *übrig sein auch*) to be left; **wieder ~** to be back; **ich bin gleich wieder da** I'll be right or straight back; **sind Sie schon lange da?** have you been here/there long?; **ist Post/sind Besucher für mich da?** is there any mail/are there visitors for me?; **war der Briefträger schon da?** has the postman (*Brit*) or mailman (*US*) been here/there today?; **für jdn ~** to be there or available for sb; **ein Arzt, der immer für seine Patienten da ist** a doctor who always has time for his patients; **voll ~** (inf) to be all there (inf); **so etwas ist noch nie da gewesen** it's quite unprecedented; **es ist alles schon mal da gewesen** it's all been done before; **das übertrifft alles bisher da Gewesene** that beats everything; **ein nie da gewesener Erfolg** an unprecedented success

Da̱|sein NT (= *Leben, Existenz, Philos*) existence; (= *das Anwesendsein*) presence; **der Kampf ums ~** the struggle for existence; **etw ins ~ rufen** (liter) to bring sth into existence, to call sth into being

Da̱|seins-: in cpds of existence; **Da̱|seins|angst** F (Philos) existential fear, angst; **Da̱|seins|be|din|gun|gen** PL living conditions pl; **Da̱|seins|be|rech|ti|gung** F right to exist; **hat die UNO noch eine ~?** can the UN still justify its existence?; **Da̱|seins|form** F form of life or existence; **Da̱|seins|freu|de** F zest for life, joie de vivre; **Da̱|seins|kampf** M struggle for survival; **Da̱|seins|wei|se** F mode of being; **Da̱|seins|zweck** M reason for existence, raison d'être (spec)

da|se̱lbst [daˈzɛlpst] ADV (old) in said place; (*bei Quellenangaben*) ibidem, ibid abbr; **geboren 1714 zu Florenz, gestorben 1768 ~** born in Florence 1714, died there 1768

da̱+sit|zen VI *sep irreg aux haben or sein* to sit there; **wie die Kinder heutzutage ~!** the way children sit nowadays!; **ohne Hilfe/einen Cent ~** (inf) to be left without any help/without a penny (*Brit*) or cent (*US*)

da̱s|je|ni|ge [ˈdasjeːnɪɡə] DEM PRON → **derjenige**

da̱ss ▲ [das] CONJ **a** (*mit Subjektsatz*) that; **~ wir alle sterben müssen, ist sicher** that we all must die is certain (liter), it is certain (that) we all must die

b (*mit Objektsatz*) (that); **ich bin überzeugt, ~ du das Richtige getan hast** I'm sure (that) you have done the right thing; **ich verstehe nicht, ~ man ihn als Bewerber abgelehnt hat** I don't understand why he was turned down; **ich sehe nicht ein, ~ wir hungern sollen** I don't see why we should starve

c (*mit Attributivsatz*) that; **angenommen/vorausge-**

setzt, **~ ...** given/provided that ...; **ich bin mir dessen bewusst, ~ ...** I am aware (that) ..., I am aware of the fact that ...; **unter der Bedingung, ~ ...** on (the) condition that ...

d (*mit Kausalsatz*) that; **ich war böse, ~ ...** I was annoyed that ...; **ich freue mich darüber, ~ ...** I'm glad (that) ...; **das kommt daher, ~ ...** that comes because ...; **das liegt daran, ~ ...** that is because ...; **das kommt davon, ~ er niemals aufpasst** that comes from him or his never paying attention

e (*mit Konsekutivsatz*) that; **er fuhr so schnell, ~ er sich überschlug** he drove so fast that he overturned

f (geh: *mit Finalsatz*) so that; **ich gab ihm den Brief, ~ er ihn selbst lesen konnte** I gave him the letter so that he could read it himself

g (*als Einleitung eines Instrumentalsatzes*) **er verbringt seine Freizeit damit, ~ er Rosen züchtet** he spends his free time breeding roses

h (geh) (*mit Wunschsatz*) if only, would that (liter); (*in Befehl*) see that; **~ er immer da wäre!** would that he were always there (liter), if only he were always there; **~ du es mir nicht verlierst!** see that you don't lose it!

da̱s|se̱l|be [dasˈzɛlbə], **das|se̱l|bi|ge** [dasˈzɛlbɪɡə] DEM PRON → **derselbe**

da̱+ste|hen VI *sep irreg aux haben or sein* **a** (= *da sein*) to stand there; **wie stehst denn du wieder da!** what sort of a way do you call that to stand!; **steh nicht so dumm da!** don't just stand there looking stupid

b (fig) **anders/glänzend/gut/schlecht ~** to be in a different/splendid/good/bad position; **die Firma/Regierung steht wieder gut da** the company/government is doing all right again (inf) or is in a good position again; **allein ~** to be on one's own; **einzig ~** to be unique or unparalleled; **jetzt stehe ich ohne Mittel/als Lügner da** now I'm left with no money/looking like a liar; **wenn die Sache schief geht, stehst du dumm da** if things go wrong you'll be left looking stupid; **wie stehe ich jetzt da!** (*Selbstlob*) just look at me now!; (*Vorwurf*) what kind of fool do I look now!

DAT [deːˈʔaːteː, dat] NT **-, -s** DAT

Da̱|tei [daˈtai] F **-, -en** (Comput) file

Da̱|tei-: in cpds file; **Da̱|tei|na|me** M file name; **Da̱|tei|ver|wal|tung** F file management; **Da̱|tei|ver|wal|tungs|pro|gramm** NT file manager; **Da̱|tei|ver|zeich|nis** NT directory

Da̱|ten [ˈdaːtn] **a** pl von **Datum b** pl (Comput) data sing

Da̱|ten-: in cpds data; **Da̱|ten|ab|fra|ge** F (data) query; **Da̱|ten|ab|ruf** M data retrieval; **Da̱|ten|auf|be|rei|tung** F data preparation; **Da̱|ten|aus|ga|be** F data output; **Da̱|ten|aus|tausch** M data exchange or interchange; **Da̱|ten|au|to|bahn** F information highway; **Da̱|ten|band** [-bant] NT pl **-bänder** data tape; **Da̱|ten|bank** F pl **-banken** database; (= *Zentralstelle*) data bank; **da̱|ten|bank|ge|stützt** [-ɡəʃtʏtst] ADJ database-supported; **Da̱|ten|bank|pfle|ge** F database management or maintenance; **Da̱|ten|bank|ver|wal|tung** F database management; **Da̱|ten|be|stand** M database; **Da̱|ten|ein|ga|be** F data input; **Da̱|ten|er|fas|sung** F data capture; **Da̱|ten|er|he|bung** F survey; **Da̱|ten|fern|über|tra|gung** F data transmission; **Da̱|ten|fern|ver|ar|bei|tung** F teleprocessing; **Da̱|ten|fluss|plan ▲** M data flowchart; **Da̱|ten|hand|schuh** M data glove; **Da̱|ten|klau** [-klau] M **-s, -s** (inf) theft of data; **Da̱|ten|kom|pres|si|on** F data compression; **Da̱|ten|kom|pres|si|ons|pro|gramm** NT data compression program; **Da̱|ten|miss|brauch ▲** M misuse of data, data abuse; **Da̱|ten|netz** NT data network; **Da̱|ten|satz** M record; **Da̱|ten|schrott** (inf) M rubbish data; **Da̱|ten|schutz** M data protection; **Da̱|ten|schutz|be|auf|trag|te(r)** MF *decl as adj* data protection official; **Da̱|ten|schüt|zer** [-ʃʏtsɐ] M **-s, -, Da̱|ten|schüt|ze|**

rin [-ərɪn] F **-, -nen** data protectionist; **Da|ten|schutz|ge|setz** NT data protection act; **Da|ten|si|che|rung** F data storage; **Da|ten|sicht|ge|rät** NT VDU, visual display unit; **Da|ten|spei|cher** M data memory; (= *Speichermedium*) data storage medium; **Da|ten|trä|ger** M data carrier; **Da|ten|trans|fer** M data transfer; **Da|ten|ty|pist** [-typɪst] M **-en, -en**, **Da|ten|ty|pis|tin** [-pɪstɪn] F **-, -nen** keyboarder; **Da|ten|über|tra|gung** F data transmission; **Da|ten|ver|ar|bei|tung** F data processing; **Da|ten|ver|ar|bei|tungs|an|la|ge** F data processing equipment; **Da|ten|ver|ar|bei|tungs|kauf|frau** F , **Da|ten|ver|ar|bei|tungs|kauf|mann** M data processing clerk; **Da|ten|ver|bund** M data network; **Da|ten|ver|lust** M loss of data, data loss; **Da|ten|ver|wal|tung** F data management; **Da|ten|zent|ra|le** F , **Da|ten|zent|rum** NT data centre (*Brit*) or center (*US*)

da|tie|ren [da'tiːrən] ptp **datiert** VT *Brief, Fund* to date; **der Brief ist vom 20. April datiert** the letter is dated 20th April VI (= *stammen*) to date (*aus* from); **dieser Brief datiert vom 1. Januar** this letter is dated January 1st; **unsere Freundschaft datiert seit einer Reise vor zehn Jahren** our friendship dates from or dates back to a trip ten years ago

Da|tiv ['daːtiːf] M **-s, -e** [-və] (*Gram*) dative (case)

Da|tiv|ob|jekt NT (*Gram*) indirect object

DAT-Kas|set|te ['dat-] F DAT or digital audio tape cassette

DAT-Lauf|werk ['dat-] NT DAT or digital audio tape drive

da|to ADV **bis ~** (*Comm, inf*) to date

Da|to|wech|sel M (*Comm*) time bill

DAT-Re|kor|der ['dat-] M DAT or digital audio tape recorder

Dat|scha ['datʃa] F **-, Dat|schen** ['datʃn], **Dat|sche** ['datʃə] F **-, -n** country cottage; **auf seiner ~** in his country cottage

DAT-Strea|mer ['dat-] M DAT or digital audio tape streamer

Dat|tel ['datl] F **-, -n** date

Dat|tel- in cpds date; **Dat|tel|pal|me** F date palm

Dat|te|rich ['datərɪç] M (*inf*) **den ~ haben/bekommen** to have/get the shakes (*inf*)

Da|tum ['daːtʊm] NT **-s, Daten** [da:tn] a date; **was für ein ~ haben wir heute?** what is the date today?; **das heutige/gestrige/morgige ~** today's /yesterday's/tomorrow's date; **sich im ~ irren** to get the date wrong; **ein Brief gleichen ~s** a letter of the same date; **gleichen ~s übersandten wir Ihnen ...** (*form*) on the same date we sent you ...; **etw mit dem ~ versehen** to date sth; **der Brief trägt das ~ vom 1. April** the letter is dated 1st April; **ein Brief ohne ~** an undated letter; **~ des Poststempels** date as postmark; **ein Nachschlagewerk neueren/älteren ~s** a recent/an old reference work
b usu pl (= *Faktum*) fact; (= *statistische Zahlenangabe etc*) datum (*form*), piece of data; **technische Daten** technical data pl

Da|tums-: **Da|tums|gren|ze** F (*Geog*) (international) date line; **Da|tums|stem|pel** M date stamp

Dau|be ['daubə] F **-, -n** stave; (*beim Eisschießen*) tee

Dau|er ['dauɐ] F **-, no pl** (= *das Andauern*) duration; (= *Zeitspanne*) period, term; (= *Länge: einer Sendung etc*) length; **während der ~ des Vertrages/Krieges** for the duration of the contract/war; **für die ~ eines Monats** or **von einem Monat** for a period of one month; **ein Gefängnisaufenthalt von zehn Jahren** a ten-year term of imprisonment; **von ~ sein** to be long-lasting; **seine Begeisterung war nicht von ~** his enthusiasm was short-lived, his enthusiasm wasn't long-lasting; **keine ~ haben** to be short-lived; **von langer ~ sein** to last a long time; **von kur-**

zer ~ sein not to last long; **auf die ~** in the long term; **auf die ~ wird das langweilig** it gets boring in the long run; **das kann man auf die ~ nicht ertragen** you can't stand it for any length of time; **das kann auf die ~ nicht so weitergehen** it can't go on like that indefinitely; **auf ~** permanently; **auf ~ gearbeitet** made to last; **für die ~ Ihres Aufenthaltes in unserem Hause** as long as you stay with us, for the period or duration of your stay with us (*form*); **man konnte sich nicht über die ~ der Regelung einigen** they could not decide on the duration of the agreement

Dau|er- in cpds permanent; **Dau|er|arbeits|lo|se(r)** MF decl as adj long-term unemployed person; **die ~n** the long-term unemployed; **Dau|er|ar|beits|lo|sig|keit** F long-term unemployment; **Dau|er|auf|trag** M (*Fin*) standing order; **Dau|er|aus|weis** M (permanent) identity card; (= *Fahrkarte etc*) season ticket; **Dau|er|be|las|tung** F continual pressure no indef art; (*von Maschine*) constant load; **unter ~** under continual pressure/a constant load; **Dau|er|be|schäf|ti|gung** F (= *Stellung*) permanent position; **Dau|er|be|trieb** M continuous operation; **Dau|er|be|zie|hung** F permanent relationship; **Dau|er|brand|ofen** M slow-burning stove; **Dau|er|bren|ner** M a (= *Dauerbrandofen*) slow-burning stove b (*inf*) (= *Dauererfolg*) long runner; (= *Dauerthema*) long-running issue; (*hum*: = *Kuss*) long passionate kiss; **Dau|er|bü|gel|fal|te** F permanent crease; **Dau|er|ein|rich|tung** F permanent institution; **Dau|er|emit|tent** [-emitent] M **-en, -en**, **Dau|er|emit|ten|tin** [-tɛntɪn] F **-, -nen** constant issuer; **Dau|er|er|folg** M long-running success; **Dau|er|fes|tig|keit** F (*Tech*) fatigue strength; **Dau|er|feu|er** NT (*Mil*) sustained fire; **Dau|er|flug** M (*Aviat*) long haul flight; **Dau|er|frost** M freeze-up; **Dau|er|frost|bo|den** M permafrost; **Dau|er|funk|ti|on** F (*bei Schreibmaschine etc*) locking function; **Dau|er|gast** M permanent guest; (= *häufiger Gast*) regular visitor, permanent fixture (*hum*); **er scheint sich hier als ~ einrichten zu wollen** (*iro inf*) he seems to be settling down for a long stay; **Dau|er|ge|schwin|dig|keit** F cruising speed

dau|er|haft ADJ Zustand, Einrichtung, Farbe permanent; Bündnis, Frieden, Beziehung lasting attr, long-lasting, durable ADV (= *für immer*) permanently, lastingly; **durch eine Impfung sind Sie gegen diese Krankheit ~ geschützt** one vaccination gives you lasting immunity to this disease

Dau|er|haf|tig|keit ['dauɐhaftɪçkaɪt] F **-, no pl** permanence; (*von Material, Bündnis, Beziehung, Frieden*) durability

Dau|er-: **Dau|er|kar|te** F season ticket; **Dau|er|lauf** M (*Sport*) jog; (= *das Laufen*) jogging; **im ~** at a jog or trot; **einen ~ machen** to jog, to go jogging, to go for a jog; **Dau|er|laut** M (*Phon*) continuant; **Dau|er|leih|ga|be** F (*Art: für Museum*) permanent loan; **es ist eine ~** it's on permanent loan (*gen* from); **Dau|er|lut|scher** M lollipop; **Dau|er|marsch** M (*Mil*) forced march; **Dau|er|mie|te** F long lease or tenancy; **er hat das Haus in ~** he has the house on a long lease; **Dau|er|mie|ter(in)** M(F) long-term tenant; **Dau|er|milch** F long-life milk

dau|ern¹ ['dauɐn] VI a (= *andauern*) to last, to go on; **das Gewitter dauerte zwei Stunden** the thunderstorm lasted (for) or went on for two hours; **die Verhandlungen ~ schon drei Wochen** the negotiations have already been going on for three weeks; **wie lange soll dieser Zustand noch ~?** how long will this situation last or go on (for) or continue?
b (= *Zeit benötigen*) to take a while or some time; (*lange*) to take a long time; **das dauert noch** (*inf*) it'll be a while or some time yet; **warum dauert das Anziehen bei dir immer so lange?** why do you always take so long to get

dressed?; **es dauerte lange, bis er sich befreit hatte** it took him a long time to get free; **das dauert mir zu lange** it takes too long for me; **muss das so lange ~?** does it have to take so long?; **das dauert immer, bis er fertig ist** (*inf*) it always takes ages for him to get ready (*inf*); **das dauert und dauert** (*inf*) it takes forever (*inf*); **es dauert jetzt nicht mehr lange** it won't take much longer; **das dauert heute vielleicht wieder einmal** (*inf*) it's taking ages again today (*inf*)
c (*geh*: = *dauerhaft sein*) to last

dau|ern² VT (*old, liter*) **etw dauert jdn** sb regrets sth; **er/sie dauert mich** I feel sorry for him/her; **es dauert mich, dass ...** I regret or I'm sorry that ...; **es dauerte ihn im Alter, seine Jugend so vergeudet zu haben** in his old age he regretted having squandered his youth like that; **das arme Tier kann einen ~** you can't help feeling sorry for the poor animal

dau|ernd ADJ (= *anhaltend*) Frieden, Regelung lasting; (= *ständig*) Wohnsitz, Ausstellung permanent; (= *fortwährend*) Unterbrechung, Nörgelei, Sorge constant, perpetual ADV **etw ~ tun** to keep doing sth; (*stärker*) to be always or forever (*inf*) doing sth, to do sth the whole time (*inf*); **sie musste ~ auf die Toilette** she had to keep going to the toilet (*Brit*) or bathroom (*esp US*); **er beschwert sich ~ darüber** he's always or forever (*inf*) complaining about it, he complains about it the whole time (*inf*); **frag nicht ~ so dumm!** don't keep asking stupid questions

Dau|er-: **Dau|er|obst** NT fruit suitable for storing; **Dau|er|par|ker** [-parkə] M **-s, -**, **Dau|er|par|ke|rin** [-ərɪn] F **-, -nen** long-stay (*Brit*) or long-term (*US*) parker; **Parkplatz für ~** long-stay car park (*Brit*), long-term parking lot (*US*); **Dau|er|prob|lem** NT constant or permanent or ongoing problem; **Dau|er|red|ner(in)** M(F) (*pej*) interminable speaker; **Dau|er|re|gen** M continuous rain; **ein mehrtägiger ~** several days of continuous rain; **Dau|er|schlaf** M prolonged sleep; **ich fiel in einen 24-stündigen ~** I fell asleep for 24 hours solid; **Dau|er|schwing|fes|tig|keit** F (*Tech*) fatigue strength; **Dau|er|schwin|gung** F continuous oscillation; **Dau|er|sit|zung** F prolonged or lengthy session; **Dau|er|span|nung** F (*Elec*) continuous voltage; **Dau|er|spei|cher** M (*Comput*) permanent memory; **Dau|er|stel|lung** F permanent position; **in ~ beschäftigt** employed on a permanent basis; **Dau|er|streit** M permanent conflict; **Dau|er|stress** ▲ M **im ~ sein** to be in a state of permanent stress; **Dau|er|strom** M , **no pl** (*Elec*) constant current; **Dau|er|test** M long-term test; **Dau|er|the|ma** NT long-running issue; **Dau|er|ton** M pl **-töne** continuous tone; **Dau|er|wald** M permanent forest; **Dau|er|wel|le** F perm, permanent wave; **Dau|er|wir|kung** F (long-)lasting effect; **Dau|er|wohn|recht** NT permanent right of tenure; **Dau|er|wurst** F German salami; **Dau|er|zu|stand** M permanent state of affairs; **ich möchte das nicht zum ~ werden lassen** I don't want that to become permanent

Däum|chen ['dɔymçən] NT **-s, -** a dim von **Daumen** b (*inf*) **~ drehen** to twiddle one's thumbs; **und da mussten wir ~ drehen** and we were left twiddling our thumbs

Dau|men ['dauman] M **-s, -** thumb; **am ~ lutschen** to suck one's thumb; **jdm** or **für jdn die ~ drücken** or **halten** to keep one's fingers crossed for sb; **den ~ auf etw** (*acc*) **halten** (*inf*) to hold on to sth → **peilen**

Dau|men-: **Dau|men|ab|druck** M thumbprint; **Dau|men|bal|len** M ball of the/one's thumb; **dau|men|breit** ADJ as broad as your thumb; **Dau|men|brei|te** F thumb's width; **Dau|men|in|dex** M thumb index; **Dau|men|ki|no** NT flicker book; **Dau|men|lut|scher(in)** M(F) thumb-sucker; **Dau|men|na|gel** M thumbnail; **Dau|men|re|gis|ter** NT thumb index; **Dau|men|schrau|be** F (*Hist*) thumbscrew; **jdm die ~n anlegen** (*lit, fig inf*) to put the (thumb)screws on sb; **die ~n ansetzen** (fig) to put the screws on

Däum|ling ['dɔymlɪŋ] M **-s, -e a** (im Märchen) **der ~** Tom Thumb **b** (von Handschuh) thumb; (Med) thumbstall

Dau|ne ['daunə] F **-, -n** down feather; **~n** down sing; **ich schlief dort wie auf ~n** it was like sleeping on air; **weich wie ~n** as soft as down

Dau|nen-: Dau|nen|a|no|rak M down jacket, down parka (US); **Dau|nen|bett** NT , **Dau|nen|de|cke** F (down-filled) duvet (Brit) or quilt; **Dau|nen|fe|der** F down feather; **Dau|nen|ja|cke** F quilted jacket; **Dau|nen|kis|sen** NT down-filled cushion; (= Kopfkissen) down pillow; **Dau|nen|schlaf|sack** M down(-filled) sleeping bag; **dau|nen|weich** ADJ as soft as down

Dau|phin [do'fɛ̃] M **-s, -s** (Hist) dauphin

Daus¹ [daus] M **(ei) der ~!** (old) was der ~! (old) what the devil or deuce! (dated)

Daus² NT **-es, Däuse(r)** ['dɔyzə, 'dɔyzɐ] **a** (beim Würfel) deuce **b** (Cards) ace (in German pack)

Da|vid(s)|stern ['da:fɪt(s)-, 'da:vɪt(s)-] M star of David

Da|vis|cup ['de:vɪskap] M , **Da|vis|po|kal** ['de:vɪs-] M Davis cup

da|von [da'fɔn, (emph) 'da:fɔn] ADV **a** (räumlich) from there; (wenn Bezugsobjekt vorher erwähnt) from it/them; (mit Entfernungsangabe) away (from there/it/them); **weg ~!** (inf) get away from there/it/them; **~ zweigt ein Weg ab** a path branches off it → **auf**

b (fig) (in Verbindung mit n, vb siehe auch dort) **es unterscheidet sich ~ nur in der Länge** it only differs from it in the length; **nein, weit ~ entfernt!** no, far from it!; **ich bin weit ~ entfernt, Ihnen Vorwürfe machen zu wollen** the last thing I want to do is reproach you; **wenn wir einmal ~ absehen, dass ...** if for once we overlook the fact that ...; **wir möchten in diesem Fall ~ absehen, Ihnen den Betrag zu berechnen** in this case we shall not invoice you; **in ihren Berechnungen sind sie ~ ausgegangen, dass ...** they made their calculations on the basis that ...

c (fig: = dadurch) leben, abhängen on that/it/them; sterben of that/it; krank/braun werden from that/it/them; **... und ~ kommt das hohe Fieber** ... and that's where the high temperature comes from, ... and the high temperature comes from that; **das kommt ~!** that's what you get; **... und ~ hängt es ab** and it depends on that; **das hängt ~ ab, ob ...** that depends on whether ...; **~ hat man nur Ärger** you get nothing but trouble with it; **~ wird man müde** that makes you tired; **gib ihr ein bisschen mehr, ~ kann sie doch nicht satt werden** give her a bit more, that won't fill her up; **~ stirbst du nicht** it won't kill you; **was habe ICH denn ~?** what do I get out of it?; **was HABE ich denn ~?** why should I?; **was hast du denn ~, dass du so schuftest?** what do you get out of slaving away like that?

d (mit Passiv) by that/it/them; **~ betroffen werden** or **sein** to be affected by that/it/them; **e** (Anteil, Ausgangsstoff) of that/it/them; **~ essen/trinken/nehmen** to eat/drink/take some of that/it/them; **nehmen Sie doch noch etwas ~!** do have some more!; **die Hälfte ~** half of that/it/them; **das Doppelte ~** twice or double that; **zwei/ein Viertelpfund ~, bitte!** would you give me two of those/a quarter of a pound of that/those, please; **er hat drei Schwestern, ~ sind zwei älter als er** he has three sisters, two of whom are older than he is; **früher war er sehr reich, aber nach dem Krieg ist ihm nichts ~ geblieben** he used to be very rich but after the war nothing was left of his earlier wealth

f (= darüber) hören, wissen, sprechen about that/it/them; verstehen, halten of that/it/them; **genug ~!** enough of this!; **ich habe keine Ahnung ~** I've no idea about that/it; **nichts mehr ~!** no more of that!; **nichts ~ halten** not to think much of it; **ich halte viel ~** I think it is quite

good; **was wissen Sie ~!** what do you know about it anyway?

da|von-: da|von+blei|ben VI sep irreg aux sein (inf) to keep away; (= nicht anfassen) to keep one's hands off; **da|von+ei|len** VI sep aux sein (geh) to hurry or hasten away; **da|von+fah|ren** VI sep irreg aux sein **a** (Fahrer, Fahrzeug) to drive away; (auf Fahrrad etc) to ride away; (Zug) to pull away **b** jdm ~ to pull away from sb; **da|von+flie|gen** VI sep irreg aux sein to fly away; **da|von+ge|hen** VI sep irreg aux sein (geh) to walk away; **da|von+ja|gen** VT sep to chase off or away; **da|von+kom|men** VI sep irreg aux sein (= entkommen) to get away, to escape; (= nicht bestraft werden) to get away with it; (= freigesprochen werden) to get off; **mit dem Schrecken/dem Leben ~** to escape with no more than a shock/with one's life; **mit einer Geldstrafe ~** to get off with a fine; **da|von+las|sen** VT sep irreg **die Hände** or **Finger ~** (inf) to leave it/them well alone; **du sollst die Hände** or **Finger ~** keep your hands or fingers off (it/them); **da|von+lau|fen** VI sep irreg aux sein **a** (= weglaufen) to run away (jdm/vor jdm from sb); (= verlassen) to walk out (jdm on sb); **den Eltern** or **von zu Hause ~** to run away from home; **das Hausmädchen/ihr Mann ist ihr davongelaufen** (inf) the maid/her husband walked out on her; **es ist zum Davonlaufen!** (inf) it's all too much! **b** (= außer Kontrolle geraten) to get out of hand; **die Preise sind davongelaufen** prices have got out of hand; **die Preise sind uns/den Löhnen davongelaufen** prices are beyond our control/have surpassed wages; **da|von+ma|chen** VR sep to make off; **da|von+ren|nen** VI sep irreg aux sein (inf) = **davonlaufen a; da|von+schlei|chen** VIR sep irreg (vi: aux sein) to creep or slink away or off; **da|von+schwim|men** VI sep irreg aux sein jdm ~ to outswim or outstrip sb; **da|von+steh|len** VR sep irreg (geh) to steal away; **da|von+tra|gen** VT sep irreg **a** (= wegtragen) Gegenstände, Verletzte to carry away **b** (= erringen) Preis to carry off; Sieg, Ruhm to win **c** (= erleiden) Schaden, Verletzung to suffer; **da|von+zie|hen** VI sep irreg aux sein (liter) to leave; (Prozession etc) to move off; (Sport inf) to pull away (jdm from sb)

da|vor [da'fo:ɐ, (emph) 'da:fo:ɐ] ADV **a** (räumlich) in front (of that/it/them); (wenn Bezugsobjekt vorher erwähnt) in front of it/them; **ein Haus mit einem großen Rasen ~** a house with a big front lawn, a house with a big lawn in front **b** (zeitlich) (= vor einem bestimmten Datum) before that; (= bevor man etw tut) beforehand; **ist er 1950 ausgewandert? – nein, schon ~** did he emigrate in 1950? – no, before that **c** (in Verbindung mit n, vb siehe auch dort) bewahren, schützen from that/it; warnen of or about that/it; Angst haben of that/it; sich ekeln by that/it; **ich habe Angst ~, das zu tun** I'm afraid of doing that; **ich habe Angst ~, dass der Hund beißen könnte** I'm afraid that the dog might bite; **sein Ekel ~** his disgust of it; **ich warne Sie ~!** I warn you!; **ich habe ihn ~ gewarnt, sich in Gefahr zu begeben** I warned him not to get into danger

da|vor: da|vor hän|gen ▲ VT to hang in front of it/them; **sie hängte das Schloss davor** she put the lock on it; **da|vor le|gen** ▲ VT to put in front of it/them; **leg doch eine Kette davor** put a chain on it/them VR to lie down in front of it/them; **da|vor lie|gen** ▲ VI irreg aux haben or sein to lie in front of it/them; **da|vor ste|hen** ▲ VI irreg aux haben or sein to stand in front of it/them; **da|vor stel|len** ▲ VT to put in front of it/them VR to stand in front of it/them

da|wi|der [da'vi:dɐ, (emph) 'da:vi:dɐ] ADV (old) against it; **dafür und ~** for and against

DAX® [daks] M **-, no pl abbr von Deutscher Aktienindex** DAX index

DAX-Wert [daks-] M (= Einzelaktie im DAX) DAX share

da|zu [da'tsu:, (emph) 'da:tsu:] ADV **a** (räumlich) there; **wozu gehört das? – ~!** where does that belong? – there!

b (= dabei, damit) with it; (= außerdem, obendrein auch) into the bargain (inf), at the same time; **er ist dumm und ~ auch noch faul** he's stupid and lazy with it or into the bargain (inf) or as well; **sie ist hübsch und ~ nicht unintelligent** she's pretty and not unintelligent either; **noch ~** as well, too; **noch ~, wo ...** when ... too; **~ reicht** or **serviert man am besten Reis** it's best to serve rice with it; **er singt und spielt Gitarre ~** he sings and accompanies himself on the guitar

c (= dahin) to that/it; **auf dem besten Wege ~ sein, etw zu tun** to be well on the way to doing sth; **er ist auf dem besten Wege ~** he's well on the way to it; **das führt ~, dass weitere Forderungen gestellt werden** that will lead to further demands being made; **~ führt das dann** that's what it leads to; **wie konnte es nur ~ kommen?** how could that happen?; **wer weiß, wie sie ~ gekommen ist** (zu diesem Auto etc) who knows how she came by it; **wie kommen ich ~?** (empört) why on earth should I?; **... aber ich bin nicht ~ gekommen ...** but I didn't get (a)round to it

d (= dafür, zu diesem Zweck) for that/it; **~ bin ich zu alt** I'm too old for that; **~ bin zu alt, noch tanzen zu gehen** I'm too old to go dancing; **~ habe ich dich nicht studieren lassen, dass du ...** I didn't send you to university so that you could ... or for you to ...; **ich habe ihm ~ geraten** I advised him to (do that); **Sie sind/die Maschine ist ~ wie geschaffen** it's as if you were/the machine was made for it; **~ fähig sein, etw zu tun** to be capable of doing sth; **~ bereit sein, etw zu tun** to be prepared to do sth; **er war nicht ~ fähig/bereit** he wasn't capable of it/prepared to; **~ gehört viel Geld** that takes a lot of money; **~ ist er da** that's what he's there for, that's why he's there; **die Erlaubnis/die Mittel/das Recht ~** permission/the means/the right to do it; **ich habe keine Lust ~** I don't feel like it; **ich habe keine Lust ~, mitzugehen** I don't feel like going along; **~ habe ich keine Zeit** I haven't the time (for that); **ich habe keine Zeit ~, die Fenster zu putzen** I haven't (the) time to clean the windows; **ich bin nicht ~ in der Lage** I'm not in a position to

e (= darüber, zum Thema) about that/it; **was sagst/meinst du ~?** what do you say to/think about that?; **meine Gedanken/Meinung ~** my thoughts about/opinion of that; **..., hören Sie jetzt einen Kommentar** ... we now bring you a commentary; **das Hauptthema war die Inflation; ~ schreibt die Zeitung ...** the main subject was inflation – the paper has this to say about it ...; **er hat sich nur kurz ~ geäußert** he only commented briefly on that/it

f (in Wendungen) **im Gegensatz ~** in contrast to that; **im Vergleich ~** in comparison with that; **früher war sie nicht so hysterisch, er hat sie ~ gemacht** she never used to be so hysterical, he made her like that; **er war nicht immer Lord, er wurde erst ~ gemacht** he wasn't born a Lord, he was made or created one; **~ wird man nicht gewählt, sondern ernannt** one is appointed rather than elected to that

da|zu-: da|zu+ge|ben VT sep irreg to add → Senf; **da|zu+ge|hö|ren** ptp **dazugehört** VI sep to belong (to it/us etc); (als Ergänzung) to go with it/them; (= eingeschlossen sein) to be included (in it/them); **bei einer Familienfeier gehört Onkel Otto auch dazu** Uncle Otto should be part of any family gathering too; **das gehört**

mit dazu that belongs to/goes with/is included in it; (= *versteht sich von selbst*) it's all part of it; **es gehört schon einiges dazu** that takes a lot; **es gehört schon einiges dazu, das zu tun** it takes a lot to do that; **da|zu|ge|hö|rig** ADJ *attr* which goes/go with it/them; *Schlüssel etc* belonging to it/them; (= *zu dieser Arbeit gehörend*) *Werkzeuge, Material* necessary; **da|zu+kom|men** VI *sep irreg aux sein* **a** (= *ankommen*) to arrive (on the scene); **er kam zufällig dazu** he happened to arrive on the scene **b** (= *hinzugefügt werden*) to be added; **es kommen laufend neue Bücher dazu** new books are always being added; **es kamen noch mehrere Straftaten dazu** there were several other offences (*Brit*) or offenses (*US*); **kommt noch etwas dazu?** is there or will there be anything else?; **es kommt noch dazu, dass er faul ist** on top of that he's lazy, in addition to that he's lazy **c** (*Aus, Sw*: = *Zeit dafür finden*) to get (a)round to it; **da|zu+le|gen** *sep* VT to add to it; **jdm/sich noch ein Stückchen Fleisch ~** to give sb/oneself another piece of meat; **leg die Sachen ruhig dazu** just put the things with it/them VR to lie down with him/them *etc*; **da|zu+ler|nen** VT *sep viel/nichts ~* to learn a lot more/nothing new; **man kann immer was ~** there's always something to learn; **schon wieder was dazugelernt!** you learn something (new) every day!

da|zu|mal ['da:tsuma:l] ADV (*old*) in those days → **anno**

da|zu-: da|zu+rech|nen VT *sep* **a** *Kosten, Betrag, Zahl* to add on **b** (= *mit berücksichtigen*) to consider also; **da|zu+schau|en** VI *sep* (*Aus*) = *zusehen*; **da|zu+schrei|ben** VT *sep irreg* to add; **da|zu+set|zen** *sep* VT **a** **können wir den Jungen hier noch ~?** could the boy sit here too? **b** (= *dazuschreiben*) to add VR to join him/us *etc*; **komm, setz dich doch dazu** come and sit with us, come and join us; **da|zu+tun** VT *sep irreg* (*inf*) to add; **Da|zu|tun** NT **er hat es ohne dein ~ geschafft** he managed it without your doing/saying anything; **ohne dein ~ hätte er es nicht geschafft** he wouldn't have managed it if you hadn't done/said something *or* without your doing/saying anything; **da|zu+ver|die|nen** VTI *sep* to earn sth extra; **seine Frau muss ~** his wife has to earn a bit on the side as well

da|zwi|schen [da'tsvɪʃn, (*emph*) 'da:tsvɪʃn] ADV (*räumlich, zeitlich*) in between; (*in der betreffenden Menge, Gruppe*) amongst them, in with them; **die Betten standen dicht nebeneinander, es hing nur ein Vorhang ~** the beds were very close together, there was only a curtain between them

da|zwi|schen-: da|zwi|schen+fah|ren VI *sep irreg aux sein* **a** (= *eingreifen*) to step in and put a stop to things, to intervene **b** (= *unterbrechen*) to break in, to interrupt; **jdm ~** to interrupt sb; **da|zwi|schen+fun|ken** VI *sep* (*Rad*) to jam the signal; (*inf*: = *eingreifen*) to put one's oar in (*inf*); (*inf*: = *vereiteln*) to put a spoke in it (*inf*); **da|zwi|schen+kom|men** VI *sep irreg aux sein* **a** **mit der Hand/der Hose** *etc* **~** to get one's hand/trousers *etc* caught in it/them **b** (= *störend erscheinen*) to get in the way; **... wenn nichts dazwischenkommt!** ... if all goes well; **leider ist** *or* **mir ist leider etwas dazwischengekommen, ich kann nicht dabei sein** something has come *or* cropped up, I'm afraid I can't be there; **da|zwi|schen+le|gen** VT *sep* to put in between; **da|zwi|schen|lie|gend** ADJ *attr* **die ~ Seiten/Monate/Bahnhöfe/Farbtöne** *etc* the pages/months/stations/shades *etc* in between; **da|zwi|schen+re|den** VI *sep* **a** (= *unterbrechen*) to interrupt (*jdm* sb) **b** = **dreinreden**; **da|zwi|schen+ru|fen** VTI *sep irreg* to yell out; **da|zwi|schen+schla|gen** VI *sep irreg* to wade in, to lam in (*esp US inf*); **da|zwi|schen+ste|hen** VI *sep irreg aux haben* or *sein* **a** (*lit*) to be amongst *or* (*zwischen zweien*) between them **b** (*zwischen den Parteien*) to be neutral **c** (*geh:*

hindernd) to be in the way; **da|zwi|schen+tre|ten** VI *sep irreg aux sein* **a** (*schlichtend*) to intervene; **sein Dazwischentreten** his intervention **b** (*geh: störend*) to come between them

DB [de:'be:] F - *abbr von* **Deutsche Bahn** von **Deutsche Bundesbahn**

DCC [de:tse:'tse:] F -, -s *abbr von* **Digitale Compact Cassette** DCC®

DD-Dis|ket|te [de:'de:-] F (*Comput*) DD diskette

DDR [de:de:'ɛr] F - (*Hist*) *abbr von* **Deutsche Demokratische Republik** GDR, German Democratic Republic, East Germany

---

DDR

DDR is the abbreviated name of the former East Germany (**Deutsche Demokratische Republik**). The **DDR** was created in 1949 out of the Soviet occupation zone in Germany and evolved into a Warsaw Pact state. Its economy, government and society were closely based on those of the Soviet Union.
In 1961 the **DDR** cut itself off even further from West Germany and the West in general with the construction of the Berlin Wall. By the end of the 1980s increasing numbers of civil rights groups were protesting against the harsh regime and were demanding reforms. The huge pressure exerted by this "velvet revolution" brought about the collapse of the economically weak socialist system in the autumn of 1989. On October 3rd 1990 Germany was re-unified and the **DDR** became part of the **Bundesrepublik Deutschland** → **BRD**

DDR-Bür|ger(in) [de:de:'ɛr-] M(F) (*Hist*) East German, citizen of the German Democratic Republic

DDT® [de:de:'te:] NT - *abbr von* **Dichlordiphenyltrichloräthan** DDT

Deal [di:l] M -s, -s (= *Geschäft etc, inf*: = *Drogengeschäft*) deal

dea|len ['di:lən] (*inf*) VI **er dealt** he is a dealer; **mit etw ~** to deal in sth VT to deal in; *Drogen auch* to push

Dea|ler ['di:lɐ] M -s, -, **Dea|le|rin** ['di:lərɪn] F -, -nen (*inf*) (drug) dealer, pusher; (*international*) trafficker, dealer

De|ba|kel [de'ba:kl] NT -s, - debacle; **ein ~ erleiden** (*Stück etc*) to be a debacle; **damit hat die Regierung ein ~ erlitten** that turned into something of a debacle for the government

De|bat|te [de'batə] F -, -n debate; **etw in die ~ werfen** to throw sth into the discussion; **etw zur ~ stellen** to put sth up for discussion *or* (*Parl*) debate; **was steht zur ~?** what is being discussed *or* is under discussion?; (*Parl*) what is being debated?; **das steht hier nicht zur ~** that's not the issue; **sich in** *or* **auf eine ~ (über etw** *acc***) einlassen** to enter into a discussion (about sth)

de|bat|te|los ADJ (*Parl*) without debate

de|bat|tie|ren [deba'ti:rən] *ptp* **debattiert** VTI to debate; **über etw** (*acc*) **(mit jdm) ~** to discuss sth (with sb); **mit ihm kann man schlecht ~** you can't have a good discussion with him

De|bat|tier|klub M debating society

De|bet ['de:bɛt] NT -s, -s (*Fin*) debits *pl*

De|bet|sei|te F (*Fin*) debit side

de|bil [de'bi:l] ADJ (*Med*) feeble-minded

De|bi|li|tät [debili'tɛːt] F -, *no pl* (*Med*) feeble-mindedness

de|bi|tie|ren [debi'ti:rən] *ptp* **debitiert** VT (*Fin*) to debit; **jdn mit einem Betrag ~** to debit an amount to sb, to debit sb with an amount

De|bi|tor ['de:bito:ɐ] M -s, **Debitoren** [-'to:rən], **De|bi|to|rin** [-'to:rɪn] F -, -nen (*Fin*) debtor

De|bi|to|ren [debi'to:rən] PL (*Econ, Fin*) accounts *pl* receivable

De|büt [de'by:] NT -s, -s debut; **sein ~ als etw geben** to make one's debut as sth

De|bü|tant [deby'tant] M -en, -en *person making his debut* (*fig*: = *Anfänger, Neuling*) novice

De|bü|tan|tin [deby'tantɪn] F -, -nen **a** *person making her debut* (= *Anfänger*) novice **b** (*in der Gesellschaft*) debutante, deb (*inf*)

De|bü|tan|tin|nen|ball M debutantes' ball

de|bü|tie|ren [deby'ti:rən] *ptp* **debütiert** VI (*Theat, fig*) to make one's debut

De|cha|nat [dɛça'na:t] NT -(e)s, -e (*Eccl*) deanery

De|cha|nei [dɛça'nai] F -, -en (*Eccl*) deanery, dean's residence

De|chant [dɛ'çant, 'dɛçant] M -en, -en (*Eccl*) dean

de|chiff|rie|ren [deʃɪ'fri:rən] *ptp* **dechiffriert** VT to decode; *Text, Geheimschrift auch* to decipher

De|chiff|rie|rung F -, -en decoding; (*von Text, Geheimschrift*) deciphering

Deck [dɛk] NT -(e)s, -s deck; (*in Parkhaus*) level; **auf ~** on deck; **an ~ gehen** to go on deck; **alle Mann an ~!** all hands on deck!; **unter** *or* **von ~ gehen** to go below deck

Deck-: Deck|ad|res|se F accommodation *or* cover (*US*) address; **Deck|an|strich** M top *or* final coat; **Deck|auf|bau|ten** PL (*Naut*) superstructure *sing*; **Deck|bett** NT feather quilt; **Deck|blatt** NT (*Bot*) bract; (*von Zigarre*) wrapper; (= *Schutzblatt*) cover; (= *Einlageblatt*) overlay

Deck|chen ['dɛkçən] NT -s, - mat; (*auf Tablett*) tray cloth; (= *Tortendeckchen*) doily; (*auf Sessel etc*) antimacassar; (*für Lehne*) arm cover

Deck|dienst M (*Naut*) deck duty

De|cke ['dɛkə] F -, -n **a** cloth; (= *Wolldecke*) blanket; (*kleiner*) rug; (= *Steppdecke*) quilt; (= *Bettdecke*) cover; **unter die ~ kriechen** to pull the bedclothes (*Brit*) *or* bedcovers up over one's head; **sich nach der ~ strecken** (*fig*) to cut one's coat according to one's cloth; **mit jdm unter einer ~ stecken** (*fig*) to be in league *or* in cahoots (*inf*) *or* hand in glove with sb **b** (= *Zimmerdecke*) ceiling; (*Min*) roof; **es tropft von der ~** there's water coming through the ceiling; **an die ~ gehen** (*inf*) to hit the roof (*inf*); **vor Freude an die ~ springen** (*inf*) to jump for joy; **mir fällt die ~ auf den Kopf** (*fig inf*) I don't like my own company **c** (= *Schicht*) layer; (= *Schneedecke, Staubdecke etc*) blanket; (= *Straßendecke*) surface; (= *Reifendecke*) outer tyre (*Brit*) *or* tire (*US*) *or* cover *or* casing **d** (*Hunt*) skin

De|ckel ['dɛkl] M -s, - lid; (*von Schachtel, Glas auch, von Flasche*) top; (= *Buchdeckel, Uhrdeckel*) cover; (*inf*: = *Hut, Mütze*) titfer (*Brit inf*), hat; **eins auf den ~ kriegen** (*inf*) (= *geschlagen werden*) to get hit on the head; (= *ausgeschimpft werden*) to be given a (good) talking-to (*inf*); **jdm eins auf den ~ geben** (*inf*) (= *schlagen*) to hit sb on the head; (= *ausschimpfen*) to give sb a (good) talking-to (*inf*); **etw unter dem** *or* **unterm ~ halten** to keep the lid on sth → **Topf**

de|ckeln ['dɛkln] VT **a** *mit einem Deckel versehen*) to put a/the lid on; (*fig*: = *nach oben begrenzen*) to impose an upper limit on; **wir müssen die Kosten ~** we'll have to keep a lid on the costs **b** (*inf*: = *rügen*) **jdn ~** to carpet sb (*Brit inf*), to tear sb off a strip (*Brit inf*), to chew sb out (*US inf*)

de|cken ['dɛkn] VT **a** (= *zudecken*) to cover; **ein Dach mit Schiefer/Ziegeln** to cover a building with slate/tiles; **ein Dach mit Stroh/Reet ~** to thatch a roof (with straw/reeds) → *auch* **gedeckt b** (= *zurechtmachen*) *Tisch, Tafel* to set, to lay; **es ist für vier Personen gedeckt** the table is laid *or* set for four (people); **sich an einen gedeckten Tisch setzen** (*lit*) to find one's meal ready and waiting; (*fig*) to be handed everything on a plate

c (= *breiten*) **die Hand/ein Tuch über etw** (*acc*) ~ to cover sth with one's hand/a cloth, to put one's hand/a cloth over sth

d (= *schützen*) to cover; (*Ftbl*) *Spieler auch* to mark; *Komplizen* to cover up for

e *Kosten, Schulden, Bedarf* to cover, to meet; **mein Bedarf ist gedeckt** I have all I need; (*fig inf*) I've had enough (to last me some time); **damit ist unser Bedarf gedeckt** that will meet or cover our needs

f (*Comm, Fin*: = *absichern*) *Scheck, Darlehen* to cover; *Defizit* to offset; **der Schaden wird voll durch die Versicherung gedeckt** the cost of the damage will be fully met by the insurance

g (= *begatten*) *Stute, Ziege* to cover

VI to cover; (*Ftbl*: = *Spieler decken*) to mark; (*Boxen*) to guard; (= *Tisch decken*) to lay a/the table; **du musst besser ~** (*Ftbl*) you must mark your opponent better; (*Boxen*) you must improve your guard; **es ist gedeckt** luncheon/dinner *etc* is served

VR a (*Standpunkte, Interessen, Begriffe*) to coincide; (*Aussagen*) to correspond, to agree; (*Math: Dreiecke, Figur*) to be congruent; **sich ~de Dreiecke** congruent triangles; **sich ~de Begriffe/Interessen** concepts/interests which coincide

b (= *sich schützen*) to defend oneself; (*mit Schild etc*) to protect oneself; (*Boxer etc*) to cover oneself; (= *sich absichern*) to cover oneself

Decken-: Decken|bal|ken M ceiling beam; **Decken|be|leuch|tung** F ceiling lighting; **Decken|ge|mäl|de** NT ceiling fresco; **Decken|ge|wöl|be** NT (*Archit*) vaulting; **Decken|hei|zung** F overhead heating; **Decken|kon|struk|ti|on** F roof construction; **Decken|lam|pe** F ceiling light; **Decken|ma|le|rei** F ceiling fresco; **Decken|strah|ler** M uplighter; **Decken|trä|ger** M ceiling girder

Deck-: Deck|far|be F opaque watercolour (*Brit*) or watercolor (*US*); **Deck|flü|gel** M (*Zool*) wing case; **Deck|fracht** F (*Naut*) deck cargo; **Deck|geld** NT (*Agr*) stud fee; **Deck|glas** NT (*Opt*) cover glass; **Deck|haar** NT top hair; **Deck|haus** NT (*Naut*) deckhouse; **Deck|hengst** M stud (horse), stallion; **Deck|man|tel** M (*fig*) mask, blind; **unter dem ~ von ...** under the guise of ...; **Deck|na|me** M assumed name; (*Mil*) code name; **Deck|of|fi|zier(in)** M(F) (*Naut*) ≈ warrant officer; **Deck|pas|sa|gier(in)** M(F) (*Naut*) first-class passenger; **Deck|pla|ne** F (*Aut*) tarpaulin; **Deck|plat|te** F (*Build*) slab; (*von Mauer*) coping stone; (*von Grab*) covering stone or slab; **Deck|sa|lon** M (*Naut*) first-class lounge; **Deck|schicht** F surface layer; (*von Straße*) surface; (*Geol*) top layer or stratum; **Deck|sta|ti|on** F stud (farm); **Deck|stein** M (*Build*) coping stone; (*von Grab*) covering stone

Deckung F ['dɛkʊŋ] **-en a** (= *Schutz*) cover; (*Ftbl, Chess*) defence (*Brit*), defense (*US*); (*Boxen, Fechten*) guard; **in ~ gehen** to take cover; **~ suchen** to seek cover; **volle ~!** (*Mil*) take cover!; **jdm ~ geben** to cover sb; (= *Feuerschutz auch*) to give sb cover

b (= *Verheimlichung*) **die ~ von etw** covering up of sth; **er kann mit ~ durch den Minister rechnen** he can count on the minister covering up for him

c (*Comm, Fin*) (*von Scheck, Wechsel*) cover; (*von Darlehen*) security; (= *das Decken*) covering; (= *das Begleichen*) meeting; **der Scheck ist ohne ~** the cheque (*Brit*) or check (*US*) is not covered; **ein Darlehen ohne ~** an unsecured loan; **zur ~ seiner Schulden** to meet or cover his debts; **als ~ für seine Schulden** as security or surety for his debts; **dafür ist auf meinem Konto keine ~** there are no funds to cover that in my account; **die Versicherung übernahm die ~ des Schadens** the insurance company agreed to meet or cover the cost of the damage

d (= *Befriedigung*) meeting; **eine ~ der Nachfrage ist unmöglich** demand cannot possibly be met

---

e (= *Übereinstimmung*) (*Math*) congruence; **zur ~ bringen** (*Math*) to make congruent; **lassen sich diese Standpunkte/Interessen zur ~ bringen?** can these points of view/interests be made to coincide?; **diese beiden Zeugenaussagen lassen sich schwer zur ~ bringen** these two statements can't be made to agree

Deckungs-: Deckungs|auf|la|ge F (*Typ*) breakeven quantity; **Deckungs|bei|trag** M (*Econ*) contribution margin, profit contribution; **Deckungs|feh|ler** M (*Ftbl*) error by the defence (*Brit*) or defense (*US*); **Deckungs|feu|er** NT (*Mil*) covering fire; **im ~ der Kameraden** under covering fire from their *etc* comrades; **deckungs|gleich** ADJ (*Math*) congruent; **~ sein** (*fig*) to coincide; (*Aussagen*) to agree; **Deckungs|gleich|heit** F (*Math*) congruence; **wegen der ~ der Ansichten/Aussagen** because of the degree to which these views coincide/these statements agree; **Deckungs|gra|ben** M (*Mil*) shelter trench; **Deckungs|ka|pi|tal** NT (*Insur*) covering funds *pl*; **Deckungs|loch** NT (*Mil*) foxhole; **Deckungs|lü|cke** F (*Fin*) shortfall *no pl*, deficit; **Deckungs|sum|me** F (*Insur*) sum or amount insured; **Deckungs|zu|sa|ge** F (*von Versicherung*) cover note

Deck-: Deck|weiß NT opaque white; **Deck|wort** NT *pl* **-wörter** code word

De|co|der [de'ko:dɐ] M **-s, -** decoder

de|co|die|ren [deko'di:rən] *ptp* **decodiert** VT = **dekodieren**

Dé|col|le|té [dekɔl'te:] NT **-s, -s** = **Dekolleté**

de|cou|ra|giert [dekura'ʒi:ɐt] ADJ (*dated geh*) disheartened, dispirited

De|cres|cen|do [dekre'ʃɛndo] NT (*Mus*) diminuendo

De|di|ka|ti|on [dedika'tsio:n] F **-, -en** (*geh*) **a** (= *Widmung*) dedication **b** (= *Schenkung*) gift

De|di|ka|ti|ons|exem|plar NT presentation copy

de|di|zie|ren [dedi'tsi:rən] *ptp* **dediziert** VT (*geh*) **a** (= *widmen*) to dedicate **b** (= *schenken*) **jdm etw ~** to present sth to sb

De|duk|ti|on [dedʊk'tsio:n] F **-, -en** deduction

de|duk|tiv [dedʊk'ti:f] ADJ deductive ADV deductively

de|du|zie|ren [dedu'tsi:rən] *ptp* **deduziert** VT to deduce (*aus* from)

Deern [de:ɐn] F **-, -s** (*N Ger inf*) lass(ie) (*dial inf*), girl

De|es|ka|la|ti|on [deˌɛskala'tsio:n] F (*Mil*) de-escalation

de|es|ka|lie|ren [deˌɛska'li:rən] *ptp* **deeskaliert** VT to de-escalate VI *aux sein* to de-escalate

Deez [de:ts] M **-es, -e** (*hum inf*) bonce (*Brit inf*), head

de fac|to [de 'fakto] ADV de facto

De-fac|to-An|er|ken|nung F (*Pol*) de facto recognition

de|fä|kie|ren [defɛ'ki:rən] *ptp* **defäkiert** VI (*form*) to defecate

De|fä|tis|mus [defɛ'tɪsmʊs] M **-**, *no pl* defeatism

De|fä|tist [defɛ'tɪst] M **-en, -en, De|fä|tis|tin** [-'tɪstɪn] F **-, -nen** defeatist

de|fä|tis|tisch [defɛ'tɪstɪʃ] ADJ defeatist *no adv*

de|fä|zie|ren [defɛ'tsi:rən] *ptp* **defäziert** VI (*form*) to defecate

de|fekt [de'fɛkt] ADJ *Gerät etc* faulty, defective; *Gen* defective; **geistig/moralisch ~ sein** to be mentally/morally deficient

De|fekt [de'fɛkt] M **-(e)s, -e** fault, defect; (*Med*) deficiency; **körperlicher ~** physical defect; **geistiger ~** mental deficiency; **einen ~ haben** to be faulty or defective; (*inf: Mensch*) to be a bit lacking (*inf*)

de|fek|tiv [defɛk'ti:f] ADJ (*Gram*) defective

De|fek|ti|vum [defɛk'ti:vʊm] NT **-s, Defektiva** [-va] (*Gram*) defective

---

de|fen|siv [defɛn'zi:f] ADJ *Maßnahmen, Taktik* defensive; *Fahrweise* non-aggressive; *Forschungen* into defensive systems ADV defensively; **sich ~ verhalten** to be on the defensive

De|fen|siv- *in cpds* defensive; **De|fen|siv|bünd|nis** NT defence (*Brit*) or defense (*US*) alliance

De|fen|si|ve [defɛn'zi:və] F **-, (rare) -n** defensive; **in der ~ bleiben** to remain on the defensive; **jdn in die ~ drängen** to force sb onto the defensive

De|fen|si|vi|tät [defɛnzivi'tɛ:t] F **-**, *no pl* defensiveness; (*von Fahrweise*) lack of aggression (+*gen* in), defensiveness (*US*) (+*gen* of)

De|fen|siv-: De|fen|siv|krieg M defensive warfare; **De|fen|siv|spiel** NT defensive game; **De|fen|siv|stel|lung** F defensive position, position of defence (*Brit*) or defense (*US*)

De|fi|bril|la|tor [defibri'la:to:ɐ] M **-s, -en** [-la'to:rən] (*Med*) defibrillator

De|fi|lee [defi'le:] NT **-s, -s** *or* **-n** [-'le:ən] (*Mil*) march past; (*fig*) parade

de|fi|lie|ren [defi'li:rən] *ptp* **defiliert** VI *aux haben or sein* (*Mil*) to march past; (*fig*) to parade past

de|fi|nier|bar ADJ definable; **schwer/leicht ~** hard/easy to define

de|fi|nie|ren [defi'ni:rən] *ptp* **definiert** VT to define; **etw neu ~** to redefine sth

De|fi|ni|ti|on [defini'tsio:n] F **-, -en** definition

de|fi|ni|tiv [defini'ti:f] ADJ definite ADV (= *bestimmt*) definitely

de|fi|ni|to|risch [defini'to:rɪʃ] (*geh*) *Frage, Problem* of definition ADV **ein ~ schwieriges Problem** a problem which is hard to define

de|fi|zi|ent [defi'tsiɛnt] ADJ deficient

De|fi|zit ['de:fitsɪt] NT **-s, -e** (= *Fehlbetrag*) deficit; (= *Mangel*) deficiency (*an* +*dat* of)

de|fi|zi|tär [defitsi'tɛ:ɐ] ADJ in deficit; **die ~e Entwicklung der Organisation** the trend in the organization to run to a deficit; **eine ~e Haushaltspolitik führen** to follow an economic policy which can only lead to deficit ADV **das Bankwesen entwickelt sich immer ~er** the banks have a larger deficit every year

De|fla|ti|on [defla'tsio:n] F **-, -en** (*Econ*) deflation

de|fla|ti|o|när [deflatsio'nɛ:ɐ], **de|fla|ti|o|nis|tisch** [deflatsio'nɪstɪʃ] ADJ deflationary *no adv*

De|fla|ti|ons|po|li|tik F deflationary policy

de|fla|to|risch [defla'to:rɪʃ] ADJ (*Econ*) = **deflationär**

De|flo|ra|ti|on [deflora'tsio:n] F **-, -en** defloration

de|flo|rie|ren [deflo'ri:rən] *ptp* **defloriert** VT to deflower

De|for|ma|ti|on [defɔrma'tsio:n] F deformation, distortion; (= *Missbildung*) deformity; (= *Entstellung*) disfigurement

de|for|mie|ren [defɔr'mi:rən] *ptp* **deformiert** VT (*Tech*) to deform, to contort; (*lit, fig*: = *missbilden*) to deform; (= *entstellen*) to disfigure; **in einer Schlägerei haben sie ihm die Nase deformiert** they flattened his nose (for him) in a fight; **eine deformierte Nase** a misshapen nose

De|for|mie|rung F **a** (= *das Deformieren*) deformation; (= *Entstellung*) disfigurement **b** = **Deformation**

De|for|mi|tät [defɔrmi'tɛ:t] F **-, -en** (*Med*) deformity

De|fros|ter [de'frɔstɐ] M **-s, -** (*Aut*) heated windscreen (*Brit*) or windshield (*US*), defroster (*US*); (= *Sprühmittel*) de-icer; (*im Kühlschrank*) defroster

def|tig ['dɛftɪç] ADJ **a** (= *derb, urwüchsig*) *Witz, Humor* ribald **b** (= *kräftig*) *Lüge* whopping (*inf*), huge; *Mahlzeit, Wurst etc* substantial, good solid *attr*; *Ohrfeige* cracking (*inf*); *Preis* extortionate; **~e Hausmannskost** good plain cooking, good honest fare (*esp Brit*) ADV (= *tüchtig*) really; **~**

---

schmecken to taste well-seasoned; **sich ~ aus-drücken** to speak bluntly

Def|tig|keit F -, no pl (= Derbheit, Urwüchsigkeit) ribaldry

de|ga|gie|ren [dega'ʒiːrən] ptp **degagiert** VT (Fechten) to disengage

De|gen ['deːgn̩] M -s, - rapier; (Sportfechten) é-pée; **mit bloßem** or **nacktem ~** with one's rapier drawn → **kreuzen** VT

De|ge|ne|ra|ti|on [degenera'tsioːn] F degeneration

De|ge|ne|ra|ti|ons|er|schei|nung F sign of degeneration

de|ge|ne|ra|tiv [degenera'tiːf] ADJ Schäden, Krankheit degenerative

de|ge|ne|rie|ren [degene'riːrən] ptp **degeneriert** VI aux sein to degenerate (zu into)

de|ge|ne|riert [degene'riːrət] ADJ degenerate

De|gen-: De|gen|fech|ten NT -s, no pl épée fencing; **De|gen|klin|ge** F rapier blade; **De|gen|knauf** M pommel; **De|gen|korb** M guard; **De|gen|stoß** M thrust from one's/a rapier

de|gou|tant [degu'tant] ADJ (geh) distasteful, disgusting

de|gou|tie|ren [degu'tiːrən] ptp **degoutiert** VT (geh) to disgust

De|gra|da|ti|on [degrada'tsioːn] F (Phys) **~ der Energie** degradation of energy

de|gra|die|ren [degra'diːrən] ptp **degradiert** VT (Mil) to demote (zu to); (fig = herabwürdigen) to degrade; **jdn/etw zu etw ~** (fig) to lower sb/sth to the level of sth

De|gra|die|rung F -, -en (Mil) demotion (zu to); (fig) degradation; **diese Behandlung emp-fand er als (eine)** ~ he felt such treatment to be degrading

De|gres|si|on [degrɛ'sioːn] F -, -en (Fin) degression

de|gres|siv [degrɛ'siːf] ADJ (Fin) degressive

De|gus|ta|ti|on [degʊsta'tsioːn] F -, -en (esp Sw) tasting

de|gus|tie|ren [degʊs'tiːrən] ptp **degustiert** VTI (esp Sw) Wein to taste

dehn|bar ADJ (lit) elastic; (fig auch) flexible; Stoff stretch attr, stretchy (inf), elastic; Metall ductile; **ein ~er Vokal** a vowel which can be lengthened

Dehn|bar|keit F -, no pl (lit) elasticity; (fig auch) flexibility; (von Stoff) stretchi-ness (inf), elasticity; (von Metall) ductility; **Eisen hat eine geringere ~ als Blei** iron is less ductile than lead; **die ~ der Vokale** the degree or ex-tent to which the vowels can be lengthened

deh|nen ['deːnən] VT to stretch; (Med auch) to dilate; Laut, Silbe to lengthen; **seine gedehnte Sprechweise** his drawling way of speaking; **Vo-kale gedehnt aussprechen** to pronounce one's vowels long VR to stretch; **er dehnte und streckte sich** he had a good stretch; **die Minu-ten dehnten sich zu Stunden** (geh) the minutes seemed like hours; **vor ihnen dehnte sich der Ozean** (geh) the ocean stretched out before them; **der Weg dehnte sich endlos** the road seemed to go on for ever

Dehn- ['deːn-] (Ling): **Dehn|strich** M length mark; **Dehn|stu|fe** F lengthened grade, dehn-stufe (form)

Deh|nung F -, -en stretching; (Med auch) dila-tion; (von Laut, Silbe) lengthening

Dehnungs- (Ling): **Dehnungs-h** [-haː] NT h with a lengthening effect on the preceding vowel; **Dehnungs|strich** M length mark

de|hyd|rie|ren [dehy'driːrən] ptp **dehydriert** VT (Chem) to dehydrate

De|hyd|rie|rung F -, -en (Chem) dehydration

Dei|bel ['daibl] M -s, - (N Ger inf) → **Teufel, pfui**

Deich [daiç] M -(e)s, -e dyke (Brit), dike (esp US)

Deich-: Deich|bau M , no pl dyke (Brit), dike (esp US); (= das Bauen) dyke (Brit) or dike (esp US) building; **Deich|bruch** M breach in the dyke (Brit) or dike (esp US); **Deich|ge|nos-sen|schaft** F association of owners of dyked land; **Deich|graf** M , **Deich|haupt|mann** M dyke (Brit) or dike (esp US) reeve (old) or warden; **Deich|kro|ne** F dyke (Brit) or dike (esp US) top

Deich|sel ['daiksl] F -, -n shaft, whiffletree (US); (= Doppeldeichsel) shafts pl; **ein Pferd in der ~** a horse in or between the shafts; **Ochsen an die ~ spannen** to yoke oxen into or between the shafts

Deich|sel-: Deich|sel|bruch M broken shaft/shafts; **Deich|sel|kreuz** NT **a** handle **b** (Rel) Y-shaped cross

deich|seln ['daiksln̩] VT (inf) to wangle (inf); **das werden wir schon ~** we'll wangle it some-how (inf)

Deich-: Deich|ver|band M association of owners of dyked land; **Deich|vogt** M (old) dyke (Brit) or dike (esp US) reeve (old); **Deich|vor|land** NT land to the seaward side of a dyke

De|i|fi|ka|ti|on [deifika'tsioːn] F -, -en (Philos) deification

de|i|fi|zie|ren [deifi'tsiːrən] ptp **deifiziert** VT (Philos) to deify

dein [dain] POSS PRON **a** (adjektivisch) your, thy (obs, dial); **~ doofes/schönes Gesicht** that stu-pid/beautiful face of yours, your stupid/beauti-ful face; **rauchst du immer noch ~e 20 Zigaret-ten pro Tag?** are you still smoking your 20 ci-garettes a day?; **herzliche Grüße, ~e Elke** with best wishes, yours or (herzlicher) love Elke; **stets** or **immer ~ Otto** yours ever, Otto; **Dein Wille geschehe** (Bibl) Thy will be done **b** (old: substantivisch) yours; **behalte, was ~ ist** keep what is yours PERS PRON gen von **du** (old, poet) **ich werde ewig ~ gedenken** I shall remember you forever

dei|ner ['dainɐ] PERS PRON gen von **du** (geh) of you; **wir werden ~ gedenken** we will remember you

dei|ne(r, s) ['dainə] POSS PRON (substantivisch) yours; **der/die/das ~** or **Deine** (geh) yours; **tu du das ~** or **Deine** (geh) you do your bit or part (esp US); **stets** or **immer der ~** or **Deine** (form) yours ever; **die ~n** or **Deinen** (geh) your family, your people; **du und die ~n** or **Deinen** (geh: = Familie) you and yours; **das ~** or **Deine** (geh: = Besitz) what is yours

dei|ner|seits ['dainɐ'zaits] ADV (= auf deiner Seite) for your part; (= von deiner Seite) on your part; **den Vorschlag hast du ~ gemacht** you made the suggestion yourself

dei|nes|glei|chen ['dainəs'glaiçn̩] PRON inv people like you or yourself; (pej auch) your sort or type, the likes of you; **an Schönheit ist keine ~** (liter) in beauty there is none to equal you (li-ter)

dei|net-: dei|net|hal|ben ['dainət'halbn̩] (dat-ed), **dei|net|we|gen** ['dainət've:gn̩] ADV (= wegen dir) because of you, on account of you, on your account; (= dir zuliebe) for your sake; (= um dich) about you; (= für dich) on your be-half; **dei|net|wil|len** ['dainət'vilən] ADV **um ~** for your sake

dei|ni|ge ['dainiɡə] POSS PRON (old, geh) **der/die/das ~** or **Deinige** yours; **die ~n** or **Deinigen** your family or friends; **das ~** or **Deinige** (= Be-sitz) what is yours; **tu du das ~** or **Deinige** you do your bit or part (esp US)

deins [dains] POSS PRON yours

De|in|stal|la|ti|on [de:ɪnstala'tsioːn] F -, -en (Comput: von Software) de-installation

de|in|stal|lie|ren [de:ɪnsta'liːrən] ptp **deinstal-liert** VT (Comput) Software to de-install

De|is|mus [de:'ɪsmʊs] M -, no pl (Philos) deism

De|ist [de:'ɪst] M -en, -en, **De|is|tin** [-'ɪstɪn] F -, -nen (Philos) deist

de|is|tisch [de:'ɪstɪʃ] ADJ (Philos) deistic

Dei|wel ['daivl] M -s, - (N Ger), **Dei|xel** ['daiksl] M -s, - (S Ger) = **Teufel**

Dé|jà-vu-Er|leb|nis [deʒa'vyː-] NT (Psych) sense or feeling of déjà vu

de ju|re [deː 'juːrə] ADV de jure

De-ju|re-An|er|ken|nung F de jure recogni-tion

De|ka ['dɛka] NT -(s), - (Aus) = **Dekagramm**

De|ka|de [de'kaːdə] F -, -n (= 10 Tage) ten days, ten-day period; (= 10 Jahre) decade

de|ka|dent [deka'dɛnt] ADJ decadent

De|ka|denz [deka'dɛnts] F -, no pl decadence

De|ka|denz|er|schei|nung F sign of deca-dence

de|ka|disch [de'kaːdɪʃ] ADJ Zahlensystem deci-mal; **~er Logarithmus** common logarithm

De|ka-: De|ka|eder [deka'le:dɐ] M -s, - decahe-dron; **De|ka|gon** [deka'goːn] NT -s, -e deca-gon; **De|ka|gramm** [deka-, 'dɛka-] NT deca-gram(me); **10 ~ Schinken** (Aus) 100 grams of ham; **De|ka|li|ter** ['deka-, 'dɛka-] M decalitre (Brit), decaliter (US)

De|ka|log [deka'loːk] M -(e)s [-ɡəs] (Bibl) deca-logue

De|ka|me|ron [de'kaːmerɔn] NT -s Decameron

De|ka|me|ter ['deka-, 'dɛka-] M decametre (Brit), decameter (US)

De|kan [de'kaːn] M -s, -e (Univ, Eccl) dean

De|ka|nat [deka'naːt] NT -(e)s, -e **a** (Univ, Eccl: = Amt, Amtszeit) deanship (= Amtssitz) (Univ) office of the dean; (Eccl) deanery

De|ka|nei [deka'nai] F -, -en (Eccl) deanery

De|ka|nin [de'kaːnɪn] F -, -nen (Univ) dean

de|kan|tie|ren [dekant'iːrən] ptp **dekantiert** VT Wein to decant

de|kar|bo|ni|sie|ren [dekarboni'ziːrən] ptp **de-karbonisiert** VT to decarbonize; (Aut) to de-coke

de|kar|tel|lie|ren [dekarte'liːrən] ptp **dekartel-liert**, **de|kar|tel|li|sie|ren** [dekarteli'ziːrən] ptp **dekartellisiert** VT to decartelize

De|kla|ma|ti|on [deklama'tsioːn] F -, -en decla-mation; **~en** (pej) (empty) rhetoric sing

de|kla|ma|to|risch [deklama'toːrɪʃ] ADJ de-clamatory, rhetorical

de|kla|mie|ren [dekla'miːrən] ptp **deklamiert** VTI to declaim

De|kla|ra|ti|on [deklara'tsioːn] F -, -en (alle Be-deutungen) declaration

de|kla|rie|ren [dekla'riːrən] ptp **deklariert** VT (alle Bedeutungen) to declare

De|kla|rie|rung F -, -en declaration

de|klas|sie|ren [dekla'siːrən] ptp **deklassiert** VT **a** (Sociol, = herabsetzen) to downgrade **b** (Sport: = weit übertreffen) to outclass

De|klas|sie|rung F -, -en (Sociol) downgrading; (Sport) outclassing

de|kli|na|bel [dekli'naːbl] ADJ (Gram) declina-ble

De|kli|na|ti|on [deklina'tsioːn] F -, -en **a** (Gram) declension **b** (Astron, Phys) declination

de|kli|nier|bar ADJ (Gram) declinable

de|kli|nie|ren [dekli'niːrən] ptp **dekliniert** VT (Gram) to decline

de|ko|die|ren [deko'diːrən] ptp **dekodiert** VT to decode

De|ko|die|rung F -, -en decoding

De|kol|le|té [dekɔl'teː] NT -s, -s, **De|kol|le|tee** ▲ NT -s, -s low-cut or décolleté neckline, dé-colletage; **ein Kleid mit einem tiefen/gewagten ~** a very/daringly low-cut or décolleté dress; **ihr ~ war so tief, ...** she was wearing such a low--cut or plunging neckline ...

de|kol|le|tie|ren [dekɔl'tiːrən] ptp **dekolletiert** VT to give a or cut with a low neckline

de|kol|le|tiert [dekɔl'tiːɐt] ADJ *Kleid* low-cut, décolleté; **eine ~e Dame** a woman in a low-cut dress

De|ko|lo|ni|sa|ti|on [dekoloniza'tsioːn] F decolonization

de|ko|lo|ni|sie|ren [dekoloni'ziːrən] *ptp* **dekolonisiert** VT to decolonize

De|kom|po|si|ti|on [dekɔmpozi'tsioːn] F decomposition

De|kom|po|si|tum [dekɔm'poːzitʊm] NT (*Ling*) (= *zusammengesetztes Wort*) mutiple compound, decomposite (*form*), decompound (*form*); (= *Ableitung*) compound derivative

De|kom|pres|si|on [dekɔmprɛ'sioːn] F decompression

De|kom|pres|si|ons|kam|mer F decompression chamber

de|kom|pri|mie|ren [dekɔmpri'miːrən] *ptp* **dekomprimiert** VT (*Comput*) to decompress

De|kon|ta|mi|na|ti|on [dekɔntamina'tsioːn] F decontamination

de|kon|ta|mi|nie|ren [dekɔntami'niːrən] *ptp* **dekontaminiert** VT to decontaminate

De|kon|zent|ra|ti|on [dekɔntsentra'tsioːn] F deconcentration, decentralization

De|kor [de'koːɐ] M OR NT **-s, -s** *or* **-e a** decoration; (*von Raum auch*) décor; (= *Muster*) pattern **b** (*Theat, Film etc*) décor

De|ko|ra|teur [dekora'tøːɐ] M **-s, -e**, **De|ko|ra|teu|rin** [-'tøːrɪn] F **-, -nen** (= *Schaufensterdekorateur*) window-dresser; (*von Innenräumen*) interior designer

De|ko|ra|ti|on [dekora'tsioːn] F **-, -en a** *no pl* (= *das Ausschmücken*) decorating, decoration **b** (= *Einrichtung*) décor *no pl*; (= *Fensterdekoration*) window-dressing *or* decoration; (*Theat*: = *Bühnenbild*) set; **zur ~ dienen** to be decorative; **zu Weihnachten haben viele Kaufhäuser schöne ~en** many department stores are beautifully decorated for Christmas **c** (= *Orden, Ordensverleihung*) decoration

De|ko|ra|ti|ons-: De|ko|ra|ti|ons|ar|bei|ten PL decorating *no pl*; **De|ko|ra|ti|ons|ma|ler(in)** M(F) (interior) decorator; (*Theat*) scene painter; **De|ko|ra|ti|ons|stoff** M (*Tex*) furnishing fabric; **De|ko|ra|ti|ons|stück** NT piece of the décor; **das ist nur ein ~** that's just for decoration

de|ko|ra|tiv [dekora'tiːf] ADJ decorative ADV decoratively; **~ wirken** *or* **aussehen** to look decorative

de|ko|rie|ren [deko'riːrən] *ptp* **dekoriert** VT to decorate; *Schaufenster* to dress

De|ko|rie|rung F **-, -en** decoration; (*von Schaufenster*) dressing

De|ko|rum [de'koːrʊm] NT **-s**, *no pl* (*liter*) propriety, decorum; **das ~ wahren** to maintain *or* observe the proprieties; **das ~ verletzen** to go against *or* infringe the proprieties

De|ko|stoff ['deko-] M furnishing fabric

Dek|ret [de'kreːt] NT **-(e)s, -e** decree

dek|re|tie|ren [dekre'tiːrən] *ptp* **dekretiert** VT to decree

de|kuv|rie|ren [deku'vriːrən] *ptp* **dekuvriert** (*geh*) VT *Skandal, Machenschaften* to expose, to uncover; *Person, Betrüger etc* to expose VR to reveal oneself

De|le|a|tur(zei|chen) [dele'aːtʊr-] NT **-s, -** (*Typ*) deletion mark

De|le|gat [dele'gaːt] M **-en, -en**, **De|le|ga|tin** [-'gaːtɪn] F **-, -nen** delegate

De|le|ga|ti|on [delega'tsioːn] F **-, -en** (*alle Bedeutungen*) delegation

De|le|ga|ti|ons|chef(in) M(F) head of a delegation; **der koreanische ~** the head of the Korean delegation

de|le|gie|ren [dele'giːrən] *ptp* **delegiert** VT (*alle Bedeutungen*) to delegate (*an +acc* to)

De|le|gier|ten|kon|fe|renz F , **De|le|gier|ten|ver|samm|lung** F delegates' conference

De|le|gier|te(r) [dele'giːɐtə] MF *decl as adj* delegate

de|lek|tie|ren [delɛk'tiːrən] *ptp* **delektiert** (*geh*) VR **sich an etw** (*dat*) **~** to delight in sth VT **jdn mit etw ~** to delight sb with sth; **sie delektierten den Sultan mit Tänzen** they danced for the sultan's delectation (*liter*)

Del|fin *etc* ▲ [dɛl'fiːn] = **Delphin** *etc*

Delf|ter ['dɛlftɐ] ADJ *attr Porzellan etc* Delft

de|li|kat [deli'kaːt] ADJ **a** (= *wohlschmeckend*) exquisite, delicious **b** (= *behutsam*) delicate; *Andeutung auch* gentle **c** (= *heikel*) *Problem, Frage* delicate, sensitive; (= *gewagt*) risqué **d** (*geh*: = *empfindlich*) delicate ADV *zubereitet* exquisitely; **~ schmecken** to taste exquisite *or* delicious

De|li|ka|tess- ▲ [delika'tɛs] *in cpds* (top-)quality

De|li|ka|tes|se [delika'tɛsə] F **-, -n a** (= *Leckerbissen, fig*) delicacy; **ein Geschäft für Obst und ~n** a fruit shop and delicatessen **b** *no pl* (*geh*: = *Feinfühligkeit*) delicacy, sensitivity

De|li|ka|tes|sen|ge|schäft NT delicatessen, deli (*inf*)

De|li|ka|tess-: De|li|ka|tess|gur|ke ▲ F gherkin; **De|li|ka|tess|la|den** ▲ M = **Delikatessengeschäft**; **De|li|ka|tess|senf** ▲ M (top-)quality mustard

De|likt [de'lɪkt] NT **-(e)s, -e** (*Jur*) offence (*Brit*), offense (*US*); (*schwerer*) crime

de|lin|quent [delɪŋ'kvɛnt] ADJ (*Sociol, Psych*) delinquent

De|lin|quent [delɪŋ'kvɛnt] M **-en, -en**, **De|lin|quen|tin** [-'kvɛntɪn] F **-, -nen** (*geh*) offender

De|lin|quenz [delɪŋ'kvɛnts] F **-**, *no pl* (*Sociol, Psych*) delinquency

de|li|rie|ren [deli'riːrən] *ptp* **deliriert** VI (*geh, Med*) to be delirious; **er delirierte im Fieber** he was delirious with fever

De|li|ri|um [de'liːriʊm] NT **-s, Delirien** [-riən] delirium; **im ~ sein** to be delirious, to be in a state of delirium; (*inf*: = *betrunken*) to be paralytic (*inf*); **im ~ redete der Kranke wirr und konfus** the sick man raved deliriously; **in seinen Delirien** whenever he was delirious; (= *betrunken*) whenever he was paralytic (*inf*); **~ tremens** delirium tremens, the DT's

de|li|zi|ös [deli'tsiøːs] (*liter*) ADJ most delectable ADV *schmecken, duften* delectable, delicious

Del|le ['dɛlə] F **-, -n a** (*inf*) dent; **eine ~ bekommen** to get a dent, to get *or* be dented **b** (= *Bodendelle*) hollow, dip

de|lo|gie|ren [delo'ʒiːrən] *ptp* **delogiert** VT (*Aus*) *Mieter* to evict

De|lo|gie|rung F **-, -en** (*Aus*) eviction

Del|phi ['dɛlfi] NT **-s** Delphi; **das Orakel von ~** the Delphic oracle, the oracle of Delphi

Del|phin¹ [dɛl'fiːn] M **-s, -e** (*Zool*) dolphin

Del|phin² NT **-s**, *no pl* (= *Delphinschwimmen*) butterfly (stroke)

Del|phi|na|ri|um [dɛlfi'naːriʊm] NT **-s, Delphinarien** [-riən] dolphinarium

Del|phin|schwim|men NT butterfly (stroke)

del|phisch ['dɛlfɪʃ] ADJ Delphic; **das Delphische Orakel** the Delphic oracle

Del|ta¹ ['dɛlta] NT **-s, -s** *or* **Delten** ['dɛltn] (*Geog*) delta

Del|ta² NT **-(s), -s** (= *Buchstabe*) delta

Del|ta-: del|ta|för|mig ADJ delta-shaped, deltaic (*rare*); *Muskel* deltoid; **Del|ta|mün|dung** F delta estuary; **Del|ta|mus|kel** M deltoid; **Del|ta|strah|len** PL (*Phys*) delta rays *pl*

de Luxe [də 'lyks] ADJ (*Comm*) de luxe

De-Luxe-Aus|füh|rung F (*Comm*) de luxe version

dem [deːm] DEF ART *dat von* **der** *von* **das a** to the; (*mit Präposition*) the **b** **es ist nicht an ~** that is not the case, that is not how it is; **wenn ~ so ist** if that is the way it is; **wie ~ auch sei** be that as it may DEM PRON *dat von* **der** *von* **das a** *attr* to that; (*mit Präposition*) that **b** (*substan-*

tivisch) to that one; that one; (*Menschen*) to him; him; (*von mehreren*) to that one; that one REL PRON *dat von* **der** *von* **das** to whom, that *or* who(m) ... to; (*mit Präposition*) who(m); (*von Sachen*) to which, which *or* that ... to; which; **~ der Fehler unterlaufen ist, ...** whoever made that mistake ...

De|ma|go|ge [dema'goːgə] M **-n, -n**, **De|ma|go|gin** [-'goːgɪn] F **-, -nen** demagogue

De|ma|go|gie [demago'giː] F **-, -n** [-'giːən] demagogy, demagoguery

de|ma|go|gisch [dema'goːgɪʃ] ADJ *Rede etc* demagogic ADV **leider lassen sich die Wähler immer noch ~ beeinflussen** sadly voters can still be swayed by demagogues *or* by demagogic ploys; **er hat in seiner Rede die Tatsachen ~ verzerrt** in his speech he twisted the facts to demagogic ends

de|man|ten [de'mantn] ADJ (*poet*) = **diamanten**

De|mar|che [de'marʃə] F **-, -n** (*Pol*) (diplomatic) representation, démarche; **eine ~ unternehmen** to lodge a diplomatic protest

De|mar|ka|ti|on [demarka'tsioːn] F **-, -en** demarcation

De|mar|ka|ti|ons|li|nie F (*Pol, Mil*) demarcation line; **die ~ des Waffenstillstands** the cease-fire line

de|mar|kie|ren [demar'kiːrən] *ptp* **demarkiert** VT *Grenze, Bereiche* to demarcate

de|mas|kie|ren [demas'kiːrən] *ptp* **demaskiert** VT to unmask, to expose; **jdn als etw ~** to expose sb as sth VR to unmask oneself, to take off one's mask; **sich als etw ~** to show oneself to be sth

De|men|ti [de'mɛnti] NT **-s, -s** denial

de|men|tie|ren [demɛn'tiːrən] *ptp* **dementiert** VT to deny VI to deny it

De|men|tie|rung F **-, -en** denial, denying

dem|ent|spre|chend ['deːmʔɛnt'ʃprɛçnt] ADV correspondingly; (= *demnach*) accordingly; *bezahlt* commensurately ADJ appropriate; *Bemerkung auch* apposite (*form*); *Gehalt* commensurate; *Vertrag* on this matter; **er nennt sich Christ, aber sein Verhalten ist nicht ~** he says he is a Christian but he does not behave accordingly *or* correspondingly

De|menz [de'mɛnts] F **-, -en** (*Med*) dementia

dem-: dem|ge|gen|über ['deːmgeˑgnˈʔyːbɐ] ADV (= *wohingegen*) on the other hand; (= *im Vergleich dazu*) in contrast; **dem|ge|mäß** ['deːmgeˑmɛːs] ADV = **dementsprechend**

de|mi|li|ta|ri|sie|ren [demilitari'ziːrən] *ptp* **demilitarisiert** VT to demilitarize

De|mi|li|ta|ri|sie|rung F **-, -en** demilitarization

De|mi|mon|de [dəmi'mõːd] F **-**, *no pl* (*pej geh*) demimonde

De|mis|si|on [demɪ'sioːn] F (*Pol*) (= *Rücktritt*) resignation; (= *Entlassung*) dismissal; **um seine ~ bitten** to ask to be relieved of one's duties; **er wurde zur ~ gezwungen** he was forced to resign

de|mis|si|o|nie|ren [demɪsio'niːrən] *ptp* **demissioniert** VI (*Pol, Sw*: = *kündigen*) to resign

De|mis|si|ons|an|ge|bot NT offer of resignation *or* to resign

De|mi|urg [demi'ʊrk] M **-en** *or* **-s**, *no pl* (*Myth, liter*) demiurge

dem-: dem|nach ['deːmnaːx] ADV therefore; (= *dementsprechend*) accordingly; **dem|nächst** ['deːmnɛːçst, deːm'nɛːçst] ADV soon; **~ (in diesem Kino)** coming soon

De|mo ['deːmo] F **-s, -s** (*inf*) demo (*inf*)

De|mo|bi|li|sa|ti|on [demobiliza'tsioːn] F **-, -en** (*Mil*) demobilization

de|mo|bi|li|sie|ren [demobili'ziːrən] *ptp* **demobilisiert** VT to demobilize; *Soldaten* to demobilize, to demob (*Brit inf*) VI to demobilize; (*Sol-*

dat) to demobilize, to get *or* be demobbed (*Brit inf*)

De|mo|bi|li|sie|rung F -, -en demobilization; (*von Soldaten*) demobilization, demob (*Brit inf*)

De|mo-CD F (*inf*) demo CD

dé|mo|dé [de:mo'de:] ADJ *attr* (*geh*) outmoded

De|mo|dis|ket|te ['de:mo-] F (*Comput*) demo disk

De|mo|du|la|ti|on [demodula'tsio:n] F -, -en (*Tech*) demodulation

De|mo|graf ▲ [demo'graːf] M -en, -en, **De|mo|gra|fin** ▲ [-'graːfɪn] F -, -nen demographer

De|mo|gra|fie ▲ [demogra'fiː] F -, -n [-'fiːən] demography

de|mo|gra|fisch ▲ [demo'graːfɪʃ] ADJ demographic

De|mo|krat [demo'kraːt] M -en, -en, **De|mo|kra|tin** [-'kraːtɪn] F -, -nen democrat; (*US Pol*) Democrat

De|mo|kra|tie [demokra'tiː] F -, -n [-'tiːən] democracy

De|mo|kra|tie-: De|mo|kra|tie|be|griff M concept of democracy; **De|mo|kra|tie|ver|ständ|nis** NT understanding of (the meaning of) democracy

de|mo|kra|tisch [demo'kraːtɪʃ] ADJ democratic
ADV democratically

de|mo|kra|ti|sie|ren [demokrati'ziːrən] ptp **de|mo|kra|ti|siert** VT to democratize, to make democratic

De|mo|kra|ti|sie|rung F -, -en democratization

De|mo|kra|ti|sie|rungs|pro|zess ▲ M democratization *or* democratic process

de|mo|lie|ren [demo'liːrən] ptp **demoliert** VT to wreck, to smash up; (*Rowdy auch*) to vandalize; **nach dem Unfall war das Auto total demoliert** after the accident the car was a complete wreck; **er sah ganz schön demoliert aus** (*inf*) he was a real mess, he looked pretty badly bashed about (*inf*)

De|mo|lie|rung F -, -en wrecking, smashing-up; (*durch Rowdy auch*) vandalizing

De|monst|rant [demon'strant] M -en, -en, **De|monst|ran|tin** [-'strantɪn] F -, -nen demonstrator

De|monst|ra|ti|on [demonstra'tsio:n] F -, -en (*alle Bedeutungen*) demonstration; **zur ~ seiner Friedfertigkeit ...** as a demonstration of *or* to demonstrate his peaceful intentions ...; **eine ~ für/gegen etw** a demonstration in support of/against sth

De|monst|ra|ti|ons-: De|monst|ra|ti|ons|frei|heit F freedom *or* right to demonstrate, freedom to hold demonstrations; **De|monst|ra|ti|ons|marsch** M march; **De|monst|ra|ti|ons|ma|te|ri|al** NT teaching material *or* aids *pl*; **De|monst|ra|ti|ons|ob|jekt** NT teaching aid; **De|monst|ra|ti|ons|recht** NT right to demonstrate, right to hold demonstrations; **De|monst|ra|ti|ons|straf|recht** NT criminal law as it relates to demonstrations; **De|monst|ra|ti|ons|ver|bot** NT ban on demonstrations; **De|monst|ra|ti|ons|zug** M demonstration, (protest) march

de|monst|ra|tiv [demonstra'tiːf] ADJ demonstrative (*auch Gram*); Beifall acclamatory; Protest, Fehlen pointed; Beispiel clear; **war seine Abwesenheit ~ oder reiner Zufall?** was his absence a deliberate *or* pointed gesture or pure chance? ADV pointedly; **der Botschafter verließ während der Rede ~ den Saal** during the speech the ambassador pointedly left the room; **~ Beifall spenden** to make a point of applauding

De|monst|ra|tiv|pro|no|men NT (*Gram*) demonstrative pronoun

de|monst|rie|ren [demon'striːrən] ptp **demonstriert** VTI (*alle Bedeutungen*) to demonstrate; **für/gegen etw ~** to demonstrate in support of/against sth; **die Regierung hat ihre Entschlossenheit demonstriert** the government gave a demonstration of *or* demonstrated its determination

De|mon|ta|ge [demon'taːʒə] F (*lit, fig*) dismantling

de|mon|tie|ren [demon'tiːrən] ptp **demontiert** VT (*lit, fig*) to dismantle; Räder to take off

De|mo|ra|li|sa|ti|on [demoraliza'tsio:n] F -, (*rare*) -en (= *Entmutigung*) demoralization; (= *Sittenverfall*) moral decline

de|mo|ra|li|sie|ren [demorali'ziːrən] ptp **demoralisiert** VT (= *entmutigen*) to demoralize; (= *korrumpieren*) to corrupt; **die römische Gesellschaft war am Ende so demoralisiert, dass ...** ultimately Roman society had suffered such a moral decline that ...

De|mo|ra|li|sie|rung F -, -en (= *Entmutigung*) demoralization

De|mo|skop [demo'skoːp] M -en -en, **De|mo|sko|pin** [-'skoːpɪn] F -, -nen (opinion) pollster

De|mo|sko|pie [demosko'piː] F -, *no pl* (public) opinion research

de|mo|sko|pisch [demo'skoːpɪʃ] ADJ Daten, Erkenntnisse opinion poll *attr*; Veränderungen in (public) opinion research; **~es Institut** (public) opinion research institute; **alle ~en Voraussagen waren falsch** all the predictions in the opinion polls were wrong; **eine ~e Untersuchung** a (public) opinion poll

De|mo|ver|si|on F (*inf: auf CD etc*) demo version

dem-: dem|sel|ben [de:m'zɛlbn] dat von derselbe *von* dasselbe; **dem|un|er|acht|et** △ ['de:mlʊnlɛɐˈlaxtət, 'de:m'lʊn-], **dem|un|ge|ach|tet** △ ['de:mlʊngəˈlaxtət, 'de:m'lʊn-] ADV (*old*) → **dessen REL PRON**

De|mut ['de:muːt] F -, *no pl* humility; **in ~** with humility

de|mü|tig ['de:myːtɪç] ADJ Bitte, Blick humble ADV humbly

de|mü|ti|gen ['de:myːtɪgn] VT Gefangenen, Besiegten, Volk to humiliate; (= *eine Lektion erteilen*) stolzen Menschen etc to humble VR to humble oneself (*vor +dat* before)

De|mü|ti|gung F -, -en humiliation; **jdm ~en/eine ~ zufügen** to humiliate sb

De|muts-: De|muts|ge|bär|de F, **De|muts|hal|tung** F (*esp Zool*) submissive posture; **de|muts|voll** ADJ Person, Geste, Entschuldigung, Respekt humble

dem|zu|fol|ge ['de:mtsuːˈfɔlgə] ADV therefore

den [de:n] DEF ART a acc von **der** b dat pl von **der** von **die** von **das**; to the; **den** DEM PRON acc von **der** a attr that b (*substantivisch*) that one; (*Menschen*) him; (*von mehreren*) that one REL PRON acc von **der** who(m), that; (*von Sachen*) which, that

de|na|tu|ra|li|sie|ren [denaturali'ziːrən] ptp **denaturalisiert** VT to denaturalize

de|na|tu|rie|ren [denatu'riːrən] ptp **denaturiert** VT to denature VI **zu etw ~** (*fig geh*) to degenerate into sth

Dend|rit [dɛn'driːt] M -en, -en (*Geol, Med*) dendrite

de|nen ['de:nən] DEM PRON dat pl von **der** von **die** von **das** to them; (*mit Präposition*) them REL PRON dat pl von **der** von **die** von **das** to whom, that *or* who(m) ... to; (*mit Präposition*) whom; (*von Sachen*) to which, that *or* which ... to; which

den|geln ['dɛŋln] VT Sense to sharpen, to hone

Den Haag [de:n 'haːk] NT -s (= *Stadt*) The Hague

De|nim® ['de:nɪm, de'niːm] M OR NT -(s), *no pl* (*Tex*) denim

Denk- ['dɛŋk-]: **Denk|an|satz** M starting point; **Denk|an|stoß** M something to start one thinking; **jdm Denkanstöße geben** to give sb something to think about, to give sb food for thought; **Denk|art** F way of thinking; **eine edle ~** high-mindedness; **eine niedrige ~** low-mindedness; **Denk|auf|ga|be** F brain-teaser; **denk|bar** ADJ conceivable; **es ist durchaus ~, dass er kommt** it's very possible *or* likely that he'll come ADV extremely; (= *ziemlich*) rather; **den ~ schlechtesten/besten Eindruck machen** to make the worst/best possible impression; **Denk|bla|se** F (*Comics*) thought bubble

Den|ke ['dɛŋkə] F -, *no pl* (*inf*) (way of) thinking

---

den|ken ['dɛŋkən]
pret **dachte** ['daxtə] ptp **gedacht** [gə'daxt]
☼ 28.1, 29, 33.1, 39.1, 48.1

| 1 INTRANSITIVES VERB | 2 TRANSITIVES VERB |

1 – INTRANSITIVES VERB

a = überlegen to think; **das gibt einem zu denken** it makes you think; **das gab mir zu denken** it made me think; **ich denke, also bin ich** I think, therefore I am; **langsam/schnell denken** to be a slow/quick thinker; **bei sich denken** to think to oneself; **solange ich denken kann** (for) as long as I can remember; **sie dachte hin und her und kam schließlich zu dem Ergebnis, sich doch noch für die Prüfung anzumelden** she thought a lot about it *or* she had a good think about it, and finally decided to sit (*Brit*) *or* take the exam after all; **wo denken Sie hin!** what an idea!; **der Mensch denkt, (und) Gott lenkt** (*Prov*) man proposes, God disposes (*Prov*)

b = urteilen to think (*über +acc* about); **was denken Sie über die Lage im Balkan?** what do you think about the situation in the Balkans?; **wie denken Sie darüber?** what do you think about it?; **schlecht von jdm** *or* **über jdn denken** to think badly of sb; **ich denke genauso** I think the same (way); **so darf man eben nicht denken** you shouldn't think like that; **wie viel soll ich spenden? – wie Sie denken** how much should I give? – it's up to you; **ich dächte, ...** I would have thought ...; **ich denke schon** I think so; **ich denke nicht** I don't think so

c = gesinnt sein to think; **edel denken** to be noble-minded; **kleinlich denken** to be petty-minded; **alle, die liberal denken** all liberally-minded people; **da muss man etwas großzügiger denken** one must be more generous-minded

♦ **denken an** to think of *or* about; **ich denke an eine rote Decke für mein Sofa** I'm thinking of *or* about (getting) a red cover for my sofa; **ich denke oft an meine alte Tante und frage mich, wie es ihr wohl geht** I often think about my old aunt and wonder how she is; **denk mal an mich, wenn du wieder einmal nach Paris fährst** think of me when you go back to Paris; **an das Geld habe ich gar nicht mehr gedacht** I had forgotten about the money; **denken Sie zum Beispiel an England im 19. Jahrhundert** look at England in the 19th century, for example; **wenn ich so an früher denke** when I think back; **denken Sie mal an die Kriegsjahre, da hatten wir nur manchmal Elektrizität** think back to the war years when we only had electricity from time to time; **und dann dachte sie an Josef als Babysitter** and then she thought of Josef as a babysitter; **an die Prüfung morgen denke ich mit gemischten Gefühlen** I've got mixed feelings about the exam tomorrow; **das Erste, woran ich dachte** the first thing I thought of; **daran ist gar nicht zu denken** that's (quite) out of the question; **ich denke nicht daran!** no way! (*inf*); **ich denke nicht daran, das zu tun** there's no way I'm going to do that (*inf*); **die viele Arbeit, ich darf gar nicht daran denken** all that work, it doesn't bear thinking about (*esp Brit*) *or* I don't dare think about it; **denk daran!** don't forget!

2 – TRANSITIVES VERB

a to think; **sagen was man denkt** to say what one thinks; **was denkst du jetzt?** what are you thinking (about)?; **ich denke gar nichts** I'm not thinking about anything; **was sie dafür bezahlt hat, das wage ich kaum zu denken** I hardly dare think how much she paid for it; **er war der Erste, der diesen Gedanken gedacht hat** he was the first to have this idea; **wie viel Trinkgeld gibt man? – so viel, wie Sie denken** how big a tip does one give? – it's up to you

♦ **für jdn/etw gedacht sein** (= *vorgesehen*) to be intended *or* meant for sb/sth; **so war das nicht gedacht** that wasn't what I/he *etc* had in mind

b = annehmen, glauben to think; **was sollen bloß die Leute denken!** what will people think!; **wer hätte das (von ihr) gedacht!** who'd have thought it (of her)!; **(nur) Schlechtes/Gutes von jdm denken** to think ill/well of sb; **denkste!** (*inf*) that's what you think!

♦ **sich** (*dat*) **etw denken** to imagine sth; **ich denke mir einen schönen Garten** I imagine a beautiful garden; **sich** (*dat*) **etw bei etw denken** to mean sth by sth; **was hast du dir bei dieser Bemerkung bloß gedacht?** what did you mean by that remark?; **ich habe mir nichts Böses dabei gedacht** I meant no harm (by it); **das kann ich mir denken** I can imagine; **wie viel soll ich Ihnen zahlen? – was Sie sich** (*dat*) **so gedacht haben** how much shall I pay you? – whatever you think; **ich könnte ihn mir gut als Direktor denken** I can just imagine him as director; **wie denkst du dir das eigentlich?** (*inf*) what's the big idea? (*inf*); **ich habe mir das so gedacht ...** this is what I'd thought ...; **das habe ich mir gleich gedacht** I thought that from the first; **das habe ich mir gedacht** I thought so; **das habe ich mir beinahe gedacht** I thought as much; **dachte ich mirs doch!** I knew it!; **ich denke mir mein Teil** I have my own thoughts on the matter; **das lässt sich denken** that's very likely; **sie läuft zu Hause immer nackt herum und denkt sich nichts dabei** she runs around the house with no clothes on and thinks nothing of it → **gedacht**

Den|ken NT -s, *no pl* **a** (= *Gedankenwelt*) thought; (= *Denkweise*) thinking; **ich kann seinem ~ nicht folgen** I can't follow his thinking *or* his train of thought; **im ~ Goethes** in Goethe's thought; **im ~ der Aufklärung** in the thinking of the Enlightenment; **abstraktes ~** abstract thought *or* thinking; **klares ~** clear thinking, clarity of thought; **positives ~** positive thinking **b** (= *Gedanken*) thoughts *pl*, thinking **c** (= *Denkvermögen*) mind

Den|ker ['dɛŋkɐ] M -s, -, **Den|ke|rin** [-ərɪn] F -, **-nen** thinker; **das Volk der Dichter und ~** the nation of poets and philosophers

Den|ker|fal|te F *usu pl* (*hum*) furrow on one's brow; **er zog seine Stirn in ~n** (*acc*) he furrowed his brow

den|ke|risch ['dɛŋkərɪʃ] ADJ intellectual

Den|ker|stirn F (*hum*) lofty brow

Denk-: Denk|fab|rik F think tank; **denk|fä|hig** ADJ capable of thinking; **nicht mehr ~** incapable of thinking (straight) (any more); **als ~er Mensch** as an intelligent person; **Denk|fä|hig|keit** F ability to think; **denk|faul** ADJ (mentally) lazy; **sei nicht so ~!** get your brain working!; **Denk|faul|heit** F mental laziness; **Denk|feh|ler** M mistake in the/one's logic, flaw in the/one's reasoning; **ein ~ in der Beurteilung der Lage** an error in the assessment of the situation; **Denk|ge|wohn|heit** F *usu pl* habitual way of thinking; **Denk|hem|mung** F mental block; **Denk|hil|fe** F clue, hint; (= *Merkhilfe*) reminder; **Denk|ho|ri|zont** M mental horizon; **Denk|in|halt** M idea; **Denk|ka|te|go|rie** F *usu pl* thought category; **in veralteten ~n erzogen** brought up to think in outmoded categories; **Denk|kraft** F mental capacity

Denk|mal ['dɛŋkmaːl] NT -s, **-e** (*liter*) *or* **=er** [-mɛːlə] **a** (= *Gedenkstätte*) monument, memo-

rial (*für* to); (= *Standbild*) statue; **die Stadt hat ihm ein ~ gesetzt** the town put up *or* erected a memorial/statue to him; **er hat sich** (*dat*) **ein ~ gesetzt** he has left a memorial (to himself) **b** (= *Zeugnis: literarisch etc*) monument (+*gen* to)

denk|mal|ge|schützt ADJ *Gebäude, Monument* listed (on a historic register); *Baum etc* protected; **das ist ein ~es Haus** this (house) is a listed building, this house is listed on a historic register (*US*)

Denk|mal(s)-: Denk|mal(s)|kun|de F study of historical monuments; **Denk|mal(s)|pfle|ge** F preservation of historical monuments; **Denk|mal(s)|pfle|ger(in)** M(F) curator of monuments; **Denk|mal(s)|schän|dung** F defacing a monument *no art*; **~en** defacing monuments; **Denk|mal(s)|schutz** M protection of historical monuments; **etw unter ~ stellen** to classify sth as a historical monument; **unter ~ stehen** to be listed *or* under a preservation order *or* classified as a historical monument; **Denk|mal(s)|schüt|zer(in)** M(F) preservationist

Denk-: Denk|mo|dell NT (= *Entwurf*) plan for further discussion; (*wissenschaftlich*) working hypothesis; (= *Denkmuster*) thought pattern; **Denk|mus|ter** NT thought pattern; **Denk|pau|se** F break, adjournment; **eine ~ einlegen** to have a break *or* to adjourn to think things over; **Denk|pro|zess** ▲ M thought-process; **Denk|psy|cho|lo|gie** F psychology of thought; **Denk|schab|lo|ne** F (*pej*) (set *or* hackneyed) thought pattern; **Denk|sche|ma** NT thought pattern; **Denk|schrift** F memorandum, memo (*inf*); **Denk|schritt** M step (in one's/sb's thinking); **Denk|spiel** NT mental *or* mind game; **Denk|sport** M mental exercise; **„Denksport"** "puzzle corner"; **er ist ein Liebhaber des ~s** he loves doing puzzles and brain-teasers; **Denk|sport|auf|ga|be** F brain-teaser; **Denk|spruch** M motto

denks|te ['dɛŋkstə] INTERJ → **denken 2 b**

Denk-: Denk|sys|tem NT system of thought; **Denk|übung** F mental exercise

Den|kungs|art F , **Den|kungs|wei|se** F = **Denkart**

Denk-: Denk|ver|mö|gen NT capacity for thought, intellectual capacity; **Denk|vers** M mnemonic (verse); **Denk|vor|gang** M thought process; **Denk|wei|se** F = **Denkart**; **denk|wür|dig** ADJ memorable, notable; **Denk|wür|dig|keit** ['dɛŋkvʏrdɪçkaɪt] F -, **-en a** *no pl* (*von Ereignis*) memorability, notability **b** (*liter*: = *Ereignis*) memorable *or* notable event; **Denk|zen|trum** NT thought centre (*Brit*) *or* center (*US*); **Denk|zet|tel** M (*inf*) warning; **jdm einen ~ verpassen** to give sb a warning

denn [dɛn] CONJ **a** (*kausal*) because, for (*esp liter*)

b (*geh*: *vergleichend*) than; **schöner ~ je** more beautiful than ever

c (*konzessiv*) **es sei ~, (dass)** unless; **..., du segnest mich ~** (*Bibl*) ... except thou blessest me (*obs, Bibl*) → **geschweige**

ADV a (*verstärkend*) **wann/woran/wer/wie/wo ~?** when/why/who/how/where?; **ich habe ihn gestern gesehen – wo ~?** I saw him yesterday – oh, where?; **wieso ~?** why?, how come?; **warum ~ nicht?** why not?; **wie gehts ~?** how are you *or* things then?, how's it going then?; **wo bleibt er ~?** where has he got to?; **was soll das ~?** what's all this then?; **das ist ~ doch die Höhe!** (well,) that really is the limit!

b (*N Ger inf*: = *dann*) then; **na, ~ man los!** right then, let's go!; **na, ~ prost!** well, cheers (then)

den|noch ['dɛnɔx] ADV nevertheless, nonetheless, still; **~ liebte er sie** yet he still loved her, he loved her nevertheless; **er hat es ~ getan** (but *or* yet) he still did it, he did it nonetheless *or* nevertheless; **und ~, ... and** yet ...; **schön und ~ hässlich** beautiful and yet ugly

De|no|mi|na|tiv ['deːnominatiːf] NT -s, **-e** [-və] (*Ling*) denominative

De|no|tat [deno'taːt] NT -s, **-e** (*Ling*) denotation

De|no|ta|ti|on [denota'tsioːn] F (*Ling*) denotation

den|sel|ben [deːn'zɛlbn] DEM PRON *acc von* **derselbe** *dat von* **dieselben**

den|tal [dɛn'taːl] ADJ (*Med, Ling*) dental

Den|tal(laut) [dɛn'taːl-] M -s, **-e** (*Ling*) dental

Den|tal|la|bor [dɛn'taːl-] NT (*Med*) dental laboratory

Den|tist [dɛn'tɪst] M -en, **-en**, **Den|tis|tin** [-'tɪstɪn] F -, **-nen** (*dated*) dentist

De|nun|zi|ant [denʊn'tsiant] M -en, **-en**, **De|nun|zi|an|tin** [-'tsiantɪn] F -, **-nen** (*pej*) informer

De|nun|zi|an|ten|tum [denʊn'tsiantntuːm] NT -s, *no pl* (*pej*) informing

De|nun|zi|a|ti|on [denʊntsia'tsioːn] F -, **-en** (*pej*) informing *no pl* (*von* on, against); (= *Anzeige*) denunciation (*von* of)

de|nun|zie|ren [denʊn'tsiːrən] *ptp* **denunziert** VT (*pej*) **a** (= *verraten*) to inform on *or* against, to denounce (*bei* to) **b** (*geh*: = *verunglimpfen*) to denounce, to condemn

Deo ['deːo] NT -(s), -s *abbr von* **Deodorant**

De|o|do|rant [deodo'rant] NT -s, -s *or* **-e** deodorant

De|o|do|rant|spray NT OR M deodorant spray

de|o|do|rie|rend [deodo'riːrənt] ADJ deodorant

Deo-: De|o|rol|ler M roll-on (deodorant); **De|o|spray** NT OR M deodorant spray; **De|o|stift** M stick deodorant

De|par|te|ment [departə'mãː] NT -s, -s (*esp Sw*) department

De|pen|dance [depã'dãːs] F -, **-n a** (*geh*) branch **b** (= *Hoteldependance*) annexe (*Brit*), annex (*US*)

De|pen|denz [depɛn'dɛnts] F -, **-en** (*Philos*) dependence

De|pen|denz|gram|ma|tik F dependence grammar

De|per|so|na|li|sa|ti|on [depɛrzonaliza'tsioːn] F -, **-en** (*Psych*) depersonalization

De|pe|sche [de'pɛʃə] F -, **-n** (*dated*) dispatch

de|pla|ciert [depla'siːɐt], **de|plat|ziert** ▲ [depla'tsiːɐt], **de|pla|ziert** △ [depla'tsiːɐt] ADJ out of place

De|po|nie [depo'niː] F -, **-n** [-'niːən] dump, disposal site

de|po|nie|ren [depo'niːrən] *ptp* **deponiert** VT (*geh*) to deposit

De|po|nie|rung F -, **-en** (*geh*) depository

De|por|ta|ti|on [depɔrta'tsioːn] F -, **-en** deportation

de|por|tie|ren [depɔr'tiːrən] *ptp* **deportiert** VT to deport

De|por|tier|te(r) [depɔr'tiːɐtə] MF *decl as adj* deportee

De|po|si|tar [depozi'taːr] M -s, **-e**, **De|po|si|ta|rin** [-'taːrɪn] F -, **-nen**, **De|po|si|tär** [depozi'tɛːr] M -s, **-e**, **De|po|si|tä|rin** [-'tɛːrɪn] F -, **-nen** (*Fin*) depositary

De|po|si|ten [depo'ziːtn] PL (*Fin*) deposits *pl*

De|po|si|ten- (*Fin*): **De|po|si|ten|bank** F *pl* **-banken** deposit bank; **De|po|si|ten|gel|der** PL deposits *pl*, deposit(ed) money; **De|po|si|ten|ge|schäft** NT deposit banking; **De|po|si|ten|kon|to** NT deposit account

De|pot [de'poː] NT -s, -s **a** depot; (= *Aufbewahrungsort auch, Wertpapierdepot*) depository; (*in Bank*) strongroom; (= *Wertpapierkonto*) securities account; (= *aufbewahrte Gegenstände*) deposits *pl*; (= *Guthaben*) deposit; (= *Schließfach*) safety deposit box; (*Med*) deposit **b** (*Sw*: = *Pfand*) deposit

De|pot-: De|pot|aus|zug M (*Fin*) statement of deposited securities; **De|pot|be|hand|lung** F (*Med*) depot treatment; **De|pot|ef|fekt** M

(*Pharm*) controlled release; **De|pot|fett** NT (*Med*) adipose fat; **De|pot|ge|bühr** F (*Fin*) safe custody charge(s *pl*); **De|pot|ge|schäft** NT (*Fin*) security deposit business; **De|pot|stimm|recht** NT (*Fin*) voting power for deposited shares

Depp [dɛp] M -en *or* -s, -e(n) (*S Ger, Aus, Sw: pej*) twit (*inf*)

dep|pert ['dɛpɐt] (*S Ger, Aus: inf*) **ADJ** dopey (*inf*) **ADV** sich ~ benehmen to be dopey (*inf*); ~ fragen to ask dopey questions (*inf*); ~ schauen to have a dopey look on one's face (*inf*)

de|pra|viert [depra'viːɐt] ADJ (*geh*) depraved

De|pres|si|on [deprɛ'sioːn] F (*alle Bedeutungen*) depression; ~en haben to suffer from depression

de|pres|siv [depre'siːf] ADJ depressive; (*Econ*) depressed

De|pres|si|vi|tät [depresivi'tɛːt] F -, *no pl* depressiveness

de|pri|mie|ren [depri'miːrən] *ptp* **deprimiert** VT to depress

de|pri|mie|rend ADJ depressing ADV depressingly

de|pri|miert [depri'miːɐt] ADJ depressed

De|pri|miert|heit F -, *no pl* depression

De|pri|va|ti|on [depriva'tsioːn] F -, -en (*Psych*) deprivation

de|pri|vie|ren [depri'viːrən] *ptp* **depriviert** VT (*Psych*) to deprive

De|pu|tat [depu'taːt] NT -(e)s, -e **a** (*esp Agr*) payment in kind **b** (*Sch*) teaching load

De|pu|ta|ti|on [deputa'tsioːn] F -, -en deputation

de|pu|tie|ren [depu'tiːrən] *ptp* **deputiert** VT to deputize

De|pu|tier|ten|kam|mer F (*Pol*) Chamber of Deputies

De|pu|tier|te(r) [depu'tiːɐtə] MF *decl as adj* deputy

der[1] [deːɐ] **DEF ART a** *gen sing, pl von* **die** of the; **das Miauen ~ Katze** the miaowing of the cat, the cat's miaowing **b** *dat sing von* **die** to the; (*mit Präposition*) the **DEM PRON** *dat sing von* **die a** (*adjektivisch*) to that; (*mit Präpositionen*) that **b** (*substantivisch*) to her; her **REL PRON** *dat sing von* **die** to whom, that *or* who(m) ... to; (*mit Präposition*) who(m); (*von Sachen*) to which, which ... to; which

der[2] [deːɐ], **das** [das] *pl* **die** **DEF ART** *gen* **des, der, des,** *pl* **der**; *dat* **dem, der, dem,** *pl* **den**; *acc* **den, die, das,** *pl* **die** the; **~/die Arme!** the poor man/woman *or* girl; **die Toten** the dead *pl*; **die Engländer** the English *pl*; ~ **Engländer** (*dated inf: = die Engländer*) the Englishman; ~ **Faust** Faust; ~ **Hans** (*inf*) Hans; ~ **kleine Hans** little Hans; ~ **Rhein** the Rhine; ~ **Michigansee** Lake Michigan; **die Domstraße** Cathedral Street; **die „Bismarck"** the "Bismarck"; ~ **Lehrer/die Frau** (*im Allgemeinen*) teachers *pl*/women *pl*; ~ **Tod/die Liebe/das Leben** death/love/life; ~ **Tod des Sokrates** the death of Socrates; **das Viktorianische England** Victorian England; **in dem England, das ich kannte** in the England (that *or* which) I knew; **er liebt den Jazz/die Oper/das Kino** he likes jazz/(the) opera/the cinema; **das Singen macht ihm Freude** singing gives him pleasure; **das Singen meines Opas** my grandpa's singing; **mir fiel das Atmen schwer** I found breathing difficult; **das Herstellen von Waffen ist ...** manufacturing weapons is ..., the manufacturing of weapons is ...; **die Callas** Callas; ~ **spätere Wittgenstein** the later Wittgenstein; **er war nicht mehr ~ Hans, ~ ...** he was no longer the Hans who ...; **er hat sich den Fuß verletzt** he has hurt his foot; **wascht euch** (*dat*) **mal das Gesicht!** wash your faces; **er nimmt den Hut ab** he takes his hat off; **ein Euro das Stück** one euro apiece *or* each; **20 Euro die Stunde** 20 euros an *or* per hour; ~ **und ~ Wissenschaftler** such and such a

scientist

DEM PRON *gen* **dessen** *or* (*old*) **des, deren, dessen,** *pl* **deren**; *dat* **dem, der, dem,** *pl* **denen**; *acc* **den, die, das,** *pl* **die a** (*attr*) (= *jener, dieser*) that; (*pl*) those, them (*inf*); **zu ~ und ~ Zeit** at such and such a time; **an dem und dem Ort** at such and such a place

b (*substantivisch*) he/she/it; (*pl*) those, them (*inf*); ~/**die war es** it was him/her; ~/**die mit ~ großen Nase** the one *or* him/her (*inf*) with the big nose; **die** *pl* **mit den roten Haaren** those *or* them (*inf*) with red hair; **deine Schwester, die war nicht da** (*inf*) your sister, she wasn't there; ~ **und schwimmen?** him, swimming?, swimming, (what) him?; ~/**die hier** (*von Menschen*) he/she, this man/woman *etc*; (*von Gegenständen*) this (one); (*von mehreren*) this one; ~/**die da** (*von Menschen*) he/she, that man/woman *etc*; (*von Gegenständen*) that (one); (*von mehreren*) that one; **die hier/da** *pl* they, these/those men/women *etc*, these/those, them (*inf*); ~, **den ich meine** the one I mean; ~ **und ~/die und die** so-and-so; **das und das** such and such

REL PRON *decl as dem pron* (*Mensch*) who, that; (*Gegenstand, Tier*) which, that

REL + DEM PRON *decl as dem pron* ~/**die dafür verantwortlich ist,** the man/woman who was responsible for it; **die so etwas tun, ...** those *or* people who do that sort of thing ...

de|ran|giert [derã'ʒiːɐt] ADJ (*geh*) Kleidung untidy, messed up; *Haar auch* dishevelled (*Brit*), disheveled (*US*), mussed up (*inf*)

der|art ['deːɐ'|aːɐt] ADV (*Art und Weise*) in such a way; **er hat sich ~ benommen, dass ...** he behaved so badly that ...; **sein Benehmen war ~, dass ...** his behaviour (*Brit*) *or* behavior (*US*) was so bad that ...; ~ **vorbereitet, ...** thus prepared ...; **b** (*Ausmaß*) (*vor adj*) so; (*vor vb*) so much, to such an extent; **ein ~ unzuverlässiger Mensch** such an unreliable person, so unreliable a person; **er hat mich ~ geärgert, dass ...** he annoyed me so much that ...; **es hat ~ geregnet, dass ...** it rained so much that ...

der|ar|tig ['deːɐ'|aːɐtɪç] ADJ such, of that kind; **bei ~en Versuchen** in such experiments, in experiments of that kind; (*etwas*) **Derartiges** something like that, something of the kind **ADV** = derart

derb [dɛrp] ADJ **a** (= *kräftig*) strong; *Stoff, Leder auch* tough; *Schuhe auch* stout; *Kost coarse* **b** (= *grob*) coarse; *Manieren, Kerl auch* uncouth; *Sprache, Witz, Ausdrucksweise* crude **c** (= *unfreundlich*) gruff **ADV a** (= *heftig*) roughly; **jdn ~ anfassen** to manhandle sb; (*fig*) to be rough with sb **b** (= *grob*) crudely; **um mich einmal ~ auszudrücken ...** to put it crudely ...

Derb|heit F -, -en **a** (= *Kräftigkeit*) strength; (*von Stoff, Leder*) toughness, strength **b** (= *Grobheit*) coarseness; (*von Manieren, Kerl*) uncouthness, coarseness; (*von Witz, Sprache, Ausdrucksweise*) crudeness; ~en crudities **c** (= *Unfreundlichkeit*) gruffness

Der|by ['dɛrbi] NT -s, -s horse race for three-year-olds, derby (*US*); (*fig* = *sportliche Begegnung*) derby; **das (englische)** ~ the Derby

Der|by|ren|nen NT = Derby

de|re|gu|lie|ren [deregu'liːrən] *ptp* **dereguliert** VT (*Econ*) to deregulate

De|re|gu|lie|rung F (*Econ*) deregulation

der|einst [deːɐ'|ainst] ADV (*liter*) **a** (= *in der Zukunft*) one day **b** (*rare*: = *früher*) at one time, once

der|eins|tig [deːɐ'|ainstɪç] ADJ (*liter*) **a** (= *künftig*) future, tomorrow's; **im ~en vereinten Europa** in tomorrow's united Europe, in the united Europe of tomorrow **b** (= *damalig*) of former times

de|ren ['deːrən] **DEM PRON** *gen pl von* **der** *von* **die** *von* **das** their **REL PRON a** *gen sing von* **die** whose **b** *gen pl von* **der** *von* **die** *von* **das** whose, of whom; (*von Sachen*) of which

de|rent|hal|ben ['deːrənt'halbn] (*dated*), **de|rent|we|gen** ['deːrənt'veːgn] ADV (= *weswegen*) because of whom, on whose account; (*von Sachen*) because of which, on account of which; (= *welcher zuliebe auch*) for whose sake; (*von Sachen*) for the sake of which; (= *um welche*) about whom; (*von Sachen*) about which; (= *für welche*) on whose behalf

de|rent|wil|len ['deːrənt'vɪlən] ADV **a** um ~ (*rel*) for whose sake; (*von Sachen*) for the sake of which **b** um ~ (*dem*) (*sing*) for her/its sake; (*pl*) for their sake

de|rer ['deːrɐ] **DEM PRON** *gen pl von* **der** *von* **die** *von* **das** of those; **das Geschlecht ~ von Hohenstein** (*geh*) the von Hohenstein family

de|ret- *in cpds* = derent-

der|ge|stalt ['deːɐgə'ʃtalt] ADV (*geh*) in such a way; (*Ausmaß*) to such an extent; ~ **ausgerüstet, ...** thus equipped ...; **dann gab er dem Pferde die Sporen ~, dass ...** then he spurred his horse on so forcefully that ...

der|glei|chen ['deːɐ'glaiçn] *inv* **DEM PRON a** (*adjektivisch*) of that kind, such, like that; ~ **Dinge** things of that kind, things like that; such things **b** (*substantivisch*) that sort of thing; **nichts** ~ nothing of that kind, nothing like it; **er tat nichts** ~ he did nothing of the kind; **und** ~ (**mehr**) and suchlike **REL PRON** (*old*) of the kind that; **Juwelen,** ~ **man selten sieht** jewels whose like *or* the like of which one rarely sees

De|ri|vat [deri'vaːt] NT -(e)s, -e (*Chem, Ling, Fin*) derivative

De|ri|va|ti|on [deriva'tsioːn] F -, -en (*Ling*) derivation

De|ri|va|tiv [deriva'tiːf] NT -s, -e [-və] (*Ling*) derivative

der|je|ni|ge ['deːɐje|nɪgə], **die|je|ni|ge, das|je|ni|ge** *pl* **die|je|ni|gen** DEM PRON **a** (*substantivisch*) the one; (*pl*) those; **sie ist immer diejenige, welche** (*inf*) it's always her; **du warst also ~, welcher!** (*inf*) so it was you!, so you're the one! **b** (*adjektivisch*) the; (*pl*) those

der|lei ['deːɐ'lai] DEM PRON *inv* **a** (*adjektivisch*) such, like that, that kind of; ~ **Probleme** problems like that, that kind of problems, such problems **b** (*substantivisch*) that sort *or* kind of thing; **und** ~ (**mehr**) and suchlike

der|ma|len ['deːɐ'maːlən, deːɐ'maːlən] ADV (*old, Aus form*) presently, at present, now

der|ma|lig ['deːɐ'maːlɪç, deːɐ'maːlɪç] ADJ (*old, Aus form*) present, actual

der|ma|ßen ['deːɐ'maːsn] ADV (*mit adj*) so; (*mit vb*) so much; ~ **dumm** so stupid; **ein ~ dummer Kerl** such a stupid fellow; **sie hatte ~ Angst, dass ...** she was so afraid that ...; **er hat sich geärgert und zwar ~, dass ...** he was angry, so much so that ...

Der|ma|to|lo|ge [dermato'loːgə] M -en, -en, **Der|ma|to|lo|gin** [-'loːgɪn] F -, -nen dermatologist

Der|ma|to|lo|gie [dermatolo'giː] F -, *no pl* dermatology

Der|ma|to|plas|tik [dermato'plastɪk] F plastic surgery, dermatoplasty (*spec*)

Der|nier Cri ▲ [dɛrnje 'kri] M - -, -s -s dernier cri

de|ro ['deːro] **POSS PRON** (*obs*) her; (*pl*) their; **Dero Gnaden** Your Grace

der|sel|be [deːɐ'zɛlbə], **die|sel|be, das|sel|be** *pl* **die|sel|ben** DEM PRON **a** (*substantivisch*) the same; (*old*: = *er, sie, es*) he/she/it; (*inf*: = *der, die, das gleiche*) the same; **er sagt in jeder Vorlesung dasselbe** he says the same (thing) in every lecture; **jedes Jahr kriegen dieselben mehr Geld** every year the same people get more money; **sie ist immer noch ganz dieselbe** she is still exactly the same; **es sind immer dieselben** it's always the same ones *or* people; **noch mal dasselbe, bitte!** (*inf*) same again, please **b** (*adjektivisch*) the same; **ein und ~ Mensch** one and the same person

der|sel|bi|ge etc [deːɐˈzɛlbɪɡə] DEM PRON (old) = **derselbe** etc

der|weil [ˈdeːɐˈvail], **der|wei|len** [ˈdeːɐˈvailən] **ADV** in the meantime, meanwhile **CONJ** (old) whilst, while

Der|wisch [ˈdɛrvɪʃ] M **-es, -e** dervish

der|zeit [ˈdeːɐˈtsait] ADV **a** (= jetzt) at present, at the moment **b** (dated: = damals) at that or the time, then

der|zei|tig [ˈdeːɐˈtsaitɪç] ADJ attr **a** (= jetzig) present, current **b** (dated: = damalig) of that or the time

des¹ [dɛs] DEF ART **a** gen von **der** von **das** of the; **das Bellen ~ Hundes** the barking of the dog, the dog's barking **b** (old) = **dessen**

des² [dɛs] NT **-, -**, **Des** NT **-, -** (Mus) D flat

De|sas|ter [deˈzastɐ] NT **-s, -** disaster

de|sas|trös [dezaˈstrøːs] ADJ (geh) disastrous

des|a|vou|ie|ren [dɛsavuˈiːrən, deza-] ptp **desavouiert** VT (geh) to disavow; Bemühungen, Pläne to compromise

De|sen|si|bi|li|sa|tor [dezɛnzibiliˈzaːtoːɐ] M (Phot) desensitizer

de|sen|si|bi|li|sie|ren [dezɛnzibiliˈziːrən] ptp **desensibilisiert** VT (Phot, Med) to desensitize

De|ser|teur [dezɛrˈtøːɐ] M **-s, -e**, **De|ser|teu|rin** [-ˈtøːrɪn] F **-, -nen** (Mil, fig) deserter

de|ser|tie|ren [dezɛrˈtiːrən] ptp **desertiert** VI aux sein or (rare) haben (Mil, fig) to desert

De|ser|ti|on [dezɛrˈtsioːn] F **-, -en** (Mil, fig) desertion

des|glei|chen [ˈdɛsˈɡlaiçn] **ADV** (= ebenso) likewise, also; **er ist Vegetarier, ~ seine Frau** he is a vegetarian, as is his wife **DEM PRON** inv (old: = dasselbe) the same; **~ habe ich noch nie gehört** I have never heard the like **REL PRON** inv (old) the like of which

des|halb [ˈdɛsˈhalp] ADV, CONJ therefore; (= aus diesem Grunde, darüber) because of that; (= dafür) for that; **es ist schon spät, ~ wollen wir anfangen** it is late, so let us start; **~ bin ich hergekommen** that is what I came here for, that is why I came here; **ich bin ~ hergekommen, weil ich dich sprechen wollte** what I came here for was to speak to you, the reason I came here was that I wanted to speak to you; **~ also!** so that's why or the reason!; **~ muss er nicht dumm sein** that does not (necessarily) mean (to say) he is stupid; **~ frage ich ja** that's exactly why I'm asking

de|si|de|ra|bel [dezideˈraːbl] ADJ (geh) desirable

De|si|de|rat [dezideˈraːt] NT **-(e)s, -e**, **De|si|de|ra|tum** [dezideˈraːtʊm] NT **-s, Desiderata** [-ta] desideratum; (= Anschaffungsvorschlag) suggestion

De|sign [diˈzain] NT **-s, -s** design

De|si|gnat [deziˈɡnaːt] NT **-(e)s, -e** (Philos, Ling) referendum

De|si|gna|ti|on [deziɡnaˈtsioːn] F **-, -en** designation

De|si|gna|tor [deziˈɡnaːtoːɐ] M **-s, Designatoren** [-ˈtoːrən] (Philos, Ling) referens

de|si|gnen [diˈzainən] ptp **designt** [diˈzaint] VT to design

De|si|gner [diˈzainɐ] M **-s, -**, **De|si|gne|rin** [diˈzainərɪn] F **-, -nen** designer

De|si|gner- [diˈzainɐ] in cpds designer attr; **De|si|gner|bril|le** F designer glasses pl or spectacles pl, designer specs pl (inf); **De|si|gner|dro|ge** F designer drug; **De|si|gner|jeans** PL designer jeans pl; **De|si|gner|mö|bel** PL designer furniture sing; **De|si|gner|mo|de** F designer fashion

de|si|gnie|ren [deziˈɡniːrən] ptp **designiert** VT to designate (jdn zu etw sb as sth)

de|si|gniert [deziˈɡniːɐt] ADJ attr der **~e Vorsitzende** the chairman elect or designate

des|il|lu|sio|nie|ren [dɛsɪluzioˈniːrən, dezɪ-] ptp **desillusioniert** VT to disillusion

Des|il|lu|si|o|nie|rung F **-, -en** disillusionment

Des|in|fek|ti|on [dɛsɪnfɛkˈtsioːn, dezɪ-] F disinfection

Des|in|fek|ti|ons-: **Des|in|fek|ti|ons|lö|sung** F antiseptic solution; **Des|in|fek|ti|ons|mit|tel** NT disinfectant

des|in|fi|zie|ren [dɛsɪnfiˈtsiːrən, dezɪ-] ptp **desinfiziert** VT Zimmer, Bett etc to disinfect; Spritze, Gefäß etc to sterilize

des|in|fi|zie|rend prp von **desinfizieren** ADJ disinfectant; **eine ~e Wirkung haben** to act as a disinfectant

Des|in|fi|zie|rung F **-, -en** (von Zimmer, Bett) disinfection; (von Spritze, Gefäß) sterilization

Des|in|for|ma|ti|on [dɛsɪnfɔrmaˈtsioːn, dezɪ-] F (Pol) disinformation no pl

Des|in|for|ma|ti|ons|kam|pag|ne F campaign of disinformation

Des|in|te|gra|ti|on [dɛsɪnteɡraˈtsioːn, dezɪ-] F (Sociol, Psych) disintegration

Des|in|te|res|se [dɛsɪntəˈrɛsə, dezɪ-] NT lack of interest (an +dat in)

des|in|te|res|siert [dɛsɪntərɛˈsiːɐt, dezɪ-] ADJ uninterested; Gesicht bored

De|skrip|ti|on [deskrɪpˈtsioːn] F (geh) **-, -en** description

de|skrip|tiv [deskrɪpˈtiːf] ADJ descriptive

Desk|top-Pub|li|shing ▲ [ˈdɛsktɔpˈpablɪʃɪŋ] NT **-, no pl**, **Desk|top|pub|li|shing** ▲ NT **-, no pl** desktop publishing, DTP

Des|o|do|rant [dɛsodoˈrant, dezo-] NT **-s, -s** or **-e** deodorant

de|so|lat [dezoˈlaːt] ADJ (geh) desolate; Zustand, wirtschaftliche Lage desperate; **die ~en Staatsfinanzen** the desperate state of the public finances

Des|or|ga|ni|sa|ti|on [dɛsɔrɡanizaˈtsioːn, dezɔ-] F disorganization; (= Auflösung auch) disruption; **auf der Tagung herrschte eine völlige ~** there was complete chaos at the conference

des|or|ga|ni|sie|ren [dɛsɔrɡaniˈziːrən, dezɔ-] ptp **desorganisiert** VT to disorganize

des|ori|en|tie|ren [dɛsorienˈtiːrən, dezo-] ptp **desorientiert** VT to disorient(ate)

Des|ori|en|tiert|heit F **-, no pl**, **Des|ori|en|tie|rung** F disorientation

Des|oxy|ri|bo|nuk|le|in|säu|re [dɛsɔksyribonukleˈiːnzyːrə, dezɔ-] F (abbr **DNS**) deoxyribonucleic acid, DNA

des|pek|tier|lich [despɛkˈtiːɐlɪç] ADJ (old, hum) disrespectful

Des|pek|tier|lich|keit F **-, -en** (old, hum) disrespect; **~en** disrespectful comments

Des|pe|ra|do [despeˈraːdo] M **-s, -s** desperado

des|pe|rat [despeˈraːt] ADJ (geh) desperate

Des|pe|ra|ti|on [despeɾaˈtsioːn] F **-, -en** (geh) desperation

Des|pot [dɛsˈpoːt] M **-en, -en**, **Des|po|tin** [-ˈpoːtɪn] F **-, -nen** despot

des|po|tie [despoˈtiː] F **-, -n** [-ˈtiːən] despotism

des|po|tisch [dɛsˈpoːtɪʃ] **ADJ** despotic **ADV** despotically

Des|po|tis|mus [despoˈtɪsmʊs] M **-, no pl** despotism

des|sel|ben [dɛsˈzɛlbn] DEM PRON gen von **derselbe** von **dasselbe**

des|sen [ˈdɛsn] **DEM PRON** gen von **der²** von **das** his; (von Sachen, Tieren) its **REL PRON** gen von **der²** von **das** whose; (von Sachen) of which, which … of; **~ ungeachtet** (geh) nevertheless, notwithstanding (this)

des|sent|hal|ben [ˈdɛsnˈthalbn] (dated), **des|sent|we|gen** [ˈdɛsnˈveːɡn] = **derenthalben** etc

des|sent|wil|len [ˈdɛsnˈvɪlən] ADV **a** um **~** (rel) for whose sake **b** um **~** (dem) for his/its sake

des|sen|un|ge|ach|tet △ [ˈdɛsnˈʊŋəˌʔaxtət, ˈdɛsnˈʊŋəaxtət] ADV → **dessen REL PRON**

Des|sert [dɛˈsɛːɐ] NT **-s, -s** dessert

Des|sert- [dɛˈseːɐ] in cpds dessert; **Des|sert|löf|fel** M dessertspoon; **Des|sert|wein** M dessert or pudding wine

Des|sin [dɛˈsɛ̃ː] NT **-s, -s** (Tex) pattern, design

Des|sous [dɛˈsuː] NT **-, -** [dɛˈsuːs] usu pl (dated) undergarment, underwear no pl

de|sta|bi|li|sie|ren [destabiliˈziːrən, -ʃt-] ptp **destabilisiert** VT to destabilize

De|sta|bi|li|sie|rung F **-, -en** destabilization

Des|til|lat [dɛstɪˈlaːt] NT **-(e)s, -e** (Chem) distillation, distillate; (fig) distillation

Des|til|la|teur [dɛstɪlaˈtøːɐ] M **-s, -e**, **Des|til|la|teu|rin** [-ˈtøːrɪn] F **-, -nen** distiller

Des|til|la|ti|on [dɛstɪlaˈtsioːn] F **-, -en a** (Chem) distillation **b** (= Branntweinbrennerei) distillery **c** (dated dial: = Großgaststätte) drinking establishment, ≈ gin palace (old), ≈ brandy shop (old)

Des|til|la|ti|ons-: **Des|til|la|ti|ons|an|la|ge** F distilling or distillation plant; **Des|til|la|ti|ons|pro|dukt** NT distillate

Des|til|le [dɛsˈtɪlə] F **-, -n a** (dial inf: = Gaststätte) (big) pub (Brit), bar **b** (= Brennerei) distillery

des|til|lie|ren [dɛstɪˈliːrən] ptp **destilliert** VT to distil (Brit), to distill (US); (fig) to condense

Des|til|lier|kol|ben [dɛstɪˈliːɐ-] M (Chem) retort

des|to [ˈdɛsto] CONJ **~ mehr/besser** all the more/better; **~ grausamer** all the more cruel; **~ schneller** all the faster; **~ wahrscheinlicher ist es, dass wir …** that makes it all the more probable that we … → **je¹ CONJ a**

De|struk|ti|on [destrʊkˈtsioːn] F **-, -en** destruction

De|struk|ti|ons|trieb M (Psych) destructive instinct

de|struk|tiv [destrʊkˈtiːf] ADJ destructive

De|struk|ti|vi|tät [destrʊktiviˈtɛːt] F **-, no pl** destructiveness

des|un|ge|ach|tet △ [ˈdɛsʊŋəˌʔaxtət, ˈdɛsˈʊŋəaxtət] ADV (old) = **dessen ungeachtet** → **dessen REL PRON**

des|we|gen [ˈdɛsˈveːɡn] ADV = **deshalb**

des|zen|dent [destsɛnˈdɛnt] ADJ (Astron) descendent (spec), setting

Des|zen|dent [destsɛnˈdɛnt] M **-en, -en im ~en sein** (Astrol) to be in the descendent

Des|zen|denz [destsɛnˈdɛnts] F **-, -en a** (= Abstammung) descent; (= Nachkommenschaft) descendants pl **b** (Astron) descendence (spec), setting

Des|zen|denz|the|o|rie F (Biol) theory of evolution

des|zen|die|ren [destsɛnˈdiːrən] ptp **deszendiert** VI aux sein (Astron, liter) to descend

De|tail [deˈtai, deˈtaːj] NT **-s, -s** detail; (= Filmeinstellung) big close-up; **ins ~ gehen** to go into detail(s); **im ~** in detail; **bis ins kleinste ~** (right) down to the smallest or last detail; **in allen ~s** in the greatest detail; **etw mit allen ~ berichten** to report sth in full detail, to give a fully detailed account of sth; **die Schwierigkeiten liegen im ~** it is the details that are most difficult → **Teufel b**

De|tail- [deˈtai-, deˈtaːj-]: **De|tail|be|richt** M detailed report; **De|tail|fra|ge** F question of detail; **de|tail|ge|nau**, **de|tail|ge|treu** **ADJ** accurate in every detail pred, accurate down to the last detail pred **ADV** etw **~ nachbauen** to make or build an exact or a faithful copy of sth; **De|tail|han|del** M (dated) = **Einzelhandel**; **De|tail|händ|ler(in)** M(F) (dated) retailer, retail trader; **De|tail|kennt|nis|se** PL detailed knowledge no pl

de|tail|lie|ren [detaˈjiːrən] ptp **detailliert** VT (= genau beschreiben) to specify, to give full particulars of; **etw genauer ~** to specify sth more precisely

de|tail|liert [deta'ji:ɐt] **ADJ** detailed **ADV** in detail; **~er** in greater or more detail

De|tail|liert|heit F -, no pl detail

De|tail- [de'tai-, de'ta:j-]: **de|tail|reich ADJ** highly detailed **ADV** **etw ~ schildern** to describe sth in great detail; **De|tail|reich|tum** M wealth of detail; **De|tail|schil|de|rung** F detailed account; **die beiden Versionen unterscheiden sich in der ~** the two versions differ in their account of the details; **De|tail|ver|kauf** M (dated Comm) retail sale; (= das Verkaufen) retailing, retail selling; **De|tail|zeich|nung** F detail drawing

De|tek|tei [detɛk'tai] F -, -en (private) detective agency, firm of (private) investigators; „**Detektei R. B. von Halske**" "R.B. von Halske, private investigator"

De|tek|tiv [detɛk'ti:f] M -s, -e [-və], **De|tek|ti|vin** [-'ti:vɪn] F -, -nen private investigator or detective or eye (inf)

De|tek|tiv|bü|ro NT = Detektei

de|tek|ti|visch [detɛk'ti:vɪʃ] **ADJ** Arbeit, Aufgabe detective attr; **man braucht dazu ~en Scharfsinn/~e Neugierde** you need the astuteness/inquisitiveness of a detective for this; **in ~er Kleinarbeit** with detailed detective work **ADV** like a detective; aufdecken through detailed detective work; **bei etw ~ vorgehen** to go about sth like a detective

De|tek|tiv|ro|man M detective novel

De|tek|tor [de'tɛkto:ɐ] M -s, Detektoren [-'to:rən] (Tech) detector

De|tek|tor|emp|fän|ger M (Rad) crystal set

Dé|tente [de'tã:t] F -, no pl (rare: Pol) détente

De|ter|mi|nan|te [detɛrmi'nantə] F -, -n (Math, Biol) determinant

de|ter|mi|nie|ren [detɛrmi'ni:rən] ptp **determiniert** VT to (pre)determine; (Gram) to govern

De|ter|mi|nis|mus [detɛrmi'nɪsmʊs] M -, no pl (Philos) determinism

De|ter|mi|nist [detɛrmi'nɪst] M -en, -en, **De|ter|mi|nis|tin** [-'nɪstɪn] F -, -nen (Philos) determinist

de|ter|mi|nis|tisch [detɛrmi'nɪstɪʃ] ADJ (Philos) deterministic

De|to|na|ti|on [detona'tsio:n] F -, -en explosion, blast; **etw** (acc) **zur ~ bringen** to detonate sth

De|to|na|ti|ons|wel|le F blast, shock wave(s pl); (Auswirkung) impact of the blast

de|to|nie|ren [deto'ni:rən] ptp **detoniert** VI aux sein to explode, to go off

Deu|bel ['dɔybl] M -s, - (dial) = **Teufel**

deucht [dɔyçt] 3. pers sing pres von **dünken**

Deus ex Ma|chi|na ▲ ['de:ʊs ɛks 'maxina] M - - -, Dei - - ['de:i] (rare) deus ex machina

Deut ['dɔyt] M **um keinen ~** not one jot (Brit) or iota; **seine Ratschläge sind keinen ~ wert** his advice is not worth tuppence (Brit) or a dime (US); **er versteht nicht einen ~ davon** he does not know the first thing about it; **daran ist kein ~ wahr** there is not a grain of truth in it; **du bist keinen ~ besser** you're not one jot (Brit) or iota better

deut|bar ADJ interpretable; **..., ob Nietzsche theologisch ~ ist** ... whether Nietzsche can be interpreted or understood theologically; **nicht/schwer ~** impossible/difficult to interpret; **es ist nicht anders ~** it cannot be explained in any other way

Deu|te|lei [dɔytə'lai] F -, -en (pej geh) quibbling, quibbles pl, cavilling (Brit), caviling (US)

deu|teln ['dɔytln] VI (geh) to quibble, to cavil; **an jedem Wort ~** to quibble over every word; **daran gibt es nichts zu ~!** there are no ifs and buts about it! (Brit), there are no ifs, ands or buts about it! (US)

deu|ten ['dɔytn] **VT** (= auslegen) to interpret; Zukunft auch to read; sich (dat) **etw ~** (geh) to understand sth; **etw falsch ~** to misinterpret sth **VI** a (= zeigen) (**mit dem Finger**) **auf etw** (acc) **~** to point (one's finger) at sth b (fig: = hinweisen) to indicate; **alles deutet auf Regen/Schnee** all the signs are that it is going to rain/snow, everything points to rain/snow; **alles deutet darauf, dass ...** all the indications are that ..., everything indicates that ...

Deu|ter¹ ['dɔytɐ] M -s, - (Aus: = Wink) sign

Deu|ter² ['dɔytɐ] M -s, -, **Deu|te|rin** [-ərɪn] F -, -nen interpreter

deut|lich ['dɔytlɪç] **ADJ** a (= klar) clear b (= unmissverständlich) clear, plain; **eine ~e Sprache mit jdm reden** to speak plainly or bluntly with sb; **~ werden** to make oneself clear or plain; **das war ~!** (= taktlos) that was clear or plain enough; **muss ich ~er werden?** have I not made myself clear or plain enough? **ADV** a (= klar) sehen, unterscheiden, sprechen clearly; erkennbar, hörbar, wahrnehmbar clearly, plainly; **~ zu erkennen/sehen/hören** easy to recognize/see/hear; **~ fühlen** to feel distinctly; **ich fühle ~, dass ...** I have the distinct feeling that ... b (= unmissverständlich) sich ausdrücken, sagen explicitly; **jdm etw ~ vor Augen führen** to make sth perfectly clear or plain to sb; **sich ~ ausdrücken** to make oneself clear or plain; **ich muss es einmal ~ sagen** let me make myself perfectly clear; **jdm ~ zu verstehen geben, dass ...** to make it clear or plain to sb that ...

Deut|lich|keit F -, no pl clarity; **etw mit aller ~ sagen** to make sth perfectly clear or plain; **seine Antwort ließ an ~ nichts zu wünschen übrig** his answer was perfectly clear or plain and left no possible doubt

deut|lich|keits|hal|ber ADV for the sake of clarity

deutsch [dɔytʃ] **ADJ** a German; **~e Schrift** Gothic script; **Deutscher Schäferhund** Alsatian (Brit), German shepherd; **~e Gründlichkeit** etc German or Teutonic efficiency etc; **die Deutsche Bucht** the German Bight; **Deutsche Mark** (Hist) Deutschmark, German mark; **der Deutsche Orden** (Hist) the Teutonic Order (of Knights) b (in Bezug auf Sprache) German; **er hat ~, nicht englisch gesprochen** he spoke German not English; **mit jdm ~ reden** (fig inf: deutlich) to speak bluntly with sb **ADV** **etw ~ aussprechen** to pronounce sth as it is said in German, to give sth a German pronunciation; **~ denken** to think in German; **sich ~ unterhalten** to speak (in) German; **der Text ist ~ geschrieben** the text is written in German

Deutsch [dɔytʃ] NT -(s), dat -, no pl German; **das ~ Thomas Manns** Thomas Mann's German; **gut(es) ~ sprechen** to speak good German; (Ausländer auch) to speak German well; **~ sprechend** German-speaking; **~ lernen/verstehen** to learn/understand German; **sich auf ~ unterhalten** to speak (in) German; **auf** or **zu ~ heißt das ...** in German it means ...; **der Text ist in ~ geschrieben** the text is written in German; **der Vortrag wird in** or **auf ~ gehalten** the lecture will be given in German; **der Unterricht in ~** German lessons pl; **die Schulnote in ~** school mark (Brit) or grade (US) in or for German; **auf gut ~ (gesagt)** (fig inf) in plain English → auch **deutsch** ADJ b

Deutsch-: **Deutsch|ame|ri|ka|ner(in)** M(F) German American; **deutsch|ame|ri|ka|nisch** ADJ German-American; **deutsch-deutsch** ADJ Vereinigung etc German; **die ~e Grenze** (Hist) the intra-German border

Deutsch(e) NT -n, dat -n, no pl a (Ling) German; **aus dem ~en/ins ~e übersetzt** translated from/into (the) German; **das ~(e) des Mittelalters** medieval German, the German of the Middle Ages; **die Aussprache des ~en** the pronunciation of German, German pronunciation

b (= Charakteristik) Germanness; **manchmal kommt noch das ~e in ihm durch** sometimes the German in him or his Germanness shows through

Deut|sche De|mo|kra|ti|sche Re|pub|lik F (abbr **DDR**) (Hist) German Democratic Republic, East Germany no art, GDR

Deut|schen-: **Deut|schen|feind(in)** M(F) , **Deut|schen|fres|ser(in)** M(F) (inf) anti-German, Germanophobe; **Deut|schen|freund(in)** M(F) Germanophile

deutsch-eng|lisch ADJ a (Pol) Anglo-German b (Ling) German-English

Deut|schen-: **Deut|schen|hass** ▲ M Germanophobia; **Deut|schen|has|ser** [-hasɐ] M -s, -, **Deut|schen|has|se|rin** [-ərɪn] F -, -nen Germanophobe, German-hater

Deut|sche(r) ['dɔytʃə] MF decl as adj **er ist ~r** he is (a) German; **die ~n** the Germans; **der hässliche ~** the obnoxious German

---

DEUTSCHE WELLE

Deutsche Welle is a radio station controlled by the Federal Government and financed exclusively from Federal funds. It has a legal responsibility to produce radio programmes for broadcast to foreign countries. The aim is to provide a comprehensive picture of political, cultural and economic life in Germany, as well as to present and explain Germany's position on important national and international questions.

Deutsch-: **deutsch|feind|lich** ADJ anti-German, Germanophobic; **Deutsch|feind|lich|keit** F Germanophobia; **deutsch-fran|zö|sisch** ADJ a (Pol) Franco-German; **der Deutsch-Französische Krieg** the Franco-Prussian war b (Ling) German-French; **deutsch|freund|lich** ADJ pro-German, Germanophile; **Deutsch|freund|lich|keit** F Germanophilia; **deutsch|ge|sinnt** ADJ **~ sein** to feel oneself to be German, to think of oneself as being German; **Deutsch|her|ren** ['dɔytʃhɛrən] PL (Hist) Teutonic Knights pl; **Deutsch|her|ren|or|den** M (Hist) Teutonic Order of Knights; **Deutsch|kennt|nis|se** PL (a knowledge sing of) German, German language skills pl; **gute ~** a good command of German, fluent German; **gute ~ Voraussetzung** (in Annoncen) German essential; **Deutsch|kurs** M German course, German lessons pl; **einen ~ machen** to do a German course, to take German lessons

Deutsch|land ['dɔytʃlant] NT -s Germany; **die beiden ~(s)** (Hist) the two Germanys

Deutsch|land-: **Deutsch|land|bild** NT (fig, von Ausländern) image of the Germans; **Deutsch|land|fra|ge** F (Pol Hist) German question; **Deutsch|land|lied** NT (West) German national anthem; **Deutsch|land|po|li|tik** F home or domestic policy; (von fremdem Staat) policy on or toward(s) Germany; **Deutsch|land|tour|nee** F tour of Germany

Deutsch-: **Deutsch|leh|rer(in)** M(F) German teacher; **deutsch|na|ti|o|nal** ADJ (Hist) German National; **Deutsch|or|dens|rit|ter** M (Hist) Teutonic Knight; **Deutsch|rit|ter|or|den** M (Hist) Teutonic Order of Knights; **Deutsch|schweiz** F **die ~** German-speaking Switzerland; **Deutsch|schwei|zer(in)** M(F) German Swiss; **deutsch|schwei|ze|risch** ADJ German-Swiss; **deutsch|spra|chig** ADJ Bevölkerung, Gebiete German-speaking; Zeitung, Ausgabe German language; Literatur German; **Deutsch|spra|chig|keit** F -, no pl use of the German language; (= Fähigkeit) ability to speak German; **deutsch|sprach|lich** ADJ German(-language); **Deutsch|spre|chen** NT -s, no pl speaking German; **deutsch|spre|chend** △ ADJ → Deutsch; **deutsch|stäm|mig** ADJ of German origin or stock; **Deutsch|stäm|mi|ge(r)** [-ʃtɛmɪgə] MF decl as adj ethnic German; **Deutsch|stun|de** F German lesson;

Deutsch|tum ['dɔytʃtuːm] NT **-s**, *no pl* Germanness; (= *die Deutschen*) Germans *pl*; **Deutsch|tü|me|lei** [dɔytʃtyːmə'laɪ] F **-, -en** (*pej*) hyper-Germanness; **Deutsch|un|ter-richt** M German lessons *pl*, German classes *pl*; (= *einzelne Stunde*) German lesson or class; (= *das Unterrichten*) teaching German, the teaching of German

Deu|tung ['dɔytʊŋ] F **-, -en** interpretation; **eine falsche ~** a misinterpretation

Deu|tungs|ver|such M attempt at an interpretation; **er unternimmt einen neuen ~ des ...** he attempts a new interpretation of ...

De|vi|se [de'viːzə] F **-, -n** a (= *Wahlspruch*) maxim, motto; (*Her auch*) device b **Devisen** PL (*Fin*) foreign exchange or currency

De|vi|sen-: **De|vi|sen|ab|kom|men** NT foreign exchange agreement; **De|vi|sen|aus-gleich** M foreign exchange offset; **De|vi|sen|be|schrän|kun|gen** PL foreign exchange restrictions *pl*; **De|vi|sen|be|stim|mun|gen** PL foreign exchange control regulations *pl*; **De|vi|sen|be|wirt|schaf|tung** F foreign exchange control; **De|vi|sen|bi|lanz** F foreign exchange balance; **De|vi|sen|bör|se** F foreign exchange market; **De|vi|sen|brin|ger** [-brɪŋɐ] M **-s**, - (= *Geschäft etc*) earner of foreign exchange or currency; **De|vi|sen|ein|nah|men** PL (foreign currency) receipts *pl*; **De|vi|sen|ge|schäft** NT foreign exchange dealing; **De|vi|sen|han|del** M foreign currency or exchange dealings *pl*, sale and purchase of currencies; **De|vi|sen|knapp|heit** F shortage of foreign exchange; **De|vi|sen|kurs** M exchange rate, rate of exchange; **De|vi|sen|markt** M foreign exchange market; **De|vi|sen|po|li|tik** F foreign exchange policy; **De|vi|sen|re|ser|ven** PL foreign exchange reserves *pl*; **De|vi|sen|schmug|gel** M currency smuggling; **de|vi|sen|schwach** ADJ **~e Länder** countries with limited foreign currency reserves; **De|vi|sen|ter|min|ge|schäft** NT forward exchange; **De|vi|sen|ver|ge|hen** NT breach of exchange control regulations; **De|vi|sen|vor|schrif|ten** PL foreign exchange control regulations *pl*

de|vot [de'voːt] ADJ (*geh*) a (*pej*: = *unterwürfig*) obsequious b (*old*: = *demütig*) humble

De|vo|ti|on [devo'tsioːn] F **-, -en** (*geh*) a (*pej*: = *Unterwürfigkeit*) obsequiousness b (*old*: = *Demut*) humility

De|vo|ti|o|na|li|en [devotsio'naːliən] PL devotional objects *pl*

Dext|ro|se [dɛks'troːzə] F **-**, *no pl* (*Chem*) dextrose

Dez [deːts] M **-es, -e** (*dial inf*) bonce (*Brit inf*), head

De|zem|ber [de'tsɛmbɐ] M **-(s)**, - December → *auch* **März**

De|zen|ni|um [de'tsɛniʊm] NT **-s**, **Dezennien** [-niən] (*geh*) decade, decennium (*form*)

de|zent [de'tsɛnt] ADJ discreet; *Kleidung* subtle; *Einrichtung* refined ADV **andeuten, hinweisen** discreetly; **~ gekleidet sein** to be dressed unobtrusively; **~ eingerichtet sein** to have refined furnishings

de|zen|tral [detsɛn'traːl] ADJ decentralized ADV **verwalten** decentrally; **Müll ~ entsorgen** to have a decentralized waste disposal system

De|zent|ra|li|sa|ti|on [detsɛntraliza'tsioːn] F decentralization

de|zent|ra|li|sie|ren [detsɛntrali'ziːrən] ptp **de-zentralisiert** VT to decentralize

De|zent|ra|li|sie|rung F decentralization

De|zenz [de'tsɛnts] F **-**, *no pl* (*geh*) a (*old*: = *Anstand*) sense of decency b (*von Geschmack, Kleidung etc*) discreetness; (*von Benehmen auch*) discretion

De|zer|nat [detsɛr'naːt] NT **-(e)s, -e** (*Admin*) department

De|zer|nent [detsɛr'nɛnt] M **-en, -en**, **De|zer-nen|tin** [-'nɛntɪn] F **-, -nen** (*Admin*) head of department

De|zi|bel ['deːtsibɛl, -'bɛl] NT **-s**, - (*Phys*) decibel

de|zi|diert [detsi'diːɐt] (*geh*) ADJ firm, determined ADV firmly

De|zi- [de'tsi-] (*Aus*): **De|zi|gramm** NT decigram(me); **De|zi|li|ter** M OR NT decilitre (*Brit*), deciliter (*US*)

de|zi|mal [detsi'maːl] ADJ decimal

De|zi|mal|bruch M decimal fraction

De|zi|ma|le [detsi'maːlə] F **-(n), -n** decimal

de|zi|ma|li|sie|ren [detsimali'ziːrən] ptp **dezi-malisiert** VT to decimalize; **als in Großbritan-nien dezimalisiert wurde** when Great Britain went decimal

De|zi|ma|li|sie|rung F **-, -en** decimalization

De|zi|mal-: **De|zi|mal|klas|si|fi|ka|ti|on** F decimal classification; **De|zi|mal|kom|ma** NT (*englischsprachige Länder*) decimal point; (*deutschsprachige Länder etc*) decimal comma; **De|zi|mal|maß** NT decimal measure; **De|zi|mal|rech|nung** F decimals *pl*; **De|zi|mal-stel|le** F decimal place; **auf zwei ~n genau** correct to two decimal places; **De|zi|mal|sys-tem** NT decimal system; **De|zi|mal|waa|ge** F decimal balance; **De|zi|mal|zahl** F decimal number

De|zi|me ['deːtsimə, de'tsiːmə] F **-, -n** (*Mus*) tenth

De|zi|me|ter [detsi'meːtɐ, 'deːtsimeːtɐ] M OR NT decimetre (*Brit*), decimeter (*US*)

de|zi|mie|ren [detsi'miːrən] ptp **dezimiert** (*fig*) VT to decimate VR to be decimated

De|zi|mie|rung F **-, -en** (*fig*) decimation

DFB [deːʔɛf'beː] M **-s** *abbr von* **Deutscher Fußball--Bund** German Football Association

DFÜ [deːʔɛf'yː] F - *abbr von* **Datenfernübertragung**

DGB [deːgeː'beː] M **-s** *abbr von* **Deutscher Ge-werkschaftsbund** Federation of German Trade Unions

dgl. *abbr von* **dergleichen** *von* **desgleichen** the like

d. Gr. *abbr von* **der Große**

d. h. *abbr von* **das heißt** i.e.

d. i. *abbr von* **das ist** i.e.

Dia ['diːa] NT **-s, -s** (*Phot*) slide, transparency

Dia|be|tes [dia'beːtɛs] M **-**, *no pl* diabetes

Dia|be|ti|ker [dia'beːtikɐ] M **-s**, -, **Dia|be|ti-ke|rin** [-ərɪn] F **-, -nen** diabetic

Dia|be|ti|ker|kost F diabetic food

dia|be|tisch [dia'beːtɪʃ] ADJ diabetic

Dia|be|trach|ter M slide viewer

Dia|bo|lik [dia'boːlɪk] F **-**, *no pl* (*geh*) diabolical-ness, fiendishness

dia|bo|lisch [dia'boːlɪʃ] (*geh*) ADJ diabolical, fiendish ADV diabolically

dia|chron [dia'kroːn] ADJ diachronic

Dia|chro|nie [diakro'niː] F **-**, *no pl* (*Ling*) dia-chrony

dia|chro|nisch [dia'kroːnɪʃ] ADJ diachronic

Di|a|dem [dia'deːm] NT **-s, -e** diadem

Di|a|do|chen [dia'dɔxn] PL (*Hist*) diadochi *pl*; (*fig*) rivals *pl* in a power struggle

Di|a|do|chen|kämp|fe PL (*fig*) power struggle

Di|ag|no|se [dia'gnoːzə] F **-, -n** diagnosis; **eine ~ stellen** to make a diagnosis

Di|ag|no|se-: **Di|ag|no|se|stand** M diagnostic test bay; **Di|ag|no|se|ver|fah|ren** NT diag-nostic method, method of diagnosis; **Di|ag-no|se|zent|rum** NT diagnostic centre (*Brit*) or center (*US*)

Di|ag|nos|tik [dia'gnɔstɪk] F **-**, *no pl* diagnosis

Di|ag|nos|ti|ker [dia'gnɔstikɐ] M **-s**, -, **Di|ag-nos|ti|ke|rin** [-ərɪn] F **-, -nen** diagnostician

di|ag|nos|tisch [dia'gnɔstɪʃ] ADJ diagnostic

di|ag|nos|ti|zie|ren [diagnɔsti'tsiːrən] ptp **dia-gnostiziert** VTI (*Med, fig*) to diagnose; **(auf) etw** (*acc*) **~** to diagnose sth

di|a|go|nal [diago'naːl] ADJ diagonal ADV diag-onally; **ein Buch ~ lesen** (*inf*) to skim or flick through a book

Di|a|go|na|le [diago'naːlə] F **-, -n** diagonal

Di|a|go|nal|rei|fen M (*Aut*) cross-ply (tyre (*Brit*) or tire (*US*))

Di|a|gramm NT *pl* **-gramme** diagram

Di|a|gramm-: **Di|a|gramm|form** F **in ~** dia-grammatically; **Di|a|gramm|pa|pier** NT graph paper

Di|a|kon [dia'koːn, (*Aus*) 'diːakoːn] M **-s** or **-en**, **-e(n)** (*Eccl*) deacon

Di|a|ko|nat [diako'naːt] NT **-(e)s, -e** (*Eccl*) a (= *Amt*) deaconry, deaconship, diaconate b (= *Wohnung*) deacon's house

Di|a|ko|nie [diako'niː] F **-**, *no pl* (*Eccl*) social welfare work

Di|a|ko|nie|sta|ti|on F (church) community care centre (*Brit*) or center (*US*)

Di|a|ko|nin [dia'koːnɪn] F **-, -nen** (*Eccl*) deacon (-ess)

Di|a|ko|nis|se [diako'nɪsə] F **-, -n**, **Di|a|ko|nis-sin** [-'nɪsɪn] F **-, -nen** (*Eccl*) deaconess

dia|kri|tisch [dia'kriːtɪʃ] ADJ diacritic; **~e Zei-chen** diacritics, diacritic(al) marks or signs

Di|a|lekt [dia'lɛkt] M **-(e)s, -e** dialect

di|a|lek|tal [dialɛk'taːl] ADJ dialectal

Di|a|lekt-: **Di|a|lekt|fär|bung** F accent, dia-lect features *pl*; **Di|a|lekt|for|scher(in)** M(F) dialectologist, dialectician; **Di|a|lekt|for-schung** F dialect research, dialectology; **di|a-lekt|frei** ADJ dialect-free ADV **~ sprechen** to speak standard German/English *etc*

Di|a|lek|tik [dia'lɛktɪk] F **-**, *no pl* (*Philos*) dialec-tics *sing or pl*

Di|a|lek|ti|ker [dia'lɛktikɐ] M **-s**, -, **Di|a|lek|ti-ke|rin** [-ərɪn] F **-, -nen** (*Philos*) dialectician

di|a|lek|tisch [dia'lɛktɪʃ] ADJ a (*Philos*) dialec-tic(al); **~er Materialismus** dialectical material-ism b (*Ling*) = **dialektal**

Di|a|lek|tis|mus [dialɛk'tɪsmʊs] M **-**, *no pl* (*Ling*) dialecticism

Di|a|log [dia'loːk] M **-(e)s, -e** [-gə] dialogue (*Brit*), dialog (*US*)

Di|a|log-: **Di|a|log|au|tor(in)** M(F) (*Film*) scriptwriter; **di|a|log|be|reit** ADJ **~ sein** to be willing to negotiate or to have talks; **Di|a|log-be|reit|schaft** F willingness to negotiate or to have talks, openness for talks; **Di|a|log|be-trieb** M (*Comput*) conversation mode; **di|a-log|fä|hig** ADJ (*Comput*) **~ sein** to be capable of two-way communication; **Di|a|log|fä|hig-keit** F ability to engage in meaningful conver-sation; (*Comput*) two-way communication ca-pability; **Di|a|log|fens|ter** NT (*Comput*) dia-logue (*Brit*) or dialog (*US*) box; **Di|a|log|form** F dialogue (*Brit*) or dialog (*US*) form

dia|lo|gisch [dia'loːgɪʃ] ADJ dialogue *attr* (*Brit*), dialog *attr* (*US*)

Di|a|log-: Di|a|log|re|gie F (Film) script supervision; **Di|a|log|stück** NT (Theat) dialogue (Brit) or dialog (US) play

Di|a|ly|se [dia'ly:zə] F -, -n (Med) dialysis

Di|a|ly|se-: Di|a|ly|se|ge|rät [dia'ly:zə-] NT (Med) dialysis or kidney machine; **Di|a|ly|se|zent|rum** NT (Med) (kidney) dialysis centre (Brit) or center (US), (kidney) dialysis clinic

Di|a|ma|ga|zin NT (Phot) slide tray

Di|a|mant¹ [dia'mant] M -en, -en diamond

Di|a|mant² F -, no pl (Typ) four-point, diamond (4½ point)

di|a|mant|be|setzt ADJ attr diamond-studded

di|a|man|ten [dia'mantn] ADJ attr diamond; **von ~er Härte** as hard as diamond; **~er Glanz** adamantine lustre (Brit liter) or luster (US liter); **~e Hochzeit** diamond wedding

Di|a|mant-: Di|a|mant|kol|li|er [-kɔ'lie:] NT diamond necklace; **Di|a|mant|na|del** F a diamond brooch b (an Tonarm) diamond (stylus); **Di|a|mant|schlei|fer(in)** M(F) diamond polisher; **Di|a|mant|schliff** M diamond polishing; **Di|a|mant|schmuck** M diamond jewellery (Brit) or jewelry (US); **Di|a|mant|stahl** M diamond plate; **Di|a|mant|staub** M diamond dust

Di|a|me|ter [dia'me:tɐ] M (Geometrie) diameter

di|a|met|ral [diame'tra:l] ADJ diametral; (fig) Ansichten diametrically opposed; Gegensatz exact ◆ ADV ~ **entgegengesetzt sein, sich ~ gegenüberliegen** to be diametrically opposite; **~ entgegengesetzt** (fig) diametrically opposed

Di|a|na ['dia:na] F -s (Myth) Diana

Di|a|phrag|ma [dia'fragma] NT -s, Diaphragmen [-mən] (Tech, Med) diaphragm

Dia- (Phot): **Di|a|po|si|tiv** NT slide, transparency; **Di|a|pro|jek|tor** M slide projector; **Di|a|rah|men** M slide frame; **Di|a|show** F slide show; (= Diavortrag) slide talk

Di|ar|rhö(e) [dia'rø:] F -, -(e)n (Med) diarrhoea (Brit), diarrhea (US)

Di|as|po|ra F -, no pl (Eccl) diaspora

Di|as|to|le [di'astole, dia'sto:lə] F -, -n (Med) diastole

di|as|to|lisch [dia'sto:lɪʃ] ADJ diastolic

di|ät △ [di'ɛ:t] ADV → **Diät**

Di|ät [di'ɛ:t] F -, -en (Med) diet; **~ kochen** to cook according to a diet; **~ essen** to eat according to a diet; **~ halten** to keep to or observe a diet; **nach einer ~ leben** to be on a diet or (wegen Krankheit) special diet; **jdn auf ~ setzen** (inf) to put sb on a diet; **auf ~ sein** (inf) to be on a diet

Di|ät-: Di|ät|as|sis|tent(in) M(F) dietician; **Di|ät|bier** NT diet beer

Di|ä|ten PL (Parl) parliamentary allowance

Di|ä|ten-: Di|ä|ten|an|pas|sung F (euph) adjustment of parliamentary (Brit) or congressional (US) allowances; **Di|ä|ten|er|hö|hung** F increase in parliamentary (Brit) or congressional (US) allowances

Di|ä|te|tik [diɛ'te:tɪk] F -, -en dietetics sing

di|ä|te|tisch [diɛ'te:tɪʃ] ADJ dietetic

Di|ät|fahr|plan M (hum) dieting course or schedule

Di|a|thek [dia'te:k] F -, -en slide collection or library

Di|ä|tist [diɛ'tɪst] M -en, -en, **Di|ä|tis|tin** [-'tɪs-tɪn] F -, -nen dietician

Di|ät-: Di|ät|kost F dietary foods pl; **~ bekommen** to be on a special diet; **Di|ät|kur** F dietary or dietetic treatment

Di|a|to|nik [dia'to:nɪk] F -, no pl (Mus) diatonicism

di|a|to|nisch [dia'to:nɪʃ] ADJ (Mus) diatonic

Di|a|vor|trag M slide presentation or talk or show

---

dich [dɪç] PERS PRON acc von **du** you; (obs, dial) thee REFL PRON yourself; **wie fühlst du ~?** how do you feel?

Di|cho|to|mie [dɪçoto'mi:] F -, -n [-'mi:ən] dichotomy

dicht [dɪçt] ADJ a Gefieder, Haar, Hecke thick; Laub, Nebel thick, dense; Wald, (Menschen)menge, Gewühl dense; Verkehr heavy, dense; Gewebe close; Stoff closely-woven; (fig: = konzentriert) Stil dense; Szene full, compact; **in ~er Folge** in rapid or quick succession; **sie standen in ~en Reihen** they were standing row upon row close together

b (= undurchlässig) Vorhänge thick, heavy; Rollladen heavy; (= wasserdicht) watertight; (= luftdicht) airtight; **~ machen** to seal, to make watertight; airtight; Fenster to seal; **er ist nicht ganz ~** (inf) he's crackers (Brit inf) or nuts (inf)

c (inf: = zu) shut, closed

d (sl: = betrunken, high) off one's face (Brit inf), out of it (inf)

◆ ADV a (= nahe) closely; (~ an) ~ **stehen** to stand close together; **~ gefolgt von** closely followed by

b (= fest) zuziehen, schließen tightly; weben densely; **~ halten** to be watertight; **~ verhängen** to curtain heavily

c (= sehr stark) bevölkert, bepflanzt densely; bewaldet densely, thickly; **~ bewachsen** (Baumstämme) grown over with moss and lichen; Ufer thickly covered with vegetation; Landstrich rich in vegetation; **~ mit Efeu bewachsen** overgrown with ivy; **~ mit etw übersät** covered with sth; **~ behaart** very hairy; **~ belaubt** thick with leaves, densely foliated; **~ bewölkt** heavily overcast; **~ gedrängt** closely packed; Programm packed

d (mit Präpositionen) **~ an/bei** close to; **~ dahinter/darüber/davor** right behind/above/in front; **~ daneben** right or close beside it; **~ bevor** right before; **~ daran** hard by it; **~ hintereinander** close(ly) or right behind one another; **~ beieinander** or **beisammen** close together; **~ am Winde halten** (Naut) to sail close to the wind, to hug the wind; **~ hinter jdm her sein** to be right or hard or close behind sb

dicht-: dicht|auf ['dɪçt'lauf] ADV closely; **~ folgen** to follow close behind or closely; **dicht|be|haart** △ [-bəha:ɐt] ADJ attr → **dicht** ADV c; **dicht|be|laubt** △ [-bəlaupt] ADJ attr → **dicht** ADV c; **dicht|be|völ|kert** △ [-bəfœlkɐt] ADJ attr → **dicht** ADV c; **dicht|be|wach|sen** △ ADJ attr → **dicht** ADV c; **dicht|be|wölkt** △ ADJ attr → **dicht** ADV c

Dich|te ['dɪçtə] F -, -n, no pl a (von Gefieder, Haar, Hecke) thickness; (von Laub, Nebel, Wald, Menschenmenge) denseness; (von Verkehr) heaviness; (von Gewebe) closeness; (von Stoff) close weave; (fig: = Konzentriertheit, von Stil) denseness b (Phys) density c (Comput) Diskette mit einfacher/doppelter ~ single-density/double-density diskette

Dich|te|mes|ser M -s, - (Phys) densimeter

dich|ten¹ ['dɪçtn] VT to write, to compose; **sein Glückwunsch war gedichtet** his congratulations were (written) in verse ◆ VI to write poems/a poem

dich|ten² VT (= undurchlässig machen) to seal; (Naut auch) to caulk

Dich|ter ['dɪçtɐ] M -s, -, **Dich|te|rin** [-ərɪn] F -, -nen poet; (= Schriftsteller) writer, author

Dich|ter|fürst(in) M(F) prince/princess among poets

dich|te|risch ['dɪçtərɪʃ] ADJ poetic; (= schriftstellerisch) literary; **~e Freiheit** poetic licence (Brit) or license (US)

Dich|ter-: Dich|ter|kreis M circle of poets; **Dich|ter|le|sung** F reading (by a poet/writer from his own works); **Dich|ter|ling** ['dɪçtɐlɪŋ] M -s, -e (pej) rhymester (pej), poetaster (pej); **Dich|ter|schu|le** F → **Dichter** school of poets/ writers; **Dich|ter|spra|che** F poetic language; **Dich|ter|wort** NT pl -worte (literary) quotation

Dich|ter-: Dich|ter|kreis (see above)

Dich|ter-: dicht|ge|drängt △ ADJ attr → **dicht** ADV c; **dicht+hal|ten** VI sep irreg (inf) to hold one's tongue (inf), to keep one's mouth shut (inf); **Dicht|heit** F -, no pl = Dichte a; **Dicht|kunst** F art of poetry; (= Schriftstellerei) creative writing; **dicht+ma|chen** VTI sep (inf) Laden etc to shut up, to close; Fabrik, Betrieb etc to close or shut down; **(den Laden) ~** to shut up shop (and go home) (inf); **er hat (sich) völlig dichtgemacht** (fig inf) he's pulled down the shutters (inf)

Dich|tung¹ ['dɪçtʊŋ] F -, -en a no pl (= Dichtkunst, Gesamtwerk) literature; (in Versform) poetry; **~ und Wahrheit** (Liter) poetry and truth; (fig) fact and fantasy or fiction b (= Dichtwerk) poem, poetic work; literary work; **dramatische ~** dramatic poem

Dich|tung² F -, -en (Tech) seal; (in Wasserhahn etc) washer; (Aut: von Zylinder, Vergaser) gasket; (= das Abdichten) sealing

Dich|tungs-: Dich|tungs|art F , **Dich|tungs|gat|tung** F literary genre; **Dich|tungs|man|schet|te** F seal; **Dich|tungs|mas|se** F sealant; **Dich|tungs|ma|te|ri|al** NT , **Dich|tungs|mit|tel** NT sealing compound; **Dich|tungs|ring** M , **Dich|tungs|schei|be** F seal, sealing ring; (in Wasserhahn) washer

dick [dɪk] ADJ a thick; Mensch, Körperteil, Band, Buch, Brieftasche fat; Baum, Stamm big, large, thick; (inf) Gehalt, Belohnung, Rechnung, Gewinn fat, hefty; (inf) Tränen, Geschäft big; **einen ~en Mercedes fahren** (inf) to drive a big Mercedes; **eine ~e Zigarre** a fat cigar; (fig) = Berta **Big Bertha; ein ~er Brocken** (inf) a hard or tough nut (to crack); **~e Dinger** (sl: = Busen) knockers pl (Brit inf), hooters pl (US inf); **ein ~es Fell haben** (inf) to have (a) thick skin, to be thick-skinned; **eine ~e Lippe riskieren** (inf) to be cheeky (Brit), to act fresh (US inf); **~ machen** (Speisen) to be fattening; **~ werden** (Mensch: = zunehmen) to get fat

b (nach Maßangaben) thick; Erdschicht deep; **3 m ~e Wände** walls 3 metres (Brit) or meters (US) thick, 3-metre (Brit) or meter (US) thick walls

c (inf: = schwerwiegend) Fehler, Verweis big; **das ist ein ~er Tadel/ein ~es Lob** that's heavy criticism/high praise; **das ist ein ~er Hund** or **ein ~es Ei** (inf: = unerhört) that's a bit much (inf); **ach, du ~es Ei!** (inf) for goodness' sake! (inf); **das ~e Ende kommt noch** (prov) the worst is yet to come

d (= geschwollen) Backe, Beine, Finger, Mandeln swollen; Beule big; **ein ~er Kopf** (inf) a thick head (inf) → **Bauch**

e (= zähflüssig, dicht) thick; **eine ~e Suppe** (inf: = Nebel) a real peasouper (Brit inf), very thick fog; **~e Milch** sour milk; **durch ~ und dünn** through thick and thin → **Luft**

f (inf: = herzlich) Freundschaft, Freund close; **mit jdm ~e sein** to be thick with sb (inf)

◆ ADV a (= warm) warmly; **sich/jdn ~ anziehen** to wrap up/sb up warmly

b anstreichen, unterstreichen heavily

c (= reichlich) auftragen, schmieren, bestreichen thickly; **etw ~ mit Butter bestreichen** to spread butter thickly on sth; **~(e)** (inf: = ausreichend) easily; **er hat es ~(e)** (= hat es satt) he's had enough of it; (= hat viel) he's got enough and to spare; **jdn/etw ~(e) haben** (= von jdm/etw genug haben) to have had one's fill of sb/sth (inf), to have had sb/sth up to here (inf) → **auftragen** VI b, **Faxen** a

d (inf: = sehr) **~ satt sein** to be stuffed (inf); **jdm etw ~ ankreiden** to hold sth against sb; **~ im Geschäft sein** to make it big (inf); **~(e) kommen** (inf) to come thick and fast

e (inf: = eng) **mit jdm ~ befreundet sein** to be thick with sb (inf)

Dick-: dick|bau|chig ADJ Vase, Krug bulbous; Mann potbellied; **dick|bäu|chig** [-bɔyçɪç] ADJ Mensch potbellied; (krankhaft auch) swollen-bellied; **Dick|darm** M (Anat) colon

di|cke ['dɪkə] ADV (inf) → **dick** ADJ f ADV c, d

Di|cke ['dɪkə] F -, -n a (= *Stärke, Durchmesser*) thickness; (*bei Maßangaben auch*) depth b (*von Menschen, Körperteilen*) fatness

Di|cken-: Di|cken|mes|ser M -s, - thickness gauge; **Di|cken|wachs|tum** NT lateral growth

Di|cke(r) ['dɪkə] MF *decl as adj* (*inf*) fatty (*inf*), fatso (*inf*)

Di|cker|chen ['dɪkəçən] NT -s, - (*inf*) chubby chops (*Brit inf*), chubby

di|cke+tun VR *sep irreg* (*inf*) = **dicktun**

Dick-: dick|fel|lig [-fɛlɪç] ADJ (*inf*) thick-skinned; **Dick|fel|lig|keit** F -, *no pl* (*inf*) insensitivity, rhinoceros hide (*inf*); **dick|flüs|sig** ADJ thick, viscous (*Tech*); **Dick|flüs|sig|keit** F thickness, viscosity (*Tech*); **Dick|häu|ter** [-hɔytɐ] M -s, - pachyderm; (*fig*) thick-skinned person; **dick|häu|tig** ADJ (*fig*) thick-skinned

Di|ckicht ['dɪkɪçt] NT -(e)s, -e (= *Gebüsch*) thicket; (*fig*) jungle, maze

Dick-: Dick|kopf M a (= *Starrsinn*) obstinacy, stubbornness, mulishness; **einen ~ haben** to be obstinate *or* stubborn *or* mulish; **sie setzt ihren ~ immer durch** she always gets what she wants b (= *Mensch*) mule (*inf*); **dick|köp|fig** ADJ (*fig*) stubborn; **Dick|köp|fig|keit** F -, *no pl* stubbornness; **dick|lei|big** [-laɪbɪç] ADJ *Buch* massive; *Mensch* corpulent; **Dick|lei|big|keit** F -, *no pl* (*von Mensch*) corpulence; **dick|lich** ['dɪklɪç] ADJ plump; *Mensch auch* plumpish, tubby (*inf*); **Dick|milch** F (*Cook*) sour milk; **Dick|schä|del** M (*inf*) = Dickkopf; **dick|schä|lig** [-ʃaːlɪç] ADJ thick-skinned, with a thick skin *or* peel; **Dick|sein** NT fatness; **Dick|tu|e|rei** F (*inf*) swanking *no pl*; **dick+tun** VR *sep irreg* (*inf*) to swank (*inf*); **(sich) mit etw ~** to swank about sth (*inf*); **dick|wan|dig** ADJ *Gebäude, Bunker etc* with thick walls, thick-walled; *Gefäß, Schale* with thick sides, thick; **Dick|wanst** M (*pej inf*) fatso (*inf*)

Di|dak|tik [di'daktɪk] F -, -en didactics *sing* (*form*), teaching methods *pl*

Di|dak|ti|ker [di'daktikɐ] M -s, -, **Di|dak|ti|ke|rin** [-ərɪn] F -, -nen (*Univ*) lecturer in teaching methods; **er ist ein miserabler ~** his teaching methods are terrible

di|dak|tisch [di'daktɪʃ] ADJ didactic ADV didactically

di|del|dum [diːdl'dʊm], **di|del|dum|dei** [diːdl-dʊm'daɪ] INTERJ tum-ti-tum

die [diː] → **der** [2]

Dieb [diːp] M -(e)s, -e [-bə], **Die|bin** ['diːbɪn] F -, -nen thief; **haltet den ~!** stop thief!; **sich wie ein ~ davonschleichen** to steal *or* slink away like a thief in the night

Die|be|rei [diːbə'raɪ] F -, -en thievery *no pl*, thieving *no pl*

Die|bes-: Die|bes|ban|de F gang of thieves; **Die|bes|ge|sin|del** NT (*pej*) thieving riff-raff (*pej*); **Die|bes|gut** NT , *no pl* stolen property *or* goods *pl*; **Die|bes|höh|le** F thieves' den; **Die|bes|nest** NT den of thieves; **Die|bes|pack** NT (*pej*) thieving riffraff (*pej*) *or* trash (*pej*); **die|bes|si|cher** ADJ thief-proof

Die|bin F -, -nen thief

die|bisch ['diːbɪʃ] ADJ a *Gesindel, Elster* thieving *attr* b (*inf*) *Freude, Vergnügen* impish, mischievous

Dieb|stahl ['diːpʃtaːl] M -(e)s, ⁀e [-ʃteːlə] theft; (*Jur auch*) larceny; **einfacher/schwerer ~** petty/grand larceny; **bewaffneter ~** armed robbery; **geistiger ~** plagiarism

Dieb|stahl-: dieb|stahl|si|cher ADJ theft-proof; **Dieb|stahl|si|che|rung** F (*Aut*) anti-theft device; **Dieb|stahl|ver|si|che|rung** F insurance against theft

die|je|ni|ge ['diːjeːnɪɡə] DEM PRON → **derjeni|ge**

Die|le ['diːlə] F -, -n a (= *Fußbodenbrett*) floorboard b (= *Vorraum*) hall, hallway → **Eisdiele**, **Tanzdiele** c (*N Ger*: = *Tenne*) threshing floor

die|len ['diːlən] VT *Zimmer* to lay floorboards in

Die|len|brett NT floorboard

die|nen ['diːnən] VI a (= *Dienste tun, sich einsetzen*) to serve (*jdm sb*); (*old*: = *angestellt sein*) to be in service (*bei* with); **bei Hof ~** to serve *or* wait at court; **bei der Messe** *or* **am Altar ~** to serve at mass b (*Mil*) (= *beim Militär sein*) to serve; (= *Militärdienst leisten*) to do (one's) military service; **bei der Kavallerie/unter jdm ~** to serve in the cavalry/under sb; **ein gedienter Soldat** an ex-soldier → *auch* **gedient**, **Pike** c (= *fördern*) (*einer Sache dat*) sth) to serve; **dem Fortschritt, der Erforschung** to aid; *dem Verständnis* to promote; (= *nützlich sein*) to be of use *or* service (*jdm* to sb); **es dient einem guten Zweck** it serves a useful purpose; **es dient einer guten Sache** it is in *or* for a good cause; **der Verbesserung der Arbeitsbedingungen ~** to serve to improve working conditions; **das wird dir später ~** that will be *or* come in useful to you later d (= *behilflich sein*) to help (*jdm* sb), to be of help or service (*jdm* to sb); **womit kann ich Ihnen ~?** what can I do for you?; (*im Geschäft auch*) can I help you?; **damit kann ich leider nicht ~** I'm afraid I can't help you there; **damit ist mir wenig gedient** that's no use *or* good to me e (= *verwendet werden*) **als/zu etw ~** to serve *or* be used as/for sth; **lass dir das als Warnung ~!** let that serve as *or* be a warning to you!

Die|ner ['diːnɐ] M -s, - a (= *Mensch* lit, fig) servant; (= *Lakai auch*) valet; **~ Gottes** servant of God; **Ihr ergebenster ~** (*old*: *in Briefen*) your (most) obedient servant → **stumm** ADJ a b (*inf*: = *Verbeugung*) bow

Die|ne|rin ['diːnərɪn] F -, -nen maid, maidservant (*old*)

die|nern ['diːnɐn] VI (*vor* +dat to) (*lit*) to bow; (*fig pej*) to bow and scrape

Die|ner|schaft ['diːnɐʃaft] F -, -en servants *pl*, domestic staff

dien|lich ['diːnlɪç] ADJ useful, helpful; (= *ratsam*) expedient, advisable; **jdm/einer Sache ~ sein** to help sb/sth, to be of use *or* help to sb/sth

Dienst [diːnst] M -(e)s, -e a (= *Arbeitsverhältnis, Tätigkeitsbereich*) service; (= *Arbeitsstelle*) position; **diplomatischer/öffentlicher ~** diplomatic/civil service; **bei jdm in ~(en) sein** *or* **stehen**, **in jds ~(en)** (*dat*) **sein** *or* **stehen** to be in sb's service; **jdn in (seinen) ~ nehmen** to engage sb; **in jds ~(e)** (*acc*) **treten** to enter sb's service; **Oberst** *etc* **außer ~** (*abbr* **a. D.**) retired colonel *etc*; **den ~ quittieren, aus dem ~ (aus)scheiden** to resign one's post; (*Mil*) to leave the service; **~ mit der Waffe** (*Mil*) armed service; **nicht mehr im ~ sein** to have left the service; **im ~ ergraut sein** to have many years of faithful service behind one b (= *Berufsausübung, Amtspflicht*) duty; (= *Arbeit, Arbeitszeit*) work; **im ~ sein, ~ haben** (*Arzt, Feuerwehrmann etc*) to be on duty; (*Apotheke*) to be open; **~ habend** (*Arzt, Offizier etc*) duty *attr*, on duty; **im ~ sein** (*Angestellter etc*) to be working; **außer ~ sein** to be off duty; **nach ~** after work; **zum ~ gehen** to go to work; **~ tun** to serve (*bei* in, *als* as); **~ tuend** (*Arzt*) duty *attr*, on duty; **jdn vom ~ beurlauben** to grant sb leave of absence; **jdn vom ~ befreien** to exempt sb from his duties; **Tellerwäscher/Kindermädchen vom ~** (*hum*) resident dishwasher/babysitter (*hum*); **~ nach Vorschrift** work to rule; **~ ist ~ und Schnaps ist Schnaps** (*Prov inf*) you can't mix business with pleasure, there's a time for everything c (= *Tätigkeit, Leistung, Hilfe*) service; **im ~(e) einer Sache/der Menschheit** in the service of sth/humanity; **sich in den ~ der Sache stellen** to embrace the cause; **jdm einen ~/einen schlechten ~ erweisen** to do sb a good/bad turn, to do sb a service/disservice; **jdm gute ~e leisten** *or* **tun** to serve sb well; **jdm den ~ verweigern** to refuse to work for sb; **die Stimme** *etc* **versagte ihr den ~** her voice *etc* failed (her) *or* gave way;

~ am Vaterland service to one's country; **~ am Kunden** customer service; **etw in ~ stellen** to put sth into commission *or* service; **jdm zu ~en** *or* **zu jds ~en stehen** to be at sb's disposal; (*Mensch auch*) to be at sb's service; **(ich stehe) zu ~en!** (*old*) at your service!; **was steht zu ~en?** (*old*) you wish, sir/madam? d (= *Einrichtung*) service e (*Archit*) engaged column *or* shaft

-dienst M *suf in cpds* service; (*für Hausarbeit etc*) duty; **Militärdienst** military service; **Küchendienst haben** to be on kitchen duty

Dienst-: Dienst|ab|teil NT (*Rail*) ≈ guard's compartment, ≈ conductor's car (*US*); **Dienst|adel** M (*Hist*) *nobility whose titles derive from being in the king's service*

Diens|tag ['diːnstaːk] M Tuesday; **~ Abend/Morgen/Nachmittag** (on) Tuesday evening/morning/afternoon; **~ abends/nachts/vormittags** on Tuesday evenings/nights/mornings; **am ~** on Tuesday; **an einem ~, eines ~s** one Tuesday; **hast du ~ Zeit?** have you time on Tuesday?; **heute ist ~, der 10. Juni** today is Tuesday the tenth of June *or* Tuesday June the tenth; **jeden ~, alle -e** every Tuesday; **des ~s** (*geh*) on Tuesdays; **die Nacht von ~ auf** *or* **zum Mittwoch** the night of Tuesday to Wednesday; **den (ganzen) ~ über** all (day) Tuesday, the whole of Tuesday (*esp Brit*); **ab nächsten** *or* **nächstem ~** from next Tuesday; **~ in acht Tagen** *or* **in einer Woche** a week on Tuesday, Tuesday week (*esp Brit*); **seit letzten** *or* **letztem ~** since last Tuesday; **~ vor einer Woche** *or* **vor acht Tagen** a week (ago) last Tuesday

Diens|tag-: Diens|tag|abend M Tuesday evening; **Diens|tag|nach|mit|tag** M Tuesday afternoon

diens|tags ['diːnstaːks] ADV on Tuesdays, on a Tuesday; **~ abends** on Tuesday evenings, on a Tuesday evening

diens|tags|nach|mit|tags ADV on Tuesday afternoons

Dienst-: Dienst|al|ter NT length of service; **Dienst|äl|tes|te(r)** MF *decl as adj* longest-serving member of staff; **dienst|äl|tes|te(r, s)** ADJ longest-serving; **Dienst|an|tritt** M assumption of one's duties; (*jeden Tag*) commencement of work; **bei ~** on taking up one's duties; on commencing work; **Dienst|an|wei|sung** F instructions *pl*, regulations *pl*; **Dienst|an|zug** M (*Mil*) service uniform *or* dress; **Dienst|auf|fas|sung** F conception of one's duties; **was ist denn das für ~!** have you no sense of duty?; **Dienst|auf|sicht** F supervision; **die ~ über etw** (*acc*) **haben** to be in charge of sth; **Dienst|auf|sichts|be|schwer|de** F complaint about a ruling; **Dienst|aus|weis** M company ID (card); **dienst|bar** ADJ a (*Hist*) subject b (*fig*: = *helfend*) **~er Geist** helpful soul; **~e Geister** willing hands; **sich** (*dat*) **etw ~ machen** to utilize sth; **Dienst|bar|keit** ['diːnstbaːrkaɪt] F -, -en a (*Jur, Hist*) servitude; **etw in seine ~ bringen** (*fig geh*) to utilize sth b (= *Gefälligkeit, Tätigkeit als Diener*) service; **dienst|be|flis|sen** ADJ zealous, assiduous; **Dienst|be|flis|sen|heit** F zealousness, assiduity; **Dienst|be|frei|ung** F (*Mil*) leave, furlough (*US*); **Dienst|be|ginn** M start of work; **~ ist um 8 Uhr** work starts at 8 o'clock; **dienst|be|reit** ADJ a (= *geöffnet*) *Apotheke* open *pred*; *Arzt* on call *pred*; *Mitarbeiter* on duty *pred* b (= *hilfsbereit*) willing to be of service, obliging; **Dienst|be|reit|schaft** F a **~ haben** (*Arzt*) to be on call; (*Mitarbeiter*) to be on duty; **in ~ sein** (*Apotheke*) to be open; **welche Apotheke hat dieses Wochenende ~?** which chemist (*Brit*) *or* pharmacy is open this weekend? b (= *Hilfsbereitschaft*) helpfulness, willingness to be of service; **Dienst|be|spre|chung** F (official) meeting; **Dienst|be|zü|ge** PL salary *sing*; **Dienst|bo|te** M , **Dienst|bo|tin** F servant; **Dienst|bo|ten|ein|gang** M tradesmen's *or* service entrance; **Dienst|eid** M oath of ser-

---

vice; **Dienst|ei|fer** M zeal; **dienst|eif|rig** ADJ zealous, assiduous; **dienst|fä|hig** ADJ fit for work; (*Mil*) fit for duty; **Dienst|fä|hig|keit** F fitness for work; (*Mil*) fitness for duty; **Dienst|fahrt** F business trip; (*von Beamten auch*) official trip; **dienst|fer|tig** ADJ zealous, assiduous; **dienst|frei** ADJ free; **~er Tag** day off, free day; **~ haben/bekommen** to have/be given a day off; **Dienst|ge|brauch** M (*Mil, Admin*) **nur für den ~** for official use only; **Dienst|ge|heim|nis** NT official secret; **Dienst|ge|spräch** NT business call; (*von Beamten*) official call; **Dienst|grad** M (*Mil*) **a** (= *Rangstufe*) rank **b** (= *Mensch*) **ein höherer ~** a person of higher rank, a higher ranking person; **Dienst|grad|ab|zei|chen** NT (*Mil*) insignia; **dienst|ha|bend** △ ADJ attr **~ Dienst b**; **Dienst|ha|ben|de(r)** MF decl as adj **der ~** (*Mil*) the duty officer; **Dienst|herr(in)** M(F) employer; **Dienst|jahr** NT usu pl (*Mil, Admin*) year of service; **Dienst|klei|dung** F working dress, uniform; (*Mil*) service dress; **Dienst|leis|ter** [-laistɐ] M **-s, -** (*Person*) service provider; (= *Firma*) service company; **wir arbeiten viel mit ~n** we use a lot of contractors; **die Datenerfassung haben wir an ~ vergeben** we've outsourced our data acquisition; **Dienst|leis|tung** F service; **Dienst|leis|tungs|abend** M late-closing night; **Dienst|leis|tungs|be|ruf** M job in a service industry; **Dienst|leis|tungs|be|trieb** M service company; **Dienst|leis|tungs|ge|sell|schaft** F service society; **Dienst|leis|tungs|ge|wer|be** NT services trade; **dienst|lich** ['diːnstlɪç] ADJ *Angelegenheiten* business attr; *Schreiben, Befehl* official; **~ werden** (*inf*) to become businesslike ADV on business; **wir haben hier ~ zu tun** we have business here; **Dienst|mäd|chen** NT maid; **Dienst|mann** M **a** pl **-männer** or **-leute** (= *Gepäckträger*) porter **b** pl **-mannen** or **-leute** (*Hist:* = *Vasall*) liegeman, vassal; **Dienst|mar|ke** F ID badge; **Dienst|müt|ze** F uniform cap; **Dienst|ord|nung** F (*Admin*) official regulations pl; (*Mil*) service regulations pl; **Dienst|per|so|nal** NT staff, personnel; **Dienst|pflicht** F compulsory service; **dienst|pflich|tig** [-pflɪçtɪç] ADJ liable for compulsory service; **Dienst|pflich|ti|ge(r)** MF decl as adj person/man/woman liable for compulsory service; **Dienst|pis|to|le** F service revolver or pistol; **Dienst|plan** M duty rota (*Brit*) or roster; **Dienst|rang** M grade; (*Mil*) rank; **Dienst|rei|se** F business trip; (*von Beamten auch*) official trip; **auf ~** on a business trip; **Dienst|sa|che** F (*Post*) **gebührenfreie ~** official matter sent postage paid; **Dienst|schluss** ▲ M end of work; **nach ~** (*von Arbeiter etc*) after work; (*von Büro, Firma etc auch*) after working hours; **wir haben jetzt ~** we finish work now; **Dienst|sie|gel** NT , **Dienst|stem|pel** M official stamp; **Dienst|stel|le** F (*Admin*) department; (*Mil*) section; **Dienst|stun|den** PL working hours pl; **dienst|taug|lich** ADJ (*Mil*) fit for duty; **Dienst|taug|lich|keit** F (*Mil*) fitness for duty; **dienst|tu|end** △ [-tuənt] ADJ **~ Dienst b**; **dienst|un|fä|hig** ADJ unfit for work; (*Mil*) unfit for duty; **Dienst|un|fä|hig|keit** F unfitness for work; (*Mil*) unfitness for duty; **dienst|un|taug|lich** ADJ (*Mil*) unfit for duty; **Dienst|un|taug|lich|keit** F (*Mil*) unfitness for duty; **Dienst|ver|ge|hen** NT breach of duty; **Dienst|ver|hält|nis** NT **im ~ stehen** to be a public employee; **in ein ~ übernommen werden** to become a public employee; **dienst|ver|pflich|ten** ptp **dienstverpflichtet** VT insep to call up or draft (*US*) for essential service; **Dienst|ver|trag** M contract of employment; **Dienst|vor|schrift** F official regulations pl; (*Mil*) service regulations pl; **Dienst|waf|fe** F service weapon; **Dienst|wa|gen** M company car; (*von Beamten*) official car; (*Mil*) staff car; (*Rail*) ≈ guard's carriage, ≈ conductor's car (*US*); **Dienst|weg** M **den ~ einhalten** to go through the proper or official channels pl; **dienst|wil|lig** ADJ willing to be of service; (*Mil*) willing

do one's duty; **Dienst|woh|nung** F police/army etc house, house provided by the police/army etc; **Dienst|zeit** F **a** period of service **b** (= *Arbeitszeit*) working hours pl; (*Mil*) hours pl of duty; **Dienst|zeug|nis** NT testimonial

dies [diːs] DEM PRON inv this; (pl) these; **~ sind** these are; **~ und das** this and that; **~ alles, alles ~** all this/that → **dieser**

dies|be|züg|lich (*form*) ADJ relating to or regarding this ADV **sich ~ äußern** to give one's views regarding this or on this matter

die|se ['diːzə] DEM PRON → **dieser**

Die|sel ['diːzl] M **-s, -** (*inf*) diesel; **mf**

Die|sel|an|trieb M diesel drive; **mit ~** diesel-driven

die|sel|be [diːˈzɛlbə], **die|sel|bi|ge** [diːˈzɛlbɪgə] DEM PRON → **derselbe**

Die|sel-: die|sel|elekt|risch ADJ diesel-electric; **Die|sel|lok** F , **Die|sel|lo|ko|mo|ti|ve** F diesel locomotive; **Die|sel|mo|tor** M diesel engine; **Die|sel|öl** NT diesel oil

die|ser ['diːzɐ], **die|se**, **die|ses** pl **die|se** DEM PRON **a** (*substantivisch*) this; (pl) these; (= *dieser dort, da*) that; (pl) those; **diese(r, s) hier** this (one); **diese hier** or **these** (ones); **diese(r, s) da** that (one); **diese da** pl those (ones); **wer hat es getan? – ~!** which one did it? – this/that one!; **~ ist es!** this/that is the one!; **~ ..., jener ...** the latter ..., the former ...; **schließlich fragte ich einen Polizisten; ~ sagte mir ...** in the end I asked a policeman, he told me ...; **dieses und jenes** this and that; **~ und jener** this person and that; **~ oder jener** someone or other; **... oder dem Überbringer dieses** (*form*) ... or to the bearer of this

 b attr this; (pl) these; (= *dieser dort, da*) that; (pl) those; **gib mir dieses Buch** give me that book; **dieses Jahr** this year; **~ Monat** this month; **Anfang dieses Jahres/Monats** at the beginning of the or this or the current (*form*) year/month; **in diesen Wochen/Jahren habe ich viel erlebt** I experienced a lot in those weeks/years; **ich fahre diese Woche/dieses Jahr noch weg** I'm going away this week/year; **am 5. dieses Monats** on the 5th of this month; (*in Briefen auch*) on the 5th inst (*form*); **~ Tage** (*vergangen*) the other day; (*zukünftig*) one of these days; **(nur) dieses eine Mal** just this/that once; **~ Maier** (*inf*) that or this Maier → **Nacht**

die|ser|art ['diːzɐˌaːɐt] ADV (*Aus, old*) thus, in this way

die|ses ['diːzəs] DEM PRON → **dieser**

die|sig ['diːzɪç] ADJ *Wetter, Luft* hazy, misty

Die|sig|keit F **-,** no pl haziness, mistiness

dies-: dies|jäh|rig ADJ attr this year's; **die ~e Ernte** this year's harvest; **dies|mal** ADV this time; **dies|ma|lig** [-maːlɪç] ADJ attr **der ~e Preis** the price this time; **dies|sei|tig** [-zaitɪç] ADJ **a** *Ufer* near(side) attr, (on) this side **b** (= *irdisch*) of this world; *Leben* in this world; **dies|seits** ['diːszaits] PREP +gen on this side of; **Dies|seits** ['diːszaits] NT **-,** no pl **das ~** this life; **im ~** in this life, on earth

Diet|rich ['diːtrɪç] M **-s, -e** picklock, skeleton key

die|weil [diːˈvail] (*obs*) ADV meanwhile, in the meantime, the while; (*dial*) CONJ whilst, while

Dif|fa|ma|ti|on [dɪfamaˈtsioːn] F **-, -en** (= *das Diffamieren*) defamation (of character); (= *Bemerkung etc*) defamatory statement

dif|fa|mie|ren [dɪfaˈmiːrən] ptp **diffamiert** VT to defame

dif|fa|mie|rend ADJ defamatory

Dif|fa|mie|rung F **-, -en** (= *das Diffamieren*) defamation (of character); (= *Bemerkung etc*) defamatory statement

Dif|fa|mie|rungs|kam|pag|ne F smear campaign

Dif|fe|ren|ti|al [dɪfərɛnˈtsiaːl] NT **-s, -e** = **Differenzial**

Dif|fe|ren|ti|al- in cpds = **Differenzial-**: **Dif|fe|ren|ti|al|rech|nung** F = **Differenzialrechnung**

Dif|fe|renz [dɪfəˈrɛnts] F **-, -en a** (= *Unterschied, fehlender Betrag, Math*) difference; (= *Abweichung*) discrepancy **b** usu pl (= *Meinungsverschiedenheit*) difference (of opinion), disagreement

Dif|fe|renz|be|trag M difference, balance

Dif|fe|ren|zi|al ▲ [dɪfəˈrɛntsiaːl] NT **-s, -e a** (*Math*) differential **b** (*Aut: auch* **Differenzialgetriebe**) differential (gear)

Dif|fe|ren|zi|al- in cpds (*Tech, Math*) differential; **Dif|fe|ren|zi|al|glei|chung** ▲ F (*Math*) differential equation; **Dif|fe|ren|zi|al|rech|nung** ▲ F (*Math*) differential calculus

dif|fe|ren|zie|ren [dɪfərɛnˈtsiːrən] ptp **differenziert** VT **a** (= *unterscheiden*) to make distinctions/a distinction in; *Behauptung, Urteil* to be discriminating in; (= *abändern*) to make changes/a change in, to modify; **die Gesetze wurden immer stärker differenziert** the laws became more and more sophisticated **b** (*Math*) to differentiate VI to make distinctions/a distinction (*zwischen +dat* between, *bei* in); (= *den Unterschied verstehen*) to differentiate (*zwischen +dat* between, *bei* in); (*bei Behauptung, Urteil*) to be discriminating, to discriminate (*bei* in); **~de Methoden** discriminative methods; **zwischen zwei Dingen ~** to differentiate between two things; **genau ~** to make a precise distinction VR to become sophisticated; (= *sich auseinander entwickeln*) to become differentiated

dif|fe|ren|ziert [dɪfərɛnˈtsiːɐt] ADJ (= *fein unterscheidend*) subtly differentiated; (= *verfeinert*) sophisticated; *Charakter, Mensch, Gefühlsleben* complex; (= *verschiedenartig*) *Farbgebung, Anschauungen* subtly diversified; *Warenangebot diverse* ADV gestalten, sich ausdrücken in a sophisticated manner; **ein Problem ~ sehen/betrachten** to look at/examine a problem from all angles; **ich sehe das etwas ~er** I think it's a bit more complex than that

Dif|fe|ren|ziert|heit F **-,** no pl differentiation, sophistication; (*von Charakter, Mensch, Gefühlsleben*) complexity; (= *Verschiedenartigkeit: von Warenangebot*) diversity

Dif|fe|ren|zie|rung F **-, -en a** (= *Unterscheidung*) distinction; (*zwischen zwei Dingen*) differentiation; (= *Abänderung*) modification **b** (*Math*) differentiation

dif|fe|rie|ren [dɪfəˈriːrən] ptp **differiert** VI (*geh*) to differ

dif|fi|zil [dɪfiˈtsiːl] ADJ (*geh*) difficult, awkward; *Mensch* complicated

dif|fus [dɪˈfuːs] ADJ *Licht* diffuse; *Gedanken, Ausdrucksweise* confused; *Rechtslage* unclear

Dif|fu|si|on [dɪfuˈzioːn] F diffusion

di|gi|tal [digiˈtaːl] ADJ digital ADV digitally

Di|gi|tal- in cpds digital; **Di|gi|tal-A|nalog-Wand|ler** [-vantlɐ] M (*Tech*) digital-analog converter; **Di|gi|tal|auf|nah|me** F (*Tech*) digital recording; (= *Foto*) digital photo or shot; **Di|gi|tal|band** [-bant] NT pl **-bänder** digital tape; **Di|gi|tal|bau|stein** M integrated circuit element; **Di|gi|tal|fern|se|hen** NT digital television

di|gi|ta|li|sie|ren [digitaliˈziːrən] ptp **digitalisiert** VT to digitalize

Di|gi|ta|li|sie|rung F **-, -en** digitalization

Di|gi|tal-: Di|gi|tal|ka|me|ra F (*Tech*) digital camera; **Di|gi|tal|rech|ner** M (*Comput*) digital calculator; **Di|gi|tal|tech|nik** F (*Comput*) digital technology; **Di|gi|tal|ton|band** NT (*abbr* **DAT**) digital audio tape; **Di|gi|tal|uhr** F digital clock; (= *Armbanduhr*) digital watch

Dik|ta (*geh*) pl von **Diktum**

Dik|ta|fon ▲ [dɪktaˈfoːn] NT **-s, -e**, **Dik|ta|phon** NT **-s, -e** Dictaphone®

Dik|tat [dɪkˈtaːt] NT **-(e)s, -e a** dictation (*also Sch*); **ein ~ schreiben** (*Sch*) to do (a) dictation; **etw nach ~ schreiben** to write sth from dictation; **Frau Wengel, bitte zum ~!** take a letter please, Ms Wengel; **nach ~ verreist** dictated by X and signed in his/her absence **b** (*fig: = Gebot*) dictate; (*Pol*) dictate, diktat

Dik|ta|tor [dɪk'taːtɔːɐ] M **-s**, **Diktatoren** [-'toːrən], **Dik|ta|to|rin** [-'toːrɪn] F **-, -nen** dictator

dik|ta|to|risch [dɪkta'toːrɪʃ] ADJ dictatorial

Dik|ta|tur [dɪkta'tuːɐ] F **-, -en** dictatorship

dik|tie|ren [dɪk'tiːrən] *ptp* **diktiert** VT (*lit, fig*) *Brief, Bedingungen* to dictate

Dik|tier|ge|rät NT , **Dik|tier|ma|schi|ne** F dictating machine

Dik|ti|on [dɪk'tsioːn] F **-, -en** style

Dik|ti|o|när [dɪktsio'nɛːɐ] NT OR M **-s, -e** (*old*) dictionary

Dik|tum ['dɪktʊm] NT **-s**, **Dikta** [-ta] (*geh*) dictum, adage

Di|la|ta|ti|on [dilata'tsioːn] F **-, -en** (*Med*) dilatation, dilation

Dil|do ['dɪldo] M **-s, -s** dildo

Di|lem|ma [di'lɛma] NT **-s, -s** *or* (*geh*) **-ta** [-ta] dilemma

Di|let|tant [dile'tant] M **-en, -en**, **Di|let|tan|tin** [-'tantɪn] F **-, -nen** amateur; (*pej auch*) dilettante

di|let|tan|tisch [dile'tantɪʃ] ADJ amateurish ADV amateurishly; **~ vorgehen** to act like an amateur

Di|let|tan|tis|mus [dilɛtan'tɪsmʊs] M **-**, *no pl* amateurism

di|let|tie|ren [dile'tiːrən] *ptp* **dilettiert** VI (*geh*) to dabble (*in +dat* in)

Dill [dɪl] M **-(e)s, -e**, **Dil|le** [dɪlə] F **-, -en** (*Aus*) (*Bot, Cook*) dill

di|lu|vi|al [dilu'viaːl] ADJ (*Geol*) diluvial

Di|lu|vi|um [di'luːviʊm] NT **-s**, *no pl* (*Geol*) glacial epoch, ice age

Di|men|si|on [dimɛn'zioːn] F **-, -en** (*Phys, Math, fig*) dimension

-di|men|si|o|nal [dimɛnzionaːl] ADJ *suf* -dimensional; **dreidimensional** three-dimensional

Di|mi|nu|en|do [dimi'nuɛndo] NT **-s, -s** (*Mus*) diminuendo

di|mi|nu|tiv [diminu'tiːf] ADJ *Form, Endung* diminutive (*zu, von* of)

Di|mi|nu|tiv [diminu'tiːf] NT **-s, -e** [-və] diminutive (*zu, von* of)

Di|mi|nu|tiv|form F diminutive form

Di|mi|nu|ti|vum [diminu'tiːvʊm] NT **-s, Diminutiva** [-va] diminutive (*zu, von* of)

Dim|mer ['dɪmɐ] M **-s, -** dimmer (switch)

DIN¹® [dɪn, diːn] F **-,** *no pl abbr von* **Deutsche Industrie-Norm** German Industrial Standard; **~ A4** A4; **~-Format** German standard paper size

DIN² [diːn] NT **-(s)**, *no pl* (*Phot*) DIN; **~-Grad** DIN-speed

di|na|risch [di'naːrɪʃ] ADJ *Rasse* Dinaric; **Dinarisches Gebirge** Dinaric Alps

Di|ner [di'neː] NT **-s, -s** (*form*) (= *Mittagessen*) luncheon; (= *Abendessen*) dinner

Ding¹ [dɪŋ] NT **-(e)s, -e** *or* (*inf*) **-er a** (= *Sache, Gegenstand*) thing; *Gläser, Flaschen und ähnliche ~e* glasses, bottles and that sort of thing *or* and things of that kind; **die Welt der ~e** (*Philos*) the world of material objects; **das ~ an sich** (*Philos*) the thing-in-itself; **das ist ein ~ der Unmöglichkeit** that is quite impossible; **das ist nicht sein ~** (*inf*) that's not really his thing (*inf*); **guter ~e sein** (*geh*) to be in good spirits, to be of good cheer (*old*); **die ~e beim (rechten) Namen nennen** to call a spade a spade (*Brit prov*), to be frank; **jedes ~ hat zwei Seiten** (*prov*) there are two sides to everything; **gut ~ will Weile haben** (*Prov*) it takes time to do a thing well → **drei**

b (= *Gegebenheit*) thing; (= *Angelegenheit, Thema auch*) matter; (= *Ereignis auch*) event; **in diesen ~en** about these things *or* matters; **vergangene**

~e past events; **berufliche ~e** professional matters; **reden wir von andern ~en** let's talk about something else; **wir harrten der ~e, die da kommen sollten** we waited to see what would happen; **die ~e sind nun mal nicht so** things aren't like that; **so wie die ~e liegen** as things are, as matters lie; **wie ich die ~e sehe** as I see things *or* matters; **über den ~en stehen** to be above things; **die ~e stehen schlecht** things are bad; **nach Lage der ~e** the way things are; **vor allen ~en** above all (things), first and foremost; **es müsste nicht mit rechten ~en zugehen, wenn ...** it would be more than a little strange if ... → **Lauf b, Natur d, unverrichtet** *etc*

c (*inf: auch* **Dings**) (= *unbestimmtes Etwas*) thing; (= *Vorrichtung auch*) gadget; **was ist das für ein ~?** what's that thing?; **das ~(s) da** (*inf*) that thing (over) there; **das ist ein ~!** now there's a thing! (*inf*); **ein tolles ~!** great! (*inf*); **das ~ ist gut!** that's a good one! (*inf*) → *auch* **Dings**

d *pl* **-er** (*inf:* = *Verbrechen*) job; **sich** (*dat*) **ein ~ leisten** to get (*Brit*) *or* be up to something; **da hast du dir aber ein ~ geleistet** that was quite something you got (*Brit*) *or* were up to (*inf*); **~er machen** to get (*Brit*) *or* be up to all sorts of tricks (*inf*); **was macht ihr bloß für ~er?** the things you do! (*inf*); **das war vielleicht ein ~** (*inf*) that was quite something (*inf*) → **drehen** VT, **krumm b**

e (= *Mädchen*) thing, creature

f (*inf:* = *Penis*) tool (*sl*), dong (*US sl*)

g (*sl:* = *Busen*) pair (*hum inf*), boobs *pl* (*inf*)

Ding² NT **-(e)s, -e** (*Hist*) thing

din|gen ['dɪŋən] *pret* **dingte** ['dɪŋtə], *ptp* **gedungen** [gə'dʊŋən] VT (*old*) *Diener* to hire, to engage; **gedungener Mörder** hired assassin

Din|gens ['dɪŋəns] NT **-, -** (*dial inf*) = **Ding¹ a, c**

ding|fest ADJ **jdn ~ machen** to take sb into custody, to arrest sb

Din|gi ['dɪŋgi] NT **-s, -s** dinghy

ding|lich ['dɪŋlɪç] ADJ material; **~er Anspruch** (*Jur*) claim in rem; **~e Klage** (*Jur*) action in rem; **~er Arrest** (*Jur*) distraint ADV (*Fin*) **~ gesicherte Forderungen** claims *pl* covered by assets

Ding|lich|keit F **-,** *no pl* materiality

Dings [dɪŋs] NT **-,** *no pl*, **Dings|bums** ['dɪŋsbʊms] NT **-,** *no pl*, **Dings|da** ['dɪŋsdaː] NT **-,** *no pl* (*inf*) (= *Sache*) whatsit, doodah, thingummy (-bob), thingummyjig (*all inf*); **der/die ~** (= *Person*) what's-his/her-name (*inf*)

Ding|wort NT *pl* **-wörter** (*Gram*) noun

di|nie|ren [di'niːrən] *ptp* **diniert** VI (*geh*) to dine (*form*)

Din|kel ['dɪŋkl] M **-s, -** (*Bot*) spelt

Din|ner ['dɪnɐ] NT **-s, -** (*geh*) dinner

Di|no|sau|ri|er [dino-] M (*lit, fig*) dinosaur

Di|o|de [di'oːdə] F **-, -n** diode

di|o|ny|sisch [dio'nyːzɪʃ] ADJ Dionysian

Di|op|ter [di'ɔptɐ] NT **-s, -** (*old*) (*Phot*) viewfinder; (*am Gewehr*) (peep) sight

Di|opt|rie [diɔp'triː] F **-, -n** [-'triːən] (*Opt*) (*abbr* **dpt**) diopter; **wie viel ~n hast du?** what's your diopter strength?, what strength of glasses do you need?

Di|o|ra|ma [dio'raːma] NT **-s, Dioramen** [-mən] diorama

Di|os|ku|ren [diɔs'kuːrən] PL (*Myth*) heavenly twins *pl* (*auch fig*), Dioscuri *pl* (*form*)

Di|o|xid [diɔ'ksiːt] NT **-s, -e** [-də] dioxide

Di|o|xin [diɔ'ksiːn] NT **-s, -e** dioxin

di|o|xin-: **di|o|xin|be|las|tet** ADJ dioxin-contaminated *attr*, dioxin-polluted *attr*; contaminated *or* polluted with dioxin *pred*; **di|o|xin|hal|tig** ADJ dioxinated

Di|o|xyd ['diːɔksyːt, diɔ'ksyːt] NT **-s, -e** [-də] dioxide

Di|ö|ze|san [diøtse'zaːn] M **-en, -en** diocesan

Di|ö|ze|san|bi|schof [diøtse'zaːn-] M (*Eccl; katholisch*) diocesan bishop, bishop of a/the diocese

Di|ö|ze|se [diø'tseːzə] F **-, -n** diocese; **die ~ Münster** the diocese of Münster

Diph|the|rie [dɪfte'riː] F **-, -n** [-'riːən] diphtheria

Diph|the|rie|(schutz)imp|fung F diphtheria immunization; (*eine Impfung*) diphtheria injection

Diph|thong [dɪf'tɔŋ] M **-s, -e** diphthong

diph|thon|gie|ren [dɪftɔŋ'giːrən] *ptp* **diphthongiert** VT to diphthongize

Diph|thon|gie|rung F **-, -en** diphthongization

diph|thon|gisch [dɪf'tɔŋɪʃ] ADJ diphthongized ADV **~ aussprechen** to pronounce as a diphthong

Dipl. *abbr von* **Diplom**

Dipl.-Ing. *abbr von* **Diplomingenieur**

Dipl.-Kfm. *abbr von* **Diplomkaufmann**

Dip|lom [di'ploːm] NT **-s, -e** diploma; (= *Zeugnis auch*) certificate; **ein ~ machen** to take (*esp Brit*) *or* do one's diploma

> ## DIPLOM
>
> The **Diplom** is an academic degree in natural sciences, technology, social sciences or economics. To attain the **Diplom**, students must undertake a period of study lasting at least eight semesters, submit a substantial dissertation, and take a final examination. The **Diplom** is presented at a fairly informal ceremony which varies from university to university. The holder is permitted to use the title **Dipl.-Ing.**, **Dipl.-Kfm.** etc.
> In the former East Germany the **Diplom** was the standard degree for all subjects, as well as being used as a title.

Dip|lom- *in cpds* (*vor Berufsbezeichnung*) qualified

Dip|lo|mand [diplo'mant] M **-en, -en** [-dn], **Dip|lo|man|din** [-'mandɪn] F **-, -nen** student about to do his/her diploma

Dip|lom|ar|beit F dissertation (*submitted for a diploma*)

Dip|lo|mat [diplo'maːt] M **-en, -en**, **Dip|lo|ma|tin** [-'maːtɪn] F **-, -nen** diplomat

Dip|lo|ma|ten-: **Dip|lo|ma|ten|kof|fer** M executive case; **Dip|lo|ma|ten|vier|tel** NT (= *Wohngebiet*) diplomatic quarter

Dip|lo|ma|tie [diploma'tiː] F **-,** *no pl* (*lit, fig*) diplomacy

dip|lo|ma|tisch [diplo'maːtɪʃ] ADJ (*Pol, fig*) diplomatic ADV diplomatically; **sie hat sich nicht sehr ~ verhalten** she wasn't very diplomatic; **ein Land ~ anerkennen** to recognize a country diplomatically

dip|lo|miert [diplo'miːɐt] ADJ qualified

Dip|lom-: **Dip|lom|in|ge|ni|eur(in)** M(F) qualified engineer; **Dip|lom|kauf|frau** F , **Dip|lom|kauf|mann** M business school graduate

Di|pol [di'poːl] M **-s, -e a** (*Phys*) dipole **b** (*auch* **Dipolantenne**) dipole (aerial (*esp Brit*) *or* antenna)

dip|pen ['dɪpn] VT (*Naut*) *Flagge* to dip

DIP-Schal|ter ['dɪp-] M (*Comput*) dip switch

dir [diːɐ] PERS PRON *dat von* **du** to you; (*obs, dial*) to thee; (*nach Präpositionen*) you; (*obs, dial*) thou → *auch* **ihm**

Dir. *abbr von* **Direktion** *von* **Direktor** *von* **Dirigent**

di|rekt [di'rɛkt] ADJ **a** (= *unmittelbar, gerade*) direct; *Erledigung* immediate; **eine ~e Verbindung** (*mit Zug*) a through train; (*mit Flugzeug*) a direct flight; **~e Rede** direct speech **b** (= *unverblümt*) *Mensch, Frage, Ausdrucksweise* direct, blunt; (= *genau*) *Hinweis* plain; *Vorstellungen, Antwort, Auskunft* clear **c** (*inf:* = *ausgesprochen*) perfect, sheer; **es war keine ~e Katastrophe** it wasn't exactly a catastrophe

ADV **a** (= *unmittelbar*) directly; (= *geradewegs auch*) straight; ~ **aus** *or* **von/zu** *or* **nach** straight *or* direct from/to; ~ **an/neben/unter/über** directly *or* right by/next to/under/over; ~ **gegenüber** right *or* directly *or* straight opposite; **jdm ~ ins Gesicht/in die Augen sehen** to look sb straight in the face/the eyes; ~ **übertragen** *or* **senden** to transmit live; **ich kann von hier nicht ~ telefonieren** I can't dial direct from here **b** (= *unverblümt*) bluntly; **jdm etw ~ ins Gesicht sagen** to tell sb sth (straight) to his face; ~ **fragen** to ask outright, to ask straight out **c** (*inf*: = *geradezu*) really; **nicht ~** not exactly *or* really

Di|rekt- in cpds direct; (*Rad, TV*) live; **Di|rekt|bank** F *pl* -banken (*Fin*) direct bank; **Di|rekt|flug** M direct flight; **Di|rekt|heit** F -, *no pl* directness

Di|rek|ti|on [dirɛk'tsi̯oːn] F -, -en **a** (= *Leitung*) management, administration; (*von Schule*) headship (*Brit*), principalship (*esp US*) **b** (= *Direktoren, Vorstand*) management **c** (= *Direktionsbüro*) manager's office

Di|rek|ti|ons|recht NT right to give directives

Di|rek|ti|ve F -, -n (*geh*) directive

Di|rekt-: Di|rekt|kan|di|dat(in) M(F) (*Pol*) candidate with a direct mandate; **Di|rekt|man|dat** NT (*Pol*) direct mandate; **Di|rekt|mar|ke|ting** NT (*Comm*) direct marketing

Di|rek|tor [di'rɛktoːɐ] M -s, **Direktoren** [-'toːrən], **Di|rek|to|rin** [-'toːrɪn] F -, -nen director; (*von Gefängnis*) governor, warden (*US*); (*von Krankenhaus*) ≈ senior consultant; (*von Hochschule*) principal; (*von Schule*) head (teacher), headmaster/-mistress (*esp Brit*), principal (*esp US*); **geschäftsführender ~** (*Univ*) head of department; ~ **der Bank von England** governor of the Bank of England

Di|rek|to|rat [dirɛkto'raːt] NT -(e)s, -e **a** (= *Amt*) directorship; (*von Schule*) headship (*Brit*), principalship (*esp US*); (*von Gefängnis*) governorship, wardenship (*US*) **b** (= *Diensträume*) (*von Firma, Museum*) director's office; (*von Hochschule etc*) principal's office; (*von Schule*) head(master/mistress)'s *or* principal's (*esp US*) study *or* room; (*von Gefängnis*) governor's *or* warden's (*US*) office **c** (= *Abteilung*) department

Di|rek|to|ri|um [dirɛk'toːri̯ʊm] NT -s, **Direktorien** [-ri̯ən] **a** board of directors, directorate **b** (*Hist*) Directory, Directoire (*Brit*)

Di|rek|tri|ce [dirɛk'triːsə] F -, -n manageress

Di|rekt-: Di|rekt|strah|lung F direct radiation; **Di|rekt|über|tra|gung** F (*Rad, TV*) live transmission; **Di|rekt|ver|bin|dung** F (*Rail*) through train; (*Aviat*) direct flight; **Di|rekt|ver|mark|tung** F (*Comm*) direct marketing; **Di|rekt|ver|si|che|rung** F (*Insur*) direct insurance; (= *Police*) direct insurance policy; **Di|rekt|ver|trieb** M direct marketing; **Di|rekt|zu|griff** M direct access; **Di|rekt|zu|griffs|spei|cher** M random access memory, RAM

Di|rex ['diːrɛks] M -, -e (*Sch sl*) head, principal (*esp US*)

Di|ri|gent [diri'gɛnt] M -en, -en, **Di|ri|gen|tin** [-'gɛntɪn] F -, -nen (*Mus*) conductor; (*fig*) leader

Di|ri|gen|ten-: Di|ri|gen|ten|pult NT conductor's stand *or* desk; **Di|ri|gen|ten|stab** M (*inf*), **Di|ri|gen|ten|stock** M (conductor's) baton

di|ri|gie|ren [diri'giːrən] *ptp* **dirigiert** VT **a** *auch* vi (*Mus*) to conduct; (*fig*) to lead **b** (= *leiten, einweisen*) Verkehr etc to direct

Di|ri|gis|mus [diri'gɪsmʊs] M -, *no pl* (*Pol*) dirigism

di|ri|gis|tisch [diri'gɪstɪʃ] ADJ Maßnahmen dirigiste

Dirn [dɪrn] F -, -en **a** (*S Ger, Aus*: = *Magd*) maid **b** (*N Ger*: = *Mädchen*) girl, lass (*dial inf*)

Dirndl ['dɪrndl] NT -s, - **a** (*auch* **Dirndlkleid**) dirndl **b** (*S Ger, Aus*: = *Mädchen*) girl, lass (*dial inf*)

Dir|ne ['dɪrnə] F -, -n **a** (= *Prostituierte*) prostitute, hooker (*esp US inf*) **b** (*obs*: = *Mädchen*) lass (*old, dial*)

Dir|nen-: Dir|nen|mi|li|eu NT red light district, prostitution scene; **im ~** (*auch*) among prostitutes; **Dir|nen|vier|tel** NT red light district

dis NT -, -, **Dis** [dɪs] NT -, - (*Mus*) D sharp

Dis|agio [dɪs'laːdʒo, dɪs'laːʒi̯o] NT -s, -s *or* **Disagien** [-'laːdʒən, -laːʒi̯ən] (*Fin*) discount

Disc-Ka|me|ra ['dɪsk-] F disc camera

Disc|man® ['dɪskmən] M -s, -s Discman®

Dis|co ['dɪsko] F -, -s disco

Dis|count- [dɪs'kaʊnt] in cpds discount

Dis|coun|ter¹ [dɪs'kaʊntɐ] M -s, - (*inf*: = *Laden*) discount shop

Dis|coun|ter² [dɪs'kaʊntɐ] M -s, -, **Dis|coun|te|rin** [-ərɪn] F -, -nen (*inf*: = *Händler*) discount dealer

Dis|count- [dɪs'kaʊnt-]: **Dis|count|händ|ler(in)** M(F) discount dealer; **Dis|count|la|den** M discount shop

Di|seur [di'zøːɐ] M -s, -e diseur

Di|seu|se [di'zøːzə] F -, -n diseuse

Dis|har|mo|nie [dɪs-] F (*Mus*) discord, dissonance, disharmony; (*fig*: = *Unstimmigkeit*) discord *no pl*, friction *no pl*, disagreement; (*von Farben*) clash

dis|har|mo|nie|ren [dɪs-] *ptp* **disharmoniert** VI (*geh*) (*Mus*) to be discordant *or* dissonant; (*Farben*) to clash; (*Menschen*) to be at variance, to disaccord (*form*); **die beiden ~ so offensichtlich** the two of them are so obviously out of tune with one another

dis|har|mo|nisch [dɪs-] ADJ Akkord discordant, dissonant, disharmonious; Farbzusammenstellung clashing; Ehe, Verbindung, Atmosphäre discordant

Dis|kant [dɪs'kant] M -s, -e (= *Stimmlage*) treble; (= *Gegenstimme*) descant

Dis|kant|schlüs|sel M soprano clef

Dis|ket|te [dɪs'kɛtə] F -, -n disk, diskette

Dis|ket|ten|lauf|werk NT disk drive

Disk|jo|ckey ['dɪskdʒɔke] M -s, -s disc jockey, deejay (*inf*), DJ (*inf*)

Dis|ko ['dɪsko] F -, -s disco

Dis|kont [dɪs'kɔnt] M -s, -e (*Fin*) discount

Dis|kon|ten [dɪs'kɔntn̩] PL (*Fin*) discounted bills *pl*

dis|kon|tie|ren [dɪskɔn'tiːrən] *ptp* **diskontiert** VT (*Fin*) to discount

dis|kon|ti|nu|ier|lich [dɪs-] ADJ (*geh*) discontinuous

Dis|kon|ti|nu|i|tät [dɪs-] F (*geh*) discontinuity

Dis|kont|satz M (*Fin*) discount rate (*Brit*), bank rate (*US*)

Dis|ko|thek [dɪsko'teːk] F -, -en **a** (= *Tanzbar*) discotheque, disco **b** (= *Plattensammlung*) record collection

dis|kre|di|tie|ren [dɪs-] *ptp* **diskreditiert** VT (*geh*) to discredit

Dis|kre|panz [dɪskre'pants] F -, -en discrepancy

dis|kret [dɪs'kreːt] ADJ **a** (= *taktvoll, unaufdringlich*) discreet; (= *vertraulich*) Angelegenheit, Gespräch confidential; **er ist sehr ~** (= *verschwiegen*) he's not one to betray a confidence *or* to betray something told in confidence; **du musst lernen, etwas ~er zu sein** you must learn to be more discreet about confidential matters **b** (*Math*) discrete **ADV** discreetly

Dis|kre|ti|on [dɪskre'tsi̯oːn] F -, *no pl* discretion; (= *vertrauliche Behandlung*) confidentiality; ~ **üben** to be discreet; **strengste ~ wahren** to preserve the strictest confidence; **jdn um ~ in einer Angelegenheit bitten** to ask sb to treat an affair as a matter of confidence; ~ **ist Ehrensache!** you can count on my discretion

---

Dis|kri|mi|nan|te [dɪskrimi'nantə] F -, -n (*Math*) discriminant

dis|kri|mi|nie|ren [dɪskrimi'niːrən] *ptp* **diskriminiert** VT to discriminate against

dis|kri|mi|nie|rend ADJ discriminatory

Dis|kri|mi|nie|rung F -, -en discrimination

Dis|kri|mi|nie|rungs|ver|bot NT ban on discrimination

Dis|kurs [dɪs'kʊrs] M (*geh*) discourse

dis|kur|siv [dɪskʊr'ziːf] ADJ (*Philos*) discursive

Dis|kus ['dɪskʊs] M -, -se *or* **Disken** ['dɪskn̩] discus

Dis|kus|si|on [dɪskʊ'si̯oːn] F -, -en discussion; **zur ~ stehen** to be under discussion; **etw zur ~ stellen** to put *or* bring sth up for discussion; **sich mit jdm auf eine ~ einlassen** to be drawn *or* to get into discussion with sb; **da gibts gar keine ~, ja ...** I'm not having any discussion about it, you ...

Dis|kus|si|ons-: Dis|kus|si|ons|be|darf M need for discussion; **es besteht ~** we *etc* need to talk about this; **Dis|kus|si|ons|bei|trag** M contribution to the discussion; **Dis|kus|si|ons|lei|ter(in)** M(F) moderator, anchorman/-woman/-person (*US*); **Dis|kus|si|ons|red|ner(in)** M(F) speaker (in a discussion); **Dis|kus|si|ons|run|de** F round of discussions; (= *Personen*) discussion group *or* panel; **Dis|kus|si|ons|stoff** M something to talk about; ~ **liefern** to provide a subject/subjects for discussion; **für ~ war gesorgt** there was plenty to discuss *or* talk about; **Dis|kus|si|ons|teil|neh|mer(in)** M(F) participant (in a discussion)

Dis|kus-: Dis|kus|wer|fen NT -s, *no pl* throwing the discus; **Dis|kus|wer|fer(in)** M(F) discus thrower

dis|ku|ta|bel [dɪsku'taːbl̩], **dis|ku|tier|bar** ADJ worth discussing; **das ist überhaupt nicht ~** that's not even worth talking about

Dis|ku|tant [dɪsku'tant] M -en, -en, **Dis|ku|tan|tin** [-'tantɪn] F -, -nen participant (in a discussion)

dis|ku|tie|ren [dɪsku'tiːrən] *ptp* **diskutiert** VTI to discuss; **über etw** (*acc*) ~ to discuss sth; **darüber lässt sich ~** that's debatable; **er diskutiert gern** he's a great one for discussing (everything); **wir haben stundenlang diskutiert** we've spent hours in discussion; **was gibts denn da zu ~?** what is there to talk about *or* to discuss?

Dis|ney|land® ['dɪzni-] NT -s Disneyland

Dis|pa|ri|tät [dɪs-] F disparity

Dis|pat|cher [dɪs'pɛtʃɐ] M -s, -, **Dis|pat|che|rin** [dɪs'pɛtʃərɪn] F -, -nen (*Comm*) dispatcher

Dis|pens [dɪs'pɛns] F -, -en *or* m -es, -e [-zə] (*Eccl*) dispensation

dis|pen|sie|ren [dɪspɛn'ziːrən] *ptp* **dispensiert** VT **a** jdn to excuse (*von* from); (*Eccl*) to dispense **b** (= *zubereiten*) Arznei to dispense

Dis|per|si|on [dɪspɛr'zi̯oːn] F -, -en (*Chem, Opt*) dispersion

Dis|per|si|ons|far|be F emulsion (paint)

Dis|play [dɪs'pleː] NT -s, -s (*Comput, von Waren*) display

Dis|po|kre|dit ['dɪspokrediːt] M (*Fin inf*) overdraft

Dis|po|nent [dɪspo'nɛnt] M -en, -en, **Dis|po|nen|tin** [-'nɛntɪn] F -, -nen (*bei Transportunternehmen*) dispatcher; (*Comm*) managing clerk (*Brit*), manager; (*Theat*) manager

dis|po|ni|bel ADJ available

dis|po|nie|ren [dɪspo'niːrən] *ptp* **disponiert** VI (*geh*) **a** (= *verfügen*) **über jdn ~** to command sb's services (*form*); **willkürlich über jdn ~** to deal with sb high-handedly; **ich kann nicht über sie ~** I can't tell her what to do; **über etw** (*acc*) (**frei**) ~ to do as one wishes *or* likes with sth; **über etw** (*acc*) ~ **können** (= *zur Verfügung haben*) to have sth at one's disposal; **ich kann über meine Zeit frei ~** my time is my own (to

---

do with as I wish) **b** (= *planen*) to make arrangements *or* plans

dis|po|niert [dɪspoˈniːɐt] ADJ **a** (*geh*) **gut/ schlecht ~ sein** to be on/off form (*Brit*), to be in good/bad form, to be in/out of form; **zu** *or* **für etw ~ sein** (*Med*) to be prone to sth; **so ~e Leute** people with this kind of disposition **b** *Gelder* available

Dis|po|si|ti|on [dɪs-] F (*geh*) **a** (= *Verfügung*) **zur ~ stehen** to be up for consideration; **jdm zur** *or* **zu jds ~ stehen** to be at sb's disposal; **jdm etw zur ~ stellen** to place sth at sb's disposal; **etw zur ~ stellen** to put sth up for consideration; **etw zur ~ haben** to have sth at one's disposal **b** (= *Anordnung*) arrangement, provision; **seine ~en treffen** to make (one's) arrangements *or* plans **c** (= *Gliederung*) layout, plan **d** (*Med:* = *Anlage*) susceptibility, proneness (*zu* to)

Dis|po|si|ti|ons|kre|dit [-krediːt] M (*Fin*) overdraft

dis|pro|por|ti|o|niert [dɪsproˈportsioniːɐt] ADJ ill-proportioned

Dis|put [dɪsˈpuːt] M -(e)s, -e (*geh*) dispute

dis|pu|ta|bel [dɪspuˈtaːbl] ADJ (*dated*) disputable

Dis|pu|tant [dɪspuˈtant] M -en, -en, **Dis|pu|tan|tin** [-ˈtantɪn] F -, -nen disputant

Dis|pu|ta|ti|on [dɪspuˈtaˈtsioːn] F -, -en (*old*) disputation

dis|pu|tie|ren [dɪspuˈtiːrən] *ptp* **disputiert** VI (*geh*) to dispute (*über etw acc* sth)

Dis|qua|li|fi|ka|ti|on [dɪs-] F disqualification

dis|qua|li|fi|zie|ren [dɪs-] *ptp* **disqualifiziert** VT to disqualify

Dis|qua|li|fi|zie|rung F -, -en disqualification

Dis|sens [drsɛns] M -es, -e [-zə] (*Jur*) dissent, disagreement *no indef art*

Dis|ser|ta|ti|on [dɪsɛrtaˈtsioːn] F -, -en dissertation; (= *Doktorarbeit*) (doctoral) thesis

dis|ser|tie|ren [dɪsɛrˈtiːrən] *ptp* **dissertiert** VI → **Dissertation** to write a dissertation/(doctoral) thesis (*über +acc* on)

Dis|si|dent [dɪsiˈdɛnt] M -en, -en, **Dis|si|den|tin** [-ˈdɛntɪn] F -, -nen dissident

Dis|si|den|ten|be|we|gung F dissident movement

Dis|si|mi|la|ti|on [dɪsimilaˈtsioːn] F -, -en (*Ling*) dissimilation; (*Biol auch*) catabolism

dis|si|mi|lie|ren [dɪsimiˈliːrən] *ptp* **dissimiliert** VT (*Ling*) *Laut* to dissimilate; (*Biol*) *Stoffe* to break down

dis|so|nant [dɪsoˈnant] ADJ dissonant; (*fig*) *Persönlichkeit* lacking harmony

Dis|so|nanz [dɪsoˈnants] F -, -en (*Mus*) dissonance; (*fig*) (note of) discord

dis|so|zi|al [dɪsoˈtsiaːl] ADJ (*Psych*) (socially) dysfunctional

Dis|tanz [dɪsˈtants] F -, -en **a** (*lit*) distance; (*fig*) (= *Abstand, Entfernung*) detachment; (= *Zurückhaltung*) reserve; **~ halten** *or* **wahren** (*lit, fig*) to keep one's distance; (**zu jdm/etw**) **auf ~ gehen** (*fig*) to distance oneself (from sb/sth); **die nötige ~ zu etw finden/haben** to become/be sufficiently detached from sth **b** (*Sport*) distance

dis|tan|zie|ren [dɪstanˈtsiːrən] *ptp* **distanziert** VR **sich von jdm/etw ~** to distance oneself from sb/sth; (= *jdn/etw zurückweisen*) to dissociate oneself from sb/sth VT (*Sport*) to outdistance

dis|tan|ziert [dɪstanˈtsiːɐt] ADJ *Verhalten* distant ADV **sich ~ verhalten** to act distant; **~ wirken** to seem distant

Dis|tan|ziert|heit F -, *no pl* distance

Dis|tanz|waf|fe F (*Mil*) long-range weapon

Dis|tel [ˈdɪstl] F -, -n thistle

Dis|tel|fink M goldfinch

Dis|ti|chon [ˈdɪstiçɔn] NT -s, Distichen [-çn] (*Poet*) distich

dis|tin|gu|iert [dɪstɪŋˈgiːɐt, dɪstɪŋguˈiːɐt] ADJ (*geh*) distinguished

Dis|tin|guiert|heit [dɪstɪŋˈgiːɐt-, dɪstɪŋguˈiːɐt-] F -, *no pl* distinction

dis|tinkt [dɪsˈtɪŋkt] ADJ (*old*) distinct, clear

Dis|tink|ti|on [dɪstɪŋkˈtsioːn] F -, -en (*geh*) **a** (= *Auszeichnung*) distinction **b** (= *Rang*) distinction; (*Aus:* = *Rangabzeichen*) insignia *pl*

dis|tri|bu|ti|on [dɪstribuˈtsioːn] F -, -en distribution

dis|tri|bu|tiv [dɪstribuˈtiːf] ADJ (*Gram, Math*) distributive

Dis|trikt [dɪsˈtrɪkt] M -(e)s, -e district

Dis|zi|plin [dɪstsiˈpliːn] F -, -en **a** *no pl* (= *Zucht, Ordnung*) discipline; **~ halten** (*Lehrer*) to keep *or* maintain discipline; (*Klasse*) to behave in a disciplined manner **b** (= *Fachrichtung, Sportart*) discipline

Dis|zi|pli|nar- [dɪstsipliˈnaːɐ] *in cpds* disciplinary; **Dis|zi|pli|nar|ge|setz** NT disciplinary code; **Dis|zi|pli|nar|ge|walt** F disciplinary powers *pl*

dis|zi|pli|na|risch [dɪstsipliˈnaːrɪʃ] ADJ disciplinary ADV **jdn ~ bestrafen, ~ gegen jdn vorgehen** to take disciplinary action against sb; **sein Regelverstoß wurde ~ geahndet** he was disciplined for an infringement of the rules; **jdm unterstellt sein** to be answerable to sb

Dis|zi|pli|nar-: Dis|zi|pli|nar|maß|nah|me F disciplinary measure *or* action; **Dis|zi|pli|nar|stra|fe** F punishment; **mit einer ~ rechnen** to expect disciplinary action; **eine ~ bekommen** to be disciplined; **Dis|zi|pli|nar|ver|fah|ren** NT disciplinary proceedings *pl*

dis|zi|pli|nie|ren [dɪstsipliˈniːrən] *ptp* **diszipliniert** VT to discipline VR to discipline oneself

dis|zi|pli|niert [dɪstsipliˈniːɐt] ADJ disciplined ADV in a disciplined manner

Dis|zi|pli|niert|heit F -, *no pl* discipline

Dis|zi|plin-: dis|zi|plin|los ADJ undisciplined ADV in an undisciplined manner; **Dis|zi|plin|lo|sig|keit** F -, -en lack *no pl* of discipline

di|to [ˈdiːto] ADV (*Comm, hum*) ditto

Di|va [ˈdiːva] F -, -s *or* **Diven** [ˈdiːvn] star; (*Film*) screen goddess

di|ver|gent [divɛrˈgɛnt] ADJ divergent

Di|ver|genz [divɛrˈgɛnts] F -, -en **a** *no pl* divergence **b** *usu pl* (= *Meinungsverschiedenheit*) difference (of opinion)

di|ver|gie|ren [divɛrˈgiːrən] *ptp* **divergiert** VI to diverge

di|ver|gie|rend [divɛrˈgiːrənd] PREP *von* divergieren diverging ADJ divergent

di|vers [diˈvɛrs] ADJ *attr* various; **die ~esten ...** the most diverse ...; **~es Angebot von ...** an assortment of ...; **~e** (= *mehrere der gleichen Art*) several; „**Diverses**" "miscellaneous"; **wir haben noch Diverses zu erledigen** we still have various *or* several things to see to

Di|ver|sant [divɛrˈzant] M -en, -en, **Di|ver|san|tin** [-ˈzantɪn] F -, -nen (*Hist*) subversive

Di|ver|si|fi|ka|ti|on [divɛrzifikaˈtsioːn] F -, -en diversification

di|ver|si|fi|zie|ren [divɛrzifiˈtsiːrən] *ptp* **diversifiziert** VTI to diversify

Di|ver|ti|men|to [divɛrtiˈmɛnto] NT -s, -s *or* **Di|ver|ti|men|ti** [-ti], **Di|ver|tis|se|ment** [divɛrtɪsəˈmãː] NT -s, -s (*Mus*) divertimento, divertissement

Di|vi|dend [diviˈdɛnt] M -en, -en [-dn] (*Math*) dividend

Di|vi|den|de [diviˈdɛndə] F -, -n (*Fin*) dividend

Di|vi|den|den-: Di|vi|den|den|aus|schüt|tung F (*Fin*) distribution of dividends; **Di|vi|den|den|er|trag** M (*Fin*) dividend yield

di|vi|die|ren [diviˈdiːrən] *ptp* **dividiert** VTI to divide (*durch* by)

di|vi|na|to|risch [divinaˈtoːrɪʃ] ADJ (*geh*) divinatory

Di|vis [diˈviːs] NT -es, -e [-zə] (*Typ*) hyphen

Di|vi|si|on [diviˈzioːn] F -, -en (*Math, Mil*) division

Di|vi|si|o|när [divizioˈnɛːɐ] M -s, -e, **Di|vi|si|o|nä|rin** [-ˈnɛːrɪn] F -, -nen (*Sw*) divisional commander

Di|vi|si|ons- *in cpds* (*Math*) division; (*Mil*) divisional; **Di|vi|si|ons|stab** M (*Mil*) divisional headquarters *pl*; **Di|vi|si|ons|zei|chen** NT (*Math*) division sign

Di|vi|sor [diˈviːzoːɐ] M -s, Divisoren [-ˈzoːrən] (*Math*) divisor

Di|wan [ˈdiːvaːn] M -s, -e divan

d. J. *abbr* **a** *von* **dieses Jahres** of this year **b** *von* **der Jüngere** jun.

DJH [deːjɔtˈhaː] NT -(s) *abbr von* **Deutsches Jugendherbergswerk** German Youth Hostel Association

DKP [deːkaːˈpeː] F - *abbr von* **Deutsche Kommunistische Partei**

DLG [deːʔɛlˈgeː] F - *abbr von* **Deutsche Landwirtschafts-Gesellschaft** German Agricultural Society

DM [deːˈʔɛm] *no art* -, - (*Hist*) *abbr von* **Deutsche Mark** DM

d. M. *abbr von* **dieses Monats** inst

D-Mark [ˈdeːmark] F *pl* -**Mark** (*Hist*) Deutschmark, German mark

DNA[1] [deːʔɛnˈʔaː] F - = **DNS**

DNA[2] [deːʔɛnˈʔaː] *abbr von* **Deutscher Normenausschuss** German Committee of Standards

D-Netz [ˈdeː-] NT (*Telec*) digital cellular phone network

DNS [deːʔɛnˈʔɛs] F - *abbr von* **Desoxyribonukleinsäure** DNA

DNS- [deːʔɛnˈʔɛs-]: **DNS-Kode** M DNA code; **DNS-Strick|lei|ter** F DNA ladder; **DNS-Zei|le** F line of DNA

Do|ber|mann [ˈdoːbɐman] M -(s), -männer Doberman (Pinscher)

doch [dɔx] CONJ (= *aber, allein*) but; (= *jedoch, trotzdem*) but still, yet; **und ~ hat er es getan** but he still did it, but still he did it

ADV **a** (*betont*) (= *dennoch*) after all; (= *trotzdem*) anyway, all the same; (= *sowieso*) anyway; **jetzt ist er ~ nicht gekommen** now he hasn't come after all; **..., doch am ich ~ hingegangen** ... but I went anyway *or* all the same *or* after all; **du weißt es ja ~ besser** you always know better than I do anyway; **das geht denn ~ zu weit!** that really is going too far; **und ~, ...** and yet ...

b (*betont:* = *tatsächlich*) really; **ja ~!** of course!, sure! (*esp US*); **nein ~!** of course not!, certainly not!; **also ~!** so it IS/so he DID! *etc*; **er hat es gestohlen – also ~!** he stole it – so it WAS him!; **er hat es also ~ gesagt** so he DID say it; **es ist ~ so, wie ich vermutet hatte** so it (really) IS as I thought; **das ist er ~!** (why,) that IS him!; **das ist ~ interessant, was er da sagt** what he's saying is really interesting; **was es ~ alles für Leute gibt!** the people you get!

c (*als bejahende Antwort*) yes I do/it does *etc*; **hat es dir nicht gefallen? – (~,) ~!** didn't you like it? – (oh) yes I did! *or* oh I did, I did!; **will er nicht mitkommen? – ~!** doesn't he want to come? – (oh) yes, he does; **~, schon, aber ...** yes it does/I do *etc*, but ...

d (*auffordernd: nicht übersetzt, aber emphatisches „to do" wird oft gebraucht*) **komm ~** do come; **kommen Sie ~ bitte morgen wieder** won't you come back tomorrow?; **gib ~ mal her** (come on,) give it to me; **seid ~ endlich still!** do keep quiet!, keep quiet, can't you?; **sei ~ nicht so frech!** don't you be so cheeky (*Brit*) *or* fresh (*US inf*)!; **lass ihn ~!** just leave him!; **soll er ~!** well let him!, let him then!; **nicht ~!** don't (do that)!

e (*verstärkend*) but; (*Bestätigung erwartend*) isn't it/haven't you *etc*?; **sie ist ~ noch so jung** but she's still so young; **es wäre ~ schön, wenn ...**

(but) it WOULD be nice if ...; **dass sie ~ immer widersprechen muss!** why must she always contradict everything?; **das ist ~ die Höhe** or **das Letzte!** well, that's the limit!, that really is the limit!; **das ist ~ gar nicht wahr!** (but) that's just not true!; **das ist ~ wohl nicht wahr?** that's not true, is it?; **du hast ~ nicht etwa ...?** you haven't ..., have you?, surely you haven't or you haven't by any chance ...(, have you)?; **ich habe ~ (aber) gefragt** (but) I did ask

f (= *eigentlich*) really, actually; **es war ~ ganz interessant** it was really or actually quite interesting; **hier ist es ~ ganz nett** it's actually quite nice here

g (*als bekannt Angenommenes wiederholend: nicht übersetzt*) **Sie wissen ~, wie das so ist** (well, you know how it is, don't you?; **du kennst dich ~ hier aus, wo ist denn ...?** you know your way around here, where is ...?; **wie war ~ Ihr Name?** (I'm sorry,) WHAT was your name?; **hier darf man ~ nicht rauchen** you can't smoke here(, you know)

h (*in Wunschsätzen*) **wenn ~** if only; **o wäre es ~ schon Frühling!** oh if only it were spring!; **dass dich ~ der Teufel holte!** (oh) go to blazes! (*inf*), the devil take you (*old*)

i (*geh: begründet*) but then; **er sprach etwas verwirrt, war er ~ eben erst aus dem Bett aufgestanden** he spoke in a somewhat confused manner, but then he had only just got out of bed

Docht [dɔxt] M **-(e)s, -e** wick

Docht-: Docht|hal|ter M wick holder; **Docht|sche|re** F wick trimmer

Dock [dɔk] NT **-s, -s** or **-e** dock

Dock|ar|bei|ter(in) M(F) docker, dockworker

Do|cke ['dɔkə] F **-, -n a** (*aus Korn*) stook; (*aus Wolle, Garn*) hank, skein; (*aus Tabak*) bundle **b** (*dial:* = *Puppe*) doll

do|cken¹ ['dɔkn] VTI to dock

do|cken² VT *Korn etc* to stook; *Wolle etc* to wind into a hank or skein; *Tabak* to bundle

Do|cker ['dɔkɐ] M **-s, -, Do|cke|rin** [-ərɪn] F **-, -nen** docker

Do|cking ['dɔkɪŋ] NT **-s, -s** (*Space*) docking

Do|ge ['do:ʒə] M **-n, -n** (*Hist*) doge

Do|gen|pa|last M Doge's Palace

Dog|ge ['dɔgə] F **-, -n** mastiff; **Englische ~** (English) mastiff; **Deutsche ~** great Dane

Dog|ger¹ ['dɔgɐ] M **-s, -** (*Naut*) dogger

Dog|ger² M **-s** (*Geol*) Middle Jurassic, Dogger; (= *Gestein*) dogger

Dog|ger|bank F, *no pl* (*Geog*) **die ~** the Dogger Bank

Dog|ma ['dɔgma] NT **-s, Dogmen** [-mən] dogma; **etw zum ~ erheben** to make sth into dogma

Dog|ma|tik [dɔ'gma:tɪk] F **-, -en** dogmatics *sing*; (*fig: usu pej*) dogmatism

Dog|ma|ti|ker [dɔ'gma:tɪkɐ] M **-s, -, Dog|ma|ti|ke|rin** [-ərɪn] F **-, -nen** dogmatist

dog|ma|tisch [dɔ'gma:tɪʃ] ADJ (*Rel, fig*) dogmatic

dog|ma|ti|sie|ren [dɔgmati'zi:rən] ptp **dogmatisiert** [VT] to make into a dogma, to dogmatize [VI] (*fig pej*) to be dogmatic

Dog|ma|tis|mus [dɔgma'tɪsmʊs] M **-, no pl** (*pej*) dogmatism

Doh|le¹ ['do:lə] F **-, -n** (*Orn*) jackdaw

Doh|le² F **-, -n** (= *Abfluss*) drain

Döhn|kes ['dø:nkəs] PL (*N Ger*) stories *pl*, anecdotes *pl*

Dok|tor ['dɔkto:ɐ] M **-s, Doktoren** [-'to:rən], **Dok|to|rin** [-'to:rɪn, 'dɔktorɪn] F **-, -nen** (*auch inf:* = *Arzt*) doctor; **ja, Herr/Frau ~** yes, Doctor; **er ist ~ der Philosophie/Theologie** he is a doctor of philosophy/theology; **sie ist ~** she has a doctorate or PhD, she is a PhD; **den** or **seinen ~ machen** or **bauen** (*inf*) to do a doctorate or PhD; **zum ~ promoviert werden** to

receive one's doctorate or PhD; **~ spielen** (*inf*) to play doctors and nurses

Dok|to|rand [dɔkto'rant] M **-en, -en** [-dn], **Dok|to|ran|din** [-'randɪn] F **-, -nen** graduate student studying for a doctorate

Dok|tor|ar|beit F doctoral or PhD thesis

Dok|to|rat [dɔkto'ra:t] NT **-(e)s, -e a** (*dated*) doctorate **b** (*Aus:* = *Prüfung*) examination for a/one's doctorate

Dok|tor-: Dok|tor|dip|lom NT doctor's diploma; **Dok|tor|exa|men** NT examination for a/one's doctorate; **Dok|tor|grad** M doctorate, doctor's degree, PhD; **den ~ erwerben** to obtain one's doctorate; **Dok|tor|hut** M doctor's cap; (*fig*) doctorate

Dok|to|rin F doctor → *auch* **Doktor**

Dok|tor-: Dok|tor|prü|fung F examination for a/one's doctorate; **Dok|tor|schrift** F (*inf:* = *Handschrift*) doctor's or illegible handwriting; **Dok|tor|spie|le** PL doctors and nurses *sing*; **Dok|tor|ti|tel** M the title of doctor; **den ~ führen** to have the title of doctor; **jdm den ~ verleihen** to confer a doctorate or the degree of doctor (up)on sb; **Dok|tor|va|ter** M (*Univ*) supervisor; **Dok|tor|wür|de** F doctorate; **jdm die ~ verleihen** to confer a doctorate or the degree of doctor (up)on sb

Dokt|rin [dɔk'tri:n] F **-, -en** doctrine

dokt|ri|när [dɔktri'nɛ:ɐ] ADJ doctrinal; (*pej:* = *stur*) doctrinaire

Do|ku|ment [doku'mɛnt] NT **-(e)s, -e** document; (*fig:* = *Zeugnis*) record

Do|ku|men|tar [dokumɛn'ta:ɐ] M **-s, -e, Do|ku|men|ta|rin** [-'ta:rɪn] F **-, -nen** documentalist

Do|ku|men|tar- *in cpds* documentary; **Do|ku|men|tar|film** M documentary (film)

do|ku|men|ta|risch [dokumɛn'ta:rɪʃ] ADJ documentary; **von ~em Interesse sein** to be of interest as documentation [ADV] (= *mit Dokumenten*) with documents; **etw ~ belegen/festhalten** to provide documentary evidence for or of sth; **etw ~ festhalten** to document sth

Do|ku|men|tar-: Do|ku|men|tar|li|te|ra|tur F documentary literature; **Do|ku|men|tar|sen|dung** F documentary; **Do|ku|men|tar|spiel** NT docudrama

Do|ku|men|ta|ti|on [dokumɛnta'tsio:n] F **-, -en** documentation; (= *Sammlung auch*) records *pl*

Do|ku|men|ten-: do|ku|men|ten|echt, do|ku|men|ten|fest ADJ *Tinte* waterproof; **~e Computerausdrucke** document-quality computer print-outs; **~es Papier** = **Dokumentenpapier**; **Do|ku|men|ten|echt|heit** F (*von Drucker*) document quality; **Do|ku|men|ten|pa|pier** NT good quality paper used for documents, certificates etc

do|ku|men|tie|ren [dokumɛn'ti:rən] ptp **dokumentiert** [VT] to document; (*fig:* = *zu erkennen geben*) to reveal, to show [VR] (*fig*) to become evident

Do|ku|ment|vor|la|ge F (*Comput*) template

Dol|ce Vi|ta ▲ ['dɔltʃə 'vi:ta] NT OR F **-, -**, *no pl* life of ease, dolce vita; **Dolce vita machen** (*inf*) to live a life of ease

Dolch [dɔlç] M **-(e)s, -e** dagger; (*inf:* = *Messer*) knife

Dolch|stich M , **Dolch|stoß** (*esp fig*) M stab (*auch fig*), dagger thrust; **ein ~ (von hinten)** (*fig*) a stab in the back

Dolch|stoß|le|gen|de F (*Hist*) myth of the stab in the back (*betrayal of Germany in the first World War by its own politicians*)

Dol|de ['dɔldə] F **-, -n** umbel

Dol|den-: Dol|den|blüt|ler [-bly:tlɐ] M **-s, -** umbelliferous plant; **dol|den|för|mig** ADJ umbellate; **Dol|den|ge|wächs** NT umbellifer; **die ~e** the Umbelliferae

Do|le ['do:lə] F **-, -n** drain

Do|li|ne [do'li:nə] F **-, -n** (*Geol*) doline, dolina, sinkhole

doll [dɔl] (*dial, inf*) ADJ **a** = **toll** ADJ **b** (= *unerhört*) incredible [ADV] **a** = **toll** ADV **b** (= *sehr*) really; **das hat ~ wehgetan** that hurt like hell (*inf*)

Dol|lar ['dɔlar] M **-(s), -s** or (*nach Zahlenangaben*) **-** dollar; **hundert ~** a hundred dollars

Dol|lar-: Dol|lar|kurs M dollar rate; **Dol|lar|no|te** F dollar bill; **dol|lar|sen|si|bel** ADJ dollar-sensitive; **dollarsensible Werte** *pl* dollar-sensitive securities *pl*; **Dol|lar|zei|chen** NT dollar sign

Doll|bord ['dɔl-] NT (*Naut*) gunwale

Dol|le ['dɔlə] F **-, -n** (*Naut*) rowlock, oarlock (*US*)

Dol|ly ['dɔli] M **-(s), -s** (*Film*) dolly

Dolm [dɔlm] M **-s, -** (*Aus*) idiot, clot (*Brit inf*)

Dol|men ['dɔlmən] M **-s, -** (*Archeol*) dolmen

Dol|metsch ['dɔlmɛtʃ] M **-(e)s, -e a** (*Aus, old*) interpreter **b** (*geh:* = *Fürsprecher*) spokesman (+*gen, von* for)

dol|met|schen ['dɔlmɛtʃn] VTI to interpret; **jdm** or **für jdn ~** to interpret for sb

Dol|met|scher ['dɔlmɛtʃɐ] M **-s, -, Dol|met|sche|rin** [-ərɪn] F interpreter

Dol|met|scher-: Dol|met|scher|in|sti|tut NT school or institute of interpreting; **Dol|met|scher|ka|bi|ne** F interpreter's booth; **Dol|met|scher|schu|le** F school or institute of interpreting

Do|lo|mit [dolo'mi:t] M **-s, -e** (*Geol, Chem*) dolomite

Do|lo|mi|ten [dolo'mi:tn] PL (*Geog*) **die ~** the Dolomites *pl*

Dom [do:m] M **-(e)s, -e a** cathedral **b** (*fig poet*) vault (*poet*), dome (*poet*)

Do|main [do'me:n] F **-, -s** (*Comput, Internet*) domain; **eine ~ (auf seinen Namen) registrieren lassen** to register a domain (in one's name)

Do|main|na|me [do'me:n-] M (*Comput, Internet*) domain name

Do|mä|ne [do'mɛ:nə] F **-, -n** (*Hist, Jur*) demesne; (*fig*) domain, province

Do|mes|tik [domɛs'ti:k] M **-en, -en** = **Domestike**

Do|mes|ti|ka|ti|on [domɛstika'tsio:n] F **-, -en** domestication

Do|mes|ti|ke [domɛs'ti:kə] M **-n, -n a** (*pej old*) (domestic) servant, domestic **b** (*Sport*) pacemaker

do|mes|ti|zie|ren [domɛsti'tsi:rən] ptp **domestiziert** VT to domesticate; (*fig auch*) to tame

Dom-: Dom|frei|heit F (*Hist*) cathedral close or precincts *pl*; **Dom|herr** M (*Eccl*) canon

Do|mi|na ['do:mina] F **-, -s** dominatrix

do|mi|nant [domi'nant] ADJ dominant (*auch Biol*), dominating

Do|mi|nant- *in cpds* (*Mus*) dominant

Do|mi|nant|ak|kord M (*Mus*) dominant chord

Do|mi|nan|te [domi'nantə] F **-, -n a** (*Mus*) dominant **b** (= *wichtigster Faktor*) dominant or dominating feature

Do|mi|nanz [domi'nants] F **-, -en** (*Biol, Psych*) dominance

do|mi|nie|ren [domi'ni:rən] ptp **dominiert** [VI] (= *vorherrschen*) to be (pre)dominant, to predominate; (*Mensch*) to dominate [VT] to dominate

do|mi|nie|rend ADJ dominating, dominant

Do|mi|ni|ka|ner [domini'ka:nɐ] M **-s, -, Do|mi|ni|ka|ne|rin** [-ərɪn] F **-, -nen a** (*Eccl*) Dominican **b** (*Geog*) Dominican

Do|mi|ni|ka|ner-: Do|mi|ni|ka|ner|klos|ter NT Dominican monastery; **Do|mi|ni|ka|ner|or|den** M Order of St Dominic, Dominicans *pl*

do|mi|ni|ka|nisch [domini'ka:nɪʃ] ADJ **a** (Eccl) Dominican **b** (Geog) **die Dominikanische Republik** the Dominican Republic

Do|mi|no¹ ['do:mino] M -s, -s domino

Do|mi|no² NT -s, -s (= Spiel) dominoes sing

Do|mi|no-: Do|mi|no|ef|fekt M domino effect; **dann tritt ein ~ ein** then the domino theory comes into play; **einen ~ auslösen** to have a knock-on (Brit) or domino effect; **Do|mi|no|spiel** NT dominoes sing; (= Spielmaterial) set of dominoes; (= Partie) game of dominoes; **Do|mi|no|stein** M **a** domino **b** (Cook) small chocolate biscuit with layers of marzipan and gingerbread

Do|mi|zil [domi'tsi:l] NT -s, -e domicile (form)

Dom-: Dom|ka|pi|tel NT cathedral chapter; **Dom|ka|pi|tu|lar** [-kapitula:ɐ] M -s, -e canon; **Dom|pfaff** ['do:mpfaf] M -en or -s, -en (Orn) bullfinch; **Dom|propst** M dean of a/the cathedral

Domp|teur [dɔmp'tø:ɐ] M -s, -e, **Domp|teur|in** [-'tørɪn] F -, -nen, **Domp|teu|se** [-'tø:zə] F -, -n trainer; (von Raubtieren) tamer

Don [dɔn] M -(s) (Geog) Don

Do|nar ['do:nar] M -s Thor

Do|nau ['do:nau] F **die ~** the (river) Danube

Do|nau|mo|nar|chie F (Hist) Austria-Hungary, Austro-Hungarian Empire

Do|nau|schwa|ben PL Swabian settlers on the Danube in Hungary

Dö|ner ['dø:nɐ] M -s, -, **Dö|ner|ke|bab** [dønɐkə'bap] M -(s), -s doner kebab

Don Ju|an [dɔn 'xuan, dɔn 'ju:an] M -s, - - Don Juan

Dön|kes ['dœŋkəs] PL (N Ger) stories pl, anecdotes pl

Don|ko|sa|ken ['dɔn-] PL Don Cossacks pl

Don|ner ['dɔnɐ] M -s, (rare) - (lit, fig) thunder no indef art, no pl; (= Donnerschlag) peal or clap of thunder; **wie vom ~ gerührt** (fig inf) thunderstruck; **~ und Doria** or **Blitz!** (dated inf) by thunder! (dated inf), by Jove! (dated inf)

Don|ner-: Don|ner|bal|ken M (Mil sl) thunderbox (sl); **Don|ner|blech** NT (Theat) thunder sheet; **Don|ner|büch|se** F (hum dated) shotgun; **Don|ner|ge|pol|ter** NT , **Don|ner|ge|tö|se** NT thunderous or deafening crash; **mit Donnergetöse** with a thunderous or deafening crash; **Don|ner|gott** M god of thunder; **Don|ner|grol|len** NT -s, no pl rolling thunder; **Don|ner|keil** M (Geol) thunderstone; (Archeol) flintstone; (Myth, poet) thunderbolt; **~!** (dated) Donnerkeil! (dated) my word!, heavens!; **Don|ner|ma|schi|ne** F (Theat) thunder machine

don|nern ['dɔnɐn] VI impers to thunder; **es donnerte in der Ferne** there was (the sound of) thunder in the distance VI aux haben or (bei Bewegung) sein to thunder; **gegen etw ~** (= prallen) to crash into sth; (= schlagen) to hammer on sth; (= schimpfen) to thunder against sth; **er hat furchtbar gedonnert** he really thundered on VT (inf) (= brüllen) to thunder out; (= schleudern, schlagen) to slam, to crash; **jdm eine ~** to thump (Brit inf) or pound (esp US inf) sb

don|nernd ADJ (fig) Beifall, Gesänge thunderous; Hufe thundering

Don|ner-: Don|ner|rol|len NT -s, no pl rolling of thunder; **Don|ner|schlag** M peal or peal of thunder, thunderclap; **die Nachricht traf mich wie ein ~** the news left me thunderstruck

Don|ners|tag ['dɔnɐsta:k] M Thursday → auch **Dienstag**

don|ners|tags ['dɔnɐsta:ks] ADV on Thursdays

Don|ner-: Don|ner|stim|me F thunderous voice; **Don|ner|wet|ter** NT (lit old) thunderstorm; (fig inf: = Schelte) row; **das wird ein schönes ~ geben** or **setzen** (inf) all hell will be let loose (inf); **~!** (inf: anerkennend) my word!; **(zum) ~!** (inf: zornig) damn or blast (it)! (inf)

Don Qui|chotte [dɔn ki'ʃɔt] M - -s, - -s (Liter, fig) Don Quixote

Don|qui|chot|te|rie [dɔnkiʃɔtə'ri:] F -, -n [-'ri:ən] (geh) quixotism; (= Handlung) quixotic gesture or act

Don Qui|jo|te [dɔn ki'xo:tə] M - -s, - -s, **Don Qui|xo|te** [dɔn ki'xo:tə] M - -s, - -s (Liter, fig) Don Quixote

Dönt|jes ['dœntjəs, 'dø:ntjəs] PL (N Ger) stories pl, anecdotes pl

doof [do:f] (inf) ADJ daft (esp Brit inf), dumb (inf) ADV **aussehen** dumb; **~ fragen** to ask a dumb question; **~ lächeln** to give a dumb smile

Doof|heit F -, no pl (inf) daftness (esp Brit inf), dumbness (inf)

Doo|fi ['do:fi] M -(s), -s (inf) thicky, dummy, dumb-dumb (all inf); **wie Klein ~ mit Plüschohren aussehen** to look a proper charlie (Brit inf) or fool

Doof|kopp [-kɔp] M -s, **Doof|köppe** [-kœpə] (sl), **Doof|mann** M pl -männer (inf) thickhead (Brit inf), blockhead (inf)

Do|pa|min [dopa'mi:n] NT -s, no pl (Med) dopamine

Dope [do:p] NT -s, -s (sl) dope (inf)

do|pen ['dɔpn, 'do:pn] (Sport) VT to dope; **er war gedopt** he had taken drugs VIR to take drugs

Do|ping ['dɔpɪŋ, 'do:pɪŋ] NT -s, -s (Sport) drug-taking; (bei Pferden) doping

Do|ping- ['dɔpɪŋ-, 'do:pɪŋ-]: **Do|ping|kon|trol|le** F (Sport) drug(s) test; **Do|ping|mit|tel** NT (Sport) drug, doping substance; **Do|ping|skan|dal** M (Sport) doping scandal; **Do|ping|sün|der(in)** M(F) (Sport) drug-taker; **Do|ping|test** M (Sport) drug(s) test; **Do|ping|ver|dacht** M (Sport) **bei ihm besteht ~** he is suspected of having taken drugs; **Do|ping|vor|wurf** M (Sport) doping charge

Dop|pel ['dɔpl] NT -s, - **a** (= Duplikat) duplicate (copy) (+gen, zu of) **b** (Tennis etc) doubles sing; (= Mannschaft) doubles pair

Dop|pel- in cpds double; **Dop|pel|ad|ler** M double eagle; **Dop|pel|agent(in)** M(F) double agent; **Dop|pel-b** [-be:] NT (Mus) double flat; **Dop|pel|band** [-bant] M pl -bände (von doppeltem Umfang) double-sized volume; (= zwei Bände) two volumes pl; **Dop|pel|bau|er** M (Chess) doubled pawn; **Dop|pel|be|las|tung** F double or dual load or burden (+gen on); **steuerliche ~** double taxation; **Dop|pel|be|schluss** ▲ M (Pol) two-track or twin-track decision; **Dop|pel|be|steue|rung** F double taxation; **Dop|pel|be|steue|rungs|ab|kom|men** NT double taxation agreement; **Dop|pel|bett** NT double bed; (= zwei Betten) twin beds pl; **Dop|pel|bil|der** PL (Med) **~ wahrnehmen** or **sehen** to have double vision; **Dop|pel|blind|ver|such** M (Psych) experiment using a double blind; **Dop|pel|bock** NT OR M (double-strength) bock beer; **dop|pel|bö|dig** [-bø:dɪç] ADJ Koffer etc false-bottomed; (= doppeldeutig) ambiguous; **Dop|pel|bö|dig|keit** F -, -en (fig) ambiguity; **Dop|pel|bo|gen** M double sheet (of paper); **Dop|pel|brief** M letter weighing over 20 g; **Dop|pel|bruch** M (Math) compound fraction; **Dop|pel|büch|se** F double-barrelled (Brit) or double-barreled (US) gun or (Schrotbüchse) shotgun; **Dop|pel|buch|sta|be** M double letter; **Dop|pel|de|cker** [-dɛkɐ] M -s, - **a** (Aviat) biplane **b** (auch Doppeldeckerbus) double-decker (bus); **dop|pel|deu|tig** [-dɔytɪç] ADJ ambiguous; **Dop|pel|deu|tig|keit** F -, -en ambiguity; **Dop|pel|ehe** F bigamous marriage; (= Tatbestand) bigamy no pl; **eine ~ führen** to live bigamously; **Dop|pel|feh|ler** M (Tennis) double fault; (Sch) double mistake; **einen ~ machen** (Tennis) to serve a double fault, to double-fault; **Dop|pel|fens|ter** NT double window; **~ ha|ben** to have double glazing; **Dop|pel|flin|te** F double-barrelled (Brit) or double-barreled (US)

---

gun or (Schrotflinte) shotgun; **Dop|pel|funk|ti|on** F dual or twin function; **Dop|pel|gän|ger** [-gɛŋɐ] M -s, -, **Dop|pel|gän|ge|rin** [-ərɪn] F -, -nen double, doppelgänger (esp Liter); **ein ~ von Boris Becker** a Boris Becker lookalike, a double of Boris Becker; **dop|pel|ge|schlech|tig** [-gəʃlɛçtɪç] ADJ (Bot) hermaphrodite; **Dop|pel|ge|sicht** NT two faces pl; (fig) two sides pl; **dop|pel|ge|sich|tig** [-gəzɪçtɪç] ADJ two-faced, having two faces; (fig) two-sided; **Dop|pel|ge|stirn** NT double star; **dop|pel|glei|sig** ADJ (Rail) double-track, twin-track; (fig) double; **~ sein** (lit) to have two tracks ADV **~ fahren** (fig) to play a double game; **Dop|pel|griff** M (Mus) double stop; **Dop|pel|haus** NT semidetached house (Brit), semi (Brit inf), duplex (house) (US); **er bewohnt eine Hälfte eines ~es** he lives in a semi(detached house etc); **Dop|pel|haus|hälf|te** F semidetached house (Brit), duplex (house) (US); **Dop|pel|heft** NT (von Zeitschrift) double number or edition; (Sch) exercise book of double thickness; **Dop|pel|hoch|zeit** F double wedding; **Dop|pel|ka|bi|ne** F double or twin cabin or (von LKW) cab; **Dop|pel|kinn** NT double chin; **Dop|pel|kle|be|band** NT double-sided adhesive tape; **Dop|pel|klick** [-klɪk] M -s, -s (Comput) double click (auf on); **dop|pel+kli|cken** VI sep (Comput) to double-click (auf on); **Dop|pel|kol|ben|mo|tor** M two-cylinder engine; **Dop|pel|kon|so|nant** M double or geminate (spec) consonant; **Dop|pel|kopf** M German card game; **Dop|pel|korn** M type of schnapps; **Dop|pel|kreuz** NT (Mus) double sharp; (Typ) double dagger; **Dop|pel|lauf** M double barrel; **dop|pel|läu|fig** ADJ double-barrelled (Brit), double-barreled (US); **Dop|pel|laut** M (Ling) (Konsonant) double or geminate (spec) consonant; (Vokal) double vowel; (= Diphthong) diphthong; **Dop|pel|le|ben** NT double life; **Dop|pel|mo|ral** F double (moral) standard(s pl); **Dop|pel|mord** M double murder

dop|peln ['dɔpln] VT **a** (= verdoppeln) to double **b** (Aus: = besohlen) to resole

Dop|pel-: Dop|pel|naht F double-stitched seam; **Dop|pel|na|me** M (= Nachname) double-barrelled (Brit) or double-barreled (US) name; (= Vorname) double name; **Dop|pel|na|tur** F dual nature; **Dop|pel|nel|son** M (Ringen) full nelson; **Dop|pel|num|mer** F (von Zeitschrift) double issue; **Dop|pel|pack** M twin pack; **im ~** as a twin pack; **Dop|pel|part|ner(in)** M(F) (Sport) doubles partner; **Dop|pel|pass** M (Ftbl) one-two **b** (für doppelte Staatsbürgerschaft) second passport; **Dop|pel|punkt** M colon; **Dop|pel|rahm|kä|se** M full-fat cheese; **dop|pel|rei|hig** ADJ in two rows; Jacke double-breasted; **~e Perlenkette** double string of pearls; **~e Nietung** two rows of rivets; **Dop|pel|rol|le** F (Theat) double role; (fig) dual capacity; **dop|pel|schläf|rig** ADJ Bett double; **Dop|pel|schlag** M (Mus) turn; **Dop|pel|schräg|strich** M (Typ) double (forward) slash; **umgekehrter ~** double backslash; **dop|pel|sei|tig** [-zaɪtɪç] ADJ two-sided, double-sided; Diskette double-sided; Lungenentzündung double; **~e Anzeige** double page spread; **~e Lähmung** diplegia; **Dop|pel|sieg** M double victory, one-two (victory); **Dop|pel|sinn** M double meaning, ambiguity; **dop|pel|sin|nig** ADJ ambiguous; **Dop|pel|spiel** NT **a** (Tennis) (game of) doubles sing **b** (fig) double game; **Dop|pel|spiel|feld** NT (Tennis) doubles court; **dop|pel|spu|rig** [-ʃpu:rɪç] ADJ = zweispurig; **Dop|pel|steck|do|se** F double socket; **Dop|pel|ste|cker** M two-way adaptor; **Dop|pel|stern** M double star; **Dop|pel|steu|er|ab|kom|men** NT reciprocal taxation agreement; **dop|pel|stö|ckig** ADJ Haus two-storey (Brit), two-story (US), twin-storey (Brit), twin-story (US); Bus double-decker attr (hum inf) Schnaps double; **ein ~es Bett** bunk beds pl; **Dop|pel|stock|wa|gen** M (Rail) double-deck

---

carriage (*Brit*) or car (*US*); **Dop|pel|stock|-zug** M (*Rail*) double-deck train; **Dop|pel|stra|te|gie** F dual strategy; **Dop|pel|strich** M (*Mus*) double bar; **Dop|pel|stu|di|um** NT joint course (of study) (*Brit*), double major (*US*); **Dop|pel|stun|de** F (*esp Sch*) double period

dop|pelt ['dɔplt] ADJ double; (= *verstärkt*) *Enthusiasmus* redoubled; (= *mit zwei identischen Teilen*) twin *attr*; (= *zweimal so viel*) twice; (*Comm*) *Buchführung* double-entry; *Staatsbürgerschaft* dual; **die ~e Freude/Länge/Menge** double or twice the pleasure/length/amount; **~e Negation** or **Verneinung** double negative; **~er Boden** (*von Koffer*) false bottom; (*von Boot*) double bottom; **~e Moral, eine Moral mit ~em Boden** double standards *pl*, a double standard; **in ~er Hinsicht** in two respects; **ein ~es Spiel spielen** or **treiben** to play a double game → **Ausfertigung**

ADV sehen, zählen double; (= *zweimal*) twice; (*direkt vor Adjektiv*) doubly; **~ so schön/so viel** twice as nice/much; **sie ist ~ so alt wie ich** she is twice as old as I am, she is twice my age; **das/die Karte habe ich ~** I have two of them/these cards; **das freut mich ~** that gives me double or twice the pleasure; **~ gemoppelt** (*inf*) saying the same thing twice over; **sich ~ in Acht nehmen** to be doubly careful; **~ und dreifach** (*bereuen, Leid tun*) deeply; *sich entschuldigen* profusely; *prüfen* thoroughly; *versichern* absolutely; **seine Schuld ~ und dreifach bezahlen** to pay back one's debt with interest; **der Stoff liegt ~** the material is double width; (= **genäht**) **hält besser** (*prov*) ≈ better safe than sorry (*prov*)

Dop|pel|te(r) ['dɔpltə] M decl as adj (*inf*) double

Dop|pel|te(s) ['dɔpltə] NT decl as adj double; **um das ~ größer** twice as large; (*Gegenstand auch*) double the size; **auf das ~ steigen** to double; **das ~ bezahlen** to pay twice as much, to pay double the amount; **etw um das ~ erhöhen** to double sth

Dop|pelt-: dop|pelt|koh|len|sau|er ADJ doppeltkohlensaures Natron sodium bicarbonate, bicarbonate of soda; **Dop|pelt|se|hen** NT double vision

Dop|pe|lung ['dɔpəlʊŋ] F -, -en doubling

Dop|pel-: Dop|pel|ver|die|ner(in) M(F) person with two incomes; (*pl*: = *Paar*) couple with two incomes, two-income or double-income family; **Dop|pel|ver|ga|ser** M twin carburettors *pl* (*Brit*) or carburetors *pl* (*US*) or carbs *pl* (*inf*); **Dop|pel|ver|gla|sung** F double glazing; **Fenster mit ~** double-glazed window; **Dop|pel|ver|si|che|rung** F double insurance; (= *Police*) double insurance policy; **Dop|pel|vie|rer** M (*Sport*) quadruple skulls *pl*; **Dop|pel|vo|kal** M double vowel; **Dop|pel|wäh|rung** F bimetallism; **Dop|pel|zent|ner** M 100 kilos, (metric) quintal; **Dop|pel|zim|mer** NT double room; **dop|pel|zün|gig** [-tsyŋɪç] ADJ (*fig*) devious; (*stärker*) deceitful; *Mensch* two-faced, devious ADV **~ reden** to say one thing and mean another; **Dop|pel|zün|gig|keit** F -, -en a no pl (*fig*) deviousness; (*stärker*) deceitfulness b (*Äußerung*) devious remark; **Dop|pel|zwei|er** M (*Sport*) double skulls *pl*

Dopp|ler|ef|fekt ['dɔplɐ-] M (*Phys*) Doppler effect

Do|ra|do [do'ra:do] NT -s, -s El Dorado

Dorf [dɔrf] NT -(e)s, ꞋꞋer ['dœrfə] village; (*fig*) backwater; **auf dem ~(e)** (= *in einem bestimmten Dorf*) in the village; (= *auf dem Land*) in the country; **das Leben auf dem ~e** village life; **er ist vom ~(e)** he's from the/our village; (= *vom Lande*) he's from the country; **nie aus seinem ~ herausgekommen sein** (*fig*) to be parochial or insular; **das olympische ~** the Olympic Village → **böhmisch, Kirche**

Dorf- in cpds village; **Dorf|äl|tes|te(r)** MF decl as adj village elder; **Dorf|an|ger** M (*dated*) village green; **Dorf|be|woh|ner(in)** M(F) villager

Dörf|chen ['dœrfçən] NT -s, - dim von Dorf small village, hamlet

Dorf-: Dorf|er|neu|e|rung F village regeneration (scheme); **Dorf|gast|haus** NT , **Dorf|gast|hof** M village inn; **Dorf|ge|mein|de** F village community; (*Admin*) rural district; (*Eccl*) village parish; **Dorf|ge|schich|te** F a (*Liter*. = *Erzählung*) story of village life b no pl village history; **Dorf|hel|fe|rin** F domestic help employed when a farmer's wife is ill; **Dorf|ju|gend** F young people pl of the village, village youth pl; **Dorf|krug** M village inn or pub (*Brit*)

Dörf|lein ['dœrflain] NT -s, - dim von Dorf

Dörf|ler ['dœrflɐ] M -s, -, **Dörf|le|rin** [-ərɪn] F -, -nen (*dated*) villager

Dorf|leu|te PL villagers pl

dörf|lich ['dœrflıç] ADJ village attr; (= *ländlich*) rustic, rural

Dorf-: Dorf|pfar|rer(in) M(F) (*bes katholisch*) village priest, country vicar (*Brit*); **Dorf|platz** M village square; **Dorf|schaft** ['dɔrfʃaft] F -, -en (*Sw*) hamlet; **Dorf|schö|ne** F , **Dorf|schön|heit** F (*iro*) village beauty; **Dorf|schul|ze** M (*Hist*) village mayor; **Dorf|trot|tel** M (*inf*) village idiot

Do|ria ['do:ria] INTERJ → Donner

do|risch ['do:rɪʃ] ADJ (*Archit*) Doric; (*Hist auch, Mus*) Dorian

Dor|mi|to|ri|um [dɔrmi'to:riʊm] NT -s, Dormitorien [-riən] (*Eccl*) dormitory

Dorn [dɔrn] M -(e)s, -en or (*inf*) -e or ꞋꞋer ['dœrnə] a (*Bot, fig*) thorn; **das ist mir ein ~ im Auge** (*fig*) that is a thorn in my flesh (*esp Brit*) or side; (*Anblick*) I find that an eyesore b PL -e (*poet*. = *Dornbusch*) briar, thornbush c PL -e (= *Sporn*) spike; (*von Schnalle*) tongue; (*von Scharnier*) pin; (*Tech*: = *Werkzeug*) awl

Dorn|busch M briar, thornbush; **der brennende ~** (*Bibl*) the burning bush

Dor|nen-: dor|nen|ge|krönt [-gəkrø:nt] ADJ (*Bibl*) wearing a crown of thorns, crowned with thorns; **Dor|nen|ge|strüpp** NT thorny bushes pl or undergrowth; **Dor|nen|he|cke** F thorn (-y) hedge; **Dor|nen|kro|ne** F (*Bibl*) crown of thorns; **Dor|nen|pfad** M thorny path; (*fig*) path fraught with difficulties, path of tribulation; **dor|nen|reich** ADJ thorny; (*fig*) fraught with difficulty; **dor|nen|voll** ADJ (*fig*) fraught with difficulty

Dorn|fort|satz M (*Anat*) spiny or spinous (*spec*) process

dor|nig ['dɔrnıç] ADJ thorny; (*fig auch*) fraught with difficulty

Dorn-: Dorn|rös|chen [-rø:sçən] NT Sleeping Beauty; **Dorn|rös|chen|schlaf** [-rø:sçən-] M (*fig*) torpor, slumber; **Dorn|strauch** M briar, thornbush

Dör|re ['dœrə] F -, -n (*dial*) drying kiln or oven; (= *Höpfendörre, Malzdörre*) oast

dor|ren ['dɔrən] VI aux sein (*geh*) to dry; (= *austrocknen*) to dry up

dör|ren ['dœrən] VT to dry VI aux sein to dry; (= *austrocknen*) to dry up

Dörr- in cpds dried; **Dörr|fisch** M dried fish; **Dörr|fleisch** NT dried meat; **Dörr|obst** NT dried fruit; **Dörr|pflau|me** F prune

dor|sal [dɔr'za:l] ADJ (*Zool, Ling*) dorsal; *Verkrümmung, Schwäche* spinal

Dor|sal [dɔr'za:l] M -s, -e, **Dor|sal|laut** M (*Ling*) dorsal (consonant)

Dorsch [dɔrʃ] M -(e)s, -e fish of the cod group; (= *Kabeljau*) cod(fish)

Dorsch|le|ber F cod liver

dort [dɔrt] ADV there; **~ zu Lande** in that country, (over) there → **da** ADV a

dort: dort be|hal|ten ▲ VT irreg to keep there; **dort blei|ben** ▲ VI irreg aux sein to stay or remain there

dor|ten ['dɔrtn] ADV (*old, Aus*) there

dort-: dort|her [dɔrt'he:ɐ, dɔrt'he:ɐ, (*emph*) 'dɔrthe:ɐ] ADV **von ~** from there, thence (*old, liter*); **dort|he|rum** [dɔrthe'rʊm, dɔrthe'rʊm, (*emph*) 'dɔrtherʊm] ADV (a)round (there), thereabouts; **dort|hin** ['dɔrt'hın, dɔrt'hın, (*emph*) 'dɔrthın] ADV there, thither (*old, liter*); **bis ~** as far as there, up to that place; **wie komme ich ~?** how do I get there?; **dort|hi|nab** ['dɔrthı'nap, dɔrthı'nap, (*emph*) 'dɔrthınap] ADV down there; **dort|hi|nauf** ['dɔrthı'nauf, dɔrthı'nauf, (*emph*) 'dɔrthınauf] ADV up there; **dort|hi|naus** ['dɔrthı'naus, dɔrthı'naus, (*emph*) 'dɔrthınaus] ADV out there; **frech bis ~** (*inf*) really cheeky (*Brit*) or fresh (*US inf*); **das ärgert mich bis ~** (*inf*) that really gets me (*inf*), that doesn't half annoy me (*Brit inf*); **dort|hi|nein** ['dɔrthı'nain, dɔrthı'nain, (*emph*) 'dɔrthınain] ADV in there; **dort|hi|nun|ter** ['dɔrthı'nʊntɐ, dɔrthı'nʊntɐ, (*emph*) 'dɔrthınʊntɐ] ADV down there

dor|tig ['dɔrtıç] ADJ there (*nachgestellt*); **die ~en Behörden** the authorities there

dort|zu|lan|de ['dɔrttsulandə] ADV in that country, (over) there

DOS [dɔs] NT -, no pl abbr von Disk Operating System (*Comput*) DOS

Dös|chen ['dø:sgən] NT -s, - dim von Dose

Do|se ['do:zə] F -, -n a (= *Blechdose*) tin; (= *Konservendose*) can, tin (*Brit*); (= *Bierdose*) can; (*esp aus Holz*) box; (*mit Deckel*) jar; (= *Pillendose, für Schmuck*) box; (= *Butterdose*) dish; (= *Zuckerdose*) bowl; (*für Gesichtspuder*) compact; (= *Plastikdose, Streudose*) pack (*inf*); **in ~n** (*Konserven*) canned, tinned (*Brit*) b (*Elec*) socket c (*Pharm*: = *Dosis*) dose d (*sl*: = *Vagina*) hole (*sl*)

dö|sen ['dø:zn] VI (*inf*) to doze

Do|sen- in cpds canned, tinned (*Brit*); **Do|sen|bier** NT canned beer; **Do|sen|blech** NT tin for making cans or tins (*Brit*); **Do|sen|milch** F canned or tinned (*Brit*) milk, condensed milk; **Do|sen|öff|ner** M can-opener, tin-opener (*Brit*); **Do|sen|pfand** NT deposit on (drinks) cans, can deposit

do|sier|bar ADJ leichter ~ sein to be more easily measured into exact doses; **etw in ~en Mengen verabreichen** to administer sth in exact doses

do|sie|ren [do'zi:rən] ptp **dosiert** VT Arznei to measure into doses; Menge to measure out; (*fig*) Rat, Liebe, Geschenke, Lob to dispense, to measure or hand out; Stoff, Hinweise to dispense; **ein Medikament genau ~** to measure out an exact dose of a medicine; **etw dosiert verteilen** (*fig*) to dispense etc sth in small amounts or doses

Do|sie|rung F -, -en a (= *Dosis*) dosage, dose b (*von Arznei*) measuring into doses; (*von Menge*) measuring out

dö|sig ['dø:zıç] ADJ (*inf*) dozy (*inf*), drowsy

Do|si|me|ter [dosi'me:tɐ] NT -s, - dosage meter, dosimeter

Do|sis ['do:zıs] F -, Dosen ['do:zn] dose; **in kleinen Dosen** (*lit, fig*) in small doses

Dös|kopp ['dø:skɔp] M -s, Dösköppe [-kœpə] (*N Ger inf*) dozy (*Brit inf*) or stupid idiot

Dos|si|er [dɔ'sie:] M OR (DATED) NT -s, -s dossier

Do|ta|ti|on [dota'tsio:n] F -, -en endowment

Dot|com ['dɔtkɔm] F -, -s (*Comm sl*: = *Internetfirma*) dotcom

do|tie|ren [do'ti:rən] ptp **dotiert** VT Posten to remunerate (*mit* with); Preis to endow (*mit* with); **eine gut dotierte Stellung** a remunerative position

Do|tie|rung F -, -en endowment; (*von Posten*) remuneration

Dot|ter ['dɔtɐ] M OR NT -s, - yolk

Dot|ter-: Dot|ter|blu|me F globe flower; (= *Sumpfdotterblume*) marsh marigold; **dot|ter|gelb** ADJ golden yellow; **Dot|ter|sack** M (*Zool*) yolk sac

---

Deutsche Rechtschreibreform (siehe Anhang): ▲ neue Schreibung △ alte Schreibung

+ trennbare Verben

dou|beln ['du:bln] **VT** *jdn* to stand in for; *Szene* to shoot with a stand-in; **er lässt sich nie ~** he never has a stand-in; **ein Stuntman hat die Szene für ihn gedoubelt** a stuntman doubled for him in the scene **VI** to stand in; (= *als Double arbeiten*) to work as a stand-in

Dou|ble ['du:bl] NT **-s, -s** (*Film etc*) stand-in; (*für Gesang*) dubber

Doub|lé [du'ble:] NT **-s, -s = Dublee**

Doub|let|te [du'blɛtə] F **-, -n = Dublette**

doub|lie|ren [du'bli:rən] *ptp* **doubliert** VT **= dublieren**

Doug|la|sie [du'gla:ziə] F **-, -n, Doug|las|fich|te** ['du:glas-] F **, Doug|las|tan|ne** ['du:glas-] F Douglas fir *or* pine

Dow-Jones-In|dex ['dau'dʒo:nz-] M **,** *no pl* (*Econ*) Dow-Jones Index

down [daun] ADJ *pred* (*inf*) **~ sein** to be (feeling) down *or* blue (*inf*)

Down|si|zing ['daunsaizɪŋ] NT **-s,** *no pl* (*Comput*) downsizing

Down|syn|drom ['daun-] NT **,** *no pl* (*Med*) Down's syndrome; **ein Kind mit ~** a Down's (syndrome) child

Do|yen [doa'jɛ̃:] M **-s, -s** (*lit, fig*) doyen

Do|yen|ne [doa'jɛn] F **-, -n** doyenne

Doz. *abbr von* **Dozent**

Do|zent [do'tsɛnt] M **-en, -en, Do|zen|tin** [-'tsɛntɪn] F **-, -nen** lecturer (*für in*), (assistant) professor (*US*) (*für of*)

Do|zen|tur [dotsɛn'tu:ɐ] F **-, -en** lectureship (*für in*), (assistant) professorship (*US*) (*für of*)

do|zie|ren [do'tsi:rən] *ptp* **doziert** (*Univ*) **VI** to lecture (*über +acc* on, *an +dat* at); (*pej auch*) to hold forth (*über +acc* on), to pontificate (*über +acc* about) **VT** to lecture in

do|zie|rend ADJ (*pej*) pontificating, lecturing

Do|zier|ton M *pl* **-töne** (*pej*) pontificating tone

dpa [de:pe:'|a:] F **-** *abbr von* **Deutsche Presse--Agentur**

dpt *abbr von* **Dioptrie**

Dr. *abbr von* **Doktor ~ rer. nat./rer. pol./phil.** PhD; **~ theol./jur.** DD/LLD; **~ med.** MD

Dra|che ['draxə] M **-n, -n** → *auch* **Drachen** a (*Myth*) dragon b (*Astron*) Draco

Dra|chen ['draxn] M **-s, -** a (= *Papierdrachen*) kite; (*Sport:* = *Fluggerät*) hang-glider; **einen ~ steigen lassen** to fly a kite b (*pej inf:* = *zänkisches Weib*) dragon (*inf*), battle-axe (*Brit inf*), battle-ax (*US inf*) c (= *Wikingerschiff*) longship; (= *Segelschiff*) dragon class yacht

Dra|chen-: Dra|chen|blut NT (*Myth*) dragon's blood; **Dra|chen|flie|gen** NT **-s,** *no pl* (*Sport*) hang-gliding; **Dra|chen|flie|ger(in)** M(F) (*Sport*) hang-glider; **Dra|chen|saat** F (*pej geh*) seeds of discord *pl*; **Dra|chen|tö|ter** [-tø:tɐ] M **-s, -** dragon-killer

Drach|me ['draxmə] F **-, -n** (*Hist:* = *Währung*) drachma; (*Pharm old*) drachm

Dra|gee [dra'ʒe:] NT **-s, -s, Dra|gée** [dra'ʒe:] NT **-s, -s** a (= *Bonbon*) sugar-coated chocolate sweet; (= *Nussdragee, Mandeldragee*) dragee b (*Pharm*) dragee, sugar-coated pill *or* tablet

Dra|gee|form F **in ~** coated with sugar, in sugar-coated form

dra|gie|ren [dra'ʒi:rən] *ptp* **dragiert** VT (*Pharm*) to sugar-coat, to coat with sugar

Dra|go|man ['dra:goma:n] M **-s, -e** dragoman

Dra|go|ner [dra'go:nɐ] M **-s, -** (*Hist*) dragoon; (*pej: Frau*) battle-axe, dragon; **fluchen wie ein ~** (*inf*) to swear like a trooper (*inf*)

Drags|ter ['drɛgstɐ] M **-s, -** dragster

Draht [dra:t] M **-(e)s, ⸚e** ['drɛ:tə] wire; **per** *or* **über ~** by wire *or* (*ins Ausland*) cable; **auf ~ sein** (*inf*) to be on the ball (*inf*); (*wissensmäßig auch*) to know one's stuff; **du bist wohl heute nicht ganz auf ~** (*inf*) you're not quite with it today (*inf*); **jdn auf ~ bringen** (*inf*) to bring sb up to scratch (*Brit*) *or* speed; **einen guten ~ zu**

jdm haben to be on good terms with sb, to have a good relationship with sb → **heiß** ADJ e

Draht- *in cpds* wire; **Draht|aus|lö|ser** M (*Phot*) cable release; **Draht|bürs|te** F wire brush

drah|ten ['dra:tn] VT (*dated*) to wire, to cable

Draht-: Draht|esel M (*dated hum*) trusty bicycle; (*alt auch*) boneshaker (*inf*); **Draht|fern|se|hen** NT cable television; **Draht|funk** M wire or line broadcasting; **Draht|ge|flecht** NT wire mesh; **Draht|ge|we|be** NT wire gauze; **Draht|git|ter** NT wire netting; **Draht|haar-** (|-da|ckel) M wire-haired dachshund; **draht|-haa|rig** ADJ wire-haired; **Draht|haar|ter|ri|er** M wire-haired terrier

draht|ig ['dra:tɪç] ADJ *Haar, Mensch* wiry

Draht-: draht|los ADJ *Telegrafie* wireless; *Telefon, Nachrichtenübermittlung* cordless; **Draht|rol|le** F wire coil; **Draht|sai|te** F (*Mus*) steel string; **Draht|sche|re** F wire cutters *pl*; **Draht|schnei|der** M wire cutters *pl*

Draht|seil NT wire cable; **Nerven wie ~e** (*inf*) nerves of steel

Draht|seil-: Draht|seil|akt M (*lit, fig*) balancing act; **Draht|seil|bahn** F cable railway; **Draht|seil|künst|ler(in)** M(F) (= *Seiltänzer*) tightrope artist *or* walker

Draht-: Draht|sieb NT wire sieve; **Draht|stift** M panel pin; **Draht|ver|hau** M wire entanglement; (= *Käfig*) wire enclosure; **Draht|zan|ge** F wire cutters *pl*; **Draht|zaun** M wire fence; **Draht|zie|hen** NT **-s,** *no pl* wiredrawing; **Draht|zie|her** [-tsi:ɐ] M **-s, -, Draht|zie|he|rin** [-ərɪn] F **-, -nen** wiredrawer; (*fig*) wirepuller (*esp US*)

Drai|na|ge [drɛ'naʒə, drɛ'na:ʒ] F **-, -n** (*esp Aus, Sw*) drainage (*auch Med etc*)

drai|nie|ren [drɛ'ni:rən] *ptp* **drainiert** VTI (*esp Aus, Sw*) to drain (*auch Med*)

Drai|si|ne [drai'zi:nə, drɛ'zi:nə] F **-, -n** (*Rail*) trolley; (= *Fahrrad*) dandy horse (*old*)

dra|ko|nisch [dra'ko:nɪʃ] ADJ Draconian

drall [dral] ADJ *Mädchen, Arme* strapping, sturdy; *Busen, Hintern* ample; *Backen* rounded

Drall [dral] M **-(e)s, -e** a (*von Kugel, Ball*) spin; (*um Längsachse auch*) twist; (= *Abweichung von Bahn*) swerve; (*inf: von Auto*) pull; **einem Ball einen ~ geben** to give a ball (some) spin, to spin a ball; **einen ~ nach links haben** (*Auto*) to pull to the left b (*fig:* = *Hang*) tendency, inclination; **sie hat einen ~ nach links** she inclines *or* leans to the left

Dra|lon® ['dra:lɔn] NT **-(s),** *no pl* Dralon®

Dra|ma ['dra:ma] NT **-s, Dramen** [-mən] (*lit:* = *Stück, Gattung, fig:* = *dramatisches Geschehen*) drama; (*fig*) (= *Katastrophe*) disaster; (= *Aufheben*) to-do (*inf*)

Dra|ma|tik [dra'ma:tɪk] F **-,** *no pl* (*lit, fig*) drama

Dra|ma|ti|ker [dra'ma:tikɐ] M **-s, -, Dra|ma|ti|ke|rin** [-ərɪn] F **-, -nen** dramatist

dra|ma|tisch [dra'ma:tɪʃ] (*lit, fig*) ADJ dramatic; ADV dramatically; **machs nicht so ~!** don't be so dramatic!

dra|ma|ti|sie|ren [dramati'zi:rən] *ptp* **dramatisiert** VT (*lit, fig*) to dramatize

Dra|ma|ti|sie|rung F **-, -en** dramatization

Dra|ma|turg [drama'tʊrk] M **-en, -en** [-gn], **Dra|ma|tur|gin** [-'tʊrgɪn] F **-, -nen** dramaturge (*form*), literary manager

Dra|ma|tur|gie [dramatʊr'gi:] F **-, -n** [-'gi:ən] dramaturgy; (= *Abteilung*) drama department

dra|ma|tur|gisch [drama'tʊrgɪʃ] ADJ dramatic, dramaturgical (*rare*); *Abteilung* drama *attr*

dran [dran] ADV (*inf*) → *auch* **daran** a (= *an der Reihe*) **jetzt bist du ~** it's your turn now; (*beim Spielen auch*) it's your go now; (**wenn er erwischt wird,) dann ist er ~** (= *am Arsch*) (if he gets caught) he'll be for it (*inf*), (if he gets caught) he'll be for the high jump (*Brit inf*); **er war ~** (= *musste sterben*) his time had come; **morgen ist Englisch ~** we've got English tomor-

row → **drauf, drum, glauben**

b **schlecht ~ sein** to be in a bad way; (= *unglücklich auch*) to be unfortunate; **gut ~ sein** to be well off; (= *glücklich*) to be fortunate; (*gesundheitlich*) to be well; **früh/spät ~ sein** to be early/late

c **an ihm ist nichts ~** (= *sehr dünn*) he's nothing but skin and bone; (= *nicht attraktiv, nicht interessant*) there is nothing to him; **an dem Hühnchen ist nichts ~** there is no meat on that chicken; **was ist an ihm ~, dass ...?** what is there about him that ...?; **da ist alles ~!** that's got everything; **da wird schon etwas (Wahres) ~ sein** there must be some truth *or* something in that; **an den Gerüchten ist nichts ~** there's nothing in those rumours; **an dem Auto ist irgendetwas ~** there is something wrong *or* the matter with the car; **ich weiß nicht, wie ich (bei ihm) ~ bin** I don't know where I stand (with him)

Drä|na|ge [drɛ'na:ʒə] F **-, -n** drainage

dran+blei|ben VI *sep irreg aux sein* (*inf*) a (= *sich nicht entfernen*) to stay close; (*am Apparat*) to hang on; (*an der Arbeit*) to stick at it; **am Gegner/an der Arbeit ~** to stick to one's opponent/at one's work b (= *sterben*) to kick the bucket (*inf*); **er ist bei der Operation drangeblieben** the operation did for him (*inf*)

drang *pret von* **dringen**

Drang [draŋ] M **-(e)s, ⸚e** ['drɛŋə] a (= *Antrieb*) urge (*auch Physiol*), impulse; (= *Sehnsucht*) yearning (*nach* for); (*nach Wissen*) thirst (*nach* for); **~ nach Bewegung** urge *or* impulse to move; **ich habe einen ~** (*inf: zur Toilette*) I'm dying to go (*inf*) → **Sturm** a b **der ~ zum Tor** (*Sport*) the surge (*Brit*) *or* drive (*US*) toward(s) the goal; **der ~ nach Osten** the drive toward(s) the East c (*geh:* = *Druck*) pressure; **im ~ der Ereignisse** under the pressure of events

dran+ge|ben VT *sep irreg* (*inf*) a (= *zufügen*) to add (*an +acc* to); **ich geb noch 10 Minuten dran** I'll wait another ten minutes, I'll give you/him *etc* another ten minutes b (= *opfern*) to give up; *Leben auch* to sacrifice; *Geld* to fork out (*inf*); **sein Leben für etw ~** to give one's life for sth

dran+ge|hen VI *sep irreg aux sein* (*inf*) a (= *berühren, sich zu schaffen machen an*) to touch (*an etw acc* sth); **an etw** (*acc*) (**zu nahe**) **~** (= *sich nähern*) to go (too) close to sth; **das Telefon klingelte, er ging aber nicht dran** the phone rang but he didn't answer it b (= *in Angriff nehmen*) **~, etw zu tun** to get down to doing sth; **es wird Zeit, dass ich drangehe** it's time I got down to it

Drän|ge|lei [drɛŋə'lai] F **-, -en** (*inf*) pushing, jostling; (*im Verkehr*) jostling; (= *Bettelei*) pestering

drän|geln ['drɛŋln] (*inf*) **VI** to push, to jostle; (*im Verkehr*) to jostle **VTI** (= *betteln*) to pester **VR** **sich nach vorne** *etc* **~** to push one's way to the front *etc*; **sich ~, etw zu tun** (*fig*) to fall over oneself to do sth (*inf*)

drän|gen ['drɛŋən] **VI** a (*in Menge*) to push, to press; **die Menge drängte zum Ausgang** the crowd pressed toward(s) the exit

b (*Sport:* = *offensiv spielen*) to press *or* push forward

c (= *fordern*) to press (*auf +acc* for); **darauf ~, eine Antwort zu erhalten, auf Antwort ~** to press for an answer; **darauf ~, dass jd etw tut/dass etw getan wird** to press for sb to do sth/for sth to be done; **zum Aufbruch/zur Eile ~** to be insistent that one should leave/hurry

d (*zeitlich*) to be pressing, to press; **die Zeit drängt** time is pressing, time presses; **es drängt (nicht)** it's (not) pressing *or* urgent

VT a (*mit Ortsangabe*) to push

b (= *auffordern*) to press, to urge; **es drängt mich, das zu tun** I feel moved *or* the urge to do that

VR (*Menge*) to throng or crowd; (*fig: Termine etc*) to mount up; **sich nach vorn/durch die Menge ~** to push *or* force one's way to the front/through the crowd → *auch* **gedrängt**

Drän|gen NT **-s**, *no pl* urging; (= *Bitten*) requests *pl*; (= *Bestehen*) insistence

drän|gend ADJ pressing, urgent

Drang|sal ['draŋza:l] F **-**, **-e** (*old, liter*) (= *Not*) hardship; (= *Leiden*) suffering, distress

drang|sa|lie|ren [draŋza'li:rən] *ptp* **drangsaliert** VT (= *plagen*) to pester, to plague; (= *unterdrücken*) to oppress

drang|voll ADJ ~e Enge (*geh*) terrible crush (of people)

dran+hal|ten *sep irreg* (*inf*) **VT** to hold up (+*dat, an* +*acc* to); **etw näher an etw** (*acc*) ~ to hold sth closer to sth **VR** (= *sich beeilen*) to hurry up, to get a move on (*inf*); (= *sich anstrengen*) to make an effort, to get one's *or* the finger out (*Brit inf*); (= *nahe dranbleiben*) to keep close to it

dran+hän|gen *sep* (*inf*) **VT** etw an etw (*acc*) ~ to hang sth onto sth; **viel Zeit etw** ~, **etw zu tun** to put a lot of time *etc* into doing sth **VI** *irreg* an etw (*dat*) ~ to hang from sth; **es hing ein Zettel dran** a tag was attached (*an* +*dat* to) **VR** to hang on; (= *verfolgen*) to stay close behind; (= *ständig begleiten*) to latch on (*bei* to); (= *jds Beispiel folgen*) to follow suit

drä|nie|ren [drε'ni:rən] *ptp* **dräniert** VT to drain

dran+kom|men VI *sep irreg aux sein* (*inf*) **a** (= *berühren*) to touch **b** (= *erreichen können*) to be able to reach (*an etw* (*acc*) sth) **c** (= *an die Reihe kommen*) to have one's turn; (*bei Spielen*) to have one's turn *or* go; (*Sch*) (*beim Melden*) to be called; (*Frage, Aufgabe etc*) to come up; **jetzt kommst du dran** now it's your turn/go; **du kommst als Erster/Nächster dran** you're first/next; **nun kommt das Schlafzimmer dran** it's the bedroom next

dran+krie|gen VT *sep* (*inf*) jdn ~ to get sb (*inf*); (*zu einer Arbeit*) to get sb to do it/sth; (*mit Witz, Streich*) to catch sb out

Drank|ton|ne ['draŋk-] F (*N Ger*) swill bucket; (*fig inf*) walking dustbin (*hum*)

dran+las|sen VT *sep irreg* (*inf*) etw (an etw *dat*) ~ to leave sth on (sth)

dran+ma|chen *sep* (*inf*) **VR** = daranmachen **VT** etw (an etw *acc*) ~ to attach sth to sth

dran+neh|men VT *sep irreg* (*inf*) Schüler to ask, to question; *Patienten* to take, to see

dran+set|zen *sep* (*inf*) **VT** **a** (= *anfügen*) ein Stück/ein Teil (an etw *acc*) ~ to add a piece/part (to sth) **b** (= *einsetzen*) seine Kraft/sein Vermögen ~ to put one's effort/money into it; **alles** ~ to make every effort; **jdn** ~ to put sb onto the job or it **VR** **a** (*nahe an etw*) sich (an etw *acc*) ~ to sit (down) next to sth **b** (= *Arbeit anfangen*) to get down to work *or* it

drans|ten ['dranstn] ADV (*hum*) am ~ → dran

dran+wol|len VI *sep* (*inf*) (= *drankommen wollen*) to want to have one's turn; (= *probieren wollen*) to want to have a go

Dra|pe|rie [drapə'ri:] F **-**, **-n** [-'ri:ən] (*old*) drapery; (= *Faltenwurf*) drapes *pl*

dra|pie|ren [dra'pi:rən] *ptp* **drapiert** VT to drape; (= *verhüllen*) to cloak

Dra|pie|rung F **-**, **-en** **a** (= *das Drapieren*) draping; (*fig*) cloaking **b** (= *Schmuck, kunstvolle Falten*) drape; **~en** (*fig*: = *beschönigende Worte*) fine phrases *pl*

Dras|tik ['drastik] F **-**, *no pl* (= *Derbheit*) drasticness; (= *Deutlichkeit*) graphicness; **etw mit besonderer** ~ **beschreiben** to describe sth particularly graphically

dras|tisch ['drastiʃ] **ADJ** (= *derb*) drastic; (= *deutlich*) graphic **ADV** (= *energisch*) kürzen drastically; (= *deutlich*) zeigen, verdeutlichen explicitly; ~ **vorgehen** to take drastic measures; ~ **sparen** to cut spending drastically; **sich** ~ **ausdrücken** to use strong language

dräu|en ['drɔyən] VI (*poet*) = drohen VI c

drauf [drauf] ADV (*inf*) → *auch* darauf immer feste ~! get stuck in there! (*inf*), let him have

it! (*inf*); ~ **und dran sein, etw zu tun** to be on the point *or* verge of doing sth → **draufhaben**

Drauf-: drauf+be|kom|men *ptp* **draufbekommen** VT *sep irreg* (*inf*) **eins** ~ to be given a smack; **Drauf|ga|be** F **a** (*Comm*) deposit **b** (*Aus*) = Zugabe; **Drauf|gän|ger** [-gεŋe] M **-s**, **-**, **Drauf|gän|ge|rin** [-ərɪn] F **-**, **-nen** daredevil, adventurous type; (= *Mann: bei Frauen*) predator; **drauf|gän|ge|risch** [-gεŋərɪʃ] ADJ daring, adventurous; (*negativ*) reckless; (*bei Frauen*) predatory, wolfish; **Drauf|gän|ger|tum** NT **-s**, *no pl* daring, adventurousness; (*negativ*) recklessness; (*bei Frauen*) predatory ways *pl*; **drauf+ge|ben** VT *irreg sep* **a** jdm eins ~ (*inf*) to give sb a smack **b** (= *dazugeben*) noch etwas ~ to add some extra (*inf*) **c** (*Aus*: = *als Zugabe anfügen*) to sing/play *etc* as an encore; **drauf+ge|hen** VI *sep irreg aux sein* (*inf*) (= *entzweigehen*) to fall apart *or* to bits; (= *sterben*) to bite the dust (*inf*); (*Geld*) to disappear; **Drauf-geld** NT extra payment; **drauf+ha|ben** VT *sep irreg* (*inf*) Sprüche, Antwort to come out with; **er hat es drauf** he knows his stuff (*inf*); **jetzt hat sie es endlich drauf** she's finally got it; **zei-gen, was man draufhat** to show what one is made of; **den Chauvi** ~ to be a real chauvinist; **etw** ~ (*sl*: = *können*) to be able to do sth no bother (*inf*); **Kenntnisse** ~ to be well up on sth (*inf*); **Witze, Sprüche** ~ to have sth off pat (*inf*); **schwer was** ~ (*sl*) to know one's stuff (*inf*) or onions (*Brit inf*); **160 Sachen** ~ (*sl*) to be doing 160; **drauf+hal|ten** *sep irreg* (*inf*) **VT** etw (auf etw *acc*) ~ to hold sth on (sth) **VI** (= *als Ziel angehen*) to aim for it; **drauf+hau|en** *sep irreg* VI (*inf*: = *schlagen*) to hit hard; **drauf+kom|men** VI *sep irreg aux sein* (*inf*) (= *sich erinnern*) to remember; (= *begreifen*) to catch on, to get it (*inf*); **jdm** ~ to get on to sb (*inf*); **drauf+krie|gen** VT *sep* (*inf*) etw (auf etw *acc*) ~ to get or fit sth on(to sth); **eins** ~ to be given what for (*Brit inf*), to be told off; (= *geschlagen werden*) to be given a smack; (= *Schicksalsschlag erhalten*) to receive a blow; (= *besiegt werden*) to be given a thrashing (*inf*); **drauf+las|sen** VT *sep irreg* (*inf*) etw (auf etw *dat*) ~ to leave sth on (sth); **drauf+le|gen** VT **a** to lay out; **20 Euro** ~ to lay out an extra 20 euros **b** etw (auf etw *acc*) ~ to put *or* lay sth on(to sth) **VI** (= *mehr bezahlen*) to pay more

drauf|los [drauf'lo:s] ADV (*nur*) immer feste *or* munter ~! (just) keep at it!, keep it up!

drauf|los-: drauf|los+ar|bei|ten VI *sep* (*inf*) to work away, to beaver away (*Brit inf*); (= *anfangen*) to start working; **drauf|los+fah|ren** VI *sep irreg aux sein* (*auf ein Ziel*) to make or head straight for it; (*ohne Ziel*) to just set off (in any direction); **drauf|los+ge|hen** VI *sep irreg aux sein* (*inf*) (*auf ein Ziel*) to make straight for it; (*ohne Ziel*) to set off (with no special destination); (= *nicht zögern*) to set to work; **drauf|-los+ma|len** VI *sep* (*inf*) to paint away; (= *anfangen*) to start painting; **drauf|los+re|den** VI *sep* (*inf*) to talk away; (= *anfangen*) to start talking; **drauf|los+schie|ßen** VI *sep irreg* (*inf*) to fire away; **drauf|los+schla|gen** VI *sep irreg* (*inf*) to hit out, to let fly (*inf*)

drauf-: drauf+ma|chen VT *sep* (*inf*) etw (auf etw *acc*) ~ to put sth on(to sth); **einen** ~ to make a night of it (*inf*); **drauf+sat|teln** VT *sep* (*inf*) to slap on (top); **drauf sein** ▲ VI *irreg aux sein* (*inf*) to be in a bad/good mood; **wie ist der denn drauf?** what kind of trip is he on? (*inf*); **drauf+set|zen** VT *sep* (*fig inf*) **eins** ~ to go one step further; **Drauf|sicht** F top view; **drauf+ste|hen** VI *sep irreg* (*inf*) aux haben *or* (*dial*) sein etw steht **drauf** sth is on it; **auf etw** (*dat*) ~ (*Mensch, Sache*) to stand on sth; (*Aufschrift*) to be on sth; (*da*) **stehe ich nicht drauf** (*fig sl*) it doesn't turn me on (*inf*); **drauf+sto|ßen** *sep irreg* VI **a** aux sein to come or hit upon it; (= *gegen etw stoßen*) to bump or run into it; (= *finden*) to come across it **VT** jdn ~ to point it out to sb; **drauf+stür|zen** VR *sep* (*inf*) to swoop or

pounce on it/them, to rush to get one's hands on it/them; **drauf+zah|len** *sep* (*inf*) **VT** = drauflegen VT a **VI a** = drauflegen VI **b** (*fig*: = *Einbußen erleiden*) to pay the price

draus [draus] ADV = daraus

draus-: draus+brin|gen VT *sep irreg* (*dial*) jdn ~ (= *Konzentration stören*) to make sb lose track, to distract sb; (= *irremachen*) to put sb off; **draus+kom|men** VI *sep irreg aux sein* **a** (*dial, Aus*: = *aus dem Konzept kommen*) to lose track **b** (*Sw*: = *verstehen*) to see, to get it (*inf*)

drau|ßen ['drausn] ADV outside; (= *im Freien auch*) out of doors, outdoors; (= *da draußen, weit weg von hier*) out there; (= *im Ausland*) abroad; ~ **(an der Front)** out there (on the front); ~ **auf dem Lande/dem Balkon/im Garten** out in the country/on the balcony/in the garden; ~ **(auf dem Meer)** out there/here; **da/hier** ~ out there/here; **ganz da** ~ way out there; ~ **(vor der Tür)** at the door; **nach** ~ outside; (*ferner weg*) out there; **weit/weiter** ~ far/further out; ~ **bleiben/lassen** to stay/leave out (*auch fig inf*) outside; **„Hunde müssen** ~ **bleiben"** "no dogs (please)", "please leave your dog outside"; **etw** ~ **tragen** to wear sth outside

Drechs|el|bank F *pl* -bänke wood(turning) lathe

drechs|eln ['drεksln] **VT** to turn (*on a wood lathe*); (*fig pej*) to overelaborate; *Vers* to turn → *auch* **gedrechselt** **VI** to work the (wood) lathe

Drechs|ler ['drεkslɐ] M **-s**, **-**, **Drechs|le|rin** [-ərɪn] F **-**, **-nen** (wood)turner

Drechs|ler|ar|beit F (wood)turning; (= *Gegenstand*) piece turned on the lathe

Drechs|le|rei [drεkslə'rai] F **-**, **-en** (= *Werkstatt*) (wood)turner's workshop; (= *Handwerk*) (wood)turning

Dreck [drεk] M **-(e)s**, *no pl* **a** dirt; (*esp ekelhaft*) filth; (= *Schlamm*) mud; (= *Kot*) muck; (*fig*) (= *Schund*) rubbish; (= *Schmutz, Obszönes*) dirt, muck; (*stärker*) filth; (*inf*: = *schlimme Lage*) mess, jam (*inf*); ~ **machen** to make a mess; **in/mit** ~ **und Speck** (= *ungewaschen*) unwashed; **im** ~ **sit-zen** *or* **stecken** (*inf*) to be in a mess *or* jam (*inf*); **aus dem größten** *or* **gröbsten** ~ **heraus sein** (*inf*) to be through *or* past the worst; **jdn wie den letzten** ~ **behandeln** (*inf*) to treat sb like dirt; **der letzte** ~ **sein** (*inf: Mensch*) to be the lowest of the low; ~ **am Stecken haben** (*inf*) to have a skeleton in the cupboard; **etw in den** ~ **ziehen** *or* **treten** (*fig*) to drag sth through the mud → **Karren b**, **bewerfen a** **b** (*inf*) (= *Angelegenheit, Kram*) business, stuff (*inf*); (= *Kleinigkeit*) little thing; **sich einen** ~ **um jdn/etw kümmern** *or* **scheren** not to care *or* give a damn about sb/sth (*inf*); **mach deinen** ~ **alleine!** do it yourself; **die Nase in jeden** ~ **stecken** (*inf*) to poke one's nose into everyone's business *or* into everything; **das geht ihn einen** ~ **an** that's none of his business, that's got damn all to do with him (*inf*); **einen** ~ **ist er/hast du** like hell he is/you have (*inf*)

Dreck-: Dreck|ar|beit F (*inf*) **a** (*lit, fig*: = *schmutzige Arbeit*) dirty work **b** (*pej*: = *niedere Arbeit*) drudgery *no pl*; **Dreck|ei|mer** M (*im Haus*) rubbish bin (*Brit*), trash can (*US*); (*im Freien*) dustbin, trash can (*US*); **Dreck|fin|ger** PL (*lit, fig*) dirty fingers *pl*; **Dreck|fink** M (*inf*) = Dreckspatz

dre|ckig ['drεkɪç] **ADJ** (*lit, fig*) dirty; (*stärker*) filthy **ADV** (*inf*) ~ **lachen** to give a dirty laugh; **es geht mir** ~ I'm in a bad way; (*finanziell*) I'm badly off; **wenn man ihn erwischt, geht es ihm** ~ if they catch him, he'll be sorry *or* he'll be in for it (*inf*)

Dreck-: Dreck|loch NT (*pej*) hole (*inf*), hovel; **Dreck|nest** NT (*pej*) dump (*inf*), hole (*inf*); **Dreck|pfo|ten** PL (*inf: lit, fig*) dirty *or* filthy paws *pl*; **Dreck|sack** M (*pej inf*) dirty bastard (*sl*); **Dreck|sau** F (*vulg*) filthy swine (*inf*); **Dreck|schleu|der** F (*pej*) (= *Mundwerk*) foul mouth; (= *Mensch*) foul-mouthed person; (=

Kraftwerk, Auto) environmental hazard; **Dreck|schwein** NT (*inf*) dirty pig (*inf*)

Drecks|kerl M (*inf*) dirty swine (*inf*), louse (*inf*)

Dreck|spatz M (*inf*) (= *Kind*) mucky pup (*Brit inf*), grubby kid; (*Schimpfwort*) filthy beggar (*inf*)

Dreck(s)|zeug NT (*inf*) damn *or* blasted stuff (*inf*); **das ist doch ein ~** damn this stuff (*inf*)

Dreck|wet|ter NT (*inf*) filthy weather (*inf*)

Dreh [dreː] M **-s, -s** *or* **-e** **a** (= *List*) dodge; (= *Kunstgriff*) trick; **den ~ heraushaben, etw zu tun** to have got the knack of doing sth; **den (richtigen) ~ heraushaben** *or* **weghaben** (*inf*) to have got the hang of it **b** = **Drehe**

Dreh-: Dreh|ach|se F axis of rotation; **Dreh|ar|beit** F **a** (*von Dreher*) lathe work; (= *Gegenstand*) piece turned on the lathe **b** **Dreharbeiten** PL (*Film*) shooting *sing*; **Dreh|bank** F *pl* **-bänke** lathe; **dreh|bar** ADJ (*rundum*) rotating, revolving *attr*; (*um einen Festpunkt*) swivelling *attr* (*Brit*), swiveling *attr* (*US*); (= *drehgelagert*) pivoted; **~ sein** to rotate *or* revolve/swivel; **Dreh|be|ginn** M (*Film*) start of shooting; **Dreh|be|we|gung** F turn(ing motion); (*esp Tech*) rotation, rotary motion; **eine ~ machen** to turn/rotate; **Dreh|blei|stift** M propelling (*Brit*) *or* mechanical (*US*) pencil; **Dreh|brü|cke** F swing bridge; **Dreh|buch** (*Film*) screenplay, (film) script; **Dreh|buch|au|tor(in)** M(F) scriptwriter, screenplay writer; **Dreh|büh|ne** F revolving stage

Dre|he [ˈdreːə] F **-, no pl** (*inf*) **(so) um die ~** (*zeitlich*) *or* thereabouts, (a)round about then; **(so) in der ~** (*örtlich*) (there) *or* thereabouts, (a)round about there

dre|hen [ˈdreːən] **VT** to turn (*auch Tech: auf Drehbank*); (*um eine Achse auch*) to rotate; (*um Mittelpunkt auch*) to revolve, to rotate; *Stuhl* to swivel; *Kreisel* to spin; *Kopf auch* to twist; *Zwirne* to twist; *Zigaretten, Pillen* to roll; *Film* to shoot; (*fig:* = *verdrehen*) to twist; (*inf:* = *schaffen*) to fix (*inf*), to work (*inf*); **das Gas hoch/auf klein ~** to turn the gas up high/down low; **Fleisch durch den Wolf ~** to put meat through the mincer (*Brit*) *or* meat grinder (*US*); **ein Ding ~** (*sl*) to play a prank, to pull off a prank; (*Verbrecher*) to pull a job (*inf*) *or* caper (*inf*); **wie man es auch dreht und wendet** no matter how you look at it → **Däumchen b, Runde c, Strick¹ a**

VI to turn; (*Wind*) to shift, to change; (*Film*) to shoot, to film; (= *Zigaretten drehen*) to roll one's own; **an etw** (*dat*) **~** to turn sth; **am Radio ~** to turn a knob on the radio; **daran ist nichts zu ~ und deuteln** (*fig*) there are no two ways about it

VR **a** (= *sich umdrehen, kreisen*) to turn (*um a-bout*); (*um Mittelpunkt auch*) to revolve, to rotate; (*um Achse auch*) to rotate; (*sehr schnell: Kreisel*) to spin; (*Wind*) to shift, to change; **sich auf den Rücken ~** to turn on(to) one's back; **sich um etw ~** to revolve *or* rotate around sth; **sich um sich (selbst) ~** to rotate, to revolve on its own axis; (*Mensch*) to turn round (*Brit*), to turn around (*US*); (*Auto*) to spin; **sich im Kreise ~** to turn round and round (*Brit*), to turn around and around (*US*); **mir drehte sich alles** everything's spinning about me; **mir dreht sich alles im Kopf** my head is spinning *or* swimming; **sich ~ und winden** (*fig*) to twist and turn

b **sich um etw ~** (= *betreffen*) to concern sth, to be about sth; (*um zentrale Frage*) to centre (*Brit*) *or* center (*US*) on sth; **alles dreht sich um sie** everything revolves (a)round her; (*steht im Mittelpunkt*) she's the centre (*Brit*) *or* center (*US*) of attention *or* interest; **es dreht sich darum, dass ...** the point is that ...; **meine Frage dreht sich darum, ob ...** my question is whether ...; **in dieser Sendung drehte es sich um ...**, **die Sendung drehte sich um ...** the broadcast concerned ... *or* was about ...

Dre|her¹ [ˈdreːɐ] M **-s, -** (= *Tanz*) country waltz

Dre|her² [ˈdreːɐ] M **-s, -**, **Dre|he|rin** [-ərɪn] F **-, -nen** lathe operator; (= *Drechsler auch*) (wood) turner

Dreh-: Dreh|er|laub|nis F (*Film*) (*allgemein*) filming permission; (*konkret*) filming permit; **Dreh|ge|schwin|dig|keit** F rotary or rotating speed; **Dreh|ge|stell** NT (*Rail*) bogie; **Dreh|im|puls** M angular momentum; **Dreh|knopf** M knob; **Dreh|kran** M slewing or rotary crane; **Dreh|kreuz** NT turnstile; **Dreh|lei|er** F barrel-organ, hurdy-gurdy; **Dreh|lei|ter** F turntable ladder; **Dreh|ma|schi|ne** F motorized (metal-turning) lathe; **Dreh|mo|ment** NT torque; **Dreh|or|gel** F barrel organ, hurdy-gurdy; **Dreh|or|gel|spie|ler(in)** M(F) organ-grinder, hurdy-gurdy man/woman; **Dreh|ort** M *pl* **-orte** (*Film*) location; **Dreh|pau|se** F (*Film*) break in shooting; **Dreh|punkt** M pivot; **Dreh|res|tau|rant** NT revolving restaurant; **Dreh|schal|ter** M rotary switch; **Dreh|schei|be** F **a** (*Rail*) turntable **b** (= *Töpferscheibe*) potter's wheel **c** (*fig*) nerve centre (*Brit*) or center (*US*); **Dreh|strom** M three-phase current; **Dreh|stuhl** M swivel chair; **Dreh|tag** M (*Film*) day of shooting; **Dreh|tür** F revolving door; **Dreh- und An|gel|punkt** M → **Angelpunkt**

Dre|hung [ˈdreːʊŋ] F **-, -en** **a** turn; (= *ganze Drehung um eigene Achse auch*) rotation; (*um einen Punkt auch*) revolution; **eine halbe/ganze ~** a half/complete turn; **eine ~ um 180°** a 180° turn, a turn through 180° **b** (= *das Drehen*) turning; (*um eigene Achse auch*) rotation; (*um einen Punkt auch*) revolving

Dreh|wurm M (*inf*) **einen** *or* **den ~ kriegen/haben** to get/feel giddy

Dreh|zahl F number of revolutions or revs; (*pro Minute*) revolutions or revs *pl* per minute, rpm

Dreh|zahl-: Dreh|zahl|be|reich M (*Aut*) engine speed range; **im niederen/hohen ~** at low/high revs; **Dreh|zahl|mes|ser** M **-s, -** rev counter

drei [drai] NUM three; **von uns ~en** from the three of us; **die (Heiligen) Drei Könige** the Three Kings, the Magi; **die ~ Weisen aus dem Morgenland** the Three Wise Men from the East; **die ~ tollen Tage** *the last three days of Fasching in Germany* **aller guten Dinge sind ~!** (*prov*) all good things come in threes!; (*nach zwei missglückten Versuchen*) third time lucky!; **er arbeitet/isst für ~** (*inf*) he does the work of/eats enough for three; **etw in ~ Worten erklären** (*inf*) to explain sth briefly *or* in a few words; **ehe man bis ~ zählen konnte** (*inf*) in a trice (*esp Brit*), before you could say Jack Robinson (*inf*); **sie sieht aus, als ob sie nicht bis ~ zählen könnte** (*inf*) she looks pretty empty-headed; (= *unschuldig*) she looks as if butter wouldn't melt in her mouth → *auch* **vier**

Drei [drai] F **-, -en** three → *auch* **Vier**

drei-, Drei- *in cpds* three-, tri-; **Drei|ach|tel|takt** M three-eight time; **drei|ad(e)rig** [ˈdrailad(ə)rɪç] ADJ (*Elec*) three-core; **drei|bei|nig** ADJ three-legged; **Drei|bett|zim|mer** NT three-bed room, room with three beds; **drei|blätt|rig** [ˈdraiblɛtrɪç] ADJ (*Bot*) three-leaved; **~es Kleeblatt** three-leav(ed) clover; **Drei|bund** M **-, no pl** (*Hist*) Triple Alliance (*between Germany, Austria-Hungary and Italy in 1882*)

Drei-D- [drai'deː] *in cpds* 3-D; **Drei-D-Bril|le** F 3-D glasses *pl* or specs *pl*

Drei-: Drei|de|cker [-dɛkɐ] M **-s, -** (*Aviat*) triplane; (*Naut*) three-decker; **drei|di|men|sio|nal** ADJ three-dimensional; **Drei|di|men|sio|na|li|tät** F **-, no pl** three-dimensionality

Drei|eck [ˈdraiɛk] NT **-(e)s, -e** triangle; (= *Zeichendreieck*) set square; (*Sport:* = *Winkel*) top left/right hand corner of the goal; **das Goldene ~** the golden triangle

drei|eckig ADJ triangular, three-sided

Drei|ecks-: Drei|ecks|ge|schäft NT (*Econ*) three-way deal, triangular transaction (*spec*); **Drei|ecks|tuch** NT *pl* **-tücher** triangular scarf; (*um die Schultern getragen*) triangular shawl; (*Med*) triangular bandage; **Drei|ecks|ver|hält|nis** NT (*eternal*) triangle; **ein ~ haben** to be involved in an eternal triangle

drei|ei|nig [drai'ainɪç] ADJ triune, three in one *pred*; **der ~e Gott** the Holy Trinity, the Triune God

Drei|ei|nig|keit F Trinity; **die ~ Gottes** the Holy Trinity

Drei|er [ˈdraiɐ] M **-s, -** **a** (*Aus, S Ger:* = *Ziffer, Note*) three **b** (*Sport*) (*Eislauf etc*) three; (*Golf*) threesome; **ein flotter ~** (*inf: Sex*) a threesome (*inf*) **c** (*Hist:* = *Münze*) three pfennig piece, ≈ thrupence (*Brit*)

Drei|er-: Drei|er|grup|pe F group of three; **Drei|er|kon|fe|renz** F (*Telec*) three-way calling; **Drei|er|pack** NT three-pack, triple pack; **Drei|er|rei|he** F row of three; **in ~n** (*von Personen*) three abreast

drei|fach [ˈdraifax] ADJ triple, threefold (*liter*); **die ~e Menge** three times *or* triple *or* treble the amount; **ein ~es Hoch!** three cheers! → **Ausfertigung** **ADV** three times; **~ abgesichert/verstärkt** three times as *or* trebly secure/reinforced → **vierfach**

Drei|fa|che(s) [ˈdraifaxə] NT *decl as adj* **das Dreifache** three times *or* triple *or* treble the amount, three times as much; **9 ist das Dreifache von 3** 9 is *or* equals three times 3; **ein Dreifaches kosten** to cost three times as much; **er verdient das Dreifache von dem, was ich bekomme** he earns three times as much as I do *or* treble the amount that I do; **etw um das Dreifache vermehren** to multiply sth three times *or* (*Zahl auch*) by three; **auf das Dreifache steigen** to treble, to triple

Drei|fach-: Drei|fach|sieg M (*Sport*) triple victory, one-two-three victory; **Drei|fach|steck|do|se** F (*Elec*) three-way *or* triple socket; **Drei|fach|ste|cker** M three-way adapter

Drei-: drei|fal|tig [-faltɪç] ADJ = **dreieinig**; **drei|fäl|tig** [-fɛltɪç] ADJ = **dreifach**; **Drei|fal|tig|keit** F **-, no pl** Trinity; **Drei|fal|tig|keits|fest** NT, **Drei|fal|tig|keits|sonn|tag** M Trinity Sunday; **Drei|far|ben|druck** M **a** (*Verfahren*) three-colour (*Brit*) *or* three-color (*US*) printing **b** (= *Gedrucktes*) three-colour (*Brit*) *or* three-color (*US*) print; **drei|far|big**, **drei|fär|big** [-fɛrbɪç] (*Aus*) ADJ three-colour *attr* (*Brit*), three-color *attr* (*US*), three-coloured (*Brit*), three-colored (*US*), trichromatic (*form*); **Drei|fel|der|wirt|schaft** F three-field system; **Drei|fuß** M tripod; (= *Gestell für Kessel*) trivet; (= *Schemel*) three-legged stool; **drei|fü|ßig** ADJ *Vers* three-foot *attr*

Drei|gang M **, no pl** (*inf*) = **Dreigangschaltung**

Drei|gang-: Drei|gang|ge|trie|be NT three-speed gear; **Drei|gang|rad** NT three-speed bike; **Drei|gang|schal|tung** F three-speed gear; **ein Fahrrad mit ~** a three-speed bicycle

Drei-: Drei|ge|spann NT troika; (*fig*) threesome; (*an leitender Stelle*) triumvirate; **Drei|ge|stirn** NT (*lit*) triple star; (*fig geh*) big three; **drei|ge|stri|chen** ADJ (*Mus*) **das ~e C/F** the C/F two octaves above middle C; **drei|ge|teilt** ADJ (*-gətailt*) divided into three (parts); **drei|glie|de|rig** ADJ *System* three-tier *attr*; (*Math*) trinomial; **Drei|glie|de|rung** F (= *das Gegliedertsein*) three-part *or* tripartite structure; (= *das Gliedern*) division into three (parts); **drei|glied|rig** [-gliːdrɪç] ADJ (*Math*) trinomial; **Drei|gro|schen|heft(chen)** NT, **Drei|gro|schen|ro|man** M (*pej*) penny-dreadful (*dated Brit inf*), trashy paperback, dime novel (*US*)

Drei|heit F **-, no pl** trinity

Drei-: drei|hun|dert [ˈdraiˈhʊndɐt] NUM three hundred → *auch* **vierhundert**; **Drei|kampf** M three-part competition (*100m sprint, long jump and shot put*); **Drei|kant** [ˈdraikant] NT

OR M **-(e)s, -e** trihedron; **Drei|kant|schlüs-
sel** M (*Tech*) (*male*) triangular spanner (*Brit*)
or wrench (*US*); **Drei|kä|se|hoch** [drai'kɛːzə-
hoːx] M **-s, -s** (*inf*) tiny tot (*inf*); **Drei|klang** M
(*Mus*) triad; **Drei|klas|sen|wahl|sys|tem** NT
(*Hist*) three-class electoral system (*in Prussia
1850-1918*); **Drei|kö|nigs|fest** NT (feast of) Epiphany;
Drei|kö|nigs|tag M feast of Epiphany; **Drei-
län|der|eck** NT place where three countries
meet; **Drei|li|ter|au|to, Drei-Li|ter-Au|to** NT
three-litre (*Brit*) or three-liter (*US*) car; **Drei|-
mäch|te|pakt** M (*Hist*) three-power or tripar-
tite pact (*between Germany, Italy and Japan*),
Axis pact

drei|mal ['draimaːl] ADV three times, thrice
(*old*) → *auch* **viermal**

Drei-: Drei|mas|ter ['draimastɐ] M **-s, -** three-
-master; **Drei|mei|len|gren|ze** F three-mile
limit; **Drei|mei|len|zo|ne** F three-mile zone;
Drei|me|ter|brett NT three-metre (*Brit*) or
three-meter (*US*) board

drein [drain] ADV (*inf*) = **darein**

drein- *in cpds* → *auch* **darein-: drein+bli|cken**
VI *sep* **traurig** *etc* ~ to look sad *etc*; **drein+fah|-
ren** VI *sep irreg aux sein* (*dial*) to intervene;
drein+fin|den VR *sep irreg* (*inf*) → **dareinfin-
den**; **drein+fü|gen** VR *sep* to resign oneself (to
it), to come to terms with it; **drein+re|den** VI
sep (*inf*) (= *dazwischenreden*) to interrupt; (= *sich
einmischen*) to interfere (*bei, in, with*); **ich lasse
mir in dieser Angelegenheit von niemandem ~** I
won't have anyone interfering (with this); **er
ließ sich nirgends ~** he would never be told;
drein+schau|en VI *sep* (*esp dial*) **traurig** *etc* ~
to look sad *etc*; **drein+schla|gen** VI *sep irreg*
(*dial*) to weigh in (*inf*)

Drei-: Drei|pha|sen|strom M three-phase cur-
rent; **drei|po|lig** [-poːlɪç] ADJ three-pole *attr*,
with three poles; *Kabel* three-core; *Steckdose,
Stecker* three-pin; **Drei|punkt|(si|cher|heits|)-
gurt** M lap and diagonal seat belt; **Drei|rad**
NT tricycle; (*inf:* = *Auto*) three-wheeler; **drei|-
rä|de|rig, drei|räd|rig** ADJ three-wheeled;
Drei|rad|wa|gen M three-wheeled vehicle,
three-wheeler; **drei|sai|tig** ADJ (*Mus*) *Instru-
ment* three-stringed; **Drei|satz** M (*Math*) rule
of three

Drei|satz-: Drei|satz|auf|ga|be F problem
using the rule of three; **Drei|satz|rech|nung**
F calculation using the rule of three; **Drei|-
satz|tisch** M nest of tables

Drei-: drei|schif|fig [-ʃɪfɪç] ADJ *Kirche* with
three naves; **drei|spal|tig** [-ʃpaltɪç] ADJ (*Typ*)
Seite etc three-column *attr*, with three columns
(*nachgestellt*); **Drei|spitz** M three-cornered
hat, tricorn; **Drei|sprin|ger(in)** M(F) triple
jumper; **Drei|sprung** M triple jump, hop, step
and jump; **drei|spu|rig** [-ʃpuːrɪç] ADJ (*Mot*)
Fahrbahn, Verkehr etc three-lane *attr*

drei|ßig ['draisɪç] NUM thirty → *auch* **vierzig**

drei|ßig- *in cpds* → *auch* **vierzig-**

Drei|ßi|ger ['draisɪgɐ] M **-s, -, Drei|ßi|ge|rin**
[-ərɪn] F **-, -nen** thirty-year-old; (*zwischen 30
und 40*) man in his/woman in her thirties →
auch **Vierziger**[2]

drei|ßig|jäh|rig ADJ (= *dreißig Jahre dauernd*)
thirty years' *attr*, lasting thirty years; (= *dreißig
Jahre alt*) thirty years old, thirty-year-old; **der
Dreißigjährige Krieg** the Thirty Years' War

Drei|ßigs|tel[1] ['draisɪçstl] NT **-s, -** thirtieth →
auch **Viertel**[1]

Drei|ßigs|tel[2] F **-, no pl** (*Phot inf*) thirtieth (of a
second)

drei|ßigs|te(r, s) ['draisɪçstə] ADJ thirtieth

dreist [draist] ADJ bold; *Handlung auch* audacious

Dreis|tig|keit ['draistɪçkait] F **-, -en** [a] *no pl*
boldness; (*von Handlung auch*) audacity [b] (=
Bemerkung) bold remark; (= *Handlung*) bold or
audacious act

Drei-: Drei|stu|fen|plan M three-stage *or*
three-phase plan; **Drei|stu|fen|ra|ke|te** F
three-stage rocket; **drei|stu|fig** ADJ *Rakete*
three-stage *attr*, with three stages; *Plan auch*
three-phase *attr*; **eine ~e Treppe** three steps;
Drei|ta|ge|bart M stubble, three-day growth
(*esp Brit*); **Drei|tau|sen|der** M (*Berg*) 3000-
-metre (*Brit*) or -meter (*US*) peak; **drei|tei|lig**
ADJ (= *aus 3 Teilen*) *Kostüm etc* three-piece *attr*;
(= *in 3 Teile geteilt*) three-part *attr*, tripartite
(*form*); **Drei|tei|lung** F division into three;
die ~ der Streitkräfte dividing the armed forces
into three

drei vier|tel ['drai 'fɪrtl] ▲ ADJ, ADV → **viertel,
Viertel**[1]

Drei|vier|tel ['drai'fɪrtl] NT three-quarters; **in ei-
nem ~ der Zeit** in three-quarters of the time;
das ~ Saal war zu einem ~ leer the room was
three-quarters empty

Drei|vier|tel-: Drei|vier|tel|arm M (*inf*),
Drei|vier|tel|är|mel M three-quarter-(length)
sleeve; **Drei|vier|tel|ja|cke** F three-quarter-
-length coat; **Drei|vier|tel|jahr** NT nine
months *pl*, nine-month period; **drei|vier|tel-
lang** ADJ three-quarter-length; **Drei|vier|tel-
li|ter|fla|sche** F 75 cl bottle; **Drei|vier|tel-
mehr|heit** F three-quarters majority; **Drei-
vier|tel|spie|ler(in)** M(F) (*Rugby*) three-quar-
ter; **Drei|vier|tel|stun|de** F three-quarters of
an hour *no indef art*; **Drei|vier|tel|takt** M
three-four time; **im ~** in three-four time

Drei|weg- *in cpds* (*Elec*) three-way; **Drei|we|ge-
ka|ta|ly|sa|tor** M (*Aut*) three-way catalytic
converter; **geregelter ~** computer-controlled *or*
feedback three-way catalytic converter; **ungere-
gelter ~** open-loop three-way catalytic convert-
er; **Drei|weg|(laut|spre|cher)|box** F three-
-way loudspeaker system; **Drei|weg|schal|ter**
M three-way switch; **Drei|weg|ste|cker** M
three-way adapter

Drei-: drei|wer|tig ADJ (*Chem*) trivalent; (*Ling*)
three-place; **drei|wö|chent|lich** [ADV] *attr*
three-weekly ADV every three weeks, at three-
-weekly intervals; **drei|wö|chig** [-vœçɪç] ADJ
attr three-week; **Drei|zack** [-tsak] M **-s, -e** tri-
dent; **drei|za|ckig** ADJ three-pointed

drei|zehn ['draitseːn] NUM thirteen; **jetzt
schlägts aber ~** (*inf*) that's a bit much *or* thick
(*inf*) → *auch* **vierzehn**

Drei|zim|mer|woh|nung F three-room *or*
two-bedroom(ed) flat (*Brit*) *or* apartment

Dresch|bo|den M , **Dresch|die|le** F thresh-
ing floor

Dre|sche ['drɛʃə] F **-, no pl** (*inf*) thrashing; **~ krie-
gen** to get a thrashing

dre|schen ['drɛʃn] *pret* **drosch** [drɔʃ], *ptp* **gedro-
schen** [gə'drɔʃn] [VT] [a] *Korn* to thresh; (*inf*) *Phrasen* to bandy; **leeres Stroh ~** (*fig*) to talk a lot of
hot air (*inf*); **Skat ~** (*inf*) to play skat [b] (*inf:* = *prügeln*)
to thrash [c] (*Sport inf:* = *treten, schlagen*) to slam
(*inf*), to wallop (*inf*) [VI] [a] (= *Korn dreschen*) to
thresh [b] (*inf:* = *schlagen, treten*) to hit violently;
auf die Tasten ~ to thump *or* pound the keys
[VR] (*inf:* = *sich prügeln*) to have a fight

Dre|scher ['drɛʃɐ] M **-s, -, Dre|sche|rin** [-ərɪn]
F **-, -nen** thresher

Dresch-: Dresch|fle|gel M flail; **Dresch|ma|-
schi|ne** F threshing machine; **Dresch|ten|ne**
F threshing floor

Dress ▲ [drɛs] M **-es, -e,** *or* (*Aus*) f **-, -en** (*Sport*)
(sports) kit; (*für Fußball auch*) strip

Dres|seur [drɛˈsøːɐ] M **-s, -e, Dres|seu|rin**
[-ˈsøːrɪn] F **-, -nen** trainer

dres|sier|bar ADJ *Tier* trainable; (*pej*) *Mensch
auch* susceptible to conditioning; **leicht/schwer
~** easy/difficult to train/condition

dres|sie|ren [drɛˈsiːrən] *ptp* **dressiert** VT [a] *Tier*
to train; (*pej*) *Menschen auch* to condition, to
discipline; **auf jdn/etw dressiert sein** to be
trained to respond to sb/sth; **auf den Mann
dressiert sein** to be trained to attack people;

auf das Zusammentreiben von Tieren dressiert
trained to round up animals; **zu etw dressiert
sein** to be trained *etc* to do sth [b] (*Cook*) *Geflügel* to dress; *Braten* to prepare; (*esp Aus*) *Torte etc*
to decorate; *Teig, Creme* to pipe

Dres|sing ['drɛsɪŋ] NT **-s, -s** (*Cook*) dressing

Dress|man ['drɛsmən] M **-s, Dress|men** male
model

Dres|sur [drɛˈsuːɐ] F **-, -en** training; (*für Dressur-
reiten*) dressage; (*fig*) conditioning

Dres|sur-: Dres|sur|akt M performing animal
act; **Dres|sur|prü|fung** F dressage test; **Dres-
sur|rei|ten** NT **-s, no pl** dressage; **Dres|sur|-
rei|ter(in)** M(F) dressage rider

drib|beln ['drɪbln] VI to dribble; **mit dem Ball ~**
to dribble the ball

Drib|bling ['drɪblɪŋ] NT **-s, -s** dribbling; **ein ~** a
piece of dribbling

Drift [drɪft] F **-, -en** (*Naut*) drift

drif|ten ['drɪftn] VI *aux sein* (*Naut, fig*) to drift

Drill [drɪl] M **-(e)s, no pl** (*Mil, fig*) drill; (*Sch auch*)
drills *pl*

Drill|boh|rer M drill

dril|len ['drɪlən] VTI [a] (*Mil, fig*) to drill; **jdn auf
etw** (*acc*) **~** to drill sb in sth; **auf etw** (*acc*) **gedrillt sein** (*fig inf*) to be practised (*Brit*) or practiced (*US*) at doing sth [b] *Loch* to drill [c] (*Agr*)
to drill, to sow *or* plant in drills [d] (*beim Angeln*) to play

Drillich ['drɪlɪç] M **-s, -e** drill; (*für Matratzen etc*)
ticking; (*für Markisen*) canvas

Drillich-: Drillich|an|zug M overalls *pl*, dun-
garees *pl*; **Drillich|zeug** NT , *no pl* overalls *pl*

Drilling ['drɪlɪŋ] M **-s, -e** [a] triplet [b] (= *Angelhaken*) three-pronged hook [c] (= *Jagdgewehr*)
triple-barrelled (*Brit*) or triple-barreled (*US*)
shotgun

Drillings|ge|burt F triple birth

Drill-: Drill|ma|schi|ne F (*Agr*) seed drill;
Drill|übung F drill

drin [drɪn] ADV [a] (*inf*) = **darin** [b], **drinnen** [b]
(*inf*) **da ~** = **darin** [b] [c] in it; **er/es ist da ~** he/it
is in there; **in der Flasche ist noch etwas ~**
there's still something in the bottle; **hallo, ist
da jemand ~?** hello, is (there) anyone in there?
→ **drinsitzen** *etc* [d] (*inf: in Redewendungen*) **das
ist** *or* **liegt bei dem alles ~** anything's possible
with him; **bis jetzt ist** *or* **liegt noch alles ~** everything is still quite open; **~ sein** (*in der Arbeit*)
to be into it; **für sie ist doch (gegen ihn) nichts
~** she hasn't a hope (against him); **das ist doch
nicht ~** (= *geht nicht*) that's not on (*inf*)

drin|gen ['drɪŋən] *pret* **drang** [draŋ], *ptp* **gedrun-
gen** [gə'drʊŋən] VI [a] *aux sein* to penetrate, to
come through; (*fig: Nachricht, Geheimnis*) to penetrate, to get through (*an or in* +*acc* to); (**durch
etw**) **~** to come through (sth), to penetrate
(sth); **jdm ans Herz ~** (*liter*) to go to *or* touch
sb's heart; **an** *or* **in die Öffentlichkeit ~** to leak
or get out, to become public knowledge; **der
Pfeil drang ihm in die Brust** the arrow pene-
trated (into) his chest; **durch eine Menschenmenge ~** to push (one's way) through a crowd
of people; **hinter die Ursache/ein Rätsel ~** to
get to the bottom of this/a puzzle
[b] *aux sein* (*geh*) **in jdn ~** to press *or* urge sb;
mit Bitten/Fragen in jdn ~ to ply *or* press sb
with requests/questions
[c] **auf etw** (*acc*) **~** to insist on sth; **er drang darauf, einen Arzt zu holen** *or* **dass man einen
Arzt holte** he insisted that a doctor should be
sent for

drin|gend ['drɪŋənt] [ADJ] (= *eilig, wichtig*) ur-
gent, pressing; (= *nachdrücklich, zwingend*)
strong; *Abraten, Anraten* strong, strenuous; *Gründe* compelling; **etw ~ machen** (*fig*) to treat sth
as urgent; **ein ~er Fall** (*Med*) an emergency [ADV]
(= *unbedingt*) urgently; (= *nachdrücklich*) *warnen,
empfehlen, abraten* strongly; **ich muss Sie ~ sprechen** I must speak to you urgently; **jdn ~ bitten, etw zu unterlassen** to ask sb in the stron-

gest terms *or* to urge sb to stop doing sth; **~ notwendig** *or* **erforderlich** urgently needed, essential; **~ verdächtig** strongly suspected

dring|lich ['drɪŋlɪç] ADJ urgent, pressing

Dring|lich|keit F -, *no pl* urgency

Dring|lich|keits-: Dring|lich|keits|an|fra|ge F (*Parl*) emergency question; **Dring|lich|keits|an|trag** M (*Parl*) emergency motion; **Dring|lich|keits|stu|fe** F priority; **~ 1** top priority

drin+hän|gen VI *sep irreg* (*inf*) = **drinstecken b, c**

Drink [drɪŋk] M -s, -s drink

drin|nen ['drɪnən] ADV (= *in geschlossenem Raum*) inside; (= *im Haus auch*) indoors; (*fig*: = *im Inland*) internally, at home; **~ und draußen** inside and outside; (*im Inland etc*) at home and abroad; **hier/dort ~** in here/there; **ich gehe nach ~** (*inf*) I'm going in(side)

drin+sit|zen VI *sep irreg* (*inf*) to be in trouble

drin+ste|cken VI *sep* (*inf*) **a** (= *verborgen sein*) to be (contained); **auch bei ihm muss ein guter Kern ~** there must be some good even in him **b** (= *investiert sein*) **da steckt eine Menge Geld/Arbeit** *etc* **drin** a lot of money/work *etc* has gone into it **c** (= *verwickelt sein*) to be involved in it; **er steckt bis über die Ohren drin** he's up to his ears in it **d** (= *voraussehen können*) **da steckt man nicht drin** one never knows *or* one can never tell (what will happen)

drin+ste|hen VI *sep irreg aux haben or* (*dial*) *sein* (*inf*) to be in it

drischt [drɪʃt] 3. *pers sing pres von* **dreschen**

dritt [drɪt] ADV **wir kommen zu ~** three of us are coming together → *auch* **viert**

dritt- *in cpds* third; **dritt|äl|tes|te(r, s)** ADJ third oldest

Drit|tel ['drɪtl] NT -s, - third → *auch* **Viertel** [1]

drit|teln ['drɪtln] VT to divide into three (parts); *Zahl* to divide by three

Drit|tel|pa|ri|tät F equal say in decision-making for each of three groups; **die ~ verlangen** to demand an equal say in decision-making

drit|tel|pa|ri|tä|tisch ⓐ *Ausschuss, Gremium* made up of equal numbers from each of three groups ⓐⓥ *entscheiden* by giving each of three groups an equal vote; **~ zusammengesetzt** made up of equal numbers from each of three groups

Drit|ten|ab|schla|gen NT -s, *no pl children's game*, ≈ tag

drit|tens ['drɪtns] ADV thirdly → **viertens**

Drit|te(r) ['drɪtə] MF *decl as adj* third person, third man/woman *etc*; (= *Unbeteiligter*) third party; **der lachende ~** the third party who benefits from a division between two others **in dieser Angelegenheit ist er der lachende ~** he comes off best from this matter; **wenn zwei sich streiten, freut sich der ~** (*prov*) when two people quarrel a third one rejoices; **der ~ im Bunde** the third in *or* of the trio → *auch* **Vierte(r)**

drit|te(r, s) ['drɪtə] ADJ third; **der ~ Fall** (*Gram*) the dative case; **an einem ~n Ort** on neutral territory; **von ~r Seite** (**eine Neuigkeit erfahren**) (to learn a piece of news) from a third party; **Menschen ~r Klasse** third-class citizens; **ein Drittes** *a* third thing → **vierte(r, s), Reich a, Welt**

Dritt-: dritt|größ|te(r, s) ADJ third-biggest, third-largest; **dritt|höchs|te(r, s)** ADJ third-highest; **Dritt|in|te|res|se** NT interest of a third party; **dritt|klas|sig** ADJ third-rate (*pej*), third-class; **Dritt|kläss|ler** ▲ M -s, -, **Dritt|kläss|le|rin** ▲ F -, -nen (*Sch*) third-former (*Brit*), third-grader (*US*); **Dritt|land** NT third country; **dritt|letz|te(r, s)** ADJ third from

last, last but two; **an ~r Stelle** third from last, last but two; **Dritt|mit|tel** PL (*Fin*) external funds *pl*; **Dritt|per|son** F third person *or* party; **dritt|ran|gig** [-raŋɪç] ADJ third-rate; **Dritt|scha|den** M damage suffered by a third party

Drive [draɪf] M -s, -s drive

DRK [deːʔɛrˈkaː] NT - *abbr von* **Deutsches Rotes Kreuz**

drob [drɔp] ADV (*obs*) = **darob**

dro|ben ['droːbn] ADV (*old, dial*) up there; **dort ~** up there

Dro|ge ['droːgə] F -, -n drug

drö|ge ['drøːgə] ADJ (*N Ger*) = **trocken a b**

Drö|ge|ler ['drøːgələ] M -s, -, **Drö|ge|le|rin** [-ərɪn] F -, -nen (*Sw*) drug addict

Drogen-: drogen|ab|hän|gig ADJ addicted to drugs; **er ist ~** he's a drug addict; **Dro|gen|ab|hän|gi|ge(r)** MF *decl as adj* drug addict; **Dro|gen|ab|hän|gig|keit** F drug addiction *no art*; **Dro|gen|ba|ron** M (*inf*) drug baron (*inf*); **Dro|gen|be|nut|zer(in)** M(F) drug user; **Dro|gen|be|ra|tungs|stel|le** F drugs advice centre (*Brit*) *or* center (*US*); **Dro|gen|fahn|der** [-faːndɐ] M -s, -, **Dro|gen|fahn|de|rin** [-ərɪn] F -, -nen drug squad officer, narcotics officer; **Dro|gen|fahn|dungs|be|hör|de** F drug squad; **Dro|gen|ge|schäft** NT drug trade; **Dro|gen|han|del** M drug traffic *or* trade; **Dro|gen|händ|ler(in)** M(F) drug trafficker *or* dealer; **Dro|gen|kon|sum** [-kɔnzuːm] M drug consumption; **Dro|gen|ku|rier(in)** M(F) drug courier; **Dro|gen|la|bor** NT drug laboratory; **Dro|gen|miss|brauch** ▲ M drug abuse *no art*; **Dro|gen|sucht** F drug addiction; **dro|gen|süch|tig** ADJ addicted to drugs, **er ist ~** he's a drug addict; **Dro|gen|süch|ti|ge(r)** MF *decl as adj* drug addict; **Dro|gen|sze|ne** F drug scene; **Dro|gen|to|te(r)** MF *decl as adj* person who died from drug abuse; **200 ~ pro Jahr** 200 drug deaths per year; **Dro|gen|um|schlag|platz** M drug-dealing *or* drug-trafficking area

Dro|ge|rie [drogəˈriː] F -, -n [-ˈriːən] chemist's (shop) (*nondispensing*), drugstore (*US*)

Dro|gist [droˈgɪst] M -en, -en, **Dro|gis|tin** [-ˈgɪstɪn] F chemist, druggist (*US*)

Drög|ler ['drøːglɐ] M -s, -, **Drög|le|rin** [-ərɪn] F -, -nen (*Sw*) drug addict

Droh|brief M threatening letter

dro|hen ['droːən] VI **a** (= *Drohung aussprechen*) to threaten (*jdm* sb); **er drohte dem Kind mit erhobenem Zeigefinger** he raised a warning finger to the child **b** (*jdm*) **mit etw ~** to threaten (sb with) sth; **er droht mit Selbstmord** he threatens to commit suicide; (**jdm**) **~, etw zu tun** to threaten to do sth **c** (= *bevorstehen*) (*Gefahr*) to threaten; (*Gewitter*) to be imminent, to be in the offing; (*Streik, Krieg*) to be imminent *or* looming; **jdm droht etw** sb is being threatened by sth; **jdm droht Gefahr/der Tod** sb is in danger/in danger of dying; **es droht Gefahr/ein Streik** there is the threat of danger/a strike **V AUX** to threaten; **das Schiff drohte zu sinken** the ship threatened to sink, the ship was in danger of sinking

dro|hend ADJ **a** *Handbewegung, Haltung, Blick, Wolken* threatening, menacing **b** (= *bevorstehend*) *Unheil, Gefahr, Krieg, Krise* imminent, impending

Droh|ge|bär|de F threatening gesture

Drohn [droːn] M -en, -en (*form*) = **Drohne a**

Droh|ne [droːnə] F -, -n **a** drone; (*fig pej auch*) idler, parasite **b** (*Mil*) drone

dröh|nen ['drøːnən] VI **a** (*Flugzeug, Motor, Straßenlärm*) to roar; (*Donner*) to rumble; (*Lautsprecher, Musik, Bass, Stimme, Fernseher*) to boom; **etw dröhnt jdm in den Ohren/im Kopf** sth roars *etc* in sb's ears/head **b** (*Raum etc*) to resound, to echo; **mir ~ die Ohren/dröhnt der Kopf** my ears are/head is ringing **c** *aux sein* (= *sich dröhnend*

fortbewegen: Lkw etc) to rumble **d** (*sl: = high machen*) to give a buzz (*inf*)

dröh|nend ⓐⓓⓙ *Lärm, Applaus* resounding, echoing; *Musik, Stimme* booming; *Gelächter* roaring ⓐⓓⓥ **~ lachen** to roar with laughter

Droh|nen-: Droh|nen|da|sein NT (*fig pej*) idle *or* parasitic life; **droh|nen|haft** ADJ drone-like; (*fig auch*) idle, parasitic; **Droh|nen|schlacht** F (*Zool*) slaughter of the drones

Dröh|nung ['drøːnʊŋ] F -, -en (*sl*) **a** (= *laute Musik*) booming music **b** (= *Rausch*) high (*inf*); (= *Dosis*) fix (*inf*); **sich** (*dat*) **voll die ~ oder die vol|le ~ geben** to get stoned (*sl*)

Dro|hung ['droːʊŋ] F -, -en threat

Droh-: Droh|ver|hal|ten NT threatening *or* aggressive behaviour (*Brit*) *or* behavior (*US*); **Droh|wort** NT *pl* **-worte** threat

drol|lig ['drɔlɪç] ⓐ *a* funny, comical, droll **b** (= *seltsam*) odd, strange; **werd nicht ~!** don't be funny!; **ein ~er Kauz** an odd bod (*Brit inf*), an oddball (*esp US inf*)

Dro|me|dar [drome'daːɐ, 'droː-] NT -s, -e dromedary

Drop-out ['drɔpaut] M -s, -s, **Drop|out** M -s, -s **a** (= *Mensch*) dropout **b** (*in Bandaufzeichnung*) fade

Drops [drɔps] M OR NT -, - *or* **-e** fruit drop

drosch *pret von* **dreschen**

Drosch|ke ['drɔʃkə] F -, -n **a** (= *Pferdedroschke*) (hackney) cab, hackney carriage **b** (*dated*: = *Taxi*) (taxi)cab

Drosch|ken-: Drosch|ken|(hal|te)|platz M (*dated*) cab rank; **Drosch|ken|kut|scher(in)** M(F) cab driver

Dro|so|phi|la [dro'zoːfila] F -, **Drosophilae** [-lɛ] (*Biol*) drosophila

Dros|sel[1] ['drɔsl] F -, -n (*Orn*) thrush

Dros|sel[2] F -, -n (= *Drosselspule*) choking coil; (= *Drosselventil*) throttle valve

Dros|sel|klap|pe F (*Tech*) throttle valve

dros|seln ['drɔsln] VT **a** *Motor, Dampf etc* to throttle, to choke; *Heizung, Wärme* to turn down; *Strom* to reduce; *Tempo, Produktion etc* to cut down **b** (*dated*: = *würgen*) to throttle, to strangle

Dros|sel|spu|le F (*Elec*) choking coil

Dros|se|lung F -, -en (*von Motor, Dampf*) throttling, choking; (*von Heizung, Wärme*) turning down; (*von Strom*) reducing; (*von Tempo, Produktion*) cutting down

Dros|sel|ven|til NT throttle valve

Dross|lung ▲ ['drɔslʊŋ] F -, -en = **Drosselung**

drü|ben ['dryːbn] ADV over there; (= *auf der anderen Seite, inf: auf die DDR/die BRD bezogen*) on the other side; (*inf: auf Amerika bezogen*) over the water; **hier/dort ~ da ~** over here/there; **nach ~** over there; (*inf: auf die DDR/die BRD bezogen*) to the other side; **von ~** from over there; (*inf: auf die DDR/die BRD bezogen*) from the other side; **bei der Nachbarin ~** over at my neighbour's (*Brit*) *or* neighbor's (*US*); **~ über dem Rhein** on the other side of the Rhine → **hüben**

Drü|ben ['dryːbn] NT -s, *no pl* (= *Jenseits*) hereafter, next world

drü|ber ['dryːbɐ] ADV (*inf*) **a** = **darüber, hinüber b da ~** = **darüber**

Druck[1] [drʊk] M -(e)s, ≈e ['drʏkə] **a** (*Phys, fig*) pressure; **unter ~ stehen** (*lit, fig*) to be under pressure; **jdn unter ~ setzen** (*fig*) to put pressure on sb, to pressurize sb; **unter ~ geraten** to come under pressure; (*fürchterlich*) **in ~ sein** (*fig*) to be under (terrible) pressure; **~ auf jdn/etw ausüben** (*lit, fig*) to exert *or* put pressure on sb/sth; **~ machen** (*inf*) to put the pressure on (*inf*); **~ hinter etw** (*acc*) **machen** (*inf*) to put some pressure on sth; **~ und Gegendruck** pressure and resistance; **ein ~ im Kopf/Magen** a feeling of pressure in one's head/stomach; **ei|nen ~ haben** (*sl*: = *Lust auf Sex*) to be choking (*Brit*) *or* gagging (*Brit*) *or* dying for it (*sl*)

b (= *das Drücken*) pressure (+*gen* from) *no indef art*; **durch einen ~ auf den Knopf** by pressing the button **c** (*Drogen sl*) fix (*inf*); **sich** (*dat*) **einen ~ verpassen** to have a fix (*inf*)

Druck² M -(e)s, -e **a** (= *das Drucken*) printing; (*Art des Drucks*, = *Schriftart*) print; (= *Druckwerk*) copy; **~ und Satz** setting and printing; **das Buch ist im ~** the book is in the press *or* is being printed; **im ~ erscheinen** to appear in print; **in ~ gehen** to go into print; **etw in ~ geben** to send sth to press *or* to be printed; **~ und Verlag von ...** printed and published by ... **b** (= *Kunstdruck*) print **c** PL -s (*Tex*) print

Druck-: Druck|ab|fall M drop *or* fall in pressure; **Druck|an|stieg** M rise in pressure; **Druck|an|zug** M pressure suit; **Druck|aus|gleich** M pressure balance; **Druck|be|häl|ter** M pressure vessel; **Druck|be|las|tung** F pressure load; **Druck|blei|stift** M retractable pencil; **Druck|bo|gen** M (*Typ*) printed sheet; **Druck|buch|sta|be** M printed character *or* letter; **in ~n schreiben** to print

Drü|cke|ber|ger ['drʏkəbɛrɡɐ] M -s, -, **Drü|cke|ber|ge|rin** [-ərɪn] F -, -nen (*pej inf*) (= *fauler Mensch*) shirker; (*in der Schule*) shirker, skiver (*Brit inf*); (= *Feigling*) coward

Drü|cke|ber|ge|rei [drʏkəbɛrɡə'raɪ] F -, -en (*pej inf*) shirking; (*in der Schule*) shirking, skiving (*Brit inf*)

drü|cke|ber|ge|risch [drʏkəbɛrɡərɪʃ] ADJ (*pej inf*) *Mensch, Einstellung* idle; **sein ~es Verhalten** his idling *or* shirking

druck|emp|find|lich ADJ sensitive (to pressure); (*Comput*) touch-sensitive

dru|cken ['drʊkn] VTI **a** (*Typ, Tex*) to print; **ein Buch ~ lassen** to have a book printed; **ein Buch in 1000 Exemplaren/einer hohen Auflage ~** to print 1000 copies/a large edition of a book → **gedruckt b** (*dial*) = **drücken**

drü|cken ['drʏkn] VT **a** *Hand, Klinke, Hebel* to press; *Knopf* to press, to push; *Obst, Saft, Eiter* to squeeze; **jdm etw in die Hand ~** to press *or* slip sth into sb's hand; **jdn ~** to squeeze sb; (= *umarmen*) to hug sb; **jdn/etw an sich/ans Herz ~** to press *or* clasp sb/sth to one/one's breast; **jdn zur Seite/nach hinten/in einen Stuhl ~** to push sb aside/back/into a chair; **den Hut in die Stirn ~** to pull one's hat down over one's brow *or* forehead **b** (*geh*: = *bedrücken*) to weigh heavily upon; **was drückt dich denn?** what's on your mind? **c** (= *Druckgefühl erzeugen*: *Schuhe, Korsett etc*) to pinch, to nip; **jdn im Magen ~** (*Essen*) to lie *or* weigh heavily on sb's stomach; **mich drückt der Magen** my stomach feels full **d** (= *verringern, herabsetzen*) to force down; *Rekord* to beat; *Leistung, Niveau* to lower; *Steuern* to bring down **e** (*inf*: = *unterdrücken*) *jdn* to keep down; *Stimmung* to dampen **f** (*Sport*) *Gewicht* to press; *Handstand* to press into **g** (*Aviat*) to point down **h** (*Cards*) to discard **i** (*Econ*) **etw in** *or* **auf den Markt ~** to push sth

VI **a** (*auf Gegenstand, Klinke, Knopf etc*) to press; (*Wetter, Hitze*) to be oppressive; (*Brille, Schuhe, Korsett etc*) to pinch; (*Essen*) to weigh (on one's stomach); **„bitte ~"** "push"; **auf etw** (*acc*) **~** to press sth; **aufs Gemüt ~** to dampen *or* depress one's spirits, to get one down; **auf die Stimmung ~** to dampen one's mood → *auch* **gedrückt b** (= *drängeln, stoßen*) to push **c** (*bei Stuhlentleerung*) to strain, to push **d** (*inf*: = *Heroin injizieren*) to shoot up

VR **a** (*mit Ortsangabe*) (*in* +*acc* into) (*an* +*acc* against) (= *sich quetschen*) to squeeze; (*Schutz suchend*) to huddle; **sich aus dem Zimmer ~** to slip out of the room **b** (*inf*: = *kneifen*) to shirk, to dodge; (*vor Militärdienst*) to dodge; **sich vor etw** (*dat*) **~** to shirk *or* dodge sth; **sich (um etw) ~** to get out of sth; (*esp in Schule auch*) to skive off (sth) (*Brit inf*), to avoid sth

drü|ckend ADJ *Last, Steuern* heavy; *Sorgen, Probleme* serious; *Verantwortung* weighty; *Armut* grinding; *Wetter, Hitze* oppressive, close; *Enge, Atmosphäre* oppressive ADV (es ist) **~ heiß** (it's) oppressively hot

drü|ckend|heiß △ ['drʏknt'haɪs] ADJ *attr* → **drückend**

Dru|cker¹ ['drʊkɐ] M -s, - (*Comput*) printer

Dru|cker² ['drʊkɐ] M -s, -, **Dru|cke|rin** [-ərɪn] F -, -nen (= *Beruf*) printer

Drü|cker¹ ['drʏkɐ] M -s, - **a** (= *Knopf*) (push) button; (*inf*: *von Pistole etc*) trigger; (*von Klingel*) push; **die Hand am ~ haben** (*fig inf*) to be ready to act; **am ~ sein** *or* **sitzen** (*fig inf*) (*in Machtposition*) to be in a key position; (*an der Quelle*) to be ideally placed, to be in an ideal position; **auf den letzten ~** (*fig inf*) at the last minute **b** (= *Türklinke*) handle; (*von Schnappschloss*) latch

Drü|cker² ['drʏkɐ] M -s, -, **Drü|cke|rin** [-ərɪn] F -, -nen (*inf*: = *Hausierer*) hawker (*inf*)

Dru|cke|rei [drʊkə'raɪ] F -, -en **a** printing works *pl*, printery; (= *Firma*) printer's **b** (= *Druckwesen*) printing *no art*

Drü|cker|ko|lon|ne F (*inf*) door-to-door sales team

Druck|er|laub|nis F imprimatur

Dru|cker-: Dru|cker|pres|se F printing press; **Dru|cker|schwär|ze** F printer's ink; **Dru|cker|spra|che** F printer's language; **Dru|cker|trei|ber** M (*Comput*) printer driver; **Dru|cker|zei|chen** NT printer's mark

Druck-: Druck|er|zeug|nis NT printed material; **Druck|fah|ne** F galley (proof), proof; **Druck|far|be** F coloured (*Brit*) *or* colored (*US*) printing ink; **Druck|feh|ler** M misprint, typographical *or* printer's error; **Druck|feh|ler|teu|fel** M (*hum*) gremlin (*which causes misprints*); **druck|fer|tig** ADJ ready to print, ready for the press; **druck|fest** ADJ *Werkstoff* pressure-resistant; **Druck|fes|tig|keit** F pressure resistance; **Druck|form** F (*Typ*) printing form(e), quoin; **Druck|for|mat** NT (*Typ*) format; **druck|frisch** ADJ hot off the press; *Geldscheine* newly printed; **Druck|ge|fäl|le** NT (*Phys*) difference in pressure; **Druck|ge|fühl** NT feeling of pressure; **Druck|ge|schwin|dig|keit** F (*Comput*) print speed; **Druck|ka|bi|ne** F pressurized cabin; **Druck|knopf** M **a** (*Sew*) press stud, snap fastener **b** (*Tech*) push button; **Druck|kopf** M (*Comput*) print head; **Druck|kos|ten** PL printing costs *pl*; **Druck|le|gung** [-leːɡʊŋ] F -, -en printing; **mit der ~ beginnen** to begin printing, to go to press

Druck|luft F compressed air

Druck|luft-: Druck|luft|boh|rer M pneumatic drill; **Druck|luft|brem|se** F air brake

Druck-: Druck|ma|schi|ne F (*Typ*) printing press; **Druck|me|nü** NT (*Comput*) print menu; **Druck|mes|ser** M -s, - pressure gauge; **Druck|mit|tel** NT (*fig*) form of pressure, means of exerting pressure; **als politisches ~** as a form of political pressure, as a means of exerting political pressure; **Druck|mus|ter** NT print(ed pattern *or* design); **Stoffe mit ~** prints, printed materials; **Druck|ort** M *pl* -orte place of printing; **Druck|pa|pier** NT printing paper; **Druck|plat|te** F printing plate; **Druck|pos|ten** M (*inf*) cushy job *or* number (*inf*); **Druck|pres|se** F printing press; **Druck|pum|pe** F pressure pump; **druck|reif** ADJ ready for printing, passed for press; (*fig*) polished ADV **~ sprechen** to speak in a polished style; **Druck|sa|che** F (*Post*) business letter; (= *Werbematerial*) circular; (*als Portoklasse*) printed matter; **„Drucksache"** "printed matter"; **etw als ~ schicken** ≈ to send sth at printed-paper rate **b** (*Typ*: = *Auftrag*) stationery printing job **c** **Drucksachen** PL (= *Akzidenz*) stationery printing *sing*; **Druck|schal|ter** M push-button

switch; **Druck|schott** NT (*Aviat*) bulkhead; **Druck|schrift** F **a** (= *Schriftart*) printing; **in ~ schreiben** to print; **die ~ lernen** to learn printing, to learn to print **b** (= *gedrucktes Werk*) pamphlet; **Druck|sei|te** F printed page

druck|sen ['drʊksn] VI (*inf*) to hum and haw (*inf*)

Druck-: Druck|sor|ten PL (*Aus*) printed forms *pl*; **Druck|stel|le** F place or (*Mal*) mark (*where pressure has been applied*); (= *Fleck auf Pfirsich, Haut*) bruise; **Druck|stock** M (*Typ*) relief plate; **Druck|tas|te** F push button; **Druck|tech|nik** F printing technology *or* (= *Verfahren*) technique; **druck|tech|nisch** ADJ typographical; (*in Bezug auf mechanischen Vorgang*) printing *attr* ADV from a typographical/printing point of view; **~ verfeinert** improved from the printing point of view; **Druck|trom|mel** F (*Comput*) print drum; **Druck|type** F type; **druck|un|emp|find|lich** ADJ insensitive to pressure; **Druck|un|ter|schied** M difference in pressure; **Druck|ver|band** M (*Med*) pressure bandage; **Druck|ver|bot** NT printing ban; **Druck|ver|fah|ren** NT printing process; **Druck|ver|lust** M (*Tech*) loss of pressure, reduction in pressure; **Druck|vor|la|ge** F (*Typ*) setting copy; **Druck|was|ser|re|ak|tor** M pressurized water reactor; **Druck|wel|le** F shock wave; **Druck|werk** NT printed work, publication; **Druck|we|sen** NT , *no pl* printing *no art*; **Druck|zei|le** F line of print

Dru|de ['druːdə] F -, -n (*Myth*) witch

Dru|den|fuß M (*Myth*) pentagram

druff [drʊf] ADV (*dial inf*) = **drauf**

Dru|i|de [dru'iːdə] M -n, -n, **Dru|i|din** [dru'iːdɪn] F -, -nen Druid

dru|i|disch [dru'iːdɪʃ] ADJ druidic(al), druid *attr*

drum [drʊm] ADV (*inf*) around, round (*Brit*); **~ (he)rum** all (a)round; **~ (he)rumreden** to beat about the bush; **da wirst du nicht ~ (he)rumkommen** there's no getting out of it; **seis ~!** (*geh*) never mind; **das (ganze) Drum und Dran** the paraphernalia; (= *Begleiterscheinungen*) the fuss and bother; **mit allem Drum und Dran** with all the bits and pieces (*inf*); *Mahlzeit* with all the trimmings *pl* → **darum**

Drum|he|rum [drʊmhɛ'rʊm] NT -s, *no pl* trappings *pl*

Drum|mer ['dramɐ] M -s, -, **Drum|me|rin** ['dramərɪn] F -, -nen (*Mus*) drummer

drun|ten ['drʊntn] ADV (*old, dial*) down there

drun|ter ['drʊntɐ] ADV under(neath); **da kann ich mir nichts ~ vorstellen** that means nothing to me; **~ und drüber** upside down, topsy-turvy (*inf*); **alles ging** *or* **es ging alles ~ und drüber** everything was upside down *or* topsy-turvy (*inf*); **das Drunter und Drüber** the confusion, the muddle → **darunter**

Drusch [drʊʃ] M -(e)s, -e (*Agr*) threshing; (= *Produkt*) threshed corn

Drü|se ['dryːzə] F -, -n gland

Dru|se¹ ['druːzə] F -, -n (*Min, Geol*) druse

Dru|se² ['druːzə] M -n, -n, **Dru|sin** ['druːzɪn] F -, -nen (*Rel*) Druse

Drü|sen-: drü|sen|ar|tig ADJ glandular; **Drü|sen|fie|ber** NT glandular fever, mono(nucleosis) (*US*); **Drü|sen|funk|ti|on** F glandular function; **Drü|sen|krank|heit** F , **Drü|sen|lei|den** NT glandular disorder; **Drü|sen|schwel|lung** F glandular swelling, swollen glands *pl*; **Drü|sen|über|funk|ti|on** F hyperactivity *or* overactivity of the glands; **Drü|sen|un|ter|funk|ti|on** F underactivity of the glands

Dru|sin F -, -nen (*Rel*) Druse

DSB [deːʔɛs'beː] M -s *abbr von* **Deutscher Sportbund** German Sports Association

Dschun|gel ['dʒʊŋl] M -s, - (*lit, fig*) jungle; **sich im ~ der Paragrafen zurechtfinden** to wade one's way through the verbiage

Dschun|gel-: dschun|gel|ar|tig ADJ *Wald* jungle-like; **Dschun|gel|fie|ber** NT yellow fever; **Dschun|gel|ge|setz** NT law of the jungle; **Dschun|gel|krieg** M jungle warfare

Dschun|ke ['dʒʊŋkə] F -, -n (*Naut*) junk

DSG [de:ʔɛs'ge:] F - *abbr von* **Deutsche Schlafwagen- und Speisewagen-Gesellschaft**

DTP [de:te:'pe:] NT *abbr von* **Desktop Publishing** DTP

DTP- [de:te:'pe:] *in cpds* DTP; **DTP-An|wen|der(in)** M(F) DTP user; **DTP-Fach|frau** F, **DTP-Fach|mann** M DTP specialist; **DTP-Pro|fi** M (*inf*) DTP pro (*inf*) or expert; **DTP-Soft|ware** F DTP software

dt(sch). *abbr von* **deutsch**

Dtzd. *abbr von* **Dutzend**

du [du:] PERS PRON *gen* **deiner**, *dat* **dir**, *acc* **dich** you (*familiar form of address*), thou (*obs, dial*); (= *man*) you; **ich gehe heute ins Kino und du?** I'm going to the cinema today, how about you?; **du (zu jdm) sagen, jdn mit Du anreden** to use the familiar form of address (with sb), to say "du" (to sb); **du, der du es erlebt hast** you who have experienced it; **mit jdm auf Du und Du stehen** to be pals with sb; **mit jdm per du sein** to be on familiar *or* friendly terms with sb; **du bist es** it's you; **bist du es** *or* **das?** is it *or* that you?; **Vater unser, der Du bist im Himmel** our Father, who *or* which art in heaven; **mach du das doch!** YOU do it!, do it yourself!; **du, meine Heimat!** (*poet*) thou, my homeland!; **du Glücklicher!** lucky you, you lucky thing; **du Idiot!** you idiot; **du Schlingel/Schuft(, du)!** you rascal/scoundrel(, you)!; **ach du lieber Gott** *or* **liebe Güte** good Lord!, good heavens!; **du (Mutti), kannst du mir mal helfen?** hey (mummy), can you help me?; **du, ich muss jetzt aber gehen** listen, I have to go now; **du, du!** (*hum: drohend*) naughty, naughty → **mir**

Du [du:] NT -(s), -(s) "du", familiar form of address; **jdm das Du anbieten** to suggest that sb uses "du" or the familiar form of address

Du|al [du'a:l] M -s, -e, **Du|a|lis** [du'a:lɪs] M -, **Duale** [-lə] dual

du|al [du'a:l] ADJ dual

DUALES SYSTEM

The **duales System** is a waste disposal system which has operated in Germany since 1991. Packaging materials that can be recycled –paper, glass, metal, plastics – are marked with the **Grüner Punkt**. Licences for using this symbol must be obtained from **DSD** (Duales System Deutschland GmbH), the company responsible for operating the system. The recyclable waste thus marked is collected separately, then sorted and sent for recycling. Although there is no charge for collecting waste for recycling, the cost of obtaining the licence from **DSD** is often included in the retail price. Austria has a similar system, for which the company **ARA** (Altstoff Recycling Austria AG) is responsible → **GRÜNER PUNKT**

Du|a|lis|mus [dua'lɪsmʊs] M -, *no pl* (*Philos, Pol, geh*) dualism

Du|a|list [dua'lɪst] M -en, -en, **Du|a|lis|tin** [-'lɪstɪn] F -, -nen (*Philos*) dualist

du|a|lis|tisch [dua'lɪstɪʃ] ADJ (*Philos, Pol, geh*) dualistic

Du|a|li|tät [duali'tɛ:t] F -, -en (*geh*) duality

Du|al|sys|tem NT (*Math*) binary system

Dub [dab] M -, *no pl* (*Mus*) dub

Dü|bel ['dy:bl] M -s, - Rawlplug®; (= *Holzdübel*) dowel

Dü|bel|mas|se F plugging compound, filler

dü|beln ['dy:bln] VTI to plug

du|bi|os [du'bio:s], **du|bi|ös** [du'biø:s] ADJ (*geh*) dubious

Dub|lee [du'ble:] NT -s, -s rolled gold *no pl*; (= *Gegenstand*) article made of rolled gold

Dub|lee|gold NT rolled gold

Dub|let|te [du'blɛtə] F -, -n **a** (= *doppelt vorhandenes Stück, Kopie*) duplicate **b** (*Hunt*) right and left **c** (= *Edelstein*) doublet **d** (*Boxen*) one-two

dub|lie|ren [du'bli:rən] *ptp* **dubliert** VT *Metall* to coat with gold; *Garn* to twist

Dub|lin ['dablɪn] NT -s Dublin

Dub|li|ner[1] ['dablɪnɐ] ADJ *attr* Dublin

Dub|li|ner[2] ['dablɪnɐ] M -s, -, **Dub|li|ne|rin** [-ərɪn] F -, -nen Dubliner

du|cken ['dʊkn] VR to duck; (*fig pej*) to cringe, to cower; (*fig: Bäume, Häuser*) to nestle; **ich duckte mich vor dem Hieb** I ducked the blow; **sich in eine Ecke/hinter eine Deckung ~** to duck *or* dodge into a corner/behind cover → *auch* **geduckt** VT *Kopf, Menschen* to duck; (*fig*) to humiliate **b** (*fig pej*) to cower

Duck|mäu|ser ['dʊkmɔyzɐ] M -s, -, **Duck|mäu|se|rin** [-ərɪn] F -, -nen (*pej*) moral coward

Duck|mäu|se|rei [dʊkmɔyzə'rai] F -, -en (*pej*) moral cowardice; **Erziehung zur ~** bringing up to be moral cowards

duck|mäu|se|risch ['dʊkmɔyzərɪʃ] (*pej*) ADJ showing moral cowardice ADV **sich ~ verhalten** to act without integrity

duck|mäu|sern ['dʊkmɔyzɐn] VI *insep* (*pej*) to be moral cowards/a moral coward

Duck|mäu|ser|tum ['dʊkmɔyzɐtu:m] NT -s, *no pl* (*pej*) moral cowardice; **jdn zum ~ erziehen** to bring sb up to be a moral coward

Du|de|lei [dudə'lai] F -, -en (*pej*) humming; (*auf Flöte*) tooting

Du|del|kas|ten M (*pej inf*) noise box

du|deln ['du:dln] (*pej inf*) VI to hum; (*auf Flöte*) to tootle (*auf +dat* on) VT **a** *Lied* to hum; (*auf Flöte*) to tootle **b** (*dial*) **einen ~** to have a nip *or* a wee dram (*Brit dial*)

Du|del|sack M bagpipes *pl*

Du|del|sack|pfei|fer(in) M(F), **Du|del|sack|spie|ler(in)** M(F) (bag)piper

Due Di|li|gence [dju: dɪlɪtʃənts, dju: 'dɪlɪdʒənts] F -, *no pl* (*Econ*) due diligence

Du|ell [du'ɛl] NT -s, -e (*lit, fig*) duel (*um* over); **ein ~ auf Degen** a duel with swords; **ein ~ (mit jdm) austragen** to fight *or* have a duel (with sb); **jdn zum ~ (heraus)fordern, jdn ins ~ fordern** to challenge sb to a duel

Du|el|lant [due'lant] M -en, -en, **Du|el|lan|tin** [-'lantɪn] F -, -nen dueller, duellist

du|el|lie|ren [due'li:rən] **duelliert** VR to fight a) duel

Du|ell|pis|to|le F duelling pistol

Du|ett [du'ɛt] NT -(e)s, -e **a** (*Mus, fig*) duet; **im ~ singen** to sing a duet; **etw im ~ singen** to sing sth as a duet **b** (*fig inf: = Paar*) duo (*inf*)

duff [dʊf] ADJ (*N Ger*) matt; *Glas, Fenster* dull

Duf|fle|coat ['daflko:t] M -s, -s duffel coat

Duft [dʊft] M -(e)s, ⸚e ['dyftə] **a** (*pleasant*) smell, scent; (*von Blumen, Parfüm*) smell, scent, fragrance; (*von Kaffee, Kaffee etc*) smell, aroma; (= *Absonderung von Tieren*) scent; (*fig*) allure; **den ~ der großen weiten Welt verspüren** (*usu iro*) to get a taste of the big wide world **b** (*liter*: = *Dunst*) haze

Duft|drü|se F scent gland

duf|te ['dʊftə] ADJ, ADV (*dated inf*) smashing (*Brit inf*), great (*inf*)

duf|ten ['dʊftn] VI to smell; **nach etw ~** to smell of sth, to have a smell of sth **VI impers hier duftet es nach Kaffee** there is a smell of coffee here, it smells of coffee here

duf|tend ADJ *attr* nice-smelling; *Parfüm, Blumen etc* fragrant; *Kaffee, Kräuter* aromatic

duf|tig ['dʊftɪç] ADJ **a** *Kleid, Stoff* gossamery; *Spitzen* frothy; *Wolken* fluffy **b** (*poet*: = *zart dunstig*) hazy

Duf|tig|keit F -, *no pl* (*von Kleid, Stoff*) gossamer lightness; (*von Spitzen*) frothiness; (*von Wolken*) fluffiness

Duft-: Duft|kis|sen NT scented sachet; (= *parfümiertes Kopfkissen*) scented pillow; **duft|los** ADJ odourless (*Brit*), odorless (*US*), unscented; **Duft|mar|ke** F scent mark; **Duft|no|te** F (*von Parfüm*) scent; (*von Mensch*) smell; **Duft|or|gan** NT scent gland; **Duft|pro|be** F **a** (= *Vorgang*) perfume test **b** (= *Probeflasche*) free sample of perfume; **Duft|stoff** M scent; (*für Parfüm, Waschmittel etc*) fragrance; **Duft|was|ser** NT *pl* -wässer toilet water; (*hum*: = *Parfüm*) perfume, scent; **Duft|wol|ke** F (*iro*) fragrance (*iro*); (*von Parfüm*) cloud of perfume

duhn [du:n] ADJ (*N Ger inf*) sloshed (*esp Brit inf*)

Du|ka|ten [du'ka:tn] M -s, - ducat

Du|ka|ten-: Du|ka|ten|esel M (*hum*) = Dukatenscheißer; **Du|ka|ten|gold** NT fine gold; **Du|ka|ten|schei|ßer(in)** M(F) (*inf*) **ein ~ sein** to be a gold mine, to be made of money

Dü|ker ['dy:kɐ] M -s, - (*Straßenbau*) drain, culvert

Duk|tus ['dʊktʊs] M -, *no pl* (*geh*) characteristic style; (*von Handschrift*) characteristics *pl*, flow

dul|den ['dʊldn] VI (*geh*: = *leiden*) to suffer VT **a** (= *zulassen*) to tolerate; *Widerspruch auch* to countenance; **ich dulde das nicht** I won't tolerate that; **die Sache duldet keinen Aufschub** the matter cannot be delayed *or* postponed; **etw stillschweigend ~** to connive at sth **b** (= *nicht vertreiben*) to tolerate; **er ist hier nur geduldet** he's only tolerated here, he's only here on sufferance **c** (*geh*: = *erdulden*) *Not, Schmerz* to suffer

Dul|der ['dʊldɐ] M -s, -, **Dul|de|rin** [-ərɪn] F -, -nen silent sufferer

Dul|der|mie|ne F (*iro*) air of patient suffering; **mit ~** with an air of patient suffering

duld|sam ['dʊltza:m] ADJ tolerant (*gegenüber* of, *jdm gegenüber* towards sb); (= *geduldig*) forbearing ADV tolerantly; (= *geduldig*) with forbearance

Duld|sam|keit F -, *no pl* tolerance; (= *Geduld*) forbearance

Dul|dung F -, (*rare*) -en **a** toleration; **solche Zustände erlauben keine weitere ~** such conditions can be tolerated no longer; **unter** *or* **bei** *or* **mit stillschweigender ~ der Behörden** *etc* with the (tacit) connivance of the authorities *etc* **b** (= *Aufenthaltsgenehmigung*) short-term residence permit

Dul|li|äh [dʊli'ɛ:] M -, *no pl* (*Aus inf*) tipsiness (*inf*); **im ~** (when one is/was) tipsy

Dult [dʊlt] F -, -en (*S Ger, Aus*: = *Jahrmarkt*) fair

Dul|zi|nea [dʊltsi'ne:a] F -, Dulzineen [-'ne:ən] (*hum*) ladylove

Dum|dum [dʊm'dʊm] NT -(s), -(s), **Dum|dum|ge|schoss** ▲ NT dumdum (bullet)

dumm [dʊm] ADJ *comp* ⸚er ['dʏmɐ], *superl* ⸚ste(r, s) ['dʏmstə] **a** stupid, dumb (*esp US*); *Mensch* stupid, thick (*inf*), dumb (*esp US*); (= *unklug, unvernünftig*) stupid, silly, foolish; **der ~e August** (*inf*) the clown; **~e Gans** silly goose; **~es Zeug (reden)** (to talk) rubbish (*Brit*) *or* nonsense; **ein ~es Gesicht machen** to look stupid; **jdn wie einen ~en Jungen behandeln** (*inf*) to treat sb like a child; **jdn für ~ verkaufen** (*inf*) to think sb is stupid; **du willst mich wohl für ~ verkaufen** you must think I'm stupid; **ich lasse mich nicht für ~ verkaufen** I'm not so stupid (*inf*); **das ist gar nicht (so) ~** that's not a bad idea; **er ist dümmer als die Polizei erlaubt** (*inf*) he's as stupid as they come (*inf*); **das war dümmer als die Polizei erlaubt** (*inf*) that was as stupid as you can get (*inf*); **jetzt wirds mir zu ~** I've had enough; **der Krach macht mich ganz ~ (im Kopf)** the noise is making my head spin → **Bohnenstroh, Bauer**[1] → **Wäsche b** **b** (= *ärgerlich, unangenehm*) annoying; *Gefühl auch* nagging; *Sache, Geschichte, Angelegenheit*

---

auch silly; **es ist zu ~, dass er nicht kommen kann** it's too bad that he can't come; **etwas Dummes** a silly *or* stupid thing; **so etwas Dummes** how silly *or* stupid; (= *wie ärgerlich*) what a nuisance **ADV** *comp* **˚er**, *superl* **am ˚sten ~ gucken** to look stupid; **dümmer hättest du dich wirklich nicht anstellen können** you couldn't have made things worse if you'd tried; **sich ~ anstellen** to behave stupidly; **sich ~ stellen** to act stupid, to play dumb (*esp US*); **~ fragen** to ask a silly question/silly questions; **~ dastehen** to look stupid *or* foolish; **sich ~ und dämlich reden** (*inf*) to talk till one is blue in the face (*inf*); **sich ~ und dämlich suchen** (*inf*) to search high and low; **sich ~ und dämlich verdienen** (*inf*) to earn the earth (*inf*); **~ geboren, nichts dazugelernt** (*prov*) he/she *etc* hasn't got the sense he/she *etc* was born with (*prov*); **jdm ~ kommen** to get funny with sb (*inf*)

Dumm-: Dumm|bach NT -s, *no pl* (*inf*) **ich bin doch nicht aus ~** you can't fool me that easily, I'm not stupid; **Dumm|bart** M , **Dumm|beutel** M (*inf*) fool (*inf*), dumbbell (*US inf*)

Dumm|chen ['dʊmçən] NT -s, - (*inf*) silly-billy (*Brit inf*), ninny (*inf*)

dumm|dreist **ADJ** insolent; *Idee* impertinent **ADV** *grinsen, antworten* insolently, impertinently

Dumm|dreis|tig|keit F insolence

Dum|me|jun|gen|streich M silly *or* foolish *or* childish prank

Dum|men|fang M **das ist der reinste ~** that's just a con (*inf*); **auf ~ ausgehen** to try to catch fools

Dum|me(r) ['dʊmə] MF *decl as adj* (*inf*) mug (*inf*), fool, sucker (*inf*); **der ~ sein** to be left to carry the can (*inf*), to be left holding the baby (*inf*); **einen ~n finden** to find a mug (*inf*) *or* a sucker (*inf*)

Dum|mer|chen ['dʊmɐçən] NT -s, - (*inf*) silly-billy (*Brit inf*), ninny (*inf*); **mein ~** you silly-billy (*Brit inf*) *or* ninny (*inf*)

Dum|mer|jan ['dʊmɐjaːn] M -s, -e (*inf*) silly dope (*inf*)

dum|mer|wei|se ADV unfortunately; (= *aus Dummheit*) stupidly, foolishly

Dumm|heit F -, -en **a** *no pl* stupidity; **vor ~ brüllen** *or* **schreien** to be incredibly stupid *or* thick (*inf*) **b** (= *dumme Handlung*) stupid thing; **mach bloß keine ~en!** just don't do anything stupid

Dumm|kopf M (*inf*) idiot, fool

dümm|lich ['dʏmlıç] ADJ silly, stupid; *Mensch auch* foolish, dumb (*esp US*); **eine ~e Blondine** a dumb blonde

Dümm|ling ['dʏmlıŋ] M -s, -e fool

Dumm|schwät|zer(in) M(F) (*inf*) hot-air merchant (*inf*), bullshitter (*vulg*)

Dum|my ['dami] M -s, -s **a** (= *Attrappe, bei Unfalltests*) dummy **b** (= *Probeband*) demo (tape) (*inf*)

düm|peln ['dʏmpln] VI **a** (*Naut*) to bob up and down **b** (*fig*) to hover; **die Partei dümpelt bei 40%** the party is hovering around the 40% mark

dumpf [dʊmpf] **ADJ** **a** *Geräusch, Ton* muffled **b** *Luft, Geruch, Keller, Geschmack etc* musty; (*fig*) *Atmosphäre* stifling **c** *Gefühl, Ahnung, Erinnerung* vague; *Schmerz* dull; (= *bedrückend*) gloomy **d** (= *stumpfsinnig*) dull **ADV** **a** (= *hohl*) *aufprallen* with a thud; **~ klingen** to sound dull; (*weil hohl*) to sound hollow **b** (= *stumpfsinnig*) **~ glotzen** to have a mindless look on one's face; **~ vor sich hin brüten** to be completely apathetic

Dumpf|ba|cke F (*sl*) nerd (*inf*)

Dumpf|heit F -, *no pl* **a** (*von Geräusch, Ton*) muffled quality **b** (*von Luft, Geruch, Keller, Geschmack etc*) mustiness; **die ~ der Provinzatmosphäre** (*fig*) the stifling atmosphere of the provinces **c** (*von Gefühl, Ahnung, Erinnerung*) vague-

ness; (*von Schmerz*) dullness; (= *Bedrücktheit*) gloominess **d** (= *Stumpfsinnigkeit*) dullness

dump|fig ['dʊmpfıç] ADJ (= *feucht*) dank, damp; (= *muffig*) musty; (= *moderig*) mouldy (*Brit*), moldy (*US*)

Dump|fig|keit F -, *no pl* (= *Feuchte*) dankness, dampness; (= *Muffigkeit*) mustiness; (= *Moderigkeit*) mouldiness (*Brit*), moldiness (*US*)

Dum|ping ['dampıŋ] NT -s, *no pl* (*Econ*) dumping

Dum|ping|preis ['dampıŋ-] M giveaway price

dun [duːn] ADJ (*N Ger inf*) sloshed (*inf*)

Dü|ne ['dyːnə] F -, -n (sand) dune

Dü|nen-: Dü|nen|bil|dung F formation of dunes; **Dü|nen|gras** NT marram (grass); **Dü|nen|sand** M dune sand

Dung [dʊŋ] M -(e)s, *no pl* dung, manure

Dün|ge|mit|tel NT fertilizer

dün|gen ['dʏŋən] **VT** to fertilize **VI** (*Stoff*) to act as a fertilizer; (*Mensch*) to apply fertilizer; **im Garten ~** to put fertilizer on the garden

Dün|ger ['dʏŋɐ] M -s, - fertilizer

Dung-: Dung|flie|ge F dung fly; **Dung|gru|be** F manure pit; **Dung|hau|fen** M dung *or* manure heap

Dün|gung F -, -en **a** (= *das Düngen*) fertilizing **b** (= *Dünger*) fertilizer

dun|kel ['dʊŋkl] **ADJ** **a** (= *finster*) dark; (*fig auch*) black; **im Dunkeln** in the dark; **in dunkler Nacht** at dead of night; **im Zimmer ~ machen** (*inf*) to make the room dark, to darken the room
  b (*farblich*) dark; **ein Dunkles, bitte!** ≈ a brown ale (*Brit*) *or* dark beer, please
  c (= *tief*) *Stimme, Ton* deep
  d (= *unbestimmt, unklar*) vague; *Erinnerung* vague, dim; *Textstelle* unclear; **in dunkler Vergangenheit** *or* **Vorzeit** in the dim and distant past; **im Dunkeln tappen** (*fig*) to grope (about) in the dark; **jdn im Dunkeln lassen** to leave sb in the dark; **das liegt noch im Dunkeln** that remains to be seen
  e (*pej*: = *zweifelhaft, zwielichtig*) shady (*inf*), dubious
  ADV **a** (= *in dunklen Farben*) in a dark colour (*Brit*) *or* color (*US*), in dark colours (*Brit*) *or* colors (*US*); **~ gefärbt sein** to be a dark colo(u)r; **sich ~ kleiden** to dress in dark colo(u)rs; **~ gekleidet** dressed in dark(-coloured) (*Brit*) *or* dark(-colored) (*US*) clothes; **etw ~ anmalen** to paint sth a dark colo(u)r
  b **sich ~ erinnern** to remember vaguely

Dun|kel ['dʊŋkl] NT -s, *no pl* (*lit, fig*) darkness; **im ~ der Vergangenheit** in the dim and distant past; **das verliert sich im ~ der Geschichte** it is lost in the mists of history; **in ~ gehüllt sein** (*fig*) to be shrouded in mystery; **im ~ der Nacht** at dead of night

Dün|kel ['dʏŋkl] M -s, *no pl* (*pej geh*) conceit, arrogance

dun|kel- *in cpds* dark; **dun|kel|blau** ADJ dark blue; **dun|kel|blond** ADJ light brown; **dun|kel|braun** ADJ dark brown; **dun|kel|far|ben** ADJ dark-coloured (*Brit*), dark-colored (*US*); **dun|kel|ge|klei|det** △ ADJ *attr* → **dunkel** ADV **a**; **dun|kel|grau** ADJ dark grey (*Brit*), dark gray (*US*); **dun|kel|grün** ADJ dark green; **dun|kel|haa|rig** ADJ dark-haired

dün|kel|haft ADJ (*pej geh*) arrogant, conceited

Dün|kel|haf|tig|keit F -, *no pl* (*pej geh*) arrogance, conceit

Dun|kel-: dun|kel|häu|tig ADJ dark-skinned; **Dun|kel|heit** F -, (*rare*) -en (*lit, fig*) darkness; **bei Einbruch** *or* **Eintritt der ~** at nightfall; **Dun|kel|kam|mer** F (*Phot*) darkroom; **Dun|kel|kam|mer|leuch|te** F , **Dun|kel|kam|mer|lam|pe** F safelight; **Dun|kel|mann** M *pl* **-män|ner** (*pej*) **a** shady character **b** (*liter*) obscurant(ist)

dun|keln ['dʊŋkln] **VI** *impers* **es dunkelt** (*geh*) darkness is falling, it is growing dark **VI a**

(*poet: Nacht, Abend*) to grow dark **b** *aux sein* (= *dunkel werden*) to become darker, to darken

Dun|kel-: dun|kel|rot ADJ dark red; **dun|kel|weiß** ADJ (*hum*) off-white; **Dun|kel|wer|den** NT nightfall; **Dun|kel|zif|fer** F *estimated number of unreported/undetected cases*; **Dun|kel|zo|ne** F twilight zone

dün|ken ['dʏŋkn] (*geh*) *pret* **dünkte** *or* (*obs*) **deuchte** ['dʏŋktə, 'dɔɪçtə], *ptp* **gedünkt** *or* (*obs*) **gedeucht** [gə'dʏŋkt, gə'dɔɪçt] **VTI** *impers* **das dünkt mich gut, das dünkt mich** *or* **mir gut zu sein, mich dünkt, dass das gut ist** it seems good to me; **mich dünkt, er kommt nicht mehr** methinks (*obs*) *or* I think he will not come **VI** to seem, to appear **VR** to think *or* imagine (oneself); **sie dünkt sich sehr klug** she thinks herself very clever

dünn [dʏn] **ADJ** thin; *Suppe, Bier auch* watery; *Kaffee, Tee* watery, weak; (= *fein*) *Schleier, Regen, Strümpfe* fine; *Haarwuchs, Besiedlung* thin, sparse; (*fig*: = *dürftig*) thin; **sich ~ machen** (*hum*) to breathe in → **dick, dünnmachen** **ADV** *besiedelt, bevölkert* sparsely; **~ behaart** (*Mensch*) with thin hair; *Haupt* thinly covered in hair; **~ gesät** (*fig*) thin on the ground, few and far between

Dünn-: dünn|be|haart △ ADJ *attr* → **dünn** ADV; **dünn|be|sie|delt** △ [-bəzi:dlt], **dünn|be|völ|kert** △ [-bəfœlkɐt] ADJ *attr* → **dünn** ADV; **Dünn|bier** NT weak beer; **Dünn|brett|boh|rer(in)** M(F) (*pej inf*) slacker, skiver (*Brit inf*); **geistiger ~** dimwit (*inf*); **Dünn|darm** M small intestine; **Dünn|druck|aus|ga|be** F India paper edition; **Dünn|druck|pa|pier** NT India paper

dün|ne ['dʏnə] ADJ *pred* (*dial*) = **dünn**

Dün|ne ['dʏnə] F -, *no pl* = **Dünnheit**

dün|ne+ma|chen VR *sep* (*dial, inf*) to make oneself scarce (*inf*)

dün|ne|mals ['dʏnəma:ls] ADV (*dated, hum*) = **damals**

Dünn-: dünn|flüs|sig ADJ *Farbe, Öl* thin; *Teig, Honig* runny; *Stuhlgang* loose; **Dünn|flüs|sig|keit** F (*von Farbe, Öl*) thinness; (*von Teig, Honig*) runniness; (*von Stuhlgang*) looseness; **dünn|ge|sät** △ [-gəze:t] ADJ *attr* → **dünn** ADV; **dünn|häu|tig** ADJ thin-skinned; (*fig auch*) sensitive; **dünn|lip|pig** [-lıpıç] ADJ thin-lipped; **dünn+ma|chen** VR *sep* (*inf*: = *weglaufen*) to make oneself scarce; **Dünn|pfiff** M (*inf*) the runs (*inf*); **Dünn|säu|re** F dilute acid; **Dünn|säu|re|ver|klap|pung** F dumping of dilute acids; **dünn|scha|lig** [-ʃa:lıç] ADJ *Obst* thin-skinned; *Nüsse, Ei etc* thin-shelled; **Dünn|schiss** ▲ M (*inf*) the runs (*inf*); **dünn|wan|dig** ADJ *Haus, Behälter, Blutgefäße* thin-walled

Dunst [dʊnst] M -(e)s, -e [ˈdʏnstə] (= *leichter Nebel*) mist, haze; (= *Dampf*) steam; (= *Smog*) smog; (= *dumpfe Luft*) fug; (= *Geruch*) smell; **blauer ~** (*fig inf*) sheer invention; **jdm blauen ~ vormachen** (*inf*) to throw dust in sb's eyes; **sich in ~ auflösen** to go up in smoke → **blass d**

Dunst-: Dunst|ab|zugs|hau|be F extractor hood (*over a cooker*); **dunst|ar|tig** ADJ *Rauch, Nebel* vapoury (*Brit*), vapory (*US*), vaporous

duns|ten ['dʊnstn] VI **a** (= *dampfen*) to steam **b** (= *Dunst ausströmen*) to give off a smell, to smell

düns|ten ['dʏnstn] VT (*Cook*) *Gemüse, Fisch, Fleisch* to steam; *Obst* to stew

Dunst|glo|cke F , **Dunst|hau|be** F (= *Nebel*) haze; (= *Smog*) pall of smog

duns|tig ['dʊnstıç] ADJ **a** hazy, misty; *Licht* hazy **b** (= *schlecht belüftet*) stuffy; (= *verräuchert*) smoky

Dunst|kreis M atmosphere; (*von Mensch*) society

Dünst|obst NT (*Cook*) stewed fruit

Dunst-: Dunst|schicht F layer of haze *or* mist; **Dunst|schlei|er** M veil of haze *or* mist; **Dunst|schwa|den** PL clouds *pl* of haze; (= *Nebel*) haze *sing*; (= *Dampf*) clouds *pl* of steam;

(= *Rauch*) clouds *pl* of smoke; **Dunst|wol|ke** F cloud of smog

Dü|nung ['dy:nʊŋ] F -, -en (*Naut*) swell

Duo ['du:o] NT -s, -s **a** (*Mus*) (= *Musikstück*) duet, duo; (= *Ausführende*) duo **b** (= *Paar*) duo

Du|o|dez- [duo'de:ts-]: **Du|o|dez|aus|ga|be** F duodecimo edition; **Du|o|dez|band** [-bant] M *pl* -bände duodecimo volume; **Du|o|dez|fürst** M (*pej geh*) princeling, minor *or* petty prince; **Du|o|dez|fürs|ten|tum** NT (*pej geh*) minor *or* petty princedom

Du|o|de|zi|mal|sys|tem [duodetsi'ma:l-] NT duodecimal system

Du|o|dez|staat [duo'de:ts-] M (*pej geh*) miniature state

dü|pie|ren [dy'pi:rən] *ptp* **düpiert** VT (*geh*) to dupe

dü|piert [dy'pi:ɛt] ADJ (*geh*) duped

Dup|li|kat [dupli'ka:t] NT -(e)s, -e duplicate (copy)

Dup|li|ka|ti|on [duplika'tsio:n] F -, -en (*geh*) duplication

dup|li|zie|ren [dupli'tsi:rən] *ptp* **dupliziert** VT (*geh*) to duplicate

Dup|li|zi|tät [duplitsi'tɛ:t] F -, -en (*geh*) duplication

Dup|lo|stein® ['duplo-] M Duplo® brick

Dur [du:ɐ] NT -, *no pl* (*Mus*) major; **ein Stück in ~/in G-Dur** a piece in a major key/in G major

du|ra|bel [du'ra:bl] ADJ (*geh*) durable

Dur|ak|kord M major chord

durch [dʊrç] PREP +acc **a** (*räumlich*: = *hindurch*) through; **quer ~** right across; **mitten ~ die Stadt** through the middle of the town; **~ den Fluss waten** to wade across the river; **~ die ganze Welt reisen** to travel all over the world *or* throughout the world **b** (= *mittels, von*) through, by (means of); (*in Passivkonstruktion*: = *von*) by; (= *über jdn/etw, mit jds Hilfe*) through, via; (*den Grund, die Ursache nennend*) through, because of; **Tod ~ Ertrinken/den Strang** death by drowning/hanging; **Tod ~ Erfrieren/Herzschlag** *etc* death from exposure/a heart attack *etc*; **neun (geteilt) ~ drei** nine divided by three, three into nine; **~ Zufall/das Los** by chance/lot; **~ die Post** by post (*Brit*) *or* mail; **etw ~ die Zeitung bekannt geben** to announce sth in the press; **~ den Lautsprecher** through the loudspeaker **c** (= *aufgrund, infolge von*) due *or* owing to **d** (*Aus: zeitlich*) for

ADV **a** (= *hindurch*) through; **die ganze Nacht ~** all through the night, throughout the night; **es ist 4 Uhr ~** it's past *or* gone 4 o'clock; **~ und ~ (kennen)** through and through; **verlogen, überzeugt** completely, utterly; **~ und ~ ehrlich** honest through and through; **~ und ~ nass** wet through; **das geht mir ~ und ~** that goes right through me **b** (*Cook inf*) *Steak* well-done; **das Fleisch ist noch nicht ~** the meat isn't done yet → *auch* **durch sein**

durch- (*in Verbindung mit Verben*) through

durch+ackern *sep* (*inf*) VT to plough (*Brit*) *or* plow (*US*) through VR to plough (*Brit*) *or* plow (*US*) one's way through (*durch etw sth*)

durch+ar|bei|ten *sep* VT **a** *Buch, Stoff etc* to work *or* go through **b** (= *ausarbeiten*) to work out (in detail) **c** (= *durchkneten*) *Teig, Knetmasse* to work *or* knead thoroughly; *Muskeln* to massage *or* knead thoroughly VI to work through VR **sich durch etw ~** to work one's way through sth

durch|ar|bei|tet [dʊrç'arbaitət] ADJ **nach fünf ~en Nächten** after being up working five whole nights

durch+at|men¹ ['dʊrçatmən] VI *sep* to breathe deeply, to take deep breaths

durch|at|men² [dʊrç'atmən] *ptp* **durchatmet** VT *insep* (*poet*) to pervade, to inform (*liter*)

durch|aus [dʊrç'aus, 'dʊrç|aus, 'dʊrç|aus] ADV **a** (*in bejahten Sätzen*: = *unbedingt*) **das muss ~ sein** that definitely has to be; **sie wollte ~ mitgehen/ein neues Auto haben** she insisted on going too/having a new car; **wenn du das ~ willst** if you insist, if you absolutely must; **das ist ~ nötig** that is absolutely necessary; **du musst ~ mitkommen** you really must come; **muss das sein? – ja ~ is** that necessary? – yes, definitely *or* absolutely; **hat er sich anständig benommen? – ja ~** did he behave himself properly? – yes, perfectly *or* absolutely; **es musste ~ dieses Kleid sein** it absolutely had to be this dress; **er will ~ Recht haben** he (absolutely) insists that he is right

b (*bekräftigend in bejahten Sätzen*) quite; *verständlich, richtig, korrekt, möglich* quite, perfectly; *passen, annehmen* perfectly well; *sich freuen, gefallen* really; **das könnte man ~ machen, das lässt sich ~ machen** that sounds feasible, I/we *etc* could do that; **ich bin ~ Ihrer Meinung** I quite *or* absolutely agree with you; **ich hätte ~ Lust …** I would like to …; **ich hätte ~ Zeit** I would have time; **es ist mir ~ ernst damit** I am quite *or* perfectly *or* absolutely serious about it; **es ist ~ anzunehmen, dass sie kommt** it's highly likely that she'll be coming; **das ist zwar ~ möglich, aber …** that is quite *or* perfectly possible, but …

c (*in bejahten Sätzen*: = *ganz und gar*) *ehrlich, zufrieden, unerfreulich* thoroughly, completely; **ein ~ gelungener Abend** a thoroughly successful evening; **ein ~ beneidenswerter Mensch** a thoroughly enviable person

d (*in verneinten Sätzen*) **~ nicht** (*als Verstärkung*) by no means; (*als Antwort*) not at all; (*stärker*) absolutely not; **~ nicht reich/so klug** by no means rich/as clever; **etw ~ nicht tun wollen** to refuse absolutely to do sth; **das braucht ~ nicht schlecht zu sein** that does not HAVE to be bad; **das ist ~ kein Witz** that's no joke at all; **er ist ~ kein schlechter Mensch** he is by no means a bad person; **es ist ~ nicht so einfach wie …** it is by no means as easy as …

durch+ba|cken *sep* VT *Kuchen* to bake through VI (*Kuchen*) to bake thoroughly

durch|be|ben [dʊrç'be:bn] *ptp* **durchbebt** VT *insep* (*geh*) to run through

durch+bei|ßen¹ ['dʊrçbaisn] *sep irreg* VT (*in zwei Teile*) to bite through VR (*inf*) (*durch etw sth*) to struggle through; (*mit Erfolg*) to win through

durch|bei|ßen² [dʊrç'baisn] *ptp* **durchbissen** [dʊrç'bɪsn] VT *insep irreg* **jdm die Kehle ~** to tear sb's throat open

durch+be|kom|men *ptp* **durchbekommen** VT *sep irreg* (*inf*) to get through

durch+bet|teln VR *sep* to beg one's way

durch+beu|teln VT *sep* (*S Ger inf*) to shake thoroughly (*auch fig*), to give a good shaking

durch+bie|gen *sep irreg* VT *Knie* to bend VR to sag

durch+bla|sen¹ ['dʊrçbla:zn] *sep irreg* VT **a** (= *Luft etc hindurchblasen*) to blow through (*durch etw sth*); *Eileiter, Rohr, Ohren etc* to clear (by blowing) **b** (*Wind*) to blow VI to blow through (*durch etw sth*)

durch|bla|sen² [dʊrç'bla:zn] *ptp* **durchblasen** VT *insep irreg* to blow (through)

durch+blät|tern ['dʊrçblɛtɐn] *sep*, **durch|blät|tern** [dʊrç'blɛtɐn] *ptp* **durchblättert** *insep* VT *Buch etc* to leaf *or* flick through

durch+bläu|en ▲ VT *sep* (*inf*) to beat black and blue

Durch|blick M vista (*auf +acc* of); (= *Ausblick*) view (*auf +acc* of); (*fig inf*: = *Verständnis, Überblick*) knowledge; **den ~ haben** (*inf*) to know what's what (*inf*); **den ~ verlieren** to lose track (*bei* of)

durch+bli|cken VI *sep* **a** (*lit*) to look through (*durch etw sth*); (= *zum Vorschein kommen*) to shine through **b** (*fig*) **etw ~ lassen** to hint at

sth, to intimate sth **c** (*fig inf*: = *verstehen*) to understand; **blickst du da durch?** do you get it? (*inf*)

durch|blit|zen *ptp* **durchblitzt** VT *insep* to flash through; **jdn ~** to flash through sb's mind

durch|blu|ten¹ [dʊrç'blu:tn] *ptp* **durchblutet** VT *insep* to supply with blood → *auch* **durchblutet**

durch+blu|ten² [dʊrç'blu:tn] VTI *sep* **die Wunde hat durchgeblutet** the wound has bled through (the bandage), blood from the wound has soaked through (the bandage); **es blutet durch** the blood is soaking through; **der Verband ist durchgeblutet** the bandage is soaked through with blood

durch|blu|tet [dʊrç'blu:tət] ADJ supplied with blood; **gut/schlecht ~e Körperteile** parts of the body in which circulation is good/bad; **sie hat schlecht ~e Finger** she's got bad circulation in her fingers

Durch|blu|tung [dʊrç'blu:tʊŋ] F circulation (of the blood) (+gen to)

Durch|blu|tungs|stö|rung F circulatory disturbance, disturbance of the circulation

durch|boh|ren¹ [dʊrç'bo:rən] *ptp* **durchbohrt** VT *insep* *Wand, Brett* to drill through; (*mit Schwert etc*) (*Kugel*) to go through; **jdn mit Blicken ~** (*fig*) to look piercingly at sb; (*hasserfüllt*) to look daggers at sb

durch+boh|ren² ['dʊrçbo:rən] *sep* VT **etw durch etw ~** (*Loch, Tunnel*) to drill sth through sth; *Schwert etc* to run sth through sth; *Nagel* to pierce sth through sth VI to drill through (*durch etw sth*) VR (*durch etw sth*) to bore one's way through; (*Speer*) to go through

durch|boh|rend ADJ piercing; *Blicke auch* penetrating

durch+bo|xen *sep* (*fig inf*) (*durch etw sth*) VT to push *or* force through VR to fight one's way through

durch+bra|ten VTI *sep irreg* to cook through; **durchgebraten** well done

durch+brau|sen VI *sep aux sein* to tear *or* roar through (*durch etw sth*)

durch+bre|chen¹ ['dʊrçbrɛçn] *sep irreg* VT (*in zwei Teile*) to break (in two) VI *aux sein* **a** (*in zwei Teile*) to break (in two) **b** (= *einbrechen*: *Mensch*) to fall through (*durch etw sth*) **c** (= *hervorbrechen*) (*Knospen*) to appear; (*Zahn*) to come through; (*Sonne*) to break through, to appear (*durch etw sth*); (*Charakter*) to reveal itself **d** (*Med: Blinddarm etc*) to burst, to perforate

durch|bre|chen² [dʊrç'brɛçn] *ptp* **durchbrochen** [dʊrç'brɔxn] VT *insep irreg* *Schallmauer* to break; *Mauer, Blockade etc* to break through; (*fig*) to break

Durch|bre|chung [dʊrç'brɛçʊŋ] F (*der Schallmauer*) breaking; (*von Mauer, Blockade*) breaking through

durch+bren|nen VI *sep irreg* **a** (= *nicht ausgehen: Ofen, Feuer, Licht etc*) to stay alight **b** *aux sein* (*Sicherung, Glühbirne*) to blow, to burn out; (*inf*: = *davonlaufen*) to run off *or* away, to abscond; **jdm ~** (*inf*) to run away from sb

Durch|bren|ner(in) M(F) (*inf*) runaway

durch+brin|gen *sep irreg* VT **a** (*durch etw sth*) (= *durchsetzen*) *durch Prüfung, Kontrolle* to get through; (*durch Krankheit*) to pull through; (= *für Unterhalt sorgen*) to provide for, to support **b** *Geld* to get through, to blow (*inf*) **c** (*dial*: = *durchbekommen*) to get through VR (*durch etw sth*) to get by; **sich kümmerlich ~** to scrape by

durch|bro|chen [dʊrç'brɔxn] ADJ open; *Stickerei etc* openwork *attr*

Durch|bruch M **a** (*durch etw sth*) (*durch Eis*) falling through *no art*; (*von Knospen*) appearance; (*von Zahn*) coming through; (*von Sonne*) breaking through; (*von Charakter*) revelation; (*von Blinddarm etc*) bursting, perforation; **zum ~ kommen** (*fig*) (*Gewohnheit etc*) to assert *or* show itself; (*Natur*) to reveal itself

b (*Mil*) breakthrough; (*Sport auch*) break; (*fig*: = *Erfolg*) breakthrough; **eine Idee kommt zum ~** an idea comes to the fore, an idea emerges; **jdm/einer Sache zum ~ verhelfen** to help sb/sth on the road to success **c** (= *durchbrochene Stelle*) breach; (= *Öffnung*) opening; (*Geog: von Fluss*) rise, resurgence

durch+buch|sta|bie|ren *ptp* **durchbuchstabiert** VT *sep* to spell out

durch+bum|meln¹ [ˈdʊrçbʊmln] VI *sep aux sein* (*inf*) (= *durchschlendern*) to stroll through (*durch etw sth*); **die Nacht ~** to spend the night on the tiles (*inf*)

durch|bum|meln² [dʊrçˈbʊmln] *ptp* **durchbummelt** VT *insep* Nacht to spend on the tiles (*inf*)

durch+bürs|ten VT *sep* to brush thoroughly

durch+che|cken VT *sep* **a** Gepäck to check through **b** (*inf*: = *überprüfen*) to check through

durch|dacht [dʊrçˈdaxt] ADJ properly thought-out; **gut/schlecht ~** well/badly thought-out

durch|den|ken [dʊrçˈdɛŋkn̩] *ptp* **durchdacht** [dʊrçˈdaxt] VT *insep*, **durch+den|ken** [ˈdʊrçdɛŋkn̩] VT *sep irreg* to think out or through

durch+dis|ku|tie|ren *ptp* **durchdiskutiert** *sep* to discuss thoroughly, to talk through

durch+drän|geln (*inf*), **durch+drän|gen** VR *sep* to push or force one's way through (*durch etw sth*)

durch+dre|hen *sep* VT Fleisch etc to mince VI **a** (*Rad*) to spin **b** (*inf*) to do one's nut (*Brit inf*), to flip (*inf*); (*nervlich*) to crack up (*inf*); **ganz durchgedreht sein** (*inf*) to be really uptight (*inf*) or (*aus dem Gleichgewicht*) confused

durch+drin|gen¹ [ˈdʊrçdrɪŋən] VI *sep irreg aux sein* **a** (= *hindurchkommen*) to penetrate (*durch etw sth*); (*Flüssigkeit, Kälte, Sonne*) to come through (*durch etw sth*); (*Stimme, Geräusch*) to be heard (*durch etw through sth*); **bis zu jdm ~** (*fig*) to go or get as far as sb **b** (= *sich durchsetzen, sich verständlich machen*) to get through; **zu jdm ~** to get through to sb; **mit einem Vorschlag ~** to get a suggestion accepted (*bei, in +dat* by)

durch|drin|gen² [dʊrçˈdrɪŋən] *ptp* **durchdrungen** [dʊrçˈdrʊŋən] VT *insep irreg* Materie, Dunkelheit etc to penetrate; (*Gefühl, Idee, Gedanke*) to pervade → *auch* **durchdrungen**

durch|drin|gend [dʊrçˈdrɪŋənt] ADJ piercing; Kälte, Wind auch biting; Stimme, Geräusch, Blick auch penetrating; Geruch pungent, sharp

Durch|drin|gung [dʊrçˈdrɪŋʊŋ] F -, -en **a** penetration; (= *Sättigung*) saturation; (= *Verschmelzung*) fusion; (*fig*: = *Erfassen*) investigation, exploration

durch+drü|cken *sep* VT **a** (*durch Sieb*) to rub through; (*durch Presse*) to press through; Creme, Teig to pipe **b** (*fig*) Gesetz, Reformen, Neuerungen etc to push or force through; seinen Willen to get; **es ~, dass ...** to get the decision through that ... **c** Knie, Ellbogen etc to straighten **d** Wäsche to wash through VR to squeeze or push (one's way) through (*durch etw sth*); **sich in der Menge ~** to squeeze or push (one's way) through the crowd

Durch|drück|pa|ckung [ˈdʊrçdrʏk-] F (*einzelne Packung*) blister pack; **~en** *pl* blister packaging *sing*

durch|drun|gen [dʊrçˈdrʊŋən] ADJ *pred* imbued (*von* with); **ganz von einer Idee ~ sein** to be taken with an idea; **von einem Gefühl der Freude ~ sein** to be full of or imbued with a feeling of joy → *auch* **durchdringen²**

durch+dür|fen VI *sep irreg* (*inf*) to be allowed through; **darf ich mal durch?** can I get through?; **Sie dürfen hier nicht durch** you can't come through here

durch|ei|nan|der [dʊrçaiˈnandɐ] ADV mixed or muddled up, in a muddle or mess; Gemüse ~ vegetable stew; **alles ~ essen/trinken** to eat/drink indiscriminately ADJ *pred* **~ sein** (*inf*) (*Mensch*) to be confused; (= *aufgeregt*) to be in a

state (*inf*); (*Zimmer, Papier*) to be in a mess or muddle

Durch|ei|nan|der [dʊrçaiˈnandɐ, ˈdʊrçaiˌnandɐ] NT -s, no pl (= *Unordnung*) mess, muddle; (= *Wirrwarr*) confusion; **in dem Zimmer herrscht ein wüstes ~** the room is in a terrible mess or muddle

durch|ei|nan|der: durch|ei|nan|der brin|gen ▲ VT *irreg* to muddle or mix up; (= *in Unordnung bringen auch*) to get into a mess or muddle; (= *verwirren*) jdn to confuse; **durch|ei|nan|der ge|hen** ▲ VI *irreg aux sein* to get confused, to get into a muddle; **durch|ei|nan|der ge|ra|ten** ▲ VI *irreg aux sein* to get mixed or muddled up; **jetzt bin ich mit dem Datum völlig ~** now I've got completely mixed or muddled up about the date; **durch|ei|nan|der kom|men** ▲ VI *irreg aux sein* **a** (= *vermischt werden*) to get mixed or muddled up **b** (*inf*) = *durcheinander geraten*; **durch|ei|nan|der lau|fen** ▲ VI *irreg aux sein* to run about or around all over the place; **durch|ei|nan|der lie|gen** ▲ VI *irreg aux haben or sein* to be in a muddle, to be all over the place; **durch|ei|nan|der men|gen** ▲, **durch|ei|nan|der mi|schen** ▲ VT to mix (up); **durch|ei|nan|der re|den** ▲ VI to all speak or talk at once or at the same time; **durch|ei|nan|der ren|nen** ▲ VI *irreg aux sein* to run about or around all over the place; **durch|ei|nan|der ru|fen** ▲, **durch|ei|nan|der schrei|en** ▲ VI *irreg* to all shout out at once or at the same time; **durch|ei|nan|der wer|fen** ▲ VT *irreg* to muddle up; (*fig inf*: = *verwechseln*) to mix up, to confuse; **durch|ei|nan|der wir|beln** ▲ VT Blätter to whirl around; (*fig*) to shake up

durch+es|sen VR *sep irreg* **a** sich bei jdm ~ to eat at sb's expense **b** sich durch etw ~ to eat one's way through sth

durch+exer|zie|ren *ptp* **durchexerziert** VT *sep* to rehearse, to run or go through

durch+fah|ren¹ [ˈdʊrçfaːrən] VI *sep irreg aux sein* **a** (*durch einen Ort, Tunnel etc*) to go through (*durch etw sth*) **b** (= *nicht anhalten/umsteigen*) to go straight through (without stopping/changing); **er ist bei Rot durchgefahren** he jumped the lights; **die Nacht ~** to travel through the night

durch|fah|ren² [dʊrçˈfaːrən] *ptp* **durchfahren** VT *insep irreg* to travel through; (*fig: Schreck, Zittern etc*) to shoot through; **ein Gedanke durchfuhr ihn blitzartig** a (sudden) thought flashed through his mind

Durch|fahrt F **a** (= *Durchreise*) way through; **auf der ~ sein** to be passing through; **auf** *or* **bei der ~ sieht man ja nicht viel** one doesn't see much when one is just passing through **b** (= *Passage*) thoroughfare; (*Naut*) thoroughfare, channel; **~ bitte freihalten!** please keep access free **c** (= *das Durchfahren*) thoroughfare; **~ verboten!** no through road, no thoroughfare; **der Polizist gab endlich die ~ frei/gab das Zeichen zur ~** the policeman finally allowed/signalled the traffic through

Durch|fahrts-: Durch|fahrts|hö|he F headroom, clearance; **Durch|fahrts|recht** NT right of way; **Durch|fahrts|stra|ße** F through road; **Durch|fahrts|ver|bot** NT seit wann besteht hier ~? since when has this been a no through road?; **die Anwohner haben das ~ durchgesetzt** the residents managed to get through traffic banned

Durch|fall M **a** (*Med*) diarrhoea no art (*Brit*), diarrhea no art (*US*) **b** (= *Misserfolg*) failure; (*von Theaterstück auch*) flop

durch+fal|len VI *sep irreg aux sein* **a** (*durch Loch, Lücke etc*) to fall through (*durch etw sth*) **b** (*inf*: = *nicht bestehen*) to fail; (*Theaterstück etc auch*) to (be a) flop; (*Wahlkandidat*) to lose, to be defeated; **in** *or* **bei der Prüfung ~** to fail the exam; **jdn ~ lassen** to fail sb; **beim Publikum/ bei der Kritik ~** to be a failure or flop with the

public/critics; **bei der Wahl ~** to lose the election, to be defeated in the election

Durch|fall|quo|te F (*Sch etc*) failure rate

durch+fär|ben *sep* VT to dye or colour (*Brit*) or color (*US*) (evenly) VI to come or seep through (*durch etw sth*)

durch+fau|len VI *sep aux sein* to rot through

durch+fech|ten *sep irreg* VT etw ~ to fight to get sth through VR **sich (im Leben) ~** to struggle through (in life)

durch+fe|dern VI *sep* to bend one's knees

durch+fe|gen¹ [ˈdʊrçfeːgn̩] *sep* VT to sweep out VI to sweep up

durch|fe|gen² [dʊrçˈfeːgn̩] *ptp* **durchfegt** VT *insep* to sweep through

durch+fei|ern¹ [ˈdʊrçfaiɐn] VI *sep* to stay up all night celebrating

durch|fei|ern² [dʊrçˈfaiɐn] *ptp* **durchfeiert** VT *insep* **die Nacht ~** to stay up all night celebrating; **nach durchfeierter Nacht** after celebrating all night

durch+fei|len¹ [ˈdʊrçfailən] *sep*, **durch|fei|len** [dʊrçˈfailən] *ptp* **durchfeilt** *insep* VT to file through

durch|feuch|ten [dʊrçˈfɔyçtn̩] *ptp* **durchfeuchtet** VT *insep* to soak; **von etw durchfeuchtet sein** to be soaked (through) with sth

durch+fin|den VIR *sep irreg* (*lit, fig*) to find one's way through (*durch etw sth*); **ich finde (mich) hier nicht mehr durch** (*fig*) I am simply lost; **ich kann mich bei diesem Kram nicht ~** (*fig*) I can't make head nor tail of this mess

durch|flech|ten [dʊrçˈflɛçtn̩] *ptp* **durchflochten** [dʊrçˈflɔxtn̩] VT *insep irreg* etw mit etw ~ (*lit*) to thread or weave sth through sth, to intertwine sth with sth; (*fig*) to interweave sth with sth

durch+flie|gen¹ [ˈdʊrçfliːgn̩] VI *sep irreg aux sein* **a** (*mit Flugzeug*) to fly through (*durch etw sth*); (*ohne Landung*) to fly nonstop or direct **b** (*inf*, *ohne Prüfung*) to fail, to flunk (*inf*) (*durch etw, in etw* (*dat*) (in) sth)

durch|flie|gen² [dʊrçˈfliːgn̩] *ptp* **durchflogen** [dʊrçˈfloːgn̩] VT *insep irreg* Luft, Wolken to fly through; (*Luftkorridor*) to fly along; Strecke to cover; (= *flüchtig lesen*) to skim through

durch+flie|ßen¹ [ˈdʊrçfliːsn̩] VI *sep irreg aux sein* to flow or run through (*durch etw sth*)

durch|flie|ßen² [dʊrçˈfliːsn̩] *ptp* **durchflossen** [dʊrçˈflɔsn̩] VT *insep irreg* (*lit, fig*) to flow or run through

Durch|flug M flight through; (= *das Durchfliegen*) flying through (*durch etw sth*)

Durch|flugs|recht NT *usu sing* overflying rights *pl*, air transit rights *pl*

Durch|fluss ▲ M (= *das Fließen, Durchflussmenge*) flow; (= *Öffnung*) opening

durch+flu|ten¹ [ˈdʊrçfluːtn̩] VI *sep aux sein* (*geh*) to flow through (*durch etw sth*)

durch|flu|ten² [dʊrçˈfluːtn̩] *ptp* **durchflutet** VT *insep* (*geh*) (*Fluss*) to flow through; (*fig*) (*Licht, Sonne*) to flood; (*Wärme, Gefühl*) to flow or flood through; **Licht durchflutete das Zimmer** the room was flooded with or bathed in light, light flooded the room

durch+for|men VT *sep* to work out (down) to the last detail

durch|for|schen [dʊrçˈfɔrʃn̩] *ptp* **durchforscht** VT *insep* Gegend to search; Land, Wissensgebiet to explore; Akten, Bücher to search through

durch|fors|ten [dʊrçˈfɔrstn̩] *ptp* **durchforstet** *insep*, **durch+fors|ten** [ˈdʊrçfɔrstn̩] *sep* VT Wald to thin out; (*fig*) Bücher, Akten etc to go through

durch+fra|gen VR *sep* to ask one's way

durch+fres|sen¹ [ˈdʊrçfrɛsn̩] *sep irreg* VR (*durch etw sth*) (*Säure, Rost, Tier*) to eat (its way) through; **sich (bei jdm) ~** (*pej inf*) to live on sb's hospitality; **sich durch ein Buch ~** (*inf*) to plough (*Brit*) or plow (*US*) or wade through a book VT (*Rost, Maus*) to eat (its way) through;

(*Motten*) to eat holes in; **ein Loch durch etw ~** to eat a hole in sth

durch|fres|sen² [dʊrçˈfrɛsn] *ptp* **durchfressen** VT *insep irreg* to eat through; (*Motten*) to eat holes in; **ein von Motten ~er Pullover** a moth-eaten pullover

durch+fret|ten VR *sep* (*Aus, S Ger*) to eke out an existence

durch+frie|ren VI *sep irreg aux sein* (*See, Fluss*) to freeze through, to freeze solid; (*Mensch*) to get frozen stiff, to get chilled to the bone

durch|fro|ren [dʊrçˈfroːrən] ADJ = **durchgefroren**

Durch|fuhr [ˈdʊrçfuːɐ] F -, **-en** transit, passage

durch|führ|bar ADJ practicable, feasible, workable

Durch|führ|bar|keit [ˈdʊrçfyːɐˈbaːɐkait] F -, *no pl* feasibility, practicability, workability

Durch|führ|bar|keits|stu|die F feasibility study

durch+füh|ren *sep* VT **a** (= *durchleiten*) (*durch etw sth*) *jdn* to lead through, to take through; *Fluss* to lead through; *Leitung, Rohr* to run through; *Straße* to build through, to lay through; *Kanal, Tunnel* to dig through; **etw durch etw ~** to lead *etc* sth through sth; **jdn durch eine Stadt/ein Haus ~** to show sb (a)round a town/a house **b** (= *verwirklichen*) *Vorhaben, Beschluss, Plan* to carry out; *Gesetz* to implement, to enforce; (= *unternehmen, veranstalten*) *Experiment, Haussuchung, Sammlung, Untersuchung, Reform* to carry out; *Test* to run, to carry out; *Expedition, Reise* to undertake; *Messung* to take; *Kursus* to run; *Wahl, Prüfung* to hold; *Unterrichtsstunde* to take, to give **c** (= *konsequent zu Ende bringen*) to carry through; *Gedankengang* to carry through (to its conclusion) VI (*durch etw sth*) to lead through; (*Straße*) to go through; **zwischen etw** (*dat*) **~** to lead between sth; **unter etw** (*dat*) **~** to go under sth

Durch|fuhr-: **Durch|fuhr|er|laub|nis** F transit permit; **Durch|fuhr|han|del** M transit trade; **Durch|fuhr|land** NT country of transit

Durch|füh|rung F **a** (= *das Verwirklichen*) carrying out; (*von Gesetz*) implementation, enforcement; (*von Experiment, Untersuchung, Reise, Expedition*) undertaking; (*von Messung*) taking; (*von Kursus, Test*) running; (*von Wahl, Prüfung*) holding; (*von Unterrichtsstunde*) giving; **zur ~ kommen** (*form, Reform, Gesetz, Maßnahme*) to come into force; **zur ~ bringen** (*form, Reform, Gesetz, Maßnahme*) to bring into force **b** (= *konsequentes Beenden*) carrying through **c** (= *das Durchleiten*) leading; (*von Rohr*) running; (*von Straße*) building; (*von Kanal, Tunnel*) digging **d** (*Mus*) (*von Sonate*) development; (*von Fuge*) exposition

Durch|fuhr-: **Durch|fuhr|ver|bot** NT transit embargo; **Durch|fuhr|zoll** M transit duty

durch|fur|chen [dʊrçˈfʊrçn] *ptp* **durchfurcht** VT *insep* (*geh*) *Land* to plough (*Brit*), to plow (*US*); *Wogen* to plough (*Brit*) or plow (*US*) through

durch+füt|tern VT *sep* (*inf*) to feed; **sich von jdm ~ lassen** to live off sb

Durch|ga|be F **a** (*von Nachricht, Lottozahlen etc*) announcement; (*von Hinweis, Bericht*) giving; **bei der ~ von Zahlen übers Telefon kommen oft Fehler vor** when numbers are given over the telephone mistakes are often made **b** (= *Nachricht, Ankündigung*) announcement; (*telefonisch*) message (over the telephone)

Durch|gang M *pl* **-gänge a** (= *Weg, Passage*) way; (*schmal*) passage(way); (= *Torweg*) gateway **b** (= *das Durchgehen*) **kein ~!**, **~ verboten!** no right of way; **beim ~ durch das Tal** going through the valley; **der ~ zur Höhle/zum anderen Tal ist beschwerlich** it's difficult to get through to the cave/other valley; **er hat mir den ~ versperrt** he blocked my passage **c** (*von Experiment, bei Arbeit, Parl*) stage **d** (*bei Wettbe-*

werb, von Wahl, Sport) round; (*beim Rennen*) heat **e** (*Astron*) transit

Durch|gän|ger [-gɛŋɐ] M **-s, -** (= *Pferd*) bolter

durch|gän|gig ADJ universal, general; **eine ~e Eigenschaft in seinen Romanen** a constant feature in *or* of his novels ADV generally; *feststellbar* universally; **die Kandidaten wurden ~ abgelehnt** every single one of the candidates was rejected

Durch|gän|gig|keit F **a** (*von Stil, Prozess etc*) consistency **b** (*Tech, Med*) ability to penetrate

Durch|gangs-: **Durch|gangs|bahn|hof** M through station; **Durch|gangs|han|del** M transit trade; **Durch|gangs|la|ger** NT transit camp; **Durch|gangs|sta|di|um** NT transition stage; **Durch|gangs|sta|ti|on** F (*fig*) stopping-off place; **Durch|gangs|stra|ße** F through road, thoroughfare; **Durch|gangs|ver|kehr** M (*Mot*) through traffic; (= *Transitverkehr*) transit traffic

durch+ga|ren *sep* VT to cook thoroughly VI *aux sein* to cook through

durch|ge|ba|cken *ptp von* **durchbacken** ADJ *Kuchen* baked through; **nicht richtig** *or* **ganz ~** not properly cooked (through)

durch+ge|ben VT *sep irreg* **a** (= *durchreichen*) to pass through (*durch etw sth*) **b** (*Rad, TV*) *Hinweis, Meldung, Wetter, Straßenzustandsbericht* to give; *Nachricht, Lottozahlen* to announce; **jdm etw telefonisch ~** to let sb know sth by telephone, to telephone sth to sb; **ein Telegramm telefonisch ~** to telephone a telegram; **jdm ~, dass ...** to let sb know that ..., to tell sb that ...; **es wurde im Radio durchgegeben** it was announced on the radio; **wir geben (Ihnen) nun den Wetterbericht durch** and now we bring you the weather forecast

durch|ge|bra|ten *ptp von* **durchbraten** ADJ *Fleisch etc* well-done *attr*, well done *pred*; **es ist noch nicht ~** it isn't (properly) done yet → **durchbraten**

durch|ge|fro|ren ADJ *Mensch* frozen stiff, perishing (cold) (*inf*) *pred*

durch+ge|hen *sep irreg aux sein* VI **a** (*lit*) (*durch etw sth*) to go through, to walk through; (*durch Kontrolle, Zoll*) to pass through; (= *weitergehen, inf*: = *sich durchstecken lassen*) to go through; **bitte ~!** (*im Bus*) move right down (the bus) please! **b** (*Fluss, Weg, Linie etc*) (*durch etw sth*) to run through, to go through; (*fig*: *Thema*) to run through **c** (= *durchdringen*) to come through (*durch etw sth*) **d** (= *nicht zurückgewiesen werden*) (*Gesetz*) to be passed, to go through; (*Antrag*) to be carried, to be passed, to go through **e** (= *toleriert werden*) to be allowed (to pass), to be tolerated; **jdm etw ~ lassen** to let sb get away with sth, to overlook sth; **das lasse ich noch mal ~** I'll let it pass **f** (= *gehalten werden für*) **für etw ~** to pass for sth, to be taken for sth **g** (= *durchpassen*) to go through (*durch etw sth*); **zwischen/unter etw** (*dat*) **~** to go (through) between/under sth **h** (*ohne Unterbrechung*) to go straight through; (*Fußgänger*) to walk *or* go straight through; (*Flug*) to be nonstop *or* direct; (*zeitlich: Party, Unterricht*; *örtlich: Straße, Linie*) to run (right) through, to go straight through; **die ganze Nacht ~** (*Mensch*) to walk all night (long), to walk throughout the night; (*Party*) to last all night (long) **i** (*Pferd etc*) to bolt; (*inf*: = *sich davonmachen*) to run off *or* away; **mit jdm ~** to run *or* go off with sb, to elope with sb; **jdm ~** to run away from sb; **seine Frau ist ihm durchgegangen** his wife has run off and left him; **mit etw ~** to run *or* make off with sth **j** (= *außer Kontrolle geraten*) **mit jdm ~** (*Temperament, Nerven*) to get the better of sb; (*Gefühle auch*) to run away with sb

VT *auch aux haben* (= *durchsehen, -sprechen etc*) to go *or* run through, to go *or* run over VI *impers* **es geht durch/nicht durch** there's a/no way through; **wo geht es durch?** where's the way through?

durch|ge|hend ADJ *Öffnungszeiten* round-the-clock *attr* (*Brit*), around-the-clock *attr* (*US*), continuous; *Straße* straight; *Verkehrsverbindung* direct; *Zug* nonstop, through *attr*, direct; *Fahrkarte* through *attr*; *Muster* continuous; *Eigenschaft* constant; **~e Güter** goods in transit ADV throughout, right through; **~ geöffnet** open right through, open 24 hours; **~ gefüttert** fully lined, lined throughout

durch|geis|tigt [dʊrçˈɡaistɪçt] ADJ cerebral

durch|ge|knallt [-ɡəknalt] ADJ (*inf*: = *verrückt*) cuckoo (*inf*), loopy (*Brit inf*), crazy (*inf*)

durch|ge|le|gen [-ɡəleːɡn] *ptp von* **durchliegen** ADJ *Bett, Matratze* sagging, saggy, worn (down); *Rücken etc* bedsore, suffering from bedsores *pred* → *auch* **durchliegen**

durch|ge|reg|net [-ɡəreːɡnət] ADJ soaked; **ich war völlig ~** I was soaked to the skin, I was soaked through → *auch* **durchregnen**

durch|ge|schwitzt [-ɡəʃvɪtst] ADJ *Mensch* bathed in sweat; *Kleidung* soaked in sweat, sweat-soaked *attr* → *auch* **durchschwitzen**

durch+ge|stal|ten *ptp* **durchgestaltet** VT *sep* to work out (down) to the last detail

durch+gie|ßen VT *sep irreg* to pour through (*durch etw sth*); **etw durch ein Sieb ~** to strain sth, to pour sth through a sieve

durch+glie|dern VT *sep* to subdivide

durch+glü|hen¹ [ˈdʊrçɡlyːən] *sep* VI *aux sein* to glow red-hot; (*Lampe, Draht, Sicherung*) to burn out VT *Eisen* to heat until red-hot, to heat to red heat

durch|glü|hen² [dʊrçˈɡlyːən] *ptp* **durchglüht** VT *insep* (*liter*: *Gefühl*) to glow through; **von Begeisterung durchglüht** aglow with enthusiasm

durch+gra|ben *sep irreg* VT to dig through (*durch etw sth*) VR to dig one's way through (*durch etw sth*)

durch+grei|fen VI *sep irreg* to reach through (*durch etw sth*); (*fig*) to take vigorous action, to resort to drastic measures; **hier muss viel strenger durchgegriffen werden** much more vigorous action is needed here

durch|grei|fend ADJ *Änderung, Maßnahme* drastic; (= *weit reichend*) *Änderung* far-reaching, radical, sweeping *attr*

durch+gu|cken VI *sep* **a** (*durch etw sth*) (*Mensch*) to look through, to peep through; (= *durchscheinen*) to show through **b** (*fig inf*: = *verstehen*) to understand (*durch etw sth*); **guckst du da durch?** do you get it? (*inf*)

durch+ha|ben VT *sep irreg* (*inf*) **etw ~** (= *hindurchbekommen haben*) to have got (*Brit*) or gotten (*US*) sth through (*durch etw sth*); (= *durchgelesen etc haben*) to have got (*Brit*) or gotten (*US*) sth through, to have finished sth; (= *zerteilt haben*) to have got (*Brit*) or gotten (*US*) through sth, to be through sth

durch+ha|cken VT *sep* to chop *or* hack through

Durch|hal|te|ap|pell M appeal to hold out, rallying call

durch+hal|ten *sep irreg* VT (= *durchstehen*) *Zeit, Ehe, Kampf etc* to survive; *Streik* to hold out till the end of, to see through; *Belastung* to (with-)stand; (*Sport*) *Strecke* to stay; *Tempo* (= *beibehalten*) to keep up; (= *aushalten*) to stand; **das Rennen ~** to stay the course VI to hold out, to stick it out (*inf*); (= *beharren*) to persevere, to stick it out (*inf*); (*bei Rennen*) to stay the course; **bis zum Äußersten ~** to hold out or stick it out (*inf*) to the last; **eisern ~** to hold out grimly

Durch|hal|te-: **Durch|hal|te|pa|ro|le** F appeal to hold out, rallying call; **Durch|hal|te|ver|mö|gen** NT , *no pl* staying power, (powers *pl* of) endurance *no indef art*

Durch|hang M sag, slack

durch+hän|gen VI *sep irreg aux haben or sein* to sag; *(fig inf)* (= *deprimiert sein*) to be down (in the mouth) *(inf)*; (= *schlappmachen*) to wilt, to flag; (= *erschöpft sein*) to be shattered *(inf)* or knackered *(Brit inf)*; **du solltest dich nicht so ~ lassen** you shouldn't let yourself go like that

Durch|hän|ger M **-s, -** *(inf: = schlechte Phase)* bad patch; *(an bestimmtem Tag)* off day *(inf)*; **einen ~ haben** to be off form

durch+hau|en¹ [ˈdʊrçhaʊən] *sep irreg or (inf) reg* **VT** **a** (= *entzweischlagen*) to chop or hack in two; (= *spalten*) to split, to cleave **b** *(inf: = verprügeln)* **jdn ~** to give sb a thrashing or walloping *(inf)*, to thrash or wallop *(inf)* sb **VR** *(lit)* to hack one's way through *(durch etw sth)*; *(fig: = sich durchschlagen)* to get by

durch|hau|en² [dʊrçˈhaʊən] *ptp* **durchhauen** VT *insep irreg* to chop or hack in two

durch+he|cheln VT *sep* **a** *Flachs etc* to hackle **b** *(fig inf)* to gossip about, to pull to pieces *(inf)*; **in allen Zeitungen durchgehechelt** dragged through all the papers

durch+hei|zen *sep* **VT** (= *gründlich heizen*) to heat right through; (= *ohne Unterbrechung heizen*) to heat continuously, to heat day and night **VI** *(ohne Unterbrechung)* to keep the heating on

durch+hel|fen *sep irreg* **VI** **jdm (durch etw)** ~ to help sb through (sth) **VR** to get by, to get along, to manage

durch+hö|ren VT *sep* **a** **etw (durch etw)** ~ *(lit, Lärm)* to hear sth (through sth); *(fig) Gefühl, Enttäuschung auch)* to discern sth (through sth); **ich konnte ~, dass ...** I could hear or tell that ... **b** *Schallplatte, Konzert etc* to hear (all the way) through, to hear all of

durch+hun|gern VR *sep* to struggle along on the breadline, to scrape by

durch|ir|ren [dʊrçˈɪrən] *ptp* **durchirrt** VT *insep* to wander or rove or roam through

durch+ixen VT *sep (inf)* to ex out

durch+ja|gen¹ [ˈdʊrçjaːgn] *sep* **VT** **a** (= *durcheilen*) to chase through *(durch etw sth)* **b** *(fig) Gesetz, Prozess etc* to rush or push through **VI** *aux sein* to race or tear through; **zwischen/unter etw** *(dat)* ~ to race or tear between/under sth

durch|ja|gen² [dʊrçˈjaːgn] *ptp* **durchjagt** VT *insep Land etc* to race or tear through

durch+käm|men¹ [ˈdʊrçkɛmən] VT *sep* **a** *Haare* to comb out **b** (= *absuchen*) to comb (through)

durch|käm|men² [dʊrçˈkɛmən] *ptp* **durchkämmt** VT *insep* (= *absuchen*) to comb (through)

durch+kämp|fen *sep* **VT** (= *durchsetzen*) to push or force through **VR** **a** *(durch etw sth)* to fight or battle one's way through; *(fig)* to struggle through **b** = **durchringen VI** (= *Kampf nicht aufgeben) (Soldaten)* to carry on fighting; *(Sportler, Bergsteiger)* to battle on, to carry on the battle or struggle; **es wurde selbst über die Weihnachtszeit durchgekämpft** the fighting continued even over Christmas

durch+kau|en VT *sep Essen* to chew (thoroughly); *(inf: = besprechen)* to go over or through

durch+klet|tern VI *sep aux sein* to climb through *(durch etw sth)*

durch+klin|gen¹ [ˈdʊrçklɪŋən] VI *sep irreg aux haben or sein (durch etw sth)* to sound through; *(fig)* to come through *(durch etw sth)*, to come across *(durch etw through sth)*; **die Musik klang durch den Lärm durch** the music could be heard above the noise

durch|klin|gen² [dʊrçˈklɪŋən] *ptp* **durchklungen** [dʊrçˈklʊŋən] VT *insep irreg* to ring through

durch+knei|fen VT *sep irreg Draht* to snip through

durch+kne|ten VT *sep Teig etc* to knead thoroughly; *(bei Massage)* to massage thoroughly; **sich ~ lassen** to have a thorough massage

durch+knöp|fen VT *sep* to button all the way up; **ein durchgeknöpftes Kleid** a button-through *(Brit)* or button-up dress

durch+ko|chen VTI *sep* to boil thoroughly

durch+kom|men VI *sep irreg aux sein* **a** *(durch etw sth)* (= *durchfahren*) to come through; (= *vorbeikommen, passieren auch)* to come past; **er ist durch diese Straße/Stadt/unter dieser Brücke durchgekommen** he came through this street/town/under or through this bridge
  b *(durch etw sth)* to get through; *(Sonne, Wasser etc)* to come through; *(Sender, Farbe)* to come through; *(Charakterzug)* to show through, to come out or through; (= *sichtbar werden) (Sonne)* to come out; *(Blumen)* to come through; **kommst du durch?** can you get through?; **es kommt immer wieder durch, dass sie Ausländerin ist** the fact that she is a foreigner keeps showing or coming through
  c *(lit, fig: = mit Erfolg durchkommen)* to succeed *(durch etw in sth)*, to get through *(durch etw sth)*; (= *sich durchsetzen) (telefonisch)* to get through; *(finanziell)* to get by; **ich komme mit meiner Hand nicht (durch das Loch) durch** I can't get my hand through (the hole); **mit etw ~** *(mit Forderungen etc)* to succeed with sth; *mit Betrug, Schmeichelei etc* to get away with sth; **er kam (bei dem Lärm) mit seiner Stimme nicht durch** he couldn't make his voice heard (above the noise); **damit kommt er bei mir nicht durch** he won't get away with that with me
  d (= *Prüfung bestehen*) to get through, to pass
  e (= *überleben*) to come through; *(Patient auch)* to pull through
  f *(im Radio)* to be announced

durch+kom|po|nie|ren *ptp* **durchkomponiert** VT *sep* **a** *(Mus) Libretto* to set to music; *Gedicht* to set to music *(with a different setting for each stanza)* **b** *(fig) Bild, Text* to work out in detail **c** *(ohne Unterbrechung)* to compose right through

durch+kön|nen VI *sep irreg (inf)* to be able to get through *(durch etw sth)*

durch+kon|stru|ie|ren *ptp* **durchkonstruiert** VT *sep* **gut durchkonstruiert** well put together throughout

durch+kos|ten VT *sep (geh)* to taste (one after the other); *(fig) Freuden* to taste; *Leiden* to endure, to experience

durch|kreu|zen¹ [dʊrçˈkrɔʏtsn] *ptp* **durchkreuzt** VT *insep* **a** *Land, Wüste, Ozean* to cross, to travel across **b** *(fig) Pläne etc* to thwart, to foil, to frustrate

durch+kreu|zen² [ˈdʊrçkrɔʏtsn] *sep* to cross out, to cross through

Durch|kreu|zung [dʊrçˈkrɔʏtsʊŋ] F **a** *(von Land etc)* crossing **b** *(von Plänen etc)* thwarting, foiling, frustrating

durch+krie|chen VI *sep irreg aux sein* to crawl through, to creep through *(durch etw sth)*

durch+krie|gen VT *sep (inf)* to get through

durch+la|den VTI *sep irreg Gewehr* to reload

durch+lan|gen VI *sep (inf)* **VI** *(durch etw sth)* to reach through, to put one's hand through **VT** (= *durchreichen*) to pass through

Durch|lass ▲ [ˈdʊrçlas] M **-es, Durchlässe** [-lɛsə] **a** (= *Durchgang*) passage, way through; *(für Wasser)* duct **b** *no pl (geh)* permission to pass; **jdm ~ verschaffen** to obtain permission for sb to pass; *(mit Gewalt)* to force a way through for sb; **sich ~ verschaffen** to obtain permission to pass; *(mit Gewalt)* to force one's way through

durch+las|sen VT *sep irreg (durch etw sth)* (= *passieren lassen*) to allow or let through; *Licht, Wasser etc* (= *durchdringen lassen auch*) to let through, to pass; (= *eindringen lassen*) to let in; *(inf: durch Prüfung)* to let through, to pass; *(inf: = durchgehen lassen) Fehler etc* to let pass, to overlook

durch|läs|sig ADJ *Material* permeable; (= *porös*) porous; *Zelt, Regenmantel, Schuh* that lets water in; *Zelt, Schuh* leaky; *Krug, Vase* that lets water out or through; *Grenze* open; **eine ~e Stelle** *(fig)*
a leak; **die Bildungswege ~ machen** to make the elements of the education programme *(Brit)* or program *(US)* interchangeable

Durch|läs|sig|keit F permeability; (= *Porosität*) porosity; **die ~ des Zelts/Krugs** the fact that the tent/jug leaks or lets water through; **die ~ der Bildungswege** the interchangeability of the elements of the education programme *(Brit)* or program *(US)*

Durch|laucht [ˈdʊrçlaʊxt, dʊrçˈlaʊxt] F **-, -en** serenity; **Seine ~** His (Serene) Highness; **(Euer) ~** Your Highness

durch|lauch|tig [dʊrçˈlaʊxtɪç] ADJ *attr (old)* serene

Durch|lauf M **a** (= *das Durchlaufen*) flow **b** *(TV, Rad, Comput)* run, run-through **c** *(Sport)* heat

durch+lau|fen¹ [ˈdʊrçlaʊfn] *sep irreg* **VT** *Schuhe, Sohlen* to go or wear through **VI** *aux sein* **a** *(durch etw sth)* (= *durch Straße/Öffnung etc gehen*) to go through; *(Straße, Rohr etc)* to run through; *(Flüssigkeit)* to run through **b** *(ohne Unterbrechung: Mensch)* to run without stopping; **8 Stunden lang ohne Pause ~** to run for 8 hours without stopping; **der Fries/das Geländer läuft von der einen Seite des Gebäudes zur anderen durch** the frieze/railing runs uninterrupted or without a break from one end of the building to the other

durch|lau|fen² [dʊrçˈlaʊfn] *ptp* **durchlaufen** VT *insep irreg* **a** *Gebiet* to run through; *Strecke* to cover, to run; *(Astron) Bahn* to describe; *Lehrzeit, Schule, Phase* to pass or go through **b** (= *erfassen, erfüllen) (Gerücht)* to spread through; *(Gefühl)* to run through; **es durchlief mich heiß** I felt hot all over

durch|lau|fend [ˈdʊrçlaʊfnt] ADJ continuous

Durch|lauf-: Durch|lauf|er|hit|zer [-lɛhɪtsɐ] M **-s, -** continuous-flow water heater; **Durch|lauf|zeit** F *(Comput)* length of a/the run

durch+la|vie|ren [dʊrçlaˈviːrən] VR *sep* to steer or manoeuvre *(Brit)* or maneuver *(US)* one's way through *(durch etw sth)*

durch|le|ben [dʊrçˈleːbn] *ptp* **durchlebt** VT *insep Jugend, Gefühl* to go through, to experience; *Zeit* to go or live through

durch|lei|den [dʊrçˈlaidn] *ptp* **durchlitten** [dʊrçˈlɪtn] VT *insep irreg* to suffer, to endure

durch+lei|ten VT *sep* to lead through *(durch etw sth)*

durch+le|sen VT *sep irreg* to read through; **etw ganz ~** to read sth all the way through; **etw flüchtig ~** to skim or glance through sth; **etw auf Fehler (hin) ~** to read sth through (looking) for mistakes; **sich** *(dat)* **etw ~** to read sth through

durch|leuch|ten¹ [dʊrçˈlɔʏçtn] *ptp* **durchleuchtet** VT *insep* **a** (= *untersuchen*) *Patienten* to X-ray; *Eier* to candle; *(fig) Angelegenheit etc* to investigate, to probe; **jdm die Lunge ~** to X-ray sb's lungs; **sich ~ lassen** to have an X-ray *(geh: Schein, Sonne etc)* to light up, to flood with light

durch+leuch|ten² [ˈdʊrçlɔʏçtn] VI *sep* to shine through *(durch etw sth)*

Durch|leuch|tung [dʊrçˈlɔʏçtʊŋ] F **-, -en** *(Med: mit Röntgenstrahlen)* X-ray examination; *(fig: von Angelegenheit etc)* investigation

durch+lie|gen *sep irreg* **VT** *Matratze, Bett* to wear down (in the middle) **VR** to get or develop bedsores

durch|lö|chern [dʊrçˈlœçɐn] *ptp* **durchlöchert** VT *insep* to make holes in; *(Motten auch, Rost)* to eat holes in; *Socken etc* to wear holes in; *(fig)* to undermine completely; *Argumente* to shoot down, to undermine completely; **(mit Schüssen) ~** to riddle with bullets; **eine völlig durchlöcherte Leiche** a corpse riddled with bullet holes; **er hatte völlig durchlöcherte Socken/ Kleidung an** his socks/clothes were full of holes; **von Würmern durchlöchert** worm-eaten; **von Rost durchlöchert** eaten away with rust

durch+lot|sen VT *sep* (*durch etw* sth) *Schiff* to pilot through; *Autofahrer* to guide through; (*fig*) to steer through; **jdn durch etw ~** to pilot *etc* sb through sth

durch+lüf|ten¹ ['dʊrçlʏftn] VTI *sep* to air thoroughly; *Wäsche auch* to air through; **ich muss mich mal wieder ~ lassen** (*inf*) I must (go and) get some fresh air

durch|lüf|ten² [dʊrç'lʏftn] **durchlüftet** VT *insep* to air thoroughly

Durch|lüf|tung F -, *no pl* ventilation

durch+lü|gen VR *sep irreg* (*inf*) to lie one's way through (*durch etw* sth)

durch+ma|chen *sep* **VT a** (= *erdulden*) to go through; *Krankheit* to have; *Operation* to undergo, to have; **er hat viel durchgemacht** he has been *or* gone through a lot **b** (= *durchlaufen*) to go through; *Lehre* to serve; (*fig*) *Entwicklung* to undergo; *Wandlung* to undergo, to experience **c** (*inf*: = *durchbewegen, durchstecken etc*) *Faden, Nadel, Stange etc* to put through (*durch etw* sth) **d** (*inf*: = *durchtrennen*) **(in der Mitte) ~** to cut in half **e** (*inf*) (= *durcharbeiten*) to work through; **eine ganze Nacht/Woche ~** (= *durchfeiern*) to have an all-night/week-long party, to make a night/week of it (*inf*) **VI** (*inf*) (= *durcharbeiten*) to work right through; (= *durchfeiern*) to keep going all night

durch+ma|növ|rie|ren VT *sep* to manoeuvre (*Brit*) *or* maneuver (*US*) through (*durch etw* sth)

Durch|marsch M **a** march(ing) through; (*fig*: = *problemloser Durchbruch*) (*Sport, von Politiker*) walkover; (*von Partei*) landslide; **der ~ durch die Stadt** the march through the town; **auf dem ~** when marching through; **sich zum ~ entschließen** (*fig*) to resolve to push (on) through **b** (*inf*: = *Durchfall*) the runs *pl* (*inf*); **den ~ haben** to have the runs (*inf*) **c** (*Cards*) grand slam

durch+mar|schie|ren *ptp* **durchmarschiert** VI *sep aux sein* to march through (*durch etw* sth)

durch+men|gen VT *sep* to mix thoroughly

durch|mes|sen [dʊrç'mɛsn] *ptp* **durchmessen** VT *insep irreg* (*geh*) *Raum* to stride across; *Strecke* to cover

Durch|mes|ser M -s, - diameter; **120 cm im ~** 120 cm in diameter

durch+mi|schen¹ ['dʊrçmɪʃn] VT *sep* to mix thoroughly

durch|mi|schen² [dʊrç'mɪʃn] *ptp* **durchmischt** VT *insep* to (inter)mix; **etw mit etw ~** to mix sth with sth

durch+mo|geln *sep* (*inf*) **VR** to wangle (*inf*) *or* fiddle (*inf*) one's way through **VT** to fiddle through (*inf*) (*durch etw* sth)

durch+müs|sen VI *sep irreg* (*inf*) (*durch etw* sth) to have to go *or* get through; (*fig*) (*durch schwere Zeit*) to have to go through; (*durch Unannehmlichmes*) to have to go through with (*inf*); **da musst du eben durch** (*fig*) you'll just have to see it through

durch+na|gen *sep* **VT** to gnaw through **VR** to gnaw one's way through (*durch etw* sth)

durch+näs|sen¹ [dʊrç'nɛsn] *ptp* **durchnässt** VT *insep* to soak, to drench, to make wet through; **völlig durchnässt** wet through, soaking wet, drenched

durch+näs|sen² ['dʊrçnɛsn] VI *sep* (*Flüssigkeit*) to come *or* seep through (*durch etw* sth); **die Zeltplane nässt durch** wet is coming *or* seeping through the canvas; **die Wunde nässt durch** moisture from the wound is coming *or* seeping through

durch+neh|men VT *sep irreg* **a** (*Sch*) to go through, to do (*inf*) **b** (*pej inf*) to gossip about

durch+num|me|rie|ren ▲ *ptp* **durchnummeriert** VT *sep* to number consecutively (all the way through)

durch+or|ga|ni|sie|ren *ptp* **durchorganisiert** VT *sep* to organize down to the last detail

durch+or|geln VT *sep* (*sl*) *Frau* to ride (*sl*)

durch+pas|sie|ren *ptp* **durchpassiert** VT *sep* to (rub through a) sieve

durch+pau|ken VT *sep* (*inf*) **a** (*Schüler*) to cram (*inf*), to swot up (*Brit inf*); **etw mit jdm ~** to drum sth into sb (*inf*) **b** (= *durchsetzen*) *Gesetz, Änderungen* to force *or* push through **c** (= *durch Schwierigkeiten bringen*) *Schüler* to push through; **dein Anwalt wird dich schon irgendwie ~** your lawyer will get you off somehow

durch+pau|sen VT *sep* to trace

durch+peit|schen VT *sep* to flog; (*fig*) to rush through, to railroad through (*inf*)

durch+pflü|gen¹ ['dʊrçpflyːgn] *sep* **VT** to plough (*Brit*) *or* plow (*US*) thoroughly **VR** to plough (*Brit*) *or* plow (*US*) (one's way) through (*durch etw* sth)

durch|pflü|gen² [dʊrç'pflyːgn] *ptp* **durchpflügt** VT *insep* to plough (*Brit*) *or* plow (*US*) through

durch+pla|nen VT *sep* to plan (down) to the last detail

durch+plump|sen VI *sep aux sein* (*inf*) (*lit*) to fall through (*durch etw* sth); (*bei Prüfung*) to fail, to flunk (*inf*) (*durch etw, in etw* (*dat*) in) sth

durch+pres|sen VT *sep* to press through, to squeeze through; *Knoblauch* to crush; *Kartoffeln* to mash (*by pushing through a press*); *Teig* to pipe

durch+pro|ben VT *sep* to rehearse right through

durch+pro|bie|ren *ptp* **durchprobiert** VT *sep* to try one after the other

durch+prü|geln VT *sep* to thrash, to beat

durch|pul|sen [dʊrç'pʊlzn] *ptp* **durchpulst** VT *insep* (*geh*) to pulsate through; **von etw durchpulst sein** to be pulsating *or* vibrating with sth; **von Leben durchpulst** pulsating *or* throbbing with life

durch+pus|ten VT *sep* (*inf*) *Rohr, Düse* to blow through; **etw (durch etw) ~** to blow sth through (sth); **der Wind hat uns kräftig durchgepustet** the wind blew right through us

durch|que|ren [dʊrç'kveːrən] *ptp* **durchquert** VT *insep* to cross; *Land, Gebiet auch* to pass through, to traverse (*form*)

Durch|que|rung F -, -en *usu sing* crossing

durch+quet|schen *sep* (*inf*) **VT** = **durchpressen** **VR** (*inf*) to squeeze (one's way) through

durch+ra|sen¹ ['dʊrçraːzn] VI *sep aux sein* (*durch etw* sth) to race *or* tear through; (*inf*: = *durchrennen auch*) to dash through

durch|ra|sen² [dʊrç'raːzn] *ptp* **durchrast** VT *insep* to race through, to tear through; (*liter*: *Schmerz*) to shoot through

durch+ras|seln VI *sep aux sein* (*inf*) to fail, to flunk (*inf*) (*durch etw, in etw* (*dat*) in) sth

durch+rau|schen VI *sep aux sein* (*inf*) (*durch etw* sth) **a** (*durch einen Raum*) to sweep through **b** (*bei Prüfung*) to fail, to flunk (*inf*) (*durch etw, in etw* (*dat*) in) sth

durch+rech|nen VT *sep* to calculate; **eine Rechnung noch einmal ~** to go over *or* through a calculation (again)

durch+reg|nen VI *impers sep* **a** (= *durchkommen*) **hier regnet es durch** the rain is coming through here; **es regnet durchs Dach durch** the rain is coming through the roof **b** (= *ununterbrochen regnen*) to rain continuously; **während des ganzen Festivals hat es durchgeregnet** it rained throughout the whole festival; **es hat die Nacht durchgeregnet** it rained all night long, it rained all through the night → *auch* **durchgeregnet**

durch+rei|ben *sep irreg* **VT** to rub through; *Material* to wear through; **VR** (*Material*) to wear through

Durch|rei|che ['dʊrçraɪçə] F -, -n (serving) hatch, pass-through (*US*)

durch+rei|chen VT *sep* to pass *or* hand through (*durch etw* sth)

Durch|rei|se F journey through; **auf der ~ sein** to be on the way through, to be passing through

Durch|rei|se|er|laub|nis F permission to travel through

durch+rei|sen¹ ['dʊrçraɪzn] VI *sep aux sein* (*durch etw* sth) to travel through, to pass through; **wir reisen nur durch** we are just passing through, we are just on the way through

durch|rei|sen² [dʊrç'raɪzn] *ptp* **durchreist** VT *insep* to travel through, to traverse (*form*)

Durch|rei|sen|de(r) MF *decl as adj* traveller (*Brit*) *or* traveler (*US*) (passing through), transient (*US*); **~ nach München** through passengers to Munich

Durch|rei|se|vi|sum NT transit visa

durch+rei|ßen *sep irreg* **VT** to tear in two *or* in half; **etw (in der Mitte) ~** to tear sth in two *or* in half *or* down the middle **VI** *aux sein* to tear in two *or* in half; (*Seil*) to snap (in two *or* in half)

durch+rei|ten¹ ['dʊrçraɪtn] *sep irreg* **VI** *aux sein* to ride through (*durch etw* sth); **die Nacht ~** to ride through(out) the night, to ride all night long **VT** *Hose* to wear out (through riding)

durch|rei|ten² [dʊrç'raɪtn] *ptp* **durchritten** VT *insep irreg* to ride through; *Land auch* to ride across

durch+ren|nen¹ ['dʊrçrɛnən] VI *sep irreg aux sein* to run *or* race through (*durch etw* sth)

durch|ren|nen² [dʊrç'rɛnən] *ptp* **durchrannt** [dʊrç'rant] VT *insep irreg* to run *or* race through

durch+rie|seln¹ ['dʊrçriːzln] VI *sep aux sein* to trickle through (*durch etw* sth); **jdm zwischen den Fingern ~** to trickle between *or* through sb's fingers

durch|rie|seln² [dʊrç'riːzln] *ptp* **durchrieselt** VT *insep* (*fig*: *Gefühl, Schauer*) to run through

durch+rin|gen VR *sep irreg* to make up one's mind finally; **er hat sich endlich durchgerungen** after much hesitation, he has finally made up his mind *or* come to a decision; **sich zu einem Entschluss ~** to force oneself to make a decision; **sich dazu ~, etw zu tun** to bring *or* force oneself to do sth

durch+rin|nen VI *sep irreg aux sein* to run through (*durch etw* sth); (= *durchsickern*) to trickle through; (*zwischen etw* (*dat*) ~ to run between sth; **das Geld rinnt mir nur so zwischen den Fingern durch** (*fig inf*) money just runs through my fingers

Durch|ritt M ride through; **beim ~, auf dem ~** on the ride through

durch+ros|ten VI *sep aux sein* to rust through

durch+ruf|en VI *sep irreg* (*inf*) to ring

durch+rüh|ren VT *sep* to mix thoroughly

durch+rut|schen VI *sep aux sein* (*lit*) to slip through (*durch etw* sth); (*fig*) (*Fehler etc*) to slip through; (*bei Prüfung*) to scrape through; **zwischen etw** (*dat*) **~** to slip between sth; **einige Fehler sind ihm durchgerutscht** a few mistakes slipped past him, he let a few mistakes slip through

durch+rüt|teln VT *sep* to shake about

durchs [dʊrçs] *contr von* **durch das**

durch+sä|beln VT *sep* (*inf*) to hack through

durch+sa|cken VI *sep aux sein* **a** (= *durchhängen*) (*Bett etc*) to sag; (= *durchbrechen*) (*Dach, Sitz*) to give way; (= *nach unten sinken*) to sink; **durch etw ~** (*Mensch*) to fall (down) through sth **b** (*Aviat*: *Flugzeug*) to pancake

Durch|sa|ge F message; (*im Radio*) announcement; **eine ~ der Polizei** a police announcement

durch+sa|gen VT *sep* **a** = **durchgeben b b** *Parole, Losung* to pass on

durch+sä|gen VT *sep* to saw through

Durch|satz M (*Ind, Comput*) throughput

durch|sau|fen[1] [ˈdʊrçzaufn] *sep irreg* (*inf*) **VI** to booze the whole night long (*inf*); **die Nacht ~** to booze all night long (*inf*) **VR** to booze at somebody else's expense (*inf*); **sich durch etw ~** to booze one's way through sth (*inf*)

durch|sau|fen[2] [dʊrçˈzaufn] *ptp* **durchsoffen** [dʊrçˈzɔfn] VT *insep irreg* (*inf*) → **durchsoffen**

durch+sau|sen VI *sep aux sein* (*inf*) **a** (= *durchflitzen*) to rush or whizz (*inf*) through (*durch etw* sth) **b** (*inf: = nicht bestehen*) to fail, to flunk *dat* (*durch etw, in etw* (*inf*) (in) sth)

durch+schal|ten *sep* **VT** (*Elec*) to connect through **VI a** (*Elec*) to connect through **b** (*Aut*) to change through the gears

durch|schau|bar [dʊrçˈʃaubaːɐ] ADJ (*fig*) *Hintergründe, Plan, Ereignisse* clear; *Lüge* transparent; **gut** or **leicht ~** (= *verständlich*) easily comprehensible or understood; (= *erkennbar, offensichtlich*) perfectly clear; **eine leicht ~e Lüge** a lie that is easy to see through; **schwer ~er Charakter/Mensch** inscrutable or enigmatic character/person

Durch|schau|bar|keit F -, *no pl* (*von Hintergründen, Plan, Ereignissen*) clearness; (*von Lüge*) transparency

durch|schau|en[1] [dʊrçˈʃauən] *ptp* **durchschaut** VT *insep* (= *erkennen*) *Absichten, Lüge, jdn, Spiel* to see through; *Sachlage* to see clearly; (= *begreifen*) to understand, to comprehend; **du bist durchschaut!** I've/we've seen through you, I/we know what you're up to (*inf*); I/we know what your little game is (*inf*)

durch+schau|en[2] [ˈdʊrçʃauən] VTI *sep* (*esp dial*) = **durchsehen VI VT a b**

durch|schau|ern [dʊrçˈʃauɐn] *ptp* **durchschauert** VT *insep* to run through; **es durchschauert mich** a shiver or shudder runs through me

durch+schei|nen[1] [ˈdʊrçʃainən] VI *sep irreg* (*durch etw* sth) (*Licht, Sonne*) to shine through; (*Farbe, Muster*) to show through; (*fig*) to shine through

durch|schei|nen[2] [dʊrçˈʃainən] *ptp* **durchschienen** [dʊrçˈʃiːnən] VT *insep irreg* (*Sonne*) to flood with light

durch|schei|nend [ˈdʊrçʃainənt] ADJ transparent; *Porzellan, Papier auch* translucent; *Stoff auch* diaphanous; *Bluse etc* see-through

durch+scheu|ern *sep* **VT** to wear through; **sich** (*dat*) **die Haut ~** to graze one's skin; **durchgescheuert sein** to be or have worn through **VR** to wear through

durch+schie|ben *sep irreg* **VT** to push or shove (*inf*) through (*durch etw* sth) **VR** to push or shove (*inf*) (one's way) through (*durch etw* sth)

durch+schie|ßen[1] [ˈdʊrçʃiːsn] VI *sep irreg* **a** **durch etw ~** to shoot through sth; **zwischen etw** (*dat*) **~** to shoot between sth **b** *aux sein* (= *schnell fahren, rennen*) to shoot or flash through; **zwischen etw** (*dat*) **~** to shoot between sth

durch|schie|ßen[2] [dʊrçˈʃiːsn] *ptp* **durchschossen** [dʊrçˈʃɔsn] VT *insep irreg* **a** (*mit Kugeln*) to shoot through; (*fig*) to shoot or flash through; **die Lunge ~** to shoot through the lung; **ein Gedanke durchschoss mich/mein Gehirn** a thought flashed through my mind **b** (*Typ: = leere Seiten einfügen*) to interleave **c** *auch* → (*Typ: = Zeilenabstand vergrößern*) to set or space out → *auch* **durchschossen d** (*Tex*) *Stoff* to interweave

durch|schif|fen [dʊrçˈʃifn] *ptp* **durchschifft** VT *insep* to sail across, to cross

durch|schim|mern VI *sep* (*durch etw* sth) to shimmer through; (*Farbe, fig*) to show through

durch+schla|fen VI *sep irreg* to sleep through (the night)

Durch|schlaf|prob|lem NT *usu pl* sleep problem, problem with sleeping through (the night)

Durch|schlag M **a** (= *Kopie*) carbon (copy), copy **b** (= *Küchengerät*) sieve, strainer **c** (= *Lochgerät*) punch **d** (*Elec*) disruptive discharge

durch+schla|gen[1] [ˈdʊrçʃlaːgn] *sep irreg* **VT** *etw ~* (= *entzweischlagen*) to chop through sth; (= *durchtreiben*) to knock sth through (*durch etw* sth); (*Cook*) to rub sth through a sieve, to sieve sth **VI a** *aux sein* (= *durchkommen*) (*durch etw* sth) to come through; (*fig: Charakter, Eigenschaft, Untugend*) to show through; **bei ihm schlägt der Vater durch** you can see his father in him **b** *aux sein* (= *Loch verursachen*) to go through (*durch etw* sth) **c** *aux haben* (= *abführen*) to have a laxative effect; **grüne Äpfel schlagen (bei mir/ihm) durch** (*inf*) green apples run or go straight through me/him **d** *aux sein* (= *Wirkung haben*) to catch on; **auf etw** (*acc*) **~** to make one's/its mark on sth; **auf jdn ~** to rub off on sb; **alte Werte schlagen wieder voll durch** old values are reasserting themselves in a big way; **Investitionen schlagen auf die Nachfrage durch** investments have a marked effect on demand **e** *aux sein* (*Sicherung*) to blow, to go **f** *aux sein* (*Tech: Federung, Stoßdämpfer*) to seize up; **das Auto schlug durch** the suspension went **VR a** (= *sich durchbringen*) to fight one's way through; (*im Leben*) to struggle through or along **b** (= *ein Ziel erreichen*) to fight one's way through **VT** *impers* (*Elec*) **es hat die Sicherung durchgeschlagen** the fuse has blown or gone

durch|schla|gen[2] [dʊrçˈʃlaːgn] *ptp* **durchschlagen** VT *insep irreg* to blast a hole in

durch|schla|gend [ˈdʊrçʃlaːgnt] ADJ *Sieg, Erfolg* sweeping; *Maßnahmen* effective, decisive; *Argument, Beweis* decisive, conclusive; *Grund* compelling, cogent; **eine ~e Wirkung haben** to be totally effective

Durch|schlag|pa|pier NT copy paper; (= *Kohlepapier*) carbon paper

Durch|schlags-: Durch|schlags|kraft F (*von Geschoss*) penetration; (*fig*) (*von Argument*) decisiveness, conclusiveness; (*von Maßnahmen*) effectiveness; (*von Grund*) cogency; **durch-schlags|kräf|tig** ADJ (*fig*) *Argument, Beweis* decisive, conclusive; *Grund* compelling, cogent; *Maßnahme* effective, decisive

durch+schlän|geln VR *sep* (*durch etw* sth) (*Fluss*) to wind (its way) through, to meander through; (*Mensch*) to thread one's way through; (*fig*) to manoeuvre (*Brit*) or maneuver (*US*) one's way through

durch+schlei|chen VIR *sep irreg* (*vi: aux sein*) to slip through (*durch etw* sth)

durch+schlep|pen *sep* **VT** to drag or haul through (*durch etw* sth); (*fig*) jdn to drag along; *Kollegen, Mitglied etc* to carry (along) (with one) **VR** (*lit: = mühsam gehen*) to drag oneself along; (*fig*) to struggle through (*durch etw* sth)

durch+schleu|sen VT *sep* **a** **ein Schiff ~** to pass a ship through a lock **b** (*fig*) (*durch etw* sth) (*durch schmale Stelle*) to guide or lead through; (= *durchschmuggeln*) *Menschen, Gegenstand* to smuggle or get through

Durch|schlupf [ˈdʊrçʃlʊpf] M -(e)s, **Durch-schlüpfe** [-ʃlʏpfə] way through

durch+schlüp|fen VI *sep aux sein* to slip through, to creep through (*durch etw* sth); **er ist der Polizei durchgeschlüpft** he slipped through the fingers of the police; **durch Lücken im Gesetz ~** to slip through loopholes in the law

durch+schme|cken *sep* **VT** to taste; **man kann den Essig ~** one can taste the vinegar through the other flavours (*Brit*) or flavors (*US*) **VI** to

come through; **der Knoblauch schmeckt deutlich durch** the taste of the garlic comes through strongly

durch+schmug|geln VT *sep* to smuggle through (*durch etw* sth)

durch+schnei|den[1] [ˈdʊrçʃnaidn] VT *sep irreg* to cut through, to cut in two; **etw in der Mitte ~** to cut sth (down) through the middle; **etw mitten ~** to cut sth in two or in half

durch|schnei|den[2] [dʊrçˈʃnaidn] *ptp* **durchschnitten** [dʊrçˈʃnitn] VT *insep irreg* to cut through, to cut in two; (*Schiff*) *Wellen* to plough (*Brit*) or plow (*US*) through; (*Straße, Weg*) to cut through; (*fig: Schrei*) to pierce; **Wasserwege ~ das Land** the country is crisscrossed by waterways

Durch|schnitt M **a** (= *Mittelwert, Mittelmaß*) average; (*in Statistik*) mean; (*Math*) average, (arithmetic) mean; **der ~** (= *normale Menschen*) the average person; (= *die Mehrheit*) the majority; **im ~ on** average; **im ~ 100 km/h fahren** to average 100 kmph; **im ~ 8 Stunden täglich arbeiten** to work on average 8 hours a day, to average 8 hours a day; **über/unter dem ~** above/below average; **~ sein** to be· average; **guter ~ sein, zum guten ~ gehören** to be a good average **b** (*form: = Querschnitt*) (cross) section

durch|schnitt|lich [ˈdʊrçʃnitlɪç] ADJ average; *Wert auch* mean attr; (= *mittelmäßig auch*) ordinary **ADV** (= *im Durchschnitt*) verdienen, schlafen, essen etc on (an) average; **~ begabt/groß** etc of average ability/height etc; **~ gut** good on average; **die Mannschaft hat sehr ~ gespielt** the team played a very average game

Durch|schnitt|lich|keit F -, *no pl* ordinariness

Durch|schnitts- *in cpds* average; **Durch-schnitts|al|ter** NT average age; **Durch-schnitts|bil|dung** F average education; **Durch|schnitts|bür|ger(in)** M(F) average citizen; **Durch|schnitts|ehe** F average or normal marriage; **Durch|schnitts|ein|kom|men** NT average income; **Durch|schnitts|ge-schwin|dig|keit** F average speed; **Durch-schnitts|ge|sicht** NT ordinary or nondescript (*pej*) face; **Durch|schnitts|leis|tung** F average performance; **Durch|schnitts|le|ser(in)** M(F) average reader; **Durch|schnitts|mensch** M average person; **Durch|schnitts|no|te** F average mark (*Brit*) or grade (*esp US*); **Durch-schnitts|schü|ler(in)** M(F) average pupil; **Durch|schnitts|tem|pe|ra|tur** F average or mean (*spec*) temperature; **Durch|schnitts|typ** M (*Person*) average sort of person; **er ist ein ~** he's your average sort of guy (*inf*); **Durch-schnitts|wert** M average or mean (*Math*) value; **Durch|schnitts|zeich|nung** F sectional drawing; **Durch|schnitts|zeit** F average time

durch+schnüf|feln [ˈdʊrçʃnʏfln] *sep*, **durch-schnüf|feln** [dʊrçˈʃnʏfln] *ptp* **durchschnüffelt** *insep* VT (*pej inf*) *Post, Tasche* to nose through (*inf*); *Wohnung* to sniff or nose around in (*inf*); **alle Winkel ~** to poke one's nose into every corner (*inf*)

durch|schos|sen [dʊrçˈʃɔsn] ADJ (*Typ*) *Buch* interleaved; *Satz* spaced → *auch* **durch-schießen**[2]

Durch|schreib|block M *pl* -**blöcke** or -**blocks** duplicating pad

durch+schrei|ben *sep irreg* **VT** to make a (carbon) copy of; **alles wird durchgeschrieben** copies are or a copy is made of everything **VI a** (= *Kopie anfertigen*) to make a (carbon) copy **b** (= *Kopie liefern*) to print through, to produce a copy

Durch|schrei|be-: Durch|schrei|be|pa|pier NT carbon paper; **Durch|schrei|be|satz** M carbon pad

durch+schrei|ten[1] [ˈdʊrçʃraitn] VI *sep irreg aux sein* (*geh*) to stride through

durch|schrei|ten² [dʊrçˈʃraitn] *ptp* **durchschritten** [dʊrçˈʃrɪtn] VT *insep irreg* (*geh*) to stride through

Durch|schrift F (carbon) copy

Durch|schuss ▲ M **a** (= *durchgehender Schuss*) shot passing right through; **bei einem ~ ...** when a shot passes right through ... **b** (= *Loch*) bullet hole; (= *Wunde*) gunshot wound (*where the bullet has passed right through*); **ein ~ durch den Darm** a gunshot wound right through the intestine **c** (*Tex*: = *Schussfaden*) weft **d** (*Typ*: = *Zwischenraum*) leading; **ohne ~** unspaced, unleaded; **mit viel/wenig ~** widely/lightly leaded or spaced

durch|schüt|teln VT *sep Mischung* to shake thoroughly; *jdn* (*zur Strafe*) to give a good shaking; (*in Auto, Bus etc*) to shake about

durch|schwär|men [dʊrçˈʃvɛrmən] *ptp* **durchschwärmt** VT *insep* (*geh*) *Gebäude, Gelände* to swarm through; **die Nacht ~** to make a merry night of it

durch+schwe|ben¹ ['dʊrçˈʃveːbn] VI *sep aux sein* (*Vogel*) to glide through; (*Wolken auch, Ballon*) to float through

durch|schwe|ben² [dʊrçˈʃveːbn] *ptp* **durchschwebt** VT *insep* (*poet*) (*Vogel*) to glide through; (*Wolken auch*) to float through

durch|schwei|fen [dʊrçˈʃvaifn] *ptp* **durchschweift** VT *insep* (*liter*) to roam or wander through

durch+schwei|ßen VT *sep* to through-weld

durch+schwim|men¹ ['dʊrçˈʃvɪmən] VI *sep irreg aux sein* **a** (*durch etw* sth) to swim through; (*Dinge*) to float through; **unter/zwischen etw** (*dat*) ~ to swim/float under/between sth **b** (= *ohne Pause schwimmen*) to swim without stopping

durch|schwim|men² [dʊrçˈʃvɪmən] *ptp* **durchschwommen** [dʊrçˈʃvɔmən] VT *insep irreg* to swim through; *Strecke* to swim

durch+schwin|deln VR *sep* to trick or cheat one's way through

durch+schwit|zen ['dʊrçˈʃvɪtsn] *sep*, **durch-schwit|zen** [dʊrçˈʃvɪtsn] *ptp* **durchschwitzt** *insep* VT to soak with or in sweat → *auch* **durchgeschwitzt**

durch+se|geln¹ ['dʊrçˈzeːgln] VI *sep aux sein* **a** (*Schiff*) to sail through (*durch etw* sth); **unter/zwischen etw** (*dat*) ~ to sail under/between sth **b** (*inf*: = *nicht bestehen*) to fail, to flunk (*inf*) (*durch etw, bei etw* sth) **c** (*inf*: = *durchlaufen*) to sail or sweep through (*durch etw* sth)

durch|se|geln² [dʊrçˈzeːgln] *ptp* **durchsegelt** VT *insep Meer, See* to sail across; **die Meere ~** to sail (across) the seas

durch+se|hen *sep irreg* VI **a** (= *hindurchschauen*) to look through (*durch etw* sth); **ein Stoff, durch den man ~ kann** material one can see through VT **a** (= *nachsehen, überprüfen*) **etw ~** to look or check sth through or over, to have a look through sth, to go through or over sth (*auf +acc* for); **etw flüchtig ~** to glance or skim through sth **b** (*durch etw hindurch*) to see through (*durch etw* sth)

durch+sei|hen VT *sep* (*Cook*) to strain

durch sein ▲ VI *irreg aux sein* (*inf*) **a** (= *hindurchgekommen sein*) to be through (*durch etw* sth); (= *vorbeigekommen sein*) to have gone **b** (= *fertig sein*) to have finished, to be through (*esp US*); **durch etw ~** to have got (*Brit*) or gotten (*US*) through sth, to have finished sth **c** (= *durchgetrennt sein*) to be through, to be in half; (= *durchgescheuert sein*) to have worn or gone through **d** (*Gesetz, Antrag*) to have gone through **e** (= *eine Krankheit überstanden haben*) to have pulled through; (= *eine Prüfung bestanden haben*) to be through, to have got (*Brit*) or gotten (*US*) through; **durch die Krise ~** to be over the crisis **f** (*Cook*) (*Steak, Gemüse, Kuchen*) to be done

durch|setz|bar [-zɛtsbaːɐ] ADJ **schwer ~** hard to enforce; **nicht ~** unenforceable, impossible to enforce *pred*

durch+set|zen¹ ['dʊrçzɛtsn] *sep* VT *Maßnahmen, Reformen* to put or carry through; *Anspruch, Forderung* to push through; *Vorschlag, Plan, Vorhaben* to carry through; *Ziel* to achieve, to accomplish; **etw bei jdm ~** to get sb to agree to sth; **etw beim Aufsichtsrat ~** to get sth through the board; **seinen Willen (bei jdm) ~** to impose one's will (on sb), to get one's (own) way (with sb) → **Dickkopf, Kopf d** VR **a** (*Mensch*) to assert oneself (*bei jdm* with sb); (*Partei etc*) to be successful, to win through; **sich gegen etw ~** to win through against sth; **sich gegen jdn ~** to assert oneself against sb, to have one's way despite sb; **sich mit etw ~** to be successful with sth; **sich im Leben ~** to make one's way in life, to be a success in life **b** (*Idee, Meinung, Neuheit*) to be (generally) accepted, to gain acceptance, to catch on

durch|set|zen² [dʊrçˈzɛtsn] *ptp* **durchsetzt** VT *insep* **etw mit etw ~** to intersperse sth with sth; **ein Land mit Spionen ~** to infiltrate spies into a country; **die Armee war von subversiven Elementen durchsetzt** the army was infiltrated by subversive elements

durch|setzt [-ˈsetst] *ptp von* **durchsetzen²** ADJ **ein mit Unkraut ~er Rasen** a weed-ridden lawn → *auch* **durchsetzen²**

Durch|set|zung¹ ['dʊrçzɛtsʊŋ] F -, *no pl* (*von Maßnahmen, Reformen*) putting or carrying through; (*von Anspruch, Forderung*) pushing through; (*von Vorschlag, Plan, Vorhaben*) carrying through; (*von Ziel*) achievement, accomplishment

Durch|set|zung² [dʊrçˈzɛtsʊŋ] F -, **-en die ~ des Laubwaldes mit Nadelbäumen** the fact that the deciduous forest is interspersed with conifers

Durch|set|zungs|kraft ['dʊrç-] F , *no pl*, **Durch|set|zungs|ver|mö|gen** ['dʊrç-] NT , *no pl* ability to assert oneself, powers *pl* of self-assertion

durch|seu|chen [dʊrçˈzɔyçn] *ptp* **durchseucht** VT *insep* (= *verseuchen*) to infect

Durch|seu|chung [dʊrçˈzɔyçʊŋ] F -, **-en** spread of infection; **die ~ der Bevölkerung** the spread of the infection throughout the population

Durch|seu|chungs-: **Durch|seu|chungs|grad** M degree of infection; **Durch|seu|chungs|ra|te** F rate of infection

Durch|sicht F examination, inspection, check; (*von Examensarbeiten*) checking through; **jdm etw zur ~ geben/vorlegen** to give sb sth to look through or over, to give sb sth to check (through) or to examine; **bei ~ der Bücher** on checking the books

durch|sich|tig [-zɪçtɪç] ADJ *Material* transparent; *Bluse etc auch* see-through; *Wasser, Luft* clear; (*fig*) transparent; *Stil* clear, lucid

Durch|sich|tig|keit F -, *no pl* (*von Material*) transparency; (*von Wasser, Luft*) clarity; (*fig*) transparency; (*von Stil*) clarity, lucidity

durch+si|ckern VI *sep aux sein* (*lit, fig*) to trickle through, to seep through; (*fig: trotz Geheimhaltung*) to leak out or through; **Informationen ~ lassen** to leak information

durch+sie|ben¹ ['dʊrçziːbn] VT *sep* to sieve, to sift

durch|sie|ben² [dʊrçˈziːbn] *ptp* **durchsiebt** VT *insep* (*inf*) **etw (mit etw)** ~ to riddle sth with sth

durch+sit|zen *sep irreg* VT *Sessel* to wear out (the seat of); **ich habe mir die Hose durchgesessen** I've worn out or through the seat of my trousers VR (*Sessel, Polster*) to wear out; **der neue Sessel hat sich schon durchgesessen** the seat of the new armchair is or has already worn out

durch|sof|fen [dʊrçˈzɔfn] ADJ *attr* (*inf*) boozy (*inf*); **eine ~e Nacht** a night of boozing (*inf*), a boozy night (*inf*) → *auch* **durchsaufen²**

durch|sonnt [dʊrçˈzɔnt] ADJ (*poet*) sunny, sun-drenched, sun-soaked

durch+spie|len *sep* VT *Szene, Spiel, Stück* to play through; *Rolle* to act through; (*fig*) to go through VI (= *zu Ende spielen*) to play through VR (*Sport*) to get through

durch+spre|chen *sep irreg* VI **a** **durch etw ~** to speak or talk through sth **b** (= *durchgehend sprechen*) to speak without a break, to speak solidly VT **a** *Problem, Möglichkeiten, Taktik* to talk over or through, to go over or through **b** (*Theat*) *Rolle* to read through

durch+sprin|gen¹ ['dʊrçʃprɪŋən] VI *sep irreg aux sein* to jump or leap or spring through (*durch etw* sth)

durch|sprin|gen² [dʊrçˈʃprɪŋən] *ptp* **durchsprungen** [dʊrçˈʃprʊŋən] VT *insep irreg* to jump or leap or spring through

durch+spü|len VT *sep* to rinse or flush or wash (out) thoroughly; *Mund, Wäsche* to rinse (out) thoroughly

durch+star|ten *sep* VI (*Aviat*) to overshoot; (*Aut*) to accelerate off again; (*beim, vorm Anfahren*) to rev up; (*fig*) to get going again VT *Flugzeug* to pull up; *Motor, Auto* to rev (up)

durch+ste|chen¹ ['dʊrçʃtɛçn] *sep irreg* VT *Nadel, Spieß* to stick through (*durch etw* sth); *Ohren* to pierce; *Deich, Damm, Grassode* to cut through; *Kanal, Tunnel* to build or put through (*durch etw* sth) VI to pierce; (*mit einer dünnen Nadel*) to prick; **die Nadel sticht durch** the needle is sticking through

durch|ste|chen² [dʊrçˈʃtɛçn] *ptp* **durchstochen** [dʊrçˈʃtɔxn] VT *insep irreg* to pierce; (*mit Degen, Spieß etc*) to run through; (*mit Nadel*) to prick

Durch|ste|che|rei [dʊrçʃtɛçəˈrai] F (*inf*) sharp practice

durch+ste|cken VT *sep* (*durch etw* sth) to put or stick through; *Nadel etc* to stick through

durch+ste|hen ['dʊrçʃteːən] *sep*, **durch|ste|hen** [dʊrçˈʃteːən] *ptp* **durchstanden** [dʊrçˈʃtandn] *insep* VT *irreg Zeit, Prüfung* to get through; *Krankheit* to pull or come through, to get over; *Tempo, Test, Qualen* to (with)stand; *Abenteuer* to have; *Schwierigkeiten, Situation* to get through

Durch|steh|ver|mö|gen NT , *no pl* endurance, staying power

durch+stei|gen VI *sep irreg aux sein* to climb through (*durch etw* sth); (*fig inf*) to get (*inf*), to see; **da steigt doch kein Mensch durch** (*fig inf*) you couldn't expect anyone to get that (*inf*)

durch+stel|len ☼ 27.4 VT *sep* to put through; (= *durchreichen auch*) to pass through; **einen Moment, ich stelle durch** one moment, I'll put you through

Durch|stich M (= *Vorgang*) cut(ting); (= *Öffnung*) cut

Durch|stieg M passage

durch+stö|bern [dʊrçˈʃtøːbɐn] *ptp* **durchstöbert** *insep*, **durch+stö|bern** ['dʊrçʃtøːbɐn] *sep* VT to hunt through (*nach* for), to rummage through (*nach* for); *Stadt, Gegend* to scour (*nach* for); (= *durchwühlen*) to ransack (*nach* looking for, in search of)

Durch|stoß M breakthrough

durch+sto|ßen¹ [dʊrçˈʃtoːsn] *ptp* **durchstoßen** VT *insep irreg* to break through; (*Mil auch*) to penetrate

durch+sto|ßen² ['dʊrçʃtoːsn] *sep irreg* VI *aux sein* (*zu einem Ziel gelangen*) to break through (*esp Mil*) VT (= *durchbrechen*) to break through; **etw (durch etw) ~** to push sth through (sth); *Tunnel* to drive sth through (sth)

durch+strei|chen¹ [dʊrçˈʃtraiçn] VT *sep irreg* to cross out or through, to strike out, to delete

durch|strei|chen² [dʊrçˈʃtraiçn] *ptp* **durchstrichen** [dʊrçˈʃtrɪçn] VT *insep irreg* (*liter*) to roam or wander or rove through

durch|strei|fen [dʊrçˈʃtraifn̩] *ptp* **durchstreift** VT *insep* (*geh*) to roam *or* wander *or* rove through

durch+strö|men[1] [ˈdʊrçʃtrøːmən] VI *sep aux sein* (*geh*) to flow *or* run through; (*Menschenmenge*) to stream *or* pour through

durch|strö|men[2] [dʊrçˈʃtrøːmən] *ptp* **durchströmt** VT (*geh*) *insep* (*lit, fig*) to flow *or* run through

durch+struk|tu|rie|ren *ptp* **durchstrukturiert** VT *sep Aufsatz* to give a good structure to; *Gesetzesvorlage* to work out in detail; **ein gut durchstrukturierter Aufsatz** a well-structured essay

durch+sty|len VT *sep* to give style to; **durchgestylt** fully styled

durch|su|chen[1] [dʊrçˈzuːxn̩] *ptp* **durchsucht** VT *insep* (*nach* for) to search (through); *Stadt, Gegend auch* to scour; *jdn* to search, to frisk

durch|su|chen[2] [ˈdʊrçzuːxn̩] VT *sep* to search (through)

Durch|su|chung [dʊrçˈzuːxʊŋ] F -, **-en** search (*auf +dat* for)

Durch|su|chungs|be|fehl M search warrant; **richterlicher ~** official search warrant

durch+tan|zen[1] [ˈdʊrçtantsn̩] *sep* VI to dance through; **die Nacht ~** to dance through the night, to dance all night, to dance the night away VT *Schuhe* to wear out (by *or* with) dancing

durch|tan|zen[2] [dʊrçˈtantsn̩] *ptp* **durchtanzt** VT *insep* to dance through; **eine durchtanzte Nacht** a night of dancing

durch+tas|ten VR *sep* to feel *or* grope one's way through (*durch etw* sth)

durch+tes|ten VT *sep* to test out

durch+tra|gen VT *sep irreg* to carry *or* take through (*durch etw* sth)

durch+trai|nie|ren *ptp* **durchtrainiert** *sep* VT *Sportler, Mannschaft, Körper, Muskeln* to get fit; **(gut) durchtrainiert** (*Sportler*) completely *or* thoroughly fit; *Muskeln, Körper* in superb condition VI (*= ohne Pause trainieren*) to train without a break, to train nonstop

durch|trän|ken [dʊrçˈtrɛŋkn̩] *ptp* **durchtränkt** VT *insep* to soak *or* saturate (completely); **mit/von etw durchtränkt sein** (*fig geh*) to be imbued with sth

durch+trei|ben VT *sep irreg* **etw (durch etw) ~** to drive sth through (sth)

durch+tren|nen [ˈdʊrçtrɛnən] *sep*, **durch|tren|nen** [dʊrçˈtrɛnən] *ptp* **durchtrennt** *insep* VT *Stoff, Papier* to tear (through), to tear in two; (*= schneiden*) to cut (through), to cut in two; *Nerv, Sehne* to sever; *Nabelschnur* to cut (through)

Durch|tren|nung F *usu sing* (*= Zerteilung*) division; (*= Schneiden: von Nerv, Kabel etc*) cutting, severing, severance (*form*)

durch+tre|ten *sep irreg* VT **a** *Pedal* to step on; (*am Fahrrad*) to press down; *Starter* to kick **b** (*= abnutzen*) *Teppich, Schuh, Sohle* to go *or* wear through **c** (*= durchkicken*) to kick through (*durch etw* sth) VI **a** (*Aut: = Gas geben*) to step on the accelerator; (*Radfahrer*) to pedal (hard) **b** (*Ftbl*) to kick out **c** *aux sein* (*= durchsickern, durchdringen*) to come through (*durch etw* sth) **d** *aux sein* (*form: = weitergehen*) to go *or* walk through VR to wear through

durch|trie|ben [dʊrçˈtriːbn̩] ADJ cunning, sly

Durch|trie|ben|heit F -, *no pl* cunning, slyness

Durch|tritt M (*= das Durchtreten*) passage; (*= Durchtrittsstelle*) place where the gas/water *etc* comes through

durch+trop|fen VI *sep aux sein* to drip through (*durch etw* sth)

durch|wa|chen [dʊrçˈvaxn̩] *ptp* **durchwacht** VT *insep* **die Nacht ~** to stay awake all through the night

durch+wach|sen[1] [ˈdʊrçvaksn̩] VI *sep irreg aux sein* to grow through (*durch etw* sth)

durch+wach|sen[2] [dʊrçˈvaksn̩] ADJ **a** (*lit*) *Speck* streaky; *Fleisch, Schinken* with fat running through (it) **b** *pred* (*hum inf: = mittelmäßig*) so--so (*inf*), fair to middling (*Brit*); **ihm geht es ~** he's having his ups and downs

durch+wa|gen VR *sep* to venture through (*durch etw* sth)

Durch|wahl F (*Telec*) direct dialling

durch|wäh|len ✪ 27.1, 27.3 VI *sep* to dial direct; **nach London ~** to dial London direct, to dial through to London (direct)

Durch|wahl|num|mer F dialling code (*Brit*), dial code (*US*); (*in Firma*) extension

durch+wal|ken VT *sep* (*inf*) **a** (*= verprügeln*) **jdn ~** to give sb a belting (*inf*) *or* hammering (*inf*), to belt sb (*inf*) **b** (*dated: = durchkneten*) to knead thoroughly

durch+wan|dern[1] [ˈdʊrçvandɐn] VI *sep aux sein* (*durch Gegend*) to hike through (*durch etw* sth); (*= ohne Unterbrechung wandern*) to carry on *or* continue hiking

durch+wan|dern[2] [dʊrçˈvandɐn] *ptp* **durchwandert** VT *insep Gegend* to walk through; (*hum*) *Zimmer, Straßen etc* to wander through; **die halbe Welt ~** to wander halfway round the world

durch+wa|schen VT *sep irreg* to wash through

durch+wa|ten[1] [ˈdʊrçvaːtn̩] VI *sep aux sein* to wade through (*durch etw* sth)

durch|wa|ten[2] [dʊrçˈvaːtn̩] *ptp* **durchwatet** VT *insep* to wade through

durch|we|ben [dʊrçˈveːbn̩] *ptp* **durchwebt** *or* (*liter*) **durchwoben** [dʊrçˈvoːbn̩] VT *insep irreg* (*mit, von* with) to interweave; (*fig liter auch*) to intersperse

durch|weg [ˈdʊrçvɛk, dʊrçˈvɛk], **durch|wegs** [ˈdʊrçvɛks, dʊrçˈvɛks] (*esp Aus*) ADV (*bei adj*) (*= ausnahmslos*) without exception; (*= in jeder Hinsicht*) in every way *or* respect; (*bei n*) without exception; (*bei vb*) (*= völlig*) totally; (*= ausnahmslos*) without exception; **~ gut** good without exception/in every way *or* respect

durch|we|hen[1] [dʊrçˈveːən] *ptp* **durchweht** VT *insep* (*geh*) to waft through

durch+we|hen[2] [ˈdʊrçveːən] VTI *sep* to blow through; **(etw) durch etw ~** to blow (sth) through sth

durch+wei|chen[1] [ˈdʊrçvaiçn̩] *sep* VI *aux sein* (*= sehr nass werden*) to get wet through, to get soaked *or* drenched; (*= weich werden: Karton, Boden*) to go soggy VT *Kleidung, jdn* to soak, to drench; *Boden, Karton* to make soggy

durch|wei|chen[2] [dʊrçˈvaiçn̩] *ptp* **durchweicht** VT *insep* (*geh*) *Boden, Karton* to soften

durch+wer|fen VT *sep irreg* to throw through (*durch etw* sth)

durch+wet|zen VTR *sep* to wear through

durch+win|den VR *sep irreg* (*Fluss*) to wind its way, to meander (*durch etw* through sth); (*Mensch*) to thread *or* worm one's way through (*durch etw* sth); (*fig*) to worm one's way through (*durch etw* sth); **sich zwischen etw** (*dat*) **~** to wind its way/to thread *or* worm one's way between sth

durch|wir|ken [dʊrçˈvɪrkn̩] *ptp* **durchwirkt** VT *insep* (*geh*) *Gewebe* to interweave

durch+wit|schen [-vɪtʃn̩] VI *sep aux sein* (*inf*) to slip through (*durch etw* sth)

durch|wo|gen [dʊrçˈvoːgn̩] *ptp* **durchwogt** VT *insep* (*fig geh*) to surge through

durch+wol|len VI *sep* (*inf*) to want to go/come through (*durch etw* sth); **zwischen/unter etw** (*dat*) **~** to want to pass between/under sth; **der Bohrer/Faden will nicht (durch den Beton/das Öhr) durch** the drill/thread doesn't want to go through (the concrete/eye)

durch+wüh|len[1] [ˈdʊrçvyːlən] *sep* VT to rummage through, to rummage about in (*nach* for); *Zimmer, Haus auch* to ransack (*nach* looking for,

in search of) VR (*durch etw* sth) to burrow through; (*fig*) to work one's way through, to plough (*Brit*) *or* plow (*US*) through

durch|wüh|len[2] [dʊrçˈvyːlən] *ptp* **durchwühlt** VT *insep* to rummage through, to rummage about in (*nach* for); *Zimmer auch* to ransack (*nach* looking for, in search of); *Boden* to dig up

durch+wursch|teln [-vʊrʃtln̩], **durch|wurs|teln** VR *sep* (*inf*) to muddle through

durch|zäh|len *sep* VT to count through *or* up VI to count *or* number off

durch|ze|chen[1] [ˈdʊrçtseçn̩] VI *sep* to carry on drinking

durch|ze|chen[2] [dʊrçˈtseçn̩] *ptp* **durchzecht** VT *insep* **die Nacht ~** to drink through the night, to carry on drinking all night; **eine durchzechte Nacht** a night of drinking

durch+zeich|nen VT *sep* to trace

durch+zie|hen[1] [ˈdʊrçtsiːən] *sep irreg* VT **a** (*= durch etw hindurchziehen*) to pull *or* draw through (*durch etw* sth) **b** (*inf: = erledigen, vollenden*) to get through **c** (*= durchbauen*) (*durch etw* sth) *Graben* to dig through; *Mauer* to build through VI **a** *aux sein* (*= durchkommen*) (*durch etw* sth) to pass *or* go through; (*Truppe*) to march through; (*Schmerz*) to go through; (*Kälte*) to come through **b** *aux sein* to soak; **etw in etw** (*dat*) **~ lassen** to steep *or* soak sth in sth; (*in Marinade*) to marinate sth in sth **c** *aux haben* (*sl*) **kräftig ~** (*= Sex haben*) to have a good shag (*sl*) VR to run through (*durch etw* sth)

durch|zie|hen[2] [dʊrçˈtsiːən] *ptp* **durchzogen** [dʊrçˈtsoːgn̩] VT *insep irreg* (*= durchwandern*) to pass through, to go through; (*Straße, Fluss, fig: Thema*) to run through; (*Geruch*) to fill, to pervade; (*Graben*) to cut through; **sein Haar ist von grauen Fäden durchzogen** his hair is streaked with grey (*Brit*) *or* gray (*US*); **die Welt ~** to travel ((a)round) the world; **ein Feld mit Gräben ~** to crisscross a field with ditches; **ein mit Goldfäden durchzogener Stoff** material with a gold thread running through it

durch|zu|cken [dʊrçˈtsʊkn̩] *ptp* **durchzuckt** VT *insep* (*Blitz*) to flash across; (*fig: Gedanke*) to flash through

Durch|zug M **a** *no pl* (*= Luftzug*) draught (*Brit*), draft (*US*); **~ machen** to create a draught (*Brit*) *or* draft (*US*); (*zur Lüftung*) to get the air moving; (*die Ohren*) **auf ~ stellen** *or* **schalten** (*fig*) to switch off (*inf*) **b** (*durch ein Gebiet*) passage; (*von Truppen*) march through; **auf dem/beim ~ durch ein Land** while passing through a country

Durch|zugs|recht NT right of passage

dür|fen [ˈdʏrfn̩] ✪ 27.5, 28.1, 29.2, 30, 36.1, 36.3, 37.4, 45.2, 46.5, 52.2 *pret* **durfte** [ˈdʊrftə], *ptp* **gedurft** *or* (*bei modal aux vb*) **dürfen** [gəˈdʊrft, ˈdʏrfn̩] VI, MODAL AUX VB **a** (*= Erlaubnis haben*) **etw tun ~** to be allowed to do sth, to be permitted to do sth; **darf ich/man das tun?** may I/one do it?, am I/is one allowed to do it?; **darf ich? – ja, Sie ~** may I? – yes, you may; **darf ich ins Kino?** may I go to the cinema?; **er hat nicht gedurft** he wasn't allowed to **b** (*verneint*) **man darf etw nicht (tun)** (*= sollte, muss nicht*) one must not *or* mustn't do sth; (*= hat keine Erlaubnis*) one isn't allowed to do sth, one may not do sth; (*= kann nicht*) one may not do sth; **hier darf man nicht rauchen** (*= ist verboten*) smoking is prohibited here, it is prohibited to smoke here; **diesen Zug darf ich nicht verpassen** I must not miss this train; **du darfst ihm das nicht übel nehmen** you must not take offence (*Brit*) *or* offense (*US*) at him; **die Kinder ~ hier nicht spielen** the children aren't allowed to *or* may not play here; **der Patient darf noch nicht transportiert werden** the patient may not be moved yet; **das darf doch nicht wahr sein!** that can't be true!; **da darf er sich

nicht wundern that shouldn't surprise him **c** (*in Höflichkeitsformeln*) **darf ich das tun?** may I do that?; **Ruhe, wenn ich bitten darf!** quiet, (if you) please!, will you please be quiet!; **darf ich um den nächsten Tanz bitten?** may I have the (pleasure of) the next dance?; **darf ich Sie bitten, das zu tun?** may *or* could I ask you to do that?; **was darf es sein?** can I help you?, what can I do for you?; (*vom Gastgeber gesagt*) what can I get you?, what'll you have?; **dürfte ich bitte Ihren Ausweis sehen** (*als Aufforderung*) may *or* might I see your identity card, please **d** (= *Veranlassung haben, können*) **wir freuen uns, Ihnen mitteilen zu ~** we are pleased to be able to tell you; **ich darf wohl sagen, dass ...** I think I can say that ...; **man darf wohl fragen** one can *or* may ask, surely?; **Sie ~ mir das ruhig glauben** you can *or* may take my word for it **e** (*im Konjunktiv*) **das dürfte ...** (*als Annahme*) that must ...; (= *sollte*) that should *or* ought to ...; (= *könnte*) that could ...; **das dürfte Emil sein** that must be Emil; **das dürfte wohl das Beste sein** that is probably the best thing; **das dürfte reichen** that should be enough, that ought to be enough; **das Essen dürfte stärker gewürzt sein** the food could have been more highly spiced

dürf|tig ['dʏrftɪç] **ADJ** **a** (= *ärmlich*) wretched, miserable; *Essen auch* meagre (*Brit*), meager (*US*) **b** (*pej: = unzureichend*) miserable, pathetic (*inf*); *Kenntnisse* sketchy, scanty; *Ausrede* feeble, lame, pathetic (*inf*); *Ersatz* poor *attr*; (= *spärlich*) *Haarwuchs, Pflanzenwuchs* sparse; *Bekleidung* scanty, skimpy; **ein paar ~e Tannen** a few scrawny fir trees **ADV** (= *kümmerlich*) **beleuchtet** poorly; *gekleidet* scantily; **die Ernte ist ~ ausgefallen** the harvest turned out to be quite meagre (*Brit*) *or* meager (*US*)

Dürf|tig|keit F -, *no pl* **a** (= *Ärmlichkeit*) wretchedness; (*von Essen*) meagreness (*Brit*), meagerness (*US*) **b** (*von Kenntnissen*) sketchiness, scantiness; (*von Ausrede*) feebleness, lameness; (*von Ersatz*) poorness; (*von Haarwuchs, Pflanzenwuchs*) sparseness; (*von Bekleidung*) skimpiness; **die ~ seines Einkommens/seiner Leistung** (*pej*) his miserable *or* pathetic (*inf*) salary/performance

dürr [dʏr] **ADJ** **a** (= *trocken*) dry; (= *ausgetrocknet*) *Boden* arid, barren; *Ast, Strauch* dried up, withered (*pej: = mager*) scrawny, scraggy **c** (*fig: = knapp, dürftig*) *Auskunft* meagre (*Brit*), meager (*US*); *Handlung einer Oper etc* thin; **mit ~en Worten** in plain terms, plainly, bluntly; **die ~en Jahre** (*Bibl, fig*) the lean years

Dür|re ['dʏrə] F -, **-n** **a** (= *Zeit der Dürre*) drought **b** = **Dürrheit**

Dür|re-: **Dür|re|jahr** NT year of drought; **Dür|re|ka|ta|stro|phe** F catastrophic *or* disastrous drought; **Dür|re|op|fer** NT (*Person*) drought victim; **Dür|re|pe|ri|o|de** F (period of) drought; (*fig*) barren period

Dürr|heit F -, *no pl* **a** (= *Trockenheit*) dryness; (*von Boden auch*) aridity, barrenness **b** (*pej: = Magerkeit*) scrawniness, scragginess

Durst [dʊrst] M -(e)s, *no pl* (*lit, fig*) thirst (*nach* for); **~ haben** to be thirsty; **~ bekommen** *or* **kriegen** (*inf*) to get *or* become thirsty; **den ~ löschen** *or* **stillen** to quench one's thirst; **das macht ~** that makes you thirsty, that gives you a thirst; **ein Glas** *or* **einen über den ~ getrunken haben** (*inf*) to have had one too many (*inf*)

durs|ten ['dʊrstn] **VI** **a** (*geh*) to be thirsty, to thirst (*liter*); **er musste ~** he had to go thirsty **b** (*fig*) = **dürsten VI** **VT** *impers* (*liter*) = **dürsten VT**

dürs|ten ['dʏrstn] **VT** *impers* (*liter*) **es dürstet mich, mich dürstet** I thirst (*liter*); **es dürstet ihn nach Rache/Wissen/Wahrheit** he thirsts for revenge/knowledge/(the) truth → **Blut VI** (*fig*) **er dürstet nach Rache/Wahrheit** he is thirsty for revenge/truth

Durst|ge|fühl NT feeling of thirst

durs|tig ['dʊrstɪç] **ADJ** thirsty; **jdn ~ machen** to make sb thirsty, to give sb a thirst; **diese Arbeit macht ~** this is thirsty work (*inf*), this work makes you thirsty; **nach etw ~ sein** (*fig geh*) to be thirsty for sth, to thirst for sth (*liter*); **sie ist eine ~e Seele** (*hum inf*) she likes the bottle (*Brit hum*), she likes to tip the bottle (*US hum inf*)

Durst-: **durst|lö|schend, durst|stil|lend** **ADJ** thirst-quenching; **Durst|stre|cke** F hard times *pl*; (= *Mangel an Inspiration*) barren period; **Durst|streik** M thirst strike

Dur-: **Dur|ton|art** ['duːratɔn-] F major key; **Dur|ton|lei|ter** F major scale

Dusch|bad NT **a** shower (bath); **ein ~ nehmen** to have *or* take a shower (bath) **b** (= *Gel*) shower gel

Du|sche ['duʃə] F -, **-n** shower; **unter der ~ sein** *or* **stehen** to be in the shower, to be taking a shower; **eine ~ nehmen** to have *or* take a shower; **das war eine kalte ~** (*fig*) that really brought him/her *etc* down to earth (with a bump); **bei ihrem Enthusiasmus wirkten seine Worte wie eine kalte ~** (*fig*) his words poured cold water on her enthusiasm

Dusch|ecke F shower (cubicle)

du|schen ['duʃn] **VIR** to have *or* take a shower, to shower; **(sich) kalt ~** to have *or* take a cold shower **VT** **jdn ~** to give sb a shower; **jdm/sich den Kopf/Rücken ~** to spray sb's/one's head/back

Dusch-: **Dusch|gel** NT shower gel; **Dusch|ge|le|gen|heit** F shower facilities *pl*; **Dusch|hau|be** F shower cap; **Dusch|ka|bi|ne** F shower (cubicle); **Dusch|kopf** M shower head; **Dusch|raum** M shower room, showers *pl*; **Dusch|vor|hang** M shower curtain; **Dusch|wand** F shower screen; **Dusch|wan|ne** F shower tray

Dü|se ['dyːzə] F -, **-n** nozzle; (*Mech auch*) jet; (*von Flugzeug*) jet

Du|sel ['duːzl] M -s, *no pl* (*inf*) **a** (= *Glück*) luck; **~ haben** to be lucky; **da hat er (einen) ~ gehabt** his luck was in (*Brit inf*), he was lucky; **so ein ~!** that was lucky!, that was a fluke! (*inf*) **b** (= *Trancezustand*) daze, dream; (*durch Alkohol*) fuddle; **im ~** in a daze *or* dream; in a fuddle

du|se|lig ['duːzəlɪç] **ADJ** **a** (= *schlaftrunken*) drowsy; (= *benommen*) dizzy, giddy; (*esp durch Alkohol*) (be)fuddled; **mir ist ganz ~ (im Kopf), ich habe ein ~es Gefühl** my head is swimming, I feel quite dizzy *or* giddy

du|seln ['duːzln] **VI** (*inf*) to doze

dü|sen ['dyːzn] **VI** *aux sein* (*inf*) to dash; (*mit Flugzeug*) to jet; **nach Hause ~** to dash *or* whizz off home; **durch die Welt ~** to jet (a)round the world

Dü|sen-: **Dü|sen|an|trieb** M jet propulsion; **mit ~** jet-propelled, with jet propulsion; **Dü|sen|bom|ber** M jet bomber; **Dü|sen|flug|zeug** NT jet aircraft *or* plane, jet; **Dü|sen|ge|trie|ben** [-gətriːbn] **ADJ** jet-propelled, jet-powered; **Dü|sen|jä|ger** M **a** (*Mil*) jet fighter **b** (*inf*: = *Düsenflugzeug*) jet aircraft *or* plane, jet; **Dü|sen|klip|per** [-klɪpɐ] M jet airliner; **Dü|sen|ma|schi|ne** F jet (aircraft *or* plane); **Dü|sen|mo|tor** M jet engine; **Dü|sen|treib|stoff** M jet fuel; **Dü|sen|trieb|werk** NT jet power-unit

dus|lig ['duːzlɪç] **ADJ** (*inf*) = **duselig**

Dus|sel ['dʊsl] M -s, - (*inf*) twit (*Brit inf*), twerp (*inf*), dope (*inf*)

Dus|se|lei [dʊsə'lai] F -, **-en** (*inf*) stupidity

dus|se|lig ['dʊsəlɪç], **duss|lig** ▲ ['dʊslɪç] (*inf*) **ADJ** stupid **ADV** **a** (= *dumm*) **sich ~ anstellen** to be stupid **b** (= *sehr viel*) **sich ~ reden** to talk till one is blue in the face (*inf*); **sich ~ verdienen** to make a killing (*inf*); **sich ~ arbeiten** to work like a horse

Dus|se|lig|keit F -, **-en**, **Duss|lig|keit** ▲ F -, **-en** (*inf*) stupidity

dus|ter ['duːstɐ] **ADJ** = **dunkel**

düs|ter ['dyːstɐ] **ADJ** gloomy; *Nacht auch* murky; *Tag, Wetter auch* dismal, murky; *Musik auch* funereal, lugubrious; *Farbe, Gesicht auch* sombre (*Brit*), somber (*US*), dismal; *Bild, Gedanken, Zukunftsvisionen auch* sombre (*Brit*), somber (*US*), dismal, dark; *Miene, Stimmung* dark, black, gloomy; (= *unheimlich*) *Gestalten, Stadtteil* sinister, (dark and) forbidding

Düs|te|re(s) ['dyːstərə] NT *decl as adj* (*poet*) gloom, dark(ness); (*fig: von Gedanken, Stimmung*) gloominess

Düs|ter|keit F -, *no pl* gloominess; (= *Unheimlichkeit: von Stadtteil*) sinister character; (= *Dunkelheit*) gloom, darkness

Dutt [dʊt] M -(e)s, -s *or* **-e** (*dial*) bun

Dut|te ['dʊtə] F -, **-n** (*Aus*) teat, nipple

Duty-free-Shop ['djuːtɪˈfriːʃɔp] M -s, -s, **Du|ty|free|shop** ▲ M -s, -s duty-free shop

Dut|zend ['dʊtsnt] NT -s, **-e** [-də] dozen; **ein halbes ~** half-a-dozen, a half-dozen; **zwei/drei ~** two/three dozen; **ein ~ frische** *or* **frischer** (*geh*) **Eier kostet** *or* **kosten ...** a dozen fresh eggs cost(s) ...; **das ~ kostet 2 Euro** they cost 2 euros a dozen; **zu ~en** (*inf*) dozens *pl*; **sie kamen in** *or* **zu dutzenden** *or* **~en** they came in (their) dozens; **im ~ billiger** (*inf*) (*bei größerer Menge*) the more you buy, the more you save; (*bei mehr Leuten*) the more you are, the more you save (*inf*); **dutzend(e) Mal** dozens of times → **zwölf**

Dut|zend-: **dut|zend|fach** **ADJ** dozens of; **in ~en Variationen** in dozens of variations **ADV** in dozens of ways; **dut|zend|mal** △ (*inf*) → **Dutzend**; **Dut|zend|mensch** M (*pej*) ordinary *or* run-of-the-mill sort of person; **Dut|zend|preis** M price per dozen; **Dut|zend|wa|re** F (*pej*) (cheap) mass-produced item; **~n** (cheap) mass-produced goods; **dut|zend|wei|se** ADV in dozens, by the dozen

Duz|bru|der M good friend *or* pal (*inf*); **alte Duzbrüder** old friends *or* pals (*inf*)

du|zen ['duːtsn] **VT** to address with the familiar "du"-form; **wir ~ uns** we use "du" *or* the "du"-form (to each other)

DUZEN/SIEZEN

There are two ways of addressing people in German: the familiar **du** and the polite **Sie**. **Duzen** means that people say "du" to each other and use first names; whereas **siezen** means that people say "Sie" and "Herr/Frau...". **Du** is reserved for family, children and close friends; in other cases the polite form **Sie** is used. **Du** is often introduced by the elder of two people as a token of friendship. However, etiquette isn't quite so strict nowadays and young people especially say **du** to one another almost as a matter of course. Sometimes different forms of address are combined, for example when colleagues use first names but also the polite **Sie**.

Duz-: **Duz|freund(in)** M(F) good friend; **alte ~e** old friends; **Duz|fuß** M **mit jdm auf dem ~ stehen** (*inf*) to be on familiar terms with sb

DV [deːˈfau] F - *abbr von* **Datenverarbeitung** DP

DVD [deːfauˈdeː] F -, -s *abbr von* **digital video disc** DVD

DVD-Play|er [deːfauˈdeːplɛːæ] M -s, - (*Tech*) DVD player

d. Verf. *abbr von* **der Verfasser**

dwars [dvars] **ADV** (*N Ger Naut*) abeam

Dy|na|mik [dyˈnaːmɪk] F -, *no pl* **a** (*Phys*) dynamics *sing* **b** (*fig*) dynamism; **Menschen mit einer solchen ~** people with such dynamism

Dy|na|mi|ker [dyˈnaːmikɐ] M -s, -, **Dy|na|mi|ke|rin** [-ərɪn] F -, **-nen** go-getter

dy|na|misch [dyˈnaːmɪʃ] **ADJ** **a** dynamic; **~e Gesetze** laws of dynamics **b** (*fig*) dynamic;

Renten ≈ index-linked **ADV** (= *schwungvoll*) dynamically

dy|na|mi|sie|ren [dynami'ziːrən] *ptp* **dynamisiert** VT (*geh*) to make dynamic; *Debatte* to enliven; *Gesellschaft* to revitalize; (= *vorantreiben*) *Prozess, Reform* to speed up; *Renten, Sozialhilfe* ≈ to index-link

Dy|na|mi|sie|rung F -, -en (*geh*) (*von Reform etc*) speeding up; (*von Renten*) ≈ index-linking; **sie streben eine ~ ihrer Politik an** they are seeking to make their policies more dynamic

Dy|na|mit [dyna'miːt] NT -s, *no pl* (*lit, fig*) dynamite

Dy|na|mo(|ma|schi|ne) [dy'naːmo-, 'dyːnamo-] M(F) -s, -s dynamo; (*fig*) powerhouse

Dy|nast [dy'nast] M -en, -en dynast

Dy|nas|tie [dynas'tiː] F -, -n [-'tiːən] dynasty

dy|nas|tisch [dy'nastɪʃ] ADJ dynastic

Dys|pro|si|um [dʏs'proːziʊm] NT -s, *no pl* (*abbr* **Dy**) dysprosium

D-Zug ['deː-] M fast (*Brit*) or express train; (*hält nur in großen Städten*) non-stop or through train; **ein alter Mann/eine alte Frau ist doch kein ~** (*inf*) I am going as fast as I can, I can't go any faster

D-Zug- ['deː-]: **D-Zug-Tem|po** NT (*inf*) fantastic speed (*inf*); **im ~** like greased lightning (*inf*), in double-quick time (*inf*); **D-Zug-Zu|schlag** M express travel supplement (*Brit*), additional fare payable on express trains (*US*); (*inf*: = *Karte*) supplementary ticket, additional fare (*US*)

E

E, e [eː] NT **-, -** E, e

Eau de Co|logne [ˈoː də koˈlɔnjə] NT **- - -**, _no pl_ eau de Cologne

Eau de Toi|let|te [ˈoː də toaˈlɛt] NT **- - -**, _no pl_ eau de toilette

Ebbe [ˈɛbə] F **-, -n** **a** (= _ablaufendes Wasser_) ebb tide; (= _Niedrigwasser_) low tide; **~ und Flut** the tides, ebb and flow; **bei ~ baden** to swim when the tide is going out; (_bei Niedrigwasser_) to swim at low tide; **bei ~ auslaufen** to go out on the (ebb) tide; (_bei Niedrigwasser_) to go out at low tide; **mit der ~** on _or_ with the ebb tide; **die ~ tritt um 15.30 Uhr ein** the tide starts to go out _or_ turns at 3.30 p.m; **es ist ~** the tide is going out; (= _es ist Niedrigwasser_) it's low tide, the tide is out

b (_fig_) **bei mir** _or_ **in meinem Geldbeutel ist** _or_ **herrscht ~** I'm a bit hard up (_inf_) _or_ my finances are at a pretty low ebb at the moment; **in den Beziehungen der beiden Staaten herrscht zur Zeit ~** relations between the two countries are at a low ebb at the moment _or_ have fallen off recently

ebd. _abbr von_ **ebenda**

eben [ˈeːbn] ADJ **a** (= _glatt_) smooth; (= _gleichmäßig_) even; (= _gleich hoch_) level; (= _flach_) flat; (_Math_) plane; **zu ~er Erde** at ground level; **auf ~er Strecke** on the flat

ADV **a** (_zeitlich_) (= _soeben_) just; (= _schnell, kurz_) for a minute _or_ second; **das wollte ich ~ sagen** I was just about to say that; **mein Bleistift war doch ~ noch da** my pencil was there (just) a minute ago; **kommst du ~ mal mit?** will you come with me for a minute _or_ second?; **ich gehe ~ zur Bank** I'll just pop to (_Brit_) _or_ by (_US_) the bank (_inf_)

b (= _gerade_ _or_ _genau das_) exactly, precisely; **(na) ~!** exactly!, quite!, precisely!; **das ist es ja ~!** that's just _or_ precisely it!; **das ~ nicht!** no, not that!; **das ist es ~ nicht!** that's just _or_ exactly what it isn't!; **~ das wollte ich sagen** that's just _or_ exactly what I wanted to say; **nicht ~ billig/viel/angenehm** _etc_ not exactly cheap/a lot/pleasant _etc_

c (= _gerade noch_) just; **das reicht so** _or_ **nur ~ aus** it's only just enough; **wir haben den Zug ~ noch erreicht** we just caught the train

d (= _nun einmal, einfach_) just, simply; **das ist ~ so** that's just the way it is _or_ things are; **dann bleibst du ~ zu Hause** then you'll just have to stay at home → **dann**

Eben|bild NT image; **dein ~** the image of you; **das genaue ~ seines Vaters** the spitting image of his father

eben|bür|tig [ˈeːbnbʏrtɪç] ADJ **a** (= _gleichwertig_) equal; _Gegner_ evenly matched; **jdm an Kraft/Ausdauer ~ sein** to be sb's equal in strength/endurance; **sie war ihm an Kenntnissen ~** her knowledge equalled (_Brit_) _or_ equaled (_US_) his, her knowledge was equal to his; **wir sind einander ~** we are equal(s) **b** (_Hist_: = _gleichrangig_) of equal birth

Eben|bür|tig|keit F **-**, _no pl_ **a** (= _Gleichwertigkeit_) equality; **die ~ dieser beiden Gegner wurde deutlich** it became clear that the two oppo-

---

nents were evenly matched **b** (_Hist_) equality of birth

eben-: eben|da [ˈeːbnˈdaː, (_emph_) eːbnˈdaː] ADV **a** (= _gerade dort_) **~ will auch ich hin** that is exactly where I am bound too **b** (_bei Zitat_) ibid, ibidem; **eben|da|hin** [ˈeːbndaˈhɪn, (_emph_) eːbnˈdaːhɪn] ADV **~ zieht es auch mich** that is exactly where _or_ whither (_old_) I am bound too; **eben|dann** [ˈeːbnˈdan, (_emph_) eːbnˈdan] ADV **~ soll ich zum Arzt** that is exactly when I have to go to the doctor; **eben|da|rum** [ˈeːbnda-ˈrʊm, (_emph_) eːbnˈdaːrʊm] ADV that is why, for that reason; **~!** (_zu Kind_) because I say so!; **eben|der** [ˈeːbnˈdeːɐ, (_emph_) eːbnˈdeːɐ], **eben|die** [ˈeːbnˈdiː, (_emph_) eːbnˈdiː], **eben|das** [ˈeːbnˈdas, (_emph_) eːbnˈdas] PRON he; she; it; **~ hat auch gesagt, dass ...** he was also the one who said that ..., it was he who also said that ...; **eben|des|halb** [ˈeːbndɛsˈhalp, (_emph_) eːbnˈdɛshalp], **eben|des|wegen** [ˈeːbndɛs-ˈveːgn, (_emph_) eːbnˈdɛsveːgn] ADV that is exactly why; **eben|die** PRON → **ebender; eben|die|se(r, s)** [ˈeːbnˈdiːzə, (_emph_) eːbnˈdiːzə] PRON (_liter_) he; she; it; **und ~r wurde später ermordet** and this same man was later murdered ADJ this very _or_ same; **und ~n Mann hat sie geheiratet** and this was the very man she married; **eben|dort** [ˈeːbnˈdɔrt, (_emph_) eːbnˈdɔrt] ADV (_old_) at that very _or_ same place

Ebene [ˈeːbənə] F **-, -n** (= _Tiefebene_) plain; (= _Hochebene_) plateau; (_Math, Phys_) plane; (_fig_) level; **auf höchster/der gleichen ~** (_fig_) at the highest/the same level; **seine Beleidigungen liegen auf der gleichen ~ wie ...** his insults are on a par with ... → **schief**

eben|er|dig ADJ at ground level

eben|falls ADV as well, likewise; (_bei Verneinungen_) either; **er hat ~ nichts davon gewusst** he knew nothing about it either; **danke, ~!** thank you, the same to you!

Eben|heit F **-**, _no pl_ (= _Glattheit_) smoothness; (= _Gleichmäßigkeit_) evenness; (= _gleiche Höhe_) levelness; (= _Flachheit_) flatness

Eben|holz NT ebony

eben-: eben|je|ne(r, s) [ˈeːbnˈjeːnə, (_emph_) eːbnˈjeːnə] (_liter_) PRON he; she; it; **~r wurde später Präsident** this same man later became president ADJ that very _or_ same; **Eben|maß** NT (_von Gestalt, Gesichtszügen_) elegant proportions _pl_; (_von Zähnen_) evenness; (_von Versen_) even flow; **eben|mä|ßig** ADJ _Gestalt, Gesichtszüge_ elegantly proportioned; _Zähne_ even; _Verse_ evenly flowing; **~ geformt** elegantly proportioned; **Eben|mä|ßig|keit** F = **Ebenmaß**

eben|so [ˈeːbnzoː] ADV (= _genauso_) just as; (= _auch, ebenfalls_) as well; **das kann doch ~ eine Frau machen** a woman can do that just as well; **die Geschäfte sind geschlossen, ~ alle Büros** the shops are closed, as are all the offices; **viele Leute haben sich ~ wie wir beschwert** a lot of people complained just like we did _or_ just as we did _or_ just like us; **er freute sich ~ wie ich** he was just as pleased as I was; **er hat ein ~ großes Zimmer wie wir** he has just as big a room as we have; **ich mag sie ~ gern** I like her just as much, I like her equally well; **ich**

---

esse ~ gern Reis I like rice just as much, I'd just as soon eat rice; **ich komme ~ gern morgen** I'd just as soon come tomorrow; **~ gut** (just) as well; **ich kann ~ gut Französisch wie Italienisch** I can speak French (just) as well as I can speak Italian, my French is (just) as good as my Italian; **~ lang** just as long; **~ oft** _or_ **häufig** just as often _or_ frequently; **~ sehr** just as much; **~ wenig** just as little; **~ wenig, wie man dies sagen kann, kann man behaupten, ...** there is just as little ground for saying this as for claiming ...; **~ viel** just as much

eben|sol|che(r, s) [ˈeːbnˈzɔlçə] ADJ (exactly) the same

ebenso-: eben|so|oft △ [ˈeːbnzoˈlɔft] ADV → **ebenso; eben|so|sehr** △ [ˈeːbnzoˈzeːɐ] ADV → **ebenso; eben|so|viel** △ [ˈeːbnzoˈfiːl] ADV → **ebenso; eben|so|we|nig** △ [ˈeːbnzoˈveːnɪç] ADV → **ebenso**

Eber [ˈeːbə] M **-s, -** boar

Eber|esche F rowan, mountain ash

ebnen [ˈeːbnən] VT to level (off), to make level; **jdm/einer Sache den Weg ~** (_fig_) to smooth the way for sb/sth

Ebola- [eˈbola-] (_Med_): **Ebola-Epi|de|mie** F, **Ebola-Seu|che** F Ebola epidemic; **Ebola--Vi|rus** M OR NT Ebola virus

EC [eːˈtseː] M **-, -s** (_Rail_) _abbr von_ **Euro-City-Zug**

echauf|fie|ren [eʃɔˈfiːrən] _ptp_ **echauffiert** VR (_dated_) to get into a taking (_dated_), to get het up (_Brit_) _or_ worked up

Echo [ˈɛço] NT **-s, -s** echo; (_fig_) response (_auf_ +_acc_ to); **er war nur das ~ seines Chefs** (_fig_) he was only an echo of his boss; **ein starkes** _or_ **lebhaftes ~ finden** (_fig_) to meet with _or_ attract a lively _or_ positive response (_bei_ from)

echo|en [ˈɛçoən] VI (_rare_) to echo; **halloo ...!, echote es** halloo ...!, came the echo

Echo-: Echo|kar|di|o|gra|fie ▲ [ɛçokardiograˈfiː] F **-, -n** [-ˈfiːən] (_Med_) echocardiography; **Echo|lot** [ˈɛçoloːt] NT (_Naut_) echo sounder, sonar; (_Aviat_) sonic altimeter; **Echo|or|tung** F echolocation

Echse [ˈɛksə] F **-, -n** (_Zool_) lizard

echt [ɛçt] ADJ, ADV **a** real, genuine; _Gefühle_ real, genuine, sincere; _Haar, Perlen, Gold_ real; _Unterschrift, Geldschein, Gemälde_ genuine; _Haarfarbe_ natural; **das Gemälde war nicht ~** the painting was a forgery, the painting was forged

b (= _typisch_) typical; **ein ~er Bayer** a real _or_ typical Bavarian

c _Farbe_ fast

d (_Math_) **~er Bruch** proper fraction

ADV **a** (= _typisch_) typically; **~ Tiroler Trachten** original Tyrolean costumes; **~ englisch** typically English; **~ Shakespeare** typical of Shakespeare, typically Shakespearean; **~ Franz/Frau** typical of _or_ just like Franz/a woman, Franz/a woman all over (_inf_)

b (= _rein_) **der Ring ist ~ golden/silbern** the ring is real gold/silver; **~ silbern** real silver

c (_inf_: = _wirklich_) really; **meinst du das ~?** do you really _or_ honestly mean that?; **der spinnt doch ~** he must be out of his mind, he must be cracked (_Brit inf_), he must be round the

---

bend (*Brit inf*); **ich habs ~ eilig** I'm really in a hurry

Echt-: echt|gol|den ADJ *attr* → **echt** ADV **b**; **Echt|haar|pe|rü|cke** F real hair wig

Echt|heit F -, *no pl* genuineness; (*von Unterschrift, Dokument auch*) authenticity; (*von Gefühlen, Glauben auch*) sincerity; (*von Haarfarbe*) naturalness; (*von Farbe*) fastness

Echt-: echt|sil|bern ADJ *attr* → **echt** ADV **b**; **Echt|zeit** F (*Comput*) real time; **Echt|zeit|ver|ar|bei|tung** F (*Comput*) real time processing

Eck [ɛk] NT -(e)s, -e **a** (*esp Aus, S Ger*) = **Ecke a b** (*Sport*) **das kurze/lange ~** the near/far corner of the goal **c über ~** diagonally across *or* opposite; **die Schrauben über ~ anziehen** to tighten the nuts working diagonally across; **im ~ sein** (*Aus*) to be out of form; **da hats ein ~** (*Aus inf*) you've/she's *etc* got problems there

Eckart ['ɛkart] M -s **der getreue ~** (*liter*) the faithful Eckart (*mythical figure in medieval German literature*); (*fig*) the old faithful

ec-Kar|te, EC-Kar|te [e:'tse:-] F = **Eurocheckkarte**

Eck-: Eck|ba|de|wan|ne F corner bath (unit); **Eck|ball** M (*Sport*) corner; **einen ~ schießen** *or* **treten/geben** to take/give a corner; **Eck|bank** F *pl* **-bänke** corner seat; **Eck|da|ten** PL key figures *pl*

Ecke ['ɛkə] F -, -n **a** corner; (= *Kante*) edge; (*von Kragen*) point; (*Sport*: = *Eckball*) corner; **Kantstraße ~ Goethestraße** at the corner of Kantstraße and Goethestraße; **er wohnt gleich um die ~** he lives just (a)round the corner; **ein Kind in die ~ stellen** to make a child stand in the corner; **er wurde in die reaktionäre ~ gestellt** he was pigeon-holed as a reactionary; **etw in allen ~n und Winkeln suchen** to search *or* look high and low for sth; **jdn in die ~ drängen** (*fig*) to push sb into the background; **an allen ~n und Enden sparen** to pinch and scrape (*inf*); **jdn um die ~ bringen** (*inf*) to bump sb off (*inf*), to do away with sb (*inf*); **mit jdm um ein paar** *or* **um sieben ~n herum verwandt sein** (*inf*) to be distantly related to sb, to be sb's second cousin twice removed (*hum inf*); **die neutrale ~** (*Boxen*) the neutral corner; **~ und Kanten** (*fig*) rough edges → **fehlen** VI *impers* **b** (= *Käseecke, Kuchenecke*) wedge **c** (*inf*) (= *Gegend*) corner, area; (*von Stadt*) quarter, area; (= *Strecke*) way; **eine ~** (*fig:* = *viel*) quite a bit; **eine ganze ~ entfernt** quite a (long) way away, a fair way away; **eine (ganze) ~ älter/billiger/größer** (quite) a bit older/cheaper/bigger; **aus welcher ~ kommst du?** what part of the world are you from?

Ecken-: Ecken|ste|her(in) M(F) (*inf*) loafer (*inf*); **Ecken|ver|hält|nis** NT (*Ftbl*) number of corners per team; **sie liegen nach dem ~ vorn** they're ahead on corners

Ecker ['ɛkɐ] F -, -n (*Bot*) beechnut

Eck-: Eck|fah|ne F (*Sport*) corner flag; **Eck|fens|ter** NT corner window; **Eck|grund|stück** NT corner plot; **Eck|haus** NT house at or on the corner; (= *Reiheneckhaus*) end house

eckig ['ɛkɪç] ADJ angular; *Tisch, Brot, Klammer, Kinn, Mund* square; (= *spitz*) sharp; (*fig*) *Bewegung, Gang* jerky

-eckig *suf* (*fünf- und mehreckig*) -cornered; **achteckig** eight-cornered → **dreieckig, viereckig**

Eck-: Eck|knei|pe F (*inf*) pub (*Brit*) or bar on the corner; **Eck|la|den** M shop on a corner, corner shop; **Eck|lohn** M basic rate of pay; **Eck|pfei|ler** M corner pillar; (*fig*) cornerstone; **Eck|pfos|ten** M corner post; **Eck|platz** M (*in Zug etc*) corner seat; (*in Theater etc*) end seat, seat at the end of a row; **Eck|schrank** M corner cupboard; **Eck|stein** M **a** (*lit, fig*) cornerstone **b** (*Cards*) diamonds *pl*; **Eck|stoß** M (*Sport*) corner; **einen ~ ausführen** to take a corner; **Eck|stun|de** F (*Sch*) first/last lesson of the day; **~n** lessons at the start and end of the

day; **Eck|tisch** M corner table; **Eck|turm** M corner tower; **Eck|wert** M (*Econ*) benchmark figure; (*fig*) basis; **Eck|wurf** M (*beim Handball*) corner (throw); **Eck|zahn** M canine tooth; **Eck|zim|mer** NT corner room; **Eck|zins** M (*Fin*) minimum lending rate

Ec|lair [e'klɛːɐ] NT -s, -s (*Cook*) eclair

E|co|no|my|klas|se [i'kɔnəmi-] F economy class; (*Aviat auch*) coach class (*esp US*); **~ flie|gen** to fly coach

EC-Scheck [e:'tse:-] M = **Euroscheck**

Ecs|ta|sy ['ɛkstazi] NT -, *no pl* (= *Droge*) ecstasy

Ecs|ta|sy-Tab|let|te F ecstasy tablet

E|cu [e:'ku:] M -(s), (-s) ecu

E|cu|a|dor [ekua'doːɐ] NT -s Ecuador

e|cu|a|do|ri|a|nisch [ekuado'riaːnɪʃ] ADJ Ecuadorian

ed. *abbr von* **edidit** = **herausgegeben**

Ed. *abbr von* **Edition**

E|da|mer (Kä|se) ['eːdamɐ] M -s, - Edam (cheese)

edc-Ser|vice [e:de:'tse:zøːɐvɪs, -zœrvɪs] M (*Fin*) edc service

Ed|da ['ɛda] F -, **Edden** ['ɛdn] (*Liter*) Edda

e|del ['eːdl] ADJ **a** (*attr* = *vornehm, adlig*) noble **b** (= *hochwertig*) precious; *Hölzer* precious, fine; *Rosen, Speisen* fine; *Wein* noble, fine; *Pferd* thoroughbred **c** (= *edel geformt, harmonisch*) noble; *Nase* regal, aristocratic **d** (*fig*) *Gesinnung, Mensch, Tat* noble; (= *großherzig*) noble, generous → **Spender(in)** ADV *eingerichtet* classically; *dinieren* exclusively; **~ gestylt** with a classic design; **~ geformte Züge** classic features; **er denkt ~** he has noble thoughts

Edel- *in cpds* **a** (= *hochwertig*) high-grade **b** (*pej*) fancy (*pej inf*), posh (*inf*); **Edel|fäu|le** F (*bei Weintrauben*) noble rot; (*bei Käse*) (veins *pl* of) mould (*Brit*) *or* mold (*US*); **Edel|frau** F (*Hist*) noblewoman; **Edel|fräu|lein** NT (*Hist*) unmarried noblewoman; **Edel|gas** NT rare gas; **Edel|holz** NT high-grade wood

E|de|ling ['eːdəlɪŋ] M -s, -e (*Hist*) (Germanic) nobleman

Edel-: Edel|kas|ta|nie F sweet *or* Spanish chestnut; **Edel|kitsch** M (*iro*) pretentious rubbish *or* kitsch; **Edel|knap|pe** M (*Hist*) squire; **Edel|me|tall** NT precious metal; **Edel|mut** M (*liter*) magnanimity; **edel|mü|tig** [-myːtɪç] ADJ (*liter*) magnanimous; **Edel|nut|te** F (*iro*) high-class tart; **Edel|pilz** M mushroom; (*in Käse, auf Weintrauben*) mould (*Brit*), mold (*US*); **Edel|pilz|kä|se** M blue (vein) cheese, mould-ripened (*Brit*) *or* mold-ripened (*US*) cheese (*spec*); **Edel|reis** NT scion; **Edel|rost** M patina; **Edel|schnul|ze** F (*iro*) sentimental schmaltz; **Edel|stahl** M high-grade steel; **Edel|stein** M precious stone; (*geschliffener auch*) jewel, gem; **e|del|süß** ADJ **~er Wein/Paprika** sweet wine/paprika; **Edel|tan|ne** F noble fir; **Edel|weiß** ['eːdlvaɪs] NT -(es), -e edelweiss

E|den ['eːdn] NT -s, *no pl* Eden; **der Garten ~** (*Bibl*) the Garden of Eden

e|die|ren [e'diːrən] *ptp* **ediert** VT to edit

E|dikt [e'dɪkt] NT -(e)s, -e (*Hist*) edict

e|di|tier|bar ADJ editable

e|di|tie|ren [edi'tiːrən] *ptp* **editiert** VT to edit

E|di|tier|funk|ti|on F (*Comput*) editing function

E|di|ti|on [edi'tsioːn] F -, -en (= *das Herausgeben*) editing; (= *die Ausgabe*) edition

E|di|tor¹ ['ɛditoːɐ] M -s, -en [-'toːrən] (*Comput*) editor

E|di|tor² [e'diːtoːɐ] M -s, -en [-'toːrən], **E|di|to|rin** [-'toːrɪn] F -, -nen editor

E|di|to|ri|al [editoˈriaːl] NT -s, -s editorial

e|di|to|risch [editoˈrɪʃ] ADJ editorial

Ed|le(r) ['eːdlə] MF *decl as adj* **a** (= *Mann*) noble(man); (= *Frau*) noblewoman **b** (*in Namen*) **Ulf ~r von Trautenau** Lord Ulf von Trautenau; **Johanna ~ von Fürstenberg** Lady Johanna von Fürstenberg **c** (*fig geh:* = *edler Mensch*) noble person

E|du|ard ['eːduart] M -s Edward

E|du|tain|ment [edu'teːnmənt] NT -s, *no pl* edutainment

EDV [e:de:'fau] F - *abbr von* **elektronische Datenverarbeitung** EDP

EDV- [e:de:'fau-]: **EDV-An|la|ge** F EDP *or* computer system; **EDV-Bran|che** F data-processing business; **EDV-Fach|frau** F , **EDV-Fach|mann** M computer specialist; **EDV-Kennt|nis|se** PL computing expertise *sing or* know-how *sing* (*inf*); **~ haben** to be computer-literate

EEG [e:|eː'ɡeː] NT -, -s *abbr von* **Elektroenzephalogramm** EEG

E|feu ['eːfɔy] M -s, *no pl* ivy; **mit ~ bewachsen** covered in ivy, ivy-clad (*liter*), ivy-covered

e|feu|be|wach|sen ADJ ivy-covered, covered in ivy *pred*, ivy-clad (*liter*)

Eff|eff [ɛf'|ɛf, 'ɛf|ɛf, 'ɛf|ɛf] NT -, *no pl* (*inf*) **etw aus dem ~ können** to be able to do sth standing on one's head (*inf*) *or* just like that (*inf*); **etw aus dem ~ beherrschen/kennen** to know sth inside out

Ef|fekt [ɛ'fɛkt] M -(e)s, -e effect; **der ~ war gleich null** the effect was absolutely nil (*Brit*) *or* zero (*US*), it had no effect whatsoever

Ef|fekt|be|leuch|tung F special lighting; (*Theat*) special effect lighting

Ef|fek|ten [ɛ'fɛktn] PL (*Fin*) stocks and bonds *pl*

Ef|fek|ten-: Ef|fek|ten|bör|se F stock exchange; **Ef|fek|ten|han|del** M stock dealing; **im ~ lässt sich viel Geld verdienen** there's a lot of money to be made in dealing on the stock exchange; **Ef|fek|ten|mak|ler(in)** M(F) stockbroker; **Ef|fek|ten|markt** M stock market

Ef|fekt|ha|sche|rei [-haʃəˈraɪ] F -, -en (*inf*) cheap showmanship

ef|fek|tiv [ɛfɛk'tiːf] ADJ **a** effective **b** (= *tatsächlich*) actual; **~e Verzinsung** *or* **Rendite** net yield ADV (= *bestimmt*) actually; **ich weiß ~, dass ...** I know for a fact that ...; **nicht/kein ~** absolutely not/no

Ef|fek|tiv|ge|schäft NT (*Comm*) spot transaction

Ef|fek|ti|vi|tät [ɛfɛktiviˈtɛːt] F -, *no pl* effectiveness

Ef|fek|tiv-: Ef|fek|tiv|lohn M actual wage; **Ef|fek|tiv|ver|zin|sung** F redemption yield

ef|fekt|voll ADJ effective

ef|fe|mi|niert [ɛfemiˈniːɐt] ADJ (*geh*) effeminate

Ef|fet [ɛ'feː] M OR NT -s, -s (*Billard*) side; **den Ball mit ~ schießen** to put side on a ball

ef|fi|zi|ent [ɛfiˈtsiɛnt] ADJ efficient ADV efficiently

Ef|fi|zi|enz [ɛfiˈtsiɛnts] F -, -en efficiency

EFTA ['ɛfta] F *abbr von* **European Free Trade Association** EFTA

EG [e:'ɡeː] F - *abbr von* **Europäische Gemeinschaft** EC

e|gal [e'ɡaːl] ⊘ 34.5 ADJ, ADV **a** *pred* (= *gleichgültig*) **das ist ~** that doesn't matter, that doesn't make any difference; **das ist mir ganz ~** it's all the same to me; (= *beides ist mir gleich*) I don't mind (either way), it doesn't make any difference to me; (= *es kümmert mich nicht*) I don't care, I couldn't care less; **ob du willst oder nicht, das ist mir ganz ~** I don't care whether you want to or not; **~ ob/wo/wie** it doesn't matter whether/where/how, no matter whether/where/how; **ihm ist alles ~** he doesn't care about anything

b (inf) (= gleichartig) the same, identical; (= gleich groß) the same size; (= gleichmäßig) Rocksaum even; ~ **gearbeitet sein** to be the same, to match; **die Bretter ~ schneiden** to cut the planks (to) the same size **c** (inf: = glatt) Holzfläche smooth **ADV** (dial inf: = ständig) non-stop

e|ga|li|sie|ren [egali'ziːrən] ptp **egalisiert** VT (Sport) Rekord to equal; **er egalisierte den Vorsprung des Gegners** he levelled (Brit) or leveled (US) with his opponent, he closed his opponent's lead

e|ga|li|tär [egali'tɛːɐ] ADJ (geh) egalitarian

E|ga|li|tät [egali'tɛːt] F , no pl (liter) equality

e|gal|weg ADV (dial inf) = egal ADV

EG- [eː'geː-]: **EG-Be|am|te(r)** M decl as adj, **EG-Be|am|tin** F EC official; **EG-Be|hör|de** F EC institution; **EG-ein|heit|lich** ADJ harmonized within the EC

E|gel ['eːɡl] M -s, - (Zool) leech

E|ger|ling ['eːɡəlɪŋ] -s, -e (Bot: = Champignon) mushroom; **brauner ~** chestnut or brown-cap mushroom

Eg|ge ['ɛɡə] F -, -n **a** (Agr) harrow **b** (Tex) selvedge

eg|gen ['ɛɡn] VT (Agr) to harrow

EG- [eː'geː-]: **EG-Kom|mis|si|on** F EC Commission; **EG-Mi|nis|ter|rat** M Council of Ministers; **EG-Mit|glieds|land** NT EC member state; **EG-Norm** F EC standard

E|go ['eːɡo] NT -s, -s (Psych) ego

E|go|is|mus [ego'ɪsmʊs] M -, **Egoismen** [-mən] ego(t)ism

E|go|ist [ego'ɪst] M -en, -en, **E|go|is|tin** [-'ɪstɪn] F -, -nen ego(t)ist

e|go|is|tisch [ego'ɪstɪʃ] ADJ ego(t)istical **ADV** ego(t)istically, like an egoist

E|go-: **E|go|ma|ne** [eɡo'maːnə] M -n, -n, **E|go|ma|nin** [-'maːnɪn] F -, -nen egomaniac; **E|go|ma|nie** [eɡoma'niː] F , no pl egomania; **E|go|trip** ['eːɡo-] M (inf) ego trip (inf); **E|go|zent|rik** [eɡo'tsɛntrɪk] F -, no pl egocentricity; **E|go|zent|ri|ker** [eɡo'tsɛntrike] M -s, -, **E|go|zent|ri|ke|rin** [-ərɪn] F -, -nen egocentric; **e|go|zent|risch** [eɡo'tsɛntrɪʃ] ADJ egocentric; **e|go|zent|ris|mus** M -, no pl egocentrism

EG-Staat [eː'geː-] M EC country

eh [eː] **INTERJ** hey **CONJ** = **ehe ADV a** (= früher, damals) **seit eh und je** since the year dot (Brit inf), for ages (inf); **wie eh und je** just as or like before; **es war alles wie eh und je** everything was just as it always had been **b** (esp S Ger, Aus: = sowieso) anyway; **ich komme eh nicht dazu** I won't get (a)round to it anyway

e. h., eh. abbr von **ehrenhalber**

e|he ['eːə] CONJ (= bevor) before, ere (old, liter); **~ ich es vergesse ...** before I forget ...; **wir können nichts tun, ~ wir (nicht) Nachricht haben** we can't do anything until or before we get some news; **~ (dass) ich mich auf andere verlasse, mache ich lieber alles selbst** rather than rely on others, I would prefer to do everything myself

E|he ['eːə] F -, -n marriage; **er versprach ihr die ~** he promised to marry her; **in den Stand der ~ treten** (form) **die ~ eingehen** (form) to enter into matrimony (form); **mit jdm die ~ eingehen** or **schließen** (form) to marry sb, to enter into marriage with sb (form); **die ~ vollziehen** to consummate a/their/the marriage; **eine glückliche/ unglückliche ~ führen** to have a happy/an unhappy marriage; **die ~ brechen** (form) to commit adultery; **die ~ zur linken Hand** (Hist) morganatische ~ (Hist) morganatic or left-handed marriage; **sie hat drei Kinder aus erster ~** she has three children from her first marriage; **Kinder in die ~ mitbringen** to bring children into the marriage; **ein außerhalb der ~ geborenes Kind** a child born out of wedlock; **er ist in zweiter ~ mit einer Adligen verheiratet** his second wife is an aristocrat; **in zweiter ~ war er**

mit Uta Schwarz verheiratet his second marriage was to Uta Schwarz, his second wife was Uta Schwarz; **ihre ~ ist 1975 geschieden worden** they were divorced in 1975; **sie leben in wilder ~** (dated, hum) they are living in sin; ~ **ohne Trauschein** common-law marriage; **sie leben in einer ~ ohne Trauschein** they live together; **eine offene ~** an open marriage → **Hafen** [1] **b, Bund** [1] **a**

E|he-: **e|he|ähn|lich** ADJ (form) similar to marriage; **in einer ~en Gemeinschaft leben** to cohabit (form), to live together as man and wife; **E|he|an|bah|nung** F marriage-broking; (= Institut) marriage bureau; **E|he|an|bah|nungsin|sti|tut** NT marriage bureau; **E|he|be|rater(in)** M(F) marriage guidance counsellor (Brit) or counselor (US); **E|he|be|ra|tung** F (= das Beraten) marriage guidance (counselling (Brit) or counseling (US)), couples therapy (US); (= Stelle) marriage guidance council (Brit), marriage counseling center (US); **E|hebe|ra|tungs|stel|le** F marriage guidance council (Brit), marriage counseling center (US); **E|he|bett** NT double bed; (fig) marital bed; **e|he|bre|chen** VI (infin only) to commit adultery; **E|he|bre|cher** M adulterer; **E|hebre|che|rin** F adulteress; **e|he|bre|che|risch** [-brɛçərɪʃ] ADJ adulterous; **E|he|bruch** M adultery; **E|he|bund** M pl -bünde, **E|hebünd|nis** NT (form) bond of matrimony

e|he|dem ['eːə'deːm] ADV (old) formerly; **seit ~** since time immemorial

E|he-: **e|he|fä|hig** ADJ (Jur) marriageable, fit to marry pred; **E|he|fä|hig|keit** F , no pl (Jur) marriageability; **E|he|fä|hig|keits|zeug|nis** NT (Jur) certificate of marriageability; **E|hefrau** F wife; **~en haben es nicht leicht** married women have a hard time; **E|he|gat|te** M (form) husband, spouse (form); **E|he|gat|tensplit|ting** NT (Steuerrecht) taxation of the total income of a married couple on the basis of equal halves; **E|he|gat|tin** F (form) wife, spouse (form); **E|he|ge|mein|schaft** F (form) wedlock (form), matrimony; **E|he|ge|spons** M OR NT (hum) spouse (hum); **E|he|glück** NT married bliss or happiness; **E|he|ha|fen** M (hum) **in den ~ einlaufen** to plight one's troth (old, hum); **E|he|hälf|te** F (hum inf) **meine bessere ~** my better half (inf); **E|he|hin|dernis** NT (Jur) impediment to marriage; **E|hekan|di|dat(in)** M(F) (inf) prospective husband/wife; (kurz vor Eheschließung) husband-to-be/wife-to-be; **E|he|ko|mö|die** F marital comedy; **E|he|krach** M marital row; **E|he|krieg** M marital feud; **E|he|kri|se** F marital crisis; **E|he|krüp|pel** M (hum inf) casualty of married life (hum); **E|he|le|ben** NT married life; **E|he|leu|te** PL (form) married couple; **ich vermiete diese Wohnung an die ~ A. und P. Meier** I hereby let this apartment to Mr and Mrs Meier; **die jungen ~** the young couple

e|he|lich ['eːəlɪç] ADJ marital; Pflichten, Rechte auch conjugal; Kind legitimate; **für ~ erklären** to (declare or make) legitimate; **das ~e Leben** married life; **die ~en Freuden** the joys of marriage

e|he|li|chen ['eːəlɪçn] VT (old, hum) to wed (old), to espouse (old, form)

E|he|lich|keit F , no pl (von Kind) legitimacy

E|he|lich|keits|er|klä|rung F (Jur) declaration of legitimacy

e|he|los ADJ unmarried, single

E|he|lo|sig|keit F , no pl unmarried state; (Rel) celibacy; **~ hat auch ihre Vorteile** being single or unmarried also has its advantages

ehem., ehm. abbr von **ehemals**

e|he|ma|lig ['eːəmaːlɪç] ADJ attr former; **die Ehemaligen einer Schulklasse** the ex-pupils or former pupils of a class; **die Ehemaligen seiner Klasse** his former classmates; **ein ~er Häftling** an ex-convict; **ein Ehemaliger** (inf) an old lag (Brit inf), an ex-con (inf); **mein Ehemaliger/ meine Ehemalige** (hum inf) my ex (inf)

e|he|mals ['eːəmals] ADV (form) formerly, previously; **die ~ deutschen Ostgebiete** the eastern territories which were formerly German

E|he-: **E|he|mann** M pl -männer husband; **seitdem er ~ ist** since he has been married; **e|hemü|de** ADJ tired of married life pred; **e|hemün|dig** ADJ (Jur) of marriageable age; **E|hemün|dig|keit** F , no pl (Jur) marriageable age; **die ~ tritt im Alter von 18 Jahren ein** a person becomes legally marriageable at the age of 18; **E|he|na|me** M married name; **E|he|paar** NT (married) couple; **E|he|part|ner(in)** M(F) (= Ehemann) husband; (= Ehefrau) wife; **beide ~** both partners (in the marriage)

e|her ['eːɐ] ADV **a** (= früher) earlier, sooner; **je ~, je** or **desto lieber** the sooner the better; **nicht ~ als/bis/als** not until/before **b** (= lieber) rather, sooner; (= wahrscheinlicher) more likely; (= leichter) more easily; **alles ~ als das!** anything but that!; **~ verzichte ich** or **will ich verzichten, als dass ...** I would rather or sooner do without than ...; **umso ~, als** the more so or all the more because or as; **das lässt sich schon ~ hören** that sounds more like it (inf), that sounds better; **das könnte man schon ~ sagen, das ist ~ möglich** that is more likely or probable; **diese Prüfung kannst du ~ bestehen** this exam will be easier for you to pass **c** (= vielmehr) more; **er ist ~ faul als dumm** he's more lazy than stupid, he's lazy rather than stupid; **er ist alles ~ als das/ein Engel/dumm** he's anything but that/an angel/stupid

E|he-: **E|he|recht** NT marriage law; **E|he|ring** M wedding ring

e|hern ['eːɐn] ADJ (liter) (lit) made of ore; (fig) iron; **mit ~er Stirn** boldly; (= tollkühn auch) brazenly

E|he-: **E|he|ro|man** M novel about marriage; **E|he|sa|che** F (Jur) matrimonial matter; **E|he|sak|ra|ment** NT marriage sacrament, sacrament of marriage; **E|he|schei|dung** F divorce; **E|he|schei|dungs|kla|ge** F (= Prozess) divorce case; **die ~ einreichen** to file a divorce petition, to file a petition for divorce; **e|hescheu** ADJ marriage-shy, not keen on marriage or getting married pred, wedding-shy (US inf); **E|he|schlie|ßung** F marriage ceremony, wedding

e|hest ['eːəst] ADV (Aus) as soon as possible

E|he-: **E|he|stand** M , no pl matrimony, marriage; **E|he|stands|dar|le|hen** NT low interest bank loan given to newly married couples

e|hes|tens ['eːəstns] ADV **a** (= frühestens) ~ **morgen** tomorrow at the earliest; **ich kann ~ heute Abend kommen** the earliest I can come is this evening **b** (Aus: = baldigst) as soon as possible, at the earliest opportunity

e|hes|te(r, s) ['eːəstə] **ADJ** **bei ~r Gelegenheit** at the earliest opportunity **ADV** **am ~n** (= am liebsten) best of all; (= am wahrscheinlichsten) most likely; (= am leichtesten) the easiest; (= zuerst) first; **am ~n würde ich mir ein Auto kaufen** what I'd like best (of all) would be to buy myself a car; **keins der Kleider gefällt mir so richtig, am ~n würde ich noch das rote nehmen** I don't really like any of the dresses, but if I had to choose I'd take the red one; **das geht wohl am ~n** that's probably the best way; **er ist am ~n gekommen** he was the first (person) to come

E|he-: **E|he|stif|ter(in)** M(F) matchmaker; **E|he|streit** M marital row or argument; **E|hetra|gö|die** F marital tragedy; **E|he|ver|kündi|gung** F , **E|he|ver|kün|dung** F (Sw) marriage announcement; **E|he|ver|mitt|ler(in)** M(F) (= Person) marriage broker; (= Büro) marriage bureau; **E|he|ver|mitt|lung** F marriage-broking; (= Büro) marriage bureau; **E|he|vermitt|lungs|in|sti|tut** NT marriage bureau; **Ehe|ver|spre|chen** NT (Jur) promise to marry; **Bruch des ~s** breach of promise; **E|he|ver|trag** M marriage contract, prenuptial agreement, prenups (*US inf*); **E|he|weib** NT (*old*: = *Ehefrau*) wife; (*hum inf*) old woman (*inf*); **e|he|wid|rig** ADJ (*form*) *Beziehungen* extramarital, adulterous; *Verhalten* constituting a matrimonial offence (*Brit*) or offense (*US*)

Ehr|ab|schnei|der(in) M(F) calumniator (*form*)

Ehr|auf|fas|sung F concept of honour (*Brit*) or honor (*US*)

ehr|bar ADJ (= *achtenswert*) respectable; (= *ehrenhaft*) honourable (*Brit*), honorable (*US*); *Beruf* reputable, respectable

Ehr|bar|keit ['eːrbaːrkait] F -, *no pl* (= *Geachtetheit*) respectability; **die ~ dieses Mannes steht außer Zweifel** there can be no doubt that this is an honourable (*Brit*) or honorable (*US*) man

Ehr|be|griff M sense of honour (*Brit*) or honor (*US*)

Eh|re ['eːrə] ✪ 52.1 F -, -n honour (*Brit*), honor (*US*); (= *Ruhm*) glory; **etw in ~n halten** to treasure or cherish sth; **damit/mit ihm können Sie ~ einlegen** that/he does you credit, that/he is a credit to you; **er wollte mit dieser Rede ~ einlegen** he wanted to gain kudos with this speech; **für jdn/etw ~ einlegen** to bring honour (*Brit*) on sb/sth; **bei jdm mit etw ~ einlegen** to make a good impression on sb with sth; **jdm ~ machen** to do sb credit; **jdm wenig ~ machen** not to do sb any credit; **jdm/einer Sache zur ~ gereichen** to do sb/sth credit; **auf ~!** (*obs*) **bei meiner ~!** (*obs*) by my troth! (*obs*), 'pon my oath! (*obs*); **auf ~ und Gewissen** on my/his *etc* hono(u)r; **auf ~ und Gewissen?** cross your heart? (*inf*), on your hono(u)r?; **auf ~ und Gewissen: ich bin es nicht gewesen!** cross my heart (*inf*) or I promise you, it wasn't me; **zu seiner ~ muss ich sagen, dass ...** in his favour (*Brit*) or favor (*US*) I must say (that) ...; **etw um der ~ willen tun** to do sth for the hono(u)r of it; **das musst du schon um deiner ~ willen machen** you should do that as a matter of hono(u)r; **ein Mann von ~** a man of hono(u)r; **keine ~ im Leib haben** (*dated*) to have not a shred of self-respect; **er ist in ~n ergraut** (*geh*) **er ist in ~n alt geworden** he has had a long and hono(u)rable life; **sein Wort/seine Kenntnisse in allen ~n, aber ...** I don't doubt his word/his knowledge, but ...; **sich** (*dat*) **etw zur ~ anrechnen** to count sth an hono(u)r; **sich** (*dat*) **es zur ~ anrechnen, dass ...** to feel hono(u)red that ..., to count it an hono(u)r that ...; **das rechne ich ihm zur ~ an** I consider that a point in his hono(u)r or favour (*Brit*) or favor (*US*); **mit wem habe ich die ~?** (*iro, form*) with whom do I have the pleasure of speaking? (*form*); **was verschafft mir die ~?** (*iro, form*) to what do I owe the hono(u)r (of your visit)?; **es ist mir eine besondere ~, ...** (*form*) it is a great hono(u)r for me ...; **um der Wahrheit die ~ zu geben ...** (*geh*) to be perfectly honest ..., to tell you the truth ...; **wir geben uns die ~, Sie zu ... einzuladen** (*form*) we request the hono(u)r of your company at ... (*form*); **zu ~n** (*+gen*) in hono(u)r of; **darf ich um die ~ bitten, Sie zu begleiten?** (*form*) may I have the hono(u)r of accompanying you? (*form*), would you do me the hono(u)r of allowing me to accompany you? (*form*); **Habe die ~!** (*dated Aus*) (*als Gruß*) hello; (*beim Abschied*) goodbye; (*als Ausdruck des Erstaunens*) good heavens; **~, wem ~ gebührt** (*prov*) credit where credit is due (*prov*); **~ sei Gott in der Höhe** (*Bibl*) glory to God in the highest → **Feld, letzte(r, s) a, militärisch**

eh|ren ['eːrən] VT (= *Achtung erweisen, würdigen*) to honour (*Brit*), to honor (*US*); **etw ehrt jdn** sth does sb credit or hono(u)r; **dein Besuch/Ihr Vertrauen ehrt mich** I am hono(u)red by your visit/trust; **der Präsident ehrte den Preisträger in einer Rede** the president made a speech in hono(u)r of the prizewinner; **der Preisträger wurde in einer Rede geehrt** a speech was made or there was a speech in hono(u)r of the prizewinner; **jdm ein ~des Andenken bewahren** to

treasure sb's memory; **du sollst Vater und Mutter ~** (*Bibl*) hono(u)r thy father and thy mother → *auch* **geehrt**

Ehren-: Eh|ren|amt NT honorary office or position; **eh|ren|amt|lich** ADJ honorary; *Helfer, Tätigkeit* voluntary; **~er Richter** ≈ member of the jury **ADV** in an honorary capacity; **Eh|ren|amt|lich|keit** F (= *ehrenamtlicher Charakter*) voluntary nature; **Eh|ren|be|zei|gung** [-bətsaigʊŋ] F -, -en, **Eh|ren|be|zeu|gung** [-bətsɔygʊŋ] F -, -en (*Mil*) salute; **jdm eine ~ erweisen/verweigern** to salute/refuse to salute sb

Eh|ren|bür|ger(in) M(F) freeman (*Brit*), honorary citizen; **er wurde zum ~ der Stadt ernannt** he was given the freedom of the city

Eh|ren|bür|ger|recht NT freedom; **die Stadt verlieh ihm das ~** he was given the freedom of the city

Ehren-: Eh|ren|dok|tor(in) M(F) honorary doctor; **Eh|ren|dok|tor|wür|de** F honorary doctorate; **ihm wurde die ~ der Universität Wien verliehen** he was made an honorary doctor of or given an honorary doctorate by the University of Vienna; **Eh|ren|er|klä|rung** F (*von Beleidiger*) (formal) apology; (*von dritter Seite*) statement in defence of (*of sb's honour*) **ich werde eine ~ für Sie abgeben** I will make a statement in your defence (*Brit*) or defense (*US*); (*nach erfolgter Beleidigung*) I will make (you) a formal apology; **Eh|ren|for|ma|tion** F guard of honour (*Brit*) or honor (*US*), honour (*Brit*) or honor (*US*) guard; **Eh|ren|gar|de** F guard of honour (*Brit*) or honor (*US*); **Eh|ren|gast** M guest of honour (*Brit*) or honor (*US*); **Eh|ren|ge|leit** NT guard of honour (*Brit*) or honor (*US*); **Eh|ren|ge|richt** NT tribunal; **eh|ren|haft** ADJ honourable (*Brit*), honorable (*US*); **Eh|ren|haf|tig|keit** ['eːrənhaftɪçkait] F -, *no pl* sense of honour (*Brit*) or honor (*US*); **eh|ren|hal|ber** ADV **er wurde ~ zum Vorsitzenden auf Lebenszeit ernannt** he was made honorary president for life; **Doktor ~** (*abbr* **e. h.**) Doctor honoris causa (*form*), honorary doctor; **Eh|ren|han|del** M *pl* **-händel** (*old*) **eine Form des ~s war das Duell** the duel was one way of settling an affair of honour (*Brit*) or honor (*US*); **Eh|ren|kar|te** F complimentary ticket; **Eh|ren|ko|dex** M code of honour (*Brit*) or honor (*US*); **Eh|ren|kom|pa|nie** F (*Mil*) guard of honour (*Brit*) or honor (*US*); **Eh|ren|krän|kung** F insult, affront; **Eh|ren|le|gi|on** F legion of honour (*Brit*) or honor (*US*); **Eh|ren|lo|ge** F VIP box; (*für königliche Gäste*) royal box; (*in Stadion*) directors' box; **Eh|ren|mal** NT *pl* **-male** or **-mäler** memorial; **Eh|ren|mann** M *pl* **-männer** man of honour (*Brit*) or honor (*US*); **ein sauberer ~** (*pej*) a blackguard (*pej*), a scoundrel; **Eh|ren|me|dail|le** F medal of honour (*Brit*) or honor (*US*); **Eh|ren|mit|glied** NT honorary member; **Eh|ren|mit|glied|schaft** F honorary membership; **Eh|ren|na|del** F badge of honour (*Brit*) or honor (*US*); **Eh|ren|pflicht** F bounden duty; **Eh|ren|platz** M (*lit*) place or seat of honour (*Brit*) or honor (*US*); (*fig*) special place; **Eh|ren|prä|si|dent(in)** M(F) honorary president; **Eh|ren|preis[1]** M (= *Auszeichnung*) prize; (= *Anerkennung*) consolation prize; **Eh|ren|preis[2]** M OR NT **-es, -** (*Bot*) speedwell, veronica; **Eh|ren|rech|te** PL (*Jur*) civil rights *pl*; **Verlust/Aberkennung der bürgerlichen ~** loss/forfeiture of one's civil rights; **Eh|ren|ret|tung** F, *no pl* retrieval of one's honour (*Brit*) or honor (*US*); **eine ~ versuchen** to attempt to retrieve one's hono(u)r; **zu seiner ~ sei gesagt, dass ...** in his favour (*Brit*) or favor (*US*) it must be said that ...; **eh|ren|rüh|rig** ADJ defamatory; **etw als ~ empfinden** to regard sth as an insult to one's honour (*Brit*) or honor (*US*); **Eh|ren|run|de** F (*Sport*) lap of honour (*Brit*) or honor (*US*); (*fig inf*: = *wiederholtes Schuljahr*) repeat year; **Eh|ren|sa|che** F matter of honour (*Brit*) or honor (*US*); **~!** (*inf*) you can count on me; **das ist für mich ~!** that's a matter of hono(u)r for me; **Eh|-**

ren|sa|lut M , **Eh|ren|sal|ve** F salute; **Eh|ren|schuld** F debt of honour (*Brit*) or honor (*US*); **Eh|ren|sold** M honorarium; **Eh|ren|ta|fel** F **a** (= *Tisch*) top table **b** (= *Gedenktafel*) roll of honour (*Brit*) or honor (*US*); **Eh|ren|tag** M (= *Geburtstag*) birthday; (= *großer Tag*) big or great day; **zum heutigen ~** on this special day; **Eh|ren|ti|tel** M honorary title; **Eh|ren|tor** NT , **Eh|ren|tref|fer** M (*Sport*) consolation goal; **Eh|ren|tri|bü|ne** F VIP rostrum (*Brit*) or platform; **Eh|ren|ur|kun|de** F certificate (*for outstanding performance in sport*); **eh|ren|voll** ADJ *Friede, Beruf, Niederlage* honourable (*Brit*), honorable (*US*); *Aufgabe auch* noble; **Eh|ren|vor|sit|zen|de(r)** MF *decl as adj* honorary chairman/-woman; **Eh|ren|wa|che** F guard of honour (*Brit*) or honor (*US*); **eh|ren|wert** ADJ *Mensch, Absichten* honourable (*Brit*), honorable (*US*), worthy; **die ~e Gesellschaft** (*hum*) the Mafia; **Eh|ren|wort** NT *pl* **-worte** word of honour (*Brit*) or honor (*US*); **(großes) ~!** (*inf*) cross my heart (and hope to die)! (*inf*); **~?** (*inf*) cross your heart? (*inf*); **mein ~!** you have my word; **sein ~ geben/halten/brechen** to give/keep/break one's word; **Urlaub auf ~** parole; **eh|ren|wört|lich** ADV *Versprechen* solemn, faithful **ADV** on one's honour (*Brit*) or honor (*US*); **Eh|ren|zei|chen** NT decoration

Ehr-: ehr|er|bie|tig ['eːrɛɐbiːtɪç] ADJ respectful, deferential; **Ehr|er|bie|tung** ['eːrɛɐbiːtʊŋ] F -, *no pl* respect, deference

Ehr|furcht F great or deep respect (*vor +dat* for); (= *fromme Scheu*) reverence (*vor +dat* for); **vor jdm/etw ~ haben** to respect/revere sb/sth, to have (great) respect for sb/sth; **von ~ ergriffen** overawed; **~ gebietend** awe-inspiring; *Stimme, Geste* authoritative; **er ist eine ~ gebietende Persönlichkeit** he's the kind of person who commands (one's) respect

ehr|furcht|ge|bie|tend △ [-gəbiːtnt] ADJ → **Ehrfurcht**

ehr|fürch|tig [-fʏrçtɪç], **ehr|furchts|voll** ADJ reverent; *Distanz* respectful

ehr|furchts|los ADJ irreverent

Ehr|furchts|lo|sig|keit F -, -en irreverence

Ehr|ge|fühl NT sense of honour (*Brit*) or honor (*US*); (= *Selbstachtung*) self-respect; **etw aus falschem ~ heraus tun** to do sth out of a misplaced sense of hono(u)r

Ehr|geiz ✪ 35.2, 35.4 M ambition

ehr|gei|zig ADJ ambitious

Ehr|geiz|ling ['eːrgaitslɪŋ] M -s, -e (*pej inf*) pusher (*inf*)

ehr|lich ['eːrlɪç] **ADJ, ADV** honest; *Name* good; *Absicht, Zuneigung* sincere; **der ~e Finder bekommt 50 Euro** a reward of 50 euros will be given to anyone finding and returning this; **eine ~e Haut** (*inf*) an honest soul; **ich hatte die ~e Absicht zu kommen** I honestly did intend to come; **er hat ~e Absichten** (*inf*) his intentions are honourable (*Brit*) or honorable (*US*); **~ währt am längsten** (*Prov*) honesty is the best policy (*Prov*)

ADV a (= *ohne Betrug*) **~ verdientes Geld** hard-earned money; **~ teilen** to share fairly; **~ gesagt ...** quite frankly or honestly ..., to be quite frank ...; **er meint es ~ mit uns** he is being honest with us; **~ spielen** (*Cards*) to play straight **b** (= *wirklich*) honestly, really (and truly), truly; **ich bin ~ begeistert** I'm really thrilled; **~, ich habe nichts damit zu tun** honestly, I've got nothing to do with it; **~!** honestly!, really!

ehr|li|cher|wei|se ['eːrlɪçɐvaizə] ADV honestly, truly, in all honesty

Ehr|lich|keit F -, *no pl* honesty; (*von Absicht, Zuneigung*) sincerity; **sie zweifelte an der ~ seiner Absichten** she doubted the sincerity of his intentions; (*in Bezug auf Heirat*) she doubted that his intentions were honourable (*Brit*) or honorable (*US*)

Ehr-: ehr|los ADJ dishonourable (*Brit*), dishonorable (*US*); **Ehr|lo|sig|keit** F -, *no pl* (=

Schlechtigkeit) infamy; **die ~ seines Verhaltens** his dishonourable (*Brit*) *or* dishonorable (*US*) conduct; **ehr|pus|se|lig** [-pʊsəlɪç], **ehr|puss|lig ▲** [-pʊslɪç] ADJ (*inf*) sensitive about one's reputation; **ehr|sam** ['eːɛzaːm] ADJ (*old*) = **ehrbar**; **Ehr|sucht** F (*old*) inordinate ambitiousness *or* ambition; **ehr|süch|tig** ADJ (*old*) inordinately ambitious

Eh|rung ['eːrʊŋ] F -, -en honour (*Brit*), honor (*US*)

Ehr-: ehr|ver|let|zend ADJ (*geh*) insulting; **Ehr|ver|let|zung** F (*geh*) insult (to one's honour (*Brit*) *or* honor (*US*)); **Ehr|ver|lust** M loss of honour (*Brit*) *or* honor (*US*); (*Jur*) loss of one's civil rights

Ehr|wür|den ['eːɐvyrdn] M -s, *no pl* Reverend; **Euer ~** Reverend Father; (*zu Äbtissin*) Reverend Mother

ehr|wür|dig ['eːɐvyrdɪç] ADJ venerable; **~e Mutter** (*Eccl*) Reverend Mother; **~er Vater** (*Eccl*) Reverend Father

Ehr|wür|dig|keit F venerability

ei [ai] INTERJ (*zärtlich*) there (there); (*old*) (*spöttisch*) well; (*bekräftigend*) oh; (*bei einem Kind/ Tier*) **ei ei machen** to pet a child/an animal; **ei freilich** *or* **gewiss!** (*old*) but of course!

Ei [ai] NT -(e)s, -er **a** (= *Vogelei, Schlangenei*) egg; (*Physiol*) egg, ovum; **das Ei des Kolumbus** to come up with just the thing; **das ist das Ei des Kolumbus** that's just the thing *or* just what we want; **das Ei will klüger sein als die Henne** you're trying to teach your grandmother to suck eggs (*prov*); **jdn wie ein rohes Ei behandeln** (*fig*) to handle sb with kid gloves; **wie auf Eiern gehen** (*inf*) to step gingerly; **wie aus dem Ei gepellt aussehen** (*inf*) to look spruce; **sie gleichen sich** *or* **einander wie ein Ei dem anderen** they are as alike as two peas (in a pod); **kümmere dich nicht um ungelegte Eier!** (*inf*) don't cross your bridges before you come to them! (*prov*); **das sind ungelegte Eier!** (*inf*) we'll cross that bridge when we come to it (*prov*) → **dick** **b** **Eier** PL (*dated sl*) (= *Geld*) euros; (*in GB*) quid (*inf*); (*in US*) bucks (*inf*); **das kostet seine 50 Eier** that'll cost a good 50 euros **c** **Eier** PL (*sl*) (= *Hoden*) balls *pl* (*sl*); **ein Tritt in die Eier** a kick in the balls (*sl*); **dicke Eier haben** (*sl*: = *Lust auf Sex*) to be choking (*Brit*) *or* gagging (*Brit*) *or* dying for it (*sl*) **d** (*Rugby sl*) ball, pill (*inf*)

ei|a|po|peia [aiapoˈpaia, ˈaiapoˈpaia] INTERJ lullaby baby

Ei|be ['aibə] F -, -n (*Bot*) yew

Ei|bisch ['aibɪʃ] M -(e)s, -e (*Bot*) marshmallow

Eich-: Eich|amt NT ≈ Weights and Measures Office (*Brit*), ≈ Bureau of Standards (*US*); **Eich|baum** M oak tree; **Eich|blatt|sa|lat** M oak-leaf lettuce

Ei|che ['aiçə] F -, -n oak; (= *Baum auch*) oak tree

Ei|chel ['aiçl] F -, -n **a** (*Bot*) acorn **b** (*Anat*) glans **c** (*Cards*) *suit in German playing cards equivalent to clubs*

Ei|chel|hä|her M jay

ei|chen¹ ['aiçn] ADJ oak, oaken (*old*)

ei|chen² VT to calibrate; **darauf bin ich geeicht!** (*inf*) that's right up my street (*inf*)

Ei|chen-: Eich|baum M oak tree; **Ei|chen|holz** NT oak; **ein Tisch aus ~** an oak table; **Ei|chen|laub** NT oak leaves *pl* → **Ritterkreuz**; **Ei|chen|sarg** M oak(en) coffin; **Ei|chen|wald** M oakwood

Eich|hörn|chen NT , **Eich|kätz|chen** NT squirrel; **mühsam nährt sich das ~** (*inf*) one struggles on and little by little

Eich-: Eich|maß NT standard measure; (= *Gewicht*) standard weight; **Eich|pfahl** M calibrated pole marking the maximum safe water level of a reservoir etc; **Eich|stem|pel** M verification stamp; **Eich|strich** M official calibration; (*an Gläsern*) line measure; **ein Glas mit ~** a lined glass

Ei|chung ['aiçʊŋ] F -, -en calibration

Eid [ait] M -(e)s, -e [-də] oath; **einen ~ ablegen** *or* **leisten** *or* **schwören** to take *or* swear an oath; **einen ~ auf die Bibel/Verfassung leisten** to swear an oath on the Bible/the constitution; **darauf kann ich einen ~ schwören** I can swear to that, I can take my oath on that; **ich nehme es auf meinen ~, dass ...** I would be prepared to swear that ...; **jdm den ~ abnehmen** to administer the oath to sb, to take the oath from sb; **unter ~** under *or* on oath; **eine Erklärung an ~es statt abgeben** (*Jur*) to make a declaration in lieu of oath; **ich erkläre an ~es statt, dass ...** I do solemnly declare that ...

Ei|dam ['aidam] M -(e)s, -e (*obs*) son-in-law

Eid-: Eid|bruch M breach of one's oath; **einen ~ begehen** to break one's oath; **eid|brü|chig** ADJ **~ werden** to break one's oath

Ei|dech|se ['aidɛksə] F (*Zool*) lizard; (*Astron*) Lacerta; (*inf*: = *Hubwagen*) fork-lift truck

Ei|der- ['aidɐ-]: **Ei|der|dau|nen** PL eiderdown *no pl*; **Ei|der|en|te** F eider (duck)

Ei|des- ['aidəs-]: **Ei|des|be|leh|rung** F (*Jur*) caution as to the consequences of committing perjury; **Ei|des|for|mel** F wording of the oath; **die ~ nachsprechen** to repeat the oath; **Ei|des|leis|tung** F swearing of the oath; **niemand kann zur ~ gezwungen werden** no-one can be forced to swear *or* take the oath; **ei|des|statt|lich** ADJ **eine ~e Erklärung** *or* **Versicherung abgeben** to make a declaration in lieu of an oath, to declare in lieu of an oath; **etw ~ erklären** to declare sth in lieu of an oath

Ei|de|tik [ai'deːtɪk] F -, *no pl* (*Psych*) eidetic ability

Ei|de|ti|ker [ai'deːtikɐ] M -s, -, **Ei|de|ti|ke|rin** [-ərɪn] F -, -nen eidetic, eidetiker

ei|de|tisch [ai'deːtɪʃ] ADJ eidetic

Eid|ge|nos|se ['ait-] M , **Eid|ge|nos|sin** F confederate; (= *Schweizer Eidgenosse*) Swiss citizen

Eid|ge|nos|sen|schaft F confederation; **Schweizerische ~** Swiss Confederation

eid|ge|nös|sisch [-gənœsɪʃ] ADJ confederate; (= *schweizerisch*) Swiss

eid|lich ['aitlɪç] ADJ sworn *attr*, given on *or* under oath; **er gab eine ~e Erklärung ab** he made a declaration on *or* under oath; (*schriftlich*) he swore an affidavit ADV on *or* under oath; **~ gebunden** bound by (one's) oath

Ei|dot|ter M OR NT egg yolk

Ei|er-: Ei|er|be|cher M eggcup; **Ei|er|bri|kett** NT ovoid (*of coal*); **Ei|er|far|be** F paint used to decorate Easter eggs; **Ei|er|frucht** F (*Bot*) aubergine, eggplant (*US*); **Ei|er|hand|gra|na|te** F (*Mil*) (pineapple) hand grenade, pineapple (*inf*); **Ei|er|ko|cher** M egg boiler; **Ei|er|kog|nak** M advocaat; **Ei|er|kopf** M (*inf: hum* or *pej*) **a** (*lit*) egg-shaped head **b** (= *Intellektueller*) egghead (*inf*), boffin (*esp Brit inf*); **Ei|er|ku|chen** M pancake; (= *Omelette*) omelette made with a mixture containing flour; **Ei|er|lau|fen** NT -s, *no pl* egg and spoon race; **~ machen** to have an egg and spoon race; **Ei|er|li|kör** M advocaat; **Ei|er|löf|fel** M eggspoon

ei|ern ['aiɐn] VI (*inf*) to wobble

Ei|er-: Ei|er|nu|deln PL (*Cook*) (egg) noodles *pl*; **Ei|er|pflau|me** F (large oval) plum; **Ei|er|scha|le** F eggshell; **er hat noch die ~n hinter den Ohren** (*inf*) he's still wet behind the ears (*inf*); **ei|er|schalen|far|ben** ADJ cream, off-white; **Ei|er|schaum** M , **Ei|er|schnee** M (*Cook*) beaten egg white; **Ei|er|schnei|der** M egg slicer; **Ei|er|schwamm** M (*esp Aus*), **Ei|er|schwam|merl** M (*S Ger, Aus*) (*Bot*) chanterelle; **Ei|er|spei|se** F **a** egg dish **b** (*Aus: = Rührei*) scrambled egg; **Ei|er|stock** M (*Anat*) ovary; **Ei|er|tanz** M tortuous manoeuvring (*Brit*) *or* maneuvering (*US*); **einen regelrechten ~ aufführen** (*fig inf*) to go through all kinds of contortions; **Ei|er|uhr** F egg timer; **Ei|er|wär|mer** [-vɛrmə] M -s, - egg cosy

Ei|fer ['aifɐ] M -s, *no pl* (= *Begeisterung*) enthusiasm; (= *Eifrigkeit*) eagerness, keenness; **mit ~** enthusiastically; eagerly, keenly; **mit ~ arbeiten** to work with a will, to work with great zeal; **in ~ geraten** to get agitated, to get into a state; **mit großem ~ bei der Sache sein** to put one's heart into it; **im ~ des Gefechts** (*fig inf*) in the heat of the moment → **blind a**

Ei|fe|rer ['aifərɐ] M -s, -, **Ei|fe|rin** [-ərɪn] F -, -nen (*liter*) fanatic; (*Rel auch*) zealot

ei|fern ['aifɐn] VI (*liter*) **a** **gegen jdn/etw ~** to rail *or* inveigh (*liter*) against sb/sth; **für etw ~** to crusade *or* campaign for sth **b** (= *streben*) **nach etw ~** to strive for sth **c** (= *wetteifern*) **um etw ~** to compete *or* vie for sth

Ei|fer|sucht F jealousy (*auf +acc* of); **aus/vor (lauter) ~** out of/for (pure) jealousy

Ei|fer|süch|te|lei [aifɐzʏçtəˈlai] F -, -en petty jealousy

ei|fer|süch|tig ADJ jealous (*auf +acc* of)

Ei|fer|suchts-: Ei|fer|suchts|sze|ne F **ihr Mann hat ihr wieder eine ~ gemacht** her husband's jealousy caused another scene; **Ei|fer|suchts|tat** F act of jealousy, jealous act; **Ei|fer|suchts|tra|gö|die** F „Eifersuchtstragödie in München" "jealousy causes tragedy in Munich"

ei|för|mig ADJ egg-shaped, oval

eif|rig ['aifrɪç] ADJ eager; *Befürworter auch* keen; *Leser, Sammler, Kinobesucher* keen, avid; *Schüler* industrious; **die Eifrigen** the eager beavers (*inf*) ADV üben religiously; **an die Arbeit gehen** enthusiastically; *teilnehmen* gladly; **~ lernen** to apply oneself; **~ bemüht sein** to make a sincere effort; **er putzte gerade ~ sein Auto, als ich ankam** he was busy *or* busily cleaning his car when I arrived; **sie diskutierten ~** they were involved in an animated discussion

Eif|rig|keit F -, *no pl* (*von Schüler*) industriousness

Ei|gelb NT -s, -e *or* (*bei Zahlenangabe*) - egg yolk; **vier ~** the yolks of four eggs, four egg yolks

ei|gen ['aign] ADJ **a** own; (= *selbstständig*) separate; **seine ~e Wohnung/Meinung haben** to have a flat/an opinion of one's own, to have one's own flat/opinion; **etw sein Eigen nennen** (*geh*) to have sth to one's name, to have sth to call one's own; **er ist stolz, zwölf Kinder sein Eigen nennen zu können** he is proud of having been blessed with twelve children; **jdm etw zu Eigen geben** (*liter*) to give sb sth; **meiner Mutter zu Eigen** (*liter*) for *or* (dedicated) to my mother; **~er Bericht** (*Press*) from *or* by our (own) correspondent; **Zimmer mit ~em Eingang** room with its own *or* a separate entrance; **San Marino ist ein ~er Staat** San Marino is an independent *or* a separate state; **sich** (*dat*) **etw zu Eigen machen** to adopt sth; (= *zur Gewohnheit machen*) to make sth a habit, to make a habit of sth; **übergeben Sie diesen Brief dem Anwalt zu ~en Händen** (*form*) give this letter to the lawyer in person; **ich habe das Papier auf ~e Rechnung gekauft** I paid for the paper myself; **ich möchte kurz in ~er Sache sprechen** I would like to say something on my own account → **Fuß, Nest, Tasche** **b** (= *typisch, kennzeichnend*) typical; **das ist ihm ~** that is typical of him; **er antwortete mit dem ihm ~en Zynismus** he answered with (his) characteristic cynicism; **ein Menschenschlag von ganz ~er Prägung** a race apart **c** (= *seltsam*) strange, peculiar; **es ist eine Landschaft von ganz ~em Reiz** the country is strangely attractive in its own way *or* has its own strange attraction → **Ding** **d** (= *ordentlich*) particular; (= *übergenau*) fussy; **in Gelddingen** *or* **was Geld anbetrifft ist er sehr ~** he is very particular about money matters

Eigen-: Ei|gen|an|teil M (*Insur*) own share, excess (*Brit*); **Ei|gen|an|trieb** M Fahrzeuge **mit ~** self-propelled vehicles; **~ haben** to be self-propelled; **Ei|gen|art** F (= *Besonderheit*) peculiarity; (= *Eigenschaft*) characteristic; (= *Individualität*) individuality; (= *Eigentümlichkeit von Personen*) idiosyncrasy; **das gehört zur ~ der Bayern** that's a typically Bavarian characteristic; **ei|gen|ar|tig** ADJ peculiar; (= *sonderbar auch*) strange; (= *persönlich kennzeichnend*) idiosyncratic ADV peculiarly, strangely; **~ aussehen/klingen** to look/sound strange or peculiar; **ei|gen|ar|ti|ger|wei|se** ADV strangely or oddly enough; **Ei|gen|ar|tig|keit** F **a** *no pl* strangeness **b** (= *Gebaren*) idiosyncrasy; **Ei|gen|bau** M , *no pl* **Tabak/Gemüse im ~ züchten** to grow one's own tobacco/vegetables; **er fährt ein Fahrrad Marke ~** (*hum inf*) he rides a home-made bike; **er raucht Zigaretten Marke ~** (*hum inf*) he smokes home-grown cigarettes (*hum*); **Ei|gen|be|darf** M (*von Mensch*) personal use; (*von Staat*) domestic requirements *pl*; **zum ~** for (one's own) personal use; **der Hausbesitzer machte ~ geltend** the landlord showed that he needed the house/flat (*Brit*) or apartment for himself; **Ei|gen|be|richt** M (*Press*) **diese Zeitung bringt kaum ~e** this paper rarely carries articles by its own journalists; **Ei|gen|be|tei|li|gung** F (*Insur*) own share, excess (*Brit*); **Ei|gen|be|we|gung** F (*Astron*) proper motion; **Ei|gen|blut** NT (*Med*) (own) blood; **dem Patienten wird ~ abgenommen** some of the patient's (own) blood is taken; **Ei|gen|blut|be|hand|lung** F (*Med*) autohaemotherapy (*Brit*), autohemotherapy (*US*); **Ei|gen|blut|trans|fu|si|on** F (*Med*) own or autologous (*spec*) blood transfusion; **Ei|gen|brö|te|lei** [aignbrøːtəˈlai] F -, -*en* (*inf*) eccentricity; (= *Einzelgängertum*) solitary ways *pl*; **Ei|gen|bröt|ler** [ˈaignbrøːtlɐ] M -s, -, **Ei|gen|bröt|le|rin** [-ərɪn] F -, -*nen* (*inf*) loner, lone wolf; (= *komischer Kauz*) queer fish (*inf*), oddball (*inf*); **ei|gen|bröt|le|risch** [ˈaignbrøːtlərɪʃ] ADJ (*inf*) solitary; (= *komisch*) eccentric; **Ei|gen|dün|kel** M sense of superiority; **Ei|gen|dy|na|mik** F momentum; **eine ~ entwickeln** to gather momentum; **Ei|gen|fi|nan|zie|rung** F self-financing; **wir bauen die neue Fabrik in ~** we are financing the building of the new factory ourselves; **ei|gen|ge|nutzt** ADJ (*form*) *Wohnung etc* owner-occupied; **ei|gen|ge|setz|lich** ADJ autonomous ADV **jede Revolution entwickelt sich ~** every revolution develops according to laws of its own; **Ei|gen|ge|setz|lich|keit** F autonomous laws *pl*; **sein Handeln folgte einer geheimnisvollen ~** his behaviour (*Brit*) or behavior (*US*) followed its own mysterious laws; **Ei|gen|ge|wicht** NT (*von LKW etc*) unladen weight; (*Comm*) net weight; (*Sci*) dead weight; **Ei|gen|goal** NT (*Aus Sport*) own goal; **Ei|gen|grup|pe** F (*Sociol*) in-group; **ei|gen|hän|dig** ADJ *Brief, Unterschrift etc* in one's own hand, handwritten; *Übergabe* personal; **ein ~es Werk Rembrandts** a work from Rembrandt's own hand or by Rembrandt himself ADV oneself, with one's own hands; **eine Arbeit ~ machen** to do a job oneself or personally or with one's own hands

Ei|gen|heim NT one's own home; **sparen Sie für ein ~!** save for a home of your own!

Ei|gen|heim-: Ei|gen|heim|för|de|rung F ≈ state support for home-buying; **Ei|gen|heim|zu|la|ge** F ≈ state subsidy available to people buying a home

Ei|gen|heit [ˈaignhait] F -, -*en* = **Eigenart**

Eigen-: Ei|gen|i|ni|ti|a|ti|ve F initiative of one's own; **auf ~** on one's own initiative; **Ei|gen|in|te|res|se** NT vested interest, self-interest; (*von Firma*) **aus ~** out of self-interest, to serve one's own interests; **Ei|gen|ka|pi|tal** NT (*von Person*) personal capital; (*von Firma*) company capital; **10.000 Euro ~** 10,000 euros of one's own capital; **Ei|gen|le|ben** NT , *no pl* one's own life; (= *selbstständige Existenz*) independent existence; (= *Privatleben*) private life; **Ei|gen|leis|tung** F (*Fin*: *bei Hausbau*) borrower's own funding, personal contribution; **Ei|gen|lie|be**

F *amour-propre*, (= *Selbstverliebtheit*) self-love, love of self; **Ei|gen|lob** NT self-importance, vaingloriousness; **~ stinkt!** (*inf*) don't blow your own trumpet! (*prov*); **ei|gen|mäch|tig** ADJ (= *selbstherrlich*) high-handed; (= *eigenverantwortlich*) taken/done *etc* on one's own authority; (= *unbefugt*) unauthorized; **~e Abwesenheit** (*Mil*) absence without leave ADV high-handedly; (entirely) on one's own authority; without any authorization; **ei|gen|mäch|ti|ger|wei|se** ADV (= *selbstherrlich*) high-handedly; (= *unbefugt*) without any authorization; **Ei|gen|mäch|tig|keit** F -, -*en* (= *Selbstherrlichkeit*) high-handedness *no pl*; (= *unbefugtes Handeln*) unauthorized behaviour (*Brit*) or behavior (*US*) *no pl*; **die ~ seines Vorgehens wurde von allen kritisiert** everyone criticized him for having acted high-handedly/without authorization; **Ei|gen|mit|tel** PL (*form*) one's own resources; **die ~ der Körperschaft** the corporation's (own) resources; **man braucht nur 20% ~** you only need to find 20% yourself or from your own resources; **Ei|gen|na|me** M proper name; **Ei|gen|nutz** [-nʊts] M -*es*, *no pl* self-interest; **das habe ich ohne jeden ~ getan** I did that with no thought of myself or of furthering my own interests; **ei|gen|nüt|zig** [-nʏtsɪç] ADJ selfish; **Ei|gen|nüt|zig|keit** F -, *no pl* = **Eigennutz**; **Ei|gen|nut|zung** F -, *no pl* (*von Wohnung etc*) owner-occupation; **Ei|gen|pro|duk|ti|on** F **das ist eine ~** we/they *etc* made it ourselves/themselves *etc*; **etw in ~ herstellen** to make sth oneself, to make one's own sth; **aus ~** (= *hausgemacht*) home-made; *Tabak etc* home-grown; **das war eine ~ des Irischen Fernsehens** that was one of Irish Television's own productions

ei|gens [ˈaigns] ADV (e)specially, (= *ausdrücklich auch*) specifically

Ei|gen|schaft [ˈaignʃaft] F -, -*en* (= *Attribut*) quality; (*Chem, Phys etc*) property; (= *Merkmal*) characteristic, feature; (= *Funktion*) capacity

Ei|gen|schafts|wort NT *pl* -*wörter* adjective

Eigen-: Ei|gen|schwin|gung F (*Sci*) free vibration; **Ei|gen|sinn** M , *no pl* stubbornness, obstinacy; (*inf*: = *Trotzkopf*) stubborn child; **ei|gen|sin|nig** ADJ stubborn, obstinate; **Ei|gen|sin|nig|keit** F -, -*en* stubbornness, obstinacy; **~en** *pl* stubborn or obstinate behaviour (*Brit*) or behavior (*US*); **ei|gen|staat|lich** ADJ sovereign; **Ei|gen|staat|lich|keit** F -, *no pl* [-ʃtaːtlɪç-] sovereignty; **ei|gen|stän|dig** ADJ original; (= *unabhängig*) independent; (= *eigengesetzlich*) autonomous; **Ei|gen|stän|dig|keit** [-ʃtɛndɪç-] F -, *no pl* originality; (= *Unabhängigkeit*) independence; (= *Eigengesetzlichkeit*) autonomy; **Ei|gen|sucht** F , *no pl* selfishness; (= *Egotismus auch*) self-centredness (*Brit*), self-centeredness (*US*); **ei|gen|süch|tig** ADJ selfish; (= *zum Egotismus neigend*) self-centred (*Brit*), self-centered (*US*)

ei|gent|lich [ˈaigntlɪç] ADJ (= *wirklich, tatsächlich*) real, actual; *Wert* true, real; (= *ursprünglich*) original; **im ~en Sinne bedeutet das ...** that really means ...; **im ~en Sinne des Wortes ...** in the original meaning of the word ... ADV actually, (= *tatsächlich, wirklich*) really; (= *überhaupt*) anyway; **~ wollte ich nur fünf Minuten bleiben** actually I was only or I was really only going to stay five minutes; **was willst du hier?** what do you want here anyway?; **wissen Sie ~, wer ich bin?** do you know who I am?; **was ist ~ mit dir los?** what's the matter with you (anyway)?; **ich bin ~ froh, dass ...** really or actually I'm happy that ...; **~ müsstest du das wissen** you should really know that; **~ dürftest du das nicht tun** you shouldn't really do that

Ei|gent|lich|keit F -, *no pl* (*Philos*) essentiality

Ei|gen|tor NT (*Sport, fig*) own goal; **ein ~ schießen** to score an own goal

Ei|gen|tum [ˈaigntuːm] NT -s, *no pl* property; **bewegliches ~** movables *pl*, movable property; **unbewegliches ~** immovables *pl*, real property; **~ an etw** (*dat*) **erwerben** to acquire possession

of sth; **~ an den Produktionsmitteln** ownership of the means of production

Ei|gen|tü|mer [ˈaigntyːmɐ] M -s, -, **Ei|gen|tü|me|rin** [-ərɪn] F -, -*nen* owner

ei|gen|tüm|lich [ˈaigntyːmlɪç] ADJ **a** (= *sonderbar, seltsam*) strange, curious, odd **b** (*geh*: = *typisch*) **jdm/einer Sache ~ sein** to be characteristic or typical of sb/sth

ei|gen|tüm|li|cher|wei|se ADV strangely or curiously or oddly enough

Ei|gen|tüm|lich|keit F -, -*en* **a** (= *Kennzeichen, Besonderheit*) characteristic **b** (= *Eigenheit*) peculiarity

Ei|gen|tums-: Ei|gen|tums|an|spruch M claim of ownership; **einen ~ auf etw** (*acc*) **geltend machen** to claim ownership of sth; **Ei|gen|tums|be|griff** M concept of property; **Ei|gen|tums|bil|dung** F private acquisition of property; **Ei|gen|tums|de|likt** NT (*Jur*) offence against property; **Ei|gen|tums|den|ken** NT (= *Theorie*) property ethic; (= *Gesinnung*) property-mindedness; **Ei|gen|tums|recht** NT right of ownership; (= *Urheberrecht*) copyright; **Ei|gen|tums|streu|ung** F dispersal of property; **Ei|gen|tums|über|tra|gung** F (*Jur*) transfer of ownership or title; **Ei|gen|tums|ur|kun|de** F (*Jur*) title deed; **Ei|gen|tums|ver|ge|hen** NT (*Jur*) offence against property; **Ei|gen|tums|ver|hält|nis|se** PL distribution *sing* of property; **Ei|gen|tums|vor|be|halt** M (*Jur*) reservation of proprietary rights; **Ei|gen|tums|woh|nung** F owner-occupied flat (*Brit*) or apartment, ≈ condominium (*US*); **er kaufte sich** (*dat*) **eine ~** he bought a flat (*Brit*) or an apartment (of his own); **~en bauen** to build flats (*Brit*) or apartments for owner-occupation

Eigen-: ei|gen|ver|ant|wort|lich ADJ autonomous ADV on one's own authority; **für etw sorgen müssen** to be personally responsible for sth; **er hat ~ dafür gesorgt** he saw to it personally or himself; **Ei|gen|ver|ant|wort|lich|keit** F autonomy; **jds ~ für etw** sb's personal responsibility for sth; **Ei|gen|ver|lag** M private publisher; **sein im ~ erschienenes Buch** the book which he published himself; **Ei|gen|wär|me** F body heat; **Ei|gen|wer|bung** F self-advertising or -publicity; **~ treiben** to promote oneself; **Ei|gen|wert** M intrinsic value; **ei|gen|wil|lig** ADJ with a mind of one's own; (= *eigensinnig*) self-willed; (= *unkonventionell*) unconventional, original; **sie ist in allem recht ~** she has a mind of her own in everything; **Ei|gen|wil|lig|keit** F -, -*en* (= *Eigensinnigkeit*) self-will; (= *Unkonventionalität*) unconventionality, originality; **Ei|gen|zeit** F (*Phys*) proper time

eig|nen [ˈaignən] VR to be suitable (*für, zu* for, *als* as); **er würde sich nicht zum Lehrer ~** he wouldn't make a good teacher → *auch* **geeignet** VI (*geh*) **ihm eignet der Charme des Österreichers** he has or possesses all the charm of an Austrian; **seinen Büchern eignet ein präziser Prosastil** his books are characterized by a precise narrative style

Eig|ner [ˈaignɐ] M -s, -, **Eig|ne|rin** [-ərɪn] F -, -*nen* (*form*) owner

Eig|nung [ˈaignʊŋ] F -, -*en* suitability; (= *Befähigung*) aptitude

Eig|nungs|prü|fung F , **Eig|nungs|test** M aptitude test

eigtl. *abbr von* **eigentlich**

Ei|klar [ˈaiklaːɐ] NT -s, - (*Aus, S Ger*) egg white

Ei|land [ˈailant] NT -(e)s, -e [-də] (*liter*) isle (*liter*)

Eil-: Ei|l|an|ge|bot NT (*Comm*) express offer; **Eil|auf|trag** M (*Comm*) rush order; **Eil|bo|te** M , **Eil|bo|tin** F messenger; **per** or **durch ~n** express; **Eil|brief** M express letter; **ich schicke diesen Brief als ~** I am sending this letter express

Ei|le [ˈailə] F -, *no pl* hurry; **in ~ sein** to be in a hurry; **~ haben** (*Mensch*) to be in a hurry or rush; (*Sache*) to be urgent; **damit hat es keine**

~, **das hat keine ~** there is no hurry or rush about it, it's not urgent; **er trieb uns zur ~ an** he hurried us up; **in aller ~** hurriedly, hastily; **in höchster ~ laufen/fahren** to rush/drive in a tremendous hurry; **mit ~/mit fieberhafter ~ arbeiten** to work very quickly/feverishly; **in der ~** in the hurry; **in meiner ~** in my haste; **nur keine ~!** don't rush!

Ei|lei|ter M (Anat) Fallopian tube

Ei|lei|ter|schwan|ger|schaft F ectopic pregnancy

ei|len ['ailən] **VI** **a** aux sein to rush, to hasten (liter), to hurry; **er eilte dem Ertrinkenden zu Hilfe** he rushed or hastened to help the drowning man; **eile mit Weile** (Prov) more haste less speed (Prov) **b** (= dringlich sein) to be urgent or pressing; **eilt!** (auf Briefen etc) urgent; **die Sache eilt** it's urgent, it's an urgent matter **VR** (inf) to rush **VI** impers **es eilt** it's urgent or pressing; **damit eilt es nicht** there's no great hurry or rush about it; **mit dieser Arbeit eilt es sehr/nicht** this work is very/is not urgent

ei|lends ['ailənts] ADV hurriedly, hastily

Eil-: eil|fer|tig ADJ (geh) zealous; **Eil|fer|tig-keit** F, no pl (geh) zeal, zealousness; **Eil|-fracht** F, **Eil|gut** NT, no pl express freight; **etw als ~ senden** to send sth express freight

ei|lig ['ailiç] **ADJ** **a** (= schnell, rasch) quick, hurried, hasty; **es ~ haben** to be in a hurry or rush; **nur nicht so ~!** don't be in such a hurry or rush! **b** (= dringend) urgent; **er hatte nichts Eiligeres zu tun, als ...** (iro) he had nothing better to do than ... (iro) **ADV** as quickly as possible; **sich ~ auf den Weg machen** to hurry; **er bat den Arzt, ~st zu kommen** he asked the doctor to come as quickly as possible

Eil-: Eil|marsch M (Mil) fast march; **Eil|mel-dung** F (Press) flash; **Eil|pa|ket** NT express parcel; **Eil|sen|dung** F express delivery or letter/parcel; **~en** or express mail or post (Brit); **Eil|tem|po** NT **etw im ~ machen** to do sth in a real rush; **er kam im ~ auf mich zugerannt** he came rushing or tearing up to me; **Eil|ver|fah-ren** NT (Jur) summary proceeding(s pl); **etw im ~ durchnehmen** (fig) to rush through sth; **etw im ~ herstellen** or **produzieren** to rush sth off; **Eil|zug** M (Aus) fast stopping train; **Eil|zu|stel|lung** F special delivery; **mit ~** (by) special delivery

Ei|mer M **-s, -** **a** bucket, pail; (= Milcheimer) pail; (= Mülleimer) (rubbish) bin (Brit), garbage can (US); **ein ~ (voll) Wasser** a bucket(ful) of water; **es gießt wie mit** or **aus ~n** (inf) it's bucketing down (Brit inf), it's coming down in buckets (US inf), it's raining cats and dogs (inf) **b** **im ~ sein** (inf) to be up the spout (Brit inf), to be down the drain or tubes (US inf); (= kaputt sein auch) to be bust (inf)

Ei|mer|wei|se ADV in bucketfuls, by the bucket(ful)

ein¹ [ain] ADV (an Geräten) **Ein/Aus** on/off; **~ und aus gehen** to come and go; **er geht bei uns ~ und aus** he is always (a)round at our place; **ich weiß (mit ihm) nicht mehr ~ noch aus** I'm at my wits' end (with him)

ein², **ei|ne**, **ein** NUM one; **das kostet nur ~en Euro** it only costs one euro; **~ Uhr** one (o'clock); **~ Uhr zwanzig** twenty past one; **~ für alle Mal** once and for all; **~ und derselbe/die-selbe/dasselbe** one and the same; **er ist ihr Ein und Alles** he means or is everything to her → auch **eins**

INDEF ART a; (vor Vokalen) an; **~ Mann** a man; **~e Frau** a woman; **~ Kind** a child; **~ Europäer** a European; **~ Hotel** a or an hotel; **der Sohn ~es Lehrers** the son of a teacher, a teacher's son; **nur ~ Hegel konnte das schreiben** only a Hegel could have written that; **~e Hitze ist das hier!** the or some heat here!; **was für ~ Wetter/Lärm!** some weather/noise, what a noise; **wir hatten ~en Durst!** (inf) we were parched!, were we thirsty! → auch **eine(r, s)**

ein|ach|sig ['ain|aksıç] ADJ two-wheeled, single-axle attr

Ein|ak|ter ['ain|aktɐ] M **-s, -** (Theat) one-act play

ei|nan|der [ai'nandɐ] PRON one another, each other; **zwei ~ widersprechende Zeugenberichte** two (mutually) contradictory eyewitness reports

ein+ar|bei|ten sep **VR** to get used to the work; **sie muss sich in ihr neues Gebiet ~** she has to get used to her new area of work **VT** **a** **jdn** to train **b** (= einfügen) to incorporate, to include **c** (= einnähen) to sew in; Futter, Polster auch to attach

Ein|ar|bei|tung ['ain|arbaitʊŋ] F **-, -en** **a** (von Menschen) training **b** (= Einfügung) incorporation, inclusion **c** (= das Einnähen) sewing in; (von Futter, Polster auch) attachment

Ein|ar|bei|tungs|zeit F training period

ein|ar|mig ADJ one-armed; Turnübungen single-arm; **~er Bandit** one-armed bandit

ein+äschern ['ain|ɛʃɐn] VT sep Leichnam to cremate; Stadt etc to burn to the ground, to burn down, to reduce to ashes

Ein|äsche|rung F **-, -en** (von Leichnam) cremation; (von Stadt etc) burning down

ein+at|men VTI sep to breathe in

ein+ät|zen VT sep to etch (in)

ein|äu|gig ADJ one-eyed; Spiegelreflexkamera single-lens

Ein|äu|gi|ge(r) MF decl as adj one-eyed person/man/woman etc

Ein|bahn-: Ein|bahn|stra|ße F one-way street; **Ein|bahn|ver|kehr** M one-way traffic

ein+bal|sa|mie|ren ptp **einbalsamiert** VT sep to embalm

Ein|bal|sa|mie|rung F **-, -en** embalming, embalmment

Ein|band [-bant] M pl **-bände** book cover, case (spec)

ein|bän|dig ADJ one-volume attr, in one volume

ein|ba|sisch ADJ (Chem) monobasic

Ein|bau M pl **-bauten** **a** no pl (= das Einbauen) installation **b** (usu pl: = Schrank etc) fixture

ein+bau|en VT sep to install, to put in; Motor auch to fit; (inf: = einfügen) Zitat etc to work in, to incorporate; **eingebaute Möbel** built-in furniture; **eingebauter Belichtungsmesser** built-in exposure meter

Ein|bau|kü|che F (fully-)fitted kitchen

Ein|baum M dug-out (canoe)

Ein|bau-: Ein|bau|mö|bel PL built-in or fitted furniture; (= Schränke) fitted cupboards pl; **Ein|-bau|schrank** M built-in or fitted cupboard

ein+be|grif|fen ['ainbəgrıfn] ADJ included

ein+be|hal|ten ptp **einbehalten** VT sep irreg to keep back

ein|bei|nig ADJ one-legged

Ein|be|kennt|nis NT (geh) admission

ein+be|rech|nen ptp **einberechnet** VT sep to allow for (in one's calculations); **~, dass ...** to allow for the fact that ...

ein+be|ru|fen ptp **einberufen** VT sep irreg Parlament to summon; Versammlung to convene, to call; (Mil) to call up, to conscript, to draft (US); **Leute zu einer Versammlung ~** to summon or call people to a meeting

Ein|be|ru|fe|ne(r) ['ainbəruːfənə] MF decl as adj (Mil) conscript, draftee (US)

Ein|be|ru|fung F **a** (einer Versammlung) convention, calling; (des Parlaments) summoning **b** (Mil) conscription; (= Einberufungsbescheid) call-up, draft (US)

Ein|be|ru|fungs|be|scheid M, **Ein|be|ru|fungs|be|fehl** M (Mil) call-up or draft (US) papers pl

ein+be|schrie|ben ['ainbəʃriːbn] ADJ (Math) Kreis inscribed; **einer Sache** (dat) **~** encompassed by sth

ein+be|to|nie|ren ptp **einbetoniert** VT sep to cement in (in +acc -to)

ein+bet|ten VT sep to embed (in +acc in); Rohr, Kabel to lay (in +acc in) → auch **eingebettet**

Ein|bett-: Ein|bett|ka|bi|ne F (Naut) single-berth cabin; **Ein|bett|zim|mer** NT single room

ein+beu|len VT sep to dent (in)

ein+be|zie|hen ptp **einbezogen** VT sep irreg to include (in +acc in)

Ein|be|zie|hung F inclusion; **unter ~ von etw** including sth; **unter ~ sämtlicher Gesichts-punkte** having regard to all points

ein+bie|gen sep irreg **VI** aux sein to turn (off) (in +acc into); **du musst hier links ~** you have to turn (off to the) left here; **diese Straße biegt in die Hauptstraße ein** this road joins the main road **VT** to bend in

ein+bil|den VT sep **a** **sich** (dat) **etw ~** to imagine sth; **er bildet sich** (dat) **ein, dass ...** he's got hold of the idea that ...; **sich** (dat) **steif und fest ~, dass ...** (inf) to get it fixed in one's head that ... (inf); **das bildest du dir nur ein** that's just your imagination; **du bildest dir nicht ein, ich sei ...** I don't have any illusions about being ..., I'm not pretending to be ...; **er bildet sich** (dat) **viel ein!** he imagines a lot of things!; **bilde dir (doch) nichts ein!** don't kid (inf) or delude yourself!; **was bildest du dir eigentlich ein?** what's got (Brit) or gotten (US) into you?; **bil-de dir bloß nicht ein, dass ich das glaube!** don't kid yourself (inf) or don't go thinking that I believe that!

   b (= stolz sein) **sich** (dat) **viel auf etw** (acc) **~** to be conceited about or vain about sth; **darauf kann ich mir etwas ~** (iro) praise indeed!; **darauf können Sie sich etwas ~!** that's something to be proud of!, that's a feather in your cap!; **darauf brauchst du dir nichts einzubilden!** that's nothing to crow about (inf) or be proud of; **auf diesen bescheidenen Erfolg brauchst du dir nichts einzubilden** don't go getting any big ideas just because of this little success → auch **eingebildet**

Ein|bil|dung F **a** (= Vorstellung) imagination; (= irrige Vorstellung) illusion; **das sind ~en** that's pure imagination; **das ist alles nur ~** it's all in the mind, it's just (your/his) imagination; **krank ist er bloß in seiner ~** he just imagines or thinks he's ill **b** (= Dünkel) conceit; **an ~en lei-den** (hum inf) to be (pretty) stuck on oneself (esp US inf), to really fancy oneself (Brit inf); **~ ist auch eine Bildung** (hum inf) he's/she's too conceited for words

Ein|bil|dungs|kraft F, **Ein|bil|dungs|ver|-mö|gen** NT, no pl (powers pl of) imagination

ein+bim|sen VT sep (inf) **jdm etw ~** to drum or din sth into sb (inf)

ein+bin|den VT sep irreg Buch to bind; (in Schutzhülle) to cover; (fig: = einbeziehen) to integrate; **neu ~** to rebind

Ein|bin|dung F (fig) integration

ein+bla|sen VT sep irreg to blow in (in +acc -to); Kaltluft auch to blast in (in +acc -to); (Mus) Blasinstrument to play or blow (inf) in; **Gott blies Adam den Lebenshauch ein** God breathed the breath of life into Adam; **jdm etw ~** (fig inf) to whisper sth to sb

ein+bläu|en ▲ VT sep (inf) **jdm etw ~** (durch Schläge) to beat sth into sb; (= einschärfen) to drum sth into sb, to ram sth into sb's head (inf); **ich habe ihm eingebläut, das ja nicht zu vergessen** I told him time and again not to forget it

ein+blen|den sep (Film, TV, Rad) **VT** to insert, to slot in; (allmählich) to fade in; (nachträglich) Musik etc to dub over **VR** **sich in etw** (acc) **~** to link up with sth; **sich bei jdm/etw ~** to go over to sb/sth

Ein|blen|dung F (Film, TV, Rad) insert; (= das Einblenden) insertion; (von Musik) overdub

ein+bleu|en △ VT sep → **einbläuen**

Ein|blick M **a** (*rare*: = *Blick in etw hinein*) view (*in +acc* of) **b** (*fig*: = *Kenntnis*) insight; **~ in etw** (*acc*) **gewinnen** to gain an insight into sth; **~ in die Akten nehmen** to look at *or* examine the files; **jdm ~ in etw** (*acc*) **gewähren** to allow sb to look at sth; **er hat ~ in diese Vorgänge** he has some knowledge of these events; **~e in etw** (*acc*) **eröffnen** to give insights *or* an insight into sth

ein|bre|chen *sep irreg* VT *Tür, Wand etc* to break down

VI **a** *aux sein* (= *einstürzen*) to fall *or* cave in; **er ist (auf dem Eis) eingebrochen** he went *or* fell through the ice

b *aux sein or haben* (= *Einbruch verüben*) to break in; **in unser** *or* **unserem Haus sind Diebe eingebrochen** thieves broke into our house; **bei mir ist eingebrochen worden, man hat bei mir eingebrochen** I've had a break-in, I've been burgled *or* (*US*) burglarized; **in neue Absatzmärkte** etc **~** to make inroads into new markets *etc*

c *aux sein* (*Nacht, Dämmerung, Dunkelheit*) to fall; (*Winter*) to set in; **bei ~der Nacht** at nightfall

d *aux sein* (*inf*: = *Verluste machen*) to come a cropper (*Brit inf*), to fall apart (*US*)

Ein|bre|cher(in) M(F) burglar

Ein|bre|cher|ban|de F gang of burglars

ein+bren|nen *sep irreg* VT *Mal* to brand; **Buchstaben/Muster in Holz ~** to burn letters/patterns into wood VR (*liter*) to engrave *or* etch itself

ein+brin|gen VT *sep irreg* **a** (*Parl*) *Gesetz* to introduce

b (= *Ertrag bringen*) *Geld, Nutzen* to bring in; *Ruhm* to bring; *Zinsen* to earn; **jdm etw ~** to bring/earn sb sth; **das bringt nichts ein** (*fig*) it's not worth it

c **etw in die Ehe ~** to bring sth into the marriage; **etw in die Firma ~** to put sth into the firm

d (= *hineinbringen, -schaffen*) to put in (*in +acc* -to); *Schiff* to bring in (*in +acc* -to); *Ernte* to bring *or* gather in

e (*Typ*) *Zeilen* to take in

f sich in etw (*acc*) **~** to play a part in sth; **jdn in etw** (*acc*) **~** to get sb involved in sth; **sie brachte ihre Kenntnisse in die Diskussion ein** she brought her knowledge to bear in the discussion

ein+bro|cken VT *sep* to crumble (*in +acc* into); **jdm/sich etwas ~** (*inf*) to land sb/oneself in it (*inf*) *or* in the soup (*inf*); **da hast du dir etwas Schönes eingebrockt!** (*inf*) you've really let yourself in for it there; **was man sich eingebrockt hat, das muss man auch auslöffeln** (*prov*) you've made your bed, now you must lie on (*Brit*) *or* in it (*prov*) → **Suppe**

Ein|bruch M **a** (= *Einbruchdiebstahl*) burglary (*in +acc* into), breaking and entering (*form*); **ein ~ in die Bank** the bank break-in **b** (*von Wasser*) penetration; **~ kühler Meeresluft** (*Met*) a stream of cold air moving inland **c** (= *Einsturz: einer Mauer etc*) collapse; (*Geol*) rift valley; (= *Verlust*) setback; **der Kurse/der Konjunktur** (*Fin*) stock exchange/economic crash **d** (*fig*) (*der Nacht*) fall; (*des Winters*) onset; **bei/vor ~ der Nacht/Dämmerung** at/before nightfall/dusk

Ein|bruch(s)-: **Ein|bruch(s)|dieb|stahl** M (*Jur*) burglary, breaking and entering (*form*); **Ein|bruch(s)|se|rie** F series of break-ins *or* burglaries; **ein|bruch(s)|si|cher** ADJ burglar-proof; **Ein|bruch(s)|stel|le** F (*im Damm*) breach; (*im Eis*) hole; **Ein|bruch(s)|tal** NT (*Geol*) rift valley; **Ein|bruch(s)|ver|si|che|rung** F burglary insurance; **Ein|bruch(s)|werk|zeug** NT housebreaking *or* burglary tool

ein+buch|ten [ˈainbʊxtn] VT *sep* (*lit*) to indent; (*inf*) to put away (*inf*), to lock up

Ein|buch|tung F -, **-en** indentation; (= *Bucht*) inlet, bay

ein+bud|deln *sep* (*inf*) VT to bury (*in +acc* in) VR **sich (in den Sand) ~** to dig oneself in(to the sand)

ein+bür|gern [ˈainbʏrgɐn] *sep* VT *Person* to naturalize; *Fremdwort, Gewohnheit, Pflanze* to introduce; **er ist in die** *or* **der Türkei eingebürgert worden** he has become a naturalized Turk VR (*Person*) to become *or* be naturalized; (*Brauch, Tier, Pflanze*) to become established; (*Fremdwort*) to gain currency, to become established; **das hat sich so eingebürgert** (*Brauch*) it's just the way we/they *etc* have come to do things; (*Wort*) it's been adopted into the language; **es hat sich bei uns so eingebürgert, dass wir uns abwechseln** we've got into the habit of taking turns

Ein|bür|ge|rung F -, **-en** (*von Menschen*) naturalization; (*von Fremdwort, Pflanze*) introduction

Ein|bür|ge|rungs|an|trag M application *or* petition for naturalization; **einen ~ stellen** to apply for naturalization

Ein|bu|ße F loss (*an +dat* to); **der Skandal hat seinem Ansehen schwere ~ getan** he lost a considerable amount of respect because of the scandal

ein+bü|ßen *sep* VT to lose; (*durch eigene Schuld*) to forfeit VI to lose something; **an Klarheit** (*dat*) **~** to lose some of its clarity

Ein|cent|stück [ainˈ(t)sɛnt-] NT one-cent piece

ein+che|cken VTI *sep* (*am Flughafen*) to check in (*an +dat* at); (*im Hotel auch*) to register

Ein|che|cken NT **-s**, *no pl* (*am Flughafen*) checking in, check-in; (*im Hotel auch*) registration; **beim ~** as I *etc* was checking in; **das ~ dauert immer furchtbar lange** it always takes ages to check in

ein+cre|men [ˈainkreːmən] VT *sep* to put cream on; *Gesicht etc auch* to cream

ein+däm|men VT *sep* *Fluss* to dam; (*fig*) (= *halten, vermindern*) to check, to stem; (= *im Zaum halten*) to contain

Ein|däm|mung F **a** (= *Damm*) dam **b** (= *das Eindämmen*) damming; (= *Verminderung*) checking, stemming; (*von Gefühlen*) containing

ein+damp|fen VT *sep* to evaporate

ein+de|cken *sep* VR **sich (mit etw) ~** to stock up (with sth); (*für den Haushalt*) to get in supplies (of sth); **wir haben uns ausreichend mit Geld eingedeckt** we've got enough money; **ich bin gut eingedeckt, ich habe mich eingedeckt** I am well supplied VT a (*Build, Mil, fig*) to cover; **ein Dach mit Ziegeln/Stroh ~** to tile/thatch a roof **b** (*inf*: = *überhäufen*) to inundate; **mit Arbeit eingedeckt sein** to be snowed under with *or* inundated with work

Ein|de|cker [ˈaindɛkɐ] M **-s**, **-** (*Aviat*) monoplane; (= *Autobus*) single decker

ein+dei|chen [ˈaindaiçn] VT *sep* to dyke (*Brit*), to dike (*US*); *Fluss auch* to embank

ein+del|len [ˈaindɛlən] VT *sep* (*inf*) to dent (in)

ein|deu|tig [ˈaindɔytɪç] ADJ clear; *Beweis auch* definite; (= *nicht zweideutig*) unambiguous; *Witz* explicit ADV a (= *unmissverständlich*) *formulieren* unambiguously; *sich ausdrücken* clearly; **jdm etw ~ sagen** to tell sb sth quite plainly, to tell sb sth straight (*inf*) **b** (= *klar*) clearly; **das ist ~ der Fall** it's clearly *or* obviously the case

Ein|deu|tig|keit F -, *no pl* clearness; (= *Unzweideutigkeit*) unambiguity; (*von Witz*) explicitness

ein+deut|schen [ˈaindɔytʃn] VT *sep* *Fremdwort* to Germanize; **Clips, ~d auch Klips** Clips, sometimes Germanized as Klips

Ein|deut|schung F -, **-en** Germanization

ein|di|cken [ˈaindɪkn] VTI *sep* (*vi: aux sein*) to thicken

ein|di|men|si|o|nal ADJ one-dimensional, unidimensional

Ein|di|men|si|o|na|li|tät F -, *no pl* one-dimensionality

ein+do|sen [ˈaindoːzn] VT *sep* to can, to tin (*Brit*)

ein+dö|sen VI *sep aux sein* (*inf*) to doze off, to drop off (*inf*)

ein+drän|gen *sep* VR to crowd in (*in +acc* -to); (*fig*) to intrude (*in +acc* upon); (= *sich einmischen*) to interfere, to meddle (*inf*) VI *aux sein* (*lit, fig*) to crowd in (*auf +acc* on)

ein+dre|cken [ˈaindrɛkn] VT *sep* (*inf*) to get dirty *or* muddy

ein+dre|hen VT *sep* a (= *einschrauben*) to screw in (*in +acc* -to) **b** *Haar* to put in rollers

ein+dre|schen VI *sep irreg* (*inf*) **auf jdn ~** to lay into sb (*inf*)

ein+dril|len VT *sep* (*inf*) **jdm etw ~** to drill sb in sth; *Verhalten, Manieren etc* to din *or* drum sth into sb (*inf*)

ein+drin|gen VI *sep irreg aux sein* **a** (= *einbrechen*) **in etw** (*acc*) **~** to force one's way into sth; (*Dieb etc auch*) to force an entry into sth; **in unsere Linien/das Land ~** (*Mil*) to penetrate our lines/into the country

b **in etw** (*acc*) **~** to go into sth, to penetrate (into); (*Wasser, Gas auch*) to get into *or* find its way into sth; (*Fremdwort, Amerikanismus*) to find its way into sth; **der Nagel drang tief ins Holz ein** the nail went deep into the wood; **eine Stimmung in sich ~ lassen** to let oneself be carried away by a mood

c (= *bestürmen*) **auf jdn ~** to go for *or* attack sb (*mit* with); (*mit Fragen, Bitten etc*) to besiege sb

ein|dring|lich ADJ (= *nachdrücklich*) insistent; (= *dringend auch*) urgent; *Schilderung* vivid; **mit ~en Worten** insistently, with insistence; vividly, in vivid words ADV *warnen* urgently, strongly; **ich habe ihn ~ gebeten, zu Hause zu bleiben** I urged him to stay at home; **jdm ~ nahe legen, etw zu tun** to urge sb *or* advise sb most strongly to do sth

Ein|dring|lich|keit F (= *Nachdrücklichkeit*) insistence; (= *Dringlichkeit auch*) urgency; (*von Schilderung*) vividness

Ein|dring|ling [ˈaindrɪŋlɪŋ] M **-s**, **-e** intruder; (*in Gesellschaft etc*) interloper

Ein|druck ✪ 33.2, 45.4, 53.4 M *pl* **-drücke** a impression; **den ~ erwecken, als ob** *or* **dass ...** to give the impression that ...; **die Eindrücke, die wir gewonnen hatten** our impressions; **ich habe den ~, dass ..., ich kann mich des ~s nicht erwehren, dass ...** (*geh*) I have the impression that ..., I can't help thinking that ... (*inf*); **großen ~ auf jdn machen** to make a great *or* big impression on sb; **er macht einen heiteren ~/den ~ eines heiteren Menschen** he gives the impression of being cheerful/of being a cheerful person; **die Rede hat ihren ~ auf ihn nicht verfehlt** the speech made a strong impression on him; **er will ~ (bei ihr) machen** *or* **schinden** (*inf*) he's out to impress (her); **ich stehe noch ganz unter dem ~ des Ereignisses** I'm still too close to it all; **viele (neue) Eindrücke sammeln** to gain a whole host of new impressions; **du solltest einmal neue Eindrücke sammeln** you should broaden your horizons

b (*rare*: = *Spur*) impression, imprint

ein+drü|cken *sep* VT **a** *Fenster* to break; *Tür, Mauer* to push down; (*Sturm, Explosion*) to blow in/down; (= *einbeulen*) to dent, to bash in (*inf*); *Brustkorb* to crush; *Nase* to flatten **b** *Fußspuren etc* to impress VR to make *or* leave an impression

Ein|drucks-: **ein|drucks|fä|hig** ADJ receptive; **Ein|drucks|fä|hig|keit** F, *no pl* receptiveness; **ein|drucks|los** ADJ unimpressive; **ein|drucks|voll** ADJ impressive

ein+dru|seln [ˈaindruːzln] VI *sep aux sein* (*inf*) to doze off, to drop off (*inf*)

ein+dü|beln VT *sep Haken* to plug (*in +acc* in-to)

ein+du|seln VI *sep aux sein* (*inf*) to doze off, to drop off (*inf*)

ei|ne [ˈainə] → **ein²**, **eine(r,s)**

ein+eb|nen VT *sep* (*lit*) to level (off); (*fig*) to level (out)

Ein|eb|nung F -, -en levelling (*Brit*), leveling (*US*)

Ein|ehe F monogamy

ein|ei|ig ['ain|aiɪç] ADJ *Zwillinge* identical

ein|ein|halb ['ain|ain'halp] NUM one and a half; ~ **Mal** one and a half times → *auch* anderthalb

ein|ein|halb|mal △ ['ain|ain'halpma:l] ADV → eineinhalb

Ein|e|l|tern|(teil)|fa|mi|lie F single-parent family

ei|nen ['ainən] VTR (*geh*) to unite

ein+en|gen ['ain|ɛŋən] VT *sep* (*lit*) to constrict; (*fig*) *Begriff* to restrict, to narrow down; *Freiheit* to curb, to restrict; **sich (in seiner Freiheit) eingeengt fühlen** to feel cramped *or* restricted; **jdn in seiner Freiheit ~** to curb sb's freedom; **eingeengt sitzen/stehen/liegen** to sit/stand/lie (all) squashed up

ein|en|gend ADJ (*lit*) constricting; (*fig*) restrictive ADV **einen Begriff ~ interpretieren** to interpret a concept narrowly

Ein|en|gung F -, -en (*lit*) constriction; (*fig*) restriction

ei|ner ['ainɐ] ADV (*Aus*) = **herein**

Ei|ner ['ainɐ] M -s, - **a** (*Math*) unit **b** (= *Ruderboot*) single scull; **Weltmeister im ~** world champion in the single sculls

ei|ne(r, s) ['ainɐ] INDEF PRON **a** one; (= *jemand*) somebody, someone; **der/die/das Eine** the one; **das ~ Buch habe ich schon gelesen** I've already read one of the books *or* the one book; **das ~ Gute war ...** the one good thing was ...; **sein ~r Sohn** (*inf*) one of his sons; **weder der ~ noch der andere** neither (one) of them; **die ~n sagen so, die anderen gerade das Gegenteil** some (people) say one thing and others *or* some say just the opposite; **~r für alle, alle für ~n** (*Prov*) all for one and one for all (*Prov*); **dumm/intelligent** *etc* **wie nur ~r** (*dated*) thick/intelligent *etc* as they come (*inf*); **das ist ~r!** (*inf*) he's a (right) one! (*inf*); **du bist mir vielleicht ~r!** (*inf*) you're a fine *or* right one (*inf*); **sieh mal ~r an!** (*iro*) well what do you know! (*inf*), surprise, surprise! (*inf*); **alles in ~m abmachen** to do everything in one go; **in ~m fort** (*inf*) **in ~r Tour** (*inf*) non-stop → andere(r, s)

b (= *man*) one (*form*), you; **und das soll ~r glauben!** (*inf*) and we're/you're meant to believe that!; **wie kann ~r nur so unklug sein!** how could anybody be so stupid!; **wenn ~m so etwas gegeben wird** if such a thing is given (to) one (*form*) *or* (to) you

c **~s** (*auch* **eins**) one thing; **~s gefällt mir nicht an ihm** (there's) one thing I don't like about him; **~s sag ich dir** I'll tell you one thing; **noch ~s!** another one!; (*Lied etc*) more!; **noch ~s, bevor ichs vergesse** (there's) something else *or* one other thing before I forget; **es kam ~s nach dem** *or* **zum anderen** it was (just) one thing after another; **es läuft alles auf ~s hinaus, es kommt alles auf ~s heraus** it all comes to the same (thing) in the end

d (*inf*) **sich** (*dat*) **~n genehmigen** to have a quick one (*inf*) *or* drink; **jdm ~ kleben** to thump sb one (*Brit inf*), to punch sb → **abbrechen** VT **a**

Ei|ner|ka|jak M single seater *or* one-man canoe *or* kayak; (= *Disziplin*) single kayak *or* canoe

ei|ner|lei ['ainɐ'lai] ADJ *inv* **a** *pred* (= *gleichgültig*) all the same; **das ist mir ganz ~** it's all the same *or* all one to me; **was du machst ist mir ~** it's all the same to me what you do; **~ ob er kommt** no matter whether he comes or not; **was/wer ...** it doesn't matter what/who ...; **b** *attr* (= *gleichartig*) **Stoff von ~ Farbe** self-coloured (*Brit*) *or* self--colored (*US*) material; **sie kocht immer nur ~ Essen** she always cooks the same kind *or* sort of food; **es gab für alle nur ~ zu essen** everyone had to eat the same thing

Ei|ner|lei ['ainɐ'lai] NT -s, *no pl* monotony

---

ei|ner|seits ['ainɐzaits] ✪ 53.5 ADV ~ ... **andererseits** ... on the one hand ... on the other hand ...

Ei|ner|stel|le F (*Math*) unit (place)

ei|nes|teils ['ainəstails] ADV ~ ... **ander(e)nteils** ... on the one hand ... on the other hand

Ein|eu|ro|stück [ain'ɔyro-] NT one-euro piece

Ei|ne-Welt-La|den M ≈ OXFAM shop (*Brit*), ≈ thrift store (*US*), ≈ charity shop for the Third World

ein|fach ['ainfax] ADJ **a** simple; *Mensch* ordinary; *Essen* plain

b (*nicht doppelt*) *Knoten, Schleife* simple; *Fahrkarte, Fahrt* one-way, single (*Brit*); *Rockfalten* knife; *Buchführung* single-entry; **einmal ~!** (*in Bus etc*) single please (*Brit*), one-way ticket please (*US*); **das ist nicht so ~ zu verstehen** that is not so easy to understand, that is not so easily understood

ADV **a** (= *schlicht*) *leben, essen, sich kleiden* simply

b (= *nicht doppelt*) once, simply; **~ gefaltet** folded once; **die Wolle ~ nehmen** to use one strand of wool

c (*verstärkend*: = *geradezu*) simply, just; **~ gemein** downright mean; **das ist doch ~ dumm** that's (just) plain stupid

d (= *ohne weiteres*) just

e (= *mit Verneinung*) just

Ein|fach|heit F -, *no pl* simplicity; (*von Mensch*) ordinariness; (*von Essen*) plainness; **der ~ halber** for the sake of simplicity

ein+fä|deln *sep* VT **a** *Nadel, Faden* to thread (*in +acc* through); *Nähmaschine* to thread up; *Film* to thread **b** (*inf*) *Intrige, Plan etc* to set up (*inf*) VR **sich in eine Verkehrskolonne ~** to filter into a stream of traffic

ein+fah|ren *sep irreg* VI *aux sein* (*Zug, Schiff*) to come in (*in +acc* -to); (*Hunt: Fuchs, Dachs etc*) to go to earth; **in die Grube/den Schacht ~** (*Min*) to go down (to the face); **auf Bahnsteig 2 fährt der Zug aus München ein** the train from Munich is arriving at *or* coming in at platform 2

VT **a** (= *kaputtfahren*) *Mauer, Zaun* to knock down

b *Ernte* to bring in

c *Fahrgestell, Periskop* to retract

d (= *ans Fahren etc gewöhnen*) to break in; *Wagen* to run in (*Brit*), to break in (*US*); **„wird eingefahren"** "running in" (*Brit*), "being broken in" (*US*)

e *Verluste* to make; *Gewinne auch* to bring in

VR to get used to driving; **ich muss mich erst mit dem neuen Auto ~** I have to get used to (driving) the new car; **das hat sich so eingefahren** (*fig*) it has just become a habit → *auch* **eingefahren**

Ein|fahr|sig|nal NT (*Rail*) home signal

Ein|fahrt F **a** *no pl* (= *das Einfahren*) entry (*in +acc* to); (*Min*) descent; **Vorsicht bei (der) ~ des Zuges!** stand well back, the train is arriving; **der Schnellzug hat ~ auf Gleis 3** the express is arriving at platform 3; **der Zug hat noch keine ~** the train can't enter the station **b** (= *Eingang*) entrance; (= *Toreinfahrt*) entry; (*Hunt*) tunnel; **„Einfahrt freihalten"** "keep clear"

Ein|fall M **a** (*fig*) (= *plötzlicher Gedanke*) idea; (= *Grille, Laune*) notion; **jdn auf den ~ bringen, etw zu tun** to give sb the idea of doing sth; **auf den ~ kommen, etw zu tun** to get the idea of doing sth; **es war ein bloßer** *or* **nur so ein ~** it was just an idea; **er hat Einfälle wie ein altes Haus** (*hum inf*) he has some weird ideas **b** (*Mil*) invasion (*in +acc* of) **c** (*des Lichts*) incidence (*spec*); **je nach (dem) ~ des Lichts** according to how the light falls **d** (*liter*) (*der Nacht*) fall; (*des Winters*) onset; **vor ~ der Nacht** before nightfall

ein+fal|len ✪ 39.3, 41 VI *sep irreg aux sein* **a** (*Gedanke*) **jdm ~** to occur to sb; **das ist mir nicht eingefallen** I didn't think of that, that didn't occur to me; **mir fällt nichts ein, was ich schreiben kann** I can't think of anything to write; **jetzt fällt mir ein, wie/warum ...** I've just

---

thought of how/why ..., it's just occurred to me how/why ...; **ihm fällt immer eine Ausrede ein** he can always think of an excuse; **das fällt mir nicht im Traum ein!** I wouldn't dream of it!; **sich** (*dat*) **etw ~ lassen** to think of sth, to come up with sth; **hast du dir etwas ~ lassen?** have you had any ideas?, have you thought of anything?; **da musst du dir schon etwas anderes/Besseres ~ lassen!** you'll really have to think of something else/better; **was fällt Ihnen ein!** what are you thinking of!

b (= *in Erinnerung kommen*) **jdm ~** to come to sb; **dabei fällt mir mein Onkel ein, der ...** that reminds me of my uncle, who ...; **es fällt mir jetzt nicht ein** I can't think of it at the moment, it won't come to me at the moment; **es wird Ihnen schon wieder ~** it will come back to you

c (= *einstürzen*) to collapse, to cave in; (*Gesicht, Wangen*) to become sunken *or* haggard → *auch* **eingefallen**

d (= *eindringen*) **in ein Land ~** to invade a country; **in die feindlichen Reihen ~** to penetrate the enemy lines; **Wölfe sind in die Schafherde eingefallen** (*liter*) wolves fell upon the flock of sheep (*liter*)

e (*Lichtstrahlen*) to fall, to be incident (*spec*); (*in ein Zimmer etc*) to come in (*+acc* -to)

f (= *mitsingen, mitreden*) to join in; (= *einsetzen: Chor, Stimmen*) to come in; (= *dazwischenreden*) to break in (*+acc* into)

g (*liter*) (*Nacht*) to fall; (*Winter*) to set in

h (*Hunt: Federwild*) to come in, to settle

Ein|falls-: ein|falls|los ADJ unimaginative; **Ein|falls|lo|sig|keit** F -, *no pl* unimaginativeness; **ein|falls|reich** ADJ imaginative; **Ein|falls|reich|tum** M , *no pl* imaginativeness; **Ein|falls|tor** NT gateway

Ein|fall|stra|ße F access road

Ein|falls|win|kel M (*Phys*) angle of incidence

Ein|falt ['ainfalt] F -, *no pl* (= *Arglosigkeit*) simplicity, naivety; (= *Dummheit*) simple-mindedness, simpleness

ein|fäl|tig ['ainfɛltɪç] ADJ (= *arglos*) simple, naive; (= *dumm*) simple(-minded)

Ein|fäl|tig|keit F -, *no pl* simple-mindedness, simpleness

Ein|falts|pin|sel M (*inf*) simpleton

Ein|fa|mi|li|en|haus NT single-family house

ein+fan|gen VT *sep irreg* (*lit, fig*) to catch, to capture

ein+fär|ben VT *sep* **a** *Stoff, Haar* to dye **b** (*Typ*) *Druckwalze* to ink

ein|far|big, (*Aus*) **ein|fär|big** ADJ all one colour (*Brit*) *or* color (*US*); (*Tex*) self-coloured (*Brit*), self-colored (*US*)

ein+fas|sen VT *sep* **a** (= *umsäumen*) *Beet, Grab* to border, to edge; *Kleid, Naht, Knopfloch* to trim **b** **ein Grundstück (mit einem Zaun/einer Mauer/Hecke) ~** to put a fence/wall/hedge (a)round a plot of land **c** *Edelstein* to set (*mit* in); *Bild* to mount; *Quelle* to put a wall (a)round

Ein|fas|sung F **a** (*von Beet, Grab*) border, edging; (*von Kleid, Naht, Knopfloch*) trimming **b** (= *Zaun*) fence; (= *Mauer*) wall; (= *Hecke*) hedge **c** (*von Edelstein*) setting; (*von Bild*) mount

ein+fet|ten VT *sep* to grease; *Leder, Schuhe* to dubbin; *Haut, Gesicht* to cream, to rub cream into

ein+fin|den VR *sep irreg* to come; (= *eintreffen*) to arrive; (*zu Prüfung etc*) to present oneself; **ich bitte sie, sich pünktlich in meinem Büro einzufinden** I would ask you all to be in my office punctually; **ich werde mich also um 10 Uhr bei euch ~** I'll be *or* arrive at your place at 10 o'clock

ein+flech|ten VT *sep irreg* *Band, Blumen* to twine; (*fig: ins Gespräch etc*) to work in (*in +acc* -to), to introduce (*in +acc* in, into); **darf ich an dieser Stelle kurz ~, dass ...** I would just like to say at this point that ...; **in das Buch sind viele witzige Anekdoten eingeflochten** many

---

amusing anecdotes have been woven into the book

ein+flie|gen *sep irreg* **VT** **a** *Flugzeug* to test-fly **b** *Proviant, Truppen* to fly in (*in +acc* -to) **c** *Verluste* to make; *Gewinne* to bring in, to make **VI** *aux sein* to fly in (*in +acc* -to)

ein+flie|ßen **VI** *sep irreg aux sein* to flow in; (*Gelder auch*) to pour in; (*Wasser auch*) to run in; (*fig*) to have some influence (*in +acc* on), to leave its mark (*in +acc* on); **er ließ nebenbei ~, dass er Professor sei** he let it drop that he was a professor

ein+flö|ßen **VT** *sep* **jdm etw ~** to pour sth down sb's throat; *Medizin auch* to give sb sth; *Ehrfurcht, Mut etc* to instil (*Brit*) or instill (*US*) sth into sb, to instil (*Brit*) or instill (*US*) sb with a sense of sth

Ein|flug M **er beobachtete das Flugzeug beim ~** he watched the plane coming in; **er wurde beim ~ in Feindgebiet abgeschossen** he was shot down when flying into enemy territory

Ein|flug|schnei|se F (*Aviat*) approach path

Ein|fluss ▲ M **a** influence; **unter dem ~ von jdm/etw** under the influence of sb/sth; **~ auf jdn haben/ausüben** to have/exert an influence on sb; **~ nehmen** to bring an influence to bear; **seinen ~ geltend machen** to make one's influence felt; **das Wetter steht unter dem ~ eines atlantischen Tiefs** the weather is being affected or influenced by an Atlantic depression; **auf die Entscheidung hat es keinen ~** it has no influence or bearing on the decision, it won't influence the decision; **darauf habe ich keinen ~** I can't influence that, I've no influence over that **b** (*lit: = das Einfließen*) (*von Luft, fig*) influx; (*von Gas, Abwässern*) inflow

Ein|fluss-: **Ein|fluss|be|reich** ▲ M , **Ein|fluss|ge|biet** ▲ NT sphere of influence; **England liegt im ~ eines atlantischen Tiefs** England is being affected by an Atlantic depression; **ein|fluss|los** ▲ ADJ uninfluential; **Ein|fluss|lo|sig|keit** ▲ F -, *no pl* lack of influence; **Ein|fluss|mög|lich|keit** ▲ F influence; **unsere ~en sind begrenzt** we don't have much scope for influence; **Ein|fluss|nah|me** ▲ [-na:mə] F -, (*rare*) **-n** exertion of influence (+*gen* by); **ein|fluss|reich** ▲ ADJ influential; **Ein|fluss|sphä|re** ▲ F sphere of influence

ein+flüs|tern VT *sep* **jdm etw ~** to whisper sth to sb; (*fig*) to insinuate sth to sb

Ein|flüs|te|rung ['ainflʏstərʊŋ] F -, **-en** (*fig*) insinuation

ein+for|dern VT *sep Schulden* to demand payment of, to call (in); *Recht* to demand; *Versprechen, Zusage* to demand fulfilment (*Brit*) or fulfillment (*US*) of; *Unterstützung, Gerechtigkeit* to demand, to call for

ein|för|mig ADJ uniform; (= *eintönig*) monotonous

Ein|för|mig|keit F -, **-en** uniformity; (= *Eintönigkeit*) monotony

ein+fres|sen VR *sep irreg* to eat in (*in +acc* -to); **der Hass hatte sich tief in ihn eingefressen** hate had eaten deep into his heart

ein+frie|den ['ainfri:dn] VT *sep* (*geh*) to enclose

Ein|frie|dung F -, **-en** (*geh*) fence; wall; hedge

ein+frie|ren *sep irreg* **VI** *aux sein* to freeze; (*Wasserleitung, Schiff*) to freeze up; **im Eis eingefroren** frozen into the ice; **die Beziehungen ~ lassen** to suspend relations **VT** (*lit, auch fig*) *Nahrungsmittel, Löhne etc* to freeze; (*Pol*) *Beziehungen* to suspend; **sich ~ lassen** to allow oneself to be put into deep-freeze

Ein|frie|rung F -, **-en** (*fig*) (*von Löhnen etc*) freezing; (*von Beziehungen*) suspension

Ein|fü|ge|mo|dus M (*Comput*) insert mode

ein+fü|gen *sep* **VT** *Steine, Maschinenteile* to fit (*in +acc* into); (*Comput*) to insert (*in +acc* in); (= *nachtragen*) to add (*in +acc* in); **darf ich an dieser Stelle ~, dass ...** may I add at this point

that ... **VR** to fit in (*in +acc* -to); (= *sich anpassen*) to adapt (*in +acc* to); (*Haus in Umgebung etc*) to fit in (*in +acc* with)

Ein|fü|ge|tas|te F (*Comput*) insert key

Ein|fü|gung F insertion, addition

ein+füh|len VR *sep* **sich in jdn ~** to empathize with sb; (*Theat*) to feel oneself into (the role of) sb; **er kann sich gut in andere Leute ~** he's good at putting himself in other people's shoes (*inf*) or places, he's good at empathizing with other people; **sich in etw** (*acc*) **~** to understand sth; **sich in die Atmosphäre des 17. Jahrhunderts ~** to get into or project oneself into the atmosphere of the 17th century; **sich in ein Gedicht ~** to experience a poem

Ein|fühl|sam ['ainfy:lza:m] **ADJ** *Interpretation* sensitive; *Mensch auch* understanding, empath(et)ic (*form*) **ADV** sensitively

Ein|fühl|sam|keit F -, *no pl* sensitivity; (*von Mensch auch*) understanding

Ein|füh|lung F understanding (*in +acc* of); (*in einen Menschen auch*) empathy (*in +acc* with); (*einer Interpretation*) sensitivity

Ein|füh|lungs|ver|mö|gen NT , *no pl* capacity for understanding, empathy; **ein Buch mit großem ~ interpretieren** to interpret a book with a great deal of sensitivity

Ein|fuhr ['ainfu:r] F -, **-en** import; (= *das Einführen*) importing

Ein|fuhr- *in cpds* import; **Ein|fuhr|ar|ti|kel** M import; **ein ~ sein** to be imported; **Ein|fuhr|be|schrän|kun|gen** PL import restrictions *pl*; **Ein|fuhr|be|stim|mun|gen** PL import regulations *pl*

ein+füh|ren *sep* **VT** **a** (= *hineinstecken*) to insert, to introduce (*in +acc* into) **b** (= *bekannt machen*) to introduce (*in +acc* into); (*Comm*) *Firma, Artikel* to establish; **ein Amt ~** to install sb (in office); **jdn in seine Arbeit ~** to introduce sb to his work; **jdn bei Hofe ~** to present sb at court; **~de Worte** introductory words, words of introduction **c** (*als Neuerung*) to introduce, to bring in; *neue Mode* to set, to start; *Sitte* to start **d** (*Comm*) *Waren, Devisen* to import **e** (*St Ex*) to list, to introduce (*an +dat* on) **VR** to introduce oneself; **sich gut/nicht gut ~** to make a good/bad (initial) impression, to get off to a good/bad start (*inf*)

Ein|fuhr-: **Ein|fuhr|er|laub|nis** F , **Ein|fuhr|ge|neh|mi|gung** F import licence (*Brit*) or license (*US*); **Ein|fuhr|ha|fen** M port of entry; **Ein|fuhr|kon|tin|gent** NT import quota; **Ein|fuhr|land** NT importing country; **Ein|fuhr|sper|re** F = Einfuhrstopp; **Ein|fuhr|stopp** M ban on imports, import ban; **ein ~ für etw a** ban on the import of sth

Ein|füh|rung 53.1 F introduction (*in +acc* to); (= *Amtseinführung*) installation; (*bei Hof*) presentation; (= *Börseneinführung*) listing, introduction; (= *das Hineinstecken*) insertion (*in +acc* into)

Ein|füh|rungs- *in cpds* introductory; **Ein|füh|rungs|an|ge|bot** NT (*Comm: bei Ladeneröffnung, neuer Ware etc*) introductory offer; **Ein|füh|rungs|kurs** M (*Univ etc*) introductory course; (*St Ex*) introductory rate; **Ein|füh|rungs|preis** M introductory price

Ein|fuhr-: **Ein|fuhr|ver|bot** NT ban on imports; **ein ~ für etw** a ban on the import of sth; **Ein|fuhr|zoll** M import duty

ein+fül|len VT *sep* to pour in; **etw in Flaschen/Säcke/Fässer ~** to put sth into bottles/sacks/barrels, to bottle/sack/barrel sth

Ein|füll-: **Ein|füll|öff|nung** F opening; **Ein|füll|stut|zen** M (*Aut*) filler pipe

Ein|ga|be F **a** (*form: = Gesuch*) petition (*an +acc* to) **b** (*von Medizin*) administration **c** (*Comput: von Daten*) input

Ein|ga|be-: **Ein|ga|be|da|ten** PL input data *sing*; **Ein|ga|be|feh|ler** M (*Comput*) input er-

ror; **Ein|ga|be|frist** F time limit for the filing of petitions; **Ein|ga|be|ge|rät** NT input device; **Ein|ga|be|mas|ke** F (*Comput*) input mask; **Ein|ga|be|tas|te** F (*Comput*) enter key

Ein|gang M *pl* **-gänge** **a** entrance (*in +acc* to); (= *Zutritt, Aufnahme*) entry; **„kein ~!"** "no entrance"; **jdn ~ in etw** (*acc*)/**zu etw verschaffen** to gain entry into/to sth; **in etw** (*acc*) **~ finden** to find one's way into sth **b** (*Comm*) (= *Wareneingang, Posteingang*) delivery; (= *Erhalt*) receipt; **wir bestätigen den ~ Ihres Schreibens vom ...** we acknowledge receipt of your communication of the ...; **die Waren werden beim ~ gezählt** the goods are counted on delivery; **den ~** or **die Eingänge bearbeiten** to deal with the in-coming post (*Brit*) or mail **c** (= *Beginn*) start, beginning; **zum ~ möchte ich bemerken ...** I would like to start by saying ...

ein|gän|gig ADJ *Melodie, Spruch* catchy; *Theorie* neat

Ein|gän|gig|keit F -, *no pl* (*von Melodie, Spruch*) catchiness

ein|gangs ['aingaŋs] **ADV** at the start or beginning **PREP** +*gen* (*form*) at the start or beginning of

Ein|gangs-: **Ein|gangs|be|reich** M (*von Gebäude*) entrance area, lobby; (*von Theater, Oper etc*) foyer; **Ein|gangs|be|stä|ti|gung** F (*Comm*) acknowledgement of receipt; **Ein|gangs|buch** NT (*Comm*) receipt book, book of receipts; **Ein|gangs|da|tum** NT date of receipt; **Ein|gangs|for|mel** F (*Jur*) preamble; (*in Brief*) opening phrase; **Ein|gangs|hal|le** F entrance hall; **Ein|gangs|pfor|te** F (*lit, fig*) gateway; **Ein|gangs|stem|pel** M (*Comm*) receipt stamp; **mit einem ~ versehen** stamped with the date of receipt; **Ein|gangs|tor** NT entrance, main gate; **Ein|gangs|tür** F entrance, door; **Ein|gangs|ver|merk** M (*Comm*) notice of receipt

ein+ge|ben VT *sep irreg* **a** (= *verabreichen*) to give; **jdm das Essen ~** to feed sb **b** (*Comput*) *Text, Befehl* to enter; (= *eintippen auch*) to key in; **Daten in den Computer ~** to feed or enter data into the computer **c** (*dated: = einreichen*) *Gesuch etc* to submit (*an +acc* to) **d** (*liter*) **jdm etw ~** (*Gedanken etc*) to inspire sb with sth; **das hat uns Gott eingegeben** it comes from God

ein|ge|bet|tet [-gebɛtət] ADJ embedded; **in** or **zwischen Wäldern/Hügeln ~** nestling among the woods/hills → *auch* **einbetten**

ein|ge|bil|det ADJ **a** (= *hochmütig*) conceited **b** (= *imaginär*) imaginary; *Schwangerschaft* phantom; **ein ~er Kranker** a hypochondriac → *auch* **einbilden**

Ein|ge|bil|det|heit F -, *no pl* conceit

ein|ge|bo|ren ADJ (= *einheimisch*) native; (= *angeboren*) innate, inborn (+*dat* in); **Gottes ~er Sohn** the only begotten Son of God

Ein|ge|bo|re|nen|spra|che F native language

Ein|ge|bo|re|ne(r) ['aingəbo:rənə] MF *decl as adj* native (*auch hum*)

Ein|ge|bo|re|nen|stamm M native or indigenous tribe or people

Ein|ge|bung F ['ainge:bʊŋ] F -, **-en** inspiration

ein|ge|denk ['aingədɛŋk] (*old, liter*) **PREP** +*gen* bearing in mind, remembering; **~ dessen, dass ...** bearing in mind that ..., remembering that ... **ADJ** *pred* **einer Sache** (*gen*) **~ sein** to bear sth in mind, to be mindful of sth (*old liter*)

ein|ge|fah|ren [-gefa:rən] ADJ *Verhaltensweise* well-worn; **die Diskussion bewegte sich in ~en Gleisen** the discussion stayed in the same old groove or covered the same old well-worn topics → *auch* **einfahren**

ein|ge|fal|len ADJ *Wangen* hollow, sunken; *Augen* sunken, deep-set; *Gesicht* haggard, gaunt; *Schultern* drooping → *auch* **einfallen**

ein|ge|fleischt [-gəflaiʃt] ADJ **a** *attr* (= *überzeugt*) confirmed; (= *unverbesserlich*) dyed-in-

-the-wool; **~er Junggeselle** (*hum*) confirmed bachelor **b** (= *zur zweiten Natur geworden*) ingrained, deep-rooted

ein+ge|hen ◊ 53.2 *sep irreg aux sein* **VI a** (= *ankommen*) (*Briefe, Waren etc*) to arrive, to be received; (*Meldung, Spenden, Bewerbungen*) to come in, to be received; **~de Post/Waren** incoming mail/goods; **eingegangene Post/Spenden** mail/donations received

b (*old*: = *eintreten*) to enter (*in +acc* into); (= *Aufnahme finden: Wort, Sitte*) to be adopted (*in +acc* in); **in die Geschichte ~** to go down in (the annals of) history; **in die Unsterblichkeit ~** to attain immortality; **zur ewigen Ruhe** *or* **in den ewigen Frieden ~** to go to (one's) rest

c *etw geht jdm ein* (= *wird verstanden*) sb grasps *or* understands sth; **wann wird es dir endlich ~, dass ...?** when will it finally sink in *or* when will you finally understand that ...?; **es will mir einfach nicht ~, wie ...** it's beyond me how ..., I just cannot understand how ...

d (= *wirken*) **diese Musik geht einem leicht ein** this music is very catchy; **diese Worte gingen ihm glatt ein** these words were music to his ears

e (*fig*: = *einfließen*) to leave its mark, to have some influence (*in +acc* on); **die verschiedensten Einflüsse sind in das Werk eingegangen** there have been the most diverse influences on his work

f (= *einlaufen: Stoff*) to shrink

g (= *sterben: Tiere, Pflanze*) to die (*an +dat* of); (*inf: Firma etc*) to fold; **bei dieser Hitze/Kälte geht man ja ein!** (*inf*) this heat/cold is just too much (*inf*) *or* is killing (*inf*)

h auf etw (*acc*) **~** (= *behandeln, auf Frage, Punkt etc*) to go into sth; **darauf gehe ich noch näher ein** I will go into that in more detail; **niemand ging auf meine Frage/mich ein** nobody took any notice of my question/me

i (= *sich widmen, einfühlen*) **auf jdn/etw ~** to give (one's) time and attention to sb/sth

j (= *zustimmen*) **auf einen Vorschlag/Plan ~** to agree to *or* fall in with a suggestion/plan

VT (= *abmachen, abschließen*) to enter into; *Risiko* to take; *Wette* to make; **er gewinnt, darauf gehe ich jede Wette ein** I bet you anything he wins; **einen Vergleich ~** (*Jur*) to reach a settlement

ein|ge|hend **ADJ** (= *ausführlich*) detailed; (= *gründlich*) thorough; *Bericht, Studien, Untersuchungen in-depth attr* **ADV** (= *ausführlich*) in detail; (= *gründlich*) thoroughly

ein|ge|keilt ['aıngəkaılt] **ADJ** hemmed in; *Auto* hemmed in, boxed in; (*Sport*) boxed in; (*fig*) trapped → *auch* **einkeilen**

ein|ge|legt ['aıngəlekt] *ptp von* **einlegen ADJ a** (*Cook*) *Gemüse* preserved; (*in Essig*) *auch Hering* pickled **b** (= *mit Intarsien verziert*) **~er Schrank** inlaid cupboard **c** (*Mot*) **mit ~em Gang parken** to park with the car *etc* in gear → *auch* **einlegen**

Ein|ge|mach|te(s) ['aıngəmaxtə] **NT** *decl as adj* bottled fruit/vegetables; (= *Marmelade*) preserves *pl*; (*inf*: = *Erspartes*) one's own resources *pl*; **ans ~ gehen** (*fig inf*) to dig deep into one's reserves

ein+ge|mein|den ['aıngəmaındn] *ptp* **eingemeindet VT** *sep* to incorporate (*in +acc, nach* into)

Ein|ge|mein|dung **F** -, **-en** incorporation

ein|ge|nom|men ['aıngənɔmən] **ADJ für jdn/ etw ~ sein** to be taken with sb/sth, to be enamoured (*Brit*) *or* enamored (*US*) of sb/sth; **gegen jdn/etw ~ sein** to be prejudiced *or* biased against sb/sth; **er ist sehr von sich** (*dat*) **selbst ~** he thinks a lot of himself, he really fancies himself (*Brit inf*) → *auch* **einnehmen**

Ein|ge|nom|men|heit **F** -, *no pl* partiality (*für, von* to)

ein|ge|schlech|tig ['aıngəʃlɛçtıç] **ADJ** (*Bot*) unisexual, diclinous (*form*)

ein|ge|schlecht|lich **ADJ** *Gruppe* single-sex

ein|ge|schlos|sen [-ʃlɔsn] *ptp von* **einschließen ADJ a** (= *eingesperrt*) *Wertsachen etc* locked up; *Person* locked in **b** (= *umgeben*) *Grundstück, Haus etc* enclosed **c** (= *umzingelt*) surrounded, encircled **d** (= *nicht extra zu zahlen*) **im Preis ~** included in the price; **es ist alles mit ~** it's all--inclusive → *auch* **einschließen**

ein|ge|schnappt [-ʃnapt] **ADJ** (*inf*) cross; **~ sein** to be in a huff; **sie ist immer gleich ~** she always goes into a huff → *auch* **einschnappen**

ein|ge|schos|sig, (*Aus, S Ger*) **ein|ge|scho-ßig ADJ** *Haus* single-storey (*Brit*), single-story (*US*)

ein|ge|schränkt [-ʃrɛŋkt] **ADJ** (= *eingeengt*) restricted, limited; (= *sparsam*) careful; **in ~en Verhältnissen leben** to live in straitened circumstances → *auch* **einschränken**

Ein|ge|schränkt|heit **F** -, *no pl* restriction; (*finanziell*) straitened circumstances *pl*

ein|ge|schrie|ben [-ʃriːbn] **ADJ** *Mitglied, Brief* registered → *auch* **einschreiben**

ein|ge|schwo|ren [-ʃvoːrən] **ADJ** confirmed; *Gemeinschaft* close; **auf etw** (*acc*) **~ sein** to swear by sth; **auf etw** (*acc*) **~ sein** to be committed to a policy; **er ist auf diese Art von Malerei ~** he is a great fan of this type of painting; **die beiden sind aufeinander ~** the two of them are very close (to one another) → *auch* **einschwören**

ein|ge|ses|sen [-gəzɛsn] **ADJ** established; **die Firma/Familie ist dort seit Generationen ~** the firm/family has been (established) there for generations; **die Eingesessenen** the established inhabitants/families *etc* → *auch* **einsitzen**

Ein|ge|sot|te|ne(s) ['aıngəzɔtənə] **NT** *decl as adj* (*Aus*) bottled fruit

ein|ge|spannt **ADJ** busy → *auch* **einspannen**

ein|ge|spielt [-gəʃpiːlt] **ADJ** *Mannschaft* used to playing together; *Arbeitsteam, Kollegen* used to working together; **aufeinander ~ sein** to be used to one another → *auch* **einspielen**

ein|ge|stan|de|ner|ma|ßen ['aıngəʃtandənə-'maːsn], **ein|ge|stand|ner|ma|ßen** ['aıngə-ʃtandnə'maːsn] **ADV** admittedly

Ein|ge|ständ|nis **NT** admission, confession

ein+ge|ste|hen *ptp* **eingestanden VT** *sep irreg* to admit, to confess; **sie hat den Diebstahl eingestanden** she admitted (to) *or* confessed to the theft; **sich** (*dat*) **~, dass ...** to admit to oneself that ...

ein|ge|stellt **ADJ** **materialistisch/fortschrittlich ~ sein** to be materialistically/progressively minded, to be materialistic/progressive; **links/ rechts ~ sein** to have leanings to the left/right; **die links/rechts Eingestellten** leftists/rightists, left-/right-wingers; **wer so ~ ist** anyone who thinks as he does, anyone like him; **gegen jdn ~ sein** to be set against sb; **ich bin im Moment nicht auf Besuch ~** I'm not prepared for visitors; **wir sind nur auf kleinere Reisegesell-schaften ~** we can only cater for small parties; **auf Export ~ sein** to be geared to exports, to be tailored to the export market → *auch* **einstellen**

ein|ge|stri|chen [-gəʃtrıçn] **ADJ** (*Mus*) **das ~e C** middle C; **das ~e A** the A above middle C

ein|ge|tra|gen [-gətraːgn] **ADJ** *Mitglied, Warenzeichen, Verein* registered → *auch* **eintragen**

Ein|ge|wei|de ['aıngəvaıdə] **NT** **-s, -** *usu pl* entrails *pl*, innards *pl*; **der Schreck fuhr mir bis in die ~** (*liter*) my blood froze

Ein|ge|wei|de|bruch **M** (*Med*) hernia

Ein|ge|weih|te(r) ['aıngəvaıtə] **MF** *decl as adj* initiate; **seine Lyrik ist nur ~n verständlich** his poetry can only be understood by the initiated; **ein paar ~** a chosen few

ein+ge|wöh|nen *ptp* **eingewöhnt VR** *sep* to settle down *or* in (*in +dat* in)

Ein|ge|wöh|nung **F** settling down *or* in

Ein|ge|wöh|nungs|zeit **F** settling-in *or* settling-down period

ein|ge|wur|zelt [-gəvʊrtslt] **ADJ** deep-rooted, deep-seated; **tief bei jdm ~ sein** to be deeply ingrained in sb

Ein|ge|zo|ge|ne(r) ['aıngatsoːgənə] **MF** *decl as adj* (*Mil*) conscript, draftee (*US*)

ein|ge|zwängt [-gətsvɛŋt] *ptp von* **einzwängen ADJ** packed *or* jammed (*in +dat* into); (*fig*) straitjacketed; **sich ~ fühlen** (*in Ehe*) to feel constricted *or* trapped; (*in Kleidung*) to feel constricted → *auch* **einzwängen**

ein+gie|ßen VT *sep irreg* (= *hineinschütten*) to pour in (*in +acc* -to); (= *einschenken*) to pour (out); **darf ich Ihnen noch Kaffee ~?** can I give you *or* pour you some more coffee?

ein+gip|sen VT *sep Arm, Bein* to put in plaster; *Dübel etc* to plaster in (*in +acc* -to)

Ein|glas **NT** (*dated*) monocle

ein|glei|sig **ADV** single-track; **der Zug fährt hier nur ~** the railway (*Brit*) *or* railroad (*US*) line is only single-track here; **die Straßenbahn fährt hier nur ~** the tram (*Brit*) *or* streetcar (*US*) line is only single-track here; **er denkt sehr ~** (*fig*) he's completely single-minded

Ein|glei|sig|keit ['aınglaızıçkaıt] **F** -, *no pl* (*fig*) single-mindedness

ein+glie|dern *sep* **VT** *Firma, Gebiet* to incorporate (*+dat* into, with); *jdn* to integrate (*in +acc* into); (= *einordnen*) to include (*unter +acc* under, in) **VR** to fit in (*+dat, in +acc* -to, in), to integrate oneself (*+dat, in +acc* into) (*form*)

Ein|glie|de|rung **F** (*von Firma, Gebiet*) incorporation; (*von Behinderten, Straffälligen*) integration

Ein|glie|de|rungs|hil|fe **F** (*für Behinderte, Spätaussiedler etc*) assistance with social integration

ein+gra|ben *sep irreg* **VT** *Pfahl, Pflanze* to dig in (*in +acc* -to); (= *vergraben*) *Schatz, Leiche* to bury (*in +acc* in); **eine Inschrift in Granit ~** (= *geh*) to carve an inscription into granite **VR** to dig oneself in (*auch Mil*); **der Fluss hat sich ins Gestein eingegraben** the river carved itself a channel in the rock; **dieses Erlebnis hat sich seinem Gedächtnis eingegraben** this experience has carved itself on his memory

ein+gra|vie|ren *ptp* **eingraviert VT** *sep* to engrave (*in +acc* in)

ein+grei|fen VI *sep irreg* **a** (*Tech*) to mesh (*in +acc* with) **b** (= *einschreiten, Mil*) to intervene; **in jds Rechte** (*acc*) **~** to intrude (up)on sb's rights; **wenn nicht sofort ein Arzt eingreift, ...** without immediate medical intervention ...; **Eingreifen** intervention

Ein|greif|trup|pe **F** (*Mil*) strike force

ein+gren|zen VT *sep* (*lit*) to enclose; (*fig*) *Problem, Thema* to delimit, to circumscribe; (= *verringern*) to narrow *or* cut down

Ein|gren|zung ['aıngrɛntsʊŋ] **F** -, **-en** enclosure; (*von Problem, Thema*) delimitation, circumscription; (= *Verringerung*) narrowing down

Ein|griff **M a** (*Med*) operation; **ein verbotener ~** an illegal abortion **b** (= *Übergriff*) intervention; **ein ~ in jds Rechte/Privatsphäre** an intrusion (up)on sb's rights/privacy **c** (*von Herrenunterhose*) fly

Ein|griffs|mög|lich|keit **F** possibility of intervention

ein+grup|pie|ren *ptp* **eingruppiert VT** *sep* to group (*in +acc* in)

Ein|grup|pie|rung **F** grouping

ein+ha|cken VI *sep* to peck (*auf +acc* at); **auf jdn ~** (*fig*) to pick on sb

ein+ha|ken *sep* **VT** to hook in (*in +acc* -to) **VI** (*inf*: = *Punkt aufgreifen*) to intervene; (*in Unterhaltung auch*) to break in; **wenn ich an diesem Punkt vielleicht ~ darf** if I might just take up that point **VR** **sie hakte sich bei ihm ein** she put *or* slipped her arm through his; **eingehakt gehen** to walk arm in arm

Ein|halt M , *no pl* **jdm/einer Sache ~ gebieten** to stop *or* halt sb/sth; *einem Missbrauch auch* to put an end *or* a stop to sth

ein+hal|ten *sep irreg* **VT a** (= *beachten*) to keep; *Spielregeln* to follow; *Diät, Vertrag* to keep to; *Verpflichtungen* to carry out; **die Zeit ~** to keep to time *or* schedule; **den Kurs ~** (*Aviat, Naut*) to maintain (its/one's) course, to stay on course; **er hält seine Zahlungsverpflichtungen immer pünktlich ein** he's always prompt about payments **b** (*old: = aufhalten*) *Schwungrad* to stop **c** (*Sew*) to gather **VI a** (*geh*) (= *aufhören*) to stop, to halt; (= *innehalten*) to pause; **halt ein!** stop! **b** (*dial: = Harn, Stuhlgang zurückhalten*) to wait

Ein|hal|tung F (= *Beachtung*) keeping (+*gen* of); (*von Spielregeln*) following (+*gen* of); (*von Diät, Vertrag*) keeping (+*gen* to); (*von Verpflichtungen*) carrying out (+*gen* of); **ich werde ihn zur ~ des Vertrages zwingen** I will force him to keep (to) the contract

ein+häm|mern *sep* **VT** *Nagel etc* to hammer in (*in +acc* -to); *Inschrift etc* to chisel in (*in +acc* -to), to engrave (*in +acc* into); **jdm etw ~** (*fig*) to hammer *or* drum sth into sb **VI auf etw** (*acc*) **~** to hammer on sth; **auf jdn ~** (*lit, fig*) to pound sb

ein+hams|tern VT *sep* (*inf*) to collect

ein+han|deln VT *sep* **a** (*gegen, für* for) to trade, to swap, to exchange **b** (= *bekommen*) **sich** (*dat*) **etw ~** (*inf*) to get sth

ein+hän|dig ADJ one-handed

ein+hän|di|gen ['ainhɛndɪgn] VT *sep* (*form*) to hand in, to submit (*form*)

Ein|hän|di|gung F -, -en (*form*) handing in, submission (*form*)

Ein|hand|seg|ler¹ M (= *Boot*) single-handed yacht, single-hander

Ein|hand|seg|ler²(in) M(F) single-handed yachtsman/-woman; **als ~ um die Welt fahren** to sail single-handed (a)round the world

ein+hän|gen *sep* **VT** *Tür* to hang; *Fenster* to put in **VR sich bei jdm ~** to slip *or* put one's arm through sb's; **sie gingen eingehängt** they walked arm in arm

ein+hau|chen VT *sep* (*liter*) **jdm/einer Sache etw ~** to breathe sth into sb/sth; **einer Sache** (*dat*) **neues Leben ~** to breathe new life into sth, to bring new life to sth

ein+hau|en *sep irreg* **VT a** *Nagel etc* to knock *or* drive *or* bash (*inf*) in (*in +acc* -to) **b** (= *zertrümmern*) to smash *or* bash (*inf*) in **c** (= *einmeißeln*) *Kerbe* to cut in (*in +acc* -to); *Inschrift etc auch* to carve in (*in +acc* -to) **VI a auf jdn ~** to lay into sb, to go for sb; **auf etw** (*acc*) **~** to go at sth **b** (*inf: beim Essen*) to tuck *or* pitch in (*inf*)

ein+he|ben VT *sep irreg* (*esp Aus*) *Steuern* to levy; *Geld* to collect

Ein|he|bung F (*esp Aus*) (*von Steuern*) levying; (*von Geldern*) collection

ein+hef|ten VT *sep* **a** *Buchseiten* to stitch in; (*mit Heftmaschine*) to staple in; (*Sew*) *Futter* to tack in **b** (= *einordnen*) *Akten etc* to file

ein+he|gen VT *sep* to enclose

ein|hei|misch ['ainhaimɪʃ] ADJ *Mensch, Tier, Pflanze* native, indigenous; *Produkt, Industrie, Mannschaft* local

Ein|hei|mi|sche(r) ['ainhaimɪʃə] MF *decl as adj* local

ein+heim|sen VT *sep* (*inf*) to collect; *Erfolg, Ruhm auch* to walk off with; *Geld auch* to rake in (*inf*); **er hat den Ruhm für sich allein eingeheimst** he took the credit himself

Ein|hei|rat F marriage (*in +acc* into)

ein+hei|ra|ten VI *sep* **in einen Betrieb ~** to marry into a business

Ein|heit ['ainhait] F -, -en **a** (*von Land etc, Einheitlichkeit*) unity; (= *das Ganze*) whole; **die drei ~en** (*Liter*) the three unities; **eine geschlossene**

~ bilden to form an integrated whole; **~ von Forschung und Lehre** indivisibility of teaching and research; **die (deutsche) ~** (German) unity **b** (*Mil, Sci, Telec*) unit

---

TAG DER DEUTSCHEN EINHEIT

The **Tag der deutschen Einheit** is the national holiday of the Federal Republic of Germany. It is celebrated on October 3rd, the day on which the two parts of Germany were re-unified in 1990. The tone of the day is political – serious speeches are made at official commemorative events – although people try to make it a day of rejoicing. The national holiday was formerly on June 17th, a day when the victims of the division of Germany were commemorated.

---

ein|heit|lich ['ainhaitlɪç] ADJ (= *gleich*) the same, uniform; (= *genormt*) standard(ized); (= *in sich geschlossen*) unified ADV uniformly; **~ gekleidet** dressed alike *or* the same; **wir müssen ~ vorgehen** we must act consistently with one another; **alle Spielplätze sind ~ gestaltet** all the playgrounds are built on the same lines; **die Pausenzeiten sind in allen Werken ~ geregelt** the times of breaks are laid down to be the same in all the works

Ein|heit|lich|keit F -, *no pl* (= *Gleichheit*) uniformity; (= *Genormtheit*) standardization; (= *innere Geschlossenheit*) unity

Ein|heits-: **Ein|heits|brei** M (*pej*) **es ist so ein ~** it's all so samey (*pej*); **Ein|heits|for|mat** NT standard format; **Ein|heits|fraß** M (*pej*) **wir bekommen einen ~** we all get the same disgusting food; **Ein|heits|front** F (*Pol*) united front; (= *Volksfront*) popular front; **Ein|heits|ge|werk|schaft** F unified trade *or* labor (*US*) union; **Ein|heits|klei|dung** F uniform; **Ein|heits|kurz|schrift** F standard shorthand; **Ein|heits|lis|te** F (*Pol*) single *or* unified list of candidates; **Ein|heits|par|tei** F united party; **in einigen Staaten gibt es nur eine ~** in some countries there is only a single *or* only one political party; **Ein|heits|preis** M standard *or* flat price; **Ein|heits|schu|le** F comprehensive (school); **Ein|heits|so|zi|a|list(in)** M(F) (*DDR*) SED member; **Ein|heits|staat** M (*Pol*) united state; **Ein|heits|ta|rif** M flat rate; **Ein|heits|wert** M (*von Immobilien*) ≈ rateable value

ein+hei|zen *sep* **VI** to put the heating on; **bei dieser Kälte muss man tüchtig ~** you have to have the heating going full blast in this cold weather; **jdm (tüchtig) ~** (*inf*) (= *die Meinung sagen*) to haul sb over the coals; (= *zu schaffen machen*) to make things hot for sb **VT** *Ofen* to put on; *Zimmer* to heat (up)

ein+hel|fen VI *sep irreg* (*dial*) to help out

ein|hel|lig ['ainhɛlɪç] ADJ unanimous ADV unanimously

Ein|hel|lig|keit F unanimity

ein|her [ain'heːɐ] ADV (*Aus*) = **herein**

ein|her- PREF (= *entlang*) along; (= *hin und her*) up and down; **einherreiten** to ride along/up and down

ein|her+ge|hen VI *sep irreg aux sein* (= *umhergehen*) to go around; **mit etw ~** (*fig: mit sich bringen*) to be accompanied by sth

ein|her+re|den VTI *sep* = **daherreden**

ein|her+stol|zie|ren *ptp* **einherstolziert** VI *sep aux sein* (*dated*) to strut along; (*auf jdn zu*) to come strutting along

ein|hin [ain'hɪn] ADV (*Aus*) = **hinein**

ein|hö|cke|rig, **ein|höck|rig** ADJ *Kamel* one-humped

ein+ho|len VT *sep* **a** (= *einziehen*) *Boot, Netz, Tau* to pull *or* haul in; *Fahne, Segel* to lower, to take down **b** *Rat, Gutachten, Erlaubnis* to obtain; **bei jdm Rat ~** to obtain sb's advice *or* advice from sb **c** (= *erreichen, nachholen*) *Laufenden, Auto* to catch up; *Vorsprung, Versäumtes, Zeit*

to make up; *Verlust* to make good; **der Alltag/ die Vergangenheit hat mich eingeholt** the daily routine/the past has caught up with me **d** *auch vi* (*dial*) = **einkaufen**

Ein|hol- (*dial*): **Ein|hol|netz** NT string bag; **Ein|hol|ta|sche** F shopping bag

Ein|ho|lung ['ainhoːlʊŋ] F -, -en **a** (*von Fahne*) lowering **b** (*von Rat, Gutachten etc*) obtaining

Ein|horn NT (*Myth, Astron*) unicorn

Ein|hu|fer ['ainhuːfɐ] M -s, - (*Zool*) solidungulate (*spec*)

ein|hu|fig [-huːfɪç] ADJ solidungulate (*spec*)

ein+hül|len *sep* **VT** *Kind, Leichnam* to wrap (up), to swathe (*liter*) (*in +acc* in); **in Nebel/Wolken eingehüllt** shrouded *or* enveloped in mist/ clouds **VR** (*geh*) to wrap oneself up

ein|hun|dert ['ain'hʊndɐt] NUM (*form*) = **hundert**

ein+hü|ten VI *sep* (*N Ger*) to keep house (*bei* for); (= *Kinder hüten*) to babysit (*bei* for)

ei|ni ['aini] ADV (*Aus*) = **hinein**

ei|nig ['ainɪç] ✪ 38.1 ADJ **a** (= *geeint*) united **b** (= *einer Meinung*) agreed, in agreement (*über +acc* on, about, *in +dat* on); **ich weiß mich in dieser Sache mit ihm ~** (*geh*) I know I am in agreement with him on this; **sich** (*dat*) **über etw** (*acc*) **~ werden** to agree on sth; **darüber** *or* **darin sind wir uns ~, dass ...** we are agreed that ...; **wir werden schon miteinander ~ werden** we will manage to come to an agreement; **ich bin mir selbst noch nicht ganz ~, was ...** I am still somewhat undecided as to what ...

ei|ni|ge ['ainɪgə] INDEF PRON = **einige(r, s)**

ein+igeln ['ainiːgln] VR *sep* (*Mil*) to take up a position of all-round defence (*Brit*) *or* all-round defense (*US*); (*fig*) to hide (oneself) away

ei|ni|ge|mal △ ['ainɪgəmaːl, 'ainɪgə'maːl] ADV → **einige(r, s)** b

ei|ni|gen ['ainɪgn] VT *Volk etc* to unite; *Streitende* to reconcile **VR** to reach (an) agreement (*über +acc* about); **sich über den Preis/eine gemeinsame Politik ~** to reach agreement *or* to agree on the price/a common policy; **sich auf einen Kompromiss/Vergleich ~** to agree to a compromise/settlement; **sich dahin (gehend) ~, dass ...** to agree that ...

Ei|ni|ger ['ainɪgɐ] M -s, -, **Ei|ni|ge|rin** [-ərɪn] F -, -nen (*geh*) unifier

ei|ni|ge(r, s) ['ainɪgə] INDEF PRON **a** *sing* (= *etwas*) some; (= *ziemlich viel*) quite some; **in ~r Entfernung** some distance away; **nach ~r Zeit** after a while *or* some time; **ich könnte dir ~s über ihn erzählen, was ...** I could tell you a thing *or* two about him that ...; **das wird ~s kosten** that will cost something; **dazu ist noch ~s zu sagen** there are still one or two things to say about that; **dazu gehört schon ~s** that really takes something; **dazu gehört schon ~ Frechheit/~r Mut** that takes some cheek (*Brit*) *or* nerve/some courage; **mit ~m guten Willen** (= *mit Anstrengung*) with a bit of effort; **mit ~m guten Willen hätte der Richter ihn freisprechen können** the judge could have given him the benefit of the doubt and acquitted him **b** *pl* some; (= *mehrere*) several; (= *ein paar*) a few, some; **mit ~n anderen** with several/a few others; **~ wenige** a few; **mit Ausnahme ~r weniger** with a few exceptions; **~ Mal(e)** a few times, several times; **~ hundert** *or* **Hundert Menschen** a few hundred people; **~ hunderte** *or* **Hunderte von Flaschen** hundreds of bottles, several hundred bottles; **an ~n Stellen** in some places; **in ~n Tagen** in a few days; **vor ~n Tagen** the other day, a few days ago

ei|ni|ger|ma|ßen ['ainɪgɐ'maːsn] ADV (= *ziemlich*) rather, somewhat; (*vor adj*) fairly; (= *ungefähr*) to some extent or degree; **ein ~ gutes Angebot** a fairly good offer, not a bad offer; **~ Bescheid wissen** to have a fair idea; **er hat die Prüfung so ~ geschafft** he did so-so in (*Brit*) *or* on (*US*) the exam; **wie gehts dir? – ~** how are you? – all right *or* so-so *or* not too bad **ADJ** *pred* (*inf*: = *leidlich*) all right, fair, reasonable; **wie ist denn das Hotel? – na ja, ~** what's the hotel like? – oh, fair *or* all right

ei|ni|ges ['aɪnɪɡəs] INDEF PRON = **einige(r, s)**

ei|nig ge|hen ▲ VI *irreg aux sein* to agree, to be agreed (*in* +*dat* on); **ich gehe mit ihm darin einig, dass ...** I am agreed with him that ...; **wir gehen einig in der Überzeugung, dass ...** we are one in our conviction that ...

Ei|nig|keit F -, *no pl* (= *Eintracht*) unity; (= *Übereinstimmung*) agreement; **in diesem** *or* **über diesen Punkt herrschte** *or* **bestand ~** there was agreement on this point; **~ macht stark** (*Prov*) unity gives strength, strength through unity (*prov*)

Ei|ni|gung F -, -en **a** (*Pol*) unification **b** (= *Übereinstimmung*) agreement; (*Jur*: = *Vergleich*) settlement; **über etw** (*acc*) **~ erzielen** to come to *or* reach agreement on sth

Ei|ni|gungs-: Ei|ni|gungs|be|stre|bun|gen PL (*Pol*) unification efforts *pl*, unification movement *sing*; **Ei|ni|gungs|ver|such** M attempt to reach agreement; **Ei|ni|gungs|ver|trag** M (*Pol*) Unification Treaty

ein+imp|fen VT *sep* **jdm etw ~** (*lit*) to inject *or* inoculate sb with sth; **er hat seinen Kindern diese Ansichten eingeimpft** he drummed these ideas into his children

ein+ja|gen VT *sep* **jdm Furcht ~** to frighten sb; **jdm einen Schrecken ~** to give sb a fright *or* a shock

ein|jäh|rig ADJ *Kind, Tier* one-year-old; *Pflanze* annual; *Amtszeit, Studium* one-year *attr*; **nach ~er Pause** after a break of one *or* a year; **eine ~e Frist/Dauer** a period of one *or* a year

Ein|jäh|ri|ge(r) ['aɪnjɛːrɪɡə] M *decl as adj*, **Ein|jäh|rig-Frei|wil|li|ge(r)** ['aɪnjɛːrɪɡə] M *decl as adj* (*Mil Hist*) one-year army volunteer

Ein|jäh|ri|ge(s) ['aɪnjɛːrɪɡə] NT *decl as adj* (*old Sch*) ≈ lower school certificate (*old*)

ein+kal|ku|lie|ren *ptp* **einkalkuliert** VT *sep* to reckon with *or* on; *Kosten* to include, to take into account

Ein|kam|mer|sys|tem NT (*Pol*) single-chamber *or* unicameral (*form*) system

ein+kap|seln ['aɪnkapsln] VR *sep* (*Med*) to encapsulate (*form*); (*fig*) to withdraw *or* go into one's shell

ein+kas|sie|ren *ptp* **einkassiert** VT *sep* **a** *Geld, Schulden* to collect; **die Polizei hat den Dieb einkassiert** the police nabbed the criminal (*inf*); **er hat eine Ohrfeige einkassiert** he earned himself a clip on the ear **b** (*inf*: = *wegnehmen*) to take

ein+kas|teln ['aɪnkastln] VT *sep* (*inf*: *Aus, S Ger*) *Straftäter* to put away (*inf*), to lock up

Ein|kauf M **a** (= *das Einkaufen*) buying (*auch Comm*), purchase; **der Sommer ist die beste Zeit für den ~ von Kohlen** summer is the best time to buy *or* for buying (in) coal; **Einkäufe machen** to go shopping; **ich muss noch ein paar Einkäufe machen** I still have a few things to buy, I still have a few purchases to make **b** (*usu pl*: = *Gekauftes*) purchase; **ein guter** *or* **vorteilhafter/schlechter ~** a good/bad buy; **sie packte ihre Einkäufe aus** she unpacked her shopping **c** *no pl* (*Comm*: = *Abteilung*) buying (department) **d** (*in Altersheim, Firma etc*) **durch den ~ in ein Seniorenheim** by buying oneself into an old people's home; **er versucht durch Einkäufe in diese Firma in Europa Fuß zu fassen** he is trying to get a foothold in Europe by buying up shares in this firm **e** (*Ftbl*) transfer

ein+kau|fen *sep* **VT** to buy; *Vorräte* to buy (in) **VI** to shop; (*Comm*) to buy, to do the buying; **~ gehen** to go shopping; **ich kaufe nur bei Müller ein** I only shop at Müllers **VR** to buy one's way (*in* +*acc* into)

Ein|käu|fer(in) M(F) (*Comm*) buyer

Ein|kaufs- *in cpds* shopping; **Ein|kaufs|bum|mel** M shopping spree; **einen ~ machen** to go on a shopping spree; **Ein|kaufs|ge|nos|sen|schaft** F consumers' cooperative society; **Ein|kaufs|korb** M shopping basket; **Ein|kaufs|lei|ter(in)** M(F) (*Comm*) chief buyer; **Ein|kaufs|lis|te** F shopping list; **Ein|kaufs|mög|lich|keit** F **mit guten ~en** with good shopping facilities; **Ein|kaufs|netz** NT string bag, shopping net; **Ein|kaufs|pas|sa|ge** F shopping arcade; **Ein|kaufs|preis** M wholesale price; (= *Kaufpreis*) purchase price; **Ein|kaufs|quel|le** F **eine gute ~ für etw** a good place to buy sth; **Ein|kaufs|stra|ße** F shopping street; **Ein|kaufs|ta|sche** F shopping bag; **Ein|kaufs|vier|tel** NT shopping area; **Ein|kaufs|wa|gen** M shopping trolley (*Brit*) *or* cart (*US*); **Ein|kaufs|zent|rum** NT shopping centre (*Brit*) *or* center (*US*); **Ein|kaufs|zet|tel** M shopping list

Ein|kehr ['aɪnkeːɐ] F -, *no pl* **a** (*in Gasthaus*) stop; **in einem Gasthaus ~ halten** to (make a) stop at an inn **b** (*geh*: = *Besinnung*) self-examination, reflection; **bei sich ~ halten** to look into *or* search one's heart

ein+keh|ren VI *sep aux sein* **a** (*in Gasthof*) to (make a) stop, to stop off (*in* +*dat* at); (*bei Freunden*) to call on **b** (*Ruhe, Friede*) to come (*bei* to); (*Not, Sorge*) to come (*bei* upon, to); **wieder ~** to return (*bei* to)

ein+kei|len VT *sep* to hem in; *Mensch auch, Auto* to box in; (*fig*) to box in, to trap → *auch* **eingekeilt**

ein+kel|lern ['aɪnkɛlɐn] VT *sep* to store in a cellar

ein+ker|ben VT *sep* to cut a notch/notches in, to notch; (= *schnitzen*) to cut, to chip

Ein|ker|bung F notch

ein+ker|kern ['aɪnkɛrkɐn] VT *sep* to incarcerate

Ein|ker|ke|rung F -, -en incarceration

ein+kes|seln ['aɪnkɛsln] VT *sep* to encircle, to surround

Ein|kes|se|lung F -, -en encirclement, surrounding

ein+kit|ten VT *sep* to fix with putty (*in* +*acc* in)

ein|klag|bar ADJ *Schulden* (legally) recoverable; *Anspruch, Recht* (legally) enforceable

ein+kla|gen VT *sep Schulden* to sue for (the recovery of); *Anspruch, Recht* to take legal action to enforce

ein+klam|mern VT *sep* to put in brackets *or* parentheses, to put brackets (a)round; (*fig*) *Thema, Frage* to leave aside

Ein|klang M **a** (*Mus*) unison **b** (*geh*: = *Übereinstimmung*) harmony; **in ~ bringen** to bring into line; **in** *or* **im ~ mit etw stehen** to be in accord with sth; **seine Worte und Taten stehen nicht miteinander im** *or* **in ~** his words and deeds were at variance *or* not in accord with one another

Ein|klas|sen|schu|le F one-class school

ein|klas|sig ADJ *Schule* one-class *attr*

ein+kle|ben VT *sep* to stick in (*in* +*acc* -to)

ein+klei|den VT *sep Soldaten* to fit *or* kit out (with a uniform); *Novizen* to accept (as a novice); (*fig*) *Gedanken* to couch; **jdn/sich völlig neu ~** to buy sb/oneself a completely new wardrobe

Ein|klei|dung F **a** (= *das Einkleiden*) fitting out; *acceptance as a novice*; (*von Gedanken*) couching **b** (= *Verhüllung*) veil; **in mystischer ~** veiled in mysticism

ein+klem|men VT *sep* **a** (= *quetschen*) to jam; *Finger etc* to catch, to get caught; **er hat sich/mir die Hand in der Tür eingeklemmt** he caught his/my hand in the door; **der Fahrer war hinter dem Steuer eingeklemmt** the driver was pinned behind the wheel **b** (= *festdrücken*) to clamp; **der Hund klemmte den Schwanz ein** the dog

put his tail between his legs; **eingeklemmter Bruch** (*Med*) strangulated hernia

ein+klin|ken ['aɪnklɪŋkn] *sep* **VT** *Tür etc* to latch; *Segelflugzeug, Leine* to hitch up; **die Tür ist eingeklinkt** the door is on the latch **VI** (*Verschluss, Sicherheitsgurt*) to click shut; (*Tech*: = *einrasten*) to engage **VR** **sich in etw** (*acc*) **~** to link up with sth

ein+klop|fen VT *sep Nagel etc* to knock in (*in* +*acc* -to); *Hautcreme etc* to pat in (*in* +*acc* -to)

ein+knei|fen VT *sep irreg Schwanz* (*lit*) to put between its legs; **mit eingekniffenem Schwanz** (*lit, fig inf*) with his *etc* tail between his *etc* legs

ein+kni|cken *sep* **VT** *Papier* to crease (over); *Streichholz, Äste* to snap **VI** *aux sein* (*Strohhalm*) to get bent; (*Äste*) to snap; (*Knie*) to give way, to buckle; (*fig*: = *umfallen*) to give way; **er knickt immer mit den Knien ein** his knees are always giving way; **mein Knöchel** *or* **Fuß knickt dauernd ein** I'm always going over on my ankle (*Brit*), I'm always turning my ankle (*esp US*)

ein|knöpf|bar ADJ *Futter* attachable

ein+knöp|fen VT *sep Futter* to button in

ein+knüp|peln VT *sep* **auf jdn ~** to beat sb (up) with cudgels; (*Polizei*) to beat sb (up) with batons *or* truncheons; (*fig*) to lash sb

ein+ko|chen *sep* **VT** *Gemüse* to preserve; *Marmelade* to make **VI** *aux sein* (*Marmelade etc*) to boil down; (*Wasser*) to boil away; (*Soße*) to thicken

Ein|koch|topf M preserving pan

ein+kom|men VI *sep irreg aux sein* (*form*) **a** **(bei jdm) um etw ~** to apply (to sb) for sth **b** (*Sport, Naut*) to come in

Ein|kom|men ['aɪnkɔmən] NT -s, - income

Ein|kom|mens-: Ein|kom|mens|aus|fall M loss of income *no pl*; **Ein|kom|mens|ein|bu|ße** F *usu pl* loss of income *no pl*; **Ein|kom|mens|ge|fäl|le** NT income differential; **Ein|kom|mens|gren|ze** F income limit; **Ein|kom|mens|grup|pe** F income bracket; **Ein|kom|mens|klas|se** F income bracket; **Ein|kom|mens|los** ADJ (*form*) without an income; **~ sein** to have no income, to be without an income; **Ein|kom|mens|schicht** F income bracket; **Ein|kom|mens|schwach** ADJ low-income *attr*; **ein|kom|mens|stark** ADJ high-income *attr*; **die Einkommensstarken** people in a high-income bracket

Ein|kom|men(s)|steu|er F income tax

Ein|kom|men(s)|steu|er-: Ein|kom|men(s)|steu|er|be|scheid M income tax assessment; **Ein|kom|men(s)|steu|er|er|klä|rung** F income tax return; **ein|kom|men(s)|steu|er|pflich|tig** [-pflɪçtɪç] ADJ liable to income tax; **Ein|kom|men(s)|steu|er|ver|an|la|gung** F income tax coding

Ein|kom|mens-: Ein|kom|mens|ver|hält|nis|se PL (level of) income; **Ein|kom|mens|ver|tei|lung** F distribution of income; **Ein|kom|mens|zu|wachs** M increase in income

ein+köp|fen VTI *sep* (*Ftbl*) to head in (*in* +*acc* -to); **Müller köpfte zum 1:0 ein** Müller's header made the score 1-0

ein+kra|chen VI *sep aux sein* (*inf*) to crash down

ein+krei|sen VT *sep Feind, Wild* to surround; (*fig*) *Frage, Problem* to consider from all sides; (*Pol*) to isolate

Ein|krei|sung ['aɪnkraɪzʊŋ] F -, -en surrounding; (*von Frage, Problem*) systematic consideration; (*Pol*) isolation

Ein|krei|sungs|po|li|tik F policy of isolation

ein+kre|men ['aɪnkreːmən] VT *sep* = **eincremen**

ein+krie|gen *sep* (*inf*) **VT** to catch up **VR** **sie konnte sich gar nicht mehr darüber ~, wie/dass ...** she couldn't get over how/the fact that ...; **krieg dich mal wieder ein!** control yourself!

Ein|künf|te ['aɪnkʏnftə] PL income *sing*; (*einer Firma auch*) receipts *pl*

---

ein+kup|peln sep **VI** (Aut) to let the clutch in, to engage the clutch **VT** Eisenbahnwaggon to couple (up)

ein+la|den ❂ 52 VT sep irreg **a** Waren to load (in +acc into) **b** to invite; **jdn zu einer Party ~** to invite or ask sb to a party; **jdn ins Kino ~** to ask sb to the cinema; **jdn auf ein Bier ~** to invite sb for a beer; **lass mal, ich lade dich ein** come on, this one's on me; **wir sind heute Abend eingeladen** we've been invited out this evening; **er traut sich nicht, das Mädchen einzuladen** he doesn't dare ask the girl out; **dieses hübsche Plätzchen lädt zum Bleiben ein** it's very tempting to linger in this pretty spot; **das lädt ja geradezu zum Stehlen/Einbrechen ein** that's inviting theft/a break-in, that's asking to be stolen/broken into **c** (Sw) = **auffordern**

ein|la|dend ADJ inviting; Speisen appetizing

Ein|la|dung ❂ 52 F **a** invitation; **einer ~ Folge leisten** (form) to accept an invitation; **eine ~ aussprechen** (sl: = aufs Klo gehen) to go for a Jimmy (Brit) or Jerry (US) Riddle (sl) **b** (Sw) = **Aufforderung**

Ein|la|dungs-: **Ein|la|dungs|kar|te** F invitation (card); **Ein|la|dungs|schrei|ben** NT (official) invitation

Ein|la|ge F **a** (= Zahneinlage) temporary filling **b** (= Schuheinlage) insole; (zum Stützen) (arch) support **c** (Sew) padding; (= Versteifung) interfacing **d** (in Brief, Paket) enclosure; **einen Prospekt als ~ beilegen** to enclose a pamphlet **e** (Cook) noodles, vegetables, egg etc added to a clear soup **f** (= Zwischenspiel) interlude **g** (Fin: = Kapitaleinlage) investment; (= Spareinlage auch) deposit; (= Spieleinlage) stake

ein+la|gern sep **VT** to store **VR** to become deposited (in +acc or dat in); (Met) to settle

Ein|la|ge|rung F **a** storage **b** (Geol) deposit

ein|la|gig ADJ one-ply attr

ein+lan|gen VI sep aux sein (Aus) to arrive

Ein|lass ▲ ['ainlas] M **-es, ⸚e** [-lɛsə] **a** no pl (= Zutritt) admission; **jdm ~ gewähren** to admit sb; **sich** (dat) **~ in etw** (acc) **verschaffen** to gain entry or admission to sth **b** (Tech: = Öffnung) inlet, opening

ein+las|sen sep irreg **VT a** (= eintreten lassen) to let in, to admit **b** (= einlaufen lassen) Wasser to run in (in +acc into); **er ließ sich** (dat) **ein Bad ein** he ran himself a bath **c** (= einpassen, einfügen) to let in (in +acc -to); (in Holz, Metall auch) to set in (in +acc -to); **ein eingelassener Schrank** a built-in cupboard, a cupboard built into the wall; **eingelassene Schraube** countersunk screw **d** (Aus) Boden, Möbel to varnish **VR a sich auf etw** (acc) **~** (auf Angelegenheit, Abenteuer, Diskussion, Liebschaft) to get involved in sth; auf Streit, zwielichtiges Unternehmen auch to get mixed up in sth, to get into sth; (= sich zu etw verpflichten) to let oneself in for sth; **sich auf einen Kompromiss ~** to agree to a compromise; **sich in ein Gespräch ~** to get into (a) or get involved in a conversation; **ich lasse mich auf keine Diskussion ein** I'm not having any discussion about it; **darauf lasse ich mich nicht ein!** (bei Geschäft, Angelegenheit) I don't want anything to do with it; (bei Kompromiss, Handel etc) I'm not agreeing to that; **lasse dich in keine Schlägerei ein!** don't you go getting mixed up in any rough stuff; **da habe ich mich aber auf etwas eingelassen!** I've let myself in for something there! **b sich mit jdm ~** (pej: = Umgang pflegen mit) to get mixed up or involved with sb; **er ließ sich mit diesem Flittchen ein** he was carrying on with this floozy (pej inf) or tarty little bit (Brit pej inf); **sie lässt sich mit jedem ein!** she'll go with anyone **c** (Jur: = sich äußern) to testify (zu on)

Ein|las|sung ['ainlasʊŋ] F **-, -en** statement; (Jur) testimony

Ein|lass|zeit ▲ F opening time; (für Veranstaltung) timed entry; (bei vorgebuchter Zeit) entry time; (= Öffnungszeit) opening hours pl; **~ 9.30 Uhr** doors open at 9.30 a.m.

Ein|lauf M **a** no pl (Sport) (am Ziel) finish; (ins Stadion etc) entry; **beim ~ in die Zielgerade ...** coming into the final straight ... **b** (Med) enema; **jdm einen ~ machen** to give sb an enema **c** (Cook) (= Einlaufsuppe) soup with egg and/or beurre manié added **d** (Comm: = Post) = **Eingang b e** (rare: = Einlauföffnung) opening

ein+lau|fen sep irreg **VI** aux sein **a** (= hineinlaufen) to come in (in +acc -to); (= ankommen auch) to arrive (in +acc -to); (Sport) (ins Stadion) to come or run in (in +acc -to), to enter (in etw acc sth); (durchs Ziel) to finish; **das Schiff läuft (in den Hafen) ein** the ship is coming into or entering the harbour (Brit) or harbor (US) **b** (= hineinlaufen: Wasser) to run in (in +acc -to) **c** (= eintreffen) (Post) to arrive; (Bewerbungen, Spenden) to be received, to come in **d** (= eingehen: Stoff) to shrink; **garantiert kein Einlaufen** guaranteed non-shrink **VT** Schuhe to wear in **VR** (Motor, Maschine) to run in (Brit), to be broken in (US); (Sport) to warm or limber up

Ein|lauf|wet|te F (Pferderennen) three-way bet

ein+läu|ten VT sep Sonntag etc to ring in; (Sport) Runde to sound the bell for; (fig: = den Anfang darstellen von) Revolution to herald the start of; Wende to usher in

ein+le|ben VR sep to settle down (in or an +dat in); (fig: = sich hineinversetzen) to immerse oneself (in +acc in)

Ein|le|ge|ar|beit F inlay work no pl

ein+le|gen VT sep **a** (in Holz etc) to inlay; **eingelegte Arbeit** inlay work **b** (= hineintun) to insert (in +acc in), to put in (in +acc -to); Film to load (in +acc into); (in Brief) to enclose (in +acc in); **einen Pfeil (in den Bogen) ~** to fit an arrow (into the bow) **c** (= einfügen) Sonderschicht, Spurt, Sonderzug to put on; Lied, Kunststück, Pause to have; (Aut) Gang to engage; (Hist) Lanze to couch **d** (Fin: = einzahlen) to pay in, to deposit **e** (fig: = geltend machen) Protest to register; **ein gutes Wort für jdn ~** to put in a good word for sb (bei with); **sein Veto ~** to exercise or use one's veto → **Ehre, Berufung f** (Cook) Heringe, Gurken etc to pickle **g** Haare to set, to put in rollers

Ein|le|ger ['ainle:ɡɐ] M **-s, -**, **Ein|le|ge|rin** [-ərɪn] F **-, -nen** investor

Ein|le|ge-: **Ein|le|ge|soh|le** F insole; **Ein|le|ge|tisch** M inlaid table

ein+lei|ten sep **VT a** (= in Gang setzen) to initiate; Maßnahmen, Schritte to introduce, to take; neues Zeitalter to mark the start of, to inaugurate; (Jur) Verfahren to institute; (Med) Geburt to induce **b** (= beginnen) to start; (= eröffnen) Buch (durch Vorwort) to write an introduction to, to introduce; (Mus) to prelude **c** Abwässer etc to discharge (in +acc into) **VI** to give an introduction (in +acc to)

ein|lei|tend ADJ introductory; Worte auch of introduction **ADV** er sagte ~, **dass ...** he said by way of introduction that ...

Ein|lei|ter M (= Einleitungsrohr) discharge pipe; (= Einleitungsverursacher) discharger

Ein|lei|tung F **a** (= Vorwort) introduction; (Mus) prelude **b** (= das Einleiten) initiation; (von Maßnahmen, von Schritten) introduction; (von neuem Zeitalter) inauguration; (von Verfahren) institution; (von Geburt) induction **c** (von Abwässern) discharge (in +acc into)

Ein|lei|tungs|teil M (von Buch, Vortrag etc) introductory section

ein+len|ken VI sep (= nachgeben) to yield, to give way; **jdn zum Einlenken bewegen** to get sb to change his/her mind

ein+le|sen sep irreg **VR** **sich in ein Buch/Gebiet** etc ~ to get into a book/subject etc **VT** Daten to read in (in +acc -to)

ein+leuch|ten VI sep to be clear (jdm to sb); **der Grund seiner Abneigung leuchtet mir nicht ein** I don't see or understand or it's not clear to me why he doesn't like me; **ja, das leuchtet mir ein!** yes, I see that, yes, that's clear (to me); **das will mir nicht ~** I just don't understand or see that

ein|leuch|tend ADJ reasonable, plausible

ein+lie|fern VT sep Waren to deliver; **jdn ins Krankenhaus ~** to admit sb to hospital; **jdn ins Gefängnis ~** to put sb in prison, to commit sb to prison; **ein Paket bei der Post ~** to take a parcel to the post (Brit), to take a package to the post office

Ein|lie|fe|rung F (von Waren) delivery; (ins Krankenhaus) admission (in +acc to); (ins Gefängnis) committal (in +acc to); (von Briefen etc) sending; **die ~ von Paketen ist nur bis 17.00 Uhr möglich** parcels (Brit) or packages are not accepted after 5 pm

Ein|lie|fe|rungs|schein M certificate of posting (Brit) or mailing (esp US)

ein|lie|gend ADJ pred (form) enclosed; **~ erhalten Sie ...** please find enclosed ...

Ein|lie|ger|woh|nung F granny annexe (Brit) or flat (Brit), in-law apartment (US)

ein+lo|chen VT sep **a** (inf: = einsperren) to lock up, to put behind bars **b** (Golf) to hole out

ein+log|gen ['ainlɔɡn] VR (Comput) to log in or on; **sich in das System ~** to log into or onto the system

ein+lo|gie|ren ['ainloʒiːrən] ptp **einlogiert** sep **VT** to put up, to lodge **VR** **sich (bei jdm) ~** to lodge (with sb); (Mil) to be billeted (with or on sb)

ein|lös|bar ADJ redeemable; **Versprechen, die nicht ~ sind** promises that can't be kept

ein+lö|sen VT sep Pfand to redeem; Scheck, Wechsel to cash (in); (fig) Wort, Versprechen to keep; **in der Praxis lässt sich das nicht problemlos ~** in practice that cannot easily be realized

Ein|lö|sung F (von Pfand) redemption; (von Scheck, Wechsel) cashing (in); (von Wort, Versprechen) keeping

ein+lö|ten VT sep to solder in (in +acc -to)

ein+lul|len ['ainlʊlən] VT sep (inf) Kind to lull to sleep; (fig) Misstrauen, Wachsamkeit to allay, to quiet; **jdn mit Versprechungen/schönen Worten ~** to lull sb with (soothing) promises/soft words

Ein|mach ['ainmax] F **-, no pl**, **Ein|ma|che** ['ainmaxə] F **-, no pl** (Aus Cook) roux

ein+ma|chen VT sep Obst, Gemüse to preserve; (in Gläser auch) to bottle; (in Dosen) to can, to tin (Brit)

Ein|mach-: **Ein|mach|glas** NT bottling or preserving jar, canning jar (US); **Ein|mach|gum|mi** M (inf) rubber ring (for a preserving or canning jar); **Ein|mach|topf** M preserving pan; **Ein|mach|zu|cker** M preserving sugar

ein+mah|nen VT sep (form) to demand payment of

ein|mal ['ainma:l] ADV **a** (= ein einziges Mal) once; (= erstens) first of all, firstly, for a start; **~ eins ist eins** once one is one, one times one is one; **~ sagt er dies, ~ das** sometimes he says one thing, sometimes another; **~ sagte sie, wir sollten bleiben, ~ wir sollten gehen** first of all she says that we should stay, then that we should go; **auf ~** (= plötzlich) suddenly, all of a sudden, all at once; (= zugleich) at once; **~ mehr** once again; **~ und nicht** or **nie wieder** once and never again; **noch ~** again; **versuchs noch ~** (= wieder) try once more, try again; **noch ~ so**

groß wie as big again as; **wenn sie da ist, ist es noch ~ so schön** it's twice as nice when she's there; **~ ist keinmal** (*Prov*) (= *schadet nicht*) once won't hurt *or* do any harm; (= *zählt nicht*) once doesn't count **b** (= *früher, vorher*) once; (= *später, in Zukunft*) one *or* some day; **waren Sie schon ~ in Rom?** have you ever been to Rome?; **er hat schon ~ bessere Zeiten gesehen** he has seen better days; **sie waren ~ glücklich, aber jetzt ...** they were happy once *or* at one time, but now ...; **es war ~ ...** once upon a time there was ...; **das war ~!** that was then; **besuchen Sie mich doch ~!** come and visit me some time!; **das wird ~ anders werden** things will be different some *or* one day **c** (*verstärkend, eingrenzend: meist nicht übersetzt*) **nicht ~** not even; **auch ~** also, too; **wieder ~** again; **ich bin/die Frauen sind nun ~ so** that's the way I am/women are, I'm just/women are like that; **wie die Lage nun ~ ist** with things as *or* the way they are; **wenn er nun ~ hier ist ...** seeing he's here ...; **alle ~ herhören!** listen everyone!; **sag ~, ist das wahr?** tell me, is it true? → **erst a**

Ein|mal|eins [ainma:l'ains] NT -, *no pl* (multiplication) tables *pl*; (*fig*) ABC, basics *pl*; **das ~ lernen/aufsagen** to learn/say one's tables; **das kleine/große ~** (multiplication) tables up to/over ten

Ein|mal-: **Ein|mal|hand|schu|he** PL disposable gloves *pl*; **Ein|mal|hand|tuch** NT disposable towel

ein|ma|lig ['ainma:lıç, (*emph*) 'ain'ma:lıç] ADJ **a** *Gelegenheit, Angebot, Fall, Leistung* unique **b** (= *nur einmal erforderlich*) single; *Anschaffung, Zahlung* one-off *attr*; **beim ~en Durchlesen des Textes** on a single reading of the text, on reading the text through once **c** (*inf*: = *hervorragend*) fantastic, amazing; **dieser Film ist etwas Einmaliges** this film is really something (*inf*); **der Bursche ist wirklich ~** that guy is really something (*inf*) ADV (*inf*: = *besonders*) absolutely; **~ gut/schlecht** incredibly good/bad

Ein|ma|lig|keit ['ainma:lıçkait] F -, *no pl* uniqueness; **alle lobten die ~ dieses Films** everyone said how fantastic the film was

Ein|mal-: **Ein|mal|ka|me|ra** F disposable *or* single-use camera; **Ein|mal|sprit|ze** F = **Einwegspritze**

Ein|mann- [ain'man-]: **Ein|mann|be|trieb** M **a** one-man business *or* band (*inf*) **b** **die Busse auf ~ umstellen** to convert the buses for one-man operation; **Ein|mann|bus** M one--man bus, driver-operated bus; **Ein|mann|ka|pel|le** F one-man band; **Ein|mann|wa|gen** M one-man tram (*esp Brit*) *or* streetcar (*US*)

Ein|mark|stück [ain'mark-] NT (*Hist*) one-mark piece

Ein|marsch M entry (*in +acc* into); (*in ein Land*) invasion (*in +acc* of)

ein+mar|schie|ren *ptp* **einmarschiert** VI *sep aux sein* to march in (*in +acc* -to)

ein+mas|sie|ren *ptp* **einmassiert** VT *sep* to massage *or* rub in (*in +acc* -to)

Ein|mas|ter ['ainmastɐ] M -s, - (*Naut*) single--masted ship, single-master

ein|mas|tig [-mastıç] ADJ single-masted

ein+mau|ern VT *sep* **a** (= *ummauern*) to wall in, to immure (*in +acc* in) **b** (= *einfügen*) to fix into the wall

ein+mei|ßeln VT *sep* to chisel in (*in +acc* -to)

Ein|me|ter|brett [ain'me:tɐ-] NT one-metre (*Brit*) *or* one-meter (*US*) (diving) board

ein+mie|ten *sep* VT (*Agr*) to clamp VR **sich bei jdm ~** to take lodgings with sb; **er hat sich in der Wohnung unter uns eingemietet** he has taken the apartment below us

ein+mi|schen VR *sep* to interfere (*in +acc* in), to stick one's oar in (*inf*); **sie muss sich bei allem ~** she has to interfere *or* meddle in every-

thing; **wenn ich mich kurz ~ darf ...** if I can butt in a moment ...

Ein|mi|schung F interference, meddling (*in +acc* in)

ein|mo|na|tig ADJ *attr* one-month

ein|mo|nat|lich ADJ monthly

ein+mon|tie|ren *ptp* **einmontiert** VT *sep* to slot in (*in +acc* -to); (*Tech*) to fit in (*in +acc* -to)

ein|mo|to|rig ADJ *Flugzeug* single-engine(d)

ein+mot|ten ['ainmɔtn] VT *sep Kleider etc* to put in mothballs; (*fig auch*) to mothball; *Schiff, Flugzeug* to mothball

ein+mum|meln ['ainmʊmln], **ein+mum|men** ['ainmʊmən] VT *sep* to muffle up

ein+mün|den VI *sep aux sein* (*Fluss*) to flow in (*in +acc* -to); (*Straße*) to run *or* lead in (*in +acc* -to); **in etw** (*acc*) **~** to join sth; (*fig*) to end up in sth; (*Elemente, Einflüsse*) to go into sth

Ein|mün|dung F (*von Fluss*) confluence; (*von Straße*) junction; **die ~ der Isar in die Donau** the confluence of the Isar and the Danube

ein|mü|tig ['ainmy:tıç] ADJ unanimous ADV unanimously; **~ zusammenstehen** to stand together as one

Ein|mü|tig|keit F -, *no pl* unanimity; **darüber besteht ~** there is complete agreement on that

ein+nach|ten VI *impers sep* (*Sw*) **es nachtet ein** it's getting dark

ein+na|geln VT *sep* to nail in (*in +acc* -to); (= *einhämmern*) to hammer in (*in +acc* -to)

ein+nä|hen VT *sep* to sew in (*in +acc* -to); (= *enger machen*) to take in

Ein|nah|me ['ainna:mə] F -, -n **a** (*Mil*) seizure; (*einer Stellung, Stadt auch*) capture **b** (= *Ertrag*) receipt **c** **Einnahmen** PL income *sing*; (= *Geschäftseinnahme*) takings *pl*; (*aus Einzelverkauf*) proceeds *pl*; (= *Gewinn*) earnings *pl*; (*eines Staates*) revenue *sing*; **~n und Ausgaben** income and expenditure **d** (= *das Einnehmen*) taking; **durch ~ von etw** by taking sth

Ein|nah|me-: **Ein|nah|me|aus|fall** M loss of income; (*von Geschäften*) loss of takings; **Ein|nah|me|buch** NT (*Comm*) book of receipts, receipt book; **Ein|nah|me|pos|ten** M item of receipt; **Ein|nah|me|quel|le** F source of income; (*eines Staates*) source of revenue

ein+näs|sen *sep* (*form*) VT to wet VR to wet oneself; (*nachtsüber*) to wet the bed

ein+ne|beln *sep* VT (*Mil*) to put up a smoke-screen (a)round; (*fig*) to befog, to obfuscate (*liter*) VR (*Mil*) to put up a smokescreen (a-round oneself); **es nebelt sich ein** (*Met*) it's getting misty, there's a mist coming down

ein+neh|men VT *sep irreg* **a** *Geld* (*Geschäft etc*) to take; (*Freiberufler*) to earn; *Steuern* to collect; **die eingenommenen Gelder** the takings **b** (*Mil*: = *erobern*) to take; *Stadt, Festung* to capture, to take **c** (*lit, fig*) *Platz etc* to take (up), to occupy; *Stelle* (= *innehaben*) to have, to occupy (*form*); *Haltung, Standpunkt etc* to take up; **er nimmt vorübergehend die Stelle des Chefs ein** he is acting for the boss; **bitte, nehmen Sie Ihre Plätze ein!** (*form*) please take your seats!; **die Plätze ~** (*Sport*) to take one's marks **d** (= *zu sich nehmen*) *Mahlzeit, Arznei* to take **e** **er nahm uns alle für sich ein** he won us all over; **er hat alle für seine Pläne eingenommen** he won everyone over to his plans; **jdn gegen sich/jdn/etw ~** to set *or* put sb against oneself/sb/sth; **das nimmt mich sehr für sie ein** that makes me think highly of her → *auch* **eingenommen**

ein+neh|mend ADJ likeable (*Brit*), likable; *Atmosphäre* agreeable, pleasant; **er hat etwas Einnehmendes** there is something lik(e)able about him; **er hat ein ~es Wesen** (= *gewinnend*) he's a lik(e)able character; (*hum inf*: = *habgierig*) he likes to acquire things

Ein|neh|mer(in) M(F) (*old*) collector

ein+ni|cken VI *sep aux sein* (*inf*) to doze *or* nod off

ein+nis|ten VR *sep* (*lit*) to nest; (*Parasiten, Ei*) to lodge; (*fig*) to park oneself (*bei* on); **in unserem Land haben sich so viele Kriminelle eingenistet** so many criminals have settled in our country; **in ihm hatte sich tiefes Misstrauen eingenistet** he was filled with a deep mistrust

Ein|öd ['ain|ø:t] F -, -en [-dn] (*Aus*) = **Einöde**

Ein|öd|bauer M *pl* -bauern, **Ein|öd|bäu|e|rin** F farmer of an isolated farm

Ein|öde ['ain|ø:də] F *Moore und ~* moors and wasteland; **Wüsten und ~** deserts and barren wastes *pl*; **die weiße ~ der Antarktis** the white wastes of the Antarctic; **er lebt in der ~ des schottischen Hochlands** he lives in the wilds of the Scottish Highlands; **er verließ die ~ seines Schwarzwaldhofes** he left the isolation of his Black Forest farm

Ein|öd|hof M ≈ croft

ein+ölen *sep* VT to oil VR to rub oneself with oil, to oil oneself

ein+ord|nen *sep* VT **a** (*der Reihe nach*) *Bücher etc* to (put in) order; *Akten, Karteikarten* to file **b** (= *klassifizieren*) to classify; *Begriff, Theorie, Denker auch* to categorize VR **a** (*in Gemeinschaft etc*) to fit in (*in +acc* -to) **b** (*Aut*) to get in(to) lane; **sich links/rechts ~** to get into the left/right lane; **„Einordnen"** "get in lane"

ein+pa|cken *sep* VT **a** (= *einwickeln*) to wrap (up) (*in +acc* in); **jdn warm ~** (*fig*) to wrap sb up warmly **b** (= *hineintun*) to pack (*in +acc* in) **c** (= *packen*) *Paket* to pack up VI to pack, to do one's packing; **dann können wir ~** (*inf*) in that case we may as well pack it all in (*inf*) *or* give up

ein+par|ken VTI *sep* to park; **(in eine Parklücke) ~** to get into a parking space; **eingeparkt** (*Auto*, = *abgestellt*) parked; (= *zugeparkt*) blocked in (by parked cars)

Ein|par|tei|en- [ainpar'taiən] *in cpds* one-party, single-party; **Ein|par|tei|en|staat** M one-party *or* single-party state

ein+pas|sen *sep* VT to fit in (*in +acc* -to) VR to adjust, to adapt oneself (*in +acc* to)

ein+pau|ken VT *sep* (*inf*) to mug up (on) (*Brit inf*), to cram; **jdm etw ~** to drum sth into sb

Ein|pau|ker(in) M(F) (*inf*) crammer (*pej*)

Ein|peit|scher ['ainpaitʃɐ] M -s, -, **Ein|peit|sche|rin** [-ərın] F -, -nen (*Pol*) whip (*Brit*), floor leader (*US*); (*inf*: = *Antreiber*) slave driver (*inf*)

ein+pen|deln *sep* VI to commute in (*in +acc* -to) VR (*fig*) to settle down; (*Währung, Preise etc*) to find its level, to level off

Ein|pend|ler(in) M(F) commuter

ein+pen|nen VI *sep aux sein* (*sl*) to doze off, to drop off (*inf*)

Ein|per|so|nen- [ainpɛr'zo:nən-]: **Ein|per|so|nen|haus|halt** M single-person household; **Ein|per|so|nen|stück** NT (*Theat*) one-man play

Ein|pfen|nig|stück [ain'pfɛnıç-] NT (*Hist*) one-pfennig piece

ein+pfer|chen VT *sep Vieh* to pen in (*in +acc* -to); (*fig*) to coop up (*in +acc* in); **eingepfercht stehen** to be hemmed in

ein+pflan|zen VT *sep* to plant (*in +dat* in); (*Med*) to implant (*jdm* in(to) sb); **jdm eine fremde Niere ~** to give sb a kidney transplant; **jdm etw ~** (*fig*) to imbue sb with a sense of sth, to instil (*Brit*) *or* instill (*US*) (a sense of) sth into sb

Ein|pha|sen|strom [ain'fa:zn-] M , **Ein|pha|sen|wech|sel|strom** M single-phase current

ein|pha|sig ADJ single-phase

ein+pin|seln VT *sep Wunde, Mandeln* to paint; (*Cook*) to brush

ein+pla|nen VT *sep* to plan (on), to include in one's plans; *Verzögerungen, Verluste* to allow for; *Baby* to plan

ein+pö|keln VT *sep Fisch, Fleisch* to salt; **eingepökeltes Rindfleisch** salt beef

ein|po|lig ['ainpo:lıç] ADJ single-pole

ein+prä|gen *sep* **VT** *Muster, Spuren* to imprint, to impress; *Inschrift* to stamp; **ein Muster in Papier ~** to emboss paper with a pattern; **sich** *(dat)* **etw ~** to remember sth; (= *auswendig lernen*) to memorize sth, to commit sth to memory **VR** **sich jdm ins Gedächtnis ~** to make an impression on sb's mind; **sich jdm ~** to make an impression on sb; **die Worte haben sich mir unauslöschlich eingeprägt** the words made an indelible impression on me

ein|präg|sam ['ainprɛ:kza:m] ADJ easily remembered; *Slogan, Melodie auch* catchy ADV **er kann sehr ~ formulieren** he can put things in a way that is easy to remember

ein+pras|seln VI *sep aux sein* **auf jdn ~** to rain down on sb, to come pouring down on sb; *(Fragen)* to be showered upon sb; **von allen Seiten prasselten Geschosse auf uns ein** we were caught in a hail of shots from all sides

ein+pres|sen VT *sep* to press in (*in +acc* -to)

ein+pro|ben VT *sep* to rehearse

ein+pro|gram|mie|ren *ptp* **einprogrammiert** VT *sep Daten* to feed in; *(fig)* to take into account; **jdm etw ~** *(fig)* to inculcate sth in sb

ein+prü|geln *sep* **VT** **jdm etw ~** to din (*inf*) or drum sth into sb **VI** **auf jdn ~** to lay into sb

ein+pu|dern *sep* **VR** to powder oneself **VT** to powder

ein+pup|pen ['ainpʊpn] VR *sep (Zool)* to pupate

ein+quar|tie|ren ['ainkvarti:rən] *ptp* **einquartiert** *sep* **VT** to quarter; *(Mil auch)* to billet; **Gäste bei Freunden ~** to put visitors up with friends **VR** to be quartered (*bei* with); *(Mil auch)* to be billeted (*bei* on); *(Gäste)* to stop (*bei* with) (*inf*); **er hat sich bei uns anscheinend für ewig einquartiert** he seems to have dumped himself on us for good (*inf*)

Ein|quar|tie|rung F -, -en **a** (= *das Einquartieren*) quartering; *(Mil auch)* billeting **b** **wir haben ~** (*inf*) (= *Soldaten*) we have soldiers billeted on us; (= *Besuch*) we've got people staying or stopping (*inf*) (with us)

ein+quet|schen VT *sep* = **einklemmen a**

Ein|rad NT unicycle

ein|rä|de|rig, ein|räd|rig ADJ one-wheeled

ein+rah|men VT *sep (lit, fig)* to frame; **von zwei Schönen eingerahmt** with a beauty on either side; **das kannst du dir ~ lassen!** (*inf*) you ought to get that framed!

ein+ram|men VT *sep Stadttor* to batter down or in; *Pfähle* to ram in (*in +acc* -to)

ein+ras|ten VTI *sep (vi: aux sein)* to engage

ein+räu|chern VT *sep* **a** (= *in Rauch hüllen*) to envelop in smoke; **die Polizei räucherte die Demonstranten mit Tränengas ein** the police used tear gas against the demonstrators **b** (*inf*) *Zimmer* to fill with smoke, to smoke up; *Gardinen* to make reek of smoke

ein+räu|men VT *sep* **a** *Wäsche, Bücher etc* to put away; *Schrank, Regal etc* to fill; *Wohnung, Zimmer* to arrange; *Möbel* to move in (*in +acc* -to); **Bücher ins Regal/in den Schrank ~** to put books on the shelf/in the cupboard; **er war mit beim Einräumen behilflich** he helped me sort things out; *(der Wohnung)* he helped me move in **b** (= *zugestehen*) to concede, to admit; *Freiheiten etc* to allow; *Frist, Kredit* to give, to grant, to allow; **jdm das Recht ~, etw zu tun** to give or grant sb the right to do sth, to allow sb to do sth; **~de Konjunktion** concessive conjunction

Ein|räu|mungs|satz M *(Gram)* concessive clause

ein+rech|nen VT *sep* to include; **ihn (mit) eingerechnet** including him; **Mehrwertsteuer eingerechnet** including VAT, inclusive of VAT

Ein|re|de F *(form)* objection

ein+re|den *sep* **VT** **jdm etw ~** to talk sb into believing sth, to persuade sb of sth; **sie hat ihm eingeredet, er sei dumm** she persuaded him that or talked him into believing that he was stupid; **das lasse ich mir nicht ~** you're not going to make me believe that; **wer hat dir denn diesen Unsinn eingeredet?** who put that rubbish (*Brit inf*) or nonsense into your head?; **er will mir ~, dass ...** he'd have me believe that ..., he wants me to believe that ...; **sich** *(dat)* **etw ~** to talk oneself into believing sth, to make oneself believe sth; **das redest du dir nur ein!** you're only imagining it **VI** **auf jdn ~** to keep on and on at sb

ein+reg|nen *sep* **VI** *aux sein (Mensch)* to get soaked (through) **VR** **es hat sich eingeregnet** the rain has set in

ein+rei|ben VT *sep irreg* **er rieb sich** *(dat)* **das Gesicht mit Schnee/Creme ein** he rubbed snow over/cream into his face

Ein|rei|bung F **-en verordnen** to prescribe embrocation or liniment

ein+rei|chen VT *sep* **a** *Antrag, Unterlagen* to submit (*bei* to); *(Jur) Klage* to file → **Abschied b** **b** (= *bitten um*) *Versetzung, Pensionierung* to apply for, to request

Ein|rei|chung ['ainraiçʊŋ] F -, *(rare)* -en *(von Antrag, Unterlagen)* submission; *(Jur: von Klage)* filing

ein+rei|hen *sep* **VT** (= *einordnen, einfügen*) to put in (*in +acc* -to); (= *klassifizieren*) to class, to classify; **dieses Buch verdient, in die bedeutendste medizinische Fachliteratur eingereiht zu werden** this book deserves to be awarded a place amongst the most important works of medical literature; **er wurde in den Arbeitsprozess eingereiht** he was fitted into or given a place in the work process **VR** **sich in etw** *(acc)* **~** to join sth

Ein|rei|her ['ainraiɐ] M -s, - (= *Anzug*) single-breasted suit; (= *Jackett*) single-breasted jacket; (= *Mantel*) single-breasted coat

ein|rei|hig ADJ *Anzug, Jackett, Mantel* single-breasted

Ein|rei|se F entry (*in +acc* into, to); **bei der ~ in die Schweiz** when entering Switzerland, on entry to Switzerland

Ein|rei|se-: **Ein|rei|se|er|laub|nis** F entry permit; **Ein|rei|se|for|ma|li|tä|ten** PL entry formalities *pl*; **Ein|rei|se|for|mu|lar** NT form for entry into the country; **Ein|rei|se|ge|neh|mi|gung** F entry permit

ein+rei|sen VI *sep aux sein* to enter the country; **er reiste in die Schweiz ein** he entered Switzerland; **ein- und ausreisen** to enter and leave the country

Ein|rei|se-: **Ein|rei|se|ver|bot** NT refusal of entry; **~ haben** to have been refused entry; **Ein|rei|se|vi|sum** NT entry visa

ein+rei|ßen *sep irreg* **VT** **a** *Papier, Stoff, Nagel* to tear; **ich habe mir einen Splitter in den Zeh eingerissen** I've got a splinter in my toe **b** *Gebäude, Zaun, Barrikaden* to tear or pull down **VI** *aux sein (Papier)* to tear; *(fig inf: Unsitte etc)* to catch on (*inf*), to get to be a habit (*inf*)

ein+rei|ten *sep irreg* **VT** *Pferd* to break in **VI** *aux sein (in die Manege etc)* to ride in (*in +acc* -to) **VR** to warm up; **sich mit einem Pferd ~** to get used to riding a particular horse

ein+ren|ken ['ainrɛŋkn] VT *sep Gelenk, Knie* to put back in place, to reduce *(spec)*; *(fig inf)* to sort out **VR** *(fig inf)* to sort itself out

ein+ren|nen VT *sep irreg (inf) Mauer, Tür etc* to batter or break down; **sich** *(dat)* **den Kopf an der Wand ~** to bang or bash *(inf)* one's head against the wall → **offen**

ein+rich|ten *sep* **VT** **a** (= *möblieren*) *Wohnung, Zimmer* to furnish; (= *ausstatten*) *Hobbyraum, Spielzimmer, Praxis, Labor* to equip, to fit out *(Brit)*; **ein Haus antik/modern ~** to furnish a house in an old/a modern style; **sein Haus neu ~** to refurnish one's house; **Wohnungen im Dachgeschoss ~** to convert the attic into flats *(Brit)* or apartments **b** (= *gründen, eröffnen*) to set up; *Lehrstuhl* to establish; *Konto* to open; *Buslinie etc* to start **c** (= *einstellen*) *Maschine* to set up; *Motor* to set *(auf +acc* for); *(Mil) Geschütz* to aim *(auf +acc* at) **d** (= *bearbeiten*) *Musikstück* to arrange; *Theaterstück* to adapt **e** *(fig: = arrangieren)* to arrange, to fix *(inf)*; **ich werde es ~, dass wir um zwei Uhr da sind** I'll see to it that we're there at two; **das lässt sich ~** that can be arranged; **das Leben/die Welt ist nun einmal nicht so eingerichtet** life/the world isn't like that; **auf Tourismus eingerichtet sein** to be geared to tourism; **auf warme Speisen eingerichtet sein** to be equipped for hot meals **f** *(Med) Arm, Knochen* to set **VR** **a** (= *sich möblieren*) **sich ~/neu ~** to furnish/refurnish one's house/one's flat *(Brit)* or apartment → **häuslich** **b** (= *sich der Lage anpassen*) to get along or by, to manage; (= *sparsam sein*) to cut down; **er hat sich im bürgerlichen Leben eingerichtet** he has settled down into middle-class life **c** **sich auf etw** *(acc)* **~** to prepare oneself for sth; **sich auf eine lange Wartezeit ~** to be prepared for a long wait

Ein|rich|tung F **a** (= *das Einrichten*) *(von Wohnung, Zimmer)* furnishing; *(von Hobbyraum, Spielzimmer, Labor, Praxis)* equipping, fitting-out *(Brit)*; *(von Maschine)* setting-up; *(von Geschütz)* aiming; *(Med)* setting **b** (= *Bearbeitung*) *(Mus)* arrangement; *(Theat)* adaptation **c** (= *Wohnungseinrichtung*) furnishings *pl*; (= *Geschäftseinrichtung etc*) fittings *pl*; *(von Laboreinrichtung etc)* equipment *no pl* **d** (= *Gründung, Eröffnung*) setting-up; *(von Lehrstuhl)* establishment; *(von Konto)* opening; *(von Katalog, Busverkehr)* starting **e** *(behördlich, wohltätig, = Gewohnheit)* institution; (= *Schwimmbäder, Transportmittel etc*) facility; **zur ständigen ~ werden** (= *Gewohnheit*) to become an institution

Ein|rich|tungs-: **Ein|rich|tungs|ge|gen|stand** M item of furniture; (= *Geschäftseinrichtung*) fitment *(Brit)*, fixture; **Ein|rich|tungs|haus** NT furnishing house

ein+rie|geln ['ainri:gln] VTR *sep* **jdn/sich ~** to lock sb/oneself in (*in +dat* -to)

Ein|ritt M entry (*in +acc* into)

ein+rit|zen VT *sep* to carve in (*in +acc* -to)

ein+rol|len *sep* **VT** (= *einwickeln*) to roll up (*in +acc* -to); *(Hockey)* to roll on (*in +acc* -to) **VI** *aux sein* to roll in (*in +acc* -to) **VR** to roll up; *(Tier etc auch)* to roll oneself up

ein+ros|ten VI *sep aux sein* to rust up; *(fig: Glieder)* to stiffen up; **mein Latein ist ziemlich eingerostet** my Latin has got pretty rusty

ein+rü|cken *sep* **VT** *Zeile* to indent; *Anzeige (in Zeitung)* to insert **VI** *aux sein (Mil)* **a** *(in ein Land)* to move in (*in +acc* -to); (= *wieder einrücken*) to return (*in +acc* -to) **b** (= *eingezogen werden*) to report for duty; *(nach Urlaub etc)* to report back

ein+rüh|ren VT *sep* to stir or mix in (*in +acc* -to); *(Cook) Ei* to beat in (*in +acc* -to)

ein+rüs|ten VT *sep Haus* to put scaffolding around

eins [ains] NUM one; **es ist/schlägt ~** it's one/just striking one (o'clock); **um ~** at one (o'clock); **gegen ~** at around one (o'clock); **~, zwei, drei** *(lit)* one, two, three; *(fig)* in a trice *(Brit)*, in an instant, in no time; **das ist ~, zwei, drei geschehen** *(fig)* it doesn't take a second; **~ zu ~** *(Sport)* one all; **~ mit jdm sein** to be one with sb; (= *übereinstimmen*) to be in agreement with sb; **sich mit jdm ~ wissen** to know one is in agreement with sb; **das ist doch alles ~** (*inf*) it's all one, it's all the same; **es ist mir alles ~** (*inf*) it's all one *or* all the same to me; **sehen und handeln waren ~** to see was to act; **~ a** (*inf*) A 1 (*inf*), first-rate (*inf*) → *auch* **ein²**, **eine(r, s)**, **vier**

Eins [ains] F **-, -en** one; (*Sch auch*) A, alpha; **er würfelte zwei ~en** he threw (*Brit*) *or* rolled two ones; **eine ~ schreiben/bekommen** to get an A *or* alpha *or* a one → *auch* **Vier**

ein+sa|cken¹ VT *sep* **a** (= *in Säcke füllen*) to put in sacks, to sack **b** (*inf*) (= *erbeuten*) to grab (*inf*); *Geld, Gewinne* to rake in (*inf*)

ein+sa|cken² VI *sep aux sein* (= *einsinken*) to sink; (*Bürgersteig, Boden etc auch*) to subside

ein+sa|gen *sep* (*dial*) **VI** **jdm ~** to prompt sb; **jdm etw ~** to whisper sth to sb

ein+sal|ben VT *sep* to rub with ointment; *Wunde, Hände auch* to rub ointment into

ein+sal|zen VT *sep irreg Fisch, Fleisch* to salt

ein|sam ['ainzaːm] **ADJ** **a** *Mensch, Leben, Gefühl* (= *allein, verlassen*) lonely; (= *einzeln*) solitary; **sich ~ fühlen** to feel lonely *or* lonesome (*esp US*); **ein ~es Boot** a lone *or* solitary boat; **ein ~er Schwimmer** a lone *or* solitary swimmer; **um sie wird es ~** she is becoming a lonely figure **b** (= *abgelegen*) *Haus, Insel* secluded; *Dorf* isolated; (= *menschenleer*) empty; *Strände* lonely, empty **c** (*inf*: = *hervorragend*) **~e Klasse** *or* **Spitze** absolutely fantastic (*inf*), really great (*inf*) **ADV** **a** (= *allein*) lonely; **~ leben** to live a lonely/solitary life; **~ überragt dieser Gipfel die anderen** this peak towers over the others in solitary grandeur **b** (= *abgelegen*) isolated; **~ liegen** to be secluded/isolated

Ein|sam|keit F **-, no pl a** (= *Verlassenheit*) loneliness; (= *das Einzelnsein*) solitariness; **er liebt die ~** he likes solitude; **die ~ vieler alter Leute** the loneliness of many old people **b** (= *Abgelegenheit*) (*von Haus, Insel*) seclusion; (*von Dorf*) isolation; (= *Menschenleere*) emptiness; (*von Strand*) loneliness; **die ~ der Bergwelt** the solitude of the mountains

Ein|sam|keits|ge|fühl NT feeling of loneliness

ein+sam|meln VT *sep* to collect (in); *Obst to* gather (in)

ein+sar|gen ['ainzargn] VT *sep* to put in a coffin; **lass dich (doch) ~!** (*inf*) (go and) take a running jump! (*inf*), get stuffed! (*Brit inf*)

Ein|satz M **a** (= *Einsatzteil*) inset; (= *Schubladeneinsatz, Koffereinsatz*) tray; (= *Topfeinsatz*) compartment; (= *Bluseneinsatz*) *false blouse collar and neck to wear under pullover* (= *Hemdeinsatz*) dicky (*dated*) **b** (= *Spieleinsatz*) stake; (= *Kapitaleinsatz*) investment; **den ~ erhöhen** to raise the stakes; **mit dem ~ herauskommen, den ~ heraushaben** (*inf*) to recover one's stake **c** (*Mus*) entry; (*Theat*) entrance; **der Dirigent gab den ~** the conductor raised his baton and brought in the orchestra/solist *etc*; **der Dirigent gab den Geigern den ~** the conductor brought in the violins; **der ~ der Streicher war verfrüht** the strings came in too early **d** (= *Verwendung*) use; (*esp Mil*) deployment; (*von Arbeitskräften*) employment; **im ~** in use; **die Ersatzspieler kamen nicht zum ~** the reserves weren't put in *or* used; **unter ~ von Schlagstöcken** using truncheons; **unter ~ aller Kräfte** by making a supreme effort **e** (= *Aktion*) (*Mil*) action, operation; (*von Polizei, Feuerwehr*) operation; **im ~** in action; **wo war er im ~?** where did he see action?; **zum ~ kommen** to go into action; **bei seinem ersten ~** the first time he went into action; **sich zum ~ melden** to report for duty; **die Pfadfinder halfen in freiwilligen Einsätzen** the scouts helped on a voluntary basis

f (= *Hingabe*) commitment; **in selbstlosem ~ ihres Lebens** with a complete disregard for her own life; **etw unter ~ seines Lebens tun** to risk one's life to do sth, to do sth at the risk of one's life; **den ~ des eigenen Lebens nicht scheuen** (*geh*) not to hesitate to sacrifice one's own life

Ein|satz-: **Ein|satz|be|fehl** M order to go into action; **Ein|satz|be|reit** ADJ ready for use; (*Mil*) ready for action; *Rakete etc* operational; **Ein|satz|be|reit|schaft** F readiness for use; (*Mil*) readiness for action; (= *Bereitschaftsdienst*) stand-by; **Ein|satz|be|spre|chung** F briefing; (*nach dem Einsatz*) debriefing; **ein|satz|fä|hig** ADJ fit for use; (*Mil*) fit for action; *Sportler* fit; **Ein|satz|fä|hig|keit** F fitness for use; (*Mil*) fitness for action; (*von Sportler*) fitness; **Ein|satz|fahr|zeug** NT = **Einsatzwagen**; **Ein|satz|freu|de** F willing application; **ein|satz|freu|dig** ADJ eager (for action), enthusiastic; **Ein|satz|ge|biet** NT (*Mil*) operational area; (= *Betätigungsfeld*) field of activity; **Ein|satz|grup|pe** F , **Ein|satz|kom|man|do** (*Mil*) NT mobiles Einsatzkommando mobile task force; **Ein|satz|lei|ter(in)** M(F) head of operations; (*von Diplomat etc*) posting; **Ein|satz|plan** M plan of action; **Ein|satz|stück** NT (*Tech*) insert; (= *Zubehörteil*) attachment; **Ein|satz|wa|gen** M (*von Polizei*) police car; (*von Feuerwehr*) fire engine; (= *Krankenwagen*) ambulance; (= *Straßenbahn/Bus*) extra tram (*esp Brit*) *or* street-car (*US*)/bus; **Ein|satz|zen|tra|le** F centre (*Brit*) *or* center (*US*) of operations, nerve centre (*Brit*) *or* center (*US, inf*)

ein+sau|gen VT *sep* (*lit, fig*) to soak up, to absorb; (*durch Strohhalm etc*) to suck; (= *einatmen*) to breathe in; *frische Luft* to draw *or* suck in → **Muttermilch**

ein+säu|men VT *sep* (*Sew*) to hem; (*fig*) to edge, to line

ein+scha|len [-ʃaːlən] VT *sep* (*Build*) to board, to shutter

ein+schal|ten *sep* **VI** **a** *Licht, Radio, Gerät* to switch *or* turn *or* put on; *Sender* to tune in to **b** (= *einfügen*) to interpolate; *Zitat, Erklärung etc auch* to include (*in +acc* in) **c** **jdn ~** to call sb in; **jdn in etw** (*acc*) **~** to bring sb into sth *or* in on sth **VR** **sich ~** to intervene; (= *teilnehmen*) to join in; **wir schalten uns jetzt in die Sendungen von Radio Bremen ein** we now go over to *or* join Radio Bremen

Ein|schalt-: **Ein|schalt|he|bel** M starting lever *or* handle; **Ein|schalt|quo|te** F (*Rad, TV*) viewing figures *pl*

Ein|schal|tung F **a** (*von Licht, Motor etc*) switching *or* turning on **b** (*von Nebensatz etc*) interpolation; (*von Zitat*) inclusion **c** (*von Person, Organisation*) calling *or* bringing in

Ein|scha|lung F , **Ein|scha|lungs|ar|beit** F (*Build*) formwork

ein+schär|fen VT *sep* **jdm etw ~** to impress sth (up)on sb; *Höflichkeit, Rücksichtnahme etc* to inculcate sth in sb; **er hat uns Vorsicht eingeschärft** he impressed on us the need for caution; **ich habe den Kindern eingeschärft, Fremden gegenüber vorsichtig zu sein** I have impressed upon the children to be careful of strangers; **schärf dir das ein!** get that firmly fixed in your mind

ein+schar|ren VT *sep* to cover with earth

ein|schät|zen ☼ 33.1 VT *sep* to assess (*auch Fin*), to evaluate; (= *schätzen auch*) to estimate; **falsch ~** to misjudge; (= *falsch schätzen*) to miscalculate; **wie ich die Lage einschätze** as I see the situation; **jdn sehr hoch/niedrig ~** to have a very high/low opinion of sb; **etw zu hoch/niedrig ~** to overestimate/underestimate sth; **jdn/sich zu hoch/niedrig ~** to overrate/underrate sb/oneself, to have too high/low an opinion of sb/oneself

Ein|schät|zung F assessment (*auch Fin*), evaluation; (= *Schätzung auch*) estimation; **falsche ~**

misjudgement; (= *falsche Schätzung*) miscalculation; **nach meiner ~** in my estimation

ein+schäu|men *sep* **VT** **a** (= *mit Schaum behandeln*) to lather **b** (*Tech*) to pack in plastic foam **VR** to lather oneself

ein+schen|ken VT *sep* to pour (out); **darf ich Ihnen noch Wein ~?** can I give *or* pour you some more wine?

ein+sche|ren *sep* **VI** *aux sein* to get back **VT** *Tau* to reeve

ein+schich|tig [-ʃɪçtɪç] ADJ **a** single-layered **b** *Arbeitstag* single-shift **ADV** **unsere Fabrik arbeitet ~** our factory works a single shift

ein+schi|cken VT *sep* to send in (*an +acc* to)

ein+schie|ben VT *sep irreg* **a** (= *hineinschieben*) to put in (*in +acc* -to) **b** (= *einfügen*) to put in; *Sonderzüge* to put on; (= *dazwischenschieben*) *Diskussion, Schüler, Patienten* to fit *or* squeeze (*inf*) in (*in +acc* -to); **eine Pause ~** to have a break

Ein|schieb|sel NT **-s, -** insertion

Ein|schie|nen|bahn [-ʃiːnən-] F monorail

ein+schie|ßen *sep irreg* **a** (= *zertrümmern*) *Fenster* to shoot in; (*mit Ball etc*) to smash (in) **b** *Gewehr* to try out and adjust **c** (*Tech*) *Dübel* to insert **d** *Fäden* to weave in; **ein Gewebe mit eingeschossenen Goldfäden** a fabric shot with gold (thread) **e** (*Typ*) *Seiten, Blätter* to interleave **f** *Fußball* to kick in; **Müller schoss den Ball zum 2:0 ein** Müller scored to make it 2-0 **g** (*Comm*) *Geld* to inject (*in +acc* into); **VR** to find one's range, to get one's eye in; **sich auf ein Ziel ~** to get the range of a target; **sich auf jdn ~** (*fig*) to line sb up for the kill **VI** **a** (*Sport*) to score; **er schoss zum 1:0 ein** he scored to make it 1-0 **b** *aux sein* (*Med*) **die Milch schießt in die Brust ein** the milk comes in **c** **auf jdn ~** to shoot at sb

ein+schif|fen *sep* **VT** to ship **VR** to embark; **er schiffte sich in London nach Amerika ein** he boarded a ship in London for America

Ein|schif|fung F **-, -en** (*von Personen*) boarding, embarkation; (*von Gütern*) loading

ein+schir|ren ['ainʃɪrən] VT *sep* *Pferd* to harness

einschl. *abbr von* **einschließlich** incl

ein+schla|fen VI *sep irreg aux sein* to fall asleep, to go to sleep, to drop off (*inf*); (*Bein, Arm*) to go to sleep; (*euph*: = *sterben*) to pass away; (*fig*: *Gewohnheit, Freundschaft*) to peter out, to tail off; **ich kann nicht ~** I can't get to sleep; **bei** *or* **über seiner Arbeit ~** to fall asleep over one's work; **vor dem Einschlafen zu nehmen** (*Medizin*) to be taken before retiring

ein+schlä|fe|rig [-ʃleːfərɪç] ADJ *Bett* single

ein+schlä|fern ['ainʃleːfɐn] VT *sep* **a** (= *zum Schlafen bringen*) to send to sleep; (= *schläfrig machen*) to make sleepy *or* drowsy; (*fig*) *Gewissen* to soothe, to quiet; **das kann uns unsere Wachsamkeit nicht ~** that won't lull us into a false sense of security **b** (= *narkotisieren*) to give a soporific **c** (= *töten*) *Tier* to put to sleep, to put down, to destroy

ein|schlä|fernd ADJ soporific; (= *langweilig*) monotonous; **ein ~es Mittel** a soporific (drug)

Ein|schlaf|stö|rung F problem in getting to sleep

Ein|schlag M **a** (*von Geschoss*) impact; (*von Blitz*) striking; **dieses Loch ist der ~ eines Geschosses** this hole was made by a bullet; **der ~ der Granate war deutlich zu sehen** the place where the grenade had landed was clearly visible **b** (*Sew*) hem **c** (*Tex*) weft, woof **d** (*von Bäumen*) felling; (= *gefällte Bäume*) timber **e** (*Aut*: *des Lenkrads*) lock; **das Lenkrad bis zum (vollen) ~ drehen** to put the wheel on full lock **f** (= *Zusatz, Beimischung*) element; **einen stark(en) autoritären/südländischen ~ haben** to have more than a hint of authoritarianism/the Mediterranean about it/him/her *etc*

---

ein+schla|gen *sep irreg* **VT** **a** *Nagel* to hammer or knock in; *Pfahl* to drive in **b** (= *zertrümmern*) to smash (in); *Tür* to smash down; *Schädel* to smash (in), to bash in (*inf*); *Zähne* to knock out; **mit eingeschlagenem Schädel** with one's head bashed in (*inf*) **c** *Bäume* to fell **d** (= *einwickeln*) *Ware* to wrap up; *Buch* to cover **e** (= *umlegen*) *Stoff, Decke* to turn up **f** (*Aut*) *Räder* to turn **g** (= *wählen*) *Weg* to take; *Kurs* (*lit*) to follow; (*fig*) to pursue, to adopt; *Laufbahn etc* to enter on; **das Schiff änderte den eingeschlagenen Kurs** the ship changed from its previous course; **die Regierung schlägt einen weicheren/härteren Kurs ein** the government is taking a softer/harder line **VI** **a** (**in etw** *acc*) **~** (*Blitz*) to strike (sth); (*Geschoss etc auch*) to hit (sth); **es muss irgendwo eingeschlagen haben** something must have been struck by lightning; **gut ~** (*inf*) to go down well, to be a big hit (*inf*); (*Schüler, Arbeiter*) to get on all right **b auf jdn/etw ~** to hit out at sb/sth **c** (*zur Bekräftigung*) to shake on it

ein|schlä|gig [ˈaɪnʃlɛːgɪç] **ADJ** **a** appropriate; *Literatur, Paragraf auch, Erfahrung* relevant **b** (= *zwielichtig*) *Lokal* dubious **ADV** **er ist ~ vorbestraft** (*Jur*) he has a previous conviction for a similar offence (*Brit*) or offense (*US*); **in der Drogenszene ~ bekannt** well-known especially on the drugs scene

Ein|schlag|kra|ter M (*von Meteorit*) impact crater

ein+schlei|chen VR *sep irreg* (in +*acc* -to) to creep in; (*lit auch*) to steal or sneak (*inf*) in; (*fig: Fehler auch*) to slip in; **sich in jds Vertrauen ~** (*fig*) to worm one's way into sb's confidence

ein+schlei|fen VT *sep irreg* to grind; (= *eingravieren*) to cut in (in +*acc* -to); **eingeschliffene Reaktionen/Verhaltensweisen** (*Psych, geh*) established reactions/patterns of behaviour (*Brit*) or behavior (*US*)

ein+schlep|pen VT *sep* (*Naut*) *Schiff* to tow in (in +*acc* -to); (*fig*) *Krankheit, Ungeziefer* to bring in

Ein|schlep|pung [ˈaɪnʃlɛpʊŋ] F **-, -en** (*fig*) introduction, bringing-in

ein+schleu|sen VT *sep* to smuggle in (in +*acc*, *nach* -to)

ein+schlie|ßen VT *sep irreg* **a** (= *wegschließen*) to lock up (in +*acc* in); (*mil*) to confine to quarters; **er schloss sich/mich in dem** or **das Zimmer ein** he locked himself/me in the room **b** (= *umgeben*) to surround; (*Mil*) *Stadt, Feind auch* to encircle; **einen Satz in Klammern ~** to put a sentence in brackets or parentheses **c** (*fig: einbegreifen, beinhalten*) to include

ein|schließ|lich [ˈaɪnʃliːslɪç] **PREP** +*gen* including, inclusive of; **~ Porto** postage included; **Preis ~ Porto** price including postage, price inclusive of postage **ADV** **er hat das Buch bis S. 205 ~ gelesen** he has read up to and including p205; **vom 1. bis ~ 31. Oktober** or **bis 31. Oktober ~ geschlossen** closed from 1st to 31st October inclusive

Ein|schlie|ßung F (*esp Mil*) confinement

ein+schlum|mern VI *sep aux sein* (*geh*) to fall asleep; (*euph: = sterben*) to pass away

Ein|schluss ▲ M **a** (*von Gefangenen*) locking of the cells **b mit** or **unter ~ von** (*form*) with the inclusion of, including **c** (*Geol*) inclusion

ein+schmei|cheln VR *sep* **sich bei jdm ~** to ingratiate oneself with sb, to insinuate oneself into sb's good graces; **~de Musik** enticing music; **~de Stimme** silky voice

Ein|schmei|che|lung [ˈaɪnʃmaɪçəlʊŋ] F **-, -en**, **Ein|schmeich|lung** [ˈaɪnʃmaɪçlʊŋ] F **-, -en** attempt to ingratiate oneself

ein+schmei|ßen VT *sep irreg* **a** (*inf*) *Fenster* to smash (in) **b** (*sl: = nehmen*) **eine Pille ~** to take

or pop a pill (*inf*); **Ecstasy ~** to do (*inf*) or drop (*sl*) ecstasy

ein+schmel|zen *sep irreg* **VT** to melt down; (*fig: = integrieren*) to put in the melting pot **VI** *aux sein* to melt

Ein|schmel|zung [ˈaɪnʃmɛltsʊŋ] F **-, -en** melting (down); (*fig*) coalescence

ein+schmie|ren VT *sep* **a** (*mit Fett*) to grease; (*mit Öl*) to oil; *Gesicht* (*mit Creme*) to cream, to put cream on; **er schmierte mir den Rücken mit Heilsalbe/Sonnenöl ein** he rubbed my back with ointment/suntan lotion **b** (*inf: = beschmutzen*) to get dirty; **er hat sich ganz mit Dreck/Marmelade eingeschmiert** he has covered himself in dirt/jam

ein+schmug|geln VT *sep* to smuggle in (in +*acc* -to); **er hat sich in den Saal eingeschmuggelt** he sneaked into the hall

ein+schnap|pen VI *sep aux sein* **a** (*Schloss, Tür*) to click shut **b** (*inf: = beleidigt sein*) to take offence (*Brit*) or offense (*US*), to go into a huff (*inf*); **er schnappt wegen jeder Kleinigkeit ein** he takes offence (*Brit*) or offense (*US*) at every little thing → *auch* **eingeschnappt**

ein+schnei|den *sep irreg* **VT** **a** *Stoff, Papier* to cut; **er schnitt das Papier an den Ecken einige Zentimeter ein** he cut a few centimetres (*Brit*) or centimeters (*US*) into the corners of the paper; **die Fesseln schneiden mir die Handgelenke ein** the bonds are cutting into my wrists **b** (= *einkerben*) *Namen, Zeichen* to carve (in +*acc* in, into); **der Fluss hat ein Tal in das Gestein eingeschnitten** the river has carved out or cut a valley in the rock; **tief eingeschnittene Felsen** steep cliffs; **eine tief eingeschnittene Schlucht** a deep ravine **c** (*Cook*) **Zwiebeln in die Suppe ~** to cut up some onions and put them in the soup **d** (*Film*) to cut in (in +*acc* -to) **VI** to cut in (in +*acc* -to)

ein|schnei|dend ADJ (*fig*) drastic, radical; *Maßnahmen auch* trenchant; *Bedeutung, Wirkung, Folgen* far-reaching

ein+schnei|en VI *sep aux sein* to get snowed up; (*Auto, Mensch auch*) to get snowed in; **eingeschneit sein** to be snowed up/in

Ein|schnitt M cut; (*Med*) incision; (*im Tal, Gebirge*) cleft; (= *Zäsur*) break; (*im Leben*) decisive point

ein+schnit|zen VT *sep* to carve (in +*acc* into)

ein+schnü|ren *sep* **VT** **a** (= *einengen*) to cut into; *Taille* (*im Mieder*) to lace in; **dieser Kragen schnürt mir den Hals ein** this collar is nearly choking or strangling me **b** (= *zusammenbinden*) *Paket* to tie up **VR** to lace oneself up or in

ein+schrän|ken [ˈaɪnʃrɛŋkn̩] *sep* **VT** to reduce, to cut back or down; *Bewegungsfreiheit, Recht* to limit, to restrict; *Wünsche* to moderate; *Behauptung* to qualify; **jdn in seinen Rechten ~** to limit or restrict sb's rights; **das Rauchen/Trinken/Essen ~** to cut down on smoking/on drinking/on what one eats **VR** (= *sparen*) to economize; **sich im Essen/Trinken ~** to cut down on what one eats/on one's drinking → *auch* **eingeschränkt**

ein+schrän|kend [ˈaɪnʃrɛŋknd̩] *ptp von* **einschränken** **ADJ** qualifying; (*Ling*) restrictive **ADV** **~ möchte ich sagen, dass ...** I'd like to qualify that by saying ... → *auch* **einschränken**

Ein|schrän|kung F **-, -en** **a** (= *das Einschränken*) reduction; (*von Bewegungsfreiheit, Recht*) limitation, restriction; (*von Wünschen*) moderation; (*von Behauptung*) qualification; (= *Vorbehalt*) reservation; **ohne ~** without reservation, unreservedly **b** (= *Sparmaßnahme*) economy; (= *das Einsparen*) saving

ein+schrau|ben VT *sep* to screw in (in +*acc* to)

Ein|schreib- = Einschreibe-

Ein|schrei|be-: **Ein|schrei|be|brief** M recorded delivery (*Brit*) or certified (*US*) letter; **Ein|schrei|be|ge|bühr** F **a** (*Post*) charge for

recorded delivery (*Brit*) or certified mail (*US*) **b** (*Univ*) registration fee **c** (*für Verein*) membership fee

ein+schrei|ben *sep irreg* **VT** (= *eintragen*) to enter; *Post* to send recorded delivery (*Brit*) or certified mail (*US*) → *auch* **eingeschrieben VR** (*in Verein, für Abendkurse etc*) to enrol (*Brit*), to enroll (*US*); (*Univ*) to register; **er schrieb sich in die Liste ein** he put his name on the list

ein|schrei|ben NT recorded delivery (*Brit*) or certified (*US*) letter/parcel (*Brit*) or package; **~ pl** recorded delivery (*Brit*) or certified (*US*) mail *sing*; **einen Brief als** or **per ~ schicken** to send a letter recorded delivery (*Brit*) or certified mail (*US*)

Ein|schrei|be|sen|dung F letter/package sent recorded delivery (*Brit*) or certified mail (*US*)

Ein|schrei|bung F enrolment (*Brit*), enrollment (*US*); (*Univ*) registration

ein+schrei|en VI *sep irreg* **auf jdn ~** to yell or bawl at sb

ein+schrei|ten VI *sep irreg aux sein* to take action (*gegen* against); (= *dazwischentreten*) to intervene, to step in

Ein|schrei|ten NT **-s**, *no pl* intervention

ein+schrum|peln (*inf*), **ein+schrump|fen** VI *sep aux sein* to shrivel (up)

Ein|schub M insertion

ein+schüch|tern [ˈaɪnʃʏçtɐn] VT *sep* to intimidate

Ein|schüch|te|rung F **-, -en** intimidation

Ein|schüch|te|rungs-: **Ein|schüch|te|rungs-tak|tik** F scare or intimidatory tactics *pl*; **Ein|schüch|te|rungs|ver|such** M attempt at intimidation

ein+schu|len VT *sep* **eingeschult werden** (*Kind*) to start school; **wir müssen unseren Sohn dieses Jahr ~** our son has to start school this year; **wir schulen dieses Jahr weniger Kinder ein** we have fewer children starting school this year

Ein|schu|lung F first day at school; **die ~ findet im Alter von 6 Jahren statt** children start school at the age of 6

Ein|schuss ▲ M **a** (= *Einschussstelle*) bullet hole; (*Med*) point of entry; **Tod durch ~ in die Schläfe** death caused by a shot or a bullet through the side of the head **b** (*Space*) **nach ~ der Rakete in die Erdumlaufbahn** after the rocket had been launched into orbit (a)round the earth **c** (*Ftbl*) shot into goal **d** (*Tex*) weft, woof **e** (*St Ex*) margin

Ein|schuss-: **Ein|schuss|loch** ▲ NT bullet hole; **Ein|schuss|stel|le** ▲ F bullet hole; (*Med*) point of entry; **Ein|schuss|win|kel** ▲ M **a** (*Ftbl, Hockey etc*) shooting or scoring angle; **ein günstiger/ungünstiger ~** an easy/difficult shooting angle **b** (*von Geschoss*) entry angle, angle of entry

ein+schüt|ten VT *sep* to tip in (in +*acc* -to); *Flüssigkeiten* to pour in (in +*acc* -to); **dem Pferd Futter ~** to give the horse some fodder; **er hat sich** (*dat*) **noch etwas Kaffee eingeschüttet** (*inf*) he poured himself (out) or gave himself some more coffee

ein+schwär|zen VT *sep* to blacken, to make black

ein+schwe|ben VI *sep aux sein* to glide in (in +*acc* -to)

ein+schwei|ßen VT *sep* (*Tech*) (= *hineinschweißen*) to weld in (in +*acc* -to); (= *zuschweißen*) *Buch, Schallplatte* to shrink-wrap, to heat-seal (*spec*)

Ein|schweiß|fo|lie F shrink-wrapping

ein+schwen|ken VI *sep aux sein* to turn or swing in (in +*acc* -to); **links/rechts ~** (*Mil*) to wheel left/right; **auf etw** (*acc*) **~** (*fig*) to fall in with sth, to go along with sth

ein+schwö|ren VT *sep irreg* **jdn auf etw** (*acc*) **~** to swear sb to sth → *auch* **eingeschworen**

|

ein+seg|nen VT *sep* **a** (= *konfirmieren*) to confirm **b** *Altar, Kirche* to consecrate; *Feld, Haus, Gläubige* to bless

Ein|seg|nung F (= *Konfirmation*) confirmation; (*von Altar, Kirche*) consecration; (*von Feld, Haus, Gläubigen*) blessing

ein|seh|bar ADJ **a** (= *verständlich*) understandable **b** *Akten, Dateien etc* accessible; *Straße, Kreuzung, Eingang* visible

ein+se|hen *sep irreg* **VT** **a** *Gelände* to see; (*Mil*) to observe **b** (= *prüfen*) *Akte* to see, to look at **c** (= *verstehen, begreifen*) to see; *Fehler, Schuld auch* to recognize; **das sehe ich nicht ein** I don't see why; (= *verstehe ich nicht*) I don't see that; **es ist schwer einzusehen, warum/dass ...** it is hard to see why/that ...; **es ist nicht einzusehen, warum/dass ...** it is incomprehensible why/that ... ; **VI** **a** **in etw** (*acc*) **~** to see sth; (*Mil*) to observe sth **b** (= *prüfen*) to look (*in +acc* at)

Ein|se|hen NT **ein ~ haben** to have some understanding (*mit, für* for); (= *Vernunft, Einsicht*) to see reason or sense; **hab doch ein ~!** have a heart!, be reasonable!; **hast du kein ~?** can't you see sense?

ein+sei|fen VT *sep* to soap; (*inf*: = *betrügen*) to con, to take for a ride (*inf*); (*inf*: *mit Schnee*) to rub with snow

ein|sei|tig ['ainzaitıç] ADJ **a** on one side; (*Jur, Pol*) *Erklärung, Kündigung, Maßnahmen* unilateral; (*Comput*) single-sided; **~e Lungenentzündung** single pneumonia; **~e Lähmung** hemiplegia (*form*), paralysis of one side of the body **b** *Freundschaft, Zuneigung* one-sided **c** (= *beschränkt*) *Ausbildung* one-sided; (= *parteiisch*) *Bericht, Standpunkt, Zeitung* biased; *Ernährung* unbalanced; **~e Kürzungen im Etat** reductions in one area of the budget only **ADV** **a** (= *auf einer Seite*) on one side **b** (= *unausgewogen*) **sich ~ ernähren** to have an unbalanced diet; **jdn ~ ausbilden** to give sb a one-sided education; **etw ~ schildern** to give a one-sided portrayal of sth, to portray sth one-sidedly **c** (= *parteiisch*) subjectively; **jdn ~ informieren** to give sb biased information

Ein|sei|tig|keit F -, (*rare*) **-en** (*fig*) one-sidedness; (*von Ernährung*) imbalance

ein+sen|den VT *sep irreg* to send in, to submit (*an +acc* to)

Ein|sen|der(in) M(F) sender; (*bei Preisausschreiben*) competitor; **wir bitten die ~ von Artikeln ...** we would ask those (people) who send in or submit articles ...

Ein|sen|de|schluss ▲ M last date for entries, closing date

Ein|sen|dung F **a** *no pl* (= *das Einsenden*) sending in, submission **b** (= *das Eingesandte*) letter/article/manuscript *etc*; (*bei Preisausschreiben*) entry

ein+sen|ken *sep* **VT** *sep* to sink in (*in +acc* -to) **VR** (*liter*) **dieses Bild senkte sich tief in seine Seele ein** this image made a deep impression on him or his mind

Ein|ser ['ainze] M -s, - (*esp S Ger inf*) (*Sch*) A (grade), alpha, one; (*Autobus*) (number) one; **er hat einen ~ geschrieben** he got an A

ein+set|zen *sep* **VT** **a** (= *einfügen*) to put in (*in +acc* -to); *Maschinenteil* to put in (*in +acc* -to), to insert (*in +acc* into), to fit in (*in +acc* -to); *Ärmel* to set in (*in +acc* -to); *Stück Stoff* to let in (*in +acc* -to); (= *einschreiben*) to enter (*in +acc* in), to put in (*in +acc* -to); *Stiftzahn* to put in (*in +acc* -to); *Gebiss* to fit; *Fische in einen Teich ~* to stock a pond with fish; **jdm einen Goldzahn ~** to give sb a gold tooth; **eingesetzte Taschen** pockets let in or set into the seams **b** (= *ernennen, bestimmen*) to appoint; *Ausschuss* to set up, to appoint; *Erben, Nachfolger* to name; **jdn in ein Amt ~** to appoint sb to an office; **jdn als** or **zum Richter ~** to appoint sb judge **c** (= *verwenden*) to use (*auch Sport*), to employ; *Truppen, Polizei, Feuerwehr* to deploy, to bring into action; *Schlagstöcke* to use; *Busse, Sonderzüge* to put on; (*Chess*) *König etc* to bring into play; **etw als** or **zum Pfand ~** to give sth as a deposit **d** (*beim Glücksspiel*) to stake; (*geh*) *Leben* to risk; **seine ganze Energie** or **Kraft für etw ~** to devote all one's energies to sth **VI** (= *beginnen*) to start, to begin; (*Mus*) to come in; (*am Anfang*) to start to play/sing; **die Ebbe/Flut setzt um 3 Uhr ein** the tide turns at 3 o'clock, the tide starts to go out/come in at 3 o'clock; **kurz vor Spielbeginn setzte leichter Regen ein** (*Ftbl*) it began to rain lightly shortly before kick-off; **gegen Abend setzte stärkeres Fieber ein** the fever increased toward(s) evening **VR** **a** **sich (voll) ~** to show (complete) commitment (*in +dat* to); **die Mannschaft setzte sich bis an den Rand ihrer Kraft ein** the team did their absolute utmost **b** **sich für jdn ~** to fight for sb, to support sb's cause; (= *sich verwenden für*) to give or lend sb one's support; **sie hat sich so sehr für ihn eingesetzt** she did so much for him; **sie hat sich voll für die Armen/Verwundeten eingesetzt** she lent her aid unreservedly to the poor/wounded; **sich für etw ~** to support sth; **ich werde mich dafür ~, dass ...** I will do what I can to see that ...; **er setzte sich für die Freilassung seines Bruders ein** he did what he could to secure the release of his brother

Ein|set|zung ['ainzɛtsʊŋ] F -, **-en** appointment (*in +acc* to); **die ~ des Bischofs in sein Amt** the Bishop's investiture → *auch* **Einsatz**

Ein|sicht F **a** (*in Akten, Bücher*) **~ in etw** (*acc*) **haben/nehmen/verlangen** to look/take a look/ask to look at sth; **jdm ~ in etw** (*acc*) **gewähren** to allow sb to look at or to see sth; **sie legte ihm die Akte zur ~ vor** she gave him the file to look at **b** (= *Vernunft*) sense, reason; (= *Erkenntnis*) insight; (= *Kenntnis*) knowledge; (= *Verständnis*) understanding; (*euph*: = *Reue*) remorse; **zur ~ kommen** to come to one's senses; **ich bin zu der ~ gekommen, dass ...** I have come to the conclusion that ...; **der erste Schritt zur Besserung** (*prov*) a fault confessed is half redressed (*Prov*); **haben Sie doch ~!** have a heart!; (= *seien Sie vernünftig*) be reasonable!; **jdn zur ~ bringen** to bring sb to his/her senses; **er hat ~ in die internen Vorgänge der Firma** he has some knowledge of the internal affairs of the firm

ein|sich|tig ['ainzıçtıç] ADJ **a** (= *vernünftig*) reasonable; (= *verständnisvoll*) understanding; **er war so ~, seinen Fehler zuzugeben** he was reasonable enough to admit his mistake **b** (= *verständlich, begreiflich*) understandable, comprehensible; **jdm etw ~ erklären** to explain sth clearly; **jdm etw ~ machen** to make sb understand or see sth

Ein|sicht|nah|me [-naːmə] F -, **-n** (*form*) inspection; **er bat um ~ in die Akten** he asked to see the files; **nach ~ in die Akten** after seeing or inspecting the files; **"zur ~"** "for inspection"

ein|sichts-: **ein|sichts|los** ADJ (= *unvernünftig*) unreasonable; (= *verständnislos*) lacking in understanding; **Ein|sichts|lo|sig|keit** F -, **-en** (= *Unvernünftigkeit*) unreasonableness; (= *Verständnislosigkeit*) lack of understanding; **ein|sichts|voll** ADJ = **einsichtig a**

ein+si|ckern VI *sep aux sein* to seep in (*in +acc* -to); (*fig*) to filter in (*in +acc* -to); **Spione sickerten in unser Land ein** spies infiltrated (into) our country

Ein|sie|de|lei [ainziːdəˈlai] F -, **-en** hermitage; (*fig hum*: = *einsames Haus*) country retreat or hideaway

ein+sie|den VT *sep irreg* (*S Ger, Aus*) *Obst* to bottle; *Marmelade* to make

Ein|sied|ler(in) M(F) hermit; (*fig auch*) recluse

ein|sied|le|risch ['ainziːdlərıʃ] ADJ hermit-like **ADV** *leben* like a hermit

Ein|sied|ler-: **Ein|sied|ler|krebs** M hermit crab; **Ein|sied|ler|le|ben** NT hermit's life, life of a hermit or recluse

Ein|sil|ber ['ainzılbe] M -s, - monosyllable

ein|sil|big ADJ **a** *Wort* monosyllabic; *Reim* masculine, single **b** (*fig*) *Mensch* uncommunicative; *Antwort, Erklärung* monosyllabic

Ein|sil|big|keit ['ainzılbıçkait] F -, *no pl* (*lit*) monosyllabism; (*von Reim*) masculinity; (*fig*: *von Mensch*) uncommunicativeness

Ein|silb|ler M -s, - monosyllable

ein+sin|gen VR *sep irreg* to get oneself into voice

ein+sin|ken VI *sep irreg aux sein* (*im Morast, Schnee*) to sink in (*in +acc or dat* -to); (*Boden etc*) to subside, to cave in; **er sank bis zu den Knien im Schlamm ein** he sank up to his knees in the mud; **ein Stück eingesunkenen Bodens** an area where the ground has caved in or subsided; **eingesunkene Schläfen/Wangen** sunken or hollow temples/cheeks

ein+sit|zen VI *sep irreg* (*form*) to serve a prison sentence; **drei Jahre ~** to serve three years, to serve a three-year sentence → *auch* **eingesessen**

Ein|sit|zer M single-seater

ein|sit|zig [-zıtsıç] ADJ *Fahrzeug, Flugzeug* single-seater *attr*

ein+sor|tie|ren *ptp* **ein**sortiert VT *sep* to sort and put away; *Dokumente* to file away; **in Schachteln/Körbe ~** to sort into boxes/baskets

ein|spal|tig [-ʃpaltıç] ADJ (*Typ*) single-column **ADV** **etw ~ setzen** to set sth in a single column/in single columns

ein+span|nen VT *sep* **a** (*in Rahmen*) *Leinwand* to fit or put in (*in +acc* -to); **Saiten in einen Schläger ~** to string a racket **b** (*in Schraubstock*) to clamp in (*in +acc* -to) **c** (*in Kamera*) to put in (*in +acc* -to); (*in Schreibmaschine*) to put in (*in +acc* -to), to insert (*in +acc* in, into) **d** *Pferde* to harness **e** (*fig*: = *arbeiten lassen*) to rope in (*für etw* to do sth); **jdn für seine Zwecke ~** to use sb for one's own ends → *auch* **eingespannt**

Ein|spän|ner M one-horse carriage; (*hum*: = *Junggeselle*) bachelor; (*Aus*) black coffee served in a glass with whipped cream

ein|spän|nig ADJ *Wagen* one-horse; **der Wagen ist/fährt ~** the carriage is pulled by one horse

ein+spa|ren VT *sep* to save; *Energie, Strom auch* to save or economize on; *Kosten, Ausgaben* to cut down on, to reduce; *Posten* to dispense with, to eliminate

Ein|spar|po|ten|zi|al ▲ NT (*esp Econ*) potential for economies

Ein|spa|rung F -, **-en** economy; (= *das Einsparen*) saving (*von* of); (*von Kosten, Ausgaben*) reduction; (*von Posten*) elimination

ein+spei|cheln ['ainʃpaiçln] VT *sep* to insalivate

ein+spei|chern VT *sep Daten* to feed in (*in +acc* -to), to enter (*in +acc* into)

ein+spei|sen VT *sep* to feed in (*in +acc* -to); *Daten auch* to enter (*in +acc* into)

ein+sper|ren VT *sep* to lock up (*in +acc or dat* in), to lock in (*in +acc or dat* -to); (*versehentlich*) to lock in (*in +acc or dat* -to); (*inf*: *ins Gefängnis*) to put away (*inf*), to lock up

ein+spie|len *sep* **VR** (*Mus, Sport*) to warm up; (*nach Sommerpause etc*) to get into practice; (*Regelung, Arbeit*) to work out; **... aber das spielt sich alles noch ein** ... but things should sort themselves out all right; **ich fahre jetzt mit dem Bus, das hat sich gut eingespielt** I come by bus now, it's working out well; **sich aufeinander ~** to become attuned to one another, to get used to one another → *auch* **eingespielt** **VT** **a** (*Mus, Sport*) *Instrument, Schläger* to play in **b** (*Film, Theat*) to bring in, to gross; *Kosten* to recover **c** (= *aufnehmen*) *Lied* to record; *Schallplatte* to record, to cut

d (= *einblenden*) *Bild, Video* to insert; *Musik* to play

e (*Comput*) *Daten, Software* to load

Ein|spiel|er|geb|nis NT (*von Film*) box-office takings *pl* or receipts *pl*

Ein|spie|lung F (*von Musikstück, Oper etc*) recording (*von* by)

ein+spin|nen *sep irreg* **VR** (*Spinne*) to spin a web (a)round itself; (*Larve*) to spin a cocoon (a)round itself **VT** (*Spinne*) to spin a web (a)round

Ein|spra|che F (*Aus, Sw*) = **Einspruch**

ein|spra|chig ADJ monolingual

Ein|spra|chig|keit F -, *no pl* monolingualism

ein+spre|chen VI *sep irreg* **auf jdn ~** to harangue sb

ein+spren|gen VT *sep* (*mit Wasser*) to sprinkle with water, to dampen

Ein|spreng|sel [ˈainʃprɛŋzl] NT **-s, -** (*Geol*) xenocryst (*spec*), embedded crystal; **ein Buch mit einigen lyrischen ~n** a book with the odd moment of lyricism

ein+sprin|gen *sep irreg* **VI** *aux sein* **a** (*Tech*) to lock shut, to lock into place; (*Maschinenteile*) to engage **b** (*inf*: = *aushelfen*) to stand in; (*mit Geld etc*) to help out **VR** (*Sport*) to do some practice jumps

Ein|spritz- *in cpds* (*Aut, Med*) injection

Ein|spritz|dü|se F (*Aut*) injector

ein+sprit|zen VT *sep* **a** (*Aut, Med*) to inject; **er spritzte ihr/sich Insulin ein** he gave her/himself an insulin injection, he injected her/himself with insulin **b** (= *einsprengen*) *Wäsche* to dampen, to sprinkle with water **c** (*inf: mit Schmutz*) to splash, to spray

Ein|sprit|zer M (*Aut*) fuel injection engine

Ein|spritz-: Ein|spritz|mo|tor M (*Aut*) fuel injection engine; **Ein|spritz|pum|pe** F (*Aut*) fuel injection pump

Ein|sprit|zung [ˈainʃprɪtsʊŋ] F **-, -en** injection

Ein|spruch M objection (*auch Jur*); **~ einlegen** (*Admin*) to file an objection, to register a protest; **gegen etw ~ erheben** to object to sth, to raise an objection to sth; **ich erhebe ~!** (*Jur*) objection!; **~ abgelehnt!** (*Jur*) objection overruled!; **(dem) ~ (wird) stattgegeben!** (*Jur*) objection sustained!

Ein|spruchs-: Ein|spruchs|frist F (*Jur*) period for filing an objection; **Ein|spruchs|recht** NT right to object or protest

ein|spu|rig [-ˈʃpuːrɪç] ADJ (*Rail*) single-track; (*Aut*) single-lane; *Fahrzeug* two-wheeled (*with the wheels one behind the other*) **ADV die Straße ist nur ~ befahrbar** only one lane of the road is open; **er denkt sehr ~** he has a one--track mind

Eins|sein NT (*liter*) oneness

einst [ainst] ADV **a** (= *früher, damals*) once; **Preußen ~ und heute** Prussia past and present or yesterday and today or then and now; **das Einst und das Heute** or **Jetzt** the past and the present **b** (*geh: = in ferner Zukunft*) one or some day

ein+stamp|fen VT *sep Papier, Buch, Auflage* to pulp

Ein|stand M **a** **ein guter ~** a good start to a new job; **er hat gestern seinen ~ gegeben** or **gefeiert** yesterday he celebrated starting his new job **b** (*Tennis*) deuce

Ein|stands-: Ein|stands|fei|er F (*in Firma*) celebration of a/the new job; **Ein|stands|preis** M (*Comm*) introductory price

ein+stan|zen VT *sep* to stamp in (*in +acc* -to)

ein+stau|ben *sep* **VI** *aux sein* to get covered in dust; **eingestaubt sein** to be covered in dust **VT** (*Aus*) **sich** (*dat*) **das Gesicht (mit Puder) ~** to powder one's face, to dust one's face with powder

ein+stäu|ben VT *sep* (*mit Puder*) to dust with powder, to powder; (*mit Parfüm etc*) to spray

---

ein+ste|chen *sep irreg* **VT** to pierce; *Gummi, Haut, Membran* to puncture, to pierce; *Nadel* to put or stick (*inf*) in (*in +acc* -to), to insert (*in +acc* in, into); (*Cook*) to prick; (= *eingravieren*) to engrave **VI auf jdn/etw ~** to stab at sb/sth

Ein|steck|al|bum NT (*stamp*) stock book (*spec*), stamp album

ein+ste|cken VT *sep* **a** (= *in etw stecken*) to put in (*in +acc* -to); *Stecker auch, Gerät* to plug in; *Schwert* to sheathe

b (*in die Tasche etc*) (**sich** *dat*) **etw ~** to take sth; **hast du deinen Pass/ein Taschentuch eingesteckt?** have you got your passport/a handkerchief with you?; **er steckte (sich) die Zeitung ein und ging los** he put the paper in his pocket etc and left, he took the paper and left; **warte mal, ich habe mir meine Zigaretten noch nicht eingesteckt** hang on, I haven't got my cigarettes yet (*inf*); **ich habe kein Geld eingesteckt** or (*incorrect*) **~** I haven't any money on me; **kannst du meinen Lippenstift für mich ~?** can you take my lipstick for me?; **steck deine Pistole wieder ein** put your pistol away

c (*in den Briefkasten*) to post (*Brit*), to mail (*esp US*)

d (*inf*) *Kritik etc* to take; *Beleidigung* to swallow, to take; (= *verdienen*) *Geld, Profit* to pocket (*inf*); **der Boxer musste viel ~** the boxer had to take a lot of punishment; **er steckt sie alle ein** he beats all of them (*inf*)

Ein|steck-: Ein|steck|kamm M (decorative) comb; **Ein|steck|kar|te** F (*Comput*) expansion card; **Ein|steck|tuch** NT *pl* **-tücher** breast pocket handkerchief

ein+ste|hen VI *sep irreg aux sein* **a** (= *sich verbürgen*) **für jdn/etw ~** to vouch for sb/sth; **ich stehe dafür ein, dass ...** I will vouch that ...; **er stand mit seinem Wort dafür ein** he vouched for it personally **b** **für etw ~** (= *Ersatz leisten*) to make good sth; (= *sich bekennen*) to answer for sth, to take responsibility for sth; **für jdn ~** to assume liability or responsibility for sb; **ich habe das immer behauptet und dafür stehe ich auch ein** I've always said that, and I'll stand by it

Ein|stei|ge|kar|te F (*Aviat*) boarding pass or card

ein+stei|gen VI *sep irreg aux sein* **a** (*in ein Fahrzeug etc*) to get in (*in +acc* -to); (*umständlich, mit viel Gepäck etc auch*) to climb or clamber in (*in +acc* -to); (*in Zug auch, in Bus*) to get on (*in +acc* -to); **~!** (*Rail etc*) all aboard!; **in eine Felswand ~** to attack a rock face; **er ist in die Problematik dieses Buchs noch nicht so richtig eingestiegen** he hasn't really got (*Brit*) or come to grips with the problems in this book

b (*in ein Haus etc*) to climb or get in (*in +acc* -to)

c (*inf*) **in die Politik/ins Verlagsgeschäft ~** to go into politics/publishing; **er ist mit einer Million in diese Firma eingestiegen** he put a million into this firm; **er ist ganz groß in dieses Geschäft eingestiegen** he's (gone) into that business in a big way (*inf*); **der Verlag ist jetzt in Wörterbücher eingestiegen** the publishing company has branched out into dictionaries or into the dictionary market

Ein|stei|ger(in) M(F) (*inf*) beginner; **ein Modell für PC-Einsteiger** an entry-level PC

Ein|stei|ni|um [ainˈʃtainiʊm] NT **-s**, *no pl* (*abbr* **Es**) einsteinium

ein|stell|bar ADJ adjustable

Ein|stell|be|reich M (*Aut*) adjustment range

ein+stel|len *sep* **VT** **a** (= *hineinstellen*) to put in; **das Auto in die** or **der Garage ~** to put the car in(to) the garage; **das Buch ist falsch eingestellt** the book has been put in the wrong place

b (= *anstellen*) *Arbeitskräfte* to take on; **„wir stellen ein: Sekretärinnen"** "we have vacancies for secretaries", "we are looking for secretaries"

c (= *beenden*) to stop; *Expedition, Suche* to call off; (*Mil*) *Feindseligkeiten, Feuer* to cease; (*Jur*) Pro-

---

zess, *Verfahren* to abandon; **die Arbeit ist eingestellt worden** work has stopped; (*vorübergehend auch*) work has been halted; **die Zeitung hat ihr Erscheinen eingestellt** the paper has ceased publication; **die Arbeit ~** (*Kommission etc*) to stop work; (= *in den Ausstand treten*) to withdraw one's labour (*Brit*) or labor (*US*)

d (= *regulieren*) to adjust (*auf +acc* to); *Kanone* to aim (*auf +acc* at); *Fernglas, Fotoapparat* (*auf Entfernung*) to focus (*auf +acc* on); *Wecker, Zünder* to set (*auf +acc* for); *Radio* to tune (in) (*auf +acc* to); *Sender* to tune in to; **die Steuerung auf Automatik ~** to switch over to or to put the plane on automatic pilot; **den Hebel auf Start ~** to set the lever to start

e (*fig: = abstimmen*) to tailor (*auf +acc* to)

f (*Sport*) *Rekord* to equal

VR **a** (*Besucher etc*) to appear, to present oneself; (*Fieber, Regen*) to set in; (*Symptome*) to appear; (*Folgen*) to become apparent, to appear; (*Wort, Gedanke*) to come to mind; (*Jahreszeiten*) to come, to arrive; **wenn es kalt ist, stellen sich bei mir regelmäßig heftige Kopfschmerzen ein** I always suffer from bad headaches when it's cold

b **sich auf jdn/etw ~** (= *sich richten nach*) to adapt oneself to sb/sth; (= *sich vorbereiten auf*) to prepare oneself for sb/sth → *auch* **eingestellt**

VI to take on staff; (*Fabrik*) to take on workers

ein|stel|lig ADJ *Zahl* single-digit; **ein Verlust im ~en Millionenbereich** or **in ~er Millionenhöhe** a loss of between 1 and 10 million

Ein|stell-: Ein|stell|knopf M (*an Radio etc*) tuning knob; **Ein|stell|platz** M (*auf Hof*) carport; (*in großer Garage*) (covered) parking accommodation *no indef art*; **Ein|stell|schrau|be** F adjustment screw

Ein|stel|lung F **a** (= *Anstellung*) employment **b** (= *Beendigung*) stopping; (*von Expedition, Suche*) calling-off; (*Mil*) cessation; (*Jur*) abandonment; **der Sturm zwang uns zur ~ der Suche/Bauarbeiten** the storm forced us to call off or abandon the search/to stop work on the building; **die Lackierer beschlossen die ~ der Arbeit** the paint-sprayers decided to withdraw their labour (*Brit*) or labor (*US*) or to down tools

c (= *Regulierung*) adjustment; (*von Fernglas, Fotoapparat*) focusing; (*von Wecker, Zünder*) setting; (*von Radio*) tuning (in); (*Film:* = *Szene*) take

d (= *Gesinnung, Haltung*) attitude; (*politisch, religiös etc*) views *pl*; **er hat eine falsche ~ zum Leben** he doesn't have the right attitude to or outlook on life; **das ist doch keine ~!** what kind of attitude is that!, that's not the right attitude!

Ein|stel|lungs-: Ein|stel|lungs|ge|spräch NT interview; **Ein|stel|lungs|stopp** M halt in recruitment; **Ein|stel|lungs|ter|min** M starting date; **Ein|stel|lungs|test** M recruitment test; **Ein|stel|lungs|un|ter|su|chung** F medical examination when starting a new job; **Ein|stel|lungs|vo|raus|set|zung** F job requirement

ein+stem|peln VI *sep* (*bei Arbeitsantritt*) to clock in or on

eins|tens [ˈainstns] ADV (*obs*) = **einst**

Ein|stich M (= *Einstichstelle*) puncture; (= *Vorgang*) insertion

Ein|stich|stel|le F puncture

Ein|stieg M **a** *no pl* (= *das Einsteigen*) getting in; (*in Bus*) getting on; (*von Dieb: in Haus etc*) entry; (*fig: zu einem Thema etc*) lead-in (*zu* to); **~ nur vorn!** enter only at the front; **kein ~** exit only; **er stürzte beim ~ in die Eigernordwand ab** he fell during the assault on the north face of the Eiger **b** (*von Bahn*) door; (*von Bus*) door, entrance

Ein|stiegs|dro|ge F starter drug, drug leading to further addiction

eins|tig [ˈainstɪç] ADJ *attr* former

ein+stim|men *sep* **VI** (*in ein Lied*) to join in; (*fig*) (= *beistimmen*) to agree (*in +acc* with); (= *zustimmen*) to agree (*in +acc* to); **in den Ge-**

---

sang/die Buhrufe (mit) ~ to join in the singing/ booing **VT** (*Mus*) *Instrument* to tune; **jdn/sich auf etw** (*acc*) ~ (*fig*) to get or put sb/oneself in the (right) mood for sth; *auf eine Atmosphäre etc* to attune sb/oneself to sth

ein|stim|mig **ADJ** **a** *Lied* for one voice **b** (= *einmütig*) unanimous **ADV** **a** ~ **singen** to sing in unison; **..., riefen sie** ~ ..., they called in unison **b** (= *einmütig*) unanimously

Ein|stim|mig|keit F **-, -en** unanimity

Ein|stim|mig|keits|prin|zip NT unanimity rule

Ein|stim|mung F (*Mus: von Instrumenten*) tuning; **für die richtige** ~ **der Zuhörer sorgen** (*fig*) to get the audience in the right mood

ein+stip|pen VT *sep* (*dial*) to dunk

einst|mals ['ainstmaːls] ADV = **einst**

ein|stö|ckig ADJ *Haus* two-storey (*Brit*), two-story (*US*); ~ **(gebaut) sein** to have two storeys (*Brit*) or stories (*US*)

ein+stöp|seln VT *sep* (*Elec*) to plug in (*in +acc* -to)

ein+sto|ßen VT *sep irreg Tür, Mauer* to knock or break down; *Scheibe* to push in, to break

ein+strah|len VI *sep* to irradiate (*spec*), to shine

Ein|strah|lung F (= *Sonneneinstrahlung*) irradiation (*spec*), shining

ein+strei|chen VT *sep irreg* **a** **eine Wunde (mit Salbe)** ~ to put ointment on a wound; **eine Kuchenform (mit Fett)** ~ to grease a baking tin (*Brit*) or pan (*US*) **b** (*inf*) *Geld, Gewinn* to pocket (*inf*)

ein+streu|en VT *sep* to sprinkle in (*in +acc* -to); (*fig*) *Bemerkung etc* to slip in (*in +acc* -to)

ein+strö|men VI *sep aux sein* to pour or flood in (*in +acc* -to); (*Licht, fig auch*) to stream in (*in +acc* -to); **kältere Luftschichten strömen nach Bayern ein** a stream of cooler air is moving in towards (*Brit*) or toward (*US*) Bavaria; **~de Kaltluft** a stream of cold air

ein|stro|phig ADJ one-verse *attr*

ein+stu|die|ren *ptp* **einstudiert** VT *sep Lied, Theaterstück* to rehearse; **einstudierte Antworten** (*fig*) well-rehearsed answers

Ein|stu|die|rung ['ainʃtudiːrʊŋ] F **-, -en** (*Theat*) production

ein+stu|fen VT *sep* to classify; **in eine Klasse/ Kategorie** etc ~ to put into a class/category *etc*

ein|stu|fig ADJ *Rakete* single-stage; *Verfahren auch* single-phase

Ein|stu|fung F classification; (*auf Lernniveau etc*) placement; **nach seiner** ~ **in eine höhere Gehaltsklasse** after he was put on a higher salary grade (*Brit*) or into a higher salary bracket

Ein|stu|fungs|test M placement test

ein|stün|dig ADJ *attr* one-hour; **mehr als ~e Verspätungen** delays of more than an hour; **nach ~er Pause** after an hour's or a one-hour break, after a break of an hour

ein+stür|men VI *sep aux sein* **auf jdn** ~ (*Mil*) to storm sb; (*fig*) to assail sb; **mit Fragen auf jdn** ~ to bombard or besiege sb with questions

Ein|sturz M collapse; (*von Mauer, Boden, Decke auch*) caving-in

ein+stür|zen VI *sep aux sein* to collapse; (*Mauer, Boden, Decke auch*) to cave in; (*Theorie, Gedankengebäude auch*) to crumble; **auf jdn** ~ (*fig*) to overwhelm sb; **es stürzte viel auf ihn ein** he was overwhelmed by events

Ein|sturz|ge|fahr F danger of collapse

ein|sturz|ge|fähr|det F in danger of collapsing *pred*

einst|wei|len ['ainst'vailən] ADV in the meantime; (= *vorläufig*) temporarily

einst|wei|lig ['ainst'vailɪç] ADJ *attr* temporary; **~e Verfügung/Anordnung** (*Jur*) temporary or interim injunction/order; ~ **verfügen** (*Jur*) to issue a temporary or an interim injunction

ein+sug|ge|rie|ren *ptp* **einsuggeriert** VT *sep* **jdm etw** ~ to suggest sth to sb; (*inf*) to brainwash sb into believing sth

Eins|wer|den NT (*geh*) becoming one *no art*

ein|tä|gig ADJ *attr* one-day → **viertägig**

Ein|tags|flie|ge F (*Zool*) mayfly; (*fig*) nine-day wonder; (= *Mode, Idee*) passing craze

ein+tan|zen VR *sep* to get used to dancing with sb; (*vor Turnier etc*) to dance a few practice steps

Ein|tän|zer M gigolo (*dated*), dancing partner

ein+tä|to|wie|ren *ptp* **eintätowiert** VT *sep* to tattoo (*in/auf +acc on*)

ein+tau|chen *sep* **VT** to dip (*in +acc* in, into); (*völlig*) to immerse (*in +acc* in); *Brot* (*in Kaffee etc*) to dunk (*in +acc* in) **VI** *aux sein* (*Schwimmer*) to dive in; (*Springer*) to enter the water; (*U-Boot*) to dive; **das U-Boot ist jetzt ganz eingetaucht** the submarine is now completely submerged

Ein|tausch M exchange, swap (*inf*); **„Eintausch von Gutscheinen"** "coupons exchanged here"

ein+tau|schen VT *sep* to exchange, to swap (*inf*) (*gegen, für* for); (= *umtauschen*) *Devisen* to change

ein|tau|send ['ain'tauznt] NUM (*form*) = **tausend**

ein+tei|len *sep* **VT** **a** (= *aufteilen*) to divide (up) (*in +acc* into); (= *aufgliedern*) to split (up) (*in +acc* into); (*in Grade*) *Thermometer* to graduate, to calibrate **b** (= *sinnvoll aufteilen*) *Zeit, Arbeit* to plan (out), to organize; *Geld auch* to budget; **wenn ich mir eine Flasche gut einteile, reicht sie eine Woche** if I plan it well a bottle lasts me a week **c** (= *dienstlich verpflichten*) to detail (*zu* for); **er ist heute als Aufseher eingeteilt** he has been allocated the job of supervisor today **VI** (*inf*: = *Haus halten*) to budget

Ein|tei|ler M (*Fashion*) one-piece (swimsuit)

ein|tei|lig ADJ *Badeanzug* one-piece *attr*

Ein|tei|lung F **a** (= *das Aufteilen*) division; (*in Grade*) gradation, calibration **b** (*von Zeit, Arbeit*) planning, organization; (*von Geld*) budgeting **c** (= *dienstliche Verpflichtung*) detailment (*esp Mil*), assignment

Ein|tel ['aintl] NT (*SW AUCH* M) **-s, -** (*Math*) whole

ein+tip|pen VT *sep* to type in (*in +acc* -to)

ein|tö|nig ['aintøːnɪç] **ADJ** monotonous **ADV** monotonously; ~ **reden** to talk in a monotone

Ein|tö|nig|keit F **-,** *no pl* monotony; (*von Stimme*) monotonousness

Ein|topf M stew

Ein|topf|es|sen NT , **Ein|topf|ge|richt** NT stew

Ein|tracht F , *no pl* harmony, concord; **er hat zwischen den beiden wieder** ~ **gestiftet** he restored peaceful relations between the two of them; ~ **X** (*Sport*) = X United

ein|träch|tig **ADJ** peaceable **ADV** peaceably

Ein|trag ['aintraːk] M **-(e)s, ~e** [-tre:gə] **a** (*schriftlich*) entry (*in +acc* in) **b** (*geh*) **das tut der Sache keinen** ~ that does no harm **c** (*Tex*) weft, woof **d** (= *Schadstoffeinleitung*) discharge

ein+tra|gen *sep irreg* **VT** **a** (*in Liste, auf Konto etc*) to enter; (= *amtlich registrieren*) to register; **sich** ~ **lassen** to have one's name put down → *auch* **eingetragen b** **jdm Hass/Undank/Gewinn** ~ to bring sb hatred/ingratitude/profit; **das trägt nur Schaden ein** that will only do harm **VR a** to sign; (= *sich vormerken lassen*) to put one's name down; **er trug sich ins Gästebuch ein** he signed the visitors' book; **er trug sich in die Warteliste ein** he put his name (down) on the waiting list

ein|träg|lich ['aintre:klɪç] ADJ profitable; *Geschäft, Arbeit auch* lucrative, remunerative

Ein|träg|lich|keit F **-, -en** profitability

Ein|tra|gung ['aintraːgʊŋ] F **-, -en** entry (*in +acc* in)

ein+trai|nie|ren *ptp* **eintrainiert** VT *sep* to practise (*Brit*), to practice (*US*)

ein+träu|feln VT *sep* **jdm Medizin in die Nase/ ins Ohr** ~ to put drops up sb's nose/in sb's ear; **jdm Hass** ~ (*geh*) to infuse sb with hatred

ein+tref|fen VI *sep irreg aux sein* **a** (= *ankommen*) to arrive; **„Bananen frisch eingetroffen"** "bananas - just in" **b** (*fig*: = *Wirklichkeit werden*) to come true; (*Prophezeiung*) to come true, to be fulfilled

ein|treib|bar ADJ *Schulden* recoverable; *Steuern, Zinsen* exactable

ein+trei|ben VT *sep irreg* **a** *Vieh, Nagel, Pfahl* to drive in (*in +acc* -to) **b** (= *einziehen*) *Geldbeträge* to collect; *Schulden* to recover, to collect

Ein|trei|bung ['aintraibʊŋ] F **-, -en** (*von Geldbeträgen*) collection; (*von Schulden auch*) recovery

ein+tre|ten *sep irreg* **VI** **a** *aux sein* (= *hineingehen*) (*ins Zimmer etc*) to go/come in (*in +acc* -to); (*in Verein, Partei etc*) to join (*in +acc* (*acc*)) sth); **ins Haus** ~ to go into or enter the house; **in eine Firma** ~ to go into or join a firm; **in die Politik/den diplomatischen Dienst** ~ to go into or enter politics/the diplomatic service; **ins Heer** ~ to join the army, to join up; **in den Krieg** ~ to enter the war; **in Verhandlungen** ~ (*form*) to enter into negotiations; **ins 30. Lebensjahr** ~ (*form*) to enter upon (*form*) or go into one's 30th year; **die Verhandlungen sind in eine kritische Phase eingetreten** the negotiations have entered a critical phase; **die Rakete trat in ihre Umlaufbahn ein** the rocket went into its orbit; **bitte treten Sie ein!** (*form*) (please) do come in **b** **auf jdn** ~ to boot or kick sb, to put the boot in on sb (*inf*) **c** *aux sein* (= *sich ereignen*) (*Tod*) to occur; (*Zeitpunkt*) to come; (= *beginnen*) (*Dunkelheit, Nacht*) to fall; (*Besserung, Tauwetter*) to set in; **bei Eintreten der Dunkelheit** at nightfall; **gegen Abend trat starkes Fieber ein** toward(s) evening the patient started to run a high temperature; **es ist eine Besserung eingetreten** there has been an improvement; **wenn der Fall eintritt, dass ...** if it happens that ...; **es ist der Fall eingetreten, den wir befürchtet hatten** what we had feared has in fact happened **d** *aux sein* **für jdn/etw** ~ to stand or speak up for sb/sth; **sein mutiges Eintreten für seine Überzeugung** his courageous defence (*Brit*) or defense (*US*) of his conviction or belief **e** (*Sw*) **auf etw** (*acc*) ~ to follow sth up **VT a** (= *zertrümmern*) to kick in; *Tür* to kick down or in **b** (= *hineintreten*) *Stein etc* to tread in (*in +acc* -to) **c** *Schuhe* to wear or break in **d** **sich** (*dat*) **etw (in den Fuß)** ~ to run sth into one's foot

ein+trich|tern ['aintrɪçtɐn], **ein+trim|men** VT *sep* (*inf*) **jdm etw** ~ to drum sth into sb; **jdm ~, dass ...** to drum it into sb that ...

Ein|tritt M **a** (= *das Eintreten*) entry (*in +acc* (in)to); (*ins Zimmer etc*) entry, entrance; (*in Verein, Partei etc*) joining (*in +acc* of); **beim** ~ **ins Zimmer** when or on entering the room; **„Eintritt im Sekretariat"** "entrance through the office"; **seine Beziehungen erleichterten ihm den** ~ **ins Geschäftsleben** his connections made it easier for him to get into the business world; **der** ~ **in den Staatsdienst** entry (in)to the civil service; **die Schule soll auf den** ~ **ins Leben vorbereiten** school should prepare you for going out into life; **der** ~ **in die EU** entry to the EU; **der** ~ **ins Gymnasium** starting at grammar school (*Brit*) or high school (*US*); **seit seinem** ~ **in die Armee** since joining the army, since joining up **b** (= *Eintrittsgeld*) admission (*in +acc* to); (= *Einlass*) admission, admittance (*in +acc* to); **was kostet der ~?** how much or what is the admission?; ~ **frei!** admission free; ~ **EUR 10** admission EUR 10; **„Eintritt verboten"** "no admittance"; **jdm** ~ **in etw** (*acc*) **gewähren** (*form*) to allow or permit sb to enter sth, to grant sb admission to sth (form) **c** (von Winter, Dunkelheit) onset; **bei ~ eines solchen Falles** in such an event; **der ~ des Todes** the moment when death occurs; **bei ~ der Dunkelheit** at nightfall, as darkness fell/falls

Ein|tritts-: Ein|tritts|geld NT entrance money, admission charge; **die Zuschauer verlangten ihr ~ zurück** the audience asked for their money back; **Ein|tritts|kar|te** F ticket (of admission), entrance ticket; **Ein|tritts|preis** M admission charge

ein+trock|nen VI sep aux sein (Fluss, Farbe) to dry up; (Wasser, Blut) to dry

ein+trom|meln sep (inf) **VT** = **eintrichtern** **VI auf jdn ~** (lit, fig) to pound sb

ein+trü|ben VR sep (Met) to cloud over, to become overcast

Ein|trü|bung F (Met) cloudiness no pl

ein+tru|deln VI sep aux sein (inf) to drift in (inf); **... bis alle eingetrudelt sind ...** until everyone has turned up

ein+tun|ken VT sep Brot to dunk (in +acc in)

ein+tü|ten ['ainty:tn] VT sep (form) to put into (paper) bags

ein+üben VT sep to practise (Brit), to practice (US); Theaterstück, Rolle etc to rehearse; Rücksichtnahme, Solidarität to learn or acquire (through practice); **sich** (dat) **etw ~** to practise (Brit) or practice (US) sth

Ein|übung F practice; (Theat etc) rehearsal

Ei|nung ['ainʊŋ] F -, -en (geh) unification

ein+ver|lei|ben ['ainfɛɐlaibn] ptp **einverleibt** VT sep and insep **a** Gebiet, Land to annex (dat to); Firma, Ministerium to incorporate (dat into) **b** (hum inf) sich (dat) **etw ~** (= essen, trinken) to put sth away (inf), to polish sth off (inf); (= sich aneignen, begreifen) to assimilate sth, to take sth in

Ein|ver|lei|bung F -, -en (von Gebiet, Land) annexation; (von Firma, Ministerium) incorporation

Ein|ver|nah|me ['ainfɛɐnaːmə] F -, -n (Jur: esp Aus, Sw) = **Vernehmung**

ein|ver|neh|men ptp **einvernommen** VT insep irreg (Jur: esp Aus, Sw) = **vernehmen**

Ein|ver|neh|men NT (= Eintracht) amity, harmony; (= Übereinstimmung) agreement; **in gutem** or **bestem ~ leben** to live in perfect amity or harmony; **wir arbeiten in gutem ~ (miteinander)** we work in perfect harmony (together); **im ~ mit jdm** in agreement with sb; **in gegenseitigem** or **beiderseitigem ~** by mutual agreement; **sich mit jdm ins ~ setzen** (form) to come to or reach an agreement or understanding with sb

ein|ver|nehm|lich (form) ADJ Regelung, Lösung consensual ADV consensually

Ein|ver|nehm|lich|keit F -, no pl consensus, agreement

Ein|ver|neh|mung F (Jur: esp Aus, Sw) = **Vernehmung**

ein|ver|stan|den ['ainfɛɐʃtandn] ☉ 41 ADJ ~! okay! (inf), agreed!; **~ sein** to agree, to consent, to be agreed; **ich bin ~** that's okay or all right by me (inf), I'm agreed; **mit jdm/etw ~ sein** to agree to sb/sth; (= übereinstimmen) to agree or be in agreement with sb/sth; **sie ist damit ~, dass sie nur 10% bekommt** she has agreed or consented to take only 10%; **ich bin mit deinem Verhalten/mit dir gar nicht ~** I don't approve of your behaviour (Brit) or behavior (US); **sich mit etw ~ erklären** to give one's agreement to sth

ein|ver|ständ|lich ADJ mutually agreed; Ehescheidung by mutual consent ADV **diese Frage wurde ~ geklärt** this question was settled to the satisfaction of both/all parties

Ein|ver|ständ|nis NT agreement; (= Zustimmung) consent; **wir haben uns in gegenseitigem ~ scheiden lassen** we were divorced by mutual consent; **er erklärte sein ~ mit dem Plan** he gave his agreement to the plan; **das geschieht**

mit meinem ~ that has my consent or agreement; **im ~ mit jdm handeln** to act with sb's consent

Ein|ver|ständ|nis|er|klä|rung F declaration of consent; **die schriftliche ~ der Eltern** the parents' written consent

Einw. abbr von **Einwohner**

Ein|waa|ge F , no pl (Comm) **a** (= Reingewicht) weight of contents of can or jar excluding juice etc Frucht-Einwaage/Fleisch-Einwaage 200 g fruit/meat content 200g **b** (Comm: = Gewichtsverlust) weight loss

ein+wach|sen¹ VT sep Boden, Skier to wax

ein+wach|sen² VI sep irreg aux sein (Baum, Staude) to establish itself; (Finger-, Zehennagel) to become ingrown; **der Zehennagel ist mir eingewachsen** I have an ingrowing (Brit) or ingrown toenail

Ein|wahl F (Telec, ins Internet) dial-up; **bei der ~** when dialling (Brit) or dialing (US) in

ein+wäh|len sep VR (Telec) to dial in (in +acc -to); **sich in ein Telefonnetz ~** to dial into a telephone network; **sich ins Internet ~** to log onto the Internet

Ein|wahl|kno|ten, **Ein|wähl|kno|ten** M (Telec, Comput) point of presence, POP

Ein|wand ['ainvant] ☉ 28.1, 36.1, 36.2, 38.1 M -(e)s, ⁻e [-vɛndə] objection; **einen ~ erheben** or **vorbringen** or **geltend machen** (form) to put forward or raise an objection

Ein|wan|de|rer M , **Ein|wan|de|rin** F immigrant

ein+wan|dern VI sep aux sein (nach, in +acc to) to immigrate; (Volk) to migrate

Ein|wan|de|rung F immigration (nach, in +acc to); **vor seiner ~ in die USA** before he came or immigrated to the USA

Ein|wan|de|rungs- in cpds immigration; **Ein|wan|de|rungs|be|hör|de** F immigration authorities pl; **Ein|wan|de|rungs|land** NT immigration country; **Ein|wan|de|rungs|po|li|tik** F immigration policy

ein|wand|frei ADJ **a** (= ohne Fehler) perfect; Sprache, Arbeit, Betrieb eines Systems auch faultless; Benehmen, Leumund irreproachable, impeccable; Lebensmittel perfectly fresh; **er spricht ein ~es Spanisch** he speaks perfect Spanish, he speaks Spanish perfectly; **ethisch ~** ethically acceptable **b** (= unzweifelhaft) indisputable; Beweis auch definite ADV **a** (= fehlerlos) Deutsch sprechen, funktionieren perfectly; sich verhalten impeccably; **er arbeitet sehr genau und ~** his work is very precise and absolutely faultless **b** (= unzweifelhaft) indisputably; beweisen auch definitely; **etw ~ beweisen** to prove sth beyond doubt, to give definite proof of sth; **es steht ~ fest, dass ...** it is beyond question or quite indisputable that ...; **das ist ~ Betrug/Unterschlagung** that is a clear case of fraud/embezzlement

ein|wärts ['ainvɛrts] ADV inwards; **~ gebogen** bent inwards

ein+wäs|sern VT sep (Cook) to steep

ein+we|ben VT sep irreg to weave in (in +acc -to); (fig auch) to work in (in +acc -to)

ein+wech|seln VT sep Geld to change (in +acc, gegen into); **jdm Geld ~** to change money for sb

ein+we|cken VT sep to preserve; Obst etc auch to bottle; (rare: in Büchsen) to can, to tin (Brit)

Ein|weck-: Ein|weck|glas NT preserving jar; **Ein|weck|gum|mi** M OR NT , **Ein|weck|ring** M rubber seal (for preserving jar)

Ein|weg- ['ainveːk] in cpds (= Wegwerf-) disposable; **Ein|weg|fla|sche** F non-returnable bottle; **Ein|weg|schei|be** F one-way glass; **Ein|weg|spie|gel** M one-way mirror; **Ein|weg|sprit|ze** F disposable syringe; **Ein|weg|ver|pa|ckung** F disposable packaging

ein+wei|chen VT sep to soak

ein+wei|hen VT sep **a** (= feierlich eröffnen) to open (officially); (fig) to christen, to baptize **b** **jdn in etw** (acc) **~** to initiate sb into sth; **er ist eingeweiht** he knows all about it → **Eingeweihte(r)**

Ein|wei|hung ['ainvaiʊŋ] F -, -en, **Ein|wei|hungs|fei|er** F (official) opening

ein+wei|sen VT sep irreg **a** (in Wohnung, Haus) to send, to assign (in +acc to) **b** (in Krankenhaus, Heilanstalt) to admit (in +acc to) **c** (= in Arbeit unterweisen) **jdn ~** to introduce sb to his job or work; **er wurde von seinem Vorgänger (in die Arbeit) eingewiesen** his predecessor showed him what the job involved **d** (in ein Amt) to install (in +acc in) **e** (Aut) to guide in (in +acc -to)

Ein|wei|sung F **a** (in Wohnung, Haus) accommodation (in +acc to) **b** (in Krankenhaus, Anstalt) admission (in +acc to) **c** **die ~ der neuen Mitarbeiter übernehmen** to assume responsibility for introducing new employees to their jobs or work **d** (in ein Amt) installation (in +acc in)

Ein|wei|sungs|schein M (in Krankenhaus, Anstalt) referral

ein+wen|den VT sep irreg **etwas/nichts gegen etw einzuwenden haben** to have an objection/no objection to sth, to object/not to object to sth; **dagegen lässt sich ~, dass ...** one objection to this is that ...; **dagegen lässt sich nichts ~** there can be no objection to that; **er wandte ein, dass ...** he objected or raised the objection that ...; **er hat immer etwas einzuwenden** he always finds something to object to, he always has some objection to make

Ein|wen|dung F objection (auch Jur); **gegen etw ~en erheben** or **haben** or **vorbringen** to raise objections to sth

ein+wer|fen sep irreg **VT a** Fensterscheibe etc to break, to smash **b** (Sport) Ball to throw in **c** Brief to post (Brit), to mail (esp US); Münze to insert **d** (fig) Bemerkung to make, to throw in; **er warf ein, dass ...** he made the point that ...; **ja, warf er ein** yes, he interjected **VI** (Sport) to throw in, to take the throw-in; **er hat falsch eingeworfen** he fouled when he was throwing in

ein|wer|tig ADJ (Chem) monovalent; (Ling) one place

ein+wi|ckeln VT sep **a** (= einpacken) to wrap (up); **er wickelte sich in seinen Mantel ein** he wrapped himself up well in his coat **b** (inf: = übervorteilen, überlisten) to fool (inf), to take in; (durch Schmeicheleien) to butter up (inf)

Ein|wi|ckel|pa|pier NT wrapping paper

ein+wie|gen VT sep irreg (Comm) Mehl etc to weigh out

ein+wil|li|gen VI sep (in +acc to) to consent, to agree

Ein|wil|li|gung ['ainvɪlɪgʊŋ] F -, -en (in +acc to) consent, agreement

ein+win|ken VT sep to guide or direct in

ein+win|tern VT sep to winter

ein+wir|ken sep **VI auf jdn/etw ~** to have an effect on sb/sth; (= beeinflussen) to influence sb/sth; **diese Maßnahmen wirken günstig auf die Marktsituation ein** these measures are having a favourable (Brit) or favorable (US) effect on the market situation; **etw ~ lassen** (Med) to let sth work in; (Chem) to let sth react; Beize to let sth soak or work in; **einen Anblick auf sich** (acc) **~ lassen** to take a sight in **VT** to work in (in +acc -to)

Ein|wir|kung F influence; (einer Sache auch) effect; (eines Katalysators) effect; **Bayern steht unter ~ eines atlantischen Hochs** Bavaria is being affected by an anticyclone over the Atlantic; **unter (der) ~ von Drogen** etc under the influence of drugs etc; **unter (der) ~ eines Schocks stehen** to be suffering (from) the effects of shock; **nach ~ der Salbe ...** when the ointment has worked in ...

Ein|wir|kungs|mög|lich|keit F influence; **dadurch haben wir eine gute ~** this has made it possible for us to bring some influence to bear *or* to have some influence

ein|wö|chig [-vœçɪç] ADJ one-week *attr*

Ein|woh|ner ['ainvoːnɐ] M **-s, -**, **Ein|woh|ne|rin** [-ərɪn] F **-, -nen** inhabitant

Ein|woh|ner-: Ein|woh|ner|mel|de|amt NT *residents' registration office* **sich beim ~ (an)melden** ≈ to register with the police; **Ein|woh|ner|schaft** ['ainvoːnɐʃaft] F **-,** *(rare)* **-en** population, inhabitants *pl*; **Ein|woh|ner|ver|zeich|nis** NT *list of inhabitants' names and addresses*; **Ein|woh|ner|zahl** F population, number of inhabitants

Ein|wurf M **a** (= *das Hineinwerfen*) *(von Münze)* insertion; *(von Brief)* posting *(Brit)*, mailing *(esp US)*; **~ 2 Euro** insert 2 euros **b** *(Sport)* throw-in; *(falscher ~ = Schlitz)* foul throw **c** (= *Schlitz*) slot; *(von Briefkasten)* slit **d** *(fig)* interjection; (= *Einwand*) objection

ein+wur|zeln VIR *sep (vi: aux sein) (Pflanzen)* to take root; *(fig auch)* to become rooted *(bei in)* → **eingewurzelt**

Ein|zahl F singular

ein+zah|len VT *sep* to pay in; **Geld auf ein Konto ~** to pay money into an account

Ein|zah|lung F payment; *(auf Bankkonto auch)* deposit *(auf +acc into)*

Ein|zah|lungs-: Ein|zah|lungs|be|leg M paying-in counterfoil, deposit receipt *(US)*; **Ein|zah|lungs|for|mu|lar** NT paying-in form, deposit form *(US)*; **Ein|zah|lungs|schal|ter** M *(Post)* paying-in counter; **Ein|zah|lungs|schein** M paying-in slip, deposit slip *(US)*

ein+zäu|nen ['aintsɔynən] VT *sep* to fence in

Ein|zäu|nung F **-, -en** (= *Zaun*) fence, fencing; (= *das Umzäunen*) fencing-in

ein+zeich|nen VT *sep* to draw *or* mark in; **ist der Ort eingezeichnet?** is the place marked?

Ein|zeich|nung F **a** *no pl* (= *das Einzeichnen*) drawing *or* marking in **b** (= *Markierung*) marking

Ein|zei|ler ['aintsailɐ] M **-s, -** *(Liter)* one-line poem, one-liner *(inf)*, monostich *(form)*

ein|zei|lig ADJ one-line *attr* ADV **~ geschriebene Schreibmaschinenseiten** single-spaced typewritten pages

Ein|zel ['aintsl] NT **-s, -** *(Tennis)* singles *sing*

Ein|zel-: Ein|zel|ak|ti|on F independent action; *(Sport)* solo performance *or* effort; **Ein|zel|an|trieb** M *(Tech)* independent drive; **Ein|zel|auf|hän|gung** F *(Aut)* independent suspension; **Ein|zel|auf|stel|lung** F *(Comm)* itemized list; **Ein|zel|aus|ga|be** F separate edition; **Ein|zel|be|hand|lung** F individual treatment; **Ein|zel|bei|spiel** NT isolated *or* one-off example; **Ein|zel|bett** NT single bed; **Ein|zel|blatt|ein|zug** M cut-sheet feed; **Ein|zel|dar|stel|lung** F individual treatment; **eine Geschichte unseres Jahrhunderts in ~en** a history of our century in individual portraits; **Ein|zel|er|schei|nung** F isolated occurrence; **Ein|zel|exem|plar** NT unique specimen; *(von Buch etc)* unique copy; *(von Auto)* unique model, one-off (model *or* car); **Ein|zel|fah|rer(in)** M(F) *(Motorradrennen)* solo rider; **Ein|zel|fahr|schein** M single *(Brit)* or one-way ticket

Ein|zel|fall M individual case; (= *Sonderfall*) isolated case, exception

Ein|zel|fall|stu|die F *(Sociol, Psych)* (individual) case study

Ein|zel-: Ein|zel|fer|ti|gung F special order; **in ~ hergestellt** made to order, custom-made; **Ein|zel|gän|ger** [-gɛŋɐ] M **-s, -**, **Ein|zel|gän|ge|rin** [-ərɪn] F **-, -nen** loner, lone wolf; (= *Elefant*) rogue; **Ein|zel|haft** F solitary confinement

Ein|zel|han|del M retail trade; **das ist im ~ teurer als im Großhandel** that is dearer (to buy) retail than wholesale; **im ~ erhältlich** available retail; **im ~ kostet das ...** it retails at ...

Ein|zel|han|dels-: Ein|zel|han|dels|ge|schäft NT retail shop; **Ein|zel|han|dels|kauf|frau** F trained retail saleswoman; **Ein|zel|han|dels|kauf|mann** M trained retail salesman; **Ein|zel|han|dels|ket|te** F *(von Läden)* retail chain; **Ein|zel|han|dels|preis** M retail price; **Ein|zel|han|dels|span|ne** F retail profit margin

Ein|zel-: Ein|zel|händ|ler(in) M(F) retailer, retail trader; **Ein|zel|haus** NT detached house *(Brit)*, self-contained house *(US)*; **Ein|zel|heit** ['aintslhait] F **-, -en** detail, particular; **auf ~en eingehen** to go into detail(s); **etw in allen/bis in die kleinsten ~en schildern** to describe sth in great detail/right down to the last detail; **sich in ~en verlieren** to get bogged down in details; **Ein|zel|hof** M isolated farm; **Ein|zel|ka|bi|ne** F *(individual)* cubicle; **Ein|zel|kampf** M **a** *(Mil)* single combat **b** *(Sport)* individual competition; **Ein|zel|kämp|fer(in)** M(F) **a** *(Mil, Sport)* single *or* solo combatant **b** *(fig)* lone wolf, loner; **Ein|zel|kauf|frau** F small businesswoman; **Ein|zel|kauf|mann** M small businessman; **Ein|zel|kind** NT only child

Ein|zel|ler ['aintslɐ] M **-s, -** *(Biol)* single-cell(ed) *or* unicellular organism

ein|zel|lig [-tsɛlɪç] ADJ single-cell(ed) *attr*, unicellular

ein|zeln ['aintsln] ADJ **a** individual; (= *getrennt*) separate; *(von Paar)* odd; **~e Teile des Bestecks kann man nicht kaufen** you cannot buy individual *or* separate *or* single pieces of this cutlery; **die ~en Städte, die wir besucht haben** the individual cities which we visited; **im ~en Fall** in the particular case **b** *Mensch* individual **c** (= *allein stehend*) *Baum, Haus* single, solitary; **~ stehend** solitary; **ein paar ~ stehende Bäume** a few scattered trees, a few trees here and there; **ein ~ stehender Baum** a tree (standing) all by itself, a solitary tree **d** *(mit pl n:* = *einige, vereinzelte)* some; *(Met) Schauer* scattered; **~e Firmen haben ...** some firms have ..., the odd firm has ..., a few odd firms have ...; **~e Besucher kamen schon früher** a few *or* one *or* two visitors came earlier

ADJ *(substantivisch)* **a** *(Mensch)* **der/die Einzelne** the individual; **ein Einzelner** an individual, a single person; (= *ein einziger Mensch*) one single person; **Einzelne** some (people), a few (people), one *or* two (people); **jeder Einzelne/jede Einzelne** each individual; **jeder Einzelne muss dabei helfen** (each and) every one of you/them *etc* must help; **als Einzelner kann man nichts machen** as an individual one can do nothing **b** **Einzelnes** some; **Einzelnes hat mir gefallen** I liked parts *or* some of it; **Einzelne haben mir gefallen** I liked some of them **c** **das Einzelne** the particular; **er kam vom Einzelnen zum Allgemeinen** he went from the particular to the general; **jedes Einzelne** each one; **im Einzelnen auf etw** *(acc)* **eingehen** to go into detail(s) *or* particulars about sth; **etw im Einzelnen besprechen** to discuss sth in detail; **bis ins Einzelne** right down to the last detail

ADV **a** (= *separat*) separately, individually; **~ aufführen** to list separately *or* individually *or* singly **b** (= *nicht zusammen*) individually; **wir kamen ~** we came separately; **die Gäste kamen ~ herein** the guests came in separately *or* singly *or* one by one; **bitte ~ eintreten** please come in one (person) at a time

ein|zeln|ste|hend △ ADJ *attr* → **einzeln ADJ c**

Ein|zel-: Ein|zel|num|mer F *(von Zeitung)* single issue; **Ein|zel|per|son** F single person; **für eine ~ kochen** to cook for one (person) *or* a

single person; **~en haben es auf Reisen meist schwer, ein Hotelzimmer zu bekommen** people travelling *(Brit)* or traveling *(US)* alone usually find it hard to get a hotel room; **Ein|zel|preis** M price, unit price *(Comm)*; *(von Zeitung)* price per copy; **Ein|zel|rad|auf|hän|gung** F *(Aut)* independent suspension; **Ein|zel|rei|sen|de(r)** MF *decl as adj* single traveller *(Brit)* or traveler *(US)*; **Ein|zel|rich|ter(in)** M(F) judge sitting singly; **Ein|zel|sie|ger(in)** M(F) individual winner; **Ein|zel|spiel** NT *(Tennis)* singles *sing*; **Ein|zel|staat** M individual state; **Ein|zel|ste|hen|de(r)** ['aintslʃteːəndə] MF *decl as adj* single person; **Ein|zel|stück** NT **ein schönes ~** a beautiful piece; **~e verkaufen wir nicht** we don't sell them singly; **Ein|zel|stun|de** F private *or* individual lesson; **Ein|zel|teil** NT individual *or* separate part; (= *Ersatzteil*) spare *or* replacement part; **etw in seine ~e zerlegen** to take sth to pieces, to take sth apart piece by piece *(esp US)*; **Ein|zel|the|ra|pie** F individual therapy; **Ein|zel|un|ter|richt** M private lessons *pl* or tuition; **Ein|zel|ver|bin|dungs|nach|weis** M *(Telec)* itemized call listing; **Ein|zel|ver|kauf** M *(Comm)* retail sale; *(das Verkaufen)* retailing, retail selling; **Ein|zel|ver|pa|ckung** F individual packing; **Ein|zel|wer|tung** F *(Sport)* individual placings *pl*; *(bei Kür)* individual marks *pl*; **Ein|zel|we|sen** NT individual; **Ein|zel|wett|be|werb** M *(Sport)* individual competition; **Ein|zel|zel|le** F single cell *(auch Biol)*; **Ein|zel|zim|mer** NT single room; **Ein|zel|zim|mer|zu|schlag** M *(auf Hotelpreis bei Pauschalreise)* single(-room) supplement

ein+ze|men|tie|ren *ptp* **einzementiert** VT *sep Stein* to cement; *Safe* to build *or* set into (the) concrete; *Kachel* to cement on

Ein|zieh-: ein|zieh|bar ADJ retractable; *Schulden* recoverable; **Ein|zieh|de|cke** F duvet, *(continental)* quilt

ein+zie|hen *sep irreg* VT **a** (= *hineinziehen, einfügen)* **Gummiband, Faden** to thread; *(in einen Bezug etc)* to put in; *(Build:* = *einbauen) Wand, Balken* to put in; *(Kopiergerät) Papier* to take in **b** (= *einsaugen) Flüssigkeit* to soak up; *(durch Strohhalm)* to draw up; *Duft* to breathe in; *Luft, Rauch* to draw in **c** (= *zurückziehen) Fühler, Krallen, Fahrgestell* to retract, to draw in; *Bauch, Netz* to pull *or* draw in; *Antenne* to retract; *Schultern* to hunch; *Periskop, Flagge, Segel* to lower, to take down; *Ruder* to ship, to take in; **den Kopf ~** to duck (one's head); **zieh den Bauch ein!** keep *or* tuck *(inf)* your tummy in; **der Hund zog den Schwanz ein** the dog put his tail between his legs; **mit eingezogenem Schwanz** *(lit, fig)* with its/his/her tail between its/his/her legs **d** *(Mil) (zu into) Personen* to conscript, to call up, to draft *(US)*; *Fahrzeuge etc* to requisition **e** (= *kassieren) Steuern, Gelder* to collect; *(fig) Erkundigungen* to make *(über +acc about)* **f** (= *aus dem Verkehr ziehen) Banknoten, Münzen* to withdraw (from circulation), to call in; (= *beschlagnahmen) Führerschein* to take away, to withdraw; *Vermögen* to confiscate **g** *(Typ) Wörter, Zeilen* to indent

VI *aux sein* **a** *(in Wohnung, Haus)* to move in; **wer ist im dritten Stock eingezogen?** who has moved into the third floor?; **er zog bei Bekannten ein** he moved in with friends; **ins Parlament ~** *(Partei)* to enter parliament; *(Abgeordneter)* to take one's seat (in parliament) **b** *(auch Mil:* = *einmarschieren)* to march in *(in +acc into)* **c** (= *einkehren)* to come *(in +dat to)*; **mit ihm zog eine fröhliche Stimmung bei uns ein** he brought a happy atmosphere with him; **wenn der Friede im Lande einzieht** when peace comes to our country, when we have peace; **Ruhe und Ordnung zogen wieder ein** law and order returned **d** (= *eindringen)* to soak in *(in +acc -to)*

Ein|zie|hung F **a** (*Mil*) (*von Personen*) conscription, call-up, drafting (*US*); (*von Fahrzeugen*) requisitioning **b** (= *Beschlagnahme*) (*von Vermögen, Publikationen*) confiscation; (= *Rücknahme: von Banknoten, Führerschein etc*) withdrawal **c** (= *Eintreiben: von Steuern etc*) collection

ein|zig ['aintsɪç] ADJ **a** attr only, sole; **ich sehe nur eine ~e Möglichkeit** I can see only one (single) possibility; **ich habe nicht einen ~en Brief bekommen** I haven't had a single or solitary letter; **kein** or **nicht ein ~es Mal** not once, not one single time **b** (*emphatisch*) absolute, complete; **dieses Rugbyspiel war eine ~e Schlammschlacht** this rugby match was just one big mudbath **c** pred (= *einzigartig*) unique; **es ist ~ in seiner Art** it is quite unique; **sein Können steht ~ da** his skill is unmatched, his skill is second to none ADJ (*substantivisch*) **der/die Einzige** the only one; **das Einzige** the only thing; **das ist das Einzige, was wir tun können** that's the only thing we can do; **ein Einziger hat geantwortet** only one (person) answered; **kein Einziger wusste es** nobody knew, not a single or solitary person knew; **die Einzigen, die es wussten ...** the only ones who knew ...; **er hat als Einziger das Ziel erreicht** he was the only one or the sole person to reach the finish; **Hans ist unser Einziger** Hans is our only child, Hans is our one and only ADV **a** (= *allein*) only, solely; **seine Beförderung hat er ~ dir zu verdanken** he owes his promotion entirely to you; **die ~ mögliche Lösung** the only possible solution, the only solution possible; **~ und allein** solely; **~ und allein deshalb hat er gewonnen** he owes his victory solely or entirely to that, that's the only or sole reason he won; **das ~ Wahre** or **Senkrechte** (*inf*) the only thing; (= *das beste*) the real McCoy (*inf*); **jetzt Ferien machen/ein Bier trinken, das wäre das ~ Wahre** etc to take a holiday (*esp Brit*) or vacation (*US*)/have a beer, that's just what the doctor ordered or that would be just the job (*inf*) **b** (*inf*: = *außerordentlich*) fantastically

ein|zig|ar|tig ADJ unique ADV *beleidigend, gerissen* incredibly, tremendously; **die Landschaft war ~ schön** the scenery was astoundingly beautiful

Ein|zig|ar|tig|keit F uniqueness

Ein|zig|keit F -, *no pl* uniqueness

Ein|zim|mer- *in cpds* one-room; **Ein|zim|mer|ap|par|te|ment** NT , **Ein|zim|mer|woh|nung** F one-room flat (*Brit*) or apartment, studio flat (*Brit*), efficiency or studio apartment (*US*), bedsit (*Brit inf*)

Ein|zug M **a** (*in Haus etc*) move (*in +acc* into); **vor dem ~** before moving in, before the move; **der ~ in das neue Haus** moving or the move into the new house; **der ~ ins Parlament** (*von Partei*) entering parliament; (*von Abgeordnetem*) taking one's seat (in parliament) **b** (= *Einmarsch*) entry (*in +acc* into) **c** (*fig: von Stimmung, Winter etc*) advent; **~ halten** to make an entrance; **der Winter hielt seinen ~ mit Schnee und Frost** winter arrived amid snow and frost; **der Frühling** etc **hält seinen ~** spring etc is coming **d** (*von Feuchtigkeit*) penetration; **der ~ kühlerer Meeresluft ...** a low trough moving in from the sea ... **e** (*von Steuern, Geldern*) collection; (*von Banknoten*) withdrawal, calling-in **f** (*Typ*) indentation

Ein|zugs-: Ein|zugs|auf|trag M (*Fin*) direct debit; **Ein|zugs|be|reich** M catchment area (*Brit*), service area (*US*); **Ein|zugs|er|mäch|ti|gung** F (*Fin*) direct debit instruction; **eine ~ erteilen** to set up a direct debit; **Ein|zugs|fei|er** F house-warming (party); **Ein|zugs|ge|biet** NT (*lit, fig*) catchment area (*Brit*), service

area (*US*); **Ein|zugs|ver|fah|ren** NT (*Fin*) direct debit

ein+zwän|gen VT *sep* (*lit*) to squeeze or jam or wedge in; (*fig*) jdn to constrain, to constrict

Ein|zy|lin|der|mo|tor M one-cylinder or single-cylinder engine

Ei|pul|ver NT dried or powdered egg

Eis [ais] NT **-es, -** **a** no pl (= *gefrorenes Wasser*) ice; **~ gefrieren** to freeze, to turn to ice; **vom ~ eingeschlossen sein** to be iced in, to be icebound; **~ laufen** to ice-skate; **sie läuft ~** she ice-skates; **das ~ brechen** (*fig*) to break the ice; **etw auf ~ legen** (*lit*) to chill sth, to put sth on ice; (*fig inf*) to put sth on ice, to put sth into cold storage **b** (= *Speiseeis*) ice (cream); **er kaufte 3 ~** he bought 3 ice creams or ices; **gemischtes ~** assorted ice cream; (*mit selbstgewählten Sorten auch*) your choice of ice cream; **~ am Stiel** ice(d) lolly (*Brit*), Popsicle® (*US*)

Eis-: Eis|bahn F ice rink; **Eis|bär** M polar bear; **Eis|be|cher** M (*aus Pappe*) ice-cream tub; (*aus Metall*) sundae dish; (= *Eis*) sundae; **eis|be|deckt** ADJ attr ice-covered, covered in ice; **Eis|bein** NT **a** (*Cook*) knuckle of pork (*boiled and served with sauerkraut*) **b** (*hum inf*) **wenn ich noch länger hier in dieser Kälte stehe, bekomme ich ~e** if I stand around here in this cold any longer my feet will turn to ice; **Eis|berg** M iceberg; **die Spitze des ~s** (*fig*) the tip of the iceberg; **Eis|berg|sa|lat** M (*Salatpflanzensorte*) iceberg lettuce; **Eis|beu|tel** M ice pack; **Eis|bil|dung** F **es kam zur ~ auf den Flüssen** ice formed on the rivers; **zur Verhinderung der ~ auf Fahrbahndecken** to prevent icing on or ice forming on road surfaces; **eis|blau** ADJ ice-blue; **Eis|blau** NT ice blue; **Eis|block** M pl **-blöcke** block of ice; **Eis|blu|me** F *usu pl* frost pattern; **Eis|bom|be** F (*Cook*) bombe glacée; **Eis|bre|cher** M icebreaker; **Eis|bu|de** F ice-cream stall

Eis|schnee ['ai-] M (*Cook*) beaten white of egg

Eis-: Eis|creme F ice (cream); **Eis|de|cke** F ice sheet, sheet of ice; **Eis|die|le** F ice-cream parlour (*Brit*) or parlor (*US*)

ei|sen ['aizn] VT *Tee, Wodka* to ice, to chill → auch **geeist**

Ei|sen ['aizn] NT **-s, -** **a** no pl (*Chem*) (*abbr* **Fe**) iron; **~ verarbeitend** iron-processing; **ein Mann aus ~** a man of iron; **mehrere/noch ein ~ im Feuer haben** (*fig*) to have more than one/another iron in the fire; **Muskeln von** or **aus ~ haben** to have muscles of steel; **zum alten ~ gehören** or **zählen** (*fig*) to be on the scrap heap; **jdn/etw zum alten ~ werfen** (*fig*) to throw sb/sth on the scrap heap; **man muss das ~ schmieden, solange es heiß** or **warm ist** (*Prov*) one must strike while the iron is hot (*prov*) → **Blut, heiß** ADJ d **b** (= *Bügeleisen, Golfschläger*) iron; (= *Eisenbeschlag*) iron fitting; (= *Eisenband*) iron band or hoop; (= *Hufeisen*) shoe; (= *Fangeisen*) trap; (*obs: = Fesseln*) fetters *pl* (*obs*), irons *pl*; (*obs: = Schwert*) iron (*obs*); **jdn in ~ legen** (*obs*) to put or clap sb in irons **c** (*no pl*: *Med*) iron

Ei|sen-: Ei|sen|ader F vein of iron ore; **ei|sen|ar|tig** ADJ ironlike

Ei|sen|bahn F railway (*Brit*), railroad (*US*); (= *Eisenbahnwesen*) railways *pl* (*Brit*), railroad (*US*); (*inf*: = *Zug*) train; (= *Spielzeugeisenbahn*) toy train; (= *Spielzeugeisenbahnanlage*) train set; **ich fahre lieber (mit der) ~ als (mit dem) Bus** I prefer to travel by train or rail than by bus; **Onkel Alfred arbeitet bei der ~** uncle Alfred works for the railways (*Brit*) or railroad (*US*); **es ist (aller)höchste ~** (*inf*) it's getting late

Ei|sen|bahn-: Ei|sen|bahn|ab|teil NT (railway (*Brit*) or railroad (*US*)) compartment; **Ei|sen|bahn|an|la|gen** PL railway (*Brit*) or railroad (*US*) installations *pl*; **Ei|sen|bahn|brü|cke** F railway (*Brit*) or railroad (*US*) bridge

Ei|sen|bah|ner [-baːnɐ] M **-s, -**, **Ei|sen|bah|ne|rin** [-ərɪn] F **-, -nen** railway employee (*Brit*), railroader (*US*)

Ei|sen|bahn-: Ei|sen|bahn|fäh|re F train ferry; **Ei|sen|bahn|fahr|kar|te** F rail ticket; **Ei|sen|bahn|fahrt** F train or rail journey or ride; **Ei|sen|bahn|ge|sell|schaft** F railway (*Brit*) or railroad (*US*) company; **Ei|sen|bahn|gleis** NT railway (*Brit*) or railroad (*US*) track; **Ei|sen|bahn|kno|ten|punkt** M railway (*Brit*) or railroad (*US*) junction; **Ei|sen|bahn|netz** NT railway (*Brit*) or railroad (*US*) network; **Ei|sen|bahn|schaff|ner(in)** M(F) (railway) guard (*Brit*), (railroad) conductor (*US*); **Ei|sen|bahn|schie|ne** F railway (*Brit*) or railroad (*US*) track; **Ei|sen|bahn|schwel|le** F railway sleeper (*Brit*), (railroad) tie (*US*); **Ei|sen|bahn|sig|nal** NT railway (*Brit*) or railroad (*US*) signal; **Ei|sen|bahn|sta|ti|on** F railway (*Brit*) or railroad (*US*) station; **Ei|sen|bahn|stre|cke** F railway line (*Brit*), railroad (*US*); **Ei|sen|bahn|über|füh|rung** F (railway (*Brit*) or railroad (*US*)) footbridge; **Ei|sen|bahn|un|glück** NT railway (*Brit*) or railroad (*US*) accident, train crash; **Ei|sen|bahn|un|ter|füh|rung** F railway (*Brit*) or railroad (*US*) underpass; **Ei|sen|bahn|ver|bin|dung** F rail link; (= *Anschluss*) connection; **Ei|sen|bahn|ver|kehr** M railway (*Brit*) or railroad (*US*) traffic; **Ei|sen|bahn|wa|gen** M (= *Personenwagen*) railway carriage (*Brit*), railroad car (*US*); (= *Güterwagen*) goods wagon or truck (*Brit*), freight car (*US*); **Ei|sen|bahn|we|sen** NT railway (*Brit*) or railroad (*US*) system; **Ei|sen|bahn|zug** M railway (*Brit*) or railroad (*US*) train

Ei|sen|bart(h) ['aiznbaːɐt] M **Doktor ~** (*fig*) quack, horse doctor (*inf*)

Ei|sen-: Ei|sen|be|rei|fung F iron hooping; (= *Reif*) iron hoop; **Ei|sen|berg|werk** NT iron mine; **Ei|sen|be|schlag** M ironwork no pl; (*zum Verstärken*) iron band; **ei|sen|be|schla|gen** ADJ with iron fittings; *Stiefel* steel-tipped; **Ei|sen|be|ton** M (*dated*) ferroconcrete, reinforced concrete; **Ei|sen|blech** NT sheet iron; **Ei|sen|block** M pl **-blöcke** iron block, block of iron; **Ei|sen|boh|rer** M (*Tech*) iron or steel drill; **Ei|sen|chlo|rid** NT (*FeCl₃*) ferrous chloride; (*FeCl₃*) ferric chloride; **Ei|sen|draht** M steel wire; **Ei|sen|erz** NT iron ore; **Ei|sen|fei|le** F iron file; **Ei|sen|feil|spä|ne** PL iron filings *pl*; **Ei|sen|fle|cken** PL (*in Kartoffeln*) discoloured (*Brit*) or discolored (*US*) patches *pl*; **Ei|sen|fres|ser** M (*pej*) tough guy; **Ei|sen|garn** NT steel thread; **Ei|sen|ge|halt** M iron content; **Ei|sen|gie|ße|rei** F (= *Vorgang*) iron smelting; (= *Werkstatt*) iron foundry; **Ei|sen|glanz** M , **Ei|sen|glim|mer** M ferric oxide, iron glance; **Ei|sen|guss** ▲ M iron casting; **ei|sen|hal|tig** ADJ *Gestein* iron-bearing, ferruginous (*form*); *Medikament* containing iron; **das Wasser ist ~** the water contains iron; **Ei|sen|ham|mer** M steam hammer; (= *Werkstatt*) forge; **ei|sen|hart** ADJ (*lit*) as hard as iron; **ein ~er Mann/Wille** a man/will of iron; **Ei|sen|hut** M (*Bot*) monk's hood, aconite **b** (*Hist*) iron helmet; **Ei|sen|hüt|te** F ironworks *pl* or sing, iron foundry; **Ei|sen|in|dust|rie** F iron industry; **Ei|sen|kar|bid** NT cementite (*US*); **Ei|sen|kern** M iron core; **Ei|sen|kies** M iron pyrites sing; **Ei|sen|kitt** M iron-cement; **Ei|sen|kur** F course of iron treatment; **Ei|sen|le|gie|rung** F iron alloy; **Ei|sen|man|gel** M iron deficiency; **Ei|sen|oxid** NT , **Ei|sen|oxyd** NT ferric oxide; **Ei|sen|prä|pa|rat** NT (*Med*) (*flüssig*) iron tonic; (*Tabletten*) iron tablets *pl*; **Ei|sen|sä|ge** F hacksaw; **ei|sen|schüs|sig** [-ʃʏsɪç] ADJ *Boden* iron-bearing, ferruginous (*form*); **Ei|sen|spä|ne** PL iron filings *pl*; **Ei|sen|stan|ge** F iron bar; **Ei|sen|sul|phat** NT ferric sulphate; **Ei|sen|trä|ger** M iron girder; **ei|sen|ver|ar|bei|tend** △ ADJ attr → **Eisen a**; **Ei|sen|ver|bin|dung** F (*Chem*) iron compound; **Ei|sen|ver|hüt|tung** F (*Metall*) iron production, iron smelting; **Ei|sen|vit|ri|ol** NT iron *or* ferrous sulphate, green vitriol; **Ei|sen|-wa|ren** PL ironmongery *sing* (*Brit*), hardware *sing*; **Ei|sen|wa|ren|händ|ler(in)** M(F) i-ronmonger (*Brit*), hardware dealer; **Ei|sen|-wa|ren|hand|lung** F ironmonger's (shop) (*Brit*), hardware store; **Ei|sen|werk** NT **a** (*Art*) ironwork **b** (= *Eisenhütte*) ironworks *pl or sing*, iron foundry; **Ei|sen|zeit** F , *no pl* (*Hist*) Iron Age

ei|sern ['aizən] **ADJ** **a** *attr* (= *aus Eisen*) iron; **das Eiserne Kreuz** (*Mil*) the Iron Cross; **der Eiserne Kanzler** the Iron Chancellor; **der ~e Vorhang** (*Theat*) the safety curtain; **der Eiserne Vorhang** (*Pol*) the Iron Curtain; **~e Lunge** (*Med*) iron lung; **die ~e Jungfrau** (*Hist*) the Iron Maiden; **~e Hochzeit** 65th wedding anniversary

b (= *fest, unnachgiebig*) *Disziplin* iron *attr*, strict; *Wille* iron *attr*, of iron; *Energie* unflagging, inde-fatigable; *Ruhe* unshakeable; **~e Gesundheit** i-ron constitution; **sein Griff war ~** his grip was like iron; **mit ~er Stirn** (= *unverschämt*) brazenly; (= *unerschütterlich*) resolutely; **mit ~er Faust** with an iron hand; **es ist ein ~es Gesetz, dass ...** it's a hard and fast rule that ...; **ein ~es Regiment führen** to rule with a rod of iron (*Brit*), to rule with an iron fist; **in etw** (*dat*) **~ sein/bleiben** to be/remain resolute about sth; **da bin** *or* **bleibe ich ~!** (*inf*) that's definite; **mit ~em Besen (aus)-kehren** to make a clean sweep, to be ruthless in creating order

c *attr* (= *unantastbar*) *Reserve* emergency; **~e Ra-tion** emergency *or* iron rations *pl*

ADV resolutely; *trainieren* with iron determina-tion; **er schwieg ~** he remained resolutely si-lent; **er ist ~ bei seinem Entschluss geblieben** he stuck steadfastly *or* firmly to his decision; **(aber) ~!** (*inf*) (but) of course!, absolutely!

Ei|ses|käl|te F icy cold

Eis-: **Eis|fach** NT freezer compartment, icebox; **Eis|fi|sche|rei** F fishing through ice; **Eis|flä-che** F (surface of the) ice; **die ~ des Sees** the (sheet of) ice covering the lake; **eis|frei** ADJ ice-free *attr*, free of ice *pred*; **Eis|gang** M , *no pl* ice drift; **eis|gän|sig** ADJ *Schiff* ice-bound; *Gewässer* ice-bound; **eis|ge|kühlt** ADJ chilled; **Eis|ge|tränk** NT iced drink; **eis|glatt** ADJ *Straße* icy, slippery; **Eis|glät|te** F black ice; **eis|grau** ADJ (*liter*) steel(y) grey (*Brit*) *or* gray (*US*); **Eis|hal|le** F (*Sport*) ice stadium, ice rink; **Eis|hei|li|gen** PL **die drei ~** three Saints' Days, 12th-14th May, which are usually particular-ly cold and after which further frost is rare; **Eis|ho|ckey** NT ice hockey, hockey (*US*)

ei|sig ['aizıç] **ADJ** **a** (= *kalt*) *Wasser, Wind* icy (cold); *Kälte* icy **b** (= *jäh*) *Schreck, Grauen* chill-ing **a** (*fig*: = *abweisend*) icy, glacial; *Schweigen auch* frosty, chilly; *Ablehnung* cold; *Blick* icy, cold; *Lächeln, Empfang* frosty **ADV** **a** (= *abwei-send*) icily, coldly; **~ lächeln** to give a frosty smile; **er wurde ~ empfangen** he was given a frosty reception **b** (= *jäh*) **es durchzuckte mich ~** a cold shiver ran through me

Eis-: **Eis|jacht** F ice yacht; **Eis|kaf|fee** M iced coffee; **eis|kalt** ADJ **a** icy-cold **b** = **eisig** ADJ **b c** (*fig*: = *abweisend*) icy, cold, frosty; (= *kalt und berechnend*) cold-blooded, cold and calcu-lating; (= *dreist*) cool **ADV** **a** (= *kalt*) **es durch-zuckte mich ~** an icy shiver ran through me **b** = **eisig** ADV **a c** (= *kalt und berechnend*) cold-blooded; **sie hat auf seine Drohung ~ reagiert** her reaction to his threat was ice cold **d** (*inf*: = *glattweg*) simply, just like that; **dem sag ich ~ die Meinung** I'll just tell him exactly what I think; **davor habe ich keine Angst, das mache ich ~** I'm not afraid of that, I can do it without turning a hair (*Brit*) *or* without batting an eye-lash (*US*); **machst du das? – ja! ~** will you do it? – no problem; **Eis|kap|pe** F icecap; **Eis|-kas|ten** M (*S Ger, Aus*) refrigerator, fridge (*Brit*), icebox (*US*); **Eis|kel|ler** M cold store, cold room; **unser Schlafzimmer ist ein ~** our bedroom is like an icebox; **Eis|kon|fekt** NT (*aus Eiscreme*) ice cream confectionery; **Eis|-krem** F , **Eis|kre|me** ▲ F = **Eiscreme**; **Eis|-**

kris|tall NT ice crystal; **Eis|kunst|lauf** M fig-ure skating; **Eis|kunst|läu|fer(in)** M(F) figure skater; **Eis|lauf** M ice-skating; **eis+lau|fen** △ VI *sep irreg aux sein* → **Eis a**; **Eis|läu|fer(in)** M(F) ice-skater; **Eis|män|ner** PL (*S Ger, Aus*) = **Eisheiligen**; **Eis|ma|schi|ne** F ice-cream ma-chine; **Eis|meer** NT polar sea; **Nördliches/Süd-liches ~** Arctic/Antarctic Ocean; **Eis|mo|nat** M , **Eis|mond** M (*obs*) January; **Eis|na|deln** PL ice needles *pl*; **Eis|ne|bel** M freezing fog; **Eis|pa|ckung** F (*Med*) ice pack; **Eis|pa|last** M ice rink; (*hum inf*) icebox; **Eis|pi|ckel** M ice axe (*Brit*), ice pick

Ei|sprung ['ai-] M (*Physiol*) ovulation *no art*

Eis-: **Eis|pul|ver** NT (*Cook*) ice-cream mix; **Eis|punkt** M (*Phys*) freezing point; **Eis|re|gen** M sleet; **Eis|re|vue** F ice revue, ice show; **Eis|rie|gel** M ice-cream bar; **Eis|schie|ßen** NT **-s**, *no pl* curling; **Eis|schmel|ze** F thaw; **Eis|-schnell|lauf** ▲ M speed skating; **Eis|-schnell|läu|fer(in)** ▲ M(F) speed skater; **Eis|-schol|le** F ice floe; **Eis|schrank** M refrigera-tor, fridge (*Brit*), icebox (*US*); **Eis|se|geln** NT ice-sailing; **Eis|sport** M ice sports *pl*; **Eis-(sport)sta|di|on** NT (ice) rink; **Eis|stock** M (*Sport*) curling stone; **Eis|stock|schie|ßen** NT **-s**, *no pl* curling; **Eis|sur|fen** NT ice surfing; **Eis|tanz** M , **Eis|tan|zen** NT ice dancing; **Eis|tor|te** F ice-cream cake; **Eis|ver|käu-fer(in)** M(F) ice-cream seller *or* vendor; (*Mann auch*) ice-cream man (*inf*); **Eis|vo|gel** M **a** kingfisher **b** (= *Schmetterling*) white admiral; **Eis|was|ser** NT , *no pl* icy water; (= *Getränk*) iced water

---

EISWEIN

Eiswein is a very sweet, alcoholic wine, made – as the name suggests – from grapes which have been exposed to frost. To make it, selected grapes are left on the vine in au-tumn. Then, provided there have been con-stant temperatures of below -5°C for at least a week, the frozen grapes are picked at night and immediately pressed. Care must be tak-en that they do not thaw, so that only the best part of the grape goes into the wine. Since the yield from this process is very small and there is a risk that the temperatures will not be low enough for the process to take place, **Eiswein** is very expensive.

Eis-: **Eis|wür|fel** M ice cube; **Eis|wüs|te** F (*Geog*) frozen wastes *pl*, frozen wilderness; **Eis|zap|fen** M icicle; **Eis|zeit** F Ice Age, gla-cial epoch (*form*); (*fig*) cold war; **eis|zeit|lich** ADJ ice-age, of the Ice Age

ei|tel ['aitl] **ADJ** **a** *Mensch* vain; (= *eingebildet auch*) conceited; **~ wie ein Pfau** vain as a pea-cock **b** (*liter*) *Hoffnung, Wahn, Versuch, Gerede* vain; **seine Hoffnungen erwiesen sich als ~** his hopes proved to be all in vain; **alles ist ~** (*Bibl*) all is vanity **c** *inv* (*obs: rein*) *Gold* pure; **es herrschte ~ Freude** (*obs, hum*) there was abso-lute joy; **er denkt, das ganze Leben sei ~ Freu-de und Sonnenschein** he thinks the whole of life is nothing but a bed of roses

Ei|tel|keit F **-, -en** (*von Mensch*) vanity; (*liter: von Hoffnung, Wahn, Versuch*) vainness

Ei|ter ['aitɐ] M **-s**, *no pl* pus

Ei|ter-: **Ei|ter|beu|le** F boil; (*fig*) canker; **Ei|-ter|bläs|chen** [-blɛ:sçən] NT , **Ei|ter|bla|se** F pustule; **Ei|ter|er|re|ger** M pyogenic organism (*spec*); **Ei|ter|herd** M suppurative focus (*spec*)

ei|te|rig ['aitərıç] ADJ *Ausfluss* purulent; *Wunde* festering, suppurating; *Binde* pus-covered

ei|tern ['aitɐn] VI to fester, to discharge pus, to suppurate

Ei|ter-: **Ei|ter|pfropf** M core (*of a boil*); (*von Pickel*) head; **Ei|ter|pi|ckel** M pimple (contain-ing pus)

Ei|te|rung ['aitərʊŋ] F **-, -en** discharge of pus, suppuration

eit|rig ['aitrıç] ADJ = **eiterig**

Ei|weiß ['aivais] NT **-es, -e** *or* **-** (egg) white, white of egg, albumen (*spec*); (*Chem*) protein

Ei|weiß-: **ei|weiß|arm** ADJ low in protein; **~e Kost** a low-protein diet; **Ei|weiß|be|darf** M protein requirement; **Ei|weiß|ge|halt** M pro-tein content; **ei|weiß|hal|tig** ADJ protein-con-taining *attr*; **Fleisch ist sehr ~** meat is high in protein, meat contains a lot of protein; **Ei|-weiß|haus|halt** M (*Physiol*) protein metabo-lism; **Ei|weiß|man|gel** M protein deficiency; **Ei|weiß|prä|pa|rat** NT protein preparation; **ei|weiß|reich** ADJ protein-rich *attr*, rich in protein *pred*; **~e Kost** high-protein diet; **Ei|-weiß|stoff|wech|sel** M protein metabolism

Ei|zel|le F (*Biol*) egg cell

Eja|ku|lat [ejaku'la:t] NT **-(e)s, -e** (*Med*) ejacu-lated semen, ejaculate (*spec*)

Eja|ku|la|ti|on [ejakula'tsio:n] F **-, -en** ejacula-tion

eja|ku|lie|ren [ejaku'li:rən] *ptp* **ejakuliert** VI to ejaculate

EK [e:'ka:] NT **-s, -s** *abbr von* **Eisernes Kreuz**; **EK I/II** Iron Cross First/Second Class

EKD [e:ka:'de:] F - *abbr von* **Evangelische Kirche in Deutschland**

Ekel¹ ['e:kl] M **-s**, *no pl* disgust, revulsion, loath-ing; (= *Übelkeit*) nausea; **vor jdm/etw einen ~ ha-ben** *or* **empfinden** to have a loathing of sb/sth, to loathe sb/sth; **dabei empfinde ich ~** it gives me a feeling of disgust; **~ erregend** nauseating, revolting, disgusting; **~ überkommt mich** a feel-ing of disgust *etc* overcomes me; **diese Heuche-lei ist mir ein ~** this hypocrisy is just nauseat-ing *or* disgusting, I find this hypocrisy nauseat-ing *or* disgusting; **er hat das Essen vor ~ ausge-spuckt** he spat out the food in disgust *or* revul-sion; **er musste sich vor ~ übergeben** he was so nauseated that he vomited

Ekel² NT **-s, -** (*inf*) obnoxious person, horror (*inf*)

ekel|er|re|gend △ ADJ → **Ekel¹**

ekel|haft, **eke|lig** ['e:kəlıç] **ADJ** disgusting, revolting; (*inf*) *Schmerzen, Problem, Chef* nasty, horrible **ADV** (= *widerlich*) *riechen, schmecken* disgusting, revolting; (*inf*: = *unangenehm*) *sich be-nehmen* horribly, terribly; **sei nicht so ~ zu ihr!** don't be so nasty to her

Ekel|haf|tig|keit F **-, -en a** *no pl* (*von Person*) nastiness **b** *usu pl* nasty behaviour (*Brit*) *or* behavior (*US*) *no pl*

ekeln ['e:kln] **VT** to disgust, to revolt, to nause-ate **VT** *impers* **es ekelt mich vor diesem Geruch/Anblick, mich** *or* **mir ekelt vor diesem Geruch/Anblick** the smell/sight of it fills me with dis-gust *or* revulsion, this smell/sight is disgusting *or* revolting *or* nauseating **VR** to be *or* feel disgusted *or* revolted *or* nauseated; **sich vor etw** (*dat*) **~** to find sth disgusting *or* revolting *or* nauseating

EKG, Ekg [e:ka:'ge:] NT **-s, -s** *abbr von* **Elektro-kardiogramm** ECG; **ein ~ machen lassen** to have an ECG

Ek|lat [e'kla(:)] M **-s, -s** (*geh*) (= *Aufsehen*) sensa-tion, stir; (= *Zusammenstoß*) row, (major) alter-cation (*form*); **mit großem ~** causing a great stir *or* sensation, spectacularly; **mit (großem) ~ durchfallen** to be a resounding flop *or* a spec-tacular failure

ek|la|tant [ekla'tant] ADJ (= *Aufsehen erregend*) *Fall* sensational, spectacular; (= *offenkundig*) *Bei-spiel* striking; *Verletzung* flagrant

Ek|lek|ti|ker [ɛk'lɛktikɐ, e'klɛktikɐ] M **-s, -**, **Ek|-lek|ti|ke|rin** [-ərın] F **-, -nen** eclectic

ek|lek|tisch [ɛk'lɛktıʃ, e'klɛktıʃ] ADJ eclectic

Ek|lek|ti|zis|mus [ɛklɛkti'tsısmʊs, eklɛ-] M **-**, *no pl* eclecticism

ek|lig ['e:klıç] ADJ, ADV = **ekelig**

Ek|lip|se [ɛk'lıpsə, e'klıpsə] F **-, -n** eclipse

Ek|lip|tik [ɛk'lıptık, e'klıptık] F **-, -en** ecliptic

ek|lip|tisch [ɛk'lɪptɪʃ, e'klɪptɪʃ] ADJ ecliptical

Eks|ta|se [ɛk'staːzə, ɛks'taːzə] F -, -n ecstasy; **in ~ geraten** to go into ecstasies; **jdn in ~ versetzen** to send sb into ecstasies

eks|ta|tisch [ɛk'staːtɪʃ, ɛks'taːtɪʃ] ADJ ecstatic, full of ecstasy ADV ecstatically

Ek|zem [ɛk'tseːm] NT -s, -e (Med) eczema

EL abbr von **Esslöffel** tbs, tbsp

E|la|bo|rat [elabo'raːt] NT -(e)s, -e (pej) concoction (pej)

E|lan [e'laːn, e'lãː] M -s, no pl élan, zest, vigour (Brit), vigor (US)

E|last [e'last] M -(e)s, -e rubber, elastomer (spec)

E|las|tik|bin|de [e'lastɪk-] F elasticated bandage

e|las|tisch [e'lastɪʃ] ADJ elastic; Gang springy; Metall, Holz springy, flexible; Stoff elastic, stretchy; Binde elasticated; (fig) (= spannkräftig) Muskel, Mensch strong and supple; (= flexibel) flexible, elastic ADV supply, lithely; **der Baum bog sich ~ im Wind** the tree bent supply in the wind; **er federte ~** he bent supply at the knees; **der Bügel schnellte ~ zurück** the bow sprang back

E|las|ti|zi|tät [elastitsi'tɛːt] F -, (rare) -en elasticity; (von Metall, Holz) flexibility; (= Flexibilität) flexibility, elasticity; **die ~ seines Körpers** the supple strength of his body

E|la|tiv [e'laːtiːf] M -s, -e [-və] (Gram) absolute superlative

E|lbe ['ɛlbə] F - **die ~** the (river) Elbe

E|lb|käh|ne ['ɛlp-] PL (N Ger hum) beetle-crushers pl (inf), clodhoppers pl (inf)

Elch [ɛlç] M -(e)s, -e elk, moose (esp US)

Elch-: Elch|bul|le M bull elk; (in Nordamerika) bull moose; **Elch|kalb** NT elk calf; (in Nordamerika) moose calf; **Elch|kuh** F cow elk; (in Nordamerika) cow moose; **Elch|test** M (inf) (Aut) high-speed swerve (to test a car's roadholding); (fig: = entscheidender Test) make-or-break test

El|do|ra|do [ɛldo'raːdo] NT -s, -s (lit, fig) eldorado

E|lect|ro|nic Ban|king [elɛk'trɔnɪk 'bɛŋkɪŋ] NT -, no pl electronic banking

E|lect|ro|nic Cash [elɛk'trɔnɪk 'kɛʃ] NT -, no pl electronic cash

E|le|fant [ele'fant] M -en, -en elephant; **wie ein ~ im Porzellanladen** (inf) like a bull in a china shop (prov) → Mücke

E|le|fan|ten-: E|le|fan|ten|ba|by NT (inf) baby elephant (auch fig hum); **E|le|fan|ten|bul|le** M bull elephant; **E|le|fan|ten|ge|dächt|nis** NT (fig) elephant's memory; **E|le|fan|ten|hoch|zeit** F (Comm inf) mega-merger (inf); **E|le|fan|ten|kalb** NT elephant calf; **E|le|fan|ten|kuh** F cow elephant; **E|le|fan|ten|ren|nen** NT (hum inf) duel between two lorries (Brit) or trucks; **E|le|fan|ten|rob|be** F elephant seal; **E|le|fan|ten|run|de** F (Pol) (= Koalitionsrunde) top-level meeting of coalition members; (im Fernsehen) debate between party leaders; **E|le|fan|ten|rüs|sel** M elephant's trunk; **E|le|fan|ten|schlacht** F (fig) battle of the giants

E|le|fan|ti|a|sis [elefan'tiːazɪs] F -, Elefantiasen [-'tiaːzn] (Med) elephantiasis

e|le|gant [ele'gant] ADJ elegant; **die ~e Welt** (dated) high society ADV elegantly

E|le|ganz [ele'gants] F -, no pl elegance

E|le|gie [ele'giː] F -, -n [-'giːən] elegy

E|le|gi|en|dich|ter(in) [ele'giːən-] M(F), **E|le|gi|ker** [e'leːgikɐ] M -s, -, **E|le|gi|ke|rin** [-ərɪn] F -, -nen elegist

e|le|gisch [e'leːgɪʃ] ADJ elegiac; (= melancholisch auch) melancholy ADV **~ gestimmt** in a melancholy mood

E|lei|son [e'laizɔn] NT -s, -s (Eccl) Kyrie eleison

E|lek|tri|fi|ka|ti|on [elɛktrifika'tsioːn] F -, -en (Sw) electrification

e|lek|tri|fi|zie|ren [elɛktrifi'tsiːrən] ptp **elektrifiziert** VT to electrify

E|lek|tri|fi|zie|rung F -, -en electrification

E|lek|trik [e'lɛktrɪk] F -, -en **a** (= elektrische Anlagen) electrical equipment **b** no pl (inf: = Elektrizitätslehre) electricity

E|lek|tri|ker [e'lɛktrikɐ] M -s, -, **E|lek|tri|ke|rin** [-ərɪn] F -, -nen electrician

e|lek|trisch [e'lɛktrɪʃ] ADJ electric; Entladung, Feld, Widerstand electrical; **~e Geräte** electrical appliances; **~er Schlag/Strom** electric shock/current; **der ~e Stuhl** the electric chair; **bei uns ist alles ~** we're all electric ADV electrically, by or with electricity; **sich ~ rasieren** to use an electric razor; **~ betrieben** electrically driven, driven or run by electricity, electric; **wir kochen/heizen ~** we cook/heat by or with electricity; **das geht alles ~** (inf) it's all automatic

E|lek|tri|sche [e'lɛktrɪʃə] F decl as adj (dated) tram (esp Brit), streetcar (US)

e|lek|tri|sie|ren [elɛktri'ziːrən] ptp **elektrisiert** VT (lit, fig) to electrify; (= aufladen) to charge with electricity; (Med) to treat with electricity; **ich habe mich elektrisiert** I gave myself or I got an electric shock; **die elektrisierte Atmosphäre** the electrically-charged atmosphere; **wie elektrisiert** (as if) electrified VI to give an electric shock

E|lek|tri|sier|ma|schi|ne F electrostatic generator

E|lek|tri|zi|tät [elɛktritsi'tɛːt] F -, no pl electricity

E|lek|tri|zi|täts-: E|lek|tri|zi|täts|ge|sell|schaft F electric power company; **E|lek|tri|zi|täts|leh|re** F (science of) electricity; **E|lek|tri|zi|täts|ver|sor|gung** F (electric) power supply; **E|lek|tri|zi|täts|ver|sor|gungs|un|ter|neh|men** NT electricity supplier or provider; **E|lek|tri|zi|täts|werk** NT (electric) power station; (= Gesellschaft) electric power company; **E|lek|tri|zi|täts|zäh|ler** M (form) electricity meter

E|lek|tro- [e'lɛktro] in cpds electro- (auch Sci), electric; **e|lek|tro|a|kus|tisch** [elɛktroa'kustɪʃ, e'lɛktro-] ADJ electroacoustic(al); **E|lek|tro|a|na|ly|se** [elɛktroana'lyːzə, e'lɛktro-] F electroanalysis; **E|lek|tro|an|trieb** M electric drive; **E|lek|tro|ar|ti|kel** M electrical appliance; **E|lek|tro|au|to** NT electric car; **E|lek|tro|che|mie** [elɛktroçe'miː, e'lɛktro-] F electrochemistry; **e|lek|tro|che|misch** [elɛktro'çemɪʃ, e'lɛktro-] ADJ electrochemical

E|lek|tro|de [elɛk'troːdə] F -, -n electrode

E|lek|tro|den|span|nung F electrode potential

E|lek|tro-: E|lek|tro|di|a|gnos|tik [elɛktrodia'gnɔstɪk, e'lɛktro-] F (Med) electrodiagnosis; **E|lek|tro|dy|na|mik** [elɛktrody'naːmɪk, e'lɛktro-] F electrodynamics sing; **e|lek|tro|dy|na|misch** [elɛktrody'naːmɪʃ, e'lɛktro-] ADJ electrodynamic; **E|lek|tro|en|ze|pha|lo|gramm** [elɛktroʔɛtsefalo'gram] NT (Med) electroencephalogram, EEG; **E|lek|tro|fahr|zeug** NT electric vehicle; **E|lek|tro|ge|rät** NT electrical appliance; **E|lek|tro|ge|schäft** NT electrical shop (Brit) or store (US); **E|lek|tro|gi|tar|re** F (Mus) electric guitar; **E|lek|tro|grill** M electric grill; **E|lek|tro|herd** M electric cooker; **E|lek|tro|in|dust|rie** F electrical industry; **E|lek|tro|in|ge|ni|eur(in)** M(F) electrical engineer; **E|lek|tro|in|stal|la|teur(in)** M(F) electrician; **E|lek|tro|kar|di|o|gramm** [elɛktrokardio'gram] NT (Med) electrocardiogram, ECG; **E|lek|tro|kar|ren** M small electric truck; (des Milchmannes etc) electric float; **E|lek|tro|lok** F , **E|lek|tro|lo|ko|mo|ti|ve** F electric locomotive; **E|lek|tro|ly|se** [elɛktro'lyːzə] F -, -n electrolysis; **e|lek|tro|lyt** [elɛktro'lyːt] M -en, -en electrolyte; **e|lek|tro|ly|tisch** [elɛktro'lyːtɪʃ] ADJ electrolytic; **E|lek|tro|lyt|lö|sung** [elɛktro'lyːt-]

F electrolytic solution, electrolyte; **E|lek|tro|mag|net** [elɛktroma'gneːt, e'lɛktro-] M electromagnet; **e|lek|tro|mag|ne|tisch** [elɛktroma'gneːtɪʃ, e'lɛktro-] ADJ electromagnetic; **E|lek|tro|me|cha|ni|ker(in)** M(F) electrician; **e|lek|tro|me|cha|nisch** [elɛktrome'çaːnɪʃ, e'lɛktro-] ADJ electromechanical; **E|lek|tro|meis|ter(in)** M(F) qualified electrician; **E|lek|tro|mes|ser** NT electric carving knife; **E|lek|tro|me|ter** [elɛktro'meːtɐ] NT -s, - electrometer; **E|lek|tro|mo|tor** M electric motor

E|lek|tron [e'lɛktrɔn, e'lɛktroːn, elɛk'troːn] NT -s, -en [elɛk'troːnən] electron

E|lek|tro|nen-: E|lek|tro|nen|blitz M , **E|lek|tro|nen|blitz|ge|rät** NT (Phot) electronic flash; **E|lek|tro|nen|(ge)|hirn** NT electronic brain; **E|lek|tro|nen|hül|le** F (Phys) electron shell or cloud; **E|lek|tro|nen|la|ser** M electron laser; **E|lek|tro|nen|mi|kro|skop** NT electron microscope; **E|lek|tro|nen|or|gel** F (Mus) electronic organ; **E|lek|tro|nen|rech|ner** M (electronic) computer; **E|lek|tro|nen|röh|re** F valve, electron tube (US); **E|lek|tro|nen|schale** F electron shell; **E|lek|tro|nen|schleu|der** F (Phys) electron accelerator, betatron (spec); **E|lek|tro|nen|strah|len** PL electron or cathode rays pl; **E|lek|tro|nen|the|o|rie** F electron theory

E|lek|tro|nik [elɛk'troːnɪk] F -, -en electronics sing; (= elektronische Teile) electronics pl

E|lek|tro|nik- in cpds electronic; **E|lek|tro|nik|ge|rät** NT electronic device; **E|lek|tro|nik|schrott** M electronic waste; **E|lek|tro|nik|spiel|zeug** NT electronic toys pl

e|lek|tro|nisch [elɛk'troːnɪʃ] ADJ electronic; **~e Post** electronic mail, E-mail, e-mail; **~er Brief|kasten** electronic mailbox; **~e Geldbörse** smartcard-based electronic wallet ADV **~ ge|steuert** electronically controlled

E|lek|tro-: E|lek|tro|ofen M (Metal) electric furnace; (= Heizofen) electric heater; **E|lek|tro|ra|sen|mä|her** M electric lawn mower; **E|lek|tro|ra|sie|rer** M electric shaver or razor; **E|lek|tro|schock** M (Med) electric shock, electroshock; **E|lek|tro|schock|be|hand|lung** F electric shock treatment; **E|lek|tro|schwei|ßen** NT arc welding; **E|lek|tro|schwei|ßung** F electric welding; **E|lek|tro|smog** M electromagnetic radiation; **E|lek|tro|stahl** M (Metal) electrosteel, electric steel; **E|lek|tro|sta|tik** [elɛktro'ʃtaːtɪk] F (Phys) electrostatics sing; **e|lek|tro|sta|tisch** [elɛktro'ʃtaːtɪʃ] ADJ electrostatic ADV electrostatically; **E|lek|tro|tech|nik** [elɛktro'tɛçnɪk, e'lɛktro-] F electrical engineering; **E|lek|tro|tech|ni|ker(in)** M(F) electrician; (= Ingenieur) electrical engineer; **e|lek|tro|tech|nisch** [elɛktro'tɛçnɪʃ, e'lɛktro-] ADJ electrical, electrotechnical (rare); **E|lek|tro|the|ra|pie** [elɛktrotera'piː, e'lɛktro-] F (Med) electrotherapy; **E|lek|tro|zaun** [e'lɛktro-] M electric fence

E|le|ment [ele'mɛnt] NT -(e)s, -e **a** element (auch Chem); (Elec) cell, battery; **kriminelle ~e** (pej) criminal elements; **in seinem ~ sein** to be in one's element **b** **Elemente** PL (fig: = Anfangsgründe) elements pl, rudiments pl; **das Toben der ~e** (liter) the raging of the elements

e|le|men|tar [elemɛn'taːɐ] ADJ (= grundlegend, wesentlich) elementary; (= naturhaft, urwüchsig) Gewalt, Trieb elemental; Hass strong, violent ADV **~ hervorbrechen** to erupt with elemental force

E|le|men|tar- in cpds (= grundlegend) elementary; (= naturhaft) elemental; **E|le|men|tar|be|griff** M elementary or basic concept; **E|le|men|tar|er|eig|nis** NT natural disaster; **E|le|men|tar|ge|walt** F (liter) elemental force; **E|le|men|tar|kennt|nis|se** PL elementary knowledge sing; **E|le|men|tar|la|dung** F (Phys) elementary charge; **E|le|men|tar|schu|le** F (rare) primary or elementary school; **E|le|men|tar|teil|chen** NT (Phys) elementary particle

E|len ['eːlɛn] M OR NT **-s, -** (rare: = Elch) elk

e|lend ['eːlɛnt] **ADJ a** (= unglücklich, jämmerlich, pej: = gemein) wretched, miserable; (= krank) wretched, awful (inf), ill pred; **mir ist ganz ~** I feel really awful (inf) or wretched; **mir wird ganz ~, wenn ich daran denke** I feel quite ill when I think about it, thinking about it makes me feel quite ill
b (inf: = sehr groß) Hunger, Hitze awful, dreadful; (= sehr schlecht) Wetter, Kälte, Leistung wretched, dreadful, miserable
ADV a (= schlecht) wretchedly, miserably; **~ aussehen** to look awful (inf) or wretched; **sich ~ fühlen** to feel awful (inf) or wretched
b (inf: = schlimm) dreadfully, terribly; **ich habe ~ gefroren** I was miserably or terribly cold; **da bin ich ~ betrogen worden** I was cheated terribly; **es war ~ heiß/kalt** it was awfully or dreadfully hot/miserably or dreadfully or terribly cold

E|lend ['eːlɛnt] NT **-(e)s** [-dəs] no pl (= Unglück, Not) misery, distress; (= Verwahrlosung) squalor; (= Armut) poverty, penury; **ein Bild des ~s** a picture of misery/squalor; **ins ~ geraten** to fall into poverty, to be reduced to penury, to become destitute; **im (tiefsten) ~ leben** to live in (abject) misery/squalor/poverty; **jdn/sich (selbst) ins ~ stürzen** to plunge sb/oneself into misery/poverty; **wie das leibhaftige ~ aussehen** (inf) to look really awful (inf) or terrible (inf); **(wie) ein Häufchen ~** (inf) (looking) a picture of misery; **das heulende ~** (inf) the blues pl (inf); **da kann man das heulende ~ kriegen** (inf) it's enough to make you scream (inf); **es ist ein ~ mit ihm** (inf) he makes you want to weep (inf), he's hopeless; **es ist ein ~, ...** (inf) it's heartbreaking ... → **lang ADJ b**

e|len|dig|(lich) ['eːlɛndɪk(lɪç), (emph) eːˈlɛndɪk(-lɪç)] ADV (geh) miserably, wretchedly; **~ zugrunde** or **zu Grunde gehen** or **verrecken** (sl) to come to a wretched or miserable or dismal end

E|lends-: E|lends|ge|stalt F (poor) wretch, wretched figure; **E|lends|quar|tier** NT slum (dwelling), squalid dwelling; **E|lends|vier|tel** NT slums pl, slum area

E|le|phan|ti|a|sis [elefanˈtiːazɪs] F **-, Elephantiasen** [-ˈtiaːzn] (Med) elephantiasis

E|le|ve [eˈleːvə] M **-n, -n, E|le|vin** [eˈleːvɪn] F **-, -nen** (Theat) student; (old: = Schüler) pupil

elf NUM eleven → auch **vier**

Elf¹ [ɛlf] F **-, -en** (Sport) team, eleven

Elf² [ɛlf] M **-en, -en, El|fe** ['ɛlfə] F **-, -n** elf

Elf-: Elf|eck NT undecagon, eleven-sided figure; **elf|eckig** ADJ eleven-sided

El|fen|bein ['ɛlfnbain] NT ivory

El|fen|bein|ar|beit F ivory (carving)

el|fen|bei|nern ADJ ivory, made of ivory; **~er Turm** (Rel) Tower of Ivory **ADV** ivory-like

El|fen|bein-: el|fen|bein|far|ben [-farbn], **el|fen|bein|far|big** ADJ ivory-coloured (Brit), ivory-colored (US); **El|fen|bein|küs|te** F Ivory Coast; **El|fen|bein|schnit|ze|rei** F ivory carving; (Produkt auch) ivory; **El|fen|bein|turm** M (fig) ivory tower

el|fen|haft, el|fen|haft ADJ (liter) elfish, elfin; **El|fen|reich** NT fairyland

El|fer ['ɛlfɐ] M **-s, -** (Ftbl inf) = Elfmeter

El|fer-: El|fer|pro|be F (Math) casting out of elevens; **El|fer|rat** M committee of eleven

elf-: elf|fach ['ɛlffax] ADJ elevenfold → auch **vierfach; elf|mal** ['ɛlfmaːl] ADV eleven times → auch **viermal**

Elf|me|ter [ɛlfˈmeːtɐ] M (Ftbl) penalty (kick) (für to, for); **einen ~ schießen** to take a penalty

Elf|me|ter-: Elf|me|ter|mar|ke F, **Elf|me|ter|punkt** M (Ftbl) penalty spot; **Elf|me|ter|schie|ßen** NT **-s, -** (Ftbl) penalty shoot-out; **durch ~ entschieden** decided on penalties; **Elf|me|ter|schuss ▲** M (Ftbl) penalty (kick); **Elf|me|ter|schüt|zin** F (Ftbl) penalty-taker

Elf|tel [ɛlftl] NT **-s, -** eleventh → auch **Viertel¹**

elf|tens ['ɛlftns] ADV eleventh, in the eleventh place

elf|te(r, s) ['ɛlftə] ADJ eleventh → **vierte(r, s)**

E|li|mi|na|ti|on [eliminaˈtsioːn] F **-, -en** elimination (auch Math)

e|li|mi|nie|ren [elimiˈniːrən] ptp **eliminiert** VT to eliminate (auch Math)

E|li|mi|nie|rung F **-, -en** elimination

e|li|sa|be|tha|nisch [elizabeˈtaːnɪʃ] ADJ Elizabethan

E|li|si|on [eliˈzioːn] F **-, -en** (Gram) elision

e|li|tär [eliˈtɛːɐ] ADJ elitist **ADV** in an elitist fashion

E|li|te [eˈliːtə] F **-, -n** elite

E|li|te-: E|li|te|den|ken NT elitism; **E|li|te|trup|pe** F (Mil) crack or elite troops pl

E|li|xier [eliˈksiːɐ] NT **-s, -e** elixir (liter), tonic

El|bo|gen ['ɛlboːgn] M = **Ellenbogen**

El|le ['ɛlə] F **-, -n a** (Anat) ulna **b** (Hist) (Measure) cubit; (= Maßstock) ≈ yardstick; **alles mit der gleichen** or **mit gleicher ~ messen** (fig) to measure everything by the same yardstick or standards

El|len|bo|gen ['ɛlənboːgn] M elbow; (fig) push; **er bahnte sich seinen Weg mit den ~ durch die Menge** he elbowed his way through the crowd; **die ~ gebrauchen** (fig) to use one's elbows, to be ruthless; **er hat keine ~** (fig) he's not ruthless enough, he has no push (inf)

El|len|bo|gen-: El|len|bo|gen|frei|heit F (fig) elbow room; **El|len|bo|gen|ge|sell|schaft** F dog-eat-dog society; **El|len|bo|gen|mensch** M ruthless or pushy (inf) person, pusher (inf); **El|len|bo|gen|tak|tik** F pushiness (inf); **~ anwenden** to be pushy (inf)

el|len-: el|len|lang ADJ (fig inf) incredibly long (inf); Liste, Weg auch mile-long attr (inf), a mile long pred (inf); Geschichte etc auch lengthy, interminable; Kerl incredibly tall (inf); **el|len|wei|se** ADV ≈ by the yard

El|lip|se [ɛˈlɪpsə] F **-, -n** (Math) ellipse; (Gram) ellipsis

el|lip|tisch [ɛˈlɪptɪʃ] ADJ (Math, Gram) elliptic(al)

Elms|feu|er ['ɛlms-] NT (Met) St Elmo's fire, corposant

E|lo|ge [eˈloːʒə] F **-, -n** eulogy

E-Lok ['eːlɔk] F abbr von **elektrische Lokomotive** electric locomotive or engine

e|lo|quent [eloˈkvɛnt] (geh) **ADJ** eloquent **ADV** eloquently

E|lo|quenz [eloˈkvɛnts] F **-, no pl** (geh) eloquence

El|sass ▲ ['ɛlzas] NT **- or -es das ~** Alsace

El|säs|ser¹ ['ɛlzɛsɐ] ADJ Alsatian

El|säs|ser² ['ɛlzɛsɐ] M **-s, -, El|säs|se|rin** [-ərɪn] F **-, -nen** Alsatian, inhabitant of Alsace

el|säs|sisch ['ɛlzɛsɪʃ] ADJ Alsatian

El|sass-Loth|rin|gen ▲ ['ɛlzasˈloːtrɪŋən] NT Alsace-Lorraine

el|sass-loth|rin|gisch ▲ ['ɛlzasˈloːtrɪŋɪʃ] ADJ Alsace-Lorraine attr, of Alsace-Lorraine

Els|ter ['ɛlstɐ] F **-, -n** magpie; **wie eine ~ stehlen** to be always stealing things, to have sticky fingers (Brit inf); **eine diebische ~ sein** (fig) to be a thief or pilferer; **geschwätzig wie eine ~ sein** to chatter like a magpie

El|ter ['ɛltɐ] M OR NT **-s, -n** (Sci) parent

el|ter|lich ['ɛltɐlɪç] ADJ parental

El|tern ['ɛltɐn] PL parents pl; **nicht von schlechten ~ sein** (inf) to be quite something (inf), to be a good one (inf)

El|tern-: El|tern|abend M (Sch) parents' evening; **El|tern|bei|rat** M ≈ PTA, parent-teacher association; **El|tern|haus** NT (lit, fig) (parental) home; **aus gutem ~ stammen** to come from a good home; **El|tern|i|ni|ti|a|ti|ve** F parents'

action group, parent pressure group; **El|tern|lie|be** F parental love; **el|tern|los** ADJ orphaned, parentless **ADV ~ aufwachsen** to grow up an orphan or without parents; **El|tern|pflicht** F parental duty; **die ~en pl** (auch) one's duties as a parent; **El|tern|schaft** ['ɛltɐnʃaft] F **-, -en** (= alle Eltern zusammen) parents pl; (= das Elternsein) parenthood; **El|tern|sprech|stun|de** F (Sch) consultation hour (for parents); **El|tern|sprech|tag** M open or visiting day (for parents); **El|tern|teil** M parent; **El|tern|ur|laub** M unpaid leave given to new mother or father; **El|tern|ver|tre|ter(in)** M(F) (Sch) parent governor, member of the school's governing body

E|ly|si|um [eˈlyːziʊm] NT **-s, no pl** (Myth, fig) **das ~** Elysium

E|mail [eˈmai, eˈmaːj] NT **-s, -s** enamel

E-Mail ['iːmeːl] F **-, -s** (Comput) E-mail, e-mail

E-Mail-Ad|res|se ['iːmeːl-] F (Comput) E-mail or e-mail address

E|mail|lack [eˈmailak, eˈmaːj-] M enamel paint

E|mail|le [eˈmaljə, eˈmai, eˈmaːj] F **-, -n** enamel

e|mail|lie|ren [emaˈjiːrən, emalˈjiːrən] ptp **emailliert** VT to enamel

E|mail- [eˈmai-, eˈmaːj-]: **E|mail|ma|le|rei** F enamel painting, enamelling (Brit), enameling (US); **E|mail|schmuck** M enamel jewellery (Brit) or jewelry (US)

E|ma|na|ti|on [emanaˈtsioːn] F **-, -en** (Philos, Chem) emanation

E|man|ze [eˈmantsə] F **-, -n** (usu pej) women's libber (inf)

E|man|zi|pa|ti|on [emantsipaˈtsioːn] F **-, -en** emancipation

E|man|zi|pa|ti|ons|be|we|gung F emancipation movement

e|man|zi|pa|to|risch [emantsipaˈtoːrɪʃ] ADJ emancipatory

e|man|zi|pie|ren [emantsiˈpiːrən] ptp **emanzipiert VT** to emancipate **VR** to emancipate oneself

E|man|zi|pie|rung F **-, -en** emancipation

Em|bar|go [ɛmˈbargo] NT **-s, -s** embargo; **etw mit einem ~ belegen, ein ~ über etw** (acc) **verhängen** to put or place an embargo on sth

Em|blem [ɛmˈbleːm, ãˈbleːm] NT **-(e)s, -e** emblem; (= Firmenemblem) logo

emb|le|ma|tisch [ɛmbleˈmaːtɪʃ, ãbleˈmaːtɪʃ] ADJ emblematic

Em|bo|lie [ɛmboˈliː] F **-, -n** [-ˈliːən] (Med) embolism

Em|bryo ['ɛmbryo] M (AUS AUCH NT) **-s, -s** or **-nen** [-ˈoːnən] embryo

Emb|ry|o|lo|ge [ɛmbryoˈloːgə] M **-n, -n, Emb|ry|o|lo|gin** [-ˈloːgɪn] F **-, -nen** embryologist

Emb|ry|o|lo|gie [ɛmbryoloˈgiː] F **-, no pl** embryology

emb|ry|o|nal [ɛmbryoˈnaːl] ADJ attr (Biol, fig) embryonic

Emb|ry|o|nen|schutz|ge|setz NT embryo protection law

E|men|da|ti|on [emɛndaˈtsioːn] F **-, no pl** (Liter) emendation

e|me|ri|tie|ren [emeriˈtiːrən] ptp **emeritiert VT** (Univ) to give emeritus status (to); **emeritierter Professor** emeritus professor

E|me|ri|tus [eˈmeːritʊs] M **-, Emeriti** [-ti] (Univ) emeritus

E|mi|grant [emiˈgrant] M **-en, -en, E|mi|gran|tin** [-ˈgrantɪn] F **-, -nen** emigrant; (= politischer Flüchtling) émigré

E|mi|gran|ten|schick|sal NT sein etc ~ his etc fate as an exile or refugee or émigré

E|mi|gra|ti|on [emigraˈtsioːn] F **-, -en** emigration; (= die Emigranten) emigrant community; **in der ~ leben** to live in (self-imposed) exile; **in die ~ gehen** to emigrate → **innere(r, s) a**

e|mig|rie|ren [emi'gri:rən] *ptp* **emigriert** VI *aux sein* to emigrate

e|mi|nent [emi'nɛnt] (*geh*) ADJ *Person* eminent; *Kenntnis* remarkable; **von ~er Bedeutung** of the utmost significance; **er hat Eminentes geleistet** he is a man of eminent achievements ADV eminently; **~ wichtig** of the utmost importance

E|mi|nenz [emi'nɛnts] F -, -en (*Eccl*) (*Seine/Eure*) **~** (His/Your) Eminence → **grau**

E|mir ['e:mɪr, e'mi:ɐ] M -s, -e emir

E|mi|rat [emi'ra:t] NT -(e)s, -e emirate

E|mis|sär [emi'sɛːɐ] M -s, -e, **E|mis|sä|rin** [-'sɛː-rɪn] F -, -nen (*old*) emissary

E|mis|si|on [emi'sio:n] F **a** (*Fin*) issue **b** (*Phys*) emission **c** (*Sw*: = *Radiosendung*) (radio) broadcast

E|mis|si|ons-: E|mis|si|ons|bank F *pl* -banken issuing bank; **E|mis|si|ons|kurs** M rate of issue, issuing price; **E|mis|si|ons|schutz** M emission(s) control; (*bei Auto*) exhaust emission(s) control

E|mit|tent [emi'tɛnt] M -en, -en, **E|mit|ten|tin** [emi'tɛntɪn] F -, -nen (*Fin: von Wertpapieren*) issuer, issuing company

e|mit|tie|ren [emi'ti:rən] *ptp* **emittiert** VT **a** (*Fin*) to issue **b** (*Phys*) to emit

Emm|chen ['ɛmçən] NT -s, - (*hum inf*, YYY>, *Hist*) mark, ≈ quid (*Brit inf*), ≈ buck (*US inf*)

Em|men|ta|ler ['ɛmənta:lɐ] M -s, - (= *Käse*) Ement(h)aler

E|mo|ti|con [e'mo:tikɔn] NT -s, -s (*Comput, E-Mail: = Zeichenkombination zum Ausdruck von Gefühlen*) emoticon; (*positives Gefühl*) smiley

E|mo|ti|on [emo'tsio:n] F -, -en emotion

e|mo|ti|o|nal [emotsio'na:l] ADJ emotional; *Ausdrucksweise* emotive ADV emotionally

e|mo|ti|o|na|li|sie|ren [emotsionali'zi:rən] *ptp* **emotionalisiert** VT to emotionalize

E|mo|ti|o|na|li|tät F -, -en emotionality

e|mo|ti|o|nell [emotsio'nɛl] ADJ = **emotional** ADJ

e|mo|ti|ons-: e|mo|ti|ons|arm ADJ lacking in emotion, unfeeling; **e|mo|ti|ons|frei** ADJ, ADV = **emotionslos; e|mo|ti|ons|ge|la|den** ADJ emotionally charged; **e|mo|ti|ons|los** ADJ emotionless, free of emotion, unemotional ADV unemotionally; **E|mo|ti|ons|lo|sig|keit** F -, *no pl* lack of emotion

Empf. *abbr von* **Empfänger** *von* **Empfohlen(er Preis)**

emp|fahl *pret von* **empfehlen**

emp|fand *pret von* **empfinden**

Emp|fang [ɛm'pfaŋ] M -(e)s, ⁻e [-'pfɛŋə] reception; (*von Brief, Ware etc*) receipt; (*von Sakramenten*) receiving; **jdm einen herzlichen ~ bereiten** to give sb a warm reception; **zu jds ~ kommen** (= *jdn begrüßen*) to (come to) receive sb; **einen ~ geben** or **veranstalten** to give or hold a reception; **jdn/etw in ~ nehmen** to receive sb/sth; (*Comm*) to take delivery of sth; (**zahlbar**) **nach/bei ~** (+*gen*) (payable) on receipt (of); **auf ~ bleiben** (*Rad*) to stand by; **auf ~ schalten** (*Rad*) to switch over to "receive"

emp|fan|gen [ɛm'pfaŋən] *pret* **empfing** [ɛm-'pfɪŋ], *ptp* **empfangen** VT to receive; (= *begrüßen*) to greet, to receive (*form*); (*herzlich*) to welcome; (= *abholen*) *Besuch* to meet; **die Weihen ~** (*Eccl*) to take Holy Orders; **die Polizisten wurden mit einem Steinhagel ~** the police were greeted by a shower of stones VTI (= *schwanger werden*) to conceive

Emp|fän|ger¹ [ɛm'pfɛŋɐ] M -s, - (*Rad*) receiver

Emp|fän|ger² [ɛm'pfɛŋɐ] M -s, -, **Emp|fän|ge|rin** [-ərɪn] F -, -nen recipient, receiver; (= *Adressat*) addressee; (= *Warenempfänger*) consignee; **~ unbekannt** (*auf Briefen*) not known at this address; **~ verzogen** gone away

Emp|fän|ger|ab|schnitt M receipt slip

emp|fäng|lich [ɛm'pfɛŋlɪç] ADJ (= *aufnahmebereit*) receptive (*für* to); (= *beeinflussbar, anfällig*) susceptible (*für* to)

Emp|fäng|lich|keit F -, -en (= *Aufnahmebereitschaft*) receptivity (*für* to); (= *Beeinflussbarkeit, Anfälligkeit*) susceptibility (*für* to)

Emp|fäng|nis [ɛm'pfɛŋnɪs] F -, -se conception → **unbefleckt**

Emp|fäng|nis-: emp|fäng|nis|ver|hü|tend ADJ contraceptive; **~e Mittel** *pl* contraceptives *pl*; **Emp|fäng|nis|ver|hü|tung** F contraception; **Emp|fäng|nis|ver|hü|tungs|mit|tel** NT contraceptive

Emp|fangs-: Emp|fangs|an|ten|ne F receiving aerial (*Brit*) or antenna; **emp|fangs|be|rech|tigt** ADJ authorized to receive payment/goods *etc*; **Emp|fangs|be|rech|tig|te(r)** [-bərɛçtɪçtə] MF *decl as adj* authorized recipient; **Emp|fangs|be|reich** M (*Rad, TV*) reception area; **Emp|fangs|be|schei|ni|gung** F, **Emp|fangs|be|stä|ti|gung** F (*acknowledgment of*) receipt; **Emp|fangs|chef(in)** M(F) (*von Hotel*) head porter; **Emp|fangs|da|me** F receptionist; **Emp|fangs|ge|rät** NT (*Rad, TV*) (radio/TV) set, receiver; **Emp|fangs|ko|pie** F incoming document; **Emp|fangs|schüs|sel** F (*TV, Rad, Telec*) receiving dish; **Emp|fangs|sta|ti|on** F (*Rad*) receiving station; (*Space*) tracking station; (*Comm*) destination; **Emp|fangs|stö|rung** F (*Rad, TV*) interference *no pl*; **Emp|fangs|zim|mer** NT reception room

emp|feh|len [ɛm'pfe:lən] ✪ 29.1, 40.4, 46.5 *pret* **empfahl** [ɛm'pfa:l], *ptp* **empfohlen** [ɛm-'pfo:lən] VT to recommend; (*liter:* = *anvertrauen*) to commend (*form*), to entrust; (**jdm**) **etw/jdn ~** to recommend sth/sb (to sb); **~, etw zu tun** to recommend or advise doing sth; **jdm ~, etw zu tun** to recommend or advise sb to do sth; **diese Methode/dieses Restaurant ist sehr zu ~** I would recommend this method/restaurant, this method/restaurant is to be recommended; **ich würde dir Vorsicht/Geduld ~** I would recommend caution/patience, I would advise or recommend you to be cautious/patient; **seinen Geist (dem Herrn) ~** (*liter*) to commend one's soul to the Lord; **bitte, ~ Sie mich Ihrer Frau Gemahlin** (*form*) please convey my respects to your wife (*form*) → *auch* **empfehlen** VR **a sich für Reparaturen/als Experte** *etc* **~** to offer one's services for repairs/as an expert *etc*; **diese Ware empfiehlt sich von selbst** this product is its own recommendation; **es empfiehlt sich, das zu tun** it is advisable to do that **b** (*dated, hum:* = *sich verabschieden*) to take one's leave; **ich empfehle mich!** I'll take my leave; **ich empfehle mich Ihnen** (*am Briefende*) please be sure of my best wishes (*dated form*) → **französisch**

emp|feh|lens|wert ADJ to be recommended, recommendable

Emp|feh|lung F -, -en recommendation; (= *Referenz*) testimonial, reference; (*form:* = *Gruß*) regards *pl*, respects *pl*; **auf ~ von** on the recommendation of; **mit freundlichen** or **den besten ~en** (*am Briefende*) with best regards; **meine ~ an Ihre Frau Gemahlin!** (*form*) my regards or respects to your wife (*form*)

Emp|feh|lungs|schrei|ben NT letter of recommendation, testimonial (*esp Brit*)

emp|fiehlt [ɛm'pfi:lt] 3. *pers sing pres von* **empfehlen**

emp|fin|den [ɛm'pfɪndn] *pret* **empfand** [ɛm'-pfant], *ptp* **empfunden** [ɛm'pfʊndn] VT to feel; **etw als kränkend** or **als Beleidigung ~** to feel sth as an insult, to find sth insulting; **er hat noch nie Hunger empfunden** he has never experienced or known hunger; **er empfand einen solch starken Hunger, dass ...** his hunger was so great that ...; **bei Musik Freude ~** to experience pleasure from music; **ich habe dabei viel Freude empfunden** it gave me great pleasure; **viel/nichts für jdn ~** to feel a lot/nothing for sb; **jdn als (einen) Störenfried ~** to think of

sb as a troublemaker, to feel sb to be a troublemaker

Emp|fin|den NT -s, *no pl* feeling; **meinem ~ nach** to my mind, the way I feel about it

emp|find|lich [ɛm'pfɪntlɪç] ADJ **a** sensitive (*auch Phot, Tech*); *Gesundheit, Stoff, Glas, Keramik etc* delicate; (= *leicht reizbar*) touchy (*inf*), (*over*)sensitive; **~e Stelle** (*lit*) sensitive spot; (*fig auch*) sore point; **gegen etw ~ sein** to be sensitive to sth; **Kupfer ist sehr ~** copper is easily damaged

b (= *spürbar, schmerzlich*) *Verlust, Kälte, Strafe, Niederlage* severe; *Mangel* appreciable

ADV **a** (= *sensibel*) sensitively; **~ reagieren** to be sensitive (*auf +acc* to); **wenn man ihren geschiedenen Mann erwähnt, reagiert sie sehr ~** she is very sensitive to references to her ex-husband

b (= *spürbar*) severely; **deine Kritik hat ihn ~ getroffen** your criticism cut him to the quick (*esp Brit*) or bone (*US*); **es ist ~ kalt** it is bitterly cold

Emp|find|lich|keit F -, -en sensitivity (*auch Phot, Tech*), sensitiveness; (*von Gesundheit, Stoff, Glas, Keramik*) delicateness; (= *leichte Reizbarkeit*) touchiness (*inf*), (*over*)sensitivity

emp|find|sam [ɛm'pfɪntza:m] ADJ *Mensch, Seele, Musik* sensitive; (= *gefühlvoll, Liter*) sentimental

Emp|find|sam|keit F -, *no pl* (= *Empfindlichkeit*: *von Mensch, Seele, Musik*) sensitivity; (*mit starkem Gefühlsausdruck*) sentimentality; **das Zeitalter der ~** (*Liter*) the age of sentimentalism

Emp|fin|dung F -, -en feeling; (= *Sinnesempfindung auch*) sensation; (= *Eindruck, Ahnung auch*) impression

Emp|fin|dungs-: emp|fin|dungs|los ADJ (*lit, fig*) insensitive (*für, gegen* to); *Glieder* numb, without sensation; **Emp|fin|dungs|lo|sig|keit** F -, *no pl* (*lit, fig*) insensitivity; (*der Glieder*) numbness, loss of sensation; **Emp|fin|dungs|ner|ven** PL (*Physiol*) sensory nerves *pl*; **Emp|fin|dungs|ver|mö|gen** NT , *no pl* faculty of sensation; (*in Gliedern*) sensation; (*fig*) sensitivity, ability to feel; **~ für etw** ability to feel or sense sth; (*fig*) sensitivity to sth; **Emp|fin|dungs|wort** NT *pl* -wörter (*Gram*) interjection

emp|fing *pret von* **empfangen**

emp|foh|len *ptp von* **empfehlen** ADJ (**sehr** or **gut**) **~** (highly) recommended

emp|fun|den *ptp von* **empfinden**

Em|pha|se [ɛm'fa:zə] F (*geh*) emphasis

em|pha|tisch [ɛm'fa:tɪʃ] (*geh*) ADJ emphatic ADV emphatically

Em|phy|sem [ɛmfy'ze:m] NT -s, -e (*Med*) emphysema

Em|pire¹ [ã'pi:ɐ] NT -(s), *no pl* (*Hist*) Empire; (= *Empirestil*) Empire style

Em|pire² ['ɛmpaɪɐ] NT -(s), *no pl* (British) Empire

Em|pire|stil [ã'pi:ɐ-] M Empire style

Em|pi|rik [ɛm'pi:rɪk] F -, *no pl* empirical experience

Em|pi|ri|ker [ɛm'pi:rikɐ] M -s, -, **Em|pi|ri|ke|rin** [-ərɪn] F -, -nen empiricist

em|pi|risch [ɛm'pi:rɪʃ] ADJ empirical

Em|pi|ris|mus [ɛmpi'rɪsmʊs] M -, *no pl* (*Philos, Sci*) empiricism

em|por [ɛm'po:ɐ] ADV (*liter*) upwards, up; **zum Licht ~** up(wards) toward(s) the light; **~ die Herzen/Blicke!** lift up your hearts/eyes! (*liter*) → *auch* **hinauf**

em|por-: em|por+ar|bei|ten VR *sep* (*geh*) to work one's way up; **em|por+bli|cken** VI *sep* (*liter*) to raise one's eyes; (*fig*) to look up (*zu* to)

Em|po|re [ɛm'po:rə] F -, -n (*Archit*) gallery

em|pö|ren [ɛm'pø:rən] *ptp* **empört** VT to fill with indignation, to outrage; (*stärker*) to incense → *auch* **empört** VR **a** (*über +acc* at) to be indignant or outraged; (*stärker*) to be incensed;

das ist unerhört! empörte sich der Schulmeister that's scandalous!, said the schoolmaster indignantly **b** (*liter: = sich auflehnen*) to rise (up) or rebel (*gegen* against)

em|pö|rend ADJ outrageous, scandalous

Em|pö|rer [ɛm'pøːrɐ] M **-s, -, Em|pö|re|rin** [-ərɪn] F **-, -nen** (*liter*) rebel, insurrectionist

em|pö|re|risch [ɛm'pøːrərɪʃ] ADJ (*liter*) rebellious, insurrectionary

em|por-: em|por+he|ben VT *sep irreg* (*geh*) to raise, to lift up; **jdn über andere ~** (*fig*) to raise or elevate sb above others; **em|por+kom|men** VI *sep irreg aux sein* (*geh*) to rise (up); (*fig*) (= *aufkommen*) to come to the fore; (= *vorankommen*) to go up or rise in the world, to get on; **nur an sein Emporkommen denken** (*fig*) to think only of one's advancement; **Em|por|kömm|ling** [ɛm'pøːrkœmlɪŋ] M **-s, -e** (*pej*) upstart, parvenu; **em|por+lo|dern** VI *sep aux sein or haben* (*liter*) to blaze or flare upwards; **em|por+ra|gen** VI *sep aux haben or sein* (*geh*) to tower (**über** +*acc* above); **em|por+re|cken** *sep* **VT** (*liter*) Faust to raise aloft **VR** to stretch upwards; **em|por+schau|en** VI *sep* (*geh*) to raise one's eyes; (*fig*) to look up (**zu** to); **em|por+schie|ßen** VI *sep irreg aux sein* (*geh*) **a** (= *häufig werden*) to shoot up, to spring up; (*Neubauten etc auch*) to mushroom **b** (= *aufspringen, Person, Tier*) to jump or spring or leap up or to one's feet **c** (= *schnell an Höhe gewinnen, Wasserstrahl*) to gush up; (*Flugzeug etc*) to shoot up; **em|por+schwe|ben** VI *sep aux sein* (*geh*) to float upwards or aloft (*liter*); **em|por+schwin|gen** VR *sep irreg* (*geh*) to soar upwards or aloft (*liter*); (*Turner*) to swing upwards; **sich zu etw ~** (*fig*) to (come to) achieve sth; **zu einer Stellung to reach sth**; **em|por+stei|gen** *sep irreg aux sein* (*geh*) **VT** to climb (up) **VI** to climb (up); (*Mond, Angst etc*) to rise (up); (*fig: = Karriere machen*) to climb, to rise; **em|por+stre|ben** VI *sep aux sein* (*geh*) to soar upwards; (*fig*) *aux haben* to be ambitious

em|pört [ɛm'pøːrt] ADJ **a** (highly) indignant, outraged (*über* +*acc* at); (= *schockiert*) outraged, scandalized **b** (*liter: in Auflehnung*) rebellious **ADV** indignantly → *auch* **empören**

em|por+trei|ben VT *sep irreg* (*geh*) to drive up

Em|pö|rung [ɛm'pøːrʊŋ] F **-, -en** **a** *no pl* (= *Entrüstung*) indignation (*über* +*acc* at); **über etw in ~ geraten** to become or get indignant about sth **b** (*liter: = Aufstand*) rebellion, uprising

em|por-: em|por+zie|hen *sep irreg* (*geh*) **VT** to draw or pull up **VI** *aux sein* to draw upwards; **em|por+zün|geln** VI *sep aux sein* (*liter: Flammen*) to leap up(wards) or aloft (*liter*)

em|sig ['ɛmzɪç] ADJ busy, industrious; (= *eifrig*) eager, keen; (= *geschäftig*) bustling *attr*, busy **ADV** industriously, busily; (= *eifrig*) eagerly

Em|sig|keit F **-, no pl** industry, industriousness; (= *Eifrigkeit*) eagerness, zeal; (= *Geschäftigkeit*) bustle

Emu ['eːmu] M **-s, -s** emu

Emu|la|ti|on [emulaˈtsi̯oːn] F **-, -en** (*esp Comput*) emulation

Emul|ga|tor [emʊlˈɡaːtoːɐ] M **-s, Emulgatoren** [-'toːrən] (*Chem*) emulsifier, emulsifying agent

emul|gie|ren [emʊlˈɡiːrən] *ptp* **emulgiert** VTI to emulsify

emu|lie|ren [emuˈliːrən] *ptp* **emuliert** VT (*esp Comput*) to emulate

Emul|si|on [emʊlˈzi̯oːn] F **-, -en** emulsion

Emul|si|ons-: Emul|si|ons|far|be F emulsion (paint); **Emul|si|ons|mit|tel** NT emulsifier

E-Mu|sik ['eː-] F serious music

en bloc [ã 'blɔk] ADV en bloc

End- *in cpds* final; **End|ab|neh|mer(in)** M(F) end buyer; **End|ab|rech|nung** F final account; **End|an|wen|der(in)** M(F) (*Comput*) end user; **End|aus|schei|dung** F (*Sport*) final elimination (round); **End|bahn|hof** M terminus, terminal; **End|be|nut|zer(in)** M(F) end

user; **End|be|tont** ADJ *Wort* with final stress; **End|be|trag** M final amount

End|chen ['ɛntçən] NT **-s, -** (*inf*) (small) piece, bit; (*eines Weges*) short distance, little way

En|de ['ɛndə] ◊ 53.4 NT **-s, -n** end; (*eines Jahrhunderts etc auch*) close; (= *Ausgang, Ergebnis*) outcome, result; (= *Ausgang eines Films, Romans etc*) ending; (*Hunt: = Geweihende*) point; (*inf: = Stückchen*) piece; (*inf: = Strecke*) way, stretch; (*Naut: = Tau*) (rope's) end; **~ Mai/der Woche** at the end of May/the week; **~ der zwanziger Jahre** or **Zwanzigerjahre** in the late twenties; **er ist ~ vierzig** he is in his late forties; **das ~ der Welt** the end of the world; **er wohnt am ~ der Welt** (*inf*) he lives at the back of beyond, he lives in the middle of nowhere; **bis ans ~ der Welt** to the ends of the earth; **das ~ vom Lied** the final outcome; **das ~ der Fahnenstange** (*fig inf*) the end of the road; **ein ~ mit Schrecken** a terrible or dreadful end; **lieber ein ~ mit Schrecken als ein Schrecken ohne ~** (*Prov*) it's best to get unpleasant things over and done with; **Probleme ohne ~** endless problems; **letzten ~s** when all is said and done, after all; (= *am Ende*) in the end, at the end of the day; **einer Sache** (*dat*) **ein ~ machen** to put an end to sth; (**bei** or **mit etw**) **kein ~ finden** (*inf*) to be unable to stop (sth or telling/doing etc sth); **damit muss es jetzt ein ~ haben** there has to be an end to this now, this must stop now; **ein ~ nehmen** to come to an end; **das nimmt** or **findet gar kein ~** (*inf*) there's no sign of it stopping, there's no end to it; **ein böses ~ nehmen** to come to a bad end; **kein ~ ist abzusehen** there's no end in sight; **da ist das ~ von weg!** (*N Ger inf*) it's incredible! (*inf*); **... und kein ~ ...** with no end in sight, ... without end; **es war des Staunens/Jubels etc kein ~** (*old, liter*) there was no end to the surprise/celebrations etc; **es ist noch ein gutes** or **ganzes ~** (*inf*) there's still quite a way to go (yet); **am ~** at the end; (= *schließlich*) in the end; (*inf: = möglicherweise*) perhaps; **(am) ~ des Monats** at the end of the month; **am ~ sein** (*fig*) to be at the end of one's tether (*Brit*) or rope (*US*); **mit etw am ~ sein** to be at the end of sth, to have reached the end of sth; (*Vorrat*) to have run out of sth; **ich bin mit meiner Weisheit am ~** I'm at my wits' end; **meine Geduld ist am ~** my patience is at an end; **ein Problem am richtigen/falschen** or **verkehrten ~ anfassen** to tackle a problem from the right/wrong end; **Leiden ohne ~** endless suffering, suffering without end; **das ist eine Kette** or **Schraube ohne ~** (*fig*) it's an endless spiral; **zu ~** finished, over, at an end; **etw zu ~ bringen** or **führen** to finish (off) sth; **ein Buch/einen Brief zu ~ lesen/schreiben** to finish (reading/writing) a book/letter; **etw zu einem guten ~ bringen** or **führen** to bring sth to a satisfactory conclusion; **zu ~ gehen** to come to an end; (*Vorräte*) to run low; **zu dem ~, dass ...** (*obs*) to the end that ... (*form*); **zu diesem ~** (*obs*) to this end (*form*); **~ gut, alles gut** (*Prov*) all's well that ends well (*Prov*); **es hat alles einmal ein ~** (*Prov*) everything must come to an end some time; (*angenehme Dinge*) all good things must come to an end (*Prov*) → **dick** ADJ c

End|ef|fekt M **im ~** (*inf*) in the end, in the final analysis

en|deln ['ɛndln] VT (*Aus*) *Saum* to whip, to oversew

En|de|mie [ɛndeˈmiː] F **-, -n** [-'miːən] (*Med*) endemic disease

en|de|misch [ɛnˈdeːmɪʃ] ADJ (*Med*) endemic

en|den ['ɛndn] VI to end, to finish; (*Frist auch*) to run out, to expire; (*Zug*) to terminate; (= *sterben*) to meet one's end; **auf etw** (*acc*) or **mit etw ~** (*Wort*) to end with sth; **mit den Worten ... ~** (*bei Rede*) to close with the words ...; **es endete damit, dass ...** the outcome was that ...; **der Streit endete vor Gericht** the quarrel ended up in court; **er endete im Gefängnis** he ended up

in prison; **wie wird das noch mit ihm ~?** what will become of him?; **das wird böse ~!** no good will come of it!; **er wird schlimm ~** he will come to a bad end; **nicht ~ wollend** unending

End-: End|er|geb|nis NT final result; **End|fas|sung** F (*von Text, Film*) final version; **End|ge|halt** F *(von Text, Film)* final salary; **end|geil** ADJ (*sl*) shithot (*Brit sl*), wicked (*sl*); **End|ge|rät** NT (*Telec etc*) terminal; **End|ge|schwin|dig|keit** F terminal velocity

end|gül|tig ADJ final; *Beweis auch* conclusive; *Antwort* definite; **etwas Endgültiges lässt sich noch nicht sagen** I/we *etc* cannot say anything definite at this stage **ADV** finally; **sich ~ entscheiden** to make the final decision; **damit ist die Sache ~ entschieden** that settles the matter once and for all; **das ist ~ aus** or **vorbei** that's (all) over and done with; **sie haben sich jetzt ~ getrennt** they've separated for good; **jetzt ist ~ Schluss!** that's the end!, that's it!

End|gül|tig|keit F **-, no pl** (*Math, Philos*) finality; (*von Antwort*) definitiveness

End|hal|te|stel|le F terminus, terminal, final stop (*US*)

En|di|vie [ɛnˈdiːvi̯ə] F **-, -n** endive

En|di|vi|en|sa|lat [ɛnˈdiːvi̯ən-] M **a** (*Pflanze*) endive **b** (*Salat*) endive salad

End-: End|kampf M (*Mil*) final battle; (*Sport*) final; (= *Endphase*) (*Mil*) final stages *pl* (of a battle); (*Sport*) final stages *pl* (of a contest); **End|la|ger** NT (*für Atommüll etc*) permanent (waste) disposal site; **end|la|gern** VT *insep Atommüll etc* to dispose of *sth* permanently; **End|la|ge|rung** F (*von Atommüll etc*) permanent (waste) disposal; **End|lauf** M final; **End|lauf|teil|neh|mer(in)** M(F) finalist

end|lich ['ɛntlɪç] ADJ **a** (*Math, Philos*) finite **b** (*rare: = lang erwartet, schließlich*) eventual **ADV** finally, at last; (= *am Ende*) eventually, in the end, finally; **na ~!** at (long) last!; **hör ~ damit auf!** will you stop that!; **komm doch ~!** come on, get a move on!; **~ kam er doch** he eventually came after all, in the end he came (after all)

End|lich|keit F **-, no pl** (*Math, Philos*) finiteness, finite nature

end|los ADJ endless; (= *langwierig auch*) interminable; **(sich) bis ins Endlose (erstrecken)** (to stretch) to infinity **ADV** forever; **ich musste ~ lange warten** I had to wait for an interminably long time, I had to wait for ages (*inf*)

End|lo|sig|keit F **-, no pl** endlessness, infinite nature; (= *Langwierigkeit*) interminable nature

End-: End|los|pa|pier NT **, no pl** continuous paper; **End|lö|sung** F **die ~** the Final Solution (*extermination of the Jews by the Nazis*); **End|mon|ta|ge** F final assembly; **End|mo|rä|ne** F terminal moraine

En|do- *in cpds* endo-; **en|do|gen** [ɛndoˈɡeːn] ADJ (*Biol, Psych*) endogenous; **en|do|krin** [ɛndoˈkriːn] ADJ (*Med*) endocrine; **En|do|kri|no|lo|gie** [ɛndokrinoloˈɡiː] F **-, no pl** (*Med*) endocrinology

En|dor|phin [ɛndɔrˈfiːn] NT **-s, -e** endorphin

En|do|skop [ɛndoˈskoːp] NT **-s, -e** (*Med*) endoscope

En|do|sko|pie [ɛndoskoˈpiː] F **-, -n** [-'piːən] (*Med*) endoscopy; **operative ~** endosurgery

en|do|sko|pisch [ɛndoˈskoːpɪʃ] (*Med*) ADJ endoscopic **ADV** **jdn ~ operieren/untersuchen** to operate on/examine sb using endoscopy or an endoscope

End-: End|pha|se F final stage(s *pl*); **End|preis** M final price; **End|pro|dukt** NT end or final product; **End|punkt** M (*lit, fig*) end; (*von Buslinie etc auch*) terminus, terminal, final stop (*US*); **End|reim** M (*Liter*) end rhyme; **End|re|sul|tat** NT final result

End|run|de F (*Sport*) finals *pl*; (*Leichtathletik, Autorennen*) final lap; (*Boxen, fig*) final round

End|run|den-: **End|run|den|spiel** NT final (match); **End|run|den|teil|neh|mer(in)** M(F) finalist

End-: **End|see** M (Geog) lake without an outlet; **End|sieg** M final or ultimate victory; **End|sil|be** F final syllable; **End|spiel** NT (Sport) final; (Chess) end game; **End|spurt** M (Sport, fig) final spurt; **End|sta|di|um** NT final or (Med) terminal stage; **End|stand** M (Sport: = Punktstand) final result or score; (Rennen etc) final positions pl, final ranking(s pl); **End|sta|ti|on** F (Rail etc) terminus, terminal; (fig) end of the line; **End|stel|le** F (Tech) terminal apparatus; **End|stu|fe** F final stage; **End|sum|me** F (sum) total

En|dung ['ɛndʊŋ] F -, -en (Gram) ending

en|dungs|los ADJ (Gram) without an ending

En|du|ro [ɛn'du:ro] F -, -s enduro bike

End-: **End|ur|sa|che** ['ɛntluːrzaxə] F ultimate cause; (Philos) final cause; **End|ur|teil** ['ɛntluːr-tail] NT final verdict or judgement; **End|ver-brau|cher(in)** M(F) consumer, end user; **End|vier|zi|ger(in)** M(F) (inf) man/woman in his/her late forties; **End|zeit** F last days pl; **end|zeit|lich** ADJ attr Phase final; Stimmung, Prophezeiung apocalyptic; **End|zeit|stim|mung** F apocalyptic mood; **End|ziel** NT ultimate goal or aim; **End|zif|fer** F final number; **End-zu|stand** M final state; **End|zweck** M ultimate aim or purpose

E|ner|ge|tik [enɛr'ge:tɪk] F -, no pl (Phys) energetics sing

e|ner|ge|tisch [enɛr'ge:tɪʃ] ADJ (Phys) energetic

E|ner|gie [enɛr'gi:] F -, -n [-'gi:ən] (Sci, fig) energy; (= Schwung auch) vigour (Brit), vigor (US), vitality; **~ sparend** energy-saving; **seine ganze ~ für etw einsetzen** or **aufbieten** to devote all one's energies to sth; **mit aller** or **ganzer ~** with all one's energy or energies; **kriminelle ~** criminal resolve

E|ner|gie-: **e|ner|gie|arm** ADJ Nahrung low-energy attr; **ein ~es Land** a country with few sources of energy; **E|ner|gie|auf|wand** M energy expenditure, expenditure of energy, (amount of) energy involved; **der ~ lohnt (sich) nicht** it's not worth the effort (involved); **E|ner|gie|be|darf** M energy requirement; **e|ner|gie|be|wusst** ▲ ADJ energy-conscious; **E|ner|gie|bi|lanz** F (Phys) energy budget or balance; **E|ner|gie|dich|te** F (Phys) energy density; **E|ner|gie|drink** M energy drink; **e|ner-gie|ef|fi|zi|ent** ADJ energy-efficient; **E|ner-gie|ef|fi|zi|enz** F energy efficiency; **E|ner-gie|farm** F (Tech) energy farm; **e|ner|gie|ge-la|den** ADJ full of energy, energetic; **E|ner-gie|ge|win|nung** F generation of energy; **E|ner|gie|haus|halt** M (Physiol) energy balance; **e|ner|gie|in|ten|siv** ADJ energy-intensive; **E|ner|gie|knapp|heit** F energy shortage; **E|ner|gie|kri|se** F energy crisis; **e|ner|gie-los** ADJ lacking in energy, weak; **E|ner|gie|lo-sig|keit** F -, no pl lack of energy; **E|ner|gie|po|li-tik** F energy policy; **e|ner|gie|po|li|tisch** ADJ energy-policy attr; Konsens, Parteilinie, Sprecher on energy policy; **E|ner|gie|prin|zip** NT principle of the conservation of energy; **E|ner-gie|quel|le** F energy source; **e|ner|gie|reich** ADJ Strahlung, Partikel energy-rich; **E|ner|gie-re|ser|ven** PL (Sport etc) energy reserves pl; (von Person) spare energy sing, physical reserves pl; **E|ner|gie|satz** M (Phys) principle of the conservation of energy; **E|ner|gie|spa|ren** NT -s, no pl energy saving; (Maßnahmen) energy saving measures pl; **e|ner|gie|spa|rend** △ ADJ → Energie

E|ner|gie|spar-: **E|ner|gie|spar|lam|pe** F energy-saving bulb; **E|ner|gie|spar|maß|nah-men** PL energy-saving measures pl; **E|ner-gie|spar|pro|gramm** NT energy-saving scheme or programme (Brit) or program (US); **E|ner|gie|spar|tas|te** F (von Waschmaschine, Geschirrspüler etc) energy-saving switch

E|ner|gie-: **E|ner|gie|tech|nik** F energy--producing technique; **E|ner|gie|trä|ger** M energy source; **E|ner|gie|ver|brauch** M energy consumption; **E|ner|gie|ver|schwen|dung** F waste of energy; **E|ner|gie|ver|sor|gung** F supply of energy; **E|ner|gie|ver|sor|gungs-un|ter|neh|men** NT energy supply company; **E|ner|gie|wirt|schaft** F (= Wirtschaftszweig) energy industry; **e|ner|gie|wirt|schaft|lich** ADJ relating to the energy industry; **E|ner|gie-zu|fuhr** F energy supply

e|ner|gisch [e'nɛrgɪʃ] ADJ (= voller Energie) energetic; (= entschlossen, streng) forceful, firm; Griff, Maßnahmen vigorous, firm; Worte forceful, strong; Protest energetic, strong; **einer Sache** (dat) **eine ~e Absage erteilen** to forcefully reject sth; **~ werden** to assert oneself or one's authority; **wenn das nicht aufhört, werde ich ~!** if this doesn't stop I'll have to put my foot down!

ADV dementieren strongly, strenuously, emphatically; sagen forcefully; verteidigen vigorously; **~ durchgreifen** to take vigorous or firm action, to act vigorously or firmly; **etw ~ betonen** to stress or emphasize sth strongly

e|ner|vie|ren [enɛr'vi:rən] ptp **enerviert** VT (old) to enervate (form)

en fa|mille [ã fa'mij] ADV (geh) en famille

En|fant ter|ri|ble [ãfã tɛ'ribl] NT -, -s -s (geh) enfant terrible

eng [ɛŋ] ADJ **a** (= schmal) Straße etc narrow; (= beengt) Raum cramped, confined; (= eng anliegend) Kleidung tight, close-fitting; (= ärmlich) Verhältnisse straitened, reduced; (= beschränkt) Horizont, Moralbegriff narrow, limited, restricted; **ein Kleid ~er machen** to take a dress in; **im ~eren Sinne** in the narrow sense; **in die ~ere Wahl kommen** to be put on the short list, to be short-listed; **ein ~erer Ausschuss** a select committee

b (= nah, dicht, vertraut) close; **eine Feier im ~sten Kreise** a small party for close friends; **die Hochzeit fand im ~sten Kreise der Familie statt** the wedding was celebrated with just the immediate family present; **die ~ere Heimat** one's home area, the area (where) one comes from

ADV **a** (= mit wenig Platz) **~ beieinander stehen** to stand very close to each other; **~ beisammen stehen** to stand close together; (Bäume etc) to be close together; **~ anliegend** tight(-fitting), close-fitting; **~ anliegen** to fit tightly; **~ sitzen** to be tight; **~ begrenzt** restricted, narrow; **~ ge-baut sein** (Anat) to be narrow-hipped, to have narrow hips; **~ gebaute Frauen** women with narrow hips; **in dem Zimmer standen wir sehr ~** we were very crowded in the room; **~ zusam-mengedrängt sein** to be crowded together

b (= dicht) tanzen close together; **~ bedruckt** densely printed; **~ beschrieben** closely written; **~ nebeneinander** or **zusammen** close together

c (= intim) **~ liiert** seriously involved; **sich ~ anfreunden** to become close friends; **aufs Engs-te** or **~ste befreundet sein** to be on the closest possible terms; **~ befreundet sein** to be close friends; **mit jdm ~ befreundet sein** to be a close friend of sb; **die ~ befreundeten Mädchen/Män-ner** the close friends

d (inf. = verkniffen) **das darfst du nicht so ~ se-hen** (fig inf) don't take it so seriously; **solche Dinge sehe ich sehr ~** I'm very particular about that type of thing; **sieh das doch nicht so ~!** don't take it so seriously!, don't make so much of it!; **es wird ~ für ihn** (fig inf) he doesn't have much room for manoeuvre (Brit) or maneuver (US)

En|ga|din ['ɛŋgadi:n] NT -s das ~ the Engadine

En|ga|ge|ment [ãgaʒə'mã:] NT -s, -s **a** (Theat) engagement **b** (geh: = Aktivität) involvement, engagement; (= politisches Engagement) commitment (für to)

en|ga|gie|ren [ãga'ʒi:rən] ptp **engagiert** VT to engage VR to be/become committed (für to); (in einer Beziehung) to get involved; **er hat**

sich sehr dafür engagiert, dass ... he completely committed himself to ...

en|ga|giert [ãga'ʒi:ɛt] ADJ committed; **~e Lite-ratur** (politically/socially) committed literature

En|ga|giert|heit F -, no pl commitment (für to); (in einer Beziehung) involvement

eng-: **eng|an|lie|gend** △ ADJ attr → **eng** ADV a; **eng|be|druckt** △ [-bədrʊkt] ADJ attr → **eng** ADV b; **eng|be|freun|det** △ ADJ attr → **eng** ADV c; **eng|be|grenzt** △ ADJ attr → **eng** ADV a; **eng|be|schrie|ben** △ [-bəʃriːbn] ADJ attr → **eng** ADV b; **eng|brüs|tig** [-brʏstɪç] ADJ narrow-chested

En|ge ['ɛŋə] F -, -n **a** no pl (von Straße etc) narrowness; (von Wohnung) confinement; (= Ge-drängtheit) crush; (von Kleid etc) tightness; (fig) (= Ärmlichkeit) straitened circumstances pl, poverty; (= Beschränktheit) narrowness, limited or restricted nature **b** (= Meerenge) strait; (= Eng-pass) pass, defile; **jdn in die ~ treiben** (fig) to drive sb into a corner

En|gel ['ɛŋl] M -s, - (lit, fig) angel; **ein rettender ~** (fig) a saviour (Brit) or savior (US); **ein guter ~** (fig) a guardian angel; **ich hörte die ~ im Him-mel singen** (inf) it hurt like anything (inf), it was agony; **er ist auch nicht gerade ein ~** (inf) he's no angel (inf); **wir sind alle keine ~** (prov) none of us is perfect

En|gel|chen ['ɛŋlçən] NT -s, -, **En|ge|lein** ['ɛŋəlain] NT -s, - little angel

En|gel- → auch Engels-: **en|gel|gleich** ADJ = engelsgleich; **En|gel|ma|cher(in)** M(F) (euph inf) backstreet abortionist; **En|gel|schar** F host of angels, angelic host

En|gels-: **En|gels|ge|duld** F saintly patience; **sie hat eine ~** she has the patience of a saint; **En|gels|ge|sicht** NT angelic or angel('s) face, angelic looks pl; **en|gels|gleich** ADJ angelic; **En|gels|haar** NT angel's hair; **en|gels|rein** ADJ pure as the driven snow; **En|gels|trom-pe|te** F (Bot) angel's trumpet; **En|gels|zun-gen** PL (wie) **mit ~ reden** to use all one's powers of persuasion

En|gel|wurz [-vʊrts] F -, -en (Bot) angelica

En|ger|ling ['ɛŋɐlɪŋ] M -s, -e (Zool) grub or larva of the cockchafer or May bug

Eng-: **eng|her|zig** ADJ petty, hidebound; **Eng-her|zig|keit** F -, no pl pettiness

engl. abbr von englisch

Eng|land ['ɛŋlant] NT -s England

Eng|län|der ['ɛŋlɛndɐ] M -s, - **a** Englishman; English boy; **die ~** pl the English, the Britishers (US), the Brits (inf); **er ist ~** he's English **b** (Tech) adjustable spanner (Brit), monkey wrench

Eng|län|de|rin ['ɛŋlɛndərɪn] F -, -nen Englishwoman; English girl

Eng|lein NT -s, - little angel

eng|lisch¹ ['ɛŋlɪʃ] ADJ English; Steak rare; **die ~e Krankheit** (dated Med) rickets sing; (fig) the English disease or sickness; **die Englische Kir-che** the Anglican Church, the Church of England; **die Englischen Fräulein** (Eccl) institute of Catholic nuns for the education of girls **~e Broschur** case binding → auch deutsch

eng|lisch² ADJ (Bibl) angelic; **der Englische Gruß** the Angelic Salutation, the Ave Maria, the Hail Mary

Eng|lisch(e) ['ɛŋlɪʃ] NT English → auch Deutsch(e)

Eng|lisch-: **eng|lisch-deutsch/-fran|zö|sisch** etc ADJ Anglo-German/-French etc; Wörterbuch English-German/-French etc; **Eng|lisch|horn** NT (Mus) cor anglais; **Eng|lisch|kennt|nis|se** PL (a knowledge sing of) English, English language skills pl; **seine/ihre ~** his/her knowledge of English; **gute ~ Voraussetzung** (in Annoncen) English essential; **Eng|lisch|le|der** NT (Tex) moleskin; **Eng|lisch|leh|rer(in)** M(F) English teacher; (Privatlehrer auch) English tutor; **eng-lisch|spra|chig** ADJ Gebiet, Minderheit English-

-speaking; *Zeitung* English-language *attr*; **Eng·lisch·tra·ben** NT **-s**, *no pl* rising trot; **Eng·lisch·un·ter·richt** M **a** English lessons *pl*, English classes *pl*; (= *einzelne Stunde*) English lesson *or* class **b** (*Unterrichten*) teaching of English; (*Privat-, Einzelunterricht*) English language tuition; **der ~** teaching English, the teaching of English

Eng·: eng·ma·schig [-maʃɪç] **ADJ** close-meshed; (*fig*) close; **ein ~es soziales Netz** a comprehensive social welfare network **ADV ~ stricken** to knit to a fine tension; **Eng·pass ▲** M (narrow) pass, defile; (= *Fahrbahnverengung, fig*) bottleneck

En·gramm [ɛnˈgram] NT *pl* **-gramme** (*Physiol*) engram

en gros [ã ˈgro] ADV wholesale; (*fig*) en masse

En·gros- [ã·gro] *in cpds* = **Großhandels-**

En·gros·sist(in) [ãgroˈsɪst(ɪn)] M(F) (*Aus*) wholesale dealer, wholesaler

Eng·stel·le F narrow place, constriction; (= *Fahrbahnverengung, fig*) bottleneck

eng·stir·nig [ˈɛŋʃtɪrnɪç] ADJ (= *intolerant*) narrow-minded; (= *mit begrenztem Horizont*) insular; (*im politischen Denken*) parochial

Eng·stir·nig·keit F (= *Intoleranz*) narrow-mindedness; (= *begrenzter Horizont*) insularity; (*im politischen Denken*) parochialism

e·nig·ma·tisch [eniˈgma:tɪʃ] ADJ (*liter*) enigmatic

En·jam·be·ment [ãʒãbəˈmãː] NT **-s, -s** (*Poet*) enjambment

En·kel¹ [ˈɛŋkl] M **-s, -** (= *Enkelkind*) grandchild; (= *Enkelsohn*) grandson; (= *Nachfahr*) descendant; (*fig*) heir; **er ist ~ eines berühmten Geschlechts** (*geh*) he comes from a famous family or line

En·kel² M **-s, -** (*dial*) ankle

En·ke·lin [ˈɛŋkəlɪn] F **-, -nen** granddaughter

En·kel-: En·kel·kind NT grandchild; **En·kel·sohn** M grandson; **En·kel·toch·ter** F granddaughter

En·kla·ve [ɛnˈkla:və] F **-, -n** enclave

en masse [ã ˈmas] ADV en masse

en mi·ni·a·ture [ã minjaˈtyːr] ADV (*geh*) in miniature

e·norm [eˈnɔrm] **ADJ** (= *riesig*) enormous; (*inf: = herrlich, kolossal*) tremendous (*inf*); **~e Hitze/Kälte** tremendous heat/cold **ADV** (= *riesig*) enormously; (*inf: = herrlich, kolossal*) tremendously; (= *enorm viel*) an enormous amount; **er verdient ~** (*inf*) **er verdient ~ viel (Geld)** (*inf*) he earns an enormous amount (of money)

en pas·sant [ã paˈsã] ADV en passant, in passing

En·que·te [ãˈkeːt(ə), ãˈkɛːt(ə)] F **-, -n** (*form*) survey; (*Aus: = Arbeitstagung*) symposium

En·que·te·kom·mis·si·on [ãˈkeːt-, ãˈkɛːt-] F commission of inquiry, select committee

En·sem·ble [ãˈsãːbl] NT **-s, -s** ensemble; (= *Besetzung*) cast

En·sem·ble·spiel [ãˈsãːbl-] NT (*Theat*) ensemble

ent·ar·ten [ɛntˈartn] *ptp* **entartet** VI *aux sein* to degenerate (*zu* into)

ent·ar·tet [ɛntˈartət] ADJ degenerate

Ent·ar·tung F **-, -en** degeneration

Ent·ar·tungs·er·schei·nung F symptom *or* sign of degeneration

ent·äu·ßern [ɛntˈɔysən] *ptp* **entäußert** VR **sich einer Sache** (*gen*) **~** (*geh*) to relinquish sth, to divest oneself of sth (*form*); **sich ~** (*Philos*) to be realized

ent·beh·ren [ɛntˈbeːrən] *ptp* **entbehrt** VT **a** (= *vermissen*) to miss; (*auch vi: = verzichten*) to do or manage without; (= *zur Verfügung stellen*) to spare **b** *auch vi* (= *verzichten*) to do or manage without; **wir haben jahrelang ~ müssen** for years we had/we have had to do or go without;

wir **können ihn heute nicht ~** we cannot spare him/it today **VI** (= *fehlen*) **einer Sache** (*gen*) **~** (*geh*) to lack sth, to be devoid of sth

ent·behr·lich [ɛntˈbeːɐlɪç] ADJ dispensable

Ent·behr·lich·keit F **-**, *no pl* dispensability

Ent·beh·rung F **-, -en** privation, deprivation, want *no pl*; **~en auf sich** (*acc*) **nehmen** to make sacrifices

ent·beh·rungs·reich, ent·beh·rungs·voll ADJ full of privation; **die ~en Kriegsjahre** the deprivation of the war years

ent·bei·nen [ɛntˈbainən] *ptp* **entbeint** VT *Fleisch* to bone

ent·bie·ten [ɛntˈbiːtn] *ptp* **entboten** [ɛntˈboːtn] VT *irreg* (*form*) (**jdm) seinen Gruß ~** (*old*) to present one's compliments (to sb) (*form*); **der Vorsitzende entbot der Delegation herzliche Willkommensgrüße** the Chairman *or* the Chair welcomed the delegation cordially

ent·bin·den [ɛntˈbɪndn] *ptp* **entbunden** [ɛntˈbʊndn] *irreg* **VT a** *Frau* to deliver; **sie ist von einem Sohn entbunden worden** she has given birth to a son, she has been delivered of a son (*liter, old*) **b** (= *befreien: von Versprechen, Amt etc*) to release (*von* from) **VI** (*Frau*) to give birth

Ent·bin·dung F delivery, birth; (*von Amt etc*) release

Ent·bin·dungs-: Ent·bin·dungs·heim NT maternity home *or* hospital; **Ent·bin·dungs·kli·nik** F maternity clinic; **Ent·bin·dungs·pfle·ger(in)** M(F) obstetric nurse; **Ent·bin·dungs·sta·ti·on** F maternity ward

ent·blät·tern [ɛntˈblɛtn] *ptp* **entblättert** VT to strip (of leaves) **VR** to shed its/their leaves; (*hum inf*) to strip, to shed one's clothes

ent·blö·den [ɛntˈbløːdn] *ptp* **entblödet** VR (*geh*) **sich nicht ~, etw zu tun** to have the effrontery *or* audacity to do sth, to do sth unashamedly

ent·blö·ßen [ɛntˈbløːsn] *ptp* **entblößt** VT (*form*) **a** *Körperteil* to bare, to expose (*auch Mil*); *Kopf* to bare, to uncover; *Schwert* to draw, to unsheathe; (*fig*) *sein Innenleben* to lay bare, to reveal; **er hat sich entblößt** (*Exhibitionist*) he exposed himself; (*seinen wahren Charakter*) he showed his true colours (*Brit*) *or* colors (*US*) **b** (*liter. = des Schutzes berauben*) to divest, to denude (*form*)

ent·blößt [ɛntˈbløːst] ADJ bare

Ent·blö·ßung F **-, -en** (*von Körperteil etc*) baring, exposure; (*Mil*) exposure; (*von Innenleben*) laying bare, revelation

ent·bren·nen [ɛntˈbrɛnən] *ptp* **entbrannt** [ɛntˈbrant] VI *irreg aux sein* (*liter*) (*Kampf, Streit, Zorn*) to flare up, to erupt; (*Leidenschaft, Liebe*) to be (a)roused; **in heißer Liebe zu jdm ~ für jdm ~** to fall passionately in love with sb; **in** *or* **von Leidenschaft/Wut ~** to become inflamed with passion/anger

ent·bü·ro·kra·ti·sie·ren [ɛntbyrokratiˈziːrən] *ptp* **entbürokratisiert** VT to free of *or* from bureaucracy, to debureaucratize

Ent·bü·ro·kra·ti·sie·rung F **-, -en** freeing from bureaucracy, debureaucratization

Ent·chen [ˈɛntçən] NT **-s, -** *dim von* **Ente** duckling

ent·de·cken [ɛntˈdɛkn] *ptp* **entdeckt** VT **a** (= *finden*) to discover; *Fehler* to discover, to detect, to spot; (*in der Ferne*) to discern, to spot; (*in einer Menge*) to spot **b** (*old: = offenbaren*) **jdm etw ~** to reveal *or* discover (*obs*) sth to sb **VR** **sich jdm ~** (*old*) to reveal *or* discover (*obs*) oneself to sb (*form*)

Ent·de·cker [ɛntˈdɛkɐ] M **-s, -**, **Ent·de·cke·rin** [-ərɪn] F **-, -nen** discoverer

Ent·de·cker·freu·de F joy(s *pl*) *or* thrill of discovery

Ent·de·ckung F discovery; (*von Fehler auch*) detection, spotting; (= *etw Entdecktes auch*) find

Ent·de·ckungs·fahrt F, **Ent·de·ckungs·rei·se** F voyage of discovery; (*zu Lande*) expedition of discovery; **auf ~ gehen** (*hum inf*) to go exploring

ent·dra·ma·ti·sie·ren [ɛntdramatiˈziːrən] *ptp* **entdramatisiert** VT (*lit, fig*) to defuse, to take the heat out of (*inf*)

En·te [ˈɛntə] F **-, -n** duck; (*Press inf*) canard, hoax, false report; (*Aut inf*) Citroën 2CV, deux-chevaux → **lahm**

ent·eh·ren [ɛntˈeːrən] *ptp* **entehrt** VT to dishonour (*Brit*), to dishonor (*US*); (= *entwürdigen*) to degrade; (= *verleumden*) to defame; (= *entjungfern*) to deflower; **~d** degrading; **sich ~** to degrade *or* disgrace oneself

Ent·eh·rung F dishonouring (*Brit*), dishonoring (*US*); (= *Entwürdigung*) degradation; (= *Verleumdung*) defamation; (= *Entjungferung*) defloration

ent·eig·nen [ɛntˈaignən] *ptp* **enteignet** VT to expropriate; *Besitzer* to dispossess

Ent·eig·nung F expropriation; (*von Besitzer*) dispossession

ent·ei·len [ɛntˈailən] *ptp* **enteilt** VI *aux sein* (*old*) to hasten away (*liter*); (*liter: Zeit*) to fly by

ent·ei·sen [ɛntˈaizn] *ptp* **enteist** VT to de-ice; *Kühlschrank* to defrost

ent·ei·sent [ɛntˈaizt] ADJ *Mineralwasser* iron-reduced

Ent·ei·sung F **-, -en** de-icing; (*von Kühlschrank*) defrosting

Ent·ei·sungs-: Ent·ei·sungs·an·la·ge F de-icing unit; **Ent·ei·sungs·mit·tel** NT de-icer

ent·emo·ti·o·na·li·sie·ren [ɛntemotionaliˈziːrən] *ptp* **entemotionalisiert** VT to de-emotionalize

En·ten-: En·ten·bra·ten M roast duck; **En·ten·brust** F breast of duck; **En·ten·ei** [-lai] NT duck's egg; **En·ten·flott** NT, **En·ten·grieß** M, **En·ten·grün** NT, **En·ten·grüt·ze** F duckweed; **En·ten·klein** NT **-s**, *no pl* (*Cook*) duck's giblets *pl* (and trimmings *pl*); **En·ten·kü·ken** NT duckling

En·ten·te [ã·tãːt(ə)] F **-, -n** (*Pol*) entente

En·ter·beil [ˈɛntɐ-] NT boarding axe (*Brit*) *or* ax (*US*)

ent·er·ben [ɛntˈɛrbn] *ptp* **enterbt** VT to disinherit

En·ter·brü·cke [ˈɛntɐ-] F boarding plank

Ent·er·bung F **-, -en** disinheriting

En·ter·ha·ken [ˈɛntɐ-] M grappling iron *or* hook

En·te·rich [ˈɛntərɪç] M **-s, -e** drake

en·tern [ˈɛntɐn] **VT a** (= *stürmen*) *Schiff, Haus* to storm **b** (*fig*) (= *betreten*) to enter; (= *erobern*) *Markt, Land* to conquer **VI** *aux sein* (*Naut*) to board

En·ter·tai·ner [ɛntɐˈteːnɐ] M **-s, -**, **En·ter·tai·ne·rin** [-ərɪn] F **-, -nen** entertainer

En·ter-Tas·te [ˈɛntɐ-] F (*Comput*) enter key

entf. *abbr von* **entfällt** n/a

ent·fa·chen [ɛntˈfaxn] *ptp* **entfacht** VT (*geh*) *Feuer* to kindle; *Leidenschaft, Begierde* to arouse, to kindle (the flames of); *Krieg, Streit* to provoke

ent·fah·ren [ɛntˈfaːrən] *ptp* **entfahren** VI *irreg aux sein* **jdm ~** to escape sb's lips; **Blödsinn! entfuhr es ihm** nonsense, he cried inadvertently; **ihr ist ein kleiner Furz ~** (*inf*) she accidentally let off a little fart (*sl*)

ent·fal·len [ɛntˈfalən] *ptp* **entfallen** VI *irreg aux sein +dat* **a** (*fig: aus dem Gedächtnis*) **jdm ~** to slip sb's mind, to escape sb; **der Name ist mir ~** the name has slipped my mind, the name escapes me **b** (= *nicht in Betracht kommen*) not to apply, to be inapplicable; (= *wegfallen*) to be dropped; (= *erlöschen*) to lapse; **dieser Punkt der Tagesordnung entfällt** this point on the agenda has been dropped

c auf jdn/etw ~ (Geld, Kosten) to be allotted or apportioned to sb/sth; **auf jeden ~ 100 Euro** (= erhalten) each person will receive 100 euros; (= bezahlen müssen) each person will pay 100 euros

d (form: = herunterfallen) jds Händen ~ to slip or fall or drop from sb's hands; **das Glas entfiel ihm** he dropped the glass

ent|fal|ten [ɛnt'faltn] ptp **entfaltet** **VT** **a** (= auseinander legen) to unfold, to open or spread out

b (fig) (= entwickeln) Kräfte, Begabung, Theorie to develop; (= beginnen) Tätigkeit to launch into; (= darlegen) Plan, Gedankengänge to set forth or out, to unfold, to expound; **seine Fähigkeiten voll ~** to develop one's abilities to the full

c (fig: = zeigen) Pracht, Prunk to display, to exhibit

VR (Knospe, Blüte) to open, to unfold; (fig) to develop, to unfold, to blossom (out); **der Garten hat sich zu voller Pracht entfaltet** the garden blossomed (out) into its full magnificence; **hier kann ich mich nicht ~** I can't make full use of my abilities here, I'm held back here

Ent|fal|tung F -, -en (von Blüte auch) opening; (fig) (= Entwicklung) development; (einer Tätigkeit) launching into; (= Darstellung) (eines Planes, Gedankens) exposition, setting out, unfolding; (von Prunk, Tatkraft) display; **zur ~ kommen** to develop, to blossom

Ent|fal|tungs|mög|lich|kei|ten PL scope sing or opportunity for (personal) development

ent|fär|ben [ɛnt'fɛrbn] ptp **entfärbt** **VT** to take the colour (Brit) or color (US) out of, to decolour (Brit Tech), to decolor (US Tech), to decolorize (Tech); (= bleichen) to bleach; **das Entfärben** the removal of colour (Brit) or color (US), decolorization (Tech) **VR** (Stoff, Blätter) to lose (its/their) colour (Brit) or color (US)

Ent|fär|ber M , **Ent|fär|bungs|mit|tel** NT colour (Brit) or color (US) remover, dye remover, decolorant (Tech)

ent|fer|nen [ɛnt'fɛrnən] ptp **entfernt** **VT** to remove (von, aus from); **jdn aus der Schule ~** to expel sb from school; **das entfernt uns (weit) vom Thema** that takes us a long way from our subject

VR **a** sich (von or aus etw) ~ (= weggehen) to go away (from sth), to leave (sth); (= abfahren, abziehen) to move off (from sth), to depart (from sth); **sich von seinem Posten/Arbeitsplatz ~** to leave one's post/position; **sich unerlaubt von der Truppe ~** (Mil) to go absent without leave; **sich zu weit ~** to go too far away

b (fig) (von from) (von jdm) to become estranged; (von Thema) to depart, to digress; (von Wahrheit) to depart, to deviate; **er hat sich sehr weit von seinen früheren Ansichten entfernt** he has come a long way from his earlier views

ent|fernt [ɛnt'fɛrnt] **ADJ** Ort, Verwandter distant; (= abgelegen) remote; (= gering) Ähnlichkeit distant, remote, vague; **10 km ~ von** 10km (away) from; **das Haus liegt 2 km ~** the house is 2km away; **aus den ~esten Ländern** from the furthest corners of the globe; **ich hatte nicht den ~esten Verdacht** I didn't have the slightest or remotest suspicion → **weit**

ADV remotely, slightly; **nicht einmal ~ (so gut/hübsch etc)** not even remotely (as good/pretty etc); **~ verwandt** distantly related; **er erinnert mich ~ an meinen Onkel** he reminds me slightly or vaguely of my uncle; **das hat nur ~ mit dieser Angelegenheit zu tun** that has only a distant bearing on this matter, that is only vaguely related to this matter; **nicht im Entferntesten!** not in the slightest or least!

Ent|fer|nung F -, -en **a** distance; (Mil: bei Waffen) range; **man hört das Echo auf große ~ (hin)** you can hear the echo from a great distance or a long way away; **aus or in der ~ (hörte er ...)** in the distance (he heard ...); **aus kurzer/großer ~ (schießen)** (to fire) at or from close/long range; **aus einiger ~** from a distance; **in einiger**

~ at a distance; **etw auf eine ~ von 50 Meter treffen** to hit sth at a distance of 50 metres; **in acht Kilometer(n) ~** eight kilometres (Brit) or kilometers (US) away

b (= das Entfernen) removal; (aus der Schule) expulsion; **unerlaubte ~ (von der Truppe)** absence without leave; **unerlaubte ~ von der Schule/vom Posten etc** absence from school/one's post etc without permission

Ent|fer|nungs|mes|ser M -s, - (Mil, Phot) rangefinder

Ent|fer|nungs|tas|te F (Comput) delete key

ent|fes|seln [ɛnt'fɛsln] ptp **entfesselt** VT (fig) to unleash

ent|fes|selt [ɛnt'fɛslt] ADJ unleashed; Leidenschaft, Trieb unbridled, uncontrolled; Mensch wild; Naturgewalten raging; **vor Zorn/Begeisterung ~** wild with rage/enthusiasm; **der ~e Prometheus** Prometheus Unbound

ent|fet|ten [ɛnt'fɛtn] ptp **entfettet** VT to remove the grease from, to degrease (Tech); Wolle to scour

Ent|fet|tung F -, -en **a** (= das Entfetten) removal of grease (from), degreasing; (von Wolle) scouring **b** (= Gewichtsabnahme) losing fat

Ent|fet|tungs|kur F = Schlankheitskur

ent|feuch|ten [ɛnt'fɔyçtn] ptp **entfeuchtet** [-tət] VT Luft to dehumidify; Mauer to dry out

ent|flamm|bar ADJ inflammable; (fig) Hass easily aroused

Ent|flamm|bar|keit F -, no pl inflammability

ent|flam|men [ɛnt'flamən] ptp **entflammt** **VT** (fig) to (a)rouse; Leidenschaft, Hass auch to inflame; Begeisterung to fire **VR** to be (a)roused or fired or inflamed **VI** aux sein to burst into flames, to catch fire, to ignite (Chem etc); (fig) (Zorn, Streit) to flare up; (Leidenschaft, Liebe) to be (a)roused or inflamed; **für etw entflammt sein** to be fired with enthusiasm for sth; **in Liebe ~/entflammt sein** to fall/be passionately in love

ent|flech|ten [ɛnt'flɛçtn] ptp **entflochten** [ɛnt-'flɔxtn] VT irreg Konzern, Kartell etc to break up

Ent|flech|tung F -, -en (von Konzern, Kartell) breaking up

ent|fle|cken [ɛnt'flɛkn] ptp **entfleckt** VT to remove the stain(s) from

ent|fleu|chen [ɛnt'flɔyçn] ptp **entfleucht** VI aux sein (obs: = wegfliegen) to fly away; (hum: = weggehen) to be off (inf)

ent|flie|gen [ɛnt'fliːgn] ptp **entflogen** [ɛnt-'floːgn] VI irreg aux sein to fly away, to escape (+dat or aus from)

ent|flie|hen [ɛnt'fliːən] ptp **entflohen** [ɛnt-'floːən] VI irreg aux sein (geh) **a** (= entkommen) to escape, to flee (+dat or aus from); **dem Lärm/der Unrast etc ~** to escape or flee (from) the noise/unrest etc **b** (geh: = vergehen: Zeit, Jugend etc) to fly past

ent|frem|den [ɛnt'frɛmdn] ptp **entfremdet** VT to alienate (auch Sociol, Philos), to estrange; **jdn einem Menschen/einer Sache** (dat) **~** to alienate or estrange sb from sb/sth; **die lange Trennung ließ die Freunde (einander) entfremdet** the long separation made the two friends strangers to each other; **entfremdete Arbeit** (Sociol) alienated work; **etw seinem Zweck ~** to use sth for the wrong purpose, not to use sth for its intended purpose

VR to become alienated or estranged (dat from); **er hat sich seiner Frau ganz entfremdet** he has become completely alienated from his wife, he has become a complete stranger to his wife; **durch die lange Abwesenheit habe ich mich or bin ich der Stadt ganz entfremdet** my long absence has made me a stranger to the city

Ent|frem|dung F -, -en estrangement; (Sociol, Philos) alienation

ent|fros|ten [ɛnt'frɔstn] ptp **entfrostet** VT to defrost

Ent|fros|ter [ɛnt'frɔstɐ] M -s, - defroster

ent|füh|ren [ɛnt'fyːrən] ptp **entführt** VT jdn to abduct, to kidnap; Beute etc to carry off, to make off with; LKW, Flugzeug to hijack; Mädchen (mit Zustimmung zur Heirat) to elope with, to run off with; (hum inf: = wegnehmen) to borrow (often hum); **sie ließ sich von ihrem Liebhaber ~** she eloped with her lover; **wer hat mir denn meinen Bleistift entführt?** (inf) who's made off with my pencil? (inf)

Ent|füh|rer(in) M(F) **a** abductor, kidnapper **b** (von Fahrzeug) hijacker; (von Flugzeug) hijacker, skyjacker (inf)

Ent|füh|rung F abduction, kidnapping; (von Flugzeug, LKW) hijacking; (von Mädchen mit Zustimmung zur Heirat) elopement; **„Die ~ aus dem Serail"** "The Abduction from the Seraglio"

ent|ga|sen [ɛnt'gaːzn] ptp **entgast** VT (Chem) to degas

ent|ge|gen [ɛnt'geːgn] **ADV** (geh) **dem Licht/der Zukunft etc ~!** on toward(s) the light/future etc!; **neuen Ufern/Abenteuern ~!** on to new shores/adventures! **PREP** +dat contrary to, against; **~ meiner Bitte** contrary to my request; **~ allen Erwartungen, allen Erwartungen ~** contrary to all or against all expectation(s)

ent|ge|gen+ar|bei|ten VI sep +dat to oppose, to work against

ent|ge|gen+bli|cken VI sep = entgegensehen

ent|ge|gen+brin|gen VT sep irreg jdm etw ~ to bring sth to sb; (fig) Achtung, Freundschaft etc to show or evince sth for sb

ent|ge|gen+ei|len VI sep aux sein +dat (geh) to rush toward(s); (um jdn zu treffen) to rush to meet

ent|ge|gen+fah|ren VI sep irreg aux sein +dat to travel toward(s), to approach; (um jdn zu treffen) to travel to meet; (mit dem Auto) to drive toward(s)/to meet

ent|ge|gen+fie|bern VI sep (inf) einer Sache ~ to feverishly await sth; (ängstlich) to wait for or to await sth with bated breath or stärker fear and trembling

ent|ge|gen+ge|hen VI sep irreg aux sein +dat to go toward(s), to approach; (um jdn zu treffen) to go to meet; (fig) einer Gefahr, dem Tode, der Zukunft to face; **dem Ende ~** (Leben, Krieg) to draw to a close, to approach its end; **seinem Untergang/Schwierigkeiten ~** to be heading for disaster/difficulties; **seiner Vollendung ~** to near or approach completion

ent|ge|gen|ge|setzt **ADJ** Richtung, Meinung opposite; Charakter auch contrasting; (fig: = einander widersprechend) Interessen, Meinungen opposing attr, opposed, conflicting attr; **einander ~e Interessen/Meinungen etc** opposing or conflicting interests/views etc **ADV** **genau ~ denken/handeln etc** to think/do etc exactly the opposite

ent|ge|gen+hal|ten VT sep irreg +dat **a** jdm etw ~ to hold sth out toward(s) sb **b** (fig) einer Sache ~, dass ... to object to sth that ...; **dieser Ansicht muss man ~, dass ...** against this view it must be objected that ...

ent|ge|gen+han|deln VI sep = zuwiderhandeln

ent|ge|gen+kom|men VI sep irreg aux sein +dat to come toward(s), to approach; (um jdn zu treffen) to (come to) meet; (fig) to accommodate; Wünschen, Bitten to accommodate, to meet, to comply with; **jdm auf halbem Wege ~** (lit, fig) to meet sb halfway; **das kommt unseren Plänen/Vorstellungen etc sehr entgegen** that fits in very well with our plans/ideas etc; **Ihr Vorschlag kommt mir sehr entgegen** I find your suggestion very congenial; **können Sie uns preislich etwas ~?** can you adjust your price a little?

Ent|ge|gen|kom|men NT (= Gefälligkeit) kindness, obligingness; (= Zugeständnis) concession, accommodation

ent|ge|gen|kom|mend ADJ **a** *Fahrzeug* oncoming **b** *(fig)* obliging, accommodating

ent|ge|gen|kom|men|der|wei|se ADV obligingly, accommodatingly; *(als Zugeständnis)* as a concession

ent|ge|gen+lau|fen VI *sep irreg aux sein +dat* to run toward(s); *(um jdn zu treffen)* to run to meet; *(fig)* to run contrary *or* counter to

Ent|ge|gen|nah|me [-na:mə] F -, *no pl (form)* (= *Empfang*) receipt; (= *Annahme*) acceptance; **bei ~** on receipt/acceptance

ent|ge|gen+neh|men VT *sep irreg* (= *empfangen*) to receive; (= *annehmen*) to accept; **nehmen Sie meinen Dank entgegen** *(form)* please accept my thanks

ent|ge|gen+schau|en VI *sep (esp dial)* = **entgegensehen**

ent|ge|gen+schla|gen VI *sep irreg aux sein +dat (Geruch, Hass)* to confront, to meet; *(Flammen auch)* to leap toward(s); *(Jubel, Begeisterung)* to meet, to greet; **ihm schlug Jubel entgegen** he was greeted with jubilation; **ihm schlug ein widerlicher Geruch entgegen** he was confronted by a nauseating smell

ent|ge|gen+se|hen VI *sep irreg* **a** **jdm ~** to see sb coming **b** *(fig)* **einer Sache** *(dat)* **~** to await sth; *(freudig)* to look forward to sth; **einer Sache ~ müssen** to have to expect *or* face sth; **Ihrer baldigen Antwort ~d** *(form)* in anticipation of *or* looking forward to your early reply

ent|ge|gen+set|zen VT *sep +dat* **etw einer Sache ~** to set sth against sth; **wir können diesen Forderungen nichts ~** we have nothing to counter these claims with; **einer Sache Alternativen ~** to put *or* pose alternatives to sth; **dem habe ich entgegenzusetzen, dass ...** against that I'd like to say that ...; **die Gewerkschaften hatten den Regierungsvorschlägen nichts entgegenzusetzen** the unions had nothing to offer in reply to the government's suggestions; **jdm/einer Sache Widerstand ~** to put up *or* offer resistance to sb/sth; **ihren Anklagen konnte er nichts ~** he could find no reply to her accusations → **entgegengesetzt**

ent|ge|gen+ste|hen VI *sep irreg +dat (fig)* to stand in the way of, to be an obstacle to; **dem steht entgegen, dass ...** what stands in the way of that is that ...; **dem steht nichts entgegen** there's no obstacle to that, there's nothing against that; **was steht dem entgegen?** what obstacle is there to that?

ent|ge|gen+stel|len *sep +dat* VT = **entgegensetzen** VR **sich jdm/einer Sache ~** to resist sb/ sth, to oppose sb/sth

ent|ge|gen+stem|men VR *sep* **sich jdm/einer Sache ~** to pit oneself against sb/sth, to oppose sb/sth

ent|ge|gen+stre|cken VT *sep* **jdm etw ~** to hold out sth to sb

ent|ge|gen+stür|zen VI *sep aux sein +dat* to fall upon; (= *zueilen auf*) to rush toward(s)

ent|ge|gen+tre|ten VI *sep aux sein +dat* to step *or* walk up to; **dem Feind** to go into action against; **einer Politik, Forderungen** to oppose; **Behauptungen, Vorurteilen** to counter; **einer Gefahr, Unsitten** to take steps against, to act against

ent|ge|gen+wir|ken VI *sep +dat* to counteract

ent|geg|nen [ɛntˈgeːgnən] *ptp* **entgegnet** VTI to reply; *(kurz, barsch)* to retort *(auf +acc* to); **er entgegnete nichts** he made no reply; **darauf wusste er nichts zu ~** he didn't know what to reply to that

Ent|geg|nung F -, -en reply; *(kurz, barsch)* retort

ent|ge|hen [ɛntˈgeːən] *ptp* **entgangen** [ɛntˈgaŋən] VI *irreg aux sein +dat* **a** (= *entkommen*) *Verfolgern, dem Feind* to elude, to escape (from); *dem Schicksal, der Gefahr, Strafe* to escape, to avoid **b** *(fig: = nicht bemerkt werden)* **dieser Fehler ist mir entgangen** I failed to notice *or* I missed this mistake, this mistake escaped my notice; **mir ist kein Wort entgangen** I didn't miss a word (of it); **es ist meiner Aufmerksamkeit nicht entgangen, dass ...** it has not escaped my attention that ...; **ihr entgeht nichts** she doesn't miss anything *or* a thing; **es ist ihm nicht entgangen, dass ...** he didn't fail to notice that ..., it didn't escape him that ...; **sich** *(dat)* **etw ~ lassen** to miss sth

ent|gei|stert [ɛntˈgaɪstɐt] ADJ dumbfounded, thunderstruck, flabbergasted *(inf); Lachen* astonished ADV **er starrte mich ganz ~ an** he stared at me quite dumbfounded *or* thunderstruck *or* flabbergasted *(inf);* **er reagierte ~** he reacted with complete astonishment

Ent|gelt [ɛntˈgɛlt] NT -(e)s, -e *(form)* **a** (= *Bezahlung*) remuneration *(form);* (= *Entschädigung*) recompense *(form)*, compensation; (= *Anerkennung*) reward **b** (= *Gebühr*) fee, consideration; **gegen ~** for a fee *or* consideration; **jdm etw gegen ~ abgeben** to give sb sth for a consideration

ent|gel|ten [ɛntˈgɛltn] *ptp* **entgolten** [ɛntˈgɔltn] VT *irreg (geh)* **a** (= *büßen*) to pay for; **jdn etw ~ lassen** to make sb pay *or* suffer for sth **b** (= *vergüten*) **jdm etw ~** to repay sb for sth

ent|gif|ten [ɛntˈgɪftn] *ptp* **entgiftet** VT to decontaminate; *(Med)* to detoxicate, to detoxify

Ent|gif|tung F -, -en decontamination; *(Med)* detoxication, detoxification

Ent|gif|tungs|sta|ti|on F *(Med)* detox(ification) centre *(Brit) or* center *(US)*

ent|glei|sen [ɛntˈglaɪzn] *ptp* **entgleist** VI *aux sein* **a** *(Rail)* to be derailed; **einen Zug zum Entgleisen bringen** *or* **~ lassen** to derail a train **b** *(fig: Mensch)* to misbehave; (= *einen Fauxpas begehen*) to commit a faux pas, to drop a clanger *(Brit inf)* **c** *(inf)* to put one's foot in it

Ent|glei|sung F -, -en derailment; *(fig)* faux pas, gaffe, clanger *(Brit inf)*

ent|glei|ten [ɛntˈglaɪtn] *ptp* **entglitten** [ɛntˈglɪtn] VI *irreg aux sein +dat* to slip; **jdm** *or* **jds Hand ~** to slip from *or* out of sb's grasp; **jdm/einer Sache ~** *(fig)* to slip away from sb/sth

ent|got|ten [ɛntˈgɔtn] *ptp* **entgottet**, **ent|göt|tern** [ɛntˈgœtɐn] *ptp* **entgöttert** VT *(liter)* to remove god(s) from; **die entgötterte Welt** the godless world, the world without god(s)

Ent|göt|te|rung F -, -en, **Ent|got|tung** F -, -en *(liter)* removal of god(s) (+gen from); **die ~ des Olymp** the banishing of the gods from Olympus

ent|grä|ten [ɛntˈgrɛːtn] *ptp* **entgrätet** VT *Fisch* to fillet, to bone

ent|haa|ren [ɛntˈhaːrən] *ptp* **enthaart** VT to remove unwanted hair from, to depilate *(form)*

Ent|haa|rungs-: **Ent|haa|rungs|creme** F depilatory *or* hair removal cream; **Ent|haa|rungs|mit|tel** NT depilatory, hair removal agent

ent|hal|ten [ɛntˈhaltn] *ptp* **enthalten** *irreg* VT to contain; **(mit) ~ sein** *(+dat)* to be included in VR **a** *(geh)* **sich einer Sache** *(gen)* **~** to abstain from sth; **sich nicht ~ können, etw zu tun** to be unable to refrain from doing sth; **sich einer Bemerkung nicht ~ können** to be unable to refrain from making a remark **b** **sich (der Stimme) ~** to abstain

ent|halt|sam [ɛntˈhaltzaːm] ADJ abstemious; *(sexuell)* chaste; (= *mäßig*) moderate ADV **~ leben** to be abstinent; (= *sexuell*) to be celibate

Ent|halt|sam|keit F -, *no pl* abstinence; *(sexuell)* chastity, abstinence; (= *Mäßigkeit*) moderation

Ent|hal|tung F abstinence; (= *Stimmenthaltung*) abstention

ent|här|ten [ɛntˈhɛrtn] *ptp* **enthärtet** VT *Wasser* to soften

Ent|här|ter M (water) softener

Ent|här|tung F *(von Wasser)* softening; *(von Metall)* annealing

Ent|här|tungs|mit|tel NT (water) softener

ent|haup|ten [ɛntˈhauptn] *ptp* **enthauptet** VT to decapitate; *(als Hinrichtung auch)* to behead

Ent|haup|tung F -, -en decapitation; *(als Hinrichtung auch)* beheading

ent|häu|ten [ɛntˈhɔytn] *ptp* **enthäutet** VT to skin; *(als Folter etc)* to flay

ent|he|ben [ɛntˈheːbn] *ptp* **enthoben** [ɛntˈhoːbn] VT *irreg* **jdn einer Sache** *(gen)* **~** to relieve sb of sth

ent|hei|li|gen [ɛntˈhaɪlɪgn] *ptp* **entheiligt** VT to desecrate, to profane

Ent|hei|li|gung F -, -en desecration, profanation

ent|hem|men [ɛntˈhɛmən] *ptp* **enthemmt** VTI **jdn ~** to make sb lose his inhibitions, to free sb from his inhibitions; **Alkohol wirkt ~d** alcohol has a disinhibiting effect; *(moralisch etc)* **völlig enthemmt sein** to have no (moral *etc*) inhibitions whatsoever, to have lost one's (moral *etc*) inhibitions

ent|hemmt [ɛntˈhɛmt] *ptp von* **enthemmen** ADJ uninhibited, free of inhibitions → *auch* **enthemmen**

Ent|hemmt|heit [ɛntˈhɛmthaɪt] F -, *no pl* loss of inhibitions

ent|hül|len [ɛntˈhʏlən] *ptp* **enthüllt** VT to uncover, to reveal; *Skandal, Lüge auch* to expose; *Denkmal, Gesicht* to unveil; *Geheimnis, Plan, Hintergründe* to reveal VR *(lit, hum)* to reveal oneself; **er hat sich in seiner ganzen Gemeinheit enthüllt** he revealed himself for the villain he was

Ent|hül|lung F -, -en uncovering, revealing; *(von Skandal, Lüge auch)* exposure; *(von Denkmal, Gesicht)* unveiling; **noch eine sensationelle ~** another sensational revelation *or* disclosure

Ent|hül|lungs- *in cpds* investigative; **Ent|hül|lungs|au|tor(in)** M(F) investigative author; **Ent|hül|lungs|blatt** NT (= *Zeitung*) scandal sheet; **Ent|hül|lungs|buch** NT exposé; **Ent|hül|lungs|jour|na|lis|mus** M investigative journalism; **Ent|hül|lungs|jour|na|list(in)** M(F) investigative journalist

ent|hül|sen [ɛntˈhʏlzn] *ptp* **enthülst** VT to shell; *Getreide* to husk

En|thu|si|as|mus [ɛntuˈziasmʊs] M -, *no pl* enthusiasm

En|thu|si|ast [ɛntuˈziast] M -en, -en, **En|thu|si|as|tin** [-ˈziastɪn] F -, -nen enthusiast

en|thu|si|as|tisch [ɛntuˈziastɪʃ] ADJ enthusiastic ADV enthusiastically

ent|ideo|lo|gi|sie|ren [ɛntideologiˈziːrən] *ptp* **entideologisiert** VT to free from ideology VR *(Partei)* to dispense with one's ideology

Ent|ideo|lo|gi|sie|rung F freeing from ideology; (= *das Entideologisiertwerden*) decreasing ideological commitment

En|ti|tät [ɛntiˈtɛːt] F -, -en *(Philos)* entity

ent|jung|fern [ɛntˈjʊŋfɐn] *ptp* **entjungfert** VT to deflower

Ent|jung|fe|rung F -, -en defloration

ent|kal|ken [ɛntˈkalkn] *ptp* **entkalkt** VT to decalcify

ent|kei|men [ɛntˈkaɪmən] *ptp* **entkeimt** VT (= *keimfrei machen*) to sterilize

ent|ker|nen [ɛntˈkɛrnən] *ptp* **entkernt** VT **a** *Orangen etc* to remove the pips from; *Kernobst* to core; *Steinobst* to stone; *(Biol) Zellen* to denucleate **b** *Gebäude* to gut; *Wohngebiet* (= *Dichte reduzieren*) to reduce the density of; (= *dezentralisieren*) to decentralize, to disperse

Ent|ker|ner [ɛntˈkɛrnɐ] M -s, - *(für Kernobst)* corer; *(für Steinobst)* stoner

ent|klei|den [ɛntˈklaɪdn] *ptp* **entkleidet** *(geh)* VT to undress; **jdn einer Sache** *(gen)* **~** *(fig)* to strip *or* divest sb of sth VR to undress, to take one's clothes off

ent|kno|ten [ɛntˈknoːtn] *ptp* **entknotet** VT to untie, to undo; *(fig: = entwirren)* to unravel

ent|kof|fe|i|niert [ɛntkɔfeiˈniːɐt] ADJ decaffeinated

ent|ko|lo|ni|a|li|sie|ren [ɛntkolonialiˈziːrən] *ptp* **entkolonialisiert** VT to decolonialize

Ent|ko|lo|ni|a|li|sie|rung F decolonialization

ent|kom|men [ɛntˈkɔmən] *ptp* **entkommen** VI *irreg aux* sein to escape, to get away (+*dat*, *aus* from)

Ent|kom|men NT escape

Ent|kon|ser|vie|rung F (*von Auto*) de-waxing

ent|kor|ken [ɛntˈkɔrkn] *ptp* **entkorkt** VT *Flasche* to uncork

ent|kör|per|licht [ɛntˈkœrpəlɪçt] ADJ (*liter*) incorporeal

ent|kräf|ten [ɛntˈkrɛftn] *ptp* **entkräftet** VT (= *schwächen*) to weaken, to debilitate, to enfeeble; (= *erschöpfen*) to exhaust, to wear out; (*fig*: = *widerlegen*) *Behauptung etc* to refute, to invalidate

Ent|kräf|tung F -, -en weakening, debilitation, enfeeblement; (= *Erschöpfung*) exhaustion; (*fig*: = *Widerlegung*) refutation, invalidation

ent|kramp|fen [ɛntˈkrampfn] *ptp* **entkrampft** VT (*fig*) to relax, to ease; *Lage* to ease; **eine entkrampfte Atmosphäre** a relaxed atmosphere

Ent|kramp|fung F -, -en (*fig*) relaxation, easing

ent|kri|mi|na|li|sie|ren [ɛntkriminaliˈziːrən] *ptp* **entkriminalisiert** VT to decriminalize

Ent|kri|mi|na|li|sie|rung [ɛntkriminaliˈziːrʊŋ] F (*von Haschischkonsum etc*) decriminalization

ent|la|den [ɛntˈlaːdn] *ptp* **entladen** *irreg* **VT** to unload; *Batterie etc* to discharge **VR** (*Gewitter*) to break; (*Schusswaffe*) to go off, to discharge (*form*); (*elektrische Spannung, Batterie etc*) to discharge; (*langsam*) to run down; (*Sprengladung*) to explode, to go off; (*fig: Emotion*) to vent itself; **sein Zorn entlud sich über mir** he vented his anger on me

Ent|la|dung F **a** (= *das Entladen*) unloading **b** (*von Gewitter*) breaking; (*von Schusswaffe, elektrisch*) discharge; (*von Sprengladung*) explosion; (*von Emotionen*) venting; **etw zur ~ bringen** (*Mil, fig*) to detonate sth

ent|lang [ɛntˈlaŋ] **PREP** +*acc*, +*dat* or (*rare*) +*gen* along; **den** or (*rare*) **dem Fluss ~, ~ dem Fluss** or (*rare*) **des Flusses** along the river **ADV** along; **am Bach ~** along (by the side of) the stream; **am Haus ~** along (by the side of) the house; **hier ~** this way

ent|lang- **PREF** along; **ent|lang|ge|hen** VTI *sep irreg aux* sein to walk along, to go along (*auch fig*); **am Haus ~** to walk along by the side of the house; **ent|lang|schram|men** VI (*fig*) to scrape by; **haarscharf an etw** (*dat*) **~ to escape sth by the skin of one's teeth

ent|lar|ven [ɛntˈlarfn] *ptp* **entlarvt** VT (*fig*) *Spion, Dieb etc* to unmask, to expose; *Pläne, Betrug etc* to uncover, to expose; **sich ~** to reveal one's true colours (*Brit*) or colors (*US*) or character; **sich als Schuft** etc **~** to reveal or show oneself to be a scoundrel etc

Ent|lar|vung F -, -en (*von Spion, Dieb*) unmasking, exposure; (*von Plänen, Betrug*) uncovering, exposure

ent|las|sen [ɛntˈlasn] *ptp* **entlassen** VT *irreg* (*aus* from) (= *gehen lassen, kündigen*) to dismiss; (*nach Streichungen*) to make redundant (*Brit*), to lay off; (*aus dem Krankenhaus*) to discharge; *Soldaten* to discharge; (= *in den Ruhestand versetzen*) to retire, to pension off (*Brit*); (*aus dem Gefängnis, aus Verpflichtungen*) to release, to discharge, to free; (*aus der Schule: als Strafe*) to expel, to exclude; **aus der Schule ~ werden** to leave school; (*als Strafe*) to be expelled or excluded from school; **jdn mit ein paar freundlichen Worten ~** to dismiss sb or send sb away with a few kind words; **jdn in den Ruhestand ~** to retire sb, to pension sb off (*Brit*); **Soldaten ins Zivilleben ~** to demobilize soldiers; **jdn aus der Verantwortung ~** to free sb from responsibility

Ent|las|sung F -, -en dismissal; (*aus dem Krankenhaus, von Soldaten*) discharge; (*aus dem Gefängnis, aus Verpflichtungen*) release, discharge; **um seine ~ einreichen** to tender one's resignation; **es gab 20 ~en** there were 20 redundancies (*esp Brit*) or lay-offs

Ent|las|sungs-: **Ent|las|sungs|fei|er** F (*Sch*) (school-)leaving (*Brit*) or graduation (*US*) ceremony, final prize day (at school) (*Brit*); **Ent|las|sungs|ge|such** NT (letter of) resignation; (*Jur*) petition for release; **ein ~ stellen** or **einreichen** to tender one's resignation; (*Jur*) to petition for one's/sb's release; **Ent|las|sungs|schein** M certificate of discharge; (*Mil auch*) discharge papers *pl*; **Ent|las|sungs|wel|le** F (= *Massenentlassungen*) wave of redundancies (*Brit*) or job losses (*US*); **Ent|las|sungs|zeug|nis** NT (*Sch*) school leaving certificate

ent|las|ten [ɛntˈlastn] *ptp* **entlastet** VT *Achse, Telefonleitungen etc* to relieve the strain or load on; *Herz* to relieve the strain on; *Gewissen* to relieve; (*Mil, Rail*) to relieve; *Verkehr* to ease; *Stadtzentrum* to relieve congestion in; (= *Arbeit abnehmen*) *Chef, Mitarbeiter, Hausfrau* to take some of the load off, to relieve; (*Jur*) *Angeklagten* (*völlig*) to exonerate; (*teilweise*) to support the case of; (*Comm*: = *gutheißen*) *Vorstand* to approve the activities of; (*von Verpflichtungen, Schulden*) *jdn* to discharge, to release; *jds finanziell* ~ to ease sb's financial burden; **jds Konto um einen Betrag ~** to credit sb or sb's account with a sum, to credit a sum to sb's account

Ent|las|tung F -, -en relief (*auch Mil, Rail etc*); (*von Achse etc, Herz*) relief of the strain (+*gen* on); (*Jur*) exoneration; (*Comm: von Vorstand*) approval; (*Fin*) credit; (*von Verpflichtungen etc*) release, discharge; **zu jds ~** (in order) to take some of the load off sb; (*Mil*) (in order) to relieve sb; **eine Aussage zur ~ des Angeklagten** a statement supporting the case of the defendant; **zu seiner ~ führte der Angeklagte an, dass ...** in his defence (*Brit*) or defense (*US*) the defendant stated that ...

Ent|las|tungs-: **Ent|las|tungs|ma|te|ri|al** NT (*Jur*) evidence for the defence (*Brit*) or defense (*US*); **Ent|las|tungs|zeu|ge** M , **Ent|las|tungs|zeu|gin** F (*Jur*) witness for the defence (*Brit*) or defense (*US*), defence (*Brit*) or defense (*US*) witness; **Ent|las|tungs|zug** M relief train

ent|lau|ben [ɛntˈlaubn] *ptp* **entlaubt** VT to strip of leaves; (*Sci*) to defoliate

Ent|lau|bung F -, -en defoliation

Ent|lau|bungs|mit|tel NT defoliant

ent|lau|fen [ɛntˈlaufn] *ptp* **entlaufen** VI *irreg aux* sein to run away (+*dat*, von from); **ein ~er Skla-ve/-es Kind** etc a runaway slave/child etc; **ein ~er Sträfling** an escaped convict; **ein ~er Hund** a lost or missing dog; „**Hund ~**" "dog missing"

ent|lau|sen [ɛntˈlauzn] *ptp* **entlaust** VT to delouse

Ent|lau|sung F -, -en delousing

ent|le|di|gen [ɛntˈleːdɪgn] *ptp* **entledigt** (*form*) **VR** **sich einer Person/einer Sache** (*gen*) **~** to rid oneself of sb/sth; **sich einer Pflicht** (*gen*) **~** to discharge a duty; **sich eines Komplizen** (*euph*) to dispose of or eliminate an accomplice (*euph*); **sich seiner Schulden** **~** to discharge one's debts (*form*), to pay off one's debts; **sich seiner Kleidung ~** to remove one's clothes **VT** **jdn einer Pflicht** (*gen*) **~** to release sb from a duty

ent|lee|ren [ɛntˈleːrən] *ptp* **entleert** VT to empty; *Darm* to evacuate; (*Sci*) *Glasglocke* to evacuate

Ent|lee|rung F emptying; (*von Darm, Glasglocke*) evacuation

ent|le|gen [ɛntˈleːgn] ADJ *Ort, Haus* (= *abgelegen*) remote, out-of-the-way; (= *weit weg*) far away or off, remote; (*fig*) *Gedanke etc* odd, out-of-the-way

Ent|le|gen|heit F -, *no pl* remoteness; (*fig*) oddness

ent|leh|nen [ɛntˈleːnən] *ptp* **entlehnt** VT (*fig*) to borrow (+*dat*, von from)

Ent|leh|nung F -, -en (*fig*) borrowing

ent|lei|ben [ɛntˈlaibn] *ptp* **entleibt** VR (*obs*) to take one's own life

ent|lei|hen [ɛntˈlaiən] *ptp* **entliehen** VT *irreg* to borrow (*von, aus* from)

Ent|lei|her [ɛntˈlaiɐ] M -s, -, **Ent|lei|he|rin** [-ərɪn] F -, -nen borrower

Ent|lei|hung F -, -en borrowing

Ent|lein [ˈɛntlain] NT -s, - duckling; **das hässliche ~** the Ugly Duckling

ent|lo|ben [ɛntˈloːbn] *ptp* **entlobt** VR to break off one's engagement

Ent|lo|bung F -, -en breaking off of one's engagement; **eine ~** a broken engagement

ent|lo|cken [ɛntˈlɔkn] *ptp* **entlockt** VT **jdm/einer Sache etw ~** to elicit sth from sb/sth; (*durch Überredung auch*) to coax sth out of sb; (*durch ständige Befragung auch*) to worm sth out of sb

ent|loh|nen [ɛntˈloːnən] *ptp* **entlohnt**, (*Sw*) **ent|löh|nen** [ɛntˈløːnən] *ptp* **entlöhnt** VT to pay; (*fig*) to reward

Ent|loh|nung F -, -en, (*Sw*) **Ent|löh|nung** F -, -en pay(ment); (*fig*) reward; **etw gegen ~ tun** to do sth for payment

ent|lüf|ten [ɛntˈlYftn] *ptp* **entlüftet** VT to ventilate, to air; *Bremsen, Heizung* to bleed

Ent|lüf|ter M ventilator

Ent|lüf|tung F ventilation, airing; (*von Bremsen, Heizung*) bleeding

Ent|lüf|tungs-: **Ent|lüf|tungs|an|la|ge** F ventilation system; **Ent|lüf|tungs|ven|til** NT (*Tech*) ventilation valve; (*von Motor, Heizung etc*) bleed(er) valve

ent|mach|ten [ɛntˈmaxtn] *ptp* **entmachtet** VT to deprive of power

Ent|mach|tung F -, -en deprivation of power

ent|mag|ne|ti|sie|ren [ɛntmagnetiˈziːrən] *ptp* **entmagnetisiert** VT to demagnetize

ent|man|nen [ɛntˈmanən] *ptp* **entmannt** VT to castrate; (*fig*) to emasculate, to unman

Ent|man|nung F -, -en castration; (*fig*) emasculation

ent|ma|te|ri|a|li|sie|ren [ɛntmateriaˈliˈziːrən] *ptp* **entmaterialisiert** VT to dematerialize

ent|mensch|li|chen [ɛntˈmɛnʃlɪçn] *ptp* **entmenschlicht** VT to dehumanize

ent|menscht [ɛntˈmɛnʃt] ADJ bestial, inhuman

ent|mie|ten [ɛntˈmiːtn] *ptp* **entmietet** VT (*form*) to clear or evict tenants from

Ent|mie|tung F -, -en (*form*) clearance

ent|mi|li|ta|ri|sie|ren [ɛntmilitaˈriˈziːrən] *ptp* **entmilitarisiert** VT to demilitarize

Ent|mi|li|ta|ri|sie|rung F -, -en demilitarization

ent|mi|nen [ɛntˈmiːnən] *ptp* **entmint** VT (*Mil*) to clear of mines

ent|mot|ten [ɛntˈmɔtn] *ptp* **entmottet** VT (*fig*) to take out of mothballs

ent|mün|di|gen [ɛntˈmYndɪgn] *ptp* **entmündigt** VT (*Jur*) to (legally) incapacitate, to declare incapable of managing one's own affairs; (*wegen Geisteskrankheit auch*) to certify; **das Fernsehen entmündigt die Zuschauer, wenn ...** television takes away the viewer's right to form an independent opinion when ...

Ent|mün|di|gung F -, -en (*legal*) incapacitation; (*wegen Geisteskrankheit auch*) certification

ent|mu|ti|gen [ɛntˈmuːtɪgn] *ptp* **entmutigt** VT to discourage, to dishearten; **sich nicht ~ lassen** not to be discouraged or disheartened

Ent|mu|ti|gung F -, -en discouragement

ent|mys|ti|fi|zie|ren [ɛntmystifiˈziːrən] *ptp* **entmystifiziert** VT to demystify, to take the mystique out of, to debunk

ent|my|tho|lo|gi|sie|ren [ɛntmytologiˈziːrən] *ptp* **entmythologisiert** VT to demythologize

Ent|nah|me [ɛnt'naːmə] F -, -n (form) removal, taking out; (von Blut) extraction; (von Geld) withdrawal; **vor ~ einer Sache** (gen) before removing/extracting/withdrawing sth

ent|na|zi|fi|zie|ren [ɛntnatsifi'tsiːrən] ptp **entnazifiziert** VT to denazify

Ent|na|zi|fi|zie|rung -, -en F denazification

ent|neh|men [ɛnt'neːmən] ptp **entnommen** [ɛnt'nɔmən] VT irreg (aus +dat) to take out (of), to take (from); (aus Kasse) Geld to withdraw (from); (einem Buch etc) Zitat to take (from); (fig: = erkennen, folgern) to infer (from), to gather (from); **wie ich Ihren Worten entnehme, ...** I gather from what you say that ...

ent|ner|ven [ɛnt'nɛrfn] ptp **entnervt** VT to unnerve; **~d** unnerving; (= nervtötend) nerve-racking

ent|nervt [ɛnt'nɛrft] ptp von **entnerven** ADJ unnerved, nervous, enervated; **ich bin völlig ~** my nerves are shot (inf) ADV enervated; **er hat ~ aufgegeben** he had reached the end of his tether (Brit) or rope (US) and give up → auch entnerven

En|to|derm [ɛnto'dɛrm] NT -s, -e (Biol) endoderm, endoderm

ent|ölen [ɛnt'øːlən] ptp **entölt** VT Kakao to extract the oil from

En|to|mo|lo|gie [ɛntomolo'giː] F -, no pl entomology

en|to|mo|lo|gisch [ɛntomo'loːgɪʃ] ADJ entomological

En|tou|ra|ge [ãtuˈraːʒ(ə)] F -, no pl (geh) entourage

ent|pa|cken [ɛnt'pakn] VT ptp **entpackt** (Comput) Daten to unpack

ent|per|sön|li|chen [ɛntpɛr'zøːnlɪçn] ptp **entpersönlicht** VT to depersonalize

ent|pflich|ten [ɛnt'pflɪçtn] ptp **entpflichtet** VT (form) Pfarrer, Professor to retire

ent|po|li|ti|sie|ren [ɛntpoliti'ziːrən] ptp **entpolitisiert** VT to depoliticize

Ent|po|li|ti|sie|rung F depoliticizing, depoliticization

ent|pri|va|ti|sie|ren [ɛntprivati'ziːrən] ptp **entprivatisiert** VT to deprivatize, to (re-)nationalize

ent|pup|pen [ɛnt'pupn] ptp **entpuppt** VR (Schmetterling) to emerge from its cocoon or chrysalis; **sich als Betrüger** etc **~** to turn out to be a cheat etc; **mal sehen, wie er sich entpuppt** we'll see how he turns out

ent|rah|men [ɛnt'raːmən] ptp **entrahmt** VT Milch to remove the cream from, to skim; (mit Zentrifuge) to separate; **entrahmte Milch** skimmed milk

Ent|rah|mung F -, -en skimming; (mit Zentrifuge) separation

ent|ra|ten [ɛnt'raːtn] ptp **entraten** VI irreg (geh, old) **einer Sache** (gen) **~** to be devoid of sth; **einer Person/Sache** (gen) **~/nicht ~ können** to be able/unable to dispense with sb/sth

ent|rät|seln [ɛnt'rɛːtsln] ptp **enträtselt** VT to solve; Sinn to work out; Schrift to decipher

ent|rech|ten [ɛnt'rɛçtn] ptp **entrechtet** VT jdn **~** to deprive sb of his rights; **die Entrechteten** those who have lost their rights, those who have been deprived of their rights

Ent|rech|tung F -, -en deprivation of rights; **die ~ des Parlaments** depriving parliament of its rights

Ent|ree [ã'treː] NT -s, -s (dated: = Eingang) entrance; (obs: = Vorraum) (entrance) hall; (= Eintrittsgeld) entrance or admission fee; (Mus: = Vorspiel) introduction; (Cook: = Vorspeise) entrée; (Theat: = Auftritt) solo entrance

ent|rei|ßen [ɛnt'raisn] ptp **entrissen** [ɛnt'rɪsn] VT irreg **jdm etw ~** (lit, fig liter) to snatch sth (away) from sb; **jdn dem Tode ~** (liter) to snatch sb from the jaws of death

ent|rich|ten [ɛnt'rɪçtn] ptp **entrichtet** VT (form) to pay

Ent|rich|tung F (form) payment

ent|rie|geln [ɛnt'riːgln] ptp **entriegelt** VT to unbolt, to unlock; (Comput, Handy etc) Tastatur to unlock

ent|rin|den [ɛnt'rɪndn] ptp **entrindet** VT to remove the bark from, to decorticate (form)

ent|rin|gen [ɛnt'rɪŋən] ptp **entrungen** [ɛnt'ruŋən] irreg **VT** (geh) **jdm etw ~** to wrench or wrest sth from sb; **jdm ein Geheimnis** etc **~** to wring a secret etc out of sb, to wrest a secret etc from sb **VR** (liter) **sich jds Lippen** (dat) **~** to escape from sb's lips; **ein Seufzer entrang sich seiner Brust** he heaved a sigh

ent|rin|nen [ɛnt'rɪnən] ptp **entronnen** [ɛnt'rɔnən] VI irreg aux sein (geh) **a** +dat to escape from; **dem Tod** to escape; **es gibt kein Entrinnen** there is no escape **b** (= entfliehen: Zeit) to fly by

ent|rol|len [ɛnt'rɔlən] ptp **entrollt** **VT** Landkarte etc to unroll; Fahne, Segel to unfurl; **ein Bild des Schreckens ~** (fig) to reveal a picture of horror **VR** (sich: Fahne, Segel) to unroll; (Bild, fig) **ein Bild des Schreckens entrollte sich** (fig) a picture of horror unfolded **VI** aux sein +dat (rare) to roll out of

En|tro|pie [ɛntro'piː] F -, -n [-'piːən] (Phys) entropy

ent|ros|ten [ɛnt'rɔstn] ptp **entrostet** VT to derust

Ent|ros|ter [ɛnt'rɔstɐ] M -s, -, **Ent|ros|tungsmit|tel** NT deruster

ent|rü|cken [ɛnt'rʏkn] ptp **entrückt** VT (geh) **jdn jdm/einer Sache ~** (lit, fig) to carry or bear (liter) sb away from sb/sth, to transport sb (away) from sb/sth; **jdn (in den Himmel) ~** (Rel) to translate sb (into heaven); **der Tod hat sie allen Sorgen entrückt** death has put her beyond all tribulation; **einer Sache** (dat) **weit entrückt sein** (fig) to be far removed from sth; **jdn jds Blicken ~** to remove sb from sb's sight; **jds Blicken entrückt (sein)** (to be) out of (sb's) sight

ent|rückt [ɛnt'rʏkt] ADJ (geh) (= verzückt) enraptured, transported; (= versunken) lost in reverie, rapt

Ent|rückt|heit F -, -en (geh) reverie

Ent|rü|ckung F -, -en (geh) rapture, ecstasy; (= Versunkenheit) rapt absorption; (Rel: = Versetzung) translation

ent|rüm|peln [ɛnt'rʏmpln] ptp **entrümpelt** VT to clear out; (fig) to tidy up

Ent|rüm|pe|lung F -, -en, **Ent|rümp|lung** F -, -en clear-out; (= das Entrümpeln) clearing out; (fig) tidying up

ent|rüs|ten [ɛnt'rʏstn] ptp **entrüstet** **VT** (= empören) to fill with indignation, to outrage; (= zornig machen) to incense, to anger; (= schockieren) to outrage, to scandalize **VR** **sich ~ über** (+acc) (= sich empören) to be filled with indignation at, to be outraged at; (= zornig werden) to be incensed at; (= schockiert sein) to be outraged or scandalized at; **das ist unerhört!, entrüstete sich die alte Dame** that is scandalous!, said the old lady incensed

ent|rüs|tet [ɛnt'rʏstət] ADJ (= empört) (highly) indignant, outraged; (= zornig) incensed; (= schockiert) outraged, scandalized ADV indignantly, outraged

Ent|rüs|tung F (über +acc at) indignation; (= Zorn) anger; **ein Sturm der ~ brach los** a storm of indignation broke out

ent|saf|ten [ɛnt'zaftn] ptp **entsaftet** VT to extract the juice from

Ent|saf|ter [ɛnt'zaftɐ] M -s, - juice extractor

ent|sa|gen [ɛnt'zaːgn] ptp **entsagt** VI +dat (geh) to renounce; **der Welt ~** to renounce the world; **sie hat vielen Freuden ~ müssen** she had to forgo many pleasures; **dem muss ich ~** I shall have to forgo that

Ent|sa|gung F -, -en (geh: von der Welt etc) renunciation (of worldly things); **Armut und ~ sind die Grundprinzipien des Klosterlebens** poverty and the renunciation of worldly things are the basic principles of monastic life

ent|sa|gungs|voll ADJ (geh) Leben (full) of privation; Blick, Geste resigned

ent|sal|zen [ɛnt'zaltsn] ptp **entsalzt** VT irreg to desalinate

Ent|sal|zung F -, -en desalination

Ent|sal|zungs|an|la|ge F desalination plant

Ent|satz [ɛnt'zats] M -es, no pl (Mil) relief

ent|schä|di|gen [ɛnt'ʃɛːdɪgn] ptp **entschädigt** **VT** (für for) (lit, fig) to compensate, to recompense, to indemnify (form); (für Dienste etc) to reward; (esp mit Geld) to remunerate; (= Kosten erstatten) to reimburse, to indemnify (form); **das Theaterstück entschädigte uns für das lange Warten** the play made up for the long wait **VR** **sich (für etw) ~** to compensate oneself for sth; **ihr Mann ist fremdgegangen, aber sie hat sich reichlich dafür entschädigt** her husband was unfaithful to her but she got her own back with a vengeance

Ent|schä|di|gung F compensation, recompense, indemnification (form); (für Dienste) reward; (mit Geld) remuneration; (= Kostenerstattung) reimbursement; **jdm eine ~ zahlen** to pay sb compensation

Ent|schä|di|gungs-: **Ent|schä|di|gungs|klage** F claim for compensation; **Ent|schä|digungs|sum|me** F amount of compensation; **Ent|schä|di|gungs|zah|lung** F (Zahlen) compensation payment; (Betrag) damages pl, compensation

ent|schär|fen [ɛnt'ʃɛrfn] ptp **entschärft** VT **a** Bombe etc to defuse, to deactivate **b** (fig) Kurve to straighten out; Krise, Lage to defuse; Argument to neutralize; Buch, Film to tone down

Ent|scheid [ɛnt'ʃait] M -(e)s, -e [-də] (Sw, form) = Entscheidung

ent|schei|den [ɛnt'ʃaidn] ✪ 35.2 pret entschied [ɛnt'ʃiːt], ptp **entschieden** [ɛnt'ʃiːdn] **VT** to decide; **das Gericht entschied, dass ...** the court decided or ruled that ...; **~ Sie, wie es gemacht werden soll!** you decide how it is to be done; **das Spiel/die Wahl ist entschieden/schon entschieden** the game/election has been decided/is already decided; **den Kampf/Krieg (um etw) für sich ~** to secure victory in the struggle/battle (for sth); **das hat das Spiel zu unseren Gunsten entschieden** that decided the game in our favour (Brit) or favor (US); **es ist noch nichts entschieden** nothing has been decided (as) yet → auch **entschieden**
VI (über +acc) to decide (on); (Jur auch) to rule (on); **darüber habe ich nicht zu ~** that is not for me to decide; **der Richter hat für/gegen den Kläger entschieden** the judge decided or ruled for/against the plaintiff
VR (Mensch) to decide, to make up one's mind, to come to a decision; (Angelegenheit) to be decided; **sich für etw ~** to decide in favour (Brit) or favor (US) of sth, to decide on sth; **sich für jdn ~** to decide in favour (Brit) or favor (US) of sb; **sich gegen jdn/etw ~** to decide against sb/sth; **jetzt wird es sich ~, wer der Schnellere ist** now we'll see or settle who is the quicker

ent|schei|dend ADJ decisive; Faktor auch deciding attr; Argument, Aussage auch conclusive; Augenblick auch crucial, critical; Fehler, Irrtum auch crucial; **die ~e Stimme** (bei Wahlen etc) the deciding or casting vote; **für jdn/etw ~ sein** to be decisive or crucial for sb/sth; **der alles ~e Augenblick** the all-decisive moment; **das Entscheidende** the decisive or deciding factor ADV schlagen, schwächen decisively; **~ zu etw beitragen** to be a crucial or decisive factor in sth

Ent|schei|der M -s, -, **Ent|schei|de|rin** F -, -nen decision-maker

Ent|schei|dung F decision; (*Jur auch*) ruling; (*der Geschworenen auch*) verdict; **um die ~ spielen** (*Sport*) to play the deciding game *or* the decider (*Brit*); (*bei gleichem Tor-, Punktverhältnis auch*) to play off; **Spiel um die ~** (*Sport*) deciding game, decider (*Brit*); play-off; **mit den finanziellen ~en habe ich nichts zu tun** I have nothing to do with the financial decision-making *or* decisions; **wie ist die ~ ausgefallen?** which way did the decision go?; **es geht um die ~** it's going to be decisive, it's going to decide things; **die Lage drängt zur ~** the situation is coming to a head; **die Frage kommt heute zur ~** the question will be decided today

Ent|schei|dungs-: Ent|schei|dungs|be|darf M need for a decision; **Ent|schei|dungs|be|fug|nis** F decision-making powers *pl*; **Ent|schei|dungs|fin|dung** F -, -en decision-making; **Ent|schei|dungs|fra|ge** F (*Gram*) yes-no question; **Ent|schei|dungs|frei|heit** F freedom to decide; **ent|schei|dungs|freu|dig** ADJ able to make decisions, decisive; **Ent|schei|dungs|freu|dig|keit** F -, *no pl* decisiveness; **Ent|schei|dungs|gre|mi|um** NT decision-making body; **Ent|schei|dungs|hil|fe** F aid to decision-making; **Ent|schei|dungs|kampf** M decisive encounter, show-down (*inf, auch fig*); (*Sport*) decider (*Brit*); deciding round/game *etc*; **Ent|schei|dungs|kri|te|ri|um** NT deciding factor; **Ent|schei|dungs|schlacht** F decisive battle; (*fig*) show-down (*inf*); **ent|schei|dungs|schwach** ADJ indecisive; **Ent|schei|dungs|schwä|che** F indecisiveness; **Ent|schei|dungs|spiel** NT deciding game, decider (*Brit*); (*bei gleichem Punkt-, Torverhältnis auch*) play-off; **Ent|schei|dungs|spiel|raum** M room for manoeuvre (*Brit*) *or* maneuver (*US*) in making a decision; **wir haben hierbei keinen ~** we don't have much choice in this; **Ent|schei|dungs|trä|ger(in)** M(F) decision-maker; **ent|schei|dungs|un|fä|hig** ADJ unable to make decisions; **Ent|schei|dungs|un|fä|hig|keit** F inability to make decisions, indecision

ent|schied *pret von* entscheiden

ent|schie|den [ɛntˈʃiːdn] *ptp von* **entscheiden** ADJ **a** (= *entschlossen*) determined, resolute; *Befürworter* staunch; *Ablehnung* firm **b** *no pred* (= *eindeutig*) decided, distinct; **er ist ein ~er Könner in seinem Fach** he is unquestionably an expert in his subject ADV **a** (= *strikt*) **ablehnen** firmly; **bekämpfen** resolutely; **von sich weisen, zurückweisen** staunchly; **das geht ~ zu weit** that's definitely going too far **b** (= *eindeutig*) definitely

Ent|schie|den|heit F -, -en (= *Entschlossenheit*) determination, resolution; (*von Befürworter*) staunchness; (*von Ablehnung*) firmness; **etw mit aller ~ dementieren** to deny sth categorically; **etw mit aller ~ ablehnen** to reject sth flatly

ent|schla|cken [ɛntˈʃlakn] *ptp* **entschlackt** VT (*Metal*) to remove the slag from; (*Med*) *Körper* to purify

Ent|schla|ckung F -, -en (*Metal*) removal of slag (+*gen* from); (*Med*) purification

ent|schla|fen [ɛntˈʃlaːfn] *ptp* **entschlafen** VI *irreg aux sein* (*geh*) to fall asleep; (*euph auch:* = *sterben*) to pass away; **der/die Entschlafene** the deceased, the departed

ent|schlei|ern [ɛntˈʃlaɪɐn] *ptp* **entschleiert** VT to unveil; (*fig auch*) to uncover, to reveal VR to unveil (oneself); (*hum*) to strip, to disrobe (*hum, form*)

ent|schlie|ßen [ɛntˈʃliːsn] *pret* **entschloss** [ɛntˈʃlɔs], *ptp* **entschlossen** [ɛntˈʃlɔsn] VR to decide (**für, zu** on); **sich ~, etw zu tun** to decide *or* determine *or* resolve to do sth; **ich entschloss mich zum Kauf dieses Hauses** I decided to buy this house; **ich weiß nicht, wozu ich mich ~ soll** I don't know what to decide; **sich anders ~** to change one's mind; **sich zu nichts ~ können** to be unable to make up one's mind; **zu allem**

entschlossen sein to be ready for anything → *auch* **entschlossen**

Ent|schlie|ßung F resolution

Ent|schlie|ßungs|an|trag M (*Pol*) resolution proposal

ent|schloss *pret von* **entschließen**

ent|schlos|sen [ɛntˈʃlɔsn] ⚙ 35.2 *ptp von* **entschließen** ADJ determined, resolute; **ich bin fest ~** I am absolutely determined; **er ist zum Schlimmsten ~** he will stop at nothing, he's prepared to do anything; **kurz ~** straight away, without further ado ADV resolutely; **~ handeln** to act resolutely *or* with determination; **schnell und ~** fast and decisively

Ent|schlos|sen|heit F -, *no pl* determination, resolution; **in wilder ~** with fierce determination

ent|schlum|mern [ɛntˈʃlʊmɐn] *ptp* **entschlummert** VI *aux sein* (*liter, auch euph:* = *sterben*) to fall asleep

ent|schlüp|fen [ɛntˈʃlʏpfn] *ptp* **entschlüpft** VI *aux sein* to escape (+*dat* from), to slip away (+*dat* from); (*Küken*) to be hatched; (*fig: Wort etc*) to slip out (+*dat* from); **mir ist eine unüberlegte Bemerkung entschlüpft** I let slip an ill--considered remark

Ent|schluss ▲ M (= *Entscheidung*) decision; (= *Vorsatz*) resolution, resolve; **zu keinem ~ kommen können** to be unable to make up one's mind *or* to come to a decision; **mein ~ ist gefasst** my decision is made, my mind is made up; **aus eigenem ~ handeln** to act on one's own initiative; **seinen ~ ändern** to change one's mind; **es ist mein fester ~ ...** it is my firm intention ..., I firmly intend ...; **ein Mann von schnellen Entschlüssen sein** to be good at decision-making, to be able to decide quickly

ent|schlüs|seln [ɛntˈʃlʏsln] *ptp* **entschlüsselt** VT to decipher; *Funkspruch auch* to decode

Ent|schlüs|se|lung F -, -en deciphering; (*von Funkspruch auch*) decoding

Ent|schluss-: ent|schluss|freu|dig ▲ ADJ decisive; **Ent|schluss|freu|dig|keit** ▲ [-frɔydɪç-kaɪt] F , *no pl* decisiveness, decision-making zeal; **Ent|schluss|kraft** ▲ F decisiveness, determination; **ent|schluss|los** ▲ ADJ indecisive, irresolute; **Ent|schluss|lo|sig|keit** ▲ F -, -en indecisiveness, irresoluteness

ent|schuld|bar [ɛntˈʃʊltbaːɐ] ADJ excusable, pardonable

ent|schul|den [ɛntˈʃʊldn] *ptp* **entschuldet** VT to free of debts

ent|schul|di|gen [ɛntˈʃʊldɪgn] ⚙ 45.1 *ptp* **entschuldigt** VT to excuse; **etw mit etw ~** to excuse sth as due to sth; **das ist durch nichts zu ~!, das lässt sich nicht ~!** that is inexcusable!; **der Lehrer entschuldigte das Kind** the teacher excused the child (from attendance); **das entschuldigt nicht, dass er sich so benimmt** that is no excuse for *or* doesn't excuse his behaving like that; **jdn bei jdm/einem Treffen ~** to make *or* present sb's excuses *or* apologies to sb/a meeting; **einen Schüler ~ lassen** *or* ~ to ask for a pupil to be excused; **ich möchte meine Tochter für morgen ~ lassen** I would like to have my daughter excused for tomorrow; **ich bitte mich zu ~** I beg (*Brit*) *or* ask to be excused; **bitte entschuldigt die Störung, aber ...** please excuse *or* forgive the interruption, but ...

VI **entschuldige/~ Sie (bitte)!** (do *or* please) excuse me!, sorry!; (*bei Bitte, Frage etc*) excuse me (please), pardon me (*US*); **(na) ~ Sie/entschuldige mal!** excuse me!

VR **sich (bei jdm) (wegen** *or* **für etw) ~** (= *um Verzeihung bitten*) to apologize (to sb) (for sth); **sich (bei jdm) ~** (= *sich abmelden, sich rechtfertigen*) to excuse oneself, to make one's excuses (to sb); (= *sich bei Lehrer, Chef abmelden*) to ask (sb) to be excused; **sich (von jdm) ~ lassen** to send *or* convey (*form*) one's excuses *or* apologies (via sb); **sich mit Krankheit ~** to excuse oneself on account of illness

ent|schul|di|gend ADJ apologetic ADV apologetically

Ent|schul|di|gung ⚙ 45.1, 45.2 F -, -en (= *Grund*) excuse; (= *Bitte um Entschuldigung*) apology; (*Sch:* = *Brief*) letter of excuse, note; **~!** excuse me!; (*Verzeihung auch*) sorry!; **als** *or* **zur ~ für ...** as an excuse/apology for ..., in excuse of ... (*form*); **zu seiner ~ sagte er ...** he said in his defence (*Brit*) *or* defense (*US*) that ...; **ohne ~ fehlen** to be absent without an excuse; (**jdn**) **(wegen einer Sache) um ~ bitten** to apologize (to sb) (for sth); **ich bitte vielmals um ~(, dass ich mich verspätet habe)!** I do apologize (for being late)!

Ent|schul|di|gungs-: Ent|schul|di|gungs|brief M letter of apology; (*Sch*) excuse note; **Ent|schul|di|gungs|grund** M excuse

ent|schwe|ben [ɛntˈʃveːbn] *ptp* **entschwebt** VI *aux sein* (*geh, hum:* = *weggehen*) to float *or* waft away (+*dat* from)

ent|schwe|feln [ɛntˈʃveːfln] *ptp* **entschwefelt** VT to desulphurize

Ent|schwe|fe|lung F -, -en desulphurization

Ent|schwe|fe|lungs|an|la|ge F desulphurization plant

ent|schwin|den [ɛntˈʃvɪndn] *ptp* **entschwunden** [ɛntˈʃvʊndn] VI *irreg aux sein* (*geh: lit, fig*) to vanish, to disappear (+*dat* from, *in* +*acc* into); **dem Gedächtnis ~** to fade from one's memory; **die Tage entschwanden wie im Flug** the days flew by *or* raced by

ent|seelt [ɛntˈzeːlt] ADJ (*liter*) lifeless, dead

ent|sen|den [ɛntˈzɛndn] *ptp* **entsandt** *or* **entsendet** [ɛntˈzant, ɛntˈzɛndət] VT *irreg or reg Abgeordnete etc* to send; *Boten auch* to dispatch

Ent|sen|dung F sending; (*von Boten auch*) dispatch

ent|set|zen [ɛntˈzɛtsn] *ptp* **entsetzt** VT **a** (= *in Grauen versetzen*) to horrify, to appal (*Brit*), to appall (*US*) **b** (*Mil*) *Truppen* to relieve VR **sich über jdn/etw ~** to be horrified *or* appalled at *or* by sb/sth; **sich vor etw (dat) ~** to be horrified *or* appalled at sth → *auch* **entsetzt**

Ent|set|zen [ɛntˈzɛtsn] NT -s, *no pl* horror; (= *Bestürzung auch*) dismay; (= *Erschrecken*) terror; **von ~ erfasst** *or* **ergriffen** *or* **gepackt werden** to be seized with horror/dismay/terror, to be horror-stricken; **zu meinem größten ~ bemerkte ich, dass ...** to my horror *or* great dismay I noticed that ...; **mit ~ sehen/hören, dass ...** to be horrified/dismayed/terrified to see/hear that ...

Ent|set|zens|schrei M cry of horror

ent|setz|lich [ɛntˈzɛtslɪç] ADJ dreadful, appalling, hideous; (*inf:* = *sehr unangenehm auch*) terrible, awful ADV **a** (= *schrecklich*) **wehtun, schreien** dreadfully, terribly, awfully; **~ aussehen** to look dreadful *or* appalling *or* hideous **b** (*inf:* = *sehr*) awfully; **~ viel (Geld)** an awful lot (of money) (*inf*)

Ent|setz|lich|keit F -, -e dreadful *or* appalling *or* terrible nature

ent|setzt [ɛntˈzɛtst] ADJ horrified, appalled (**über** +*acc* at, by); **ein ~er Schrei** a horrified scream, a cry *or* scream of horror ADV in horror; **jdn ~ anstarren** to give sb a horrified look → *auch* **entsetzen**

Ent|set|zung F -, -en (*Mil*) relief

ent|seu|chen [ɛntˈzɔyçn] *ptp* **entseucht** VT (= *desinfizieren*) to disinfect; (= *dekontaminieren*) to decontaminate

Ent|seu|chung F -, -en decontamination

ent|si|chern [ɛntˈzɪçɐn] *ptp* **entsichert** VT **eine Pistole ~** to release the safety catch of a pistol; **eine entsicherte Pistole** a pistol with the safety catch off, a pistol with an unlocked safety catch (*esp US*)

ent|sin|nen [ɛntˈzɪnən] *ptp* **entsonnen** [ɛntˈzɔnən] VR *irreg* (*einer Sache (gen), an etw (acc)* sth) to remember, to recall, to recollect; **wenn ich mich recht entsinne** if my memory serves me correctly *or* right

ent|sor|gen [ɛntˈzɔrgn] *ptp* **entsorgt** **VT** *Abfälle, Schutt, Brennstäbe, Chemikalien, Medikamente* to dispose of; *Ölplattform, Altautos* to break up; **eine Stadt ~** to dispose of a town's refuse and sewage **VI** to dispose of refuse and sewage

Ent|sor|gung F -, -en waste disposal; **die ~ von Chemikalien** the disposal of chemicals

Ent|sor|gungs-: **Ent|sor|gungs|nach|weis** M proof of disposal; **Ent|sor|gungs|not|stand** M waste (disposal) emergency; **Ent|sor|gungs|park** M (nuclear) waste dump

ent|span|nen [ɛntˈʃpanən] *ptp* **entspannt** **VT** *Muskeln, Nerven etc* to relax; *Bogen* to unbend; *Seil* to slacken, to untighten; *Wasser* to reduce the surface tension of; (*fig*) *Lage, Beziehungen* to ease (up) **VR** to relax (*auch fig*); (= *ausruhen*) to rest; (*nach der Arbeit etc*) to unwind, to unbend; (*Lage etc*) to ease; (*Feder etc*) to lose tension

ent|spannt [ɛntˈʃpant] ADJ relaxed; **die Lage ist wieder etwas ~er** the situation is now less tense again

Ent|spannt|heit F -, *no pl* (*der Lage*) lack of tension (+*gen* in); **meine mangelnde ~** the fact that I wasn't relaxed

Ent|span|nung F relaxation (*auch fig*); (*von Lage, Fin: an der Börse*) easing(-up); (*Pol*) easing or reduction of tension (+*gen* in), détente; (*des Wassers*) reduction of surface tension; (*von Seil etc*) slackening, untightening; **nach der Arbeit sehe ich zur ~ etwas fern** after work I watch television for a bit to help me unwind

Ent|span|nungs-: **Ent|span|nungs|be|mü|hun|gen** PL efforts *pl* aimed at easing (political) tension; **Ent|span|nungs|po|li|tik** F policy of détente; **Ent|span|nungs|übun|gen** PL (*Med etc*) relaxation exercises *pl*

ent|spie|gelt [ɛntˈʃpiːɡlt] ADJ *Brillengläser, Bildschirm* anti-reflective

ent|spin|nen [ɛntˈʃpɪnən] *ptp* **entsponnen** [ɛntˈʃpɔnən] VR *irreg* (*geh*) to develop, to arise

entspr. *abbr von* **entsprechend**

ent|spre|chen [ɛntˈʃprɛçn] ⊕ 32.4, 38.1, 53.6 *ptp* **entsprochen** [ɛntˈʃprɔxn] VI *irreg* +*dat* to correspond to; *der Wahrheit* to be in accordance with; *den Tatsachen auch* to fit, to be in accordance with; (= *genügen*) *Anforderungen, Kriterien* to fulfil (*Brit*), to fullfill (*US*), to meet; *einem Anlass* to be in keeping with; *Erwartungen* to come or live up to; *einer Beschreibung* to answer, to fit; *einer Bitte, einem Wunsch etc* to meet, to comply with; **sich** *or* **einander ~** to correspond (with each other), to tally; **ihre Ausrüstung entsprach nicht den alpinen Bedingungen** her outfit wasn't suitable for the alpine conditions; **seinem Zweck ~** to fulfil (*Brit*) or fulfill (*US*) its purpose

ent|spre|chend **ADJ** corresponding; (= *zuständig*) relevant; (= *angemessen*) appropriate; **der Film war besonders geschmacklos, und die Kritiken waren dann auch ~** the film was particularly tasteless and the reviews of it were correspondingly harsh; **ein der Leistung ~es Gehalt** a salary commensurate with one's performance

ADV accordingly; (= *ähnlich, gleich*) correspondingly; **er wurde ~ bestraft** he was suitably *or* appropriately punished; **etw ~ würdigen** to show suitable appreciation for sth

PREP +*dat* in accordance with, according to; (= *ähnlich, gleich*) corresponding to; **er wird seiner Leistung ~ bezahlt** he is paid according to output; **er hat sich den Erwartungen ~ entwickelt** he has progressed as we had hoped → **Umstand**

Ent|spre|chung F -, -en (= *Äquivalent*) equivalent; (= *Gegenstück*) counterpart; (= *Analogie*) parallel; (= *Übereinstimmung*) correspondence

ent|sprie|ßen [ɛntˈʃpriːsn] *ptp* **entsprossen** [ɛntˈʃprɔsn] VI *irreg aux sein* (*liter: lit, fig*) **einer Sache** (*dat*) *or* **aus etw ~** to spring forth from

sth (*liter*); (*old, hum*) *aus Ehe, Familie etc* to issue from sth (*old, form*)

ent|sprin|gen [ɛntˈʃprɪŋən] *ptp* **entsprungen** [ɛntˈʃprʊŋən] VI *irreg aux sein* **a** (*Fluss*) to rise **b** (= *entfliehen*) to escape (+*dat, aus* from) **c** (= *sich herleiten von*) +*dat* to spring from, to arise from

ent|staat|li|chen [ɛntˈʃtaːtlɪçn] *ptp* **entstaatlicht** VT to denationalize

Ent|sta|li|ni|sie|rung [ɛntʃtaliniˈziːrʊŋ] F -, -en destalinization

ent|stam|men [ɛntˈʃtamən] *ptp* **entstammt** VI *aux sein* +*dat* to stem or come from; *einer Familie auch* to be descended from; (*fig auch*) to originate in *or* from

ent|stauben [ɛntˈʃtaubn] *ptp* **entstaubt** VT to remove the dust from, to free from dust

ent|ste|hen [ɛntˈʃteːən] *ptp* **entstanden** [ɛntˈʃtandn] VI *irreg aux sein* (= *ins Dasein treten*) to come into being; (= *seinen Ursprung haben*) to originate; (= *sich entwickeln*) to arise, to develop (*aus, durch* from); (= *hervorkommen*) to emerge (*aus, durch* from); (= *verursacht werden*) to result (*aus, durch* from); (*Chem: Verbindungen*) to be produced (*aus* from, *durch* through, via); (*Kunstwerk*: = *geschrieben/gebaut etc werden*) to be written/built etc; **das Feuer war durch Nachlässigkeit entstanden** the fire was caused by negligence; **bei Entstehen eines Feuers** in the event of (a) fire; **wir wollen nicht den Eindruck ~ lassen, ...** we don't want to give (rise to) the impression that ..., we don't want to let the impression emerge that ...; **im Entstehen begriffen sein** to be in the process of formation or development, to be emerging; **für ~den** *or* **entstandenen Schaden** for damages incurred

Ent|ste|hen NT -s, *no pl* → **Entstehung** → *auch* **entstehen**

Ent|ste|hung F -, -en (= *das Werden*) genesis, coming into being; (= *das Hervorkommen*) emergence; (= *Ursprung*) origin; (= *Bildung*) formation

Ent|ste|hungs-: **Ent|ste|hungs|ge|schich|te** F genesis; (*Bibl*) Genesis; **Ent|ste|hungs|ort** M *pl* -orte place of origin; **Ent|ste|hungs|ur|sa|che** F original cause; **Ent|ste|hungs|zeit** F time of origin

ent|stei|gen [ɛntˈʃtaign] *ptp* **entstiegen** [ɛntˈʃtiːɡn] VI *irreg aux sein* +*dat* (*geh*) *einem Wagen* to alight from (*form*); *dem Wasser, dem Bad* to emerge from; (*fig: Dampf etc*) to rise from

ent|stei|nen [ɛntˈʃtainən] *ptp* **entsteint** VT to stone

ent|stel|len [ɛntˈʃtɛlən] *ptp* **entstellt** VT (= *verunstalten*) *Gesicht* to disfigure; (= *verzerren*) *Gesicht(szüge)* to distort, to contort; (*fig*) *Bericht, Wahrheit etc* to distort; **etw entstellt wiedergeben** to distort or misrepresent sth; **sein von Hass/Schmerz entstelltes Gesicht** his face distorted or contorted with hate/pain

ent|stel|lend *prp von* **entstellen** ADJ *Narbe etc* disfiguring

Ent|stel|lung F disfigurement; (*fig*) distortion; (*der Wahrheit*) perversion, distortion

ent|stem|peln [ɛntˈʃtɛmpln] *ptp* **entstempelt** VT (*Aut*) to cancel the registration of

Ent|sti|ckung [ɛntˈʃtɪkʊŋ] F -, -en denitrification

Ent|sti|ckungs|an|la|ge F denitrification plant

ent|stie|len [ɛntˈʃtiːlən] *ptp* **entstielt** VT *Obst* to remove the stalk(s) from

ent|stoff|li|chen [ɛntˈʃtɔflɪçn] *ptp* **entstofflicht** VT to dematerialize

ent|stö|ren [ɛntˈʃtøːrən] *ptp* **entstört** VT *Radio, Telefon* to free from interference; *Auto, Staubsauger* to fit a suppressor to, to suppress

Ent|stö|rer M , **Ent|stör|ge|rät** NT (*für Auto etc*) suppressor; (*für Radio, Telefon*) anti-interference device

Ent|stö|rung F (*von Radio, Telefon*) freeing from interference, suppression of interference; (*von*

Auto, Staubsauger) fitting of a suppressor (+*gen* to), suppressing

Ent|stö|rungs|dienst M , **Ent|stö|rungs|stel|le** F telephone maintenance service

ent|strö|men [ɛntˈʃtrøːmən] *ptp* **entströmt** VI *aux sein* to pour or gush out (+*dat, aus* of); (*Gas, Geruch etc*) to issue or escape (+*dat, aus* from)

Ent|sub|li|mie|rung F (*Psych, Sociol*) repressive ~ repressive desublimation

ent|ta|bu|i|sie|ren [ɛnttabuiˈziːrən] *ptp* **enttabuisiert** VT to free from taboos, to remove the taboos from

Ent|ta|bu|i|sie|rung F -, -en removal of taboos (+*gen* of)

ent|tar|nen [ɛntˈtarnən] *ptp* **enttarnt** VT *Spion* to blow the cover of (*inf*); (*fig*: = *entlarven*) to expose; **er wurde enttarnt** (*Spion*) his cover was blown, he was exposed

Ent|tar|nung F exposure

ent|täu|schen [ɛntˈtɔyʃn] *ptp* **enttäuscht** **VT** to disappoint; *Vertrauen* to betray; **enttäuscht sein über** (+*acc*)**/von** to be disappointed at/by or in; **er ging enttäuscht nach Hause** he went home disappointed; **sie ist im Leben oft enttäuscht worden** she has had many disappointments in life; **du hast uns sehr enttäuscht** you have really let us down *or* disappointed us; **angenehm enttäuscht sein** (*hum*) to be pleasantly surprised

VI **unsere Mannschaft hat sehr enttäuscht** our team were very disappointing; (= *hat schlecht gespielt*) our team played very disappointingly; **der neue Wagen hat enttäuscht** the new car is a disappointment *or* let-down (*inf*)

Ent|täu|schung F disappointment; **das Theaterstück war eine große ~** the play was a big disappointment *or* let-down (*inf*); **jdm eine ~ bereiten** to disappoint sb

ent|thro|nen [ɛntˈtroːnən] *ptp* **entthront** VT (*lit, fig*) to dethrone

Ent|thro|nung F -, -en (*lit, fig*) dethronement, dethroning

ent|trüm|mern [ɛntˈtrʏmɛn] *ptp* **enttrümmert** **VT** to clear of rubble **VI** to clear the rubble (away)

ent|völ|kern [ɛntˈvœlkɛn] *ptp* **entvölkert** VT to depopulate

ent|völ|kert [ɛntˈvœlkɛt] *ptp von* **entvölkern** ADJ depopulated; (= *leer*) deserted, unpopulated

Ent|völ|ke|rung F -, -en depopulation

entw. *abbr von* **entweder**

ent|wach|sen [ɛntˈvaksn] *ptp* **entwachsen** VI *irreg aux sein* +*dat* **a** (*geh*: = *herauswachsen aus*) to spring from **b** (= *zu groß werden für*) to outgrow, to grow out of

ent|waff|nen [ɛntˈvafnən] *ptp* **entwaffnet** VT (*lit, fig*) to disarm

ent|waff|nend ADJ (*fig*) disarming

Ent|waff|nung F -, -en disarming; (*eines Landes*) disarmament

ent|wal|den [ɛntˈvaldn] *ptp* **entwaldet** VT to deforest

ent|wan|zen [ɛntˈvantsn] *ptp* **entwanzt** VT to debug

ent|war|nen [ɛntˈvarnən] *ptp* **entwarnt** VI to sound or give the all-clear

Ent|war|nung F sounding of the all-clear; (= *Signal*) all-clear

ent|wäs|sern [ɛntˈvɛsən] *ptp* **entwässert** VT *Grundstück, Moor, Keller* to drain; *Gewebe, Ödem, Körper* to dehydrate

Ent|wäs|se|rung F drainage; (*Chem*) dehydration

Ent|wäs|se|rungs-: **Ent|wäs|se|rungs|an|la|ge** F drainage system; **Ent|wäs|se|rungs|gra|ben** M drainage ditch; **Ent|wäs|se|rungs|ka|nal** M drainage channel

ent|we|der [ˈɛntveːdɐ, ɛntˈveːdɐ] CONJ ~ ... **oder ...** either ... or ...; ~ **oder!** make up your mind (one way or the other)!, yes or no; ~ **gleich oder gar nicht**, ~ **jetzt oder nie** it's now or never

Ent|we|der-o-der ▲ [ˈɛntveːdɐˈʔoːdɐ] NT -, - **hier gibt es kein** ~ there is no alternative; **hier gibt es nur ein** ~ there has to be a definite decision one way or the other

ent|wei|chen [ɛntˈvaiçn] ptp **entwichen** [ɛntˈviçn] VI irreg aux sein (geh: = fliehen) to escape (+dat, aus from), to run away (+dat, aus from); (= sich verflüchtigen: Gas, Flüssigkeit) to leak or escape (+dat, aus from, out of)

ent|wei|hen [ɛntˈvaian] ptp **entweiht** VT to violate (auch fig); (= entheiligen) to profane, to desecrate

Ent|wei|hung F -, -en violation; (= Entheiligung) profanation, desecration

ent|wen|den [ɛntˈvɛndn] ptp **entwendet** VT (form) **jdn etw/etw aus etw** ~ to steal or purloin (hum, form) sth from sb/sth

Ent|wen|dung F (form) theft, stealing, purloining (hum, form)

ent|wer|fen [ɛntˈvɛrfn] ptp **entworfen** [ɛntˈvɔrfn] VT irreg **a** (= zeichnen, gestalten) Zeichnung etc to sketch; Muster, Modell etc to design **b** (= ausarbeiten) Gesetz, Vortrag, Schreiben etc to draft, to draw up; Plan to devise, to draw up **c** (fig) (= darstellen, darlegen) Bild to depict, to draw; (= in Umrissen darstellen) to outline

ent|wer|ten [ɛntˈveːɐtn] ptp **entwertet** VT **a** (= im Wert mindern) to devalue, to depreciate; Zeugenaussage, Argument etc auch to undermine **b** (= ungültig machen) to make or render invalid; Münzen to demonetize; Briefmarke, Fahrschein to cancel

Ent|wer|ter [ɛntˈveːɐtɐ] M -s, - (ticket-)cancelling (Brit) or (ticket-)canceling (US) machine

Ent|wer|tung F **a** (= Wertminderung) devaluation, depreciation **b** (von Zeugenaussagen, Argumenten) undermining **c** (= Ungültigmachung) invalidation; (von Briefmarke, Fahrschein) cancellation

ent|wi|ckeln [ɛntˈvɪkln] ptp **entwickelt** VT to develop (auch Phot); (Phot) esp Diapositive to process; Methode, Verfahren to develop, to evolve; (Math) Formel to expand, to develop; (Chem) Gas etc to produce, to generate; Mut, Energie to show, to display; **jdm etw** ~ to set out or expound sth to sb; **etw zu etw** ~ to develop sth into sth
VR to develop (zu into); (Chem: Gase etc) to be produced or generated; **das Projekt/der neue Angestellte entwickelt sich gut** the project/the new employee is coming along or shaping up nicely; **das Kind entwickelt sich gut** the child is doing well; **er hat sich ganz schön entwickelt** (inf) he's turned out really nicely

Ent|wick|ler [ɛntˈvɪklɐ] M -s, - (Phot) developer

Ent|wick|ler|bad NT (Phot) developing bath

Ent|wick|lung F -, -en development; (von Methoden, Verfahren, Gattung auch) evolution; (Math: von Formel auch) expansion; (= Erzeugung, Chem: von Gasen etc) production, generation; (von Mut, Energie) show, display; (Phot) developing; (esp von Diapositiven) processing; **das Flugzeug ist noch in der** ~ the plane is still being developed, the plane is still in the development stage; **Jugendliche, die noch in der** ~ **sind** young people who are still in their adolescence or still developing

Ent|wick|lungs-: **Ent|wick|lungs|al|ter** NT adolescence; **Ent|wick|lungs|ar|beit** F development (work); **Ent|wick|lungs|be|schleu|ni|gung** F (Physiol) acceleration (in development); **Ent|wick|lungs|bio|lo|gie** F evolutionary biology; **ent|wick|lungs|bio|lo|gisch** ADJ Prozesse of evolutionary biology; **Ent|wick|lungs|dienst** M voluntary service overseas (Brit), VSO (Brit), Peace Corps (US); **ent|wick|lungs|fä|hig** ADJ capable of devel-

opment; **der Plan/die Idee ist durchaus** ~ this plan/idea is definitely worth following up or expanding; **diese Stelle ist** ~ this position has prospects; **Ent|wick|lungs|fä|hig|keit** F capability of development, capacity for development; (einer Stelle) prospects pl; **Ent|wick|lungs|gang** M pl -gänge development; **Ent|wick|lungs|ge|biet** NT development area; **Ent|wick|lungs|ge|schich|te** F developmental history, evolution; **ent|wick|lungs|ge|schicht|lich** ADJ evolutionary attr, with respect to evolution; **Ent|wick|lungs|hel|fer(in)** M(F) person doing Voluntary Service Overseas (Brit), VSO worker (Brit), Peace Corps worker (US); **ent|wick|lungs|hem|mend** ADJ restricting or impeding development; **Ent|wick|lungs|hil|fe** F foreign aid; **Ent|wick|lungs|jah|re** PL adolescent or formative (auch fig) years, adolescence; **Ent|wick|lungs|kos|ten** PL development costs pl; **Ent|wick|lungs|land** NT developing or third-world country; **Ent|wick|lungs|mög|lich|keit** F possibility for development; **Ent|wick|lungs|pha|se** F (Psych) developmental stage; **Ent|wick|lungs|po|li|tik** F development aid policy; **ent|wick|lungs|po|li|tisch** ADJ development aid policy attr, Sprecher on development aid policy; **Ent|wick|lungs|psy|cho|lo|gie** F developmental psychology; **Ent|wick|lungs|ro|man** M (Liter) novel showing the development of a character; **Ent|wick|lungs|sta|di|um** NT stage of development; (der Menschheit etc) evolutionary stage; **Ent|wick|lungs|stö|rung** F developmental disturbance, disturbance in development; **Ent|wick|lungs|stu|fe** F stage of development; (der Menschheit etc) evolutionary stage; **Ent|wick|lungs|zeit** F period of development; (Biol, Psych) developmental period; (Phot) developing time

ent|win|den [ɛntˈvɪndn] ptp **entwunden** [ɛntˈvʊndn] VT irreg (geh) **jdm etw** ~ to wrest sth from sb

ent|wirr|bar ADJ schwer ~ sein (lit, fig) to be hard to untangle or unravel

ent|wir|ren [ɛntˈvɪrən] ptp **entwirrt** VT (lit, fig) to untangle, to unravel

ent|wi|schen [ɛntˈvɪʃn] ptp **entwischt** VI aux sein (inf) to escape, to get away (+dat, aus from)

ent|wöh|nen [ɛntˈvøːnən] ptp **entwöhnt** VT Säugling, Jungtier to wean; **jdn** ~ (einer Gewohnheit, Sucht) to break sb of the habit (+dat, von of), to cure sb (+dat, von of), to wean sb (+dat, von from); **sich einer Sache** (gen) ~ (geh) to wean oneself off sth, to disaccustom oneself from sth (form)

Ent|wöh|nung F -, -en (von Drogen) withdrawal; (von Säugling, Jungtier) weaning

Ent|wöh|nungs|kur F (von Drogen) withdrawal treatment or therapy

ent|wöl|ken [ɛntˈvœlkn] ptp **entwölkt** VR (lit, fig liter) to clear

ent|wür|di|gen [ɛntˈvʏrdɪgn] ptp **entwürdigt** VT to degrade; (= Schande bringen über) to disgrace
VR to degrade or abase oneself

ent|wür|di|gend ADJ degrading

Ent|wür|di|gung F degradation, abasement; (= Entehrung) disgrace (+gen to)

Ent|wurf M **a** (= Skizze, Abriss) outline, sketch; (= Design) design; (Archit, fig) blueprint **b** (von Plan, Gesetz etc, = Vertragsentwurf, Konzept) draft (version), framework; (einer Theorie auch) outline; (Parl: = Gesetzentwurf) bill; **das Bild ist im** ~ **fertig** the sketch for the picture is finished; **die Doktorarbeit ist im** ~ **fertig** the framework for the PhD is finished

Ent|wurfs|sta|di|um NT sich im ~ befinden to be in the planning stage, to be on the drawing board

ent|wur|men [ɛntˈvʊrmən] ptp **entwurmt** VT Katze etc to worm

ent|wur|zeln [ɛntˈvʊrtsln] ptp **entwurzelt** VT (lit, fig) to uproot

Ent|wur|ze|lung F -, -en (lit, fig: = das Entwurzeln) uprooting; (fig: = das Entwurzeltsein) rootlessness

ent|zau|bern [ɛntˈtsaubɐn] ptp **entzaubert** VT **jdn/etw** ~ to break the spell on sb/sth; (fig auch) to deprive sb/sth of his/her/its mystique; **ihre romantischen Vorstellungen wurden entzaubert** her romantic illusions were shattered

Ent|zau|be|rung F -, -en breaking of the/a spell (+gen on); (fig auch) deprivation of mystique; (von Vorstellungen) shattering, destruction

ent|zer|ren [ɛntˈtseːrən] ptp **entzerrt** VT to correct, to rectify

Ent|zer|rung F correction, rectification; **zeitli|che** ~ staggering

ent|zie|hen [ɛntˈtsiːən] ptp **entzogen** [ɛntˈtsoːgn] irreg VT (+dat from) to withdraw, to take away; Gunst etc to withdraw; Flüssigkeit to draw, to extract; (Chem) to extract; **jdm Alkohol/Nikotin** ~ to deprive sb of alcohol/nicotine; **die Ärzte versuchten ihn zu** ~ (inf) the doctors tried to cure him of his addiction; **jdm die Erlaubnis** etc ~ to withdraw or revoke sb's permit etc, to take sb's permit etc away; **jdm die Rente** etc ~ to cut off or stop sb's pension etc; **jdm sein Vertrauen** ~ to withdraw one's confidence or trust in sb; **dem Redner das Wort** ~ to ask the speaker to stop
VR **sich jdm/einer Sache** ~ to evade or elude sb/sth; (= entkommen auch) to escape (from) sb/sth; **sich seiner Verantwortung** ~ to shirk one's responsibilities; **sich jds Verständnis/Kontrolle** ~ to be beyond sb's understanding/control; **das entzieht sich meiner Kenntnis/Zuständigkeit** that is beyond my knowledge/authority; **das hat sich meiner Aufmerksamkeit entzogen** that escaped my attention; **sich jds Blicken** ~ to be hidden from sight
VI (inf) to undergo treatment for (drug) addiction; (Alkoholiker) to dry out (inf)

Ent|zie|hung F **a** (von Lizenz etc) withdrawal, revocation (form) **b** (von Drogen etc) (= Wegnahme) withdrawal, deprivation; (= Behandlung) treatment for drug addiction; (gegen Alkoholismus) treatment for alcoholism

Ent|zie|hungs-: **Ent|zie|hungs|an|stalt** F (für Drogenabhängige) rehabilitation or treatment centre (Brit) or center (US) for drug addicts, detoxification or detox (inf) clinic; (für Alkoholiker) rehabilitation or treatment centre (Brit) or center (US) for alcoholics, rehab centre (Brit inf) or center (US inf), drying-out clinic (Brit inf); **Ent|zie|hungs|kur** F withdrawal treatment; (für Drogenabhängige auch) cure for drug addiction; (für Alkoholiker auch) cure for alcoholism

ent|zif|fer|bar ADJ decipherable; Funkspruch etc decodable

ent|zif|fern [ɛntˈtsɪfɐn] ptp **entziffert** VT to decipher; Geheimschrift, verschlüsselte Botschaft, DNS-Struktur to decode; **ich kann den Namen nicht** ~ I can't make out the name

Ent|zif|fe|rung F -, -en deciphering; (von Funkspruch etc) decoding

ent|zü|cken [ɛntˈtsʏkn] ptp **entzückt** VT to delight; **von jdm/über etw** (acc) **entzückt sein** to be delighted by sb/at sth

Ent|zü|cken [ɛntˈtsʏkn] NT -s, no pl delight, joy; **zu meinem (größten)** ~ to my (great) delight or joy; **in** ~ **geraten** to go into raptures; **jdn in (helles)** ~ **versetzen** to send sb into raptures

ent|zü|ckend ADJ delightful, charming; **das ist ja ~!** how delightful or charming!

Ent|zü|ckung F -, -en = Entzücken

Ent|zug M , no pl **a** (einer Lizenz etc) withdrawal, revocation (form) **b** (Med) (von Drogen etc) withdrawal; (= Entziehungskur) (für Drogenabhängige) cure for drug addiction; (für Alkoholiker) cure for alcoholism; **er ist auf** ~ (Med inf) (Drogenabhängiger) he is being treated for drug addiction; (*Alkoholiker*) he is being dried out (*inf*); **kalter ~** (*sl: von Drogen*) cold turkey (*inf*)

Ent|zugs|er|schei|nung F , **Ent|zugs|symp|tom** NT withdrawal symptom

ent|zünd|bar ADJ (*lit, fig*) inflammable; **leicht ~** highly inflammable; (*fig*) easily roused *or* excited

Ent|zünd|bar|keit [ɛntˈtsʏntbaːɐkait] F -, *no pl* inflammability

ent|zün|den [ɛntˈtsʏndn] *ptp* **entzündet** ⓥ **a** *Feuer* to light; *Holz etc auch* to set light to, to ignite (*esp Sci, Tech*); *Streichholz* to light, to strike; (*fig*) *Streit etc* to start, to spark off; *Hass* to inflame; *Fantasie to* fire; *Begeisterung* to fire, to kindle **b** (*Med*) to inflame ⓥⓡ **a** (= *zu brennen anfangen*) to catch fire, to ignite (*esp Sci, Tech*); (*fig*) (*Streit*) to be sparked off; (*Hass*) to be inflamed; (*Fantasie*) to be fired; (*Begeisterung*) to be kindled **b** (*Med*) to become inflamed

ent|zün|det [ɛntˈtsʏndət] *ptp von* **entzünden** ADJ (*Med*) inflamed; *Augen auch* sore

ent|zünd|lich [ɛntˈtsʏntlɪç] ADJ *Gase, Brennstoff* inflammable; (*Med*) inflammatory; **~e Haut** skin which easily becomes inflamed; **ein leicht ~es Temperament** a highly inflammable temper

Ent|zün|dung F **a** (*Med*) inflammation **b** ignition (*esp Sci, Tech*); **Funken führten zur ~ des Heus** sparks led to the hay catching fire

Ent|zün|dungs- (*Med*): **ent|zün|dungs|hem|mend** ADJ anti-inflammatory, antiphlogistic (*form*); **Ent|zün|dungs|hem|mer** M -s, - antiphlogistic (*form*); **Ent|zün|dungs|herd** M focus of inflammation

ent|zwei [ɛntˈtsvai] ADJ *pred* in two (pieces), in half, asunder (*old, poet*); (= *kaputt*) broken; (= *zerrissen*) torn

ent|zwei+bre|chen VTI *sep irreg* (*vi: aux sein*) to break in two; (= *zerbrechen*) to break

ent|zwei|en [ɛntˈtsvaiən] *ptp* **entzweit** ⓥ to turn against each other, to divide, to set at variance ⓥⓡ **sich (mit jdm)** (= *sich streiten auch*) to quarrel (with sb)

ent|zwei-: **ent|zwei+ge|hen** VI *sep irreg aux sein* to break (in two *or* half), to break asunder (*poet*); **ent|zwei+rei|ßen** VT *sep irreg* to tear *or* rend in two *or* in half *or* asunder (*poet*); (= *zerreißen*) to tear to pieces; **ent|zwei+schla|gen** VT *sep irreg* to strike in half *or* in two *or* asunder (*poet*); (= *zerschlagen*) to smash (to pieces); **ent|zwei+schnei|den** VT *sep irreg* to cut in two *or* half; (= *zerschneiden*) to cut to pieces

Ent|zwei|ung F -, -en (*fig*) (= *Bruch*) split, rupture, break; (= *Streit*) quarrel

en vogue [ã ˈvoːk] ADJ *pred* (*geh*) in vogue *or* fashion

En|ze|pha|lo|gramm [ɛntsefaloˈgram] NT *pl* **-gramme** (*Med*) encephalogram

En|ze|pha|lo|pa|thie [ɛntsefalopaˈtiː] F -, -n [-ˈtiːən] (*Med*) encephalopathy

En|zi|an [ˈɛntsiaːn] M -s, -e gentian; (= *Branntwein*) spirit distilled from the roots of gentian

En|zyk|li|ka [ɛnˈtsyːklika] F -, **Enzykliken** [-kn] (*Eccl*) encyclical

En|zyk|lo|pä|die [ɛntsyklopɛˈdiː] F -, -n [-ˈdiːən] encyclop(a)edia

en|zyk|lo|pä|disch [ɛntsykloˈpɛːdɪʃ] ADJ encyclop(a)edic

En|zym [ɛnˈtsyːm] NT -s, -e enzyme

eo ip|so [ˈeːo ˈɪpso] ADV (*geh*) ipso facto

E|pau|let|te [epoˈlɛtə] F -, -n *usu pl* epaulette; (*US auch*) epaulet

E|pen *pl von* **Epos**

E|phe|be [eˈfeːbə] M -n, -n (*Hist*) ephebe, ephebus

e|phe|mer [efeˈmeːɐ], **e|phe|me|risch** [efeˈmeːrɪʃ] ADJ (*geh*) ephemeral

E|phe|ser [ˈeːfezɐ] M -s, -, **E|phe|se|rin** [-ərɪn] F -, -nen Ephesian

E|phe|ser|brief M Epistle to the Ephesians, Ephesians *sing*

E|pi|de|mie [epideˈmiː] F -, -n [-ˈmiːən] (*Med, fig*) epidemic

E|pi|de|mi|o|lo|ge [epidemioˈloːgə] M -n, -n, **E|pi|de|mi|o|lo|gin** [-ˈloːgɪn] F -, -nen epidemiologist

E|pi|de|mi|o|lo|gie [epidemioloˈgiː] F -, *no pl* epidemiology

e|pi|de|mi|o|lo|gisch [epidemioˈloːgɪʃ] ADJ epidemiological

e|pi|de|misch [epiˈdeːmɪʃ] ADJ (*Med, fig*) epidemic ADV **sich ~ ausbreiten** (*Med*) to spread as an epidemic; (*fig*) to spread like an epidemic

E|pi|der|mis [epiˈdɛrmɪs] F -, **Epidermen** [-ˈdɛrmən] epidermis

E|pi|di|a|skop [epidiaˈskoːp] NT -s, -e epidiascope

E|pi|go|ne [epiˈgoːnə] M -n, -n, **E|pi|go|nin** [-ˈgoːnɪn] F -, -nen epigone (*liter*); (= *Nachahmer*) imitator

e|pi|go|nen|haft ADJ epigonic (*liter, rare*); (= *nachahmend*) imitative

E|pi|gramm [epiˈgram] NT *pl* **-gramme** epigram

e|pi|gram|ma|tisch [epigraˈmaːtɪʃ] ADJ epigrammatic

E|pi|graf ▲ [epiˈgraːf] NT -s, -e epigraph

E|pik [ˈeːpɪk] F -, *no pl* epic poetry

E|pi|ker [ˈeːpikɐ] M -s, -, **E|pi|ke|rin** [-ərɪn] F -, -nen epic poet

E|pi|kur [epiˈkuːɐ] M -s Epicurus

E|pi|ku|re|er [epikuˈreːɐ] M -s, -, **E|pi|ku|re|e|rin** [-ˈreːərɪn] F -, -nen (*Philos*) Epicurean; (*fig*) epicure(an)

e|pi|ku|re|isch [epikuˈreːɪʃ] ADJ (*Philos*) Epicurean; (*fig*) epicurean

E|pi|lep|sie [epilɛˈpsiː] F -, -n [-ˈpsiːən] epilepsy

E|pi|lep|ti|ker [epiˈlɛptikɐ] M -s, -, **E|pi|lep|ti|ke|rin** [-ərɪn] F -, -nen epileptic

e|pi|lep|tisch [epiˈlɛptɪʃ] ADJ epileptic

E|pi|log [epiˈloːk] M -s, -e [-gə] epilogue

e|pisch [ˈeːpɪʃ] ADJ (*lit, fig*) epic

E|pi|skop [epiˈskoːp] NT -s, -e episcope

E|pis|ko|pat [epɪskoˈpaːt] M OR NT -(e)s, -e episcopacy, episcopate

E|pi|so|de [epiˈzoːdə] F -, -n episode

E|pi|so|den|film M film in instalments (*Brit*) *or* installments (*US*), serial film

e|pi|so|den|haft, **e|pi|so|disch** [epiˈzoːdɪʃ] ADJ episodic

E|pis|tel [eˈpɪstl] F -, -n epistle (*auch inf*); (*old*: = *Lesung*) lesson; **jdm die ~ lesen** (*old inf*) to read sb the riot act (*inf*)

E|pis|te|mo|lo|gie [epɪstemoloˈgiː] F -, *no pl* epistemology

E|pi|taph [epiˈtaːf] NT -s, -e (*liter*) epitaph

E|pi|the|ton [eˈpiːtetɔn] NT -s, **Epitheta** [-ta] (*Poet*) epithet

E|pi|zent|rum [epiˈtsɛntrom] NT epicentre (*Brit*), epicenter (*US*)

e|po|chal [epɔˈxaːl] ADJ **a** epochal **b** (= *Epoche machend*) epoch-making, era-making

E|po|che [eˈpɔxə] F -, -n epoch; **~ machen** to be epoch-making, to mark a new epoch or era; **~ machend** epoch-making

e|po|che|ma|chend △ ADJ → **Epoche**

E|pos [ˈeːpɔs] NT -, **Epen** [ˈeːpn] epic (poem), epos

E|po|xyd|harz [epɔˈksyːt-] NT epoxy resin

Ep|rou|vet|te [epruˈvɛt] F -, -n (*Aus Chem*) test tube

E|qua|li|zer [ˈiːkvəlaizɐ] M -s, - (*Tech*) equalizer

E|qui|pa|ge [ek(v)iˈpaːʒə] F -, -n (*old*) equipage

E|qui|pe [eˈkɪp] F -, -n team

er [eːɐ] PERS PRON *gen* **seiner**, *dat* **ihm**, *acc* **ihn** he; (*von Dingen*) it; (*von Hund etc*) it, he; (*vom Mond*) it, she (*poet*); **wenn ich er wäre** if I were

him *or* he (*form*); **er ist es** it's him, it is he (*form*); **wer hat das gemacht/ist der Täter? – er/ er (ist es)!** who did that/is the person responsible? – he did/is!, him (*inf*)!; **er war es nicht, ich wars** it wasn't him, it was me; **sie ist größer als er** she is taller than he is *or* him; **Er** (*obs*) you; (*Bibl*) He; **ein Er und eine Sie** (*hum inf*) a he and a she

er|ach|ten [ɛɐˈʔaxtn] *ptp* **erachtet** VT (*geh*) **jdn/ etw für** *or* **als etw ~** to consider *or* deem (*form*) sb/sth (to be) sth

Er|ach|ten [ɛɐˈʔaxtn] NT -s, *no pl* **meines ~s, nach meinem ~** in my opinion

er|ah|nen [ɛɐˈʔaːnən] *ptp* **erahnt** VT = **ahnen**

er|ar|bei|ten [ɛɐˈʔarbaitn] *ptp* **erarbeitet** VT **a** (= *erwerben*) *Vermögen etc* to work for; *Wissen etc* to acquire **b** (= *erstellen*) *Entwurf etc* to work out, to elaborate

Er|ar|bei|tung [ɛɐˈʔarbaitoŋ] F -, -en *usu sing* **a** (*von Lernstoff etc*) mastering; (*von Wissen*) acquisition **b** (= *Erstellung*) development, creation

Erb- [ˈɛrp-]: **Erb|adel** M hereditary nobility; **Erb|an|la|ge** F *usu pl* hereditary factor(s *pl*); **Erb|an|spruch** M claim to an/the inheritance; **Erb|an|teil** M share *or* portion of an/the inheritance

er|bar|men [ɛɐˈbarmən] *ptp* **erbarmt** ⓥ **jdn ~** to arouse sb's pity, to move sb to pity; **es kann einen ~** it's pitiable; **er sieht zum Erbarmen aus** he's a pitiful sight; **das ist zum Erbarmen** it's pitiful; **sie singt zum Erbarmen** she sings appallingly, she's an appalling singer; **es möchte einen Hund ~** (*inf*) it would melt a heart of stone ⓥⓡ **+gen** to have *or* take pity (on) (*auch hum inf*); (= *verzeihen, verschonen*) to have mercy (on); **Herr, erbarme dich (unser)!** Lord, have mercy (upon us)!

Er|bar|men [ɛɐˈbarmən] NT -s, *no pl* (= *Mitleid*) pity, compassion (*mit* on); (= *Gnade*) mercy (*mit* on); **aus ~** out of pity; **ohne ~** pitiless(ly), merciless(ly); **er kennt kein ~** he knows no mercy; **kein ~ mit jdm kennen** to be merciless with sb, to show sb no mercy

er|bar|mens|wert ADJ pitiable, wretched, pitiful

er|bärm|lich [ɛɐˈbɛrmlɪç] ADJ (= *erbarmenswert, pej*: = *dürftig*) pitiful, wretched; (= *gemein, schlecht*) wretched, miserable; (*inf*: = *furchtbar*) *Kälte* terrible, hideous ADV *sich verhalten* abominably, wretchedly; (= *sehr schlecht*) *singen* miserably, appallingly; (*inf*: = *furchtbar*) *frieren, wehtun* terribly; **~ aussehen** to look wretched *or* terrible

Er|bärm|lich|keit F -, -en (= *Elend*) wretchedness, misery; (*fig*: = *Dürftigkeit, Gemeinheit etc*) wretchedness

Er|bar|mungs-: **er|bar|mungs|los** (*lit, fig*) ADJ pitiless, merciless ADV pitilessly, mercilessly; **Er|bar|mungs|lo|sig|keit** F -, *no pl* (*lit, fig*) pitilessness, mercilessness; **er|bar|mungs|voll** ADJ compassionate, full of pity; **er|bar|mungs|wür|dig** ADJ = **erbarmenswert**

er|bau|en [ɛɐˈbauən] *ptp* **erbaut** ⓥ **a** (*lit, fig*: = *errichten*) to build **b** (*fig*: = *seelisch bereichern*) to edify, to uplift; **wir waren von der Nachricht nicht gerade erbaut** (*inf*) we weren't exactly delighted by the news; **der Chef ist von meinem Plan nicht besonders erbaut** (*inf*) the boss isn't particularly enthusiastic about my plan ⓥⓡ **sich ~ an** (+*dat*) to be uplifted *or* edified by; **abends erbaut er sich an bachschen Kantaten** in the evenings he is uplifted by Bach's cantatas

Er|bau|er [ɛɐˈbauɐ] M -s, -, **Er|bau|e|rin** [-ərɪn] F -, -nen builder; (*fig auch*) architect

er|bau|lich [ɛɐˈbaulɪç] ADJ edifying (*auch iro*), uplifting; (*Rel*) *Buch, Schriften* devotional

Er|bau|lich|keit F -, *no pl* edification *no pl*, uplift *no pl*

Er|bau|ung F -, -en **a** building **b** (*fig: seelisch*) edification; **zur ~** for one's edification

Erb-: Erb|bau|er M pl **-bauern, Erb|bäu|e|rin** F *farmer with a hereditary right to his/her property;* **Erb|bau|recht** NT *(Jur)* inheritable or hereditary building rights pl; **Erb|be|gräb|nis** NT family grave or (= *Gruft*) vault; **erb|be|rech|tigt** ADJ entitled to inherit; **die Erbberechtigten** the legal heirs; **erb|bi|o|lo|gisch** ADJ genetic; **~es Gutachten** *(Jur)* blood test (*to establish paternity*)

Er|be¹ ['ɛrbə] M **-n, -n** *(lit, fig)* heir (*einer Person (gen)* of or to sb, *einer Sache (gen)* to sth); **gesetzlicher ~** legal heir, heir at law *(Jur)*, heir apparent *(Jur)*; **leiblicher ~** blood-related heir, heir according to bloodright; **direkter ~** direct or lineal heir, heir of the body *(Jur)*; **mutmaßlicher ~** presumptive heir, heir presumptive *(Jur)*; **jdn zum** or **als ~n einsetzen** to appoint sb as or to make sb one's heir → **Erbin**

Er|be² NT **-s**, *no pl* inheritance; *(fig)* heritage; (*esp Unerwünschtes*) legacy; **das ~ des Faschismus** the legacy of fascism

er|be|ben [ɛʁˈbeːbn] ptp **erbebt** VI *aux sein (geh: Erde, Mensch etc)* to tremble, to shake, to shudder

er|bei|gen ['ɛrp|aign] ADJ (= *geerbt, vererbt*) inherited; (= *erblich*) hereditary

Erb|ei|gen|schaft F hereditary characteristic

er|ben ['ɛrbn] VT *(lit, fig)* to inherit (*von* from); *Vermögen auch* to come into; (*inf: = geschenkt bekommen*) to get, to be given; **bei ihm ist nichts zu ~** (*inf*) he won't leave you anything; **bei ihm kann man nichts ~** (*inf*) you won't get anything or a sausage *(Brit inf)* out of him VI to inherit

Er|ben|ge|mein|schaft F community of heirs

er|bet|teln [ɛʁˈbɛtln] ptp **erbettelt** VT to get by begging; **die Kinder müssen alles auf der Straße ~** the children have to go begging on the streets for everything; **seine Möbel hat er (sich** dat) **alle des seinen Bekannten erbettelt** he cadged (*esp Brit inf*) or mooched (*US inf*) all his furniture off his friends; **die Kinder erbettelten sich die Erlaubnis, ...** the children managed to wheedle permission ...

er|beu|ten [ɛʁˈbɔytn] ptp **erbeutet** VT *(Tier)* Opfer to carry off; *(Dieb)* to get away with; (*im Krieg*) to capture, to take

Erb-: erb|fä|hig ADJ *(Jur)* entitled to inherit, heritable *(spec)*; **Erb|fä|hig|keit** F *(Jur)* entitlement to inherit, heritability *(spec)*; **Erb|faktor** M *(Biol)* (hereditary) factor, gene; **Erb|fall** M *(Jur)* **im ~** in the case of inheritance; **Erb|fehler** M *(lit, fig)* hereditary defect; **Erb|feind(in)** M(F) traditional or arch enemy; **der ~** (= *Teufel*) the Arch-Fiend; **Erb|fol|ge** F (line of) succession; **Erb|fol|ge|krieg** M war of succession

Erb|gut NT **a** pl **-güter** (= *Hof*) ancestral estate **b** no pl (= *Nachlass*) estate, inheritance; *(fig)* heritage **c** no pl *(Biol)* genotype, genetic make-up

erb|gut-: erb|gut|schä|di|gend ADJ genetically harmful; **erb|gut|ver|än|dernd** ADJ *Stoff* causing genetic changes; **das hat eine ~e Wirkung** it causes genetic changes

er|bie|ten [ɛʁˈbiːtn] ptp **erboten** [ɛʁˈboːtn] VR *irreg (geh)* **sich ~, etw zu tun** to offer or volunteer to do sth; **sich zu etw ~** to offer one's services for sth

Er|bin ['ɛrbɪn] F **-, -nen** heiress → **Erbe¹**

Erb|in|for|ma|ti|on ['ɛrp-] F genetic information

er|bit|ten [ɛʁˈbɪtn] ptp **erbeten** [ɛʁˈbeːtn] VT *irreg* to ask for, to request; **sich ~/nicht ~ lassen** to be/not to be prevailed upon

er|bit|tern [ɛʁˈbɪtɐn] ptp **erbittert** VT to enrage, to incense

er|bit|tert [ɛʁˈbɪtɐt] ADJ *Widerstand, Gegner, Diskussion etc* bitter ADV bitterly

Er|bit|te|rung F **-**, *no pl* rage; (*rare: = Heftigkeit*) fierceness, bitterness

Er|bi|um ['ɛrbiʊm] NT **-s**, *no pl (abbr* **Er**) erbium

Erb|krank|heit ['ɛrp-] F hereditary disease

er|blas|sen [ɛʁˈblasn] ptp **erblasst** VI *aux sein* to (go or turn) pale, to blanch; **vor Neid ~** to turn or go (*esp Brit*) green with envy

Erb|las|ser ['ɛrplasə] M **-s, -, Erb|las|se|rin** [-ərɪn] F **-, -nen** **a** person who leaves an inheritance **b** (= *Testator*) testator/testatrix

Erb|last F negative inheritance or heritage, burden from the past; (= *Probleme*) inherited problem(s pl)

er|blei|chen [ɛʁˈblaiçn] VI *aux sein* **a** ptp **erbleicht** *(geh)* to (go or turn) pale, to blanch **b** pret **erblich** [ɛʁˈblɪç], ptp **erblichen** [ɛʁˈblɪçn] (*obs, liter: = sterben*) to expire

erb|lich ['ɛrplɪç] ADJ hereditary ADV **er ist ~ belastet, auch kam Vater hatte ...** (*bei Eigenschaft*) it's inherited, his father also had ...; (*bei Krankheit*) it runs in the family, his father also had ...; **er ist ~ schwer (vor)belastet** it runs in the family; **etw ist ~ bedingt** sth is an inherited condition; **etw wird ~ von jdm weitergegeben** sth is passed on as a hereditary trait

Erb|lich|keit F **-**, *no pl* heritability, hereditability

er|bli|cken [ɛʁˈblɪkn] ptp **erblickt** VT *(geh)* to see, to perceive; (= *erspähen*) to spot, to catch sight of; **in jdm/etw eine Gefahr** etc **~** to see sb/ sth as a danger etc, to see a danger etc in sb/ sth → **Licht a**

er|blin|den [ɛʁˈblɪndn] ptp **erblindet** VI *aux sein* to go blind, to lose one's sight

Er|blin|dung F **-, -en** loss of sight

er|blon|den [ɛʁˈblɔndn] ptp **erblondet** VI *aux sein (hum)* to go blond(e)

er|blü|hen [ɛʁˈblyːən] ptp **erblüht** VI *aux sein (geh)* to bloom, to blossom; **zu voller Schönheit ~** *(fig)* to blossom out

Erb-: Erb|mas|se F estate, inheritance; *(Biol)* genotype, genetic make-up; **Erb|on|kel** M (*inf*) rich uncle

er|bo|sen [ɛʁˈboːzn] ptp **erbost** *(geh)* VT to infuriate, to anger; **erbost sein über** (+acc) to be furious or infuriated at VR **sich ~ über** (+acc) to get or become furious or infuriated about

er|bö|tig [ɛʁˈbøːtɪç] ADJ **~ sein, etw zu tun** *(obs)* to be willing or prepared to do sth

Erb-: Erb|pacht F hereditary lease(hold); **Erb|pächter(in)** M(F) hereditary leaseholder; **Erb|pfle|ge** F eugenics sing; **Erb|prinz** M hereditary prince; (= *Thronfolger*) heir to the throne; **Erb|prin|zes|sin** F hereditary princess; (= *Thronfolgerin*) heiress to the throne

er|bre|chen [ɛʁˈbreçn] ptp **erbrochen** [ɛʁˈbrɔxn] *irreg* VT **a** (= *ausspucken*) to vomit, to bring up **b** (*liter*) *Schloss, Siegel* to break open; *Tür auch* to force (open) VR *(sich) ~ (Med)* to vomit, to be sick; **etw bis zum Erbrechen tun** *(fig)* to do sth ad nauseam; **etw zum Erbrechen satt haben** *(fig)* to be absolutely sick of sth

Erb|recht ['ɛrp-] NT law of inheritance; (= *Erbanspruch*) right of inheritance (*auf* +acc) to)

er|brin|gen [ɛʁˈbrɪŋən] ptp **erbracht** [ɛʁˈbraxt] VT *irreg* to produce, to furnish, to adduce

Erb|bro|che|ne(s) [ɛʁˈbrɔxənə] NT decl as adj, no pl vomit

Erb|scha|den ['ɛrp-] M hereditary defect

Erb|schaft ['ɛrpʃaft] F **-, -en** inheritance; **eine ~ machen** or **antreten** to come into an inheritance; **die ~ des Faschismus** the legacy of fascism

Erb|schafts-: Erb|schafts|aus|ei|nan|derset|zung F dispute over an inheritance; **Erb|schafts|kla|ge** F *(Jur)* action for recovery of an/the inheritance; **Erb|schafts|steu|er** F estate or death duty or duties pl

Erb-: Erb|schein M certificate of inheritance; **Erb|schlei|cher(in)** M(F) legacy-hunter; **Erb|schlei|che|rei** F legacy-hunting; **Erb|schuld** F inherited debt

Erb|se ['ɛrpsə] F **-, -n** pea; **gelbe** or **getrocknete ~n** dried peas

Erb|sen-: erb|sen|groß ADJ pea-size, the size of a pea; **Erb|sen|pü|ree** NT ≈ pease pudding (*esp Brit*); **Erb|sen|sup|pe** F pea soup; **Erbsen|zäh|ler** M **-s, -, Erb|sen|zäh|le|rin** F **-, -nen** *(pej inf)* bean-counter *(pej inf)*; **Erb|senzäh|le|rei** F [-tseː|ləˈrai] F **-**, *no pl (pej inf)* bean-counting *(pej inf)*

Erb-: Erb|strei|tig|keit F usu pl inheritance dispute, quarrel over a will or legacy; **Erb|stück** NT heirloom; **Erb|sün|de** F *(Rel)* original sin

Erbs|wurst ['ɛrps-] F pea meal compressed into the form of a sausage

Erb-: Erb|tan|te F (*inf*) rich aunt; **Erb|teil** NT **a** *(Jur)* auch M (portion of an/the) inheritance **b** (= *Veranlagung*) inherited trait; **Erb|tei|lung** F usu pl division of an/the estate (*on succession (to the estate)*); **Erb|ver|trag** M testamentary contract, agreement or contract of inheritance *(US)*; **Erb|ver|zicht** M renunciation of one's claim to an inheritance; **Erb|walter** ['ɛrpvaltɐ] M **-s, -, Erb|wal|te|rin** [-ərɪn] F **-, -nen** *(geh)* trustee

Erd|ach|se ['eːrt-] F earth's axis

er|dacht [ɛʁˈdaxt] ADJ *Geschichte* made-up → *auch* **erdenken**

Erd- ['eːrt-]: **Erd|al|ter|tum** NT *(Geol)* Palaeozoic; **Erd|an|zie|hung** F **-**, *no pl* gravitational pull of the earth; **Erd|ap|fel** M *(Aus, S Ger)* potato; **Erd|ar|bei|ten** PL excavation(s pl), earthwork sing; **Erd|at|mo|sphä|re** F earth's atmosphere; **Erd|bahn** F orbit of the earth, earth's orbit; **Erd|ball** M *(liter)* globe, world

Erd|be|ben NT earthquake, quake

Erd|be|ben-: Erd|be|ben|ge|biet NT earthquake area; **erd|be|ben|ge|fähr|det** ADJ at risk from earthquakes; **Erd|be|ben|gür|tel** M earthquake belt or zone; **Erd|be|ben|herd** M seismic focus, seismic centre *(Brit)* or center *(US)*; **Erd|be|ben|mes|ser** M **-s, -, Erd|beben|mess|ge|rät** ▲ NT seismograph, seismometer; **Erd|be|ben|op|fer** NT earthquake victim or casualty; **Erd|be|ben|schutz** M earthquake protection; **erd|be|ben|si|cher** ADJ *Gebäude etc* earthquake-proof; *Gebiet* not prone to earthquakes; **Erd|be|ben|si|cherheit** F (*von Gebäude etc*) resistance to earthquakes; **die ~ dieses Gebiets** the fact that this area is not prone to earthquakes; **Erd|beben|war|te** F seismological station

Erd-: Erd|bee|re F strawberry; **erd|beer|farben** [-farbn] ADJ strawberry-colour(ed) *(Brit)*, strawberry-color(ed) *(US)*; **Erd|be|stat|tung** F burial, interment; **Erd|be|völ|ke|rung** F population of the earth, earth's population; **Erd|be|woh|ner(in)** M(F) inhabitant of the earth; (*gegenüber Marsbewohnern etc*) terrestrial, earthling *(hum)*; **Erd|bir|ne** F *(dial)* potato; **Erd|bo|den** M ground, earth; **etw dem ~ gleichmachen** to level sth, to raze sth to the ground; **vom ~ verschwinden** to disappear from or off the face of the earth; **als hätte ihn der ~ verschluckt** as if the earth had swallowed him up; **Erd|bro|cken** M clod (of earth)

Er|de ['eːrdə] F **-, -n** **a** (= *Welt*) earth, world; **unsere Mutter ~** *(liter)* Mother Earth; **auf ~n** (*old, liter*) on earth; **auf der ganzen ~** all over the world; **niemand auf der ganzen ~** nobody in the whole world **b** (= *Boden*) ground; **in fremder/heimatlicher ~ ruhen** *(liter)* to lie or rest in foreign/native soil (*liter*); **unter der ~** underground, below ground; *(fig)* beneath the soil; **du wirst mich noch unter die ~ bringen** (*inf*) you'll be the death of me yet (*inf*); **über der ~** above ground; **auf die ~ fallen** to fall to the ground; **auf nackter** or **bloßer ~** on the bare ground; **mit beiden Beinen** or **Füßen (fest) auf der ~ stehen** *(fig)* to have both feet firmly on the ground → **eben** ADV **c** (= *Erdreich, Bodenart*) soil, earth (*auch*

Chem); **fette/trockene ~** rich/dry soil; **zu ~ werden** to turn to dust; **~ zu ~** (*Eccl*) dust to dust; **seltene ~n** (*Chem*) rare earths

　d (*Elec*: = *Erdung*) earth, ground (*US*)

er|den ['eːɐdn] VT　(*Elec*) to earth, to ground (*US*)

Erden-: **Er|den|bür|ger(in)** M(F)　(*geh*) mortal; **ein neuer ~** a new addition to the human race; **er|den|fern** ADJ　(*liter*) far from the earth; **Er|den|glück** NT　(*liter*) earthly happiness

er|den|ken [ɛɐˈdɛŋkn] *ptp* **erdacht** [ɛɐˈdaxt] VT *irreg* to devise, to think up → *auch* **erdacht**

Er|den|kind NT　(*geh*) child of the earth (*liter*)

er|denk|lich [ɛɐˈdɛŋklɪç] ADJ *attr* conceivable, imaginable; **alles ~(e) Gute** all the very best; **sich** (*dat*) **alle** *or* **jede ~e Mühe geben** to take the greatest (possible) pains; **alles Erdenkliche tun** to do everything conceivable or imaginable

Er|den-: (*liter*) **Er|den|leben** NT earthly life, life on earth; **Er|den|rund** [-rʊnt] NT **-s**, *no pl* world

Erd-: **erd|far|ben** [-farbn], **erd|far|big** ADJ earth-coloured (*Brit*), earth-colored (*US*); **erd|fern** ADJ　(*Astron*) far from the earth; **Erd|fer|ne** F　(*Astron*) apogee; **Erd|fern|er|kun|dungs|sa|tel|lit** M long-distance reconnaissance satellite; **Erd|gas** NT natural gas; **Erd|ge|bo|re|ne(r)** ['eːɐtɡəboːrənə] MF *decl as adj* (*liter*) mortal; **erd|ge|bun|den** ADJ **a** (*liter*) earthbound **b** *Teleskop, Observatorium* on (the) earth; *Telefonnetz* underground; **Erd|geist** M earth-spirit; **Erd|ge|ruch** M earthy smell; **Erd|ge|schich|te** F geological history, history of the earth; **erd|ge|schicht|lich** ADJ *no pred* geological; **Erd|ge|schoss** ▲ NT , **Erd|ge-schoß** NT (*S Ger, Aus*) ground floor, first floor (*US*); **im ~** on the ground *or* first (*US*) floor; **erd|hal|tig** ADJ containing earth; **Erd|harz** NT bitumen; **Erd|hau|fen** M mound of earth; **Erd|hörn|chen** NT ground squirrel

er|dich|ten [ɛɐˈdɪçtn] *ptp* **erdichtet** VT to invent, to fabricate, to make up; **das ist alles erdichtet und erlogen** it's all pure fabrication

er|dig ['eːɐdɪç] ADJ earthy

Erd-: **Erd|in|ne|re(s)** ['eːɐtɪnərə] NT *decl as adj* interior *or* bowels *pl* of the earth; **Erd|ka|bel** NT underground cable; **Erd|kar|te** F map of the earth; **Erd|käs** ['eːɐtkɛːs] M (*Sch sl*: = *Erdkunde*) geography; **Erd|kern** M earth's core; **Erd|klum|pen** M clod of earth; **Erd|kreis** M globe, world; **auf dem ganzen ~** all over the world; **Erd|krüm|mung** F (the) earth's curvature, curvature of the earth; **Erd|krus|te** F earth's crust; **Erd|ku|gel** F world, earth, globe; **Erd|kun|de** F geography; **erd|kund|lich** ['eːɐtkʊntlɪç] ADJ geographical; **Erd|lei|tung** F (*Elec*) earth *or* ground (*US*) (connection); (= *Kabel*) underground wire; **Erd|loch** NT (*Mil*) foxhole; **erd|mag|ne|tisch** ADJ geomagnetic; **Erd|mag|ne|tis|mus** M geomagnetism; **Erd|männ|chen** NT (*Zool*) meerkat; **Erd|man|tel** M mantle; **Erd|me|tal|le** PL earth metals *pl*; **Erd|mit|tel|al|ter** NT (*Geol*) Mesozoic; **erd|nah** ADJ (*Astron*) near to the earth; (*fig*) down--to-earth; **Erd|nä|he** F (*Astron*) perigee; **Erd|nuss** ▲ F peanut, groundnut; **Erd|nuss|but|ter** ▲ F peanut butter; **Erd|ober|flä|che** F surface of the earth, earth's surface

Erd|öl ['eːɐtøːl] NT (mineral) oil, petroleum; **~ exportierend** oil-exporting, petroleum-exporting

erd|dol|chen [ɛɐˈdɔlçn] *ptp* **erdolcht** VT to stab (to death); **jdn mit Blicken ~** to look daggers at sb

Erdöl-: **erd|öl|ex|por|tie|rend** △ ADJ *attr* → **Erdöl**; **Erd|öl|feld** NT oil field; **Erd|öl|ge-sell|schaft** F oil company; **Erd|öl|lei|tung** F oil pipeline; **Erd|öl|prei|se** PL oil prices *pl*; **Erd|öl|raf|fi|na|ti|on** F petroleum refining; **Erd|öl|raf|fi|ne|rie** F oil refinery; **Erd|öl|ver-ar|bei|tung** F processing of crude oil

---

Erd-: **Erd|pech** NT bitumen, asphalt, mineral pitch; **Erd|pol** M (*Geog*) (terrestrial) pole; **Erd|reich** NT soil, earth

er|dreis|ten [ɛɐˈdraɪstn] *ptp* **erdreistet** VR **sich ~, etw zu tun** to have the audacity to do sth; **wie können Sie sich ~!** how dare you!; **er hat sich zu dieser Eigenmächtigkeit erdreistet** he had the audacity to act in this high-handed way

Erd|rin|de ['eːɐt-] F earth's crust

er|dröh|nen [ɛɐˈdrøːnən] *ptp* **erdröhnt** VI *aux sein* (*geh*) to boom out, to thunder out; (*Kanonen auch*) to roar; (*Luft, Raum*) to resound (*von* with)

er|dros|seln [ɛɐˈdrɔsln] *ptp* **erdrosselt** VT to strangle, to throttle

Erd|ros|se|lung F strangulation, throttling

er|drü|cken [ɛɐˈdrʏkn] *ptp* **erdrückt** VT to crush (to death); (*fig*: = *überwältigen*) to overwhelm; **ein ~des Gefühl** a stifling feeling; **~de Über-macht** overwhelming superiority; **~des Beweis-material** overwhelming evidence; **die Schuld er-drückte ihn beinahe** the sense of guilt oppressed him *or* weighed down on him

Erd-: **Erd|rutsch** M landslide, landslip; **politi-scher ~** political upheaval; (= *überwältigender Wahlsieg*) (political) landslide; **erd|rutsch|ar-tig** ADJ *Sieg* landslide *attr*; *Niederlage* devastating; **Erd|rutsch|sieg** M landslide (victory); **Erd|sa|tel|lit** M earth satellite; **Erd|schat|ten** M shadow of the earth; **Erd|schicht** F layer (of the earth), stratum; **Erd|schluss** ▲ M (*Elec*) accidental earth *or* ground (*US*); **Erd|schol|le** F clod of earth; **Erd|sicht** F (*Aviat*) ground visibility; **Erd|spal|te** F crevice; **Erd-stoß** M (seismic) shock; **Erd|strah|len** PL field lines *pl*; **Erd|strich** M region, area; **Erd-teil** M continent; **Erd|tra|bant** M moon

er|dul|den [ɛɐˈdʊldn] *ptp* **erduldet** VT to endure, to suffer

Erd-: **Erd|um|dre|hung** F rotation *or* revolution of the earth; **Erd|um|fang** M circumference of the earth; **Erd|um|krei|sung** F (*durch Satelliten*) orbit(ing) of the earth; **Erd|um|lauf-bahn** F earth orbit; **Erd|um|run|dung** F (*durch Satelliten*) orbit(ing) of the earth; **Erd-um|se|ge|lung** F voyage around the world, circumnavigation of the globe; **Erd|um|seg-ler(in)** M(F) round-the-world sailor, circumnavigator of the globe

Er|dung ['eːɐdʊŋ] F **-**, **-en** (*Elec*) earth(ing), ground(ing) (*US*)

Erd-: **erd|ver|bun|den**, **erd|ver|wach|sen** ADJ *Mensch, Volksstamm* close to the earth; **Erd|wall** M earthwork, earth bank *or* wall; **Erd|wär|me** F natural heat of the earth; **erd|wärts** ['eːɐtvɛrts] ADV earthward(s); **Erd|zeit|al|ter** NT geological era

er|ei|fern [ɛɐˈʔaɪfn] *ptp* **ereifert** VR to get excited *or* worked up (*über* +*acc* over)

er|eig|nen [ɛɐˈʔaɪɡnən] *ptp* **ereignet** VR to occur, to happen

Er|eig|nis [ɛɐˈʔaɪɡnɪs] NT **-ses**, **-se** event, occurrence; (= *Vorfall*) incident, event; (*besonderes*) occasion, event → **freudig** ADJ b

er|eig|nis-: **er|eig|nis|los** ADJ uneventful; **Er-eig|nis|lo|sig|keit** F **-**, *no pl* uneventfulness; **er|eig|nis|reich** ADJ eventful

er|ei|len [ɛɐˈʔaɪlən] *ptp* **ereilt** VT　(*geh*) to overtake

e|rek|til [erɛkˈtiːl] ADJ (*Physiol*) erectile

E|rek|ti|on [erɛkˈtsɪoːn] F **-**, **-en** (*Physiol*) erection

E|re|mit [ereˈmiːt] M **-en**, **-en**, **E|re|mi|tin** [-ˈmiː-tɪn] F **-**, **-nen** hermit

E|re|mi|ta|ge [eremiˈtaːʒə] F **-**, **-n** hermitage

er|er|ben [ɛɐˈʔɛrbən] *ptp* **ererbt** VT to inherit

er|fah|ren[1] [ɛɐˈfaːrən] *ptp* **erfahren** *irreg* VT **a** *Nachricht etc* to learn, to find out; (= *hören*) to hear (*von* about, of); **wenn der Chef das erfährt, wird er wütend** if the boss gets to hear about it *or* finds that out he'll be furious; **etw zu ~ su-**

---

chen to try to find out sth; **darf man Ihre Ab-sichten ~?** might one inquire as to your intentions? **b** (= *erleben*) to experience; (= *erleiden auch*) *Rückschlag* to suffer; (= *empfangen*) *Liebe, Verständnis* to receive; *Veränderungen etc* to undergo **VI** to hear (*von* about, of)

er|fah|ren[2] [ɛɐˈfaːrən] ADJ experienced

Er|fah|ren|heit F **-**, *no pl* experience

Er|fah|rung ✪ 38.1, 46.2 F **-**, **-en** experience; (= *Übung auch*) practical knowledge; (*Philos auch*) empirical knowledge; **aus (eigener) ~** from (one's own) experience; **nach meiner ~** in my experience; **~en sammeln** to gain experience; **die ~ hat gezeigt, dass ...** experience has shown that ...; **etw in ~ bringen** to learn *or* to find out sth; **eine ~ machen** to have an experience; **seine ~ machen** to learn (things) the hard way; **jeder muss seine ~en selber machen** everyone has to learn by experience; **ich habe die ~ gemacht, dass ...** I have found that ...; **mit dieser neuen Maschine/Mitarbeitern haben wir nur gute/schlechte ~en gemacht** we have found this new machine/employee (to be) completely satisfactory/unsatisfactory; **was für ~en haben Sie mit ihm/damit gemacht?** how did you find him/it?; **ich habe mit der Ehe nur schlechte ~en gemacht** I've had a very bad experience of marriage (*esp Brit*), I've had very bad experience with marriage (*US*); **durch ~ wird man klug** (*Prov*) one learns by experience

Er|fah|rungs-: **Er|fah|rungs|aus|tausch** M (*Pol*) exchange of experiences; **er|fah|rungs-ge|mäß** ADV **~ ist es ...** experience shows ...; **Er|fah|rungs|me|di|zin** F alternative medicine; **Er|fah|rungs|tat|sa|che** F empirical fact; **Er|fah|rungs|wert** M figure based on experience, empirically established figure; **Er|fah-rungs|wis|sen|schaft** F empirical science

er|fass|bar ▲ ADJ recordable; **ein nicht ~es Le-bensgefühl** an indefinable feeling of being alive

Er|fass|bar|keit ▲ [ɛɐˈfasbaːɐkaɪt] F **-**, *no pl* ability to be recorded

er|fas|sen [ɛɐˈfasn] *ptp* **erfasst** VT **a** (= *mitrei-ßen*: *Auto, Strömung*) to catch

　b (*Furcht, Verlangen etc*) to seize; **Angst erfasste sie** she was seized by fear; **Mitleid erfasste sie** she was filled with compassion

　c (= *begreifen*) to grasp, to comprehend, to understand; **er hats endlich erfasst** he's caught on at last

　d (= *einbeziehen*) to include; (= *registrieren*) to record, to register; *Daten* to capture; **alle Fälle werden statistisch erfasst** statistics of all cases are being recorded; **das ist noch nicht statis-tisch erfasst worden** there are no statistics on it yet

　e (*rare*: = *ergreifen*) to seize, to catch (hold of)

Er|fas|sung F registration, recording; (*von Da-ten*) capture; (= *Miteinbeziehung*) inclusion

er|fech|ten [ɛɐˈfɛçtn] *ptp* **erfochten** [ɛɐˈfɔxtn] VT *irreg Sieg* to gain; *Rechte* to fight for and win

er|fin|den [ɛɐˈfɪndn] *ptp* **erfunden** [ɛɐˈfʊndn] VT *irreg* to invent; (= *erdichten auch*) to make up, to fabricate; **das hat sie glatt erfunden** she made it all up; **frei erfunden** completely fictitious; **er hat die Arbeit auch nicht erfunden** (*inf*) he's not exactly crazy about work (*inf*) → **Pulver**

Er|fin|der(in) M(F) inventor

Er|fin|der|geist M inventive genius

er|fin|de|risch [ɛɐˈfɪndərɪʃ] ADJ inventive; (= *fantasievoll auch*) imaginative; (= *findig auch*) ingenious → **Not**

Er|fin|der|schutz M (*Jur*) protection of inventors

Er|fin|dung F **-**, **-en** invention; (= *Erdichtung, Lü-ge auch*) fiction, fabrication; **eine ~ machen** to invent something

Er|fin|dungs-: **Er|fin|dungs|ga|be** F , *no pl*, **Er|fin|dungs|kraft** F , *no pl* inventiveness, inventive talent *or* genius; (*der Menschheit*) power of invention; **er|fin|dungs|reich** ADJ = **er-**

---

finderisch; **Er|fin|dungs|reich|tum** M inventiveness, ingenuity

er|fle|hen [ɛɐˈfleːən] ptp **erfleht** VT (geh) to beg for; **etw von jdm ~** to beg or beseech (liter) sb for sth, to beg sth of sb

Er|folg [ɛɐˈfɔlk] M -(e)s, -e success; (= Ergebnis, Folge) result, outcome; (Sport: = Sieg) victory, success; **mit ~** successfully; **ohne ~** without success, unsuccessfully; **viel ~!** good luck!; **~ haben** to be successful; **keinen ~ haben** to have no success, to be unsuccessful; **ohne ~ bleiben** or **sein** to be unsuccessful; **~ versprechend** promising; **ein voller ~** a great success; (Stück, Roman, Vorschlag etc auch) a hit; **ein kläglicher ~** not much of a success, a bit of a failure; **~(e) bei Frauen haben** to be successful with women; **sie warnte mich mit dem ~, dass ...** the effect or result of her warning me was that ...

er|fol|gen [ɛɐˈfɔlgn] ptp **erfolgt** VI aux sein (form) (= folgen) to follow, to ensue; (= sich ergeben) to result; (= vollzogen werden) to be effected (form) or carried out; (= stattfinden) to take place, to occur; (Zahlung) to be effected (form) or made; **nach erfolgter Zahlung** after payment has been effected (form) or made; **es erfolgte keine Antwort** no answer was forthcoming

Er|folg-: **er|folg|ge|krönt** ADJ (ultimately) successful or triumphant, successful in the end pred; **ihre Stücke waren weltweit ~** her plays enjoyed success around the world; **Er|folg|ha|sche|rei** [-haʃəˈraɪ] F -, -en (pej) striving or angling for success; **er|folg|los** ADJ unsuccessful, without success ADV unsuccessfully; **~ verlaufen** to be unsuccessful; **Er|folg|lo|sig|keit** F -, no pl lack of success; **er|folg|reich** ADJ successful ADV successfully; **~ verlaufen** to be successful; **sich um etw ~ bewerben** to succeed in getting sth

Er|folgs-: **er|folgs|ab|hän|gig** ADJ success-related; (Econ) profit-related; **ein ~er Sportler** a sportsman who is depending on victory or success; **er|folgs|arm** ADJ short on success; **Er|folgs|aus|sicht** F prospect of success; **Er|folgs|au|tor(in)** M(F) successful author; **Er|folgs|be|tei|li|gung** F (Comm) profit-sharing; **Er|folgs|bi|lanz** F record of success; **Er|folgs|buch** NT bestseller, successful book; **Er|folgs|den|ken** NT positive way of thinking; **Er|folgs|druck** M , no pl pressure to succeed; **Er|folgs|er|leb|nis** NT feeling of success, sense of achievement; **Er|folgs|film** M successful or hit film; **er|folgs|ge|wohnt** ADJ used to success pred; **Er|folgs|ho|no|rar** NT performance-related or success-related fee; **Er|folgs|kurs** M success; **auf ~ liegen** to be on course for success; **Er|folgs|kur|ve** F success curve; **Er|folgs|lei|ter** F (fig) ladder to success; **Er|folgs|mar|ke** F successful brand; **Er|folgs|mel|dung** F news sing of success; **endlich eine ~!** good news at last!; **Er|folgs|mensch** M success, successful person; **als einem ~en widerstrebt ihm so etwas** being used to success or succeeding, he reacts against that sort of thing; **er|folgs|ori|en|tiert** [-ɔriɛntiːɐt] ADJ achievement-oriented; **Er|folgs|prä|mie** F (Comm) efficiency bonus, incentive payment; **Er|folgs|re|zept** NT recipe for success; **Er|folgs|ro|man** M successful novel; **Er|folgs|se|rie** F string of successes; **Er|folgs|stra|te|gie** F strategy for success

er|folg|ver|spre|chend △ ADJ → Erfolg

er|for|der|lich [ɛɐˈfɔrdəlɪç] ADJ necessary, required, requisite; **es ist dringend ~, dass ...** it is a matter of urgent necessity that ...; **etw ~ machen** to make sth necessary, to necessitate sth; **unbedingt ~** (absolutely) essential or imperative

er|for|der|li|chen|falls ADV (form) if required, if necessary, if need be

er|for|dern [ɛɐˈfɔrdən] ptp **erfordert** VT to require, to demand, to call for

Er|for|der|nis [ɛɐˈfɔrdənɪs] NT -ses, -se requirement; (= Voraussetzung auch) prerequisite

er|for|schen [ɛɐˈfɔrʃn] ptp **erforscht** VT a Land, Weltraum etc to explore b Probleme etc to explore, to investigate, to inquire into; (in der Wissenschaft auch) to research into; Thema etc to research; Lage, Meinung, Wahrheit to ascertain, to find out; **sein Gewissen ~** to search or examine one's conscience

Er|for|scher(in) M(F) (eines Landes) explorer; (in Wissenschaft) investigator, researcher

Er|for|schung F a (von Land, Weltraum etc) exploration b (von Problemen) investigation, inquiry (+gen into); (wissenschaftlich) research (+gen into); (von Thema) researching (von Lage, Meinung, Wahrheit) ascertaining

er|fra|gen [ɛɐˈfraːgn] ptp **erfragt** VT Weg to ask, to inquire; Einzelheiten etc to obtain, to ascertain; **Einzelheiten zu ~ bei ...** for details apply to ..., details can be obtained from ...

er|fre|chen [ɛɐˈfrɛçn] ptp **erfrecht** VR **sich ~, etw zu tun** to have the audacity to do sth; **wie können Sie sich zu so einer Behauptung ~?** how dare you (have the audacity to) claim such a thing!

er|freu|en [ɛɐˈfrɔyən] ptp **erfreut** VT to please, to delight; Herz to gladden; **sehr erfreut!** (dated: bei Vorstellung) pleased to meet you!, delighted! (dated); **er wollte damit die Menschen ~** he wanted to give people pleasure; **ja, sagte er erfreut** yes, he said delighted(ly); **über jdn/etw erfreut sein** to be pleased or delighted about or at sb/sth VR **sich einer Sache** (gen) **~** (geh) to enjoy sth; **sich an etw** (dat) **~** to enjoy sth, to take pleasure in sth

er|freu|lich [ɛɐˈfrɔylɪç] ADJ pleasant; Neuerung, Besserung etc welcome; (= befriedigend) gratifying; **es ist wenig ~, dass wir ...** it's not very satisfactory that we ...; **es wäre ~, wenn die Regierung ...** it would be good or nice if the government ...; **ich habe diesmal keine Rüge bekommen – das ist ja sehr ~** I didn't get a rebuke this time – that's good to hear or I'm so glad; **sehr ~!** very nice! ADV fortunately; **er hat sich ~ wenig beklagt** it was pleasant or nice how little he complained

er|freu|li|cher|wei|se ADV happily; **wir haben ~ einmal ein Spiel gewonnen** I'm pleased or glad to say that we've won a game at last

er|frie|ren [ɛɐˈfriːrən] ptp **erfroren** [ɛɐˈfroːrən] VI irreg aux sein to freeze to death, to die of exposure; (Pflanzen) to be killed by frost; **erfrorene Glieder** frostbitten limbs VT **sich** (dat) **die Füße/Finger ~** to suffer frostbite in one's feet/fingers

Er|frie|rung F -, -en usu pl frostbite no pl; **Tod durch ~** death from exposure

er|fri|schen [ɛɐˈfrɪʃn] ptp **erfrischt** VT to refresh VI to be refreshing VR to refresh oneself; (= sich waschen) to freshen up

er|fri|schend ADJ (lit, fig) refreshing ADV refreshingly; **~ wirken** to be refreshing

Er|fri|schung F -, -en refreshment

Er|fri|schungs-: **Er|fri|schungs|ge|tränk** NT refreshment; **Er|fri|schungs|raum** M refreshment room, cafeteria, snack bar; **Er|fri|schungs|tuch** NT pl -tücher towelette, refreshing towel

er|fül|len [ɛɐˈfylən] ptp **erfüllt** VT a Raum etc to fill; **Hass/Liebe/Ekel etc erfüllte ihn** he was full of hate/love/disgust etc, he was filled with hate/love/disgust etc; **Schmerz erfüllte ihn** he was grief-stricken; **Freude erfüllte ihn** his heart was full of or filled with joy; **er/sein Leben war von einem starken Pflichtgefühl erfüllt** he/his life was impregnated with a strong sense of duty; **es erfüllt mich mit Genugtuung, dass ...** it gives me great satisfaction to see that ...; **ein erfülltes Leben** a full life

b (= ausführen, einhalten) to fulfil (Brit), to fulfil (US); Bedingungen to meet, to comply with, to fulfil(l); Wunsch, Bitte to fulfi(l), to carry out; Pflicht, Aufgabe to fulfil(l), to carry out, to perform; Erwartungen to come up to, to fulfil(l); (Jur) Soll to achieve; Plan to carry through; Formalitäten to comply with; Zweck, Funktion to serve; **die Fee erfüllte ihm seinen Wunsch** the fairy granted him his wish; **ihr Wunsch nach einem Kind wurde erfüllt** their wish for a child came true or was granted; **erfüllst du mir einen Wunsch?** will you do something for me? → **Tatbestand**

VR (Wunsch, Voraussagung) to be fulfilled, to come true; **als er diesen Titel bekam, hatte sich sein Leben erfüllt** when he received this title his life had reached fulfilment (Brit) or fulfillment (US)

VI (Jur) to discharge one's debts

Er|fül|lung F fulfilment (Brit), fulfillment (US); (einer Bitte, eines Wunsches auch) carrying out; (einer Pflicht, Aufgabe auch) performance; (von Erwartungen) realization; (eines Solls) achievement; (eines Plans) execution; (Jur: = Tilgung) discharge; **in ~ gehen** to be fulfilled; **in etw** (dat) **~ finden** to find fulfil(l)ment in sth

Er|fül|lungs-: **Er|fül|lungs|ge|hil|fe** M , **Er|fül|lungs|ge|hil|fin** F (Jur) = agent; (= Helfershelfer) henchman (pej); **Er|fül|lungs|ort** M pl -orte (Jur) (von Vertrag) place where a contract is to be fulfilled (von Scheck) place of payment; **Er|fül|lungs|po|li|tik** F (Hist) policy of fulfilment (Brit) or fulfillment (US); (pej) (policy of) appeasement; **Er|fül|lungs|po|li|ti|ker(in)** M(F) (Hist) politician supporting the policy of fulfilment (Brit) or fulfillment (US); (pej) appeaser

Erg [ɛrk] NT -s, - (Sci) erg

erg. abbr von **ergänze** supply, add

er|gän|zen [ɛɐˈgɛntsn] ptp **ergänzt** VT to supplement; (= vervollständigen) to complete; Fehlendes to supply; Lager, Vorräte to replenish; Bericht to add (sth) to; Ausführungen to amplify; Worte, Summe to add; Gesetz, Gesetzentwurf to amend; **seine Sammlung ~** to add to or build up one's collection; **ergänzte Ausgabe** expanded edition; **einander** or **sich ~** to complement one another; **um das Team zu ~** to make up the numbers of the team

er|gän|zend prp von **ergänzen** ADJ (= komplementär) complementary; (= nachträglich) supplementary; (= zusätzlich) additional; (= zum Ganzen gehörig) integral; **~er Satz** (Ling) completive clause ADV **~ hinzufügen** or **bemerken** to add (zu to); **~ möchte ich noch hinzufügen, dass ...** (as a rider to that) I would like to add that ..., I would amplify that by saying ...; **~ muss noch gesagt werden, dass ...** it should also be added or said that ... → auch **ergänzen**

Er|gän|zung F -, -en a (= das Ergänzen) supplementing; (= Vervollständigung) completion; (von Fehlendem) supply(ing); (eines Berichts) addition (+gen to); (von Summe) addition; (von Gesetz) amendment; (von Lager, Vorräten) replenishment; **zur ~ meiner Sammlung** to add to or build up my collection; **zur ~ des vorher Gesagten möchte ich hinzufügen, dass ...** let me amplify the previous remarks by adding that ...; **zur ~ des Teams** to make up the numbers of the team b (= Zusatz: zu Buch etc) supplement; (= Hinzugefügtes, Person) addition; (zu einem Gesetz) amendment; (Gram) complement

Er|gän|zungs-: **Er|gän|zungs|ab|ga|be** F supplementary tax; **Er|gän|zungs|an|trag** M (Parl) amendment; **Er|gän|zungs|band** [-bant] M pl -bände supplement(ary volume); **Er|gän|zungs|bin|de|strich** M hyphen; **Er|gän|zungs|men|ge** F (Math) complementary set; **Er|gän|zungs|satz** M (Gram) complementary clause

er|gat|tern [ɛɐˈgatɐn] ptp **ergattert** VT (inf) to get hold of

er|gau|nern [ɛɐˈgaunɐn] ptp **ergaunert** VT (inf) **(sich** dat) **etw ~** to get sth by dishonest means

er|ge|ben¹ [ɛɐˈgeːbn] ptp **ergeben** irreg VT to yield, to produce; (= zum Ergebnis haben) to result in; (= *zeigen*) to reveal; *Betrag, Summe* to amount to, to come to

VR **a** (= *kapitulieren*) (+*dat* to) to surrender, to yield, to capitulate; **sich auf Gnade oder Ungnade ~** to surrender unconditionally; **sich in etw** (*acc*) **~** to submit to sth

b **sich einer Sache** (*dat*) **~** (= *sich hingeben*) to take to sth, to give oneself up to sth; *der Schwermut* to sink into sth; *dem Dienst etc* to devote oneself to sth; **sich dem Suff** (*inf*) **~** to take to drink (*Brit*) or the bottle (*inf*)

c (= *folgen*) to result, to arise, to ensue (*aus* from); **daraus können sich Nachteile ~** this could turn out to be disadvantageous; **das eine ergibt sich aus dem anderen** the one (thing) follows from the other

d (= *sich herausstellen*) to come to light; **es ergab sich, dass unsere Befürchtungen ...** it turned out that our fears ...

er|ge|ben² [ɛɐ̯'geːbn] ADJ **a** (= *hingegeben, treu*) devoted; (= *demütig*) humble; (= *unterwürfig*) submissive; **einem Laster ~ sein** to be addicted to a vice; **Ihr (sehr) ~er ...** (*old form*) **Ihr ~ster ...** (*old form*) respectfully yours ... (*form*), your (most) obedient or humble servant ... (*old form*) → **treu** ADV

Er|ge|ben|heit F -, no pl (= *Hingabe, Treue*) devotion; (= *Demut*) humility; (= *Unterwürfigkeit*) submissiveness

Er|geb|nis [ɛɐ̯'geːpnɪs] NT **-ses, -se** result; (= *Auswirkung auch*) consequence, outcome; **im ~** (= *folglich*) as a result; **die Verhandlungen führten zu keinem ~** the negotiations led nowhere, the negotiations were inconclusive; **die Verhandlungen führten zu dem ~, dass ...** the negotiations led to the conclusion that ...; **zu einem ~ kommen** to come to or reach a conclusion; **unsere Anstrengungen blieben ohne ~** our efforts produced no results

er|geb|nis|los ADJ unsuccessful, without result, fruitless; *Verhandlungen auch* inconclusive **ADV ~ bleiben/verlaufen** to come to nothing; **Verhandlungen ~ abbrechen** to break off negotiations without having reached any conclusions

Er|geb|nis|lo|sig|keit F -, no pl lack of success, fruitlessness; (*von Verhandlungen auch*) inconclusiveness

er|geb|nis|of|fen ADJ *Diskussion* open and unbiased **ADV** **etw ~ diskutieren** to discuss sth in an open and unbiased way

Er|ge|bung F -, -en (*Mil, fig*) surrender, capitulation; (*fig: = Demut*) humility

er|ge|hen [ɛɐ̯'geːən] ptp **ergangen** [ɛɐ̯'gaŋən] irreg **VI** aux sein **a** (*form*) (*an* +*acc* to) = *erteilt, erlassen werden*) to go out, to be issued; (*Einladung*) to go out, to be sent; (*Gesetz*) to be enacted; **~ lassen** to issue; to send; to enact

b **etw über sich** (*acc*) **~ lassen** to let sth wash over one (*Brit*), to let sth roll off one's back (*US*); **sie ließ seine Vorwürfe/alles über sich** (*acc*) **~** she let his reproaches/everything simply wash over her (*Brit*) or roll off her back (*US*); **sie ließ seine Zärtlichkeiten über sich** (*acc*) **~** she submitted to his intimacies

VI impers aux sein **es ist ihm schlecht/gut ergangen** he fared badly/well; **es wird ihm schlecht ~** he will suffer; **wie ist es ihm in der Prüfung ergangen?** how did he fare in (*Brit*) or on (*US*) the exam?

VR **a** (*geh*) to go for a walk or stroll, to take the air (*Brit*)

b (*fig*) **sich in etw** (*dat*) **~** to indulge in sth; **er erging sich in Lobreden** he indulged in lavish or profuse praise; **er erging sich in Schmähungen** he let out a stream of abuse; **sich (in langen Reden) über ein Thema ~** to hold forth at length on sth, to expatiate on sth

Er|ge|hen NT (*geh*) (state of) health

er|gie|big [ɛɐ̯'giːbɪç] ADJ (*lit, fig*) productive; *Geschäft* profitable, lucrative; *Thema* productive, fertile; *Kupfervorkommen, Goldmine etc* high-yield

---

attr, rich; *Regenfälle* abundant; (= *fruchtbar*) fertile; (= *sparsam im Verbrauch*) economical

Er|gie|big|keit F -, no pl (*lit, fig*) productiveness, productivity; (*von Geschäft*) profitability; (*von Regenfällen*) abundance; (= *Fruchtbarkeit*) fertility; (= *Sparsamkeit im Verbrauch*) economy; **die ~ der Goldmine** the high yield of the gold mine; **die erhöhte ~ dieses Waschmittels** the washing powder's new economical or economy formula

er|gie|ßen [ɛɐ̯'giːsn] ptp **ergossen** [ɛɐ̯'gɔsn] irreg **VT** (*liter*) to pour (out or forth (*liter*)) **VR** (*geh*) to pour forth (*liter*) or out (*auch fig*)

er|glän|zen [ɛɐ̯'glɛntsn] ptp **erglänzt** VI aux sein (*geh*) to shine, to gleam; (*Licht auch*) to shine out

er|glü|hen [ɛɐ̯'glyːən] ptp **erglüht** VI aux sein (*liter*) to glow; (*fig*) (*vor Scham, Zorn*) to burn; (*vor Freude*) to glow; **in Liebe für jdn ~** (*liter*) to fall passionately in love with sb

er|go ['ɛrgo] CONJ therefore, ergo (*liter, hum*)

Er|go|me|ter [ɛrgo'meːtɐ] NT ergometer

Er|go|no|mie [ɛrgono'miː] F -, no pl ergonomics *sing*

er|go|no|misch [ɛrgo'noːmɪʃ] ADJ ergonomic **ADV** ergonomically

Er|go|the|ra|peut(in) [ɛrgotera'pɔyt(ɪn)] M(F) ergotherapist

Er|go|the|ra|pie [ɛrgotera'piː] F ergotherapy

er|göt|zen [ɛɐ̯'gœtsn] ptp **ergötzt** **VT** to delight; **zum Ergötzen aller** to everyone's delight **VR** **sich an etw** (*dat*) **~** to be amused by sth, to take delight in sth; (*schadenfroh auch, böswillig*) to gloat over sth

er|götz|lich [ɛɐ̯'gœtslɪç] ADJ delightful

er|grau|en [ɛɐ̯'grauən] ptp **ergraut** VI aux sein to turn or go grey (*Brit*) or gray (*US*) → **Dienst a, Ehre**

er|grei|fen [ɛɐ̯'graifn] ptp **ergriffen** [ɛɐ̯'grɪfn] VT irreg **a** (= *packen*) (= *fassen auch*) to grasp, to grip; *Feder, Schwert auch* to take up; *Verbrecher* to seize, to apprehend; (*Krankheit*) to overcome; **das Feuer ergriff den ganzen Wald** the fire engulfed the whole forest → **Besitz a**

b (*fig*) *Gelegenheit, Macht* to seize; *Beruf* to take up; *Maßnahmen* to take, to resort to; **er ergriff das Wort** he began to speak; (*Parl, bei Versammlung etc*) he took the floor → **Flucht a, Partei c**

c (*fig*) *jdn* (= *packen*) to seize, to grip; (= *bewegen*) to move; **von Furcht/Sehnsucht etc ergriffen werden** to be seized with fear/longing etc → *auch* **ergriffen**

er|grei|fend ADJ (*fig*) moving, touching (*auch iro*)

er|grif|fen [ɛɐ̯'grɪfn] ADJ (*fig*) moved → *auch* **ergreifen**

Er|grif|fen|heit F -, no pl emotion

er|grim|men [ɛɐ̯'grɪmən] ptp **ergrimmt** (*old, liter*) **VI** aux sein to become angry or furious **VT** to incense, to anger

er|grün|den [ɛɐ̯'grʏndn] ptp **ergründet** VT *Sinn etc* to fathom; *Geheimnis auch* to penetrate; *Ursache, Motiv* to discover; **ich muss ~, ob ...** I have to discover whether ...

Er|guss ▲ M effusion; (= *Bluterguss*) bruise, contusion (*form*); (= *Samenerguss*) ejaculation, emission; (*fig*) outpouring, effusion

er|ha|ben [ɛɐ̯'haːbn] ADJ **a** *Druck, Muster* raised, embossed

b (*fig*) *Gedanken, Stil* lofty, elevated, exalted; *Schönheit, Anblick* sublime; *Augenblick* solemn; *Herrscher* illustrious, eminent; **das Erhabene** the sublime; **vom Erhabenen zum Lächerlichen ist nur ein Schritt** it is but a step from the sublime to the ridiculous

c (= *überlegen*) superior; **er dünkt sich über alles/alle ~** he thinks himself to be above it all/ superior to everybody; **über etw** (*acc*) **~ (sein)** (to be) above sth; **über jeden Tadel/Verdacht ~ sein** to be above or beyond reproach/suspicion

---

ADV **~ lächeln** to smile in a superior way; **~ tun** to act superior

Er|ha|ben|heit F -, -en **a** (*rare*: = *Erhöhung*) elevation, relief **b** (*fig*) (*von Gedanken, Stil*) loftiness, elevation; (*von Schönheit, Anblick*) sublimity; (*von Augenblick*) solemnity; (*von Herrscher*) illustriousness, eminence **c** (= *Überlegenheit*) superiority

Er|halt M , no pl receipt; (= *das Erhalten*) preservation; **der ~ der Macht** the preservation of power

er|hal|ten [ɛɐ̯'haltn] ptp **erhalten** irreg **VT** **a** (= *bekommen*) to get, to receive; *Preis, Orden* to get, to receive, to be awarded; *Strafe, neuen Namen, fünf Jahre Gefängnis* to get, to be given; *Resultat, Produkt, Genehmigung* to obtain, to get; **das Wort ~** to receive permission to speak; **(Betrag) dankend ~** (*form*) received with thanks (the sum of...) → **Besuch a, Kenntnis b**

b (= *bewahren*) *Gebäude, Natur* to preserve; *Gesundheit etc auch* to maintain; **jdn am Leben/bei guter Laune ~** to keep sb alive/in a good mood; **ich hoffe, dass du uns noch lange bleibst** I hope you'll be with us for a long time yet; (= *nicht sterben*) I hope you'll have many more happy days; **erhalte dir deinen Frohsinn/Optimismus** stay cheerful/optimistic; **er hat sich** (*dat*) **seinen Frohsinn/Optimismus ~** he kept up or retained his cheerfulness/optimism; **unser Kind ist uns ~ geblieben** our child was spared; **gut ~** well preserved (*auch hum inf*), in good condition; **von der Altstadt sind nur noch ein paar Kirchen ~** of the old town only a few churches remain or still stand

c (= *unterhalten*) *Familie* to support, to keep, to maintain

VR (*Brauch etc*) to be preserved, to remain; **sich frisch und gesund ~** to keep or stay bright and healthy

er|hal|tens|wert [ɛɐ̯'haltnsveːɐ̯t] ADJ worth preserving *pred*

Er|hal|ter(in) M(F) preserver, maintainer; (*der Familie*) breadwinner, supporter

er|hält|lich [ɛɐ̯'hɛltlɪç] ADJ obtainable, available; **schwer ~** difficult to obtain, hard to come by

Er|hal|tung F -, -en (= *Bewahrung*) preservation; (= *Unterhaltung*) support; **die ~ der Energie** (*Phys*) the conservation of energy

er|han|deln [ɛɐ̯'handln] ptp **erhandelt** VT to get by bargaining, to bargain for

er|hän|gen [ɛɐ̯'hɛŋən] ptp **erhängt** VT to hang; **Tod durch Erhängen** death by hanging; **sich ~** to hang oneself

er|här|ten [ɛɐ̯'hɛrtn] ptp **erhärtet** **VT** to harden; (*fig*) *Behauptung* to substantiate, to corroborate; *Verdacht* to harden; **etw durch Eid ~** to affirm sth on oath **VR** (*fig: Verdacht*) to harden

Er|här|tung F (*von Behauptung*) substantiation, corroboration; (*von Verdacht*) hardening

er|ha|schen [ɛɐ̯'haʃn] ptp **erhascht** VT to catch (*auch fig*), to seize, to grab

er|he|ben [ɛɐ̯'heːbn] ✪ 36.2 ptp **erhoben** [ɛɐ̯'hoːbn] irreg **VT** **a** (= *hochheben*) to raise (*auch Math*), to lift (up); *Glas, Stimme* to raise; **die Hand zum Gruß ~** to raise one's hand in greeting; **seinen** or **den Blick ~** to look up; **jdn in den Adelsstand ~** to raise or elevate sb to the peerage; **etw zu einem Prinzip/einer Regel etc ~** to make sth into a principle/a rule etc, to raise or elevate sth to (the level of) a principle/a rule etc; **jdn zum Herrscher ~** to install sb as a/the ruler → **Anklage a, Anspruch a, c, Einspruch, Geschrei, Potenz b**

b *Gebühren* to charge, to levy; *Steuern* (= *einziehen*) to raise, to levy; (= *auferlegen*) to impose

c *Fakten, Daten* to ascertain

d (*liter*: = *loben*) to laud (*liter*), to extol (*liter*)

VR **a** (= *aufstehen*) to get up, to rise; (*Flugzeug, Vogel*) to rise

b (= *sich auflehnen*) to rise (up) (in revolt), to revolt

---

c (= aufragen) to rise (über +dat above) **d** sich über eine Schwierigkeit ~ to rise above or overcome a difficulty; sich über andere ~ to elevate or place oneself above others **e** (= aufkommen) (Wind etc, form: Frage etc) to a-rise

er|he|bend ADJ elevating, uplifting; (= beeindruckend) impressive; (= erbaulich) edifying

er|heb|lich [ɛɐˈheːplɪç] **ADJ** (= beträchtlich) considerable; (= wichtig) important; (= relevant) relevant, pertinent; Verletzung serious, severe **ADV** (= beträchtlich) considerably; beschädigen, verletzen severely

Er|he|bung F **a** (= Bodenerhebung) elevation **b** (= Aufstand) uprising, revolt; (= Meuterei) mutiny **c** (von Gebühren) levying, imposition **d** (= amtliche Ermittlung) investigation, inquiry; (= Umfrage) survey; ~ en machen or anstellen über (+acc) to make inquiries about or into **e** (= das Erheben) raising; (in den Adelsstand) elevation; (zum Herrscher) installation (zu as); ~ ins Quadrat squaring; ~ in die dritte Potenz cubing, raising to the power of three **f** (fig: = Erbauung) uplift, elevation

Er|he|bungs|zeit|raum M (von Umfrage, Daten etc) survey period

er|hei|schen [ɛɐˈhaɪʃn] ptp erheischt VT (old, liter) to require, to demand; Achtung to command

er|hei|tern [ɛɐˈhaɪtɐn] ptp erheitert **VT** to cheer (up); (= belustigen) to entertain, to amuse **VR** to be amused (über +acc by); (Gesicht) to brighten, to cheer up

Er|hei|te|rung F -, -en amusement; zur allgemeinen ~ to the general amusement

er|hel|len [ɛɐˈhɛlən] ptp erhellt **VT** to light up (auch fig), to illuminate; (fig: = klären) to elucidate, to illuminate; Geheimnis to shed light on **VR** (lit, fig) to brighten; (plötzlich) to light up **VI** (geh: = hervorgehen) to be evident or manifest; daraus erhellt, dass ... from that it is evident or manifest that ...

Er|hel|lung F -, -en (fig) elucidation, illumination

er|hit|zen [ɛɐˈhɪtsn] ptp erhitzt **VT** to heat (up) (auf +acc to); die Gemüter ~ to inflame passions, to whip up feeling **VR** to get hot, to heat up; (fig: = sich erregen) to become heated (an +dat over); (Fantasie etc) to be inflamed or aroused (an +dat at); die Gemüter erhitzten sich feelings were running high; erhitzt aussehen to look hot; (fig) to look hot and bothered; vom Tanzen erhitzt hot from the dancing

Er|hit|zung F -, -en heating up; (fig) (= Erregung) excitement; (der Gemüter, Fantasie) inflammation

er|hof|fen [ɛɐˈhɔfn] ptp erhofft VT to hope for; sich (dat) etw ~ to hope for sth (von from); was erhoffst du dir davon? what do you hope to gain from it?

er|hofft [ɛɐˈhɔft] ptp von erhoffen ADJ hoped-for, looked-for (inf)

er|hö|hen [ɛɐˈhøːən] ptp erhöht **VT** to raise; Preise, Miete etc auch to increase, to put up; Zahl auch, Produktion, Kraft to increase; Wirkung, Schönheit to heighten, to enhance; Spannung to increase, to heighten; (Mus) Note to sharpen; die Mauern wurden um zwei Meter erhöht the walls were made two metres (Brit) or meters (US) higher, the walls were raised (by) two metres (Brit) or meters (US); etw um 10% ~ to raise or put up or increase sth by 10%; etw um das Doppelte ~ to increase by twice as much again; erhöhte Temperatur haben to have a temperature; erhöhte Wachsamkeit/Anstrengungen etc increased vigilance/efforts etc **VR** to rise, to increase; (Spannung etc auch) to heighten, to intensify; wer sich selbst erhöht, der wird erniedrigt (werden) (Bibl) whosoever shall exalt himself shall be abased

Er|hö|hung F -, -en **a** (= das Erhöhen) raising; (von Preisen, Miete etc) increase, putting up; (von Zahl auch, von Produktion, Kraft) increase; (von

Wirkung) heightening, enhancement; (von Spannung) heightening, intensification **b** (= Lohnerhöhung) rise (Brit), raise (US); (= Preiserhöhung) increase **c** (= Hügel) hill, elevation

Er|hö|hungs|zei|chen NT (Mus) sharp (sign)

er|ho|len [ɛɐˈhoːlən] ptp erholt VR (von from) to recover; (von Krankheit auch) to recuperate; (= sich entspannen auch) to relax, to have a rest; (fig: Preise, Aktien) to recover, to rally, to pick up; er hat sich von dem Schreck(en) noch nicht erholt he hasn't got over the shock yet; du siehst sehr erholt aus you look very rested

er|hol|sam [ɛɐˈhoːlzaːm] ADJ restful, refreshing

Er|ho|lung F -, no pl recovery; (von Krankheit auch) recuperation; (= Entspannung) relaxation, rest; (der Wirtschaft) recovery, rallying; der Direktor ist zur ~ in der Schweiz the director has gone to Switzerland for a holiday (esp Brit) or a vacation (US) and a rest; (zur Genesung) the director is convalescing in Switzerland; zur ~ an die See fahren to go to the seaside in order to recover or recuperate or convalesce; er braucht dringend ~ he badly needs a holiday (esp Brit) or a vacation (US) or a break; Urlaub ist zur ~ da holidays (esp Brit) or vacations (US) are for relaxation; gute ~! have a good rest

Er|ho|lung|su|chen|de(r) [-zuːxndə] MF decl as adj holiday-maker (esp Brit), vacationer (esp US), vacationist (esp US)

Er|ho|lungs-: **Er|ho|lungs|auf|ent|halt** M holiday (esp Brit), vacation (US); **er|ho|lungs|be|dürf|tig** ADJ in need of a rest, run-down; **Er|ho|lungs|ge|biet** NT recreation area; **Er|ho|lungs|heim** NT rest home; (= Ferienheim) holiday home; (= Sanatorium) convalescent home; **Er|ho|lungs|kur** F rest-cure; **Er|ho|lungs|ort** M pl -orte spa, health resort; **Er|ho|lungs|pau|se** F break; **Er|ho|lungs|rei|se** F holiday (esp Brit) or vacation (US) trip; **Er|ho|lungs|ur|laub** M holiday (esp Brit), vacation (US); (nach Krankheit) convalescent leave; **Er|ho|lungs|wert** M recreational value

er|hö|ren [ɛɐˈhøːrən] ptp erhört VT Gebet etc to hear; Bitte, Liebhaber to yield to

E|rie|see [ˈeːri-] M Lake Erie no art

e|ri|gi|bel [eriˈgiːbl] ADJ (Physiol) erectile

e|ri|gie|ren [eriˈgiːrən] ptp erigiert VI to become erect

e|ri|giert [eriˈgiːɐt] ADJ erect

E|ri|ka [ˈeːrika] F -, Eriken [-kn] (Bot) heather

er|in|ner|lich [ɛɐˈɪnɐlɪç] ADJ soviel mir ~ ist as far as I (can) remember or recall; die letzte uns ~e Postkarte kam aus Deutschland the last postcard we (can) remember came from Germany

er|in|nern [ɛɐˈɪnɐn] ptp erinnert **VT** jdn an etw (acc) ~ to remind sb of sth; jdn daran ~, etw zu tun/dass ... to remind sb to do sth/that ...; etw ~ (dial, sl) to remember or recall sth **VR** sich an jdn/etw ~, sich einer Sache (gen) ~ (old) to remember or recall or recollect sb/sth; sich nur noch dunkel ~ an (+acc) to have only a faint or dim recollection or memory of; soweit or soviel ich mich ~ kann as far as I remember etc, to the best of my recollection; wenn ich mich recht erinnere, ... if my memory serves me right or correctly ..., if I remember rightly ... **VI** **a** ~ an (+acc) to be reminiscent of, to call to mind, to recall; sie erinnert sehr an ihre Mutter she reminds one very much of her mother **b** (= erwähnen) daran ~, dass ... to point out that ...

Er|in|ne|rung F -, -en **a** (an +acc of) memory, recollection; (euph: = Mahnung) reminder; (= Andenken) memento, remembrance, keepsake; zur ~ an (+acc) in memory of; (an Ereignis) in commemoration of; (als Andenken) as a memento of; jdn/etw in guter/schlechter ~ haben or behalten to have pleasant/unpleasant memories of sb/sth; sich (dat) etw in die ~ zurückru-

fen to call sth to mind; jdm etw in ~ bringen to remind sb of sth; ich muss ihm mal schreiben, um mich bei ihm in ~ zu bringen I'll have to write to him so that he doesn't forget me; wenn mich meine ~ nicht täuscht if my memory doesn't deceive me **b** **Erinnerungen** PL (= Lebenserinnerungen) reminiscences pl; (Liter) memoirs pl; ~en austauschen to reminisce

Er|in|ne|rungs-: **Er|in|ne|rungs|bild** NT visual memento (an +acc of); **Er|in|ne|rungs|fei|er** F commemoration; **Er|in|ne|rungs|fo|to** NT (von Urlaub, Ereignis etc) souvenir photo or snapshot; (von Verstorbenen) cherished photo (-graph); **Er|in|ne|rungs|lü|cke** F gap in one's memory; **Er|in|ne|rungs|schrei|ben** NT (Comm) reminder; **Er|in|ne|rungs|stück** NT keepsake (an +acc from); **Er|in|ne|rungs|ta|fel** F commemorative plaque; **Er|in|ne|rungs|ver|mö|gen** NT , no pl memory, powers pl of recollection; **Er|in|ne|rungs|wert** M sentimental value

E|rin|ny|en [eˈrɪnyən] PL (Myth) Furies pl, Erin(n)yes pl

E|rit|rea [eriˈtreːa] NT -s Eritrea

E|rit|re|er [eriˈtreːɐ] M -s, -, **E|rit|re|e|rin** [-ərɪn] F -, -nen Eritrean

e|rit|re|isch [eriˈtreːɪʃ] ADJ Eritrean

er|ja|gen [ɛɐˈjaːɡn] ptp erjagt VT to bag, to catch; (fig: = ergattern) to get hold of, to hunt down; um sich dort Reichtum zu ~ to make his fortune

er|kal|ten [ɛɐˈkaltn] ptp erkaltet VI aux sein (lit, fig) to cool (down or off), to go cold

er|käl|ten [ɛɐˈkɛltn] ptp erkältet **VR** to catch a cold; (= esp sich verkühlen) to catch a chill; sich stark or sehr/leicht erkältet haben to have (caught) a bad/slight cold/chill **VT** sich (dat) die Blase ~ to catch a chill in one's bladder (Brit), to get a bladder infection

er|käl|tet [ɛɐˈkɛltət] ADJ with a cold; (stark) ~ sein to have a (bad) cold; wir sind alle ~ we all have colds

Er|käl|tung F -, -en cold; (leicht) chill; sich (dat) eine ~ zuziehen to catch a cold/chill

Er|käl|tungs|krank|hei|ten PL coughs and sneezes pl

er|kämp|fen [ɛɐˈkɛmpfn] ptp erkämpft VT to win, to secure; sich (dat) etw ~ to win sth; hart erkämpft hard-won; er hat sich (dat) seine Position hart erkämpft he fought hard for his position or to secure his position

er|kau|fen [ɛɐˈkaufn] ptp erkauft VT to buy; etw teuer ~ to pay dearly for sth; den Erfolg mit seiner Gesundheit ~ to pay for one's success with one's health, to buy success at the price of one's health

er|kenn|bar ADJ (= wieder erkennbar) recognizable; (= sichtbar) visible; (= wahrnehmbar, ersichtlich) discernible

Er|kenn|bar|keit [ɛɐˈkɛnbaːɐkait] F -, no pl (= Wiedererkennbarkeit) being recognizable; (= Sichtbarkeit) visibility; (= Wahrnehmbarkeit, Ersichtlichkeit) discernibility

er|ken|nen [ɛɐˈkɛnən] ptp erkannt [ɛɐˈkant] irreg **VT** **a** (= wieder erkennen, anerkennen, einsehen) to recognize (an +dat by); (= wahrnehmen) to see, to make out, to discern; Unterschied to see; Situation to see, to understand; ich erkannte die Lage sofort I immediately realized what the situation was; er hat erkannt, dass das nicht stimmte he realized that it wasn't right; kannst du ~, ob das da drüben X ist? can you see or tell if that's X over there?; jdn für schuldig ~ (Jur) to find sb guilty; (jdm) etw zu ~ geben to indicate sth (to sb); jdm zu ~ geben, dass ... to give sb to understand that ...; sich zu ~ geben to reveal oneself (als to be), to disclose one's identity; ~ lassen to show, to reveal; erkenne dich selbst! know thyself!; du bist erkannt! I see what you're after, I know your game **b** (Bibl, obs) to know (Bibl)

VI ~ **auf** (+*acc*) (*Jur, auf Freispruch*) to grant; *auf Strafe* to impose, to inflict; (*Sport*) *auf Freistoß etc* to give, to award; **auf drei Jahre Haft ~** to impose a sentence of three years' imprisonment

er|kennt|lich [ɛɐ̯'kɛntlɪç] ADJ **a** **sich (für etw) ~ zeigen** to show one's gratitude or appreciation (for sth) **b** (*rare*) = **erkennbar**

Er|kennt|lich|keit F -, -en (= *Dankbarkeit*) gratitude; (= *Gegenleistung*) token of one's gratitude or appreciation

Er|kennt|nis¹ [ɛɐ̯'kɛntnɪs] F (= *Wissen*) knowledge *no pl*; (= *das Erkennen*) recognition, realization; (*Philos, Psych*) cognition *no pl*; (= *Einsicht*) insight, realization; (= *Entdeckung*) finding, discovery; **zur ~ kommen** to see the light; **zu der ~ kommen** *or* **gelangen, dass ...** to come to the realization that ..., to realize that ...

Er|kennt|nis² NT -ses, -se (*Aus, Sw: Jur*) decision, finding; (= *Urteil*) judg(e)ment; (*der Geschworenen*) verdict

Er|kennt|nis-: **Er|kennt|nis|drang** M thirst for knowledge; **Er|kennt|nis|fähig|keit** F cognitive faculty; **Er|kennt|nis|la|ge** F level of knowledge; **Er|kennt|nis|leh|re** F epistemology, theory of knowledge; **Er|kennt|nis|schub** M wealth of new knowledge; **Er|kennt|nis|stand** M level of knowledge; **er|kennt|nis|the|o|re|tisch** ADJ epistemological; **Er|kennt|nis|the|o|rie** F epistemology, theory of knowledge; **Er|kennt|nis|ver|mö|gen** NT cognitive capacity

Er|ken|nung F recognition, identification

Er|ken|nungs-: **Er|ken|nungs|dienst** M police records department; **er|ken|nungs|dienst|lich** ADV **jdn ~ behandeln** to fingerprint and photograph sb; **Er|ken|nungs|mar|ke** F identity disc (*Brit*), identity (*Brit*) *or* identification (*US*) tag; **Er|ken|nungs|me|lo|die** F signature tune; **Er|ken|nungs|wort** NT *pl* **-wörter** password; **Er|ken|nungs|zei|chen** NT identification; (*Mil:* = *Abzeichen*) badge; (*Aviat*) markings *pl*; (*Med*) sign (*für or* of); **das ist mein ~** that's what you'll recognize me by

Er|ker ['ɛrkɐ] M -s, - bay; (= *kleiner Vorbau*) oriel

Er|ker-: **Er|ker|fens|ter** NT bay window; oriel window; **Er|ker|zim|mer** NT room with a bay *or* oriel window (recess)

er|kie|sen [ɛɐ̯'kiːzn] *pret* **erkor** [ɛɐ̯'koːɐ̯], *ptp* **erko|ren** [ɛɐ̯'koːrən] VT (*obs, liter*) to choose, to elect (*zu* as, to be)

er|klär|bar ADJ explicable, explainable; **leicht ~** easily explained; **schwer ~** hard to explain; **nicht ~** inexplicable

er|klä|ren [ɛɐ̯'klɛːrən] *ptp* **erklärt** **VT** **a** (= *erläutern*) to explain (*jdm etw* sth to sb); (= *begründen*) to account for, to explain; **ich kann mir nicht ~, warum ...** I can't understand why ...; **wie erklärt ihr euch das?** how can *or* do you explain that?, what do you make of that?; **ich erkläre mir die Sache so: ...** the way I see it, ...
b (= *äußern, bekannt geben*) to declare (*als* to be); (*Rücktritt*) to announce; (*Politiker, Pressesprecher etc*) to say; **einem Staat den Krieg ~** to declare war on a country; **er erklärte ihr seine Liebe** he declared his love for her; **eine Ausstellung etc für** *or* **als eröffnet ~** to declare an exhibition etc open; **jdn für schuldig/tot/gesund etc ~** to pronounce sb guilty/dead/healthy *etc*
VR **a** (*Sache*) to be explained; **das erklärt sich daraus, dass ...** it can be explained by the fact that ...; **damit hat sich die Sache von selbst erklärt** the affair thereby explained itself; **das erklärt sich (von) selbst** that's self-explanatory
b (*Mensch*) to declare oneself; (= *Liebe gestehen auch*) to declare one's love; **sich für bankrott etc ~** to declare oneself bankrupt *etc*; **sich für gesund/diensttauglich ~** to pronounce *or* declare oneself healthy/fit for service; **sich für/gegen jdn/etw ~** to declare oneself *or* come out for/against sb/sth → *auch* **erklärt**
VI to explain; **er kann sehr gut ~** he's very good at explaining things

er|klä|rend ADJ explanatory; **einige ~e Worte** a few words of explanation ADV **er fügte ~ hinzu ...** he added in explanation ...

er|klär|lich [ɛɐ̯'klɛːrlɪç] ADJ **a** = **erklärbar** **b** (= *verständlich*) understandable; **ist Ihnen das ~?** can you find an explanation for that?; **mir ist einfach nicht ~, wie ...** I simply cannot understand how ...

er|klär|li|cher|wei|se ADV understandably

er|klärt [ɛɐ̯'klɛːɐ̯t] ADJ *attr Ziel* professed; *Gegner auch* avowed; *Favorit, Liebling* acknowledged → *auch* **erklären**

er|klär|ter|ma|ßen [ɛɐ̯'klɛːɐ̯tɐ'maːsn], **er|klär|ter|wei|se** [ɛɐ̯'klɛːɐ̯tɐ'waɪsə] ADV avowedly

Er|klä|rung F **a** explanation **b** (= *Mitteilung, Bekanntgabe*) declaration; (*eines Politikers, Pressesprechers etc*) statement; **eine ~ (zu etw) abgeben** to make a statement (about *or* concerning sth)

Er|klä|rungs-: **er|klä|rungs|be|dürf|tig** ADJ in need of (an) explanation; **das ist ~** that needs (further) explanation; **Er|klä|rungs|frist** F period of time granted to sb to explain sth *to a commission etc*; **Er|klä|rungs|not|stand** M **im ~ sein** to have a lot of explaining to do; **Er|klä|rungs|ver|such** M attempt at explanation *or* at explaining *sth*

er|kleck|lich [ɛɐ̯'klɛklɪç] ADJ considerable

er|klet|tern [ɛɐ̯'klɛtɐn] *ptp* **erklettert** VT to climb (up); *Berg auch* to scale; *Alpengebiet* to climb

er|klim|men [ɛɐ̯'klɪmən] *ptp* **erklommen** [ɛɐ̯'klɔmən] VT *irreg* (*geh*) to scale; (*fig*) *Spitze, höchste Stufe* to climb to; (*fig*) *Leiter* to climb *or* ascend to the top of

er|klin|gen [ɛɐ̯'klɪŋən] *ptp* **erklungen** [ɛɐ̯'klʊŋən] VI *irreg* (*geh*) *aux sein* to ring out, to resound; **eine Harfe/ein Glöckchen/Stimmchen erklang** (the sound of) a harp/bell/voice was heard, I *etc* heard (the sound of) a harp/bell/voice; **ein Lied ~ lassen** to burst (forth) into song; **die Gläser ~ lassen** to clink glasses

er|kor *pret von* **erkiesen** *von* **erküren**

er|ko|ren *ptp von* **erkiesen** *von* **erküren**

er|kran|ken [ɛɐ̯'kraŋkn] *ptp* **erkrankt** VI *aux sein* (= *krank werden*) to be taken ill (*Brit*) *or* sick, to get sick (*US*), to fall ill (*an* +*dat* with); (*Organ, Pflanze, Tier*) to become diseased (*an* +*dat* with); **erkrankt sein** (= *krank sein*) to be ill/diseased; **die an Krebs erkrankten Menschen** people with *or* suffering from cancer; **die erkrankten Stellen** the diseased *or* affected areas

Er|kran|kung F -, -en illness; (*von Organ, Pflanze, Tier*) disease; **wegen einer plötzlichen ~ des Viehbestandes** because the livestock suddenly became diseased

Er|kran|kungs|fall M case of illness; **im ~** in case of illness

er|küh|nen [ɛɐ̯'kyːnən] *ptp* **erkühnt** VR (*old, liter*) **sich ~, etw zu tun** to dare to do sth, to make so bold as to do sth

er|kun|den [ɛɐ̯'kʊndn] *ptp* **erkundet** VT (*esp Mil*) *Gelände, Stellungen* to reconnoitre (*Brit*), to reconnoiter (*US*), to scout; (= *feststellen*) to find out, to establish, to ascertain

er|kun|di|gen [ɛɐ̯'kʊndɪgn] **36.1, 48.1** *ptp* **erkundigt** VR **sich (nach etw/über jdn) ~** to ask *or* inquire (about sth/sb); **sich nach jdm ~** to ask after (*Brit*) *or* about sb; **sich bei jdm (nach etw) ~** to ask sb (about sth); **ich werde mich ~** I'll find out

Er|kun|di|gung F -, -en inquiry; (= *Nachforschung auch*) investigation; **~en einholen** *or* **einziehen** to make inquiries

Er|kun|dung F -, -en (*Mil*) reconnaissance

Er|kun|dungs|gang M *pl* **-gänge** (*Mil, fig*) reconnaissance expedition

er|kü|ren [ɛɐ̯'kyːrən] *pret* **erkor** [ɛɐ̯'koːɐ̯], *ptp* **erkoren** [ɛɐ̯'koːrən] VT (*obs, liter*) to choose, to elect (*zu* as, to be)

Er|lag|schein [ɛɐ̯'laːk-] M (*Aus*) giro transfer form

er|lah|men [ɛɐ̯'laːmən] *ptp* **erlahmt** VI *aux sein* to tire, to grow weary; (*Kräfte, fig: Interesse, Eifer*) to flag, to wane

er|lan|gen [ɛɐ̯'laŋən] *ptp* **erlangt** VT to attain, to achieve; *Alter, Ziel auch* to reach; *Bedeutung auch, Eintritt* to gain

Er|lan|gung F -, *no pl* attainment

Er|lass ▲ [ɛɐ̯'las] M -es, -e *or* (*Aus*) ∸e [-'lɛsə] **a** (= *Verfügung*) decree, edict; (*der Regierung*) enactment, edict **b** (= *Straferlass, Schuldenerlass, Sündenerlass etc*) remission

er|las|sen [ɛɐ̯'lasn] *ptp* **erlassen** VT *irreg* **a** *Verfügung* to pass; *Gesetz* to enact; *Embargo etc* to impose; *Dekret* to issue **b** (*von etw entbinden*) *Strafe, Schulden etc* to remit; *Gebühren* to waive; **jdm etw ~** (*Schulden etc*) to release sb from sth; *Gebühren* to waive sth for sb; **bitte ~ Sie es mir, darüber zu sprechen** please don't ask me to talk about that; **jdm die Strafarbeit ~** to let sb off a punishment; **jdm eine Pflicht ~** to release sb from a duty; **ich erlasse ihm den Rest (des Geldes)** I'll waive the rest (of the money), I'll let him off paying the rest (of the money)

er|lau|ben [ɛɐ̯'laubn] ☯ **36.3** *ptp* **erlaubt** VT **a** (= *gestatten*) to allow, to permit; **jdm etw ~** to allow *or* permit sb (to do) sth; **mein Vater erlaubt mir nicht, dass ich mit Mädchen ausgehe** my father doesn't *or* won't allow me to go out with girls; **es ist mir nicht erlaubt, das zu tun** I am not allowed *or* permitted to do that; **du erlaubst deinem Kind zu viel** you allow your child too much freedom; **~ Sie? (**form**) Sie ~?** (*form*) may I?; **~ Sie, dass ich das Fenster öffne?** do you mind if I open the window?; **~ Sie, dass ich mich vorstelle** allow *or* permit me to introduce myself; **~ Sie mal!** do you mind!; **soweit es meine Zeit/das Wetter erlaubt** (*form*) time/weather permitting; **erlaubt ist, was gefällt** (*prov*) a little of what you fancy does you good (*prov*); **erlaubt ist, was sich ziemt** (*prov*) you must only do what is proper
b **sich** (*dat*) **etw ~** (= *gestatten, sich gönnen*) to allow *or* permit oneself sth; (= *wagen*) *Bemerkung, Vorschlag* to venture sth; (= *sich leisten*) to afford sth; **sich** (*dat*) **~, etw zu tun** (= *so frei sein*) to take the liberty of doing sth; (= *sich leisten*) to afford to do sth; **darf ich mir ~ ...?** might I possibly ...?; **wenn ich mir die folgende Bemerkung ~ darf ...** if I might venture *or* be allowed the following remark ...; **sich** (*dat*) **Frechheiten ~** to take liberties, to be cheeky (*Brit*) *or* fresh (*US*); **sich** (*dat*) **einen Scherz ~** to have a joke; **was die Jugend sich heutzutage alles erlaubt!** the things young people get up to nowadays!; **was ~ Sie sich (eigentlich)!** how dare you!

Er|laub|nis [ɛɐ̯'laupnɪs] ☯ **36** F -, (*rare*) **-se** permission; (= *Schriftstück*) permit; **mit Ihrer (freundlichen) ~** (*form*) with your (*kind*) permission, by your leave (*form*); **du brauchst eine elterliche ~** you need your parents' (written) permission; (*jdn*) **um ~ bitten** to ask (sb) for permission, to ask *or* beg leave (of sb) (*form*); **jdm zu etw die ~ geben** *or* **erteilen** (*form*) to give sb permission *or* leave (*form*) for sth

Er|laub|nis|schein M permit

er|laucht [ɛɐ̯'lauxt] ADJ (*obs, iro*) illustrious; **ein ~er Kreis** a select circle

Er|laucht [ɛɐ̯'lauxt] F -, -en (*Hist*) Lordship

er|läu|tern [ɛɐ̯'lɔytɐn] *ptp* **erläutert** VT to explain, to elucidate; (= *klarstellen auch*) to clarify; *Text* to comment on; **~d** explanatory; **~d fügte er hinzu** he added in explanation *or* clarification; **etw anhand von Beispielen ~** to illustrate sth with examples

Er|läu|te|rung F explanation, elucidation; (= *Klarstellung auch*) clarification; (*zu Text*) comment, commentary; **zur ~** in explanation

Er|le ['ɛrlə] F -, -n alder

er|le|ben [ɛɐˈleːbn] ptp **erlebt** VT to experience; (= noch lebend erreichen) to live to see; (= durchmachen) schwere Zeiten, Sturm to go through; Aufstieg, Abenteuer, Enttäuschung to have; Erfolg to have, to enjoy; Misserfolg, Niederlage to have, to suffer; Aufführung to have, to receive; Jahrhundertwende, erste Mondlandung to see; Schauspieler to see (perform); Musik, Gedicht, Fußballspiel, Landschaft to experience; **im Ausland habe ich viel erlebt** I had an eventful time abroad; **was haben Sie im Ausland erlebt?** what sort of experiences did you have abroad?; **Deutschland, wie ich es erlebt habe, war …** I remember Germany as being …; **wir haben wunderschöne Tage in Spanien erlebt** we had a lovely time in Spain; **etwas Angenehmes** etc ~ to have a pleasant etc experience; **er hat schon viel Schlimmes erlebt** he's had a lot of bad times or experiences; **wir haben mit unseren Kindern viel Freude erlebt** our children have given us much pleasure; **ich habe es oft erlebt …** I've often known or seen it happen …; **so wütend habe ich ihn noch nie erlebt** I've never seen or known him so furious; **unser Land hat schon bessere Zeiten erlebt** our country has seen or known better times; **ich möchte mal ~, dass du rechtzeitig kommst** I'd like to see you come on time; **er hat gesagt, er möchte helfen – das möchte ich ~!** he said he'd like to help – that I'd like to see!; **das werde ich nicht mehr ~** I won't live to see that; **er möchte mal etwas ~** he wants to have a good time; **er hat viel erlebt** he has been around (inf), he has experienced a lot; **das muss man erlebt haben** you've got to have experienced it (for) yourself; **erlebte Rede** (Liter) interior monologue; **na, der kann was ~!** (inf) he's going to be (in) for it! (inf); **hat man so (et)was schon (mal) erlebt!** (inf) I've never heard anything like it!; **dass ich das noch ~ darf!** I never thought I'd see the day!; **so was Dummes habe ich noch nie erlebt!** I've never seen/heard anything so stupid in all my life!

Er|le|bens|fall M **im ~** in case of survival; **Versicherung auf den ~** pure endowment insurance

Er|leb|nis [ɛɐˈleːpnɪs] NT -ses, -se experience; (= Abenteuer) adventure; (= Liebschaft) affair; **(jdm) zu einem ~ werden** to be (quite) an experience (for sb)

Er|leb|nis-: **Er|leb|nis|auf|satz** M (Sch) essay based on personal experience; **Er|leb|nis|bad** NT adventure pool; **Er|leb|nis|dich|te** F richness of experience; **er|leb|nis|fä|hig** ADJ receptive, able to experience things pred; **Er|leb|nis|fä|hig|keit** F receptivity, capacity for experience; **Er|leb|nis|gast|ro|no|mie** F gastronomic experience (with entertainment or in a theme restaurant); **er|leb|nis|hung|rig** ADJ thirsty for experience pred; (nach Abenteuer) thirsty for adventure pred; **Er|leb|nis|ly|rik** F poetry based on personal experience; **Er|leb|nis|pä|da|go|gik** F system of education through practical experience rather than classroom studies; **Er|leb|nis|park** M adventure park, theme park; **er|leb|nis|reich** ADJ eventful

er|le|di|gen [ɛɐˈleːdɪgn] ptp **erledigt** VT a Angelegenheit to deal with, to take care of; Akte etc to process; (= ausführen) Auftrag to carry out; (= beenden) Arbeit to finish off, to deal with; Sache to settle; Einkäufe ~ to do the shopping; **ich habe noch einiges in der Stadt zu ~** I've still got a few things to do in town; **ich muss noch schnell was ~** I've just got something to do; **die Sache/er ist für mich erledigt** as far as I'm concerned the matter's closed/I'm finished with him; **erledigt!** (Stempel) dealt with, processed; **erledigt, reden wir nicht mehr darüber!** OK, let's say no more about it!; **das ist (damit) erledigt** that's settled, that's taken care of; **wird erledigt!** shall (Brit) or will do! (inf), right-ho! (Brit inf), sure thing! (US inf); **zu ~** (Vermerk auf Akten) for attention; **schon erledigt!** I've alread-

y done it; (= mache ich sofort) consider it done b (inf: = ermüden) to wear or knock (inf) out; (inf: = ruinieren) to finish, to ruin; (inf: = töten) to do in (inf); (inf: = k.o. schlagen) to finish off, to knock out

VR **damit erledigt sich das Problem** that disposes of or settles the problem; **das hat sich erledigt** that's all settled; **sich von selbst ~** to take care of itself

er|le|digt [ɛɐˈleːdɪçt] ADJ a (inf) (= erschöpft) shattered (Brit inf), done in pred (Brit inf), all in (inf); (= ruiniert) finished, ruined; **wenn jetzt die Bullen kommen, sind wir ~** if the cops come now, we've had it (inf) b (obs) Stelle vacant

Er|le|di|gung F -, -en (= Ausführung) execution, carrying out; (= Durchführung, Beendung) completion; (einer Sache, eines Geschäfts) settlement; **ich habe noch einige ~en** I still have a few items of business to attend to; **einige ~en in der Stadt** a few things to do in town; **die ~ von Einkäufen** (form) shopping; **die ~ meiner Korrespondenz** dealing with my correspondence; **sie betraute ihn mit der ~ ihrer Geschäfte** she entrusted him with (the execution of) her business affairs; **um rasche ~ wird gebeten** please give this your immediate attention; **in ~ Ihres Auftrages** (form) in execution of your order (form); **in ~ Ihrer Anfrage** (form) further to your inquiry

Er|le|di|gungs|ver|merk M actioned stamp

er|le|gen [ɛɐˈleːgn] ptp **erlegt** VT a Wild to shoot, to bag (Hunt) b (Aus, Sw: = bezahlen) to pay

er|leich|tern [ɛɐˈlaɪçtɐn] ptp **erleichtert** VT (= einfacher machen) to make easier; (fig) Last, Los to lighten; (= beruhigen) to relieve; (= lindern) Not, Schmerz etc to relieve, to alleviate; **sein Herz/Gewissen** vor jdm (dat) **das Gewissen ~** to unburden one's heart/conscience; **es würde mein Gewissen ~, wenn …** it would ease my mind or conscience if …; **jdm etw ~** to make sth easier for sb; **jdn um etw ~** (hum) to relieve sb of sth VR (old) to relieve oneself

er|leich|tert [ɛɐˈlaɪçtɐt] ptp von **erleichtern** ADJ relieved (über +acc about, to hear that) ADV **~ aufatmen** to breathe or heave a sigh of relief

Er|leich|te|rung F -, -en (von Last etc) lightening; (= Linderung) relief, alleviation; (= Beruhigung) relief; (= Zahlungserleichterung) facility; **das trägt zur ~ meiner Aufgabe bei** it makes my work easier; **einem Kranken ~ verschaffen** to give relief to a sick person

er|lei|den [ɛɐˈlaɪdn] ptp **erlitten** [ɛɐˈlɪtn] VT irreg to suffer; Verluste, Schaden auch to sustain, to incur; **den Tod ~** (old) to suffer death (old) → Schiffbruch

Er|len|mei|er|kol|ben [ˈɛrlənmaɪɐ-] M (Phys) Erlenmeyer flask

er|lern|bar ADJ easily learned

er|ler|nen [ɛɐˈlɛrnən] ptp **erlernt** VT to learn

er|le|sen [ɛɐˈleːzn] ADJ exquisite; **ein ~er Kreis** a select circle

Er|le|sen|heit F -, no pl exquisite nature; (von Kreis) selectness

er|leuch|ten [ɛɐˈlɔʏçtn] ptp **erleuchtet** VT to light (up), to illuminate; (fig) to enlighten, to inspire; **Herr, erleuchte uns!** Lord, let thy light shine upon us; **hell erleuchtet** brightly lit; Stadt brightly illuminated

Er|leuch|tung F -, -en (= Eingebung) inspiration; (religiöse auch) enlightenment no pl

er|lie|gen [ɛɐˈliːgn] ptp **erlegen** VI irreg aux sein +dat (lit, fig) to succumb to; einem Irrtum to be the victim of; **zum Erliegen kommen/bringen** to come/bring to a standstill

er|lischt [ɛɐˈlɪʃt] 3. PERS SING pres von **erlöschen**

er|lo|gen [ɛɐˈloːgn] ptp von **erlügen** ADJ not true pred; (= erfunden) made-up attr, made up pred; **das ist erstunken und ~** that's a rotten lie; **das ist von Anfang bis Ende ~** there's not a word of

truth in it, it's a pack of lies (inf) → auch **erlügen**

Er|lös [ɛɐˈløːs] M -es, -e [-zə] proceeds pl

er|lö|schen [ɛɐˈløʃn] pres **erlischt** [ɛɐˈlɪʃt], pret **erlosch** [ɛɐˈlɔʃ], ptp **erloschen** [ɛɐˈlɔʃn] VI aux sein (Feuer) to go out; (Gefühle, Interesse) to die; (Vulkan) to become extinct; (Leben) to come to an end; (Vertrag, Anspruch etc) to expire, to lapse; (Garantie, Mandat) to expire; (Hirnfunktionen) to cease; (Geschlecht, Name) to die out; **ein erloschener Vulkan** an extinct volcano; **mit ~der Stimme** (liter) in a dying voice; **seine Augen waren erloschen** (liter) his eyes were lifeless

er|lö|sen [ɛɐˈløːzn] ptp **erlöst** VT a (= retten) to save, to rescue (aus, von from); (Rel) to redeem, to save; (von Sünden, Qualen) to deliver (esp Bibl); to release; **erlöse uns von dem Bösen** (Rel) deliver us from evil b (Comm: aus Verkauf) Geld to realize

er|lö|send ADJ relieving, liberating; **sie sprach das ~e Wort** she spoke the word he/she/everybody etc was waiting for ADV **~ wirken** to come as a relief; **er empfand es beinahe ~, als …** it was almost a relief for him when …

Er|lö|ser [ɛɐˈløːzɐ] M -s, -, **Er|lö|se|rin** [-ərɪn] F -, -nen (= Befreier) saviour (Brit), savior (US); **der ~** (Rel) the Redeemer

Er|lö|sung F release, deliverance; (= Erleichterung) relief; (Rel) redemption; **der Tod war für sie eine ~** death was a release for her

er|lü|gen [ɛɐˈlyːgn] ptp **erlogen** [ɛɐˈloːgn] VT irreg to fabricate, to make up, to invent; **eine erlogene Geschichte** a fabrication, a fiction

er|mäch|ti|gen [ɛɐˈmɛçtɪgn] ptp **ermächtigt** VT to authorize, to empower (zu etw to do sth)

er|mäch|tigt [ɛɐˈmɛçtɪçt] ADJ authorized, empowered; **zur Unterschrift ~** authorized to sign

Er|mäch|ti|gung F -, -en authorization

Er|mäch|ti|gungs|ge|setz NT (Pol) Enabling Act (esp that of Nazis in 1933)

er|mah|nen [ɛɐˈmaːnən] ptp **ermahnt** VT to exhort (form), to admonish, to urge; (warnend) to warn; (Jur) to caution; **jdn zum Fleiß/zur Aufmerksamkeit** etc **~** to exhort (form) or urge sb to work hard/to be attentive etc; **muss ich dich immer erst ~?** do I always have to remind or tell you first?; **jdn im Guten ~** to give sb a friendly warning

Er|mah|nung F exhortation, admonition, urging; (warnend) warning; (Jur) caution

er|man|geln [ɛɐˈmaŋəln] ptp **ermangelt** VI einer Sache (gen) **~** (geh) to lack sth

Er|man|ge|lung [ɛɐˈmaŋəlʊŋ] F -, no pl, **Er|mang|lung** [ɛɐˈmaŋlʊŋ] F -, no pl (geh) **in ~** +gen because of the lack of; **in ~ eines Besseren** for lack of something better

er|man|nen [ɛɐˈmanən] ptp **ermannt** VR to pluck up courage

er|mä|ßi|gen [ɛɐˈmɛːsɪgn] ptp **ermäßigt** VT to reduce VR to be reduced

er|mä|ßigt [ɛɐˈmɛːsɪçt] ptp von **ermäßigen** ADJ reduced; **zu ~en Preisen** at reduced prices; (Fahrkarten, Eintritt etc) at reduced rates

Er|mä|ßi|gung F -, -en reduction; (= Steuerermäßigung) relief

Er|mä|ßi|gungs|fahr|schein M concessionary (Brit) or reduced ticket

er|mat|ten [ɛɐˈmatn] ptp **ermattet** (geh) VT to tire, to exhaust VI aux sein to tire, to become exhausted

er|mat|tet [ɛɐˈmatət] ADJ (geh) exhausted, weary

Er|mat|tung F -, no pl (geh) exhaustion, weariness, fatigue

er|mes|sen [ɛɐˈmɛsn] ptp **ermessen** VT irreg (= einschätzen) Größe, Weite, Wert to gauge, to estimate; (= erfassen, begreifen können) to appreciate, to realize

Er|mes|sen [ɛɐˈmɛsn] NT -s, no pl (= Urteil) judgement, estimation; (= Gutdünken) discretion; **nach meinem ~** in my estimation; **nach menschlichem ~** as far as anyone can judge; **nach bestem ~ handeln** to act according to one's best judgement; **nach freiem ~** at one's discretion; **nach eigenem ~ handeln** to act on one's own discretion; **etw in jds ~** (*acc*) **stellen**, **etw jds ~** (*dat*) **anheim stellen** to leave sth to sb's discretion; **in jds ~** (*dat*) **liegen** or **stehen** to be within sb's discretion

Er|mes|sens-: Er|mes|sens|ent|schei|dung F (*Jur*) discretionary decision; **Er|mes|sens|fra|ge** F matter of discretion; **Er|mes|sens|frei|heit** F powers *pl* of discretion, discretionary powers *pl*; **Er|mes|sens|miss|brauch** ▲ M abuse of (one's powers of) discretion; **Er|mes|sens|spiel|raum** M discretionary powers *pl*

er|mit|teln [ɛɐ̯ˈmɪtln] *ptp* **ermittelt** **VT** to determine (*auch Chem, Math*), to ascertain; *Person* to trace; *Tatsache, Identität* to establish **VI** to investigate; **gegen jdn ~** to investigate sb; **in einem Fall ~** to investigate a case

Er|mitt|ler(in) M(F) investigator; **verdeckter ~** undercover investigator

Er|mitt|lung F -, -en **a** (*esp Jur*: = *Erkundigung*) investigation, inquiry; **~en anstellen** to make inquiries (*über +acc* about) **b** *no pl* (= *das Ermitteln*) determination, ascertaining; (*von Person*) tracing; (*von Tatsache, Identität*) establishing, establishment

Er|mitt|lungs-: Er|mitt|lungs|aus|schuss ▲ M committee of inquiry (*Brit*), investigative committee (*US*); **Er|mitt|lungs|rich|ter(in)** M(F) (*Jur*) examining magistrate; **Er|mitt|lungs|stand** M stage of the investigation; **Er|mitt|lungs|ver|fah|ren** NT (*Jur*) preliminary proceedings *pl*

er|mög|lichen [ɛɐ̯ˈmøːklɪçn] *ptp* **ermöglicht** VT to facilitate, to make possible; **jdm etw ~** to make sth possible for sb, to facilitate sth for sb; **es jdm ~, etw zu tun** to make it possible for sb to do sth, to enable sb to do sth; **um uns den freien Austausch von Informationen zu ~** to facilitate the free exchange of information, to make it possible for us or to enable us to exchange information freely; **jdm das Studium/eine Reise ~** to make it possible for sb to study/to go on a journey; **(nur) wenn Sie es ~ können** (*form*) (only) if you are able to; **können Sie es ~, morgen zu kommen?** (*form*) would it be possible for you to or are you able to come tomorrow?

er|mor|den [ɛɐ̯ˈmɔrdn] *ptp* **ermordet** VT to murder; (*esp aus politischen Gründen*) to assassinate

Er|mor|dung F -, -en murder; (*esp politisch*) assassination

er|mü|den [ɛɐ̯ˈmyːdn] *ptp* **ermüdet** **VT** to tire **VI** *aux sein* to tire, to become tired; (*Tech*) to fatigue

er|mü|dend ADJ tiring

Er|mü|dung F -, (*rare*) -en fatigue (*auch Tech*), tiredness, weariness

Er|mü|dungs-: Er|mü|dungs|er|schei|nung F sign or symptom of fatigue; **Er|mü|dungs|zu|stand** M feeling of tiredness

er|mun|tern [ɛɐ̯ˈmʊntɐn] *ptp* **ermuntert** **VT** (= *ermutigen*) to encourage; (*jdn zu etw* sb to do sth); (= *beleben, erfrischen*) to liven up, to stimulate, to invigorate; (= *aufmuntern*) to cheer up; **seine Gegenwart wirkt ~d auf mich** his presence has an enlivening effect on me, his presence stimulates me **VR** (*rare*) to wake up, to rouse oneself

Er|mun|te|rung F -, -en encouragement; (= *Belebung*) enlivening, stimulation; (= *Aufmunterung*) cheering-up

er|mu|ti|gen [ɛɐ̯ˈmuːtɪgn] *ptp* **ermutigt** VT (= *ermuntern*) to encourage; (= *Mut geben*) to give courage, to embolden (*form*); **jdn zu etw ~** to encourage sb to do sth, to give sb the courage or embolden sb (*form*) to do sth

Er|mu|ti|gung F -, -en encouragement

Ern [eːɐ̯n] M -(e)s, -e (*dial*: = *Hausflur*) (entrance) hall, hallway

er|näh|ren [ɛɐ̯ˈnɛːrən] *ptp* **ernährt** **VT** to feed; (= *unterhalten*) to support, to keep, to maintain; **schlecht ernährt** undernourished; **gut ernährt** well-nourished, well-fed; **dieser Beruf ernährt seinen Mann** you can make a good living in this profession **VR** to eat; **sich gesund ~** to eat healthily, to have a healthy diet; **der Arzt klärte ihn auf, wie er sich ~ sollte** the doctor advised him on his diet; **sich von etw ~** to live or subsist on sth; **sich von Übersetzungen ~** to earn one's living by doing translations; **sich selbst ~ müssen** to have to earn one's own living

Er|näh|rer [ɛɐ̯ˈnɛːrɐ] M -s, -, **Er|näh|re|rin** [-ərɪn] F -, -nen breadwinner, provider

Er|näh|rung F -, *no pl* (= *das Ernähren*) feeding; (= *Nahrung*) food, nourishment, nutrition (*esp Med*); (= *Unterhalt*) maintenance; **auf vernünftige ~ achten** to eat sensibly; **die ~ einer großen Familie** feeding a big family; **falsche/richtige/pflanzliche ~** the wrong/a proper/a vegetarian diet

Er|näh|rungs- *in cpds* nutritional; **Er|näh|rungs|be|ra|ter(in)** M(F) nutritional or dietary adviser; **Er|näh|rungs|be|ra|tung** F nutritional or dietary advice; (= *Beratungsstelle*) nutritional or dietary advice centre (*Brit*) or center (*US*); **er|näh|rungs|be|wusst** ▲ ADJ nutrition-conscious; **Er|näh|rungs|feh|ler** M bad or unhealthy eating habit; **~ machen** to eat unhealthily or an unhealthy diet; **Er|näh|rungs|for|schung** F nutritional research; **Er|näh|rungs|ge|wohn|hei|ten** PL eating habits *pl*; **Er|näh|rungs|krank|heit** F nutritional disease; **Er|näh|rungs|wei|se** F diet, form of nutrition; **Er|näh|rungs|wis|sen|schaft** F dietetics *sing*; **Er|näh|rungs|wis|sen|schaft|ler(in)** M(F) dietician, nutritionist; **Er|näh|rungs|zu|stand** M nutritional state; **in einem guten/schlechten ~ sein** to be well/poorly nourished or fed

er|nen|nen [ɛɐ̯ˈnɛnən] *ptp* **ernannt** [ɛɐ̯ˈnant] VT *irreg* to appoint; **jdn zu etw ~** to make or appoint sb sth

Er|nen|nung F appointment (*zu* as)

Er|nen|nungs-: Er|nen|nungs|schrei|ben NT letter of appointment; **Er|nen|nungs|ur|kun|de** F certificate of appointment

er|neu|er|bar ADJ renewable

Er|neu|e|rer [ɛɐ̯ˈnɔʏ̯ɐrɐ] M -s, -, **Er|neu|e|rin** [-ərɪn] F -, -nen innovator

er|neu|ern [ɛɐ̯ˈnɔʏ̯ɐn] *ptp* **erneuert** VT to renew; *Forderung, Kritik* to reiterate; (= *renovieren*) to renovate; (= *restaurieren*) to restore; (= *auswechseln*) *Öl* to change; *Maschinenteile* to replace; (= *wieder beleben*) to revive; **einen Vertrag ~** to renew a contract

Er|neu|e|rung F renewal; (= *Renovierung*) renovation; (= *Restaurierung*) restoration; (= *Auswechslung*) (*von Öl*) changing; (*von Maschinenteil*) replacement; (= *Wiederbelebung*) revival

Er|neu|e|rungs-: er|neu|e|rungs|be|dürf|tig ADJ in need of renewal or replacement *pred*; **Er|neu|e|rungs|be|we|gung** F (*in Politik*) reform movement; (*in Religion*) revivalist movement

er|neut [ɛɐ̯ˈnɔʏ̯t] ADJ *attr* renewed **ADV** (once) again, once more

er|nied|ri|gen [ɛɐ̯ˈniːdrɪgn] *ptp* **erniedrigt** **VT** (= *demütigen*) to humiliate; (= *herabsetzen*) to degrade; (*Mus*) to flatten, to flat (*US*) **VR** to humble oneself; (*pej*) to demean or lower oneself

Er|nied|ri|gung F -, -en humiliation; (= *Herabsetzung*) degradation; (*Mus*) flattening, flatting (*US*)

Er|nied|ri|gungs|zei|chen NT (*Mus*) flat (sign)

ernst [ɛrnst] ADJ serious; (= *bedenklich, bedrohlich, würdevoll auch*) grave; (= *eifrig, ernsthaft*) *Mensch, Gesinnung* earnest; (= *feierlich, elegisch*) solemn; **~e Absichten haben** (*inf*) to have honourable (*Brit*) or honorable (*US*) intentions; **es ist nichts Ernstes** it's nothing serious; **~ bleiben** to remain or be serious; (= *sich das Lachen verbeißen*) to keep a straight face **ADV** *reden, zuhören* earnestly; **es (mit jdm/etw) meinen** to be serious (about sb/sth); **~ gemeint** serious; **jdn/etw ~ nehmen** to take sb/sth seriously; **es steht ~ um ihn** things look bad for him; (*wegen Krankheit*) he's in a bad way; **ich muss mal ganz ~ mit ihr reden** I have to have a serious talk with her

Ernst¹ [ɛrnst] M -s (= *Name*) Ernest

Ernst² M -(e)s, *no pl* seriousness; (= *Bedenklichkeit auch*) gravity; (= *Dringlichkeit, Ernsthaftigkeit von Gesinnung*) earnestness; **feierlicher ~** solemnity; **im ~** seriously; **allen ~es** in all seriousness, quite seriously; **meinen Sie das allen ~es?, ist das Ihr ~?** are you (really) serious?, you're not serious, are you?; **das kann doch nicht dein ~ sein!** you can't mean that seriously!, you can't be serious!; **das ist mein (völliger** or **voller) ~** I'm quite serious; **dieses Angebot ist im ~ gemeint** this offer is meant seriously; **es ist mir ~ damit** I'm serious about it, I'm in earnest; **mit etw ~ machen** to put sth into action; **wir sollten endlich ~ machen** let's get down to business; **mit einer Drohung ~ machen** to carry out a threat; **der ~ des Lebens** the serious side of life, the real world; **damit wird es jetzt ~** now it's serious, now it's for real (*inf*); **mit ~ bei der Sache sein** to do sth seriously

Ernst-: Ernst|fall M emergency; **im ~** in case of emergency; **ernst|ge|meint** △ [-gəmaɪnt] ADJ *attr* → **ernst** ADV; **ernst|haft** ADJ serious; (= *bedenklich, gewichtig auch*) grave; (= *eindringlich, eifrig*) earnest **ADV a** (= *wirklich*) annehmen, glauben, wollen, sich verlieben seriously; (= *mit Ernst*) tun seriously, in earnest **b** (= *schwer*) krank, erkranken, sich verschlimmern seriously **c** (= *eindringlich*) jdn ~ ermahnen/warnen to give sb a serious warning; **Ernst|haf|tig|keit** [ˈɛrnsthaftɪçkaɪt] F -, *no pl* seriousness; (= *Bedenklichkeit, Gewichtigkeit auch*) gravity; (= *Eindringlichkeit, Eifrigkeit*) earnestness; **ernst|lich** [ˈɛrnstlɪç] ADJ serious; (= *bedrohlich auch*) grave; (*attr.* = *eindringlich auch*) earnest **ADV** besorgt um seriously or gravely concerned about; **~ böse werden** to get really angry

Ern|te [ˈɛrntə] F -, -n **a** (= *das Ernten*) (*von Getreide*) harvest(ing); (*von Kartoffeln*) digging; (*von Äpfeln etc*) picking **b** (= *Ertrag*) harvest (*an +dat* of); (*von Kartoffeln etc auch, von Äpfeln, fig*) crop; **die ~ bergen** (*form*) or **einbringen** to bring in the harvest, to harvest the crop(s); **die ~ seines Fleißes** the fruits of his hard work; **der Tod hielt grausige ~** (*liter*) death took a heavy toll; **du siehst aus, als sei dir die ganze ~ verhagelt** (*fig inf*) you look as though you've lost a shilling and found sixpence

Ern|te-: Ern|te|ar|bei|ter(in) M(F) (*von Getreide*) reaper, harvester; (*von Kartoffeln, Obst, Hopfen*) picker; **Ern|te|aus|fall** M crop shortfall (*spec*) or failure; **Ern|te(dank)|fest** NT harvest festival; **Ern|te|ma|schi|ne** F reaper, harvester

ern|ten [ˈɛrntn] VT **a** *Getreide* to harvest, to reap; *Kartoffeln* to dig, to get in; *Äpfel, Erbsen* to pick; **ich muss jetzt meinen Apfelbaum ~** it's time I picked my apples **b** (*fig*) *Früchte, Lohn, Unfrieden* to reap; *Undank, Applaus, Spott* to get

Ern|te|zeit F harvest (time)

er|nüch|tern [ɛɐ̯ˈnʏçtɐn] *ptp* **ernüchtert** VT to sober up; (*fig*) to bring down to earth, to sober; **~d** sobering

Er|nüch|te|rung F -, -en sobering-up; (*fig*) disillusionment

Er|obe|rer [ɛɐ̯ˈoːbərɐ] M -s, -, **Er|obe|rin** [-ərɪn] F -, -nen conqueror

er|obern [ɛɐ̯ˈoːbɐn] *ptp* **erobert** VT to conquer; *Festung, Stadt* to take, to capture; (*fig*) *Sympathie etc* to win, to capture; *neue Märkte* to win, to move into; *Herz, Mädchen* to conquer; (*inf*: = *er-*

gattern) to get hold of; **im Sturm ~** (*Mil, fig*) to take by storm

Er|obe|rung F **-, -en** (*lit, fig*) conquest; (*einer Festung, Stadt*) capture, taking; **eine ~ machen** (*fig inf*) to make a conquest; **auf ~en ausgehen** (*fig inf*) to be out to make conquests

Er|obe|rungs-: Er|obe|rungs|krieg M war of conquest; **Er|obe|rungs|zug** M campaign of conquest

er|öff|nen [ɛʁˈœfnən] *ptp* **eröffnet** ▼ⓣ **a** (= *beginnen*) to open (*auch Fin, Mil etc*); *Ausstellung* to open, to inaugurate (*form*); *Konkursverfahren* to institute, to initiate; *Testament* to open; **etw für eröffnet erklären** to declare sth open **b** (*Med*) *Geschwür* to lance **c** (*hum, geh*) **jdm etw ~** to disclose *or* reveal sth to sb; **ich habe dir etwas zu ~** I have something to tell you ▼ⓡ **a** (*Aussichten etc*) to open up, to present itself/themselves **b** (*geh*) **sich jdm ~** to open one's heart to sb ▼ⓘ (*Währungskurs*) to open (*mit at*)

Er|öff|nung F **a** (= *Beginn*) opening; (*von Ausstellung*) opening, inauguration; (*von Konkursverfahren*) institution, initiation **b** (*Med: von Geschwür*) lancing **c** (*hum, geh*) disclosure, revelation; **jdm eine ~ machen** to disclose *or* reveal sth to sb; **ich habe dir eine ~ zu machen** I have something to tell you

Er|öff|nungs-: Er|öff|nungs|an|spra|che F inaugural *or* opening address; **Er|öff|nungs|fei|er|lich|kei|ten** PL opening ceremony; (*Sportereignisse auch*) opening ceremonies *pl*; **Er|öff|nungs|kurs** M opening price; **Er|öff|nungs|we|hen** PL (*Med*) first stage contractions *pl*

e|ro|gen [eroˈgeːn] ADJ erogenous

er|ör|tern [ɛʁˈœrtən] ✪ 53.1 *ptp* **erörtert** VT to discuss (in detail)

Er|ör|te|rung F **-, -en** discussion; **zur ~ stehen** (*form*) to be under discussion

E|ros [ˈeːrɔs] M **-, no pl** (*esp Philos*) Eros

E|ros-Cen|ter [ˈeːrɔsɛntɐ] NT **-s, -** eros centre (*Brit*) *or* center (*US*)

E|ro|si|on [eroˈzioːn] F **-, -en** (*Geol, Med*) erosion

E|ro|si|ons|schä|den [eroˈzioːnsʃɛːdn] PL (*Geol*) erosion damage, damage *sing* caused by erosion

E|ro|ten [eˈroːtn] PL (*Art*) Cupids *pl*

E|ro|tik [eˈroːtɪk] F **-, no pl** eroticism

E|ro|ti|ka [eˈroːtika] PL (*Liter*) erotica *sing*

E|ro|ti|ker [eˈroːtikɐ] M **-s, -, E|ro|ti|ke|rin** [-ərɪn] F **-, -nen** eroticist

e|ro|tisch [eˈroːtɪʃ] ADJ erotic

E|ro|to|ma|ne [erotoˈmaːnə] M **-n, -n** sex maniac

E|ro|to|ma|nie [erotomaˈniː] F (*Psych*) erotomania (*spec*)

E|ro|to|ma|nin [erotoˈmaːnɪn] F **-, -nen** nymphomaniac

Er|pel [ˈɛrpl] M **-s, -** drake

er|picht [ɛʁˈpɪçt] ADJ **auf etw** (*acc*) **~ sein** to be keen (*Brit*) *or* bent (*US*) on sth; **er ist nur auf Geld ~** he's only after money

er|press|bar ▲ ADJ **~ sein** to be susceptible to blackmail; **~e Politiker** politicians who are susceptible to blackmail; **sich ~ machen** to lay oneself open to blackmail

er|pres|sen [ɛʁˈprɛsn] *ptp* **erpresst** VT *Geld etc* to extort (*von* from); *jdn* to blackmail; **die Kidnapper haben den Vater erpresst** the kidnappers tried to extort money from the father

Er|pres|ser [ɛʁˈprɛsɐ] M **-s, -, Er|pres|se|rin** [-ərɪn] F **-, -nen** blackmailer; (*bei Entführung*) kidnapper

Er|pres|ser|brief M blackmail letter

er|pres|se|risch [ɛʁˈprɛsərɪʃ] ADJ blackmailing *attr*; **~er Menschenraub** (*Jur*) kidnapping

Er|pres|ser|me|tho|den PL blackmail *sing*

Er|pres|sung F **-, -en** (*von Geld, Zugeständnissen*) extortion; (*eines Menschen*) blackmail; **die Kid-**

napper hatten keinen Erfolg mit ihrer ~ the kidnappers failed to get their ransom money, the kidnappers failed in their ransom attempt

Er|pres|sungs|ver|such M blackmail attempt; (*durch Gewaltandrohung*) attempt at obtaining money by menaces; (*bei Entführung*) attempt at getting a ransom

er|pro|ben [ɛʁˈproːbn] *ptp* **erprobt** VT to test; (*fig*) to (put to the) test

er|probt ADJ tried and tested, proven; (= *zuverlässig*) reliable; (= *erfahren*) experienced

Er|pro|bung F **-, -en** *usu sing* testing, trial(s *pl*)

Er|pro|bungs|pha|se F test phase

er|qui|cken [ɛʁˈkvɪkn] *ptp* **erquickt** VT (*old, liter*) to refresh

er|quick|lich [ɛʁˈkvɪklɪç] ADJ (= *angenehm*) pleasant; (= *anregend*) stimulating

Er|qui|ckung F **-, -en** (*old*) refreshment

Er|ra|ta [ɛˈraːta] PL (*Typ*) errata *pl*

er|ra|ten [ɛʁˈraːtn] *ptp* **erraten** VT *irreg* to guess; *Rätsel* to guess (the answer to); **du hast es ~!** how did you guess?, you guessed!

er|ra|tisch [ɛˈraːtɪʃ] ADJ (*Geol*) erratic; **ein ~er Block** an erratic

er|rech|nen [ɛʁˈrɛçnən] *ptp* **errechnet** VT to calculate, to work out

er|reg|bar ADJ excitable; (*sexuell*) easily aroused; (= *empfindlich*) sensitive; **schwer ~** not easily aroused

Er|reg|bar|keit [ɛʁˈreːkbaːʁkait] F **-, no pl** excitability; (= *Empfindlichkeit*) sensitivity

er|re|gen [ɛʁˈreːgn] *ptp* **erregt** ▼ⓣ **a** (= *aufregen*) *jdn, Nerven etc* to excite; (*sexuell auch*) to arouse; (= *erzürnen*) to infuriate, to annoy; **er war vor Wut ganz erregt** he was in a rage *or* fury; **in der Debatte ging es erregt zu** feelings ran high in the debate, the debate was quite heated; **erregte Diskussionen** heated discussions; **erregt lief er hin und her** he paced back and forth in a state of agitation; **freudig erregt** excited → **Gemüt b**
b (= *hervorrufen, erzeugen*) to arouse; *Zorn* to provoke; *Leidenschaften* to arouse, to excite; *Aufsehen, öffentliches Ärgernis, Heiterkeit* to cause, to create; *Aufmerksamkeit* to attract; *Zweifel* to raise ▼ⓡ to get worked up *or* excited (*über +acc* a-bout, over); (= *sich ärgern*) to get annoyed (*über +acc* at)

Er|re|ger [ɛʁˈreːgɐ] M **-s, -** (*Med*) cause, causative agent (*spec*); (= *Bazillus etc*) pathogene (*spec*)

Er|regt|heit [ɛʁˈreːkthait] F **-, no pl** (*esp angenehm*) excitement; (*sexuell auch*) arousal; (= *Beunruhigung*) agitation; (= *Wut*) rage

Er|re|gung F **a** *no pl* (= *das Aufregen*) excitation; (*sexuell auch*) arousal, arousing; (= *das Erzürnen*) infuriation, infuriating **b** *no pl* (= *Erzeugung*) arousal, arousing; (*von Aufsehen, Heiterkeit*) causing, creating; (*von Aufmerksamkeit*) attracting → **Ärgernis a c** (= *Zustand*) (*esp angenehm*) excitement; (*sexuell auch*) arousal; (= *Beunruhigung*) agitation; (= *Wut*) rage; (*liter: des Meeres, der Wellen*) turbulence; **in ~ geraten** to get excited/aroused/agitated/into a rage; **jdn in ~ versetzen** to get sb excited/aroused/agitated; **das Meer in ~ versetzen** to make the sea churn

er|reich|bar ADJ reachable, able to be reached; (= *nicht weit*) within reach; (*Telec*) obtainable; *Glück, Ziel* attainable; **leicht ~** easily reached; within easy reach; easily attainable; **schwer ~ sein** (*Ort*) not to be very accessible; (*Mensch*) to be difficult to get hold of; (*Gegenstand*) to be difficult to reach; **zu Fuß ~** able to be reached on foot; (= *nicht weit*) within walking distance; **in ~er Nähe** near at hand (*+gen* to); **der Direktor ist nie ~** the director is never available; (*telefonisch*) the director can never be reached; **sind Sie morgen zu Hause ~?** can I get in touch with you at home tomorrow?, are you contactable at home tomorrow? → **telefonisch**

Er|reich|bar|keit [ɛʁˈraiçbaːʁekait] F **-, no pl** (*von Ort, Mensch*) accessibility; (*Telec*) obtainability

er|rei|chen [ɛʁˈraiçn] *ptp* **erreicht** VT to reach; *Ort auch* to get to, to arrive at; *Festland, Hafen auch* to make; *Zug* to catch; *Alter, Geschwindigkeit* to reach, to attain; *Absicht, Zweck* to achieve, to attain; (= *einholen*) to catch up with; (= *sich in Verbindung setzen mit*) *jdn, Büro etc* to contact, to get, to reach; **ein hohes Alter ~** to live to a ripe old age; **vom Bahnhof leicht zu ~** within easy reach of the station; **zu Fuß zu ~** able to be reached on foot; (= *nicht weit*) within walking distance; **wann kann ich Sie morgen ~?** when can I get in touch with you tomorrow?; **du erreichst damit nur, dass ...** all you'll achieve that way is that ...; **wir haben nichts erreicht** we achieved nothing; **bei ihm war nichts zu ~** you couldn't get anywhere with him *or* anything out of him

Er|rei|chung F **-, no pl** (*form*) attainment; (*eines Ziels auch*) achievement; **bei ~ des 60. Lebensjahres** on reaching the age of 60

er|ret|ten [ɛʁˈrɛtn] *ptp* **errettet** VT (*liter, esp Rel*) to save, to deliver (*liter*)

Er|ret|ter(in) M(F) (*liter, esp Rel*) saviour (*Brit esp Rel*), savior (*US esp Rel*), deliverer (*liter*)

Er|ret|tung F (*liter*) rescue, deliverance (*liter*); (*Rel*) salvation

er|rich|ten [ɛʁˈrɪçtn] *ptp* **errichtet** VT to erect (*auch Math*), to put up; (*fig:* = *gründen*) to establish, to set up

Er|rich|tung F erection, construction; (*fig:* = *Gründung*) establishment, setting-up

er|rin|gen [ɛʁˈrɪŋən] *ptp* **errungen** [ɛʁˈrʊŋən] VT *irreg* to gain, to win; *den 3. Platz, Erfolg* to gain, to achieve; *Rekord* to set; **ein hart errungener Sieg** a hard-won victory

Er-Ro|man [ˈeːɐ-] M (*Liter*) third-person novel

er|rö|ten [ɛʁˈrøːtn] *ptp* **errötet** VI *aux sein* (*über +acc* at) to flush; (*esp aus Verlegenheit, Scham*) to blush; (*Gesicht*) to go *or* turn red, to redden; **jdn zum Erröten bringen** to make sb flush/blush

Er|run|gen|schaft [ɛʁˈrʊŋənʃaft] F **-, -en** achievement; (*inf:* = *Anschaffung*) acquisition

Er|satz [ɛʁˈzats] M **, no pl** substitute (*auch Sport*); (*für Altes, Zerbrochenes, Mitarbeiter*) replacement; (*inf:* = *die Ersatzspieler*) substitutes *pl*; (*Mil:* = *Ersatztruppen*) replacements *pl*; (= *Reserveheer*) reserves *pl*; (= *das Ersetzen*) replacement, substitution; (*durch Geld*) compensation; (*von Kosten*) reimbursement; **als** *or* **zum ~** as a substitute/replacement; **zum ~ der beschädigten Ware verpflichtet** obliged to replace the damaged item; **als ~ für jdn einspringen** to stand in for sb; **für etw ~ leisten** (*Jur*) to pay *or* provide compensation *or* restitution for sth; **~ schaffen für** to find replacements/a replacement for, to replace

Er|satz-: Er|satz|an|spruch M (*Jur*) entitlement to compensation; **~ haben** to be entitled to compensation; **Er|satz|bank** F *pl* **-bänke** (*Sport*) substitutes' bench; **Er|satz|be|frie|di|gung** F (*Psych*) vicarious satisfaction; **das Rauchen ist eine ~** smoking is a substitute; **Er|satz|bril|le** F spare (pair of) glasses *pl or* spectacles *pl* (*Brit*); **Er|satz|dienst** M alternative *or* community service (*for conscientious objectors*); **Er|satz|dienst|leis|ten|de(r)** [-laistndə] M *decl as adj* (civilian) alternative service worker; **Er|satz|droge** F substitute drug; **Er|satz|frau** F replacement; (*Sport*) substitute; **Er|satz|hand|lung** F (*Psych*) substitute (act); **Er|satz|kaf|fee** M coffee substitute; **Er|satz|kas|se** F state health insurance scheme; **er|satz|los** ADJ **~e Streichung** (*von Stelle, Steuer, Regelung*) abolition; (*von Sendung, Veranstaltung*) cancellation ADV **etw ~ streichen** (*Stelle, Steuer, Regelung*) to abolish sth; *Sendung, Veranstaltung* to cancel sth; **Er|satz|mann** M *pl* **-männer** *or* **-leute** replacement; (*Sport*) substitute; **Er|satz|mi|ne** F refill; **Er|satz|ob|jekt** NT (*Psych*) substitute, surrogate; **Er|satz|-**

pflicht F liability to pay compensation; **er|satz|pflich|tig** [-pflɪçtɪç] ADJ liable to pay compensation; **Er|satz|rad** NT (Aut) spare wheel; **Er|satz|rei|fen** M (Aut) spare tyre (Brit) or tire (US); **Er|satz|spie|ler(in)** M(F) (Sport) substitute; **Er|satz|teil** NT spare (part); **Er|satz|trup|pen** PL replacements pl, (= Reserveheer) reserve troops pl, reserves pl; **er|satz|wei|se** ADV as an alternative

er|sau|fen [ɛɐˈzaufn] ptp **ersoffen** [ɛɐˈzɔfn] VI irreg aux sein (inf) a (= ertrinken) to drown, to be drowned b (= überschwemmt werden, Aut) to be flooded, to flood

er|säu|fen [ɛɐˈzɔyfn] ptp **ersäuft** VT to drown; **seinen Kummer im Alkohol ~** (inf) to drown one's sorrows (in drink (Brit) or alcohol) (inf)

er|schaf|fen [ɛɐˈʃafn] pret **erschuf** [ɛɐˈʃuːf], ptp **erschaffen** VT to create

Er|schaf|fer(in) M(F) creator

Er|schaf|fung F creation

er|schal|len [ɛɐˈʃalən] pret **erscholl** or **erschallte** [ɛɐˈʃɔl, ɛɐˈʃaltə], ptp **erschollen** or **erschallt** [ɛɐˈʃɔlən, ɛɐˈʃalt] VI aux sein (geh) (Stimme, Lachen) to ring out; (Trompete) to sound

er|schau|dern [ɛɐˈʃaudɐn] ptp **erschaudert** VI aux sein (geh) to shudder (bei at)

er|schau|en [ɛɐˈʃauən] ptp **erschaut** VT (liter) to see, to espy (liter)

er|schau|ern [ɛɐˈʃauɐn] ptp **erschauert** VI aux sein (geh) (vor Kälte) to shiver; (vor Erregung, Ehrfurcht) to tremble, to shudder

er|schei|nen [ɛɐˈʃainən] ☼ 53.3 ptp **erschienen** [ɛɐˈʃiːnən] VI irreg aux sein to appear; (= vorkommen, wirken wie auch) to seem (+dat to); (= sich sehen lassen: auf Party etc auch) to put in an appearance (auf +dat at); (zur Arbeit auch) to turn up (zu for); (Buch auch) to come out; **in einem anderen Licht ~** to appear in a different light; **es scheint (mir) wünschenswert** it seems or appears desirable (to me); **das Buch ist in** or **bei einem anderen Verlag erschienen** the book was published by or brought out by another publisher; **das Buch erscheint nicht mehr** the book is no longer published

Er|schei|nen [ɛɐˈʃainən] NT -s, no pl appearance; (von Geist auch) apparition; (von Buch auch) publication; **um rechtzeitiges ~ wird gebeten** you are kindly requested to attend punctually; **er dankte den Besuchern für ihr (zahlreiches) ~** he thanked his (many) guests for coming; **mit seinem ~ hatte ich nicht mehr gerechnet** I no longer reckoned on his turning up or appearing

Er|schei|nung F -, -en a no pl (= das Erscheinen) appearance; **das Fest der ~** (Eccl) (the Feast of) the Epiphany; **in ~ treten** (Merkmale) to appear, to manifest themselves (form); (Gefühle) to show themselves, to become visible or obvious; **sie tritt (persönlich) fast nie in ~** she hardly ever appears (in person) b (= äußere Erscheinung) appearance; (Philos auch, = Naturerscheinung, Vorkommnis) phenomenon; (= Krankheitserscheinung, Alterserscheinung) symptom; (= Zeichen) sign, manifestation; **es ist eine bekannte ~, dass ...** it is (a) well-known (phenomenon) that ... c (= Gestalt) figure; **seiner äußeren ~ nach** judging by his appearance; **er ist eine stattliche ~** he is a fine figure of a man; **eine elegante ~ sein** to cut an elegant figure d (= Geistererscheinung) apparition; (= Traumbild) vision

Er|schei|nungs-: Er|schei|nungs|bild NT (Biol) phenotype; (fig) image; **sein äußeres ~** his outward appearance; **Er|schei|nungs|da|tum** NT (von Buch, Zeitung) publication date; (von Video, Film) release date; **Er|schei|nungs|form** F manifestation; **Er|schei|nungs|jahr** NT (von Buch) year of publication; **Er|schei|nungs|ort** M pl **-orte** (von Buch) place of publication; **Er|schei|nungs|wei|se** F (von Zeitschrift) publi-

cation dates pl, **~: monatlich** appearing monthly

er|schie|ßen [ɛɐˈʃiːsn] ptp **erschossen** [ɛɐˈʃɔsn] irreg VT to shoot (dead) VR to shoot oneself; **dann kannst du dich ~** you might as well stick your head in a gas oven → auch **erschossen**

Er|schie|ßung F -, -en shooting; (Jur: als Todesstrafe) execution; **die Verurteilten wurden zur ~ abgeführt** the condemned were led off to be shot; **er drohte mit ~ der Geiseln** he threatened to shoot the hostages; **Tod durch ~** (Jur) death by firing squad

Er|schie|ßungs|kom|man|do NT firing squad

er|schlaf|fen [ɛɐˈʃlafn] ptp **erschlafft** VI aux sein (= ermüden) to tire, to grow weary; (= schlaff werden) to go limp; (Seil) to slacken, to go slack; (Interesse, Eifer) to wane, to flag VT to tire; (Medikament) to relax

Er|schlaf|fung F -, no pl tiredness, weariness; (= das Schlaffwerden) limpness; (von Interesse, Eifer) waning, flagging

er|schla|gen¹ [ɛɐˈʃlaːgn] ptp **erschlagen** VT irreg to kill, to strike dead (liter); **vom Blitz ~ werden** to be struck (dead) by lightning

er|schla|gen² [ɛɐˈʃlaːgn] ADJ **~ sein** (inf) (= todmüde) to be worn out, to be dead beat (Brit inf); (= erstaunt) to be flabbergasted (inf)

er|schlei|chen [ɛɐˈʃlaiçn] ptp **erschlichen** [ɛɐˈʃlɪçn] VT irreg (sich dat) etw ~ to obtain sth by devious means or in an underhand way; **sich (dat) jds Gunst/Vertrauen ~** to worm oneself into sb's favour (Brit) or favor (US) or good graces/into sb's confidence

er|schlie|ßen [ɛɐˈʃliːsn] ptp **erschlossen** [ɛɐˈʃlɔsn] irreg VT a Gebiet, Absatzmarkt, Baugelände to develop, to open up; Einnahmequelle to find, to acquire; Rohstoffquellen, Bodenschätze to tap; Wählergruppen to tap into; **erschlossen** (Gebiet) developed b (= folgern) to deduce, to infer (aus from); Gedicht to decipher, to work out the meaning of; **daraus ist zu ~, dass ...** it can be deduced or inferred from this, that ... c (Ling, Liter) to reconstruct VR (liter) (Blüte) to open (out); **sich jdm ~** (= verständlich werden) to disclose itself to sb (liter)

Er|schlie|ßungs|kos|ten PL development costs pl

er|scholl pret von **erschallen**

er|schol|len ptp von **erschallen**

er|schöpf|bar ADJ exhaustible

er|schöp|fen [ɛɐˈʃœpfn] ptp **erschöpft** VT Mittel, Thema, Geduld to exhaust; (= ermüden auch) to tire out; **in erschöpftem Zustand** in a state of exhaustion VR a (körperlich) to exhaust oneself b (fig) **sich in etw (dat) ~** to amount to nothing more than sth; **darin erschöpft sich seine Bildung** that's the sum total of his education; **ein Schriftsteller, der sich erschöpft hat** an author who has run out of ideas or expended his talent

er|schöp|fend ADJ a (= ermüdend) exhausting b (= ausführlich) exhaustive ADV exhaustively

er|schöpft [ɛɐˈʃœpft] ptp von **erschöpfen** ADJ exhausted; **meine Geduld ist (endgültig) ~** my patience has (finally) run out → **erschöpfen**

Er|schöp|fung F a (= völlige Ermüdung) exhaustion, fatigue; **bis zur ~ arbeiten** to work to the point of exhaustion b (der Mittel, Vorräte etc) exhaustion

Er|schöp|fungs|zu|stand M state of exhaustion no pl

er|schos|sen [ɛɐˈʃɔsn] ADJ (inf) **(völlig) ~ sein** to be whacked (Brit inf), to be dead (inf) (Brit inf), to be exhausted → auch **erschießen**

er|schrak pret von **erschrecken** VIR

er|schre|cken [ɛɐˈʃrɛkn] pret **erschreckte**, ptp **erschreckt** VT to frighten, to scare; (= bestürzen) to startle, to give a shock or a start; (= zusammenzucken lassen) to make jump, to give a start, to startle; **es hat mich erschreckt, wie schlecht**

er aussah it gave me a shock or a start or it startled me to see how bad he looked pret **erschreckte** or **erschrak** [ɛɐˈʃrɛktə, ɛɐˈʃraːk], ptp **erschreckt** or **erschrocken** [ɛɐˈʃrɛkt, ɛɐˈʃrɔkn] VIR (vi: aux sein) to be frightened (vor +dat by); (= bestürzt sein) to be startled; (= zusammenzucken) to jump, to start; **ich bin erschrocken, wie schlecht er aussah** it gave me a shock or a start or I was shocked or startled to see how bad he looked; **sie erschrak bei dem Gedanken, dass ...** the thought that ... gave her a start or a scare; **sie erschrak bei dem Knall** the bang made her jump; **~ Sie nicht, ich bins nur** don't be frightened or afraid, it's only me; **~ Sie nicht, wenn Sie ihn sehen, er ist sehr alt geworden** don't be alarmed when you see him, he's aged terribly → auch **erschrocken**

Er|schre|cken NT -s, no pl fright, shock

er|schre|ckend ADJ alarming, frightening ADV **~ aussehen** to look dreadful or terrible; **~ wenig Leute** alarmingly few people; **~ viele** an alarmingly large number

er|schrickt [ɛɐˈʃrɪkt] 3. pers sing pres von **erschrecken**

er|schro|cken [ɛɐˈʃrɔkn] ptp von **erschrecken** VIR ADJ frightened, scared; (= bestürzt) startled ADV **~ hochspringen/zusammenzucken** to jump, to (give a) start

er|schuf pret von **erschaffen**

er|schüt|tern [ɛɐˈʃʏtɐn] ptp **erschüttert** VT Boden, Gebäude, Vertrauen, Glauben etc to shake; (fig) Glaubwürdigkeit to cast doubt upon; (fig) Gesundheit to unsettle, to upset; (= bewegen, Schock versetzen) to shake severely; **jdn in seinem Glauben ~** to shake or shatter sb's faith; **sie war von seinem Tod tief erschüttert** she was severely shaken by his death; **seine Geschichte hat mich erschüttert** I was shattered (inf) by his story; **über etw (acc) erschüttert sein** to be shaken or shattered (inf) by sth; **mich kann nichts mehr ~** nothing surprises me any more; **er lässt sich durch nichts ~, ihn kann nichts ~** he always keeps his cool (inf)

er|schüt|ternd ADJ shattering (inf); Nachricht auch distressing; Verhältnisse auch shocking

Er|schüt|te|rung F -, -en (des Bodens etc) tremor, vibration; (fig) (der Ruhe, Wirtschaftslage) disruption; (des Selbstvertrauens) blow (+gen to); (= seelische Ergriffenheit) emotion, shock; **bei der ~ des Gebäudes** when the building shook; **die Krise kann zu einer ~ des Staates führen** the crisis could rock the state; **ihr Tod löste allgemeine ~ aus** her death shocked everyone

er|schwe|ren [ɛɐˈʃveːrən] ptp **erschwert** VT to make more difficult; Sachlage auch to aggravate; Fortschritt etc auch to impede, to hinder; **jdm etw ~** to make sth more difficult for sb; **~de Umstände** (Jur) aggravating circumstances; **es kommt noch ~d hinzu, dass ...** to compound matters, ...

Er|schwer|nis [ɛɐˈʃveːɐnɪs] F -, -se difficulty

Er|schwer|nis|zu|la|ge F hardship allowance

Er|schwe|rung F -, -en impediment (+gen to), obstruction (+gen to); **das bedeutet eine ~ meiner Arbeit** that will make my job more difficult

er|schwin|deln [ɛɐˈʃvɪndln] ptp **erschwindelt** VT to obtain by fraud; **sich (dat) (von jdm) etw ~** to swindle or do (inf) sb out of sth

er|schwin|gen [ɛɐˈʃvɪŋən] ptp **erschwungen** [ɛɐˈʃvʊŋən] VT irreg to afford

er|schwing|lich [ɛɐˈʃvɪŋlɪç] ADJ Preise within one's means, reasonable; **das Haus ist für uns nicht ~** the house is not within our means

er|se|hen [ɛɐˈzeːən] ptp **ersehen** VT irreg (form) **etw aus etw ~** to see or gather sth from sth

er|seh|nen [ɛɐˈzeːnən] ptp **ersehnt** VT (geh) to long for

er|sehnt [ɛɐˈzeːnt] ADJ longed-for; **heiß** or **lang ~** much-longed-for

er|sẹtz|bar ADJ replaceable; *Schaden* reparable

er|sẹt|zen [ɛɐˈzɛtsn̩] *ptp* **ersẹtzt** VT to replace (*auch Comput*); (= *als Ersatz dienen für, an die Stelle treten von auch*) to take the place of; **niemand kann Kindern die Mutter ~** no-one can take the place of a child's mother, no-one can replace a child's mother; **diese Vase kannst du mir nie ~** you'll never be able to replace that vase

Er|sẹt|zung F -, *no pl* replacing; (*von Schaden, Verlust*) compensation, reparation (+*gen* for); (*von Unkosten*) reimbursement, repayment

er|sịcht|lich [ɛɐˈzɪçtlɪç] ADJ obvious, clear, apparent; **ohne ~en Grund** for no apparent reason; **hieraus ist klar ~, dass ...** it is obvious *etc* from this that ..., this shows clearly that ...

er|sịn|nen [ɛɐˈzɪnən] *ptp* **ersọnnen** [ɛɐˈzɔnən] VT *irreg* to devise, to think up; (= *erfinden*) to invent

er|sịt|zen [ɛɐˈzɪtsn̩] *ptp* **ersẹssen** [ɛɐˈzɛsn̩] VT *irreg* (*Jur*) *Anspruch* to acquire by prescription

er|spä|hen [ɛɐˈʃpɛːən] *ptp* **erspäht** VT to catch sight of, to spot, to espy (*liter*)

er|spa|ren [ɛɐˈʃpaːrən] *ptp* **erspart** VT *Kosten, Zeit, Kummer etc* to save; **jdm/sich etw ~** to spare *or* save sb/oneself sth; **ich kann mir jeglichen Kommentar ~** I don't think I need to comment; **jdm eine Demütigung ~** to spare sb humiliation; **~ Sie sich die Mühe!** save *or* spare yourself the trouble; **Sie können sich alles Weitere ~** you don't need to say any more; **ihr blieb auch nichts erspart** she was spared nothing; **das Ersparte** the savings *pl* VR to be superfluous *or* unnecessary

Er|spar|nis [ɛɐˈʃpaːenɪs] F -, -se *or* (*Aus*) nt -ses, -se a *no pl* (*an Zeit etc*) saving (*an* +*dat* of) b *usu pl* savings *pl*

er|spie|len [ɛɐˈʃpiːlən] *ptp* **erspielt** VT (*Sport*) *Punkte, Sieg* to win, to gain; **sich** (*dat*) **etw ~** (*Sympathien, guten Ruf*) to gain sth; *Berühmtheit* to achieve sth; **sich** (*dat*) **Torchancen ~** to create chances (to score)

er|sprieß|lich [ɛɐˈʃpriːslɪç] ADJ (= *förderlich*) beneficial, advantageous; (= *nützlich*) fruitful, profitable; (= *angenehm*) pleasant

erst [eːɐst] ADV a first; (= *anfänglich*) at first; **mach ~ (ein)mal die Arbeit fertig** finish your work first; **~ mal ist das gar nicht wahr ...** first *or* for one thing it's just not true ...; **~ einmal musst du an deine Pflicht denken** you should consider your duty first; **wenn du das ~ einmal hinter dir hast** once you've got that behind you; **~ wollte er, dann wieder nicht** first he wanted to, then he didn't → **Arbeit** b (= *nicht mehr als, bloß*) only; (= *nicht früher als auch*) not until; **eben** *or* **gerade ~** just; **~ gestern** only yesterday; **~ jetzt** (= *gerade eben*) only just; **~ jetzt verstehe ich ...** I have only just understood ...; **~ jetzt wissen wir ...** it is only now that we know ...; **~ morgen** not until *or* before tomorrow; **~ vor kurzem** only a short time ago; **es ist ~ 6 Uhr** it is only 6 o'clock; **wir fahren ~ übermorgen/~ später** we're not going until the day after tomorrow/until later; **sie war ~ 6 Jahre** she was only 6; **~ als** only when, not until; **~ wenn** only when, not until

c (*emph: = gar, nun gar*) **da gings ~ richtig los** then it really got going; **was wird Mutter ~ sagen!** whatever will mother say!; **was dann ~ passieren?** whatever will happen then?; **sie ist schon ziemlich blöd, aber ~ ihre Schwester!** she is fairly stupid, but you should see her sister!; **da fange ich ~ gar nicht an** I simply won't (bother to) begin; **wie wird er sich ~ ärgern, wenn er das noch erfährt** he really will be annoyed when he finds out about that; **jetzt ~ recht/nicht!** that just makes me all the more determined; **da tat er es ~ recht!** so he did it deliberately; **das macht es ~ recht schlimm** that makes it even worse *or* all the worse; **da habe ich mich ~ recht geärgert** then I really did get annoyed d **wäre er doch ~ zurück!** if only he were

back!; **diese Gerüchte darf man gar nicht ~ aufkommen lassen** these rumours (*Brit*) *or* rumors (*US*) mustn't even be allowed to start

er|star|ken [ɛɐˈʃtarkn̩] *ptp* **erstarkt** VI *aux sein* (*geh*) to gain strength, to become stronger

er|star|ren [ɛɐˈʃtarən] *ptp* **erstarrt** VI *aux sein* (*Finger*) to grow stiff *or* numb; (*Flüssigkeit*) to solidify; (*Gips, Zement etc*) to set, to solidify; (*Blut, Fett etc*) to congeal; (*fig*) (*Blut*) to freeze, to run cold; (*Lächeln*) to freeze; (*vor Schrecken, Entsetzen etc*) to be paralyzed *or* petrified (*vor* +*dat* with); (*Haltung, Meinung*) to become rigid *or* fixed; (*Ideen, Kunstform etc*) to ossify, to become rigid; **erstarrte Formen** fossilized forms

Er|star|rung F -, *no pl* (*von Fingern*) stiffness, numbness; (*von Flüssigkeit, Gips, Zement*) solidification; (*von Blut, Fett*) congelation, congealment; (*vor Schrecken, Entsetzen*) paralysis, petrification

er|stat|ten [ɛɐˈʃtatn̩] *ptp* **erstattet** VT a *Unkosten* to refund, to reimburse b (*form*) (*Straf)anzeige gegen jdn ~** to report sb; **Meldung ~** to report; **Bericht ~** to (give a) report (*über* +*acc* on)

Er|stat|tung F -, *no pl* (*von Unkosten*) refund, reimbursement

Erst- [eːɐst-]: **erst|auf+füh|ren** *ptp* **erstaufgeführt** VT *infin, ptp only* (*Theat*) to give the first public performance of; **Erst|auf|füh|rung** F (*Theat*) first performance *or* night, première; **Erst|auf|la|ge** F first printing

er|stau|nen [ɛɐˈʃtaunən] *ptp* **erstaunt** VT to astonish, to amaze → *auch* **erstaunt** VI a *aux sein* (*old: = überrascht sein*) to be astonished *or* amazed b (= *Erstaunen erregen*) to cause astonishment *or* amazement, to astonish *or* amaze (people); **seine Körperbeherrschung erstaunt immer wieder** his physical control never fails to amaze

Er|stau|nen [ɛɐˈʃtaunən] NT astonishment, amazement; **jdn in ~ (ver)setzen** to astonish *or* amaze sb

er|staun|lich [ɛɐˈʃtaunlɪç] ADJ astonishing, amazing ADV astonishingly, amazingly; **für sein Alter kann er ~ gut lesen** he can read astonishingly *or* amazingly well for his age

er|staunt [ɛɐˈʃtaunt] ADJ astonished, amazed (*über* +*acc* about) ADV in astonishment, in amazement; **~ blicken** to look astonished → *auch* **erstaunen**

Erst- [eːɐst-]: **Erst|aus|ga|be** F first edition; **erst|bes|te(r,s)** ADJ *attr* → **erste(r, s)** b; **Erst|be|stei|gung** F first ascent; **Erst|druck** M *pl* **-drucke** first edition

er|ste|chen [ɛɐˈʃtɛçn̩] *ptp* **erstochen** [ɛɐˈʃtɔxn̩] VT *irreg* to stab to death

er|ste|hen [ɛɐˈʃteːən] *ptp* **erstanden** [ɛɐˈʃtandn̩] *irreg* VT (*inf: = kaufen*) to buy, to get VI *aux sein* (*form*) to arise; (*Städte*) to rise up; (*Bibl: = auferstehen*) to rise

Ers|te-Hil|fe-: **Ers|te-Hil|fe-Kof|fer** [eːɐstəˈhɪlfə-] M first-aid kit; **Ers|te-Hil|fe-Kurs** [eːɐstəˈhɪlfə-] M first-aid course; **Ers|te-Hil|fe-Leis|tung** [eːɐstəˈhɪlfə-] F administering first aid

er|stei|gen [ɛɐˈʃtaign̩] *ptp* **erstiegen** [ɛɐˈʃtiːgn̩] VT *irreg* to climb; *Felswand auch, Stadtmauer* to scale

er|stei|gern [ɛɐˈʃtaigɐn] *ptp* **ersteigert** VT to buy at an auction

Er|stei|gung F ascent; (*von Felswand auch, von Stadtmauer*) scaling

Erst|ein|satz [ˈeːɐst-] M **~ (von Atomwaffen)** first strike

er|stel|len [ɛɐˈʃtɛlən] *ptp* **erstellt** VT a (= *bauen*) to construct, to erect b (= *anfertigen*) *Liste etc* to draw up, to make out

Er|stel|lung F a (= *Bau*) construction, erection b (*von Liste etc*) drawing up, making out

ers|te|mal △ [ˈeːɐstəmaːl] ADV → **erste(r, s)**

ers|ten|mal △ [ˈeːɐstnmaːl] ADV → **erste(r, s)**

ers|tens [ˈeːɐstns] ADV first(ly), in the first place

Ers|te(r) [ˈeːɐstə(r)] MF *decl as adj* first; **die drei ~n** the first three; **der ~ in der Klasse** the top of *or* best in the class; **die ~n werden die Letzten sein** (*Bibl*) the first shall be last; **~r unter Gleichen** first among equals; **der ~ des Monats** the first (day) of the month; **vom nächsten ~n an** as of the first of next month; **er kam als ~r** he was the first to come

ers|te(r, s) [ˈeːɐstə] ADJ a first; (*fig: = führend auch*) best, foremost; *Seite der Zeitung* front; **~r Stock** ~ **Etage** first floor, second floor (*US*); **die ~ Klasse** (*Rail*) the first class (compartment); **~r Klasse fahren** to travel first class; **das ~ Mal** the first time; **das tue ich das ~ Mal** I'm doing this for the first time, it's the first time I've done this; **zum ~n Mal** for the first time; **der ~ Rang** (*Theat*) the dress circle, the (first) balcony (*US*); **~ Güte** *or* **Qualität** top quality; **~ Hilfe** first aid; **die ~n drei** the first three (from each group); **~ Kontakte anknüpfen** to establish preliminary contacts; **am ~n** first; **an ~r Stelle** in the first place; **dieses Thema steht an ~r Stelle unserer Tagesordnung** this subject comes first on our agenda; **in ~r Linie** first and foremost → **Blick, Hand, Mal** → *auch* **vierte(r, s)** b **nimm das ~ Beste!** take anything!; **er hat das erstbeste Auto gekauft** he bought the first car he saw, he bought any old car (*inf*) → **beste(r, s)**

er|ster|ben [ɛɐˈʃtɛrbn̩] *ptp* **erstorben** [ɛɐˈʃtɔrbn̩] VI *irreg aux sein* (*liter*) to die; (*Lärm, Wort*) to die away

ers|te|re(r, s) [ˈeːɐstərə] ADJ the former; **der/die/das Erstere** the former

Ers|te(r)-Klas|se- [eːɐstəˈklasə-, - ɛːɐstəˈklasə-] (*Rail*) first class; **Ers|te(r)-Klas|se-Ab|teil** NT first class compartment; **Ers|te(r)-Klas|se-Wa|gen** M first class carriage (*Brit*) *or* car (*US*)

Ers|te(s) [ˈeːɐstə(s)] MF *decl as adj* **das ~** the first thing; **das ist das ~, was ich höre** that's the first I've heard of it; **als ~** first of all; **fürs ~** for the time being, for the present; **zum ~n, zum Zweiten, zum Dritten** (*bei Auktionen*) going, going, gone!

Erst-: **Erst|ge|bä|ren|de** [ˈeːɐstgəbɛːrəndə] F *decl as adj* primigravida (*spec*); **erst|ge|bo|ren** [ˈeːɐstgəboːrən] ADJ *attr* first-born; **Erst|ge|bo|re|ne(r)** [ˈeːɐstgəboːrənə] MF *decl as adj* first-born (child); **Erst|ge|burt** F (= *Kind*) first-born (child); (= *Tier*) first young; (*Hist: auch* **Erstgeburtsrecht**) birthright, right of primogeniture (*Jur*); **erst|ge|nannt** [-gənant] ADJ *attr* first-mentioned; (= *wichtigster*) first to be mentioned

er|sti|cken [ɛɐˈʃtɪkn̩] *ptp* **erstickt** VT *jdn* to suffocate, to smother; *Feuer* to smother; *Geräusche* to stifle, to smother; (*fig: = unterdrücken*) *Aufruhr etc* to suppress; **mit erstickter Stimme** in a choked voice VI *aux sein* to suffocate; (*Feuer*) to die, to go out; (*Stimme*) to become choked; **an etw** (*dat*) **~** to be suffocated by sth; **an einer Gräte ~** to choke (to death) on a fish bone; **vor Lachen ~** to choke with laughter; **das Kind erstickt förmlich unter der Liebe der Mutter** the child is smothered by motherly love; **unsere Städte ~ im Verkehr** our cities are being choked by traffic; **in der Arbeit ~** (*inf*) to be snowed under with (*Brit*) *or* in (*US*) work, to be up to one's neck in work (*inf*); **er erstickt im Geld** (*inf*) he's rolling in money (*inf*); **die Luft im Zimmer war zum Ersticken** the air in the room was suffocating *or* stifling

Er|sti|ckung F -, *no pl* suffocation, asphyxiation

Er|sti|ckungs-: **Er|sti|ckungs|ge|fahr** F danger of suffocation; **Er|sti|ckungs|tod** M death from *or* by suffocation, asphyxia

erst|in|stanz|lich [ˈeːɐstɪnstantslɪç] ADJ (*Jur*) first-instance

erstkl. *abbr von* **erstklassig**

Erst-: Erst|kläs|ser ['eːrstklɛsə] M **-s, -, Erst|kläs|se|rin** [-ərɪn] F **-, -nen** year 1 or reception pupil (*Brit*), first-grader (*US*); **erst|klas|sig** ADJ first-class, first-rate; (= *in erster Spielklasse*) *Mannschaft* first-division *attr* ADV spielen excellently; **~ schmecken** or **munden** to taste excellent; **~ gekleidet sein** to be perfectly dressed; **das Auto fährt sich ~** that car drives like a dream; **Erst|klas|sig|keit** F **-**, *no pl* excellence; **Erst|kläss|ler** ▲ ['eːrstklɛslə] M **-s, -, Erst|kläss|le|rin** ▲ [-ərɪn] F **-, -nen** (*esp S Ger, Sw*) pupil in the first class of primary school, first-grader (*US*); **Erst|kom|mu|ni|on** F first communion; **Erst|la|ge|rung** F (*von Atommüll*) initial storage

Erst|li|gist ['eːrstlɪgɪst] M **-s, -en** (*Sport*) first-league or first-division team, team in the top division

Erst|ling ['eːrstlɪŋ] M **-s, -e** (= *Kind*) first (child); (= *Tier*) first young; (= *Werk*) first work or baby (*inf*)

Erst|lings-: Erst|lings|film M debut film; **Erst|lings|ro|man** M first or debut novel; **Erst|lings|werk** NT first work

erst|ma|lig ['eːrstmaːlɪç] ADJ first ADV for the first time

erst|mals ['eːrstmals] ADV for the first time

er|strah|len [ɛɐ̯'ʃtraːlən] *ptp* **erstrahlt** VI *aux sein* (*liter*) to shine; **im Lichterglanz ~** to be aglitter (with lights)

erst|ran|gig ['eːrstraŋɪç] ADJ **a** (= *sehr bedeutsam*) of top priority, priority *attr*; (*Fin:* = *ersten Ranges*) *Gläubiger* preferential; *Schuldner* primary; *Hypothek* first; **von ~er Bedeutung** of paramount importance **b** (= *erstklassig*) first-rate, first-class

er|stre|ben [ɛɐ̯'ʃtreːbn] *ptp* **erstrebt** VT to strive for or after, to aspire to

er|stre|bens|wert ADJ worthwhile, desirable; *Beruf* desirable

er|stre|cken [ɛɐ̯'ʃtrɛkn] *ptp* **erstreckt** VR to extend (*auf, über +acc* over); (*räumlich auch*) to reach, to stretch (*auf, über +acc* over); (*zeitlich auch*) to carry on, to last (*auf, über +acc* for); **sich auf jdn/etw ~** (= *betreffen*) to apply to sb/sth

Erst-: Erst|schlag M (*mit Atomwaffen*) first strike; **Erst|schlag|waf|fe** F first-strike weapon; **Erst|se|mes|ter** NT first-year student, fresher (*Brit inf*); (*männlich auch*) freshman; **Erst|sen|dung** F (*Rad, TV*) first broadcast; **Erst|stim|me** F first vote

Erst-: Erst|tags|brief M first-day cover; **Erst|tags|stem|pel** M date stamp or postmark from a first-day cover; **Erst|tä|ter(in)** M(F) first offender

er|stun|ken [ɛɐ̯'ʃtʊŋkn] ADJ **das ist ~ und erlogen** (*inf*) that's a pack of lies

er|stür|men [ɛɐ̯'ʃtʏrmən] *ptp* **erstürmt** VT (*Mil*) to (take by) storm; (*liter*) *Gipfel* to conquer

Er|stür|mung F **-, -en** (*Mil*) storming

Erst-: Erst|ver|öf|fent|li|chung F first publication; **Erst|wäh|ler(in)** M(F) first-time voter

er|su|chen [ɛɐ̯'zuːxn] *ptp* **ersucht** VT (*form*) to request (*jdm um etw* sth of sb)

Er|su|chen [ɛɐ̯'zuːxn] NT **-s, -** (*form*) request; **auf ~ von** at the request of; **ein ~ an jdn richten** or **stellen** to make a request of sb

er|tap|pen [ɛɐ̯'tapn] *ptp* **ertappt** VT to catch; **jdn/sich bei etw ~** to catch sb/oneself at or doing sth; **ich habe ihn dabei ertappt** I caught him at it or doing it

er|tas|ten [ɛɐ̯'tastn] *ptp* **ertastet** VT to feel, to make out by touch(ing); (*um zu finden*) to feel for

er|tei|len [ɛɐ̯'tailən] *ptp* **erteilt** VT to give; *Genehmigung auch* to grant; *Auftrag auch* to place (*jdm* with sb); *Lizenz* to issue; **jdm einen Verweis ~** to reproach sb; *Unterricht* ~ to teach, to give lessons → **Wort c**

Er|tei|lung F giving; (*von Genehmigung auch*) granting; (*von Auftrag auch*) placing; (*von Lizenz*) issuing; **für die ~ von Auskünften zuständig** responsible for giving information

er|tö|nen [ɛɐ̯'tøːnən] *ptp* **ertönt** VI *aux sein* (*geh*) to sound, to ring out; **von etw ~** to resound with sth; **~ lassen** to sound; **er ließ seine tiefe Bassstimme ~** his deep bass voice rang out

Er|trag [ɛɐ̯'traːk] M **-(e)s, ⸚e** [-'trɛːgə] (*von Acker*) yield; (= *Ergebnis einer Arbeit*) return; (= *Einnahmen*) proceeds *pl*, return; **~ abwerfen** or **bringen** to bring in a return; **vom ~ seiner Bücher/seines Kapitals leben** to live on the proceeds from one's books/the return on one's capital

er|tra|gen [ɛɐ̯'traːgn] ⊘ 34.3 *ptp* **ertragen** VT *irreg* to bear; *Schmerzen, Leiden, Schicksal auch* to endure; *Ungewissheit, Zweifel auch* to tolerate; (*esp in Frage, Verneinung auch*) to stand; **das ist nicht mehr zu ~** it's unbearable or intolerable; **wie erträgt du nur seine Launen?** how do you put up with or stand his moods?

er|träg|lich [ɛɐ̯'trɛːklɪç] ADJ bearable, endurable; (= *leidlich*) tolerable

er|trag-: er|trag|los ADJ *Acker* unproductive, infertile; *Geschäft* unprofitable; *Vermögen* providing no return; **er|trag|reich** ADJ *Acker* productive, fertile; *Pflanzensorte, Nutztier* productive; *Geschäft, Markt* profitable, lucrative

Er|trags-: er|trags|arm ADJ *Boden* poor; **Er|trags|aus|schüt|tung** F dividend distribution; **Er|trags|kraft** F , *no pl* earning power or potential; **Er|trags|la|ge** F , *no pl* returns *pl*, profits *pl*, profit situation; **Er|trags|min|de|rung** F decrease in profit(s) or return(s); **Er|trags|schein** M dividend coupon; **Er|trags|stei|ge|rung** F increase in profit(s) or return(s); **Er|trags|steu|er** F profit(s) tax, tax on profit(s); **Er|trags|wert** M → **Ertrag** capitalized value of potential yield/return(s)

er|trän|ken [ɛɐ̯'trɛŋkn] *ptp* **ertränkt** VT to drown; **seinen Kummer** or **seine Sorgen im Alkohol ~** to drown one's sorrows VR to drown oneself

er|träu|men [ɛɐ̯'trɔymən] *ptp* **erträumt** VT to dream of, to imagine; **eine erträumte Welt** an imaginary world; **das war alles nur erträumt** it was all in the mind; **sich (dat) etw ~** to dream of sth, to imagine sth

er|trin|ken [ɛɐ̯'trɪŋkn] *ptp* **ertrunken** [ɛɐ̯'trʊŋkn] VI *irreg aux sein* to drown, to be drowned

Er|trin|ken [ɛɐ̯'trɪŋkn] NT **-s**, *no pl* drowning

er|trot|zen [ɛɐ̯'trɔtsn] *ptp* **ertrotzt** VT (*geh*) **(sich dat) etw ~** to obtain sth by sheer obstinacy or defiance

er|tüch|ti|gen [ɛɐ̯'tʏçtɪgn] *ptp* **ertüchtigt** (*geh*) VT to toughen up, (*Brit*), to harden (*US*) VR to keep fit, to train

Er|tüch|ti|gung F **-, -en** (*geh*) getting in (good) trim (*Brit*), toughening up; **körperliche ~** physical training

er|üb|ri|gen [ɛɐ̯'yːbrɪgn] *ptp* **erübrigt** VT *Zeit, Geld* to spare VR to be unnecessary or superfluous; **jedes weitere Wort erübrigt sich** there's nothing more to be said

e|ru|ie|ren [eru'iːrən] *ptp* **eruiert** VT (*form*) *Sachverhalt* to investigate, to find out; (*esp Aus*) *Person* to trace

E|rup|ti|on [erʊp'tsioːn] F **-, -en** (*Geol, Med, fig*) eruption

E|rup|tiv|ge|stein [erʊp'tiːf-] NT volcanic rock

erw. *abbr von* **erweitert** extended

er|wa|chen [ɛɐ̯'vaxn] *ptp* **erwacht** VI *aux sein* to awake, to wake (up); (*aus Ohnmacht etc*) to come to or round (*aus* from); (*fig: Gefühle, Verdacht*) to be aroused; (*liter: Tag*) to dawn; **von etw ~** to be awoken or woken up by sth; **ein böses Erwachen** (*fig*) a rude awakening

er|wach|sen [ɛɐ̯'vaksn] *ptp* **erwachsen** VI *irreg aux sein* (*geh*) to arise, to develop; (*Vorteil, Kosten etc*) to result, to accrue; **daraus erwuchsen ihm Unannehmlichkeiten** that caused him some trouble; **daraus wird ihm kein Nutzen ~** no advantage will accrue to him (from this); **mir sind Zweifel ~** I have come to have doubts ADJ grown-up, adult; **~ sein** (*Mensch*) to be grown-up or an adult

Er|wach|se|nen-: Er|wach|se|nen|al|ter NT **im ~** in adulthood, as an adult; **Er|wach|se|nen|bil|dung** F adult education; **Er|wach|se|nen|tau|fe** F adult baptism

Er|wach|se|ne(r) [ɛɐ̯'vaksənə] MF *decl as adj* adult, grown-up

er|wä|gen [ɛɐ̯'vɛːgn] *ptp* **erwogen** [ɛɐ̯'voːgn] VT *irreg* (= *überlegen*) to consider, to deliberate; (= *prüfen*) to consider, to examine; (= *in Betracht ziehen*) to consider, to take into consideration

er|wä|gens|wert ADJ worthy of consideration, worth considering

Er|wä|gung F **-, -en** consideration; **aus folgenden ~en (heraus)** for the following reasons or considerations; **etw in ~ ziehen** to consider sth, to take sth into consideration

er|wäh|len [ɛɐ̯'vɛːlən] *ptp* **erwählt** VT to choose

er|wäh|nen [ɛɐ̯'vɛːnən] ⊘ 53.2 *ptp* **erwähnt** VT to mention, to refer to, to make mention of or reference to; **ich möchte nur kurz erwähnt haben, dass ...** I would just briefly like to mention that ...; **davon hat er nichts erwähnt, das hat er mit keinem Wort erwähnt** he did not mention it or refer to it at all, he made no mention of or reference to it; **beiläufig** or **nebenbei ~** to mention in passing, to make a passing reference to

er|wäh|nens|wert ADJ worth mentioning

Er|wäh|nung F **-, -en** mention (+*gen* of), reference (+*gen* to); **~ finden** (*form*) to be mentioned, to be referred to

er|wan|dern [ɛɐ̯'vandən] *ptp* **erwandert** VT **er hat sich (dat) die ganze Insel erwandert** he's walked all over the island and knows it inside out

er|wär|men [ɛɐ̯'vɛrmən] *ptp* **erwärmt** VT to warm, to heat; (*fig*) to warm VR to warm up; **sich für jdn/etw ~** (*fig*) to take to sb/sth; **ich kann mich für Goethe/Geometrie nicht ~** Goethe/geometry leaves me cold

Er|wär|mung F **-, -en** warming; **globale ~** global warming; **~ der Erdatmosphäre** warming of the earth's atmosphere

er|war|ten [ɛɐ̯'vartn] ⊘ 35.4, 37.3, 43.2, 47.3 *ptp* **erwartet** VT *Gäste, Ereignis* to expect; **etw von jdm/etw ~** to expect sth from or of sb/sth; **ein Kind** or **Baby ~** to be expecting a child or baby; **das war zu ~** that was to be expected; **etw sehnsüchtig ~** to long for sth; **sie kann den Sommer kaum noch ~** she can hardly wait for the summer, she's really looking forward to the summer; **sie kann es kaum ~, dass Vater heimkommt** she can hardly wait for father to come home, she's really looking forward to father coming home; **was mich da wohl erwartet?** I wonder what awaits me there; **von ihr ist nicht viel Gutes zu ~** no good can come of her; **da hast du (et)was zu ~!** (*iro*) then you'll have something to think about!; **es steht zu ~, dass**

... (*form*) it is to be expected that ...; **über Erwarten** beyond expectation → **wider**

Er|war|tung F expectation; (= *Spannung, Ungeduld*) anticipation; **in ~ einer Sache** (*gen*) in anticipation of sth; **in ~ Ihrer baldigen Antwort** (*form*) in anticipation of *or* looking forward to *or* awaiting your early reply; **zu großen ~en berechtigen** to show great promise; **den ~en entsprechen** *or* **gerecht werden** to come up to expectations; (= *Voraussetzung erfüllen*) to meet the requirements; **hinter den ~en zurückbleiben** not to come up *or* meet expectations

Er|war|tungs-: Er|war|tungs|druck M , *no pl* **unter ~ sein** *or* **stehen** to be under pressure as a result of people's expectations; **erwar|tungs|ge|mäß** ADV as expected; **Er|war|tungs|hal|tung** F expectations *pl*; **Er|war|tungs|ho|ri|zont** M level of expectations; **er|war|tungs|voll** ADJ expectant

er|we|cken [ɛɐ̯'vɛkn] *ptp* **erweckt** VT **a** (*liter: aus Schlaf, Lethargie*) to wake, to rouse; (*Bibl: vom Tode*) to raise (from the dead); **etw zu neuem Leben ~** to resurrect *or* revive sth **b** (*fig*) *Freude, Begeisterung etc* to arouse; *Hoffnungen, Zweifel* to raise; *Erinnerungen* to bring back; **(bei jdm) den Eindruck ~, als ob ...** to give (sb) the impression that ...

Er|we|ckung F -, -en (*Bibl: vom Tode*) resurrection, raising (from the dead); (*Rel*) revival; (*fig*) arousal, awakening

Er|we|ckungs|be|we|gung F (*Rel*) revivalist movement, revivalism

Er|we|ckungs|pre|di|ger(in) M(F) (*Rel pej*) revivalist preacher

er|weh|ren [ɛɐ̯'veːrən] *ptp* **erwehrt** VR +*gen* (*geh*) to ward *or* fend off; **er konnte sich kaum der Tränen ~** he could hardly keep *or* hold back his tears → **Eindruck a**

er|wei|chen [ɛɐ̯'vaɪçn] *ptp* **erweicht** VT to soften; (*fig: = überreden auch*) to move; **jds Herz ~** to touch sb's heart; **sich (durch Bitten) nicht ~ lassen** to be unmoved (by entreaties), not to give in *or* yield (to entreaties)

Er|weis [ɛɐ̯'vaɪs] M -es, -e [-zə] (*form*) proof

er|wei|sen [ɛɐ̯'vaɪzn] *ptp* **erwiesen** [ɛɐ̯'viːzn] *irreg* **VT** **a** (= *nachweisen*) to prove; **eine erwiesene Tatsache** a proven fact; **es ist noch nicht erwiesen** it has not been proved *or* proven yet **b** (= *zuteil werden lassen*) to show; **jdm einen Gefallen/Dienst ~** to do sb a favour (*Brit*) *or* favor (*US*)/service; **jdm Achtung ~** to pay respect to sb; **jdm Gutes ~** to be good to sb; **wir danken für die erwiesene Anteilnahme** we thank you for the sympathy you have shown **VR** **sich als etw ~** to prove to be sth, to turn out to be sth; **sich als zuverlässig ~** to prove to be reliable, to prove oneself reliable; **sich jdm gegenüber dankbar ~** to show *or* prove one's gratitude to sb, to show *or* prove oneself grateful to sb; **es hat sich erwiesen, dass ...** it turned out that ...

er|weis|lich [ɛɐ̯'vaɪslɪç] (*geh*) ADJ provable, demonstrable ADV **das ist ~ falsch** that is demonstrably false

er|wei|ter|bar ADJ (*auch Comput*) expandable

Er|wei|ter|bar|keit F -, -en (*auch Comput*) expandability

er|wei|tern [ɛɐ̯'vaɪtɐn] *ptp* **erweitert** VTR to widen, to enlarge; *Absatzgebiet auch, Geschäft, Abteilung* to expand; *Kleid* to let out; (*Med*) to dilate; (*Math*) *Bruch* to make up to the lowest common denominator; (*fig*) *Interessen, Kenntnisse, Horizont* to broaden; *Macht* to extend; **im erweiterten Sinn** in a broader sense

Er|wei|te|rung F -, -en widening, enlargement; (*von Absatzgebiet auch, von Geschäft, Abteilung*) expansion; (*Med*) dilation; (*Math: von Bruch*) taking to the lowest common denominator; (*fig*) (*von Interessen, Kenntnissen, Horizont*) broadening; (*von Macht*) extension

Er|wei|te|rungs|bau M *pl* **-bauten** extension

Er|werb [ɛɐ̯'vɛrp] M -(e)s, -e [-bə] **a** *no pl* acquisition; (= *Kauf*) purchase; **beim ~ eines Autos** when buying a car **b** (= *Broterwerb, Beruf*) living; (= *Verdienst, Lohn*) earnings *pl*, income; **einem ~ nachgehen** to follow a trade *or* (*akademisch*) profession

er|wer|ben [ɛɐ̯'vɛrbn] *ptp* **erworben** [ɛɐ̯'vɔrbn] VT *irreg* to acquire; *Achtung, Ehre, Vertrauen* to earn, to gain, to win; *Pokal* to win; (*Sport*) *Titel* to win, to gain; (*käuflich*) to purchase; **sich** (*dat*) **etw ~** to acquire *etc* sth; **er hat sich** (*dat*) **große Verdienste um die Firma erworben** he has done great service for the firm → *auch* **erworben**

Er|wer|ber|mo|dell NT *scheme by which tax relief is obtained on investment in property*

Er|werbs-: Er|werbs|ar|beit F gainful employment; **er|werbs|be|hin|dert** ADJ (*form*) incapable of gainful employment, partially disabled; **er|werbs|fä|hig** ADJ (*form*) capable of gainful employment; **Er|werbs|fä|hi|ge(r)** [-fɛːɪɡə] MF *decl as adj* (*form*) person capable of gainful employment; **Er|werbs|fä|hig|keit** F (*form*) ability to work; **er|werbs|ge|min|dert** [-ɡəmɪndɐt] ADJ suffering a reduction in (one's) earning capacity; **Er|werbs|kampf** M rat race; **Er|werbs|le|ben** NT working life; **er|werbs|los** ADJ = **arbeitslos**; **Er|werbs|min|de|rung** F reduction in (one's) earning capacity; **Er|werbs|per|son** F (*form*) person capable of gainful employment; **Er|werbs|quel|le** F source of income; **er|werbs|tä|tig** ADJ (gainfully) employed; **Er|werbs|tä|ti|ge(r)** MF *decl as adj* person in gainful employment; **Er|werbs|tä|tig|keit** F gainful employment; **er|werbs|un|fä|hig** ADJ (*form*) incapable of gainful employment, incapacitated; **Er|werbs|un|fä|hi|ge(r)** MF *decl as adj* person incapable of gainful employment; **Er|werbs|un|fä|hig|keit** F inability to work; **Er|werbs|un|fä|hig|keits|ren|te** F disability pension; **Er|werbs|zweig** M line of business

Er|wer|bung F acquisition

er|wi|dern [ɛɐ̯'viːdɐn] *ptp* **erwidert** VT **a** (= *antworten*) to reply (*auf* +*acc* to); (*schroff*) to retort; **darauf konnte er nichts ~** he couldn't answer that, he had no answer to that; **auf meine Frage erwiderte sie, dass ...** in reply *or* answer to my question, she said that ... **b** (= *entgegnen, entgelten*) *Besuch, Grüße, Komplimente, Gefühle* to return, to reciprocate; *Blick* to return; (*Mil*) *Feuer* to return

Er|wi|de|rung F -, -en **a** (= *Antwort*) reply, answer; (*schroff*) retort, rejoinder; **in ~ Ihres Schreibens vom ...** (*form*) in reply *or* answer to your letter of the ... **b** (= *das Erwidern*) return, reciprocation; (*von Gefühlen*) reciprocation; (*Mil: des Feuers*) return; **ihre Liebe fand bei ihm keine ~** he did not return her love

er|wie|se|ner|ma|ßen [ɛɐ̯'viːznɐ'maːsn] ADV as has been proved (*esp Brit*) *or* proven *or* shown; **er hat dich ~ betrogen** it has been proved (*esp Brit*) *or* proven *or* shown that he has deceived you; **der Angeklagte ist ~ schuldig** the accused has been proved (*esp Brit*) *or* proven guilty

er|wir|ken [ɛɐ̯'vɪrkn] *ptp* **erwirkt** VT (*form*) to obtain

er|wirt|schaf|ten [ɛɐ̯'vɪrtʃaftn] *ptp* **erwirtschaftet** VT to make *or* obtain through good *or* careful management; **Gewinne ~** to make profits; **seine Frau hat ein kleines Auto erwirtschaftet** his wife has bought a little car with her savings

er|wi|schen [ɛɐ̯'vɪʃn] *ptp* **erwischt** VT (*inf*) (= *erreichen, ertappen*) to catch; (= *ergattern*) to get (hold of); **jdn beim Stehlen ~** to catch sb stealing; **du darfst dich nicht ~ lassen** you mustn't get caught; **ihn hats erwischt!** (*verliebt*) he's got it bad (*inf*); (*krank*) he's got it, he's caught it; (*gestorben*) he's had it (*inf*); **die Kugel/der Hund hat ihn am Bein erwischt** the bullet got *or* caught/the dog got him in the leg

er|wor|ben [ɛɐ̯'vɔrbn] ADJ acquired (*auch Med, Jur*) → *auch* **erwerben**

er|wünscht [ɛɐ̯'vʏnʃt] ADJ *Wirkung etc* desired; *Eigenschaft, Kenntnisse* desirable; (= *willkommen*) welcome; **persönliche Vorstellung** applications should be made in person; **du bist hier nicht ~!** you're not welcome *or* wanted here!

er|wür|gen [ɛɐ̯'vʏrɡn] *ptp* **erwürgt** VT to strangle, to throttle

E|ryth|ro|zyt [eritro'tsyːt] M -en, -en *usu pl* (*Med*) erythrocyte

Erz [eːɐ̯ts, ɛrts] NT -es, -e ore; (= *Bronze*) bronze

erz-, Erz- *in cpds* **a** [eːɐ̯ts, ɛrts] (*Geol*) mineral, ore **b** [ɛrts] (= *ausgemacht*) out-and-out; **ein Erzverbrecher** an out-and-out criminal; **sein Erzrivale** his arch-rival **c** [ɛrts] (*Rang bezeichnend*) arch-

Erz- [eːɐ̯ts-, ɛrts-]: **Erz|ab|bau** [eːɐ̯ts-, ɛrts-] M ore extraction; **Erz|ader** [eːɐ̯ts-, ɛrts-] F mineral vein, vein of ore

Erzähl- (*Liter*): **Er|zähl|ab|sicht** F narrative intent; **Er|zähl|ebe|ne** F narrative level

er|zäh|len [ɛɐ̯'tsɛːlən] *ptp* **erzählt** VT **a** *Geschichte, Witz etc* to tell; (= *berichten*) *Traum, Vorfall, Erlebnis etc auch* to relate, to recount, to give an account of; **er hat seinen Traum/den Vorfall erzählt** he told (us *etc*) about his dream/the incident; **jdm etw ~** to tell sth to sb; **man erzählt sich, dass ...** people say that ..., it is said that ...; **erzähl mal, was/wie ...** tell me/us what/how ...; **Mutti, erzähl mir was** tell me a story, mummy (*Brit*) *or* mommy (*US*); **erzähl mal was** (*inf*) say something; **wem ~ Sie das!** (*inf*) you're telling me!; **das kannst du einem anderen ~** (*inf*) pull the other one (*inf*), tell that to the marines (*inf*); **mir kannst du viel ~ nichts ~** (*inf*) don't give *or* tell me that! (*inf*); **davon kann ich etwas ~!** (*inf*) I can tell you a thing or two about it; **dem werd ich was ~!** (*inf*) I'll have something to say to him, I'll give him a piece of my mind (*inf*) → **Großmutter** **b** (*Liter*) to narrate; **~de Dichtung** narrative fiction; **Grundformen des Erzählens** basic forms of narrative; **erzählte Zeit** narrated time **VI a** to tell (*von* about, *of* (*liter*)); **er kann gut ~** he tells good stories, he's a good storyteller; **er hat die ganze Nacht erzählt** he told stories all night **b** (*Liter*) to narrate

er|zäh|lens|wert ADJ worth telling

Er|zäh|ler(in) M(F) narrator (*auch Liter*); (= *Geschichtenerzähler*) storyteller; (= *Schriftsteller*) narrative writer

er|zäh|le|risch [ɛɐ̯'tsɛːlərɪʃ] ADJ narrative

Er|zäh|ler|stand|punkt M (*Liter*) point of view of the narrator

Er|zähl-: Er|zähl|for|men PL (*Liter*) narrative forms *pl*; **Er|zähl|per|spek|ti|ve** F (*Liter*) narrative perspective

Er|zäh|lung F (*Liter*) story, tale; (= *das Erzählen*) narration, relation; (= *Bericht, Schilderung*) account; **in Form einer ~** in narrative form; **Dialog und ~ wechseln sich ab** dialogue (*Brit*) *or* dialog (*US*) alternates with narrative

Er|zähl-: Er|zähl|wei|se F (*Liter*) narrative style; **Er|zähl|zeit** F (*Liter*) narrative time

Erz-: Erz|berg|bau M ore mining; **Erz|berg|werk** NT mineral *or* ore mine; **Erz|bi|schof** M archbishop; **erz|bi|schöf|lich** ADJ *attr* archiepiscopal; **Erz|bis|tum** NT archbishopric; **Erz|bö|se|wicht** M arrant rogue (*old*), archvillain; **Erz|di|akon** M archdeacon; **Erz|di|ö|ze|se** F archbishopric; **erz|dumm** ADJ (*inf*) extremely stupid; **Erz|dumm|heit** F (*inf*) extremely stupid thing; **eine ~ sein** to be an extremely stupid thing to do, to be extremely stupid

er|zei|gen [ɛɐ̯'tsaɪɡn] *ptp* **erzeigt** VR (*geh*) **sich dankbar ~** to show *or* prove oneself grateful

er|zen ['eːɐ̯tsn] ADJ (*liter*) bronze

Erz|en|gel M archangel

er|zeu|gen [ɛɐˈtsɔygn̩] ptp **erzeugt** VT (Chem, Elec, Phys) to generate, to produce; (Comm) Produkt to produce, to manufacture; Wein, Butter etc to produce; (rare) Kinder to beget (old); (fig: = bewirken) to cause, to engender, to give rise to; **Misstrauen/Angst** etc **in** or **bei jdm ~** to give rise to or produce or engender a sense of mistrust/fear etc in sb; **der Autor versteht es, Spannung zu ~** the author knows how to create or generate tension

Er|zeu|ger¹ [ɛɐˈtsɔygɐ] M -s, - (form: = Vater) begetter (old), progenitor (form)

Er|zeu|ger² [ɛɐˈtsɔygɐ] M -s, -, **Er|zeu|ge|rin** [-ərɪn] F -, -nen (Comm) producer, manufacturer; (von Naturprodukten) producer

Er|zeu|ger-: Er|zeu|ger|land NT country of origin; **Er|zeu|ger|preis** M manufacturer's price

Er|zeug|nis NT product; (= Industrieprodukt auch) manufacture (esp Comm); (Agr) produce no indef art, no pl; (fig: geistiges, künstlerisches) creation, product; **deutsches ~** made in Germany; **~ seiner Fantasie** figment of his imagination

Er|zeu|gung F (Chem, Elec, Phys) generation, production; (von Waren) manufacture, production; (rare: eines Kindes) procreation (form); (geistige, künstlerische) creation

Er|zeu|gungs|gram|ma|tik F (Ling) generative grammar

Erz-: erz|faul ADJ bone idle (Brit inf); **Erz|feind(in)** M(F) arch-enemy; (Theologie auch) arch-fiend; **Erz|gau|ner(in)** M(F) (inf) cunning or sly rascal (inf)

Erz- [ˈeːɐts-, ˈɛrts-]: **Erz|ge|bir|ge** NT Erzgebirge; **Erz|ge|halt** M usu sing (Min) ore content; **Erz|gie|ßer(in)** M(F) brass-founder; **Erz|gie|ße|rei** F brass-foundry; **Erz|gru|be** F ore mine; **erz|hal|tig** ADJ ore-bearing, metalliferous (spec)

Erz-: Erz|her|zog M archduke; **Erz|her|zo|gin** F archduchess; **erz|her|zog|lich** ADJ attr archducal; **Erz|her|zog|tum** NT archduchy

Erz|hüt|te [ˈeːɐts-, ˈɛrts-] F smelting works sing or pl

er|zieh|bar ADJ Kind educable; Tier trainable; **schwer ~** (Kind) difficult; Hund difficult to train; **das Kind ist schwer ~** he/she is a problem child or a difficult child; **ein Heim für schwer ~e Kinder** a home for problem or difficult children

er|zie|hen [ɛɐˈtsiːən] ptp **erzogen** VT irreg Kind to bring up; Tier, Körper, Gehör to train; (= ausbilden) to educate; **ein Tier/ein Kind zur Sauberkeit** etc **~** to train an animal/to bring up or teach a child to be clean etc; **jdn zu einem tüchtigen Menschen ~** to bring sb up to be a fine, upstanding person; **ein gut/schlecht erzogenes Kind** a well-brought-up/badly-brought-up child, a well-bred/an ill-bred child

Er|zie|her [ɛɐˈtsiːɐ] M -s, -, **Er|zie|he|rin** [-ərɪn] F -, -nen educator, teacher; (in Kindergarten) nursery school teacher; (= Privatlehrer) tutor; (Frau auch, = Gouvernante) governess; **der Vater war ein strenger ~** the father brought his children up strictly

er|zie|he|risch [ɛɐˈtsiːərɪʃ] ADJ educational; **ein Vater mit wenig ~em Können** a father with little skill in bringing up children; **~e Maßnahmen ergreifen** to impose discipline; **verschiedene ~e Methoden** different ways of bringing up children ADV **~ wertvoll** educationally valuable; **~ falsch** educationally unsound

Er|zie|hung F , no pl upbringing; (= Ausbildung) education; (= das Erziehen) bringing up; (von Tieren, Körper, Gehör) training; (= Manieren) upbringing, (good) breeding; **die ~ zu(r) Höflichkeit** teaching (sb) politeness or good manners; (durch Eltern auch) bringing (sb) up to be polite or well-mannered

Er|zie|hungs-: Er|zie|hungs|an|stalt F approved school (Brit dated), borstal (Brit dated), reformatory (US); **Er|zie|hungs|bei|hil|fe**

F (dated) → **Ausbildungsbeihilfe; Er|zie|hungs|be|ra|tung** F educational guidance or counselling (Brit) or counseling (US); **er|zie|hungs|be|rech|tigt** ADJ having parental authority; **Er|zie|hungs|be|rech|tig|te(r)** [-bəˈrɛçtɪçtə] MF decl as adj parent or (legal) guardian; **Er|zie|hungs|feh|ler** PL wrong upbringing (+gen on the part of); **Er|zie|hungs|geld** NT ≈ child benefit; **Er|zie|hungs|ge|walt** F parental authority; **Er|zie|hungs|heim** NT approved school (Brit dated), borstal (Brit dated), reformatory (US); **Er|zie|hungs|jahr** NT (nach Geburt) year off for bringing up one's child/children; (im Rentenrecht) year of credited contributions (for each child); **Er|zie|hungs|me|tho|de** F educational method; **Er|zie|hungs|mit|tel** NT educational aid; **Er|zie|hungs|ur|laub** M paid leave for new parent; (für Mutter auch) extended maternity leave; (für Vater auch) extended paternity leave; **Er|zie|hungs|we|sen** NT , no pl educational system; **Er|zie|hungs|wis|sen|schaft** F educational science; **Er|zie|hungs|wis|sen|schaft|ler(in)** M(F) educationalist

er|zie|len [ɛɐˈtsiːlən] ptp **erzielt** VT Erfolg, Ergebnis to achieve, to attain, to obtain; Kompromiss, Einigung to reach, to arrive at; Geschwindigkeit to reach; Gewinn to make, to realize; Preis (Mensch) to secure; (Gegenstand) to fetch; (Sport) Tor, Punkte to score; Rekord to set; **was willst du damit ~?** what do you hope to achieve by that?

er|zit|tern [ɛɐˈtsɪtɐn] ptp **erzittert** VI aux sein (liter) to tremble, to shake, to quake

Erz-: erz|kon|ser|va|tiv ADJ ultraconservative; **Erz|kon|ser|va|ti|ve(r)** MF decl as adj archconvservative, dyed-in-the-wool conservative, true blue (Brit); **Erz|la|ger** [ˈeːɐts-, ˈɛrts-] NT ore deposit; **Erz|lüg|ner(in)** M(F) (inf) inveterate or unmitigated liar; **Erz|re|ak|ti|o|när(in)** M(F) ultrareactionary

er|zür|nen [ɛɐˈtsyrnən] ptp **erzürnt** (geh) VT to anger, to incense VR to become or grow angry (über +acc about)

Erz|va|ter M (Bibl) patriarch; (fig) forefather

er|zwin|gen [ɛɐˈtsvɪŋən] ptp **erzwungen** [ɛɐˈtsvʊŋən] VT irreg to force; (gerichtlich) to enforce; **etw von jdm ~** to force sth from or out of sb; **sie erzwangen den Zutritt zur Wohnung mit Gewalt** they forced entry into the flat

es¹ [ɛs] PERS PRON gen seiner, dat ihm, acc es **a** (auf Dinge bezogen) it; (auf männliches Wesen bezogen) (nom) he; (acc) him; (auf weibliches Wesen bezogen) (nom) she; (acc) her
b (auf vorangehende Substantive, Adjektive bezüglich) **wer ist da? – es ist er** who's there? – it's me or I (form); **sie ist klug, er ist es auch** she is clever, so is he; **ich höre jemanden klopfen, es sind die Kinder** I can hear somebody knocking, it's the children; **wer ist die Dame? – es ist meine Frau** who's the lady? – it's or she's my wife
c (auf vorangehenden Satzinhalt bezüglich) **das Glas wurde zerbrochen, keiner will es getan haben** the glass had been broken, but nobody will admit to doing it; **alle dachten, dass das ungerecht war, aber niemand sagte es** everyone thought it was unjust, but nobody said so
d (rein formales Subjekt) **es ist kalt/8 Uhr/Sonntag** it's cold/8 o'clock/Sunday; **es friert mich** I am cold; **es freut mich, dass ...** I am pleased or glad that ...; **es sei denn, dass ...** unless ...
e (rein formales Objekt) **ich halte es für richtig, dass ...** I think it (is) right that ...; **ich hoffe es** I hope so; **ich habe es satt, zu** (+infin), **ich bin es müde, zu** (+infin) I've had enough of (+prp), I'm tired of (+prp)
f (bei unpersönlichem Gebrauch des Verbs) **es gefällt mir** I like it; **es klopft** there's a knock (at the door); **es regnet** it's raining; **es sich** (dat) **schön machen** to have a good time; **bei dem Licht liest es sich gut** this light is good for reading; **es sitzt sich bequem hier** it's comfortable sitting here; **es darf geraucht werden**

smoking is permitted; **es wurde gesagt, dass ...** it was said that ...; **es wurde getanzt** there was dancing; **er lässt es nicht zu, dass ich länger bleibe** he won't allow me to stay any longer
g (Einleitewort mit folgendem Subjekt) **es geschah ein Unglück** there was an accident; **es gibt viel Arbeit** there's a lot of work; **es gibt viele Leute, die ...** there are of people who ...; **es kamen viele Leute** a lot of people came; **es lebe der König!** long live the king!; **es meldete sich niemand** nobody replied; **es war einmal eine Königin** once upon a time there was a queen

es² NT -, - (Mus) E flat
Es NT -, - **a** (Mus: Dur) E flat **b** (Psych) id, Id
Es|cape-Tas|te [ɛsˈkeːp-] F (Comput) escape key
Es|cha|to|lo|gie [ɛʃatoloˈgiː] F -, -n [-ˈgiːən] (Rel) eschatology
E|sche [ˈɛʃə] F -, -n ash-tree; (= Holz) ash
E|schen|holz NT ash
E|sel [ˈeːzl̩] M -s, - donkey, ass (old, esp Bibl); (inf: = Dummkopf) (silly) ass; **du alter ~!** you are an ass (inf) or a fool; **ich ~!** I am an ass (inf) or a fool!, silly (old) me!; **störrisch wie ein ~** as stubborn as a mule; **der ~ nennt sich selbst zuerst** (prov) it's rude to put yourself first; **ein ~ schimpft den andern Langohr** (prov) (it's a case of) the pot calling the kettle black (prov); **wenn es dem ~ zu wohl wird, geht er aufs Eis (tanzen)** (Prov) complacency makes one or you reckless
E|se|lei [eːzəˈlai] F -, -en (inf) stupidity; (= Streich) silly prank
E|se|lin [ˈeːzəlɪn] F -, -nen she-ass
E|sels-: E|sels|brü|cke F (= Gedächtnishilfe) mnemonic, aide-mémoire; (gereimt) jingle; **E|sels|ohr** NT (fig) dog-ear, turned-down corner; **ein Buch mit ~en** a dog-eared book
Es|ka|la|ti|on [ɛskalaˈtsioːn] F -, -en escalation
es|ka|lie|ren [ɛskaˈliːrən] ptp **eskaliert** VTI (vi: aux sein) to escalate
Es|ka|lie|rung F -, -en escalation
Es|ka|mo|ta|ge [ɛskamoˈtaːʒə] F -, -n sleight of hand
es|ka|mo|tie|ren [ɛskamoˈtiːrən] ptp **eskamotiert** VT to spirit or conjure away
Es|ka|pa|de [ɛskaˈpaːdə] F -, -n (von Pferd) caper; (fig) escapade
Es|ka|pis|mus [ɛskaˈpɪsmʊs] M -, no pl (Psych, Sociol) escapism
Es|ki|mo [ˈɛskimo] M -s, -s Eskimo
Es|ki|mo|frau F Eskimo (woman)
es|ki|mo|tie|ren [ɛskimoˈtiːrən] ptp **eskimotiert** VI (Sport) to roll
es|komp|tie|ren [ɛskõˈtiːrən] ptp **eskomptiert** VT (Fin) (= diskontieren) to discount; (St Ex) to preempt
Es|kor|te [ɛsˈkɔrtə] F -, -n (Mil) escort
es|kor|tie|ren [ɛskɔrˈtiːrən] ptp **eskortiert** VT to escort
E|so|te|rik [ezoˈteːrɪk] F -, no pl esotericism
E|so|te|ri|ker [ezoˈteːrɪkɐ] M -s, -, **E|so|te|ri|ke|rin** [-ərɪn] F -, -nen esoteric
e|so|te|risch [ezoˈteːrɪʃ] ADJ esoteric
Es|pe [ˈɛspə] F -, -n aspen; (Holz auch) aspen wood
Es|pen|laub NT aspen leaves pl; **zittern wie ~** to shake like a leaf
Es|pe|ran|to [ɛspeˈranto] NT -s, no pl Esperanto
Es|pres|so¹ [ɛsˈprɛso] M -(s), -s or **Espressi** [-si] espresso
Es|pres|so² NT -(s), -(s), **Es|pres|so|bar** F (= Café) coffee or espresso bar
Es|pres|so|ma|schi|ne F espresso machine
Es|prit [ɛsˈpriː] M -s, no pl wit; **ein Mann von ~** a wit, a witty man
Ess|ap|fel ▲ M eating apple, eater
Es|say [ˈɛse, ˈɛseː] M OR NT -s, -s (Liter) essay

Es|say|ist [ɛseˈɪst] M **-en, -en, Es|say|is|tin** [-ˈɪstɪn] F **-, -nen** (*Liter*) essayist

es|say|is|tisch [ɛseˈɪstɪʃ] ADJ (*Liter*) *Roman* essayistic; **das ~e Werk Thomas Manns** the essays of Thomas Mann

Ess-: ess|bar ▲ ADJ edible, eatable; *Pilz* edible; **habt ihr irgend etwas Essbares im Haus?** have you got anything to eat in the house?; **nicht ~** inedible, uneatable; **Ess|be|steck** ▲ NT knife, fork and spoon, eating irons *pl* (*Brit hum*); **Ess-Brech|sucht** ▲ [-ˈbrɛçzʊxt] F **-, *no pl* bulimia

Es|se [ˈɛsə] F **-, -n** (*dial: = Schornstein*) chimney; (*von Schmiede*) hearth

Ess|ecke ▲ F eating area

es|sen [ˈɛsn] *pret* **aß** [aːs], *ptp* **gegessen** [ɡəˈɡɛsn] VTI to eat; **gut/schlecht ~** (= *Appetit haben*) to have a good/poor appetite; **in dem Restaurant kann man gut ~** that's a good restaurant; **die Franzosen ~ gut** the French eat well, French food is good; **da isst es sich gut** the food is good there, you can eat well there, they do good food there; **warm/kalt ~** to have a hot/cold meal; **tüchtig** *or* **ordentlich ~** to eat well *or* properly; **iss mal tüchtig!** tuck in! (*Brit inf*), eat up!; **sich satt ~** to eat one's fill; **sich krank ~** to overeat, to overindulge (in food); **jdn arm ~** to eat sb out of house and home; **den Teller leer ~** to eat everything up, to empty one's plate; ~ **Sie gern Äpfel?** do you like apples?; **wer hat davon gegessen?** who has been eating that?; **wer hat von meinem Teller gegessen?** who's been eating off my plate?; **gerade ~, beim Essen sein** to be in the middle of eating *or* of a meal; ~ **gehen** (*auswärts*) to eat out, to go out to eat; **wann gehst du ~?** when are you going to eat?; (*normalerweise*) when do you eat?; **ich bin ~** (*inf*) I've gone to eat; **nach der Vorstellung gingen wir noch ~** after the performance we went for a meal; **das Thema ist schon lange/noch nicht gegessen** (*fig inf*) the subject is dead and buried/still alive; **selber ~ macht fett** (*prov*) I'm all right, Jack (*Brit prov*), it's not my problem; **Essen und Trinken hält Leib und Seele zusammen** (*prov*) food and drink keep body and soul together → **heiß** ADV a, **Tisch**

Es|sen [ˈɛsn] NT **-s, -** (= *Mahlzeit*) meal; (= *Nahrung*) food; (= *Küche*) cooking; (= *Mittagessen*) lunch; (= *Abendessen*) dinner; **bleib doch zum ~** stay for lunch/dinner, stay for a meal; **das ~ kochen** *or* **machen** (*inf*) to cook *or* get the meal; **jdn zum ~ einladen** to invite sb for a meal; **das ~ ist fertig!** (*bitte) zum ~** lunch/dinner is ready; ~ **auf Rädern** meals on wheels → **ruhen** VI a

Es|sen(s)-: Es|sen(s)|aus|ga|be F serving of meals; (*Stelle*) serving counter; **ab 12.30 Uhr ist in der Kantine ~** meals are served in the canteen from 12.30; **Es|sen(s)|mar|ke** F meal voucher (*Brit*) *or* ticket (*US*); **Es|sen(s)|zeit** F mealtime; **bei uns ist um 12.00 Uhr ~** we have lunch at 12; **die Kinder müssen abends zur ~ zu Hause sein** the children have to be at home in time for their evening meal; **Es|sen(s)|zu|schuss** ▲ M meal subsidy

Es|sen|tial [ɪˈsɛnʃəl] NT **-s, -s** essential

es|sen|ti|ell [ɛsɛnˈtsiɛl] ADJ **= essenziell**

Es|senz [ɛˈsɛnts] F **-, -en** a *no pl* (*Philos*) essence b (*Cook etc*) essence

es|sen|zi|ell ▲ [ɛsɛnˈtsiɛl] ADJ (*auch Biol, Chem, Philos*) essential

Es|ser [ˈɛsɐ] M **-s, -, Es|se|rin** [-ərɪn] F **-, -nen** diner; (*pl auch*) people eating; **ein guter** *or* **starker/schlechter ~ sein** to be a good *or* great/poor eater; **auf einen ~ mehr kommt es nicht an** one more person won't make any difference

Es|se|rei [ɛsəˈraɪ] F **-, -en** (*inf*) guzzling (*inf*); (= *Mahl*) blowout (*Brit inf*), nosh-up (*Brit inf*), feast (*US inf*); **die ~ im Stehen ist nicht gut** it's not good to eat standing up

Ess-: Ess|ge|schirr ▲ NT dinner service; (*Mil*) mess tin; **Ess|ge|wohn|hei|ten** ▲ PL eating habits *pl*

Es|sig [ˈɛsɪç] M **-s, -e** [-ɡə] vinegar; **damit ist es ~** (*inf*) it's all off, it's up the spout (*Brit inf*)

Es|sig-: Es|sig|äther M ethyl acetate; **Es|sig|es|senz** F vinegar concentrate; **Es|sig|es|ter** M ethyl acetate; **Es|sig|gur|ke** F (pickled) gherkin; **es|sig|sau|er** ADJ (*Chem*) acetic; **essigsaure Tonerde** aluminium acetate; **Es|sig|säu|re** F acetic acid

Ess-: Ess|kas|ta|nie ▲ F sweet chestnut; **Ess|kul|tur** ▲ F gastronomic culture; **Ess|löf|fel** ▲ M (*für Suppe*) soup spoon; (*für Nachtisch*) dessert spoon; (*in Rezept*) tablespoon; **ess|löf|fel|wei|se** ▲ ADV in tablespoonfuls; (*inf*) by the spoonful; **Ess|lust** ▲ F appetite; **Ess|stäb|chen** ▲ PL chopsticks *pl*; **Ess|stö|rung** ▲ F *usu pl* eating disorder; **Ess|tisch** ▲ M dining table; **Ess|un|lust** ▲ F loss of appetite; **Ess|wa|ren** PL food *sing*, provisions *pl*; **Ess|zim|mer** ▲ NT dining room; **Ess|zwang** ▲ M (*Psych*) compulsive eating; **an ~ leiden** to be a compulsive eater

Es|tab|lish|ment [ɪsˈtɛblɪʃmənt] NT **-s, -s** (*Sociol, Press*) establishment

Es|te [ˈeːstə, ˈɛstə] M **-n, -n, Es|tin** [ˈeːstɪn, ˈɛstɪn] F **-, -nen** Est(h)onian

Es|ter [ˈɛstɐ] M **-s, -** (*Chem*) ester

Est|land [ˈɛstlant, ˈɛst-] NT **-s** Est(h)onia

est|län|disch [ˈɛstlɛndɪʃ, ˈɛst-], **est|nisch** [ˈɛstnɪʃ, ˈɛst-] ADJ Est(h)onian

Est|ni|sch(e) [ˈɛstnɪʃ, ˈɛst-] NT Est(h)onian → *auch* **Deutsch(e)**

Est|ra|de [ɛsˈtraːdə] F **-, -n** a podium b (*auch* **Estradenkonzert**) concert of light music etc, *especially performed out of doors*

Est|ra|gon [ˈɛstragɔn] M **-s,** *no pl* tarragon

Est|rich [ˈɛstrɪç] M **-s, -e** a stone floor b (*Sw: = Dachboden*) attic

Es|zett [ɛsˈtsɛt] NT **-, -** eszett, ß

e|tab|lie|ren [etaˈbliːrən] *ptp* **etabliert** VT (*dated*) to establish VR to establish oneself; (*als Geschäftsmann auch*) to set up

e|tab|liert [etaˈbliːɐt] ADJ established; **er gehört jetzt zu den Etablierten** he is now part of the establishment; **die ~e Oberschicht** the upper echelons of the establishment

E|tab|lie|rung [etaˈbliːrʊŋ] F **-,** *no pl* establishment

E|tab|lis|se|ment [etablɪsəˈmãː] NT **-s, -s** establishment

E|ta|ge [eˈtaːʒə] F **-, -n** floor; **in** *or* **auf der 2. ~** on the 2nd *or* 3rd (*US*) floor; **er bewohnt im 5. Stock die ganze ~** he lives in *or* occupies the whole of the 5th *or* 6th (*US*) floor

E|ta|gen-: E|ta|gen|bad NT (*im Hotel*) shared bath; **E|ta|gen|bett** NT bunk bed; **E|ta|gen|du|sche** F (*im Hotel*) shared shower; **E|ta|gen|hei|zung** F *heating system which covers one floor of a building*; **E|ta|gen|kell|ner(in)** M(F) waiter/waitress on room service; **E|ta|gen|woh|nung** F *apartment occupying the whole of one floor of a building*

E|ta|ge|re [etaˈʒɛːrə] F **-, -n** (*dated*) étagère

E|tap|pe [eˈtapə] F **-, -n** a (= *Abschnitt, Stufe, beim Radrennen*) stage; (*einer Strecke auch*) leg b (*Mil*) communications zone; **in der ~ liegen** *or* **sein** to be behind the lines

E|tap|pen-: E|tap|pen|hengst M , **E|tap|pen|schwein** NT (*Mil sl*) base wallah (*Mil sl*); **E|tap|pen|sieg** M (*Sport*) stage win; (*fig*) partial victory; **E|tap|pen|sie|ger(in)** M(F) (*Sport*) stage winner; **e|tap|pen|wei|se** ADJ step-by-step, stage-by-stage ADV step by step, stage by stage

E|tat [eˈta] M **-s, -s** budget

E|tat-: E|tat|jahr NT financial year; **e|tat|mä|ßig** ADJ a (*Admin*) budgetary b *Stürmer, Quarterback etc* regular ADV **das Geld wurde ~ aus-**

gegeben the money was spent as budgeted; **nicht ~ erfasst** not in the budget, not budgeted for; **E|tat|pos|ten** M item in the budget, budgetary item; **E|tat|über|schrei|tung** [-yːbɐʃraɪtʊŋ] F overspending, spending over budget

etc [ɛtˈtseːtera] *abbr von* **et cetera** etc, et cetera

etc pp [ɛtˈtseːteraˈpeːˈpeː] ADV (*hum*) and so on and so forth

e|te|pe|te|te [eːtəpeˈteːtə] ADJ *pred* (*inf*) fussy, finicky (*inf*), pernickety (*inf*)

E|ter|nit® [eterˈniːt] M OR NT **-s,** *no pl* fibre (*Brit*) *or* fiber (*US*) cement

E|than [eˈtaːn] NT **-s** (*Chem*) ethane

E|thik [ˈeːtɪk] F **-, -en** ethics *pl*; (= *Fach*) ethics *sing*; **die ~ Kants** Kantian ethics; **die christliche ~** the Christian ethic, Christian ethics

E|thi|ker [ˈeːtɪkɐ] M **-s, -, E|thi|ke|rin** [-ərɪn] F **-, -nen** moral philosopher

E|thik-: E|thik|kom|mis|si|on F ethics committee; **E|thik|un|ter|richt** M (*Sch*) (teaching of) ethics

e|thisch [ˈeːtɪʃ] ADJ ethical

eth|nisch [ˈɛtnɪʃ] ADJ ethnic; **~e Säuberung** ethnic cleansing

Eth|no- [ɛtno] *in cpds* ethno-

Eth|no|graf ▲ [ɛtnoˈɡraːf] M **-en, -en, Eth|no|gra|fin** ▲ [-ˈɡraːfɪn] F **-, -nen** ethnographer

Eth|no|gra|fie ▲ [ɛtnoɡraˈfiː] F **-, -n** [-ˈfiːən] ethnography

eth|no|gra|fisch ▲ [ɛtnoˈɡraːfɪʃ] ADJ ethnographic

Eth|no|lo|ge [ɛtnoˈloːɡə] M **-n, -n, Eth|no|lo|gin** [-ˈloːɡɪn] F **-, -nen** ethnologist

Eth|no|lo|gie [ɛtnoloˈɡiː] F **-, -n** [-ˈɡiːən] ethnology

Eth|no|rock [ˈɛtnorɔk] M , *no pl* (*Mus*) ethnic rock

E|tho|lo|ge [ɛtoˈloːɡə] M **-n, -n, E|tho|lo|gin** [-ˈloːɡɪn] F **-, -nen** ethologist

E|tho|lo|gie [ɛtoloˈɡiː] F **-,** *no pl* ethology

E|thos [ˈeːtɔs] NT **-,** *no pl* ethos; (= *Berufsethos*) professional ethics *pl*

E|ti|kett [etiˈkɛt] NT **-(e)s, -e** (*lit, fig*) label

E|ti|ket|te [etiˈkɛtə] F **-, -n** a etiquette; **gegen die ~ (bei Hofe) verstoßen** to offend against (court) etiquette, to commit a breach of (court) etiquette b (*Aus: = Etikett*) label

E|ti|ket|ten|schwin|del M (*Pol*) juggling with names; **es ist reinster ~, wenn ...** it is just playing *or* juggling with names if ...

e|ti|ket|tie|ren [etikɛˈtiːrən] *ptp* **etikettiert** VT (*lit, fig*) to label

E|ti|ket|tier|ge|rät NT (*Tech*) labelling (*Brit*) *or* labeling (*US*) machine

et|li|che|mal △ [ˈɛtlɪçəˈmaːl] ADV → **etliche(r, s)**

et|li|che(r, s) [ˈɛtlɪçə] INDEF PRON a *sing attr* quite a lot of; **nachdem ~ Zeit verstrichen war** after quite some time; **~ Mal** quite a few times b **etliche** PL (*substantivisch*) quite a few, several people/things; (*attr*) several, quite a few c **etliches** SING (*substantivisch*) quite a lot; **ich habe ~s daran auszusetzen, aber im Großen und Ganzen ...** I have one *or* two objections to make but by and large ...; **um ~s älter als ich** quite a lot *or* considerably older than me

Et|ru|ri|en [eˈtruːriən] NT **-s** (*Hist*) Etruria

Et|rus|ker [eˈtrʊskɐ] M **-s, -, Et|rus|ke|rin** [-ərɪn] F **-, -nen** Etruscan

et|rus|kisch [eˈtrʊskɪʃ] ADJ Etruscan

Etsch [ɛtʃ] F - Adige

E|tü|de [eˈtyːdə] F **-, -n** (*Mus*) étude

E|tui [ɛtˈviː, eˈtyi] NT **-s, -s** case

E|tui|kleid [ɛtˈviː-, eˈtyi-] NT box dress

et|wa [ˈɛtva] ADV a (= *ungefähr, annähernd*) about, approximately; **so ~, ~ so** roughly *or* more *or* less like this; **wann ~ ...?** about *or* approximately *or* roughly when ...?

ⓑ (= *zum Beispiel*) for instance; **wenn man ~ behauptet, dass ...** for instance if one maintains that ...

ⓒ (*entrüstet, erstaunt*) **hast du ~ schon wieder kein Geld dabei?** don't tell me *or* you don't mean to say you haven't got any money again!; **soll das ~ heißen, dass ...?** is that supposed to mean ...?; **willst du ~ schon gehen?** (surely) you don't want to go already!

ⓓ (*zur Bestätigung*) **Sie kommen doch, oder ~ nicht?** you are coming, aren't you?; **das haben Sie wohl nicht mit Absicht gesagt, oder ~ doch?** surely you didn't say that on purpose, you didn't say that on purpose - or did you?; **sind Sie ~ nicht einverstanden?** do you mean to say that you don't agree?; **ist das ~ wahr?** (surely) it's not true!, (surely) it can't be true!; **ist das ~ nicht wahr?** do you mean to say it's not true?

ⓔ (*in Gegenüberstellung, einschränkend*) **nicht ~, dass ...** (it's) not that ...; **er ist nicht ~ dumm, sondern nur faul** it's not that he's stupid, he's simply lazy; **das hat Fritz getan und nicht ~ sein Bruder** Fritz did it and not his brother; **ich wollte dich nicht ~ beleidigen** I didn't intend to insult you

et|wa|ig ['ɛtvaɪç, ɛt'va:ɪç] ADJ *attr* possible; **~e Einwände/Unkosten** any objections/costs arising *or* which might arise; **bei ~en Beschwerden/ Schäden** *etc* in the event of (any) complaints/ damage *etc*; **ein Zimmer für ~e Besucher** a room for possible visitors, a room in case there should be visitors

et|was ['ɛtvas] INDEF PRON **ⓐ** (*substantivisch*) something; (*fragend, bedingend auch, verneinend*) anything; (*unbestimmter Teil einer Menge*) some; any; **kannst du mir ~ (davon) leihen?** can you lend me some (of it)?; **ohne ~ zu erwähnen** without saying anything; **~ habe ich doch vergessen** there is something I've forgotten; **~ anderes** something else; **das ist ~ (ganz) anderes** that's something (quite) different; **er ist ~** (*inf*) he is somebody; **~ werden** (*inf*) **es zu ~ bringen** (*inf*) to make something of oneself, to get somewhere (*inf*); **aus ihm wird nie ~** (*inf*) he'll never become anything; **er kann ~** he's good; **das ist immerhin ~** at least that's something; **sein Wort gilt ~ beim Chef** what he says counts for something with the boss; **hast du ~?** is (there) something wrong *or* the matter (with you)?; **sie hat ~ mit ihm** (*inf*) she's got something going on with him; **das ist sicher, wie nur ~** (*inf*) that's as sure as (sure) can be (*inf*); **er hat ~ von einem** *or* **vom Schulmeister an sich** he has *or* there is something of the schoolmaster about him; **da ist ~ (Richtiges) dran** there's something in that; **da ist ~ Wahres dran** there is some truth in that

ⓑ (*adjektivisch*) some; (*fragend, bedingend auch*) any; **~ Salz?** some salt?; **kannst du mir vielleicht ~ Geld leihen?** could you possibly lend me some money?; **~ Nettes** something nice; **~ Schöneres habe ich noch nie gesehen** I have never seen anything more beautiful

ⓒ (*adverbial*) somewhat, a little

Et|was ['ɛtvas] NT **-**, *no pl* something; **das gewisse ~** that certain something; **ein winziges ~** a tiny little thing

E|ty|mo|lo|ge [etymo'lo:gə] M **-n, -n**, **E|ty|mo|lo|gin** [-'lo:gɪn] F **-, -nen** etymologist

E|ty|mo|lo|gie [etymolo'gi:] F **-, -n** [-'gi:ən] etymology

e|ty|mo|lo|gisch [etymo'lo:gɪʃ] ADJ etymological

Et-Zei|chen ['ɛt-] NT ampersand

Et|zel ['ɛtsl] M **-s** Attila the Hun

EU [e:'|u:] F *- abbr von* **Europäische Union** EU

EU- [e:|u:-]: **EU-Be|am|te(r)** [e:'|u:-] M *decl as adj*, **EU-Be|am|tin** [e:'|u:-] F EU official; **EU-Be|hör|de** [e:'|u:-] F EU institution; **EU-Bei|hil|fe** [e:'|u:-] F EU subsidy; **EU-Be|stim|mung** [e:'|u:-] F EU regulation

euch [ɔyç] PERS PRON *dat, acc von* **ihr** you; (*dat auch*) to/for you; (*refl*) yourselves; **ein Freund von ~** a friend of yours; **wascht ~!** wash yourselves; **setzt ~!** sit (yourselves (*inf*)) down!; **vertragt ~!** stop quarrelling (*Brit*) *or* quarreling (*US*)!

Eu|cha|ris|tie [ɔyçarɪs'ti:] F **-, -n** [-'ti:ən] (*Eccl*) Eucharist

Eu|cha|ris|tie|fei|er [ɔyçarɪs'ti:-] F (*Eccl*) Eucharist, Eucharistic mass

eu|cha|ris|tisch [ɔyça'rɪstɪʃ] ADJ Eucharistic

EU-ein|heit|lich [e:'|u:-] ADJ standardized within the EU ADV **etw ~ regeln** to regulate sth uniformly throughout the EU

eu|er ['ɔyɐ] POSS PRON **ⓐ** (*adjektivisch*) your; **Euer** (*Briefschluss*) yours; **viele Grüße, ~ Hans** best wishes, yours, Hans; **das sind ~e** *or* **eure Bücher** those are your books; **ist das ~ Haus?** is that your house?; **Euer** *or* **Eure Gnaden/Exzellenz/Majestät** your Grace/Excellency/Majesty **ⓑ** (*old: substantivisch*) yours; **behaltet, was ~** *or* **Euer ist** keep what is yours PERS PRON *gen von* **ihr** (*geh*) **wir werden ~ gedenken** we will think of you; **~ beider gemeinsame Zukunft** your common future; **~ aller heimlicher Wunsch** the secret wish of all of you

eu|e|re(r, s) ['ɔyərə] POSS PRON = **eure(r, s)**

eu|ers|glei|chen ['ɔyɐs'glaɪçn] PRON *inv* = **euresgleichen**

eu|ert- ['ɔyɐt] *in cpds* = **euret-**

Eu|ge|nik [ɔy'ge:nɪk] F **-**, *no pl* (*Biol*) eugenics *sing*

eu|ge|nisch [ɔy'ge:nɪʃ] ADJ (*Biol*) eugenic

EU-Gip|fel [e:'|u:-] M (*inf.* = *Gipfelkonferenz*) EU summit

Eu|ka|lyp|tus [ɔyka'lyptʊs] M **-,** Eukalypten [-tn] (= *Baum*) eucalyptus (tree); (= *Öl*) eucalyptus oil

Eu|ka|lyp|tus|bon|bon M OR NT eucalyptus sweet (*Brit*) *or* candy (*US*)

Euk|lid [ɔy'kli:t] M **-s** Euclid

euk|li|disch [ɔy'kli:dɪʃ] ADJ Euclidean

EU- [e:|u:-]: **EU-Kom|mis|si|on** [e:'|u:-] F EU Commission; **EU-Land** [e:'|u:-] NT EU country *or* member

Eu|le ['ɔylə] F **-, -n** owl; (*pej*: = *hässliche Frau*) crow; **~n nach Athen tragen** (*prov*) to carry coals to Newcastle (*Brit prov*), to do something unnecessary

Eu|len|spie|gel ['ɔylənʃpi:gl] M **Till ~** (*lit*) Till Eulenspiegel; **unser Sohn ist ein richtiger ~** (*fig*) our son is a real scamp (*inf*) *or* rascal (*inf*)

Eu|len|spie|ge|lei [ɔylənʃpi:gə'laɪ] F **-, -en**, **Eu|len|spie|gel|streich** M trick, caper

EU- [e:|u:-]: **EU-Mi|nis|ter|rat** [e:'|u:-] M Council of Ministers; **EU-Mit|glied** [e:'|u:-] NT , **EU--Mit|glieds|land** [e:'|u:-] NT EU member (state); **EU-Norm** [e:'|u:-] F EU standard

Eu|nuch [ɔy'nu:x] M **-en, -en** eunuch

Eu|phe|mis|mus [ɔyfe'mɪsmʊs] M **-,** Euphemismen [-mən] euphemism

eu|phe|mis|tisch [ɔyfe'mɪstɪʃ] ADJ euphemistic ADV euphemistically

Eu|pho|rie [ɔyfo'ri:] F **-, -n** [-'ri:ən] euphoria

eu|pho|risch [ɔy'fo:rɪʃ] ADJ euphoric

Euph|rat ['ɔyfrat] M **-(s)** Euphrates

Eu|ra|si|en [ɔy'ra:ziən] NT **-s** Eurasia

Eu|ra|si|er [ɔy'ra:ziɐ] M **-s, -**, **Eu|ra|si|e|rin** [-iərɪn] F **-, -nen** Eurasian

eu|ra|sisch [ɔy'ra:zɪʃ] ADJ Eurasian

Eu|ra|tom [ɔyra'to:m] *abbr von* **Europäische Atomgemeinschaft** European Atomic Community, Euratom

eu|re(r, s) ['ɔyrə] POSS PRON **ⓐ** (*substantivisch*) yours; **der/die/das ~** *or* **Eure** (*geh*) yours; **tut ihr das ~** *or* **Eure** (*geh*) you do your bit (*Brit*) *or* part (*US*); **stets** *or* **immer der ~** *or* **Eure** (*form*) yours ever; **die ~n** *or* **Euren** (*geh*) your family, your people; **ihr und die ~n** *or* **Euren** (*geh*: = Fa-

milie) you and yours; **der/die ~** *or* **Eure** (*old*: = *Ehepartner*) your spouse (*old*); **das ~** *or* **Eure** (*geh*: = *Besitz*) what is yours **ⓑ** (*adjektivisch*) → **euer POSS PRON a**

eu|rer|seits ['ɔyrɐ'zaits] ADV (= *auf eurer Seite*) for your part; (= *von eurer Seite*) from *or* on your part; **den Vorschlag habt ihr ~ gemacht** you made the suggestion yourselves

eu|res|glei|chen ['ɔyrəs'glaɪçn] PRON *inv* people like you *or* yourselves; (*pej auch*) the likes of you, your sort

eu|ret|hal|ben ['ɔyrət'halbn] (*dated*), **eu|ret|we|gen** ['ɔyrət've:gn] ADV (= *wegen euch*) because of you, on account of you, on your account; (= *euch zuliebe auch*) for your sake; (= *um euch*) about you; (= *für euch*) on your behalf

eu|ret|wil|len ['ɔyrət'vɪlən] ADV **um ~** for your sake

Eu|rhyth|mie [ɔyryt'mi:] F **-**, *no pl* eurythmics *sing*

eu|ri|ge ['ɔyrɪgə] POSS PRON (*old, geh*) **der/die/ das ~** *or* **Eurige** yours; **die Eurigen** your families; **das Eurige** (= *Besitz*) what is yours; **tut ihr das ~** *or* **Eurige** you do your bit (*Brit*) *or* part (*US*)

Eu|ro ['ɔyro] M **-, -** (= *Währung*) euro; **vier ~ zwanzig** four euros twenty (cents); **das kostet zehn ~** that's ten euros; **mit jedem ~ rechnen, den** *or* **jeden ~ umdrehen** to think twice before spending anything; **mit jedem ~ rechnen müssen** to have to count every penny

eu|ro-, Eu|ro- *in cpds* Euro-; **Eu|ro|cent** M euro cent; **Eu|ro|cent|mün|ze** F euro cent coin; **Eu|ro|cheque** ['ɔyroʃɛk] M **-s, -s** Eurocheque (*Brit*), Eurocheck (*US*); **Eu|ro-Ci|ty-Zug** [-'sɪti-] M European Inter-City train; **Eu|ro|dol|lar** M eurodollar; **Eu|ro|korps** NT (*Mil*) Euro-corps

Eu|ro|krat [ɔyro'kra:t] M **-en, -en**, **Eu|ro|kra|tin** [-'kra:tɪn] F **-, -nen** Eurocrat

Eu|ro-: Eu|ro|land NT **ⓐ** *no pl* (*inf*: = *Eurozone*) Euroland (*inf*) **ⓑ** **-(e)s, ⸚er** (= *Mitgliedsstaat der EU*) euro country; **Eu|ro|mün|ze** F euro coin; **Eu|ro|norm** F European standard

Eu|ro|pa [ɔy'ro:pa] NT **-s** Europe

Eu|ro|pa|cup [-kap] M European cup

Eu|ro|pä|er [ɔyro'pɛ:ɐ] M **-s, -**, **Eu|ro|pä|e|rin** [-ərɪn] F **-, -nen** European

eu|ro|pä|isch [ɔyro'pɛ:ɪʃ] ADJ European; **Europäischer Binnenmarkt** European Internal Market; **die Europäische Gemeinschaft** the European Community; **Europäischer Gerichtshof** European Court of Justice; **Europäische Kommission** European Commission; **Europäische Kulturhauptstadt** European City of Culture; **das Europäische Parlament** the European Parliament; **Europäische Union** European Union; **Europäisches Währungssystem** European Monetary System; **Europäische Währungsunion** European Monetary Union; **Europäische Wirtschaftsgemeinschaft** European Economic Community, Common Market; **Europäischer Wirtschaftsraum** European Economic Area; **Europäische Zentralbank** European Central Bank

eu|ro|pä|i|sie|ren [ɔyropɛi'zi:rən] *ptp* **europäisiert** VT to Europeanize

Eu|ro|pa-: Eu|ro|pa|meis|ter(in) M(F) (*Sport*) European champion; (= *Team, Land*) European champions *pl*; **Eu|ro|pa|meis|ter|schaft** F European championship; **eu|ro|pa|müde** ADJ (*Pol*) Euro-fatigued, tired of Europe *pred*; **Eu|ro|pa|par|la|ment** NT European Parliament; **Eu|ro|pa|pass ▲** M European passport; **Eu|ro|pa|po|kal** M (*Sport*) European cup; **~ der Pokalsieger** (*Football*) European Cup-Winners' Cup; **Eu|ro|pa|rat** M Council of Europe; **Eu|ro|pa|stra|ße** F European route; **Eu|ro|pa|wah|len** PL European elections *pl*; **eu|ro|pa|weit** ADJ Europe-wide ADV throughout Europe

eu|ro|pid [ɔyro'pi:t] ADJ *Rasse* Caucasian

Eu|ro|pi|de(r) [ɔyro'pi:də] MF *decl as adj* Caucasian

Eu|ro|pi|um [ɔy'ro:piʊm] NT **-s**, *no pl* (*abbr* **Eu**) europium

Euro-: Eu|ro|pol ['ɔyropo:l] F **-**, *no pl* Europol; **Eu|ro|scheck** M Eurocheque (*Brit*), Eurocheck (*US*); **Eu|ro|scheck|kar|te** F Eurocheque (*Brit*) or Eurocheck (*US*) card; **Eu|ro|ste|cker** M flat two-pinned plug; **Eu|ro|stück** NT (one-)euro coin; **Eu|ro|tun|nel** M (= *Kanaltunnel*) Eurotunnel; **Eu|ro|vi|si|on** F , *no pl* Eurovision; **Eu|ro|vi|si|ons|sen|dung** F Eurovision broadcast or programme (*Brit*) or program (*US*); **Eu|ro|zei|chen** NT , *no pl* euro symbol or sign

Eu|ryth|mie [ɔyryt'mi:] F **-**, *no pl* eurythmics *sing*

EU-Staat [e:'ʔu:-] M EU country

eus|ta|chi|sche Röh|re [ɔys'taxɪʃə] F (*Anat*) Eustachian tube

Eu|ter ['ɔytɐ] NT **-s, -** udder

Eu|tha|na|sie [ɔytanaˈzi:] F **-**, *no pl* euthanasia

EU-weit [e:'ʔu:-] ADJ, ADV EU-wide

e. V., E. V. *abbr von* **eingetragener Verein**

ev. *abbr von* **evangelisch**

E|va ['e:fa, 'e:va] F **-s** Eve; **sie ist eine echte ~** (*hum*) she is the archetypal woman

e|va|ku|ie|ren [evaku'i:rən] *ptp* **evakuiert** VT to evacuate

E|va|ku|ier|te(r) [evaku'i:ɐtə] MF *decl as adj* evacuee

E|va|ku|ie|rung F **-**, **-en** evacuation

e|va|lu|ie|ren [evalu'i:rən] *ptp* **evaluiert** VT (*geh*) to evaluate

E|van|ge|li|ar [evaŋgeli'a:ɐ] NT **-s, -e**, **E|van|ge|li|en|buch** [evaŋˈge:liən-] NT book of the Gospels, Gospel

e|van|ge|li|kal [evaŋgeli'ka:l] ADJ evangelical

E|van|ge|li|ka|le(r) [evaŋgeli'ka:lə] MF *decl as adj* evangelical

e|van|ge|lisch [evaŋˈge:lɪʃ] ADJ Protestant **ADV ~ denken** to have Protestant beliefs; **~ heiraten** to be married in the Protestant church; **~ beerdigt werden** to be buried as a Protestant; **~ beeinflusst** influenced by Protestantism; **seine Kinder ~ erziehen** to raise one's children as Protestants

E|van|ge|list [evaŋgeˈlɪst] M **-en, -en**, **E|van|ge|lis|tin** [-'lɪstɪn] F **-**, **-nen** evangelist

E|van|ge|li|um [evaŋˈge:liʊm] NT **-s, Evangelien** [-liən] Gospel; (*fig*) gospel; **alles, was er sagt, ist für sie (ein) ~** (*fig*) everything he says is gospel to her

e|va|po|rie|ren [evapo'ri:rən] *ptp* **evaporiert** VI *aux sein* to evaporate

E|va(s)|kos|tüm NT (*dated hum*) **im ~** in the altogether (*Brit hum*), in her birthday suit (*hum*)

E|vas|toch|ter ['e:fas-, 'e:vas-] F (*dated hum*) coquette

E|ven|tu|al- [eventu'a:l-]: **E|ven|tu|al|fall** M eventuality; **E|ven|tu|al|haus|halt** M (*Parl*) emergency or contingency budget

E|ven|tu|a|li|tät [eventuali'tɛ:t] F **-**, **-en** eventuality, contingency

e|ven|tu|ell [even'tuɛl] **ADJ** *attr* possible **ADV** possibly, perhaps; **~ rufe ich Sie später an** I may possibly call you later; **ich komme ~ ein bisschen später** I might (possibly) come a little later

E|ver|green ['ɛvɐgri:n] M **-s, -s** evergreen

e|vi|dent [evi'dɛnt] ADJ (*geh*: = *offenbar*) obvious, clear

E|vi|denz [evi'dɛnts] F **-**, **-en** a (*Philos*) evidence b (*Aus*) **etw in ~ halten** to keep a current record of sth, to keep sth up-to-date

E|vi|denz|bü|ro NT (*Aus*) registry

ev.-luth. *abbr von* **evangelisch-lutherisch** Lutheran Protestant

E|vo|lu|ti|on [evolu'tsio:n] F **-**, **-en** evolution

e|vo|lu|ti|o|när [evolutsio'nɛ:ɐ], **e|vo|lu|ti|o|nis|tisch** [evolutsio'nɪstɪʃ] ADJ evolutionary

E|vo|lu|ti|ons|the|o|rie F theory of evolution

evtl. *abbr von* **eventuell**

E-Werk ['e:-] NT *abbr von* **Elektrizitätswerk** generating or power station

EWG [e:ve:'ge:] F **-** *abbr von* **Europäische Wirtschaftsgemeinschaft** EEC, Common Market

e|wig ['e:vɪç] **ADJ** eternal; *Leben auch* everlasting; *Eis, Schnee* perpetual; (*inf*) *Nörgelei etc* never-ending; **der Ewige Jude** the Wandering Jew; **das ~e Licht** (*Eccl*) **die ~e Lampe** (*Eccl*) the sanctuary lamp; **in den ~en Frieden** or **die ~e Ruhe eingehen** to find eternal peace; **die Ewige Stadt** the Eternal City; **(Gott,) der Ewige** God, the Eternal → **Jagdgründe**

ADV for ever, eternally; **auf ~** for ever; **das dauert ja ~ (und drei Tage** (*hum*)) it goes on for ever (and a day); **das dauert ja ~, bis …** it'll take ages until … (*inf*); **er muss sich ~ beklagen** he's eternally or for ever complaining; **es ist ~ schade, dass …** (*inf*) it's an enormous pity or shame that …; **~ dankbar** eternally grateful; **ich habe Sie ~ lange nicht gesehen** (*inf*) I haven't seen you for absolutely ages (*inf*) or for an eternity → **immer**

E|wig|gest|ri|ge(r) ['e:vɪçˈgestrɪgə] MF *decl as adj* person living in the past; (*gegen alles Neue*) stick-in-the-mud (*inf*)

E|wig|keit ['e:vɪçkait] F **-**, **-en** eternity; (*der Naturgesetze*) immutability; (*inf*) ages; **in die ~ eingehen** to go to eternal rest; **bis in alle ~ amen, von ~ zu ~ amen** for ever and ever, amen; **bis in alle ~** for ever, for all eternity (*liter*); **eine ~** or **eine halbe ~** (*hum*) **dauern** (*inf*) to last an age or an eternity; **es dauert eine ~** or **eine halbe ~** (*hum*), **bis …** (*inf*) it'll take absolutely ages until … (*inf*); **ich habe sie seit ~en** or **einer ~ nicht gesehen** (*inf*) I haven't seen her for ages

e|wig|lich ['e:vɪklɪç] (*liter*) **ADJ** *attr* eternal, everlasting **ADV** eternally, for ever, to the end of time (*liter*)

E|wig|weib|li|che(s) ['e:vɪçˈvaiplçə] NT **-n**, *no pl decl as adj* (*geh*) eternal feminine

EWR [e:ve:'ʔɛr] M **-** *abbr von* **Europäischer Wirtschaftsraum** EEA

EWS [e:ve:'ʔɛs] NT **-** *abbr von* **Europäisches Währungssystem** EMS

EWU [e:ve:'ʔu:] F **-** *abbr von* **Europäische Währungsunion** EMU

e. Wz. *abbr von* **eingetragenes Warenzeichen**

ex [ɛks] ADV (*inf*) a (= *leer*) **(trink) ex!** down the hatch! (*esp Brit inf*); **etw (auf) ex trinken** to drink sth in one go or down in one b (*Schluss, vorbei*) (all) over, finished; **ex und hopp** here today, gone tomorrow

Ex- *in cpds* ex-; **ihr Exmann** her ex-husband

e|xakt [ɛ'ksakt] **ADJ** exact; **eine ~e Wissenschaft** an exact science **ADV** exactly; **~ arbeiten** to work accurately

E|xakt|heit F **-**, *no pl* exactness, precision

e|xal|tiert [ɛksal'ti:ɐt] ADJ effusive

E|xal|tiert|heit F **-**, **-en** effusiveness

E|xa|men [ɛ'ksa:mən] NT **-s, -** or **Examina** [-mina] exam, examination; (*Univ*) final examinations, finals *pl*; **~ machen** to do or take one's exams or finals; **das ~ mit Eins machen** to get top marks in an exam (*Brit*), to get the best grade in an exam (*US*); (*Univ*) ≈ to get a First (*Brit*), ≈ to get an A (*US*); **mündliches/schriftliches ~** oral/written examination

E|xa|mens-: E|xa|mens|angst F exam nerves *pl*; **E|xa|mens|ar|beit** F dissertation (*Brit*), thesis; **E|xa|mens|kan|di|dat(in)** M(F) candidate (for an examination), examinee

e|xa|mi|nie|ren [ɛksami'ni:rən] *ptp* **examiniert** VT (*geh*) to examine; **jdn über etw** (*acc*) **~** (*lit, fig*) to question sb about sth

E|xe|ge|se [ɛkse'ge:zə] F **-**, **-n** exegesis

E|xe|get [ɛkse'ge:t] M **-en, -en**, **E|xe|ge|tin** [-'ge:tɪn] F **-**, **-nen** exegete

e|xe|ge|tisch [ɛkse'ge:tɪʃ] ADJ exegetic(al)

e|xe|ku|tie|ren [ɛkseku'ti:rən] *ptp* **exekutiert** VT (*form*) to execute; **jdn ~** (*Aus*: = *pfänden*) to seize or impound sb's possessions

E|xe|ku|ti|on [ɛkseku'tsio:n] F **-**, **-en** execution; (*Aus*: = *Pfändung*) seizing, impounding

E|xe|ku|ti|ons|kom|man|do NT firing squad

e|xe|ku|tiv [ɛkseku'ti:f] ADJ executive

E|xe|ku|tiv|aus|schuss ▲ M executive committee

E|xe|ku|ti|ve [ɛkseku'ti:və] F **-**, **-n**, **E|xe|ku|tiv|ge|walt** F executive; (*Aus*) forces *pl* of law and order

E|xe|ku|tor [ɛkse'ku:to:ɐ] M **-s, Exekutoren** [-'to:rən], **E|xe|ku|to|rin** [-'to:rɪn] F **-**, **-nen** (*Aus*) bailiff

E|xem|pel [ɛ'ksɛmpl] NT **-s, -** (*geh*) example; (*dated Math*: = *Rechenexempel*) example (*dated*); **die Probe aufs ~ machen** to put it to the test → **statuieren**

E|xem|plar [ɛksɛm'pla:ɐ] NT **-s, -e** specimen; (= *Buchexemplar, Zeitschriftenexemplar*) copy

e|xem|pla|risch [ɛksɛm'pla:rɪʃ] **ADJ** exemplary; **~es Lehren/Lernen** teaching/learning by example; **das Urteil wurde ~ für alle folgenden Fälle** the verdict set a precedent for all subsequent cases **ADV ~ durcharbeiten** to work through sth as an example; **jdm etw ~ zeigen** to give sb a perfect example of sth; **jdn ~ bestrafen** to punish sb as an example (to others)

E|xem|pli|fi|ka|ti|on [ɛksɛmplifika'tsio:n] F **-**, **-en** (*geh*) exemplification

e|xem|pli|fi|zie|ren [ɛksɛmplifi'tsi:rən] *ptp* **exemplifiziert** VT (*geh*) to exemplify

e|xer|zie|ren [ɛksɛr'tsi:rən] *ptp* **exerziert** VTI to drill; (*fig*) to practise (*Brit*), to practice (*US*)

E|xer|zier|platz M (*Mil*) parade or drill ground

E|xer|zi|ti|en [ɛksɛr'tsi:tsiən] PL (*Eccl*) spiritual exercises *pl*

Ex|hi|bi|ti|o|nis|mus [ɛkshibitsio'nɪsmʊs] M **-**, *no pl* exhibitionism

Ex|hi|bi|ti|o|nist [ɛkshibitsio'nɪst] M **-en, -en**, **Ex|hi|bi|ti|o|nis|tin** [-'nɪstɪn] F **-**, **-nen** exhibitionist

ex|hi|bi|ti|o|nis|tisch [ɛkshibitsio'nɪstɪʃ] ADJ exhibitionist

ex|hu|mie|ren [ɛkshu'mi:rən] *ptp* **exhumiert** VT to exhume

Ex|hu|mie|rung F **-**, **-en** exhumation

E|xil [ɛ'ksi:l] NT **-s, -e** exile; **im (amerikanischen) ~ leben** to live in exile in (America); **ins ~ gehen** to go into exile

E|xi|lier|te(r) [ɛksi'li:ɐtə] MF *decl as adj* exile

Exil-: E|xil|li|te|ra|tur F literature written in exile (*esp by Germans exiled during the 3rd Reich*); **E|xil|re|gie|rung** F government in exile

e|xis|tent [ɛksɪs'tɛnt] ADJ (*geh*) existing, existent

E|xis|ten|ti|a|lis|mus [ɛksɪstɛntsia'lɪsmʊs] M **-**, *no pl* = **Existenzialismus**

E|xis|ten|ti|a|list [ɛksɪstɛntsia'lɪst] M **-en, -en**, **E|xis|ten|ti|a|lis|tin** [-'lɪstɪn] F **-**, **-nen** = **Existenzialist**

e|xis|ten|ti|a|lis|tisch [ɛksɪstɛntsia'lɪstɪʃ] ADJ = **existenzialistisch**

E|xis|ten|ti|al|phi|lo|so|phie [ɛksɪstɛn'tsia:l-] F = **Existenzialphilosophie**

e|xis|ten|ti|ell [ɛksɪstɛn'tsiɛl] ADJ = **existenziell**

E|xis|tenz [ɛksɪs'tɛnts] F **-**, **-en** existence; (= *Lebensgrundlage, Auskommen*) livelihood; (*pej inf*: = *Person*) character, customer (*inf*); **eine gescheiterte** or **verkrachte ~** (*inf*) a failure; **sich eine (neue) ~ aufbauen** to make a (new) life for oneself; **keine sichere ~ haben** to have no secure livelihood

E|xis|tenz-: E|xis|tenz|angst F (*Philos*) existential fear, angst; (*wirtschaftlich*) fear for one's livelihood *or* existence; **E|xis|tenz|be|rech|ti|gung** F right to exist; **hat die UNO noch eine ~?** can the UN still justify its existence?; **e|xis|tenz|fä|hig** ADJ able to exist; *Firma* viable; **E|xis|tenz|fä|hig|keit** F ability to exist; (*von Firma*) viability; **E|xis|tenz|grün|der(in)** M(F) (*Econ*) founder of a new business; **E|xis|tenz|grund|la|ge** F basis of one's livelihood; **E|xis|tenz|grün|dung** F **a** (= *Gründungsvorgang*) establishing a livelihood; (*Econ*) founding of a new business, starting (up) a new *or* one's own business **b** (*Econ*: = *neu gegründete Firma*) start-up (business); **E|xis|tenz|grün|dungs|dar|le|hen** NT , **E|xis|tenz|grün|dungs|kre|dit** [-kreːdiːt] M start-up loan, loan to found a new business

E|xis|ten|zia|lis|mus ▲ [ɛksɪstentsiaˈlɪsmʊs] M -, *no pl* existentialism

E|xis|ten|zia|list ▲ [ɛksɪstentsiaˈlɪst] M -en, -en, **E|xis|ten|zia|lis|tin** ▲ [-ˈlɪstɪn] F -, -nen existentialist

e|xis|ten|zia|lis|tisch ▲ [ɛksɪstentsiaˈlɪstɪʃ] ADJ existential(ist)

E|xis|ten|zi|al|phi|lo|so|phie ▲ [ɛksɪsten'tsiaːl-] F existential(ist) philosophy

e|xis|ten|zi|ell ▲ [ɛksɪsten'tsiɛl] ADJ (*geh*) existential; **das Problem der Umweltverschmutzung ist ~** the problem of environmental pollution is of vital significance; **von ~er Bedeutung** of vital significance

E|xis|tenz-: E|xis|tenz|kampf M struggle for survival; **E|xis|tenz|mi|ni|mum** NT subsistence level; (= *Lohn*) minimal living wage *or* income; **das Gehalt liegt noch unter dem ~** that salary is not enough to live on, that is not even a living wage; **er verdient nicht einmal das ~** he does not even earn enough to live on, he does not even earn a living wage; **das gibt uns gera-de das ~** we just have enough to get by on; **E|xis|tenz|phi|lo|so|phie** F existentialism; **E|xis|tenz|si|che|rung** F securing one's livelihood

e|xis|tie|ren [ɛksɪsˈtiːrən] *ptp* **existiert** VI to exist; (*Gesetz, Schule etc auch*) to be in existence

E|xi|tus [ˈɛksitʊs] M -, *no pl* (*Med*) death

exkl. *abbr von* **exklusive**

Ex|kla|ve [ɛksˈklaːvə] F -, -n (*Pol*) exclave

ex|klu|siv [ɛkskluˈziːf] ADJ exclusive

Ex|klu|siv|be|richt M (*Press*) exclusive (report)

ex|klu|si|ve [ɛkskluˈziːvə] **PREP** +*gen* exclusive of, excluding **ADV** *Getränke* ~ excluding drinks; **bis zum 20.** ~ to the 20th exclusively

Ex|klu|siv|in|ter|view NT (*Press*) exclusive interview

Ex|klu|si|vi|tät [ɛkskluziviˈtɛːt] F -, *no pl* exclusiveness

Ex|klu|siv|recht NT exclusive rights *pl*

Ex|kom|mu|ni|ka|ti|on F (*Eccl*) excommunication

ex|kom|mu|ni|zie|ren [ɛkskɔmuniˈtsiːrən] *ptp* **exkommuniziert** VT to excommunicate

Ex|kre|ment [ɛkskreˈmɛnt] NT -(e)s, -e *usu pl* (*geh*) excrement *no pl*, excreta *pl*

Ex|kre|ti|on [ɛkskreˈtsioːn] F -, -en (*Med*) excretion

ex|kul|pie|ren [ɛkskulˈpiːrən] *ptp* **exkulpiert** VT (*Jur*) *Person* to exculpate; *Verbrechen* to excuse

Ex|kurs [ɛksˈkʊrs] M digression

Ex|kur|si|on [ɛkskʊrˈzioːn] F -, -en (study) trip

Ex|lib|ris [ɛksˈliːbrɪs] NT -, - ex-libris, bookplate

Ex|mat|ri|ku|la|ti|on [ɛksmatrikulaˈtsioːn] F -, -en (*Univ*) being taken off the university register

ex|mat|ri|ku|lie|ren [ɛksmatrikuˈliːrən] *ptp* **exmatrikuliert** VT (*Univ*) to take off the university register; **sich ~ lassen** to withdraw from the university register

ex|mit|tie|ren [ɛksmɪˈtiːrən] *ptp* **exmittiert** VT (*Admin*) *Mieter* to evict

Ex|mit|tie|rung F -, -en (*Admin*) eviction

E|xo|dus [ˈɛksodʊs] M - (*Bibl, fig*) exodus

e|xo|gen [ɛksoˈgeːn] ADJ (*Biol, Geol*) exogenous

e|xor|bi|tant [ɛksɔrbiˈtant] ADJ (*geh*) *Preise* exorbitant; *Alkoholwerte* excessive; **es kam zu ei-ner ~en Überschreitung der Strahlengrenzwerte** radiation levels were greatly exceeded

e|xor|zie|ren [ɛksɔrˈtsiːrən] *ptp* **exorziert**, **e|xor|zi|sie|ren** [ɛksɔrtsiˈziːrən] *ptp* **exorzisiert** VT to exorcize

E|xor|zis|mus [ɛksɔrˈtsɪsmʊs] M -, **Exorzismen** [-mən] exorcism

E|xor|zist [ɛksɔrˈtsɪst] M -en, -en, **E|xor|zis|tin** [-ˈtsɪstɪn] F -, -nen exorcist

E|xot [ɛˈksoːt] M -en, -en, **E|xo|te** [ɛˈksoːtə] M -n, -n, **E|xo|tin** [ɛˈksoːtɪn] F -, -nen exotic *or* tropical animal/plant *etc*; (*Mensch*) exotic foreigner

E|xo|tik [ɛˈksoːtɪk] F -, *no pl* exoticism

e|xo|tisch [ɛˈksoːtɪʃ] ADJ exotic

Ex|pan|der [ɛksˈpandɐ] M -s, - (*Sport*) chest expander

ex|pan|die|ren [ɛkspanˈdiːrən] *ptp* **expandiert** VI to expand

Ex|pan|si|on [ɛkspanˈzioːn] F -, -en (*Phys, Pol*) expansion

Ex|pan|si|ons-: Ex|pan|si|ons|kurs M (*Comm*) expansion(ary) strategy; **auf ~ sein** to be expanding *or* growing; **Ex|pan|si|ons|po|li|tik** F expansionism, expansionist policies *pl*

ex|pan|siv [ɛkspanˈziːf] ADJ *Politik* expansionist; *Wirtschaftszweige* expanding; *Gase* expansile, expansive

ex|pat|ri|ie|ren [ɛkspatriˈiːrən] *ptp* **expatriiert** VT to expatriate

Ex|pe|di|ent [ɛkspeˈdiɛnt] M -en, -en, **Ex|pe|di|en|tin** [-ˈdiɛntɪn] F -, -nen (*Comm*) dispatch clerk

ex|pe|die|ren [ɛkspeˈdiːrən] *ptp* **expediert** VT to dispatch, to send (off)

Ex|pe|di|ti|on [ɛkspediˈtsioːn] F -, -en **a** (= *Forschungsexpedition, Mil*) expedition **b** (= *Versendung*) dispatch; (= *Versandabteilung*) dispatch office

Ex|pe|ri|ment [ɛksperiˈmɛnt] NT -(e)s, -e experiment; **~e machen** *or* **anstellen** to carry out *or* do experiments

Ex|pe|ri|men|tal- [ɛksperimɛnˈtaːl] *in cpds* experimental; **Ex|pe|ri|men|tal|film** M experimental film

ex|pe|ri|men|tell [ɛksperimɛnˈtɛl] **ADJ** experimental **ADV** experimentally; **~ vorgehen** to work experimentally, to do experimental work; **etw ~ nachweisen** to prove sth by experiment

ex|pe|ri|men|tie|ren [ɛksperimɛnˈtiːrən] *ptp* **experimentiert** VI to experiment (*mit* with)

Ex|pe|ri|men|tier|freu|de [ɛksperiˈmɛnt] F , *no pl* eagerness to experiment, love of experimentation, great desire to try out new things

ex|pe|ri|men|tier|freu|dig [ɛksperimɛnˈtiː-ɐ-] ADJ **sie ist sehr ~** she likes *or* loves to experiment, she likes *or* loves to try out new things

Ex|per|te [ɛksˈpɛrtə] M -n, -n, **Ex|per|tin** [-ˈpɛr-tɪn] F -, -nen expert (*für* in)

Ex|per|tin F -, -nen expert (*für* in)

Ex|per|ti|se [ɛkspɛrˈtiːzə] F -, -n (expert's) report

Expl. *abbr von* **Exemplar**

Ex|pli|ka|ti|on [ɛksplikaˈtsioːn] F -, -en (*geh*) explication (*form*)

ex|pli|zie|ren [ɛkspliˈtsiːrən] *ptp* **expliziert** VT (*geh*) to explicate (*form*)

ex|pli|zit [ɛkspliˈtsiːt] (*geh*) **ADJ** explicit **ADV** explicitly

ex|pli|zi|te [ɛkspliˈtsiːtə] ADV (*geh*) explicitly

ex|plo|die|ren [ɛksploˈdiːrən] *ptp* **explodiert** VI *aux sein* (*lit, fig*) to explode

Ex|plo|ra|ti|on [ɛksploraˈtsioːn] F -, -en (*eines Landes*) exploration; (*Psych*) examination

Ex|plo|ra|ti|ons|fonds M exploratory investment

ex|plo|rie|ren [ɛksploˈriːrən] *ptp* **exploriert** VT *Gelände* to explore

Ex|plo|si|on [ɛksploˈzioːn] F -, -en explosion; **etw zur ~ bringen** to detonate *or* explode sth

Ex|plo|si|ons-: ex|plo|si|ons|ar|tig ADJ *Geräusch, Wirkung* explosive; *Wachstum, Zunahme* phenomenal **ADV** explosively; **das Gerücht ver-breitete sich ~** the rumour (*Brit*) *or* rumor (*US*) spread like wildfire; **Ex|plo|si|ons|ge|fahr** F danger of explosion; **Ex|plo|si|ons|mo|tor** M internal combustion engine; **Ex|plo|si|ons|wel|le** F blast (wave); (*Auswirkung*) impact of the blast

ex|plo|siv [ɛksploˈziːf] ADJ (*lit, fig*) explosive

Ex|plo|siv [ɛksploˈziːf] M -s, -e [-və], **Ex|plo|siv|laut** M (*Ling*) plosive

Ex|plo|siv|stoff M explosive

Ex|po|nat [ɛkspoˈnaːt] NT -(e)s, -e exhibit

Ex|po|nent[1] [ɛkspoˈnɛnt] M -en, -en (*Math*) exponent

Ex|po|nent[2] [ɛkspoˈnɛnt] M -en, -en, **Ex|po|nen|tin** [-ˈnɛntɪn] F -, -nen (*fig*) exponent, spokesman/-woman

Ex|po|nen|ti|al- [ɛksponɛnˈtsiaːl-]: **Ex|po|nen|ti|al|funk|ti|on** F (*Math*) exponential function; **Ex|po|nen|ti|al|glei|chung** F (*Math*) exponential equation

ex|po|nen|ti|ell [ɛksponɛnˈtsiɛl] (*Math*) **ADJ** exponential **ADV** exponentially; **~ anwachsen** (*Bevölkerung etc*) to rise at an exponential rate

Ex|po|nen|tin F -, -nen (*fig*) → **Exponent**[2]

ex|po|nie|ren [ɛkspoˈniːrən] *ptp* **exponiert** **VT** (= *herausheben, dated Phot*) to exponier; **jdn zu sehr ~** to overexpose sb **VR** (= *sich auffällig be-nehmen*) to behave boisterously; (*in der Politik*) to take a prominent stance; (*in Diskussion*) to make one's presence felt, to come on strong (*inf*); **die Studenten wollen sich nicht mehr ~** the students are keeping a low profile

ex|po|niert [ɛkspoˈniːrt] *ptp von* **exponieren** ADJ *Lage etc* exposed → **exponieren**; **an ~er Stelle stehen** to be in an exposed position

Ex|port [ɛksˈpɔrt] M -(e)s, -e export (*an* +*dat* of); (= *Exportwaren*) exports *pl*

Ex|port- *in cpds* export; **Ex|port|ab|tei|lung** F export department; **Ex|port|an|reiz** M export incentive; **Ex|port|ar|ti|kel** M export; **Ex|port|aus|füh|rung** F export model; **Ex|port|be|schrän|kun|gen** PL export restraints *pl*

Ex|por|teur [ɛkspɔrˈtøːɐ] M -s, -e, **Ex|por|teu|rin** [-ˈtøːrɪn] F -, -nen exporter

Ex|port-: Ex|port|ge|schäft NT **a** (= *Firma*) export business **b** (= *Handel*) export business *or* trade; **Ex|port|han|del** M export business *or* trade

ex|por|tie|ren *ptp* **exportiert** VTI (*auch Com-put*) to export

Ex|port-: Ex|port|kauf|frau F , **Ex|port|kauf|mann** M exporter; **Ex|port|quo|te** F export ratio; **Ex|port|wa|re** F export

Ex|po|sé [ɛkspoˈzeː] NT -s, -s, **Ex|po|see** ▲ NT -s, -s (*für Film, Buch etc*) outline, plan; (= *Denkschrift*) memo(randum)

Ex|po|si|ti|on F (*Liter, Mus*) exposition; (= *Gliederung eines Aufsatzes*) outline, plan

Ex|po|si|tur F (*Aus*) = *Zweigstelle*) branch; (*Sch*) annexe (*Brit*), annex (*US*)

ex|press ▲ [ɛks'prɛs] ADV *(dated)* quickly, expeditiously *(form)*; *(Post)* express

Ex|press ▲ [ɛks'prɛs] M **-es, -e** *(Rail)* express (train)

Ex|press-: Ex|press|brief ▲ M express letter; **Ex|press|gut** ▲ NT express goods *pl*

Ex|pres|si|o|nis|mus [ɛkspresio'nɪsmʊs] M **-**, *no pl* expressionism

Ex|pres|si|o|nist [ɛkspresio'nɪst] M **-en, -en**, **Ex|pres|si|o|nis|tin** [-'nɪstɪn] F **-, -nen** expressionist

ex|pres|si|o|nis|tisch [ɛkspresio'nɪstɪʃ] ADJ expressionist *no adv*, expressionistic

ex|pres|sis ver|bis [ɛks'prɛsi:s 'vɛrbi:s] ADV *(geh)* explicitly, expressly

ex|pres|siv [ɛksprɛ'si:f] ADJ expressive

Ex|pres|si|vi|tät [ɛksprɛsivi'tɛ:t] F **-**, *no pl* expressiveness

Ex|press-: Ex|press|rei|ni|gung ▲ F express dry-cleaning service; **Ex|press|zug** ▲ M *(old, Aus)* express (train)

Ex|prop|ri|a|ti|on [ɛkspropria'tsio:n] F **-, -en** *(geh)* expropriation

ex|qui|sit [ɛkskvi'zi:t] *(geh)* ADJ exquisite **ADV** exquisitely; **~ schmecken** to taste exquisite

ex|tem|po|rie|ren [ɛkstɛmpo'ri:rən] ptp **extemporiert** VTI *(geh)* to improvise, to extemporize, to ad-lib

ex|ten|siv [ɛkstɛn'zi:f] ADJ *(auch Agr)* extensive

ex|tern [ɛks'tɛrn] **ADJ** external; *Fachleute auch* outside *attr*; **ein ~er Schüler** a day boy **ADV die Prüfung fürs Diplom ~ ablegen** to take an external examination to get one's diploma

Ex|ter|ne(r) [ɛks'tɛrnə] MF *decl as adj (Sch)* day boy/girl

Ex|ter|nist [ɛkstɛr'nɪst] M **-en, -en**, **Ex|ter|nis|tin** [-'nɪstɪn] F **-, -nen** *(Aus)* **a** *(= Schüler)* day boy/girl **b** *pupil educated by private tuition, not at school*

ex|ter|ri|to|ri|al [ɛksterito'ria:l] ADJ extraterritorial

Ex|ter|ri|to|ri|a|li|tät [ɛksteritoriali'tɛ:t] F **-**, *no pl* extraterritoriality

ext|ra ['ɛkstra] **ADJ** *inv (inf)* extra; **etwas Extraes** *(inf)* something special **ADV** *(= besonders, außerordentlich)* extra, (e)specially; *(= eigens, ausschließlich)* (e)specially, just; *(= gesondert)* separately; *(= zusätzlich)* extra, in addition; *(inf: = ab-*

sichtlich) on purpose, deliberately; **etw ~ legen** to put sth in a separate place; **ich gebe Ihnen noch ein Exemplar ~** I'll give you an extra copy; **jetzt tu ichs ~!** *(inf)* just for that I will do it!

Ext|ra ['ɛkstra] NT **-s, -s** extra

Ext|ra-: Ext|ra|aus|ga|be F special edition; **Ext|ra|aus|stat|tung** F extras *pl*; **Ext|ra|blatt** NT special edition; *(= zusätzlich zur Zeitung)* special supplement; **ext|ra|fein** **ADJ** superfine **ADV ~ gemahlener Kaffee** very finely ground coffee

ext|ra|hie|ren [ɛkstra'hi:rən] ptp **extrahiert** VT to extract

Ext|ra|klas|se F **ein Wagen/Film der ~** a top (-of-the-)line model/a first-rate film *or* movie *(esp US)*; **Service etc der ~** top-flight service /etc=; **das ist ~** that's brilliant *or* fantastic

Ex|trakt [ɛks'trakt] M (MED, PHARM AUCH NT) **-(e)s, -e** extract; *(von Buch etc)* synopsis; **etw im ~ wiedergeben** to summarize sth, to give a summary of sth

Ext|ra|or|di|na|ri|us [ɛkstra'ɔrdi'na:riʊs] M *(Univ)* ≈ reader *(Brit)*, ≈ associate professor *(US)*

Ext|ra|po|la|ti|on [ɛkstrapola'tsio:n] F **-, -en** *(Math, fig)* extrapolation

ext|ra|po|lie|ren [ɛkstrapo'li:rən] ptp **extrapoliert** VTI *(Math, fig)* to extrapolate

ext|ra|ter|res|trisch ADJ extraterrestrial

Ext|ra|tour F *(fig inf)* special favour *(Brit)* or favor *(US)*; **er will immer eine ~** he always wants something different *or* special

ext|ra|ute|rin [ɛkstra|ute'ri:n] ADJ extra-uterine

ext|ra|va|gant [ɛkstrava'gant] ADJ extravagant; *Kleidung auch* flamboyant **ADV** extravagantly

Ext|ra|va|ganz [ɛkstrava'gants] F **-, -en** extravagance; *(von Kleidung auch)* flamboyance

ext|ra|ver|tiert [ɛkstraver'ti:rt] ADJ *(Psych)* extrovert

Ext|ra|wurst F **a** *(inf: = Sonderwunsch)* special favour *(Brit)* or favor *(US)*; **jdm eine ~ braten** to make an exception of *or* for sb; **er will immer eine ~ (gebraten haben)** he always wants something different *or* special **b** *(Aus: = Lyoner)* type of pork *or* veal sausage

ext|rem [ɛks'tre:m] **ADJ** extreme; *Belastung* excessive; **du bist immer so ~** you always go to extremes; **ist ja ~!** *(sl)* it's way out *(inf)* **ADV**

kalt, rechts, primitiv extremely; *sich verbessern, sich verschlechtern, sinken, steigen* radically; **~ schlecht/gut** *etc* extremely badly/well *etc*; **ich habe mich ~ beeilt** I hurried as much as I could

Ext|rem [ɛks'tre:m] NT **-s, -e** extreme; **von einem ~ ins andere fallen** to go from one extreme to the other

Ext|rem|fall M extreme (case)

Ext|re|mist [ɛkstre'mɪst] M **-en, -en**, **Ext|re|mis|tin** [-'mɪstɪn] F **-, -nen** extremist

ext|re|mis|tisch [ɛkstre'mɪstɪʃ] ADJ extremist

Ext|re|mi|tät [ɛkstremi'tɛ:t] F **-, -en** *usu pl* extremity *usu pl*

Ext|rem-: Ext|rem|si|tu|a|ti|on F extreme situation; **Ext|rem|sport** M , **Ext|rem|sport|art** F extreme sport; **Ext|rem|wert** M extreme (value)

ext|ro|ver|tiert [ɛkstrover'ti:rt] ADJ = **extravertiert**

Ex-und-Hopp NT **-**, *no pl (pej)* throwaway mentality

Ex-und-hopp- *in cpds (pej)* throwaway; **~Mentalität** throwaway mentality

ex|zel|lent [ɛkstse'lɛnt] *(geh)* **ADJ** excellent **ADV ~ schmecken** to taste excellent; **~ speisen** to have an excellent meal; **sich ~ fühlen** to feel fantastic

Ex|zel|lenz [ɛkstse'lɛnts] F **-, -en** Excellency

ex|zent|risch [ɛks'tsɛntrɪʃ] ADJ *(Math, fig)* eccentric

Ex|zent|ri|zi|tät [ɛkstsɛntritsi'tɛ:t] F **-, -en** *(Math, Tech, fig)* eccentricity

ex|zer|pie|ren [ɛkstser'pi:rən] ptp **exzerpiert** VT to select *or* extract *(aus* from)

Ex|zerpt [ɛks'tsɛrpt] NT **-(e)s, -e** excerpt

Ex|zess ▲ [ɛks'tsɛs] M **-es, -e a** excess; **bis zum ~** excessively, to excess; **etw bis zum ~ treiben** to take sth to excess *or* extremes; **gesteigerter Hass** excessive hate **b** *usu pl (= Ausschreitung)* excess

ex|zes|siv [ɛkstse'si:f] ADJ excessive

Eye|li|ner ['ailainɐ] M **-s, -** eyeliner

EZB [e:tsɛt'be:] F *abbr von* **Europäische Zentralbank** ECB

E-Zug ['e:-] M *abbr von* **Eilzug**

F

F, f [ɛf] NT **-, -** F, f; **nach Schema F** (*inf*) in the usual way

F *abbr von* **Fahrenheit** *von* **Farad** *von* **Fernschnellzug**

f. *abbr von* **und folgende(r, s)**

fa [faː] INTERJ (*Mus*) fa(h)

Fa. *abbr von* **Firma**

Fa|bel ['faːbl] F **-, -n** **a** fable **b** (*inf*) fantastic story **c** (*Liter.* = *Handlung*) plot

Fa|bel-: Fa|bel|buch NT book of fables; **Fa|bel|dich|ter(in)** M(F) writer of fables, fabulist (*form*)

Fa|be|lei [faːbə'laɪ] F **-, -en** **a** (= *das Fabeln*) romancing **b** (= *Geschichte*) fantastic story

Fa|bel-: Fa|bel|ge|schöpf NT , **Fa|bel|ge|stalt** F mythical creature; **fa|bel|haft** ADJ splendid, magnificent; (*inf:* = *unglaublich groß*) fantastic, fabulous **ADV** splendidly, magnificently; (*inf:* = *sehr, überaus*) fantastically, fabulously

fa|beln ['faːbln] VI to romance **VT** Unsinn to concoct, to fabricate

Fa|bel-: Fa|bel|tier NT mythical creature; **der Fuchs als ~** the fox (as he appears) in fables; **Fa|bel|welt** F world *or* realm of fantasy; **Fa|bel|we|sen** NT mythical creature

Fab|rik [fa'briːk] F **-, -en** factory; (= *Papier-, Baumwollfabrik*) mill; **in die ~ gehen** (*inf*) to work in a factory; **(Preis) ab ~** (price) ex factory *or* works

Fab|rik|an|la|ge F (manufacturing) plant; (= *Fabrikgelände*) factory premises *pl*

Fab|ri|kant [fabri'kant] M **-en, -en**, **Fab|ri|kan|tin** [-'kantɪn] F **-, -nen** **a** (= *Fabrikbesitzer*) industrialist **b** (= *Hersteller*) manufacturer

Fab|rik-: Fab|rik|ar|beit F , *no pl* factory work; **das ist ~** that is factory-made; **Fab|rik|ar|bei|ter(in)** M(F) factory worker

Fab|ri|kat [fabri'kaːt] NT **-(e)s, -e** **a** (= *Marke*) make; (*von Nahrungs- und Genussmitteln*) brand **b** (= *Produkt*) product; (= *Ausführung*) model

Fab|ri|ka|ti|on [fabrika'tsioːn] F **-, -en** manufacture, production

Fab|ri|ka|ti|ons-: Fab|ri|ka|ti|ons|feh|ler M manufacturing fault; **Fab|ri|ka|ti|ons|stät|te** F manufacturing *or* production plant

Fab|rik-: Fab|rik|bau M *pl* **-bauten** factory (building); **Fab|rik|di|rek|tor(in)** M(F) managing director (of a factory); **fab|rik|frisch** ADJ straight from the factory; **Fab|rik|ge|bäu|de** NT factory building; **Fab|rik|ge|län|de** NT factory site; **Fab|rik|hal|le** F factory building

Fab|rik|ler [fa'briːklɐ] M **-s, -**, **Fab|rik|le|rin** [-ərɪn] F **-, -nen** (*Sw*) factory worker

fab|rik-: fab|rik|mä|ßig ADJ **~e Herstellung** mass production; **~er Massenmord** systematic mass murder **ADV** **~ hergestellt** mass-produced; **fab|rik|neu** ADJ straight from the factory; (= *nagelneu*) brand-new **ADV** **~ aussehen** to be in mint condition

Fab|riks- *in cpds* (*Aus*) = **Fabrik-**

Fab|rik-: Fab|riks|schiff NT factory ship; **Fab|rik|ver|kauf** M (= *Laden mit Fabrikware*) factory

shop *or* outlet; **Fab|rik|wa|re** F (*einzelner Artikel*) manufactured article; (*Gesamtheit von Artikeln*) manufactured goods *pl or* articles *pl*

fab|ri|zie|ren [fabri'tsiːrən] *ptp* **fabriziert** VT **a** (*dated*) (= *industriell produzieren*) to manufacture, to produce, to fabricate (*dated*) **b** (*inf*) Möbelstück *etc* to make; *geistiges Produkt* to produce; *Alibi, Lügengeschichte* to concoct, to fabricate **c** (*inf:* = *anstellen*) to get up to (*inf*)

Fa|bu|lant [fabu'lant] M **-en, -en**, **Fa|bu|lan|tin** [-'lantɪn] F **-, -nen** (*geh*) **a** (= *Erzähler*) romancer, storyteller

fa|bu|lie|ren [fabu'liːrən] *ptp* **fabuliert** VI (*geh*) **a** (*pej:* = *schwätzen*) to romance **b** (= *fantasievoll erzählen*) to spin a yarn; **er fabulierte, wie ...** he spun some yarns about how ...

Fa|bu|lie|rer [fabu'liːrɐ] M **-s, -**, **Fa|bu|lie|re|rin** [-ərɪn] F **-, -nen** (*geh*) romancer, storyteller

fa|bu|lös [fabu'løːs] ADJ (*geh*) fabulous (*liter*); (= *unglaubwürdig, hum:* = *großartig*) fantastic

Face|lif|ting ['feːslɪftɪŋ] NT **-s, -s** (*lit, fig*) face-lift

Fa|cet|te [fa'sɛtə] F **-, -n** facet

Fa|cet|ten-: fa|cet|ten|ar|tig ADJ facet(t)ed **ADV** *schleifen* in facets; **Fa|cet|ten|au|ge** NT compound eye; **Fa|cet|ten|schliff** M facet(t)ing; **ein Amethyst mit ~** a facet(t)ed amethyst

fa|cet|tie|ren [fasɛ'tiːrən] *ptp* **facettiert** VT to facet; **facettiert** (*lit, fig*) facet(t)ed

Fach [fax] NT **-(e)s, ⸚er** **a** compartment; (*in Tasche, Brieftasche, Portemonnaie etc auch*) pocket; (*in Schrank, Regal etc*) shelf; (*für Briefe etc*) pigeonhole **b** (= *Wissens-, Sachgebiet*) subject; (= *Gebiet*) field; (= *Handwerk*) trade; **ein Mann vom ~** an expert; **sein ~ verstehen** to know one's stuff (*inf*) *or* one's subject/trade; **das ~ Medizin** *etc* medicine *etc* **c** (*Theat*) mode

-fach [fax] ADJ *suf* (= *-mal*) times; **dreifach** three times; **für die dreifache Summe** for three times the amount → **vierfach** *etc*

Fach-: Fach|abi|tur NT (*Sch*) examination entitling the successful candidate to study at a *Fachhochschule* or certain subjects at a university; **Fach|arbei|ter(in)** M(F) skilled worker; **Fach|arbei|ter|brief** M certificate of proficiency; **Fach|arzt** M , **Fach|ärz|tin** F specialist (*für* in); **fach|ärzt|lich** ADJ *Weiterbildung* specialist *attr*; *Untersuchung, Behandlung* by a specialist; **ein ~es Attest** a certificate from *or* signed by a specialist; **ein ~es Gutachten** a specialist's opinion; **Fach|aus|bil|dung** F specialist training; **Fach|aus|druck** M technical *or* specialist term; **Fach|aus|schuss** ▲ M committee of experts; **Fach|be|griff** M technical *or* specialist term; **Fach|be|ra|ter(in)** M(F) technical consultant; **Fach|be|reich** M **a** (= *Fachgebiet*) (special) field **b** (*Univ*) school, faculty; **fach|be|zo|gen** ADJ specifically related to one's/the subject; (= *fachlich beschränkt*) *Job, Weiterbildung, Kenntnisse* specialized; **Fach|bib|li|o|thek** F specialist library; **Fach|blatt** NT (specialist) journal; **ein medizinisches ~** a medical journal; **Fach|buch** NT reference book; **wasserbautechnische Fachbücher** specialist books on hydraulic engineering; **Fach|buch|hand|lung** F specialist bookshop; **~ für Medi-**

zin/Mathematik *etc* bookshop specializing in medical/mathematical *etc* books; **Fach|buch|ver|lag** M specialist publishing company; **~ für Geografie/Fremdsprachen** *etc* publisher of geography/modern language *etc* books; **Fach|chi|ne|sisch** NT , *no pl* (*inf*) technical jargon *or* mumbo-jumbo (*inf*)

fä|cheln ['fɛçln] (*geh*) VT to fan; *Blätter etc* to stir **VI** to stir

Fä|cher ['fɛçɐ] M **-s, -** fan; (*fig*) range, array

Fä|cher-: fä|cher|ar|tig ADJ fanlike **ADV** like a fan; **Fä|cher|be|sen** M (*Hort*) wire rake; **fä|cher|för|mig** ADJ fan-shaped **ADV** like a fan; **Fä|cher|ge|wöl|be** NT fan vaulting; **ein ~** a fan vault; **Fä|cher|kom|bi|na|ti|on** F (*Sch, Univ*) combination of subjects

fä|chern ['fɛçɐn] VT to fan (out); (*fig*) to diversify; **gefächert** diverse; *Auswahl auch* varied; *Unterricht* diversified **VR** to fan out

Fä|cher|pal|me F fan palm

fä|cher|über|grei|fend ADJ, ADV = **fachübergreifend**

Fä|che|rung F **-, -en** variety, range, diversity

Fach-: Fach|frau F expert; **fach|fremd** ADJ *Mitarbeiter* with no background in the subject; *Leser auch* uninitiated; *Aufgaben etc* unconnected (with the/one's subject); *Methode* foreign to the subject **ADV** → **Fach b** outside one's own subject/field, in another subject/field; **Fach|ge|biet** NT (special) field; **fach|ge|bun|den** ADJ → **Fach b** related (to the field/subject); **Fach|ge|lehr|te(r)** MF *decl as adj* specialist; **fach|ge|mäß**, **fach|ge|recht** ADJ expert; *Ausbildung* specialist *attr* **ADV** expertly; **nicht ~** incompetently, incorrectly; **Fach|ge|schäft** NT specialist shop, specialty store (*US*); **~ für Lederwaren** leather shop *or* store (*esp US*), shop *or* store (*esp US*) specializing in leather goods; **Fach|ge|spräch** NT professional *or* technical discussion; **Fach|grö|ße** F authority; **Fach|grup|pe** F professional group; (*Univ*) study group; (= *Gruppe von Experten*) team of specialists; **Fach|han|del** M specialist shops *pl*, specialty stores *pl* (*US*); **Fach|händ|ler(in)** M(F) specialist supplier; **Fach|hoch|schul|ab|schluss** ▲ M diploma (*from a higher education institution*); **Fach|hoch|schu|le** F higher education institution

FACHHOCHSCHULE

Fachhochschulen, or **FH** for short, are higher education institutions which generally offer relatively focused and practical courses of study. They were set up principally to cover the areas of technology, social and natural sciences, and art.
A **Fachabitur** is the minimum requirement for admission to a **FH**, although many **Fachhochschulen** require students to take an aptitude test as well.
Austria and Switzerland have similar systems.

Fach-: Fach|idi|ot(in) M(F) (*inf*) person who can think of nothing but his/her subject, philosophy/chemistry *etc* freak (*inf*); **Fach|jar|gon** M technical jargon; **Fach|kennt|nis|se**

PL specialized knowledge; **Fach|kol|le|ge** M , **Fach|kol|le|gin** F professional colleague; **Fach|kraft** F qualified employee; **Fach|krei|se** PL in ~n among experts; **fach|kun|dig** ADJ informed; (= erfahren) with a knowledge of the subject; (= fachmännisch) proficient ADV jdn ~ **beraten** to give sb informed advice; ~ **betreut werden** to receive expert service; **fach|kund|lich** [-kʊntlɪç] ADJ **~er Unterricht** teaching of technical subjects; **Fach|leh|rer(in)** M(F) specialist subject teacher; **Fach|lei|ter(in)** M(F) head of department

fach|lich ['faxlɪç] ADJ technical; Ausbildung specialist; Spezialisierung in one aspect of a/the subject; (= beruflich) professional ADV **ein ~ ausgezeichneter Lehrer** a teacher who is academically excellent; ~ **hervorragend sein** to be excellent in one's field; ~ **hochqualifizierte Mitarbeiter** staff members who are highly qualified in their field; **sich ~ qualifizieren** to gain qualifications in one's field; ~ **auf dem Laufenden bleiben** to keep up to date in one's subject; **das ~ zuständige Ressort** the department responsible for such matters

Fach-: Fach|li|te|ra|tur F specialist or technical literature; **Fach|mann** M pl **-leute** or (rare) **-männer** expert; **fach|män|nisch** [-mɛnɪʃ] ADJ expert ADV expertly; ~ **ausgeführt** expertly done; **Fach|ober|schu|le** F College of Further Education; **Fach|per|so|nal** NT specialist staff; **Fach|pres|se** F specialist or technical publications pl; **die medizinische/philologische etc ~** the medical/philological etc publications pl; **Fach|prü|fung** F professional examination; **Fach|re|dak|teur(in)** M(F) (special) editor; ~ **für Sport/Naturwissenschaft etc** sports/science etc editor; **Fach|rich|tung** F subject area; **die ~ Mathematik** mathematics; **Fach|schaft** ['faxʃaft] F -, -en (Univ) students pl of the/a department; **Fach|schu|le** F technical college; **Fach|schul|rei|fe** F entrance qualification for a technical college; **Fach|sim|pe|lei** [faxzɪmpə'laɪ] F -, -en (inf) shoptalk; **fach|sim|peln** ['faxzɪmpl̩n] VI insep (inf) to talk shop; **fach|spe|zi|fisch** ADJ technical, specialist attr ADV **ausbilden** in the field; arbeiten in one's own field; **Fach|spra|che** F technical terminology; **fach|sprach|lich** ADJ technical ADV in technical terminology; **Fach|stu|di|um** NT course of study at a technical college; **Fach|ter|mi|nus** M technical term; **Fach|text** NT specialist text; **fach|über|grei|fend** ADJ Problematik, Lernziel etc inter-disciplinary, which extends across the disciplines ADV across the disciplines; **Fach|ver|band** M (im Handel) trade association; (von Ärzten etc) association; **Fach|ver|mitt|lungs|dienst** M professional placement agency; **Fach|vo|ka|bu|lar** NT technical vocabulary; **Fach|welt** F experts pl; **Fach|werk** NT , no pl half-timbering; **Fach|werk|bau** M a (= Fachwerkhaus) half-timbered building or house b no pl (auch **Fachwerkbauweise**) half-timbering; **Fach|werk|haus** NT half-timbered house; **Fach|wirt(in)** M(F) business administrator; **Fach|wis|sen** NT (specialized) knowledge of the/one's subject; **Fach|wis|sen|schaft|ler(in)** M(F) specialist or expert (in a particular subject); **fach|wis|sen|schaft|lich** ADJ technical; Publikation, Interesse auch specialist attr; **Fach|wort** NT pl **-wörter** specialist or technical term; **Fach|wör|ter|buch** NT specialist dictionary; (wissenschaftliches auch) technical dictionary; **Fach|wort|schatz** M technical or specialized vocabulary; **Fach|zeit|schrift** F specialist journal; (technisch) technical journal; (naturwissenschaftlich) scientific journal; (für Berufe) trade journal

Fa|ckel ['fakl̩] F -, -n (lit, fig) torch; (der Revolution auch, des Glaubens) flame

Fa|ckel|lauf M torch race

fa|ckeln ['fakl̩n] VI (inf) to shillyshally (esp Brit inf); **nicht lange gefackelt!** no shillyshallying! (esp Brit inf); **da wird nicht lange gefackelt** there won't be any shillyshallying (esp Brit inf)

Fa|ckel-: Fa|ckel|schein M torchlight; **im ~** by torchlight; **im ~ sah man ...** you could see by the light of the torches ...; **Fa|ckel|zug** M torchlight procession

Fac|to|ring ['fɛktərɪŋ] NT -s, no pl (Fin) factoring

fad [faːt] ADJ pred a = fade ADJ a, b ADV b (Aus, S Ger) (= zimperlich) soft, wet, soppy (all inf)

Fäd|chen ['fɛːtçən] NT -s, - dim von Faden¹

fa|de ['faːdə] ADJ a Geschmack insipid; Essen auch tasteless b (fig: = langweilig) dull c (Aus, S Ger) = fad b ADV ~ **schmecken** to have not much of a taste

fä|deln ['fɛːdl̩n] VT to thread (auf etw acc onto sth) VR **sich durch etw ~** to thread one's way through sth

Fa|den¹ ['faːdn̩] M -s, ⸚ ['fɛːdn̩] a (lit, fig) thread; (an Marionetten) string; (Med) stitch; **der rote ~** (fig) the leitmotif, the central theme; **den ~ verlieren** (fig) to lose the thread; **alle Fäden laufen hier zusammen** this is the hub of the whole business; **er hält alle Fäden (fest) in der Hand** he holds the reins; **sein Leben hing an einem (dünnen or seidenen) ~** his life was hanging by a thread; **keinen guten ~ an jdm/etw lassen** (inf) to tear sb/sth to shreds (inf) or pieces (inf) b (= Spinnenfaden etc) thread; (= Bohnenfaden) string; **der Klebstoff zieht Fäden** the glue is tacky (Brit) or gummy (US); **der Käse zieht Fäden** the cheese has gone stringy; **die Bohnen haben Fäden** the beans are stringy

Fa|den² M -s, - (Naut) fathom

Fa|den-: fa|den|för|mig ADJ thread-like; **Fa|den|hef|tung** [-hɛftʊŋ] F -, -en (Typ) (thread-)stitching; **Fa|den|kreuz** NT crosshair; **jdn/etw im ~ haben** to have sb/sth in one's sights; **ins ~ (+gen) geraten** to come into the firing line of; **Fa|den|nu|deln** PL vermicelli sing; **fa|den|schei|nig** [-ʃaɪnɪç] ADJ a threadbare b (fig) Argument, Grund flimsy; Moral threadbare no adv; Ausrede transparent; Trost poor; **Fa|den|schlag** M (Sw Sew) basted or tacked seam; **Fa|den|wurm** M threadworm

Fad|heit F -, -en a (von Essen) tastelessness b (fig: = Langeweile) dullness

Fa|ding ['fɛːdɪŋ] NT -(s), no pl (Rad) fading

fa|di|sie|ren [fadi'ziːrən] ptp **fadisiert** VR (Aus) = **langweilen** VR

Fa|gott [fa'gɔt] NT -(e)s, -e bassoon

Fa|gott|blä|ser(in) M(F) , **Fa|got|tist** [fagɔ'tɪst] M -en, -en, **Fa|got|tis|tin** [-'tɪstɪn] F -, -nen bassoonist

Fä|he ['fɛːə] F -, -n (Hunt) (= Füchsin) vixen; (= Dächsin) sow

fä|hig ['fɛːɪç] ADJ a (= tüchtig) Mensch, Mitarbeiter etc capable, competent, able; **sie ist ein ~er Kopf** she has an able mind b pred (= befähigt, bereit) capable (zu, +gen of); (dazu) ~ **sein, etw zu tun** to be capable of doing sth; **bei dem Lärm bin ich keines klaren Gedankens ~** I can't think straight or hear myself think with all this noise; **zu allem ~ sein** to be capable of anything

Fä|hig|keit F -, -en a (= Begabung) ability; (= Tüchtigkeit auch) capability; (= Geschicklichkeit auch) aptitude; (= praktisches Können) skill; **die ~ haben, etw zu tun** to be capable of doing sth; **eine Frau von großen ~en** a woman of great ability; **bei deinen ~en ...** with your talents ...

fahl [faːl] ADJ pale; Mondlicht auch wan (liter)

fahl|gelb ADJ pale yellow

Fahl|heit F -, no pl paleness; (von Mondlicht auch) wanness (liter)

Fähn|chen ['fɛːnçən] NT -s, - a dim von Fahne → **Wind a** b (= Wimpel) pennant c (inf, usu pej) flimsy dress

fahn|den ['faːndn̩] VI (inf) to search (nach for)

Fahn|der ['faːndɐ] M -s, -, **Fahn|de|rin** ['faːndə-rɪn] F -, -nen investigator

Fahn|dung F -, -en search

Fahn|dungs-: Fahn|dungs|ak|ti|on F search; **Fahn|dungs|buch** NT wanted (persons) list; **Fahn|dungs|dienst** M CID (Brit), detective branch; **Fahn|dungs|lis|te** F wanted (persons) list

Fah|ne ['faːnə] F -, -n a flag; (von Verein etc auch) banner; (Mil, von Pfadfinder etc auch) colours pl (Brit), colors pl (US); **die ~ hochhalten** (fig) to keep the flag flying; **die ~ des Glaubens etc hochhalten** (fig geh) to hold aloft the flag or banner of faith etc; **etw auf seine ~ schreiben** (fig) to take up the cause of sth; **mit fliegenden ~n** with beat of drum and flourish of trumpets (liter), with flying colors (US); **mit fliegenden or wehenden ~n untergehen** to go down with all flags flying; **zu den ~n eilen** (old, geh) to join the colours (Brit) or colors (US, old); **jdn zu den ~n rufen** (old, geh) to call sb up for military service); **unter der ~ stehen** (old, geh) der ~ **folgen** (old, geh) to follow the flag (old), to serve with the colours (Brit) or colors (US, old); **unter jds ~n fechten** or **kämpfen** (old, geh) to fight under sb's flag → **Wind a** b (inf) **eine ~ haben** to reek of alcohol; **man konnte seine ~ schon aus drei Meter Entfernung riechen** you could smell the alcohol on his breath ten feet away c (Typ) galley (proof)

Fah|nen-: Fah|nen|ab|zug M (Typ) galley (proof); **Fah|nen|eid** M oath of allegiance; **Fah|nen|flucht** F (Mil, fig) desertion; **fah|nen|flüch|tig** ADJ ~ **sein** (Mil, fig) to be a deserter, to have deserted; ~ **werden** (Mil, fig) to desert; **ein ~er Soldat** a deserter; **Fah|nen|flüch|ti|ge(r)** MF decl as adj (Mil, fig) deserter; **fah|nen|ge|schmückt** [-gəʃmʏkt] ADJ beflagged, decorated with flags; **Fah|nen|jun|ker** M a (Mil: = Offiziersanwärter) officer cadet b (Mil Hist) colour (Brit) or color (US) sergeant; **Fah|nen|mast** M flagpole; **Fah|nen|schmuck** M drapery of flags and bunting; **im ~** decked out with flags and bunting; **Fah|nen|stan|ge** F flagpole; **Fah|nen|trä|ger(in)** M(F) standard-bearer, colour-bearer (Brit), color-bearer (US); **Fah|nen|tuch** NT a pl -tuche (Tex) bunting b pl -tücher (= Fahne) flag; **Fah|nen|wei|he** F consecration of the flag

Fähn|lein ['fɛːnlaɪn] NT -s, - a dim von Fahne b (= kleine Gruppe) troop

Fähn|rich ['fɛːnrɪç] M -s, -e (Hist) standard-bearer; (Mil) sergeant; ~ **zur See** petty officer

Fahr|aus|weis M a (Sw, form) ticket b (Sw) = Führerschein

Fahr|bahn F carriageway (Brit), highway (US), roadway; (= Fahrspur) lane; **„Betreten der ~ verboten"** "pedestrians keep off the road"

Fahr|bahn-: Fahr|bahn|mar|kie|rung F road marking; **Fahr|bahn|ver|en|gung** F lane closures pl; (auf Schildern) "road narrows"; **Fahr|bahn|ver|schmut|zung** F dirt on the road

Fahr-: fahr|bar ADJ a Liege, Ständer etc on casters; Kran, Abschussrampe etc mobile; **~er Untersatz** (hum) wheels pl (hum) b (dated) = **befahrbar**; **Fahr|be|reit** ADJ in running order; **etw ~ machen** to get sth in(to) running order; **Fahr|be|reit|schaft** F a chauffeur-driven carpool; ~ **haben** to be the driver on duty b (eines Fahrzeugs) good running order

Fähr-: Fähr|be|trieb M ferry service; **es herrschte reger ~** there were a lot of ferries running; **Fähr|boot** NT ferry (boat)

Fahr-: Fahr|bü|che|rei F mobile library; **Fahr|damm** M (dial) carriageway (Brit), highway (US), roadway; (= Fahrspur) lane; **Fahr|dienst** M a ~ **haben** to have crew duty b (Rail) rail service

Fähr|dienst ['fɛːɐ-] M ferry service

Fähr|dienst|lei|ter(in) M(F) area manager

Fahr|draht M (Rail etc) overhead contact wire or line

Fäh|re ['fɛːrə] F -, -n ferry

Fahr|ei|gen|schaft F *usu pl* handling characteristic; **die ~en eines Wagens** the handling of a car; **der Wagen hat hervorragende ~en** the car handles excellently

---

fah|ren ['faːrən]
pret **fuhr** [fuːɐ̯], *ptp* **gefahren** [gə'faːrən]

1 INTRANSITIVES VERB	3 REFLEXIVES VERB
2 TRANSITIVES VERB	

1 – INTRANSITIVES VERB

a = sich fortbewegen (*aux sein*) (*Fahrzeug, Fahrgast*) to go; (*Autofahrer*) to drive; (*Zweiradfahrer*) to ride; (*Schiff*) to sail; (*Kran, Kamera, Rolltreppe etc*) to move; **mit dem Auto fahren** to go by car; **mit dem Zug fahren** to go by train *or* rail; **mit dem Rad fahren** to cycle, to go by bike; **mit dem Motorrad/Taxi fahren** to go by motorbike/taxi; **mit dem Bus fahren** to go by bus, to ride the bus (*US*); **mit dem Aufzug fahren** to take the lift, to ride *or* take the elevator (*US*); **ich fuhr mit dem Fahrrad/Auto in die Stadt** I cycled/drove into town, I went into town on my bike/in the car; **möchtest du lieber mit dem Fahrrad oder mit dem Auto fahren?** would you rather go by bike or by car?; **wir sind mit dem Auto gekommen, und meine Frau ist gefahren** we came by car and my wife drove; **wollen wir fahren oder zu Fuß gehen?** shall we go by car or walk?; **links/rechts fahren** to drive on the left/right; **wie lange fährt man von hier nach Basel?** how long does it take to get to Basle from here?; **ich fahre mit dem Auto nach Schweden** I'm taking the car to Sweden, I'm going to Sweden by car; **mein Chor fährt nächstes Jahr wieder nach Schottland** next year my choir is going to Scotland again; **wie fährt man von hier zum Bahnhof?** how do you get to the station from here?; **wie fährt man am schnellsten zum Bahnhof?** what is the quickest way to the station?; **ich fahre lieber in der Stadt** I prefer driving *or* to drive in town; **zweiter Klasse fahren** to travel *or* go second class; **per Anhalter** *or* **Autostopp fahren** to hitch (-hike); **gegen einen Baum fahren** to drive *or* go into a tree; **über den See fahren** to cross the lake; **die Lok fährt elektrisch/mit Dampf** the engine is powered by electricity/is steam-driven; **der Wagen fährt sehr ruhig** the car is very quiet; **gen Himmel fahren** (*liter*) to ascend into heaven; **zur Hölle fahren** (*liter*) to descend into hell; **fahr zur Hölle** *or* **zum Teufel!** (*old*) the devil take you! (*old*) → **fahrend, Grube** *etc*

b = losfahren (*aux sein*) (*Verkehrsmittel, Fahrer, Mitfahrer*) to go, to leave; **wann fährt der nächste Bus nach Bamberg?** when does the next bus to Bamberg go *or* leave?; **wann fährst du morgen nach Glasgow? fährst du früh?** when are you leaving for Glasgow tomorrow? are you leaving early in the morning?; **einen fahren lassen** (*inf*) to let off (*inf*)

c = verkehren (*aux sein*) **es fahren täglich zwei Fähren** there are two ferries a day; **fahren da keine Züge?** don't any trains go there?; **fahren Sie bis Walterplatz?** do you go as far as Walterplatz?; **der Bus fährt alle fünf Minuten** there's a bus every five minutes

d = rasen, schießen (*aux sein*) **es fuhr ihm durch den Kopf, dass ...** the thought flashed through his mind that ...; **was ist (denn) in dich gefahren?** what's got into you?; **in die Kleider fahren** to throw on one's clothes; **ich bin hastig in die Kleider gefahren** I hastily pulled on my clothes; **der Blitz fuhr in die Eiche** the lightning struck the oak; **die Katze fuhr ihm ins Gesicht** the cat leapt *or* sprang at his face; **der Hexenschuss fuhr ihm durch den Rücken** a twinge of lumbago shot up his back

e = zurechtkommen (*aux sein*) **(mit jdm) gut fahren** to get on well (with sb); **mit etw gut fahren** to be OK with sth (*inf*); **mit ihm sind wir gut/schlecht gefahren** we made a good/bad choice when we picked him; **mit diesem teuren Modell fahren Sie immer gut** you'll always be OK

with this expensive model (*inf*); **mit der Billigreise nach Tunesien sind wir schlecht gefahren** the cheap trip to Tunisia turned out badly; **(bei etw) gut/schlecht fahren** to do well/badly (with sth); **du fährst besser, wenn ... you** would do better if ...

f = streichen (*aux sein or haben*) **er fuhr mit der Hand/einem Tuch über den Tisch** he ran his hand/a cloth over the table; **ihre Hand fuhr sanft über sein Haar** she gently ran her hand over his hair; **jdm/sich durchs Haar fahren** to run one's fingers through sb's/one's hair; **sich** (*dat*) **mit der Hand über die Stirn fahren** to pass one's hand over one's brow

g Film (*aux haben*) (= eine Kamerafahrt machen) to track; **die Kamera fuhr auf seine Hand** the camera tracked to his hand

2 – TRANSITIVES VERB

a = lenken (*aux haben*) *Auto, Bus, Zug etc* to drive; *Fahrrad, Motorrad* to ride; **schrottreif** *or* **zu Schrott fahren** (*durch Unfall*) to write off; (*durch Verschleiß*) to drive into the ground

b = benutzen: Straße, Strecke etc (*aux sein*) to take; **welche Strecke fährt die Linie 59?** which way does the number 59 go?; **einen Umweg fahren** to go a long way round, to go out of one's way; **wir sind die Umleitung gefahren** we followed the diversion *or* detour; **ich fahre lieber Autobahn** I prefer (driving on) motorways (*Brit*) *or* freeways (*US*); **diesen steilen Berg musst du im ersten Gang fahren** you have to go up *or* take this steep hill in first gear; **eine so gebirgige Strecke darfst du im Winter nicht ohne Schneeketten fahren** you shouldn't drive such a mountainous route in winter without snow chains → **Eisenbahn, Karussell, Schlitten a**

c = benutzen: Kraftstoff etc (*aux haben*) to use; *Reifen* to drive on

d = befördern (*aux haben*) to take; (= hierher fahren) to bring; *Personen* to drive, to take; **Kinder in die Schule fahren** to take children to school; **jemanden ins Krankenhaus fahren** to take sb to hospital; **die Spedition fährt Fisch von der Nordsee nach Nürnberg** the haulage firm transports *or* takes fish from the North Sea to Nuremberg; **wer hat Sie hierher ins Krankenhaus gefahren?** who brought you to the hospital?; **ich fahre dich nach Hause** I'll take *or* drive you home; **jdn in den Tod fahren** (*geh*) to kill sb

e Geschwindigkeit (*aux sein*) to do; **er fuhr über 80 km/h** he did over 80 km/h, he drove at over 80 km/h; **in der Stadt darf man nur Tempo 50 fahren** in town the speed limit is 50 km/h

f Sport (*aux haben or sein*) *Rennen* to take part in; *Runde etc* to do; *Zeit, Rekord etc* to clock up

g Tech (*aux haben*) (= steuern, betreiben) to run; (= abspielen) *Platten, Tonbandspulen etc* to play; (= senden) to broadcast; (= durchführen) *Überstunden* to do, to work; *Angriff* to launch; **ein Experiment fahren** to run an experiment; **einen Versuch fahren** to run a test; **eine Sonderschicht fahren** to put on an extra shift; **Überstunden fahren** to do overtime; **eine Aufnahme fahren** to do a shot; **einen harten Kurs fahren** (*fig*) to take a hard line

3 – REFLEXIVES VERB

♦ **sich gut fahren** **mit diesem Wagen fährt es sich gut** it's good driving this car; **bei solchem Wetter/auf dieser Straße fährt es sich gut** it's good driving in that kind of weather/on this road; **der neue Wagen fährt sich gut** the new car is nice to drive; **mit dem neuen Belag fährt sich die Straße gut** the road is good to drive on since it's been resurfaced

fah|rend ADJ itinerant; *Musikant auch* travelling (*Brit*), traveling (*US*); *Zug, Auto* in motion; **~es Volk** travelling (*Brit*) *or* traveling (*US*) people; **ein ~er Sänger** a wandering minstrel; **ein unter panamaischer Flagge ~es Schiff** a ship sailing under a Panamanian flag

Fah|ren|heit ['faːrənhait] *no art* Fahrenheit

Fah|ren|heit|ska|la ['faːrənhait-] F , *no pl* Fahrenheit scale

fah|ren las|sen ▲ *ptp* **fahren lassen** *or* (*rare*) **fahren gelassen** VT *irreg* (*lit*) to let go of, to relinquish one's hold on; (*fig*) to abandon → **fahren 1 c**

Fah|rer ['faːrɐ] M **-s, -, Fah|re|rin** [-ərɪn] F **-, -nen a** driver; (= Chauffeur) chauffeur/chauffeuse, driver **b** (*Sport inf*) (= Radfahrer) cyclist; (= Motorradfahrer) motorcyclist

Fah|rer|air|bag M , **Fah|rer-Air|bag** M (*Aut*) driver airbag

Fah|re|rei [faːrə'rai] F **-, -en** driving

Fahrer-: Fah|rer|flucht F hit-and-run driving; **~ begehen** to fail to stop after being involved in an accident, to be a hit-and-run driver; **fah|rer|flüch|tig** ADJ (*form*) hit-and-run *attr*; **~ sein** to have failed to stop after being involved in an accident, to be a hit-and-run driver; **Fah|rer|haus** NT (driver's) cab

Fah|re|rin F → **Fahrer**

fah|re|risch ['faːrərɪʃ] ADJ driving *attr* ADV **er ist mir ~ weit überlegen** he is a far better driver than I am; **eine ~ anspruchsvolle Tour** a tour involving a lot of demanding driving

Fahr|er|laub|nis F (*form*) driving licence (*Brit*), driver's license (*US*)

Fahr|er|sitz M driver's seat

Fahr|gast M passenger

Fahrgast-: Fahr|gast|auf|kom|men NT number *or* volume of passengers; **Fahr|gast|raum** M (*von Auto*) interior; (*Rail etc*) compartment; **Fahr|gast|schiff** NT passenger boat; **Fahr|gast|zel|le** F (*Mot*) passenger cell

Fahr-: Fahr|ge|fühl NT **unser neues Modell vermittelt Ihnen ein völlig neues ~** our new model offers you a completely new driving experience; **Fahr|geld** NT *no pl* fares *pl*; (*für einzelne Fahrt*) fare; **„das ~ bitte passend** *or* **abgezählt bereithalten"** "please tender exact fare" (*form*), "please have the exact fare ready"; **Fahr|ge|le|gen|heit** F transport *no indef art*, means of transport; **Fahr|ge|mein|schaft** F carpool; **Fahr|ge|schwin|dig|keit** F (*form*) speed; **Fahr|ge|stell** NT **a** (*Aut*) chassis **b** (*Aviat*) undercarriage (*esp Brit*), landing gear **c** (*hum inf*) legs *pl*; **ein hohes ~** long legs

Fähr- ['fɛːɐ-]: **Fähr|ha|fen** M ferry terminal; **Fähr|haus** NT ferry house

fah|rig ['faːrɪç] ADJ nervous; (= unkonzentriert) distracted

Fah|rig|keit F **-, no pl** nervousness; (= Unkonzentriertheit) distractedness, distraction

Fahr|kar|te F **a** ticket; (= Zeitfahrkarte, Streckenkarte) season ticket; (*fig*) passport (*nach* to); **mit diesem Sieg hatten sie die ~ zum Endspiel in der Tasche** this victory was their passport to the final **b** (*Schießsport*) miss

Fahrkarten-: Fahr|kar|ten|aus|ga|be F ticket office; **Fahr|kar|ten|au|to|mat** M ticket machine; **Fahr|kar|ten|kon|trol|le** F ticket inspection; **Fahr|kar|ten|kon|trol|leur(in)** M(F) ticket inspector; **Fahr|kar|ten|schal|ter** M ticket office

Fahr-: Fahr|kom|fort M (motoring) comfort; **Fahr|kos|ten** PL travelling (*Brit*) *or* traveling (*US*) expenses *pl*; **Fahr|küns|te** PL driving skills *pl*; **fahr|läs|sig** ADJ negligent (*auch Jur*) → **Körperverletzung, Tötung** ADV negligently; **~ handeln** to be guilty of negligence, to be negligent; **Fahr|läs|sig|keit** F **-, -en** negligence (*auch Jur*); **Fahr|leh|rer(in)** M(F) driving instructor; **Fahr|leis|tung** F road performance

Fähr|mann ['fɛːɐ-] M *pl* **-männer** *or* **-leute** ferryman

Fahr|nis ['faːrnɪs] F **-, -se** (*Jur*) chattels *pl*, moveables *pl*

Fähr|nis ['fɛːɐnɪs] F **-, -se** (*obs*) peril

Fahr|per|so|nal NT drivers and conductors pl; (Rail) footplatemen pl (Brit), railroad crews pl (US); (von Einzelfahrzeug) bus/tram/train crew

Fahr|plan M timetable, schedule (US); (fig) schedule

Fahr|plan-: Fahr|plan|aus|zug M (Rail) timetable, schedule (US, for a particular service); **fahr|plan|mä|ßig** ADJ scheduled attr, pred ADV ~ **verkehren/ankommen** to run/arrive on schedule; **es verlief alles** ~ everything went according to schedule; **Fahr|plan|wech|sel** M (Rail) change in (the) timetable (Brit) or schedule (US)

Fahr-: Fahr|pra|xis F , no pl driving experience no indef art

Fahr|preis M fare

Fahr|preis-: Fahr|preis|an|zei|ger M taxi meter; **Fahr|preis|er|mä|ßi|gung** F fare reduction

Fahr|prü|fung F driving test

Fahr|rad NT bicycle, cycle, bike (inf)

Fahr|rad-: Fahr|rad|an|hän|ger M bicycle trailer; **Fahr|rad|er|go|me|ter** NT bicycle ergometer; **Fahr|rad|fah|rer(in)** M(F) cyclist, bicyclist (form); **Fahr|rad|ge|schäft** NT bicycle or cycle shop, bike shop (inf); **Fahr|rad|händ|ler(in)** M(F) bicycle dealer; **gibt es hier einen ~?** is there a cycle shop around here?; **Fahr|rad|helm** M cycle helmet; **Fahr|rad|ku|rier(in)** M(F) cycle courier; **Fahr|rad|rik|scha** F trishaw, pedicab; **Fahr|rad|stän|der** M (bi)cycle stand; **Fahr|rad|weg** M cycle path, cycleway (esp Brit)

Fahr|rin|ne F (Naut) shipping channel, fairway

Fahr|schein M ticket

Fahr|schein-: Fahr|schein|au|to|mat M ticket machine; **Fahr|schein|block** M pl **-blöcke** or **-blocks** book of tickets; **Fahr|schein|ent|wer|ter** M automatic ticket stamping machine (in bus/trams etc); **Fahr|schein|heft** NT book of tickets

Fähr|schiff ['fɛːɐ-] NT ferry(boat)

Fahr-: Fahr|schu|le F driving school; **Fahr|schü|ler(in)** M(F) a (bei Fahrschule) learner (driver), student (driver) (US) b pupil who has to travel some distance to and from school; **Fahr|schul|leh|rer(in)** M(F) driving instructor; **Fahr|si|cher|heit** F a safe driving or motoring (esp Brit) no art; **erhöhte** ~ safer driving or motoring (esp Brit) b (von Auto) driver safety; (von Skilift, Drahtseilbahn) operational safety; **Fahr|spur** F lane; **Fahr|stil** M style of driving; **Fahr|strei|fen** M lane; **Fahr|stuhl** M lift (Brit), elevator (US); **Fahr|stuhl|schacht** M lift or elevator (US) shaft; **Fahr|stun|de** F driving lesson

Fahrt [faːɐt] F -, **-en a** (= das Fahren) journey; „**während der** ~ **nicht hinauslehnen**" "do not lean out of the window while the train/bus etc is in motion"; **nach zwei Stunden** ~ after travelling (Brit) or traveling (US) for two hours; (mit dem Auto auch) after two hours' drive → **frei 1 a** b (= Fahrgeschwindigkeit) speed; **volle/halbe** ~ **voraus!** (Naut) full/half speed ahead!; **30 Knoten** ~ **machen** to do 30 knots; ~ **aufnehmen** to pick up speed; **jdn in** ~ **bringen** to get sb going; **in** ~ **kommen** or **geraten/sein** to get/have got going **c** (= Reise) journey; **was kostet eine ~/eine einfache** ~ **nach London?** how much is it/is a one-way ticket or a single (Brit) to London?; **gute** ~! bon voyage!, safe journey!; **auf** ~ **gehen** (dated) to take to the road **d** (= Ausflug, Wanderung) trip; **eine** ~ **machen** to go on a trip **e** (Naut) voyage; (= Überfahrt) crossing; **für große/kleine** ~ **zugelassen sein** to be licensed for long/short voyages **f** (Film) tracking shot

fährt ['fɛːɐt] 3. pers sing pres von **fahren**

Fahrt|an|tritt M start of the journey

Fahr-: fahr|taug|lich ADJ fit to drive; Wagen etc roadworthy; **Fahr|taug|lich|keit** F fitness to drive; (von Wagen etc) roadworthiness; **jdm die** ~ **bescheinigen** to certify sb fit to drive

Fahrt|dau|er F time for the journey; **bei einer** ~ **von fünf Stunden** on a five-hour journey; **man muss für diese Strecke mit einer** ~ **von drei Stunden rechnen** you have to allow three hours for this stretch

Fähr|te ['fɛːɐtə] F -, **-n** tracks pl; (= Witterung) scent; (= Spuren) trail; **auf der richtigen/falschen** ~ **sein** (fig) to be on the right/wrong track; **jdn auf die richtige** ~ **bringen** (fig) to put sb on the right track; **jdn auf eine falsche** ~ **locken** (fig) to put sb off the scent; **eine** ~ **verfolgen** (fig) to follow up (on) a lead; **eine falsche** ~ **verfolgen** (fig) to be on the wrong track

Fahr-: Fahr|tech|nik F driving technique; **fahr|tech|nisch** ADJ Können, Fähigkeiten driving attr; **eine gute ~e Ausbildung bekommen** to learn to drive well ADV **eine ~ schwierige Strecke** a difficult stretch of road (to drive); ~ **vollwertige Öko-Autos** environment-friendly cars that drive as well as other cars

Fahr|ten-: Fahr|ten|buch NT **a** (= Kontrollbuch) driver's log **b** (= Wandertagebuch) diary of a trip; **Fahr|ten|mes|ser** NT sheath knife; **Fahr|ten|schrei|ber** M tachograph (Brit), trip recorder; **Fahr|ten|schwim|mer(in)** M(F) person who has passed an advanced swimming test **seinen** ~ **machen** (inf) to do one's advanced swimming test

Fahr|test M road test

Fahrt-: Fahrt|kos|ten PL travelling (Brit) or traveling (US) expenses pl; **Fahrt|rich|tung** F direction of travel; (im Verkehr) direction of the traffic; **entgegen der** ~ (im Zug) with one's back to the engine; (im Bus etc) facing backwards; **in** ~ (im Zug) facing the engine; (im Bus etc) facing the front; **die Züge in** ~ **Norden/Süden** etc the northbound/southbound etc trains; **in** ~ **Norden sind Stauungen zu erwarten** long delays are affecting northbound traffic; **die Autobahn ist in** ~ **Norden gesperrt** the northbound carriageway of the motorway is closed (Brit), the northbound lanes of the freeway are closed (US); **Fahrt|rich|tungs|an|zei|ger** M (Aut) indicator (Brit), turn signal (US); **Fahrt|rou|te** F route; **Fahrt|schrei|ber** M tachograph (Brit), trip recorder

Fahr-: fahr|tüch|tig ADJ fit to drive; Wagen etc roadworthy; **Fahr|tüch|tig|keit** F fitness to drive; (von Wagen etc) roadworthiness

Fahrt-: Fahrt|un|ter|bre|chung F break in the journey, stop; **Fahrt|wind** M airstream

Fahr-: fahr|un|taug|lich ADJ unfit to drive; Wagen etc unroadworthy; **Fahr|un|taug|lich|keit** F unfitness to drive; (von Wagen etc) unroadworthiness

Fähr|ver|bin|dung F (Naut) ferry service

Fahr-: Fahr|ver|bot NT loss of one's licence (Brit) or license (US), driving ban; **jdn mit** ~ **belegen** to ban sb from driving, to take sb's licence (Brit) or license (US) away; ~ **für Privatwagen** ban on private vehicles; **Fahr|ver|hal|ten** NT (von Fahrer) behaviour (Brit) or behavior (US) behind the wheel; (von Wagen) road performance

Fähr|ver|kehr ['fɛːɐ-] M ferry traffic

Fahr-: Fahr|was|ser NT , no pl **a** (Naut) shipping channel, fairway **b** (fig) **in jds** ~ **geraten** to get in with sb; **in ein gefährliches** ~ **geraten** to get onto dangerous ground; **in ein politisches/kommunistisches** ~ **geraten** to get tied up with politics/communism; **in jds** ~ **segeln** or **schwimmen** to follow in sb's wake; **in seinem** or **im richtigen** ~ **sein** to be in one's element; **Fahr|wei|se** F **seine** ~ his driving, the way he drives; **Fahr|werk** NT **a** (Aviat) undercarriage (esp Brit), landing gear **b** (Aut) chassis; **Fahr|wind** M **a** (Naut) wind **b** (= Fahrtwind) airstream; **Fahr|zeit** F = **Fahrtdauer**

Fahr|zeug NT pl **-zeuge** vehicle; (= Luftfahrzeug) aircraft; (= Wasserfahrzeug) vessel

Fahr|zeug-: Fahr|zeug|aus|fall M vehicle breakdown; **Fahr|zeug|aus|stat|tung** F vehicle accessories pl; **Fahr|zeug|brief** M (vehicle) title document, log book (Brit inf); **Fahr|zeug|füh|rer(in)** M(F) (form) driver of a vehicle; **Fahr|zeug|hal|ter(in)** M(F) keeper of the vehicle; **Fahr|zeug|ko|lon|ne** F **a** (= Schlange) queue (Brit) or line of vehicles etc **b** (auch **Fahrzeugkonvoi**) convoy; (bei Staatsbesuchen etc) motorcade; **Fahr|zeug|len|ker(in)** M(F) (form) driver of a vehicle; **Fahr|zeug|pa|pie|re** PL vehicle documents pl; **Fahr|zeug|park** M (form) fleet; **Fahr|zeug|schein** M (vehicle) registration document, car or vehicle license (Brit) or licence (US)

Faib|le ['fɛːbl] NT -s, -s (geh) liking; (= Schwäche auch) weakness; (= Vorliebe auch) penchant

fair [fɛːɐ] ADJ fair (gegen to) ADV fairly; ~ **spie|len** (Sport) to play fairly; (fig) to play fair

Fair|ness ▲ ['fɛːɐnɛs] F -, no pl fairness

Fair|play ▲ ['fɛːɐ 'pleː] NT -, no pl, **Fair Play** ▲ NT -, no pl fair play

fä|kal [fɛˈkaːl] ADJ (geh) faecal (Brit), fecal (US)

Fä|kal|dün|ger M natural manure, dung

Fä|ka|li|en [fɛˈkaːliən] PL faeces pl (Brit), feces pl (US)

Fä|kal|spra|che F scatological language, scatology

Fa|kir ['faːkiːɐ] M -s, -e fakir

Fak|si|mi|le [fakˈziːmilə] NT -s, -s facsimile

Fak|si|mi|le-: Fak|si|mi|le|aus|ga|be F facsimile edition; **Fak|si|mi|le|druck** M **a** pl **-drucke** printed facsimile **b** no pl (= Verfahren) autotype; **Fak|si|mi|le|stem|pel** M signature stamp; **Fak|si|mi|le|un|ter|schrift** F facsimile signature

fak|si|mi|lie|ren [fakzimiˈliːrən] ptp **faksimiliert** VT to make a facsimile of, to reproduce in facsimile, to facsimile

Fakt [fakt] NT or M -(e)s, -en fact; ~ **ist, dass ...** the fact is that ...

Fak|ten pl von **Fakt** von **Faktum**

Fak|ten-: Fak|ten|ma|te|ri|al NT , no pl facts pl; **Fak|ten|samm|lung** F collection of facts; **Fak|ten|wis|sen** NT factual knowledge

fak|tisch ['faktɪʃ] ADJ attr actual, real ADV **a** in actual fact, actually **b** (esp Aus inf: = praktisch) more or less

fak|ti|tiv [faktiˈtiːf, 'faktitiːf] ADJ (Gram) factitive

Fak|ti|tiv ['faktitiːf] NT -s, -e [-və], **Fak|ti|ti|vum** [faktiˈtiːvʊm] NT -s, **Faktitiva** [-va] (Gram) factitive verb

Fak|ti|zi|tät [faktitsiˈtɛːt] F -, -en (geh) factuality

Fak|tor ['faktoːɐ] M -s, **Faktoren** [-ˈtoːrən] factor (auch Math)

Fak|to|rei [faktoˈrai] F -, -en (Comm) trading post

Fak|to|ren|ana|ly|se F factor analysis

Fak|to|tum [fakˈtoːtʊm] NT -s, -s or **Faktoten** [-ˈtoːtn] factotum

Fak|tum ['faktʊm] NT -s, **Fakten** ['faktn] fact

Fak|tur [fakˈtuːɐ] F -, -en **a** (dated) invoice **b** (Mus) structure

Fak|tu|ra [fakˈtuːra] F -, **Fakturen** [-rən] (Aus, dated) invoice

fak|tu|rie|ren [faktuˈriːrən] ptp **fakturiert** VT (Comm) to invoice

Fak|tu|rist [faktuˈrɪst] M -en, -en, **Fak|tu|ris|tin** [-ˈrɪstɪn] F -, -nen **a** (Comm) book-keeper **b** (Aus: = Rechnungsprüfer) invoice clerk

Fa|kul|tas [faˈkʊltas] F -, **Fakultäten** [-ˈtɛːtn] **die** ~ **für ein Fach haben** to be qualified to teach a subject

Fa|kul|tät [fakʊlˈtɛːt] F -, -en **a** (Univ: = Fachbereich) faculty; (**ein Kollege**) **von der anderen** ~ **sein** (hum inf) (= homosexuell sein) to be one of them (*Brit dated inf*), to be the other way round (*Brit dated inf*), to be queerer than a three dollar bill (*US inf*); (*rare*: = *eine andere Weltanschauung haben*) to be of another school of thought **b** (*obs*: = *Begabung*) faculty **c** (*Math*) factorial

fa|kul|ta|tiv [fakʊlta'tiːf] ADJ (*geh*) optional

Fa|lan|ge [fa'laŋɡə] F -, *no pl* (*Pol*) Falange

Fa|lan|gist [falaŋ'ɡɪst] M **-en, -en, Fa|lan|gis|tin** F **-, -nen** (*Pol*) Falangist

falb [falp] ADJ (*geh*) Pferd dun

Fal|be ['falbə] M **-n, -n** dun

Fal|ke ['falkə] M **-n, -n** falcon; (*fig*) hawk

Fal|ken-: Fal|ken|au|ge NT (*Miner*) hawk's--eye; **Fal|ken|bei|ze** F , **Fal|ken|jagd** F falconry

Falk|land- ['falklant-, 'fɔːklɛnt-]: **Falk|land|in|seln** PL Falkland Islands *pl*; **Falk|land|krieg** M Falklands War

Falk|ner ['falknɐ] M **-s, -, Falk|ne|rin** [-ərɪn] F **-, -nen** falconer

Falk|ne|rei [falknə'raɪ] F **-, -en a** falconry **b** (= *Anlage*) falcon house

Fall¹ [fal] M **-(e)s, ≈ e** ['fɛlə] **a** (= *das Hinunterfallen*) fall; **im/beim ~ hat er ...** when/as he fell he ... → **frei 1 a**
b (= *das Zufallkommen*) fall; (*fig*) (*von Menschen, Regierung*) downfall; (*von Plänen, Gesetz etc*) failure; **zu ~ kommen** (*lit geh*) to fall; **über die Affäre ist er zu ~ gekommen** (*fig*) the affair was or caused his downfall; **zu ~ bringen** (*lit geh*) to make fall, to trip up; (*fig*) *Menschen* to cause the downfall of; *Regierung* to bring down; *Gesetz, Plan etc* to thwart; *Tabu* to break down **c** (*fig*: = *Untergang, Sturz*) fall **d** (*von Kurs, Temperatur*) drop, fall (+*gen* in) **e** (*von Gardine etc*) hang, drape

Fall² ⊗ 29, 34.3, 36, 37.4, 39.1, 40.2, 40.3 M **-(e)s, ≈ e** ['fɛlə] **a** (= *Umstand*) **gesetzt den ~** assuming or supposing (that); **für den ~, dass ich ... in case I ...; für den ~ meines Todes, im ~e meines Todes** in case I die; **für alle Fälle** just in case; **in jedem ~(e)** always; **in keinem ~(e)** never; **auf jeden ~** at any rate, at all events; **auf keinen ~** on no account; **auf alle Fälle** in any case, anyway; **für solche Fälle** for such occasions; **im äußersten ~(e)** if the worst comes to the worst; **im anderen ~(e)** if, if that is not the case; **im günstigsten/schlimmsten ~(e)** at best/worst; **im ~e eines ~es** if it comes to it; **wenn dieser ~ eintritt** if this should be the case, if this should arise **b** (= *gegebener Sachverhalt*) case; **in diesem ~** in this case or instance; **ein ~ von ...** a case or an instance of ...; **von ~ zu ~** from case to case, from one case to the next; (*hin und wieder*) periodically; **in diesem ~(e) will ich noch einmal von einer Bestrafung absehen, aber ...** I won't punish you on this occasion, but ...; **jds ~ sein** (*inf*) to be sb's cup of tea (*inf*); **klarer ~!** (*inf*) sure thing! (*esp US inf*), you bet! (*inf*) **c** (*Jur, Med*: = *Beispiel, Person*) case; **ein hoffnungsloser ~** a hopeless case **d** (*Gram*: = *Kasus*) case; **der erste/zweite/dritte/vierte ~** the nominative/genitive/dative/accusative case; **der fünfte ~** (= *Ablativ*) the ablative case; (= *Instrumental*) the instrumental case; **der sechste ~** (= *Vokativ*) the vocative case; (= *Präpositiv*) the prepositional case

Fall³ NT **-(e)s, -en** (*Naut*) halyard

fäll|bar ADJ (*Chem*) precipitable

Fall-: Fall|beil NT guillotine; **Fall|bei|spiel** NT case study; **Fall|be|richt** M case report; **Fall|be|schleu|ni|gung** F gravitational acceleration, acceleration due to gravity; **Fall|bö(e)** F down gust; **Fall|brü|cke** F drawbridge; (= *Enterbrücke*) gangplank

Fal|le ['falə] F **-, -n a** (*lit, fig*) trap; **~n legen** or **stellen** to set traps; **in eine ~ geraten** or **gehen** (*lit*) to get caught in a trap; (*fig*) to fall into a trap; **jdm in die ~ gehen, in jds ~ geraten** to walk or fall into sb's trap; **in der ~ sitzen** to be

trapped; **jdn in eine ~ locken** (*fig*) to trick sb; **jdm eine ~ stellen** (*fig*) to set a trap for sb **b** (*Tech*) catch, latch **c** (*inf*: = *Bett*) bed; **in der ~ sein** or **liegen** to be in bed; **sich in die ~ hauen, in die ~ gehen** to hit the hay (*inf*), to turn in; **ab (mit euch) in die ~!** off to bed!

fal|len ['falən] *pret* **fiel** [fiːl], *ptp* **gefallen** [ɡə'falən] VI *aux sein* **a** (= *hinabfallen, umfallen*) to fall; (*Gegenstand, Wassermassen*) to drop; (*Theat: Vorhang*) to fall, to come down; (*Klappe*) to come down, to drop; **etw ~ lassen** to drop sth; **über etw** (*acc*) **~** to trip over sth; **sich ~ lassen** to drop; to give up; **durch eine Prüfung etc ~** to fail an exam *etc*; **ein gefallener Engel** a fallen angel; **ein gefallenes Mädchen** (*dated*) a fallen woman (*dated*) → *auch* **Groschen b, Nase a**
b (= *hängen*: *Vorhang, Kleid etc*) to hang; (= *reichen*) to come down (*bis auf* +*acc* to); **die Haare ~ ihr bis auf die Schultern/über die Augen/ins Gesicht/in die Stirn** her hair comes down to or reaches her shoulders/falls into her eyes/face/onto her forehead
c (= *abfallen, sinken*) to drop; (*Wasserstand, Preise, Fieber auch, Thermometer*) to go down; (*Fluss, Kurse, Wert, Aktien auch, Barometer*) to fall; (*Nachfrage, Ansehen*) to fall off, to decrease; **im Preis/Wert ~** to go down or drop or fall in price/value; **im Kurs ~** to go down, to drop
d (= *im Krieg ums Leben kommen*) to fall, to be killed; **gefallen** killed in action; **er ist gefallen** he was killed in action; **mein Mann ist (im Krieg) gefallen** my husband was killed in the war
e (= *erobert werden*: *Festung, Stadt etc*) to fall
f (*fig*) (*Gesetz, Passus etc*) to be dropped; (*Tabu, Brauch etc*) to disappear
g (*mit schneller Bewegung*) **jdm ins Lenkrad ~** to grab the steering wheel from sb; **einem Pferd in die Zügel ~** to grab a horse's reins; **die Tür fällt ins Schloss** the door clicks shut; **die Tür ins Schloss ~ lassen** to let the door shut; **der Löwe fiel dem Gnu in die Flanke** the lion pounced on (the flank of) the gnu → **Hals ¹ a, Wort c**
h (= *treffen*: *Wahl, Verdacht*) to fall, to light (*form*) (*auf* +*acc* (up)on); **das Licht fällt durch die Luke** the light comes in through the skylight; **das Los, das zu tun, fiel auf ihn** it fell to his lot to do that
i (= *stattfinden, sich ereignen*: *Weihnachten, Datum etc*) to fall (*auf* +*acc* on); (= *gehören*) to come (*unter* +*acc* under, *in* +*acc* within, under); **in eine Zeit ~** to belong to an era; **unter einen Begriff ~** to be part of a concept; **aus einer Gruppe/Kategorie etc ~** to come outside a group/category *etc*, to be excluded from a group/category *etc*
j (= *zufallen*: *Erbschaft etc*) to go (*an* +*acc* to); **das Elsass fiel an Frankreich** Alsace fell to France; (*nach Verhandlungen*) Alsace went to France
k (= *gemacht, erzielt werden*) (*Entscheidung*) to be made; (*Urteil*) to be passed or pronounced; (*Schuss*) to be fired; (*Sport: Tor*) to be scored
l (*Wort*) to be uttered or spoken; (*Name*) to be mentioned; (*Bemerkung*) to be made
m (= *geraten*) **in Schlaf ~** to fall asleep; **in eine andere Tonart ~** to speak in or (*absichtlich*) adopt a different tone (of voice); **in eine andere Sprache ~** to lapse or drop into another language; **in eine andere Gangart ~** to change one's pace → **Opfer b, Rahmen b, Rolle e**
n (= *sein*) **das fällt ihm leicht/schwer** he finds that easy/difficult → **Last b, lästig**

fäl|len ['fɛlən] VT **a** (= *umschlagen*) to fell **b** (*fig*) *Entscheidung* to make, to come to; *Urteil* to pass, to pronounce **c** (= *zum Angriff senken*) *Lanze* to lower, to level; **mit gefälltem Bajonett** with bayonet(s) at the ready **d** (*Chem*) to precipitate **e** (*Math*) **das Lot ~** to drop a perpendicular

fal|len las|sen ▲ *ptp* **fallen lassen** or (*rare*) **fal-len gelassen** VT *irreg* **a** (= *aufgeben*) *Plan, Mitarbeiter* to drop **b** (= *äußern*) *Bemerkung* to let

drop; **hat er irgend etwas darüber ~?** (*inf*) has he let anything drop about it?

Fal|len|stel|ler [-ʃtɛlɐ] M **-s, -, Fal|len|stel|le|rin** [-ərɪn] F **-, -nen** (*Hunt*) trapper

Fall-: Fall|gat|ter NT portcullis; **Fall|ge|schwin|dig|keit** F (*Phys*) speed of fall; **Fall|ge|setz** NT (*Phys*) law of falling bodies; **Fall|git|ter** NT portcullis; **Fall|gru|be** F (*Hunt*) pit; (*fig rare*) pitfall; **Fall|ham|mer** M pile-driver; **Fall|hö|he** F (*Phys*) (height or depth of) drop; (*beim Wasserkraftwerk*) head

fall|lie|ren [fa'liːrən] *ptp* **falliert** VI (*Fin*) to fail, to go bankrupt

fäl|lig ['fɛlɪç] ADJ due *pred*; (*Fin*) *Rechnung, Betrag etc auch* payable; *Wechsel* mature(d); **längst ~** long overdue; **die ~en Zinsen** the interest due; **~ werden** to become or fall due; (*Wechsel*) to mature; **am Wochenende ist endlich Rasenmähen ~** the lawn is about due for a cut at the weekend; **am Wochenende ist eine Party ~** a party is about due at the weekend; **der Kerl ist ~** (*inf*) he's for it (*inf*)

Fäl|lig|keit F **-, -en** (*Fin*) settlement date; (*von Wechseln*) maturity; **zahlbar bei ~** payable by settlement date; payable at or on maturity

Fäl|lig|keits|tag M , **Fäl|lig|keits|ter|min** M settlement date; (*von Wechsel*) date of maturity

Fall|obst ['falʔoːpst] NT windfalls *pl*; **ein Stück ~** a windfall

Fall-out ▲ ['fɔːlʔaut] M **-s, -s, Fall|out** M **-s, -s** fallout

Fall-: Fall|reep NT (*Naut*) rope ladder; (= *Treppe*) gangway; **Fall|rohr** NT drainpipe, downpipe (*form*); **Fall|rück|zie|her** M (*Ftbl*) overhead kick, bicycle kick

falls [fals] CONJ (= *wenn*) if; (= *für den Fall, dass*) in case; **~ möglich** if possible; **~ du Lust hast** if you (happen to) want to, if you should (happen to) want to; **gib mir deine Telefonnummer, ~ ich mich verspäten sollte** give me your phone number in case I'm late; **~ ich mich verspäten sollte, rufe ich vorher an** if I'm late or in the event of my being late (*form*) I'll phone you first

Fall|schirm M parachute; **mit dem ~ abspringen** to parachute, to make a parachute jump; **mit dem ~ über Frankreich abspringen** to parachute out over France; (*in Kriegszeit*) to parachute into France; **etw mit dem ~ abwerfen** to drop sth by parachute

Fall|schirm-: Fall|schirm|ab|sprung M parachute jump; **Fall|schirm|jä|ger(in)** M(F) (*Mil*) paratrooper; **die ~** (= *Einheit*) the paratroop(er)s; **Fall|schirm|sprin|gen** NT parachuting; **Fall|schirm|sprin|ger(in)** M(F) parachutist; **Fall|schirm|trup|pe** F (*Mil*) paratroop(er)s *pl*

Fall-: Fall|strick M (*fig*) trap, snare; **jdm ~e** or **einen ~ legen** to set a trap or snare for sb (to walk into); **Fall|stu|die** F case study; **Fall|sucht** F , *no pl* (*old*) falling sickness (*old*); **fall|süch|tig** ADJ (*old*) epileptic; **Fall|süch|ti|ge(r)** MF *decl as adj* (*old*) epileptic

fällt [fɛlt] 3. *pers sing pres von* **fallen**

Fall|tür F trapdoor

Fäl|lung ['fɛlʊŋ] F **-, -en a** (*von Bäumen etc*) felling **b** (*Jur*: *eines Urteils*) pronouncement; (*einer Entscheidung*) reaching **c** (*Chem*) precipitation

Fäl|lungs|mit|tel NT (*Chem*) precipitant

Fall-: fall|wei|se ADV **a** from case to case **b** (*esp Aus*: = *gelegentlich*) now and again, occasionally **ADJ** case-by-case *attr*; **Fall|wind** M katabatic (*form*) or fall wind; **Fall|wurf** M (*Sport*) diving throw

falsch [falʃ] **ADJ a** (= *verkehrt, fehlerhaft*) wrong; (*in der Logik etc*) false; **richtig oder ~** right or wrong; **wahr oder ~** true or false; **wie mans macht, ist es ~** (*inf*) whatever I/you *etc* do it's bound to be wrong; **mach dir keine ~en Vorstellungen darüber/davon** don't get the wrong idea (*inf*) or any misconceptions about it; **du**

machst dir völlig ~e Vorstellungen you have or you've got quite the wrong idea or some misconceptions; **~es Bewusstsein** (*Philos, Sociol*) false consciousness; **~er Alarm** (*lit, fig*) false alarm; **Sie sind hier ~** you're in the wrong place; **bei jdm an den Falschen geraten** or **kommen** to pick the wrong person in sb; **am ~en Ort** or **Platz sein** to have come to the wrong place; **im ~en Film sein** (*sl*) to be on another planet (*inf*) → **Licht, Pferd**

b (= *unecht, nachgemacht*) *Zähne etc* false; *Perlen auch* fake; *Würfel* loaded; (= *gefälscht*) *Pass etc* forged, fake; *Geld* counterfeit; (= *betrügerisch*) bogus, fake; **~er Zopf** hairpiece, switch

c (= *unaufrichtig, unangebracht*) *Gefühl, Freund, Scham, Pathos etc* false; **ein ~er Hund** (*inf*) **eine ~e Schlange** (*inf*) a snake-in-the-grass; **ein ~es Spiel (mit jdm) treiben** to play (sb) false, to play an underhand game (with sb); **unter ~er Flagge segeln** (*lit, fig*) to sail under false colours (*Brit*) or colors (*US*) → **Bescheidenheit**

d (*dial*: = *tückisch*) nasty

ADV a (= *nicht richtig*) wrongly, incorrectly; **alles ~ machen** to do everything wrong; **etw ~ verstehen** to misunderstand sth, to get sth wrong (*inf*); **jdn/etw ganz ~ verstehen** to completely misunderstand sb/sth; **~ verstandene Freundschaft** misinterpreted friendship; **etw ~ schreiben/aussprechen** to spell/pronounce sth wrongly or incorrectly, to misspell/mispronounce sth; **jdn ~ informieren** to misinform sb; **die Uhr geht ~** the clock is wrong; **Kinder ~ erziehen** to bring children up badly; **~ spielen** (*Mus*) to play the wrong note/notes; (= *unrein*) to play off key, to play out of tune; (*Cards*) to cheat; **~ singen** to sing out of tune, to sing off key; **~ liegen** (*inf*) to be wrong (*bei, in +dat* about, *mit* in); **~ verbunden sein** to have the wrong number

b (= *unaufrichtig*) falsely, insincerely; **~ lachen** to give a false laugh

Falsch [falʃ] M (*old*) **ohne ~ sein** to be without guile or artifice

Falsch|aus|sa|ge F (*Jur*) (*uneidliche*) **~** false statement, false evidence

Falsch|eid M (*Jur*) (*unintentional*) false statement or oath

fäl|schen ['fɛlʃn] VT to forge, to fake; *Geld, Briefmarken auch* to counterfeit; (*Comm*) *Bücher* to falsify; *Geschichte, Tatsachen* to falsify → *auch* **gefälscht**

Fäl|scher ['fɛlʃɐ] M **-s, -**, **Fäl|sche|rin** [-ərɪn] F **-, -nen** forger; (*von Geld, Briefmarken auch*) counterfeiter

Falsch-: Falsch|fah|rer(in) M(F) ghost-driver (*esp US inf*), person driving the wrong way on the motorway; **Falsch|geld** NT counterfeit or forged money; **falsch|gläu|big** ADJ (*old Rel*) heterodox; **Falsch|heit** F **-, no pl** falsity, falseness; (*von Menschen*) nastiness

fälsch|lich ['fɛlʃlɪç] ADJ false; *Behauptung auch* erroneous; *Annahme, Glaube auch* mistaken, erroneous **ADV** wrongly, falsely; *behaupten, annehmen, glauben auch* mistakenly, erroneously; (*versehentlich*) by mistake

fälsch|li|cher|wei|se ['fɛlʃlɪçɐ'vaizə] ADV wrongly, falsely; *behaupten, annehmen, glauben auch* mistakenly, erroneously

Falsch-: Falsch|mel|dung F (*Press*) false report; **Falsch|mün|zer** [-mʏntsɐ] M **-s, -**, **Falsch|mün|ze|rin** [-ərɪn] F **-, -nen** forger, counterfeiter; **Falsch|mün|ze|rei** [-mʏntsə'rai] F **-, -en** forgery, counterfeiting; **Falsch|par|ken** [-parkn] NT **-s, no pl** illegal parking; **Falsch|par|ker** [-parkɐ] M **-s, -**, **Falsch|par|ke|rin** [-ərɪn] M **-, -nen** parking offender; **falsch spie|len** ▲ VI (*Cards*) to cheat; **Falsch|spie|ler(in)** M(F) (*Cards*) cheat; (*professionell*) cardsharp(er)

Fäl|schung ['fɛlʃʊŋ] F **-, -en a no pl** (= *das Fälschen*) forgery, forging, faking; (*von Geld, Briefmarken*) counterfeiting, forgery **b** (= *gefälschter Gegenstand*) forgery, fake

fäl|schungs|si|cher ADJ forgery-proof; *Fahrtenschreiber* tamper-proof

Fäl|schungs|si|cher|heit F forgery-proof nature; (*von Fahrtenschreiber*) tamper-proof nature

Fal|sett [fal'zɛt] NT **-(e)s, -e** falsetto; **~ singen, mit ~stimme singen** to sing falsetto

Fal|si|fi|kat [falzifi'ka:t] NT **-(e)s, -e** forgery, fake

Fal|si|fi|ka|ti|on [falzifika'tsio:n] F **-, -en** falsification

fal|si|fi|zie|ren [falzifi'tsi:rən] ptp **falsifiziert** VT to falsify

Falt-: falt|bar ADJ foldable; (= *zusammenklappbar*) collapsible; *Stuhl, Tisch, Fahrrad* folding attr, collapsible; **Falt|blatt** NT leaflet; (*in Zeitschrift etc auch*) insert; **Falt|boot** NT collapsible boat

Fält|chen ['fɛltçən] NT **-s, -** *dim von* **Falte**

Fal|te ['faltə] F **-, -n a** (*in Stoff, Papier*) fold; (= *Knitterfalte, Bügelfalte*) crease; **in ~n legen** to fold; **~n schlagen** to get creased, to crease; **~n werfen** to fall in folds, to drape **b** (*in Haut*) wrinkle; **strenge ~n** harsh lines; **die Stirn in ~n ziehen** or **legen** to knit or furrow one's brow **c** (*Geol*) fold

fäl|teln ['fɛltln] VT to pleat

fal|ten ['faltn] **VT** to fold; **die Stirn ~** to knit one's brow **VR** to fold

Falten-: fal|ten|frei ADJ = **faltenlos**; **Fal|ten|ge|bir|ge** NT fold mountains pl; **fal|ten|los** ADJ *Gesicht* unlined; *Haut auch* smooth; *Stoff* uncreased; *Rock* unpleated; **fal|ten|reich** ADJ *Haut* wrinkled; *Gesicht auch* lined; *Kleid, Mantel* tightly pleated; **Fal|ten|rock** M pleated skirt; **Fal|ten|wurf** M fall of the folds

Fal|ter ['faltɐ] M **-s, -** (= *Tagfalter*) butterfly; (= *Nachtfalter*) moth

fal|tig ['faltɪç] ADJ (= *zerknittert*) creased; (= *in Falten gelegt*) hanging in folds; *Gesicht, Stirn, Haut* wrinkled **ADV ~ fallen** to hang in folds; **~ gerafft sein** to be gathered into folds

Falt-: Falt|ka|len|der M fold-out planner; **Falt|kar|te** F folding or fold-up map; **Falt|kar|ton** M collapsible box; **Falt|kin|der|wa|gen** M collapsible pram (*Brit*), collapsible baby carriage (*US*); (= *Sportwagen*) baby buggy (*Brit*), stroller (*US*); **Falt|pla|ner** M fold-out planner; **Falt|pros|pekt** M leaflet; **Falt|schach|tel** F collapsible box; **Falt|tür** F folding door

Falz [falts] M **-es, -e** (= *Kniff, Faltlinie*) fold; (*zwischen Buchrücken und -deckel*) joint; (*Tech*) rabbet; (*zwischen Blechrändern*) join, lock seam (*spec*); (= *Briefmarkenfalz*) hinge

fal|zen ['faltsn] VT *Papierbogen* to fold; *Holz* to rabbet; *Blechränder* to join with a lock seam

Fam. *abbr von* **Familie**

fa|mi|li|är [fami'liɛːɐ] ADJ **a** family attr (= *zwanglos*) informal; (= *freundschaftlich*) close; (*pej*: = *plump-vertraulich*) familiar; **ein ~er Ausdruck** a colloquialism **ADV mit jdm ~ verkehren** to be on close terms with sb; **da geht es so ~ zu** it's so informal there

Fa|mi|li|a|ri|tät [familiari'tɛːt] F **-, -en** (= *Zwanglosigkeit*) informality; (= *Freundschaftlichkeit*) closeness; (*pej*: = *plumpe Vertraulichkeit*) familiarity

Fa|mi|lie [fa'mi:liə] F **-, -n** family; **~ Müller** the Müller family; **~ Otto Francke** (*als Anschrift*) Mr & Mrs Otto Francke and family; **eine ~ gründen** to start a family; **~ haben** (*inf*) to have a family; **aus guter ~ sein** to come from a good family; **es liegt in der ~** it runs in the family; **zur ~ gehören** to be one of the family; **es bleibt in der ~** it'll stay in the family → **beste(r, s) ADJ a**

Familien- *in cpds* family; **Fa|mi|li|en|ähn|lich|keit** F family resemblance; **Fa|mi|li|en|an|ge|hö|ri|ge(r)** MF *decl as adj* family member, relative; **Fa|mi|li|en|an|schluss** ▲ M Unterkunft/Stellung mit **~** accommodation/job where one is treated as part of the family; **~**

suchen to wish to be treated as one of the family; **Fa|mi|li|en|an|zei|gen** PL personal announcements pl; **Fa|mi|li|en|aus|weis** M family pass; **Fa|mi|li|en|be|ra|tungs|stel|le** F family planning office; **Fa|mi|li|en|be|sitz** M family property; **in ~ sein** to be owned by the family; **Fa|mi|li|en|be|trieb** M family concern or business; **Fa|mi|li|en|buch** NT *book of family events with some legal documents*; **Fa|mi|li|en|feier** F , **Fa|mi|li|en|fest** NT family party; **Fa|mi|li|en|for|schung** F genealogy; **Fa|mi|li|en|fo|to** NT family photo, family photo; **fa|mi|li|en|freund|lich** ADJ *Politik* pro-family attr, favourable (*Brit*) or favorable (*US*) to families pred; *Hotel etc* family attr, that welcomes families pred; **Fa|mi|li|en|glück** NT happy family life; **Fa|mi|li|en|grab** NT family grave; **Fa|mi|li|en|gruft** F family vault; **Fa|mi|li|en|klün|gel** M (*inf*) *der ganze* ~ the whole tribe (*inf*); **Fa|mi|li|en|kreis** M family circle; **die Trauung fand im engsten ~ statt** only the immediate family were present at the wedding; **Fa|mi|li|en|le|ben** NT family life; **Fa|mi|li|en|mit|glied** NT member of the family; **Fa|mi|li|en|nach|rich|ten** PL births, marriages and deaths, personal announcements pl; **Fa|mi|li|en|na|me** M surname, family name (*US*); **Fa|mi|li|en|ober|haupt** NT head of the family; **Fa|mi|li|en|pa|ckung** F family(-size) pack; **Fa|mi|li|en|pass** ▲ M family passport; **Fa|mi|li|en|pla|nung** F family planning; **Fa|mi|li|en|rat** M family council; **Fa|mi|li|en|recht** NT family law; **Fa|mi|li|en|ro|man** M (family) saga; **Fa|mi|li|en|schmuck** M family jewels pl; **Fa|mi|li|en|se|rie** F (*TV*) family series; **Fa|mi|li|en|sinn** M sense of family; **Fa|mi|li|en|stand** M marital status; **Fa|mi|li|en|tref|fen** NT family gathering or get-together, family affair (*inf, iro*); (= *Wiedersehen*) family reunion; **Fa|mi|li|en|un|ter|halt** M family upkeep or maintenance; **den ~ verdienen** to support the family; **Fa|mi|li|en|va|ter** M father (of a family); **Fa|mi|li|en|ver|hält|nis|se** PL family circumstances pl or background sing; **aus was für ~ kommt sie?** what is her family background?, what kind of family does she come from?; **Fa|mi|li|en|vor|stand** M (*form*) head of the family; **Fa|mi|li|en|wap|pen** NT family arms pl; **Fa|mi|li|en|zu|la|ge** F dependants' allowance (*in unemployment benefit*); **Fa|mi|li|en|zu|sam|men|füh|rung** F (*Pol*) principle of allowing families to be united; **Fa|mi|li|en|zu|wachs** M addition to the family

fa|mos [fa'mo:s] ADJ (*dated inf*) capital (*dated inf*), splendid

Fa|mu|la F **-, Famulä** → **Famulus**

Fa|mu|la|tur [famula'tuːɐ] F **-, -en** *period when a medical student does practical work in a hospital*, clinical practice

fa|mu|lie|ren [famu'li:rən] ptp **famuliert** VI (*Med*) to do some practical work

Fa|mu|lus ['fa:mulʊs] M **-, Famuli** [-li], **Fa|mu|la** ['fa:mula] F **-, Famulä** [-lɛ] **a** (*Med*) *student doing practical work* **b** (*old*) professor's assistant, student

Fan [fɛn] M **-s, -s** fan; (*Ftbl auch*) supporter

Fa|nal [fa'na:l] NT **-s, -e** (*liter*) signal (+gen for)

Fa|na|ti|ker [fa'na:tikɐ] M **-s, -**, **Fa|na|ti|ke|rin** [-ərɪn] F **-, -nen** fanatic

-fa|na|ti|ker(in) M(F) *suf in cpds* fanatic; **ein Fitnessfanatiker** a fitness fanatic or freak (*inf*)

fa|na|tisch [fa'na:tɪʃ] ADJ fanatical **ADV** fanatically

fa|na|ti|siert [fanati'zi:ɐt] ADJ (*geh*) rabid

Fa|na|tis|mus [fana'tɪsmʊs] M **-, no pl** fanaticism

Fan|club ['fɛnklʊp] M → **Fanklub**

fand *pret von* **finden**

Fan|fa|re [fan'fa:rə] F **-, -n a** (*Mus*) fanfare **b** (*Aut*) horn

Fan|fa|ren-: Fan|fa|ren|stoß M flourish (of trumpets), fanfare; **Fan|fa|ren|zug** M trumpeters *pl*

Fang [faŋ] M -(e)s, ⸚ e [ˈfɛŋə] **a** *no pl* (= *das Fangen*) hunting; (*mit Fallen*) trapping; (= *Fischen*) fishing; **auf ~ gehen** to go hunting/trapping/fishing; **zum ~ auslaufen** to go fishing **b** *no pl* (= *Beute*) (*lit, fig*) catch; (*Wild*) catch, bag; (*fig: Gegenstände*) haul; **einen guten ~ machen** to make a good catch/get a good bag/haul **c** *no pl* (*Hunt: = Todesstoß*) coup de grâce **d** *usu pl* (*Hunt*) (= *Kralle*) talon; (= *Reißzahn*) fang; **in den Fängen** +*gen* (*fig*) in the clutches of

Fang-: Fang|arm M (*Zool*) tentacle; **Fang|ball** M catch; **Fang|ei|sen** NT (*Hunt*) gin trap

Fan|ge|mein|de [ˈfɛn-] F fan club *or* community

fan|gen [ˈfaŋən] *pret* **fing** [fɪŋ], *ptp* **gefangen** [gəˈfaŋən] **VT** *Tier, Fisch, Verbrecher* to catch; *Wild* to catch, to bag; (*mit Fallen*) to trap; (*fig: = überlisten*) (*durch geschickte Fragen*) to trap; (*durch Versprechungen etc*) to trick; (**sich** *dat*) **eine (Ohrfeige etc) ~** (*inf*) to catch it (*Brit inf*), to get one (*US inf*) → *auch* **gefangen**
VI to catch; **Fangen spielen** to play tag
VR (*in einer Falle*) to get caught; **er hat sich in der eigenen Schlinge** *or* **Falle gefangen** (*fig*) he was hoist with his own petard **b** (= *das Gleichgewicht wieder finden*) to steady oneself; (*beim Reden etc*) to recover oneself; (*Flugzeug*) to straighten out; (*seelisch*) to get on an even keel again **c** (= *sich verfangen*) to get caught (up); (*Wind*) to get trapped; **ich mich mit dem Rock in der Fahrradkette** I got my skirt caught (up) in the bicycle chain

Fän|ger [ˈfɛŋɐ] M -s, -, **Fän|ge|rin** [-ərɪn] F -, -nen **a** (= *Tierfänger*) hunter; (*mit Fallen*) trapper; (= *Walfänger*) whaler; (= *Robbenfänger*) sealer **b** (*Sport*) catcher

Fang-: Fang|flot|te F fishing fleet; **Fang|fra|ge** F catch *or* trick question; **fang|frisch** ADJ *Fisch* freshly caught, fresh-caught, fresh; **Fang|grün|de** PL fishing grounds *pl*; **Fang|korb** M lifeguard, cowcatcher (*inf*); **Fang|lei|ne** F **a** (*Naut*) hawser **b** (*Aviat*) arresting gear cable **c** (*von Fallschirm*) rigging line; **Fang|mes|ser** NT hunting knife; **Fang|netz** NT **a** (*Hunt, Fishing*) net **b** (*Aviat*) arresting gear

Fan|go [ˈfaŋɡo] M -s, *no pl* fango

Fan|go|pa|ckung F fango pack

Fang-: Fang|quo|te F (fishing) quota; **Fang|schal|tung** F (*Telec*) interception circuit; **Fang|schiff** NT fishing boat; (*mit Netzen*) trawler; (= *Walfangschiff*) whaler; **Fang|schnur** F (*Mil*) aiguillette; **Fang|schuss** M (*Hunt, fig*) coup de grâce (*with a gun*); **fang|si|cher** ADJ **ein ~er Torwart** a goalkeeper with a safe pair of hands; **~ sein** to have a safe pair of hands; **Fang|stoß** M coup de grâce (*with a knife*)

fängt [fɛnt] 3. *pers sing pres von* **fangen**

Fang-: Fang|tuch NT *pl* -tücher life-net (*US*), jumping-sheet, blanket (*inf*); **fang|un|si|cher** ADJ butter-fingered; **Fang|ver|bot** NT (*Fishing*) fishing ban; (*von Walen*) whaling ban; **Fang|vor|rich|tung** F arresting device; **Fang|zahn** M canine (tooth), fang; (*von Eber*) tusk

Fan- [ˈfɛn-]: **Fan|klub** M fan club; (*Ftbl auch*) supporters' club; **Fan|post** [ˈfɛn-] F fan mail; (*einzelner Brief*) (a) fan letter

Fant [fant] M -(e)s, -e (*old pej*) jackanapes (*old*)

Fan|ta|sie¹ ▲ [fantaˈziː] F -, -n [-ˈziːən] **a** *no pl* (= *Einbildung*) imagination; **er hat ~** he's got imagination; **eine schmutzige ~ haben** to have a dirty mind; **in seiner ~** in his mind *or* imagination; **er spielt ohne ~** he plays unimaginatively *or* without any imagination; **seiner ~ freien Lauf lassen** to give free rein to one's imagination **b** *usu pl* (= *Trugbild, Vorstellung*) fantasy

Fan|ta|sie² F -, -n (*Mus*) fantasia

Fan|ta|sie-: fan|ta|sie|arm ▲ ADJ unimaginative, lacking in imagination; **fan|ta|sie|be|gabt** ▲ ADJ imaginative; **Fan|ta|sie|bild** ▲ NT fantasy (picture); **Fan|ta|sie|ge|bil|de** ▲ NT **a** (= *fantastische Form*) fantastic form **b** (= *Einbildung*) figment of the *or* one's imagination; **fan|ta|sie|los** ▲ ADJ unimaginative, lacking in imagination; **Fan|ta|sie|lo|sig|keit** ▲ F -, *no pl* lack of imagination, unimaginativeness; **Fan|ta|sie|preis** ▲ M astronomical price (*inf*); **fan|ta|sie|reich** ▲ ADJ, ADV = **fantasievoll**

fan|ta|sie|ren ▲ [fantaˈziːrən] *ptp* **fantasiert** **VI** to fantasize (*von* about); (*von Schlimmem*) to have visions (*von* of); (*Med*) to be delirious; (*Mus*) to improvise; **er fantasiert von einem großen Haus auf dem Lande** he has fantasies about a big house in the country
VT *Geschichte* to dream up; (*Mus*) to improvise; **was fantasierst du denn da?** (*inf*) what are you (going) on about? (*inf*); **er hat das alles fantasiert** that's all just (in) his imagination; **er fantasiert, dass die Welt untergeht** he has visions of the world coming to an end; **sie fantasiert, dass sie auswandern will** she fantasizes about emigrating

fan|ta|sie|voll ▲ ADJ highly imaginative ADV highly imaginatively; *reden, antworten* imaginatively

Fan|ta|sie|vor|stel|lung ▲ F figment of the imagination

Fan|tast ▲ [fanˈtast] M -en, -en, **Fan|tas|tin** ▲ [-ˈtastɪn] F -, -nen dreamer, visionary

Fan|tas|te|rei ▲ [fantastəˈrai] F -, -en fantasy

fan|tas|tisch ▲ [fanˈtastɪʃ] ADJ fantastic; (= *unglaublich auch*) incredible; **~e Literatur** fantasy literature ADV fantastically; **~ schmecken/aussehen** to taste/look fantastic; **~ klingen** to sound fantastic; (*unglaublich auch*) to sound incredible; **sie verdient ~** she earns a fantastic amount

Fan|ta|sy|film [ˈfɛntəzi-] M fantasy film

Fan|zine [ˈfɛnziːn] NT -s, -s (*inf*) fanzine

Fa|rad [faˈraːt] NT -(s), - farad

fa|ra|daysch ▲ [faraˈdeːʃ] ADJ **~er Käfig** Faraday cage

Farb- *in cpds* colour (*Brit*), color (*US*); **Farb|ab|stim|mung** F colo(u)r scheme; (*TV*) colo(u)r adjustment; **Farb|ab|stu|fung** F colo(u)r gradation; **Farb|auf|nah|me** F colo(u)r photo(-graph); **Farb|bad** NT dye-bath; **Farb|band¹** [-bant] NT *pl* -bänder (*von Schreibmaschine*) (typewriter) ribbon; **Farb|band²** [-bant] M *pl* -bände (= *Buch*) book with colo(u)r illustrations; **Farb|band|kas|set|te** F typewriter ribbon cassette

färb|bar ADJ colourable (*Brit*), colorable (*US*)

Farb-: Farb|be|richt M (*Press, TV*) report in colo(u)r; (*in Zeitschriften auch*) colo(u)r feature; **Farb|beu|tel** M paint bomb; **Farb|bild** NT (*Phot*) colo(u)r photo(graph); **Farb|druck** M *pl* -drucke colo(u)r print; **Farb|dru|cker** M colo(u)r printer

Far|be [ˈfarbə] F -, -n **a** (= *Farbton, Tönung*) colour (*Brit*), color (*US*); **~ bekommen** to get a bit of colo(u)r, to catch the sun (*inf*); **~ verlieren** to go pale; **in ~** in colo(u)r; **einer Sache** (*dat*) **mehr ~ geben** (*fig*) to give sth more colo(u)r; **etw in den dunkelsten** *or* **schwärzesten ~n schildern** *or* **ausmalen** to paint a black picture of sth; **etw in den glänzendsten ~n schildern** *or* **ausmalen** to paint a rosy picture of sth, to paint sth in glowing colo(u)rs
b (= *Malerfarbe, Anstrichfarbe*) paint; (*für Farbbad*) dye; (= *Druckfarbe*) ink
c (*auch fig*) (= *Fahne, Univ*) colo(u)rs *pl*; **~n tragende Studenten/Verbindung** students belonging to a fraternity/student fraternity with traditional heraldic colours **d** (*Cards*) suit; **~ bedienen** to follow suit; **~ bekennen** (*fig*) to lay one's cards on the table; (= *klaren Standpunkt beziehen*) to nail one's colo(u)rs to the mast

---

farb|echt ADJ colourfast (*Brit*), colorfast (*US*); (*Comput*) true-colour *attr* (*Brit*), true-color *attr* (*US*)

Farb|echt|heit F colourfastness (*Brit*), colorfastness (*US*); (*Comput*) true colour (*Brit*) *or* color (*US*)

Färb|e|mit|tel NT dye

farb|emp|find|lich ADJ (*Phot*) colour-sensitive (*Brit*), color-sensitive (*US*)

fär|ben [ˈfɛrbn] **VT** to colour (*Brit*), to color (*US*); *Stoff, Haar* to dye → *auch* **gefärbt** **VI** (= *abfärben*) to run (*inf*) **VR** to change colo(u)r; **ihre Wangen färbten sich leicht** she coloured (*Brit*) *or* blushed slightly; **sich grün/blau** *etc* **~** to turn green/blue *etc*

Farben- *in cpds* colour (*Brit*), color (*US*); **far|ben|blind** ADJ colo(u)r-blind; **Far|ben|blind|heit** F colo(u)r-blindness; **Far|ben|druck** M, *no pl* (*Typ*) colo(u)r printing; **far|ben|freu|dig** ADJ colo(u)rful; *Mensch* fond of bright colo(u)rs; **far|ben|froh** ADJ colo(u)rful; **far|ben|kräf|tig** ADJ (very) colo(u)rful, in strong colo(u)rs; **Far|ben|leh|re** F theory of colo(u)r; (= *Fach auch*) chromatics *sing*; **Far|ben|pracht** F blaze of colo(u)r; **in seiner ganzen ~** in all its glory; **far|ben|präch|tig** ADJ gloriously colo(u)rful; **far|ben|reich** ADJ (*auch Mus*) colo(u)rful; **Far|ben|reich|tum** M (*auch Mus*) wealth of colo(u)rs; **Far|ben|sinn** M sense of colo(u)r (*auch Biol*), colo(u)r sense; **Far|ben|spiel** NT play *or* kaleidoscope of colo(u)rs; **far|ben|tra|gend** △ ADJ (*Univ*) → **Farbe c**; **Far|ben|zu|sam|men|stel|lung** F colo(u)r combination

Fär|ber [ˈfɛrbə] M -s, -, **Fär|be|rin** [-ərɪn] F -, -nen dyer

Fär|be|rei [fɛrbəˈrai] F -, -en **a** (= *Betrieb*) dyeing works *sing* or *pl* **b** *no pl* (= *Verfahren*) dyeing

Farb-: Farb|fern|se|hen NT colour (*Brit*) or color (*US*) television or TV; **Farb|fern|se|her** M , **Farb|fern|seh|ge|rät** NT colo(u)r television (set); **Farb|film** M colo(u)r film; **Farb|fil|ter** M (*Phot*) colo(u)r filter; **Farb|fleck** M paint spot *or* stain; **Farb|fo|to** NT colo(u)r photo(graph); **Farb|fo|to|gra|fie** F (= *Verfahren*) colo(u)r photography; (= *Bild*) colo(u)r photo(graph); **Farb|ge|bung** [-ɡeːbʊŋ] F -, -en colo(u)ring, coloration

far|big [ˈfarbɪç] ADJ **a** coloured (*Brit*), colored (*US*); (*fig*) *Schilderung* vivid, colourful (*Brit*), colorful (*US*); **ein ~er Druck** a colo(u)r print; **eine ~e Postkarte** a colo(u)r postcard **b** *attr Hautfarbe* colo(u)red ADV (= *in Farbe*) anstreichen in a colo(u)r; (= *anschaulich*) *schildern* colo(u)rfully, vividly; **~ fotografieren** to take colo(u)r photographs, to photograph in colo(u)r

fär|big [ˈfɛrbɪç] ADJ (*Aus*) = **farbig a**

Far|bi|ge(r) [ˈfarbɪɡə] MF *decl as adj* coloured (*Brit*) or colored (*US*) man/woman/person *etc*; **die ~n** the colo(u)reds *pl*, colo(u)red people *pl*

Farb-: Farb|kas|ten M paintbox; **Farb|kis|sen** NT inkpad; **Farb|klecks** M blob of paint, paint spot; **Farb|kom|bi|na|ti|on** F colo(u)r combination; (= *Farbzusammenstellung*) colo(u)r scheme; **Farb|ko|pie|rer** M colour (*Brit*) or color (*US*) copier; **farb|lich** [ˈfarplɪç] ADJ colo(u)r *attr* ADV **die Fotokopie ist ~ einwandfrei** the colo(u)rs in this photocopy are excellent; **zwei Sachen ~ aufeinander abstimmen** to match two things up for colo(u)r; **~ harmonisch** in harmonious colo(u)rs; **farb|los** ADJ (*lit, fig*) colo(u)rless; **Farb|lo|sig|keit** F -, *no pl* (*lit, fig*) colo(u)rlessness; **Farb|mi|ne** F colo(u)red-ink cartridge; **Farb|mi|schung** F (= *gemischte Farbe*) mixture of colo(u)rs; **Farb|rol|ler** M paint roller; **Farb|sinn** M sense of colo(u)r (*auch Biol*), colo(u)r sense; **Farb|stich** M (*Phot, TV*) colo(u)r fault; **Farb|stift** M colo(u)red pen; (= *Buntstift*) crayon, colo(u)red pencil; **Farb|stoff** M (= *Lebensmittelfarbstoff*) (artificial) colo(u)ring; (= *Hautfarbstoff*) pigment; (*für Textilien etc*) dye; **Farb|ta|fel** F col-

---

o(u)r plate; (= *Tabelle*) colo(u)r chart; **Farb|ton** M *pl* **-töne** shade, hue; (= *Tönung*) tint; **Farb|tup|fer** M spot of colo(u)r

Fär|bung ['fɛrbʊŋ] F -, **-en** (= *das Färben, Farbgebung*) colouring (*Brit*), coloring (*US*); (= *Tönung*) tinge, hue; (*fig*) slant, bias

Farb-: Farb|wie|der|ga|be F (*TV etc*) colo(u)r reproduction; **Farb|zu|sam|men|stel|lung** F colo(u)r scheme

Far|ce ['farsə] F -, **-n** a (*Theat, fig*) farce b (*Cook*) stuffing

far|cie|ren [far'siːrən] *ptp* **farciert** VT (*Cook*) to stuff

Farm [farm] F -, **-en** farm

Far|mer ['farmɐ] M -s, -, **Far|me|rin** [-ərɪn] F -, **-nen** farmer

Farm|haus NT farmhouse

Farn [farn] M **-(e)s, -e**, **Farn|kraut** NT fern; (= *Adlerfarn*) bracken

Fä|rö|er [fɛˈrøːɐ, ˈfɛːrøɐ] PL Faroes *pl*, Faroe Islands *pl*

Fär|se ['fɛrzə] F -, **-n** heifer

Fa|san [faˈzaːn] M -s, **-e** *or* **-en** pheasant

Fa|sa|ne|rie [fazanəˈriː] F -, **-n** [-ˈriːən] pheasant-house; (*im Freien*) pheasant-run

Fa|sche ['faʃə] F -, **-n** (*Aus*) bandage

fa|schen ['faʃən] VT (*Aus*) to bandage

fa|schie|ren [faˈʃiːrən] *ptp* **faschiert** VT (*Aus Cook*) to mince; **Faschiertes** mince, minced meat, ground meat (*US*); **faschiertes Laiberl** *or* **Laibchen** hamburger

Fa|schi|ne [faˈʃiːnə] F -, **-n** fascine

Fa|sching ['faʃɪŋ] M -s, **-e** *or* **-s** Shrovetide carnival, Fasching

Faschings- *in cpds* carnival; **Fa|schings|diens|tag** M Shrove Tuesday; **Fa|schings|kos|tüm** NT carnival costume, fancy dress *sing or pl*; **Fa|schings|prinz** M carnival prince; **Fa|schings|prin|zes|sin** F carnival princess; **Fa|schings|zeit** F carnival period

Fa|schis|mus [faˈʃɪsmʊs] M -, *no pl* fascism

Fa|schist [faˈʃɪst] M **-en, -en**, **Fa|schis|tin** [-ˈʃɪstɪn] F -, **-nen** fascist

fa|schis|tisch [faˈʃɪstɪʃ] ADJ fascist

fa|schis|to|id [faʃɪstoˈiːt] ADJ fascistic

Fas|cho [ˈfaʃo] M -s, **-s** (*sl*) fascist

Fa|se ['faːzə] F -, **-n** bevel, chamfer

Fa|se|lei [faːzəˈlai] F -, **-en** (*pej*) twaddle (*inf*), drivel (*inf*)

Fa|se|ler [ˈfaːzəlɐ] M -s, -, **Fa|se|le|rin** [-ərɪn] F -, **-nen** (*pej*) drivelling (*Brit*) *or* driveling (*US*) idiot (*pej*)

fa|seln ['faːzln] (*pej*) VI to drivel (*inf*) VT **Blödsinn ~** to talk drivel (*inf*); **das ist alles gefaselt** that's drivel (*inf*), that's just (so much) twaddle (*inf*); **was hat er gefaselt?** what was he drivelling (*Brit*) *or* driveling (*US*) (on) about? (*inf*)

Fa|se|nacht ['faːzənaxt] F -, *no pl* (*S Ger, Sw*) Shrovetide carnival, Fasenacht

Fa|ser ['faːzɐ] F -, **-n** fibre (*Brit*), fiber (*US*); **ein Pullover aus synthetischen ~n** a pullover made of synthetic fibre (*Brit*) *or* fiber (*US*); **er hat keine trockene ~ am Leib** he's soaked through *or* drenched; **mit allen ~n des Herzens** (*liter*) with every fibre (*Brit*) *or* fiber (*US*) of one's being (*liter*)

Faser-: fa|ser|ar|tig ADJ fibrous; **Fa|ser|ge|we|be** NT (*Biol*) fibrous tissue

fa|se|rig ['faːzərɪç] ADJ fibrous; *Fleisch, Spargel auch* stringy (*pej*); (= *zerfasert*) frayed

fa|sern ['faːzɐn] VI to fray

Faser-: fa|ser|nackt ADJ = **splitter(faser)nackt**; **Fa|ser|op|tik** F fibre (*Brit*) *or* fiber (*US*) optics *sing*; **Fa|ser|pflan|ze** F fibre (*Brit*) *or* fiber (*US*) plant; **Fa|ser|plat|te** F fibreboard (*Brit*), fiberboard (*US*); **fa|ser|scho|nend** ADJ gentle (*to fabrics*); **Fa|ser|schrei|ber** M (= *Schreibstift*) felt-tip pen, fibretip (*Brit*) *or* fibertip (*US*) pen; **Fa|ser|stoff** M fibrous material

Fas|ler ['faːslɐ] M -s, -, **Fas|le|rin** [-ərɪn] F -, **-nen** (*pej*) = **Faseler**

Fas|nacht ['fasnaxt] F, *no pl* = **Fastnacht**

fas|rig ['faːzrɪç] ADJ = **faserig**

Fass ▲ [fas] NT **-es, ̈er** ['fɛsɐ] barrel; (= *kleines Bierfass*) keg; (*zum Gären, Einlegen*) vat; (*zum Buttern*) (barrel) churn; (*für Öl, Benzin, Chemikalien*) drum; **etw in Fässer füllen** to put sth into barrels/drums, to barrel sth; **drei Fässer/~ Bier** three barrels of beer; **vom ~** on tap; *Bier auch* on draught (*Brit*) *or* draft (*US*); *Sherry, Wein auch* from the wood (*esp Brit*); **er trinkt nur Bier vom ~** he only drinks draught (*Brit*) *or* draft (*US*) beer; **ein ~ ohne Boden** (*fig*) a bottomless pit; **ein ~ aufmachen** (*fig inf*) to kick up a shindy (*Brit inf*) *or* a storm (*US inf*); **das schlägt dem ~ den Boden aus** (*inf*) that beats everything!, that takes the biscuit! (*Brit inf*); **das brachte das ~ zum Überlaufen** (*fig*) that was the last straw (*prov*), that was the straw that broke the camel's back (*prov*)

Fas|sa|de [faˈsaːdə] F -, **-n** (*lit, fig*) façade; (*inf*: = *Gesicht*) face; **das ist doch nur ~** (*fig*) that's just a façade

Fassaden-: Fas|sa|den|klet|te|rer M , **Fas|sa|den|klet|te|rin** F cat burglar; **Fas|sa|den|rei|ni|gung** F exterior cleaning

Fass-: Fass|band ▲ [-bant] NT *pl* **-bänder** hoop (of a barrel); **fass|bar** ['fasbaːɐ] ▲ ADJ comprehensible, understandable; **das ist doch nicht ~!** that's incomprehensible!; **Fass|bar|keit** ▲ F -, *no pl* comprehensibility; **Fass|bier** ▲ NT draught (*Brit*) *or* draft (*US*) beer; **Fass|bin|der(in)** ▲ M(F) (*old, Aus*) cooper

Fäss|chen ▲ ['fɛsçən] NT -s, - *dim von* **Fass** cask

Fass|dau|be ▲ F stave

fas|sen ['fasn] VT a (= *ergreifen*) to take hold of; (*hastig, kräftig*) to grab, to seize; (= *festnehmen*) *Einbrecher etc* to apprehend (*form*), to seize; (*Mil*) *Munition* to draw; **jdn beim** *or* **am Arm ~** to take/grab sb by the arm; **er fasste ihre Hand** he took her hand; **Schauder/Grauen/Entsetzen fasste ihn** he was seized with horror; **fass!** seize! b (*fig*) *Beschluss, Entschluss* to make, to take; *Mut* to take; **Vertrauen zu jdm ~** to come to trust sb; **den Gedanken ~, etw zu tun** to form *or* have the idea of doing sth; **den Vorsatz ~, etw zu tun** to make a resolution to do sth → *Auge* a, *Fuß* a, *Herz* d c (= *begreifen*) to grasp, to understand; **es ist nicht zu ~** it's unbelievable *or* incredible; **ich fasse es nicht** I don't believe it d (= *enthalten*) to hold e (= *aufnehmen*) *Essen* to get; (*Rail, Naut*) *Wasser, Kohlen* to take on; **Essen ~!** come and get it! f (= *einfassen*) *Edelsteine* to set; *Bild* to frame; *Quelle* to surround; (*fig*: = *ausdrücken*) to express; **in Verse/Worte ~** to put into verse/words; **neu ~** (*Manuskript, Rede, Erzählung*) to revise; **etw weit/eng ~** to interpret sth broadly/ *auch* **gefasst**

VI a (= *nicht abrutschen*) to grip; (*Zahnrad*) to bite b (= *greifen*) **an/in etw** (*acc*) **~** to feel sth; (= *berühren*) to touch sth; **fass mal unter den Tisch** feel under the table; **sich** (*dat*) **an den Kopf ~** (*fig*) to shake one's head in disbelief; **da fasst man sich** (*dat*) **an den Kopf** (*inf*) you wouldn't believe it, would you?

VR (= *sich beherrschen*) to compose oneself; **fass dich!** pull yourself together!; **sich vor Freude kaum ~ können** to be beside oneself with joy; **sich in Geduld ~** to be patient, to possess one's soul in patience; **sich kurz ~** to be brief → *auch* **gefasst**

fäs|ser|wei|se ADV (= *in großen Mengen*) by the gallon; (= *in Fässern*) by the barrel

Fas|set|te *etc* ▲ [faˈsɛtə] F -, **-n** = **Facette** *etc*

fass|lich ▲ ['faslɪç] ADJ comprehensible, understandable

Fass|lich|keit ▲ F -, *no pl* comprehensibility

Fas|son [faˈsõː] F -, **-s** (*von Kleidung*) style; (*von Frisur*) shape; **aus der ~ geraten** (*lit*) to go out of shape, to lose its shape; (*dated*: = *dick werden*) to get fat; **jeder soll nach seiner ~ selig werden** (*prov*) everyone has to find his own salvation

fas|so|nie|ren [fasoˈniːrən] *ptp* **fassoniert** VT (*Aus*) *Haare* to (cut and) shape

Fas|son|schnitt [faˈsõː-] M *style in which the hair is shaped back into the neck* (*für Herren*) short back and sides

Fass|reif ▲ M , **Fass|rei|fen** ▲ M hoop

Fas|sung ['fasʊŋ] F -, **-en** a (*von Juwelen*) setting; (*von Bild*) frame; (*Elec*) holder b (= *Bearbeitung, Wortlaut*) version; **ein Film in ungekürzter ~** the uncut version of a film; **ein Buch in ungekürzter ~** the unabridged version of a book; **ein Film in deutscher ~** a film with German dubbing c *no pl* (= *Ruhe, Besonnenheit*) composure; **die ~ bewahren** *or* **behalten** to maintain one's composure; **etw mit ~ tragen** to take sth calmly *or* with equanimity; **die ~ verlieren** to lose one's composure; **völlig außer ~ geraten** to lose all self-control; **jdn aus der ~ bringen** to disconcert *or* throw (*inf*) sb; *Redner auch* to put sb off

Fassungs-: Fas|sungs|kraft F (*liter*) (powers of) comprehension *or* understanding; **die menschliche ~ übersteigen** to be beyond human understanding; **fas|sungs|los** ADJ stunned, bewildered in bewilderment; **Fas|sungs|lo|sig|keit** F -, *no pl* bewilderment; **Fas|sungs|ver|mö|gen** NT (*lit, fig*) capacity; **das übersteigt mein ~** that's beyond me, that's beyond the limits of my comprehension

Fass-: Fass|wein ▲ M wine from the wood; **fass|wei|se** ▲ ADV by the barrel; (= *in Fässern*) in barrels

fast [fast] ADV almost, nearly; **~ nie** hardly ever, almost never; **~ nichts** hardly anything, almost nothing; **ich wäre ~ überfahren worden** I was almost *or* nearly run over

fas|ten ['fastn] VI to fast

Fas|ten-: Fas|ten|kur F diet; **eine ~ machen/ anfangen** to be/go on a diet; **Fas|ten|zeit** F period of fasting; (*Eccl*) Lent

Fast|food ▲ [faːst'fuːd] NT -, *no pl*, **Fast Food** ▲ NT -, *no pl* fast food

Fast|nacht ['fastnaxt] F, *no pl* (= *Fasching*) *Shrovetide carnival* (= *Faschingsdienstag*) Shrove Tuesday

---

FASTNACHT

Fastnacht is another word for **Karneval**. However, **Karneval** is celebrated in the Rhine area very differently from the way **Fastnacht** is celebrated in the Swabian-Alemannic region of Germany and in Switzerland. Here the period of celebration extends beyond Ash Wednesday; indeed **Fastnacht** in Basle does not even begin until after Ash Wednesday. The customs date back over 400 years and have their origin in ancient rites for the banishing of winter. Strict care is taken that only traditional costumes and wooden masks appear in the processions. Drums and bells are used to drive out the winter, while participants dressed as witches, goblins and other fantastic creatures play pranks on the spectators, sometimes even during the night or at the first light of dawn → KARNEVAL

Fastnachts-: Fast|nachts|narr M , **Fast|nachts|när|rin** F *disguised figure in Shrove Tuesday celebrations*; **Fast|nachts|spiel** NT (*Liter*) Shrovetide play; **Fast|nachts|um|zug** M Shrove Tuesday procession

Fast|tag M day of fasting

Fas|zi|kel [fasˈtsiːkl] M -s, - (*old, form*) section of manuscript, fascicle (*spec*)

Fas|zi|na|ti|on [fastsinaˈtsi̯oːn] F -, **-en** fascination; **~ ausstrahlen** to radiate charm; **jds ~** (*dat*)

erlegen sein to succumb to sb's fascinating power

fas|zi|nie|ren [fastsi'niːrən] *ptp* **fasziniert** VTI to fascinate (*an* +*dat* about); **~d** fascinating; **mich fasziniert der Gedanke, das zu tun** I'm very attracted by *or* to the idea of doing that

fa|tal [fa'taːl] ADJ (*geh*) (= *verhängnisvoll*) fatal, fateful, dire; (= *peinlich*) embarrassing, awkward

Fa|ta|lis|mus [fata'lɪsmʊs] M -, *no pl* fatalism

Fa|ta|list [fata'lɪst] M -en, -en, **Fa|ta|lis|tin** [-'lɪstɪn] F -, -nen fatalist

fa|ta|lis|tisch [fata'lɪstɪʃ] ADJ fatalistic

Fa|ta|li|tät [fatali'tɛːt] F -, -en great misfortune

Fa|ta Mor|ga|na ['faːta mɔr'gaːna] F -, - -s *or* **Morganen** [mɔr'gaːnən] (*lit, fig*) Fata Morgana (*liter*), mirage

Fat|sche ['fatʃə] F -, -n (*Aus*) bandage

fat|schen ['fatʃn] VT (*Aus*) to bandage

Fatz|ke ['fatska] M -n *or* -s, -n *or* -s (*inf*) stuck-up twit (*Brit inf*) *or* twerp (*inf*)

fau|chen ['fauxn] VTI to hiss

faul [faul] ADJ **a** (= *verfault*) bad; *Lebensmittel* off *pred* (*Brit*), bad *pred*; *Eier, Obst* rotten, bad; *Holz, Gesellschaftsordnung* rotten; *Geschmack, Geruch* foul, putrid; *Zahn* bad, decayed; *Laub* rotting; *Wasser* foul
b (= *verdächtig*) fishy (*inf*), suspicious, dubious; (*Comm*) *Wechsel, Scheck* dud (*inf*); *Kredit* bad; (= *fadenscheinig*) *Ausrede* flimsy, feeble; *Kompromiss* uneasy; *Friede* empty; (= *dumm*) *Witz* bad; **hier ist etwas ~** (*inf*) there's something fishy here (*inf*); **etwas ist ~ daran** (*inf*) there's something fishy about the whole business (*inf*); **etwas ist ~ im Staate Dänemark** (*prov*) there's something rotten in the State of Denmark (*prov*)
c (= *träge*) lazy, idle; **wie die Sünde** i-dle (*Brit inf*), very lazy; **nicht ~** (= *reaktionsschnell*) quick as you please; **er hat seinen ~en Tag** (= *müßiger Tag*) he's having a lazy day; (= *faule Stimmung*) he's in a lazy mood → **Haut**, **Strick**[1]

Fäu|le F -, *no pl* **a** (*Vet*) (liver) rot **b** = **Fäulnis**

fau|len ['faulən] VI *aux sein or haben* to rot; (*Aas auch*) to putrefy; (*Zahn*) to decay; (*Lebensmittel*) to go bad

fau|len|zen ['faulɛntsn] VI to laze *or* loaf (*esp pej inf*) about

Fau|len|zer[1] ['faulɛntsɐ] M -s, - (*Aus*: = *Linienblatt*) sheet of ruled paper

Fau|len|zer[2] ['faulɛntsɐ] M -s, -, **Fau|len|ze|rin** [-ərɪn] F -, -nen layabout

Fau|len|ze|rei [faulɛntsə'rai] F -, (*rare*) -en lazing *or* loafing (*esp pej inf*) about

Faul|heit F -, *no pl* laziness, idleness; **er stinkt vor ~** (*inf*) he's bone idle (*Brit inf*) *or* a lazybones (*inf*)

fau|lig ['faulɪç] ADJ going bad; *Lebensmittel* going bad, going off (*Brit*); *Eier, Obst* going bad, going rotten; *Wasser* stale; (*in Teich, See etc*) stagnating; *Geruch, Geschmack* foul, putrid ADV **~ schmecken/riechen** to taste/smell bad; (*Wasser*) to taste/smell foul

Fäul|nis ['fɔylnɪs] F -, *no pl* rot; (*von Fleisch auch*) putrefaction; (*von Zahn*) decay; (*fig*) decadence, degeneracy; **~ erregend** putrefactive; **von ~ befallen** rotting, decaying

Fäul|nis|er|re|ger M putrefier

Faul-: Faul|pelz M (*inf*) lazybones *sing* (*inf*); **Faul|schlamm** M sapropel (*spec*), sludge; **Faul|tier** NT sloth; (*inf*: = *Mensch*) lazybones *sing* (*inf*)

Faun [faun] M -(e)s, -e (*Myth*) faun

Fau|na ['fauna] F -, **Faunen** ['faunən] fauna

Faust [faust] F -, **Fäuste** ['fɔystə] fist; **die (Hand zur) ~ ballen** to clench one's fist; **jdm eine ~ machen** (*inf*) to shake one's fist at sb; **jdm mit der ~ ins Gesicht schlagen** to punch sb in the face; **jdm die ~ unter die Nase halten** to shake one's fist in sb's face *or* under sb's nose; **mit**

der ~ auf den Tisch schlagen (*lit*) to thump on the table (with one's fist); (*fig*) to take a hard line, to put one's foot down; **etw aus der ~ essen** to eat sth with one's hands; **ein Butterbrot auf die ~** a sandwich in one's hand; **die ~/Fäuste in der Tasche ballen** (*fig*) to bottle up *or* choke back one's anger; **mit geballten Fäusten zusehen müssen** (*fig*) to watch in helpless anger; **das passt wie die ~ aufs Auge** (= *passt nicht*) it's all wrong; (*Farbe*) it clashes horribly; (= *ist fehl am Platz*) it's completely out of place; (= *passt gut*) it's just the thing (*inf*) *or* job (*inf*); **jds ~ im Nacken spüren** (*fig*) to have sb breathing down one's neck; **auf eigene ~** (*fig*) off one's own bat (*Brit inf*), on one's own initiative; **reisen, fahren** under one's own steam → **eisern ADJ b**

Faust-: Faust|ab|wehr F (*Sport*) save using the fists; **herrlich, diese ~ des Torwarts!** the goalkeeper punches the ball clear beautifully!; **Faust|ball** M *form of volleyball*

Fäust|chen ['fɔystçən] NT -s, - *dim von* **Faust** **sich** (*dat*) **ins ~ lachen** to laugh up (*Brit*) *or* in (*US*) one's sleeve; (*bei finanziellem Vorteil*) to laugh all the way to the bank (*inf*)

faust|dick (*inf*) ADJ **eine ~e Lüge** a whopper (*inf*), a whopping (great) lie (*inf*); **eine ~e Überraschung** a huge surprise ADV **das ist ~ gelogen** that's a whopping lie (*inf*), that's a whopper (*inf*); **er hat es ~ hinter den Ohren** he's a sly *or* crafty one (*inf*); **~ auftragen** to lay it on thick (*inf*)

Fäus|tel ['fɔystl] M OR NT -s, - sledgehammer

faus|ten ['faustn] VT *Ball* to punch; (*Ftbl auch*)

Faust-: Faust|feu|er|waf|fe F handgun; **faust|groß** ADJ as big as a fist, the size of a fist; **Faust|hand|schuh** M mitt(en)

faus|tisch ['faustɪʃ] ADJ Faustian

Faust-: Faust|kampf M fist-fight; **Faust-kämp|fer(in)** M(F) (*old*) pugilist (*old*); **Faust|keil** M hand-axe (*Brit*), hand-ax (*US*)

Fäust|ling ['fɔystlɪŋ] M -s, -e mitt(en)

Faust-: Faust|pfand NT security; **Faust|recht** NT , *no pl* law of the jungle; **Faust|re|gel** F rule of thumb; **Faust|schlag** M punch

Fau|teuil [fo'tøːj] M -s, -s (*old, Aus*) leather armchair

Faux|pas [fo'pa] M -, - gaffe, faux pas

fa|vo|ri|sie|ren [favori'ziːrən] *ptp* **favorisiert** VT to favour (*Brit*), to favor (*US*); **die Wettbüros ~ X als Sieger** the betting shops show X as favourite (*Brit*) *or* favorite (*US*), the betting shops have X to win; **favorisiert werden** to be favourite (*Brit*) *or* favorite (*US*)

Fa|vo|rit [favo'riːt] M -en, -en, **Fa|vo|ri|tin** [-'riːtɪn] F -, -nen favourite (*Brit*), favorite (*US*)

Fa|vo|ri|ten|rol|le [favo'riːtn-] F role as favourite (*Brit*) *or* favorite (*US*), favourite (*Brit*) *or* favorite (*US*) tag

Fax [faks] NT -, -e fax

Fax|ab|ruf M fax polling

fa|xen ['faksn] VT to fax, to send by fax

Fa|xen ['faksn] PL **a** (*inf*: = *Alberei*) fooling about (*Brit*) *or* around; **~ machen** to fool about (*Brit*) *or* around; **die ~ dicke haben** to be fed up with all the nonsense **b** (= *Grimassen*) **~ schneiden** to pull faces

Fax-: Fax|ge|rät NT fax machine; **Fax|num|mer** F fax number

Fa|yence [fa'jãːs] F -, -n faïence

FAZ [ɛfla'tsɛt, fats] F - *abbr von* **Frankfurter Allgemeine Zeitung**

Fa|zit ['faːtsɪt] NT -s, -s *or* -e **das ~ der Untersuchungen war ...** on balance the result of the investigations was ...; **wenn wir aus diesen vier Jahren das ~ ziehen** if we take stock of these four years; **wenn ich das ~ ziehen müsste, würde ich sagen ...** on balance I would say ...

FCKW [ɛftseːka'veː] M -s, -s *abbr von* **Fluorchlorkohlenwasserstoff** CFC

FCKW-frei [ɛftseːka'veː-] ADJ CFC-free

FDGB [ɛfdeːgeː'beː] M -(s) (*DDR*) *abbr von* **Freier Deutscher Gewerkschaftsbund** Free German Trades Union Congress

FDJ [ɛfdeː'jɔt] F - (*DDR*) *abbr von* **Freie Deutsche Jugend** Free German Youth

FDJler [ɛfdeː'jɔtlɐ] M -s, -, **FDJle|rin** [-ərɪn] F -, -nen (*DDR*) member of the Free German Youth

FDP [ɛfdeː'peː] F - *abbr von* **Freie Demokratische Partei**

FDP

The **FDP** (Freie Demokratische Partei) was founded in Germany in 1948. It is a central party supporting liberal views. Although a relatively small party, as a coalition partner of both **CDU** and **SPD** it plays a part in many decisions both at Federal and **Land** level → CDU, SPD

Fea|ture ['fiːtʃɐ] NT -s, -s (*Rad, TV*) feature programme (*Brit*) *or* program (*US*)

Fe|ber ['feːbɐ] M -s, - (*Aus*) February → *auch* **März**

Feb|ru|ar ['feːbruaːɐ] M -(s), -e February → *auch* **März**

Fecht|bahn F (*Sport*) piste

fech|ten ['fɛçtn] *pret* **focht** [fɔxt], *ptp* **gefochten** [gə'fɔxtn] VI (*Sport*) to fence; (*geh*: = *kämpfen*) to fight; **das Fechten** fencing VT **Degen/Florett ~** to fence with épées/foils; **einen Gang ~** to fence a bout

Fech|ter ['fɛçtɐ] M -s, -, **Fech|te|rin** [-ərɪn] F -, -nen fencer

Fech|ter|stel|lung F fencing stance

Fecht-: Fecht|hand|schuh M fencing glove; **Fecht|hieb** M (*fencing*) cut; **Fecht|kunst** F art of fencing; (= *Geschick*) skill in fencing; **Fecht|meis|ter(in)** M(F) fencing master; **Fecht|sport** M fencing

Fe|der ['feːdɐ] F -, -n **a** (= *Vogelfeder*) feather; (= *Gänsefeder etc*) quill; (= *lange Hutfeder*) plume; **leicht wie eine ~** as light as a feather; **~n lassen müssen** (*inf*) not to escape unscathed; **in den ~n stecken** (*inf*) to be in one's bed *or* pit (*inf*); **jdn aus den ~n holen** (*inf*) to drag sb out of bed (*inf*); **raus aus den ~n!** (*inf*) rise and shine! (*inf*), show a leg! (*inf*) → **fremd a**
b (= *Schreibfeder*) quill; (*an Federhalter*) nib; **ich greife zur ~ ...** I take up my pen ...; **aus jds ~ fließen** to flow from sb's pen; **dieser Text stammt nicht aus meiner ~** this text was not written by me; **eine scharfe** *or* **spitze ~ führen** to wield a wicked *or* deadly pen; **mit spitzer ~** with a deadly pen, with a pen dipped in vitriol (*liter*); **ein Mann der ~** (*dated geh*) a man of letters
c (*Tech*) spring
d (*in Holz*) tongue

Fe|der-: Fe|der|an|trieb M clockwork; **mit ~** clockwork-driven, driven by clockwork; **Fe|der|ball** M (= *Ball*) shuttlecock, birdie (*US inf*); (= *Spiel*) badminton; **Fe|der|bein** NT (*Tech*) suspension strut; **Fe|der|be|sen** M feather duster; **Fe|der|bett** NT continental quilt, duvet; **Fe|der|blatt** NT leaf of a spring; **Fe|der|busch** M (*von Vögeln*) crest; (*von Hut, Helm*) plume; **Fe|der|de|cke** F continental quilt, duvet; **Fe|der|fuch|ser** [-fʊksɐ] M -s, -, **Fe|der|fuch|se|rin** [-ərɪn] F -, -nen (*pej*) petty-minded pedant (*pej*); (= *Schreiberling*) pettifogging penpusher (*pej*) *or* pencilpusher (*US pej*); **fe|der|füh|rend** ADJ *Behörde etc* in overall charge (*für* of); **Fe|der|füh|rung** F **unter der ~** +*gen* under the overall control of; **die ~ haben** to be in charge, to have overall charge; **Fe|der|ge|wicht** NT (*Sport*) featherweight (class); **Fe|der|ge|wicht|ler** [-gəvɪçtlɐ] M -s, -, **Fe|der|ge|wicht|le|rin** [-ərɪn] F -, -nen (*Sport*) featherweight; **Fe|der|hal|ter** M (dip) pen; (=

Füllfederhalter) (fountain) pen; (*ohne Feder* pen(holder); **Fe|der|hut** M plumed hat; **Fe|der|kas|ten** M (*Sch*) pencil box; **Fe|der|kern|mat|rat|ze** F interior sprung mattress, inner-spring mattress (*US*); **Fe|der|kiel** M quill; **Fe|der|kis|sen** NT feather cushion; (*in Bett*) feather pillow; **Fe|der|kleid** NT (*liter*) plumage; **Fe|der|krieg** M (*fig*) war of words; **fe|der|leicht** ADJ light as a feather; (*fig*) *Musik, Töne* floating; **Fe|der|le|sen** NT -s, *no pl* **nicht viel ~s mit jdm/etw machen** to waste no time on sb/sth, to make short work of sb/sth; **ohne langes ~, ohne viel ~s** without ceremony, without any (further) ado; **Fe|der|mäpp|chen** NT , **Fe|der|map|pe** F pencil case; **Fe|der|mes|ser** NT penknife

fe|dern ['feːdən] **VI a** (*Eigenschaft*) to be springy **b** (= *hochfedern, zurückfedern*) to spring back; (*Fahrzeug*) to bounce (up and down); (*Springer, Turner:* = *hochgeschleudert werden*) to bounce; (**in den Knien**) – (*Sport*) to bend or give at the knees **c** (*Kissen etc*) to shed (feathers); (*Vogel*) to moult (*Brit*), to molt (*US*), to shed its feathers **VT** to spring; *Rad, Räder* to fit with suspension; **ein Auto hydraulisch ~** to fit a car with hydraulic suspension → *auch* **gefedert**

fe|dernd ADJ (*Tech*) sprung; (*fig*) jaunty; **~e Radaufhängung** spring suspension; **einen ~en Gang haben** to have a jaunty or springy step or gait; **mit ~en Schritten** with a spring in one's step

Fe|der-: Fe|der|pen|nal ['feːdɐpɛnaːl] NT -s, -e (*Aus*) pencil case; **Fe|der|ring** M spring washer; **Fe|der|schmuck** M feather trimming; (*von Indianern etc*) headdress; (= *Federbusch*) plume; (*von Vogel*) plumage; **Fe|der|skiz|ze** F pen-and-ink sketch; **Fe|der|spiel** NT (*Hist*) lure; **Fe|der|strich** M pen-stroke, stroke of the pen; **mit einem** or **durch einen ~** with a single stroke of the pen

Fe|de|rung ['feːdərʊŋ] F -, -en springs *pl*, springing; (*Aut auch*) suspension

Fe|der-: Fe|der|vieh NT poultry; **Fe|der|waa|ge** F spring balance; **Fe|der|wei|ße(r)** M *decl as adj* (*dial*) new wine

FEDERWEISSER

Federweißer (also known as **Sauser, Bitzler** or – in Austria – **Sturm**) is new wine. It is only partially fermented and so still contains carbon dioxide and yeast, which accounts for its typical cloudiness. **Federweißer** is a very popular drink at grape-harvest time and is often enjoyed with a piece of **Zwiebelkuchen** → WEIN

Fe|der-: Fe|der|wild NT (*Hunt*) game birds *pl*; **Fe|der|wisch** M (*old*) feather duster; **Fe|der|wölk|chen** NT , **Fe|der|wol|ke** F fleecy cloud; **Fe|der|zeich|nung** F pen-and-ink drawing

Fee [feː] F -, -n ['feːən] fairy

Feed-back ▲ ['fiːdbɛk] NT -s, -s, **Feed|back** NT -s, -s feedback

Fee|ling ['fiːlɪŋ] NT (*inf*) -s, -s feeling (*für* for)

feen|haft ['feːən-] ADJ (*liter*) fairylike

Fe|ge|feu|er ['feːgə-] NT das ~ purgatory

fe|gen ['feːgn] **VT a** (*mit Besen*) to sweep; (= *auffegen*) to sweep up; (*Sw* = *wischen*) to wipe; (*mit Bürste*) to scrub; **den Schmutz von etw ~** to sweep sth (clean) **b** (*Hunt*) *Geweih* to fray **VI a** (= *ausfegen*) to sweep (up) **b** *aus sein* (*inf:* = *jagen*) to sweep; (*Wind auch*) to race

Fe|ger ['feːgɐ] M -s, - **a** (*inf*) brush **b** (*inf:* = *Mädchen*) girl

Feh|de ['feːdə] F -, -n (*Hist*) feud; **mit jdm eine ~ ausfechten** to feud with sb, to carry on a feud with sb; **mit jdm in ~ liegen** (*lit, fig*) to be feuding with sb, to be in a state of feud with sb

Feh|de|hand|schuh M jdm den ~ hinwerfen (*lit, fig*) to throw down the gauntlet to sb; **den ~ aufheben** (*lit, fig*) to take up the gauntlet

fehl [feːl] ADJ **~ am Platz(e)** out of place

Fehl [feːl] M (*old, liter*) **ohne ~** without (a) blemish

Fehl-: Fehl|an|flug M (*Aviat*) failed approach (to landing); **Fehl|an|pas|sung** F **a** (*Psych*) maladjustment **b** (*Elec*) mismatch; **Fehl|an|zei|ge** F (*inf*) dead loss (*inf*); **~!** wrong!; **Fehl|auf|schlag** M (*Sport*) fault; **einen ~ machen** to serve a fault; **fehl|bar** ADJ fallible; (*Sw*) guilty; **Fehl|bar|keit** F -, *no pl* fallibility; (*Sw*) guilt; **Fehl|be|darf** M uncovered demand; **Fehl|be|die|nung** F (*von Geräten*) operating error; **Fehl|be|le|gung** F (*von Sozialwohnungen*) inappropriate occupation (*of a subsidized accommodation*); **Fehl|be|le|gungsab|ga|be** F tax levied on those inappropriately occupying subsidized accommodation; **fehl+be|set|zen** *ptp* **fehlbesetzt** VT *sep* to miscast; **Fehl|be|set|zung** F miscasting; **eine ~ a** piece or bit of miscasting; **Fehl|be|stand** M deficiency; **Fehl|be|trag** M (*form*) deficit, shortfall; **Fehl|bil|dung** F (*Biol*) malformation; (= *Missbildung*) deformity; **Fehl|bit|te** F (*form*) vain request; **Fehl|deu|tung** F misinterpretation; **Fehl|di|ag|no|se** F wrong or false diagnosis; **Fehl|dis|po|si|ti|on** F miscalculation; **Fehl|druck** M *pl* **-drucke** (*Typ*) misprint; **Fehl|ein|schät|zung** F false estimation; (*der Lage*) misjudgement

feh|len ['feːlən] **VI a** (= *mangeln*) to be lacking; (= *nicht vorhanden sein*) to be missing; (*in der Schule etc*) to be away or absent (*in +dat* from); (= *schmerzlich vermisst werden*) to be missed; **entschuldigt ~** to be absent; **unentschuldigt ~** (*Sch*) to play truant; **das Geld fehlt** (= *ist nicht vorhanden*) there is no money; (= *ist zu wenig vorhanden*) there isn't enough money; **etwas fehlt** there's something missing; **jdm fehlt etw** sb lacks sth, sb doesn't have sth; (= *wird schmerzlich vermisst*) sb misses sth; **mir fehlt Geld** I'm missing some money; **mir ~ 20 Cent am Fahrgeld** I'm 20 cents short for my fare, I'm short of 20 cents for my fare; **mir ~ die Worte** words fail me; **meine Bibliothek fehlt/du fehlst mir sehr** I miss my library/you a lot; **der/das hat mir gerade noch gefehlt!** (*inf*) he/that was all I needed (*iro*); **das durfte nicht ~** that had to happen **b** (= *los sein*) **was fehlt dir?** what's the matter or what's up (with you)?; **fehlt dir (et)was?** is something the matter (with you)?; **mir fehlt nichts** there's nothing the matter (with me); **dem Hund scheint etwas zu ~** the dog seems to have something the matter with it, there seems to be something wrong or the matter with the dog **c** (*old:* = *etwas falsch machen*) to err **VI** *impers* **es fehlt etw** or **an etw** (*dat*) there is a lack of sth; (*völlig*) there is no sth, sth is missing; **es ~ drei Messer** there are three knives missing; **es fehlt jdm an etw** (*dat*) sb lacks sth; **es an etw** (*dat*) **~ lassen** to be lacking in sth, to lack sth; **er ließ es uns an nichts ~** (*geh*) he let us want for nothing; **es fehlt hinten und vorn(e), es fehlt an allen Ecken und Enden** or **Kanten** we/they etc are short of everything; (*bei Kenntnissen*) he/she etc has a lot to learn, he/she etc has a long way to go; (*bei Klassenarbeit etc*) it's a long way from perfect; **wo fehlt es?** what's the trouble?, what's up? (*inf*); **es fehlte nicht viel und ich hätte ihn verprügelt** I almost hit him; **es fehlt(e) nur noch, dass wir sonntags arbeiten sollen** working Sundays is all we need (*iro*) **VT** (*old Hunt*) to miss; **weit gefehlt!** (*fig*) you're way out! (*inf*); (*ganz im Gegenteil*) far from it!

Fehl-: Fehl|ent|schei|dung F wrong decision; **Fehl|ent|wick|lung** F mistake; **um ~en zu vermeiden** to stop things going off course or taking a wrong turn

Fehler ['feːlɐ] ✪ 45.2 M -s, - **a** (= *Irrtum, Unrichtigkeit*) mistake, error; (*Sport*) fault; **einen ~ machen** or **begehen** to make a mistake or error; **ihr ist ein ~ unterlaufen** she's made a mistake;

~! (*Sport*) fault! **b** (= *Mangel*) fault, defect; (= *Charakterfehler auch*) failing; **einen ~ aufweisen** to prove faulty; **jeder hat seine ~** we all have our faults, nobody's perfect; **das ist nicht mein ~** that's not my fault; **einen ~ an sich** (*dat*) **haben** to have a fault; **er hat den ~ an sich, immer dazwischenzureden** or **dass er immer dazwischenredet** the trouble with him is that he's always interrupting; **in den ~ verfallen, etw zu tun** to make the mistake of doing sth

Feh|ler-: Feh|ler|ana|ly|se F error analysis; **feh|ler|an|fäl|lig** ADJ error-prone; **Feh|leran|fäl|lig|keit** F proneness to errors; **Feh|leran|zei|ge** F (*Comput*) error message; **Feh|lerfrei** ADJ perfect; *Ware auch* in perfect condition; *Arbeit, Aussprache, Kür etc auch* faultless, flawless; *Messung, Rechnung* correct; **~er Lauf/ Sprung** (*Sport*) clear round/jump; **Feh|ler|freiheit** F (*von Ware*) perfect condition; **Feh|lergren|ze** F margin of error; **feh|ler|haft** ADJ (*Mech, Tech*) faulty, defective; *Ware* substandard, imperfect; *Messung, Rechnung, Bescheide* incorrect; *Arbeit, Aussprache auch* poor; **Feh|ler|haf|tigkeit** ['feːlɐhaftɪçkaɪt] F -, *no pl* (*Mech, Tech*) defectiveness; (*von Ware*) substandard condition; (*von Messung, Rechnung, Bescheiden*) incorrectness; (*von Arbeit, Aussprache*) poorness; **Feh|lerko|de** M error code; **Feh|ler|kor|rek|tur** F **a** (*Sch*) correction of mistakes; (*eines einzelnen Fehlers*) correction **b** (*Comput* = *Rechtschreibkorrektur*) spell check; (*für Computerprogramme*) debugging program **c** (*Tech: in CD-Spieler etc*) error correction or concealment; **Feh|ler|korrek|tur|pro|gramm** M (*Comput*) **a** (*Rechtschreibkorrekturprogramm*) spellchecker, spelling checker **b** (*für Computerprogramme*) debugging program; **feh|ler|los** ADJ = **fehlerfrei**; **Feh|ler|mel|dung** F (*Comput*) error message

Feh|ler|näh|rung ['feːl-] F malnutrition

Feh|ler-: Feh|ler|quel|le F cause of the fault; (*in Statistik*) source of error; **Feh|ler|quo|te** F error rate; **Feh|ler|su|che** F troubleshooting; (*Tech*) fault detection; (= *Suche nach möglichen Fehlern*) checking for faults; **Feh|ler|ver|zeichnis** NT errata *pl*

Fehl-: Fehl|far|be F (*Cards*) missing suit; (= *Nicht-Trumpf*) plain or side suit; (= *Zigarre*) cigar with a discoloured (*Brit*) or discolored (*US*) wrapper; **Fehl|ge|burt** F miscarriage

fehl+ge|hen VI *sep irreg aux sein* **a** (*geh:* = *sich verirren*) to go wrong, to miss the way; (*Schuss*) to go wide **b** (= *sich irren*) to be wrong or mistaken, to err (*form*); **ich hoffe, ich gehe nicht fehl in der Annahme, dass ...** I trust I am not mistaken in assuming that ...

Fehl-: fehl|ge|steu|ert [-gə'ʃtɔʏɐt] ADJ misdirected; (*fig*) mismanaged; **Fehl|griff** M mistake; **einen ~ tun** to make a mistake; **Fehl|infor|ma|ti|on** F incorrect information *no pl*; **Fehl|in|ter|pre|ta|ti|on** F misinterpretation; **Fehl|in|ves|ti|ti|on** F bad investment; **Fehlkal|ku|la|ti|on** F miscalculation; **Fehl|konstruk|ti|on** F bad design; **der Stuhl ist eine ~** this chair is badly designed; **Fehl|lan|dung** F bad landing; **Fehl|leis|tung** F slip, mistake; **freudsche ~** Freudian slip; **fehl+lei|ten** VT *sep* to misdirect; **die Akte wurde fehlgeleitet** the file was sent to the wrong place; **Fehl|lei|tung** F misdirection; **Fehl|pass ▲** M (*Ftbl*) bad pass; **Fehl|pla|nung** F misplanning, bad planning; **eine ~** a piece of misplanning or bad planning; **fehl|plat|ziert ▲** [-platsiːɐt] ADJ *Empörung etc* misplaced; **Fehl|prä|gung** F (*einer Münze*) mis-strike; **Fehl|prog|no|se** F incorrect prognosis; **Fehl|re|ak|ti|on** F incorrect response; **Fehl|schal|tung** F faulty circuit; **fehl+schie|ßen** VI *sep irreg* to shoot wide; **Fehl|schlag** M (*fig*) failure; **fehl+schla|gen** VI *sep irreg aux sein* to go wrong; (*Hoffnung*) to be misplaced, to come to nothing; **Fehlschluss ▲** M false conclusion; **Fehl|schuss ▲** M miss; **fehl|sich|tig** [-zɪçtɪç] ADJ (*form*) with defective vision; **Fehl|sich|tig|keit** F -, *no pl* (*form*) defective vision; **Fehl|spe|ku|la|ti|on** F bad speculation; **Fehl|start** M false start; (*Space*) faulty launch; **Fehl|stoß** M (*Ftbl*) miskick; (*Billard*) miscue; **fehl+sto|ßen** VI *sep irreg* (*Ftbl*) to miskick; (*Billard*) to miscue; **fehl+tre|ten** VI *sep irreg aux sein* (*geh*) to miss one's footing, to stumble; (*fig*) to err, to lapse; **Fehl|tritt** M (*geh*) false step; (*fig* = *Vergehen*) slip, lapse; (= *Affäre*) indiscretion; **Fehl|ur|teil** NT miscarriage of justice; **Fehl|ver|hal|ten** NT inappropriate behaviour (*Brit*) or behavior (*US*), (*Psych*) abnormal behaviour (*Brit*) or behavior (*US*); **Fehl|ver|such** M unsuccessful or abortive attempt; **fehl+ver|wen|den** *ptp* fehlverwendet VT *sep* to misappropriate; **Fehl|wurf** M (*Sport*) misthrow, bad throw; (*ungültig*) no-throw; **Fehl|zei|ten** PL working hours *pl* lost; **Fehl|zug** M (*Chess*) bad move; **Fehl|zün|dung** F misfiring *no pl*; **eine ~** a backfire; **das war bei mir eine ~** (*fig inf*) I got hold of the wrong end of the stick (*inf*)

fei|en ['faiən] VT (*old*) to protect (*gegen* from), to make proof (*gegen* against) → *auch* **gefeit**

Fei|er ['faiɐ] F -, -n celebration; (= *Party*) party; (= *Zeremonie*) ceremony; (= *Hochzeitsfeier*) reception; **zur ~ von etw** to celebrate sth; **zur ~ des Tages** in honour (*Brit*) or honor (*US*) of the occasion

Fei|er|abend M a (= *Arbeitsschluss*) finishing time; (= *Geschäftsschluss*) closing time; **~ machen** to finish work, to knock off (work) (*inf*); (*Geschäfte*) to close; **ich mache jetzt ~** I think I'll call it a day (*inf*), I think I'll knock off now (*inf*); **um 16.00 Uhr ~ haben** to finish work at 4 o'clock; **~!** (*in Gaststätte*) time, please!; **nach ~** after work; **jetzt ist aber ~!** (*fig inf*) enough is enough; **damit ist jetzt ~** (*fig inf*) that's all over now; **dann ist ~** (*fig inf*) then it's all over, then it's the end of the road; **für mich ist ~** (*fig inf*) I've had enough **b** (= *Zeit nach Arbeitsschluss*) evening; **schönen ~!** have a nice evening!

fei|er|lich ['faiɐlıç] ADJ (= *ernsthaft, würdig*) solemn; (= *festlich*) festive; (= *förmlich*) ceremonial; **das ist ja nicht mehr ~** (*inf*) that's beyond a joke (*inf*) ADV solemnly; **einen Tag ~ begehen** to celebrate a day

Fei|er|lich|keit F -, -en a (= *Ernsthaftigkeit, Würde*) solemnity; (= *Festlichkeit*) festiveness; (= *Förmlichkeit*) ceremony **b** *usu pl* (= *Veranstaltungen*) celebrations *pl*, festivities *pl*

fei|ern ['faiɐn] VT a *Ereignis* to celebrate; *Party, Fest, Orgie* to hold; **das muss gefeiert werden!** that calls for a celebration; **Triumphe ~** to achieve a great triumph, to make one's mark **b** (= *umjubeln*) to fête → *auch* **gefeiert** VI a (= *eine Feier abhalten*) to celebrate; **die ganze Nacht ~** to make a night of it **b** (= *nicht arbeiten*) to stay off work

Fei|er-: **Fei|er|schicht** F cancelled (*Brit*) or canceled (*US*) shift; **eine ~ fahren/einlegen** to miss/cancel a shift; **Fei|er|stun|de** F ceremony; **Fei|er|tag** M holiday; **fei|er|täg|lich** ADJ holiday *attr* (*esp Brit*), vacation *attr* (*US*); **~e Stimmung** holiday mood; **das ~e Ruhegebot** rule discouraging any activity likely to disturb the quietness of Sundays and public holidays ADV **~ angezogen** in one's Sunday best

Fei|er|tags|stim|mung F holiday mood

feig [faik], **fei|ge** ['faigə] ADJ cowardly; **~ wie er war** like the coward he was ADV in a cowardly way; **er zog sich ~ zurück** he retreated like a coward

Fei|ge ['faigə] F -, -n fig

Fei|gen-: **Fei|gen|baum** M fig tree; **Fei|gen|blatt** NT fig leaf; **ein ~ für etw** (*fig*) a front to hide sth; **als demokratisches ~** (*fig*) to give a veneer of democracy; **Fei|gen|kak|tus** M prickly pear

Feig|heit F -, *no pl* cowardice, cowardliness

Feig|ling ['faiklıŋ] M -s, -e coward

---

feil [fail] ADJ (*old, geh*) (up) for sale; **der Ring war ihr um** or **für nichts auf der Welt ~** not for all the world would she have sold the ring

feil+bie|ten VT *sep irreg* (*old*) to offer for sale

Fei|le ['failə] F -, -n file

fei|len ['failən] VT to file VI to file; (*fig*) to make some improvements; **an etw** (*dat*) **~** (*lit*) to file (away at) sth; (*fig*) to hone sth, to polish sth up

feil+hal|ten VT *sep irreg* (*old*) to offer for sale → **Maulaffen**

feil|schen ['failʃn] VI (*pej*) to haggle (*um* over)

Feil-: **Feil|span** M filing; **Feil|staub** M (fine) filings *pl*

fein [fain] ADJ a (= *nicht grob*) fine; *Humor, Ironie* delicate; *Unterschied* subtle; (*fig* = *listig*) cunning **b** (= *erlesen*) excellent, choice *attr*; *Geruch, Geschmack* delicate; *Gold, Silber* refined; *Mensch, Charakter* thoroughly nice; (= *prima*) great (*inf*), splendid, swell (*esp US inf*); (*iro*) fine; **ein ~er Kerl** a great guy (*inf*), a splendid person; **~!** great! (*inf*), marvellous! (*Brit*), marvelous! (*US*); (= *in Ordnung*) fine!; **~, dass ...** great that ... (*inf*), (I'm) so glad that ...; **das ist etwas Feines** that's really something (*inf*) or nice; **das ist nicht die ~e englische Art** that's not the proper way to go about things; **vom Feinsten sein** to be first-rate; **italienisches Design vom Feinsten** Italian design at its finest **c** (= *scharf*) sensitive, keen; *Gehör, Gefühl auch* acute **d** (= *vornehm*) refined, fine (*esp iro*), posh (*inf*); **nicht ~ genug sein** not to be good enough; **dazu ist sie sich** (*dat*) **zu ~** that's beneath her ADV a (= *nicht grob*) *gemahlen, passiert, gesponnen, schleifen, geädert* finely; **ein ~ gestreiftes Hemd** a shirt with very thin stripes; **sie hat ein ~ geschnittenes Gesicht** she has fine features; **~ geschwungene Augenbrauen** finely arched eyebrows **b** (= *gut*) **~ säuberlich** (nice and) neat; **etw ~ machen** to do sth beautifully; **das war von dir aber wieder ~ bemerkt** you have such a nice way of putting things; **~ (he)raus sein** to be sitting pretty **c** (= *genau*) **etw ~ einstellen** to adjust sth precisely **d** (= *elegant*) **er hat sich ~ gemacht** he's dressed to kill (*inf*); **sie hat sich ~ gemacht** she's all dolled up **e** (*baby-talk*) just; **du gehst jetzt ~ nach Hause** now just you go straight home; **sei jetzt mal ~ still** now keep nice and quiet or very very quiet

Fein-: **Fein|ab|stim|mung** F (*Rad, TV*) fine tuning; **Fein|ar|beit** F precision work; **Fein|aus|gleich** M (*Comput*) microspacing; **Fein|bä|cke|rei** F cake shop, patisserie; **Fein|blech** NT thin sheet metal

feind △ [faint] ADJ *pred* → **Feind**

Feind [faint] M -(e)s, -e [-də], **Fein|din** ['faindın] F -, -nen enemy, foe (*liter*); **jdn zum ~ haben** to have sb as an enemy; **sich** (*dat*) **jdn zum ~ machen** to make an enemy of sb; **sich** (*dat*) **~e schaffen** to make enemies; **er war ein ~ jeden Fortschritts** he was opposed to progress in any shape or form; **ran an den ~** (*inf*) let's get stuck in (*inf*); **der böse ~** (*Bibl*) the Evil One, the Enemy; **liebet eure ~e** (*Bibl*) love thine enemy (*Bibl*); **jdm/einer Sache ~ sein** to be hostile to sb/sth

-feind(in) M(F) *suf in cpds* -hater; **eine Männerfeindin** a man-hater

Feind- *in cpds* enemy; **Feind|be|rüh|rung** F contact with the enemy; **Feind|bild** NT concept of an/the enemy; **Feind|ein|wir|kung** F (*Mil form*) **durch ~** as a result of enemy action; **er verletzte sich ohne ~** his injury was self-inflicted

Fein|des-: **Fein|des|hand** F (*old, liter*) the hands of the foe (*liter*); **Fein|des|land** NT (*old, liter*) enemy territory

---

Fein|din F → **Feind**

feind|lich ['faintlıç] ADJ a (*Mil*: = *gegnerisch*) enemy; **im ~en Lager** (*lit, fig*) in the enemy camp **b** (= *feindselig*) hostile ADV **jdm/einer Sache ~ gegenüberstehen** to be hostile to sb/sth; **einer Sache ausgesprochen ~ gegenüberstehen** to be vehemently opposed to sth, to be extremely hostile to sth

-feind|lich ADJ *suf* anti-; **deutschfeindlich** anti-German

Feind|macht F enemy power; **eine ~ unseres Landes** an enemy of our country

Feind|schaft ['faintʃaft] F -, -en hostility, enmity; **sich** (*dat*) **jds ~ zuziehen** to make an enemy of sb; **mit jdm in ~ liegen** to be at daggers drawn with sb, to live in enmity with sb; **eine ~ auf Leben und Tod** mortal enmity

feind|se|lig ADJ hostile ADV hostilely; **jdn ~ ansehen** to give sb a hostile look

Feind|se|lig|keit F -, -en hostility; **~en** hostilities

Fein-: **Fein|ein|stel|lung** F (*Tech*) fine adjustment; (*Radio, Kurzwelle*) fine tuning; **fein|füh|lend** [-fy:lıç] ADJ sensitive; (= *taktvoll*) tactful; **Fein|füh|lig|keit** F -, *no pl* sensitivity; (= *Takt*) tact(fulness); **Fein|ge|bäck** NT cakes and pastries *pl*; **Fein|ge|fühl** NT , *no pl* sensitivity; (= *Takt*) delicacy, tact(fulness); **jds ~ verletzen** to hurt sb's feelings; **fein|ge|mah|len** △ [-gəma:lən] ADJ *attr* → **fein** ADV a; **fein|glie|drig** [-gli:drıç], **fein|glied|rig** [-gli:drıç] ADJ *Person, Hände* slender; **Fein|gold** NT refined gold

Fein|heit F -, -en a (= *Zartheit*) fineness; **die ~ des britischen Humors** the delicate British humour (*Brit*) or humor (*US*) **b** (= *Erlesenheit*) excellence; (*von Gold, Silber*) refinement; **die ~ des Geschmacks** the delicate flavour (*Brit*) or flavor (*US*) **c** (= *Schärfe*) keenness; (*von Gehör, Gefühl auch*) acuteness **d** (= *Vornehmheit*) refinement, poshness (*inf*) **e** **Feinheiten** PL niceties *pl*, finer points *pl*; (= *Nuancen*) subtleties *pl*; **das sind eben die ~en** it's the little things that make the difference

Fein-: **Fein|koh|le** F slack; **fein|kör|nig** ADJ *Film* fine-grain; *Sand, Salz auch* fine; **Fein|kost** F delicacies *pl*; „**Feinkost**" "Delicatessen"; **Fein|kost|ge|schäft** NT delicatessen; **fein|ma|schig** [-maʃıç] ADJ with a fine mesh; *Strickwaren* finely knitted; **Fein|me|cha|nik** F precision engineering; **Fein|me|cha|ni|ker(in)** M(F) precision engineer; **Fein|mess|ge|rät** ▲ NT precision instrument; **fein|ner|vig** ADJ sensitive; **Fein|po|si|ti|o|nie|rung** F microjustification; **Fein|schliff** M fine finish(ing); **Fein|schme|cker** [-ʃmɛkɐ] M -s, -, **Fein|schme|cke|rin** [-ərın] F -, -nen gourmet, epicure; (*fig*) connoisseur; **Fein|schme|cker|lo|kal** NT gourmet restaurant; **Fein|schnitt** M (= *Tabak*) fine cut; (*Film*) final editing; **Fein|sil|ber** NT refined silver; **fein|sin|nig** ADJ sensitive; *Unterscheidung* subtle; **Fein|sin|nig|keit** F -, *no pl* sensitivity

Feins|lieb|chen ['fains'li:pçən] NT -s, - (*poet*) lady-love (*poet*), sweetheart

Fein-: **Fein|struk|tur** F fine structure; **Fein|un|ze** F troy ounce; **Fein|waa|ge** F precision balance; **Fein|wä|sche** F delicates *pl*; **Fein|wasch|mit|tel** NT mild(-action) detergent

feist [faist] ADJ fat; *Mensch auch* gross, obese; **ein ~es Lachen** an obscene chuckle

Feist|heit F -, *no pl*, **Feis|tig|keit** ['faistıçkait] F -, *no pl* fatness; (*von Mensch auch*) grossness, obesity

Fei|tel ['faitl] M -s, - (*Aus*) penknife

fei|xen ['faiksn] VI (*inf*) to smirk

Fel|chen ['fɛlçn] M -s, - whitefish

Feld [fɛlt] NT -(e)s, -er [-dɐ] a (= *offenes Gelände*) open country; **auf freiem ~** in the open country → **Wald** **b** (= *Acker*) field **c** (= *Flächenstück: auf Spielbrett*) square; (*an Ziel-*

scheibe) ring; (Her) field

d (Sport: = Spielfeld) field, pitch; **das ~ beherrschen** to be on top

e (= Kriegsschauplatz) (battle)field; **ins ~ ziehen** or **rücken** (old) to take the field, to march into battle; **auf dem ~e der Ehre fallen** (euph old) to fall on the field of honour (Brit) or honor (US); **gegen jdn/etw zu ~e ziehen** (fig) to crusade against sb/sth; **Argumente ins ~ führen** to bring arguments to bear; **das ~ behaupten** (fig) to stand or stay one's ground; **jdn aus dem ~ schlagen** (fig) to eliminate sb; **das ~ räumen** (fig) to quit the field, to bow out; **jdm/einer Sache das ~ überlassen** or **räumen** to give way or yield to sb/sth; (freiwillig) to hand over to sb/ sth

f (fig: = Bereich) field, area

g (Ling, Min, Phys, Comput) field

h (Sport: = Gruppe) field; **er ließ das ~ hinter sich** (dat) he left the rest of the field behind (him); **das ~ ist geschlossen** the field is bunched (up)

Feld- in cpds field; **Feld|ar|beit** F (Agr) work in the fields; (Sci, Sociol) fieldwork; **Feld|ar|bei|ter(in)** M(F) fieldworker; **Feld|arzt** M (old Mil) army doctor; **Feld|be|steck** NT knife, fork and spoon, eating irons pl (Brit hum); **Feld|bett** NT campbed, cot (US); **Feld|bin|de** F **a** (old: = Schärpe) sash **b** (Med Mil) Red Cross armband; **Feld|blu|me** F wild flower; **Feld|dienst** M (old Mil) active service; **Feld|elek|tro|nen** PL (Elec) field electrons pl; **Feld|ener|gie** F (Phys) field energy

Fel|der|wirt|schaft F (Agr) crop rotation

Feld-: **Feld|fla|sche** F canteen (Mil), water bottle; **Feld|flug|platz** M (military) airstrip (near the front); **Feld|for|schung** F , no pl (esp Sociol) field research, fieldwork; **Feld|frucht** F (Agr) agricultural crop; **Feld|geist|li|che(r)** M decl as adj (old Mil) army chaplain, padre; **Feld|gen|dar|me|rie** F (old Mil) military police; **Feld|glei|chung** F (Math) field equation; **Feld|got|tes|dienst** M (Mil) camp service; **Feld|hand|ball** M European (outdoor) handball; **Feld|ha|se** M European hare; **Feld|hau|bit|ze** F (Mil) (field) howitzer; **Feld|heer** NT (Mil) army in the field; **Feld|herr(in)** M(F) commander; **Feld|herrn|kunst** F (old) strategy; **Feld|herrn|stab** M (old) (general's) baton, (general's) swagger stick; **Feld|heu|schre|cke** F grasshopper; (schädlich) locust; **Feld|huhn** NT partridge; **Feld|hü|ter** M watchman (in charge of fields); **Feld|jä|ger(in)** M(F) **a** (old Mil) (= Kurier) courier; (= Infanterist) infantryman **b** ~ (Mil) military police; (bei der Marine) shore patrol; **Feld|kon|stan|te** F (Phys) space constant; **Feld|kraft** F (Phys) field intensity or strength; **Feld|krä|he** F rook; **Feld|kü|che** F (Mil) field kitchen; **Feld|la|ger** NT (old Mil) camp, encampment; **Feld|la|za|rett** NT (Mil) field hospital; **Feld|ler|che** F skylark; **Feld|li|nie** F (Phys) line of force; **Feld|mark** F pl **-marken** (von Gemeinde) parish land; (von Gut) estate; **Feld|mar|schall** M (old) field marshal; **Feld|maus** F field mouse, common vole (spec); **Feld|mes|ser** [-mɛsɐ] M **-s, -**, **Feld|mes|se|rin** [-ərɪn] F **-, -nen** (land) surveyor; **Feld|pflan|ze** F agricultural crop; **Feld|post** F (Mil) forces' postal service; **Feld|post|brief** M (Mil) forces' letter; **Feld|rain** M edge of the field; **Feld|sa|lat** M lamb's lettuce; **Feld|schlacht** F (old) battle; **Feld|schütz** [-ʏts] M **-es, -e** (Mil) watchman (in charge of fields); **Feld|spat** M (Geol) fel(d)spar; **Feld|spie|ler(in)** M(F) (Sport) player (on the field); **Feld|stär|ke** F (Phys) field strength or intensity; (Rad, TV) strength of the signal; **Feld|ste|cher** [-ʃtɛçɐ] M **-s, -** (pair of) binoculars, (pair of) field glasses; **Feld|stu|die** F (esp Sociol) field study; **Feld|stuhl** M folding stool; **Feld|te|le|fon** NT (Mil) field telephone; **Feld|te|le|graf** M (Mil) field telegraph; **Feld|the|o|rie** F (Ling, Phys, Psych) field theory; **Feld|ver|such** M field test;

Feld|ver|weis M = Platzverweis; **Feld|wa|che** F (old Mil) outpost

Feld-Wald-und-Wie|sen- in cpds (inf) common-or-garden (Brit), garden-variety (esp US), run-of-the-mill; **ein ~Arzt** a common-or-garden (Brit) or garden-variety (esp US) or run-of-the--mill doctor; **ein ~Thema** a run-of-the-mill subject

Feld-: **Feld|we|bel** ['fɛltveːbl] M **-s, -**, **Feld|we|be|lin** [-bəlɪn] F **-, -nen** sergeant; (fig inf) sergeant-major (type); **Feld|weg** M track across the fields; **Feld|wei|bel** ['fɛltvaibl] M **-s, -**, **Feld|wei|be|lin** [-bəlɪn] F **-, -nen** (Sw) sergeant; **Feld|zei|chen** NT (old Mil) standard, ensign; **Feld|zug** M (old, fig) campaign

Felg|auf|schwung ['fɛlk-] M (Sport) upward circle forwards

Fel|ge ['fɛlgə] F **-, -n** **a** (Tech) (wheel) rim **b** (Sport) circle

Fel|gen|brem|se F calliper brake

Felg|um|schwung ['fɛlk-] M (Sport) circle

Fell [fɛl] NT **-(e)s, -e** **a** fur; (von Schaf, Lamm) fleece; (von toten Tieren) skin, fell; **ein gesundes ~ haben** a healthy coat; **einem Tier das ~ abziehen** to skin an animal; **ihm sind alle** or **die ~e weggeschwommen** (fig) all his hopes were dashed **b** (fig inf: = Menschenhaut) skin, hide (inf); **ein dickes ~ haben** to be thick-skinned, to have a thick skin; **jdm das ~ gerben** or **versohlen** to tan sb's hide (inf); **jdm das ~ über die Ohren ziehen** to dupe sb, to pull the wool over sb's eyes; **ihn** or **ihm juckt das ~** he's asking for a good hiding; **das ~ versaufen** to hold the wake **c** (von Trommel) skin

Fell- in cpds fur; (Schaffell- etc) sheepskin etc; **eine Fellmütze** a fur/sheepskin hat; **eine Felljacke** a fur/sheepskin jacket

Fell|la|che [fɛˈlaxə] M **-n, -n**, **Fell|la|chin** [-ˈlaxɪn] F **-, -nen** fellah

Fell|la|tio [fɛˈlaːtsio] F **-, Fellationes** [fɛlaˈtsioːnəs] fellatio

Fell-: **Fell|ei|sen** NT (obs) knapsack; **Fell|han|del** M trade in skins

Fels [fɛls] M **-en, -en** [ˈfɛlzn] rock; (= Klippe) cliff

Fels- in cpds (von Felsen-:) **Fels|bild** NT rockscape; **Fels|block** M pl **-blöcke** boulder; **Fels|bro|cken** M (lump of) rock

Fel|sen ['fɛlzn] M **-s, -** rock; (= Klippe) cliff

Fel|sen- in cpds → auch Fels-: **Fel|sen|burg** F mountain fortress; **fel|sen|fest** ADJ firm ADV ~ **überzeugt sein** to be absolutely or firmly convinced; **sich ~ auf jdn verlassen** to put one's complete trust in sb; **Fel|sen|ge|bir|ge** NT **a** rocky mountain range **b** (Geog) Rocky Mountains pl, Rockies pl; **Fel|sen|grab** NT rock tomb; **Fel|sen|grund** M rockbed; (poet: = Tal) rocky vale (poet) or glen; **Fel|sen|höh|le** F rock cave; **Fel|sen|nest** NT mountain lair or hideout; **Fel|sen|riff** NT (rocky) reef; **Fel|sen|schlucht** F rocky valley or glen; **Fel|sen|tor** NT arch in the rock

Fels-: **Fels|for|ma|ti|on** F (Geol) rock formation; **Fels|ge|stein** NT (Geol) (solid) rock; **Fels|glim|mer** M (Geol) mica; **Fels|grat** M (rocky) ridge

fel|sig ['fɛlzɪç] ADJ rocky; (= steil abfallend) Küste cliff-lined, cliffy

Fels-: **Fels|kes|sel** M corrie; **Fels|klip|pe** F rocky cliff; (im Meer) stack; **Fels|ma|le|rei** F rock painting; **Fels|mas|siv** NT rock massif; **Fels|na|se** F rock overhang or shelf; **Fels|spal|te** F crevice; **Fels|vor|sprung** M ledge; **Fels|wand** F rock face; **Fels|wüs|te** F rock desert; **Fels|za|cke** F crag

Fe|lu|ke [feˈluːkə] F **-, -n** felucca

Fe|me ['feːmə] F **-, -n**, **Fe|me|ge|richt** NT (Hist) Vehmgericht; (= Bandengericht) kangaroo court

Fe|me|mord M (Hist) killing ordered by a Vehmgericht (fig) lynch-law killing; (unter Gangstern) underworld killing

Fem|ge|richt ['feːm-] NT = Feme(gericht)

Fe|mi|nat [femiˈnaːt] NT **-(e)s, -e** female power base

fe|mi|nin [femiˈniːn] ADJ **a** (Gram) feminine **b** (= fraulich) feminine; (pej) effeminate

Fe|mi|ni|num ['feːminiːnʊm] NT **-s, Feminina** [-na] (Gram) feminine noun

Fe|mi|nis|mus [femiˈnɪsmʊs] M **-, Feminismen** [-mən] feminism

Fe|mi|nist [femiˈnɪst] M **-en, -en**, **Fe|mi|nis|tin** [-ˈnɪstɪn] F **-, -nen** feminist

fe|mi|nis|tisch [femiˈnɪstɪʃ] ADJ feminist ADV ~ **orientiert sein** to have feminist tendencies

Femme fa|tale [fam faˈtal] F **- -, -s -s** femme fatale

Fem|to|gramm [fɛmtoˈgram] NT femtogram(me)

Fen|chel ['fɛnçl] M **-s, no pl** fennel

Fen|chel- in cpds fennel; **Fen|chel|holz** NT sassafras wood; **Fen|chel|tee** M fennel tea

Fen|der ['fɛndɐ] M **-s, -** fender

Fens|ter ['fɛnstɐ] NT **-s, -** window (auch Comput, fig); **weg vom ~** (inf) out of the game (inf), finished; **~ der Gelegenheit** window of opportunity → **Geld a**

Fens|ter- in cpds window; **Fens|ter|bank** F pl **-bänke**, **Fens|ter|brett** NT window-sill, window ledge; **Fens|ter|brief|um|schlag** M window envelope; **Fens|ter|flü|gel** M side of a window; **Fens|ter|front** F glass façade; **Fens|ter|glas** NT window glass; (in Brille) plain glass; **Fens|ter|griff** M window catch (Brit) or knob (US); **Fens|ter|he|ber** M (Aut) window winder (Brit) or raiser (US); (elektronisch) electric windows pl; **Fens|ter|kitt** M (window) putty; **Fens|ter|klap|pe** F fanlight; **Fens|ter|kreuz** NT mullion and transom (of a cross window); **Fens|ter|kur|bel** F window handle (for winding car windows); **Fens|ter|la|den** M shutter; **Fens|ter|le|der** NT chamois, shammy (leather)

fens|terln ['fɛnstɐln] VI (S Ger, Aus) to climb through one's sweetheart's bedroom window

Fens|ter-: **fens|ter|los** ADJ windowless; **Fens|ter|pfos|ten** M mullion; **Fens|ter|platz** M seat by the window, window seat; **Fens|ter|put|zer** [-pʊtsɐ] M **-s, -**, **Fens|ter|put|ze|rin** F **-, -nen** window cleaner; **Fens|ter|rah|men** M window frame; **Fens|ter|re|de** F soapbox speech; **Fens|ter|rei|ni|ger¹** M **-s, -** (Putzmittel) window or glass cleaner; **Fens|ter|rei|ni|ger²** M **-s, -**, **Fens|ter|rei|ni|ge|rin** [-gərɪn] F **-, -nen** window cleaner; **Fens|ter|ro|se** F rose window; **Fens|ter|schei|be** F window pane; **Fens|ter|sims** M window ledge, windowsill; **Fens|ter|stock** M window frame; **Fens|ter|sturz** M **a** (Build) window lintel **b** (Hist) **der Prager ~** the Prague defenestration; **Fens|ter|tech|nik** F (Comput) windowing technique; **Fens|ter|um|schlag** M window envelope

Fer|ge ['fɛrgə] M **-n, -n** (poet) ferryman

Fe|ri|al- [feˈriaːl] in cpds (Aus) = Ferien-

Fe|ri|en ['feːriən] PL holidays pl (Brit), vacation sing (US, Univ); (= Ferienreise) holiday sing (esp Brit), vacation sing (US); (= Parlamentsferien, Jur) recess sing; **die großen ~** the summer holidays (esp Brit), the long vacation (US, Univ); **~ haben** to be on holiday (esp Brit) or vacation (US); **~ machen** to have or take a holiday (esp Brit) or vacation (US); **vom Ich machen** to get away from it all; **in die ~ gehen** or **fahren** to go on holiday (esp Brit) or vacation (US)

Fe|ri|en- in cpds holiday (esp Brit), vacation (US); **Fe|ri|en|an|la|ge** F holiday (esp Brit) or vacation (US) complex; **Fe|ri|en|dorf** NT holiday village; **Fe|ri|en|gast** M holiday-maker (Brit), vacationer (US); (= Besuch) person staying on holiday (esp Brit) or vacation (US); **Fe|ri|en|haus** NT holiday home; **Fe|ri|en|kind** NT child from a town on a state-subsi-

dized holiday; **Fe|ri|en|ko|lo|nie** F children's holiday (*esp Brit*) or vacation (*US*) camp; **Fe|ri|en|kurs** M vacation course; (*im Sommer auch*) summer course; **Fe|ri|en|la|ger** NT holiday (*esp Brit*) or vacation (*US*) camp; (*für Kinder, im Sommer*) summer camp; **ins ~ fahren** to go to a holiday (*esp Brit*) or vacation (*US*) camp; (*im Sommer*) to go to summer camp; **Fe|ri|en|ord|nung** F holiday dates *pl*; **Fe|ri|en|ort** M *pl* **-orte** holiday (*esp Brit*) or vacation (*US*) resort; **Fe|ri|en|rei|se** F holiday (*esp Brit*) or vacation (*US*); **Fe|ri|en|tag** M day of one's holidays (*Brit*) or vacation (*US*); **Fe|ri|en|woh|nung** F holiday flat (*Brit*), vacation apartment (*US*); **Fe|ri|en|zeit** F holiday (*esp Brit*) or vacation (*US*) period

Fer|kel ['ferkl] NT **-s, -** piglet; (*fig*) (*unsauber*) pig, mucky pup (*Brit inf*); (*unanständig*) dirty pig (*inf*)

Fer|ke|lei [ferkə'laɪ] F **-, -en** (*inf*) (= *Schmutz*) mess; (= *Witz*) dirty joke; (= *Handlung*) dirty or filthy or disgusting thing to do

fer|keln ['ferkln] VI **a** (*Zool*) to litter **b** (*inf*) (= *Schmutz verursachen*) to make a mess; (= *schmutzige Witze erzählen*) to tell dirty jokes; (= *sich unanständig benehmen*) to be dirty or filthy or disgusting

Fer|ma|te [fer'maːtə] F **-, -n** (*Mus*) fermata, pause

Fer|ment [fer'ment] NT **-s, -e** enzyme

Fer|men|ta|ti|on [fermenta'tsi̯oːn] F **-, -en** fermentation

Fer|men|ter [fer'mentɐ] M **-s, -** fermenter

fer|men|tie|ren [fermen'tiːrən] *ptp* **fermentiert** VT to ferment

Fer|ment|man|gel M enzyme deficiency

Fer|mi|um ['fermiʊm] NT **-s,** *no pl* (*abbr* **Fm**) fermium

fern [fern] **ADJ** **a** (*räumlich*) distant, far-off, faraway; **~ von hier** a long way (away) from here, far away from here; **von ~(e) betrachtet** seen from a distance; **sich ~ sein** (*fig*) to be not at all close (to one another); **der Ferne Osten** the Far East; **von ~(e) kennen** (*fig*) to know (only) slightly; **das sei ~ von mir** (*fig*) nothing is further from my thoughts, heaven forbid; **von ~ her** (*old*) from afar (*old, liter*) **b** (*zeitlich entfernt*) far-off; **~e Vergangenheit** (*dim and*) distant past; **in nicht (all)zu ~er Zeit** in the not-too-distant future; **der Tag ist nicht mehr ~, wo ... the day is not far off when ... **PREP** *+gen* far (away) from; **~ der Heimat** far from home; **unrasiert und ~ der Heimat** (*hum inf*) down on one's luck and a long way from home

Fern-: fern|ab [fern'lap] **ADV** far away; **~ gelegen** far away; **Fern|ab|fra|ge** F (*Telec*) remote control facility; **Fern|amt** NT (telephone) exchange; **das Gespräch wurde vom ~ vermittelt** the call was connected by the operator; **Fern|auf|nah|me** F (*Phot*) long shot; **Fern|aus|lö|ser** M (*Phot*) cable release; **Fern|bahn** F (*Rail*) main-line service; **Fern|be|ben** NT distant earthquake; **Fern|be|die|nung** F remote control; **fern+blei|ben** VI *sep irreg aux sein* to stay away (*+dat, von* from); **Fern|blei|ben** NT **-s,** *no pl* absence (*von* from); (= *Nichtteilnahme*) non-attendance; **Fern|blick** M good view; **ein herrlicher ~** a splendid view for miles around

fer|ne ['fernə] **ADJ** (*poet, geh*) = **fern ADJ**

Fer|ne ['fernə] F **-, -n** **a** (*räumlich*) distance; (*liter: = ferne Länder*) distant lands *pl* or shores *pl* (*liter*); **in der ~** in the distance; **aus der ~** from a distance; **in die ~ ziehen** (*liter*) to seek out far-off shores, to seek out distant climes (*liter*) **b** (*zeitlich*) (= *Zukunft*) future; (= *Vergangenheit*) (distant) past; **in weiter ~ liegen** to be a long time off, to be in the distant future

Fern|emp|fang M (*Rad, TV*) long-distance reception

fer|ner ['fernɐ] **ADJ** *comp von* **fern** further; **Ihre ~en Aufträge** (*Comm*) your future or further or-

ders; **für die ~e Zukunft** for the long term **ADV** **a** further; **~ liefen ...** (*Sport*) also-rans ...; **unter ~ liefen rangieren** or **kommen** (*inf*) to be among the also-rans **b** (= *künftig*) in future; (**auch**) **~ etw machen** to continue to do sth; **auch ~ im Amt bleiben** to continue in office

fer|ner|hin ['fernɐhɪn, ˌfernɐ'hɪn] **ADV** = **ferner ADV b**

fer|ner lie|gen ▲ VI *irreg* (*fig*) **nichts läge mir ferner, als ...** nothing could be further from my thoughts or mind than ...; **kein Gedanke könnte ~ als ...** nothing could be further from my thoughts than ...

Fern-: Fern|ex|press ▲ M (*Rail*) long-distance express train; **Fern|fah|rer(in)** M(F) long-distance lorry (*Brit*) or truck driver, trucker (*US*); **Fern|fah|rer|lo|kal** NT transport café (*Brit*), truckstop (*US*); **Fern|flug** M long-distance or long-haul flight; **Fern|gas** NT *gas piped over a long distance*; **fern|ge|lenkt** [-gəleŋkt] **ADJ** remote-controlled; (*fig*) manipulated (*von* by) → *auch* **fernlenken**; **Fern|ge|schütz** NT (*Mil*) long-range weapon; **Fern|ge|spräch** NT trunk (*Brit*) or long-distance call; **fern|ge|steu|ert** [-gəʃtɔʏɐt] **ADJ** remote-controlled; (*durch Funk auch*) radio-controlled; (*fig*) manipulated (*von* by) → *auch* **fernsteuern**; **Fern|glas** NT (pair of) binoculars *pl*, (pair of) field glasses *pl*

fern hal|ten ▲ *irreg* **VT** to keep away **VR** to keep or stay away

Fern-: Fern|hei|zung F district heating (*spec*); **Fern|heiz|werk** NT district heating plant (*spec*); **fern|her** ['fern'heːɐ] **ADV** (*old*) from afar (*old, liter*) → *auch* **fern ADJ a**; **Fern|ko|pie** F (*Telec*) fax; **Fern|ko|pie|rer** M fax (machine); **Fern|kurs** M **,** **Fern|kur|sus** **M** correspondence course

Fern|las|ter M long-distance lorry (*Brit*) or truck, juggernaut (*Brit*)

Fern|last-: Fern|last|fah|rer(in) M(F) (*inf*) long-distance lorry (*Brit*) or truck driver, trucker (*US*); **Fern|last|ver|kehr** M long-distance goods traffic; **Fern|last|zug** M long-distance truck-trailer

Fern-: Fern|lehr|gang M correspondence course; **Fern|lei|tung** F **a** (*Telec*) trunk (*Brit*) or long-distance line(s) **b** (= *Röhren*) pipeline; **fern+len|ken** VT *sep* to operate by remote control → *auch* **ferngelenkt**; **Fern|len|kung** F remote control; **Fern|lenk|waf|fen** PL (*Mil*) guided missiles; **Fern|licht** NT (*Aut*) full or main or high (*esp US*) beam; **mit ~ fahren**, (*das*) **~ anhaben** to be or drive on full or main or high (*esp US*) beam; **fern lie|gen** ▲ VI *irreg* (*fig*) (*jdm*) ~ to be far from sb's thoughts or mind; **es liegt mir fern, das zu tun** far be it from me to do that → **ferner liegen**

Fern|mel|de-: Fern|mel|de|amt NT telephone exchange; **Fern|mel|de|dienst** M telecommunications service; (= *Telefondienst*) telephone service; **Fern|mel|de|ge|heim|nis** NT (*Jur*) secrecy of telecommunications

Fern|mel|der M (*form*) telephone

Fern|mel|der(in) M(F) (*Mil inf*) signaller (*Brit*), signaler (*US*)

Fern|mel|de-: Fern|mel|de|sa|tel|lit M communications satellite; **Fern|mel|de|tech|nik** F telecommunications engineering; (= *Telefontechnik*) telephone engineering; **Fern|mel|de|trup|pe** F (*Mil*) signals corps *sing*; **Fern|mel|de|we|sen** NT **,** *no pl* telecommunications *sing*

Fern-: Fern|mes|sung F telemetering; **fern|münd|lich** (*form*) **ADJ** telephone *attr* **ADV** by telephone

Fern|ost ['fern'ɔst] *no art* **aus/in/nach ~** from/in/to the Far East

Fern|ost|ex|por|te PL exports *pl* to the Far East

Fern|ost|han|del M trade with the Far East

fern|öst|lich ['fern'lœstlɪç] **ADJ** Far Eastern *attr*

Fern|ost|rei|se F journey to the Far East

Fern-: Fern|ra|ke|te F long-range missile; **Fern|rei|se** F long-haul journey; **Fern|rohr** NT telescope; **Fern|ruf** M (*form*) telephone number; **~ 68190** Tel. 68190; **Fern|schal|ter** M (*Elec*) remote-control switch; **Fern|schnell|zug** M long-distance express (train); **Fern|schrei|ben** NT telex; **Fern|schrei|ber** M teleprinter; (*Comm*) telex(-machine); **Fern|schrei|ber(in)** M(F) teleprinter operator; (*Comm*) telex operator; **Fern|schreib|netz** NT telex network; **fern|schrift|lich** **ADJ, ADV** by telex

Fern|seh- *in cpds* television, TV; **Fern|seh|an|sa|ger(in)** M(F) television announcer; **Fern|seh|an|spra|che** F television speech; **Fern|seh|an|stalt** F television company; **Fern|seh|an|ten|ne** F television or TV aerial or antenna; **Fern|seh|ap|pa|rat** M television or TV set; **Fern|seh|de|bat|te** F televised debate; **Fern|seh|emp|fän|ger** M (*form*) television receiver

fern+se|hen VI *sep irreg* to watch television or TV or telly (*Brit inf*)

Fern|se|hen NT **-s,** *no pl* television, TV, telly (*Brit inf*); **~ haben** (*Familie etc*) to have a television; (*Staat etc*) to have television or TV; **beim ~ arbeiten** to work or be in television; **vom ~ übertragen werden** to be televised; **im** or (*Sw*) **am ~** on television or TV or (the) telly (*Brit inf*); **was kommt heute Abend im** or (*Sw*) **am ~?** what's on television or TV or (the) telly (*Brit inf*) tonight?; **das ~ bringt etw** sth is on television, they're showing sth on television

Fern|se|her M (*inf: = Gerät*) television, TV, telly (*Brit inf*)

Fern|se|her(in) M(F) (*inf: = Zuschauer*) (television) viewer

Fern|seh-: Fern|seh|film M television or TV film (*Brit*), television or TV movie (*US*); **Fern|seh|ge|büh|ren** PL television licence (*Brit*) or license (*US*) fee; **Fern|seh|ge|neh|mi|gung** F television licence (*Brit*) or license (*US*); **Fern|seh|ge|rät** NT television or TV set; **fern|seh|ge|recht** **ADJ** suitable for television **ADV** **etw ~ aufbereiten** to adapt sth for television; **Fern|seh|jour|na|list(in)** M(F) television or TV reporter; **Fern|seh|ka|me|ra** F television or TV camera; **wir haben Herr Schmidt vor die ~ gebeten** we've asked Herr Schmidt to speak to us; **Fern|seh|ka|nal** M (television) channel; **Fern|seh|kon|ser|ve** F (tele)recording; **Fern|seh|norm** F television standard; **Fern|seh|pro|gramm** NT **a** (= *Kanal*) channel, station (*US*) **b** (= *Sendung*) programme (*Brit*), program (*US*); (= *Sendefolge*) programmes *pl* (*Brit*), programs *pl* (*US*) **c** (= *Fernsehzeitschrift*) (television) programme (*Brit*) or program (*US*) guide, TV guide; **Fern|seh|pub|li|kum** NT television viewers *pl*, viewing public; **Fern|seh|rech|te** PL television rights *pl*; **Fern|seh|sa|tel|lit** M TV satellite; **Fern|seh|schirm** M television or TV screen; **Fern|seh|sen|der** M television transmitter; **Fern|seh|sen|dung** F television programme (*Brit*) or program (*US*); **Fern|seh|spiel** NT television play; **Fern|seh|spot** M **a** (= *Werbespot*) TV ad(vertisement) **b** (= *Kurzfilm*) TV short; **Fern|seh|spre|cher(in)** M(F) television announcer; **Fern|seh|teil|neh|mer(in)** M(F) (*form*) television viewer; **Fern|seh|tru|he** F cabinet TV; **Fern|seh|turm** M television tower; **Fern|seh|über|tra|gung** F television broadcast; (*von außerhalb des Studios*) outside broadcast; **Fern|seh|über|tra|gungs|wa|gen** M outside broadcast vehicle or van; **Fern|seh|wer|bung** F **,** *no pl* **a** (= *Werbung im Fernsehen*) television or TV advertising or commercials *pl* **b** (= *Werbespot*) television or TV commercial or ad (*inf*); **Fern|seh|zeit|schrift** F TV guide; **Fern|seh|zu|schau|er(in)** M(F) (television) viewer

Fern|sicht F clear view; (**eine**) **gute ~ haben** to be able to see a long way

---

| German spelling reform (see supplement): ▲ new spelling △ old spelling

Fẹrn|sprech- in cpds (form) telephone → auch Telefon-; **Fẹrn|sprech|an|schluss** ▲ M telephone; **15 Fernsprechanschlüsse haben** to have 15 lines; **Fẹrn|sprech|ap|pa|rat** M telephone; **Fẹrn|sprech|auf|trags|dienst** NT telephone services pl; **Fẹrn|sprech|buch** NT telephone directory, telephone book

Fẹrn|spre|cher M (form) (public) telephone

Fẹrn|sprech-: **Fẹrn|sprech|ge|büh|ren** PL telephone charges pl; **Fẹrn|sprech|ge|heim|nis** NT (Jur) secrecy of telecommunications; **Fẹrn|sprech|lei|tung** F (per Draht) (telephone) line; (per Radio, Satellit) telephone link; **Fẹrn|sprech|netz** NT telephone system; **Fẹrn|sprech|teil|neh|mer(in)** M(F) (form) telephone subscriber; **Fẹrn|sprech|ver|kehr** M telephone traffic; **Fẹrn|sprech|we|sen** NT , no pl telephone system; **Fẹrn|sprech|zel|le** F (form) (tele)phone box or (US) booth, call box (Brit); **Fẹrn|sprech|zent|ra|le** F telephone exchange

Fẹrn-: **fẹrn ste|hen** ▲ VI irreg jdm/einer Sache ~ to have no connection with sb/sth; **ich stehe ihm ziemlich fern** I'm not on very close terms with him; **fẹrn+steu|ern** VT sep to operate by remote control; (per Funk auch) to control by radio → auch **ferngesteuert**; **Fẹrn|steu|e|rung** F remote control; (per Funk auch) radio control; ~ **haben** to be remote-controlled/radio-controlled; **Fẹrn|stra|ße** F trunk or major road, highway (US); **Fẹrn|stu|di|um** NT correspondence degree course (with radio, TV etc), ≈ Open University course (Brit)

FERNSTUDIUM

A **Fernstudium** is a university-level adult education course that does not require the student to attend a particular place of study. The best-known establishment for this type of correspondence course is the university at Hagen, which is a **Gesamthochschule**.
The expression **Fernstudium** is also used colloquially for any sort of teaching where the student does not attend regular classes. This is most commonly done by educational broadcasts on radio and television, which are developed by the broadcasting corporations in close cooperation with, amongst others, the **Deutsches Institut für Fernstudien** in Tübingen → GESAMTHOCHSCHULE

Fẹrn-: **Fẹrn|tou|ris|mus** M long-haul tourism; **Fẹrn|trau|ung** F marriage by proxy; **Fẹrn|über|wa|chung** F remote monitoring; **Fẹrn|uni|ver|si|tät** F ≈ Open University (Brit), ≈ correspondence school (US); **Fẹrn|un|ter|richt** M correspondence course also using radio, TV, multimedia etc; **Fẹrn|ver|kehr** M **a** (Transport) long-distance traffic **b** (Telec) trunk (Brit) or long-distance traffic; **Fẹrn|ver|kehrs|stra|ße** F trunk (Brit) or major road, highway (US); **Fẹrn|ver|mitt|lung(s|stel|le)** F telephone exchange; **Fẹrn|ver|sor|gung** F long-distance supply; **Fẹrn|wär|me** F district heating (spec); **Fẹrn|weh** NT wanderlust; **Fẹrn|wir|kung** F (Phys) long-distance effect; **Fẹrn|ziel** NT long-term goal; **Fẹrn|zug** M long-distance train; **Fẹrn|zün|dung** F long-range or remote ignition

Fẹr|rat [fɛˈraːt] NT -s, -e (Chem) ferrate

Fẹr|rit [fɛˈriːt] M -s, -e (Chem) ferrite

Fẹr|ro- [fɛro] in cpds ferro-; **Fẹr|ro|mag|ne|tis|mus** [feromagneˈtɪsmʊs] M ferromagnetism

Fẹr|se [ˈfɛrzə] F -, -n heel; **jdm (dicht) auf den ~n sein** or **folgen/bleiben** to be/stay hard or close on sb's heels → **heften** VR b

Fẹr|sen-: **Fẹr|sen|au|to|ma|tik** F (Ski) automatic heel release; **Fẹr|sen|bein** NT (Anat) heel bone, calcaneus (spec); **Fẹr|sen|geld** NT ~ **geben** to take to one's heels

fẹr|tig [ˈfɛrtɪç] **ADJ a** (= abgeschlossen, vollendet) finished; (= ausgebildet) qualified; (= reif) Mensch, Charakter mature; **mit der Ausbildung ~**

---

sein to have completed one's training; ~ **ist die Laube** (inf) or **der Lack** (inf) (and) there we are!, (and) Bob's your uncle! (Brit inf) **b** (= zu Ende) finished; **wird das/werden wir rechtzeitig ~ werden?** will it/we be finished in time?; **mit etw ~ sein, etw ~ haben** to have finished sth; **mit jdm ~ sein** (fig) to be finished or through with sb/sth; **ich werde damit nicht ~** I can't cope with it; **du darfst nicht gehen, ~!** you're not going and that's that or and that's the end of it! **c** (= bereit) ready; ~ **zur Abfahrt** ready to go or leave; **bist du/ist das Essen ~?** are you/is the meal ready? → **Achtung, Platz** **d** (inf) (= erschöpft) shattered (Brit inf), all in (inf); (= ruiniert) finished; (= erstaunt) knocked for six (Brit inf) or for a loop (US inf); **mit den Nerven ~ sein** to be at the end of one's tether (Brit) or rope (US); **da bin ich ~!** (= erstaunt) my God!, well I never! → **fix**
ADV ~ **duschen** to finish having a shower; **etw ~ kaufen** to buy sth ready-made; Essen to buy sth ready to eat or ready-prepared; ~ **ausgebildet** fully qualified; ~ **essen/lesen** to finish eating/reading

Fẹr|tig- in cpds finished; (Build) prefabricated; **Fẹr|tig|bau** M (Build) (no pl, = Bauweise) prefabricated building pl -**bauten** (= Gebäude) prefabricated building, prefab; **Fẹr|tig|bau|wei|se** F (Build) prefabricated building or construction

fẹr|tig be|kom|men ▲ VT irreg to finish, to get finished

Fẹr|tig|be|ton M (Build) ready-mixed concrete

fẹr|tig brin|gen ▲ VT irreg **a** (= vollenden) to get done **b** (= imstande sein) to manage; (iro) to be capable of; **ich habe es nicht fertig gebracht, ihr die Wahrheit zu sagen** I couldn't bring myself to tell her the truth; **er bringt das fertig** (iro) I wouldn't put it past him; **er bringt es fertig, und sagt ihr das** he's quite capable of saying that to her

fẹr|ti|gen [ˈfɛrtɪɡn̩] VT (form) to manufacture

Fẹr|tig-: **Fẹr|ti|ger|zeug|nis** NT finished product; **Fẹr|tig|fab|ri|kat** NT finished product; **Fẹr|tig|ge|richt** NT ready-to-serve meal; **Fẹr|tig|haus** NT prefabricated house

Fẹr|tig|keit F -, -en skill; **wenig/eine große ~ in etw** (dat) **haben** not to be very/to be very skilled at or in sth

Fẹr|tig-: **fẹr|tig krie|gen** ▲ VT (inf) = **fertig bringen**; **fẹr|tig ma|chen** ▲ VT **a** (= vollenden) to finish **b** (= bereit machen) to get ready; **sich ~** to get ready; **~!** get ready!; (Sport) get set!, steady! **c** (inf) **jdn ~** (= erledigen) to do for sb; (= ermüden) to take it out of sb; (= deprimieren) to get sb down; (= abkanzeln) to tear sb off a strip (Brit inf), to lay into sb (inf); **sich ~** to do oneself in; **Fẹr|tig|pro|dukt** NT finished product; **fẹr|tig stel|len** ▲ VT to complete; **Fẹr|tig|stel|lung** F completion; **Fẹr|tig|teil** NT finished part

Fẹr|ti|gung [ˈfɛrtɪɡʊŋ] F -, -en production; **in der ~ arbeiten** to work in production or in the production department

Fẹr|ti|gungs- in cpds production; **Fẹr|ti|gungs|hal|le** F assembly shop; **Fẹr|ti|gungs|stra|ße** F production or assembly line; **Fẹr|ti|gungs|tech|nik** F production engineering

Fẹr|tig|wa|re F finished product

Fẹs¹ [fɛs] NT -, -, **fẹs** NT -, - (Mus) F flat

Fẹs² [fɛs] M -(es), -(e) [-zə] fez

fẹsch [fɛʃ] ADJ (S Ger, Aus: inf) (= modisch) smart; (= hübsch) attractive; **das ist ~** that's great (inf); **sei ~!** (Aus) (= sei brav) be good; (= sei kein Frosch) be a sport (inf)

Fẹs|sel [ˈfɛsl] F -, -n (meist pl) (= Bande) (lit, fig) bond, fetter, shackle; (= Kette) chain; **sich von den ~n befreien** to free oneself, to loose (Brit liter) or loosen (US liter) one's bonds; **jdm ~n anlegen** to fetter or shackle sb; **jdn in ~n legen** to fetter or shackle sb; (= anket-

---

ten) to put sb in chains; **jdn in ~n schlagen** (liter, fig) to put sb in fetters, to enchain sb (liter); **die ~n der Ehe/Liebe** the shackles of marriage/love **b** (Anat) (von Huftieren) pastern; (von Menschen) ankle

Fẹs|sel-: **Fẹs|sel|bal|lon** M captive balloon; **Fẹs|sel|ge|lenk** NT pastern; (von Menschen) ankle joint; **Fẹs|sel|griff** M lock

fẹs|seln [ˈfɛsln̩] VT **a** (mit Tau etc) to tie (up), to bind; (Hist: mit Handfesseln, Fußfesseln) to fetter; (mit Handschellen) to handcuff; (mit Ketten) to chain (up); **jdn (an Händen und Füßen) ~** to tie/fetter/chain sb (hand and foot); **jdm die Hände auf dem Rücken ~** to tie sb's hands behind his back; **der Gefangene wurde gefesselt vorgeführt** the prisoner was brought in handcuffed/in chains; **jdn ans Bett ~** (fig) to confine sb to (his) bed, to keep sb in bed; **jdn ans Haus ~** (fig) to tie sb to the house; **jdn an jdn/sich ~** (fig) to bind sb to sb/oneself **b** (= faszinieren) to grip; Aufmerksamkeit to hold; **seine Vorstellung fesselte die Zuschauer** his performance gripped the audience

fẹs|selnd ADJ gripping

fẹst [fɛst] **ADJ a** (= hart) solid; **~e Nahrung** solid food, solids pl; **~e Form** or **Gestalt annehmen** (fig) to take shape **b** (= stabil) solid; Gewebe, Schuhe tough, sturdy; (Comm, Fin) stable; Zuneigung strong → **Boden** **c** (= sicher, entschlossen) firm; Plan firm, definite; Stimme steady; **eine ~e Meinung von etw haben** to have definite views on sth; **etw ist ~** (= steht fest) sth is definite **d** (= kräftig) firm; Schlag hard, heavy **e** (= nicht locker) tight; Griff firm; (fig) Schlaf sound **f** (= ständig) regular; Freund(in) steady; Bindung, Stellung, Mitarbeiter permanent; Kosten, Tarif, Einkommen fixed; Redewendung set; **in ~en Händen sein, sich in ~en Händen befinden** (Besitz) to be in private hands; (inf: Mädchen) to be spoken for; **seinen ~en Platz gewinnen** to establish oneself; **sie hat keinen ~en Platz im Büro** she doesn't have her own desk in the office; **er hat einen ~en Platz in ihrem Herzen** he has a special place in her affections → auch **Platz**
ADV a (= kräftig) anpacken, packen firmly; drücken, umarmen tightly; (inf: tüchtig, kräftig) helfen, arbeiten with a will; ~ **zuschlagen** to hit hard **b** (= nicht locker) anziehen, zudrehen, verknoten tight; ~ **kochende Kartoffeln** waxy potatoes; ~ **verwurzelt** deep-rooted, deep-seated; Tradition long-established; ~ **umrissen** clear-cut; **die Handbremse ~ anziehen** to put the handbrake on firmly; **die Tür ~ schließen** to shut the door tight; **er hat schon ~ geschlafen** he was sound asleep; **jdn ~ in der Hand haben** to have sb under one's thumb; **etw ~ in der Hand haben** to have sth firmly under control **c** (= sicher) versprechen faithfully; zusagen definitely; **sie sind an den Vertrag ~ gebunden** their contract is binding; ~ **verankert** (lit) firmly or securely anchored; (fig) firmly rooted; ~ **entschlossen sein** to be absolutely determined **d** (= dauerhaft) permanently; **Gehälter sind im Tarifvertrag ~ geregelt** salaries are set in the pay agreement; ~ **befreundet sein** to be good friends; (Freund und Freundin) to be going steady; **jdn ~ anstellen** to employ sb as a regular member of staff; ~ **angestellt** employed on a regular basis; ~ **besoldet** on a regular salary; **Geld ~ anlegen** to tie up money

Fẹst [fɛst] NT -(e)s, -e **a** (= Feier) celebration; (= historische Begebenheit) celebrations pl; (= Party) party; (= Hochzeitsfest) reception; (= Bankett) banquet, feast (old); (= Ballfest) ball; (= Kinderfest, Schützenfest) carnival; **ein ~ zum hundertjährigen Bestehen des Vereins** the club's centenary celebrations, celebrations to mark the club's centenary; **das war ein ~!** (inf) it was great fun; **man soll die ~e feiern, wie sie fallen** (prov) make hay while the sun shines (prov) **b** (= kirchlicher Feiertag) feast, festival; (= Weih-

---

nachtsfest) Christmas; **bewegliches/unbewegliches ~** movable/immovable feast; **frohes ~!** Merry *or* Happy (*esp Brit*) Christmas!

Fest-: Fest|akt M ceremony; **fest|an|ge|stellt** △ ADJ → **fest** ADV d; **Fest|an|ge|stell|te(r)** MF *decl as adj* regular member of staff; **Fest|an|spra|che** F speech; **Fest|an|stel|lung** F permanent post *or* appointment; **Fest|auf|füh|rung** F festival production; **fest+ba|cken** VI *sep irreg aux sein* (*dial*: = *festkleben*) to stick (firmly) (*an +dat* (on)to); **Fest|ban|kett** NT ceremonial banquet; **fest+bei|ßen** VR *sep irreg* (*Hund etc*) to get a firm hold with its teeth (*an +dat* on); (*Zecke etc*) to attach itself firmly (*an +dat* to); (*fig: = nicht weiterkommen*) to get bogged down (*an +dat* in); **der Hund biss sich an ihrem Bein fest** the dog sank its teeth firmly into her leg; **Fest|be|leuch|tung** F festive lighting *or* lights *pl*; (*inf: im Haus*) blazing lights *pl*; **was soll denn diese ~?** (*inf*) why is the place lit up like a Christmas tree? (*inf*); **fest|be|sol|det** △ [-bəzɔldət] ADJ → **fest** ADV d; **fest+bin|den** VT *sep irreg* to tie up; **jdn/etw an etw** (*dat*) ~ to tie sb/sth to sth; **fest+blei|ben** VI *sep irreg aux sein* to stand firm, to remain resolute; **fest+dre|hen** VT *sep* to screw up tightly; **fest+drü|cken** VT *sep* to press in/down/together firmly

fes|te ['fɛstə] ADV (*inf*) = **fest** ADV immer ~ **druff!** let him/her *etc* have it! (*inf*), give it to him/her *etc*! (*inf*)

Fes|te ['fɛstə] F -, -n (*old*) a (= *Festung*) fortress; (= *Burgfeste*) castle **b** (= *Erde*) dry land, terra firma; **die ~ des Himmels** (*Bibl*) the firmament

Fest-: Fest|es|sen NT banquet, Christmas dinner; **fest+fah|ren** VR *sep irreg* (*fig*) to get bogged down; (*lit auch*) to get stuck, to stick fast; **fest+fres|sen** VR *sep irreg* to seize up; **fest+frie|ren** VI *sep irreg aux sein* to freeze solid; **Fest|ga|be** F a (= *Geschenk*) presentation gift **b** (= *Festschrift*) commemorative paper, festschrift (*esp Brit*); **Fest|ge|dicht** NT celebratory *or* occasional poem; **Fest|ge|la|ge** NT banquet; **Fest|ge|läu|te** NT festive peal of bells; **Fest|geld** NT (*Fin*) time deposit; **Fest|ge|wand** NT (*liter*) festive garb (*liter*); **fest|ge|wur|zelt** [-gəvʊrtslt] ADJ **wie ~** rooted to the spot; **Fest|got|tes|dienst** M festival service; **fest+gur|ten** *sep* VR to strap oneself in VT to strap in; **fest+ha|ken** *sep* VT to hook up (*an +dat* on) VR to get caught (up) (*an +dat* on); **Fest|hal|le** F festival hall

fest+hal|ten *sep irreg* VT a (= *nicht loslassen*) to keep a firm hold on, to keep hold of, to hold on to; **jdn am Arm/Rockzipfel ~** to hold on to sb's arm/the hem of sb's coat

b (= *bemerken*) to stress, to emphasize

c (= *inhaftieren*) to hold, to detain

d (= *speichern*) to record; **Atmosphäre** *etc* to capture; **etw schriftlich ~** to record sth; **etw im Gedächtnis ~** to bear sth firmly in mind; **etw in Wort und Bild ~** to record sth in words and pictures

VI **an etw** (*dat*) **~** to hold *or* stick (*inf*) to sth; **am Glauben ~** to hold to the faith

VR to hold on (*an +dat* to); **sich irgendwo ~** to hold on to something; **halt dich fest!** (*lit*) hold tight!; **halt dich fest und hör dir das an!** (*inf*) brace yourself and listen to this!

fest+hän|gen VI *sep irreg aux haben or sein* (*lit, fig*) to be stuck (*an +dat* on, *in +dat* in)

fest+hef|ten VT *sep* (*mit Nadel*) to pin (*an +dat* (on)to); (*mit Faden*) to tack (*an +dat* (on)to)

fes|ti|gen ['fɛstɪgn] VT to strengthen; *Freundschaft, Macht, Ruf auch* to consolidate → *auch* **gefestigt** VR to become stronger; (*Freundschaft, Macht, Ruf auch*) to consolidate

Fes|ti|ger ['fɛstɪgɐ] M -s, - setting lotion

Fes|tig|keit ['fɛstɪçkaɪt] F -, *no pl* (*von Material*) strength; (*fig*) steadfastness; (*von Meinung*) firmness; (*von Stimme*) steadiness; **die ~ seines Charakters** his moral strength, his strength of character

---

Fes|ti|gung ['fɛstɪgʊŋ] F -, -en strengthening; (*von Freundschaft, Macht, Ruf auch*) consolidation

Fes|ti|val ['fɛstɪvəl, 'fɛstɪval] NT -s, -s festival

Fes|ti|vi|tät [fɛstiviˈtɛːt] F -, -en (*old, hum inf*) celebration, festivity

Fest-: fest+kei|len VT *sep* to wedge; **fest+klam|mern** *sep* VT to clip on (*an +dat* to); **Wäsche an** *or* **auf der Leine ~** to peg washing on the line VR to cling (*an +dat* to); **fest+kle|ben** VTI *sep* (*vi: aux sein*) to stick (firmly) (*an +dat* (on)to); **Fest|kleid** NT formal dress; **die Stadt legte ihr ~ an** (*liter*) the town decked itself out in all its finery; **fest+klem|men** *sep* VT to wedge fast; (*mit Klammer, Klemme*) to clip; **festgeklemmt werden** (*aus Versehen*) to get stuck *or* jammed VIR (*vi: aux sein*) to jam, to stick (fast); **fest+klop|fen** VT *sep* to pack down; **fest+kno|ten** VT *sep* = **festbinden**; **Fest|kom|ma** NT (*auch Comput*) fixed point; **Fest|kör|per** M (*Phys*) solid; **Fest|kör|per|phy|sik** F solid-state physics *sing*; **fest+kral|len** VR *sep* (*Tier*) to dig one's claws in (*an +dat* -to); (*Mensch*) to dig one's nails in (*an +dat* -to); (*fig*) to cling (*an +dat* to)

Fest|land NT (*nicht Insel*) mainland; (*nicht Meer*) dry land; (= *europäisches Festland*) Continent (*Brit*), Europe

fest|län|disch [-lɛndɪʃ] ADJ mainland *attr*; Continental, European

Festlands-: Fest|lands|mas|se F continent; **Fest|lands|so|ckel** M continental shelf

fest+lau|fen *sep irreg* VR (*Schiff*) to run aground; (*fig*) (*Verhandlungen*) to founder; **die Stürmer liefen sich (an der Verteidigung) immer wieder fest** the forwards kept coming up against a solid line of defence (*Brit*) *or* defense (*US*) VI *aux sein* (*Schiff*) to run aground

fest+le|gen *sep* VT a (= *festsetzen*) *Reihenfolge, Termin, Kurs etc* to fix (*auf +acc, bei* for); *Grenze auch* to establish; *Sprachgebrauch* to establish, to lay down; (= *bestimmen*) *Regelung, Arbeitszeiten* to lay down; (= *feststellen*) *Geburtsdatum* to determine; **etw schriftlich/testamentarisch ~** to stipulate *or* specify sth in writing/in one's will

b **jdn auf etw** (*acc*) **~/darauf ~, etw zu tun** (= *festnageln*) to tie sb (down) to sth/to doing sth; (= *einschränken auch*) to restrict *or* limit sb to sth/to doing sth; (= *verpflichten*) to commit sb to sth/to doing sth

c *Geld* to put on time deposit, to tie up

VR a (= *verbindlich sein*) to tie oneself down (*auf +acc* to); (= *sich verpflichten*) to commit oneself (*auf +acc* to); **ich kann mich darauf nicht ~, ich kann mich auch irren** I can't swear to it, I might be wrong; **sich darauf ~, etw zu tun** to tie oneself down/commit oneself to doing sth

b (= *einen Entschluss fassen*) to decide (*auf +acc* on); **sich darauf ~, etw zu tun** to decide on doing sth *or* to do sth

Fest|le|gung F -, -en (= *Festsetzung*) fixing; (*von Grenze*) establishing; (*von Regelung, Arbeitszeiten*) laying-down

fest|lich ['fɛstlɪç] ADJ festive; (= *feierlich*) solemn; (= *prächtig*) splendid, magnificent; **ein ~er Tag** a special *or* red-letter day (*Fin: Geld*) to be on a time deposit ADV **geschmückt** festively; **gekleidet** formally; **etw ~ begehen** to celebrate sth

Fest|lich|keit F -, -en celebration; (= *Stimmung*) festiveness

Fest-: fest+lie|gen VI *sep irreg* a (= *festgesetzt sein*) to have been fixed; (*Sprachgebrauch, Grenze*) to have been established; (*Arbeitszeiten, Regelung*) to have been laid down (*Fin: Geld*) to be on a time deposit, to be tied up **c** (= *nicht weiterkönnen*) to be stuck; (*Naut*) to be aground; **fest+ma|chen** *sep* VT a (= *befestigen*) to fix on (*an +dat* -to); (= *festbinden*) to fasten (*an +dat* (on)to); (*Naut*) to moor **b** (= *vereinbaren*) to arrange; **ein Geschäft ~** to clinch a deal **c** (*Hunt: = aufspüren*) to bring to bay **d** (= *beweisen, zeigen*) to demonstrate, to exemplify; **etw an etw/jdm ~** (*fig*) to link sth to sth/sb VI

(*Naut*) to moor; **Fest|mahl** NT (*geh*) banquet, feast; **Fest|me|ter** M OR NT cubic metre (*Brit*) *or* meter (*US*) of solid timber; **fest+na|geln** VT *sep* a *Gegenstand* to nail (down/up/on); **etw an/auf etw** (*dat*) **~** to nail sth to sth **b** (*fig inf*) *jdn* to tie down (*auf +acc* to); **fest+nä|hen** VT *sep* to sew up; (= *annähen*) to sew on; **Fest|nah|me** [-naːmə] F -, -n arrest, apprehension; **vorläufige ~** temporary custody; **fest+neh|men** VT *sep irreg* to apprehend, to arrest; **vorläufig ~** to take into custody; **Sie sind festgenommen** you are under arrest; **Fest|netz** NT (*Telec*) fixed-line network; **Fest|netz|an|schluss** ▲ M (*Telec*) fixed-line *or* permanent connection; **Fest|of|fer|te** F (*Comm*) firm offer; **Fest|plat|te** F (*Comput*) hard disk; **Fest|plat|ten|lauf|werk** NT hard disk drive; **Fest|platz** M festival ground; (*für Volksfest*) fairground; **Fest|pre|digt** F feast-day sermon; **Fest|preis** M (*Comm*) fixed price; **Fest|pro|gramm** NT festival programme (*Brit*) *or* program (*US*); **Fest|punkt** M (*auch Comput*) fixed point; **Fest|re|de** F speech; **eine ~ halten** to make a speech on a special occasion; **fest+re|den** VR *sep* to get involved in a conversation; **Fest|red|ner(in)** M(F) (main) speaker; **fest+ren|nen** VR *sep irreg* (*inf*) to get bogged down; **unsere Spieler rannten sich (an der gegnerischen Abwehr) fest** our players came up against the solid line of the opponents' defence (*Brit*) *or* defense (*US*); **Fest|saal** M hall; (= *Speisesaal*) banqueting hall; (= *Tanzsaal*) ballroom; **fest+sau|fen** VR *sep irreg* (*inf*) to get stuck in (*inf*), to make a night of it (*inf*); **fest+sau|gen** VR *sep* to attach itself firmly (*an +dat* to); **Fest|schmaus** M (*old*) banquet, feast; **Fest|schmuck** M festive decorations *pl*; **im ~** festively decorated; **fest+schnal|len** VTR *sep* = **anschnallen**; **fest+schnü|ren** VT *sep* = **festbinden**; **fest+schrau|ben** VT *sep* to screw (in/on/down/up) tight; **fest+schrei|ben** VT *sep irreg* (*fig*) to establish; (*Jur*) to enact; **Fest|schrei|bung** F establishment; (*Jur*) enactment; **Fest|schrift** F commemorative publication; (*für Gelehrten*) commemorative paper, festschrift (*esp Brit*)

fest+set|zen *sep* VT a (= *bestimmen*) *Preis, Rente, Grenze* to fix (*bei, auf +acc* at); *Ort, Termin auch* to arrange (*auf +acc, bei* for); *Frist auch* to set; *Arbeitszeiten* to lay down; **der Beginn der Veranstaltung wurde auf zwei Uhr festgesetzt** the event was scheduled to begin at 2 o'clock

b (= *inhaftieren*) to detain VR (*Staub, Schmutz*) to collect; (*Rost, Ungeziefer, unerwünschte Personen*) to get a foothold; (*Mil*) to take up one's position; (*fig: Gedanke*) to take root, to implant itself

Fest|set|zung F -, -en a (*von Preis, Rente, Grenze*) fixing; (*von Ort, Termin*) arrangement; (*von Frist*) setting; (*von Arbeitszeiten*) laying-down **b** (= *Inhaftierung*) detention

fest+sit|zen VI *sep irreg* a (= *klemmen, haften*) to be stuck; (*Schmutz*) to cling; (*in Zwischenräumen*) to be trapped **b** (= *stecken geblieben sein*) to be stuck (*bei* on); (*Naut*) to be aground

Fest|spei|cher M (*Comput*) read-only memory, ROM

Fest|spiel NT a (= *einzelnes Stück*) festival production **b** ~**e** (= *Veranstaltung*) festival *sing*

Fest|spiel-: Fest|spiel|haus NT festival theatre (*Brit*) *or* theater (*US*); **Fest|spiel|stadt** F festival city

fest-: fest+stamp|fen VT *sep* to pound down; (*mit den Füßen auch*) to stamp *or* tread down; **fest+ste|cken** *sep* VT to pin (*an +dat* (on)to, *in +dat* in); *Haare, Rocksaum* to pin up VI (= *stecken geblieben sein*) to be stuck; **fest+ste|hen** VI *sep irreg* (= *sicher sein*) to be certain; (= *beschlossen sein*) to have been settled *or* fixed; (= *unveränderlich sein*) to be definite; **fest steht** *or* **eines steht fest, dass ...** one thing's (for) certain *or* sure and that is that ...; **so viel steht fest** this *or* so much is certain; **fest|ste|hend**

ADJ **a** (*Mech*) fixed **b** *attr* (= *bestimmt, verbindlich*) definite; *Redewendung, Begriff, Reihenfolge* set; *Brauch* (well-)established; *Terminplan* fixed; **fest|stell|bar** ADJ **a** (*Mech*: = *arretierbar*) **der Wagen der Schreibmaschine ist ~** the typewriter carriage can be locked in position **b** (= *herausfinden*) ascertainable; (= *wahrnehmbar, erkennbar*) discernible

fest+stel|len ⚫ 53.5, 53.6 VT *sep* **a** (*Mech*) to lock (fast)

b (= *ermitteln*) to ascertain, to find out; *Personalien, Sachverhalt, Datum etc* to establish; *Ursache, Grund* to establish, to determine; *Schaden* to assess; *Krankheit* to diagnose; **einen Totalschaden an einem Wagen ~** to assess a car as a total write-off; **der Arzt konnte nur noch den Tod ~** the doctor found him to be dead

c (= *erkennen*) to tell (*an +dat* from); *Fehler, Unterschied* to find, to detect; (= *bemerken*) to discover; (= *einsehen*) to realize; **wir mussten ~, dass wir uns geirrt hatten** we were forced to realize that we had made a mistake; **ich musste entsetzt/überrascht etc ~, dass ...** I was horrified/surprised *etc* to find that ...

d (= *aussprechen*) to stress, to emphasize

Fest|stell|tas|te F shift lock

Fest|stel|lung F **a** (= *Ermittlung*) ascertainment; (*von Personalien, Sachverhalt, Datum, Ursache, Grund*) establishment; (*von Schaden*) assessment; (*von Krankheit*) diagnosis

b (*Erkenntnis*) conclusion; **zu der ~ kommen** or **gelangen, dass ...** to come to the conclusion that ...

c (= *Wahrnehmung*) observation; **die ~ machen** or **treffen dass ...** to realize that ...; **wir mussten leider die ~ machen, dass ...** (*form*) it has come to our notice that ...; **ist das eine Frage oder eine ~?** is that a question or a statement (of fact)?

d (= *Bemerkung*) remark, comment, observation; **die abschließende ~** one's closing remarks; **die ~ machen, dass ...** to remark or observe that ...

Fest|stel|lungs|kla|ge F action for a declaratory judgement

Fest-: Fest|stim|mung F festive atmosphere; (= *Festlaune*) festive mood; **Fest|stoff|ra|ke|te** F solid-fuel rocket; **Fest|ta|fel** F banquet table; (*bei Familienanlässen*) (dinner) table

Fest|tag M **a** (= *Ehrentag*) special or red-letter day **b** (= *Feiertag*) holiday, feast (day) (*Eccl*); **angenehme ~e!** Happy (*esp Brit*) or Merry Christmas/Happy Easter *etc*!

fest|täg|lich ADJ holiday *attr* (*esp Brit*), vacation *attr* (*US*) ADV **~ gestimmt sein** to be in a festive or holiday mood; **~ gekleidet** festively dressed

Fest|tags-: Fest|tags|klei|dung F **~ tragen** to be festively dressed; **Fest|tags|lau|ne** F festive mood; **Fest|tags|stim|mung** F festive atmosphere; **in ~** in a festive mood

Fest-: Fest|treib|stoff|ra|ke|te F solid-fuel rocket; **fest+tre|ten** *sep irreg* VT to tread down; (*in Teppich etc*) to tread in (*in +acc -to*) VR to get trodden down/in; **das tritt sich fest!** (*hum inf*) don't worry, it's good for the carpet (*hum*); **fest+trock|nen** VI *aux sein* to dry (on); **fest|um|ris|sen** △ [-lʊmrɪsn̩] ADJ *attr* → **fest** ADV **b**; **Fest|um|zug** M procession

Fes|tung ['fɛstʊŋ] F -, -en (= *Befestigung*) fortress; (= *Burgfeste*) castle

Fes|tungs-: Fes|tungs|gra|ben M moat; **Fes|tungs|haft** F imprisonment in a fortress; **Fes|tungs|wall** M rampart

Fest-: Fest|ver|an|stal|tung F function; **Fest|ver|samm|lung** F assembled company; **fest|ver|wur|zelt** △ ADJ *attr* → **fest** ADV **b**; **fest|ver|zins|lich** ADJ fixed-interest *attr*; **Fest|vor|stel|lung** F gala performance; **Fest|vor|trag** M lecture, talk; **fest+wach|sen** VI *sep irreg aux sein* = **anwachsen a**; **Fest|wert|spei|cher** M (*Comput*) read-only memory; **Fest|wie|se** F festival ground; (*für Volksfest*) fair-

ground; **Fest|wo|che** F festival week; **die ~n** the festival *sing*; **fest+wur|zeln** VI *sep aux sein* to take root → **festgewurzelt**; **Fest|zeit** F holiday (*esp Brit*) or vacation (*US*) period; (= *Festspielzeit*) festival (period); **Fest|zelt** NT carnival marquee; **fest+zie|hen** VT *sep irreg* to pull tight; *Schraube* to tighten (up); **Fest|zins** M fixed interest; **Fest|zins|satz** M fixed rate of interest; **Fest|zug** M carnival procession; **fest+zur|ren** VT *sep* (*Naut*) to lash up; (*fig*: = *endgültig bestimmen*) *Entscheidung etc* to finalize

fe|tal [fe'taːl] ADJ *attr* foetal (*Brit*), fetal (*US*)

Fe|te ['feːtə] F -, -n party; **eine ~ feiern** (*als Gastgeber*) to have or give or throw a party; (*als Gast*) to go to a party

Fe|ten *pl von* **Fetus**

Fe|tisch ['feːtɪʃ] M -(e)s, -e fetish

fe|ti|schi|sie|ren [fetɪʃiˈziːrən] *ptp* **fetischisiert** VT (*geh*) to make a fetish of

Fe|ti|schis|mus [fetɪˈʃɪsmʊs] M -, *no pl* fetishism

Fe|ti|schist [fetɪˈʃɪst] M -en, -en, **Fe|ti|schis|tin** [-ˈʃɪstɪn] F -, -nen fetishist

fett [fɛt] ADJ **a** (= *fetthaltig*) *Speisen, Kost* fatty; (*fig inf*: = *ölig*) *Stimme* fat; **ein ~er Bissen** or **Brocken** or **Happen** (*lit*) a juicy morsel; (*fig*) a lucrative deal

b (= *dick*) fat; (*Typ*) *Überschrift, Schlagzeilen* bold

c (= *üppig*) *Boden, Weide, Klee* rich, luxuriant; (*fig inf*) rich; *Beute, Gewinn* fat; *Geschäft* lucrative; **~e Jahre** fat years; **ein ~er Posten** (*inf*) a cushy job or number (*inf*) → **sieben²**

d (*Aut*) *Gemisch etc* rich

e (*sl*: = *toll*) wicked (*sl*); **das ist voll ~** that's really wicked (*sl*); **~e Teile** (= *Busen*) tits *pl* (*sl*) ADV **a** (= *fetthaltig*) **~ essen** to eat fatty food; **~ kochen** to cook fatty food; (= *viel Fett gebrauchen*) to use a lot of fat

b (= *dick*) **~ gedruckt** (*Typ*) in bold(face); **sich dick und ~ fressen** (*inf*) to stuff oneself (*inf*) or one's face (*inf*); **~ dasitzen** (*inf*) to sit there like a sack of potatoes (*inf*); **sich ~ hinsetzen** (*inf*) to plump oneself down like a sack of potatoes (*inf*)

Fett [fɛt] NT -(e)s, -e fat; (*zum Schmieren*) grease; **tierische/pflanzliche ~e** animal/vegetable fats; **~ ansetzen** to put on weight, to get fat; (*Tiere*) to fatten up; **mit heißem ~ übergießen** to baste (with hot fat); **in schwimmendem ~ backen** to deep-fry; **sein ~ bekommen** (*inf*) or **kriegen** (*inf*)/**weghaben** (*inf*) to get/have got what was coming to one (*inf*), to get/have got one's comeuppance (*inf*); **ein ~ lösendes Mittel** a grease-cutting agent; **~ schwimmt oben** (*prov hum*: *Dicke im Wasser*) fat floats → **abschöpfen, schmoren** VI **a**

Fett-: Fett|ab|sau|gung [-apzaugʊŋ] F -, -en (*Med*) liposuction; **Fett|ab|la|ge|rung** F deposition of fat; **~en** fatty deposits; **Fett|an|satz** M layer of fat; **zu ~ neigen** to tend to corpulence; **fett|arm** ADJ *Speisen* low-fat, with a low fat content ADV **~ essen** to eat foods with a low fat content or which are low in fat; **~ kochen** to cook low-fat meals; **Fett|au|ge** NT globule of fat; **Fett|bauch** M paunch; (*inf*: = *fetter Mann*) fatso (*inf*); **fett|bäu|chig** [-bɔyçɪç] ADJ paunchy, fat-bellied (*inf*); **Fett|be|darf** M fat requirements *pl*; **Fett|creme** F skin cream with oil; **Fett|druck** M , *no pl* (*Typ*) bold type

Fett|e Hen|ne F (*Bot*) stonecrop

Fett|em|bo|lie F (*Med*) fat-embolism

fet|ten ['fɛtn̩] VT to grease VI to be greasy; (= *Fett absondern*) to get greasy

Fett-: Fett|film M greasy film; **Fett|fleck** M , **Fett|fle|cken** M grease spot, greasy mark; **fett|frei** ADJ fat-free; *Milch* non-fat; *Kost* non-fatty; *Creme* non-greasy ADV **~ kochen** to cook fat-free meals; **~ essen** to eat no fats; **fett füt|tern** △ VT to fatten up; **fett gedruckt** △ ADJ *attr* → **fett** ADV **b**; **Fett|ge|halt** M fat content; **Fett|ge|schwulst** F (*Med*) fatty tumour (*Brit*) or tumor (*US*); **Fett|ge|we|be** NT

(*Anat*) fat(ty) tissue; **fett|glän|zend** ADJ *Hinterkopf* shiny and greasy; **die ~en Ringer** the wrestlers with their oiled bodies glistening; **fett|hal|tig**, (*Aus*) **fett|häl|tig** ADJ fatty; **Fett|haus|halt** M fat balance; **ein gestörter ~** a fat imbalance

Fett|heit F -, *no pl* (*inf*: = *Dickheit*) fatness; (= *Fetthaltigkeit*) fattiness

fet|tig ['fɛtɪç] ADJ *Haare, Finger, Speisen* greasy; *Haut auch* oily

Fet|tig|keit F -, *no pl* greasiness; (*von Haut auch*) oiliness

Fett-: Fett|klops M (*pej inf*), **Fett|kloß** M (*pej*) fatty (*inf*), dumpling (*inf*); **Fett|klum|pen** M globule of fat; **Fett|le|ber** F fatty liver; **fett|lei|big** [-laibɪç] ADJ (*geh*) obese, corpulent; **Fett|lei|big|keit** F -, *no pl* (*geh*) obesity, corpulence; **fett|los** ADJ fat-free ADV **völlig ~ essen** to eat no fats at all; **~ kochen** to cook fat-free meals; **fett|lö|send** △ ADJ → **Fett**; **fett|lös|lich** ADJ fat-soluble; **Fett|mas|sen** PL (*inf*) mass *sing* of fat; **Fett|mops** M (*inf*) roly-poly (*inf*), dumpling (*inf*); **Fett|näpf|chen** [-nɛpfçən] NT -s, - (*inf*) **ins ~ treten** to put one's foot in it (*bei jdm with sb*), to drop a clanger (*Brit inf*); **Fett|pols|ter** NT (*Anat*) (layer of) subcutaneous fat; (*hum inf*) flab *no pl*, padding *no pl*; **~ haben** to be well-padded; **Fett|pöls|ter|chen** NT padding *no pl*; **Fett|pres|se** F grease gun; **fett|reich** ADJ high-fat, with a high fat content; *Haut* oily ADV **~ essen** to eat foods with a high fat content or which are high in fat; **~ kochen** to use a lot of fat in cooking; **Fett|sack** M (*inf*) fatso (*inf*); **Fett|sal|be** F fat-based ointment; **Fett|sau** F (*vulg*) fat slob (*inf*); **Fett|säu|re** F (*Chem*) fatty acid; **Fett|schicht** F layer of fat; **Fett|schrift** F bold (type or face); **Fett|steiß** M (*Anat*) steatopygia (*spec*); **Fett|stift** M grease pencil, lithographic crayon; (*für Lippen*) lip salve; **Fett|sucht** F , *no pl* (*Med*) obesity; **fett|süch|tig** ADJ (*Med*) obese; **fett|trie|fend** ADJ greasy, dripping with fat; **Fett|wanst** M (*pej*) potbelly; (= *Mensch*) paunchy man, fatso (*inf*); **Fett|zel|le** F (*Physiol*) fat cell, adipose cell (*spec*)

Fe|tus ['feːtʊs] M - or -sses, -sse or **Feten** ['feːtn̩] foetus (*Brit*), fetus (*US*)

fet|zen ['fɛtsn̩] VI *aux sein* (= *rasen*) to tear (*inf*); **gegen jdn/etw ~** to tear into sb/sth VT to rip; **der Sturm fetzte das Dach vom Haus** the storm tore the roof off the house VR (*inf*: = *sich streiten*) to quarrel viciously; **die beiden ~ sich den ganzen Tag** they are tearing into each other all day long

Fet|zen ['fɛtsn̩] M -s, - **a** (*abgerissen*) shred; (*zerrissen auch*) tatter; (= *Stofffetzen, Papierfetzen, Gesprächsfetzen*) scrap; (= *Kleidung*) rag; (= *Nebelfetzen*) wisp; **in ~ sein, nur noch ~ sein** to be in tatters or shreds; **in ~ gekleidet** dressed in rags; **das Kleid ist in ~ gegangen** the dress has fallen to pieces; **etw in ~ (zer)reißen** to tear sth to shreds; **etw in tausend ~ (zer)reißen** to tear sth into a thousand pieces; **..., dass die ~ fliegen** (*inf*) ... like mad (*Brit inf*) or crazy (*inf*) **b** (*Aus*: = *Scheuertuch*) rag

Fet|zen|ball M (*Aus*: = *Maskenball*) masked ball

fet|zig ['fɛtsɪç] ADJ (*dated sl*) wild, crazy (*inf*); *Musik auch* hot; *Rede* rousing

feucht [fɔyçt] ADJ damp; (= *schlüpfrig*) moist; (= *feuchtheiß*) *Klima* humid; *Jahreszeit* wet, rainy; *Luftmassen* rain-bearing, rain-bringing; *Hände* sweaty; *Tinte, Farbe* wet; **sich ins ~e Element stürzen** (*hum*) to plunge into the water; **sie kriegte/hatte ~e Augen** her eyes moistened/were moist; **ein ~er Abend** (*hum*) a boozy or drunken night (*inf*); **eine ~e Aussprache haben** (*hum inf*) to splutter when one speaks; **das geht dich einen ~en Kehricht an** (*inf*) that's none of your goddamn (*inf*) or bloody (*Brit inf*) business; **~er Traum** (*inf*) wet dream → **Ohr**

Feucht|bi|o|top NT damp biotope

Feuch|te ['fɔyçtə] F -, *no pl* dampness; (*von Luft*) humidity

Feucht-: feucht|fröh|lich ADJ (*hum*) merry, convivial; **ein ~er Abend** an evening of convivial drinking; **Feucht|ge|biet** NT marshland; **feucht|heiß** ADJ hot and damp, muggy

Feuch|tig|keit ['fɔyçtɪçkait] F -, *no pl* **a** dampness; (= *Schlüpfrigkeit*) moistness; (*von Klima*) humidity; (*von Händen*) sweatiness **b** (= *Flüssigkeit*) moisture; (= *Luftfeuchtigkeit*) humidity

Feuch|tig|keits-: Feuch|tig|keits|creme F moisturizer, moisturizing cream; **Feuch|tig|keits|ge|halt** M , **Feuch|tig|keits|grad** M moisture level *or* content; **Feuch|tig|keits|mes|ser** M -s, - hygrometer

feucht-: feucht|kalt ADJ *Luft, Nacht, Wand* cold and damp; *Höhle, Keller etc auch* dank; **feucht|warm** ADJ *Klima, Luft* muggy, humid; *Boden* warm and damp

feu|dal [fɔy'daːl] ADJ **a** (*Pol, Hist*) feudal **b** (*inf*: = *prächtig*) plush (*inf*); *Mahlzeit* slap-up *attr* (*Brit inf*), lavish

Feu|dal- *in cpds* feudal; **Feu|dal|herr|schaft** F feudalism

Feu|da|lis|mus [fɔyda'lɪsmʊs] M -, *no pl* feudalism

feu|da|lis|tisch [fɔyda'lɪstɪʃ] ADJ feudalistic

Feu|da|li|tät [fɔydali'tɛːt] F -, *no pl* **a** (*Hist*) feudality **b** (*inf*) plushness (*inf*)

Feu|dal|sys|tem NT , **Feu|dal|we|sen** NT , *no pl* feudalism, feudal system

Feu|del ['fɔydl] M -s, - (*N Ger*) (floor)cloth

feu|deln ['fɔydln] VT (*N Ger*) to wash, to wipe

Feu|er ['fɔyɐ] NT -s, - **a** (= *Flamme, Kaminfeuer*) fire; (= *olympisches Feuer*) flame; **am ~** by the fire; **~ machen** to light a/the fire; **~ schlagen** to make fire, to strike a spark; **~ speien** to spew flames *or* fire; **~ speiend, ~ sprühend** (*liter, Drache*) fire-breathing; *Berg* spewing (forth) fire; **das brennt wie ~** (*fig*) that burns; **~ hinter etw** (*acc*) **machen** (*fig*) to chase sth up; **jdm ~ unterm Hintern** (*inf*) *or* **Arsch** (*sl*) **machen** to put a bomb under sb; **mit dem ~ spielen** (*fig*) to play with fire; **sie sind wie ~ und Wasser** they're as different as chalk and cheese **b** (= *Funkfeuer*) beacon; (*von Leuchtturm*) light **c** (= *Herd*) fire; **auf offenem ~ kochen** to cook on an open fire; **sie stellte die Kartoffeln aufs ~** she put the potatoes on **d** (*für Zigarette etc*) light; **haben Sie ~?** have you got a light?; **jdm ~ geben** to give sb a light **e** (= *Brand*) fire; **~! fire!**; **~ legen** to start a fire; **an etw** (*acc*)**/in etw** (*acc*) **~ legen** to set fire to sth; **~ fangen** to catch fire; **für jdn durchs ~ gehen** to go through fire and water for sb **f** (= *Schwung*) (*von Frau*) passion; (*von Liebhaber auch*) ardour (*Brit*), ardor (*US*); (*von Pferd*) mettle; (*von Wein*) vigour (*Brit*), vigor (*US*); **~ haben** to be passionate/ardent/mettlesome/full of vigo(u)r; **~ fangen** to be really taken (*bei* with); **bei jdm ~ fangen** to fall for sb; **~ und Flamme sein** (*inf*) to be dead keen (*Brit inf*) (*für* on), to be very enthusiastic (*für* about) **g** (*liter*: = *Glanz*) sparkle, glitter; **das ~ ihrer Augen** her flashing *or* fiery eyes **h** (= *Schießen*) fire; **~! fire!**; **~ frei!** open fire!; **~ geben, das ~ eröffnen** to open fire; **das ~ einstellen** to cease fire *or* firing; **etw unter ~** (*acc*) **nehmen** to open fire on sth; **unter ~** (*dat*) **liegen** to be under fire; **zwischen zwei ~** (*acc*) **geraten** (*fig*) to be caught between the Devil and the deep blue sea (*prov*)

Feuer- *in cpds* fire; **Feu|er|alarm** M fire alarm; **Feu|er|an|zün|der** M firelighter; **Feu|er|ba|ke** F (*Naut*) light beacon; **Feu|er|ball** M fireball; **Feu|er|be|fehl** M (*Mil*) order to fire; **Feu|er|be|kämp|fung** F fire-fighting; **Feu|er|be|reich** M (*Mil*) firing range; **feu|er|be|reit** ADJ (*Mil*) *Soldat, Waffe* ready to fire; **feu|er|be|stän|dig** ADJ fire-resistant; **Feu|er|be|stat|tung** F cremation; **Feu|er|ei|fer** M zeal; **mit ~ spielen/diskutieren** to play/discuss with

zest; **Feu|er|ei|mer** M fire bucket; **Feu|er|ein|stel|lung** F cessation of fire; (= *Waffenstillstand*) ceasefire; **feu|er|fest** ADJ fireproof; *Geschirr* heat-resistant; **~er Ton** fire clay; **~er Ziegel** firebrick; **Feu|er|fres|ser(in)** M(F) fire-eater; **Feu|er|gar|be** F burst of fire; **Feu|er|gas|se** F fire lane; **Feu|er|ge|fahr** F fire hazard *or* risk; **bei ~** in the event of fire; **feu|er|ge|fähr|lich** ADJ (highly) (in)flammable *or* combustible; **Feu|er|ge|fähr|lich|keit** F (in)flammability, combustibility; **Feu|er|ge|fecht** NT gun fight, shoot-out (*inf*); **Feu|er|geist** M (*liter*) volatile young genius, fireball; **Feu|er|glo|cke** F fire bell; **Feu|er|gott** M god of fire; **Feu|er|ha|ken** M poker; **Feu|er|holz** NT , *no pl* firewood; **Feu|er|kä|fer** M cardinal beetle; **Feu|er|kopf** M (*fig geh*) hothead; **Feu|er|kult** M (*Rel*) fire cult; **Feu|er|land** ['fɔyɐlant] NT -s Tierra del Fuego; **Feu|er|län|der** ['fɔyɐlɛndɐ] M -s, -, **Feu|er|län|de|rin** [-ərɪn] F -, -nen Fuegian; **Feu|er|lei|ter** F (*am Haus*) fire escape; (*bei Feuerwehrauto*) (fireman's) ladder; (*fahrbar*) turntable ladder; **Feu|er|li|nie** F (*Mil*) firing line

Feu|er|lösch|boot NT fireboat

Feu|er|lö|scher M -s, - **a** fire extinguisher **b** (*sl*: = *Penis*) tool (*sl*)

Feu|er|lösch-: Feu|er|lösch|ge|rät NT fire-fighting appliance; **Feu|er|lösch|teich** M emergency water reserve; **Feu|er|lösch|übung** F fire drill; **Feu|er|lösch|zug** M convoy of fire engines, set of appliances (*form*)

Feuer-: Feu|er|mal NT (*Med*) port-wine stain; **Feu|er|meer** NT sea of flames, blazing inferno; **Feu|er|mel|der** M fire alarm; **er hat ein Gesicht wie ein ~(, so schön zum Reinschlagen)** (*sl*) he's got the kind of face that just makes you want to hit it

feu|ern ['fɔyɐn] VI **a** (= *heizen*) **mit Öl/Gas ~** to have oil/gas heating; **mit Holz ~** to use wood for one's heating **b** (*Mil*) to fire VT **a** *Ofen* to light; **Öl ~** to have oil heating; **Briketts ~** to use briquettes for one's heating **b** (*inf*) (= *werfen*) to fling (*inf*), to sling (*inf*); (*Ftbl*) *Ball* to slam (*inf*); (*ins Tor*) to slam home (*inf*) *or* in (*inf*) **c** (*inf*: = *entlassen*) to fire (*inf*), to sack (*inf*); **ge-feuert werden** to get the sack, to be fired *or* sacked (*all inf*)

Feuer-: Feu|er|ofen M (*Bibl*) fiery furnace; **Feu|er|pat|sche** F fire-beater; **Feu|er|pau|se** F break in the firing; (*vereinbart*) ceasefire; **feu|er|po|li|zei|lich** ADJ *Bestimmungen* laid down by the fire authorities; **~e Notrufleitungen** emergency lines to the fire station ADV **~ verboten** prohibited by order of the fire authorities; **Feu|er|pro|be** F (*Hist*: = *Gottesurteil*) ordeal by fire; **die ~ bestehen** (*fig*) to pass the (acid) test; **das war seine ~** (*fig*) that was the acid test for him; **Feu|er|qual|le** F stinging jellyfish; **Feu|er|rad** NT fire-wheel; (= *Feuerwerkskörper*) catherine (*Brit*) *or* pin (*US*) wheel; **feu|er|rot** ADJ fiery red; *Haar auch* flaming; *Kleidung, Auto* scarlet; **~ werden** (*vor Verlegenheit etc*) to turn crimson *or* scarlet; **Feu|er|sa|la|man|der** M fire *or* European salamander; **Feu|er|säu|le** F (*Bibl*) pillar of fire

Feu|ers|brunst F (*geh*) conflagration

Feuer-: Feu|er|scha|den M fire damage *no pl*; **Feu|er|schein** M glow of the fire; **Feu|er|schiff** NT lightship; **Feu|er|schlu|cker** [-ʃlʊkɐ] M -s, -, **Feu|er|schlu|cke|rin** [-ərɪn] F -, -nen fire-eater; **feu|er|schnau|bend** ADJ *attr* (*poet*) fire-breathing; **Feu|er|schnei|se** F fire break; **Feu|er|schutz** M **a** (= *Vorbeugung*) fire prevention **b** (*Mil*: = *Deckung*) covering fire; **Feu|er|schutz|tür** F fire door; **Feu|er|schweif** M fiery tail; **feu|er|si|cher** ADJ = feuerfest; **Feu|er|si|re|ne** F fire siren

Feu|ers|not F (*liter*) fiery peril (*poet*)

Feuer-: feu|er|spei|end △ ADJ *attr* → **Feuer a**; **Feu|er|sprit|ze** F fire hose; **feu|er|sprühend** △ ADJ (*liter*) → **Feuer a**; **Feu|er|stät|te** F (*form*) **a** (= *Koch-, Heizstelle*) fireplace, hearth

b (= *Brandstelle*) scene of the fire; **Feu|er|stein** M flint; **Feu|er|stel|le** F campfire site; (= *Spuren eines Feuers*) burned spot, remains *pl* of a fire; (= *Herd*) fireplace; **Feu|er|stel|lung** F (*Mil*) firing position; **Feu|er|stoß** M burst of fire; **Feu|er|strahl** M (*geh*) jet of flame *or* fire; (*poet*: = *Blitz*) thunderbolt; **Feu|er|stuhl** M (*inf*) (motor)bike; **Feu|er|sturm** M fire storm; **Feu|er|tau|fe** F baptism of fire; **die ~ bestehen/erhalten** to go through/have one's baptism of fire; **Feu|er|teu|fel** M (*inf*) firebug (*inf*); **Feu|er|tod** M (*Hist*) (death at) the stake; **den ~ erleiden** to be burned *or* to die at the stake; **Feu|er|trep|pe** F fire escape; **Feu|er|tür** F fire door; **Feu|er|über|fall** M armed attack

Feu|e|rung ['fɔyərʊŋ] F -, -en **a** (= *das Beheizen*) heating **b** (= *Brennstoff*) fuel **c** (= *Heizanlage*) heating system

Feuer-: Feu|er|ver|hü|tung F fire prevention; **Feu|er|ver|si|che|rung** F fire insurance; **feu|er|ver|zinkt** [-fɛtsɪŋkt] ADJ (hot-dip) galvanized; **Feu|er|wa|che** F fire station; **Feu|er|waf|fe** F firearm; **Feu|er|wal|ze** F swath of fire; **Feu|er|was|ser** NT , *no pl* (*inf*) firewater (*inf*); **Feu|er|wech|sel** M exchange of fire

Feu|er|wehr F fire brigade (*Brit*), fire department (*US*); **fahren wie die ~** (*inf*) to drive like the clappers (*Brit inf*) *or* like a bat out of hell (*US inf*); **~ spielen** (*fig*: = *Schlimmes verhindern*) to act as a troubleshooter, to troubleshoot

Feu|er|wehr-: Feu|er|wehr|au|to NT fire engine; **Feu|er|wehr|ball** M firemen's ball; **Feu|er|wehr|frau** F firewoman; **Feu|er|wehr|mann** M *pl* -leute *or* -männer fireman; **Feu|er|wehr|schlauch** M fire hose; **Feu|er|wehr|übung** F fire-fighting exercise; **Feu|er|wehr|wa|gen** M fire engine

Feuer-: Feu|er|werk NT fireworks *pl*; (= *Schauspiel auch*) firework display; (*fig*) cavalcade; **Feu|er|wer|ker** [-vɛrkɐ] M -s, -, **Feu|er|wer|ke|rin** [-ərɪn] F -, -nen firework-maker; **Feu|er|werks|kör|per** M firework; **Feu|er|zan|ge** F fire tongs *pl*; **Feu|er|zan|gen|bow|le** F red wine punch (*containing rum which has been set alight*)

FEUERZANGENBOWLE

A **Feuerzangenbowle** is a hot drink made from wine, with rum and sometimes fruit juice added. It is prepared by clamping a sugar loaf into a device like a pair of fire tongs over a punch bowl filled with red wine, into which orange or lemon juice and a cinnamon stick are sometimes added. The sugar is then soaked with rum and set alight. The sugar slowly melts, caramelizes, and drips into the wine, giving the punch its characteristic taste.

Feu|er|zei|chen NT **a** (= *Signal*) beacon **b** (*Astrol*) fire sign

Feu|er|zeug NT *pl* -zeuge (cigarette) lighter

Feu|er|zeug|ben|zin NT lighter fuel

Feu|er|zeug|gas NT lighter gas

Feu|er|zo|ne F (*Mil*) firing zone

Feu|er|zun|ge F (*Bibl*) tongue of flame

Feuil|le|ton [fœjə'tõː, 'fœjətõ] NT -s, -s (*Press*) **a** (= *Zeitungsteil*) feature pages *pl* or section **b** (= *Artikel*) feature (article)

Feuil|le|to|nis|mus [fœjəto'nɪsmʊs] M -, *no pl* style of writing used in feature articles, often regarded as facile

Feuil|le|to|nist [fœjəto'nɪst] M -en, -en, **Feuil|le|to|nis|tin** [-'nɪstɪn] F -, -nen feature writer

feuil|le|to|nis|tisch [fœjəto'nɪstɪʃ] ADJ **dieser Journalist ist ein ~es Talent** this journalist has a natural flair for writing feature articles; **dieser Aufsatz ist zu ~** (*pej*) this essay is too glib *or* facile

Feuil|le|ton- [fœjətõː-, -'fœjətõ-]: **Feuil|le|ton|schreiber(in)** M(F) feature writer; **Feuil|le-**

ton|stil M style used in feature articles; (*pej*) facile *or* glib style

feu|rig ['fɔyrɪç] ADJ *Pferd, Liebhaber, Rede* fiery; (*old*: = *glühend*) glowing

feu|rio ['fɔyrio] INTERJ (*old*) fire(, fire)!

Fex [fɛks] M **-es** *or* **-en, -e** *or* **-en** (*S Ger, Aus*) enthusiast

Fez¹ [fe:ts, fɛ:s] M **-(es), -(e)** (= *Hut*) fez

Fez² [fe:ts] M **-(e)s**, *no pl* (*dated inf*) larking about (*Brit inf*), fooling around (*esp US inf*); ~ **machen** to lark about (*Brit inf*), to fool around (*esp US inf*)

ff [ɛf|ɛf] ADJ *inv* first-class, top-grade → **Effeff**

ff. *abbr von* **folgende Seiten**

Ffm. *abbr von* **Frankfurt am Main**

FH [ɛf|ha:] F **-, -s** *abbr von* **Fachhochschule**

Fi|a|ker ['fiakɐ] M **-s, -** (*Aus*) **a** (= *Kutsche*) (hackney) cab **b** (= *Kutscher*) cab driver, cabby (*inf*)

Fi|a|le ['fia:lə] F **-, -n** (*Archit*) pinnacle

Fi|as|ko ['fiasko] NT **-s, -s** (*inf*) fiasco; **mit seinem Buch erlebte er ein ~** his book was a complete failure *or* flop (*inf*) *or* fiasco; **dann gibt es ein ~** it'll be disastrous *or* a fiasco

Fi|bel¹ ['fi:bl] F **-, -n** (*Sch*) primer

Fi|bel² F **-, -n** (*Archeol*) fibula (*spec*), clasp

Fi|ber ['fi:bɐ] F **-, -n** fibre (*Brit*), fiber (*US*)

Fib|rin [fi'bri:n] NT **-s**, *no pl* (*Physiol*) fibrin

Fib|rom [fi'bro:m] NT **-s, -e** (*Med*) fibroma (*spec*)

fib|rös [fi'brø:s] ADJ (*Med*) fibrous

Fiche [fi:ʃ] M OR NT **-(s), -s** **a** (micro)fiche **b** (*Sw*: = *Akte*) file

ficht [fɪçt] *3. pers sing pres von* **fechten**

Fich|te ['fɪçtə] F **-, -n** (*Bot*) spruce; (*Holz auch*) spruce wood

fich|ten ['fɪçtn] ADJ spruce(wood)

Fich|ten- *in cpds* spruce; **Fich|ten|na|del|ex|-trakt** M pine essence; **Fich|ten|zap|fen** M spruce cone

Fick [fɪk] M **-s, -s** (*vulg*) fuck (*vulg*)

fi|cken ['fɪkn] VTI (*vulg*) to fuck (*vulg*); **mit jdm ~** to fuck sb (*vulg*)

fi|cke|rig ['fɪkərɪç], **fick|rig** ['fɪkrɪç] ADJ (*dial*) fidgety

Fick|teu|fel M (*vulg*: = *Penis*) dick (*sl*), cock (*sl*)

Fi|cus ['fi:kʊs] M **-, Fici** ['fi:tsi] (= *Zierpflanze*) weeping fig

Fi|de|i|kom|miss ▲ [fideiko'mɪs, 'fi:dei-] NT **-es, -e** (*old Jur*) entail (*form*), entailed estate

fi|del [fi'de:l] ADJ jolly, merry

Fi|del ['fi:dl] F **-, -n** fiddle

Fi|di|bus ['fi:dibʊs] M **-** *or* **-ses, -** *or* **-se** spill

Fid|schi¹ ['fɪdʒi] NT **-s** Fiji

Fid|schi² M **-s, -s** (*pej sl*: = *Exot*) gook (*pej sl*)

Fid|schi|a|ner [fɪ'dʒia:nɐ] M **-s, -, Fid|schi|a|ne|rin** [-ərɪn] F **-, -nen** Fijian

Fid|schi|in|seln ['fɪdʒi-] PL Fiji Islands *pl*

Fie|ber ['fi:bɐ] NT **-s,** (*rare*) **-** **a** temperature; (*sehr hoch, mit Fantasieren*) fever; ~ **haben** to have *or* be running a temperature; **to be feverish** *or* running a fever; **40°** ~ **haben** to have a temperature of 40; **(jdm) das ~ messen** to take sb's temperature; **im ~ seiner Leidenschaft** in a fever of passion **b** (= *Krankheit*) fever

Fie|ber-: Fie|ber|an|fall M attack *or* bout of fever; **Fie|ber|bläs|chen** NT fever blister; **Fie|ber|fan|ta|si|en** ▲ PL feverish *or* febrile (*form*) wanderings *pl or* ravings *pl*; **Fie|ber|fle|cken** PL fever spots *pl*; **fie|ber|frei** ADJ free of fever; **Fie|ber|frost** M feverish shivering; **fie|ber|haft** ADJ **a** (= *fieberig*) feverish, febrile (*form*) **b** (= *hektisch*) feverish ADV feverishly

fie|be|rig ['fi:bərɪç] ADJ feverish, febrile (*form*); **in ~er Eile** with feverish haste

Fie|ber-: Fie|ber|kur|ve F temperature curve; **Fie|ber|mes|ser** M **-s, -** (*dated, Sw*) thermometer; **Fie|ber|mit|tel** NT anti-fever drug, antipyretic (*spec*); **Fie|ber|mü|cke** F malarial mosquito

fie|bern ['fi:bɐn] VI **a** (*Kranker*) to have a fever *or* temperature; (*schwer*) to be feverish *or* febrile (*form*) **b** (*fig*) **nach etw ~** to long feverishly for sth; **vor Ungeduld/Erregung** (*dat*) ~ to be in a fever of impatience/excitement

Fie|ber-: Fie|ber|phan|ta|si|en PL = Fieberfantasien; **fie|ber|sen|kend** ADJ fever-reducing; **Fie|ber|sen|kung** F reduction of fever; **ein Mittel zur ~** a medicine for reducing fever; **Fie|ber|ta|bel|le** F temperature chart; **Fie|ber|ther|mo|me|ter** NT (clinical) thermometer; **Fie|ber|wahn** M (feverish *or* febrile) delirium; **Fie|ber|zäpf|chen** NT (*Pharm, Med*) fever-reducing *or* antipyretic (*spec*) suppository

fieb|rig ['fi:brɪç] ADJ = fieberig

Fie|del ['fi:dl] F **-, -n** fiddle

Fie|del|bo|gen M fiddle bow

fie|deln ['fi:dln] VTI (*hum, pej*) to fiddle; **ein Liedchen ~** to play a song on the fiddle

fie|dern ['fi:dɐn] VR (*Orn*) to acquire its plumage → *auch* **gefiedert**

Fie|de|rung ['fi:dərʊŋ] F **-, -en** **a** (*Orn*) plumage **b** (*Bot*) pinnation (*spec*)

Fied|ler ['fi:dlɐ] M **-s, -, Fied|le|rin** [-ərɪn] F **-, -nen** (*hum, pej*: = *Geiger*) fiddler

fiel *pret von* **fallen**

fie|pen ['fi:pn] VI (*Reh*) to call; (*Hund, Mensch*) to whimper; (*Vogel*) to cheep

Fie|rant [fiə'rant] M **-en, -en, Fie|ran|tin** [fiə'rantɪn] F **-, -nen** (*S Ger, Aus*) (street) market trader

fie|ren ['fi:rən] VT (*Naut*) *Segel, Last* to lower; *Tau* to pay out

fies [fi:s] (*inf*) ADJ (= *abstoßend, unangenehm*) *Mensch, Gesicht, Geruch, Arbeit* nasty, horrid, horrible; (= *gemein*) *Charakter, Methoden auch* mean → **Möpp** ADV (= *abstoßend, ekelhaft*) *sich benehmen, lachen* nastily, horribly; (= *gemein*) *handeln, reagieren* in a nasty way; ~ **aussehen** to look horrible; ~ **riechen** to smell horrible; **benimm dich nicht so ~!** don't be so horrid!; (= *ordinär*) don't behave so horribly!

Fies|heit F **-, -en** *usu pl* (*inf*) mean trick

Fies|ling ['fi:slɪŋ] M **-s, -e** (*inf*) (= *abstoßender Mensch*) slob (*inf*); (= *gemeiner Mensch*) sod (*Brit sl*), bastard (*sl*)

Fi|fa ['fi:fa] F **-, FIFA** F - FIFA

fif|ty-fif|ty ['fɪftɪ'fɪftɪ] ADV (*inf*) fifty-fifty (*inf*); ~ **machen** to go fifty-fifty (*inf*); **die Sache steht** ~ there's a fifty-fifty chance (*inf*)

Fi|ga|ro ['fi:garo] M **-s, -s** (*hum*) hairdresser

Fight [fait] M **-s, -s** fight

figh|ten ['faitn] VI to fight

Figh|ter ['faitɐ] M **-s, -, Figh|te|rin** ['faitərɪn] F **-, -nen** fighter

Fi|gur [fi'gu:ɐ] F **-, -en** **a** (= *Bildwerk, Abbildung, Math*) figure; (*gedankenlos hingezeichnet*) doodle **b** (= *Gestalt, Persönlichkeit*) figure; (= *Körperform*) (*von Frauen*) figure; (*von Männern*) physique; (*inf*: = *Mensch*) character; **in ganzer ~** (*Phot, Art*) full-figure; **auf seine ~ achten** to watch one's figure; **eine gute/schlechte/traurige ~ machen** *or* **abgeben** to cut a good/poor/sorry figure **c** (= *Romanfigur, Filmfigur etc*) character **d** (*Sport, Mus*) figure; (= *rhetorische Figur*) figure of speech

fi|gu|ral [figu'ra:l] ADJ (*Art*) figured

Fi|gu|ral|mu|sik F figural *or* florid music

Fi|gu|ra|ti|on [figura'tsio:n] F **-, -en** figuration

fi|gu|ra|tiv [figura'ti:f] ADJ figurative ADV figuratively; (*geh*: = *gegenständlich*) representationally

fi|gur|be|tont ADJ figure-hugging

Fi|gür|chen [fi'gy:ɐçən] NT **-s,** *dim von* **Figur**

Fi|gu|ren|lau|fen NT **-s**, *no pl* figure skating

fi|gu|rie|ren [figu'ri:rən] ptp **figuriert** VI (*geh*) to figure VT (*Mus*) to figure

Fi|gu|ri|ne [figu'ri:nə] F **-, -n** (*Art*) figure; (= *kleine Statue*) figurine; (*Theat*) costume design *or* sketch

fi|gür|lich [fi'gy:ɐlɪç] ADJ **a** (= *übertragen*) figurative **b** (= *figurmäßig*) as regards the/her figure; (*von Männern*) as regards physique **c** (*Art*) figurative ADV **a** (= *figurmäßig*) in terms of the/one's figure; (= *übertragen*) figuratively

Fi|gur|prob|lem NT problem with one's figure, weight problem

Fik|ti|on [fɪk'tsio:n] F **-, -en** fiction

fik|tiv [fɪk'ti:f] ADJ fictitious

Fi|let [fi'le:] NT **-s, -s** **a** (*Cook*) (= *Schweinefilet, Geflügelfilet, Fischfilet*) fillet; (= *Rinderfilet*) fillet steak; (*zum Braten*) piece of sirloin *or* tenderloin (*US*) **b** (*Tex*) netting

Fi|let|ar|beit [fi'le:-] F (*Tex*) netting

fi|le|tie|ren [file'ti:rən] ptp **filetiert** VT to fillet

Fi|let-: [fi'le:-] **Fi|let|steak** NT fillet steak; **Fi|let|stück** NT (*Cook*) piece of sirloin *or* tenderloin (*US*); (*fig inf*: = *lohnendes Investitionsobjekt etc*) prime investment choice

Fi|lia ['fi:lia] F **-, Filiae** ['fi:liɛ] (*hum*) daughter, offspring (*hum*)

Fi|li|al|be|trieb [fi'lia:l-] M branch

Fi|li|a|le [fi'lia:lə] F **-, -n** branch

Fi|li|al-: [fi'lia:l-]: **Fi|li|al|ge|ne|ra|ti|on** F (*Biol*) (first) filial generation; **Fi|li|al|ge|schäft** NT branch; **Fi|li|al|kir|che** F daughter church; **Fi|li|al|lei|ter(in)** M(F) branch manager/manageress; **Fi|li|al|netz** NT network of branches

Fi|li|bus|ter¹ [fili'bʊstɐ] M **-s, -** (*old, fig*) buccaneer

Fi|li|bus|ter² [fili'bastɐ] NT **-(s), -** (*Pol*) filibuster

fi|li|gran [fili'gra:n] ADJ filigree

Fi|li|gran [fili'gra:n] NT **-s, -e** filigree

Fi|li|gran|ar|beit F filigree work; (= *Schmuckstück*) piece of filigree work

Fi|li|pi|na [fili'pi:na] F **-, -s** Filipina

Fi|li|pi|no¹ [fili'pi:no] M **-s, -s** Filipino

Fi|li|pi|no² [fili'pi:no] NT **-,** *no pl* (*Ling*) Filipino, Tagalog

Fi|li|us ['fi:liʊs] M **-, -se** (*hum*) son, offspring (*hum*)

Film [fɪlm] M **-(e)s, -e** **a** (*alle Bedeutungen*) film; (= *Spielfilm*) film, movie (*esp US*), motion picture (*US*); (= *Dokumentarfilm*) documentary (film); **ein ~ nach dem Roman von E. Marlitt** a film of *or* based on the novel by E. Marlitt; **in einen ~ gehen** to go and see a film, to go to a film; **da ist bei mir der ~ gerissen** (*fig inf*) I had a mental blackout (*inf*) **b** (= *Filmbranche*) films *pl*, movie (*esp US*) *or* motion-picture (*esp US*) business; **zum ~ gehen/kommen** to go/get *or* break into films *or* movies (*esp US*); **beim ~ arbeiten** *or* **sein** (*inf*) to work in films *or* in the movie business (*esp US*)

Film- *in cpds* film, movie (*esp US*); **Film|ama|teur(in)** M(F) home-movie enthusiast *or* buff (*inf*); **Film|ar|chiv** NT film archives *pl*; **Film|ate|li|er** NT film studio; **Film|auf|nah|me** F **a** (*Einzelszene*) shot, take **b** (= *das Drehen*) **die ~n** *pl* shooting; **Film|au|tor(in)** M(F) scriptwriter, screen-writer; **Film|ball** M film festival ball; **Film|bau|ten** PL film sets *pl*; **Film|be|ar|bei|tung** F (screen) adaptation; **Film|be|richt** M film report; **Film|be|wer|tungs|stel|le** F ≈ board of film classification; **Film|bio|gra|fie** ▲ F biopic; **Film|büh|ne** F (*dated*) picture house (*dated*), movie house (*US*); **Film|di|va** F (*dated*) screen goddess; **Film|dra|ma** NT film drama

Fil|me|ma|cher(in) M(F) film-maker

Film|emp|find|lich|keit F film speed

fil|men ['fɪlmən] VTI to film

Film-: Film|ent|wick|ler M developer; **Film|epos** NT epic film

Fil|mer ['fɪlmɐ] M **-s, -, Fil|me|rin** [-ərɪn] F **-, -nen** (*inf*) film or movie (*esp US*) director

Fil|me|rei [fɪlmə'raɪ] F **-, -en** (*inf*) filming

Film-: Film|fes|ti|val NT , **Film|fest|spie|le** PL film festival; **Film|för|de|rungs|ge|setz** NT *law on film subsidies*; **Film|for|mat** NT (*für Fotoapparat*) film size; (*für Filmkamera*) film gauge; **Film|frit|ze** M (*inf*) film or movie (*esp US*) guy (*inf*); **film|ge|recht** ADJ filmable ADV der Roman muss ~ bearbeitet werden the novel will have to be adapted for the cinema or for film; **Film|ge|schäft** NT film or movie (*esp US*) or motion-picture (*esp US*) industry; **Film|ge|schich|te** F history of the cinema; ~ **machen** to make film or movie (*esp US*) or motion-picture (*esp US*) history; **Film|grö|ße** F (= *Filmstar*) great star of the screen, great movie star (*esp US*); **Film|held** M screen or movie (*esp US*) hero; **Film|hel|din** F screen or movie (*esp US*) heroine

fil|misch ['fɪlmɪʃ] ADJ cinematic; ~es Porträt film portrait; eine ~e Dokumentation der Aufführung a record on film of the production ADV cinematically

Film-: Film|ka|me|ra F film or movie (*esp US*) camera; (= *Schmalfilmkamera*) cine camera (*Brit*), movie camera (*Brit*); **Film|kas|set|te** F film cassette; **Film|kom|po|nist(in)** M(F) composer of film music; **Film|kri|tik** F film or movie (*esp US*) criticism or reviewing; (= *Artikel*) film or movie (*esp US*) review; (= *Kritiker*) film or movie (*esp US*) critics *pl*; **Film|ku|lis|se** F setting for a film or movie (*esp US*); **Film|kunst** F cinematic art; **Film|lein|wand** F screen; **Film|ma|te|ri|al** NT film; **Film|mu|sik** F film music, movie soundtrack (*esp US*); **die originale ~** the original soundtrack

Fil|mo|gra|fie [fɪlmogra'fi:] F **-, -n** [-'fi:ən] filmography

Fil|mo|thek [fɪlmo'te:k] F **-, -en** film or movie (*esp US*) library or archive

Film-: Film|pa|last M picture or movie (*esp US*) palace; **Film|preis** M film or movie (*esp US*) award; **Film|pro|du|zent(in)** M(F) film or movie (*esp US*) producer; **Film|pro|jek|tor** M film or movie (*esp US*) projector; **Film|prüf|stel|le** F film censorship office; **Film|pub|li|kum** NT filmgoing or moviegoing (*esp US*) public; **Film|rech|te** PL film or movie (*esp US*) rights *pl*; **Film|re|gie** F direction of a/the film or movie (*esp US*); **Film|re|gis|seur(in)** M(F) film or movie (*esp US*) director; **Film|re|por|ta|ge** F film report; **Film|riss** ▲ M (*lit*) tear in a film; (*fig inf*) mental blackout (*inf*); **Film|rol|le** F (= *Spule*) spool of film; (*für Fotoapparat*) roll of film; (= *Part*) film part or role, movie role (*esp US*); **Film|satz** M (*Typ* = *Lichtsatz*; **Film|schaf|fen|de(r)** MF *decl as adj* film-maker, movie-maker (*esp US*); **Film|schau|platz** M setting of a film or movie (*esp US*); **Film|schau|spie|ler** M film or movie (*esp US*) actor; **Film|schau|spie|le|rin** F film or movie (*esp US*) actress; **Film|schön|heit** F screen beauty; **Film|se|rie** F (*auch TV*) film series *sing*; **Film|spu|le** F film spool; **Film|star** M filmstar, movie star (*esp US*); **Film|stern|chen** NT starlet; **Film|stu|dio** NT film or movie (*esp US*) studio; **Film|sze|ne** F scene of a film; **Film|thea|ter** NT (*form*) cinema, movie theater (*US*); **Film|trans|port|he|bel** F film advance lever; **Film- und Fern|seh|aka|de|mie** F , **Film- und Fern|seh|hoch|schu|le** F college of film and television technology; **Film|ver|leih** M film or movie (*esp US*) distributors *pl*; **Film|vor|füh|rer(in)** M(F) projectionist; **Film|vor|stel|lung** F film or movie (*esp US*) show; **Film|welt** F film or movie (*esp US*) world; **Film|zen|sur** F film censorship; (= *Zensoren*) film censors *pl*

Fi|lou [fi'lu:] M **-s, -s** (*dated inf*) devil (*inf*)

Fil|ter ['fɪltɐ] NT OR M **-s, -** filter; **eine Zigarette mit/ohne ~** a (filter-)tipped/plain cigarette

Fil|ter-: Fil|ter|an|la|ge F filter; **Fil|ter|ein|satz** M filter pad; **fil|ter|fein** ADJ finely ground ADV ~ **mahlen** to grind finely; **Fil|ter|glas** NT tinted glass; **Fil|ter|kaf|fee** M filter or drip (*US*) coffee; **Fil|ter|mund|stück** NT filter-tip

fil|tern ['fɪltɐn] VTI to filter

Fil|ter-: Fil|ter|pa|pier NT filter paper; **Fil|ter|rück|stand** M residue (*after filtering*); **Fil|ter|staub** M filter dust; **Fil|ter|tuch** NT *pl* **-tücher** filter cloth; **Fil|ter|tü|te** F filter bag

Fil|te|rung ['fɪltərʊŋ] F **-, -en** filtering

Fil|ter|zi|ga|ret|te F tipped or filter(-tipped) cigarette

Filt|rat [fɪl'tra:t] NT **-(e)s, -e** filtrate

Filt|ra|ti|on [fɪltra'tsio:n] F **-, -en** filtration

filt|rier|bar ADJ filterable

filt|rie|ren [fɪl'tri:rən] *ptp* **filtriert** VT to filter

Filt|rie|rung F **-, -en** filtering

Filz [fɪlts] M **-es, -e** a (*Tex*) felt; (*inf*: = *Filzhut*) felt hat; (*inf*: = *Bierdeckel*) beer mat (*Brit*) or coaster (*US*) c (*inf*) (= *Korruption*) corruption; (*Pol pej*) sleaze (*inf*)

fil|zen ['fɪltsn] VI (*Tex*) to felt, to go felty VT (*inf*) (= *durchsuchen*) jdn to frisk, to search; *Gepäck etc* to search, to go through; (= *berauben*) to do over (*inf*)

Filz|hut M felt hat

fil|zig ['fɪltsɪç] ADJ a (= *wie Filz*) felty, feltlike b (*inf*) (= *korrupt*) corrupt; (*Pol pej*) sleazy (*inf*)

Filz-: Filz|lat|schen M (*inf*) carpet slipper; **Filz|laus** F crab louse

Fil|zo|krat [fɪltso'kra:t] M **-en, -en, Fil|zo|kra|tin** [-'kra:tɪn] F **-, -nen** (*Pol pej*) corrupt nepotist

Fil|zo|kra|tie [fɪltsokra'ti:] F **-, -n** [-'ti:ən] (*Pol pej*) web of patronage and nepotism, spoils system (*US*)

fil|zo|kra|tisch [fɪltso'kra:tɪʃ] ADJ (*Pol pej*) nepotically corrupt

Filz-: Filz|pan|tof|fel M (carpet) slipper; **Filz|schrei|ber** M felt(-tip) pen, felt-tip; **Filz|soh|le** F felt insole; **Filz|stie|fel** M felt boot; **Filz|stift** M felt(-tip) pen, felt-tip

Fim|mel ['fɪml] M **-s, -** (*inf*) a (= *Tick*) mania; **er hat diesen ~ mit dem Unkrautjäten** he's got this thing about weeding (*inf*) b (= *Spleen*) obsession (*mit* about); **du hast wohl einen ~!** you're crazy (*inf*) or mad (*inf*)!

fi|nal [fi'na:l] ADJ final → **Rettungsschuss**

Fi|na|le [fi'na:lə] NT **-s, -s** or **-** (*Mus*) finale; (*Sport*) final, finals *pl*

Fi|na|list [fina'lɪst] M **-en, -en, Fi|na|lis|tin** [-'lɪstɪn] F **-, -nen** finalist

Fi|na|li|tät [finali'tɛt] F **-, -en** (*Philos*) finality

Fi|na|li|prin|zip NT principle of finality

Final-: Fi|nal|satz M final clause; **Fi|nal|spiel** NT (*Sport*) final

Fi|nan|cier [finã'sie:] M **-s, -s** financier

Fi|nanz [fi'nants] F **-, no pl** financial world; **die hohe ~** the world of high finance; **Kreise der ~** financial circles

Fi|nanz- *in cpds* financial; **Fi|nanz|adel** M plutocrats *pl*, plutocracy; **Fi|nanz|ak|ro|bat(in)** M(F) (*pej inf*) financial juggler; **Fi|nanz|amt** NT tax office; **Fi|nanz|aris|to|kra|tie** F plutocrats *pl*, plutocracy; **Fi|nanz|aus|gleich** M redistribution of income between Bund, Länder and Gemeinden; **Fi|nanz|aus|schuss** ▲ M finance committee; **Fi|nanz|au|to|no|mie** F financial autonomy; **Fi|nanz|be|am|te(r)** M *decl as adj*, **Fi|nanz|be|am|tin** F tax official; **Fi|nanz|be|hör|de** F tax authority; **Fi|nanz|buch|hal|ter(in)** M(F) financial accountant; **Fi|nanz|din|ge** PL financial matters *pl*

Fi|nan|zen [fi'nantsn] PL finances *pl*; **das übersteigt meine ~** that's beyond my means

Fi|nan|zer [fi'nantse] M **-s, -, Fi|nan|ze|rin** [-ərɪn] F **-, -nen** (*Aus*: = *Zollbeamter*) customs officer or official

Fi|nanz-: Fi|nanz|fra|ge F question of finance; **Fi|nanz|ge|ba|ren** NT management of public finances; **Fi|nanz|ge|nie** NT financial genius or wizard (*inf*); **Fi|nanz|ge|richt** NT *tribunal dealing with tax and other financial matters*; **Fi|nanz|hai** M (*pej*) (financial) shark (*inf*); **Fi|nanz|hil|fe** F financial aid; **Fi|nanz|ho|heit** F financial autonomy

fi|nan|zi|ell [finan'tsiɛl] ADJ financial ADV financially; **sich ~ an etw** (*dat*) **beteiligen** to take a (financial) stake in sth

Fi|nan|zi|er [finan'tsie:] M **-s, -s** financier

fi|nan|zier|bar [finan'tsi:ɐba:ɐ] ADJ financeable; **es ist (nicht) ~** it can(not) be funded or financed, the money can(not) be found

fi|nan|zie|ren [finan'tsi:rən] *ptp* **finanziert** VT to finance, to fund; **frei ~** to finance privately; **ich kann einen Urlaub nicht ~** I can't afford a holiday (*esp Brit*) or vacation (*US*)

Fi|nan|zie|rung F **-, -en** financing; **zur ~ von etw** to finance sth; **die ~ meines Projekts ist noch nicht gesichert** it isn't certain whether I will have the money for this project

Fi|nan|zie|rungs-: Fi|nan|zie|rungs|be|darf M funding or borrowing requirement; **Fi|nan|zie|rungs|de|fi|zit** NT budget deficit; **Fi|nan|zie|rungs|ge|sell|schaft** F finance company; **Fi|nan|zie|rungs|loch** NT , **Fi|nan|zie|rungs|lü|cke** F financing gap; **Fi|nan|zie|rungs|plan** M finance plan or scheme

Fi|nanz-: Fi|nanz|jahr NT financial year; **Fi|nanz|jong|leur(in)** M(F) (*pej inf*) financial juggler; **Fi|nanz|kraft** F , *no pl* financial strength, financial clout (*inf*); **fi|nanz|kräf|tig** ADJ financially strong; **Fi|nanz|kri|se** F financial crisis; **Fi|nanz|mi|nis|ter(in)** M(F) ≈ Chancellor of the Exchequer (*Brit*), ≈ Treasury Secretary (*US*), finance minister; **Fi|nanz|plan** M financial plan; **Fi|nanz|pla|nung** F financial planning; **Fi|nanz|platz** M financial centre (*Brit*) or center (*US*); **Fi|nanz|po|li|tik** F financial policy; (= *Wissenschaft, Disziplin*) politics of finance; **fi|nanz|po|li|tisch** ADJ *Fragen, Probleme, Maßnahmen, Entscheidung* relating to financial policy ADV in terms of financial policy; ~ **unklug** unwise as regards financial policy; **Fi|nanz|recht** NT financial law; **fi|nanz|schwach** ADJ financially weak; **Fi|nanz|schwä|che** F financial weakness; **Fi|nanz|sprit|ze** F injection of capital; **ich brauche eine kleine ~** I need something to boost my cash flow, I could do with a little cash; **fi|nanz|stark** ADJ financially strong; **Fi|nanz|stär|ke** F financial strength; **Fi|nanz|welt** F financial world; **Fi|nanz|we|sen** NT , *no pl* financial system; **ein Ausdruck aus dem ~** a financial term

fi|nas|sie|ren [fina'si:rən] *ptp* **finassiert** VI (*pej*) to machinate, to do some finagling (*inf*)

Fin|del|kind ['fɪndl-] NT (*old*) foundling (*old*)

fin|den ['fɪndn] ☯ 27.1, 34.3, 40.2, 40.3 *pret* **fand** [fant], *ptp* **gefunden** [gə'fʊndn] VT a (= *entdecken*) to find; **ich finde es nicht** I can't find it; **es war nicht/nirgends zu ~** it was not/nowhere to be found; **das muss zu ~ sein** it must be somewhere (to be found); **es ließ sich niemand ~** we/they *etc* couldn't find anybody, there was nobody to be found; **der Grund/die Ursache lässt sich nicht ~** we/they *etc* couldn't find the reason/cause; **etwas an jdm ~** to see something in sb; **nichts dabei ~** to think nothing of it → *auch* **gefunden**

b (= *vorfinden*) to find; **jdn schlafend/bei der Arbeit ~** to find sb asleep/working

c (*in Verbindung mit n siehe auch dort*) *Trost, Hilfe, Ruhe, Schlaf etc* to find; *Anklang, Zustimmung auch* to meet with; *Beifall* to meet or be met with; *Berücksichtigung, Beachtung* to receive; **(den) Mut/ (die) Kraft ~, etw zu tun** to find the courage/ strength to do sth; **(bei jdm) Anerkennung ~** to find recognition (with sb); **Bestätigung ~** to be confirmed

d (= *ansehen, betrachten*) to think; **es kalt/**

warm/ganz erträglich *etc* ~ to find it cold/warm/quite tolerable *etc*; **etw gut/zu teuer/eine Frechheit** *etc* ~ to think (that) sth is good/too expensive/a cheek *etc*; **jdn blöd/nett** *etc* ~ to think (that) sb is stupid/nice *etc*; **wie findest du das?** what do you think?; **wie finde ich denn das?** what do I think (of that)?

VI (*lit, fig*: = *den Weg finden*) to find one's way; **er findet nicht nach Hause** (*lit*) he can't find his or the way home; (*fig*) he can't tear or drag himself away (*inf*); **zu sich selbst** ~ to sort oneself out

VTI (= *meinen*) to think; ~ **Sie (das?)** do you think so?; **ich finde (das) nicht** I don't think so; ~ **Sie (das) nicht auch?** don't you agree?, don't you think so too?; **ich finde, wir sollten/dass wir …** I think we should/that we …; **ich kann das** or **das kann ich nicht** ~ I don't think so; **ich fände es besser, wenn …** I think it would be better if …

VR **a** (= *zum Vorschein kommen*) to be found; (= *wieder auftauchen auch*) to turn up; (= *sich befinden auch*) to be; **das wird sich (alles)** ~ it will (all) turn up; (= *sich herausstellen*) it'll come out (*inf*); **es fand sich niemand, der sich freiwillig gemeldet hätte** there was nobody who volunteered **b** (*Angelegenheit etc*: = *in Ordnung kommen*) to sort itself out; (*Mensch*: = *zu sich finden*) to sort oneself out; **das wird sich alles** ~ it'll all sort itself out **c** (= *sich fügen*) **sich in etw** (*acc*) ~ to reconcile oneself to sth, to become reconciled to sth **d** (= *sich treffen*) (*lit*) to find each other; (*fig*) to meet; **da haben sich aber zwei gefunden!** (*iro*) they'll make a fine pair

Fin|der ['fɪndɐ] M **-s, -**, **Fin|de|rin** [-ərɪn] F **-, -nen** finder

Fin|der|lohn M reward for the finder

Fin de Siè|cle ▲ [fɛ d'sjɛkl] NT **- - -**, *no pl* fin de siècle; **die Kunst des** ~ fin de siècle art

fin|dig ['fɪndɪç] ADJ resourceful

Fin|dig|keit F **-**, *no pl* resourcefulness

Find|ling ['fɪntlɪŋ] M **-s, -e** **a** (*Geol*) erratic (boulder) **b** (= *Findelkind*) foundling (*old*)

Fine|li|ner ['faɪnlaɪnɐ] M **-s, -** (= *Stift*) fineliner

Fi|nes|se [fi'nɛsə] F **-, -n** **a** (= *Feinheit*) refinement; (*no pl*: = *Kunstfertigkeit*) finesse; **mit allen ~n** with every refinement **b** (= *Trick*) trick

fi|nes|sen|reich ADJ artful

fing *pret von* **fangen**

Fin|ger ['fɪŋɐ] M **-s, -** finger; **der kleine** ~ one's little finger, one's pinkie (*US, Scot*); **mit dem ~ auf jdn/etw zeigen** or **weisen** (*geh*) to point to sb/sth; **mit ~n auf jdn zeigen** (*fig*) to look askance at sb; **jdm mit dem ~ drohen** to wag one's finger at sb; **jdm eins auf die ~ geben** to give sb a rap across the knuckles; **jdm was auf die ~ geben** to rap sb across the knuckles; **jdm auf die ~ schlagen** or **hauen** or **klopfen** (*lit, fig*) to rap sb's knuckles, to give sb a rap on the knuckles; **zwei ~ breit** the width of two fingers, two fingers wide; **(nimm/lass die) ~ weg!** (get/keep your) hands off!; **sich** (*dat*) **nicht die ~ schmutzig machen** (*lit, fig*) not to get one's hands dirty, not to dirty one's hands; **das kann sich jeder an den (fünf** or **zehn) ~n abzählen** (*inf*) it sticks out a mile (to anybody) (*inf*); **das lässt er nicht mehr aus den ~n** he won't let it out of his hands; **jdn/etw in die ~ bekommen** or **kriegen** (*inf*) to get one's hands on sb/sth, to get hold of sb/sth; **bei etw die ~ drinhaben** (*inf*) to have a hand in sth; **er hat überall seine ~ drin** (*inf*) he has a finger in every pie (*inf*); **sich** (*dat*) **die ~ abschreiben** or **wund schreiben/wund arbeiten** *etc* to write/work *etc* one's fingers to the bone; **wenn man ihm/dem Teufel den kleinen ~ gibt, (dann) nimmt er (gleich) die ganze Hand** (*prov*) give him an inch and he'll take a mile (*inf*); **lange ~ machen** (*hum inf*) to be light-fingered; **jdm in** or **zwischen die ~ geraten** or **fallen** to fall into sb's hands or clutches; **die ~ von jdm/etw lassen** (*inf*) to keep

away from sb/sth; **sich** (*dat*) **bei** or **an etw** (*dat*) **die ~ verbrennen** to burn one's fingers in sth, to get one's fingers burned in sth; **jdm (scharf) auf die ~ sehen** to keep an eye or a close eye on sb; **sich** (*dat*) **etw aus den ~n saugen** to conjure sth up (*inf*), to dream sth up (*inf*); **sich** (*dat*) **die** or **alle ~ nach etw lecken** (*inf*) to be panting or dying for sth (*inf*); **für jdn keinen ~ rühren** not to lift a finger to help sb; **keinen ~ krumm machen** (*inf*) not to lift a finger (*inf*); **den ~ auf eine/die Wunde legen** to touch on a sore point; **mich** or **mir juckt es in den ~n(, etw zu tun)** (*inf*) I'm itching or dying to (do sth); **da hast du dich in den ~ geschnitten** (*inf*) you've made a big mistake; **er hat eine** or **zehn an jedem ~** he's got a woman for every day of the week; **jdn um den kleinen ~ wickeln** to twist sb round one's little finger; **etw im kleinen ~ haben** (= *perfekt beherrschen*) to have sth at one's fingertips; (= *sicher im Gefühl haben*) to have a feel for sth; **man zeigt nicht mit nacktem ~ auf angezogene Leute** (*inf*) it's rude to point → **spitz a**

Fin|ger-: Fin|ger|ab|druck M fingerprint; **jds Fingerabdrücke nehmen** to take sb's fingerprints, to fingerprint sb; **genetischer ~** genetic fingerprint; **Fin|ger|al|pha|bet** NT manual alphabet; **fin|ger|breit** ADJ the width of a finger; **Fin|ger|breit** M **-, -** finger's breadth, fingerbreadth; (*fig*) inch; **keinen ~ nachgeben** or **weichen** not to give an inch; **fin|ger|dick** ADJ as thick as a finger; **Fin|ger|druck** M *pl* **-drü|cke** touch of the finger; **Fin|ger|far|be** F finger paint; **fin|ger|fer|tig** ADJ nimble-fingered, dexterous; **Fin|ger|fer|tig|keit** F dexterity; **fin|ger|för|mig** ADJ finger-shaped **ADV** **die Halbinseln ragen ~ ins Meer hinein** the peninsulas stick out into the sea like fingers; **Fin|ger|ge|lenk** NT finger joint; **Fin|ger|glied** NT phalanx (of the finger) (*form*); **Fin|ger|ha|keln** NT **-s**, *no pl* finger-wrestling; **Fin|ger|hand|schuh** M glove; **Fin|ger|hut** M **a** (*Sew*) thimble; **ein ~ (voll)** (*fig*) a thimbleful **b** (*Bot*) foxglove; **Fin|ger|kno|chen** M , **Fin|ger|knö|chel** M knucklebone; **Fin|ger|kup|pe** F fingertip; **fin|ger|lang** ADJ *Narbe etc* the length of a finger; **Fin|ger|ling** ['fɪŋɐlɪŋ] M **-s, -e** fingerstall

fin|gern ['fɪŋɐn] **VI** **an** or **mit etw** (*dat*) ~ to fiddle with sth; **nach etw ~** to fumble (around) for sth; **… als eine Hand über die Decke fingerte** … as a hand moved over the bedclothes **VT** (= *hervorholen*) to fumble around and produce (*inf*); (= *manipulieren*) to fiddle (*inf*); (*inf*: = *bewerkstelligen*) *Projekt* to wangle (*inf*)

Fin|ger-: Fin|ger|na|gel M fingernail; **Fingernägel kauen** to bite one's (finger)nails; **Fin|ger|ring** M ring (for one's finger); **Fin|ger|scha|le** F finger bowl; **Fin|ger|spit|ze** F fingertip, tip of one's finger; **er ist musikalisch bis in die ~n** he's musical right down to his fingertips or the tips of his fingers; **das muss man in den ~n haben** you have to have a feel for it; **mir juckt** or **kribbelt es in den ~n, das zu tun** I'm itching to do that; **Fin|ger|spit|zen|ge|fühl** NT , *no pl* (= *Einfühlungsgabe*) instinctive feel or feeling; (*im Umgang mit Menschen*) tact and sensitivity, fine feeling; **Fin|ger|spra|che** F manual alphabet, sign language; **Fin|ger|übung** F (*Mus*) finger exercise; (= *Übungsstück*) étude; (*fig*) (= *erste Arbeit*) first stage of one's apprenticeship; (= *Anfangswerk*) apprentice piece; **Fin|ger|zeig** [-tsaɪk] M **-s, -e** [-gə] hint; **etw als ~ Gottes/des Schicksals empfinden** to regard sth as a sign from God/as meant

fin|gie|ren [fɪŋ'giːrən] *ptp* **fingiert** VT (= *vortäuschen*) to fake; (= *erdichten*) to fabricate

fin|giert [fɪŋ'giːɐt] ADJ (= *vorgetäuscht*) bogus; (= *erfunden*) fictitious

fi|ni ['fiːni] ADJ *pred* (*inf*) **jetzt/dann ist ~** that's it, finito (*inf*)

Fi|nish ['fɪnɪʃ] NT **-s, -s** **a** (= *Endverarbeitung*) finish; (= *Vorgang*) finishing **b** (*Sport*: = *Endspurt*) final spurt

fi|nit [fi'niːt] ADJ (*Gram*) finite

Fink [fɪŋk] M **-en, -en** finch

Fin|ken ['fɪŋkn] M **-s, -** (*Sw*: = *warmer Hausschuh*) (fleece-lined) slipper; **die ~ klopfen** (*inf*: = *sich davonmachen*) to clear off (*inf*), to leg it (*inf*)

Fin|ken|schlag M , *no pl* finch's song

Fin|ne¹ ['fɪnə] F **-, -n** **a** (*Zool*: = *Stadium des Bandwurms*) bladder worm, cysticercus (*form*) **b** (*Med*: = *Mitesser*) pimple **c** (= *Rückenflosse*) fin **d** (*von Hammer*) peen

Fin|ne² M **-n, -n** Finn, Finnish man/boy

Fin|nin ['fɪnɪn] F **-, -nen** Finn, Finnish woman/girl

fin|nisch ['fɪnɪʃ] ADJ Finnish; **der Finnische Meerbusen** the Gulf of Finland

Fin|nisch(e) ['fɪnɪʃ] NT Finnish → *auch* **Deutsch(e)**

fin|nisch-ug|risch ['fɪnɪʃ'uːgrɪʃ] ADJ = **finno-ugrisch**

Finn|land ['fɪnlant] NT **-s** Finland

Finn|län|der ['fɪnlɛndɐ] M **-s, -**, **Finn|län|de|rin** [-ərɪn] F **-, -nen** Finn

finn|län|disch ['fɪnlɛndɪʃ] ADJ Finnish

finn|lan|di|sie|ren [fɪnlandi'ziːrən] *ptp* **finnlandisiert** VT (*Pol sl*) to Finlandize

Finn|lan|di|sie|rung F **-**, *no pl* (*Pol sl*) Finlandization

Finn|mark ['fɪnmark] F *pl* **-mark** (*Hist*: = *Währung*) Finnish mark, markka (*form*)

fin|no|ug|risch [fɪno'uːgrɪʃ] ADJ Finno-Ugric, Finno-Ugrian

Fin|no|ug|ris|tik [fɪnou'grɪstɪk] F **-**, *no pl* Finno-Ugric studies *pl*

Finn|wal ['fɪnvaːl] M finback, finwhale

fins|ter ['fɪnstɐ] ADJ **a** (= *ohne Licht*) dark; *Zimmer, Wald, Nacht* dark (and gloomy); **im Finstern** in the dark; **im Finstern liegen** to be in darkness **b** (= *dubios*) shady **c** (= *mürrisch, verdrossen, düster*) grim; *Wolken* dark, black **d** (*fig*: = *unaufgeklärt*) dark; **das ~(st)e Mittelalter** the Dark Ages *pl* **e** (= *unheimlich*) *Gestalt, Blick, Gedanken, Drohung, Verschwörung* sinister **ADV** (= *mürrisch*) grimly; **es sieht ~ aus** (*fig*) things look bleak; ~ **entschlossen sein** to be grimly determined; **jdn ~ ansehen** to give sb a black (*Brit*) or dirty (*US*) look **b** (= *unheimlich*) **das alte Haus sah ziemlich ~ aus** the old house looked quite sinister

Fins|ter|ling ['fɪnstɐlɪŋ] M **-s, -e** sinister character; (= *Dunkelmann*) obscurantist

Fins|ter|nis ['fɪnstɛnɪs] F **-, -se** **a** (= *Dunkelheit, Bibl*: = *Hölle*) darkness **b** (*Astron*) eclipse

Fin|te ['fɪntə] F **-, -n** **a** (*Sport*) feint; (*im Rugby*) dummy **b** (= *List*) ruse, subterfuge

fin|ten|reich ADJ artful, crafty; (*inf*: = *Mensch*) a cunning or sly devil (*inf*) or fox

fin|ze|lig ['fɪntsəlɪç], **finz|lig** ['fɪntslɪç] ADJ (*N Ger inf*) **a** (= *winzig*) *Schrift* tiny, weeny (*inf*) **b** (= *knifflig*) fiddly

Fips [fɪps] M **-es, -e** (*dial*) little chap (*Brit inf*) or fellow (*inf*)

fip|sig ['fɪpsɪç] ADJ (*dial*) titchy (*inf*)

Fire|wall ['faɪəwɔːl] F **-, -s** (*Comput*) firewall

Fir|le|fanz ['fɪrləfants] M **-es**, *no pl* (*inf*) **a** (= *Kram*) frippery, trumpery **b** (= *Albernheit*) clowning or fooling around; ~ **machen** to play the fool, to clown or fool around

firm [fɪrm] ADJ *pred* **ich bin noch nicht ~** I don't really know it yet; **in einem Fachgebiet ~ sein** to have a sound knowledge of an area

Fir|ma ['fɪrma] F **-, Firmen** ['fɪrmən] **a** company, firm; (= *Kleinbetrieb*) business; **die ~ Wahlster/Lexomat** Wahlster(s)/Lexomat; **die ~ dankt** (*hum*) much obliged (to you) **b** (= *Geschäfts- or Handelsname*) **eine ~ löschen** to strike a company's name/the name of a business from the register;

eine ~ eintragen to register a company name/the name of a business; **unter der ~ Smith** under the name of Smith; **unter eigener ~** under one's own name

Fir|ma|ment [fɪrmaˈmɛnt] NT **-s**, *no pl* (*liter*) heavens *pl* (*liter*), firmament (*Bibl*)

fir|men [ˈfɪrmən] VT (*Rel*) to confirm

Fir|men *pl von* **Firma**

Firmen-: Fir|men|an|ge|hö|ri|ge(r) MF *decl as adj* member of staff, company employee; **Fir|men|auf|druck** M company stamp; **Fir|men|bü|cher** PL books *pl*, accounts *pl*; **Fir|men|chef(in)** M(F) head of the company, (company) president (*esp US*); **fir|men|ei|gen** ADJ company *attr*; **~ sein** to belong to the company; **Fir|men|ge|län|de** NT company site; **Fir|men|grün|der(in)** M(F) founder of a/the business, company founder; **Fir|men|grün|dung** F (= *Gründung*) formation or founding of a company; (= *neu gegründete Firma*) business start-up; **Fir|men|grup|pe** F group (of companies), conglomerate; **Fir|men|in|ha|ber(in)** M(F) owner of the company; **fir|men|in|tern** ADJ within the company *attr*; *Weiterbildung, Berater auch* in-house *attr*; **~ sein** to be an internal company matter ADV; **~ geregelt** decided within the company; **Fir|men|kopf** M company letterhead; **Fir|men|lo|go** NT company logo; **Fir|men|na|me** M company name; **Fir|men|phi|lo|so|phie** F company philosophy; **Fir|men|re|gis|ter** NT register of companies; **Fir|men|schild** NT company plaque; **Fir|men|schlie|ßung** F closing down (of a firm); **Fir|men|stem|pel** M company stamp; **Fir|men|ver|zeich|nis** NT trade directory; **Fir|men|wa|gen** M company car; **Fir|men|wert** M (*Comm*) goodwill; **Fir|men|zei|chen** NT trademark

fir|mie|ren [fɪrˈmiːrən] *ptp* **firmiert** VI **als** *or* **mit ... ~** (*Comm, fig*) to trade under the name of ...

Firm|ling [ˈfɪrmlɪŋ] M **-s**, **-e** (*Rel*) candidate for confirmation

Firm|pa|te M , **Firm|pa|tin** F sponsor

Fir|mung F **-**, **-en** (*Rel*) confirmation; **jdm die ~ erteilen** to confirm sb

Firm|ware [ˈføːɛmwɛːɐ, ˈfœrm-] F (*Comput*) firmware

firn [fɪrn] ADJ *Wein* old

Firn [fɪrn] M **-(e)s**, **-e** névé, firn

Fir|ne [ˈfɪrnə] F **-**, **-n** well-seasoned taste

fir|nig [ˈfɪrnɪç] ADJ *Schnee* névé *attr*

Fir|nis [ˈfɪrnɪs] M **-ses**, **-se** (= *Ölfirnis*) oil; (= *Lackfirnis*) varnish

fir|nis|sen [ˈfɪrnɪsn] VT (*mit Ölfirnis*) to oil; (*mit Lackfirnis*) to varnish

Firn|schnee M névé, firn

First [fɪrst] M **-(e)s**, **-e** a (= *Dachfirst*) (roof) ridge b (*geh*: = *Gebirgskamm*) crest, ridge

First-: First|fei|er F (*Aus*) topping-out ceremony; **First|zie|gel** M ridge tile

Fis [fɪs] NT **-**, **-**, **fis** [fɪs] NT **-**, **-** (*Mus*) F sharp; **in ~** in F sharp major/minor

Fisch [fɪʃ] M **-(e)s**, **-e** a (*Zool, Cook*) fish; **~e/drei ~e fangen** to catch fish/three fish(es); **~ verarbeitend** fish-processing; **das sind kleine ~e** (*fig inf*) that's child's play (*inf*) (*für* to, for); **ein großer** *or* **dicker ~** (*fig inf*) a big fish; **ein kleiner ~** one of the small fry; **ein paar kleine ~e** some of the small fry; (*kalter*) **~ sein** (*fig*) to be a cold fish; **munter** *or* **gesund sein wie ein ~ im Wasser** to be in fine fettle; **sich wohl fühlen wie ein ~ im Wasser** to be in one's element; **stumm wie ein ~ sein** (= *sich zu einem Thema nicht äußern*) to keep stumm (*inf*); **er war den ganzen Abend stumm wie ein ~** he didn't open his mouth all night (*inf*); **weder ~ noch Fleisch** neither fish nor fowl; **die ~e füttern** (*hum*) to be sick; **~ will schwimmen** (*prov*) fish gives you a thirst; **der ~ stinkt vom Kopf her** the problems are at the top

b (*Astrol*) Pisces *sing*; **die ~e** (*Astron*) Pisces *sing*,

the Fish *sing*; **ein ~ sein** to be Pisces or a Piscean

c (*Typ*) character from the wrong fount

Fisch- *in cpds* fish; **Fisch|ad|ler** M osprey; **fisch|ähn|lich** ADJ fish-like; **fisch|arm** ADJ *Gewässer* low in fish; **Fisch|ar|mut** F scarcity of fish; **fisch|ar|tig** ADJ (*Zool*) fish-like; *Geschmack, Geruch* fishy; **Fisch|au|ge** NT (*Phot*) fish-eye lens; **fisch|äu|gig** ADJ fish-eyed; **Fisch|be|cken** NT fishpond; **Fisch|bein** NT , *no pl* whalebone; **Fisch|be|stand** M fish population; **Fisch|be|steck** NT (*einzelnes Set*) fish knife and fork; (*kollektiv*) fish knives and forks *pl*; **Fisch|bla|se** F a (*Zool*) air bladder, swim bladder b (*Archit*) foil; **Fisch|blut** NT (*fig*) **~ in den Adern haben** to be a cold fish; **Fisch|bra|te|rei** [-braːtəˈraɪ] F **-**, **-en**, **Fisch|brat|kü|che** F fish and chip shop; **Fisch|bröt|chen** NT fish roll (*Brit*) or sandwich (*US*); **Fisch|brut** F fry *pl*, young fish *pl*; **Fisch|bu|de** F stand selling fish and various snacks, ≈ fish and chip stand (*Brit*); **Fisch|bu|let|te** F fish cake; **Fisch|damp|fer** M trawler

fi|schen [ˈfɪʃn] VTI (*lit, fig*) to fish; **mit (dem) Netz ~** to trawl; **(auf) Heringe ~** to fish for herring → **trüb(e)** a

Fi|scher [ˈfɪʃɐ] M **-s**, **-**, **Fi|sche|rin** [-ərɪn] F **-**, **-nen** fisherman/-woman

Fischer-: Fi|scher|boot NT fishing boat; **Fi|scher|dorf** NT fishing village

Fi|sche|rei [fɪʃəˈraɪ] F **-**, **-en** a (= *das Fangen*) fishing b (= *Fischereigewerbe*) fishing industry, fisheries *pl*

Fischerei- *in cpds* fishing; **Fi|sche|rei|fre|vel** M (*Jur*) poaching; **Fi|sche|rei|ge|rät** NT fishing tackle; (= *einzelnes Stück*) piece of fishing tackle; **Fi|sche|rei|gren|ze** F fishing limit; **Fi|sche|rei|ha|fen** M fishing port; **Fi|sche|rei|recht** NT , *no pl* a fishing rights *pl* b (*Jur*) law on fishing; **Fi|sche|rei|schutz|boot** NT fishery protection vessel; **Fi|sche|rei|we|sen** NT , *no pl* fishing *no art*; **Ministerium für ~** ministry of fisheries

Fi|sche|rin F **-**, **-nen** fisherwoman

Fischer-: Fi|scher|netz NT fishing net; **Fi|scher|ring** M (*Rel*) Ring of the Fisherman

Fisch|fang M , *no pl* **vom ~ leben** to live by fishing; **zum ~ auslaufen** to set off for the fishing grounds

Fischfang-: Fisch|fang|flot|te F fishing fleet; **Fisch|fang|ge|biet** NT fishing grounds *pl*

Fisch-: Fisch|farm F fish farm; **Fisch|fi|let** NT fish fillet; **Fisch|fri|ka|del|le** F fishcake; **Fisch|fut|ter** NT fish food; **Fisch|ge|ruch** M smell of fish, fishy smell; **Fisch|ge|schäft** NT fishmonger's (shop) (*Brit*), fish shop (*Brit*) or dealer (*US*); **Fisch|grä|te** F fish bone; **Fisch|grä|ten|mus|ter** NT herringbone (pattern); **Fisch|grün|de** PL fishing grounds *pl*, fisheries *pl*; **Fisch|hal|le** F fish market hall; **Fisch|händ|ler(in)** M(F) fishmonger (*Brit*), fish dealer (*US*); (= *Großhändler*) fish merchant; **Fisch|kö|der** M bait; **Fisch|kon|ser|ve** F canned *or* tinned (*Brit*) fish; **Fisch|kopf** M , (*N Ger*) **Fisch|kopp** M (*hum inf*) northerner (*from the German coastal region*); **Fisch|kut|ter** M fishing cutter; **Fisch|la|den** M fish shop (*Brit*) or dealer (*US*); **Fisch|le|der** NT shagreen; **Fisch|leim** M isinglass; **Fisch|markt** M fish market; **Fisch|mehl** NT fish meal; **Fisch|milch** F milt, soft roe; **Fisch|ot|ter** M otter; **fisch|reich** ADJ *Gewässer* rich in fish; **Fisch|rei|her** M grey heron; **Fisch|reu|se** F fish trap, weir basket; **Fisch|ro|gen** M (hard) roe; **Fisch|schup|pe** F (fish) scale; **Fisch|schup|pen|krank|heit** F ichthyosis (*spec*); **Fisch|schwarm** M shoal of fish; **Fisch|stäb|chen** NT fish finger (*Brit*), fish stick (*US*); **Fisch|ster|ben** NT death of fish; **Fisch|sup|pe** F (*Cook*) fish soup; **Fisch|teich** M fishpond; **Fisch|tran** M train oil; **Fisch|traw|ler** [-trɔːlɐ] M **-s**, **-** trawler; **Fisch|ver|ar|bei|tend**

△ ADJ *attr* → **Fisch** a; **Fisch|ver|ar|bei|tung** F fish processing; **Fisch|wa|ren** PL fish products *pl*; **Fisch|was|ser** NT , *no pl* (*Cook*) fish stock; **Fisch|wehr** NT fish weir; **Fisch|weib** NT (*dated*) fish seller, fishwoman; (*pej*) fishwife; **Fisch|wil|de|rei** F poaching; **Fisch|wirt|schaft** F fishing industry; **Fisch|zaun** M fish weir; **Fisch|zucht** F fish-farming; (*inf: auch* **Fischzuchtanstalt**) fish farm; **Fisch|zug** M a (*Bibl*) **der ~ des Petrus**, **Petri ~** the miraculous draught of fishes (*Brit*), the miraculous catch of fish (*US*) b (*fig*: = *Beutezug*) raid, foray

Fi|si|ma|ten|ten [fizimaˈtɛntn] PL (*inf*) (= *Ausflüchte*) excuses *pl*; (= *Umstände*) fuss; (= *Albernheiten*) nonsense; **~ machen** to make excuses/a fuss/to get up to some silly things; **mit jdm/etw ~ machen** to mess about with sb/sth (*inf*)

fis|ka|lisch [fɪsˈkaːlɪʃ] ADJ fiscal

Fis|kal- [fɪsˈkaːl-]: **Fis|kal|po|li|tik** F , *no pl* fiscal policy; **fis|kal|po|li|tisch** ADJ politico-economic

Fis|kus [ˈfɪskʊs] M **-**, **-se** *or* **Fisken** [ˈfɪskn] (= *Staatsvermögen*) treasury, exchequer (*Brit*); (*fig*: = *Staat*) Treasury

Fi|so|len [fiˈzoːlən] PL (*Aus*) green beans *pl*

fis|se|lig [ˈfɪsəlɪç] ADJ (*dial*) fine; (= *empfindlich zu handhaben*) fiddly

Fis|sel|re|gen [ˈfɪsl-] M (*dial*) drizzle

Fis|si|on [fɪsiˈoːn] F **-**, **-en** fission

Fis|sur [fɪˈsuːɐ] F **-**, **-en** (*Anat*) fissure; (*Med*) crack

Fis|tel [ˈfɪstl] F **-**, **-n** (*Med*) fistula (*spec*)

fis|teln [ˈfɪstln] VI to speak in a falsetto (voice) or piping voice

Fis|tel|stim|me F a (*Mus*) falsetto b (= *hohes Sprechstimmchen*) falsetto (voice), piping voice

fit [fɪt] ADJ fit; **sich ~ halten/machen** to keep/get fit

Fit|ness ▲ [ˈfɪtnɛs] F **-**, *no pl* physical fitness

Fitness-: Fit|ness|cen|ter ▲ NT , **Fit|ness|stu|dio** ▲ NT fitness centre (*Brit*) or center (*US*); **Fit|ness|trai|ning** ▲ NT fitness training

fit|ten [ˈfɪtn] VT (*Tech*) to fit

Fit|tich [ˈfɪtɪç] M **-(e)s**, **-e** (*liter*) wing, pinion (*liter*); **jdn unter seine ~e nehmen** (*hum*) to take sb under one's wing (*fig*)

Fit|ting [ˈfɪtɪŋ] M **-s**, **-s** (*Tech*) fitting

Fitz|chen [ˈfɪtsçən] NT **-s**, **-** (*dial*), **Fit|zel** [ˈfɪtsl] M OR NT **-s**, **-**, **Fit|zel|chen** [ˈfɪtslçən] NT **-s**, **-** little bit

fix [fɪks] ADJ a (*inf*) (= *flink*) quick; (= *intelligent*) quick, bright, smart; **in etw** (*dat*) **~ sein** to be quick at sth

b (*inf*) **~ und fertig sein** (= *nervös*) to be at the end of one's tether (*Brit*) or rope (*US*); (= *erschöpft*) to be worn out, to be done in (*inf*), to be all in (*inf*); (*emotional, seelisch*) to be shattered; (= *ruiniert*) to be done for (*inf*); **jdn ~ und fertig machen** (= *nervös machen*) to drive sb mad (*Brit*) or crazy (*US*); (= *erschöpfen*) to wear sb out, to do sb in (*inf*); (*emotional, seelisch*) to shatter sb; (*in Prüfung, Wettbewerb, Kampf etc*) to give sb a thrashing (*inf*); (= *ruinieren*) to do for sb (*inf*)

c (= *feststehend*) fixed; **~e Idee** obsession, idée fixe

ADV (*inf*: = *schnell*) quickly; **mach ~!** be quick!, look lively! (*inf*); **das geht ganz ~** that won't take long at all; **geht das nicht ~er?** does it have to take so long?

Fi|xa *pl von* **Fixum**

fi|xen [ˈfɪksn] VI a (*inf*: = *Drogen spritzen*) to fix (*inf*), to shoot (up) (*inf*) b (*St Ex*) to bear

Fi|xer [ˈfɪksɐ] M **-s**, **-**, **Fi|xe|rin** [-ərɪn] F **-**, **-nen** a (*inf*) fixer (*inf*) b (*St Ex*) bear

Fixer-: Fi|xer|be|steck NT (*inf*: = *Nadel*) needle; **Fi|xer|stu|be** F (*inf*) junkies' centre (*Brit*) or center (*US*, *inf*)

Fix|ge|schäft NT (*Comm*) transaction for delivery by a fixed date; (*St Ex*) time bargain

Fi|xier|bad [fɪˈksiːɐ-] NT fixer

fi|xier|bar ADJ specifiable, definable

fi|xie|ren [fɪˈksiːrən] *ptp* **fixiert** VT **a** (= *anstarren*) **jdn/etw (mit seinem Blick/seinen Augen) ~** to fix one's gaze/eyes on sb/sth **b** (= *festlegen*) to specify, to define; *Gehälter, Termin etc* to set (*auf +acc* for); (= *schriftlich niederlegen*) to record; **er ist zu stark auf seine Mutter fixiert** (*Psych*) he has a mother fixation; **seine Interessen sind auf Fußball fixiert** he has a fixation about football **c** (= *haltbar machen*) to fix **d** (*Gewichtheben*) to lock; (*Ringen*) to get in a lock

Fi|xier- [fɪˈksiːɐ-]: **Fi|xier|mit|tel** NT fixer, fixative; **Fi|xier|nat|ron** NT , **Fi|xier|salz** NT hypo

Fi|xie|rung F -, -en **a** (= *Festlegung*) specification, definition; (*von Gehältern, Terminen*) setting; (= *schriftliche Niederlegung*) recording; (*Psych*) fixation **b** (= *das Anstarren*) fixing of one's gaze (*+gen* on)

Fi|xig|keit [ˈfɪksɪçkaɪt] F -, *no pl* (*inf*) speed

Fi|xing [ˈfɪksɪŋ] NT -s, *no pl* (*Fin*) fixing

Fix-: **Fix|kos|ten** PL fixed costs *pl*; **Fix|punkt** M fixed point; **Fix|stern** M fixed star

Fi|xum [ˈfɪksʊm] NT -s, **Fixa** [ˈfɪksa] basic salary, basic

Fix|zeit F core time

Fjord [fjɔrt] M -(e)s, -e [-də] fiord

FKK [ɛfkaːˈkaː] *no art* – *abbr von* **Freikörperkultur**

FKK-An|hän|ger(in) [ɛfkaːˈkaː-] M(F) nudist, naturist

FKKler [ɛfkaːˈkaːlɐ] M -s, -, **FKKle|rin** [ɛfkaːˈkaːlərɪn] F (*inf*) -, -nen nudist, naturist

FKK-Strand [ɛfkaːˈkaː-] M nudist beach

Fla [flaː] F -, *no pl* (*Mil*) *abbr von* **Flugabwehr**

Flab [flap] F -, *no pl* (*Sw*) *abbr von* **Fliegerabwehr** anti-aircraft or ack-ack unit

flach [flax] **ADJ a** (= *eben, platt, niedrig*) flat; *Gebäude* low; *Abhang* gentle; *Boot* flat-bottomed; **die ~e Klinge/Hand** the flat of the blade/one's hand; **eine ~e Brust** a hollow chest; (*Busen*) a flat chest; **auf dem ~en Land** in the middle of the country **b** (= *untief*) shallow **c** (= *nichts sagend*) flat; *Geschmack* insipid; (= *oberflächlich*) shallow **ADV** ~ **atmen** to take shallow breaths; **sich ~ hinlegen** to lie down; ~ **liegen** to lie flat; ~ **schlafen** to sleep without a pillow

Flach [flax] NT -(e)s, -e (*Naut*) shallows *pl*

Flach-: **Flach|bau** M *pl* **-bauten** low building; **Flach|bau|wei|se** F low style of building; **Flach|bild|schirm** M (*TV*) flat screen; **flach|brüs|tig** [-brʏstɪç] ADJ flat-chested; **Flach|dach** NT flat roof; **Flach|druck** M **a** *no pl* (= *Verfahren*) planography **b** *pl* **-drucke** (= *Produkt*) planograph; **Flach|dru|cker** M planographic printer

Flä|che [ˈflɛçə] F -, -n (= *Ausdehnung, Flächeninhalt, Math*) area; (= *Oberfläche*) surface; (*von Würfel*) face; (= *Gelände, Landfläche/Wasserfläche*) expanse (of ground/water)

Flach|ei|sen NT flat bar; (= *Werkzeug*) flat-bladed chisel

Flä|chen-: **Flä|chen|aus|deh|nung** F surface area; **Flä|chen|brand** M extensive fire; **sich zu einem ~ ausweiten** (*fig*) to spread to epidemic proportions; **flä|chen|de|ckend** ADJ extensive; **die ~e Versorgung der Bevölkerung mit Gas** a comprehensive or extensive gas supply for the population **ADV** extensively, over a wide area; **wir müssen ~ arbeiten** we need blanket coverage; **Flä|chen|er|trag** M yield per acre/hectare *etc*; **flä|chen|gleich** ADJ (*Math*) equal in area; **Flä|chen|haft** ADJ two-dimensional; (= *ausgedehnt*) extensive; **Flä|chen|in|halt** M area; **Flä|chen|land** NT state (*as opposed to city state*); **Flä|chen|maß** NT unit of square measure; **Flä|chen|nut|zung** F land utilization; **Flä|chen|nut|zungs|plan** M

zoning plan, land development plan; **Flä|chen|staat** M state (*as opposed to city state*); **flä|chen|treu** ADJ *Projektion* equal-area

Flach-: **flach+fal|len** VI *sep irreg aux sein* (*inf*) not to come off; (*Regelung*) to end; **Flach|fei|le** F flat file; **Flach|glas** NT sheet glass; **Flach|hang** M gentle slope

Flach|heit F -, -en **a** (= *Plattheit*) flatness; (*von Gebäude*) lowness; (*von Abhang*) gentleness **b** (= *mangelnder Tiefgang*) flatness; (*von Geschmack*) insipidity, insipidness; (= *Oberflächlichkeit*) shallowness

flä|chig [ˈflɛçɪç] ADJ *Gesicht* flat; *Aufforstungen* extensive; (*Art*) two-dimensional

Flä|chig|keit F -, *no pl* (*Art*) two-dimensionality

Flach-: **Flach|kopf** M (*inf*) dunderhead (*inf*), numskull (*inf*); **Flach|kopf|schrau|be** F countersunk (*Brit*) or flat-head (*US*) screw; **Flach|küs|te** F flat coast; **Flach|land** NT lowland; (= *Tiefland*) plains *pl*; **Flach|län|der** [-lɛndɐ] M -s, -, **Flach|län|de|rin** [-ərɪn] F -, -nen lowlander; **Flach|land|ti|ro|ler(in)** M(F) (*inf*) would-be mountain dweller; **flach|le|gen** *sep* VT **a** (*inf*: = *nicht stellen*) to lay out **b** (*sl*) *Frau* to lay (*sl*) VR (*inf*) to lie down; **flach+lie|gen** VI *sep irreg* (*inf*) to be laid up (*inf*); **Flach|mann** M *pl* **-männer** (*inf*) hip flask; **Flach|mei|ßel** M flat chisel; **Flach|moor** NT fen; **Flach|pass** ▲ M (*Ftbl*) low pass; **Flach|re|li|ef** NT bas-relief; **Flach|ren|nen** NT flat race; (*Pferd*) (= *race*)

Flachs [flaks] M -es, *no pl* **a** (*Bot, Tex*) flax **b** (*inf*: = *Neckerei, Witzelei*) kidding (*inf*); (= *Bemerkung*) joke; ~ **machen** to kid around (*inf*); **das war nur ~** I/he *etc* was only kidding (*inf*); **jetzt mal ganz ohne ~** = joking or kidding (*inf*) apart

flachs|blond ADJ flaxen

Flach|schuss ▲ M (*Ftbl*) low shot

Flach|se [ˈflaksə] F -, -n (*Aus*) tendon

flach|sen [ˈflaksn] VI (*inf*) to kid around (*inf*); **mit jdm ~** to kid sb (on) (*inf*)

Flachs|e|rei [flaksəˈraɪ] F -, -en (*inf*) = **Flachs b**

Flachs|far|ben [ˈflaksfarbn] ADJ flaxen

Flachs|haar NT flaxen hair

Flachs|sinn M , *no pl* shallowness

Flachs|kopf [ˈflaks-] M (= *Kind*) flaxen-haired child; (= *Jugendlicher*) flaxen-haired youth

Flach-: **Flach|was|ser** NT , *no pl* shallow water, shallows *pl*; **Flach|zan|ge** F flat-nosed pliers *pl*

fla|ckern [ˈflakɐn] VI (*lit, fig*) to flicker

Fla|cker|schein M flicker, flickering light

Fla|den [ˈflaːdn] M -s, - **a** (*Cook*) round flat dough-cake **b** (*inf*: = *Kuhfladen*) cowpat (*Brit*), cow dung

Fla|den|brot NT unleavened bread; **ein ~** an unleavened loaf

fla|dern [ˈflaːdɐn] VTI (*Aus inf*) to steal, to nick (*Brit inf*)

Fläd|li|sup|pe [ˈflɛːtli-] F (*Sw*) pancake soup

Fla|gel|lant [flagəˈlant] M -en, -en, **Fla|gel|lan|tin** [-ˈlantɪn] F -, -nen flagellant

Fla|gel|lan|ten|tum [flagəˈlantntuːm] NT -s, *no pl* (*Rel*) self-flagellation, flagellantism

Fla|gel|lan|tis|mus [flagəlanˈtɪsmʊs] M -, *no pl* (*Psych*) flagellantism

Fla|gel|lat [flagəˈlaːt] M -en, -en (*Biol*) flagellate

Fla|gel|la|ti|on [flagɛlaˈtsioːn] F -, -en (*Psych*) flagellation

Fla|geo|lett [flaʒoˈlɛt] NT -s, -s *or* -e (*Mus*) **a** (*Ton*) harmonic **b** (*Instrument*) flageolet

Flag|ge [ˈflagə] F -, -n flag; **die belgische ~ führen** to fly the Belgian flag or colours (*Brit*) or colors (*US*); **unter deutscher ~ fahren** to sail under a German flag; **die ~ streichen** (*lit*) to strike the flag; (*fig*) to capitulate, to show the white flag; ~ **zeigen** to nail one's colours (*Brit*) or colors (*US*) to the mast

flag|gen [ˈflagn] VI to fly flags/a flag; **geflaggt haben** to fly flags/a flag → **halbmast, Topp**

Flag|gen-: **Flag|gen|al|pha|bet** NT semaphore *no art*; **Flag|gen|gruß** M dipping of the flag; **Flag|gen|lei|ne** F (flag) halyard; **Flag|gen|mast** M flagpole, flagstaff; **Flag|gen|pa|ra|de** F morning/evening colours (*Brit*) or colors (*US*) *sing*; **Flag|gen|sig|nal** NT flag signal; **Flag|gen|tuch** NT , *no pl* bunting

Flagg-: [ˈflak-]: **Flagg|lei|ne** F (flag) halyard; **Flagg|of|fi|zier(in)** M(F) flag officer; **Flagg|schiff** NT (*lit, fig*) flagship

flag|rant [flaˈgrant] ADJ flagrant → **in flagranti**

Flair [flɛːɐ] NT OR (RARE) M -s, *no pl* (*geh*) atmosphere; (= *Nimbus*) aura; (= *Gespür*) Sw: *Gespür*) flair

Flak [flak] F -, -(s) *abbr von* **Flug(zeug)abwehrka|none a** anti-aircraft or ack-ack gun **b** (= *Einheit*) anti-aircraft or ack-ack unit

Flak-: **Flak|bat|te|rie** F anti-aircraft or ack-ack battery; **Flak|hel|fer(in)** M(F) (*Hist*) anti-aircraft auxiliary

Fla|kon [flaˈkõː] NT OR M -s, -s bottle, flacon

Flak|stel|lung F anti-aircraft or ack-ack artillery position

Flam|beau [flãˈboː] M -s, -s (*geh*) chandelier

flam|bie|ren [flamˈbiːrən] *ptp* **flambiert** VT (*Cook*) to flambé

flam|biert [flamˈbiːɐt] (*Cook*) *ptp von* **flambieren** ADJ flambé (*nachgestellt*); (*bei Plural*) flambés (*nachgestellt*); **~es Steak** steak flambé

flam|bo|yant [flãboaˈjãː] ADJ (*geh, Archit*) flamboyant

Flam|bo|yant|stil [flãboaˈjãː-] M flamboyant style

Fla|me [ˈflaːmə] M -n, -n Fleming, Flemish man/boy

Fla|men|co [flaˈmɛŋko] M -(s), -s flamenco

Fla|min [ˈflaːmɪn] F -, -nen, **Flä|min** [ˈflɛːmɪn] F -, -nen Fleming, Flemish woman/girl

Fla|min|go [flaˈmɪŋgo] M -s, -s flamingo

flä|misch [ˈflɛːmɪʃ] ADJ Flemish

Flä|misch(e) [ˈflɛːmɪʃ] NT Flemish → *auch* **Deutsch(e)**

Flämm|chen [ˈflɛmçən] NT -s, - *dim von* **Flamme**

Flam|me [ˈflamə] F -, -n **a** (*lit, fig*) flame; **mit ruhiger/flackernder ~ brennen** to burn with a steady/flickering flame; **in ~n aufgehen** to go up in flames; **in (hellen) ~n stehen** to be ablaze, to be in flames; **etw den ~n übergeben** (*liter*) to consign sth to the flames; **etw auf kleiner ~ kochen** (*lit*) to cook sth on a low flame; (*fig*) to let sth just tick over (*Brit*), to let sth ride; **etw auf großer ~ kochen** to cook sth fast **b** (= *Brennstelle*) flame, burner **c** (*dated inf*: = *Geliebte*) flame (*inf*)

flam|men [ˈflamən] VI (*old, fig*) to blaze → *auch* **flammend, geflammt**

flam|mend ADJ fiery; *Zorn* burning; **mit ~em Gesicht** blazing; **~ rot** (*geh*) flame (*Brit*) or flaming red, blazing red

Flam|men-: **Flam|men|meer** NT sea of flames; **Flam|men|tod** M death by burning; **den ~ erleiden** to be burned to death; **jdn zum ~ verurteilen** to sentence sb to be burned to death; **Flam|men|wer|fer** M flame-thrower; **Flam|men|zei|chen** NT (*geh*) beacon

Flan|dern [ˈflandɐn] NT -s Flanders *sing*

fländ|risch [ˈflandrɪʃ] ADJ Flemish

Fla|nell [flaˈnɛl] M -s, -e flannel

fla|nell|en [flaˈnɛlən] ADJ *attr* flannel

Fla|nell|hemd NT flannel shirt

Fla|neur [flaˈnøːɐ] M -s, -e, **Fla|neu|rin** [-ˈnøːrɪn] F -, -nen (*geh*) stroller

fla|nie|ren [flaˈniːrən] *ptp* **flaniert** VI to stroll, to saunter

Flan|ke [ˈflaŋkə] F -, -n **a** (*Anat, Mil, Chess*) flank; (*von Bus, Lastzug etc*) side; **dem Feind in die ~n fallen** to attack the enemy on the flank **b** (*Sport*) (*Turnen*) flank-vault; (*Ftbl*) cross; (= *Spielfeldseite*) wing

flan|ken ['flaŋkn] VI *(Turnen)* to flank-vault; *(Ftbl)* to centre *(Brit)*, to center *(US)*

Flan|ken-: Flan|ken|an|griff M *(Mil, Chess)* flank attack; **Flan|ken|ball** M *(Ftbl)* cross, centre *(Brit)*, center *(US)*; **Flan|ken|de|ckung** F *(Mil)* flank defence *(Brit)* or defense *(US)*; **Flan|ken|schutz** M *(Mil)* protection on the flank; **jdm ~ geben** *(fig)* to give sb added support; **Flan|ken|si|che|rung** F *(Mil)* flank defence *(Brit)* or defense *(US)*

flan|kie|ren [flaŋ'kiːrən] ptp **flankiert** VT *(Mil, Chess, fig)* to flank; *(fig: = ergänzen)* to accompany; **~de Maßnahmen** supporting measures

Flansch [flanʃ] M -(e)s, -e flange

Flap|pe ['flapə] F -, -n *(dial)* pout; **eine ~ ziehen** to look petulant, to pout

flap|pen ['flapn] VI *(N Ger)* to flap

Flaps [flaps] M -es, -e *(dial inf: = Flegel)* lout, yob *(Brit inf)*; *(= Kind)* brat *(inf)*

flap|sig ['flapsɪç] ADJ *(inf)* Benehmen cheeky *(Brit)*, fresh *(US)*; Bemerkung offhand

Fläsch|chen ['flɛʃçən] NT -s, - bottle

Fla|sche ['flaʃə] F -, -n a bottle; **einem Baby die ~ geben** to give a baby its bottle; **mit der ~ aufziehen** to bottle-feed; **das Kind bekommt die ~** *(momentan)* the child is having its bottle; *(generell)* the child is bottle-fed; **eine ~ Wein/Bier** etc a bottle of wine/beer etc; **aus der ~ trinken** to drink (straight) from or out of the bottle; **zur ~ greifen** *(fig)* to take to the bottle b *(inf: = Versager)* dead loss *(Brit inf)*, complete loser *(inf)*; **du ~!** you're a dead loss *(Brit inf)* or complete loser *(inf)*!

Fla|schen-: Fla|schen|bat|te|rie F array of bottles; **Fla|schen|bier** NT bottled beer; **Fla|schen|bürs|te** F bottlebrush; **Fla|schen|eti|kett** NT label on a/the bottle; **Fla|schen|gä|rung** F fermentation in the bottle; **Fla|schen|ge|stell** NT wine rack; **fla|schen|grün** ADJ bottle-green; **Fla|schen|hals** M neck of a bottle; *(fig)* bottleneck; **Fla|schen|kind** NT bottle-fed baby; **er ist ein ~** *(hum)* he's a straight-from-the-bottle man *(inf)*, he always drinks straight from the bottle; **Fla|schen|kür|bis** M calabash, bottle gourd; **Fla|schen|milch** F bottled milk; **Fla|schen|nah|rung** F baby milk; **Fla|schen|öff|ner** M bottle opener; **Fla|schen|pfand** NT deposit on a/the bottle; **Fla|schen|post** F message in a bottle; **mit der ~ in a bottle; Fla|schen|re|gal** NT wine rack; **fla|schen|reif** ADJ Wein ready for bottling; **Fla|schen|ver|schluss** ▲ M bottle top; **Fla|schen|wein** M bottled wine; **fla|schen|wei|se** ADV by the bottle; **Fla|schen|zug** M block and tackle

Flasch|ner ['flaʃnɐ] M -s, -, **Flasch|ne|rin** [-ərɪn] F -, -nen *(S Ger)* plumber

Flash [flɛʃ] M -s, -s *(Film)* flash, intercut scene *(form)*; *(= Rückblende)* flashback; *(inf)* flash *(inf)*

Flat|ter-: Flat|ter|geist M butterfly; **flat|ter|haft** ADJ butterfly attr, fickle; **sie ist ziemlich ~** she's a bit of a butterfly; **Flat|ter|haf|tig|keit** ['flatɐhaftɪçkaɪt] F -, no pl fickleness

flat|te|rig ['flatərɪç] ADJ fluttery; Puls fluttering

Flat|ter|mann M pl -männer *(inf)* a **einen ~ haben** *(= Zittern der Hände)* to have the shakes; *(= Lampenfieber)* to have stage fright b *(hum: = Hähnchen)* chicken

flat|tern ['flatɐn] VI bei Richtungsangabe aux sein *(lit, fig)* to flutter; *(= mit den Flügeln schlagen)* to flap its wings; *(Fahne, Segel beim Sturm, Hose)* to flap; *(Haar)* to stream, to fly; *(Blick)* to flicker; *(inf: Mensch)* to be in a flap *(inf)*; *(Lenkung, Autorad)* to wobble; **ein Brief flatterte mir auf den Schreibtisch** a letter turned up or arrived on my desk

Flat|ter|satz M *(Typ)* unjustified print, ragged right/left

Fla|tu|lenz [flatu'lɛnts] F -, -en *(Med)* flatulence

---

flau [flau] ADJ a Brise, Wind slack b Geschmack insipid; Stimmung flat; *(Phot inf)* Negativ flat; Farbe weak c *(= übel)* queasy; *(vor Hunger)* faint; **mir ist ~ (im Magen)** I feel queasy d *(Comm)* Markt, Börse, Konjunktur slack; **in meiner Kasse sieht es ~ aus** *(inf)* my finances aren't too healthy *(inf)*

Flau|heit F -, no pl a *(von Farbe)* weakness; *(von Stimmung)* flatness; *(Phot inf: von Negativ)* flatness b *(= Übelkeit)* queasiness; *(vor Hunger)* faintness c *(Comm: von Markt, Börse, Konjunktur)* slackness

Flaum [flaum] M -(e)s, no pl a *(= Flaumfedern, Härchen, auf Obst)* down b *(dial: = Schweinebauchfett)* lard

Flaum-: Flaum|bart M downy beard, bum-fluff no indef art *(Brit inf)*, peach fuzz *(US inf)*; **Flaum|fe|der** F down feather, plumule *(spec)*

flau|mig ['flaumɪç] ADJ downy; Pullover, Schneedecke fleecy; *(Aus: = flockig)* light and creamy

flaum|weich ADJ Haut (as) soft as thistledown; *(fig inf)* Mensch soft; Haltung milk-and-water attr, lukewarm

Flausch [flauʃ] M -(e)s, -e fleece

flau|schig ['flauʃɪç] ADJ fleecy; *(= weich)* soft

Flau|sen ['flauzn] PL *(inf)* *(= Unsinn)* nonsense; *(= Illusionen)* fancy ideas pl *(inf)*; **macht keine ~!** don't try anything! *(inf)*

Flau|te ['flautə] F -, -n a *(Met)* calm; **das Schiff geriet in eine ~** the ship was becalmed b *(fig)* *(Comm)* lull, slack period; *(der Stimmung)* fit of the doldrums *(inf)*; *(der Leistung)* period of slackness

Fla|xe ['flaksə] F -, -n *(Aus)* tendon

Fläz [flɛːts] M -es, -e *(dial inf)* lout, roughneck

flä|zen ['flɛːtsn] VR *(inf)* to sprawl *(in +acc in)*

Flech|se ['flɛksə] F -, -n tendon

flech|sig ['flɛksɪç] ADJ Fleisch stringy *(inf)*, sinewy

Flecht|ar|beit F wickerwork, basketwork; *(aus Rohr)* canework

Flech|te ['flɛçtə] F -, -n a *(Bot, Med)* lichen b *(geh: = Zopf)* plait, braid

flech|ten ['flɛçtn] pret **flocht** [flɔxt], ptp **geflochten** [gə'flɔxtn] VT Haar to plait, to braid; Kranz, Korb, Matte to weave, to make; Seil to make; Stuhl to cane; **sich/jdm das Haar zu Zöpfen** or **in Zöpfe ~** to plait or braid one's/sb's hair; **Zitate in eine Rede ~** to punctuate a speech with quotations → **Rad a**

Flecht|werk NT a *(Art)* interlace b **= Geflecht**

Fleck [flɛk] M -(e)s, -e or -en a *(= Schmutzfleck)* stain; **Zeug macht ~en** this stuff stains *(in/auf etw (acc)* sth; **einen ~ auf der (weißen) Weste haben** *(fig)* to have blotted one's copybook; **einen ~ auf der Ehre haben** to have a stain on one's honour *(Brit)* or honor *(US)*

b *(= Farbfleck)* splodge *(Brit)*, splotch, blob; *(auf Arm etc)* blotch; *(auf Obst)* blemish; **ein grüner/gelber ~** a patch of green/yellow etc, a green/yellow etc patch; **weißer ~** white patch; *(auf Stirn von Pferd)* star, blaze; *(auf Landkarte)* blank area → **blau a**

c *(= Stelle)* spot, place; **auf demselben ~** in the same place; **sich nicht vom ~ rühren** not to move or budge *(inf)*; **nicht vom ~ kommen** not to get any further; **er hat das Herz auf dem rechten ~** *(fig)* his heart is in the right place; **am falschen ~** *(fig)* in the wrong way; sparen in the wrong places; **vom ~ weg** on the spot, right away

d *(dial: = Flicken)* patch

e *(Cook dial: = Kaldaune)* entrails pl

Fleck|chen ['flɛkçən] NT -s, - a dim von **Fleck** b **ein schönes ~ (Erde)** a lovely little spot

fle|cken ['flɛkn] VI *(dial)* to stain → auch **gefleckt**

Fle|cken ['flɛkn] M -s, - a *(old: = Marktflecken)* small town b **= Fleck a, b, d**

Fle|cken-: Fle|cken|ent|fer|ner [-ɛntfɛrnɐ] M -s, - stain remover; **fle|cken|los** ADJ *(lit, fig)* spotless

Fleck|ent|fer|ner [-ɛntfɛrnɐ] M -s, -, **Fleck|ent|fer|nungs|mit|tel** NT stain remover

Fle|cken|was|ser NT pl -wässer stain-remover

Fle|ckerl|tep|pich ['flɛkɐl-] M *(S Ger, Aus)* rag rug

Fleck|fie|ber NT typhus fever

fle|ckig ['flɛkɪç] ADJ marked; *(mit Flüssigkeit auch)* stained; Obst blemished; Tierfell speckled; Gesichtshaut blotchy

Fleck-: Fleck|ty|phus M typhus fever; **Fleck|vieh** NT spotted cattle

Fled|de|rer ['flɛdərɐ] M -s, -, **Fled|de|rin** [-ərɪn] F -, -nen person who robs dead people; *(fig)* vulture

fled|dern ['flɛdɐn] VT Leichen to rob; *(inf: = durchwühlen)* to rummage or ferret *(inf)* through

Fle|der- ['fleːdɐ-]: **Fle|der|maus** F bat; **Fle|der|maus|är|mel** M *(Fashion)* Mantel mit ~ batwing coat; **Fle|der|wisch** M feather duster

Fleet [fleːt] NT -(e)s, -e *(N Ger)* canal

Fle|gel ['fleːgl] M -s, - a *(= Lümmel)* lout, yob *(Brit inf)*; *(= Kind)* brat *(inf)* b *(= Dreschflegel, old: = Kriegsflegel)* flail

Fle|gel|al|ter NT awkward adolescent phase

Fle|ge|lei [fleːgə'laɪ] F -, -en uncouthness; *(= Benehmen)* uncouth behaviour *(Brit)* or behavior *(US) no pl*; *(= Bemerkung)* uncouth remark; **so eine ~!** how rude or uncouth!

Fle|gel-: fle|gel|haft ADJ uncouth ADV sich benehmen uncouthly; **Fle|gel|haf|tig|keit** ['fleːgl-haftɪçkaɪt] F -, -en uncouthness; **Fle|gel|jah|re** PL awkward adolescent phase

fle|geln ['fleːgln] VR to loll, to sprawl; **sich in die Bank/den Sessel ~** to loll or sprawl all over the bench/in the armchair

fle|hen ['fleːən] VI *(geh)* to plead *(um +acc for, zu with)*; **..., flehte er zu Gott ...,** he beseeched or besought God *(liter, old)*

fle|hent|lich ['fleːəntlɪç] ADJ imploring, pleading, beseeching *(liter, old)*; **eine ~e Bitte** an earnest entreaty or plea ADV imploringly, pleadingly, beseechingly *(liter, old)*; **jdn ~ bitten** to plead with sb; **jdn ~ bitten, etw zu tun** to entreat or implore sb to do sth

Fleisch [flaɪʃ] NT -(e)s, no pl a *(= Gewebe, Muskelfleisch)* flesh; **nacktes ~** *(lit, fig hum)* bare flesh; **vom ~ fallen** to lose (a lot of) weight; **sich** *(dat or acc)* **ins eigene ~ schneiden** to cut off one's nose to spite one's face; **den Weg allen ~es gehen** *(liter)* to go the way of all flesh; **Menschen von ~ und Blut** flesh and blood; **sein eigen ~ und Blut** *(geh)* his own flesh and blood; **jdm in ~ und Blut übergehen** to become second nature to sb; **und das Wort ward ~** *(Bibl)* and the Word was made flesh; **~ geworden** *(liter)* incarnate; **der ~ gewordene Sohn Gottes** the Son of God incarnate

b *(= Nahrungsmittel)* meat; *(= Fruchtfleisch)* flesh; **~ fressende Pflanzen** carnivorous plants, carnivores; **~ fressende Tiere** carnivores, carnivorous animals; **~ verarbeitend** meat-processing

Fleisch- in cpds *(Cook)* meat; *(Anat)* flesh; **Fleisch|ab|fäl|le** PL *(meat)* scraps pl; **fleisch|arm** ADJ containing little meat; **~ sein** to contain little meat; **Fleisch|berg** M *(pej inf)* mountain of flesh; **Fleisch|be|schau** F a meat inspection b *(hum inf)* cattle market *(inf)*; **Fleisch|be|schau|er(in)** M(F) meat inspector; **Fleisch|bro|cken** M lump of meat; **Fleisch|brü|he** F *(= Gericht)* bouillon; *(= Fond)* meat stock; **Fleisch|brüh|wür|fel** M *(meat)* stock cube; **Fleisch|ein|la|ge** F meat; **Fleisch|ein|waa|ge** F meat content, weight of meat

Flei|scher ['flaɪʃɐ] M -s, -, **Flei|sche|rin** [-ərɪn] F -, -nen butcher; *(pej inf: = Chirurg)* sawbones sing *(inf)*

Flei|scher|beil NT meat cleaver

Flei|sche|rei [flaɪʃə'raɪ] F **-, -en** butcher's (shop) (*Brit*), butcher (shop) (*US*)

Flei|scher-: Flei|scher|ha|ken M meat hook; **Flei|scher|hand|werk** NT butcher's trade, butchery; **Flei|scher|hund** M (*lit*) butcher's dog; (*fig*) brute of a dog; **ein Gemüt wie ein ~ haben** (*inf*) to be a callous brute

Flei|sche|rin F → Fleischer

Flei|scher-: Flei|scher|in|nung F butchers' guild; **Flei|scher|la|den** M butcher's (shop); **Flei|scher|mes|ser** NT butcher's knife

Flei|scher|ne(s) NT *decl as adj* (*S Ger*) meat

Flei|sches|lust F (*old liter*) carnal lust, lusts *pl* of the flesh

Fleisch-: Fleisch|es|ser(in) M(F) meat-eater; **Fleisch|ex|trakt** M beef extract; **Fleisch|far|be** F flesh colour (*Brit*) or color (*US*); **fleisch|far|ben** [-farbn], **fleisch|far|big** ADJ flesh-coloured (*Brit*), flesh-colored (*US*); **Fleisch|flie|ge** F flesh-fly; **fleisch|fres|send** △ ADJ → Fleisch b; **Fleisch|fres|ser(in)** M(F) (*Zool*) carnivore; **Fleisch|ge|nuss** M (*form*) consumption of meat; **fleisch|ge|wor|den** △ ADJ *attr* → Fleisch a; **Fleisch|hau|er(in)** M(F) (*Aus*) butcher; **Fleisch|hau|e|rei** F (*Aus*) butcher's (shop) (*Brit*), butcher (shop) (*US*)

flei|schig [flaɪʃɪç] ADJ fleshy

Fleisch-: Fleisch|kä|se M meat loaf; **Fleisch|klop|fer** M steak hammer; **Fleisch|kloß** M , **Fleisch|klöß|chen** NT a meatball b (*pej inf*) mountain of flesh; **Fleisch|kon|ser|ve** F can *or* tin (*Brit*) of meat; (*in Glas*) pot *or* jar of meat; **Fleisch|kon|ser|ven** PL (*als Gattung*) canned *or* tinned (*Brit*) meat *sing*; (*in Glas*) potted (*Brit*) *or* jarred (*US*) meat *sing*; **Fleisch|lai|berl** [-laibəl] NT **-s, -n** (*Aus*: = Frikadelle) meatball

fleisch|lich [flaɪʃlɪç] ADJ *attr* Speisen, Kost meat; (*liter*) Lüste, Genüsse, Begierden carnal, of the flesh

Fleisch-: fleisch|los ADJ a (= ohne Fleisch) meatless; Kost, Ernährung vegetarian b (= mager) thin, lean ADV ~ **essen** to eat no meat; ~ **kochen** to cook without meat; **Fleisch|ma|schi|ne** F (*Aus, S Ger*) mincer, meat grinder (*esp US*); **Fleisch|pas|te|te** F meat vol-au-vent; **Fleisch|pflan|zerl** [-pflantsəl] NT **-s, -n** (*S Ger*: = Frikadelle) meatball; **Fleisch|res|te** PL left-over meat *sing*; **Fleisch|saft** M meat juices *pl*; **Fleisch|sa|lat** M meat salad with mayonnaise; **Fleisch|spieß** M (*Cook*) meat skewer; **Fleisch|stück(chen)** NT piece of meat; **Fleisch|sup|pe** F meat soup; **Fleisch|to|ma|te** F beef tomato; **Fleisch|ton** M (*Art*) flesh colour (*Brit*) or color (*US*); **Fleisch|topf** M a (*Cook*) meat pan b **Fleischtöpfe** (*Bibl*) fleshpots *pl*; (*fig*) good life; **fleisch|ver|ar|bei|tend** △ ADJ *attr* → Fleisch b; **Fleisch|ver|gif|tung** F food poisoning (*from meat*); **Fleisch|wa|ren** PL meat products *pl*; **Fleisch|wer|dung** F **-, *no pl* (*Rel, liter*) incarnation; **Fleisch|wolf** M mincer, meat grinder (*esp US*); **Rekruten/Prüflinge durch den ~ drehen** (*inf*) to put new recruits/exam candidates through the mill; **Fleisch|wun|de** F flesh wound; **Fleisch|wurst** F pork sausage

Fleiß [flaɪs] M **-(e)s, *no pl* diligence; (= eifriges Tätigsein) industry; (= Beharrlichkeit) application; (als Charaktereigenschaft) industriousness; ~ **auf|wenden** to apply oneself; **ihm fehlt der ~** he lacks application; **mit ~ kann es jeder zu etwas bringen** anybody can succeed if they work hard; **er hat die Prüfung ausschließlich durch ~ geschafft** he passed the exam by sheer hard work *or* simply by working hard; **mit ~ bei der Sache sein** to work hard; **mit ~** (*S Ger*), **zu ~** (*N Ger*) (= absichtlich) deliberately, on purpose; **ohne ~ kein Preis** (*Prov*) no pain, no gain

Fleiß-: Fleiß|ar|beit F industrious piece of work; (*nichts als Fleiß erfordernd*) laborious task; **eine (reine)** ~ (*pej*) an industrious but uninspired piece of work; **Fleiß|auf|ga|be** F (*Sch*) voluntary extra task

flei|ßig [flaɪsɪç] ADJ a (= arbeitsam) hard-working *no adv*, industrious, diligent; ~ **wie die Bienen sein** to work like beavers; **~e Hände** busy hands; **Fleißiges Lieschen** (*Bot*) busy Lizzie b (= Fleiß zeigend) diligent, painstaking c (*inf*: = unverdrossen) Theaterbesucher, Sammler etc keen (*esp Brit*), enthusiastic ADV a (= arbeitsam) industriously, diligently; ~ **studieren/arbeiten** to study/work hard b (*inf*: = unverdrossen) trinken quite a bit; trainieren, Diät halten like a good boy/girl; ~ **zulangen** to get stuck in (*inf*); **wir haben immer ~ bis 12 Uhr getrunken** we were drinking away till 12 o'clock

flek|tier|bar ADJ (in)flectional (*form*); Verb conjugable; Substantiv, Adjektiv declinable

flek|tie|ren [flɛk'tiːrən] ptp **flektiert** VT to inflect (*form*); Substantiv, Adjektiv to decline; Verb to conjugate VI to inflect; to be declined; to be conjugated; **„schwimmen" flektiert stark** "schwimmen" is (conjugated as) a strong verb

flen|nen ['flɛnən] VI (*pej inf*) to blub(ber) (*inf*)

Flen|ne|rei [flɛnə'raɪ] F **-, -en** (*pej inf*) blub(ber)ing (*inf*)

flet|schen ['flɛtʃn] VT **die Zähne ~** to bare *or* show one's teeth

fleucht [flɔʏçt] (*obs, poet*) 3. *pers sing pres von* fliegen → kreucht

Fleu|rop® ['flɔʏrɔp, 'fløːrɔp, flɔʏ'roːp, fløˈroːp] F - Interflora®

fle|xi|bel [flɛ'ksiːbl] ADJ (*lit, fig*) flexible; Holz, Kunststoff auch pliable ADV flexibly

Fle|xi|bi|li|sie|rung [flɛksibili'ziːrʊŋ] F **-, -en ~ der Arbeitszeit** transition to flexible working hours

Fle|xi|bi|li|tät [flɛksibili'tɛːt] F **-, *no pl* (*lit, fig*) flexibility; (von Holz, Kunststoff auch) pliability

Fle|xi|on [flɛ'ksi̯oːn] F **-, -en** (*Gram*) inflection

Fle|xi|ons-: Fle|xi|ons|en|dung F inflectional ending *or* suffix; **fle|xi|ons|fä|hig** ADJ = flektierbar; **fle|xi|ons|los** ADJ uninflected

Fli|bus|tier [fli'bʊstiɐ] M **-s, -** (*old, fig*) buccaneer

flicht [flɪçt] 3. *pers sing pres von* flechten

Flick|ar|beit ['flɪk-] F (*Sew*) mending

fli|cken ['flɪkn] VT to mend; Wäsche (= stopfen auch) to darn; (mit Flicken) to patch → Zeug d

Fli|cken ['flɪkn] M **-s, -** patch; **eine Jacke mit ~** a patched jacket; (*als Schmuck*) a patchwork jacket

Fli|cken|tep|pich M rag rug

Flick-: Flick|flack ['flɪkflak] M **-s, -s** (*Sport*) backflip; **Flick|schnei|der(in)** M(F) (*dated*) mender; (*pej*) bungler (*inf*), bungling tailor; **Flick|schus|ter(in)** M(F) (*old*) cobbler; (*fig pej*) bungler (*inf*), botcher (*inf*); **Flick|schus|te|rei** F (*old*) cobbler's (shop); **das ist ~** (*fig pej*) that's a patch-up job; **Flick|wä|sche** F mending; **Flick|werk** NT the reform war seines **tes ~** the reform had been carried out piecemeal; **Flick|wort** NT *pl* -wörter filler; **Flick|zeug** NT *pl* (*Sew*) sewing kit; (*für Reifen*) (puncture) repair kit

Flie|der ['fliːdɐ] M **-s, -** a lilac b (*dial*: = Holunder) elder b (*Aus inf*: = Geld) money

Flie|der-: Flie|der|bee|re F (*dial*) elderberry; **Flie|der|busch** M lilac; **flie|der|far|ben** [-farbn], **flie|der|far|big** ADJ lilac; **Flie|der|tee** M elderflower tea

Flie|ge ['fliːgə] F **-, -n** a fly; **sie fielen um wie die ~n** they went down like ninepins (*Brit*), they dropped like flies; **sie starben wie die ~n** they fell like flies; **er tut keiner ~ etwas zuleide** *or* **zu Leide** (*fig*) **er würde keiner ~ ein Bein ausreißen** (*fig*) he wouldn't hurt a fly; **zwei ~n mit einer Klappe schlagen** (*prov*) to kill two birds with one stone (*prov*); **ihn stört die ~ an der Wand, er ärgert sich über die ~ an der Wand** every little thing irritates him; **die 'ne ~ ma|chen** (*sl*) to beat it (*inf*) b (= Bärtchen) imperial c (= Schlips) bow tie

flie|gen ['fliːgn] pret **flog** [floːk], ptp **geflogen** [gə'floːgn] VI *aux* sein a (durch die Luft, mit Flugzeug) to fly; (Raumschiff, Raumfahrer) to go, to travel (*form*); **mit General Air ~** to fly (with *or* by) General Air; **in den Urlaub ~** to fly on holiday (*Brit*) *or* vacation (*US*); **nach Köln fliegt man zwei Stunden** it takes two hours to fly to Cologne, it's a two-hour flight to Cologne; **ich kann doch nicht ~!** I haven't got wings (*inf*) b (= eilen) to fly; **jdm/einander in die Arme ~** to fly into sb's/each other's arms; **jdm an den Hals ~** to hurl oneself at sb; **ein Lächeln flog über sein Gesicht** a brief smile lit up his face; **die Zeit fliegt** time flies; **auf jdn/etw ~** (*inf*) to be mad *or* wild about sb/sth (*inf*) c (*inf*: = fallen) to fall; **von der Leiter ~** to fall off the ladder; **durchs Examen ~** to fail *or* flunk (*inf*) one's exam d (*inf*: = hinausgeworfen werden) to be chucked *or* slung *or* kicked out (*inf*) (aus, von of); **aus der Firma ~** to get the sack *or* the boot (*inf*); **von der Schule ~** to be chucked out of school (*inf*) e (= bewegt werden) (Fahne, Haare) to fly; (*Puls*) to race f (= geworfen werden) to be thrown *or* flung (*inf*) *or* chucked (*inf*); **geflogen kommen** to come flying; **in den Papierkorb ~** to go into the wastepaper basket, to be immediately consigned to the wastepaper basket; **die Tür flog ins Schloss** the door flew shut; **ein Schuh flog ihm an den Kopf** he had a shoe flung at him; **der Hut flog ihm vom Kopf** his hat flew off his head; **aus der Kurve ~** to skid off the bend → Luft a VT Flugzeug, Güter, Personen, Route, Einsatz etc to fly VR **in dieser Maschine/nachts fliegt es sich angenehm** flying in this plane/at night is pleasant; **das Flugzeug fliegt sich leicht/schwer** this plane is easy/difficult to fly, flying this plane is easy/difficult → *auch* fliegend

flie|gend ADJ *attr* Fische, Untertasse, Start flying; Personal flight; Würstchenstand, Büchertisch mobile; **Fliegender Hund** flying fox; **in ~er Eile** *or* **Hast** in a tremendous hurry; **~er Händler** travelling (*Brit*) *or* traveling (*US*) hawker; (*mit Lieferwagen*) mobile trader; **~er Teppich** flying carpet; **Der Fliegende Holländer** The Flying Dutchman; **~e Hitze** hot flushes *pl* (*Brit*) *or* flashes *pl* (*US*); **~e Blätter** loose leaves *or* sheets; (*Hist*) broadsheets → **Fahne**

Flie|gen-: Flie|gen|draht M wire mesh; **Flie|gen|dreck** M fly droppings *pl*; **Flie|gen|fän|ger** M (= Klebestreifen) flypaper; **Flie|gen|fens|ter** NT wire-mesh window; **Flie|gen|ge|wicht** NT (*Sport, fig*) flyweight; **Flie|gen|ge|wicht|ler** [-gəvɪçtlɐ] M **-s, -, Flie|gen|ge|wicht|le|rin** [-ərɪn] F **-, -nen** (*Sport*) flyweight; **Flie|gen|git|ter** NT fly screen; **Flie|gen|klat|sche** F fly swat; **Flie|gen|kopf** M (*Typ*) turn; **Flie|gen|netz** NT fly net; **Flie|gen|pilz** M fly agaric; **Flie|gen|ru|te** F fly rod; **Flie|gen|schiss** ▲ M (*inf*) **sich wegen jedem ~ an der Wand aufregen** to get one's knickers in a twist about nothing (*Brit*), to get upset about nothing

Flie|ger ['fliːgɐ] M **-s, -** a (= Pilot) airman, aviator (*dated*), flier (*dated*); (*Mil: Rang*) aircraftman (*Brit*), airman basic (*US*); **er ist bei den ~n** (*dated*) he's in the air force b (*inf*: = Flugzeug*) plane c (= Vogel) flier d (*Radrennen*) sprinter e (*Pferderennen*) flier

Flie|ger- (*Mil*): Flie|ger|ab|wehr F air defence (*Brit*) *or* defense (*US*); **Flie|ger|ab|zei|chen** NT wings *pl*; **Flie|ger|alarm** M air-raid warning; **Flie|ger|an|griff** M air raid; **Flie|ger|bom|be** F aerial bomb

Flie|ge|rei [fliːgə'raɪ] F **-, *no pl* flying

Flie|ger|horst M (*Mil*) military airfield *or* aerodrome (*Brit*)

Flie|ge|rin ['fliːgərɪn] F **-, -nen** **a** (= *Pilotin*) airwoman, aviatrix (*dated*), flier (*dated*) **b** (*Radrennen*) s

flie|ge|risch ['fliːgərɪʃ] ADJ *attr* aeronautical

Flie|ger-: Flie|ger|ja|cke F bomber jacket; **Flie|ger|kar|te** F aviation chart; **Flie|ger|of|fi|zier(in)** M(F) (*Mil, Aviat*) air force officer; **Flie|ger|schu|le** F flying school; **Flie|ger|spra|che** F pilots' jargon; **Flie|ger|staf|fel** F (*Mil*) (air force) squadron; **Flie|ger|trup|pe** F (*Mil*) air corps line

Flieh|burg F refuge

flie|hen ['fliːən] *pret* **floh** [floː], *ptp* **geflohen** [gə'floːən] **VI** *aux* sein to flee (*vor +dat* from); (= *entkommen*) to escape (*aus* from); **vor jdm/dem Krieg/der Polizei/einem Gewitter ~** to flee from sb/war/the police/before a storm; **aus dem Lande ~** to flee the country → **fliehend VT** (*liter*) (= *meiden*) to shun; (= *entkommen*) to flee from; **jds Gegenwart ~** to shun/flee sb's presence

flie|hend ADJ *Kinn* receding; *Stirn* sloping; *Schrift* sloping, slanting

Flieh-: Flieh|kraft F centrifugal force; **Flieh|kraft|kupp|lung** F centrifugal clutch

Flie|se ['fliːzə] F **-, -n** tile; **~n legen** to lay tiles; **etw mit ~n auslegen** to tile sth

flie|sen ['fliːzn] VT to tile

Flie|sen-: Flie|sen(fuß)bo|den M tiled floor; **Flie|sen|le|ger** [-leːgɐ] M **-s, -**, **Flie|sen|le|ge|rin** [-ərɪn] **F** **-, -nen** tiler

Fließ|band [-bant] NT *pl* **-bänder** conveyor belt; (*als Einrichtung*) assembly *or* production line; **am ~ arbeiten** *or* **stehen** (*inf*) to work on the assembly *or* production line

Fließband-: Fließ|band|ar|beit F assembly-line work; **Fließ|band|fer|ti|gung** F belt production

flie|ßen ['fliːsn] *pret* **floss** [flɔs], *ptp* **geflossen** [gə'flɔsn] VI *aux* sein to flow; (*Verkehr, Luftmassen auch*) to move; (*Fluss auch, Tränen*) to run; **es ist genug Blut geflossen** enough blood has been shed *or* spilled; **der Schweiß floss ihm von der Stirn** sweat was pouring off his forehead; **die Steuergelder flossen in dunkle Kanäle** the taxes were diverted along rather dubious channels; **die Mittel für Jugendarbeit ~ immer spärlicher** less and less money is being made available for youth work; **aus der Feder ~** (*geh*) to flow from the pen; **Nachrichten ~ spärlich** the flow of news is minimal; **alles fließt** (*Philos*) all is in a state of flux → **Strom a**

flie|ßend **ADJ** flowing; *Leitungswasser, Gewässer* running; *Verkehr* moving; *Rede, Vortrag, Sprache* fluent; *Grenze, Übergang* fluid; **sie spricht ein ~es Französisch** she speaks fluent French, she speaks French fluently **ADV** *sprechen* fluently; **~ warm und kalt Wasser** running hot and cold water

Fließ-: Fließ|heck NT fastback; **Fließ|kom|ma** NT (*auch Comput*) floating point; **Fließ|laut** M liquid; **Fließ|punkt** M (*auch Comput*) floating point; **Fließ|satz** M (*Typ*) wordwrap; **Fließ|stra|ße** F (*Tech*) assembly *or* production line; **Fließ|text** M (*Typ*) running text; **Fließ|was|ser** NT , *no pl* (*esp Aus*) running water

Flim|mer ['flɪmɐ] M **-s, -** **a** (*Anat*) cilium **b** *no pl* (*liter*. = *zitternder Glanz*) shimmer

Flim|mer-: flim|mer|frei ADJ (*Opt, Phot*) flicker-free; **Flim|mer|här|chen** NT cilium; **Flim|mer|kas|ten** M , **Flim|mer|kis|te F** (*inf*) TV (*inf*), (goggle)box (*Brit inf*), telly (*Brit inf*), (boob) tube (*US inf*)

flim|mern ['flɪmɐn] **VI** to shimmer; (*Film, TV*) to flicker; **es flimmert mir vor den Augen** everything is swimming *or* dancing before my eyes; **über den Bildschirm ~** (*inf*) to be on the box (*Brit inf*) *or* on the tube (*US inf*) *or* on TV (*inf*)

VT (*dial*: = *blank putzen*) to polish, to shine (*inf*)

Flim|mern ['flɪmɐn] NT **-s**, *no pl* (*von Luft, Wasser*) shimmering; (*von Bildschirm etc*) flickering; (*von Sternen*) twinkling; (*Med*: = *Herzflimmern*) fibrillation; **ein ~ vor den Augen** flickering in front of one's eyes

flink [flɪŋk] **ADJ** (= *geschickt*) nimble; *Bewegung, Finger auch* deft; (= *schnell, dated*: = *aufgeweckt*) quick; *Mundwerk, Zunge* quick, ready; *Augen* sharp **ADV** *arbeiten, sich bewegen* quickly; *springen* nimbly; **ein bisschen ~!** (*inf*) get a move on!, make it snappy! (*inf*); **mit etw ~ bei der Hand sein** to be quick (off the mark) with sth

Flink|heit F **-**, *no pl* (= *Geschicktheit*) nimbleness; (*von Bewegung, Finger auch*) deftness; (= *Schnelligkeit*) quickness

Flint [flɪnt] M **-(e)s, -e** (*old*) flint

Flin|te ['flɪntə] F **-, -n** (= *Schrotflinte*) shotgun; **jdn/etw vor die ~ bekommen** (*fig*) to get hold of sb/sth; **wenn der mir vor die ~ kommt ...** (*fig*) just wait till I get hold of him ...; **die ~ ins Korn werfen** (*fig*) to throw in the sponge (*Brit*) *or* towel

Flinten-: Flin|ten|lauf M (shot)gun barrel; **Flin|ten|weib** NT (*pej*) gunwoman

Flint|glas NT flint glass

Flip [flɪp] M **-s, -s** (*Eiskunstlauf*) flip

Flip|chart **▲** ['flɪptʃaːɐt] F **-, -s** flip chart

Flip|flop|schal|tung ['flɪpflɔp-] F flip-flop circuit

Flip|per ['flɪpɐ] M **-s, -**, **Flip|per|au|to|mat** M pinball machine

flip|pern ['flɪpɐn] **VT** to flip **VI** to play pinball

flip|pig ['flɪpɪç] (*inf*) **ADJ** way-out (*inf*); **er ist ein ~er Typ** he's way-out (*inf*) **ADV** way-out (*inf*)

flir|ren ['flɪrən] VI to whirr; (*Luft, Hitze*) to shimmer

Flirt [flɪrt, flœːɐt, flœrt] M **-s, -s** **a** (= *Flirten*) flirtation **b** (*dated*) (= *Schwarm*) flame (*dated*); (= *Mann auch*) beau (*dated*)

flir|ten ['flɪrtn, 'flœːɐtn, 'flœrtn] VI to flirt; **mit einem Gedanken ~** (*inf*) to toy with an idea

Flit|scherl ['flɪtʃɐl] NT **-s, -(n)** (*Aus pej inf*) slut

Flitt|chen ['flɪtçən] NT **-s, -** (*pej inf*) slut

Flit|ter ['flɪtɐ] M **-s, -** **a** (= *Flitterschmuck*) sequins *pl*, spangles *pl* **b** *no pl* (*pej*: = *Tand*) trumpery

Flit|ter|gold NT gold foil

flit|tern ['flɪtɐn] VI (*hum*) to honeymoon

Flitter-: Flit|ter|werk NT , *no pl* (*pej*: = *Tand*) trumpery; **Flit|ter|wo|chen** PL honeymoon *sing*; **in die ~ fahren/in den ~ sein** to go/be on one's honeymoon; **Flit|ter|wöch|ner** [-vœçnɐ] M **-s, -**, **Flit|ter|wöch|ne|rin** [-ərɪn] F **-, -nen** (*hum*) honeymooner; **die ~** the honeymoon couple

Flitz|bo|gen ['flɪts-] M , **Flit|ze|bo|gen** ['flɪtsə-] M bow and arrow; **ich bin gespannt wie ein ~** (*inf*) the suspense is killing me (*inf*); **gespannt wie ein ~ sein, ob ...** to be on tenterhooks waiting to see whether ...

Flit|ze ['flɪtsə] F **die ~ machen** (*sl*: = *verschwinden*) to bolt (*sl*)

flit|zen ['flɪtsn] VI *aux* sein (*inf*) **a** (= *sich schnell bewegen*) to whizz (*inf*), to dash **b** (= *nackt rennen*) to streak; **(das) Flitzen** streaking

Flit|zer¹ ['flɪtsɐ] M **-s, -** (*inf*: = *Fahrzeug*) sporty little job (*Brit inf*) *or* number (*US inf*)

Flit|zer² ['flɪtsɐ] M **-s, -**, **Flit|ze|rin** [-ərɪn] F **-, -nen** (*inf*) **a** (= *Schnellläufer*) streak of lightning (*inf*) **b** (= *nackter Läufer*) streaker

floa|ten ['floːtn] VTI (*Fin*) to float; **~ (lassen)** to float

Floa|ting ['floːtɪŋ] NT **-s, -s** (*Fin*) floating

F-Loch ['ɛf-] NT (*Mus*) f-hole

flocht *pret von* **flechten**

Flöck|chen ['flœkçən] NT **-s, -** *dim von* **Flocke**

Flo|cke ['flɔkə] F **-, -n** **a** (= *Wollflocke*) piece of wool; (= *Schaumflocke*) blob (of foam); (= *Staubflocke*) ball of (fluff) **b** **Flocken** PL (*inf*: = *Geld*) dough (*inf*)

flo|ckig ['flɔkɪç] ADJ (*lit*) fluffy; (*fig*) lively

flog *pret von* **fliegen**

floh *pret von* **fliehen**

Floh [floː] M **-(e)s, ⸚e** ['fløːə] (*Zool*) flea; **von Flöhen zerbissen** *or* **zerstochen** flea-bitten *attr*, bitten by fleas; **es ist leichter, einen Sack Flöhe zu hüten, als ...** I'd as soon jump in the lake as ...; **jdm einen ~ ins Ohr setzen** (*inf*) to put an idea into sb's head; **die Flöhe husten hören** (*inf*) to imagine things

Floh|biss ▲ M fleabite

flö|hen ['fløːən] VT **jdn/sich ~** to get rid of sb's/one's fleas, to debug sb/oneself (*inf*)

Floh-: Floh|hals|band NT flea collar; **Floh|hüp|fen** NT **-s**, *no pl* tiddl(e)ywinks *sing, no art*; **Floh|ki|no** NT (*inf*) local fleapit (*inf*); **Floh|markt** M flea market; **Floh|spiel** NT tiddl(e)ywinks *sing, no art*; **Floh|zir|kus** M flea circus

Flo|ka|ti [flo'kaːti] M **-s, -s** flokati

Flom [floːm] M , *no pl*, **Flo|men** ['floːmən] M **-s**, *no pl* (*Cook*) lard

Flop [flɔp] M **-s, -s** flop (*inf*)

Flop|py|disk ▲ ['flɔpi-] F **-, -s**, **Flop|py Disk** F **-, -, -s** floppy disk

Flor¹ [floːɐ] M **-s, -e** (*liter*) array of flowers; **in ~ stehen** to be in full bloom

Flor² M **-s, -e** *or* (*rare*) **⸚e** ['fløːrə] **a** (= *dünnes Gewebe*) gauze; (= *Trauerflor*) crêpe; (*liter*: = *Schleier*) veil **b** (= *Teppichflor, Samtflor*) pile

Flo|ra ['floːra] F **-, Floren** ['floːrən] flora

Flo|ren|ti|ner¹ [floren'tiːnɐ] ADJ *attr* Florentine

Flo|ren|ti|ner² [floren'tiːnɐ] M **-s, -** **a** (*Cook*) Florentine **b** (*auch* **Florentinerhut**) picture hat

Flo|ren|ti|ner³ [floren'tiːnɐ] M **-s, -**, **Flo|ren|ti|ne|rin** [-ərɪn] F **-, -nen** Florentine

flo|ren|ti|nisch [floren'tiːnɪʃ] ADJ Florentine

Flo|renz [flo'rents] NT **-'** *or* **-ens** Florence

Flo|rett [flo'rɛt] NT **-(e)s, -e** **a** (= *Waffe*) foil; **~ fechten** to fence with a foil **b** (*auch* **Florett-fechten**) foil-fencing

Flor|flie|ge F lacewing

flo|rie|ren [flo'riːrən] *ptp* **floriert** VI to flourish, to bloom

Flo|rist [flo'rɪst] M **-en, -en**, **Flo|ris|tin** [-'rɪstɪn] F **-, -nen** florist

Flos|kel ['flɔskl] F **-, -n** set phrase; **eine höfliche/abgedroschene ~** a polite but meaningless/a hackneyed (*Brit*) *or* clichéd phrase

flos|kel|haft ADJ *Stil, Rede, Brief* cliché-ridden; *Phrasen, Ausdrucksweise* stereotyped

floss ▲ *pret von* **fließen**

Floß [floːs] NT **-es, ⸚e** ['fløːsə] raft; (*Fishing*) float

flöß|bar ADJ navigable by raft

Floß|brü|cke F floating bridge

Flos|se ['flɔsə] F **-, -n** **a** (*Zool*) (= *Fischflosse*) fin; (= *Walflosse, Robbenflosse*) flipper **b** (*Aviat, Naut*: = *Leitwerk*) fin **c** (= *Taucherflosse*) flipper **d** (*inf*: = *Hand*) paw (*inf*), mauler (*inf*); **~n hoch!** hands up!

flö|ßen ['fløːsn] VTI to raft

Flö|ßer ['fløːsɐ] M **-s, -**, **Flö|ße|rin** [-ərɪn] F **-, -nen** raftsman/-woman (*Brit*), rafter (*US*)

Flö|ße|rei [fløːsə'raɪ] F **-**, *no pl* rafting

Floß|fahrt F raft trip

Flö|te ['fløːtə] F **-, -n** **a** pipe; (= *Querflöte, Orgelflöte, in Zusammensetzungen*) flute; (= *Blockflöte*) recorder; (= *Pikkoloflöte*) piccolo; (*des Pan*) pipes *pl*; (*dial*: = *Pfeife, Kesselflöte*) whistle; **die ~ or auf der ~ spielen** *or* **blasen** to play the pipe *etc* **b** (= *Kelchglas*) flute glass **c** (*Cards*) flush

flö|ten ['fløːtn] **VT** (*Mus*) to play on the flute; (*auf Blockflöte*) to play on the recorder **VI** (*Mus*) to play the flute; (= *Blockflöte spielen*) to play the recorder **VTI a** (*Vogel*) to warble; (*dial*: = *pfeifen*) to whistle **b** (*hum inf*: = *süß sprechen*) to flute, to warble

Flö|ten-: Flö|ten|blä|ser(in) M(F) = **Flötenspieler(in)**; **flö|ten ge|hen ▲** VI *aux sein* (*inf*) to go west (*esp Brit inf*), to go for a burton (*dated Brit sl*), to go to the dogs (*inf*); **Flö|ten|kes|sel** M whistling kettle; **Flö|ten|re|gis|ter** NT flue stop; **Flö|ten|spiel** NT pipe-/flute- *etc* playing; (= *Flötenmusik*) pipe/flute *etc* music; **Flö|ten|spie|ler(in)** M(F) piper; (*von Querflöte*) flautist; (*von Blockflöte*) recorder player; (*von Pikkoloflöte*) piccolo player; **Flö|ten|ton** M *pl* **-töne a** (*lit*) sound of flutes/a flute **b** (*inf*) **jdm die Flötentöne beibringen** to teach sb what's what (*inf*); **Flö|ten|werk** NT flue-work

Flö|tist [fløˈtɪst] M **-en, -en, Flö|tis|tin** [-ˈtɪstɪn] F **-, -nen** = **Flötenspieler(in)**

flott [flɔt] **ADJ a** (= *zügig*) Fahrt quick; *Tempo, Geschäft* brisk; *Arbeiter, Bedienung* speedy (*inf*), quick and efficient; *Tänzer* good; (= *flüssig*) *Stil, Artikel* racy (*inf*); (= *schwungvoll*) *Musik* lively; **den ~en Otto** or **Heinrich haben** (*hum inf*) to have the runs (*inf*)
b (= *schick*) smart
c (= *lebenslustig*) fun-loving, fast-living; **~ le-ben, ein ~es Leben führen** to be a fast liver
d *pred* **-/wieder ~ werden** *Schiff* to be floated off/refloated; (*fig inf*) (*Auto etc*) to be/get back on the road; (*Flugzeug etc*) to be working/working again; (*Mensch*) to be out of the woods/back on top; (*Unternehmen*) to be/get back on its feet; **wieder ~ sein** (*Schiff*) to be afloat again; (*fig inf*) (*Auto etc*) to be back on the road; (*Flugzeug*) to be working again; (*Mensch*) (*gesundheitlich*) to be in the pink again (*inf*); (*finanziell*) to be in funds or in the money again; (*Unternehmen*) to be back on its feet
ADV a (= *zügig*) quickly, speedily; **ich komme ~ voran mit meiner Arbeit** I'm making speedy progress with my work; **aber ein bisschen ~!** and look lively!, and make it snappy! (*inf*)
b (= *schick*) stylishly; **~ aussehen** to look stylish; **~ auftreten** to cut a dash (*Brit*), to look stylish

Flott [flɔt] NT **-(e)s,** *no pl* **a** (*N Ger*) skin of the milk **b** (= *Entenflott*) duckweed

flott+be|kom|men *ptp* **flottbekommen** VT *sep irreg Schiff* to float off; (*fig inf*) *Auto etc* to get on the road; *Flugzeug* to get working; *Unternehmen* to get on its feet

Flot|te [ˈflɔtə] F **-, -n a** (*Naut, Aviat*) fleet **b** (*Tex*) (= *Färbebad*) dye (solution); (= *Bleichlösung*) bleach (solution); (= *Einweichlösung*) soaking solution

Flot|ten-: Flot|ten|ab|kom|men NT naval treaty; **Flot|ten|ba|sis** F naval base; **Flot|ten|chef(in)** M(F) commander-in-chief of the fleet; **Flot|ten|kom|man|do** NT fleet command; **Flot|ten|pa|ra|de** F naval review; **die ~ abnehmen** to review the fleet; **Flot|ten|stütz|punkt** M naval base; **Flot|ten|ver|band** M naval unit

Flot|til|le [flɔˈtɪl(j)ə] F **-, -n** (*Mil*) flotilla; (= *Fischfangflottille*) fleet

Flot|til|len|ad|mi|ral(in) M(F) (*Mil*) commodore

flott-: flott+krie|gen (*inf*), **flott+ma|chen** VT *sep* = **flottbekommen**; **flott|weg** [ˈflɔtvɛk] ADV (*inf*) non-stop; **das geht immer ~** there's no hanging about (*inf*)

Flöz [fløːts] NT **-es, -e** (*Min*) seam

Fluch [fluːx] M **-(e)s, ̈-e** [ˈflyːçə] curse; (= *Schimpfwort auch*) oath; **ein ~ liegt über** or **lastet auf diesem Haus** there is a curse on this house, this house lies under a curse; **~ dem Alkohol!** a curse on alcohol!; **das (eben) ist der ~ der bösen Tat** (*prov*) evil begets evil (*prov*)

fluch|be|la|den [-bəlaːdn] ADJ (*liter*) accursed, cursed

flu|chen [ˈfluːxn] VI (= *Flüche ausstoßen, schimpfen*) to curse (and swear); **auf** or **über jdn/etw ~** to curse sb/sth VT (*old*) **jdm/etw ~** to curse sb/sth

Flucht [flʊxt] F **-, -en a** (= *Fliehen*) flight (*vor +dat* from); (*geglückt*) escape, flight; **die ~ ergreifen** to take flight, to flee; (*erfolgreich auch*) to (make one's) escape; **ihm glückte die ~** he escaped, he succeeded in escaping; **auf der ~ sein** to be fleeing; (*Gesetzesbrecher*) to be on the run; **jdn/etw in die ~ treiben** or **jagen** or **schlagen** to put sb/sth to flight; **in wilder** or **heilloser ~ davonjagen** or **stampede**; **jdm zur ~ verhelfen** to help sb to escape; **auf der ~ erschossen werden** to be shot while attempting to escape; **sein Heil in der ~ suchen** (*geh*) to take refuge in flight; **die ~ nach vorn antreten** to take the bull by the horns; **die ~ in die Anonymität/die Krankheit antreten** to take refuge in anonymity/illness; **die ~ in den Trotz antreten** to resort to defiance; **die ~ in** or **an die Öffentlichkeit antreten** to resort to going public; **die ~ nach Ägypten** (*Bibl*) the flight into Egypt
b (*Hunt*) leap, bound; **eine ~ machen** to make a leap or bound
c (= *Häuserflucht*) row; (= *Fluchtlinie*) alignment
d (= *Zimmerflucht*) suite

Flucht-: flucht|ar|tig ADJ hasty, hurried, precipitate (*form*); **in ~er Eile** in great haste **ADV** hastily, hurriedly; **Flucht|au|to** NT escape car; (*von Gesetzesbrecher*) getaway car; **Flucht|burg** F refuge

fluch|ten [ˈflʊxtn] (*Archit*) VT to align VI to be aligned

flüch|ten [ˈflʏçtn] VI **a** *aux sein* (= *davonlaufen*) to flee (*vor +dat* from); (*erfolgreich*) to escape, to flee; **aus dem Land/Südafrika ~** to flee the country/from South Africa; **vor der Wirklichkeit ~** to escape reality; **sich in (den) Alkohol ~** to take refuge in alcohol; **sich in Ausreden ~** to resort to excuses **b** *auch vr* (*vi: aux sein*) (= *Schutz suchen*) to take refuge

Flucht-: Flucht|fahr|zeug NT escape vehicle; (*von Gesetzesbrecher*) getaway vehicle; **Flucht|ge|fahr** F risk of escape, risk of an escape attempt; **Flucht|ge|schwin|dig|keit** F (*Phys*) escape velocity; **Flucht|hel|fer(in)** M(F) escape helper; **Flucht|hil|fe** F escape aid; **~ leisten** to aid an escape; **Flucht|hil|fe|or|ga|ni|sa|ti|on** F escape organization

flüch|tig [ˈflʏçtɪç] **ADJ a** (= *geflüchtet*) fugitive; **~ sein** to be still at large; **ein ~er Verbrecher** a criminal who hasn't been caught; **ein ~er Fahrer** (*nach Unfall*) a hit-and-run driver **b** (= *kurz, schnell vorübergehend*) fleeting, brief; *Gruß* brief **c** (= *oberflächlich*) cursory, sketchy **d** (*Chem*) volatile **e** (*Comput*) **~er Speicher** volatile memory **ADV a** (= *kurz*) fleetingly, briefly; **~ erwähnen** to mention in passing **b** (= *oberflächlich*) cursorily, superficially; **etw ~ lesen** to glance or skim through sth; **~ arbeiten** to work hurriedly or hastily; **jdn ~ kennen** to have met sb briefly

Flüch|ti|ge(r) [ˈflʏçtɪgə] MF *decl as adj* fugitive; (= *Ausbrecher*) escaper

Flüch|tig|keit F **-, -en a** (= *Kürze*) briefness, brevity **b** (= *Oberflächlichkeit*) hurried nature, sketchiness; (= *Flüchtigkeitsfehler*) careless mistake **c** (= *Vergänglichkeit*) fleeting nature, briefness **d** (*Chem*) volatility

Flüch|tig|keits|feh|ler M careless mistake; (*beim Schreiben auch*) slip of the pen

Flucht|ka|pi|tal NT (*Fin*) flight capital

Flücht|ling [ˈflʏçtlɪŋ] M **-s, -e** refugee

Flücht|lings- *in cpds* refugee → *auch* **Vertriebenen-; Flücht|lings|aus|weis** F refugee's identity card; **Flücht|lings|camp** NT refugee camp; **Flücht|lings|hil|fe** F aid to refugees; (*inf*: = *Flüchtlingsorganisation*) (refugee) relief agency; **Flücht|lings|la|ger** NT refugee camp; **Flücht|lings|wel|le** F wave or tide of refugees

Flucht-: Flucht|li|nie F alignment; (*einer Straße*) building line; **Flucht|punkt** M vanishing point; **Flucht|tun|nel** M escape tunnel; **Flucht|ver|dacht** M *bei:* if an attempt to abscond is thought likely; **es besteht ~** there are grounds for suspecting that he/she *etc* will try to abscond; **flucht|ver|däch|tig** ADJ suspected of planning to abscond; **Flucht|ver|such** M escape attempt or bid; **Flucht|weg** M escape route

fluch|wür|dig ADJ (*liter*) dastardly (*old*) *no adv*, execrable (*liter*)

Flug [fluːk] M **-(e)s, ̈-e** [ˈflyːgə] (*alle Bedeutungen*) flight; (= *Skiflug*) jump; **im ~(e)** in the air; (*bei Vögeln auch*) in flight, on the wing; **einen ~ antreten** to take off (*nach* for); **einen ~ stornieren** to cancel a booking; **der ~ zum Mond** (= *Fliegen*) travel to the moon; (= *spezifische Fahrt*) the moon flight or trip; **wie im ~(e)** (*fig*) in a twinkling or flash

Flug|ab|wehr F air defence (*Brit*) or defense (*US*)

Flug|ab|wehr-: Flug|ab|wehr|ka|no|ne F anti-aircraft gun; **Flug|ab|wehr|kör|per** M air defence (*Brit*) or defense (*US*) missile; **Flug|ab|wehr|ra|ke|te** F anti-aircraft missile

Flug-: Flug|an|gel F fly rod; **Flug|angst** F fear of flying; **Flug|ap|pa|rat** M flying machine; **Flug|asche** F flying ashes *pl*; **Flug|auf|kom|men** NT air traffic; **Flug|bahn** F (*von Vogel, Flugzeug*) flight path; (*von Rakete, Satelliten auch, von Kugel*) trajectory; (= *Kreisbahn*) orbit; **Flug|ball** M (*Sport*) high ball; (*Tennis etc*) volley; **Flug|ba|sis** F (*Mil*) air base; **Flug|be|glei|ter(in)** M(F) flight attendant; **Flug|be|gleit|per|so|nal** NT cabin crew; **Flug|ben|zin** NT aviation fuel; **Flug|be|reich** M operational range *no pl*; **flug|be|reit** ADJ ready for take-off; **Flug|be|reit|schaft** F readiness for take-off; **Flug|be|trieb** M air traffic; **den ~ auf einem Flughafen einstellen** to close an airport; **Flug|be|we|gun|gen** PL aircraft movements *pl*; **Flug|bild** NT (*Zool*) flight silhouette

Flug|blatt NT leaflet; (= *Werbung auch*) handbill

Flug|blatt-: Flug|blatt|ak|ti|on F leafleting campaign; **Flug|blatt|ver|tei|ler(in)** M(F) distributor of leaflets or (*für Werbung*) handbills

Flug-: Flug|boot NT flying boat; **Flug|buch** NT logbook, flight log; **Flug|da|ten|schrei|ber** M flight recorder; **Flug|dau|er** F flying time; **Flug|deck** NT flight deck; **Flug|dich|te** F density of air traffic; **Flug|dienst** M air traffic services *pl*; (= *Flugverkehr*) air service; **Flug|dra|chen** M hang-glider; **Flug|ech|se** F pterosaur; **die ~n** the Pterosauria; **Flug|ei|gen|schaft** F *usu pl* handling characteristic

Flü|gel [ˈflyːgl] M **-s, -** (*Anat, Aviat*) wing; **mit den ~n schlagen** to beat or flap its wings; **einem Vogel/jdm die ~ stutzen** or **beschneiden** to clip a bird's/sb's wings; **die ~ hängen lassen** (*fig inf*: = *mutlos sein*) to be despondent or dejected; **die Hoffnung/der Gedanke verlieh ihm ~** (*liter*) hope/the thought lent him wings (*liter*)
b (*von Hubschrauber, Ventilator*) blade; (= *Propellerflügel auch*) vane; (= *Windmühlenflügel*) sail, vane
c (= *Altarflügel*) sidepiece, wing; (= *Fensterflügel*) casement (*form*), side; (= *Türflügel*) door (of *double doors*), leaf (*form*); (= *Lungenflügel*) lung; (= *Nasenflügel*) nostril
d (*Pol, Mil, Sport*) wing; **der linke/rechte ~** the left/right wing
e (= *Gebäudeflügel*) wing
f (= *Konzertflügel*) grand piano, grand (*inf*); **auf dem ~ spielen** to play the piano; **am ~: ...** at or on the piano: ...

Flü|gel-: Flü|gel|ad|ju|tant M (*Mil, Hist*) aide-de-camp (*often to a general*); **Flü|gel|al|tar** M winged altar; **Flü|gel|är|mel** M hanging sleeve; **Flü|gel|fens|ter** NT casement window; (= *Verandafenster*) French window (*Brit*), French door (*US*); **flü|gel|för|mig** ADJ wing-shaped; **Flü|gel|frau** F (*Ftbl*) wing forward, winger; (Pol) person on the wing of a party; **Flü|gel|hau|be** F pinner, cap with upturned lappets; **Flü|gel|horn** NT (Mus) flugelhorn; **Flü|gel|kampf** M (Pol) factional dispute, party in-fighting; **Flü|gel|klap|pe** F (Aviat) wing flap, aileron (spec); **flü|gel|lahm** ADJ with injured wings/an injured wing; (fig) Industrie etc ailing; Mensch feeble; ~ **sein** (lit) to have an injured wing/its wings injured; (fig: = mutlos) to be dejected or despondent; **einen Vogel ~ schießen** to wing a bird; **eine ~e Ente** (fig) a lame duck; **flü|gel|los** ADJ wingless; **Flü|gel|mann** M pl **-männer** or **-leute** (Ftbl) wing forward, winger; (Mil) flank man; (Pol) person on the wing of a party; **Flü|gel|mut|ter** F pl **-muttern** wing or butterfly nut; **Flü|gel|ross ▲** NT (Myth) winged horse; **Flü|gel|schlag** M (liter) beat of its wings; **den ~ der Zeit spüren** (liter) to feel the life-pulse of history; **flü|gel|schla|gend** ADJ beating its wings; **Flü|gel|schrau|be** F **a** wing bolt **b** (= Flügelmutter) wing or butterfly nut; **Flü|gel|span|ne** F , **Flü|gel|spann|wei|te** F wing span; **Flü|gel|stür|mer** M (Sport) wing forward; **Flü|gel|tür** F leaved door (form); (mit zwei Flügeln) double door; (= Verandatür) French window (Brit), French door (US)

Flug-: Flug|en|te F (Cook) muscovy duck; **Flug|ent|fer|nung** F air or flying distance; **Flug|er|fah|rung** F flying experience; **flug|er|probt** [-ɛːproːpt] ADJ flight-tested; **flug|fä|hig** ADJ able to fly; Flugzeug (= in Ordnung) airworthy; **Flug|fä|hig|keit** F ability to fly; (von Flugzeug) airworthiness; **Flug|feld** NT airfield; **Flug|fre|quenz** F frequency of flights; **Flug|fuchs** M (Indian) flying fox; **Flug|funk** M air radio

Flug|gast M (airline) passenger

Flug|gast-: Flug|gast|kon|trol|le F airport security check; **Flug|gast|raum** M passenger cabin

flüg|ge ['flʏgə] ADJ fully-fledged; (fig) Jugendlicher independent; **~ werden** (lit) to be able to fly; (fig) to leave the nest

Flug-: Flug|ge|län|de NT airfield; **Flug|ge|päck** NT baggage; **erlaubtes ~ 15 Kilo** baggage allowance 15 kilos; **Flug|ge|rät** NT , no pl aircraft; **Flug|ge|schwin|dig|keit** F (von Vögeln, Insekten) speed of flight; (von Flugzeug) flying speed; (von Rakete, Geschoss, Ball) velocity; **Flug|ge|sell|schaft** F airline (company); **Flug|ge|wicht** NT all-up weight

Flug|ha|fen M airport; (Mil) aerodrome (Brit), airdrome (US); **der ~ Hamburg** Hamburg airport; **auf dem ~** at the airport

Flug|ha|fen-: Flug|ha|fen|bus M airport bus; **Flug|ha|fen|feu|er|wehr** F airport fire fighting service; **Flug|ha|fen|ge|bühr** F airport charges pl; **Flug|ha|fen|ge|län|de** NT airport grounds pl; **Flug|ha|fen|nä|he** F in ~ near or in the vicinity of the/an airport; **Flug|ha|fen|steu|er** F airport tax

Flug-: Flug|hö|he F flying height (auch Orn); (Aviat) altitude; **unsere** or **die ~ beträgt 10.000 Meter** we are flying at an altitude of 10,000 metres (Brit) or meters (US); **die ~ erreichen** to reach one's cruising altitude or flying height; **Flug|hörn|chen** NT flying squirrel; **Flug|hund** M flying fox; **Flug|in|ge|ni|eur(in)** M(F) flight engineer; **Flug|kan|zel** F cockpit; **Flug|ka|pi|tän(in)** M(F) captain of an/the aircraft); **Flug|kar|te** F **a** (= Luftfahrtkarte) flight or aviation chart **b** (rare: = Flugschein) plane ticket; **Flug|ki|lo|me|ter** M (air) kilometre (Brit) or kilometer (US); **Flug|kör|per** M flying object; **Flug|kor|ri|dor** M air corridor; **Flug|kunst** F airmanship, flying skill; **Flug|küns|te** PL flying skills pl; (= Kunststücke) aerobatic feats pl; **Flug|lärm** M aircraft noise; **Flug|la|ge** F flying position or attitude (spec); **Flug|leh|rer(in)** M(F) flying instructor; **Flug|leit|sys|tem** NT flight control system; **Flug|lei|tung** F air-traffic or flight control; **Flug|li-**

nie F **a** (= Strecke) airway, air route **b** (= Fluggesellschaft) airline (company); **Flug|loch** NT entrance hole; (bei Bienenstock) (hive) entrance; **Flug|lot|se** M , **Flug|lot|sin** F air-traffic or flight controller; **Flug|ma|nö|ver** NT aerial manoeuvre (Brit) or maneuver (US); **Flug|mel|de|dienst** M (Mil) enemy aircraft warning service; **Flug|me|te|o|ro|lo|gie** F aeronautical meteorology; **Flug|mi|nu|te** F nach **fünf ~n** after flying for five minutes; **dreißig ~n von hier** thirty minutes by air from here; **Flug|mis|si|on** F space mission; **Flug|mo|tor** M aircraft engine; **Flug|netz** NT network of air routes; **Flug|num|mer** F flight number; **Flug|ob|jekt** NT **ein unbekanntes ~** an unidentified flying object, a UFO; **Flug|ord|nung** F flight formation; **Flug|pas|sa|gier(in)** M(F) (airline) passenger; **Flug|per|so|nal** NT flight personnel pl; **Flug|plan** M flight schedule; **Flug|platz** M airfield; (größer) airport; **Flug|pra|xis** F flying experience; **Flug|preis** M air fare; **Flug|prü|fung** F examination for one's pilot's licence (Brit) or license (US); **Flug|rei|se** F flight; **eine ~ machen** to travel by air; **Flug|rei|sen|de(r)** MF decl as adj (airline) passenger; **Flug|rich|tung** F direction of flight; **die ~ än|dern** to change one's flight course; **Flug|rou|te** F air route

flugs [flʊks] ADV without delay, speedily

Flug-: Flug|sand M drifting sand; **Flug|sau|ri|er** M pterodactyl; **die ~** the Pterosauria; **Flug|schan|ze** F (Sport) ski jump; **Flug|schau** F air or flying display; **Flug|schein** M **a** pilot's licence (Brit) or license (US) **b** (= Flugticket) plane or air ticket; **Flug|schnei|se** F flight path; **Flug|schrei|ber** M flight recorder; **Flug|schrift** F pamphlet; **Flug|schü|ler(in)** M(F) trainee pilot; **Flug|si|cher|heit** F air safety; **Flug|si|cher|heits|be|hör|de** F air safety authority; **Flug|si|che|rung** F air traffic control; **Flug|si|mu|la|tor** M flight simulator; **Flug|sport** M flying, aviation; **Flug|staub** M flue dust; **Flug|steig** M gate; **Flug|stre|cke** F **a** flying distance; **eine große ~ zurücklegen** to fly a long distance **b** (= Route) route; **Flug|stun|de** F **a** flying hour; **zehn ~n entfernt** ten hours away by air **b** (= Unterricht) flying lesson; **flug|taug|lich** ADJ Pilot fit to fly; Flugzeug airworthy; **Flug|taug|lich|keit** F (von Pilot) fitness to fly; (von Flugzeug) airworthiness; **Flug|tech|nik** F **a** aircraft engineering (b = Flugfertigkeit) flying technique; **flug|tech|nisch** ADJ aeronautical; Bedeutung, Entwicklung, Prinzipien auch aerotechnical; Erfahrung, Fehler flying attr; **eine ~e Ausbildung haben** to have been trained in flying ADV from an aeronautical point of view; **~ ist er perfekt** his flying is perfect; **Flug|ti|cket** NT plane ticket; **Flug|tou|ris|tik** F holiday (esp Brit) or vacation (US) air travel; **flug|tüch|tig** ADJ airworthy; **Flug|tüch|tig|keit** F airworthiness; **flug|un|fä|hig** ADJ unable to fly; Flugzeug (= nicht in Ordnung) not airworthy; **flug|un|taug|lich** ADJ Pilot unfit to fly; Flugzeug not airworthy; **Flug|un|taug|lich|keit** F (von Pilot) unfitness to fly; (von Flugzeug) lack of airworthiness; **Flug|un|ter|bre|chung** F stop; (mit Übernachtung auch) stopover; **flug|un|tüch|tig** ADJ not airworthy; **Flug|ver|an|stal|tung** F air display or show; **Flug|ver|bin|dung** F air connection; **es gibt auch eine ~** there are flights there too; **Flug|ver|bot** NT flying ban; **nachts besteht ~ auf dem Flughafen** the airport is closed to air traffic at night; **ein ~ erlassen** to ground; (über bestimmten Gebieten) to ban from flying; **Flug|ver|kehr** M air traffic; **Flug|ver|such** M attempt to fly or at flight; **Flug|warn|dienst** M (Mil) enemy aircraft warning service; **Flug|we|sen** NT , no pl aviation no art; (mit Ballons etc) aeronautics sing, no art; **Flug|wet|ter** NT flying weather; **Flug|zeit** F flying time; **Flug|zet|tel** M (Aus) leaflet; (= Werbung auch) handbill

Flug|zeug NT pl **-zeuge** plane, aircraft, aeroplane (Brit), airplane (US); (= Düsenflugzeug auch) jet; (= Segelflugzeug) glider; **im** or **mit dem** or **per ~** by air or plane; **ein ~ der Lufthansa** a Lufthansa plane/jet

Flug|zeug- in cpds aircraft; **Flug|zeug|ab|sturz** M plane or air crash; **Flug|zeug|ab|wehr** F (Mil) air defence (Brit) or defense (US); **Flug|zeug|bau** M , no pl aircraft construction no art; **Flug|zeug|be|sat|zung** F air or plane crew; **Flug|zeug|ent|füh|rer(in)** M(F) (aircraft) hijacker, skyjacker; **Flug|zeug|ent|füh|rung** F (aircraft) hijacking, skyjacking; **Flug|zeug|füh|rer(in)** M(F) (aircraft) pilot; **Flug|zeug|hal|le** F (aircraft) hangar; **Flug|zeug|ka|ta|stro|phe** F air disaster; **Flug|zeug|mo|dell** NT model plane; **Flug|zeug|park** M fleet of aircraft; **Flug|zeug|rumpf** M fuselage; **Flug|zeug|schleu|der** F catapult; **Flug|zeug|start** M aeroplane (Brit) or airplane (US) takeoff; **Flug|zeug|trä|ger** M aircraft carrier; **Flug|zeug|typ** M model of aircraft; **Flug|zeug|un|glück** NT plane or air crash; **Flug|zeug|ver|band** M (Mil) aircraft formation; **Flug|zeug|wrack** NT wreckage of a/the plane

Flug|ziel NT destination

Flu|i|dum ['fluːidʊm] NT pl **-s, Fluida** [-da] **a** (fig) aura; (von Städten, Orten) atmosphere; **von ihr ging ein geheimnisvolles ~ aus** she was surrounded by an aura of mystery **b** (Chem) fluid

Fluk|tu|a|ti|on [flʊktuaˈtsi̯oːn] F -, **-en** fluctuation (+gen in)

fluk|tu|ie|ren [flʊktuˈiːrən] ptp **fluktuiert** VI to fluctuate

Flun|der ['flʊndɐ] F -, **-n** flounder; **da war ich platt wie eine ~** (inf) you could have knocked me down with a feather (inf)

Flun|ke|rei [flʊŋkəˈrai] F -, **-en** **a** no pl (= Flunkern) storytelling **b** (= kleine Lüge) story

Flun|ke|rer ['flʊŋkərɐ] M -s, -, **Flun|ke|rin** [-ərɪn] F -, **-nen** (inf) storyteller

flun|kern ['flʊŋkɐn] (inf) VI to tell stories VT to make up

Flunsch [flʊnʃ] M OR F -(e)s, -e (inf) pout; **ei|ne(n) ~ ziehen** or **machen** to pout

Flu|or¹ ['fluːoːɐ] M , no pl (abbr **F**) fluorine; (= Fluorverbindung) fluoride

Flu|or² M -s, no pl (Med) (vaginal) discharge

Flu|or|chlor|koh|len|was|ser|stoff M chlorofluorocarbon

Flu|o|res|zenz [fluores'tsɛnts] F -, no pl fluorescence

Flu|o|res|zenz|far|be F luminous paint

flu|o|res|zie|ren [fluores'tsiːrən] ptp **fluoresziert** VI to be luminous, to fluoresce (form)

Flu|o|rid [fluoˈriːt] NT -(e)s, -e [-də] (Chem) fluoride

Flu|o|rit [fluoˈriːt] M -s, -e fluorspar, fluorite (US)

Flu|or|koh|len|was|ser|stoff M fluorocarbon

Flur¹ [fluːɐ] M -(e)s, -e corridor; (= Hausflur) hall

Flur² F -, **-en** (liter) (= unbewaldetes Land) open fields pl; (= Wiese) meadow, mead (poet); (Agr) agricultural land of a community **durch Wald/Feld und ~** through woods/fields and meadows; **allein auf weiter ~ stehen** (fig) to be out on a limb

Flur-: Flur|be|leuch|tung F corridor light/lights pl; (von Hausflur) hall light/lights pl; **Flur|be|rei|ni|gung** F reparcelling of the agricultural land of a community; **Flur|fens|ter** NT corridor window; (von Hausflur) hall window; **Flur|form** F layout of the agricultural land of a community; **Flur|gar|de|ro|be** F hall stand; **Flur|gren|ze** F boundary of village lands; **Flur|licht** NT corridor light; (von Hausflur) hall light; **Flur|na|me** M field-name; **Flur|scha|den** M damage to an agricultural area (fig) damage; **Flur|toi|let|te** F toilet on the landing; **Flur|tür** F door to the corridor, hall door

Flu|se ['fluːzə] F -, -n bit of fluff; (= *Wollfluse*) bobble; **~n** fluff; bobbles

Fluss ▲ [flʊs] M -es, ⸗e ['flʏsə] **a** (= *Gewässer*) river; **am ~** by the river; *Stadt* on the river; **unten an ~** down by the river(side); **den ~ aufwärts/abwärts fahren** to go upstream or upriver/downstream or downriver

b no pl (*Tech*: = *Schmelzfluss*) molten mass; **im ~ sein** to be molten

c (= *kontinuierlicher Verlauf: von Verkehr, Rede, Strom, Elektronen*) flow; (*von Verhandlungen auch*) continuity; **etw in ~** (*acc*) **bringen** to get sth moving or going; **etw kommt or gerät in ~** sth gets underway or going; (= *sich verändern*) sth moves into a state of flux; **im ~ sein** (= *sich verändern*) to be in a state of flux; (= *im Gange sein*) to be in progress, to be going on

Fluss- ▲ in cpds river; **Fluss|aal** ▲ M common eel; **fluss|ab(wärts)** ▲ [flʊsˈlap(vɛrts)] ADV downstream, downriver; **Fluss|arm** ▲ M arm of a/the river; **fluss|auf|wärts** ▲ [flʊsˈlaufvɛrts] ADV upstream, upriver; **Fluss|bau** ▲ M pl -bauten river control no art, no pl; **Fluss|bett** ▲ NT riverbed; **Fluss|bie|gung** ▲ F bend in the river

Flüss|chen ▲ ['flʏsçən] NT -s, - little river

Fluss-: Fluss|dia|gramm ▲ NT flow chart or diagram; **Fluss|ebe|ne** ▲ F fluvial plain; **Fluss|fisch** ▲ M river or freshwater fish; **Fluss|ge|biet** ▲ NT river basin; **Fluss|ge|fäl|le** ▲ NT gradient of a/the river; **Fluss|ge|schie|be** ▲ NT silt; **Fluss|ha|fen** ▲ M river port

flüs|sig ['flʏsɪç] ADJ **a** (= *nicht fest*) liquid; *Honig, Lack* runny; (= *geschmolzen*) *Glas, Metall* molten; *Butter* melted; **~e Nahrung** liquids pl, liquid food; **~ machen** to liquefy; *Glas, Metall, Wachs, Fett* to melt; **~ werden** to turn or become liquid, to liquefy; (*Lack*) to become runny; (*Glas, Metall*) to become molten; (*Wachs, Fett*) to melt

b (= *fließend*) *Stil, Spiel* flowing, fluid; **die Polizei meldete ~en Verkehr** the police reported that the traffic was flowing smoothly; **den Verkehr ~ halten** to keep the traffic flowing

c (= *verfügbar*) *Geld* available; **~es Vermögen** liquid assets pl; **ich bin im Moment nicht ~** (*inf*) I'm out of funds at the moment; **wenn ich wieder ~ bin** when I'm in funds again

ADV **a** **~ ernährt werden** to be fed on liquids **b** (= *fließend*) fluently; **~ lesen/schreiben/sprechen** to read/write/talk fluently

Flüs|sig|gas NT liquid gas

Flüs|sig|keit F -, -en **a** (= *flüssiger Stoff*) liquid **b** no pl (von Metall, Glas, Wachs etc) liquidity; (*von Geldern*) availability; (*von Stil*) fluidity

Flüs|sig|keits-: Flüs|sig|keits|auf|nah|me F fluid or liquid intake; **Flüs|sig|keits|be|darf** M fluid requirement; **Flüs|sig|keits|maß** NT liquid measure; **Flüs|sig|keits|men|ge** F quantity or amount of liquid

Flüs|sig-: Flüs|sig|kris|tall M liquid crystal; **Flüs|sig|kris|tall|an|zei|ge** F liquid-crystal display, LCD; **flüs|sig ma|chen** ▲ VT to realize; (= *in Geld umwandeln auch*) to convert (into cash); **Flüs|sig|spreng|stoff** M liquid explosive

Fluss-: Fluss|krebs ▲ M crayfish (*Brit*), crawfish (*US*); **Fluss|land|schaft** ▲ F countryside by a/the river; (*Art*) riverscape; **Fluss|lauf** ▲ M course of a/the river; **Fluss|mün|dung** ▲ F river mouth; (*von Gezeitenfluss*) estuary; **Fluss|nie|de|rung** ▲ F fluvial plain; **Fluss|ni|xe** ▲ F river sprite; **Fluss|pferd** ▲ NT hippopotamus; **Fluss|re|ge|lung** ▲ F, **Fluss|re|gu|lie|rung** ▲ F river control no art, no pl; **Fluss|sand** ▲ M river or fluvial sand; **Fluss|schiff** ▲ NT river boat; **Fluss|schiff|fahrt** ▲ F, no pl river navigation; (= *Verkehr*) river traffic; **Fluss|spat** ▲ M fluorspar, fluorite (*US*); **Fluss|stahl** ▲ M ingot steel; **Fluss|ufer** ▲ NT river bank

Flüs|ter-: Flüs|ter|ga|le|rie F , **Flüs|ter|ge|wöl|be** NT whispering gallery; **Flüs|ter|kam|pag|ne** F whispering campaign; **Flüs|ter|laut** M whisper

flüs|tern ['flʏstɐn] VTI to whisper; (= *etwas lauter tuscheln*) to mutter; **jdm etw ins Ohr ~** to whisper sth in sb's ear; **sich ~d unterhalten** to talk in whispers; **miteinander ~** to whisper together; **wer hat da geflüstert?** who was that whispering?; **das kann ich dir ~** (*inf*) take it from me (*inf*); (*Zustimmung heischend auch*) I can tell you (*inf*); **dem werde ich was ~** (*inf*) I'll tell him a thing or two (*inf*)

Flüs|ter-: Flüs|ter|pa|ro|le F rumour (*Brit*), rumor (*US*), whisper (*inf*); **Flüs|ter|pro|pa|gan|da** F underground rumours (*Brit*) or rumors (*US*) pl; **Flüs|ter|stim|me** F whisper; **mit ~ sprechen** to talk in a whisper or in whispers; **Flüs|ter|ton** M , no pl whisper; **sich im ~ unterhalten** to talk in whispers; **Flüs|ter|tü|te** F (*hum*) megaphone

Flut [fluːt] F -, -en **a** (= *ansteigender Wasserstand*) incoming or flood tide; (= *angestiegener Wasserstand*) high tide; **es ist ~** the tide is coming in; it's high tide, the tide's in; **die ~ kommt or steigt** (*form*) the tide's coming in or rising; **bei ~ baden** to swim when the tide is coming in/at high tide; **bei ~ einlaufen** to come in on the tide/at high tide; **mit der ~** with the tide or flood tide (*spec*); **die ~ tritt um 16.30 Uhr ein** the tide starts to come in or turns at 4.30 p.m.; **die ~ geht zurück** the tide has started to go out, the tide has turned → Ebbe a

b usu pl (= *Wassermasse*) waters pl; **sich in die kühlen ~en stürzen** (*hum*) to plunge into the water

c (*fig*: = *Menge*) flood; **eine ~ von Tränen** floods of tears

flu|ten ['fluːtn] VI aux sein (*geh*) (*Wasser, Licht*) to flood, to stream, to pour; (*Verkehr*) to stream, to pour; (*Musik*) to flood, to pour; **~des Licht** streaming light VT (*Naut*) to flood

Flut-: Flut|ha|fen M tidal harbour (*Brit*) or harbor (*US*); **Flut|ka|ta|stro|phe** F flood disaster; **Flut|kraft|werk** NT tidal power plant or station; **Flut|licht** NT floodlight

Flut|licht-: Flut|licht|an|la|ge F floodlights pl, floodlighting; **Flut|licht|spiel** NT match played by floodlight, floodlit match

flut|schen ['flʊtʃn] VI (*inf*) **a** aux sein (*N Ger*: = *rutschen*) to slide **b** (= *funktionieren*) to go smoothly or well or swimmingly (*dated inf*)

Flut-: Flut|tor NT floodgate; **Flut|ven|til** NT antiflood valve; **Flut|wel|le** F tidal wave

fl. W. abbr von **fließendes Wasser**

focht pret von **fechten**

Fock [fɔk] F -, -en (*Naut*) foresail

Fock-: Fock|mast M foremast; **Fock|rah** F , **Fock|ra|he** F foreyard; **Fock|se|gel** NT foresail

fö|de|ral [fødeˈraːl] ADJ federal

Fö|de|ra|lis|mus [føderaˈlɪsmʊs] M -, no pl federalism

Fö|de|ra|list [føderaˈlɪst] M -en, -en, **Fö|de|ra|lis|tin** [-ˈlɪstɪn] F -, -nen federalist

fö|de|ra|lis|tisch [føderaˈlɪstɪʃ] ADJ federalist

Fö|de|ra|ti|on [føderaˈtsi̯oːn] F -, -en federation

fö|de|ra|tiv [føderaˈtiːf] ADJ federal

fö|de|rie|ren [fødeˈriːrən] ptp **föderiert** VR to federate; **föderierte Staaten** federated states

foh|len ['foːlən] VI to foal

Foh|len ['foːlən] NT -s, - foal; (*männliches Pferd auch*) colt; (*weibliches Pferd auch*) filly

Föhn [føːn] M -(e)s, -e **a** (= *Wind*) foehn, föhn; **wir haben ~** the foehn is blowing **b** ▲ (= *Haartrockner*) hairdryer

föh|nen [ˈføːnən] VT to dry

Föhn|fri|sur F blow-dried hair

föh|nig [ˈføːnɪç] ADJ foehn attr; **es ist ~** there's a foehn (wind)

Föh|re [ˈføːrə] F -, -n Scots pine (tree)

fo|kal [foˈkaːl] ADJ focal

Fo|kus [ˈfoːkʊs] M -, -se focus

fo|kus|sie|ren [fokuˈsiːrən] ptp **fokussiert** VTI to focus

Fol|ge [ˈfɔlgə] F -, -n **a** (= *Reihenfolge*) order; (= *Aufeinanderfolge*) succession; (= *zusammengehörige Reihe, Math*) sequence; (*Cards*) run, sequence; (= *Lieferung einer Zeitschrift*) issue; (= *Fortsetzung*) instalment; (*TV, Rad*) episode; (= *Serie*) series; **in chronologischer/zwangloser ~** in chronological/no particular order; **in rascher/dichter ~** in rapid or quick/close succession; **Musik in bunter ~** a musical potpourri; **in der or für die ~** (*form*: = *in Zukunft*) in future

b (= *Ergebnis*) consequence; (= *unmittelbare Folge*) result; (= *Auswirkung*) effect; **als ~ davon** in consequence, as a result (of that); **dies hatte zur ~, dass ...** the consequence or result of this was that ...; **dies hatte seine Entlassung zur ~** this resulted in his dismissal or in his being dismissed; **bedenke die ~n!** think of the consequences!; **die ~n werden nicht ausbleiben** there will be repercussions; **die ~n für den Tourismus** the effect on tourism, the consequences for tourism; **für die ~n aufkommen** to take the consequences; **an den ~n eines Unfalls/einer Krankheit sterben** to die as a result of an accident/illness; **das wird ~n haben** that will have serious consequences; **ohne ~n bleiben** to have no consequences; **ihr Verhältnis blieb nicht ohne ~n** (*euph*) their relationship was not exactly unfruitful

c (*form*) **einem Befehl ~ leisten** to comply with or obey an order; **einer Einladung** (*dat*) **~ leisten** to accept an invitation

Folge-: Folge|ein|rich|tung F facility or utility (*US*) for the community; **Fol|ge|er|schei|nung** F result, consequence; **Fol|ge|kos|ten** PL subsequent costs pl; **Fol|ge|las|ten** PL resultant costs pl

fol|gen [ˈfɔlgn] VI aux sein **a** (= *kommen nach*) to follow (*jdm/einer Sache* sb/sth); **auf etw** (*acc*) **~** to follow sth, to come after sth; **auf jdn (im Rang) ~** to come or rank after sb; **~ Sie mir (bitte/unauffällig)!** come with me please; **es folgt nun or nun folgt ein Konzert** we now have a concert, a concert now follows; **... dann ~ die Meldungen im Einzelnen** ... followed by the news in detail; **dem** (*liter*) **auf den Frühling folgt der Sommer** spring is followed by summer; **Fortsetzung folgt** (to be) continued; **wie folgt** as follows → Tod

b (= *verstehen*) to follow (*jdm/einer Sache* sb/sth); **können Sie mir ~?** are you with me? (*inf*), do you follow (me)?

c (= *gehorchen*) to do as or what one is told; **einem Befehl/einer Anordnung ~** to follow an order/instruction; **jdm ~** (*inf*) to do what sb tells one

d +dat (= *sich richten nach*) einer Mode, einem Vorschlag to follow; **jdm ~** to agree with, to go along with (*inf*)

e (= *hervorgehen*) to follow (*aus* from); **was folgt daraus für die Zukunft?** what are the consequences of this for the future?

fol|gend ADJ following; **Folgendes** the following; **er schreibt Folgendes or das Folgende** he writes (as follows or the following); **im Folgenden** in the following; (*schriftlich auch*) below; **es handelt sich um Folgendes** it's like this; (*schriftlich*) it concerns the following

fol|gen|der|ma|ßen [ˈfɔlgndɐˈmaːsn], **fol|gen|der|wei|se** [ˈfɔlgndɐˈvaɪzə] (*rare*) ADV like this, as follows; **wir werden das ~ machen** we'll do it like this or in the following way

Folgen-: fol|gen|los ADJ without consequences; (= *wirkungslos*) ineffective; **~ bleiben** not to have any consequences; to be ineffective; **das konnte nicht ~ bleiben** that was bound to have serious consequences/could not fail to be effective; **fol|gen|reich** ADJ (= *bedeutsam*) momentous; (= *folgenschwer*) serious;

(= *wirkungsvoll*) effective; **fol|gen|schwer** ADJ serious; **die Maßnahme erwies sich als ~** the measure had serious consequences; **Fol|gen|schwe|re** F seriousness

Fol|ge-: Fol|ge|prob|lem NT resultant problem; **die ~e einer Sache** (*gen*) the problems arising from or out of sth; **fol|ge|recht** (*rare*), **fol|ge|rich|tig** ADJ (logically) consistent; **das einzig Folgerichtige in dieser Situation** the only logical or consistent thing to do in this situation; **Fol|ge|rich|tig|keit** F logical consistency

fol|gern ['fɔlɡɐn] VT to conclude; **aus diesem Brief lässt sich ~, dass ...** it can be concluded or we can conclude from this letter that ... VI to draw a/the conclusion; **logisch ~ lernen** to learn to think logically

Fol|ge|rung ['fɔlɡərʊŋ] F -, -en conclusion; **daraus ergibt sich die ~, dass ...** from this it can be concluded that ...

Fol|ge-: Fol|ge|satz M (*Gram*) consecutive clause; **Fol|ge|ton|horn** NT (*Aus*) = **Martinshorn**; **fol|ge|wid|rig** ADJ (*geh*) logically inconsistent; **Fol|ge|wid|rig|keit** F (*geh*) logical inconsistency; **Fol|ge|wir|kung** F consequence, effect; **eine ~ war ...** one effect or result (it had) was ...; **Fol|ge|zeit** F following period, period following

folg|lich ['fɔlklɪç] ADV, CONJ consequently, therefore

folg|sam ['fɔlkzaːm] ADJ obedient

Folg|sam|keit F -, *no pl* obedience

Fo|li|ant [fo'liant] M -en, -en folio (volume); (= *dicker Band*) tome

Fo|lie ['foːliə] F -, -n a (= *Plastikfolie*) film; (*für Projektor*) transparency; (= *Metallfolie, Typ, Cook*) foil; (= *Schicht*) layer of film/foil; **eine ~ aus Kupfer** a thin layer of copper b (*fig* = *Hintergrund*) background; **etw als ~ benutzen** to use sth as a model

Fo|li|en *pl von* **Folie** *von* **Folio**

Fo|li|en-: Fo|li|en|kar|tof|fel F (*Cook*) jacket (*Brit*) or baked (*US*) potato (*baked in foil*); **Fo|li|en|schrei|ber** M marker pen (*for overhead projector transparencies*); **fo|li|en|ver|packt** ADJ wrapped in foil; (*in Alufolie*) aluminium-wrapped (*Brit*), aluminum-wrapped (*US*); (*in Plastikfolie*) wrapped in cling film (*Brit*), plastic-wrapped (*US*)

Fo|lio ['foːlio] NT -s, -s or **Folien** [-liən] folio

Folk|lo|re [fɔlk'loːrə, 'fɔlkloːrə] F -, *no pl* folklore; (= *Volksmusik*) folk music

Folk|lo|rist [fɔlklo'rɪst] M -en, -en, **Folk|lo|ris|tin** [-'rɪstɪn] F -, -nen folklorist

folk|lo|ris|tisch [fɔlklo'rɪstɪʃ] ADJ folkloric; *Kleidung* ethnic; **~e Musik** folk music

Folk-: Folk|sän|ger ['fɔːk-]**(in)** M(F) folk singer; **Folk|song** ['fɔːk-] M (*Mus*) folk song

Fol|li|kel ['fɔlikl] M -s, - follicle

Fol|li|kel|sprung M ovulation

Fol|säu|re ['foːl-] F, *no pl* (*Chem*) folic acid

Fol|ter ['fɔltə] F -, -n a (*lit, fig*) torture; (*fig auch*) torment; **die ~ anwenden** to use torture b (*old:* = *Folterbank*) rack; **jdn auf die ~ spannen** (*fig*) to keep sb on tenterhooks, to keep sb in an agony of suspense

Fol|ter|bank F *pl* -**bänke** rack

Fol|te|rer ['fɔltərə] M -s, -, **Fol|te|rin** [-ərɪn] F -, -nen torturer

Fol|ter-: Fol|ter|ge|rät NT, **Fol|ter|in|stru|ment** NT instrument of torture; **Fol|ter|kam|mer** F, **Fol|ter|kel|ler** M torture chamber; **Fol|ter|knecht** M torturer; **Fol|ter|me|tho|de** F method of torture

fol|tern ['fɔltɐn] VT to torture; (= *quälen auch*) to torment; **jdn ~ lassen** to have sb tortured VI to use torture

Fol|ter|qual F (*lit*) agony of torture; (*fig*) agony of torment

Fol|te|rung ['fɔltərʊŋ] F -, -en torture

Fol|ter|werk|zeug NT instrument of torture

Fon¹ ▲ [foːn] M NT -s, -s = **Phon**

Fon² [foːn] *abbr von* **Telefon** Tel

Fön® [føːn] M -(e)s, -e hairdryer → *auch* **Föhn** b

Fond [fõː] M -s, -s a (*geh:* = *Wagenfond*) back, rear b (= *Hintergrund*) (*Art*) background; (*Tex*) (back)ground; **im ~ der Bühne** (*Theat*) at the back of the stage c (*geh:* = *Basis*) foundation (*zu* for) d (*Cook:* = *Fleischsaft*) meat juices *pl*

Fon|dant [fõ'dãː] M OR (AUS) NT -s, -s (*Cook*) fondant

Fonds [fõː] M -, - a (= *Geldreserve, fig geh*) fund; **keinen ~ für etw haben** to have no funds for sth b (*Fin:* = *Schuldverschreibung*) government bond

Fonds|bör|se ['fõː-] F , **Fonds|ge|schäft** NT (*Fin*) market of government bonds

Fon|due [fõ'dyː] NT -s, -s or F -, -s fondue

fö|nen △ ['føːnən] VT → **föhnen**

Fön|fri|sur △ F → **Föhnfrisur**

Fo|no- ▲ ['foːno-, foːno-] → **Phono-**

Font M (*Comput*) font

Fon|tä|ne [fɔn'tɛːnə] F -, -n jet, fount (*poet*); (*geh:* = *Springbrunnen*) fountain, fount (*poet*)

Fon|ta|nel|le [fɔnta'nɛlə] F -, -n (*Anat*) fontanelle

fop|pen ['fɔpn] VT (*inf*) **jdn ~** to make a fool of sb; (= *necken*) to pull sb's leg (*inf*); **er fühlte sich gefoppt** he felt he'd been made a fool of

Fop|pe|rei [fɔpə'rai] F -, -en (*inf*) leg-pulling *no pl* (*inf*)

Fo|ra (*Hist*) *pl von* **Forum**

for|cie|ren [fɔr'siːrən] *ptp* **forciert** VT to push; *Entwicklung auch, Tempo* to force; *Konsum, Produktion* to push or force up; **seine Anstrengungen ~** to increase one's efforts

for|ciert [fɔr'siːɐt] ADJ forced

För|de ['fœrdə] F -, -n firth (*esp Scot*), *narrow coastal inlet*

För|der-: För|der|an|la|ge F conveyor; **För|der|band** [-bant] NT *pl* -**bänder** conveyor belt; **För|der|be|trag** M (*Univ*) grant; **För|der|be|trieb** M (*Min*) production; **den ~ aufnehmen** to start production

För|de|rer ['fœrdərə] M -s, -, **För|de|rin** [-ərɪn] F -, -nen sponsor; (= *Gönner*) patron

För|der-: För|der|gel|der PL grants *pl*, funding *sing*; **För|der|klas|se** F (*Sch*) special class; **För|der|koh|le** F run of mine (coal), through-and-through coal (*Brit*); **För|der|korb** M mine cage; **För|der|kreis** M **~ für ...** society for the promotion of ...; **För|der|kurs** M , **För|der|kur|sus** M (*Sch*) special classes *pl*; **För|der|land** NT producing country; **För|der|leis|tung** F output

för|der|lich ['fœrdəlɪç] ADJ beneficial (+*dat* to); **guten Beziehungen ~ sein** to be conducive to good relations; **der Krebsbekämpfung ~ sein** to help in the fight against cancer; **ein der Weiterbildung ~er Kursus** a course which contributes to one's further education

För|der-: För|der|ma|schi|ne F winding engine; **För|der|men|ge** F output; **För|der|mit|tel** PL aid *sing*; **for|dern** ['fɔrdn] VT a (= *verlangen*) to demand; *Preis* to ask; (*in Appell, Aufrufen etc,* = *erfordern*) to call for; (= *Anspruch erheben auf*) *Entschädigung, Lohnerhöhung* to claim; **viel/zu viel von jdm ~** to ask or demand a lot/too much of sb, to make too many demands on sb → **Rechenschaft** b (*fig:* = *kosten*) *Menschenleben, Opfer* to claim c (*lit, fig:* = *herausfordern*) to challenge; **er ist noch nie im Leben richtig gefordert worden** he has never been faced with a real challenge d (*Sport*) to make demands on; (= *das Äußerste abverlangen*) to stretch VI to make demands; **er fordert nur, ohne selbst zu geben** he demands everything as a right, without giving anything himself; **för|dern** ['fœrdn] VT a (= *unterstützen*) *Handel, Projekt, Entwicklung, Arbeit, Kunst, Wissenschaft*

to support; (= *propagieren*) to promote; (*finanziell*) *bestimmtes Projekt* to sponsor; *Nachwuchs, Künstler* to support, to help; *jds Talent, Kunstverständnis, Neigung* to encourage, to foster; (= *voranbringen*) *Freundschaft, Frieden* to foster, to promote; *Verdauung* to aid; *Appetit* to stimulate; *Untersuchung, Wahrheitsfindung* to further; **jdn beruflich ~** to help sb in his career b (= *steigern*) *Wachstum* to promote; *Umsatz, Absatz, Produktion, Verbrauch* to boost, to increase c *Bodenschätze* to extract; *Kohle, Erz* to mine; **för|dernd** ADJ *Verhalten, Ruf* imperious; *Persönlichkeit, Aufgabe* demanding

För|der-: För|der|platt|form F (*Min*) production platform; **För|der|quo|te** F (*Min*) production level; **För|der|schacht** M (*Min*) winding shaft; **För|der|schu|le** F (*Sch*) special school; **För|der|seil** NT (*Min*) winding rope; **För|der|soh|le** F (*Min*) haulage level; **För|der|staa|ten** PL (*Min*) producing countries *pl*; **För|der|stu|fe** F (*Sch*) mixed ability class(es) *intended to foster the particular talents of each pupil*; **För|der|turm** M (*Min*) winding tower; (*auf Bohrstelle*) derrick

For|de|rung ['fɔrdərʊŋ] F -, -en a (= *Verlangen*) demand (*nach* for); (= *Lohnforderung, Entschädigungsforderung etc*) claim (*nach* for); (*in Appell, Aufrufen etc*) call (*nach* for); **~en an jdn stellen** to make demands on sb; **hohe ~en an jdn stellen** to demand a lot of sb; **eine ~ nach etw erheben** to call for sth; **jds ~ erfüllen** to meet sb's demand/claim b (*geh:* = *Erfordernis*) requirement c (*Comm:* = *Anspruch*) claim (*an* +*acc, gegen* on, against); **eine ~ einklagen** to sue for payment of a debt; **eine ~ eintreiben** or **einziehen** to collect a debt d (= *Herausforderung*) challenge

För|de|rung ['fœrdərʊŋ] F -, -en a (= *Unterstützung*) support; (*finanziell*) sponsorship; (*von Nachwuchs, Künstler*) support, help; (*von Talent*) encouragement, fostering; (*von Freundschaft, Frieden*) fostering, promotion; (*von Verdauung*) aid (*gen* to); (*von Appetit*) stimulation; **Maßnahmen zur ~ des Fremdenverkehrs** measures to promote tourism or for the promotion of tourism b (*inf:* = *Förderungsbetrag*) grant c (= *Gewinnung*) extraction; (*von Kohle, Erz auch*) mining

For|de|rungs|ab|tre|tung F (*Jur*) assignment of a claim

För|de|rungs-: För|de|rungs|maß|nah|me F supportive measure; **För|de|rungs|maß|nah|men** PL assistance *sing*; **För|de|rungs|mit|tel** PL aid *sing*; **För|de|rungs|pro|gramm** NT aid programme (*Brit*) or program (*US*); **för|de|rungs|wür|dig** ADJ deserving support; **För|de|rungs|wür|dig|keit** F **wir waren von der ~ des Projekts nicht überzeugt** we were not convinced that the project deserved support

För|der|un|ter|richt M special instruction

För|der|wa|gen M (*Min*) tram, mine car

Fo|rel|le [fo'rɛlə] F -, -n trout → **blau**

Fo|rel|len-: Fo|rel|len|teich M trout hatchery; **Fo|rel|len|zucht** F trout farming; (= *Anlage*) trout farm

Fo|ren *pl von* **Forum**

fo|ren|sisch [fo'rɛnzɪʃ] ADJ *Medizin, Psychologie, Gutachten* forensic; (*old:* = *rhetorisch*) oratorical

For|ke ['fɔrkə] F -, -n (*N Ger*) pitch fork

Form [fɔrm] F -, -en a form; (= *Gestalt, Umriss*) shape; **in ~ von Regen/Steuerermäßigungen** in the form of rain/tax reductions; **in ~ von Dragees/Salbe** in pill/cream form, in the form of pills/cream; **in ~ eines Dreiecks** shaped like a triangle, in the shape of a triangle; **eine bestimmte ~ haben** to be in a certain form; to be a certain shape; **seine ~ verlieren, aus der ~ geraten** to lose its shape; (*Kleidung auch*) to go out of shape; **einer Sache** (*dat*) **~ (und Gestalt) geben** to give sth form; (*fig*) to give sth a coherent shape; **Sie müssen Ihr Gesuch in die geeignete ~ kleiden** your application must be in the proper form; **feste ~ annehmen** (fig) to take shape; **hässliche/gewalttätige ~en annehmen** (fig) to become ugly/violent; **(weibliche) ~en** feminine figure → **bringen e** **b** (= Gestaltung) form; **~ und Inhalt** form and content **c** **Formen** PL (= Umgangsformen) manners pl; **die ~ wahren** to observe the proprieties; **der ~ wegen** or **halber**, **um der ~ zu genügen** for form's sake, as a matter of form; **in aller ~** formally; **ein Mann mit/ohne ~en** a well-mannered/ill-mannered gentleman **d** (= Kondition) form; **in bester ~ sein** to be in great form or shape; **in ~ bleiben/kommen** to keep/get (oneself) fit or in condition; (Sportler) to keep/get in form; **hoch in ~** in great form or shape; **außer ~** out of condition **e** (= Gießform) mould (Brit), mold (US); (= Kuchenform, Backform) baking tin (Brit) or pan (US); (= Hutform, Schuhform) block

for|mal [fɔrˈmaːl] ADJ **a** formal; **~~ästhetisch** formal aesthetic **b** (= äußerlich) Besitzer, Fehler, Grund technical ADV **a** formally **b** (= äußerlich) technically

For|mal|aus|bil|dung F drill

For|mal|de|hyd [ˈfɔrmaldehyːt, fɔrmˈaldeˈhyːt] M -s, no pl formaldehyde

For|ma|lie [fɔrˈmaːliə] F -, -n usu pl formality; (= Äußerlichkeit) technicality

For|ma|lin® [fɔrmaˈliːn] NT -s, no pl formalin

for|ma|li|sie|ren [fɔrmaliˈziːrən] ptp **formalisiert** VT to formalize

For|ma|lis|mus [fɔrmaˈlɪsmʊs] M -, no pl formalism no pl

For|ma|list [fɔrmaˈlɪst] M -en, -en, **For|ma|lis|tin** [-ˈlɪstɪn] F -, -nen formalist

for|ma|lis|tisch [fɔrmaˈlɪstɪʃ] ADJ formalistic

For|ma|li|tät [fɔrmaliˈtɛːt] F -, -en formality; (= Äußerlichkeit) technicality; **alle ~en erledigen** to go through all the formalities

for|ma|li|ter [fɔrmaˈliːtɐ] ADV (geh) in form; (= äußerlich) technically

for|mal|ju|ris|tisch, **for|mal|recht|lich** ADJ technical

For|mans [ˈfɔrmans] NT -, **Formanzien** [fɔrˈmantsiən] or **Formantia** [fɔrˈmantsia] (Ling) formative (element)

For|mat [fɔrˈmaːt] NT -(e)s, -e **a** (= Größenverhältnis) size; (von Zeitung, Papierbogen, Fotografie, Film) format; (von Buch) trim size, trim (inf); **im ~ DIN A4** in A4 (format) **b** (= Rang, Persönlichkeit) stature **c** (fig: = Niveau) class (inf), quality; **internationales ~ haben** to be of international quality

for|ma|tie|ren [fɔrmaˈtiːrən] ptp **formatiert** VTI (Comput) to format

For|ma|tie|rung F -, -en (Comput) formatting

For|ma|ti|on [fɔrmaˈtsioːn] F -, -en formation; (= Gruppe) group

For|ma|tions|flug M (Mil) formation flying

for|ma|tiv [fɔrmaˈtiːf] ADJ formative

For|ma|tiv [fɔrmaˈtiːf] NT -s, -e [-və] (Ling) syntactic morpheme; (= Formans) formative (element)

For|mat|vor|la|ge F (Comput) style (sheet)

Form-: form|bar ADJ (lit, fig) malleable; **Form|bar|keit** [ˈfɔrmbaːɐkait] F -, no pl (lit, fig) malleability; **form|be|stän|dig** ADJ **a** **~ sein** to hold or retain its shape **b** (Sport) consistent in form; **Form|blatt** NT form; **Form|brief** M form letter

Förm|chen [ˈfœrmçən] NT -s, - (im Sandkasten) (plastic) mould (Brit) or mold (US); (Cook) baking dish

Form|ei|sen NT structural steel

For|mel [ˈfɔrml] F -, -n formula; (von Eid etc) wording; (= Floskel) set phrase; **etw auf eine ~ bringen** to reduce sth to a formula

For|mel-1-Ren|nen [fɔrml̩ˈʔains-] NT Formula-1 race

Form|ele|ment NT (esp Art) formal element, element of form

For|mel-: for|mel|haft ADJ **a** (= floskelhaft) Sprache, Stil stereotyped; **~e Wendung** set phrase **b** (= als Formel) formulistic ADV (= floskelhaft) sich ausdrücken, schreiben in clichés; **~ klingen** to sound clichéd; **~ reden** to talk in set phrases; **For|mel|haf|tig|keit** [ˈfɔrml̩haftɪçkait] F -, no pl (= formelhafte Art) stereotyped nature; (einer Wendung) setness

for|mell [fɔrˈmɛl] ADJ formal ADV (= offiziell) formally, officially; **als Bürgermeister musste er den Vorfall ~ verurteilen** as mayor he had to deplore the incident as a matter of form

For|mel-: For|mel|samm|lung F (Math) formulary; **For|mel|spra|che** F system of notation

for|men [ˈfɔrmən] VT to form, to shape; Charakter auch, Eisen to mould (Brit), to mold (US); Wörter to articulate; **schön geformte Glieder** beautifully shaped limbs; **der Krieg hat ihn geformt** the war shaped him or his character; **~de Kraft** formative power VR (lit) to form or shape itself; (fig) to mature

For|men-: For|men|fül|le F wealth of forms; **For|men|leh|re** F morphology; (Mus) theory of musical form; **for|men|reich** ADJ with a great variety or wealth of forms; **~ sein** to have a great variety or wealth of forms; **For|men|reich|tum** M wealth of forms; **For|men|sinn** M sense of form, feeling for form; **For|men|spra|che** F (geh) use of forms

For|mer [ˈfɔrmɐ] M -s, -, **For|me|rin** [-ərɪn] F -, -nen (Brit), molder (US)

For|me|rei [fɔrməˈrai] F -, -en moulding (Brit) or molding (US) shop

Form-: Form|feh|ler M irregularity; (gesellschaftlich) breach of etiquette; **Form|fleisch** NT pressed meat; **Form|ge|bung** [-geːbʊŋ] F -, -en (geh) design; **Form|ge|fühl** NT sense of form; **form|ge|recht** ADJ (lit, fig) correct, proper; **Form|ge|stal|ter(in)** M(F) (geh) designer; **Form|ge|stal|tung** F design; **form|ge|wandt** ADJ urbane, suave

for|mi|da|bel [fɔrmiˈdaːbl] ADJ (dated) formidable

for|mie|ren [fɔrˈmiːrən] ptp **formiert** VT Truppen to draw up; Kolonne, Zug to form (into), to fall into; (= bilden) to form VR to form up

For|mie|rung F -, -en formation; (Mil: von Truppen) drawing-up

-för|mig [fœrmɪç] ADJ suf -shaped; **sternförmig** star-shaped

Form|kri|se F (esp Sport) loss of form

förm|lich [ˈfœrmlɪç] ADJ **a** (= formell) formal **b** (= regelrecht) positive ADV **a** (= formell) formally **b** (= regelrecht) positively; **ich hätte ~ weinen können** I really could have cried

Förm|lich|keit F -, -en **a** no pl (von Benehmen) formality **b** usu pl (= Äußerlichkeit) social convention; **bitte keine ~en!** please don't stand on ceremony

form|los ADJ **a** (= ohne Form) shapeless; Vortrag, Aufsatz, Roman unstructured **b** (= zwanglos) informal, casual **c** (Admin) Antrag unaccompanied by a form/any forms

Form|lo|sig|keit F -, no pl **a** (= Gestaltlosigkeit) shapelessness, lack of shape; (von Vortrag, Aufsatz, Roman) lack of structure **b** (= Zwanglosigkeit) informality, casualness

Form-: Form|sa|che F matter of form, formality; **form|schön** ADJ elegant, elegantly proportioned; **Form|schön|heit** F elegant proportions pl, elegance; **Form|schwä|che** F poor form; **~n zeigen** to be in or on poor form; **Form|stren|ge** F strict observance of form; **Form|tief** NT loss of form; **sich in einem ~ befinden** to be badly off form; **form|treu** ADJ = formbeständig

For|mu|lar [fɔrmuˈlaːɐ] NT -s, -e form

For|mu|lar|vor|schub M (Comput) form feed

for|mu|lie|ren [fɔrmuˈliːrən] ptp **formuliert** VT to word, to phrase, to formulate; **... wenn ich es mal so ~ darf** ... if I might put it like that VI to use words skilfully (Brit) or skillfully (US); **..., wie der Kanzler formulierte** ... as the chancellor put it; **wenn ich mal so ~ darf** if I might put it like that

For|mu|lie|rung F -, -en wording, phrasing no pl, formulation

For|mung [ˈfɔrmʊŋ] F -, -en **a** no pl (= Formen) forming, shaping; (von Eisen) moulding (Brit), molding (US); (von Charakter) moulding (Brit), molding (US), shaping, formation; (von Wörtern) articulation; **zur ~ muss das Eisen erhitzt werden** the iron has to be heated before it can be moulded (Brit) or molded (US) **b** (= Form) shape; (von Felsen, Dünen etc auch) formation

Form-: Form|ver|än|de|rung F change in the form; (einer Sprache) change in the forms; (= Gestaltveränderung) change in the shape; **eine kleine ~ vornehmen** to make a small modification; **Form|ver|stoß** M breach of form; **form|voll|en|det** ADJ perfect; Vase etc perfectly shaped; Gedicht, Musikstück perfectly structured ADV **er verabschiedete/verneigte sich ~** he took his leave/bowed with perfect elegance; **Form|vor|schrift** F formal requirement; **form|wid|rig** ADJ incorrect; (Admin, Jur) irregular; Urkunde incorrectly drawn up; **Form|wil|le** M (geh) striving for form

forsch [fɔrʃ] ADJ brash; (dated: = schneidig) dashing (dated) ADV brashly; **eine Sache ~ anpacken** to attack sth energetically or with vigour (Brit) or vigor (US)

for|schen [ˈfɔrʃn] VI **a** (= suchen) to search (nach for), to seek (liter) (nach jdm/etw sb/sth); **in alten Papieren ~** to search in old papers; **nach der Wahrheit ~** to seek or search after truth **b** (= Forschung betreiben) to research; **über etw** (acc) **~** to research on or into sth VT (Sw) = erforschen b

for|schend ADJ Blick searching ADV searchingly; **etw ~ betrachten** to look at sth very closely; **jdn ~ ansehen** to look at sb searchingly, to give sb a searching look

For|scher [ˈfɔrʃɐ] M -s, -, **For|sche|rin** [-ərɪn] F -, -nen **a** (= Wissenschaftler) researcher; (in Medizin, Naturwissenschaften) research scientist **b** (= Forschungsreisender) explorer

For|scher-: For|scher|ar|beit F research; **For|scher|blick** M , no pl (geh) scientific eye; **For|scher|drang** M , no pl (geh) intellectual curiosity; (als Entdecker) urge to explore; **For|scher|geist** M (geh) inquiring mind; (= Entdeckungsreisender) explorer; (= Entdeckergeist) exploratory spirit; **der Mensch in seinem angeborenen ~ ist bestrebt, ...** man, with his inquiring mind, strives ...

For|sche|rin F → **Forscher**

for|sche|risch [ˈfɔrʃərɪʃ] ADJ research attr; Begeisterung for research; Ehrgeiz in the field of research; **eine ~e Höchstleistung** a triumph for research

Forsch|heit F -, -en brashness

For|schung [ˈfɔrʃʊŋ] F -, -en research no pl; **eingehende ~en** intensive research; **ältere/verschiedene ~en** older/various studies; **~en betreiben** to research, to be engaged in research **b** (= Wissenschaft) research no art; **~ und Lehre** research and teaching; **~ und Entwicklung** research and development, R&D

For|schungs- in cpds research; **For|schungs|ar|beit** F research; **For|schungs|auf|ga|be** F research assignment; (= Forschungsauftrag eines Wissenschaftlers) research duty; **For|schungs|auf|trag** M research assignment or contract; **For|schungs|bal|lon** M observation balloon; **For|schungs|be|reich** M = **Forschungsgebiet**; **For|schungs|be|richt** M research report; **For|schungs|drang** M exploratory urge; **For|schungs|er|geb|nis** NT result of the research; **neueste ~se** results of the latest research; **For|**

schungs|ge|biet NT field of research; **ein/das ~ der Medizin** a/the field of medical research; **For|schungs|ge|gen|stand** M object of research; **For|schungs|ge|mein|schaft** F research council; **For|schungs|me|tho|de** F method of research; **For|schungs|mi|nis|ter(in)** M(F) minister of science; **For|schungs|mi|nis|te|ri|um** NT ministry of research and development; **For|schungs|ob|jekt** NT object of research; **For|schungs|rei|se** F expedition; **For|schungs|rei|sen|de(r)** MF decl as adj explorer; **For|schungs|sa|tel|lit** M research satellite; **For|schungs|schiff** NT research vessel; **For|schungs|se|mes|ter** NT sabbatical term; **For|schungs|sta|ti|on** F research station; **For|schungs|sti|pen|di|um** NT research fellowship; **For|schungs|tä|tig|keit** F research no indef art; **For|schungs|vor|ha|ben** NT research project; **For|schungs|zent|rum** NT research centre (Brit) or center (US); **For|schungs|zweig** M branch of research; **For|schungs|zweck** M purpose of the or our etc research; **für ~e** pl, **zu ~en** pl for research purposes pl

Forst [fɔrst] M **-(e)s, -e(n)** forest

Forst-: Forst|aka|de|mie F school of forestry; **Forst|amt** NT forestry office; **Forst|as|ses|sor(in)** M(F) graduate forestry official who has completed the probationary period; **Forst|be|am|te(r)** M decl as adj, **Forst|be|am|tin** F forestry official

fors|ten ['fɔrstn] VT (form) to forest

Förs|ter ['fœrstə] M **-s, -**, **Förs|te|rin** [-ərɪn] F **-, -nen** forest warden or ranger (US)

Förs|te|rei [fœrstə'rai] F **-, -en** forest warden's or ranger's (US) lodge

Forst-: Forst|fre|vel M (Jur) offence (Brit) or offense (US) against the forest laws; **Forst|haus** NT forester's lodge; **Forst|meis|ter(in)** M(F) forestry commissioner, chief (forest) ranger (US); **Forst|recht** NT forest law; **Forst|re|vier** NT forestry district; **Forst|scha|den** M forest damage no pl; **Forst|schäd|ling** M forest pest; **Forst|schu|le** F school of forestry; **Forst|ver|wal|tung** F forestry commission; **Forst|we|sen** NT , no pl forestry no art; **Forst|wirt(in)** M(F) graduate in forestry; **Forst|wirt|schaft** F forestry; **forst|wirt|schaft|lich** ADJ forestry attr; **nach ~en Ge-sichtspunkten** from the point of view of good forestry management; **Forst|wis|sen|schaft** F forestry

For|sy|thie [fɔr'zy:tsiə, (Aus) fɔr'zy:tiə] F **-, -n** forsythia

fort [fɔrt] ADV **a** (= weg) away; (= verschwunden) gone; **~ mit ihm/damit!** away with him/it!, take him/it away!; **etw ist ~** sth has gone or disappeared; **es war plötzlich ~** it suddenly disappeared; **die Katze ist schon seit gestern ~** the cat has been missing since yesterday; **er ist ~** he has left or gone; (dial: = ist nicht zu Hause) he isn't here; **weit ~** far away, a long way away; **von zu Hause ~** away from home; **wann sind Sie von zu Hause ~?** (dial) when did you leave home?; **nur ~ von hier!** (geh) let us begone (old); **~ von hier!** (geh) begone! (old), hence! (old)
b (= weiter) on; **und so ~** and so on, and so forth; **das ging immer so weiter und so ~ und so ~** (inf) that went on and on and on; **in einem ~, ~ und ~** (old) incessantly, continually

Fort [fo:ɐ] NT **-s, -s** fort

fort- PREF in cpd vbs (= weg) away → auch **weg-**

Fort-: fort|ab [fɔrt'ap] (rare), **fort|an** [fɔrt'lan] (geh) ADV from this time on, henceforth (old, liter), henceforward (old); **fort|be|ge|ben** ptp **fortbegeben** VR sep irreg (geh) to depart, to leave; **sich aus dem Schloss** etc **~** to depart from (form) or to leave the castle etc; **Fort|be|stand** M , no pl continuance; (von Staat, Institution) continued existence; (von Gattung etc) survival; **fort|be|ste|hen** ptp **fortbestanden** VI sep irreg to continue; (Staat, Institution) to

continue in existence; (Zustand) to continue (to exist); **fort|be|we|gen** ptp **fortbewegt** sep **VT** to move away **VR** to move; **Fort|be|we|gung** F , no pl locomotion; **Fort|be|we|gungs|mit|tel** NT means sing of locomotion; **fort|bil|den** VT sep jdn/sich **~** to continue sb's/one's education; (= weiterbilden) to further one's education; **Fort|bil|dung** F , no pl further education; berufliche **~** further vocational training

Fort|bil|dungs-: Fort|bil|dungs|kurs M in-service training course; **Fort|bil|dungs|maß|nah|me** F continuing or further education (esp Brit) provision

Fort-: fort|blei|ben VI sep irreg aux sein to stay away; **Fort|blei|ben** NT **-s**, no pl absence; **fort|brin|gen** VT sep irreg to take away; (zur Reparatur, Reinigung etc) to take in; Brief, Paket etc to post (Brit), to mail (esp US); (= zurückbringen) to take back; (= bewegen) to move; **Fort|dau|er** F continuance, continuation; **fort|dau|ern** VI sep to continue; **fort|dau|ernd** ADJ continuing; (in der Vergangenheit) continued ADV constantly, continuously

for|te ['fɔrtə] ADV (Mus, Pharm) forte

For|te ['fɔrtə] NT **-s, -s** or Forti [-ti] forte

Fort-: fort|ei|len VI sep (geh) to hurry or hasten away; **fort|ent|wi|ckeln** ptp **fortentwickelt** sep **VT** to develop; (to develop; **Fort|ent|wick|lung** F , no pl development; **fort|exis|tie|ren** ptp **fortexistiert** VI sep = **fortbestehen**; **fort|fah|ren VI a** (= wegfahren) to go away; (= abfahren) to leave, to go; (= einen Ausflug machen) to go out **b** aux haben or sein (= weitermachen) to continue; **~, etw zu tun** to continue doing sth or to do sth; **in einer Tätigkeit ~** to continue with an activity; **ich fahre fort...** as I was about to say ... **VT** (= wegbringen) to take away; Wagen to drive away; **Fort|fall** M discontinuance; **fort|fal|len** VI sep irreg aux sein to cease to exist; (= nicht mehr zutreffend sein) to cease to apply; (Zuschuss etc) to be discontinued or stopped; (= abgeschafft werden) to be abolished; **fort|flie|gen** VI sep aux sein to fly away or off; **fort|füh|ren** sep **VT a** (= fortsetzen) to continue, to carry on **b** (= wegführen) to take away; (zu Fuß, fig) to lead away **VI** (fig) to lead away; **Fort|füh|rung** F continuation; **Fort|gang** M , no pl **a** (= Weggang) departure (aus from); **bei seinem ~** when he left, on his departure; **nach seinem ~** after he had left, after his departure **b** (= Verlauf) progress; **seinen ~ nehmen** to progress; **fort|ge|hen** VI sep aux sein **a** (= weggehen) to leave; **von zu Hause ~** to leave home; **geh fort!** go away!; **geh nicht fort!** don't go (away)! **b** (= weitergehen) to go on; **fort|ge|schrit|ten** ADJ advanced; **zu ~er Stunde wurden sie fröh|lich** as the night wore on they got quite merry; **er kam zu ~er Stunde** he came at a late hour → auch **fortschreiten; Fort|ge|schrit|te|nen|kurs** M advanced course; **Fort|ge|schrit|te|ne(r)** ['fɔrtgəʃrɪtnə] MF decl as adj advanced student; **fort|ge|setzt** ADJ continual, constant, incessant; Betrug, Steuerhinterziehung, Handlung repeated → auch **fortsetzen; fort|hin** [fɔrt'hɪn] ADV (dated) from this time on, henceforth (old, liter), henceforward (old)

For|ti pl von **Forte**

For|ti|fi|ka|ti|on [fɔrtifika'tsio:n] F **-, -en** (old Mil) fortification

For|tis|si|mo [fɔr'tɪsimo] NT **-s, -s** or Fortissimi [-mi] fortissimo; **im ~ spielen** to play fortissimo

Fort-: fort|ja|gen sep **VT** Menschen to throw out (aus, von of); Tier, Kinder to chase out (aus, von of) **VI** aux sein to race or career off; **fort|kom|men** VI aux sein **a** (= wegkommen) to get away; (= weggebracht werden) to be taken away; **mach, dass du fortkommst!** begone! (old), be off! **b** (= abhanden kommen) to disappear, to vanish **c** (= vorankommen) to get on well; **im Leben ~** to get on in life or in the world; **Fort|kom|men** NT **a** (lit, fig: = Weiter-kommen) progress; **jdn am ~ hindern** to hold sb back, to hinder sb's progress **b** (= Auskommen)

sein ~ finden to find a means of earning one's living; **fort|kön|nen** VI sep irreg to be able to get away; **fort|las|sen** VT sep irreg **a** (= weg-gehen lassen) **jdn ~** to let sb go, to allow sb to go **b** (= auslassen) to leave out, to omit; **fort|lau|fen** VI sep irreg aux sein to run away; **der Hund ist mir fortgelaufen** the dog has run away from me; **meine Freundin ist mir fortge-laufen** my girlfriend has (gone off and) left me; **fort|lau|fend** ADJ Handlung ongoing; Erscheinen serial attr; Zahlungen regular; (= andauernd) continual **ADV** (= andauernd) continually; **die Handlung geht ~ weiter** the storyline unfolds steadily; **~ nummeriert** (Geldscheine, Motoren) serially numbered; Blätter, Seiten consecutively numbered; **fort|le|ben** VI sep (liter) to live on; **fort|lo|ben** VT jdn auf einen Posten **~** to kick sb upstairs; **fort|lo|cken** VT sep to lure away; **fort|ma|chen** VR sep (inf) to clear out or off (inf); **fort|müs|sen** VI sep irreg to have to go or leave; (= ausgehen müssen) to have to go out; (Brief) to have to go (off); **fort|neh|men** VT sep irreg to take away (jdm from sb); **fort|pflan|zen** VR sep (Mensch, Tier) to repro-duce; (Pflanzen auch) to propagate (itself); (Schall, Wellen, Licht) to travel, to be transmitted; (Gerücht) to spread

Fort|pflan|zung F , no pl reproduction; (von Pflanzen) propagation

Fort|pflan|zungs-: fort|pflan|zungs|fä|hig ADJ capable of reproduction; Pflanze capable of propagation; **Fort|pflan|zungs|fä|hig|keit** F reproductive capacity; (von Pflanze) capacity for propagation; **Fort|pflan|zungs|ge|schwin|dig|keit** F (Phys) speed of propagation; **Fort|pflan|zungs|me|di|zin** F reproductive medi-cine; **Fort|pflan|zungs|or|gan** NT reproduc-tive organ; **Fort|pflan|zungs|trieb** M re-productive instinct; **fort|pflan|zungs|un|fä|hig** ADJ incapable of reproduction; Pflanze in-capable of propagation

Fort-: fort|räu|men VT sep (lit, fig) to clear a-way; **fort|rei|sen** VI sep aux sein to go away; **fort|rei|ßen** VT sep irreg to snatch or tear a-way; (Menge, Flut, Strom) to sweep or carry a-way; (fig) to carry away; **jdn/etw mit sich ~** (lit) to carry or sweep sb/sth along; **fort|ren|nen** VI sep irreg aux sein to race or tear (inf) off or away; **fort|rü|cken** sep **VT** to move away **VI** aux sein to move away; **Fort|satz** M (Anat) process; **fort|schaf|fen** VT sep to remove; **fort|sche|ren** VR sep (inf) to clear off (inf) (aus out of), to clear out (inf) (aus of); **fort|schi|cken** VT sep to send away; Brief etc to send off; **fort|schlei|chen** VIR sep irreg (inf) to slink or creep away; **fort|schlep|pen** sep **VT** to drag away; (fig) Fehler, Traditionen to perpetuate **VR** to drag oneself along; (fig) (Feh-ler, Traditionen) to be perpetuated; (Beziehung, Unterhaltung) to limp along; **fort|schrei|ben** VT sep irreg **a** Statistik etc to extrapolate **b** (= weiterführend aktualisieren) Programm etc to con-tinue; **Fort|schrei|bung** F (von Statistik) extra-polation; (von Programm) continuation; **fort|schrei|ten** VI sep irreg aux sein (= vorwärts schreiten) to progress; (= weitergehen) to contin-ue; (Entwicklung, Sprache) to develop; (Wissen-schaft) to advance; (Zeit) to go or march (liter) on; **die Ausbreitung der Epidemie schreitet weiter fort** the epidemic is continuing to spread → auch **fortgeschritten; fort|schrei-tend** ADJ progressive; Alter, Wissenschaft ad-vancing

Fort|schritt M advance; (esp Pol) progress no pl; **gute ~e machen** to make good progress, to get on (inf) or progress well; **~e erzielen** to make progress; **~e in der Medizin** advances in medicine; **das ist ein wesentlicher ~** that's a considerable step forward; **dem ~ dienen** to further progress

fort|schritt|lich ['fɔrtʃrɪtlɪç] ADJ progressive (auch Pol); Mensch, Ideen auch forward-looking **ADV** progressively; **~ eingestellt sein** or **denken** to be progressive or forward-looking

Fort|schritt|lich|keit F -, *no pl* progressiveness

Fort|schritts-: Fort|schritts|fa|na|ti|ker(in) M(F) fanatical progressive; **fort|schritts|feind|lich** ADJ anti-progressive; **Fort|schritts|feind|lich|keit** F anti-progressiveness; **Fort|schritts|glau|be** M belief in progress; **fort|schritts|gläu|big** ADJ ~ **sein** to believe in progress; **das ~e 19. Jahrhundert** the 19th century with its belief in progress; **Fort|schritts|gläu|big|keit** F naïve belief in progress; **Fort|schritts|op|ti|mis|mus** M belief in progress

fort-: fort+seh|nen VR *sep* to long *or* yearn to be away (*aus* from); **fort+set|zen** *sep* VT to continue; (*nach Unterbrechung auch*) to resume; **den Weg zu Fuß ~** to continue on foot; „**wird fortgesetzt**" "to be continued" → *auch* **fortgesetzt** VR (*zeitlich*) to continue; (*räumlich*) to extend

Fort|set|zung ['fɔrtzɛtsʊŋ] F -, -en a *no pl* (= *das Fortsetzen*) continuation; (*esp nach Unterbrechung*) resumption b (= *folgender Teil*) (*Rad, TV*) episode; (*eines Romans*) instalment (*Brit*), installment (*US*); **ein Film in drei ~en** a film in three parts; „**Fortsetzung folgt**" "to be continued" c (= *Anschlussstück*) continuation

Fort|set|zungs-: Fort|set|zungs|ge|schich|te F serial; **Fort|set|zungs|ro|man** M serialized novel; **Fort|set|zungs|se|rie** F series

fort-: fort+steh|len VR *sep irreg* (*geh*) to steal *or* slip away; **sich aus etw ~** to steal *or* slip out of sth; **fort+stre|ben** VI *sep* (*geh*) to attempt *or* try to get away (*aus* from); **fort+stür|zen** VI *sep aux sein* (*geh*) to rush off *or* away; (*Pferd*) to bolt; **fort+trei|ben** *sep irreg* VT a (= *verjagen*) to drive away b (= *weitertragen*) to carry away c (*fig: = weitermachen*) to go *or* keep *or* carry on with; **wenn er es weiter so forttreibt wie bisher …** if he goes *or* keeps *or* carries on as he has been (doing) … VI *aux sein* to be carried away

For|tu|na [fɔr'tuːna] F - (*Myth*) Fortuna; (*fig*) Fortune

For|tune [fɔr'tyːn] F -, *no pl* (*geh*), **For|tü|ne** [fɔr'tyːnə] F -, *no pl* good fortune; **politische ~ haben** to have good fortune in politics; **keine ~ haben** to have no luck

fort-: fort+wäh|ren VI *sep* (*geh*) to continue, to persist; **fort|wäh|rend** ADJ *no pred* constant, continual, incessant; ADV constantly, continually, incessantly; **fort+wäl|zen** VT *sep* to roll away; **mit sich ~** to carry away (with it); **fort|weg** ['fɔrtvɛk] ADV (*rare*) the whole time, all the time; **er hat ~ geschwatzt** he was chattering the whole time *or* all the time; **fort+wir|ken** VI *sep* to continue to have an effect; **das wirkt noch bis heute fort** that still has an effect today; **das Gesehene wirkte noch lange in ihm fort** what he had seen affected him *or* went on having an effect on him for a long time; **das Fortwirken klassischer Ideale** the continued effect of classical ideals; **fort+wol|len** VI *sep* to want to get away (*aus* from); **fort+wol|len** VI *sep* to want to get away (*aus* from); **Fort|zah|lung** F (*von Lohn, Gehalt*) continued payment; **fort+zeu|gen** VI *sep* (*liter*) to continue to have an effect; **fort+zie|hen** *sep irreg* VT to pull away; (*mit großer Anstrengung*) to drag away; (*Strom, Strudel*) to carry away VI *aux sein* a (= *weiterziehen*) to move on; (*Vögel*) to migrate b (*von einem Ort*) to move away (*aus* from); (*aus einer Wohnung*) to move out (*aus* of)

Fo|rum ['foːrʊm] NT -s, **Foren** *or* (*Hist*) **Fora** ['foːrən, 'foːra] forum; **etw vor das ~ der Öffentlichkeit bringen** to bring sth before the forum of public opinion

Fo|rums|dis|kus|si|on F , **Fo|rums|ge|spräch** NT forum (discussion)

For|ward ['fɔːwəd, 'fɔːɛvart] M -(s), -s (*esp Aus Ftbl*) forward

Forz [fɔrts] M -es, -e (*dial inf*) = **Furz**

Fos|bu|ry|flop ▲ ['fɔsbərıflɔp] M Fosbury flop

fos|sil [fɔ'siːl] ADJ *attr* fossil *attr*, fossilized; *Brennstoff, Energie* fossil *attr*; ~ **beheizte** *or* ~**e Kraftwerke** fossil-fuelled (*Brit*) *or* fossil-fueled (*US*) power stations

Fos|sil [fɔ'siːl] NT -s, -ien [-liən] (*lit, fig*) fossil

fö|tal [fø'taːl] ADJ foetal (*Brit*), fetal (*US*)

Fö|ten *pl von* **Fötus**

Fo|to¹ ['foːto] NT -s, -s photo(graph), snap (-shot) (*inf*); **ein ~ machen** to take a photo (-graph) → *auch* **Photo¹**

Fo|to² M -s, -s (*dial inf*) camera

Fo|to- *in cpds* (*Sci*) photo → *auch* **Photo-; Fo|to|al|bum** NT photograph album; **Fo|to|ama|teur(in)** M(F) amateur photographer; **Fo|to|ap|pa|rat** M camera; **Fo|to|ar|bei|ten** PL photographic work *sing*; **Fo|to|ar|chiv** NT photo archives *pl*; **Fo|to|ar|ti|kel** PL photographic equipment *sing*; **Fo|to|ate|li|er** NT (photographic) studio; **Fo|to|aus|rüs|tung** F photographic equipment *sing*; **Fo|to|au|to|mat** M (*für Passbilder*) photo booth; **Fo|to-CD** [-tseːdeː] F Photo CD®; **fo|to|che|misch** ADJ photochemical; **Fo|to|ecke** F corner; **Fo|to|fi|nish** NT (*Sport*) photo finish

fo|to|gen [foto'geːn] ADJ photogenic

Fo|to|ge|schäft NT photographic shop

Fo|to|graf [foto'graːf] M -en, -en, **Fo|to|gra|fin** [-'graːfɪn] F -, -nen photographer

Fo|to|gra|fie [fotogra'fiː] F -, -n [-'fiːən] a photography b (= *Bild*) photo(graph)

fo|to|gra|fie|ren [fotogra'fiːrən] *ptp* **fotografiert** VT to photograph, to take a photo(graph) of; **sich ~ lassen** to have one's photo(graph) *or* picture taken; **sie lässt sich gut ~** she photographs well, she comes out well in photos VI to take photos *or* photographs

Fo|to|gra|fie|ren [fotogra'fiːrən] -s, *no pl* (= *Fotografie*) photography; (*als Handlung*) taking (of) photographs *or* pictures (*inf*)

fo|to|gra|fisch [foto'graːfɪʃ] ADJ photographic ADV photographically

Fo|to-: Fo|to|in|dust|rie F photographic industry; **Fo|to|jour|na|list(in)** M(F) photojournalist; **Fo|to|ko|pie** F photocopy; **fo|to|ko|pie|ren** [fotoko'piːrən] *ptp* **fotokopiert** VT *insep* to photocopy, to make a photocopy of; **Fo|to|ko|pie|rer** M , **Fo|to|ko|pier|ge|rät** NT photocopier; **Fo|to|la|bor** NT photo lab; **Fo|to|la|bo|rant(in)** M(F) photographic lab(oratory) assistant; **Fo|to|ma|te|ri|al** NT photographic materials *pl*; **fo|to|me|cha|nisch** ADJ photomechanical; **Fo|to|mo|dell** NT photographic model; **Fo|to|mon|ta|ge** F photomontage; **Fo|to|pa|pier** NT photographic paper; **Fo|to|re|por|ta|ge** F photo reportage *or* feature; **Fo|to|re|por|ter(in)** M(F) press photographer; **Fo|to|ro|man** M photo book; **Fo|to|satz** M (*Typ*) = Lichtsatz; **Fo|to|ta|sche** F camera bag; (*größer*) camera holdall; **Fo|to|ter|min** M photo call

Fo|to|thek [foto'teːk] F -, -en photographic collection

Fo|to|zeit|schrift F photographic magazine

Fö|tus ['føːtʊs] M - *or* -ses, **Föten** *or* -se foetus (*Brit*), fetus (*US*)

Fot|ze ['fɔtsə] F -, -n (*vulg*) cunt (*vulg*)

Föt|zel ['fœtsl] M -s, - (*Sw*) scoundrel, rogue

foul [faul] ADJ (*Sport*) **das war aber ~** (*inf*) that was a foul ADV ~ **spielen** to foul

Foul [faul] NT -s, -s (*Sport*) foul

Foul|elf|me|ter ['faul-] M (*Ftbl*) penalty (kick)

fou|len ['faulən] VI/VT (*Sport*) to foul; **es wurde viel gefoult** there was a lot of fouling

Foul|spiel ['faul-] NT (*Sport*) foul play

Fou|ra|ge [fu'raːʒə] F -, *no pl* (*Mil old*) forage

Fox [fɔks] M -(es), -e, **Fox|ter|ri|er** M fox terrier

Fox|trott ['fɔkstrɔt] M -s, -e *or* -s foxtrot

Fo|yer [foa'jeː] NT -s, -s foyer; (*in Hotel auch*) lobby, entrance hall

FPÖ [ɛfpeː'øː] F - *abbr von* **Freiheitliche Partei Österreichs**

Fr. *abbr von* **Frau**

Fracht [fraxt] F -, -en a (= *Ladung*) freight *no pl*; (*von Flugzeug, Schiff auch*) cargo; (= *Güter auch*) payload; **etw per ~ schicken** to send sth freight, to freight sth b (= *Frachtpreis*) freight *no pl*, freightage *no pl*; (*bei Lastwagen*) carriage *no pl*; (= *Frachttarif*) freight/carriage rate

Fracht|brief M consignment note, waybill

Fracht|damp|fer M (*dated*) cargo *or* freight steamer

Frach|ten|bahn|hof M (*Aus*) freight *or* goods (*esp Brit*) depot

Frach|ter ['fraxtɐ] M -s, - freighter

Fracht-: Fracht|flug|zeug NT cargo *or* freight plane, (air) freighter; **fracht|frei** ADJ, ADV carriage paid *or* free; **Fracht|füh|rer(in)** M(F) (*form*) carrier; **Fracht|geld** NT freight, freightage; (*bei Lastwagen*) carriage; **Fracht|gut** NT (*ordinary*) freight *no pl*; **etw als ~ schicken** to send sth freight *or* as ordinary freight; **Fracht|kos|ten** PL freight charges *pl*; **Fracht|ma|schi|ne** F (*Aviat*) cargo *or* freight plane, (air) freighter; **Fracht|post|zen|trum** NT parcel depot; **Fracht|raum** M hold; (= *Ladefähigkeit*) cargo space; **Fracht|schiff** NT cargo ship, freighter; **Fracht|schiff|fahrt** ▲ F cargo shipping; **Fracht|sen|dung** F freight load; (*Aviat, Naut*) cargo *of* freight; **als ~** (as) freight; **Fracht|ta|rif** M freight rate *or* charge; **Fracht|ver|kehr** M goods traffic; **Fracht|zen|trum** NT (*für Gütertransport*) freight *or* goods (*esp Brit*) depot; (*von Post*) parcel depot; **Fracht|zet|tel** M consignment note, waybill

Frack [frak] M -(e)s, -e *or* ⸚e ['frɛkə] tails *pl*, tail coat; **im ~** in tails

Frack-: Frack|hemd NT dress shirt; **Frack|ho|se** F dress trousers *pl* (*esp Brit*) *or* pants *pl* (*esp US*); **Frack|ja|cke** F tails *pl*, tail coat; **Frack|sau|sen** NT ~ **haben** (*inf*) to be in a funk (*inf*); **Frack|schoß** M coat-tail; **Frack|ver|leih** M dress hire (service); **Frack|wes|te** F waistcoat *or* vest (*US, worn with tails*); **Frack|zwang** M requirement to wear tails; (**es herrscht**) ~ tails are obligatory, you have to wear tails, it is white tie; „**Frackzwang**" "tails", "white tie"

Fra|ge ['fraːgə] ✪ 39.3, 42.1, 43.3, 53.1, 53.2, 53.5, 53.6 F -, -n question; (= *Rückfrage, Zwischenfrage auch*) query; (= *Problem auch*) problem; (= *Angelegenheit auch*) matter, issue (*esp Pol*); **eine ~ zu etw** a question on sth; **jdm eine ~ stellen, an jdn eine ~ stellen** *or* **richten** to ask sb a question; **an jdn eine ~ haben** to have a question for sb; **gestatten Sie mir eine ~?** (*form*) might I ask a question?; (*in Diskussionen auch*) permit me to ask you a question (*form*); **auf eine ~ mit Ja oder Nein antworten** to answer a question with a straight yes *or* no; **sind noch ~n?, hat jemand noch eine ~?** does anyone have any further questions?, are there any more *or* any further questions?; **auf eine dumme ~ (bekommt man) eine dumme Antwort** (*prov*) ask a silly question (get a silly answer) (*prov*); **die deutsche ~** the German question *or* issue; **das ist (doch sehr) die ~** that's (just *or* precisely) the question/problem, that's the whole question/problem; **das ist die große ~** that's the big *or* sixty-four thousand dollar (*inf*) question; **das ist gar keine ~, natürlich dürfen Sie heute freinehmen** you don't even need to ask, of course you can take today off; **das ist gar keine ~, das steht** *or* **ist außer ~** there's no question *or* doubt about it; **dass …, steht außer ~** that … is beyond question, …, there's no question *or* doubt about it; **ohne ~** without question *or* doubt; **in ~ kommen** to be possible; *Bewerber* to be worth considering; **sollte er für diese Stelle in ~ kommen, …** if he should be considered for this position …; **in ~ kommende**

Möglichkeiten possible opportunities; **für jdn/ etw nicht in ~ kommen** to be out of the question for sb/sth; **das kommt (überhaupt) nicht in ~!** that's (quite) out of the question; **etw in ~ stellen** to question sth, to query sth, to call sth into question; **eine ~ der Zeit/des Geldes** a question or matter of time/money → *auch* **infrage**

-fra|ge F *suf in cpds* question of; (= *Problem auch*) problem of; **die Arbeitslosenfrage** the unemployment issue; **eine Zeit- und Kostenfrage** a question of time and money

Fra|ge-: **Fra|ge|bo|gen** M questionnaire; (= *Formular*) form; **Fra|ge|bo|gen|ak|ti|on** F poll; **Fra|ge|für|wort** NT interrogative pronoun

fra|gen ['fraːɡn] ❂ 28.1, 29, 33.2 **VTI** to ask; **nach** *or* **wegen** (*inf*) **jdm ~** to ask after sb; (*in Hotel etc*) to ask for sb; **ich fragte sie nach den Kindern** I asked her how the children were doing; **nach jds Namen/Alter/dem Weg ~** to ask sb's name/age/the way; **nach Arbeit/Post ~** to ask whether there is/was any work/mail; **nach den Ursachen ~** to inquire as to the causes; **ich fragte sie nach ihren Wünschen** I asked her what she wanted; **ich habe nicht nach Einzelheiten gefragt** I didn't ask any details; **nach den Folgen ~** to bother or care about the consequences; **er fragte nicht danach, ob ...** he didn't bother or care whether ...; **wegen etw ~** to ask about sth; **frag (mich/ihn) lieber nicht** you'd better not ask (me/him) that; **das frage ich dich!** I could ask you the same; **da fragst du noch?** you still have to ask?, you still don't know?; **frag nicht so dumm!** don't ask silly questions; **du fragst zu viel** you ask too many questions; **da fragst du mich zu viel** (*inf*) I really couldn't say; **man wird ja wohl noch ~ dürfen** (*inf*) I was only asking (*inf*), there's no law against asking, is there? (*inf*); **wenn ich (mal) ~ darf** if I may or might ask; **ohne lange zu ~** without asking a lot of questions → *auch* **gefragt**

VR to wonder; **das/da frage ich mich** I wonder; **das frage ich mich auch** that's just what I was wondering; **ja, das fragt man sich** yes, that's the question; **es fragt sich, ob ...** it's debatable or questionable whether or if ...; **man fragt sich, ob ...** one wonders whether or if ...; **da muss man sich ~, ob ...** you or one can't help wondering whether or if ...; **ich frage mich, wie/wo ...** I'd like to know how/where ..., I really wonder how/where ...

fra|gend **ADJ** Blick questioning, inquiring; (*Gram*) interrogative **ADV** jdn **~ ansehen** to give sb a questioning look

Fra|gen-: **Fra|gen|ka|ta|log** M package or slew (*US inf*) of questions; **ein ganzer ~** a long list of questions; **Fra|gen|kom|plex** M , **Fra|gen|kreis** M set of questions

Fra|ger ['fraːɡɐ] M -s, -, **Fra|ge|rin** [-ərɪn] F -, -nen questioner; **wer ist denn der lästige ~?** who is this wretched person who keeps asking questions?

Fra|ge|rei [fraːɡə'raɪ] F -, -en questions pl

Fra|ge-: **Fra|ge|satz** M (*Gram*) interrogative sentence; (= *Nebensatz*) interrogative clause; **Fra|ge|stel|ler** [-ʃtɛlɐ] M -s, -, **Fra|ge|stel|le|rin** [-ərɪn] F -, -nen questioner; (= *Interviewer*) interviewer; **Fra|ge|stel|lung** F **a** formulation of a question; **das ist eine falsche ~** the question is wrongly put or stated or formulated **b** (= *Frage*) question; **Fra|ge|stun|de** F (*Parl*) question time *no art* (*Brit*); **Fra|ge-und-Ant|wort-Spiel** NT question and answer game; **Fra|ge|wort** NT pl -wörter interrogative (particle); **Fra|ge|zei|chen** NT question mark (*auch fig*), interrogation mark or point (*form*); **hinter diese Behauptung muss man ein dickes** or **großes ~ setzen** (*fig*) this statement should be taken with a large pinch of salt; **dastehen/ dasitzen wie ein ~** to slouch

fra|gil [fra'ɡiːl] ADJ (*geh*) fragile

Fra|gi|li|tät [fraɡili'tɛːt] F -, no pl (*geh*) fragility

---

frag|lich ['fraːklɪç] ❂ 53.6 ADJ **a** (= *zweifelhaft*) uncertain; (= *fragwürdig*) doubtful, questionable; **eine ~e Sache** a moot point **b** *attr* (= *betreffend*) in question; *Angelegenheit* under discussion; **zu der ~en Zeit** at the time in question

Frag|lich|keit F -, no pl (= *Zweifelhaftigkeit*) uncertainty; (= *Fragwürdigkeit*) doubtfulness

frag|los ADV undoubtedly, unquestionably

Frag|ment [fraɡ'mɛnt] NT -(e)s, -e fragment; **~ bleiben** to remain a fragment

frag|men|ta|risch [fraɡmɛn'taːrɪʃ] **ADJ** fragmentary **ADV** **die Manuskripte sind nur ~ erhalten** only fragments of the manuscript have been preserved; **~ überlieferte Texte** fragmentary texts

frag|wür|dig ADJ **a** doubtful, dubious **b** (*pej*) *Lokal, Mensch, Kreise, Geschäfte* dubious

Frag|wür|dig|keit F -, -en **a** doubtful or dubious nature, doubtfulness **b** (*pej: von Lokal, Mensch, Kreisen, Geschäften*) dubious nature

frais ['frɛːz], **frai|se** ['frɛːzə] ADJ inv (*Aus Fashion*) strawberry(-coloured) (*Brit*), strawberry(-colored) (*US*)

Frai|sen ['fraɪzn] PL (*Aus Med*) **die ~** (infant) spasms pl

Frak|tal [frak'taːl] NT -s, -e fractal

Frak|ti|on [frak'tsioːn] F -, -en **a** (*Pol*) ≈ parliamentary or congressional (*US*) party; (*von mehreren Parteien*) ≈ coalition party; (= *Sondergruppe*) group, faction **b** (*Aus*: = *Ortsteil*) area **c** (*Chem*) fraction

frak|ti|o|nell [fraktsio'nɛl] (*Pol*) **ADJ** **~e Gruppen** factions within the parliamentary etc party **ADV** **~ entschieden** decided by the parliamentary etc party

frak|ti|o|nie|ren [fraktsio'niːrən] ptp **fraktioniert** VT (*Chem*) to fractionate

Frak|ti|ons- *in cpds* (*Pol*) party; **Frak|ti|ons|bil|dung** F formation of factions/a faction; **Frak|ti|ons|füh|rer(in)** M(F) party whip, floor leader (*US*); **frak|ti|ons|los** ADJ Abgeordneter independent; **Frak|ti|ons|mit|glied** NT member of a parliamentary etc party; **Frak|ti|ons|sit|zung** F party meeting; **Frak|ti|ons|spal|tung** F party split; (*auf Dauer*) split into two parties; **Frak|ti|ons|spre|cher(in)** M(F) party spokesperson; **Frak|ti|ons|stär|ke** F **a** numerical strength of a/the parliamentary etc party **b** (= *erforderliche Mitgliederzahl*) numerical strength required for recognition of a parliamentary party; **Frak|ti|ons|sta|tus** M party status; **Frak|ti|ons|vor|sit|zen|de(r)** MF decl as adj party whip, floor leader (*US*); **Frak|ti|ons|vor|stand** ≈ party executive; **Frak|ti|ons|zwang** M requirement to vote in accordance with party policy; **unter ~ stehen** to be under the whip

Frak|tur [frak'tuːɐ] F -, -en **a** (*Typ*) Gothic print, Fraktur; **(mit jdm) ~ reden** (*inf*) to be blunt (with sb) **b** (*Med*) fracture

Frak|tur|schrift F Gothic script

Franc [frãː] M -, -s (*Hist*) franc

Fran|chise [frɛnt'faɪz] M -, no pl franchise

Fran|chise- ['frɛntʃaɪz-]: **Fran|chise-Ge|ber(in)** M(F) franchisor; **Fran|chise-Neh|mer(in)** M(F) franchisee

Fran|chi|sing ['frɛntʃaɪzɪŋ] NT -s, no pl franchising

Fran|ci|um ['frantsiʊm] NT -s, no pl (abbr **Fr**) francium

frank [fraŋk] ADV **~ und frei** frankly, openly

Fran|ke ['fraŋkə] M -n, -n (*Geog*) Franconian; (*Hist*) Frank

Fran|ken[1] ['fraŋkn] NT -s Franconia

Fran|ken[2] M -s, - (*Schweizer*) ~ (Swiss) franc

Fran|ken|wein M Franconian wine

Frank|furt ['fraŋkfʊrt] NT -s ~ **(am Main)** Frankfurt (on the Main); ~ **(Oder)** Frankfurt on the Oder

---

Frank|fur|ter[1] ['fraŋkfʊrtɐ] ADJ Frankfurt attr; ~ **Buchmesse** Frankfurt book fair

Frank|fur|ter[2] ['fraŋkfʊrtɐ] M -s, - (*inf*: = *Würstchen*) frankfurter

Frank|fur|ter[3] ['fraŋkfʊrtɐ] M -s, -, **Frank|fur|te|rin** [-ərɪn] F -, -nen (= *Einwohner Frankfurts*) Frankfurter

frank|fur|te|risch ['fraŋkfʊrtərɪʃ] (*inf*), **frank|fur|tisch** ['fraŋkfʊrtɪʃ] ADJ Frankfurt attr; **er spricht Frankfurterisch** or **Frankfurtisch** he speaks the Frankfurt dialect

fran|kie|ren [fraŋ'kiːrən] ptp **frankiert** VT to stamp; (*mit Maschine*) to frank

Fran|kier|ma|schi|ne F franking machine

Fran|kie|rung F -, -en franking; (= *Porto auch*) postage

Frän|kin ['frɛŋkɪn] F -, -nen Franconian (woman)

frän|kisch ['frɛŋkɪʃ] ADJ Franconian

Fränk|ler ['frɛŋklɐ] M -s, -, **Fränk|li** ['frɛŋkli] NT -s, - (*inf*) (*Sw*) franc (piece)

fran|ko ['fraŋko] ADV (*Comm*) carriage paid; (*von Postsendungen*) post-free (*Brit*), postpaid

Fran|ko-: **Fran|ko|ka|na|dier(in)** M(F) French-Canadian; **fran|ko|ka|na|disch** ADJ French-Canadian; **Fran|ko|ma|nie** F (*geh*) Francomania; **fran|ko|phil** [fraŋko'fiːl] ADJ (*geh*) Francophile; **Fran|ko|phi|le(r)** [fraŋko-'fiːlə] MF decl as adj Francophile; **Fran|ko|phi|lie** [fraŋkofi'liː] F -, no pl (*geh*) Francophilia; **fran|ko|phob** [fraŋko'foːp] ADJ (*geh*) Francophobe; **Fran|ko|pho|bie** [fraŋkofo'biː] F , no pl (*geh*) Francophobia; **fran|ko|phon** [fraŋko-'foːn] ADJ francophone; **Fran|ko|pho|nie** [fraŋkofo'niː] F -, no pl francophonia

Frank|reich ['fraŋkraiç] NT -s France

Fräns|chen ['frɛnsçən] NT -s, - dim von Franse

Fran|se ['franzə] F -, -n (lose) (loose) thread; (*von Haar*) strand of hair; **~n** (= *Pony*) fringe (*Brit*), bangs pl (*US*); **ein mit ~n besetzter Schal** a shawl with a fringe, a fringed shawl

fran|sen ['franzn] VI to fray (out)

fran|sig ['franzɪç] ADJ (*Sew*) fringed no adv; *Haar* straggly no adv; (= *ausgefasert*) frayed no adv

Franz[1] [frants] M -' or -ens Francis; (*bei Deutschen*) Franz

Franz[2] [frants] NT -, no pl (*Sch inf*: = *Französisch*) French

Franz-: **Franz|band** [-bant] M pl -bände leather binding; **ein ~-Buchrücken** a leather spine; **Franz|brannt|wein** M alcoholic liniment

Fran|zis|ka|ner [frantsɪs'kaːnɐ] M -s, - (*Eccl*) Franciscan (friar)

Fran|zis|ka|ne|rin [frantsɪs'kaːnərɪn] F -, -nen (*Eccl*) Franciscan (nun)

Fran|zis|ka|ner|or|den M (*Eccl*) Franciscan Order, Order of St. Francis

Franz|mann ['frants-] M pl -männer (dated sl) Frenchie (*inf*), frog (pej inf)

Fran|zo|se [fran'tsoːzə] M -n, -n **a** Frenchman/French boy; **er ist ~** he's French; **die ~n** the French **b** (= *Werkzeug*) adjustable spanner, monkey wrench

Fran|zo|sen-: **fran|zo|sen|feind|lich** ADJ anti-French; **Fran|zo|sen|krank|heit** F (old) French disease (old), syphilis

Fran|zö|sin [fran'tsøːzɪn] F -, -nen Frenchwoman/French girl; **sie ist ~** she's French

fran|zö|sisch [fran'tsøːzɪʃ] ADJ French; **die ~e Schweiz** French-speaking Switzerland; **die Französische Revolution** the French Revolution; **die ~e Krankheit** (old) the French disease (old), syphilis; **~es Bett** double bed; **~e Spielkarten** ordinary playing cards; **~ kochen** to do French cooking; **(auf) ~ Abschied nehmen** to leave without saying goodbye; **sich (auf) ~ empfehlen** to leave without saying goodbye; (= *ohne zu zahlen*) to leave without paying; (= *sich unerlaubt entfernen*) to take French leave; **es auf**

Französisch or ~ **machen** (inf) to have oral sex → auch **deutsch**

Fran|zö|sisch(e) [fran'tsøːzɪʃ] NT French → auch **Deutsch(e)**

fran|zö|sisch|spra|chig [-ʃpraːxɪç] ADJ French-speaking, francophone → auch **deutschsprachig**

frap|pant [fra'pant] (geh) ADJ Schnelligkeit, Entdeckung remarkable, astounding; Verbesserung, Wirkung, Ähnlichkeit, Beispiele auch striking ADV remarkably; **auf jdn ~ wirken** to astound sb

frap|pie|ren [fra'piːrən] ptp **frappiert** VT (= verblüffen) to astound, to astonish, to amaze VI (Sache) to be astounding or astonishing

frap|pie|rend ADJ astonishing, astounding

Frä|se ['frɛːzə] F -, -n a (= Werkzeug) milling cutter; (für Holz) moulding (Brit) or molding (US) cutter; (= Bodenfräse) rotary hoe b (= Bart) chinstrap (beard)

frä|sen ['frɛːzn] VT to mill, to mill-cut; Holz to mould (Brit), to mold (US)

Frä|ser[1] ['frɛːzɐ] M -s, - milling cutter; (für Holz) moulding (Brit) or molding (US) cutter

Frä|ser[2] ['frɛːzɐ] M -s, -, **Frä|se|rin** [-ərɪn] F -, -nen milling cutter

Fräs|ma|schi|ne F milling machine

fraß pret von **fressen**

Fraß [fraːs] M -es, -e a food; (pej inf) muck (inf) no pl; **etw einem Tier zum ~ vorwerfen** to feed sth to an animal; **jdn den Kritikern zum ~ vorwerfen** to throw sb to the critics b (= Abfressen) **vom ~ befallen** eaten away

Fra|ter ['fraːtɐ] M -s, **Fratres** ['fraːtreːs] (Eccl) Brother

fra|ter|ni|sie|ren [fraterni'ziːrən] ptp **fraternisiert** VI to fraternize

Fra|ter|ni|sie|rung F -, -nen fraternization

Fratz [frats] M -es, -e or (Aus) -en, -en a (pej) brat b (= schelmisches Mädchen) rascal, scallywag (inf)

Frätz|chen ['frɛtsçən] NT -s, - dim von **Fratz** von **Fratze**

Frat|ze ['fratsə] F -, -n a grotesque face b (= Grimasse) grimace; (inf: = Gesicht) face, phiz (Brit dated inf); (fig: = Zerrbild) caricature; **jdm eine ~ schneiden** to pull or make a face at sb; **eine ~ ziehen, das Gesicht zu einer ~ verziehen** to pull or make a face, to grimace

frat|zen|haft ADJ grotesque

frau [frau] INDEF PRON proposed feminist alternative to "man" → **man**[1]

Frau [frau] F -, -en a (= weiblicher Mensch) woman; **zur ~ werden** to become a woman; **von ~ zu ~** woman to woman; **Unsere Liebe ~** (Eccl) our blessed Lady, the blessed Virgin b (= Ehefrau) wife; **sich** (dat) **eine ~ nehmen** (dated) to marry, to take a wife (old); **willst du meine ~ werden?** will you marry me?, will you be my wife?; **jdn zur ~ haben** to be married to sb; **seine zukünftige ~** his bride-to-be; **seine geschiedene ~** his ex-wife c (= Anrede) madam; (mit Namen) Mrs; (für eine unverheiratete Frau) Miss, Ms; **liebe ~!** (dated) my dear lady!; ~ **Doktor** doctor; **Ihre (liebe) ~ Mutter/Schwester** (form) your good mother/sister; ~ **Nachbarin** (old) neighbour (Brit old) or neighbor (US old)

Frau|chen ['frauçən] NT -s, - dim von **Frau** (inf: von Hund) mistress; **geh zum ~** go to your mistress

Frau|en- in cpds women's; (einer bestimmten Frau) woman's; (Sport) ladies', women's; **Frau|en|an|teil** M percentage or proportion of women; **Frau|en|ar|beit** F a (= Arbeit für Frauen, von Frauen) female or women's labour (Brit) or labor (US); **das ist keine ~** that's no job for a woman; **niedrig bezahlte ~** badly paid jobs for women b (= Arbeit zugunsten der Frau) work among women; **in der ~ tätig sein** to be involved in work among women; **Frau|en|art** F

nach ~ (dated) as women do; **Frau|en|arzt** M, **Frau|en|ärz|tin** F gynaecologist (Brit), gynecologist (US); **Frau|en|be|auf|trag|te(r)** MF decl as adj (in Gewerkschaft etc) women's representative; (= Beamter) officer for women's issues; **Frau|en|be|ruf** M career for women; **frau|en|be|wegt** ADJ feminist; **Frau|en|be|weg|te(r)** [-bəveːktə] MF decl as adj feminist; **Frau|en|be|we|gung** F women's (auch Hist) or feminist movement; **Frau|en|blatt** NT women's magazine; **Frau|en|buch** NT women's book; **Frau|en|chor** M ladies' or female choir; **Frau|en|eman|zi|pa|ti|on** F female emancipation no art, emancipation of women; (in der heutigen Zeit auch) women's lib(eration); **Frau|en|fach|schu|le** F domestic science college; **Frau|en|feind** M misogynist; **frau|en|feind|lich** ADJ anti-women pred; Mensch, Verhalten auch misogynous; **Frau|en|feind|lich|keit** F misogyny; (im Berufsleben) discrimination against women; **Frau|en|fra|ge** F question of women's rights; **frau|en|freund|lich** ADJ pro-women pred; **Frau|en|freund|lich|keit** F positive attitude toward(s) women; **Frau|en|front** F women's front; **Frau|en|funk** M woman's radio, ≈ Woman's Hour (Brit); **Frau|en|ge|fäng|nis** NT women's prison; **Frau|en|ge|schich|te** F affair with a woman; ~n (= Affären) womanizing; (= Erlebnisse) sexploits pl (hum inf), experiences with women pl; **Frau|en|ge|stalt** F female figure; (Liter, Art) female character; **Frau|en|grup|pe** F women's group; **Frau|en|haar** NT a woman's hair b (Bot) maidenhair (fern); **frau|en|haft** ADJ womanly no adv; **Frau|en|hand** F **von (zarter) ~ by** a woman's fair hand; **Frau|en|has|ser** [-hasɐ] M -s, - misogynist, woman-hater; **Frau|en|haus** NT a women's refuge b (Ethnologie) women's house; **Frau|en|heil|kun|de** F gynaecology (Brit), gynecology (US); **Frau|en|held** M lady-killer; **Frau|en|ken|ner** M connoisseur of women; **Frau|en|klei|der** PL women's clothes pl or clothing sing; **Frau|en|kli|nik** F gynaecological (Brit) or gynecological (US) hospital or clinic; **Frau|en|klos|ter** NT convent, nunnery (old); **Frau|en|krank|heit** F, **Frau|en|lei|den** NT gynaecological (Brit) or gynecological (US) disorder; **Facharzt für ~en und Geburtshilfe** gynaecologist (Brit) or gynecologist (US) and obstetrician; **Frau|en|li|te|ra|tur** F women's literature; (emanzipatorisch) feminist writings pl or literature; **Frau|en|man|tel** M (Bot) lady's mantle; **Frau|en|mör|der(in)** M(F) murderer (of women/a woman); **Frau|en|or|den** M (Eccl) women's order; **Frau|en|po|li|tik** F feminist politics sing or pl; **Frau|en|quo|te** F quota for women; **Frau|en|recht|ler** [-reçtlɐ] M -s, -, **Frau|en|recht|le|rin** [-ərɪn] F -, -nen feminist; **frau|en|recht|le|risch** [-reçtlərɪʃ] ADJ feminist ADV **sich ~ betätigen** to be involved in women's rights or (in der heutigen Zeit auch) Women's Lib; **Frau|en|re|fe|rat** NT women's department; **Frau|en|re|fe|rent(in)** M(F) consultant on women's issues; **Frau|en|sa|che** F a (= Frauenangelegenheit) women's affair; **das ist ~** that's women's business b (euph: = Menstruation) women's curse; **Frau|en|schän|der** [-ʃɛndɐ] M -s, - rapist; **Frau|en|schuh** M, no pl (Bot) lady's slipper no pl

Frau|ens- ['frauəns-]: **Frau|ens|leu|te** PL (hum inf) womenfolk pl; **Frau|ens|per|son** F female person; (hum inf) female (inf), broad (US inf)

Frau|en-: **Frau|en|sport** M women's sport; **Frau|en|sta|ti|on** F women's ward; **Frau|en|stim|me** F woman's voice; (Parl) woman's vote; ~n (= Stimmen) women's voices/votes; **Frau|en|stimm|recht** NT vote for women, female suffrage no art; **Frau|en|tausch** M wife-swapping; (Anthropologie) exchange of partners; **Frau|en|treff** M (inf) women's meeting place or haunt (inf) or hangout (inf); **Frau|en|typ** M a feminine type (of woman); **mütterlicher ~**

motherly type of woman b (inf) ladies' man; **Frau|en|über|schuss** ▲ M surplus of women; **Frau|en|ver|band** M, **Frau|en|ver|ein** M women's association or society; **Frau|en|wahl|recht** NT vote for women, female suffrage no art; **Frau|en|zeit|schrift** F women's magazine; **Frau|en|zent|rum** NT women's advice centre (Brit) or center (US); **Frau|en|zim|mer** NT (old, dated) woman; (hum) woman, female (inf), broad (US inf)

Fräu|lein ['frɔylaɪn] NT -s, - or (inf) -s (dated) a (= unverheiratete weibliche Person) young lady; **ein altes** or **älteres ~** an elderly spinster b (= Anrede) Miss; **Ihr ~ Tochter/Braut** your daughter/bride c (= weibliche Angestellte) young lady; (= Verkäuferin) assistant; (= Kellnerin) waitress; (= Lehrerin) teacher, mistress; ~! Miss!; (= Kellnerin auch) waitress!; **das ~ vom Amt** the operator, the switchboard girl

Fräu|lein|wun|der NT girl wonder

frau|lich ['fraulɪç] ADJ feminine; (= reif) womanly no adv

Frau|lich|keit F -, no pl femininity; (= frauliche Reife) womanliness

Freak ['friːk] M -s, -s (inf) freak (inf)

frea|kig ['friːkɪç] ADJ (inf) freaky (inf)

frech [frɛç] ADJ a (= unverschämt) cheeky (esp Brit), fresh pred (esp US), impudent; Lüge brazen, bare-faced no adv; ~ **werden** to get cheeky etc; **halt deinen ~en Mund!** (inf) shut up and stop being cheeky etc; ~ **wie Oskar** (inf) or **wie ein Spatz sein** (inf) to be a cheeky little devil (Brit inf), to be a little monkey b (= herausfordernd) Kleidung, Texte etc saucy (inf) ADV **lachen** impudently; **anlügen** brazenly; **jdm ~ kommen** to get cheeky etc with sb; **sich ~ benehmen** to be cheeky etc

Frech|dachs M (inf) cheeky monkey (Brit inf) or devil (Brit inf), monkey, smart aleck (US)

Frech|heit F -, -en a no pl (= Verhalten) impudence; (esp von Kindern) cheekiness (esp Brit), impudence; **das ist der Gipfel der ~** that's the height of impudence; **die ~ haben** or **besitzen, ... zu ...** to have the cheek (esp Brit) or nerve (inf) or impudence to ... b (= Äußerung, Handlung) piece or bit of cheek (esp Brit) or impudence; **sich** (dat) **einige ~en erlauben** or **herausnehmen** to be a bit cheeky (esp Brit) or fresh (esp US); **solche ~en** what cheek (esp Brit) or impudence

Free|sie ['freːziə] F -, -n freesia

Free|ware ['friːwɛːɐ] F -, -s (Comput) freeware

Fre|gat|te [fre'gatə] F -, -n frigate

Fre|gat|ten|ka|pi|tän(in) M(F) commander

Fre|gatt|vo|gel [fre'gat-] M frigate bird

frei [fraɪ]	
1 ADJEKTIV	2 ADVERB

1 – ADJEKTIV

a = unbehindert free; **frei von etw** free of sth; **sich von etw frei machen** to free oneself from sth; **die Straße frei machen** to clear the road; **sie hatte einen freien Blick aufs Meer** she had a clear view of the sea; **der Film ist frei (für Jugendliche) ab 16 (Jahren)** this film is suitable for persons aged 16 years and over; **frei sein** (Sport) to be free or not marked; **ich bin so frei** (form) may I?

♦ **frei + Substantiv**

Siehe auch unter dem Eintrag für das jeweilige Substantiv.

freier Durchgang thoroughfare; **von Kiel nach Hamburg hatten wir freie Fahrt** we had a clear run from Kiel to Hamburg; **einem Zug freie Fahrt geben** to give a train the "go" signal; **der Polizist gab uns freie Fahrt** the policeman signalled (Brit) or signaled (US) us on; **für etw freie Fahrt geben** (fig) to give sth the go-ahead; **der freie Fall** (Phys) free fall; **auf freiem Fuß sein** to be free; **freie Hand haben** to have a free hand; **jdm freie Hand lassen** to give sb free rein, to give sb a free hand; **das Recht der freien Rede** or **auf freie Rede** the right of free speech, the right to freedom of speech; **freie Rhythmen** free verse; **aus freien Stücken** of one's own free will; **jdm zur freien Verfügung stehen** to be completely at sb's disposal; **aus freiem Willen** of one's own free will; **freier Zugang** unlimited or unrestricted access; **freier Zutritt** unrestricted access → **frank, Lauf**

b = unabhängig free; *Schriftsteller, Journalist etc* freelance; (= *nicht staatlich*) private

♦ **frei + Substantiv**

> Siehe auch unter dem Eintrag für das jeweilige Substantiv.

freier Beruf independent profession; **Freie Demokratische Partei** Free Democratic Party; **Freie Deutsche Jugend** (*DDR*) *youth wing of the former East German Socialist Unity Party* **Freier Deutscher Gewerkschaftsbund** (*DDR*) *Trades Union Congress of the former East Germany* **Freie Hansestadt Bremen** Free Hansa Town of Bremen; **Freie und Hansestadt Hamburg** Free Hansa Town of Hamburg; **freier Markt** free market; **freie Marktwirtschaft** free-market economy; **freier Mitarbeiter** freelance, freelancer; **freier Mitarbeiter sein** to be freelance; **als freier Mitarbeiter arbeiten** to work freelance; **freie Reichsstadt** (*Hist*) free city of the Empire; **freie Tankstelle** independent petrol (*Brit*) or gas (*US*) station; **die freie Wirtschaft** private enterprise; **in die freie Wirtschaft gehen** to go into the private sector

c = verfügbar *Mittel, Geld* available; *Zeit* free; **Herr Mayer ist jetzt frei** Mr Mayer is free now; **ich bin jetzt frei für ihn** I can see him now; (*am Telefon*) I can speak to him now

d = arbeitsfrei **morgen/Mittwoch ist frei** tomorrow/Wednesday is a holiday → **freihaben, freinehmen**

e = ohne Hilfsmittel **etw aus freier Hand zeichnen** to draw sth freehand; **ein Vortrag in freier Rede** an extempory talk

f = unbesetzt *Zimmer, Toilette* vacant; *Taxi* for hire; **ist hier noch frei?, ist dieser Platz noch frei?** is anyone sitting here?, is this seat free?; **im Kino/Flugzeug waren noch zehn freie Plätze** in the cinema/plane there were still ten seats free; **„frei"** (*an Taxi*) "for hire"; (*an Toilettentür*) "vacant"; **„Zimmer frei"** "vacancies"; **haben Sie noch etwas frei?** (*in Hotel*) do you have any vacancies?; **bei HarperCollins sind einige Stellen frei** there are some vacancies at HarperCollins; **einen Platz frei machen** (= *aufstehen*) to vacate a seat; (= *leer räumen*) to clear a seat; **einen Platz für jdn frei lassen** to keep a seat for sb; **für etw Platz frei lassen/machen** to leave/make room for sth; **eine Wohnung frei machen** to vacate a flat → **Bahn, Ring, freimachen**

g = offen **unter freiem Himmel** in the open air; **im freien Raum** (*Astron*) in (outer) space; **auf freier Strecke** (*Rail*) between stations; **eine Frage/Aussage im freien Raum stehen lassen** to leave a question/statement hanging in mid-air → **Freie(s), Feld**

h = kostenlos free; **Eintritt frei** admission free; **frei Schiff** free on board → **Haus**

i = unkonventionell *Sitten, Erziehung* liberal; **freie Liebe** free love

j = unbekleidet bare; **mit freiem Oberkörper** stripped to the waist

k = ungeschützt *Autor* out of copyright; **seit die Rechte an Karl May frei geworden sind** since Karl May's books have been out of copyright

2 – ADVERB

a = ungehindert freely; *sprechen* openly; **frei beweglich** free-moving; **frei erfunden** purely fictional; **er hat das frei erfunden** he made it up; **frei schalten und walten** to do what one wants; **das ist frei wählbar** you can choose as you please, it's completely optional; **frei definierbare Zeichen** (*Comput*) user-definable characters

---

♦ **frei (herum)laufen frei laufend** (*Hunde, Katzen*) feral; *Huhn* free-range; **Eier von frei laufenden Hühnern** free-range eggs; **frei herumlaufen** (*inf*) to be free, to be running around free (*inf*); **der Verbrecher läuft immer noch frei herum** the criminal is still at large

♦ **frei lebend** *Wölfe, Mustangherden etc* living in the wild; *Katzen, Stadttauben* feral; *Mikroorganismen* free-living

♦ **frei stehen** (*Haus*) to stand by itself; (*Sport*) to be free or not marked; **ein frei stehendes Gebäude** a free-standing building → *auch* **c**

♦ **frei nach** based on; **frei nach Goethe** (*Zitat*) as Goethe didn't say

b = ungezwungen **sich frei und ungezwungen verhalten, frei und locker auftreten** to have a relaxed manner, to be easy-going; **sie benimmt sich etwas zu frei** she's rather free in her behaviour (*Brit*) or behavior (*US*); **frei atmen können** (= *erleichtert sein*) to be able to breathe easy

c = ohne Hilfsmittel unaided, without help; **das Kind kann frei stehen** the child can stand on its own or without any help; **frei schwimmen** to swim unaided; **frei in der Luft schweben** to hang in mid-air; **frei sprechen** to speak without notes; **frei finanziert** (*Wohnungsbau*) privately financed

Frei-: Frei|an|la|ge F (*im Zoo*) outdoor or open-air enclosure; (*Sport*) sports ground, playing fields *pl*; (= *Park*) park grounds *pl*; **Frei|bad** NT open-air (swimming) pool, lido; **Frei|bal|lon** M free balloon; **Frei|bank** F (*rare*) *pl* **-bänke** *stall or shop selling substandard meat*; **frei+be|kom|men** *ptp* **freibekommen** VT *sep irreg* **a** (= *befreien*) **jdn ~** to get sb freed or released; **etw ~** to get sth free, to free sth **b** **einen Tag/eine Woche ~** to get a day/a week off; **Frei|be|ruf|ler** [-bərʊːflɐ] M **-s, -**, **Frei|be|ruf|le|rin** [-ərɪn] F **-, -nen** freelance, freelancer; **frei|be|ruf|lich** ADJ freelance ADV **~ arbeiten** to work freelance; **tätig sein** to do freelance work, to freelance; **Frei|be|trag** M tax allowance; **Frei|beu|ter** [-bɔytɐ] M **-s, -**, **Frei|beu|te|rin** F **-, -nen** pirate, buccaneer, freebooter (*old*); (*fig*) exploiter; **Frei|beu|te|rei** [-bɔytəˈraɪ] F **-, -en** piracy, buccaneering, free-booting (*old*); (*fig*) exploitation; **frei|be|weg|lich** △ **frei 2 a**; **Frei|bier** NT free beer; **frei|blei|bend** ADJ subject to alteration; **Frei|bord** M (*Naut*) freeboard; **Frei|brief** M **a** (*Hist*) (= *Privileg*) royal charter; (= *Freilassung*) letter of manumission **b** (*fig*) licence (*Brit*), license (*US*)

Frei|burg [ˈfraɪbʊrk] NT **-s a** (*in Deutschland*) Freiburg **b** (*in der Schweiz: Kanton, Stadt*) Fribourg

Frei-: Frei|deck NT uncovered level (*of multi-storey car park*); **Frei|den|ker(in)** M(F) freethinker; **frei|den|ke|risch** ADJ freethinking

frei|en [ˈfraɪən] (*old*) VT to wed (*old, liter*) VI **um ein Mädchen ~** to woo (*old*) or court (*dated*) a girl; **jung gefreit hat nie gereut** (*Prov*) marry young and you'll never regret it

Freie(r) [ˈfraɪə] MF *decl as adj* (*Hist*) freeman

Frei|er [ˈfraɪə] M **-s, - a** (*dated, hum*) suitor **b** (*inf: von Dirne*) (prostitute's) client, john (*US inf*)

Frei|ers|fü|ße PL **auf ~n gehen** (*hum*) to be courting (*dated*)

Freie(s) [ˈfraɪ] NT *decl as adj* **das ~** the open (air); **im ~n** in the open (air); **ins ~ gehen** to go outside or into the open (air); **ins ~ gelangen** to get out; **im ~n übernachten** to sleep out in the open

Frei-: Frei|exem|plar NT free copy; **Frei|fahr|schein** M free ticket; **Frei|fahrt** F free journey; **~ haben** to travel free; **frei|fi|nan|ziert** △ [-finantsiːɐt] → **frei 2 c**; **Frei|flä|che** F open space; **Frei|flug** M free flight; **Frei|frau** F baroness (*by marriage*); **Frei|fräu|lein** NT baron-

---

ess (*in her own right*); **Frei|ga|be** F release; (*von Preisen, Wechselkursen*) decontrol, lifting of control (+*gen* on); (*von Straße, Strecke, Flugbahn*) opening; (*von Film*) passing; (*Ftbl: von Ball*) putting back into play; **Frei|gang** M (*von Strafgefangenen*) day release; **~ bekommen** to be let out on parole; **während des ~s** while on parole; **Frei|gän|ger** [-gɛŋɐ] M **-s, -**, **Frei|gän|ge|rin** [-ərɪn] F **-, -nen** day release prisoner; **frei+ge|ben** *sep irreg* VT to release (*an* +*acc* to); *Gefangene, Ehepartner auch* to set free; *Preise, Wechselkurse* to decontrol, to lift controls on; *Straße, Strecke, Flugbahn* to open; *Film* to pass; (*Ftbl*) *Ball* to put back into play; *Spieler* to release; **etw zum Verkauf ~** to allow sth to be sold on the open market; **jdm den Weg ~** to let sb past or by VI **jdm ~** to give sb a holiday (*Brit*), to give sb vacation (*US*); **jdm zwei Tage ~** to give sb two days off; **frei|ge|big** [ˈfraɪɡəˌbɪç] ADJ generous; **Frei|ge|big|keit** F **-, *no pl*** generosity; **Frei|ge|he|ge** NT open-air or outdoor enclosure; **Frei|geist** M freethinker; **frei|geis|tig** ADJ freethinking; **Frei|ge|län|de** NT open-air exhibition ground; **Frei|ge|las|se|ne(r)** [-gəlasnə] MF *decl as adj* (*Hist*) freedman/-woman; (= *ex-Gefangener*) released prisoner; **Frei|ge|päck** NT baggage allowance; **Frei|ge|richt** NT (*Hist*) Vehmgericht; **frei|ge|stellt** PTP *von* freistellen ADJ **a** (*wahlweise*) optional **b** (= *befreit*) **~ sein von** to be exempt from → *auch* freistellen; **frei|gie|big** [ˈfraɪɡiːbɪç] ADJ generous; **Frei|graf** M (*Hist*) Vehmic judge; **Frei|gren|ze** F (*bei Steuer*) tax exemption limit; **frei+ha|ben** VI *sep irreg* to have a holiday (*Brit*), to have vacation (*US*); **ich habe heute/zwei Tage frei** I have today/two days off; **eine Stunde ~** (*Sch*) to have a free period; **die sechste Stunde ~** (*Sch*) to have the sixth period free; **er hat mittags eine Stunde frei** he has an hour free at midday; **fünf Minuten ~** to have five minutes (free); **Frei|ha|fen** M free port; **frei+hal|ten** VT *sep irreg* **a** (= *nicht besetzen*) to keep free or clear **b** (= *reservieren*) to keep, to save **c** (= *jds Zeche begleichen*) to pay for; **sich von jdm ~ lassen** to let sb pay for one VR **sich von etw ~** to avoid sth; *von Vorurteilen etc* to be free of sth; *von Verpflichtungen* to keep oneself free of sth; **Frei|hand|bü|che|rei** F open-shelf library; **Frei|han|del** M free trade; **Frei|han|dels|zo|ne** F free trade area; **die kleine ~** EFTA, the European Free Trade Area; **frei|hän|dig** ADJ, ADV *Zeichnung* freehand; *Radfahren* without hands, (with) no hands; *Schießen* offhand (*spec*), without support; *Vergabe von Aufträgen* private; **Frei|hand|zeich|nung** F freehand drawing; **frei|hän|gend** ADJ *attr* suspended

Frei|heit [ˈfraɪhaɪt] F **-, -en a** *no pl* freedom; **die ~** freedom; (= *persönliche Freiheit als politisches Ideal*) liberty; **~, Gleichheit, Brüderlichkeit** liberty, equality, fraternity; **persönliche ~** personal freedom; **in ~** (*dat*) **sein** to be free; (*Tier*) to be in the wild; **in ~ leben** (*Tier*) to live in the wild; **in ~ geboren** born free; **jdn/etw in ~** (*acc*) **setzen** to set sb/sth free; **jdm die ~ schenken** to give sb his/her etc freedom, to free sb; **der Weg in die ~** the path to freedom

b (= *Vorrecht*) freedom *no pl*; **dichterische ~** poetic licence (*Brit*) or license (*US*); **alle ~en haben** to have all the freedom possible; **die ~ haben** or **genießen** (*geh*), **etw zu tun** to be free or at liberty to do sth, to have or enjoy the freedom to do sth; **sich** (*dat*) **die ~ nehmen, etw zu tun** to take the liberty of doing sth; **sich** (*dat*) **zu viele ~en erlauben** to take too many liberties

frei|heit|lich [ˈfraɪhaɪtlɪç] ADJ liberal; *Verfassung* based on the principle of liberty; *Demokratie* free; **die ~-demokratische Grundordnung** the free democratic constitutional structure ADV **erziehen** liberally; **~ gesinnt** or **eingestellt** liberal

Frei|heit|li|che(r) [ˈfraɪhaɪtlɪçə] MF *decl as adj* (*Aus Pol*) member of the (Austrian) Freedom Party; **die ~n** *pl* the (Austrian) Freedom Party

---

Frei|heits-: Frei|heits|be|griff M concept of freedom; **Frei|heits|be|rau|bung** F (*Jur*) wrongful deprivation of personal liberty; **Frei-heits|be|we|gung** F liberation movement; **Frei|heits|de|likt** NT (*Jur*) offence (*Brit*) or offense (*US*) against personal liberty; **Frei-heits|drang** M , *no pl* urge or desire for freedom; **Frei|heits|ent|zug** M imprisonment; **frei|heits|feind|lich** ADJ operating against freedom; *Kräfte auch* anti-freedom *attr*; **Frei-heits|kampf** M fight for freedom; **Frei|heits-kämp|fer(in)** M(F) freedom fighter; **Frei-heits|krieg** M war of liberation; **Frei|heits-lie|be** F love of liberty; **frei|heits|lie|bend** ADJ freedom-loving; **Frei|heits|rech|te** PL civil rights and liberties *pl*; **Frei|heits|sta|tue** F Statue of Liberty; **Frei|heits|stra|fe** F prison sentence; **er erhielt eine ~ von zwei Jahren** he was given a two-year prison sentence, he was sentenced to two years' imprisonment

Frei-: frei|he|raus [fraihe'raus] ADV candidly, frankly; **Frei|herr** M baron; **frei|herr|lich** ADJ *attr* baronial

Frei|in ['fraiɪn] F -, **-nen** baroness (*in her own right*)

Frei-: frei+kämp|fen *sep* VT to get free; (*durch Gewaltanwendung*) to free by force VR to get free; to free oneself by force; **Frei|kar|te** F free or complimentary ticket; **frei+kau|fen** VT *sep jdn/sich* ~ to buy sb's/one's freedom; **Frei-kir|che** F Free Church; **Frei|klet|tern** NT free climbing; **frei+kom|men** VI *sep irreg aux sein* **a** (= *entkommen*) to get out (*aus* of); (= *befreit werden*) to be released or freed (*aus, von* from) **b** (= *sich bewegen lassen: Boot*) to come free; **Frei|kon|zert** NT (*Sw*) open-air concert; **Frei|kör|per|kul|tur** F , *no pl* nudism, naturism; **Frei|korps** NT (*Mil*) volunteer corps *sing*

Frei|land NT , *no pl* (*Hort*) open beds *pl*; **auf/im ~** outdoors

Frei|land-: Frei|land|an|bau M outdoor cultivation; **Frei|land|ge|mü|se** NT outdoor vegetables *pl*; **Frei|land|hal|tung** F , *no pl* free--range husbandry; **Eier/Hühner aus** ~ free-range eggs/chickens; **Frei|land|kul|tur** F outdoor cultivation; **Frei|land|ver|such** M outdoor trial

Frei-: frei|las|sen VT *sep irreg* to set free, to free; (*aus Haft, Gefangenschaft auch*) to release; *Hund* to let off the lead or leash; **Frei|las|sung** F -, **-en** release; (*von Sklaven*) setting free; **Frei-lauf** M (*Aut*) neutral; (*bei Fahrrad*) freewheel; **im ~ fahren** to coast (in neutral); to freewheel; **frei+lau|fen** VR *sep irreg* (*Sport*) to get free; **frei|lau|fend** △ ADJ → **frei 2 a**; **frei|le|bend** △ ADJ → **frei 2 a**; **frei+le|gen** VT *sep* to expose; *Ruinen, Trümmer* to uncover; (*fig*) to lay bare, to expose; **Frei|le|gung** F -, **-en** (*lit, fig*) exposure; (*von Ruinen, Trümmern*) uncovering; **Frei|lei|tung** F overhead cable

frei|lich ['frailɪç] ADV **a** (= *allerdings*) admittedly; **es scheint ~ nicht leicht zu sein** admittedly or certainly it doesn't seem easy **b** (*esp S Ger: = natürlich*) of course, certainly, sure (*esp US*); **aber ~!** (of) course!; **ja ~** yes of course

Frei|licht- ['frailɪçt] *in cpds* open-air; **Frei|licht-büh|ne** F open-air theatre (*Brit*) or theater (*US*); **Frei|licht|ki|no** NT open-air cinema; (= *Autokino*) drive-in cinema; **Frei|licht|mu|se|um** NT open-air museum

Frei-: Frei|los NT free lottery ticket; (*Sport*) bye; **frei+ma|chen** *sep* VT to stamp; (*mit Frankiermaschine*) to frank; **einen Brief mit 55 Cent ~** to put stamps to the value of 55 cents on a letter → *auch* **frei a, b** VR **a** (= *freie Zeit einplanen*) to arrange to be free **b** (= *sich entkleiden*) to take one's clothes off, to strip; **Frei|ma|chung** [-maxʊŋ] F, *no pl* (*von Brief etc*) stamping; (*mit Frankiermaschine*) franking; **Frei|mar|ke** F (*postage*) stamp; **Frei|mau|rer** M Mason, Freemason; **Frei|mau|re|rei** [-maurə'rai] F -, *no pl* Freemasonry; **frei|mau|re|risch** [-maurərɪʃ] ADJ Masonic; **Frei|mau|rer|lo|ge** F Masonic Lodge

Frei|mut M , *no pl* frankness, honesty, openness; **mit allem** ~ perfectly frankly or honestly or openly

frei|mü|tig ['fraimy:tɪç] ADJ frank, honest, open ADV frankly, honestly, openly

Frei|mü|tig|keit F -, *no pl* frankness, honesty, openness

Frei-: frei|neh|men VT *sep irreg* **einen Tag ~** to take a day off; **Frei|platz** M **a** free or complimentary seat **b** (*Univ*) scholarship; (*Sch auch*) free place; **frei+pres|sen** VT *sep jdn* ~ to obtain sb's release, to get sb set free; **versuchen, jdn freizupressen** to demand sb's release; **Frei-raum** M (*fig*) freedom *no art, no pl* (*zu* for); ~ **brauchen, in dem man sich entwickeln kann** to need freedom to develop or in which to develop; **die Universität ist kein gesellschaftlicher ~** university isn't a social vacuum; **frei|re|li|gi-ös** ADJ non-denominational; **Frei|sass** ▲ ['fraizas] M **-en, -en**, **Frei|sas|se** ['fraizasə] M **-n, -n** (*Hist*) yeoman; **Frei|schaf|fen|de(r)** [-ʃafndə] MF *decl as adj* freelance, freelancer; **frei+schal|ten** VT *sep* (*Telec*) *Leitung* to clear; *Handy* to connect, to enable; **Frei|schar** F (*Hist*) (irregular) volunteer corps *sing*; **Frei|schär|ler** [-ɛːɐlɐ] M **-s, -**, **Frei|schär|le|rin** [-ərɪn] F -, **-nen** guerrilla; (*Hist*) irregular (volunteer); **frei+schau|feln** VT *sep* to clear, to dig clear; **frei+schie|ßen** VT *sep irreg* **sich** (*dat*) **den Weg ~** to shoot one's way out; **jdn ~** to shoot sb free; **Frei|schuss** ▲ M free shot; **frei+schwim|men** VR *sep irreg* (*Sport*) *to pass a test by swimming for 15 minutes* (*fig*) to learn to stand on one's own two feet; **Frei|schwim|men** NT *15-minute swimming test*

FREISCHWIMMER

The **Freischwimmer** badge is awarded to swimmers who can swim for 15 minutes without holding onto the side of the pool and dive from the lower diving board. Children without the **Freischwimmer** badge displayed on their trunks or swimsuit are not allowed to use the deep end of a public swimming pool unless supervised. The next level up is the **Fahrtenschwimmer**, which entails a 30-minute swimming test, beginning with a dive from the higher diving board.

Frei-: Frei|schwin|ger [-ʃvɪŋɐ] M **-s, -** **a** (= *Sessel*) cantilevered chair **b** (= *Uhr*) caseless pendulum clock; **frei+set|zen** VT *sep* to release; (*euph*) *Arbeitskräfte* to make redundant; (*vorübergehend*) to lay off; **Frei|set|zung** F -, **-en** release; (*euph*) dismissal; (*vorübergehend*) laying off; **Frei|sinn** M , *no pl* (*dated*) liberalism; **frei-sin|nig** ADJ (*dated*) liberal; **Freisinnige Partei** (*Sw*) Swiss Liberal Party; **Frei|spiel** NT free game; **frei+spie|len** *sep* VR **a** (*Sport*) to get into space **b** (*Theat, Film*) to get over one's stage fright VT (*Sport*) **jdn ~** to play sb clear, to create space for sb; **Frei|sprech|an|la|ge** F hands-free (headset); (*im Auto*) hands-free (car kit); **frei+spre|chen** VT *sep irreg* **a** *Angeklagten, Beschuldigten* to acquit; **jdn von einer Schuld ~** (*Jur*) to find sb not guilty; **jdn von einem Verdacht ~** to clear sb of suspicion; **jdn wegen erwiesener Unschuld ~** to prove sb not guilty **b** (*Handwerk*) *Auszubildende* to qualify; **Frei|spruch** M acquittal; **es ergeht ~** the verdict is "not guilty"; **auf ~ plädieren** to plead not guilty; **Frei|staat** M free state; **der ~ Bayern/Sachsen** the Free State of Bavaria/Saxony

FREISTAAT

During the Weimar Republic most **Länder** were called **Freistaat**, although after the Second World War the majority chose other ways of describing themselves. Prior to re-unification only Bavaria kept the name **Freistaat**, as a sign of its independence

within the federation. Today two of the new **Länder**, Saxony and Thuringia, also bear the title.

Frei-: Frei|statt [-ʃtat] F -, **-en**, **Frei|stät|te** F (*liter*) sanctuary; **frei+ste|hen** VI *sep irreg* **a** (= *überlassen sein*) **es steht jdm frei, etw zu tun** sb is free or at liberty to do sth; **das steht Ihnen völlig frei** that is completely up to you; **es steht Ihnen frei, ob ...** it is up to you whether ... **b** (= *leer stehen*) to stand empty; **frei+stel-len** VT *sep* **a** (= *anheim stellen*) **jdm etw ~** to leave sth (up) to sb **b** (= *zur Verfügung stellen*) *Mittel* to make available; *Personal* to release **c** (= *befreien*) to exempt; **einen Schüler vom Unterricht ~** to excuse a pupil from a lesson/his lessons; **Frei|stem|pel** M frank

Frei|stil- *in cpds* freestyle; **Frei|stil|rin|gen** NT all-in or freestyle wrestling

Frei-: Frei|stoß M (*Ftbl*) free kick (*für* to, for); **Frei|stück** NT free copy; **Frei|stun|de** F free hour; (*Sch*) free period

Frei|tag ['fraita:k] M Friday; **der Schwarze ~** *the day of the Wall Street crash* **ein schwarzer ~** a black day → *auch* **Dienstag**

frei|täg|lich ADJ *attr* Friday

frei|tags ['fraita:ks] ADV on Fridays, on a Friday

Frei-: Frei|tisch M free meals *pl*; **Frei|tod** M suicide; **den ~ wählen** or **suchen** to decide to put an end to one's life; **frei+tra|gend** ADJ self-supporting; *Konstruktion, Brücke, Flügel* cantilever *attr*; *Treppe* hanging, cantilever *attr*; **Frei-trep|pe** F (flight of) steps (+*gen* leading up to); **Frei|übung** F exercise; **~en machen** to do one's exercises; **Frei|um|schlag** M stamped addressed envelope, s.a.e.

frei|weg ['fraivɛk] ADV openly; (= *freiheraus*) straight out, frankly; **er fing an, ~ zu erzählen** he started talking away

Frei-: Frei|wild NT (*fig*) fair game; **frei|wil|lig** ADJ voluntary; (*Jur*) *Gerichtsbarkeit auch* non--contentious; (= *freigestellt*) *Versicherung, Unterricht* optional; **~e Feuerwehr** voluntary fire brigade (*Brit*) or fire department (*US*) ADV voluntarily; **sich ~ melden** to volunteer (*zu, für* for); **etw ~ machen** to do sth voluntarily, to do sth of one's own free will; **~ in den Tod gehen** to take one's own life; **sich ~ verpflichten** (*bei Militär*) to enlist; **Frei|wil|li|ge(r)** [-vɪlɪɡə] MF *decl as adj* volunteer; **~ vor!** volunteers, one pace forwards!; **Frei|wil|li|gen|ar|mee** F volunteer army; **Frei|wil|lig|keit** F voluntary nature, voluntariness; **Frei|wurf** M free throw; **Frei|zei|chen** NT (*Telec*) ringing tone; **Frei|zeich|nungs-klau|sel** F (*Jur, Comm*) exemption from liability clause

Frei|zeit F **a** (= *arbeitsfreie Zeit*) free or spare or leisure time **b** (= *Zusammenkunft*) weekend or holiday course; (*Eccl*) retreat

Frei|zeit-: Frei|zeit|an|ge|bot NT leisure activity; **ein breites ~ bereitstellen** to offer a wide range of leisure activities; **Frei|zeit|an-zug** M jogging suit; **Frei|zeit|aus|gleich** M time off in lieu (*Brit*), time off instead of pay (*US*); **Frei|zeit|be|klei|dung** F casual clothes *pl*; (*als Warengattung*) leisurewear *no pl*; **Frei-zeit|be|schäf|ti|gung** F leisure pursuit or activity; **Frei|zeit|for|scher(in)** M(F) researcher in leisure activities; **Frei|zeit|ge|stal|tung** F organization of one's leisure time; **das Problem der ~** the leisure problem; **Frei|zeit|heim** NT (*für Jugendliche*) hostel for groups of young people with organized leisure activities; **Frei|zeit|hemd** NT sports shirt; **Frei|zeit|in-dust|rie** F leisure industry; **Frei|zeit|klei-dung** F casual clothes *pl*; (= *Warengattung*) leisurewear *no pl*; **Frei|zeit|park** M amusement park; **Frei|zeit|pro|blem** NT problem of leisure, leisure problem; **Frei|zeit|ver|hal|ten** NT recreational behaviour (*Brit*) or behavior (*US*), recreational patterns *pl*; **Frei|zeit|wert** M **München hat einen hohen ~** Munich has a lot to offer in the way of recreational and leisure facilities

Frei-: frei│zü│gig ADJ **a** (= *reichlich*) *Gebrauch, Anwendung* liberal **b** (*in moralischer Hinsicht*) permissive **c** (= *den Wohnort frei wählen könnend*) free to move ADV **a** (= *reichlich*) freely, liberally; **~ Geld ausgeben** to spend money freely or liberally **b** (= *moralisch locker*) **sich ~ benehmen** to be loose; **~ gekleidet** provocatively dressed; **Frei│zü│gig│keit** [-tsy:gɪçkaɪt] F **-**, *no pl* **a** (= *Großzügigkeit*) liberality **b** (*in moralischer Hinsicht*) permissiveness **c** (= *Beweglichkeit: von Waren, freie Wahl des Wohnorts etc*) freedom of movement

fremd [frɛmt] ADJ **a** (= *andern gehörig*) someone else's; *Bank, Bibliothek, Firma* different; (*Comm, Fin, Pol*) *attr*; **ohne ~e Hilfe** without anyone else's/outside help, without help from anyone else/outside; **ich schlafe nicht gern in ~en Betten** I don't like sleeping in strange beds; **~es Eigentum** someone else's property, property not one's own (*form*); **das ist nicht für ~e Ohren** that is not for other people to hear; **etw geht in ~e Hände über** sth passes into the hands of strangers or into strange hands; **sich mit ~en Federn schmücken** to claim all the glory for oneself **b** (= *fremdländisch*) foreign, alien (*esp Admin, Pol*) **c** (= *andersartig*) strange; *Planeten* other; *Welt* different **d** (= *unvertraut*) strange; **jdm ~ sein** (= *unbekannt*) to be unknown to sb; (= *unverständlich*) to be foreign or alien to sb; (= *nicht in jds Art*) to be foreign or alien to sb or to sb's nature; **es ist mir ~, wie …** I don't understand how …; **das ist eine mir ~e Seite seines Wesens** that is a side of his character which I haven't seen before; **ich bin hier/in London ~** I'm a stranger here/to London; **meine Heimat ist mir ~ geworden** I've become a stranger in my own country, my own country has become quite foreign or alien to me; **sich ~ einander** (*dat*) **~ werden** to grow apart, to become strangers (to one another); **sich ~ fühlen** to feel alien, to feel like a stranger; **~ tun** to be reserved

Fremd-: Fremd│ar│bei│ter(in) M(F) foreign worker; **fremd│ar│tig** ADJ strange; (= *exotisch*) exotic ADV **~ aussehen/klingen/anmuten** to look/sound/seem strange or exotic; **Fremd│ar│tig│keit** F, *no pl* strangeness; (= *Exotik*) exoticism; **Fremd│be│stäu│bung** F cross-fertilization; **fremd│be│stimmt** ADJ heteronomous ADV **~ handeln** to act under orders; **Fremd│be│stim│mung** F heteronomy

Frem│de ['frɛmdə] F **-**, *no pl* (*liter*) **die ~** foreign parts *pl*; **in die ~ gehen** to go to foreign parts, to go abroad; **in der ~ sein** to be in foreign parts, to be abroad

frem│de(l)n ['frɛmd(l)n] VI (*S Ger, Sw*) to be scared of strangers

Frem│den-: Frem│den│bett NT spare or guest bed; (*in Hotel*) hotel bed; **frem│den│feind│lich** ADJ hostile to strangers; (= *ausländerfeindlich*) hostile to foreigners, xenophobic; **Frem│den│feind│lich│keit** F xenophobia; **Frem│den│füh│rer** M guide(book); **Frem│den│füh│rer(in)** M(F) (*tourist*) guide; **Frem│den│has│ser** ▲ M xenophobe; **Frem│den│has│ser** [-hasɐ] M **-s**, **-**, **Frem│den│has│se│rin** [-hasərɪn] F **-**, **-nen** xenophobe (*form*); **er ist ein ~** he hates foreigners; **Frem│den│le│gion** F Foreign Legion; **Frem│den│le│gio│när** M Foreign Legionnaire; **Frem│den│pass** ▲ M alien's passport; **Frem│den│po│li│zei** F aliens branch (of the police); (*Aviat*) aliens office

Frem│den│ver│kehr M tourism *no def art*

Frem│den│ver│kehrs-: Frem│den│ver│kehrs│amt NT tourist office; **Frem│den│ver│kehrs│ort** M *pl* **-orte** tourist resort, tourist centre (*Brit*) or center (*US*); **Frem│den│ver│kehrs│ver│ein** M tourist association

Frem│den│zim│mer NT guest room

Frem│de(r) ['frɛmdə] MF *decl as adj* (= *Unbekannter, Ortsfremder*) stranger; (= *Ausländer*) foreigner; (*Admin, Pol*) alien; (= *Tourist*) visitor

Fremd-: Fremd│fi│nan│zie│rung F outside financing; **fremd│ge│hen** VI *sep irreg aux sein* (*inf*) to be unfaithful; **Fremd│heit** F, (*rare*) **-en** (= *ausländische Natur*) foreignness; (= *Unvertrautheit*) strangeness; (= *Entfremdung*) alienation; (*zwischen Menschen*) reserve; **Fremd│herr│schaft** F, *no pl* foreign rule; **Fremd│ka│pi│tal** NT outside capital; **Fremd│kör│per** M foreign body; (*fig*) alien element; **sich als ~ fühlen** to feel out of place; **fremd│län│disch** [-lɛndɪʃ] ADJ foreign *no adv*; (= *exotisch*) exotic; **Fremd│ling** ['frɛmtlɪŋ] M **-s**, **-e** (*liter*) stranger

Fremd│spra│che F foreign language; **eine Begabung für ~n** a gift for languages

Fremd│spra│chen-: Fremd│spra│chen│kor│res│pon│dent(in) M(F), **Fremd│spra│chen│sek│re│tär(in)** M(F) bilingual secretary; **Fremd│spra│chen│un│ter│richt** M language teaching; **~ haben/erteilen** to have/give language classes

Fremd-: fremd│spra│chig ADJ in a foreign language; *Fähigkeiten* (foreign) language; **die ~e Bevölkerung** non-English/non-German *etc* speakers; **fremd│sprach│lich** ADJ foreign; **~er Unterricht** language teaching; **Fremd│stoff** M foreign matter *no pl* or substance; **Fremd│ver│schul│den** NT third-party responsibility; **Fremd│wäh│rung** F foreign currency; **Fremd│wort** NT *pl* **-wörter** borrowed or foreign word, borrowing; **Rücksichtnahme ist für ihn ein ~** (*fig*) he's never heard of the word consideration; **Fremd│wör│ter│buch** NT dictionary of borrowed or foreign words

fre│ne│tisch [freˈneːtɪʃ] ADJ frenetic, frenzied; *Beifall auch* wildly

fre│quen│tie│ren [frekvɛnˈtiːrən] *ptp* **frequentiert** VT (*geh*) to frequent

Fre│quenz [freˈkvɛnts] F **-**, **-en** **a** (= *Häufigkeit*) frequency (*auch Phys*); (*Med*) (pulse) rate **b** (= *Stärke*) numbers *pl*; (= *Verkehrsdichte*) volume of traffic

Fre│quenz- *in cpds* frequency; **Fre│quenz│be│reich** M (*Rad*) frequency range

Fres│ke ['frɛskə] F **-**, **-n** (*rare*), **Fres│ko** ['frɛsko] NT **-s**, **Fresken** [-kn] fresco

Fres│sa│li│en [frɛˈsaːliən] PL (*inf*) grub *sing* (*sl*), eats *pl* (*inf*)

Fress│beu│tel ▲ M (*für Pferd*) nosebag

Fres│se ['frɛsə] F **-**, **-n** (*vulg*) (= *Mund*) trap (*inf*), gob (*Brit inf*), cakehole (*Brit inf*); (= *Gesicht*) mug (*inf*); **die ~ halten** to shut one's trap or gob or face (*all inf*); **eine große ~ haben** (*sl*) to be a loud-mouth (*inf*); **jdn** or **jdm in die ~ hauen, jdm die ~ polieren** to smash sb's face in (*inf*); **ach du meine ~!** (*sl*) bloody hell! (*Brit inf*), Jesus Christ! (*sl*)

fres│sen ['frɛsn] *pret* **fraß** [fraːs], *ptp* **gefressen** [gəˈfrɛsn] VI **a** (= *essen*) to feed, to eat; (*sl: Menschen*) to eat, to nosh (*Brit inf*), to guzzle (*inf*); **jdm aus der Hand ~** (*lit, fig inf*) to eat out of sb's hand; **für drei ~** to eat enough for a whole army (*inf*); **er isst nicht, er frisst** (*wie ein Schwein*) he eats like a pig → **Vogel, Scheunendrescher**

b (= *zerstören*) to eat away (*an etw* *dat*) sth)

VT **a** (= *verzehren*) (*Tier, sl: Mensch*) to eat; (= *sich ernähren von*) to feed or live on; (*sl: = gierig essen*) to guzzle (*inf*), to scoff (*Brit inf*), to scarf down (*US inf*); **etwas zu ~** something to eat; **den Napf leer ~** (*Tiere*) to lick the bowl clean; (*Menschen*) to polish everything off (*inf*); **jdn arm ~, jdm die Haare vom Kopf ~** to eat sb out of house and home → **Bauer** [1] **a, Not a**

b (*in Wendungen*) **Kilometer ~** to burn up the kilometres (*Brit*) or kilometers (*US*); **Löcher in etw** (*acc*) **~** (*lit*) to eat holes in sth; **ein Loch in den Geldbeutel ~** to make a big hole in one's pocket; **ich habe dich zum Fressen gern** (*inf*) you're good enough to eat (*inf*); **ich könnte**

dich ~ (*inf*) I could eat you (*inf*); **ich will dich doch nicht ~** (*inf*) I'm not going to eat you (*inf*); **ich fresse einen Besen** or **meinen Hut, wenn …** (*inf*) I'll eat my hat if …; **jdn/etw gefressen haben** (*inf*) to have had one's fill or as much as one can take of sb/sth; **jetzt hat er es endlich gefressen** (*inf*) he's got it or got there at last (*inf*), at last the penny's dropped; **einen Narren** or **Affen an jdm/etw gefressen haben** to dote on sb/sth → **Weisheit a**

c (= *verbrauchen*) *Benzin, Ersparnisse* to eat or gobble up; *Zeit* to take up

d (*geh: Neid, Hass*) to eat up

VR **a** (= *sich bohren*) to eat one's way (*in* +*acc* into, *durch* through)

b **sich voll** or **satt ~** (*Tier*) to gorge itself; (*sl: Mensch*) to stuff oneself or one's face (*inf*); **von diesem Futter wird sich Ihr Hund krank ~** this food will make your dog sick

Fres│sen NT **-s**, *no pl* food; (*sl*) grub (*sl*); (*sl: = Schmaus*) blow-out (*inf*) → **gefunden** ADJ

Fres│ser ['frɛsɐ] M **-s**, **-**, **Fres│se│rin** [-ərɪn] F **-**, **-nen** (*Tier*) eater

-fres│ser(in) M(F) *suf in cpds* **a** (= *Esser von etw*) eater **b** (= *Bekämpfer von jdm*) -basher (*inf*)

Fres│se│rei [frɛsəˈraɪ] F **-**, **-en** (*inf*) **a** *no pl* (= *übermäßiges Essen*) guzzling (*inf*); (= *Gefräßigkeit*) piggishness (*inf*), gluttony (*inf*) **b** (= *Schmaus*) blow-out (*inf*), nosh-up (*Brit inf*)

Fress-: Fress│feind ▲ M (*Zool*) predator; **Fress│gier** ▲ F voraciousness; (*pej: von Menschen*) gluttony, piggishness (*inf*); **Fress│korb** ▲ M (*inf*) (*für Picknick*) picnic hamper or basket; (= *Geschenkkorb*) food hamper or basket; **Fress│lust** ▲ F **a** (*Zool*) appetite **b** → **Fressgier**; **Fress│napf** ▲ M feeding bowl; **Fress│pa│ket** ▲ NT (*inf*) food parcel (*Brit*) or package; **Fress│sack** ▲ M (*sl*) greedy guts (*Brit inf*), glutton; **Fress│sucht** ▲ F (*inf*) gluttony; (*krankhaft*) craving for food; **Fress│wel│le** ▲ F (*hum inf*) wave of gluttony; **Fress│werk│zeu│ge** ▲ PL feeding equipment *no pl* or organs *pl*; (*von Insekten*) mouthpart; **Fress│zel│le** ▲ F (*Med*) = **Makrophage**

Frett│chen ['frɛtçən] NT **-s**, **-** ferret

Freu│de ['frɔydə] F **-**, **-n** **a** *no pl* pleasure; (*innig*) joy (*über* +*acc* at); (= *Erfreutheit*) delight (*über* +*acc* at); **~ an etw** (*dat*) **haben** to get or derive pleasure from sth; **er hat ~ an seinen Kindern** his children give him pleasure; **~ am Leben haben** to enjoy life; **wenn man an der Arbeit keine ~ hat** if you don't get any pleasure out of your work, if you don't enjoy your work; **vor ~** with joy; **die ~ an der Natur** the joy one gets from nature; **der Garten ist seine ganze ~** the garden is his pride and joy; **daran hat er seine ~** that gives him pleasure; (*iro*) he thinks that's fun; **es ist eine (wahre** or **reine) ~** … it's a (real) joy or pleasure to …; **es war eine reine ~, das mit anzusehen** it was a joy to see; **es ist keine (reine) ~, das zu tun** (*iro*) it's not exactly fun doing that; **es ist mir eine ~, zu …** it's a real pleasure for me to …; **jdm ~ machen** to give sb pleasure; **das Kind macht seinen Eltern viel/nur ~** the child gives his parents a lot of/nothing but joy; **er macht ihnen keine/wenig ~** he's no joy/not much of a joy to them; **es macht ihnen keine/wenig ~** they don't enjoy it (at all)/much; **jdm eine ~ machen** or **bereiten** to make sb happy; **jdm eine ~ machen wollen** to want to do something to please sb; **zu meiner großen ~** to my great delight; **zu unserer größten ~ können wir Ihnen mitteilen …** we are pleased to be able to inform you …; **Sie hätten seine ~ sehen sollen** you should have seen how happy he was; **aus ~ an der Sache** for the love of it or the thing; **aus Spaß an der ~** (*inf*) for the fun or hell (*inf*) of it or the thing; **in Freud und Leid zu jdm halten** (*dated*) to stand by sb come rain, come shine

b (= *Vergnügen*) joy; **die kleinen ~n des Lebens** the pleasures of life; **herrlich und in ~n le-**

---

ben to live a life of ease; **mit ~n** with pleasure; **da kommt ~ auf** this is where the fun starts

Freu|den-: Freu|den|bot|schaft F good news sing, glad tidings pl (old, Bibl); **Freu|den|fest** NT celebration; **Freu|den|feu|er** NT bonfire; **Freu|den|ge|heul** NT , **Freu|den|ge|schrei** NT shrieks pl of joy; **Freu|den|haus** NT (dated, hum) house of pleasure or ill-repute; **Freu|den|jun|ge** M (hum) male prostitute; **Freu|den|mäd|chen** NT (dated, hum) lady of easy virtue (euph), prostitute; **Freu|den|mahl** NT celebration meal, banquet (old), feast; **freu|den|reich** ADJ (geh) joyful, joyous; **Freu|den|ruf** M , **Freu|den|schrei** M joyful cry, cry of joy; **Freu|den|sprung** M joyful leap; **ei-nen ~ machen** to jump for joy; **Freu|den|tag** M happy or joyful (esp liter) day; **Freu|den|tanz** M dance of joy; **einen ~ aufführen** or **vollführen** to dance with joy; **Freu|den|tau|mel** M ecstasy (of joy); **Freu|den|trä|nen** PL tears pl of joy; **freu|den|voll** ADJ = freudvoll

freu|de-: freu|de|strah|lend ADJ no pred beaming with delight; Gesicht auch beaming ADV beaming with delight; **freu|de|trun|ken** ADJ (liter) delirious with joy

Freu|di|a|ner [frɔyˈdiːanɐ] M -s, -, **Freu|di|a|ne|rin** [-ərɪn] -, **-nen** Freudian

freu|dig [ˈfrɔydɪç] ADJ a (= froh gestimmt) joyful; (= gern bereit) willing; (= begeistert) enthusiastic; **jdn ~ stimmen** to raise sb's spirits b (= beglückend) happy, joyful (liter); **eine ~e Nachricht** some good or joyful (liter) news, some glad tidings pl (old, Bibl); **ein ~es Ereignis** (euph) a happy or blessed event (euph) ADV happily, joyfully; **einen Vorschlag ~ begrüßen** to greet a suggestion with delight; **etw ~ erwar-ten** to look forward to sth with great pleasure; **~ überrascht sein** to be pleasantly surprised

Freud- [ˈfrɔyt-]: **freud|los** ADJ joyless, cheerless ADV **~ dahinleben** to lead a joyless or cheerless existence; **Freud|lo|sig|keit** F -, no pl joylessness, cheerlessness

freudsch ▲ [frɔytʃ] ADJ attr Freudian → **Fehl-leistung**

freud|voll ADJ (geh) joyful, joyous (liter); Tage, Leben filled with joy

freu|en [ˈfrɔyən] ✪ 31, 38.3, 46.4, 47.5, 48.1, 48.2, 51.1, 51.2, 52.2, 52.3 VR a (= froh sein) to be glad or pleased (über +acc, (geh) +gen a-bout); **sich über ein Geschenk ~** to be pleased with a present; **sich sehr** or **riesig** (inf) ~ to be delighted or ever so pleased (inf) (über +acc a-bout); **sich habe es bekommen, freute sie sich** I've got it, she said happily or (stärker) joyfully; **sich an etw** (dat) ~ to get or derive a lot of pleasure from sth; **er freut sich sehr an sei-nen Kindern** his children give him a lot of pleasure; **sich für jdn ~** to be glad or pleased for sb or for sb's sake; **sich mit jdm ~** to share sb's happiness; **sich seines Lebens ~** to enjoy life; **ich freue mich, Ihnen mitteilen zu können, ...** I'm pleased to be able to tell you ... → **Kind** b **sich auf jdn/etw ~** to look forward to seeing sb/to sth; **sich auf das Kind ~** to look forward to the child being born or to the child's birth; **sich zu früh ~** to get one's hopes up too soon VT impers to please; **es freut mich/ihn, dass ...** I'm/he's pleased or glad that ...; **es freut mich/ihn sehr, dass ...** I'm/he's delighted or very pleased or very glad that ...; **das freut mich** I'm really pleased; **es freut mich sehr/es hat mich sehr gefreut, Ihre Bekanntschaft zu machen** (form) (I'm) pleased to meet/have met you

Freund [frɔynt] M -(e)s, -e [-də] a (= Kamerad) friend; **wir sind schon seit 1954 ~e** we've been friends since 1954; **mit jdm gut ~ sein** to be good friends with sb; **das habe ich ihm unter ~en gesagt** that was just between ourselves; **10 Euro unter ~en** 10 euros to a friend; **~ und Feind** friend and foe; **dein/Ihr ~ und Helfer** your friend and helper; **ein schöner ~** (iro inf) a fine friend; **jdn zum ~ haben** to have sb for or as a friend; **guter ~!** (liter) my dear man; **jdm ~ sein/**

bleiben/werden (old) to be/remain/become sb's friend → **alt a**

b (= Liebhaber) boyfriend; (esp älter) gentle-man-friend

c (fig) (= Anhänger) lover; (= Förderer) friend; **ein ~ der Kunst** an art lover; **ich bin kein ~ von Hunden** I'm no lover of dogs; **er ist kein ~ von vielen Worten** he's not one for talking much, he's a man of few words; **ich bin kein ~ von so etwas** I'm not keen on that sort of thing; **ein ~ des Alkohols sein** to like one's drink

-freund(in) M(F) suf in cpds a (= Kamerad) friend; **ein Schulfreund von mir** a school friend of mine b (fig = Liebhaber) lover of; **eine Mu-sikfreundin** a music-lover, a lover of music

Freund|chen [ˈfrɔyntçən] NT -s, - (inf) my friend (iro); **~, ~!** watch it, mate (Brit inf) or my friend!

Freun|des-: Freun|des|hand F (geh) **jdm die ~ reichen** to extend the hand or arm of friend-ship to sb; **von ~** by the hand of a friend; **Freun|des|kreis** M circle of friends; **etw im engsten ~ feiern** to celebrate sth with one's closest friends

Freund-Feind-Den|ken NT attitude that if you're not for us you're against us

Freun|din [ˈfrɔyndɪn] F -, -nen a friend; (= Lieb-haberin) girlfriend; (esp älter) lady-friend b (fig: = Anhängerin, Förderin) → **Freund c**

-freundin F suf in cpds = **-freund(in)**

freund|lich [ˈfrɔyntlɪç] ADJ a (= wohlgesinnt) friendly no adv; **bitte recht ~!** say cheese! (inf), smile please!; **mit ~en Grüßen, mit ~em Gruß** (with) best wishes

b (= liebenswürdig) kind (zu to); **würden Sie bitte so ~ sein und das tun?** would you be so kind or good as to do that?, would you be so kind or good enough to do that?; **das ist sehr ~ von Ihnen** that's very kind or good of you

c (= ansprechend) Aussehen, Landschaft, Wetter etc pleasant; Atmosphäre, Einrichtung, Farben cheerful; Atmosphäre friendly, congenial; (Fin, Comm: = günstig) favourable (Brit), favorable (US) ADV (= wohlwollend) bitten, fragen nicely; **jdn ~ anschauen** to give sb a friendly look; **jdm ~ be-handeln** to be friendly toward(s) sb; **einem Vor-schlag ~ gegenüberstehen** to be in favour (Brit) or favor (US) of a suggestion, to be well-disposed to a suggestion

-freund|lich ADJ suf a (= wohlgesinnt) pro-; **ei-ne israelfreundliche Politik** a pro-Israel policy b (= liebend) fond of; **er ist sehr kinderfreund-lich** he is very fond of children c (= geeignet) -friendly; **umweltfreundlich** eco-friendly d (= schonend) kind to; **ein magenfreundlicher Kaffee** a coffee which is kind to or gentle on the stomach

freund|li|cher|wei|se [ˈfrɔyntlɪçɐˈvaizə] ADV kindly; **er trug uns ~ die Koffer** he was kind e-nough to carry our cases for us, he kindly car-ried our cases (for us)

Freund|lich|keit F -, -en a no pl (= Wohlgeson-nenheit) friendliness; (= Liebenswürdigkeit) kind-ness; (von Aussehen, Landschaft, Wetter etc) pleas-antness; (von Zimmer, Einrichtung, Farben) cheer-fulness; (von Atmosphäre) friendliness, congeni-ality; **würden Sie (wohl) die ~ haben, das zu tun?** would you be so kind or good as to do that?, would you be kind or good enough to do that?; **die ~ des Investitionsklimas** the fa-vourable (Brit) or favorable (US) climate for in-vestment

b (= freundliche Handlung, Gefälligkeit) kindness, favour (Brit), favor (US); **jdm ~en erweisen** to be kind to sb; **jdm ein paar ~en sagen** to say a few kind words to sb; (iro) to say a few choice words to sb

Freund|schaft [ˈfrɔyntʃaft] F -, -en a (= freund-schaftliches Verhältnis) friendship; **mit jdm ~ schließen** to make or become friends with sb, to form a friendship with sb; **jdm die ~ anbie-ten** to offer sb's friendship; **in aller ~** in all

friendliness; **da hört die ~ auf** (inf) friendship doesn't go that far; **in Geldsachen hört die ~ auf** friendship doesn't extend to money matters → **kündigen** VT, Geschenk b no pl (dial: = Ver-wandtschaft) relatives pl, relations pl c (DDR) the Pioneer groups in one school

freund|schaft|lich [ˈfrɔyntʃaftlɪç] ADJ friendly no adv; **~e Gefühle** feelings of friendship ADV **jdm ~ verbunden sein** to be friends with sb; **mit jdm ~ verkehren** to be on friendly terms with sb; **jdm ~ gesinnt sein** to feel friendly toward(s) sb; **jdm ~ auf die Schulter klopfen** to give sb a friendly slap on the back

Freund|schafts-: Freund|schafts|ban|de PL (liter) ties pl of friendship; **Freund|schafts-be|such** M (Pol) goodwill visit; **Freund|schafts|bund** M pl -bünde friendly alliance; **Freund|schafts|dienst** M favour (Brit) or fa-vor (US) to a friend; **jdm einen ~ erweisen** to do sb a favo(u)r; **Freund|schafts|preis** M (special) price for a friend; **er überließ mir sein Auto zu einem ~/einem ~ von 800 Euro** he let me have his car cheaply/for 800 euros because we're friends; **ich mache dir einen ~** (inf) seeing we're friends I'll let you have it for a special price; **Freund|schafts|spiel** NT (Sport) friendly game or match, friendly (inf); **Freund|schafts|ver|trag** M (Pol) treaty of friendship

Fre|vel [ˈfreːfl] M -s, - (geh) sin (gegen against); (= Tat auch) heinous deed (liter); (fig) crime (an +dat against)

Fre|vel-: fre|vel|haft ADJ (geh) (= verwerflich) sinful; Leichtsinn, Verschwendung wanton; **Fre|vel|haf|tig|keit** [ˈfreːflhaftɪçkait] F -, no pl (geh) (= Verwerflichkeit) sinfulness; (von Leichtsinn, Ver-schwendung) wantonness

fre|veln [ˈfreːfln] VI (liter) to sin (gegen, an +dat against)

Fre|vel|tat F (liter) heinous deed (liter)

Frev|ler [ˈfreːflɐ] M -s, -, **Frev|le|rin** [-ərɪn] F -, -nen (liter) sinner; **die Strafe für den ~ an der Natur/gegen Gott** the punishment for someone who sins against nature/God

frev|le|risch [ˈfreːflərɪʃ] ADJ (liter) = frevelhaft

fri|de|ri|zi|a|nisch [frideriˈtsiaːnɪʃ] ADJ of Fred-erick the Great

Frie|de [ˈfriːdə] M -ns, -n (old) peace; **der ~ der Natur** the tranquillity of nature; **~ auf Erden** peace on earth; **~ sei mit euch** peace be with you; **~ seiner Asche** God rest his soul; **~, Freu-de, Eierkuchen** (inf) everything is rosy

Frie|den [ˈfriːdn] M -s, - a peace; **ein langer, ungestörter ~** a long period of uninterrupted peace; **im ~** in peacetime, in time of peace; **in ~ und Freiheit leben** to live at peace and in freedom; **im tiefsten ~** (living) in perfect tran-quillity; **seit letztem Jahr herrscht in dieser Ge-gend ~** this region has been at peace since last year; **~ schließen** to make one's peace; (Pol) to conclude (form) or make peace; **seinen ~ mit jdm/etw machen** to make one's peace with sb/ sth; **~ stiften** to make peace (zwischen +dat be-tween)

b (= Friedensschluss) peace; (= Vertrag) peace treaty; **der Westfälische ~** (Hist) the Peace of Westphalia; **den ~ diktieren** to dictate the peace terms; **über den ~ verhandeln** to hold peace negotiations; **den ~ einhalten** to keep the peace, to keep to the peace agreement

c (= Harmonie) peace, tranquillity; **sozialer ~** social harmony; **der häusliche ~** domestic har-mony; **in ~ und Freundschaft** or **Eintracht leben** to live in peace and harmony or tranquillity

d (= Ruhe) peace; **jdn in ~ lassen** to leave sb in peace; **um des lieben ~s willen** (inf) for the sake of peace and quiet; **sein schlechtes Gewissen ließ ihn keinen ~ mehr finden** his guilty con-science gave him no peace; **ich traue dem ~ nicht** (inf) something (fishy) is going on (inf); **(er) ruhe in ~** rest in peace

Frie|dens- in cpds peace; **Frie|dens|ak|ti-vist(in)** M(F) peace activist; **Frie|dens|ap-pell** M call for peace; **Frie|dens|be|din-**

gun|gen PL peace terms *pl*; **Frie|dens|be-mü|hung** F *usu pl* peace effort; (= *Friedensangebot*) peace move; **frie|dens|be|wegt** ADJ *Gruppen* campaigning for peace; *Aktivität* peace *attr*; **Frie|dens|be|weg|te(r)** [-bəvɛːktə] MF *decl as adj* peace activist; **Frie|dens|be-we|gung** F peace movement; **Frie|dens-bruch** M violation of the peace; **Frie|dens-en|gel** M (*lit, fig*) angel of peace; **Frie|dens-fahrt** F *international cycling race through eastern Europe*; **Frie|dens|for|scher(in)** M(F) peace researcher; **Frie|dens|for|schung** F peace studies *sing*; **Frie|dens|füh|ler** PL die ~ **ausstrecken** (*inf*) to make a tentative move toward(s) peace (*in Richtung* with); **Frie|dens-ini|ti|a|ti|ve** F peace initiative; **Frie|dens-kämp|fer(in)** M(F) pacifist; **Frie|dens|kon-fe|renz** F peace conference; **Frie|dens|kuss** ▲ (*Eccl*) pax, kiss of peace; **Frie|dens|la-ger** NT (*Hist*) nations of the Socialist bloc; **Frie|dens|lie|be** F love of peace; **Frie|dens-marsch** M peace march; **Frie|dens|no|bel-preis** M Nobel peace prize; **Frie|dens|ord-nung** F (*Pol*) peace framework; **Frie|dens-pfei|fe** F peace pipe; **mit jdm die ~ rauchen** (*lit*) to smoke a peace pipe with sb; (*fig*) to make (one's) peace *or* to bury the hatchet with sb; **miteinander die ~ rauchen** (*fig*) to bury the hatchet; **Frie|dens|pflicht** F (*Ind*) obligation binding on employers and unions to avoid industrial action during wages negotiations; **Frie|dens|plan** M peace plan; **Frie|dens|po-li|tik** F policy of peace; **Frie|dens|preis** F peace prize *or* award; **der ~ des deutschen Buchhandels** the peace prize of the German book trade; **Frie|dens|pro|duk|ti|on** F peacetime production; **Frie|dens|pro|zess** ▲ M peace process; **Frie|dens|rich|ter(in)** M(F) justice of the peace, JP; **Frie|dens|schluss** ▲ M peace agreement; **frie|dens|si|chernd** ADJ *Streitkräfte* peacekeeping; **~e Maßnahmen** measures to ensure peace; **Frie|dens|si|che|rung** F maintenance of peace; **Maßnahmen zur ~** measures to ensure peace; **Frie|dens|stär|ke** F (*Mil*) peacetime strength; **frie|dens|stif-tend** ADJ peacemaking; **Frie|dens|stif-ter(in)** M(F) peacemaker; **Frie|dens|tau|be** F dove of peace; **Frie|dens|trup|pen** PL peacekeeping forces *pl*; **Frie|dens|ver|hand-lun|gen** PL peace negotiations *pl*; **Frie|dens-ver|trag** M peace treaty; **Frie|dens|vor-schlag** M peace proposal; **Frie|dens|wil|le** M desire *or* wish for peace; **Frie|dens|wirt-schaft** F peacetime economy; **Frie|dens|zeit** F period of peace; **in ~en** in peacetime, in times of peace; **Frie|dens|zu|stand** M state of peace; **im ~** at peace

fried|fer|tig ['friːtfɛrtɪç] ADJ *Mensch* peaceable; *Miteinander* peaceful; *Hund* placid; **selig sind die Friedfertigen** (*Bibl*) blessed are the peacemakers

Fried|fer|tig|keit F *, no pl* peaceable nature; (*von Hund*) placidness; **in seiner ~ hat er …** peaceable as he is, he …; **aus reiner ~ hat er …** because of his peaceable nature, he …; **sie wur-den von den Polizeibeamten zur ~ ermahnt** they were warned by the police officers to keep the peace

Fried|hof ['friːthoːf] M (= *Kirchhof*) graveyard; (= *Stadtfriedhof etc*) cemetery; **auf dem ~** in the graveyard/cemetery

Fried|hofs-: **Fried|hofs|at|mos|phä|re** F gloomy atmosphere; **im Haus herrscht eine ~** the house is like a graveyard; **Fried|hofs-gärt|ne|rei** F cemetery flower shop; **Fried-hofs|ka|pel|le** F cemetery chapel; **Fried-hofs|ru|he** F (*lit*) → Friedhof peace of the graveyard/cemetery; (*fig*) deathly quiet

fried|lich ['friːtlɪç] ADJ **a** (= *nicht kriegerisch, gewaltlos*) *Lösung, Demonstration* peaceful; (= *friedfertig*) *Mensch* peaceable; (= *sanftmütig*) *Tier* placid; **etw auf ~em Wege lösen** to find a peaceful solution to sth, to solve sth peacefully *or* by peaceful means; **damit er endlich ~ ist** (*inf*) to keep him happy; **nun sei doch endlich ~!** (*fig*

inf) give it a rest! (*inf*); **sei ~, ich will keinen Streit** take it easy *or* calm down, I don't want any trouble; **die ~e Nutzung der Kernenergie** the use of nuclear power for peaceful purposes
b (= *friedvoll*) peaceful
ADV **a** (= *in Frieden*) peacefully
b ~ **sterben** *or* **einschlafen** (*euph*) to die peacefully; **jetzt kann ich ~ sterben** now I can die in peace

Fried|lich|keit F *-, no pl* **a** (= *Gewaltfreiheit*: *von Demonstration, Volk, Zeiten*) peacefulness; (= *Friedfertigkeit*: *von Mensch*) peaceable nature; (= *Sanftmut*) placidity **b** (= *friedvolle Atmosphäre*) peacefulness

fried- ['friːt-]: **fried|lie|bend** ADJ peace-loving; **fried|los** ADJ **a** (*liter.* = *ruhelos*) *Leben, Europa* without peace; *Mensch* unable to find peace **b** (*Hist*) *Person* outlawed; **fried|sam** ['friːtzaːm] ADJ (*old*) = friedlich

Fried|rich ['friːdrɪç] M -s Frederick; **~ der Gro-ße** Frederick the Great; **seinen ~ Wilhelm unter etw** (*acc*) **setzen** (*inf*) to put one's signature *or* moniker (*Brit inf*) to sth, to put one's John Hancock on sth (*US inf*)

frie|ren ['friːrən] *pret* **fror** [froːɐ], *ptp* **gefroren** [gəˈfroːrən] **VI** **a** *auch vt impers* (= *sich kalt füh-len*) to be cold; **ich friere, mich friert, es friert mich** (*geh*) I'm cold; **wie ein Schneider ~** (*inf*) to be frozen to the bone (*inf*); **mir** *or* **mich ~ die Zehen, mich friert es** *or* **ich friere an den Zehen** my toes are cold **b** *aux sein* (= *gefrieren*) to freeze; (*Fluss auch*) to freeze over **VI** *impers* to freeze; **heute Nacht hat es gefroren** it was below freezing last night

Fries [friːs] M -es, -e [-zə] (*Archit, Tex*) frieze

Frie|se ['friːzə] M -n, -n, **Frie|sin** ['friːzɪn] F -, -nen Fri(e)sian

Frie|sen|nerz ['friːzn-] M (*inf hum*) oilskin jacket

frie|sisch ['friːzɪʃ] ADJ Fri(e)sian → *auch* deutsch

Frie|sisch(e) ['friːzɪʃ] NT Fri(e)sian → *auch* Deutsch(e)

Fries|land ['friːslant] NT -s Friesland

fri|gid [friˈgiːt], **fri|gi|de** [friˈgiːdə] ADJ frigid

Fri|gi|di|tät [frigidiˈtɛːt] F -, *no pl* frigidity

Fri|ka(n)|del|le [frika(n)ˈdɛlə] F -, -n (*Cook*) ris-sole

Fri|kas|see [frikaˈseː] NT -s, -s (*Cook*) fricassee

fri|kas|sie|ren [frikaˈsiːrən] *ptp* **frikassiert** VT (*Cook*) to fricassee

Fri|ka|tiv [frikaˈtiːf] M -s, -e [-və], **Fri|ka|tiv-laut** M (*Ling*) fricative

Frik|ti|on [frɪkˈtsi̯oːn] F -, -en (*Tech, fig geh*) fric-tion *no pl*

Fris|bee® ['frɪsbi] NT -, -s Frisbee®; **~ spielen** to play (with a) Frisbee®

Fris|bee|schei|be ['frɪsbi-] F Frisbee®

frisch [frɪʃ] ADJ **a** fresh; *Wäsche, Kleidung* clean; (= *feucht*) *Farbe, Fleck* wet; **~es Obst** fresh fruit; **~e Eier** new-laid (*Brit*) *or* freshly-laid eggs; **sich ~ machen** to freshen up; **mit ~en Kräften** with renewed vigour (*Brit*) *or* vigor (*US*) *or* strength; **~en Mut fassen** to gain new courage; **~e Luft schöpfen** to get some fresh air; **jdn an die ~e Luft setzen** (*inf*) to show sb the door; **jdn auf ~er Tat ertappen** (*inf*) to catch sb in the act, to catch sb red-handed
b (= *munter*) *Wesen, Art* bright, cheery; *Erzäh-lung, Farbe* cheerful; (= *gesund*) *Aussehen, Ge-sichtsfarbe* fresh; *Mädchen* fresh-looking; **und munter sein** (*inf*) to be bright and lively; **~, fromm, fröhlich, frei** (*prov*) motto of a 19th century gymnastic movement (*iro*) cheerfully, gaily
c (= *kühl*) cool, chilly; *Luft, Wind auch* fresh; **es weht ein ~er Wind** (*lit*) there's a fresh wind; (*fig*) the wind of change is blowing
ADV **a** (= *neu*) freshly; **~ von** *or* **aus etw** fresh from sth; **Bier ~ vom Fass** beer (straight) from the tap; **~ gestrichen** newly *or* freshly painted;

(*auf Schild*) wet paint; **~ geschlachtet** fresh(ly) slaughtered; *Geflügel* fresh(ly) killed; **~ gefalle-ner Schnee** freshly *or* newly fallen snow; **~ ge-backen** (*inf, Ehepaar, Ehemann, Ehefrau*) newly-wed; *Diplom-Ingenieur etc* newly-qualified; *Minis-ter, Pressesprecher etc* newly-appointed; **~ gewa-schen** (*Kind*) clean; *Hemd etc auch* freshly washed *or* laundered; **das Bett ~ beziehen** to change the bed, to make the bed up with fresh sheets; **das ist mir noch ~ in Erinnerung** that is still fresh in my mind *or* memory
b (= *munter*) **immer ~ drauflos!** don't hold back!; **er geht immer ~ drauflos** he doesn't hang about; **er redet/schreibt immer ~ drauflos** he just talks/writes away; **~ begonnen, halb gewonnen** (*prov*) **~ gewagt ist halb gewonnen** (*Prov*) a good start is half the battle

frisch|auf [frɪʃˈʔauf] INTERJ (*old*) let us away (*old*)

Fri|sche ['frɪʃə] F -, *no pl* **a** freshness; **wegen der ~ der Farbe** because the paint is/was still wet (*von Wesen*) brightness; (*von Erzählung, Farbe*) cheerfulness; (= *gesundes Aussehen*) fresh-ness; **in voller körperlicher und geistiger ~** in perfect health both physically and mentally; **in alter ~** (*inf*) as always **c** (= *Kühle*) coolness, chilliness; (*von Luft, Wind*) freshness, chilliness

Fri|sche|da|tum NT sell-by date

Frisch|ei ['frɪʃʔai] NT new-laid (*Brit*) *or* freshly--laid egg

fri|schen ['frɪʃn] VT *Metall* to refine **VI** (*Wild-schwein*) to farrow

Frisch-: **Frisch|fisch** M fresh fish; **Frisch|-fleisch** NT fresh meat; **frisch-fröh|lich** ADJ bright and cheerful; **frisch|ge|ba|cken** △ [-gəbakn] ADJ → frisch ADV a; **Frisch|ge|mü-se** NT fresh vegetables *pl*

Frisch|hal|te-: **Frisch|hal|te|beu|tel** M air--tight bag; **Frisch|hal|te|box** F air-tight container; **Frisch|hal|te|da|tum** NT sell-by date; **Frisch|hal|te|fo|lie** F clingfilm; **Frisch|-hal|te|pa|ckung** F airtight pack

Frisch-: **Frisch|kä|se** M cream cheese; **Frisch|-ling** ['frɪʃlɪŋ] M -s, -e **a** (*Hunt*) young wild boar **b** (*hum:* = *Neuling*) complete beginner

Frisch|luft F fresh air

Frisch|luft-: **Frisch|luft|fa|na|ti|ker(in)** M(F) fresh air fiend *or* fanatic; **Frisch|luft|zu|fuhr** F fresh air supply

Frisch-: **Frisch|milch** F fresh milk; **Frisch|-was|ser** NT *, no pl* fresh water; **frisch|weg** [frɪʃˈvɛk] ADV (= *ohne Hemmungen*) straight out (*inf*); **die Kinder fingen ~ an zu singen** the chil-dren started to sing right off (*inf*); **Frisch|-wurst** F sausage (*unsmoked, undried etc*); **Frisch|zel|le** F (*Med*) live cell; **Frisch|zel-len|kur** F , **Frisch|zel|len|the|ra|pie** F (*Med*) live-cell *or* cellular therapy

Fri|seur [friˈzøːɐ] M -s, -e hairdresser; (= *Herren-friseur auch*) barber; (= *Geschäft*) hairdresser's; barber's

Fri|seu|rin [friˈzøːrɪn] F -, -nen (female) hairdresser

Fri|seur|sa|lon [friˈzøːɐ-] M hairdresser's, hairdressing salon

Fri|seu|se [friˈzøːzə] F -, -n (female) hairdresser

Fri|sier|creme F hair cream

fri|sie|ren [friˈziːrən] *ptp* **frisiert** VT **a** (= *käm-men*) **jdn ~, jdm das Haar ~** to do sb's hair; (*nach dem Legen*) to comb sb's hair out; **ihr ele-gant frisierter Kopf** her elegant hairdo; **sie ist stets gut frisiert** her hair is always beautifully done; **eine modisch frisierte Dame** a lady with a fashionable hairstyle *or* hairdo **b** (*inf:* = *ab-ändern*) *Abrechnung* to fiddle; *Bericht, Meldung* to doctor (*inf*); **die Bilanzen ~** to cook the books (*inf*) *Auto, Motorrad, Motor* to soup up (*inf*) **VR** to do one's hair

Fri|sier-: **Fri|sier|hau|be** F (= *Trockner*) hair-dryer hood; (*beim Friseur*) hairdryer; **Fri|sier-kom|mo|de** F dressing table; **Fri|sier|sa|lon**

M hairdressing salon; (*für Herren*) barber's shop; **Fri|sier|spie|gel** M dressing (table) mirror; **Fri|sier|stab** M styling brush; **Fri|sier|tisch** M dressing table; **Fri|sier|um|hang** M hairdressing cape

Fri|sör [fri'zøːɐ] M **-s, -e**, **Fri|sö|se** [-'zøːzə] F **-, -n = Friseur, Friseuse**

frisst ▲ [frɪst] 3. *pers sing pres von* **fressen**

Frist [frɪst] F **-, -en a** (= *Zeitraum*) period; (= *Kündigungsfrist*) period of notice; **eine ~ von vier Tagen/Wochen** *etc* four days/weeks *etc*; **eine ~ einhalten** to meet a deadline; (*bei Rechnung*) to pay within the period stipulated; **jds ~ verlängern**, **jdm die ~ verlängern** to give sb more time; **jds ~** *or* **jdm die ~ um zwei Tage verlängern** to give sb two more days; **die Bibliothek hat mir die ~ für die Rückgabe der Bücher verlängert** the library extended the loan-period on my books; **eine ~ verstreichen lassen** to let a deadline pass; (*bei Rechnung*) not to pay within the period stipulated; **innerhalb kürzester ~** without delay **b** (= *Zeitpunkt*) deadline (*zu* for); (*bei Rechnung*) last date for payment; **eine ~ versäumen** *or* **verpassen** to miss a deadline/the last date for payment **c** (= *Aufschub*) extension, period of grace; **jdm eine ~ von vier Tagen/Wochen geben** to give sb four days'/weeks' grace

Frist|ab|lauf M **nach ~** after the deadline has/had expired; (*bei Rechnung*) after expiry of the stipulated period

fris|ten ['frɪstn] VT **sein Leben** *or* **Dasein ~/mit etw ~** to eke out an existence/one's existence with sth; **ein kümmerliches Dasein ~** to eke out a miserable existence; (*Partei, Institution*) to exist on the fringes; **die Bauern mussten in Armut ihr Leben ~** the peasants barely managed to scrape a living

Fris|ten|lö|sung F , **Fris|ten|re|ge|lung** F *law allowing the termination of a pregnancy within the first three months*

Frist-: frist|ge|mäß, frist|ge|recht ADJ, ADV within the stated period; **jdm fristgerecht kündigen** to fire sb with (proper) notice (*inf*); **fristgerecht kündigen** to give proper notice; **frist|los** ADV instant, without notice; **frist|los** ADV **entlassen**, **kündigen** without notice; **Frist|ver|län|ge|rung** F extension

Fri|sur [fri'zuːɐ] F **-, -en** hairstyle

Fri|teu|se △ [fri'tøːzə] F **-, -n** → **Fritteuse**

fri|tie|ren △ [fri'tiːrən] *ptp* **fritiert** VT → **frittieren**

Frit|ta|ten [frɪ'taːtn] PL (*Aus*) pancake strips *pl*, strips *pl* of pancake

Frit|ten ['frɪtn] PL (*inf*) chips *pl* (*Brit*), fries *pl* (*esp US inf*)

Frit|ten|bu|de F (*inf*) chip shop (*Brit*), chippie (*Brit inf*), ≈ hotdog stand

Frit|teu|se ▲ [frɪ'tøːzə] F **-, -n** chip pan (*Brit*), deep-fat fryer

frit|tie|ren ▲ [frɪ'tiːrən] *ptp* **frittiert** VT to (deep-)fry

Frit|tü|re ▲ [frɪ'tyːrə] F **-, -n a** (= *Fritteuse*) chip pan (*Brit*), deep-fat fryer **b** (= *Fett*) fat **c** (= *Speise*) fried food

-frit|ze [frɪtsə] M *suf in cpds* **-n, -n** (*inf*) chap (*Brit inf*), guy (*inf*); **Computerfritze** computer chap (*Brit inf*) or guy (*inf*)

fri|vol [fri'voːl] ADJ (= *leichtfertig*) frivolous; (= *anzüglich*) *Witz, Bemerkung* risqué, suggestive; (= *verantwortungslos*) irresponsible

Fri|vo|li|tät [frivoli'tɛːt] F **-, -en a** *no pl* (= *Leichtfertigkeit*) frivolity; (= *Anzüglichkeit*) *Bemerkung* suggestiveness; (= *Verantwortungslosigkeit*) irresponsibility **b** (= *Bemerkung*) risqué remark

Fri|vo|li|tä|ten|ar|beit F (*Sew*) tatting

Frl. *abbr von* **Fräulein**

froh [froː] ADJ **a** (= *heiter*) happy; (= *dankbar*) glad, happy; (= *erfreut*) glad, pleased, happy;

über etw (*acc*) **~ sein** to be pleased with sth; (**darüber**) **~ sein, dass ...** to be glad *or* pleased that ...; **um etw ~ sein** to be grateful for sth; **~ gelaunt** joyful (*liter*), cheerful, happy; **~ gestimmt** (*geh*) happy, joyful (*liter*); **~en Mutes** *or* **Sinnes sein** (*old, geh*) to be cheerful, to be of good cheer (*old*); **~en Mutes machte sie sich an die Arbeit** (*old, geh*) cheerfully *or* with a light heart she set herself to work; **seines Lebens nicht (mehr) ~ werden** not to enjoy life any more; **da wird man seines Lebens nicht mehr ~!** it makes your life a misery **b** (= *erfreulich*) happy, joyful; *Nachricht* good, happy; **~e Ostern!** Happy Easter!; **~e Weihnachten!** Happy (*esp Brit*) *or* Merry Christmas!; **die Frohe Botschaft** the Gospel

froh-: froh|ge|launt △ ADJ → **froh a**; **froh|ge|mut** [-gəmuːt] ADJ (*old*) with a cheerful heart; **froh|ge|stimmt** △ ADJ → **froh a**

fröh|lich ['frøːlɪç] ADJ happy, cheerful, merry; *Lieder, Lachen, Stimme auch* gay (*dated*); **~e Weihnachten!** Happy (*esp Brit*) *or* Merry Christmas!; **~es Treiben** gaiety ADV (= *unbekümmert*) merrily, blithely, gaily; **er kam einfach so ~ ins Zimmer marschiert** he came waltzing into the room (*inf*)

Fröh|lich|keit F **-**, *no pl* happiness; (= *fröhliches Wesen*) happy *or* cheerful nature; (= *gesellige Stimmung*) merriment, gaiety

froh|lo|cken [froːˈlɔkn] *ptp* **frohlockt** VI (*geh*) to rejoice (*über +acc* over, at); (*vor Schadenfreude auch*) to gloat (*über +acc* over, *bei* at)

Froh-: Froh|na|tur F (*geh*) **a** (= *Mensch*) happy *or* cheerful soul *or* person **b** (= *Wesensart*) happy *or* cheerful nature; **Froh|sinn** M , *no pl* cheerfulness; (= *fröhliches Wesen*) cheerful nature; **froh|sin|nig** ADJ cheerful

fromm [frɔm] ADJ *comp* **~er** *or* **-er** ['frœmɐ], *superl* **~ste(r, s)** ['frœmstə] **a** (= *gläubig*) religious; *Christ* devout; *Werke* good; *Leben, Tun* godly, pious; (= *scheinheilig*) pious, sanctimonious; **~ werden** to become religious, to turn to *or* get (*inf*) religion; **mit ~em Augenaufschlag** *or* **Blick** looking as if butter wouldn't melt in his/her *etc* mouth; **~e Sprüche** pious words **b** (*old*: = *rechtschaffen*) *Bürger, Leute, Denkart* god-fearing, upright; **es kann der Frömmste nicht in Frieden leben, wenn es dem bösen Nachbarn nicht gefällt** (*Prov*) you can't be on good terms with a bad neighbour (*Brit*) *or* neighbor (*US*), however hard you try **c** (*old*: = *gehorsam*) meek, docile; *Tier* quiet, docile; **~ wie ein Lamm sein** to be as meek *or* (*Tier*) gentle as a lamb **d** (*fig*) **eine ~e Lüge, ein ~er Betrug** self-deception; **das ist ja wohl nur ein ~er Wunsch** that's just a pipe dream

Fröm|me|lei [frœməˈlai] F **-, -en** (*pej*) false piety

fröm|meln ['frœmln] VI (*pej*) to act piously, to affect piety

from|men ['frɔmən] VI (*old*) **jdm ~** to avail sb (*form*); **jdm nichts ~** to avail sb naught (*old*); **was frommt ihm das Geld?** of what avail is the money to him? (*form*)

Fröm|mig|keit ['frœmɪçkait] F **-**, *no pl* (= *Gläubigkeit*) religiousness; (*von Christ*) devoutness; (*von Leben, Tun, Schriften, Werken*) godliness, piousness; (*old*: = *Rechtschaffenheit*) uprightness

Frömm|ler ['frœmlɐ] M **-s, -**, **Fömm|le|rin** [-ərɪn] F **-, -nen** (*pej*) sanctimonious hypocrite

fömm|le|risch ['frœmlərɪʃ] ADJ (*pej*) pious, sanctimonious

Fron [froːn] F **-, -en**, **Fron|ar|beit** F (*Hist*) socage *no pl*; (*fig*) drudgery *no pl*; (= *Sklavenarbeit*) slavery

Fron|de ['frõːdə] F **-, -n** (*Pol*) faction

Fron|deur [frõ'døːɐ] M **-s, -e**, **Fron|deu|rin** [-'døːrɪn] F **-, -nen** factionist

Fron|dienst M (*Hist*) socage *no pl*; **jdm ~e leisten** to do socage (work) for sb

---

fro|nen ['froːnən] VI (*Hist*) to labour (*Brit*) *or* labor (*US*) for one's feudal lord; (*fig geh*) to labour (*Brit*), to labor (*US*)

frö|nen ['frøːnən] VI +*dat* (*geh*) to indulge in; **seiner Eitelkeit** to indulge

Fron|leich|nam [froːnˈlaiçnaːm] *no art* **-(e)s**, *no pl* (the Feast of) Corpus Christi; **zu** *or* **an ~** at the Feast of Corpus Christi, on Corpus Christi

Fron|leich|nams-: Fron|leich|nams|fest NT Feast of Corpus Christi; **Fron|leich|nams|pro|zes|si|on** F , **Fron|leich|nams|zug** M Corpus Christi procession

Front [frɔnt] F **-, -en a** (= *Vorderseite*) front; (= *Vorderansicht*) frontage; **die hintere ~** the back; **der General schritt die ~ der wartenden Truppen ab** the general inspected the waiting troops **b** (= *Kampflinie, -gebiet*) front; **in vorderster ~ stehen** to be in the front line; **auf breiter ~** along a wide front; **an der ~** at the front; **klare ~en schaffen** (*fig*) to clarify the/one's position **c** (*Met*) front **d** (= *Einheit*) ranks *pl*; (*in Namen*) front; **sich einer geschlossenen ~ gegenübersehen** to be faced with a united front; **~ gegen jdn/etw machen** to make a stand against sb/sth **e** (*Sport*: = *Führung*) **in ~ liegen** to be in the lead; **in ~ gehen** to go into *or* take the lead

Front|ab|schnitt M section of the front

fron|tal [frɔnˈtaːl] ADJ *no pred Angriff* frontal; *Zusammenstoß* head-on; *Position* at the front ADV *angreifen* (*Mil*) from the front; (*fig*) head-on; *zusammenstoßen* head-on; *darstellen* front-on

Frontal-: Fron|tal|an|griff M frontal attack; **Fron|tal|un|ter|richt** M (*Sch*) didactic teaching, chalk and talk (*inf*); **Fron|tal|zu|sam|men|stoß** M head-on collision

Front-: Front|an|sicht F front(al) view; **Front|an|trieb** M (*Aut*) front-wheel drive; **Front|be|gra|di|gung** F straightening of the front; (*fig*) streamlining operation; **Front|be|richt** M report from the front; **Front|dienst** M , **Front|ein|satz** M service at the front; **er wurde zum ~ nach Rumänien abkommandiert** he was posted to serve on the Romanian front

Fron|ten|sys|tem NT (*Met*) frontal system

Fron|tis|piz [frɔntiˈspiːts] NT **-es, -e** (*Archit, Typ*) frontispiece

Front-: Front|kämp|fer(in) M(F) frontline soldier; **Front|la|der** [-laːdɐ] M **-s, -** front loader; **Front|mo|tor** M front-mounted engine; **Front|schei|be** F (*Mot*) (front) windscreen (*Brit*), (front) windshield (*US*); **Front|schwein** NT (*sl*), **Front|sol|dat(in)** M(F) frontline soldier; **Front|spoiler** M (*Aut*) front spoiler; **Front|stadt** F frontier town; **Front|ur|laub** M leave from the front; **Front|wand** F frontage; **Front|wech|sel** M (*fig*) about-turn; **Front|zu|la|ge** F supplement for service at the front

Fron|vogt M (*Hist*) (socage) overseer

fror *pret von* **frieren**

Frosch [frɔʃ] M **-(e)s, ~e** ['frœʃə] frog; (= *Feuerwerkskörper*) (fire)cracker, jumping jack (*Brit*); **einen ~ in der Kehle** *or* **im Hals haben** (*inf*) to have a frog in one's throat; **sei kein ~!** (*inf*) be a sport!

Frosch-: Frosch|au|ge NT (*fig inf*) pop eye; **er hat ~n** he has pop eyes, he is pop-eyed; **Frosch|biss** ▲ M (*Bot*) frogbit; **Frosch|hüp|fen** NT **-s**, *no pl* leapfrog; **Frosch|kö|nig** M Frog Prince; **Frosch|kon|zert** NT (*hum*) frog chorus; **Frosch|laich** M frogspawn; **Frosch|lurch** M salientian (*form*), member of the frog family; **Frosch|mann** M *pl* **-männer** frogman; **Frosch|maul** M (*fig*) pout; **Frosch|per|spek|ti|ve** F worm's-eye view; (*fig*) blinkered view; **etw aus der ~ fotografieren/sehen** to take/get a worm's-eye view of sth; **etw aus der ~ betrachten** (*fig*) to have a blinkered view of sth; **Frosch|schen|kel** M frog's leg; **Frosch|test** M (*Med*) Bickenbach (pregnancy) test

---

Frost [frɔst] M -(e)s, ∺e ['frœstə] **a** frost; **es herrscht strenger/klirrender ~** there's a hard or heavy/crisp frost; **bei eisigem ~** in heavy frost; **~ (ab)bekommen** (Hände, Ohren) to get frostbitten; **~ vertragen (können)** to be able to stand (the) frost **b** (Med: = Schüttelfrost) fit of shivering or the shivers (inf); **er wurde von einem heftigen ~ geschüttelt** he shivered violently

Frost-: frost|an|fäl|lig ADJ susceptible to frost; **Frost|an|fäl|lig|keit** F susceptibility to frost; **Frost|auf|bruch** M frost damage; **frost|be|stän|dig** ADJ frost-resistant; **Frost|beu|le** F chilblain; **Frost|bo|den** M frozen ground; (ständig gefroren) permafrost; **Frost|ein|bruch** M sudden frost

frös|te|lig ['frœstəlıç] ADJ (inf) chilly; **er ist ein ~er Mensch** he's a chilly mortal (inf), he feels the cold

frös|teln ['frœstln] VI to shiver; (vor Angst auch) to tremble; (vor Entsetzen auch) to shudder; **im Fieber ~** to shiver feverishly VT impers **es fröstelte mich** I shivered/trembled/shuddered

frost|emp|find|lich ADJ Pflanzen etc frost-sensitive attr, sensitive to frost pred, delicate, not hardy pred

frös|ten ['frɔstn] VT to freeze

Fros|ter ['frɔstɐ] M -s, - (im Kühlschrank) icebox (Brit), freezer compartment; (= Gefriertruhe) freezer, deep-freeze

Frost-: frost|frei ADJ frost-free, free from or of frost; **die Nacht war ~** there was no frost overnight; **Frost|ge|fahr** F danger of frost; **Frost|gren|ze** F (Met) frost line

fros|tig ['frɔstıç] ADJ (lit, fig) frosty; **ein ~er Hauch** an icy draught (Brit) or draft (US) ADV **jdn ~ begrüßen** to give sb a frosty greeting; **~ klingen** to sound frosty; **jdn ~ empfangen** to give sb a frosty reception, to receive sb frostily; **jdn ~ abfertigen** to be very frosty to sb

Fros|tig|keit F -, no pl (lit, fig) frostiness

Frost-: frost|klar ADJ clear and frosty; **frost|klir|rend** ADJ attr (liter) crisp and frosty

fröst|lig ['frœstlıç] ADJ = fröstelig

Frost-: Frost|scha|den M frost damage; **Frost|schutz** M protection against frost; **Frost|schutz|mit|tel** NT (Aut) antifreeze; **frost|si|cher** ADJ frostproof; Ort free of frost; **Frost|war|nung** F frost warning; **Frost|wet|ter** NT frosty weather

Frot|tee [frɔ'te:] NT OR M -s, -s terry towelling (Brit), terry-cloth toweling (US); **ein Kleid aus ~ a** towelling (Brit) or terry-cloth (US) dress

Frot|tee-: Frot|tee|hand|tuch NT (terry) towel (Brit), terry-cloth towel (US); **Frot|tee|kleid** NT towelling (Brit) or terry-cloth (US) dress; **Frot|tee|tuch** NT pl **-tücher** (terry) towel (Brit), terry-cloth towel (US)

frot|tie|ren [frɔ'tiːrən] ptp **frottiert** VT Haut to rub; **jdn, sich** to rub down

Frot|tier- [frɔ'tiːɐ-]: **Frot|tier|hand|tuch** NT (terry) towel (Brit), terry-cloth towel (US); **Frot|tier|tuch** NT pl **-tücher** (terry) towel (Brit), terry-cloth towel (US)

Frot|ze|lei [frɔtsə'laı] F -, -en (inf) teasing; (= Bemerkung) teasing remark

frot|zeln ['frɔtsln] VTI (inf) to tease; **über jdn/etw ~** to make fun of sb/sth

Frucht [frʊxt] F -, ∺e ['frʏçtə] (Bot, fig) fruit; (= Embryo) foetus (Brit), fetus (US); (no pl: = Getreide) crops pl; **Früchte** (= Obst) fruit sing; **Früchte tragen** (lit, fig) to bear fruit; **die Früchte des Feldes** (liter) the fruits of the earth (liter); **verbotene Früchte** forbidden fruits; **eine ~ der Liebe** (old euph) a love child; **an ihren Früchten sollt ihr sie erkennen** (Bibl) by their fruits ye shall know them (Bibl)

Frucht|an|satz M (Bot) fruit buds pl

frucht|bar ADJ (lit, fig: = zeugungsfähig, reiche Frucht bringend) fertile **a** (lit, fig: = Boden **a b** (lit, fig: = viele Nachkommen zeugend, viel schaffend) prolific; (Bibl) fruitful **c** (fig: = nutzbringend) fruitful,

productive; etw für jdn/etw ~ machen to use sth for the good of sb/sth, to use sth to benefit sb/sth → **mehren** VR

Frucht|bar|keit ['frʊxtbaːɐkaıt] F -, no pl **a** (lit, fig: = Zeugungsfähigkeit, Ergiebigkeit) fertility **b** (lit, fig: = viele Nachkommen zeugend, Schaffensreichtum) prolificness **c** (fig: = Nutzen) fruitfulness, productiveness

Frucht|bar|keits-: Frucht|bar|keits|göt|tin F fertility goddess; **Frucht|bar|keits|kult** M fertility cult; **Frucht|bar|keits|sym|bol** NT fertility symbol; **Frucht|bar|keits|zau|ber** M fertility rite

Frucht|bar|ma|chung [-maxʊŋ] F -, -en (von Wüste) reclamation

Frucht-: Frucht|be|cher M fruit sundae; (Bot) cupule (spec), cup; **Frucht|bla|se** F amniotic sac; **Frucht|bon|bon** M OR NT fruit drop; **frucht|brin|gend** ADJ (geh) fruitful, productive

Frücht|chen ['frʏçtçən] NT -s, - dim von Frucht (inf) (= Tunichtgut) good-for-nothing; (= Kind) rascal (inf); **du bist mir ein sauberes** or **nettes ~** (iro) you're a right one (inf)

Früch|te|brot NT fruit loaf

Frucht|ein|waa|ge F net weight of fruit

fruch|ten ['frʊxtn] VI to bear fruit; **nichts ~** to be fruitless

Früch|te|tee M fruit tea or infusion

Frucht-: Frucht|fleisch NT flesh (of a fruit); **Frucht|flie|ge** F fruit fly; **Frucht|fol|ge** F (Agr) rotation of crops

fruch|tig ['frʊxtıç] ADJ fruity

Fruch|tig|keit F -, no pl fruitiness

Frucht-: Frucht|kap|sel F (Bot) capsule; **Frucht|kno|ten** M (Bot) ovary; **frucht|los** ADJ (fig) fruitless; **Frucht|lo|sig|keit** F -, no pl (fig) fruitlessness; **Frucht|mark** NT (Cook) fruit pulp; **Frucht|pres|se** F fruit press or squeezer; **Frucht|saft** M fruit juice; **Frucht|säu|re** F fruit acid; **Frucht|stand** M (Bot) multiple fruit; **frucht|tra|gend** ADJ attr fruit-bearing; **Frucht|was|ser** NT , no pl (Physiol) amniotic fluid; **das ~ ist vorzeitig abgegangen** her waters broke early; **Frucht|was|ser|un|ter|su|chung** F (Med) amniocentesis; **Frucht|wech|sel** M crop rotation; **Frucht|zu|cker** M fructose

fru|gal [fru'gaːl] (geh) ADJ frugal ADV frugally

früh [fry:] ADJ early; **am ~en Morgen** early in the morning, **in der ~e des Morgens** in one's early morning; **in ~er Jugend** in one's early youth; **in ~er Kindheit** in one's early childhood; **in ~ester Kindheit** very early in one's childhood; **der ~e Goethe** the young Goethe; **ein Werk des ~en Picasso** an early work by Picasso; **ein ~er Picasso** an early Picasso

ADV **a** early; (= in jungen Jahren) young, at an early age; (in Entwicklung) early on; **von ~ auf** from an early age; **es ist noch ~ am Tag/im Jahr** it is still early in the day/year; **von ~ bis spät** from morning till night, from dawn to dusk; **er hat schon ~ erkannt, dass ...** he recognized early on that ...; **du hast dich nicht ~ genug angemeldet** you didn't apply early or soon enough; **zu ~ starten** to start too soon; **ein ~ vollendeter Maler/Dichter** etc (liter) a young artist/poet etc whose genius reached its climax early; **~ übt sich, was ein Meister werden will** (Prov) there's nothing like starting young

b **Freitag/morgen ~** Friday/tomorrow morning; **heute ~** this morning

Früh- in cpds early; **Früh|an|ti|ke** F early classical period; **früh|auf** △ ['fry:lauf] ADV → **früh** ADV a; **Früh|auf|ste|her** [-lauf∫te:ɐ] M -s, -, **Früh|auf|ste|he|rin** [-ərın] F -, -nen early riser, early bird (inf); **Früh|beet** NT cold frame; **Früh|be|hand|lung** F early or prompt treatment no indef art

Früh|chen ['fry:çən] NT -s, - (inf) premature baby, prem (inf), pre(e)mie (US inf)

Früh-: früh|christ|lich ADJ early Christian; **Früh|di|ag|no|se** F early diagnosis; **Früh|dienst** M early duty; **~ haben** to be on early duty

Frü|he ['fry:ə] F -, no pl (liter: = Frühzeit) dawn; **in der ~ des Tages** in the early morning **b** (= Morgen) **in der ~** early in the morning; **in aller ~, gleich in der ~** at (the) crack of dawn

Früh-: Früh|ehe F young marriage; **Früh|ent|wick|ler(in)** M(F) early developer

frü|her ['fry:ɐ] comp von früh ADJ **a** earlier; **in ~en Jahren/Zeiten** in the past; **in ~en Zeitaltern** in past ages

b (= ehemalig) former; (= vorherig) Besitzer, Wohnsitz previous; **der Kontakt zu seinen ~en Freunden ist abgebrochen** he lost contact with his old friends

ADV **a** earlier; **~ als 6 Uhr/Freitag kann ich nicht kommen** I can't come earlier than 6 o'clock/earlier or sooner than Friday; **~ gehts nicht** (= kann nicht früher gemacht werden) it can't be done any earlier or sooner; (= ich kann nicht früher kommen) I can't make it any earlier or sooner; **~ am Abend hat er gesagt ...** earlier (on) in the evening he said ...; **alle, die sich ~ angemeldet haben, werden zuerst berücksichtigt** the first to apply will be the first to be considered; **das hättest du ~ sagen müssen/wissen sollen** you should have said that before or sooner/known that before; **~ oder später** sooner or later

b (= in jüngeren Jahren, in vergangenen Zeiten) **Herr X, ~ Direktor eines Industriebetriebs** Herr X, formerly director of an industrial concern; **ich habe ihn ~ mal gekannt** I used to know him; **~ habe ich so etwas nie gemacht** I never used to do that kind of thing; **~ stand hier eine Kirche** there used to be a church here; **~ war alles besser/war das alles anders** things were better/different in the old days, things used to be better/different; **genau wie ~** just as it/he etc used to be; **Erzählungen von/Erinnerungen an ~** stories/memories of times gone by or of bygone days (liter); **das habe ich noch von ~** I had it before; **ich kannte ihn von ~** I knew him before; **ich kenne ihn von ~** I've known him some time; **wir kennen uns noch von ~** we got to know each other some time ago; **meine Freunde von ~** my old friends

Früh|er|ken|nung F (Med) early diagnosis

frü|hes|tens ['fry:əstns] ADV at the earliest; **~ am Sonntag** on Sunday at the earliest; **wann kann das ~ fertig sein?** what is the earliest that can be ready?

frü|hes|te(r, s) ['fry:əstə] ADJ superl von früh

frü|hest|mög|lich ['fry:əst'mø:klıç] ADJ attr earliest possible

Früh-: Früh|ge|bo|re|ne(s) [-gəbo:rənə] NT decl as adj premature baby or infant (form); **Früh|ge|burt** F premature birth; (= Kind) premature baby; **sie hatte/meine Tochter war eine ~** her baby/my daughter was premature or born prematurely; **Früh|ge|mü|se** NT early vegetables pl; **Früh|ge|schich|te** F early history; **Früh|got|tes|dienst** M early service; **Früh|herbst** M early autumn or fall (US); **früh|herbst|lich** ADJ early autumn or fall (US) attr; **Früh|in|va|li|de(r)** MF decl as adj premature invalid; **Früh|in|va|li|di|tät** F early retirement due to ill health

Früh|jahr NT spring

Früh|jahrs-: Früh|jahrs|bo|te M (liter) harbinger of spring (liter); **Früh|jahrs|mü|dig|keit** F springtime lethargy; **Früh|jahrs|putz** M spring-cleaning

Früh-: Früh|ka|pi|ta|lis|mus M early capitalism; **Früh|kar|tof|feln** PL early potatoes pl; **früh|kind|lich** ADJ (Psych) of early childhood; Sexualität, Entwicklung in early childhood; Trauma, Erlebnisse from early childhood; **Früh|kon|zert** NT early morning concert; (von Vögeln) dawn chorus; **Früh|kul|tur** F **a** early culture **b** (Hort) propagated seedlings pl

Früh|ling ['fry:lɪŋ] M **-s, -e** spring; **es wird ~, der ~ kommt** spring is coming; **im ~** in spring; **die Stadt des ewigen ~s** (*poet*) the springtime city (*liter*); **im ~ des Lebens stehen** (*poet*) to be in the prime of one's life (*liter*); **einem neuen ~ entgegengehen** (*fig*) to start to flourish again; **seinen zweiten ~ erleben** to go through one's second adolescence

Früh|lings- *in cpds* spring; **Früh|lings|an|fang** M first day of spring; **Früh|lings|bo|te** M (*liter*) harbinger of spring (*liter*); **Früh|lings|fest** NT spring festival; **Früh|lings|ge|füh|le** PL (*hum inf*) ~ **haben/bekommen** to be/get frisky (*hum inf*); **wenn sich ~ (bei ihm) regen** when he starts to feel frisky (*hum inf*), when the sap starts to rise (*hum*); **früh|lings|haft** ADJ springlike **ADV** ~ **sich ~ kleiden** to dress in spring clothes; **es ist schon ~ warm** it's as warm as it is in spring; **Früh|lings|rol|le** F (*Cook*) spring roll; **Früh|lings|sup|pe** F spring vegetable soup; **Früh|lings|zeit** F springtime, springtide (*liter*); **Früh|lings|zwie|bel** F spring (*Brit*) or green (*US*) onion

Früh-: **Früh|mes|se** F early mass; **früh|mor|gend|lich** ADJ early morning; **früh|mor|gens** ADV early in the morning; **Früh|ne|bel** M early morning mist; **Früh|neu|hoch|deutsch** NT Early New High German; **früh|pen|sio|nie|ren** *insep* VT **jdn ~** to give sb early retirement; **Früh|pen|sio|nie|rung** F early retirement; **früh|reif** ADJ precocious; (*körperlich*) mature at an early age; **Früh|rei|fe** F precociousness; (*von Körper*) early maturity; **Früh|rent|ner(in)** M(F) person who has retired early; **Früh|schicht** F early shift; **ich gehöre zur ~** (*inf*) I'm on the early shift; **Früh|schop|pen** M morning or (*mittags*) lunchtime drinking; **zum ~ gehen** to go for a morning/lunchtime drink

---

FRÜHSCHOPPEN

A **Frühschoppen** is a social gathering in the morning, when friends sit together over a **Schoppen**. Depending on the region, this may be a glass of wine or a beer and schnapps. The custom of enjoying a **Frühschoppen** on Sundays between church and midday meal is still popular, particularly in rural areas.

Früh-: **Früh|som|mer** M early summer; **früh|som|mer|lich** ADJ early summer *attr*; **das Wetter ist schon ~** the weather is already quite summery; **Früh|sport** M early morning exercise; **~ treiben** to get some early morning exercise; **Früh|sta|di|um** NT early stage; **im ~** in the early stages; **Früh|start** M false start

Früh|stück NT **-s, -e** breakfast; (= *Frühstückspause*) morning or coffee break; **zweites ~** ≈ elevenses (*Brit inf*), ≈ midmorning snack; **um 9 Uhr ist ~** breakfast is at 9 o'clock; **was isst du zum ~?** what do you have for breakfast?; **die ganze Familie saß beim ~** the whole family were having breakfast

früh|stü|cken ['fry:ʃtʏkn] *insep* VI to have breakfast, to breakfast VT to breakfast on

Früh|stücks-: **Früh|stücks|brett** NT wooden platter; **Früh|stücks|brot** NT sandwich (*for one's morning snack*); **Früh|stücks|buf|fet** NT , **Früh|stücks|büf|fet** NT (*esp Aus*) breakfast buffet; **Früh|stücks|di|rek|tor(in)** M(F) (*pej*) figurehead; **Früh|stücks|fern|se|hen** NT breakfast television; **Früh|stücks|fleisch** NT luncheon meat; **Früh|stücks|pau|se** F morning or coffee break; **~ machen** to have one's morning or coffee break; **Früh|stücks|tel|ler** M dessert plate; **Früh|stücks|zim|mer** NT breakfast room

Früh-: **früh|ver|ren|ten** [-fɛɐrɛntn] *ptp* **früh|verrentet** VT *insep* **jdn ~** to give sb early retirement; **Früh|ver|ren|tung** F early retirement; **früh|voll|en|det** △ ADJ *attr* (*liter*) → **früh** ADV **a**; **Früh|voll|en|de|te(r)** MF *decl as adj* **ein ~r** a

young artist/poet *etc* whose genius reached its climax early; **Früh|warn|sys|tem** NT early warning system; **Früh|werk** NT early work; **Früh|zeit** F early days *pl*; **die ~ des Christentums** early Christian times; **die ~ der Menschheit** the early days of mankind; **früh|zei|tig** ADJ early; (= *vorzeitig auch*) premature; *Tod auch* premature, untimely ADV early; (= *vorzeitig*) prematurely; (= *zu guter Zeit*) in good time, early; (= *ziemlich am Anfang*) early on; **Früh|zug** M early train; **Früh|zün|dung** F (*Aut*) pre-ignition

Frust [frʊst] M **-(e)s**, *no pl* (*inf*) frustration *no art*; **das ist der totale ~, wenn ...** it's totally frustrating when ...

frus|ten ['frʊstn] VTI (*inf*) **von etw gefrustet sein** to be frustrated by sth; **das frustet** it's frustrating

Frust|kauf M (*inf*) retail therapy *no pl*

Frust|ra|ti|on [frʊstraˈtsi̯oːn] F **-, -en** frustration

frust|rie|ren [frʊsˈtriːrən] *ptp* **frustriert** VT to frustrate; (*inf*: = *enttäuschen*) to upset

frz. *abbr von* **französisch**

F-Schlüs|sel ['ɛf-] M (*Mus*) F or bass clef

FU [ɛfˈuː] F - *abbr von* **Freie Universität (Berlin)**

Fuchs [fʊks] M **-es, =e** ['fʏksə] **a** (= *Tier*) fox; (*fig auch*) cunning devil (*inf*); **er ist ein alter** or **schlauer ~** (*inf*) he's a cunning old devil (*inf*) or fox (*inf*); **schlau wie ein ~** as cunning as a fox; **wo sich ~ und Hase** or **die Füchse gute Nacht sagen** (*hum*) in the back of beyond (*esp Brit*), in the middle of nowhere **b** (= *Fuchspelz*) fox (fur) **c** (= *Pferd*) chestnut; (*mit hellerem Schwanz und Mähne*) sorrel; (*inf*: = *Mensch*) redhead **d** (*Univ*) new member of a student fraternity

Fuchs-: **Fuchs|band|wurm** M fox tapeworm; **Fuchs|bau** M *pl* **-baue** fox's den; **Fuchs|ei|sen** NT (*Hunt*) fox trap

fuch|sen ['fʊksn] (*inf*) VT to vex, to annoy VR to be annoyed or cross

Fuch|sie ['fʊksi̯ə] F **-, -n** (*Bot*) fuchsia

fuch|sig ['fʊksɪç] ADJ (*inf*) **a** (= *rotblond*) *Haar* ginger, carroty (*inf*) **b** (= *wütend*) mad (*inf*)

Füch|sin ['fʏksɪn] F **-, -nen** vixen

Fuchs-: **Fuchs|jagd** F fox-hunting; (= *einzelne Jagd*) fox hunt; **Fuchs|loch** NT foxhole; **Fuchs|pelz** M fox fur; **fuchs|rot** ADJ *Fell* red; *Pferd* chestnut; *Haar* ginger, carroty (*inf*); **Fuchs|schwanz** M **a** fox's tail; (*Hunt*) (fox's) brush **b** (*Bot*) love-lies-bleeding, amaranth **c** (*Tech*: = *Säge*) handsaw; **fuchs|teu|fels|wild** ADJ (*inf*) hopping mad (*inf*)

Fuch|tel ['fʊxtl] F **-, -n** **a** (*Hist*: = *Degen*) broadsword; (*fig inf*: = *Knute*) control; **unter jds ~** under sb's thumb; **er ist unter ihre ~ gekommen** or **geraten** she's got or gotten (*US*) him under her thumb; **er steht unter der ~** he's not his own master **b** (*Aus, S Ger inf*: = *zänkische Frau*) shrew, vixen

fuch|teln ['fʊxtln] VI (*inf*) **(mit den Händen) ~** to wave one's hands about (*inf*); **mit etw ~** to wave sth about or around; (*drohend*) to brandish sth

fuch|tig ['fʊxtɪç] ADJ (*inf*) (hopping) mad (*inf*)

Fu|der ['fuːdɐ] NT **-s, - a** (= *Wagenladung*) cartload **b** (= *Hohlmaß für Wein*) tun

fu|der|wei|se ADV by the cartload; **~ Salat essen** (*hum*) to eat tons of salad (*inf*)

Fud|schi|ja|ma [fʊdʒiˈjaːma] M **-s** Fujiyama

Fuf|fi ['fʊfi] M **-s, -s** (*hum inf*: = *Fünfzigeuroschein*) fifty (*inf*) (big ones *pl*)

fuff|zehn ['fʊftseːn] NUM (*dial*) fifteen

Fuff|zi|ger ['fʊftsɪɡɐ] M **-s, -** (*dial*) (= *Fünfzigeuroschein*) fifty-euro note (*Brit*) or bill (*US*); (= *Fünfzigcentstück*) fifty-cent piece; **er ist ein falscher ~** (*inf*) he's a real crook (*inf*)

Fug [fuːk] M (*geh*) **mit ~ und Recht** with complete justification; **etw mit ~ und Recht tun** to be completely justified in doing sth

Fu|ge ['fuːɡə] F **-, -n a** joint; (= *Ritze*) gap, crack; **in allen ~n krachen** to creak at the joints; **aus den ~n gehen** or **geraten** (*Auto etc*) to come apart at the seams; **die Welt ist/die Zeiten sind aus den ~n geraten** (*geh*) the world is/the times are out of joint (*liter*) **b** (*Mus*) fugue

fu|gen ['fuːɡn] VT to joint

fü|gen ['fyːɡn] VT **a** (= *setzen, einfügen*) to put, to place; (*geh*) *Worte, Satz* to formulate; **Wort an Wort ~** to string words together **b** (*geh*: = *bewirken*) to ordain; (*Schicksal*) to ordain, to decree; **der Zufall fügte es, dass ...** fate decreed that ... VR (= *sich unterordnen*) to be obedient, to obey; **sich jdm/einer Sache** or **in etw** (*acc*) (*geh*) ~ to bow to sb/sth; *Anordnungen etc* to obey sth; **sich dem** or **in das Schicksal ~** to accept one's fate, to bow to one's fate **b** *impers* (*geh*: = *geschehen*) **es hat sich so gefügt** it was decreed by fate; **es fügte sich, dass ...** it so happened that ...

Fu|gen-: **fu|gen|los** ADJ *Übergang* smooth; **Fu|gen-s** [-ləs] NT (*Ling*) linking "s"; **Fu|gen|zei|chen** NT (*Ling*) linking letter

füg|lich ['fyːklɪç] ADV (*liter*) justifiably, reasonably

füg|sam ['fyːkzaːm] ADJ *Mensch, Tier* obedient; *Haar* manageable

Füg|sam|keit F -, *no pl* (*von Mensch, Tier*) obedience

Fü|gung ['fyːɡʊŋ] F **-, -en a** (= *Bestimmung*) chance, stroke of fate; **eine glückliche ~** a stroke of good fortune, a happy chance (*Brit*); **göttliche ~** divine providence; **eine ~ Gottes/des Schicksals** an act of divine providence/of fate; **eine seltsame ~ wollte es, dass er ...** by some or a strange chance he ... **b** (*Ling*: = *Wortgruppe*) construction

fühl|bar ADJ (= *spürbar*) perceptible; (= *beträchtlich auch*) marked; **bald wird die Krise auch bei uns ~** the crisis will soon be felt here too

füh|len ['fyːlən] VT **a** (= *spüren, empfinden*) to feel; **Mitleid mit jdm ~** to feel sympathy for sb **b** (= *ertasten*) *Beule, Erhebung* to feel; *Puls* to feel, to take VI **a** (*geh*: = *empfinden*) to feel **b** **nach etw ~** to feel for sth VR **a** (= *empfinden, sich halten für*) to feel; **sich krank/beleidigt/verantwortlich ~** to feel ill (*Brit*) or sick (*esp US*)/insulted/responsible; **wie ~ Sie sich?** how are you feeling?, how do you feel?; **er fühlte sich als Held** he felt (like) a hero **b** (*inf*: = *stolz sein*) to think one is so great (*inf*)

Füh|ler ['fyːlɐ] M **-s, -** (*Zool*) feeler, antenna; (*von Schnecke*) horn; **seine ~ ausstrecken** (*fig inf*) to put out feelers (*nach towards*)

Füh|ler|leh|re F feeler gauge

fühl|los ADJ (*geh*) = **gefühllos**

Fühl|lo|sig|keit F -, *no pl* (*geh*) = **Gefühllosigkeit**

Füh|lung ['fyːlʊŋ] F **-, -en** contact; **mit jdm in ~ bleiben/stehen** to remain or stay/be in contact or touch with sb

Füh|lung|nah|me [-naːmə] F **-, -n die erste ~ der beiden Parteien** the initial contact between the two parties

fuhr *pret von* **fahren**

Fuhr-: **Fuhr|amt** NT (*form*) cleansing department; **Fuhr|be|trieb** M haulage business

Fuh|re ['fuːrə] F **-, -n** (= *Ladung*) load; (= *Taxieinsatz*) fare; **eine ~ Stroh** a (cart- or wagon-)load of straw; **wir müssen die Leute in zwei ~n zum Bahnhof bringen** we'll have to take the people to the station in two loads

füh|ren ['fyːrən] VT **a** (= *geleiten*) to take; (= *vorangehen, -fahren*) to lead; **eine alte Dame über die Straße ~** to help an old lady over the road; **sie hat uns den richtigen Weg geführt** she showed us the right way; **er führte uns durch das Schloss** he showed us (a)round the castle; **er führte uns durch Italien** he was our guide in

---

Italy; **eine Klasse zum Abitur ~** ≈ to see a class through to A-levels (*Brit*) or to their high school diploma (*US*); **jdn zum (Trau)altar ~** to lead sb to the altar

b (= *leiten*) *Geschäft, Betrieb etc* to run; *Gruppe, Expedition etc* to lead, to head; *Schiff* to captain; *Armee etc* to command

c (= *in eine Situation bringen*) to get (*inf*), to lead; (= *veranlassen zu kommen/gehen*) to bring/ take; **der Hinweis führte die Polizei auf die Spur des Diebes** that tip put the police on the trail of the thief; **das führt uns auf das Thema ...** that brings or leads us (on)to the subject ...; **was führt Sie zu mir?** (*form*) what brings you to me?; **ein Land ins Chaos ~** to reduce a country to chaos

d (= *registriert haben*) to have a record of; **wir ~ keinen Meier in unserer Kartei** we have no (record of a) Meier on our files

e (= *handhaben*) *Pinsel, Bogen, Kamera etc* to wield; **den Löffel zum Mund/das Glas an die Lippen ~** to raise one's spoon to one's mouth/ one's glass to one's lips; **die Hand an die Mütze ~** to touch one's cap

f (= *entlangführen*) *Leitung, Draht* to carry

g (*form:* = *steuern*) *Kraftfahrzeug* to drive; *Flugzeug* to fly, to pilot; *Kran, Fahrstuhl* to operate; *Schiff* to sail

h (= *transportieren*) to carry; (= *haben*) *Autokennzeichen, Wappen, Namen* to have, to bear; *Titel* to have; (= *selbst gebrauchen*) to use; **Geld/seine Papiere bei sich ~** (*form*) to carry money/one's papers on one's person; **der Fluss führt Hochwasser** the river is running high

i (= *im Angebot haben*) to stock, to carry (*spec*), to keep; **etw ständig im Munde ~** to be always talking about sth; **er führt diesen Spruch ständig im Munde** he is always using that phrase

VI a (= *in Führung liegen*) to lead; (*bei Wettkämpfen*) to be in the lead, to lead; **die Mannschaft führt mit 10 Punkten Vorsprung** the team has a lead of 10 points, the team is in the lead or is leading by 10 points; **die Firma XY führt in Videorekordern** XY is the leading firm for video recorders

b (= *verlaufen*) (*Straße*) to go; (*Kabel, Pipeline etc*) to run; (*Spur*) to lead; **das Rennen führt über 10 Runden/durch ganz Frankreich** the race takes place over 10 laps/covers France; **die Straße führt nach Kiel/am Rhein entlang** the road goes to Kiel/runs or goes along the Rhine; **die Brücke führt über die Elbe** the bridge crosses or spans the Elbe; **der Waldweg führt zu einem Gasthof** the forest path leads or goes to an inn

c (= *als Ergebnis haben*) **zu etw ~** to lead to sth, to result in sth; **das führt zu nichts** that will come to nothing; **es führte zu dem Ergebnis, dass er entlassen wurde** it resulted in or led to his being dismissed; **das führt dazu, dass noch mehr Stellen abgebaut werden** it'll lead to or end in further staff reductions or job cuts; **wohin soll das alles nur ~?** where is it all leading (us)?

VR (*form:* = *sich benehmen*) to conduct oneself, to deport oneself (*form*)

füh|rend ADJ leading *attr*; *Rolle, Persönlichkeit auch* prominent; **diese Firma ist im Stahlbau ~** that is one of the leading firms in steel construction; **die Amerikaner sind in der Leichtathletik ~** the Americans lead the world or are the world leaders in athletics

Füh|rer¹ ['fyːrɐ] M -s, - (= *Buch*) guide; **~ durch England** guide to England

Füh|rer² ['fyːrɐ] M -s, -, **Füh|re|rin** [-ərɪn] F -, -nen **a** (= *Leiter*) leader; (= *Oberhaupt*) head; **der ~** (*Hist*) the Führer or Fuehrer **b** (= *Fremdenführer, Bergführer*) guide **c** (*form:* = *Lenker*) driver; (*von Flugzeug*) pilot; (*von Kran, Fahrstuhl*) operator; (*von Schiff*) person in charge

Füh|rer-: Füh|rer|haus NT cab; (*von Kran auch*) cabin; **füh|rer|los** ADJ *Gruppe, Partei* leaderless *no adv*, without a leader; *Wagen* driverless *no adv*, without a driver; *Flugzeug* pilotless *no adv*, without a pilot; *Schiff* with no-one at the

helm; **Füh|rer|na|tur** F (*fig*) born or natural leader; **Füh|rer|rol|le** F role of a/the leader, leadership role

Füh|rer|schein M (*für Auto*) driving licence (*Brit*), driver's license (*US*); (*für Motorboot*) motorboat licence (*Brit*) or license (*US*); **den ~ machen** (*Aut*) to learn to drive; (= *die Prüfung ablegen*) to take one's (driving) test; **jdm den ~ entziehen** to take away sb's driving licence (*Brit*) or driver's license (*US*), to disqualify sb from driving; **ihm ist der ~ abgenommen worden** he's lost his licence (*Brit*) or license (*US*); **~ auf Probe** probationary driving licence (*Brit*) or driver's license (*US*)

Füh|rer|schein-: Füh|rer|schein|ent|zug M disqualification from driving; **Füh|rer|schein|prü|fung** F driving test; **praktische ~** practical (part of the) driving test; **theoretische ~** theoretical (part of the) driving test, driving theory test

Füh|rer|stand M (*von Zug*) cab; (*von Kran auch*) cabin

Fuhr-: Fuhr|geld NT delivery charge; **Fuhr|ge|schäft** NT haulage business

füh|rig ['fyːrɪç] ADJ *Schnee* good (for skiing)

Fuhr-: Fuhr|knecht M (*old*) carter; (= *Kutscher*) coachman; **Fuhr|leu|te** *pl von* **Fuhrmann**; **Fuhr|lohn** M delivery charge; **Fuhr|mann** M *pl* **-leute** carter (*Brit*), carrier; (= *Kutscher*) coachman; **der ~** (*Astron*) Auriga, the Charioteer; **Fuhr|park** M fleet (of vehicles)

Füh|rung ['fyːrʊŋ] F -, *en* **a** *no pl* guidance, direction; (*von Partei, Expedition etc*) leadership; (*Mil*) command; (*eines Unternehmens etc*) management; **unter der ~** under the direction/leadership/command/management of, directed/led or headed/commanded/managed by; **wer hat hier die ~?** (*Mil*) who is in command here?

b *no pl* (= *die Führer*) leaders *pl*, leadership *sing*; (*Mil*) commanders *pl*; (*eines Unternehmens etc*) directors *pl*

c (= *Besichtigung*) guided tour (*durch* of)

d *no pl* (= *Vorsprung*) lead; **die klare ~ haben** (*bei Wettkämpfen*) to have a clear lead; **die Firma hat eine klare ~ auf diesem Gebiet** the firm clearly leads the field in this area; **in ~ gehen/ liegen** to go into/be in the lead

e *no pl* (= *Betragen*) conduct; **wegen guter ~ vorzeitig aus der Haft entlassen werden** to be released from prison early for good behaviour (*Brit*) or behavior (*US*)

f *no pl* (= *Handhabung*) touch

g (*Mech*) guide, guideway

h (*form:* = *Lenken*) **zur ~ eines Kraftfahrzeugs/ Wasserfahrzeugs/Flugzeugs berechtigt sein** to be licensed to drive a motor vehicle/be in charge of a vessel/fly or pilot an aircraft

i *no pl* (= *Betreuung*) running; **die ~ der Akten/ Bücher** keeping the files/books

Füh|rungs-: Füh|rungs|an|spruch M claims *pl* to leadership; **seinen ~ anmelden** to make a bid for the leadership; **Füh|rungs|auf|ga|be** F executive duty; **Füh|rungs|eta|ge** F (*von Partei, Verband*) leadership; (*von Unternehmen*) management; **Füh|rungs|kraft** F (*Person*) executive; **Füh|rungs|kri|se** F leadership crisis; (*Comm*) management crisis; **Füh|rungs|offi|zier(in)** M(F) (*DDR*) commanding officer; **Füh|rungs|qua|li|tät** F *usu pl* leadership qualities *pl*; **Füh|rungs|rie|ge** F leadership; **Füh|rungs|rol|le** F role of leader; **Füh|rungs|schicht** F ruling classes *pl*; **Füh|rungs|schie|ne** F guide rail; **füh|rungs|schwach** ADJ *Partei, Chef* weak; **Füh|rungs|schwä|che** F weak leadership; **Füh|rungs|spit|ze** F highest echelon of the leadership; (*eines Unternehmens etc*) top management; **Füh|rungs|stab** M (*Mil*) command *no pl*; (*Comm*) top management; **Füh|rungs|stär|ke** F strong leadership; **Füh|rungs|stil** M style of leadership; (*Comm auch*) management style; **Füh|rungs|tor** NT (*Ftbl*) goal which gives/gave a/the team the

lead; **Füh|rungs|wech|sel** M change of leadership; **Füh|rungs|zeug|nis** NT → **polizeilich**

Fuhr-: Fuhr|un|ter|neh|men NT haulage business; **Fuhr|un|ter|neh|mer(in)** M(F) haulier (*Brit*), haulage contractor, carrier, trucking operator (*US*); **Fuhr|werk** NT wagon; (= *Pferdefuhrwerk*) horse and cart; (= *Ochsenfuhrwerk*) oxcart; **fuhr|wer|ken** ['fuːɐverkn] VI *insep* **a** (*inf*) in der Küche to bustle around in the kitchen; **mit den Armen ~** to wave one's arms about **b** (*S Ger, Aus*) to drive a cart; **Fuhr|we|sen** NT , *no pl* cartage business

Fül|le ['fʏlə] F -, *no pl* **a** (= *Körpermasse*) corpulence, portliness **b** (= *Stärke*) fullness; (*von Stimme, Klang auch*) richness; (*von Wein auch*) full-bodiedness; (*von Haar auch*) body **c** (= *Menge*) wealth; **eine ~ von Fragen/Eindrücken** *etc* a whole host of questions/impressions *etc*; **in ~** in abundance → **Hülle e**

fül|len ['fʏlən] VT **a** (= *mit Inhalt füllen*) to fill; (*Cook*) to stuff; **etw in Flaschen ~** to bottle sth; **etw in Säcke ~** to put sth into sacks → *auch* **gefüllt b** (= *in Anspruch nehmen*) to fill, to occupy; *Regal* to fill, to take up **VR** (*Theater, Badewanne*) to fill up; **ihre Augen füllten sich mit Tränen** her eyes filled with tears

Fül|len ['fʏlən] NT -s, - = **Fohlen**

Fül|ler ['fʏlɐ] M -s, - **a** (= *Füllfederhalter*) fountain pen **b** (*Press*) filler

Füll-: Füll|fe|der|hal|ter M fountain pen; **Füll|ge|wicht** NT **a** (*Comm*) weight at time of packing; (*auf Dosen*) net weight **b** (*von Waschmaschine*) maximum load, capacity; **Füll|horn** NT (*liter*) cornucopia, (*fig auch*) horn of plenty

fül|lig ['fʏlɪç] ADJ *Mensch* corpulent, portly; *Figur, Busen* generous, ample; *Frisur* bouffant *attr*

Füll-: Füll|mas|se F filler, filling material; (= *Zahnfüllmasse*) filling compound; **Füll|ma|te|ri|al** NT filler, filling material

Füll|sel ['fʏlzl] NT -s, - (*in Paket etc*) packing; (*in Geschriebenem*) (= *Wort*) filler; (= *Floskel*) padding

Full|time|job ▲, **Full-Time-Job** ▲ ['fʊltaim-dʒɔp] M full-time job

Fül|lung ['fʏlʊŋ] F -, *en* filling; (= *Geflügelfüllung, Fleischfüllung, Stofftierfüllung, Polsterfüllung*) stuffing; (= *Türfüllung*) panel; (*von Pralinen*) centre (*Brit*), center (*US*)

Füll|wort NT *pl* **-wörter** filler (word)

ful|mi|nant [fʊlmiˈnant] ADJ (*geh*) brilliant

Fum|mel ['fʊml] M -s, - (*inf*) rag; **im ~** (*sl:* = *in Frauenkleidung*) in drag (*inf*)

Fum|me|lei [fʊməˈlai] F -, *en* (*inf*) fidgeting, fiddling; (= *Petting*) petting, groping (*inf*)

Fum|mel|kram M (*inf*) fiddle (*inf*), fiddly job (*inf*)

fum|meln ['fʊmln] VI (*inf*) to fiddle; (= *hantieren*) to fumble; (*erotisch*) to pet, to grope (*inf*); **an etw** (*dat*) or **mit etw ~** to fiddle (about)/fumble around with sth

Fund [fʊnt] M -(e)s, -e [-də] find; (= *das Entdecken*) discovery, finding; **einen ~ machen** to make a find

Fun|da|ment [fʊndaˈmɛnt] NT -(e)s, -e (*lit, fig*) foundation (*usu pl*); **das ~ zu etw legen** (*fig*) **das ~ für etw schaffen** (*fig*) to lay the foundation for sth

fun|da|men|tal [fʊndamɛnˈtaːl] ADJ fundamental **ADV** fundamentally

Fun|da|men|ta|lis|mus [fʊndamɛntaˈlɪsmʊs] M -, *no pl* fundamentalism

Fun|da|men|ta|list [fʊndamɛntaˈlɪst] M -en, -en, **Fun|da|men|ta|lis|tin** [-lɪstɪn] F -, -nen fundamentalist

fun|da|men|ta|lis|tisch [fʊndamɛntaˈlɪstɪʃ] ADJ fundamentalist

fun|da|men|tie|ren [fʊndamɛnˈtiːrən] *ptp* **fundamentiert** VT to lay the foundations

Fund-: Fund|amt NT , **Fund|bü|ro** NT lost property office (*Brit*), lost and found (*US*);

Fund|gru|be F (fig) treasure trove; **eine ~ des Wissens** a treasury of knowledge

Fun|di ['fʊndi] M -s, -s or f -, -s (Pol inf) fundamentalist (of the Green party)

fun|die|ren [fʊn'diːrən] ptp **fundiert** VT (fig) to back up

fun|diert [fʊn'diːet] ADJ sound; **schlecht ~** unsound

fün|dig ['fʏndɪç] ADJ (Min) Sohle rich; **~ werden** to make a strike; (fig) to strike it lucky; **~e Mitbürger sollen ...** anyone who finds it/them should ...

Fund-: Fund|ort M pl **-orte der ~ von etw** (the place) where sth is/was found; **Fund|sa|chen** PL lost property sing; **Fund|stät|te** F, **Fund|stel|le** F **die ~ von etw** (the place) where sth is/was found

Fun|dus ['fʊndʊs] M -, - (lit, fig) fund; (Theat) basic equipment; **der ~ seines reichen Wissens** his rich fund of knowledge

fünf [fʏnf] NUM five; **es ist ~ Minuten vor zwölf** (lit) it's five to twelve; (fig) it's almost too late; **sie warteten bis ~ Minuten vor zwölf** (fig) they waited till the eleventh hour; **seine ~ Sinne beieinander haben** or **beisammenhaben** to have all one's wits about one; **seine ~ Sinne zusammennehmen** to gather one's wits together; **man musste seine ~ Sinne zusammennehmen** you had to have your wits about you; **~(e) gerade sein lassen** (inf) to turn a blind eye, to look the other way → auch **Finger**, **vier**

Fünf [fʏnf] F -, -en five → auch **Vier**

Fünf- in cpds five → auch **Vier-**; **Fünf|cent|stück** [fʏnf'(t)sɛnt-] NT five-cent piece; **Fünf|eck** NT pentagon; **fünf|eckig** ADJ pentagonal, five-cornered

Fün|fer ['fʏnfɐ] M -s, - (inf) (= Fünfcentmünze) five-cent piece; (= Fünfeuroschein) five-euro note (Brit) or bill (US) → auch **Vierer**

Fünf-: Fünf|eu|ro|schein [fʏnf'ɔyro-] M five-euro note (Brit) or bill (US); **fünf|fach** ['fʏnf-fax] ADJ fivefold → auch **vierfach**; **fünf|fü|ßig** ADJ (Poet) pentametrical; **~er Jambus** iambic pentameter; **Fünf|gang|ge|trie|be** NT five-speed gearbox; **Fünf|gang|schal|tung** F five-speed gears pl; **fünf|hun|dert** ['fʏnf'hʊndɐt] NUM five hundred → auch **vierhundert**; **Fünf|jah|res|plan** M five-year plan; **fünf|jäh|rig** ADJ Frist, Plan, Amtszeit etc five-year, quinquennial (form); Kind five-year-old; **eine ~e Zeitspanne** a period of five years, a quinquennium (form) → auch **vierjährig**; **Fünf|kampf** M (Sport) pentathlon

Fünf|ling ['fʏnflɪŋ] M -s, -e quintuplet

Fünf-: fünf|mal ['fʏnfmaːl] ADV five times → auch **viermal**; **Fünf|mark|schein** [fʏnf'mark-] M (Hist) five-mark note (Brit) or bill (US); **Fünf|mark|stück** NT (Hist) five-mark piece; **Fünf|me|ter|raum** M (Ftbl) six-yard box; **Fünf|pfen|nig|stück** [fʏnf'pfɛnɪç-] NT (Hist) five-pfennig piece

Fünf|pro|zent- [fʏnfpro'tsɛnt-]: **Fünf|pro|zent|gren|ze** F (Parl) five-percent barrier; **Fünf|pro|zent|hür|de** F (Parl) five-percent hurdle; **Fünf|pro|zent|klau|sel** F five-percent rule

---

FÜNFPROZENTKLAUSEL

Electoral law in Germany contains a **Fünfprozentklausel**, meaning that only those parties that manage to poll at least 5% of the votes over an entire electoral area may have a stake in the allocation of seats. This rule was introduced after the Second World War to guard against the fragmentation of parties, which was seen as one of the causes of the collapse of the Weimar Republic.

Fünf-: fünf|sei|tig [-zaitɪç] ADJ (Geometrie) five-sided; Brief five-page attr → auch **vierseitig**; **Fünf|strom|land** [fʏnf'ʃtroːm-] NT , no pl (Geog) Punjab; **Fünf|ta|ge|wo|che** [fʏnf'taːgə-]

F , no pl five-day week; **fünf|tä|gig** ADJ five-day attr; **fünf|tau|send** ['fʏnf'tauznt] NUM five thousand → auch **viertausend**; **Fünf|tau|send|me|ter|lauf, 5000-m-Lauf** [fʏnftauznd'meːtɐ-] M five thousand metres (Brit) or meters (US)

Fünf|tel ['fʏnftl] NT -s, - fifth → auch **Viertel** [1]

fünf|tens ['fʏnftns] ADV fifth(ly), in the fifth place

fünf|te(r, s) ['fʏnftə] ADJ fifth; **die ~ Kolonne** the fifth column → auch **vierte(r, s)**, **Rad**

Fünf-: Fünf|uhr|tee M afternoon tea; **Fünf|und|drei|ßig|stun|den|wo|che** F thirty-five-hour week; **fünf|und|zwan|zig** NUM twenty-five; **fünf|zehn** ['fʏnftseːn] NUM fifteen

fünf|zig ['fʏnftsɪç] NUM fifty → auch **vierzig**

Fünf|zig ['fʏnftsɪç] F -, -en fifty → auch **Vierzig**

Fünf|zig|cent|stück [fʏnftsɪç'(t)sɛnt-] NT fifty-cent piece

Fünf|zi|ger[1] ['fʏnftsɪgɐ] M -s, - (inf) (= Fünfzigeuroschein) fifty-euro note (Brit) or bill (US); (= Fünfzigcentstück) fifty-cent piece → auch **Fuffziger**

Fünf|zi|ger[2] ['fʏnftsɪgɐ] M -s, -, **Fünf|zi|ge|rin** [-ərɪn] F -, -nen (inf: = Fünfzigjähriger) fifty-year-old → auch **Vierziger[2]**

Fünf|zi|ger|jah|re, fünf|zi|ger Jah|re ['fʏnftsɪgɐ-] PL fifties pl

Fünf|zig-: Fünf|zig|eu|ro|schein [fʏnftsɪç'ɔy-ro-] M fifty-euro note (Brit) or bill (US); **fünf|zig|jäh|rig** ADJ Person fifty-year-old attr; Zeitspanne fifty-year; **er ist ~ verstorben** he died at (the age of) fifty; **Fünf|zig|mark|schein** [fʏnftsɪç'mark-] M (Hist) fifty-mark note (Brit) or bill (US); **Fünf|zig|pfen|nig|stück** [fʏnftsɪç'pfɛnɪç-] NT (Hist) fifty-pfennig piece

fun|gie|ren [fʊn'giːrən] ptp **fungiert** VI to function (als as a)

Fun|gi|zid [fʊŋgi'tsiːt] NT -(e)s, -e [-də] fungicide

Funk[1] [fʊŋk] M -s, no pl radio, wireless (dated); **über** or **per ~** by radio; **er arbeitet beim ~** he works in radio or broadcasting

Funk[2] [faŋk] M -s, no pl funk

-funk suf in cpds broadcasts pl, programmes pl (Brit), programs pl (US); **Hausfrauenfunk** housewives' broadcasts pl, programmes pl (Brit) or programs pl (US) for housewives

Funk-: Funk|ama|teur(in) M(F) radio ham, amateur radio enthusiast; **Funk|an|la|ge** F radio set or transceiver; **Funk|auf|klä|rung** F (Mil) radio intelligence; **Funk|aus|stel|lung** F radio and television exhibition; **Funk|ba|ke** F radio beacon; **Funk|bild** NT telephotograph (spec), radio picture; **Funk|brü|cke** F radio bridge

Fünk|chen ['fʏŋkçən] NT -s, - dim von **Funke ein ~ Wahrheit** a grain of truth; **kein ~ Wahrheit** not a grain of truth

Funk|dienst M radio communication service

Fun|ke ['fʊŋkə] M -ns, -n [a] (lit, fig) spark; **~n sprühen** to spark, to send out or emit sparks; **~n sprühend** giving off or emitting sparks; (fig) Diskussion lively; Augen flashing attr, fiery; **ihre Augen sprühten ~n** her eyes flashed; **der zündende ~** (fig) the vital spark; **der ~ der Begeisterung sprang auf die Zuschauer über** the audience was infected by his/her etc enthusiasm; **arbeiten, dass die ~n fliegen** or **sprühen** (inf) to work like mad (inf) or crazy (inf); **zwischen den beiden sprang der ~ über** (inf) something clicked between them (inf)

[b] (= ein bisschen) scrap; (von Hoffnung auch) gleam, ray, glimmer; (von Anstand) scrap, spark

Funk|ein|rich|tung F radio (equipment); **mit ~ versehen** radio-equipped, equipped with radio

fun|keln ['fʊŋkln] VI to sparkle; (Sterne auch) to twinkle; (Edelsteine auch) to glitter; (Edelmetall) to gleam; (Augen) (vor Freude) to gleam, to twinkle; (vor Zorn) to glitter, to flash

fun|kel|na|gel|neu ['fʊŋkl'naːgl'nɔy] ADJ (inf) brand-new

fun|ken ['fʊŋkn] VT Signal to radio; **SOS ~** to send out or radio an SOS VI [a] (= senden) to radio [b] (= Funken sprühen) to give off or emit sparks, to spark; (fig inf: = funktionieren) to work VI impers **endlich hat es bei ihm gefunkt** (inf) it finally clicked (with him) (inf), the light finally dawned (on him)

Fun|ken ['fʊŋkn] M -s, - = **Funke**

Fun|ken-: Fun|ken|ent|la|dung F spark discharge; **Fun|ken|flug** M **der Brand wurde durch ~ von einer Lokomotive verursacht** the fire was caused by sparks from a locomotive; **Fun|ken|git|ter** NT fireguard; **fun|ken|sprü|hend** △ ADJ → **Funke a**

Funk|ent|stö|rung ['fʊŋk|ɛnt-] F suppression of interference

funk|ent|stört ['fʊŋk|ɛntʃtøːɐt] ADJ (radio noise-)suppressed

Fun|ker ['fʊŋkɐ] M -s, -, **Fun|ke|rin** [-ərɪn] F -, -nen radio or wireless operator

Funk-: Funk|fern|steu|e|rung F radio control; (= Anlage) radio-control equipment no pl; **Funk|feu|er** NT radio beacon; **Funk|ge|rät** NT [a] no pl radio equipment [b] (= Sprechfunkgerät) radio set, walkie-talkie; **Funk|haus** NT broadcasting centre (Brit) or center (US), studios pl

fun|kig ['faŋkɪç] ADJ (inf) funky (inf)

Funk-: Funk|kol|leg NT educational radio broadcasts pl; **Funk|kon|takt** M radio contact; **Funk|mess|ge|rät** ▲ NT radar (equipment) no pl; **Funk|na|vi|ga|ti|on** F radio navigation; **Funk|netz** NT radio network; (= Funktelefonnetz) radio telephone network; **Funk|or|tung** F radiolocation; **Funk|pei|lung** F radio direction finding; **Funk|ruf** M [a] radio call [b] (Telec) (radio) paging; **Funk|ruf|dienst** M (Telec) (radio) paging service; **Funk|ruf|emp|fänger** M (radio) pager; **Funk|ruf|netz** NT (Telec) (radio) paging network; **Funk|sig|nal** NT radio signal; **Funk|sprech|ge|rät** NT radio telephone; (tragbar) walkie-talkie; **Funk|sprech|ver|kehr** M radiotelephony; **Funk|spruch** M radio signal; (= Mitteilung) radio message; **Funk|sta|ti|on** F radio station; **funk|still** ADJ non-transmitting; **Funk|stil|le** F radio silence; (fig) silence; **Funk|strei|fe** F police radio patrol; **Funk|strei|fen|wa|gen** M police radio patrol or squad car; **Funk|ta|xi** NT radio taxi or cab; **Funk|tech|nik** F radio technology; **Funk|te|le|fon** NT radio telephone; **Funk|te|le|fon|netz** NT (Telec) radio telephone network

Funk|ti|on [fʊŋk'tsioːn] F -, -en (= Zweck, Aufgabe, Math) function; (no pl: = Tätigkeit) functioning; (= Amt) office; (= Stellung) position; **in ~ treten** to come into operation; (Organ, Maschine etc) to start to function; **in ~ sein** to be in operation; (Organ, Maschine etc) to be functioning; **etw außer ~ setzen** to stop sth functioning; **dieser Bolzen hat die ~, den Apparat senkrecht zu halten** the function of this bolt is to hold the machine upright

funk|ti|o|nal [fʊŋktsio'naːl] ADJ = **funktionell**

Funk|ti|o|na|lis|mus [fʊŋktsiona'lɪsmʊs] M -, no pl functionalism

funk|ti|o|na|li|sie|ren [fʊŋktsionali'ziːrən] ptp **funktionalisiert** VT to make functional, to give a functional design (etw to sth)

funk|ti|o|na|lis|tisch [fʊŋktsiona'lɪstisch] ADJ functionalist

Funk|ti|o|na|li|tät [fʊŋktsionali'tɛːt] F -, -en practicality

Funk|ti|o|när [fʊŋktsio'nɛːɐ] M -s, -e, **Funk|ti|o|nä|rin** [-'nɛːrɪn] F -, -nen functionary, official

funk|ti|o|nell [fʊŋktsio'nɛl] ADJ functional (auch Med), practical

---

Deutsche Rechtschreibreform (siehe Anhang): ▲ neue Schreibung △ alte Schreibung

+ trennbare Verben

funk|ti|o|nie|ren [fʊŋktsio'niːrən] *ptp* **funktioniert** VI to work; (*Maschine etc auch*) to function, to operate; (*inf*: = *gehorchen*) to obey

Funk|ti|ons-: Funk|ti|ons|bild NT , *no pl* job profile; **funk|ti|ons|fä|hig** ADJ able to work; *Maschine etc auch* in working order; **Funk|ti|ons|fä|hig|keit** F ability to work; **die ~ einer Maschine überprüfen** to check if a machine is in working order; **Funk|ti|ons|leis|te** F (*Comput*) toolbar; **Funk|ti|ons|prü|fung** F (*Med*) function test; **Funk|ti|ons|stö|rung** F (*Med*) malfunction, functional disorder; **Funk|ti|ons|tas|te** F (*Comput*) function key; **funk|ti|ons|tüch|tig** ADJ in working order; *Organ* sound; **Funk|ti|ons|tüch|tig|keit** F ability to operate; (*von Organ*) soundness; **Funk|ti|ons|verb** NT (*Ling*) empty verb; **Funk|ti|ons|wei|se** F -, -n mode of operation

Funk-: Funk|turm M radio tower; **Funk|uhr** F radio-controlled clock; **Funk|uni|ver|si|tät** F educational radio broadcasts *pl*; **Funk|ver|bin|dung** F radio contact; **Funk|ver|kehr** M radio communication *or* traffic; **Funk|wa|gen** M radio car; **Funk|weg** M **auf dem ~** by radio; **Funk|wer|bung** F radio advertising; **Funk|we|sen** NT , *no pl* radio; (= *Sendesystem*) broadcasting system; **Funk|zent|ra|le** F (radio) call centre (*Brit*) *or* center (*US*)

Fun|sel ['fʊnzl] F -, -n, **Fun|zel** ['fʊntsl] F -, -n (*inf*) dim light, gloom

für [fyːɐ] PREP +*acc* **a** for; **~ was ist denn dieses Werkzeug?** (*inf*) what is this tool (used) for?; **kann ich sonst noch etwas ~ Sie tun?** will there be anything else?; **~ mich** for me; (= *meiner Ansicht nach*) in my opinion *or* view; **diese Frage muss jeder ~ sich (alleine) entscheiden** everyone has to decide this question for *or* by themselves; **das ist gut ~ Migräne** that's good for migraine; **~ zwei arbeiten** (*fig*) to do the work of two people; **~ einen Deutschen ...** for a German ...; **~s Erste** for the moment; **~s nächste Mal** next time

b (*Zustimmung*) for, in favour (*Brit*) *or* favor (*US*) of; **sich ~ etw entscheiden** to decide in favo(u)r; **was Sie da sagen, hat etwas ~ sich** there's something in what you're saying; **er hat was ~ sich** he's not a bad person; **das hat was ~ sich** it's not a bad thing

c (*Gegenleistung*) (in exchange) for; **das hat er ~ zehn Pfund gekauft** he bought it for ten pounds

d (*Ersatz*) for, instead of, in place of; **~ jdn einspringen** to stand in for sb

e (*Aufeinanderfolge*) **Tag ~ Tag** day after day; **Schritt ~ Schritt** step by step

f (*in Verbindung mit vb, adj siehe auch dort*) **etw ~ sich behalten** to keep sth to oneself; **~ etw bekannt sein** to be famous *or* known for sth; **ich halte sie ~ intelligent** I think she is intelligent

g **was ~ was** →**was**

ADV (*old poet*) **~ und ~** for ever and ever

Für ['fyːɐ] NT **das ~ und Wider** the pros and cons *pl*

Fu|ra|ge [fu'raːʒə] F -, *no pl* (*Mil old*) forage

für|bass ▲ [fyːɐ'bas] ADV (*obs*) onwards; **~ gehen** *or* **schreiten** to continue on one's way

Für|bit|te F (*Eccl, fig*) intercession; **er legte beim Kaiser ~ für die Gefangenen ein** he interceded with the Emperor on behalf of the prisoners

Für|bit|ten NT -s, *no pl* (*Eccl*) prayers *pl*; (*fig*) pleading

Fur|che ['fʊrçə] F -, -n (= *Ackerfurche, Gesichtsfalte*) furrow; (= *Wagenspur*) rut; **ein von ~n durchzogenes Gesicht** a deeply furrowed *or* lined face

fur|chen ['fʊrçn] VT to furrow; (*Zeit, Sorge etc*) *Gesicht etc auch* to line; **die Spuren des Traktors furchten den Weg** the tractor made ruts *or* furrows in the road → *auch* **gefurcht**

fur|chig ['fʊrçɪç] ADJ *Stirn* furrowed; (*durch Wagenspuren etc auch*) rutted

Furcht [fʊrçt] F -, *no pl* fear; **aus ~ vor jdm/etw** for fear of sb/sth; **ohne ~ sein** to be fearless, to be without fear; **~ vor jdm/etw haben** *or* **empfinden** to be afraid of sb/sth, to fear sb/sth; **~ ergriff** *or* **packte ihn** fear seized him, he was seized with fear; **jdn in ~ versetzen**, **jdm ~ einflößen** to frighten *or* scare sb; **~ einflößend**, **~ erregend** terrifying, fearful; **ohne ~ und Tadel** without fear or reproach

furcht|bar ADJ terrible, awful, dreadful; **ich habe einen ~en Hunger** I'm ever so hungry (*inf*), I'm terribly hungry (*inf*) ADV terribly (*inf*), awfully (*inf*); **wir haben ~ gelacht** we laughed ourselves silly (*inf*)

Furcht|bar|keit F -, -en **a** *no pl* (= *Furchtbarsein, von Zorn*) awesomeness; **die ~ der Armut/Zustände in diesem Land** the dreadful poverty/conditions in this country **b** *usu pl* (= *furchtbare Geschehnisse*) terrible *or* awful *or* dreadful things *pl*

furcht|ein|flö|ßend △ ADJ → **Furcht**

fürch|ten ['fʏrçtn] VT **jdn/etw ~** to be afraid of sb/sth, to fear sb/sth; **das Schlimmste ~** to fear the worst; **~, dass ...** to be afraid *or* to fear that ...; **es war schlimmer, als ich gefürchtet hatte** it was worse than I had feared; **Gott ~** to fear God → *auch* **gefürchtet** VR to be afraid (*vor* +*dat* of); **sich im Dunkeln ~** to be afraid *or* scared of the dark VI **für** *or* **um jdn/jds Leben/etw ~** to fear for sb/sb's life/sth; **zum Fürchten aussehen** to look frightening *or* terrifying; **da kannst du das Fürchten lernen** that will scare you stiff; **jdm das Fürchten lehren** to put the fear of God into sb

fürch|ter|lich ['fʏrçtɐlɪç] ADJ, ADV = **furchtbar**

Furcht-: furcht|er|re|gend △ ADJ → **Furcht**; **furcht|los** ADJ *Person* fearless, intrepid; *Entschlossenheit* fearless; **Furcht|lo|sig|keit** F -, *no pl* fearlessness, intrepidity; **furcht|sam** ['fʊrçtzaːm] ADJ timid, timorous; **Furcht|sam|keit** F -, (*rare*) -en timidity, timorousness

Fur|chung ['fʊrçʊŋ] F -, -en (*Biol*) cleavage

für|der(hin) ['fʏrdɐ(hɪn)] ADV (*obs*) hereafter (*old*), in future

für|ei|nan|der [fyːɐai'nandɐ] ADV for each other, for one another

Fu|rie ['fuːriə] F -, -n (*Myth*) fury; (*fig*) hellcat (*esp Brit*), termagant; **wie von ~n gejagt** *or* **gehetzt** (*liter*) as though the devil himself were after him/them *etc*; **sie gingen wie ~n aufeinander los** they went for each other like cats *or* wild things

fu|ri|os [fu'rioːs] ADJ high-energy, dynamic

Fur|nier [fʊr'niːɐ] NT -s, -e veneer

fur|nie|ren [fʊr'niːrən] *ptp* **furniert** VT to veneer; **mit Mahagoni furniert** with a mahogany veneer

Fu|ro|re [fu'roːrə] F - *or* nt -s, *no pl* sensation; **~ machen** (*inf*) to cause a sensation

Für|sor|ge F , *no pl* **a** (= *Betreuung*) care; (= *Sozialfürsorge*) welfare **b** (*inf*: = *Sozialamt*) welfare (*inf*), welfare services; **der ~ zur Last fallen** to be a burden on the state **c** (*inf*: = *Sozialunterstützung*) social security (*Brit*), welfare (*US*); **von der ~ leben** to live on social security (*Brit*) *or* welfare (*US*)

Für|sor|ge-: Für|sor|ge|amt NT (church) welfare office; **Für|sor|ge|be|ruf** M job in one of the welfare services; **Für|sor|ge|er|zie|hung** F education in a special school; **Für|sor|ge|pflicht** F (*Jur*) employer's obligation to provide for the welfare of his employees

Für|sor|ger ['fyːɐzɔrgɐ] M -s, -, **Für|sor|ge|rin** [-ərɪn] F -, -nen welfare worker

für|sor|ge|risch ['fyːɐzɔrgərɪʃ] ADJ welfare *attr* ADV **alte Menschen ~ betreuen** to look after the welfare of old people

Für|sor|ge-: Für|sor|ge|satz M rate of social security (benefit) (*Brit*), rate of welfare (*US*); **Für|sor|ge|staat** M welfare state; **Für|sor|ge|un|ter|stüt|zung** F social security benefit (*Brit*), welfare (*US*)

für|sorg|lich ['fyːɐzɔrklɪç] ADJ caring; *Mensch auch* solicitous; **~e Pflege** attentive care ADV **jdn sehr ~ behandeln** to lavish care on sb

Für|sorg|lich|keit F -, *no pl* **die ~, mit der er sie pflegte** how caring he looked after her; **gerührt von der ~ meines Chefs** touched by how caring my boss was

Für|spra|che F recommendation; **für jdn ~ einlegen** to recommend sb (*bei* to), to put in a word for sb (*inf*) (*bei* with); **auf ~ von jdm** on sb's recommendation

Für|sprech ['fyːɐʃprɛç] M -s, -e **a** (*old*: = *Rechtsbeistand*) counsel **b** (*Sw*: = *Rechtsanwalt*) barrister (*Brit*), lawyer

Für|spre|cher(in) M(F) **a** advocate **b** (*Sw*: = *Rechtsanwalt*) barrister (*Brit*), lawyer

Fürst [fʏrst] M -en, -en prince; (= *Herrscher*) ruler; **geistlicher ~** prince bishop; **wie ein ~ leben** to live like a lord *or* king; **der ~ der Finsternis** *or* **dieser Welt** (*liter*) the Prince of Darkness *or* of this world (*Bibl*)

Fürst|bi|schof M (*Hist*) prince bishop

Fürs|ten-: Fürs|ten|ge|schlecht NT , **Fürs|ten|haus** NT royal house; **Fürs|ten|stand** M royal rank; **jdn in den ~ erheben** to create sb prince; **Fürs|ten|tum** ['fʏrstntuːm] NT -s, **Fürstentümer** [-tyːmɐ] principality, princedom (*old*); **das ~ Monaco/Liechtenstein** the principality of Monaco/Liechtenstein

Fürs|tin ['fʏrstɪn] F -, -nen princess; (= *Herrscherin*) ruler

fürst|lich ['fʏrstlɪç] ADJ (*lit*) princely *no adv*; (*fig auch*) handsome, lavish ADV **jdn ~ bewirten** to entertain sb right royally; **jdn ~ belohnen** to reward sb handsomely; **~ leben** to live like a king *or* lord

Fürst|lich|keit F -, -en **a** *no pl* princeliness **b** (*form*: = *fürstliche Persönlichkeit*) royal personage (*form*)

Furt [fʊrt] F -, -en ford

Fu|run|kel [fu'rʊŋkl] NT OR M -s, - boil

für|wahr [fyːɐ'vaːɐ] ADV (*old*) forsooth (*old*), in truth (*old*)

Für|wort NT *pl* -wörter (*Gram*) pronoun

Furz [fʊrts] M -(e)s, -e ['fʏrtsə] fart (*inf*); **einen ~ (fahren) lassen** to let off (a fart) (*inf*)

fur|zen ['fʊrtsn] VI (*inf*) to fart (*inf*)

Fu|sel ['fuːzl] M -s, - (*pej*) rotgut (*inf*), hooch (*esp US inf*)

Fu|sel|öl NT fusel oil

Fü|si|lier [fyzi'liːɐ] M -s, -e (*old Mil, Sw*) fusilier

fü|si|lie|ren [fyzi'liːrən] *ptp* **füsiliert** VT (*old Mil*) to execute by firing squad

Fu|si|on [fu'zioːn] F -, -en amalgamation; (*von Unternehmen auch*) merger; (*von Atomkernen, Zellen*) fusion

fu|si|o|nie|ren [fuzio'niːrən] *ptp* **fusioniert** VTI to amalgamate; (*Unternehmen auch*) to merge

Fu|si|o|ni|tis [fuzio'niːtɪs] F -, *no pl* (*hum pej*: = *Comm*) merger mania

Fu|si|ons|re|ak|tor M fusion reactor

Fuß [fuːs] M -es, **Füße** ['fyːsə] **a** (= *Körperteil*) foot; (*S Ger, Aus*: = *Bein*) leg; **zu ~** on *or* by foot; **zu ~ gehen/kommen** to walk, to go/come on foot; **er ist gut/schlecht zu ~** he is steady/not so steady on his feet; **sich jdm zu Füßen werfen** to prostrate oneself before sb; **jdm zu Füßen fallen/liegen/sitzen** to fall/lie/sit at sb's feet; **jdm zu Füßen sinken** to sink to the ground at sb's feet; **jdm zu Füßen fallen** *or* **sinken** (*fig*: *Bittsteller*) to go down on one's knees to *or* before sb; **das Publikum lag/sank ihm zu Füßen** he had the audience at his feet; **den ~ in** *or* **zwischen die Tür stellen** to get *or* put one's foot in the door; **den ~ auf die Erde/den Mond setzen** to set foot on the earth/the moon; **über seine eigenen Füße stolpern** to trip over one's own feet; (*fig*) to get tied up in knots; **kalte Füße bekommen** (*lit, fig*) **sich** (*dat*) **kalte Füße holen** (*lit, fig*) to get cold feet; **so schnell/weit ihn seine**

Füße trugen as fast/far as his legs would carry him; **bei ~!** heel!; **jdm zwischen die Füße geraten** or **kommen** to get under sb's feet; **jdm etw vor die Füße werfen** or **schmeißen** (inf) (lit) to throw sth at sb; (fig) to tell sb to keep or stuff (inf) sth; **jdn mit Füßen treten** (fig) to walk all over sb; **etw mit Füßen treten** (fig) to treat sth with contempt; **(festen) ~ fassen** (lit, fig) to gain a foothold; (= sich niederlassen) to settle down; **auf eigenen Füßen stehen** (lit) to stand by oneself; (fig) to stand on one's own two feet; **jdn auf freien ~ setzen** to release sb, to set sb free; **jdn auf dem falschen ~ erwischen** (fig) to catch sb on the wrong foot; **auf großem ~ leben** to live the high life; **mit jdm auf gutem ~ stehen** to be on good terms with sb; **jdm/einer Sache auf dem ~e folgen** (lit) to be hot on the heels of sb/sth; (fig) to follow hard on sb/sth; **mit einem ~ im Grab stehen** to have one foot in the grave → **Boden a, Hand g, Gewehr, frei 1 a**
b (von Gegenstand) base; (= Tisch-, Stuhlbein) leg; (von Schrank, Gebirge) foot; **auf schwachen** or **tönernen Füßen stehen** to be built on sand
c (Poet) foot
d (von Strumpf) foot
e pl - (Längenmaß) foot; **12 ~ lang** 12 foot or feet long

Fuß-: Fuß|ab|druck M footprint; **Fuß|ab|strei|fer** [-laɒʃtraife] M **-s, -** footscraper; (= Matte) doormat; **Fuß|ab|tre|ter** M doormat; **Fuß|an|gel** F (lit) mantrap; (fig) catch, trap; **Fuß|ar|beit** F, no pl (Sport) footwork; **Fuß|bad** NT foot bath

Fuß|ball M **a** (no pl: = Fußballspiel) football (esp Brit), soccer **b** (= Ball) football (esp Brit), soccer ball

Fuß|bal|ler [-balɐ] M **-s, -**, **Fuß|bal|le|rin** [-ərɪn] F **-, -nen** (inf) footballer (esp Brit), soccer player

fuß|bal|le|risch ['fuːsbalərɪʃ] **ADJ** Leistungen etc footballing (esp Brit), soccer-playing (US) **ADV** **~ überlegen sein** to have superior football(ing) (esp Brit) or soccer(-playing) (US) skills

Fuß|ball-: Fuß|ball|mann|schaft F football (esp Brit) or soccer team; **Fuß|ball|match** NT (Aus) football (esp Brit) or soccer match; **Fuß|ball|meis|ter|schaft** F football (esp Brit) or soccer league championship; **Fuß|ball|platz** M football pitch (esp Brit), soccer field (US); **Fuß|ball|row|dy** M football (esp Brit) or soccer hooligan; **Fuß|ball|schuh** M football boot (esp Brit), soccer shoe (US); **Fuß|ball|spiel** NT football (esp Brit) or soccer match; (= Sportart) football (esp Brit), soccer; **Fuß|ball|spie|ler(in)** M(F) football (esp Brit) or soccer player; **Fuß|ball|sta|di|on** NT football (esp Brit) or soccer (US) stadium; **Fuß|ball|to|to** M or NT football (esp Brit) or soccer (US) pools pl; **Fuß|ball|ver|ein** M football (esp Brit) or soccer club

Fuß|bank F pl **-bänke** footstool

Fuß|bo|den M floor

Fuß|bo|den-: Fuß|bo|den|be|lag M floor covering; **Fuß|bo|den|hei|zung** F (under-)floor heating

Fuß-: fuß|breit ADJ a foot wide; **Fuß|breit** M **-, no pl** foot; **keinen ~ weichen** (lit, fig) not to budge an inch (inf); **Fuß|brem|se** F foot brake; **Fuß|ei|sen** NT mantrap

Fus|sel ['fʊsl] F **-, -n** or m **s,-** - fluff no pl; **ein(e) ~** some fluff, a bit of fluff

fus|se|lig ['fʊsəlɪç] **ADJ** (= von Fusseln bedeckt) covered with fluff; (= fusselnd) giving off fluff; (= ausgefranst) frayed; **sich** (dat) **den Mund ~ reden** (inf) to talk till one is blue in the face

fus|seln ['fʊsln] VI to give off fluff

fü|ßeln ['fyːsln] VI to play footsie (inf) (mit with)

fu|ßen ['fuːsn] VI to rest, to be based (auf +dat on)

Fuß-: Fuß|en|de NT (von Bett) foot; **Fuß|fall** M = Kniefall; **fuß|fäl|lig** ADJ, ADV = kniefällig; **Fuß|fes|sel** F **a** **~n** pl (= Knebel) shackles pl **b** elektronische ~ electronic tag

Fuß|gän|ger [-gɛŋɐ] M **-s, -**, **Fuß|gän|ge|rin** [-ərɪn] F **-, -nen** pedestrian

Fuß|gän|ger-: Fuß|gän|ger|am|pel F pedestrian lights pl; **Fuß|gän|ger|brü|cke** F footbridge; **Fuß|gän|ger|in|sel** F traffic island; **Fuß|gän|ger|über|gang** M pedestrian crossing; **Fuß|gän|ger|über|weg** M pedestrian crossing (Brit), crosswalk (US); (auch **Fußgängerüberführung**) pedestrian bridge; **Fuß|gän|ger|un|ter|füh|rung** F underpass, pedestrian subway (Brit); **Fuß|gän|ger|zo|ne** F pedestrian precinct or zone

Fuß-: Fuß|ge|her(in) M(F) (Aus) pedestrian; **Fuß|ge|lenk** NT ankle; **fuß|hoch** ADJ ankle-deep ADV up to one's ankles

-fü|ßig [fyːsɪç] ADJ suf **a** -legged; **ein dreifüßiger Tisch** a three-legged table **b** (Poet) -foot; **fünffüßiger Jambus** iambic pentameter

Fuß-: fuß|kalt ADJ **das Haus ist immer ~** the floor in that house is always cold; **fuß|krank** ADJ **~ sein** to have bad feet or trouble with one's feet; (fig) to be lagging behind; **Fuß|kran|ke(r)** MF decl as adj person with bad feet; (fig) laggard; **Fuß|lap|pen** M footcloth; **Fuß|lei|den** NT foot complaint; **Fuß|leis|te** F skirting (board) (Brit), baseboard (US)

fuss|lig ▲ ADJ = fusselig

Füß|ling ['fyːslɪŋ] M **-s, -e** (von Strumpf) foot; (= Socke) sockette (dated Brit)

Fuß-: Fuß|marsch M walk; (Mil) march; **Fuß|mat|te** F doormat; **Fuß|no|te** F footnote; **Fuß|pfad** M footpath; **Fuß|pfle|ge** F chiropody; **zur ~ gehen** to go to the chiropodist; **Fuß|pfle|ger(in)** M(F) chiropodist; **Fuß|pilz** M (Med) athlete's foot; **Fuß|pu|der** M foot powder; **Fuß|punkt** M **a** (Astron) nadir **b** (Math) foot (of a perpendicular); **Fuß|re|flex|zo|nen|mas|sa|ge** F = Reflexzonenmassage; **Fuß|schweiß** M foot perspiration; **Fuß|soh|le** F sole of the foot; **Fuß|sol|dat** M (Mil old) foot soldier; **Fuß|spit|ze** F toes pl; **sich auf die ~n stellen** to stand on tiptoe; **Fuß|sprung** M **einen ~ machen** to jump feet-first; **Fuß|spur** F footprint; **Fuß|stap|fe** F, **Fuß|stap|fen** M footprint; **in jds ~n (pl) treten** (fig) to follow in sb's footsteps; **Fuß|steig** M **a** (= Weg) footpath **b** (S Ger: = Bürgersteig) pavement (Brit), sidewalk (US); **Fuß|stüt|ze** F footrest; **fuß|tief** ADJ ankle-deep; **Fuß|tritt** M (= Geräusch) footstep; (= Spur auch) footprint; (= Stoß) kick; **jdm einen ~ geben** or **versetzen** to kick sb, to give sb a kick; **jdn mit einem ~ hinausbefördern** to kick sb out; **einen ~ bekommen** (fig) to be kicked out; **Fuß|trup|pe** F infantry no

pl; **Fuß|volk** NT, no pl **a** (Mil old) footmen pl **b** (fig) **das ~** the rank and file; **Fuß|wan|de|rung** F walk; **Fuß|wa|schung** F foot-washing; **die ~ Christi** the washing of Christ's feet; **Fuß|weg** M **a** (= Pfad) footpath **b** (= Entfernung) **es sind nur 15 Minuten ~** it's only 15 minutes' walk; **Fuß|wur|zel** F (Anat) tarsus; **Fuß|zei|le** F (Comput) footer

Fu|ton ['fuːtɔn] M **-s, -s** futon

Fu|ton|mat|rat|ze F futon

futsch [fʊtʃ] ADJ pred (inf) (= weg) gone, vanished; (S Ger: = kaputt) bust (inf), broken

Fut|ter ['fʊtɐ] NT **-s, - a** no pl (animal) food or feed; (esp für Kühe, Pferde etc) fodder; **gut im ~ sein** to be well-fed **b** (= Auskleidung, Kleiderfutter, Briefumschlagfutter) lining; (= Türfutter) casing **c** (= Spannfutter) chuck

Fut|te|ral [fʊtəˈraːl] NT **-s, -e** case

Futter-: Fut|ter|ge|trei|de NT forage cereal; **Fut|ter|häus|chen** [-hɔysçən] NT birdhouse; **Fut|ter|krip|pe** F manger; **an der ~ sitzen** (inf) to be well-placed; **Fut|ter|mit|tel** NT animal feed no pl; **Fut|ter|mit|tel|in|dus|trie** F (animal) feed industry

fut|tern ['fʊtɐn] (hum inf) VI to stuff oneself (inf) VT to scoff (Brit inf), to scarf or chow (US inf)

füt|tern ['fʏtɐn] VT **a** Tier, Kind, Kranke to feed; **„Füttern verboten"** "do not feed the animals" **b** Kleidungsstück to line

Futter-: Fut|ter|napf M bowl; **Fut|ter|neid** M (fig) green-eyed monster (hum), jealousy; **Fut|ter|pflan|ze** F forage plant; **Fut|ter|rü|be** F root vegetable used to feed animals; **Fut|ter|sack** M nosebag; **Fut|ter|stoff** M lining (material); **Fut|ter|su|che** F search for food; **auf ~ sein** to be searching for food; **Fut|ter|trog** M feeding trough

Füt|te|rung ['fʏtərʊŋ] F **-, -en** feeding; **die ~ der Nilpferde findet um 17.00 Uhr statt** feeding time for the hippos is 5 pm

Fut|ter|ver|wer|ter [-fɛɐvɛɐtɐ] M **-s, -**, **Fut|ter|ver|wer|te|rin** [-ərɪn] **-, -nen** (inf: Mensch) **er ist ein guter ~** he looks like he can really pack it away (inf)

Fu|tur [fuˈtuːɐ] NT **-(e)s, -e** (Gram) future (tense)

Fu|tu|ra pl von Futurum

fu|tu|risch [fuˈtuːrɪʃ] ADJ (Gram) future

Fu|tu|ris|mus [futuˈrɪsmʊs] M **-, no pl** futurism

fu|tu|ris|tisch [futuˈrɪstɪʃ] ADJ **a** (= zukunftsweisend) futuristic **b** (= den Futurismus betreffend) futurist

Fu|tu|ro|lo|ge [futuroˈloːgə] M **-n, -n**, **Fu|tu|ro|lo|gin** [-ˈloːgɪn] F **-, -nen** futurologist

Fu|tu|ro|lo|gie [futuroloˈgiː] F **-, no pl** futurology

fu|tu|ro|lo|gisch [futuroˈloːgɪʃ] ADJ futurological

Fu|tu|rum [fuˈtuːrʊm] NT **-s, Futura** [-ra] (Gram) future (tense)

Fux [fʊks] M **-es, ^e** ['fʏksə] (Univ) new member of a student fraternity

Fux|ma|jor M (Univ) student in charge of the new members of a fraternity

fu|zeln ['fuːtsln] VI (Aus) to write small

Fuz|zi ['fʊtsi] M **-s, -s** (inf) freak (inf)

G

G, g [ge:] NT -, - G, g

g abbr von **Gramm**

gab pret von **geben**

Ga|bar|di|ne [ˈgabardiːn, gabarˈdiːn(ə)] M -s or f -, no pl gaberdine, gabardine

Ga|be [ˈgaːbə] F -, -n **a** (dated: = Geschenk) gift, present (+gen of, from); (= Schenkung) donation (+gen from); (Eccl: = Opfer) offering → **mild(e)** ADJ **b** b (= Begabung) gift; **die ~ haben, etw zu tun** to have a natural or (auch iro) (great) gift for doing sth **c** (Med) (= das Verabreichen) administering; (= Dosis) dose

Ga|bel [ˈgaːbl] F -, -n fork; (= Heugabel, Mistgabel) pitchfork; (= Deichsel) shafts pl; (Telec) rest, cradle; (Hunt: = Geweih mit zwei Enden) two--pointed antler; (= zwei Enden des Geweihs) branch, fork

Ga|bel-: Ga|bel|bis|sen M canapé; **Ga|bel|bock** M (Hunt: = Rehbock) two-pointer; (= Gabelantilope) pronghorn (antelope); **Ga|bel|deich|sel** F shafts pl; **ga|bel|för|mig** ADJ forked no adv ADV **sich ~ teilen** to fork; **Ga|bel|früh|stück** NT ≈ mid-morning snack; **Ga|bel|hirsch** M (Hunt: = Rothirsch) two--pointer; (= Andenhirsch) guemal

ga|be|lig [ˈgaːbəlɪç] ADJ, ADV = **gabelförmig**

ga|beln [ˈgaːbln] VR to fork → auch **gegabelt**

Ga|bel|stap|ler [-ʃtaplɐ] M -s, - fork-lift truck

Ga|be|lung F -, -en fork

Ga|ben|tisch M table for Christmas or birthday presents

Ga|bun [gaˈbuːn] NT -s Gabon

G8, G-8 [geːˈlaxt] F - G8

G8-Staat, G-8-Staat M G8 nation

ga|ckern [ˈgakɐn] VI (lit, fig) to cackle

Ga|do|li|ni|um [gadoˈliːniʊm] NT -s, no pl (abbr **Gd**) gadolinium

Gaf|fel [ˈgafl] F -, -n (Naut) gaff

Gaf|fel-: Gaf|fel|scho|ner M (Naut) fore-and--aft schooner; **Gaf|fel|se|gel** NT (Naut) gaff--sail

gaf|fen [ˈgafn] VI to gape, to gawp (inf), to stare (nach at), to rubberneck (esp US inf); **gaff nicht, hilf mir lieber!** don't just stand there staring, come and help!

Gaf|fer [ˈgafɐ] M -s, -, **Gaf|fe|rin** [-ərɪn] F -, -nen gaper, gawper (inf), starer, rubbernecker (esp US inf); **die neugierigen ~ bei einem Unfall** the nosy people standing staring at an accident, the rubbernecks at an accident (esp US inf)

Gaf|fe|rei [gafəˈrai] F -, no pl gaping, gawping (inf), staring, rubbernecking (esp US inf)

Gag [gɛ(ː)k] M -s, -s (= Filmgag) gag; (= Werbegag) gimmick; (= Witz) joke; (inf: = Spaß) laugh

ga|ga [gaga] ADJ pred inv (inf) gaga (inf)

Ga|gat [gaˈgaːt] M -(e)s, -e, **Ga|gat|koh|le** F jet

Ga|ge [ˈgaːʒə] F -, -n (esp Theat) fee; (= regelmäßige Gage) salary

gäh|nen [ˈgɛːnən] VI (lit, fig) to yawn; **~de Leere** total emptiness; **im Kino herrschte ~de Leere** the cinema was (totally) deserted; **ein ~der Ab-** grund a yawning abyss; **ein ~des Loch** a gaping hole; **ein Gähnen** a yawn; **das Gähnen unterdrücken** to stop oneself (from) yawning; **das Gähnen der Schüler** the pupils' yawning; **das war zum Gähnen (langweilig)** it was one big yawn (inf)

GAL [geːlaːˈʔɛl] F - abbr von **Grün-Alternative Liste** electoral pact of Greens and alternative parties

Ga|la [ˈgala, ˈgaːla] F -, -s formal or evening or gala dress; (Mil) full or ceremonial or gala dress; **sich in ~ werfen** to get all dressed up (to the nines (esp Brit inf)), to put on one's best bib and tucker (Brit inf)

Ga|la- [ˈgala, ˈgaːla] in cpds formal, evening; (Mil) full ceremonial, gala; (Theat) gala; **Ga|la|abend** M gala evening; **Ga|la|an|zug** M formal or evening dress; (Mil) full or ceremonial or gala dress; **Ga|la|di|ner** NT formal dinner; **Ga|la|emp|fang** M formal reception

ga|lak|tisch [gaˈlaktɪʃ] ADJ galactic

Ga|lan [gaˈlaːn] M -s, -e (old) gallant; (hum auch) beau

ga|lant [gaˈlant] (dated) ADJ gallant; **die ~e Dichtung** galant poetry; **~es Abenteuer** affair of the heart, amatory adventure ADV gallantly

Ga|lan|te|rie [galantəˈriː] F -, -n [-ˈriːən] (dated) gallantry

Ga|lan|te|rie|wa|ren PL (old) fashion accessories pl

Ga|la- [ˈgala, ˈgaːla]: **Ga|la|uni|form** F (Mil) full dress or ceremonial or gala uniform; **Ga|la|vor|stel|lung** F (Theat) gala performance

Gä|le [ˈgɛːlə] M -n, -n, **Gä|lin** [ˈgɛːlɪn] F -, -nen Gael

Gal|ee|re [gaˈleːrə] F -, -n galley

Gal|ee|ren|skla|ve M , **Gal|ee|ren|sträf|ling** M galley slave

Gal|e|o|ne [galeˈoːnə] F -, -n (Hist) galleon

Ga|le|rie [galəˈriː] F -, -n [-ˈriːən] **a** (= Empore, Gang, Kunstgalerie, Mil, Naut) gallery; **auf der ~** in the gallery **b** (= Geschäftspassage) arcade

Ga|le|rist [galəˈrɪst] M -en, -en, **Ga|le|ris|tin** [-ˈrɪstɪn] F -, -nen gallery owner

Gal|gen [ˈgalgn] M -s, - gallows pl, gibbet; (Film) boom; (Tech) crossbeam; (= Spiel) hangman; **jdn an den ~ bringen** to bring sb to the gallows; **an den ~ mit ihm!** let him swing!, to the gallows with him!; **jdn am ~ hinrichten** to hang sb (from the gallows)

Gal|gen-: Gal|gen|frist F (inf) reprieve; **jdm eine ~ geben** to give sb a reprieve, to reprieve sb; **Gal|gen|hu|mor** M gallows humour (Brit) or humor (US); **sagte er mit ~** he said with a macabre sense of humo(u)r; **Gal|gen|strick** M , **Gal|gen|vo|gel** M (inf) gallows bird (inf)

Ga|li|ci|en [gaˈliːtsiən] NT -s, no pl Galicia

Ga|li|läa [galiˈlɛːa] NT -s, no pl Galilee

Ga|li|lä|er [galiˈlɛːɐ] M -s, -, **Ga|li|lä|e|rin** [-ərɪn] F -, -nen Galilean

ga|li|lä|isch [galiˈlɛːɪʃ] ADJ Galilean

Gä|lin F [ˈgɛːlɪn] -, -nen Gael

Ga|li|on [gaˈliːoːn] NT -s, -s (Hist) cutwater

Ga|li|ons|fi|gur F figurehead

gä|lisch [ˈgɛːlɪʃ] ADJ Gaelic

Gall|ap|fel [ˈgal-] M gallnut; (an Eichen) oak apple, oak gall

Gal|le [ˈgalə] F -, -n (Anat) (= Organ) gall bladder; (= Flüssigkeit) bile, gall; (Bot, Vet) gall; (fig: = Bosheit) gall, virulence; **bitter wie ~** bitter as gall; **seine ~ verspritzen** (fig) to pour out one's venom; **jdm kommt die ~ hoch** sb's blood begins to boil; **die ~ läuft ihm über** (inf) he's seething or livid → **Gift**

gal|le|bit|ter ADJ very bitter; Wein, Geschmack auch acid, acrid; Bemerkung caustic

Gal|len- in cpds gall; **gal|len|bit|ter** ADJ = **gallebitter**; **Gal|len|bla|se** F gall bladder; **Gal|len|gang** M pl -gänge bile duct; **Gal|len|grieß** M small gallstones pl; **Gal|len|ko|lik** F gallstone colic; **Gal|len|lei|den** NT trouble with one's gall bladder; **Gal|len|stein** M gallstone

Gal|lert [ˈgalɛrt, ˈgalɐt] NT -(e)s, -e jelly (Brit), Jell-O® (US)

gal|lert|ar|tig ADJ jelly-like (Brit), Jell-O-like® (US), gelatinous

Gal|ler|te [gaˈlɛrtə, ˈgalɐtə] F -, -n jelly (Brit), Jell-O® (US)

Gal|li|en [ˈgaliən] NT -s Gaul

Gal|li|er [ˈgaliɐ] M -s, -, **Gal|li|e|rin** [-iərɪn] F -, -nen Gaul

gal|lig [ˈgalɪç] ADJ gall-like attr; (fig) Mensch, Bemerkung, Humor caustic, acerbic ADV (fig) caustically

gal|lisch [ˈgalɪʃ] ADJ Gallic

Gal|li|um [ˈgaliʊm] NT -s, no pl (abbr **Ga**) gallium

Gal|li|zis|mus [galiˈtsɪsmʊs] M -, **Gallizismen** [-mən] (Ling) Gallicism

Gal|lo|ne [gaˈloːnə] F -, -n gallon

Gall|sei|fe [ˈgal-] F ox-gall soap

Ga|lopp [gaˈlɔp] M -s, -s or -e gallop; (= Tanz) galop; **im ~** (lit) at a gallop; (fig) at top or high speed; **langsamer ~** canter; **gestreckter/kurzer ~** full/checked gallop; **in den ~ verfallen** to break into a gallop; **das Pferd sprang in fliegendem ~ über die Mauer** the horse flew or soared over the wall in mid-gallop

ga|lop|pie|ren [galɔˈpiːrən] ptp **galoppiert** VI aux haben or sein to gallop; **~de Inflation** galloping inflation

Ga|lopp-: Ga|lopp|renn|bahn F racecourse, racetrack; **Ga|lopp|ren|nen** NT horse race (on the flat); **zum ~ gehen** to go to the races

Ga|lo|sche [gaˈlɔʃə] F -, -n galosh usu pl, overshoe

galt pret von **gelten**

gal|va|nisch [galˈvaːnɪʃ] ADJ galvanic

Gal|va|ni|seur [galvaniˈzøːɐ] M -s, -e, **Gal|va|ni|seu|rin** [-ˈzøːrɪn] F -, -nen electroplater

Gal|va|ni|sier|an|stalt F electroplating works sing or pl

gal|va|ni|sie|ren [galvaniˈziːrən] ptp **galvanisiert** VT to electroplate; (mit Zink auch) to galvanize

Gal|va|ni|sie|rung F -, -en electroplating; (*mit Zink auch*) galvanizing

Gal|va|nis|mus [galva'nɪsmʊs] M -, *no pl* galvanism

Gal|va|no [gal'va:no] NT -s, -s (*Typ*) electrotype, electro (*inf*)

Gal|va|no-: Gal|va|no|me|ter NT -s, - galvanometer; **Gal|va|no|plas|tik** F (*Tech*) electroforming, galvanoplasty (*form*); (*Typ*) electrotype

Ga|ma|sche [ga'maʃə] F -, -n gaiter; (= *kurze Gamasche*) spat; (= *Wickelgamasche*) puttee; **sie hat ~n vor ihm/davor** (*dated inf*) he/it makes her shake in her shoes (*inf*)

Ga|ma|schen|ho|se F (pair of) leggings *pl*

Gam|be ['gambə] F -, -n viola da gamba

Gam|bia ['gambia] NT -s (the) Gambia

Game|boy® ['ge:mbɔy] M -(s), -s (*Comput*) Gameboy®

Game|show ['ge:mʃo:] F game show

Gam|ma ['gama] NT -(s), -s gamma

Gam|ma|strah|len ['gama-] PL gamma rays *pl*

Gam|ma|strah|lung F gamma radiation

Gam|mel ['gaml] M -s, *no pl* (*dial*) junk (*inf*), rubbish

Gam|mel|dienst M (*Mil sl*) lazy spell of duty

gam|me|lig ['gaməlɪç] ADJ (*inf*) *Lebensmittel* old, ancient (*inf*); *Kleidung* tatty (*inf*); *Auto* decrepit; **das Fleisch ist ja schon ganz ~** the meat has already gone off (*Brit*) or bad

Gam|mel|le|ben NT (*inf*) loafing or bumming around *no art* (*inf*)

gam|meln ['gamln] VI (*inf*) to laze about, to loaf about (*Brit*) or around (*inf*), to bum around (*inf*)

Gamm|ler ['gamlɐ] M -s, -, **Gamm|le|rin** [-ərɪn] F -, -nen long-haired layabout (*Brit*) or bum (*inf*)

Gams [gams] F -, -(en) [-zn] (*Aus, S Ger, Hunt*) chamois

Gäms|bart ▲ M , **Gams|bart** M tuft of hair from a chamois worn as a hat decoration, shaving brush (*hum inf*)

Gäms|bock ▲ M , **Gams|bock** M chamois buck

Gäm|se ▲ ['gɛmzə] F -, -n chamois

Gäms|le|der ▲ NT , **Gams|le|der** NT chamois (leather)

gang [gaŋ] ADJ **~ und gäbe sein** to be the usual thing, to be quite usual

Gang¹ [gaŋ] M -(e)s, ⁻e ['gɛŋə] **a** (*no pl*: = *Gangart*) walk, way of walking, gait; (*eines Pferdes*) gait, pace; **einen leichten ~ haben** to be light on one's feet, to walk lightly; **einen schnellen ~ haben** to be a fast walker; **jdn an seinem** or **am ~ erkennen** to recognize sb's walk or sb by the way he walks; **jdn am aufrechten ~ erkennen** to recognize sb from his upright carriage; **in aufrechtem ~** (*fig*) with one's head held high; **seinen ~ verlangsamen** to slow down; **seinen ~ beschleunigen** to speed up, to hasten one's step (*liter*)
b (= *Besorgung*) errand; (= *Spaziergang*) walk; **einen ~ machen** or **tun** to go on an errand/for a walk; **einen ~ zum Anwalt/zur Bank machen** to go to one's lawyer/the bank, to pay a visit to one's lawyer/the bank; **einen schweren ~ tun** to do something difficult; **das war für ihn immer ein schwerer ~** it was always hard for him; **ich muss einen schweren ~ tun** I have a difficult thing to do; **sein erster ~ war ...** the first thing he did was ...; **den ~ nach Canossa** or **Kanossa antreten** (*fig*) to eat humble pie; **der ~ nach Canossa** or **Kanossa** (*Hist*) the pilgrimage to Canossa; **der ~ an die Börse** flotation (on the stock exchange)
c (*no pl*) (*Bewegung eines Motors*) running; (*einer Maschine*) running, operation; (= *Ablauf*) course; (*eines Dramas*) development; **der Motor hat einen leisen ~** the engine runs quietly; **der ~ der Ereignisse/der Dinge** the course of events/

things; **seinen (gewohnten) ~ gehen** (*fig*) to run its usual course; **etw in ~ bringen** or **setzen** to get or set sth going; (*fig auch*) to get sth off the ground or under way; **etw in ~ halten** (*lit, fig*) to keep sth going; *Maschine, Motor auch* to keep sth running; **in ~ kommen** to get going; (*fig auch*) to get off the ground or under way; **in ~ sein** to be going; (*Maschine auch*) to be in operation, to be running; (*Motor auch*) to be running; (*fig*) to be off the ground or under way; (= *los sein*) to be going on or happening; **in vollem ~ in full swing; es ist etwas im ~(e)** (*inf*) something's up (*inf*) → **tot c**
d (= *Arbeitsgang*) operation; (*eines Essens*) course; (*Fechten, im Zweikampf*) bout; (*beim Rennen*) heat; **ein Essen von** or **mit vier Gängen** a four-course meal
e (= *Verbindungsgang*) passage(way); (*Rail, in Gebäuden*) corridor; (= *Hausflur*) (*offen*) passage (-way), close (*Scot*); (*hinter Eingangstür*) hallway; (*im oberen Stock*) landing; (*zwischen Sitzreihen, in Geschäft*) aisle; (= *Tunnel: in Stadion, zu Flugzeug*) gangway; (= *Säulengang*) colonnade, passage; (= *Bogengang*) arcade, passage; (= *Wandelgang*) walk; (*in einem Bergwerk*) tunnel, gallery; (= *Durchgang zwischen Häusern*) passage(way); (*Anat*) duct; (= *Gehörgang*) meatus; (*Min*: = *Erzgang*) vein; (*Tech: eines Gewindes*) thread
f (*Mech*) gear; (*bei Fahrrad*) gear, speed; **den ersten ~ einschalten** or **einlegen** to engage first (gear); **auf** or **in den dritten ~ schalten** to change (*Brit*) or shift (*US*) into third (gear); **in die Gänge kommen** (*fig*) to get started or going

Gang² [gɛŋ] F -, -s gang

Gang|art F **a** walk, way of walking, gait; (*von Pferd*) gait, pace; (= *Haltung*) carriage, bearing; (*fig*) stance; **Menschen haben eine aufrechte ~** humans walk upright; **eine leicht nach vorne gebeugte ~** to walk with one's body bent slightly forward; **eine schnellere ~ vorlegen** to walk faster; **eine harte ~** (*fig*) a tough stance or line **b** (*Min*) gangue, matrix

gang|bar ADJ (*lit*) *Weg, Brücke etc* passable; (*fig*) *Lösung, Weg* practicable; **nicht ~** impassable; impracticable

Gän|gel|band [-bant] NT *pl* -**bänder jdn am ~ führen** (*fig*) (*Lehrer etc*) to spoon-feed sb; (*Ehefrau, Mutter*) to keep sb tied to one's apron strings

Gän|ge|lei [gɛŋə'lai] F -, -en spoon-feeding; **warum wehrt er sich nicht gegen die ~ seiner Mutter/Frau?** why doesn't he fight against being tied to his mother's/wife's apron strings?

gän|geln ['gɛŋln] VT (*fig*) **jdn ~** to spoon-feed sb, to treat sb like a child; (*Mutter, Ehefrau*) to keep sb tied to one's apron strings

Gang|he|bel M (*Tech*) gear lever

gän|gig ['gɛŋɪç] ADJ **a** (= *üblich*) common; (= *aktuell*) current; *Münze* current; (= *vertretbar*) possible; **~e Praxis sein** to be common practice **b** (= *gut gehend*) *Waren* popular, in demand; **die ~ste Ausführung** the best-selling model **c** (*rare*: = *gut laufend*) **~ sein** (*Pferd*) to be a good goer; (*Hund*) to be well-trained; **ein ~es/schlecht ~es Gespann** a fast/slow team; **einen Hund ~ machen** (*Hunt*) to train a dog

Gang|li|en ['gaŋ(g)liən] PL (*Anat*) ganglia *pl*

Gang|li|en-: Gang|li|en|sys|tem NT gangliar or ganglionic system; **Gang|li|en|zel|le** F gangliocyte, ganglion cell

Gang|grän [gaŋ'grɛ:n] NT -s, -e, **Gan|grä|ne** [gaŋ'grɛ:nə] F -, -n (*Med*) gangrene

Gang|schal|tung F gears *pl*

Gangs|ter ['gɛŋstɐ, 'gaŋstɐ] M -s, - gangster

Gangs|ter- ['gɛŋstɐ, 'gaŋstɐ]: **Gangs|ter|boss** ▲ M gang boss; **Gangs|ter|braut** F (*inf*) (gangster's) moll (*inf*); **Gangs|ter|film** M gangster film or movie (*esp US*); **Gangs|ter|me|tho|den** PL strong-arm tactics *pl*

Gang|way ['gɛŋwe:] F -, -s (*Naut*) gangway; (*Aviat*) steps *pl*

Ga|no|ve [ga'no:və] M -n, -n (*inf*) crook; (*hum*: = *listiger Kerl*) sly old fox → *auch* **Ganovin**

Ga|no|ven-: Ga|no|ven|eh|re F honour (*Brit*) or honor (*US*) among(st) thieves; **das verbietet mir meine ~** even crooks have some honour (*Brit*) or honor (*US*); **Ga|no|ven|spra|che** F underworld slang

Ga|no|vin [ga'no:vɪn] F -, -nen (*inf*) crook

Gans [gans] F -, ⁻e ['gɛnzə] goose; **wie die Gänse schnattern** to cackle away, to cackle like a bunch of old hens (*inf*)

Gäns- in cpds (*Aus*) = **Gänse-**

Gäns|chen ['gɛnsçən] NT -s, - gosling; (*fig inf*) little goose (*inf*)

Gän|se- in cpds goose; **Gän|se|blüm|chen** NT , **Gän|se|blu|me** F daisy; **Gän|se|bra|ten** M roast goose; **Gän|se|brust** F (*Cook*) breast of goose; **Gän|se|fe|der** F (goose-)quill; **Gän|se|fett** NT goose-fat; **Gän|se|füß|chen** PL (*inf*) inverted commas *pl*, quotation marks *pl*, sixty-sixes and ninety-nines *pl* (*inf*); **Gän|se|haut** F (*fig*) goose pimples *pl* (*Brit*), goose flesh (*Brit*), goose bumps *pl*; **eine ~ bekommen** or **kriegen** (*inf*) to get goose pimples (*Brit*) or goose flesh (*Brit*) or goose bumps, to go all goose-pimply (*Brit inf*); **Gän|se|kiel** M (goose-)quill; **Gän|se|klein** NT -s, *no pl* goose pieces *pl*; (= *Innereien*) goose giblets *pl*; **Gän|se|le|ber|pas|te|te** F pâté de foie gras, goose-liver pâté; **Gän|se|marsch** M **im ~** in single or Indian file

Gän|se|rich ['gɛnzərɪç] M -s, -e, (*Aus*) **Gan|ser** ['ganzɐ] M -s, - gander

Gän|se-: Gän|se|schmalz NT goose dripping; **Gän|se|wein** M (*hum*) Adam's ale (*hum*), water

Gan|ter ['gantɐ] M -s, - (*N Ger*) gander

ganz [gants] ADJ **a** whole, entire; (= *vollständig*) complete; *Wahrheit* whole; **eine ~e Zahl** a whole number, an integer; **eine ~e Note** (*Mus*) a semibreve (*Brit*), a whole note (*US*); **eine ~e Pause** (*Mus*) a semibreve (*Brit*) or whole note (*US*) rest; **die ~e Mannschaft war ...** the whole or entire team was ..., all the team were ...; **die ~en Tassen/Kinder** (*inf*) all the cups/children; **der ~e Vordergrund** the whole or entire foreground, the whole of the foreground, all the foreground; **~ England/London** the whole of England/London (*Brit*), all (of) England/London; **wir fuhren durch ~ England** we travelled (*Brit*) or traveled (*US*) all over England; **in ~ England/London** in the whole of (*Brit*) or in all England/London; **die ~e Zeit** all the time, the whole time; **der ~e Kram** the whole lot (*Brit*), all the stuff (*US*); **eine ~e Menge** quite a lot; **sein ~es Geld/Vermögen** all his money/fortune, his entire or whole fortune; **seine ~en Sachen** all his things; **seine ~e Kraft** all his strength; **sie ist seine ~e Freude** (*inf*) she's the apple of his eye (*inf*); **du bist ja mein ~es Leben** you're my whole life; **du hast mir den ~en Spaß verdorben** you've spoiled all my fun; **ein ~er Mann** a real or proper man → **Arbeit**
b Käse/eine Sammlung ~ or **im Ganzen kaufen** to buy a whole cheese/a collection as a whole; **im (Großen und) Ganzen (genommen)** on the whole, by and large, (taken) all in all
c (*inf*: = *unbeschädigt*) intact; **etw wieder ~ machen** to mend sth; **wieder ~ sein** to be mended
d (*inf*: = *nicht mehr als*: = *mit Zahl*) **ich verdiene im Monat ~e 1000 EUR** I earn all of 1000 euros a month; **noch ~e zehn Minuten** all of ten minutes

ADV (= *völlig*) quite; (= *vollständig, ausnahmslos*) completely; (= *ziemlich, leidlich*) quite; (= *sehr*) really; (= *genau*) exactly, just; **~ hinten/vorn** right at the back/front; **nicht ~** not quite; **~ gewiss!** most certainly, absolutely; **ein ~ gutes Buch** (= *ziemlich*) quite a good book; (= *sehr gut*) a very or really good book; **ich habe mich ~ riesig gefreut** (*inf*) I was really pleased; **du hast ihn ~ fürchterlich beleidigt** you've really insulted him very badly; **ein ~ billiger Trick/böser Kerl** a really cheap trick/evil character; **du bist ein ~ Schlauer** you're really a crafty one; **das war ~ lieb von dir** that was really nice of you; **das ist mir ~ gleich** it's all the same or all one to me; **er hat ~ Recht** he's quite or absolutely right; **~ mit Ruß bedeckt** all or completely covered with soot; **~ allein** all alone; **du bist ja ~ nass** you're all wet; **so ~ vergnügt/traurig** etc so very happy/sad etc; **~ Aufmerksamkeit/Demut** etc **sein** to be all attention/humility etc; **etwas ~ Intelligentes/Verrücktes** etc something really clever/mad etc; **es ist ~ aus** it's all over; **wie Sie meinen** just as you think (best); **~ gleich wer** it doesn't matter who, no matter who; **eine Zeitschrift ~ lesen** to read a magazine right through, to read a magazine from cover to cover; **das habe ich nicht ~ gelesen** I haven't read it all yet, I haven't finished reading it yet; **ein ~ ~ hoher Berg** a very very or really really high mountain; **~ und gar** completely, utterly; **~ und gar nicht** not at all, not in the least; **noch nicht ~ zwei Uhr** not quite two o'clock yet; **ich habe ~ den Eindruck, dass ...** I've rather got the impression that ...; **ein ~ klein wenig** just a little or tiny bit; **das mag ich ~ besonders gerne** I'm particularly or especially fond of that; **sie ist ~ die Mutter** she's just or exactly like her mother; **etw ~ oder gar nicht machen** to do sth properly or not at all

Ganz|auf|nah|me F (Phot) full-length photo (-graph)

Gän|ze ['gɛntsə] F -, no pl (form, Aus) entirety; **zur ~** completely, fully, in its entirety

Gan|ze(s) ['gantsə] NT decl as adj whole; (= alle Sachen zusammen) lot; (= ganzer Satz, ganze Ausrüstung) complete set; **etw als ~s sehen** to see sth as a whole; **das ~ kostet ...** altogether it costs ...; **das ~ alleine machen** to do the whole thing or it all on one's own; **das ~ halt!** (Mil) parade, halt!; **das ist nichts ~s und nichts Halbes** that's neither one thing nor the other; **das ~ gefällt mir gar nicht** I don't like it at all, I don't like anything about it; **aufs ~ gehen** (inf) to go all out; **es geht ums ~** everything's at stake

Ganz|heit F -, (rare) -en (= Einheit) unity; (= Vollständigkeit) entirety; **als ~** as an integral whole; **in seiner ~** in its entirety

ganz|heit|lich ['gantshaitlɪç] ADJ (= umfassend einheitlich) integral; Lernen integrated; Medizin holistic ADV **ein Problem ~ betrachten/darstellen** to view/present a problem in its entirety

Ganz|heits-: Ganz|heits|me|di|zin F holistic medicine; **Ganz|heits|me|tho|de** F look-and-say method; **Ganz|heits|psy|cho|lo|gie** F holism

Ganz-: Ganz|jah|res|rei|fen ['gantsjaːrəs-] M (Mot) all-season tyre (Brit) or tire (US); **ganz|jäh|rig** ADJ, ADV all (the) year round; **Ganz|le|der** NT **ein Buch in ~** a leather-bound book, a book with a leather binding; **Ganz|le|der|band** M leather-bound volume; **ganz|le|dern** ADJ leather-bound, bound in leather; **Ganz|lei|nen** NT **a** (= Stoff) pure linen **b** (= Ganzeinband) **ein Buch in ~** a cloth-bound book, a book with a cloth binding; **Ganz|lei|nen|band** M cloth-bound volume

ganz|lich ['gɛntslɪç] ADV completely, totally ADJ (rare) complete, total

Ganz-: ganz|sei|den ADJ pure silk; **ganz|sei|tig** [-zaitɪç] ADJ Anzeige etc full-page; **ganz|tä|gig** ADJ all-day; Arbeit, Stelle full-time; **ein ~er Ausflug** a day trip ADV **~ arbeiten** to work full-time; **sie ist jetzt ~ zu Hause** she's at home all day now; **das Schwimmbad ist ~ geöffnet** the swimming pool is open all day

ganz|tags ['gantstaːks] ADV arbeiten full-time

Ganz-: ganz|tags-: Ganz|tags|be|schäf|ti|gung F full-time occupation; **Ganz|tags|be|treu|ung** F all-day or all-day care; **Ganz|tags|schu|le** F all-day schooling no pl or schools pl; (= Gebäude) all-day school; **Ganz|tags|stel|le** F full-time job

Ganz-: Ganz|ton M pl -töne (Mus) (whole) tone; **ganz|wol|len** ADJ all-wool

gar [gaːɐ] ADV **a** (= überhaupt) at all; **~ keines** none whatsoever, none at all; **~ kein Grund** no reason whatsoever, no reason at all; **~ niemand** not a soul, nobody at all or whatsoever; **~ nichts** nothing at all or whatsoever; **~ nicht schlecht** or **übel** not bad at all, not at all bad **b** (old, S Ger, Aus: zur Verstärkung) **es war ~ so kalt/warm** it was really or so cold/warm; **er wäre ~ zu gern noch länger geblieben** he would really or so have liked to stay longer; **es ist ~ zu dumm, dass er nicht gekommen ist** (S Ger, Aus) it's really or so or too stupid that he didn't come → **ganz** ADV **c** (geh, S Ger, Aus: = sogar) even; **er wird doch nicht ~ verunglückt sein?** he hasn't had an accident, has he?; **du hast das doch nicht ~ meinem Mann erzählt?** you haven't told my husband, have you?; **warum nicht ~?** (and) why not?, why not indeed?; **und nun will sie ~ ...** and now she even wants ...; **hast du eine Wohnung, oder ~ ein eigenes Haus?** do you have a flat (Brit) or apartment, or perhaps even a house of your own? **d** (obs, Aus, S Ger: = sehr) really, indeed; **ein ~ feiner Mensch** a really splendid person, a splendid person indeed; **~ schön** passing fair (obs); **er kommt ~ oft** he comes really frequently or very frequently indeed; **~ mancher** many a person; **~ manchmal** many a time, many a time and oft (old) ADJ **a** Speise done pred, cooked; **das Steak ist ja nur halb ~** this steak is only half-cooked **b** (form) Leder tanned, dressed; (Agr) Boden well-prepared **c** (S Ger, Aus) (= verbraucht) used up, finished; (= zu Ende) at an end, over; **das Öl wird ja nie ~** we'll never use all this oil

Ga|ra|ge [ga'raːʒə] F -, -n garage; (= Hochgarage, Tiefgarage) car park (Brit), parking garage (US); **das Auto in einer ~ unterstellen** to garage one's car (Brit), to park one's car in a garage (esp US)

Ga|ra|gen|tor [ga'raːʒn-] NT garage door

ga|ra|gie|ren [gara'ʒiːrən] ptp **garagiert** VT (Aus, Sw) to park

Ga|rant [ga'rant] M -en, -en, **Ga|ran|tin** [-'rantɪn] F -, -nen guarantor

Ga|ran|tie [garan'tiː] F -, -n [-'tiːən] (lit, fig) guarantee; (auf Auto) warranty; **die Uhr hat ein Jahr ~** the watch is guaranteed for a year or has a year's guarantee; **drei Jahre ~ auf etw gewähren** or **geben** to give a three-year guarantee/warranty on sth; **das fällt noch unter die ~, das geht noch auf ~** that comes under or is covered by the guarantee/warranty; **ich gebe dir meine ~ darauf** (fig inf) I guarantee (you) that; **unter ~** under guarantee/warranty; (fig: = garantiert) guaranteed

Ga|ran|tie-: Ga|ran|tie|an|spruch M → **Garantie** right to claim under guarantee/warranty; **Ga|ran|tie|frist** F → **Garantie** guarantee/warranty period; **Ga|ran|tie|lohn** M guaranteed minimum wage

ga|ran|tie|ren [garan'tiːrən] ptp **garantiert** VT to guarantee (jdm etw sb sth); **der Name dieser Firma garantiert Qualität** the name of this firm is a guarantee of good quality or guarantees good quality; **er konnte mir nicht ~, dass ...** he couldn't give me any guarantee that ... VI to give a guarantee; **für etw ~** guarantee sth; **er konnte für nichts ~** he couldn't guarantee anything

ga|ran|tiert [garan'tiːɐt] ADV guaranteed; (inf) I bet (inf); **er kommt ~ nicht** I bet he won't come (inf), he's bound not to come

Ga|ran|tie|schein M guarantee, certificate of guarantee (form); (für Auto) warranty

Ga|ran|tin F [ga'rantɪn] -, -nen guarantor

Gar|aus ['gaːɐlaus] M (inf) **jdm den ~ machen** to do sb in (inf), to bump sb off (inf); **einer Sache** (dat) **den ~ machen** to put an end or a stop to sth

Gar|be ['garbə] F -, -n (= Korngarbe) sheaf; (= Lichtgarbe) beam; (Mil: = Schussgarbe) burst of fire; (Metal) faggot; **das Getreide wurde in ~ zu ~n gebunden** the corn was bound into sheaves

Gar|ben|bin|de|ma|schi|ne F (Agr) sheaf-binder, sheaf-binding machine

Gär|bot|tich ['gɛːɐ-] M fermenting vat

Gar|çon|ni|ère [garsɔ'niːrə] F -, -n (Aus) one-room flat (Brit) or apartment, efficiency (US)

Gar|de ['gardə] F -, -n guard; **zu Fuß** (Hist) Foot Guards pl; **bei der ~** in the Guards; **die alte/junge ~** (fig) the old/young guard

Garde-: Gar|de|maß NT height required for eligibility for the Guards **~ haben** (inf) to be as tall as a tree; **Gar|de|of|fi|zier(in)** M(F) Guards officer; **Gar|de|re|gi|ment** NT Guards regiment

Gar|de|ro|be [gardə'roːbə] F -, -n **a** (= Kleiderbestand) wardrobe (Brit); **eine umfangreiche ~ haben** to have a large wardrobe, to have a great many clothes **b** (= Kleiderablage) hall stand; (im Theater, Kino etc) cloakroom (Brit), checkroom (US); **seinen Mantel an der ~ abgeben** to leave one's coat in the cloakroom (Brit) or checkroom (US) **c** (Theat: = Umkleideraum) dressing room

Gar|de|ro|ben-: Gar|de|ro|ben|frau F cloakroom (Brit) or checkroom (US) attendant; **Gar|de|ro|ben|ha|ken** M coat hook; **Gar|de|ro|ben|mann** M pl -männer cloakroom (Brit) or checkroom (US) attendant; **Gar|de|ro|ben|mar|ke** F, **Gar|de|ro|ben|schein** M cloakroom (Brit) or checkroom (US) ticket; **Gar|de|ro|ben|schrank** M hall cupboard; **Gar|de|ro|ben|stän|der** M hat stand (Brit), hat tree (US)

Gar|de|ro|bi|er [gardəro'bieː] M -s, -s **a** (Theat: für Kostüme) wardrobe master; (im Umkleideraum) dresser **b** (an der Abgabe) cloakroom (Brit) or checkroom (US) attendant

Gar|de|ro|bi|e|re [gardəro'bieːrə] F -, -n **a** (Theat: für Kostüme) wardrobe mistress; (im Umkleideraum) dresser **b** (an der Abgabe) cloakroom (Brit) or checkroom (US) attendant

gar|dez [gar'deː] INTERJ (Chess) gardez

Gar|di|ne [gar'diːnə] F -, -n curtain (Brit), drape (US); (= Scheibengardine) net (Brit) or café (US) curtain, curtain → **schwedisch**

Gar|di|nen-: Gar|di|nen|band [-bant] NT pl -bänder curtain tape; **Gar|di|nen|blen|de** F pelmet (Brit), valance (esp US); **Gar|di|nen|pre|digt** F (inf) dressing-down (Brit), talking-to; **jdm eine ~ halten** to give sb a dressing-down (Brit) or a talking-to; **Gar|di|nen|rol|le** F, **Gar|di|nen|röll|chen** NT curtain runner; **Gar|di|nen|stan|ge** F curtain rail; (zum Ziehen) curtain rod

Gar|dist [gar'dɪst] M -en, -en (Mil) guardsman

Gar|dis|tin [gar'dɪstɪn] F -, -nen (Mil) guardswoman

ga|ren ['gaːrən] (Cook) VTI to cook; (auf kleiner Flamme) to simmer

gä|ren ['gɛːrən] pret **gor** or **gärte**, ptp **gegoren** or **gegärt** VI aux **haben** or **sein** to ferment; (Hefe) to work; (fig: Gefühle etc) to seethe; **die Wut/das Unrecht gärte in ihm** he was seething with anger/a sense of injustice; **in ihm gärt es** he is in a state of inner turmoil VT to ferment

Gä|ren NT -s, no pl fermentation; **ins ~ kommen** to start fermenting

Gär|ret|te [ga'rɛtə] F -, -n (Sw: = Schubkarren) barrow

Gär|fut|ter ['gɛːɐ-] NT (Agr) silage no pl

Gar- ['gaːɐ-]: **gar ko|chen** ▲ VT sep etw ~ to cook sth through; **Gar|kü|che** F hot food stall

Gär|mit|tel ['gɛːɐ-] NT ferment

Garn [garn] NT -(e)s, -e **a** thread; (= Baumwollgarn) thread, cotton; (= Häkelgarn, fig: = See-

mannsgarn) yarn; **ein ~ spinnen** (*fig*) to spin a yarn **b** (= *Netz*) net; **jdm ins ~ gehen** (*fig*) to fall into sb's snare, to fall *or* walk into sb's trap

Gar|ne|le [garˈneːlə] F -, -n (*Zool*) prawn; (= *Granat*) shrimp

gar|ni [garˈni] ADJ → **Hotel garni**

gar|nie|ren [garˈniːrən] *ptp* **garniert** VT *Kuchen, Kleid* to decorate; *Gericht* to garnish; (*fig*) *Reden etc* to garnish

Gar|nie|rung F -, -en **a** (= *das Garnieren*) decoration; (*von Gericht, fig: von Rede*) garnishing **b** (= *Material zur Garnierung*) decoration; (*von Gericht*) garnish; **Zitate als ~ einer Rede** quotations to garnish a speech

Gar|ni|son [garniˈzoːn] F -, -en (*Mil*) garrison; **mit ~ belegen** to garrison; **in ~ liegen** to be garrisoned

Garni|son(s)- *in cpds* garrison; **Gar|ni|son(s)|kir|che** F garrison church; **Gar|ni|son(s)|stadt** F garrison town

Gar|ni|tur [garniˈtuːɐ] F -, -en **a** (= *Satz*) set; (= *Unterwäsche*) set of (matching) underwear; **die erste ~** (*fig*) the pick of the bunch, the top-notches *pl* (*inf*); **erste/zweite ~ sein, zur ersten/zweiten ~ gehören** to be first-rate *or* first-class/second-rate **b** (= *Besatz*) trimming **c** (*Mil*: = *Uniform*) uniform; **erste ~** number one uniform *or* dress

Garn-: **Garn|knäu|el** M OR NT ball of thread *or* yarn; **Garn|rol|le** F spool; (*von Baumwolle, Nähgarn*) cotton reel; **Garn|spin|ne|rei** F spinning mill

Ga|rot|te [gaˈrɔtə] F -, -n garrotte

ga|rot|tie|ren [garɔˈtiːrən] *ptp* **garottiert** VT to garrotte

gars|tig [ˈgarstɪç] ADJ (*dated*) nasty, horrible

Gars|tig|keit F -, -en (*dated*) **a** *no pl* nastiness **b** ~**en** (= *garstige Äußerungen*) nasty *or* horrible remarks *pl*

Gär|stoff [ˈgɛːɐ-] M ferment

Gar|ten [ˈgartn] M -s, ¨ [ˈgɛrtn] garden; (= *Obstgarten*) orchard; **öffentlicher/botanischer/zoologischer ~** public/botanic(al)/zoological gardens *pl*; **im ~ arbeiten** to work in the garden, to do some gardening

Gar|ten- *in cpds* garden; **Gar|ten|ab|fäl|le** PL garden waste *sing*; **Gar|ten|ar|beit** F gardening *no pl*; **Gar|ten|ar|chi|tekt(in)** M(F) landscape gardener; **Gar|ten|bau** M , *no pl* horticulture

Gar|ten|bau-: **Gar|ten|bau|aus|stel|lung** F horticultural exhibition; **Gar|ten|be|trieb** M market garden, truck farm (*US*)

Gar|ten-: **Gar|ten|beet** NT flower *or* vegetable bed; **Gar|ten|blu|me** F garden *or* cultivated flower; **Gar|ten|ge|rät** NT gardening tool *or* implement; **Gar|ten|haus** NT summer house; (*für Geräte*) garden shed; (= *Hinterhaus*) back *or* rear building; **Gar|ten|ko|lo|nie** F allotments *pl*; **Gar|ten|lau|be** F (= *Gartenhäuschen*) summer house; (*aus Blattwerk*) arbour (*Brit*), arbor (*US*), bower; (*für Geräte*) garden shed; **Gar|ten|lo|kal** NT beer garden; (= *Restaurant*) garden café; **Gar|ten|mö|bel** PL garden furniture; **Gar|ten|sche|re** F secateurs *pl* (*Brit*), pruning shears *pl*; (= *Heckenschere*) shears *pl*; **Gar|ten|schlauch** M garden hose; **Gar|ten|tür** F garden gate; **Gar|ten|zwerg** M garden gnome; (*pej inf*) squirt (*inf*)

Gärt|ner [ˈgɛrtnɐ] M -s, -, **Gärt|ne|rin** [-ərɪn] F -, -nen gardener → **Bock¹ a**

Gärt|ne|rei [gɛrtnəˈrai] F -, -en **a** (= *Baumschule, für Setzlinge*) nursery; (*für Obst, Gemüse, Schnittblumen*) market garden (*Brit*), truck farm (*US*) **b** *no pl* (= *Gartenarbeit*) gardening; (= *Gartenbau*) horticulture

gärt|ne|risch [ˈgɛrtnərɪʃ] ADJ *attr* gardening; *Betrieb, Erzeugnisse auch*, *Ausbildung* horticultural; **~e Gestaltung** landscaping; **die ~en Kosten** the cost of the landscaping ADV **einen Park ~ ge-**

---

stalten to landscape a park; **~ ausgebildet** trained in horticulture

gärt|nern [ˈgɛrtnɐn] VI to garden

Gä|rung [ˈgɛːrʊŋ] F -, -en fermentation; (*fig*) ferment, turmoil; **in ~ kommen** to start fermenting; **in ~ sein** (*fig*) to be in ferment *or* in a turmoil

Gä|rungs-: **Gä|rungs|er|re|ger** M ferment; **Gä|rungs|pro|zess** ▲ M process of fermentation

Gar|zeit [ˈgaːɐ-] F cooking time

Gas [gaːs] NT -es, -e [-zə] gas; (*Aut*: = *Gaspedal*) accelerator, gas pedal (*esp US*); **~ geben** (*Aut*) to accelerate, to put one's foot down (*inf*), to step on the gas (*inf*); (*auf höhere Touren bringen*) to rev up; **~ wegnehmen** (*Aut*) to decelerate, to ease one's foot off the accelerator *or* gas (*inf*), to throttle back (*US*); **mit ~ vergiften** to gas

Gas- *in cpds* gas; **Gas|an|griff** M (*Mil*) gas attack; **Gas|ba|de|ofen** M gas(-fired) water heater; **Gas|be|häl|ter** M gas holder, gasometer; **gas|be|heizt** ADJ gas-heated; **gas|be|trie|ben** [-bətriːbn] ADJ (*Tech*) gas-driven, gas-powered; **Gas|dich|te** F (*Phys*) density of a/the gas; **Gas|er|zeu|gung** F generation of gas; (*Ind*) gas production; **Gas|ex|plo|si|on** F gas explosion; **Gas|fern|ver|sor|gung** F (= *System*) long-distance gas supply; **Gas|feu|er|zeug** NT gas lighter; **Gas|fla|sche** F bottle of gas, gas canister; **gas|för|mig** ADJ gaseous, gasiform; **Gas|ge|ruch** M smell of gas; **Gas|hahn** M gas tap; **den ~ aufdrehen** (*fig*) to put one's head in the gas oven; **Gas|he|bel** M (*Aut*) accelerator (pedal), gas pedal (*esp US*); (= *Handgashebel*) (hand) throttle; **Gas|hei|zung** F gas (central) heating; **Gas|herd** M gas cooker; **Gas|hül|le** F atmosphere; **Gas|in|stal|la|teur(in)** M(F) gas fitter; **Gas|kam|mer** F gas chamber; **Gas|ko|cher** M camping stove; **Gas|kraft|werk** NT gas-fired power station; **Gas|krieg** M chemical *or* gas warfare; **Gas|la|ter|ne** F gas (street-)lamp; **Gas|lei|tung** F (= *Rohr*) gas pipe; (= *Hauptrohr*) gas main; **Gas|licht** NT gaslight; (= *Beleuchtung*) gas lighting; **Gas|mann** M *pl* **-männer** gasman; **Gas|mas|ke** F gas mask; **Gas|ofen** M (= *Heizofen*) gas fire *or* heater; (= *Heizungsofen*) gas(-fired) boiler; (= *Backofen*) gas oven; (= *Herd*) gas cooker *or* stove

Ga|so|lin [gazoˈliːn] NT -s, *no pl* petroleum ether

Ga|so|me|ter [gazoˈmeːtɐ] M gasometer

Gas-: **Gas|pe|dal** NT (*Aut*) accelerator (pedal), gas pedal (*esp US*); **Gas|pis|to|le** F tear gas gun; **Gas|plas|ma** NT gas plasma; **Gas|rohr** NT gas pipe; (= *Hauptrohr*) gas main

Gäss|chen ▲ [ˈgɛsçən] NT -s, - alley(way)

Gas|se [ˈgasə] F -, -n lane; (= *Durchgang*) alley (-way); (*S Ger, Aus*: = *Stadtstraße*) street; (*Rugby*) line-out; **die schmalen ~n der Altstadt** the narrow streets and alleys of the old town; **eine ~ bilden** to clear a passage; (*Rugby*) to form a line-out; **eine ~ für jdn bilden** to make way *or* clear a path for sb; **sich** (*dat*) **eine ~ bahnen** to force one's way; **auf der ~** (*S Ger, Aus*) on the street; **etw über die ~ verkaufen** (*Aus*) to sell sth to take away

Gas|sen-: **Gas|sen|hau|er** M (*old, inf*) popular melody; **Gas|sen|jar|gon** M gutter language; **Gas|sen|jun|ge** M , **Gas|sen|mäd|chen** NT (*pej*) street urchin, street Arab (*inf*), street kid (*inf*); **Gas|sen|schän|ke** ▲ F , **Gas|sen|schen|ke** F (*S Ger*) off-sales (*Brit*), package store (*US*)

Gas|si [ˈgasi] ADV (*inf*) **~ gehen** to go walkies (*Brit inf*), to go for a walk; **mit einem Hund ~ gehen** to take a dog (for) walkies (*Brit inf*), to take a dog out for a walk

Gast¹ [gast] M -es, ¨e [ˈgɛstə] guest; (= *Besucher auch, Tourist*) visitor; (*in einer Gaststätte*) customer; (*Theat*) guest (star); (*Univ*: = *Gasthörer*) observer, auditor (*US*); **Vorstellung vor gelade-**

---

nen Gästen performance before an invited audience; **ungeladener ~** uninvited guest; (*bei einer Party auch*) gatecrasher (*esp Brit*), party-crasher (*US*); **jdn zu ~ bitten** (*form*) to request the pleasure of sb's company (*form*); **wir haben heute Abend Gäste** we're having people round (*Brit*) or around *or* we're having company this evening; **bei jdm zu ~ sein** to be sb's guest(s); **in einem anderen Ort zu ~ sein** to visit another place

Gast² M -(e)s, -en (*Naut*) (= *Signalgast*) signalman; (= *Radiogast*) operator

Gast-: **Gast|ar|bei|ter(in)** M(F) immigrant *or* foreign worker; **Gast|do|zent(in)** M(F) visiting *or* guest lecturer

Gäs|te-: **Gäs|te|bett** NT spare *or* guest bed; **Gäs|te|buch** NT visitors' book

Gas|tech|nik F gas engineering

Gäs|te-: **Gäs|te|hand|tuch** NT guest towel; **Gäs|te|haus** NT guest house; **Gäs|te|heim** NT (*dated*) guest house, boarding house; **Gäs|te|lis|te** F guest list; **Gäs|te-WC** NT guest toilet; **Gäs|te|zim|mer** NT guest *or* spare room

Gast-: **Gast|fa|mi|lie** F host family; **gast|frei**, **gast|freund|lich** ADJ hospitable **ADV** hospitably; **Gast|freund|lich|keit** F -, *no pl*, **Gast|freund|schaft** F -, *no pl* hospitality; **gast|ge|bend** ADJ *attr Land, Theater* host *attr*; *Mannschaft* home *attr*; **Gast|ge|ber** M host; **Gast|ge|be|rin** F hostess; **Gast|ge|schenk** NT present (*brought by a guest*); **Gast|haus** NT , **Gast|hof** M inn; **Gast|hö|rer(in)** M(F) (*Univ*) observer, auditor (*US*)

gas|tie|ren [gasˈtiːrən] *ptp* **gastiert** VI to guest, to make a guest appearance

Gast-: **Gast|land** NT host country; **gast|lich** [ˈgastlɪç] ADJ hospitable **ADV** hospitably; **Gast|lich|keit** F -, *no pl* hospitality; **Gast|mahl** NT (*old*) banquet; **Platos „Gastmahl"** Plato's "Symposium"

Gas|tod M death by gassing; **den ~ sterben** to be gassed

Gast-: **Gast|pro|fes|sor(in)** M(F) visiting professor; **Gast|recht** NT right to hospitality; **Gast|red|ner(in)** M(F) guest speaker

gast|risch [ˈgastrɪʃ] ADJ (*Med*) gastric

Gas|tri|tis [gasˈtriːtɪs] F -, **Gastritiden** [-ˈtiːdn] gastritis

Gast|rol|le F (*Theat*) guest role; **eine ~ geben** *or* **spielen** (*lit*) to make a guest appearance; (*fig*) to put in *or* make a fleeting *or* brief appearance

Gast|ro|nom [gastroˈnoːm] M -en, -en, **Gast|ro|no|min** [-ˈnoːmɪn] F -, -nen (= *Gastwirt*) restaurateur; (= *Koch*) cuisinier, cordon bleu cook (*esp Brit*)

Gast|ro|no|mie [gastronoˈmiː] F -, *no pl* (*form*: = *Gaststättengewerbe*) catering trade; (*geh*: = *Kochkunst*) gastronomy

gast|ro|no|misch [gastroˈnoːmɪʃ] ADJ gastronomic

Gast|ro|sko|pie [gastroskoˈpiː] F -, -n [-ˈpiːən] (*Med*) gastroscopy

Gast-: **Gast|spiel** NT (*Theat*) guest performance; (*Sport*) away match; **ein ~ geben** (*lit*) to give a guest performance; (*fig inf*) to put in *or* make a fleeting *or* brief appearance; **Gast|spiel|rei|se** F (*Theat*) tour; **auf ~** on tour; **Gast|stät|te** F (= *Restaurant*) restaurant; (= *Trinklokal*) pub (*Brit*), bar; **Gast|stät|ten|ge|wer|be** NT catering trade; **Gast|stu|be** F lounge

Gas|tur|bi|ne F gas turbine

Gast-: **Gast|vor|le|sung** F (*Univ*) guest lecture; **Gast|vor|stel|lung** F (*Theat*) guest performance; **eine ~ geben** to give a guest performance; **Gast|vor|trag** M g; **Gast|wirt** M (*Besitzer*) restaurant owner *or* proprietor; (*Pächter*) restaurant manager; (*von Kneipe*) landlord; **Gast|wir|tin** F (*Besitzerin*) restaurant owner *or* proprietress; (*Pächterin*) restaurant manageress;

(*von Kneipe*) landlady; **Gast|wirt|schaft** F = Gaststätte; **Gast|zim|mer** NT guest room

Gas-: **Gas|uhr** F gas meter; **Gas|ver|brauch** M gas consumption; **Gas|ver|gif|tung** F gas poisoning; **Gas|ver|sor|gung** F (= *System*) gas supply (+*gen* to); (= *Gasverwaltung*) gas board; **Gas|werk** NT gasworks *sing or pl*; **Gas|wol|ke** F gas cloud; **Gas|zäh|ler** M gas meter; **Gas|-zent|ral|hei|zung** F gas central heating

Gatt [gat] NT -(e)s, -en *or* -s (*Naut*) (= *Speigatt*) scupper; (= *Heckform*) stern; (= *kleiner Raum*) locker; (= *Loch*) clew; (= *enge Durchfahrt*) strait

GATT [gat] NT -s GATT

Gat|te ['gatə] M -n, -n (*form*) husband, spouse (*form*); **die (beiden) ~n** both partners, husband and wife → *auch* **Gattin**

Gat|ten-: **Gat|ten|lie|be** F (*form*) married *or* conjugal (*form*) love; **Gat|ten|mord** M (*form*) murder of one's husband/wife; **Gat|ten|wahl** F (*Biol*) choice of mate; **das Ritual der ~** the complicated ritual of choosing a mate

Gat|ter ['gatɐ] NT -s, - **a** (= *Tür*) gate; (= *Zaun*) fence; (= *Rost*) grating, grid **b** (*Tech: auch* **Gat-tersäge**) gangsaw, framesaw

Gat|tin ['gatɪn] F -, -nen (*form*) wife, spouse (*form*)

Gat|tung ['gatʊŋ] F -, -en (*Biol*) genus; (*Liter, Mus, Art*) genre, form; (*fig* = *Sorte*) type, kind

Gat|tungs-: **Gat|tungs|be|griff** M generic concept; **Gat|tungs|na|me** M generic term

Gau [gau] M OR NT -(e)s, -e **a** (*Hist*) gau, *a trib-al district, later an administrative district under the Nazis* **b** (= *Bezirk*) district, region, area

GAU [gau] M -(s) *abbr von* **größter anzunehmen-der Unfall** MCA, maximum credible accident; (*fig inf*) worst-case scenario

Gau|be ['gaubə] F -, -n dormer window

Gau|dee [gau'de:] F -, -n [-'de:ən] (*Aus*) fun *no pl*; **auf der ~ sein** to be out gallivanting (*inf*)

Gau|di ['gaudi] NT -s *or* (*S Ger, Aus*) f -, *no pl* (*inf*) fun; **das war eine ~** that was great fun; **das war eine ~ auf die Party** the party was great fun

Gau|di|um ['gaudiʊm] NT -s, *no pl* (*old*) amuse-ment, entertainment

Gau|ke|lei [gaukə'lai] F -, -en trickery *no pl*; ~**en** tricks *pl*, trickery

gau|keln ['gaukln] VI (*liter*) (*Schmetterling*) to flutter; (*fig*) to flit

Gau|kel|spiel NT (*liter*) illusion; **ein ~ mit jdm treiben** to play sb false (*liter*), to deceive sb

Gauk|ler¹ ['gauklɐ] M -s, - (*Orn*) bateleur eagle

Gauk|ler² ['gauklɐ] M -s, -, **Gauk|le|rin** [-ərɪn] F -, -nen (*liter*) travelling (*Brit*) *or* traveling (*US*) entertainer; (*fig*) storyteller

Gaul [gaul] M -(e)s, **Gäule** ['gɔylə] (*pej*) nag, hack; (*rare:* = *Arbeitspferd*) workhorse → **Schwanz a**, **schenken** VT **a**, **scheu**

Gau|lei|ter(in) M(F) (*Pol*) Gauleiter, *head of a Nazi administrative district*

Gaul|lis|mus [go'lɪsmʊs] M -, *no pl* Gaullism

Gaul|list [go'lɪst] M -en, -en, **Gaul|lis|tin** [-'lɪs-tɪn] F -, -nen Gaullist

gaul|lis|tisch [go'lɪstɪʃ] ADJ Gaullist *no adv*

Gau|men ['gaumən] M -s, - palate (*auch fig*), roof of the/one's mouth; **die Zunge klebte ihm vor Durst am ~** his tongue was hanging out (with thirst); **einen feinen ~ haben** (*fig*) to be (something of) a gourmet, to enjoy good food; **das kitzelt mir den ~** (*fig*) that tickles my taste buds *or* my palate

Gau|men-: **Gau|men|freu|den** PL culinary delights *pl*; **Gau|men|kit|zel** M (*inf*) delight for the taste buds; **Gau|men|laut** M palatal (sound); **Gau|men|man|del** F (*Anat*) (pala-tine) tonsil; **Gau|men|plat|te** F (dental) plate; **Gau|men|se|gel** NT soft palate, velum (*spec*); **Gau|men|zäpf|chen** NT uvula

Gau|ner ['gaunɐ] M -s, - rogue, rascal, scoun-drel; (= *Betrüger*) crook; (*hum inf:* = *Schelm auch*) scamp, scallywag (*Brit inf*); (*inf:* = *gerissener Kerl*) cunning devil (*inf*), sly customer (*inf*); **kleine ~** (= *Kriminelle*) small-time crooks → *auch* **Gaunerin**

Gau|ner|ban|de F → **Gauner** bunch of rogues *or* rascals *or* scoundrels/crooks; (*hum: Kinder auch*) bunch of scamps *or* scallywags (*Brit inf*) *or* rascals

Gau|ne|rei [gaunə'rai] F -, -en swindling *no pl*, cheating *no pl*

gau|ner|haft ADJ rascally *no adv*

Gau|ne|rin ['gaunərɪn] F -, -nen rascal; (= *Betrü-gerin*) crook → *auch* **Gauner**

gau|nern ['gaunɐn] VI (*inf*) (= *betrügen*) to swin-dle, to cheat; (= *stehlen*) to thieve; **er hat sich durchs Leben gegaunert** he cheated his way through life

Gau|ner-: **Gau|ner|spra|che** F underworld jargon; **Gau|ner|zin|ken** M *tramp's or gypsy's sign written on wall etc*

Ga|vot|te [ga'vɔt(ə)] F -, -n (*Mus*) gavotte

Ga|za|strei|fen ['ga:za-] M Gaza Strip

Ga|ze ['ga:zə] F -, -n gauze; (= *Drahtgaze auch*) (wire) mesh

Ga|ze|bin|de ['ga:zə-] F gauze bandage

Ga|zel|le [ga'tsɛlə] F -, -n gazelle

Ga|zet|te [ga'tsɛtə, ga'zɛtə] F -, -n (*old, pej*) ga-zette (*old*), (news)paper, rag (*pej inf*)

GB NT *abbr* **a** *von* **Gigabyte** Gb **b** *von* **Großbri-tannien** GB

g-Druck ['ge:-] M *pl* -drücke (*Aviat*) g-force

Ge|äch|te|te(r) [gə'ɛçtətə] MF *decl as adj* out-law; (*fig*) outcast

Ge|äch|ze [gə'ɛçtsə] NT -s, *no pl* groaning *no pl*, groans *pl*

ge|ädert [gə'ɛːdɐt] ADJ veined

ge|ar|tet [gə'aːɐtət] ADJ **gutmütig ~ sein** to be good-natured; **freundlich ~ sein** to have a friendly nature; **er ist (eben) so ~** (*, dass ...*) it's (just) his nature (to ...); **sie ist ganz anders ~** she has a completely different nature, she's quite different; **so ~e Probleme** problems of this nature; **das Problem ist so ~, dass ...** the nature of the problem is such that ...; **eine wie auch immer ~e Erklärung** a statement of any kind whatsoever → *auch* **arten**

Ge|äst [gə'ɛst] NT -(e)s, *no pl* branches *pl*, boughs *pl* (*liter*); (*von Adern etc*) branches *pl*

geb. *abbr von* **geboren**

Ge|bab|bel [gə'babl] NT -s, *no pl* (*inf*) babbling

Ge|bäck [gə'bɛk] NT -(e)s, -e (= *Kekse*) biscuits *pl* (*Brit*), cookies *pl* (*US*); (= *süße Teilchen*) pas-tries *pl*; (= *rundes Hefegebäck*) buns *pl*; (= *Tört-chen*) tarts *pl*, tartlets *pl*; **allerlei (Kuchen und) ~** all kinds of cakes and pastries

ge|ba|cken *ptp von* **backen**¹

Ge|bälk [gə'bɛlk] NT -(e)s, -e timberwork *no pl*, timbers *pl*; (*Archit:* = *Verbindung zu Säulen*) entablature; **ein Partisan im ~** (*inf*) a nigger in the woodpile (*Brit pej*) → **knistern**

ge|ballt [gə'balt] ADJ (= *konzentriert*) Energie, Kraft, Ladung concentrated (*auch fig*); Stil, Be-richterstattung concise; Banalität, Naivität un-diluted, unmitigated; Beschuss massed; **eine ~e Ladung Salz** a pile of salt ADV **es kommt alles ~ auf einmal** everything happens at once; **die Probleme treten jetzt ~ auf** the problems are piling up now → *auch* **ballen**

ge|bannt [gə'bant] ADJ spellbound; **vor Schreck ~** rigid with fear; (*wie*) ~ fascinated, in fascina-tion; (*stärker*) spellbound → *auch* **bannen**

ge|bar *pret von* **gebären**

Ge|bär|de [gə'bɛːɐdə] F -, -n gesture; (*lebhafte auch*) gesticulation

ge|bär|den [gə'bɛːɐdn] *ptp* **gebärdet** VR to be-have, to conduct oneself (*form*)

Ge|bär|den-: **Ge|bär|den|dol|met|scher(in)** M(F) sign-language interpreter; **Ge|bär|den-spiel** NT , *no pl* gestures *pl*, gesticulation(s *pl*); **das ~ der Sänger** the singers' use of ges-ture; **Ge|bär|den|spra|che** F gestures *pl*; (= *Zeichensprache*) sign language; (*in Stummfilmen etc*) gesturing; (= *unbewusste Gebärdensprache*) body language

ge|ba|ren [gə'ba:rən] *ptp* **gebart** VR (*rare*) to behave, to conduct oneself (*form*)

Ge|ba|ren [gə'ba:rən] NT -s, *no pl* **a** behaviour (*Brit*), behavior (*US*) **b** (*Comm:* = *Geschäftsge-baren*) conduct

ge|bä|ren [gə'bɛːrən] *pres* **gebärt** *or* (*geh*) **gebiert** [gə'bi:ɐt], *pret* **gebar** [gə'ba:ɐ], *ptp* **geboren** [gə'bo:rən] VT to give birth to; Kind *auch* to bear (*old, form*), to be delivered of (*old*); (*fig li-ter:* = *erzeugen*) to breed; **jdm ein Kind ~** to bear *or* give sb a child; **geboren werden** to be born; **wo sind Sie geboren?** where were you born?; **aus der Not geborene Ideen** ideas springing *or* stemming from necessity → *auch* **geboren** VI to give birth

ge|bär-: **ge|bär|fä|hig** ADJ Alter child-bearing; Frau capable of bearing children; **ge|bär|freu|dig** ADJ Frau who has/had given birth many times; Tier prolific; **ein ~es Becken haben** to have child-bearing hips

Ge|bär|mut|ter F *pl* -mütter (*Anat*) womb, ute-rus

Ge|bär|mut|ter-: **Ge|bär|mut|ter|hals** M neck of the womb *or* uterus, cervix; **Ge|bär-mut|ter|krebs** M cancer of the uterus; **Ge|bär|mut|ter|mund** M mouth of the uterus

Ge|ba|rung F -, -en (*Aus Comm:* = *Geschäftsgeba-ren*) conduct

Ge|ba|rungs- (*Aus Comm*): **Ge|ba|rungs|be-richt** M financial report; **Ge|ba|rungs|jahr** NT financial year; **Ge|ba|rungs|kon|trol|le** F audit

ge|bauch|pin|selt [gə'bauxpɪnzlt] ADJ (*hum inf*) **sich ~ fühlen** to feel flattered

Ge|bäu|de [gə'bɔydə] NT -s, - building; (= *Prachtgebäude*) edifice; (*fig:* = *Gefüge*) structure; (*von Ideen*) edifice; (*von Lügen*) web

Ge|bäu|de-: **Ge|bäu|de|kom|plex** M build-ing complex; **Ge|bäu|de|rei|ni|ger(in)** M(F) cleaner; (= *Fensterputzer*) window cleaner; (= *Fassadenreiniger*) building cleaner; **Ge|bäu|de-rei|ni|gung** F (= *das Reinigen*) commercial cleaning; (= *Firma*) cleaning contractors *pl*; **Ge|bäu|de|scha|den** M damage to a/the building; **Ge|bäu|de|teil** M part of the build-ing; **Ge|bäu|de|trakt** M part of the building; **einen neuen ~ errichten** to add an extension to the/a building; **Ge|bäu|de|ver|si|che|rung** F buildings insurance

ge|baut [gə'baut] ADJ built; **gut ~ sein** to be well-built; **stark ~ sein** to have a broad frame; **... so, wie du ~ bist** (*inf*) ... a big man/woman like you; **ein gut ~es Stück** a well-constructed play → *auch* **bauen**

ge|be|freu|dig ADJ generous, open-handed

Ge|be|freu|dig|keit ['ge:bəfrɔydɪçkait] F -, *no pl* generosity, open-handedness

Ge|bein [gə'baɪn] NT **a** skeleton; **der Schreck fuhr ihm ins ~** (old) his whole body trembled with fear **b** **Gebeine** PL (geh) bones pl, mortal remains pl (liter); (esp von Heiligen etc) relics pl

Ge|bell [gə'bɛl] NT -s, no pl, **Ge|bel|le** [gə'bɛlə] NT -s, no pl barking; (von Jagdhunden) baying; (fig inf: = Geschimpfe) bawling (inf)

---

ge|ben ['ge:bn]
pret **gab** [ga:p], *ptp* **gegeben** [gə'ge:bn]

1 TRANSITIVES VERB	3 UNPERSÖNLICHES
2 INTRANSITIVES VERB	VERB
	4 REFLEXIVES VERB

1 – TRANSITIVES VERB

a to give; (= reichen) to give, to pass; Schatten, Kühle to provide; **wer hat dir das gegeben?** who gave you that?; **gibs mir!** give it to me!, give me it!; **was darf ich Ihnen geben?** what can I get you?; **könnten Sie mir die Butter/den Korkenzieher geben?** could you pass me the butter/the corkscrew?; **geben Sie mir bitte zwei Flaschen Bier** I'd like two bottles of beer, please; **ich gebe dir das Auto für 500 Euro** (= verkaufen) I'll let you have the car for 500 euros; **ich gebe dir das Auto für zwei Tage** (= überlassen) I'll let you have the car for two days; **sich** (dat) **(von jdm) etw geben lassen** to ask (sb) for sth; **geben Sie mir bitte Herrn Braun** (Telec) can I speak to Mr Braun please?; **man kann nicht für alles geben** (= spenden) you can't give to everything; **geben** or **Geben ist seliger denn nehmen** or **Nehmen** (Bibl) it is more blessed to give than to receive; **ich gäbe viel darum, zu ...** I'd give a lot to ...; **sie würde ihr Leben für ihre Kinder geben** she'd give her life for her children; **sie gaben ihr Leben fürs Vaterland** they gave or laid down their lives for their country; **jdm einen Tritt geben** to give sb a kick; (fig inf) to give sb the boot (inf); **gibs ihm (tüchtig)!** (inf) let him have it! (inf); **ein gutes Beispiel geben** to set a good example; **jdm etw zu verstehen geben** to make sth known to sb; **jdn/etw verloren geben** to give sb/sth up for lost; **das Buch hat mir viel gegeben** I got a lot out of the book → auch **gegeben**

b = Cards to deal; **er hat mir drei Asse und zwei Buben gegeben** he dealt me three aces and two jacks; **da hast du mir aber ein lausiges Blatt gegeben** you've given or dealt me a lousy hand

c = gewähren, verleihen to give; Thema, Aufgabe, Problem to set; **jdm einen Preis geben** to give sb a prize; **einen Elfmeter/einen Freistoß geben** to give a penalty kick/a free kick; **gebe Gott, dass ...** God grant that ...; **Taktgefühl ist ihm nicht gegeben** he's not over-endowed with tact; **es war ihm nicht gegeben, seine Eltern lebend wiederzusehen** he was not to see his parents alive again

d = schicken, übergeben to send; (dial: = tun) to put; **in die Post geben** to post (Brit), to mail (esp US); **ein Auto in Reparatur geben** to have a car repaired; **ein Kind in Pflege geben** to put a child in care; **Zucker über etw** (acc) **geben** (dial) to sprinkle sugar over sth; **Milch an den Teig geben** (dial) to add milk to the dough → **Bescheid d, Nachricht a**

e = ergeben, erzeugen to produce; **die Kuh gibt Milch** the cow produces milk; **die Kuh gibt 25 Liter** the cow produces or gives 25 litres (Brit) or liters (US); **2 + 2 gibt 4** 2 + 2 makes 4; **fünf Manuskriptseiten geben eine Druckseite** five pages of manuscript equal or make one page of print; **ein Pfund gibt fünf Klöße** a pound will make five dumplings; **Rotwein gibt Flecken** red wine leaves stains; **das gibt Ärger/Probleme** that will cause trouble/problems; **was wird das noch geben?** where will it end?

f = veranstalten Konzert, Fest to give; Theaterstück etc to do; **am Schillertheater geben sie wieder „Maria Stuart"** they are doing "Maria Stuart" at the Schillertheater again; **was wird heute im Theater gegeben?** what's on at the theatre (Brit) or theater (US) today?

g = unterrichten to teach; **Englisch/Deutsch geben** to teach English/German; **er gibt Nachhilfeunterricht/Tanzstunden** he gives private tuition/dancing lessons (Brit), he does tutoring/gives dancing lessons

h andere Wendungen

♦ **viel/nicht viel auf etw** (acc) **geben** to set great/little store by sth; **auf die Meinung der Lehrer braucht du nichts zu geben** you needn't bother about what the teachers think; **ich gebe nicht viel auf seinen Rat** I don't think much of his advice

♦ **etw von sich geben** Laut, Worte, Flüche to utter; Meinung to express; **was er gestern von sich gegeben hat, war wieder einmal völlig unverständlich** what he was going on about yesterday was, as ever, completely incomprehensible

2 – INTRANSITIVES VERB

a Cards to deal; **der links von mir Sitzende gibt** the person sitting on my left deals; **wer gibt?** whose deal is it?, whose turn is it to deal?

b Sport (= Aufschlag haben) to serve; **wer gibt?** whose serve is it?

3 – UNPERSÖNLICHES VERB

♦ **es gibt** (+sing) there is; (+pl) there are; **es gibt da noch ein Problem** there's still one problem; **es gibt dieses Jahr viele Äpfel** there are a lot of apples this year; **gibt es einen Gott?** is there a God?; **gibt es den Osterhasen?** is there really an Easter Bunny?; **heute gibts noch Regen** it's going to rain today; **es wird noch Ärger geben** there'll be trouble (yet); **darauf gibt es 10% Rabatt** you get 10% discount on it; **was gibts zum Mittagessen?** what's for lunch?; **freitags gibt es bei uns immer Fisch** we always have fish on Fridays; **wann gibts was zu essen?** – **es gibt gleich was** when are we going to get something to eat? – it's on its way; **es gibt gleich Mittagessen!** it's nearly time for lunch!; **jetzt gibt es keine Süßigkeiten mehr** (you're getting) no more sweets now; **was gibts?** what's the matter?, what is it?; **ein Mensch mit zwei Köpfen? das gibts nicht!** a two-headed person? there's no such thing!; **das gibts doch nicht, dass ein Vegetarier Metzger wird** it's impossible, a vegetarian wouldn't become a butcher, it's inconceivable that a vegetarian would become a butcher; **so was gibts also!** (inf) who'd have thought it! (inf); **das gibts doch nicht!** I don't believe it!; **das darf es doch nicht geben!** I don't believe it!; **das hat es ja noch nie gegeben!** it's unbelievable!; **so was gibts bei uns nicht!** (inf) that's just not on! (inf); **da gibts nichts** (inf) there's no two ways about it (inf); **was es nicht alles gibt!** it's a funny old world!; **hat es sonst noch etwas gegeben?** was there anything else?; **gleich gibts was!** (inf) there's going to be trouble!

4 – REFLEXIVES VERB

♦ **sich geben**

a = nachlassen (Regen) to ease off; (Schmerzen) to ease, to lessen; (Leidenschaft, Begeisterung) to lessen, to cool; (freches Benehmen) to lessen

b = aufgeben, ergeben **sich gefangen geben** to give oneself up; **sich verloren geben** to give oneself up for lost → **schlagen VT a, erkennen VT a**

c = sich erledigen to sort itself out; (= aufhören) to stop; **das wird sich schon geben** it'll all work out; **machen Sie erst mal die dringendsten Sachen, der Rest wird sich (von alleine) geben** do the most urgent things first, the rest will sort itself out; **gibt sich das bald?** (inf) cut it out! (inf)

d = sich benehmen to behave; **sich als etw geben** to play sth; **sich freundlich geben** to behave in a friendly way, to be friendly; **sich als große Dame geben** to play the great lady; **sich von oben herab geben** to behave condescendingly, to be condescending; **sich von der bes-** ten Seite geben to show one's best side; **nach außen gab er sich heiter** outwardly he seemed quite cheerful; **sie gibt sich, wie sie ist** she's completely genuine, there's no pretence (Brit) or pretense (US) with her

---

Ge|be|ne|dei|te [gəbene'daɪtə] F decl as adj no pl (Eccl) **die ~** the Blessed Virgin

Ge|ber ['ge:bɐ] M -s, -, **Ge|be|rin** [-ərɪn] F -, -nen giver; (Cards) dealer

Ge|ber-: Ge|ber|land NT donor country; **Ge|ber|lau|ne** F generous mood; **in ~ sein** to be feeling generous, to be in a generous mood

Ge|bet [gə'be:t] NT -(e)s, -e prayer; **ein ~ sprechen** to say a prayer; **sein ~ sprechen** or **verrichten** to say one's prayers; **das ~ des Herrn** the Lord's Prayer; **die Hände zum ~ falten** to join one's hands in prayer; **jdn ins ~ nehmen** (fig) to take sb to task; (iro: bei Polizeiverhör etc) to put the pressure on sb

Ge|bet|buch NT prayer book, missal (US)

ge|be|ten ptp von **bitten**

Ge|bet|läu|ten NT -s, no pl (Aus) angelus

Ge|bets-: Ge|bets|man|tel M prayer shawl, tallith; **Ge|bets|müh|le** F prayer wheel; **ge|bets|müh|len|haft** ADJ constant, continual ADV constantly, continually; **Ge|bets|rie|men** M phylactery; **Ge|bets|stät|te** F place of prayer; **Ge|bets|tep|pich** M prayer mat or rug

Ge|bet|tel [gə'bɛtl] NT -s, no pl begging

ge|beugt [gə'bɔʏkt] ADJ **a** Haltung stooped; Kopf bowed; Beine bent; Schultern sloping **b** (Gram) Verb, Substantiv inflected ADV **~ sitzen/stehen** to sit/stand hunched over → auch **beugen**

ge|biert [gə'biːɐt] (geh) 3. pers sing pres von **gebären**

Ge|biet [gə'biːt] NT -(e)s, -e **a** area, region; (= Fläche, Stadtgebiet) area; (= Staatsgebiet) territory **b** (fig: = Fach) field; (= Teilgebiet) branch; **auf diesem ~** in this field

ge|bie|ten [gə'biːtn] pret **gebot** [gə'boːt], ptp **geboten** [gə'boːtn] (geh) VT **a** (= verlangen) to demand; (= befehlen) to command; **jdm etw ~** to command sb to do sth; **der Ernst der Lage gebietet sofortiges Handeln** the seriousness of the situation demands immediate action → **Einhalt, Ehrfurcht** VI **a** (liter: = herrschen) to have command (über +acc over); **über ein Land/Volk ~** to have dominion over a country/nation **b** (geh: = verfügen) **über etw** (acc) **~** (über Geld etc) to have sth at one's disposal; **über Wissen ~** to have sth at one's command → auch **geboten**

Ge|bie|ter [gə'biːtɐ] M -s, - (liter) master, lord; (über Heer) commander (über +acc of); **(mein) Herr und ~** (old) (my) lord and master

Ge|bie|te|rin [gə'biːtərɪn] F -, -nen mistress, lady; (über Heer) commander

ge|bie|te|risch [gə'biːtərɪʃ] (geh) ADJ imperious; (= herrisch) domineering; Ton peremptory ADV imperiously; (= unbedingt) absolutely

Ge|biets-: Ge|biets|ab|tre|tung F (form) cession of territory; **Ge|biets|an|spruch** M territorial claim; **Ge|biets|er|wei|te|rung** F territorial expansion; **Ge|biets|ho|heit** F territorial sovereignty; **Ge|biets|kör|per|schaft** F regional administrative body; **Ge|biets|lei|ter(in)** M(F) (Comm) regional manager; **Ge|biets|re|form** F local government reform; **Ge|biets|teil** M area (of territory); **ge|biets|wei|se** ADV (= nach Gebieten) locally; (= in einzelnen Gebieten) in some areas

Ge|bil|de [gə'bɪldə] NT -s, - (= Ding) thing; (= Gegenstand) object; (= Bauwerk) construction; (= Schöpfung) creation; (= Muster) pattern; (= Form) shape; (= Einrichtung) organization; (der Fantasie) figment

ge|bil|det [gə'bɪldət] ADJ educated; (= gelehrt) learned, erudite; (= wohlerzogen) well-bred; (= kultiviert) cultured, cultivated; (= belesen) well-

---

-read; *Manieren* refined **ADV** **sich ~ unterhalten** to have a cultured conversation → *auch* **bilden**

Ge|bil|de|te(r) [gə'bɪldətə] MF *decl as adj* educated person; **die ~n** the intellectuals

Ge|bim|mel [gə'bɪml] NT **-s**, *no pl* (*inf*) ting-a--ling (*inf*)

Ge|bin|de [gə'bɪndə] NT **-s, -** (= *Blumengebinde*) arrangement; (= *Sträußchen*) posy; (= *Blumenkranz*) wreath; (= *Getreidegarbe*) sheaf **b** (*von Garn*) skein

Ge|bir|ge [gə'bɪrgə] NT **-s, -** **a** mountains *pl*, mountain range; **im/ins ~** in/into the mountains **b** (*Min*) rock

ge|bir|gig [gə'bɪrgɪç] ADJ mountainous

Ge|birg|ler [gə'bɪrklɐ] M **-s, -**, **Ge|birg|le|rin** [-ərɪn] F **-, -nen** mountain-dweller, highlander

Ge|birgs- *in cpds* mountain; **Ge|birgs|bach** M mountain stream; **Ge|birgs|bahn** F mountain railway (*Brit*) or railroad (*US*) (*crossing a mountain range*); (*in Alpen*) transalpine railway (*Brit*) or railroad (*US*); **Ge|birgs|blu|me** F mountain flower, flower growing in the mountains; **Ge|birgs|jä|ger(in)** M(F) (*Mil*) mountain soldier; (*pl auch*) mountain troops *pl*; **Ge|birgs|land|schaft** F (= *Gegend*) mountainous region; (= *Gemälde*) mountainscape; (= *Ausblick*) mountain scenery; **Ge|birgs|mas|siv** NT massif; **Ge|birgs|rü|cken** M mountain ridge; **Ge|birgs|stock** M massif; **Ge|birgs|stra|ße** F mountain road; **Ge|birgs|trup|pen** PL mountain troops *pl*; **Ge|birgs|wand** F mountain face; **Ge|birgs|zug** M mountain range

Ge|biss ▲ [gə'bɪs] NT **-es, -e** **a** (= *die Zähne*) (set of) teeth *pl*; (= *künstliches Gebiss*) dentures *pl*; **ich habe noch mein ganzes ~** I still have all my teeth **b** (*am Pferdezaum*) bit

Ge|biss-: Ge|biss|ab|druck ▲ M impression; **Ge|biss|ano|ma|lie** ▲ F deformity of the teeth

ge|bis|sen *ptp von* **beißen**

Ge|blä|se [gə'blɛːzə] NT **-s, -** fan, blower; (= *Motorgebläse*) supercharger; (= *Verdichter*) compressor

Ge|blä|se-: Ge|blä|se|luft F air from a blower; **Ge|blä|se|mo|tor** M supercharger (engine)

ge|bla|sen *ptp von* **blasen**

ge|bli|chen *ptp von* **bleichen**

ge|blie|ben *ptp von* **bleiben**

Ge|blö|del [gə'bløːdl] NT **-s**, *no pl* (*inf*) nonsense; (= *blödes Gerede auch*) twaddle (*inf*), baloney (*inf*); (*von Komiker*) patter; **die Unterhaltung artete in allgemeines ~ aus** the conversation degenerated into silliness

Ge|blök [gə'bløːk] NT **-(e)s**, *no pl*, **Ge|blö|ke** [gə'bløːkə] NT **-s**, *no pl* (*von Schaf, Kalb*) bleating; (*von Kuh*) lowing; (*inf: von Mensch*) bawling (*inf*)

ge|blümt [gə'blyːmt], (*Aus*) **ge|blumt** [gə'bluːmt] ADJ flowered; (*Liter, fig*) *Stil* flowery

Ge|blüt [gə'blyːt] NT **-(e)s**, *no pl* (*geh*) (= *Abstammung*) descent, lineage; (*fig*: = *Blut*) blood; (*liter*: = *Geschlecht*) family; **von edlem ~** of noble blood

ge|bo|gen [gə'boːgn] *ptp von* **biegen** ADJ *Nase* curved

ge|bo|ren [gə'boːrən] *ptp von* **gebären** ADJ born; **blind ~** to have been born blind; **er ist blind ~** he was born blind; **-er Engländer/Londoner sein** to be English/a Londoner by birth; **er ist der ~e Erfinder** he's a born inventor; **Hanna Schmidt ~e** or **geb. Müller** Hanna Schmidt, née Müller; **sie ist eine ~e Müller** she was born Müller, her maiden name was Müller

Ge|bo|ren|zei|chen NT asterisk used to denote "date of birth"

ge|bor|gen [gə'bɔrgn] *ptp von* **bergen** ADJ **sich ~ fühlen** to feel secure or safe; **~ sein** to be secure or safe

Ge|bor|gen|heit F **-**, *no pl* security

ge|bors|ten *ptp von* **bersten**

---

ge|bot *pret von* **gebieten**

Ge|bot [gə'boːt] NT **-(e)s, -e** **a** (= *Gesetz*) law; (= *Regel, Vorschrift*) rule; (*Bibl*) commandment; (= *Grundsatz*) precept; (*old*: = *Verordnung*) decree; (*old*: = *Befehl*) command **b** (*geh*: = *Erfordernis*) requirement; **das ~ der Stunde** the needs of the moment; **Besonnenheit ist das ~ der Stunde** what is called for now is calm; **das ~ der Vernunft** the dictates of reason; **das ~ der Vernunft verlangt, dass ...** reason dictates that ... **c** (= *Verfügung*) command; **jdm zu ~e stehen** to be at sb's command or (*Geld etc*) disposal **d** (*Comm*: *bei Auktionen*) bid

ge|bo|ten [gə'boːtn] *ptp von* **gebieten** *von* **bieten** ADJ (= *ratsam, angebracht*) advisable; (= *notwendig*) necessary; (= *dringend geboten*) imperative; **bei aller ~en Achtung** with all due respect

Ge|bots|schild NT *pl* **-schilder**, **Ge|bots|zei|chen** NT mandatory sign; (*Mot also*) traffic sign (giving an instruction)

Gebr. *abbr von* **Gebrüder** Bros

Ge|brab|bel [gə'brabl] NT **-s**, *no pl* (*inf*) jabbering (*inf*), prattling (*inf*)

ge|bracht *ptp von* **bringen**

ge|brannt [gə'brant] *ptp von* **brennen** ADJ **~er Kalk** quicklime; **~e Mandeln** *pl* burnt (*Brit*) or baked (*US*) almonds *pl*; **~er Ton** fired clay; **~es Kind scheut das Feuer** (*Prov*) once bitten, twice shy (*Prov*)

ge|bra|ten *ptp von* **braten**

Ge|bra|te|ne(s) [gə'braːtnə] NT *decl as adj* fried food

Ge|bräu [gə'brɔy] NT **-(e)s, -e** brew; (*pej*) strange concoction; (*fig*) concoction (*aus of*)

Ge|brauch [gə'braux] M **-(e)s, Gebräuche** [gə'brɔyçə] (= *Benutzung*) use; (*eines Wortes*) usage; (= *Anwendung*) application; (= *Brauch, Gepflogenheit*) custom; **falscher ~** misuse; (= *falsche Anwendung*) misapplication; **von etw ~ machen** to make use of sth; **in ~ sein** to be used, to be in use; **etw in ~ (dat) haben** to use sth; *Auto etc* to run sth; **allgemein in ~** (*dat*) in general use; **etw in ~ nehmen** (*form*) to put sth into use; **zum äußeren/inneren ~** to be taken externally/internally; **vor ~ (gut) schütteln** shake (well) before use

ge|brau|chen [gə'brauxn] *ptp* **gebraucht** VT (= *benutzen*) to use; (= *anwenden*) to apply; **sich zu etw ~ lassen** to be useful for sth; (= *missbrauchen*) to be used as sth; **nicht mehr zu ~ sein** to be no longer any use, to be useless; **er/das ist zu nichts zu ~** he's/that's (of) no use to anybody, he's/that's absolutely useless; **das kann ich gut ~** I can make good use of that, I can really use that; **ich könnte ein neues Kleid/einen Whisky ~** I could use a new dress/a whisky; **Geld kann ich immer ~** money's always useful → **gebraucht**

ge|bräuch|lich [gə'brɔyçlɪç] ADJ (= *verbreitet*) common; (= *gewöhnlich*) usual, customary; (= *herkömmlich*) conventional; **nicht mehr ~** (*Ausdruck etc*) no longer used

Ge|bräuch|lich|keit F **-**, *no pl* (= *Herkömmlichkeit*) conventionality; **die ~ dieses Wortes/Verfahrens** how common this word/procedure is

Ge|brauchs-: Ge|brauchs|an|lei|tung F (*form*), **Ge|brauchs|an|wei|sung** F (*für Arznei*) directions *pl*; (*für Geräte etc*) instructions *pl* (for use); **Ge|brauchs|ar|ti|kel** M article for everyday use; (*pl: esp Comm*) basic consumer goods *pl*; **ge|brauchs|fä|hig** ADJ in working order, usable; **etw ~ machen** to put sth into working order; **ge|brauchs|fer|tig** ADJ ready for use; *Nahrungsmittel auch* instant; **Ge|brauchs|ge|gen|stand** M commodity; (= *Werkzeug, Küchengerät*) utensil; **Ge|brauchs|gra|fik** F commercial art; **Ge|brauchs|gra|fi|ker(in)** ▲ M(F) commercial artist; **Ge|brauchs|gut** NT *usu pl* consumer item; **Kon-sum- und Gebrauchsgüter** consumer and utility goods; **Ge|brauchs|li|te|ra|tur** F functional

---

writing; **Ge|brauchs|ly|rik** F everyday poetry; **Ge|brauchs|mö|bel** PL utility furniture *no pl*; **Ge|brauchs|mu|sik** F functional music; **Ge|brauchs|mus|ter** NT (*Jur*) utility model; **Ge|brauchs|mus|ter|schutz** M protection of utility models; **Ge|brauchs|wert** M utility value

ge|braucht [gə'brauxt] ADJ *Auto* second-hand, used; *Kleidung, Computer etc* second-hand; *Verpackung* used **ADV** **etw ~ kaufen** to buy sth second-hand → *auch* **brauchen**

Ge|braucht|wa|gen M used or second-hand car

Ge|braucht|wa|gen-: Ge|braucht|wa|gen|händ|ler(in) M(F) used or second-hand car dealer; **Ge|braucht|wa|gen|markt** M used or second-hand car market

Ge|braucht|wa|ren PL second-hand goods *pl*

Ge|braucht|wa|ren-: Ge|braucht|wa|ren|händ|ler(in) M(F) dealer in second-hand goods; **Ge|braucht|wa|ren|hand|lung** F second-hand shop

ge|bräunt [gə'brɔynt] ADJ (= *braun gebrannt*) (sun-)tanned → *auch* **bräunen**

ge|bre|chen [gə'brɛçn] *ptp* **gebrochen** VI *irreg* (*old liter*) **es gebricht an etw** (*dat*) sth is lacking; **es gebricht ihm an Mut** he lacks courage

Ge|bre|chen [gə'brɛçn] NT **-s, -** (*geh*) affliction; (*fig*) weakness; **die ~ des Alters** the afflictions or infirmities of old age

ge|brech|lich [gə'brɛçlɪç] ADJ frail; (= *altersschwach*) infirm; (*fig*: = *unvollkommen*) weak

Ge|brech|lich|keit F **-**, *no pl* frailty; (= *Altersschwäche*) infirmity; (*fig*: = *Unvollkommenheit*) weakness

ge|bro|chen [gə'brɔxn] *ptp von* **brechen** ADJ broken; *Mensch auch* crushed; **~e Zahl** (*Math*) fraction; **mit ~em Herzen, mit ~en Herzens** broken-hearted; **an ~em Herzen** of a broken heart **ADV** **~ Deutsch sprechen** to speak broken German

Ge|brü|der [gə'bryːdɐ] PL (*Comm*) Brothers *pl*; **~ Müller** Müller Brothers

Ge|brüll [gə'brʏl] NT **-s**, *no pl* (*von Rind*) bellowing; (*von Esel*) braying; (*von Löwe*) roar; (*in Todesangst*) screaming; (*von Mensch*) yelling; **auf ihn mit ~!** (*inf*) go for him!, at him!

Ge|brumm [gə'brʊm] NT **-(e)s**, *no pl*, **Ge|brum|me** [gə'brʊmə] NT **-s**, *no pl* buzzing; (*von Motor, von Bass, Singen*) droning; (*inf*: = *Gebrummel*) grumping (*inf*)

Ge|brum|mel [gə'brʊml] NT **-s**, *no pl* grumping

ge|bückt [gə'bʏkt] ADJ **eine ~e Haltung** a stoop **ADV** **~ sitzen** to stoop; **~ stehen** to stand stooped → *auch* **bücken**

ge|bü|gelt [gə'byːglt] ADJ (*inf*: = *perplex*) knocked flat (*inf*) → *auch* **bügeln** → **geschniegelt**

Ge|bühr [gə'byːɐ] F **-, -en** **a** charge; (= *Postgebühr*) postage *no pl*; (= *Honorar, Beitrag*) fee; (= *Schulgebühr, Studiengebühr*) fees *pl*; (= *Vermittlungsgebühr*) commission; (= *Straßenbenutzungsgebühr*) toll; **~en erheben** to make or levy (*form*) a charge, to charge postage/a fee etc; **zu ermäßigter ~** at a reduced rate; **eine ~ von 50 Euro bezahlen**, **50 Euro ~ bezahlen** to pay a fee/charge etc of 50 euros; **~ (be)zahlt Empfänger** postage to be paid by addressee; **die ~en für Rundfunk/Fernsehen werden erhöht** radio/television licences (*Brit*) are going up **b** (= *Angemessenheit*) **nach ~** suitably, properly; **über ~** excessively

ge|büh|ren [gə'byːrən] *ptp* **gebührt** (*geh*) **VI** to be due (+*dat* to); **ihm gebührt Anerkennung/Achtung** he deserves or is due recognition/respect; **das gebührt ihm** (= *steht ihm zu*) it is his (just) due; (= *gehört sich für ihn*) it befits him **VR** to be proper or seemly or fitting; **wie es sich gebührt** as is proper

Ge|büh|ren-: Ge|büh|ren|an|he|bung F increase in charges; **Ge|büh|ren|an|zei|ger** M call-fee indicator (*Brit*), tollcharge meter (*US*)

---

ge|büh|rend ADJ (= *verdient*) due; (= *angemessen*) suitable; (= *geziemend*) proper; **das ihm ~e Gehalt** the salary he deserves; **jdm die ~e Achtung erweisen/verweigern** to pay/deny sb the respect due to him ADV duly, appropriately, suitably; **etw ~ feiern** to celebrate sth in a fitting manner; **etw ~ zu schätzen/würdigen wissen** to appreciate sth; **jdn ~ loben** to give sb due credit

Ge|büh|ren-: **Ge|büh|ren|ein|heit** F (*Telec*) (tariff) unit; **Ge|büh|ren|er|hö|hung** F increase in charges; **Ge|büh|ren|er|lass ▲** M remission of charges; **Ge|büh|ren|er|mä|ßi|gung** F reduction in charges; **ge|büh|ren|frei** ADJ free of charge; *Brief, Paket* post-free (*Brit*), postpaid; *Telefonnummer* Freefone® (*Brit*), toll-free (*US*) ADV free of charge; **Ge|büh|ren|frei|heit** F exemption from charges; **Ge|büh|ren|mar|ke** F revenue stamp; **ge|büh|ren|ord|nung** F scale of charges, tariff; **ge|büh|ren|pflich|tig** [-pflɪçtɪç] ADJ subject or liable to a charge, chargeable; *Autobahnbenutzung* subject to a toll; **~e Verwarnung** (*Jur*) fine; **~e Autobahn** toll road (*Brit*), turnpike (*US*) ADV **jdn ~ verwarnen** to fine sb; **Ge|büh|ren|satz** M rate (of charge); **Ge|büh|ren|zäh|ler** M meter

ge|bühr|lich [ɡəˈbyːɐlɪç] ADJ, ADV = **gebührend**

Ge|bums [ɡəˈbʊms] NT **-es**, *no pl*, **Ge|bum|se** [ɡəˈbʊmzə] NT **-s**, *no pl* (*inf*: = *Gepolter*) thumping, thudding

ge|bün|delt [ɡəˈbʏndlt] ADJ *Strahlen* bundled; (*fig*) joint → *auch* **bündeln**

ge|bun|den [ɡəˈbʊndn] *ptp von* **binden** ADJ tied (*an* +*acc* to); (*durch Verpflichtungen etc*) tied down; *Kapital* tied up; *Preise* controlled; (*Ling, Phys, Chem*) bound; *Buch* cased, hardback; *Wärme* latent; (*Mus*) legato; **in ~er Rede** in verse; **sozial ~e Mietwohnungen** fixed-rent flats (*Brit*) *or* apartments; **zeitlich ~ sein** to be restricted as regards time; **vertraglich ~ sein** to be bound by contract; **anderweitig ~ sein** to be otherwise engaged

Ge|bun|den|heit F **-**, *no pl* (*von Kapital, Preisen etc*) restriction; **auf Grund der ~ unseres Kapitals** because our capital is tied up; **ein Gefühl der ~** a feeling of being tied down; **die ~ an jdn/etw/einen Ort** being tied to sb/sth/a place

Ge|burt [ɡəˈbuːɐt] ⊘ 51.1 F **-**, **-en** (*lit, fig*) birth; (*fig*: = *Produkt*) fruit, product; **von ~** by birth; **von ~ an** from birth; **von hoher/adliger ~** of good/noble birth; **bei der ~ sterben** (*Mutter*) to die in childbirth; (*Kind*) to die at birth; **das war eine schwere ~!** (*fig inf*) that took some doing (*inf*); **die Gnade der späten ~** the good fortune of being born too late (*and so free from association with the Nazi era*)

Ge|bur|ten-: **Ge|bur|ten|be|schrän|kung** F population control; **Ge|bur|ten|buch** NT register of births; **Ge|bur|ten|kon|trol|le** F , **Ge|bur|ten|re|ge|lung** F birth control; **Ge|bur|ten|ra|te** F birthrate; **Ge|bur|ten|rück|gang** M drop in the birthrate; **ge|bur|ten|schwach** ADJ *Jahrgang* with a low birthrate; **ge|bur|ten|stark** ADJ *Jahrgang* with a high birthrate; **Ge|bur|ten|sta|tis|tik** F birth statistics *pl*; **Ge|bur|ten|über|schuss ▲** M excess of births over deaths; **Ge|bur|ten|zah|len** PL , **Ge|bur|ten|zif|fer** F number of births, birthrate; **Ge|bur|ten|zu|wachs** M increase in the birthrate

ge|bür|tig [ɡəˈbʏrtɪç] ADJ **~er Londoner sein, aus London ~ sein** to have been born in London, to be London-born, to be a native Londoner

Ge|burts-: **Ge|burts|adel** M hereditary nobility; **er stammt aus altem ~** he comes from a long line of nobility; **Ge|burts|an|zei|ge** F birth announcement; **Ge|burts|da|tum** NT date of birth; **Ge|burts|feh|ler** M congenital defect; **Ge|burts|haus** NT **das ~ Kleists** the house where Kleist was born; **Ge|burts|hel|fer(in)** M(F) (*Med*) (= *Arzt*) obstetrician; (=

Hebamme) midwife; (*fig*) midwife; **Ge|burts|hil|fe** F a assistance at a birth; **~ leisten** to assist at a birth; **bei etw ~ leisten** (*fig*) to help sth see the light of day b (*als Fach*) obstetrics *sing*; (*von Hebamme auch*) midwifery; **Ge|burts|jahr** NT year of birth; **Ge|burts|la|ge** F presentation; **Ge|burts|land** NT native country; **Ge|burts|na|me** M birth name, name at birth; (*einer Frau auch*) maiden name; **Ge|burts|ort** M *pl* **-orte** birthplace; **Ge|burts|stadt** F native town; **Ge|burts|stät|te** F (*geh*) birthplace

Ge|burts|tag ⊘ 50.3 M birthday; (*auf Formularen*) date of birth; **herzlichen Glückwunsch zum ~!** happy birthday!, many happy returns (of the day)!; **jdm zum ~ gratulieren** to wish sb (a) happy birthday, to wish sb many happy returns (of the day); **heute habe ich ~** it's my birthday today; **~ feiern** to celebrate one's/sb's birthday; **jdm etw zum ~ schenken** to give sb sth for his/her birthday

Ge|burts|tags- *in cpds* birthday; **Ge|burts|tags|fei|er** F birthday party; **Ge|burts|tags|gruß** M birthday greeting; **Ge|burts|tags|kind** NT birthday boy/girl

Ge|burts-: **Ge|burts|ur|kun|de** F birth certificate; **Ge|burts|we|hen** PL labour (*Brit*) *or* labor (*US*) pains *pl*; (*fig auch*) birth pangs *pl*; **Ge|burts|zan|ge** F (pair of) forceps *pl*

Ge|büsch [ɡəˈbʏʃ] NT **-(e)s**, **-e** bushes *pl*, (= *Unterholz*) undergrowth, brush

Geck [ɡɛk] M **-en**, **-en** (*pej*) fop (*dated esp Brit*), dandy, dude

ge|cken|haft ADJ (*pej*) foppish (*dated esp Brit*), dandyish

Ge|cko [ˈɡɛko] M **-s**, **-s** (*Zool*) gecko

ge|dacht [ɡəˈdaxt] *ptp von* **denken** *von* **gedenken** ADJ *Linie, Größe, Fall* imaginary; **als Kapitalanlage ~e Lebensversicherung** life assurance intended *or* meant as a capital investment

Ge|dächt|nis [ɡəˈdɛçtnɪs] NT **-ses**, **-se** memory; (= *Andenken auch*) remembrance; **etw aus dem ~ hersagen** to recite sth from memory; **das ist seinem ~ entfallen** it went out of his mind; **jdm im ~ bleiben** to stick in sb's mind; **im ~ bleiben** to be remembered; **etw im ~ behalten** to remember sth; **sich** (*dat*) **etw ins ~ zurückrufen** to recall sth, to call sth to mind; **wenn mich mein ~ nicht trügt** if my memory serves me right; **noch frisch in jds ~** (*dat*) **sein** to be still fresh in sb's mind; **zum ~ der** *or* **an die Toten** in memory *or* remembrance of the dead

Ge|dächt|nis-: **Ge|dächt|nis|feh|ler** M lapse of memory; **Ge|dächt|nis|fei|er** F commemoration; (*kirchliche*) memorial *or* commemorative service; **Ge|dächt|nis|hil|fe** F memory aid, mnemonic; **er machte sich ein paar Notizen als ~** he made a few notes to aid his memory; **Ge|dächt|nis|kon|zert** NT memorial concert; **Ge|dächt|nis|lü|cke** F gap in one's memory; (*Psych*) localized amnesia; **da habe ich eine ~** I just don't remember anything about it; **Ge|dächt|nis|pro|to|koll** NT minutes *pl* written from memory; **Ge|dächt|nis|ren|nen** NT memorial race; **Ge|dächt|nis|schu|lung** F memory training; **Ge|dächt|nis|schwund** M amnesia, loss of memory; **Ge|dächt|nis|stö|rung** F partial *or* (*vorübergehend*) temporary amnesia; **Ge|dächt|nis|stüt|ze** F memory aid, mnemonic; **Ge|dächt|nis|übung** F memory training exercise; **Ge|dächt|nis|ver|lust** M loss of memory; **Ge|dächt|nis|zel|le** F (*Med*) memory cell

ge|dämpft [ɡəˈdɛmpft] ADJ a (= *vermindert*) *Geräusch* muffled; *Farben, Musikinstrument, Stimmung* muted; *Optimismus* cautious; *Licht, Freude* subdued; *Wut* suppressed; *Entwicklung, Wachstum* restrained; (*Tech*) *Schwingung* damped; **mit ~er Stimme** in a low voice b (*Cook*) steamed → *auch* **dämpfen**

Ge|dan|ke [ɡəˈdaŋkə] ⊘ 35.2, 39.2 M **-ns**, **-n** thought (*über* +*acc* on, about); (= *Idee, Plan, Einfall*) idea; (= *Konzept*) concept; (= *Betrachtung*)

reflection (*über* +*acc* on); **der bloße ~ an ...** the mere thought of ...; **da kam mir ein ~** then I had an idea, then something occurred to me; **einen ~n fassen** to formulate an idea; **bei diesem Lärm kann man ja keinen ~n fassen** you can't hear yourself think in this noise; **seine ~n beisammenhaben** to have one's mind *or* thoughts concentrated; **in ~n vertieft** *or* **versunken/verloren sein** to be deep *or* sunk/lost in thought; **in ~n, Worten und Werken sündigen** to sin in thought, word and deed; **in ~n bin ich bei dir** in thought I am with you, my thoughts are with you; **jdn auf andere ~n bringen** to take sb's mind off things; **schwarzen ~n nachhängen** to think gloomy *or* dismal thoughts; **wo hat er nur seine ~n?** whatever is he thinking about?; **sich** (*dat*) **über etw** (*acc*) **~n machen** to think about sth; (= *sich sorgen*) to worry *or* be worried about sth; **mach dir keine ~n (darüber)!** don't worry about it!; **man macht sich** (*dat*) **so seine ~n** (*inf*) I've got my ideas; **daran würde ich keinen ~n verschwenden** I wouldn't even give it a thought; **kein ~ (daran)!** (= *stimmt nicht*) not a bit of it! (*inf*); (= *kommt nicht infrage*) (that's) out of the question; **etw ganz in ~n** (*dat*) **tun** to do sth (quite) without thinking; **jds ~n lesen** to read sb's mind *or* thoughts; **ich kann doch nicht ~n lesen!** I'm not a mind-reader!; **auf einen ~n kommen** to have *or* get an idea; **wie kommen Sie auf den ~n?** what gives you that idea?, what makes you think that?; **auf dumme ~n kommen** (*inf*) to get up to mischief; **jdn auf den ~n bringen, etw zu tun** to give sb the idea of doing sth; **sich mit dem ~n tragen, etw zu tun** (*geh*) **mit dem ~n spielen, etw zu tun** to toy with *or* consider the idea of doing sth; **der europäische/olympische ~** the European/Olympic idea

Ge|dan|ken-: **Ge|dan|ken|ar|mut** F lack of thought; (= *Ideenarmut*) lack of originality; **Ge|dan|ken|aus|tausch** M (*Pol*) exchange of ideas; **Ge|dan|ken|blitz** M (*inf*) sudden inspiration, brainwave (*inf*); **Ge|dan|ken|flug** M (*geh*) flight(s *pl*) of thought; **Ge|dan|ken|fol|ge** F reasoning; **Ge|dan|ken|frei|heit** F freedom of thought; **Ge|dan|ken|fül|le** F wealth of ideas; **Ge|dan|ken|gang** M *pl* **-gän|ge** train of thought; **Ge|dan|ken|ge|bäu|de** NT edifice *or* construct of ideas; **Ge|dan|ken|gut** NT , *no pl* body of thought; **Ge|dan|ken|ket|te** F chain of thought; **Ge|dan|ken|le|sen** NT **-s**, *no pl* mind-reading; **ge|dan|ken|los** ADJ (= *unüberlegt*) unthinking; (= *zerstreut*) absent-minded; (= *rücksichtslos*) thoughtless ADV (= *unüberlegt*) unthinkingly; (= *rücksichtslos*) thoughtlessly; **etw ~ tun** to do sth without thinking; **Ge|dan|ken|lo|sig|keit** F **-**, **-en** (= *Unüberlegtheit*) lack of thought; (= *Zerstreutheit*) absent-mindedness; (= *Rücksichtslosigkeit*) thoughtlessness; **Ge|dan|ken|ly|rik** F reflective poetry; **ge|dan|ken|reich** ADJ full of ideas; **Ge|dan|ken|reich|tum** M wealth of ideas; **Ge|dan|ken|rei|he** F chain of thought; **ge|dan|ken|schwer** ADJ *Buch, Lektüre etc* deep, heavy; *Person* weighed down with his *or* her thoughts *pred*; **Ge|dan|ken|spiel** NT intellectual game; (*fantasierend*) game of make-believe; (*als psychologische Taktik*) mind game; **Ge|dan|ken|split|ter** M aphorism; **Ge|dan|ken|sprung** M mental leap, jump from one idea to another; **Ge|dan|ken|strich** M dash; **Ge|dan|ken|tie|fe** F depth of thought; **Ge|dan|ken|über|tra|gung** F telepathy (*auch fig*), thought transference; **Ge|dan|ken|ver|bin|dung** F , **Ge|dan|ken|ver|knüp|fung** F association of ideas; **ge|dan|ken|ver|lo|ren** ADJ, ADV lost in thought; **ge|dan|ken|voll** ADJ (= *nachdenklich*) thoughtful, pensive; **Ge|dan|ken|welt** F world of thought *or* ideas; **die römische ~** (= *Ideenwelt*) (the world of) Roman thought; **er lebt in seiner eigenen ~** he lives in a world of his own

ge|dank|lich [ɡəˈdaŋklɪç] ADJ intellectual; (= *vorgestellt*) imaginary; **sich** (*dat*) ~ *or* **in ~er Hin-**

sicht näher kommen to find a common way of thinking; **in ~er Hinsicht übereinstimmen** to have an affinity of mind; **die große ~e Klarheit in seinem Werk** the great clarity of thought in his work **ADV** intellectually; **sie leben ~ in einer anderen Welt** in their minds *or* imagination they live in another world

Ge|därm [gə'dɛrm] NT -(e)s, -e, **Ge|där|me** [gə'dɛrmə] NT -s, - (*old, liter*) **a** bowels *pl*, entrails *pl* **b Gedärme** PL intestines *pl*; **da drehen sich einem ja die ~e um!** it's enough to make your insides *or* stomach turn over!

Ge|deck [gə'dɛk] NT -(e)s, -e **a** (= *Tischgedeck*) cover; **ein ~ auflegen** to lay (*Brit*) *or* set a place; **ein ~ für drei Personen** places *or* covers for three people; **eine Tafel mit zehn ~en** a table laid (*Brit*) *or* set for ten (people) **b** (= *Menü*) set meal, table d'hôte **c** (*im Nachtklub*) cover charge

ge|deckt [gə'dɛkt] ADJ *Farben* muted; *Basar, Gang, Dach* covered; *Tisch* set *or* laid (*Brit*) for a meal → *auch* **decken**

Ge|deih [gə'dai] M **auf ~ und Verderb** for better *or* (for) worse; **jdm auf ~ und Verderb ausgeliefert sein** to be completely and utterly at sb's mercy

ge|dei|hen [gə'daiən] *pret* **gedieh** [gə'di:], *ptp* **gediehen** [gə'di:ən] VI *aux* sein to thrive; (*wirtschaftlich auch*) to prosper, to flourish; (*geh*: = *sich entwickeln*) to develop; (*fig*: = *vorankommen*) to make progress *or* headway, to progress; **die Sache ist so weit gediehen, dass ...** the matter has reached the point *or* stage where ...

Ge|dei|hen [gə'daiən] NT -s, *no pl* thriving; (*wirtschaftlich auch*) prospering, flourishing; (= *Gelingen*) success; **zum ~ dieses Vorhabens braucht es Geduld und Glück** if this plan is to succeed patience and luck will be called for

ge|deih|lich [gə'dailiç] ADJ (*geh*) (= *vorteilhaft*) beneficial, advantageous; (= *erfolgreich*) successful

Ge|denk|aus|stel|lung F commemorative exhibition

ge|den|ken [gə'dɛŋkn] ⟳ 35.3 *pret* **gedachte** [gə'daxtə], *ptp* **gedacht** [gə'daxt] VI *irreg* +*gen* **a** (*geh*) (= *denken an*) to remember, to think of; (= *erwähnen*) to recall; **in seiner Rede gedachte er der Toten** in his speech he remembered the dead **b** (= *feiern*) to commemorate, to remember **c ~, etw zu tun** to propose to do sth

Ge|den|ken [gə'dɛŋkn] NT -s, *no pl* memory (*an* +*acc* of); **zum** *or* **im ~ an jdn** in memory *or* remembrance of sb; **etw in gutem ~ behalten** to treasure the memory of sth; **jdm ein ehrendes ~ bewahren** to remember sb with honour (*Brit*) *or* honor (*US*)

Ge|denk-: Ge|denk|fei|er F commemoration; **Ge|denk|got|tes|dienst** M memorial *or* commemorative service; **Ge|denk|mar|ke** F commemorative stamp; **Ge|denk|mi|nu|te** F minute's silence; **Ge|denk|mün|ze** F commemorative coin; **Ge|denk|re|de** F commemorative speech; **Ge|denk|stät|te** F memorial; **Ge|denk|stein** M commemorative *or* memorial stone; **Ge|denk|stun|de** F hour of commemoration; **Ge|denk|ta|fel** F plaque; **Ge|denk|tag** M commemoration day; **Ge|denk|ver|an|stal|tung** F commemoration (ceremony)

Ge|dicht [gə'diçt] NT -(e)s, -e poem; **die ~e Enzensbergers** Enzensberger's poetry *or* poems; **dieses Kleid/der Nachtisch ist ein ~** (*fig inf*) this dress/the dessert is sheer poetry

Ge|dicht-: Ge|dicht|band *pl* **-bände** M book of poems *or* poetry; **Ge|dicht|form** F poetic form; **in ~** in verse; **Ge|dicht|samm|lung** F collection of poems; (*von mehreren Dichtern auch*) anthology; **Ge|dicht|zyk|lus** M cycle of poems, poem cycle

ge|die|gen [gə'di:gn] ADJ **a** *Metall* pure, native (*Min*) **b** (*von guter Qualität*) high-quality; (= *geschmackvoll*) tasteful; (= *rechtschaffen*) upright;

Verarbeitung solid; *Kenntnisse* sound **c** (*inf*: = *wunderlich*) peculiar

Ge|die|gen|heit F -, *no pl* **a** (*von Metall*) purity **b** (= *gute Qualität*) high quality; (= *geschmackvolle Atmosphäre*) tastefulness; (= *Rechtschaffenheit*) uprightness; (*von Verarbeitung*) solidity; (*von Kenntnissen*) soundness

ge|dieh *pret von* **gedeihen**

ge|die|hen *ptp von* **gedeihen**

ge|dient [gə'di:nt] ADJ **ein ~er Soldat sein** to have completed one's (military) service → *auch* **dienen**

Ge|din|ge [gə'dɪŋə] NT -s, - (*Miner*) **im ~ arbeiten** to work on a piece-rate basis

Ge|döns [gə'dø:ns] NT -es [-zəs] *no pl* (*dial inf*) fuss, hullabaloo (*inf*)

ge|dopt [gə'do:pt] *ptp von* **dopen** ADJ **sie war ~** she had taken drugs; **die ~en Schwimmer wurden disqualifiziert** the swimmers who had taken drugs were disqualified → *auch* **dopen**

gedr. *abbr von* **gedruckt**

Ge|drän|ge [gə'drɛŋə] NT -s, *no pl* (= *Menschenmenge*) crowd, crush; (= *Drängeln*) jostling; (*Sport*) bunching; (*Rugby*) scrum(mage); **vor der Theaterkasse herrschte ~** there was a big crowd at the ticket office; **ein offenes ~** (*Rugby*) a loose scrum; **ins ~ kommen** *or* **geraten** (*fig*) to get into a fix (*inf*)

Ge|drän|gel [gə'drɛŋl] NT -s, *no pl* (*inf*) (= *Menschenmenge*) crush; (= *Drängeln*) shoving (*inf*)

ge|drängt [gə'drɛŋt] ADJ packed; (*fig*) *Stil* terse; **~e Übersicht** synopsis **ADV ~ voll** packed full, jam-packed (*inf*); **~ stehen** to be crowded together → *auch* **drängen**

Ge|drängt|heit F -, *no pl* (*von Stil*) terseness; (*von Übersicht*) conciseness

ge|drech|selt [gə'drɛkslt] ADJ (*pej*) *Rede, Sätze, Stil* stilted; **wie ~ reden** to speak stiltedly; **kunstvoll ~e Sätze** nicely turned phrases → *auch* **drechseln**

Ge|dröhn [gə'drø:n] NT -(e)s, *no pl*, **Ge|dröh|ne** [gə'drø:nə] NT -s, *no pl* (*von Motoren*) droning; (*von Kanonen, Lautsprecher, Hämmern etc*) booming

ge|dro|schen *ptp von* **dreschen**

ge|druckt [gə'drʊkt] ADJ printed; **~e Schaltung** printed circuit board, PCB; **lügen wie ~** (*inf*) to lie right, left and centre (*Brit inf*) *or* center (*US inf*) → *auch* **drucken**

ge|drückt [gə'drʊkt] ADJ *Stimmung* depressed, dejected; *Schweigen* gloomy; *Konjunktur, Preise* depressed; **~er Stimmung sein** to be in low spirits, to feel depressed → *auch* **drücken**

Ge|drückt|heit F -, *no pl* depression, dejection

ge|drun|gen [gə'drʊŋən] *ptp von* **dringen** ADJ *Person, Gestalt* stocky; *Gebäude, Form* squat

Ge|drun|gen|heit F -, *no pl* stockiness; (*von Gebäude, Form*) squatness

ge|duckt [gə'dʊkt] ADJ *Haltung, Mensch* crouching; *Kopf* lowered; *Haus* low; **hinter einer Hecke ~ crouching** down behind a hedge **ADV ~ sitzen** to sit hunched up (*Brit*) *or* over (*US*) → *auch* **ducken**

Ge|du|del [gə'du:dl] NT -s, *no pl* (*inf*) (*von Klarinette etc*) tootling; (*von Dudelsack*) droning, whining; (*von Radio*) noise

Ge|duld [gə'dʊlt] F -, *no pl* patience; **mit jdm/etw ~ haben** to be patient *or* have patience with sb/sth; **sich mit ~ wappnen** to possess one's soul in patience; **mir geht die ~ aus, mir reißt die ~, ich verliere die ~** my patience is wearing thin, I'm losing my patience; **meine ~ mit dir ist erschöpft** you've exhausted my patience; **jds ~ auf eine harte Probe stellen** to try sb's patience

ge|dul|den [gə'dʊldn] *ptp von* **geduldet** VR to be patient

ge|dul|dig [gə'dʊldiç] ADJ patient; **~ wie ein Lamm** meek as a lamb → **Papier a** **ADV** patiently

Ge|dulds-: Ge|dulds|ar|beit F job calling for patience; **Ge|dulds|fa|den** M **jetzt reißt mir aber der ~!** (*inf*) I'm just about losing my patience; **einen langen ~ haben** to have a lot of patience, to have the patience of Job; **Ge|dulds|pro|be** F trial of (one's) patience; **das war eine harte ~** it was enough to try anyone's patience *or* to try the patience of a saint; **Ge|dulds|spiel** NT puzzle

ge|dun|gen *ptp von* **dingen**

ge|dun|sen [gə'dʊnzn] ADJ bloated

ge|durft *ptp von* **dürfen**

ge|ehrt [gə'e:ɐt] ADJ honoured (*Brit*), honored (*US*), esteemed; **sehr ~e Damen und Herren!** Ladies and Gentlemen!; **sehr ~er Herr Kurz!** dear Mr Kurz; **Sehr ~e Damen und Herren** (*in Briefen*) Dear Sir or Madam → *auch* **ehren**

ge|eig|net [gə'laignət] ADJ **a** (= *passend*) suitable; (= *richtig*) right; **sie ist für diesen Posten nicht ~** she's not the right person for this job; **er ist nicht der ~e Mann für meine Tochter** he's not the right *or* a suitable man for my daughter; **im ~en Augenblick** at the right moment; **er ist zu dieser Arbeit nicht ~** he's not suited to this work; **er wäre zum Lehrer gut/schlecht ~** he would/wouldn't make a good teacher → *auch* **eignen**

ge|eig|ne|ten|orts [gə'laignətn'|ɔrts] ADV (*form*) in an appropriate place

Ge|eig|net|heit F -, *no pl* (= *Passen*) suitability; (= *Richtigkeit*) rightness

ge|eist [gə'laist] ADJ *Früchte, Getränke, Suppe* iced → *auch* **eisen**

Geest [ge:st] F -, -en, **Geest|land** NT *coastal sandy moorlands of N.W. Germany*

Ge|fahr [gə'fa:ɐ] F -, -en **a** danger (*für* to, for); (= *Bedrohung*) threat (*für* to, for); **die ~en des Dschungels/Verkehrs/dieses Berufs** the dangers *or* perils *or* hazards of the jungle/traffic/this job; **~ bringend** dangerous; **in ~ sein** *or* **schweben** to be in danger *or* jeopardy; (= *bedroht*) to be threatened; **in ~ geraten** to be under threat; **außer ~** (= *nicht gefährdet*) not in danger; (= *nicht mehr gefährdet*) out of danger; *Patient* out of danger, off the danger list; **sich ~en** *or* **einer ~ aussetzen** to expose oneself to danger, to put oneself in danger; **es besteht die ~, dass ...** there's a risk *or* the danger that ...; **er liebt die ~** he likes living dangerously; **(nur) bei ~ (bedienen)!** to be used only) in case of emergency!; **wer sich in ~ begibt, kommt darin um** (*Prov*) if you play with fire, you must expect to get your fingers burned **b** (= *Wagnis, Risiko*) risk (*für* to, for); **auf eigene ~** at one's own risk *or* (*stärker*) peril; **auf die ~ hin, etw zu tun/dass jd etw tut** at the risk of doing sth/of sb doing sth; **~ laufen, etw zu tun** to run the risk of doing sth; **unter ~ seines eigenen Lebens** at the risk of one's own life; **auf eigene Rechnung und ~** (*Comm*) at one's own account and risk

ge|fahr|brin|gend △ ADJ → **Gefahr a**

ge|fähr|den [gə'fɛ:ɐdn] *ptp von* **gefährdet** VT to endanger; *Position, Wirtschaft, Chancen etc auch* to jeopardize; (= *bedrohen*) to threaten; (= *aufs Spiel setzen*) to put at risk; **Versetzung** *or* **Vorrücken gefährdet** (*Sch*) comment on a school report *indicating that the pupil may have to repeat a year*

ge|fähr|det [gə'fɛ:ɐdət] ADJ *Tierart* endangered; *Ehe, Jugend, Bevölkerungsgruppe, Unternehmen, Gebiet* at risk *pred*; **von Erdbeben ~** at risk from earthquakes; **Gefährdete** people at risk

Ge|fähr|dung F -, -en **a** (= *das Gefährden*) endangering; (*von Position, Wirtschaft, Chancen*) endangering, jeopardizing; (= *das Riskieren*) risking **b** (= *Gefahr*) danger (+*gen* to)

Ge|fähr|dungs|haf|tung F risk liability

ge|fah|ren *ptp von* **fahren**

Ge|fah|ren|be|reich M danger zone; **Ge|fah|ren|herd** M danger area; **Ge|fah|ren|mo|ment**[1] NT potential danger; **Ge|-**

fah|ren|mo|ment² M (= Schrecksekunde) moment of danger; **Ge|fah|ren|quel|le** F source of danger; **Ge|fah|ren|stel|le** F danger spot; **Ge|fah|ren|zo|ne** F danger zone or area; **Ge|fah|ren|zu|la|ge** F danger money; **eine ~ von 200 Euro** 200 euros' danger money

Ge|fahr-: Ge|fahr|gut NT hazardous materials pl; **Ge|fahr|gut|trans|port** M transport of hazardous materials

ge|fähr|lich [gəˈfɛːʀlɪç] ADJ dangerous; (= gewagt auch) risky; (= lebensgefährlich auch) perilous; **das ~e Alter** (fig) the dangerous age ADV dangerously; (= gewagt auch) recklessly

Ge|fähr|lich|keit F -, no pl dangerousness; (= Gewagtheit auch) riskiness; (= Lebensgefahr auch) perilousness

Ge|fahr-: ge|fahr|los ADJ safe; (= harmlos) harmless ADV safely; (= harmlos) harmlessly; **Ge|fahr|lo|sig|keit** F -, no pl safety; (= Harmlosigkeit) harmlessness; **Ge|fahr|stel|le** F danger spot

Ge|fährt [gəˈfɛːɐt] NT -(e)s, -e (dated) wagon, carriage; (hum) jalopy (inf)

Ge|fähr|te [gəˈfɛːɐtə] M -n, -n, **Ge|fähr|tin** [gəˈfɛːɐtɪn] F -, -nen (geh) (lit, fig) companion; (= Lebensgefährte auch) partner (through life)

Ge|fahr-: ge|fahr|voll ADJ dangerous, full of danger; **Ge|fahr|zei|chen** NT danger sign

Ge|fäl|le [gəˈfɛlə] NT -s, - **a** (= Neigung) (von Fluss) drop, fall; (von Land, Straße) slope; (= Neigungsgrad) gradient; **das Gelände hat ein starkes ~** the land slopes down steeply; **der Fluss hat ein starkes ~** the river drops suddenly; **ein ~ von 10%** a gradient of 10%; **starkes ~!** steep hill **b** (fig: = Unterschied) difference; **das Nord-Süd-Gefälle** the North-South divide

ge|fal|len¹ [gəˈfalən] ♦ 34.3, 34.4, 40.2 pret **ge|fiel** [gəˈfiːl], ptp **gefallen** [gəˈfalən] VI to please (jdm sb); **es gefällt mir (gut)** I like it (very much or a lot); **es gefällt ihm, wie sie spricht** he likes the way she talks; **das gefällt mir gar nicht, das will mir gar nicht ~** (dated) I don't like it at all or one little bit; **das könnte dir so ~!** (inf) no way! (inf); **das Stück hat ~** (geh) the play was well received; **das gefällt mir schon besser** (inf) that's more like it (inf); **er gefällt mir gar nicht** (inf: gesundheitlich) I don't like the look of him (inf); **sich (dat) in einer Rolle ~** to fancy oneself in a role; **er gefällt sich in der Rolle des Leidenden** he likes playing the martyr; **sich** (dat) **etw ~ lassen** (= dulden) to put up with sth, to tolerate sth; **er lässt sich alles ~** he'll put up with anything; **das lasse ich mir (von Ihnen/denen) nicht ~!** I won't stand for or put up with that (from you/them)!; **das lasse ich mir ~!** that's just the job (inf) or thing (inf), there's nothing I'd like better

ge|fal|len² [gəˈfalən] ptp von **fallen** von **gefallen¹**

Ge|fal|len¹ [gəˈfalən] NT -s, no pl (geh) pleasure; **an etw** (dat) **~ finden** to derive or get pleasure from sth, to delight in sth; **an jdm/aneinander (großes) ~ finden** to take a (great) fancy to sb/each other; **bei jdm ~ finden** to appeal to sb

Ge|fal|len² M -s, - favour (Brit), favor (US); **jdn um einen ~ bitten** to ask sb a favo(u)r; **jdm einen ~ erweisen**, **jdm einen ~ tun** to do sb a favo(u)r; **tun Sie mir den ~ und schreiben Sie** would you do me a favo(u)r and write, would you do me the favo(u)r of writing; **Sie würden mir einen ~ tun, wenn ...** you'd be doing me a favo(u)r if ...; **jdm etw zu ~ tun** (geh) to do sth to please sb; **ihm zu ~** to please him

Ge|fal|le|nen|denk|mal NT war memorial

Ge|fal|le|ne(r) [gəˈfalənə] MF decl as adj soldier killed in action; **die ~n und die Toten des Krieges** the soldiers and civilians who died in the war; **ein Denkmal für die ~n des Krieges** a memorial to those killed in the war

Ge|fäl|le|stre|cke F incline

ge|fäl|lig [gəˈfɛlɪç] ADJ **a** (= hilfsbereit) helpful, obliging; **sich ~ zeigen** to show oneself willing to oblige; **jdm ~ sein** to oblige or help sb **b** (=

ansprechend) pleasing; (= freundlich) pleasant **c** **Zigarette ~?** (form) would you care for a cigarette? → **gefälligst**

Ge|fäl|lig|keit F **a** (= Gefallen) favour (Brit), favor (US); **jdm eine ~ erweisen** to do sb a favo(u)r **b** no pl (= gefälliges Wesen) pleasantness; (= Entgegenkommen) helpfulness; **etw aus ~ tun** to do sth out of the kindness of one's heart

Ge|fäl|lig|keits|ak|zept NT , **Ge|fäl|lig|keits|wech|sel** M (Fin) accommodation bill or paper

ge|fäl|ligst [gəˈfɛlɪçst] ADV (inf) kindly; **sei ~ still!** kindly keep your mouth shut! (inf)

Ge|fäll|stre|cke F incline

Ge|fall-: Ge|fall|sucht F craving for admiration; **ge|fall|süch|tig** ADJ desperate to be admired

ge|fällt [gəˈfɛlt] 3. pers sing pres von **gefallen¹**

ge|fälscht [gəˈfɛlʃt] ADJ forged

ge|fan|gen [gəˈfaŋən] ptp von **fangen** ADJ (= gefangen genommen) captured; (fig) captivated; **sich ~ geben** to give oneself up, to surrender

Ge|fan|ge|nen-: Ge|fan|ge|nen|auf|se|her(in) M(F) guard; **Ge|fan|ge|nen|aus|tausch** M exchange of prisoners; **Ge|fan|ge|nen|be|frei|ung** F rescue of a prisoner/prisoners; (als Delikt) aiding and abetting the escape of a prisoner; **Ge|fan|ge|nen|für|sor|ge** F prison welfare; (inf: = Dienst) prison welfare service; **Ge|fan|ge|nen|haus** NT (Aus) prison; **Ge|fan|ge|nen|hilfs|or|ga|ni|sa|ti|on** F prisoners' rights organization; **Ge|fan|ge|nen|la|ger** NT prison camp; **Ge|fan|ge|nen|miss|hand|lung** ▲ F mistreatment of prisoners; **Ge|fan|ge|nen|wär|ter(in)** M(F) prison officer or guard, (prison) warder (Brit), jailer (old inf)

Ge|fan|ge|ne(r) [gəˈfaŋənə] MF decl as adj captive; (= Sträfling, Kriegsgefangene, fig) prisoner; **500 ~ machen** (Mil) to take 500 prisoners; **keine ~n machen** (Mil) to take no prisoners (alive)

Ge|fan|gen-: ge|fan|gen hal|ten ▲ VT irreg to hold prisoner; Geiseln to hold; Tiere to keep in captivity; (fig) to captivate; **Ge|fan|gen|haus** NT (form, Aus) prison; **Ge|fan|gen|nah|me** [-naːmə] F -n capture; (= Verhaftung) arrest; **bei der ~** on one's capture/arrest; **ge|fan|gen neh|men** ▲ VT irreg Mensch to take captive; (= verhaften) to arrest; (Mil) to take prisoner; (fig) to captivate; **Ge|fan|gen|schaft** [gəˈfaŋənʃaft] F -, -en captivity; **in ~ geraten** to be taken prisoner; **ge|fan|gen set|zen** ▲ VT to take into captivity; (= verhaften) to imprison

Ge|fäng|nis [gəˈfɛŋnɪs] NT -ses, -se prison, jail, gaol (Brit); (= Gefängnisstrafe) imprisonment; **im ~ sein** or **sitzen** (inf) to be in prison; **ins ~ kommen** to be sent to prison; **zwei Jahre ~ bekommen** to get two years' imprisonment, to get two years in prison; **auf Meineid steht ~** perjury is punishable by imprisonment or by a prison sentence

Ge|fäng|nis- in cpds prison; **Ge|fäng|nis|auf|ent|halt** M prison term, time in prison; **Ge|fäng|nis|auf|se|her(in)** M(F) warder (Brit), prison officer or guard, jailer (old inf); **Ge|fäng|nis|di|rek|tor(in)** M(F) prison governor, prison warden (esp US); **Ge|fäng|nis|ge|bäu|de** NT prison; **Ge|fäng|nis|geist|li|che(r)** MF decl as adj prison chaplain; **Ge|fäng|nis|haft** F imprisonment; **Ge|fäng|nis|hof** M prison yard; **Ge|fäng|nis|in|sas|se** M , **Ge|fäng|nis|in|sas|sin** F inmate; **Ge|fäng|nis|re|vol|te** F prison riot(s pl); **Ge|fäng|nis|stra|fe** F prison sentence; **eine ~ von zehn Jahren** ten years' imprisonment; **er wurde zu einer ~ verurteilt** he was sent to prison, he was given a prison sentence; **Ge|fäng|nis|tor** NT prison gate usu pl; **für ihn öffneten sich die ~e** the prison gates were opened for him; **Ge|fäng|nis|wär|ter(in)** M(F) warder (Brit), prison officer or guard, jailer (old inf); **Ge|fäng|nis|zel|le** F prison cell

ge|färbt [gəˈfɛrpt] ADJ dyed; Lebensmittel artificially coloured (Brit) or colored (US); (fig) Aussprache tinged; Bericht biased; **ihre Sprache ist schottisch ~** her accent has a Scottish tinge or ring to it; **konservativ ~ sein** to have a conservative bias; **rot ~es Haar** dyed red hair, hair dyed red → auch **färben**

Ge|fa|sel [gəˈfaːzl] NT -s, no pl (pej) twaddle (inf), drivel (inf)

Ge|fäß [gəˈfɛːs] NT -es, -e vessel (auch Anat, Bot); (= Behälter) receptacle; (= Degenkorb) coquille

Ge|fäß-: Ge|fäß|chi|rur|gie F (Med) vascular surgery; **ge|fäß|er|wei|ternd** ADJ vasodilatory; **Ge|fäß|er|wei|te|rung** F vasodilation, vascular dilatation; **Ge|fäß|lei|den** NT angiopathy, vascular disease

ge|fasst ▲ [gəˈfast] ADJ (= ruhig) composed, calm; Stimme calm; Lächeln composed; **einen sehr ~en Eindruck machen** to appear cool, calm and collected; **auf etw** (acc) **~ sein** to be prepared or ready for sth; **sich auf etw** (acc) **~ machen** to prepare oneself for sth; **er kann sich auf etwas ~ machen** (inf) I'll give him something to think about (inf) ADV (= beherrscht) calmly → auch **fassen**

Ge|fasst|heit ▲ F -, no pl composure, calm (-ness)

Ge|fäß-: ge|fäß|ver|en|gend ADJ vasoconstrictive; **Ge|fäß|ver|en|gung** F vasoconstriction, vascular constriction; **Ge|fäß|ver|schluss** ▲ M , **Ge|fäß|ver|stop|fung** F embolism; **Ge|fäß|wand** F vascular wall

Ge|fecht [gəˈfɛçt] NT -(e)s, -e (lit, fig) battle; (Mil) encounter, engagement; (= Scharmützel) skirmish; **ein hartes ~** fierce fighting; **das ~ abbrechen/einleiten** to cease/open combat; **jdn/etw außer ~ setzen** (lit, fig) to put sb/sth out of action; **mit diesen Argumenten setzte er seinen Gegner außer ~** he shot down his opponents with these arguments; **Argumente ins ~ führen** to advance arguments; **im Eifer** or **in der Hitze des ~s** (fig) in the heat of the moment; **klar zum ~!** (Naut) clear for action!; (fig) clear the decks!

Ge|fechts-: Ge|fechts|ab|schnitt M battle zone; **Ge|fechts|auf|klä|rung** F tactical reconnaissance; **Ge|fechts|aus|bil|dung** F combat training; **ge|fechts|be|reit** ADJ ready for action or battle; (= einsatzfähig) (fully) operational; **Ge|fechts|be|reit|schaft** F readiness for action or battle; **in ~** fully operational; **Ge|fechts|feld** NT battleground; **Ge|fechts|feld|waf|fe** F battleground weapon; **ge|fechts|klar** ADJ (Naut) cleared for action; **ein Schiff ~ machen** to clear a ship for action; **Ge|fechts|kopf** M warhead; **Ge|fechts|lärm** M noise of battle; **ge|fechts|mä|ßig** ADJ combat attr, under combat conditions; **Ge|fechts|pau|se** F break in the fighting; **Ge|fechts|stand** M command post; **Ge|fechts|stär|ke** F fighting strength; **Ge|fechts|übung** F field exercise, manoeuvres pl (Brit), maneuvers pl (US)

ge|fe|dert [gəˈfeːdɐt] ADJ Matratze sprung; Karosserie spring-suspended; Sohlen cushion attr; **ein gut ~es Auto** a car with good suspension; **eine gut ~e Kutsche** a well-sprung carriage → auch **federn**

ge|fei|ert [gəˈfaiɐt] ADJ celebrated → auch **feiern**

Ge|feil|sche [gəˈfailʃə] NT -s, no pl (inf) haggling

ge|feit [gəˈfait] ADJ **gegen etw ~ sein** to be immune to sth; **niemand ist gegen den Tod ~** nobody is immortal; **dagegen ist keiner ~** that could happen to anyone → auch **feien**

ge|fes|tigt [gəˈfɛstɪçt] ADJ Tradition, Verhältnisse established; Charakter steady; Bindungen firm; **sittlich ~ sein** to have a sense of moral responsibility → auch **festigen**

Ge|fie|del [gə'fiːdl] NT -s, no pl (inf) fiddling (inf), scraping (pej)

Ge|fie|der [gə'fiːdɐ] NT -s, - plumage, feathers pl; (old: von Pfeil) flight

ge|fie|dert [gə'fiːdɐt] ADJ feathered; Blatt pinnate; **die ~en Sänger** (poet) the feathered songsters (poet); **unsere ~en Freunde** (geh) our feathered friends → auch **fiedern**

ge|fiel pret von **gefallen**[1]

Ge|fil|de [gə'fɪldə] NT -s, - (old, liter) realm; **die ~ der Seligen** the Elysian fields; **die heimatlichen ~** (hum) home pastures

ge|fin|kelt [gə'fɪŋklt] ADJ (esp Aus) cunning, crafty

Ge|fla|cker [gə'flakɐ] NT -s, no pl flickering

ge|flammt [gə'flamt] ADJ Marmor waved, rippled; Holz wavy-grained; Stoff watered → auch **flammen**

Ge|flat|ter [gə'flatɐ] NT -s, no pl fluttering; (von Fahne etc: bei starkem Wind) flapping

Ge|flecht [gə'flɛçt] NT -(e)s, -e (lit, fig) network; (= Gewebe) weave; (= Rohrgeflecht) wickerwork, basketwork; (von Haaren) plaiting (Brit), braiding (US)

ge|fleckt [gə'flɛkt] ADJ spotted; Blume, Vogel speckled; Haut blotchy

Ge|flenn [gə'flɛn] NT -(e)s, no pl, **Ge|flen|ne** [gə'flɛnə] NT -s, no pl (pej inf) blubbering (inf)

Ge|flim|mer [gə'flɪmɐ] NT -s, no pl shimmering; (Film, TV) flicker(ing); (durch heiße Luft) heat haze; (von Stern) twinkling

Ge|flis|sen|heit [gə'flɪsnhait] F -, no pl (geh) = **Beflissenheit**

ge|flis|sent|lich [gə'flɪsntlɪç] (geh) ADJ deliberate, intentional; **zur ~en Beachtung** (form) for your attention ADV deliberately, intentionally

ge|floch|ten ptp von **flechten**

ge|flo|gen ptp von **fliegen**

ge|flo|hen ptp von **fliehen**

ge|flos|sen ptp von **fließen**

Ge|flü|gel [gə'flyːgl] NT -s, no pl (Zool, Cook) poultry no pl; (= Vögel auch) fowl

Ge|flü|gel- in cpds (Cook) chicken/turkey etc; (allgemein) poultry; **Ge|flü|gel|creme|sup|pe** F cream of chicken/turkey etc soup; **Ge|flü|gel|farm** F poultry farm, chicken or turkey etc farm; **Ge|flü|gel|fleisch** NT poultry; **Ge|flü|gel|händ|ler(in)** M(F) poulterer, poultry dealer; **Ge|flü|gel|hand|lung** F poulterer's; **Ge|flü|gel|klein** NT -s, no pl giblets pl; **Ge|flü|gel|le|ber** F chicken/turkey etc liver; **Ge|flü|gel|sa|lat** M chicken/turkey etc salad; **Ge|flü|gel|sche|re** F poultry shears pl

ge|flü|gelt [gə'flyːglt] ADJ winged; **~e Worte** familiar or standard quotations; **er spricht immer in ~en Worten** he always speaks in quotations

Ge|flü|gel|zucht F poultry farming

Ge|flun|ker [gə'flʊŋkɐ] NT -s, no pl (inf) fibbing (inf); **das ist alles ~** it's all lies or fibs (inf)

Ge|flüs|ter [gə'flʏstɐ] NT -s, no pl whispering; (von Bäumen, Blättern auch) rustling

ge|foch|ten ptp von **fechten**

Ge|fol|ge [gə'fɔlgə] NT -s, - retinue, entourage; (= Trauergefolge) cortege; (fig) wake; **im ~** in the wake (+gen of); **etw im ~ haben** (fig) to result in sth, to bring sth in its wake

Ge|folg|schaft [gə'fɔlkʃaft] F -, -en **a** (= die Anhänger) following; (NS: = Betriebsgefolgschaft) workforce; (Hist: = Gefolge) retinue, entourage **b** (= Treue) fealty (Hist), allegiance (auch Hist), loyalty

Ge|folg|schafts|treue F fealty (Hist), allegiance (auch Hist), loyalty

Ge|folgs|mann M pl **-leute** or **-männer**, **Ge|folgs|frau** F follower; (Hist) liegeman/-woman

Ge|fra|ge [gə'fraːgə] NT -s, no pl (inf) questions pl; **hör auf mit deinem ~!** stop pestering me with (your) questions!

---

ge|fragt [gə'fraːkt] ADJ Waren, Sänger etc in demand pred → auch **fragen**

ge|frä|ßig [gə'frɛːsɪç] ADJ gluttonous; (fig geh) voracious; Flammen, Feuer all-enveloping; **~e Stille** (hum) the silence of people who enjoy their food

Ge|frä|ßig|keit F -, no pl gluttony; (fig geh) voracity

Ge|frei|te(r) [gə'fraitə] MF decl as adj (Mil) lance corporal (Brit), private first class (US); (Naut) able seaman (Brit), seaman apprentice (US); (Aviat) leading aircraftman (Brit), airman first class (US)

ge|fres|sen [gə'frɛsn] ptp von **fressen**

Ge|frett [gə'frɛt] NT -s, no pl (Aus) worry

Ge|frier-: **Ge|frier|beu|tel** M (Cook) freezer bag; **Ge|frier|box** F freezer box; **Ge|frier|brand** M (Cook) freezer burn; **Ge|frier|chi|rur|gie** F cryosurgery

ge|frie|ren ptp **gefroren** VI irreg aux sein (lit, fig) to freeze → **Blut**

Ge|frier-: **Ge|frier|fach** NT freezer or ice compartment, icebox (esp US); **Ge|frier|fleisch** NT frozen meat; **Ge|frier|ge|mü|se** NT frozen vegetables pl; **ge|frier|ge|trock|net** [-gətrɔknət] ADJ freeze-dried; **Ge|frier|kost** F frozen food; **Ge|frier|punkt** M freezing point; (von Thermometer) zero; **auf dem ~ stehen** to be at freezing point/zero; **Temperaturen unter dem ~** temperatures below zero, temperatures below freezing (point); **Ge|frier|raum** M deep-freeze room; **Ge|frier|schrank** M (upright) freezer; **Ge|frier|schutz|mit|tel** NT (Aut) antifreeze; **Ge|frier|tem|pe|ra|tur** F freezing temperature; **Ge|frier|trock|nung** F -, no pl freeze-drying; **Ge|frier|tru|he** F freezer, deep-freeze; **Ge|frier|ver|fah|ren** NT freezing process

ge|fro|ren ptp von **frieren** von **gefrieren**

Ge|fuch|tel [gə'fʊxtl] NT -s, no pl gesticulating

Ge|fü|ge [gə'fyːgə] NT -s, - (lit, fig) structure; (= Baugefüge auch) construction; (= Aufbau) structure, make-up

ge|fü|gig [gə'fyːgɪç] ADJ (= willfährig) submissive; (= gehorsam) obedient; **jdn ~ machen** to make sb bend to one's will

Ge|fü|gig|keit F -, no pl (= Willfährigkeit) submissiveness; (= Gehorsamkeit) obedience

Ge|fühl [gə'fyːl] NT -(e)s, -e **a** (= Sinneswahrnehmung) feeling; **etw im ~ haben** to have a feel for sth; **sie hat mehr ~ in den Fingern als ich** she has a better sense of touch than I do; **er hat kein ~ für heiß und kalt** he can't tell or feel the difference between hot and cold

b (= seelische Empfindung, Ahnung) feeling; (= Emotionalität) sentiment; **ich habe das ~, dass ...** I have the feeling that ...; **ich habe ein ~, als ob ...** I feel as though ...; **es geht gegen mein ~ ...** I don't like ...; **mein ~ täuscht mich nie** my instinct is never wrong; **jds ~e erwidern** to return sb's affection; **jds ~e verletzen** to hurt sb's feelings; **ein Mensch ohne ~** (= hartherzig) a person without any feelings; (= gefühlskalt) a person without any emotions; **er ist zu keinem menschlichen ~ fähig** he is incapable of (feeling) any human emotion; **~ und Verstand** emotion and reason, sense and sensibility; **die Romantik war das Zeitalter des ~s** romanticism was the age of sensibility; **das höchste der ~e** (inf) the ultimate

c (= Verständnis) feeling; (= Sinn) sense; **ein ~ für Zahlen/Musik** a feeling for figures/music; **ein ~ für Gerechtigkeit/Anstand/Proportionen/Rhythmus** a sense of justice/decency/proportion/rhythm; **Tiere haben ein ~ dafür, wer sie mag** animals can sense who likes them; **einen Apparat mit ~ behandeln** to treat an appliance sensitively

ge|füh|lig [gə'fyːlɪç] ADJ (pej geh) mawkish

Ge|füh|lig|keit F -, no pl (pej geh) mawkishness

---

ge|fühl|los ADJ (= unempfindlich, hartherzig) insensitive; (= mitleidlos) callous, unfeeling; Glieder numb, dead pred; **ich habe ganz ~e Finger** my fingers are completely numb, my fingers have gone dead ADV coldly, callously; **sich ~ verhalten** to be cold

Ge|fühl|lo|sig|keit F -, -en (= Unempfindlichkeit, Hartherzigkeit) insensitivity; (= Mitleidlosigkeit) callousness; (von Gliedern) numbness, deadness

Ge|fühls-: **Ge|fühls|an|wand|lung** F (fit of) emotion; **ge|fühls|arm** ADJ unemotional; **Ge|fühls|ar|mut** F lack of emotion or feeling; **Ge|fühls|auf|wal|lung** F , **Ge|fühls|ausbruch** M emotional outburst; **Ge|fühls|ausdruck** M , **Ge|fühls|äu|ße|rung** F expression of one's emotions; **ge|fühls|be|dingt** ADJ emotional; **ge|fühls|be|stimmt** ADJ emotional; **ge|fühls|be|tont** ADJ emotional; Rede, Äußerung auch emotive; **Ge|fühls|din|ge** PL emotional matters pl; **Ge|fühls|du|se|lei** F -, -en (pej) mawkishness; **ge|fühls|echt** ADJ Lied, Gedicht emotionally honest; Kondom ultrasensitive; **ge|fühls|ge|la|den** ADJ (very) emotional, emotionally charged; Wort etc auch emotive; **ge|fühls|kalt** ADJ cold; **Ge|fühls|käl|te** F coldness; **Ge|fühls|krüp|pel** M (pej) emotional cripple; **Ge|fühls|la|ge** F emotional state; **Ge|fühls|le|ben** NT emotional life; **ge|fühls|mä|ßig** ADJ (= gefühlsgesteuert) instinctive; (= gefühlbetont) emotional ADV instinctively, emotionally; **Ge|fühls|mensch** M emotional person; **Ge|fühls|nerv** M sensory nerve; **Ge|fühls|re|gung** F stir of emotion; (= seelische Empfindung) feeling; **ge|fühls|roh** ADJ hard-hearted; **Ge|fühls|sa|che** F matter of feeling; **Kochen ist zum großen Teil ~** cooking is largely something you have a feel for; **Ge|fühls|schwel|ge|rei** F wallowing no pl in one's emotions; **ge|fühls|se|lig** ADJ sentimental; **Ge|fühls|se|lig|keit** F sentimentality; **ge|fühls|tief** ADJ intense; **Ge|fühls|tie|fe** F emotional depth, depth of feeling; **Ge|fühls|über|schwang** M flood of emotions; **Ge|fühls|wal|lung** F emotional outburst; **Ge|fühls|welt** F emotions pl

ge|fühl|voll ADJ **a** (= empfindsam) sensitive; (= ausdrucksvoll) expressive; Volleystopp etc delicate **b** (= liebevoll) loving ADV with (so much) feeling; (= ausdrucksvoll) expressively; **sehr ~ singen** to sing with feeling

ge|füllt [gə'fʏlt] ADJ Paprikaschoten etc stuffed; Brieftasche full; **~e Pralinen** chocolates with soft centres (Brit), candies with soft centers (US) → auch **füllen**

Ge|fum|mel [gə'fʊml] NT -s, no pl (inf) fiddling (inf); (= Hantieren) fumbling (inf); (erotisch) groping (inf); **diese Arbeit ist ein furchtbares ~** this work is a terrible fiddle (Brit inf), this work is very tricky

ge|fun|den [gə'fʊndn] ptp von **finden** ADJ **das war ein ~es Fressen für ihn** that was handing it to him on a plate

Ge|fun|kel [gə'fʊŋkl] NT -s, no pl (von Sonne, Glas, Wein etc) sparkling; (von Sternen auch) twinkling; (von Augen) gleaming, twinkling; (vor Freude) gleaming, twinkling; (vor Zorn) flashing; (von Edelsteinen) glittering; (von Edelmetall) gleaming

ge|furcht [gə'fʊrçt] ADJ Stirn, Sand, Acker furrowed; eine von Sorgen **~e Stirn** a careworn brow → auch **furchen**

ge|fürch|tet [gə'fʏrçtət] ADJ dreaded usu attr; **~ sein** to be feared → auch **fürchten**

ge|ga|belt [gə'gaːblt] ADJ forked, bifurcate (spec); Zunge forked → auch **gabeln**

Ge|ga|cker [gə'gakɐ] NT -s, no pl (lit, fig) cackle, cackling

ge|gan|gen ptp von **gehen**

ge|ge|ben [gə'geːbn] ptp von **geben** ADJ **a** (= bekannt) given **b** (= vorhanden) given attr; (Philos: = real) factual; Bedingung, Voraussetzung fulfilled pred; **im ~en Fall ...** should the situation

---

arise ...; **bei den ~en Tatsachen/der ~en Situation** given these facts/this situation; **etw als ~ voraussetzen** to assume sth **c** (= *günstig*) **zu ~er Zeit** in due course

ge|ge|be|nen|falls [gəˈgeːbnənˈfals] ADV should the situation arise; (= *wenn nötig*) if need be, if necessary; (= *eventuell*) possibly; (*Admin*) if applicable

Ge|ge|ben|heit [gəˈgeːbnhait] F **-, -en** *usu pl* (actual) fact; (= *Realität*) actuality; (= *Zustand*) condition; **sich mit den ~en abfinden** to come to terms with the facts as they are

ge|gen [ˈgeːgn] PREP +acc **a** (= *wider*) against; **X ~ Y** (*Sport, Jur*) X versus Y; **für oder ~** for or against; **~ seinen Befehl** contrary to or against his orders; **haben Sie ein Mittel ~ Schnupfen?** do you have anything for colds?; **etwas/nichts ~ jdn/etw haben** to have something/nothing against sb/sth; **~ etw sein** to be against sth, to be opposed to sth; **10 ~ 1 wetten** to bet 10 to 1

b (= *in Richtung auf*) towards, toward (*US*); (= *nach*) to; (= *an*) against; **~ einen Baum rennen/ prallen** to run/crash into a tree; **er pochte ~ das Tor** he hammered on the gate; **etw ~ das Licht halten** to hold sth to or against the light; **~ Osten** etc **fahren** to travel eastwards (*Brit*) or eastward (*US*) etc, to travel to(wards) the east etc; **es wird ~ Abend kühler** it grows cooler toward(s) evening

c (= *ungefähr*) round about, around; (= *nicht mehr als*) getting on for; (= *nicht später als*) towards; **~ 5 Uhr** around 5 o'clock

d (= *gegenüber*) towards, to; **sie ist immer fair ~ mich gewesen** she's always been fair to me

e (= *im Austausch für*) for; **~ bar** for cash; **~ Bezahlung/Quittung** against payment/a receipt

f (= *verglichen mit*) compared with, in comparison with

Gegen-: Ge|gen|ak|ti|on F counteraction; **Ge|gen|an|ge|bot** NT counteroffer; **Ge|gen|an|griff** M (*Mil, fig*) counterattack; **Ge|gen|an|sicht** F opposite opinion; **Ge|gen|an|trag** M countermotion; (*Jur*) counterclaim; **Ge|gen|an|zei|ge** F (*Med*) contraindication; **Ge|gen|ar|gu|ment** NT counterargument; **Ge|gen|aus|sa|ge** F counterstatement; **Ge|gen|be|din|gung** F countercondition, counterstipulation; **Ge|gen|be|fehl** M (*Mil*) countermand, countercommand; **Ge|gen|be|haup|tung** F counterclaim; **Ge|gen|bei|spiel** NT counterexample; **Ge|gen|be|such** M return visit; **jdm einen ~ machen** to return sb's visit; **Ge|gen|be|we|gung** F (*Tech, fig*) countermovement; (*Mus*) contramotion; **Ge|gen|be|weis** M counterevidence *no indef art, no pl*; **den ~ zu etw erbringen** or **antreten** to produce evidence to counter sth; **bis zum ~ müssen wir ...** until we have evidence to the contrary we must ...; **Ge|gen|bu|chung** F cross entry

Ge|gend [ˈgeːgnt] F **-, -en** [-dn] area; (= *Wohngegend auch*) neighbourhood (*Brit*), neighborhood (*US*), district; (= *geografisches Gebiet, Körpergegend*) region; (= *Richtung*) direction; (*inf:* = *Nähe*) area; **die ~ von London, die Londoner ~** the London area; **er wohnt in der ~ des Bahnhofs** he lives in the area near the station; **Neuwied liegt in einer schönen ~** Neuwied is in a beautiful area; **eine schöne ~ Deutschlands** a beautiful part of Germany; **hier in der ~** (a)round here, in this area, hereabouts; **ungefähr in dieser ~** somewhere in this area; **die ganze ~ spricht davon** it's the talk of the neighbourhood (*Brit*) or neighborhood (*US*); **ein bisschen durch die ~ laufen** (*inf*) to have a stroll (a)round; **sie warfen die leeren Bierflaschen einfach in die ~** (*inf*) they just threw the empty beer bottles around anywhere; **brüll nicht so durch die ~** (*inf*) don't scream your head off (*inf*)

Gegen-: Ge|gen|dar|stel|lung F reply; **Ge|gen|de|mons|tra|ti|on** F counterdemonstration; **Ge|gen|dienst** M favour (*Brit*) or favor

(*US*) in return; **jdm einen ~ leisten** or **erweisen** to return the favo(u)r, to do sb a favo(u)r in return; **Ge|gen|drei|er** M (*Sport*) bracket; **Ge|gen|druck** M , *no pl* (*Tech*) counterpressure; (*fig*) resistance → **Druck¹** a

ge|gen|ei|nan|der [geːgnaiˈnandɐ] ADV against each other or one another; (= *zueinander*) to(wards) each other or one another; (= *im Austausch*) for each other or one another; **sich ~ aufheben** to cancel each other or one another out; **sie haben etwas ~** they've got something against each other

Ge|gen|ei|nan|der [geːgnaiˈnandɐ] NT **-s**, *no pl* conflict

ge|gen|ei|nan|der: ge|gen|ei|nan|der hal|ten ▲ VT *irreg* (*lit*) to hold together; (*fig*) to compare; **ge|gen|ei|nan|der pral|len** ▲ VI *aux sein* (*lit*) to collide; **ge|gen|ei|nan|der ste|hen** ▲ VI *irreg* (*fig*) to be on opposite sides; **im Wettbewerb ~** to be opponents; **ge|gen|ei|nan|der stel|len** ▲ VT (*lit*) to put together; (*fig*) to compare; **ge|gen|ei|nan|der sto|ßen** ▲ VI *irreg aux sein* to bump into each other; (= *kollidieren*) to collide

Ge|gen-: Ge|gen|ent|wurf M alternative plan; **Ge|gen|er|klä|rung** F counterstatement; (= *Dementi*) denial, disclaimer; **Ge|gen|fahr|bahn** F oncoming carriageway (*Brit*) or highway (*US*) or (= *Spur*) lane; **Ge|gen|feu|er** NT backfire; **Ge|gen|for|de|rung** F counterdemand; (*Comm*) counterclaim; **Ge|gen|fra|ge** F counterquestion; **darf ich mit einer ~ antworten?** may I answer your question with another (of my own)?; **jdm eine ~ stellen** to ask sb a question in reply (to his); **Ge|gen|ga|be** F (*geh*) = Gegengeschenk; **Ge|gen|ge|ra|de** F (*Sport*) back straight, backstretch (*US*); **Ge|gen|ge|schenk** NT present or gift in return; **jdm etw als ~ überreichen** to give sb sth in return; **Ge|gen|ge|walt** F counterviolence; **Ge|walt mit ~ beantworten** to counter violence with violence; **Ge|gen|ge|wicht** NT counterbalance (*auch fig*), counterweight, counterpoise; **als (ausgleichendes) ~ zu etw wirken** (*lit, fig*) to counterbalance sth; **Ge|gen|gift** NT antidote (*gegen* to); **Ge|gen|gleis** NT opposite track; **Ge|gen|grund** M reason against; **Gründe und Gegengründe (für etw)** reasons for and against (sth); **Ge|gen|gut|ach|ten** NT opposing opinion, counter-opinion; **ge|gen+hal|ten** VI *sep* (= *sich wehren*) to counter; (= *standhalten*) to stand one's ground; **Ge|gen|kai|ser** M (*Hist*) anti-emperor; **Ge|gen|kan|di|dat(in)** M(F) rival candidate; **als ~ zu jdm aufgestellt werden** to be put up as a candidate against sb; **Ge|gen|kla|ge** F (*Jur*) countercharge; **~ gegen jdn erheben** to put in a countercharge against sb, to countercharge sb; **Ge|gen|klä|ger(in)** M(F) (*Jur*) bringer of a countercharge; **Ge|gen|kö|nig** M (*Hist*) anti-king; **Ge|gen|kraft** F (*lit, fig*) counterforce; **Ge|gen|kul|tur** F alternative culture; **Ge|gen|kurs** M (*lit, fig*) opposite course; **einen ~ steuern** to take an opposing course of action; **ge|gen|läu|fig** ADJ (*Tech*) Bewegung contrarotating; (*fig*) Tendenz, Entwicklung, Meinung contrary, opposite; **Ge|gen|leis|tung** F service in return; **als ~ für etw** in return for sth; **ich erwarte keine ~** I don't expect anything in return; **ge|gen+len|ken** VI *sep* (*Aut*) to steer in the opposite direction; **ge|gen+le|sen** VTI *sep irreg* to countercheck

Ge|gen|licht NT **bei ~ Auto fahren** to drive with the light in one's eyes; **etw bei ~** or **im ~ aufnehmen** (*Phot*) to take a backlit or contre-jour photo(graph) of sth

Ge|gen|licht- (*Phot*): **Ge|gen|licht|auf|nah|me** F backlit or contre-jour photo(graph) or shot; **Ge|gen|licht|blen|de** F lens hood

Ge|gen-: Ge|gen|lie|be F requited love; (*fig:* = *Zustimmung*) approval; **sie fand keine ~** (*lit*) her love was not returned or reciprocated; (*fig*) she met with no approval; **auf ~/wenig stoßen**

(*fig*) to be welcomed/hardly welcomed with open arms; **Ge|gen|macht** F hostile power; **Ge|gen|maß|nah|me** F countermeasure; **~n zur Bekämpfung der Inflation** measures to counter inflation; **Ge|gen|mei|nung** F opposite view or opinion; **Ge|gen|mit|tel** NT (*Med*) antidote (*gegen* to); **Ge|gen|mut|ter** F pl **-muttern** (*Tech*) locknut; **Ge|gen|of|fen|si|ve** F (*lit, fig*) counteroffensive; **Ge|gen|papst** M (*Hist*) antipope; **Ge|gen|part** M (= *Theat, Mus*) opposite number; **Ge|gen|par|tei** F other side; (*Sport*) opposing side; (*Jur*) opposing party; **Ge|gen|pol** M counterpole; (*fig*) antithesis (*zu* of, to); **Ge|gen|po|si|ti|on** F opposite standpoint; **Ge|gen|pro|be** F crosscheck; **die ~ zu etw machen** to carry out a crosscheck on sth, to crosscheck sth; **Ge|gen|pro|pa|gan|da** F counterpropaganda; **Ge|gen|re|ak|ti|on** F counter-reaction; **Ge|gen|rech|nung** F **a** (*Math:* = *Gegenprobe*) crosscheck **b** (*Comm*) set-off; (= *Gegenschuld*) offset; **die ~ auf|machen** (*fig*) to present one's own reckoning; **Ge|gen|re|de** F (= *Antwort*) reply; (= *Widerrede*) contradiction; **eine ~ zu jds Rede halten** to reply to sb's speech; **keine ~!** no contradiction!; **Rede und ~** dialogue (*Brit*), dialog (*US*); **eine Diskussion, in der Rede und ~ einander abwechseln** a discussion with a lively exchange between the speakers; **Ge|gen|re|for|ma|ti|on** F (*Hist*) Counter-Reformation; **Ge|gen|re|gie|rung** F rival government; **Ge|gen|re|vo|lu|ti|on** F counter-revolution; **Ge|gen|rich|tung** F opposite direction; **Ge|gen|ru|der** NT opposed control surfaces pl

Ge|gen|satz ☼ **32.1** M (= *konträrer Gegensatz*) contrast; (= *kontradiktorischer Gegensatz, Gegenteil*) opposite; (= *Unvereinbarkeit*) conflict; (= *Unterschied*) difference; (*Philos*) antithesis; (*Mus*) countersubject; **Gegensätze** (= *Meinungsverschiedenheiten*) differences *pl*; **im ~ zu** unlike, in contrast to; **Marx, im ~ zu ...** Marx, as against ...; **er, im ~ zu mir, ...** unlike me, he ...; **einen krassen ~ zu etw bilden** to contrast sharply with sth; **Gegensätze ziehen einander** or **sich an** (*prov*) opposites attract; **im ~ zu etw stehen** to conflict with sth; **Gegensätze ausgleichen** to even out differences; **unüberbrückbare Gegensätze** irreconcilable differences

ge|gen|sätz|lich [ˈgeːgnzetslıç] ADJ (= *konträr*) contrasting; (= *widersprüchlich*) opposing; (= *unterschiedlich*) different; (= *unvereinbar*) conflicting; **Schwarz und Weiß sind ~e Begriffe** black and white are opposites; **eine ~e Meinung** a conflicting view ADV **sie verhalten sich völlig ~** they behave in totally different ways; **~ veranlagt sein** to have contradictory characteristics

Ge|gen|sätz|lich|keit F **-, -en** (+gen between) (= *Kontrast*) contrast; (= *Widersprüchlichkeit*) opposition; (= *Unterschiedlichkeit*) difference; (= *Unvereinbarkeit*) conflict; **die ~ dieser beiden Systeme** the contrast between or contrasting nature of these two systems; **bei aller ~ ...** in spite of all (the) differences ...

Ge|gen|satz|paar NT pair of opposites

Ge|gen-: Ge|gen|schlag M (*Mil*) reprisal; (*fig*) retaliation *no pl*; **einen ~ (gegen jdn) führen** to strike back (at sb); **zum ~ ausholen** to prepare to retaliate; **Ge|gen|sei|te** F (*lit, fig*) other side; (= *gegenüberliegende Seite auch*) opposite side; **ge|gen|sei|tig** [ˈgeːgnzaitıç] ADJ mutual; (= *wechselseitig auch*) reciprocal; **in ~em Einverständnis** by mutual agreement ADV each other, one another; **sie beschuldigten sich ~** they (each) accused one another or each other; **sich ~ bedingen** to be contingent (up)on one another or each other; **sich ~ ausschließen** to be mutually exclusive, to exclude one another; **Ge|gen|sei|tig|keit** F **-,** *no pl* mutuality; (= *Wechselseitigkeit auch*) reciprocity; **ein Abkommen/Vertrag auf ~** a reciprocal agreement/treaty; **Versicherung auf ~** mutual insurance; **das beruht auf ~** the feeling is mutual; **Ge|gen|sei|tig|keits|prin|zip** NT , *no pl* (*Pol etc*) principle of reciprocity, reciprocity principle; **Ge|**

gen|sinn M , *no pl* **im ~** in the opposite direction; **ge|gen|sin|nig** ADJ (*Tech*) in the opposite direction; (= *widersprüchlich*) contradictory; **Ge|gen|spie|ler(in)** M(F) opponent; (*bei Mannschaftsspielen auch*) opposite number; (*Liter*) antagonist; **Ge|gen|spi|o|na|ge** F counterespionage, counterintelligence; **Ge|gen|sprech-|an|la|ge** F (two-way) intercom; (*Telec*) duplex (system); **Ge|gen|sprech|ver|kehr** M two--way communication

Ge|gen|stand M (= *Ding*) object, thing; (*Econ*: = *Artikel*) article; (= *Thema, Angelegenheit, Stoff*) subject; (*von Gespräch, Diskussion*) subject, topic; (*der Neugier, des Hasses etc, Philos*) object; (*Aus*: = *Schulfach*) subject; **ein harter ~ fiel ihm auf den Kopf** something hard or a hard object fell on his head; **sie wurde mit einem stumpfen ~ erschlagen** she was killed by a blow from a blunt instrument; **~ des Gespötts** laughing stock, object of ridicule; (*Mensch auch*) figure of fun

ge|gen|ständ|lich [ˈgeːgn̩ʃtɛntlɪç] ADJ concrete; (*Philos*) objective; (*Art*) representational; (= *anschaulich*) graphic(al); **die ~e Welt** the world of objects

Ge|gen|ständ|lich|keit F -, *no pl* concreteness; (*Philos*) objectivity; (*Art*) representationalism; (= *Anschaulichkeit*) graphic(al)ness

Ge|gen|stand|punkt M opposite point of view

Ge|gen|stands-: ge|gen|stands|los ADJ (= *überflüssig*) redundant, unnecessary; (= *grundlos*) unfounded, groundless; (= *hinfällig*) irrelevant; (*Art*) non-representational, abstract; **bitte betrachten Sie dieses Schreiben als ~, falls ...** please disregard this notice if ...; **Ge|gen|stands|lo|sig|keit** F -, *no pl* (*Art*) abstraction; **Ge|gen|stands|wort** NT *pl* -wörter concrete noun

Ge|gen-: ge|gen+steu|ern VI *sep* (*Aut*) to steer in the opposite direction; (*fig*) to take countermeasures; **Ge|gen|stim|me** F (*Parl*) vote against; **der Antrag wurde mit 250 Stimmen bei** or **und 30 ~n angenommen** the motion was carried by 250 votes to 30; **der Antrag wurde ohne ~n angenommen** the motion was carried unanimously; **Ge|gen|stoß** M (*Mil, Sport*) counterattack; **Ge|gen|stra|te|gie** F (*Mil, Pol, Sport*) counterstrategy; **Ge|gen|strö|mung** F (*lit, fig*) countercurrent; **Ge|gen|stück** NT opposite; (= *passendes Gegenstück*) counterpart

Ge|gen|teil NT , *no pl* opposite (*von* of); (= *Umkehrung*) reverse (*von* of); **im ~!** on the contrary!; **ganz im ~** quite the reverse; **das ~ bewirken** to have the opposite effect; (*Mensch*) to achieve the exact opposite; **ins ~ umschlagen** to swing to the other extreme; **eine Äußerung ins ~ umkehren** or **verkehren** to twist a statement to mean just the opposite

ge|gen|tei|lig ADJ *Ansicht, Wirkung, Erfahrung* opposite, contrary; **eine ~e Meinung** a contrary opinion; **~e Aussagen** contradictory statements; **~e Behauptungen** statements to the contrary; **ich habe nichts Gegenteiliges gehört** I've heard nothing to the contrary ADV **sich ~ entscheiden** to come to a different decision **Ge|gen|teils|be|weis** M (*Jur*) evidence to the contrary

Ge|gen|tor NT (*esp Ftbl, Sport*) **sie konnten ein ~ verhindern** they managed to stop any goals being scored against them; **ein ~ hinnehmen müssen** to concede a goal; **ein ~ erzielen** to score

Ge|gen|tref|fer M (*Sport*) = Gegentor

ge|gen|über [geːgnˈʔyːbɐ] PREP +dat **a** (*örtlich*) opposite; **er wohnt mir ~** he lives opposite me, he lives across from me; **er saß mir genau/schräg ~** he sat directly opposite or facing me/ diagonally across from me **b** (= *zu*) to; (= *in Bezug auf*) with regard or respect to, as regards; (= *angesichts, vor*) in the face of; (= *im Vergleich zu*) in comparison with, compared with; **mir ~ hat er das nicht geäußert** he didn't say that to me; **allem Politischen ~ ist**

---

er misstrauisch he's distrustful of anything political, he's distrustful as far as anything political is concerned; **er ist allem Neuen ~ wenig aufgeschlossen** he's not very open-minded about anything new or where anything new is concerned

ADV opposite; **der Park ~** the park opposite; **die Leute von ~** (*inf*) the people opposite

Ge|gen|über [geːgnˈʔyːbɐ] NT **-s, -** (*bei Kampf*) opponent; (*bei Diskussion*) opposite number; **mein ~ im Zug/am Tisch** the person (sitting) opposite me in the train/at (the) table; **wir haben einen freien Ausblick und kein ~** we've an open view with no building opposite

ge|gen|über-: ge|gen|über+lie|gen VI *sep ir-reg +dat* to be opposite, to face; **sich** (*dat*) **~** to face each other; **ge|gen|über|lie|gend** ADJ *attr* opposite; **das ~e Grundstück** the plot of land opposite; **der der Hypotenuse ~e Winkel** the angle opposite or facing the hypotenuse; **ge|gen|über+se|hen** VR *sep irreg +dat* **sich einer Aufgabe ~** to be faced or confronted with a task; **ge|gen|über+sit|zen** VI *sep irreg +dat* to sit opposite or facing; **ge|gen|über+ste|hen** VI *sep irreg +dat* to be opposite, to face, (*fig*) to stand opposite or facing; **jdm feindlich/freundlich/desinteressiert ~** to have a hostile/friendly/disinterested attitude toward(s) sb; **einem Plan freundlich ~** to be favourably (*Brit*) or favorably (*US*) disposed to a plan; **einer Gefahr ~** to be faced with a danger; **ge|gen|über+stel|len** *sep* (= *konfrontieren mit*) to confront (+*dat* with); (*fig*: = *vergleichen*) to compare (+*dat* with); **sich einer Sache** (*dat*) **gegenübergestellt sehen** to be faced or confronted with sth; **Ge|gen|über|stel|lung** F confrontation; (*fig*: = *Vergleich*) comparison; **ge|gen|über+tre|ten** VI *sep irreg aux sein* **jdm ~** to face sb

Ge|gen-: Ge|gen|ver|kehr M oncoming traffic; **Ge|gen|vor|schlag** M counterproposal

Ge|gen|wart [ˈgeːgnvart] F -, *no pl* **a** (= *jetziger Augenblick*) present; (= *heutiges Zeitalter*) present (time or day); (*Gram*) present (tense); **in der ~ leben** to live in the present; (= *den Augenblick genießen*) to live for the present or for today; **die Literatur/Musik der ~** contemporary literature/music; **die Probleme der ~** the problems of today, today's problems; **in der ~ stehen** (*Gram*) to be in the present (tense) **b** (= *Anwesenheit*) presence; **in ~ +gen** in the presence of

ge|gen|wär|tig [ˈgeːgnvɛrtɪç, geːgnˈvɛrtɪç] ADJ **a** *attr* (= *jetzig*) present; (= *heutig*) present, current, present-day; **der ~e Minister** the present minister; **der ~e Preis** the current price **b** (*geh*: = *anwesend*) present *pred*; **es ist mir im Moment nicht ~** I can't recall it at the moment ADV **a** (= *augenblicklich*) at present, at the moment; (= *heutzutage*) at present, currently **b** **sich** (*dat*) **etw ~ halten** (*geh*) to bear sth in mind

Ge|gen|wär|tig|keit F -, *no pl* **a** (= *Anwesenheit*) presence **b** (*mit Bezug zur Gegenwart*) present-day relevance

Ge|gen|warts-: ge|gen|warts|be|zo|gen [-bɒtsoːgn̩] ADJ relevant to present times; **ein sehr ~er Mensch** a person whose life revolves very much (a)round the present; **Ge|gen|warts|be|zug** M relevance (to present times); **Ge|gen|warts|deutsch** NT modern German; **Ge|gen|warts|form** F (*Gram*) present (tense); **ge|gen|warts|fremd** ADJ out-of-touch (with reality); **Ge|gen|warts|kunst** F contemporary art; **ge|gen|warts|nah, ge|gen|warts|na|he** ADJ relevant to the present; **Ge|gen|warts|nä|he** F relevance (to the present); **Ge|gen|warts|prob|lem** NT current or topical problem; **Ge|gen|warts|ro|man** M contemporary novel; **Ge|gen|warts|schaf|fen** NT contemporary scene; **Ge|gen|warts|spra|che** F present-day language; **die englische ~** modern English

Ge|gen-: Ge|gen|wehr F resistance; **Ge|gen|wert** M equivalent; **es wurden Waren im ~ von**

8.000 Euro entwendet goods to the value of or worth 8,000 euros were taken; **Ge|gen|wind** M headwind; **wir hatten starken ~** there was a strong headwind; **Ge|gen|win|kel** M (*Geom*) opposite angle; (*korrespondierend*) corresponding angle; **Ge|gen|wir|kung** F reaction, counteraction; **diese Tabletten können eine ~ haben** these tablets can have the opposite effect; **ge|gen+zeich|nen** VT *sep* to countersign; **Ge|gen|zeich|nung** F (= *Unterschrift*) countersignature; (= *das Unterschreiben*) countersigning; **Ge|gen|zeu|ge** M , **Ge|gen|zeu|gin** F witness for the other side; **Ge|gen|zug** M **a** countermove; **im ~ zu etw** as a countermove to sth **b** (= *Luftzug*) cross-draught (*Brit*), cross--draft (*US*) **c** (*Rail*) corresponding train in the other direction; (= *entgegenkommender Zug*) oncoming train

ge|ges|sen *ptp von* **essen**

ge|gli|chen *ptp von* **gleichen**

ge|glie|dert [gəˈgliːdɐt] ADJ jointed; (*fig*) structured; (= *organisiert*) organized; **das ~e Schulwesen** the tiered school system → *auch* **gliedern**

ge|glit|ten *ptp von* **gleiten**

Ge|glit|zer [gəˈglɪtsɐ] NT **-s**, *no pl* glitter(ing)

ge|glom|men *ptp von* **glimmen**

Geg|ner [ˈgeːgnɐ] M , **Geg|ne|rin** [-ərɪn] F -, **-nen** opponent (*auch Sport*), adversary; (= *Rivale*) rival; (= *Feind*) enemy; **ein ~ der Todesstrafe sein** to be against or opposed to capital punishment

geg|ne|risch [ˈgeːgnərɪʃ] ADJ *attr* opposing; (*Mil*: = *feindlich*) enemy *attr*, hostile; *Übermacht* of the enemy; **das ~e Tor** the opponents' goal

Geg|ner|schaft [ˈgeːgnɐʃaft] F -, **-en** opposition

ge|gol|ten *ptp von* **gelten**

ge|go|ren *ptp von* **gären**

ge|gos|sen *ptp von* **gießen**

gegr. *abbr von* **gegründet** established, est.

ge|gra|ben *ptp von* **graben**

ge|grif|fen *ptp von* **greifen**

Ge|grin|se [gəˈgrɪnzə] NT **-s**, *no pl* (*inf*) grin (-ning)

Ge|grö|le [gəˈgrøːlə] NT **-s**, *no pl* (*inf*) raucous bawling (*inf*)

Ge|grü|bel [gəˈgryːbl̩] NT **-s**, *no pl* (*inf*) worrying

Ge|grun|ze [gəˈgrʊntsə] NT **-s**, *no pl* grunting

Ge|ha|be [gəˈhaːbə] NT **-s**, *no pl* (*inf*) affected behaviour (*Brit*) or behavior (*US*)

ge|ha|ben [gəˈhaːbn̩] *ptp* **gehabt** VR (*old, Aus*) to behave, to deport oneself (*old, form*); **gehab dich wohl!** (*old, dial*) farewell! (*old*)

ge|habt [gəˈhaːpt] *ptp von* **haben**

Ge|hack|te(s) [gəˈhaktə] NT *decl as adj* mince (*Brit*), minced (*Brit*) or ground (*US*) meat

Ge|halt¹ [gəˈhalt] M **-(e)s, -e** **a** (= *Anteil*) content; **der ~ an Eiweiß/Kohlenhydraten** the protein/carbohydrate content; **ein hoher ~ an Kohlenmonoxid** a high carbon monoxide content **b** (*fig*) (= *Inhalt*) content; (= *Substanz*) substance; **~ und Gestalt** (*Liter*) form and content

Ge|halt² NT OR (AUS) M **-(e)s, ⸚er** [gəˈhɛltɐ] salary; (*esp Eccl*) stipend

ge|hal|ten [gəˈhaltn̩] *ptp von* **halten** ADJ **~ sein, etw zu tun** (*form*) to be required to do sth

Ge|halt-: ge|halt|los ADJ *Nahrung* non-nutritious; (*fig*) empty; (= *oberflächlich*) shallow, empty; **dieses Brot ist ziemlich ~** there's not much nourishment in this bread; **ge|halt|reich** ADJ **a** *Erz* high-yield **b** = gehaltvoll

Ge|halts-: Ge|halts|ab|rech|nung F salary statement; **die ~ ist abgeschlossen** the salaries have been worked out; **Ge|halts|ab|zug** M salary deduction; **Ge|halts|an|glei|chung** F salary adjustment; **Ge|halts|an|spruch** M salary claim; **Ge|halts|auf|bes|se|rung** F salary increase; **Ge|halts|be|schei|ni|gung** F salary declaration; **Ge|halts|emp|fän|ger(in)** M(F) salary-earner; **~ sein** to receive a salary, to be

---

salaried; **die Firma hat 500 ~** the firm has 500 employees *or* salaried staff; **Ge|halts|er|hö-hung** F salary increase, rise (*Brit*) *or* raise (*esp US*); (*regelmäßig*) increment; **Ge|halts|for|de|rung** F salary claim; **Ge|halts|fort|zah|lung** F continued payment of salary; **Ge|halts|grup|pe** F , **Ge|halts|klas|se** F salary bracket; **er ist in der ~ 6** he's on grade 6 on the salary scale; **Ge|halts|kon|to** NT current account (*Brit*), checking account (*US*); **Ge|halts|kür|zung** F cut in salary; **Ge|halts|mit|tei|lung** F salary statement; **Ge|halts|nach|zah|lung** F back payment; **Ge|halts|pfän|dung** F deduction of salary (at source); **Ge|halts|strei|fen** M salary slip; **Ge|halts|stu|fe** F = Gehaltsgruppe; **Ge|halts|ver|hand|lung** F salary negotiations *pl*; **Ge|halts|vor|rü|ckung** F -, -en (*Aus*) = Gehaltserhöhung; **Ge|halts|vor|stel|lung** F , **Ge|halts|wunsch** M salary requirement; **Ge|halts|zah|lung** F salary payment; **der Tag der ~ ist der 28.** salaries are paid on the 28th; **Ge|halts|zet|tel** M (*inf*) pay slip; **Ge|halts|zu|la|ge** F (= Gehaltserhöhung) salary increase, rise (*Brit*) *or* raise (*esp US*) in salary; (*regelmäßige*) increment; (= Extrazulage) salary bonus

ge|halt|voll ADJ *Speise* nutritious, nourishing; *Wein* full-bodied; (*fig*) rich in content; **ein ~es Buch** a book which says a great deal

Ge|häm|mer [gə'hɛmɐ] NT -s, *no pl* hammering

ge|han|di|kapt [gə'hɛndikɛpt] ADJ handicapped (*durch* by) → *auch* **handikapen**

Ge|hän|ge [gə'hɛŋə] NT -s, - **a** garland; (= Ohrgehänge) drop, pendant **b** (= Wehrgehänge) ammunition belt **c** (*Min*: = Abhang) declivity, incline **d** (*Build*) system of fascines **e** (*sl*: = Geschlechtsorgane) goolies *pl* (*Brit inf*), balls *pl* (*inf*)

ge|han|gen *ptp von* **hängen**

Ge|häng|te(r) [gə'hɛŋtə] MF *decl as adj* hanged man/woman; **die ~n** the hanged

Ge|hän|sel [gə'hɛnzl] NT -s, *no pl* (*inf*) mocking; **hört auf mit dem ~!** stop making fun of me/him *etc*!

ge|har|nischt [gə'ha:rnɪʃt] ADJ (*Hist*: = gepanzert) armour-clad (*Brit*), armor-clad (*US*); (*fig*) *Brief, Abfuhr etc* strong; *Antwort* sharp, sharply-worded; **ein ~er Ritter** a knight in armour (*Brit*) *or* armor (*US*)

ge|häs|sig [gə'hɛsɪç] ADJ spiteful ADV spitefully; **~ von jdm reden** to say nasty things about sb

Ge|häs|sig|keit F -, -en spite, spitefulness; **~en** spiteful things; **jdm ~en sagen** to be spiteful to sb

Ge|haue [gə'hauə] NT -s, *no pl* (*inf*) fisticuffs (*inf*); **Schluss mit dem ewigen ~!** stop fighting all the time!

ge|hau|en *ptp von* **hauen**

ge|häuft [gə'hɔyft] ADJ *Löffel* heaped; **ein ~er Teelöffel Salz** a heaped teaspoonful of salt; **das ~e Auftreten bestimmter Krankheiten** the frequent occurrence of certain diseases ADV in large numbers; **dieser Fehler tritt ~ auf** this error occurs more and more frequently → *auch* **häufen**

Ge|häu|se [gə'hɔyzə] NT -s, - **a** case; (= Radiogehäuse, Kameragehäuse, Uhrgehäuse, Kompassgehäuse) case, casing; (= Lautsprechergehäuse) box; (= großes Lautsprechergehäuse, Radiogehäuse) cabinet **b** (= Schneckengehäuse) shell **c** (= Obstgehäuse) core

geh|be|hin|dert ['ge:bəhɪndɐt] ADJ unable to walk properly

Geh|be|hin|der|te(r) ['ge:bəhɪndɐtə] MF *decl as adj* person with walking difficulties, physically challenged person (*esp US*)

Ge|he|ge [gə'he:gə] NT -s, - reserve; (*im Zoo*) enclosure, compound; (= Wildgehege) preserve; **jdm ins ~ kommen** (*fig inf*) to get under sb's feet (*inf*); (= ein Recht streitig machen) to poach on sb's preserves

---

ge|hei|ligt [gə'haɪlɪçt] ADJ *Brauch, Tradition, Recht, Prinzip, Symbol* sacred; *Räume* sacrosanct; **sein ~es Mittagsschläfchen** (*inf*) his precious afternoon nap → *auch* **heiligen**

ge|heim [gə'haɪm] ADJ secret; **seine ~sten Gefühle/Wünsche/Gedanken** his innermost *or* most private feelings/wishes/thoughts; **streng ~** top secret; **die ~en Verführer** the hidden persuaders; **Geheimer Rat** privy council; (*Mitglied*) privy councillor; **~ bleiben** to remain (a) secret; **im Geheimen** in secret, secretly ADV secretly; **~ abstimmen** to vote by secret ballot

Ge|heim- *in cpds* secret; **Ge|heim|agent(in)** M(F) secret agent; **Ge|heim|bund** M *pl* -bünde secret society; **Ge|heim|dienst** M secret service; **Ge|heim|dienst|ler** [-di:nstlɐ] M -s, -, **Ge|heim|dienst|le|rin** [-ərɪn] F -, -nen (*inf*) man/woman from the secret service; **Ge|heim|fach** NT secret compartment; (= Schublade) secret drawer; **Ge|heim|fa|vo|rit** M personal favourite (*Brit*) *or* favorite (*US*); **ge|heim hal|ten** ▲ VT *irreg* **etw (vor jdm) ~** to keep sth a secret (from sb)

Ge|heim|hal|tung F , *no pl* secrecy; **zur ~ von etw verpflichtet sein** to be sworn to secrecy about sth

Ge|heim|hal|tungs-: Ge|heim|hal|tungs|pflicht F obligation to maintain secrecy; **Ge|heim|hal|tungs|stu|fe** F security classification

Ge|heim-: Ge|heim|kon|to NT private *or* secret account; **Ge|heim|leh|re** F esoteric doctrine

Ge|heim|nis [gə'haɪmnɪs] NT -ses, -se secret; (= rätselhaftes Geheimnis) mystery; **das ~ der Schönheit/des Erfolgs** the secret of beauty/success; **das ~ der Auferstehung/des Lebens** the mystery of the Resurrection/of life; **ein offenes** *or* **öffentliches** (*rare*) **~** an open secret; **das ist das ganze ~** (*inf*) that's all there is to it; **aus etw ein/kein ~ machen** to make a big secret about sth/no secret of sth; **sie hat ein süßes ~** (*inf*) she's expecting a happy event

Ge|heim|nis-: Ge|heim|nis|krä|mer(in) M(F) (*inf*) secretive person; **Ge|heim|nis|krä|me|rei** [-krɛːmə'raɪ] F -, -en (*inf*) secretiveness; **Ge|heim|nis|trä|ger(in)** M(F) bearer of secrets; **Ge|heim|nis|tu|er** [-tuːɐ] M -s, -, **Ge|heim|nis|tu|e|rin** [-ərɪn] F -, -nen secretive person; **Ge|heim|nis|tu|e|rei** F secretiveness; **ge|heim|nis|tu|e|risch** [-tuːərɪʃ] ADJ secretive; **ge|heim|nis|um|wit|tert** ADJ (*geh*) shrouded in mystery (*liter*); **Ge|heim|nis|ver|rat** M ≈ offence under the Official Secrets Act (*Brit*), ≈ treason against the State (*US*); **ge|heim|nis|voll** ADJ mysterious; **~ tun** to be mysterious; **mit etw ~ tun** to make a big mystery of sth

Ge|heim-: Ge|heim|num|mer F secret number (*auch Telec*); (= Geheimzahl, PIN) PIN (number), personal identification number; **Ge|heim|po|li|zei** F secret police; **Ge|heim|po|li|zist(in)** M(F) member of the secret police; **Ge|heim|rat** M , **Ge|heim|rä|tin** F privy councillor; **Ge|heim|rats|ecken** PL (*inf*) receding hairline *sing*; **er hat ~** he has a receding hairline; **Ge|heim|re|zept** NT secret recipe; **Ge|heim|schloss** ▲ NT combination lock; **Ge|heim|schrift** F code, secret writing; **Ge|heim|tin|te** F invisible ink; **Ge|heim|tipp** ▲ M (personal) tip; **Ge|heim|trep|pe** F secret staircase; **ge|heim tun** ▲ VI *irreg* to be secretive; **mit etw ~** to be secretive about sth; **Ge|heim|tür** F secret door; **Ge|heim|waf|fe** F secret weapon; **Ge|heim|wis|sen|schaft** F secret *or* esoteric lore; **Ge|heim|zahl** F PIN (number), personal identification number; **Ge|heim|zei|chen** NT secret sign; (= Chiffre) cipher

Ge|heiß [gə'haɪs] NT -es, *no pl* (*geh*) behest (*old, form*) *no pl*; **auf jds ~** (*acc*) at sb's behest *or* bidding

ge|hei|ßen *ptp von* **heißen**

---

ge|hemmt [gə'hɛmt] ADJ *Mensch* inhibited; *Benehmen* self-conscious ADV *sich benehmen* in an inhibited way, self-consciously; **~ sprechen** to have inhibitions in speaking → *auch* **hemmen**

> ## ge|hen ['ge:ən] *aux sein*
> *pret* **ging** [gɪŋ], *ptp* **gegangen** [gə'gaŋən]
> ✪ 43.4, 53.1
>
> | | |
> |---|---|
> | 1 INTRANSITIVES VERB | 3 UNPERSÖNLICHES VERB |
> | 2 TRANSITIVES VERB | 4 REFLEXIVES VERB |

1 – INTRANSITIVES VERB

a to go; **wo er geht und steht, singt er** everywhere he goes, he sings; **gehen wir!** let's go!; **ich muss gehen** I must go *or* be off; **bitte gehen Sie!** (= verlassen Sie das Zimmer) please leave!; (Vortritt gewährend) after you!; **geh doch!** go on (then)!; **geh schon!** go on!; **wie geht man dorthin?** how do you get there?; **er ist gegangen worden** (*hum inf*) he was given the push (*hum inf*); **er ist von uns gegangen** (*euph*) he has passed away; **der Schmerz ging sehr tief** the pain went very deep

♦ **gehen + Infinitiv schwimmen/tanzen gehen** to go swimming/dancing; **spielen gehen** to go and play; **schlafen gehen** to go to bed

b = zu Fuß gehen to go, to walk; **das Kind lernt gehen** the baby is learning to walk; **am Stock (dat) gehen** to walk with a stick; **an Krücken (dat) gehen** to walk with *or* on crutches; **auf Stelzen (dat) gehen** to walk on stilts; **wie lange geht man bis zum Bus?** how long a walk is it to the bus?; **er ging im Zimmer auf und ab** he walked up and down the room; **das Pferd geht (im Schritt)** the horse is walking; **das Pferd geht Trab** the horse is trotting

c mit Präposition

> In Verbindung mit Präpositionen siehe auch unter dem Eintrag für die Präposition.

♦ **gehen + als** (= sich verkleiden) to go as sth; **als Schreiner gehen** (dial: = arbeiten) to work as a carpenter

♦ **gehen + an er ging an den Tisch** he went to the table; **gehen Sie (mir) nicht an meine Sachen!** don't touch my things!; **er ist an meine Geldbörse gegangen** he went into my purse; **das Erbe ging an ihn** the inheritance went to him → *auch* **b**

♦ **gehen + auf sie gingen auf den Berg** they went up the mountain; **sie ging auf die Straße** she went out into the street; **auf die andere Seite gehen** to cross to the other side, to go over to the other side; **das Fenster geht auf den Hof** the window overlooks the yard; **diese Tür geht auf den Balkon** this door leads onto the balcony; **das geht auf sein Konto** *or* **auf ihn** he's responsible for that; **das ging auf Sie!** that was aimed at you!; **das Bier geht auf mich** (*inf*) the beer's on me; **auf wen geht das Bier?** (*inf*) who's paying for the beer? → *auch* **b**

♦ **gehen + aus sie ging aus dem Zimmer** she went out of *or* left the room; **er ist wieder ohne Schirm aus dem Haus gegangen** he's gone out without his umbrella again; **jdm aus dem Licht/Weg gehen** to get out of sb's light/way

♦ **gehen + bis er ging bis zum Zaun** he went up to the fence; **er ging bis zur Straße** he went as far as the street; **das Wasser ging ihm bis zum Bauch** the water went up to his waist; **der Rock ging ihr bis zum Knöchel** the skirt went down to her ankles

♦ **gehen + durch wir gingen durch den Wald** we went through the wood; **das Klavier geht nicht durch die Tür** the piano won't go *or* fit through the door

♦ **gehen + gegen das geht gegen meine Prinzipien** *or* **meine Überzeugung** it's against my principles

♦ **gehen + in geh mal in die Küche** go into the kitchen; **du kannst unmöglich in einem roten Mantel zu einer Beerdigung gehen** you can't possibly go to a funeral in a red coat, you

---

can't possibly wear a red coat to a funeral; **ins Kloster gehen** (*Mann*) to enter a monastery; (*Frau*) to enter a convent; **in die Industrie/Politik gehen** to go into industry/politics; **in die Gewerkschaft/Partei gehen** to join the union/party; **wie viele Leute gehen in deinen Wagen?** how many people can you get in your car?; **in diesen Saal gehen 300 Leute** this hall holds 300 people; **in diesen Krug geht ein ganzer Liter** this jug holds a whole litre (*Brit*) or liter (*US*); **3 geht in 9 dreimal** 3 into 9 goes 3; **das will mir nicht in den Kopf gehen** I just can't understand it; **in die tausende** or **Tausende gehen** to run into (the) thousands; **er geht ins siebzigste Jahr** he's getting on for seventy; **in sich** (*acc*) **gehen** to stop and think

♦ **gehen + mit** **mit jdm gehen** to go with sb; (= *befreundet sein*) to go out with sb, to be with sb; **mit der Zeit gehen** to move with the times; **mit der Mode gehen** to follow fashion

♦ **gehen + nach** **er ging nach München** he went to Munich; **diese Straße geht nach Hannover** this road goes to Hanover; **diese Tür geht nach draußen/nach nebenan** this door leads to the outside/into the next room; **das Schiff geht nach Harwich** the boat is going to Harwich; **nach einer Regel gehen** to follow a rule; **wenn man nach seiner Aussage gehen kann** (= *urteilen*) if his statement is anything to go by; **man darf nicht nur nach dem Äußeren gehen** (= *urteilen*) you shouldn't judge or go just by appearances

♦ **gehen + über** **über die Straße gehen** to cross the road; **über die Brücke gehen** to go over the bridge; **die Brücke geht dort über den Fluss** the bridge crosses the river there; **die Reise geht über Dresden** we/they *etc* are going via Dresden; **das geht über meine Kräfte** that's more than I can manage; (*seelisch*) that's more than I can handle; **sein Garten geht ihm über alles** his garden is the thing that means most to him; **nichts geht über** (+*acc*) **...** there's nothing to beat ...

♦ **gehen + unter** **unter Menschen gehen** to mix with people; **jetzt ist er unter die Dichter gegangen** he's now joined the poetic fraternity

♦ **gehen + um** → (11)

♦ **gehen + zu** **zur Post gehen** to go to the post office; **zum Metzger gehen** to go to the butcher's; **zur Schule gehen** to go to school; **zu jdm gehen** to go to see sb; **geh mal zu deiner Oma in die Küche** go to your granny in the kitchen, go and see granny in the kitchen; **zur See gehen** to go to sea; **zum Militär gehen** to join the army; **zum Theater gehen** to go on the stage; **zur Universität gehen** to go to university

d 〔= sich bewegen〕 **ich hörte, wie die Tür ging** I heard the door (go); **diese Tür/Schublade geht schwer** this door/drawer is very stiff; **mein Rasenmäher geht schwer** my lawnmower is hard to push; **heute geht ein scharfer Wind** there's a bitter wind today; **die See geht hoch** the sea is running high

e 〔= ertönen〕 (*Klingel, Glocke, Telefon*) to ring, to go; **ständig geht bei ihr das Telefon** the phone is constantly going or ringing in her house; **wie geht das Lied/Gedicht?** how does the song/poem go?

f 〔= funktionieren〕 to work; (*Auto, Uhr*) to go; **mein Computer geht schon wieder nicht** my computer's not working again; **dieses Programm geht nur, wenn man dieses Betriebssystem hat** this program only works if you've got this operating system; **mein Auto geht mal, mal nicht** my car sometimes goes and sometimes doesn't; **die Uhr geht gut** the clock keeps good time; **die Uhr geht falsch/richtig** the clock is wrong/right; **so geht das, das geht so** this is the way to do it; **wir bauen uns aus Pappkartons ein Haus, und das geht so:** we're making a house out of cardboard boxes, and this is how: ...

g 〔= florieren〕 (*Geschäft*) to do well; (= *verkauft werden*) to sell; **das Milchgeschäft an der Lessingstraße geht gut, seit dort eine Schule er-**

öffnet wurde the dairy on Lessingstraße has been doing well since a school opened there; **mein Geschäft geht gut, aber ich könnte noch mehr Umsatz brauchen** my business is doing well, but I could do with a bigger turnover; **wie gehen die Geschäfte?** how's business?; **seit es im Fernsehen diskutiert wurde, geht das Buch besser** the book is selling better since it was discussed on TV; **das geht wie warme Semmeln** it's selling like hot cakes

h 〔= dauern〕 to go on; **wie lange geht das denn noch?** how much longer is it going to go on?; **es geht schon eine halbe Stunde** it's been going (on) for half an hour; **mein Kurs geht vom 2. bis 28. Juni** my course is from the 2nd to the 28th of June

i 〔= aufgehen〕 (*Hefeteig*) to rise; **Hefeteig muss; zwei- bis dreimal gehen** yeast dough has to rise two or three times

j 〔= sich kleiden〕 **ohne Hut gehen** not to wear a hat; **an einem Tag wie heute geht man einfach nicht ohne Hut/Schirm** on a day like this you simply can't go out without a hat/umbrella; **sorgfältig gekleidet gehen** to be carefully dressed

k 〔= betreffen〕 **der Artikel ging gegen ...** the article criticized ...; **das Buch ging um ...** the book was about ...; **die Wette geht um 50 Euro** the bet is for 50 euros; **mein Vorschlag geht dahin, dass ...** my suggestion is that ...

l 〔= möglich, gut sein〕 to be all right, to be OK (*inf*); **Montag geht** Monday's all right; **das geht gut** Monday's fine; **geht morgen? – ja, morgen geht gut** is tomorrow all right? – yes, tomorrow's fine; **das geht doch nicht** that's not on (*Brit*) or not OK; **Dienstag geht auch nicht** (*inf*) Tuesday's no good either

m 〔andere Redewendungen〕 **(ach) geh (doch), das darf doch nicht wahr sein!** (*inf*) get away with you (*Brit*) or come on, that can't be true! (*inf*); **(ach) geh, so schlimm ist das nicht!** (*inf*) (oh) come on, it's not that bad!; **gehen Sie (mir) doch mit Ihren Ausreden!** (*inf*) I don't want any of your excuses!; **geh!** (*Aus inf: erstaunt*) get away! (*Brit inf*), get out of here! (*US inf*)

♦ **vor sich gehen** **was geht hier vor sich?** what's going on here?; **ich weiß nicht, wie das vor sich geht** I don't know the procedure

♦ **so/zu weit gehen** to go so/too far; **er ging so weit, ihr eine Gehaltserhöhung zu versprechen** he went so far as to promise her a rise (*Brit*) or raise (*esp US*); **das geht einfach zu weit** this is just going too far

2 – TRANSITIVES VERB

er ging eine Meile he walked a mile; **ich gehe immer diesen Weg/diese Straße** I always go this way/along this road

3 – UNPERSÖNLICHES VERB

a 〔= ergehen〕 **wie geht es Ihnen?** how are you?; (*zu Patient*) how are you feeling?; **wie gehts?** how are things?; (*bei Arbeit etc*) how's it going?; **wie gehts sonst?** (*inf*) how are things otherwise?; **wie gehts denn (so)? – es geht** (*inf*) how are things? – all right or not too bad (*inf*); **danke, es geht** (*inf*) all right, thanks, not too bad, thanks (*inf*); **es geht ihm gut/schlecht** he's fine/not well; **es geht mir (wieder) besser** I'm better now; **nach einem Bad gings mir gleich besser** once I'd had a bath I felt better; **sonst gehts dir gut?** (*iro*) are you sure you're feeling all right? (*iro*); **wie war denn die Prüfung? – ach, es ging ganz gut** how was the exam? – oh, it went quite well; **mir ist es genauso gegangen** (= *ich habe dasselbe erlebt*) it was just the same or just like that for me; (= *ich habe dasselbe empfunden*) I felt the same way; **lass es dir gut gehen** look after yourself, take care of yourself; **so geht es (eben)** (= *so ist das Leben*) that's how it goes, that's the way things go

b 〔= sich machen lassen, möglich sein〕 **es geht** it is possible; (= *funktioniert*) it works; **solange es geht** as long as possible; **geht es?** (*ohne Hilfe*) can you manage?; **es geht nicht** (= *ist nicht*

möglich) it's impossible; (= *kommt nicht in Frage*) it's not on; **das wird schon gehen** I'll/he'll *etc* manage; (= *wird sich machen lassen*) it'll be all right; **wir müssen uns damit abfinden, es geht eben nicht anders** we'll just have to put up with it, there's no other way; **so geht es nicht** that's not the way to do it; (*entrüstet*) it just won't do; **morgen geht es nicht** tomorrow's no good

c 〔= führen〕 **dann geht es immer geradeaus** then it's straight on (*Brit*) or ahead; **Sie nehmen die erste rechts, und dann geht es immer geradeaus bis zur Ampel** you take the first right and then it's straight on (*Brit*) or ahead till you get to the traffic lights; **dann ging es nach Süden/ins Gebirge** (= *gingen wir/sie etc*) then we/they *etc* set off for the south/the mountains; **wohin geht es diesmal in Urlaub?** where are you going on holiday (*Brit*) or vacation (*US*) this time?

d 〔andere Wendungen〕 **es geht ein starker Wind** there's a strong wind (blowing); **es geht das Gerücht, dass er kündigen will** the rumour (*Brit*) or rumor (*US*) is going (a)round that he's going to hand in his notice; **es geht auf 9 Uhr** it is approaching 9 o'clock; **es ging schon auf den Winter** (*geh*) winter was approaching

♦ **es geht um** (= *betrifft*) **es geht um seinen Vertrag** it's about his contract; **worum gehts denn?** what's it about?; **ich weiß nicht, worum es geht** I don't know what this is about; **worum geht es in diesem Film/bei eurem Streit?** what is this film/your argument about?; **es geht um Leben und Tod** it's a matter of life and death; **es geht um meinen Ruf** my reputation is at stake; **es geht ihm nur um eins** he's only interested in one thing; **darum geht es mir nicht** (= *habe ich nicht gemeint*) that's not my point; (= *spielt keine Rolle für mich*) that doesn't matter to me; **es geht bei diesem Geschäft um 5 Millionen** (= *sind im Spiel*) the deal involves 5 million; (= *stehen auf dem Spiel*) 5 million are at stake in the deal; **wenn es ums Schauspielern geht, reicht ihm so schnell keiner das Wasser** when it comes to acting, there's nobody to touch him; **wenn es an die Kleinigkeiten geht, fängt der Ärger erst an** when it comes to the details the trouble starts

♦ **es geht nach jdm** it's up to sb; **wenn es nach mir ginge ...** if it were or was up to me ...; **es kann nicht immer alles nach dir gehen** you can't expect to have your own way all the time

4 – REFLEXIVES VERB

♦ **sich gehen** **es geht sich schlecht hier** it's not nice walking here; **mit den hochhackigen Schuhen geht es sich auf diesem steinigen Weg schlecht** it's not nice walking on this stony path in high heels; **in diesen Schuhen geht es sich bequem** these shoes are comfortable to walk in

Ge|hen NT **-s**, *no pl* (= *Zu-Fuß-Gehen*) walking; (= *Abschied*) leaving; (*Sport*) (= *Disziplin*) walking; (= *Wettbewerb*) walk

Ge|henk [gə'hɛŋk] NT **-(e)s**, **-e** (*Hist*) (*für Schwert*) sword belt; (*für Degen*) knife belt; (*für Pistolen*) gun belt

Ge|henk|te(r) [gə'hɛŋktə] MF *decl as adj* hanged man/woman; **die ~n** the hanged

ge|hen las|sen ▲ *ptp* **gehen lassen** or (*rare*) **gehen gelassen** *irreg* **VT** (= *in Ruhe lassen*) to leave alone **VR a** (= *sich nicht beherrschen*) to lose one's self-control, to lose control of oneself **b** (= *nachlässig sein*) to let oneself go

Ge|her ['ɡeːɐ] M **-s**, **-**, **Ge|he|rin** [-ərɪn] F **-**, **-nen** (*Sport*) walker; **er ist Weltmeister der ~** he's the world champion in walking

Ge|het|ze [gə'hɛtsə] NT **-s**, *no pl* (*inf*) **a** (= *Eile*) mad rush or dash **b** (*pej*: = *das Aufhetzen*) backbiting (*pej inf*)

ge|hetzt [gə'hɛtst] ADJ harassed → *auch* **hetzen**

ge|heu|er [gə'hɔyɐ] ADJ **nicht ~** (= beängstigend) scary (inf); (= spukhaft) eerie, creepy (inf), spooky; (= verdächtig) dubious, fishy; (= unwohl) uneasy; **es ist mir nicht ganz ~** it is scary (inf); it is eerie etc or gives me the creeps (inf); it seems a bit dubious or fishy to me; I feel uneasy about it; **mir ist es hier nicht ~** (= mir ist unheimlich) this place gives me the creeps (inf); (= mir ist unwohl) I have got an uneasy feeling about this place

Ge|heul [gə'hɔyl] NT **-(e)s**, no pl, **Ge|heu|le** [gə'hɔylə] NT **-s**, no pl howling

Geh|ge|rät NT Zimmer® (Brit), walker (US)

Geh|hil|fe M **-**, **-n** (Gestell etc) walking aid

Ge|hil|fe [gə'hɪlfə] M **-n**, **-n**, **Ge|hil|fin** ['-hɪlfɪn] F **-**, **-nen a** (dated: = Helfer) assistant, helper **b** (= kaufmännischer Gehilfe) trainee **c** (Jur) accomplice

Ge|hil|fen|brief M diploma

Ge|hil|fen|schaft [gə'hɪlfnʃaft] F **-**, no pl (Sw) aiding and abetting

Ge|hil|fin F → Gehilfe

Ge|hirn [gə'hɪrn] NT **-(e)s**, **-e** brain; (= Geist) mind; **das ist nicht seinem ~ entsprungen** (inf) he didn't think of that himself; **hast du denn kein ~ im Kopf?** (inf) haven't you got any brains or a brain in your head? (inf)

Ge|hirn- in cpds → auch Hirn-: **Ge|hirn|akro|ba|tik** F (inf) mental acrobatics pl; **ge|hirn|am|pu|tiert** [-lamputiɐt] ADJ (pej sl) dead from the neck up (inf); **Ge|hirn|blu|tung** F brain or cerebral haemorrhage (Brit) or hemorrhage (US); **Ge|hirn|chi|rurg(in)** M(F) brain surgeon; **Ge|hirn|chi|rur|gie** F brain surgery; **Ge|hirn|er|schüt|te|rung** F concussion; **Ge|hirn|er|wei|chung** [-lɛɐvaiçʊŋ] F **-**, **-en** (lit, fig inf) softening of the brain; **Ge|hirn|haut|ent|zün|dung** F (Med) meningitis; **Ge|hirn|kas|ten** M (inf) thick skull; **Ge|hirn|lap|pen** M (Anat) lobe of the brain, brain lobe; **Ge|hirn|nerv** M cranial nerve; **Ge|hirn|rin|de** F cerebral cortex; **Ge|hirn|schlag** M stroke; **Ge|hirn|schwund** M atrophy of the brain; **Ge|hirn|sub|stanz** F brain matter; **graue ~** grey (Brit) or gray (US) matter; **Ge|hirn|tod** M (Med) brain death; **ge|hirn|tot** ADJ **~ hirntot; Ge|hirn|tu|mor** M (Med) brain tumour (Brit) or tumor (US); **Ge|hirn|wä|sche** F brainwashing no pl; **jdn einer ~ unterziehen** to brainwash sb (inf); **Ge|hirn|zel|le** F brain cell

gehl [geːl] ADJ (dial) yellow

gehn [geːn] = gehen

ge|ho|ben [gə'hoːbn] ptp von heben ADJ Sprache, Ausdrucksweise elevated, lofty; (= anspruchsvoll) Ausstattung, Unterhaltungsprogramm sophisticated; Stellung senior, high; Stimmung elated; Ansprüche high; Mittelschicht upper; **ein Hotel der ~en Kategorie** a luxury hotel; **Güter des ~en Bedarfs** semi-luxuries; **~er Dienst** professional and executive levels of the civil service ADV **sich ~ ausdrücken** to use elevated language

Ge|höft [gə'hœft, gə'høːft] NT **-(e)s**, **-e** farm (-stead)

ge|hol|fen ptp von helfen

Ge|hol|per [gə'hɔlpɐ] NT **-s**, no pl, **Ge|hol|pe|re** [gə'hɔlpərə] NT **-s**, no pl bumping

Ge|hölz [gə'hœlts] NT **-es**, **-e** (geh) copse, coppice, spinney; (= Dickicht) undergrowth

Ge|hol|ze [gə'hɔltsə] NT **-s**, no pl (Sport inf) bad play; (unfair) rough play

Ge|hop|pel [gə'hɔpl] NT **-s**, no pl, **Ge|hop|pe|le** [gə'hɔplə] NT **-s**, no pl hopping

Ge|hör [gə'høːɐ] NT **-(e)s**, (rare) **-e a** (= Hörvermögen) hearing; (Mus) ear; **kein musikalisches ~ haben** to have no ear for music; **ein schlechtes ~ haben** to be hard of hearing, to have bad hearing; (Mus) to have a bad ear (for music); **nach dem ~ singen/spielen** to sing/play by ear; **absolutes ~** perfect pitch; **das ~ verlieren** to go or become deaf

b (geh: = Anhörung) **ein Musikstück zu ~ bringen** to perform a piece of music; **~ finden** to gain a hearing; **jdm ~/kein ~ schenken** to listen/not to listen to sb; **schenkt mir ~!** (old) lend me your ears (old); **um ~ bitten** to request a hearing; **sich** (dat) **~ verschaffen** to obtain a hearing; (= Aufmerksamkeit) to gain attention

Ge|hör|bil|dung F aural training

ge|hor|chen [gə'hɔrçn] ptp **gehorcht** VI to obey (jdm sb); (Wagen, Maschine etc) to respond (jdm/einer Sache to sb/sth); **seine Stimme gehorchte ihm nicht mehr** he lost control over his voice; **der Junge gehorcht überhaupt nicht** the boy is always disobedient, the boy is never obedient → Wort f

ge|hö|ren [gə'høːrən] ptp **gehört** VI **a** jdm ~ (= jds Eigentum sein) to belong to sb, to be sb's; **das Haus gehört ihm** he owns the house, the house belongs to him; **ihm gehört meine ganze Liebe** he is the only one I love, he has all my love; **ihr Herz gehört einem anderen** her heart belongs to another

b (= den richtigen Platz haben) to go; (Mensch) to belong; (= gehören) to deserve; **das gehört nicht hierher** (Gegenstand) it doesn't go here; (Vorschlag) it is irrelevant here; **das Buch gehört ins Regal** the book belongs in or goes on the bookshelves; **das gehört nicht zur Sache/zum Thema** that is off the point, that is irrelevant; **dieser Betrag gehört unter die Rubrik „Einnahmen"** this sum comes or belongs under the heading "credits"; **er gehört ins Bett** he should be in bed; **er gehört verprügelt** (dial) he needs a thrashing, he ought to be thrashed

c ~ zu (= zählen zu) to be amongst, to be one of; (= Bestandteil sein von) to be part of; (= Mitglied sein von) to belong to; **es gehört zu seiner Arbeit/zu seinen Pflichten** it's part of his work/one of his duties; **zur Familie ~** to be one of the family; **zu diesem Kleid gehört ein blauer Hut** (= ist Bestandteil von) a blue hat goes with or belongs to this dress; (= würde dazu passen) a blue hat would go with this dress; **zum Wild gehört einfach Rotwein** red wine is a must with venison

d ~ zu (= Voraussetzung sein, nötig sein) to be called for by; **zu dieser Arbeit gehört viel Konzentration** this work calls for or takes a lot of concentration; **dazu gehört Mut** that takes courage; **dazu gehört nicht viel** it doesn't take much; **dazu gehört (schon) einiges** or **etwas** that takes some doing (inf); **dazu gehört mehr** there's more to it than that

VR to be (right and) proper; **das gehört sich einfach nicht** that's just not done; **wie es sich gehört** (= wie es sich schickt) as is (right and) proper; (= wie es zünftig ist) comme il faut; **benimm dich, wie es sich gehört!** behave yourself properly

Ge|hör-: Ge|hör|feh|ler M **ein ~** a hearing defect, defective hearing; **Ge|hör|gang** M pl **-gänge** auditory canal

ge|hör|ge|schä|digt ADJ hearing-impaired

ge|hö|rig [gə'høːrɪç] ADJ **a** (geh) jdm/zu etw ~ belonging to sb/sth; **zu etw ~ sein** to belong to sth; **nicht zur Sache ~** irrelevant; **alle nicht zum Thema ~en Vorschläge** all suggestions not pertaining to or relevant to the topic

b attr (= gebührend) proper; (= notwendig auch) necessary, requisite; **er behandelt seinen Vater nicht mit dem ~en Respekt** he doesn't treat his father with proper respect or with the respect due to him

c (inf: = beträchtlich, groß) good attr, good and proper (inf), well and truly; **eine ~e Achtung vor jdm haben** to have a healthy respect for sb; **eine ~e Tracht Prügel** a good or proper thrashing

ADV (inf: = ordentlich) ausschimpfen severely; verwarnen sharply; **ich habs ihm ~ gegeben** (inf) I showed him what's what (inf), I gave him what for (inf); (mit Worten) I gave him a piece of my mind (inf); **jdm ~ Bescheid stoßen** to give sb a piece of one's mind (inf); **jdn ~ verprügeln** to give

sb a good beating; **ich habe mich in ihm ~ getäuscht** I was totally wrong about him; **da hast du dich ~ getäuscht!** you're badly or terribly mistaken; **sich ~ verspäten** to be terribly late

ge|hör|los ADJ (form) deaf; **~ sein** to have no hearing

Ge|hör|lo|sen|schu|le F (form) school for the deaf

Ge|hör|lo|se(r) [gə'høːɐloːzə] MF decl as adj (form) deaf person

Ge|hörn [gə'hœrn] NT **-(e)s**, **-e** (Hunt) antlers pl, set of antlers

Ge|hör|nerv M auditory nerve

ge|hörnt [gə'hœrnt] ADJ horned; (= mit Geweih) antlered; **ein ~er Ehemann** (hum inf) a cuckold; **der Gehörnte** Satan

ge|hor|sam [gə'hoːɐzaːm] ADJ obedient; **Ihr ~ster Diener** (old) your most obedient servant (old), yours obediently (old); ADV obediently; **melde ~st** reporting, sir; **ich bitte ~st** (old) I respectfully beg → melden

Ge|hor|sam [gə'hoːɐzaːm] M **-s**, no pl obedience; **jdm den ~ verweigern** to refuse to obey sb

Ge|hor|sam|keit F **-**, no pl obedience

Ge|hor|sams-: Ge|hor|sams|pflicht F duty to obey; **Ge|hor|sams|ver|wei|ge|rung** F (Mil) insubordination, refusal to obey orders

Ge|hör-: Ge|hör|schutz M ear protectors pl, earmuffs pl; **Ge|hör|sinn** M sense of hearing; **Ge|hör|sturz** M (temporary) loss of hearing

geh|ren ['geːrən] VTI (Tech) to mitre (Brit), to miter (US)

Geh|rock M frock coat

Geh|rung ['geːrʊŋ] F **-**, **-en** (Tech) (= das Gehren) mitring; (= Eckfuge) mitre (Brit) or miter (US) joint

Geh|steig M pavement (Brit), sidewalk (US)

Geh|stö|rung F problem (with) walking, impaired walking

Geht|nicht|mehr ['geːtnɪçtmeːɐ] NT **trinken/tanzen bis zum ~** to drink/dance till one drops (inf); **sich bis zum ~ verschulden** to get up to one's ears in debt (inf)

Ge|hu|pe [gə'huːpə] NT **-s**, no pl (inf) hooting, honking

Ge|hus|te [gə'huːstə] NT **-s**, no pl (inf) coughing

Geh-: Geh|ver|band M (Med) walking cast; **Geh|ver|such** M **a** (von Kind, nach Unfall, Verletzung) attempt at walking; **erste ~e** first attempts at walking **b** (fig) tentative step; **Geh|wa|gen** M wheeled Zimmer® (Brit), walker (US); **Geh|weg** M footpath

Gei [gai] F **-**, **-en** (Naut) stay

Gei|er ['gaiɐ] M **-s**, **-** (lit, fig) vulture; **weiß der ~!** (inf) God knows!

Gei|fer ['gaifɐ] M **-s**, no pl slaver; (= Schaum vor dem Mund) froth, foam; (fig pej) venom; **seinen ~ (gegen etw) verspritzen** to pour out one's venom (on sth)

gei|fern ['gaifɐn] VI to slaver; (= Schaum vor dem Mund haben) to foam at the mouth; (fig pej) to be full of spite; **vor Wut ~** to be spitting with rage; **vor Neid ~** to be drooling with envy; **gegen jdn/etw ~** to revile sb/sth

Gei|ge ['gaigə] F **-**, **-n** violin, fiddle (inf); **die erste/zweite ~ spielen** (lit) to play first/second violin; (fig) to call the tune/play second fiddle; **nach jds ~ tanzen** (fig) to dance to sb's tune

gei|gen ['gaign] VI to play the violin, to (play the) fiddle (inf) VT Lied to play on a/the violin or fiddle (inf); **jdm die Meinung ~** (inf) to give sb a piece of one's mind (inf)

Gei|gen-: Gei|gen|bau M , no pl violin-making; **Gei|gen|bau|er(in)** M(F) pl **-bauer(innen)** violin-maker; **Gei|gen|bo|gen** M violin bow; **Gei|gen|harz** NT rosin; **Gei|gen|kas|ten** M **a** violin case **b** **Geigenkästen** PL (hum inf) clodhoppers pl (inf); **Gei|gen|sai|te** F violin string; **Gei|gen|strich** M stroke of the violin bow

Gei|ger ['gaigɐ] M **-s, -, Gei|ge|rin** [-ərɪn] F **-, -nen** violinist, fiddler (*inf*); **erster ~** first violin

Gei|ger|zäh|ler M Geiger counter

geil [gail] ADJ **a** randy (*Brit*), horny; (*pej*: = *lüstern*) lecherous; **auf jdn ~ sein** to be lusting after sb **b** (*Agr*) Boden rich, fertile; (= *üppig*) luxuriant; *Vegetation* rank **c** (*sl*: = *prima*) brilliant (*inf*), wicked (*inf*); **der Typ ist ~** he's a cool guy (*inf*) ADV **a** (= *lüstern*) lecherously; **jdn ~ ansehen** to give sb a lecherous look **b** (*sl*: = *prima*) spielen, tanzen brilliantly; **~ aussehen** to look cool (*inf*)

Geil|heit F **-, no pl a** randiness (*Brit*), horniness; (*pej*: = *Lüsternheit*) lecherousness **b** (*Agr*) (von Boden) richness, fertility; (= *Üppigkeit*) luxuriance; (von Vegetation) rankness

Gei|sel ['gaizl] F **-, -n** hostage; **jdn als ~ nehmen** to take sb hostage; **~n stellen** to produce hostages

Gei|sel-: Gei|sel|be|frei|ung F (= *Befreiungsaktion*) freeing of the hostages; (= *Freilassung*) release of the hostages; **Gei|sel|dra|ma** NT hostage crisis; **Gei|sel|gangs|ter** M (*Press sl*) hostage taker; **Gei|sel|haft** F captivity (as a hostage); **Gei|sel|nah|me** [-na:mə] F **-, -n** hostage-taking; **mit ~ der Besatzung** with the crew taken hostage; **Gei|sel|neh|mer(in)** M(F) hostage-taker

Gei|ser ['gaizɐ] M **-s, -** geyser

Gei|sha ['ge:ʃa] F **-, -s** geisha (girl)

Geiß [gais] F **-, -en a** (*S Ger, Aus, Sw*: = *Ziege*) (nanny-)goat **b** (von Rehwild etc) doe

Geiß-: Geiß|bart M (*Bot*) goatsbeard; (*esp S Ger inf*: = *Spitzbart*) goatee (beard); **Geiß|blatt** NT honeysuckle, woodbine; **Geiß|bock** M billy goat

Gei|ßel ['gaisl] F **-, -n a** (*lit, fig*) scourge; (*dial*: = *Peitsche*) whip **b** (*Biol*) flagellum

Gei|ßel|bru|der M (*Eccl*) flagellator

gei|ßeln ['gaisln] VT **a** (= *peitschen*) to whip, to flagellate (*esp Rel*) **b** (*fig* = *kasteien*) to chastise; (= *anprangern*) to castigate; (= *heimsuchen*) to scourge

Gei|ßel|tier|chen NT flagellate

Gei|ße|lung F **-, -en a** (= *das Peitschen*) whipping, flagellation (*esp Rel*) **b** (= *Kasteiung*) chastisement; (= *Anprangerung*) castigation

Geiß-: Geiß|fuß M (= *Gehreisen*) parting tool; (= *Brechstange*) crowbar; **Geiß|hirt(in)** M(F) goatherd; **Geiß|kitz** NT (female) kid; **Geiß|lein** ['gaislain] NT **-s, -** kid

Geiß|ler ['gaislɐ] M **-s, -** (*Rel*) flagellator

Geiß|lung ['gaislʊn] F **-, -en** = Geißelung

Geist [gaist] M **-(e)s, -er a** no pl (= *Denken, Vernunft*) mind; **der menschliche ~, des Menschen** the human mind; **~ und Materie** mind and matter; **mit ~ begabt** endowed with a mind; **„Phänomenologie des ~es"** "Phenomenology of the Spirit" **b** (*Rel*: = *Seele, außerirdisches Wesen*) spirit; (= *Gespenst*) ghost; **~ und Körper** mind and body; **seinen ~ aufgeben** or **aushauchen** (*liter, iro*) to give up the ghost; **der ~ ist willig, aber das Fleisch ist schwach** (*prov*) the spirit is willing, but the flesh is weak; **der Heilige ~** the Holy Ghost or Spirit; **der ~ Gottes** the Spirit of God; **der böse ~** the Evil One; **der ~ der Finsternis** the Prince of Darkness; **gute/böse ~er** good/evil spirits; **die Stunde der ~er** the witching hour; **der gute ~ des Hauses** (*geh*) the moving spirit in the household; **von allen guten ~ern verlassen sein** (*inf*) to have taken leave of one's senses (*inf*); **jdm auf den ~ gehen** (*inf*) to get on sb's nerves; **in dem Schloss gehen ~er um** the castle is haunted, the castle is walked by ghosts (*liter*) → **empfehlen** VT **c** (no pl: = *Intellekt*) intellect, mind; (*fig*: = *Denker, Genie*) mind; **~ haben** to have a good mind or intellect; (*Witz*) to show wit; **einen regen/leb-**

haften ~ haben to have an active/lively mind; **ein Mann von großem ~** a man of great intellect, a man with a great mind; **die Rede zeugte nicht von großem ~** the speech was not particularly brilliant; **das geht über meinen ~** (*inf*) that's way over my head (*inf*), that's beyond me (*inf*); **hier scheiden sich die ~er** this is the parting of the ways; **seinen ~ anstrengen** (*inf*) to use one's brains (*inf*); **sie sind verwandte ~er** they are kindred spirits; **kleine ~er** (*iro*: *ungebildet*) people of limited intellect; (*kleinmütig*) small-minded or petty-minded people → **unruhig** **d** no pl (= *Wesen, Sinn, Gesinnung*) spirit; **in kameradschaftlichem ~** in a spirit of comradeship; **in diesem Büro herrscht ein kollegialer ~** this office has a friendly atmosphere; **in seinem/ihrem ~** in his/her spirit; **in jds ~ handeln** to act in the spirit of sb; **der ~ der Zeit/der russischen Sprache** the spirit or genius (*liter*) of the times/of the Russian language; **nach dem ~ des Gesetzes, nicht nach seinem Buchstaben gehen** to go by the spirit rather than the letter of the law; **daran zeigt sich, wes ~es Kind er ist** that (just) shows what kind of person he is **e** no pl (= *Vorstellung*) mind; **etw im ~(e) vor sich sehen** to see sth in one's mind's eye; **sich im ~(e) als etw/als jd/an einem Ort sehen** to see or picture oneself as sth/as sb/in a place; **im ~e bin ich bei euch** I am with you in spirit, my thoughts are with you

Geis|ter-: Geis|ter|bahn F ghost train; **Geis|ter|be|schwö|rer** [-bəʃvø:rɐ] M **-s, -, Geis|ter|be|schwö|re|rin** [-ərɪn] F **-, -nen a** (*der Geister herbeiruft*) necromancer **b** (*der Geister austreibt*) exorcist; **Geis|ter|be|schwö|rung** F **a** (= *Herbeirufung*) necromancy **b** (= *Austreibung*) exorcism; **Geis|ter|bild** NT (*TV*) ghost image; **~er** ghosting no pl; **Geis|ter|er|schei|nung** F (ghostly) apparition; (*im Traum etc*) vision; **eine ~ haben** to see a ghost or an apparition; (*im Traum etc*) to have a vision; **Geis|ter|fah|rer(in)** M(F) (*inf*) ghost-driver (*US inf*), person driving the wrong way on the motorway; **Geis|ter|ge|schich|te** F ghost story; **Geis|ter|glau|be** M belief in the supernatural; **geis|ter|haft** ADJ ghostly no adv, unearthly no adv; (= *übernatürlich*) supernatural; **Geis|ter|hand** F **wie von** or **durch ~** as if by magic; **Geis|ter|haus** NT (= *Spukhaus*) haunted house **b** (*Rel*: = *Sitz von Geistern*) spirit house

geis|tern ['gaistɐn] VI aux sein to wander like a ghost; **der Gedanke geisterte in seinem Hirn** or **durch sein Hirn** the thought haunted him or his mind; **Lichter geisterten hinter den Fenstern** ghostly lights shone through the windows; **Schatten geisterten an der Wand** ghostly or ghostlike shadows played on the wall

Geis|ter-: Geis|ter|se|her(in) M(F) visionary; **Geis|ter|stadt** F ghost town; **Geis|ter|stim|me** F ghostly voice; **Geis|ter|stun|de** F witching hour; **Geis|ter|welt** F spirit world; **Geis|ter|zug** M empty train (speeding along)

Geis|tes-: geis|tes|ab|we|send ADJ absent-minded ADV absent-mindedly; **~ blicken** to have an absent-minded look on one's face; **jdn ~ ansehen** to give sb an absent-minded look; **Geis|tes|ab|we|sen|heit** F absent-mindedness; **Geis|tes|an|stren|gung** F mental effort; **Geis|tes|ar|beit** F brainwork (*inf*); **Geis|tes|ar|bei|ter(in)** M(F) brain-worker (*inf*); **Geis|tes|ar|mut** F dullness, intellectual poverty; (von Mensch auch) poverty of mind; **Geis|tes|art** F disposition; **Geis|tes|blitz** M brainwave (*Brit*), brainstorm (*US*), flash of inspiration; **Geis|tes|ga|be** F intellectual gift; **Geis|tes|ge|gen|wart** F presence of mind; **geis|tes|ge|gen|wär|tig** ADJ quick-witted ADV quick-wittedly; **~ duckte er sich unter das Steuer** with great presence of mind he ducked below the steering wheel; **Geis|tes|ge|schich|te** F, no pl history of ideas; **die ~ der Goethezeit** the intellectual history of Goethe's

time; **geis|tes|ge|schicht|lich** ADJ relating to the history of ideas pred (*nachgestellt*); **geis|tes|ge|stört** ADJ mentally disturbed or (*stärker*) deranged; **du bist wohl ~!** (*inf*) are you out of your mind? (*inf*); **Geis|tes|ge|stör|te(r)** MF decl as adj a mentally disturbed/deranged person; **Geis|tes|ge|stört|heit** F **-, no pl** mental instability or (*stärker*) derangement; **Geis|tes|grö|ße** F **a** no pl (= *Genialität*) greatness of mind **b** (= *genialer Mensch*) great mind, genius; **Geis|tes|hal|tung** F attitude of mind; **geis|tes|krank** ADJ mentally ill; **Geis|tes|kran|ke(r)** MF decl as adj mentally ill person; **die ~n** the mentally ill; **Geis|tes|krank|heit** F mental illness; (= *Wahnsinn*) insanity; **geis|tes|schwach** ADJ feebleminded; **Geis|tes|stö|rung** F mental disturbance or (*stärker*) derangement; **Geis|tes|ver|fas|sung** F frame or state of mind; **geis|tes|ver|wandt** ADJ spiritually akin (*mit* to); **die beiden sind ~** they are kindred spirits; **Geis|tes|ver|wand|te(r)** MF decl as adj kindred spirit; **Geis|tes|ver|wandt|schaft** F spiritual affinity (*mit* to); **Geis|tes|ver|wir|rung** F mental confusion; **Geis|tes|welt** F (*liter*) world of thought; **Geis|tes|wis|sen|schaft** F arts subject; **die ~en** the arts; (als Studium) the humanities; **Geis|tes|wis|sen|schaft|ler(in)** M(F) arts scholar; (= *Student*) arts student; **geis|tes|wis|sen|schaft|lich** ADJ Fach, Studium, Fakultät arts attr; **~e Psychologie** humanistic psychology ADV **er ist mehr ~ orientiert** he is more orientated toward(s) the arts; **Geis|tes|zu|stand** M mental condition; **jdn auf seinen ~ untersuchen** to give sb a psychiatric examination; **du musst dich mal auf deinen ~ untersuchen lassen** (*inf*) you need your head examined (*inf*)

Geist-: geist|feind|lich ADJ anti-intellectual; **Geist|feind|lich|keit** F anti-intellectualism; **Geist|hei|ler(in)** M(F) faith healer

geis|tig ['gaistɪç] ADJ **a** (= *unkörperlich*) Wesen, Liebe, Existenz spiritual; **ein ~es Band** a spiritual bond; **~-moralisch** spiritual and moral; **~-moralische Erneuerung** spiritual and moral renewal; **~-seelisch** mental and spiritual **b** (= *intellektuell*) intellectual; (*Psych*) mental; **~e Arbeit** intellectual work, brainwork (*inf*); **~e Nahrung** intellectual nourishment; **~er Diebstahl** plagiarism no pl; **~es Eigentum** intellectual property; **der ~e Vater** the spiritual father **c** (= *imaginär*) **jds ~es Auge** sb's mind's eye; **etw vor seinem ~en Auge sehen** to see sth in one's mind's eye **d** attr (= *alkoholisch*) spirituous ADV (= *intellektuell*) intellectually; (*Med*) mentally; **~ anspruchsvoll/anspruchslos** intellectually demanding/undemanding, highbrow/lowbrow (*inf*); **~ nicht mehr folgen können** to be unable to understand or follow any more; **~ behindert/zurückgeblieben** mentally handicapped or deficient or disabled/retarded

Geis|tig|keit F **-, no pl** intellectuality

geis|tig-see|lisch ADJ mental and spiritual ADV mentally and spiritually

geist|lich ['gaistlɪç] ADJ Angelegenheit, Einstellung, Führer, Beistand spiritual; (= *religiös*) Drama, Dichtung, Schrift religious; Musik religious, sacred; (= *kirchlich*) ecclesiastical; Gewand ecclesiastical, clerical; **~es Amt** religious office; **~er Orden** religious order; **~es Recht** canon law; **der ~e Stand** the clergy; **die ~en Weihen empfangen** to take holy orders

Geist|li|che ['gaistlɪçə] F decl as adj woman priest; (von Freikirchen) woman minister

Geist|li|che(r) ['gaistlɪçə] M decl as adj clergyman; (= *Priester*) priest; (= *Pastor, von Freikirchen*) minister; (= *Gefängnisgeistliche, Militärgeistliche etc*) chaplain

Geist|lich|keit F **-, no pl** clergy; (= *Priester*) priesthood; (= *Pastoren; von Freikirchen*) ministry

Geist-: geist|los ADJ (= *dumm*) stupid; (= *langweilig*) dull; (= *einfallslos*) unimaginative; (= *trivial*) inane; **Geist|lo|sig|keit** F **-, -en a** no *pl* (= *Dummheit*) stupidity; (= *Langweiligkeit*) dullness; (= *Einfallslosigkeit*) unimaginativeness; (= *Trivialität*) inanity **b** (= *geistlose Äußerung*) inane remark; **geist|reich** ADJ (= *witzig*) witty; (= *klug*) intelligent; (= *einfallsreich*) ingenious; *Beschäftigung, Gespräch, Unterhaltung* intellectually stimulating; (= *schlagfertig*) quick-witted; **das war sehr ~** (*iro*) that was bright (*iro*); **geist|-sprü|hend** ADJ *attr* (*geh*) scintillatingly *or* brilliantly witty; **geist|tö|tend** ADJ soul-destroying; **geist|voll** ADJ *Mensch, Äußerung* wise, sage; *Buch, Gespräch, Beschäftigung* intellectual

Gei|tau ['gaitau] NT (*Naut*) stay

Geiz [gaits] M **-es**, *no pl* meanness (*esp Brit*), stinginess (*inf*); (= *Sparsamkeit, Knauserei auch*) miserliness

gei|zen ['gaitsn] VI to be mean (*esp Brit*) *or* stingy (*inf*); (= *sparsam, knausrig sein auch*) to be miserly; (*mit Worten, Zeit*) to be sparing; **mit etw ~** to be mean *etc* with sth; **sie geizt nicht mit ihren Reizen** she doesn't mind showing what she's got; **nach etw ~** (*old*) to crave (for) sth

Geiz|hals M miser

gei|zig ['gaitsɪç] ADJ mean (*esp Brit*), stingy (*inf*); (= *sparsam, knausrig auch*) miserly; (*mit Geld auch*) tight-fisted; „**Der Geizige**" "The Miser"

Geiz|kra|gen M (*inf*) skinflint

Ge|jam|mer [gə'jame] NT **-s**, *no pl* moaning (and groaning); (*inf*: = *Klagen auch*) bellyaching (*inf*), griping (*inf*)

Ge|jauch|ze [gə'jauxtsə] NT **-s**, *no pl* jubilation, exultation (*liter*), rejoicing

Ge|jau|le [gə'jaulə] NT **-s**, *no pl* howling; (*von Tieren auch*) yowling

Ge|joh|le [gə'jo:lə] NT **-s**, *no pl* howling; (*von Betrunkenen etc*) caterwauling

gek. *abbr von* **gekürzt** abbreviated

ge|kannt *ptp von* **kennen**

Ge|kei|fe [gə'kaifə] NT **-s**, *no pl* carping, nagging

Ge|ki|cher [gə'kɪçe] NT **-s**, *no pl* giggling, tittering; (*spöttisch*) sniggering, snickering

Ge|kläff [gə'klɛf] NT **-(e)s**, *no pl* yapping (*auch fig pej*), yelping

Ge|klap|per [gə'klape] NT **-s**, *no pl* clatter(ing)

Ge|klat|sche [gə'klatʃə] NT **-s**, *no pl* (*inf*) **a** (*von Händen*) clapping **b** (*pej*: = *Tratscherei*) gossiping, tittle-tattling (*Brit inf*)

ge|klei|det [gə'klaidət] *ptp von* **kleiden** ADJ **a** (= *angezogen*) **gut/schlecht ~** well/badly dressed; **korrekt ~** correctly dressed; **weiß/ schwarz ~ sein** to be dressed in white/black; **in Lumpen ~** dressed in rags **b** (*fig*) **eine in freundliche Worte ~e Kränkung** an insult cloaked in friendly words (*form*), a backhanded compliment → *auch* **kleiden**

Ge|klim|per [gə'klɪmpe] NT **-s**, *no pl* (*inf*) (= *Klaviergeklimper*) tinkling; (*stümperhaft*) plonking (*inf*); (= *Banjogeklimper etc*) twanging; (*von Geld*) jingling; (*von Wimpern*) fluttering

Ge|klin|gel [gə'klɪŋl] NT **-s**, *no pl* ringing; (*von Motor*) pinking, knocking

Ge|klirr [gə'klɪr] NT **-(e)s**, *no pl*, **Ge|klir|re** [gə'klɪrə] NT **-s**, *no pl* clinking; (*von Gläsern auch*) tinkling; (*von Fensterscheiben*) rattling; (*von Ketten etc*) clanging, clanking; (*von Waffen*) clashing; (*von Lautsprecher, Mikrofon*) crackling; (*von Eis*) crunching

ge|klom|men *ptp von* **klimmen**

Ge|klön [gə'klø:n] NT **-(e)s**, *no pl*, **Ge|klö|ne** [gə'klø:nə] NT **-s**, *no pl* (*inf*) natter (*inf*)

Ge|klop|fe [gə'klɔpfə] NT **-s**, *no pl* knocking; (*von Fleisch, Teppich*) beating; (*des Spechts*) tapping, hammering; (*des Motors*) knocking, pinking

ge|klun|gen *ptp von* **klingen**

Ge|knall [gə'knal] NT **-(e)s**, *no pl*, **Ge|knal|le** [gə'knalə] NT **-s**, *no pl* banging; (*von Tür auch*) slamming; (*bei Feuerwerk*) banging; (*von Pfropfen*) popping; (*von Peitsche*) cracking; **das ununterbrochene ~ von Schüssen** the constant sound of shots being fired

Ge|knarr [gə'knar] NT **-(e)s**, *no pl*, **Ge|knar|re** [gə'knarə] NT **-s**, *no pl* creaking; (*von Stimme*) rasping, grating

Ge|knat|ter [gə'knate] NT **-s**, *no pl* (*von Motorrad*) roaring; (*von Presslufthammer*) hammering; (*von Maschinengewehr*) rattling, chattering; (*von Schüssen*) rattling (out)

ge|knickt [gə'knɪkt] ADJ (*inf*) glum, dejected → *auch* **knicken**

Ge|knickt|heit F **-**, *no pl* (*inf*) dejection

ge|knif|fen *ptp von* **kneifen**

Ge|knip|se [gə'knɪpsə] NT **-s**, *no pl* (*inf*) snap-taking (*inf*)

Ge|knis|ter [gə'knɪstə] NT **-s**, *no pl* crackling, crackle; (*von Papier, Seide*) rustling

ge|knüp|pelt [gə'knʏplt] ADV **~ voll** (*inf*) packed (out), chock-a-block (*inf*) → *auch* **knüppeln**

ge|kom|men *ptp von* **kommen**

ge|konnt [gə'kɔnt] *ptp von* **können** ADJ masterly **ADV** in a masterly fashion

Ge|krächz [gə'krɛçts] NT **-es**, *no pl*, **Ge|kräch|ze** [gə'krɛçtsə] NT **-s**, *no pl* croaking

Ge|kra|kel [gə'kra:kl] NT **-s**, *no pl* (*inf*) scrawl, scribble; (= *Krakeln*) scrawling, scribbling

ge|kränkt [gə'krɛŋkt] *ptp von* **kränken** ADJ hurt, offended (*über +acc* at, by); *Stolz* injured → *auch* **kränken**

Ge|krat|ze [gə'kratsə] NT **-s**, *no pl* scratching

Ge|kreisch [gə'kraiʃ] NT **-(e)s**, *no pl*, **Ge|krei|sche** [gə'kraiʃə] NT **-s**, *no pl* screeching; (*von Vogel auch*) squawking; (*von Reifen, Bremsen auch*) squealing; (*von Mensch auch*) shrieking, squealing

Ge|kreu|zig|te(r) [gə'krɔytsɪçtə] MF *decl as adj* crucified (person); **Jesus der ~** Jesus the Crucified

Ge|krie|che [gə'kri:çə] NT **-s**, *no pl* (*inf*) crawling, creeping

ge|kri|schen (*old, hum*) *ptp von* **kreischen**

Ge|krit|zel [gə'krɪtsl] NT **-s**, *no pl* **a** scribbling, scrawling; (= *Männchenmalen*) doodling **b** (= *Gekritzeltes*) scribble, scrawl; doodle

ge|kro|chen *ptp von* **kriechen**

Ge|krö|se [gə'krø:zə] NT **-s**, **-** (*Anat*) mesentery; (= *Kutteln*) tripe; (= *essbare Eingeweide*) chitterlings *pl*; (*von Geflügel*) giblets *pl*

ge|krümmt [gə'krʏmt] *ptp von* **krümmen** ADJ curved; (= *hakenartig*) hooked; (= *gebogen, gebeugt*) bent; (= *verzogen, verworfen*) warped → *auch* **krümmen**

ge|kühlt [gə'ky:lt] **ADJ** *Getränke* chilled; *Räume* air-conditioned **ADV** **etw ~ servieren** to serve sth chilled → *auch* **kühlen**

ge|küns|telt [gə'kʏnstlt] **ADJ** artificial; *Sprache, Benehmen auch* affected **ADV** affectedly; **er spricht sehr ~** his speech is very affected; **~ la-chen** to give an affected laugh, to laugh affectedly

Gel [ge:l] NT **-s, -e** gel

Ge|la|ber [gə'la:bɐ] NT **-s**, *no pl*, **Ge|la|be|re** [gə'la:bərə] NT **-s**, *no pl* (*inf*) jabbering (*inf*), prattling (*inf*)

Ge|läch|ter [gə'lɛçtɐ] NT **-s, -** laughter; **in ~ aus-brechen** to burst into laughter, to burst out laughing; **sich dem ~ aussetzen** to make oneself a laughing stock, to expose oneself to ridicule; **jdn dem ~ preisgeben** (*geh*) to make sb a laughing stock

ge|lack|mei|ert [gə'lakmaiɐt] ADJ (*inf*) duped, conned (*inf*); **~ sein, der Gelackmeierte sein** (= *hintergangen worden sein*) to have been duped *or* conned (*inf*); (= *dumm dastehen*) to look a right fool (*Brit inf*), to look like a complete fool

ge|la|den [gə'la:dn] *ptp von* **laden**[1] *von* **laden**[2] ADJ **a** loaded; (*Phys, fig*) *Atmosphäre* charged;

(*inf*: = *wütend*) (hopping (*inf*)) mad; **der Chef war mächtig ~** (*inf*) the boss was absolutely hopping mad (*inf*); **mit Spannung ~** charged with tension **b** **~ haben** (*inf*) to be tanked up (*inf*)

Ge|la|ge [gə'la:gə] NT **-s, -** feast, banquet; (= *Zechgelage*) carouse

ge|la|gert [gə'la:gɐt] ADJ **ähnlich ~** similar; **in anders/ähnlich/besonders ~en Fällen** in different/similar/exceptional cases; **anders ~ sein** to be different → *auch* **lagern**

ge|lähmt [gə'lɛ:mt] ADJ (*lit, fig*) paralysed; **er ist seit seinem Unfall ~** his accident left him paralysed, he's been paralysed since his accident; **er hat ~e Beine** his legs are paralysed, he's paralysed in the legs; **er ist an beiden Beinen ~** he is paralysed in both legs; **er ist von der Hüfte abwärts ~** he is paralysed from the waist down; **vor Angst wie ~ sein** to be petrified, to be paralysed with fear → *auch* **lähmen**

Ge|län|de [gə'lɛndə] NT **-s, -**, **-a** (= *Land*) open country; (*Mil*: = *Gebiet, Terrain*) ground; **offenes ~** open country; **schwieriges ~** difficult terrain *or* country; **das ~ erkunden** (*Mil*) to reconnoitre (*Brit*), to reconnoiter (*US*) **b** (= *Gebiet*) area **c** (= *Grundstück*) site; (= *Fabrikgelände, Schulgelände etc*) grounds *pl*; (= *Baugelände*) site; (= *Ausstellungsgelände*) exhibition centre (*Brit*) *or* center (*US*)

Ge|län|de-: **Ge|län|de|fahrt** F cross-country drive; **für ~en gut geeignet** well-suited to cross-country driving *or* to driving cross-country; **Ge|län|de|fahr|zeug** NT cross-country *or* all-terrain vehicle; **ge|län|de|gän|gig** ADJ *Fahrzeug* suitable for cross-country driving; **Ge|län|de|gän|gig|keit** [-gɛŋkait] F **-**, *no pl* suitability for cross-country driving; **Ge|län|de|lauf** M cross-country run; (= *Wettbewerb*) cross-country race; **er macht gerne ~e** he enjoys cross-country running; **Ge|län|de|marsch** M cross-country march; **einen ~ machen** to march cross-country

Ge|län|der [gə'lɛndɐ] NT **-s, -** railing(s *pl*); (= *Treppengeländer*) banister(s *pl*)

Ge|län|de-: **Ge|län|de|rad** NT all-terrain bike, mountain bike; **Ge|län|de|rei|fen** M (*Mot*) off-road *or* cross-country tyre (*Brit*) *or* tire (*US*); **Ge|län|de|ren|nen** NT cross-country race; **Ge|län|de|ritt** M cross-country riding; **ein ~** a cross-country ride; **für ~e ungeeignet** unsuitable for cross-country riding; **Ge|län|de|spiel** NT scouting game; (*Mil*) field exercise; **Ge|län|de|übung** F field exercise; **Ge|län|de|wa|gen** M cross-country *or* general-purpose vehicle

ge|lang *pret von* **gelingen**

ge|lan|gen [gə'laŋən] *ptp* **gelangt** VI *aux sein* **an/auf** *etc* **etw** (*acc*)**/zu etw ~** (*lit, fig*) to reach sth; (*fig*: *mit Mühe*) to attain sth; (= *erwerben*) to acquire sth; **zum Ziel ~** to reach one's goal; (*fig auch*) to attain one's end *or* goal; **in jds Besitz ~** to come into sb's possession; **in die richtigen/falschen Hände ~** to fall into the right/wrong hands; **zu Reichtum ~** to come into a fortune; (*durch Arbeit*) to make a *or* one's fortune; **zu Ruhm ~** to achieve *or* acquire fame; **zur Reife ~** to reach *or* attain (*form*) maturity; **zu einer Überzeugung ~** to become convinced; **zum Abschluss ~** (*form*) to reach a conclusion; **zur Abstimmung ~** (*form*) to be put to the vote; **zur Durchführung/Aufführung ~** (*form*) to be carried out/performed; **zur Auszahlung ~** (*form*) to be paid out; **an die Macht ~** to come to power

ge|lang|weilt [gə'laŋvailt] **ADJ** bored **ADV** **die Zuschauer saßen ~ da** the audience sat there looking bored; **er hörte ihr ~ zu** he was bored listening to her → *auch* **langweilen**

ge|lappt [gə'lapt] ADJ *Blatt* lobate, lobed

Ge|lär|me [gə'lɛrmə] NT **-s**, *no pl* (*inf*) = **Lärm**

ge|las|sen [gə'lasn] *ptp von* **lassen** **ADJ** (= *ruhig*) calm; (= *gefasst auch*) cool, composed *no adv*; **~ bleiben** to keep calm *or* cool **ADV** calmly;

etw ~ hinnehmen to take sth calmly *or* with composure; **~ blicken** to have a calm look on one's face; **sie blickte mich ~ an** she looked at me calmly

Ge|las|sen|heit F **-**, *no pl* (= *Ruhe*) calmness; (= *Gefasstheit auch*) coolness, composure

Ge|la|ti|ne [ʒelaˈtiːnə] F **-**, *no pl* gelatine

ge|la|ti|nie|ren [ʒelatiˈniːrən] *ptp* **gelatiniert** VTI to gelatinize

Ge|läuf [gəˈlɔyf] NT **-(e)s, -e** **a** (*Hunt*) tracks *pl* (*of game birds*) **b** (*von Pferderennbahn*) turf

Ge|lau|fe [gəˈlaufə] NT **-s**, *no pl* (*inf*) running about; **das war ein ~** that was a real run-around (*inf*)

ge|lau|fen *ptp von* **laufen**

ge|läu|fig [gəˈlɔyfɪç] ADJ (= *üblich*) common; (= *vertraut*) familiar; (*dated*: = *redegewandt*) fluent; **eine ~e Redensart** a common saying; **das ist mir nicht ~** I'm not familiar with that, that isn't familiar to me

Ge|läu|fig|keit F **-**, *no pl* (= *Häufigkeit*) frequency; (= *Leichtigkeit*) ease; (*dated*: = *Redegewandtheit*) fluency

ge|launt [gəˈlaunt] ADJ *pred* **gut ~** good-tempered, good-humoured (*Brit*), good-humored (*US*); (*vorübergehend*) in a good mood; **schlecht ~** bad-tempered, ill-humoured (*Brit*), ill-humored (*US*); (*vorübergehend*) in a bad mood; **wie ist er ~?** what sort of mood is he in?

Ge|läut [gəˈlɔyt] NT **-(e)s**, *no pl*, **Ge|läu|te** [gəˈlɔytə] NT **-s**, *no pl* **a** (= *Glockenläuten*) ringing; (*harmonisch auch*) chiming (= *Läutwerk*) chime **b** (*Hunt*) baying

gelb [gɛlp] ADJ yellow; (*bei Verkehrsampel*) amber; **die Blätter werden ~** the leaves are turning (yellow); **~er Fleck** (*Anat*) yellow spot; **Gelbe Rübe** carrot; **die ~e Rasse** the yellow race, the Orientals *pl*; **die ~e Gefahr** (*Pol pej*) the yellow peril; **der Gelbe Fluss** the Yellow River; **das Gelbe Meer** the Yellow Sea; **~e Karte** (*Ftbl*) yellow card; **die Gelben Seiten** the Yellow Pages®; **die ~e Post** the postal service (*excluding telecommunications and banking services*); **~er Sack** yellow bag (*for the collection of recyclable packaging material*); **~ vor Neid** green with envy; **Löwenzahn blüht ~** the dandelion has a yellow flower → **grün**

Gelb [gɛlp] NT **-s, -** *or* (*inf*) **-s** yellow; (*von Verkehrsampel*) amber; **die Ampel stand auf ~** the lights were amber, the lights had turned amber; **bei ~ stehen bleiben** to stop on amber

Gelb|be(r) [ˈgɛlbə] MF *decl as adj* Oriental

Gelb|be(s) [ˈgɛlbə] NT *decl as adj* (*vom Ei*) yolk; **das ist nicht gerade das ~ vom Ei** (*inf*) it's not exactly brilliant

Gelb-: **Gelb|fie|ber** NT yellow fever; **Gelb|fil|ter** M (*Phot*) yellow filter; **gelb|grün** ADJ yellowish-green; **Gelb|kör|per|hor|mon** NT gestagen; **Gelb|kreuz** NT (*Chem*) mustard gas

gelb|lich [ˈgɛlplɪç] ADJ yellowish, yellowy; *Gesichtsfarbe* sallow

Gelb|ling [ˈgɛlplɪŋ] M **-s, -e** (*Bot*) chanterelle

Gelb-: **Gelb|sucht** F jaundice; **gelb|süch|tig** ADJ jaundiced; **er ist ~** he has jaundice; **Gelb|wurz** [-vʊrts] F **-**, *no pl* turmeric

Geld [gɛlt] NT **-(e)s, -er** [-dɐ] **a** *no pl* (= *Zahlungsmittel*) money; **bares ~** cash; **großes ~** notes *pl* (*Brit*), bills *pl* (*US*); **kleines ~** change; **~ und Gut** wealth and possessions; **alles für unser ~!** and we're paying for it!; **~ aufnehmen** to raise money; **aus etw ~ machen** to make money out of sth; **zu ~ machen** to sell off; **(mit etw) ~ machen** (*inf*) to make money (from sth); **um ~ spielen** to play for money; **ins ~ gehen** (*inf*) *or* **laufen** (*inf*) to cost a pretty penny (*inf*); **das kostet ein (wahnsinniges) ~** (*inf*) that costs a fortune *or* a packet (*Brit inf*) *or* a bunch (*US inf*); **etw für teures ~ kaufen** to pay a lot for sth; **das habe ich für billiges ~ gekauft** I got it cheaply, I didn't pay much for it; **ich stand ohne ~ da** I was left penniless *or*

without a penny; **in** *or* **im ~ schwimmen** (*inf*) to be rolling in it (*inf*), to be loaded (*inf*); **er hat ~ wie Heu** (*inf*) he's got stacks of money (*inf*), he's filthy *or* stinking rich (*inf*); **das ~ auf die Straße werfen** (*inf*) to spend money like water (*inf*) *or* like it was going out of fashion (*inf*); **da hast du das ~ zum Fenster hinausgeworfen** (*inf*) that's money down the drain (*inf*); **mit ~ um sich werfen** *or* **schmeißen** (*inf*) to chuck one's money around (*inf*); **gutes ~ dem schlechten hinterherwerfen** *or* **nachwerfen** (*inf*) to throw good money after bad; **jdm das ~ aus der Tasche ziehen** *or* **lotsen** (*inf*) to get *or* squeeze money out of sb; **am ~ hängen** *or* **kleben** to be tight with money; **hinter ~ her sein** (*inf*) to be a money-grubber (*Brit inf*), to be money-crazy (*US inf*); **das ist nicht für ~ zu haben** (*inf*) that can't be bought; **sie/das ist nicht mit ~ zu bezahlen** (*inf*) she/that is priceless; **nicht für ~ und gute Worte** (*inf*) not for love nor money; **~ allein macht nicht glücklich(, aber es beruhigt)** (*prov*) money isn't everything(, but it helps) (*prov*); **~ oder Leben!** your money or your life!; **~ stinkt nicht** (*Prov*) there's nothing wrong with money; **~ regiert die Welt** (*Prov*) money makes the world go round (*prov*)

b **Gelder** PL (= *Geldsummen*) money; **tägliche ~er** day-to-day money *or* loans *pl*; **staatliche/öffentliche ~er** state/public funds *pl* *or* money

c (*St Ex*: = *Geldkurs*) buying rate, bid price

Geld-: **Geld|ab|wer|tung** F currency devaluation; **Geld|adel** M **der ~** the money aristocracy; (*hum*: = *die Reichen*) the rich *pl*; **Geld|an|ge|le|gen|heit** F financial matter; **jds ~en** sb's financial affairs; **Geld|an|la|ge** F (financial) investment; **Geld|an|le|ger(in)** M(F) (financial) investor; **Geld|an|wei|sung** F money order; **Geld|aris|to|kra|tie** F **die ~** the money aristocracy; **Geld|auf|wer|tung** F currency revaluation; **Geld|aus|ga|be** F (financial) expenditure; **Geld|aus|ga|be|au|to|mat** M cash machine *or* dispenser (*Brit*), money machine, ATM; **Geld|au|to|mat** M (*zum Geldabheben*) cash machine *or* dispenser (*Brit*), money machine, ATM; (*zum Geldwechseln*) change machine; **Geld|be|trag** M amount (of money), sum (of money); **Geld|beu|tel** M wallet, billfold (*US*); (*für Münzen*) purse (*Brit*), wallet (*US*); **tief in den ~ greifen** (*inf*) to dig deep (into one's pocket) (*inf*); **Geld|bom|be** F strongbox; **Geld|bör|se** F wallet, billfold (*US*); (*für Münzen*) purse (*Brit*), wallet (*US*); **Geld|bo|te** M , **Geld|bo|tin** F security guard; **Geld|brief** M registered letter (*containing money*); **Geld|brief|trä|ger(in)** M(F) postman/-woman who delivers money orders; **Geld|bu|ße** F (*Jur*) fine; **eine hohe ~** a heavy fine; **Geld|din|ge** PL financial matters *pl*; **Geld|ein|la|ge** F capital invested *no pl*; **Geld|ein|wurf** M slot; **Sie müssen Sie ... beim ~ ent- serting the money you should ...; **Geld|ent|wer|tung** F (= *Inflation*) currency depreciation; (= *Abwertung*) currency devaluation; **Geld|er|werb** M **zum ~ arbeiten** to work to earn money; **etw zum ~ machen** to make money out of sth; **Geld|fäl|schung** F counterfeiting; **Geld|ge|ber(in)** M(F) financial backer; (*esp Rad, TV*) sponsor; (*hum*: = *Arbeitgeber*) employer; **Geld|ge|schäft** NT financial transaction; **Geld|ge|schenk** NT gift of money; **Geld|gier** F avarice; **geld|gie|rig** ADJ avaricious; **Geld|hahn** M **(jdm) den ~ zudrehen** *or* **abdrehen** to cut off sb's money supply; **den ~ öffnen** to loosen the purse strings; **Geld|hei|rat** F **das war eine reine ~** she/he *etc* just got married for the money; **Geld|herr|schaft** F plutocracy

gel|dig [ˈgɛldɪç] ADJ (*esp Aus*) moneyed, monied

Geld-: **Geld|in|sti|tut** NT financial institution; **Geld|kar|te** F (*aufladbar*) charge card; **Geld|kas|set|te** F cash box; **Geld|kat|ze** F (*Hist*)

money pouch; (= *Gürtel*) money belt; **Geld|knapp|heit** F shortage of money; **Geld|kurs** M (*St Ex*) buying rate, bid price

geld|lich [ˈgɛltlɪç] ADJ financial **ADV** financially

Geld-: **Geld|man|gel** M lack of money; **Geld|markt** M money market; **Geld|men|ge** F money supply; **Geld|mit|tel** PL funds *pl*; **Geld|not** F (= *Geldmangel*) lack of money; (= *Geldschwierigkeiten*) financial difficulties *pl*; **Geld|po|li|tik** F financial policy; **etwas von ~ verstehen** to know something about the politics of finance; **Geld|prä|mie** F bonus; (*als Auszeichnung*) (financial) award; (*als Belohnung*) (financial) reward; **Geld|preis** M cash prize; **Geld|quel|le** F source of income; **Geld|rol|le** F roll of money *or* coins; **Geld|rück|ga|be** F **a** (*als Handlung*) returning the money **b** (*Aufschrift auf Automaten*) coin return; **keine ~** no change given; **Geld|sa|che** F money *or* financial matter; **in ~n hört die Gemütlichkeit auf** (*prov*) business is business (*prov*); **Geld|sack** M money bag; (*pej inf*: = *reicher Mann*) moneybags *sing*; **auf dem ~ sitzen** (*inf*) to be sitting on a pile of money (*inf*); **Geld|sä|ckel** M (*dial*) money bag; (*fig*: *von Kanton, Staat etc*) coffers *pl*; **Geld|schein** M banknote (*esp Brit*), bill (*US*); **Geld|schöp|fung** F (*Fin*) money creation; **Geld|schrank** M safe; **Geld|schrank|kna|cker(in)** M(F) (*inf*) safeblower; **Geld|schuld** F (financial) debt; **Geld|schwie|rig|kei|ten** PL financial difficulties *pl*; **Geld|se|gen** M (*fig*) windfall, bonanza, financial godsend; **Geld|sen|dung** F cash remittance; **Geld|sor|gen** PL financial worries *pl*, money troubles *pl*; **~ haben, in ~ sein** to have financial worries, to have money troubles; **Geld|sor|te** F (*Fin*) (type of) currency; **Geld|spen|de** F donation, gift of money; **Geld|spiel|au|to|mat** M slot machine; **Geld|sprit|ze** F (*inf*) injection of money; **Geld|stra|fe** F fine; **jdn zu einer ~ verurteilen**, **jdn mit einer ~ belegen** to fine sb, to impose a fine on sb; **Geld|stück** NT coin; **Geld|sum|me** F sum of money; **Geld|ta|sche** F purse (*Brit*), wallet (*US*); (*für Herren*) wallet, billfold (*US*); (*sackartig*) money bag; **Geld|trans|port** M transport of money; **einen ~ sichern** to safeguard an armoured (*Brit*) *or* armored (*US*) car (*carrying money*); **Geld|trans|por|ter** M armoured (*Brit*) *or* armored (*US*) car (*for transporting money*); **Geld|um|lauf** M circulation of money; **Geld|um|tausch** M = **Geldwechsel**; **Geld|ver|die|ner(in)** M(F) (*inf*) moneymaker (*inf*); **Geld|ver|kehr** M money transactions *pl*; **Geld|ver|knap|pung** F financial restraint; **Geld|ver|le|gen|heit** F financial embarrassment *no pl*; **in ~ sein** to be short of money; **jdm aus einer ~ helfen** to help sb out of his financial difficulties; **Geld|ver|lei|her(in)** M(F) moneylender; **Geld|ver|schwen|dung** F waste of money; **Geld|vo|lu|men** NT (*Fin*) money supply; **Geld|wasch|an|la|ge** F money-laundering outfit; **Geld|wä|sche** F money laundering; **Geld|wech|sel** M exchange of money; **beim ~ muss man eine Gebühr bezahlen** there is a charge for changing money; „Geldwechsel" "bureau de change" (*Brit*), exchange counter (*US*); **Geld|wech|sel|au|to|mat** M change machine; **Geld|wechs|ler** M (= *Automat*) change machine; **Geld|wechs|ler(in)** M(F) moneychanger; **geld|wert** ADJ **~er Vorteil** perk, payment in kind; **~e Leistung** payment in kind; **Geld|wert** M cash value; (*Fin*: = *Kaufkraft*) (currency) value; **innerer/äußerer ~** internal/external value of currency; **Geld|wert|sta|bi|li|tät** F stability of a/the currency; **Geld|we|sen** NT , *no pl* monetary system; **Geld|wirt|schaft** F money economy; **Geld|zu|wen|dun|gen** PL money *sing*; (= *Geldgeschenk*) gifts *pl* of money; (= *regelmäßiges Geldgeschenk*) allowance *sing*; **private ~ erhalten** to receive a private income

ge|leckt [gə'lɛkt] ADJ slick; **wie ~ aussehen** (*Mann*) to be spruced up; (*Zimmer, Boden etc*) to be spick and span → *auch* **lecken²**

Ge|lee [ʒe'le:] M OR NT **-s, -s** jelly

Ge|le|ge [gə'le:gə] NT **-s, -** (= *Vogelgelege*) clutch (of eggs); (*Froschgelege*) spawn *no pl*; (*von Reptilien*) eggs *pl*

ge|le|gen [gə'le:gn] *ptp von* **liegen** ADJ **a** (= *befindlich, liegend*) *Haus, Ort* situated; *Grundstück auch* located; **ein herrlich ~er Ort** a place in a magnificent area **b** (= *passend*) opportune; **zu ~er Zeit** at a convenient time **c** *pred* (= *wichtig*) **mir ist viel/nichts daran ~** it matters a great deal/doesn't matter to me; (*es ist*) **wenn ich nicht ~ komme, gehe ich gleich wieder** if it's not convenient, I'll go immediately; **du kommst mir gerade ~** you've come at just the right time; (*iro*) **du pick your time well; es kommt mir sehr/nicht sehr ~** it comes just at the right/wrong time

Ge|le|gen|heit [gə'le:gnhait] F **-, -en** **a** (= *günstiger Umstand, Zeitpunkt*) opportunity; **bei ~** some time (or other); **bei passender ~** when the opportunity arises; **bei passender ~ werde ich ...** when I get the opportunity or chance I'll ...; **bei der ersten (besten) ~** at the first opportunity; (**die**) **~ haben** to get an or the opportunity or a or the chance (*etw zu tun* to do sth); **jdm** (**die**) **~ geben** or **bieten** to give sb an or the opportunity or a or the chance (*etw zu tun* to do sth); **~ macht Diebe** (*Prov*) opportunity makes a thief

b (= *Anlass*) occasion; **bei dieser ~** on this occasion; **ein Kleid für alle ~en** a dress suitable for all occasions → **Schopf**

c (*Comm*) bargain

Ge|le|gen|heits-: **Ge|le|gen|heits|ar|beit** F **a** casual work *no pl* **b** (*eines Autors*) minor work; **Ge|le|gen|heits|ar|bei|ter(in)** M(F) casual labourer (*Brit*) or laborer (*US*); **Ge|le|gen|heits|dich|ter(in)** M(F) occasional poet; **Ge|le|gen|heits|dieb(in)** M(F) opportunistic or sneak thief; **Ge|le|gen|heits|ge|dicht** NT occasional poem; **Ge|le|gen|heits|kauf** M bargain; **Ge|le|gen|heits|rau|cher(in)** M(F) occasional smoker; **Ge|le|gen|heits|trin|ker(in)** M(F) occasional drinker

ge|le|gent|lich [gə'le:gntlɪç] ADJ *attr* occasional; **von – an Ausnahmen abgesehen** except for the odd occasion ADV (= *manchmal*) occasionally, now and again; (= *bei Gelegenheit*) some time (or other); **wenn Sie ~ dort sind** if you happen to be there; **lassen Sie ~ etwas von sich hören!** keep in touch PREP *+gen* (*geh*) **~ seines 60. Geburtstags** on the occasion of his 60th birthday

ge|leh|rig [gə'le:rɪç] ADJ *Schüler, Tier* quick and eager to learn ADV **sich bei etw ~ anstellen** to be quick to grasp sth

Ge|leh|rig|keit F **-,** *no pl* quickness and eagerness to learn

ge|lehr|sam [gə'le:rza:m] ADJ **a** (*old*) = **gelehrt** ADJ **b** (*rare*) = **gelehrig**

Ge|lehr|sam|keit F **-,** *no pl* (*geh*) learning, erudition

ge|lehrt [gə'le:rt] ADJ *Mensch* learned, erudite; (= *wissenschaftlich*) *Mensch, Literatur, Anmerkungen* scholarly; **~e Gesellschaft** (*old*) learned society → *auch* **lehren**

Ge|lehr|ten-: **Ge|lehr|ten|fa|mi|lie** F family of scholars; **Ge|lehr|ten|kopf** M scholarly profile; **Ge|lehr|ten|streit** M dispute amongst the scholars; **Ge|lehr|ten|welt** F world of learning

Ge|lehr|te(r) [gə'le:rtə] MF *decl as adj* scholar; **darüber sind sich die ~n noch nicht einig, darüber streiten sich die ~n** that's a moot point

Ge|lehrt|heit F **-,** *no pl* learning, erudition

Ge|lei|er [gə'laiɐ] NT **-s,** *no pl* droning

Ge|lei|se [gə'laizə] NT **-s, -** (*geh, Aus*) = **Gleis**

Ge|leit [gə'lait] NT **-(e)s, -e** (*Hist:* = *Gefolge*) retinue, entourage; (= *Begleitung, Mil*) escort; (*Naut*)

---

convoy, escort; (= *Leichenzug*) cortege; **freies** or **sicheres ~** safe-conduct; **jdm das ~ geben** to escort or accompany sb; **„zum ~"** "preface" → **letzte(r, s) a**

Ge|leit-: **Ge|leit|boot** NT escort or convoy ship; **Ge|leit|brief** M (*Hist*) letter of safe-conduct

ge|lei|ten [gə'laitn] *ptp* **geleitet** VT (*geh*) to escort; (= *begleiten auch*) to accompany; (*Naut*) to convoy, to escort

Ge|leit-: **Ge|leit|fahr|zeug** NT escort vehicle; (*Naut*) escort vessel; **Ge|leit|schiff** NT escort or convoy ship; **Ge|leit|schutz** M escort; (*Naut auch*) convoy; **jdm ~ gewähren** or **geben** to give sb an escort/a convoy; (*persönlich*) to escort/convoy sb; **im ~ (von Polizeifahrzeugen)** under (police) escort; **Ge|leit|wort** NT *pl* **-worte** (*geh*) preface; **Ge|leit|zug** M (*Mil, Naut*) convoy; **im ~ fahren** to drive in convoy; (*Naut*) to sail under convoy

ge|lenk [gə'lɛŋk] ADJ (*old*) = **gelenkig**

Ge|lenk [gə'lɛŋk] NT **-(e)s, -e** joint; (= *Handgelenk*) wrist; (= *Fußgelenk*) ankle; (= *Kettengelenk*) link; (= *Scharniergelenk*) hinge

Ge|lenk-: **Ge|lenk|bus** M articulated bus; **Ge|lenk|ent|zün|dung** F arthritis; **Ge|lenk|fahr|zeug** NT articulated vehicle

ge|len|kig [gə'lɛŋkɪç] ADJ agile; (= *geschmeidig*) supple ADV **~ verbunden sein** (*Tech*) to be jointed; (*zusammengefügt*) to be articulated; (*mit Kettengelenk*) to be linked; (*mit Scharniergelenk*) to be hinged

Ge|len|kig|keit F **-,** *no pl* agility; (= *Geschmeidigkeit*) suppleness

Ge|lenk-: **Ge|lenk|kopf** M , **Ge|lenk|ku|gel** F (*Anat*) head of a bone, condyle (*spec*); **Ge|lenk|leuch|te** F Anglepoise® (lamp); **Ge|lenk|om|ni|bus** M articulated bus; **Ge|lenk|pfan|ne** F (*Anat*) glenoid cavity; **Ge|lenk|plas|tik** F (*Med*) arthroplasty; **Ge|lenk|pup|pe** F jointed doll; **Ge|lenk|rheu|ma|tis|mus** M rheumatic fever

Ge|lenks- *in cpds* (*Aus*) = **Gelenk-**

Ge|lenk-: **Ge|lenk|schmie|re** F (*Anat*) synovial fluid; **Ge|lenk|stan|ge** F (*Tech*) toggle link; **Ge|lenk|wel|le** F (*Tech*) cardan shaft; **Ge|lenk|zug** M articulated train

ge|lernt [gə'lɛrnt] ADJ trained; *Arbeiter* skilled → *auch* **lernen**

ge|le|sen *ptp von* **lesen**

ge|liebt ADJ dear, beloved (*liter, Eccl*) → *auch* **lieben**

Ge|lieb|te [gə'li:ptə] F *decl as adj* sweetheart; (= *Mätresse*) mistress; (*liter: als Anrede*) beloved (*liter*)

Ge|lieb|te(r) [gə'li:ptə] M *decl as adj* sweetheart, lover (*old*); (= *Liebhaber*) lover; (*liter: als Anrede*) beloved (*liter*)

ge|lie|fert [gə'li:fɐt] ADJ **~ sein** (*inf*) to have had it (*inf*); **jetzt sind wir ~** that's the end (*inf*) → *auch* **liefern**

ge|lie|hen *ptp von* **leihen**

ge|lie|ren [ʒe'li:rən] *ptp* **geliert** VI to gel

Ge|lier- [ʒe'li:ɐ-]: **Ge|lier|mit|tel** NT gelling agent; **Ge|lier|zu|cker** M preserving sugar

ge|lin|de [gə'lɪndə], **ge|lind** [gə'lɪnt] ADJ **a** (*geh*) (= *mäßig, mild*) mild; (= *schonend, vorsichtig*) gentle; *Wind, Frost, Regen* light; *Klima, Anhöhe* gentle **b** (*inf: = heftig*) awful (*inf*); **da packte mich ~ Wut** I got pretty angry ADV **~ gesagt** putting it mildly, to put it mildly

ge|lin|gen [gə'lɪŋən] *pret* **gelang** [gə'laŋ], *ptp* **gelungen** [gə'lʊŋən] VI *aux sein* (= *glücken*) to succeed; (= *erfolgreich sein*) to be successful; **es gelang ihm, das zu tun** he succeeded in doing it; **es gelang ihm nicht, das zu tun** he failed to do it, he didn't succeed in doing it; **dem Häftling gelang die Flucht** the prisoner managed to escape, the prisoner succeeded in escaping; **dein Plan wird dir nicht ~** you won't succeed with your plan; **es will mir nicht ~** I can't seem to

---

manage it; **es will mir nicht ~ ... zu ...** I can't seem to manage to ...; **das Bild ist ihr gut/schlecht gelungen** her picture turned out well/badly → *auch* **gelungen**

Ge|lin|gen [gə'lɪŋən] NT **-s,** *no pl* (*geh*) (= *Glück*) success; (= *erfolgreiches Ergebnis*) successful outcome; **gutes ~ für Ihren Plan!** good luck with your plan!; **auf gutes ~!** to success!

Ge|lis|pel [gə'lɪspl] NT **-s,** *no pl* (= *das Lispeln*) lisping; (= *Geflüster*) whispering

ge|lit|ten *ptp von* **leiden**

gell¹ [gɛl] ADJ shrill, piercing

gell², **gel|le** ['gɛlə] INTERJ (*S Ger, Sw*) = **gelt**

gel|len ['gɛlən] VI to shrill; (= *von lauten Tönen erfüllt sein*) to ring; **der Lärm gellt mir in den Ohren** the noise makes my ears ring; **ein schriller Schrei gellte durch die Nacht** a shrill scream pierced the night

gel|lend ADJ shrill, piercing; **ein ~es Pfeifkonzert** a shrill barrage of catcalls ADV **~ um Hilfe schreien** to scream for help

ge|lo|ben [gə'lo:bn] *ptp* **gelobt** VT (*geh*) to vow, to swear; **die Fürsten gelobten dem König Treue** the princes pledged their loyalty or vowed loyalty to the king; **ich habe mir gelobt, das Rauchen aufzugeben** I've vowed or made a pledge or sworn to give up smoking; **das Gelobte Land** (*Bibl*) the Promised Land; **ich schwöre und gelobe, ...** I (do) solemnly swear and promise ...

Ge|löb|nis [gə'lø:pnɪs] NT **-ses, -se** (*geh*) vow; **ein** or **das ~ ablegen** to take a vow

Ge|löb|nis|fei|er F swearing-in ceremony

Ge|lo|der [gə'lo:dɐ] NT **-s,** *no pl* (*geh*) blaze

ge|lo|gen *ptp von* **lügen**

ge|löst [gə'lø:st] ADJ relaxed; **danach war sie ~ und entspannt** afterwards she felt calm and relaxed → *auch* **lösen**

Ge|löst|heit F **-,** *no pl* relaxed feeling; (= *gelöste Stimmung*) relaxed mood

Gel|se ['gɛlzə] F **-, -n** (*Aus*) gnat, mosquito

gelt [gɛlt] INTERJ (*S Ger*) right; **morgen kommst du wieder, ~?** you'll be back tomorrow, won't you or right?; **~, du leihst mir 5 Euro?** you'll lend me 5 euros, won't you or right?; **ich werde es mal versuchen, ~?** well, I'll give it a try; **es ist schön heute – ~?** it's nice today – isn't it just?

gel|ten ['gɛltn] *pret* **galt** [galt], *ptp* **gegolten** [gə'gɔltn] VI **a** (= *gültig sein*) to be valid; (*Gesetz*) to be in force; (*Preise*) to be effective; (*Münze*) to be legal tender; (= *erlaubt sein*) to be allowed or permitted; (= *zählen*) to count; **die Wette gilt!** the bet's on!, it's a bet!; **was ich sage, gilt!** what I say goes!; **das gilt nicht!** that doesn't count!; (= *ist nicht erlaubt*) that's not allowed!; **das Gesetz gilt für alle** the law applies to everyone; **diese Karte gilt nur für eine Person** this ticket only admits one → **geltend**

b *+dat* (= *bestimmt sein für*) to be meant for or aimed at

c *+dat* (*geh: = sich beziehen auf*) to be for; **seine ganze Liebe galt der Musik** music was his only love; **sein letzter Gedanke galt seinem Volk** his last thought was for his people

d (= *zutreffen*) **für jdn/etw ~** to hold (good) for sb/sth, to go for sb/sth; **das gleiche gilt auch für ihn/von ihm** the same goes for him too/is true of him too

e **~ als** or **für** (*rare*) to be regarded as; **es gilt als sicher, dass ...** it seems certain that ...

f **~ lassen** to accept; **das lasse ich ~!** I'll agree to that!, I accept that!; **für diesmal lasse ich es ~** I'll let it go this time; **etw als etw ~ lassen** to accept sth as sth; **er lässt nur seine eigene Meinung ~** he won't accept anybody's opinion but his own

VTI *impers* (*geh*) **es gilt, ... zu ...** it is necessary to ...; **jetzt gilt es, Mut zu zeigen/zusammenzuhalten** it is now a question of courage/of sticking together; **jetzt gilts!** this is it!; **was gilts?** (*bei Wette*) what do you bet?; **es gilt!** done!,

---

you're on!, it's a deal!

VT (= *wert sein*) to be worth; (= *zählen*) to count for; **was gilt die Wette?** what do you bet?

gel|tend ADJ *attr Preise, Tarife* current; *Gesetz, Regelung* in force; (= *vorherrschend*) *Meinung etc* currently accepted, prevailing; **~ machen** (*form*) to assert; **einen Einwand ~ machen** to raise an objection; **~es Recht sein** to be the law of the land

Gel|tend|ma|chung [-maxʊŋ] F -, *no pl* (*form*) enforcement

Gel|tung ['gɛltʊŋ] F -, -en (= *Gültigkeit*) validity; (*von Münzen*) currency; (= *Wert*) value, worth; (= *Einfluss*) influence; (= *Ansehen*) prestige; **~ haben** to have validity; (*Münzen*) to be legal tender, to have currency; (*Gesetz*) to be in force; (*Preise*) to be effective; (*Auffassung etc*) to be prevalent; (= *Einfluss haben*) to carry weight; (= *angesehen sein*) to be recognized; **an ~ verlieren** to lose prestige; **einer Sache** (*dat*) **~ verschaffen** to enforce sth; **sich** (*dat*) **~ verschaffen** to establish one's position; **etw zur ~ bringen** to show sth (off) to advantage; (*durch Kontrast*) to set sth off; **zur ~ kommen** to show to advantage; (*durch Kontrast*) to be set off; **in diesem Konzertsaal kommt die Musik voll zur ~** the music can be heard to its best advantage in this concert hall

Gel|tungs-: Gel|tungs|be|dürf|nis NT , *no pl* need for admiration; **Gel|tungs|be|dürf|tig** ADJ desperate for admiration; **Gel|tungs|be|dürf|tig|keit** F need for admiration; **Gel|tungs|be|reich** M *der ~ einer Fahrkarte/eines Gesetzes* the area within which a ticket is valid/a law is operative; **Gel|tungs|dau|er** F (*einer Fahrkarte etc*) period of validity; **die ~ eines Vertrages/einer Genehmigung** the period during which a contract is in force/a licence (*Brit*) or license (*US*) is valid; **Gel|tungs|drang** M , **Gel|tungs|stre|ben** NT need for admiration; **Gel|tungs|sucht** F craving for admiration; **gel|tungs|süch|tig** ADJ craving admiration; **Gel|tungs|trieb** M (= *Geltungsbedürfnis*) need for admiration; (= *Geltungssucht*) craving for admiration

Ge|lüb|de [gə'lʏpdə] NT -s, - (*Rel, geh*) vow; **ein/das ~ ablegen** or **tun** to take a vow

Ge|lump [gə'lʊmp] NT -(e)s, *no pl*, **Ge|lum|pe** [gə'lʊmpə] NT -s, *no pl* (*inf*: = *Plunder, Sachen*) junk, trash; (*pej*: = *Gesindel*) trash

ge|lun|gen [gə'lʊŋən] *ptp von* **gelingen** ADJ *attr* **a** (= *geglückt*) successful; **ein gut ~er Abend** a very successful evening; **ein gut ~er Braten** a roast that turned out very well; **eine nicht so recht ~e Überraschung** a surprise that didn't quite come off **b** (*inf*: = *drollig*) priceless (*inf*); **du bist mir ein ~er Bursche** you're priceless (*inf*), you ARE a funny chap (*Brit*)

Ge|lüst [gə'lʏst] NT -(e)s, -e, **Ge|lüs|te** [gə'lʏstə] NT -s, - (*geh*) desire; (= *Sucht*) craving (*auf +acc, nach* for)

ge|lüs|ten [gə'lʏstn] *ptp* **gelüstet** VT *impers* (*liter, iro*) **es gelüstet mich** or **mich gelüstet nach …** I am overcome by desire for …; (= *süchtig sein nach*) I have a craving for …; **es gelüstet mich, das zu tun** I'm more than tempted to do that, I'm sorely tempted to do that

Ge|lüs|ten [gə'lʏstn] NT -s, *no pl* desire; (= *Sucht*) craving (*nach* for)

GEMA ['ge:ma] F -, *no pl abbr von* **Gesellschaft für musikalische Aufführungs- und mechanische Vervielfältigungsrechte** *musical copyright watchdog body*

ge|mach [gə'ma:x] ADV (*old*) slowly; **~!** not so fast!; (= *nichts übereilen*) one mustn't rush things!

Ge|mach [gə'ma:x] NT -(e)s, ̈er [gə'mɛ:çɐ] (*geh*) chamber (*old, form*); **sich in seine Gemächer zurückziehen** to repair to one's chamber (*old, hum*)

ge|mäch|lich [gə'mɛ:çlɪç] ADJ leisurely; *Mensch* unhurried; **ein ~es Leben führen** to lead a quiet

life **ADV** *erledigen, frühstücken* leisurely; **er wanderte ~ durch die Wiesen** he strolled through the meadows, he took a leisurely stroll through the meadows; **ein ~ fließender Strom** a gently flowing river

Ge|mäch|lich|keit F -, *no pl* leisureliness; (= *Ruhe*) peace

ge|macht [gə'maxt] ADJ **a** made; **für etw ~ sein** to be made for sth; **ein ~er Mann sein** to be made, to be a made man → **Bett b** (= *gewollt, gekünstelt*) false, contrived **c** (*ist*) **~!** (*inf*) done! (*inf*) → *auch* **machen**

Ge|mäch|te [gə'mɛçtə] NT -s, - (*old, hum*) private parts *pl*, privates *pl* (*inf*)

GEMA-Ge|büh|ren ['ge:ma-] PL royalties *pl* (*payable to the GEMA*)

Ge|mahl¹ [gə'ma:l] M -s, -e (*geh, form*) spouse (*old, form*), husband; (= *Prinzgemahl*) consort; **bitte grüßen Sie Ihren Herrn ~** please give my regards to your husband

Ge|mahl² NT - or -(e)s, -e (*obs*) spouse (*old, form*), wife

Ge|mah|lin [gə'ma:lɪn] F -, -nen (*geh, form*) spouse (*old, form*), wife; (*von König auch*) consort; **bitte empfehlen Sie mich Ihrer Frau ~** please give my regards to your wife (*form*) or to your good lady (*Brit*)

ge|mah|nen [gə'ma:nən] *ptp* **gemahnt** VT (*geh*) **jdn an jdn/etw ~** to remind sb of sb/sth, to put sb in mind of sb/sth

Ge|mäl|de [gə'mɛ:ldə] NT -s, - painting; (*fig*: = *Schilderung*) portrayal

Ge|mäl|de-: Ge|mäl|de|aus|stel|lung F exhibition of paintings; **Ge|mäl|de|ga|le|rie** F picture gallery; **Ge|mäl|de|samm|lung** F collection of paintings; (= *Gemäldegalerie*) art collection

Ge|man|sche [gə'manʃə] NT -s, *no pl* (*dial*) mush; **hör auf mit dem ~!** stop messing around with it!

Ge|mar|kung [gə'markʊŋ] F -, -en (*dated, form*) (= *Feldmark*) bounds *pl*; (= *Gemeindegebiet*) district

ge|ma|sert [gə'mazɐt] ADJ *Holz* grained → *auch* **masern**

ge|mäß [gə'mɛːs] PREP +*dat* in accordance with; **Ihren Anordnungen ~** as per your instructions, in accordance with your instructions; **~ den Bestimmungen** under the regulations; **~ § 209** under § 209 **ADJ** appropriate (+*dat* to); **dieser Umgang ist seiner sozialen Stellung nicht ~** the company is keeping ill befits or does not befit his social position; **eine ihren Fähigkeiten ~e Arbeit** a job suited to her abilities; **das einzig Gemäße** the only fitting thing

ge|mä|ßigt [gə'mɛːsɪçt] ADJ moderate; *Klima, Zone* temperate; *Optimismus etc* qualified → *auch* **mäßigen**

Ge|mäu|er [gə'mɔʏɐ] NT -s, - (*geh*) masonry, walls *pl*; (= *Ruine*) ruins *pl*

Ge|mau|schel [gə'mauʃl] NT -s, *no pl* (*pej inf*) scheming

Ge|me|cker [gə'mɛkɐ] NT -s, *no pl*, **Ge|me|cke|re** [gə'mɛkərə] NT -s, *no pl*, **Ge|me|ck|re** [gə'mɛkrə] NT -s, *no pl* (*von Ziegen*) bleating; (*inf*: = *Nörgelei*) moaning, bellyaching (*inf*); (= *meckerndes Lachen*) cackling

ge|mein [gə'main] **⏺** 32.5 **ADJ** **a** *pred no comp* (= *gemeinsam*) **etw ~ mit jdm/etw haben** to have sth in common with sb/sth; **jdm/einer Sache** (*dat*) **~ sein** (*geh*) to be common to sb/sth; **nichts mit jdm ~ haben wollen** to want nothing to do with sb; **das ist beiden ~** it is common to both of them
b *attr no comp* (*Biol, old*: = *üblich, verbreitet, öffentlich*) common; (= *Bruch* (*Math*) vulgar fraction; **~es Recht** common law; **ein ~er Soldat** a common soldier, a private (*US*); **das ~e Volk/Wohl** the common people/good or weal (*old*); **der ~e Mann** the ordinary man
c (= *niederträchtig*) mean; (= *roh, unverschämt*)

mean, nasty; *Verräter, Lüge* contemptible; **das war ~ von dir!** that was mean or nasty of you; **ein ~er Streich** a dirty or rotten trick; **alles ins Gemeine ziehen** to cheapen or debase everything

d (= *ordinär*) vulgar; *Bemerkung, Witz* vulgar, dirty, coarse
e (*inf*: = *unangenehm*) horrible, awful **ADV a** (= *niederträchtig*) *behandeln* meanly; *betrügen, hintergehen* despicably; **er hat sie ~ im Stich gelassen** he abandoned her in a despicable way
b (*inf*: = *unangenehm*) horribly, awfully; **die Prüfung war ~ schwer** the exam was horribly or awfully difficult; **das hat ~ wehgetan** it hurt terribly

Ge|mein|be|sitz M common property

Ge|mein|de [gə'maində] F -, -n **a** (= *Kommune*) municipality; (= *Gemeindebewohner auch*) community; (*inf*: = *Gemeindeamt*) local authority; **die ~ Burg** the municipality of Burg **b** (= *Pfarrgemeinde*) parish; (= *Gläubige auch*) parishioners *pl*; (*beim Gottesdienst*) congregation **c** (= *Anhängerschaft*) (*von Theater etc*) patrons *pl*; (*von Schriftsteller etc*) following

Ge|mein|de-: Ge|mein|de|ab|ga|ben PL local taxes *pl*; **Ge|mein|de|am|mann** M (*Sw*) **a** = **Gemeindevorsteher(in) b** (= *Gerichtsvollzieher*) bailiff; **Ge|mein|de|amt** NT local authority; (= *Gebäude*) local administrative office; **Ge|mein|de|bau** M *pl* -bauten (*Aus*) subsidized housing; **Ge|mein|de|be|am|te(r)** M *decl as adj*, **Ge|mein|de|be|am|tin** F local government officer; **Ge|mein|de|be|hör|de** F local authority; **Ge|mein|de|be|schluss** ▲ M local government decision; **Ge|mein|de|be|zirk** M district; (*Aus*) ward; **im ~ Dumfries** in the district of Dumfries; **Ge|mein|de|bü|che|rei** F public or local (*Brit*) library; **Ge|mein|de|die|ner(in)** M(F) (*dated*) beadle; **ge|mein|de|ei|gen** ADJ local authority *attr*; (*esp städtisch*) municipal; **Ge|mein|de|ei|gen|tum** NT communal property; **Ge|mein|de|glied** NT (*Eccl*) parishioner; **Ge|mein|de|haus** NT (*Eccl*) parish rooms *pl*; (*von Freikirchen*) church rooms *pl*; (*katholisch*) parish house; **Ge|mein|de|hel|fer(in)** M(F) (*Eccl*) parish worker; **Ge|mein|de|mit|glied** NT (*Eccl*) parishioner; **Ge|mein|de|ord|nung** F bylaws *pl*, ordinances *pl* (*US*); **Ge|mein|de|prä|si|dent(in)** M(F) (*Sw*) mayor; **Ge|mein|de|rat¹** M local council; **Ge|mein|de|rat²** M , **Ge|mein|de|rä|tin** F local councillor (*Brit*), councilman/-woman (*US*); **Ge|mein|de|rats|wahl** F local elections *pl*, elections *pl* for the local council; **Ge|mein|de|saal** M (*Eccl*) church hall; **Ge|mein|de|schwes|ter** F district nurse; (*Eccl*) *nun working in a parish as a nurse or social worker*; **Ge|mein|de|spi|tal** NT (*Aus*) local hospital; **Ge|mein|de|steu|er** F local tax

ge|mein|deutsch ADJ standard German

Ge|mein|de-: Ge|mein|de|vä|ter PL (*hum*) venerable councillors (*Brit*) or councilors (*US*) *pl* (*hum*); **Ge|mein|de|ver|tre|tung** F district council; **Ge|mein|de|ver|wal|tung** F local administration or government; **Ge|mein|de|vor|stand** M ≈ aldermen *pl*; **Ge|mein|de|vor|ste|her(in)** M(F) head of the local council; (≈ *Bürgermeister*) mayor; **Ge|mein|de|wahl** F local election; **Ge|mein|de|zen|trum** NT community centre (*Brit*) or center (*US*); (*Eccl*) parish rooms *pl*; (*von Freikirchen*) church rooms *pl*; (*katholisch*) parish house

Ge|mein|ei|gen|tum NT common property

Ge|mei|ne(r) [gə'mainə] M *decl as adj* **a** (*dated*: = *Soldat*) common soldier, private (*US*); **die ~n** the ranks *pl* **b** (*Typ*) lower-case letter; **in ~n** in lower case

Ge|mein-: ge|mein|ge|fähr|lich ADJ dangerous to the public, constituting a public danger; **ein ~er Verbrecher** a dangerous criminal **ADV** **~ handeln** to endanger public safety; **Ge|mein|ge|fähr|lich|keit** F danger to the public; **Ge|mein|geist** M public spirit; **ge|mein|-gül|tig** ADJ = **allgemein** ADV; **Ge|mein|gut** NT , no pl (lit, fig) common property; **Schumanns Lieder gehören zum ~ der Deutschen** Schumann's Lieder are part of the German heritage

Ge|mein|heit F -, -en **a** no pl (= Niedertracht) meanness; (= Rohheit, Unverschämtheit auch) nastiness **b** no pl (= Vulgarität) vulgarity; (von Bemerkung, Witz) vulgarity, coarseness **c** (= Tat) mean or dirty trick; (= Behandlung) nasty treatment no pl; (= Worte) mean thing; **das war eine ~** (= Handlung) that was a mean thing to do; (= Bemerkung) that was a mean thing to say **d** (inf: = ärgerlicher Umstand) (blasted (Brit inf)) nuisance

Ge|mein-: ge|mein|hin [gə'mainhɪn] ADV generally; **Ge|mein|kos|ten** PL overheads pl, overhead costs pl; **Ge|mein|nutz** [-nʊts] M -es, no pl public or common good; ~ **geht vor Eigennutz** (dated prov) service before self (Prov); **ge|mein|nüt|zig** ADJ of benefit to the public pred; (= wohltätig) charitable; **~er Verein** charitable or non-profit-making organization; **~e Einrichtung** charitable or non-profit-making institution; **er wurde zu 80 Stunden ~er Arbeit verurteilt** he was sentenced to 80 hours' community service; **Ge|mein|nüt|zig|keit** [-nʏtsɪk-kait] F -, no pl benefit to the public; **die ~ einer Organisation** the charitable status of an organization; **Ge|mein|platz** M commonplace

ge|mein|sam [gə'mainza:m] ADJ **a** (= mehreren gehörend) Eigenschaft, Interesse, Zwecke, Politik common; Konto joint; Freund mutual; (= von mehreren unternommen) Aktion, Ausflug, Nutzung joint; **sie haben vieles ~, ihnen ist vieles ~** they have a great deal in common; **die Firma ist ~es Eigentum** or **das ~e Eigentum der beiden Brüder** the firm belongs jointly to or is the joint property of the two brothers; **unser ~es Leben** our life together; **der Gemeinsame Markt** the Common Market; **die ~e (europäische) Währung** the single (European) currency; **mit jdm ~e Sache machen** to make common cause with sb; **er betonte das Gemeinsame** he stressed all that we/they had in common

ADV together; **etw ~ haben** to have sth in common; **es gehört den beiden ~** it belongs jointly to the two of them

Ge|mein|sam|keit F -, -en **a** (= gemeinsame Interessen, Eigenschaft etc) common ground no pl; **die ~en zwischen ihnen sind sehr groß** they have a great deal in common **b** no pl (= gemeinsames Besitzen) joint possession; (von Freunden, Interessen) mutuality; **uns verbindet die ~ unserer Interessen** we are united by common interests

Ge|mein|schaft [gə'mainʃaft] F -, -en community; (= Gruppe) group; (= Zusammensein) company; (= Zusammengehörigkeitsgefühl) sense of community; **die ~ Unabhängiger Staaten** the Commonwealth of Independent States; **in ~ mit** jointly with, together with; **in ~ mit jdm leben** to live in close companionship with sb; **die ~ der Heiligen/der Gläubigen** the communion of saints/of the faithful; **eheliche ~** (Jur) matrimony

ge|mein|schaft|lich [gə'mainʃaftlɪç] ADJ **a** = **gemeinsam b** (Jur) **~e Straftat** joint offence (Brit) or offense (US)

Ge|mein|schafts-: Ge|mein|schafts|ak|ti|on F cooperative or joint action; **Ge|mein|schafts|an|schluss** ▲ (Telec) party line; **Ge|mein|schafts|an|ten|ne** F block or party aerial or antenna (esp US); **Ge|mein|schafts|ar|beit** F teamwork; **das Buch ist eine ~** the book is a team effort; (von zwei Personen) the book is a joint effort; **Ge|mein|schafts|auf|ga|be** F joint task; (= Aufgabe des Bundes) federal project; **Ge|mein|schafts|beich|te** F (Eccl) general confession; **Ge|mein|schafts|be|sitz** M (= Besitzrechte) joint ownership; (= konkretes Objekt) joint property; **in ~** jointly

owned; **Ge|mein|schafts|bil|dend** ADJ community-building; (= einigend) unifying; **Ge|mein|schafts|de|pot** NT (Fin) joint security deposit; **Ge|mein|schafts|ehe** F group or communal marriage; **Ge|mein|schafts|er|zie|hung** F coeducation; (= soziale Erziehung) social education; **Ge|mein|schafts|fä|hig** ADJ capable of living in a community; **Ge|mein|schafts|ge|fühl** NT sense of community; (= Uneigennützigkeit) public-spiritedness; **Ge|mein|schafts|geist** M community spirit, esprit de corps; **Ge|mein|schafts|grab** NT communal grave; **Ge|mein|schafts|haft** F group confinement; **Ge|mein|schafts|kü|che** F (= Kantine) canteen; (= gemeinsame Kochgelegenheit) communal or (kleiner) shared kitchen; **Ge|mein|schafts|kun|de** F social studies pl; **Ge|mein|schafts|le|ben** NT community life; **Ge|mein|schafts|leis|tung** F collective achievement; **Ge|mein|schafts|pra|xis** F joint practice; **Ge|mein|schafts|pro|duk|ti|on** F **a** (= Gemeinschaftsarbeit) teamwork **b** (Rad, TV, Film) co-production; **Ge|mein|schafts|raum** M common room; **ge|mein|schafts|schä|di|gend**, **ge|mein|schafts|schäd|lich** ADJ Verhalten antisocial; **Ge|mein|schafts|schu|le** F interdenominational school; **Ge|mein|schafts|sen|dung** F simultaneous broadcast; **Ge|mein|schafts|sinn** M community spirit, esprit de corps; **ge|mein|schafts|stif|tend** ADJ promoting a sense of community; **Ge|mein|schafts|un|ter|neh|men** NT (Econ) joint venture; **Ge|mein|schafts|wer|bung** F joint advertising no pl; **~ machen** to advertise jointly, to run a joint advertisement; **Ge|mein|schafts|woh|nung** F shared flat (Brit) or apartment; **Ge|mein|schafts|zel|le** F communal cell

Ge|mein-: Ge|mein|schuld|ner(in) M(F) (Jur) bankrupt; **Ge|mein|sinn** M , no pl public spirit; **Ge|mein|spra|che** F standard language; **ge|mein|sprach|lich** ADJ standard language attr; **ge|mein|ver|ständ|lich** ADJ generally comprehensible ADV **sich ~ ausdrücken** to make oneself generally understood; **wissenschaftliche Probleme ~ darstellen** to present scientific problems in such a way that they can be generally understood; **Ge|mein|werk** NT (Sw) voluntary work; **Ge|mein|we|sen** NT community; (= Staat) polity; **Ge|mein|wil|le** M collective will; **Ge|mein|wirt|schaft** F cooperative economy; **ge|mein|wirt|schaft|lich** ADJ cooperative; **Ge|mein|wohl** NT public welfare; **das dient dem ~** it is in the public interest

Ge|men|ge [gə'mɛŋə] NT -s, **a** (= Mischung) mixture (aus of); (Agr) mixed crop; (fig) mixture; (= wirres Durcheinander) jumble (aus of) **b** (= Gewühl) bustle; (= Handgemenge) scuffle; **mit jdm ins ~ kommen** to come to blows with sb

ge|mes|sen [gə'mɛsn] ptp von **messen** ADJ **a** (= würdevoll) measured, studied; **~en Schrittes** with measured tread **b** (dated: = zurückhaltend) reticent **c** attr (= angemessen) Abstand, Entfernung respectful

Ge|mes|sen|heit F -, no pl **a** (= Würde) measuredness, studiedness **b** (dated: = Zurückhaltung) reticence

Ge|met|zel [gə'mɛtsl] NT -s, - bloodbath; (= Massaker auch) slaughter, massacre

ge|mie|den ptp von **meiden**

Ge|misch [gə'mɪʃ] NT -(e)s, -e **a** (lit, fig) mixture (aus of) **b** no pl (= Durcheinander) jumble (aus of)

ge|mischt [gə'mɪʃt] ADJ mixed; (inf: = nicht sehr gut auch) patchy; **mit ~en Gefühlen** with mixed feelings; **~er Teller** (mit verschiedenen Speisen) mixed platter or plate; **~es Eis** assorted ice cream; (mit selbstgewählten Sorten auch) your choice of ice cream; **~es Doppel** (Sport) mixed doubles pl → auch **Hautevolee**

Ge|mischt-: Ge|mischt|bau|wei|se F composite construction; **ge|mischt|ras|sig** ADJ of

mixed race; **Ehe** mixed-race; (mit mehreren Rassen) multi-racial; **ge|mischt|spra|chig** ADJ multilingual; **Ge|mischt|wa|ren|hand|lung** F (dated) grocery and general store

ge|mit|telt [gə'mɪtlt] ADJ average

Gem|me ['gɛmə] F -, -n (erhaben) cameo; (vertieft) intaglio

ge|mocht ptp von **mögen**

ge|mol|ken ptp von **melken**

ge|mop|pelt [gə'mɔplt] ADJ → **doppelt**

Ge|mo̱t|ze [gə'mɔtsə] NT -s, no pl (inf) moaning, fault-finding

Gems-: Gems|bart △ M → **Gamsbart**, **Gäms-bart**; **Gems|bock** △ M → **Gämsbock**

Gem|se △ ['gɛmzə] F -, -n → **Gämse**

Gems|le|der △ NT → **Gämsleder**

Ge|mun|kel [gə'mʊŋkl] NT -s, no pl rumours pl (Brit), rumors pl (US); (= Klatsch) gossip

Ge|murks [gə'mʊrks] NT -s, no pl (inf pej) **a** (als Tätigkeit) messing around **b** (= Ergebnis von Pfuscharbeit) mess

Ge|mur|mel [gə'mʊrml] NT -s, no pl murmuring; (= unverständliches Reden auch) mumbling; **zustimmendes ~ ging durch den Saal** a murmur of approval ran through the hall

Ge|mur|re [gə'mʊrə] NT -s, no pl (inf) grumbling (inf)

Ge|mü|se [gə'my:zə] NT -s, (rare) - vegetables pl; **frisches ~** fresh vegetables; **ein ~** a vegetable; **junges ~** (hum inf) whippersnappers pl (inf), green young things pl (inf)

Ge|mü|se-: Ge|mü|se|(an)|bau M , no pl vegetable-growing; (für den Handel) market gardening (Brit), truck farming (US); **Ge|mü|se|beet** NT vegetable bed or patch; **Ge|mü|se|bei|la|ge** F vegetables pl; **nach Wunsch ~** a choice of vegetables; **Ge|mü|se|brü|he** F **a** (= Gemüse-suppe) vegetable soup **b** (= Gemüsepulver, -brühwürfel) vegetable stock; **Ge|mü|se|ein|topf** M vegetable stew; **Ge|mü|se|fach** NT vegetable compartment; **Ge|mü|se|frau** F (inf) vegetable woman (inf); **Ge|mü|se|frit|ze** M (inf) vegetable seller; **Ge|mü|se|gar|ten** M vegetable or kitchen garden; **quer durch den ~** (hum inf) a real assortment; **in dem Geschäft dort gibt es alles quer durch den ~** they have everything but the kitchen sink in that shop there (esp Brit inf); **Ge|mü|se|händ|ler(in)** M(F) greengrocer (esp Brit), vegetable salesman/saleswoman (US); (= Großhändler) vegetable supplier; **Ge|mü|se|hand|lung** F greengrocer's (shop) (esp Brit), produce shop (US); **Ge|mü|se|kon|ser|ve** F tinned (Brit) or canned vegetables pl; (in Gläsern) preserved vegetables pl; **Ge|mü|se|la|den** M greengrocer's (shop) (esp Brit), produce shop (US); **Ge|mü|se|markt** M vegetable market; **Ge|mü|se|pflan|ze** F vegetable; **Ge|mü|se|plat|te** F (Cook) eine ~ assorted vegetables pl; **Ge|mü|se|saft** M vegetable juice; **Ge|mü|se|sor|te** F kind or type of vegetable; **Ge|mü|se|stand** M (= Marktstand) vegetable stall or stand; **Ge|mü|se|sup|pe** F vegetable soup; **Ge|mü|se|zwie|bel** F Spanish onion

ge|mü̱ßigt [gə'my:sɪçt] ADV = **bemüßigt**

ge|musst ▲ ptp von **müssen**

ge|mus|tert [gə'mʊstet] ADJ patterned → auch **mustern**

Ge|müt [gə'my:t] NT -(e)s, -er **a** (= Geist) mind; (= Charakter) nature, disposition; (= Seele) soul; (= Gefühl) feeling; (= Gutmütigkeit) warm-heartedness; **viel ~ haben** to be very warm-hearted; **die Menschen hatten damals mehr ~** people had more soul in those days; **das denkst du (dir) so einfach in deinem kindlichen ~!** that's what you think in your innocence; **etwas fürs ~** (hum) something for the soul; (Film, Buch etc) something sentimental; **jds ~ bewegen** (liter) to stir sb's heart or emotions; **sich (dat) etw zu ~e führen** (= beherzigen) to take sth to heart; (hum inf) Glas Wein, Speise, Buch etc to indulge in sth;

das ist ihr aufs ~ geschlagen that made her worry herself sick (*inf*)

b (*fig*: = *Mensch*) person; (*pl*) people; **sie ist ein ängstliches ~** she's a nervous soul, she has a nervous disposition; **die ~er erregen** to cause a stir; **wir müssen warten, bis sich die ~er beruhigt haben** we must wait until feelings have cooled down

ge|müt|lich [ɡəˈmyːtlɪç] **ADJ** **a** (= *bequem, behaglich*) comfortable, comfy (*inf*); (= *freundlich*) friendly *no adv*; (= *zwanglos*) informal; (= *klein und intim*) cosy (*Brit*), cozy (*US*), snug; *Schwatz, Beisammensein etc* cosy (*Brit*), cozy (*US*); **wir verbrachten einen ~en Abend** we spent a very pleasant evening

b *Mensch* good-natured, pleasant; (= *leutselig*) approachable, friendly; (= *gelassen*) easy-going *no adv*, relaxed *no adv*

c (= *gemächlich*) unhurried, leisurely; **in ~em Tempo** at a comfortable *or* leisurely speed

ADV **a** (= *behaglich*) leisurely; *einrichten* comfortably; **wir wollen das Wochenende ~ gestalten** we plan to have a leisurely weekend; **es sich/jdm ~ machen** to make oneself/sb comfortable

b (= *gemächlich*) leisurely; **er arbeitete ~ vor sich hin** he worked away at a leisurely pace, he worked away unhurriedly

Ge|müt|lich|keit F -, *no pl* **a** (= *Bequemlichkeit, Behaglichkeit*) comfort; (*von Lokal, Wohnung*) comfortable ambience; (= *Freundlichkeit*) friendliness; (= *Zwanglosigkeit*) informality; (= *Intimität*) cosiness (*Brit*), coziness (*US*), snugness

b (*von Mensch*) good nature, pleasantness; (= *Leutseligkeit*) approachability, friendliness; (= *Gelassenheit*) easy-going nature; **da hört doch die ~ auf!** (*inf*) that's going too far; **da hört bei mir die ~ auf** I won't stand for that; **ein Prosit der ~!** happy days!

c (= *Gemächlichkeit*) unhurriedness, leisureliness; **in aller ~** at one's leisure; **ich sitze da in aller ~, und ich arbeite wie ein Verrückter** you sit there as though there were all the time in the world and I'm working like mad

Ge|müts-: ge|müts|arm ADJ emotionally impoverished; **Ge|müts|ar|mut** F emotional impoverishment; **Ge|müts|art** F disposition, nature; **ein Mensch von heiterer ~** a person of cheerful disposition *or* nature; **Ge|müts|be|we|gung** F emotion; **bist du zu keiner ~ fähig?** can't you show some emotion?; **ge|müts|kalt** ADJ cold; **ge|müts|krank** ADJ emotionally disturbed; **Ge|müts|kran|ke(r)** MF *decl as adj* emotionally disturbed person; **Ge|müts|krank|heit** F emotional disorder *or* disturbance; **Ge|müts|krüp|pel** M (*inf*) emotional cripple; **Ge|müts|la|ge** F mood; **je nach ~** as the mood takes me/him *etc*; **Ge|müts|le|ben** NT emotional life; **Ge|müts|lei|den** NT emotional disorder *or* disturbance; **Ge|müts|mensch** M good-natured, phlegmatic person; **du bist vielleicht ein ~!** (*iro inf*) you're a fine one! (*inf*); (= *das ist unmöglich*) you'll be lucky! (*inf*); **Ge|müts|re|gung** F = Gemütsbewegung; **Ge|müts|ru|he** F calmness; (= *Kaltblütigkeit*) sang-froid, composure, coolness; (= *Phlegma*) placidness; **in aller ~** (*inf*) (as) cool as a cucumber (*inf*) *or* as you please (*inf*); (= *gemächlich*) at a leisurely pace; (= *aufreizend langsam*) as if there were all the time in the world; **du hast eine ~!** you take everything so calmly; **deine ~ möchte ich haben!** (*iro*) I like your cool! (*Brit inf*), I'd like to have your composure; **Ge|müts|ver|fas|sung** F, **Ge|müts|zu|stand** M frame *or* state of mind

ge|müt|voll ADJ sentimental; (= *warmherzig*) warm-hearted

gen [ɡɛn] PREP +*acc* (*old, liter*) towards, toward; **~ Norden/Osten** *etc* northwards/eastwards *etc*; **~ Himmel blicken** to look up to the sky, to look heavenwards

Gen [ɡeːn] NT -s, -e gene

Gen- *in cpds* genetic; (= *genmanipuliert*) genetically modified *or* engineered

ge|nannt *ptp von* **nennen**

ge|nant [ʒeˈnant] ADJ (*dated*) (= *schüchtern*) bashful, shy; (= *peinlich*) embarrassing

ge|narbt [ɡəˈnarpt] ADJ *Leder* grained

ge|nas *pret von* **genesen**

Ge|nä|sel [ɡəˈnɛːzl] NT -s, *no pl* nasal voice

ge|nau [ɡəˈnau] ✪ 28.2, 40.2, 43.1, 43.1, 52.5, 53.1, 53.3, 53.6 ADJ exact; (= *richtig auch*) accurate; (= *präzis auch*) precise; (= *sorgfältig auch*) meticulous; (= *förmlich genau auch*) punctilious; **haben Sie die ~e Zeit?** have you got (*esp Brit*) *or* do you have the right *or* exact time?; **Genaueres** further details *pl or* particulars *pl*; **Genaueres weiß ich nicht** I don't know any more than that; **man weiß nichts Genaues über ihn** no-one knows anything definite about him

ADV **~!** (*inf*) exactly!, precisely!, quite!; **~ dasselbe** just *or* exactly the same; **~ das Gegenteil** just *or* exactly the opposite; **~ in der Mitte** right in the middle; **~ das wollte ich sagen** that's just *or* exactly what I wanted to say; **ich kenne ihn ~** I know just *or* exactly what he's like; **etw ~ wissen** to know sth for certain *or* for sure; **etw ~ nehmen** to take sth seriously; **~ genommen** strictly speaking; **er nimmt es sehr/nicht sehr ~** he's very/not very particular (*mit etw* about sth); **einen Entschluss ~ überlegen** to think a decision over very carefully; **meine Uhr geht ~** my watch keeps accurate time; **es stimmt auf den Millimeter ~** it's right to the millimetre (*Brit*) *or* millimeter (*US*); **die Schuhe passten mir ~** the shoes fitted me perfectly; **das reicht ~** that's just enough; **~estens, aufs ~este** *or* **Genaueste** (right) down to the last (little) detail; **~ entgegengesetzt** diametrically opposed; **~ auf die Minute** dead (*inf*) *or* exactly on time; **so ~ wollte ich es (nun auch wieder) nicht wissen!** (*iro*) you can spare me the details → **Wahrheit**

ge|nau|ge|nom|men △ ADV → **genau** ADV

Ge|nau|ig|keit F -, *no pl* (= *Exaktheit*) exactness; (= *Richtigkeit*) accuracy; (= *Präzision*) precision; (= *Sorgfalt*) meticulousness

ge|nau|so [ɡəˈnauzoː] ADV (*vor Adjektiv*) just as; (*allein stehend*) just *or* exactly the same

Gen|bank F *pl* **-banken** gene bank

Gen|darm [ʒanˈdarm, ʒãˈdarm] M -en, -en (*old, Aus*) gendarme

Gen|dar|me|rie [ʒandarməˈriː, ʒã-] F -, -n [-ˈriːən] (*old, Aus*) gendarmerie

Gen|da|tei F (*Jur, Polizei*) DNA profile

Ge|ne|a|lo|ge [geneaˈloːɡə] M -n, -n, **Ge|ne|a|lo|gin** [-ˈloːɡɪn] F -, -nen genealogist

Ge|ne|a|lo|gie [genealoˈɡiː] F -, -n [-ˈɡiːən] genealogy

ge|ne|a|lo|gisch [geneaˈloːɡɪʃ] ADJ genealogical

ge|nehm [ɡəˈneːm] ADJ (*geh*) acceptable; **eine ihm ~e Antwort** an answer acceptable to him; **jdm ~ sein** to be acceptable to sb; **ist es so ~?** is that agreeable *or* acceptable to you?; **wenn es ~ ist** if you are agreeable

ge|neh|mi|gen [ɡəˈneːmɪɡn] *ptp* **genehmigt** VT *Baupläne, Antrag, Veränderungen* to approve; (= *erlauben*) to sanction; (= *Lizenz erteilen*) to license; *Durchreise, Aufenthalt* to authorize; (= *zugestehen*) to grant; *Bitte* to agree to, to assent to, to grant; **wer kann mir die Teilnahme ~?** from whom do I get permission to take part?; **„genehmigt"** "approved"; (*inf*) permission granted (*hum*); **sich** (*dat*) **etw ~** to indulge in sth; (= *kaufen*) to lash *or* splash out on sth; **sich** (*dat*) **einen ~** (*hum inf*) to have a little drink

Ge|neh|mi|gung F -, -en **a** (*von Bauplan, Antrag, Veränderungen*) approval; (= *Lizenzerteilung*) licensing; (*von Durchreise, Aufenthalt*) authorization; (= *das Zugestehen*) granting **b** (= *Erlaubnis*) approval; (= *Lizenz*) licence (*Brit*), license (*US*); (*für Durchreise, Aufenthalt*) authorization; (= *Be-*

rechtigungsschein) permit; **mit freundlicher ~ von** by kind permission of

Ge|neh|mi|gungs-: Ge|neh|mi|gungs|pflicht F (*form*) licence (*Brit*) *or* license (*US*) requirement; **ge|neh|mi|gungs|pflich|tig** [-ˌpflɪçtɪç] ADJ (*form*) requiring official approval; (*mit Visum, Stempel, Marke*) requiring official authorization; (*mit schriftlicher Genehmigung*) requiring a licence (*Brit*) *or* license (*US*); **Radiosender sind ~** a licence (*Brit*) *or* license (*US*) is required for radio transmitters

ge|neigt [ɡəˈnaikt] ADJ (*geh*) *Zuhörer, Publikum* willing; *Aufmerksamkeit* kind; (*obs*: = *huldvoll*) gracious; **~er Leser!** gentle reader; **jdm/einer Sache ~ sein** to be well-disposed *or* favourably (*Brit*) *or* favorably (*US*) disposed to sb/sth; **~ sein, etw zu tun** to be inclined to do sth; **nicht ~ sein, etw zu tun** not to be inclined to do sth → *auch* **neigen, Ohr**

Ge|neigt|heit F -, *no pl* (*geh*) (= *Bereitwilligkeit*) inclination; (= *Wohlwollen*) goodwill (*gegenüber* towards); (= *Huld*) favour (*Brit*), favor (*US*) (*genüber* to)

Ge|ne|ra *pl von* **Genus**

Ge|ne|ral [ɡenəˈraːl] M -(e)s, -e *or* ⸚e [-ˈrɛːlə], **Ge|ne|ra|lin** [-ˈraːlɪn] F -, -nen **a** (*Mil, Eccl*) general; **Herr ~** General **b** (*inf*: = *Generaldirektor*) head

Ge|ne|ral-: Ge|ne|ral|ab|so|lu|ti|on F general absolution; **Ge|ne|ral|agent(in)** M(F) general agent; **Ge|ne|ral|agen|tur** F general agency; **Ge|ne|ral|am|nes|tie** F general amnesty; **Ge|ne|ral|an|griff** M (*Mil, fig*) general attack; **Ge|ne|ral|an|walt** M, **Ge|ne|ral|an|wäl|tin** F (*Jur: des Europäischen Gerichtshofs*) advocate general; **Ge|ne|ral|bass** M (basso) continuo; **Ge|ne|ral|beich|te** F general confession; **Ge|ne|ral|be|voll|mäch|tig|te(r)** MF *decl as adj* plenipotentiary; (*Comm*) general representative; **Ge|ne|ral|bun|des|an|walt** M, **Ge|ne|ral|bun|des|an|wäl|tin** F Chief Federal Prosecutor; **Ge|ne|ral|di|rek|ti|on** F head office; **Ge|ne|ral|di|rek|tor(in)** M(F) chairman/-woman, president (*US*), CEO; **Ge|ne|ral|feld|mar|schall(in)** M(F) field marshal, general of the army (*US*); **Ge|ne|ral|gou|ver|neur(in)** M(F) governor general

Ge|ne|ra|lin F -, -nen → **General**

Ge|ne|ral-: Ge|ne|ral|in|spek|teur(in) M(F) inspector general; **Ge|ne|ral|in|ten|dant(in)** M(F) (*Theat, Mus*) director

ge|ne|ra|li|sie|ren [ɡenəraliˈziːrən] *ptp* **generalisiert** VI to generalize

Ge|ne|ra|li|sie|rung F -, -en generalization

Ge|ne|ra|lis|si|mus [ɡenəraˈlɪsɪmʊs] M -, **Generalissimi** *or* -**se** generalissimo

Ge|ne|ra|list [ɡenəraˈlɪst] M -en, -en, **Ge|ne|ra|lis|tin** [-ˈlɪstɪn] F -, -nen generalist

Ge|ne|ra|li|tät [ɡenəraliˈtɛːt] F -, (*rare*) -en (*Mil*) generals *pl*

Ge|ne|ral-: Ge|ne|ral|klau|sel F general *or* blanket clause; **Ge|ne|ral|kon|sul(in)** M(F) consul general; **Ge|ne|ral|kon|su|lat** NT consulate general; **Ge|ne|ral|leut|nant** M lieutenant general (*Brit*), major general (*US*); (*Brit Aviat*) air marshal; **Ge|ne|ral|ma|jor(in)** M(F) major general (*Brit*), brigadier general (*US*); (*Brit Aviat*) air vice-marshal; **Ge|ne|ral|mu|sik|di|rek|tor(in)** M(F) (chief) musical director; **Ge|ne|ral|nen|ner** M (*Math, fig*) common denominator; **Ge|ne|ral|obe|re(r)** [-ˈloːbərə] M *decl as adj* (*Eccl*) general (*of a religious order*); **Ge|ne|ral|obe|rin** F (*Eccl*) general (*of a women's order*); **Ge|ne|ral|oberst** M (*Hist*) senior general; **Ge|ne|ral|pau|se** F (*Mus*) general rest; **Ge|ne|ral|prä|ven|ti|on** F (*Jur*) general deterrence; **Ge|ne|ral|pro|be** F (*Theat, fig*) dress rehearsal; (*Mus*) final rehearsal; **Ge|ne|ral|re|prä|sen|tanz** F (*esp Aus*) sole *or* exclusive agency *or* distribution; **Ge|ne|ral|sek|re|tär(in)** M(F) secretary-general; **Ge|ne|ral|staats|an|walt** M, **Ge|ne|ral|staats|an|-**

wäl|tin F *public prosecutor for a provincial court,* ≈ *district attorney (US);* **Ge|ne|ral|stab** M general staff; **Ge|ne|ral|stabs|kar|te** F ≈ Ordnance Survey map (*Brit*), detailed map (*on the scale 1:100 000*); **ge|ne|ral|stabs|mä|ßig** **ADJ** *Aktion* planned with military precision; **ADV** *planen, organisieren* with military precision; **Ge|ne|ral|stabs|of|fi|zier(in)** M(F) general staff officer; **Ge|ne|ral|streik** M general strike; **Ge|ne|ral|sy|no|de** F general synod; **Ge|ne|ral|über|ho|len** *ptp* **generalüberholt** VT *infin, ptp only* **etw** ~ to give sth a general o-verhaul; **etw ~ lassen** to have sth generally overhauled; **Ge|ne|ral|über|ho|lung** F -, -en complete overhaul; **Ge|ne|ral|ver|samm|lung** F general meeting; **Ge|ne|ral|ver|tre|ter(in)** M(F) general representative; **Ge|ne|ral|ver|tre|tung** F sole agency; **Ge|ne|ral|vi|kar** M vicar general; **Ge|ne|ral|voll|macht** F general or full power of attorney

Ge|ne|ra|ti|on [genəra'tsio:n] F -, -en generation; **ein technisches Gerät der ersten ~** a piece of first-generation technology; **~ X/@** generation X/@

Ge|ne|ra|ti|o|nen-: **Ge|ne|ra|ti|o|nen|kon|flikt** M generation gap; **ge|ne|ra|ti|o|nen|lang** **ADJ** age-long **ADV** for generations; **Ge|ne|ra|ti|o|nen|ver|trag** M (*Econ*) system whereby old people receive a pension from contributions being made by current working population

Ge|ne|ra|ti|ons-: **Ge|ne|ra|ti|ons|kon|flikt** M generation gap; **Ge|ne|ra|ti|ons|problem** NT problem of one generation; **ein ~ der Jugend** a problem of the younger generation; **Ge|ne|ra|ti|ons|wech|sel** M (*Biol*) alternation of generations; **wir brauchen einen ~ in der Regierung** we need a new generation in government

ge|ne|ra|tiv [genəra'ti:f] ADJ generative; **~e Zellen** reproductive cells; **~e (Transformations-) Grammatik** (transformational) generative grammar

Ge|ne|ra|tor [genə'ra:tɔr] M -s, Generatoren generator; (= *Gasgenerator auch*) producer

Ge|ne|ra|tor|gas NT producer gas

ge|ne|rell [genə'rɛl] **ADJ** general **ADV** in general; (= *normalerweise*) normally; **~ kann man sagen, dass ...** generally or in general one can say that ...

ge|ne|rie|ren [genə'ri:rən] *ptp* **generiert** VT (*Ling, geh*) to generate

Ge|ne|ri|kum [ge'ne:rikʊm] NT -s, Generika [-ka] generic drug

ge|ne|rös [genə'rø:s] ADJ (*geh*) generous; (= *freigebig auch*) munificent (*liter*)

Ge|ne|ro|si|tät [genərozi'tɛ:t] F -, (*rare*) -en (*geh*) generosity; (= *Freigebigkeit auch*) munificence (*liter*)

Ge|ne|se [ge'ne:zə] F -, -n (*Biol, fig*) genesis

ge|ne|sen [ge'ne:zn] *pret* **genas** [ge'na:s], *ptp* **genesen** [ge'ne:zn] VI *aux sein* (*geh*) to convalesce; (*fig*) to recuperate

Ge|ne|sen|de(r) [ge'ne:zndə] MF *decl as adj* convalescent

Ge|ne|sis [ge'ne:zɪs, 'genɛzɪs] F -, *no pl* genesis; **die ~** (*Bibl*) (the Book of) Genesis

Ge|ne|sung [ge'ne:zʊŋ] ✪ 50.4 F -, (*rare*) -en convalescence, recovery (*auch fig*); **auf dem Wege der ~** on the road to recovery; **ich wünsche baldige ~** I wish you a speedy recovery; **er fuhr zur ~ ins Sanatorium** he went into a sanatorium (*esp Brit*) or sanitarium (*US*) to convalesce

Ge|ne|sungs-: **Ge|ne|sungs|heim** NT (*dated*) convalescent home; **Ge|ne|sungs|pro|zess** ▲ M convalescence; **der ~ hat sich verzögert** his *etc* convalescence was protracted; **Ge|ne|sungs|ur|laub** M convalescent leave

Ge|ne|tik [ge'ne:tɪk] F -, *no pl* genetics *sing*

Ge|ne|ti|ker [ge'ne:tikə] M -s, -, **Ge|ne|ti|ke|rin** [-ərɪn] F -, -nen geneticist

ge|ne|tisch [ge'ne:tɪʃ] **ADJ** genetic; *Vater* biological **ADV** genetically

Ge|ne|za|reth [ge'ne:tsarɛt] **der See** ~ the Sea of Galilee

Genf [gɛnf] NT -s Geneva

Gen|fer[1] ['gɛnfə] ADJ *attr* Genevan; **der ~ See** Lake Geneva; **~ Konvention** Geneva Convention

Gen|fer[2] ['gɛnfə] M -s, -, **Gen|fe|rin** [-ərɪn] F -, -nen Genevan, native or (= *Einwohner*) inhabitant of Geneva

Gen-: **Gen|for|scher(in)** M(F) genetic researcher; **Gen|for|schung** F genetic research

ge|ni|al [ge'nia:l] ADJ *Entdeckung, Einfall, Mensch* brilliant; *Künstler, Stil auch* inspired; (= *erfinderisch*) ingenious; **ein ~er Mensch, ein Genialer** a genius; **ein ~es Werk** a work of genius; **das war eine ~e Idee** that idea was or showed a stroke of genius

ge|ni|a|lisch [ge'nia:lɪʃ] ADJ (*geh*) brilliant; (= *unkonventionell*) eccentric

Ge|ni|a|li|tät [geniali'tɛ:t] F -, *no pl* (*von Künstler, Musiker etc*) genius; (*von Idee, Lösung etc*) brilliance; (= *Erfindungsreichtum*) ingenuity

Ge|nick [gə'nɪk] NT -(e)s, -e neck; **jdn am ~ packen** to grab sb by the scruff of the neck; **ein Schlag ins ~** a blow on the back of the neck; **seinen Hut ins ~ schieben** to push one's hat back (on one's head); **sich** (*dat*) **das ~ brechen** to break one's neck; (*fig*) to kill oneself; **jdm/einer Sache das ~ brechen** (*fig*) to finish sb/sth

Ge|nick-: **Ge|nick|schuss** ▲ M shot in the neck; **Ge|nick|star|re** F stiffness of the neck; (*Med*) (cerebral) meningitis; **~ haben** (*inf*) to have a stiff neck

Ge|nie[1] [ʒe'ni:] NT -s, -s genius; **er ist ein ~** he's a (man of) genius; **er ist ein ~ im Taktieren** he's a genius when it comes to tactics, he has a genius for tactics

Ge|nie[2] F -, -s (*Sw Mil*) engineer corps

Ge|ni|en *pl von* **Genius**

ge|nie|ren [ʒe'ni:rən] *ptp* **geniert** **VR** to be embarrassed; **sich vor Fremden ~** to be shy of or with strangers; **~ Sie sich nicht!** don't be shy!; **dabei geniere ich mich** I get embarrassed doing it; **ich geniere mich, das zu sagen** I don't like to say it; **er genierte sich (gar) nicht, das zu tun** it didn't bother him (at all) to do that → *auch* **geniert** **VT** **jdn ~** (= *peinlich berühren*) to embarrass sb; (*old, dial:* = *stören*) to bother or disturb sb; **das geniert mich wenig!** that doesn't bother or worry me

ge|nier|lich [ʒe'ni:ɐlɪç] ADJ **a** (*inf:* = *lästig*) bothersome; (= *genant*) embarrassing **b** (*dated:* = *schüchtern*) shy, bashful

ge|niert [ʒe'ni:ɐt] **ADJ** embarrassed **ADV** with embarrassment → *auch* **genieren**

ge|nieß|bar ADJ (= *essbar*) edible; (= *trinkbar*) drinkable; (*fig:* = *annehmbar*) acceptable; **er ist heute nicht ~** (*fig inf*) he is unbearable today

Ge|nieß|bar|keit [gə'ni:sba:ɐkait] F -, *no pl* (= *Essbarkeit*) edibility; (= *Trinkbarkeit*) drinkability; (*fig*) acceptability

ge|nie|ßen [gə'ni:sn] *pret* **genoss** ▲ [gə'nɔs] *ptp* **genossen** [gə'nɔsn] VT **a** (*lit, fig:* = *sich erfreuen an*) to enjoy; **den Wein muss man ~** this is a wine to be savoured (*Brit*) or savored (*US*); **er ist heute nicht zu ~** (*inf*) he is unbearable today **b** (= *essen*) to eat; (= *trinken*) to drink; **das Essen ist kaum zu ~** the meal is scarcely edible; **der Wein ist kaum zu ~** the wine is scarcely drinkable → **Vorsicht, Kavalier a**

Ge|nie|ßer [gə'ni:sə] M -s, -, **Ge|nie|ße|rin** [-ərɪn] F -, -nen connoisseur; (*des Lebens*) pleasure-lover; (= *Feinschmecker*) gourmet, epicure; **er ist ein stiller ~** he really knows how to enjoy life in his quiet way

ge|nie|ße|risch [gə'ni:sərɪʃ] **ADJ** appreciative; **sein ~er Ausdruck** his expression of pleasure

ADV appreciatively; (= *mit Behagen*) pleasurably; **~ schmatzte er mit den Lippen** he smacked his lips with relish; **~ zog er an seiner Zigarre** he puffed at his cigar with relish

Ge|nie- [ʒe'ni:-]: **Ge|nie|streich** M stroke of genius; **Ge|nie|trup|pe** F (*Sw Mil*) engineer corps

ge|ni|tal [geni'ta:l] ADJ genital

Ge|ni|tal- *in cpds* genital; **Ge|ni|tal|be|reich** M genital area

Ge|ni|ta|le [geni'ta:lə] NT -s, **Genitalien** [-liən] genital; **die Genitalien** the genitals or genitalia (*form*)

Ge|ni|tiv [ge'ni:ti:f] M -s, -e [-və] (= *Fall*) genitive (case); (= *Form*) genitive (form); **im ~** in the genitive

Ge|ni|tiv|ob|jekt NT genitive object

Ge|ni|us ['ge:niʊs] M -, **Genien** ['ge:niən] **a** (*Myth*) genius, guardian spirit **b** (= *Genie*) genius; **~ loci** (*geh*) genius loci **c** (*Art*) genius

Gen-: **Gen|la|bor** NT genetics laboratory; **Gen|ma|ni|pu|la|ti|on** F genetic manipulation; **gen|ma|ni|pu|liert** [-manipuli:ɐt] ADJ genetically engineered or modified; **Gen|mu|ta|ti|on** F gene mutation

Ge|nom [ge'no:m] NT -s, -e genome

Ge|nom|ana|ly|se F genome analysis

ge|nom|men *ptp von* **nehmen**

ge|noppt [gə'nɔpt] ADJ *Teppich, Stoff, Wolle* nubbly; *Gummi* pimpled → *auch* **noppen**

Ge|nör|gel [gə'nœrgl] NT -s, *no pl* (*inf*) moaning, grumbling, carping

ge|noss ▲ *pret von* **genießen**

Ge|nos|se [gə'nɔsə] M -n, -n, **Ge|nos|sin** [-'nɔsɪn] F -, -nen comrade; (*dated:* = *Gefährte auch*) companion; (= *Mitglied einer Genossenschaft*) member of a cooperative; (*pej:* = *Kumpan*) mate (*Brit inf*), buddy (*US inf*), pal (*inf*); **X und ~n** (*Jur*) X and others; (*pej*) X and co (*inf*)

ge|nos|sen *ptp von* **genießen**

Ge|nos|sen-: **Ge|nos|sen|schaft** [gə'nɔsnʃaft] F -, -en cooperative; **Ge|nos|sen|schaf|ter** [-ʃaftə] M -s, -, **Ge|nos|sen|schaf|te|rin** [-ərɪn] F -, -nen, **Ge|nos|sen|schaft|ler** [-ʃaftlə] M -s, -, **Ge|nos|sen|schaft|le|rin** [-ərɪn] F -, -nen member of a cooperative; **ge|nos|sen|schaft|lich** [-ʃaftlɪç] **ADJ** cooperative **ADV** **~ organisiert** organized as a cooperative

Ge|nos|sen|schafts-: **Ge|nos|sen|schafts|bank** F *pl* -banken cooperative bank; **Ge|nos|sen|schafts|bau|er** M, **Ge|nos|sen|schafts|bäu|e|rin** F cooperative farmer; **Ge|nos|sen|schafts|be|trieb** M cooperative; **Ge|nos|sen|schafts|we|sen** NT , *no pl* cooperative system

Ge|nos|sin F → **Genosse**

ge|nö|tigt [gə'nø:tɪçt] ADJ **~ sein, etw zu tun** to be forced or obliged to do sth; **sich ~ sehen, etw zu tun** to feel (oneself) obliged to do sth → *auch* **nötigen**

Ge|no|typ [geno'ty:p] M , **Ge|no|ty|pus** [geno'ty:pʊs] M genotype

ge|no|ty|pisch [geno'ty:pɪʃ] ADJ genotypic

Ge|no|zid [geno'tsi:t] M OR NT -(e)s, -e or -ien [-də, -diən] (*geh*) genocide

Gen|re ['ʒã:rə] NT -s, -s genre

Gen|re- ['ʒã:rə-]: **Gen|re|bild** NT genre picture; **Gen|re|ma|ler(in)** M(F) genre painter; **Gen|re|ma|le|rei** F , *no pl* genre painting

Gent [gɛnt] NT -s Ghent

Gen-: **Gen|tech|nik** F genetic engineering; **Gen|tech|ni|ker(in)** M(F) genetic engineer; **gen|tech|nik|frei** ADJ *Lebensmittel etc* GM-free, not genetically modified *pred*; **gen|tech|nisch** **ADJ** *Fortschritte etc* in genetic engineering **ADV** *manipulieren, verändern* genetically; *produzieren, herstellen* by means of genetic engineering; **~ vermehren** to reproduce through genetic engineering; **~ veränderte Organismen** genetically manipulated organisms; **Gen|tech|no|lo|gie**

F genetic engineering; **gen|tech|no|lo|gisch** **ADJ** *Verfahren, Zeitalter* of genetic engineering **ADV** ~ **hergestellte Arzneimittel** drugs produced by means of genetic engineering; **Gen|the|ra|pie** F gene therapy; **Gen|trans|fer** M genetic transfer

Ge|nua ['geːnua] NT **-s** Genoa

Ge|nu|e|se [genuˈeːzə] M **-n, -n**, **Ge|nu|e|sin** [-ˈeːzɪn] F **-, -nen**, **Ge|nu|e|ser** [genuˈeːzə] M **-s, -**, **Ge|nu|e|se|rin** [-ərɪn] F **-, -nen** Genoese

ge|nu|e|sisch [genuˈeːzɪʃ] **ADJ** Genoese

ge|nug [ɡəˈnuːk] **ADV** enough; ~ **Platz, Platz** ~ enough or sufficient room; **groß/alt/reich** ~ big/old/rich enough; ~ **davon** enough of that; ~ **der vielen Worte!** enough of words!; **danke, das ist** ~ that's enough, thank you; **das ist wenig** ~ that's precious little; **und damit noch nicht** ~ and that's not all; **sie sind jetzt ~, um ...** there are enough of them now to ...; **sag, wenns ~ ist!** (*beim Einschenken etc*) say when!; **jetzt ist(s) aber ~!** that's enough, that does it!; **(von etw)** ~ **haben** to have (got) enough (of sth); (= *einer Sache überdrüssig sein*) to have had enough (of sth); **er kann nicht ~ bekommen** or **kriegen** he can't get enough; **nicht ~, dass er sein ganzes Geld verspielt, außerdem ... er ...** not only does he gamble away all his money, he also ...; **er konnte sich nicht ~ darin tun, ihre Gastfreundschaft zu loben** (*geh*) he could not praise her hospitality enough or sufficiently; **sich** (*dat*) **selbst ~ sein** to be sufficient unto oneself; (= *gern allein sein*) to be content with one's own company; **Manns ~ sein, um zu ...** to be man enough to ...

Ge|nü|ge [ɡəˈnyːɡə] F **-, *no pl* zur ~** enough; **das habe ich zur ~ getan/gehört/gesehen** I have done/heard/seen it often enough or (*stärker, abwertend*) quite often; **etw zur ~ kennen** to know sth well enough; (*abwertender*) to know sth only too well, to be only too familiar with sth; **jdm ~ tun** (*geh*) to satisfy sb; **jds Forderungen** (*dat*) ~ **tun** (*geh*) to satisfy or meet sb's demands; **jds Erwartungen** (*dat*) ~ **tun** (*geh*) to fulfil (*Brit*) or fulfill (*US*) sb's expectations

ge|nü|gen [ɡəˈnyːɡn̩] *ptp* **genügt** VI **a** (= *ausreichen*) to be enough or sufficient (+*dat* for); **das genügt (mir)** that's enough or sufficient (for me), that will do (for me); **dieses Haus genügt uns** we're happy with this house; **dieses Haus genügt für uns** this house is enough for us **b** +*dat* (= *befriedigen, gerecht werden*) **den Anforderungen** to satisfy; **jds Wünschen, Erwartungen** to fulfil (*Brit*), to fulfill (*US*)

ge|nü|gend **ADJ a** *inv* (= *ausreichend*) enough, sufficient **b** (= *befriedigend*) satisfactory **ADV** (= *reichlich*) enough, sufficiently; **ich habe ~ oft versucht, zu ...** I have tried often enough or sufficiently often to ...

ge|nug|sam [ɡəˈnuːkzaːm] **ADV** (*geh*) enough; **es ist ~ bekannt** it is sufficiently well-known

ge|nüg|sam [ɡəˈnyːkzaːm] **ADJ** (= *anspruchslos*) *Tier, Pflanze* undemanding; *Mensch auch* modest; **ein ~es Leben führen** to live modestly **ADV** *leben* modestly; **sich ~ ernähren** to live on or to have a simple diet

Ge|nüg|sam|keit F **-, *no pl* (*von Mensch*) undemanding nature; **die ~ einer Pflanze/eines Tieres** the modest requirements of a plant/an animal; **seine bewundernswerte ~** his admirably undemanding nature

ge|nug|tun VI *sep irreg* +*dat* (*dated*) to satisfy; **er konnte sich** (*dat*) **nicht ~, ihre Schönheit zu preisen** he couldn't praise her beauty enough, he never tired of praising her beauty

Ge|nug|tu|ung [ɡəˈnuːktuːʊŋ] F **-, (*rare*) -en** satisfaction (*über* +*acc* at); **für etw ~ leisten** to make amends for sth; ~ **verlangen** or **fordern** to demand satisfaction; **ich hörte mit ~, dass ...** it gave me great satisfaction to hear that ...; **das hat mir ~ verschafft** that gave me a sense of satisfaction

ge|nu|in [genuˈiːn] **ADJ** (*geh*) genuine

Ge|nus ['geːnʊs, 'ɡɛnʊs] NT **-, Genera** ['geːnera, 'ɡɛnera] **a** (*Biol*) genus **b** (*Gram*) gender; ~ **ver|bi** voice of the verb

Ge|nuss ▲ [ɡəˈnʊs] M **-es, -̈e** [ɡəˈnʏsə] **a** *no pl* (= *das Zusichnehmen*) consumption; (*von Drogen*) taking, use; (*von Tabak*) smoking; **der ~ von Alkohol ist Kindern verboten** children are forbidden to drink or consume (*form*) alcohol; **der übermäßige ~ von Tabak ist gesundheitsschädlich** excessive smoking is injurious to one's health; **nach dem ~ der Pilze** after eating the mushrooms **b** (= *Vergnügen*) pleasure; **die Genüsse des Lebens** the pleasures or joys of life; **etw mit ~ essen** to eat sth with relish; **den Wein hat er mit ~ getrunken** he really enjoyed the wine **c** *no pl* (= *Nutznießung*) **in den ~ von etw kommen** (*von Vergünstigungen*) to enjoy sth; (*von Rente, Prämie etc*) to be in receipt of sth

Ge|nuss-: ge|nuss|freu|dig ▲ **ADJ** (*geh*) pleasure-loving *no adv*; **Ge|nuss|gift** ▲ NT (*form*) social drug

ge|nüss|lich ▲ [ɡəˈnʏslɪç] **ADJ** pleasurable **ADV** with pleasure; **er grunzte ~** he grunted with obvious enjoyment; **er schmatzte ~** he smacked his lips with relish

Ge|nuss-: Ge|nuss|mensch ▲ M hedonist; (*auf Essen und Trinken bezogen*) bon vivant; **Ge|nuss|mit|tel** ▲ NT semi-luxury foods and tobacco; **ge|nuss|reich** ▲ **ADJ** enjoyable; **Ge|nuss|schein** ▲ M (*Fin*) profit-participation certificate; **ge|nuss|sucht** ▲ F pursuit of pleasure; **ge|nuss|süch|tig** ▲ **ADJ** pleasure-seeking; **ge|nuss|voll** ▲ **ADJ** *Aufenthalt, Urlaub, Erlebnis, Abend* delightful; *Schmatzen* appreciative; *Lächeln* gratified **ADV** with obvious enjoyment

Ge|o|dä|sie [geodɛˈziː] F **-, *no pl* geodesy, geodetics *sing*

Ge|o|dät [geoˈdɛːt] M **-en, -en**, **Ge|o|dä|tin** [-ˈdɛːtɪn] F **-, -nen** geodesist

Ge|o|drei|eck [ˈgeo-] NT (*inf*) set square

Ge|o|graf ▲ [geoˈgraːf] M **-en, -en**, **Ge|o|gra|fin** ▲ [-ˈgraːfɪn] F **-, -nen** geographer

Ge|o|gra|fie ▲ [geograˈfiː] F **-, *no pl* geography

ge|o|gra|fisch ▲ [geoˈgraːfɪʃ] **ADJ** *no pred* geographic(al)

Ge|o|lo|ge [geoˈloːɡə] M **-n, -n**, **Ge|o|lo|gin** [-ˈloːɡɪn] F **-, -nen** geologist

Ge|o|lo|gie [geoloˈɡiː] F **-, *no pl* geology

ge|o|lo|gisch [geoˈloːɡɪʃ] **ADJ** *no pred* geological

Ge|o|me|ter [geoˈmeːtɐ] M **-s, -**, **Ge|o|me|te|rin** [-ərɪn] F **-, -nen a** surveyor **b** (*old*) geometrician

Ge|o|met|rie [geomeˈtriː] F **-, *no pl* geometry

ge|o|met|risch [geoˈmeːtrɪʃ] **ADJ** geometric; **~er Ort** locus

Ge|o|mor|pho|lo|gie F geomorphology

Ge|o|phy|sik F geophysics *sing*

Ge|o|po|li|tik F geopolitics *pl* or (*als Fachgebiet*) *sing*

ge|o|po|li|tisch **ADJ** *no pred* geopolitical

ge|ord|net [ɡəˈʔɔrdnət] **ADJ** *Leben, Zustände* well-ordered; **in ~en Verhältnissen leben** to live a well-ordered life; **Kinder aus ~en Verhältnissen** children from well-ordered backgrounds; **~e Verhältnisse schaffen** to put things on an orderly basis → *auch* **ordnen**

Geor|gette [ʒɔrˈʒɛt] F **-, -s**, *or nt* **-s, -s** georgette

Ge|or|gi|en [geˈɔrgiən] NT **-s** Georgia (*in Caucasia*)

Ge|or|gi|er [geˈɔrgiɐ] M **-s, -**, **Ge|or|gi|e|rin** [-iərɪn] F **-, -nen** Georgian

ge|or|gisch **ADJ** Georgian

Ge|o-: ge|o|sta|ti|o|när **ADJ** geostationary; **ge|o|stra|te|gisch** **ADJ** geostrategic; **Ge|o|wis|sen|schaft** F earth science; **ge|o|zent|risch** **ADJ** geocentric

ge|paart [ɡəˈpaːɐt] *ptp von* **paaren** **ADJ** (*fig*) **Bosheit ~ mit Dummheit** maliciousness coupled or combined with stupidity → *auch* **paaren**

Ge|päck [ɡəˈpɛk] NT **-(e)s**, *no pl* luggage *no pl* (*Brit*), baggage *no pl*; (*Mil*: = *Marschgepäck*) baggage; (*von Soldat, Pfadfinder etc*) kit; (*von Bergsteiger*) pack; **mit leichtem ~ reisen** to travel light

Ge|päck-: Ge|päck|ab|fer|ti|gung F (= *Vorgang*) (*am Bahnhof*) luggage (*Brit*) or baggage processing; (*am Flughafen*) checking-in of luggage (*Brit*) or baggage; (= *Stelle*) (*am Bahnhof*) luggage (*Brit*) or baggage office; (*am Flughafen*) luggage (*Brit*) or baggage check-in; **Ge|päck|ab|la|ge** F luggage (*Brit*) or baggage rack; **Ge|päck|an|nah|me** F (= *Vorgang*) checking-in of luggage (*Brit*) or baggage; (*auch* **Gepäck-annahmestelle**) (*am Bahnhof*) (*zur Beförderung*) luggage (*Brit*) or baggage office; (*zur Aufbewahrung*) left-luggage office (*Brit*), baggage checkroom (*US*); (*am Flughafen*) luggage (*Brit*) or baggage check-in; **Ge|päck|auf|be|wah|rung** F (= *das Aufbewahren*) looking after left luggage *no art* (*Brit*) or baggage *no art*; (*auch* **Ge-päckaufbewahrungsstelle**) left-luggage office (*Brit*), baggage checkroom (*US*); **Ge|päck|auf|be|wah|rungs|schein** M left-luggage ticket (*Brit*), check number (*US*); **Ge|päck|auf|kle|ber** M luggage (*Brit*) or baggage sticker; **Ge|päck|aus|ga|be** F (*auch* **Ge-päckausgabestelle**) (*am Bahnhof*) (*zur Beförderung*) (out-counter of the) luggage (*Brit*) or baggage office; (*zur Aufbewahrung*) (out-counter of the) left-luggage office (*Brit*) or baggage checkroom (*US*); (*am Flughafen*) luggage (*Brit*) or baggage reclaim; **wir müssen noch zur ~** we still have to collect our luggage (*Brit*) or baggage; **Ge|päck|band** [-bant] NT *pl* **-bänder** luggage (*Brit*) or baggage conveyor belt; **Ge|päck|er|mitt|lung** F luggage (*Brit*) or baggage tracing; **Ge|päck|iden|ti|fi|zie|rung** F luggage (*Brit*) or baggage identification; **Ge|päck|kar|ren** M luggage (*Brit*) or baggage trolley, cart (*US*); **Ge|päck|kon|trol|le** F luggage (*Brit*) or baggage control or check; **Ge|päck|marsch** M (*Mil*) pack march; **Ge|päck|netz** NT luggage (*Brit*) or baggage rack; **Ge|päck|raum** M (*Aut*) boot (*Brit*), trunk (*US*)

Ge|päcks- (*Aus*) *in cpds* = **Gepäck-**

Ge|päck-: Ge|päck|schal|ter M = **Gepäckannahme**; **Ge|päck|schein** M luggage (*Brit*) or baggage ticket; **Ge|päck|schließ|fach** NT luggage (*Brit*) or baggage locker; **Ge|päck|stück** NT piece or item of luggage (*Brit*) or baggage; **Ge|päck|trä|ger** M (*am Fahrrad*) carrier; **Ge|päck|trä|ger(in)** M(F) porter (*Brit*), baggage handler (*Brit*) or carrier; **Ge|päck|ver|si|che|rung** F luggage (*Brit*) or baggage insurance; **Ge|päck|wa|gen** M luggage van (*Brit*), baggage car (*US*)

ge|pan|zert [ɡəˈpantsɐt] *ptp von* **panzern** **ADJ** *Fahrzeug* armoured (*Brit*), armored (*US*); *Tier* mailed; (*mit Hornhaut*) sclerodermic (*spec*) → *auch* **panzern**

Ge|pard ['geːpart] M **-s, -e** [-də] cheetah

ge|pfef|fert [ɡəˈpfɛfɐt] **ADJ** (*inf*) (= *hoch*) *Preise, Mieten* steep; (= *schwierig*) *Fragen, Prüfung* tough; (= *hart*) *Kritik* biting; *Strafpredigt* tough; (= *anzüglich*) *Witz, Geschichte* spicy; **jdm eine ~e Ohrfeige geben** to give sb a clout (*inf*), to clout sb one (*inf*) → *auch* **pfeffern**

Ge|pfei|fe [ɡəˈpfaifə] NT **-s**, *no pl* whistling

ge|pfif|fen *ptp von* **pfeifen**

ge|pflegt [ɡəˈpfleːkt] **ADJ a** (= *nicht vernachlässigt*) well looked after; *Garten auch* well-tended; *Parkanlagen auch* well-kept; *Mensch, Äußeres, Hund* well-groomed; *Aussehen* well-groomed, soigné (*liter*) → *auch* **pflegen** **b** (= *kultiviert, niveauvoll*) civilized; *Atmosphäre, Restaurant* sophisticated; *Ausdrucksweise, Gespräche* cultured; *Sprache, Stil* cultured, refined; *Umgangsformen* refined; (= *angenehm*) *Abend* pleasant; **ein ganz ~es Bad nehmen** to have a nice long bath

c (= *erstklassig*) *Speisen, Weine* excellent; (*inf*: = *von guter Qualität*) decent; „**gepflegte Küche**" "excellent cuisine"

ADV a (= *kultiviert*) **sich ~ unterhalten** to have a civilized conversation; **sich ~ ausdrücken** to have a cultured way of speaking; **drück dich gefälligst ein bisschen ~er aus** don't be so crude; **sehr ~ wohnen** to live in style; **so richtig ~ essen gehen** (*inf*) to go to a really nice restaurant

b (*inf*: = *gut, gründlich*) **sich ganz ~ ausruhen** to have a good long rest

Ge|pflegt|heit F -, *no pl* **a die ~ des Gartens/ Rasens** the well-tended garden/well-kept lawn; **die ~ ihrer Hände erstaunte mich** I was amazed at how beautifully looked-after her hands were; **die ~ seines Aussehens** his well-groomed appearance **b die ~ ihrer Aussprache/ihres Stils** her refined *or* cultured accent/style

ge|pflo|gen (*old*) *ptp von* **pflegen**

Ge|pflo|gen|heit [gə'pfloːgnhaɪt] F -, **-en** (*geh*) (= *Gewohnheit*) habit; (= *Verfahrensweise*) practice; (= *Brauch*) custom, tradition

Ge|plän|kel [gə'plɛŋkl] NT **-s, -** skirmish; (*fig*) squabble

Ge|plap|per [gə'plapɐ] NT **-s**, *no pl* babbling; (*fig*: = *Geschwätz auch*) chatter(ing)

Ge|plärr [gə'plɛr] NT **-(e)s**, *no pl*, **Ge|plär|re** [gə'plɛrə] NT **-s**, *no pl* bawling; (*von Radio*) blaring

Ge|plät|scher [gə'plɛtʃɐ] NT **-s**, *no pl* splashing; (*pej inf*: = *Unterhaltung*) babbling

ge|plät|tet [gə'plɛtət] ADJ *pred* (*inf*) floored (*inf*); **ich bin ganz ~** (*inf*) I'm flabbergasted (*inf*) → *auch* **plätten**

Ge|plau|der [gə'plaudɐ] NT **-s**, *no pl* (*geh*) chatting

ge|pols|tert [gə'pɔlstɐt] *ptp von* **polstern** ADJ *Möbel etc* upholstered; *Kleidung etc* padded; **sie ist gut ~** (*inf, euph*) she's well-padded → *auch* **polstern**

Ge|pol|ter [gə'pɔltɐ] NT **-s**, *no pl* (= *Krach*) din; (*an Tür etc*) banging, thudding; (*von Kutsche etc*) clattering; (*inf*: = *Geschimpfe*) ranting; **die Fässer fielen mit ~ die Treppe hinunter** the barrels went thudding down the stairs

gepr. *abbr von* **geprüft**

Ge|prä|ge [gə'prɛːgə] NT **-s**, *no pl* (*auf Münzen*) strike; (*fig*: = *Eigentümlichkeit*) character; (= *Aura*) aura; **das hat den 60er Jahren ihr ~ gegeben** *or* **verliehen** it has left its mark *or* stamp on the sixties

Ge|prah|le [gə'praːlə] NT **-s**, *no pl* (*inf*) boasting, bragging

Ge|prän|ge [gə'prɛŋə] NT **-s**, *no pl* (*geh*) splendour (*Brit*), splendor (*US*), magnificence

Ge|pras|sel [gə'prasl] NT **-s**, *no pl* clatter(ing), rattle, rattling; (*von Regen, Hagel*) drumming; (*von Feuer*) crackle, crackling

ge|prie|sen *ptp von* **preisen**

ge|puf|fert [gə'pʊfɐt] ADJ (*Chem, Comput*) buffered

ge|punk|tet [gə'pʊŋktət] ADJ *Linie* dotted; *Stoff, Kleid* spotted; (*regelmäßig*) polka-dot → *auch* **punkten**

Ge|qua|ke [gə'kvaːkə] NT **-s**, *no pl* croaking; (*pej inf*: = *Geschwätz*) chatter

Ge|quä|ke [gə'kvɛːkə] NT **-s**, *no pl* (*inf*) (*von Kind*) whining; (*von Radio*) blaring

ge|quält [gə'kvɛːlt] ADJ *Lächeln* forced; *Miene, Ausdruck* pained; *Gesang, Stimme* strained → *auch* **quälen**

Ge|quas|sel [gə'kvasl] NT **-s**, *no pl* (*pej inf*) chattering

Ge|quat|sche [gə'kvatʃə] NT **-s**, *no pl* (*pej inf*) gabbing (*inf*); (= *Blödsinn*) twaddle (*inf*)

Ge|quen|gel [gə'kvɛŋl] NT **-s**, *no pl*, **Ge|quen|ge|le** [gə'kvɛŋələ] NT **-s**, *no pl* whining

Ge|quie|ke [gə'kviːkə] NT **-s**, *no pl* squealing

Ge|quiet|sche [gə'kviːtʃə] NT **-s**, *no pl* squeaking; (*von Reifen, Mensch*) squealing

ge|quol|len *ptp von* **quellen**

Ger [geːɐ] M **-(e)s, -e** (*old*) javelin (*used by the ancient Germanic peoples*)

ge|ra|de [gə'raːdə] ADJ straight; *Zahl* even; (= *aufrecht*) *Haltung* upright; (*fig*: = *aufrichtig*) *Charakter* honest; *Mensch* upright, upstanding; **eine ~ Körperhaltung haben** to hold oneself up straight; **in ~r Linie von jdm abstammen** to be directly descended from sb; **seinen ~n Weg gehen** (*fig*) to maintain one's integrity; **jdn mit ~m und offenem Blick ansehen** to look sb straight in the face; **das ~ Gegenteil** the exact *or* very opposite, exactly *or* just the opposite → **fünf**

ADV a (= *nicht krumm*) straight; **~ gewachsen sein** (*Mensch*) to be clean-limbed; (*Baum*) to be straight; **~ sitzen/stehen** to sit up/stand up straight

b (= *im Augenblick, soeben*) just; **wenn Sie ~ Zeit haben** if you have time just now; **wo Sie ~ da sind** just while you're here; **er wollte ~ aufstehen** he was just about to get up; **der Zug war ~ weg** the train had just gone; **~ erst** only just; **da wir ~ von Geld sprechen, ...** talking of money ...; **es macht uns ~ so viel Spaß** we're just enjoying it so much

c (= *knapp*) just; **so viel, dass er davon leben kann** just enough for him to live on; **sie hat die Prüfung ~ so bestanden** she just about passed the exam; **~ noch** only just; **~ noch zur rechten Zeit** just in time; **das hat ~ noch gefehlt!** (*iro*) that's all we wanted!

d (= *genau*) just; (= *direkt*) right; **es ist ~ 8 Uhr** it's just 8 o'clock; **~ zur rechten Zeit** at just *or* exactly the right time, just at the right time; **~ heute hab ich an dich gedacht** I was thinking of you just *or* only today; **jdm ~ in die Augen sehen** to look sb straight *or* right in the eyes; **~ deshalb** that's just *or* exactly why; **~ umgekehrt, ~ das Gegenteil** exactly *or* just the opposite; **das ist es ja ~!** that's just *or* exactly it!; **so ist es ~ richtig** that's just *or* exactly right

e (= *speziell, besonders*) especially; **~, weil ...** just because ...; **du solltest dafür Verständnis haben** you should be particularly understanding; **sie ist nicht ~ eine Schönheit** she's not exactly a beauty; **das war nicht ~ schön/interessant** that wasn't particularly *or* exactly nice/interesting; **du kannst dich ~ beklagen** (*iro*) what are you complaining about?, you've got a lot to complain about (*iro*)

f (= *ausgerechnet*) **warum ~ das?** why that of all things?; **warum ~ heute?** why today of all days?; **warum ~ ich?** why me of all people?; **warum ~ im Winter?** why in winter of all times?; **warum ~ in Venedig?** why in Venice of all places?; **~ diesem Trottel musste ich begegnen** of all people I would have to meet that idiot

g (*inf*: = *erst recht*) **nun ~!** you try and stop me now! (*inf*); **jetzt** *or* **nun ~ nicht!** I'll be damned if I will! (*inf*)

Ge|ra|de [gə'raːdə] F **-n, -n a** (*Math*) straight line **b** (*Sport*) (*von Renn-, Laufbahn*) straight; (*Boxen*) straight left/right; **seine rechte ~ traf ihn genau am Kinn** he hit him with a right to the chin

ge|ra|de-: **ge|ra|de|aus** [gəraːdə'laus] ADV straight ahead; *gehen, fahren* straight on (*Brit*) *or* ahead; **ge|ra|de bie|gen** ▲ VT *irreg* to straighten out; **ge|ra|de+bie|gen** VT *sep irreg* (*fig inf*) to straighten out, to put straight, to sort out; **ge|ra|de hal|ten** ▲ *irreg* VT to hold straight VR to hold oneself (up) straight; **ge|ra|de|he|raus** [gəraːdəhɛ'raus] (*inf*) ADJ *pred* forthright, frank, plain-spoken ADV frankly; **~ gesagt** quite frankly; **ge|ra|de le|gen** ▲ VT to put straight; **ge|ra|de ma|chen** ▲ VT to straighten (out); **ge|ra|den|wegs** [gə'raːdn̩veːks] ADV = **gerade(s)wegs**; **ge|ra|de rich|ten** ▲ VT to straighten up; (*horizontal*) to straighten out

---

ge|rä|dert [gə'rɛːdɐt] ADJ (*inf*) **wie ~ sein, sich wie ~ fühlen** to be *or* feel (absolutely) whacked (*inf*) → *auch* **rädern**

ge|ra|de-: **ge|ra|de sit|zen** ▲ VI *irreg aux haben or sein* to sit up straight; **ge|ra|de|so** [gə'raːdəzoː] ADV = **ebenso**; **ge|ra|de|so|gut** △ ADV → **ebenso**; **ge|ra|de|so|viel** △ ADV → **ebenso**; **ge|ra|de ste|hen** ▲ VI *irreg aux haben or sein* (= *aufrecht stehen*) to stand up straight; **ge|ra|de+ste|hen** VI *sep irreg aux haben or sein* **für jdn/etw ~** (*fig*) to be answerable *or* to answer for sb/sth; **ge|ra|de(s)wegs** [gə'raːdə(s)veːks] ADV straight; **~ auf etw** (*acc*) **losgehen** (*fig*) to get straight down to sth; **ge|ra|de|zu** [gə'raːdətsuː, gəraːdə'tsuː] **ADV a** (= *beinahe*) virtually, almost; (= *wirklich, durchaus*) really; **das ist doch ~ Selbstmord** that's nothing short of suicide, that's absolute suicide; **das ist ja ~ verblüffend/lächerlich!** that is absolutely amazing/ridiculous! **b** (= *ohne Umschweife*) frankly; **er sagte mir ~, dass ...** he told me straight out *or* frankly that ...; **~ aufs Ziel zusteuern** (*fig*) to go straight to the point **ADJ** *pred* (*inf*) (= *ehrlich*) frank, candid; (= *unverblümt*) blunt

Ge|rad-: **Ge|rad|füh|rung** F (*Tech*) guide; **Ge|rad|heit** F -, *no pl* (*fig*) (= *Aufrichtigkeit*) rectitude; (= *Freimut*) frankness, candour (*Brit*), candor (*US*); **ge|rad|li|nig** [-liːnɪç] ADJ straight; *Abkomme, Abstammung* direct; *Entwicklung etc* linear; (*fig*: = *aufrichtig*) straight ADV **~ denken/handeln** to be straight; **~ verlaufen** to run in a straight line; **die Straße verläuft ~ durch die Wiesen** the road runs in a straight line through the meadows; **Ge|rad|li|nig|keit** F -, *no pl* straightness; **sie ist für ihre ~ bekannt** she is known for coming straight to the point; **ge|rad|sin|nig** ADJ (*geh*) upright

Ge|raf|fel [gə'rafl] NT **-s**, *no pl* (*Aus, S Ger*) junk

ge|ram|melt [gə'ramlt] ADV **~ voll** (*inf*) (jam-)packed (*inf*), chock-a-block (*inf*) → *auch* **rammeln**

Ge|ran|gel [gə'raŋl] NT **-s**, *no pl* (= *Balgerei*) scrapping; (*fig*: = *zäher Kampf*) wrangling; **ein kurzes ~ der beiden Spieler** a short scrap between the two players; **das ~ um die Sonderangebote** the tussle over the bargains

Ge|ra|nie [gə'raːniə] F -, **-n** geranium

ge|rann *pret von* **gerinnen**

ge|rannt *ptp von* **rennen**

Ge|rant [ʒeˈrant] M **-en, -en**, **Ge|ran|tin** [-'rantɪn] F -, **-nen** (*Sw*) manager/manageress

Ge|ra|schel [gə'raʃl] NT **-s**, *no pl* rustle, rustling

Ge|ras|sel [gə'rasl] NT **-s**, *no pl* rattle, rattling

ge|rät [gə'rɛːt] 3. *pers sing pres von* **geraten** [1]

Ge|rät [gə'rɛːt] NT **-(e)s, -e a** piece of equipment; (= *Vorrichtung*) device; (= *Apparat*) gadget; (= *landwirtschaftliches Gerät*) implement; (= *elektrisches Gerät*) appliance; (= *Radiogerät, Fernsehgerät, Telefon*) set; (= *Messgerät*) instrument; (= *Küchengerät*) utensil; (= *Werkzeug, Gartengerät*) tool; (= *Turngerät*) piece of apparatus; (*inf*: = *Penis*) tool (*sl*) **b** *no pl* (= *Ausrüstung*) equipment *no pl*; (*von Handwerker*) tools *pl*

Ge|rä|te-: **Ge|rä|te|an|bie|ter(in)** M(F) (= *Leasinganbieter*) lessor (of the equipment); **Ge|rä|te|me|di|zin** F (*usu pej*) high-tech(nology) medicine

ge|ra|ten [1] [gə'raːtn] *pret* **geriet** [gə'riːt], *ptp* **geraten** [gə'raːtn] VI *aux sein* **a** (= *zufällig gelangen*) to get (*in +acc* into); **an jdn ~** (= *jdn kennen lernen*) to come across sb; (= *jdn bekommen*) to find sb, to dig sb up (*pej*); **an etw** (*acc*) **~** to get sth, to come by sth; **an einen Ort ~** to come to a place; **an den Richtigen/Falschen ~** to come to the right/wrong person; **unter ein Fahrzeug ~** to fall under a vehicle; **mit der Hand in eine Maschine ~** to get one's hand caught in a machine; **in Gefangenschaft ~** to be taken prisoner; **das Schiff ist in einen Sturm ~** the boat got caught in a storm; **in Bewegung ~** to begin to move; **ins Stocken ~** to come to a halt; **ins Schleudern ~** to go into a skid; **in Brand ~** to

---

catch fire; **in Angst/Begeisterung/Schwierigkeiten ~** to get scared/enthusiastic/into difficulties; **in Vergessenheit ~** to fall into oblivion; **aus der Bahn ~** (*lit*) to come off *or* leave the track; (*fig*) to go off the rails; **auf krumme Wege** *or* **die schiefe Bahn ~** to stray from the straight and narrow; **aus der Fassung/der Form ~** to lose one's composure/one's shape; **außer sich ~ (vor etw** *dat*) to be beside oneself (with sth); **unter schlechten Einfluss ~** to come under a bad influence → **Abweg, Haar**

b (= *sich entwickeln, gelingen, ausfallen*) to turn out; **ihm gerät einfach alles** everything he does turns out well *or* is a success, everything always goes right for him; **mein Aufsatz ist mir zu lang ~** my essay turned out too long; **der Junge/Kaktus ist gut ~** the boy/cactus turned out well; **nach jdm ~** to take after sb

ge|ra|ten² *ptp von* **raten**, *von* **geraten ¹** ADJ (*geh*: = *ratsam*) advisable; **ich halte es für ~** I think it would be advisable

Ge|rä|te-: Ge|rä|te|raum M equipment room; **Ge|rä|te|schup|pen** M tool shed; **Ge|rä|te|tur|nen** NT apparatus gymnastics *no pl*

Ge|ra|te|wohl NT **aufs ~** on the off-chance; (*aussuchen, auswählen etc*) at random; **er hat die Prüfung einfach aufs ~ versucht** he decided to have a go at the exam just on the off chance of passing; **er ist aufs ~ nach Amerika ausgewandert** he emigrated to America just like that; **wir schlugen aufs ~ diesen Weg ein** we decided to trust to luck and come this way

Ge|rät|schaf|ten PL (= *Ausrüstung*) equipment *sing*; (= *Werkzeug*) tools *pl*

Ge|rat|ter [gəˈratɐ] NT **-s**, *no pl* clatter(ing), rattle, rattling; (*von Maschinengewehr*) chatter(ing)

Ge|räu|cher|te(s) [gəˈrɔʏçətə] NT , *no pl decl as adj* smoked meat (*especially bacon and ham*)

ge|raum [gəˈraum] ADJ *attr* **vor ~er Zeit** some time ago; **seit ~er Zeit** for some time; **es dauerte eine ~e Weile** it took some time; **in/aus ~er Entfernung** at/from some distance; **ein ~es Maß an Arbeit/Zeit** a good deal of work/time

ge|räu|mig [gəˈrɔʏmɪç] ADJ *Haus, Zimmer, Auto* spacious, roomy; *Schrank, Koffer, Kofferraum auch* capacious

Ge|räu|mig|keit F **-**, *no pl* (*von Haus, Zimmer, Auto*) spaciousness, roominess; (*von Schrank, Koffer, Kofferraum auch*) capaciousness

Ge|rau|ne NT **-s**, *no pl* (*liter*) whispering

Ge|raun|ze [gəˈrauntsə] NT **-s**, *no pl* (*S Ger, Aus: inf*) grousing (*esp Brit inf*), grouching (*inf*)

Ge|räusch [gəˈrɔʏʃ] NT **-(e)s**, **-e** sound; (*esp unangenehm*) noise; **der Arzt horchte meine Brust auf ~e ab** the doctor listened to my chest for any unusual sounds; **die ~e des Verkehrs** the noise of the traffic; **aus dem Keller hörte man verdächtige ~e** suspicious noises came from the cellar; **mit einem dumpfen ~** with a dull thud

Ge|räusch-: ge|räusch|arm ADJ quiet; **Ge|räusch|ar|mut** F quietness; **ge|räusch|däm|mend** [-dɛmənt], **ge|räusch|dämp|fend** [-dɛmpfənt] ADJ noise-reducing, noise-insulating; **Ge|räusch|dämp|fung** F sound damping; (*stärker*) deadening of sound; **ge|räusch|emp|find|lich** ADJ sensitive to noise; (*Tech*) sound-sensitive; **Ge|räusch|ku|lis|se** F background noise; (*Film, Rad, TV*) sound effects *pl*; **ge|räusch|los** ADJ silent; **sie fanden eine ~e Lösung des Problems** (*fig*) they found out how to solve the problem quietly *or* without a lot of fuss ADV silently, without a sound; (*fig*) quietly, without a lot of fuss; **Ge|räusch|lo|sig|keit** F **-**, *no pl* quietness, noiselessness; (*fig*) lack of fuss; **Ge|räusch|mes|ser** M **-s**, **-** sound level recorder; **Ge|räusch|pe|gel** M sound level; **ge|räusch|voll** ADJ (= *laut*) loud; (= *lärmend*) noisy ADV (= *laut*) loudly; (= *lärmend*) noisily; **weniger ~** with less noise

Ge|räus|per [gəˈrɔʏspɐ] NT **-s**, *no pl* throat-clearing

ger|ben [ˈɡɛrbn] VT to tan; **vom Wetter gegerbte Haut** weather-beaten skin → **Fell**

Ger|ber [ˈɡɛrbɐ] M **-s**, **-**, **Ger|be|rin** [-ərɪn] F **-**, **-nen** tanner

Ger|be|ra [ˈɡɛrbera] F **-**, **-(s)** (*Bot*) gerbera

Ger|be|rei [ɡɛrbəˈrai] F **-**, **-en** **a** *no pl* (= *Gerben*) tanning **b** (= *Werkstatt*) tannery

Ger|be|rin [ˈɡɛrbərɪn] F **-**, **-nen** tanner

Ger|ber|lo|he F tanbark

Gerb|säu|re F tannic acid

Gerb|stoff M tanning agent

Ger|bung F **-**, **-en** tanning

ge|recht [gəˈrɛçt] ADJ **a** (= *rechtgemäß, verdient*) just; (= *unparteiisch auch*) fair; (= *rechtschaffen*) upright; **~ gegen jdn sein** to be fair *or* just to sb; **~er Lohn für alle Arbeiter!** fair wages for all workers!; **seinen ~en Lohn bekommen** (*fig*) to get one's just deserts *or* reward; **das ist nur ~** that's only fair *or* right *or* just; **~er Gott** *or* **Himmel!** (*inf*) good heavens (above)!; **die Gerechten** the just; **Gott, der Gerechte** God the righteous; **der Gerechte muss viel leiden** (*prov*) no rest for the wicked (*iro prov*); **den Schlaf des Gerechten schlafen** (*usu hum*) to sleep the sleep of the just

b (= *berechtigt*) just, legitimate; **~er Zorn** righteous anger; **sich für eine ~e Sache einsetzen** to fight for a just cause

c **jdm/einer Sache ~ werden** to do justice to sb/sth; **den Bedingungen ~ werden** to fulfil (*Brit*) *or* fulfill (*US*) the conditions; **jds Erwartungen** (*dat*) **~ werden** to come up to *or* fulfil (*Brit*) *or* fulfill (*US*) sb's expectations → **Sattel**

ADV fairly; (= *rechtgemäß*) justly

-ge|recht ADJ *suf* suitable for; **behinderten|ge|recht** suitable for disabled people

ge|rech|ter|wei|se [gəˈrɛçtɐˈvaizə] ADV to be fair

ge|recht|fer|tigt [gəˈrɛçtfɛrtɪçt] ADJ justified

Ge|rech|tig|keit F **-**, *no pl* **a** justice; (= *das Gerechtsein*) justness; (= *Unparteilichkeit*) fairness; (= *Rechtschaffenheit*) righteousness; **die ~ nahm ihren Lauf** justice took its course; **jdm/einer Sache ~ widerfahren lassen** to be just to sb/sth; (*fig*) to do justice to sb/sth **b** (*geh*: = *Gerechtsbarkeit*) justice; **jdn (den Händen) der ~ ausliefern** to bring sb to justice

Ge|rech|tig|keits-: Ge|rech|tig|keits|fim|mel M (*pej inf*) thing about justice (*inf*); **Ge|rech|tig|keits|ge|fühl** NT sense of justice; **Ge|rech|tig|keits|lie|be** F love of justice; **ge|rech|tig|keits|lie|bend** ADJ **ein ~er Mensch** a lover of justice, a person with a love of justice; **~ sein** to have a love of justice; **Ge|rech|tig|keits|sinn** M , *no pl* sense of justice

Ge|recht|sa|me [gəˈrɛçtzaːmə] F **-**, **-n** (*Hist*) rights *pl*

Ge|re|de [gəˈreːdə] NT **-s**, *no pl* talk; (= *Klatsch*) gossip(ing); **ins ~ kommen** *or* **geraten** to get oneself talked about; **jdn ins ~ bringen** to get sb talked about; **kümmere dich nicht um das ~ der Leute** don't worry about what people say

ge|re|gelt [gəˈreːɡlt] ADJ *Arbeit(szeiten), Mahlzeiten* regular; *Leben* well-ordered; **~er Katalysator** computer-controlled *or* feedback catalytic converter; **~er Markt** (*St Ex*) over-the-counter *or* official market → *auch* **regeln**

ge|rei|chen [gəˈraiçn] *ptp* **gereicht** VI (*geh*) **jdm zur Ehre ~** to do sb honour (*Brit*) *or* honor (*US*), to redound to sb's honour (*Brit form*) *or* honor (*US form*); **jdm zum Schaden/Nutzen ~** to be damaging/beneficial to sb, to redound to sb's benefit (*form*); **jdm/einer Sache zum Vorteil ~** to be an advantage to sb/sth, to redound to sb's advantage (*form*); (= *vorteilhaft erscheinen lassen*) to be advantageous for sb/sth

ge|reift [gəˈraift] ADJ (*fig*) mature; *Produkt, Technologie* fully developed → *auch* **reifen**

Ge|reift|heit F **-**, *no pl* (*fig*) maturity

ge|reizt [gəˈraitst] ADJ (= *verärgert*) irritated; (= *reizbar*) irritable, touchy; (= *nervös*) tetchy (*esp Brit inf*), edgy; **im Zimmer herrschte ~e Stimmung** there was a strained atmosphere in the room ADV (= *verärgert*) irritably → *auch* **reizen**

Ge|reizt|heit F **-**, *no pl* (= *Verärgertheit*) irritation; (= *Reizbarkeit*) irritability, touchiness; (= *Nervosität*) tetchiness (*esp Brit inf*), edginess; **die ~ der Atmosphäre** the strained atmosphere

Ge|ren|ne NT **-s**, *no pl* (*inf*) running, racing; (= *das Umherlaufen*) running *or* racing about (*Brit*) *or* around

ge|reu|en [gəˈrɔʏən] *ptp* **gereut** (*old, geh*) VT *impers* **es gereut mich, dass ...** I regret that ..., I am sorry that ...; **es wird Sie nicht ~** you will not regret it VT **meine Tat gereut mich** I regret my action

Ger|fal|ke [ˈɡeːɐ-] M gyrfalcon, gerfalcon

Ge|ri|a|ter [ɡeˈriaːtɐ] M **-s**, **-**, **Ge|ri|a|te|rin** [-ərɪn] F **-**, **-nen** geriatrician

Ge|ri|at|rie [ɡeriaˈtriː] F **-**, *no pl* geriatrics *sing*

ge|ri|at|risch [ɡeˈriaːtrɪʃ] ADJ geriatric

Ge|richt¹ [gəˈrɪçt] NT **-(e)s**, **-e** (= *Speise*) dish; **leckere ~e** delicious meals

Ge|richt² NT **-(e)s**, **-e** **a** (= *Behörde*) court (of justice); (= *Gebäude*) court(house), law courts *pl*; (= *die Richter*) court, bench; **Hohes ~!** My Lord! (*Brit*), Your Honor! (*US*); **vor ~ erscheinen/aussagen** to appear/testify in court; **vor ~ kommen** (*Fall*) to come to court; (*Mensch*) to come *or* appear before a/the court; **vor ~ stehen** to stand trial; **jdn vor ~ laden** to summon *or* call sb to appear in court; **jdn/einen Fall vor ~ bringen** to take sb/a case to court; **mit etw vor ~ gehen** to go to court about sth, to take legal action about sth; **jdn bei ~ verklagen** to take sb to court; **jdn/einen Fall vor ~ vertreten** to represent sb/a case in court; **das ~ zieht sich zur Beratung zurück** the court will adjourn **b** **das Jüngste** *or* **Letzte ~** the Last Judgement; **über jdn/etw ~ halten** to pronounce judgement on sb/sth; **über jdn zu ~ sitzen** (*fig*) to sit in judgement on sb; **mit jdm (scharf) ins ~ gehen** (*fig*) to judge sb harshly

ge|richt|lich [gəˈrɪçtlɪç] ADJ *attr* judicial; *Bestimmung, Entscheidung etc* court; *Medizin, Psychologie* forensic; *Verhandlung* legal; **~e Schritte gegen jdn einleiten** to initiate legal proceedings against sb; **laut ~em Beschluss** according to the decision of a/the court, according to a/the court decision; **ein ~es Nachspiel** a court sequel; **ein ~es Nachspiel haben** to finish up in court; **eine Sache ~** *or* **auf ~em Weg klären** to settle a matter in court or by litigation ADV *anerkannt* by a court; *durchsetzbar* legally, by the court; *klären* in court; **jdn ~ belangen** (= *strafrechtlich*) to prosecute sb; (= *zivilrechtlich*) to bring legal proceedings against sb; **~ gegen jdn vorgehen** to take legal action against sb, to litigate against sb; **jdn ~ vertreten** to represent sb in and out of court; **Schulden ~ beitreiben** to enforce the payment of debts; **jdm etw ~ untersagen lassen** to get an injunction against sb doing sth; **jdn ~ für tot erklären lassen** to have sb declared legally dead; **~ vereidigter Dolmetscher** court-appointed interpreter; **~ angeordnet** ordered by the courts

Ge|richts-: Ge|richts|ak|ten PL court records *pl*; **Ge|richts|arzt** M , **Ge|richts|ärz|tin** F court doctor; **Ge|richts|as|ses|sor(in)** M(F) ≈ junior barrister *or* lawyer (*Brit*), assistant judge (*US*)

Ge|richts-: Ge|richts|be|richt|er|stat|ter(in) M(F) legal correspondent; **Ge|richts|be|schluss** ▲ M decision of a/the court, court decision; **Ge|richts|be|zirk** M juridical district; **Ge|richts|die|ner(in)** M(F) (*old*) court usher; **Ge|richts|ent|scheid** M , **Ge|richts|ent|schei|dung** F court decision; **Ge|richts|fe|ri|en** PL court vacation, recess; **Ge|richts-**

ge|bäu|de NT law court(s *pl*), courthouse (*US*); **Ge|richts|ge|büh|ren** PL = **Gerichts-kosten**; **Ge|richts|herr** M (*Hist*) lord of the manor; **Ge|richts|hof** M court (of justice), law court; **Oberster ~** Supreme Court (of Justice); **der hohe ~** the high court; **Ge|richts|-ho|heit** F jurisdiction; **Ge|richts|kas|se** F **den Betrag von 200 Euro an die ~ zahlen** to pay the court 200 euros; **Ge|richts|kos|ten** PL court costs *pl*; **jdn zum Tragen der ~ verurteilen** (*form*) **jdm die ~ auferlegen** (*form*) to order sb to pay costs; **ge|richts|kun|dig** ADJ = **gerichtsnotorisch**; **Ge|richts|me|di|zin** F forensic medicine, medical jurisprudence; **Ge|richts|me|di|zi|ner(in)** M(F) forensic doctor; **ge|richts|me|di|zi|nisch** ADJ forensic medical *attr* ADV **die Leiche wurde ~ untersucht** the body was examined by an expert in forensic medicine; **ge|richts|no|to|risch** ADJ known to the court; **Ge|richts|ord|nung** F rules *pl* of the court; **Ge|richts|ort** M *pl* **-orte** town etc with a court; **~ ist Stuttgart** (*Vertragsbedingung*) any legal case arising from this contract shall be heard in Stuttgart; **Ge|richts|präsi|dent(in)** M(F) president of the court; **Ge|richts|re|fe|ren|dar(in)** M(F) *law student who has passed the first State Examination,* ≈ articled barrister (*Brit*), ≈ law graduate (*US*); **Ge|richts|re|por|ter(in)** M(F) legal correspondent; **Ge|richts|saal** M courtroom; **Ge|richts|schrei|ber(in)** M(F) clerk of the court (*Brit*), registrar (*US*); **Ge|richts|spra|che** F language of the courts; **Ge|richts|stand** M (*form*) court of jurisdiction; **Ge|richts|ta|fel** F court notice board; (*für öffentliche Bekanntmachungen*) ≈ public notice board; **Ge|richts|tag** M court day; **Montag ist ~** the court sits on Mondays, the court is in session on Mondays; **Ge|richts|ter|min** M date of a/the trial; (*für Zivilsachen*) date of a/the hearing; **einen ~ ansetzen** to fix a date for a/the trial/hearing; **Ge|richts|ver|fah|ren** NT court or legal proceedings *pl*; **ein ~ gegen jdn einleiten** to institute legal proceedings against sb; (*zivil auch*) to litigate against sb; **er wurde ohne ordentliches ~ verurteilt** he was sentenced without a proper trial; **Ge|richts|ver|fas|sung** F legal constitution; **Ge|richts|ver|hand|lung** F trial; (*zivil*) hearing; **Ge|richts|voll|zie|her** [-fɔltsiːɐ] M **-s, -**, **Ge|richts|voll|zie|he|rin** F **-, -nen** bailiff; **Ge|richts|weg** M **auf dem ~** through the courts; **Ge|richts|we|sen** NT, *no pl* judiciary, judicial system

ge|rie|ben [gəˈriːbn] *ptp von* **reiben** ADJ (*fig inf*) smart, sharp; (= *verschlagen auch*) tricky, sly, fly (*Brit inf*); **der ist verdammt ~** (*inf*) there are no flies on him (*Brit inf*), you can't pull the wool over his eyes

ge|rie|ren [geˈriːrən] *ptp* **geriert** VR (*geh*) to project an image

Ge|rie|sel [gəˈriːzl] NT **-s**, *no pl* (*von Sand*) trickling; (*von Schnee*) floating down

ge|riet *pret von* **geraten** [1]

ge|rif|felt [gəˈrɪflt] *ptp von* **riffeln** ADJ *Glas, Säule* etc grooved, fluted; (= *gerippt*) ribbed; (= *eng gewellt*) corrugated → *auch* **riffeln**

ge|ring [gəˈrɪŋ] ADJ **a** (= *nicht sehr groß, niedrig*) *Temperatur, Luftdruck, Leistung, Produktion* low; *Gehalt, Preis* low, modest; *Menge, Vorrat, Betrag, Entfernung* small; *Wert* little *attr*; (= *kurz*) *Zeit, Entfernung* short; **mit ~en Ausnahmen** with few exceptions; **Berge von ~er Höhe** low hills; **etw in ~er Höhe anbringen** to fix sth fairly low down; **seine Leistung erhielt eine zu ~e Bewertung** his achievement wasn't rated highly enough

b (= *unbedeutend, unerheblich*) slight; *Chance auch* small, slim; *Bedeutung, Rolle* minor; **die ~ste Kleinigkeit** the least or smallest or slightest little thing; **das ist meine ~ste Sorge** that's the least of my worries; **die Kosten sind nicht ~** the costs are not inconsiderable; **nicht das Geringste** nothing at all; **nicht im Geringsten** not in the least or slightest; **das Geringste** the least thing; **nichts Geringeres als ...** nothing less

than ... **c** (= *unzulänglich*) *Qualität, Kenntnisse* poor; (= *abschätzig*) *Meinung* low, poor

d *attr* (*fig geh*) *Familie, Herkunft* humble; **(auch)** **der Geringste** even the most humble person; **kein Geringerer als Freud ...** no less a person than Freud

ADV **a** (= *wenig*) **~ gerechnet** at a conservative estimate

b (= *abschätzig*) **~ von jdm sprechen** to speak badly of sb; **~ von jdm denken** to have a low opinion of sb

ge|ring ach|ten ▲ VT = **gering schätzen**

ge|rin|gelt [gəˈrɪŋlt] ADJ **a** *Muster* ringed; *Socken* hooped **b** (= *lockig*) *Haare* curly

Ge|ring-: ge|ring|fü|gig [-fyːgɪç] ADJ (= *unwichtig*) insignificant; *Verbesserung, Unterschied* slight; *Vergehen, Verletzung* minor; *Einzelheiten* minor, trivial; *Betrag* small; **~e Beschäftigung** part-time employment ADV slightly; **sein Zustand hat sich ~ gebessert** his condition is marginally or slightly improved; **Ge|ring|fü|gig|keit** F **-, -en a** (*Jur*) **ein Verfahren wegen ~ einstellen** to dismiss a case because of the trifling nature of the offence (*Brit*) or offense (*US*) **b** (*von Betrag*) insignificance **c** (= *Kleinigkeit*) little or small thing, trifle; **Ge|ring|fü|gig|keits|gren|ze** F lower earnings limit; **ge|ring schät|zen** ▲ VT (= *verachten*) *Menschen, Leistung* to think little of, to have a poor or low opinion of; *Erfolg, Reichtum* to set little store by (*Brit*) or in (*US*), to place little value on; *menschliches Leben* to have scant regard for, to place little value on; (= *missachten*) *Gefahr, Folgen* to disregard; **eine Tugend, die man nicht ~ sollte** a virtue not to be despised; **ge|ring|-schät|zig** [-ʃetsɪç] ADJ contemptuous; *Bemerkung auch* disparaging ADV contemptuously; **Ge|ring|schät|zig|keit** F **-**, *no pl* contemptuousness; **Ge|ring|schät|zung** F **-**, *no pl* (= *Ablehnung*) disdain; (*von Bemerkung*) disparagement (*für, +gen* of); (= *schlechte Meinung*) poor or low opinion (*für, +gen* of); (*für Erfolg, Reichtum, menschliches Leben*) low regard (*für, +gen* for)

ge|rings|ten|falls ADV (*geh*) at (the very) least

ge|ring|wer|tig ADJ (*rare*) inferior; *Nahrung* low-value

ge|rinn|bar ADJ = **gerinnungsfähig**

ge|rin|nen [gəˈrɪnən] *pret* **gerann** [gəˈran], *ptp* **ge-ron|nen** [gəˈrɔnən] VI *aux sein* to coagulate; (*Blut auch*) to clot; (*Milch auch*) to curdle; **mir gerann (vor Schreck) das Blut in den Adern** (*fig*) my blood ran cold; **zu etw ~** (*fig geh*) to develop into sth

Ge|rinn|sel [gəˈrɪnzl] NT **-s, - a** (= *Blutgerinnsel*) clot, coagulum (*spec*) **b** (*geh*: = *Rinnsal*) rivulet, trickle

Ge|rin|nung F **-, -en** coagulation; (*von Blut auch*) clotting; (*von Milch auch*) curdling

Ge|rin|nungs-: ge|rin|nungs|fä|hig ADJ coagulable; **Ge|rin|nungs|fä|hig|keit** F coagulability; **ge|rin|nungs|hem|mend** ADJ (*Med*) anticoagulant; **Ge|rin|nungs|hem|mer** M **-s, -** (*Med*) anticoagulant

Ge|rip|pe [gəˈrɪpə] NT **-s, -** skeleton; (*von Schiff, Flugzeug auch, von Schirm, Gebäude*) frame; (*von Blatt auch*) ribbing; (*fig*: = *Grundplan*) framework; **er ist nur noch ein ~** he's nothing but skin and bones

ge|rippt [gəˈrɪpt] ADJ ribbed *no adv*; *Säule* fluted *no adv*; **~e Sohlen** grip soles → *auch* **rippen**

Ge|riss ▲ [gəˈrɪs] NT **-es**, *no pl* (*Aus inf*) crush

ge|ris|sen [gəˈrɪsn] *ptp von* **reißen** ADJ crafty, cunning

Ge|ris|sen|heit F **-**, *no pl* cunning

ge|rit|ten *ptp von* **reiten**

ge|ritzt [gəˈrɪtst] ADJ *pred* (*inf*) **die Sache ist ~** everything's fixed up or settled → *auch* **ritzen**

Germ [gɛrm] M OR F **-**, *no pl* (*Aus*) baker's yeast

Ger|ma|ne [gɛrˈmaːnə] M **-n, -n**, **Ger|ma|nin** [-ˈmaːnɪn] F **-, -nen** Teuton; **die alten ~n** the Teutons

Ger|ma|nen|tum [gɛrˈmaːnəntuːm] NT **-s**, *no pl* Teutonicism; (= *Kultur*) Teutonism; (= *Gesamtheit der Germanen*) Teutonic world, Teutons *pl*

ger|ma|nisch [gɛrˈmaːnɪʃ] ADJ Germanic; **~es Seminar** Institute of Germanic Studies

ger|ma|ni|sie|ren [gɛrmaniˈziːrən] *ptp* **germani-siert** VT to Germanize

Ger|ma|ni|sie|rung F **-, -en** Germanization

Ger|ma|nis|mus [gɛrmaˈnɪsmʊs] M **-, Germanis-men** [-mən] (*Ling*) Germanism

Ger|ma|nist [gɛrmaˈnɪst] M **-en, -en**, **Ger|ma|-nis|tin** [-ˈnɪstɪn] F **-, -nen** Germanist; (= *Student auch*) German student; (= *Wissenschaftler auch*) German specialist

Ger|ma|nis|tik [gɛrmaˈnɪstɪk] F **-**, *no pl* German (studies *pl*); **~ studieren** to do German studies, to study German; **Professor der ~** professor of German studies or German

ger|ma|nis|tisch [gɛrmaˈnɪstɪʃ] ADJ German; *Zeitschrift* on German studies

Ger|ma|ni|um [gɛrˈmaːniʊm] NT **-s**, *no pl* (*abbr* **Ge**) germanium

ger|ma|no|phil [gɛrmanoˈfiːl] ADJ Germanophile

Ger|ma|no|phi|lie [gɛrmanofiˈliː] F **-**, *no pl* Germanophilia

ger|ma|no|phob [gɛrmanoˈfoːp] ADJ Germanophobe

Ger|ma|no|pho|bie [gɛrmanofoˈbiː] F Germanophobia

gern [gɛrn], **ger|ne** [ˈgɛrnə] ADV *comp* **lieber**, *superl* **am liebsten a** (= *freudig*) with pleasure; (= *bereitwillig*) with pleasure, willingly, readily; **(aber) ~!** of course!; **ja, ~!** (yes) please; **kommst du mit? – ja, ~** are you coming too? – oh yes, I'd like to; **darf ich das? – ja, ~** can I do that? – (yes,) of course; **~ geschehen!** you're welcome! (*esp US*), not at all!, my pleasure!; **„Witwer, 61, sucht Partnerin, ~ älter/mit Kindern"** "widower, aged 61, seeks partner, age not important/children not a problem"; **von mir aus kann er ja ~ älter sein** I don't mind if he's older; **etw ~ tun** to like doing sth or to do sth (*esp US*); **etw ~ essen/trinken** to like sth; **sie isst am liebsten Spargel** asparagus is her favourite (*Brit*) or favorite (*US*) food; **~ ins Kino gehen** to like or enjoy going to the cinema; **das tue ich für mein Leben ~** I adore doing that; **etw ~ sehen** to like sth; **das sähe ich ~** I would welcome it; **das wird nicht ~ gesehen** that's frowned (up)on; **er sieht es nicht ~, wenn wir zu spät kommen** he doesn't like us arriving late; **ein ~ gesehener Gast** a welcome visitor; **das glaube ich ~** I can quite or well believe it, I'm quite willing to believe it; **das würde ich zu ~ tun** I'd really love to do that; **er macht seine Arbeit ~ und mit Freude** he does his work willingly and gets a lot of pleasure out of it; **ich stehe ~ zu Ihren Diensten** (*old form*) I am happy or pleased to be of service to you; **ich bin ~ dazu bereit** I'm quite willing or happy to do it; **jdn/etw ~ haben** or **mögen** to like sb/sth, to be fond of sb/sth; **das kannst du ~ haben** you're welcome to it, you can have it with pleasure; **er hat es ~, wenn man ihm schmeichelt** he likes being flattered, he likes it when you flatter him; **ich hätte** or **möchte ~ ...** I would like ...; **ich hätte ~ Herrn Kurtz gesprochen** could I speak to Mr Kurtz?, I would like to speak to Mr Kurtz, please; **wie hätten Sies (denn) ~?** how would you like it?; **du kannst/er kann mich mal ~ haben!** (*inf*) (you can)/(he can) go to hell! (*inf*), stuff you/him! (*Brit inf*), screw you/him (*sl*) → **gut** ADV, **lieber**

b (= *gewöhnlich, oft*) **etw ~ tun** to tend to do sth; **Weiden wachsen ~ an Flüssen** willows tend to grow by rivers; **morgens lässt er sich ~ viel Zeit** he likes to leave himself a lot of time in the mornings

Ger|ne|groß ['gɛrnəgroːs] M -, -e (hum) **er war schon immer ein kleiner ~** he always did like to act big (inf)

Ge|rö|chel [gə'rœçl] NT -s, no pl groans pl; (von Sterbenden) (death) rattle

ge|ro|chen ptp von **riechen**

Ge|röll [gə'rœl] NT -(e)s, -e, **Ge|röl|le** [gə'rœlə] NT -s, - (rare) detritus no pl; (im Gebirge auch) scree no pl; (größeres) boulders pl

Ge|röll-: Ge|röll|hal|de F scree (slope); **Ge|röll|la|wi|ne** ▲ F scree avalanche; **Ge|röll|schutt** M rock debris

ge|ron|nen ptp von **rinnen** von **gerinnen**

Ge|ron|to|kra|tie [gerɔntokra'tiː] F -, -n [-tiːən] (Pol) gerontocracy

Ge|ron|to|lo|ge [gerɔnto'loːgə] M -n, -n, **Ge|ron|to|lo|gin** [-'loːgɪn] F -, -nen (Med) gerontologist

Ge|ron|to|lo|gie [gerɔntolo'giː] F -, no pl (Med) gerontology

ge|ron|to|lo|gisch [gerɔnto'loːgɪʃ] ADJ (Med) gerontological

Ge|rös|te|te [gə'rœstətə, gə'røːstətə] PL decl as adj (S Ger, Aus: Cook) sauté potatoes pl

Gers|te ['gɛrstə] F -, -n barley

Gers|ten- in cpds barley; **Gers|ten|grau|pen** PL pearl barley sing; **Gers|ten|grüt|ze** F barley groats pl; (= Brei) barley porridge; **Gers|ten|korn** NT -(e)s **-körner** a barleycorn b (Med) stye; **Gers|ten|saft** M (hum) beer; **Gers|ten|zu|cker** M barley sugar

Ger|te ['gɛrtə] F -, -n switch; (= Reitgerte auch) crop; **sie ist schlank wie eine ~** she is slim and willowy, she is as slender as a reed

ger|ten|schlank ADJ slim and willowy

Ge|ruch [gə'rʊx] M -(e)s, ⁺e [gə'rʏçə] a smell, odour (Brit), odor (US) (nach of); (= Duft) fragrance, scent, perfume (nach of); (von Kuchen etc) aroma (nach of); (unangenehm) stench (nach of); **der starke ~ nach Alkohol/Knoblauch** b no pl (= Geruchssinn) sense of smell c no pl (fig = Ruf) reputation; **in den ~ von etw kommen** to get a reputation for sth

Ge|ruch-: ge|ruch|los ADJ odourless (Brit), odorless (US); (= duftlos) scentless; **~ sein** not to have a smell, to be odourless (Brit) or odorless (US); (Blumen) not to smell, to have no scent; **Ge|ruch|lo|sig|keit** F -, no pl lack of smell

Ge|ruchs-: Ge|ruchs|be|läs|ti|gung F das ist eine ~ the smell is a real nuisance; **ge|ruchs|bin|dend** ADJ deodorizing no adv; **ge|ruchs|emp|find|lich** ADJ sensitive to smell; **~ sein** to have a sensitive nose; **Ge|ruchs|emp|fin|dung** F a (= Riechempfindung) smell b (= Geruchssinn) sense of smell; **Ge|ruchs|nerv** M olfactory nerve; **ge|ruchs|neut|ral** ADJ = geruchlos; **Ge|ruchs|or|gan** NT organ of smell, olfactory organ; **Ge|ruchs|sinn** M no pl sense of smell; **Ge|ruchs|ver|schluss** ▲ M (Tech) odour (Brit) or odor (US) trap; **Ge|ruchs|werk|zeu|ge** PL olfactory organs pl

Ge|rücht [gə'rʏçt] NT -(e)s, -e rumour (Brit), rumor (US); **es geht das ~, dass ...** there's a rumo(u)r (going (a)round) that ..., it's rumo(u)red that ...; **das halte ich für ein ~** (inf) I have my doubts about that

Ge|rüch|te-: Ge|rüch|te|kü|che F (inf) gossip factory (inf); **die Pressestelle ist eine wahre ~** the press office is filled with rumour-mongers (Brit) or rumor-mongers (US); **Ge|rüch|te|ma|cher(in)** M(F) rumour-monger (Brit), rumor-monger (US); **ge|rüch|te|wei|se** ADV **etw ~ hören** to hear sth rumoured (Brit) or rumored (US); **es ist bekannt geworden, dass ...** rumour (Brit) or rumor (US) has it that ...; **ich habe ~ erfahren, dass ...** I've heard a rumour (Brit) or rumor (US) that ...; **das ist mir ~ zu Ohren gekommen** I've heard it rumoured (Brit) or rumored (US)

ge|ruch|til|gend ADJ deodorizing no adv, deodorant attr

ge|rücht|wei|se ADV = gerüchteweise

Ge|ru|ckel [gə'rʊkl] NT -s, no pl jerking, jolting

Ge|ru|fe [gə'ruːfə] NT -s, no pl calling

ge|ru|fen ptp von **rufen**

ge|ru|hen [gə'ruːən] ptp **geruht** VT ~, **etw zu tun** (dated form) to deign or condescend to do sth (auch iro), to be pleased to do sth

ge|ru|hig [gə'ruːɪç] ADJ, ADV (old) = ruhig

ge|ruh|sam [gə'ruːzaːm] ADJ peaceful; Spaziergang etc ADV leisurely; **~ essen** to eat in peace (and quiet)

Ge|ruh|sam|keit F -, no pl peacefulness; (von Spaziergang etc) leisureliness

Ge|rum|pel [gə'rʊmpl] NT -s, no pl rumbling, rumble

Ge|rüm|pel [gə'rʏmpl] NT -s, no pl junk

Ge|run|di|um [ge'rʊndiʊm] NT -s, **Gerundien** [-diːən] gerund

Ge|run|div [gerʊn'diːf] ADJ gerundival

Ge|run|div [gerʊn'diːf] NT -s, -e [-və] gerundive

ge|run|di|visch [gerʊn'diːvɪʃ] ADJ = gerundiv

Ge|run|di|vum [gerʊn'diːvʊm] NT -s, **Gerundiva** [-va] gerundive

ge|run|gen ptp von **ringen**

Ge|rüst [gə'rʏst] NT -(e)s, -e scaffolding no pl; (= Gestell) trestle; (= Brückengerüst, Dachgerüst) truss; (= Hängegerüst) cradle; (fig = Gerippe) framework (zu of); **ein ~ aufstellen** to put up or erect scaffolding

Ge|rüst-: Ge|rüst|bau M , no pl erection of scaffolding; **„W. Friedrich GmbH, ~"** "W. Friedrich Ltd, Scaffolders"; **Ge|rüst|bau|er(in)** M(F) pl **-bauer(innen)** scaffolder; **Ge|rüst|stan|ge** F scaffolding pole

Ge|rüt|tel [gə'rʏtl] NT -s, no pl shaking (about); (im Zug, Wagen etc) jolting (about)

ge|rüt|telt [gə'rʏtlt] ADJ **ein ~es Maß von** or **an etw** (dat) a fair amount of sth; **er besitzt ein ~es Maß (an) Unverschämtheit** he has more than his fair share of impudence ADV **~ voll** chock-a-block (esp Brit inf), jam-packed (inf), chock-full → auch **rütteln**

Ges [gɛs] NT -, -, **Ges** NT -, - (Mus) G flat

Ge|salb|te(r) [gə'zalptə] M decl as adj (Rel) **der ~** the Lord's Anointed

ge|sal|zen [gə'zaltsn] ptp von **salzen** ADJ (fig inf) Witz spicy; Preis, Rechnung steep, fancy (inf), stiff

Ge|sal|ze|ne(s) [gə'zaltsnə] NT decl as adj (Cook) salted meat

ge|sam|melt [gə'zamlt] ADJ Aufmerksamkeit, Kraft collective; Werke collected → auch **sammeln**

ge|samt [gə'zamt] ADJ attr whole, entire; **die ~e Familie** all the family, the whole or entire family; **die ~en Lehrkräfte** all the teachers; **im ~en** in all; **die ~en Kosten** the total costs

Ge|samt [gə'zamt] NT -s, no pl (liter) = Gesamtheit

Ge|samt-: Ge|samt|an|sicht F general or overall view; **Ge|samt|auf|la|ge** F (von Zeitung etc) total circulation; (von Buch) total edition; **bisherige ~ 300.000 Stück** sales totalling (Brit) or totaling (US) 300,000; **Ge|samt|aus|fuhr** F total exports pl; **Ge|samt|aus|ga|be** F complete edition; **Ge|samt|be|darf** M complete needs pl; **Ge|samt|be|stand** M (an Tieren, Pflanzen etc) total stock; **Ge|samt|be|trag** M total (amount); **Ge|samt|bild** NT general or overall picture; **ge|samt|deutsch** ADJ all-German; **Ministerium für ~e Fragen** (Hist) Ministry for all-German Affairs; **Ge|samt|deutsch|land** NT all Germany; **ein ~ hat auch schon von 1871 bis 1945 bestanden** there was also a united Germany from 1871 to 1945; **Ge|samt|ein|druck** M general or overall impression; **Ge|samt|ein|fuhr** F total imports pl; **Ge|samt|ein|kom|men** NT total income; **Ge|samt|er|geb|nis** NT overall result; **Ge|samt|er|lös** M total proceeds pl; **Ge|samt|er|trag** M total yield; **Ge|samt|flä|che** F total area; **Ge|samt|ge|sell|schaft** F (Sociol) society as a whole; **ge|samt|ge|sell|schaft|lich** ADJ (Sociol) Problem, Kosten relating to society as a whole; Produktion, Solidarität by society as a whole; **Ge|samt|ge|wicht** NT total weight; (eines LKWs etc auch) laden weight; **Ge|samt|gläu|bi|ger** PL (Jur) joint creditors pl; **ge|samt|haft** (esp Sw) ADJ = gesamt ADV = insgesamt; **Ge|samt|haf|tung** F (Jur) joint liability

Ge|samt|heit F -, no pl totality; **die ~ der ...** all the ...; (= die Summe) the totality of ...; **die ~ (der Bevölkerung)** the population (as a whole); **die ~ der Studenten/Arbeiter** the entire student population/workforce, all the students/workers; **die ~ der Delegierten** all the delegates; **in seiner ~** in its entirety; **das Volk in seiner ~** the nation as a whole

ge|samt|heit|lich ADJ overall ADV as a whole

Ge|samt|hoch|schu|le F ≈ polytechnic (Brit), ≈ college

GESAMTHOCHSCHULE

A **Gesamthochschule** is an institution of higher education which combines **Hochschulen** and **Fachhochschulen** and provides a wider choice of subjects. Within each subject area a range of courses are available that vary in emphasis and length and which lead to different final qualifications, depending on the student's objectives. In addition, it is easier to change between subjects at a **Gesamthochschule** than it is at a conventional university → Fachhochschule

---

Ge|samt-: Ge|samt|in|te|res|se NT general interest; **Ge|samt|ka|pi|tal** NT total capital; **Ge|samt|ka|ta|log** M central catalogue (Brit) or catalog (US); **Ge|samt|klas|se|ment** NT (Sport) overall placings pl; **Ge|samt|kon|zept** NT overall plan or idea or design, master plan; **Ge|samt|kos|ten** PL total or overall costs pl; **Ge|samt|kunst|werk** NT (bei Wagner) synthesis of the arts; (= Show, Happening) multimedia performance or show; **Ge|samt|la|ge** F general situation; **Ge|samt|mas|se** F (Comm) total assets pl; **Ge|samt|no|te** F (Sch) overall mark (Brit) or grade (US); **Ge|samt|nut|zungs|dau|er** F useful life; **Ge|samt|pla|nung** F overall planning; **Ge|samt|preis** M total price, all-in price (inf); **Ge|samt|scha|den** M total damage; **ein ~ von 5.000 Euro** damage totalling (Brit) or totaling (US) 5,000 euros; **Ge|samt|schau** F synopsis (über +acc of); **Ge|samt|schuld|ner** PL (Jur) (joint) debtors pl; **Ge|samt|schu|le** F comprehensive school

---

GESAMTSCHULE

The **Gesamtschulen**, created during the educational reforms of the 1970s, were intended to replace the traditional three-way division of schools into **Hauptschule**, **Realschule** and **Gymnasium** with a single system. Pupils have the chance to learn a subject at a level appropriate to them: for example, if their lack of ability at mathematics has meant they cannot go to a **Gymnasium**, they may still study, say, languages to a high level at the **Gesamtschule**. In addition, pupils who may not initially have been considered suitable to take their **Abitur** can still have the opportunity to take it → Abitur, Gymnasium, Hauptschule, Realschule

---

Ge|samt-: Ge|samt|sie|ger(in) M(F) (Sport) overall winner; **Ge|samt|stär|ke** F total strength; **Ge|samt|stim|men|zahl** F total number of votes cast; **Ge|samt|stra|fe** F (Jur) overall sentence (for a series of offences, longer than the maximum sentence for the most serious one but less than the total sentences taken consecutively); **Ge|samt|sum|me** F total amount; **Ge|samt|über|sicht** F general survey (über +acc of); **Ge|samt|um|satz** M total turnover; **Ge|samt|ver|mö|gen** NT total assets pl; **Ge|samt|werk** NT complete works pl; **Ge|samt|wert** M total value; **im ~ von ...** totalling (Brit) or totaling (US) ... in value; **Ge|samt|wer|tung** F (Sport) overall placings pl; **er liegt in der ~ vorn** he's leading overall, he has the overall lead; **Ge|samt|wir|kung** F general or overall effect; **Ge|samt|wirt|schaft** F national economy; **ge|samt|wirt|schaft|lich** ADJ national economic attr ADV **~ nicht ver-tretbar** not justifiable from the point of view of the national economy; **Ge|samt|zahl** F total number; **eine ~ von 8.000 Punkten** a total of 8,000 points; **Ge|samt|zu|sam|men|hang** M general view

ge|sandt ptp von **senden** ¹

Ge|sand|te(r) [gəˈzantə] M decl as adj, **Ge|-sand|tin** [gəˈzantɪn] F -, -nen envoy, legate; (inf: = Botschafter) ambassador; **päpstlicher ~r** (papal) nuncio

Ge|sandt|schaft [gəˈzantʃaft] F -, -en legation; (inf: = Botschaft) embassy; (= päpstliche Gesandt-schaft) nunciature

Ge|sang [gəˈzaŋ] M -(e)s, ⸚e [gəˈzɛŋə] **a** (= Lied, Vogelgesang) song; (= Preislied) hymn; (= gregoria-nischer Gesang etc) chant; **erster ~ der Ilias** first book of the Iliad; **erster ~ von Dantes Inferno** first canto of Dante's Inferno; **geistliche Ge-sänge** religious hymns and chants **b** no pl (= das Singen) singing; (von Mönchen etc) chanting

Ge|sang-: Ge|sang|buch NT (Eccl) hymn-book; **das richtige/falsche ~ haben** (inf) to be-long to the right/wrong denomination; **Ge|-sang|leh|rer(in)** M(F) singing teacher

ge|sang|lich [gəˈzaŋlɪç] ADJ vocal; Begabung for singing

Ge|sangs- in cpds (Aus) = Gesang-

Ge|sangs|ein|la|ge F vocal number

Ge|sangs|kunst F singing technique

Ge|sang-: Ge|sang|stun|de F singing lesson; **Ge|sang(s)|un|ter|richt** M singing lessons pl; **Ge|sang(s)|ver|ein** M choral society (Brit), glee club (US); **mein lieber Herr Gesangverein!** (hum) ye gods and little fishes! (hum)

Ge|säß [gəˈzɛːs] NT -es, -e seat, bottom, posteri-or (hum)

Ge|säß-: Ge|säß|ba|cke F buttock, cheek; **Ge|säß|mus|kel** M gluteal muscle (spec); **Ge|säß|spal|te** F (form) cleft between the buttocks; **Ge|säß|ta|sche** F back pocket

ge|sät|tigt [gəˈzɛtɪçt] ADJ (Chem) saturated → auch **sättigen**

Ge|säu|sel [gəˈzɔyzl] NT -s, no pl (von Blättern) rustling, rustle, whisper; (vom Wind) mur-mur(ing), whisper(ing), sigh(ing); (fig iro: von Menschen) purring

gesch. abbr von **geschieden** divorced

Ge|scha|cher [gəˈʃaxɐ] NT -s, no pl (pej) hag-gling (um about)

Ge|schä|dig|te(r) [gəˈʃɛːdɪçtə] MF decl as adj victim

ge|schaf|fen ptp von **schaffen** ¹

ge|schafft ptp von **schaffen** ² ADJ (inf: = er-schöpft) shattered, whacked (inf); **ich bin ~** I've had it (inf) → auch **schaffen** ²

Ge|schäft [gəˈʃɛft] NT -(e)s, -e **a** (= Gewerbe, Handel) business no pl; (= Geschäftsabschluss) (business) deal or transaction; **~ ist ~** business is business; **wie geht das ~?, wie gehen die ~e?** how's business?; **mit jdm ins ~ kommen** to do business with sb; **mit jdm ~e machen** to do business with sb, to have business dealings with sb; **im ~ sein** to be in business; **für jdn die ~e führen** to act for sb; (im Gewerbe, Handel) to run the business for sb; **ein ~ tätigen** to do a deal, to make a transaction, to carry out a transaction; **dunkle ~e treiben** to be involved

in some shady dealings or business; **ein gutes/ schlechtes ~ machen** to make a good/bad deal; **dabei hat er ein ~ gemacht** he made a profit by it; **~e mit etw machen** to make money out of sth; **das ~ mit der Lust** the sex industry; **Boule-vardzeitungen leben von dem ~ mit der Angst** the popular press make their living by trading on people's fears

b (= Aufgabe) duty; **das gehört zu den ~en des Ministers** that is one of the minister's duties, that is part of the minister's work; **seinen ~en nachgehen** to go about one's business

c (= Firma) business; (= Laden) shop (Brit), store; (inf: = Büro) office; **die ~e schließen um 17.30 Uhr** the shops (esp Brit) or stores close at 5.30; **ich gehe um 8 Uhr ins ~** I go to work or to the office at 8.00; **im ~** at work, in the of-fice; (im Laden) in the shop

d (baby-talk: = Notdurft) **kleines/großes ~** little/ big job (baby-talk), number one/two (baby--talk); **ein ~ machen** to do a job (baby-talk); **sein ~ verrichten** to do one's business (euph)

Ge|schäfte-: ge|schäf|te|hal|ber ADV (= in Geschäften) on business; (= wegen Geschäften) because of business; **Ge|schäf|te|ma|cher(in)** M(F) (pej) profiteer; **Ge|schäf|te|ma|che|rei** [-maxəˈrai] F -, -en (pej) profiteering no indef art

ge|schäf|tig [gəˈʃɛftɪç] ADJ (= betriebsam) busy; Stadt auch bustling; **~es Treiben, ~es Hin und Her** hustle and bustle, bustling activity ADV busily; **~ hin und her laufen** to bustle (a)round (busily); **~ tun, sich ~ geben** to try to look bus-y

Ge|schäf|tig|keit F -, no pl busyness; (= ge-schäftiges Treiben) (hustle and) bustle; **eine enorme ~ entfalten** or **an den Tag legen** to get incredibly busy

Ge|schaftl|hu|ber [gəˈʃaftlhuːbɐ] M -s, -, **Ge|-schaftl|hu|be|rin** [-ərɪn] F -, -nen (S Ger) bus-ybody

ge|schäft|lich [gəˈʃɛftlɪç] ADJ (= das Geschäft betreffend) business attr; (= sachlich) Ton busi-nesslike; **ich habe mit ihm etwas Geschäftliches zu besprechen** I have some business or busi-ness matters to discuss with him ADV (= in Geschäften) on business; (= wegen Geschäften) because of business; (= geschäftlich gesehen) from a business point of view; **er hat morgen ~ in Berlin zu tun** he has business in Berlin to-morrow, he has to be in Berlin on business to-morrow; **~ verhindert** prevented by business; **~ verreist** away on business; **~ mit jdm verkehren** to have business dealings with sb

Ge|schäfts-: Ge|schäfts|ab|lauf M course of business; **Ge|schäfts|ab|schluss** ▲ M busi-ness deal or transaction; **Ge|schäfts|adres-se** F business address; **Ge|schäfts|an|ge|le-gen|heit** F business matter or affair; **Ge|-schäfts|an|teil** M share of a/the business; **Ge|schäfts|auf|ga|be** F , **Ge|schäfts|auf|-lö|sung** F closure of a/the business; **Räu-mungsverkauf wegen ~** closing-down sale; **Ge|-schäfts|aus|la|ge** F window display; **Ge|-schäfts|au|to** NT company car; **Ge|schäfts|-bank** F pl -banken commercial bank; **Ge|-schäfts|be|din|gun|gen** PL terms pl of busi-ness; **Ge|schäfts|be|reich** M (Parl) responsi-bilities pl; **Minister ohne ~** minister without portfolio; **Ge|schäfts|be|richt** M report; (ei-ner Gesellschaft) company report; **Ge|schäfts|-be|sit|zer(in)** M(F) = Geschäftsinhaber(in); **Ge|schäfts|be|zie|hun|gen** PL business con-nections pl (zu with); **Ge|schäfts|brief** M business letter; **Ge|schäfts|bü|cher** PL books pl, accounts pl; **Ge|schäfts|er|öff|nung** F o-pening of a shop (Brit) or store; **Ge|schäfts|-es|sen** NT business lunch etc; **ge|schäfts|fä-hig** ADJ **a** (Jur) capable of contracting (form), competent (form); **voll/beschränkt ~ sein** to have complete/limited competence **b** Firma, System able to function; **Ge|schäfts|fä|hig-keit** F **a** (Jur) (legal) competence **b** (von Fir-ma, System) ability to function; **Ge|schäfts|-**

frau F businesswoman; **Ge|schäfts-freund(in)** M(F) business associate; **ge|-schäfts|füh|rend** ADJ attr executive; (= stell-vertretend) acting; (= Regierung) caretaker; **Ge|-schäfts|füh|rer(in)** M(F) (von Laden) manag-er/manageress; (von Unternehmen) managing di-rector, CEO; (von Verein) secretary; (von Partei) whip; **Ge|schäfts|füh|rung** F management; **mit der ~ beauftragt** (abbr **m.d.G.b.**) in charge of administration; **Ge|schäfts|gang** M **a** no pl business no art **b** pl -gänge (= Be-sorgung) errand; **Ge|schäfts|ge|ba|ren** NT business methods pl or practices pl; **Ge|-schäfts|ge|heim|nis** NT business secret; **Ge|-schäfts|geist** M business sense or acumen; **Ge|schäfts|haus** NT **a** (= Gebäude) business premises pl; (mit Büros) office block **b** (= Firma) house, firm; **Ge|schäfts|herr(in)** M(F) (Sw) owner (of a business); **Ge|schäfts|idee** F business idea; **Ge|schäfts|in|ha|ber(in)** M(F) owner (of a business); (von Laden, Restaurant) proprietor/proprietress, owner; **Ge|schäfts|-in|te|res|se** NT business interest; **Ge|-schäfts|jahr** NT financial year; **Ge|schäfts|-ju|bi|lä|um** NT company anniversary; (kleineres Geschäft) business anniversary; **Ge|schäfts|-ka|pi|tal** NT working capital; **Ge|schäfts|-kos|ten** PL business expenses pl; **das geht al-les auf ~** it's all on expenses; **Ge|schäfts|la|ge** F **a** (= Wirtschaftslage) business situation **b** in erstklassiger ~ in a good business location; **Ge|schäfts|le|ben** NT business life; **er steht noch im ~** he's still active in the world of busi-ness; **Ge|schäfts|lei|tung** F management; **Ge|schäfts|lis|te** F (Sw) = Tagesordnung; **Ge|schäfts|mann** M pl -leute businessman; **ge|schäfts|mä|ßig** ADJ businesslike ADV klin-gen businesslike; erledigen, gekleidet sein in a businesslike manner; **Ge|schäfts|mä|ßig|keit** F businesslike manner; **Ge|schäfts|me|tho-den** PL business methods pl; **Ge|schäfts|-ord|nung** F standing orders pl; **zur ~!** point of order!; **eine Frage zur ~** a question on a point of order; **Ge|schäfts|pa|pie|re** PL busi-ness papers pl; **Ge|schäfts|part|ner(in)** M(F) business partner; (= Geschäftsfreund) business associate; **Ge|schäfts|räu|me** PL (business) premises pl; (= Büroräume) offices pl; **in den ~n** on the premises; in the offices; **Ge|schäfts|-rei|se** F business trip; **auf ~ sein** to be on a business trip; **Ge|schäfts|rück|gang** M de-cline in business; **Ge|schäfts|sa|che** F busi-ness matter or affair; **ge|schäfts|schä|di-gend** ADJ bad for business; **~es Verhalten** = Geschäftsschädigung; **Ge|schäfts|schä|di-gung** F conduct no art injurious to the inter-ests of the company (form); **Ge|schäfts|-schluss** ▲ M close of business; (von Läden) closing time; **nach ~** out of office or working hours/after closing time; **Ge|schäfts|sinn** M , no pl business sense or acumen; **Ge|schäfts|-sitz** M place of business; **Ge|schäfts|stel|le** F offices pl; (von Gericht) administrative office; **Ge|schäfts|stra|ße** F shopping street; **Ge|-schäfts|stun|den** PL office or working hours pl; (von Läden) (shop (esp Brit) or store) open-ing hours pl; „Geschäftsstunden" "hours of o-pening"; **Ge|schäfts|tä|tig|keit** F business activity; **Ge|schäfts|trä|ger(in)** M(F) (Pol) chargé d'affaires, representative (US); **ge|-schäfts|tüch|tig** ADJ business-minded; **Ge|-schäfts|tüch|tig|keit** F business sense; **Ge|-schäfts|über|nah|me** F takeover of a/the business; (eines Ladens) takeover of a/the shop (esp Brit) or store; **ge|schäfts|un|fä|hig** ADJ (Jur) not capable of contracting (form), (legally) incompetent (form); **Ge|schäfts|un|fä|hig-keit** F (Jur) (legal) incompetence; **Ge|-schäfts|ver|bin|dung** F business connection; **in ~ mit jdm stehen** to have business connec-tions with sb; **Ge|schäfts|ver|kehr** M **a** business no art; **in regem ~ mit einer Firma ste-hen** to do a considerable amount of business with a firm **b** (= Straßenverkehr) business traf-fic; **Ge|schäfts|vier|tel** NT **a** (= Geschäftsge-

gend) shopping area **b** (= *Banken- und Versicherungsviertel*) business or commercial district; **Ge|schäfts|vo|lu|men** NT volume of trade; **Ge|schäfts|wa|gen** M company car; **Ge|schäfts|welt** F world of business, business world; **Ge|schäfts|wert** M value of a/the business; **Ge|schäfts|zeit** F business or office hours *pl*; (*von Läden*) (shop) (*esp Brit* or store) opening hours *pl*; **Ge|schäfts|zim|mer** NT office; **Ge|schäfts|zweig** M branch of a/the business

ge|schah *pret von* **geschehen**

Ge|schä|ker [gə'ʃɛːkɐ] NT -s, *no pl* (*inf*) flirting

ge|scha|mig [gə'ʃaːmɪç] ADJ (*esp Aus inf*) = **gschamig**

ge|schätzt *ptp von* **schätzen** ADJ (*fig, = angesehen*) respected, esteemed (*form*); *Freund etc* valued; (= *beliebt*) well-liked

Ge|schau|kel [gə'ʃaʊkl] NT -s, *no pl* (*im Schaukelstuhl*) swinging; (*in Bus, Wagen*) lurching; (*in Boot*) pitching, rolling

ge|scheckt [gə'ʃɛkt] ADJ spotted; *Pferd* skewbald, pinto (*US*)

ge|sche|hen [gə'ʃeːən] *pret* **geschah** [gə'ʃaː], *ptp* **geschehen** [gə'ʃeːən] VI *aux sein* to happen (*jdm* to sb); (= *vorkommen auch*) to occur; (= *stattfinden auch*) to take place; (= *ausgeführt werden*) to be done; (*Verbrechen*) to be committed; **ihr Selbstmord geschah aus Verzweiflung** her despair led her to commit suicide; **es ist nun einmal ~** what's done is done; **Dein Wille geschehe** (*Bibl*) Thy or Your will be done; **es wird ihm nichts ~** nothing will happen to him; **das geschieht ihm (ganz) recht** it serves him right; **ihm ist ein Unrecht ~** he has been wronged; **ihm ist ein Missgeschick ~** he had a mishap; **er wusste nicht, wie ihm geschah** he didn't know what was going on or happening; **was soll mit ihm/damit ~?** what is to be done with him/it?; **als er sie sah, war es um ihn ~** he was lost the moment he set eyes on her; **da war es um meine Seelenruhe ~** that was an end to my peace of mind; **es kann ~, dass …** it could happen that …; **und so geschah es, dass …** and so it happened or came about that …; **es muss etwas ~** something must be done; **so ~ am …** such was the case on …; **Geschehenes ruhen lassen** (*geh*) to let bygones be bygones → **gern a**

Ge|sche|hen [gə'ʃeːən] NT -s, (*rare*) - events *pl*, happenings *pl*

Ge|scheh|nis [gə'ʃeːnɪs] NT -ses, -se (*geh*) event; (= *Vorfall auch*) incident

ge|scheit [gə'ʃaɪt] ADJ **a** clever; *Mensch, Idee* clever, bright; (= *vernünftig*) sensible; **du bist wohl nicht recht ~?** you must be out of your mind or off your head; **sei ~!** be sensible; **es wäre ~er …** it would be wiser or more sensible …; **jetzt bin ich so ~ wie vorher** I'm none the wiser now **b** (*S Ger*: = *tüchtig, ordentlich*) proper, good; **ich habe ihm ~ die Meinung gesagt** (*S Ger*) I really gave him a piece of my mind; **wie ~** (*Aus inf*) like mad or crazy (*inf*)

Ge|schenk [gə'ʃɛŋk] NT -(e)s, -e present, gift; (= *Schenkung*) gift; **jdm ein ~ machen** to give sb a present; **jdm etw zum ~ machen** to make sb a present of sth, to give sb sth (as a present); **ein ~ seiner Mutter** a present or gift from his mother; **ein ~ Gottes** a gift from or of God; **das war ein ~ des Himmels** it was a godsend; **kleine ~e erhalten die Freundschaft** (*prov*) little presents keep a friendship alive

Ge|schenk- *in cpds* gift; **Ge|schenk|ar|ti|kel** M gift; **Ge|schenk|gut|schein** M gift voucher; **Ge|schenk|idee** F gift idea; **Ge|schenk|korb** M (gift) hamper, gift basket; **Ge|schenk|pa|ckung** F gift pack or box; (*von Pralinen*) gift box; **Ge|schenk|pa|pier** NT wrapping paper, giftwrap; **etw in ~ einwickeln** to giftwrap sth

Ge|schenks- [gə'ʃɛŋks] (*Aus*) *in cpds* = **Geschenk-**

Ge|schenk|sen|dung F gift parcel (*esp Brit*) or package

Ge|scher|te(r) [gə'ʃeːɐtə] MF *decl as adj* (*Aus inf*) idiot

Ge|schicht|chen [gə'ʃɪçtçən] NT -s, - little story

Ge|schich|te [gə'ʃɪçtə] F -, -n **a** *no pl* (= *Historie*) history; **~ des Altertums/der Neuzeit, Alte/Neue ~** ancient/modern history; **die ~ Spaniens/der Menschheit** the history of Spain/mankind; **~ machen** to make history; **das ist längst ~** that's past history
  b (= *Erzählung, Lügengeschichte*) story; (= *Märchen, Fabel etc*) tale, story; (= *Kurzgeschichte*) short story; **das sind alles bloß ~n** that's all just made up, that's just a story; **~n erzählen** to tell stories
  c (*inf*: = *Angelegenheit, Sache*) affair, business *no pl*; **das sind alte ~n** that's old hat (*inf*); **das ist (wieder) die alte ~** it's the same old or the old old story (all over again); **alte ~n wieder aufwärmen** to rake up the past; **die ganze ~** the whole business; **eine schöne ~!** (*iro*) a fine how-do-you-do! (*inf*); **das sind ja nette ~n!** (*iro*) this is a fine thing; **die ~ mit seinem Magen** the trouble or business with his stomach; **als er damals diese ~ mit der Tänzerin hatte** when he was having that affair with the dancer; **mach keine ~n!** don't be silly! (*inf*); (= *Dummheiten*) don't do anything silly!

Ge|schich|ten-: Ge|schich|ten|buch NT storybook; **Ge|schich|ten|er|zäh|ler(in)** M(F) (*lit, fig*) storyteller

ge|schicht|lich [gə'ʃɪçtlɪç] ADJ (= *historisch*) historical; (= *bedeutungsvoll*) historic ADV historically; **~ bedeutsam** historic; **~ denken** to think in terms of history; **etw ~ betrachten** to consider sth from the historical point of view; **~ belegt** or **nachgewiesen sein** to be a historical fact; **~ bewandert sein** to be well-versed in history, to be familiar with history

Ge|schichts-: Ge|schichts|at|las M historical atlas; **Ge|schichts|auf|fas|sung** F, **Ge|schichts|be|trach|tung** F conception of history; **Ge|schichts|be|wäl|ti|gung** F, *no pl* coming to terms with the past; **Ge|schichts|be|wusst|sein** NT awareness of history, historical awareness; **Ge|schichts|buch** NT history book; **Ge|schichts|deu|tung** F interpretation of history; **Ge|schichts|dra|ma** NT historical drama; **Ge|schichts|epo|che** F period of history; **Ge|schichts|fäl|schung** F falsification of history; **Ge|schichts|for|scher(in)** M(F) historian; **Ge|schichts|for|schung** F historical research; **Ge|schichts|kennt|nis** F knowledge of history *no pl*, historical knowledge *no pl*; **Ge|schichts|klit|te|rung** F historical misrepresentation; **Ge|schichts|leh|rer(in)** M(F) history teacher; **ge|schichts|los** ADJ *Land, Stadt* with no history; *Zeit* with no historical records; *Volk* with no sense of history, ahistorical; *Politik, Weltanschauung* ahistorical; **Ge|schichts|lo|sig|keit** F -, *no pl* (*von Land, Stadt*) lack of history; (*von Zeit*) absence of historical records (+*gen* for); (*von Volk*) historical unawareness; (*von Politik, Weltanschauung*) ahistoricity (*form*); **Ge|schichts|phi|lo|soph(in)** M(F) philosopher of history; **Ge|schichts|phi|lo|so|phie** F philosophy of history; **ge|schichts|phi|lo|so|phisch** ADJ *Schrift etc* on the philosophy of history; *Interesse, Studien* in the philosophy of history; **Ge|schichts|schrei|ber(in)** M(F) historian, historiographer; **Ge|schichts|schrei|bung** F historiography; **Ge|schichts|ver|ständ|nis** NT , *no pl* conception or reading of history; **Ge|schichts|werk** NT historical work; **Ge|schichts|wis|sen|schaft** F (science of) history; **Ge|schichts|wis|sen|schaft|ler(in)** M(F) historian; **Ge|schichts|zahl** F (historical) date

Ge|schick¹ [gə'ʃɪk] NT -(e)s, -e (*geh*) (= *Schicksal*) fate; (= *politische etc Entwicklung, Situation*) for-

tune; **ein gütiges ~** good fortune, providence; **ein schlimmes/schweres/trauriges ~** a sad fate

Ge|schick² NT -s, *no pl* skill

Ge|schick|lich|keit [gə'ʃɪklɪçkaɪt] F -, *no pl* skill, skilfulness (*Brit*), skillfulness (*US*); (= *Taktik auch*) cleverness, adroitness; (= *Fingerfertigkeit auch*) dexterity; (= *Beweglichkeit*) agility; **für** or **zu etw ~ haben** or **zeigen** to be clever at sth

Ge|schick|lich|keits-: Ge|schick|lich|keits|fah|ren NT -s, *no pl* (*Sport*) skill tests *pl*; (*Aut*) manoeuvring (*Brit*) or maneuvering (*US*) tests *pl*; **Ge|schick|lich|keits|spiel** NT game of skill; **Ge|schick|lich|keits|übung** F exercise in skill; (= *Beweglichkeitsübung*) exercise in agility

ge|schickt [gə'ʃɪkt] ADJ **a** skilful (*Brit*), skillful (*US*); (= *taktisch auch*) clever, adroit; (= *fingerfertig auch*) dexterous; (= *beweglich*) agile **b** (*S Ger*) = **praktisch** ADJ ADV (= *clever*) cleverly; **~ agieren** to be clever

Ge|schickt|heit F -, *no pl* = **Geschicklichkeit**

Ge|schie|be [gə'ʃiːbə] NT -s, *no pl* **a** (*Geol*) debris; (*in Flüssen*) deposit **b** (= *Gedränge*) pushing and shoving (*inf*)

ge|schie|den [gə'ʃiːdn] *ptp von* **scheiden** ADJ divorced; **eine ~e Frau** a divorced woman, a divorcee; **Uta Schwarz, ~e Böhme** Uta Schwarz, former married name Böhme; **von dem Moment an waren wir (zwei) ~e Leute** (*inf*) after that it was the parting of the ways for us (*inf*)

Ge|schie|de|ne F *decl as adj* divorcee, divorced woman; **seine ~** (*inf*) his ex (*inf*)

Ge|schie|de|ne(r) [gə'ʃiːdnə] M *decl as adj* divorced man, divorcé; **ihr ~r** (*inf*) her ex (*inf*)

ge|schie|nen *ptp von* **scheinen**

ge|schimp|fe [gə'ʃɪmpfə] NT -s, *no pl* (*inf*) cursing; (*tadelnd*) scolding

Ge|schirr [gə'ʃɪr] NT -(e)s, -e **a** *no pl* (= *Haushaltsgefäße*) crockery (*Brit*), tableware; (= *Küchengeschirr*) pots and pans *pl*, kitchenware; (= *Teller etc*) china; (*zu einer Mahlzeit benutzt*) dishes *pl*; **(das) ~ (ab)spülen** to wash or do the dishes (*Brit*), to wash up; **feuerfestes ~** ovenware
  b (= *Service*) (dinner/tea *etc*) service; (= *Glasgeschirr*) set of glasses; (= *feuerfestes Geschirr*) set of ovenware; **das gute ~** the best china
  c (*old*) (= *Gefäß*) vessel, pot; (= *Nachtgeschirr*) chamber pot
  d (*von Zugtieren*) harness; **einem Pferd das ~ anlegen** to harness (up) a horse; **sich ins ~ legen** or **werfen** (*Pferde, Ochsen*) to pull hard; (*fig*) to put one's shoulder to the wheel, to put one's back into it

Ge|schirr-: Ge|schirr|auf|zug M dumb waiter; **Ge|schirr|hand|tuch** NT tea towel (*Brit*), dishtowel (*US*); **Ge|schirr|ma|cher(in)** M(F) harness-maker; **Ge|schirr|schrank** M china cupboard (*Brit*) or cabinet (*US*); **Ge|schirr|spü|len** NT -s, *no pl* washing-up; **Ge|schirr|spü|ler** M , **Ge|schirr|spül|ma|schi|ne** F dishwasher; **Ge|schirr|spül|mit|tel** NT washing-up liquid (*Brit*), dishwashing liquid (*US*); **Ge|schirr|tuch** NT *pl* **-tücher** tea towel (*Brit*), dishtowel (*US*)

Ge|schiss ▲ [gə'ʃɪs] NT -es, *no pl* (*inf*) fuss and bother

ge|schis|sen *ptp von* **scheißen**

Ge|schlab|ber [gə'ʃlabɐ] NT -s, *no pl* (*inf*) slurping

ge|schla|fen *ptp von* **schlafen**

ge|schla|gen *ptp von* **schlagen**

ge|schlaucht *ptp von* **schlauchen** ADJ (*inf*) whacked (*inf*), dead beat (*inf*) → *auch* **schlauchen**

Ge|schlecht [gə'ʃlɛçt] NT -(e)s, -er **a** sex; (*Gram*) gender; **Jugendliche beiderlei ~s** young people of both sexes; **das andere ~** the opposite sex; **das schwache/schöne/starke ~** the weaker/fair/stronger sex; **das dritte ~** transvestites *pl*; (= *Homosexuelle*) homosexuals *pl* **b** (*geh*: = *Geschlechtsteil*) sex (*liter*) **c** (*liter*) (= *Gat-*

tung) race; (= *Generation*) generation; (= *Sippe*) house; (= *Abstammung*) lineage; **das menschliche ~, das ~ der Menschen** the human race; **das ~ der Götter** the gods; **er ist vornehmen ~s** he is of noble lineage

Ge|schlech|ter-: Ge|schlech|ter|fol|ge F line; **Ge|schlech|ter|kampf** M battle of the sexes; **Ge|schlech|ter|kun|de** F genealogy; **Ge|schlech|ter|tren|nung** F segregation of the sexes

ge|schlęcht|lich [gəˈʃlɛçtlɪç] ADJ sexual; **~e Erziehung** sex education ADV **mit jdm ~ verkehren** to have sexual intercourse with sb; **sich ~ vermehren** (*Biol*) to reproduce sexually

Ge|schlęcht|lich|keit F -, *no pl* sexuality

Ge|schlęchts-: ge|schlęchts|ab|hän|gig ADJ sexually determined; **Ge|schlęchts|akt** M sex(ual) act; **Ge|schlęchts|be|stim|mung** F sex determination; **Ge|schlęchts|chro|mo|som** NT sex chromosome; **Ge|schlęchts|drang** M sex(ual) urge; **Ge|schlęchts|drü|se** F sex gland; **Ge|schlęchts|er|zie|hung** F sex(ual) education; **ge|schlęchts|ge|bun|den** ADJ = **geschlechtsabhängig**; **Ge|schlęchts|ge|nos|se** M , **Ge|schlęchts|ge|nos|sin** F person of the same sex; **jds ~n** those *or* people of the same sex as sb; **Ge|schlęchts|hor|mon** NT sex hormone; **ge|schlęchts|krank** ADJ suffering from a sexually transmitted disease, suffering from VD (*dated*) *or* a venereal disease (*dated*); **ein Geschlechtskranker** a person with VD (*dated*) *or* with a sexually transmitted disease; **Ge|schlęchts|krank|heit** F sexually transmitted disease, venereal disease (*dated*); **eine ~ haben** to have a sexually transmitted disease, to have VD (*dated*); **Ge|schlęchts|le|ben** NT sex life; **Ge|schlęchts|lei|den** NT sexually transmitted disease, venereal disease (*dated*); **ge|schlęchts|los** ADJ asexual (*auch Biol*), sexless; **Ge|schlęchts|lo|sig|keit** F -, *no pl* asexuality (*auch Biol*), sexlessness; **Ge|schlęchts|lust** F (*geh*) lust; **Ge|schlęchts|merk|mal** NT sex(ual) characteristic; **ge|schlęchts|or|gan** NT sex(ual) organ; **ge|schlęchts|reif** ADJ sexually mature; **Ge|schlęchts|rei|fe** F sexual maturity; **Ge|schlęchts|rol|le** F (*Sociol*) sex role; **ge|schlęchts|spe|zi|fisch** ADJ (*Sociol*) sex-specific; **Ge|schlęchts|teil** NT genitals *pl*; **Ge|schlęchts|trieb** M sex(ual) urge; sex(ual) drive; **Ge|schlęchts|um|wand|lung** F sex change; **Ge|schlęchts|un|ter|schied** M difference between the sexes; **Ge|schlęchts|ver|ir|rung** F sexual perversion; **Ge|schlęchts|ver|kehr** M sexual intercourse; **Ge|schlęchts|wort** NT *pl* **-wörter** (*Gram*) article; **Ge|schlęchts|zel|le** F sexual cell

ge|schli|chen *ptp von* **schleichen**

ge|schlif|fen [gəˈʃlɪfn] *ptp von* **schleifen**[2] ADJ *Manieren, Ausdrucksweise* polished, refined; *Sätze* polished; *Edelstein* facetted

Ge|schlif|fen|heit F -, (*rare*) **-en** (= *Feinheit*) refinement; (= *Schliff*) polish

ge|schlos|sen [gəˈʃlɔsn] *ptp von* **schließen** ADJ closed; (= *vereint*) united, unified; **in sich** (*dat*) **~** self-contained; *Mensch, Charakter* well-rounded; *Buch, Handlung* well-knit; *Systeme, Produktionskreisläufe* closed; **es war eine ~e Wolkendecke vorhanden** the sky was completely overcast; **ein ~es Ganzes** a unified whole; **~e Gesellschaft** closed society; (= *Fest*) private party; **in ~er Sitzung** in closed session; (*Jur*) in camera; **ein ~er Wagen** a saloon car (*Brit*), a sedan (*US*); **~e Ortschaft** built-up area; **in ~er Formation** (*Aviat*) in close formation

ADV **~ für etw sein/stimmen** to be/vote unanimously in favour (*Brit*) *or* favor (*US*) of sth; **wir protestierten ~ gegen das neue Gesetz** we were unanimous in our protest against the new law; **~ hinter jdm stehen** to stand solidly behind sb; **wir gingen ~ mit der ganzen Klasse ins Kino** the whole class went to the cinema

en masse *or* as a body; **dieses zwölfbändige Lexikon wird nur ~ abgegeben** this twelve-volume encyclopedia is only sold as a complete set; **dieser Vokal wird ~ ausgesprochen** this vowel has closed articulation

Ge|schlos|sen|heit F -, *no pl* unity

Ge|schluch|ze [gəˈʃlʊxtsə] NT -s, *no pl* sobbing

ge|schlun|gen *ptp von* **schlingen**[1] *von* **schlingen**[2]

Ge|schlür|fe [gəˈʃlʏrfə] NT -s, *no pl* (*inf*) slurping

Ge|schmack [gəˈʃmak] M -(e)s, **¨e** *or* (*hum, inf*) **¨er** [gəˈʃmɛkə, gəˈʃmɛkɐ] (*lit, fig*) taste; (= *Aroma auch*) flavour (*Brit*), flavor (*US*); (*S Ger.* = *Geruch*) smell; (*no pl:* = *Geschmackssinn*) sense of taste; **je nach ~** to one's own taste; **Salz (je) nach ~ hinzufügen** add salt to taste; **seinen ~ bilden** *or* **entwickeln** (*lit*) to develop one's sense of taste; (*fig*) to acquire a sense of the aesthetic; **an etw** (*dat*) **~ finden** to acquire a taste for sth; **auf den ~ kommen** to acquire a taste for it; **einen guten ~ haben** (*Essen*) to taste good; **er hat einen guten ~** (*fig*) he has good taste; **für meinen ~** for my taste; **das ist nicht mein/nach meinem ~** that's not my/to my taste; **die Geschmäcker sind verschieden** tastes differ; **über ~ lässt sich (nicht) streiten** (*prov*) there's no accounting for taste(s) (*prov*)

ge|schmäck|le|risch [gəˈʃmɛklərɪʃ] ADJ highly elaborate

ge|schmack|lich [gəˈʃmaklɪç] ADJ (*lit, fig*) as regards taste; **ausgezeichnete ~e Qualitäten** (*form*) exquisite flavour (*Brit*) *or* flavor (*US*), exquisite taste ADV **~ besser/hervorragend/Spitzenklasse sein** to taste better/fantastic/excellent; **etw ~ verbessern** to improve the taste of sth

ge|schmack|los ADJ (*lit, fig*) tasteless; (= *taktlos auch*) in bad taste

Ge|schmack|lo|sig|keit F -, **-en** a *no pl* (*lit, fig*) tastelessness, lack of taste; (= *Taktlosigkeit auch*) bad taste b (= *Beispiel der Geschmacklosigkeit*) example of bad taste; (= *Bemerkung*) remark in bad taste; **das ist eine ~!** that is the most appalling bad taste!

Ge|schmacks-: ge|schmacks|bil|dend ADJ aesthetically formative; **Ge|schmacks|bil|dung** F formation of good taste; **Ge|schmacks|emp|fin|dung** F sense of taste; **keine ~ haben** to be unable to taste anything; **Ge|schmacks|fra|ge** F matter *or* question of (good) taste; **Ge|schmacks|knos|pen** taste buds *pl*; **Ge|schmacks|mus|ter** NT (*Jur*) registered design; **Ge|schmacks|nerv** M taste bud; **ge|schmacks|neut|ral** ADJ tasteless; **Ge|schmacks|rich|tung** F taste; **in sieben neuen ~en** in seven new flavours (*Brit*) *or* flavors (*US*); **Ge|schmacks|sa|che** F matter of taste; **das ist ~** it's (all) a matter of taste; **Ge|schmacks|sinn** M , *no pl* sense of taste; **Ge|schmacks|trä|ger** M (*Cook*) flavour (*Brit*) *or* flavor (*US*) carrier; **Ge|schmacks|ver|ir|rung** F unter ~ leiden (*iro*) to have no taste; **der Hut ist eine ~** that hat is an aberration; **Ge|schmacks|ver|stär|ker** M (*Chem, Cook*) flavour (*Brit*) *or* flavor (*US*) enhancer

ge|schmack|voll ADJ tasteful; **~e Kleider tragen** to dress tastefully; **das war eine nicht sehr ~e Bemerkung** that remark was not in very good taste ADV tastefully

Ge|schmat|ze [gəˈʃmatsə] NT -s, *no pl* (*inf*) noisy eating

Ge|schmei|de [gəˈʃmaidə] NT -s, - (*geh*) jewellery *no pl* (*Brit*), jewelry *no pl* (*US*); **ein ~** a piece of jewel(le)ry

ge|schmei|dig [gəˈʃmaidɪç] ADJ a *Leder, Haut* supple; *Körper, Bewegung auch* lithe, lissom(e); *Fell* sleek; (= *weich*) *Handtuch, Haar* soft; *Teig* workable; *Wachs* malleable; (= *anschmiegsam*) soft and clinging; **er hat einen ~en Gang** he moves with supple grace b (*fig*) (= *anpassungsfähig*) adaptable, flexible; (= *wendig*) adroit; *Zun-*

ge, *Worte* glib, smooth ADV (= *wendig*) smoothly, supply; (*in Bezug auf Tanzen*) lithely; **~ glitt die Katze vom Stuhl** the cat slid off the chair with feline grace

Ge|schmei|dig|keit F -, *no pl* a (*von Leder, Haut*) suppleness; (*von Körper, Bewegung auch*) litheness; (*von Fell*) sleekness; (= *Weichheit*) (*von Handtuch, Haar*) softness; (*von Wachs*) malleability; (= *Anschmiegsamkeit*) clinging softness b (*fig*) (= *Anpassungsfähigkeit*) flexibility; (= *Wendigkeit*) adroitness; (*von Zunge, Worten*) glibness

Ge|schmeiß [gəˈʃmais] NT -es, *no pl* a (*old lit, fig*) vermin *pl* b (*Hunt*) droppings *pl*

Ge|schmet|ter [gəˈʃmɛtɐ] NT -s, *no pl* flourish

Ge|schmier [gəˈʃmiːɐ] NT -(e)s, *no pl*, **Ge|schmie|re** [gəˈʃmiːrə] NT -s, *no pl* (*inf*) mess; (= *Handschrift*) scrawl; (= *Geschriebenes*) scribble; (= *schlechtes Bild*) daub

ge|schmis|sen *ptp von* **schmeißen**

ge|schmol|zen *ptp von* **schmelzen**

Ge|schmor|te(s) [gəˈʃmoːɐtə] NT *decl as adj* (*Cook*) braised meat

Ge|schmun|zel [gəˈʃmʊntsl̩] NT -s, *no pl* smiling

Ge|schmus [gəˈʃmuːs] NT -es, *no pl*, **Ge|schmu|se** [gəˈʃmuːzə] NT -s, *no pl* (*inf*) cuddling; (*von Pärchen*) cuddling, canoodling (*Brit inf*)

Ge|schnä|bel [gəˈʃnɛːbl̩] NT -s, *no pl* billing; (*hum = Küsserei*) billing and cooing

Ge|schnat|ter [gəˈʃnatɐ] NT -s, *no pl* (*lit*) cackle, cackling; (*fig*) jabber, jabbering

Ge|schnet|zel|te(s) [gəˈʃnɛtsltə] NT *decl as adj* (*esp Sw Cook*) meat cut into strips stewed to produce a thick sauce

ge|schnie|gelt [gəˈʃniːglt] ADJ (*pej*) flashy; **~ und gebügelt** *or* **gestriegelt** spruced up → *auch* **schniegeln**

ge|schnit|ten *ptp von* **schneiden**

ge|schno|ben *ptp von* **schnauben**

Ge|schnüf|fel [gəˈʃnʏfl̩] NT -s, *no pl* sniffing; (*fig*) nosing *or* sniffing about (*Brit*) *or* around

ge|scho|ben *ptp von* **schieben**

ge|schol|len (*old*) *ptp von* **schallen**

ge|schol|ten *ptp von* **schelten**

Ge|schöpf [gəˈʃœpf] NT -(e)s, **-e** (= *Geschaffenes*) creation; (= *Lebewesen*) creature; **wir sind alle ~e Gottes** we are all God's creatures; **sie ist sein ~** (*geh*) she is his creature

ge|scho|ren *ptp von* **scheren**[1]

Ge|schoss[1] ▲ [gəˈʃɔs] NT -es, -e, **Ge|schoß**[1] [gəˈʃoːs] (*Aus, S Ger*) NT -es, -e projectile (*form*); (= *Wurfgeschoss, Rakete etc auch*) missile; (= *Kugel auch*) bullet; (*fig inf*: = *scharf geschossener Ball*) shot; **ferngelenktes ~** guided missile

Ge|schoss[2] ▲ NT -es, -e, **Ge|schoß**[2] (*Aus, S Ger*) NT -es, -e (= *Stockwerk*) floor, storey (*Brit*), story (*US*); **im ersten ~** on the first (*Brit*) *or* second (*US*) floor; **das Haus hat vier ~e** the house has four storeys (*Brit*) *or* storys (*US*); **das Kaufhaus hat vier ~e** the department store has four floors

Ge|schoss|bahn ▲ F trajectory; (*einer Rakete auch*) flight path

ge|schos|sen *ptp von* **schießen**

Ge|schoss-: Ge|schoss|gar|be ▲ F burst of fire; **Ge|schoss|ha|gel** ▲ M hail of bullets

-ge|schos|sig [gəˈʃɔsɪç], (*Aus, S Ger*) **-ge|scho|ßig** [gəˈʃoːsɪç] *suf* -storey *attr* (*Brit*), -story *attr* (*US*), -storeyed (*Brit*), -storied (*US*); **mehrgeschossig** multistorey *etc*

ge|schraubt [gəˈʃraupt] ADJ (*pej*) *Stil, Redeweise* pretentious → *auch* **schrauben**

Ge|schrei [gəˈʃrai] NT -s, *no pl* shouts *pl*, shouting; (*von Kindern, Fußballfans, Streitenden auch*) yells *pl*, yelling; (*von Verletzten, Babys, Popfans*) screams *pl*, screaming; (= *schrilles Geschrei*) shrieks *pl*, shrieking; (*fig*: = *Aufhebens*) fuss, todo (*inf*); **viel ~ um etw machen** to kick up (*inf*) or make a big fuss about sth; **ein großes ~ erheben** to set up a cry; (*fig*) to raise an outcry

Ge|schreib|sel [gəˈʃraipsl] NT **-s,** *no pl* (*inf*) scribble; (*fig*: = *Schreiberei*) scribblings *pl*

ge|schrie|ben *ptp von* **schreiben**

ge|schrie|en, ge|schrien *ptp von* **schreien**

ge|schrit|ten *ptp von* **schreiten**

ge|schult *ptp von* **schulen** ADJ hervorragend **~e Mitarbeiter** outstandingly trained employees; **ein ~es Auge/Ohr haben** to have a practised (*Brit*) or practiced (*US*) or an expert eye/ear → *auch* **schulen**

ge|schun|den *ptp von* **schinden** ADJ *Land, Volk* ravaged, devastated; **der ~e Leib Christi** the broken body of Christ

Ge|schütz [gəˈʃyts] NT **-es, -e** gun; **schweres ~** heavy artillery; **eine Kanone ist ein ~** a cannon is a piece of artillery; **ein ~ auffahren** to bring up a gun; **schweres** or **grobes ~ auffahren** (*fig*) to bring up one's big guns

Ge|schütz-: Ge|schütz|be|die|nung F gunnery; (= *Personal*) gun crew; **Ge|schütz|don|ner** M roar or booming of (the) guns; **Ge|schütz|feu|er** NT shell fire; **Ge|schütz|rohr** NT gun barrel; **Ge|schütz|stand** M , **Ge|schütz|stel|lung** F gun emplacement

ge|schützt [gəˈʃytst] ADJ *Winkel, Ecke* sheltered; *Pflanze, Tier* protected; **ein ~er Platz** a sheltered spot or place; **~er Feiertag** unpaid statutory holiday (*Brit*) or vacation (*US*) → *auch* **schützen**

Ge|schütz|turm M gun turret

Geschw. *abbr von* **Geschwister**

Ge|schwa|der [gəˈʃvaːdɐ] NT **-s, -** squadron

Ge|schwa|der-: Ge|schwa|der|kom|man|deur(in) M(F) (*Naut*) commodore; **Ge|schwa|der|kom|mo|do|re** M (*Aviat*) squadron leader (*Brit*), major (*US*)

Ge|schwa|fel [gəˈʃvaːfl] NT **-s,** *no pl* (*inf*) waffle (*Brit inf*), blather (*inf*)

Ge|schwal|le [gəˈʃvalə] NT **-s,** *no pl* (*pej inf*) waffle (*Brit inf*), blather (*inf*)

ge|schwänzt [gəˈʃvɛntst] ADJ *Peitsche* with tails; *Haar* in a ponytail

Ge|schwätz [gəˈʃvɛts] NT **-es,** *no pl* (*pej*) prattle; (= *Klatsch*) tittle-tattle (*Brit inf*), gossip

Ge|schwat|ze [gəˈʃvatsə] NT **-s,** *no pl,* (*S Ger*) **Ge|schwät|ze** [gəˈʃvɛtsə] NT **-s,** *no pl* (*inf*) chattering, nattering (*inf*)

ge|schwät|zig [gəˈʃvɛtsɪç] ADJ talkative, garrulous; (= *klatschsüchtig*) gossipy

Ge|schwät|zig|keit F **-,** *no pl* talkativeness, garrulousness; (= *Klatschsucht*) constant gossiping; **das haben wir deiner ~ zu verdanken** we've you and your eternal chattering/gossiping to thank for that

ge|schweift [gəˈʃvaift] ADJ **a** curved; **~e Klammer** (*Typ*) curly bracket, brace → *auch* **schweifen b** *Stern* with a tail

ge|schwei|ge [gəˈʃvaigə] CONJ **~ (denn)** let or leave alone, never mind

ge|schwie|gen *ptp von* **schweigen**

ge|schwind [gəˈʃvɪnt] ADJ (*old, S Ger*) swift, quick, fast *no adv*; **~!** quick(ly)!, hurry!; **~en Schrittes** (*geh*) with rapid steps; **~ wie der Wind** (*geh*) as swift as the wind

Ge|schwin|dig|keit [gəˈʃvɪndɪçkait] F **-, -en** speed; (= *Schnelligkeit auch*) swiftness, quickness; (*Phys: von Masse*) velocity; **mit einer ~ von ...** at a speed of ...; **mit höchster ~** at top speed; **mit rasender ~ fahren** to belt or tear along (*inf*); **eine zu große ~ draufhaben** (*inf*) to be going too fast; **an ~ zunehmen** to gather or pick up speed; (*Phys: Masse*) to gain momentum; **die ~ steigern/verringern** to increase/decrease one's speed, to speed up/slow down

Ge|schwin|dig|keits-: Ge|schwin|dig|keits|ab|fall M (*Phys*) loss of speed; **Ge|schwin|dig|keits|be|gren|zung** F , **Ge|schwin|dig|keits|be|schrän|kung** F speed

limit; **gegen die ~ verstoßen** to exceed the speed limit; **Ge|schwin|dig|keits|kon|trol|le** F speed check; **Ge|schwin|dig|keits|mes|ser** M **-s, -** tachometer; (*Aut auch*) speedometer, speedo (*Brit inf*); **Ge|schwin|dig|keits|über|schrei|tung** [-ly:bəˈʃraitʊŋ] F **-, -en, Ge|schwin|dig|keits|über|tre|tung** F exceeding the speed limit, speeding; **Ge|schwin|dig|keits|zu|nah|me** F (*Phys*) increase in velocity

Ge|schwirr [gəˈʃvɪr] NT **-s,** *no pl* (*von Insekten*) buzzing; (*von Pfeilen*) whizzing

Ge|schwis|ter¹ [gəˈʃvɪstɐ] PL brothers and sisters *pl*, siblings *pl*; **wir sind drei ~** there are three of us in my or our family; **haben Sie noch ~?** do you have any brothers or sisters?

Ge|schwis|ter² NT **-s, -** (*form, Sw*) sibling (*form*); (= *Bruder*) brother; (= *Schwester*) sister

Ge|schwis|ter|chen [gəˈʃvɪsteçən] NT **-s, -** little brother/sister

ge|schwis|ter|lich [gəˈʃvɪstɐlɪç] ADJ brotherly/sisterly ADV in a brotherly/sisterly way; **sie leben ~ zusammen** they live together as brother and sister

Ge|schwis|ter-: Ge|schwis|ter|lie|be F brotherly/sisterly love; (*gegenseitig*) love between a brother and a sister; **ge|schwis|ter|los** ADJ who have no brothers or sisters ADV **~ aufwachsen** to grow up as an only child; **Ge|schwis|ter|paar** NT brother and sister *pl*; **die beiden sind ein reizendes ~** the children are a lovely pair

ge|schwol|len [gəˈʃvɔlən] *ptp von* **schwellen** ADJ (*pej*) turgid, pompous, bombastic ADV (*pej*) turgidly, pompously, bombastically

ge|schwom|men *ptp von* **schwimmen**

ge|schwo|ren [gəˈʃvoːrən] *ptp von* **schwören**

Ge|schwo|re|nen-: Ge|schwo|re|nen|bank F *pl* **-bänke** jury box; (= *die Geschworenen*) jury; **Ge|schwo|re|nen|ge|richt** NT = Schwurgericht; **Ge|schwo|re|nen|lis|te** F panel

Ge|schwo|re|ne(r) [gəˈʃvoːrənə] MF *decl as adj* juror; **die ~n** the jury *sing or pl*

Ge|schwor|ne(r) [gəˈʃvoːrnə] MF *decl as adj* (*Aus*) = Geschworene(r)

Ge|schwulst [gəˈʃvʊlst] F **-, ⁻e** [gəˈʃvylstə] growth; (= *Hirngeschwulst, Krebsgeschwulst etc auch*) tumour (*Brit*), tumor (*US*)

Ge|schwulst-: ge|schwulst|ar|tig ADJ growth-like; tumorous; **Ge|schwulst|kno|ten** M growth

ge|schwun|den *ptp von* **schwinden**

ge|schwun|gen *ptp von* **schwingen** ADJ curved; **eine leicht ~e Nase** a slightly curved nose; **eine kühn ~e Nase** an aquiline nose; **~e Klammer** (*Typ*) curly bracket, brace

Ge|schwür [gəˈʃvyːɐ] NT **-s, -e** ulcer; (= *Hautgeschwür auch*) sore; (= *Furunkel*) boil; (*fig*) running sore, ulcer

ge|schwür|ar|tig ADJ ulcerous ADV **sich ~ verändern** to become ulcerous, to ulcerate; **~ wachsen** (*fig*) to spread like a cancer

ge|seg|net [gəˈzeːgnət] ADJ (*geh*) **mit etw ~ sein** to be blessed with sth; **~en Leibes sein** (*old, Bibl*) to be great with child (*old, Bibl*); **~es neues Jahr!** Happy New Year!; **~e Mahlzeit!** for what we are about to receive may the Lord make us truly thankful; **im ~en Alter von 84 Jahren** at the ripe old age of 84; **einen ~en Schlaf haben** to be a sound sleeper; **einen ~en Appetit haben** to have a healthy appetite → *auch* **segnen**

ge|se|hen *ptp von* **sehen**

Ge|seich [gəˈzaiç] NT **-s,** *no pl* (*sl*) claptrap (*inf*)

Ge|sei|er [gəˈzaiɐ] NT **-s,** *no pl,* **Ge|sei|re** [gəˈzairə] NT **-s,** *no pl* (*pej inf*) **a** (= *Gejammer*) moaning, bellyaching (*inf*) **b** (= *Geschwafel*) claptrap (*inf*)

Ge|selch|te(s) [gəˈzɛlçtə] NT *decl as adj* (*S Ger, Aus*) *salted and smoked meat*

Ge|sel|le [gəˈzɛlə] M **-n, -n, Ge|sell** [gəˈzɛl] M **-en, -en** (*obs*) **a** (= *Handwerksgeselle*) journeyman **b** (*old inf: = Bursche*) fellow **c** (*dated:* = *Kamerad*) companion

ge|sel|len [gəˈzɛlən] *ptp* **gesellt** VR **sich zu jdm ~** to join sb; **dazu gesellte sich noch, dass ...** (*geh*) in addition to this was the fact that ..., this was accompanied by the fact that ... → **gleich 1**

Ge|sel|len-: Ge|sel|len|brief M journeyman's certificate; **Ge|sel|len|jah|re** PL years *pl* as a journeyman; **Ge|sel|len|prü|fung** F examination to become a journeyman; **Ge|sel|len|stück** NT journeyman's piece; **Ge|sel|len|zeit** F period as a journeyman

ge|sel|lig [gəˈzɛlɪç] ADJ sociable, convivial; *Tier* gregarious; *Verkehr* social; **der Mensch ist ein ~es Tier** man is a social creature or animal; **~es Beisammensein** social gathering, get-together (*inf*); **sie genehmigten sich in ~er Runde ein paar Bierchen** they had a friendly little get-together over a couple of beers ADV **sie saßen ~ bei einer Flasche Wein zusammen** they were sitting together over a friendly bottle of wine

Ge|sel|lig|keit F **-, -en a** *no pl* sociability, conviviality; (*von Tieren*) gregariousness; (= *geselliges Leben*) social intercourse; **die ~ lieben** to be sociable, to enjoy company **b** (= *Veranstaltung*) social gathering

Ge|sel|lin [gəˈzɛlɪn] F **-, -nen** (= *Handwerksgesellin*) journeyman

Ge|sell|schaft [gəˈzɛlʃaft] F **-, -en a** (*Sociol, fig:* = *Oberschicht*) society; **die ~ verändern** to change society; **eine Dame der ~** a society lady; **die ~ der Stadt** the high society of the town; **jdn in die ~ einführen** to introduce sb into society

b (= *Vereinigung*) society; (*Comm*) company; **die ~ der Freunde** the Society of Friends; **~ des bürgerlichen Rechts** private company or corporation (*US*); **~ mit beschränkter Haftung** limited company (*Brit*) or corporation (*US*)

c (= *Abendgesellschaft*) reception, party; (= *Gäste*) guests *pl*, party; **geschlossene ~** private party; **eine erlesene ~ hatte sich eingefunden** a select group of people had gathered

d (*in Restaurant etc*) function

e (= *Umgang, Begleitung*) company, society (*old, form*); **zur ~** to be sociable; **in schlechte ~ geraten** to get into bad company; **da befindest du dich in guter ~** then you're in good company; **jdm ~ leisten** to keep sb company

f (= *Kreis von Menschen*) group of people; (*pej*) pack, bunch, crowd (*all inf*); **diese Familie/Abteilung ist eine komische ~** that family/department are an odd bunch (*inf*); **wir waren eine bunte ~** we were a mixed bunch

Ge|sell|schaf|ter [gəˈzɛlʃaftɐ] M **-s, -, Ge|sell|schaf|te|rin** [-ərɪn] F **-, -nen a** (= *Unterhalter*) companion; (*euph:* = *Prostituierte*) escort; **ein guter ~ sein** to be good company; **er ist nicht der Typ des ~s** he's not good company; **mit einem so anregenden ~ ...** with somebody who is such good company ... **b** (*Comm*) (= *Teilhaber*) shareholder; (= *Partner*) partner; **stiller ~** sleeping (*Brit*) or silent (*US*) partner

ge|sell|schaft|lich [gəˈzɛlʃaftlɪç] ADJ social; (*Sociol auch*) societal; **~e Produktion** production by society ADV **er ist ~ erledigt** he's ruined socially; **sich ~ unmöglich machen** or **daneben benehmen** to disgrace oneself socially

Ge|sell|schafts-: Ge|sell|schafts|abend M social evening; **Ge|sell|schafts|an|teil** M (*Comm*) share of the business; **Ge|sell|schafts|an|zug** M formal dress; **Ge|sell|schafts|auf|bau** M , *no pl* structure of society; **Ge|sell|schafts|bild** NT (*Sociol*) view of society; **Ge|sell|schafts|da|me** F (*old*) (lady's) companion; **ge|sell|schafts|fä|hig** ADJ *Verhalten, Gedankengut, Kunstrichtung* socially acceptable; *Mensch, Aussehen auch* presentable; **ge|sell|schafts|feind|lich** ADJ hostile to society; **Ge|sell|schafts|form** F social system;

Ge|sell|schafts|for|ma|ti|on F (*Sociol*) development of society; **Ge|sell|schafts|ka|pi|tal** NT (*Comm*) company's capital; **Ge|sell|schafts|klas|se** F (*Sociol*) social class; **Ge|sell|schafts|klatsch** M society gossip; **Ge|sell|schafts|klei|dung** F formal dress; **Ge|sell|schafts|kri|tik** F social criticism, criticism of society; **Ge|sell|schafts|kri|ti|ker(in)** M(F) social critic; **ge|sell|schafts|kri|tisch** ADJ critical of society; **die ~e Funktion einer Zeitung** the function of a newspaper as a critic of society *or* social critic ADV **sich ~ äußern** to be critical of society; **~ denken** to have a critical attitude toward(s) society; **Ge|sell|schafts|leh|re** F (*dated*) sociology; (*Sch*) social studies *pl*; **Ge|sell|schafts|ord|nung** F social system; **Ge|sell|schafts|po|li|tik** F social politics *sing*; **Ge|sell|schafts|raum** M function room; **Ge|sell|schafts|ro|man** M social novel; **Ge|sell|schafts|schicht** F stratum of society, social stratum; **Ge|sell|schafts|spiel** NT party game, parlour (*Brit*) *or* parlor (*US*) game; **Ge|sell|schafts|struk|tur** F structure of society; (*bestimmte auch*) social structure; **Ge|sell|schafts|stück** NT (*Theat*) comedy of manners; (*Art*) genre painting; **Ge|sell|schafts|sys|tem** NT social system; **Ge|sell|schafts|tanz** M ballroom dance; **Ge|sell|schafts|ver|än|de|rung** F social change; **Ge|sell|schafts|ver|trag** M (*Philos*) social contract; (*Comm*) articles *pl* of partnership, partnership agreement; **Ge|sell|schafts|wis|sen|schaf|ten** PL social sciences *pl*; **ge|sell|schafts|wis|sen|schaft|lich** ADJ sociological

Ge|senk [gə'zɛŋk] NT -(e)s, -e a (*Tech*) die b (*Min*) blind shaft, winze

Ge|senk|schmie|de F (*Tech*) drop forge

ge|ses|sen ptp von **sitzen**

Ge|setz [gə'zɛts] NT -es, -e (*Jur, = Naturgesetz, Prinzip*) law; (*= Gesetzbuch*) statute book; (*Parl: = Vorlage*) bill; (*nach Verabschiedung*) act; (*= Satzung, Regel*) rule; **das Copyrightgesetz** the Copyright Act; (**zum**) **~ werden** to become law, to pass into law; **auf Grund des ~es, nach dem ~** under the law (*über +acc* on); **vor dem ~** in (the eyes of the) law; **im Sinne des ~es** within the meaning of the act; **steht etwas davon im ~?** is there any law about it?; **ich kann nichts im ~ finden, wonach das verboten wäre** I can't find any law forbidding it; **das ~ der Schwerkraft** the law of gravity; **das ~ des Dschungels** the law of the jungle; **das erste** *or* **oberste ~ (der Wirtschaft etc)** the golden rule (of industry etc); **das ~ Mose** (*Bibl*) the Law of Moses, the Mosaic Law; **ein ungeschriebenes ~** an unwritten rule; **wenn uns das ~ des Handelns aufgezwungen wird** if we are forced to take the initiative *or* the first step

Ge|setz-: Ge|setz|blatt NT law gazette; **Ge|setz|buch** NT statute book; **Bürgerliches ~** Civil Code; **Ge|setz|ent|wurf** M (draft) bill

Ge|set|zes-: Ge|set|zes|än|de|rung F change in the law; **Ge|set|zes|bre|cher(in)** M(F) law-breaker; **Ge|set|zes|hü|ter(in)** M(F) (*iro*) guardian of the law; **Ge|set|zes|ini|ti|a|ti|ve** F legislative initiative; (*Sw: = Volksbegehren*) petition for a referendum; **Ge|set|zes|kraft** F the force of law; **~ erlangen** to become law; **~ haben** to be law; **ge|set|zes|kun|dig** ADJ (well-)versed in the law; **Ge|set|zes|la|ge** F **wie ist die ~?** what is the legal position?; **Ge|set|zes|lü|cke** F legal loophole; **Ge|set|zes|no|vel|le** F amendment; **Ge|set|zes|samm|lung** F compendium of laws (*zu* on); **Ge|set|zes|ta|feln** PL (*Bibl*) tablets *pl* (*on which the Ten Commandments were written*); **Ge|set|zes|text** M wording of a/the law; **Ge|set|zes|treu** ADJ *Person* law-abiding; *Verhalten* in accordance with the law; **Ge|set|zes|treue** F **seine ~ wurde angezweifelt** it was questioned how law-abiding he was; **Ge|set|zes|über|tre|tung** F infringement of a/the law; **Ge|set|zes|vor|la|ge** F

(draft) bill; **Ge|set|zes|werk** NT corpus of laws; **ge|set|zes|wid|rig** ADJ illegal; (*unrechtmäßig*) unlawful ADV illegally; (*= unrechtmäßig*) unlawfully; **Ge|set|zes|wid|rig|keit** F a no pl illegality; (*= Unrechtmäßigkeit*) unlawfulness b pl (*= gesetzeswidrige Handlungen*) illegal acts pl

Ge|setz-: ge|setz|ge|bend ADJ attr legislative, law-making; **die ~e Gewalt** the legislature; **Ge|setz|ge|ber** M legislature, legislative body; **Ge|setz|ge|ber(in)** M(F) legislator, lawmaker; **ge|setz|ge|be|risch** [-ge:bərɪʃ] ADJ attr legislative

Ge|setz|ge|bung [-ge:bʊŋ] F -, -en legislation no pl

Ge|setz|ge|bungs-: Ge|setz|ge|bungs|ho|heit F legislative sovereignty; **Ge|setz|ge|bungs|not|stand** M legislative state of emergency

ge|setz|kun|dig ADJ = **gesetzeskundig**

ge|setz|lich [gə'zɛtslɪç] ADJ *Verpflichtung, Bestimmungen, Vertreter, Zahlungsmittel* legal; *Feiertag, Rücklage, Zinsen, Regelungen* statutory; (*= rechtmäßig*) lawful, legitimate; **~e Krankenversicherung** statutory health insurance; **auf ~em Wege zur Macht gelangen** to come to power by legal means ADV legally; (*= durch Gesetze auch*) by law; (*= rechtmäßig*) lawfully, legitimately; **~ zu etw verpflichtet sein** to be required by law to do sth, to be legally required to do sth → **schützen**

Ge|setz|lich|keit F -, no pl a (*= Regel*) law b (*= das Gesetzlichsein*) legality; (*= Rechtmäßigkeit*) lawfulness, legitimacy; (*= Rechtsordnung*) law

Ge|setz-: ge|setz|los ADJ *Gruppe, Zeit* lawless; **Ge|setz|lo|sig|keit** F -, -en lawlessness; **ge|setz|mä|ßig** ADJ a (*= gesetzlich*) legal; (*= rechtmäßig*) lawful, legitimate b (*= einem Naturgesetz folgend*) following a set pattern; (*rare: = regelmäßig*) regular ADV a (*= dem Gesetz entsprechend*) legally b (*= regelmäßig*) **~ ablaufen** to follow a set pattern; **Ge|setz|mä|ßig|keit** F -, -en a (*= gesetzlich*) b (*= rechtmäßig*) law; **unser Seelenleben folgt vielleicht uns unbekannten ~en** perhaps the life of the mind runs in accordance with laws which are unknown to us b no pl (*= Gesetzlichkeit*) legality; (*= Rechtmäßigkeit*) lawfulness, legitimacy; (*= Regelmäßigkeit*) regularity

ge|setzt [gə'zɛtst] ADJ (*= reif*) sedate, sober; **ein Herr im ~en Alter** a man of mature years → *auch* **setzen** CONJ **~ den Fall, ...** assuming (that) ...

Ge|setzt|heit F -, no pl (*= Reife*) sedateness

Ge|setz-: ge|setz|wid|rig ADJ, ADV = **gesetzeswidrig**; **Ge|setz|wid|rig|keit** F = **Gesetzeswidrigkeit**

Ge|seuf|ze [gə'zɔyftsə] NT -s, no pl sighing

ges. gesch. abbr von **gesetzlich geschützt** reg'd

ge|si|chert [gə'zɪçɐt] ADJ *Einkommen, Existenz* secure; *Fakten, Erkenntnisse* definite, solid; **~es Gewehr** gun with the safety catch on → *auch* **sichern**

Ge|sicht¹ [gə'zɪçt] NT -(e)s, -er a face; **ein ~ machen** *or* **ziehen** (*inf*) to make *or* pull a face; **ein intelligentes/trauriges/böses/wütendes ~ machen** to look intelligent/sad/cross/angry; **ein langes ~ machen** to make *or* pull a long face; **was machst du denn heute für ein ~?** what's up with you today?; **jdm ein ~ schneiden** (*inf*) to make *or* pull a face at sb; **jdm ins ~ spucken** to spit in sb's face; **jdm ins ~ lachen** to laugh in sb's face; **jdm ins ~ lügen** to lie to sb's face; **jdm ins ~ sehen** to look sb in the face; **den Tatsachen ins ~ sehen** to face facts; **jdm etw ins ~ sagen** to tell sb sth to his face; **mir schien das Sonne ins ~** the sun was (shining) in my eyes; **es stand ihm im** *or* **ins ~ geschrieben** it was written all over his face; **jdm ins ~ springen** (*fig inf*) to go for sb; **aufs ~ fallen** to fall on one's face; (*fig inf: Brot etc*) to fall sticky side down; **sein wahres ~ zeigen** to show (one-

self in) one's true colours (*Brit*) or colors (*US*); **neue ~er sehen** to see some new faces; **das sieht man ihm am ~ an** you can see *or* tell (that) from his face; **sich** (*dat*) **eine (Zigarette) ins ~ stecken** (*inf*) to stick a cigarette in one's face (*inf*) *or* mouth; **jdm wie aus dem ~ geschnitten sein** to be the spitting image of sb; **der Hut steht ihr gut zu ~** (*dated*) her hat is very becoming, her hat becomes her; **dieses Verhalten steht dir nicht zu ~** (*dated*) such behaviour (*Brit*) *or* behavior (*US*) ill becomes you, it ill becomes you to behave like that; **das** *or* **sein ~ verlieren** to lose face; **das ~ wahren** *or* **retten** to save face → **Schlag a**

b (*fig*) (*= Aussehen*) look, appearance; (*einer Stadt, Landschaft etc*) face, appearance; (*geh: = Charakter*) character; **ein anderes/freundlicheres ~ bekommen** to look quite different/more friendly; **die Sache bekommt ein anderes ~** the matter takes on a different complexion; **das gibt der Sache ein neues ~** that puts a different complexion on the matter *or* on things

c no pl (*old: = Sehvermögen*) sight; (*Med: = das zweite ~*) second sight; **jdn aus dem ~ verlieren** (*lit*) to lose sight of sb; (*fig*) to lose touch with sb; **etw aus dem ~ verlieren** (*lit, fig*) to lose sight of sth; **jdn/etw zu ~ bekommen** to set eyes on sb/sth, to see sb/sth; **jdm zu ~ kommen** (*geh*) to be seen by sb

Ge|sicht² NT -(e)s, -e **~e haben** to have visions

Ge|sichts-: Ge|sichts|aus|druck M (facial) expression; (*= Mienenspiel auch*) face; **einen ängstlichen ~ haben** to look scared, to have a scared look *or* expression on one's face; **Ge|sichts|bil|dung** F (*geh*) features *pl*; **Ge|sichts|creme** F face cream; **Ge|sichts|far|be** F complexion; **Ge|sichts|feld** NT field of vision, visual field; **Ge|sichts|hälf|te** F side *or* half of the face; **seine linke ~** the left side *or* half of his face; **Ge|sichts|haut** F facial skin; **Ge|sichts|kon|trol|le** F face check (*carried out by bouncers*); **Ge|sichts|kreis** M a (*dated*) (*= Umkreis*) field of vision; (*= Horizont*) horizon; **jds ~** (*dat*) **entschwinden** to disappear from (sb's) sight, to be lost to sight; **jdn aus dem** *or* **seinem ~ verlieren** to lose sight of sb b (*fig*) horizons *pl*, outlook; **Ge|sichts|läh|mung** F facial paralysis; **ge|sichts|los** ADJ (*fig*) faceless; **Ge|sichts|lo|sig|keit** F -, no pl facelessness; **Ge|sichts|mas|ke** F face mask; (*eines Chirurgen*) mask; **Ge|sichts|mas|sa|ge** F facial massage, facial; **Ge|sichts|milch** F face lotion; **Ge|sichts|mus|kel** M facial muscle; **Ge|sichts|nerv** M facial nerve; **Ge|sichts|ope|ra|ti|on** F operation to one's face; **sich einer ~ unterziehen** to undergo facial surgery; **Ge|sichts|pa|ckung** F face pack; **Ge|sichts|par|tie** F part of the/one's face; **Ge|sichts|pfle|ge** F care of one's face; **Ge|sichts|plas|tik** F facial *or* cosmetic surgery; **Ge|sichts|pu|der** M face powder; **Ge|sichts|punkt** M (*= Betrachtungsweise*) point of view, standpoint; (*= Einzelheit*) point; **unter diesem ~ betrachtet** looked at from this point of view *or* standpoint; **Ge|sichts|ro|se** F (*Med*) facial erysipelas (*spec*); **Ge|sichts|schä|del** M (*Anat*) facial bones *pl*; **Ge|sichts|schnitt** M features *pl*; **ein ovaler ~** an oval face; **ein feiner ~** delicate features *pl*; **Ge|sichts|sinn** no pl (*spec*) M sense of sight *or* vision; **Ge|sichts|straf|fung** [-ʃtrafʊŋ] F facelift; **Ge|sichts|ver|lust** M loss of face; **Ge|sichts|was|ser** NT pl -wässer face lotion; **Ge|sichts|win|kel** M visual angle; (*fig*) angle, point of view; **Ge|sichts|zü|ge** PL features *pl*

Ge|sims [gə'zɪms] NT -es, -e [-zə] ledge

Ge|sin|de [gə'zɪndə] NT -s, - (*old*) servants *pl*; (*= Bauerngesinde*) (farm)hands *pl*

Ge|sin|del [gə'zɪndl] NT -s, no pl (*pej*) riffraff *pl*

Ge|sin|de-: Ge|sin|de|ord|nung F (*Hist*) *rules governing relations between servant and master*; **Ge|sin|de|stu|be** F (*old*) servants' room

Ge|sin|ge [ɡəˈzɪŋə] NT **-s**, *no pl* (*inf*) singing

ge|sinnt [ɡəˈzɪnt] ADJ *usu pred* **jdm gut/günstig/ übel ~ sein** to be well/favourably (*Brit*) or favorably (*US*)/ill disposed to(wards) sb; **jdm freundlich/feindlich ~ sein** to be friendly/hostile to(wards) sb; **sozial/fortschrittlich ~ sein** to be socially/progressively minded; **er ist anders ~ als wir** his views are different from ours, he holds different views from us; **die so ~en Mitglieder** the members holding or taking this view

Ge|sin|nung [ɡəˈzɪnʊŋ] F **-**, **-en** (= *Charakter*) cast of mind; (= *Ansichten*) views *pl*, basic convictions *pl*; (= *Einstellung*) fundamental attitude; (= *Denkart*) way of thinking; (*einer Gruppe*) ethos; **eine liberale ~** liberal-mindedness; **eine edle ~** noble-mindedness; **anständige ~** decency; **seiner ~ treu bleiben** to remain loyal to one's basic convictions; **wegen seiner ~ verfolgt werden** to be persecuted because of one's views or basic convictions or way of thinking; **seine wahre ~ zeigen** to show (oneself in) one's true colours (*Brit*) or colors (*US*)

Ge|sin|nungs-: Ge|sin|nungs|freund(in) M(F), **Ge|sin|nungs|ge|nos|se** M, **Ge|sin|nungs|ge|nos|sin** F like-minded person; **Herr Klein und seine Gesinnungsgenossen von der Opposition** Mr Klein and people from the Opposition who think as he does or who share his views; **ge|sin|nungs|los** (*pej*) ADJ unprincipled ADV **sich ~ verhalten** to behave in an unprincipled manner, to show a total lack of principle; **Ge|sin|nungs|lo|sig|keit** F **-**, *no pl* lack of principles; **Ge|sin|nungs|lump** M (*pej*) timeserver (*pej inf*); **Ge|sin|nungs- schnüf|fe|lei** F (*pej*) **~ betreiben** to snoop around and find out people's political convictions; **Ge|sin|nungs|tä|ter(in)** M(F) person motivated by moral convictions; (*aus politischen Gründen*) person motivated by political convictions; **ge|sin|nungs|treu** ADJ true to one's convictions; **Ge|sin|nungs|treue** F loyalty to one's convictions; **Ge|sin|nungs|wan|del** M, **Ge|sin|nungs|wech|sel** M conversion

ge|sit|tet [ɡəˈzɪtət] ADJ a (= *wohlerzogen*) well- -mannered, well-behaved b (= *zivilisiert, kultiviert*) civilized ADV **die Kinder benahmen sich sehr ~** the children were very well-behaved or well-mannered; **die Demonstration lief ~ ab** it was an orderly demonstration

Ge|sit|tung [ɡəˈzɪtʊŋ] F **-**, *no pl* (*geh*) (= *zivilisiertes Verhalten*) civilized (mode of) behaviour (*Brit*) or behavior (*US*); (= *Gesinnung*) ethos

Ge|socks [ɡəˈzɔks] NT **-es**, *no pl* (*pej inf*) riffraff *pl*

Ge|söff [ɡəˈzœf] NT **-(e)s**, **-e** (*inf*) muck (*inf*), swill (*inf*)

ge|sof|fen *ptp von* **saufen**

ge|so|gen *ptp von* **saugen**

ge|son|dert [ɡəˈzɔndɐt] ADJ separate ADV separately; **dieses Thema wird ~ behandelt** this subject will be dealt with separately; **~ berücksichtigt werden** to receive special consideration → *auch* **sondern** ²

ge|son|nen [ɡəˈzɔnən] *ptp von* **sinnen** ADJ a **~ sein, etw zu tun** to be of a mind to do sth b (*incorrect*) = **gesinnt**

ge|sot|ten [ɡəˈzɔtn] *ptp von* **sieden** ADJ (*dial*) boiled; **Gesottenes** boiled meat

ge|spal|ten [ɡəˈʃpaltn] *ptp von* **spalten** ADJ *Bewusstsein* split; *Lippe, Rachen* cleft; *Huf* cloven; *Zunge* forked; *Gesellschaft, Nation, Konjunktur* divided; **mit ~er Zunge reden** (*old, liter*) to talk falsely; (*esp in Indianergeschichten*) to talk with forked tongue; **bei dieser Frage sind die Meinungen ~** opinions are divided on this question

Ge|spann [ɡəˈʃpan] NT **-(e)s**, **-e** a (= *Zugtiere*) team; (= *zwei Ochsen*) yoke b (= *Wagen und Zugtiere*) oxcart, ox-drawn cart; (= *Ochsengespann*) oxcart, ox-drawn cart; (= *Pferdegespann*) horse and cart; (*zur Personenbeförderung*) horse and carriage; (*fig inf:* =

Paar) pair; **ein gutes ~ abgeben** to make a good team

ge|spannt [ɡəˈʃpant] ADJ a *Seil, Schnur* taut b (*fig*) *Lage* tense; *Beziehungen auch* strained; **seine Nerven waren aufs Äußerste** or **äußerste ~** his nerves were at breaking point c (= *neugierig*) curious; (= *begierig*) eager; *Aufmerksamkeit* close; **in ~er Erwartung** in eager or keen anticipation; **ich bin ~, wie er darauf reagiert** I wonder how he'll react to that, I'd like to see how he reacts to that; **ich bin sehr ~, was ich zu Weihnachten bekomme** I'm longing or dying to know what I'm getting for Christmas; **ich bin schon sehr auf diesen Film ~** I'm dying to see this film; **ich bin auf seine Reaktion sehr ~** I'm longing or dying to see how he reacts; **ich bin ~ wie ein Regenschirm** (*hum inf*) or **Flitzbogen** (*hum inf*) I'm dying to know/see/ find out, I'm on tenterhooks (*esp Brit*) or on pins and needles (*US*); **da bin ich aber ~!** I'm looking forward to that; (*iro*) (oh really?) that I'd like to see!

ADV intently; **~ zuhören/zusehen** to be engrossed with what's going on; **~ in seinem Buch lesen** to be engrossed in one's book → *auch* **spannen**

Ge|spannt|heit F **-**, *no pl* a (*von Seil, Schnur*) tension b (*fig*) (*von Lage*) tension; (*von Beziehungen auch*) tension c (= *Neugierde*) eager anticipation; **es herrscht große ~** everyone is on tenterhooks (*esp Brit*) or on pins and needles (*US*)

ge|spa|ßig [ɡəˈʃpaːsɪç] ADJ (*S Ger, Aus*) = **spaßig**

Ge|spenst [ɡəˈʃpɛnst] NT **-(e)s**, **-er** ghost, spectre (*Brit liter*), specter (*US liter*); (*fig:* = *Gefahr*) spectre (*Brit*), specter (*US*); **~er sehen** (*fig inf*) to imagine things; **er sieht wie ein ~ aus** (*inf*) he looks like a ghost

ge|spens|ter-: Ge|spens|ter|ge|schich|te F ghost story; **Ge|spens|ter|glau|be** M belief in ghosts; **ge|spens|ter|haft** ADJ ghostly *no adv*; (*fig*) eerie, eery ADV eerily; **er sah ~ bleich aus** he was deadly or deathly pale, he looked like a ghost; **~ wirken/aussehen** to seem/look ghostly or eerie

ge|spens|tern [ɡəˈʃpɛnstɐn] *ptp* **gespenstert** VI *aux sein* (*rare*) = **geistern**

Ge|spens|ter-: Ge|spens|ter|schiff NT phantom ship; **Ge|spens|ter|stun|de** F witching hour

ge|spens|tig [ɡəˈʃpɛnstɪç] (*rare*), **ge|spens|tisch** [ɡəˈʃpɛnstɪʃ] ADJ, ADV a = **gespensterhaft** b (*fig:* = *bizarr, unheimlich*) eerie, eery; **es ist gespenstisch ruhig** there is an eerie calm

ge|spickt [ɡəˈʃpɪkt] *ptp von* **spicken** ADJ (*inf*) **mit Fehlern ~** riddled with mistakes; **seine Brieftasche war ~ (voll)** his wallet was bulging, he was loaded (*inf*) → *auch* **spicken**

ge|spie|en *ptp von* **speien**

Ge|spie|le [ɡəˈʃpiːlə] M **-n**, **-n** (*old liter, hum*), **Ge|spie|lin** [ɡəˈʃpiːlɪn] F **-**, **-nen** (*old liter, hum*) playmate

ge|spielt [ɡəˈʃpiːlt] ADJ feigned; **mit ~em Interesse** with a pretence (*Brit*) or pretense (*US*) of being interested → *auch* **spielen**

ge|spien *ptp von* **speien**

ge|spie|sen (*hum*) *ptp von* **speisen**

Ge|spinst [ɡəˈʃpɪnst] NT **-(e)s**, **-e** a (*Tex*) weave; (= *gedrehtes Garn*) thread, spun yarn; (*von Spinne*) web; (*von Raupe*) cocoon b (*fig geh*) web; (*von Lügen*) tissue, web; (*der Fantasie*) product, fabrication

Ge|spinst|fa|ser F (*Tex*) spinning fibre (*Brit*) or fiber (*US*)

ge|splis|sen *ptp von* **spleißen**

ge|spon|nen *ptp von* **spinnen**

Ge|spons [ɡəˈʃpɔns] M **-es**, **-e** [-zə] (*old, hum*) spouse (*hum, form*)

ge|spornt [ɡəˈʃpɔrnt] ADJ → **gestiefelt**

Ge|spött [ɡəˈʃpœt] NT **-(e)s**, *no pl* mockery; (*höhnisch auch*) derision, ridicule; (= *Gegenstand des Spotts*) laughing stock; **jdn/sich zum ~ der Leute machen** to make sb/oneself a laughing stock or an object of ridicule; **zum ~ werden** to become a laughing stock; **zum ~ der ganzen Welt werden** to become the laughing stock of the whole world; **mit jdm sein ~ treiben** to poke fun at sb

Ge|spräch [ɡəˈʃprɛːç] ✪ 27 NT **-(e)s**, **-e** a (= *Unterhaltung*) conversation; (= *Diskussion*) discussion; (= *Dialog*) dialogue (*Brit*), dialog (*US*); **~e** (*Pol*) talks; **ich habe ein sehr interessantes ~ mit ihm geführt** I had a very interesting conversation or talk with him; **ein ~ unter vier Augen** a confidential or private talk; **ein ~ unter Freunden** a conversation between friends; **mit jdm ein ~ anknüpfen** to start a conversation with sb; **das ~ auf etw** (*acc*) **bringen** to bring or steer the conversation *etc* (a)round to sth; **im ~ sein** (*lit*) to be being discussed, to be being talked about; (*in der Schwebe*) to be under discussion; **mit jdm ins ~ kommen** to get into conversation with sb; (*fig*) to establish a dialogue (*Brit*) or dialog (*US*) with sb

b (= *Gesprächsstoff*) **das ~ des Tages** the topic of the hour; **das ~ der Stadt** the talk of the town; **zum ~ werden** to become a talking point c (*Telec:* = *Anruf*) (telephone) call; **wir haben in unserem gestrigen ~ vereinbart, dass ...** we agreed in our telephone conversation yesterday that ...; **ein ~ für dich** a call for you; **stundenlange ~e führen** to be on the telephone for hours

ge|sprä|chig [ɡəˈʃprɛːçɪç] ADJ talkative, chatty (*inf*); (= *mitteilsam*) communicative; **jdn ~ machen** to make sb talk, to loosen sb's tongue ADV **~ von etw erzählen** to talk volubly or expansively about sth

Ge|sprä|chig|keit F **-**, *no pl* talkativeness, chattiness (*inf*); (= *Mitteilsamkeit*) communicativeness; **von unglaublicher ~ sein** to be incredibly talkative or chatty (*inf*)

Ge|sprächs-: ge|sprächs|be|reit ADJ (*esp Pol*) ready to talk; **Ge|sprächs|be|reit|schaft** F (*esp Pol*) readiness to talk; **Ge|sprächs- dau|er** F a (*Telec*) call time b **nach vierstündiger ~** after four hours of talks; **Ge|sprächs- ein|heit** F (*Telec*) unit; **Ge|sprächs|fa|den** M line of communication (*zu* with); **den ~ weiterspinnen** to pursue the line of conversation; **Ge|sprächs|fet|zen** M scrap or snippet of conversation; **Ge|sprächs|form** F **in ~** in dialogue (*Brit*) or dialog (*US*) form; **Ge|sprächs- ge|bühr** F (*Telec*) charge for a/the call; **Ge|sprächs|ge|gen|stand** M topic; **der Skandal ist ~ Nummer eins** the scandal is the number one topic; **damit die Leute endlich einen ~ haben** so that people at last have something to talk about; **Ge|sprächs|kli|ma** NT mood of the discussion or conversation; (*Pol*) atmosphere of the talks; **Ge|sprächs|part|ner(in)** M(F) interlocutor (*form*); **~ bei der Diskussion sind die Herren X, Y und Z** taking part in the discussion are Mr X, Mr Y and Mr Z; **mein ~ bei den Verhandlungen** my opposite number at the talks; **er ist nicht gerade ein anregender ~** he's not exactly an exciting conversationalist; **wer war dein ~?** who did you talk with?; **mein ~ heute Abend ist ...** with me this evening is ...; **Ge|sprächs|pau|se** F break in a/the conversation; (*bei Verhandlungen*) break in the talks; **eine ~ einlegen** to have a break, to break off (for a while); **Ge|sprächs|run|de** F discussion(s *pl*); (*Pol*) round of talks; **Ge|sprächs- stoff** M topics *pl*; (= *Diskussionsstoff*) topics to discuss; **Ge|sprächs|teil|neh|mer(in)** M(F) participant in a/the discussion; (*bei Fernsehserien etc*) panellist (*Brit*), panelist (*US*); **Ge|sprächs|the|ma** NT = **Gesprächsgegenstand**; **Ge|sprächs|the|ra|pie** F (*Psych*) counselling (*Brit*), counseling (*US*); **Ge|sprächs|um|lei|tung** F (*Telec*) call routing system; **ge|sprächs|wei|se** ADV in conversation

ge|spreizt [gəˈʃpraitst] (*fig*) **ADJ** affected, unnatural **ADV** *reden, sich ausdrücken* affectedly, unnaturally → *auch* **spreizen**

Ge|spreizt|heit F -, *no pl* affectation; **von unerträglicher ~** unbearably affected

ge|spren|kelt [gəˈʃprɛŋklt] **ADJ** speckled; **schwarz ~** speckled with black → *auch* **sprenkeln**

Ge|spritz|te(r) [gəˈʃprɪtstə] M *decl as adj* (*S Ger, Aus*) spritzer, wine with soda water

ge|spro|chen *ptp von* **sprechen**

ge|spros|sen *ptp von* **sprießen** *von* **sprossen**

ge|sprun|gen *ptp von* **springen**

Ge|spür [gəˈʃpyːɐ] NT -s, *no pl* feel(ing)

gest. *abbr von* **gestorben**

Ge|sta|de [gəˈʃtaːdə] NT -s, - (*liter*) strand (*poet*)

Ge|sta|gen [gɛstaˈgeːn] NT -s, -e (*Med*) gestagen

Ge|stalt [gəˈʃtalt] F -, -en **a** (*lit, fig*) form; (= *Umriss auch*) shape; **in ~ von** (*fig*) in the form of; **(feste) ~ annehmen** *or* **gewinnen** to take shape; **einer Sache** (*dat*) **~ geben** *or* **verleihen** to shape sth; **das Abendmahl in beiderlei ~** (*Eccl*) Communion under both kinds; **sich in seiner wahren ~ zeigen** (*fig*) to show (oneself in) one's true colours (*Brit*) *or* colors (*US*); **~ geworden** (*liter*) made flesh *pred* → **Ritter a b** (= *Wuchs*) build **c** (= *Person, Persönlichkeit, Traumgestalt*) figure; (*in Literaturwerken auch, pej:* = *Mensch*) character

ge|stal|ten [gəˈʃtaltn] *ptp* **gestaltet** **VT** *Text, Wohnung* to lay out; *Programm, Abend, Layout* to arrange; *Arbeitsplatz, Benutzeroberfläche* to organize; *Arbeitszeit, Freizeit, Abend* to organize, to structure; *Schaufenster* to dress; *Zukunft, Beziehung, Gesellschaft, Politik* to shape; **etw rationeller/effizienter/flexibler ~** to make sth more rational/efficient/flexible; **ich gestalte mein Leben so, wie ich will** I live *or* organize my life the way I want to; **etw interessanter/moderner** *etc* **~** to make sth more interesting/modern *etc*; **der Umbau wurde nach den ursprünglichen Plänen gestaltet** the conversion was carried out in accordance with the original plans; **die Gastgeber haben den Abend sehr lebendig gestaltet** our hosts laid on a very lively evening; **etw künstlerisch ~** to give artistic form to sth; **schöpferisches Gestalten** creative expression; **einen historischen Stoff zu einem Roman ~** to fashion *or* mould (*Brit*) *or* mold (*US*) a historical subject into a novel; **einen Stoff literarisch ~** to give literary form to one's material **VR** (= *werden*) to become; (= *sich entwickeln*) to turn *or* develop (*zu* into); **sich schwierig ~** (*Verhandlungen etc*) to run into difficulties; **sich zu einem Erfolg ~** to turn out to be a success

Ge|stal|ter [gəˈʃtaltɐ] M -s, -, **Ge|stal|te|rin** [-ərɪn] F -, -nen creator; (*Tech: rare*) designer

ge|stal|te|risch [gəˈʃtaltərɪʃ] **ADJ** creative

Ge|stalt-: Ge|stalt|leh|re F (*dated*) morphology; **ge|stalt|los ADJ** formless, shapeless, amorphous; **Ge|stalt|psy|cho|lo|gie** F gestalt psychology; **Ge|stalt|the|ra|pie** F (*spec*) gestalt therapy

Ge|stal|tung F -, -en **a** (= *das Gestalten*) shaping, forming, fashioning (*zu* into); (*von Wohnung*) layout; (*von Abend, Programm*) arrangement; (*von Schaufenster*) dressing; (*von Freizeit*) structuring; **wir bemühen uns um eine möglichst interessante ~ des Sprachunterrichts** we are trying to structure our language-teaching as interestingly as possible **b** (*liter*: = *Gestaltetes*) creation

Ge|stal|tungs-: Ge|stal|tungs|form F form; **Ge|stal|tungs|kraft** F creative power; **Ge|stal|tungs|mit|tel** NT artistic means *sing*; **verschiedene ~** different artistic methods; **Ge|stal|tungs|prin|zip** NT formal principle

Ge|stam|mel [gəˈʃtaml] NT -s, *no pl* stammering, stuttering

ge|stand *pret von* **gestehen**

---

ge|stan|den *ptp von* **stehen** *von* **gestehen** **ADJ** *attr Seefahrer, Fachmann etc* experienced; **ein ~er Mann, ein ~es Mannsbild** a mature and experienced man

ge|stän|dig [gəˈʃtɛndɪç] **ADJ** **~ sein** to have confessed; **ein ~er Mörder** a murderer who confessed

Ge|stän|dig|keit F **die ~ des Angeklagten** the fact that the accused confesses/has confessed *etc*

Ge|ständ|nis [gəˈʃtɛntnɪs] NT -ses, -se confession; **ein ~ ablegen** to make a confession; **jdm ein ~ machen** to make a confession to sb; **jdn zu einem ~ zwingen** to force sb to make a confession

Ge|stän|ge [gəˈʃtɛŋə] NT -s, - (*von Gerüst*) bars *pl*, struts *pl*; (*von Maschine*) linkage; (*Min*: = *Bohrgestänge*) drill stem

Ge|stank [gəˈʃtaŋk] M -(e)s, *no pl* stink, stench

Ge|stän|ker [gəˈʃtɛŋkɐ] NT -s, *no pl* (*inf*) troublemaking, stirring (*inf*)

Ge|sta|po [geˈstaːpo, gəˈʃtaːpo] F -, *no pl* Gestapo

ge|stat|ten [gəˈʃtatn] ✪ 30, 36, 37.4 *ptp* **gestattet** **VT** to allow, to permit; (= *einwilligen in*) to agree *or* consent to; **jdm etw ~** to allow sb sth; **jdm ~, etw zu tun** to allow *or* permit sb to do sth; **~ Sie eine Frage?** may I ask you something *or* a question?; **sich** (*dat*) **~, etw zu tun** (*geh*) to take the liberty of doing sth, to be *or* make so bold as to do sth (*dated, hum*); **sich** (*dat*) **etw ~** to permit *or* allow oneself sth; **wenn ich mir eine Frage/Bemerkung ~ darf ...** (*geh*) if I might be permitted a question/comment, if I may make *or* be so bold *or* free as to ask a question/make a remark ...; **mein Gehalt gestattet mir das nicht** (*geh*) my salary won't permit it; **wenn es die Umstände ~ ...** (*geh*) circumstances permitting ...
VI **~ Sie?(, darf ich ...), ~ Sie, dass ich ...?** may I ...?, would you mind if I ...?; **wenn Sie ~ ...** with your permission ...

Ges|te [ˈgɛstə, geˈstə] F -, -n (*lit, fig*) gesture

Ge|steck [gəˈʃtɛk] NT -(e)s, -e flower arrangement

ge|steckt [gəˈʃtɛkt] **ADV** **~ voll** (*dial*) chock-a-block (*esp Brit inf*), jam-packed (*inf*) → *auch* **stecken**

ge|ste|hen [gəˈʃteːən] *pret* **gestand** [gəˈʃtant], *ptp* **gestanden** [gəˈʃtandn] **VTI** to confess (*jdm etw* sth to sb); **offen gestanden ...** to be frank ..., quite frankly ...

Ge|ste|hungs|kos|ten [gəˈʃteːʊŋs-] PL , **Ge|ste|hungs|preis** M (*Comm*) production costs *pl*

Ge|stein [gəˈʃtain] NT -(e)s, -e rock(s *pl*); (= *Schicht*) rock stratum

Ge|steins-: Ge|steins|ader F vein of rock; **Ge|steins|art** F type of rock; **Ge|steins|boh|rer** M , **Ge|steins|bohr|ma|schi|ne** F rock drill; **Ge|steins|bro|cken** M rock; **Ge|steins|kun|de** F petrography; **Ge|steins|mas|se** F mass of rock; **Ge|steins|mehl** NT mineral powder; **Ge|steins|pro|be** F rock sample; **Ge|steins|schicht** F rock layer *or* stratum

Ge|stell [gəˈʃtɛl] NT -(e)s, -e **a** stand; (= *Regal*) shelf; (= *Ablage*) rack; (= *Rahmen, Bettgestell, Brillengestell, Tischgestell*) frame; (*auf Böcken*) trestle; (= *Wäschegestell*) clothes dryer; (*aus Holz*) clotheshorse; (= *Fahrgestell*) chassis; (= *Flugzeuggestell*) undercarriage (*esp Brit*), landing gear; (*Tech: von Hochofen*) hearth **b** (*fig, inf:* = *Beine*) pins *pl* (*inf*); **langes ~** beanpole (*inf*)

Ge|stel|lung F **a** (*old, Mil*) muster **b** (*form*) furnishing (*form*), making available; **ich bitte um ~ von zwei Fahrzeugen** I request that two vehicles be made available

Ge|stel|lungs|be|fehl M (*Mil*) call-up (*Brit*), draft papers *pl* (*US*)

---

ge|stelzt [gəˈʃteltst] **ADJ** stilted **ADV** *reden, sich ausdrücken* stiltedly → *auch* **stelzen**

Ge|stelzt|heit F -, *no pl* stiltedness *no pl*

ges|tern [ˈgɛstɐn] **ADV** yesterday; **~ Abend** (*früh*) yesterday evening; (*spät*) last night; **die Zeitung von ~** yesterday's paper; **Ansichten von ~** outdated views, opinions of yesteryear (*liter*); **er ist nicht von ~** (*inf*) he wasn't born yesterday; **~ vor acht Tagen** a week (ago) yesterday, yesterday week; **~ in acht Tagen** a week (from) yesterday

Ges|tern [ˈgɛstɐn] NT -, *no pl* yesterday; **das ~** yesterday, yesteryear (*liter*); **im ~** in the past

Ge|sti|chel [gəˈʃtɪçl] NT -s, *no pl* snide remarks *pl*

ge|stie|felt [gəˈʃtiːflt] **ADJ** **a** wearing boots, in boots; **der Gestiefelte Kater** Puss-in-Boots **b** **~ und gespornt** (*fig inf*) ready and waiting, ready for the off (*Brit inf*)

ge|stie|gen *ptp von* **steigen**

ge|stielt [gəˈʃtiːlt] **ADJ** stemmed (*auch Bot*)

Ges|tik [ˈgɛstɪk, ˈgɛstɪk] F -, *no pl* gestures *pl*

Ges|ti|ku|la|ti|on [gɛstikulaˈtsioːn] F -, -en gesticulation(s *pl*)

ges|ti|ku|lie|ren [gɛstikuˈliːrən] *ptp* **gestikuliert** **VI** to gesticulate

Ges|ti|ku|lie|ren NT -s, *no pl* gesticulation(s *pl*), gesticulating

ge|stimmt [gəˈʃtɪmt] **ADJ** **froh/düster ~** in a cheerful/sombre (*Brit*) *or* somber (*US*) mood → *auch* **stimmen**

Ge|stimmt|heit F -, -en mood

Ge|stirn [gəˈʃtɪrn] NT -(e)s, -e star, heavenly body

ge|stirnt [gəˈʃtɪrnt] **ADJ** *attr* (*geh*) starry, star-studded (*liter*)

ges|tisch [ˈgɛstɪʃ, ˈgeːstɪʃ] **ADJ** gestural **ADV** **etw ~ und mimisch zum Ausdruck bringen** to express sth using gestures and mime; **all seine Worte waren ~ untermalt** everything he said was underlined by gesture

ge|sto|ben *ptp von* **stieben**

Ge|stö|ber [gəˈʃtøːbɐ] NT -s, - (*leicht*) snow flurry; (*stark*) snowstorm

ge|sto|chen [gəˈʃtɔxn] *ptp von* **stechen** **ADJ** *Handschrift, Zeichnung* clear, neat **ADV** **~ scharfe Fotos** needle-sharp photographs; **wie ~ schreiben** to write clearly *or* in a neat hand

ge|stockt [gəˈʃtɔkt] **ADJ** (*S Ger*) *Milch* soured

ge|stoh|len [gəˈʃtoːlən] *ptp von* **stehlen** **ADJ** **der/das kann mir ~ bleiben** (*inf*) he/it can go hang (*inf*)

Ge|stöhn [gəˈʃtøːn] NT -(e)s, *no pl*, **Ge|stöh|ne** [gəˈʃtøːnə] NT -s, *no pl* moaning, groaning

ge|stopft [gəˈʃtɔpft] **ADV** **~ voll** (*inf*) jam-packed (*inf*) → *auch* **stopfen**

ge|stor|ben *ptp von* **sterben**

ge|stört [gəˈʃtøːɐt] **ADJ** disturbed; *Schlaf auch* broken; *Verhältnis auch* troubled; *Rundfunkempfang* poor, with a lot of interference; *Einverständnis* troubled, disrupted; **seelisch/geistig ~ sein** to be (psychologically/mentally) unbalanced *or* disturbed; **~er Kreislauf** circulation problems; **Kinder aus ~en Familien** children from problem families → *auch* **stören**

ge|sto|ßen *ptp von* **stoßen**

Ge|stot|ter [gəˈʃtɔtɐ] NT -s, *no pl* stuttering, stammering

Ge|stram|pel [gəˈʃtrampl] NT -s, *no pl* kicking about (*Brit*) *or* around; (*beim Radfahren*) pedalling (*Brit*), pedaling (*US*)

Ge|sträuch [gəˈʃtrɔyç] NT -(e)s, -e shrubbery, bushes *pl*; (= *Dickicht*) thicket

ge|streckt [gəˈʃtrɛkt] **ADJ** *Galopp* full; *Winkel, Flugbahn* elongated → *auch* **strecken**

ge|streift [gəˈʃtraift] **ADJ** striped; **eine rot-grün ~e Bluse** a red and green striped blouse → *auch* **streifen**

Ge|strei|te [gəˈʃtraitə] NT -s, no pl (inf) bickering (inf), quarrelling (Brit), quarreling (US)

ge|streng [gəˈʃtrɛŋ] ADJ (old) strict, stern; **~er Herr!** gracious master or Lord; **die Gestrengen Herren** → **Eisheiligen**

ge|stresst [gəˈʃtrɛst] ptp von **stressen** ADJ stressed, under stress; **~ sein** to be under stress, to be suffering from stress → auch **stressen**

ge|stri|chen [gəˈʃtrɪçn] ptp von **streichen** ADJ (= genau voll) **ein ~es Maß** a level measure; **ein ~er Teelöffel voll** a level teaspoon(ful) ADV **~ voll** level; (= sehr voll) full to the brim; **er hat die Hosen ~ voll** (inf) he's wetting (inf) or shitting (sl) himself; **ich habe die Nase ~ voll** (inf) I'm fed up (to the back teeth with it) (inf)

ge|strie|gelt [gəˈʃtriːɡlt] ADJ **~ und gebügelt** dressed up to the nines → auch **striegeln**

gest|rig [ˈɡɛstrɪç] ADJ attr yesterday's; **unser ~es Gespräch** our conversation (of) yesterday; **unser ~es Schreiben** our letter of yesterday; **am ~en Abend** (geh) (früh) yesterday evening; (spät) last night; **am ~en Tage** (geh) yesterday

ge|strit|ten ptp von **streiten**

Ge|strüpp [gəˈʃtrʏp] NT -(e)s, -e undergrowth, brushwood; (fig) jungle

ge|stuft [gəˈʃtuːft] ADJ (= in Stufen) terraced; Haarschnitt layered; (fig) (= abgestuft) graded; (zeitlich) staggered → auch **stufen**

Ge|stühl [gəˈʃtyːl] NT -(e)s, -e seating

Ge|stüm|per [gəˈʃtʏmpɐ] NT -s, no pl (pej inf) bungling; **sein erbärmliches ~ auf dem Klavier** his pathetic plonking away on the piano (inf)

ge|stun|ken ptp von **stinken**

Ges|tus [ˈɡɛstʊs] M -, no pl (geh) **a** (= Gestik) gestures pl **b** (fig: = Ausdruck) air

Ge|stüt [gəˈʃtyːt] NT -(e)s, -e stud; (= Anlage auch) stud farm

Ge|stüt|buch NT stud book

Ge|stüts-: **Ge|stüts|brand** M stud brand; **Ge|stüts|hengst** M stud (horse); **Ge|stüts|pferd** NT horse at stud; **Ge|stüts|zei|chen** NT stud brand

Ge|such [gəˈzuːx] NT -(e)s, -e petition (auf +acc, um for); (= Antrag) application (auf +acc, um for); **ein ~ einreichen** or **stellen** to make or lodge a petition/an application

Ge|such|stel|ler [-ˌʃtɛlɐ] M -s, -, **Ge|such|stel|le|rin** [-ərɪn] F -, -nen (dated) petitioner; (= Antragsteller) applicant

ge|sucht [gəˈzuːxt] ADJ (= begehrt) sought after; **sehr ~** (very) much sought after; **Ingenieure sind ~e Arbeitskräfte** engineers are much sought after → auch **suchen**

Ge|su|del [gəˈzuːdl] NT -s, no pl (pej) = **Sudelei**

Ge|sül|ze [gəˈzʏltsə] NT -s, no pl (inf) claptrap (inf)

Ge|summ [gəˈzʊm] NT -(e)s, no pl humming, droning

Ge|sums [gəˈzʊms] NT -es [-zəs] no pl (inf) fuss

ge|sund [gəˈzʊnt] ADJ comp -er or ̈-er [gəˈzʏndɐ], superl -este(r, s) or ̈-este(r, s) [gəˈzʏndəstə] (allgemein) healthy; (= arbeits-, leistungsfähig) fit; Unternehmen, Politik sound; (= heilsam) Lehre salutary; **frisch und ~, ~ und munter, ~ wie ein Fisch (im Wasser)** in the pink (Brit), hale and hearty (esp Brit), (as) sound as a bell; **ich fühle mich nicht ganz ~** I don't feel very or too well; **sonst bist du ~?** (iro inf) are you feeling all right? (iro), you need your head examined (inf); **wieder ~ werden** to get better, to get well again, to recover; **Äpfel sind ~** apples are good for you, apples are good for your health; **bleib (schön) ~!** look after yourself

ADV comp ̈-er or -er, superl **am** ̈-esten or -esten **~ leben** to have a healthy lifestyle; **sich ~ ernähren** to have a healthy diet; **~ essen** to eat healthily; **jdn ~ pflegen** to nurse sb back to health → **gesundschreiben**

Ge|sund-: **ge|sund+be|ten** VT sep to heal through prayer; **Ge|sund|be|ten** NT -s, no pl faith healing; **Ge|sund|be|ter** [-beːtɐ] M -s, -, **Ge|sund|be|te|rin** [-ərɪn] F -, -nen faith healer; **Ge|sund|be|te|rei** [-beːtəˈrai] F -, no pl (pej inf) praying; **Ge|sund|brun|nen** M -, no pl (fig) **das ist ein wahrer ~** it's like a fountain of youth

ge|sun|den [gəˈzʊndn] ptp **gesundet** VI aux sein (geh) to recover (auch fig), to regain one's health

Ge|sun|de(r) [gəˈzʊndə] MF decl as adj healthy person

Ge|sund|heit F -, no pl (= seelisches, körperliches Wohlbefinden) health; (= gesunder Zustand) healthiness; (= Arbeits-, Leistungsfähigkeit) fitness; (von Unternehmen, Politik) healthiness, soundness; (von Klima, Lebensweise etc) healthiness; **bei guter ~** in good health; **bei bester ~** in the best of health; **mit meiner ~ steht es mit Besten** I'm not in the best of health, my health is not all (that) it might be; **~!** bless you; **auf Ihre ~!** your (very good) health; **eine robuste/eiserne/zarte ~ haben** to have a robust/an iron/a delicate constitution

ge|sund|heit|lich [gəˈzʊnthaitlɪç] ADJ **~e Schäden** damage to one's health; **sein ~er Zustand** (the state of) his health; **aus ~en Gründen** for health reasons ADV **~ geht es mir nicht besonders** my health is not particularly good; **in ~ schlechtem Zustand** in a poor state of health; **wie geht es Ihnen ~?** how is your health?; **sie ist ~ angeschlagen** she is in poor health; **sich ~ wohl fühlen** to feel physically well

Ge|sund|heits-: **Ge|sund|heits|amt** NT public health department; **Ge|sund|heits|apos|tel** M (iro) health freak (inf) or nut (inf); **Ge|sund|heits|at|test** NT health certificate; **Ge|sund|heits|be|hör|de** F health authorities pl; **ge|sund|heits|be|wusst** ▲ ADJ health-conscious; **Ge|sund|heits|dienst** M health service; **Ge|sund|heits|fa|na|ti|ker(in)** M(F) health freak (inf) or nut (inf); **ge|sund|heits|för|dernd** ADJ healthy, good for the health; **Ge|sund|heits|för|de|rung** F promotion of good health; **Ge|sund|heits|für|sor|ge** F health care; **ge|sund|heits|ge|fähr|dend** [-ɡəfɛːdnt] ADJ unhealthy, bad for one's health; **~ sein** (auch) to be a health hazard; **ge|sund|heits|hal|ber** ADV for health reasons; **Ge|sund|heits|pfle|ge** F hygiene; Ratschläge zur ~ health advice; **öffentliche ~** public health (care); **Ge|sund|heits|scha|den** M health defect; **Gesundheitsschäden** damage to one's health; **viele Arbeiter haben dabei einen ~ davongetragen** the health of many workers has suffered as a result; **ge|sund|heits|schä|di|gend**, **ge|sund|heits|schäd|lich** ADJ unhealthy, damaging to (one's) health; **Ge|sund|heits|schäd|lich|keit** F unhealthiness; **Ge|sund|heits|sys|tem** NT public health system; **Ge|sund|heits|tee** M herbal tea; **Ge|sund|heits|vor|sor|ge** F health care, healthcare (US); **Ge|sund|heits|we|sen** NT , no pl health service; **Ge|sund|heits|zeug|nis** NT certificate of health, health certificate; **Ge|sund|heits|zu|stand** M , no pl state of health

ge|sund-: **ge|sund+ma|chen** VR sep (fig inf) to grow fat (an +dat on); **ge|sund+schrei|ben** ▲ VT sep irreg jdn ~ to certify sb (as) fit; **ge|sund+schrump|fen** sep VT (fig) to trim down, to streamline VR to be trimmed down or streamlined; **Ge|sund|schrump|fung** F trimming down, streamlining; **ge|sund+sto|ßen** VR sep irreg (sl) to line one's pockets (inf)

Ge|sun|dung [gəˈzʊndʊŋ] F -, no pl (lit, fig) recovery; (= Genesung) convalescence, recuperation; **seine ~ macht Fortschritte** he's progressing well

ge|sun|gen ptp von **singen**

ge|sun|ken ptp von **sinken**

Ge|surr [gəˈzʊr] NT -(e)s, no pl, **Ge|sur|re** [gəˈzʊrə] NT -s, no pl humming

Ge|tä|fel [gəˈtɛːfl] NT -s, no pl, (Sw) **Ge|tä|fer** [gəˈtɛːfɐ] NT -s, no pl panelling (Brit), paneling (US)

ge|tan [gəˈtaːn] ptp von **tun** ADJ **nach ~er Arbeit** when the day's work is done

Ge|tän|del [gəˈtɛndl] NT -s, no pl (dated, geh) dalliance (old, liter)

Ge|tier [gəˈtiːɐ] NT -s, no pl **a** (= Tiere, esp Insekten) creatures pl **b** (einzelnes) creature

ge|ti|gert [gəˈtiːɡɐt] ADJ (mit Streifen) striped; (mit Flecken) piebald; **~e Katze** tabby (cat)

Ge|to|be [gəˈtoːbə] NT -s, no pl (inf) chasing about

ge|tönt [gəˈtøːnt] ADJ Glas, Scheibe, Brille tinted → auch **tönen**²

Ge|to|se [gəˈtoːzə] NT -s, no pl raging

Ge|tö|se [gəˈtøːzə] NT -s, no pl din, racket, row; (von Auto, Beifall etc) roar; **mit ~** with a din etc

ge|tra|gen [gəˈtraːɡn] ptp von **tragen** ADJ (fig) Melodie, Tempo etc stately no adv

Ge|tra|gen|heit F -, no pl stateliness

Ge|trä|ller [gəˈtrɛlə] NT -s, no pl trilling

Ge|tram|pel [gəˈtrampl] NT -s, no pl trampling; (= Beifallsgetrampel, Protestgetrampel) stamping

Ge|tränk [gəˈtrɛŋk] NT -(e)s, -e drink, beverage (form); **er gibt viel für ~e aus** he spends a lot on drink

Ge|trän|ke-: **Ge|trän|ke|au|to|mat** M drinks machine or dispenser (Brit), beverage machine or dispenser (US); **Ge|trän|ke|do|se** F drinks can (Brit), beverage can (US); **Ge|trän|ke|kar|te** F (in Café) list of beverages; (in Restaurant) wine list; **Ge|trän|ke|ki|osk** M (Brit) or beverage (US) stand; **Ge|trän|ke|markt** M drinks cash-and-carry (Brit), beverage store (US); **Ge|trän|ke|stand** M drinks (Brit) or beverage (US) stand; **Ge|trän|ke|steu|er** F alcohol tax

Ge|trap|pel [gəˈtrapl] NT -s, no pl patter; (= Hufgetrappel) clop

Ge|tratsch [gəˈtraːtʃ] NT -(e)s, no pl, **Ge|trat|sche** [gəˈtraːtʃə] NT -s, no pl (pej) gossip, gossiping

ge|trau|en [gəˈtrauən] ptp **getraut** VR to dare; **getraust du dich or dir** (inf) **das?** do you dare do that?; **ich getraue mich nicht dorthin** I don't dare (to) go there, I daren't go there; **ich getraue mich zu behaupten, dass ...** (geh) **ich getraue mir die Behauptung, dass ...** (geh) I would venture to say that ...

Ge|trei|de [gəˈtraidə] NT -s (form) - grain, cereal; **in diesem Klima wächst kein ~** grain doesn't or cereals don't grow in this climate; **das ~ steht gut** the grain or cereal crop is doing well

Ge|trei|de-: **Ge|trei|de|(an)bau** M , no pl cultivation of grain or cereals; **Ge|trei|de|art** F cereal; **Ge|trei|de|bör|se** F grain or corn (Brit) exchange; **Ge|trei|de|ern|te** F grain harvest; **Ge|trei|de|feld** NT grain field, cornfield (Brit); **Ge|trei|de|flo|cke** F usu pl cereal; **Ge|trei|de|gar|be** F sheaf of grain; **Ge|trei|de|han|del** M grain trade; **Ge|trei|de|händ|ler(in)** M(F) grain or corn (Brit) merchant; **Ge|trei|de|kam|mer** F granary; **Ge|trei|de|korn** NT -körner grain; **Ge|trei|de|land** NT **a** grain-growing land, cornland (Brit) **b** no pl (= Getreidefelder) grain fields pl, cornfields pl (Brit); **Ge|trei|de|lie|fe|run|gen** PL grain supply sing or supplies pl (an +dat to); **Ge|trei|de|müh|le** F (= Müllereibetrieb, Gerät) flour mill; **Ge|trei|de|pflan|ze** F cereal (plant); **Ge|trei|de|pro|dukt** NT cereal product; **Ge|trei|de|si|lo** NT OR M , **Ge|trei|de|spei|cher** M silo; **Ge|trei|de|wirt|schaft** F grain cultivation; **Indiens ~ ist fast autark** India is almost self-supporting in terms of grain cultivation

ge|trennt [gəˈtrɛnt] ADJ separate; **sie führten ~e Kasse** they each paid for themselves → **Tisch** ADV **~ wohnen** not to live together, to live separately; **~ leben** to be separated, to live apart;

~ schlafen not to sleep together, to sleep in different rooms → *auch* **trennen, marschieren**

Ge|trennt|ge|schlech|tig [-gəʃlɛçtıç] ADJ (*Bot*) di(o)ecious

Ge|trennt|schrei|bung F writing as two/three *etc* words; **zu beachten ist die ~ von „wie viel"** remember that "wie viel" is written as two (separate) words

ge|tre|ten *ptp von* **treten**

ge|treu [gə'trɔy] ADJ a (= *genau, entsprechend*) faithful, true *no adv* b (*liter, dated*) faithful, loyal, trusty (*old*) PREP +*dat* true to; **~ dem Motto ...** true to the motto ...

Ge|treue(r) [gə'trɔyə] MF *decl as adj* (faithful or trusty) follower

ge|treu|lich [gə'trɔylıç] ADJ = **getreu** a

Ge|trie|be [gə'tri:bə] NT **-s, -** a (*Tech*) gears *pl*; (= *Getriebekasten*) gearbox; (= *Antrieb*) drive; (*von Uhr*) movement, works *pl* → **Sand** b (= *lebhaftes Treiben*) bustle, hurly-burly

Ge|trie|be- *in cpds* (*Tech*) gear

ge|trie|ben *ptp von* **treiben**

Ge|trie|be-: Ge|trie|be|öl NT gear(box) oil; **Ge|trie|be|scha|den** M gearbox trouble *no indef art*

Ge|tril|ler [gə'trılɐ] NT **-s,** *no pl* warbling

Ge|trip|pel [gə'trıpl] NT **-s,** *no pl* tripping along; (*affektiert*) mincing

ge|trof|fen *ptp von* **treffen**

ge|tro|gen *ptp von* **trügen**

Ge|trom|mel [gə'trɔml] NT **-s,** *no pl* drumming

ge|trost [gə'tro:st] ADJ confident; **du kannst ~ sein, sei ~** rest assured, never fear; **er war ~en Mutes** (*old*) his mind was reassured ADV a (= *vertrauensvoll*) confidently; **~ sterben** to die in peace b (= *bedenkenlos*) **wenn er frech ist, darfst du ihm ~ eine runterhauen** if he's naughty, feel free to *or* don't hesitate to hit him; **du kannst dich ~ auf ihn verlassen** you need have no fears about relying on him; **man kann ~ behaupten/annehmen, dass ...** one need have no hesitation in *or* about asserting/assuming that ...

ge|trübt [gə'try:pt] *ptp von* **trüben** VR ADJ **ein ~es Verhältnis zu jdm haben** to have an unhappy relationship with sb; **er hat ein ~es Verhältnis zur Wirklichkeit** he doesn't have a very good grip on reality → *auch* **trüben**

ge|trun|ken *ptp von* **trinken**

Get|to ['gɛto] NT **-s, -s** ghetto

Get|to|blas|ter [-bla:stɐ] M **-s, -** (*inf*) ghetto blaster (*inf*), boom box (*esp US inf*)

get|to|i|sie|ren [gɛtoʔiˈzi:rən] *ptp* **gettoisiert** VT to ghettoize

Ge|tue [gə'tu:ə] NT **-s,** *no pl* (*pej*) to-do (*inf*), fuss, (= *geheuchelte Höflichkeit*) affectation; **ein ~ machen** to make a to-do (*inf*) *or* fuss; (= *überhöflich sein, sich wichtig machen*) to put on airs

Ge|tüm|mel [gə'tyml] NT **-s,** *no pl* turmoil; **das ~ des Kampfes** the tumult of battle; **sich ins ~ stürzen** to plunge into the tumult *or* hurly-burly

ge|tüp|felt [gə'typfəlt] ADJ *Kleid etc* spotted; (= *mit kleinen Tupfen*) dotted → *auch* **tüpfeln**

Ge|tu|schel [gə'tʊʃl] NT **-s,** *no pl* whispering

ge|übt [gə'y:pt] ADJ *Auge, Ohr, Griff* practised (*Brit*), practiced (*US*); *Fahrer, Segler etc* proficient; **mit ~em Auge** with a practised (*Brit*) *or* practiced (*US*) eye; **~ sein** to be experienced; **im Schreiben/Reden ~ sein** to be a proficient writer/talker → *auch* **üben**

Ge|vat|ter [gə'fatɐ] M **-s** *or* **-n, -n** (*obs*) godfather; (*fig*) brother; **~ Tod** (Death) the Reaper (*liter*)

Ge|vat|te|rin [gə'fatərın] F **-, -nen** (*obs*) godmother; (*fig*) sister (*old*)

Ge|viert [gə'fi:ɐt] NT **-s, -e** (*old*: = *Quadrat*) square; (*Min*) crib; (*Typ*) quad(rat); **5 Meter im ~** (*old*) 5 metres (*Brit*) *or* meters (*US*) square

GEW [ge:ʔe:'ve:] F *abbr von* Gewerkschaft Erziehung und Wissenschaft ≈ NUT (*Brit*), teachers' union

Ge|wächs [gə'vɛks] NT **-es, -e** a (= *Pflanze*) plant; **er ist ein seltsames ~** (*dated*) he is an odd specimen (*inf*) b (= *Weinjahrgang*) wine c (*Med*) growth

ge|wach|sen [gə'vaksn] *ptp von* **wachsen** [1] ADJ a (= *von allein entstanden*) evolved; **diese in Jahrtausenden ~en Traditionen** these traditions which have evolved over the millennia b **jdm ~ sein** to be a match for sb; **einer Sache** (*dat*) **~ sein** to be up to sth; **er ist seinem Bruder (an Stärke/Intelligenz) durchaus ~** he is his brother's equal in strength/intelligence

Ge|wächs|haus NT greenhouse; (= *Treibhaus*) hothouse

Ge|wa|ckel [gə'vakl] NT **-s,** *no pl* (*inf*) (*von Tisch, Stuhl etc*) wobbling; **~ mit den Hüften** wiggling one's hips

ge|wagt [gə'va:kt] ADJ a (= *kühn*) daring; (= *gefährlich*) risky b (= *moralisch bedenklich*) risqué → *auch* **wagen**

ge|wagt|heit F **-, -en** a *no pl* (= *Kühnheit*) daring; (= *Gefährlichkeit*) riskiness; (= *moralische Bedenklichkeit*) risqué nature b (= *gewagte Äußerung*) daring remark

ge|wählt [gə've:lt] ADJ *Sprache* refined, elegant ADV **sich ~ ausdrücken** to express oneself elegantly, to express oneself in a refined manner → *auch* **wählen**

Ge|wählt|heit F **-,** *no pl* elegance

ge|wahr [gə'va:ɐ] ADJ *pred* **etw** *or* **einer Sache** (*gen*) **~ werden** (*geh*) to become aware of sth

Ge|währ [gə've:ɐ] F **-,** *no pl* guarantee; **jdm ~ dafür geben, dass ...** to guarantee (sb *or* to sb) that ...; **dadurch ist die ~ gegeben, dass ...** that guarantees that ...; **(die) ~ für etw bieten** to offer a guarantee for sth; **keine ~ für etw bieten** to offer no guarantee for sth; **die ~ für jds Zahlungsfähigkeit übernehmen** to guarantee sb's ability to pay; **die Angabe erfolgt ohne ~** this information is supplied without liability; **„ohne ~"** (*auf Fahrplan, Preisliste*) "subject to change"; (*bei Lottozahlen, statistischen Angaben*) "no liability assumed"; **für etw ~ leisten** to guarantee sth

ge|wah|ren [gə'va:rən] *ptp* **gewahrt** VT (*liter*) to become aware of

ge|wäh|ren [gə've:rən] *ptp* **gewährt** VT to grant; *Rabatt, Vorteile* to give; *Sicherheit, Trost, Schutz* to afford, to give; **jdm Unterstützung ~** to provide sb with support, to support sb; **jdn ~ lassen** (*geh*) not to stop sb

ge|währ|leis|ten [gə've:ɐlaıstn] *ptp* **gewährleistet** VT *insep* (= *sicherstellen*) to ensure (*jdm etw* sb sth); (= *garantieren*) to guarantee (*jdm etw* sb sth)

Ge|währ|leis|tung F guarantee; **zur ~ der Sicherheit** to ensure safety

Ge|wahr|sam [gə'va:ɐza:m] M **-s,** *no pl* a (= *Verwahrung*) safekeeping; **etw in ~ nehmen/haben** to take sth into/have sth in safekeeping; **etw (bei jdm) in ~ geben** to hand sth over (to sb) for safekeeping b (= *Haft*) custody; **jdn in ~ nehmen** to take sb into custody; **in ~ sein, sich in ~ befinden** to be in custody

Ge|währs-: Ge|währs|frau F, **Ge|währs|mann** M *pl* **-männer** *or* **-leute** source; **Ge|währs|trä|ger(in)** M(F) (*Fin*) guarantor

Ge|wäh|rung F, *no pl* granting; (*von Rabatt, Vorteilen*) giving; (*von Sicherheit, Schutz*) affording

Ge|walt [gə'valt] F **-, -en** a (= *Machtbefugnis, Macht, Herrschaft*) power; **die drei ~en** (*Pol*) the three powers; **die ausübende** *or* **vollziehende/ gesetzgebende/richterliche ~** the executive/ legislature/judiciary; **elterliche ~** parental authority; **jdn/etw in seine ~ bringen** to bring sb/ sth under one's control; **jdn in seiner ~ haben** to have sb in one's power; **~ über jdn haben** to have power over sb; **etw in der ~ haben** (= *übersehen*) to have control of sth; (=

steuern können) to have sth under control; (= *entscheiden können*) to have sth in one's power; **sich in der ~ haben** to have oneself under control; **in jds ~** (*dat*) **sein** *or* **stehen** to be in sb's power; **unter jds ~** (*dat*) **sein** *or* **stehen** to be under sb's control; **die ~ über etw** (*acc*) **verlieren** to lose control of sth; **~ über Leben und Tod (haben)** (to have) power over life and death

b *no pl* (= *Zwang*) force; (= *Gewalttätigkeit*) violence; **~ anwenden** to use force; **höhere ~** acts/ an act of God; **nackte ~** brute force; **mit ~** by force; **mit aller ~** (*inf*) for all one is worth; **jdm/ einer Sache ~ antun** to do violence to sb/sth; **einer Frau ~ antun** to violate a woman; **sich** (*dat*) **~ antun** (*fig*: = *sich überwinden*) to force oneself; **~ geht vor Recht** (*Prov*) might is right (*Prov*)

c *no pl* (= *Heftigkeit, Wucht*) force; (= *elementare Kraft auch*) power; **die ~ der Explosion/des Sturmes** the force of the explosion/storm; **er warf sich mit ~ gegen die Tür** he hurled himself violently against the door

Ge|walt-: Ge|walt|akt M act of violence; **Ge|walt|an|dro|hung** F threat of violence; **unter ~** under threat of violence; **Ge|walt|an|wen|dung** F use of force *or* violence; **ge|walt|be|ja|hend** ADJ condoning violence; **ge|walt|be|reit** ADJ ready to use violence, violent; **Ge|walt|be|reit|schaft** F propensity to violence; **Ge|walt|ein|wir|kung** F violence

Ge|wal|ten|tei|lung F, **Ge|wal|ten|tren|nung** F separation of powers

Ge|walt-: ge|walt|frei ADJ, ADV = **gewaltlos**; **Ge|walt|frei|heit** F non-violence; **Ge|walt|frie|de(n)** M dictated peace; **ge|walt|ge|neigt** ADJ inclined toward(s) violence, violent; **Ge|walt|herr|schaft** F, *no pl* tyranny; **Ge|walt|herr|scher(in)** M(F) tyrant

ge|wal|tig [gə'valtıç] ADJ a (= *heftig*) *Sturm etc* violent b (= *groß, riesig*) colossal, immense; (= *wuchtig auch*) massive; *Anblick* tremendous; *Stimme, Töne* powerful; (*inf*: = *sehr groß*) *Unterschied, Hitze etc* tremendous, colossal (*inf*); *Summe* huge c (*geh*: = *mächtig*) powerful; **die Gewaltigen der Erde** the mighty rulers of the world ADV (*inf*: = *sehr*) enormously; **sich ~ irren** to be very much mistaken, to be very wrong, to be way out (*inf*); **du musst dich ~ ändern** you'll have to change one hell of a lot (*inf*); **er hat sich ~ in meine Schwester verknallt** he's really got it bad for my sister (*inf*)

Ge|wal|tig|keit F **-,** *no pl* a (= *Heftigkeit*) violence b (= *gewaltige Größe*) colossal *or* immense size; (= *Wuchtigkeit*) massiveness

Ge|walt-: Ge|walt|kri|mi|na|li|tät F violent crime(s *pl*); **Ge|walt|kur** F drastic measures *pl*; (= *Hungerdiät*) crash diet; **Ge|walt|leis|tung** F feat of strength, tour de force; **ge|walt|los** ADJ non-violent ADV (= *ohne Zwang*) without force; (= *ohne Gewaltanwendung*) without violence; **Ge|walt|lo|sig|keit** F **-,** *no pl* non-violence; **Ge|walt|marsch** M forced march; **im ~** at a cracking pace (*inf*); **Ge|walt|maß|nah|me** F (*fig*) drastic measure; **jdm mit ~n drohen** to threaten to use force against sb; (*fig*) to threaten sb with drastic action; **Ge|walt|mensch** M pusher (*inf*); (= *brutaler Mensch*) brute; **Ge|walt|mo|no|pol** NT monopoly on the use of force; **Ge|walt|or|gie** F orgy of violence; **ge|walt|sam** [gə'valtza:m] ADJ forcible; *Tod, Auseinandersetzung, Aufstand* violent ADV forcibly, by force; **Ge|walt|sam|keit** F **-, -en** a *no pl* violence b (= *gewaltsame Handlung*) act of violence; **Ge|walt|spi|ra|le** F spiral of violence (and counter-violence); **Ge|walt|streich** M (*Mil*) storm; (*fig*) coup (de force); **Ge|walt|tat** F act of violence; **Ge|walt|tä|ter(in)** M(F) violent criminal; **ge|walt|tä|tig** ADJ violent; **Ge|walt|tä|tig|keit** F (*no pl*: = *Brutalität*) violence; (= *Handlung*) act of violence; **Ge|walt|ver|bre|chen** NT crime of violence; **Ge|walt|ver|bre|cher(in)** M(F) violent criminal; **ge|walt|ver|herr|li|chend**

ADJ glorifying violence *pred*; **Ge|walt|ver|herr|li|chung** F glorification of violence

Ge|walt|ver|zicht M non-aggression

Ge|walt|ver|zichts-: Ge|walt|ver|zichts|ab|kom|men NT non-aggression treaty; **Ge|walt|ver|zichts|er|klä|rung** F declaration renouncing the use of force, non-aggression declaration

Ge|walt|vi|deo NT violent video, video nasty (*Brit*)

Ge|wand [gə'vant] NT -(e)s, =er [gə'vɛndə] (*geh*: = *Kleidungsstück*) garment; (*weites, langes*) robe, gown; (*Eccl*) vestment, robe; (*old*: = *Kleidung*) garb, garments *pl*, apparel (*old*); (*fig*: = *Maske*) guise; **ein altes Buch in neuem ~** an old book with a new look *or* appearance *or* livery, an old book dressed up

ge|wan|det [gə'vandət] ADJ (*old, hum*) clad, apparelled (*Brit old*), appareled (*US old*); **blau/gelb ~** clad in blue/yellow

ge|wandt [gə'vant] ptp von **wenden** ADJ skilful (*Brit*), skillful (*US*); (*körperlich*) nimble; (= *geschickt*) deft, dexterous; *Auftreten, Redner, Stil* elegant ADV elegantly

Ge|wandt|heit F -, no pl skilfulness (*Brit*), skillfulness (*US*); (*von Körper*) nimbleness; (= *Geschicktheit*) deftness, dexterity; (*von Stil*) elegance

ge|wann pret von **gewinnen**

ge|wapp|net [gə'wapnət] ADJ armed (*gegen* against), prepared (*gegen* for) → *auch* **wappnen**

ge|wär|tig [gə'vɛrtɪç] ADJ pred (*geh*) prepared (+*gen* for); **~ sein, dass ...** to be prepared for the possibility that ...

ge|wär|ti|gen [gə'vɛrtɪgn] ptp **gewärtigt** VTR (*geh*) to expect; (= *sich einstellen auf auch*) to be prepared for; **~, dass ...** to expect that ...; to be prepared for the possibility that ...; **etw ~ müssen** to have to be prepared for sth, to have to expect sth

Ge|wäsch [gə'vɛʃ] NT -(e)s, no pl (*pej inf*) twaddle (*inf*), claptrap (*inf*)

ge|wa|schen ptp von **waschen**

Ge|wäs|ser [gə'vɛsɐ] NT -s, - stretch of water; **~** pl inshore waters *pl*, lakes, rivers and canals *pl*; **ein fließendes/stehendes ~** a stretch of running/standing water

Ge|wäs|ser-: Ge|wäs|ser|kun|de F hydrography; **Ge|wäs|ser|schutz** M prevention of water pollution

Ge|we|be [gə've:bə] NT -s, - (= *Stoff*) fabric, material; (= *Gewebeart*) weave; (*Biol*) tissue; (*fig*) web

Ge|we|be- in cpds → *auch* Gewebs-: **Ge|we|be|flüs|sig|keit** F (*Physiol*) tissue *or* lymph fluid; **Ge|we|be|pro|be** F (*Med*) tissue sample; **ge|we|be|scho|nend** ADJ (*Comm*) kind to fabrics; (*Med*) tissue-conserving

Ge|webs-: Ge|webs|flüs|sig|keit F (*Med*) lymph; **Ge|webs|trans|plan|ta|ti|on** F (*Med*) tissue graft

Ge|wehr [gə've:ɐ] NT -(e)s, -e (= *Flinte*) rifle; (= *Schrotbüchse*) shotgun; **~ ab!** (*Mil*) order arms!; **das ~ über!** (*Mil*) shoulder arms!; **an die ~e!** (*Mil*) to arms!; (*dated inf*) let's get cracking (*inf*) *or* started; **präsentiert das ~!** (*Mil*) present arms!; **das ~ or mit dem ~ (auf jdn) anlegen** to aim (at sb); (*Mil*) to train a gun (on sb); **~ bei Fuß stehen** (*Mil*) to stand at order arms; (*fig inf*) to be at the ready

Ge|wehr-: Ge|wehr|griff M rifle position; **~e üben** to do rifle drill; **Ge|wehr|kol|ben** M (*von Flinte*) rifle butt; (*von Schrotbüchse*) butt of a shotgun; **Ge|wehr|ku|gel** F rifle bullet; **Ge|wehr|lauf** M (*von Flinte*) rifle barrel; (*von Schrotbüchse*) barrel of a shotgun; **Ge|wehr|mün|dung** F (*von Flinte/Schrotbüchse*) muzzle (of a rifle/shotgun); **Ge|wehr|rie|men** M (*von Flinte*) rifle sling; (*von Schrotbüchse*) gunsling; **Ge|wehr|sal|ve** F volley of gunfire

Ge|weih [gə'vai] NT -(e)s, -e antlers *pl*; **das ~** the antlers; **ein ~** a set of antlers

Ge|weih-: Ge|weih|en|de [-lɛndə] NT point *or* tine (*spec*) of an antler; **Ge|weih|schau|fel** F palm (of an antler)

Ge|wei|ne [gə'vainə] NT -s, no pl (*inf*) crying

Ge|wer|be [gə'vɛrbə] NT -s, - trade; **Handel und ~** trade and industry; **das älteste ~ der Welt** (*hum*) the oldest profession in the world (*hum*); **ein dunkles ~** a shady business; **einem dunklen ~ nachgehen** to be in a shady trade, to have a shady occupation; **seinem ~ nachgehen** to carry on *or* practise (*Brit*) *or* practice (*US*) one's trade; **ein ~ (be)treiben** *or* **ausüben** to practise (*Brit*) *or* practice (*US*) a trade **b** (*Sw*: = *Bauerngehöft*) farm

Ge|wer|be-: Ge|wer|be|amt NT ≈ factory inspectorate; **Ge|wer|be|auf|sicht** F ≈ health and safety control; **Ge|wer|be|auf|sichts|amt** NT ≈ factory inspectorate (*Brit*); **Ge|wer|be|be|trieb** M commercial enterprise; **Ge|wer|be|flä|che** F commercial space; **Ge|wer|be|frei|heit** F freedom of trade; **Ge|wer|be|ge|biet** NT industrial area; (*eigens angelegt*) trading estate (*esp Brit*); **Ge|wer|be|leh|rer(in)** M(F) teacher in a trade school; **Ge|wer|be|müll** M commercial waste; **Ge|wer|be|ord|nung** F trading regulations *pl*; **Ge|wer|be|schein** M trading licence (*Brit*) *or* license (*US*); **Ge|wer|be|schu|le** F trade school; **Ge|wer|be|steu|er** F trade tax; **Ge|wer|be|tä|tig|keit** F commercial activity; **ge|wer|be|trei|b(end)** [-traibnd] trading, engaged in a trade *pred*; **Ge|wer|be|trei|ben|de(r)** [-traibndə] MF decl as adj trader; **Ge|wer|be|ver|ein** M (*old*) trade association; **Ge|wer|be|zweig** M branch of a/the trade

ge|werb|lich [gə'vɛrplɪç] ADJ commercial; *Lehrling, Genossenschaft* trade *attr*; (= *industriell*) industrial; **~e Arbeiter** industrial workers; **die ~e Wirtschaft** industry; **~er Rechtsschutz** legal protection of industrial property; **die ~en Berufe** the trades ADV **diese Räume dürfen nicht ~ genutzt werden** these rooms are not to be used for commercial purposes

ge|werbs|mä|ßig ADJ professional; **der ~e Vertrieb von etw** selling sth as a business; **~e Unzucht** (*form*) prostitution ADV professionally, for gain

Ge|werk|schaft [gə'vɛrkʃaft] F -, -en (trade *or* trades *or* labor (*US*)) union

Ge|werk|schaf|ter [gə'vɛrkʃaftɐ] M -s, -, **Ge|werk|schaf|te|rin** [-ərɪn] F -, -nen, **Ge|werk|schaft|ler** [gə'vɛrkʃaftlɐ] M -s, -, **Ge|werk|schaft|le|rin** [-ərɪn] F -, -nen trade *or* labor (*US*) unionist

ge|werk|schaft|lich [gə'vɛrkʃaftlɪç] ADJ (trade *or* labor (*US*)) union *attr*; **~er Vertrauensmann** (*im Betrieb*) shop steward (*esp Brit*) ADV **wir haben uns ~ organisiert** we organized ourselves into a union; **~ organisierter Arbeiter** union member; **~ engagiert** involved in the (trade *or* labor (*US*)) union movement; **~ tätig sein** to be active in the union

Ge|werk|schafts- in cpds (trade *or* labor (*US*)) union; **Ge|werk|schafts|bank** F pl -banken trade *or* labor (*US*) union bank; **Ge|werk|schafts|be|we|gung** F (trade *or* labor (*US*)) union movement; **Ge|werk|schafts|boss** ▲ M (*usu pej*) (trade *or* labor (*US*)) union boss; **Ge|werk|schafts|bund** M pl -bünde federation of trade *or* labor (*US*) unions, ≈ Trades Union Congress (*Brit*), ≈ Federation of Labor (*US*); **ge|werk|schafts|ei|gen** ADJ owned by a (trade *or* labor (*US*)) union; **ge|werk|schafts|feind|lich** ADJ anti-(trade) union *attr*; **Ge|werk|schafts|füh|rer(in)** M(F) (trade *or* labor (*US*)) union leader; **Ge|werk|schafts|kon|gress** ▲ M trade *or* labor (*US*) union conference; **Ge|werk|schafts|mit|glied** NT member of a/the (trade *or* labor (*US*)) union; **Ge|werk|schafts|tag** M trade *or* labor (*US*) union conference; **Ge|werk|**

schafts|ver|band M federation of trade *or* labor (*US*) unions; **Ge|werk|schafts|ver|samm|lung** F (trade) union meeting; **Ge|werk|schafts|vor|sit|zen|de(r)** MF decl as adj (trade *or* labor (*US*)) union president; **Ge|werk|schafts|we|sen** NT , no pl (trade *or* labor (*US*)) union movement

ge|we|sen [gə've:zn] ptp von **sein** [1] ADJ attr former

ge|wi|chen ptp von **weichen** [2]

ge|wichst [gə'vɪkst] ADJ (*inf*) fly (*Brit inf*), crafty → *auch* **wichsen**

Ge|wicht [gə'vɪçt] NT -(e)s, -e **a** no pl (*lit, fig*) weight; **dieser Stein hat ein großes ~** this rock is very heavy; **dieser Stein hat ein ~ von 100 kg** this rock weighs 100 kg; **er hat sein ~ gehalten** he has stayed the same weight; **er brachte zu viel ~ auf die Waage** he weighed in too heavy; **spezifisches ~** specific gravity; **das hat ein ~!** (*inf*) it isn't half heavy! (*Brit inf*), it's very heavy!; **etw nach ~ verkaufen** to sell sth by weight; **~ haben** (*lit*) to be heavy; (*fig*) to carry weight; **ins ~ fallen** to be crucial; **nicht ins ~ fallen** to be of no consequence; **auf etw** (*acc*) **~ legen, einer Sache** (*dat*) **~ beilegen** *or* **beimessen** to set (great) store by sth, to lay stress on sth → **Waagschale** **b** (*Metallstück zum Beschweren etc, Sport*) weight

ge|wich|ten [gə'vɪçtn] ptp **gewichtet** VT (*Statistik*) to weight; (*fig*) to evaluate

Ge|wicht-: Ge|wicht|he|ben NT -s, no pl (*Sport*) weightlifting; **Ge|wicht|he|ber(in)** M(F) weightlifter

ge|wich|tig [gə'vɪçtɪç] ADJ **a** (*dated*: = *schwer*) heavy, hefty (*inf*); **eine ~e Persönlichkeit** (*hum inf*) a personage of some weight **b** (*fig*) (= *wichtig*) weighty; (= *wichtigtuerisch*) self-important; (= *einflussreich*) influential

Ge|wich|tig|keit F -, no pl (*fig*) (= *Wichtigkeit*) weightiness; (= *Wichtigtuerei*) self-importance; (= *Einflussreichtum*) influence

Ge|wichts-: Ge|wichts|ab|nah|me F loss of weight; **Ge|wichts|ana|ly|se** F (*Chem*) gravimetric analysis; **Ge|wichts|an|ga|be** F indication of weight; **die Hersteller von Fleischwaren sind zur ~ verpflichtet** the manufacturers of meat products are obliged to show the weight; **Ge|wichts|ein|heit** F unit of weight; **Ge|wichts|klas|se** F (*Sport*) weight (category); **Ge|wichts|kon|trol|le** F weight check; **ge|wichts|los** ADJ weightless; (*fig*) lacking substance; **Ge|wichts|proble|me** PL weight problems *pl*; **Ge|wichts|satz** M set of weights; **Ge|wichts|ver|la|ge|rung** F shifting of weight; (*fig*) shift of *or* in emphasis; **Ge|wichts|ver|lust** M loss of weight, weight loss; **Ge|wichts|ver|schie|bung** F shifting of weight; (*fig*) shift of *or* in emphasis; **Ge|wichts|zu|nah|me** F increase in weight

Ge|wich|tung [gə'vɪçtʊŋ] F -, -en (*Statistik*) weighting; (*fig*) evaluation

ge|wieft [gə'vi:ft] ADJ (*inf*) fly (*inf*), crafty (*in* +*dat* at)

ge|wiegt [gə'vi:kt] ADJ shrewd, slick (*inf*), canny (*esp Scot inf*) → *auch* **wiegen** [1]

Ge|wie|her [gə'vi:ɐ] NT -s, no pl whinnying; (*fig*) guffawing, braying

ge|wie|sen ptp von **weisen**

ge|willt [gə'vɪlt] ADJ **~ sein, etw zu tun** to be willing to do sth; (= *entschlossen*) to be determined to do sth

Ge|wim|mel [gə'vɪml] NT -s, no pl swarm, milling mass; (= *Menge*) crush, throng

Ge|wim|mer [gə'vɪmɐ] NT -s, no pl whimpering

Ge|win|de [gə'vɪndə] NT -s, - (*Tech*) thread

Ge|win|de- (*Tech*): **Ge|win|de|boh|rer** M (screw) tap; **Ge|win|de|bol|zen** M threaded bolt; **Ge|win|de|frä|sen** NT -s, no pl thread milling; **Ge|win|de|gang** M pl -gänge pitch (of screw thread); **Ge|win|de|schnei|den** NT

-s, *no pl* thread cutting; *(für Innengewinde)* tapping

ge|win|kelt [gə'vɪŋklt] ADJ angled

Ge|winn [gə'vɪn] M **-(e)s, -e a** (= *Ertrag*) profit; **~ abwerfen** *or* **bringen** to make a profit; **~ bringend** profitable; **~ erzielen** to make a profit; **aus etw ~ schlagen** *(inf)* to make a profit out of sth; **etw mit ~ verkaufen** to sell sth at a profit → *auch* **gewinnbringend**
b (= *Preis, Treffer*) prize; *(bei Wetten, Glücksspiel)* winnings *pl*; **einen großen ~ machen** to win a lot; **jedes Los ist ein ~** every ticket a winner; **er hat im Lotto einen ~ gehabt** he had a win on the lottery
c *no pl (fig*: = *Vorteil*) gain; **das ist ein großer ~ (für mich)** I have gained a lot from this, that is of great benefit to me); **ein ~ für die Abteilung** a valuable addition to the department

Ge|winn-: Ge|winn|an|teil M **a** (*Comm*) dividend **b** (*beim Wetten etc*) share; **Ge|winn|aus|schüt|tung** F prize draw; **Ge|winn|be|tei|li|gung** F **a** (*Ind*) (= *Prinzip*) profit-sharing; (= *Summe*) (profit-sharing) bonus **b** (= *Dividende*) dividend; **ge|winn|brin|gend** ADJ (*lit, fig*) profitable ADV profitably; **~ wirtschaften** to make a profit; **Ge|winn|chan|ce** F chance of winning; **~n** (*beim Wetten*) odds; **Ge|winn|ein|bruch** M (big) drop in profits

ge|win|nen [gə'vɪnən] *pret* **gewann** [gə'van], *ptp* **gewonnen** [gə'vɔnən] VT **a** (= *siegen in*) to win; (= *erwerben, bekommen*) to gain, to win; *Preis, jds Herz* to win; **jdn (für etw) ~** to win sb over (to sth); **jdn für sich ~** to win sb over (to one's side); **jdn zum Freund ~** to win sb as a friend; **es gewinnt den Anschein, als ob ...** (*form*) it would appear that ...; **das Ufer ~** (*liter*) to reach *or* gain (*liter*) the bank; **Zeit ~** to gain time; **was ist damit gewonnen?** what good is that?; **was ist damit gewonnen, wenn du das tust?** what is the good *or* use of you *or* your doing that?; **wie gewonnen, so zerronnen** (*Prov*) easy come easy go (*prov*)
b (*als Profit*) to make (a profit of)
c (= *erzeugen*) to produce, to obtain; *Erze etc* to mine, to extract; to win (*liter*); *(aus Altmaterial*) to reclaim, to recover
VI **a** (= *Sieger sein*) to win (*bei, in +dat* at)
b (= *sich verbessern*) to gain; (= *profitieren*) to gain something; **an Bedeutung ~** to gain (in) importance; **an Boden ~** (*fig*) to gain ground; **an Höhe ~** to gain height; **an Geschwindigkeit ~** to pick up *or* gain speed; **an Klarheit ~** to gain in clarity; **sie gewinnt durch ihre neue Frisur** her new hairstyle does something for her; **sie gewinnt bei näherer Bekanntschaft** she improves on closer acquaintance → **wagen** VT

ge|win|nend ADJ (*fig*) winning, winsome

Ge|win|ner [gə'vɪnɐ] M **-s, -, Ge|win|ne|rin** [-ərɪn] F **-, -nen** winner

Ge|win|ner|stra|ße F (*inf*) **auf der ~ sein** to be headed for a win, to be on the way to victory

Ge|winn-: Ge|winn|er|war|tung F anticipated profit; **Ge|winn|er|zie|lungs|ab|sicht** F (*Comm*) profit motive; **Ge|winn|ge|mein|schaft** F (*Comm*) profit pool; **Ge|winn|klas|se** F prize category; **Ge|winn|lis|te** F list of winners, winners list; **Ge|winn|los** NT winning ticket; **Ge|winn|ma|xi|mie|rung** F maximization of profit(s); **Ge|winn|mit|nah|me** F (*Fin*) profit taking; **Ge|winn|num|mer** ▲ F winning number; **Ge|winn|satz** M (*Tennis etc*) **mit drei Gewinnsätzen spielen** to play the best of five sets; **der dritte Satz war sein ~** the third set was the winning set for him; **Ge|winn|schuld|ver|schrei|bung** F (*Fin*) income bond; **Ge|winn|schwel|le** F (*Econ*) breakeven point; **Ge|winn|span|ne** F profit margin; **Ge|winn|spiel** NT competition; (*TV*) game show; **Ge|winn|stre|ben** NT pursuit of profit; **Ge|winn|sucht** F profit-seeking; **aus ~** for motives of (material) gain; *(finanziell)* for motives of (financial) gain; **ge|winn|süch|tig** ADJ

profit-seeking *attr*; **ge|winn|träch|tig** ADJ profitable

Gewinnummer △ F → **Gewinnnummer**

Ge|winn- und Ver|lust|rech|nung F (*Fin*) profit-and-loss account

Ge|win|nung [gə'vɪnʊŋ] F **-,** (*rare*) **-en** (*von Kohle, Öl*) extraction; (*von Energie, Plutonium*) production

Ge|winn-: Ge|winn|warnung F (*Comm euph*) profit warning; **Ge|winn|zahl** F winning number; **Ge|winn|zo|ne** F **die ~ erreichen** to move into profit; **in der ~ sein** to be in profit

Ge|win|sel [gə'vɪnzl] NT **-s,** *no pl* (*lit, fig*) whining

Ge|winst [gə'vɪnst] M **-(e)s, -e** (*old*) = **Gewinn**

Ge|wir|bel [gə'vɪrbl] NT **-s,** *no pl* whirl(ing)

Ge|wirr [gə'vɪr] NT **-(e)s,** *no pl* tangle; (*fig*: = *Durcheinander*) jumble; (*von Paragrafen, Klauseln etc*) maze, confusion; (*von Gassen*) maze; (*von Stimmen*) confusion, babble

Ge|wis|per [gə'vɪspɐ] NT **-s,** *no pl* whispering

ge|wiss ▲ [gə'vɪs] ADJ **a** (= *sicher*) certain, sure (*+gen* of); **ich bin dessen ~** (*geh*) I'm certain *or* sure of it; **das ist so ~, wie die Nacht dem Tag folgt** (*geh*) as sure as night follows day; **darüber weiß man noch nichts Gewisses** nothing certain is known as yet
b *attr* certain; **ein ~er Herr Müller** a certain Herr Müller; **in ~em Maße** to some *or* a certain extent; **in ~em Sinne** in a (certain) sense → **Etwas**
ADV (*geh*) certainly; **Sie denken ~, dass ...** no doubt you think that ...; **ich weiß es ganz ~** I'm certain *or* sure of it; **eins ist (ganz) ~** one thing is certain *or* sure; **eins weiß ich (ganz) ~** there's one thing I know for certain *or* sure; **(ja) ~!** certainly, sure (*esp US*); **(aber) ~ (doch)!** (but) of course; **darf ich ...? – (aber) ~ (doch)!** may I ...? – but, of course, may I ...? – by all means

Ge|wis|sen [gə'vɪsn] NT **-s,** *no pl* conscience; **ein schlechtes ~** a guilty *or* bad conscience; **jdn/etw auf dem ~ haben** to have sb/sth on one's conscience; **das hast du auf dem ~** it's your fault; **jdm ins ~ reden** to have a serious talk with sb; **jdm ins ~ reden, etw zu tun** to get *or* persuade sb to do sth; **das musst du vor deinem ~ verantworten** you'll have to answer to your own conscience for that; **ein gutes ~ ist ein sanftes Ruhekissen** (*Prov*) I *etc* just want to have a clear conscience, I *etc* just want to be able to sleep nights (*esp US*) → **Ehre, Wissen**

Ge|wis|sen-: ge|wis|sen|haft ADJ *Mensch, Arbeit, Politik* conscientious ADV conscientiously; **Ge|wis|sen|haf|tig|keit** [gə'vɪsnhaftɪçkait] F **-,** *no pl* conscientiousness; **ge|wis|sen|los** ADJ unprincipled, without conscience, unscrupulous; (= *verantwortungslos*) irresponsible; **~ sein** to have no conscience; **wie kann man so ~ sein und ...** how could anybody be so unscrupulous/irresponsible as to ... ADV unscrupulously; **sich unmenschlich und ~ verhalten** to behave inhumanly and immorally; **Ge|wis|sen|lo|sig|keit** F **-,** *no pl* unscrupulousness; (= *Verantwortungslosigkeit*) irresponsibility

Ge|wis|sens-: Ge|wis|sens|angst F pangs *pl* of conscience; **Ge|wis|sens|bis|se** PL pangs *pl* of conscience; **mach dir deswegen keine ~!** there's nothing for you to feel guilty about; **~ bekommen** to get a guilty conscience; **ohne ~** without compunction, without feeling guilty; **Ge|wis|sens|ent|schei|dung** F question of conscience, matter for one's conscience to decide; **Ge|wis|sens|er|for|schung** F examination of one's conscience; **Ge|wis|sens|fra|ge** F matter of conscience; **Ge|wis|sens|frei|heit** F freedom of conscience; **Ge|wis|sens|grün|de** PL conscientious reasons *pl*; **Ge|wis|sens|kon|flikt** M moral conflict; **Ge|wis|sens|not** F moral dilemma; **Ge|wis|sens|qual** F (*geh*) pangs *pl* of conscience; **Ge|wis|sens|sa|che** F matter of conscience; **Ge|wis|-**

sens|zwang M , *no pl* moral constraint(s *pl*); **Ge|wis|sens|zwei|fel** M moral doubt

ge|wis|ser|ma|ßen [gə'vɪsɐ'maːsn] ADV (= *sozusagen*) so to speak, as it were; (= *auf gewisse Weise*) in a way, to an extent

Ge|wiss|heit ▲ ◑ 43.1 F **-, -en** certainty; **mit ~** with certainty; *wissen* for certain *or* sure; **~ erlangen** to achieve certain knowledge; **(zur) ~ werden** to become a certainty → **verschaffen b**

ge|wiss|lich ▲ [gə'vɪslɪç] ADV (*old, geh*) = **gewiss** ADV

Ge|wit|ter [gə'vɪtɐ] NT **-s, -** thunderstorm; (*fig*) storm

Ge|wit|ter-: Ge|wit|ter|flie|ge F thunder fly; **Ge|wit|ter|front** F (*Met*) storm front; **Ge|wit|ter|him|mel** M stormy sky, thunderclouds *pl*

ge|wit|te|rig [gə'vɪtərɪç] ADJ thundery; **~e Schwüle** thundery (and oppressive) air ADV **~ schwül** thundery (and oppressive)

Ge|wit|ter|luft F thundery atmosphere; **es ist ~** there's thunder in the air *or* about

ge|wit|tern [gə'vɪtɐn] *ptp* **gewittert** VI *impers* **es gewittert** it's thundering

Ge|wit|ter-: Ge|wit|ter|nei|gung F (*Met*) likelihood of thunderstorms; **Ge|wit|ter|re|gen** M , **Ge|wit|ter|schauer** M thundery shower; **ge|wit|ter|schwül** ADJ = **gewitterig**; **Ge|wit|ter|schwü|le** F thundery (and oppressive) atmosphere; **Ge|wit|ter|stim|mung** F (*fig*) stormy atmosphere; **Ge|wit|ter|sturm** M thunderstorm; **Ge|wit|ter|wand** F wall *or* mass of thunderclouds; **Ge|wit|ter|wol|ke** F thundercloud; (*fig inf*) storm cloud; **Vater hatte ~n auf der Stirn** Father's face was as black as thunder; **Ge|wit|ter|zie|ge** F (*pej inf*) sour old hag

ge|wit|trig [gə'vɪtrɪç] ADJ, ADV = **gewitterig**

Ge|wit|zel [gə'vɪtsl] NT **-s,** *no pl* joking, jokes *pl*

ge|witzt [gə'vɪtst] ADJ crafty, cunning

Ge|witzt|heit F **-,** *no pl* craftiness, cunning

ge|wo|ben *ptp von* **weben**

Ge|wo|ge [gə'voːgə] NT **-s,** *no pl* surging; (*von Kornfeld*) waving; (*hum: von Busen*) surging

ge|wo|gen[1] [gə'voːgn] *ptp von* **wägen** *von* **wiegen**[2]

ge|wo|gen[2] ADJ (*geh*) well-disposed, favourably (*Brit*) *or* favorably (*US*) disposed (*+dat* towards)

Ge|wo|gen|heit F **-,** *no pl* (*geh*) favourable (*Brit*) *or* favorable (*US*) attitude

ge|wöh|nen [gə'vøːnən] *ptp* **gewöhnt** VT **jdn an etw** (*acc*) **~** to make sb used *or* accustomed to sth, to accustom sb to sth; **einen Hund an Sauberkeit ~** to house-train a dog; **Sie werden sich noch daran ~ müssen, dass ...** you'll have to get used to *or* have to accept the fact that ...; **an jdn/etw gewöhnt sein, jdn/etw gewöhnt sein** (*inf*) to be used to sb/sth; **daran gewöhnt sein, etw zu tun** to be used to doing sth
VR **sich an jdn/etw ~** to get *or* become used to sb/sth, to accustom oneself to sb/sth; **du musst dich an Ordnung/Pünktlichkeit ~** you must get used to being orderly/punctual, you must get into the habit of being orderly/punctual; **sich daran ~, etw zu tun** to get used *or* accustomed to doing sth; **das bin ich gewöhnt** I'm used to it

Ge|wohn|heit [gə'voːnhait] F **-, -en** habit; **aus (lauter) ~** from (sheer) force of habit; **die ~ haben, etw zu tun** to have a habit of doing sth; **wie es seine ~ war, nach alter ~** as was his wont *or* custom; **das ist ihm zur ~ geworden** it's become a habit with him; **sich** (*dat*) **etw zur ~ machen** to make a habit of sth

Ge|wohn|heits-: ge|wohn|heits|ge|mäß, ge|wohn|heits|mä|ßig ADJ habitual ADV (= *ohne nachzudenken*) automatically; **Ge|wohn|heits|mensch** M creature of habit; **Ge|wohn|heits|recht** NT (*Jur*) **a** (*im Einzelfall*) established *or* customary right **b** (*als Rechtssys-*

tem) common law; **ge|wohn|heits|recht|lich** ADJ *Recht* unwritten; **Ge|wohn|heits|sa|che** F question of habit; **Ge|wohn|heits|tä|ter(in)** M(F) habitual *or* persistent offender; **Ge|wohn|heits|tier** NT der Mensch ist ein ~ (*inf*) man is a creature of habit; **Ge|wohn|heits|trin|ker(in)** M(F) habitual drinker; **Ge|wohn|heits|ver|bre|cher(in)** M(F) habitual criminal

ge|wöhn|lich [gə'vøːnlıç] **ADJ** **a** attr (= *allgemein, üblich*) usual, customary; (= *normal*) normal; (= *durchschnittlich*) ordinary; (= *alltäglich*) everyday; **ein ~er Sterblicher** an ordinary mortal; **~er Bruch** (*Math*) vulgar fraction **b** (*pej*: = *ordinär*) common **ADV** normally, usually; **wie ~** as usual, as per usual (*Brit inf*); **sie zieht sich immer so ~ an** she always wears such plain clothes

Ge|wöhn|lich|keit F -, *no pl* (*pej*) commonness

ge|wohnt [gə'voːnt] ADJ usual; **etw** (*acc*) **~ sein** to be used to sth; **ich bin es ~, früh aufzustehen** I am used to getting up early

ge|wohn|ter|ma|ßen [gə'voːntə'maːsn] ADV usually

Ge|wöh|nung [gə'vøːnʊŋ] F -, *no pl* (= *das Sichgewöhnen*) habituation (*an +acc* to); (= *das Angewöhnen*) training (*an +acc* in); (= *Sucht*) habit, addiction; **die ~ an den Kindergarten kann bei einigen Kindern ziemlich lange dauern** it can take a fairly long time for some children to get used to kindergarten

ge|wöh|nungs|be|dürf|tig ADJ ... that takes (some) time to get used to; **die neue Software ist ~** the new software takes some time to get used to *or* takes some getting used to

Ge|wöl|be [gə'vœlbə] NT -s, - (= *Deckengewölbe*) vault; (= *Kellergewölbe auch*) vaults *pl*

Ge|wöl|be-: Ge|wöl|be|bo|gen M arch (of a vault); **Ge|wöl|be|pfei|ler** M pier (of a vault)

ge|wölbt [gə'vœlpt] ADJ *Stirn* domed; *Himmel, Decke, Dach* vaulted; *Brust* bulging; *Nase* aquiline → *auch* **wölben**

ge|wölkt [gə'vœlkt] ADJ (*liter*) *Stirn* o'erclouded (*poet*)

Ge|wöl|le [gə'vœlə] NT -s, - (*Zool*) cast, pellet

ge|wollt [gə'vɔlt] ADJ **a** (= *gekünstelt*) forced, artificial **b** (= *erwünscht*) desired → *auch* **wollen**[2]

ge|won|nen ptp von **gewinnen**
ge|wor|ben ptp von **werben**
ge|wor|den ptp von **werden**
ge|wor|fen ptp von **werfen**
ge|wrun|gen ptp von **wringen**

Ge|wühl [gə'vyːl] NT -(e)s, *no pl* **a** (*pej*: = *das Wühlen*) (in *Kisten, Schubladen etc*) rummaging around; (*im Schlamm etc*) wallowing (about) **b** (= *Gedränge*) crowd, throng; (= *Verkehrsgewühl*) chaos, snarl-up (*Brit inf*)

ge|wun|den [gə'vʊndn] ptp von **winden**[1] ADJ *Weg, Fluss etc* winding; *Erklärung* roundabout *no adv*, tortuous

ge|wun|ken (*dial*) ptp von **winken**

ge|wür|felt [gə'vʏrflt] ADJ *Stoff, Kleidungsstück etc* check(ed) → *auch* **würfeln**

Ge|wür|ge [gə'vʏrgə] NT -s, *no pl* (vor dem *Erbrechen*) retching

Ge|würm [gə'vʏrm] NT -(e)s, *no pl* worms *pl*; (= *Kriechtiere*) creeping animals *pl*, creepy-crawlies *pl* (*inf*); (*fig*) vermin

Ge|würz [gə'vʏrts] NT -es, -e spice; (= *Kräutersorte*) herb; (= *Pfeffer, Salz*) condiment

Ge|würz-: Ge|würz|bord NT spice rack; **Ge|würz|es|sig** M spiced vinegar; (= *Kräuteressig*) herb vinegar; **Ge|würz|gur|ke** F pickled gherkin; **Ge|würz|kraut** NT potherb; **Ge|würz|ku|chen** M spice cake; **Ge|würz|mi|schung** F mixed herbs *pl*; (= *Gewürzsalz*) herbal salt; **Ge|würz|nel|ke** F clove; **Ge|würz|pap|ri|ka** M paprika; **Ge|würz|pflan|ze** F spice plant;

(= *Kräuterpflanze*) herb; **Ge|würz|re|gal** NT spice rack; **Ge|würz|stän|der** M cruet (set)

Ge|wu|sel [gə'vuːzl] NT -s, *no pl* (*dial*) = **Gewimmel**

ge|wusst ▲ ptp von **wissen**

Gey|sir ['gaizɪr] M -s, -e geyser

gez. *abbr von* **gezeichnet**

ge|zackt [gə'tsakt] ADJ *Fels* jagged; *Hahnenkamm* toothed; *Blatt* serrated, dentate (*spec*) → *auch* **zacken**

ge|zahnt [gə'tsaːnt], **ge|zähnt** [gə'tsɛːnt] ADJ serrated; (*Bot*) serrated, dentate (*spec*); (*Tech*) cogged; *Briefmarke* perforated → *auch* **zähnen**

Ge|zänk [gə'tsɛŋk] NT -(e)s, *no pl*, **Ge|zan|ke** [gə'tsaŋkə] NT -s, *no pl* (*inf*) quarrelling (*Brit*), quarreling (*US*)

Ge|zap|pel [gə'tsapl] NT -s, *no pl* (*inf*) wriggling

ge|zeich|net [gə'tsaiçnət] ADJ marked; (*als Straffälliger auch*) branded; **vom Tode ~ sein, ein vom Tod Gezeichneter sein** to have the mark of death on one; **sein Gesicht war von Krankheit ~** one could see from his face how ill he was → *auch* **zeichnen**

Ge|zei|ten [gə'tsaitn] PL tides *pl*

Ge|zei|ten-: Ge|zei|ten|e|ner|gie F tidal energy; **Ge|zei|ten|kraft|werk** NT tidal power plant *or* station; **Ge|zei|ten|strom** M , **Ge|zei|ten|strö|mung** F tidal current; **Ge|zei|ten|ta|fel** F table of (the) tides; **Ge|zei|ten|wech|sel** M turn of the tide

Ge|zer|re [gə'tsɛrə] NT -s, *no pl* tugging

Ge|ze|ter [gə'tseːtɐ] NT -s, *no pl* (*inf*) (*lit*) nagging; (*fig*) clamour (*Brit*), clamor (*US*); **in ~** (*acc*) **ausbrechen** (*fig*) to set up *or* raise a clamour (*Brit*) *or* clamor (*US*)

Ge|zie|fer [gə'tsiːfɐ] NT -s, *no pl* (*obs*) vermin

ge|zie|hen ptp von **zeihen**

ge|zielt [gə'tsiːlt] **ADJ** purposeful; *Schuss* well-aimed; *Frage, Maßnahme, Forschung etc* specific; *Werbung* selective, targeted; *Hilfe* well-directed; *Indiskretion* deliberate **ADV** vorgehen, ansetzen directly; *forschen, planen, helfen* specifically; *werben* selectively; **~ schießen** to shoot to kill; **er hat sehr ~ gefragt** he asked very specific questions → *auch* **zielen**

ge|zie|men [gə'tsiːmən] ptp **geziemt** (*old, geh*) **VI** +*dat* to befit; **dieses Verhalten geziemt ihm nicht** such behaviour (*Brit*) or behavior (*US*) ill befits him **VR** to be proper; **wie es sich geziemt** as is proper; **wie es sich für ein artiges Kind geziemt** as befits a well-behaved child

ge|zie|mend ADJ proper

ge|ziert [gə'tsiːɐt] **ADJ** affected **ADV** affectedly → *auch* **zieren**

Ge|zirp [gə'tsɪrp] NT -(e)s, *no pl*, **Ge|zir|pe** [gə'tsɪrpə] NT -s, *no pl* chirruping, chirping

Ge|zisch [gə'tsɪʃ] NT -es, *no pl*, **Ge|zi|sche** [gə'tsɪʃə] NT -s, *no pl* hiss(ing)

Ge|zi|schel [gə'tsɪʃl] NT -s, *no pl* (*fig*: *Klatsch*) gossip, tittle-tattle (*Brit inf*)

ge|zo|gen [gə'tsoːgn] ptp von **ziehen** ADJ *Gewehrlauf etc* rifled; *Soldat* conscript(ed); **ein Gezogener** (*Mil inf*) a conscript

Ge|zücht [gə'tsʏçt] NT -(e)s, -e (*obs*) (*pej*: = *Brut*) brood; (*inf*: = *Gesindel*) riffraff *pl*, rabble *pl*

ge|zu|ckert [gə'tsʊkɐt] ADJ sugared; **zu stark ~ sein** to have too much sugar in it → *auch* **zuckern**

Ge|zün|gel [gə'tsʏŋl] NT -s, *no pl* (*geh*) (von *Schlange*) darting *or* flicking of its tongue; (von *Flamme*) flickering

Ge|zweig [gə'tsvaik] NT -(e)s [-gəs] *no pl* (*geh*) branches *pl*

Ge|zwin|ker [gə'tsvɪŋkɐ] NT -s, *no pl* winking

Ge|zwit|scher [gə'tsvɪtʃɐ] NT -s, *no pl* chirruping, twitter(ing)

ge|zwun|gen [gə'tsvʊŋən] ptp von **zwingen** **ADJ** (= *nicht entspannt*) forced; *Atmosphäre* strained; *Stil, Benehmen* stiff **ADV** stiffly; **~ lachen** to give

a forced *or* strained laugh; **~ wirken** to seem stiff *or* strained

ge|zwun|ge|ner|ma|ßen [gə'tsvʊŋənɐ'maːsn] ADV of necessity; **etw ~ tun** to be forced to do sth, to do sth of necessity

Ge|zwun|gen|heit F -, *no pl* artificiality; (*von Atmosphäre*) constraint; (*von Stil, Benehmen*) stiffness

Gfrett [kfrɛt] NT -s, *no pl* (*Aus*) = **Gefrett**

ggf. *abbr von* **gegebenenfalls**

Gha|na ['gaːna] NT -s Ghana

Gha|na|er ['gaːnaɐ] M -s, -, **Gha|na|e|rin** [-ərɪn] F -, -nen Ghanaian

gha|na|isch ['gaːnaɪʃ] ADJ Ghanaian

Ghet|to ['gɛto] NT -s, -s ghetto

Ghost|wri|ter ['goːstraitɐ] M -s, -, **Ghost|wri|te|rin** [-ərɪn] F -, -nen ghostwriter; **er ist der ~ des Premiers** he ghosts *or* ghostwrites for the PM

gib [giːp] IMPER *sing von* **geben**

Gib|bon ['gɪbɔn] M -s, -s gibbon

gibt [giːpt] 3. *pers sing pres von* **geben**

Gicht [gɪçt] F -, -en **a** *no pl* (*Med, Bot*) gout **b** (*Metal*) throat (of a/the furnace)

Gicht-: Gicht|an|fall M attack of gout; **Gicht|gas** NT (*Metal*) top gas; **Gicht|kno|ten** M gouty deposit, tophus (*form*); **gicht|krank** ADJ gouty; **Gicht|kran|ke(r)** MF *decl as adj* gout sufferer

Gi|ckel ['gɪkl] M -s, - (*dial*) cock; (*jünger*) cockerel

Gie|bel ['giːbl] M -s, - gable; (= *Türgiebel, Fenstergiebel*) pediment

Gie|bel-: Gie|bel|dach NT gabled roof; **Gie|bel|feld** NT tympanum (*spec*); **Gie|bel|fens|ter** NT gable window; **Gie|bel|haus** NT gabled house

gie|be|lig ['giːbəlɪç] ADJ gabled

Gie|bel-: Gie|bel|sei|te F gable end; **Gie|bel|wand** F gable end *or* wall; **Gie|bel|zim|mer** NT attic room

gieb|lig ['giːblɪç] ADJ gabled

Gie|per ['giːpɐ] M -s, *no pl* (*dial*) craving (*auf +acc* for)

Gier [giːɐ] F -, *no pl* (*nach* for) greed; (*nach Geld auch*) avarice, lust; (*nach Macht, Ruhm auch*) craving, lust; (= *Lüsternheit*) lust

gie|ren[1] ['giːrən] VI (*pej*) to lust (*nach* for)

gie|ren[2] VI (*Naut*) to yaw

gie|ren[3] VI (*Sw*: = *quietschen*) (*Tür, Scharnier etc*) to creak

gie|rig ['giːrɪç] **ADJ** greedy; (*nach Geld*) avaricious; (= *lüstern*) lustful; **~ nach etw sein** to be greedy for sth; *nach Vergnügen auch* to crave sth; *nach Wissen auch* to be avid for sth; (*sexuell*) to lust for sth **ADV** greedily; **etw ~ verschlingen** (*lit, fig*) to devour sth greedily

Gieß|bach M (mountain) torrent

gie|ßen ['giːsn] pret **goss** ▲ [gɔs] ptp **gegossen** [gə'gɔsn] **VT** **a** *Flüssigkeit* to pour; (= *verschütten*) to spill; *Pflanzen, Garten etc* to water; (*liter*) *Licht* to shed; **gieß das Glas nicht so voll!** don't fill the glass so full! **b** *Glas* to found (*zu* in(*to*)); *Metall auch* to cast (*zu* into) **VI** *impers* to pour; **es gießt in Strömen** or **wie aus Eimern** it's pouring down, it's bucketing down (*Brit inf*), it's coming down in buckets (*US inf*)

Gie|ßer[1] ['giːsɐ] M -s, - (an *Kanne*) pourer

Gie|ßer[2] ['giːsɐ] M -s, -, **Gie|ße|rin** [-ərɪn] F -, -nen (*Metal*) caster, founder

Gie|ße|rei [giːsə'rai] F -, -en **a** *no pl* (= *Gießen*) casting, founding **b** (= *Werkstatt*) foundry

Gie|ße|rei-: Gie|ße|rei|ar|bei|ter(in) M(F) foundry worker; **Gie|ße|rei|be|trieb** M foundry; **Gie|ße|rei|tech|nik** F foundry practice

Gie|ße|rin F -, -nen (*Metal*) caster, founder

Gieß-: Gieß|form F mould (*Brit*), mold (*US*); **Gieß|gru|be** F foundry pit; **Gieß|kan|ne** F watering can; **Gieß|kan|nen|prin|zip** NT (*inf*) principle of indiscriminate all-round (*Brit*) or all-around (*US*) distribution; **Gieß|kel|le** F , **Gieß|löf|fel** M casting ladle; **Gieß|ofen** M foundry furnace; **Gieß|pfan|ne** F casting ladle

giet|zig ['giːtsɪç] ADJ (*Sw*) = geizig

Gift [gɪft] NT -(e)s, -e (*lit, fig*) poison; (= *Bakteriengift*) toxin; (= *Schlangengift, fig*: = *Bosheit*) venom; ~ **nehmen** to poison oneself; **das ist (wie) ~ für ihn** (*inf*) that is very bad for him; **darauf kannst du ~ nehmen** (*inf*) you can bet your bottom dollar *or* your life on that (*inf*); **sein ~ verspritzen** to be venomous; **~ und Galle spucken** (*inf*) *or* **speien** to be fuming, to be in a rage

Gift-: Gift|am|pul|le F poison capsule; **Gift|be|cher** M cup of poison; **Gift|cock|tail** M (*fig*) toxic *or* poisonous cocktail; **Gift|drü|se** F venom gland

gif|ten ['gɪftn] VI (*inf*) to be nasty (*gegen* about)

Gift-: Gift|fass ▲ NT toxic waste drum; **Gift|fracht** F , *no pl* toxic cargo; **gift|frei** ADJ non--toxic, non-poisonous; **Gift|gas** NT poison gas; **Gift|gas|wol|ke** F cloud of poison gas, poison gas cloud; **gift|grün** ADJ bilious green; **gift|hal|tig**, (*Aus*) **gift|häl|tig** ADJ containing poison, poisonous, toxic; **Gift|hauch** M (*liter*) miasma (*liter*)

gif|tig ['gɪftɪç] ADJ **a** (= *Gift enthaltend*) poisonous; *Stoff, Chemikalien etc auch* toxic **b** (*fig*) (= *boshaft, hasserfüllt*) venomous; (= *zornig*) vitriolic → **Zunge c** (= *grell*) bilious ADV **b** (= *böse*) venomously **b** (= *grell*) **etw ist ~ grün/gelb** sth is a bilious green/yellow

Gif|tig|keit F -, *no pl* **a** poisonous nature; (*von Stoff, Chemikalien etc auch*) toxicity **b** (*fig*) (= *Boshaftigkeit*) venom; (= *Zornigkeit*) vitriol

Gift-: Gift|kü|che F devil's workshop; **Gift|mi|scher** [-mɪʃɐ] M -s, -, **Gift|mi|sche|rin** [-ərɪn] F -, -nen preparer of poison; (*fig*) troublemaker, stirrer (*inf*); (*hum*: = *Apotheker*) chemist; **Gift|mord** M poisoning; **Gift|mör|der(in)** M(F) poisoner; **Gift|müll** M toxic waste; **Gift|müll|de|po|nie** F toxic waste dump; **Gift|not|ruf|zent|ra|le** F poison information *or* control centre (*Brit*) *or* center (*US*); **Gift|nu|del** F (*hum inf*) **a** (= *Zigarre, Zigarette*) cancer tube (*hum inf*) **b** (= *gehässige Frau*) vixen, shrew; **Gift|pfeil** M poisoned arrow; **Gift|pflan|ze** F poisonous plant; **Gift|pilz** M poisonous toadstool; **Gift|schlan|ge** F poisonous snake; **Gift|schrank** M poison cabinet; **Gift|stoff** M poisonous *or* toxic substance; **Gift|wir|kung** F effect of (the) poison; **die ~ machte sich nach ein paar Sekunden bemerkbar** the poison took effect after a few seconds; **Gift|zahn** M fang; **jdm die Giftzähne ausbrechen** (*fig inf*) to draw sb's fangs; **Gift|zwerg** M (*inf*) spiteful little devil (*inf*)

Gi|ga|byte ['giga-] NT (*Comput*) gigabyte

gi|gamp|fen ['giː|gampfn] *ptp* **gigampft** VI (*Sw*) to swing

Gi|gant [gi'gant] M -en, -en, **Gi|gan|tin** [-'gantɪn] F -, -en giant; (*Myth*) Titan; (*fig auch*) colossus

gi|gan|tisch [gi'gantɪʃ] ADJ gigantic, colossal

Gi|gan|tis|mus [gigan'tɪsmʊs] M -, *no pl* (*Med*) gigantism; (*fig*) giantism

Gi|gan|to|ma|nie [gigantoma'niː] F , *no pl* (*geh*) love of things big

Gi|ga|watt ['giga-] NT (*Elec*) gigawatt

Gi|gerl ['giː|gɐl] M OR NT -s, -(n) (*Aus, inf*) dandy, peacock (*inf*)

Gi|go|lo ['ʒiː|golo, 'ʒigolo] M -s, -s gigolo

gil|ben ['gɪlbn] VI *aux sein* (*liter*) to yellow

Gil|de ['gɪldə] F -, -n guild

Gil|de|haus NT guildhall

Gi|let [ʒi'leː] NT -s, -s (*Aus, Sw*) waistcoat (*Brit*), vest (*US*)

---

gilt [gɪlt] 3. *pers sing pres von* **gelten**

Gim|pel ['gɪmpl] M -s, - (*Orn*) bullfinch; (*inf*: = *Einfaltspinsel*) ninny (*inf*)

Gin [dʒɪn] M -s, -s gin; ~ **Tonic** gin and tonic

Gin|fizz ▲ ['dʒɪnfɪs] M -, -, **Gin-Fizz** M -, - gin-fizz

ging *pret von* **gehen**

Gin|seng ['gɪnzɛŋ, 'ʒɪnzɛŋ] M -s, -s (*Bot*) ginseng

Gin|seng|wur|zel ['gɪnzɛŋ-, 'ʒɪnzɛŋ-] F (*Bot*) ginseng root

Gins|ter ['gɪnstɐ] M -s, - (*Bot*) broom; (= *Stechginster*) gorse

Gip|fel ['gɪpfl] M -s, - **a** (= *Bergspitze*) peak; (= *höchster Punkt eines Berges*) summit; (*old*: = *Baumgipfel*) top, tip **b** (*fig*: = *Höhepunkt*) height; (*des Ruhms, der Karriere*) height, peak; (*der Vollkommenheit*) epitome; **er hat den ~ seiner Wünsche/Träume erreicht** all his wishes/dreams have been fulfilled *or* have come true; **das ist der ~!** (*inf*) that's the limit, that takes the biscuit (*Brit*) *or* cake (*inf*) **c** (= *Gipfelkonferenz*) summit **d** (*Sw*: = *Croissant*) croissant

Gip|fel|ge|spräch NT (*Pol*) summit talks *pl*

Gip|fe|li ['gɪpfəli] NT -s, - (*Sw*: = *Croissant*) croissant

Gip|fel-: Gip|fel|kon|fe|renz F (*Pol*) summit conference; **Gip|fel|kreuz** NT cross on the summit of a/the mountain; **Gip|fel|leis|tung** F crowning achievement

gip|feln ['gɪpfln] VI to culminate (*in* +*dat* in)

Gip|fel-: Gip|fel|punkt M (*lit*) zenith; (*fig*) high point; **Gip|fel|stür|mer(in)** M(F) conqueror of a/the peak; **Gip|fel|teil|neh|mer(in)** M(F) (*Pol inf*) summiteer; **Gip|fel|tref|fen** NT (*Pol*) summit (meeting)

Gips [gɪps] M -es, -e **a** plaster, (= *gebrannter Gips, Art*) plaster (of Paris); (*Chem*) gypsum **b** (= *Gipsverband*) plaster; **einen Arm in ~ legen** to put an arm in plaster (*Brit*) *or* in a cast; **er lag sechs Wochen in ~** he was in plaster (*Brit*) *or* in a cast for six weeks

Gips- *in cpds* plaster; **Gips|ab|druck** M , **Gips|ab|guss** ▲ M plaster cast; **Gips|be|cher** M plaster mixing cup; **Gips|bein** NT (*inf*) leg in plaster (*Brit*) *or* in a cast

gip|sen ['gɪpsn] VT to plaster; *Arm, Bein* to put in plaster (*Brit*) *or* in a cast

Gip|ser ['gɪpsɐ] M -s, -, **Gip|se|rin** [-ərɪn] F -, -nen plasterer

gip|sern ['gɪpsɐn] ADJ *attr* plaster

Gips-: Gips|fi|gur F plaster (of Paris) figure; **Gips|form** F plaster (of Paris) mould (*Brit*) *or* mold (*US*); **Gips|kopf** M (*inf*) blockhead, dimwit, num(b)skull (*all inf*); **Gips|kor|sett** NT (*Med*) plaster jacket; **Gips|kra|wat|te** F (*Med*) plaster collar; **Gips|mo|dell** NT (*Art, Archit etc*) plaster model; **Gips|ver|band** M (*Med*) plaster cast *or* bandage (*form*); **er trug den Arm im ~** he had his arm in plaster (*esp Brit*) *or* in a plaster cast, he had his arm in a cast

Gi|raf|fe [gi'rafə] F -, -n giraffe

Gi|ri ['ʒiːri] (*Aus*) *pl von* **Giro**

Girl [gøːɐl, gœrl] NT -s, -s (*inf*) girl; (= *Revuegirl etc*) chorus girl

Gir|lan|de [gɪr'landə] F -, -n garland (*aus* of); **etw mit ~n schmücken** to garland sth, to decorate sth with garlands

Girl|ie [gøːɐli, gœrli] NT -s, -s (*inf*) girlie (*inf*)

Gir|litz ['gɪrlɪts] M -es, -e (*Orn*) serin (finch)

Gi|ro ['ʒiːro] NT -s, -s *or* (*Aus*) **Giri** ['ʒiːri] (*Fin*) (bank) giro; (= *Indossament*) endorsement; **durch ~** by giro

Gi|ro-: Gi|ro|bank F *pl* -banken clearing bank; **Gi|ro|ge|schäft** NT (bank) giro transfer; **Gi|ro|kon|to** NT current account; **Gi|ro|über|wei|sung** F giro transfer; **Gi|ro|ver|kehr** M giro system; (= *Girogeschäft*) giro transfer (business); **Gi|ro|zent|ra|le** F clearing house

gir|ren ['gɪrən] VI (*lit, fig*) to coo

---

gis [gɪs] NT -, -, **Gis** NT -, - (*Mus*) G sharp; **Gis--Dur** G sharp major; **~-Moll** G sharp minor

Gischt [gɪʃt] M -(e)s, -e *or* f , -en spray

Gi|tar|re [gi'tarə] F -, -n guitar

Gi|tar|re(n)-: Gi|tar|re(n)|spiel NT guitar--playing; **Gi|tar|re(n)|spie|ler(in)** M(F) guitarist, guitar-player

Gi|tar|rist [gita'rɪst] M -en, -en, **Gi|tar|ris|tin** [-'rɪstɪn] F -, -nen guitarist

Git|ter ['gɪtɐ] NT -s, - bars *pl*; (*engstäbig, vor Türen, Schaufenstern*) grid; (*in Fußboden, Straßendecke*) grid, grating; (*für Gewächse etc*) lattice, trellis; (= *feines Drahtgitter*) (wire-)mesh; (= *Kamingitter*) fireguard; (= *Geländer*) railing *usu pl*; (*Phys, Chem*: = *Kristallgitter*) lattice; (*Elec, Geog*) grid; **hinter ~n** (*fig inf*) behind bars

Git|ter-: Git|ter|bett NT cot (*Brit*), crib (*US*); **Git|ter|elekt|ro|de** F (*Elec*) grid (electrode); **Git|ter|fens|ter** NT barred window; **Git|ter|mast** M (*Elec*) (lattice) pylon; **Git|ter|netz** NT (*Geog*) grid; **Git|ter|rost** M grid, grating; **Git|ter|span|nung** F (*Elec*) grid voltage; **Git|ter|stab** M bar; **Git|ter|struk|tur** F (*Chem*) lattice structure; **Git|ter|tor** NT (paled) gate; **Git|ter|tüll** M latticework tulle; **Git|ter|tür** F (paled) gate; **Git|ter|ver|schlag** M crate; **Git|ter|zaun** M paling; (*mit gekreuzten Stäben*) lattice fence

Gk F , *no pl abbr von* **Gemeinschaftskunde** (*Sch inf*) social studies *pl*

Glace ['glasə] F -, -n (*Sw*) ice (cream)

Gla|cé- [gla'seː], **Gla|cee-** ▲: **Gla|cé|hand|schuh** M , **Gla|cee|hand|schuh** ▲ M kid glove; **jdn mit ~en anfassen** (*fig*) to handle sb with kid gloves; **Gla|cé|le|der** NT , **Gla|cee|le|der** ▲ NT glacé leather

gla|cie|ren [gla'siːrən] *ptp* **glaciert** VT (*Cook*) to glaze

Gla|cis [gla'siː] NT -, - [-'siː(s), -'siːs] (*Mil*) glacis

Gla|di|a|tor [gla'diaːtoːɐ] M -s, **Gladiatoren** *ptp* gladiator

Gla|di|o|le [gla'dioːlə] F -, -n (*Bot*) gladiolus

Gla|mour ['glɛmɐ] M OR NT -s, *no pl* (*Press sl*) glamour (*Brit*), glamor (*US*)

Gla|mour|girl ['glɛmɐ-] NT glamour (*Brit*) *or* glamor (*US*) girl

gla|mou|rös [glamu'røːs] ADJ glamorous

Glanz [glants] M -es, *no pl* gleam; (*von Oberfläche auch*) shine; (= *Funkeln*) sparkle, glitter; (*von Augen*) sparkle; (*von Haaren*) sheen, shine; (*von Seide, Perlen*) sheen, shine; (*von Farbe*) gloss; (*blendender: von Sonne, Scheinwerfer etc*) glare; (*fig*) (*der Schönheit, Jugend*) radiance; (*von Ruhm, Erfolg*) glory; (= *Gepränge, Pracht*) splendour (*Brit*), splendor (*US*); **mit ~ und Gloria** (*iro inf*) in grand style; **eine Prüfung mit ~ bestehen** (*inf*) to pass an exam with flying colours (*Brit*) *or* colors (*US*); **den ~ verlieren** *or* **einbüßen** (*Metall, Leder, Möbel*) to lose its shine; (*Diamanten, Augen, fig*) to lose its/one's/their sparkle; **welch ~ in dieser Hütte!** (*iro*) to what do I owe the honour (*Brit*) *or* honor (*US*) (of this visit)? (*iro*)

Glanz|ab|zug M (*Phot*) glossy *or* gloss print

glän|zen ['glɛntsn] VI (*lit, fig*) to shine; (*polierte Oberfläche auch*) to gleam; (= *glitzern*) to glisten; (= *funkeln*) to sparkle; (= *blenden*) to glare; (*Hosenboden, Ellbogen, Nase*) to be shiny; **vor jdm ~ wollen** to want to shine in front of sb; **ihr Gesicht glänzte vor Freude** her face shone with joy, her face was radiant with joy → **Gold**

glän|zend ADJ shining; *Haar, Seide auch* lustrous; *Metall, Leder, Holz auch* gleaming; (= *strahlend*) radiant; (= *blendend*) dazzling; (= *glitzernd*) glistening; (= *funkelnd*) sparkling, glittering; *Papier* glossy, shiny; *Stoff, Nase, Hosenboden, Ellbogen* shiny; (*fig*) brilliant; *Erfolg* brilliant, dazzling; *Aussehen, Fest* dazzling; *Zukunft* brilliant, glittering; *Gesellschaft* glittering; (= *erstklassig*) marvellous (*Brit*), marvelous (*US*), splendid; **~ in Form** (*inf*) in splendid form; **ein ~er Reinfall**

(*iro*) a glorious failure **ADV** (= *sehr gut*) brilliantly; **wir haben uns ~ amüsiert** we had a marvellous (*Brit*) or marvelous (*US*) or great (*inf*) time; **mir geht es ~** I'm just fine; **~ miteinander auskommen** to get a-long fantastically or brilliantly

Glanz-: Glanz|form F , *no pl* (*inf*) brilliant form; **Glanz|gras** NT canary grass; **Glanz|idee** F (*inf*) brilliant idea; **Glanz|koh|le** F glance coal; **Glanz|lack** M gloss (paint); **Glanz|le|der** NT patent leather; **Glanz|lein|wand** F (*Tex*) glazed taffeta; **Glanz|leis|tung** F brilliant achievement; **eine wissenschaftliche ~** a brilliant scientific achievement; **Glanz|licht** NT **a** (*Art*, *fig*) highlight **b** (*Phys*) reflected light; **glanz|los** ADJ (*lit*, *fig*) dull; *Augen*, *Haar*, *Vorstellung auch*, *Sieg* lacklustre (*Brit*), lackluster (*US*); *Lack*, *Oberfläche* matt; **Glanz|num|mer** F big number, pièce de résistance; **Glanz|pa|pier** NT glossy paper; **Glanz|pa|ra|de** F (*Sport*) brilliant save; **Glanz|pe|ri|o|de** F heyday; **Glanz|po|li|tur** F gloss polish; **Glanz|punkt** M (*fig*) highlight, high spot; **Glanz|rol|le** F star role; **Glanz|stück** NT pièce de résistance; **glanz|voll** ADJ (*fig*) brilliant; *Zukunft auch* glittering; *Darstellung*, *Unterhaltung auch* sparkling; *Sieg auch* dazzling; (= *prachtvoll*) glittering; **Glanz|zeit** F heyday; **sei-ne ~ ist vorüber** he has had his day

Gla|rus ['glaːrʊs] NT - Glarus

Glas¹ [glaːs] NT **-es, ⸚er** ['glɛːzə] or (*als Maßangabe*) **-** **a** (= *Stoff*, *Gefäß*) glass; (= *Konservenglas*) jar; **buntes** or **farbiges** or **gefärbtes ~** coloured (*Brit*) or colored (*US*) glass; (*von Fenstern*) stained glass; **„Vorsicht ~!"** "glass – handle with care"; **ein ~ Milch** a glass of milk; **ein ~ Marmelade** a pot (*Brit*) or jar of jam; **ein ~ Gurken** a jar of gherkins; **zwei ~ Wein** two glasses of wine; **zu tief ins ~ gucken** (*inf*) or **schauen** (*inf*) **ein ~ über den Durst trinken** (*inf*) to have one too many, to have one over the eight (*Brit inf*); **unter ~** behind glass; (*Gewächs*) under glass

b (= *Brillenglas*) lens *sing*; (= *Fernglas*) binoculars *pl*, (field) glasses *pl*, (= *Opernglas*) opera glasses *pl*; **Gläser** (*old*: = *Brille*) spectacles *pl*, glasses *pl*

Glas² [glaːs] NT **-es, -en** ['glaːzn] (*Naut*: = *halbe Stunde*) bell; **es schlägt acht ~en** it's eight bells

Glas- *in cpds* glass; **Glas|bal|lon** M carboy; **Glas|bau** M *pl* **-bauten** glass structure; **Glas|bau|stein** M glass block; **glas+bla|sen** VI *sep irreg* to blow glass; **Glas|blä|ser(in)** M(F) glass-blower; **Glas|blä|se|rei** [-blɛːzə'raɪ] F **-, -en** *no pl* (= *Handwerk*) glass-blowing **b** (= *Werkstatt*) glassworks *sing* or *pl*; **Glas|bruch** M broken glass

Gläs|chen ['glɛːsçən] NT **-s, -** *dim von* **Glas¹** (= *Getränk*) little drink; **darauf müssen wir ein ~ trinken** we must drink to that, that calls for a little drink

Glas-: Glas|con|tai|ner M bottle bank; **Glas|dach** NT glass roof

Gla|ser ['glaːzə] M **-s, -**, **Gla|se|rin** [-ərɪn] F **-, -nen** glazier

Gla|se|rei [glaːzə'raɪ] F **-, -en** **a** *no pl* (= *Handwerk*) glazing **b** (= *Werkstatt*) glazier's workshop

Glas-: Gla|ser|hand|werk NT glazing; **Gla|ser|kitt** M glazier's putty

Gläser|klang M (*dated*) the clink of glasses

Glas|er|meis|ter(in) M(F) master glazier

glä|sern ['glɛːzən] ADJ glass; (*liter.*: = *starr*) glassy; (*fig*: = *durchschaubar*) transparent; *Verwaltung* o-pen; **der ~e Bürger** the citizen under the eye of Big Brother **ADV** **sich ~ anfühlen** to feel like glass

Glas-: Glä|ser|tuch NT *pl* **-tücher** glass-cloth; **glä|ser|wei|se** ADV by the glassful

Glas|fab|rik F glassworks *sing* or *pl*

Glas|fa|ser F glass fibre (*Brit*) or fiber (*US*), fibreglass (*Brit*), fiberglass (*US*)

Glas|fa|ser-: Glas|fa|ser|ka|bel NT optical fibre (*Brit*) or fiber (*US*) cable; **Glas|fa|ser|op|tik** F fibre optics *sing* (*Brit*), fiber optics *sing* (*US*); **Glas|fa|ser|pa|pier** NT fibreglass (*Brit*) or fiberglass (*US*) paper; **glas|fa|ser|ver|stärkt** [-fɛɐʃtɛɐkt] ADJ fibreglass-reinforced (*Brit*), fiberglass-reinforced (*US*)

Glas-: Glas|fi|ber F glass fibre (*Brit*) or fiber (*US*), fibreglass (*Brit*), fibreglass (*US*); **Glas|fi|ber|stab** M (*Sport*) glass fibre (*Brit*) or fiber (*US*) pole; **Glas|flüg|ler** [-flyːglə] M **-s, -** (*Zool*) clearwing; **Glas|ge|schirr** NT glassware; **Glas|glo|cke** F glass cover or dome; (*als Lampenschirm*) glass ball; **Glas|har|fe** F musical glasses *pl*; **Glas|har|mo|ni|ka** F musical glasses *pl*, glass harmonica; **glas|hart** ADJ brittle; *Stimme* steely; *Nein* definite; *wirtschaftliche Positionen* unequivocal; *Koalitionsfrage* clear-cut **ADV** verhandeln without compromise; **diese Frage stellt sich ~** this issue is clear-cut; **Glas|haus** NT greenhouse; (*in botanischen Gärten etc*) glasshouse; **wer (selbst) im ~ sitzt, soll nicht mit Steinen werfen** (*Prov*) people who live in glass houses shouldn't throw stones (*Prov*); **Glas|hüt|te** F glassworks *sing* or *pl*

gla|sie|ren [gla'ziːrən] *ptp* **glasiert** VT to glaze; *Kuchen* to ice (*Brit*), to frost (*esp US*)

gla|sig ['glaːzɪç] ADJ *Blick* glassy; (*Cook*) *Kartoffeln* waxy; *Speck*, *Zwiebeln* transparent

Glas-: Glas|in|dust|rie F glass industry; **Glas|kas|ten** M glass case; (*in Fabrik*, *Büro*) glass box; (*Hort*) cold frame; **glas|klar** ADJ (*lit*) clear as glass; (*fig*) crystal-clear; **Glas|kol|ben** M glass flask; (*von Glühlampe*, *Radioröhre etc*) glass bulb; **Glas|ku|gel** F glass ball; (= *Murmel*) marble; **Glas|ma|le|rei** F glass painting; **Glas|mas|se** F molten glass

Glas|nost ['glasnɔst] F **-, *no pl*** (*Pol*) glasnost

Glas-: Glas|nu|del F fine Chinese noodle; **Glas|pa|pier** NT glasspaper; **Glas|per|le** F glass bead; **Glas|plat|te** F glass top; **Glas|rei|ni|ger** M **a** (= *Glasreinigungsmittel*) glass cleaner **b** (*Beruf*) window cleaner; **Glas|röhr|chen** NT small glass tube; **Glas|röh|re** F glass tube; **Glas|schei|be** F sheet of glass; (*von Fenster*) pane of glass; **Glas|scher|be** F fragment of glass, piece of broken glass; **~n** broken glass; **Glas|schlei|fer(in)** M(F) (*Opt*) glass grinder; (*Art*) glass cutter; **Glas|schliff** M (*Opt*) glass grinding; (*Art*) glass cutting; **Glas|schmel|ze** F glass melt; **Glas|schnei|der** (*Gerät*) glass cutter; **Glas|schrank** M glass-fronted cupboard; **Glas|split|ter** M splinter of glass

Glast [glast] M **-(e)s, *no pl*** (*poet*) = **Glanz**

Gla|sur [gla'zuːə] F **-, -en** glaze; (*Metal*) enamel; (= *Zuckerguss*) icing (*Brit*), frosting (*esp US*)

Glas-: Glas|ve|ran|da F glass veranda, sun room or parlor (*US*); **Glas|ver|si|che|rung** F glass insurance; **Glas|wa|ren** PL glassware *sing*; **glas|wei|se** ADJ, ADV by the glass; **Glas|wol|le** F glass wool; **Glas|zie|gel** M (*für Wand*) glass brick; (*für Dach*) glass tile; **Glas|zy|lin|der** M glass cylinder; (*von Petroleumlampe*) glass chimney

glatt [glat] ADJ *comp* **-er** or **⸚er** ['glɛːtə], *superl* **-es-te(r, s)** or **⸚este(r, s)** ['glɛːtəstə] **a** (= *eben*) smooth; *Meer auch* unruffled; *Haar* straight; (*Med*) *Bruch* clean; *Stoff* (= *faltenlos*) uncreased; (= *ungemustert*) plain; (*Aus*) *Mehl* finely ground

b (= *schlüpfrig*) slippery; **auf dem ~en Parkett der Außenpolitik ausrutschen** to come a cropper (*Brit inf*) or to blunder in the tricky area of foreign policy

c (*fig*) *Landung*, *Ablauf* smooth; **eine ~e Eins** (*Sch*) a straight A

d *attr* (*inf*: = *klar*, *eindeutig*) outright; *Lüge*, *Unsinn etc* downright, outright; *Absage auch* flat; **das kostet ~e 1.000 Euro** it costs a good 1,000 euros

e (*pej*: = *allzu gewandt*) smooth, slick

ADV *comp* **-er** or **⸚er**, *superl* **am -esten** or **⸚esten** **a** (= *eben*) bügeln, hobeln, walzen (till) smooth;

polieren highly; *rühren* till smooth; *schneiden* straight; **~ rasieren** to shave; **~ rasiert** (*Mann*, *Kinn*) clean-shaven; *Beine* shaved; **~ stricken** to knit garter stitch → *auch* **glatt kämmen**, **glatt le-gen** *etc*

b (= *problemlos*) smoothly; **er hat sich ~ aus der Affäre gezogen** he wriggled his way neatly out of the whole affair → *auch* **glatt gehen**

c (*inf*: = *einfach*) completely; *leugnen*, *ablehnen* flatly; *vergessen* clean; **jdm etw ~ ins Gesicht sa-gen** to tell sb sth to his/her face; **das ist doch ~ gelogen** that's a downright lie; **die Rechnung ist ~ aufgegangen** the sum works out exactly; **es kostete ~ EUR 10.000** it cost a good 10,000 euros

Glät|te ['glɛtə] F **-, *no pl*** **a** (= *Ebenheit*) smooth-ness; (*von Haar*) sleekness **b** (= *Schlüpfrigkeit*) slipperiness **c** (= *Politur*) polish **d** (*fig*) (*des Auftretens*) smoothness, slickness; (*des Stils*) pol-ish

Glatt|eis NT ice; **„Vorsicht ~!"** "danger, black ice"; **sich auf ~ begeben** (*fig*) aufs ~ geraten (*fig*) to skate on thin ice; **jdn aufs ~ führen** (*fig*) to take sb for a ride

Glatt|eis|bil|dung F formation of black ice

Glätt|ei|sen ['glɛt-] NT (*Sw*) iron, smoothing i-ron (*old*)

Glatt|eis|ge|fahr F danger of black ice

glät|ten ['glɛtn] **VT** (= *glatt machen*) to smooth out; (= *glatt streichen*) *Haar*, *Tuch* to smooth; (*esp Sw*: = *bügeln*) to iron; (*fig*: = *stilistisch glätten*) to polish up **VR** to smooth out; (*Wellen*, *Meer*, *fig*) to subside

Glät|ter ['glɛtə] M **-s, -**, **Glät|te|rin** [-ərɪn] F **-, -nen** (*esp Sw*) presser

glatt-: glatt ge|hen ▲ VI *irreg aux sein* to go smoothly or OK (*inf*); **glatt ho|beln** ▲ VT to plane smooth; **glatt käm|men** ▲ VT to comb straight; (*mit Haarpomade*) to sleek down; **glatt le|gen** ▲ VT to fold up carefully; **glatt ma|chen** ▲ VT (= *glatt streichen*) to smooth out; *Haare* to smooth (down); (*mit Kamm*) to comb straight; **glatt+ma|chen** VT *sep* (*inf*: = *begleichen*) to settle; **glatt po|lie|ren** ▲ VT to pol-ish highly; **glatt ra|sie|ren** ▲ VT to shave; **glatt|ra|siert** △ [-raziːɐt] ADJ → **glatt** ADV **a**; **glatt rüh|ren** ▲ VT to stir till smooth; **glatt schlei|fen** ▲ VT *irreg* to rub smooth; *Linsen*, *Diamanten etc* to grind smooth; *Felsen etc* to wear smooth; **glatt strei|chen** ▲ VT *irreg* to smooth out; *Haare* to smooth (down); **glatt wal|zen** ▲ VT to roll smooth; **glatt|weg** ['glatvɛk] ADV (*inf*) simply, just, just like that (*inf*); **er hat meinen Vorschlag ~ abgelehnt** he simply turned my suggestion down, he turned my suggestion down just like that (*inf*); **das ist ~ erlogen** that's a blatant lie; **glatt|zün|gig** [-tsʏnɪç] ADJ (*pej geh*) glib, smooth-tongued

Glat|ze ['glatsə] F **-, -n** **a** bald head; (*rare*: = *kahle Stelle*) bald patch or spot; **eine ~ bekom-men/haben** to go/be bald; **er zeigt Ansätze zu einer ~** he shows signs of going bald; **ein Mann mit ~** a bald(-headed) man, a man with a bald head; **sich** (*dat*) **eine ~ schneiden lassen** to have one's head shaved **b** (*inf*: = *Skinhead*) skin (*inf*)

Glatz-: Glatz|kopf M bald head; (*inf*: = *Mann mit Glatze*) baldie (*inf*); **glatz|köp|fig** ADJ bald(-headed); **Glatz|köp|fig|keit** [-kœpfɪk-kaɪt] F **-, *no pl*** baldness

Glau|be ['glaʊbə] M **-ns, *no pl*** (= *Vertrauen*, *religiöse Überzeugung*, *Konfession*) faith (*an* +*acc* in); (= *Überzeugung*, *Meinung*) belief (*an* +*acc* in); **~, Liebe, Hoffnung** faith, hope and charity; **im gu-ten** or **in gutem ~n** in good faith; **(bei jdm) ~n finden** to be believed (by sb); (*Bericht*, *Aussage etc auch*) to find credence (with sb); **den ~n an jdn/etw verlieren** to lose faith in sb/sth; **jdm ~n schenken** to believe sb, to give credence to sb; **jdn in dem ~n (be)lassen, dass ...** to let sb be-lieve that ...; **lass ihn bei seinem ~n!** let him keep his illusions; **er ist katholischen ~ns** he is of the Catholic faith → **Treue**

glau|ben ['glaubn] ✪ 33.2, 39.1, 53.5, 53.6 VTI (= *Glauben schenken, überzeugt sein, vertrauen*) to believe (*an +acc* in); (= *meinen, annehmen, vermuten*) to think; **jdm ~** to believe sb; **das glaube ich dir gerne/nicht** I quite/don't believe you; **glaube es mir** believe me; **diese Geschichte/das soll ich dir ~?** do you expect me to believe that story/that?; **er glaubte mir jedes Wort** he believed every word I said; **ich glaube kein Wort davon** I don't believe a word of it; **jdm (etw) aufs Wort ~** to take sb's word (for sth); **ich glaube dir jedes Wort (einzeln)** (*iro*) pull the other one (*inf*); **d(a)ran ~ müssen** (*inf*: = *sterben*) to cop it (*Brit inf*), to bite the dust (*US inf*), to buy it (*inf*); **das glaubst du doch selbst nicht!** you can't be serious; **das will ich ~!** (*dated*: *als Antwort*) I'm sure!, I can well believe it; **jdn etw ~ machen wollen** to try to make sb believe sth; **das glaube ich kaum** I can't believe that of him; **ob du es glaubst oder nicht, ...** believe it or not ...; **wers glaubt, wird selig** (*iro*) a likely story (*iro*); **wer hätte das je geglaubt!** who would have thought it?; **ich glaubte ihn zu kennen, doch ...** I thought I knew him, but ...; **ich glaubte ihn tot/in Sicherheit** I thought he was dead/safe; **ich glaubte ihn in Berlin** I thought he was in Berlin; **er glaubte sich unbeobachtet** he thought nobody was watching him; **man glaubte ihm den Fachmann** one could well believe him to be an expert; **es ist nicht zu ~** it's incredible or unbelievable; **ich glaube, ja** I think so; **ich glaube, nein** I don't think so, I think not

Glau|ben ['glaubn] M **-s**, *no pl* = Glaube

Glau|bens-: **Glau|bens|ar|ti|kel** M article of faith; **Glau|bens|be|kennt|nis** NT creed; **Glau|bens|be|we|gung** F religious movement; **Glau|bens|bru|der** M co-religionist (*form*), brother in faith, fellow Buddhist/Christian/Jew *etc* → *auch* Glaubensschwester; **Glau|bens|din|ge** PL matters *pl* of faith; **Glau|bens|ei|fer** M religious zeal; **Glau|bens|fra|ge** F question of faith; **Glau|bens|frei|heit** F freedom of worship, religious freedom; **Glau|bens|ge|mein|schaft** F religious sect; (*christliche auch*) denomination; **Glau|bens|ge|nos|se** M , **Glau|bens|ge|nos|sin** F co-religionist (*form*); **Glau|bens|kampf** M religious battle; **Glau|bens|krieg** M religious war; **Glau|bens|leh|re** F dogmatics *sing*; (*pej*: = *Doktrin*) doctrine, dogma; **Glau|bens|rich|tung** F (religious) persuasion, religious orientation; **Glau|bens|sa|che** F matter of faith; **Glau|bens|satz** M dogma, doctrine; **Glau|bens|schwes|ter** F co-religionist (*form*), fellow Buddhist/Christian/Jew *etc* → *auch* Glaubensbruder; **Glau|bens|spal|tung** F schism; **glau|bens|stark** ADJ deeply religious; **Glau|bens|streit** M religious controversy; **glau|bens|ver|wandt** ADJ **jdm ~ sein** to be of a similar faith to sb; **Glau|bens|wech|sel** M change of faith or religion; **zum ~ bereit sein** to be prepared to change one's faith or religion; **Glau|bens|zwei|fel** M *usu pl* religious doubt; **Glau|bens|zwist** M religious controversy

Glau|ber|salz ['glaubɐ-] NT (*Chem*) Glauber('s) salt

glaub|haft ADJ credible, believable; (= *einleuchtend*) plausible; **(jdm) etw (überzeugend) ~ machen** to substantiate sth (to sb), to satisfy sb of sth ADV believably, credibly

Glaub|haf|tig|keit ['glauphaftɪçkait] F **-**, *no pl* credibility; (= *Evidenz*) plausibility

Glaub|haft|ma|chung ['glauphaftmaxʊŋ] F **-**, *no pl* (*Jur*) substantiation

gläu|big ['glɔybɪç] ADJ Katholik etc devout; (= *vertrauensvoll*) trusting ADV **~ hörten sie meiner Geschichte zu** they listened to and believed my story

Gläu|bi|ge(r) ['glɔybɪɡə] MF *decl as adj* believer; **die ~n** the faithful

Gläu|bi|ger ['glɔybɪɡɐ] M **-s, -** (*Comm*) creditor

Gläu|bi|ger-: **Gläu|bi|ger|an|sprü|che** PL creditors' claims *pl*; **Gläu|bi|ger|aus|schuss** ▲ M committee or board of creditors; **Gläu|bi|ger|bank** F *pl* **-banken** creditor bank

Gläu|bi|ge|rin ['glɔybɪɡərɪn] F **-**, **-nen** (*Comm*) creditor

Gläu|bi|ger-: **Gläu|bi|ger|land** NT , **Gläu|bi|ger|staat** M creditor nation or state; **Gläu|bi|ger|ver|samm|lung** F meeting of creditors

Gläu|big|keit F **-**, *no pl* devoutness; (= *Vertrauen*) trust

glaub|lich ['glauplɪç] ADJ **kaum ~** scarcely credible

glaub|wür|dig ADJ Mensch, Beweise credible; **~e Quellen** reliable sources ADV credibly; **sich ~ verhalten** to be reliable or credible

Glaub|wür|dig|keit F **-**, *no pl* credibility

Glau|kom [glau'ko:m] NT **-s, -e** (*Med*) glaucoma

gla|zi|al [gla'tsia:l] ADJ (*Geol*) glacial

Gla|zi|al [gla'tsia:l] NT **-s, -e** (*Geol*) glacial epoch or episode

gleich [glaiç]	
1 ADJEKTIV	3 PRÄPOSITION
2 ADVERB	4 BINDEWORT

1 – ADJEKTIV

a = identisch, ähnlich same; **das gleiche, aber nicht dasselbe Auto** a similar car, but not the same one; **der/die/das gleiche ... wie** the same ... as; **in gleicher Weise** in the same way; **die beiden Briefe kamen mit der gleichen Post** the two letters arrived in the same post (*Brit*) or mail; **zur gleichen Zeit** at the same time; **die beiden haben gleiches Gewicht** they are both the same weight, they both weigh the same; **ich fahre den gleichen Wagen wie Sie** I drive the same car as you; **das kommt** or **läuft aufs Gleiche hinaus** it amounts to the same thing; **wir wollten alle das Gleiche** we all wanted the same thing; **es ist genau das Gleiche** it's exactly the same; **es waren die Gleichen, die ... ihr Männer seid doch alle gleich!** you men are all the same!; **es ist mir (alles** or **ganz) gleich** it's all the same to me; **ein Gleiches tun** (*geh*) to do the same; **Gleich und Gleich gesellt sich gern** (*Prov*) birds of a feather flock together (*Prov*); **Gleiches mit Gleichem vergelten** to pay someone back in the same coin (*Brit*), to pay sb back in kind; **ganz gleich wer/was** *etc* no matter who/what *etc* → Boot, Münze, Strang

b = gleichwertig, gleichberechtigt equal; **in gleichem Abstand** at an equal distance; **zu gleichen Teilen** in equal parts; **zwei mal zwei (ist) gleich vier** two times are four, two times two is four; **vier plus/durch/minus zwei ist gleich ...** four plus/divided by/minus two is ...; **jdm (an etw** *dat*) **gleich sein** to be sb's equal (in sth); **gleicher Lohn für gleiche Arbeit** equal pay for equal work; **gleiche Rechte, gleiche Pflichten** equal rights, equal responsibilities; **mit jdm in einem Ton von gleich zu gleich reden** (*geh*) to talk to sb as an equal; **alle Menschen sind gleich, nur einige sind gleicher** (*hum*) all men are equal, but some are more equal than others; **wir sind in gleicher Weise daran schuld** we are equally to blame

2 – ADVERB

a = ohne Unterschied equally; (= *auf gleiche Weise*) alike, the same; **der Lehrer behandelt alle Kinder gleich** the teacher treats all the children equally; **gleich gekleidet** dressed alike or the same; **sie sind gleich groß/alt/schwer** they are the same size/age/weight

♦ **gleich bleibend** Kurs constant, steady; Temperatur (von Wetter) steady; (in Brutkasten etc) constant; **gleich bleibend sein** to remain the same; (Temperatur) (von Wetter) to remain steady; (in Brutkasten etc) to remain constant; **mehr**

Urlaub bei gleich bleibendem Gehalt more holidays (*esp Brit*) or vacation (*US*) with the same pay; **in gleich bleibendem Abstand** always at the same distance; **unter gleich bleibenden Umständen** if things remain as they are; **gleich bleibend gute Qualität** consistent(ly) good quality; **er ist immer gleich bleibend zuvorkommend** he is always equally helpful

♦ **gleich geartet** of the same kind; (= *ähnlich*) similar

♦ **gleich gesinnt** or **denkend** like-minded

♦ **gleich gestimmt** (*Mus*) in tune (+*dat* with); (*fig*) in harmony (+*dat* with)

♦ **gleich lautend** identical; **gleich lautende Abschrift** duplicate (copy); **gleich lautende Wörter** homophones; (= *gleich buchstabiert*) homonyms

b räumlich right, just; **das Wohnzimmer ist gleich neben der Küche** the living room is right or just next to the kitchen; **gleich hinter dem Haus ist ein großer Garten** there's a big garden just behind the house

c zeitlich (= *sofort*) immediately; (= *bald*) in a minute; **ich komme gleich** I'm just coming; **ich komme gleich wieder** I'll be right back; **du kriegst gleich eine Ohrfeige** you'll get a slap in a minute; **es muss nicht gleich sein** there's no hurry; **es ist gleich drei Uhr** it's almost or very nearly three o'clock; **das mache ich gleich heute** I'll do that today; **gleich zu** or **am Anfang** right at the beginning, at the very beginning; **gleich danach** straight or right afterwards; **ich werde ihn gleich morgen besuchen** I'll go and see him tomorrow; **gleich zu Beginn der Vorstellung** right at the beginning of the performance; **habe ich es nicht gleich gesagt!** what did I tell you?; **das habe ich mir gleich gedacht** I thought that straight away; **warum nicht gleich so?** why didn't you say/do that in the first place?; **na kommen schon! – gleich!** come along! – I'm just coming! or – I'll be right there; **wann machst du das? – gleich!** when are you going to do it? – right away or in just a moment; **gleich als** or **nachdem er ...** as soon as he ...; **so wirkt das Bild gleich ganz anders** suddenly, the picture has changed completely; **wenn das stimmt, kann ich ja gleich aufgeben** if that's true I might as well give up right now; **deswegen brauchst du nicht gleich zu weinen** there's no need to start crying because of that; **er ging gleich in die Küche/vor Gericht** he went straight to the kitchen/to court; **sie hat sich gleich zwei Hüte gekauft** she went and bought TWO hats; **bis gleich!** see you later!

d in Fragesätzen again; **wie war doch gleich die Nummer/Ihr Name?** what was the number/your name again?

3 – PRÄPOSITION (+*dat*)

(*liter*) like; **einer Epidemie gleich, gleich einer Epidemie** like an epidemic

4 – BINDEWORT

(*old, liter*) **ob er gleich ...** although he ...; **wenn er gleich ...** even if he ...

Gleich-: **gleich|alt|rig** ADJ (of) the same age; **die beiden sind ~** they are both the same age; **Gleichaltrige** people/children (of) the same age; **gleich|ar|mig** ADJ (*Phys*) Hebel equal-armed; **gleich|ar|tig** ADJ of the same kind (+*dat* as); (= *ähnlich*) similar (+*dat* to); (= *homogen*) homogeneous (+*dat* with) ADV in the same way; similarly; homogeneously; **Gleich|ar|tig|keit** F similarity; (= *Homogenität*) homogeneity; **gleich|auf** ['glaiç'lauf] ADV (*esp Sport*) equal; **~ liegen** to be lying equal, to be equal, to be level-pegging (*Brit*); **gleich|be|deu|tend** ADJ synonymous (*mit* with); (= *so gut wie*) tantamount (*mit* to); **Gleich|be|hand|lung** F equal treatment; **Gleich|be|hand|lungs|grund|satz** M principle of equal treatment; **gleich|be|rech|tigt** ADJ with equal *or* the same rights; *Partner, Möglichkeiten, Dialog* equal; *Amtssprache* equally recognized *or* valid; **~ sein** to have equal rights; **Gleich|be|rech|ti|gung** F equal rights *sing or pl*, equality (+*gen* for); **gleich blei|ben ▲** VI *irreg aux sein* to stay *or* remain the same; (*Temperaturen, Geschwindigkeit, Kurs auch*) to remain constant; **sich** (*dat*) **~** (*Mensch*) to stay *or* remain the same; **das bleibt sich gleich** it doesn't matter; **gleich|blei|bend** △ ADJ → **gleich 2 a**; **gleichen|kend** △ ADJ → **gleich 2 a**

glei|chen ['glaɪçn̩] *pret* **glich** [glɪç], *ptp* **geglichen** [gə'glɪçn̩] VI **jdm/einer Sache ~** to be like sb/ sth; **sich ~** to be alike *or* similar; **jdm an Erfahrung/Schönheit ~** to be sb's equal *or* to equal sb in experience/beauty

glei|chen|tags ['glaɪçn̩taːks] ADV (*esp Sw*) (on) the same day

glei|cher|ma|ßen ['glaɪçe'maːsn̩] ✪ 53.5 ADV, **glei|cher|wei|se** ['glaɪçe'vaɪzə] ADV equally; **~ ... und ...** both ... and ...

Gleich-: gleich|falls ADV (= *ebenfalls*) likewise; (= *auch*) also; (= *zur gleichen Zeit*) at the same time; **danke ~!** thank you, (and) the same to you; **gleich|far|big** ADJ (of) the same colour (*Brit*) *or* color (*US*); **gleich|för|mig** ADJ of the same shape; (= *einheitlich*, fig: = *eintönig*) uniform (*auch Phys*); (= *ähnlich*) similar; **Gleich|för|mig|keit** ['glaɪçfœrmɪçkaɪt] F, *no pl* similarity of shape; (= *Einheitlichkeit*, fig: = *Eintönigkeit*) uniformity (*auch Phys*); (= *Ähnlichkeit*) similarity; **gleich|ge|ar|tet** △ ADJ → **gleich 2 a**; **gleich|ge|schlech|tig** [-gəʃlɛçtɪç] ADJ (*Biol, Zool*) of the same sex, same-sex *attr*; (*Bot*) homogamous; **gleich|ge|schlecht|lich** ADJ **a** homosexual **b** = **gleichgeschlechtig**; **Gleich|ge|schlecht|lich|keit** F homosexuality *no def art*; **gleich|ge|sinnt** △ ADJ → **gleich 2 a**; **Gleich|ge|sinnt|heit** F [-gəzɪnthaɪt], *no pl* like-mindedness; **gleich|ge|stellt** ADJ equal (+*dat* to, with), on a par (+*dat* with); **er spricht nur mit Gleichgestellten** he only speaks to his equals; **rechtlich ~** equal in law → *auch* **gleichstellen**; **gleich|ge|stimmt** △ ADJ → **gleich 2 a**

Gleich|ge|wicht NT, *no pl* (*lit*) balance, equilibrium (*auch Phys, Chem*); (fig) (= *Stabilität*) balance; (= *seelisches Gleichgewicht*) equilibrium; **im ~** (*lit*) balanced, in equilibrium; **(wieder) ins ~ kommen** (fig) to become more balanced again; to regain one's equilibrium; **das ~ verlieren, aus dem ~ kommen** to lose one's balance *or* equilibrium (*auch fig*); **das ~ behalten** (*lit*) to keep one's balance *or* equilibrium; (fig) to retain one's equilibrium; **jdn aus dem ~ bringen** to throw sb off balance; (fig *auch*) to disturb sb's equilibrium; **das ~ einer Sache wiederherstellen** to get sth back into balance *or* equilibrium; **das ~ zwischen ... (dat) und ... halten** to maintain a proper balance between ... and ...; **diese Dinge müssen sich** (*dat*) **das ~ halten** (fig) these things should balance each other out; **das ~ der Kräfte** the balance of power

gleich|ge|wich|tig ADJ (= *ausgeglichen*) *Verhältnis* balanced; (= *gleich wichtig*) equal in weight ADV **die Kommission ist nicht ~ zusammengesetzt** the commission is not properly balanced

Gleich|ge|wichts-: Gleich|ge|wichts|emp|fin|den NT, **Gleich|ge|wichts|ge|fühl** NT sense of balance; **Gleich|ge|wichts|la|ge** F (fig) equilibrium; **Gleich|ge|wichts|or|gan** NT organ of equilibrium; **Gleich|ge|wichts|sinn** M sense of balance; **Gleich|ge|wichts|stö|rung** F impaired balance, disturbance of the sense of balance; **Gleich|ge|wichts|übung** F (*Sport*) balancing exercise; **Gleich|ge|wichts|zu|stand** M equilibrium

gleich|gül|tig, gleich|gil|tig [-gɪltɪç] (*old*) ADJ indifferent (*gegenüber, gegen* to, towards); (= *uninteressiert*) apathetic (*gegenüber, gegen* towards); (= *unwesentlich*) trivial, immaterial, unimportant; **das ist mir ~** it's a matter of (complete)

indifference to me; **Politik ist ihm ~** he doesn't care about politics; **~, was er tut** no matter what he does, irrespective of what he does; **es ist mir ~, was er tut** I don't care what he does; **er war ihr nicht ~ geblieben** she had not remained indifferent to him

Gleich|gül|tig|keit F indifference (*gegenüber, gegen* to, towards); (= *Desinteresse*) apathy (*gegenüber, gegen* towards)

Gleich|heit F -, -en **a** *no pl* (= *gleiche Stellung*) equality; (= *Identität*) identity; (= *Übereinstimmung*) correspondence; (*Ind*) parity **b** (= *Ähnlichkeit*) similarity

Gleich|heits-: Gleich|heits|grund|satz M, **Gleich|heits|prin|zip** NT principle of equality; **Gleich|heits|zei|chen** NT (*Math*) equals sign

Gleich-: Gleich|klang M (fig) harmony, accord; **gleich+kom|men** VI *sep irreg aux sein* +*dat* **a** (= *die gleiche Leistung etc erreichen*) to equal (*an* +*dat* for), to match (*an* +*dat* for, in); **niemand kommt ihm an Dummheit gleich** no-one can equal *or* match him for stupidity **b** (= *gleichbedeutend sein mit*) to be tantamount *or* equivalent to, to amount to; **Gleich|lauf** M, *no pl* (*Tech*) synchronization; **gleich|lau|fend** ADJ parallel (*mit* to); (*Tech*) synchronized; **gleich|lau|tend** △ ADJ → **gleich 2 a**; **gleich+ma|chen** VT *sep* to make the same, to level out → **Erdboden**; **Gleich|ma|cher(in)** M(F) (*pej*) leveller (*Brit pej*), leveler (*US pej*), egalitarian; **Gleich|ma|che|rei** [-maxə'raɪ] F -, -en (*pej*) levelling down (*Brit pej*), leveling down (*US pej*), egalitarianism; **gleich|ma|che|risch** [-maxərɪʃ] ADJ levelling (*Brit pej*), leveling (*US pej*), egalitarian; **Gleich|maß** NT, *no pl* **a** (= *Ebenmaß*) evenness; (*von Proportionen auch*) symmetry **b** (geh: = *Regelhaftigkeit*) monotony (*pej*), regularity; **gleich|mä|ßig** ADJ even, regular; *Puls* steady, regular; *Abstände* regular; *Proportionen* symmetrical ADV **a** (= *regelmäßig*) regularly; **er ist immer ~ freundlich** he is always consistently friendly **b** (= *in gleicher Stärke, Größe, Anzahl*) evenly; **sie hat die Äpfel ~ unter die Kinder verteilt** she distributed the apples evenly among the children; **die Farbe ~ auftragen** apply the paint evenly; **Gleich|mä|ßig|keit** F evenness, regularity; (*von Puls*) steadiness, regularity; (*von Abständen*) regularity; (*von Proportionen*) symmetry; **mit** *or* **in schöner ~** (*iro*) with monotonous regularity; **Gleich|mut** M equanimity, serenity, composure; **gleich|mü|tig** [-myːtɪç] ADJ serene, composed; *Stimme* calm ADV **etw ~ sagen** to say sth calmly; **Gleich|mü|tig|keit** F, *no pl* equanimity, composure; **gleich|na|mig** [-naːmɪç] ADJ of the same name; (*Math*) with a common denominator; **Brüche ~ machen** to reduce fractions to a common denominator

Gleich|nis ['glaɪçnɪs] NT -ses, -se **a** (*Liter*) simile **b** (= *Allegorie*) allegory; (*Bibl*) parable

gleich|nis|haft ADJ (*Liter*) as a simile; (= *allegorisch*) allegorical; (= *biblisch*) parabolic ADV (*Liter*) in a simile; (= *allegorisch*) allegorically; (= *biblisch*) in a parable

Gleich-: gleich|ran|gig [-raŋɪç] ADJ *Beamte etc* equal in rank *or* status (*mit* to), at the same level (*mit* as); *Straßen etc* of the same grade (*mit* as), equally graded; *Probleme, Regelungen etc* equally important, of equal status; **Gleich|ran|gig|keit** F -, *no pl* equal status; (*von Straßen*) equal grading; **gleich+rich|ten** VT *sep* (*Elec*) to rectify; **Gleich|rich|ter** M (*Elec*) rectifier; **Gleich|rich|ter|röh|re** F (*Elec*) rectifier tube (*esp US*) *or* valve; **Gleich|rich|tung** F (*Elec*) rectification

gleich|sam ['glaɪçzaːm] ADV (*geh*) as it were, so to speak; **~, als ob** just as if

Gleich-: gleich+schal|ten *sep* (*Pol, NS: pej*) VT to bring *or* force into line VR to conform, to step into line; **Gleich|schal|tung** F (*Pol, NS: pej*) bringing *or* forcing into line; (*unter Hitler auch*) gleichschaltung; **er wehrte sich gegen ei-**

ne ~ he refused to be brought *or* forced into line; **gleich|schen|ke|lig** [-ʃeŋkəlɪç], **gleich|schen|k|lig** [-ʃeŋklɪç] ADJ *Dreieck* isosceles; **Gleich|schritt** M, *no pl* (*Mil*) marching in step; **im ~** (*lit, fig*) in step; **im ~, marsch!** forward march!; **im ~ marschieren** to march in step; **~ halten** (*lit, fig*) to keep in step; **gleich+se|hen** VI *sep irreg* **jdm/einer Sache ~** to look like sb/ sth; **gleich|sei|tig** [-zaɪtɪç] ADJ *Dreieck* equilateral; **gleich+set|zen** VT *sep* (= *als dasselbe ansehen*) to equate (*mit* with); (= *als gleichwertig ansehen*) to treat as equivalent (*mit* to); **nichts ist mit echter Wolle gleichzusetzen** there's nothing to compare with pure wool; **Gleich|set|zung** F -, -en **die ~ der Arbeiter mit den Angestellten** treating workers as equivalent to office employees; **gleich|sil|big** ADJ with the same number of syllables; **Gleich|stand** M, *no pl* **a** (*Sport*) **den ~ erzielen** to draw level; **beim ~ von 1:1** with the scores level (*Brit*) *or* equal at 1 all **b** (*Pol*) equal stage of development; **gleich+ste|hen** VI *sep irreg* to be equal (+*dat* to *or* with), to be on a par (+*dat* with); (*Sport*) to be level (*Brit*) *or* equal (+*dat* with); **er steht im Rang einem Hauptmann gleich** he is equal in rank to a captain; **Gleichstehende** equals, people on an equal footing; **gleich+stel|len** VT *sep* **a** (*rechtlich etc*) to treat as equal, to give parity of treatment (to); **dass Frauen und Männer arbeitsrechtlich gleichzustellen sind** that men and women should be treated as equals *or* equally *or* given parity of treatment as far as work is concerned → *auch* **gleichgestellt b** = **gleichsetzen**; **Gleich|stel|lung** F **a** (*rechtlich etc*) equality (+*gen* of, for), equal status (+*gen* of, for), parity **b** = **Gleichsetzung**; **Gleich|stel|lungs|be|auf|trag|te(r)** MF *decl as adj* equal rights representative; **Gleich|strom** M (*Elec*) direct current, DC; **Gleich|tritt** M = **Gleichschritt**; **gleich+tun** VT *impers sep irreg* **es jdm ~** to equal *or* match sb; **es jdm im Laufen *etc* ~** to equal *or* match sb at *or* in running *etc*

Glei|chung ['glaɪçʊŋ] F -, -en equation; **eine ~ ersten/zweiten Grades** a simple *or* linear/quadratic equation, an equation of the first/second degree (*form*)

Gleich-: gleich|viel ADV (*geh*) nonetheless; **~ ob** no matter whether; **~ wie** however; **~ wohin** no matter where; **gleich|wer|tig** ADJ of the same value; (= *gleich zu bewerten*) *Leistung, Qualität* equal (+*dat* to); *Gegner* equally *or* evenly matched; *Partner* equal; (*Chem*) equivalent; **Gleich|wer|tig|keit** F, *no pl* equal value; (= *von gleich zu bewertender Leistung, Qualität*) equality; (*Chem*) equivalence, equivalency; **gleich|wie** ADV (*old*) (just) as; **gleich|win|ke|lig**, **gleich|wink|lig** ADJ (*Geometrie*) equiangular (*form*), with (all) angles equal; **gleich|wohl** ADV (*geh*) nevertheless, nonetheless; **gleich|zei|tig** ADJ simultaneous ADV simultaneously, at the same time; (= *ebenso, sowohl*) at the same time; **ihr sollt nicht alle ~ reden** you mustn't all speak at the same time; **Gleich|zei|tig|keit** ['glaɪçzaɪtɪçkaɪt] F -, *no pl* simultaneity; **gleich+zie|hen** VI *sep irreg* (*inf*) to catch up (*mit* with)

Gleis [glaɪs] NT -es, -e [-zə] (*Rail*) line, track, rails *pl*; (= *einzelne Schiene*) rail; (= *Bahnsteig*) platform; (fig) rut; **~ 6** platform *or* track (*US*) 6; **„Überschreiten der ~e verboten"** "passengers must not cross the line (*Brit*) *or* tracks"; **ein totes ~** (*lit*) a siding; (fig) a dead end; **jdn/etw aufs tote ~ schieben** to put sb/sth on ice (*inf*); **aus dem ~ springen** to jump the rails; **aus dem ~ kommen** (fig) to go off the rails (*Brit inf*), to get off the track (*US inf*); **etw ins (rechte) ~ bringen** (fig) to straighten *or* sort sth out; **jdn aus dem ~ bringen** (fig) to put sb off his stroke (*Brit*), to throw sb off track (*US*); **wieder im richtigen ~ sein** (fig) to be back on track *or* on the rails (*Brit inf*) *or* on the right lines (*Brit inf*); **wieder ins richtige ~ kommen** (fig) to get back on track *or* on the rails (*Brit inf*) *or* on the right lines (*Brit inf*)

Gleis-: Gleis|an|la|gen PL railway (*Brit*) or railroad (*US*) lines pl; **Gleis|an|schluss** ▲ M works siding; **Gleis|ar|bei|ten** PL work on the line, line or track repairs pl; **Gleis|bau** M , no pl railway (*Brit*) or railroad (*US*) construction; **Gleis|bau|stel|le** F place where work is being done on the line; **überall auf der Strecke waren ~n** work was being done all along the line; **Gleis|bett** NT ballast; **Gleis|brem|se** F rail brake; **Gleis|drei|eck** NT triangular junction

-glei|sig [glaizɪç] ADJ suf (lit, fig) -track; **eingleisig** single-track; **mehrgleisig** multi-track; **eine eingleisige Denkweise** a narrow-minded way of thinking

Gleis-: Gleis|ket|te F caterpillar® track; **Gleis|ket|ten|fahr|zeug** NT caterpillar® vehicle; **Gleis|kör|per** M railway (*Brit*) or railroad (*US*) embankment

Gleis|ner ['glaisnɐ] M -s, -, **Gleis|ne|rin** [-ərɪn] F -, -nen (old) hypocrite, dissembler (liter)

gleis|ne|risch ['glaisnərɪʃ] ADJ (old) dissembling (liter), hypocritical

glei|ßen ['glaisn] VI (liter) to gleam, to glisten

Gleit-: Gleit|boot NT hydroplane; **Gleit|bü|gel** M (Elec) pantograph, current collector

glei|ten ['glaitn] pret **glitt** [glɪt], ptp **geglitten** [gə'glɪtn] VI **a** aux sein (Vogel, Flugzeug, Tänzer, Boot, Skier, Schlange) to glide; (Blick) to pass, to range; (Hand) to slide, to glide; **ein Lächeln glitt über ihr Gesicht** a smile flickered across her face; **sein Auge über etw** (acc) **~ lassen** to cast an eye over sth; **die Finger über etw** (acc) **~ lassen** to glide or slide one's fingers over or across sth **b** aux sein (= rutschen) to slide; (Auto) to skid; (= entgleiten: Gegenstand) to slip; (geh: = ausrutschen) to slip; **zu Boden ~** to slip to the ground; (auf den Fußboden) to slip to the floor; **ins Wasser ~** to slide or slip into the water; **ins Gleiten kommen** to start to slide or slip **c** (Ind inf: = gleitende Arbeitszeit haben) to have flex(i)time

glei|tend ADJ **~e Löhne** or **Lohnskala** sliding wage scale; **~e Arbeitszeit** flexible working hours pl, flex(i)time; **~er Übergang** gradual transition; **~er Ruhestand** gradual retirement

Glei|ter ['glaitɐ] M -s, - (Aviat) glider

Gleit-: Gleit|flug M glide; **im ~ niedergehen** to glide or plane down; **Gleit|flug|zeug** NT glider; **Gleit|klau|sel** F (Comm) escalator clause; **Gleit|kom|ma** NT floating point; **Gleit|ku|fe** F (Aviat) landing skid; **Gleit|mit|tel** NT (Med) lubricant; **Gleit|schirm** M paraglider; **Gleit|schirm|flie|gen** NT -s, no pl paragliding; **Gleit|schirm|flie|ger(in)** M(F) paraglider; **Gleit|schutz** M (Aut) anti-skid(-ding) device; **Gleit|se|geln** NT , no pl hanggliding; **Gleit|segler** M (Fluggerät) hang-glider; **Gleit|segler(in)** M(F) hang-glider; **Gleit|sicht|bril|le** F varifocals pl; **Gleit|tag** M flexiday; **Gleit|wachs** NT (für Skier) wax; **Gleit|win|kel** M gliding angle; **Gleit|zeit** F flex(i)time

Glen|check ['glɛntʃɛk] M -(s), -s glencheck

Glet|scher ['glɛtʃɐ] M -s, - glacier

Glet|scher-: glet|scher|ar|tig ADJ glacial; **Glet|scher|bach** M glacial stream; **Glet|scher|brand** M glacial sunburn; **Glet|scher|bril|le** F sunglasses pl; **Glet|scher|eis** NT glacial ice; **Glet|scher|feld** NT glacier; **Glet|scher|for|schung** F glaciology; **Glet|scher|müh|le** F (Geol) moulin; **Glet|scher|ski|fah|ren** NT glacier skiing; **Glet|scher|spal|te** F crevasse; **Glet|scher|tor** NT mouth (of glacier); **Glet|scher|was|ser** NT , no pl glacier water; **Glet|scher|zun|ge** F glacier snout

Glib|ber ['glɪbɐ] M -s, no pl (inf) slime

glib|be|rig ['glɪbərɪç] ADJ (inf) slimy

glich pret von **gleichen**

Glied [gliːt] NT -(e)s, -er [-dɐ] **a** (= Körperteil) limb, member (form); (= Fingerglied, Zehenglied) joint; **seine ~er recken** to stretch (oneself); **an allen ~ern zittern** to be shaking all over; **der Schreck fuhr ihm in alle ~er** the shock made him shake all over; **der Schreck sitzt** or **steckt ihr noch in den ~ern** she is still shaking with (Brit) or from (esp US) the shock; **sich** (dat) **alle ~er brechen** to break every bone in one's body **b** (= Penis) penis, organ (form) **c** (= Kettenglied, fig) link **d** (= Teil) section, part; (von Grashalm) segment **e** (= Mitglied) member; (Mil etc) rank; (Bibl) generation; (Math) term; **aus dem ~ treten** (Mil) to step forward (out of the ranks); **ins ~ zurücktreten** (Mil) to step back into the ranks

Glie|der-: Glie|der|arm|band NT (von Uhr) expanding bracelet; **Glie|der|bau** M , no pl limb structure; (= Körperbau) build; **Glie|der|füßer** [-fyːsɐ] M -s, - usu pl (Zool) arthropod; **glie|der|lahm** ADJ heavy-limbed, weary; **ich bin ganz ~** my limbs are so stiff

glie|dern ['gliːdɐn] VT **a** (= ordnen) to structure, to order, to organize **b** (= unterteilen) to (sub)divide (in +acc into) → auch **gegliedert** VR (= zerfallen in) **sich ~ in** (+acc) to (sub)divide into; (= bestehen aus) to consist of

Glie|der-: Glie|der|pup|pe F jointed doll; (= Marionette) (string) puppet, marionette; (Art) lay figure; **Glie|der|rei|ßen** NT rheumatic pains pl; **Glie|der|satz** M (Ling) period; **Glie|der|schmer|zen** PL painful limbs pl (and joints pl); **Glie|der|schwe|re** F heaviness in one's limbs; **Glie|der|tier** NT articulate

Glie|de|rung ['gliːdərʊŋ] F -, -en **a** (= das Gliedern) structuring, organization; (= das Unterteilen) subdivision **b** (= Aufbau) structure; (= Unterteilung, von Organisation) subdivision **c** (= Aufstellung in Reihe etc) formation

Glie|der-: Glie|der|zu|cken NT -s, no pl twitching of the limbs; **Glie|der|zug** M articulated train

Glied-: Glied|kir|che F member church; **Glied|ma|ßen** PL limbs pl; **Glied|satz** M (Ling) subordinate clause; **Glied|staat** M member or constituent state; **glied|wei|se** ADV (Mil) in ranks

glim|men ['glɪmən] pret **glomm** or (rare) **glimmte** [glɔm, 'glɪmtə], ptp **geglommen** or (rare) **geglimmt** [gə'glɔmən, gə'glɪmt] VI to glow; (Feuer, Asche auch) to smoulder (Brit), to smolder (US); **~der Hass** (geh) smouldering (Brit) or smoldering (US) hatred; **noch glomm ein Funken Hoffnung in ihm** (geh) a ray of hope still glimmered within him

Glim|mer ['glɪmɐ] M -s, - **a** (Min) mica **b** (rare: = Schimmer) gleam, glint

glim|mern ['glɪmɐn] VI to glimmer

Glim|mer|schie|fer M (Min) mica schist

Glimm-: Glimm|lam|pe F glow lamp; **Glimm|stän|gel** ▲ M (dated inf) fag (esp Brit inf), cigarette, butt (US inf)

glimpf|lich ['glɪmpflɪç] ADJ (= mild) mild, light, lenient; Unfall minor; Verletzungen slight, light; Folgen negligible; **wegen des ~en Ausgangs des Unfalls** because the accident wasn't too serious; **einen ~en Ausgang nehmen** to pass off without serious consequences ADV bestrafen mildly; **~ bestraft werden** to receive a mild punishment; **~ davonkommen** to get off lightly; **mit jdm ~ umgehen** or verfahren to treat sb mildly or leniently; **mit Gefangenem ~ umgehen** to treat sb humanely; **~ abgehen** or ablaufen or verlaufen to pass (off) without serious consequences; **die Sache ist für sie ~ abgegangen** or verlaufen they got off lightly

Glitsch|bahn F (dial) slide

glit|schen ['glɪtʃn] VI aux sein (inf) to slip (aus out of)

glit|schig ['glɪtʃɪç] ADJ (inf) slippery, slippy (inf)

glitt pret von **gleiten**

Glit|zer- ['glɪtsɐ] in cpds glitzy (inf)

glit|zern ['glɪtsɐn] VI to glitter; (Stern auch) to twinkle

Glit|zer|welt ['glɪtsɐ-] F (usu pej) glitzy world, glitz; (der Schickeria) (world of the) glitterati; (des Films etc) wonder world

glo|bal [glo'baːl] ADJ **a** (= weltweit) global, world-wide; **~e Erwärmung** global warming **b** (= ungefähr, pauschal) general ADV **a** (= weltweit) world-wide; **~ verbreitet** global, world-wide **b** (= pauschal) **sich** (dat) **etw ~ vorstellen** to have a general idea of sth; **jdm etw ~ erläutern** to give sb a general idea of sth; **~ gerechnet** in round figures

glo|ba|li|sie|ren [globali'ziːrən] ptp **globalisiert** VT to globalize

Glo|ba|li|sie|rung F -, no pl globalization

Glo|ba|li|sie|rungs|geg|ner(in) M(F) anti-globalization protester, antiglobalist

Global-: Glo|bal|steu|e|rung F overall control; **Glo|bal|stra|te|gie** F (Pol) global or worldwide strategy

Glo|ben pl von **Globus**

Glo|be|trot|ter ['gloːbətrɔtɐ, gloˈptrɔtɐ] M -s, -, **Glo|be|trot|te|rin** [-ərɪn] F -, -nen globetrotter

Glo|bu|li ['gloːbuli] PL (Pharm) globules pl

Glo|bus ['gloːbʊs] M - or -ses, **Glo|ben** or -se globe; (inf: = Kopf) nut (inf)

Glöck|chen ['glœkçən] NT -s, - (little) bell

Glo|cke ['glɔkə] F -, -n **a** (auch Blüte) bell; (= Käseglocke etc) cover; (= Florettglocke) coquille; (in Labor) bell jar; (= Taucherglocke) (diving) bell; (= Damenhut) cloche; (inf: = Herrenhut) bowler; **nach den ~n von Big Ben** after the chimes from Big Ben, after Big Ben strikes; **etw an die große ~ hängen** (inf) to shout sth from the rooftops; **wissen, was die ~ geschlagen hat** (inf) to know what one is in for (inf), to know what's in store for one; **über der Stadt wölbte sich eine dichte ~ von Rauch** a thick pall of smoke hung over the city **b** (sl: = Hoden) **Glocken** PL balls pl

Glocken-: Glo|cken|bal|ken M (bell) yoke; **Glo|cken|blu|me** F bellflower, campanula; **Glo|cken|bron|ze** F bell metal; **glo|cken|för|mig** ADJ bell-shaped; **Glo|cken|ge|läut** NT , **Glo|cken|ge|läu|te** NT (peal of) bells pl; **Glo|cken|gie|ßer(in)** M(F) bellfounder; **Glo|cken|gie|ße|rei** F bellfoundry; **Glo|cken|guss** ▲ M bell-founding; **glo|cken|hell** ADJ (geh) bell-like; Stimme auch as clear as a bell; **Glo|cken|helm** M top of a/the bell; **Glo|cken|klang** M ringing or (esp hell auch) pealing (of bells); **Glo|cken|klöp|pel** M clapper, tongue (of a/the bell); **Glo|cken|läu|ten** NT -s, no pl (peal of) bells pl; **Glo|cken|man|tel** M cope (for founding bell); **glo|cken|rein** ADJ (geh) bell-like; Stimme auch as clear as a bell; **Glo|cken|rock** M flared skirt; **Glo|cken|schlag** M stroke of a/the bell; (von Uhr auch) chime; **es ist mit dem ~ 6 Uhr** on the stroke it will be 6 o'clock; **auf den** or **mit dem ~** on the stroke of eight/nine etc; (= genau pünktlich) on the dot; **Glo|cken|spei|se** F bell metal; **Glo|cken|spiel** NT (in Turm) carillon; (automatisch auch) chimes pl; (= Instrument) glockenspiel; **Glo|cken|strang** M bell-rope; **Glo|cken|stu|be** F belfry; **Glo|cken|stuhl** M bell cage; **Glo|cken|ton** M pl -töne sound of a/the bell; **Glo|cken|turm** M belltower, belfry; **Glo|cken|wei|he** F consecration of a/the bell; **Glo|cken|zei|chen** NT ring of a/the bell; **auf ein ~ erschien der Butler** a ring on the bell summoned the butler; **Glo|cken|zug** M (= Glockenstrang) bell rope; (= Klingelschnur) bell pull, bell cord

glo|ckig ['glɔkɪç] ADJ bell-shaped; Kleid, Rock flared

Deutsche Rechtschreibreform (siehe Anhang): ▲ neue Schreibung △ alte Schreibung   + trennbare Verben

Glöck|ner ['glœknə] M **-s**, **-**, **Glöck|ne|rin** [-ərɪn] F **-**, **-nen** bell-ringer; „Der ~ von Notre--Dame" "The Hunchback of Notre Dame"

glomm *pret von* **glimmen**

Glo|ria[1] ['gloːriaː] NT **-s**, **-s** (*Eccl*) gloria, Gloria → **Glanz**

Glo|ria[2] F - *or* nt -s, *no pl* (*usu iro*) glory

Glo|rie ['gloːriə] F **-**, **-n** **a** *no pl* (= *Ruhm*) glory, splendour (*Brit*), splendor (*US*) **b** (= *Heiligenschein*) halo

Glo|ri|en|schein M halo; (*fig*) aura

glo|ri|fi|zie|ren [gloːrifiˈtsiːrən] *ptp* **glorifiziert** VT to glorify

Glo|ri|fi|zie|rung F **-**, **-en** glorification

Glo|ri|o|le [gloˈrioːlə] F **-**, **-n** halo; (*fig*) aura

glo|ri|os [gloˈrioːs] ADJ (*oft iro*) glorious, magnificent

glor|reich ['gloːrɐ-] **ADJ** glorious; der ~e Rosenkranz (*Eccl*) the Glorious Mysteries *pl* **ADV** zurückkehren, herrschen victoriously; ~ siegen to have *or* achieve a glorious victory; seine Laufbahn ~ beenden to bring one's career to a glorious conclusion

Gloss [glɔs] NT **-**, **-** gloss

Glos|sar [glɔˈsaːɐ] NT **-s**, **-e** glossary

Glos|se ['glɔsə] F **-**, **-n** **a** (*Liter*) gloss (zu on) **b** (*Press, Rad etc*) commentary **c** **Glossen** PL (*inf*) snide *or* sneering comments; seine ~n über jdn/etw machen (*inf*) to make snide comments about sb/sth

Glos|sen|schrei|ber(in) M(F) (*Press*) commentator

glos|sie|ren [glɔˈsiːrən] *ptp* **glossiert** VT **a** (*Liter*) to gloss, to write a gloss/glosses on **b** (= *bespötteln*) to sneer at **c** (*Press, Rad etc*) to do a commentary on, to commentate on

Glotz-: Glotz|au|ge NT **a** (*usu pl: inf*) staring *or* goggle (*inf*) eye; ~n machen to stare (goggle--eyed), to gawp **b** (*Med*) exophthalmia (*spec*); **glotz|äu|gig** ADJ, ADV (*inf*) goggle-eyed (*inf*)

Glot|ze ['glɔtsə] F **-**, **-n** **a** (= *Fernseher*) gogglebox (*Brit inf*), one-eyed monster (*Brit pej inf*), boob tube (*US inf*) **b** (= *Bildschirm*) screen

glot|zen ['glɔtsn] VI (*pej inf*) (auf, in +acc at) to stare, to gawp, to gape

Glo|xi|nie [glɔˈksiːniə] F **-**, **-n** (*Bot*) gloxinia

Glubsch|au|ge ['glʊpʃ-] NT (*inf*) = **Glotzauge a**

gluck [glʊk] INTERJ **a** (*von Huhn*) cluck **b** (*von Flüssigkeit*) glug; ~ ~, weg war er (*inf*) glug glug, and he'd gone

Glück [glʏk] ⊘ 50.5 NT **-(e)s**, (*rare*) **-e** **a** luck; ein seltenes ~ a funny stroke *or* piece of luck; ~/kein ~ haben to be lucky/unlucky; er hat das ~ gehabt, zu ... he was lucky enough to ..., he had the good fortune to ...; ~ gehabt! that was lucky; auf gut ~ (= *aufs Geratewohl*) on the off chance; (= *unvorbereitet*) trusting to luck; (= *wahllos*) at random; ein ~! how lucky!, what a stroke *or* piece of luck!; ein ~, dass ... it is/was lucky that ...; es ist ein wahres ~, dass ... it's really lucky that ...; du hast ~ im Unglück gehabt it could have been a great deal worse (for you); in ~ und Unglück in good times and in bad, through thick and thin; viel ~ (bei ...)! good luck (with ...)!, the best of luck (with ...)!; bei Frauen haben to be successful with women; jdm ~ für etw wünschen to wish sb luck for sth; jdm ~ wünschen zu ... to congratulate sb on ...; er wünscht dir ~ bei deiner Prüfung he wishes you (good) luck in (*Brit*) *or* on (*US*) your exam; ich wünsche dir ~ bei deiner Prüfung good luck in (*Brit*) or on (*US*) your exam; jdm zum neuen Jahr/zum Geburtstag ~ wünschen to wish sb (a) Happy New Year/ happy birthday; zum ~ luckily, fortunately; zu seinem ~ luckily *or* fortunately for him; das ist dein ~! that's lucky for you!; ~ auf! (*Min*) good luck!; mehr ~ als Verstand haben to have more luck than brains; sie weiß noch nichts von ihrem ~ (*iro*) she doesn't know anything about it

yet; damit wirst du bei ihr kein ~ haben you won't have any joy with her (with that) (*inf*), that won't work with her; ~ bringend lucky; ~ verheißend (*liter, Religion, Gesichtsausdruck*) which holds out a promise of happiness; *Zeichen etc* propitious (*form*), auspicious; sein ~ machen to make one's fortune; sein ~ probieren *or* versuchen to try one's luck; er kann von ~ reden *or* sagen, dass ... he can count himself lucky that ..., he can thank his lucky stars that ... (*inf*); sein ~ mit Füßen treten to turn one's back on fortune; ~ muss der Mensch haben (*inf*) my/your *etc* luck is in; das war das ~ des Tüchtigen he/she deserved the break (*inf*), he/ she deserved his/her good luck; das hat mir gerade noch zu meinem ~ gefehlt! (*iro*) that was all I wanted; man kann niemanden zu seinem ~ zwingen (*prov*) you can lead a horse to water but you can't make him drink (*Prov*); ein Kind des ~s sein (*geh*) to have been born under a lucky star; ein Stiefkind des ~s sein (*geh*) to be a born loser; jeder ist seines ~es Schmied (*Prov*) life is what you make it (*prov*), everyone is the architect of his own future **b** (= *Freude*) happiness; eheliches ~ wedded *or* marital bliss; er ist ihr ganzes ~ she is her whole life; das Streben nach ~ the pursuit of happiness; ~ und Glas, wie leicht bricht das! (*Prov*) happiness is such a fragile thing

Glück-: Glück|auf [glʏkˈʔaʊf] NT **-s**, *no pl* (cry of) "good luck"; **glück|brin|gend** △ ADJ → **Glück**

Glu|cke ['glʊkə] F **-**, **-n** (= *Bruthenne*) broody *or* sitting hen; (*mit Jungen*) mother hen; wie eine ~ ist sie ständig um ihre Kinder herum she fusses (a)round her children like a mother hen

glu|cken ['glʊkn] VI **a** (= *brüten*) to brood; (= *brüten wollen*) to go broody; (*fig inf*) to sit around **b** (= *Küken rufen*) to cluck

glü|cken ['glʏkn] VI *aux sein* to be a success, to be successful; nicht ~ to be a failure, not to be a success; (*Plan auch*) to miscarry; ihm glückt alles/nichts everything/nothing he does is a success, he succeeds/fails at whatever he does; geglückt (*Feier, Experiment, Aktion*) successful; *Wahl* lucky; *Überraschung* real; dieses Bild/die Torte ist dir gut geglückt your picture/cake has turned out very well; endlich ist es ihm geglückt at last he managed it; es wollte nicht ~ it wouldn't go right

glu|ckern ['glʊkɐn] VI to glug

glück|haft ADJ (*geh*) *Erinnerung, Ergebnis, Augenblick* happy

Gluck|hen|ne ['glʊk-] F = **Glucke**

glück|lich ['glʏklɪç] ⊘ 41, 50.2 **ADJ** **a** (= *erfolgreich, vom Glück begünstigt*) lucky, fortunate; (= *vorteilhaft, treffend, erfreulich*) happy; ~e Reise! bon voyage!, pleasant journey!; er kann sich ~ schätzen(, dass ...) he can count *or* consider himself lucky (that ...); wer ist der/die Glückliche? who is the lucky man/woman/girl *etc*? → Hand h **b** (= *froh, selig*) happy; ein ~es Ende, ein ~er Ausgang a happy ending; ~ machen to bring happiness; jdn ~ machen to make sb happy, to bring sb happiness **ADV** **a** (= *mit Glück*) by *or* through luck; (= *vorteilhaft, treffend, erfreulich*) happily; ~ zurückkommen (= *in Sicherheit*) to come back safely **b** (= *froh, selig*) happily; die ~-heiteren Tage der Kindheit the bright and happy days of childhood

glück|li|cher|wei|se ['glʏklɪçɐˈvaɪzə] ADV luckily, fortunately

Glück-: glück|los ADJ hapless, luckless; **Glück|sa|che** F = **Glückssache**

Glücks-: Glücks|au|to|mat M (*fig*) gaming machine; **Glücks|bo|te** M , **Glücks|bo|tin** F bearer of (the) glad *or* good tidings; **Glücks|bot|schaft** F glad *or* good tidings *pl*; **Glücks|brin|ger**[1] [-brɪŋɐ] M **-s**, **-** (= *Talisman*) lucky charm; **Glücks|brin|ger**[2] [-brɪŋə] M **-s**, **-**, **Glücks|brin|ge|rin** [-ərɪn] F **-**, **-nen** bearer

of (the) glad tidings; **Glücks|bu|de** F try--your-luck stall

glück|se|lig [glʏkˈzeːlɪç] ADJ blissfully happy, blissful; *Lächeln, Gesichtsausdruck auch* rapturous

Glück|se|lig|keit F bliss, rapture (*liter*)

gluck|sen ['glʊksn] VI **a** (= *lachen*) (*Kleinkind*) to gurgle; (*Erwachsener*) to chortle **b** (= *gluckern*) to glug

Glücks-: Glücks|fall M piece *or* stroke of luck; durch einen ~ by a lucky chance; im ~ kannst du mit einer Geldstrafe rechnen if you're lucky you'll get away with a fine; **Glücks|fee** F (*fig hum*) good fairy, fairy godmother; **Glücks|ge|fühl** NT feeling of happiness; **Glücks|göt|tin** F goddess of luck; die ~ ist mir nicht hold (*hum, geh*) (*Dame*) Fortune has deserted me; **Glücks|ha|fen** M (*S Ger, Aus*) try-your-luck stall; **Glücks|kind** NT child of Fortune; **Glücks|klee** M four--leaf(ed) clover; **Glücks|li|nie** F line of fortune *or* luck; **Glücks|pfen|nig** M (*fig*) lucky penny, (*shiny*) coin supposed to bring luck; **Glücks|pil|le** F (*inf*) (get-)happy pill; **Glücks|pilz** M lucky beggar (*Brit inf*) *or* devil (*inf*); **Glücks|rad** NT wheel of fortune; **Glücks|rit|ter** M adventurer; **Glücks|sa|che** F das ist ~ it's a matter of luck; ich hab gedacht ... – Denken ist ~ (*inf*) I thought ... – you thought?; **Glücks|schwein(|chen)** NT pig *as a symbol of good luck*; **Glücks|spiel** NT game of chance; **Glücks|spie|ler(in)** M(F) gambler; **Glücks|stern** M lucky star; **Glücks|sträh|ne** F lucky streak; eine ~ haben to be on a lucky streak; **Glücks|tag** M lucky day

glück|strah|lend ADJ beaming with happiness; *Kind, Frau auch* radiant (with happiness)

Glücks-: Glücks|tref|fer M stroke of luck; (*beim Schießen, Ftbl*) lucky shot, fluke (*inf*); **Glücks|um|stand** M fortunate circumstance; **Glücks|zahl** F lucky number

glück|ver|hei|ßend △ ADJ → **Glück**

Glück|wunsch M 50.6, 51.1, 51.2, 51.3 M congratulations *pl* (zu on); herzlichen ~ congratulations; herzlichen ~ zum Geburtstag! happy birthday, many happy returns of the day; Glückwünsche zur Verlobung/zur bestandenen Prüfung congratulations on your engagement/on passing your examination

Glück|wunsch-: Glück|wunsch|ad|res|se F message of congratulations, congratulatory message; **Glück|wunsch|kar|te** F greetings card; **Glück|wunsch|schrei|ben** NT letter of congratulations; **Glück|wunsch|te|le|gramm** NT greetings telegram

Glüh- (*Elec*): **Glüh|bir|ne** F (electric) light bulb; **Glüh|draht** M filament

glü|hen ['glyːən] **VI** to glow; (*fig auch*) to be a-glow; der Ofen/die Sonne glüht, dass man es nicht aushalten kann the fire/sun is too hot to bear; vor Fieber/Scham ~ to be flushed with fever/shame; vor Verlangen *etc* ~ (*liter*) to burn with desire *etc* **VT** to heat until red-hot

glü|hend **ADJ** glowing; (= *heiß glühend*) *Metall* red-hot; *Hitze* blazing; (*fig* = *leidenschaftlich*) ardent; *Hass* burning; *Wangen* flushed, burning **ADV** lieben madly, passionately; ~ heiß scorching; *Sonne auch* blazing hot; jdn ~ beneiden to be consumed by envy for sb; jdn ~ verehren to worship sb; sich ~ hassen to have a burning hatred for one another

Glüh-: Glüh|fa|den M (*Elec*) filament; **Glüh|ker|ze** F (*Aut*) heater *or* incandescent plug; **Glüh|lam|pe** F (*form*) electric light bulb; **Glüh|ofen** M (*Metal*) annealing furnace; **Glüh|strumpf** M (gas) mantle; **Glüh|wein** M glühwein, mulled wine, glogg (*US*); **Glüh|würm|chen** NT glow-worm; (*fliegend*) firefly

Glu|ko|se [gluˈkoːzə] F **-**, **-n** glucose

Glupsch|au|ge ['glʊpʃ-] NT (*N Ger inf*) = **Glotzauge a**

glup|schen ['glʊpʃn̩] **VI** (*N Ger inf*) (*auf, in +acc at*) to gawp, to gape

Glut [gluːt] **F -, -en a** (= *glühende Masse, Kohle*) embers *pl*; (= *Tabaksglut*) burning ash; (= *Hitze*) heat **b** (*fig liter*) (= *glühende Farbe, Hitze*) glow; (*auf Gesicht*) flush, redness; (= *Leidenschaft*) ardour (*Brit*), ardor (*US*)

Glu|ta|mat [gluːta'maːt] **NT -(e)s, -e** glutamate

Glu|ta|min [gluːta'miːn] **NT -s, -e** glutamine

Glu|ta|min|säu|re **F** glutamic acid

Glut-: glut|äu|gig **ADJ** (*geh*) with smouldering (*Brit*) or smoldering (*US*) eyes; **Glut|ball** **M** (*poet*) fiery orb (*poet*); **Glu|ten** [gluː'teːn] **NT -s, no pl** (*Chem, Physiol*) gluten

Glu|ten-: glu|ten|frei **ADJ** *Lebensmittel* gluten-free; **glu|ten|hal|tig** **ADJ** *Lebensmittel* gluten-containing, containing gluten *pred*

Glut-: Glut|hauch **M** (*liter*) torrid or sweltering heat; **glut|heiß** **ADJ** (*geh*) swelteringly hot; *Sand, Gesicht* red-hot; **Glut|hit|ze** **F** sweltering heat; **glut|rot** **ADJ** (*liter*) fiery red; **Glut|rö|te** **F** (*liter*) fiery red; **glut|voll** **ADJ** passionate; **Glut|wind** **M** (*liter*) torrid wind

Gly|ce|rin [glytse'riːn] **NT** = **Glyzerin**

Gly|kol [gly'koːl] **NT -s, -e** glycol

Gly|ze|rin [glytse'riːn] **NT -s, no pl** (*Chem*) glycerin(e)

Gly|zi|nie [gly'tsiːniə] **F -, -n** wisteria

GmbH [geːɛmbeː'haː] **F -, -s** *abbr von* **Gesellschaft mit beschränkter Haftung** limited company, Ltd

Gna|de ['gnaːdə] **F -, -n** (= *Barmherzigkeit*) mercy; (= *heilig machende Gnade*) grace; (= *Gunst*) favour (*Brit*), favor (*US*); (= *Verzeihung*) pardon; **um ~ bitten** to ask for or crave (*liter*) mercy; **jdn um ~ für seine Sünden bitten** to ask sb to pardon (one for) one's sins; **jds ~ finden, bei jdm** or **vor jdm ~ finden** to find favo(u)r with sb or in sb's eyes; **~ vor** or **für Recht ergehen lassen** to temper justice with mercy; **etw aus ~ und Barmherzigkeit tun** to do sth out of the kindness of one's heart; **ohne ~** without mercy; **~!** mercy!; **bei jdm in (hohen) ~n stehen** (*old*) to stand high in sb's favo(u)r; **von jds ~n** by the grace of sb; **Fürst von Gottes ~n** (*Hist*) by the Grace of God, Prince; **jdn in ~n entlassen** to allow to go unpunished; **jdn in ~n wieder aufnehmen** to restore sb to favo(u)r; **sich** (*dat*) **eine ~ erbitten** (*geh*) to ask or crave (*liter*) a favo(u)r; **jdm eine ~ gewähren** (*geh*) to grant sb a favo(u)r; **Euer ~n!** (*Hist*) Your Grace; **die Jungfrau der ~n** (*Eccl*) Our Lady of Mercy; **die ~ haben, etw zu tun** (*iro*) to graciously consent to do sth

gna|den ['gnaːdn̩] **VI (dann) gnade dir Gott!** (then) God help you, (then) heaven have mercy on you

Gna|den-: Gna|den|akt **M** act of mercy; **Gna|den|bild** **NT** (*Eccl*) picture or (= *Figur*) statue with miraculous powers; **Gna|den|brot** **NT**, *no pl* **jdm das ~ geben** to keep sb in his/her old age; **einem Pferd das ~ geben** to put a horse out to grass; **das ~ bei jdm essen** to be provided for by sb (in one's old age); **Gna|den|er|lass** ▲ **M** (*Jur*) general pardon; **Gna|den|frist** **F** (*temporary*) reprieve; **eine ~ von 24 Stunden** a 24 hour(s') reprieve, 24 hours' grace; **Gna|den|ge|such** **NT** plea for clemency; **Gna|den|kraut** **NT** hedge hyssop; **gna|den|los** ▣ADJ merciless ▣ADV mercilessly; **Gna|den|lo|sig|keit** **F -, no pl** mercilessness; **Gna|den|mit|tel** **PL** (*Eccl*) means *pl* of grace; **gna|den|reich** **ADJ** (*old, Eccl*) gracious; **Maria, die Gnadenreiche** Our Gracious Lady; **Gna|den|schuss** ▲ **M** coup de grâce (*by shooting*); **Gna|den|stoß** **M** coup de grâce (*with sword etc*) (*auch fig*); **Gna|den|tod** **M** (*geh*) mercy killing, euthanasia; **Gna|den|ver|hei|ßung** **F** promise of grace; **gna|den|voll** **ADJ** (*old, Eccl*) gracious; **Gna|den|weg** **M**, *no pl* **auf dem ~** by a pardon; **jedem Häftling steht der ~**

offen every prisoner is at liberty to ask for a pardon

gnä|dig ['gnɛːdɪç] ▣ADJ (= *barmherzig*) merciful; (= *gunstvoll, herablassend*) gracious; *Strafe* lenient; (= *freundlich*) kind; **das ~e Fräulein** (*form*) the young lady; **die ~e Frau** (*form*) the mistress, madam; **der ~e Herr** (*old*) the master; **darf ich das ~e Fräulein zum Tanz bitten?** (*dated*) may I have the pleasure of this dance? (*form*); **~es Fräulein** (*dated*) madam; (= *jüngere Dame*) miss; **~e Frau** (*form*) madam, ma'am; **~er Herr** (*old*) sir; **meine Gnädige** (*dated*) or **Gnädigste** (*dated*) my dear madam; **~er Gott!** (*inf*) merciful heavens! (*inf*); **Gott sei uns ~!** (*geh*) (may the good) Lord preserve us; **sei doch so ~ und mach mal Platz!** (*iro*) would you be so good as to make some room?
▣ADV (= *milde*) urteilen leniently; *zensieren* generously; (= *herablassend*) lächeln, nicken graciously; **~ davonkommen** to get off lightly; **es ~ machen** to be lenient, to show leniency; **machen wir s ~ mit dem Hausputz** let's take it easy with the cleaning

gnat|zig ['gnatsɪç] **ADJ** (*dial*) bearish (*inf*), bad-tempered

Gnat|zig|keit **F -, no pl** (*dial*) bearishness (*inf*), bad temper

Gneis [gnais] **M -es, -e** [-zə] (*Geol*) gneiss

Gnom [gnoːm] **M -en, -e** gnome

gno|men|haft **ADJ** gnomish

Gno|sis ['gnoːzɪs] **F -, no pl** (*Rel*) gnosis

Gnos|tik ['gnɔstɪk] **F -, no pl** (*Rel*) gnosticism

Gnos|ti|ker ['gnɔstɪkɐ] **M -s, -, Gnos|ti|ke|rin** [-ərɪn] **F -, -nen** (*Rel*) gnostic

gnos|tisch ['gnɔstɪʃ] **ADJ** (*Rel*) gnostic

Gnos|ti|zis|mus [gnɔsti'tsɪsmʊs] **M -, no pl** (*Rel*) Gnosticism

Gnu [gnuː] **NT -s, -s** (*Zool*) gnu, wildebeest

Go [goː] **NT -, no pl** go (*Japanese board game*)

Goal [goːl] **NT -s, -s** (*Aus, Sw: Sport*) goal

Goal- [goːl-] (*Aus, Sw*): **Goal|get|ter** [-gɛtɐ] **M -s, -, Goal|get|te|rin** [-ərɪn] **F -, -nen** scorer; **Goal|kee|per** [-kiːpə] **M -s, -, Goal|kee|pe|rin** [-ərɪn] **F -, -nen**, **Goal|mann** **M** *pl* **-männer** goalkeeper, goalie (*inf*); **Goal|stan|ge** **F** crossbar

Go|be|lin [gobə'lɛ̃ː] **M -s, -s** tapestry, Gobelin; (= *Webart*) tapestry weave

Go|ckel ['gɔkl̩] **M -s, -** (*esp S Ger, baby-talk*) cock; (*fig*) old goat (*inf*)

Gode|mi|ché [goːdmiˈʃeː] **M -, -s** dildo

Go|derl ['goːdɐl] **NT -s, -n jdm das ~ kratzen** (*Aus inf*) to butter sb up (*inf*)

Goe|the ['gøːtə] **M -s** Goethe

goe|thesch ['gøːtəʃ], **goe|thisch** ['gøːtɪʃ] **ADJ** Goethean

Go-go-Girl ['goːgoː-] **NT** go-go dancer or girl

Goi ['goːi] **M -(s), Gojim** ['goːjiːm, goˈjiːm] goy, Gentile

Go-in [goːˈɪn] **NT -(s), -s die Versammlung wurde durch ein ~ gestört** the meeting was disrupted (by demonstrators); **ein ~ veranstalten** to disrupt a/the meeting

Go|kart ▲ ['goːkaːt] **M -(s), -s** kart, go-cart

Go|lan [goˈlaːn] **M -s der** ~ the Golan

Go|lan|hö|hen **PL**, **Go|lan-Hö|hen** **PL** Golan Heights *pl*

Gold [gɔlt] **NT -(e)s, -[dəs] no pl** (*abbr* **Au**) (*lit, fig*) gold; **nicht mit ~ zu bezahlen** or **aufzuwiegen sein** to be worth one's weight in gold; **nicht für alles ~ der Welt** (*liter*) not for all the money in the world; **er hat ein Herz aus ~** he has a heart of gold; **er hat ~ in der Kehle** he has a golden voice; **zehnmal olympisches ~ holen** to win ten golds in the Olympics; **es ist nicht alles ~, was glänzt** (*Prov*) all that glitters or glisters is not gold (*Prov*) → **Morgenstunde, treu ADJ**

Gold- *in cpds* gold; (*von Farbe, Zool*) golden; **Gold|ader** **F** vein of gold; **Gold|am|mer** **F** yellowhammer; **Gold|am|sel** **F** golden oriole; **Gold|ar|beit** **F** goldwork; **Gold|bar|ren** **M** gold ingot; **Gold|barsch** **M** (= *Rotbarsch*) redfish; (= *Kaulbarsch*) ruff; **Gold|ba|sis** **F** gold basis; **eine Währung auf ~** a gold-based currency; **gold|be|stickt** [-bəʃtɪkt] **ADJ** embroidered with gold (*thread*); **gold|be|tresst** ▲ [-bətrɛst] **ADJ** trimmed with gold braid; **Gold|blech** **NT** gold foil; **gold|blond** **ADJ** golden blond; **Gold|bor|te** **F** gold edging *no pl*; **Gold|broi|ler** **M** (*dial Cook*) roast chicken; **Gold|de|ckung** **F** (*Fin*) gold backing; **Gold|doub|lé** **NT** gold-plated metal; **Gold|druck** **M a** *pl* **-drucke** gold print **b** *no pl* (= *Schrift*) gold lettering; **gold|durch|wirkt** [-dʊrçvɪrkt] **ADJ** shot with gold thread

gol|den ['gɔldn̩] ▣ADJ *attr* (*lit, fig*) golden; (= *aus Gold*) gold, golden (*liter*); **~e Schallplatte** gold disc; **~er Humor** irrepressible sense of humour (*Brit*) or humor (*US*); **~e Worte** wise words, words of wisdom; **ein ~es Herz haben** to have a heart of gold; **~e Berge versprechen** to promise the moon (and the stars); **die ~e Mitte** or **den ~en Mittelweg wählen** to strike a happy medium; **sich** (*dat*) **eine ~e Nase verdienen** to make a mint; **~er Schnitt** (*Math, Art*) golden section; **das Goldene Buch** the visitors' book; **die Goldene Stadt** (*geh*) Prague; **die Goldene Horn** (*Geog*) the Golden Horn; **die Goldene Horde** (*Hist*) the Golden Horde; **das ~e Zeitalter** (*Myth, fig*) the golden age; **das Goldene Vlies** (*Myth*) the Golden Fleece; **das Goldene Kalb** (*Bibl*) the golden calf; **der Tanz ums Goldene Kalb** (*fig*) the worship of Mammon (*fig*) → **Brücke**
▣ADV like gold; **~ schimmern** to shimmer like gold

Gold-: Gold|esel **M** (*Liter*) gold-ass; **leider habe ich keinen ~** (*fig*) money doesn't grow on trees, I'm afraid; **Gold|fa|den** **M** gold thread; **gold|far|ben** [-farbn̩], **gold|far|big** **ADJ** golden, gold-coloured (*Brit*), gold-colored (*US*); **Gold|fe|der** **F** gold nib; **Gold|fie|ber** **NT** (*fig*) gold fever; **Gold|fisch** **M** goldfish; **sich** (*dat*) **einen ~ angeln** (*hum inf*) to make a rich catch, to marry money; **Gold|fuchs** **M a** (= *Pferd*) golden chestnut (*horse*) **b** (*old inf*) gold piece; **Gold|fül|lung** **F** (*Med*) gold filling; **gold|ge|fasst** ▲ **ADJ** *Brille* gold-rimmed; *Edelstein* set in gold; **gold|gelb** **ADJ** golden brown, old gold; **gold|ge|lockt** **ADJ** (*dated*) with golden locks; **gold|ge|rän|dert** [-gərɛndɐt] **ADJ** edged with gold; *Brille* gold-rimmed; **~e Bilanzen** highly profitable results; **Gold|ge|wicht** **NT** gold weight, ≈ troy weight; **Gold|glanz** **M** (*liter*) golden gleam; **gold|glän|zend** **ADJ** (*liter*) gleaming gold; **Gold|grä|ber** [-grɛːbɐ] **M -s, -, Gold|grä|be|rin** [-ərɪn] **F -, -nen** gold-digger; **Gold|grä|ber|stim|mung** **F** gold-rush mood; **Gold|gru|be** **F** (*lit, fig*) gold mine; **Gold|grund** **M**, *no pl* (*Art*) gold ground; **gold|hal|tig**, (*Aus*) **gold|häl|tig** **ADJ** gold-bearing, auriferous (*spec*); **Gold|hams|ter** **M** (*golden*) hamster

gol|dig ['gɔldɪç] **ADJ a** (*fig inf*: = *allerliebst*) sweet, cute; **du bist vielleicht ~!** (*iro*) the ideas you get! **b** (*poet*: = *golden*) golden; **~e Zeiten** golden days

Gold-: Gold|jun|ge **M** (*inf*) blue-eyed boy (*Brit inf*), golden boy (*inf*); (*Sport*) gold medallist (*Brit*) or medalist (*US*); **Gold|kä|fer** **M** (*inf*: = *reiches Mädchen*) rich girl; **Gold|kehl|chen** [-keːlçən] **NT -s, -** (*inf*) singer with a/the golden voice; **Gold|kind** **NT** (*inf*) little treasure (*inf*), dear child; **mein ~** (= *als Anrede*) (*my*) pet or precious; **Gold|klum|pen** **M** gold nugget; **Gold|küs|te** **F** (*Geog*) Gold Coast; **Gold|lack** **M a** (*Bot*) wallflower **b** (= *Glanzlack*) gold lacquer; **Gold|mäd|chen** **NT** (*inf*) blue-eyed girl (*Brit inf*), golden girl (*inf*);

(*Sport*) gold medallist (*Brit*) or medalist (*US*); **Gold|mark** F *pl* **-mark** (*Hist*) gold mark

Gold|me|dail|le F gold medal

Gold|me|dail|len|ge|win|ner(in) M(F) gold medallist (*Brit*) or medalist (*US*)

Gold-: Gold|mi|ne F gold mine; **Gold|mund|stück** NT gold tip; **Gold|mün|ze** F gold coin; **Gold|pa|pier** NT gold foil; **Gold|pa|ri|tät** F (*Fin*) gold parity; **Gold|preis** M gold price, price of gold; **Gold|pro|be** F assay (for gold); **Gold|rah|men** M gilt frame; **Gold|rand** M gold edge; **mit ~** with a gold edge; **Gold|rausch** M gold fever; **Gold|re|gen** M (*Bot*) laburnum; (= *Feuerwerkskörper*) Roman candle; (*fig*) riches *pl*; **gold|reich** ADJ rich in gold; **Gold|reif** M (*geh*) circlet of gold; (= *Ring*) gold ring; (= *Armband*) gold bracelet; **Gold|re|ser|ve** F (*Fin*) gold reserves *pl*; **gold|rich|tig** (*inf*) ADJ absolutely or dead (*inf*) right; *Mensch* all right (*inf*) ADV exactly right; *sich verhalten, machen, tun* perfectly; **du liegst (damit) ~** you're absolutely or dead (*inf*) right (there); **sie hat ~ gehandelt** what she did was absolutely right; **Gold|schatz** M golden treasure; (*von Geld*) hoard of gold; (*Kosewort*) treasure

Gold|schmied(in) M(F) goldsmith

Gold|schmie|de-: Gold|schmie|de|ar|beit F (= *Handwerk*) gold work; (= *Gegenstand*) worked gold article; **Gold|schmie|de|hand|werk** NT , **Gold|schmie|de|kunst** F gold work

Gold-: Gold|schmuck M gold jewellery (*Brit*) or jewelry (*US*); **Gold|schnitt** M , *no pl* gilt edging; **Gold|schnitt|aus|ga|be** F gilt-edged edition; **Gold|schrift** F gold lettering; **Gold|stück** NT piece of gold; (= *Münze*) gold coin or piece, piece of gold (*old*); (*fig inf*) jewel, treasure; **Gold|su|che** F search for gold; **Gold|su|cher(in)** M(F) gold-hunter; **Gold|ton** M *pl* **-töne** golden colour (*Brit*) or color (*US*); **Gold|to|pas** M yellow topaz; **Gold|tres|se** F gold braid; **Gold|über|zug** M layer of gold plate; **Gold|uhr** F gold watch; **gold|um|rän|dert, gold|um|ran|det** [-lʊmrandət] ADJ = goldgerändert; **Gold|vor|kom|men** NT gold deposit; **Gold|vor|rat** M (*Fin*) gold reserves *pl*; **Gold|waa|ge** F gold or bullion balance; **jedes Wort or alles auf die ~ legen** (= *sich vorsichtig ausdrücken*) to weigh one's words; (= *überempfindlich sein*) to be hypersensitive; **Gold|wäh|rung** F gold standard; **eine ~** a currency on the gold standard; **Gold|wa|ren** PL gold articles *pl*; **Gold|wä|scher(in)** M(F) gold panner; **Gold|wert** M , *no pl* value in gold; (= *Wert des Goldes*) value of gold; **Gold|zahn** M gold tooth

Go|lem ['goːlɛm] M **-s**, *no pl* golem

Golf[1] [gɔlf] M **-(e)s, -e** (= *Meerbusen*) gulf; **der ~ von Biskaya** the Bay of Biscay; **der (Persische) ~** the (Persian) Gulf

Golf[2] NT **-s**, *no pl* (*Sport*) golf

Golf- *in cpds* (*Sport*) golf; (*Geog, Pol*) Gulf

Golf|ball M golf ball

Gol|fer ['gɔlfɐ] M **-s, -**, **Gol|fe|rin** [-ərɪn] F **-, -nen** (*inf*) golfer

Golf-: Golf|klub M golf club; **Golf|krieg** M Gulf War; **Golf|platz** M golf course; **Golf|rat** M (*Pol*) Gulf Council; **Golf|schlä|ger** M golf club; **Golf|spiel** NT **das ~** golf; **Golf|spie|ler(in)** M(F) golfer; **Golf|staa|ten** PL **die ~** the Gulf States *pl*; **Golf|strom** M (*Geog*) Gulf Stream; **Golf|ta|sche** F golf bag, caddie; **Golf|wa|gen** M (*Golf*) caddie cart

Gol|ga|tha ['gɔlgata] NT **-s** (*Bibl*) Golgotha

Go|li|ath ['goːliat] M **-s, -s** (*Bibl, fig*) Goliath

Go|na|de [goˈnaːdə] F **-, -n** (*Biol*) gonad

Gon|del [gɔndl] F **-, -n** gondola; (*von Sessellift etc auch*) (cable) car

---

Gon|del-: Gon|del|bahn F cable railway; **Gon|del|fahrt** F trip in a gondola; **Gon|del|füh|rer(in)** M(F) gondolier

gon|deln ['gɔndln] VI *aux sein* (*inf*) (= *reisen*) to travel (a)round; (= *herumfahren*) to drive (a)round; **nach Schönefeld und zurück ~** to travel to Schönefeld and back; **durch die Welt ~** to go globetrotting (*inf*)

Gon|do|lie|re [gɔndoˈlieːrə] M **-, Gondolieri** [-ri] gondolier

Gong [gɔŋ] M **-s, -s** gong; (*bei Boxkampf etc*) bell; **der ~ zur dritten Runde** the bell for the third round

gon|gen ['gɔŋən] VI impers **es hat gegongt** the gong has gone or sounded; **es gongte zum Essen** the gong went or sounded for dinner *etc* VI to ring or sound a/the gong

Gong|schlag M stroke of the gong

gön|nen ['gœnən] VT **jdm etw ~** not to (be)grudge sb sth; (= *zuteil werden lassen*) to grant or allow sb sth; **jdm etw nicht ~** to (be)grudge sb sth; not to grant or allow sb sth; **sich** (*dat*) **etw ~** to allow oneself sth; **jdm ~, dass ...** not to (be)grudge sb the fact that ...; **er gönnte mir keinen Blick** he didn't spare me a single glance; **er gönnt ihr nicht die Luft zum Atmen** he (be)grudges her the very air she breathes; **ich gönne ihm diesen Erfolg/seine Frau von ganzem Herzen** I'm delighted for him that he's had this success/that he has such a nice wife; **das sei ihm gegönnt** I don't (be)grudge him that; **man gönnt sich ja sonst nichts** (*hum inf*) you've got to spoil yourself sometimes

Gön|ner ['gœnɐ] M **-s, -**, **Gön|ne|rin** [-ərɪn] F **-, -nen** patron; (*Frau auch*) patroness

Gön|ner-: gön|ner|haft (*pej*) ADJ patronizing ADV patronizingly; **~ tun, sich ~ geben** to play the big benefactor; **Gön|ner|haf|tig|keit** ['gœnɐhaftɪçkaɪt] F **-**, *no pl* (*pej*) patronizing; **Gön|ner|mie|ne** F (*pej*) patronizing air; **Gön|ner|schaft** ['gœnɐʃaft] F **-**, *no pl* (= *Förderung*) patronage

Go|no|kok|kus [gonoˈkɔkʊs] M **-, Gonokokken** [-ˈkɔkn] (*Med*) gonococcus

Go|nor|rhö [gonɔˈrøː] F **-, -en** [-ˈrøːən], **Go|nor|rhöe** [gonɔˈrøː] F **-, -n** [-ˈrøːən] (*Med*) gonorrhoea (*Brit*), gonorrhea (*US*); **er hat die ~** he has gonorrh(o)ea

Good|will ['gʊdwɪl] M **-s**, *no pl* (*auch Econ*) goodwill, good will

Good|will-: Good|will|be|such ['gʊdwɪl-] M goodwill visit; **Good|will|rei|se** ['gʊdwɪl-] F , **Good|will|tour** ['gʊdwɪl-] F goodwill journey or trip

gor *pret von* **gären**

Gör [gøːr] NT **-(e)s, -en** (*inf*) **a** (= *kleines Kind*) brat (*pej inf*), kid (*inf*) **b** (= *Mädchen*) (cheeky (*Brit*) or fresh (*US*) or saucy) little miss

gor|disch ['gɔrdɪʃ] ADJ **der Gordische Knoten** (*Myth*) the Gordian knot; **ein ~er Knoten** (*fig*) a Gordian knot

Gö|re ['gøːrə] F **-, -n** **a** (= *kleines Mädchen*) (cheeky (*Brit*) or fresh (*US*)) little miss **b** (= *kleines Kind*) brat (*pej inf*), kid (*inf*)

Gore-Tex® ['gɔːrəˈtɛks] NT **-**, *no pl* Gore-Tex®

Gor|gon|zo|la [gɔrgɔnˈtsoːla] M **-s, -s** gorgonzola (cheese)

Go|ril|la [goˈrɪla] M **-s, -s** gorilla; (*inf*: = *Leibwächter*) heavy (*Brit inf*), goon (*US inf*); (*sl*: = *Türsteher*) bouncer (*inf*)

Go|sche ['gɔʃə] F **-, -n** (*S Ger inf*) gob (*inf*), mouth; **eine freche ~ haben** to have the cheek of the devil (*Brit inf*), to be fresh (*US*); **halt die ~!** shut your mouth or gob (*inf*) or trap (*inf*)

Go|schen ['gɔʃn] F **-**, (*S Ger, Aus: pej*) = **Gosche**

Gos|pel ['gɔspl] NT OR M **-s, -s**, **Gos|pel|song** M gospel song

goss ▲ *pret von* **gießen**

Gos|se ['gɔsə] F **-, -n** **a** (= *Rinnstein*) gutter; (*rare*: = *Abfluss, Gully*) drain **b** (*fig*) gutter; **in der ~**

---

enden or **landen** to end up in the gutter; **jdn aus der ~ holen** or **ziehen** to take sb from the gutter, to pull sb out of the gutter; **jdn** or **jds Namen durch die ~ ziehen** or **schleifen** to drag sb's name through the mud

Gos|sen-: Gos|sen|aus|druck M *pl* **-ausdrücke** vulgarity; **Gos|sen|jar|gon** M , **Gos|sen|spra|che** F gutter language, language of the gutter

Gote ['goːtə] M **-n, -n**, **Go|tin** ['goːtɪn] F **-, -nen** Goth

Gö|te|borg ['gøːtəbɔrk] NT **-s** Gothenburg

Go|tha ['goːta] M **-s, -s** *directory of the German nobility*; ≈ Debrett's (Peerage) (*Brit*)

Go|tik ['goːtɪk] F **-**, *no pl* (*Art*) Gothic (style); (= *gotische Epoche*) Gothic period; **ein Meisterwerk der ~** a masterpiece of Gothic architecture *etc*; **typisch für die ~** typical of Gothic

Go|tin F **-, -nen** Goth

go|tisch ['goːtɪʃ] ADJ Gothic; **~e Schrift** (*Typ*) Gothic (script)

Gott [gɔt] M **-es**, **⸚er** ['gœtɐ] **a** god; (*als Name*) God; **~ der Herr** the Lord God; **~ (der) Vater** God the Father; **~ der Allmächtige** Almighty God, God (the) Almighty; **der liebe ~** the good or dear Lord; **an ~ glauben** to believe in God; **zu ~ beten** or **flehen** (*liter*) to pray to God; **er ist ihr ~** she worships him like a god; **bei ~ schwören** to swear by Almighty God
b **in ~ entschlafen** (*liter*) to pass away or on; **dein Schicksal liegt in ~es Hand** you are or your fate is in God's hands; **dich hat ~ im Zorn erschaffen!** God left something out when he put you together! (*hum*); **dem lieben ~ den Tag stehlen** to laze the day(s) away; **den lieben ~ einen guten** or **frommen Mann sein lassen** (*inf*) to take things as they come; **er ist wohl (ganz und gar) von ~** or **von den Göttern verlassen** (*inf*) he's (quite) taken leave of his senses; **~ ist mein Zeuge** (*liter*) as God is my witness; **wie ihn geschaffen hat** (*hum inf*) as naked as the day (that) he was born; **ein Anblick** or **Bild für die Götter** (*hum inf*) a sight for sore eyes; **das wissen die Götter** (*inf*) heaven or God (only) knows; **~ weiß** (*inf*) heaven knows (*inf*), God knows (*inf*); **er hat ~ weiß was erzählt** (*inf*) he said God knows what (*inf*); **ich bin weiß ~ nicht prüde, aber ...** heaven or God knows I'm no prude but ...; **so ~ will** (*geh*) God willing, DV (*esp Brit*); **vor ~ und der Welt** before the whole world; **~ und die Welt** (*fig*) everybody; **über ~ und die Welt reden** (*fig*) to talk about everything under the sun, to talk about anything and everything; **im Namen ~es** in the name of God; **dann mach es eben in ~es Namen** just do it then; **warum in ~es Namen ...?** why in God's name ...?; **leider ~es** unfortunately, alas; **was ~ tut, das ist wohl getan** God does all things well; **~es Mühlen mahlen langsam** (*hum*) the mills of God grind slowly (but they grind exceeding fine); **ein Leben wie ~ in Frankreich führen**, **wie ~ in Frankreich leben** (*inf*) to be in clover (*esp Brit*), to be in the lap of luxury, to live the life of Riley (*Brit inf*); **was ~ zusammengefügt hat, soll der Mensch nicht scheiden** what God has joined together let no man put asunder
c (*in Ausrufen*) **grüß ~!** (*esp S Ger, Aus*) hello, good morning/afternoon/evening; **~ zum Gruß!** (*old*) God be with you (*old*); **~ sei mit dir!** (*old*) God be with you (*old*); **~ mit dir!** (*old*) God bless you; **vergelts ~!** (*dated*) God bless you, may you be rewarded; **wollte** or **gebe ~, dass ...** (*old*) (may) God grant that ...; **~ soll mich strafen, wenn ...** (*old*) may God strike me dumb if ...; **~ steh mir bei!** (*old*) God help me!; **~ hab ihn selig!** God have mercy on his soul; **in ~es Namen!** for heaven's or goodness sake!; **ach (du lieber) ~!** (*inf*) oh Lord! (*inf*), oh heavens! (*inf*); **mein ~!, ach ~!** (*my*) God! (*inf*); (*als Leerformel in Antworten*) (oh) well, (oh) you know; **großer ~!** good Lord or God!; **~ im Himmel!** (*dated*) heavens above!; **bei ~!** by God!; **~ behüte** or **bewah-**

re!, **da sei ~ vor!** God *or* Heaven forbid!; **um ~es willen!** for heaven's *or* God's sake!; **~ sei Dank!** thank God!

Gott-: gott|ähn|lich ADJ godlike ADV **verehren** as a god; **gott|be|gna|det** [-bəgna:dət] ADJ divinely gifted; **gott|be|hü|te** [gɔtbəˈhyːtə] (*esp Aus*), **gott|be|wah|re** [gɔtbəˈvaːrə] ADV heaven *or* God forbid

Gott|chen [ˈgɔtçən] NT **(ach) ~!** (*inf*) gosh! (*inf*), golly! (*inf*)

Gott|er|bar|men NT **zum ~** (*inf*) pitiful(ly), pathetic(ally) (*inf*)

Göt|ter-: Göt|ter|bild NT idol; **Göt|ter|bo|te** M (*Myth*) messenger of the gods; **Göt|ter|däm|me|rung** F götterdämmerung, twilight of the gods; **Göt|ter|epos** NT epic of the gods; **Göt|ter|gat|te** M (*dated hum*) lord and master (*hum*), better half (*inf*)

Gott-: gott|er|ge|ben ADJ (= *demütig*) meek; (= *fromm*) pious ADV meekly; **Gott|er|ge|ben|heit** F meekness

Göt|ter-: Göt|ter|ge|stalt F god; **göt|ter|gleich** ADJ godlike; **Göt|ter|sa|ge** F myth about the gods/a god; (*als Literaturform*) mythology of the gods; **Göt|ter|spei|se** F (*Myth*) food of the gods; (*Cook*) jelly (*Brit*), Jell-O® (*US*); **Göt|ter|trank** M (*Myth*) drink of the gods; **Göt|ter|va|ter** M (*Myth*) father of the gods; **Göt|ter|welt** F (*Myth*) realm of the gods; (= *alle Götter zusammen*) the gods *pl*

Got|tes-: Got|tes|acker M (*old*) God's acre; **Got|tes|an|be|te|rin** F (*Zool*) praying mantis; **Got|tes|be|griff** M conception of God; **Got|tes|be|weis** M proof of the existence of God; **der ontologische** *etc* **~** the ontological *etc* argument

Got|tes|dienst M **a** (= *Gottesverehrung*) worship **b** (*Eccl*) service; **zum ~ gehen** to go to church; **dem ~ beiwohnen** (*form*) to attend church

Got|tes|dienst|be|such M church attendance

Got|tes-: Got|tes|frau F (*old, iro*) woman of God; **Got|tes|frie|de** M (*Hist*) (= *Pax Dei*) Peace of God; (= *Treuga Dei*) Truce of God; **Got|tes|furcht** F (*geh*) fear of God; **jdn zur ~ erziehen** to teach sb to fear God; **got|tes|fürch|tig** [-fʏrçtɪç] ADJ God-fearing; **Got|tes|ga|be** F gift of *or* from God; **Got|tes|ge|richt** NT **a** punishment of God **b** (*Hist*: = *Gottesurteil*) trial by ordeal; **Got|tes|ge|schenk** NT gift of *or* from God; **Got|tes|gna|den|tum** NT , *no pl* (*Hist*) doctrine of divine right; **Got|tes|haus** NT place of worship; **Got|tes|lamm** NT (*Rel*) Lamb of God; **Got|tes|läs|te|rer** M , **Got|tes|läs|te|rin** F blasphemer; **got|tes|läs|ter|lich** ADJ blasphemous ADV blasphemously; **Got|tes|läs|te|rung** F blasphemy; **Got|tes|leug|ner** [-lɔygnɐ] M **-s,** - , **Got|tes|leug|ne|rin** F **-,** **-nen** (*dated*) unbeliever; **Got|tes|lohn** M , *no pl* (*old*) reward from God; **etw für einen ~ tun** to do sth for love; **Got|tes|mann** M *pl* **-männer** (*old, iro*) man of God; **Got|tes|mut|ter** F , *no pl* (*Rel*) Mother of God; **Maria, die ~** Mary (the) Mother of God; **Got|tes|sohn** M (*Rel*) Son of God; **Got|tes|staat** M theocracy; **Augustins „Gottesstaat"** Augustine's "City of God"; **Got|tes|ur|teil** NT (*Hist*) trial by ordeal

Gott-: gott|froh ADJ (*esp Sw*) = **heilfroh**; **gott|ge|fäl|lig** (*old*) ADJ godly, pleasing in the sight of God (*form*) ADV **~ leben** to live in a manner pleasing in the sight of God; **gott|ge|ge|ben** ADJ god-given; **etw als ~ hinnehmen** to take *or* accept sth as god-given; **gott|ge|sandt** [-gəzant] ADJ (*old, liter*) sent from God; **gott|ge|weiht** [-gəvait] ADJ (*liter*) dedicated to God; **gott|ge|wollt** ADJ willed by God; **gott|gläu|big** ADJ religious; (*NS*) non-denominational

Gott|hard|chi|ne|se [ˈgɔthart-] M (*Sw pej*) Eyetie (*Brit pej sl*), Italian

Gott|heit [ˈgɔthait] F **-,** **-en** **a** *no pl* (= *Göttlichkeit*) divinity, godhood, godship; **die ~** (= *Gott*) the Godhead **b** (= *esp heidnische Göttergestalt*) deity; **jdn wie eine ~ verehren** to worship sb like a god

Göt|tin [ˈgœtɪn] F **-,** **-nen** goddess

Gott|kö|nig M god-king

gött|lich [ˈgœtlɪç] ADJ (*lit, fig*) divine; **du bist ja ~!** (*dated*) you (really) are a one (*dated Brit inf*), you're a little dickens (*dated US inf*); **das Göttliche im Menschen** the divine in Man ADV **wir haben uns ~ amüsiert** (= *lustig gemacht*) we were terribly amused; (= *gut unterhalten*) we had a wonderful time

Gött|lich|keit F **-,** *no pl* divinity

Gott-: gott|lob [gɔtˈloːp] INTERJ thank God *or* heavens *or* goodness; **er ist ~ wieder gesund** he has recovered now, thank God *or* heavens *or* goodness; **gott|los** ADJ godless; (= *verwerflich*) ungodly; **Gott|lo|sig|keit** F **-,** *no pl* godlessness; **Gott|sei|bei|uns** [gɔtzaiˈbaiʊns, gɔtˈzai-] M **-,** *no pl* (*euph*) **der ~** the Evil One, the Tempter

Gotts-: gotts|er|bärm|lich (*inf*) ADJ dreadful, godawful (*inf*) ADV dreadfully; **Gotts|öbers|te(r)** [ˈgɔtsˌøːbəstə] M *decl as adj* (*Aus iro*) his lordship (*iro*), my noble lord (*iro*); **die ~n** the noble lords

Gott-: Gott|su|cher(in) M(F) seeker after God; **Gott|va|ter** M , *no pl* God the Father; **gott|ver|dam|mich** [gɔtfɛɐˈdamɪç] INTERJ (*inf*) bloody hell (*Brit inf*), God Almighty (*inf*); **gott|ver|dammt**, **gott|ver|flucht** ADJ *attr* (*inf*) goddamn(ed) (*inf*), damn(ed) (*inf*), bloody (*Brit inf*); **gott|ver|ges|sen** ADJ **a** godless **b** (= *gottverlassen*) godforsaken; **gott|ver|las|sen** ADJ godforsaken ADV **~ allein** utterly alone; **Gott|ver|trau|en** NT trust *or* faith in God; **dein ~ möch|te ich haben!** I wish I had your faith; **gott|voll** ADJ (*fig inf*) divine; **du bist ja ~!** you're a right one! (*dated Brit inf*), you're a little dickens (*dated US inf*); **Gott|we|sen** NT (*liter*) god(head)

Göt|ze [ˈgœtsə] M **-n,** **-n** (*lit, fig*) idol

Göt|zen-: Göt|zen|an|be|ter(in) M(F) idolater; (*fig*) worshipper; **Göt|zen|bild** NT idol, graven image (*Bibl*); **Göt|zen|die|ner(in)** M(F) idolater/idolatress; (*fig*) worshipper; **Göt|zen|dienst** M , **Göt|zen|glau|be** M , **Göt|zen|ver|eh|rung** F idolatry

Götz von Ber|li|chin|gen [gœts fɔn ˈbɛrlɪçɪŋən] M (*euph*) **er beschimpfte ihn mit ~** he used a few four-letter words to (*Brit*) *or* with (*US*) him

Götz|zi|tat NT **das ~** ≈ the V-sign (*Brit*), ≈ the finger (*US*)

Gou|ache [guˈa(ː)ʃ] F **-,** **-n** (*Art*) gouache

Gour|mand [gʊrˈmãː] M **-s,** **-s** glutton, gourmand

Gour|met [gʊrˈme, -ˈmeː] M **-s,** **-s** gourmet

gou|tie|ren [guˈtiːrən] *ptp* **goutiert** VT (*geh*) **a** (*fig*) (= *Gefallen finden an*) to appreciate; (= *gutheißen*) to approve (of) **b** (*rare*: = *kosten, genießen*) to taste, to partake of (*liter*)

Gou|ver|nan|te [gʊvɛrˈnantə] F **-,** **-n** governess; (*pej*) schoolmarm

gou|ver|nan|ten|haft ADJ schoolmarmish

Gou|ver|ne|ment [gʊvɛrnəˈmãː] NT **-s,** **-s** **a** (*Hist* = *Regierung*) government; (= *Verwaltung*) administration **b** province

Gou|ver|neur [gʊvɛrˈnøːɐ] M **-s,** **-e**, **Gou|ver|neu|rin** F **-,** **-nen** governor

Grab [graːp] NT **-(e)s,** **-er** [ˈgrɛːbɐ] grave; (= *Gruft*) tomb, sepulchre (*Brit*), sepulcher (*US*); (*fig*: = *Untergang*) end, ruination; **das Heilige ~** the Holy Sepulchre (*Brit*) *or* Sepulcher (*US*); **jdn zu ~e tragen** to bear sb to his grave; **ins ~ sinken** (*old liter*) to be laid in the earth (*liter*); **ein frühes ~ finden** (*geh*) to go to an early grave; **ein ~ in fremder Erde finden** (*geh*) to be buried in foreign soil; **ein feuchtes** *or* **nasses ~**

finden (*liter*) **sein ~ in den Wellen finden** (*liter*) to go to a watery grave, to meet a watery end; **ein Geheimnis mit ins ~ nehmen** to take a secret with one to the grave; **treu bis ans ~** faithful to the end, faithful unto death (*liter*); **(bis) über das ~ hinaus** in death, beyond the grave; **verschwiegen wie ein** *or* **das ~** (as) silent as the grave; **er würde sich im ~e umdrehen, wenn …** he would turn in his grave if …; **du bringst mich noch ins ~** *or* **an den Rand des ~es!** you'll be the death of me yet (*inf*), you'll send me to an early grave; **mit einem Bein** *or* **Fuß im ~e stehen** (*fig*) to have one foot in the grave; **sich** (*dat*) **selbst sein** *or* **sich** (*dat*) **sein eigenes ~ graben** *or* **schaufeln** (*fig*) to dig one's own grave; **seine Hoffnungen** *etc* **zu ~e tragen** (*geh*) to abandon *or* bury one's hopes *etc* → *auch* **Grabmal**

Grab|bei|ga|be F (*Archeol*) burial object

Grab|be|lei [grabəˈlai] F **-,** **-en** (*inf*) groping *or* rummaging (around) (*inf*)

grab|beln [ˈgrabln] VI (*inf*) to grope about (*Brit*) *or* around, to rummage (around)

Grab|bel|tisch M (*inf*) cheap goods table *or* counter

Gräb|chen [ˈgrɛːpçən] NT **-s,** - *dim von* **Grab**

Grab|denk|mal NT monument

gra|ben [ˈgraːbn] *pret* **grub** [gruːp], *ptp* **gegraben** [gəˈgraːbn] VT (*in Erde etc*) to dig; **seine Zähne/Nägel in etw** (*acc*) **~** to sink one's teeth/nails into sth **b** (*auch Archeol*) to dig; **nach Gold/Erz ~** to dig for gold/ore; **in etw** (*dat*) **~** (*fig*: in Archiven, Quellen, jds Vergangenheit) to dig around in **b** **sich in etw** (*acc*) **~** (*Zähne, Krallen*) to sink into sth; **der Fluss hat sich in den Fels gegraben** the river has eaten its way into the rock; **das hat sich mir tief ins Gedächtnis gegraben** (*geh*) it has imprinted itself firmly on my memory; **sich durch etw ~** to dig one's way through sth → **Grube**

Gra|ben [ˈgraːbn] M **-s,** **-** [ˈgrɛːbn] ditch; (= *trockener Graben, Mil*) trench; (*Sport*) ditch; (*Sport*: = *Wassergraben*) water jump; (= *Burggraben*) moat; (*Geol*) rift (valley), graben (*spec*); **im ~ liegen** (*Mil*) to be in the trenches

Gra|ben-: Gra|ben|bruch M (*Geol*) (rift) valley, graben (*spec*); **Gra|ben|kampf** M , **Gra|ben|krieg** M (*Mil*) trench warfare *no pl*, *no indef art*; **Gra|ben|sen|ke** F (*Geol*) (rift) valley, graben (*spec*)

Grä|ber *pl von* **Grab**

Grä|ber-: Grä|ber|feld NT cemetery, burial ground; **Grä|ber|fund** M grave find

Grabes- (*liter*): **Gra|bes|dun|kel** NT sepulchral darkness; **Gra|bes|käl|te** F grave-like cold; **Gra|bes|luft** F grave-like air; **Gra|bes|rand** M **am ~** on the very brink of the grave; **Gra|bes|ru|he** F , **Gra|bes|stil|le** F deathly hush *or* silence; **Gra|bes|stim|me** F sepulchral voice

Grab-: Grab|fund M grave find; **Grab|ge|läu|te** NT **a** (*death*) knell **b** = **Grabgesang** b; **Grab|ge|leit** NT (*geh*) **jdm das ~ geben** to accompany *or* follow sb's coffin; **Grab|ge|sang** M **a** funeral hymn, dirge **b** (*fig*) **der ~ einer Sache** (*gen*) **sein** to sound the death knell for sth; **Grab|ge|wölbe** NT vault; (*von Kirche, Dom*) crypt; **Grab|hü|gel** M mound (*over a grave*); (*Archeol*) barrow, tumulus (*form*); **Grab|in|schrift** F epitaph, inscription (*on gravestone etc*); **Grab|kam|mer** F burial chamber; **Grab|kreuz** NT (*cross-shaped*) gravestone, cross; **Grab|le|gung** F [-leːgʊŋ] **-,** **-en** burial, interment

Gräb|lein [ˈgrɛːplain] NT **-s,** - *dim von* **Grab**

Grab-: Grab|licht NT candle (*on a grave*); **Grab|mal** NT *pl* **-mäler** *or* (*geh*) **-male** monument; (= *Grabstein*) gravestone; **das ~ des Unbekannten Soldaten** the tomb of the Unknown Warrior *or* Soldier; **Grab|ni|sche** F burial niche; **Grab|pfle|ge** F care of the grave(s)/of graves; **Grab|plat|te** F memorial slab; **Grab|re|de** F funeral oration; **Grab|schän|der**

[-fɛndɐ] M **-s**, **-**, **Grab|schän|de|rin** [-ərɪn] F **-**, **-nen** defiler of the grave(s)/of graves; **Grab|schän|dung** F defilement of graves

grab|schen ['grapʃn] VTI = **grapschen**

Grab-: Grab|schmuck M plants pl (on a grave); (= Kränze) wreaths pl (on a grave); **Grab|schrift** F epitaph, inscription (on gravestone etc); **Grab|spruch** M epitaph, inscription (on gravestone etc); **Grab|stät|te** F grave; (= Gruft) tomb, sepulchre (Brit), sepulcher (US); **Grab|stein** M gravestone, tombstone; **Grab|stel|le** F (burial) plot; **Grab|sti|chel** M (Art) burin

gräbt [grɛːpt] 3. pers sing pres von **graben**

Gra|bung F **-**, **-en** (Archeol) excavation

Grabungs-: Gra|bungs|ar|bei|ten PL (Archeol) (archaeological (Brit) or archeological (US)) excavations pl or dig sing; **Gra|bungs|fund** M (Archeol) (arch[a]eological) find; **Gra|bungs|stät|te** F (Archeol) arch(a)eological site

Grab-: Grab|ur|ne F funeral urn; **Grab|werk|zeug** NT (Zool) claw

Grac|chen ['graxn] PL die ~ (Hist) the Gracchi

Gracht [graxt] F **-**, **-en** canal

grad [graːt] (inf) = **gerade**

Grad [graːt] M **-(e)s**, **-e** [-də] (Sci, Univ, fig) degree; (Mil) rank; (Typ: = Schriftgrad) size; **ein Winkel von 45** ~ an angle of 45 degrees, a 45-degree angle; **unterm 32.** ~ **nördlicher Breite** latitude 32 degrees north; **4** ~ **Kälte** 4 degrees below freezing point or zero, 4 degrees below; **4** ~ **Wärme** 4 degrees above freezing point or zero; **20** ~ **Fahrenheit/Celsius** 20 (degrees) Fahrenheit/centigrade or Celsius; **um 5** ~ **wärmer sein** to be 5 degrees warmer; **Wasser auf 80** ~ **erhitzen** to heat water to 80 degrees; **es kocht bei 100** ~ boiling occurs at 100 degrees; **in ~e einteilen** to calibrate, to graduate; **ein Verwandter zweiten/dritten ~es** a relative once/twice removed; **Vetter zweiten ~es** second cousin; **Verbrennungen ersten/zweiten ~es** (Med) first-/second-degree burns; **in einem or bis zu einem gewissen ~(e)** up to a certain point, to a certain degree; **in hohem ~(e)** to a great or large extent; **im höchsten ~(e)** extremely → **Gleichung**

grad- = **gerade-**

Gra|da|ti|on [grada'tsioːn] F **-**, **-en** gradation

Grad|bo|gen M (Surv, Mil) quadrant

gra|de ['graːdə] (inf) = **gerade**

Grad|ein|tei|lung F calibration, graduation

Gra|di|ent [gra'diɛnt] M **-en**, **-en** (Sci) gradient

gra|die|ren [gra'diːrən] ptp **gradiert** VT **a** (= in Grade einteilen) to calibrate, to graduate **b** (= abstufen) to grade

Grad-: Grad|kreis M (Math) graduated circle; **grad|mä|ßig** ADJ = **graduell** ADJ; **Grad|mes|ser** M **-s**, **-** (fig) gauge (+gen, für of); **Grad|netz** NT (Geog) latitude and longitude grid; **Grad|ska|la** F scale (of degrees)

gra|du|ell [gra'duɛl] ADJ (= allmählich) gradual; (= gering) slight ADV (= geringfügig) slightly; (= allmählich) gradually

gra|du|ie|ren [gradu'iːrən] ptp **graduiert** VT **a** (= in Grade einteilen) to calibrate, to graduate **b** (Univ) to confer a degree upon, to graduate; **graduierter Ingenieur** engineer with the diploma of a School of Engineering, engineering graduate VI (Univ) to graduate

Gra|du|ier|te(r) [gradu'iːrtə] MF decl as adj graduate

Gra|du|ie|rung F **-**, **-en** (Univ) graduation

Grad-: Grad|un|ter|schied M difference of degree; **grad|wei|se** ADJ, ADV by degrees

Grae|cum ['grɛːkʊm] NT **-s**, no pl (Univ, Sch) examination in Greek

Graf [graːf] M **-en**, **-en** count; (als Titel) Count; (britischer Graf) earl; (als Titel) Earl; ~ **Koks** or

Rotz (inf) Lord Muck (Brit hum inf), His Highness (hum inf)

Gra|fem [gra'feːm] NT **-s**, **-e** (Ling) = **Graphem**

Gra|fen-: Gra|fen|fa|mi|lie F , **Gra|fen|ge|schlecht** NT → **Graf** family of counts/earls; **Gra|fen|kro|ne** F → **Graf** (count's/earl's) coronet; **Gra|fen|stand** M → **Graf** (Hist) (= Rang) rank of count; earldom; (= Gesamtheit der Grafen) counts pl/earls pl; **jdn in den** ~ **erheben** to confer the rank of count/earl upon sb

Graf|fel ['grafl] NT **-s**, no pl (Aus, S Ger inf) junk

Graf|fi|ti [gra'fiːti] NT **-s**, **-s** graffiti

Graf|fi|ti-Spra|yer(in) M(F) graffiti sprayer

Graf|fi|to [gra'fiːto] M OR NT **-(s)**, **Graffiti** [-'fiːti] (Art) graffito

Gra|fie ▲ [gra'fiː] F **-**, **-n** [-fiːən] = **Graphie**

Gra|fik ['graːfɪk] F **-**, **-en** **a** no pl (Art) graphic arts pl; (= Technik) graphics sing; (= Entwurf) design **b** (Art: = Darstellung) graphic; (= Druck) print; (= Schaubild) illustration; (= technisches Schaubild) diagram

Grafik-: Gra|fik|be|schleu|ni|ger M (Comput) graphics accelerator; **Gra|fik|bild|schirm** M (Comput) graphics screen; **Gra|fik|de|sign** NT , no pl (Fach) graphic design; **Gra|fik|dru|cker** M graphics printer

Gra|fi|ker ['graːfɪkɐ] M **-s**, **-**, **Gra|fi|ke|rin** [-ərɪn] F **-**, **-nen** graphic artist; (= Illustrator) illustrator; (= Gestalter) (graphic) designer

Grafik- (Comput): **gra|fik|fä|hig** ADJ ~ **sein** to be able to do graphics; **Gra|fik|fä|hig|keit** F graphics capability; **Gra|fik|kar|te** F graphics card; **Gra|fik|mo|dus** M graphics mode; **Gra|fik|mög|lich|keit** F graphics facility; **gra|fik|ori|en|tiert** [-lorɪɛntiːrt] ADJ graphics-orientated, graphics-oriented; **Gra|fik|pro|gramm** NT graphics program

Grä|fin ['grɛːfɪn] F **-**, **-nen** countess

gra|fisch ['graːfɪʃ] ADJ graphic; (= schematisch) diagrammatic, schematic; **~es Gewerbe** graphic trades pl ADV graphically, with a graph/graphs; **eine Funktion** ~ **darstellen** (Math) to show a function on a graph

Gra|fit etc ▲ [gra'fiːt] M **-s**, **-e** = **Graphit** etc

gräf|lich ['grɛːflɪç] ADJ count's/earl's; **das ~e Schloss** the count's/earl's castle; **ein ~er Diener** one of the count's/earl's servants

Gra|fo|lo|ge ▲ [grafo'loːgə] M **-n**, **-n**, **Gra|fo|lo|gin** ▲ [-'loːgɪn] F **-**, **-nen** graphologist

Gra|fo|lo|gie ▲ [grafolo'giː] F **-**, no pl graphology

Graf|schaft ['graːfʃaft] F **-**, **-en** land of a count; earldom; (Admin) county

Gra|ham|brot ['graː.ham-] NT (type of) wholemeal bread

grä|ko- ['grɛːko], **Grä|ko-** PREF graeco-, greco- (esp US), Graeco-, Greco- (esp US); **~roma|nisch** Graeco-Roman, Greco-Roman (esp US)

Gral [graːl] M **-s**, no pl (Liter) **der (Heilige)** ~ the (Holy) Grail

Grals- in cpds of the (Holy) Grail; **Grals|hü|ter(in)** M(F) (lit) keeper of the (Holy) Grail; (fig) guardian; **Grals|su|che** F quest for the (Holy) Grail

gram [graːm] ADJ pred (geh) **jdm** ~ **sein** to bear sb ill will

Gram [graːm] M **-(e)s**, no pl (geh) grief, sorrow; **vom** or **von** ~ **gebeugt** bowed down with grief or sorrow

grä|men ['grɛːmən] VR **sich über jdn/etw** ~ to grieve over sb/sth; **sich zu Tode** ~ to die of grief or sorrow VT to grieve

gram|er|füllt [-lɛɐfʏlt] ADJ (geh) grief-stricken, woebegone

Gram|fär|bung ▲ ['gram-] F (Med) Gram's method

gram|ge|beugt ADJ (geh) bowed down with grief or sorrow

gräm|lich ['grɛːmlɪç] ADJ morose, sullen; Gedanken morose

Gramm [gram] NT **-s**, **-e** or (nach Zahlenangabe) - gram(me); **100** ~ **Mehl** 100 gram(me)s of flour

Gram|ma|tik [gra'matɪk] F **-**, **-en** grammar; (= Grammatikbuch) grammar (book)

gram|ma|ti|ka|lisch [gramati'kaːlɪʃ] ADJ grammatical ADV grammatically

Gram|ma|ti|ker [gra'matɪkɐ] M **-s**, **-**, **Gram|ma|ti|ke|rin** [-ərɪn] F **-**, **-nen** grammarian

Gram|ma|tik|re|gel F grammatical rule

gram|ma|tisch [gra'matɪʃ] ADJ grammatical ADV grammatically

Gramm|atom ['gram.atoːm] NT gram(me) atom

Gram|mel ['graml] F **-**, **-n** (S Ger, Aus: Cook) ≈ crackling no indef art, no pl (Brit), ≈ cracklings pl (US), ≈ greaves pl

Gramm|mo|le|kül ▲ NT gram(me) molecule

Gramm|mo|fon ▲ [gramo'foːn] NT **-s**, **-e**, **Gram|mo|phon®** NT **-s**, **-e** (dated) gramophone (dated), phonograph (dated)

gram- [gram-] (Med): **gram|ne|ga|tiv** [-'neːgatiːf] ADJ Gram-negative; **gram|po|si|tiv** [-'poːzitiːf] ADJ Gram-positive

gram|voll ADJ (geh) grief-stricken, sorrowful

Gran [graːn] NT **-(e)s**, **-e** or (nach Zahlenangabe) - (old) **a** (= Apothekergewicht) grain **b** (= Edelmetallgewicht) grain

Grän [grɛːn] NT **-(e)s**, **-e** (= Edelmetallgewicht) grain

Gra|nat [gra'naːt] M **-(e)s**, **-e** or (Aus) **-en** **a** (Miner) garnet **b** (N Ger: = Garnele) shrimp

Gra|nat|ap|fel M pomegranate

Gra|na|te [gra'naːtə] F **-**, **-n** (Mil) (= Geschoss) shell; (= Handgranate) grenade

Granat-: Gra|nat|feu|er NT shelling, shellfire; **unter heftigem** ~ **liegen** to be under heavy shellfire or shelling; **Gra|nat|split|ter** M → Granate shell/grenade splinter; **Gra|nat|trich|ter** M shell crater; **Gra|nat|wer|fer** M mortar

Grand [grãː] M **-s**, **-s** (Cards) grand; ~ **ouvert** open grand; ~ **Hand** grand solo

Gran|de ['grandə] M **-n**, **-n** grandee

Gran|deur [grã'døːɐ] F **-**, no pl (geh) grandeur

Gran|dez|za [gran'dɛtsa] F **-**, no pl grandeur

Grand|ho|tel ['grã-hotɛl] NT luxury hotel

gran|di|os [gran'dioːs] ADJ magnificent, superb; (hum) fantastic (inf), terrific (inf) ADV (= hervorragend) magnificently, superbly, fantastically; **sich** ~ **amüsieren** to have a magnificent or fantastic time; **sich** ~ **erholen** to make a splendid recovery

Gran|di|o|si|tät [grandiozi'tɛːt] F **-**, no pl magnificence

Grand Prix [grã 'priː] M **- -**, **- -** Grand Prix

Grand|seig|neur [grãsɛn'jøːɐ] M **-s**, **-s** or **-e** (geh) nobleman

Grand-Tou|ris|me-Wa|gen [grãtu'rism-] M , **GT-Wagen** [ge:'teː-] M (Aut) GT (model)

Gra|nit [gra'niːt] M **-s**, **-e** granite; **auf** ~ **beißen (bei …)** to bang one's head against a brick wall (with …)

gra|ni|ten [gra'niːtn] ADJ attr granite, granitic (spec); (fig) rigid

Gran|ne ['granə] F **-**, **-n** **a** (= Ährenborste) awn, beard **b** (bei Tieren) long coarse hair

Grant [grant] M **-s**, no pl (inf: S Ger, Aus) **einen** ~ **haben** to be mad (inf) or cross (wegen about, auf jdn at sb)

gran|teln ['grantln] VI (inf: S Ger, Aus) **a** (= schlechte Laune haben) to be in a bad mood, to be grumpy, to have the hump (Brit inf) **b** (= meckern, herumnörgeln) to grumble, to be cross (inf)

gran|tig ['grantɪç] (inf: S Ger, Aus) ADJ grumpy ADV grumpily

Grant|ler ['grantlɐ] M **-s**, **-**, **Grant|le|rin** ['grantlərɪn] F **-**, **-nen** (*inf: S Ger, Aus*) cross-patch, (old) grouch

Grant|hu|ber ['grantlhuːbɐ] M **-s**, **-** (*inf: S Ger, Aus*) crosspatch, (old) grouch

Gra|nu|lat [granu'laːt] NT **-(e)s**, **-e** granules *pl*

gra|nu|lie|ren [granu'liːrən] *ptp* **granuliert** VTI to granulate

Grape|fruit ['greːpfruːt] F **-**, **-s** grapefruit

Grape|fruit|saft ['greːpfruːtzaft] NT grapefruit juice

Graph[1] [graːf] M **-en**, **-en** (*Sci*) graph

Graph[2] NT **-s**, **-e** (*Ling*) graph

Gra|phem [gra'feːm] NT **-s**, **-e** (*Ling*) grapheme

Gra|phie [gra'fiː] F **-**, **-n** [-fiːən] (*Ling*) written form

Gra|phik ['graːfɪk] F **-**, **-en** = **Grafik**

gra|phisch ['graːfɪʃ] ADJ, ADV = **grafisch**

Gra|phit [gra'fiːt] M **-s**, **-e** graphite

Graphit-: gra|phit|grau ADJ dark grey (*Brit*) or gray (*US*); **Gra|phit|stab** NT (*Tech*) graphite rod; **Gra|phit|stift** M lead pencil

Gra|pho|lo|ge [grafo'loːgə] M **-n**, **-n**, **Gra|pho|lo|gin** [-'loːgɪn] F **-**, **-nen** graphologist

Gra|pho|lo|gie [grafolo'giː] F **-**, *no pl* graphology

Grap|pa ['grapa] M **-s**, **-s** or f **-**, **-s** grappa

grap|schen ['grapʃn], **grap|sen** ['grapsn] (*inf*) VT **sich** (*dat*) **etw ~** to grab sth; (*S Ger, Aus: hum = stehlen*) to pinch (*inf*) or swipe (*inf*) sth VI **a nach etw ~** to make a grab at sth **b** (= *fummeln*) to grope (*inf*)

Grap|scher ['grapʃɐ] M **-s**, **-** (*inf*) **a** (= *Person*) groper (*inf*) **b** (= *Griff*) grab

Gras [graːs] NT **-es**, ̈**-er** ['greːzə] grass; **ins ~ bei-ßen** (*inf*) to bite the dust (*inf*); **das ~ wachsen hören** to be highly perceptive, to have a sixth sense; (= *zu viel hineindeuten*) to read too much into things; **über etw** (*acc*) **~ wachsen lassen** (*fig*) to let the dust settle on sth; **darüber ist viel ~ gewachsen** (*fig*) that's dead and buried; **wo er zuschlägt, wächst kein ~ mehr** (*inf*) he packs quite a punch; **wo er hinlangt, da wächst kein ~ mehr** once he gets his hands on something you'll never recognize it any more

Gras- *in cpds* grass; **gras|be|deckt**, **gras|be|wach|sen** ADJ grassy, grass-covered; **Gras|bü|schel** M tuft of grass

Gräs|chen ['greːsçən] NT **-s**, **-** *dim von* **Gras**

gra|sen ['graːzn] VI to graze

Gras-: Gras|flä|che F grassland; (= *Rasen*) piece or patch of grass; **Gras|fleck** M **a** grassy spot **b** (*auf Kleidern etc*) grass stain; **Gras|fres|ser** M herbivore; **Gras|frosch** M grass frog; **gras|grün** ADJ grass-green; **Gras|halm** M blade of grass; **Gras|hüp|fer** M (*inf*) grasshopper

gra|sig ['graːzɪç] ADJ grassy

Gras-: Gras|land NT , *no pl* grassland; **Gras|mäh|ma|schi|ne** F mower; **Gras|mü|cke** F (*Orn*) warbler; **Gras|nar|be** F turf; **Gras|nel|ke** F (*Bot*) thrift; **Gras|pflan|ze** F grass or graminaceous (*form*) plant

Grass [gras] NT **-**, *no pl* (*sl*) grass (*inf*)

Gras|sa|men M grass seed

gras|sie|ren [gra'siːrən] *ptp* **grassiert** VI to be rife; (*Krankheit auch*) to be rampant, to rage

gräss|lich ▲ ['grɛslɪç] ADJ **a** hideous; *Verbre-chen auch* heinous, abominable **b** (= *intensiv, unangenehm*) terrible, dreadful, awful; *Mensch* horrible, awful ADV **a** (= *schrecklich*) horribly **b** (*inf = äußerst*) terribly, dreadfully, awfully; **~ müde** terribly or dreadfully or awfully tired

Gräss|lich|keit ▲ F **-**, **-en** hideousness; (*von Verbrechen auch*) heinousness **b** (= *grässliche Tat etc*) atrocity

Gras-: Gras|so|de F (*esp N Ger*) turf, sod; **Gras|step|pe** F savanna(h); **Gras|strei|fen** M strip of grass, grassy strip; **Gras|tep|pich** M

M (*geh*) sward *no indef art, no pl* (*liter*); **gras|über|wach|sen** [-ly:bəvaksn], **gras|über|wu|chert** [-ly:bəvu:xɐt] ADJ overgrown with grass; **Gras|wuchs** M grass

Grat [graːt] M **-(e)s**, **-e** (= *Berggrat*) ridge; (*Tech*) burr; (*Archit*) hip (*of roof*); (*fig*) (dividing) line, border

Grä|te ['greːtə] F **-**, **-n** (fish) bone

Gra|ti|fi|ka|ti|on [gratifika'tsioːn] F **-**, **-en** bonus

gra|ti|nie|ren [grati'niːrən] *ptp* **gratiniert** VT (*Cook*) to brown (the top of); **gratinierte Zwie-belsuppe** onion soup au gratin

gra|tis ['graːtɪs] ADV free; (*Comm*) free (of charge); **~ und franko** (*dated*) free of charge

Gratis- *in cpds* free; **Gra|tis|ak|tie** F bonus share; **Gra|tis|exem|plar** NT free or compli-mentary copy; **Gra|tis|pro|be** F free sample

Grät|sche ['greːtʃə] F **-**, **-n** (*Sport*) straddle

grät|schen ['greːtʃn] VI *aux sein* to do a straddle (vault) VT *Beine* to straddle, to put apart

Grätsch-: Grätsch|sitz M straddle position; **Grätsch|sprung** M straddle vault; **Grätsch|stel|lung** F straddle (position); **in ~ gehen** to take up a straddle position

Gra|tu|lant [gratu'lant] M **-en**, **-en**, **Gra|tu|lan|tin** [-'lantɪn] F **-**, **-nen** well-wisher; **er war der erste ~** he was the first to offer his congra-tulations

Gra|tu|la|ti|on [gratula'tsioːn] F **-**, **-en** congra-tulations *pl*; **zur ~ bei jdm erscheinen** to call on sb to congratulate him/her

Gratulations-: Gra|tu|la|ti|ons|be|such M congratulatory visit; **Gra|tu|la|ti|ons|cour** [-kuːɐ] F **-**, **-en** congratulatory reception; **Gra|tu|la|ti|ons|kar|te** F congratulations card; **Gra|tu|la|ti|ons|schrei|ben** NT letter of con-gratulation

gra|tu|lie|ren [gratu'liːrən] ✪ 40.4, 50.6 *ptp* **gratuliert** VI **jdm** (**zu einer Sache**) **~** to congrat-ulate sb (on sth); **jdm zum Geburtstag ~** to wish sb many happy returns (of the day); **(ich) gratuliere!** congratulations!; **Sie können sich** (*dat*) **dass alles gut gegangen ist** you can count yourself lucky that everything went off all right

Grat|wan|de|rung F (*lit*) ridge walk; (*fig*) bal-ancing act, tightrope walk

grau [grau] ADJ grey (*Brit*), gray (*US*); *Ge-sicht(sfarbe) auch* ashen; (= *trostlos*) gloomy, dark, bleak; **~e Haare bekommen**, **~ werden** (*inf*) to go grey (*Brit*) or gray (*US*); **der Himmel** or **es sieht ~ in ~ aus** the sky or it is looking very grey (*Brit*) or gray (*US*); **er malte die Lage ~ in ~** (*fig*) he painted a gloomy or dark or bleak picture of the situation; **~e Eminenz** émi-nence grise; **der ~e Markt** (*Comm*) the grey (*Brit*) or gray (*US*) market; **die (kleinen) ~en Zellen** (*hum*) the little grey (*Brit*) or gray (*US*) cells; **die ~e Substanz** (*Anat*) the grey (*Brit*) or gray (*US*) matter; **der ~e Alltag** dull or drab re-ality, the daily round or grind; **in ~er Vorzeit** (*fig*) in the dim and distant past; **das liegt in ~er Ferne** (*fig*) it's in the dim and distant future; **~ ist alle Theorie** (*prov*) theory is no use with-out practice; **das ist bloß ~e Theorie** that's all very well in theory; **Graue Panther** Gray (*US*) Panthers (*US*), old people's action group ADV (= *mit grauer Farbe*) anstreichen, färben grey (*Brit*), gray (*US*); *tapezieren auch*, einrichten, sich kleiden in grey (*Brit*) or gray (*US*); **~ gestreift** grey-striped (*Brit*), gray-striped (*US*); **~ meliert** flecked with grey (*Brit*) or gray (*US*); *Haar auch* greying (*Brit*), graying (*US*)

Grau [grau] NT **-s**, **-(s)** grey (*Brit*), gray (*US*); (*fig*) dullness, drabness

Grau-: grau|äu|gig ADJ grey-eyed (*Brit*), gray-eyed (*US*); **grau|blau** ADJ grey-blue (*Brit*), gray-blue (*US*); **grau|braun** ADJ greyish-brown (*Brit*), grayish-brown (*US*); **Grau|brot** NT bread made from more than one kind of flour

Grau|bün|den [grau'byndn] NT **-s** (*Geog*) the Grisons

Grau|bünd|ner [grau'byndnɐ] M **-s**, **-**, **Grau|bünd|ne|rin** [-ərɪn] F **-**, **-nen** inhabitant of the Grisons

Gräu|el ▲ ['grɔyəl] M **-s**, **-** **a** *no pl* (= *Grauen, Abscheu*) horror; **~ vor etw** (*dat*) **haben** to have a horror of sth **b** (= *Gräueltat*) atrocity **c** (= *Gegenstand des Abscheus*) abomination; **sie/er/es ist mir ein ~** I loathe or detest her/him/it; **die Prüfung ist mir ein ~** I'm really dreading the ex-am; **es ist mir ein ~, das zu tun** I loathe or de-test or cannot bear doing that

Gräuel-: Gräu|el|ge|schich|te ▲ F , **Gräu|el|mär|chen** ▲ NT horror story; **Gräu|el|mel|dung** ▲ F , **Gräu|el|nach|richt** ▲ F re-port of an atrocity/atrocities; **Gräu|el|pro|pa|gan|da** ▲ F atrocity propaganda, horror sto-ries *pl*; **Gräu|el|tat** ▲ F atrocity

grau|en[1] ['grauən] VI (*geh: Tag*) to dawn; **es be-gann zu ~** dawn began to break

grau|en[2] VI *impers* **mir graut vor etw** (*dat*), **es graut mir vor etw** (*dat*) I dread sth; **mir graut vor ihm** I'm terrified of him

Grau|en ['grauən] NT **-s**, *no pl* **a** horror (*vor* of); **mich überlief ein ~** I shuddered with hor-ror; **~ erregend** atrocious, terrible **b** (= *grauen-haftes Ereignis*) horror

grau|en|er|re|gend △ → **Grauen a**

grau|en|haft, **grau|en|voll** ADJ terrible, atro-cious; *Schmerz* terrible; (*inf*) *Durcheinander* appal-ling, horrendous ADV *sich benehmen* atro-ciously, horrendously, appallingly; *wehtun* hor-rendously, atrociously; **~ aussehen** to look ghastly; **die Wohnung war ~ durcheinander** the apartment was in an appalling or horrendous mess

Grau-: Grau|fuchs M grey (*Brit*) or gray (*US*) fox; **Grau|gans** F grey(lag) (*Brit*) or gray(lag) (*US*) goose; **grau|ge|streift** △ ADJ → **grau ADV**; **grau|grün** ADJ grey-green (*Brit*), gray--green (*US*); **Grau|guss** ▲ M (*Tech*) grey (*Brit*) or gray (*US*) iron; **grau|haa|rig** ADJ grey--haired (*Brit*), gray-haired (*US*); **Grau|hörn|chen** NT (*Zool*) grey (*Brit*) or gray (*US*) squir-rel; **Grau|kopf** M (*fig*) grey-haired (*Brit*) or gray-haired (*US*) man/woman; **grau|köp|fig** ADJ grey-haired (*Brit*), gray-haired (*US*)

grau|len ['graulən] (*inf*) VI *impers* **davor grault mir** I dread it; **mir grault vor ihm** I'm scared or frightened of him VR **sich vor jdm/etw ~** to be scared or frightened of sb/sth VT to drive out (*aus* of)

grau|lich[1] ['graulɪç], **gräu|lich**[1] ▲ ['grɔylɪç] ADJ = **grässlich**

grau|lich[2], **gräu|lich**[2] ADJ (= *Farbe*) greyish (*Brit*), grayish (*US*)

Grau|markt M grey (*Brit*) or gray (*US*) market

Grau|markt|ti|cket NT (*Aviat*) bucket shop ticket

grau|me|liert △ ADJ *attr* → **grau ADV**

Grau|pe ['graupə] F **-**, **-n** grain of pearl barley; **~n** pearl barley *sing*

Grau|pel ['graupl] F **-**, **-n** (small) hailstone; **~n** soft hail *sing*, graupel *sing* (*spec*)

grau|pe|lig ['graupəlɪç] ADJ *Schauer* of soft hail; **~er Schnee** snow mixed with fine hail; **~er Ha-gel** soft hail

grau|peln ['graupln] VI *impers* **es graupelt** a soft hail is falling

Graupel-: Grau|pel|re|gen M , **Grau|pel|schau|er** M sleet; **Grau|pel|wet|ter** NT soft hail

Grau|pen|sup|pe F barley broth or soup

graup|lig ['grauplɪç] ADJ = **graupelig**

Grau|rei|her M (*Zool*) grey (*Brit*) or gray (*US*) heron

graus [graus] ADJ (*old*) afeared (*old, liter*)

Graus [graus] M **-es** [-zəs] *no pl* horror; **es war ein ~ zu sehen, wie …** it was terrible to see how ...; **es ist ein ~ mit ihm!** he's impossible!, he's the limit!, will he never learn!; **o ~!** (old, hum) oh horror! (old, hum), (alack and) alas! (old, iro)

grau|sam ['grauza:m] **ADJ** **a** (= gefühllos, roh) cruel (gegen, zu to) **b** (inf) terrible, awful, dreadful **ADV** **a** (= auf schreckliche Weise) cruelly; **~ ums Leben kommen** to die a cruel death; **sich – für etw rächen** to take (a) cruel revenge for sth **b** (inf: = furchtbar) terribly, horrendously, dreadfully

Grau|sam|keit F -, -en **a** no pl cruelty **b** (= grausame Tat) act of cruelty; (stärker) atrocity

Grau-: **Grau|schim|mel** M **a** (= Pferd) grey (Brit) or gray (US) (horse) **b** (= Pilz) grey mould (Brit), gray mold (US); **Grau|schlei|er** M (von Wäsche) grey(ness) (Brit), gray(ness) (US); (fig) veil; **grau|schwarz** ADJ greyish--black (Brit), grayish-black (US)

grau|sen ['grauzn] VI impers **mir graust vor** or **es graust mir vor der Prüfung** I am dreading the exam

Grau|sen ['grauzn] NT -s, no pl **a** = Grauen a **b** (inf) **da kann man das große** or **kalte ~ kriegen** it's enough to give you the creeps (inf) or willies (Brit inf)

grau|sig ['grauzıç] ADJ, ADV = grauenhaft

graus|lich ['grauslıç] ADJ, ADV (dial) = grässlich

Grau-: **Grau|specht** M grey-headed (Brit) or gray-headed (US) woodpecker; **Grau|stu|fe** F shade of grey (Brit) or gray (US); **Grau|tier** NT (hum inf) (jack)ass, donkey, mule; **Grau|ton** M pl -töne grey colour (Brit), gray color (US); **Grau|wal** M grey (Brit) or gray (US) whale; **grau|weiß** ADJ greyish (Brit) or grayish (US) white; **Grau|zo|ne** F (fig) grey (Brit) or gray (US) area

Gra|veur [gra'vø:ɐ] M -s, -e, **Gra|veu|rin** [-'vø:rɪn] F -, -nen engraver

Gra|vier|: [gra'vi:ɐ-]: **Gra|vier|an|stalt** F engraving establishment; **Gra|vier|ar|beit** F engraving

gra|vie|ren [gra'vi:rən] ptp **graviert** VT to engrave

gra|vie|rend ADJ serious, grave

Gra|vier|: **Gra|vier|ma|schi|ne** F engraving machine; **Gra|vier|na|del** F graver, burin

Gra|vie|rung [gra'vi:rʊŋ] F -, -en engraving

Gra|vi|met|rie [gravime'tri:] F -, no pl gravimetry

gra|vi|met|risch [gravi'me:trɪʃ] ADJ gravimetric

Gra|vis ['gra:vɪs] M -, - (Gram) grave accent

Gra|vi|ta|ti|on [gravita'tsio:n] F -, no pl gravitation, gravitational pull

Gra|vi|ta|ti|ons|: **Gra|vi|ta|ti|ons|feld** NT gravitational field; **Gra|vi|ta|ti|ons|ge|setz** NT law of gravity; **Gra|vi|ta|ti|ons|kraft** F gravitational force

gra|vi|tä|tisch [gravi'tɛ:tɪʃ] ADJ grave, solemn

gra|vi|tie|ren [gravi'ti:rən] ptp **gravitiert** VI (Phys, fig) to gravitate (zu towards)

Gra|vur [gra'vu:ɐ] F -, -en, **Gra|vü|re** [gra'vy:rə] F -, -n engraving

Gra|zie ['gra:tsiə] F -, -n **a** (Myth) Grace; (hum) beauty, belle **b** no pl (= Liebreiz) grace(fulness)

gra|zil [gra'tsi:l] **ADJ** delicate; (rare: = geschmeidig) nimble **ADV** **~ gebaut sein** to have a delicate figure

gra|zi|ös [gra'tsiø:s] **ADJ** graceful; (= lieblich) charming **ADV** gracefully

Grä|zis|mus [grɛ'tsɪsmʊs] M -, **Grä|zis|men** [-mən] (Ling) Graecism, Grecism (esp US)

Grä|zist [grɛ'tsɪst] M -en, -en, **Grä|zis|tin** [-'tsɪstɪn] F -, -nen Greek scholar, Hellenist

Grä|zis|tik [grɛ'tsɪstɪk] F -, no pl Greek studies pl

Green|horn ['gri:nhɔːɐn] NT -s, -s (inf) greenhorn (inf)

Green|peace ['gri:npi:s] NT no art Greenpeace

Green|pea|cer ['gri:npi:sɐ] M -s, -, **Green|pea|ce|rin** [-ərɪn] F -, -nen (inf) member of Greenpeace

Green|wich-Zeit ['grɪnɪdʒ-, -ɪtʃ-] F , **Green|wi|cher Zeit** ['grɪnɪdʒɐ-] F (die) ~ GMT, Greenwich Mean Time

Gre|gor ['gre:go:ɐ] M -s Gregory

Gre|go|ri|a|nik [grego'ria:nɪk] F -, no pl Gregorian music

gre|go|ri|a|nisch [grego'ria:nɪʃ] ADJ Gregorian; **~er Gesang** Gregorian chant, plainsong

Greif [graif] M -(e)s or -en, -e(n) (Myth) (Vogel) ~ griffin, griffon, gryphon

Greif-: **Greif|arm** M claw arm; **greif|bar** ADJ (= konkret) tangible, concrete; (= erreichbar) available; **Ware available, in stock** pred; **~e Gestalt** or **~e Formen annehmen** to take on (a) concrete or tangible form; **~ nahe,** in **~er Nähe** within reach; **Greif|be|we|gung** F grasping movement

grei|fen ['graifn] pret **griff** [grɪf], ptp **gegriffen** [gə'grɪfn] **VT** **a** (= nehmen, packen) to take hold of, to grasp; (= grapschen) to seize, to grab; **Saite to stop,** to hold down; **Akkord to strike; eine Oktave ~** to stretch or reach an octave; **diese Zahl ist zu hoch/zu niedrig gegriffen** (fig) this figure is too high/low; **zum Greifen nahe sein** (Sieg) to be within reach; (Folgerung) to be obvious (to anyone); **die Gipfel waren zum Greifen nahe** you could almost touch the peaks; **aus dem Leben gegriffen** taken from life

b (= fangen) to catch; **Greifen spielen** to play catch or tag; **sich** (dat) **jdn/etw ~** to grab sb/sth; **den werde ich mir mal ~** (inf) I'm going to tell him a thing or two (inf) or a few home truths (Brit)

VI **a** **hinter sich** (acc) **~** to reach behind one; **um sich ~** (fig) to spread, to gain ground; **unter etw** (acc) **~** to reach under sth; **in etw** (acc) **~** to put one's hand into sth, to reach into sth; **nach einer Sache ~** to reach for sth; (um zu halten) to clutch or (hastig) grab at sth; **an etw** (acc) **~** (= fassen) to take hold of sth, to grasp sth; (= berühren) to touch sth; **zu etw ~** (zu Pistole) to reach for sth; (fig) zu Methoden, Mitteln to turn or resort to sth; **zur Flasche ~** to take or turn to the bottle; **er greift gern nach einem guten Buch** he likes to settle down with a good book; **tief in die Tasche ~** (fig) to dig deep in one's pocket(s); **in die Saiten/Tasten ~** to strike up a tune; **nach den Sternen ~** to reach for the stars; **nach dem rettenden Strohhalm ~** to clutch at a straw; **zum Äußersten ~** to resort to extremes; **nach der Macht ~** to try to seize power; **die Geschichte greift ans Herz** the story really tears or tugs at one's heartstrings

b (= fassen: nicht rutschen, einrasten) to grip; (fig) (= wirksam werden) to take effect; (= zum Ziel/Erfolg führen) to achieve its ends; (= zutreffen) (Gesetz, Vorschrift) to apply; (Vergleich, Unterscheidung) to hold; **zu kurz ~** to fall short

Grei|fer ['graifɐ] M -s, - (Tech) grab

Greif-: **Greif|fuß** M prehensile foot; **Greif|re|flex** M gripping reflex or response; **Greif|trupp** M riot squad; **Greif|vo|gel** M bird of prey, raptor (spec); **Greif|werk|zeug** NT prehensile organ; **Greif|zan|ge** F (pair of) tongs pl; **Greif|zir|kel** M (outside) callipers pl (Brit) or calipers pl (US)

grei|nen ['grainən] VI (pej) to whine, to whimper

greis [grais] ADJ aged; (= ehrwürdig) venerable; (= altersgrau) grey (Brit), gray (US), hoary (liter, hum); **sein ~es Haupt schütteln** (usu iro) to shake one's wise old head

Greis [grais] M -es, -e [-zə] old man; **ein neunzigjähriger ~** an old man of ninety, a ninety--year-old man

Grei|sen-: **Grei|sen|al|ter** NT extreme old age; **grei|sen|haft** ADJ very old, aged attr; (von jüngerem Menschen) Gesicht, Ansicht, Aussehen aged attr; **das ~e Verhalten dieser Kinder** the

way these children behave like old people; **Grei|sen|haf|tig|keit** ['graiznhaftıçkait] F -, no pl **sie zeigt keine Anzeichen von ~** she shows no signs of old age; **verfrühte ~** premature ageing; **die ~ dieser Kindergesichter** the little old men's faces of these children; **Grei|sen|haupt** NT (geh) hoary head; (iro) wise old head

Grei|sin ['graizɪn] F -, -nen old lady; **eine neunzigjährige ~** an old lady of ninety, a ninety--year-old lady

grell [grɛl] **ADJ** Stimme, Schrei, Ton shrill, piercing; Licht, Sonne glaring, dazzling; Farbe garish, gaudy, loud; Kleidung, Mode loud, flashy; Gegensatz sharp; (stärker) glaring; (fig) Inszenierung, Szene lurid **ADV** (= sehr hell) scheinen brightly; (= schrill) shrilly; (= auffallend) garishly; **~ beleuchtet** or **erleuchtet** dazzlingly bright; **~ leuchten** to be garish; **~ klingen/tönen** to sound shrill; **ihre Stimme klang ~** her voice sounded shrill; **~ gegen etw** (acc) **abstechen** to contrast very sharply with sth

grell-: **grell|be|leuch|tet** [-bə'lɔyçtət], **grell|er|leuch|tet** △ [-ɛɐ'lɔyçtət] ADJ attr → grell **ADV**; **grell|bunt** ADJ gaudily coloured (Brit) or colored (US); Farbe gaudy

Grel|le ['grɛlə] F -, no pl, **Grell|heit** F -, no pl (von Stimme, Schrei, Ton) shrillness; (von Licht, Sonne) glare; (von Farbe) garishness, gaudiness

grell|rot **ADJ** garish or gaudy red **ADV** **~ geschminkt** painted a garish or gaudy red

Gre|mi|um ['gre:miʊm] NT -s, **Gremien** ['gre:miən] body; (= Ausschuss) committee

Gre|na|dier [grena'di:ɐ] M -s, -e (Mil) **a** (Hist) grenadier **b** (= Infanterist) infantryman

Grenz- in cpds border, frontier; **Grenz|ab|fer|ti|gung** F border or frontier clearance; **Grenz|ab|schnitt** M sector of the/a border or frontier; **Grenz|an|la|gen** PL border installations pl; **Grenz|baum** M (= Schlagbaum) frontier barrier; **Grenz|be|gra|di|gung** F straightening of the border/a border/borders; **Grenz|be|reich** M frontier or border zone or area; (fig) limits pl; **im ~ liegen** (fig) to lie at the limits; **Grenz|be|völ|ke|rung** F inhabitants pl of the/a border zone; (esp in unwegsamen Gebieten) frontiersmen pl; **Grenz|be|woh|ner(in)** M(F) inhabitant of the/a border zone; (esp in unwegsamen Gebieten) frontiersman/-woman; **Grenz|be|zirk** M border district; **Grenz|durch|bruch** M breaking through the/a border or frontier

Gren|ze ['grɛntsə] F -, -n border; (= Landesgrenze auch) frontier; (= Stadtgrenze, zwischen Grundstücken) boundary; (fig: zwischen Begriffen) dividing line, boundary; (fig: = äußerstes Maß, Schranke) limits pl, bounds pl; **die ~ zwischen Spanien und Frankreich** the Spanish-French border or frontier; **die ~ zu Österreich** the border with Austria, the Austrian border; **über die ~ gehen/fahren** to cross the border; **(bis) zur äußersten ~ gehen** (fig) to go as far as one can; **jdm ~n setzen** to lay down limits for sb; **einer Sache** (dat) **~n setzen** or **stecken** to set a limit or limits to sth; **keine ~n kennen** (fig) to know no bounds; **seine ~n kennen** to know one's limitations; **seiner Großzügigkeit sind keine ~n gesetzt** there is no limit to his generosity; **hart an der ~ des Möglichen** bordering or verging on the limits of what is possible; **innerhalb seiner ~n bleiben** (fig) to stay within one's limits; (finanziell) to live within one's means; **jdn in seine ~n verweisen** (fig) to put sb in his place; **die ~n einhalten** to stay within the limits; **sich in ~n halten** (fig) to be limited; **die ~n des Möglichen** the bounds of possibility; **die oberste/unterste ~** (fig) the upper/lower limit; **die ~ seines Amtes überschreiten** to exceed one's office; **über die ~(n)** (+gen) **... hinaus** (fig) beyond the bounds of ...; **an ~n stoßen** (fig) to come up against limiting factors; **alles hat seine ~n** there is a limit or there are limits to everything

gren|zen ['grɛntsn] VI **an etw** (acc) **~** (lit) to border (on) sth; (fig) to border or verge on sth

Gren|zen-: gren|zen|los ADJ (lit, fig) boundless; **sich ins Grenzenlose verlieren** to disappear into the distance; (fig) to go too far ADV boundlessly; (fig) immensely; **Gren|zen|lo|sig|keit** F -, no pl boundlessness; (fig) immensity

Gren|zer ['grɛntsɐ] M -s, -, **Gren|ze|rin** [-ərɪn] F -, -nen **a** (= Zöllner) customs man/woman; (= Grenzsoldat) border or frontier guard **b** = Grenzbewohner(in)

Grenz-: Grenz|fall M borderline case; **Grenz|fluss** ▲ M river forming a/the border or frontier; **Grenz|for|ma|li|tä|ten** PL border formalities pl; **Grenz|gän|ger** [-gɛŋɐ] M -s, -, **Grenz|gän|ge|rin** [-ərɪn] F -, -nen (= Arbeiter) international commuter (across a local border); (= heimlicher Grenzgänger) illegal border or frontier crosser; (= Schmuggler) smuggler; **Grenz|ge|biet** NT border or frontier area or zone; (fig) border(ing) area; **Grenz|kon|flikt** M border or frontier dispute; **Grenz|kon|trol|le** F border or frontier control; **Grenz|land** NT border or frontier area or zone

Grenz|ler ['grɛntslɐ] M -s, -, **Grenz|le|rin** [-ərɪn] F -, -nen (= Grenzbewohner(in)

Grenz-: Grenz|li|nie F border; (Sport) line; **Grenz|mark** F pl -marken (Hist) border or frontier area or zone; **grenz|nah** ADJ close to the border or frontier; **Grenz|nä|he** F closeness to the border or frontier; **in ~ zur Ukraine** close to the border or frontier with the Ukraine; **Grenz|nut|zen** M (Econ) marginal utility; **Grenz|pfahl** M boundary post; **Grenz|pos|ten** M border guard; **Grenz|schutz** M **a** no pl protection of the border(s) or frontier(s) **b** (= Truppen) border or frontier guard(s); **Grenz|si|che|rungs|an|la|gen** PL border or frontier protection sing; **Grenz|si|tu|a|ti|on** F borderline situation; **Grenz|sol|dat(in)** M(F) border or frontier guard; **Grenz|sper|re** F border or frontier barrier; (fig: des Grenzverkehrs) ban on border traffic; **Grenz|stadt** F border town; **Grenz|stein** M boundary stone; **Grenz|strei|tig|keit** F boundary dispute; (Pol) border or frontier dispute; **Grenz|über|gang** M **a** (= Stelle) border or frontier crossing(-point) **b** (= Grenzübertritt) crossing of the border; **grenz|über|schreit|end** ADJ attr across the border or frontier/(the) borders or frontiers, cross-border; **Grenz|über|schrei|tung** F -, -en (lit) crossing (of) a/the border; (fig) boundary crossing, crossing boundaries; **Grenz|ver|kehr** M border or frontier traffic; **kleiner ~** regular border traffic; **Grenz|ver|lauf** M boundary line (between countries); **Grenz|ver|let|zer** [-fɛɛltsɐ] M -s, -, **Grenz|ver|let|ze|rin** [-ərɪn] F -, -nen border or frontier violator; **Grenz|ver|let|zung** F violation of the/a border or frontier; **Grenz|wa|che** F border guard; **Grenz|wacht** F (Sw) border or frontier guard; **Grenz|wall** M border rampart; **Grenz|wert** M limit; **Grenz|zei|chen** NT boundary marker; **Grenz|zie|hung** F drawing up of the/a border or frontier; **Grenz|zwi|schen|fall** M border incident or clash

Gret|chen|fra|ge ['gre:tçən-] F (fig) crunch question (inf), sixty-four-thousand-dollar question (inf)

Greu|el △ ['grɔyəl] M -s, - → **Gräuel**

Greu|el- △ → **Gräuel-**

greu|lich △ ['grɔylɪç] ADJ, ADV → **gräulich** [1]

Grey|er|zer ['graiɛtsɐ] M -s, - ~ (Käse) Gruyère

Grie|be ['gri:bə] F -, -n ≈ crackling no indef art, no pl (Brit); ≈ cracklings pl (US); ≈ greaves pl

Grie|ben|schmalz NT ≈ dripping with crackling etc

Griebs(ch) [gri:ps, gri:pʃ] M -es, -e (dial) **a** (= Apfelgriebs(ch), Birnengriebs(ch)) core **b** (= Gurgel) throat, gullet

Grie|che ['gri:çə] M -n, -n, **Grie|chin** ['gri:çɪn] F -, -nen Greek; **zum ~n gehen** to go to a or the Greek restaurant

Grie|chen|land ['gri:çnlant] NT -s Greece

Grie|chen|tum ['gri:çntu:m] NT -s, no pl das ~ **a** (= Volkstum) Greekness, Hellenism **b** (= Zivilisation) Hellenism, (the) Greek civilization; (= Kultur) Greek culture, things pl Greek **c** (= Gesamtheit der Griechen) the Greeks pl

Grie|chin F -, -nen Greek (woman/girl)

grie|chisch ['gri:çɪʃ] ADJ Greek; Kleidung, Architektur, Vase, Stil, Profil auch Grecian; **die ~e Tragödie** Greek tragedy; **~es Feuer** Greek fire; **~-orthodox** Greek Orthodox; **~-römisch** Graeco-Roman, Greco-Roman (esp US) → auch **deutsch**

Grie|chisch(e) ['gri:çɪʃ] NT Greek → auch **Deutsch(e)**

grie|nen ['gri:nən] VI (N Ger inf) to smirk (inf)

Gries|gram ['gri:sgra:m] M -(e)s, -e grouch (inf), misery

gries|grä|mig ['gri:sgrɛ:mɪç] ADJ grumpy, grouchy (inf) ADV grumpily, grouchily (inf); **~ aussehen** to look grumpy or grouchy (inf); **er guckte ~ in die Gegend** he looked around with a grumpy expression on his face

Grieß [gri:s] M -es, -e **a** semolina; (= Reisgrieß) ground rice **b** (= Kies) gravel (auch Med); (= Sand) grit

Grieß-: Grieß|brei M semolina; **Grieß|kloß** M , **Grieß|klöß|chen** NT semolina dumpling; **Grieß|no|ckerl** NT -s, -(n) (S Ger, Aus, Cook) semolina dumpling; **Grieß|pud|ding** M semolina pudding

griff pret von **greifen**

Griff [grɪf] M -(e)s, -e **a** (= das Greifen) der ~ an etw (acc) taking hold of sth, grasping sth; (= Berührung) touching sth; **der ~ nach etw** reaching for sth; **einen ~ in die Kasse tun** to put one's hand in the till; **einen tiefen ~ in den Geldbeutel tun** (fig) to dig deep in one's pocket; **der ~ nach der Droge/der Flasche** turning or taking to drugs/the bottle; **der ~ nach der Macht** the bid for power; **das ist ein ~ nach den Sternen** that's just reaching for the stars **b** (= Handgriff) grip, grasp; (beim Ringen, Judo, Bergsteigen) hold; (beim Turnen) grip; (Mus: = Fingerstellung) fingering; (inf: = Akkord) chord; (vom Tuch: = Anfühlen) feel, texture; **mit festem ~** firmly; **einen ~ ansetzen** (Ringen) to put on or apply a hold; **jdn/etw im ~ haben** (fig) to have sb/sth under control, to have the upper hand of sb/sth; (geistig) to have a good grasp of sth; **ein falscher ~** (fig) a false move; **jdn/etw in den ~ bekommen** (fig) to get the upper hand of sb/sth, to gain control of sb/sth; (geistig) to get a grasp of sth; **(mit jdm/etw) einen guten or glücklichen ~ tun** to make a wise choice (with sb/sth), to get on to a good thing (with sb/sth) (inf); **etw mit einem ~ tun** (fig) to do sth in a flash **c** (= Stiel, Knauf) handle; (= Pistolengriff) butt; (= Schwertgriff) hilt; (an Saiteninstrumenten) neck **d** usu pl (Hunt: = Kralle) talon **e** **Griffe** PL (Mil) rifle positions pl; **~e üben** or **kloppen** (inf) to do rifle drill

Griff-: griff|be|reit ADJ ready to hand, handy; **etw ~ halten** to keep sth handy, to keep sth to (Brit) or on hand; **Griff|brett** NT (Mus) fingerboard

Grif|fel ['grɪfl] M -s, - slate pencil; (Bot) style

Grif|fel|kas|ten M pencil case or box

grif|fig ['grɪfɪç] ADJ Boden, Fahrbahn etc that has a good grip; Rad, Sohle, Profil that grips well; Gewebe firm; (fig) Ausdruck useful, handy; Slogan pithy; Formulierung, Theorie concise; (Aus) Mehl coarse-grained; **etw auf eine ~e Formel bringen** to break sth down into a simple phrase ADV (= eingängig) darstellen, formulieren pithily, concisely

Grif|fig|keit F -, no pl grip; (von Slogan) pithiness

Griff|loch NT finger hole

Grill [grɪl] M -s, -s grill; (Aut: = Kühlergrill) grille

Grill|a|bend M (evening) barbecue, barbecue or BBQ night

Grill|a|de [grɪ'ja:də] F -, -n (Cook) grill

Grill|le ['grɪlə] F -, -n **a** (Zool) cricket **b** (dated inf: = Laune) silly notion or idea; **~n im Kopf haben** to be full of big ideas; **~n fangen** to be moody

grill|len ['grɪlən] VT to grill VR **sich ~ (lassen)** (inf) to roast (inf)

grill|len|haft ADJ (dated) (= trübsinnig) moody; (= sonderbar) strange, extraordinary

Grill- (Cook): **Grill|fest** NT barbecue party; **Grill|ge|richt** NT grill; **Grill|koh|le** F charcoal; **Grill|platz** M barbecue area; **Grill|res|tau|rant** NT , **Grill|room** [-ru:m] M -s, -s, **Grill|stu|be** F grillroom, grill and griddle

Gri|mas|se [gri'masə] F -, -n grimace; **~n schneiden** or **ziehen** or **machen** to grimace, to make or pull faces; **sein Gesicht zu einer ~ verziehen** to twist one's face into a grimace

Gri|mas|sen|schnei|der(in) M(F) face-puller

grimm [grɪm] ADJ (old) = **grimmig**

Grimm [grɪm] M -(e)s, no pl (old) fury, wrath (old, liter), ire (old, liter) (auf +acc against)

Grimm|darm M colon

Grim|men ['grɪmən] NT -s, no pl (S Ger) griping pains pl

grim|mig ['grɪmɪç] ADJ **a** (= zornig) furious, wrathful (liter); Gegner fierce; Miene grim; **~er Humor** grim or morbid humour (Brit) or humor (US) **b** (= sehr groß, heftig) Kälte, Spott etc severe, harsh ADV furiously, grimly; **~ lächeln** to smile grimly

Grind [grɪnt] M -(e)s, -e [-də] scab; (inf: Sw, S Ger: = Kopf) bonce (Brit inf), head

Grind|wal M pilot whale

grin|sen ['grɪnzn] VI to grin; (vor Schadenfreude, Dreistigkeit, höhnisch auch) to smirk

Grin|sen NT -s, no pl grin; (schadenfroh, dreist, höhnisch auch) smirk

grip|pal [grɪ'pa:l] ADJ (Med) influenzal; **~er Infekt** influenza infection

Grip|pe ['grɪpə] F -, -n 'flu, influenza; (= Erkältung) cold

Grip|pe- in cpds 'flu, influenza; **Grip|pe|kran|ke(r)** MF decl as adj 'flu sufferer, person with (the) 'flu; **Grip|pe|(schutz)|imp|fung** F influenza vaccination; **Grip|pe|vi|rus** NT OR M 'flu virus; **Grip|pe|wel|le** F wave of 'flu or influenza

grip|pös [grɪ'pø:s] ADJ attr influenzal

Grips [grɪps] M -es, -e (inf) nous (Brit inf), brains pl (inf), sense; **nun strengt mal euren ~ an** use your nous (Brit inf), use your common sense; **~ zu etw haben** to have the nous (Brit inf) or brains (inf) or common sense to do sth

Gris|li|bär ▲ ['grɪsli-] M , **Grizz|ly|bär** ['grɪsli-] M grizzly (bear)

Griss ▲ [grɪs] NT -es, no pl (Aus inf) crush

grob [gro:p] ADJ comp **~er** ['grø:bɐ], superl **~ste(r, s)** ['grø:psta] **a** (= nicht fein) Material, Oberfläche etc coarse; Arbeit dirty attr **b** (= ungefähr) rough; **in ~en Umrissen** roughly **c** (= schlimm, groß) gross (auch Jur); **den gröbsten Schmutz habe ich schon weggeputzt** I have already cleaned off the worst of the dirt; **ein ~er Fehler** a bad mistake, a gross error; **wir sind aus dem Gröbsten heraus** we're out of the woods (now), we can see the light at the end of the tunnel (now); **~e Fahrlässigkeit** gross negligence **d** (= brutal, derb) rough; (fig: = derb) coarse; Antwort rude; (= unhöflich) ill-mannered; **~ gegen jdn werden** to become offensive (towards sb); **auf einen ~en Klotz gehört ein ~er Keil** (Prov) one must answer rudeness with rudeness → **Geschütz** ADV comp **~er**, superl **am ~sten** **a** (= nicht fein) **zerkleinern/hacken** to chop coarsely; **etw ~ schneiden** to cut sth in large pieces; Käse to cut sth in thick slices; **~ gemahlen** coarsely ground; **~ mahlen** to grind coarsely

b (= *ungefähr*) **~ geschätzt/gemessen/gerechnet** approximately, roughly, at a rough estimate; **etw ~ umreißen/skizzieren** to give a rough idea of sth; **etw ~ wiedergeben** to give a superficial *or* an approximate account of sth

c (= *schlimm*) **~ fahrlässig handeln** to commit an act of gross negligence

d (= *brutal*) *anfassen, behandeln* roughly; *massieren* hard, roughly; (= *unhöflich*) rudely; (= *barsch*) curtly; **~ mit jdm umspringen** to rough sb up; **jdm ~ kommen** (*inf*) to get coarse with sb

grob-, Grob- *in cpds* coarse

Gro|be(s) ['gro:bə] NT *decl as adj* (*fig*) dirty work; **ein Mann fürs ~** (*inf*) a man who does the dirty work

grob|fa|se|rig, grob|fas|rig ADJ coarse-fibred (*Brit*), coarse-fibered (*US*)

grob|ge|mah|len △ [-gəmaːlən] ADJ *attr* → **grob** ADV a

Grob|heit F -, **-en** **a** (= *Beschimpfung, Ausdrucksweise*) foul language *no pl* **b** (= *Manieren*) bad manners *pl* **c** (*von Material*) coarseness; (*von Gerät*) crudeness

Gro|bi|an ['gro:biaːn] M **-(e)s, -e** brute

grob-: grob|klot|zig ADJ (*pej*) *Benehmen, Kerl etc* clumsy, hamfisted; **grob|kno|chig** ADJ big-boned; **grob|kör|nig** ADJ coarse-grained

gröb|lich ['grø:plɪç] ADJ **a** (*form:* = *schlimm*) gross **b** (*geh:* = *heftig, derb*) gross ADV **a** (*form:* = *schwerwiegend*) grossly; *missachten* grossly, largely **b** (*geh:* = *derb*) badly; *beleidigen, kränken* deeply, badly; **jdn ~ beschimpfen** to call sb rude names

Grob-: grob|ma|schig [-maʃɪç] ADJ large-meshed; (= *grob gestrickt*) loose-knit *attr* ADV coarsely; **grob|schläch|tig** [-ʃlɛçtɪç] ADJ coarse; *Mensch* big-built, heavily built; (*fig*) unrefined; **Grob|schläch|tig|keit** F -, *no pl* coarseness; (*von Mensch*) heavy *or* big build; (*fig*) lack of refinement; **Grob|schnitt** M (= *Tabak*) coarse cut; **Grob|strick** M coarse knit

Grö|faz ['grø:fats] M -' (*iro*) **der ~** the Big Chief (*hum*), the great General (*iro*)

Grog [grɔk] M **-s, -s** grog

grog|gy ['grɔgi] ADJ *pred* (*Boxen*) groggy; (*inf:* = *erschöpft*) all-in (*inf*)

grö|len ['grø:lən] VTI (*pej*) to bawl; **~de Stimme/Menge** raucous voice/crowd; **~d durch die Straßen ziehen** to roam rowdily through the streets

Grö|le|rei [grø:lə'rai] F -, **-en** (*pej*) bawling *no pl*

Groll [grɔl] M **-(e)s**, *no pl* (= *Zorn*) anger, wrath (*liter*); (= *Erbitterung*) resentment; **einen ~ gegen jdn hegen** to harbour (*Brit*) *or* harbor (*US*) a grudge against sb

grol|len ['grɔlən] VI (*geh*) **a** (= *dröhnen*) to rumble; (*Donner auch*) to roll, to peal (*liter*) **b** (= *böse sein*) **(jdm) ~** to be annoyed (with sb); **(mit) seinem Schicksal ~** to bemoan one's fate

Grön|land ['grø:nlant] NT **-s** Greenland

Grön|län|der ['grø:nlɛndɐ] M **-s, -, Grön|län|de|rin** [-ərɪn] F -, **-nen** Greenlander

grön|län|disch ['grø:nlɛndɪʃ] ADJ Greenland *attr*

Grön|land|wal M bowhead (whale)

groo|ven ['gruːvn] VI (*Mus sl*) **das groovt** it's grooving

Gros¹ [gro:] NT **-, -** [gro:s] (= *Mehrzahl*) major *or* greater part, majority, bulk → **en gros**

Gros² [grɔs] NT **-ses, -se** *or* (*bei Zahlenangaben*) - (= *Measure*) gross

Gro|schen ['grɔʃn] M **-s, - a** (*Aus: Hist*) groschen; (*in Polen*) grosz; (*Hist*) groschen **b** (*Hist inf*) 10-pfennig piece; (*fig*) penny, cent (*US*); **seine paar ~ zusammenhalten** to scrape together a few pence *or* pennies/cents (*US*); **sich** (*dat*) **ein paar ~ verdienen** to earn (oneself) a few pence *or* pennies/cents (*US*), to earn

(oneself) a bit of pocket money; **der ~ ist gefallen** (*hum inf*) the penny has dropped (*inf*); **bei ihm fällt der ~ pfennigweise** he's pretty slow on the uptake, it takes him a while to catch on

Gro|schen-: Gro|schen|blatt NT (*pej*) (cheap) rag (*inf*), sensational (news)paper; **die Groschenblätter** the gutter press (*Brit pej*), the yellow press (*US*); **Gro|schen|grab** NT (*hum:* = *Spielautomat*) one-armed bandit; **diese Parkuhr ist ein richtiges ~** this parking meter just swallows *or* eats up your money; **Gro|schen|heft** NT (*pej*) pulp magazine; (= *Krimi auch*) penny dreadful (*dated*); **Gro|schen|ro|man** M (*pej*) cheap *or* dime-store (*US*) novel

groß [gro:s]

1 ADJEKTIV	2 ADVERB

1 – ADJEKTIV

comp **=er** ['grø:sɐ], *superl* **=te(r, s)** ['grø:stə]

a big; *Fläche, Raum, Haus, Hände* big, large; *Höhe, Breite* great; *Größe, Tube, Dose, Packung etc* large; (*Typ*) *Buchstabe* capital; **ein ganz großes Haus/ Buch** a great big house/book; **der große (Uhr-) Zeiger** the big *or* minute hand; **x ist größer als 10** (*Math*) x is greater than 10; **die Wiese ist 10 Hektar groß** the field measures 10 hectares; **ein 2 Hektar großes Grundstück** a 2-hectare plot of land; **ein Loch größer machen** to make a hole bigger; **ein großes Bier, ein Großes** (*inf*) ≈ a pint (of beer) (*Brit*), a large beer; **großes Geld** notes *pl* (*Brit*), bills *pl* (*US*); **ich habe nur großes Geld** I haven't got any change on me; **die große Masse** (*fig*) the vast majority; **im Großen und Ganzen (gesehen)** by and large; **im Großen einkaufen** to buy in bulk *or* quantity → **Glocke**

b = *hoch, hoch gewachsen* tall; **ein großer Mann** a tall man; **wie groß bist du?** how tall are you?; **er ist 1,80 Meter groß** he's one metre (*Brit*) *or* meter (*US*) eighty (tall); **du bist groß geworden** you've grown

c = *älter* *Bruder, Schwester* big; **unsere Große** our eldest *or* oldest (daughter); (*von zweien*) our elder daughter; **unser Großer** our eldest *or* oldest (son); (*von zweien*) our elder son; **Groß und Klein** young and old (alike); **mit etw groß geworden sein** to have grown up with sth; **die Großen** (= *Erwachsene*) the grown-ups; (= *ältere Kinder*) the older children; **zu groß für etw sein** to be too big for sth; **er ist ein großes Kind** he's a big *or* a great big (*inf*) baby

d *zeitlich* *Verzögerung, Rede* big, long; **die große Pause** (*Sch*) the long *or* lunch break; **die großen Ferien** the summer holidays (*Brit*) *or* holiday (*US*)

e = *beträchtlich, wichtig, bedeutend* great; *Erfolg, Enttäuschung, Hoffnung, Eile* great, big; *Gewinn, Ereignis* big; *Katastrophe, Schreck* terrible; *Summe* large; *Geschwindigkeit* high; **er hat Großes geleistet** he has achieved great things; **die größten Erfindungen unseres Jahrhunderts** the greatest inventions of our century; **ein großer Dichter wie Goethe** a great poet like Goethe; **eine große Dummheit machen** to do something very *or* really stupid; **großen Durst haben** to be very thirsty; **er ist kein großer Esser** (*inf*) he's not a big eater; **eine der größeren Firmen** one of the major companies; **die großen Fragen unserer Zeit** the great *or* big questions of our time; **das große Ganze** the broader *or* wider view; **große Gefühle** strong feelings; **vor meinem Haus war** *or* **herrschte ein großer Lärm** there was a lot of noise outside my house; **großen Hunger haben** to be very hungry; **ich habe große Lust zu verreisen** I'd really like to go away (on holiday (*Brit*) *or* vacation (*US*)); **sie hatte große Lust, sich zu verkleiden** she really wanted to get dressed up; **ich habe keine große Lust** I don't particularly want to; **die große Mode sein** to be all the rage (*inf*); **einen großen Namen haben** to be a big name; **die große Nummer** (*im Zirkus*) the big number, the star turn (*esp Brit*); **ich bin**

kein großer Redner (*inf*) I'm no great speaker; **ich bin kein großer Opernfreund** (*inf*) I'm not a great opera fan; **im größten Regen/Schneesturm** in the middle of a downpour/snowstorm; **jds große Stunde** sb's big moment; **eine größere Summe** a biggish *or* largish sum; **er ist kein großer Trinker** (*inf*) he's not a big drinker; **die große Welt** (= *die Fremde*) the big wide world; (= *die oberen zehntausend*) high society, the upper crust; **große Worte** big words; **große Worte machen** to use grand words

f = *großartig, bewundernswert* (*iro*) great; **das ist** *or* **finde ich ganz groß** (*inf*) that's really great (*inf*)

g *in Eigennamen* Great; **die Großen Seen** the Great Lakes; **der Große Ozean** the Pacific; **Karl der Große** Charlemagne; **Alfred/Friedrich der Große** Alfred/Frederick the Great

h *Mus* **große Sexte** major sixth

2 – ADVERB

comp **=er**, *superl* **am =ten**

a = *nicht klein* **groß gewachsen** tall; **groß gemustert** large-print, with a large print; **groß kariert** large-check(ed); **groß machen** (*baby-talk*) to do number two (*baby-talk*), to do a poo (*Brit baby-talk*); **groß daherreden** (*inf*) to talk big (*inf*) → **großschreiben**

b = *in großem Ausmaß* **groß einkaufen gehen** to go on a spending spree, to splash out (*Brit inf*); **groß ausgeben** to go out somewhere expensive; **groß feiern** to have a big celebration; **groß aufgemacht** dressed up to the nines; **groß angelegt** large-scale; **groß und breit** (*fig*) at great length

c = *besonders* **jdn groß anblicken** to give sb a hard stare; **groß in Mode sein** to be all the rage (*inf*); **was ist das schon groß?** (*inf*) big deal! (*inf*), so what? (*inf*); **was soll man da schon groß machen/sagen?** (*inf*) what can you do/say?; **er hat sich nicht gerade groß für unsere Belange eingesetzt** (*inf*) he didn't exactly put up a big fight for us; **ich habe mich nicht groß um Politik gekümmert** (*inf*) I've never been a great one for politics (*inf*); **ich kümmere mich nicht groß darum** (*inf*) I don't take much notice; **ganz groß rauskommen** (*inf*) to make the big time (*inf*)

Groß- PREF (*vor Namen von Ballungsräumen*) Greater; **~Berlin** Greater Berlin

Groß-: Groß|ab|neh|mer(in) M(F) (*Comm*) bulk purchaser *or* buyer; **Groß|ad|mi|ral** M (*Naut Hist*) Grand Admiral, ≈ Admiral of the Fleet; **Groß|ak|ti|o|när(in)** M(F) major *or* principal shareholder; **Groß|alarm** M red alert; **~ geben** to give a red alert; **groß|an|ge|legt** △ ADJ *attr* → **groß 2 b**; **Groß|an|griff** M large-scale *or* major attack; **Groß|an|lass** ▲ M (*Sw*) = Großveranstaltung; **groß|ar|tig** ADJ wonderful, superb, splendid; *Erfolg* tremendous; (= *prächtig*) *Bauwerk etc* magnificent, splendid; **er hat Großartiges geleistet** he has achieved great things; **eine ~e Frau** a wonderful *or* fine woman ADV wonderfully, splendidly, magnificently; **ha, ~** (*iro*) wonderful!, that's just great *or* wonderful; **~ tun** (*pej*) to show off, to give oneself airs; **Groß|ar|tig|keit** F magnificence, splendour (*Brit*), splendor (*US*); **Groß|auf|nah|me** F (*Phot, Film*) close-up; **Groß|auf|trag** M (*Comm*) large-scale *or* major order; **Groß|bank** F *pl* **-banken** major *or* big bank; **Groß|bau|er** M *pl* **-bauern, Groß|bäu|e|rin** F -, **-nen** (*Sw*) big purchaser *or* buyer; **Groß|bild** NT blow-up; **Groß|bild|ka|me|ra** F plate camera; **Groß|bild|schirm** M large screen; **Groß|bour|geoi|sie** F (*Sociol, Pol*) upper classes *pl*, upper bourgeoisie; **Groß**-**brand** M enormous blaze, major *or* big fire; **Groß**|**bri**|**tan**|**ni**|**en** [gro:sbri'taniən] NT (Great) Britain; **groß**|**bri**|**tan**|**nisch** [gro:sbri-'taniʃ] ADJ (Great) British, Britannic (*rare*); **Groß**|**buch**|**sta**|**be** M capital (letter), upper case letter (*Typ*); **Groß**|**bür**|**ger(in)** M(F) (*Soziol*) member of the upper classes; **groß**|**bür**|**ger**|**lich** ADJ (*Sociol*) upper-class; **Groß**|**bür**|**ger**|**tum** NT (*Sociol*) upper classes *pl*; **Groß**|**com**|**pu**|**ter** M mainframe (computer); **Groß**|**de**|**mons**|**tra**|**ti**|**on** F mass demonstration; **groß**|**deutsch** ADJ (*Hist*) Pan-German; **das Großdeutsche Reich** (*NS*) the Reich; **Groß**|**deutsch**|**land** NT (*NS*) Greater Germany; **Groß**|**druck** M *, no pl* large print; **ein Buch im ~** a large-print book

Grö|**ße** ['grø:sə] F *-, -n* **a** (= *Format, Maßeinheit*) size; **nach der ~** according to size; **er trägt** *or* **hat ~ 48** he takes *or* is size 48 **b** (= *Höhe, Körpergröße*) height; (= *Flächeninhalt*) size, area, dimensions *pl*; (= *Dimension*) size, dimensions *pl*; (*Math, Phys*) quantity; (*Astron*) magnitude; **nach der ~** according to height/size; **eine unbekannte ~** (*lit, fig*) an unknown quantity; **ein Stern erster ~** a star of the first magnitude **c** *no pl* (= *Ausmaß*) extent; (= *Bedeutsamkeit*) significance **d** *no pl* (= *Erhabenheit*) greatness (= *bedeutender Mensch*) leading light, important figure

Groß-: **Groß**|**ein**|**kauf** M bulk purchase, bulk purchasing *no indef art, no pl*; **Groß**|**ein**-**satz** M ~ **der Feuerwehr/Polizei** *etc* large-scale operation by the fire brigade/police *etc*; **der ~ von Truppen** the large-scale use *or* deployment of troops; **groß**|**el**|**ter**|**lich** ADJ *attr* of one's grandparents; **im ~en Haus wohnen** to live in one's grandparents' house; **Groß**|**el**|**tern** PL grandparents *pl*

Grö|**ßen**|**an**|**ga**|**be** F (indication *or* specification of) size

Groß-: **Groß**|**en**|**kel** M great-grandchild; (= *Junge*) great-grandson; **Groß**|**en**|**ke**|**lin** F great-granddaughter

Grö|**ßen**-: **Grö**|**ßen**|**klas**|**se** F (*Astron*) magnitude; (*Comm*) (size) class; **Grö**|**ßen**|**ord**|**nung** F scale; (= *Größe*) magnitude; (*Math*) order (of magnitude); **ich denke in anderen ~en** I think on a different scale

gro|**ßen**|**teils** ['gro:sn'tails] ADV mostly, for the most part; **er macht seine Arbeit ~ selbstständig** he does his work mostly on his own, he does his work on his own for the most part

Grö|**ßen**-: **Grö**|**ßen**|**un**|**ter**|**schied** M (*im Format*) difference in size; (*in der Höhe, im Wuchs*) difference in height; (*in der Bedeutung*) difference in importance; **Grö**|**ßen**|**ver**|**hält**|**nis** NT proportions *pl* (+*gen* between); (= *Maßstab*) scale; **im ~ 1:100** on the scale 1:100; **etw im richtigen ~ sehen** to see sth in perspective; **Grö**|**ßen**|**wahn**(**sinn**) M megalomania, delusions *pl* of grandeur; **grö**|**ßen**|**wahn**|**sin**|**nig** ADJ *Mensch, Bauten etc* megalomaniac(al); **er ist ~** he is a megalomaniac; **Grö**|**ßen**|**wahn**|**sin**-**ni**|**ge(r)** MF *decl as adj* megalomaniac

grö|**ßer** *comp von* **groß**

grö|**ße**|**ren**|**teils** ['grø:sərən'tails] ADV = **größenteils**

Groß-: **Groß**|**fahn**|**dung** F large-scale manhunt; **Groß**|**fa**|**mi**|**lie** F extended family; **Groß**|**feu**|**er** NT major fire, enormous blaze; **groß**|**flä**|**chig** ADJ extensive; *Gemälde, Muster etc* covering a large area; *Gesicht* flat-featured; **Groß**|**flug**|**ha**|**fen** M major airport; **Groß**-**flug**|**zeug** NT large-capacity aircraft; **Groß**-**for**|**mat** NT large size; (*bei Büchern, Fotos auch*) large format; **ein … im ~** a large-size …/large-format …; **groß**|**for**|**ma**|**tig** ADJ [-fɔrma:tɪç] large-size; *Bücher, Fotos auch* large-format; **Groß**|**fo**|**to** NT giant photo(graph); **Groß**-**fürst** M (*Hist*) grand prince; **Groß**|**fürs**|**ten**-**tum** NT (*Hist*) grand principality; **Groß**|**fürs**-**tin** F (*Hist*) grand princess; **groß**+**füt**|**tern**

VT *sep* to raise, to rear; **Groß**|**ga**|**ra**|**ge** F large (underground) car park (*Brit*) *or* parking garage (*US*); **Groß**|**ge**|**mein**|**de** F municipality with several villages *or* districts; **groß**|**ge**-**mus**|**tert** △ ADJ → **groß 2 c**; **groß**|**ge**|**wach**-**sen** △ ADJ → **groß 2 c**; **Groß**|**grund**|**be**|**sitz** M **a** large-scale land-holding **b** (= *die Großgrundbesitzer*) big landowners *pl*; **Groß**|**grund**-**be**|**sit**|**zer(in)** M(F) big landowner

Groß|**han**|**del** M wholesale trade, wholesaling *no art*; **etw im ~ kaufen** to buy sth wholesale

Groß|**han**|**dels**- *in cpds* wholesale; **Groß**|**han**-**dels**|**kauf**|**frau** F , **Groß**|**han**|**dels**|**kauf**-**mann** M wholesaler; **Groß**|**han**|**dels**|**preis** M wholesale price; **Groß**|**han**|**dels**|**ra**|**batt** M bulk discount

Groß-: **Groß**|**händ**|**ler(in)** M(F) wholesaler; (*inf*: = *Großhandlung*) wholesaler's; **Groß**-**hand**|**lung** F wholesale business; **groß**|**her**-**zig** ADJ *Mensch, Geschenk, Angebot* generous, magnanimous; **~e Motive** the best of motives; **Groß**|**her**|**zig**|**keit** [-hertsıçkait] F *-, no pl* generosity, magnanimity; **Groß**|**her**|**zog** M grand duke; (**der**) **~ Roland** Grand Duke Roland; **Groß**|**her**|**zo**|**gin** F grand duchess; **groß**-**her**|**zog**|**lich** ADJ grand ducal; **Groß**|**her**-**zog**|**tum** NT grand duchy; **das ~ Luxemburg** the Grand Duchy of Luxembourg; **Groß**|**hirn** NT cerebrum; **Groß**|**hirn**|**rin**|**de** F cerebral cortex; **Groß**|**in**|**dust**|**rie** F major *or* big industry; **groß**|**in**|**dust**|**ri**|**ell** ADJ major industrial *attr*; **Groß**|**in**|**dust**|**ri**|**el**|**le(r)** M *decl as adj* major *or* big industrialist; **die französischen ~n** the major *or* big French industrialists; **Groß**|**in**|**qui**|**si**|**tor** M (*Hist*) Grand Inquisitor; **Groß**|**in**|**te**|**gra**|**ti**|**on** F (*Comput*) large-scale integration

Gros|**sist** [grɔ'sıst] M *-en, -en*, **Gros**|**sis**|**tin** [-'sıstın] F *-, -nen* wholesaler; (*inf*: = *Großhandlung*) wholesaler's

Groß-: **groß**|**jäh**|**rig** ADJ (*dated*) of age, major (*form*); **~ werden** to come of age, to reach the age of majority; **groß**|**ka**|**li**|**be**|**rig** [-kali:bərıç], **groß**|**ka**|**lib**|**rig** [-kali:brıç] ADJ large-calibre (*Brit*), large-caliber (*US*)

Groß|**kampf**-: **Groß**|**kampf**|**schiff** NT capital ship; **Groß**|**kampf**|**tag** M (*Mil*) day of a/the great battle; **Montag ist bei uns im Büro meist ~** (*hum*) it's usually all systems go on Monday in the office (*inf*)

Groß-: **Groß**|**ka**|**pi**|**tal** NT **das ~** big business; **Groß**|**ka**|**pi**|**ta**|**list(in)** M(F) big capitalist; **was, du willst 50 Euro? ich bin doch kein ~!** what - you want 50 euros? I'm not made of money! (*inf*); **groß**|**ka**|**riert** △ ADJ → **groß 2 c**; **Groß**|**kat**|**ze** F big cat; **Groß**|**kind** NT (*Sw*) grandchild; **Groß**|**ki**|**no** NT multiplex cinema; **Groß**|**kli**|**ma** NT macroclimate; **Groß**|**knecht** M (*old*) chief (farm)hand; **Groß**|**kon**|**zern** M big *or* large combine; **Groß**|**kopf**|**e(r)**|**te(r)** [-ko:pfətə, -kəpfətə] MF *decl as adj* (*Aus, S Ger: pej*) bigwig (*inf*), bigshot (*inf*); **Groß**|**kotz** ['gro:skɔts] M *-es, -e* (*pej inf*) swank (*inf*); **groß**|**kot**|**zig** ['gro:skɔtsıç] (*pej inf*) ADJ swank (*inf*), ADV swankily (*inf*), pretentiously; **~ auftreten** to act swankily *or* pretentiously, to be swanky (*inf*) *or* pretentious; **Groß**|**kot**|**zig**|**keit** F *-, -en* (*pej inf*) swank (*inf*) *no pl*; **Groß**|**kraft**|**werk** NT large power plant; **Groß**|**kreuz** NT Grand Cross; **Groß**|**kü**|**che** F canteen kitchen; **Groß**|**kun**-**de** M , **Groß**|**kun**|**din** F (*Comm*) major client; **Groß**|**kund**|**ge**|**bung** F mass rally; **Groß**|**lein**|**wand** F (*Film*) big screen; **Groß**-**macht** F (*Pol*) big *or* great power

Groß|**macht**-: **Groß**|**macht**|**po**|**li**|**tik** F (big-)power politics; **Groß**|**macht**|**stel**|**lung** F great-power *or* big-power status

Groß-: **Groß**|**ma**|**ma** [-mama:] F grandmama (*dated*), grandma; **Groß**|**manns**|**sucht** F , *no pl* (*pej*) craving for status; **Groß**|**markt** M hypermarket (*Brit*), large supermarket; **groß**-**ma**|**schig** [-maʃıç] ADJ, ADV = **grobmaschig**

Groß|**mast** M mainmast; **Groß**|**maul** NT (*pej inf*) bigmouth (*inf*), loudmouth (*inf*); **groß**|**mäu**|**lig** [-mɔylıç] (*pej inf*) ADJ big-mouthed *attr* (*inf*), loudmouthed (*inf*); **~ Erklärungen, Worte** boastful (*inf*); **~ verkünden, dass …** to brag *or* boast that …; **Groß**-**mäu**|**lig**|**keit** F *-, no pl* (*pej inf*) big mouth (*inf*); **Groß**|**meis**|**ter** M Grand Master; **Groß**|**mo**-**gul** M (*Hist*) Great Mogul; **Groß**|**muf**|**ti** M (*Hist*) grand mufti; **Groß**|**mut** F *-, no pl* magnanimity; **groß**|**mü**|**tig** [-my:tıç] ADJ magnanimous ADV magnanimously; **Groß**|**mü**|**tig**-**keit** F *-, no pl* magnanimity; **Groß**|**mut**|**ter** F grandmother; **das kannst du deiner ~ erzählen!** (*inf*) you can tell that one to the marines (*Brit inf*), pull the other one (*inf*); **groß**|**müt**|**ter**-**lich** ADJ *attr* **a** (= *von der Großmutter*) of one's grandmother; **im ~en Haus wohnen** to live in one's grandmother's house; **das ~ Erbe** one's inheritance from one's grandmother **b** (= *in der Art einer Großmutter*) grandmotherly; **groß**-**müt**|**ter**|**li**|**cher**|**seits** ADV on one's grandmother's side; **Groß**|**nef**|**fe** M great-nephew; **Groß**|**nich**|**te** F great-niece; **Groß**|**of**|**fen**|**si**-**ve** F (*Mil*) major offensive; **Groß**|**ok**|**tav** [-lɔk-ta:f] NT *-s, no pl* large octavo; **Groß**|**on**|**kel** M great-uncle; **Groß**|**pa**|**ckung** F large *or* economy pack; **Groß**|**pa**|**pa** [-papa:] M grandpapa (*dated*), grandpa; **Groß**|**plas**|**tik** F large sculpture; **groß**|**po**|**rig** ADJ large-pored; **Groß**|**pro**|**duk**|**ti**|**on** F large-scale production; **Groß**|**pro**|**du**|**zent(in)** M(F) large-scale producer; **Groß**|**pro**|**jekt** NT large-scale project; **Groß**|**putz** M *-es, -e* thorough cleaning, ≈ spring cleaning; **Groß**|**quart** NT large quarto; **Groß**|**rat** M , **Groß**|**rä**|**tin** F (*Sw*) member of a/the Cantonal parliament

Groß|**raum** M (*einer Stadt*) **der ~ München** the Munich area *or* conurbation, Greater Munich

Groß|**raum**-: **Groß**|**raum**|**ab**|**teil** NT (*Rail*) open-plan carriage (*Brit*) *or* car (*US*); **Groß**-**raum**|**bü**|**ro** NT open-plan office; **Groß**-**raum**|**flug**|**zeug** NT large-capacity aircraft

Groß-: **groß**|**räu**|**mig** [-rɔymıç] ADJ **a** (= *mit großen Räumen*) with large rooms; **~ sein** to have large rooms **b** (= *mit viel Platz, geräumig*) roomy, spacious **c** (= *über große Flächen*) extensive **d** (= *im großen Umkreis*) **~es Umfahren eines Gebietes** making a large detour (a)round an area ADV **ein Gebiet ~ absperren** to cordon off a large area; **Ortskundige sollten den Bereich ~ umfahren** local drivers should find an alternative route well away from the area; **Groß**|**raum**|**wa**|**gen** M (*von Straßenbahn*) articulated tram (*esp Brit*) *or* streetcar (*US*); (*Rail*) open-plan carriage (*Brit*) *or* car (*US*); **Groß**|**raz**|**zia** F large-scale raid; **Groß**|**rech**-**ner** M mainframe (computer); **Groß**|**rei**|**ne**-**ma**|**chen** NT thorough cleaning, ≈ spring-cleaning; **Groß**|**schiff**|**fahrts**|**weg** ▲ M major waterway (*for seagoing ships*); **groß schrei**-**ben** ▲ VT *irreg* **groß geschrieben werden** (*fig inf*) to be stressed, to be given pride of place, to be writ large; **groß**+**schrei**|**ben** VT *sep irreg* **ein Wort ~** to write a word with a capital/in capitals; **Groß**|**schrei**|**bung** F capitalization; **Groß**|**se**|**gel** NT (*Naut*) mainsail; **groß**-**spre**|**che**|**risch** [-ʃpreçərıʃ] ADJ (*pej*) boastful, boasting *attr*, bragging *attr*; **groß**|**spu**|**rig** [-ʃpu:rıç] (*pej*) ADJ flashy (*inf*), showy (*inf*) ADV **etw ~ erklären** to make a show of saying sth; **~ reden** to speak flamboyantly; **sich ~ benehmen** to be flashy; **Groß**|**spu**|**rig**|**keit** F *-, -en* (*pej*) flashiness (*inf*) *no pl*, showiness (*inf*) *no pl*

Groß|**stadt** F city

Groß|**stadt**|**be**|**völ**|**ke**|**rung** F city population

Groß|**städ**|**ter(in)** M(F) city dweller

groß|**städ**|**tisch** ADJ big-city *attr* ADV **München wirkt ~er als Bonn** Munich has more of a big-city feel to it than Bonn

Groß|**stadt**- *in cpds* city; **Groß**|**stadt**|**kind** NT city child, city kid (*inf*); **Groß**|**stadt**|**mensch**

M city dweller; **der ~** urban man, city dwellers *pl*

Groß-: Groß|tan|te F great-aunt; **Groß|tat** F great feat; **eine medizinische ~** a great medical feat; **groß|tech|nisch** ADJ *Projekt, Anlage, Produktion, Nutzung* large-scale ADV **Kernkraft ~ erzeugen** to produce nuclear power on a large scale

Groß|teil M large part; **zum ~** in the main, for the most part; **zu einem ~** for the most part

groß|teils ['groːstaɪls], **größ|ten|teils** ['grøːstn̩taɪls] ADV in the main, for the most part

größ|te(r, s) *superl von* **groß**

Größt-: Größt|maß NT (*fig*) maximum amount (*an +dat* of); **größt|mög|lich** ADJ *attr* greatest possible

Groß-: Groß|tuer [-tuːɐ] M **-s, -**, **Groß|tue-rin** [-ərɪn] F **-, -nen** (*pej*) boaster, bragger, show-off; **Groß|tue|rei** [-tuːəˈraɪ] F (*pej*) **a** *no pl* boasting, bragging, showing off **b** (= *großtuerische Äußerung etc*) boast; **groß|tue|risch** [-tuːərɪʃ] ADJ (*pej*) boastful, bragging; **groß+tun** *sep irreg* (*pej*) VI to boast, to brag, to show off VR **sich mit etw ~** to show off *or* boast *or* brag about sth; **Groß|un|terneh-men** NT large concern; **Groß|un|terneh-mer(in)** M(F) big businessman/-woman *or* entrepreneur

Groß|va|ter M grandfather

groß|vä|ter|lich ADJ **a** (= *vom Großvater*) of one's grandfather; **er hat den ~en Betrieb übernommen** he has taken over his grandfather's business; **das ~e Erbe** one's inheritance from one's grandfather **b** (= *in der Art eines Großvaters*) grandfatherly

groß|vä|ter|li|cher|seits ADV on one's grandfather's side

Groß|va|ter-: Groß|va|ters|ses|sel M , **Groß|va|ter|stuhl** M (*inf*) fireside armchair; **Groß|va|ter|uhr** F (*inf*) grandfather clock

Groß-: Groß|ver|an|stal|tung F big event; (= *Großkundgebung*) mass rally; **eine sportliche ~** a big sporting event; **Groß|ver|brau|cher(in)** M(F) large consumer; **Groß|ver|die|ner(in)** M(F) big earner; **Groß|ver|such** M (*esp Psych*) large-scale experiment; **Groß|vieh** NT cattle and horses *pl*; **Groß|we|sir** M (*Hist*) grand vizier; **Groß|wet|ter|la|ge** F general weather situation; **die politische ~** the general political climate

Groß|wild NT big game

Groß|wild-: Groß|wild|jagd F big-game hunting; **eine ~** a big-game hunt; **auf ~ gehen** to go big-game hunting; **Groß|wild|jä|ger(in)** M(F) big-game hunter

Groß-: Groß|wör|ter|buch NT large *or* comprehensive dictionary; **groß|wüch|sig** [-vyːk-sɪç] ADJ (*form*) tall; **groß+zie|hen** VT *sep irreg* to raise; *Tier* to rear; **groß|zü|gig** ADJ generous; (= *weiträumig*) spacious; *Plan* large-scale, ambitious; (*inf*: = *ungenau*) generous, liberal ADV generously; (= *spendabel*) magnanimously; (= *weiträumig*) spaciously; **~ gerechnet** at a liberal *or* generous estimate; **Groß|zü|gig|keit** [-tsyː-gɪçkaɪt] F **-**, *no pl* generosity; (= *Weiträumigkeit*) spaciousness; (*von Plan*) (large) scale, ambitiousness; (*inf*: = *Ungenauigkeit*) generousness, liberality

gro|tesk [groˈtɛsk] ADJ grotesque ADV grotesquely; **~ wirken/aussehen** to look grotesque

Gro|tesk [groˈtɛsk] F **-**, *no pl* (*Typ*) grotesque, sans serif

Gro|tes|ke [groˈtɛskə] F **-, -n** (*Art*) grotesque (*-rie*); (*Liter*) grotesquerie

gro|tes|ker|wei|se [groˈtɛskəˈvaɪzə] ADV ironically enough

Grot|te ['grɔtə] F **-, -n a** (= *Höhle*) grotto **b** (*sl*: = *Vagina*) pussy (*sl*)

Grot|ten|olm [-ɔlm] M **-s, -e** (*Zool*) olm (*spec*)

Grou|pie ['gruːpi] NT **-s, -s** groupie

grub *pret von* **graben**

Grub|ber ['grʊbɐ] M **-s, -** (*Agr*) grubber

Grüb|chen ['gryːpçən] NT **-s, -** dimple

Gru|be ['gruːbə] F **-, -n** pit; (*klein*) hole, hollow; (*Min*) mine, pit; (*dated*: = *Gruft, Grab*) grave; **wer andern eine ~ gräbt(, fällt selbst hinein)** (*Prov*) you can easily fall into your own trap; **in die ~ (ein)fahren** to go down the pit; **in die** *or* **zur ~ fahren** (*old*) to give up the ghost

Grü|be|lei [gryːbəˈlaɪ] F **-, -en** brooding *no pl*

grü|beln ['gryːbln̩] VI to brood (*über +acc* about, over)

Gru|ben- *in cpds* pit (*Brit*), mine; **Gru|ben|ar-bei|ter(in)** M(F) pit (*Brit*) *or* mine worker; (*Mann auch*) miner, pitman (*Brit*); **Gru|ben-gas** NT firedamp; **Gru|ben|un|glück** NT mining accident *or* disaster, pit disaster; **Gru|ben|wa|gen** M mine car

Grüb|ler ['gryːblɐ] M **-s, -**, **Grüb|le|rin** [-ərɪn] F **-, -nen** brooder, brooding type

grüb|le|risch ['gryːblərɪʃ] ADJ pensive, brooding

grü|e|zi ['gryːɛtsi] INTERJ (*Sw*) hello, hi (*inf*), good morning/afternoon/evening

Gruft [grʊft] F **-, ⁼e** ['grʏftə] tomb, vault; (*in Kirchen*) crypt; (= *offenes Grab*) grave

Gruf|ti ['grʊfti] M **-s, -s a** (*inf*: = *älterer Mensch*) old fogey (*inf*) **b** (*sl*: = *Okkultist*) ≈ goth

gruf|tig ['grʊftɪç] ADJ (*inf*: = *altmodisch*) *Musik, Mode* square (*inf*), old hat (*inf*); (= *moderig*) *Keller etc* musty

grum|meln ['grʊmln̩] VI to rumble; (*inf*: = *brummeln*) to mumble

Grum|met ['grʊmət] NT **-s**, *no pl*, **Grumt** [grʊmt] NT **-s**, *no pl* (*Agr*) aftermath, rowen (*dial, US*)

grün [gryːn] ADJ (*alle Bedeutungen*) green; (*Pol auch*) ecological; **~e Heringe** fresh herrings, **Aal ~** (*Cook*) (dish of) fresh eel (*with parsley sauce*); **~er Salat** lettuce; **die Grüne Insel** the Emerald Isle; **ein ~er Junge** (*inf*) a greenhorn (*inf*); **~es Licht (für etw) geben/haben** (*fig*) to give/have got the go-ahead *or* green light (for sth); **komm an meine ~e Seite!** (*inf*) come and sit up close to me; **am ~en Tisch, vom ~en Tisch aus** from a bureaucratic ivory tower; **über die ~e Grenze fahren/kommen** (*inf*) to cross the border illegally (*in a wood etc*); **die ~e Hölle** (*fig*) the green hell of the jungle; **die ~en Lungen der Großstadt** (*fig*) the breathing spaces of the city; **~e Minna** (*inf*) Black Maria (*Brit inf*), paddy wagon (*US inf*); **der Grüne Plan** (*Pol*) Agricultural Aid Plan; **die ~e Tonne** container for recyclable waste; **wir haben ~e Weihnachten gehabt** we didn't have a white Christmas; **~e Welle** phased traffic lights; **~e Welle bei 60 km/h** traffic lights phased for 60 kmph; **~ im Gesicht werden** to go green (about the gills (*inf*)); **~e Witwe** (*inf*) lonely suburban housewife; **auf keinen ~en Zweig kommen** (*fig inf*) to get nowhere; **die beiden sind sich gar nicht ~** (*inf*) there's no love lost between them; **er ist dir nicht ~** (*inf*) you're not in his good books (*inf*) ADV (= *in grüner Farbe*) gekleidet (in) green; (= *mit grüner Farbe*) *streichen, anmalen* green; *umranden, unterstreichen* in green; **sich ~ und blau** *or* **gelb ärgern** (*inf*) to be furious; **jdn ~ und blau** *or* **gelb schlagen** (*inf*) to beat sb black and blue

Grün [gryːn] NT **-s, -** *or* (*inf*) **-s** green; (= *Grünfläche*) green spaces *pl*; (*Golf*) green; (*Cards*: = *Pik*) spades *pl*; **die Ampel steht auf ~** the light is (at (*Brit*)) green; **das ist dasselbe in ~** (*inf*) it's (one and) the same (thing)

Grün- *in cpds* green; **Grün|al|ge** F green alga; **grün|al|ter|na|tiv** ADJ (*Pol*) green alternative; **Grün|an|la|ge** F green space *or* area; **grün|äu|gig** ADJ green-eyed; **grün|blau** ADJ greenish-blue, greeny-blue; **grün|blind** ADJ suffering from red-green colour-blindness (*Brit*) *or* color-blindness (*US*); **Grün|blind|heit** F red-green colour-blindness (*Brit*) *or* color-blindness (*US*)

Grund [grʊnt] ⊕ 42.2, 44.1, 44.2, 53.2 M **-(e)s, ⁼e** ['grʏndə] **a** *no pl* (= *Erdboden*) ground; (*old, dial*: = *Erdreich*) soil, ground; **~ und Boden** land; **in ~ und Boden** (*fig, sich blamieren, schämen*) utterly; *verdammen* outright; **jdn in ~ und Boden reden** not to leave sb a leg to stand on, to shoot sb's arguments to pieces; **bis auf den ~ zerstören/abtragen** to raze to the ground **b** (*Aus*) (= *Bauplatz*) (building) plot; (= *Grundstück*) grounds *pl*, land *no pl* art, *no pl* **c** *no pl* (*esp Art*) ground; (*Her*) field **d** *no pl* (*von Gefäßen, Becken etc*) bottom; (= *Meeresgrund*) (sea)bed; (*liter*: = *Talgrund*) bottom of the/a valley; **~ suchen** (*im Wasser*) to look for a foothold, to try to find the bottom; **auf ~ sto-ßen** (*Naut*) (to run to) ground; **ein Schiff auf ~ setzen** to scuttle a ship; **das Glas/den Becher bis auf den ~ leeren** to drain the glass/tumbler **e** *no pl* (*lit, fig*: = *Fundament*) foundation(s *pl*); (= *das Innerste*) depths *pl*; **von ~ auf** *or* **aus** entirely, completely; **etw von ~ auf ändern** to change sth fundamentally *or* from top to bottom; **von ~ auf neu gebaut/geplant** rebuilt/re--planned from scratch; **ein von ~ auf aufrechter Mensch** a thoroughly honest fellow; **den ~ zu etw legen** (*lit, fig*) to lay the foundations of *or* for sth; **einer Sache** (*dat*) **auf den ~ gehen** (*fig*) to get to the bottom of sth; **im ~e seines Herzens** in one's heart of hearts; **im ~e (genommen)** basically, fundamentally **f** (= *Ursache, Veranlassung, Ausrede*) reason; (= *Beweggrund*) grounds *pl*, reason; **aus gesundheitlichen** *etc* **Gründen** for health *etc* reasons, on health *etc* grounds; **aus dem einfachen ~e, dass ...** for the simple reason that ...; **ohne ~** without reason; **auf ~** *or* **aufgrund von Zeugenaussagen** on the basis *or* strength of the witnesses' testimonies; **auf ~** *or* **aufgrund einer Verwechslung/seiner Eifersucht** owing to *or* because of a mistake/his jealousy; **ich habe ~ zu der Annahme, dass ...** I have reason to believe *or* grounds for believing that ...; **Gründe und Gegengründe** pros and cons, arguments for and against; **einen ~ zum Feiern haben** to have good cause for (a) celebration; **du hast keinen ~ zum Klagen** you have no cause to complain *or* for complaint; **die Gründe für und wider** the cases for and against; **jdm ~ (zu etw) geben** to give sb good reason *or* cause (for sth); **jdm allen ~ geben, etw zu glauben** to give sb every reason to believe *etc* sth; **aus diesem ~** for this reason; **aus guten Gründen, mit gutem ~** with good reason; **aus welchem ~(e)?** for what reason?; **aus Gründen** for reasons of; **zu ~e = zugrunde**

Grund-: Grund|ak|kord M (*Mus*) chord in root position; **Grund|an|schau|ung** F , **Grund|an|sicht** F fundamental philosophy; **grund|an|stän|dig** ADJ thoroughly decent; **Grund|an|strich** M first coat; (= *erstes Anstreichen*) application of the first coat; **Grund|aus-bil|dung** F (*Mil*) basic training; **Grund|aus-stat|tung** F basic equipment; **Grund|bau** M **a** *pl* **-bauten** (*Archit*) foundation(s *pl*) **b** *no pl* (= *Grundarbeiten*) laying of the foundations **c** *no pl* (*Univ*: = *Fach*) civil engineering; **Grund|be|deu|tung** F (*Ling*) primary *or* basic meaning; **Grund|be|griff** M basic concept; **Grund|be|sitz** M land, property; (= *das Besitzen*) ownership of land *or* property; **Grund|be|sit|zer(in)** M(F) landowner; **Grund|buch** NT land register; **Grund|buch|amt** NT land registry *or* office; **grund|ehr|lich** ADJ thoroughly honest; **Grund|ei|gen|tum** NT land, property; (= *das Besitzen*) ownership of land *or* property; **Grund|ei|gen|tü|mer(in)** M(F) landowner; **Grund|ein|stel|lung** F fundamental philosophy; **Grund|eis** NT ground ice, anchor-ice → **Arsch a**

grün|den ['grʏndn̩] VT to found; *Argument etc* to base (*auf +acc* on); *Heim, Geschäft* to set up; **gegründet 1857** established *or* founded in

1857; **eine Familie ~** to get married (and have a family) **VI** to be based or founded (in +dat on) **VR** **sich auf etw** (acc) **~** to be based or founded on sth

Grün|der ['grʏndɐ] M **-s, -, Grün|de|rin** [-ərɪn] F **-, -nen** founder

Grün|der|fi|gur F founder

Grün|der|jah|re PL **a** (Hist) years of rapid industrial expansion in Germany (from 1871) **b** (fig: von Atomzeitalter etc) early days pl

Grund-: Grund|er|werb M acquisition of land; **Grund|er|werbs|steu|er** F tax on land acquisition, land transfer tax

Grün|der|zeit F, no pl (Hist) = **Gründerjahre**

Grund-: grund|falsch ADJ utterly wrong; **Grund|far|be** F primary colour (Brit) or color (US); (= Grundierfarbe) ground colour (Brit) or color (US); **Grund|fes|ten** PL (fig) foundations pl; **etw bis in die ~ or in seinen ~ erschüttern** to shake sth to or its very foundations; **an den ~ von etw rütteln** to shake the (very) foundations of sth; **Grund|flä|che** F (Math) base; **Grund|form** F basic form (auch Gram); **Grund|frei|be|trag** M tax-free allowance; **Grund|ge|bühr** F basic or standing charge; **Grund|ge|dan|ke** M basic idea; **Grund|ge|halt** NT (= Entlohnung ohne Zulagen) basic salary; **grund|ge|scheit** ADJ extremely bright

Grund|ge|setz NT **a** (= Grundprinzip) basic law **b das ~** the (German) Constitution

---

GRUNDGESETZ

The "**Grundgesetz** of the Federal Republic of Germany" is the German Constitution, which came into force in 1949. It was actually intended only as a temporary measure until Germany could be re-united, but upon re-unification in 1990 the **Grundgesetz** was retained since people's trust in it had become so great. For changes to be made to the **Grundgesetz** a two-thirds majority is needed both in the **Bundestag** and in the **Bundesrat**. If citizens consider that their basic rights, as laid down in the **Grundgesetz**, have been violated by the state authorities, they can ask for independent arbitration from the **Bundesverfassungsgericht**, which is binding on all parties → BUNDESRAT, BUNDESTAG

Grund|ge|setz-: Grund|ge|setz|än|de|rung F amendment of the (German) Constitution; **grund|ge|setz|wid|rig** ADJ unconstitutional

Grund-: Grund|hal|tung F basic position; **grund|häss|lich** ▲ ADJ extremely or dreadfully ugly; **Grund|herr** M (Hist) lord of the manor; **Grund|herr|schaft** F (Hist) manorial system; **Grund|idee** F basic idea

grun|die|ren [grʊn'diːrən] ptp **grundiert** VT to undercoat; (Art) to ground

Grun|dier|far|be F, **Grun|dier|schicht** F undercoat

Grun|die|rung F -, -en **a** no pl (= das Grundieren) undercoating; (Art) grounding **b** (= Farbe, Fläche) undercoat; (Art) ground

Grund-: Grund|irr|tum M fundamental error; **Grund|ka|pi|tal** NT share capital; (= Anfangskapital) initial capital; **Grund|kennt|nis|se** PL basic knowledge (in +dat of), basics pl; **Grund|kurs** M (Sch, Univ) basic or base course; **Grund|la|ge** F basis; (Mus) root position; **als ~ für etw dienen** to serve as a basis for sth; **auf der ~ von** or +gen on the basis of; **die ~n einer Wissenschaft** the fundamental principles of a science; **die ~n eines Lehrfachs** the rudiments of a subject; **etw auf eine neue ~ stellen** (Beziehungen) to put sth on a different footing or basis; Organisation etc to change the basic structure(s) of sth; **jeder ~ entbehren** to be completely unfounded or without foundation; **Grund|last** F (Tech) constant load; **Grund|last|ka|pa|zi|tät** F (Tech) constant

load capacity; **grund|le|gend** ADJ fundamental, basic (für to); Werk, Textbuch standard ADV fundamentally; **das muss sich ~ verändern** that has to change fundamentally; **sich zu etw ~ äußern** to make a statement of fundamental importance on sth; **Grund|le|gung** [-leːgʊŋ] F -, -en (lit, fig) laying of the foundations; (fig: = Grundriss) outline

gründ|lich ['grʏntlɪç] ADJ thorough; Vorbereitung auch careful; Arbeit painstaking, careful ADV thoroughly; (inf: = sehr auch) really; **jdm ~ die Meinung sagen** to give sb a real piece of one's mind; **da haben Sie sich ~ getäuscht** you're completely mistaken there

Gründ|lich|keit F -, no pl thoroughness; (von Vorbereitung auch) carefulness

Grund-: Grund|li|nie F (Math, Sport) baseline; **Grund|li|ni|en|spiel** NT baseline game; **Grund|lohn** M basic pay or wage(s pl); **grund|los** ADJ **a** Tiefe etc bottomless **b** (fig: = unbegründet) groundless, unfounded; **~es Lachen** laughter for no reason (at all) ADV (fig) without reason, for no reason (at all); **Grund|mau|er** F foundation wall; **bis auf die ~n niederbrennen** to be gutted; **Grund|men|ge** F (Math) fundamental or universal set; **Grund|mo|rä|ne** F (Geol) ground moraine; **Grund|nah|rungs|mit|tel** NT basic food(stuff)

Grün|don|ners|tag [gryːn'dɔnɛstaːk] M Maundy Thursday

Grund-: Grund|ord|nung F basic order; **Grund|pfand|recht** NT encumbrance on property; **Grund|pfei|ler** M (Archit) supporting pier; (fig) cornerstone, keystone; **Grund|re|chen|art** F, **Grund|rech|nungs|art** F basic arithmetical operation; **Grund|recht** NT basic or fundamental right; **Grund|re|gel** F basic rule; (fürs Leben etc) maxim; **Grund|ren|te** F (Econ) ground rent; (Insur) basic pension; **Grund|rich|tung** F general tendency or direction; **Grund|riss** ▲ M (von Gebäude) ground or floor plan; (Math) base; (= Abriss) outline, sketch; „**Grundriss der chinesischen Grammatik**" "Outlines of Chinese Grammar"

Grund|satz M principle; **aus ~** on principle; **ein Mann mit** or **von Grundsätzen** a man of principle; **an seinen Grundsätzen festhalten, bei seinen Grundsätzen bleiben** to stand by or keep to one's principles; **es sich** (dat) **zum ~ machen, etw zu tun** to make a principle of doing sth, to make it a matter of principle to do sth

Grund|satz-: Grund|satz|de|bat|te F, **Grund|satz|dis|kus|si|on** F debate on (general) principles; **Grund|satz|ent|schei|dung** F decision of general principle; **Grund|satz|er|klä|rung** F declaration of principle; **Grund|satz|fra|ge** F basic issue; (= Schlüsselfrage) key question

grund|sätz|lich ['grʊntzɛtslɪç] ADJ fundamental; Verbot absolute; Möglichkeit in principle; Frage of principle ADV (= allgemein, im Prinzip) in principle; (= aus Prinzip) on principle; (= immer) always; (= völlig) absolutely; **sich zu etw ~ äußern** to make a statement of principle on sth; **er ist ~ anderer Meinung als sie** he always disagrees with her, he disagrees with her on principle; **ihre Meinungen sind ~ verschieden** their views are fundamentally different; **das erlaube ich Ihnen ~ nicht** I will most definitely not permit that; **das ist ~ verboten** it is absolutely forbidden; **das ist ~ möglich** it is possible in principle; **er hat ~ kein Interesse für so etwas** he has absolutely no interest in that sort of thing

Grund|sätz|lich|keit F -, no pl fundamental nature

Grund|satz-: Grund|satz|pa|pier NT (Pol) (written) statement of principles; **Grund|satz|re|fe|rat** NT speech or (schriftlich) paper setting out a basic principle; **Grund|satz|ur|teil** NT judgement that establishes a principle

Grund-: grund|schlecht ADJ thoroughly bad; **Grund|schrift** F (Typ) base type; **Grund|schuld** F mortgage; **Grund|schu|le** F primary (Brit) or elementary school; **Grund|schü|ler(in)** M(F) primary (Brit) or elementary (-school) pupil; **Grund|schul|leh|rer(in)** M(F) primary (Brit) or elementary(-school) teacher

---

GRUNDSCHULE

In Germany, all children begin school at the age of six and attend **Grundschule** for the first four years of school life. After the fourth year they take an aptitude test, which helps pupils and parents decide whether they should attend a **Gymnasium**, a **Realschule** or a **Hauptschule**. Another possibility at this stage is the **Orientierungsstufe**. In Austria the corresponding school is called a **Volksschule**. In Switzerland children attend a **Primarschule** for the first three to six years (depending on canton) as part of the **Volksschule** → GYMNASIUM, HAUPTSCHULE, ORIENTIERUNGSSTUFE, REALSCHULE

Grund-: grund|so|li|de ADJ very respectable; **grund|stän|dig** ADJ **a** (= bodenständig) indigenous **b** Schule primary attr (Brit), elementary attr **c** (Bot) basal, basilar; **Grund|stein** M (lit, fig) foundation stone; **der ~ zu etw sein** to form the foundation(s) of or for sth; **den ~ zu etw legen** (lit) to lay the foundation stone of sth; (fig) to lay the foundations of or for sth; **Grund|stein|le|gung** [-leːgʊŋ] F -, -en laying of the foundation stone; **Grund|stel|lung** F (Turnen) starting position; (Boxen) on-guard position; (Chess) initial or starting position; (Mus) root position; **Grund|steu|er** F (local) property tax, **~ rates** pl (Brit dated); **Grund|stim|me** F bass; **Grund|stim|mung** F prevailing mood; **Grund|stock** M basis, foundation; **Grund|stoff** M basic material; (= Rohstoff) raw material; (Chem) element; **Grund|stoff|in|dust|rie** F primary industry

Grund|stück NT plot (of land); (= Baugrundstück auch) site; (bebaut) property; (= Anwesen) estate; **in ~en spekulieren** to speculate in property or in real estate

Grund|stücks-: Grund|stücks|haf|tung F real estate collateral; **Grund|stücks|mak|ler(in)** M(F) estate agent (Brit), real estate agent, realtor (US); **Grund|stücks|markt** M property market; **Grund|stücks|preis** M land price; **Grund|stücks|spe|ku|lant(in)** M(F) property speculator; **Grund|stücks|spe|ku|la|ti|on** F property speculation

Grund-: Grund|stu|di|um NT (Univ) basic course; **Grund|stu|fe** F **a** first stage; (Sch) ≈ junior (Brit) or grade (US) school **b** (Gram) positive (degree); **Grund|ten|denz** F, **Grund|te|nor** M basic trend; (verborgen) underlying trend; **Grund|ton** M pl **-tö|ne** (Mus) (eines Akkords) root; (einer Tonleiter) tonic keynote; (= Grundfarbe) ground colour (Brit) or color (US); **Grund|übel** NT basic or fundamental evil; (= Nachteil) basic problem; **Grund|um|satz** M (Physiol) basal metabolism

Grün|dung F -, -en founding, foundation; (Archit = Fundament) foundation(s pl); (= das Anlegen des Fundaments) laying of the foundations; (von Heim, Geschäft) setting up; **die ~ einer Familie** getting married (and having a family)

Grün|dün|ger M (Agr) green manure

Grün|dungs-: Grün|dungs|jahr NT year of the foundation; **Grün|dungs|ka|pi|tal** NT initial capital; **Grün|dungs|rek|tor(in)** M(F) (Univ) first vice chancellor (Brit), first university president (US); **Grün|dungs|ver|samm|lung** F inaugural meeting (of a new company)

Grün|dün|gung F (Agr) green manuring

Grund-: grund|ver|kehrt ADJ completely wrong; **Grund|ver|mö|gen** NT landed proper-

---

ty, real estate; **Grund|ver|schie|den** ADJ totally *or* entirely different; **Grund|was|ser** NT , *no pl* ground water; **Grund|was|ser|spie|gel** M , **Grund|was|ser|stand** M water table, ground-water level; **Grund|wehr|dienst** M national (*Brit*) *or* selective (*US*) service; **den ~ absolvieren** *or* **leisten** to do one's national (*Brit*) *or* selective (*US*) service; **Grund|wert** M (*Philos*) fundamental value; **Grund|wer|te|ka|ta|log** M (*Philos*) index of fundamental values; **Grund|wis|sen** NT basic knowledge (*in* +*dat* of); **Grund|wort** NT *pl* -wörter (*Gram*) root; **Grund|zahl** F (*Math*) base (number); (= *Kardinalzahl*) cardinal number; **Grund|zins** M (*Hist*) feudal dues *pl* (*Hist*); (= *Feudalabgabe*) essential feature *or* trait; „**Grundzüge der Geometrie**" "Basic Geometry", "(The) Rudiments of Geometry"; **etw in seinen Grundzügen darstellen** to outline (the essentials of) sth; **dieses Werk entstand in seinen Grundzügen schon ...** the essential features *or* the essentials of this work appeared as early as ...

grü|nen ['gry:nən] VI (*geh*) to turn green; (*fig: Liebe, Hoffnung*) to blossom (forth)

Grü|nen-: **Grü|nen|ab|ge|ord|ne|te(r)** MF *decl as adj* Green MP *or* representative; **Grü|nen|frak|ti|on** F Green Party (*in Parliament/ on council*)

Grü|ne(r) ['gry:nə] MF *decl as adj* **a** (*Pol*) Green **b** (*dated inf:* = *Polizist*) cop (*inf*), copper (*Brit inf*), bluebottle (*dated Brit inf*)

DIE GRÜNEN

The political party **Die Grünen**, which is now part of Bündnis 90/Die Grünen, was founded in 1980. It grew out of the numerous citizens' action groups operating at the time, together with the women's and peace movements. Its objectives are determined by its principles, with priority being given to environmental policy, the restructuring of Germany's economic and social orders to create a more equal society for men and women, the subordination of executive bodies to grass-roots decisions, and an active peace policy with the ultimate aim of multilateral disarmament → BÜNDNIS 90/DIE GRÜNEN

Grü|ne(s) ['gry:nə] NT *decl as adj* (= *Farbe*) green; (*als Ausschmückung*) greenery; (= *Gemüse*) greens *pl*, green vegetables *pl*; (= *Grünfutter*) green stuff; **ins ~ fahren** to go to the country; **wir essen viel ~s** (*inf*) we eat a lot of greens; **~s in die Suppe tun** (*inf*) to put green vegetables in the soup

---

GRÜNE WOCHE

The International **Grüne Woche**, which takes place every year in Berlin, is a food fair focusing on food science, agriculture and horticulture. It is particularly popular with the general public, since delicacies and specialities from all over the world are on offer.

GRÜNER PUNKT

The **grüner Punkt** is a green symbol used on packaging materials which are suitable for recycling and which should therefore be discarded in the **gelbe Tonne** *or* **gelber Sack**, separate from other waste. Manufacturers wishing to use the symbol on their products must obtain a permit from DSD (**Duales System Deutschland GmbH**) → DUALES SYSTEM

Grün-: **Grün|fink** M greenfinch; **Grün|flä|che** F green space *or* area; **Grün|fut|ter** NT green fodder, greenstuff; (*inf:* = *Salat*) salad; (*inf:* = *Gemüse*) green vegetables *pl*, greens *pl* (*inf*); **grün|gelb** ADJ greenish yellow, greeny-yellow; **Grün|gür|tel** M green belt; **Grün|kern** M (= *unreifer Dinkel*) (dried) unripe spelt grain; **Grün|kohl** M (curly) kale; **Grün|land** NT

no pl meadowland *no indef art*, grassland *no indef art*; **grün|lich** ['gry:nlɪç] ADJ greenish; **Grün|pflan|ze** F non-flowering *or* foliage plant; **Grün|pha|se** F (*Mot*) green phase; **Grün|rock** M (*hum*) gamekeeper; (= *Jäger*) huntsman (*esp Brit*), hunter; **Grün|schna|bel** M (*inf*) (little) whippersnapper (*inf*); (= *Neuling*) greenhorn (*inf*); **sei still, du ~!** be quiet, you little know-all! (*Brit inf*) *or* know-it-all (*US inf*); **Grün|span** M , *no pl* verdigris; **~ ansetzen** *or* **bilden** to form verdigris; (*fig*) to grow hoary; **Grün|specht** M green woodpecker; **Grün|stich** M (*Phot*) green cast; **grün|sti|chig** [-ʃtɪçɪç] ADJ with a green cast; **Grün|strei|fen** M central reservation (*Brit*), median (strip) (*US, Austral*); (*am Straßenrand*) grass verge

grun|zen ['grʊntsn] VTI to grunt

Grün|zeug NT , *no pl* greens *pl*, green vegetables *pl*; (= *Kräuter*) herbs *pl*

Grunz|laut M grunt

Grüpp|chen ['grʏpçən] NT -s, - (*usu pej*) little group

Grup|pe ['grʊpə] F -, -n group (*auch Math*); (*von Mitarbeitern auch*) team; (*Mil*) ≈ squad; (*Aviat*) ≈ squadron (*Brit*), ≈ group (*US*); (*von Pfadfindern*) section; (= *Klasse, Kategorie*) class, group; **eine ~ Zuschauer** *or* **von Zuschauern** a group of onlookers; **eine ~ von Beispielen** a list *or* series of examples; **~n (zu je fünf/sechs) bilden** to form (into) *or* to make groups (of five/six)

Grup|pen- *in cpds* group; **Grup|pen|ar|beit** F teamwork; **Grup|pen|bild** NT group portrait; **Grup|pen|bil|dung** F group formation, formation of groups; **Grup|pen|dy|na|mik** F (*Psych*) group dynamics; **grup|pen|dy|na|misch** ADJ (*Psych*) group-dynamic; **Grup|pen|ego|is|mus** M self-interest of the/a group; **Grup|pen|füh|rer(in)** M(F) group leader; (*Mil*) squad leader; **Grup|pen|le|ben** NT group living; **Grup|pen|lei|ter(in)** M(F) group manager; **Grup|pen|mit|glied** NT member of a/the group, group member; **Grup|pen|pä|da|go|gik** F group teaching; **Grup|pen|psy|cho|lo|gie** F group psychology; **Grup|pen|rei|se** F group travel *no pl*; **Grup|pen|sex** M group sex; **Grup|pen|sieg** M (*Sport*) **den ~ erringen** to win in one's group; **Grup|pen|sie|ger(in)** M(F) (*Sport*) group winner, winner in *or* of a/the group; **grup|pen|spe|zi|fisch** ADJ group-specific; **Grup|pen|sta|tus** M (*Pol*) interest-group status; **Grup|pen|the|ra|pie** F group therapy; **Grup|pen|un|ter|richt** M group learning; **Grup|pen|ver|ge|wal|ti|gung** F multiple rape, gang bang (*inf*); **grup|pen|wei|se** ADV in groups; (*Ind, Comm, Sport auch*) in teams; (*Mil*) in squads; (*Aviat*) in squadrons; **Grup|pen|zwang** M , *no pl* (*Psych*) (peer) group pressure

grup|pie|ren [grʊˈpiːrən] *ptp* **gruppiert** VT to group VR to form a group/groups, to group

Grup|pie|rung F -, -en **a** *no pl* grouping **b** (= *Konstellation*) grouping; (= *Gruppe*) group; (*Pol*) faction

Grus [gruːs] M -es, -e [-zə] (= *Gesteinsschutt*) rubble; (= *Kohlengrus*) slack

Grusel-: **Gru|sel|ef|fekt** M horror effect; **Gru|sel|film** M horror *or* gothic film; **Gru|sel|ge|schich|te** F tale of horror, horror *or* gothic story

gru|se|lig ['gruːzəlɪç] ADJ horrifying, gruesome; *Geschichte, Film* creepy, spine-chilling

Gru|sel|mär|chen NT tale of horror, horror story

gru|seln ['gruːzln] VTI *impers* **mich** *or* **mir gruselt auf Friedhöfen** cemeteries give me an eerie feeling, cemeteries give me the creeps; **hier kann man das Gruseln lernen** this will teach you the meaning of fear VR **hier würde ich mich ~** a place like this would give me the

creeps; **sie gruselt sich vor Schlangen** snakes give her the creeps

Gru|si|cal ['gruːzikl] NT -s, -s (*hum*) comic horror *or* gothic film *or* (= *Theaterstück*) play

grus|lig ['gruːslɪç] ADJ = **gruselig**

Gruß [gruːs] ✪ 48.2 M -es, ⸚e ['gryːsə] **a** greeting; (= *Grußgeste, Mil*) salute; **zum ~** in greeting; **der deutsche ~** (*NS*) the Nazi salute; **er ging ohne ~ an mir vorbei** he walked past me without saying hello **b** (*als Zeichen der Verbundenheit*) **viele Grüße** best wishes (*an* +*acc* to); **bestell Renate bitte viele Grüße von mir** please give Renate my best wishes *or* my regards, remember me to Renate (*Brit*); **schick mir einen ~ aus Paris** drop me a line from Paris; **sag ihm einen schönen ~** say hello to him (from me); **einen (schönen) ~ an Ihre Gattin!** my regards to your wife **c** (*als Briefformel*) **mit bestem ~, mit besten Grüßen** yours; **mit brüderlichem/sozialistischem ~** (*Pol*) yours fraternally; **mit freundlichen Grüßen** *or* **freundlichem ~** (*bei Anrede Mr/Mrs/Miss X*) Yours sincerely, Yours truly (*esp US*); (*bei Anrede Sir(s)/Madam*) Yours faithfully, Yours truly (*esp US*)

Gruß|ad|res|se F , **Gruß|an|spra|che** F , **Gruß|bot|schaft** F (*Pol*) message of greeting

grü|ßen ['gryːsn] ✪ 48.2, 50.1 VT **a** (= *guten Tag sagen zu*) to greet; (*Mil*) to salute; **grüßt er dich auch nicht?** doesn't he say hello to you either?; **sei gegrüßt!** (*old, geh, iro*) greetings; **grüß dich!** (*inf*) hello there!, hi! (*inf*) **b** (= *Grüße übermitteln*) **Otto lässt dich (schön) ~** Otto sends his regards *or* best wishes, Otto asked to be remembered to you (*Brit*); **ich soll Sie von ihm ~** he sends his regards *etc*; **grüß mir deine Mutter!, grüß deine Mutter von mir!** remember me to your mother (*Brit*), give my regards to your mother; **und grüß mir Wien/den Goldenen Löwen** and say hello to Vienna/the Golden Lion for me; **grüß Gott!** (*S Ger, Aus*) hello VI to say hello, to give a greeting (*form*); (*Mil*) to salute; **Otto lässt ~** Otto sends his regards; **die Berge grüßten aus der Ferne** (*liter*) the mountains greeted us in the distance VR **ich grüße mich nicht mehr mit ihm** I don't say hello to him any more

Gruß-: **Gruß|for|mel** F form of greeting; (*am Briefanfang*) salutation; (*am Briefende*) complimentary close, ending; **gruß|los** ADV without a word of greeting, without saying hello; (*beim Abschied*) without saying goodbye; **Gruß|ord|nung** F (*Mil*) saluting hierarchy; **Gruß|pflicht** F (*Mil*) obligation to salute; **Gruß|schrei|ben** NT greeting; (*Pol*) letter of greeting; **Gruß|te|le|gramm** NT greetings telegram; (*Pol*) goodwill telegram; **Gruß|wort** NT *pl* -worte greeting

Grütz-: **Grütz|beu|tel** M (*Med*) wen; **Grütz|brei** M gruel

Grüt|ze ['grʏtsə] F -, -n **a** groats *pl*; (= *Brei*) gruel; **rote ~** *type of red fruit jelly* **b** *no pl* (*inf:* = *Verstand*) brains *pl* (*inf*); **der hat ~ im Kopf** (*inf*) he's got brains (*inf*)

Grütz|kopf M (*inf*) **a** (= *Dummkopf*) thickhead (*inf*), thickie (*inf*) **b** (= *Verstand*) thick head

Gschaftl|hu|ber ['kʃaftlhuːbɐ] M -s, -, **Gschaftl|hu|be|rin** [-ərɪn] F -, -nen (*S Ger, Aus: inf*) busybody

gscha|mig ['kʃaːmɪç] ADJ (*Aus inf*) bashful

Gscher|te(r) ['kʃeːrtɐ] MF *decl as adj* (*Aus inf*) idiot

Gschnas [kʃnaːs] NT -, *no pl* (*Aus, inf*) fancy-dress *or* costume (*US*) party

G7, **G-7** [geːˈziːbn] F - G7

G7-Staat, **G-7-Staat** [geːˈziːbn-] M G7 nation

Gspu|si ['kʃpuːzi] NT -s, -s (*S Ger, Aus: inf*) **a** (= *Liebschaft*) affair, carry-on (*inf*) **b** (= *Liebste(r)*) darling, sweetheart

Gstan|zel [kʃˈtantsl] NT **-s, -n, Gstanzl** [kʃˈtantsl] NT **-s, -n** (S Ger, Aus inf) (rude) song (containing humour, innuendo or criticism)

Gstät|ten [ˈkʃtɛtn] F -, - (Aus inf) grassy patch of land on a hillside

GTI-Mo|dell [geːteːˈʔiː-] NT (Aut) GTI model

Gu|a|no [ˈguaːno] M -s, no pl (= Dünger aus Vogelmist) guano

Gu|a|te|ma|la [guateˈmaːla] NT -s Guatemala

Gu|a|te|mal|te|ke [guatemalˈteːkə] M -n, -n, **Gu|a|te|mal|te|kin** [-ˈteːkɪn] F -, -nen Guatemalan

gu|a|te|mal|te|kisch [guatemalˈteːkɪʃ] ADJ Guatemalan

Gu|a|ve [ˈguaːvə] F -, -en guava

Gu|a|ya|na [guaˈjaːna] NT -s Guiana; (= ehem. Brit.-Guayana) Guyana

Gu|a|ya|ner [guaˈjaːnɐ] M -s, -, **Gu|a|ya|ne|rin** [-ərɪn] F -, -nen → **Guayana** Guianese/Guyanese

gu|a|ya|nisch [guaˈjaːnɪʃ] ADJ → **Guayana** Guianese/Guyanese

gu|cken [ˈgʊkn] VI (= sehen) to look (zu at); (heimlich auch) to peep, to peek; (= hervorschauen) to peep (aus out of); **lass mal ~!** let's have a look, give us a look (inf); **jdm in die Karten ~** to look or have a look at sb's cards VT (inf) **Fernsehen ~** to watch telly (Brit inf) or television (inf)

Gu|cker [ˈgʊkɐ] M -s, - (inf) a (= Fernglas) telescope; (= Opernglas) opera glass(es pl) b PL (= Augen) peepers (inf), eyes pl

Guck-: Guck|fens|ter NT small window; (in Tür) peephole, judas window; **Guck|in|die|luft** [ˈgʊklɪndiːlʊft] M → **Hans**; **Guck|kas|ten** M (inf = Fernseher) telly (Brit inf), gogglebox (Brit inf), tube (US inf); **Guck|kas|ten|büh|ne** F proscenium or fourth-wall stage; **Guck|loch** NT peephole

Gue|ril|la[1] [geˈrɪlja] F -, -s a (= Guerillakrieg) guerilla war b (= Guerillaeinheit) guerilla unit

Gue|ril|la[2] M -(s), -s (= Guerillakämpfer) guerilla

Gue|ril|la- [geˈrɪlja] in cpds guerilla; **Gue|ril|la|krieg** M guerilla war

Gue|ril|le|ro [gerɪlˈjeːro] M -s, -s, **Gue|ril|le|ra** [gerɪlˈjeːra] F -, -s guerilla fighter

Guern|sey [ˈgœːɐnzi] NT -s Guernsey

Gu|gel|hupf [ˈguːglhʊpf] M -s, -e (S Ger, Aus), **Gu|gel|hopf** [ˈguːglhɔpf] M -s, -e (Sw) (Cook) gugelhupf

Güg|ge|li [ˈgygəli] NT -s, - (Sw Cook) roast chicken

Guil|lo|ti|ne [gɪljoˈtiːnə, gijoˈtiːnə] F -, -n guillotine

guil|lo|ti|nie|ren [gɪljotiˈniːrən, gijo-] ptp **guillotiniert** VT to guillotine

Gui|nea [gɪˈneːa] NT -s (Geog) Guinea

Gui|ne|er [gɪˈneːɐ] M -s, -, **Gui|ne|e|rin** [-ərɪn] F -, -nen Guinean

gui|ne|isch [gɪˈneːɪʃ] ADJ Guinean

Gu|lag [ˈguːlak] M -(s), -s gulag

Gu|lasch [ˈguːlaʃ, ˈgʊlaʃ] NT OR M -(e)s, -e or -s goulash; **ich mache aus dir ~!** (inf) I'll beat the living daylights out of you (inf)

Gu|lasch-: Gu|lasch|ka|no|ne F (Mil sl) field kitchen; **Gu|lasch|kom|mu|nis|mus** M (pej) communism which is concerned only with material well-being; **Gu|lasch|sup|pe** F goulash soup

Gul|den [ˈgʊldn] M -s, - (Hist) (= Münze) florin; (= niederländischer Gulden) g(u)ilder, gulden

gül|den [ˈgʏldn] ADJ (poet) golden

Gül|le [ˈgʏlə] F -, no pl (S Ger, Sw) liquid manure

Gul|ly [ˈgʊli] M OR NT -s, -s drain

gül|tig [ˈgʏltɪç] ADJ valid; **nach den ~en Bestimmungen** according to current regulations; **nach dem bis Mai noch ~en Gesetz** according to the law in force until May; **ab wann ist der Fahrplan ~?** when does the timetable come into ef-

fect or force?; **~ für zehn Fahrten** valid or good for ten trips; **~ werden** to become valid; (Gesetz, Vertrag) to come into force or effect; (Münze) to become legal tender

Gül|tig|keit F -, no pl validity; (von Gesetz) legal force; **die alten Geldscheine verlieren im Herbst ihre ~** the old notes (Brit) or bills (US) cease to be legal tender in the autumn

Gül|tig|keits-: Gül|tig|keits|be|reich M range of validity; (eines Gesetzes etc) scope; **Gül|tig|keits|dau|er** F period of validity; (eines Gesetzes) period in force

Gul|yás [ˈgʊlaʃ] NT OR M -, -e (esp Aus) goulash

Gum|mi [ˈgʊmi] NT OR M -s, -s (= Material) rubber; (= Gummiarabikum) gum; (= Radiergummi) rubber (Brit), eraser; (= Gummiband) rubber or elastic (esp Brit); (in Kleidung etc) elastic; (inf = Kondom) rubber (esp US inf), Durex®

Gum|mi- in cpds rubber; **Gum|mi|an|zug** M wetsuit; **Gum|mi|a|ra|bi|kum** NT -s, no pl gum arabic; **gum|mi|ar|tig** ADJ rubbery ADV like rubber; **Gum|mi|band** [-bant] NT pl **-bänder** rubber or elastic (esp Brit) band; (in Kleidung) elastic; **Gum|mi|bär|chen** [-bɛːɐçən] NT -s, - ≈ jelly baby (Brit), gummi bear; **Gum|mi|baum** M rubber plant; **Gum|mi|be|griff** M (inf) elastic concept; **Gum|mi|boot** NT inflatable boat, rubber dinghy

gum|mie|ren [gʊˈmiːrən] ptp **gummiert** VT to gum; **gummiert** (Briefmarke, Kuvert) gummed; (Tech) rubberized

Gum|mie|rung F -, -en a (= Verfahren) gumming b (= gummierte Fläche) gum

Gum|mi-: Gum|mi|ge|schoss ▲ NT rubber bullet; **Gum|mi|hand|schuh** M rubber glove; **Gum|mi|harz** NT gum resin; **Gum|mi|ho|se** F, **Gum|mi|hös|chen** [-høːsçən] NT plastic pants pl; **Gum|mi|kis|sen** NT inflatable rubber cushion; **Gum|mi|knüp|pel** M rubber truncheon; **Gum|mi|lin|se** F (Phot) zoom lens; **Gum|mi|man|tel** M plastic raincoat, plastic mac (Brit); **Gum|mi|muf|fe** F (Comput: für Akustikkoppler) rubber cups pl; **Gum|mi|pa|ra|graf** ▲ M (inf) ambiguous clause; **Gum|mi|rei|fen** M rubber tyre (Brit) or tire (US); **Gum|mi|sau|ger** M rubber teat (Brit) or nipple (US); **Gum|mi|schlauch** M rubber hose; (bei Fahrrad etc) inner tube; **Gum|mi|schutz** M (dated) sheath; **Gum|mi|soh|le** F rubber sole; **Gum|mi|stie|fel** M rubber boot, gumboot, wellington (boot) (Brit), wellie (Brit inf); (bis zu den Oberschenkeln) wader; **Gum|mi|strumpf** M rubber or elastic stocking; **Gum|mi|tier** NT rubber animal; (aufblasbar) inflatable animal; **Gum|mi|un|ter|la|ge** F rubber sheet; **Gum|mi|wa|ren** PL rubber goods pl; **Gum|mi|wucht|ge|schoss** ▲ NT rubber bullet; **Gum|mi|zel|le** F padded cell; **Gum|mi|zug** M (piece of) elastic

Gunst [gʊnst] F -, no pl favour (Brit), favor (US); (= Wohlwollen auch) goodwill; (= Gönnerschaft auch) patronage; (des Schicksals etc) benevolence; **zu meinen/deinen ~en** in my/your favo(u)r; **jdm eine ~ erweisen** (geh) to do sb a kindness; **jdm die ~ erweisen, etw zu tun** (geh) to be so gracious as to do sth for sb; **jds ~ besitzen** or **genießen, in jds** (dat) **~ stehen** to have or enjoy sb's favo(u)r, to be in favo(u)r with sb; **zu ~en** = zugunsten

Gunst-: Gunst|be|weis M, **Gunst|be|zei|gung** [-bətsaigʊŋ] F -, -en mark of favour (Brit) or favor (US); **Gunst|ge|wer|be** NT (hum) the oldest profession in the world (hum), prostitution; **Gunst|ge|werb|le|rin** F (hum) lady of easy virtue, prostitute

güns|tig [ˈgʏnstɪç] ADJ favourable (Brit), favorable (US); (zeitlich, bei Reisen etc) convenient; Angebot, Preis etc reasonable, good; **bei ~er Witterung** weather permitting; **die Fähre um 3 Uhr ist ~er** the 3 o'clock ferry is more convenient or better; **im ~sten Fall(e)** with luck; **im ~sten Licht** (lit, fig) in the most favo(u)rable light; **mit Geschäften und Erholungsmöglichkeiten in ~er**

Lage convenient for shops and recreational facilities

ADV kaufen, verkaufen for a good price; einkaufen, beziehen at a good price; **jdm etw ~er geben** to give sb sth at a discount or for less; **jdm/einer Sache ~ gesinnt sein** (geh) to be favourably (Brit) or favorably (US) disposed toward(s) sb/sth; **es trifft sich ...** it's very lucky that ...; **~ bei etw abschneiden** to do well in sth, to come out of sth very well; **die Stadt liegt ~ (für)** the town is well situated (for); **wie komme ich am ~sten nach ...?** what's the best or easiest way to get to ...?; **„Fernseher ~ abzugeben"** "television for sale: bargain price"

güns|ti|gen|falls ADV at best; (bei Geldbeträgen auch) at (the) most

Güns|tig|keits|prin|zip NT principle of advantage

güns|tigs|ten|falls ADV at the very best; (bei Geldbeträgen auch) at (the) most

Günst|ling [ˈgʏnstlɪŋ] M -s, -e (pej) favourite (Brit), favorite (US)

Günst|lings|wirt|schaft F (pej) (system of) favouritism (Brit) or favoritism (US)

Gupf [gʊpf] M -(e)s, -e (Aus) head

Gup|py [ˈgʊpi] M -s, -s (Zool) guppy

Gur|gel [ˈgʊrgl] F -, -n throat; (= Schlund) gullet; **jdm die ~ zudrücken** or **abdrücken** or **abschnüren** or **zuschnüren** (lit, fig) to strangle sb; **dann springt** or **geht sie mir an die ~!** (inf) she'll kill me (inf); **sein Geld durch die ~ jagen** (inf) to pour all one's money down one's throat or gullet (inf); **sich** (dat) **die ~ schmieren** (hum) to oil one's throat or gullet (inf)

Gur|gel|mit|tel NT gargle

gur|geln [ˈgʊrgln] VI a (= den Rachen spülen) to gargle b (Wasser, Laut) to gurgle

Gur|gel|was|ser NT pl **-wässer** gargle

Gürk|chen [ˈgʏrkçən] NT -s, - midget gherkin (Brit), baby gherkin pickle (US)

Gur|ke [ˈgʊrkə] F -, -n a cucumber; (= Essiggurke) gherkin, saure ~n pickled gherkins b (hum inf: = Nase) hooter (inf), conk (Brit inf), nose c (sl: = Schrottauto) banger (Brit inf), jalopy (inf)

gur|ken [ˈgʊrkn] VI aux sein (sl) to drive

Gurken-: Gur|ken|ho|bel M slicer; **Gur|ken|sa|lat** M cucumber salad

gur|ren [ˈgʊrən] VI (lit, fig) to coo

Gurt [gʊrt] M -(e)s, -e (= Gürtel, Sicherheitsgurt, Ladestreifen) belt; (= Riemen) strap; (= Sattelgurt) girth; (Archit) girder

Gurt|band [-bant] NT pl **-bänder** waistband

Gür|tel [ˈgʏrtl] M -s, - (= Gurt, Zone) belt; (= Absperrkette) cordon; **den ~ enger schnallen** (lit, fig) to tighten one's belt

Gür|tel-: Gür|tel|li|nie F waist; **ein Schlag unter die ~** (lit) a blow below the belt; **das war ein Schlag unter die ~** (fig) that really was (hitting) below the belt; **Gür|tel|rei|fen** M radial (tyre (Brit) or tire (US)); **Gür|tel|ro|se** F (Med) shingles sing or pl; **Gür|tel|schnal|le** F belt buckle; **Gür|tel|ta|sche** F belt bag, pouch; **Gür|tel|tier** NT armadillo

gür|ten [ˈgʏrtn] (geh) VT to gird (old); Pferd to girth VR to gird oneself

Gurt-: Gurt|muf|fel M (inf) person who refuses to wear a seat belt; **Gurt|pflicht** F, no pl **es besteht ~** the wearing of seat belts is compulsory; **Gurt|straf|fer** [-ʃtrafe] M -s, - (Aut) seat-belt tensioner; **Gurt|zwang** M, no pl = **Gurtpflicht**

Gu|ru [ˈguːru] M -s, -s (lit, fig) guru

GUS [gʊs] F - abbr von **Gemeinschaft Unabhängiger Staaten** CIS

Gu|sche [ˈgʊʃə] F -, -n (dial) = **Gosche**

Guss [gʊs] M -es, ⸚e [ˈgʏsə] a (Metal) (no pl: = das Gießen) casting, founding; (= Gussstück) cast; **(wie) aus einem ~** (fig) a unified whole b (= Strahl) stream, gush; (inf: = Regenguss) cloudburst, downpour; **kalte Güsse** (*Med*) cold affusions **c** (= *Zuckerguss*) icing, frosting (*esp US*); (*durchsichtig*) glaze; **einen Kuchen mit einem ~ überziehen** to ice or frost (*US*) a cake

Guss-: Guss|as|phalt ▲ M poured asphalt; **Guss|be|ton** ▲ M cast concrete; **Guss|ei|sen** ▲ NT cast iron; **guss|ei|sern** ▲ ADJ cast-iron; **Guss|form** ▲ F mould (*Brit*), mold (*US*); **Guss|naht** ▲ F seam; **Guss|stahl** ▲ M cast steel

GUS-Staat ['ɡʊs-] M CIS state

gus|tie|ren [ɡʊsˈtiːrən] *ptp* **gustiert** VT **a** = **goutieren b** (*Aus*) to taste, to try

gus|ti|ös [ɡʊsˈtiøːs] ADJ (*Aus*) appetizing

Gus|to ['ɡʊsto] M -s (*rare*) -s (*geh, Aus*) **a** (= *Appetit*) **~ auf etw** (*acc*) **haben** to feel like sth **b** (*fig*: = *Geschmack*) taste; **nach jds ~** to sb's taste; **mit ~** with gusto; **nach eigenem ~** just as one/ he *etc* likes

Gus|to|stü|ckerl NT -s, -(n) (*Aus inf*) delicacy

gut [ɡuːt] ADJ *comp* **besser** ['bɛsɐ], *superl* **beste(r, s)** ['bɛstə] good; **probieren Sie unsere ~en Weine/Speisen!** try our fine wines/food; **er ist in der Schule/in Spanisch sehr ~** he's very good at school/Spanish; **~e Frau!** (*dated*) my dear lady; **er macht sich** (*dat*) **einen ~en Tag** (= *faulenzt*) he's taking things easy for a day; (= *amüsiert sich*) he's having a good day of it; **die ~e Stube** the best or good room; **das ist ~ gegen** or **für** (*inf*) **Husten** it's good for coughs; **wozu ist das ~?** (*inf*) what's that for?; **er ist immer für eine Überraschung ~** (*inf*) he's always good for a surprise; **das war Pech, aber wer weiß, wozu es ~ ist** it was bad luck, but it's an ill wind (that blows nobody any good) (*Brit prov*), it was bad luck, but every cloud has a silver lining (*prov*); **sei so ~ (und) gib mir das** would you mind giving me that; **würden Sie so ~ sein und ...** would you be good enough to ...; **jdm ~ sein** (*old*) to love sb; **sie ist ihm von Herzen ~** (*old*) her heart is his (*liter*); **bist du mir wieder ~?** (*dated*) are you friends with me again?; **dafür ist er sich zu ~** he wouldn't stoop to that sort of thing; **sind die Bilder/die Brötchen ~ geworden?** did the pictures/rolls turn out all right?; **ist dein Magen wieder ~?** is your stomach better or all right again?; **es wird alles wieder ~!** everything will be all right; **es ist ganz ~, dass ...** it's good that ...; **wie ~, dass ...** it's good that ..., how fortunate that ...; **~, dass du das endlich einsiehst** it's a good thing or job (that) you realize it at last; **so was ist immer ~** that's always useful; **ich will es damit ~ sein lassen** I'll leave it at that; **lass das ~ sein!** don't worry; **lass mal ~ sein!** (= *ist genug*) that's enough, that'll do; (= *ist erledigt*) just leave it; **jetzt ist aber ~!** (*inf*) that's enough; **das ist ja alles ~ und schön, aber ...** that's all very well but ..., that's all well and good but ...; **ein ~es Stück Weg(s)** (*dated*) a good way; **ein ~es Pfund Reis** a good pound of rice; **~e Besserung!** get well soon; **auf ~e Freundschaft!** here's to us!; **auf ~es Gelingen!** here's to success!; **~! good;** (= *in Ordnung*) (all) right, OK; **schon ~!** (it's) all right or OK; **~, ~!** all right; **also ~!** all right or OK then; **nun ~!** fair enough, all right then; **~ und schön** (*inf*) fair enough, that's all well and good; **du bist ~!** (*inf*) you're a fine one! → **drei, Ding a, Dienst c, Ende, Geist b, Gesellschaft e, Miene, Riecher**

ADV *comp* **besser**, *superl* **am besten** well; **~ aussehend** good-looking; **~ schmecken/riechen** to taste/smell good; **sie spricht ~ Schwedisch** she speaks Swedish well, she speaks good Swedish; **es ~ haben** to have a good time of it, to have it good (*esp US*); **unser Volk hat es noch nie so ~ gehabt** our people have never had it so good; **er hat es in seiner Jugend nicht ~ gehabt** he had a hard time (of it) when he was young; **du hast es ~!** you've got it made; **~ wohnen** to have a nice home; **das kann ~ sein** that may well be; **so ~ wie nichts** next to nothing; **so ~ wie nicht** hardly, scarcely; **so ~ wie**

verloren as good as lost; **so ~ ich kann** as best I can, as well as I can; **es dauert ~(e) drei Stunden** it lasts a good three hours; **nehmen Sie ~ ein Pfund Mehl** take a good pound of flour; **~ betucht** (*inf*) well-heeled (*Brit inf*), well-off (*inf*); **~ bezahlt** (*Person, Job*) highly-paid; **~ dotiert** (*Job*) well-paid; (*Vertrag*) lucrative; **~ gehend** flourishing, thriving; **~ gelaunt** cheerful, in a good mood; **~ gelungen** very successful; (*Überraschung*) wonderful; **~ gemeint** well-meaning, well-meant; **~ gesinnt** well-disposed (*dat* towards); (= *von edler Gesinnung*) right-thinking; **~ sitzend** well-fitting; **~ verdienend** with a good salary, high-income; **das ist aber ~ gewogen/eingeschenkt!** that's a generous measure; **~ und gern** easily; **das lässt sich nicht ~ machen** that wouldn't be easy; (**das hast du**) **~ gemacht!** well done!; **darauf kann man ~ verzichten** you can easily or well do without that; **machs ~!** (*inf*) cheers! (*Brit*), cheerio! (*Brit*), bye!; (*stärker*) look after yourself, take care; **pass ~ auf!** be very careful; **ich kann ihn jetzt nicht ~ im Stich lassen** I can't very well let him down now → **Gute(s), lachen VI, reden VI, beraten VT a, Besen a**

Gut [ɡuːt] NT -(e)s, ̈er ['ɡyːtɐ] **a** (= *Eigentum*) property; (*lit, fig*: = *Besitztum*) possession; **irdische Güter** worldly goods; **geistige Güter** intellectual wealth; **nicht um alle Güter der Welt** (*geh*) not for all the world; **bewegliche Güter** movables; **unbewegliche Güter** immovables **b** *no pl* (= *das Gute*) good, Good; **~ und Böse** good and evil, Good and Evil; **das höchste ~** (*Philos*) the greatest good; (= *Gesundheit etc*) one's most valuable possession **c** (= *Ware, Frachtgut*) item; **Güter** goods; (= *Frachtgut*) freight *sing*, goods (*esp Brit*) **d** *no pl* (*dated*: = *Material*) material (to be treated) **e** (= *Landgut*) estate **f** *no pl* (*Naut*) rigging, gear; **laufendes/stehendes ~** running/standing rigging or gear

-gut NT -(e)s, *no pl suf in cpds* **a** (*denotes material intended for or having undergone a process*) **Saatgut** seed; **Mahlgut** (*zum Mahlen bestimmt*) substance(s) to be ground; (*gemahlen*) ground substance(s) **b** (*often not translated in English: denotes the totality of an abstract possession*) **das deutsche Musikgut/Gedankengut** (the body of) German music/thought

Gut-: gut|ach|ten ['ɡuːtʔaxtn] VI *insep* (*usu infin, no pl*) (*esp Jur*) to act as an expert witness; **Gut|ach|ten** ['ɡuːtʔaxtn] NT -s, - report; **Gut|ach|ter** ['ɡuːtʔaxtɐ] M -s, -, **Gut|ach|te|rin** [-ərɪn] F -, **-nen** expert; (= *Schätzer auch*) valuator; (*Jur: in Prozess*) expert witness; **gut|acht|lich** (*form*) ADJ expert ADV **etw ~ feststellen** to ascertain sth in an expert's report; **gut|ar|tig** ADJ *Kind, Hund etc* good-natured; (*Med*) *Geschwulst, Geschwür* benign; **Gut|ar|tig|keit** F -, *no pl* (*von Kind, Tier etc*) good nature; (*von Geschwulst*) benignity; **gut|aus|se|hend** △ ADJ → **gut** ADV; **gut|be|tucht** △ ADJ *attr* → **gut** ADV; **gut|be|zahlt** △ ADJ *attr* → **gut** ADV; **gut|bür|ger|lich** ADJ solid middle-class; *Küche* homely (*Brit*), good plain; **gut|do|tiert** △ ADJ *attr* → **gut** ADV; **Gut|dün|ken** ['ɡuːtdʏŋkn] NT -s, *no pl* discretion; **nach (eigenem) ~** at one's own discretion, as one sees fit, as one thinks fit or best

Gü|te ['ɡyːtə] F -, *no pl* **a** (= *Herzensgüte, Freundlichkeit*) goodness, kindness; (*Gottes auch*) loving kindness; **würden Sie die ~ haben, zu ...** (*form*) would you have the goodness or kindness to ... (*form*); **ein Vorschlag zur ~** a suggestion; **in ~** amicably; **meine ~, ist der dumm!** (*inf*) my goodness, is he stupid! (*inf*); **ach du liebe** or **meine ~!** (*inf*) oh my goodness!, goodness me! **b** (*einer Ware*) quality; **ein Reinfall erster ~** (*inf*) a first-class flop, a flop of the first order or water (*inf*)

Gü|te|grad M, **Gü|te|klas|se** F   (*Comm*) grade

Gu|te|nacht-: Gu|te|nacht|ge|schich|te [ɡuːtəˈnaxt-] F bedtime story; **Gu|te|nacht|kuss** ▲ [ɡuːtəˈnaxt-] M goodnight kiss

Gu|te(r) ['ɡuːtə] MF *decl as adj* **mein ~r** (*dated*) my dear friend; (= *Ehemann*) my dear husband; **meine ~** (*old*) my dear; (= *Ehefrau*) my dear wife; **der/die ~** the dear kind soul; (*mitleidig*) the poor soul; **die ~n und die Bösen** the good and the bad; (*inf: in Westernfilmen etc*) the goodies and the baddies (*inf*)

Gü|ter-: Gü|ter|ab|fer|ti|gung F **a** *no pl* dispatch of freight or goods (*esp Brit*) **b** (= *Abfertigungsstelle*) freight or goods (*esp Brit*) office; **Gü|ter|ab|wä|gung** F choice between conflicting rights; **Gü|ter|an|ge|bot** NT range of goods for sale; **Gü|ter|bahn|hof** M freight or goods (*esp Brit*) depot; **Gü|ter|fern|ver|kehr** M long-distance haulage; **Gü|ter|ge|mein|schaft** F (*Jur*) community of property; **in ~ le|ben** to have community of property; **Gü|ter|nah|ver|kehr** M short-distance haulage (*up to 50 km*); **Gü|ter|schup|pen** M freight depot, goods shed (*Brit*); **Gü|ter|tren|nung** F (*Jur*) separation of property; **in ~ leben** to have separation of property; **Gü|ter|ver|kehr** M freight or goods (*esp Brit*) traffic; **Gü|ter|wa|gen** M (*Rail*) freight car (*US*), goods truck (*Brit*), **Gü|ter|zug** M freight or goods (*esp Brit*) train

Gu|te(s) ['ɡuːtə] NT *decl as adj* **~s tun** to do good; **es hat alles sein ~s** (*prov*) every cloud has a silver lining (*Prov*), it's an ill wind (that blows nobody any good) (*Brit Prov*); **alles ~!** all the best!, good luck!; **man hört über sie nur ~s** you hear so many good things about her; **das führt zu nichts ~m** it'll lead to no good; **jdm (viel) ~s tun** to be (very) good to sb; **des ~n zu viel tun** to overdo things; **das ist des ~n zu viel** that is too much of a good thing; **das ~ daran** the good thing about it; **das ~ siegt** Good or good shall triumph; **das ~ im Menschen** the good in man; **im ~n wie im Bösen** for better or for worse; **im ~n** (*sich trennen*) amicably; **ich sage es dir im ~n** I want to give you a friendly piece of advice

Gü|te-: Gü|te|sie|gel NT (*Comm*) stamp of quality; **Gü|te|ter|min** M, **Gü|te|ver|hand|lung** F (*Jur*) conciliation proceedings *pl*; **Gü|te|zei|chen** NT mark of quality; (*fig auch*) hallmark

Gut-: gut ge|hen ▲ *irreg aux sein* VI *impers* **es geht ihm gut** he is doing well or nicely; (= *er ist gesund*) he is well; **sonst gehts dir gut!** (*iro*) are you feeling all right?, are you in your right mind? VI **~ to go** (off) well; **das ist noch einmal gut gegangen** it turned out all right; **wenn es gut geht** with luck; **das konnte ja nicht ~ gehen** it was bound to go wrong; **wenn das man gut geht!** (*N Ger*) that's asking for trouble; **hoffentlich es mit den beiden gut!** (*inf*) I hope things will work out for the two of them; **gut|ge|hend** △ ADJ *attr* → **gut** ADV; **gut|ge|launt** △ ADJ → **gut** ADV; **gut|ge|lun|gen** △ ADJ *attr* → **gut** ADV; **gut|ge|meint** △ [-ɡəmaint] ADJ *attr* → **gut** ADV; **gut|ge|sinnt** △ ADJ → **gut** ADV; **gut|gläu|big** ADJ trusting; (= *vertrauensselig auch*) credulous; **Gut|gläu|big|keit** F trusting nature; (= *Vertrauensseligkeit auch*) credulity

Guth. *abbr von* **Guthaben**

Gut-: gut|ha|ben ['ɡuːthaːbn] VT *sep irreg* **etw ~** to be owed sth (*bei* by), to have sth coming (to one) (*bei* from) (*inf*); **Gut|ha|ben** ['ɡuːthaːbn] NT -s, - (*Fin*: = *Bankguthaben*) credit; **auf meinem Konto ist ~** my account is in credit; **ich habe ein ~ von 500 Euro** my account is 500 euros in credit; **gut|hei|ßen** ['ɡuːthaisn] VT *sep irreg* to approve of; (= *genehmigen*) to approve; **Gut|hei|ßung** F -, **-en** approval; **gut|her|zig** ADJ kind-hearted, kindly; **Gut|her|zig|keit** F -, *no pl* kind-heartedness, kindliness

gü|tig ['ɡyːtɪç] ADJ kind; (= *edelmütig*) generous, gracious; **mit Ihrer ~en Erlaubnis** (*dated form*) with your kind permission; **würden Sie so ~ sein, zu ...** (*dated form*) would you be so kind as to ...

güt|lich ['gy:tlɪç] **ADJ** amicable **ADV** amicably; **sich ~ einigen** to come to an amicable agreement; **wir haben uns ~ auf 10 000 Euro geeinigt** we reached an amicable settlement of 10,000 euros; **etw ~ schlichten** to settle sth amicably; **sich an etw** (*dat*) **~ tun** to make free with sth (*Brit*), to use sth freely

Gut-: gut+ma|chen VT *sep* **a** (= *in Ordnung bringen*) *Fehler* to put right, to correct; *Schaden* to make good; **das kann ich ja gar nicht wieder ~!** (*fig*) how on earth can I ever repay you!; **du hast viel an ihm gutzumachen** you've a lot to make up to him (for) **b** (= *gewinnen*) to make (*bei* out of, on); **gut|mü|tig** ['gu:tmy:tɪç] ADJ *Mensch, Tier* good-natured; **Gut|mü|tig|keit** F -, *no pl* good nature; **jds ~ ausnützen** to presume upon sb's good nature; **gut|nach|bar|lich** ADJ neighbourly (*Brit*), neighborly (*US*) ADV in a neighbourly (*Brit*) or neighborly (*US*) fashion, as good neighbours (*Brit*) or neighbors (*US*); **gut+sa|gen** VI *sep* (*dated*) to vouch (*für* for)

Guts|be|sit|zer(in) M(F) lord/lady of the manor; (*als Klasse*) landowner

Gut-: Gut|schein M voucher, coupon; (*für Umtausch*) credit note; **Gut|schein|heft** NT book of vouchers (*Brit*) or coupons (*US*); **gut+schrei|ben** ['gu:tʃraibn] VT *sep irreg* to credit (+*dat* to); **Gut|schrift** F **a** *no pl* (= *Vorgang*) crediting **b** (= *Bescheinigung*) credit note; (= *Betrag*) credit (item)

Guts-: Guts|haus NT manor (house); **Guts|herr** M squire, lord of the manor; **Guts|her|rin** F lady of the manor; **Guts|herr|schaft** F squire and his family; **Guts|hof** M estate

gut-: gut|si|tu|iert △ ADJ *attr* → **situiert a**; **gut|sit|zend** △ ADJ *attr* → **gut ADV**

Guts|ver|wal|ter(in) M(F) steward

Gut-: Gut|temp|ler ['gu:ttɛmplɐ] M -s, -, **Gut|temp|le|rin** [-ərɪn] F -, -nen Good Templar;

gut tun ▲ VI *irreg* **jdm ~** to do sb good; **das tut gut** that's good; **o, wie gut das tut!** oh, that's good

gut|tu|ral [gʊtu'ra:l] ADJ guttural

Gut|tu|ral [gʊtu'ra:l] M -s, -e, **Gut|tu|ral|laut** M (*Ling*) guttural (sound)

Gut-: gut|un|ter|rich|tet △ ADJ *attr* → **unterrichtet**; **gut|ver|die|nend** △ ADJ *attr* → **gut ADV**; **gut|wil|lig** ADJ willing; (= *entgegenkommend*) obliging; (= *wohlwollend*) well-meaning; **Gut|wil|lig|keit** ['gu:tvɪlɪçkait] F -, *no pl* willingness; (= *Entgegenkommen*) obliging ways *pl*; (= *Wohlwollen*) well-meaningness

Gu|ya|na [gu'ja:na] NT -s Guiana; (= *ehem. Brit.-Guyana*) Guyana

Gu|ya|ner [gu'ja:nɐ] M -s, -, **Gu|ya|ne|rin** [-ərɪn] F -, -nen → **Guyana** Guianese/Guyanese

gu|ya|nisch [gu'ja:nɪʃ] ADJ → **Guyana** Guianese/Guyanese

gym|na|si|al [gʏmna'zia:l] ADJ *attr* ≈ at grammar schools (*Brit*), ≈ at high schools (*US*); **die ~e Oberstufe** ≈ the sixth form (*Brit*), ≈ the twelfth grade (*US*)

Gym|na|si|al-: Gym|na|si|al|bil|dung F ≈ grammar school education (*Brit*), ≈ high school education (*US*); **Gym|na|si|al|leh|rer(in)** M(F), **Gym|na|si|al|pro|fes|sor(in)** (*Aus*) M(F) ≈ grammar school teacher (*Brit*), ≈ high school teacher (*US*)

Gym|na|si|ast [gʏmna'ziast] M -en, -en, **Gym|na|si|as|tin** [-'ziastɪn] F -, -nen ≈ grammar school pupil (*Brit*), ≈ high school student (*US*)

Gym|na|si|um [gʏm'na:ziʊm] NT -s, **Gymnasien** [-ziən] **a** (*Sch*) ≈ grammar school (*Brit*), ≈ high school (*US*) **b** (*Hist*) gymnasium

---

GYMNASIUM

A **Gymnasium** is a secondary school which pupils attend for nine years and which leads to the **Abitur**. The final two years at a **Gymnasium** (two and a half in some **Länder**) are known as the **Kollegstufe**. The curriculum varies according to the type of school: in a **humanistisches Gymnasium** Latin and Greek are taught; in a **neusprachliches Gymnasium** English, Latin and French or other lingua franca are taught; and in a **mathematisch-naturwissenschaftliches Gymnasium** the emphasis is on the sciences. A **Gymnasium** may offer several of these curricula, which pupils must choose from when they reach a certain class, usually the seventh or ninth.

Since nowadays many students who have taken their **Abitur** do not necessarily continue studying but undertake a period of training instead, new types of **Gymnasium** (for example **Wirtschaftsgymnasien**) have been created with an emphasis on practical work → Aʙɪᴛᴜʀ, Kᴏʟʟᴇɢꜱᴛᴜꜰᴇ

Gym|nas|tik [gʏm'nastɪk] F -, *no pl* keep-fit exercises *pl*; (= *Turnen*) gymnastics *sing*; **~ machen** to do keep-fit (exercises)/gymnastics

Gym|nas|tik|an|zug M leotard

Gym|nas|ti|ker [gʏm'nastikɐ] M -s, -, **Gym|nas|ti|ke|rin** [-ərɪn] F -, -nen gymnast

Gym|nas|tik-: Gym|nas|tik|leh|rer(in) M(F) PE *or* physical education teacher; **Gym|nas|tik|saal** M gymnasium; **Gym|nas|tik|un|ter|richt** M gymnastics *sing*

gym|nas|tisch [gʏm'nastɪʃ] ADJ gymnastic

Gy|nä|ko|lo|ge [gʏnɛko'lo:gə] M -n, -n, **Gy|nä|ko|lo|gin** [-'lo:gɪn] F -, -nen gynaecologist (*Brit*), gynecologist (*US*), gyno (*esp US inf*)

Gy|nä|ko|lo|gie [gʏnɛkolo'gi:] F -, *no pl* gynaecology (*Brit*), gynecology (*US*)

gy|nä|ko|lo|gisch [gʏnɛko'lo:gɪʃ] ADJ gynaecological (*Brit*), gynecological (*US*) ADV **sich ~ untersuchen lassen** to have a gyn(a)ecological examination; **~ betreuen/behandeln** to give/administer gyn(a)ecological treatment

Gy|ros ['gy:ros] NT -, *no pl* ≈ doner kebab

Gy|ro|skop [gyro'sko:p] NT -s, -e gyroscope

H

H, h [haː] NT **-, -** H, h; (*Mus*) B

h abbr von **hora(e)** (= *Stunde*) hr; **120 km/h** 120 km/h or kmph

ha¹ abbr von **Hektar** hectare

ha² [haː] INTERJ ha; (*triumphierend*) aha; (*überrascht, erstaunt, verärgert*) oh; (*verächtlich*) huh; **ha no** (*S Ger inf, Selbstverständliches betonend*) why not; (*ungläubig*) well, well; (*aufmunternd*) come on; (*resignierend*) oh well

hä [hɛ, hɛː] INTERJ what

Haag [haːk] M **-s der ~, Den ~** The Hague; **in** or **im ~, in Den ~** in The Hague

Haa|ger [ˈhaːgɐ] ADJ attr Hague; **~ Konventionen** Hague Conventions; **~ Schiedshof** International Court of Justice in The Hague

Haar [haːɐ] NT **-(e)s, -e** **a** (= *Menschenhaar*) hair; **sie hat schönes ~** or **schöne ~e** she has nice hair; **sich** (*dat*) **die ~e** or **das ~ schneiden lassen** to have or get one's hair cut, to have a haircut; **sich** (*dat*) **durch die ~e fahren** to run one's fingers through one's hair

b (*Bot, Zool*: = *Material*) hair

c (*in Wendungen*) **~e auf den Zähnen haben** to be a tough customer (*Brit*) or cookie (*esp US*); **~e lassen (müssen)** to suffer badly, to come off badly; **jdm kein ~ krümmen** not to harm a hair on sb's head; **darüber lass dir keine grauen ~e wachsen** don't worry your head about it, don't lose any sleep over it; **er findet immer ein ~ in der Suppe** he always finds something to quibble about; **jdm aufs ~ gleichen** to be the spitting image of sb; **sie gleichen sich** (*dat*) **aufs ~** they are the spitting image of each other, they're as alike as two peas in a pod; **das ist an den ~en herbeigezogen** that's rather far-fetched; **sich** (*dat*) **die ~e raufen** to tear one's hair out; **an jdm/etw kein** or **nicht ein gutes ~ lassen** to pick or pull sb/sth to pieces; **sich** (*dat*) **in die ~e geraten** or **kriegen** (*inf*) to quarrel, to squabble; **sich** (*dat*) **in den ~en liegen** to be at loggerheads (*Brit*), to be at daggers drawn; **jdm die ~e vom Kopf fressen** (*inf*) to eat sb out of house and home; **er hat mehr Schulden als ~e auf dem Kopf** he's up to his ears in debt; **um kein ~ besser** no better, not a bit or whit better; **um ein ~** or **ums ~** very nearly, almost; **er hat mich um ein ~ getroffen** he just missed (hitting) me by a hair's breadth → **Berg**
a

Haar-: **Haar|an|satz** M hairline; **Haar|aus|fall** M hair loss; **Haar|balg** M (*Anat*) hair follicle; **Haar|band** [-bant] NT pl **-bänder** hairband; (= *Schleife*) hair ribbon; **Haar|bo|den** M scalp; **Haar|breit** NT **nicht ein ~, um kein ~** not an inch; **Haar|bürs|te** F hairbrush; **Haar|bü|schel** NT tuft of hair

haa|ren [ˈhaːrən] VI (*Tier*) to moult (*Brit*), to molt (*US*), to lose its coat or hair; (*Pelz etc*) to shed (hair); (*Teppich*) to shed VR (*Tier*) to moult (*Brit*), to molt (*US*)

Haar-: **Haar|ent|fer|ner** [-ɛntfɛrnɐ] M **-s, -**, **Haar|ent|fer|nungs|mit|tel** NT hair remover, depilatory; **Haar|er|satz** M (*form*) hairpiece; (= *Perücke*) wig; (= *Toupet*) toupee

Haa|res|brei|te [ˈhaːrəsbraɪtə] F inv (**nur**) **um ~** almost, very nearly; **verfehlen** by a hair's

---

breadth; **er wich nicht um ~ von seiner Meinung ab** he did not change his opinion one iota

Haa|re|wa|schen NT , no pl hair-washing, shampoo(ing); (*beim Friseur*) shampoo, wash; **bei jedem ~** every time you wash your hair

Haar-: **Haar|far|be** F hair colour (*Brit*) or color (*US*); **haar|fein** ADJ **ein ~er Riss** a hairline crack; **Haar|fes|ti|ger** M (hair) setting lotion; **Haar|flech|te** F (*old, geh*) plait (*Brit*), braid (*US*); **Haar|garn** NT yarn made from hair; **Haar|ge|fäß** NT (*Anat*) capillary; **haar|ge|nau** ADJ exact; **Übereinstimmung** total ADV exactly; **die Beschreibung trifft ~ auf ihn zu** the description fits him exactly or to a T (*esp Brit inf*); **jdm etw ~ erklären** to explain sth to sb in great detail; **das trifft ~ zu** that is absolutely right

haa|rig [ˈhaːrɪç] ADJ hairy; (*inf*) (= *heikel, gefährlich*) hairy (*inf*); (= *schwierig*) nasty

Haar-: **Haar|klam|mer** F (= *Klemme*) hairgrip (*Brit*), bobby pin (*US*); (= *Spange*) hair slide (*Brit*), barrette (*US*); **Haar|kleid** NT (*geh*) coat; **haar|klein** ADJ (*inf*) Beschreibung detailed ADV in great or minute detail; **er hat mir alles ~ berechnet** he charged me for absolutely everything; **Haar|klem|me** F hairgrip (*Brit*), bobby pin (*US*); **Haar|kranz** M (*von Männern*) fringe (of hair) (*Brit*), bangs pl (*US*); (= *Frauenfrisur*) plaits fixed around one's head; **Haar|künst|ler(in)** M(F) (*usu hum*) hair artiste; **Haar|lack** M hair lacquer; **haar|los** ADJ hairless; (= *glatzköpfig*) bald; **Haar|mo|de** F hairstyle; **Haar|na|del** F hairpin; **Haar|na|del|kur|ve** F hairpin bend; **Haar|netz** NT hairnet; **Haar|öl** NT hair oil; **Haar|pfle|ge** F hair care; **zur ~** (for caring) for one's hair; **Haar|pfle|ge|mit|tel** NT hair care product; **Haar|pracht** F superb head of hair; **Haar|riss** ▲ M (*Tech*) (in Metall, Pflaster etc) hairline crack; **haar|scharf** ADJ Beschreibung, Wiedergabe exact; Gedächtnis very sharp, very clear; Unterschied very fine; Beobachtung very close ADV treffen exactly; danebentreffen, vorbeitreffen barely; folgern, schließen precisely; **die Kugel ging ~ daneben** the bullet missed by a hair's breadth; **~ an jdm vorbeizielen** to aim to just miss sb; **~ an jdm vorbeischießen** to shoot just past sb; **der Glassplitter traf ihn ~ über dem Auge** the splinter of glass only just missed his eye; **Haar|schlei|fe** F hair ribbon; **Haar|schmuck** M ornaments pl for one's hair; **Haar|schnei|de|ma|schi|ne** F , **Haar|schnei|der** M **-s, -** (= *Gerät*) electric clippers pl; **Haar|schnei|der(in)** M(F) (*inf*: = *Friseur*) barber; **Haar|schnitt** M **a** (= *Frisur*) haircut, hairstyle **b** (= *das Haarschneiden*) haircut; **Haar|schopf** M mop or shock of hair; **ihr roter ~** her mop or shock of red hair; **Haar|sei|te** F (*von Fell*) fleece side; (*von Pelz*) fur side; (*von Teppich*) pile side; **Haar|sieb** NT fine sieve; **Haar|spal|ter** [-ʃpaltɐ] M **-s, -**, **Haar|spal|te|rin** [-ərɪn] F **-, -nen** pedant, hairsplitter; **Haar|spal|te|rei** [-ʃpaltəˈraɪ] F **-, -en** splitting hairs no indef art, no pl; **eine solche ~** hairsplitting like that; **haar|spal|te|risch** [-ʃpaltərɪʃ] ADJ hairsplitting; Unterschied minute; **Haar|span|ge** F hair slide (*Brit*), barrette (*US*); **Haar|spit|ze** F end (of a hair); **gespalte-**

---

ne ~n split ends; **Haar|spray** NT OR M hairspray; **Haar|sträh|ne** F strand or (*dünner*) wisp of hair; **haar|sträu|bend** [-ʃtrɔybnt] ADJ hair-raising; (= *empörend*) shocking, terrible; (= *unglaublich*) Frechheit incredible ADV brutal hair-raisingly; schlecht painfully; obszön terribly, shockingly; frech incredibly; **sich benehmen** shockingly; **Haar|strich** M (= *dünner Strich*) hairline, hair stroke; (*von Tierfell*) growth of the hair; **Haar|stu|dio** NT hair stylist's; **Haar|teil** NT hairpiece; **Haar|tol|le** F quiff; (= *Hahnenkamm*) cockscomb; **Haar|tö|ner** [-tøːnɐ] M **-s,** **-** hair-tinting lotion; **Haar|tö|nung** F tinting; **Haar|tracht** F (*dated, geh*: = *Frisur*) hairstyle; **Haar|trans|plan|ta|ti|on** F hair transplant; (= *Vorgang*) hair transplantation; **Haar|trock|ner** [-trɔknɐ] M **-s, -** hairdryer; **Haar|wä|sche** F washing one's hair no art; **eine regelmäßige ~** washing one's hair regularly; **Haar|wasch|mit|tel** NT shampoo; **Haar|was|ser** NT pl **-wässer** hair lotion; **Haar|wech|sel** M change of coat; **Haar|wild** NT (*Hunt*) game animals pl; **Haar|wir|bel** M cowlick; (*am Hinterkopf*) crown; **Haar|wuchs** M growth of hair; **einen kräftigen ~ haben** to have a lot of hair or a full head of hair; **einen spärlichen ~ haben** to have little hair or a thin head of hair; **Haar|wuchs|mit|tel** NT hair restorer; **Haar|wur|zel** F root of a/the hair

Hab [haːp] NT **~ und Gut** possessions, belongings, worldly goods all pl

Hab|acht|stel|lung [haːpˈʔaxtʃtɛlʊŋ] F = **Habt-achtstellung**

Ha|be [ˈhaːbə] F **-**, no pl (*geh*) possessions pl, belongings pl

Ha|be|as|kor|pus|ak|te [haːbeasˈkɔrpʊs-] F (*Jur*) Act of Habeas Corpus

Ha|be|dank [ˈhaːbədaŋk, -ˈdaŋk] NT **-s**, no pl (*poet*) thanks pl; **ein herzliches ~** heartfelt thanks

---

**ha	ben** [ˈhaːbn]		
pres **hat** [hat], pret **hatte** [ˈhatə], ptp **gehabt** [gəˈhaːpt]		
1 HILFSVERB	3 UNPERSÖNLICHES	
2 TRANSITIVES VERB	VERB	
	4 REFLEXIVES VERB	

1 – HILFSVERB

ich habe/hatte gerufen I have/had called, I've/I'd called; **er will ihn gesehen haben** he says (that) he saw him; **du hättest den Brief früher schreiben können** you could have written the letter earlier; **wenn er mich angerufen hätte, wäre ich gleich gekommen** if he had phoned me, I would have come at once

2 – TRANSITIVES VERB

In Verbindung mit Substantiv siehe auch Eintrag für das jeweilige Substantiv.

Im Präsens wird im britischen Englisch oft **have got** verwendet.

a = besitzen to have; **wir haben ein Haus/Auto** we've got a house/car; **ich hatte viele Bücher** I had a lot of books; **er hat eine Brille** he's got or wears glasses; **eine böse Schwiegermutter haben** to have an awful mother-in-law; **er hat noch nie eine Frau gehabt** he's never had a woman; **was man hat, das hat man** (*inf*) what you've got, you've got; **wer hat, der hat** some people have everything; **die habens (ja)** (*inf*) they can afford it

b | = als Eigenschaft aufweisen | **sie hatte blaue Augen/lange Beine** she had blue eyes/long legs; **er hat eine große Nase/abstehende Ohren** he's got a big nose/sticking-out ears; **man hat wieder lange Haare** long hair is in fashion again

c | = bekommen, erhalten | to have; *Note* to get; (= *studieren*) *Fach* to do; **kann ich mal das Handtuch haben?** can I have the towel?; **dürfte ich die Butter haben?** could I have the butter?; **kann ich noch etwas Brot haben?** could I have some more bread?; **was möchten Sie haben?** what would you like?; **da hast du 10 Euro/das Buch** there's 10 euros/the book; **wie hätten Sie es gern?** how would you like it?; **woher hast du denn das?** where did you get that from?; **Schule/Unterricht haben** to have school/lessons; **in der ersten Stunde haben wir Englisch** (*inf*) we have English first lesson; **an unserer Schule haben wir ab dem ersten Schuljahr Französisch und Englisch** (*inf*) at our school we have *or* do French and English in the first year; **was hast du diesmal in Englisch?** what did you get in English this time?; **gute Schulnoten haben** to get good marks (*Brit*) *or* grades (*US*); **gutes/schlechtes Wetter haben** to have good/bad weather; **morgen werden wir Nebel haben** we'll have fog tomorrow; **was haben wir heute für ein Wetter?** what's the weather like today?; **heute haben wir 10°** it's 10° today; **in Australien haben sie jetzt Winter** it's winter in Australia now; **wie viel Uhr haben wir?** what's the time?; **was für ein Datum haben wir heute?, den Wievielten haben wir heute?** what's the date today?, what's today's date?

d | = verfügen über | *Zeit, Muße, Beziehungen, Erfahrung* to have; **Zeit haben, etw zu tun** to have the time to do sth; **er hat immer Zeit für seine Kinder** he always has time for his children; **ich habe jetzt keine Zeit** I haven't got time now; **wenn ich nur Zeit hätte!** if only I had time!; **die Sache hat Zeit** it's not urgent; **in diesem Job muss man Beziehungen haben** in this job you need to have connections; **mit Computern habe ich keine Erfahrung** I've got no experience of computers

e | = zeitweise ergriffen, bedrückt sein von | to have; **Durst haben** to be thirsty; **Hunger haben** to be hungry; **eine Krankheit haben** to have an illness; **Grippe/Masern/eine schreckliche Erkältung haben** to have flu/measles/a terrible cold; **Husten haben** to have a cough; **Fieber haben** to have a temperature; **ich kann heute nicht kommen, ich habe Fieber** I can't come today, I've got a temperature; **Peter hat Windpocken** Peter's got chicken pox; **Angst haben** to be afraid; **gute/schlechte Laune haben** to be in a good/bad mood; **Sorgen haben** to be worried; **erhebliche Zweifel haben** to have grave doubts; **die Hoffnung haben, dass etw geschieht** to have hopes that sth will happen; **was hat er denn?** what's the matter with him?; **hast du was?** are you all right?, is something the matter?; **ich habe nichts** I'm all right

f | = sich zusammensetzen aus | **ein Meter hat 100 cm** there are 100 cm in a meter (*Brit*) *or* meter (*US*); **ein Euro hat 100 Cent** there are 100 cents in a euro; **unser Haus hat 4 Etagen** our house has 4 storeys (*Brit*) *or* stories (*US*)

g | mit Präposition |

Für **haben** in Verbindung mit Präpositionen siehe auch unter dem Eintrag für die Präposition.

♦ **haben + an sie hat eine große Hilfe an ihren Kindern** her children are a great help to her, she gets a lot of help from her children; **sie werden schon merken, was sie an ihm haben** they'll see what an asset she is; **jd/etw hat eine nette Art an sich** (*dat*) there is something nice

about sb/sth; **das hat er/sie/es so an sich** (*dat*) that's just the way he/she/it is; **es am Herzen/Magen/an der Leber haben** (*inf*) to have heart/stomach/liver trouble

♦ **haben + für sich das hat etwas für sich** there's something to be said for that

♦ **haben + gegen etw gegen jdn/etw haben** to have sth against sb/sth; **jdn/etw gegen sich haben** to have sb/sth against one

♦ **haben + in es in den Beinen haben** (*inf*: = *leiden*) to have trouble with one's legs

♦ **haben + in sich das hat es in sich** (*inf*) (= *schwierig*) that's a tough one; (= *alkoholreich*) that's strong; (= *reichhaltig*) that's rich

♦ **haben + mit etwas mit jdm haben** (*euph*) to have a thing with sb (*inf*); **er hat es mit dem Malen/Bergsteigen** (*inf*) he has a passion for painting/mountaineering; **was hat es mit seiner Frage auf sich?** what is his question actually about?

♦ **haben + von etwas von etw haben** (*inf*) to get something out of sth; **das hast du jetzt davon!** now see what's happened!; **das hat er von seinem Leichtsinn** that's what comes of his foolishness; **die blonden Haare hat sie von ihrem Vater** she gets her blonde hair from her father; **er hat etwas von einem Hochstapler an sich** he's a bit of a con man; **sie hat etwas von einer Aristokratin an sich** there's something aristocratic about her; **mehr/weniger von etw haben** (*inf*) to get more/less out of *or* from sth; **da habe ich dann mehr davon** that way I get more out of it; **nichts davon/von etw haben** to get nothing out of it/sth; **sie hat viel von ihrem Vater/wenig von ihrer Mutter** she's very like her father/not at all like her mother; **dieses Werk von Braque hat viel von Picasso** this work by Braque owes a lot to Picasso; **Kinder haben nicht viel von ihren Eltern, wenn Mutter und Vater arbeiten** children don't see much of their parents if both the mother and the father work

♦ **haben + vor sich ich hatte gar keine Ahnung, wen ich da vor mir hatte** I had no idea who I was talking to; **wissen Sie eigentlich, wen Sie vor sich haben?** do you actually realize who you're talking to?

♦ **haben + zu er wollte sie zur Frau haben** he wanted to make her his wife → *auch* **h**

h | in anderen Verbindungen |

♦ **es haben + Adjektiv es gut/schön/bequem haben** to have it good/nice/easy; **sie hat es warm in ihrem Zimmer** it's warm in her room; **wir haben es noch weit bis nach Hause** it's still a long way home; **es schlecht haben** to have a bad time; **er hat es nicht leicht mit ihr** he has a hard time with her; **du hast es gut, du darfst schon nach Hause** it's all right for you, you can go home

♦ **haben + zu + Infinitiv** (= *verfügen über, müssen*) to have to; **nichts mehr zu essen haben** to have nothing left to eat; **ich habe zu tun** I'm busy; **ich habe nichts zu tun** I have nothing to do; **du hast zu gehorchen** you have to obey; **ich habe nicht zu fragen** I'm not to ask questions

♦ **zu haben sein etw ist zu haben** (= *erhältlich*) sth is to be had; **jd ist zu haben** (= *nicht verheiratet*) sb is single; (*sexuell*) sb is available; **für etw zu haben sein** to be ready for sth; **für Whisky ist er immer zu haben** he's always ready for a whisky; **der ist doch für jeden Ulk zu haben** he's always ready for a lark (*inf*); **er ist nicht dafür zu haben** (= *nicht interessiert*) he's not keen on it (*Brit*), he's not interested in it; (= *möchte nicht beteiligt sein*) he won't have anything to do with it

i | andere Wendungen | **ich habs!** (*inf*) I've got it!, I know!; **da hast du/haben wir's!** (*inf*) there you/we are!; **wie gehabt** as before; **ich kann das nicht haben!** (*inf*) I can't stand it!; **es nicht haben, wenn du immer den Teller ableckst** I can't stand the way you lick your plate

3 – UNPERSÖNLICHES VERB

♦ **es hat** (*dial*: = *es gibt*) (*bei Objekt im Singular*) there is; (*bei Objekt im Plural*) there are; **es hat noch Kaffee** there's still some coffee left; **hier hat es noch viele schöne alte Bauernhäuser** there are still a lot of beautiful old farmhouses here; **damit hat es noch Zeit** it's not urgent, it can wait

♦ **es hat sich** (*inf*) **und damit hat es sich** and that's that; **es hat sich was mit der Liebe!** so much for love!; **es hat sich was mit der Hoffnung!** so much for my hopes!; **hat sich was!** some hopes!

4 – REFLEXIVES VERB

♦ **sich haben**

a | = sich anstellen | (*inf*) to make a fuss; **was hast du dich denn so?** what are you making such a fuss about?; **hab dich nicht so** stop making such a fuss

b | = erledigt sein | **die Sache hat sich** that's done

Ha|ben ['haːbn̩] NT -s, *no pl* credit; **im ~ stehen** to be on the credit side

Ha|be|nichts ['haːbənɪçts] M -(es), -e have-not

Haben-: Ha|ben|sei|te F credit side; **Ha|ben|zin|sen** PL interest *sing* on credit

Ha|be|rer ['haːbərɐ] M -s, - (*Aus inf*) bloke (*Brit inf*), chap (*Brit inf*), guy (*inf*)

Ha|ber|sack ['haːbəzak] M (*old*) knapsack, haversack

Hab-: Hab|gier F greed, acquisitiveness; **hab|gie|rig** ADJ greedy, acquisitive; **hab|haft** ['haːphaft] ADJ **jds/einer Sache ~ werden** (*geh*) to get hold of sb/sth

Ha|bicht ['haːbɪçt] M -s, -e hawk; (= *Hühnerhabicht*) goshawk

Ha|bichts|na|se F hooked nose

ha|bil [ha'biːl] ADJ (*dated, geh*) skilful (*Brit*), skillful (*US*), clever

habil. *abbr von* **habilitatus** Dr. ~ doctor with postdoctoral university teaching qualification

Ha|bi|li|tand [habili'tant] M -en, -en [-dn̩], **Ha|bi|li|tan|din** [-'tandɪn] F -, -nen person writing postdoctoral thesis to qualify as a professor

Ha|bi|li|ta|ti|on [habilitatsi'oːn] F -, -en **a** (= *Festakt*) ceremony at which sb receives his/her qualification as a professor **b** (= *Lehrberechtigung*) postdoctoral lecturing qualification

Ha|bi|li|ta|ti|ons|schrift F postdoctoral thesis required for qualification as a professor

ha|bi|li|tie|ren [habili'tiːrən] ptp **habilitiert** VR to qualify as a professor VT to confer qualification as a professor on

ha|bi|li|tiert [habili'tiːɐt] ADJ qualified to assume a professorship

Ha|bit¹ [ha'biːt, 'haːbɪt] NT OR M -s, -e (= *Ordenskleid*) habit; (*geh*: = *Aufzug*) attire

Ha|bit² ['hɛbɪt] NT OR M -s, -s (*Psych*) habit

Ha|bi|tat [habi'taːt] NT -s, -e (*Zool*) habitat

ha|bi|tu|ell [habi'tuɛl] ADJ (*geh*) habitual

Ha|bi|tus ['haːbɪtʊs] M -, *no pl* (*geh, Med*) disposition

Habs|burg ['haːpsbʊrk] NT -s Hapsburg, Habsburg

Habs|bur|ger¹ ['haːpsbʊrgɐ] ADJ *attr* = **habsburgisch**

Habs|bur|ger² ['haːpsbʊrgɐ] M -s, -, **Habs|bur|ge|rin** [-ərɪn] F -, -nen Hapsburg, Habsburg

habs|bur|gisch ['haːpsbʊrgɪʃ] ADJ Hapsburg *attr*, Habsburg *attr*, of the Hapsburgs *or* Habsburgs

Hab-: Hab|schaft ['haːpʃaft] F -, -en, **Hab|se|lig|kei|ten** ['haːpzeːlɪçkaɪtn̩] PL possessions, belongings, effects (*form*) *all pl*; **Hab|sucht** ['haːpzʊxt] F greed, acquisitiveness; **hab|süch|tig** ['haːpzʏçtɪç] ADJ greedy, acquisitive

Habt|acht|stel|lung [haːptˈʔaxtʃtɛlʊŋ] F (Mil, fig) attention; **in ~ stehen** or **sein** to stand to or be at attention

hach [hax] INTERJ oh; (verächtlich) huh

Ha|chel [ˈhaxl] F -, **-n** (Aus) slicer

ha|cheln [ˈhaxln] VTI (Aus) to chop, to slice

Hach|se [ˈhaksə] F -, **-n** (dial) = **Haxe**

Hack-: Hack|bank F pl **-bänke** butcher's chopping (Brit) or cutting (US) board; **Hack|bau** M , no pl (Agr) hoe-farming; **Hack|beil** NT chopper, cleaver; **Hack|block** M pl **-blöcke** chopping block; **Hack|bra|ten** M meat loaf; **Hack|brett** NT **a** chopping board (Brit), cutting board (US) **b** (Mus) dulcimer

ha|cke [ˈhakə] ADJ (sl: = betrunken) pissed (Brit inf), plastered (inf)

Ha|cke¹ [ˈhakə] F -, **-n a** (dial: = Ferse, am Strumpf) heel **b** (dial, Mil: = Absatz) heel; **die ~n zusammenschlagen** or **zusammenklappen** (Mil) to click one's heels; **einen im** or **am ~n haben** (N Ger inf) to be pickled (inf) → **ablaufen** VT **a**

Ha|cke² F -, **-n a** (= Pickel) pickaxe (Brit), pickax (US), pick; (= Gartenhacke) hoe **b** (Aus) hatchet, axe (Brit), ax (US)

Ha|cke|beil NT chopper, cleaver

ha|cke|dicht ADJ (sl: = betrunken) pissed (Brit inf), plastered (inf)

ha|cken [ˈhakn] VT **a** (= zerkleinern) to chop; (im Fleischwolf) to mince (Brit), to grind (US) **b** Garten, Erdreich to hoe **c** (mit spitzem Gegenstand) Loch to hack, to chop; (Vogel) to peck VI **a** (mit dem Schnabel) to peck; (mit spitzem Gegenstand) to hack, to chop; **ich habe mich** or **mir in den Finger gehackt** I've cut my finger; **nach jdm/etw ~** to peck at sth/sb **b** (im Garten etc) to hoe **c** (Comput) to hack (in +acc into) VR **a** = sich verletzen) to cut (oneself)

Ha|cken [ˈhakn] M -s, - (= Ferse) heel

Ha|cken|trick M (Sport) backheel

Ha|cke|pe|ter [ˈhakəpeːtɐ] M -s, - **a** (N Ger) mince (Brit), minced (Brit) or ground (US) meat **b** (S Ger) seasoned raw meat loaf

Ha|cker [ˈhakɐ] M -s, -, **Ha|cke|rin** [-ərɪn] F -, **-nen** (Comput) hacker

ha|cke|voll ADJ (inf), **ha|cke|zu** ADJ (sl) (= betrunken) pissed (Brit inf), plastered (inf)

Hack-: Hack|fleisch NT mince (Brit), minced (Brit) or ground (US) meat; **jdn zu ~ machen** (inf) to make mincemeat of sb (inf); (= verprügeln) to beat sb up; **Hack|frucht** F root crop; **Hack|klotz** M chopping block; **Hack|ord|nung** F (lit, fig) pecking order

Häck|sel [ˈhɛksl] NT OR M -s, no pl chaff

Häck|sel|ma|schine F chaffcutter

Hack-: Hack|steak NT hamburger; **Hack|stock** M (Aus) chopping block

Ha|der [ˈhaːdɐ] M -s, no pl (geh) (= Zwist) discord; (= Unzufriedenheit) discontentment; **in ~ mit sich und der Welt leben** to be at odds with oneself and the world

Ha|de|rer [ˈhaːdərə] M -s, -, **Ha|de|rin** [-ərɪn] F -, **-nen** (geh: = unzufriedener Mensch) grumbler

Ha|der|lump M (Aus, S Ger) good-for-nothing

ha|dern [ˈhaːdɐn] VI (dated, geh) (= streiten) to quarrel, to wrangle (mit with); (= unzufrieden sein) to be at odds (mit with); **hadere nicht mit deinem Schicksal** you must accept your fate

Ha|dern [ˈhaːdɐn] PL (S Ger, Aus) rags pl (for making paper)

Ha|dern|pa|pier NT rag paper

Ha|des [ˈhaːdɛs] M -, no pl (Myth) Hades

Had|ri|an [ˈhaːdriaːn] M -s Hadrian

Had|schi [ˈhaːdʒi] M -s, -s hajji

Ha|fen¹ [ˈhaːfn] M -s, ⸚ [ˈhɛːfn] **a** harbour (Brit), harbor (US); (= Handelshafen, für große Schiffe) port; (= Jachthafen) marina; (= Hafenanlagen) docks pl; **in den ~ einlaufen** to put into harbo(u)r/port **b** (fig) haven; **im ~ der Ehe**

landen to get married; **in den ~ der Ehe einlaufen** to enter the state of matrimony

Ha|fen² M -s, ⸚ or - (dial) **a** (= Kochtopf) pot, pan; (= Schüssel) dish, bowl; (= Krug) jug **b** (= Nachttopf) chamber pot

Hä|fen [ˈhɛːfn] M -s, - (Aus) **a** (sauce)pan **b** (inf: = Gefängnis) jug (inf), clink (inf)

Ha|fen- in cpds harbour (Brit), harbor (US); (bei Handelshafen, für große Schiffe) port; **Ha|fen|amt** NT harbo(u)r/port authority; **Ha|fen|an|la|gen** PL docks pl; **Ha|fen|ar|bei|ter(in)** M(F) dockworker, docker; **Ha|fen|arzt** M , **Ha|fen|ärz|tin** F port doctor; **Ha|fen|be|cken** NT harbour (Brit) or harbor (US) basin, (wet) dock; **Ha|fen|be|hör|den** PL harbo(u)r/port authorities pl; **Ha|fen|blo|cka|de** F blockade of a harbo(u)r/port

Hä|fen|bru|der [ˈhɛːfn-] M (Aus inf) jailbird (inf)

Hafen-: Ha|fen|ein|fahrt F harbo(u)r/port entrance; **die ~ von Dover** the entrance to Dover Harbour; **Ha|fen|ge|bühr** F usu pl harbo(u)r/port dues pl; **Ha|fen|knei|pe** F (inf) dockland pub (Brit) or bar; **Ha|fen|meis|ter(in)** M(F) harbourmaster/-mistress (Brit), harbormaster/-mistress (US); **Ha|fen|meis|te|rei** F harbourmaster's (Brit) or harbormaster's (US) office; **Ha|fen|po|li|zei** F port or dock police; **Ha|fen|rund|fahrt** F (boat-)trip round the harbo(u)r; **Ha|fen|stadt** F port; (am Meer auch) seaport; **Ha|fen|vier|tel** NT dock area

Ha|fer [ˈhaːfɐ] M -s, - oats pl; **ihn sticht der ~** (inf) he's feeling his oats (inf)

Hafer-: Ha|fer|brei M porridge; **Ha|fer|flo|cken** PL rolled oats pl; **Ha|fer|grüt|ze** F porridge; **Ha|fer|kleie** F oat bran; **Ha|fer|korn** NT pl **-körner** (oat) grain

Ha|ferl [ˈhaːfɐl] NT -s, -n, **Hä|ferl** [ˈhɛːfɐl] NT -s, **-n** (S Ger, Aus inf) (= große Tasse, Becher) mug; (= Schüssel) bowl; (= Topf) pot

Ha|ferl|schuh [ˈhaːfɐl-] M type of brogue

Hafer-: Ha|fer|mehl NT oatmeal; **Ha|fer|sack** M rucksack bag; **Ha|fer|schleim** M gruel

Haff [haf] NT -(e)s, -s or **-e** lagoon

Haf|lin|ger [ˈhaːflɪŋɐ] M -s, - Haflinger (horse)

Haf|ner [ˈhaːfnɐ] M -s, -, **Haf|ne|rin** [-ərɪn] F -, **-nen**, **Häf|ner** [ˈhɛːfnɐ] M -s, -, **Häf|ne|rin** [-ərɪn] F -, **-nen** (S Ger) (= Töpfer) potter; (= Ofensetzer) stove-fitter

Haf|ne|rei [haːfnəˈrai] F -, **-en** (S Ger) (= Töpferei) pottery; (= Ofensetzerbetrieb) stove-fitter's works sing or pl

Haf|ni|um [ˈhaːfniʊm, ˈhafniʊm] NT -s, no pl (abbr **Hf**) hafnium

Haft [haft] F -, no pl (vor dem Prozess) custody; (= Haftstrafe) imprisonment; (= Haftzeit) prison sentence, term of imprisonment; (politisch) detention; **sich in ~ befinden** to be in custody/prison/detention; **eine schwere/leichte ~ verhängen** to impose a long/short term of imprisonment; **jdn aus der ~ entlassen** to release sb from custody/prison/detention; **eine ~ absitzen** (inf) to do time (inf); **in ~ sitzen** to be held in custody/prison/detention; **in ~ nehmen** to take into custody, to detain

-haft ADJ suf **a** (= -artig) -like; -ish; -ly; **kindhaft** childlike; **jungenhaft** boyish; **frauenhaft** womanly; (auf Eigenschaft bezüglich) -ly; -ive; **lebhaft** lively; **schwatzhaft** talkative **c** (in Verbaladjektiven) -ing; **wohnhaft** residing, resident **b** (Möglichkeit bezeichnend) -ible, -able; **glaubhaft** credible, believable

Haft-: Haft|an|stalt F detention centre (Brit) or center (US); **Haft|aus|schlie|ßungs|grund** M grounds pl for not imposing a prison sentence; **Haft|aus|set|zung** F suspended prison sentence; (= Unterbrechung) parole; **haft|bar** ADJ (für jdn) legally responsible; (für etw) (legally) liable; **jdn für etw ~ machen** to make or hold sb liable for sth; **Haft|bar|keit** [ˈhaftbaːɐkait] F -, no pl (für jdn) (legal) responsibility; (für

etw) (legal) liability; **Haft|be|fehl** M warrant; **einen ~ gegen jdn ausstellen** to issue a warrant for sb's arrest; **Haft|be|schwer|de** F appeal against a remand in custody; **Haft|dau|er** F term of imprisonment

Haf|tel [ˈhaftl] NT -s, - (Aus) hook and eye sing

Haf|tel|ma|cher M (Aus) **aufpassen wie ein ~** to watch like a hawk

haf|ten¹ [ˈhaftn] VI (Jur) **für jdn ~** to be (legally) responsible for sb; **für etw ~** to be (legally) liable for sth; **(jdm) für jdn/etw ~** (= verantwortlich sein) to be responsible (to sb) for sb/sth; **die Versicherung hat für den Schaden nicht gehaftet** the insurance company did not accept liability (for the damage); **für Garderobe kann nicht gehaftet werden** the management can accept no responsibility for articles deposited, all articles are left at owner's risk

haf|ten² VI **a** (= kleben) to stick (an +dat to); (Klebstoff auch, Reifen, Phys) to adhere; (= sich festsetzen: Rauch, Schmutz, Geruch) to cling (an +dat to); **an jdm ~** (fig: Makel etc) to hang over sb, to stick to sb **b** (Eindruck, Erinnerung) to stick (in one's mind); (Blick) to become fixed; **an etw** (dat) **~ (= hängen)** to be fixed on sth; **bei den Schülern haftet nichts** nothing sinks in with these pupils; **~de Eindrücke** lasting impressions

haf|ten blei|ben ▲ VI irreg aux sein to stick; (an or auf +dat to) (= sich festsetzen: Rauch, Schmutz, Geruch) to cling; (Klebstoff) to cling, to adhere; (Phys) to adhere; (Eindruck, Gelerntes) to stick

Haft-: Haft|ent|las|se|ne(r) [-ɛntlasənə] MF decl as adj released prisoner; **Haft|ent|las|sung** F → **Haft** release from custody/prison/detention; **Haft|ent|schä|di|gung** F compensation for wrongful imprisonment; **Haft|eti|kett** NT adhesive label; **haft|fä|hig** ADJ **a** Material adhesive; Reifen with good road-holding; **auf etw** (dat) **~ sein** to stick to sth **b** (Jur) fit to be kept in prison; **Haft|fä|hig|keit** F , no pl **a** (von Material) adhesive strength; (von Reifen) road-holding **b** (Jur) fitness to be kept in prison; **Haft|grund** M (Jur) grounds pl for detaining sb (in custody) **b** (Tech) base

Häft|ling [ˈhɛftlɪŋ] M -s, -e prisoner; (politisch auch) detainee

Häftlings-: Häft|lings|klei|dung F prison uniform or clothes pl; **Häft|lings|re|vol|te** F prison or prisoners' revolt

Haft-: Haft|no|tiz F Post-it®; **Haft|or|gan** NT suction pad; **Haft|pflicht** F **a** (= Schadenersatzpflicht) (legal) liability; (für Personen) (legal) responsibility; **die ~ der Versicherung erstreckt sich nicht auf Glas und Silber** the insurance does not cover glass and silver **b** (inf: = Haftpflichtversicherung) personal or public (US) liability insurance; (für Auto) ≈ third party insurance; **ich bin in keiner ~** I don't have any personal liability insurance etc; **haft|pflich|tig** [-pflɪçtɪç] ADJ liable; **haft|pflicht|ver|si|chert** [-fɛːɐzɪçɐt] ADJ **~ sein** to have personal or public (US) liability insurance; (Autofahrer) ≈ to have third-party insurance; **Haft|pflicht|ver|si|che|rung** F personal or public (US) liability insurance no indef art; (von Autofahrer) ≈ third-party insurance; **Haft|prü|fung** F review of remand in custody; **Haft|psy|cho|se** F prison psychosis no indef art; **Haft|pul|ver** NT (für Gebiss) denture fixative or adhesive; **Haft|rei|bung** F (Phys) static friction; **Haft|rich|ter(in)** M(F) magistrate; **Haft|scha|len** PL contact lenses pl; **Haft|stra|fe** F prison sentence; **haft|un|fä|hig** ADJ (Jur) unfit to be kept in prison; **Haft|un|fä|hig|keit** F , no pl (Jur) unfitness to be kept in prison (because of illness etc)

Haf|tung [ˈhaftʊŋ] ✪ 47.3 F -, **-en a** (Jur) (legal) liability; (für Personen) (legal) responsibility; **für Ihre Garderobe übernehmen wir keine ~** articles are left at owner's risk, the management accepts no responsibility for articles deposited **b** (Tech, Phys, von Reifen) adhesion

---

Haf|tungs- (Jur): **Haf|tungs|be|schrän|kung** F limitation of liability; **Haf|tungs|kla|ge** F action to establish liability

Haft-: **Haft|ur|laub** M parole; **Haft|ver|kür|zung** F shortened sentence; **Haft|ver|scho|nung** F exemption from imprisonment; **Haft|zeit** F prison sentence

Hag [ha:k] M **-(e)s, -e** [-gə] (poet, old) (= Hain) grove; (= Hecke) hedge

Ha|ge-: **Ha|ge|bu|che** ['ha:gəbu:xə] F hornbeam; **Ha|ge|but|te** ['ha:gəbʊtə] F **-, -n** rose hip; (inf: = Heckenrose) dog rose; **Ha|ge|but|ten|tee** M rose-hip tea; **Ha|ge|dorn** M pl **-dorne** hawthorn

Ha|gel [ha:gl] M **-s,** no pl **a** hail; (= Hagelschauer) hailstorm **b** (= große Menge) (von Steinen, Geschossen) hail; (von Vorwürfen, Drohungen, Anschuldigungen) stream; (von Schimpfworten) stream, torrent

Ha|gel|korn NT pl **-körner** hailstone

ha|geln ['ha:gln] **VI** impers **es hagelt** it's hailing **VI** etw hagelt auf jdn/etw (Schläge, Geschosse, Steine) sth rains down on sb/sth; (Vorwürfe, Schimpfworte) sb is showered with sth **VI** impers (lit) to hail (down); **es hagelte etw** (fig) sth rained down; Vorwürfe, Schimpfworte there was a shower of sth

Ha|gel-: **Ha|gel|scha|den** M damage caused by hail; **Ha|gel|schau|er** M (short) hailstorm; **Ha|gel|schlag** M **a** (Met) hail; (= Hagelschauer) hailstorm **b** (Cook) sugar crystals pl; **Ha|gel|schlo|ße** F **-, -n** (dial) hailstone; **Ha|gel|sturm** M hailstorm; **Ha|gel|wet|ter** NT (lit) hailstorm

ha|ger ['ha:gə] ADJ gaunt, thin; Mensch auch lean

Ha|ge|stolz ['ha:gəʃtɔlts] M **-es, -e** (old, hum) confirmed bachelor

Ha|gio- [hagio-]: **Ha|gi|o|graf** ▲ ['-gra:f] M **-en, -en**, **Ha|gi|o|gra|fin** ▲ ['-gra:fɪn] F **-, -nen** (form) hagiographer; **Ha|gi|o|gra|fen** ▲ ['-gra:fɪn] PL (Bibl) Hagiographa; **Ha|gi|o|gra|fie** ▲ ['-gra:fi:] F **-, -n** [-'fi:ən] (form) hagiography

ha|ha [ha'ha:, ha'ha], **ha|ha|ha** [haha'ha:, haha-'ha] INTERJ haha, ha, ha, ha

Hä|her ['hɛ:ɐ] M **-s, -** jay

Hahn [ha:n] M **-(e)s, ⸚e** ['hɛ:nə] **a** (= männlicher Vogel) cock; (= männliches Haushuhn auch) rooster; (jünger) cockerel; (= Wetterhahn) weathercock; **der gallische ~** the French cockerel; **~ im Korb sein** (= Mann unter Frauen) to be cock of the walk; **danach kräht kein ~ mehr** (inf) no one cares two hoots about that any more (inf); **jdm den (roten) ~ aufs Dach setzen** to set sb's house on fire **b** pl auch **-en** (Tech) tap, faucet (US); (= Zapfhahn auch) spigot; (= Schwimmerhahn) ball cock **c** (= Abzug) trigger

Hähn|chen ['hɛ:nçən] NT **-s, -** chicken; (= junger Hahn) cockerel

Hah|nen-: **Hah|nen|bal|ken** M (Build) ridge beam; **Hah|nen|fe|der** F cock's plume; **Hah|nen|fuß** M (Bot) buttercup; **Hah|nen|fuß|ge|wächs** NT buttercup; **Hah|nen|kamm** M (auch Frisur) cockscomb; **Hah|nen|kampf** M **a** cockfight; (Sport) cockfighting **b** (= Spiel) children's hopping game; **Hah|nen|schrei** M cockcrow; **beim ersten ~** (fig) at cockcrow; **Hah|nen|sporn** M pl **-sporen** cock's spur; **Hah|nen|tritt|mus|ter** NT dogtooth check

Hah|ni|um ['ha:niʊm] NT **-s,** no pl (abbr **Ha**) hahnium

Hahn|rei ['ha:nrai] M **-s, -e** (dated) cuckold; **jdn zum ~ machen** to cuckold sb

Hai [hai] M **-(e)s, -e**, **Hai|fisch** M (lit, fig) shark

Hai|fisch|flos|sen|sup|pe F shark's-fin soup

Hain [hain] M **-(e)s, -e** (poet, geh) grove

Hain|bu|che F hornbeam

Hai|ti [ha'i:ti] NT **-s** Haiti

Hai|ti|a|ner [hai'tia:nɐ] M **-s, -**, **Hai|ti|a|ne|rin** [-ərɪn] F **-, -nen** Haitian

hai|ti|a|nisch [hai'tia:nɪʃ] ADJ Haitian

Hai|ti|er [ha'i:tiɐ] M **-s, -**, **Hai|ti|e|rin** [-iərɪn] F **-, -nen** Haitian

hai|tisch [ha'i:tɪʃ] ADJ Haitian

Häk|chen ['hɛ:kçən] NT **-s, -** (Sew) (small) hook; **was ein ~ werden will, krümmt sich bei|zeiten** (Prov) there's nothing like starting young **b** (= Zeichen) tick (Brit), check (US); (auf Buchstaben) diacritic (spec), accent **c** (= Instrument) dental probe

Hä|kel|ar|beit F crochet (work) no indef art; (= das Häkeln auch) crocheting; (= Gegenstand) piece of crochet (work)

Hä|ke|lei [hɛ:kə'lai] F **-, -en** crocheting, crochet work

Hä|kel|garn NT crochet thread

ha|keln ['ha:kln] **VI** (= Fingerhakeln machen) to finger-wrestle **VTI** **a** (Ftbl, Hockey etc) to trip up **b** (Rugby) to heel **c** (beim Ringen) Gegner to get in a foot-lock

hä|keln ['hɛ:kln] VTI to crochet

Hä|kel|na|del F crochet hook

ha|ken ['ha:kn] **VI** (= klemmen) to stick; **es hakt** (fig) there's some delay, there are sticking points; **es hakt bei jdm** (inf: = versteht nicht) sb is stuck **VT** **a** (= befestigen) to hook (an +acc to) **b** (= einhängen, um etw legen) to hook (in +acc in, um around) **VTI** (Sport) to trip up

Ha|ken ['ha:kn] M **-s, -** **a** hook; (aus Holz auch) peg; **~ und Öse** hook and eye; **mit ~ und Ösen spielen** (Ftbl inf) to foul **b** (inf: = Schwierigkeit) snag, catch; **die Sache hat einen ~** there's a snag or a catch; **die Sache ist ganz ohne ~ und Ösen** there's no catch; **ein Angebot ohne ~ und Ösen** an offer with no strings attached **c** (= plötzlicher Richtungswechsel) **einen ~ schlagen** to dart sideways; **~ pl schlagen** to dart from side to side **d** (Boxen) hook **e** = Häkchen b

Ha|ken-: **ha|ken|för|mig** ADJ hooked, hook-shaped; Nase hooked; **Ha|ken|kral|le** F pinch hook; **Ha|ken|kreuz** NT swastika; **Ha|ken|kreuz|fah|ne** F swastika flag; **Ha|ken|na|se** F hooked nose, hooknose

ha|kig ['ha:kɪç] ADJ **= hakenförmig**

Hal|a|li [hala'li:] NT **-s, -(s)** (Hunt) mort

halb [halp] **ADJ** **a** (Bruchteil) half; Lehrauftrag etc part-time; **~ er Kuchen/Meter** etc half a cake/metre (Brit) or meter (US) etc; **der ~e Kuchen/Tag** etc half the cake/day etc; **eine ~e Stunde** half an hour; **jede ~e Stunde** every half hour; **ein ~es Jahr** six months pl, half a year; **ein ~es Dutzend** half a dozen; **auf ~er Höhe** at half the normal height; (zum Gipfel) halfway up; **auf ~em Weg, auf ~er Strecke** (lit) halfway; (fig) halfway through; **jdm auf ~em Weg entgegenkommen** (fig) to meet sb halfway; **das ~e Hundert** fifty, half a hundred (old); **zum ~en Preis** (at) half price; **den Apfel nur ~ essen** to eat only half the apple; **Kleid mit ~em Arm** dress with half-length sleeves

b (Mus) **eine ~e Note** a minim (Brit), a half-note (US); **ein ~er Ton** a semitone; **~e Pause** minim (Brit) or half-note (US) rest

c inv (Uhrzeit) **~ zehn** half past nine; **fünf Minuten vor/nach ~ zwei** twenty-five (minutes) past one/to two; **es schlägt ~** it's striking the half hour; **um drei Minuten nach ~** at three minutes past the half hour; **um fünf Minuten nach ~** at twenty-five-to

d inv, no art (bei geografischen Namen) **~ Deutschland/London** half of Germany/London **e** (= teilweise, stückhaft) Maßnahmen half; Reformen partial (= vermindert) Tempo half; Lächeln slight; Licht poor; **~e Arbeit leisten** to do a bad job; **die ~e Freude** half the pleasure; **die ~e Wahrheit** half of or part of the truth; **nichts Halbes und nichts Ganzes** neither one thing nor the other; **mit ~em Ohr** with half an ear; **ein ~er Mensch/eine ~e Frau sein**, **sich nur wie ein ~er Mensch/eine ~e Frau fühlen** not to feel like

a complete person/woman; (= energielos) to feel half dead; **eine ~e Sache machen** not to do it properly; **keine ~en Sachen machen** not to do things by halves

f (inf) (= große Anzahl, großer Teil) **die ~e Stadt/Welt/Arbeit** half the town/world/work; **sie ist schon eine ~e Schottin** she is already half Scottish; **ein ~er Elektriker/Mechaniker** something of an electrician/mechanic; **(noch) ein ~es Kind sein** to be hardly or scarcely more than a child

ADV **a** (= zur Hälfte) half; **~ gar** half-cooked, half-done; (fig) Idee half-baked; **~ links** (Sport, spielen) (at) inside left; (im Theater) sitzen left of centre (Brit) or center (US); **~ links abbiegen** to fork left; **die Straße ~ links** the left fork; **das Auto kam von ~ links** the car came from a/the left fork; **~ linke(r, s)** (Sport) inside left; **die linke Abzweigung/Straße** the left fork; **~ rech|te(r, s)** (Sport) inside right; **die ~ rechte Abzweigung/Straße** the right fork; **~ rechts** (Sport, spielen) (at) inside right; (im Theater) sitzen right of centre (Brit) or center (US); **~ rechts abbiegen** to fork right; **die Straße ~ rechts** the right fork; **das Auto kam von ~ rechts** the car came from a/the right fork; **~ rechts/links abzweigen** (Straße, Fahrer) to fork (off) to the right/left, to turn half right/left; **~ voll** half-filled; Behälter auch half-full; **die Zeit ist ~ vorbei** half the time has already gone

b (= nicht ganz, teilweise) half; **~ fest** (Zustand, Materie) semi-solid; Gelee half-set; **~ offen** half-open; Gefängnis open; **~ offener Vollzug** daytime release (for prisoners); **~ reif** half-ripe; **~ verdaut** (lit, fig) half-digested; **~ wach** half awake; **in ~ wachem Zustand** half awake; **~ zivilisiert** half-civilized; **~ so gut** half as good; **etw nur ~ verstehen** to only half understand sth; **ich hörte nur ~ zu** I was only half listening; **das ist ~ so schlimm** it's not as bad as all that; (Zukünftiges) that won't be too bad; **er weiß alles nur ~** he only knows about things superficially; **etw nur ~ machen** to only half-do sth (inf)

c (= fast vollständig) almost, nearly; blind, roh half; **~ fertig** half-finished; (Ind) semi-finished; (fig) immature; **ich war schon ~ fertig** I was almost or nearly finished; **~ nackt** half-naked; Arm half-covered; **~ tot** (lit) half dead; **wir haben uns ~ totgelacht** we almost died laughing; **ich hätte mich ~ totärgern können** I could have kicked myself (inf); → frisch b

d (= lachend, weinend) half laughing, half crying; **~ Mensch, ~ Pferd** half or part man, half or part horse; **Wein oder Sprudel? – ~ und ~** wine or mineral water? – half and half

e **mit jdm ~e-halbe machen** (inf) to go halves with sb (Brit), to go 50/50 with sb; **~ und ~** (inf: = beinahe) more or less; **gefällt es dir? – ~ und ~** do you like it? – sort of (inf) or so-so (inf)

Halb-: **Halb|af|fe** M prosimian; **halb|amt|lich** ADJ semi-official; **halb|au|to|ma|tisch** ADJ semi-automatic; **Halb|band** [-bant] M pl **-bän|de** half-binding; **Halb|bil|dung** F smattering of knowledge or (in Bezug auf Ausbildung) education; **halb|bit|ter** ADJ Schokolade semi-sweet; **Halb|blut** NT **a** (= Mensch) half-caste **b** (= Tier) crossbreed; **Halb|blü|ter** M **-s, -** crossbreed; **Halb|blü|ti|ge(r)** [-bly:tɪgə] MF decl as adj half-caste; **Halb|bru|der** M half-brother; **Halb|de|ckung** F (Fin) partial cover; **halb|dun|kel** ADJ half-dark, dim; **Halb|dun|kel** NT semi-darkness, half-dark; (= Dämmerung) dusk, twilight

Hal|be ['halbə] F decl as adj (esp S Ger) **= Halbe(r)**

Halb|edel|stein M semi-precious stone

Hal|be(r) ['halbə] M decl as adj half a litre (Brit) or liter (US) (of beer); **trinken Sie noch einen ~n!** ≈ have another pint! (Brit), ≈ have another beer!

hal|ber¹ ['halbə] PREP +gen (nachgestellt) (dated, geh) (= wegen) on account of; (= um … willen) for the sake of

hạl|ber² ADJ, ADV (S Ger) → **halb** ADJ c ADV b, c

-hal|ber ADV suf (= wegen) on account of; (= um ... willen) for the sake of; **gesundheitshalber** for reasons of health, for medical reasons; **vorsichtshalber** to be on the safe side, as a precaution; **sicherheitshalber** (= aus Sicherheitsgründen) for safety reasons; (= um sicher zu sein) to be on the safe side

Halb-: **halb|er|wach|sen** ADJ attr half grown (up); **Halb|er|zeug|nis** NT (Comm) semi-finished product

Hạl|be(s) ['halbə] NT decl as adj = **Halbe(r)**

Halb-: **Halb|fab|ri|kat** NT semi-finished product; **halb|fer|tig** △ ADJ attr → **halb ADV** c; **halb|fest** △ ADJ attr → **halb ADV** b; **halb|fett** **ADJ** **a** (Typ) secondary bold **b** Lebensmittel medium-fat **ADV** (Typ) in secondary bold; **Halb|fi|na|le** NT semi-final; **Halb|fin|ger|hand|schuh** M fingerless glove; **halb|gar** △ ADJ attr → **halb ADV** a; **halb|ge|bil|det** ADJ attr half-educated; **Halb|ge|schoss** ▲ NT (Archit) mezzanine floor; **Halb|ge|schwis|ter** PL half brothers and sisters pl; **Halb|glat|ze** F receding hairline; **Halb|gott** M (Myth, fig) demigod; **Halbgötter in Weiß** (iro) doctors

Halb|heit F -, -en (pej) half measure; **er ist nicht für ~en** he is not one for half measures, he doesn't do things by halves; **mach keine ~en** (inf) don't do things by halves

Halb-: **halb|her|zig** **ADJ** half-hearted **ADV** half-heartedly; **na, dieses Ja kam aber sehr ~** well, that yes sounded very half-hearted; **Halb|her|zig|keit** [-hɛrtsɪçkaɪt] F -, no pl half-heartedness no pl; **halb|hoch** **ADJ** Baum half-grown; Stern halfway up the sky; (Comput) Laufwerkschacht half-height **ADV** **den Ball ~ abspielen** to pass the ball at shoulder height; **~ fliegen** to fly at half (its/one's etc normal) height

hal|bie|ren [hal'biːrən] ptp **halbiert** VT to halve, to divide in half or two; (Geometrie) to bisect; (= in zwei schneiden) to cut in half; **eine Zahl ~** to divide a number by two

Hal|bie|rung F -, -en halving, dividing in half or two; (Geometrie) bisection

Halb-: **Halb|in|sel** F peninsula; **Halb|in|va|li|de** M , **Halb|in|va|li|din** **F** semi-invalid, partially disabled

Halb|jahr NT half-year (auch Comm), six months; **im ersten/zweiten ~** in the first/last six months of the year

Halb|jah|res-: **Halb|jah|res|be|richt** M half-yearly report; **Halb|jah|res|bi|lanz** F half-yearly figures pl; **Halb|jah|res|kurs** M six-month course; **Halb|jah|res|zeug|nis** NT (Sch) half-yearly report

Halb-: **halb|jäh|rig** ADJ attr Kind six-month-old; Lehrgang etc six-month; Kündigung six months; **halb|jähr|lich** **ADJ** half-yearly (auch Comm), six-monthly; **in ~em Wechsel** changing every six months **ADV** every six months, twice a year, twice yearly; **Halb|jahrs|aus|weis** M (Aus Sch) half-yearly report; **Halb|jahrs|kurs** M six-month course; **Halb|ju|de** M , **Halb|jü|din** F half Jew; **~ sein** to be half Jewish; **Halb|kan|ton** M sub-canton; **Halb|kon|so|nant** M semi-consonant; **Halb|kreis** M semicircle; **halb|kreis|för|mig** **ADJ** semicircular **ADV** in a semicircle; **Halb|ku|gel** F hemisphere; **nordliche/südliche ~** northern/southern hemisphere; **halb|ku|gel|för|mig** ADJ hemispherical; **halb|lang** ADJ Kleid, Rock midcalf length; Haar chin-length; **nun mach mal ~!** (inf) now wait a minute!; **halb|laut** **ADJ** low **ADV** in a low voice, in an undertone; **Halb|le|der** NT (= Verfahren) half-binding; **in ~ binden** to bind in half-leather; **Halb|le|der|band** M (= Buch) half-bound volume; (= Ausgabe) half-bound edition; **halb|lei|nen** ADJ attr Stoff made of a fifty per cent linen mixture; Bucheinband half-cloth; **Halb|lei|nen** NT Stoff fifty per cent linen material; (= Bucheinband) half-cloth; **Halb|lei|nen|band** M (= Buch)

volume bound in half-cloth; (= Ausgabe) edition bound in half-cloth; **Halb|lei|ter** M (Phys) semiconductor; **halb|lin|ke(r, s)** △ ADJ attr → **halb ADV** a; **Halb|lin|ke(r)** MF decl as adj, **Halb|links** M -, - (Sport) inside left; **halb|links** △ ADV → **halb ADV** a; **Halb|li|ter|fla|sche** F half-litre (Brit) or half-liter (US) bottle; **halb|mast** ['halpmast] ADV at half-mast; (eine Flagge) ~ **hissen** to hoist a flag to half-mast; ~ **flaggen** to fly flags/a flag at half-mast; **auf ~ stehen** to fly or be at half-mast; **seine Socken hängen auf ~** (hum: = sind verrutscht) his socks are at half-mast; **halb|matt** ADJ (Phot) semimatt; **Halb|mes|ser** M -s, - radius; **Halb|me|tall** NT semi-metal; **Halb|mo|nats|schrift** F fortnightly periodical; **Halb|mond** M (Astron) half-moon; (= Symbol) crescent; (an Fingernägeln) half-moon; **bei ~** when there is a half-moon; **wir haben ~** there's a half-moon; **halb|mo|nat|lich** **ADJ** half-monthly **ADV** half-monthly, fortnightly, biweekly (US); **halb|mond|för|mig** ADJ crescent-shaped; **halb|nackt** △ ADJ attr → **halb ADV** b; **halb|part** ['halppart] ADV ~ **machen** (bei einer Unternehmung) to go halves; (bei Gewinn) to split it fifty-fifty; **Halb|pen|si|on** F half-board; **in ~ wohnen** to have half-board; **Halb|pro|dukt** NT semi-finished product; **halb|rech|te(r, s)** △ ADJ attr → **halb ADV** a; **Halb|rech|te(r)** MF decl as adj, **Halb|rechts** M -, - (Sport) inside right; **halb|rechts** △ ADV → **halb ADV** a; **halb|reif** △ ADJ attr → **halb ADV** b; **Halb|re|li|ef** NT half-relief, mezzo-relievo; **halb|rund** ADJ attr Tisch etc semicircular; Ecke half-rounded; **Halb|rund** ['halprʊnt] NT -(e)s, (rare) -e [-də] semicircle, half-circle; **im ~** in a semicircle; **Halb|schat|ten** M half shadow; (Astron) penumbra; **Halb|schlaf** M light sleep; **im ~ sein** to be half asleep; **Halb|schritt-Tas|te** F condensed key, half-space key; **Halb|schuh** M shoe; **Halb|schwer|ge|wicht** NT **a** no pl (= Klasse) light-heavyweight division; **ein Boxkampf im ~** a light-heavyweight contest **b** (= Boxer) light-heavyweight; **Halb|schwer|ge|wicht|ler(in)** M(F) light-heavyweight; **Halb|schwes|ter** F half-sister; **Halb|sei|de** F fifty per cent (Brit) or percent (US) silk mixture; **halb|sei|den** ADJ (lit) fifty per cent (Brit) or percent (US) silk; (fig) Dame fast; Aussehen flashy; (= schwul) gay; (= zweifelhaft, undurchsichtig) dubious; ~**e Milieu, ~e Kreise** the demimonde; **halb|sei|tig** [-zaɪtɪç] ADJ Anzeige etc half-page; (Med) Kopfschmerzen in one side of one's head; ~**e Lähmung** one-sided paralysis, hemiplegia **ADV** ~ **gelähmt** paralyzed on one side, hemiplegic; **halb|staat|lich** ADJ attr partly state-run or state-controlled; **halb|stark** ADJ attr Sprache, Manieren, Jugendliche rowdy; **Halb|star|ke(r)** M decl as adj young hooligan, young rowdy (Brit); **halb|stün|dig** ADJ attr half-hour attr, lasting half an hour; **halb|stünd|lich** **ADJ** half-hourly **ADV** every half an hour, half-hourly; **Halb|stür|mer(in)** M(F) (Ftbl) half-back

halb|tä|gig **ADJ** attr half-day attr; Fahrt, Ausflug, Urlaub, Arbeit etc half a day's attr **ADV** → **halb|tags**

halb|tags ['halptaːks] ADV (= morgens) in the mornings; (= nachmittags) in the afternoons; (in Bezug auf Angestellte auch) part-time

Halb|tags-: **Halb|tags|ar|beit** F (= Arbeitsverhältnis) half-day job; (morgens auch) morning job; (nachmittags auch) afternoon job; (von Angestellten auch) part-time job; **Halb|tags|be|schäf|tig|te(r)** MF decl as adj = **Halbtagskraft**; **Halb|tags|be|schäf|ti|gung** F = Halbtagsarbeit; **Halb|tags|kraft** F worker employed for half-days only; **Halb|tags|schu|le** F half-day school

Halb-: **Halb|ton** M pl -**töne** (Mus) semitone; (Art, Phot) halftone; **Halb|ton|schritt** M semitone; **halb|tot** △ ADJ attr → **halb ADV** c; **Halb|to|ta|le** F (Film) medium shot; **Halb|trau|er** F half-mourning; **halb|tro|cken** ADJ

Wein medium-dry; **halb|ver|daut** △ [-fɛɐdaut] ADJ attr → **halb ADV** b; **Halb|vers** M half-line, hemistich; **Halb|vo|kal** M semivowel; **halb|voll** △ ADJ attr → **halb ADV** b; **halb|wach** △ ADJ attr → **halb ADV** b; **Halb|wahr|heit** F half-truth; **Halb|wai|se** F person who has lost one parent **er/sie ist** ~ he/she has lost one of his/her parents; **halb|wegs** ['halp'veːks] ADV **a** partly; gut, adäquat reasonably; annehmbar halfway; **wenn es dir wieder ~ gut geht** when you're feeling a bit better; **wenn Sie ~ eine Vorstellung haben, ...** if you have the least idea ... **b** (dated: = auf halber Strecke) halfway; **Halb|welt** F demimonde; **Halb|welt|da|me** F demimondaine; **Halb|wel|ter|ge|wicht** NT (= Klasse) light-welterweight no def art; (= Sportler) light-welterweight; **Halb|wert(s)|zeit** F (Phys) half-life; **halb|wild** ADJ attr Mensch uncivilized; Tier half wild; **wie die Halbwilden** (inf) like (a bunch of) savages; **Halb|wis|sen** NT (pej) superficial knowledge; **halb|wö|chent|lich** **ADJ** twice-weekly or twice weekly; **halb|wüch|sig** [-vyːksɪç] ADJ adolescent; **Halb|wüch|si|ge(r)** [-vyːksɪgə] MF decl as adj adolescent; **Halb|wüs|te** F semi-desert; **Halb|zei|le** F (Poet) half-line; **Halb|zeit** F (Sport) (= Hälfte) half; (= Pause) half-time

Halb|zeit-: **Halb|zeit|pfiff** M half-time whistle; **Halb|zeit|stand** M half-time score

halb|zi|vi|li|siert △ ADJ attr → **halb ADV** b

Hal|de ['haldə] F -, -n **a** (= Abfallhalde) mound, heap; (Min: = Abbauhalde) slag heap; (fig) mountain; **etw auf ~ legen** (Ware, Vorräte) to stockpile sth; Pläne etc to shelve sth **b** (geh: = Abhang) slope

half pret von **helfen**

Half-Back ['haːfbɛk] M -s, -s, **Half|back** M -s, -s (Sw) half-back

Half|pipe ['haːfpaip] F -, -s (Sport) half-pipe

Hälf|te ['hɛlftə] F -, -n **a** half; **die ~ der Kinder war abwesend** half the children were absent; **die ~ einer Sache** (gen) or **von etw** half (of) sth; **eine ~ des Apfels** half of the apple; **wir haben schon die ~ (des Vorrats) verbraucht** we have already used up half (the stocks); **die ~ ist gelogen** half of it is lies; **Rentner zahlen die ~** pensioners pay half price; **um die ~ mehr** half as much again; **um die ~ zu viel** too much by half; **um die ~ steigen** to increase by half or by fifty per cent; **um die ~ kleiner** half as small or big; **um die ~ größer** half as big again; **es ist zur ~ fertig/voll** it is half finished/full; **die Beiträge werden je zur ~ vom Arbeitgeber und Arbeitnehmer bezahlt** the employer and employee each pay half (of) the contribution; **das werde ich zur ~ bezahlen** I will pay half (of it); **meine bessere ~** (hum inf) my better half (hum inf) **b** (= Mitte: einer Fläche) middle; **auf der ~ des Weges** halfway

hälf|ten ['hɛlftn] VT (rare) = **halbieren**

Half|ter¹ ['halftə] M OR NT -s, - (für Tiere) halter

Half|ter² F -, -n or nt -s, - (= Pistolenhalfter) holster

half|tern ['halftən] VT to halter, to put a halter on

hal|ky|o|nisch [hal'kyoːnɪʃ] ADJ (liter) ~**e Tage** halcyon days

Hall [hal] M -(e)s, -e **a** reverberation, echo **b** (= Nachhall) echo

Hal|le ['halə] F -, -n hall; (= Hotelhalle) lobby, vestibule; (= Werkshalle, Fabrikhalle) shed; (= Sporthalle) (sports) hall, gym(nasium); (= Tennishalle) indoor tennis court(s pl); (= Schwimmhalle) indoor swimming pool; (= Flugzeughalle) hangar; **in der ~** (im Gegensatz zu draußen) inside, indoors; **Fußball in der ~** indoor football (esp Brit) or soccer; **in der ~ des Postamts** in the post office; **in diesen heiligen ~n** (iro) in these august surroundings (iro)

hal|le|lu|ja [hale'luːja] INTERJ halleluja(h)

Hal|le|lu|ja [haleˈluːja] NT **-s, -s** (*Rel, Mus*) halleluja(h); **das ~ aus Händels „Messias"** the Hallelujah Chorus from Handel's "Messiah"

hal|len [ˈhalən] VI to reverberate, to echo (*auch fig*), to resound

Hallen- *in cpds* (*Sport*) indoor; **Hal|len|bad** NT indoor swimming pool; **Hal|len|fuß|ball** M indoor football (*esp Brit*) or soccer; **Hal|len-kir|che** F hall church; **Hal|len|meis|ter-schaft** F (*Sport*) indoor championship(s *pl*); **Hal|len|schwimm|bad** NT indoor swimming pool; **Hal|len|sport** M indoor sport(s *pl*); **Hal|len|ten|nis** NT indoor tennis; **Hal|len-tur|nier** NT (*Sport*) indoor tournament; (*Leichtathletik auch*) indoor meeting

hal|leysch ▲ [ˈhaleʃ] ADJ **der ~e Komet** Halley's comet

Hal|lig [ˈhalɪç] F **-, -en** [-gn] *a small island off the west coast of Schleswig-Holstein*

Hal|li|masch [ˈhalimaʃ] M **-(e)s, -e** (*Bot*) honey agaric

hal|lo [haˈloː, ˈhalo] INTERJ **a** hello; (*zur Begrüßung*) hi (*inf*), hello **b** (*überrascht*) hello

Hal|lo [haˈloː, ˈhalo] NT **-s, -s** cheer *usu pl*; (= *Gruß*) hello

Hal|lo|dri [haˈloːdri] M **-s, -(s)** (*Aus, S Ger: inf*) rogue

Hall|statt|zeit [ˈhalʃtat-] F *, no pl* (*Archeol*) Hallstatt period

Hal|lu|zi|na|ti|on [halutsinaˈtsioːn] F **-, -en** hallucination; **ich leide wohl an ~en** (*fig*) I must be seeing things

hal|lu|zi|na|to|risch [halutsinaˈtoːrɪʃ] ADJ hallucinatory

hal|lu|zi|nie|ren [halutsiˈniːrən] *ptp* **halluziniert** VI to hallucinate

hal|lu|zi|no|gen [halutsinoˈgeːn] ADJ (*Med*) hallucinogenic

Hal|lu|zi|no|gen [halutsinoˈgeːn] NT **-s, -e** (*Med*) hallucinogen

Halm [halm] M **-(e)s, -e** stalk, stem; (= *Grashalm*) blade of grass; (= *Strohhalm, zum Trinken*) straw; **Getreide auf dem ~** standing grain

Hal|ma [ˈhalma] NT **-s**, *no pl* halma, Chinese chequers *sing* (*Brit*), Chinese checkers *sing* (*US*)

Hälm|chen [ˈhɛlmçən] NT **-s, -** *dim von* **Halm**

Ha|lo [ˈhaːlo] M **-(s), -s** *or* **-nen** [-ˈloːnən] (*Astron, Met*) halo; (*TV*) shadow

ha|lo|gen [haloˈgeːn] ADJ halogenous

Ha|lo|gen [haloˈgeːn] NT **-s, -e** halogen

Halogen-: **Ha|lo|gen|bir|ne** F halogen bulb; **Ha|lo|gen|(glüh)|lam|pe** F halogen lamp; **Ha|lo|gen|leuch|te** F halogen lamp; **Ha|lo-gen|licht** NT halogen light; **Ha|lo|gen-schein|wer|fer** M halogen headlamp

Hals¹ [hals] M **-es, ⸚e** [ˈhɛlzə] **a** (*von außen gesehen*) neck; **einen langen ~ machen, den ~ re-cken** to crane one's neck; **sich** (*dat*) **nach jdm/ etw den ~ verrenken** (*inf*) to crane one's neck to see sb/sth; **jdm um den ~ fallen** to fling one's arms (a)round sb's neck; **sich jdm an den ~ werfen** (*fig inf*) to throw oneself at sb; **sich** (*dat*) **den ~ brechen** (*inf*) to break one's neck; **etw kostet jdn** *or* **jdm den ~** (*inf*) **etw bricht jdm den ~** (*inf*) sth will cost sb his/her neck; **sich um den** *or* **seinen ~ reden** (*inf*) to put one's head in the noose; **~ über Kopf ab-reisen/den Koffer packen** to leave/pack one's case in a rush *or* hurry; **ihm steht das Wasser bis zum ~** (*fig*) he is up to his neck in it (*inf*); **bis über den ~** (*fig inf*) up to one's ears; **jdn auf dem** *or* **am ~ haben** (*inf*) to be lumbered (*Brit*) *or* saddled with sb (*inf*); **jdm/sich etw auf den ~ laden** (*inf*) to lumber (*Brit*) *or* saddle sb/oneself with sth (*inf*); **jdn jdm auf den ~ schicken** *or* **hetzen** (*inf*) to put sb onto sb; **jdm etw an den ~ wünschen** (*inf*) to wish sth on sb; **jdm mit etw vom ~(e) bleiben** (*inf*) not to bother sb with sth (*inf*); **sich** (*dat*) **jdn/etw vom ~e schaffen** (*inf*) to get sb/sth off one's

back (*inf*); **jdm jdn/etw vom ~ schaffen** (*inf*) to get sb/sth off sb's back (*inf*); **sich** (*dat*) **die Pest an den ~ ärgern (können)** to be mad *or* furious with oneself (*mit over*)

  b (= *Kehle, Rachen*) throat; **sie hat es am** *or* **im ~** (*inf*) she has a sore throat; **aus vollem ~(e)** at the top of one's voice; **aus vollem ~(e) la-chen** to roar with laughter; **es hängt** *or* **wächst mir zum ~ heraus** (*inf*) I'm sick and tired of it, I've had it up to here (*inf*); **sie hat es in den falschen ~ bekommen** (*inf*) (= *sich verschlucken*) it went down the wrong way; (= *falsch verstehen*) she took it wrongly; **etw bleibt jdm im ~ stecken** (*lit, fig*) sth sticks in sb's throat; **er kann den ~ nicht voll (genug) kriegen** (*fig inf*) he is never satisfied

  c (= *Flaschenhals, Geigenhals, Säulenhals*) neck; (= *Notenhals*) stem → **brechen VT a**

  d (*von Knochen*) neck; (= *Gebärmutterhals*) cervix, neck of the womb

Hals² [hals] M **-es, -en** [-zn] (*Naut*) tack

Hals-: **Hals|ab|schnei|der(in)** M(F) (*pej inf*) shark (*inf*); **hals|ab|schnei|de|risch** [ˈhalsʃap-ʃnaidərɪʃ] ADJ (*pej inf*) *Preise, Maßnahme* extortionate, exorbitant; *Mensch* cutthroat (*inf*); **Hals|an|satz** M base of the neck; **Hals|aus-schnitt** M neck(line); **Hals|band** [-bant] NT *pl* **-bänder** (= *Hundehalsband*) collar; (= *Schmuck*) necklace; (*eng anliegend*) choker; **hals|bre-che|risch** [ˈhalsbreçərɪʃ] ADJ dangerous, risky; *Tempo* breakneck; *Fahrt* hair-raising; *Weg* treacherous ADV **herumturnen, klettern** recklessly; **~ schnell/rasant/wild** at breakneck pace; **fahren** at breakneck speed; **Hals|bund** M *pl* **-bünde**, **Hals|bünd|chen** NT neckband

Häls|chen [ˈhɛlsçən] NT **-s, -** *dim von* **Hals¹**

hal|sen¹ [ˈhalzn] VT (*rare*) to embrace

hal|sen² VI (*Naut*) to wear

Hals-: **Hals|ent|zün|dung** F sore throat; **Hals|grat** M (*esp S Ger, Cook*) neck (of pork); **Hals|ket|te** F (= *Schmuck*) necklace; (*für Hund*) chain; **Hals|krau|se** F (*Fashion, Zool*) ruff; (*Med*) cervical *or* neck collar; **Hals|län|ge** F neck; (**um**) **eine ~ by a** neck; **um zwei ~n** by half a length; **hals|los** ADJ without a neck

Hals-Na|sen-Oh|ren-: **Hals-Na|sen-Oh|ren-Arzt** M , **Hals-Na|sen-Oh|ren-Ärz|tin** F ear, nose and throat specialist; **Hals-Na-sen-Oh|ren-Heil|kun|de** F ear, nose and throat medicine; **Hals-Na|sen-Oh|ren--Krank|heit** F disease of the ear, nose and throat

Hals-: **Hals|par|tie** F (*außen*) neck area, area *or* region of the neck; (*innen*) throat area, area *or* region of the throat; **Hals|schlag|ader** F carotid (artery); **Hals|schmer|zen** PL sore throat *sing*; **Hals|schmuck** M necklace; (*Sam-melbegriff*) necklaces *pl*; **hals|star|rig** [-ʃtarɪç] ADJ obstinate, stubborn; **Hals|star|rig|keit** F *-, no pl* obstinacy, stubbornness; **Hals|stück** NT (*Cook*) neck; **Hals|tuch** NT *pl* **-tücher** scarf; **Hals- und Bein|bruch** INTERJ good luck; **Hals|weh** NT sore throat; **Hals|wei|te** F neck size; **Hals|wi|ckel** M (*Med*) throat compress; **Hals|wir|bel** M cervical vertebra; **Hals-wir|bel|säu|le** F (*Anat*) cervical vertebrae *pl*

halt¹ [halt] INTERJ stop; (*Mil*) halt

halt² [halt] ADV (*dial*) **a** = **eben** ADV **d b** (*Aus*) **und so** = and so on *or* forth

Halt [halt] M **-(e)s, -e** **a** (*für Füße, Hände, Festig-keit*) hold; (*lit, fig*: = *Stütze*) support; (*fig*: = *inne-rer Halt*) security *no art*; **~ haben** (*Ding*) to hold; **jdm/einer Sache ~ geben** to support sb/sth; **dem Haar ~ geben** to give hold to one's hair; **keinen ~ haben** to have no hold/support; to be insecure; **~ suchen/finden** to look for/find a hold/a support/security; **auf dem Eis den ~ ver-lieren** to lose one's footing on the ice; **ohne in-neren ~** insecure

  b (*geh: = Anhalten*) stop; **ohne ~** non-stop, without stopping; **~ machen** to stop; **vor nichts ~ machen** (*fig*) to stop at nothing; **vor nieman-dem ~ machen** (*fig*) to spare no-one

hält [hɛlt] *3. pers sing pres von* **halten**

halt|bar ✪ 53.3 ADJ **a** (= *nicht leicht verderblich*) **~ sein** (*Lebensmittel*) to keep (well); **~e Lebens-mittel** food which keeps (well); **das ist sechs Monate ~** that will keep for six months; **etw ~ machen** to preserve sth; **~ bis 6.11.** use by 6 Nov; **nur begrenzt ~** perishable; **schlecht ~** highly perishable; **~ gemacht** artificially preserved

  b (= *widerstandsfähig*) durable; *Stoff, Kleider* hard-wearing; *Beziehung, Ehe* long-lasting

  c *Behauptung, Theorie, Annahme* tenable

  d *pred Festung* defensible; **die Stadt ist nicht mehr ~** the town can't be held any longer

  e *Position, Rang, Platz* tenable; *Zustand, Lage* tolerable; **diese Position ist nicht mehr ~** this position can't be maintained any longer

  f (*Sport*) *Ball, Wurf* stoppable; *Schuss auch* savable

halt|bar|ge|macht △ ADJ *attr* → **haltbar a**

Halt|bar|keit [ˈhaltbaːɐkait] F **-, no pl** **a** (*von Lebensmitteln*) **eine längere ~ haben** to keep longer; **Lebensmittel von kurzer ~** perishable food; **die begrenzte ~ von Fleisch** the perishability of meat **b** (= *Widerstandsfähigkeit*) durability **c** (*von Behauptung, Theorie, Annahme*) tenability

Halt|bar|keits-: **Halt|bar|keits|da|tum** NT eat-by date (*Brit*), best-before date, use-by date; **Halt|bar|keits|dau|er** F *length of time for which food may be kept* **eine kurze/lange ~** has to be/not to be perishable

Hal|te-: **Hal|te|bo|gen** M (*Mus*) tie; **Hal|te-bucht** F (*Mot*) lay-by, rest stop (*US*); **Hal|te-griff** M **a** grip, handle; (*in Bus*) strap; (*an Ba-dewanne*) handrail **b** (*Sport*) hold; **Hal|te|gurt** M seat *or* safety belt; (*an Kinderwagen*) safety harness

---

hal|ten [ˈhaltn]
pret **hielt** [hiːlt], *ptp* **gehalten** [gəˈhaltn]
✪ 28.1, 30, 33.1, 34.1, 39.2, 41

1 TRANSITIVES VERB	3 REFLEXIVES VERB
2 INTRANSITIVES VERB	

---

1 – TRANSITIVES VERB

  a = festhalten to hold; **jdm etw halten** to hold sth for sb; **jdm den Mantel halten** to hold sb's coat (for him/her); **kannst du mir bitte die Lei-ter halten?** could you please hold the ladder for me?; **sich** (*dat*) **den Kopf/Bauch halten** to hold one's head/stomach

  b = in eine bestimmte Position bringen **etw gegen das Licht halten** to hold sth up to the light; **den Arm in die Höhe halten** to hold one's arm up; **einen Fuß/einen Zeh ins Wasser halten** to put a foot/a toe in the water

  c = tragen **die drei Pfeiler halten die Brücke** the three piers support the bridge; **meinst du, der kleine Nagel hält das schwere Ölbild?** do you think this small nail will take the weight of the heavy oil painting?; **nur zwei morsche Bret-ter hielten den Balkon noch** there were only two rotten boards holding the balcony up; **zwei Schlaufen halten den Vorhang an der Sei-te** two loops hold back the curtain

  d = zurückhalten, aufhalten to hold; (*Sport*) to save; **die Wärme/Feuchtigkeit halten** to retain heat/moisture; **er kann den Urin** *or* **das Wasser nicht halten** he's incontinent; **einen Elfmeter** *or* **Strafstoß halten** to save a penalty; **das ist ein toller Torwart, der hält jeden Ball!** he's a great goalkeeper, he makes great saves!; **ich konnte ihn/es gerade noch halten** I just managed to grab hold of him/it; **haltet den Dieb!** stop thief!; **sie lässt sich nicht halten, sie ist nicht zu halten** (*fig*) there's no holding her back; **es hält mich hier nichts mehr** there's nothing to keep me here any more; **es hält dich niemand** nobody's stopping you

  e = behalten *Festung, Rekord* to hold; *Position* to hold (on to); **den Schnabel** *or* **Mund halten** (*inf*) to keep one's mouth shut (*inf*)

---

f = unterhalten, besitzen | *Chauffeur, Lehrer* to employ; *Haustier* to keep; *Auto* to run; **sich** *(dat)* **eine Geliebte halten** to keep a mistress; **sich** *(dat)* **eine Perserkatze/einen Hausfreund halten** to have a Persian cat/a live-in lover; **wir können uns kein Auto halten** we can't afford (to run) a car; **(sich** *dat)* **eine Zeitung/Zeitschrift halten** to get a paper/magazine

g = einhalten, erfüllen | to keep; **ein Versprechen halten** to keep a promise; **man muss halten, was man verspricht** a promise is a promise; **der Film hält nicht, was er/der Titel verspricht** the film doesn't live up to expectations/its title

h = beibehalten, aufrechterhalten | *Niveau* to keep up, to maintain; *Tempo, Disziplin, Temperatur* to maintain; *Kurs* to keep, to to hold; **Ruhe halten** to keep quiet; **die Balance** *or* **das Gleichgewicht halten** to keep one's balance; **den Ton halten** to stay in tune *or* in key; **die These lässt sich nicht länger halten** *or* **ist nicht länger zu halten** this hypothesis is no longer tenable; **Kontakt halten** to keep in touch; **(mit jdm) Verbindung halten** to keep in touch (with sb); **Abstand halten!** keep your distance!; **etw sauber halten** to keep sth clean; **das Essen warm halten** to keep the food warm; **viel Sport hält jung/schlank** doing a lot of sport keeps you young/slim; **er hält sein Haus immer tadellos** he keeps his house immaculate; **halten Sie die Erklärungen einfach** keep the explanations simple; **wenn es neblig ist sollten Sie den Abstand immer so groß wie möglich halten** if it's foggy you should always stay as far as possible from the car in front; **ein Land besetzt halten** to keep a country under occupation

i = behandeln | to treat; **die Gefangenen werden in diesen Gefängnissen wie Tiere gehalten** the prisoners are treated like animals in these prisons; **er hält seine Kinder sehr streng** he's very strict with his children

j = handhaben, verfahren mit | **das kannst du (so) halten, wie du willst** that's entirely up to you

♦ **es mit etw/jdm halten** wie halten Sie es mit Ihrer Steuererklärung? how do you deal with your tax return?; **wie hältst dus mit der Religion?** what's your attitude toward(s) religion?; **wir halten es mit den Abrechnungen anders** we deal with invoices in a different way; **er hält es nicht so sehr mit der Sauberkeit** he's not over-concerned about cleanliness; **es mehr** *or* **lieber mit jdm/etw halten** to prefer sb/sth

k = gestalten | **ein in Brauntönen gehaltener Raum** a room done in different shades of brown; **sie beschloss das Zimmer in Grün zu halten** she decided to do the room in green; **das Kleid ist in dunklen Tönen gehalten** it is a dark-coloured *(Brit)* *or* dark-colored *(US)* dress; **das Mobiliar ist in einem hellen Holz gehalten** the furniture is made of a light wood

l = veranstalten, abhalten | *Fest, Pressekonferenz* to give; *Rede* to make; *Gottesdienst, Zwiesprache* to hold; *Wache* to keep; **Selbstgespräche halten** to talk to oneself; **Unterricht halten** to teach; **Mittagsschlaf halten** to have an afternoon nap; **Winterschlaf halten** to hibernate

m = einschätzen, denken |

♦ **jdn/etw für etw halten** to think sb/sth sth; **ich habe das Bild für ein Original gehalten** I thought the picture was an original; **etw für angebracht/schön halten** to think *or* consider sth appropriate/beautiful; **jdn für ehrlich halten** to think *or* consider sb honest; **ich habe ihn (irrtümlich) für seinen Bruder gehalten** I (mis)took him for his brother; **wofür halten Sie mich?** what do you take me for?; **das halte ich nicht für möglich** I don't think that is possible; **ich halte es für Unsinn, alles noch einmal abzuschreiben** I think it's silly to copy everything out again

♦ **etw von jdm/etw halten** to think sth of sb/sth; **nicht viel von jdm/etw halten** not to think much of sb/sth; **nicht viel vom Beten/Sparen halten** not to be a great one for praying/saving *(inf)*; **ich halte nichts davon, das zu tun** I'm

not in favour *(Brit)* or favor *(US)* of (doing) that

♦ **etwas/viel auf etw** *(acc)* **halten** to consider sth important/very important; **er hält etwas auf gute Manieren** he considers good manners important; **der Chef hält viel auf Pünktlichkeit** the boss attaches a lot of importance to punctuality → **Stück c**

n → **gehalten**

2 – INTRANSITIVES VERB

a = festhalten | to hold; (= *haften bleiben*) to stick; *(Sport)* to make a save; **kannst du mal einen Moment halten?** can you just hold that (for) a moment?; **unser Tormann hat heute wieder großartig gehalten** our goalkeeper made some good saves again today; **kann der denn (gut) halten?** is he a good goalkeeper?

b = bestehen bleiben, haltbar sein | to last; (*Konserven*) to keep; (*Wetter*) to last, to hold; (*Frisur, Comm: Preise*) to hold; (*Stoff*) to be hard-wearing; **der Waffenstillstand hält nun schon drei Wochen** the truce has now held for three weeks; **Rosen halten länger, wenn man ein Aspirin ins Wasser tut** roses last longer if you put an aspirin in the water; **dieser Stoff hält lange** this material is hard-wearing

c = stehen bleiben, anhalten | to stop; **zum Halten bringen** to bring to a standstill; **halten lassen** *(Mil)* to call a halt

♦ **halt mal** (= *Moment mal*) hang on *(inf)*, hold on; **halt mal, stop!** *(hum)* hang on *(inf)* or hold on a minute! → **halt** [1]

d andere Redewendungen |

♦ **auf etw** *(acc)* **halten** (= *zielen*) to aim at sth; (= *steuern*) to head for sth; (= *Wert legen auf*) to attach importance to sth; **sehr auf etw halten** to attach great importance to sth

♦ **auf sich** *(acc)* **halten** (= *auf sein Äußeres achten*) to take a pride in oneself; (= *selbstbewusst sein*) to be self-confident

♦ **an sich** *(acc)* **halten** (= *sich beherrschen*) to control oneself; **ich musste an mich halten, um nicht in schallendes Gelächter auszubrechen** I had to control myself so as not to burst into fits of laughter

♦ **zu jdm halten** (= *beistehen, treu sein*) to stand by sb; (= *favorisieren*) to support sb

3 – REFLEXIVES VERB

♦ **sich halten**

a = sich festhalten | to hold on to (*an* +*dat* to); **er konnte sich gerade noch an dem Griff halten, als der Zug mit einem scharfen Ruck anfuhr** he just managed to grab hold of the strap when the train suddenly jolted forward; **sie konnte sich auf dem glatten Abhang nicht halten** she couldn't keep her footing on the slippery slope; **er konnte sich auf dem wilden Mustang nur drei Sekunden halten** he could only stay on the wild mustang three seconds

b = eine bestimmte Körperhaltung haben | to carry *or* hold oneself; **er hält sich sehr aufrecht** he holds *or* carries himself very erect; **sich (im Gleichgewicht) halten** to keep one's balance; **sich auf den Beinen halten** to stay on one's feet; **sich (nach) links halten** to keep (to the) left; **sich nach Westen halten** to keep going westwards; **der Autofahrer hielt sich ganz rechts** the driver kept to the right; **ich halte mich an die alte Methode** I'll stick to *or* with the old method; **sich an ein Versprechen halten** to keep a promise; **sich an die Tatsachen/den Text halten** to keep *or* stick to the facts/text → **Vorschrift**

c = sich nicht verändern | (*Lebensmittel, Blumen*) to keep; (*Wetter*) to last, to hold; (*Geruch, Rauch*) to linger; (*Preise*) to hold; (*Brauch, Sitte*) to continue; **der Geruch von Knoblauch hält sich ewig** the smell of garlic lingers for ages *(inf)*

d = seine Position behaupten | to hold on; (*in Kampf*) to hold out; **er hat sich in der Spitzenposition gehalten** he held on to the lead; **er hat sich im erbarmungslosen Wettbewerb prächtig gehalten** he held on amazingly in the

cut-throat competition; **das Geschäft kann sich in dieser Straße nicht halten** the shop can't continue to stay open in this street

♦ **sich gut halten** (*in Prüfung, Spiel etc*) to do well; **er hat sich ziemlich gut gehalten** (*körperlich*) he is quite well-preserved; **sie hat sich in der schweren Prüfung unerwartet gut gehalten** she did unexpectedly well in the difficult exam

e = sich beherrschen | to control oneself; **sich nicht halten können** to be unable to control oneself

f andere Wendungen |

♦ **sich halten an** (+*acc*) **sich an jdn halten** (= *sich wenden an*) to ask sb; (= *sich richten nach*) to follow sb; (= *sich gut stellen mit*) to keep in with sb; **ich halte mich lieber an den Wein** I'd rather keep *or* stick to wine

♦ **sich halten für er hält sich für einen Spezialisten/für besonders klug** he thinks he's a specialist/very clever

---

Hạl|te-: **Hạl|te|platz** M (= *Taxihalteplatz*) taxi rank *(Brit)* or stand; **Hạl|te|punkt** M *(Rail)* stop

Hạl|ter[1] [ˈhaltɐ] M **-s, -** **a** (= *Halterung*) holder **b** (= *Sockenhalter*) garter; (= *Strumpfhalter, Hüfthalter*) suspender *(Brit)* or garter *(US)* belt **c** (*rare*: = *Griff*) handle

Hạl|ter[2] [ˈhaltɐ] M **-s, -,** **Hạl|te|rin** [-ərɪn] F **-, -nen** (*Jur: von Kraftfahrzeug, Tier*) owner

Hạl|te|rie|men M strap

hạl|ter|los ADJ **~e Strümpfe** hold-ups *(Brit)*, stockings not requiring a garter belt *(US)*

Hạl|te|rung [ˈhaltərʊŋ] F **-, -en** mounting; (*für Regal etc*) support

Hạl|te-: **Hạl|te|schild** NT *pl* **-schilder** stop sign; **Hạl|te|schlau|fe** F (*in Bus etc*) strap; **Hạl|te|seil** NT safety rope; **Hạl|te|sig|nal** NT *(Rail)* stop signal; **Hạl|te|stel|le** F stop; **Hạl|te|ver|bot** NT (*absolutes* or *uneingeschränktes*) **~** no stopping; (= *Stelle*) no-stopping zone; **eingeschränktes ~** no waiting; (= *Stelle*) no-waiting zone; **hier ist ~** there's no stopping here; **im ~ stehen** to have parked in a no-stopping zone; **Hạl|te|ver|bot(s)|schild** NT *pl* **-schilder** no-stopping sign; **Hạl|te|vor|rich|tung** F mounting; (*für Regal etc*) support

-hạl|tig [haltɪç], **(Aus)** **-häl|tig** [hɛltɪç] ADJ *suf* containing; **stark alkoholhaltig** containing a lot of alcohol, with a high alcohol content

Hạlt-: **hạlt|los** ADJ (= *schwach*) insecure; (= *hemmungslos*) unrestrained; (= *unbegründet*) groundless, unfounded; **Hạlt|lo|sig|keit** F **-, no pl** (= *Schwäche*) lack of security; (= *Hemmungslosigkeit*) lack of inhibitions; (= *Unbegründetheit*) groundlessness; **hạlt+ma|chen** △ VI *sep* → **Halt b**; **Hạlt|sig|nal** NT *(Rail)* stop signal; **Hạlt|tas|te** F pause button

Hạl|tung [ˈhaltʊŋ] F **-, -en** **a** (= *Körperhaltung*) posture; (= *Stellung*) position; (*esp Sport*) stance; **~ annehmen** (*esp Mil*) to stand to attention **b** (*fig*) (= *Auftreten*) manner; (= *Einstellung*) attitude; **in majestätischer/würdiger ~** with majestic/dignified bearing **c** *no pl* (= *Beherrschtheit*) composure; **~ bewahren** to keep one's composure **d** *no pl* (*von Tieren, Fahrzeugen*) keeping

Hạl|tungs-: **Hạl|tungs|feh|ler** M **a** (*Med*) bad posture *no indef art, no pl* **b** (*Sport*) style fault; **Hạl|tungs|män|gel** PL bad posture *sing*; **Hạl|tungs|scha|den** M damaged posture *no pl*; **zu Haltungsschäden führen** to damage one's posture

Hạlt|zei|chen NT *(Rail)* stop signal

Hạ|lun|ke [haˈlʊŋkə] M **-n, -n** **a** scoundrel **b** (*hum*) rascal, scamp

Hä|ma|tit [hɛmaˈtiːt] M **-s, -e** haematite *(Brit)*, hematite *(US)*

Hä|ma|to|lo|ge [hɛmatoˈloːgə] M **-n, -n,** **Hä|ma|to|lo|gin** [-ˈloːgɪn] F **-, -nen** haematologist *(Brit)*, hematologist *(US)*

Hä|ma|to|lo|gie [hɛmatolo'giː] F -, no pl haematology (Brit), hematology (US)

hä|ma|to|lo|gisch [hɛmato'loːgɪʃ] ADJ haematological (Brit), hematological (US)

Hä|ma|tom [hɛma'toːm] NT -s, -e haematoma (Brit), hematoma (US)

Ham|burg ['hambʊrk] NT -s Hamburg

Ham|bur|ger[1] ['hambʊrgɐ] ADJ attr Hamburg

Ham|bur|ger[2] ['hambʊrgɐ] M -s, - (Cook) hamburger

Ham|bur|ger[3] ['hambʊrgɐ] M -s, -, **Ham|bur|ge|rin** [-ərɪn] F -, -nen native or (= Einwohner) inhabitant of Hamburg

Ham|bur|ger|bröt|chen NT roll or bun (for hamburger)

ham|bur|gern ['hambʊrgɐn] VI to speak with a Hamburg dialect

ham|bur|gisch ['hambʊrgɪʃ] ADJ Hamburg attr

Hä|me ['hɛːmə] F -, no pl (rare) malice

hä|misch ['hɛːmɪʃ] ADJ Lächeln malicious; Bemerkung auch spiteful ADV maliciously; bemerken auch spitefully; **er hat sich ~ gefreut** he gloated; **~ grinsen** to grin maliciously, to smirk

Ha|mit [ha'miːt] M -en, -en, **Ha|mi|tin** [-'miːtɪn] F -, -nen Hamite

ha|mi|tisch [ha'miːtɪʃ] ADJ Hamitic

Ham|mel ['haml] M -s, - or (rare) ¨ ['hɛml] **a** (Zool) wether, castrated ram **b** no pl (Cook) mutton **c** (fig pej) ass, donkey

Ham|mel-: Ham|mel|bei|ne PL **jdm die ~ lang ziehen** (hum inf) to give sb a dressing-down; **jdn bei den ~n nehmen** or **kriegen** (inf: = zur Verantwortung ziehen) to take sb to task; **Ham|mel|bra|ten** M roast mutton; **Ham|mel|fleisch** NT mutton; **Ham|mel|her|de** F herd or flock of wethers or rams; (pej inf) flock of sheep; **Ham|mel|keu|le** F (Cook) leg of mutton; **Ham|mel|sprung** M (Parl) division

Ham|mer ['hamɐ] M -s, ¨ ['hɛmɐ] **a** (= Werkzeug, von Auktionator) hammer; (= Holzhammer) mallet; **~ und Sichel** hammer and sickle; **unter den ~ kommen** to come under the hammer; **zwischen ~ und Amboss geraten** (fig) to come under attack from both sides; **das ist ein ~!** (inf) (= unerhört) that's absurd! **b** (= Sportgerät) hammer **c** (Anat) hammer, malleus **d** (= Klavierhammer, Glockenhammer) hammer

häm|mer|bar ADJ malleable

Häm|mer|chen ['hɛmɐçən] NT -s, - dim von **Hammer**

Ham|mer-: ham|mer|för|mig ADJ hammer-shaped; **Ham|mer|hai** M hammerhead (shark); **Ham|mer|kla|vier** NT (Mus Hist) pianoforte; **Ham|mer|kopf** M hammerhead; (Sport: auch **Ham|mer|kugel**)

häm|mern ['hɛmɐn] VI **a** (mit Hammer, Gegenstand) to hammer; (mit den Fäusten etc) to pound; (inf: beim Klavierspielen etc) to pound, to thump **b** (= hämmerndes Geräusch verursachen: Maschine, Motor) to make a hammering sound **c** (Puls, Herz, Blut) to pound VT **a** (= bearbeiten) to hammer; Blech, Metallgefäße, Schmuck etc to beat **b** (fig: = einprägen) **jdm etw ins Bewusstsein ~** to hammer or knock sth into sb's head (inf) VI impers **es hämmert** there's a sound of hammering

Ham|mer-: Ham|mer|schlag M **a** hammer blow; (fig) bolt from the blue **b** (Sport) (Boxen) rabbit punch; (Faustball) smash **c** (Schmiederei) hammer or mill scale; (old) person working in a hammer mill; **Ham|mer|schmied** M (old) hammer mill; **Ham|mer|stiel** M handle or shaft of a/the hammer; **Ham|mer|wer|fen** NT -s, no pl (Sport) hammer(-throwing); **Ham|mer|wer|fer(in)** M(F) (Sport) hammer-thrower; **Ham|mer|werk** NT (old) hammer mill; **Ham|mer|wurf** M (Sport) **a** hammer throw **b** (= Hammerwerfen) hammer(-throwing); **Ham|mer|ze|he** F (Med) hammertoe

Ham|mond|or|gel ['hɛmənd-] F electric organ

Hä|mo|glo|bin [hɛmoglo'biːn] NT -s, no pl haemoglobin (Brit), hemoglobin (US)

Hä|mo|phi|le(r) [hɛmo'fiːlə] MF decl as adj haemophiliac (Brit), hemophiliac (US)

Hä|mo|phi|lie [hɛmofi'liː] F -, -n [-'liːən] haemophilia (Brit), hemophilia (US)

Hä|mor|rhoi|den [hɛmɔro'iːdən] PL, **Hä|mor|ri|den** [hɛmɔri'iːdən] ▲ PL piles pl, haemorrhoids pl (Brit), hemorrhoids pl (US)

Hä|mor|rhoi|den|schau|kel F, **Hä|mor|ri|den|schau|kel** ▲ F (hum) boneshaker (inf)

Ham|pe|lei [hampə'lai] F -, -en (pej inf) (continual) fidgeting no pl

Ham|pel|mann M pl **-männer a** jumping jack **b** (inf) (= zappeliger Mensch) fidget; **er ist nur ein ~** he just lets people walk all over him; **jdn zu einem ~ machen** to walk all over sb

ham|peln ['hampln] VI to jump about; (= zappeln) to fidget

Hams|ter ['hamstɐ] M -s, - hamster

Hams|ter|ba|cken PL (fig inf) chubby cheeks pl

Hams|te|rer ['hamstərɐ] M -s, -, **Hams|te|rin** [-ərɪn] F -, -nen (fig inf) hoarder

Hams|ter-: Hams|ter|fahrt F foraging trip; **auf ~ gehen** to go foraging; **Hams|ter|kauf** M panic buying no pl; **Hamsterkäufe machen** to buy in order to hoard; (bei Knappheit) to panic-buy

hams|tern ['hamstɐn] VTI (= speichern) to hoard; (bei Hamsterfahrt) to forage; (= Hamsterkäufe machen) to panic-buy

Hams|ter-: Hams|ter|ta|sche F large shopping bag; **Hams|ter|wa|re** F → **hamstern** hoarded/foraged/panic-bought goods

Hand [hant] -, ¨e ['hɛndə]

SUBSTANTIV (F)

a allgemein hand (auch Mus, Cards); **jdm die Hand drücken/schütteln/küssen** to press/shake/kiss sb's hand; **jdm die Hand geben** or **reichen** (geh) to give sb one's hand; **die Arbeit seiner Hände** his handiwork, the work of his own hands; **sie leben von der Arbeit ihrer Hände** they make a living by working with their hands; **in die Hände klatschen** to clap one's hands; **ich hatte eine schreckliche Hand** (Cards) I had a terrible hand; **Hände hoch!** (put your) hands up!; **Hand aufs Herz** hand on heart; **Hand aufs Herz, ich wars nicht** it wasn't me, cross my heart or I swear it; **eine Hand breit** ≈ six inches wide; **zwei Hände breit** ≈ a foot wide

♦ **eine Hand voll** (lit, fig) a handful; **werfen Sie drei Hand voll Badesalz in die Wanne** sprinkle three handfuls of bath salts into the tub; **es war nur eine Hand voll Leute im Publikum** there were only a handful of people in the audience

b Sport no pl (inf: = Handspiel) handball; **das war ganz klar Hand** it was a blatant handball; **Hand machen** to handle the ball

c mit Adjektiv

Siehe auch unter dem Eintrag für das jeweilige Adjektiv.

ein Auto aus erster Hand a car which has had one previous owner; **etw aus erster Hand wissen** to have first-hand knowledge of sth; **der Chef zeigt** or **hat mit seinen Mitarbeitern eine feste Hand** the boss takes a firm hand with his employees; **in festen Händen sein** (fig) to be spoken for; **mit der flachen Hand** with the flat or palm of one's hand; **bei etw eine glückliche Hand haben** to be lucky with sth; **in guten Händen sein** to be in good hands; **besser als in die hohle Hand gespuckt** (inf) better than a slap in the face with a wet fish (Brit inf), could be worse; **mit leeren Händen** empty-handed; **mit leeren Händen dastehen** to stand

there empty-handed; **ihm fehlt die leitende** or **lenkende Hand** he lacks a guiding hand; **letzte Hand an etw** (acc) **legen** to put the finishing touches to sth; **linker Hand, zur linken Hand** on the left-hand side; **eine lockere** or **lose Hand haben** (hum inf) to lash out at the slightest provocation; **aus** or **von privater Hand** privately; **„aus privater Hand abzugeben"** "private sale"; **rechter Hand, zur rechten Hand** on or to the right(-hand side); **eine ruhige Hand** a steady hand; **der Hund ist dort in schlechten Händen** that's not a good home for the dog; **eine sichere Hand** (lit) a steady hand; (fig) a sure hand; **in sicheren Händen sein** to be in safe hands; **eine starke Hand** (fig) a firm hand; **das Geld mit vollen Händen ausgeben** to spend money hand over fist (inf); **hinter vorgehaltener Hand** on the quiet; **aus zweiter Hand** second hand; **Kleider aus zweiter Hand** second-hand clothes → **rechte(r, s) a, linke(r, s) a**

d mit Präposition

Siehe auch unter dem Eintrag für die jeweilige Präposition.

♦ **an + Hand er hatte seine kleine Tochter an der Hand** he had his little daughter by the hand; **er hat jemanden an der Hand, der mir meine Küche streichen könnte** he knows of somebody who could paint my kitchen for me; **jdn an der Hand fassen** to grab sb by the hand; **jdn an die Hand nehmen** to take sb by the hand; **jdm an die Hand gehen** to lend sb a (helping) hand; **an Hand von** or +gen → **anhand**

♦ **auf + Hand/Händen auf der Hand** (Cards) in one's hand; **das liegt auf der Hand** (inf) that's obvious; **jdn auf Händen tragen** to cherish sb

♦ **aus + Hand aus der Hand** (zeichnen, entwerfen etc) freehand; **jdm etw aus der Hand nehmen** to take sth from or off sb (auch fig), to take sth out of sb's hand; **etw aus der Hand essen** to eat sth with one's fingers; **jdm aus der Hand fressen** (lit, fig) to eat out of sb's hand; **etw aus der Hand geben** to let sth out of one's hands; **etw aus der Hand legen** to put sth aside

♦ **bei + Hand jdn bei der Hand nehmen** to take sb by the hand; **etw bei der Hand haben** to have sth ready; Ausrede, Erklärung to have sth ready; **mit etw schnell** or **gleich bei der Hand sein** (inf) to be ready with sth

♦ **durch + Hand/Hände durch jds Hände** or **Hand gehen** to pass or go through sb's hands

♦ **für + Hand Klaviersonate für vier Hände** piano sonata for four hands

♦ **in + Hand/Hände(n) er nimmt niemals ein Buch in die Hand** he never picks up a book; **Hand in Hand** hand in hand; **jdm/einer Sache in die Hände arbeiten** to play into sb's hands/the hands of sth; **jdm in die Hand** or **Hände fallen** or **geraten** or **kommen** to fall into sb's hands; **jdn/etw in die Hand** or **Hände kriegen** or **bekommen** to get one's hands on sb/sth; **jdn (fest) in der Hand haben** to have sb (well) in hand; **etw in der Hand haben** to have sth; **ich habe diese Entscheidung nicht in der Hand** the decision is out of my hands; **etw gegen jdn in der Hand haben** to have sth on sb; **diese Gebiete sind zur Zeit in serbischer Hand** these areas are in Serbian hands at the moment; **dieser Laden ist schon seit Jahren in türkischer Hand** this shop has been owned by Turks for years; **in welcher Hand ist dieses Hotel im Augenblick?** who currently owns this hotel?; **der Badestrand ist im Juli immer fest in deutscher Hand** in July this beach is always taken over by Germans; **in jds Hände** (acc) **übergehen** to pass to sb or into sb's hands; **sich in der Hand haben** to have a grip on oneself; **etw in Händen halten** (geh) to hold or have sth in one's hands; **etw in jds Hand** or **Hände legen** to put sth in sb's hands; **etw liegt** or **ist in jds Hand** sth is in sb's hands; **etw in jds Hand sein** to be in sb's hands; **etw in die Hand nehmen** to pick sth up; (fig) to take sth in hand; **jdm etw in die Hand versprechen** to promise sb sth or sth to sb; **jdm etw in die Hand** or **Hände spielen** to pass sth on to sb

♦ **mit + Hand/Händen mit der Hand** (= *in Handarbeit*) by hand; **(bei etw) mit Hand anlegen** to lend a hand (with sth); **das ist mit Händen zu greifen** (*fig*) that's obvious; **sich mit Händen und Füßen gegen etw wehren** to fight sth tooth and nail

♦ **um + Hand um jds Hand bitten** or **anhalten** to ask for sb's hand (in marriage)

♦ **unter + Hand/Händen unter der Hand** (*fig*) on the quiet; **Geld schmilzt** or **zerrinnt ihm unter den Händen** money runs through his fingers like water; **jdm unter der Hand** or **den Händen wegsterben** to die while under sb's care

♦ **von + Hand von Hand geschrieben** handwritten; **von Hand genäht** hand-sewn; **Vermittlung von Hand** (*Telec*) operator-connected calls *pl*; **von Hand zu Hand gehen** to pass from hand to hand; **von jds Hand sterben** to die at sb's hands; **die Arbeit ging ihr leicht von der Hand** she found the work easy; **die Arbeit ging ihr flott** or **schnell von der Hand** she sailed through the work; **etw lässt sich nicht von der Hand weisen, etw ist nicht von der Hand zu weisen** sth is undeniable; **von der Hand in den Mund leben** to live from hand to mouth

♦ **zu + Hand/Händen zur Hand sein** to be at hand; **etw zur Hand haben** to have sth to hand; **Ausrede, Erklärung** etc **etw zur Hand nehmen** to pick sth up; **jdm zur Hand gehen** to lend sb a (helping) hand; **zu jds Händen, zu Händen von jdm** for the attention of sb; **Klaviersonate zu vier Händen** piano sonata for four hands; **zu vier Händen spielen** (*Mus*) to play a (piano) duet → **treu ADJ**

e | **mit Verb** |

Siehe auch unter dem Eintrag für das jeweilige Verb.

sich (*dat*) **für jdn/etw die Hand abhacken lassen** (*inf*) to stake one's life on sb/sth; **die** or **seine Hand aufhalten** or **hinhalten** (*fig inf*) to hold out one's hand (for money); **darauf gaben sie sich die Hand** they shook hands on it; **man konnte die Hand nicht vor (den) Augen sehen** you couldn't see your hand in front of your face; **eine Hand wäscht die andere** you scratch my back, I'll scratch yours; **ich wasche meine Hände in Unschuld** I wash my hands of it or of the matter; **die Hände überm Kopf zusammenschlagen** to throw up one's hands in horror

♦ **Hand + haben die Hand auf etw** (*dat*) **haben** to keep a tight rein on sth; **alle Hände voll zu tun haben** to have one's hands full; **bei etw die** or **seine Hand im Spiel haben** to have a hand in sth; **dabei hatte Eifersucht die Hand im Spiel** jealousy had a part to play in this; **er hat überall seine Hand im Spiel** he has a finger in every pie; **Hand und Fuß haben** to make sense; **was er macht, hat weder Hand noch Fuß** what he's doing doesn't make any sense at all; **die Geschichte, die du mir erzählt hast, hat Hand und Fuß** the story you told me hangs together perfectly; **diese Ausrede hat weder Hand noch Fuß** this excuse doesn't stand up

♦ **Hand + halten die Hand auf etw** (*dat*) **halten** to keep a tight rein on sth; **die Hand auf der Tasche halten** (*inf*) to control the purse strings; **die** or **seine Hand über jdn halten** to protect or shield sb

♦ **Hand/Hände + legen Hand an jdn legen** (*geh*) to assault sb; **Hand an sich legen** (*geh*) to kill oneself; **seine** or **die Hand auf etw** (*acc*) **legen** (*geh*) to lay (one's) hands on sth; **die Hände in den Schoß legen** (*fig*) to sit back and do nothing; **seine** or **die Hand für jdn ins Feuer legen** to vouch for sb

♦ **Hand + reichen sich** or **einander die Hand fürs Leben reichen** to tie the knot; **sich** or **einander** (*geh*) **die Hand reichen können** (*fig*) to be tarred with the same brush; **da können wir uns die Hand reichen** snap! (*inf*)

Hand-: Hand|ab|wehr F (*Sport*) save; **durch ~ klären** to save, to clear; **Hand|ab|zug** M (*Typ*) proof pulled by hand; (*Phot*) print made by hand; **Hand|an|trieb** M hand-driven mechanism; **mit ~** hand-driven; **Hand|ap|pa|rat** M **a** reference books *pl* (*on open shelves*) **b** (*Telec*) handset

Hand|ar|beit F **a** work done by hand; (*Gegenstand*) article made by hand, handmade article; **etw in ~ herstellen** to produce or make sth by hand; **der Tisch ist ~** the table is handmade or made by hand **b** (= *körperliche Arbeit*) manual work **c** (= *Nähen, Sticken* etc, *als Schulfach*) needlework *no pl*; (= *Stricken*) knitting *no pl*; (= *Häkeln*) crochet(ing) *no pl*; **diese Tischdecke ist ~** this tablecloth is handmade; **eine ~ aus dem 18. Jahrhundert** a piece of needlework *etc* from the 18th century **d** (*kunsthandwerklich*) handicraft *no pl*; **eine ~** a piece of handicraft work

hand|ar|bei|ten VI *insep* → **Handarbeit c** to do needlework/knitting/crocheting

Hand|ar|bei|ten NT **-s**, *no pl* (*Sch*) needlework

Hand|ar|bei|ter(in) M(F) manual worker

Hand|ar|beits-: Hand|ar|beits|ge|schäft NT needlework and wool shop; **Hand|ar|beits|heft** NT sewing, knitting and crocheting manual; **Hand|ar|beits|korb** M workbasket

Hand-: Hand|auf|he|ben NT **-s**, *no pl* (*bei Wahl*) show of hands; **sich durch ~ zu Wort melden** to ask for permission to speak by raising one's hand; **Hand|auf|le|gen** NT **-s**, *no pl*, **Hand|auf|le|gung** [-lauflɛːɡʊŋ] F **-, -en** laying on of hands; **Hand|aus|ga|be** F (= *Buch*) concise edition; **Hand|ball** M **a** (= *Ball*) handball **b** *no pl* (*inf auch nt*) (= *Spiel*) handball; **Hand|bal|len** M (*Anat*) ball of the thumb; **Hand|bal|ler** [-balɐ] M **-s, -**, **Hand|bal|le|rin** [-ərɪn] F **-, -nen** handball player; **Hand|ball|spiel** NT **a** (= *Spiel*) game of handball **b** (= *Disziplin*) handball *no def art*; **Hand|ball|spie|ler(in)** M(F) handball player; **hand|be|dient** [-bədiːnt] ADJ manually operated, hand-operated; **Hand|be|die|nung** F hand or manual operation or control; **mit** or **für ~** hand-operated; **Hand|beil** NT hatchet; **Hand|be|sen** M hand brush; **Hand|be|trieb** M hand or manual operation; **für** or **mit ~** hand-operated; **hand|be|trie|ben** [-bətriːbn] ADJ hand-operated; **Hand|be|we|gung** F sweep of the hand; (= *Geste, Zeichen*) gesture; **Hand|bib|li|o|thek** F reference library or books *pl* (*on open shelves*); **Hand|boh|rer** M gimlet, auger; **Hand|bohr|ma|schi|ne** F (hand) drill; **Hand|brau|se** F shower attachment; **hand|breit** ['hantbrait] ADJ ≈ six inches wide **ADV** ≈ six inches; **Hand|breit** ['hantbrait] F **-, -**, hand's width; **Hand|brem|se** F handbrake (*Brit*), parking brake (*US*); **Hand|buch** NT handbook; (*technisch*) manual; **Hand|bü|che|rei** F reference library or books *pl* (*on open shelves*)

Händ|chen ['hɛntçən] NT **-s,** *-dim von* **Hand** little hand; **~ halten** (*inf*) to hold hands; **~ haltend** holding hands; **~ haltend gehen/sitzen** to walk/sit hand in hand; **für etw ein ~ haben** (*inf*) to have a knack for sth; (= *gut können*) to be good at sth; **~ geben** to shake hands

Händ|chen|hal|ten NT **-s,** *no pl* holding hands *no def art*

händ|chen|hal|tend △ → **Händchen**

Hand-: Hand|creme F hand cream; **Hand|deu|tung** F palmistry; **Hand|druck** M (*Typ, Tex*) **a** *pl* **-drucke** block print **b** *no pl* (= *Verfahren*) block printing; **Hand|du|sche** F shower attachment

Hän|de-: Hän|de|druck M *pl* **-drücke** handshake; **Hän|de|hand|tuch** NT hand towel

Hand|ein|stel|lung F (*Tech*) manual or hand-operated setting

Hän|de|klat|schen NT applause *no pl*

Han|del¹ ['handl] M **-s**, *no pl* **a** (= *das Handeln*) trade; (*esp mit illegaler Ware*) traffic; **~ mit etw/ei-**

nem Land trade in sth/with a country **b** (= *Warenverkehr*) trade; (= *Warenmarkt*) market; **im ~ sein** to be on the market; **etw in den ~ bringen** to put sth on the market; **etw aus dem ~ ziehen** to take sth off the market; **(mit jdm) ~ (be)treiben** to trade (with sb); **~ treibend** trading; **~ und Wandel** (*dated*) doings and dealings *pl* **c** (= *Abmachung, Geschäft*) deal, transaction; (*inf*) deal; **mit jdm in den ~ kommen** to do business with sb **d** (= *Wirtschaftszweig*) commerce, trade; (= *die Handel Treibenden*) trade **e** (*dial*: = *Handelsunternehmen*) business; **er betreibt/hat einen ~ in** or **mit Kohlen und Heizöl** he runs/has a coal and fuel oil business

Han|del² ['handl] M **-s,** ⸚ ['hɛndl] *usu pl* quarrel, argument

han|del|bar [-baːɐ] ADJ (*St Ex*) **an der Börse ~** negotiable on the stock exchange; **frei ~** freely negotiable

Hand|elf|me|ter M penalty for a handball

han|deln ['handln] **VI a** (= *Handel treiben*) to trade; **er handelt mit Gemüse** he trades or deals in vegetables, he's in the vegetable trade; **er handelt mit Drogen** he traffics in drugs; **er handelt in Gebrauchtwagen** he's in the second--hand car trade, he sells second-hand cars **b** (= *feilschen*) to bargain, to haggle (*um* about, over); (*fig*: = *verhandeln*) to negotiate (*um* about); **ich lasse schon mit mir ~** I'm open to persuasion; (*in Bezug auf Preis*) I'm open to offers **c** (= *tätig werden, agieren*) to act; **er ist ein schnell ~der Mensch** he's a quick-acting person **d** (= *sich verhalten*) to act, to behave; **gegen jdn** or **an jdm gut/als Freund ~** (*geh*) to act or behave well/as or like a friend toward(s) sb **e** (= *zum Thema haben*) **von etw ~, über etw** (*acc*) **~** to deal with sth; (*Aufsatz* etc *auch*) to be about sth

VR *impers* **a** **es handelt sich bei diesen so genannten UFOs um optische Täuschungen** these so-called UFOs are optical illusions; **es handelt sich hier/dabei um ein Verbrechen** it's a crime we are dealing with here/there; **bei dem Festgenommenen handelt es sich um X** the person arrested is X **b** (= *betreffen*) **sich um etw ~** to be about sth, to concern sth; **worum handelt es sich, bitte?** what's it about, please?; **es handelt sich darum, dass ich einen Kredit beantragen möchte** it is about or concerns a loan which I wish to apply for **c** (= *um etw gehen, auf etw ankommen*) **sich um etw ~** to be a question or matter of sth; **es handelt sich nur ums Überleben** it's simply a question of survival

VT a (= *verkaufen*) to sell (*für* at, for); (*an der Börse*) to quote (*mit* at) **b** *Preis* etc (= *hinaufhandeln*) to push up, to raise; (= *herunterhandeln*) to bring down **c** (*fig*) **er wird als der neue Außenminister gehandelt** (= *ist im Gespräch*) he is being talked about for the position of foreign minister

Han|deln NT **-s**, *no pl* **a** (= *Feilschen*) bargaining, haggling **b** (= *das Handeltreiben*) trading; **das ~ mit Antiquitäten** trading or dealing in antiques **c** (= *Verhalten*) behaviour (*Brit*), behavior (*US*) **d** (= *das Tätigwerden*) action

han|delnd ADJ **die ~en Personen in einem Drama** the characters in a drama, the dramatis personae *pl*; **das ~e Subjekt** the active subject

Han|dels-: Han|dels|ab|kom|men NT trade agreement; **Han|dels|aka|de|mie** F (*Aus*) commercial college, business school; **Han|dels|aka|de|mi|ker(in)** M(F) (*Aus*) graduate of a commercial college, business school graduate; **Han|dels|ar|ti|kel** M commodity; **Han|dels|at|ta|ché** M commercial attaché; **Han|dels|bank** F *pl* **-banken** merchant bank; **Han|dels|be|schrän|kung** F trading restriction, restriction on trade; **Han|dels|be|trieb**

M trading or business concern; **Han|dels|be|zeich|nung** F trade name; **Han|dels|be|zie|hun|gen** PL trade relations pl; **Han|dels|bi|lanz** F balance of trade; **aktive/passive ~** balance of trade surplus/deficit; **Han|dels|brauch** M trade or commercial practice; **Han|dels|de|fi|zit** NT trade deficit; **han|dels|ei|nig** ADJ pred **~ werden/sein** to agree terms, to come to an agreement; **Han|dels|em|bar|go** NT trade embargo; **han|dels|fä|hig** ADJ Güter etc marketable, merchantable; **Han|dels|fir|ma** F (commercial or business) firm; **Han|dels|flag|ge** F (Naut) merchant flag; **Han|dels|flot|te** F merchant fleet; **Han|dels|frei|heit** F a (Comm) freedom of trade no pl b (rare: = Handlungsfreiheit) freedom of action; **Han|dels|ge|sell|schaft** F commercial company; **Han|dels|ge|setz** NT commercial law; **Han|dels|ge|setz|buch** NT code of commercial law; **Han|dels|ge|wer|be** NT commerce no art; **Han|dels|gut** NT commodity; **Han|dels|ha|fen** M trading port; **Han|dels|haus** NT business house, firm; **Han|dels|hemm|nis** NT trade barrier; **Han|dels|kam|mer** F chamber of commerce; **Han|dels|ket|te** F a chain of retail shops b (= Weg der Ware) sales route (from manufacturer to buyer); **Han|dels|klas|se** F grade; **Heringe der ~ 1** grade 1 herring; **Han|dels|krieg** M trade war; **Han|dels|kri|se** F commercial crisis; **Han|dels|leh|rer(in)** M(F) teacher of commercial subjects; **Han|dels|macht** F trading nation or power; **Han|dels|mak|ler(in)** M(F) broker; **Han|dels|ma|ri|ne** F merchant navy, mercantile marine (form); **Han|dels|mar|ke** F trade name; **Han|dels|me|tro|po|le** F commercial metropolis; **Han|dels|mi|nis|ter(in)** M(F) ≈ Trade Secretary (Brit), ≈ Secretary of Commerce (US); **Han|dels|mi|nis|te|ri|um** NT ≈ Board of Trade (Brit), ≈ Department of Commerce (US); **Han|dels|mis|si|on** F trade mission; **Han|dels|na|me** M trade name; **Han|dels|na|ti|on** F trading nation; **Han|dels|nie|der|las|sung** F branch of a trading organization); **Han|dels|ob|jekt** NT commodity; **Han|dels|or|ga|ni|sa|ti|on** F trading organization; **Han|dels|part|ner(in)** M(F) trading partner; **Han|dels|platz** M trading centre (Brit) or center (US); **Han|dels|po|li|tik** F trade or commercial policy; **han|dels|po|li|tisch** ADJ relating to trade or commercial policy ADV as far as trade or commercial policy is concerned; **Han|dels|re|al|schu|le** F (esp Sw) commercial school or college; **Han|dels|recht** NT commercial law no def art, no pl; **han|dels|recht|lich** ADJ of commercial law ADV according to commercial law; **Han|dels|re|gis|ter** NT register of companies; **Han|dels|rei|sen|de(r)** MF decl as adj commercial traveller (Brit) or traveler (US); **Han|dels|schiff** NT trading ship or vessel, merchantman (old); **Han|dels|schiff|fahrt** ▲ F merchant shipping no def art; **Han|dels|schran|ke** F usu pl trade barrier; **Han|dels|schu|le** F commercial school or college; **Han|dels|schü|ler(in)** M(F) student at a commercial school or college; **Han|dels|span|ne** F profit margin; **Han|dels|sper|re** F trade embargo (gegen on); **Han|dels|spra|che** F commercial language; **Han|dels|stadt** F trading city or centre (Brit) or center (US); **Han|dels|stand** M (Sociol) merchant class; **Han|dels|stra|ße** F (Hist) trade route; **Han|dels|stütz|punkt** M trading base; **han|dels|üb|lich** ADJ usual or customary (in the trade or in commerce); **Produkt, Ware** standard; **etw zu den ~en Preisen kaufen** to buy sth at normal (trade) prices

hän|del|süch|tig ADJ (geh, old) quarrelsome

Han|dels-: **Han|dels|un|ter|neh|men** NT commercial enterprise; **Han|dels|ver|kehr** M trade; **Han|dels|ver|trag** M trade agreement; **Han|dels|ver|tre|ter(in)** M(F) commercial traveller (Brit) or traveler (US); **Han|dels|ver|**

tre|tung F trade mission; **Han|dels|volk** NT trading nation; **Han|dels|wa|re** F commodity; **keine ~** no commercial value; **Han|dels|wa|ren** PL commodities pl, merchandise sing; **Han|dels|weg** M a sales route b (Hist: = Handelsstraße) trade route; **Han|dels|wert** M market value; **Han|dels|we|sen** NT , no pl commerce, trade no def art; **Han|dels|zent|rum** NT trading or commercial centre (Brit) or center (US); **Han|dels|zweig** M branch

han|del|trei|bend △ ADJ attr → **Handel** a
Han|del|trei|ben|de(r) [-traibndə] MF decl as adj trader, tradesman/-woman

Hän|de-: **Hän|de|rin|gen** NT -s, no pl (fig) wringing of one's hands; **hän|de|rin|gend** ['hɛndərɪŋənt] ADV wringing one's hands, (fig) **um etw bitten** imploringly; **~ nach etw suchen** to search desperately for sth; **Hän|de|schüt|teln** NT -s, no pl handshaking; **Hän|de|trock|ner** [-trɔknɐ] M -s, - hand drier; **Hän|de|wa|schen** NT -s, no pl washing one's hands; **jdn zum ~ schicken** to send sb to wash his/her hands

Hand-: **Hand|fe|ger** M hand brush; **wie ein wild gewordener ~** (inf) like a wild thing; **Hand|fer|tig|keit** F dexterity; **Hand|fes|sel** F a manacle; **etw als ~ benutzen** to tie sb's hands together with sth b (= Handschelle) handcuff; **hand|fest** ADJ a (= kräftig) Mensch sturdy, robust; Essen solid, substantial b (fig) Schlägerei violent; Skandal huge; Vorschlag, Argument well-founded, solid; Beweis solid, tangible; Interesse strong; Lüge, Betrug flagrant, blatant; **Hand|feu|er|lö|scher** M hand fire extinguisher; **Hand|feu|er|waf|fe** F handgun; **Hand|flä|che** F palm or flat (of the/one's hand); **Hand|funk|ge|rät** NT walkie-talkie; **Hand|gas** NT , no pl (Aut: = Vorrichtung) hand throttle; **~ haben/geben** to have a/pull out the hand throttle; **mit ~ fahren** to use the hand throttle; **hand|ge|ar|bei|tet** ADJ handmade; Stickerei etc handworked; **hand|ge|bun|den** ADJ hand-bound; **hand|ge|fer|tigt** [-gəfɛrtɪçt] ADJ = handgearbeitet; **hand|ge|knüpft** [-gəknʏpft] ADJ Teppich hand-knotted; **Hand|geld** NT (Sport) transfer fee; (Hist) earnest money; (Mil Hist) bounty; **Hand|ge|lenk** NT wrist; **aus dem ~** (fig inf) (= ohne Mühe) with the greatest of ease, effortlessly; (= improvisiert) off the cuff; **etw aus dem ~ schütteln** (fig inf) to do sth effortlessly or with no trouble at all; **ein lockeres** or **loses ~ haben** (inf) to let fly at the slightest provocation; **hand|ge|macht** ADJ handmade; **hand|ge|malt** [-gəma:lt] ADJ hand-painted; **hand|ge|mein** ADJ **(mit jdm) ~ werden** to come to blows (with sb); **Hand|ge|men|ge** NT scuffle, fight; **hand|ge|näht** [-gənɛ:t] ADJ hand-sewn; **Hand|ge|päck** NT hand luggage no pl or baggage no pl; **Hand|ge|rät** NT (Sport) hand apparatus; **hand|ge|recht** ADJ handy; **hand|ge|schlif|fen** ADJ Edelstein, Glas hand-cut; Linse hand-ground; **hand|ge|schmie|det** [-gəʃmi:dət] ADJ hand-forged; **hand|ge|schöpft** [-gəʃœpft] ADJ Papier handmade; **hand|ge|schrie|ben** ADJ hand-written; **hand|ge|setzt** ADJ (Typ) handset, set by hand; **hand|ge|spon|nen** ADJ hand-spun; **hand|ge|steu|ert** [-gəʃtɔøɐt] ADJ (Tech) hand-operated; **hand|ge|strickt** [-gəʃtrɪkt] ADJ hand-knitted; (fig) homespun; Lösung homegrown; **Hand|ge|strick|te(s)** [-gəʃtrɪktə] NT decl as adj hand-knitted goods pl; **hand|ge|webt** [-gəve:pt] ADJ hand-woven; **Hand|gra|na|te** F hand grenade; **hand|greif|lich** ['hantgraiflɪç] ADJ a Streit, Auseinandersetzung violent; **~ werden** to become violent b (fig) (= offensichtlich) clear; Lüge blatant, flagrant ADV **etw ~ vor Augen führen** to demonstrate sth clearly; **Hand|greif|lich|keit** F -, -en a usu pl violence no pl b (fig: = Offensichtlichkeit) clarity; (von Lüge) blatancy; **Hand|griff** M a (= Bewegung) movement; (im Haushalt) chore; **keinen ~ tun** not to lift a finger; **mit einem ~** (öffnen) with one flick of the wrist; (= schnell) in no

time; **mit ein paar ~en** in next to no time b (= Gegenstand) handle; **hand|groß** ADJ hand-sized; **hand|hab|bar** ADJ manageable; **leicht/schwer ~** easy/difficult to manage; **Hand|hab|bar|keit** F -, no pl manageability; **Hand|ha|be** ['hantha:bə] F (fig) **ich habe gegen ihn keine ~** I have no hold on him; **etw als ~ (gegen jdn) benutzen** to use sth as a lever (against sb); **hand|ha|ben** VT insep to handle; Maschine auch to operate, to work; Gesetz to implement, to administer; **Hand|ha|bung** ['hantha:bʊŋ] F -, -en handling; (von Maschine auch) operation, working; (von Gesetz) implementation, administration; **Hand|har|mo|ni|ka** F concertina; **Hand|he|bel** M manually operated or hand-operated lever

Han|di|cap ['hɛndikɛp] NT → **Handikap**

-hän|dig [hɛndɪç] ADJ suf -handed; **linkshändig** left-handed

Han|di|kap ['hɛndikɛp] NT -s, -s (Sport, fig) handicap

han|di|ka|pen ['hɛndikɛpn] VT insep to handicap → auch **gehandikapt**

Han|di|kap- ['hɛndikɛp-]: **Han|di|kap|ren|nen** NT handicap (race); **Han|di|kap|spiel** NT handicap game

Hand-in-Hand-Ar|bei|ten NT -s, no pl cooperation

hän|disch ['hɛndɪʃ] ADJ (Aus) manual

Hand-: **Hand|ka|me|ra** F hand-held camera; **Hand|kan|te** F side of the/one's hand; **Hand|kan|ten|schlag** M karate chop; **Hand|kar|re** F , **Hand|kar|ren** M handcart; **Hand|kä|se** M strong-smelling round German cheese; **Hand|ka|ta|log** M ready-reference catalogue (Brit) or catalog (US); **hand|ko|lo|riert** [-koloːri:et] ADJ hand-coloured (Brit), hand-colored (US); **Hand|korb** M (small) basket; **Hand|kreis|sä|ge** F hand-held circular saw; **Hand|kur|bel** F hand crank; (Aut) starting handle; **Hand|kuss** ▲ M kiss on the hand; (Eccl) kiss (on the ring of a bishop etc); **mit ~** (fig inf) with pleasure, gladly; **zum ~ kommen** (Aus fig) to come off worse; **Hand|lam|pe** F inspection lamp; **Hand|lan|ger** ['hantlaŋɐ] M -s, - odd-job man, handyman; (fig) (= Untergeordneter) dogsbody (Brit inf), drudge (US); (pej: = Gehilfe) henchman; **Hand|lan|ger|ar|beit** F (pej) donkey-work no pl; (fig) = **Handlangerdienst** M dirty work no pl; **Hand|lan|ge|rin** ['hantlaŋərɪn] F -, -nen (lit) odd-job woman; (fig) (= Untergeordnete) dogsbody (Brit inf), drudge (US); (pej: = Gehilfin) henchman; **Hand|lauf** M (an Treppen) handrail

Händ|ler ['hɛndlɐ] M -s, -, **Händ|le|rin** [-ərɪn] F -, -nen trader, dealer; (= Autohändler) dealer; (= Ladenbesitzer) shopkeeper (Brit), store owner (US); (= Fischhändler) fishmonger (Brit), fish dealer (US); (= Fleischhändler) butcher; (= Gemüsehändler) greengrocer (Brit), produce dealer (US); **ambulanter** or **fliegender ~** street trader

Händ|ler-: **Händ|ler|preis** M trade price; **Händ|ler|ra|batt** M trade discount

Hand-: **Hand|le|se|kunst** F **(die) ~** palmistry, (the art of) reading palms; **Hand|le|ser(in)** M(F) palm reader, palmist; **Hand|leuch|te** F inspection lamp

hand|lich ['hantlɪç] ADJ a Gerät, Format, Form handy; Gepäckstück manageable, easy to manage; Auto manoeuvrable (Brit), maneuverable (US) b (Sw: = behände) handy, dexterous c (Sw: = mit der Hand) with one's hand(s)

Hand|lich|keit F -, no pl (von Gerät, Format, Form) handiness; (von Gepäckstück) manageability; (von Auto) manoeuvrability (Brit), maneuverability (US)

Hand-: **Hand|li|nie** F line (in the palm of the hand); **Hand|li|ni|en|deu|tung** F **(die) ~** palmistry; **Hand|lö|scher** [-lœʃɐ] M , **Hand|lösch|ge|rät** NT fire extinguisher (hand-held)

Hạnd|lung ['handluŋ] F -, -en **a** (= Vorgehen, Handeln) action, deed; (= Tat, Akt) act **b** (= Geschehen) action; (= Handlungsablauf) plot; **der Ort der ~** the scene of the action **c** (dated) (mit Waren) business; (= Laden) shop (esp Brit), store

Hạnd|lungs-: Hạnd|lungs|ab|lauf M plot; **hạnd|lungs|arm** ADJ thin on plot; **Hạnd|lungs|ar|mut** F lack of plot or action; **Hạnd|lungs|be|darf** M need for action; **Hạnd|lungs|be|voll|mäch|tig|te(r)** MF decl as adj authorized agent, proxy; **hạnd|lungs|fä|hig** ADJ Regierung, Bündnis capable of acting, able to act; (Jur) empowered or authorized to act; **eine ~e Mehrheit** a working majority; **Hạnd|lungs|fä|hig|keit** F (von Regierung, Bündnis) ability to act; (Jur) power to act; **Hạnd|lungs|frei|heit** F freedom of action; **Hạnd|lungs|ge|rüst** NT (Liter) framework; **hạnd|lungs|reich** ADJ action-packed, full of action; **Hạnd|lungs|reich|tum** M abundance of action; **Hạnd|lungs|rei|sen|de(r)** MF decl as adj (Comm) commercial traveller (Brit) pr traveler (US), rep, representative (dated); **Hạnd|lungs|spiel|raum** M scope (of action); **Hạnd|lungs|strang** M (Liter, Theat) strand (of the plot); **Hạnd|lungs|theo|rie** F (Sociol) theory of action; **hạnd|lungs|un|fä|hig** ADJ Regierung, Bündnis incapable of acting, unable to act; (Jur) without power to act; **Hạnd|lungs|un|fä|hig|keit** F (von Regierung, Bündnis) inability to act; (Jur) lack of power to act; **Hạnd|lungs|verb** NT transitive verb; **Hạnd|lungs|ver|lauf** M plot; **Hạnd|lungs|voll|macht** F proxy; **Hạnd|lungs|wei|se** F way of behaving, behaviour no pl (Brit), behavior no pl (US), conduct no pl; **eine selbstlose ~** unselfish behaviour (Brit) or behavior (US) or conduct; **eine edelmütige ~** noble conduct

Hạnd-: Hạnd|mehr ['hantmeːɐ] NT -s, no pl (Sw) show of hands; **Hạnd|müh|le** F handmill

Hạnd|out, Hand-out ▲ ['hɛntaut] NT -s, -s handout

Hạnd-: Hạnd|pfle|ge F care of one's hands; **Hạnd|pres|se** F (Typ) hand-press; **Hạnd|pum|pe** F hand-pump; **Hạnd|pup|pe** F glove (Brit) or hand (US) puppet; **Hạnd|pup|pen|spiel** NT (= Technik) glove (Brit) or hand (US) puppetry; (= Stück) glove (Brit) or hand (US) puppet show; **Hạnd|rei|chung** ['hantraiçʊŋ] F -, -en **a** helping hand no pl **b** (= Instruktion, Empfehlung) recommendation **c** (= Handzettel) handout; **Hạnd|rü|cken** M back of the/one's hand; **auf beiden ~** on the back of both hands; **Hạnd|sä|ge** F hand saw; **Hạnd|satz** M (Typ) hand-setting, hand-composition; **Hạnd|schal|ter** M manual switch; **Hạnd|schal|tung** F (Aut) manual controls pl; **Hạnd|schel|le** F usu pl handcuff; **jdm ~n anle|gen** to handcuff sb, to put handcuffs on sb; **in ~n** in handcuffs, handcuffed; **Hạnd|schlag** M **a** (= Händedruck) handshake; **mit** or **durch** or **per ~** with a handshake; **ein Geschäft durch ~ abschließen** to shake on a deal; **goldener ~** (fig inf) golden handshake **b** **keinen ~ tun** not to do a stroke (of work); **Hạnd|schrei|ben** NT handwritten letter; **Hạnd|schrift** F **a** handwriting; (fig) (trade)mark; **er hat eine gute/leserliche ~** he has a good/legible hand, he has good/legible handwriting; **etw trägt/ver|rät jds ~** (fig) sth bears or has sb's (trade)mark; (Kunstwerk auch) sth shows the hand of sb; **eine kräftige/gute ~ haben** or **schreiben** (fig inf) to be a hard/good hitter **b** (= Text) manuscript; **Hạnd|schrif|ten|deu|tung** F (die) ~ the study of handwriting, graphology; **hạnd|schrift|lich** ADJ handwritten ADV korrigieren, einfügen by hand; **sich bewerben** in writing; **einen Brief ~ beantworten** to answer a letter by hand

Hạnd|schuh M (= Fingerhandschuh) glove; (= Fausthandschuh) mitten, mitt (inf)

Hạnd|schuh-: Hạnd|schuh|fach NT , **Hạnd|schuh|kas|ten** M (Aut) glove compartment; **Hạnd|schuh|ma|cher(in)** M(F) glove maker

Hạnd-: Hạnd|schutz M protection no pl for the hands; (= Handschuhe) hand protection no pl; (an Maschine) hand guard; **Hạnd|set|zer(in)** M(F) (Typ) hand compositor; **hạnd|sig|niert** [-zɪgniːɐt] ADJ signed, autographed; **Hạnd|skiz|ze** F rough sketch; **Hạnd|spie|gel** M hand mirror or glass; **Hạnd|spiel** NT , no pl **a** (Sport) handball **b** (Cards) (finishing a game by) playing all one's hand at once; **Hạnd|stand** M (Sport) handstand; **Hạnd|stand|über|schlag** M (Sport) handspring; **Hạnd|steu|e|rung** F manual control; **Hạnd|streich** M **in** or **durch einen ~** in a surprise coup; (Mil) by surprise; **in einem** or **durch einen kühnen/detailliert geplanten ~** in a bold/minutely planned coup; **hạnd|streich|ar|tig** ADJ sudden and unexpected ADV suddenly and unexpectedly; **Hạnd|ta|sche** F handbag (Brit), purse (US); **Hạnd|ta|schen|raub** M bag-snatching; **Hạnd|tel|ler** M palm (of the/one's hand); **Hạnd|trom|mel** F hand drum

Hạnd|tuch NT pl -tücher towel; (= Geschirrhandtuch) tea towel, tea cloth; (= Papierhandtuch) paper towel; **das ~ werfen** (lit) to throw in the towel; (fig inf) to throw in the sponge (Brit) or towel

Hạnd|tuch- in cpds towel; **Hạnd|tuch|au|to|mat** M towel dispenser; **Hạnd|tuch|hal|ter** M towel rail (Brit) or rack (US); **Hạnd|tuch|spen|der** M towel dispenser

Hạnd-: Hạnd|um|dre|hen NT (fig) **im ~** in the twinkling of an eye; **hạnd|ver|le|sen** ADJ Obst etc hand-graded; (fig) Gesellschaft etc hand-picked; **hạnd|ver|mit|telt** [-fɛɐmɪtlt] ADJ Telefongespräch connected through or by the operator; **Hạnd|ver|mitt|lung** F connection by the operator; **eine durch ~ hergestellte Telefonver|bindung** a call connected through or by the operator; **Hạnd|voll** △ ['hantfɔl] F -, → Hand a; **Hạnd|waf|fe** F hand weapon; **Hạnd|wa|gen** M handcart; **hạnd|warm** ADJ hand-hot (Brit), warm ADV **etw ~ waschen** to wash sth in hand-hot (Brit) or warm water; **Hạnd|wasch|be|cken** NT wash-hand basin; **Hạnd|wä|sche** F washing by hand; (= Wäschestücke) hand wash; **Hạnd|web|stuhl** M hand loom

Hạnd|werk NT **a** (= Beruf) trade; (= Kunsthandwerk) craft; (fig: = Tätigkeit) business; **das Leder verarbeitende ~** the leather worker's trade; **das ~ des Bäckers** the baking trade; **das ~ des Schneiders/Schreiners** the trade of tailor/joiner; **das ~ des Töpfers** the potter's craft; **der Krieg ist das einzige ~, das er versteht** or **beherrscht** war is the only business he knows anything about; **sein ~ verstehen** or **beherrschen** (fig) to know one's job; **jdm ins ~ pfuschen** (fig) to tread on sb's toes; **jdm das ~ legen** (fig) to put a stop to sb's game (inf) or to sb **b** no pl (= Wirtschaftsbereich) trade

hạnd|wer|keln ['hantvɛɐkln] VI insep (hum) to potter (Brit) or putter (US) around (making things)

Hạnd|wer|ker ['hantvɛɐkɐ] M -s, - tradesman, (skilled) manual worker; (= Kunsthandwerker) craftsman; **wir haben seit Wochen die ~ im Haus** we've had workmen or tradesmen in the house for weeks

Hạnd|wer|ke|rin ['hantvɛɐkərɪn] F -, -nen tradeswoman, (skilled) manual worker; (= Kunsthandwerkerin) craftswoman

Hạnd|wer|ker|schaft ['hantvɛɐkɐʃaft] F -, no pl trade sing or pl

hạnd|werk|lich ['hantvɛɐklɪç] ADJ → Handwerker Ausbildung as a manual worker/craftsman/craftswoman; (fig) technical; **~er Beruf** skilled trade; **~e Ausführung des Möbelstücks** the workmanship or craftsmanship of the piece of furniture; **~es Können** craftsmanship; **~e Fähigkeiten** manual skills; **~er Betrieb** workshop; **~es Produkt** product (made by craftsmen/

craftswomen/ **~e Tätigkeit** skilled manual job **ADV das ist ~ eine Katastrophe** this is a disgraceful or an incredibly slipshod piece of work; **~ begabt sein** to be good with one's hands; **eine ~ ausgezeichnete Leistung** a masterpiece of craftsmanship; **~ ist der Fotograf perfekt** technically the photographer is perfect

Hạnd|werks-: Hạnd|werks|be|ruf M skilled trade; **Hạnd|werks|be|trieb** M workshop; **Hạnd|werks|bur|sche** M (old) travelling (Brit) or traveling (US) journeyman; **Hạnd|werks|ge|sel|le** M ; **Hạnd|werks|ge|sel|lin** F journeyman (apprentice); **Hạnd|werks|kam|mer** F trade corporation; **Hạnd|werks|mann** M pl -leute (obs) (skilled) manual worker; **Hạnd|werks|meis|ter(in)** M(F) master craftsman/-woman; **Hạnd|werks|rol|le** F register of master craftspeople; **Hạnd|werks|zeug** NT , no pl tools pl; (fig) tools of the trade pl, equipment

Hạnd-: Hạnd|werk|zeug NT hand tools pl; **Hạnd|win|de** F hand-winch; **Hạnd|wör|ter|buch** NT concise dictionary; **Hạnd|wur|zel** F (Anat) carpus; **Hạnd|wur|zel|kno|chen** M (Anat) carpal bone

Han|dy ['hɛndi] NT -s, -s (Telec) mobile (phone), cell(ular) phone (US)

Hạnd-: hạnd|zahm ADJ Tier tame enough to be handled; (fig inf) Mensch, Frage tame; **Hạnd|zei|chen** NT signal; (= Geste auch) sign; (bei Abstimmung) show of hands; **durch ~** by a show of hands; **er gab mir durch ein ~ zu verstehen, dass ich still sein sollte** he signalled (Brit) or signaled (US) to me to be quiet, he gave me a sign to be quiet; **Hạnd|zeich|nung** F **a** (= Skizze) sketch **b** (Art) drawing; **Hạnd|zet|tel** M handout, leaflet, handbill

ha|ne|bü|chen ['haːnəbyːçn] ADJ (geh) outrageous, scandalous

Hanf [hanf] M -(e)s, no pl (Pflanze, Faser) hemp; (= Samen) hemp seed

Hänf|ling ['hɛnflɪŋ] M -s, -e (Orn) linnet

Hạnf|seil NT , **Hạnf|strick** M hemp-rope

Hang [haŋ] M -(e)s, ¨e ['hɛŋə] **a** (= Abhang) slope **b** no pl (= Neigung) tendency; **er hat einen (deutlichen) ~ zur Kriminalität** he has a (marked) tendency toward(s) criminality

hang|ab|wärts ADV downhill

Han|gar ['haŋaːɐ, haŋˈgaːɐ] M -s, -s hangar, shed

Hän|ge-: Hän|ge|ba|cken PL flabby cheeks pl; **Hän|ge|bauch** M drooping belly (inf); **Hän|ge|brü|cke** F suspension bridge; **Hän|ge|brust** F , **Hän|ge|bu|sen** M (pej) sagging or droopy (inf) breasts pl or bosom no pl; **Hän|ge|dach** NT suspended roof; **Hän|ge|glei|ten** NT (Sport) hang-gliding; **Hän|ge|glei|ter** M (Sport) hang-glider; **Hän|ge|kleid** NT loose dress, smock; **Hän|ge|lam|pe** F droplight

han|geln ['haŋln] VIR (vi: aux sein or haben) **er hangelte sich an einem Tau über den Fluss** he moved hand over hand along a rope over the river; **er hangelte sich am Fels hinunter** he let himself down the cliff hand over hand; **er hangelte sich über den Abgrund** he crossed the chasm hand over hand

Hän|ge-: Hän|ge|map|pe F suspension file; **Hän|ge|mat|te** F hammock

han|gen ['haŋən] VI (obs, dial) (dial:) aux sein = hängen 1

Han|gen ['haŋən] NT **mit ~ und Bangen** with fear and trembling

hän|gen ['hɛŋən]

1 INTRANSITIVES VERB	3 REFLEXIVES VERB
2 TRANSITIVES VERB	

1 – INTRANSITIVES VERB
pret **hing** [hɪŋ], ptp **gehangen** [gəˈhaŋən]

a = herunterhängen to hang; **die Vorhänge hängen schief** the curtains don't hang straight; **die Gardinen hängen schon** the curtains are already up; **ihre Haare hängen bis auf die Schultern** her hair comes down to her shoulders; **die Haare hängen ihr ins Gesicht** her hair falls over her face; **mit hängenden Schultern** with drooping shoulders; **die Blumen ließen die Köpfe hängen** the flowers drooped; **den Kopf hängen lassen** (fig) to be downcast; **die Kleider hingen ihr in Fetzen am Leib** her clothes hung (on her) in tatters; **es sieht sehr schick aus, wenn dieses Kleid ein wenig lose hängt** this dress looks very elegant if it's a bit loose; **sie hängt den ganzen Tag aus dem Fenster** she leans or hangs out of the window all day

b = gehenkt werden to hang; **dafür wirst du hängen, Schurke!** you'll hang for this, villain!

c = befestigt, angeschlossen sein to hang; (Wohnwagen etc, Lautsprecher, Telefonapparat etc) to be connected (up) (an +dat to), to be attached (an +dat to); **der Wohnwagen hängt am Auto** the caravan is attached to the car, the caravan is on the car; **die Tür hängt in den Angeln** the door hangs on its hinges; **das Bild hängt an der Wand/am Nagel** the picture is hanging on the wall/from a nail; **die Wäsche hängt auf der Leine** the washing is hanging on the line; **das Bild hängt schief** the picture is (hanging) crooked; **der Knopf hängt nur noch an einem Faden** the button is only hanging by a thread; **der Patient hängt an der künstlichen Niere/am Tropf** the patient is on the kidney machine/on the drip; **das Kalb hing am Euter der Mutter** the calf hung on to its mother's udder; **sie hing ihm am Hals** she hung (a)round his neck; **sie hing ihm an der Schulter** she clung to his shoulder

d = festhängen to be caught (an +dat on); (= kleben) to be stuck (an +dat on); **mit einer Masche im Stacheldraht hängen** to be caught on barbed wire; **mit dem Ärmel an einem Dorn hängen** to have one's sleeve caught on a thorn; **ihre Blicke** or **Augen hingen an dem Sänger** her eyes were fixed on the singer; **sie hing am Mund** or **an den Lippen des Redners** she hung on the speaker's every word; **Ihnen hängt da eine Fluse am Kragen** there's a bit of fluff (Brit) or fuzz (US) on your collar; **manchmal hängt wegen der statischen Elektrizität noch Staub an den CDs** sometimes static electricity makes dust stick to CDs; **daran hängt viel Arbeit** there's a lot of work involved in that

e = sich aufhalten (inf) to hang around (inf); **sie hängt ständig in Diskos** she hangs around discos; **er hängt den ganzen Tag vor dem Fernseher** he sits in front of the television all day

f = behangen sein

♦ **hängen voller** or **voll** to be full of; **der Schrank hängt voll(er) Kleider** the cupboard is full of clothes; **der Baum hängt voller Früchte** the tree is laden down with fruit

g = sich neigen to lean; **in der Kurve hängen** (Motorradfahrer) to lean into the bend; **der Wagen hängt (stark) nach rechts** the car leans (badly) to the right; **häng nicht so auf dem Stuhl, sitz gerade hin!** (inf) don't slouch on your chair like that, sit up straight!

h = schweben to hang; **eine Wolke hing im Tal** a cloud hung over the valley; **eine Gefahr/ein Fluch hängt über uns** danger/a curse is hanging over us; **eine unerträgliche Spannung hing im Raum** there was unbearable tension in the room → **Luft a**

i = nicht vorankommen to be behind schedule; (Sch inf) to be behind; **der Prozeß hängt** the trial is behind schedule; **meine Examensarbeit hängt** I'm behind (schedule) with my dissertation; **er hängt in Chemie** (inf) he's behind in chemistry

j Chess **die Partie hängt** the game has been held over or adjourned; **der Springer hängt** the knight is vulnerable

k gefühlsmäßig

♦ **an jdm/etw hängen** (= lieben) to love sb/sth; (inf: = abhängen von) to depend on sb/sth; **ich hänge am Leben/an meinem Beruf** I love life/my job; **er geht nicht auf die Expedition mit, er hängt nämlich am Leben** he's not going on the expedition because he values his life; **es hängt an ihm/an unserer Abstimmung, ob wir Truppen schicken** it depends on him/on our vote whether we send troops

2 – TRANSITIVES VERB
pret **hängte** or **hing**, ptp **gehängt** or **gehangen**

a = aufhängen, henken to hang; **am nächsten Tag wurde er gehängt** they hanged him the next day; **wir müssen noch die Gardinen hängen** we still have to put up or hang the curtains; **dieses Bild sollten wir etwas höher hängen** we should hang this picture a bit higher up; **und hierher hängen wir noch einen Spiegel** and we'll hang or put a mirror here; **er hängt sich all sein Geld** or **alles auf den Leib** (inf) he spends all his money on clothes; **er hängte den Telefonhörer in die Gabel** he replaced the receiver; **er hängte die Wand voll Bilder** he hung pictures all over the wall → **Nagel, Brotkorb, Glocke**

♦ **hängen an** (+acc) (= anschließen) to connect to; (= befestigen) Wohnwagen etc to hitch up to; **das Bild an die Wand hängen** to hang the picture on the wall; **eine Notiz ans schwarze Brett hängen** to put a note on the notice board (Brit) or bulletin board (US); **das Telefon an die neue Anlage hängen** to connect the phone to the new system

b = hängen lassen to dangle; **die Füße ins Wasser hängen** to dangle one's feet in the water; **seine Nase in etw** (acc) **hängen** (inf) to stick one's nose into sth (inf)

3 – REFLEXIVES VERB

♦ **sich hängen** pret **hängte**, ptp **gehängt**
♦ **sich an etw** (acc) **hängen** (= sich festhalten) to hang on to sth; (= sich festsetzen) to stick to sth; (= sich gefühlsmäßig binden) to be fixated on sth; **er hängte sich an den untersten Ast** he hung onto the lowest branch; **er hängte sich ihr an den Hals/Arm/Rockzipfel** he hung on to or clung to her neck/arm/coat-tails; **man sollte sich nicht an Äußerlichkeiten hängen** you shouldn't be too concerned with outward appearances; **sich hängen ans Telefon** or **an die Strippe** (inf) he got on the phone; **sich an den Wasserhahn hängen** (inf) to have a drink straight from the tap; **sich an die Flasche hängen** (inf) to hit the bottle (inf); **sich an ein Fahrzeug hängen** (= dicht verfolgen) to be in hot pursuit of a vehicle

♦ **sich an jdn hängen** (= anschließen) to tag on to sb (inf), to latch on to sb (inf); (= gefühlsmäßig binden) to become attached to sb; (= verfolgen) to go after sb, to pursue sb

♦ **sich in etw** (acc) **hängen** (sl) (= sich engagieren) to be involved in sth

Hän|gen NT -s, no pl **a** **Tod durch ~** death by hanging **b** **mit ~ und Würgen** (inf) by the skin of one's teeth

hän|gen blei|ben ▲ VI irreg aux sein **a** (= sich verfangen) to get caught (an +dat on) **b** (Sport) (= zurückbleiben) to get left behind; (= nicht durch-, weiterkommen) not to get through; **der Aufschlag blieb im Netz hängen** the ball didn't get past the net; **der Angriff blieb vor dem Strafraum hängen** the attack didn't get past the front of the penalty area; **die Mannschaft blieb schon in der ersten Runde hängen** the team didn't get past or through the first round **c** (Sch inf: = nicht versetzt werden) to stay down **d** (= sich aufhalten) to stay on; **bei einer Nebensächlichkeit ~** to get bogged down with a secondary issue, to get sidetracked **e** (= sich festsetzen, haften bleiben) to get stuck or caught (in, an +dat on); (Blick, Augen) to rest

(an +dat on); **es bleibt ja doch alles an mir hängen** (fig inf) in the end it's all down to me anyhow (inf); **der Verdacht ist an ihm hängen geblieben** suspicion rested on him; **vom Lateinunterricht ist bei ihm nicht viel hängen geblieben** (fig inf) not much of his Latin stuck (inf)

hän|gend ADJ hanging; **~e Gärten** hanging gardens; **mit ~er Zunge kam er angelaufen** (fig) he came running up panting; **mit ~em Kopf** (fig) in low spirits, crestfallen; **~ befestigt sein** to be hung up; **~e Ventile** (Tech) overhead valves

hän|gen las|sen ▲ ptp **hängen lassen** or (rare) **gelassen** irreg VT **a** (= vergessen) to leave behind **b** (inf: = im Stich lassen) to let down **c** (Sch: = nicht versetzen) to keep down VR to let oneself go; **lass dich nicht so hängen!** don't let yourself go like this!, pull yourself together!; **er lässt sich furchtbar hängen** he has really let himself go

Hän|ge-: **Hän|ge|ohr** NT lop ear; **Hän|ge|par|tie** F (Chess) adjourned game; (fig) stalemate; **Hän|ge|pflan|ze** F trailing plant

Hän|ger ['hɛŋɐ] M -s, - **a** (= Anhänger) trailer **b** (= Hängekleid) loose dress, smock **c** (= Mantel) loose(-fitting) coat **d** (inf: im Text) **einen ~ haben** to go blank **e** (inf) = **Durchhänger**

Hän|gerl ['hɛŋɐl] NT -s, -(n) (Aus) **a** (= Lätzchen) bib **b** (= Geschirrhandtuch) tea towel

Hän|ge-: **Hän|ge|schloss** ▲ NT padlock; **Hän|ge|schrank** M wall cupboard; **Hän|ge|schul|tern** PL drooping shoulders pl

hän|gig ['hɛŋɪç] ADJ **a** (Sw Jur) = **anhängig** **b** (form) sloping, inclined

Hang|la|ge F sloping site; **in ~** situated on a slope

hängt [hɛŋt] 3. pers sing pres von **hängen**

Hang|tä|ter(in) M(F) (Jur) person with criminal tendencies

Han|ne|mann ['hanəman] M **~ geh du voran** (inf) you go first

Han|ni|bal ['hanibal] M -s Hannibal

Han|no|ver [ha'noːfɐ] NT -s Hanover

Han|no|ve|ra|ner[1] [hanovə'raːnɐ] M -s, - (= Pferd) Hanoverian (horse)

Han|no|ve|ra|ner[2] [hanovə'raːnɐ] M -s, -, **Han|no|ve|ra|ne|rin** [-ərɪn] F -, -nen Hanoverian

han|no|ve|risch [ha'noːfərɪʃ] (rare), **han|no|versch** [ha'noːfɐʃ], **han|nö|versch** [ha'nøːfɐʃ] (old) ADJ Hanoverian

Hans [hans] M -' or -ens [-zns] **~ Guckindieluft** Johnny Head-in-the-Air; **~ im Glück** (fig) lucky dog (inf) or devil (inf)

Han|sa ['hanza] F -, no pl (Hist) Hanseatic League, Hansa, Hanse

Han|sa|plast® [hanza'plast, 'hanza-] NT -(e)s, no pl Elastoplast® (Brit), Band-Aid® (esp US)

Häns|chen ['hɛnsçən] NT -s, - dim von **Hans** was **~ nicht lernt, lernt Hans nimmermehr** (Prov) ≈ you can't teach an old dog new tricks (Prov)

Hans|dampf [hans'dampf, 'hans-] M -(e)s, -e Jack-of-all-trades (and master of none); **er ist ein ~ in allen Gassen** he knows everybody and everything

Han|se ['hanzə] F -, no pl (Hist) Hanseatic League, Hansa, Hanse

Han|se|at [hanze'aːt] M -en, -en, **Han|se|a|tin** [hanze'aːtɪn] F -, -nen citizen of a Hansa town; (Hist) Hanseatic merchant, merchant belonging to the Hanseatic League

Han|se|a|ten|geist M Hanseatic spirit

han|se|a|tisch [hanze'aːtɪʃ] ADJ **a** (Hist) Hanseatic **b** (= hansestädtisch) Hanseatic; **~ zurückhaltend** cool and reserved

Han|se|bund M -, no pl (Hist) Hanseatic League

Han|sel ['hanzl] M -s, -, **Hän|sel** ['hɛnzl] M -s, - dim von **Hans** (dial: = Trottel) dolt, ninny (inf); **Hänsel und Gretel** Hansel and Gretel; **ein paar ~** (dial: = wenige) a few

Hän|se|lei [hɛnzə'lai] F -, -en teasing no pl

hän|seln ['hɛnzln] VT to tease

Han|se-: Han|se|stadt F Hansa or Hanseatic or Hanse town; **han|se|städ|tisch** ADJ Hanseatic

---

HANSESTADT

In the Middle Ages the **Hanse** (Hanseatic League) was a powerful alliance of independent trading centres on the Baltic and North Sea coasts. Its aim was to represent and protect the common commercial interests of its members. From the time of the Thirty Years' War up to the present the Hanseatic tradition has been continued by Lübeck, Hamburg and Bremen in particular. Bremen and Hamburg are both independent **Länder** with the titles **Freie Hansestadt Bremen** and **Freie Hansestadt Hamburg** respectively. Since re-unification other cities – Stralsund, Wismar, Greifswald and Rostock – have re-adopted the title of **Hansestadt**.

---

han|sisch ['hanzɪʃ] ADJ (Hist) Hanseatic

Hans- [hans-]: **Hans|wurst** [hans'vʊrst, 'hans-] M -(e)s, -e or (hum) **≠e** **a** buffoon, clown **b** (Theat) fool, clown; **Hans|wurs|ti|a|de** [hansvʊrs'tia:də] F -, -n **a** clowning, buffoonery **b** (Theat) ≈ harlequinade

Han|tel ['hantl] F -, -n (Sport) dumbbell

han|teln ['hantln] VI (Sport) to exercise with dumbbells

Han|tel|trai|ning NT (Sport) dumbbells training

han|tie|ren [han'ti:rən] ptp **hantiert** VI **a** (= arbeiten) to be busy **b** (= umgehen mit) **mit etw ~** to handle sth; **seine Geschicklichkeit im Hantieren mit Begriffen** (fig) his skill in handling ideas **c** (= herumhantieren) to tinker or fiddle about (an +dat with, on)

han|tig ['hantɪç] ADJ (Aus, S Ger) **a** (= bitter) bitter **b** (= barsch) brusque, abrupt

ha|pe|rig ['ha:pərɪç] ADJ, ADV (N Ger) = **stockend**

ha|pern ['ha:pɛn] VI impers (inf) **es hapert an etw** (dat) (= fehlt) there is a shortage or lack of sth; **es hapert bei jdm mit etw** (= fehlt) sb is short of sth, sb is badly off for sth; **es hapert (bei jdm) mit etw** (= klappt nicht) sb has a problem with sth; **mit der Grammatik hapert es bei ihm** he's weak in or poor at grammar

Häpp|chen ['hɛpçən] NT -s, - dim von **Happen** morsel, bit; (= Appetithappen) titbit (Brit), tidbit (US)

häpp|chen|wei|se ADV (inf: lit, fig) bit by bit

Hap|pen ['hapn] M -s, - (inf) mouthful, morsel; (= kleine Mahlzeit) bite, snack; **ein fetter ~** (fig) a good catch; **nach dem Theater aßen wir noch einen ~** after the theatre (Brit) or theater (US) we had a bite to eat (inf) or a snack; **ich habe heute noch keinen ~ gegessen** I haven't had a bite to eat all day

Hap|pe|ning ['hɛpənɪŋ] NT -s, -s (Theat) happening; (Art) action painting

hap|pig ['hapɪç] ADJ (inf) Preis, Zuwachs etc steep (inf)

hap|py ['hɛpi] ADJ inv (inf) happy

Hap|py End ▲ ['hɛpɪ'ɛnt] NT -s, -s, **Hap|py|end** ▲ NT -s, -s happy ending; **ein Film/Buch/ eine Geschichte mit Happy-End** a film/book/ story with a happy ending

Ha|ra|ki|ri [hara'ki:ri] NT -(s), -s hara-kiri

Ha|rald ['ha:ralt] M -s Harold

Ha|rass ['haras] M -es, -e, **Ha|ras|se** ['harasə] F -, -n (Aus, Sw: = Kasten, Kiste) crate

Här|chen ['hɛ:rçən] NT -s, - dim von **Haar** little or tiny hair

Hard|core- ['ha:dkɔːɐ] in cpds hard-core; **Hard|core-Por|no** M (= Film) hard-core porn film

Hard|co|ver ▲ ['ha:dkavɐ] NT -s, -s, **Hard Co|ver** NT -s, -s hardcover

Hard|li|ner ['ha:dlaɪnɐ] M -s, -, **Hard|li|ne|rin** [-ərɪn] F -, -nen (Pol) hardliner

Hard|rock ['ha:drɔk] M -s, no pl hard rock

Hardt|hö|he F Hardthöhe (German Ministry of Defence)

Hard|top ['ha:dtɔp] NT OR M -s, -s (Aut: = Wagen, Dach) hardtop; **ein Kabrio mit ~** a convertible with a hardtop

Hard|ware ['ha:dwɛːɐ] F -, -s (Comput) hardware

Ha|rem ['ha:rɛm] M -s, -s (auch hum inf) harem

Ha|rems-: Ha|rems|da|me F lady of the/a harem; **Ha|rems|wäch|ter** M harem guard

hä|ren ['hɛ:rən] ADJ (rare) **~es Gewand** hair shirt

Hä|re|sie [hɛre'zi:] F -, -en [-'zi:ən] (lit, fig) heresy

Hä|re|ti|ker [hɛ're:tikɐ] M -s, -, **Hä|re|ti|ke|rin** [-ərɪn] F -, -nen (lit, fig) heretic

hä|re|tisch [hɛ're:tɪʃ] ADJ (lit, fig) heretical

Har|fe ['harfə] F -, -n harp

Har|fe|nist [harfə'nɪst] M -en, -en, **Har|fe|nis|tin** [-'nɪstɪn] F -, -nen harpist

Har|fen-: Har|fen|klang M sound of the/a harp; **Har|fen|spiel** NT , no pl harp-playing; **Har|fen|spie|ler(in)** M(F) harp-player, harpist

Harf|ner ['harfnɐ] M -s, - (old), **Harf|ne|rin** [-ərɪn] F -, -nen (old) harp-player, harpist

Har|ke ['harkə] F -, -n (esp N Ger) rake; **jdm zeigen, was eine ~ ist** (fig inf) to show sb what's what (inf)

har|ken ['harkn] VTI (esp N Ger) to rake

Har|le|kin ['harleki:n] M -s, -e Harlequin

Har|le|ki|na|de [harleki'na:də] F -, -n = **Hanswurstiade**

Harm [harm] M -(e)s, no pl (poet, obs) sore affliction (liter), grief

här|men ['hɛrmən] VTR (old) = **grämen**

harm|los ADJ **a** (= ungefährlich) harmless; Berg, Piste, Kurve easy **b** (= unschuldig, gutartig, naiv) innocent; (= unbedenklich) harmless, innocuous; **er ist ein ~er Mensch** he's harmless (enough), he's an innocuous type ADV **a** (= ungefährlich) harmlessly **b** (= unschuldig) innocently, innocuously

Harm|lo|sig|keit F -, no pl **a** (= Ungefährlichkeit) harmlessness **b** (= Unschuld, Naivität) innocence; (= Unbedenklichkeit) harmlessness, innocuousness; **in aller ~** in all innocence

Har|mo|nie [harmo'ni:] F -, -n [-'ni:ən] (Mus, fig) harmony

Har|mo|nie-: Har|mo|nie|be|dürf|nis NT , no pl need for peace and harmony; **Har|mo|nie|ge|setz** NT usu pl rule of harmony; **Har|mo|nie|leh|re** F (= Gebiet) harmony; (= Theorie) harmonic theory; **Har|mo|nie|mu|sik** F music for wind instruments

har|mo|nie|ren [harmo'ni:rən] ptp **harmoniert** VI (Mus, fig) to harmonize; (farblich auch) to go together, to match

Har|mo|nik [har'mo:nɪk] F -, no pl harmony

Har|mo|ni|ka [har'mo:nika] F -, -s or **Harmoniken** harmonica, (= Mundharmonika auch) mouth organ; (= Ziehharmonika) accordion

Har|mo|ni|ka|tür F folding or accordion door

har|mo|nisch [har'mo:nɪʃ] ADJ (Mus, Math) harmonic; (= wohlklingend, fig) harmonious ADV harmoniously; **~ klingende Akkorde** harmonious chords; **etw ~ mischen** to make a harmonious mixture out of sth; **~ komponiert sein** to be a harmonious composition; **das klingt nicht sehr ~** that's not a very harmonious sound; **~ verlaufen** to be harmonious; **sie leben ~ zusammen** they live together in harmony

har|mo|ni|sie|ren [harmoni'zi:rən] ptp **harmonisiert** VT Musik, Steuern to harmonize; (fig) to coordinate

Har|mo|ni|sie|rung F -, -en (von Musik, Steuern) harmonization; (fig) coordination

Har|mo|ni|um [har'mo:niʊm] NT -s, Harmonien [-'ni:ən] harmonium

Harn [harn] M -(e)s, -e urine; **~ lassen** to pass water, to urinate

Harn-: Harn|bla|se F bladder; **Harn|bla|sen|ent|zün|dung** F cystitis; **Harn|drang** M (form) urge or need to pass water or to urinate

har|nen ['harnən] VI (form) to urinate, to pass water, to micturate (form)

Harn-: Harn|ent|lee|rung F urination, passing of water, micturition (form); **Harn|fla|sche** F urinal

Har|nisch ['harnɪʃ] M -(e)s, -e armour (Brit), armor (US); **in ~ sein** (fig) to be up in arms, to have one's hackles up; **jdn in ~ bringen** (fig) to get sb up in arms, to get sb's hackles up

Harn-: Harn|las|sen NT -s, no pl (form) urination, passing of water, micturition (form); **Harn|lei|ter** M ureter; **Harn|or|gan** NT urinary organ; **Harn|pro|be** F urine sample or specimen; **Harn|röh|re** F urethra; **Harn|säu|re** F (Chem) uric acid; **Harn|stein** M (Med) urinary calculus; **Harn|stoff** M (Chem) urea, carbamide; **harn|trei|bend** ADJ (form) diuretic; **Harn|un|ter|su|chung** F urine analysis, urinalysis; **Harn|ver|gif|tung** F uraemia (Brit), uremia (US); **Harn|we|ge** PL (Anat) urinary tract sing; **Harn|zu|cker** M sugar in the urine

Harp|si|chord [harpsi'kɔrt] NT -(e)s, -e [-də] (old) harpsichord, cembalo

Har|pu|ne [har'pu:nə] F -, -n harpoon

Har|pu|nen|ge|schütz NT , **Har|pu|nen|ka|no|ne** F , **Har|pu|nen|wer|fer** M harpoon gun

Har|pu|nier [harpu'ni:ɐ] M -s, -e, **Har|pu|nie|rin** [-'ni:rɪn] F -, -nen harpooner

har|pu|nie|ren [harpu'ni:rən] ptp **harpuniert** VTI to harpoon

Har|py|ie [har'py:jə] F -, -n usu pl (Myth) Harpy

har|ren ['harən] VI (geh) **jds/einer Sache ~, auf jdn/etw ~** to await sb/sth, to wait for sb/sth → **Ding** ¹ **b**

harsch [harʃ] ADJ **a** (= barsch) Worte, Kritik, Ton, Reaktion harsh **b** (= verharscht) Schnee frozen

Harsch [harʃ] M -(e)s, no pl frozen snow

har|schen ['harʃn] VI to freeze over

har|schig ['harʃɪç] ADJ Schnee frozen

Harsch|schnee M frozen snow

hart [hart] ADJ comp **≠er** ['hɛrtɐ], superl **≠este(r, s)** ['hɛrtəstə] **a** (= nicht weich, nicht sanft) hard; Matratze, Bett, Federung, Apfelschale hard, firm; Aufprall, Ruck violent, hard; Wind strong; Ei hard-boiled; **~ werden** to get hard, to harden; **Eier ~ kochen** to hard-boil eggs; **er hat einen ~en Leib** (Med old) he is constipated; **er hat einen ~en Schädel** or **Kopf** (fig) he's pig-headed or obstinate; **ein ~es Herz haben** (fig) to have a hard heart, to be hard-hearted; **~ wie Stahl/Stein** as hard as steel/stone

b (= scharf) Konturen, Kontrast, Formen sharp; (Phot) Negativ sharp; (Gesichts)züge, Konsonant hard; Licht harsh, hard; Klang, Ton, Aussprache, Akzent harsh

c (= rau) Spiel, Gegner rough; (fig) Getränke strong; Droge hard; Porno hard-core; Kriminalfilm etc, Western tough

d (= widerstandsfähig, robust) tough; **gelobt sei, was ~ macht** (prov, usu iro) treat 'em rough, make 'em tough! (inf); **er ist ~ im Nehmen** he's tough

e (= stabil, sicher) Währung, Devisen stable; **in ~en Dollars** in hard dollars

f (= streng, gnadenlos, kompromisslos) Mensch, Kampf hard; Wort strong, harsh; Winter, Frost, Vertragsbedingung hard, severe; Strafe, Urteil, Kritik severe, harsh; Maßnahmen, Gesetze, Politik, Kurs tough; *Auseinandersetzung* violent; **der ~e Kern einer Vereinigung** the hard core of an organization; **er ist durch eine ~e Schule gegangen** (*fig*) he has been through a hard school; **~ bleiben** to stand *or* remain firm; **~ mit jdm sein** to be hard on sb, to be harsh with sb; **es fielen ~e Worte** hard *or* strong *or* harsh words were used; **es geht ~ auf ~** it's a tough fight, it's a real battle

g (= *schwer zu ertragen*) *Los, Schicksal, Tatsache* hard, cruel; *Verlust* cruel; *Wirklichkeit, Wahrheit* harsh; **es war sehr ~ für ihn, dass er ...** it was very hard for him to ...; **oh, das war ~!** (*inf: Witz etc*) oh, that was painful!; **das Härteste** (*sl: = Zumutung*) a real bummer (*inf*) *or* pisser (*Brit sl*)

h (= *mühevoll, anstrengend*) *Arbeit, Leben, Zeiten* hard, tough

i (*Phys*) *Strahlen* hard

ADV comp **~er**, superl **am ~esten a** (= *nicht weich*) hard; **er schläft gerne ~** he likes sleeping on a hard surface/bed; **~ gebrannt** (*Ziegel, Keramik*) hard-baked; **~ gefroren** frozen, frozen stiff pred, frozen solid pred; **der Boden ist ~ gefroren** the ground is frozen hard *or* solid; **~ gekocht** *or* **gesotten** (*Aus*) (*Ei*) hard-boiled; *Mensch* hard-baked (*inf*), hard-boiled; **~ geworden** hard

b (= *scharf*) kontrastiert sharply; **~ klingen** (*Sprache*) to sound hard; (*Bemerkung*) to sound harsh; **er spricht manche Laute zu ~ aus** he pronounces some sounds too hard

c (= *heftig, rau*) roughly; *fallen, aufprallen, zuschlagen* hard; **er lässt die Kupplung immer so ~ kommen** he always lets the clutch out so roughly *or* violently; **~ bedrängt** hard-pressed; **~ bedrängt sein** to be put under pressure; **~ aneinander geraten** (= *sich prügeln*) to come to blows, to have a (real) set-to (*inf*); (= *sich streiten*) to get into a fierce argument, to have a (real) set-to (*inf*); **~ einsteigen** (*Sport*) to go hard at it; **jdn ~ anfahren** to bite sb's head off (*inf*); **jdm ~ zusetzen** to give sb a hard time; **etw trifft jdn ~** (*lit, fig*) sth hits sb hard; **~ diskutieren** to have a vigorous discussion; **~ spielen** (*Sport*) to play rough

d (= *streng*) severely, harshly; **~ durchgreifen** to take tough *or* rigorous action; **jdn ~ anfassen** to be hard on sb, to treat sb harshly; **man muss sie ~ anfassen** you have to keep them in line

e (= *mühevoll*) hard; **~ arbeiten** to work hard; **es kommt mich ~ an** (*geh*) I find it hard

f (= *nahe*) close (*an* +*dat* to); **das ist ~ an der Grenze der Legalität/des Zumutbaren** that's pushing legality/reasonableness to its (very) limit(s), that's on the very limits of legality/of what's reasonable; **das ist ~ an der Grenze zum Kriminellen/zum Kitsch** that's very close to being criminal/kitsch; **wir fuhren ~ am Abgrund vorbei** (*fig*) we were (very) close to disaster, we were on the (very) brink of disaster; **~ am Wind (segeln)** (*Naut*) (to sail) close to the wind; **~ auf ein Ziel zuhalten** (*Naut*) to head straight for a destination

Hart-: Hart|bahn F (*Sport*) hard track; **hart|be|drängt** [-bədrɛŋt] △ ADJ attr → hart ADV c; **Hart|be|ton** M (especially) hard concrete; **hart|blät|te|rig, hart|blätt|rig** ADJ (*Bot*) hard-leaved

Här|te ['hɛrtə] F -, -n **a** hardness; (*von Matratze*) firmness; (*von Aufprall, Ruck*) violence, hardness; (= *Härtegrad*) degree *or* grade of hardness) **b** no pl (= *Schärfe*) (*von Konturen, Kontrast, Formen*) sharpness; (*von Gesichtszügen*) hardness; (*von Licht, Klang, Akzent*) harshness **c** (= *Rauheit: von Spiel, Gegner*) roughness no pl; **sie spielten mit größter ~** they played very rough **d** no pl (= *Robustheit*) toughness **e** no pl (= *Stabilität: von Währung, Devisen*) stability **f** no pl (= *Strenge*) (*von Mensch, Kampf*) hardness; (*von Worten*) harshness; (*von Winter, Frost, Vertragsbedingungen*) hardness, severity; (*von*

Strafe, Urteil, Kritik) severity; (*von Maßnahmen, Gesetz, Politik*) toughness; (*von Auseinandersetzung*) violence; **eine Auseinandersetzung in großer ~ führen** to have a violent argument; **mit großer ~ diskutieren** to have a very heated discussion **g** (= *Belastung*) (*von Schicksal, Verlust*) cruelty; (*von Wahrheit*) harshness; **der Schicksalsschlag traf ihn in seiner ganzen ~** this blow of fate struck him with all its force *or* cruelty; **soziale ~n** (= *Fälle*) cases of social hardship; **das ist die ~** (*sl: = Zumutung*) that's a bit much *or* a real killer (*inf*) **h** (*Phys, von Strahlen*) degree of penetration

Här|te-: Här|te|aus|gleich M (*Admin*) compensation for (social) hardship; **Här|te|fall** M case of hardship; (*inf: = Mensch*) hardship case; **Här|te|fall|re|ge|lung** F hardship provision (ruling); **Här|te|fonds** M hardship fund; **Här|te|grad** M degree *or* grade of hardness; **Här|te|klau|sel** F hardship clause; **Här|te|mit|tel** NT (*Metal*) hardening agent

här|ten ['hɛrtn] **VT** to harden; *Stahl auch* to temper **VI** to harden **VR** (*Stoff*) to harden

Här|te-: Här|te|ofen M (*Metal*) tempering oven *or* furnace; **Här|te|pa|ra|graf** ▲ M paragraph dealing with cases of hardship

här|ter comp von **hart**

Här|ter ['hɛrtɐ] M -s, - (*Tech*) hardener, hardening agent

Här|te|ska|la F scale of hardness, Mohs scale

här|tes|te(r, s) superl von **hart**

Här|te-: Här|te|stu|fe F (*von Material, Wasser*) hardness grade; **Här|te|test** M endurance test; (*fig*) acid test; **Här|te|zu|stand** M hard state; **im ~ lässt sich das Material wie Metall bearbeiten** in the hard state *or* when it is hard this material can be worked like metal

Hart-: Hart|fa|ser|plat|te F hardboard, fiberboard (*US*); **hart|ge|brannt** △ ADJ attr → hart ADV a; **hart|ge|fro|ren** △ ADJ attr → hart ADV a; **hart|ge|kocht** [-gəkɔxt] △ ADJ attr → hart ADV a; **Hart|geld** NT hard cash; **hart|ge|sot|ten** ADJ hard-baked (*inf*), hard-boiled **b** (*Aus*) → hart ADV a; **hart|ge|wor|den** △ ADJ attr → hart ADV a; **Hart|gum|mi** M OR NT hard rubber; **hart|her|zig** ADJ hard-hearted; **Hart|her|zig|keit** [-hɛrtsɪçkaɪt] F -, no pl hard-heartedness; **Hart|holz** NT hardwood; **hart|hö|rig** ADJ **a** (= *nicht reagierend*) unresponsive **b** (*dated: = schwerhörig*) hard of hearing; **Hart|kä|se** M hard cheese; **Hart|laub|ge|wächs** NT (*Bot*) sclerophyllous evergreen (*spec*); **hart|lei|big** ['hartlaɪbɪç] ADJ (*Med old*) constipated; (*fig*) (= *stur*) unyielding, intransigent; (= *hartnäckig*) obdurate; **Hart|lei|big|keit** F -, no pl (*Med old*) constipation; (*fig*) (= *Sturheit*) intransigence; (= *Hartnäckigkeit*) obduracy; **hart|lö|ten** VTI sep to hard-solder; **Hart|me|tall** NT hard metal; **hart|nä|ckig** ['hartnɛkɪç] **ADJ** (= *stur*) *Mensch, Haltung* obstinate, stubborn; (= *ausdauernd*) *Widerstand, Gerücht* stubborn; *Lügner, Husten* persistent; (= *beharrlich*) dogged, persistent; (= *langwierig*) *Erkältung, Fleck* stubborn **ADV** (= *beharrlich*) persistently; (= *stur*) stubbornly; **das Gerücht hielt sich ~ the** rumour (*Brit*) *or* rumor (*US*) persisted stubbornly; **Hart|nä|ckig|keit** F -, no pl (= *Sturheit*) obstinacy, stubbornness; (= *Beharrlichkeit*) doggedness; **ein Fleck von besonderer ~** a particularly stubborn *or* persistent stain; **Hart|pa|ckung** F hard pack; **Hart|pap|pe** F cardboard; **Hart|platz** M (*Sport*) hard sports area; (*für Ballspiele*) hard pitch; (*Tennis*) hard court; **Hart|scha|len|kof|fer** M hard-sided case; **hart|scha|lig** [-ʃaːlɪç] ADJ *Frucht* hard-shelled, testaceous (*spec*); *Apfel, Traube* having a tough skin, tough-skinned; *Koffer* hard-sided; **Hart|spi|ri|tus** [-ʃpiːrɪtʊs] M methylated spirits in solid form

Har|tung ['hartʊŋ] M -s, -e (*obs*) January

Här|tung ['hɛrtʊŋ] F -, -en (*Tech*) hardening; (*von Stahl auch*) tempering

Hart-: Hart|wa|re F hardware no pl; **Hart|wei|zen** M durum wheat; **Hart|wei|zen|grieß** M semolina; **Hart|wurst** F salami-type sausage

Harz¹ [haːɐ̯ts] NT -es, -e resin

Harz² M -es (*Geog*) Harz Mountains pl

harz|ar|tig ADJ resin-like, resinous, resinoid

har|zen ['haːɐ̯tsn] **VT** *Wein* to treat with resin, to resinate **VI** (*Baum, Holz*) to secrete *or* exude resin

Har|zer¹ ['haːɐ̯tsɐ] ADJ (*Geog*) Harz; **~ Roller** (*Zool*) roller canary; (*Cook*) (roll-shaped) Harz cheese; **~ Käse** (*Cook*) (roll-shaped) Harz cheese

Har|zer² ['haːɐ̯tsɐ] M -s, - (*Cook*) Harz cheese

Har|zer³ ['haːɐ̯tsɐ] M -s, -, **Har|ze|rin** [-ərɪn] F -, -nen native *or* (= *Einwohner*) inhabitant of the Harz Mountains

harz|hal|tig ADJ *Holz* resinous, containing resin

har|zig ['haːɐ̯tsɪç] ADJ **a** *Holz, Geruch, Geschmack, Wein* resinous, resiny **b** (*Sw fig: = zähflüssig*) slow-moving

Ha|sard [ha'zart] NT -s, no pl = **Hasardspiel (mit etw) ~ spielen** (*fig geh*) to gamble (with sth)

Ha|sar|deur [hazar'døːɐ] M -s, -e, **Ha|sar|deu|se** [-'døːzə] F -, -n (*geh*) gambler

Ha|sard|spiel NT (*geh*) game of chance; (*fig geh*) gamble; **glatte Fahrbahnen machen das Autofahren zum ~** slippery roads make driving hazardous

Hasch [haʃ] NT -(s), no pl (*inf*) hash (*inf*)

Ha|schee [ha'ʃeː] NT -s, -s (*Cook*) hash

ha|schen¹ ['haʃn] (*dated, geh*) **VT** to catch; **hasch mich, ich bin der Frühling** (*hum inf*) come and get me, boys! (*hum*) **VI** **nach etw ~** to make a grab at sth; **nach Beifall/Lob** etc **~** to fish *or* angle (*Brit*) for applause/praise etc

ha|schen² VI (*inf*) to smoke (hash) (*inf*)

Ha|schen NT -s, no pl catch, tag

Häs|chen ['hɛːsçən] NT -s, - **a** dim von **Hase** young hare, leveret **b** (*inf: = Kaninchen, Playboyhäschen*) bunny (*inf*) **c** (= *Kosename*) sweetheart, sweetie(-pie)

Ha|scher ['haʃɐ] M -s, - (*inf*), **Ha|sche|rin** [-ərɪn] F -, -nen (*inf*) hash smoker

Hä|scher ['hɛʃɐ] M -s, - (*old, geh*) henchman

Ha|scherl ['haʃɐl] NT -s, -(n) (*Aus inf*) poor soul *or* thing *or* creature

ha|schie|ren [ha'ʃiːrən] ptp **haschiert** VT (*Cook*) *Fleisch* to mince (*Brit*), to grind (*US*)

Ha|schisch ['haʃɪʃ] NT OR M -(s), no pl hashish

Ha|schisch|rausch M state of euphoria produced by hashish; **im ~** under the effects of hashish

Hasch|mich ['haʃmɪç] M -s, no pl (*inf*) **einen ~ haben** to have a screw loose (*inf*), to be off one's rocker (*inf*)

Ha|se ['haːzə] M -n, -n hare; (*männlich auch*) buck; (*dial: = Kaninchen, Osterhase, in Märchen*) rabbit; **falscher ~** (*Cook*) meat loaf; **wissen/sehen, wie der ~ läuft** (*fig inf*) to know/see which way the wind blows; **alter ~** (*fig inf*) old hand; **da liegt der ~ im Pfeffer** (*inf*) that's the crux of the matter; **mein Name ist ~(, ich weiß von nichts)** I don't know anything about anything

Ha|sel [haːzl] F -, -n (*dated*) hazel

Ha|sel-: Ha|sel|huhn NT hazel grouse; **Ha|sel|kätz|chen** NT (*Bot*) (hazel) catkin, lamb's tail (*inf*); **Ha|sel|maus** F dormouse; **Ha|sel|nuss** ▲ F hazelnut, cobnut; **Ha|sel|nuss|braun** ▲ ADJ hazel; **ha|sel|nuss|groß** ▲ ADJ hazelnut-sized, the size of a hazelnut pred; **Ha|sel|ru|te** F hazel rod *or* switch; **Ha|sel|strauch** M hazel-bush

Ha|sen-: Ha|sen|bra|ten M roast hare; **Ha|sen|fuß** M **a** hare's foot **b** (*dated inf: = Feigling*) milksop (*dated*); **ha|sen|fü|ßig** ADJ (*dated inf: = feige*) chicken-hearted (*inf*), lily-livered (*inf*); **Ha|sen|herz** NT a hare's heart **b** (*dated inf*: = *Feigling*) milksop (*dated*); **Ha|sen|jagd** F hare-hunt; **auf (die) ~ gehen** to go hunting hares, to go on a hare-hunt; **Ha|sen|klein** [-klain] NT **-s**, *no pl* (*Cook*) jointed hare; **Ha|sen|pa|nier** NT **das ~ ergreifen** (*dated inf*) to turn tail (and run); **Ha|sen|pfef|fer** M (*Cook*) ≈ jugged hare; **ha|sen|rein** ADJ (*Hunt*) *Hund* trained to chase hares only on command; **jd/ etw ist nicht (ganz) ~** (*inf*) sb/sth is not (quite) above board, there's something fishy about sb/ sth (*inf*); **das ist alles ~** (*inf*) everything's above board; **Ha|sen|rü|cken** M (*Cook*) saddle of hare; **Ha|sen|schar|te** F (*Med*) harelip

Hä|sin ['hɛːzɪn] F **-, -nen** doe, female hare

Has|pel ['haspl] F **-, -n** a (= *Förderwinde*) windlass **b** (= *Garnhaspel*) reel

has|peln ['haspln] VT a (*inf*: = *hastig sprechen*) to splutter, to sputter; *Gebete, Entschuldigung* to sp(l)utter out **b** (= *wickeln*) to wind up, to reel up; (= *abwickeln*) to unwind, to reel off VI (*inf*) to splutter, to sputter

Hass ▲ [has] M **-es**, *no pl* a hatred, hate (*auf +acc, gegen* of); **Liebe und ~** love and hate *or* hatred; **sich** (*dat*) **jds ~ zuziehen, jds ~ auf sich** (*acc*) **ziehen** to incur sb's hatred **b** (*inf*: = *Wut, Ärger*) **wenn ich so etwas sehe, könnt ich einen ~ kriegen** (*inf*) when I see something like that I could get really angry; **einen ~ (auf jdn) schieben** (*inf*) *or* **haben** (*inf*) to be really sore (with sb) (*inf*)

Hass- ▲: **Hass|aus|bruch** ▲ M burst of hatred; **Hass|brief** ▲ N hate letter; **-e** *pl* (*als Sammelbegriff*) hatemail *no pl*

has|sen ['hasn] ⊘ 34.3 VT to hate, to detest, to loathe; **etw ~ wie die Pest** (*inf*) to detest sth VI to hate

has|sens|wert ADJ hateful, odious, detestable

Hass-: **hass|er|füllt** ▲ [-ɛɐfʏlt] ADJ, ADV full of hate *or* hatred; **Hass|ge|fühl** ▲ NT feeling of hatred

häss|lich ▲ ['hɛslɪç] ADJ a (= *scheußlich*) ugly; **~ wie die Nacht** *or* **die Sünde** (as) ugly as sin **b** (= *gemein*) nasty, mean; **das war ~ von ihm** that was nasty *or* mean of him **c** (= *unerfreulich*) nasty; *Vorfall, Streit* nasty, ugly ADV a (= *gemein*) **sich ~ benehmen** to be mean *or* nasty; **über jdn sprechen** to say nasty *or* mean things about sb **b** (= *nicht schön*) hideously; **~ zugerichtet sein** to be in a hideous state *or* condition; **~ grün/braun/gelb** a hideous green/ brown/yellow

Häss|lich|keit ▲ F **-, -en** a *no pl* (= *Scheußlichkeit*) ugliness **b** (= *Gemeinheit, Unfreundlichkeit*) nastiness **c** (*Bemerkung*) nasty *or* mean remark

Hass-: **Hass|lie|be** ▲ F love-hate relationship (*für* with); **~ für jdn empfinden** to have a love-hate relationship with sb; **Hass|ob|jekt** ▲ NT (object of) hate; **sein bevorzugtes ~** his pet hate; **Hass|ti|ra|de** ▲ F tirade of hatred; **hass|ver|zerrt** ▲ [-fɛɐtsert] ADJ *Gesicht* twisted (up) with hatred

hast [hast] 2. pers sing pres von **haben**

Hast [hast] F **-**, *no pl* haste; **voller ~** in great haste, in a great hurry *or* rush; **ohne ~** without haste, without hurrying *or* rushing; **mit fliegender/rasender ~** in a tearing/frantic hurry; **mit einer solchen ~** in such a hurry *or* rush, in such haste; **nur keine (jüdische) ~!** not so fast!, hold your horses! (*inf*)

has|te ['hastə] (*inf*) *contr von* **hast du (was) ~ was kannste** as quick *or* fast as possible; **~ was, bis|te was** (*prov*) money brings status

has|ten ['hastn] VI *aux sein* (*geh*) to hasten (*form*), to hurry

has|tig ['hastɪç] ADJ hasty; *Essen auch, Worte* hurried, rushed; **sein ~es Rauchen** his hasty way of smoking ADV hastily; **etw ~ tun** to do sth hastily; **nicht so ~!** not so fast!; **er schlang sein Essen ~ hinunter** he gobbled down his food

Has|tig|keit F **-**, *no pl* hurriedness; **sie isst/ schwimmt** *etc* **mit einer solchen ~** she eats/ swims *etc* in such a hasty manner

hat [hat] 3. pers sing pres von **haben**

Ha|tha-Yo|ga ['haːta-] NT hatha yoga

Hät|sche|lei [hɛtʃəˈlai] F **-, -en** (*pej*) pampering, mollycoddling

Hät|schel|kind NT (*pej*) (= *Kind*) pampered child; (*fig*: = *Liebling*) blue-eyed boy/girl (*Brit inf*), golden-haired boy/girl (*US inf*), darling

hät|scheln ['hɛtʃln] VT (= *zu weich behandeln*) to pamper, to mollycoddle; (= *bevorzugen*) to pamper, to indulge; *Industrie, Firma* to give preferential treatment to

hat|schen ['haːtʃn] VI *aux sein* (*Aus, S Ger*: *inf*) (= *schlendern*) to amble along; (= *mühsam gehen*) to trudge along; (= *hinken*) to hobble; **durch die Berge ~** to trudge through the mountains

hat|schert ['haːtʃɛt] ADJ (*Aus inf*) hobbling; **er geht ~** he hobbles (along)

hat|schi [haˈtʃiː, ˈhatʃi] INTERJ atishoo (*Brit*), achoo; **~ machen** (*baby-talk*) to sneeze

hat|te *pret von* **haben**

Hat|trick ['hɛttrɪk] M (*Sport*) hat-trick; (*fig*) masterstroke

Hatz [hats] F **-, -en** a (*Hunt, fig*) hunt **b** (*fig*: *esp S Ger, Aus*) rush

Hau [hau] M **-s, -e** (*inf*) bash (*inf*), clout (*inf*); **einen ~ haben** to be thick (*inf*)

Häub|chen ['hɔypçən] NT **-s, -** *dim von* **Haube**

Hau|be ['haubə] F **-, -n** a bonnet; (*Aus, S Ger*: = *Mütze*) (woollen) cap; (*von Krankenschwester etc*) cap; **jdn unter die ~ bringen** (*hum*) to marry sb off; **unter der ~ sein** (*hum*) to be married; **unter die ~ kommen** (*hum*) to get married **b** (*bei Vögeln*) crest **c** (*allgemein*: = *Bedeckung*) cover; (= *Trockenhaube*) (hair) dryer, drying hood (*US*); (*für Kaffee-, Teekanne*) cosy (*Brit*), cozy (*US*); (= *Motorhaube*) bonnet, hood (*US*); **der hat einiges unter der ~** (*inf*: *Wagen*) it's got quite some engine (*inf*)

Hauben-: **Hau|ben|ler|che** F crested lark; **Hau|ben|mei|se** F crested tit; **Hau|ben|tau|cher** M (*Zool*) great crested grebe

Hau|bit|ze [hauˈbitsə] F **-, -n** howitzer

Hauch [haux] M **-(e)s, -e** a (*geh*: = *Atem*) breath; (= *Luftzug*) breath of air, breeze **b** (= *Duft*) smell; (*von Parfüm*) smell, waft; **ein ~ von Frühling** (*poet*) a breath of spring **c** (= *Flair*) aura, air; **ihr Haus hat den ~ des Exotischen** their house has an exotic air (about it) *or* an aura of exoticism **d** (= *Andeutung, Anflug*) hint, touch; (*von Lächeln*) hint, ghost

hauch|dünn ADJ extremely thin; *Scheiben, Schokoladentäfelchen* wafer-thin; *Strümpfe, Strumpfhose* sheer; (*fig*) *Mehrheit* extremely narrow; *Sieg* extremely close ADV **das Make-up ~ auftragen** to apply a thin layer of foundation; **etw ~ schneiden** to cut sth paper-thin *or* wafer-thin

hau|chen ['hauxn] VI to breathe; **gegen/auf etw** (*acc*) **~** to breathe on sth VT (*lit, fig, liter*: = *flüstern*) to breathe; **jdn einen Kuss auf die Wange ~** (*liter*) to brush sb's cheek with one's lips; **das Jawort ~** (*liter*) to breathe "I will"; **jdm etw** (*acc*) **ins Ohr ~** (*liter*) to whisper sth in sb's ear; **er hauchte mir den Zigarettenrauch ins Gesicht** he blew cigarette smoke in(to) my face

Hauch-: **hauch|fein** ADJ extremely fine; **Hauch|laut** M (*Phon*) aspirate; **hauch|zart** ADJ very delicate; *Schokoladentäfelchen* wafer-thin

Hau|de|gen M (*fig*) old campaigner, (old) warhorse

Haue ['hauə] F **-, -n** a (*S Ger, Sw, Aus*) (= *Pickel*) pickaxe (*Brit*), pickax (*US*), pick; (= *Gartenhacke*) hoe **b** *no pl* (*inf*: = *Prügel*) (good) hiding (*inf*) *or* spanking; **~ kriegen** to get a good hiding (*inf*) *or* spanking

hau|en ['hauən] *pret* **haute** ['hautə], *ptp* **gehauen** *or* (*dial*) **gehaut** [gəˈhauən, gəˈhaut] VT a *pret*

auch hieb [hiːp] (*inf*: = *schlagen*) to hit, to clout (*inf*), to clobber (*inf*); **er haute den Stein in zwei Teile** he smashed the stone in two; **er haute ihr das Heft um die Ohren** he hit *or* clouted (*inf*) *or* clobbered (*inf*) her round (*Brit*) *or* around the head with the exercise book **b** (*inf*: = *verprügeln*) to hit, to belt (*inf*), to thump (*inf*); **hau(t) ihn!** let him have it! (*inf*), belt *or* thump him (one) (*inf*) **c** (= *meißeln*) *Statue, Figur* to carve; *Stufen* to cut, to hew (*form*); *Loch* to cut, to knock **d** *pret* **hieb** [hiːp] (*inf*: *mit Waffe schlagen*) to make a thrust at sb; **jdn aus dem Sattel/vom Pferd ~** to knock sb out of the saddle/from his horse **e** (*inf*: = *stoßen*) *jdn, Gegenstand* to shove (*inf*); *Körperteil* to bang, to knock (*an +acc* on, a- gainst); **das haut einen vom Stuhl** *or* **aus den Latschen** *or* **aus dem Anzug** it really knocks you sideways (*inf*) **f** (*inf*) (= *werfen*) to chuck (*inf*), to fling; *Farbe* to slap (*inf*) (*auf +acc* on); **er hat ihm eine 6 ins Zeugnis gehauen** he slammed a 6 on his report (*Brit*) *or* report card (*US*) (*inf*) **g** (*dial*) (= *fällen*) *Baum* to chop (down), to hew (down); (= *zerhacken*) *Holz, Fleisch* to chop (up) **h** (*Min*) *Erz* to cut; *Kohle* to break

VI a *pret auch* **hieb** [hiːp] (*inf*: = *schlagen*) to hit; **jdm ins Gesicht ~** to hit *or* clout (*inf*) *or* clobber (*inf*) sb in the face; **jdm auf die Schulter ~** to clap *or* slap sb on the shoulder; **hau doch nicht so (auf die Tasten)** don't thump like that; **er haute und haute** he banged *or* thumped away **b** (*inf*: = *prügeln*) **nicht ~, Papi!** don't hit *or* thump (*inf*) me, daddy!; **er haut immer gleich** he's quick to lash out **c** *pret* **hieb** [hiːp] (*geh*: *mit Waffe*) to lash out; **er hieb mit dem Degen (auf seinen Gegner)** he made a thrust (at his opponent) with his dagger; **es geht auf Hauen und Stechen** (*fig*) there's a tough battle **d** *aux sein* (*inf*: = *stoßen*) to bang, to hit; **er ist mit dem Fuß gegen einen spitzen Stein gehauen** he banged *or* hit his foot against a sharp stone

VR (*inf*) a (= *sich prügeln*) to scrap, to fight; **sich mit jdm ~** to scrap *or* fight with sb **b** (= *sich setzen, legen*) to fling oneself

Hau|er¹ ['hauɐ] M **-s, -** (*Zool*) tusk; (*hum*: = *großer Zahn*) fang

Hau|er² ['hauɐ] M **-s, -**, **Häu|e|rin** [-ərɪn] F **-, -nen** a (*Min*) face worker (*Brit*), miner **b** (*Aus*: = *Winzer*) wine-grower

Häu|er ['hɔyɐ] M **-s, -**, **Häu|e|rin** [-ərɪn] F **-, -nen** (*Aus Min*) face worker (*Brit*), miner

Hau|e|rei [hauəˈrai] F **-, -en** (*inf*) scrap, fight

Häuf|chen ['hɔyfçən] NT **-s, -** *dim von* **Haufen** small heap *or* pile; **ein ~ Unglück** a picture of misery → **Elend**

Hau|fe ['haufə] M **-ns, -n** (*rare*) = **Haufen**

häu|feln ['hɔyfln] VT a *Kartoffeln, Spargel* to hill up **b** (= *Haufen machen aus*) to heap *or* pile up

Hau|fen ['haufn] M **-s, -** a heap, pile; **jdn/ein Tier über den ~ rennen/fahren** *etc* (*inf*) to knock *or* run sb/an animal down, to run over sb/an animal; **jdn/ein Tier über den ~ schießen** (*inf*) *or* **knallen** (*inf*) to shoot sb/an animal down; **etw** (*acc*) **über den ~ werfen** *or* **schmeißen** (*inf*) (= *verwerfen*) to throw *or* chuck (*inf*) sth out; (= *durchkreuzen*) to mess sth up (*inf*); **der Hund hat da einen ~ gemacht** the dog has made a mess there (*inf*); **so viel Dummköpfe/ so viel Idiotie/so viel Geld habe ich noch nie auf einem ~ gesehen** (*inf*) I've never seen so many fools/so much idiocy/so much money in one place before **b** (*inf*: = *große Menge*) load (*inf*), heap (*inf*); **ein ~ Arbeit/Geld/Bücher** a load *or* heap of work/money/books, piles *or* loads *or* heaps of work/money/books (*all inf*); **ein ~ Unsinn** a load of (old) rubbish (*inf*), a load of nonsense (*inf*); **ein ~ Zeit** loads *or* heaps of time (*both inf*); **ich hab noch einen ~ zu tun** I still have loads *or* piles *or* heaps *or* a load to do (*all inf*); **in ~** by the ton (*inf*); **er hat einen ganzen ~ Freunde** he has a whole load of friends (*inf*), he has loads *or* heaps of friends (*both inf*)

  c (= *Schar*) crowd; (*von Vögeln*) flock; (= *Sternenhaufen*) cluster of stars; **ein ~ Schaulustige(r)** a crowd of onlookers; **dichte ~ von Reisenden** dense crowds of travellers (*Brit*) *or* travelers (*US*); **dem ~ folgen** (*pej*) to follow the crowd; **der große ~** (*pej*) the common herd, the masses *pl*

  d (= *Gruppe, Gemeinschaft*) crowd (*inf*), bunch (*inf*); (*Mil*) troop

häu|fen ['hɔyfn] 🔲 **VT** to pile up, to heap up; (= *sammeln*) to accumulate; **Bücher auf den Tisch ~** to pile books onto the table; **Lob auf jdn ~** (*fig*) to heap praise(s) (up)on sb → *auch* **gehäuft** 🔲 **VR** (*lit, fig* = *sich ansammeln*) to mount up; (= *zahlreicher werden: Unfälle, Fehler, Fachausdrücke etc*) to occur increasingly often; **das kann schon mal vorkommen, es darf sich nur nicht ~** these things happen, just as long as they don't happen too often

Hau|fen-: **Hau|fen|dorf** NT scattered village; **hau|fen|wei|se** ADV **a** (= *in Haufen*) in heaps *or* piles **b** (*inf*: = *in großer Zahl, Menge*) piles *or* heaps *or* loads of (*all inf*); **etw ~ haben** to have piles *or* heaps *or* loads of sth (*all inf*); **Hau|fen|wol|ke** F cumulus (cloud)

häu|fig ['hɔyfɪç] 🔲 **ADJ** frequent; (= *weit verbreitet auch*) common, widespread; **seine Anfälle werden ~er** his attacks are becoming more frequent 🔲 **ADV** often, frequently

Häu|fig|keit F -, -en frequency; (= *räumliche Verbreitung*) commonness

Häu|fig|keits- *in cpds* frequency-; **Häu|fig|keits|grad** M frequency rank; **Häu|fig|keits|wör|ter|buch** NT frequency dictionary; **Häu|fig|keits|zahl** F , **Häu|fig|keits|zif|fer** 🔲 frequency

Häu|fung ['hɔyfʊŋ] F -, -en **a** (*fig*: = *das Anhäufen*) accumulation, amassment **b** (= *das Sichhäufen*) increasing number; **in ähnlicher ~** in similar numbers *pl*

Haupt [haupt] NT -(e)s, Häupter ['hɔyptɐ] **a** (*geh*: = *Kopf*) head; **entblößten ~es** bareheaded; **gesenkten/erhobenen ~es** with one's head bowed/raised; **zu jds Häupten** at sb's head; **jdn aufs ~ schlagen** (*fig*: = *besiegen*) to vanquish sb; **eine Reform an ~ und Gliedern** a total *or* wide-reaching reform **b** (= *zentrale Figur*) head **c** (*poet: von Berg*) peak

Haupt- *in cpds* main, principal, chief; **Haupt|ab|neh|mer(in)** M(F) (*Comm*) biggest *or* main buyer; **Haupt|ach|se** F main *or* principal axis; (*von Fahrzeug*) main axle; **Haupt|ak|teur(in)** M(F) (*lit, fig*) leading light; (*pej*) kingpin; **Haupt|ak|ti|on** F → **Haupt- und Staatsaktion**; **Haupt|ak|ti|o|när(in)** M(F) principal *or* main shareholder; **Haupt|ak|zent** M **a** (*Ling*) main *or* primary accent *or* stress **b** (*fig*) main emphasis; **auf etw** (*acc*) **den ~ legen** to put *or* place the main emphasis on sth; **Haupt|al|tar** M high altar; **haupt|amt|lich** 🔲 **ADJ** full-time; **~e Tätigkeit** full-time office 🔲 **ADV** (on a) full-time (basis); **~ tätig sein** to work full-time; **Haupt|an|ge|klag|te(r)** MF *decl as adj* main *or* principal defendant; **Haupt|an|schluss** ▲ M (*Telec*) main extension; **nur einen ~ haben** to have a phone without extensions; **Haupt|an|teil** M main *or* principal part *or* share; **Haupt|ar|beit** F main (part of the) work; **Haupt|at|trak|ti|on** F main *or* chief attraction; (*bei Veranstaltung etc*) big draw (*inf*); **Haupt|aus|gang** M main exit; **Haupt|bahn|hof** M main *or* central station; **Haupt|be|las|tungs|zeu|ge** M , **Haupt|be|las|tungs|zeu|gin** F main *or* principal witness for the prosecution; **Haupt|be|ruf** M chief *or* main occupation *or* profession; **er ist Lehrer im ~** his main *or* chief occupation *or* profession is that of

teacher; **haupt|be|ruf|lich** 🔲 **ADJ** *Lehrer, Gärtner etc* full-time; **~e Tätigkeit** main *or* chief occupation 🔲 **ADV** full-time; **~ tätig sein** to be employed full-time, to be in full-time employment; **er ist ~ bei dieser Firma tätig** (= *voll angestellt*) he is employed full-time by this firm; (*im Gegensatz zu Nebenerwerb*) his main employment is at this firm; **Haupt|be|schäf|ti|gung** F **a** main *or* chief occupation *or* pursuit **b** (= *Hauptberuf*) main *or* chief occupation *or* job; **Haupt|be|stand|teil** M main constituent; (*Tech*) main component; **Haupt|be|trieb** M **a** (= *Zentralbetrieb*) headquarters *sing or pl* **b** (= *geschäftigste Zeit*) peak period; (= *Hauptverkehrszeit*) rush hour; **Haupt|buch** NT (*Comm*) ledger; **Haupt|bü|ro** NT head office; **Haupt|dar|stel|ler** M principal actor, leading man; **Haupt|dar|stel|le|rin** F principal actress, leading lady; **Haupt|da|ten** PL main facts *pl*; **Haupt|deck** NT main deck; **Haupt|ein|gang** M main entrance; **Haupt|ein|kaufs|zeit** F main shopping hours *pl*; **Haupt|ein|nah|me|quel|le** F main *or* chief source of income; **Haupt|ein|wand** M main *or* chief *or* principal objection (*gegen* to)

Häup|tel ['hɔyptl] NT -s, - (*Aus*) head (of lettuce *etc*)

Häup|tel|sa|lat M (*Aus*) lettuce

Haupt-: **Haupt|ent|las|tungs|zeu|ge** M , **Haupt|ent|las|tungs|zeu|gin** F main *or* principal witness for the defence (*Brit*) *or* defense (*US*); **Haupt|er|be¹** M principal heir; **Haupt|er|be²** NT principal inheritance; **Haupt|er|bin** F principal heir(ess); **Haupt|er|eig|nis** NT main *or* principal event

Haup|tes|län|ge F **jdn um ~ überragen** (*lit, fig*) to be head and shoulders above sb

Haupt-: **Haupt|fach** NT (*Sch, Univ*) main *or* principal subject, major (*US*); **etw im ~ studieren** to study sth as one's main *or* principal subject, to major in (*US*); **Haupt|feh|ler** M main *or* chief *or* principal fault; **Haupt|feind(in)** M(F) main *or* chief enemy; **Haupt|feld¹** ['hauptfɛlt] NT (*bei Rennen*) (main) pack; **Haupt|feld²** ['hauptfɛlt] M -s, -s (*sl*), **Haupt|feld|we|bel(in)** M(F) (company) sergeant major; **Haupt|fi|gur** F (*Liter*) central *or* main *or* principal character *or* figure; (*fig*) leading *or* central figure; **Haupt|film** M main film; **Haupt|for|de|rung** F main *or* chief *or* principal demand; **Haupt|fra|ge** F main *or* principal question *or* issue; **Haupt|gang** M **a** (*Archit etc*) main corridor; (*in Kirche, Theater, Kino*) central aisle **b** (*Cook*) main course; **Haupt|ge|bäu|de** NT main building; **Haupt|ge|dan|ke** M main idea; **Haupt|ge|frei|te(r)** MF *decl as adj* ≈ lance corporal (*Brit*), ≈ private first class (*US*); **Haupt|ge|gen|stand** M **a** main *or* chief topic, main subject **b** (*Aus Sch*) = **Hauptfach**; **Haupt|ge|richt** NT main course

Haupt|ge|schäft NT **a** (= *Zentrale*) head office, headquarters *sing or pl* **b** (= *Hauptverdienst*) main business, major part of one's business

Haupt|ge|schäfts-: **Haupt|ge|schäfts|stel|le** F head office, headquarters *sing or pl*; **Haupt|ge|schäfts|stra|ße** F main shopping street; **Haupt|ge|schäfts|zeit** F peak (shopping) period *or* hours *pl*

Haupt-: **Haupt|ge|sichts|punkt** M main *or* major consideration; **Haupt|ge|sprächs|the|ma** NT main topic of conversation, conversation topic number one; **Haupt|ge|wicht** NT (*lit*) major part of the weight, bulk of the weight; (*fig*) main emphasis; **Haupt|ge|winn** M first prize; **Haupt|grund** M main *or* principal *or* chief reason; **Haupt|haar** NT (*geh*) hair (of the/one's head); **Haupt|hahn** M mains cock *or* tap (*Brit*); **Haupt|hand|lung** F (*Liter etc*) main plot; **Haupt|in|te|res|se** NT main *or* chief interest; **Haupt|kampf|li|nie** F main front; **Haupt|kenn|zei|chen** NT main feature, chief *or* principal characteristic; **Haupt-**

klä|ger(in) M(F) principal plaintiff; **Haupt|last** F main load, major part of the load; (*fig*) main *or* major burden; **Haupt|leid|tra|gen|de(r)** MF *decl as adj* main victim; **die ~n** *pl* the ones to suffer most, the ones who suffer/suffered *etc* most; **Haupt|lei|tung** F mains *pl*; **Haupt|leu|te** *pl von* **Hauptmann a**; **Haupt|lie|fe|rant(in)** M(F) main *or* principal *or* chief supplier

Häupt|ling ['hɔyptlɪŋ] M -s, -e chief(tain); (*esp von Dorf*) headman; (*fig, inf:* = *Boss*) chief (*inf*)

häupt|lings ['hɔyptlɪŋs] ADV (*old, geh*) = **kopfüber**

Haupt-: **Haupt|macht** F (*Mil*) bulk *or* main body of its/the forces; **Haupt|mahl|zeit** F main meal; **Haupt|man|gel** M main deficiency, main *or* principal defect; **Haupt|mann** M *pl* **-leute a** (*Mil*) captain **b** (*Hist:* = *Führer*) leader; **Haupt|mas|se** F bulk, main body; **Haupt|me|nü** NT (*Comput*) main menu; **Haupt|merk|mal** NT main feature, chief *or* principal characteristic; **Haupt|mie|ter(in)** M(F) main tenant; **Haupt|mo|tiv** NT **a** (= *Beweggrund*) primary *or* main motive **b** (*Art, Liter, Mus*) main *or* principal motif; **Haupt|nah|rung** F staple *or* principal food, staple diet; **Haupt|nah|rungs|mit|tel** NT staple *or* principal food; **Haupt|nen|ner** M (*Math, fig*) common denominator; **Haupt|nie|der|las|sung** F head office, headquarters *sing or pl*; **Haupt|per|son** F (*lit, fig*) central figure; **Haupt|pla|ti|ne** F (*Comput*) motherboard; **Haupt|por|tal** NT main portal *or* doorway; **Haupt|post** F (*inf*), **Haupt|post|amt** NT main post office; **Haupt|pro|be** F final rehearsal; (= *Kostümprobe*) dress rehearsal; **Haupt|prob|lem** NT main *or* chief *or* principal problem; **Haupt|pro|dukt** NT main product; (*esp im Gegensatz zu Nebenprodukt*) primary product; **Haupt|pro|zes|sor** M (*Comput*) main processor; **Haupt|quar|tier** NT (*Mil, fig*) headquarters *sing or pl*; **Haupt|quel|le** F (*lit, fig*) main *or* primary source; **Haupt|rech|ner** M (*Comput*) mainframe (computer); **Haupt|rech|nungs|art** F (*Math*) basic arithmetical operation; **Haupt|red|ner(in)** M(F) main *or* principal speaker; **Haupt|re|fe|rent(in)** M(F) main *or* principal speaker; **Haupt|rei|se|zeit** F peak travelling (*Brit*) *or* traveling (*US*) time(s *pl*); **Haupt|rohr** NT (*von Gas-/Wasserleitung*) main pipe, mains pipe; **Haupt|rol|le** F (*Film, Theat*) leading *or* main role *or* part, lead; **die ~ spielen** (*fig*) to be all-important; (= *wichtigste Person sein*) to play the main role *or* part; **Haupt|run|de** F (*Sport*) main round; **Haupt|sa|che** F main thing; (*in Brief, Rede etc*) main point; **in der ~** in the main, mainly; **~, es klappt/du bist glücklich** the main thing is that it comes off/you're happy; **haupt|säch|lich** 🔲 **ADV** mainly, chiefly, principally 🔲 **ADJ** main, chief, principal; **Haupt|sai|son** F peak *or* high season; **~ haben** to have its/their peak season; **Haupt|satz** M **a** (*Gram*) (*übergeordnet*) main clause; (*alleinstehend*) sentence **b** (*Mus*) first *or* main subject **c** (*Philos*) main proposition; **Haupt|schal|ter** M (*Elec*) main *or* master switch; **Haupt|schiff** NT (*Archit*) nave; **Haupt|schlag|ader** F aorta; **Haupt|schlüs|sel** M master key; **Haupt|schul|ab|schluss** ▲ M **den ~ haben** ≈ to have completed secondary school *or* junior high (school) (*US*); **Haupt|schuld** F main blame, principal fault (*esp Jur*); **Haupt|schul|di|ge(r)** MF *decl as adj* person mainly to blame *or* at fault, main offender (*esp Jur*); **er ist der ~** he is mainly to blame *or* at fault, he is the main offender (*esp Jur*); **Haupt|schu|le** F ≈ secondary school, ≈ junior high (school) (*US*); **Haupt|schü|ler(in)** M(F) ≈ secondary school *or* junior high (school) (*US*) pupil; **Haupt|schul|leh|rer(in)** M(F) ≈ secondary school *or* junior high (school) (*US*) teacher

---

HAUPTSCHULE

A **Hauptschule** caters for the last five years (or three years after an **Orientierungsstufe**) of the compulsory nine years at school in Germany. Subsequently pupils can add on a tenth continuation year and, if their marks are good enough, obtain a **qualifizierter Hauptschulabschluss**, known colloquially as a **Quali**, which gives them a better chance in the job market and also entitles them to attend a **Fachoberschule**.

In Austria a **Hauptschule** covers school years five to eight and also offers opportunities for young people who wish to go on to higher education. In Switzerland compulsory schooling is covered by a **Volksschule** → ORIENTIE-RUNGSSTUFE

Haupt-: Haupt|schwie|rig|keit F main or chief or principal difficulty; **Haupt|se|gel** NT mainsail; **Haupt|se|mi|nar** NT (*Univ*) seminar for advanced students; **Haupt|sen|de|zeit** F (*TV*) peak viewing hours *pl*, prime time; **Haupt|si|che|rung** F (*Elec*) main fuse; **Haupt|sitz** M head office, headquarters *sing or pl*; **Haupt|sor|ge** F main or chief worry; **Haupt|spei|cher** M (*Comput*) main memory; **Haupt|stadt** F capital (city); **Haupt|städt|er(in)** M(F) citizen of the capital, metropolitan; **haupt|städ|tisch** ADJ metropolitan, of the capital (city); **Haupt|stoß|rich|tung** F (*Mil, fig*) main object of one's/the attack (*gegen* on); **Haupt|straße** F (= *Durchgangsstraße*) main or major road; (*im Stadtzentrum etc*) main street; **Haupt|stre|cke** F (*Rail*) main line; (= *Straße*) main or primary (*Admin*) route; **Haupt|streit|punkt** M (*fig*) main issue or point of contention; **Haupt|strö|mung** F (*lit, fig*) main current; **Haupt|stu|di|um** NT (*Univ*) main course (of studies); **Haupt|stüt|ze** F (*fig*) mainstay, main support or prop; **Haupt|sün|de** F (*Rel*) cardinal sin; **Haupt|tä|ter(in)** M(F) main or chief or principal culprit; **Haupt|tä|tig|keit** F main or principal or chief activity; (*beruflich*) main occupation; **Haupt|teil** M main part; (= *größter Teil auch*) major part; **Haupt|the|ma** NT main or principal topic; (*Mus, Liter*) main or principal theme; **Haupt|ton** M *pl* **-töne** (*Ling*) main or primary stress; (*Mus*) principal note; **Haupt|tref|fer** M top prize, jackpot (*inf*); **den ~ machen** (*inf*) to win the top prize, to hit the jackpot (*inf*); **Haupt|trep|pe** F main staircase or stairs *pl*; **Haupt|tri|bü|ne** F main stand; (*Sport auch*) grandstand; **Haupt|tu|gend** F cardinal virtue; **Haupt- und Staats|ak|ti|on** F **aus etw eine ~ machen** to make a great issue of sth, to make a song and dance about sth (*inf*), to make a Federal case out of sth (*US inf*); **Haupt|un|ter|schied** M main or principal difference; **Haupt|ur|sa|che** F main or chief or principal cause; **Haupt|ver|ant|wort|li|che(r)** MF *decl as adj* person mainly or chiefly responsible; **Haupt|ver|ant|wor|tung** F main responsibility; **Haupt|ver|die|ner(in)** M(F) main or principal earner; **Haupt|ver|dienst¹** M main income; **Haupt|ver|dienst²** NT chief merit; **Haupt|ver|fah|ren** NT (*Jur*) main proceedings *pl*; **Haupt|ver|hand|lung** F (*Jur*) main hearing

Haupt|ver|kehr M peak(-hour) traffic; (= *Verkehrsteilnehmer*) main traffic, bulk of the traffic

Haupt|ver|kehrs-: Haupt|ver|kehrs|ader F main highway (*US*), arterial route; **Haupt|ver|kehrs|stra|ße** F (*in Stadt*) main street; (= *Durchgangsstraße*) main thoroughfare; (*zwischen Städten*) main highway, trunk road (*Brit*); **Haupt|ver|kehrs|zeit** F peak traffic times *pl*; (*in Stadt, bei Pendlern auch*) rush hour

Haupt-: Haupt|ver|le|sen NT **-s, -** (*Sw Mil*) roll call; **Haupt|ver|samm|lung** F general meeting; **Haupt|ver|wal|tung** F head office, headquarters *sing or pl*; **Haupt|ver|zeich|nis** NT

(*Comput*) root directory; **Haupt|wa|che** F main police station; **Haupt|wä|sche** F, **Haupt|wasch|gang** M main wash; **Haupt|werk** NT a (*Art etc*) main or principal work b (= *Fabrik*) main factory or works *sing or pl*; **Haupt|wohn|sitz** M main place of residence, main domicile (*form*); **Haupt|wort** NT *pl* **-wör|ter** (*Gram*) noun; **haupt|wört|lich** ADJ (*Gram*) nominal; **Haupt|zeit** F (= *Hauptsaison*) peak times *pl*; (*in Bezug auf Obst etc*) main season; **Haupt|zeu|ge** M, **Haupt|zeu|gin** F principal or main or chief witness; **Haupt|ziel** NT main or principal aim or goal; **Haupt|zoll|amt** NT main customs office; **Haupt|zug** M a (*Rail*) scheduled train b *usu pl* (= *Charakteristikum*) main or principal feature, chief characteristic; **Haupt|zweck** M main or chief purpose or object

hau ruck [ˈhau ˈrʊk] INTERJ heave-ho
Hau|ruck [hauˈrʊk] NT **-s, -s** heave
Hau|ruck|ver|fah|ren NT **etw im ~ tun** to do sth in a great hurry

---

Haus [haus] **-es, Häuser** [ˈhɔyzɐ]

SUBSTANTIV (NT)

a = Gebäude house; **er war nicht im Haus, sondern im Garten** he wasn't indoors or in the house but in the garden; **Tomaten kann man im Haus ziehen** tomatoes can be grown indoors or in the house; **lass uns ins Haus gehen** let's go inside or into the house; **der Klavierlehrer kommt ins Haus** the piano teacher comes to the house; **aus dem Haus gehen** to leave the house; **mit jdm Haus an Haus wohnen** to live next door to sb; **wir wohnen Haus an Haus** we live next door to each other; **von Haus zu Haus gehen** to go from door to door or from house to house; **das Haus Gottes** or **des Herrn** (*geh*) the House of God or of the Lord; **Haus der Jugend** youth centre (*Brit*) or center (*US*); **das (gemeinsame) europäische Haus** the (common) European house

b = Zuhause, Heim home; **Haus und Hof** or **Herd verlassen** to leave one's home (behind), to leave house and home; **Haus und Hof verspielen** to gamble away the roof over one's head; **Haus und Hof verlieren** to lose the roof over one's head; **etw ins Haus liefern** to deliver sth to the door; **wir liefern frei Haus** we offer free delivery; **ein großes Haus führen** (*fig*) to entertain lavishly or in style; **jdm das Haus führen** to keep house for sb; **jdm das Haus verbieten** not to allow sb in the house; **aus dem Haus sein** to be away from home; **außer Haus essen** to eat out; **im Hause meiner Schwester** at my sister's (house); **er hat nichts zu essen im Haus** he has no food in the house; **jdn ins Haus nehmen** to take sb in(to one's home); **ein Fernsehgerät kommt mir nicht ins Haus!** I won't have a television set in the house!; **ins Haus stehen** (*fig*) to be on the way; **jdm steht etw ins Haus** (*fig*) sb is facing sth; **Grüße von Haus zu Haus** (*form*) regards from ourselves to you all; **Haus halten** = haushalten

♦ **nach Hause** or (*Aus, Sw*) **nachhause** (*lit, fig*) home; **jdn nach Hause bringen** to take or see sb home; **jdn nach Hause schicken** (*lit*) to send sb home; (*fig inf*) to send sb packing (*inf*)

♦ **zu Hause** or (*Aus, Sw*) **zuhause** at home; **Borussia hat zu Hause 3:1 gewonnen** Borussia have won 3-1 at home; **bei jdm zu Hause** in sb's house; **bei uns zu Hause** at home; **wie gehts zu Hause?** how are things at home?; **von zu Hause aus** from home; **heute bin ich für niemanden zu Hause** I'm not at home to anybody today; **irgendwo zu Hause sein** (*Mensch, Tier*) to live somewhere; (= *sich heimisch fühlen*) to feel at home somewhere; **dieser Brauch ist in Polen zu Hause** this custom comes from Poland; **in etw** (*dat*) **zu Hause sein** (*fig*) to be well up in sth; **sich wie zu Hause fühlen** to feel at home; **fühl dich wie zu Hause!** make yourself at

home!; **damit kannst du zu Hause bleiben** (*fig inf*) **bleib doch damit zu Hause** (*fig inf*) you can keep it/them *etc* (*inf*)

c = Unternehmen House (*form*); **das Haus Siemens** (*geh*) the House of Siemens; „**Haus Talblick**" "Talblick (House)"; **das erste Haus am Platze** (*geh*) (= *Hotel*) the best hotel in town; (= *Kaufhaus*) the best store in town; **ein gut geführtes Haus** (*geh*: = *Restaurant etc*) a well-run house; **er ist nicht im Hause** (= *in der Firma*) he's not in the building, he's not in; **in unserem Hause dulden wir keine Drogen/keinen Alkohol** (= *in unserer Firma*) we do not allow drugs/alcohol on the premises

d = Bewohnerschaft eines Hauses household; **der Herr des Hauses** (*form*) the head of the household; **ein Freund des Hauses** a friend of the family; **die Dame/Tochter** *etc* **des Hauses** (*form*) the lady/daughter *etc* of the house

e = Herkunft (*geh*) **aus gutem/bürgerlichem Haus(e)** from a good/middle-class family; **aus adligem Haus(e)** of noble birth, of or from a noble house (*form*); **von Hause aus** (= *ursprünglich*) originally; (= *von Natur aus*) naturally

f = Dynastie House; **das Haus Windsor** the House of Windsor; **das Haus Habsburg** the Hapsburg dynasty; **aus dem Haus Davids** of the House of David

g = Theater theatre (*Brit*), theater (*US*); (= *Saal, Publikum*) house; **die große/kleine Haus** the large or main/small theatre (*Brit*) or theater (*US*); **vor vollem Haus spielen** to play to a full house

h Parl House; **Hohes Haus!** (*form*) ≈ honourable (*Brit*) or honorable (*US*) members (of the House)!; **dieses hohe Haus ...** the or this House ...

i von Schnecke shell, house (*inf*)

j Astrol house

k = Kerl (*dated*) *inf* chap (*Brit inf*), fellow; **grüß dich Hans, (du) altes Haus!** (*inf*) hello Hans, old chap (*Brit inf*) or buddy (*esp US inf*)

Haus-: Haus|al|tar M family or house altar; **Haus|an|dacht** F family worship; **Haus|an|ge|stell|te(r)** MF *decl as adj* domestic servant; (*esp Frau*) domestic; **Haus|an|ten|ne** F roof aerial (*Brit*) or antenna (*US*); **Haus|an|zug** M leisure suit; **Haus|apo|the|ke** F medicine cupboard or chest; **Haus|ar|beit** F a housework *no pl* b (*Sch*) homework *no indef art, no pl*, piece of homework, assignment (*esp US*); **Haus|ar|rest** M (*im Internat*) detention; (*Jur*) house arrest; **~ haben** to be in detention/under house arrest; **Fritz kann nicht zum Spielen rauskommen, er hat ~** Fritz can't come out to play - he's grounded or being kept in; **Haus|arzt** M, **Haus|ärz|tin** F family doctor, GP; (*von Heim, Anstalt*) resident doctor; **Haus|auf|ga|be** F (*Sch*) homework *sing, no indef art*; **seine ~n machen** (*auch fig*) to do one's homework; **Haus|auf|ga|ben|be|treu|ung** F, **Haus|auf|ga|ben|über|wa|chung** F (*Sch*) homework supervision; **Haus|auf|satz** M (*Sch*) homework essay, essay for homework; **haus|ba|cken** [ˈhausbakn] ADJ (*fig*) homespun, drab, homely (*US*); *Kleidung* unadventurous; **Haus|ball** M (*private*) ball or dance; **Haus|bank** F *pl* **-banken** bank; **Haus|bar** F home bar; (= *Möbelstück*) cocktail or drinks cabinet; **Haus|bau** M a *pl* **-bauten** house building or construction b *no pl* (= *das Bauen*) building of a/the house; **Haus|berg** M (*einer Stadt*) local mountain; (= *beliebtester Berg*) favourite (*Brit*) or favorite (*US*) mountain; (*eines Sportlers*) home slopes *pl*; **Haus|be|set|zer(in)** M(F) squatter; **Haus|be|set|zung** F squatting; (*Einzug*) moving into a squat; **Haus|be|sitz** M house ownership; **~ haben** to own a house/houses; **Haus|be|sit|zer** M homeowner, house-owner; (= *Hauswirt*) landlord; **Haus|be|sit|ze|rin** F homeowner, house-owner; (= *Hauswirtin*) landlady; **Haus|be|sor|ger(in)** M(F) (*Aus*) caretaker, janitor; **Haus|be|such** M home visit; **Haus|be|woh|ner(in)** M(F)

(house) occupant or occupier; **Haus|bib|li|o|thek** F library; **Haus|bock** M (Zool) house longhorn; **Haus|boot** NT houseboat; **Haus|brand** M ▲ a house fire b (= Brennstoff) domestic or heating fuel; **Haus|brief|kas|ten** M letter box (Brit), mailbox (US); **Haus|bur|sche** M pageboy, bellboy (US), bellhop (US)

Häus|chen ['hɔysçən] NT **-s, -** ▲ dim von **Haus** b (fig inf) **ganz aus dem ~ sein vor ...** to be out of one's mind with ... (inf); **ganz aus dem ~ geraten** to go berserk (inf); **jdn (ganz) aus dem ~ bringen** to make sb go berserk (inf) c (inf: = Karo) square, block d (euph inf: = Toilette) loo (Brit inf), bathroom (US), smallest room (Brit hum inf); (= außerhalb des Gebäudes) privy, outside loo (Brit inf), outhouse (US)

Haus-: Haus|da|me F housekeeper; **Haus|de|tek|tiv(in)** M(F) house detective; (von Kaufhaus) store detective; **Haus|die|ner(in)** M(F) (in Hotel) house servant; (= Gepäckträger) (hotel) porter; **Haus|dra|chen** M (inf) dragon (inf), battle-axe (Brit inf), battle-ax (US inf); **Haus|durch|su|chung** F (Aus) = **Haussuchung**; **haus|ei|gen** ADJ belonging to a/the hotel/firm etc; **Haus|ei|gen|tü|mer(in)** M(F) homeowner; **Haus|ein|fahrt** F (Aus), **Haus|ein|gang** M (house) entrance

Häu|sel ['hɔyzl] NT **-s, -** (Aus, dial) = **Häuschen a, d**

hau|sen ['hauzn] VI ▲ a (= wohnen) to live b (= wüten) **(übel** or **schlimm) ~** to wreak or create havoc; **schrecklich ~** to wreak the most dreadful havoc; **wie die Wandalen ~** to act like vandals c (Sw, S Ger: = sparsam sein) to be economical

Hau|sen ['hauzn] M **-s, -** (Zool) sturgeon

Häu|ser ['hɔyze] M **-s, -**, **Häu|se|rin** [-ərɪn] F **-, -nen** (Aus, S Ger: = Haushälter) housekeeper

Häu|ser-: Häu|ser|block M pl **-blocks** or (rare) **-blöcke** block (of houses); **Häu|ser|flucht** F row of houses; **Häu|ser|front** F front of a terrace, front of a row of houses

Häu|se|rin F **-, -nen** (Aus, S Ger: = Haushälterin) housekeeper

Häu|ser-: Häu|ser|kampf M (Mil) house-to-house fighting; (Pol) squatting actions pl; (= einzelner Fall) squat(ting action); **Häu|ser|mak|ler(in)** M(F) estate agent (Brit), realtor (US); **Häu|ser|meer** NT mass of houses; **Häu|ser|reihe** F row of houses; (aneinandergebaut) terrace; **Häu|ser|schlucht** F **die ~en New Yorks** the urban jungle of New York; **Häu|ser|zei|le** F = **Häuserreihe**

Haus-: Haus|flag|ge F (Naut) house flag; **Haus|flur** M (entrance) hall, hallway

Haus|frau F ▲ a housewife; (= Gastgeberin) hostess b (Aus, S Ger: = Hauswirtin) landlady

Haus|frau|en-: Haus|frau|en|art F **Wurst etc nach ~** home-made-style sausage etc; **Haus|frau|en|bri|ga|de** F (DDR) housewives' brigade; **Haus|frau|en|da|sein** NT life of a housewife; **das ~ satt haben** to be fed up of being (just) a housewife; **Haus|frau|en|pflicht** F housewifely duty

Haus-: haus|frau|lich ADJ housewifely; **Haus|freund** M ▲ a (= Freund der Familie) friend of the family b (euph inf) man friend; **Haus|freun|din** F (= Freundin der Familie) friend of the family; **Haus|frie|de(n)** M domestic peace; **Haus|frie|dens|bruch** M (Jur) trespass (in sb's house); **Haus|gans** F (domestic) goose; **Haus|gast** M (von Pension etc) resident, guest; **Haus|ge|brauch** M **für den ~** (Gerät) for domestic or household use; Obst-, Gemüseanbau for one's own consumption; **sein Französisch reicht für den ~** (inf) his French is (good) enough to get by (on); **Haus|ge|burt** F home birth; **Haus|ge|hil|fe** M , **Haus|ge|hil|fin** F home help; **Haus|geist** M ▲ a household spirit; (= Gespenst) household ghost b (hum: = Hausangestellter) faithful retainer (old, hum); **haus|ge|macht** ADJ home-made; (fig) Problem

etc of one's own making; **Haus|ge|mein|schaft** F household (community); **mit jdm in ~ leben** to live together with sb (in the same household); **Haus|ge|nos|se** M , **Haus|ge|nos|sin** F fellow tenant; **Haus|göt|ter** PL (Myth) household gods pl

Haus|halt ['haushalt] M **-(e)s, -e** ▲ a (= Hausgemeinschaft) household; (= Haushaltsführung) housekeeping; **Geräte für den ~** household utensils; **den ~ führen** to run the household; **jdm den ~ führen** to keep house for sb b (fig: Biol etc) balance c (= Etat) budget

Haus|halt- in cpds = **Haushalts-**

haus+hal|ten ['haushaltn] VI sep irreg ▲ a (= sparsam wirtschaften) to be economical; **mit etw ~** (mit Geld, Zeit) to be economical with sth, to use sth economically; **mit Kräften, Vorräten** auch to conserve sth b (= den Haushalt führen) to keep house

Haus|häl|ter ['haushɛltɐ] M **-s, -**, **Haus|häl|te|rin** [-ərɪn] F **-, -nen**, **Haus|hal|ter(in)** M(F) housekeeper

haus|häl|te|risch ['haushɛltərɪʃ] ADJ thrifty, economical ADV thriftily, economically; **mit etw ~ umgehen** = **haushalten a**

Haus|halts- in cpds household; (Pol) budget; **Haus|halts|ar|ti|kel** M household item or article; **Haus|halts|buch** NT housekeeping book; **(ein) ~ führen** to keep a housekeeping book; **Haus|halts|de|bat|te** F (Parl) budget debate; **Haus|halts|de|fi|zit** NT (Pol) budget deficit; **Haus|halts|ent|wurf** M (Pol) draft budget, budget proposals pl; **Haus|halts|fra|gen** PL (Pol) budgetary questions pl; **Haus|halts|füh|rung** F housekeeping; **doppelte ~** running two homes; **Haus|halts|geld** NT housekeeping money; **Haus|halts|ge|rät** NT household appliance; **Haus|halts|hil|fe** F domestic or home help; **Haus|halts|jahr** NT (Pol, Econ) financial or fiscal year; **Haus|halts|kas|se** F household or family budget; **Haus|halts|loch** NT budget deficit; **das ~ stopfen** to cure current budget shortfalls; **Haus|halts|mit|tel** PL (Pol) budgetary funds pl; **Haus|halts|pa|ckung** F family pack; **Haus|halts|plan** M (Pol) budget; **Haus|halts|pla|nung** F (Pol) budgetary planning, planning of a budget; **Haus|halts|po|li|tik** F (Pol) budgetary policy; **haus|halts|po|li|tisch** ADJ concerning budgetary policy; Sprecher, Ausschuss on budgetary policy ADV **die Regierung hat ~ versagt** the government has failed in its budgetary policy; **Haus|halts|vor|stand** M (form: = Verantwortlicher in einem privaten Haushalt) head of a/the household; **Haus|halts|waa|ge** F kitchen scales pl; **Haus|halts|wa|ren** PL household goods pl

Haus|hal|tung F ▲ a (= das Haushaltführen) housekeeping, household management; (= das Sparsamsein) economizing (mit with) b (form: = Haushalt) household

Haus|hal|tungs-: Haus|hal|tungs|buch NT housekeeping book; **Haus|hal|tungs|kos|ten** PL household or housekeeping expenses pl; **Haus|hal|tungs|vor|stand** M (form) head of the household

Haus-: Haus|herr M ▲ a head of the household; (= Gastgeber, Sport) host b (Jur) householder c (Aus, S Ger: = Hausbesitzer) homeowner, house-owner; (= Hauswirt) landlord; **Haus|her|rin** F ▲ a lady of the house; (= Gastgeberin) hostess b (Aus, S Ger: = Hausbesitzerin) homeowner, house-owner; (= Hauswirtin) landlady; **haus|hoch** ADJ (as) high as a house/houses; (fig) Sieg crushing; **der haushohe Favorit** the hot favourite (Brit inf) or favorite (US inf) ADV high (in the sky); **jdn ~ schlagen** to give sb a hammering (inf) or thrashing (inf); **~ gewinnen** to win hands down, to win by miles (inf); **jdm ~ überlegen sein** to be head and shoulders above sb; **Haus|huhn** NT domestic fowl

hau|sie|ren [hau'ziːrən] ptp **hausiert** VI to hawk, to peddle (mit etw sth); **mit etw ~ gehen** (fig, mit Plänen etc) to hawk sth about; **mit Gerüchten** to peddle sth; **„Hausieren verboten"** "no hawkers or peddlers"

Hau|sie|rer [hau'ziːrɐ] M **-s, -**, **Hau|sie|re|rin** [-ərɪn] F **-, -nen** hawker, peddler, pedlar (Brit)

haus|in|tern ADJ = **firmenintern**

Hau|sis ['hauzɪs] PL (inf: = Hausaufgaben) homework

Haus-: Haus|ja|cke F house jacket; **Haus|ju|rist(in)** M(F) company lawyer; **Haus|ka|nin|chen** NT domestic rabbit; **Haus|ka|pel|le** F ▲ a (Rel) private chapel b (= Musikkapelle) resident band; (an Fürstenhof) resident or private orchestra; **Haus|kat|ze** F domestic cat; **Haus|kauf** M house-buying no art, house purchase; **Haus|kleid** NT housecoat; **Haus|kon|zert** NT family concert; **Haus|kor|rek|tur** F (Typ) proofreading (carried out by the publishers)

Häus|le|bau|er ['hɔyslǝbauɐ] M **-s, -** sing rare (inf) private developer

Haus-: Haus|leh|rer(in) M(F) (private) tutor; **Haus|leu|te** PL ▲ a (dial inf: = Wirtsleute) landlord and landlady b (S Ger, Sw: = Bewohner) tenants pl

häus|lich ['hɔyslɪç] ADJ Angelegenheiten, Pflichten, Friede, Umfeld domestic; Pflege home attr; (= der Familie gehörend) family attr; (= an häuslichen Dingen interessiert) domesticated; (= das Zuhause liebend) home-loving; **der ~e Herd** the family home ADV **sich ~ niederlassen** to make oneself at home; **sich ~ einrichten** to settle in

Häus|lich|keit F **-**, no pl domesticity

Haus|ma|cher-: Haus|ma|cher|art F **Wurst etc nach ~** home-made-style sausage etc; **Haus|ma|cher|kost** F home cooking; **Haus|ma|cher|wurst** F home-made sausage

Haus-: Haus|macht F (Hist) allodium; (fig) power base; **Haus|mäd|chen** NT (house-)maid; **Haus|mann** M pl **-männer** (= den Haushalt versorgender Mann) househusband; **Haus|manns|kost** F plain cooking or fare; (fig) plain fare; **Haus|man|tel** M housecoat; **Haus|mär|chen** NT folk tale; **„Haus- und Kindermärchen"** "Fairy Tales"; **Haus|mar|ke** F (= eigene Marke) own brand or label; (= bevorzugte Marke) favourite (Brit) or favorite (US) brand; **Haus|maus** F house mouse; **Haus|meis|ter** M ▲ a caretaker, janitor b (dated Sw: = Hausbesitzer) house-owner; **Haus|mit|tei|lung** F internal memo; **Haus|mit|tel** NT household remedy; **Haus|müll** M domestic rubbish (Brit) or garbage (US), domestic refuse; **Haus|mu|sik** F music at home, family music; **Haus|mut|ter** F pl **-mütter** (von Herberge etc) housemother; **Haus|müt|ter|chen** NT (hum) little mother; (pej) housewife, wife and mother; **Haus|num|mer** F street or house number; **Haus|ord|nung** F house rules pl or regulations pl; **Haus|par|tei** F tenant; (Aus) household; **Haus|post** F internal or in-house mail; **Haus|pos|til|le** [-pɔstɪlǝ] F **-, -n** (old) collection of instructional reading for the family; (fig) manual; **Haus|putz** M house cleaning; **Haus|rat** M , no pl household equipment or goods pl; **Haus|rat|ver|si|che|rung** F (household) contents insurance; **Haus|recht** NT right(s pl) as a householder (to forbid sb entrance); **von seinem ~ Gebrauch machen** to show sb the door, to tell sb to leave; **Haus|rind** NT domestic cattle pl; **Haus|samm|lung** F house-to-house or door-to-door collection; **Haus|schlach|ten** NT **-s**, no pl, **Haus|schlach|tung** F home slaughtering; **Haus|schlüs|sel** M front-door key, house key; **Haus|schuh** M slipper; **Haus|schwamm** M dry rot; **Haus|schwein** NT domestic pig

Hausse ['(h)oːs(ǝ)] F **-, -n** (Econ: = Aufschwung) boom (an +dat in); (St Ex: = Kurssteigerung) bull market; **~ haben** (St Ex) to rise on the Stock Exchange; **wenn man ~ hat, ...** (St Ex) when there's a bull market ...; **auf ~ spekulieren** (*St Ex*) to bull

Haus|se|gen M house blessing *or* benediction; **bei ihnen hängt der ~ schief** (*hum*) they're a bit short on domestic bliss (*inf*)

Hausse|spe|ku|la|ti|on ['(h)o:sə-] F (*St Ex*) bull speculation

Haus|si|er [(h)o'sie:] M **-s, -s** (*St Ex*) bull

Haus-: Haus|stand M household, home; **einen ~ gründen** to set up house *or* home; **Haus|su|chung** [-zu:xʊŋ] F **-, -en** (*in einem Haus*) house search; (*in mehreren Häusern*) house-to-house search; **Haus|su|chungs|be|fehl** M search warrant; **Haus|te|le|fon** NT internal telephone; **Haus|tier** NT domestic animal; (*aus Liebhaberei gehalten*) pet; **Haus|toch|ter** F lady's help; **Haus|trau|ung** F wedding at home; **Haus|tür** F front door; **gleich vor der ~** (*fig inf*) on one's doorstep; **Haus|tür|ge|schäft** NT door-to-door sales *pl*; **Haus|ty|rann(in)** M(F) (*inf*) domestic *or* household tyrant; **Haus|va|ter** M (*von Herberge etc*) housefather; **Haus|ver|bot** NT ban on entering the house; **jdm ~ erteilen** to bar *or* ban sb from the house, to forbid sb to enter the house; **in einem Lokal/bei jdm ~ haben** to be barred *or* banned from a pub (*Brit*) *or* bar/sb's house; **Haus|ver|samm|lung** F house meeting; **Haus|ver|wal|ter(in)** M(F) (house) supervisor; **Haus|ver|wal|tung** F property *or* house management; **Haus|wap|pen** NT family coat of arms; **Haus|wart** [-vart] M **-(e)s, -e**, **Haus|war|tin** F **-, -nen** caretaker, janitor; **Haus|wirt** M landlord; **Haus|wir|tin** F landlady

Haus|wirt|schaft F **a** (= *Haushaltsführung*) housekeeping **b** (*Sch*) home economics *sing*, domestic science (*esp Brit old*)

haus|wirt|schaft|lich ADJ domestic; **ein ~er Kurs** a course on home economics *or* domestic science (*esp Brit old*); **die ~e Versorgung von Patienten** taking care of the housework in patients' homes; **~ interessiert** interested in domestic matters

Haus|wirt|schafts-: Haus|wirt|schafts|leh|re F (*Sch*) home economics *sing*, domestic science (*esp Brit old*); **Haus|wirt|schafts|leh|rer(in)** M(F) home economics teacher, domestic science teacher (*esp Brit old*); **Haus|wirt|schafts|schu|le** F school of home economics *or* domestic science (*esp Brit old*)

Haus-: Haus|wurf|sen|dung F (house-to--house) circular; **Haus|zei|tung** F , **Haus|zeit|schrift** F company magazine; **Haus|zelt** NT frame tent; **Haus|zent|ra|le** F (*Telec*) (internal) switchboard

Haus-zu-Haus-: Haus-zu-Haus-Trans|port M , **Haus-zu-Haus-Ver|kehr** M (*Rail etc*) door-to-door service

Haut [haut] F **-, Häute** ['hɔytə] skin; (*dick, esp von größerem Tier*) hide; (= *geschälte Schale von Obst etc*) peel; (*inf*: = *Mensch*) sort (*inf*); **nass bis auf die ~** soaked to the skin; **nur ~ und Knochen sein** to be only *or* nothing but skin and bones; **viel ~ zeigen** (*hum*) to show all one's got (*hum*), to show a lot (of bare skin); **mit ~ und Haar(en)** (*inf*) completely, totally; **er ist ihr mit ~ und Haar(en) verfallen** (*inf*) he's head over heels in love with her, he's fallen for her hook, line and sinker (*inf*); **das geht** *or* **dringt unter die ~** that gets under one's skin; **in seiner ~ möchte ich nicht stecken** I wouldn't like to be in his shoes; **er fühlt sich nicht wohl in seiner ~** (*inf*) **ihm ist nicht wohl in seiner ~** (*inf*) (= *unglücklich, unzufrieden*) he's (feeling) rather unsettled; (= *unbehaglich*) he feels uneasy *or* uncomfortable; **er kann nicht aus seiner ~ heraus** (*inf*) he can't change the way he is, a leopard can't change its spots (*prov*); **aus der ~ fahren** (*inf*) (*aus Ungeduld*) to work oneself up into a sweat (*inf*); (*aus Wut*) to go through the roof (*inf*), to hit the ceiling (*inf*); **das ist zum Aus-der-Haut-Fahren!** it's enough to drive you up the wall (*inf*) *or* round the bend (*Brit inf*); **auf der faulen ~ lie-**

gen (*inf*) **sich auf die faule ~ legen** (*inf*) to sit back and do nothing, not to lift a finger (*inf*); **seine ~ zu Markte tragen** (= *sich in Gefahr begeben*) to risk one's neck *or* hide (*inf*); (*euph*: *Frau*) to sell one's charms; **seine eigene ~ retten** to save one's (own) skin; (*esp vor Prügel*) to save one's (own) hide (*inf*); **sich seiner ~ wehren** to defend oneself vigorously; **seine ~ so teuer wie möglich verkaufen** (*inf*) to sell oneself as dearly as possible → **ehrlich** ADJ

Haut- *in cpds* skin; **Haut|ab|schür|fung** F graze; **Haut|arzt** M , **Haut|ärz|tin** F skin specialist, dermatologist; **Haut|at|mung** F cutaneous respiration; **die ~ verhindern** to stop the skin from breathing; **Haut|aus|schlag** M (skin) rash *or* eruption (*form*)

Häut|chen ['hɔytçən] NT **-s, -** *dim von* **Haut** (*auf Flüssigkeit*) skin; (*Anat, Bot*) membrane; (*an Fingernägeln*) cuticle

hau|te *pret von* **hauen**

Haute Cou|ture [(h)o:t ku'ty:ɐ] F **- -, *no pl*** haute couture

häu|ten ['hɔytn] VT *Tiere* to skin VR (*Tier*) to shed its skin; (*Schlange auch*) to slough (its skin); (*hum*: *Mensch*) to peel

haut|eng ADJ skintight

Haute|vo|lee [(h)o:tvo'le:] F **-, *no pl*** upper crust

Haut-: Haut|fal|te F skin fold; **Haut|far|be** F skin colour (*Brit*) *or* color (*US*); **nur, weil er eine andere ~ hat** just because his skin is a different colo(u)r; **haut|far|ben** [-farbn] ADJ flesh-coloured (*Brit*), flesh-colored (*US*); **Haut|flüg|ler** [-fly:glɐ] M **-s, -** hymenopter (-on); **haut|freund|lich** ADJ *Stoff, Kleidung* kind to one's *or* the skin; **~es Heftpflaster** micropore tape

-häu|tig [hɔytɪç] ADJ *suf* -skinned; **dunkelhäutig** dark-skinned

Haut-: Haut|ju|cken NT **-s, *no pl*** itching; **eine Creme gegen ~** a cream for skin irritations; **Haut|kli|nik** F dermatology clinic, skin clinic; **Haut|kon|takt** M skin contact; **Haut|krank|heit** F skin disease; **Haut|krebs** M (*Med*) skin cancer; **haut|nah** ADJ **a** (*Anat*) close to the skin **b** (= *sehr eng, Sport*) (very) close **c** (*fig inf*: = *wirklichkeitsnah*) *Kontakt* (very) close; *Problem* that affects us/him *etc* directly; *Darstellung, Schilderung* deeply affecting ADV **a** (= *eng*) **~ tanzen** to dance very close(ly); ~ **in Kontakt mit jdm/etw kommen** to come into (very) close contact with sb/sth **b** (*inf*: = *direkt*) *darstellen, schildern* realistically; **etw ~ erleben** to experience sth at close quarters; **Haut|pfle|ge** F skin care; **Haut|pfle|ge|mit|tel** NT skin--care product; **Haut|pilz** M (*Med*) fungal skin infection, dermatophyte (*spec*); **haut|scho|nend** ADJ kind to the skin; *Spülmittel auch* kind to the hands; **Haut|spe|zi|a|list(in)** M(F) skin specialist, dermatologist; **Haut|trans|plan|ta|ti|on** F (= *Operation*) skin graft; (= *Verfahren*) skin grafting; **Haut|typ** M skin type; **was für ein ~ ist sie?** what's her skin type?

Häu|tung ['hɔytʊŋ] F **-, -en** skinning; (*von Schlange*) sloughing; **verschiedene ~en durchmachen** to slough several skins

Haut-: haut|ver|träg|lich ADJ non-irritating, hypoallergenic, kind to the skin *pred*; **Haut|wun|de** F superficial *or* skin wound

Ha|van|na(zi|gar|re) [ha'vana-] F **-, -s** Havana (cigar)

Ha|va|rie [hava'ri:] F **-, -n** [-'ri:ən] **a** (*Naut, Aviat*) (= *Unfall*) accident; (= *Schaden*) average (*spec*), damage *no indef art, no pl* **b** (= *Kraftfahrzeugunfall*) accident; (= *Kraftfahrzeugschaden*) damage *no indef art, no pl*

ha|va|rie|ren [hava'ri:rən] *ptp* **havariert** VI **a** (*Schiff*) to be damaged **b** (*Aus*: *Fahrzeug*) to crash

ha|va|riert [hava'ri:ɐt] ADJ *Schiff, Kraftwerk* damaged

Ha|va|rist¹ [hava'rɪst] M **-en, -en** (= *Schiff*) damaged ship

Ha|va|rist² [hava'rɪst] M **-en, -en**, **Ha|va|ris|tin** [-'rɪstɪn] F **-, -nen** (= *Reeder*) owner of a/the damaged ship

Ha|waii [ha'vaii, ha'vai] NT **-s** Hawaii

Ha|wai|i|a|ner [havaii'ia:nɐ] M **-s, -**, **Ha|wai|i|a|ne|rin** [-ərɪn] F **-, -nen** Hawaiian

Ha|wai|i|gi|tar|re [ha'vaii-, ha'vai-] F Hawaiian guitar

ha|wai|isch [ha'vaiiʃ] ADJ Hawaiian

Ha|xe ['haksə] F **-, -n** (*Cook*) leg (joint); (*S Ger inf*) (= *Fuß*) foot, plate of meat (*Brit inf*); (= *Bein*) leg; **„Haxen abkratzen!"** (*hum inf*) "wipe your feet!"

Hbf *abbr von* **Hauptbahnhof**

H-Bom|be ['ha:-] F H-bomb

h. c. [ha:'tse:] *abbr von* **honoris causa**

HD [ha:'de:] *abbr* **a** (*Comput*) *von* **High Density** **b** (*Sw*) *von* **Hilfsdienst**

HD-Dis|ket|te [ha:'de:-] F (*Comput*) HD diskette

he [he:] INTERJ hey; (*fragend*) eh

Head|hun|ter ['hɛdhantɐ] M **-s, -**, **Head|hun|te|rin** [-ərɪn] F **-, -nen** head-hunter

Hea|ring ['hiːrɪŋ] NT **-(s), -s** hearing

hea|vy ['hɛvi] ADJ *pred* (*sl*) **a** (= *schwierig*) heavy (*inf*); **das war einfach zu ~ für sie** (*Erlebnis etc*) it was simply too much for her to take **b** (= *unerhört*) beyond belief

Hea|vy|me|tal ▲ ['hɛvi'mɛtl] NT **-, *no pl*** (*Mus*) heavy metal

Heb|am|me ['he:p|amə, 'he:bamə] F **-, -n** midwife

He|be-: He|be|bal|ken M , **He|be|baum** M lever; **He|be|bock** M (*hydraulic*) jack; **He|be|büh|ne** F hydraulic ramp

He|bel ['he:bl] M **-s, -** **a** (*Phys*, = *Griff*) lever; (*an Maschinen*) handle, lever; (*fig*) leverage; **den ~ ansetzen** to position the lever; (*fig*) to tackle it, to set about it; **den ~ an der richtigen Stelle ansetzen** (*fig*) to set about *or* tackle it in the right way; **alle ~ in Bewegung setzen** (*inf*) to move heaven and earth; **am längeren ~ sitzen** (*inf*) to have the whip hand **b** (*Sport*: = *Hebelgriff*) lever hold

He|bel-: He|bel|arm M (lever) arm; **He|bel|griff** M (*Sport*) lever hold; **He|bel|kraft** F , **He|bel|wir|kung** F leverage

he|ben ['he:bn] *pret* **hob** [ho:p], *ptp* **gehoben** [gə'ho:bn] VT **a** (= *nach oben bewegen*) to lift, to raise; *Augenbraue, Kamera, Fernglas* to raise; **die Stimme ~** (= *lauter sprechen*) to raise one's voice, to speak up; (= *höher sprechen*) to raise one's/the pitch; **die Hand gegen jdn ~** (*geh*) to raise one's hand against sb; **die Faust gegen jdn ~** (*geh*) to shake one's fist at sb; **einen ~ gehen** (*inf*) to go for a drink; **er hebt gern einen** (*inf*) he likes *or* enjoys a drink → *auch* **gehoben** **b** (= *nach oben befördern, hochheben*) to lift; *Wrack* to raise, to bring up; *Schatz* to dig up; (*Sport*) *Gewicht* to lift; **er hob das Kind auf die Mauer/vom Baum** he lifted the child (up) onto the wall/ (down) from the tree; **jdn auf die Schultern ~** to hoist *or* lift sb onto one's shoulders; **den Ball in den Strafraum/ins Tor ~** to lob the ball into the penalty area/goal; **heb deine Füße!** pick your feet up! **c** (= *verbessern*) *Farbe* to bring out, to enhance; *Selbstbewusstsein, Effekt* to heighten; *Ertrag* to increase; *Geschäft* to increase, to boost; *Stimmung, Wohlstand* to improve; *Niveau* to raise, to increase; *jds Ansehen* to boost, to enhance; **jds Stimmung ~** to cheer sb up; **das hebt den Mut** that boosts *or* raises one's morale **d** (*S Ger*: = *halten*) to hold VR **a** (= *sich nach oben bewegen*) to rise; (*Vorhang*) to go up, to rise; (*Nebel, Deckel*) to lift; **sich ~ und senken** (*Schiff*) to rise and fall; (*Busen*) to heave **b** (*geh*: = *emporragen*) to tower up, to rise up

c (= *sich bessern*) (*Stimmung, Konjunktur, Handel*) to improve; **da hob sich seine Stimmung** that cheered him up

d (*S Ger: = sich halten*) to hold on (*an +dat* to) **VT** *impers* **es hebt jdn** (*inf*) sb feels sick; **es hebt mir den Magen** (*inf*) sb feels sick; **es hebt mich** *or* **es hebt mir den Magen, wenn ich das sehe** (*inf*) seeing that makes me feel sick *or* turns my stomach (*inf*)

VI **a** (*Sport*) to do weightlifting

b (*S Ger: = haltbar sein*) to hold; (*Nahrungsmittel*) to keep

He|ber[1] ['heːbɐ] M **-s, -** **a** (*Chem*) pipette **b** (*Tech*) (hydraulic) jack

He|ber[2] M **-s, -** (*Ftbl: inf*) lob

He|ber[3] ['heːbɐ] M **-s, -**, **He|be|rin** [-ərɪn] F **-, -nen** (*Sport: = Gewichtheber*) weightlifter

He|be|satz M (*Fin*) rate of assessment

Heb|rä|er [he'brɛːɐ] M **-s, -**, **Heb|rä|e|rin** [-ərɪn] F **-, -nen** Hebrew

heb|rä|isch [he'brɛːɪʃ] ADJ Hebrew

Heb|rä|isch(e) [he'brɛːɪʃ] NT Hebrew → *auch* **Deutsch(e)**

Heb|ri|den [he'briːdn] PL **die ~** the Hebrides *pl*

He|bung ['heːbʊŋ] F **-, -en** **a** (*von Schatz, Wrack etc*) recovery, raising **b** (*Geol*) elevation, rise (in the ground) **c** *no pl* (*fig: = Verbesserung*) improvement; (*von Effekt, Selbstbewusstsein*) heightening; (*von Lebensstandard, Niveau*) rise; **seine Fröhlichkeit trug zur ~ der gedrückten Stimmung bei** his cheerfulness helped to relieve the subdued mood **d** (*Poet*) stressed *or* accented syllable

he|cheln ['heçln] **VT** *Flachs, Hanf* to hatchel, to heckle **VI** **a** (*inf: = lästern*) to gossip **b** (= *keuchen*) to pant

Hecht [heçt] M **-(e)s, -e** (*Zool*) pike; (*inf: = Bursche*) chap (*inf*), bloke (*Brit inf*), guy (*inf*); **das ist ein ~** (*inf*) he's some guy (*inf*), he's quite a guy (*inf*); **er ist (wie) ein ~ im Karpfenteich** (*fig*) (= *sehr aktiv*) he certainly shakes people up; (= *sorgt für Unruhe*) he's a stirrer (*inf*)

hech|ten ['heçtn] **VI** *aux sein* (*inf*) to dive, to make a (headlong) dive; (*beim Schwimmen*) to do a racing dive; (*beim Turnen*) to do a forward dive

Hecht-: Hecht|rol|le F (*Sport*) dive roll; **Hecht|sprung** M (*beim Schwimmen*) racing dive; (*beim Turnen*) forward dive; (*Ftbl inf*) (headlong *or* full-length) dive; **Hecht|sup|pe** F **es zieht wie ~** (*inf*) it's blowing a gale (in here) (*inf*), there's a terrible draught (*Brit*) *or* draft (*US*)

Heck [hɛk] NT **-(e)s, -e** **a** *pl auch* **-s** (*Naut*) stern; (*Aviat*) tail, rear; (*Aut*) rear, back **b** (*N Ger: = Gatter*) gate

Heck|an|trieb M (*Aut*) rear-wheel drive

He|cke ['hɛkə] F **-, -n** hedge; (*am Wegrand*) hedgerow

Hecken-: Hecken|ro|se F dog rose, wild rose; **Hecken|sche|re** F hedge clippers *pl*; **Hecken|schüt|ze** M , **Hecken|schüt|zin** F sniper

Heck-: Heck|fens|ter NT (*Aut*) rear window *or* windscreen (*Brit*) *or* windshield (*US*); **Heck|flos|se** F (*Aut*) tail fin; **Heck|klap|pe** F (*Aut*) tailgate; **heck|las|tig** [-lastɪç] ADJ tail-heavy; **Heck|licht** NT (*Aviat*) tail-light

Heck|meck ['hɛkmɛk] M **-s**, *no pl* (*inf*) (= *dummes Gerede*) nonsense, rubbish (*Brit*); (= *dumme Streiche*) stupid *or* daft (*Brit inf*) things *pl*; (= *Umstände*) fuss, palaver (*inf*); (= *unnötiges Zeug*) rubbish; **mach doch keinen ~** don't be so stupid *or* daft (*Brit inf*)

Heck|mo|tor M (*Aut*) rear engine; **mit ~** rear-engined

Heck|schei|be F (*Aut*) rear windscreen (*Brit*) *or* windshield (*US*)

Heck|schei|ben-: Heck|schei|ben|hei|zung F rear windscreen (*Brit*) *or* windshield (*US*)

---

heater; **Heck|schei|ben|wi|scher** M rear windscreen (*Brit*) *or* windshield (*US*) wiper

Heck-: Heck|schüt|ze M , **Heck|schüt|zin** F rear gunner; **Heck|spoi|ler** M rear spoiler; **Heck|tür** F (*Aut*) tailgate; (*von Lieferwagen*) rear doors *pl*; **Heck|tür|mo|dell** NT hatchback (car); **Heck|wel|le** F (*Naut*) wash *no pl*

he|da ['heːda] INTERJ hey there

He|de|rich ['heːdərɪç] M **-s**, *no pl* (*Bot*) wild radish

Hedge|fonds ['hɛdʒfõ:] M (*Fin*) hedge fund

Hedge|ge|schäft ['hɛdʒ-] NT (*Fin*) hedge transaction

He|do|nis|mus [hedo'nɪsmʊs] M **-**, *no pl* hedonism

he|do|nis|tisch [hedo'nɪstɪʃ] ADJ hedonistic

Heer ['heːɐ] NT **-(e)s, -e** (*lit, fig*) army; **beim ~** in the army; **in das ~ eintreten** to join the army, to enlist in the army

Heer|bann M (*Hist*) levy

Hee|res-: Hee|res|be|richt M military communiqué *or* despatch; **Hee|res|be|stän|de** PL army stores *pl* or supplies *pl*; **Hee|res|dienst** M , *no pl* (*Hist*) military service; **Hee|resdienst|vor|schrift** F army regulations *pl*; **Hee|res|grup|pe** F army group; **Hee|res|leitung** F command; **Hee|res|zug** M (*Hist*) campaign

Heer-: Heer|füh|rer(in) M(F) (*Hist*) army commander; **Heer|la|ger** NT army camp; **der Flughafen glich einem ~** the airport was like a refugee camp; **Heer|schar** F (*liter*) legion, troop; (*fig: = große Menge*) host; **die himmlischen ~en** the heavenly hosts; **Heer|schau** F (*old*) military parade; **Heer|stra|ße** F military road; **Heer|we|sen** NT , *no pl* army

He|fe ['heːfə] F **-, -n** yeast; **die ~ des Volkes** (*geh*) (= *treibende Kraft*) the (driving) force behind the people; (*pej: = Abschaum*) the scum of the earth

He|fe-: He|fe|ge|bäck NT yeast-risen pastry; **He|fe|kranz** M ≈ savarin; **He|fe|ku|chen** M yeast cake; **He|fe|pilz** M yeast plant; **He|festück(chen)** NT *small fruit tart*, ≈ Danish pastry; **He|fe|teig** M yeast dough; **wie ein ~ auseinander gehen** (*inf*) to put on mounds of fat; **He|fe|teil|chen** NT *small fruit tart*, ≈ Danish pastry; **He|fe|zopf** M plaited *or* braided (*US*) yeast bun

Heft[1] [hɛft] NT **-(e)s, -e** (*von Werkzeug, Messer*) handle; (*von Säge, Feile auch*) grip; (*von Dolch, Schwert*) hilt; **das ~ in der Hand haben** (*fig*) to hold the reins, to be at the helm; **das ~ in der Hand behalten** (*fig*) to remain in control *or* at the helm; **das ~ aus der Hand geben** (*fig*) to hand over control *or* the reins; **jdm das ~ aus der Hand nehmen** (*fig*) to seize control from sb; **ich lasse mir nicht das ~ aus der Hand nehmen** nobody's going to take over from me

Heft[2] NT **-(e)s, -e** **a** (= *Schreibheft*) exercise book **b** (= *Zeitschrift*) magazine; (= *Comicheft*) comic; (= *Nummer*) number, issue; **„National Geographic 1998, ~ 3“** "National Geographic 1998, No 3" **c** (= *geheftetes Büchlein*) booklet

Heft|chen ['hɛftçən] NT **-s, -** *dim von* **Heft**[2] **b** (*pej: = billiger Roman*) rubbishy (*Brit*) *or* cheap or pulp novel (*pej*); (= *schlechte Zeitschrift, Comicheftchen*) rag (*pej inf*) **c** (= *Fahrkartenheftchen, Eintrittskartenheftchen*) book(let) of tickets; (= *Briefmarkenheftchen*) book of stamps

hef|ten ['hɛftn] **VT** **a** (= *nähen*) *Saum, Naht* to tack (up), to baste; *Buch* to sew, to stitch; (= *klammern*) to clip (*an +acc* to); (*mit Heftmaschine*) to staple (*an +acc* to)

b (= *befestigen*) to pin, to fix; **er heftete mit Reißzwecken eine Landkarte an die Wand** he pinned a map on the wall; **jdm ein Abzeichen an die Brust ~** to pin a decoration to sb's chest; **den Blick** *or* **die Augen auf jdn/etw ~** to gaze at sb/sth, to fix one's eyes on sb/sth, to stare fixedly at sb/sth

VR **a** (*Blick, Augen*) **sich auf jdn/etw ~** to fix on-

---

to sb/sth

b **sich an jdn ~** to latch on to sb; **sich an jds Spur** *or* **Fährte ~** to follow sb's trail; **sich an jds Fersen** *or* **Sohlen ~** (*fig*) (= *jdn verfolgen*) to dog sb's heels; (*bei Rennen etc*) to stick to sb's heels

Hef|ter ['hɛftɐ] M **-s, -** **a** (loose-leaf) file **b** (= *Heftapparat*) stapler

Heft|fa|den M , **Heft|garn** NT tacking thread

hef|tig ['hɛftɪç] ADJ **a** (= *stark, gewaltig*) violent; *Kopfschmerzen* severe; *Schmerz* intense, acute; *Erkältung* severe; *Fieber* raging, severe; *Zorn, Ärger, Hass* violent, burning *no adv*, intense; *Liebe, Sehnsucht* ardent, burning *no adv*, intense; *Leidenschaft* violent; *Abneigung* intense; *Widerstand* vehement; *Weinen* bitter; *Lachen* uproarious; *Atmen* heavy; *Kontroverse, Kampf, Wind* fierce; *Regen* lashing *no adv*, driving *no adv*, heavy; *Frost* severe, heavy; **ein ~er Regenguss** a downpour

b (= *jähzornig, ungehalten*) *Mensch* violent(-tempered); *Ton* fierce, vehement; *Worte* violent; **~ werden** to fly into a passion

c (*sl: = sehr gut*) wicked (*sl*); **das ist ganz schön ~** (*sl: = unangenehm*) that's a bummer (*sl*) *or* a pisser (*Brit sl*)

ADV *regnen, schneien, zuschlagen* hard; *verprügeln* severely; *aufprallen* with great force, hard; *schütteln, rühren* vigorously; *nicken* emphatically; *zittern* badly; *dementieren, schimpfen* vehemently; *verliebt* passionately, madly (*inf*); **es stürmt/gewittert ~** there is a violent storm/thunderstorm; **sich ~ streiten** to have a violent argument; **der Regen schlug ~ gegen die Scheiben** the rain pounded *or* beat against the windows; **sie knallte die Tür ~ ins Schloss** she slammed *or* banged the door (shut); **er hat ~ dagegen gewettert** he raged vehemently against it

Hef|tig|keit F , *no pl* (= *Stärke, Gewalt*) violence; (*von Kopfschmerzen*) severity; (*von Schmerz*) intensity, acuteness; (*von Widerstand*) vehemence; (*von Liebe, Abneigung*) intensity; (*von Kampf, Wind*) ferocity, fierceness; (*von Regen*) heaviness; (*von Frost*) severity, heaviness

Heft-: Heft|klam|mer F staple; **Heft|ma|schine** F stapler; **Heft|naht** F (*Sew*) basted *or* tacked seam; (*Tech*) tack weld; **Heft|pflas|ter** NT (sticking) plaster, adhesive tape (*US*); **Heft|ro|man** M cheap paperback novel, dime novel (*US*); **Heft|stich** M tacking stitch; **Heft|zwe|cke** F drawing pin (*Brit*), thumb tack (*US*)

He|ge|li|a|ner [heːgə'liaːnɐ] M **-s, -**, **He|ge|lia|ne|rin** [-ərɪn] F **-, -nen** Hegelian

he|ge|li|a|nisch [heːgə'liaːnɪʃ], **he|gelsch** ['heːglʃ] ADJ Hegelian

He|ge|mo|nie [hegemo'niː] F **-, -n** [-'niːən] hegemony

he|gen ['heːgn] **VT** **a** (= *pflegen*) *Wild, Pflanzen* to care for, to tend; (*geh: = umsorgen*) *jdn* to care for, to look after; **jdn ~ und pflegen** to lavish care and attention on sb **b** (= *empfinden, haben*) *Hass, Groll, Verdacht* to harbour (*Brit*), to harbor (*US*); *Misstrauen, Achtung, Abneigung* to feel; *Zweifel* to entertain; *Hoffnung, Wunsch* to cherish; *Plan, Unternehmen* to foster; **ich hege den starken Verdacht, dass ...** I have a strong suspicion that ...; **ich hege schon lange den Plan auszuwandern** for a long time I've been contemplating emigrating

He|ger ['heːgɐ] M **-s, -**, **He|ge|rin** [-ərɪn] F **-, -nen** gamekeeper

Hehl [heːl] NT OR M **kein** *or* **keinen ~ aus etw machen** to make no secret of sth

Heh|ler ['heːlɐ] M **-s, -**, **Heh|le|rin** [-ərɪn] F **-, -nen** receiver (of stolen goods), fence (*inf*); **der ~ ist schlimmer als der Stehler** (*Prov*) it is worse to condone a crime than to commit it

Heh|le|rei [heːlə'rai] F **-, -en** receiving (stolen goods)

hehr [heːɐ] ADJ (*liter*) noble, sublime

hei [hai] INTERJ wow

Heia ['haia] F **-**, *no pl* (*baby-talk*) bye-byes (*Brit baby-talk*), bye-bye (*US baby-talk*), beddy-

---

-byes (*Brit baby-talk*), beddy-bye (*US baby--talk*); **ab in die ~** off to bye-byes *etc*; **in die ~ gehen** to go bye-byes *etc*; **heia machen** to have a little nap *or* sleep

Heia|bett NT (*baby-talk*) beddy-byes (*Brit baby-talk*), beddy-bye (*US baby-talk*)

Heide¹ ['haidə] F **-, -n** a moor, heath; (= *Heideland*) moorland, heathland **b** (= *Heidekraut*) heather

Heide² ['haidə] M **-n, -n, Hei|din** ['haidɪn] F **-, -nen** heathen, pagan; (= *Nichtjude*) Gentile

Heide-: Hei|de|kraut NT heather; **Hei|de|land** NT moorland, heathland

Hei|del|bee|re F bilberry, blueberry (*esp US*)

Hei|del|beer|kraut NT , **Hei|del|beer|strauch** M bilberry *or* blueberry (*esp US*) bush

Heiden-: Hei|den|angst F **eine ~ vor etw** (*dat*) **haben** (*inf*) to be scared stiff of sth (*inf*); **Hei|den|ar|beit** F (*inf*) real slog (*inf*); **Hei|den|geld** NT (*inf*) packet (*Brit inf*), bundle (*US inf*); **Hei|den|krach** M (*inf*), **Hei|den|lärm** M (*inf*) unholy din (*inf*); **hei|den|mä|ßig** (*inf*) ADJ huge, massive ADV incredibly; **~ Geld verdienen** to earn a (real) packet (*Brit inf*) *or* bundle (*US inf*); **Hei|den|mis|si|on** F missionary work among the heathen; **Hei|den|respekt** M (*inf*) healthy respect; **Hei|den|spaß** M (*inf*) terrific fun; **einen ~ haben** to have a whale of a time (*inf*); **das macht ihm einen ~** he finds it terrific fun; **Hei|den|spek|ta|kel** M (*inf*) awful row; (= *Schimpfen*) awful fuss

Hei|den|tum ['haidntu:m] NT **-s**, *no pl* heathenism, heathendom, paganism; **das ~** (= *Menschen*) the heathen *pl*, the pagans *pl*

hei|di [hai'di:, 'haidi] INTERJ **~ ging es den Berg hinab** down the hill they/we *etc* went; **~ (, dann gehts los)** here they/we *etc* go

Hei|din F → **Heide²**

heid|nisch ['haidnɪʃ] ADJ **a** heathen; (*auf Götterkult bezüglich*) pagan ADV like a heathen *or* pagan; **~ denken** to have heathen *or* pagan beliefs; **~ geprägt** characterized by heathen *or* pagan customs; **~ leben** to live a heathen *or* pagan life

Heid|schnu|cke ['hait∫nʊkə] F **-, -n** German moorland sheep

hei|kel ['haikl] ADJ **a** (= *schwierig, gefährlich*) Angelegenheit, Situation, Thema tricky, delicate; Frage awkward, tricky **b** (*dial*) Mensch particular, pernickety (*inf*), persnickety (*US inf*) (*in Bezug auf +acc* about); (= *wählerisch*) fussy, particular; (*in Bezug aufs Essen*) fussy, choosy **c** (*dial*) Stoff, Farbe difficult; **der Stoff ist mir zu ~** that material is too much of a nuisance

heil [hail] ADJ **a** (= *unverletzt*) Mensch unhurt, uninjured; Glieder unbroken; Haut undamaged; **wieder ~ sein/werden** (= *wieder gesund*) to be/get better again; (*Wunde*) to have healed/to heal up; (*Knochen*) to have mended/to mend; **~ machen** (*inf* = *heilen*) to make better; (= *reparieren*) to fix, to mend; **Gott sei Dank sind die Glieder noch ~** thank goodness there are no broken bones; **mit ~en Gliedern** *or* **~ am Ziel ankommen** to reach the finish without breaking any bones; **mit ~er Haut davonkommen** to escape unscathed *or* (*lit auch*) in one piece **b** (*inf*: = *ganz*) intact; Kleidungsstück decent (*inf*); **die Uhr ist wieder ~** the clock's back in working order; **die ~e Welt** an ideal world (*without problems, uncertainties etc*) ADV (= *unverletzt*) all in one piece, safe and sound; (= *unbeschädigt*) in good shape, all in one piece; **~ nach Hause kommen** to get home safe and sound; **etw ~ überstehen** (*Unfall*) to come through sth without a scratch; Prüfung to get through sth

Heil [hail] NT **-s**, *no pl* **a** (= *Wohlergehen*) well-being, good; **sein ~ bei jdm versuchen** (*inf*) to try one's luck with sb; **jdm ~ und Segen wünschen** to wish sb every blessing **b** (*Eccl, fig*) salvation; **sein ~ in etw** (*dat*) **suchen** to seek one's salvation in sth; **sein ~ in der Flucht suchen** to flee for one's life; **zu jds ~(e) gereichen** (*geh*) to be sb's salvation; **im Jahr des ~s 1848** (*old*) in the year of grace 1848 (*old*) INTERJ **~!** hail! (*old*); **~ dem König!** long live *or* God save the King!; **~ Hitler!** (*NS*) heil Hitler!; **Berg/Ski/Petri ~!** good climbing/skiing/fishing!

Hei|land ['hailant] M **-(e)s, -e** [-də] (*Rel*) Saviour (*Brit*), Savior (*US*), Redeemer; (*fig geh*: = *Retter*) saviour (*Brit*), savior (*US*)

Heil-: Heil|an|stalt F nursing home; (*für Sucht- oder Geisteskranke*) home; **~ für Geisteskranke** mental home; **Heil|bad** NT (= *Bad*) medicinal bath; (= *Ort*) spa, watering-place (*old*); **heil|bar** ADJ curable; **Heil|bar|keit** ['hailba:ɐkait] F **-**, *no pl* curability; **heil|brin|gend** ADJ (*Rel*) redeeming; Wirkung, Kur beneficial; Kräuter medicinal; **sie warteten auf den ~en Regen** they were waiting for the vitally needed rain

Heil|butt M halibut

hei|len ['hailən] VI *aux sein* (Wunde, Bruch) to heal (up); (Entzündung) to clear up VT Kranke, Krankheiten to cure; Wunde to heal; (*Rel*) to heal; **als geheilt entlassen werden** to be discharged with a clean bill of health; **Jesus heilt uns von unseren Sünden** Jesus redeems us from our sins; **jdn von etw ~** (*lit, fig*) to cure sb of sth; **von jdm/etw geheilt sein** (*fig*) to have got over sb/sth; **die Zeit heilt alle Wunden** (*Prov*) time heals all wounds (*prov*)

hei|lend ADJ healing

Hei|ler ['hailɐ] M **-s, -, Hei|le|rin** [-ərɪn] F **-, -nen** (*geh*) healer

Heil-: Heil|er|de F healing earth; **Heil|er|folg** M success; **zum ~ führen** to lead to a successful cure; **Heil|fas|ten** NT **-s**, *no pl* therapeutic fasting; **Heil|fleisch** NT **ich habe gutes ~** I heal quickly *or* easily; **heil|froh** ADJ (*inf*) ecstatic; **Heil|gym|nas|tik** F physiotherapy; **Heil|haut** F **eine gute/schlechte ~ haben** to have skin that heals quickly/doesn't heal quickly

hei|lig ['hailiç] ADJ **a** holy; (= *geweiht, geheiligt*) sacred, holy; (*bei Namen von Heiligen*) Saint; (*old*: = *fromm*) devout, saintly; (*pej*) holier-than-thou; **jdm ~ sein** (*lit, fig*) to be sacred to sb; **bei allem, was ~ ist** by all that is sacred, by all that I hold sacred; **die ~e Veronika** Saint Veronica; **der ~e Augustinus** Saint Augustine; **Heiliger Abend** Christmas Eve; **das ~e Abendmahl, die ~e Kommunion** Holy Communion; **die Heilige Dreifaltigkeit/Familie/Stadt** the Holy Trinity/Family/City; **die Heilige Jungfrau** the Blessed Virgin; **Heilige Maria** Holy Mary; **der Heilige Geist/Vater/Stuhl** the Holy Spirit/Father/See; **die Heiligen Drei Könige** the Three Kings *or* Wise Men, the Magi; **das Heilige Land** the Holy Land; **die Heilige Schrift** the Holy Scriptures *pl*; **das Heilige Römische Reich** the Holy Roman Empire; **die Heilige Allianz** the Holy Alliance; **das Heiligste** (*lit, fig*) the holy of holies **b** (*fig*: = *ernst*) Eid, Pflicht sacred, solemn; Recht sacred; Eifer, Zorn righteous; (*von Ehrfurcht erfüllt*) Stille, Schauer awed; (= *unantastbar*) Würde, Gefühl, Gewohnheit sacred; **~e Kuh** sacred cow; **~e ist mein ~er Ernst** I am deadly serious (*Brit*), I am in dead earnest **c** (*inf*: = *groß*) incredible (*inf*); Respekt healthy, incredible (*inf*); **mit jdm/etw seine ~e Not haben** to have a hard time with sb/sth; **von einer ~en Angst gepackt werden** to be scared out of one's wits **d** (*inf*: *in Ausrufen*) **(ach du) ~er Bimbam** *or* **Strohsack!, ~es Kanonenrohr!** holy smoke! (*inf*), hell's bell's! (*inf*)

Hei|lig|abend [hailiç'|a:bnt] M Christmas Eve

dition, the presents are brought – especially in Protestant areas – by the **Christkind**, a mythical figure somewhere between an angel and the baby Jesus. Around midnight candle-lit **Christmetten** take place. These are festive Christmas services in celebration of Jesus' birth. A traditional meal – commonly goose, turkey or carp – is eaten on Christmas Day.

---

hei|li|gen ['hailɪgn] VT (= *weihen*) to hallow, to sanctify; (= *heilig halten*) to hallow, to keep holy; Sonntag etc to keep holy, to observe; **der Zweck heiligt die Mittel** the end justifies the means; **durch die Zeit geheiligt** time-honoured (*Brit*), time-honored (*US*) → *auch* **geheiligt**

Hei|li|gen-: Hei|li|gen|bild NT holy picture; **Hei|li|gen|fi|gur** F figure *or* statue of a saint; **Hei|li|gen|le|gen|de** F life *or* story of the saints; **Hei|li|gen|schein** M halo; **jdn mit einem ~ umgeben** (*fig*) to put sb on a pedestal; **sich mit einem ~ umgeben** (*fig*) to be holier--than-thou; **Hei|li|gen|ver|eh|rung** F veneration of the saints

Hei|li|ge(r) ['hailɪgə] MF *decl as adj* (*lit, fig*) saint; **ein sonderbarer** *or* **wunderlicher ~r** (*inf*) a queer fish (*Brit inf*), an odd bird (*US inf*)

Hei|lig-: hei|lig hal|ten ▲ VT *irreg* to keep holy; Andenken etc to keep sacred; Sonntag *auch* to observe; **Hei|lig|keit** F **-**, *no pl* holiness; (= *Geweihtheit, Geheiligtheit auch, von Eigentum*) sacredness; (*von Zorn*) righteousness; **Eure/Seine ~** your/his Holiness; **im Geruch der ~ stehen** to be surrounded by an aura of sanctity; **hei|lig spre|chen** ▲ VT *irreg* to canonize; **Hei|lig|spre|chung** [-ʃpreçʊŋ] F **-, -en** canonization; **Hei|lig|tum** ['hailiçtu:m] NT **-s, -tümer** [-ty:mə] (= *Stätte*) shrine; (= *Gegenstand*) (holy) relic; **Schändung eines ~s** sacrilege; **jds ~ sein** (*inf*) (*Zimmer*) to be sb's sanctum; (*Gegenstand etc*) to be sacrosanct (to sb)

Hei|li|gung F , *no pl* **die ~ des Sonntags** Lord's day *or* Sunday observance; **die ~ des Sabbats** the observance of the Sabbath

Heil-: Heil|kli|ma NT healthy climate; **heil|kli|ma|tisch** ADJ Kurort with a curative climate (*nachgestellt*); **Heil|kraft** F healing power; **heil|kräf|tig** ADJ Pflanze, Tee medicinal; Wirkung curative; **ein ~es Mittel** a curative; **Heil|kraut** NT *usu pl* medicinal herb; **Heil|kun|de** F medicine; **heil|kun|dig** ADJ skilled in the art of healing, skilled in medicine; **Heil|kun|di|ge(r)** [-kʊndɪgə] MF *decl as adj* person skilled in medicine *or* in the art of healing, healer; **heil|los** ADJ unholy (*inf*); Durcheinander, Verwirrung *auch* hopeless; Schreck terrible, frightful ADV **sich ~ verirren** to get hopelessly lost; **~ verschuldet sein** to be up to one's ears in debt; **die Partei war ~ zerstritten** the party was hopelessly divided; **Heil|me|tho|de** F cure; **Heil|mit|tel** NT (*lit, fig*) remedy, cure; (= *Medikament*) medicine; **Heil|pä|da|go|gik** F remedial education; **Heil|pflan|ze** F medicinal plant; **Heil|prak|ti|ker|in** M(F) non-medical practitioner; **Heil|quel|le** F medicinal spring; **Heil|sal|be** F (medicated) ointment; **heil|sam** ['hailza:m] ADJ **a** (*dated*: = *heilend*) Wirkung healing; Arznei curative, healing; Klima salutary, beneficial **b** (*fig*: = *förderlich*) Erfahrung, Strafe, Einfluss, Schock salutary

Heils-: Heils|ar|mee F Salvation Army; **Heils|bot|schaft** F message of salvation, gospel

Heil|schlaf M healing sleep (*induced for therapeutic ends*)

Heils-: Heils|ge|schich|te F heilsgeschichte, *interpretation of history stressing God's saving grace*; **Heils|leh|re** F (*Rel, fig*) doctrine of salvation; **Heils|ord|nung** F order of salvation

Heil|stät|te F (*form*) sanatorium (*Brit*), sanitarium (*US*), clinic

Hei|lung ['haɪlʊŋ] F -, (rare) -en (= das Heilen) (von Wunde) healing; (von Krankheit, Kranken) curing; (Rel) healing; (= das Gesundwerden) cure; ~ in etw (dat) finden to find relief in sth

Hei|lungs-: Hei|lungs|chan|cen PL chances pl of recovery; **Hei|lungs|pro|zess** ▲ M healing process

Heil-: Heil|ver|fah|ren NT (course of) treatment; **Heil|was|ser** NT (aus Heilquelle) healing water(s pl); (in Flaschen) healing water; **Heil|-zweck** M zu ~en for medicinal purposes

heim [haɪm] ADV home; ~, bitte let's go home; ~ ins Reich (NS) back to the Reich (referring to formerly German areas and their inhabitants)

Heim [haɪm] NT -(e)s, -e (= Zuhause, Anstalt) home; (= Obdachlosenheim, für Lehrlinge) hostel; (= Studentenwohnheim) hall of residence, hostel, dormitory (US); (von Sportverein) clubhouse; (= Freizeitheim) recreation centre (Brit) or center (US); ~ und Herd (liter) house and home

Heim- in cpds home; **Heim|abend** M social evening; **Heim|ar|beit** F (Ind) homework no indef art, outwork no indef art; etw in ~ herstellen lassen to have sth produced by homeworkers; **Heim|ar|bei|ter(in)** M(F) (Ind) homeworker; **Heim|ar|beits|platz** M die Zahl der Heimarbeitsplätze nimmt zu more and more people work from home

Hei|mat ['haɪmaːt] F -, -en home; (= Heimatort auch) home town (Brit), hometown (US); (= Heimatland auch) native country; (Bot, Zool auch) natural habitat; die ~ verlassen to leave one's home; jdm zur ~ werden to become sb's home; politische ~ political home

Hei|mat- in cpds home; **Hei|mat|an|schrift** F home address; **Hei|mat|dich|ter(in)** M(F) regional writer; **Hei|mat|dich|tung** F regional literature; **Hei|mat|er|de** F native soil; **Hei|mat|film** M sentimental film in idealized regional setting; **Hei|mat|flug|ha|fen** M home airport; **Hei|mat|for|scher(in)** M(F) local historian; **Hei|mat|for|schung** F research into local history; **Hei|mat|ha|fen** M home port; **Hei|mat|kun|de** F (Sch) local history; **hei|mat|kund|lich** [-kʊntlɪç] ADJ local history attr; er hat ~e Interessen he is interested in local history; **Hei|mat|kunst** F regional art; **Hei|mat|land** NT native country or land; **hei|mat|lich** ['haɪmaːtlɪç] ADJ (= zur Heimat gehörend) native; Bräuche, Dialekt local; (= an die Heimat erinnernd) Gefühle, Wehmut nostalgic; Klänge of home; die ~en Berge the mountains of (one's) home; ~er Boden native soil ADV das mutet mich ~ an, das kommt mir ~ vor, das berührt mich ~ that reminds me of home; **Hei|mat|lie|be** F love of one's native country or land; **hei|mat|los** ADJ homeless; **Hei|mat|lo|se(r)** ['haɪmaːtloːzə] MF decl as adj homeless person; die ~n the homeless; **Hei|mat|lo|sig|keit** F -, no pl homelessness; **Hei|mat|muse|um** NT museum of local history; **Hei|mat|ort** M pl -orte **a** home town (Brit), hometown (US); (= Dorf) home village **b** (= Heimathafen) home port; **Hei|mat|recht** NT right of domicile; **Hei|mat|schrift|stel|ler(in)** M(F) regional writer; **Hei|mat|spra|che** F native dialect; (Baskisch etc) native language; **hei|mat|ver|trie|ben** ADJ displaced; **Hei|mat|ver|trie|be|ne(r)** MF decl as adj displaced person, expellee (esp from eastern regions of the German Empire at the end of World War II)

Heim-: heim+be|ge|ben ptp heimbegeben VR sep irreg (geh) to make one's way home; **heim+be|glei|ten** ptp heimbegleitet VT sep jdn ~ to take or see sb home; **Heim|be|woh|ner(in)** M(F) resident (of a/the home); **heim+brin|gen** VT sep irreg (= nach Hause bringen) to bring home; (= heimbegleiten) to take or see home; **Heim|bü|gler** M rotary iron

Heim|chen ['haɪmçən] NT -s, - (Zool) house cricket; ~ (am Herd) (pej: = Hausfrau) housewife

Heim-: Heim|com|pu|ter M home computer; **heim+dür|fen** VI sep irreg darf ich/sie heim? may I/she go home?; **heim+ei|len** VI sep aux sein (geh) to hurry home

hei|me|lig ['haɪməlɪç] ADJ cosy (Brit), cozy (US); Atmosphäre auch homely

Hei|me|lig|keit F -, no pl cosiness (Brit), coziness (US)

Heim-: heim+fah|ren VTI sep irreg (vi:aux sein) to drive home; **Heim|fahrt** F journey home, return journey; (Naut) return voyage, voyage home; **heim+fin|den** VI sep irreg to find one's way home; **heim+füh|ren** VT sep to take home; ein Mädchen ~ (dated) to take a girl as one's wife (dated); **Heim|gang** M pl -gänge (euph geh: = Tod) passing away; beim ~ meiner Mutter when my mother was called to her Lord or Maker (euph); **Heim|ge|gan|ge|ne(r)** [-gəganənə] MF decl as adj (euph geh) deceased; unser lieber ~r our dear departed friend/father etc; **heim+ge|hen** sep irreg aux sein **VI** to go home; (euph geh) to pass away or on **VI** impers es geht mir heim we're going home; **heim+ho|len** VT sep to fetch home; Gott hat ihn heimgeholt he has been called to his Maker; **Heim|in|dust|rie** F cottage industry

hei|misch ['haɪmɪʃ] ADJ **a** (= einheimisch) (Zool, Bot) indigenous, native (in +acc to); Rohstoffe native; (= national) Wirtschaft, Markt, Industrie domestic, home; (= ortsansässig) local; (= regional) regional; Gewässer, Landschaft native; etw ~ machen to introduce sth (in +dat to); vor ~em Publikum or vor ~er Kulisse spielen (Sport) to play in front of a home crowd **b** (= vertraut) familiar; an einem Ort ~ sein to feel at home in a place; sich ~ fühlen to feel at home; vom ~en Herd weg sein to be away from house and home; in einer Sprache etc ~ sein to be or feel at home in a language etc; sich ~ ma|chen to make oneself at home; ~ werden to become acclimatized (an, in +dat to), to settle in (an, in +dat to)

Heim-: Heim|kampf M (Sport) home match or game; (Boxen) home fight; **Heim|kehr** ['haɪmkeːɐ] F -, no pl homecoming, return; **heim+keh|ren** VI sep aux sein to return home (aus from); **Heim|keh|rer** ['haɪmkeːɐ] M -s, -; **Heim|keh|re|rin** [-ərɪn] F -, -nen homecomer; **Heim|kind** NT institution child, child brought up in a home; **Heim|ki|no** NT home movies pl; (= Ausrüstung) home movie kit; (inf: = TV) gogglebox (Brit inf), tube (US inf); **heim+kom|men** VI sep irreg aux sein to come or return home; **heim+kön|nen** VI sep irreg to be able to go home; **Heim|kunft** ['haɪmkʊnft] F -, no pl (geh) homecoming, return; **Heim|lei|ter(in)** M(F) → head or warden of a/the home/hostel; **Heim|lei|tung** F → Heim person(s) in charge of a/the home/hostel; ihr wurde die ~ übertragen she was put in charge of the home/hostel; **heim+leuch|ten** VI sep (fig inf) jdm ~ to give sb a piece of one's mind

heim|lich ['haɪmlɪç] ADJ (= geheim, verborgen) secret; Treffen auch clandestine; Benehmen secretive; Bewegungen furtive ADV secretly; treffen, tun auch in secret; lachen inwardly; er blickte sie ~ an he stole a glance at her; sich ~ entfer|nen to steal or sneak away; ~, still und leise (inf) quietly, on the quiet

Heim|lich|keit F -, -en secrecy; (= Geheimnis) secret; in aller ~ secretly, in secret; nur keine ~en! (inf) stop being (so) secretive, no secrets now!

Heim|lich-: Heim|lich|tu|er [-tuːɐ] M -s, -; **Heim|lich|tu|e|rin** [-ərɪn] F -, -nen secretive person; **Heim|lich|tu|e|rei** F secrecy, secretiveness; **heim|lich tun** ▲ VI irreg to be secretive (mit about)

Heim-: heim+müs|sen VI sep irreg to have to go home; **Heim|mut|ter** F pl -mütter warden of a/the home; (von Jugendherberge) hostel warden; **Heim|nie|der|la|ge** F (Sport) home defeat; **Heim|ord|nung** F → Heim rules pl and

regulations pl of a/the home/hostel; **Heim|or|gel** F home organ; **Heim|rei|se** F journey home, homeward journey; (Naut) voyage home, homeward voyage; **heim+rei|sen** VI sep aux sein to travel home; **Heim|sau|na** F home sauna; **heim+schi|cken** VT sep to send home; **Heim|sieg** M (Sport) home win or victory; **Heim|spiel** NT (Sport) home match or game; **Heim|statt** F (liter) home; ohne ~ without a home; **Heim|stät|te** F **a** (= Zuhause) home **b** (Jur) homestead

heim+su|chen ['haɪmzuːxn] VT sep to strike; (für längere Zeit) to plague; (Feind) to attack; (Gespenst) to haunt; (Krankheit) to afflict; (Albträume, Vorstellungen) to afflict, to haunt; (Schicksal) to overtake, to afflict; (inf: = besuchen) to descend on (inf); von Dürre heimgesucht drought-stricken; vom Streik heimgesucht strike-torn; von Krieg heimgesucht war-torn, war-ravaged; Gott suchte die Ägypter mit schweren Plagen heim God visited terrible plagues on the Egyptians

Heim|su|chung F -, -en **a** (= Schicksalsschlag) affliction; (= Katastrophe) disaster; (= Plage) plague **b** Mariä ~ the visitation of Mary

Heim|trai|ner M exercise machine; (= Trimmrad) exercise bike

Heim|trai|ner(in) M(F) personal trainer

heim+trau|en VR sep to dare to go home

Heim|tü|cke F , no pl (= Hinterlist) insidiousness; (= Boshaftigkeit) maliciousness; (von Mensch) treachery; (von Krankheit) insidiousness; (Jur) malice; (= Gefährlichkeit) treacherous nature

heim|tü|ckisch ADJ (= hinterlistig) insidious; (= boshaft) malicious; Krankheit insidious; (= gefährlich) Glatteis, Maschine treacherous ADV überfallen, verraten insidiously, treacherously

Heim-: Heim|un|ter|brin|gung F accommodation in a home; **Heim|va|ter** M warden of a/the home; (von Jugendherberge) hostel warden; **Heim|vor|teil** M (Sport, fig) home advantage; **heim|wärts** ['haɪmvɛrts] ADV (= nach Hause zu) home; (= auf dem Heimweg) on the way home; ~ ziehen/gehen to go homewards; **Heim|weg** M way home; sich auf den ~ ma|chen to set out or head for home; **Heim|weh** NT homesickness no art; ~ haben/bekommen to be/become homesick (nach for); krank vor ~ sein to be pining for home, to be very homesick; **heim|weh|krank** ADJ homesick; **Heim|wer|ken** [-vɛrkn] NT do-it-yourself (inf), DIY; **Heim|wer|ker** [-vɛrkɐ] M -s, -, **Heim|wer|ke|rin** [-ərɪn] F -, -nen do-it-yourself or DIY enthusiast, do-it-yourselfer (inf); **Heim|wer|ker|be|darf** M do-it-yourself or DIY products pl; **heim+wol|len** VI sep to want to go home; **heim+zah|len** VT sep jdm etw ~ to pay sb back for sth; **heim+zie|hen** sep irreg **VI** aux sein to return home **VT** impers es zog ihn heim he felt he wanted to go home

Hein [haɪn] M Freund ~ (old) Death

Hei|ni ['haɪni] M -s, -s (inf) bloke (Brit inf), guy (inf); (= Dummkopf) idiot, fool

Hein|zel|männ|chen ['haɪntslmɛnçən] NT brownie

Hei|rat ['haɪraːt] F -, -en marriage; (= Feier) wedding; (= Partie) match

hei|ra|ten ['haɪraːtn] ✪ 51.3 VT VR to marry VI to get married VI to get married, to marry; aufs Land/in die Stadt/nach Berlin ~ to marry or get married and settle in the country/in town/in Berlin; in eine reiche/alte Familie ~ to marry into a rich/old family; ~ müssen (euph) to have to get married; „wir ~" "we are getting married"; „geheiratet haben ..." ≈ "marriages", ≈ "marriage announcements"

Hei|ra|ten NT -s, no pl marriage, getting married no def art

Hei|rats-: Hei|rats|ab|sich|ten PL marriage plans pl; **Hei|rats|al|ter** NT marriageable or marrying age; (Jur) minimum legal age for marriage; **Hei|rats|an|non|ce** F advertisement for a marriage partner; **Hei|rats|an|trag**

M proposal (of marriage); **jdm einen ~ machen** to propose to sb; **Hei|rats|an|zei|ge** F **a** (= *Bekanntgabe*) announcement of a forthcoming marriage **b** (= *Annonce für Partnersuche*) advertisement for a marriage partner; **Hei|rats|bü|ro** NT marriage bureau; **Hei|rats|er|laub|nis** F consent (to a marriage); **hei|rats|fä|hig** ADJ **eine Frau/ein Mann im ~en Alter** a woman/man of marriageable age; **Hei|rats|in|sti|tut** NT marriage bureau; **Hei|rats|kan|di|dat** M (= *Bräutigam*) husband-to-be; (= *Ehewilliger*) eligible bachelor; **Hei|rats|kan|di|da|tin** F (= *Braut*) bride-to-be; (= *Ehewillige*) eligible woman; **hei|rats|lus|tig** ADJ eager to get married; **Hei|rats|markt** M **a** (*in Zeitung*) marriage ads *pl* **b** (= *Treff für Heiratswillige*) marriage market, cattle market (*pej inf*); **hei|rats|mü|de** ADJ (*inf*) unwilling to marry; **Hei|rats|schwin|del** M marriage proposal made under false pretences (*Brit*) or pretenses (*US*); **Hei|rats|schwind|ler(in)** M(F) person who makes a marriage proposal under false pretences (*Brit*) or pretenses (*US*); **Hei|rats|ur|kun|de** F marriage certificate; **Hei|rats|ur|laub** M leave to get married; **Hei|rats|ver|mitt|ler(in)** M(F) marriage broker; **Hei|rats|ver|mitt|lung** F (= *Büro*) marriage bureau; **diskrete ~** marriages arranged discreetly; **Hei|rats|ver|spre|chen** NT (*Jur*) promise of marriage; **Bruch des ~s** breach of promise (of marriage)

hei|sa INTERJ hey

hei|schen VT (*geh*) **a** *Beifall, Hochachtung, Aufmerksamkeit etc* to demand **b** (*dated*: = *erbitten*) to beg or ask for

hei|ser ADJ **a** hoarse; (= *dunkel klingend*) husky; *Laut* croaky ADV **~ reden** to talk hoarsely, to talk in a hoarse voice; **sich ~ schreien/reden** to shout/talk oneself hoarse

Hei|ser|keit F -, *no pl* hoarseness

heiß ADJ **a** hot; *Zone* torrid; **brennend/siedend/glühend ~** burning/boiling/scorching hot; **drückend ~** oppressively hot; **jdm ist/wird ~** sb is/is getting hot; **sie hat einen ~en Kopf** (*wegen Fieber*) she has a burning forehead; (*vom Denken*) her head is spinning; **etw ~ machen** to heat sth up; **~e Tränen weinen** to cry one's heart out; **mit der ~en Nadel genäht** thrown together; **ein Paar Heiße** (*dial*) a couple of hot sausages; **~!** (*inf*: = *fast gefunden*) you're hot → **baden**

b (= *heftig*) *Diskussion, Kampf, Auseinandersetzung* heated, fierce; *Zorn* impassioned; *Begierde* passionate, burning; (= *innig*) *Liebe, Wunsch* burning, fervent; **~en Dank** very many thanks

c (= *aufreizend*) *Musik, Sachen, Bilder* hot; (*inf*: = *sexuell erregt*) hot, randy (*Brit inf*), horny (*inf*); **~e Höschen** hot pants; **jdn ~ machen** (*inf*) to turn sb on (*inf*)

d (= *gefährlich*) *Ware, Geld* hot; (= *radioaktiv*) *Teilchen etc* hot; *Gegend, Thema* hotly-disputed; **das wird ein ~er Winter** things are going to be pretty hot this winter (*inf*); **ein ~es Eisen** a hot potato; **ein ~es Eisen anfassen** (*inf*) to grasp the nettle

e *attr* (*inf*) *Favorit, Tip, Maschine* hot; **ein ~er Ofen** a motorbike; **~er Draht** hotline; **~e Spur** firm lead

f *pred* (*inf*: = *brünstig*) **~ sein** to be on heat ADV **a** (= *nicht kalt*) **~ waschen** to wash with hot water; **etw ~ trinken** to drink sth hot; **~ baden** to have a hot bath; **~ duschen** to take a hot shower; **es überläuft mich ~ und kalt** I feel hot and cold all over; **es wird nichts so ~ gegessen, wie es gekocht wird** (*prov*) things are never as bad as they seem

b (= *heftig*) **sich** (*dat*) **etw ~ wünschen** to be dying to have sth; **~ ersehnt** much longed for; **~ geliebt** dearly beloved; **eine ~ geführte Diskussion** a passionate discussion; **es ging ~ her** things got heated; **das Gebiet/die Stadt ist ~ umkämpft** the area/town is being hotly or fiercely fought over; **ein ~ umkämpfter Markt** a fiercely contested market; **~ umstritten** (*Frage*) hotly debated; *Künstler etc* highly controversial;

jdn/etw ~ und innig lieben to love sb/sth madly; **sich die Köpfe ~ reden, sich ~ reden** or **diskutieren** to talk till one is blue in the face

hei|ßa ['haisa] INTERJ hey

heiß|blü|tig ADJ (= *erregbar*) hot-tempered; (= *leidenschaftlich*) hot-blooded; *Affäre, Tanz* passionate

hei|ßen ['haisn] *pret* **hieß** [hi:s], *ptp* **geheißen** [gə'haisn] VT **a** (= *nennen*) to call; (*old*: = *Namen geben*) *jdn, Ort* to name; **das heiße ich klug vorgehen!** that's what I call being clever; **jdn einen Lügner etc ~** to call sb a liar etc; **oder wie heißt man das?** (*inf*) ... or what do you call it?; **... oder wie man das heißt** ... or whatever it's called

b (*geh*: = *auffordern*) to tell, to bid (*form*); **jdn etw tun ~** to tell sb to do sth, to bid sb do sth; **jdn willkommen ~** to bid sb welcome

VI **a** (= *den Namen haben, bezeichnet werden*) to be called (*Brit*) or named; (= *als Titel haben*) to be titled; **wie ~ Sie/heißt die Straße?** what are you/is the street called?, what's your name/the name of the street?; **ich heiße Müller** I'm called or my name is Müller; **sie heißt jetzt anders** her name is different now, she has changed her name; **nach jdm ~** to be called after (*Brit*) or for (*US*) sb; **wie kann man nur Gotthelf/so ~?** how can anyone have a name like Gotthelf/like that?; **wie heißt das?** what is that called?; **eigentlich heißt es richtig X** actually the correct word is X; **... und wie sie alle ~** ... and the rest of them; **... so wahr ich Franz-Josef heiße** (*als Bekräftigung*) ... as sure as I'm standing here; **... dann will ich Fridolin ~** ... then I'm a Dutchman (*Brit*) or a monkey's uncle

b (= *bestimmte Bedeutung haben*) to mean; **was heißt „gut" auf Englisch?** what is the English (word) for "gut"?; **„gut" heißt auf Englisch „good"** the English (word) for "gut" is "good"; **soll** or **will ~** (*am Satzanfang*) in other words; **ich weiß, was es heißt, allein zu sein** I know what it means to be alone

c (= *lauten*) to go; (*Spruch, Gedicht etc*) to go

d **das heißt** that is; (= *in anderen Worten*) that is to say

VI *impers* **a** **es heißt, dass ...** (= *es geht die Rede*) they say that ...; **es soll nicht ~, dass ...** never let it be said that ...

b (= *zu lesen sein*) **in der Bibel/im Gesetz/in seinem Brief heißt es, dass ...** the Bible/the law/his letter says that ..., in the Bible etc it says that ...; **bei Hegel/Goethe etc heißt es ...** Hegel/Goethe says ...; **es heißt hier ...** it says here ...

c (= *es ist nötig*) **es heißt, etw zu tun** you/we/he etc must do sth; **nun heißt es handeln** now it's time to act; **da heißt es aufgepasst** or **aufpassen** you'd better watch out

Heiß-: heiß|er|sehnt △ ADJ *attr* → **heiß** ADV **b**; **heiß|ge|liebt** △ ADJ → **heiß** ADV **b**; **Heiß|hun|ger** M ravenous or voracious appetite; **etw mit ~ essen** to eat sth ravenously or voraciously; **etw mit wahrem ~ verschlingen** (*fig*) to really devour sth; **heiß|hung|rig** ADJ ravenous, voracious ADV ravenously, voraciously; **heiß|lau|fen** VI *sep irreg aux sein* (*Motor, Auto, Maschinenteil*) to overheat; (*Diskussionsteilnehmer etc*) to become heated; (*Telefonleitungen, -drähte*) to buzz

Heiß|luft F hot air; **Kochen mit ~** fan-assisted cooking

Heiß|luft-: Heiß|luft|bal|lon M hot-air balloon; **Heiß|luft|hei|zung** F hot-air heating; **Heiß|luft|herd** M fan-assisted oven; **Heiß|luft|mo|tor** M hot-air or Stirling® engine; **Heiß|luft|trock|ner** [-trɔknɐ] M -s, - hot-air dryer

Heiß-: Heiß|man|gel F (= *Gerät*) rotary iron; (= *Ort*) laundry specializing in ironing sheets *etc*; **Heiß|sporn** M *pl* **-sporne** hothead; **heiß|um|kämpft** △ [-lʊmkɛmpft] ADJ *attr* → **heiß** ADV **b**; **heiß|um|strit|ten** △ ADJ *attr* → **heiß** ADV **b**; **Heiß|was|ser|be|rei|ter**

[-bəraitɐ] M -s, - geyser, water heater; **Heiß|was|ser|spei|cher** M hot (water) tank

hei|ter ['haitɐ] ADJ (= *fröhlich*) cheerful; (= *ausgeglichen*) serene; (= *amüsant*) *Geschichte* amusing, funny; (= *leicht betrunken*) merry; (= *hell, klar*) *Farbe, Raum* bright; *Himmel, Tag* bright, clear; *Wetter* clear, fine; (*Met*) fair; **~ werden** to become cheerful; (*Gesicht*) to brighten; (*Wetter*) to brighten or clear up; **~er werden** to cheer up; (*Wetter*) to brighten up, to become brighter; **das kann ja ~ werden!** (*iro*) that sounds great (*iro*); **aus ~em Himmel** (*fig*) out of the blue

Hei|ter|keit F -, *no pl* (= *Fröhlichkeit*) cheerfulness; (*von Mensch, Wesen auch*) happiness; (= *Ausgeglichenheit*) serenity; (= *Helligkeit, Klarheit, von Himmel, Tag*) clearness; (= *heitere Stimmung*) merriment; (= *Belustigung*) amusement; **allgemeine ~ hervorrufen** to cause general merriment or amusement

Hei|ter|keits-: Hei|ter|keits|aus|bruch M fit of merriment; **Hei|ter|keits|er|folg** M **einen ~ haben** to raise a laugh

Heiz-: Heiz|an|la|ge F heating system; **Heiz|ap|pa|rat** M heater; **heiz|bar** ADJ *Heckscheibe etc* heated; *Zimmer auch* with heating; **der Saal ist schwer ~** the hall is difficult to heat → *auch* **beheizbar**; **Heiz|(bett)|de|cke** F electric blanket; **Heiz|ele|ment** NT heating element

hei|zen ['haitsn] VI (= *die Heizung anhaben*) to have the/one's heating on; (= *Wärme abgeben*) to give off heat; **der Ofen heizt gut** the stove gives (off) a good heat; **mit Holz/Strom etc ~** to use wood/electricity etc for heating; **ab November wird geheizt** the heating is put on in November VT (= *warm machen*) to heat; (= *verbrennen*) to burn; (= *beheizen*) *Lokomotive* to stoke; **den Ofen heize ich nur mit Holz** I only burn wood in the stove VR **sich gut/schlecht ~** to be easily/not easily heated, to be easy/hard to heat

Hei|zer ['haitsɐ] M -s, -, **Hei|ze|rin** [-ərɪn] F -, **-nen** boilerman; (*von Lokomotive, Schiff*) stoker

Heiz-: Heiz|flä|che F heating surface; **Heiz|gas** NT fuel gas; **Heiz|ge|rät** NT heater; **Heiz|kes|sel** M boiler; **Heiz|kis|sen** NT electric heat pad; **Heiz|kör|per** M (= *Gerät*) heater; (*von Zentralheizung*) radiator; (= *Element*) heating element; **Heiz|kör|per|ver|klei|dung** F radiator cover; **Heiz|kos|ten** PL heating costs *pl*

Heiz|kos|ten-: Heiz|kos|ten|ab|rech|nung F heating bill; **Heiz|kos|ten|pau|scha|le** F fixed heating cost

Heiz|kraft F calorific or heating power

Heiz|kraft|werk NT thermal power station

Heiz|lüf|ter M fan heater

Heiz|ma|te|ri|al NT fuel (*for heating*)

Heiz|ofen M heater

Heiz|öl NT heating or fuel oil

Heiz|plat|te F hotplate

Heiz|son|ne F electric fire

Heiz|strah|ler M electric (wall) heater

Hei|zung ['haitsʊŋ] F -, **-en** heating; (= *Heizkörper*) heater; (*von Zentralheizung*) radiator

Hei|zungs-: Hei|zungs|an|la|ge F heating system; **Hei|zungs|bau|er** M -s, -, **Hei|zungs|bau|e|rin** [-bauərn] F -, **-nen** heating engineer; **Hei|zungs|kel|ler** M boiler room; **Hei|zungs|mon|teur(in)** M(F) heating engineer; **Hei|zungs|rohr** NT heating pipe; **Hei|zungs|tech|nik** F heating engineering

Heiz|wert M calorific value

Hek|tar [hɛk'ta:ɐ, 'hɛkta:ɐ] NT OR M -s, **-e** hectare

Hek|tik ['hɛktɪk] F -, *no pl* (= *Hast*) hectic rush; (*von Großstadt etc*) hustle and bustle; (*von Leben etc*) hectic pace; **sie isst/arbeitet mit einer solchen ~** she eats/works at such a hectic pace; **nur keine ~** take it easy

hek|tisch [ˈhɛktɪʃ] **ADJ** (auch dated Med) hectic; Mensch auch frantic; Arbeiten frantic, furious **ADV** hectically; **es geht ~ zu** things are hectic; **ich lebe zur Zeit ~** my life is very hectic just now; **nur mal nicht so ~** take it easy

Hek|to-: Hek|to|gra|fie ▲ [hɛktoɡraˈfiː] F -, -n [-ˈfiːən] (= Verfahren) hectography; (= Abzug) hectograph (copy); **hek|to|gra|fie|ren** ▲ [hɛktoɡraˈfiːrən] ptp **hektografiert** VT insep to hectograph, to copy; **Hek|to|li|ter** [hɛktoˈliːtɐ, ˈhɛkto-] M OR NT hectolitre (Brit), hectoliter (US); **Hek|to|watt** [hɛktoˈvat, ˈhɛkto-] NT hectowatt

He|lan|ca® [heˈlaŋka] NT -, no pl stretch fabric

he|lau [heˈlau] INTERJ greeting used at Carnival time

Held [hɛlt] M -en, -en [-dn] hero; **der ~ des Tages** the hero of the hour; **kein ~ in etw** (dat) **sein** not to be very brave about sth; (in Schulfach etc) to be no great shakes at sth (inf); **du bist mir ein (rechter or schöner) ~!** (iro) some hero you are!; **den ~en spielen** (inf) to come or play the (great) hero

Hel|den-: Hel|den|brust F (hum) manly chest; **Hel|den|dar|stel|ler** M (Theat) heroic leading man; **Hel|den|dich|tung** F epic or heroic poetry; **Hel|den|epos** NT heroic epic; **Hel|den|fried|hof** M military cemetery; **Hel|den|ge|denk|tag** M (old) ≈ Remembrance Day, ≈ Memorial Day (US); **Hel|den|ge|stalt** F hero; **hel|den|haft ADJ** heroic, valiant **ADV** heroically, valiantly; **Hel|den|lied** NT (Liter) epic song or lay; **Hel|den|mut** M heroic courage; **hel|den|mü|tig** [-myːtɪç] ADJ, ADV = **heldenhaft**; **Hel|den|po|se** F heroic pose; **Hel|den|rol|le** F (Theat) hero's part or role; **Hel|den|sa|ge** F heroic saga; **Hel|den|stück** NT **das war kein ~** (inf) that didn't exactly cover you/him etc in glory; **Hel|den|tat** F heroic deed or feat; **Hel|den|te|nor** M heroic tenor; **Hel|den|tod** M heroic death, hero's death; **den ~ sterben** to die a hero's death; (Mil) to be killed in action; **Hel|den|tum** [ˈhɛldntuːm] NT -s, no pl heroism

Hel|din [ˈhɛldɪn] F -, -nen heroine → auch **Held**

hel|fen [ˈhɛlfn] pret **half** [half], ptp **geholfen** [ɡəˈhɔlfn] VI **a** (= Beistand geben) to help (jdm sb); (= mit anfassen) to lend a hand, to help; **jdm bei etw ~** to help sb with sth, to lend sb a hand with sth; **jdm etw tun ~** to help sb do sth; **er half ihr aus dem Mantel/einer Verlegenheit** he helped her out of her coat or off with her coat/out of a difficulty; **ihm/dir ist nicht zu ~** (fig) he is/you are beyond help; **dem Kranken ist nicht mehr zu ~** the patient is beyond help; **ich kann mir nicht ~** I can't help it; **ich kann mir nicht ~, ich muss es tun** I can't help doing it; **ich werd dir/ihm (schon) ~!** I'll give you/him what for (inf); **ich werde dir ~, die Tapeten zu beschmieren** I'll teach you to mess up the wallpaper (inf); **er weiß sich** (dat) **zu ~** he is very resourceful; **man muss sich** (dat) **nur zu ~ wissen** (prov) you just have to use your head; **er weiß sich** (dat) **nicht mehr zu ~** he is at his wits' end; **hilf dir selbst, dann or so hilft dir Gott** (Prov) God helps those who help themselves (Prov)
b auch vi impers (= dienen, nützen) to help; **es hilft nichts** it's no use or no good; **da ist nicht zu ~** there's no help for it; **da hilft alles nichts ...** there's nothing for it ...; **da hilft kein Jammern und kein Klagen** it's no use moaning; **es hilft ihm nichts, dass ...** it's no use to him that ...; **das hilft mir wenig, damit ist mir nicht geholfen** that's not much help to me; **das hat mir schon viel geholfen** that has been a great help to me; **was hilfts?** what's the use?; **was hülfe es dem Menschen, wenn ...** (Bibl) what does it profit a man if ... (Bibl)
c (= heilsam sein) to help; (= heilen: auch Arzt) to cure; **diese Arznei hilft gegen or bei Kopfweh** this medicine is good for headaches, this medicine helps to relieve headaches; **jetzt**

kann nur noch eine Operation ~ only an operation will help now or do any good now

Hel|fer [ˈhɛlfɐ] M -s, -, **Hel|fe|rin** [-ərɪn] F -, -nen helper; (= Mitarbeiter) assistant; (von Verbrecher) accomplice; (inf: = Gerät) help; **~ in Steuersachen** tax adviser; **ein ~ in der Not** a friend in need

Hel|fers|hel|fer(in) M(F) accomplice; (Jur: vor/nach begangener Tat) accessory before/after the fact

Hel|fer-: Hel|fer|syn|drom NT (Psych) (helpless) helper syndrome; **Hel|fer|zel|le** F (Med) helper cell

Hel|go|land [ˈhɛlɡolant] NT -s Heligoland

He|li [ˈheːli] M -s, - (Sw, inf) helicopter

He|li|kop|ter [heliˈkɔptɐ] M -s, - helicopter

He|li|kop|ter-Ski|ing [-skiˑɪŋ] NT -s, no pl, **He|li|kop|ter|ski|ing** ▲ NT -s, no pl helicopter skiing

He|li|port [heliˈpɔrt] M -s, -s heliport

He|li|ski|ing ▲ [-skiˑɪŋ] NT -s, no pl helicopter skiing

He|li|um [ˈheːliʊm] NT -s, no pl (abbr **He**) helium

hell [hɛl] **ADJ** **a** (optisch) light; Licht, Beleuchtung, Himmel bright; Farbe light, pale; Kleidungsstück light-coloured (Brit), light-colored (US); Haar, Teint light; Hautfarbe (von Rasse) fair, pale; (fig) Zukunft bright; **es wird ~** it's getting light; **~ bleiben** to stay light; **am ~en Tage** in broad daylight; **bis in den ~en Morgen schlafen** to sleep late; **in ~en Flammen** in flames, ablaze; **~es Bier** ≈ lager
b (akustisch) Laut, Ton, Stimme high(-pitched); Gelächter ringing
c (= klug) Junge bright, intelligent; (= geistig klar) Augenblicke lucid; **er ist ein ~er Kopf, er hat einen ~en Kopf** he has brains → **helle**
d attr (= stark, groß) great; Verwunderung etc utter; Verzweiflung, Unsinn sheer, utter; Neid pure; **in ~en Scharen** in great numbers; **seine ~e Freude an etw** (dat) **haben** to find great joy or pleasure in sth
ADV **a** (= licht) brightly; **~ leuchtend** brightly shining; Farbe bright; Kleid brightly coloured (Brit) or colored (US); **~ lodernd** blazing; **~ strahlend** brilliant, brightly shining
b (= hoch) **~ klingen** to sound high(-pitched); **~ tönen** to have a high-pitched ring
c (= sehr) absolutely; **von etw ~ begeistert/entzückt sein** to be very enthusiastic/quite delighted about sth

hell- in cpds (esp auf Farben bezüglich) light

Hel|las [ˈhɛlas] NT -' Hellas

hell-: hell|auf [ˈhɛlˈlauf] ADV completely, utterly; **~ lachen** to laugh out loud; **~ begeistert sein** to be wildly enthusiastic; **hell|blau** ADJ light blue; **hell|blond** ADJ very fair, blonde; **hell|braun** ADJ light brown; **Hell|dun|kel** NT (Art) chiaroscuro

hel|le [ˈhɛlə] ADJ pred (inf) bright, clever; **Mensch, sei ~!** use your loaf, mate! (Brit inf), use your brain, buddy! (US inf)

Hel|le [ˈhɛlə] F -, no pl = **Helligkeit**

Hel|le|bar|de [hɛləˈbardə] F -, -n (Hist) halberd

Hel|le|ne [hɛˈleːnə] M -n, -n, **Hel|le|nin** [-ˈleːnɪn] F -, -nen (ancient) Greek, Hellene

hel|le|nisch [hɛˈleːnɪʃ] ADJ Hellenic

hel|le|ni|sie|ren [hɛleniˈziːrən] ptp **hellenisiert** VT to hellenize

Hel|le|nis|mus [hɛleˈnɪsmʊs] M -, no pl Hellenism

Hel|le|nist [hɛleˈnɪst] M -en, -en, **Hel|le|nis|tin** [-ˈnɪstɪn] F -, -nen Hellenist

Hel|le|nis|tik [hɛleˈnɪstɪk] F -, no pl classical Greek studies pl

hel|le|nis|tisch [hɛleˈnɪstɪʃ] ADJ Hellenistic; **die ~e Staatenwelt** the Hellenistic World

Hel|ler [ˈhɛlɐ] M -s, - (Hist) heller; **das ist keinen (roten or lumpigen) or nicht einen ~ wert** that

isn't worth a brass farthing (Brit), that's worth nothing; **er besitzt keinen (roten or lumpigen) ~** he doesn't have a penny to his name (esp Brit), he doesn't have two pennies to rub together (esp Brit); **darauf geb ich keinen (roten) ~** I wouldn't give you tuppence (Brit) or a dime (US) for it; **auf ~ und Pfennig, bis auf den letzten ~** (down) to the last farthing (Brit) or penny (esp Brit); **stimmen** down to the last detail

Hel|le(s) [ˈhɛlə] NT decl as adj (= Bier) ≈ lager; **zwei ~, bitte** two lagers, please

hell|leuchtend △ ADJ → **hell ADV a**

hell-: hell|haa|rig ADJ fair-haired; **hell|häu|tig** ADJ fair-skinned; (von Rasse auch) pale-skinned; **hell|hö|rig** ADJ keen (Brit) or quick (US) of hearing; (Archit) poorly soundproofed; **~ sein** (fig: Mensch) to have sharp ears; **als er das sagte, wurde ich ~** when he said that I pricked up my ears; **jdn ~ machen** to make sb prick up their ears

hell|licht ADJ → **helllicht**

Hel|lig|keit F -, no pl lightness; (von Licht, Beleuchtung, Himmel) brightness; (von Farbe) lightness, paleness; (von Haar, Teint, Haut) fairness; (= helles Licht) light; (Phys, Astron) luminosity

Hel|lig|keits-: Hel|lig|keits|reg|ler M brightness control; **Hel|lig|keits|stu|fe** F brightness level

Hel|ling [ˈhɛlɪŋ] M -s, -e or f -, -en or **Helligen** [ˈhɛlɪɡn] (Naut) slipway

hell|licht ▲ [ˈhɛllɪçt] ADJ **am ~en Tage** in broad daylight; **es ist ~er Tag** it is broad daylight

hell|lodernd △ ADJ attr → **hell ADV a**

Hell-: Hell|raum|pro|jek|tor M (Sw) overhead projector; **hell|rot** ADJ bright red; **hell|se|hen** VI infin only **~ können** to have second sight, to be clairvoyant; **du kannst wohl ~!** you must be clairvoyant; **Hell|se|hen** NT clairvoyance; **Hell|se|her(in)** M(F) (lit, fig) clairvoyant; **hell|se|he|risch** ADJ attr clairvoyant; **hell|sich|tig** [ˈhɛlzɪçtɪç] ADJ shrewd; **Hell|sich|tig|keit** F -, no pl shrewdness; **hell|strah|lend** △ ADJ attr → **hell ADV a**; **hell|wach** ADJ (lit) wide-awake; (fig) alert; **Hell|wer|den** NT daybreak

Helm [hɛlm] M -(e)s, -e helmet; (Archit) helm roof

Helm-: Helm|busch M plume; **Helm|pflicht** F **es besteht ~** the wearing of crash helmets is compulsory; **Helm|schmuck** M crest; **Helm|zwang** M = **Helmpflicht**

He|lot [heˈloːt] M -en, -en Helot

He|lo|ten|tum [heˈloːtntuːm] NT -s, no pl (= Sklaverei) helotism, helotage; (= alle Heloten) helotry

Hel|sin|ki [ˈhɛlzɪŋki] NT -s Helsinki

Hel|ve|tis|mus [hɛlveˈtɪsmʊs] M -, Helvetismen [-ˈtɪsmən] (Ling) Helveticism

hem [həm, hm] INTERJ hem

Hemd [hɛmt] NT -(e)s, -en [-dn] (= Oberhemd) shirt; (= Unterhemd) vest (Brit), undershirt (US); **etw wie das or sein ~ wechseln** (fig) to change sth with monotonous regularity; **für dich gebe ich auch das letzte or mein letztes ~ her** (inf) I'd give you the shirt off my back (inf); **nass bis aufs ~** wet through, soaked to the skin; **jdn bis aufs ~ ausziehen** (fig inf) to have the shirt off sb's back (inf), to fleece sb (inf); **sich** (dat) **(wegen etw) ins ~ machen** (sl) to get one's knickers in a twist (over sth) (Brit inf), to get all worked up (about sth) (inf); **das ~ ist mir näher als der Rock** (prov) charity begins at home (Prov)

Hemd-: Hemd|är|mel M shirtsleeve; **in ~n** in one's shirtsleeves; **Hemd|blu|se** F shirt (-blouse), shirtwaist (US); **Hemd|blu|sen|kleid** NT shirtwaister (Brit) or shirtwaist (US) (dress); **Hemd|brust** F dickey

Hem|den-: Hem|den|matz M (*inf*) *small child dressed only in a vest,* ≈ Wee Willie Winkie; **Hem|den|stoff** M shirting

Hemd-: Hemd|ho|se F combinations *pl*, combs *pl* (*inf*); **Hemd|knopf** M shirt button; **Hemd|kra|gen** M shirt collar

Hemds-: Hemds|är|mel M shirtsleeve; **in ~n** in one's shirtsleeves; **hemds|är|me|lig** ADJ shirt-sleeved; (*fig inf*) down-to-earth; *Ausdrucksweise, Empfang, Einstellung* casual

He|mi|sphä|re [hemi'sfɛːrə] F hemisphere

he|mi|sphä|risch [hemi'sfɛːrɪʃ] ADJ hemispheric(al)

hem|men ['hɛmən] VT *Entwicklung, Fortschritt* to hinder, to hamper; *Lauf der Geschehnisse etc* to check; (= *verlangsamen*) to slow down; *Maschine, Rad* to check; *Wasserlauf* to stem; (*Med*) *Blut* to staunch; (*Psych*) to inhibit; *Leidenschaften* to restrain, to check; **jdn in seiner Entwicklung ~** to hinder *or* hamper sb's development → *auch* **gehemmt**

Hemm|nis ['hɛmnɪs] NT **-ses, -se** hindrance, impediment (*für* to)

Hemm-: Hemm|rad NT (*von Uhr*) escapement; **Hemm|schuh** M brake shoe; (*fig*) hindrance, impediment (*für* to); **jdm einen ~ in den Weg legen** (*fig*) to obstruct sb; **Hemm|schwel|le** F inhibition level *or* threshold; **eine ~ überwinden** to overcome one's inhibitions; **Hemm|stoff** M (*Chem*) inhibitor

Hem|mung ['hɛmʊŋ] F **-, -en a** (*Psych*) inhibition; (= *Bedenken*) scruple; **da habe ich ~en** I've got scruples about that; **an ~en leiden** to suffer from inhibitions; **keine ~en kennen** to have no inhibitions, not to feel inhibited; **nur keine ~en** don't feel inhibited **b** (*von Entwicklung, Fortschritt*) hindering, hampering; (= *Verlangsamung*) slowing down **c** (*von Gewehr*) **bei einer ~ des Gewehrs** when the gun is jammed **d** (*von Uhr*) escapement

Hemmungs-: hem|mungs|los ADJ (= *rückhaltlos*) unrestrained; (= *skrupellos*) unscrupulous; *brüllen, schreien, jubeln, weinen* without restraint; *sich hingeben, genießen* wantonly; *foltern, töten* without conscience; **jdn ~ machen** to remove sb's inhibitions; **Hem|mungs|lo|sig|keit** F **-, -en** (= *Rückhaltlosigkeit*) lack *no pl* of restraint; (= *Skrupellosigkeit*) unscrupulousness *no pl*; **Hem|mungs|nerv** M inhibitor (nerve)

Hendl ['hɛndl] NT **-s, -(n)** (*S Ger, Aus*) chicken

Hendl|bra|te|rei [-braːtərai] F **-, -en** (*S Ger, Aus*) grilled chicken place

Hengst [hɛŋst] M **-(e)s, -e** stallion; (= *Kamelhengst, Eselhengst*) male; (*sl:* = *Mann*) stud (*inf*)

Hengst|foh|len NT , **Hengst|fül|len** NT (male) foal, colt

Hen|kel ['hɛŋkl] M **-s, -** handle

Hen|kel-: Hen|kel|glas NT glass with a handle; **Hen|kel|korb** M basket with a handle; **Hen|kel|krug** M jug (with a handle); **Hen|kel|mann** M *pl* **-männer** (*inf*) set of containers *for reheating lunch at work*; **Hen|kel|oh|ren** PL (*inf*) big, sticking-out ears *pl* (*inf*); **Hen|kel|topf** M pot *or* pan with a handle/handles

hen|ken ['hɛŋkn] VT (*old*) to hang

Hen|ker ['hɛŋkɐ] M **-s, -** hangman; (= *Scharfrichter*) executioner; **zum ~** (*old inf*) hang it all (*inf*), zounds (*obs inf*); **was zum ~!** (*old inf*) what the devil (*inf*); **hols der ~!** (*old inf*) the devil take it! (*old inf*); **hol mich der ~** (*old inf*) zounds (*obs inf*); **scher dich** *or* **geh zum ~!** (*old inf*) go to the devil! (*inf*); **wie der ~ fahren** (*inf*) to drive like a maniac (*inf*)

Hen|ker(s)|beil NT executioner's axe (*Brit*) *or* ax (*US*)

Hen|kers-: Hen|kers|hand F **durch** *or* **von ~ sterben** to be executed; **Hen|kers|knecht** M (*Hist*) hangman's *or* (*von Scharfrichter*) executioner's assistant; (*fig*) torturer; (= *Handlanger*) henchman; **Hen|kers|mahl** NT , **Hen|kers|mahl|zeit** F last meal before execution; (*hum*

inf) last slap-up meal (*Brit*), final feast (*esp US, before examination etc*)

Hen|na ['hɛna] F **-** *or* nt **-(s)**, *no pl* henna; **mit ~ färben** to dye with henna, to henna

Hen|ne ['hɛna] F **-, -n** hen

He|pa|ti|tis [hepa'tiːtɪs] F **-, Hepati|tiden** [-ti-'tiːdn] hepatitis

her [heːɐ] ADV → *auch* **herkommen, hermüssen, her sein** *etc* **a** (*räumlich*) **von der Kirche/Frankreich/dem Meer ~** from the church/France/the sea; **er winkte vom Nachbarhaus ~** he waved from the house next door; **~ zu mir!** come here (to me); **um mich ~** (all) around me; **von weit ~** from a long way off *or* away, from afar (*liter*) → *auch* **hin**

b (*in Aufforderung*) **Bier/Essen ~!** bring (me/us) some beer/food (here); **~ mit dem Geld!** hand over your money!, give me your money!; **(wieder) ~ mit den alten Bräuchen** give me/us the old way of doing things, bring back the old customs, I say; **~ damit!** give me that, give that here (*inf*); **immer ~ damit!** let's have it/them (then)

c (*von etwas aus gesehen*) **von der Idee/Form ~** as for the idea/form, as far as the idea/form is concerned *or* goes; **vom finanziellen Standpunkt ~** from the financial point of view; **von den Eltern ~ gute Anlagen haben** to have inherited good qualities from one's parents

d (*zeitlich*) **ich kenne ihn von früher ~** I know him from before *or* from earlier times, I used to know him (before); **von der Schule/meiner Kindheit ~** since school/my childhood; **von der letzten Saison ~** from last season → **her sein**

he|rab [hɛ'rap] ADV down; **den Hügel/die Treppe ~** down the hill/stairs; **von oben ~** (down) from above → **oben**

he|rab- PREF → *auch* **herunter-, runter-** down; **he|rab+bli|cken** VI *sep* (*lit, fig*) to look down (*auf +acc* on); **he|rab+fle|hen** VT *sep* (*liter*) to call down; **he|rab+flie|ßen** VI *sep irreg aux sein* to flow down; **langes ~des Haar** long, flowing hair; **he|rab+kom|men** VI *sep irreg aux sein* (*geh*) to come down, to descend (*liter, form*); **he|rab+las|sen** *sep irreg* VT to let down, to lower **a** (*lit*) to let oneself down, to lower oneself **b** (*fig*) to lower oneself; **sich zu etw ~** to condescend *or* deign to do sth; **sich auf jds Ebene** (*acc*) **~** to descend to sb's level; **wenn du dich ~ könntest, mir dabei zu helfen** if you would condescend *or* deign to help me with it; **he|rab|las|send** ADJ condescending; *Verachtung* haughty ADV condescendingly; **sich ~ benehmen** to be condescending; **He|rab|las|sung** [-lasʊŋ] F **-**, *no pl* condescension; **he|rab+min|dern** VT *sep* (= *schlecht machen*) *Leistung, Qualitäten* to belittle, to disparage; (= *bagatellisieren*) *Gefahr, Problem* to minimize, to make little of; (= *reduzieren*) *Geschwindigkeit, Länge, Niveau* to reduce; **he|rab+rie|seln** VI *sep aux sein* to trickle down; (*Schneeflocken, Staub, Musik*) to float *or* waft down; **he|rab+se|hen** VI *sep irreg* (*lit, fig*) to look down (*auf +acc* on); **he|rab+sen|ken** VR *sep* (*geh: Nebel, Dunkelheit, Abend*) to fall; **he|rab+set|zen** VT *sep Ware* to reduce; *Preise, Kosten auch* to lower; *Geschwindigkeit auch* to slacken off; *Niveau* to lower, to debase; (= *schlecht machen*) *Leistungen, Fähigkeiten, jdn* to belittle, to disparage; **zu stark herabgesetzten Preisen** at greatly reduced prices; **he|rab|set|zend** ADJ disparaging ADV disparagingly; **sich ~ über jdn äußern** to speak disparagingly of sb; **He|rab|set|zung** [-zɛtsʊŋ] F **-, -en** (*von Ware*) reduction; (*von Preisen, Kosten auch*) lowering; (*von Niveau*) debasement, lowering; (*von Leistungen, Fähigkeiten*) belittling, disparagement; (= *Kränkung*) slight, snub; **he|rab+sin|ken** VI *sep irreg aux sein* to sink (down); (*liter: Nacht*) to fall, to descend (*liter*); **he|rab+stei|gen** VI *sep irreg aux sein* to get down, to descend; (*von Pferd*) to dismount; (*von Berg*) to climb down, to descend; **he|rab+sto|ßen** VI *sep irreg aux sein* to swoop (down); **he|-**

rab+stür|zen *sep* VT to push off (*von etw* sth); VI *aux sein* to fall off (*von etw* sth); (*Felsbrocken*) to fall down (*von* from); (*geh: Wasserfall*) to cascade *or* plunge down, to come rushing down; VR to jump off (*von etw* sth); **er stürzte sich vom Turm herab** he threw himself off *or* from the tower, he jumped off *or* from the tower; **he|rab+wür|di|gen** *sep* VT to belittle, to disparage; VR to degrade *or* lower oneself; **He|rab|wür|di|gung** F belittling, disparagement; **he|rab+zie|hen** VT *sep irreg* (*lit*) to pull down; *Mundwinkel* to turn down; (*fig*) *jdn* to drag down

He|ral|dik [he'raldɪk] F **-**, *no pl* heraldry

he|ral|disch [he'raldɪʃ] ADJ heraldic

he|ran [hɛ'ran] ADV **rechts/links ~!** over to the right/left; **immer** *or* **nur ~!** come on *or* along (then)!; **bis an etw** (*acc*) **~** close *or* near to sth, right by *or* beside sth; (*mit Bewegungsverb*) right up to sth

he|ran- PREF → *auch* **ran-: he|ran+ar|bei|ten** VR *sep* (= *sich nähern*) to work one's way along; **sich an jdn/etw ~** to work one's way (along *or* over) toward(s) sb/sth; **he|ran+bil|den** VT *sep* to train (up); (*in der Schule*) to educate; **he|ran+brin|gen** VT *sep irreg* (= *herbringen*) to bring over; **sein Spurt brachte ihn näher an die führenden Läufer heran** his spurt brought him up toward(s) the leader *or* brought him nearer to the leader; **die Schüler bedächtig an diese schwierigen Probleme ~** to introduce the pupils slowly to these difficult problems; **he|ran+ei|len** VI *sep aux sein* (*geh*) to rush *or* hurry over; **he|ran+fah|ren** VI *sep irreg aux sein* to drive *or* (*mit Fahrrad*) ride up (*an +acc* to); **he|ran+füh|ren** *sep* VT *jdn* to lead up; *Truppen* to bring up; **jdn an etw** (*acc*) **~** (*lit*) to lead/bring sb up to sth; (*fig*) *Frage, Problem* to lead *or* bring sb to sth; (*Lehrer etc*) to introduce sb to sth VI **an etw** (*acc*) **~** (*lit, fig*) to lead to sth; **he|ran+ge|hen** VI *sep irreg aux sein* to go up (*an +acc* to); **ich würde nicht näher ~** I wouldn't go any nearer *or* closer; **an jdn/etw ~** (*lit*) to go up to sb/sth; (*fig:* = *angreifen*) *an Problem, Aufgabe* to tackle *or* approach sth; *an Gegner* to set about sb; **he|ran+kom|men** VI *sep irreg aux sein* **a** (*räumlich*) to come *or* draw near (*an +acc* to), to approach (*an etw acc* sth); (*zeitlich*) to draw near (*an +acc* to), to approach (*an etw acc* sth); **das lasse ich mal an mich ~** (*fig auch*) I'll cross that bridge when I come to it (*prov*); **die Verfolger kamen dicht an den führenden Läufer heran** those behind were almost catching up with the leader; **unsere Verfolger kamen immer näher heran** our pursuers were gaining on us; **auf 1:3 ~** to pull up *or* back to 1-3; **er lässt alle Probleme an sich ~** he always adopts a wait-and-see attitude **b** (= *erreichen, bekommen*) **an den Chef/Motor kommt man nicht heran** you can't get hold of the boss/get at *or* to the engine; **wie komme ich nur an das Kapital heran?** how do I get hold of *or* (*wenn festgelegt*) get at the capital? **c** (= *sich messen können mit*) **an jdn ~** to be up to the standard of sb; **an etw** (*acc*) **~** to be up to (the standard of) sth; **an diesen Wissenschaftler kommt keiner heran** there's no-one who is a patch on (*Brit*) *or* a match for (*US*) this scientist; **er kommt nicht an seinen Vater heran** he's not a patch on (*Brit*) *or a match for* (*US*) his father **d an etw** (*acc*) **~** (= *grenzen an*) to verge on sth; **he|ran+ma|chen** VR *sep* (*inf*) **sich an etw** (*acc*) **~** to get down to sth, to get going on sth (*inf*); **sich an jdn ~** to approach sb, to have a go at sb (*inf*); *an Mädchen* to make up to sb, to chat sb up (*esp Brit inf*); **he|ran+na|hen** VI *sep aux sein* (*geh*) to approach; (*Katastrophe, Unwetter auch*) to be imminent; **He|ran|na|hen** NT **-s**, *no pl* (*geh*) approach; **he|ran+pir|schen** VR *sep* **sich an jdn/etw ~** to stalk up on sb/sth; **he|ran+rei|chen ✪** 32.3 VI *sep* **an jdn/etw ~** (*lit*) (*Mensch*) to reach sb/sth; (*Weg, Gelände etc*) to reach (up to) sth; (*fig:* = *sich messen können mit*) to come up to (the standard of) sb/sth, to come near sb/sth; **er reicht bei weitem nicht an**

---

mich heran (fig) he is nowhere near as good as me, he can't touch me (inf); **he|ran+rei|fen** VI sep aux sein (geh) (Obst) to ripen; (fig) (Jugendliche) to mature; (Plan, Entschluss, Idee) to mature, to ripen; **zur Frau/zum Mann/zum Erwachsenen ~** to mature into a woman/a man/an adult; **he|ran+rü|cken** sep VI aux sein (= sich nähern) to approach (an etw (acc) sth); (Truppen auch) to advance (an +acc upon, towards); (= dicht aufrücken) to move nearer or closer (an +acc to); **er rückte mit seinem Stuhl heran** he brought or drew his chair up or nearer VT to move over or up (an +acc to); **rück deinen Stuhl heran** bring or draw up your chair; **he|ran+schaf|fen** VT sep to bring (along); **he|ran+schlei|chen** VIR sep irreg (vi: aux sein) to creep up (an etw (acc) to sth, an jdn on sb); **he|ran+tas|ten** VR sep (lit) to feel or grope one's way over (an +acc to); (fig) to feel one's way; **sich an eine Frage ~** to approach a matter cautiously; **he|ran+tra|gen** VT sep irreg to bring (over), to carry over; **etw an jdn ~** (fig) to take sth to sb, to go on to sb with sth; **he|ran+tre|ten** VI sep irreg aux sein (lit) to move up (an +acc to); **näher ~** to move nearer; **bitte treten Sie näher heran!** this way!, come along!; **an jdn ~** (fig) = konfrontieren: Probleme, Zweifel, Versuchung) to confront or face sb; **mit etw an jdn ~** (= sich wenden an) to go to or approach sb with sth; **he|ran+wach|sen** VI sep irreg aux sein (geh) to grow; (Kind) to grow up; (fig: Probleme, Konkurrenz) to grow up (jdm around sb); **zu einer schönen jungen Frau ~** to grow (up) into or to be a lovely young woman; **die ~de Generation** the rising generation, the up-and-coming generation; **He|ran|wach|sen|de(r)** MF decl as adj (Jur) adolescent; **he|ran+wa|gen** VR sep to venture near, to dare to go near; **sich an etw (acc) ~** (lit) to venture near sth, to dare to go near sth; (fig) to venture to tackle sth; **er wagte sich nicht an sie heran** he did not dare to approach her; **he|ran+win|ken** VT sep to beckon or wave over; Taxi to hail; **einen Polizisten ~ to** call a policeman over

he|ran+zie|hen sep irreg VT **a** (= näher bringen) to pull over, to draw near (an +acc to)
b (= zu Hilfe holen) to call in; Literatur to consult; **jdn zur Hilfe/Unterstützung ~** to enlist sb's aid or help/support
c (= einsetzen) Arbeitskräfte, Kapital to bring in; **jdn zu einer Aufgabe ~** to enlist sb to do a task
d (= geltend machen) Recht, Paragrafen, Quelle, Zitat to call or bring into play; **etw zum Vergleich ~** to use sth by way of comparison
e (= aufziehen) Tier, Kind to raise; Pflanze to cultivate; **jdn zu etw ~** to bring sb up to be sth; **sich** (dat) **Revolutionäre/Jasager ~** (pej) to make revolutionaries/yes men for oneself
VI aux sein to approach; (Mil) to advance

He|ran|zie|hungs|be|scheid M (Admin) final notice

he|rauf [hɛˈrauf] ADV up; **vom Tal ~** up from the valley; **von unten ~** up from below; **vom Süden ~** (inf) up from the south PREP +acc up; **den Fluss/den Berg/die Treppe ~** up the river/ mountain/stairs

he|rauf- pref → auch **rauf-** up; **he|rauf+ar|bei|ten** VR sep (lit, fig) to work one's way up; **he|rauf+be|mü|hen** ptp **heraufbemüht** sep (geh) VT to trouble to come up, to ask (to come) up VR to take the trouble to come up; **he|rauf+be|schwö|ren** ptp **heraufbeschworen** VT sep irreg **a** (= wachrufen) Erinnerung, Vergangenheit to evoke **b** (= herbeiführen) Unglück, Streit, Krise to cause, to give rise to; **he|rauf+bit|ten** VT sep irreg to ask (to come) up; **he|rauf+bli|cken** VI sep (geh) to look up (zu to); **he|rauf+brin|gen** VT sep irreg to bring up; **he|rauf+däm|mern** VI sep aux sein (liter) to dawn; **he|rauf+drin|gen** VI sep irreg aux sein to rise (up) from below; (Geruch) to waft up; **ein Geräusch drang zu ihm herauf** a noise from below reached him or his ears; **he|rauf+dür|fen** VI sep irreg (inf) to be allowed up; **he|rauf+füh|-**

ren sep VT Pferd etc to lead up; jdn to show up VI (Weg etc) to lead up; **he|rauf+kom|men** VI sep irreg aux sein to come up; (in oberes Stockwerk) to come up(stairs); (auf Boot, Kutsche) to climb or come or get aboard; (Mond, Geräusch, Nebel, Wolke) to rise; (Gewitter) to approach; **he|rauf+las|sen** VT sep irreg to allow (to come) up; **er wollte mich nicht in den 2. Stock ~** he wouldn't let me come up to the 2nd (Brit) or 3rd (US) floor; **he|rauf+rei|chen** VT sep to hand or pass up VI to reach; **der Baum reicht bis zum Fenster herauf** the tree reaches (up to) or comes up to the window; **he|rauf+set|zen** sep VT Preise etc to increase, to raise VR **komm setz dich zu mir herauf** come up here and sit with me, come and sit up here with me; **he|rauf+stei|gen** VI sep irreg aux sein **a** (= heraufklettern) to climb up; (Dampf, Rauch) to rise; (Erinnerungen) to well up (in jdm in sb) **b** (liter: = anbrechen) (Tag, neue Zeit) to dawn; (Dämmerung) to break; **he|rauf+tra|gen** sep irreg VT to carry up; **he|rauf+zie|hen** sep irreg VT to pull up; **er zog ihn zu sich herauf** (lit) he pulled him up to him; (fig) he raised him to his own level VI aux sein **a** (Gewitter, Unheil etc) to approach; (liter, Nacht, Tag, Zeitalter) to draw nigh (liter) or near **b** (= nach oben umziehen) to move up

he|raus [hɛˈraus] ADV → auch **herauskommen**, **heraus sein** etc out; **~ da!** (inf) get or come out of there!; **da ~?** out of there?; **~ aus den Federn!** (inf) rise and shine! (inf); **~ mit ihm** (inf) get him out!; **~ damit!** (inf) (= gib her) hand it over!; (= heraus mit der Sprache!) out with it! (inf); **zum Fenster ~** out of the window; **nach vorn ~ wohnen** to live facing or at the front; **von innen ~** to the core, through and through; **das rostet von innen ~ durch** it's rusting through from the inside; **mir ist von innen ~ kalt** I'm cold inside; **etw von innen ~ heilen** to cure sth from inside; **aus einem Gefühl der Verlassenheit ~** out of a feeling of forlornness → **freiheraus**

he|raus- PREF → auch **raus-** out; **he|raus+ar|bei|ten** sep VT (aus Stein, Holz) to carve (aus out of); (fig) to bring out VR to work one's way out (aus of); **he|raus+be|kom|men** ptp **herausbekommen** VT sep irreg **a** Fleck, Nagel etc to get out (aus of) **b** (= ermitteln, herausfinden) Täter, Ursache, Geheimnis to find out (aus jdm from sb); Lösung, Aufgabe to work or figure out **c** Wechselgeld to get back; **Sie bekommen noch 1 Euro heraus** you still have 1 euro change to come; **he|raus+bil|den** VR sep to form, to develop (aus out of); **he|raus+bo|xen** VT sep (aus of) Ball to punch out; (inf) jdn to bail out (inf); **he|raus+brin|gen** VT sep irreg **a** (lit) to bring out (aus of) **b** (inf: = entfernen, ermitteln) = **herausbekommen a, b c** (auf den Markt bringen) to bring out; neues Modell to bring out, to launch; **jdn/etw ganz groß ~** to launch sb/sth in a big way, to give sb/sth a big build-up; **die Affäre wurde in allen Zeitungen groß herausgebracht** the affair made a big splash in the papers, they made a big splash of the affair in the papers **d** (= hervorbringen) Worte to utter, to say; **er brachte kein Wort/keinen Ton heraus** he couldn't utter a word/sound; **aus ihm war kein Wort herauszubringen** they couldn't get a (single) word out of him; **he|raus+dre|hen** VT sep Birne, Schraube to unscrew (aus from); **he|raus+drin|gen** VI sep irreg aux sein to come out (aus of); (Wasser, Information auch) to leak out (aus from); **he|raus+drü|cken** VT sep to squeeze out (aus of); die Brust ~ to stick one's chest out; **he|raus+fah|ren** sep irreg VI aux sein **a** (aus of) to come out; (Auto, Fahrer) to come or drive out; (Zug) to pull or draw out; (Radfahrer) to ride out; **aufs Land/zu Besuch herausgefahren kommen** to drive or come out to the country/for a visit **b** (= schnell herauskommen) to leap out; (= entweichen) to come out; (Wort etc) to slip out, to come out; **das Wort ist mir nur so herausgefahren** that word just came or slipped out somehow VT **a** (aus of) Zug, Auto

to drive out; Fahrrad to ride out **b** (Sport) **eine gute** or **schnelle Zeit/den Vorsprung ~** to make good time/the lead; **einen Sieg ~** to drive to victory; (bei Rad-/Motorradrennen) to ride to victory; **verlorene Minuten ~** to make up for lost time; **he|raus+fil|tern** VT sep (aus of) to filter out; (fig auch) to sift out; **he|raus+fin|den** sep irreg VT **a** Fehler, Fakten, Ursache to find out; (= herauslesen) Gesuchtes to pick out (aus from (among)), to find (aus (from) among); **er hat herausgefunden, dass ...** he has found out or discovered that ...; (= erkannt) he has found or discovered that ... VIR to find one's way out (aus of); **he|raus+fi|schen** VT sep (inf) to fish out (inf) (aus of); **sich** (dat) **etw ~** to pick sth out (for oneself); **sich immer das Beste aus allem ~** always to take the best of everything; **he|raus+flie|gen** sep irreg VI aux sein (aus of) (lit) to fly out; (inf: = herausfallen) to come flying out VT to fly out (aus of)

He|raus|for|de|rer [hɛˈrausfɔrdərɐ] M -s, -, **He|raus|for|de|rin** [-ərɪn] F -, -nen challenger

he|raus+for|dern [hɛˈrausfɔrdən] sep VT (esp Sport) to challenge (zu to); (= provozieren) to provoke (zu etw to do sth); Kritik, Protest to invite; (= heraufbeschwören) Gefahr to court; Unglück to court, to invite; **das Schicksal ~** to tempt fate or providence VI **zu etw ~** (= provozieren) to invite sth

he|raus|for|dernd ADJ provocative; (= lockend auch) inviting; Blick auch come-hither attr; (= Auseinandersetzung suchend) Reden, Haltung, Blick challenging ADV (= aggressiv, sexuell) provocatively; (= lockend) invitingly; **jdn ~ ansehen** to give sb a provocative look

He|raus|for|de|rung F challenge; (= Provokation) provocation

he|raus+füh|len VT sep (fig) to sense (aus from)

he|raus+füh|ren VTI sep (lit, fig) to lead out (aus of)

He|raus|ga|be F **a** (= Rückgabe) return, handing back; (von Personen) handing over, surrender, delivery; **Klage auf ~** action for restitution or return (für of) **b** (von Buch etc) publication

he|raus+ge|ben sep irreg VT **a** (= zurückgeben) to return, to hand or give back; Gefangene etc to hand over, to surrender, to deliver
b (= veröffentlichen, erlassen) to issue; Buch, Zeitung to publish; (= bearbeiten) to edit
c (= Wechselgeld geben) Betrag to give in or as change; **wie viel hat er dir herausgegeben?** how much change or what change did he give you (back)?; **2 EUR/zu wenig ~** to give 2 euros change/too little change
d (= herausreichen) to hand or pass out (aus of) VI (= Wechselgeld geben) to give change (auf +acc for); **er hat vergessen, mir herauszugeben** he's forgotten to give me my change; **können Sie (mir) ~?** can you give me change?, have you got the or enough change?; **falsch ~** to give the wrong change

He|raus|ge|ber(in) M(F) (= Verleger) publisher; (= Redakteur) editor

he|raus-: **he|raus+ge|hen** VI sep irreg aux sein (aus of) to go out; (Fleck, Korken etc) to come out; **aus sich ~** (fig) to come out of one's shell (fig); **he|raus+grei|fen** VT sep irreg to pick or single out (aus of); Beispiel to take; **sich** (dat) **einzelne Demonstranten ~** to pick on or single out individual demonstrators; **he|raus+ha|ben** VT sep irreg (inf) **a** (= entfernt haben) to have got out (aus of); **ich will ihn aus der Firma ~** I want him out of the firm **b** (= begriffen haben) to have got (inf); (= gelöst haben) Problem, Rätsel, Aufgabe to have solved; Geheimnis to have found out; **ich habe es jetzt heraus, wie man das am besten macht** I've got it - I know the best way to do it now; **jetzt hat er die Handhabung der Maschine heraus** he's got the knack or hang of the machine now (inf) → **Dreh a c** (= zurückbekommen haben) to have got back; **he|raus+hal|ten** sep irreg VT **a** (lit)

Hand, Gegenstand to put *or* stick out (*aus* of) **b** (= *fernhalten*) *Tiere, Eindringlinge* to keep out (*aus* of) **c** (*fig*: = *nicht verwickeln*) to keep out (*aus* of) **VR** to keep out of it; **sich aus etw ~** to keep out of sth; **halt du dich mal heraus!** you keep *or* stay out of it *or* this; **he|raus+hän|gen** *sep* **VT** to hang out (*aus* of); **den Intellektuellen ~** (*inf*) to show off about being an intellectual (*inf*) **VI** *irreg* to hang out (*aus* of); **he|raus+hau|en** *ptp* **herausgehauen** **VT** *sep* **a** (*inf: aus misslicher Lage*) **jdn ~** to get sb off the hook (*inf*) **b** (*aus Stein*) *Stufe, Figur, Relief* to carve, to cut (*aus* of); **he|raus+he|ben** *sep* *irreg* **VT** to lift out (*aus* of); (*fig*: = *betonen*) to bring out **VR** to stand out; **er hebt sich durch seine Begabung heraus** he stands out on account of his talent; **he|raus+hel|fen** **VI** *sep* *irreg* **jdm ~** (*lit, fig*) to help sb out (*aus* of); **jdm aus dem Zug ~** to help sb off the train; **he|raus+ho|len** **VT** *sep* **a** (*lit*) to get out (*aus* of) **b** *Bedingungen, Vorteil* to gain; *günstiges Ergebnis, hohe Umsätze, Vorsprung, gute Zeit, Sieg* to achieve; *Gewinn* to make; *Herstellungskosten* to recoup; **etw aus etw ~** to get sth from sth; **alles aus sich ~** to get the best from oneself; **das Letzte aus sich ~** to give one's all **c** (= *herauspauken*) to get off the hook (*inf*); **mein Anwalt wird mich da ~** my solicitor will get me off (the hook (*inf*)); **he|raus+hö|ren** **VT** *sep* (= *wahrnehmen*) to hear; (= *fühlen*) to detect, to sense (*aus* in); **he|raus+keh|ren** **VT** *sep* (*lit*) to sweep out (*aus* of); (*fig*: = *betonen*) *Bildung, Überlegenheit* to parade; **Strenge ~** to show one's sterner *or* stricter side; **den reichen Mann/Vorgesetzten ~** to parade the fact that one is rich/the boss; **he|raus+kit|zeln** **VT** *sep* (*inf*) **etw aus jdm ~** to worm sth out of sb (*inf*); **he|raus+klin|gen** **VI** *sep* *irreg* to ring out (*aus* from); (= *zum Ausdruck kommen*) to ring through (*aus etw* sth)

he|raus+kom|men **VI** *sep* *irreg* *aux* sein **a** (= *nicht innen bleiben*) to come out (*aus* of); **ich bin schon seit Tagen aus den Kleidern/dem Haus nicht herausgekommen** I haven't had these clothes off/I haven't been out of the house in days; **er ist nie aus seinem Land/Dorf herausgekommen** he has never been out of *or* has never left his country/village; **sie kommt zu wenig heraus** (*inf*) she doesn't go *or* get out enough; **aus sich ~** to come out of one's shell; **er kam aus dem Staunen/der Verwunderung nicht heraus** he couldn't get over his astonishment/amazement; **er kam aus dem Lachen nicht heraus** he couldn't stop laughing; **wie kommen wir bloß hier heraus?** how do *or* shall we get out of here?
b (*aus bestimmter Lage*) to get out (*aus* of); **aus seinen Schwierigkeiten/Sorgen ~** to get over one's difficulties/worries; **aus den Schulden ~** to get out of debt; **mit einem Gewinn ~** to get *or* win a prize
c (= *auf den Markt kommen*) to come out; (*neues Modell*) to come out, to be launched; **mit einem neuen Modell ~** to bring out a new model, to come out with a new model
d (= *bekannt gegeben werden*) to come out; (*Gesetz*) to come into force; (= *bekannt werden: Schwindel, Betrug etc*) to come to light, to come out; **es wird bald ~, dass du das Auto gestohlen hast** they'll soon find out *or* it will soon come out that you stole the car
e (= *sichtbar werden*) to come out; (*Fleck*) to appear; (= *zur Geltung kommen, hörbar werden*) to come over; **ganz groß ~** (*inf*) to make a big splash (*inf*), to have a big impact
f (= *geäußert werden*) to come out; **mit etw ~** to come out with sth; **mit der Sprache ~** to come out with it (*inf*)
g (= *Resultat haben*) **bei etw ~** to come of sth, to emerge from sth; **und was soll dabei ~?** and what is that supposed to achieve?, and where is that supposed to get us?; **bei dieser Rechenaufgabe kommt 10 heraus** this sum comes to 10, the answer to this sum is 10; **es kommt nichts dabei heraus, da kommt nichts bei heraus** (*inf*) it doesn't get us anywhere, it doesn't

achieve anything; **dabei wird nichts Gutes ~** no good will come of it; **es kommt auf eins** *or* **auf dasselbe** *or* **aufs Gleiche heraus** it comes (down) to *or* boils down to the same thing
h (*Sw*: = *ausgehen*) to turn out
i (*inf*: = *aus der Übung kommen*) to get out of practice
j (*Cards*) to lead; **wer kommt heraus?** whose lead is it?, who leads?

he|raus-: he|raus+krie|gen **VT** *sep* (*inf*) = **herausbekommen**; **he|raus+kris|tal|li|sie|ren** *ptp* **herauskristallisiert** *sep* **VT** (*Chem*) to crystallize (*aus* out of); (*fig*) *Fakten, Essenz, Punkte* to extract (*aus* from) **VR** (*Chem*) to crystallize (out); (*fig*) to crystallize, to take shape; **he|raus+las|sen** **VT** *sep* *irreg* to let out (*aus* of); **he|raus+lau|fen** **VI** *sep* *irreg* **VI** *aux* sein to run out (*aus* of) **VT** (*Sport*) *Vorsprung, Zeit, Sekunden* to gain; *Sieg, zweiten Platz auch* to win; **he|raus+le|sen** **VT** *sep* *irreg* (= *erkennen*) to gather (*aus* from); **aus seinem Brief/seiner Miene las ich Kummer heraus** from his letter/expression I could tell *or* I gathered that he was worried; **was die Kritiker aus seinem Roman alles ~ wollen** the things the critics try to read into his novel; **he|raus+lo|cken** **VT** *sep* (*aus* of) to entice out; *Gegner, Tier auch* to lure out; **etw aus jdm ~** (= *ablisten*) to get *or* worm (*inf*) sth out of sb; **jdn aus seiner Reserve ~** to draw sb out of his shell; **he|raus+lü|gen** **VR** *sep* *irreg* to lie one's way out of it; **sich aus etw ~** to lie one's way out of it; **he|raus+ma|chen** *sep* (*inf*) **VT** (*aus* of) to take out; *Fleck* to get out **VR** (= *sich gut entwickeln*) to come on (well); (*finanziell*) to do well; (*nach Krankheit*) to pick up; **sie hat sich prächtig herausgemacht** she has really blossomed *or* bloomed; **he|raus+müs|sen** **VI** *sep* *irreg* (*inf*) **a** (= *entfernt werden müssen*) to have to come out **b** (= *aufstehen müssen*) to have to get up **c** (= *gesagt werden müssen*) to have to come out; **he|raus+nehm|bar** **ADJ** removable; **he|raus+neh|men** **VT** *sep* *irreg* **a** (= *entfernen*) to take out (*aus* of); (*inf*) *Zahn* to pull out; *Kind* (*aus der Schule etc*) to take away, to remove (*aus* from); **sich** (*dat*) **die Mandeln ~ lassen** to have one's tonsils out; **den Gang ~** (*Aut*) to put the car into neutral **b** (*inf*: = *sich erlauben*) **es sich** (*dat*) **~, etw zu tun** to have the nerve to do sth (*inf*); **sich** (*dat*) **Freiheiten ~** to take liberties; **Sie nehmen sich zu viel heraus** you're going too far; **he|raus+pau|ken** **VT** *sep* (*inf*) **jdn (aus etw) ~** to bail sb out (of sth) (*inf*); **he|raus+pi|cken** **VT** *sep* (*inf*) (*Vögel*) to peck out; (*fig*) *das Beste* to pick out; **he|raus+plat|zen** **VI** *sep* *aux* sein (*inf*) (= *spontan sagen*) to blurt it out; (= *lachen*) to burst out laughing; **mit etw ~** to blurt sth out; **he|raus+pres|sen** **VT** *sep* (*aus* of) to squeeze out; *Saft etc auch* to press out; *Geld, Geständnis auch* to wring out; **he|raus+put|zen** **VT** *sep* jdn to dress up; (= *schmücken*) *Stadt, Weihnachtsbaum, Wohnung etc* to deck out; **sich prächtig ~** to get dressed up, to do oneself up (*inf*); (*Stadt*) to be decked out magnificently; **he|raus+quet|schen** **VT** *sep* (*lit, fig*) to squeeze out (*inf*); **etw aus jdm ~** to squeeze sth out of sb (*inf*); **he|raus+ra|gen** **VI** *sep* = **hervorragen**; **he|raus+ra|gend** **ADJ** **a** (*lit*: = *vorstehend*) projecting **b** (*fig*: = *ausgezeichnet*) excellent, outstanding; **he|raus+re|den** **VR** *sep* to talk one's way out of it (*inf*); **he|raus+rei|ßen** **VT** *sep* *irreg* **a** (*lit*) (*aus* of) to tear *or* rip out; *Zahn* to pull out; *Baum* to pull out *or* up **b** **jdn aus etw ~** (*aus Umgebung*) to tear sb away from sth; *aus Arbeit, Spiel, Unterhaltung* to drag sb away from sth; *aus Schlaf, Träumerei* to startle sb out of sth; *aus Lethargie, Sorgen* to shake sb out of sth; **jdn aus seinem Kummer ~** to take sb out of himself **c** (*inf: aus Schwierigkeiten*) **jdn ~** to get sb out of it (*inf*) **d** (*inf*: = *wieder gutmachen*) to save; **he|raus+rü|cken** **VT** *sep* to push out (*aus* of); (*inf*: = *hergeben*) *Geld* to cough up (*inf*); *Beute, Gegenstand* to hand over **VI** *aux* sein **a** (*lit*) to move out **b** (*inf*: = *hergeben*) **mit etw ~** (*mit Geld*) to cough sth up (*inf*); *mit Beute* to hand sth over **c** (*inf*: = *aussprechen*) **mit etw ~**

to come out with sth; **rück schon mit deinem Problem heraus!** come on (now), out with it, out with it now, what's the problem?; **mit der Sprache ~** to come out with it; **he|raus+ru|fen** *sep* *irreg* **VT** to call *or* shout out (*aus* of); **das Publikum rief den Schauspieler noch dreimal heraus** the audience called the actor back another three times **VI** to call *or* shout out (*aus* of); **he|raus+rut|schen** **VI** *sep* *aux* sein (*lit*) to slip out (*aus* of); (*fig inf*: *Bemerkung*) to slip out; **das ist mir nur so herausgerutscht** it just slipped out somehow, I just let it slip (out) somehow; **he|raus+sau|gen** **VT** *sep* to suck out (*aus* of); **he|raus+schä|len** *sep* **VT** *das Essbare etc* (*aus* of) to get out, to dig out (*inf*); (= *ausschneiden*) *schlechte Stelle auch* to scrape out; (*fig*: = *absondern*) *Fakten, Elemente* to single out; **sich aus seinen Sachen ~** (*inf*) to peel off one's clothes **VR** (*fig*: = *deutlich werden*) to become evident *or* apparent; **he|raus+schau|en** **VI** *sep* (*dial*) **a** (*Mensch*) to look out (*aus, zu* of) **b** (= *zu sehen sein*) to show **c** (*inf*) = **herausspringen** c; **he|raus+schie|ßen** **VI** *sep* *irreg* **a** (*lit*) to shoot out **aus einem Gebäude ~** to shoot from a building **b** *aux* sein (*auch* **herausgeschossen kommen**) (*aus* of) to shoot out **VT** to shoot out; **he|raus+schin|den** **VT** *sep* *irreg* (*inf*) = **herausschlagen VT** b; **he|raus+schla|gen** *sep* *irreg* **VT** **a** (*lit*) to knock out (*aus* of); **aus einem Stein Funken ~** to strike sparks from *or* off a stone **b** (*inf*: = *erreichen*) *Geld* to make; *Erlaubnis, Verzögerung, Gewinn, Vorteil* to get; *Zeit* to gain; **seine Kosten ~** to cover one's costs **VI** *aux* sein (*Flammen*) to leap *or* shoot out (*aus* of); **die Flammen schlugen zum Dach heraus** the flames were leaping through the roof; **he|raus+schleu|dern** **VT** *sep* (= *werfen*) to hurl out (*aus* of); *Piloten* to eject; (*fig*) *Fragen, Vorwürfe, wütende Worte* to burst out with; **he|raus+schlüp|fen** **VI** *sep* *aux* sein (*lit, fig*) to slip out (*aus* of); **he|raus+schme|cken** *sep* **VT** to taste **VI** to be prominent (over the other flavours (*Brit*) *or* flavors (*US*)); **he|raus+schmei|ßen** **VT** *sep* *irreg* (*inf*: *lit, fig*) to throw *or* chuck (*inf*) *or* sling (*inf*) out (*aus* of); **he|raus+schnei|den** **VT** *sep* *irreg* to cut out (*aus* of); **he|raus+schrei|ben** **VT** *sep* *irreg* *Stellen, Zitat etc* to copy out (*aus* of); **he|raus+schrei|en** **VT** *sep* *irreg* *Hass, Gefühle* to shout out

he|raus sein ▲ **VI** *irreg* *aux* sein (*inf*) **a** (= *entfernt sein*) to be out
b (= *hervorgekommen sein: Sterne, Blumen etc*) to be out
c (= *herausgekommen sein*) (*Buch, Programm etc*) to be out; (*Gesetz*) to be in force
d (= *bekannt sein*) to be known; (= *entschieden sein*) to have been *or* to be settled *or* decided
e (= *hinter sich haben*) (*aus* of) to be out, to have got out; **aus der Schule ~** to have left school; **aus dem Gröbsten** *or* **Ärgsten** *or* **Schlimmsten ~** to have got past the worst (part); (*bei Krise, Krankheit*) to be over the worst; **wenn ich nur erst aus dieser Stadt heraus wäre** if only I were out of this town ▸ **fein ADV** b
f (= *gesagt worden sein*) (*Wahrheit*) to be out; (*Worte*) to have come out

he|rau|ßen [heˈrausn] **ADV** (*S Ger, Aus*) out here

he|raus-: he|raus+sprin|gen **VI** *sep* *irreg* *aux* sein (*aus* of) **a** (*lit*) to jump *or* leap out **b** (= *sich lösen*) to come out; **aus dem Gleis ~** to jump the rails **c** (*inf*) **dabei springt ein fetter Gewinn heraus** there is a handsome profit in it; **dabei springt nichts heraus** there's nothing to be got out of it; **was springt für mich dabei heraus?** what's in it for me?; **he|raus+spru|deln** *sep* **VI** *aux* sein to bubble out (*aus* of) **VT** *Worte, Sätze* to come gushing out with; **he|raus+ste|hen** **VI** *sep* *irreg* (*S Ger: aux* sein) to stand *or* stick out, to protrude; **he|raus+stel|len** *sep* **VT** **a** (*lit*) to put outside; (*Sport*) to send off **b** (*fig*: = *hervorheben*) to emphasize, to underline; *jdn* to give prominence to **VR** (*Unschuld, Wahrheit*) to come to light; **sich als falsch/wahr/rich-**

tig/begründet ~ to show itself to be *or* to prove (to be) wrong/true/correct/well-founded; **es stellte sich heraus, dass ...** it turned out *or* emerged that ...; **es wird sich ~, wer Recht hat/ was getan werden muss** we shall see who is right/what must be done; **das muss sich erst ~** that remains to be seen; **he|raus+stre|cken** VT *sep* to stick out (*zu, aus of*); **he|raus+strei|chen** VT *sep irreg* **a** *Fehler etc* to cross out, to delete (*aus in*) **b** (= *betonen*) *Verdienste etc* to stress, to lay great stress upon; **he|raus+strö|men** VI *sep aux sein* (*aus of*) (*Flüssigkeit*) to stream *or* pour out; (*Gas*) to come out; (*geh: Menschenmenge*) to pour out; **he|raus+stür|zen** VI *sep aux sein* **a** (auch **herausgestürzt kommen**) (= *eilen*) to rush out (*aus of*) **b** (= *fallen*) to fall out; **zum Fenster ~** to fall out of the window; **he|raus+su|chen** VT *sep* to pick out; **he|raus+tre|ten** VI *sep irreg aux sein* to step *or* come out (*aus of*), to emerge (*aus from*); (*Adern etc*) to stand out, to protrude; **he|raus+trom|meln** VT *sep* (*inf*) to get out; **he|raus+wach|sen** VI *sep irreg aux sein* to grow out (*aus of*); **he|raus+wa|gen** VR *sep* to dare to come out (*aus of*), to venture out (*aus of*) *or* forth (*liter*) (*aus from*); **he|raus+win|den** VR *sep irreg* (*fig*) to wriggle out of it; **sich aus etw ~** to wriggle out of sth; **he|raus+wirt|schaf|ten** VT *sep* to make (*aus out of*); **he|raus+wol|len** VI *sep* to want to get out (*aus of*); **nicht mit etw ~** (*inf*: = *sagen wollen*) not to want to come out with sth (*inf*); **er wollte nicht mit der Sprache heraus** (*inf*) he didn't want to come out with it (*inf*); **he|raus+zie|hen** *sep irreg* **VT** to pull out (*aus of*); (= *herausschleppen*) to drag out (*aus of*); (*Chem, Med*) to extract (*aus from*); **die Essenz aus einem Buch ~** to extract the main substance from a book; **muss ich dir die Antworten einzeln ~?** (*inf*) do I have to drag answers out of you one by one? **VR** to pull oneself out (*aus of*)

herb [hɛrp] **ADJ a** *Geruch* sharp; *Geschmack* sharp, tangy; *Parfüm* tangy; *Wein* dry **b** *Enttäuschung, Verlust, Niederlage* bitter; *Erwachen* rude; *Erkenntnis, Wahrheit* cruel **c** (= *streng*) *Züge, Gesicht* severe, harsh; *Art, Wesen, Charakter, Mensch* dour; *Schönheit* severe, austere **d** (= *unfreundlich*) *Worte, Kritik* harsh **ADV** ~ **riechen** *or* **duften** to smell tangy; ~ **schmecken** to taste tangy; *Wein* to taste dry

Her|ba|rium [hɛrˈbaːriʊm] NT **-s, Herbarien** herbarium, herbary

her|bei [hɛɐ̯ˈbai] ADV (*geh*) come (here); **(alle Mann) ~!** come here(, everybody)!

her|bei-: her|bei+brin|gen VT *sep irreg* *jdn, Gegenstand* to bring over; *Indizien, Beweise* to provide; *Sachverständige* to bring in; **her|bei+ei|len** VI *sep aux sein* (*geh*) to hurry *or* rush over; **her|bei+füh|ren** VT *sep* **a** (= *bewirken*) *Entscheidung, Konfrontation etc* to bring about; (= *verursachen*) to cause; **den Tod** *etc* ~ (*Med*) to cause death *etc* (*form*) **b** (*an einen Ort*) to bring; *Schlusszeuge* to draw; **her|bei+ho|len** VT *sep* to bring; *Verstärkung* to bring in; *Arzt, Taxi, Polizisten* to fetch; **einen Arzt ~ lassen** to send for a doctor; **her|bei+kom|men** VI *sep irreg aux sein* to come *or* draw near, to approach; **her|bei+las|sen** VR *sep irreg* **sich zu etw ~, sich ~, etw zu tun** to condescend *or* deign to do sth; **her|bei+lau|fen** VI *sep irreg aux sein* to come running up; **her|bei+re|den** VT *sep* **etw ~** to bring sth about by talking about it; **Probleme ~** to create problems by talking about them; **her|bei+ru|fen** VT *sep* to call over; *Verstärkung* to call in; *Arzt, Polizei, Taxi* to call; **her|bei+schaf|fen** VT *sep* to bring; *Geld* to get, to get hold of (*inf*); *Beweise* to produce; **her|bei+seh|nen** VT *sep* to long for; **her|bei+strö|men** VI *sep aux sein* (*geh*) to come flocking, to come in (their) crowds; **her|bei+win|ken** VT *sep* to wave over, to summon; **her|bei+wün|schen** VT *sep* (**sich** *dat*) **etw ~** to long for sth; (**sich** *dat*) **jdn ~** to wish sb were *or* was here; **her|bei+zau|bern** VT *sep* to conjure

up; **her|bei+zie|hen** *sep irreg* **VT** *aux sein* to approach; **herbei+zi|tie|ren** *ptp* **herbeizitiert** VT *sep* (*inf*) to send for

her-: her+be|kom|men *ptp* **herbekommen** VT *sep irreg* (*inf*) to get; **her+be|mü|hen** *ptp* **herbemüht** *sep* (*geh*) **VT** *jdn* ~ to trouble sb to come here **VR** to take the trouble to come here; **her+be|or|dern** *ptp* **herbeordert** VT *sep* to summon, to send for

Her|ber|ge [ˈhɛrbɛrgə] F **-, -n a** *no pl* (= *Unterkunft*) lodging *no indef art*, accommodation *no indef art*; (*fig*) refuge **b** (*old: = Gasthaus*) inn; (= *Jugendherberge*) (youth) hostel

Her|bergs-: Her|bergs|el|tern PL (youth hostel) wardens *pl*; **Her|bergs|mut|ter** F *pl* **-müt|ter, Her|bergs|va|ter** M (youth hostel) warden

her-: her+be|stel|len *ptp* **herbestellt** VT *sep* to ask to come; **her+be|ten** VT *sep* (*pej*) to rattle off

Herb|heit F **-,** *no pl* **a** (*von Geruch*) sharpness; (*von Parfüm*) tanginess; (*von Geschmack*) sharpness, tanginess; (*von Wein*) dryness **b** (*von Enttäuschung, Verlust*) bitterness; (*von Erwachen*) rudeness **c** (= *Strenge*) (*von Gesicht, Zügen*) severity, harshness; (*von Art, Wesen, Charakter, Mensch*) dourness; **die ~ dieser Wahrheit/Erkenntnis** the cruel truth/realization; **ihre Schönheit ist von einer gewissen ~** she has a certain severe beauty **d** (= *Unfreundlichkeit*: *von Worten, Kritik*) harshness

her+bit|ten VT *sep irreg* to ask to come

Her|bi|zid [hɛrbiˈtsiːt] NT **-(e)s, -e** [-də] herbicide

her+brin|gen VT *sep irreg* to bring (here); **bring mir das Buch her** bring me the book (over) → *auch* **hergebracht**

Herbst [hɛrpst] M **-(e)s, -e** autumn, fall (*US*); **im ~** in autumn, in the fall (*US*); **der ~ des Lebens** (*liter*) the autumn of (one's) life (*liter*); **auch der ~ hat noch schöne Tage** (*prov*) you're never too old

Herbst- *in cpds* autumn, fall (*US*); **Herbst|an|fang** M beginning of autumn *or* fall (*US*); **Herbst|as|ter** F Michaelmas daisy

herbs|ten [ˈhɛrpstn] **VI** *impers* **es herbstet** (*liter*) autumn *or* fall (*US*) is nigh (*liter*) **VT** (*dial*) *Wein* to harvest

Herbs|tes- (*poet*) *in cpds* = **Herbst-**

Herbst- *in cpds* autumn, fall (*US*); **Herbst|far|ben** PL autumn *or* autumnal colours *pl* (*Brit*), fall colors *pl* (*US*); **Herbst|fe|ri|en** PL autumn holiday(s *pl*) (*esp Brit*) *or* vacation (*US*); (*Sch*) autumn half-term holiday(s *pl*) (*esp Brit*) *or* vacation (*US*); **Herbst|laub** NT *autumn or fall* (*US*) leaves (*US*); **herbst|lich** [ˈhɛrpstlɪç] **ADJ** autumn *attr*, (= *wie im Herbst auch*) autumnal; **das Wetter wird schon ~** autumn *or* fall (*US*) is in the air; **das Wetter ist schon ~** it's already autumn *or* fall (*US*); **herbst|lich** gefärbtes Laub leaves in autumnal colours (*Brit*) *or* fall colors (*US*); ~ **kleiden** to dress for the autumn *or* fall (*US*); **Herbst|mo|nat** M autumn month; **der ~** (*old*) September; **Herbst|ne|bel** M autumn mist; **Herbst|sturm** M autumn *or* fall (*US*) storm; **Herbst-Tag-und|nacht|glei|che** F *decl as adj* autumnal equinox; **Herbst|zeit|lo|se** [ˈhɛrpstsaitloːzə] F *decl as adj* meadow saffron

Herd [heːrt] M **-(e)s, -e** [-də] **a** (= *Küchenherd*) cooker, stove; (= *Kohleherd*) range; (*fig*: = *Heim*) home; **eigener ~ ist Goldes wert** (*Prov*) there's no place like home (*Prov*); **den ganzen Tag am ~ stehen** (*fig*) to slave over a hot stove all day **b** (*Med*: = *Krankheitsherd*) focus; (*Geol: von Erdbeben*) epicentre (*Brit*), epicenter (*US*); (*fig: von Rebellion etc*) seat **c** (*Tech*) hearth

Herd|ab|deck|plat|te F electric ring cover

Her|de [ˈheːrədə] F **-, -n** (*lit*) herd; (*von Schafen, fig geh*: = *Gemeinde*) flock; **mit der ~ laufen** (*pej*) to follow the herd; **der ~ folgen** (*pej*) to follow the herd

Her|den-: Her|den|ins|tinkt M (*lit, fig pej*) herd instinct; **Her|den|mensch** M (*pej*) sheep (*pej*), herd-follower (*pej*); **Her|den|tier** NT gregarious animal; **Her|den|trieb** M (*lit, fig pej*) herd instinct; **her|den|wei|se** ADV in herds; (*Schafe*) in flocks; (*fig*) in crowds *or* herds

Herd|plat|te F (*von Kohleherd*) (top) plate; (*von Elektroherd*) hotplate

he|rein [hɛˈrain] ADV in; **~!** come in!, come! (*form*); **nur ~!** do come in!; **immer ~!** come along in!; **hier ~!** in here!; **von (dr)außen ~** from outside; **auf dem Wege von draußen ~** on the way in

he|rein- PREF → *auch* **rein-** in; **he|rein+be|kom|men** *ptp* **hereinbekommen** VT *sep irreg* (*inf*) *Waren* to get in; *Radiosender* to get; *Unkosten etc* to recover; **he|rein+be|mü|hen** *ptp* **hereinbemüht** *sep* (*geh*) **VT** to trouble to come in **VR** to take the trouble to come in; **he|rein+bit|ten** VT *sep irreg* to ask (to come) in; **he|rein+bre|chen** VI *sep irreg aux sein* **a** (= *eindringen: Wasser, Flut, Wellen*) to gush in; **über jdn/etw ~** (*lit, fig*) to descend upon sb/sth **b** (*Gewitter*) to break; (*Krieg, Pest*) to break out; **das Unglück brach über ihn herein** misfortune overtook him **c** (*liter*: = *anbrechen*) (*Nacht, Abend*) to fall, to close in; (*Winter*) to set in **d** (*lit*: = *nach innen stürzen*) to fall in; **wie ist er herein+brin|gen** VT *sep irreg* **a** (= *nach innen bringen*) to bring in **b** (*inf*: = *wettmachen*) *Geldverlust* to make good; *Zeit-, Produktionsverluste* to make up for; *Unkosten* to get back; **he|rein+drän|gen** VIR *sep* to push one's way in; **he|rein+drin|gen** VI *sep irreg aux sein* (*Licht, Wasser*) to come in (*in +acc* -to); **ein Geräusch/Geruch drang ins Zimmer herein** a sound/smell reached the room; **he|rein+dür|fen** VI *sep irreg* (*inf*) to be allowed in; **darf ich herein?** may or can I come in?; **he|rein+fah|ren** VTI *sep irreg* (*vi: aux sein*) to drive in; (*mit Fahrrad*) to ride in; **he|rein+fal|len** VI *sep irreg aux sein* **a** (= *nach innen fallen*) to fall in (*in +acc* -to) **b** (*inf*) (= *sich täuschen lassen*) to fall for it (*inf*); (= *betrogen werden*) to be had (*inf*); **auf jdn/etw ~** to be taken in by sb/sth, to be taken for a ride (by sb) (*inf*)/to fall for sth; **mit jdm/etw ~** to have a bad deal with sb/sth; **he|rein+füh|ren** VT *sep* to show in; **he|rein+ho|len** VT *sep* to bring in (*in +acc* -to); **he|rein+kom|men** VI *sep irreg aux sein* to come in (*in +acc* -to); **wie ist er hereingekommen?** how did he get in?; **ins Haus ~** to come in *or* inside; **he|rein+krie|gen** VT *sep* (*inf*) = **hereinbekommen**; **he|rein+las|sen** VT *sep irreg* to let in (*in +acc* -to); **he|rein+le|gen** VT *sep* **a** (= *nach innen legen*) to lay (down) **b** (*inf*) *jdn ~* (= *betrügen*) to take sb for a ride (*inf*); (= *anführen*) to take sb in; **he|rein+neh|men** VT *sep irreg* to bring in (*in +acc* -to); (= *in Liste, Kollektion etc aufnehmen*) to put in, to include; (*Comm*) *Aufträge* to accept; **he|rein+nö|ti|gen** VT *sep* to urge to come in; **sie hat mich förmlich hereingenötigt** she insisted that I come in; **he|rein+plat|zen** VI *sep aux sein* (*inf*) to burst *or* come bursting in (*in +acc* -to); **bei jdm ~** to burst in on sb; **he|rein+reg|nen** VI *impers sep* **es regnet herein** the rain is coming in; **he|rein+rei|ten** *sep irreg* **VTI** (*vi: aux sein*) to ride in (*in +acc* -to) **VR** (*inf*) to land oneself in it *or* in the soup (*inf*); **he|rein+ru|fen** VT *sep irreg* to call in; **he|rein+schau|en** VI *sep* (*dial*) to look in (*in +acc* -to); **(bei jdm) ~** (*inf*) to look in on sb (*inf*), to look sb up (*inf*); **he|rein+schlei|chen** VIR *sep irreg* (*vi: aux sein*) (*in +acc* -to) to creep or slip in; (*heimlich*) to sneak in; **he|rein+schmug|geln** VT *sep* (*in +acc* -to) to smuggle in; **he|rein+schnei|en** VI *sep* *impers* **es schneit herein** the snow's coming in **VI** *aux sein* (*inf*) to drop in (*inf*); **he|rein+se|hen** VI *sep irreg* to look in (*in +acc* -to); **he|rein+spa|zie|ren** VI *sep aux sein* to breeze in (*in +acc* -to); **hereinspaziert!** come right in!; **he|rein+ste|cken** VT *sep* (*in +acc* -to) to put in; *Kopf, Hand auch* to stick in;

he|rein+strö|men VI *sep aux sein* (*in +acc* -to) to stream *or* pour in; (*geh: Menschenmassen*) to pour in; (*in +acc* -to); **he|rein+stür|men** VI *sep aux sein* to storm *or* come storming in (*in +acc* -to); **he|rein+stür|zen** VI *sep aux sein* to rush in (*in +acc* -to); **he|rein+wa|gen** VR *sep* (*in +acc* -to) to dare to come in, to venture in; **he|rein+wol|len** VI *sep* (*inf*) to want to come in

Her-: her|fah|ren *sep irreg* VI *aux sein* to come *or* get here; **hinter/vor jdm/etw ~** to drive *or* (*mit Rad*) ride (along) behind/in front of *or* ahead of sb/sth; **der Detektiv fuhr hinter dem Auto her** the detective followed *or* trailed the car VT to drive *or* bring here; **Her|fahrt** F journey here; **auf der ~** on the journey *or* way here; **her+fal|len** VI *sep irreg aux sein* **über jdn ~** to attack sb, to fall upon sb; (*mit Fragen*) to attack sb, to pitch into sb; (*esp Brit*); (= *kritisieren*) to pull sb to pieces; **über etw** (*acc*) **~** to descend upon sth; *über Geschenke, Essbares etc* to pounce upon sth; **her+fin|den** VI *sep irreg* to find one's way here

herg. *abbr von* **hergestellt** manufactured, mfd

Her|gang M *pl* (*rare*) **-gänge** (*von Schlacht*) course; **schildern Sie mir genau den ~ dieses Vorfalls** tell me exactly what happened; **der ~ des Unfalls** the way the accident happened, the details of the accident

her-: her+ge|ben *sep irreg* VT (= *weggeben*) to give away; (= *überreichen, aushändigen*) to hand over; (= *zurückgeben*) to give back; **gib das her!** give me that, let me have that; **viel/einiges ~** (*inf:* = *erbringen*) to be a lot of use/of some use; **wenig ~** (*inf*) not to be much use; **das Buch gibt nicht viel her** the book doesn't tell me/you (very) much; **das Thema gibt viel/nichts her** there's a lot/nothing to this topic; **ein Essen, das was hergibt** a fine spread; **was die Beine hergaben** as fast as one's legs would carry one; **was die Lunge/Stimme hergab** at the top of one's voice; **seinen Namen für etw ~** to lend one's name to sth VR **sich zu** *or* **für etw ~** to be (a) party to sth; **dazu gebe ich mich nicht her** I won't have anything to do with it; **eine Schauspielerin, die sich für solche Filme hergibt** an actress who allows herself to be involved in such films; **her|ge|bracht** ADJ (= *traditionell*) traditional; **in ~er Weise** as is/was traditional → *auch* **herbringen**; **her+ge|hen** *sep irreg aux sein* **a hinter/vor/neben jdm ~** to walk (along) behind/in front of *or* ahead of/beside sb **b** (*S Ger, Aus*) = **herkommen c ~ und etw tun** (= *einfach tun*) just *or* simply to (go and) do sth VI *impers* (*inf*) (= *zugehen*) **so geht es her** that's the way it goes *or* is; **es ging heiß her** things got heated (*inf*), (the) sparks flew; **hier geht es hoch her** there's plenty going on here; **her+ge|hö|ren** *ptp* **hergehört** VI *sep* to belong here; (*fig auch*) to be relevant; **her|ge|lau|fen** ADJ *attr* (*pej*) = **dahergelaufen**; **her+ha|ben** VT *sep irreg* (*inf*) **wo hat er das her?** where did he get that from?; **her+hal|ten** *sep irreg* VT to hold out VI to suffer (for it), to pay for it; **für etw ~** to pay for sth; **er muss als Sündenbock ~** he is the scapegoat; **als Entschuldigung für etw ~** to serve *or* be used as an excuse for sth; **her+ho|len** VT *sep* (*inf*) to fetch; **~ lassen** to send for; **weit hergeholt sein** (*fig*) to be far-fetched; **her+hö|ren** VI *sep* (*inf*) to listen; **alle** *or* **alles mal ~!** listen (to me) *or* listen here (*inf*) *or* pay attention everybody, everybody listen (to me)

He|ring ['heːrɪŋ] M **-s, -e a** herring; **ein gedörrter ~** a kipper; **wie die ~e zusammengedrängt** packed in like sardines (in a tin); **dünn wie ein ~** as thin as a rake (*Brit*) *or* rail (*US*) **b** (= *Zeltpflock*) (tent) peg **c** (*fig inf: schwächlicher Mensch*) weakling

He|rings-: He|rings|fän|ger M (= *Heringsfangschiff*) herring boat; **He|rings|fi|let** NT (*Cook*) herring fillet; **He|rings|topf** M pickled herring with sour cream

---

he|rin|nen [hɛˈrɪnən] ADV (*S Ger, Aus*) = **drinnen, innen**

her-: her+ja|gen *sep* VT (*auf jdn zu*) to drive *or* chase over *or* across; **jdn vor sich** (*dat*) **~** to drive sb along in front of one VI *aux sein* **hinter jdm ~** to chase after sb; **hinter etw** (*dat*) **~** to be after sth; **her+kom|men** VI *sep irreg aux sein* to come here; (= *sich nähern*) to come, to approach; (= *herstammen*) to come from; **komm her!** come here!; **von jdm/etw ~** (= *stammen*) to come from sb/sth; **ich weiß nicht, wo das herkommt** (*was der Grund ist*) I don't know why it is, I don't know what the reason is; **her|kömm|lich** ['heːrkœmlɪç] ADJ conventional; **nach ~em Brauch** according to convention; **her+krie|gen** VT *sep* (*inf*) to get; **ich kriege ihn einfach nicht her** I simply can't get him to come (here)

Her|ku|les ['hɛrkuləs] M **-', -se** (*Myth, fig*) Hercules

Her|ku|les|ar|beit F (*fig*) Herculean task

her|ku|lisch [hɛrˈkuːlɪʃ] ADJ Herculean

Her|kunft ['heːrkʊnft] F **-, ⁼e** [-kʏnftə] origin; (*soziale*) background, origins *pl*; **er ist britischer ~** (*gen*), **er ist seiner ~ nach Brite** he is of British extraction *or* descent *or* origin; **er ist aristokratischer ~** (*gen*) he comes from an aristocratic family, he is of aristocratic descent

Her|kunfts-: Her|kunfts|be|zeich|nung F (*Comm*) designation of origin; **Her|kunfts|land** NT (*Comm*) country of origin; **Her|kunfts|ort** M *pl* **-orte** place of origin

her-: her+lau|fen VI *sep irreg aux sein* to come running; **lauf doch mal her zu mir!** come over here to me; **hinter** (*lit, fig*)/**vor/neben jdm ~** to run after/ahead of/beside sb; **her+lei|ern** ['heːrlaɪɐn] VT *sep* (*inf*) to spout (*inf*); **her+lei|hen** VT *sep irreg* (*Aus, S Ger*) to lend (out); **her+lei|ten** *sep* VT **a** (= *ableiten, folgern*) to derive (*aus* from) **b** (= *an bestimmten Ort leiten*) to bring VR **sich von etw ~** to come from sth, to be derived from sth; **Her|lei|tung** F (*von Wort etc*) derivation; **her+lo|cken** VT *sep* to entice, to lure

her+ma|chen *sep* (*inf*) VR **sich über etw** (*acc*) **~** (= *in Angriff nehmen, über Arbeit, Buch, Essen*) to get stuck into sth (*inf*); (= *Besitz ergreifen*) *über Eigentum, Gegenstände* to pounce (up)on sth; **sich über jdn ~** to lay into sb (*inf*) VT **viel ~** (*inf*) to look impressive; **wenig ~** not to look very impressive; **nichts ~** not to be up to much (*inf*); **von jdm/etw viel ~** to crack sb/sth up to be quite fantastic (*inf*), to make a big thing of sb/sth (*inf*); **von jdm/etw wenig** *or* **nicht viel ~** not to make a big thing of sb/sth (*inf*); **viel von sich ~** to be full of oneself; **er macht wenig** *or* **nicht viel von sich her** he's pretty modest

Her|maph|ro|dit [hɛrmafroˈdiːt] M **-en, -en** hermaphrodite

Her|me|lin¹ [hɛrməˈliːn] NT **-s, -e** (*Zool*) ermine

Her|me|lin² M **-s, -e** (= *Pelz*) ermine

Her|me|neu|tik [hɛrməˈnɔytɪk] F **-, no pl** hermeneutics *sing*

her|me|neu|tisch [hɛrməˈnɔytɪʃ] ADJ hermeneutic(al)

Her|mes|bürg|schaft ['hɛrmɛs-] F government export credit guarantee

her|me|tisch [hɛrˈmeːtɪʃ] ADJ (*lit, fig*) hermetic; ADV **die Häftlinge sind ~ von der Außenwelt abgeschlossen** the prisoners are completely shut off from the outside world; **~ abgeriegelt** completely sealed off

her+müs|sen VI *sep irreg* (*inf*) **a das muss her** I/we have to have it **b** (= *kommen müssen*) to have to come (here); **hinter jdm ~** to have to go after sb

her|nach [hɛɐˈnaːx] ADV (*dated, dial*) afterwards

her+neh|men VT *sep irreg* **a** (= *beschaffen*) to get, to find; **wo soll ich das ~?** where am I sup-

---

posed to get that from? **b** (*dial inf*) **jdn ~** (= *stark fordern, belasten*) to make sb sweat (*inf*); (= *mitnehmen: Krankheit, Schock, Nachricht, Anstrengung*) to take it out of sb (*inf*) **c** (**sich** *dat*) **jdn ~** (*dial:* = *tadeln, verprügeln*) to give it to sb (*inf*), to let sb have it (*inf*) **d** (*dial:* = *nehmen*) to take

her|nie|der [hɛɐˈniːdɐ] ADV (*liter*) down

he|ro|ben [hɛˈroːbn̩] ADV (*Aus, S Ger*) up here

He|roe [heˈroːə] M **-n, -n** (*geh*) hero

He|ro|en|kult [heˈroːən-] M (*geh*) hero worship

He|ro|in [heroˈiːn] NT **-s, no pl** heroin

he|ro|in|ab|hän|gig ADJ addicted to heroin

He|ro|in|ab|hän|gi|ge(r) MF *decl as adj* heroin addict

He|ro|ine [heroˈiːnə] F **-, -n** (*dated Theat*) heroine

He|ro|in-: He|ro|in|han|del M (*auf der Straße*) heroin dealing; (*international*) heroin trafficking; **He|ro|in|op|fer** NT (= *Herointote(r)*) heroin victim; **he|ro|in|süch|tig** ADJ addicted to heroin; **He|ro|in|süch|ti|ge(r)** MF *decl as adj* heroin addict; **He|ro|in|to|te(r)** MF *decl as adj* heroin victim

he|ro|isch [heˈroːɪʃ] (*geh*) ADJ heroic ADV heroically

he|ro|i|sie|ren [heroiˈziːrən] *ptp* **heroisiert** VT (*geh*) **jdn** to make a hero of; **Tat** to glorify

He|ro|is|mus [heroˈɪsmʊs] M **-, no pl** (*geh*) heroism

He|rold ['heːrɔlt] M **-(e)s, -e** [-də] (*Hist:* = *Bote*) herald; (*fig:* = *Vorbote auch*) harbinger

He|ros ['heːrɔs] M **-, Heroen** [heˈroːən] hero

Her|pes ['hɛrpɛs] M **-, no pl** (*Med*) herpes

Her|pes-: Her|pes-Bläs|chen NT , **Her|pes|bläs|chen** NT herpes blister; **Her|pes-Vi|rus** NT OR M , **Her|pes|vi|rus** NT OR M herpes virus

Herr [hɛr] M **-(e)n, -en a** (= *Gebieter*) lord, master; (= *Herrscher*) lord, ruler (*über +acc* of); (*von Hund*) master; **mein ~ und Gebieter** my lord and master; **der junge ~** (*form*) the young master; **die ~en der Schöpfung** (*hum:* = *Männer*) the gentlemen; **sein eigener ~ sein** to be one's own master *or* boss; **~ im eigenen Haus sein** to be master in one's own house; **~ einer Sache** (*gen*) **sein/werden** (= *in der Hand haben*) to have/get sth under control; **~ der Lage** *or* **Situation sein/bleiben** to be/remain master of the situation, to have/keep the situation under control; **nicht mehr ~ seiner Sinne sein** not to be in control of oneself any more; **~ über Leben und Tod sein** to have the power of life and death (*gen* over); **über jdn/etw ~ werden** to master sb/sth; **man kann nicht** *or* **niemand kann zwei ~en dienen** (*prov*) no man can serve two masters (*prov*); **wie der ~, sos Gescherr!** (*Prov*) like master, like man! (*prov*) → **Land c**

b (= *Gott, Christus*) Lord; **Gott, der ~** the Lord God; **der ~ Jesus** the Lord Jesus; **der ~ der Heerscharen** the Lord of Hosts; **~, du meine Güte!** good(ness) gracious (me)!; **~ des Himmels!** good Lord!; **er ist ein großer Schwindler/Esser** etc **vor dem ~n** (*hum inf*) what a great fibber/eater etc he is

c (= *feiner Herr, Mann*) gentleman; **ein geistlicher ~** a clergyman; **ein adliger ~, ein ~ von Adel** a nobleman; „**Herren**" (= *Toilette*) "gentlemen", "gents", "men"; **den (großen) ~n spielen** *or* **markieren** to give oneself airs, to put on airs → **alt**

d (*vor Eigennamen*) Mr; (*vor Titeln*) *usu not translated* (*in Anrede ohne Namen*) sir; (**mein**) **~!** sir!; **bitte, der ~** (*beim Servieren*) there you are, sir; **der ~ wünscht?** what can I do for you, sir?; **Ihr ~ Vater** (*form*) your father; **~ Nachbar** (*old*) excuse me, sir; **~ Dr./Doktor/Professor Schmidt** Dr/Doctor/Professor Schmidt; **~ Doktor** doctor; **~ Professor** professor; **~ Präsident/Vorsitzender** Mr President/Chairman; **der ~ Präsident/Vorsitzende** the President/Chairman; **lieber** *or* **werter** (*dated*) *or* **sehr geehrter** *or* **sehr**

---

verehrter (*form*) ~ **Bell** (*in Brief*) Dear Mr Bell; **an den ~n Abgeordneten C. Schmidt** C. Schmidt, MP; **werte ~en, sehr geehrte ~en** (*in Brief*) Dear Sirs (*Brit*), to whom it may concern (*US*) **e** (*allgemein gesehen: = Tanzpartner, Begleiter*) gentleman; (*auf eine bestimmte Dame bezogen*) partner; (*bei Cocktailparty, Theaterbesuch etc*) (gentleman) companion **f** (*Sport*) **4x100m-Staffel der ~en** men's 4 x 100m relay

Herr|chen ['hɛrçən] NT **-s,** - *dim von* **Herr** (*inf: von Hund*) master; **geh zum ~** go to your master

Her-: her|rei|chen VT *sep* to hand, to pass; **Her|rei|se** F journey here; **auf der ~ von Köln** on the journey from Cologne

Her|ren- *in cpds* men's; (*auf Kleidung bezüglich auch*) gents' (*dated*); (*bei einzelnes Exemplar bezüglich*) man's, gent's; **Her|ren|abend** M stag night; **seinen/einen ~ haben** to have one's/a night out with the boys (*inf*); **Her|ren|artikel** PL gentlemen's requisites *pl* (*dated*); **Her|ren|aus|stat|ter** [-lausʃtatə] M **-s,** -, **Her|ren|aus|stat|te|rin** [-ərɪn] F **-, -nen** gents' *or* men's outfitter; **Her|ren|be|glei|tung** F ~ **erwünscht** please bring a gentleman *or* (*bei Ball*) partner; **in ~** in the company of a gentleman; **Her|ren|be|kannt|schaft** F gentleman acquaintance; **eine ~ machen** to make the acquaintance of a gentleman; **Her|ren|be|klei|dung** F menswear; **Her|ren|be|such** M (gentle)man visitor/visitors; **Her|ren|dop|pel** NT (*Tennis etc*) men's doubles *sing*; **Her|ren|ein|zel** NT (*Tennis etc*) men's singles *sing*; **Her|ren|fahr|rad** NT man's bicycle *or* bike (*inf*); **Her|ren|fri|seur(in)** M(F) men's hairdresser, barber; **Her|ren|ge|sell|schaft** F **a** (*= gesellige Runde*) stag party **b** *no pl* (*= Begleitung von Herren*) **in ~ sein** to be in the company of gentlemen/a gentleman; **Her|ren|haus** NT **a** manor house **b** (*Hist*) upper chamber; **Her|ren|jah|re** PL → **Lehrjahr**; **Her|ren|kon|fek|ti|on** F men's ready-to-wear clothes *pl*; (*= Abteilung*) menswear department; **Her|ren|le|ben** NT life of luxury and ease; **Her|ren|los** ADJ abandoned; **Hund** *etc* stray; **Her|ren|ma|ga|zin** NT (*Zeitschrift für Männer*) men's magazine; **Her|ren|man|gel** M shortage of men; **Her|ren|mensch** M member of the master race; **Her|ren|mo|de** F men's fashion; **Her|ren|par|tie** F (*= Ausflug*) men-only outing; (*= Gesellschaft*) stag party; **Her|ren|pilz** M (*Bot: = Steinpilz*) cep, porcini (*esp US*); **Her|ren|rad** NT man's bicycle *or* bike (*inf*); **Her|ren|ras|se** F master race; **Her|ren|rei|ten** NT **a,** *no pl* amateur racing; **Her|ren|rei|ter** M **a** (*Sport*) amateur jockey **b** (*iro*) stuffed shirt (*inf*); **Her|ren|sa|lon** M barber's; **Her|ren|sat|tel** M (man's) saddle; **im ~ reiten** to ride astride; **Her|ren|sau|na** M (*euph*) massage parlour (*Brit*) *or* parlor (*US*); **Her|ren|schnei|der(in)** M(F) gentlemen's tailor; **Her|ren|schnitt** M (*= Frisur*) haircut like a man's; **Her|ren|sitz** M **a** (*= Gutshof*) manor house **b** **im ~ reiten** to ride astride; **Her|ren|tie|re** PL primates *pl*; **Her|ren|toi|let|te** F men's toilet *or* restroom (*US*), gents *sing*; **Her|ren|volk** NT master race; **Her|ren|welt** F, *no pl* (*dated hum*) gentlemen *pl*; **Her|ren|win|ker** M (*hum*) kiss curl (*Brit*), spit curl (*US*); **Her|ren|witz** M dirty joke; **Her|ren|zim|mer** NT study; (*= Rauchzimmer*) smoking room

Herr|gott M (*dated inf*) (*Anrede*) God, Lord; **der ~** God, the Lord (God); (*S Ger, Aus: = Figur*) figure of the Lord; **~ (Sakrament)!** (*inf*) good God *or* Lord!; **~ noch mal!** (*inf*) damn it all! (*inf*)

Herr|gotts-: Herr|gotts|frü|he F **in aller ~** (*inf*) at the crack of dawn; **Herr|gotts|schnit|zer(in)** M(F) (*S Ger, Aus*) carver of crucifixes; **Herr|gotts|win|kel** M (*S Ger, Aus*) corner of a room with a crucifix

her|rich|ten *sep* VT **a** (*= vorbereiten*) to get ready (+*dat*, *für* for); **Bett** to make; **Tisch** to set **b** (*= instand setzen, ausbessern*) to do up (*inf*) VR (*dial*) to get dressed up

Her|rin ['hɛrɪn] F **-, -nen** (*Hist: = Herrscherin*) female ruler; (*von Hund, old: = Hausherrin*) mistress; **die ~** (*Anrede*) my lady

her|risch ['hɛrɪʃ] ADJ overbearing, imperious; **Ton** *auch* peremptory ADV imperiously, overbearingly; **auffordern** peremptorily

herr|je(h) [hɛrˈjeː], **herr|je|mi|ne** [hɛrˈjeːmiːnə] INTERJ goodness gracious

herr|lich ['hɛrlɪç] ADJ marvellous (*Brit*), marvelous (*US*); **Anblick, Tag, Wetter** *auch* magnificent, glorious, lovely; **Kleid** gorgeous, lovely; **Essen, Witz, Geschichte** marvel(l)ous, wonderful, lovely; **das ist ja ~** (*iro*) that's great ADV **du bist so ~ doof/naiv** (*iro*) you are so wonderfully stupid/naïve; **wir haben uns ~ amüsiert** we had marvel(l)ous fun *or* a marvel(l)ous time; **~ feiern** to have a marvellous time; **~ schmecken** *or* **mun|den** to taste absolutely delicious

Herr|lich|keit F **-, -en a** *no pl* (*= Schönheit, Pracht*) glory, magnificence, splendour (*Brit*), splendor (*US*); **die ~ Gottes** the glory of God; **Pracht und ~** pomp and circumstance; (*von Natur*) glory; **die ~ wird nicht lange dauern** (*iro inf*) this is too good to last; **ist das die ganze ~?** is that all there is to it?; **aus und vorbei mit der ~** here we go again **b** *usu pl* (*= prächtiger Gegenstand*) treasure **c** (*obs: Anrede*) lordship

Herr|schaft ['hɛrʃaft] F **-, -en a** *no pl* (*= Macht*) power; (*= Staatsgewalt*) rule; **zur ~ gelangen** *or* **kommen** to come to power; **sich der ~ bemächtigen** to seize power; **unter der ~** under the rule (+*gen, von* of); **unter jds ~** (*acc*) **fallen** to come under sb's rule; **während der ~** (+*gen*) in the reign of **b** *no pl* (*= Gewalt, Kontrolle*) control; **er verlor die ~ über sich** he lost his self-control; **er verlor die ~ über sein Auto** he lost control of his car, his car went out of control **c** (*old: = Dienstherrschaft*) master and mistress *pl*; **die ~en** (*= Damen und Herren*) the ladies and gentlemen; **hohe ~en** (*dated*) persons of high rank *or* standing; **meine alten ~en** (*dated inf: = Eltern*) my old man and old woman; **ältere ~en** (*iro: = alte Leute*) old folks; **würden die ~en bitte ...** ladies and gentlemen, would you please ...; **was wünschen die ~en?** what can I get you?; (*von Butler*) you rang?; **(meine) ~en!** ladies and gentlemen! **d** (*inf: Ausruf*) **~ (noch mal)** hang it (all) (*inf*) **e** (*Hist: = Landgut*) domain, estate, lands *pl*

herr|schaft|lich ['hɛrʃaftlɪç] ADJ of a person of high standing; (*= vornehm*) grand; **die ~e Kutsche** his lordship's coach

Herr|schafts-: Herr|schafts|an|spruch M claim to power; (*von Thronfolger*) claim to the throne; **Herr|schafts|be|reich** M territory; **Herr|schafts|form** F form *or* type of rule; **Herr|schafts|ge|walt** F authority, power; **herr|schafts|los** ADJ without rule *or* government; **Herr|schafts|lo|sig|keit** F, *no pl* state of being without rule *or* government; **Herr|schafts|struk|tur** F power structure; **Herr|schafts|sys|tem** NT system of rule

herr|schen ['hɛrʃn] VI **a** (*= Macht, Gewalt haben*) to rule; **König** to reign; (*fig*) (*Mensch*) to dominate; (*Geld*) to hold sway; (*Tod, Terror*) to rule, to hold sway **b** (*= vorherrschen*) (*Angst, Ungewissheit, Zweifel*) to prevail; (*Verkehr, Ruhe, Betriebsamkeit*) to be prevalent; (*Nebel, Regen, Kälte*) to be predominant; (*Krankheit, Not*) to be rampant, to rage; (*Meinung, Ansicht*) to predominate; **überall herrschte Freude/Terror** there was joy/terror everywhere; **im Zimmer herrschte bedrückende Stille** it was oppressively quiet in the room; **hier herrscht Ordnung** things are orderly (a)round here; **hier herrscht ein anderer Ton** the atmosphere is different here; **hier ~ ja Zustände!** things are in a pretty state around here! **c** (*= in herrischem Ton reden*) to snap, to bark VI *impers* **es herrscht schlechtes Wetter** the weather is bad, we're having bad weather; **es**

herrschte Schweigen silence reigned; **es herrscht Ungewissheit darüber, ob ...** there is uncertainty about whether ...

herr|schend ADJ **Partei, Klasse** ruling; **König** reigning; **Bedingungen, Verhältnisse, Meinungen** prevailing; **Mode** current; **die Herrschenden** the rulers, those in power

Herr|scher ['hɛrʃə] M **-s,** -, **Herr|sche|rin** [-ərɪn] F **-, -nen** (*über* +*acc* of) ruler; (*= König/Königin auch*) sovereign

Herr|scher-: Herr|scher|blick M imperious look; **mit ~** with an imperious look; **Herr|scher|fa|mi|lie** F ruling family; **Herr|scher|ge|schlecht** NT ruling dynasty; **Herr|scher|haus** NT ruling house *or* dynasty

Herr|sche|rin F → **Herrscher**

Herr|scher-: Herr|scher|kult M ruler cult; **Herr|scher|mie|ne** F imperious *or* commanding air; **Herr|scher|na|tur** F **a** (*= Mensch*) domineering person **b** (*= Wesensart*) domineering character; **Herr|scher|paar** NT ruler *or* sovereign and his *or* her consort

Herrsch|sucht F, *no pl* domineeringness

herrsch|süch|tig ADJ domineering

her-: her+rü|cken *sep* VT to move nearer *or* closer VI *aux sein* to move *or* come nearer *or* closer; **her+ru|fen** VT *sep irreg* to call (over); **Tier** to call; **her+rüh|ren** VI *sep* **von etw ~** to be due to sth, to stem from sth; **her+sa|gen** VT *sep* to recite; **her+schaf|fen** VT *sep* (*inf*) = **herbeischaffen**; **her+schau|en** VI *sep* (*dial*) to look here *or* this way; **zu jdm ~** to look in sb's direction; **da schau her!** (*Aus inf*) well, I never! (*inf*); **her+schen|ken** VT *sep* (*inf: = verschenken*) to give away; **her+schi|cken** VT *sep* to send; **jdn hinter jdm ~** to send sb after sb; **her+schlei|chen** VIR *sep irreg* (*VI: aux sein*) **a** (*an bestimmten Ort*) to creep up **b** (*sich*) **hinter jdm ~** to creep along behind sb; **her+se|hen** VI *sep irreg* **a** (*= hierher sehen*) to look here *or* this way; **zu jdm ~** to look in sb's direction **b** **hinter jdm/etw ~** to follow sb/sth with one's eyes; **her sein** ▲ VI *irreg aux sein* **a** (*zeitlich*) **das ist schon 5 Jahre her** that was 5 years ago; **es ist schon 5 Jahre her, dass ...** it was 5 years ago that ...; **es ist kaum ein Jahr her, dass ...** it's hardly a year since ...; **wie lange ist es her?** how long ago was it? **b** (*= herstammen*) to come from; **mit jdm/etw ist es nicht weit her** (*inf*) sb/sth is not up to much (*inf*) **c** **hinter jdm/etw ~** to be after sb/sth; **dahinter ~, dass** **jd etw tut** to be on to sb to do sth; **her+spio|nie|ren** *ptp* **herspioniert** VI *sep* **hinter jdm ~** to spy on sb; **her+stam|men** VI *sep* **a** (*= abstammen*) to come from; **wo stammst du her?** where do you come from originally? **b** (*= herrühren*) **von etw ~** to stem from sth **c** (*= herkommen*) **von jdm/etw ~** to come from sb/sth

her|stell|bar ADJ capable of being produced *or* manufactured; **schwer ~e Waren** goods which are difficult to produce *or* manufacture

her+stel|len VT *sep* **a** (*= erzeugen*) to produce; (*esp industriell*) to manufacture; **von Hand ~** to make *or* produce by hand; **in Deutschland hergestellt** made in Germany **b** (*= zustande bringen*) to establish; **Kontakt** to establish, to make; (*Telec*) **Verbindung** to make; **Stromkreis** to complete **c** (*gesundheitlich*) **jdn** to restore to health; **Gesundheit** to restore; **er ist wieder ganz hergestellt** he has quite recovered **d** (*an bestimmten Platz*) to put *or* place here; **sich (zu jdm) ~** to come over (to sb); **etw zu jdm ~** to put sth by sb

Her|stel|ler ['heːʃtɛlə] M **-s,** -, **Her|stel|le|rin** [-ərɪn] F **-, -nen** (*= Produzent*) manufacturer; (*in Verlag*) production manager, to sb by sb

Her|stel|ler-: Her|stel|ler|an|ga|be F **a** (*= Nennung der Herstellerfirma*) manufacturer's details *pl* **b** (*= Produktinformation*) **~n** *pl* product information *sing*; **Her|stel|ler|be|trieb** M, **Her|stel|ler|fir|ma** F manufacturing firm, manufacturer; **Her|stel|lung** F **a** (*= Erzeugung*) production; (*esp industriell*) manufacture

b (= *das Zustandebringen*) establishment **c** (*von Gesundheit*) restoration **d** (= *Abteilung in Verlag*) production department

Her|stel|lungs-: Her|stel|lungs|feh|ler M manufacturing defect *or* fault; **Her|stel|lungs|kos|ten** PL manufacturing *or* production costs *pl*; **Her|stel|lungs|land** NT country of manufacture; **Her|stel|lungs|preis** M cost of manufacture; **Her|stel|lungs|ver|fah|ren** NT manufacturing *or* production method

her-: her+stür|zen *sep* VI *aux sein* **a** (*auch* **hergestürzt kommen**) to come rushing up **b** **hinter jdm/etw ~** to rush after sb/sth VR sich hinter jdm ~ to throw oneself after sb; **her+tra|gen** VT *sep irreg* **a** (*an bestimmten Ort*) to carry here **b** **etw vor/hinter jdm/etw ~** to carry sth in front of/behind sb/sth; **her+trau|en** VR *sep* to dare to come here; **her+trei|ben** *sep irreg* **VT** **a** (*an bestimmten Ort*) to drive here; (*Wind*) to blow here; (*Strömung*) to wash here; **etw zu uns ~** to drive/blow/wash sth over to us **b** **jdn/etw vor jdm/etw ~** to drive (*Wind*) blow sb/sth in front of *or* before sb/sth; **jdn/etw hinter jdm/etw ~** to drive *or* (*Wind*) blow sb/sth behind sb/sth; **was treibt dich her?** what brings you here? **VI** *aux sein* to be driven (*vor +dat* in front of, before); (*Wolken*) to blow; (*in der Strömung*) to be washed; **her+tre|ten** VI *sep irreg aux sein* to step up

Hertz [hɛrts] NT **-, -** (*Phys, Rad*) hertz

he|rü|ben [hɛˈryːbn̩] ADV (*S Ger, Aus*) over here

he|rü|ber [hɛˈryːbɐ] ADV over here; (*über Fluss, Straße, Grenze etc*) across; **~ und hinüber** to and fro, back and forth; **da ~** over/across there

he|rü|ber- PREF → *auch* **rüber-** over; (*über Fluss, Straße, Grenze etc*) across; **he|rü|ber+bit|ten** VT *sep irreg* to ask (to come) over; **he|rü|ber+brin|gen** VT *sep irreg* → **herüber** to bring over/across (*über etw* (*acc*) sth); **he|rü|ber+dür|fen** VI *sep irreg* → **herüber** to be allowed (to come) over/across; **he|rü|ber+fah|ren** *sep irreg* → **herüber** **VI** *aux sein* to come *or* (*mit Auto auch*) drive over/across (*über etw* (*acc*) sth); **VT** (*über etw* (*acc*) sth) *Auto etc* to drive over/across; *Fahrgast, Güter* to take over/across; **he|rü|ber+flie|gen** VTI *sep irreg* (*vi: aux sein*) → **herüber** to fly over/across (*über etw* (*acc*) sth); **he|rü|ber+ge|ben** VT *sep irreg* to pass (*über +acc* over); **he|rü|ber+ho|len** VT *sep* to fetch; *jdn* to fetch over; **he|rü|ber+kom|men** VI *sep irreg aux sein* → **herüber** to come over/across (*über etw* (*acc*) sth); (*inf: zu Nachbarn*) to pop round (*Brit inf*), to call round; **wie sind es die Leute (über die Mauer/den Fluss) herübergekommen?** how did the people get over (the wall)/across (the river)?; **he|rü|ber+las|sen** VT *sep irreg* → **herüber** to allow (to come) over/across (*über etw* (*acc*) sth); (*aus Land*) to allow (to come) out; **he|rü|ber+lau|fen** VI *sep irreg aux sein* → **herüber** to run over/across (*über etw* (*acc*) sth); **he|rü|ber+rei|chen** *sep* **VT** to pass (*über +acc* over) **VI** to reach across (*über etw* (*acc*) sth); **he|rü|ber+ret|ten** VT *sep* **etw in die Gegenwart ~** to preserve sth; **he|rü|ber+schi|cken** VT *sep* → **herüber** to send over/across; **he|rü|ber+schwim|men** VI *sep irreg aux sein* to swim across (*über etw* (*acc*) sth); **he|rü|ber+se|hen** VI *sep irreg* → **herüber** to look over (*über etw* (*acc*) sth); **zu jdm ~** to look over/across to sb; **he|rü|ber+wech|seln** VI *sep aux sein or haben* (*Tiere*) to cross (*über etw* (*acc*) sth); **in unsere Partei/unseren Verein ~** to join our party/club, to swap parties/clubs (and join ours); **he|rü|ber+we|hen** *sep* → **herüber** (*über etw* (*acc*) sth) **VI** **a** (*Wind*) to blow over/across **b** *aux sein* (*Klang*) to be blown over/across; (*Duft*) to waft over/across; **he|rü|ber+wer|fen** VT *sep irreg* → **herüber** to throw over/across (*über etw* (*acc*) sth); **he|rü|ber+wol|len** VI *sep* → **herüber** to want to come over/across (*über etw* (*acc*) sth); **he|rü|ber+zie|hen** *sep irreg* → **herüber** (*über etw* (*acc*) sth) **VT** to pull over/across; (*fig*) to

win over **VI** *aux sein* (*Truppen, Wolken*) to move over/across; (= *umziehen*) to move

he|rum [hɛˈrʊm] ADV **a** (*örtlich richtungsangebend*) **um ... ~** (a)round; **links/rechts ~** (a)round to the left/right; **hier/dort ~** (a)round here/there; **oben ~** (*über Gegenstand, Berg*) over the top; (*in Bezug auf Körper*) (a)round the top; **sie ist oben ~ ziemlich füllig** she's quite well endowed (*hum*); **unten ~** (*unter Gegenstand*) underneath; (*um Berg, in Bezug auf Körper*) (a)round the bottom; **oben/unten ~ fahren** to take the top/lower road; **wasch dich auch unten ~** (*euph*) don't forget to wash down below; **verkehrt ~** the wrong way (a)round; (= *hinten nach vorn*) back to front; (= *links nach außen*) inside out; (= *oben nach unten*) upside down; **immer um etw ~** round and round sth (*esp Brit*), around and around sth

b (= *kreisförmig angeordnet, in der Nähe*) **um ... ~** around; **hier ~** (a)round here; (= *in der Nähe auch*) hereabouts; **alle um mich ~ wussten, dass ...** everyone (a)round me knew that ...

c **um ... ~** (*ungefähre Mengenangabe*) about, a-round; (*Zeitangabe*) (at) about *or* around → *auch* **herum sein**

he|rum- PREF → *auch* **umher-, rum-** (a)round; **he|rum+al|bern** VI *sep* (*inf*) to fool *or* lark (*inf*) around; **he|rum+är|gern** VR *sep* (*inf*) **sich mit jdm/etw ~** to keep struggling with sb/sth; **he|rum+bal|gen** VR *sep* (*inf*) to romp about; **he|rum+bal|lern** VI *sep* to fire in all directions *or* all over the place; **he|rum+bas|teln** VI *sep* (*inf*) to tinker *or* mess (*inf*) about (*an +dat* with); **he|rum+be|kom|men** VT *sep irreg* (*inf*) *jdn* to talk round (*esp Brit*) *or* around (*esp US*); **etw ~** to (manage to) get sth round (*um etw* sth); **he|rum+bes|sern** VI *sep* **an etw** (*dat*) **~** to fiddle around correcting sth; **he|rum+blät|tern** VI *sep* (**in einem Buch**) **~** to leaf *or* browse through a book; **he|rum+boh|ren** VI *sep* (*mit Stock, Finger etc*) to poke around; (*mit Bohrer*) to drill; **in der Nase ~** to pick one's nose; **he|rum+brin|gen** VT *sep irreg* (*inf*) **a** (= *überreden*) to talk round (*esp Brit*) *or* around (*esp US*) **b** *Zeit* to get through; **he|rum+brül|len** VI *sep* to yell; **he|rum+bum|meln** VI *sep* (*inf*) **a** (= *trödeln*) to mess about (*inf*) **b** *aux sein* (= *spazieren*) to stroll (a)round (*in etw* (*dat*) sth); **he|rum+deu|teln** VI *sep* (*inf*) **an etw** (*+dat*) **~** to quibble *or* to split hairs over sth; **daran ist nichts herumzudeuteln** it's perfectly plain; **he|rum+dok|tern** [hɛˈrʊmdɔktɐn] VI *sep* (*inf*) **an jdm/einer Krankheit/einer Wunde ~** to try to cure sb/an illness/to heal a wound (*unsuccessfully, using many different treatments*); **an etw** (*dat*) **~** (*fig*) to fiddle *or* tinker about with sth; **he|rum+dre|hen** *sep* **VT** *Schlüssel* to turn; (= *wenden*) *Decke, Tuch, Braten etc* to turn (over) → *Wort* VR to turn (a)round; (*im Liegen*) to turn over **VI** (*inf*) **an etw** (*dat*) **~** to fiddle *or* tinker about with sth; **he|rum+drü|cken** *sep* VR (*inf*) **a** (= *sich aufhalten*) to hang around (*inf*) (*um etw* sth) **b** (= *vermeiden*) **sich um etw ~** to dodge sth **VI** **an etw** (*dat*) **~** to squeeze sth VT *Hebel* to turn; **he|rum+druck|sen** VI *sep* (*inf*) to hum and haw (*inf*); **he|rum+er|zäh|len** *ptp* **herumerzählt** VT *sep* **etw bei jdm ~** to tell sb about sth; **erzähl das nicht herum** don't spread that (a)round; **he|rum+ex|pe|ri|men|tie|ren** *ptp* **herumexperimentiert** VI *sep* to experiment; **he|rum+fah|ren** *sep irreg* **VI** *aux sein* **a** (= *umherfahren*) to go *or* travel *or* (*mit Auto*) drive (a)round; **in der Stadt ~** to drive (a)round the town **b** (= *um etw herumfahren*) to go *or* (*mit Auto*) drive *or* (*mit Schiff*) sail (a)round **c** (= *sich rasch umdrehen*) to turn (a)round quickly, to spin (a)round **d** *aux sein* to turn *around* sich (*dat*) (*mit den Händen*) **in den Haaren ~** to run one's fingers through one's hair VT to drive (a)round; **he|rum+fin|gern** VI *sep* (*inf*) **an etw** (*dat*) **~** to fiddle about with sth; *an Körperteil* to finger sth; **he|rum+flat|tern** VI *sep aux sein* (= *umherflattern*) to flutter about; **um**

etw ~ to flutter around sth; **he|rum+fle|geln** VI *sep* to loll about *or* around; **he|rum+flie|gen** *sep irreg* **VI** *aux sein* to fly around (*um jdn/etw* sb/sth); (*inf:* = *herumliegen*) to be kicking around (*inf*) **VT** *jdn* to fly about *or* around; **he|rum+fra|gen** VI *sep* (*inf*) to ask around (*bei* a-mong); **he|rum+fuch|teln** VI *sep* (*inf*) (**mit den Händen**) **~** to wave one's hands about (*Brit*) *or* around; **mit einer Pistole ~** to wave a pistol a-round, to brandish a pistol; **he|rum+füh|ren** *sep* **VT** **a** *jdn, Tier* to lead (a)round (*um etw* sth); (*bei Besichtigung*) to take *or* show (a)round; **jdn in einer Stadt/im Haus ~** to take *or* show sb (a)round a town/the house **b** (= *leiten, dirigieren*) **jdn/einer um etw ~** to direct sb/sth around sth **c** (= *bauen*) **etw um etw ~** to build *or* take sth (a)round sth **VI** **um etw ~** to go (a)round sth; **he|rum+fuhr|wer|ken** VI *sep* (*inf*) to bustle about, to busy oneself; **he|rum+fum|meln** VI *sep* (*inf*) (*an +dat* with) to fiddle *or* fumble about; (*an Auto*) to mess about; (= *basteln*) to tinker (about); **he|rum+ge|ben** VT *sep irreg* to hand *or* pass (a)round; **he|rum+ge|hen** VI *sep irreg aux sein* (*inf*) **a** (= *um etw herumgehen*) to walk *or* go (a)round (*um etw* sth) **b** (= *ziellos umhergehen*) to go *or* wander (a)round (*in etw* (*dat*) sth); **es ging ihm im Kopf herum** it went round and round in his head **c** (= *von einem zum andern gehen: Mensch*) to go (a)round; (= *herumgereicht werden*) to be passed *or* handed (a)round; (= *weitererzählt werden*) to go (a)round (*in etw* (*dat*) sth); **etw ~ lassen** to circulate sth **d** (*zeitlich:* = *vorbeigehen*) to pass; **he|rum+geis|tern** VI *sep aux sein* (*inf*) (*Gespenster etc*) to haunt (*in etw* (*dat*) sth); (*Mensch*) to wander (a)round; **in jds Kopf ~** (*Idee*) to possess sb; **he|rum+gon|deln** VI *sep aux sein* (*inf*) to drive around; **he|rum+ha|ben** VT *sep irreg* (*inf*) **a** *Zeit* to have finished **b** (= *überredet haben*) to have talked round (*esp Brit*) *or* around (*esp US*); **he|rum+ha|cken** VI *sep* (*fig inf*) **auf jdm ~** to pick on sb (*inf*); **he|rum+hän|gen** VI *sep irreg* **a** (*inf:* = *unordentlich aufgehängt sein*) to hang around **b** (*inf:* = *sich lümmeln*) to loll a-bout **c** (*inf:* = *ständig zu finden sein*) to hang out (*inf*); **he|rum+han|tie|ren** *ptp* **herumhantiert** VI *sep* (*inf*) to fiddle (about) (*an +dat* with); **he|rum+het|zen** VI *sep aux sein* to rush a-round; **he|rum+hor|chen** VI *sep* (*inf*) to keep one's ears open; **he|rum+hu|ren** VI *sep* (*inf*) to whore around (*inf*); **he|rum+ir|ren** VI *sep aux sein* to wander (a)round; **he|rum+kno|beln** VI *sep* (*inf*) **an etw** (*dat*) **~** to rack one's brains about sth; **he|rum+kom|man|die|ren** *ptp* **herumkommandiert** *sep* (*inf*) **VT** to order about, to boss around *or* about (*Brit, inf*) **VI** to give orders; **he|rum+kom|men** VI *sep irreg aux sein* (*inf*) **a** (*um eine Ecke etc*) to come round (*Brit*) *or* around (*um etw* sth) **b** (= *herumgehen, herumfahren etc* around) to get (a)round (*um etw* sth); **mit den Armen um etw ~** to be able to get one's arms (a)round sth **c** (= *vermeiden können*) **um etw ~** to get out of sth, to avoid sth; **darum ~, etw zu machen** to get out of *or* avoid doing sth; **wir kommen um die Tatsache nicht herum, dass ...** we cannot get away from *or* overlook the fact that ... **d** (= *reisen*) to get about (*Brit*) *or* around (*um etw* sth); **er ist viel *or* weit herumgekommen** he has got around a great deal, he has seen a lot of the world; **he|rum+krab|beln** VI *sep aux sein* (*inf*) to crawl a-round *or* about; **he|rum+kra|men** VI *sep* (*inf*) to rummage about *or* around; **he|rum+kreb|sen** VI *sep* (*inf*) **a** (= *sich verzweifelt bemühen*) to struggle **b** (= *sich unwohl fühlen*) to drag oneself about (*Brit*) *or* around **c** *aux sein* (= *langsam or schwerfällig gehen*) to trudge (a)round; **he|rum+krie|chen** VI *sep irreg aux sein* (*inf*) to crawl about *or* around (*um etw* sth); **he|rum+krie|gen** VT *sep* (*inf*) = **herumbekommen**; **he|rum+kri|ti|sie|ren** *ptp* **herumkritisiert**, **he|rum+krit|teln** *ptp* VI *sep* to find fault (*an +dat* with), to pick holes (*an +dat* in); **he|rum+ku|rie|ren** *ptp* **herumkuriert** VI *sep* = **herumdok-tern**; **he|rum+kur|ven** VI *sep aux sein* (*inf*) cruise around (*in +dat* sth); **he|rụm+kut|- schie|ren** *ptp* **herumkutschiert** VTI *sep* (*vi: aux sein*) to drive around; **he|rụm+la|bo|rie|ren** *ptp* **herumlaboriert** VI *sep* (*inf*) **an etw** (*dat*) **~** to try to get rid of sth; **he|rụm+lau|fen** VI *sep irreg aux sein* (*inf*) (= *um etw herumlaufen*) to run round (*Brit*) or around (*um etw* sth); (= *umherlaufen*) to run or go about (*Brit*) or around; **so kannst du doch nicht ~** (*fig inf*) you can't run or go (a)round (looking) like that; **he|rụm+lie|- gen** VI *sep irreg* (*inf*) to lie about (*Brit*) or a-round (*um etw* sth); **he|rụm+lüm|meln** VIR *sep* (*inf*) to loll around; **he|rụm+lun|gern** VI *sep* (*inf*) to hang about (*Brit*) or (a)round; **he|- rụm+ma|chen** *sep* (*inf*) VI a (= *sich überlegen*) to consider; **da braucht man doch nicht so lan-ge herumzumachen** you don't need to think a-bout it for so long b (= *sich beschäftigen*) **an jdm ~** to fuss about sb; **an etw** (*dat*) **~** to mess about with sth; **mit jdm ~** to mess around with sb c (= *herumfingern*) **an etw** (*dat*) **~** to pick at sth; *an den Haaren* to fiddle with sth d (= *he-rumnörgeln*) **an jdm/etw ~** to go on at sb/about sth (*inf*) VT to put (a)round (*um etw* sth); **he|- rụm+mä|keln** VI *sep* (*inf*) to find fault (*an +dat* with); **he|rụm+nör|geln** VI *sep* **an jdm/etw ~** to find fault with sb/sth; **he|rụm+pfu|schen** VI *sep* (*inf*) to mess about (*inf*) (*an +dat* with); **he|rụm+pus|seln** VI *sep* (*inf*) to fiddle about (*an +dat* with); **he|rụm+quä|len** VR *sep* (*inf*) to struggle; (*mit Problemen*) to worry oneself sick (*mit* over) (*inf*); **sich mit Rheuma ~** to be plagued by rheumatism; **he|rụm+ra|ten** VI *sep irreg* (*inf*) to guess; **he|rụm+rät|seln** VI *sep* **an etw** (*dat*) **~** to (try to) figure sth out; **er rätselte herum** he tried to figure it out; **he|rụm+re|den** VI *sep* (*inf*) (= *belangloses Zeug reden*) to talk or chat away; **um etw ~** (*ausweichend*) to talk a-round sth; **he|rụm+rei|chen** VT *sep* a (= *he-rumgeben*) to pass (a)round; (*fig inf*) *Besucher* to show off b (= *lang genug sein*) to reach round (*Brit*) or around (*um etw* sth); **he|rụm+rei|sen** VI *sep aux sein* to travel about (*Brit*) or around; **he|rụm+rei|ßen** VT *sep irreg* to pull or swing (a)round (hard); **das Steuer ~** (*fig*) to change or alter course; **he|rụm+rei|ten** VI *sep irreg* a *aux sein* (= *umherreiten*) to ride about (*Brit*) or (a)round; (= *um etw herumreiten*) to ride (a)round (*um etw* sth) b (*fig inf*) **auf jdm/etw ~** to keep on at sb/about sth; **he|rụm+ren|nen** VI *sep irreg aux sein* (*inf*) (= *um etw herumrennen*) to run (a)round (*um etw* sth); (= *umherrennen*) to run about (*Brit*) or (a)round; **he|rụm+rut|- schen** VI *sep aux sein* (*inf*) to fidget about; **he|- rụm+schar|wen|zeln** *ptp* **herumscharwenzelt** VI *sep aux sein* (*inf*) to dance attendance (*um* on); **he|rụm+schi|cken** VT *sep* (*inf*) *jdn* to send round (*bei* to); *Brief etc* to circulate; **he|- rụm+schla|gen** *sep irreg* VT *Papier, Tuch etc* to wrap (a)round (*um etw* sth) VR (*inf*) **sich mit jdm ~** (*lit*) to fight or scuffle with sb; (*fig*) to fight a running battle with sb; **sich mit etw ~** (*fig*) to keep struggling with sth; **he|- rụm+schlei|chen** VI *sep irreg aux sein* to creep (a)round (*um etw* sth); **he|rụm+schlei|fen** VT *sep* (*dial inf*) to drag around; **he|rụm+schlen|- dern** VI *sep aux sein* to stroll or saunter about (*in der Stadt* (in) the town); **he|rụm+schlep|- pen** VT *sep* (*inf*) *Sachen* to lug (a)round (*inf*); *jdn* to drag (a)round; **etw mit sich ~** (*Kummer, Sorge, Problem*) to be troubled or worried by sth; *Krankheit, Infektion* to be going (a)round with sth; **he|rụm+schnüf|feln** VI *sep* (*inf*) to sniff (a)round (*in etw* (*dat*) sth); (*fig*) to snoop (a)round (*in +dat* in); **he|rụm+schrei|en** VI *sep irreg* (*inf*) to shout out loud; **he|- rụm+schwän|zeln** VI *sep aux sein* (*inf*) to dance attendance (*um* on); **he|rụm+schwir|- ren** VI *sep aux sein* (*inf*) **sie muss hier irgendwo ~** she must be floating (a)round here some-where (*inf*); **he|rụm sein** ▲ VI *irreg aux sein* (*inf*) a (= *vorüber sein*) to be past or over b (= *verbreitet worden sein*: *Gerücht, Neuigkeit, Nach-richt*) to have got (a)round c (= *in jds Nähe sein*) **um jdn ~** to be around sb d (= *um etw*

gelaufen, gefahren sein) to be around (*um etw* sth); **he|rụm+sit|zen** VI *sep irreg aux haben or sein* to sit around (*um jdn/etw* sb/sth); **he|- rụm+spa|zie|ren** VI *sep aux sein* (*inf*) to walk or stroll around (*in +dat* sth, *um jdn/etw* sb/sth); **he|- rụm+spie|len** VI *sep* (*inf*) **mit etw ~** to play a-bout (*Brit*) or around with sth; **an etw** (*dat*) **~** to fiddle about (*Brit*) or around with sth; **auf etw** (*dat*) **~** to play around on sth; **he|- rụm+spre|chen** VR *sep irreg* to get about (*Brit* or *around*) **es dürfte sich herumgesprochen ha-ben, dass ...** it has probably got out that ...; **he|rụm+spu|ken** VI *sep* to haunt; **die Idee spukt jdm im Kopf** or **in jds Kopf herum** sb has the idea; **he|rụm+stän|kern** VI *sep* (*inf*) to moan, to gripe (*inf*), to bellyache (*inf*); **he|- rụm+ste|hen** VI *sep irreg aux haben or sein* a (*Sachen*) to be lying around; **der Sessel steht blöd herum** the chair is in a stupid place b (*Menschen*) to stand (a)round (*um jdn/etw* sb/ sth); **he|rụm+stö|bern** VI *sep* (*inf*) a (= *su-chen*) to rummage about (*Brit*) or around b (= *herumschnüffeln*) to snoop (a)round; **he|- rụm+sto|chern** VI *sep* (*inf*) to poke about (*Brit*) or around; **im Essen** ~ to pick at one's food; **in den Zähnen** ~ to pick one's teeth; **he|- rụm+sto|ßen** VT *sep irreg jdn* to shove (a)round; **he|rụm+strei|chen** VI *sep irreg aux sein* (*um jdn/etw* sb/sth) to creep (a)round; (*Ver-brecher, Katze*) to prowl (a)round; **he|- rụm+strei|fen** VI *sep aux sein* to roam around; **he|rụm+strei|ten** VR *sep irreg* to squabble; **he|rụm+streu|nen**, **he|rụm+strol|chen** VI *sep aux sein* (*inf*) to prowl (a)round; **he|- rụm+stro|mern** VI *sep aux sein* (*inf*) to wander or roam about or around; **he|rụm+tan|zen** VI *sep aux sein* (*inf*) (= *umhertanzen*) to dance (a)round; **um jdn/etw ~** to dance (a)round sb/ sth; **sie tanzt ihm auf der Nase herum** she does as she pleases or likes with him; **he|rụm+tap-pen** VI *sep aux sein* (*inf*) to grope around or a-bout; **he|rụm+tas|ten** VI *sep* a (= *tastend füh-len*) to grope about (*Brit*) or around b (= *tastend gehen*) to grope about (*Brit*) or a-round; **he|rụm+to|ben** VI *sep* (*inf*) a *auch aux sein* (= *umherlaufen*) to romp about (*Brit*) or (a)round b (= *schimpfen*) to shout and scream; **he|rụm+tol|len** VI *sep aux sein* (*inf*) to romp a-bout or around; **he|rụm+tra|gen** VT *sep irreg* (*inf*) a (= *mit sich tragen*) to carry about (*Brit*) or (a)round; **um etw ~** to carry (a)round sth; **Sorgen mit sich ~** to have worries; **eine Idee mit sich ~** to be contemplating an idea, to be thinking about an idea b (= *weitererzählen*) to spread (a)round; **he|rụm+tram|peln** VI *sep aux sein* (*inf*) to trample (*auf +dat* on); **jdm auf den Nerven ~, auf jds Nerven ~** to get on sb's nerves; **auf jdm ~** (*fig*) to get at sb; **he|- rụm+trei|ben** VR *sep irreg* (*inf*) (= *herumziehen in*) to hang about (*Brit*) or (a)round (*in +dat* in) (*inf*); (*in schlechter Gesellschaft*) to hang about (*Brit*) or (a)round in bad company; **die treibt sich mal wieder irgendwo in Spanien herum** she's off gadding about (*Brit*) or roaming a-round in Spain again (*inf*); **sich mit jdm ~** to hang or knock (*Brit*) around with sb (*inf*)

He|rụm|trei|ber(in) M(F) (*pej*) a (= *Mensch ohne feste Arbeit, Wohnsitz*) tramp b (*inf*) (= *Streuner*) vagabond; (*liederlich*) good-for-nothing; (= *Frau*) tramp (*inf*)

he|rụm-: he|rụm+tre|ten VI *sep irreg* (*inf*) to trample (*auf +dat* on); **he|rụm+trö|deln** VI *sep* (*inf*) to dawdle (*inf*); **he|rụm+tur|nen** VI *sep aux sein* (*inf*) to clamber or scramble a-bout; **he|rụm+va|ga|bun|die|ren** *ptp* **herumva-gabundiert** VI *sep aux sein* (*pej*) to roam about; **he|rụm+wäl|zen** *sep* VT *Stein* to turn over VR to roll around; **sich (schlaflos) im Bett ~** to toss and turn in bed; **he|rụm+wan|dern** VI *sep aux sein* (= *umhergehen*) to wander about; **um etw ~** to wander (a)round sth; **he|rụm+wer|fen** *sep irreg* VT a (= *achtlos werfen*) to throw around (*in etw* (*dat*) sth) b (= *heftig bewegen*) *Kopf* to turn (quickly); *Steuer, Hebel* to throw around

VR to roll over; **sich (im Bett) ~** to toss and turn (in bed) VI (*inf*) **mit Bemerkungen/Geld** *etc* ~ to fling or throw remarks/one's money *etc* around; **he|rụm+wi|ckeln** VT *sep* (*um etw* sth) to wrap (a)round; *Schnur, Faden etc* to wind (a)round; **he|rụm+wir|beln** VTI *sep* (*vi: aux sein*) *jdn* ~, **mit jdm ~** to whirl or spin sb (a)round; **he|rụm+wirt|schaf|ten** VI *sep* (*inf*) to potter (*Brit*) or putter (*US*) about; **he|- rụm+wüh|len** VI *sep* (*inf*) to rummage about or around; (*Schwein*) to root around; (= *herum-schnüffeln*) to nose or snoop about or around; **he|rụm+wursch|teln** [-vʊrʃtln] VI *sep* (*inf*) → **herumwursteln**; **he|rụm+wurs|teln** VI *sep* (*inf*) to fiddle or mess (*inf*) about (*Brit*) or (a)round (*an +dat* with); **he|rụm+zan|ken** VR *sep* to squabble; **he|rụm+zap|pen** VI *sep* (*TV inf*) to zap around (*inf*); **he|rụm+zei|gen** VT *sep* to show (a)round; **he|rụm+zie|hen** *sep irreg* VI *aux sein* a (= *von Ort zu Ort ziehen*) to move a-round; (*inf*: = *sich herumtreiben in*) to go around (*in etw* (*dat*) sth); **in der Welt ~** to roam the world; **mit jdm ~** (*inf*) to go or hang around with sb b (= *um etw herumziehen*) to move (a)round (*um etw* sth) VR *sep* **sich um etw ~** (*Hecke etc*) to run (a)round sth; **he|rụm|zie|hend** ADJ *attr Händler* itinerant; *Musikant, Schauspieler* wandering, strolling; **he|rụm+zi|geu|nern** *ptp* **herumzigeunert** VI *sep aux sein* (*pej*) to roam or wander (a)round (*in etw* (*dat*) sth)

he|rụn|ten [hɛˈrʊntn̩] ADV (*S Ger, Aus*) down here

he|rụn|ter [hɛˈrʊntɐ] ADV down; ~**! get down!; ~ mit euch** get down; ~ **mit ihm** get him down; ~ **damit** get or bring it down; (*in Bezug auf Klei-der*) get or take it off; **da/hier ~** down there/ here; **den Hut ~, ~ mit dem Hut** get or take your hat off; **vom Berg ~** down the mountain; **vom Himmel ~** down from heaven; **bis ins Tal ~** down into the valley → *auch* **herunterhaben, herunter sein** *etc* PREP +*acc* (*nachgestellt*) down

he|rụn|ter- PREF → *auch* **runter-, herab-** down; **he|rụn|ter+be|kom|men** *ptp* **herunterbekom-men** VT *sep irreg* = **herunterkriegen; he|rụn|- ter+be|mü|hen** *ptp* **herunterbemüht** (*geh*) *sep* VT **jdn ~** to ask sb to come down VR to trou-ble to come down, to take the trouble to come down; **he|rụn|ter+bit|ten** VT *sep irreg* **jdn ~** to ask sb to come down; **he|rụn|ter+bren|nen** VI *sep irreg* a (*Sonne*) to burn or scorch down b *aux sein* (*Haus, Feuer, Kerze etc*) to burn down; **he|rụn|ter+brin|gen** VT *sep irreg* a (= *nach unten bringen*) to bring down b (= *zugrunde richten*) to ruin c (*inf*) = **herunterkriegen; he|- rụn|ter+drü|cken** VT *sep Hebel, Pedal* to press down; *Preise* to force or bring down; *Niveau* to lower; **he|rụn|ter+fah|ren** *sep irreg* VI *aux sein* to go down; **heruntergefahren kommen** to come down VT to bring down; *Reaktor* (= *völlig abschalten*) to shut down; (= *Leistung verringern*) to scale down; **he|rụn|ter+fal|len** VI *sep irreg aux sein* to fall down; **von etw ~** to fall off sth; **ihm fiel die Kinnlade herunter** his jaw dropped; **he|rụn|ter+flie|gen** VI *sep irreg aux sein* to fly down; (*inf*) to fall down; **he|rụn|ter+ge|ben** VT *sep irreg* to hand down; **he|rụn|ter+ge|hen** VI *sep irreg aux sein* to go down; (*Fieber, Tempera-tur auch*) to drop; (*Preise auch*) to come down, to drop; (*Flugzeug*) to descend; **von etw ~** (= *get down from sth, to get off sth; **auf etw** (*acc*) ~ (*Preise*) to go down to sth; (*Geschwindig-keit*) to slow down to sth; **mit den Preisen ~** to lower or cut one's prices; **he|rụn|ter+ge|kom-men** ADJ *Haus* dilapidated; *Stadt* run-down; *Mensch* down-at-heel; **he|rụn|ter+ha|ben** VT *sep irreg* (*inf*) (= *heruntergeholt haben*) to have got down; (= *abgenommen haben*) to have lost; **he|rụn|ter+han|deln** VT *sep* (*inf*) *Preis, Gebühren* to beat down; **etw um 20 Euro ~** to get 20 euros knocked off sth; **jdn (auf etw** *acc*) ~ to knock sb down (to sth); **he|rụn|ter+hän|gen** VI *sep irreg* to hang down; (*Haare*) to hang; **he|rụn|- ter+hau|en** VT *sep irreg* (*inf*) a **jdm eine ~** to give sb a clip round the ear (*Brit inf*), to slap sb on the side of the head **b** (= *schnell machen*) to dash *or* knock off (*inf*); **he|run|ter+he|ben** VT *sep irreg* to lift down; **he|run|ter+hel|fen** VI *sep irreg* **jdm** ~ to help sb down; **he|run|ter+ho|len** VT *sep* to fetch down; (*inf*) *Vogel* to bring down, to bag; *Flugzeug* to bring down; **he|run|ter+klap|pen** VT *sep* to turn down; *Sitz* to fold down; *Deckel* to close; **he|run|ter+klet|tern** VI *sep aux sein* to climb down; **he|run|ter+kom|men** VI *sep irreg aux sein* **a** (= *nach unten kommen*) to come down; (*inf*: = *herunterkönnen*) to get down **b** (*fig inf*: = *verfallen*) (*Stadt, Firma*) to go downhill; (*Wirtschaft*) to go to rack and ruin; (*gesundheitlich*) to become run-down; **er ist so weit heruntergekommen, dass ...** (*sittlich*) he has sunk so low that ... → **heruntergekommen** **c** (*fig inf*: = *wegkommen*: *von schlechten Noten etc*) to get over (*von etw* sth); **von Drogen/vom Alkohol** ~ to kick the habit (*inf*); **he|run|ter+kön|nen** VI *sep irreg* to be able to get down; **he|run|ter+krie|gen** VT *sep* (*inf*) **a** (= *herunterholen, schlucken können*) to get down; (= *abmachen können*) to get off **b** (= *abnehmen*) to lose; **he|run|ter+kur|beln** VT *sep Fensterscheibe* to wind down; **he|run|ter+la|den** VT *sep irreg* (*Comput*) to download (*auf +acc* onto); **he|run|ter+las|sen** *sep irreg* **VT** (= *abseilen*) *Gegenstand* to let down, to lower; *Hose* to take down; *jdn* to lower; **sie lässt mich nicht herunter** (*inf*) she won't let me down **VR** (*am Seil*) to lower oneself; **he|run|ter+lei|ern** [hɛˈrʊntəlaɪən] VT *sep* (*inf*) to reel off; **he|run|ter+le|sen** VT *sep irreg* (*pej*) to read off; **he|run|ter+ma|chen** VT *sep* (*inf*) **a** (= *schlecht machen*) to run down, to knock (*inf*) **b** (= *zurechtweisen*) to tell off **c** (= *abmachen*) to take down; *Schminke, Farbe, Dreck* to take off; **he|run|ter+neh|men** VT *sep irreg* to take down; (*inf*: *von Schule*) to take away; **etw vom Tisch etc** ~ to take sth off the table *etc*; **he|run|ter+put|zen** VT *sep* (*inf*) **jdn** ~ to tear sb off a strip (*Brit inf*), to give sb an earful (*inf*); **he|run|ter+ras|seln** VT *sep* (*inf*) to rattle *or* reel off; **he|run|ter+rei|chen** *sep* **VT** to pass *or* hand down **VI** to reach down; **he|run|ter+rei|ßen** VT *sep irreg* (*inf*) **a** (*von oben nach unten*) to pull *or* tear down **b** (= *abreißen*) *Pflaster, Tapete etc* to pull off; **he|run|ter+rut|schen** VI *sep aux sein* to slide down → **Buckel** a; **he|run|ter+schal|ten** VI *sep* (*Aut*) to change *or* shift (*US*) down (*in +acc* into); **he|run|ter+schie|ßen** *sep irreg* **VT** (*mit Geschoss*) to shoot down **VI** *aux sein* (*inf*: = *sich schnell bewegen*) to shoot down; **he|run|ter+schla|gen** VT *sep irreg* **a** *jdm den Hut etc* ~ to knock sb's hat *etc* off; **etw vom Baum** ~ to knock sth off the tree **b** *Kragen, Hutkrempe* to turn down; **he|run|ter+schlin|gen** VT *sep irreg* (*inf*) *Essen* to gobble down, to wolf down; *Getränk* to gulp down; **he|run|ter+schlu|cken** VT *sep* (*inf*) to swallow; **he|run|ter+schrau|ben** VT *sep* (*lit*) *Deckel etc* to screw off; *Petroleumlampe* to turn down; (*fig*) *Ansprüche, Niveau* to lower; **he|run|ter+se|hen** VI *sep irreg* **a** (*von oben*) to look down **b** (*fig*: = *mustern*) **an jdm** ~ to look sb up and down **c** (*fig*: = *geringschätzig behandeln*) **auf jdn** ~ to look down on sb; **he|run|ter+sein** ▲ VI *sep irreg* (*inf*) **a** (*von oben*) to be down **b** (= *heruntergelassen sein*) to be down **c** (= *abgeschnitten sein*) to be (cut) off **d** (*Fieber, Preise*) to be lower *or* down; **wenn die 5 Kilo Übergewicht herunter sind** when I/you *etc* have lost those 5 kilos excess weight **e** (*inf*) **mit den Nerven** ~ to be at the end of one's tether (*Brit*) *or* rope (*US*); **mit der Gesundheit** ~ to be run-down **f** (= *abgewirtschaftet haben*) to be in a bad way; **he|run|ter+set|zen** VT *sep* (= *herabsetzen*) **he|run|ter+spie|len** VT *sep* (*inf*) *Stück* to run through; (= *verharmlosen*) *Problem, Vorfall* to play down; **he|run|ter+sprin|gen** VI *sep irreg aux sein* to jump down; **he|run|ter+stei|gen** VI *sep irreg aux sein* to climb down; **he|run|ter+stür|zen** *sep* **VI** *aux sein* (= *herunterfallen*) to fall *or* tumble down; (*inf*: = *heruntereilen*) to rush down **VT a jdn** ~ to throw sb down **b** (*inf*:

schnell trinken*) to gulp down **VR** to throw oneself down; **he|run|ter+wer|fen** VT *sep irreg* to throw down; (*unabsichtlich*) to drop; **he|run|ter+wirt|schaf|ten** VT *sep* (*inf*) to bring to the brink of ruin; **he|run|ter+wol|len** VI *sep* (*inf*) to want to get down; **he|run|ter+zie|hen** *sep irreg* VT **a** (= *nach unten ziehen*) to pull down; *Pullover etc* to pull off; **etw von etw** ~ to pull sth off sth **b** (*fig*) **jdn auf sein Niveau** *or* **seine Ebene** *or* **zu sich** ~ to pull sb down to one's own level **c** (= *umziehen*) to move down

her|vor [hɛɐˈfoːɐ] ADV **aus etw** ~ out of sth; **hinter dem Tisch** ~ out from behind the table; ~ **mit euch** (*geh*) out you come

her|vor-: her|vor+bre|chen VI *sep irreg aux sein* (*geh*) to burst *or* break out; (*Sonne, fig: Gefühl*) to break through; (*Quelle, Flüssigkeit*) to gush out *or* forth (*liter*); **her|vor+brin|gen** VT *sep irreg* **a** (= *entstehen lassen*) to produce; *Worte* to utter **b** (= *verursachen*) *Unheil, Böses* to create; **her|vor+drin|gen** VI *sep irreg aux sein* (*geh*) to issue forth (*liter*); **her|vor+ge|hen** ✿ 53.4 VI *sep irreg aux sein* **a** (*geh*: = *entstammen*) to come (*aus* from); **aus der Ehe gingen zwei Kinder hervor** the marriage produced two children **b** (= *sich ergeben, zu folgern sein*) to follow; **daraus geht hervor, dass ...** from this it follows that ... **c** (= *etwas übersteh en*) to emerge; **als Sieger** ~ to emerge victorious; **aus etw** ~ to come out of sth; **her|vor+gu|cken** VI *sep* (*inf*) to peep out (*unter +dat* (from) under); **her|vor+he|ben** VT *sep irreg* to emphasize, to stress; **her|vor+ho|len** VT *sep* to bring out; **her|vor+keh|ren** VT *sep* (*geh*) to emphasize; **er kehrt immer den feinen Mann hervor** he always emphasizes what a gentleman he is; **her|vor+kom|men** VI *sep irreg aux sein* to come out (*hinter +dat* from behind); **her|vor+kra|men** VT *sep* (*inf*) **a** *Fotos, Besteck etc* to dig out **b** (*fig*) *Erinnerungen etc* to dredge up; **her|vor+lo|cken** VT *sep* to entice *or* lure out (*aus* from, *hinter +dat* from behind); **dein Gejammer lockt bei mir keine Träne hervor** your moaning is not going to move me; **her|vor+quel|len** VI *sep irreg aux sein* (*Wasser*) to gush forth (*aus* from) (*liter*); (*Tränen*) to well up (*aus* in); (*Blut*) to spurt out (*aus* of); (*Körperfülle*) to bulge *or* protrude (*aus* from, *unter +dat* from under); **her|vor+ra|gen** VI *sep* **a** (*Felsen, Stein etc*) to jut out, to project; (*Nase*) to protrude **b** (*fig*: = *sich auszeichnen*) to stand out; **er ragt unter den anderen/durch seine Intelligenz hervor** he stands out from the others/because of his intelligence; **her|vor|ra|gend** ADJ **a** (*lit*: = *vorstehend*) *esp Körperteil* protruding **b** (*fig*: = *ausgezeichnet*) excellent; *Mensch, Leistung etc* excellent, outstanding; **er hat Hervorragendes geleistet** his achievement was outstanding **ADV** (= *ausgezeichnet*) very well; **etw** ~ **beschreiben/interpretieren** to give an excellent description/interpretation of sth; ~ **kochen** to be an excellent cook; ~ **schmecken** to taste exquisite; **her|vor+ru|fen** ✿ 44.2 VT *sep irreg* **a** (= *rufen*) **jdn** ~ to call (to) sb to come out; (*Theat etc*) to call for sb **b** (= *bewirken*) to cause, to give rise to; *Bewunderung* to arouse; *Reaktion, Krankheit* to cause; *Eindruck* to create; **her|vor+se|hen** VI *sep irreg* (*Unterrock*) to show; (*Mensch*) to look out; **hinter etw** (*dat*) ~ (*Mensch*) to look out from behind sth; (*Mond, Sterne*) to shine out from behind sth; **her|vor+sprin|gen** VI *sep irreg aux sein* **a** (*Mensch, Tier*) to jump or leap out (*hinter +dat* from behind) **b** (*Felsen*) to project, to jut out; (*Nase*) to protrude, to stick out; **her|vor+spru|deln** VI *sep aux sein* to bubble *or* gush out; (*Worte*) to gush (out); **her|vor+ste|chen** VI *sep irreg aux sein* (*lit, fig*) to stand out; **her|vor+ste|chend** ADJ striking; **her|vor+ste|hen** VI *sep irreg aux sein* (*Spitze*) to project, to jut out; (*Nase, Ohren etc*) to stick out; **her|vor+sto|ßen** VT *sep* (*fig*) *Worte* to gasp (out); **her|vor+stür|zen** VI *sep aux sein* to rush *or* hurtle out (*hinter +dat* from behind); **her|vor+su|chen** VT *sep* (= *he-*

raussuchen*) to look out; **her|vor+trau|en** VR *sep* (*inf*) to dare to come out; **her|vor+tre|ten** VI *sep irreg aux sein* **a** (= *heraustreten*) to step out, to emerge (*hinter +dat* from behind); (*Backenknochen*) to protrude; (*Adern*) to bulge; (*Sonne, Mond*) to emerge (*hinter +dat, aus* from behind) **b** (= *sichtbar werden*) to stand out; (*fig*) to become evident **c** (= *an die Öffentlichkeit treten*) to come to the fore; **her|vor+tun** VR *sep irreg* to distinguish oneself; (*inf*: = *sich wichtig tun*) to show off (*mit etw* sth); **her|vor+wa|gen** VR *sep* to dare to come out; **her|vor+zau|bern** VT *sep* (*lit, fig*) to conjure up; **her|vor+zie|hen** VT *sep irreg* to pull out (*unter +dat* from under); **etw aus/zwischen etw** (*dat*) ~ to pull sth out of/from among sth

Her-: her+wa|gen VR *sep* to dare to come; **her|wärts** [ˈhɛːɐvɛrts] ADV on the way here; **Her|weg** M , *no pl* way here; **auf dem** ~ on the way here

Herz [hɛrts] -ens, -en

SUBSTANTIV (NT)

a = Organ heart; **ein gesundes/schwaches Herz haben** to have a healthy/weak heart; **Operation/Eingriff am offenen Herzen** open-heart surgery; **sein Herz schlägt sehr schnell** he has a very high heart rate; **mir schlug das Herz bis zum Hals** my heart was thumping *or* pounding; **sein Herz schlug höher** his heart leapt; **die Herzen höher schlagen lassen** to touch people's hearts; **er drückte sie an sein Herz** he clasped her to his breast; **sie drückte den Teddybär ans Herz** she clutched her teddy to her heart, she held her teddy tight; **komm an mein Herz** come into my arms

b = Herzform heart; **Herzen aus Teig ausstechen** to cut hearts out of pastry; **ein Herz auf das i malen** to draw a heart on (top of) the i

c Kosewort (*old*) **du, mein liebes Herz** you, my love

d Cards (= *Karte*) heart; (*no pl*: = *Farbe*) hearts *pl*; **Herz (aus)spielen** to play hearts; (*einzelne Karte*) **Herz ist Trumpf** hearts are trumps; **hast du noch Herz?** do you have any hearts left?

e = Inneres heart; **das Herz des Salats hat sehr zarte Blätter** the leaves of the lettuce heart are very tender; **das Parlament befindet sich im Herzen der Stadt** the parliament is in the heart of the city; **das Herz der Sache** the heart of the matter

f = Gemüt heart; **im Grund seines/meines Herzens** in his/my heart of hearts; **die Dame seines Herzens** the woman he has given his heart to; **ein Herz und eine Seele sein** to be the best of friends

♦ **Adjektiv + Herz mit ganzem Herzen** wholeheartedly; **er ist mit ganzem Herzen bei der Arbeit** he is putting his heart and soul into his work; **jdm von ganzem Herzen danken** to thank sb with all one's heart; **ein goldenes Herz** a heart of gold; **ein gutes Herz haben** (*fig*) to be good-hearted, to have a good heart; **sie konnte nicht leichten Herzens darauf verzichten** she couldn't easily do without it; **schweren Herzens** with a heavy heart; **mir ist das Herz schwer** I have a heavy heart; **jdm das Herz schwer machen** to grieve sb; **aus tiefstem Herzen** from the bottom of one's heart; **traurigen Herzens** with a sad heart

♦ **Präposition + Herz**

> Die in Verbindung mit **Herz** verwendeten Präpositionen sind alphabetisch angeordnet.

dieser Hund ist mir ans Herz gewachsen I have grown fond of *or* become attached to this dog; **es liegt mir am Herzen** I am very concerned about it; **es liegt mir sehr am Herzen, dass der Spielplatz gebaut wird** it's very important to me that the playground be built; **jdm etw ans Herz legen** to entrust sth to sb's care; **ich lege es dir ans Herz, das zu tun** I would ask you particularly to do that; **etw auf dem Herzen haben** to have sth on one's mind; **jdn auf Herz und Nieren prüfen** to examine sb very thoroughly; **du sprichst mir aus dem Herzen** that's just what I feel; **er hat sie in sein Herz geschlossen** he has grown fond of her; **es ging mir bis ins Herz** it cut me to the quick; (= *traurig stimmen*) it saddened me very much; **es gab mir einen Stich ins Herz** it hurt me; (= *traurig stimmen*) it saddened me; **ein Mann nach meinem Herzen** a man after my own heart; **ohne Herz** heartless; **es wurde ihr leichter ums Herz** she felt relieved; **ich weiß, wie es dir ums Herz ist** I know how you feel; **ein Kind unter dem Herzen tragen** (*Bibl, old*) to be with child (*old*); **von Herzen** with all one's heart; **etw von Herzen gern tun** to love doing sth; **jdn von Herzen gern haben** to love sb dearly; **von Herzen kommend** heartfelt; **der Applaus kam von Herzen** the applause was heartfelt; **eine schwere Last** or **eine Zentnerlast fiel ihr vom Herzen** she felt a weight lifted from her mind; **sich** (*dat*) **etw vom Herzen reden** to get sth off one's chest; **den Weg in die** or **zu den Herzen finden** to find one's way into people's hearts; **es ging mir zu Herzen** it touched me deeply; **sich** (*dat*) **etw zu Herzen nehmen** to take sth to heart

♦ **Verb + Herz**

> Die in Verbindung mit **Herz** verwendeten Verben sind alphabetisch angeordnet (siehe auch **Präposition + Herz**).

alles, was das Herz begehrt everything one's heart desires; **mir blutet das Herz, mein Herz blutet** (*auch iro*) my heart bleeds; **jds Herz brechen** to break sb's heart; **dabei dreht sich mir das Herz im Leib um** it makes me feel sick at heart; **sein Herz für etw entdecken** to start liking sth; **alle Herzen im Sturm erobern** to capture people's hearts; **sich** (*dat*) **ein Herz fassen** to take heart; **gib deinem Herzen einen Stoß!** go on!; **mein Herz gehört dir** my heart belongs to you; **mein Herz gehört der Musik** music is the love of my life; **jds Herz gewinnen** to win sb's heart; **hast du denn (gar) kein Herz?** how can you be so heartless?; **haben Sie doch ein Herz!** have a heart!; **ein Herz für jdn/etw haben** to be fond of sb/sth; **habt ein Herz für die Armen** spare a thought for the poor; **er hat das Herz auf dem** or **am rechten Fleck** his heart is in the right place; **sein Herz an jdn/etw hängen** to commit oneself heart and soul to sb/sth; **jds Herz hängt an jdm/etw** sb is committed heart and soul to sb/sth; **an Geld** sb is preoccupied with sth; **mir lacht das Herz im Leibe** my heart is leaping with joy; **seinem Herzen Luft machen** to give vent to one's feelings; **sich** (*dat*) **ein Herz nehmen** to take heart; **sein Herz in beide Hände nehmen** to take one's courage in both hands; **der Anblick rührte ihr das Herz** the sight touched her heart; **jdm sein Herz schenken** to give sb one's heart; **jds Herz stehlen** to steal sb's heart; **das Herz auf der Zunge tragen** to speak one's mind; **ihr tat das Herz im Leibe weh** she felt terribly saddened; **es zerreißt mir das Herz** it breaks my heart → *auch* **Hose**

her+zäh|len VT *sep* to count

Herz-: herz|al|ler|liebst ADJ (*old, hum*) most charming; **Herz|al|ler|liebs|te(r)** [hɛrtslalə-'li:pstə] MF *decl as adj* (*old, hum*) darling, dearest; **Herz|an|fall** M heart attack; **Herz|ass** NT ace of hearts; **Herz|at|ta|cke** F heart attack

her+zau|bern VT *sep* to produce out of thin air

Herz-: herz|be|klem|mend ADJ oppressive; **Herz|be|klem|mung** F ~en bekommen to feel as if one cannot breathe; **Herz|be|schwer|den** PL heart trouble *sing*; **Herz|beu|tel** M pericardium; **Herz|beu|tel|ent|zün|dung** F pericarditis; **herz|be|we|gend** ADJ heart-rending; **Herz|blatt** NT **a** (*Bot*) grass of Par-

nassus **b** (*dated inf*) darling; **herz|blät|rig** ADJ heart-shaped; **Herz|blut** NT (*poet*) life-blood; **mit ~** (= *leidenschaftlich*) passionately; **Herz|bu|be** M jack or knave of hearts

Herz|chen ['hɛrtsçən] NT -s, - little heart; (*inf*: *Kosewort*) (little) darling

Herz-: Herz|chi|rurg(in) M(F) heart or cardiac surgeon; **Herz|chi|rur|gie** F heart or cardiac surgery; **Herz|da|me** F **a** (*Cards*) queen of hearts **b** (*old, hum* = *Angebetete*) beloved

Her|ze|go|wi|na [hɛrtse'go:vina] F - die ~ Herzegovina, Hercegovina

her+zei|gen VT *sep* to show; **zeig (mal) her!** let me see, let's see; **das kann man ~** that's worth showing off

Her|ze|leid ['hɛrtsəlait] NT (*old*) heartache

her|zen ['hɛrtsn] VT (*dated*) to hug

Her|zens-: Her|zens|an|ge|le|gen|heit F (*dated*: = *Liebesangelegenheit*) affair of the heart; **es ist ihm eine ~** it is a matter close to his heart; **Her|zens|be|dürf|nis** NT (*dated*) **es ist mir ein ~** it is a matter dear to my heart; **Her|zens|bil|dung** F, *no pl* (*geh*) nobleness of heart; **Her|zens|bre|cher(in)** M(F) (*fig inf*) heartbreaker; **Her|zens|er|gie|ßung** [-lɛrgi:-sʊŋ] F -, -en, **Her|zens|er|guss** M (*dated, hum*) emotional outpourings *pl*; **Her|zens|freu|de** F (*dated*) **es ist mir eine ~** it warms my heart; **Her|zens|grund** M , *no pl* (*dated*) **aus tiefstem ~** from the very bottom of one's heart; **her|zens|gut** ADJ good-hearted; **Her|zens|gü|te** F good-heartedness; **Her|zens|lust** F **nach ~** to one's heart's content; **Her|zens|qual** F (*old*) *usu pl* great emotional torment *pl rare*; **Her|zens|wunsch** M dearest wish

Herz-: herz|er|freu|end ADJ heart-warming; **herz|er|fri|schend** ADJ refreshing; **herz|er|grei|fend** ADJ heart-rending; **herz|er|qui|ckend** ADJ refreshing; **herz|er|wär|mend** ADJ heart-warming; **herz|er|wei|chend** ADJ ▲ heart-rending; **Herz|er|wei|te|rung** F cardiectasis (*spec*), dilation of the heart; **Herz|feh|ler** M cardiac or heart defect; **Herz|flat|tern** NT -s, *no pl* palpitations *pl* (of the heart); **Herz|flim|mern** NT -s, *no pl* heart flutter; (= *Kammerflimmern*) (ventricular) fibrillation; **ich habe ~** (*fig*) my heart misses or skips a beat; **herz|för|mig** ADJ heart-shaped; **Herz|ge|gend** F , *no pl* cardiac region, area of the heart (*auch fig*); **Herz|ge|räu|sche** PL heartbeats *pl*

herz|haft ADJ **a** (*dated*: = *mutig*) brave **b** (= *kräftig*) hearty; *Händedruck, Griff* firm; *Geschmack* strong **c** (= *nahrhaft*) *Essen* substantial ADV **~ gähnen** to yawn loudly; **alle packten ~ an** everyone pitched in and helped; **alle griffen ~ zu** everyone got stuck in (*inf*); **das schmeckt ~** that's good honest fare; **jdn ~ küssen** to give sb a big fat kiss; **~ lachen** to laugh hard

her+zie|hen *sep irreg* VT **a** to draw or pull closer or nearer; **jdn/etw hinter sich** (*dat*) **~** to pull or drag sb/sth (along) behind one VI **a** *aux sein* (= *herankommen*) to approach; **hinter/neben/vor jdm ~** (*fig*) to move along behind/beside/in front of sb **b** *aux sein* (= *umziehen*) to move here **c** *aux sein* **über jdn/etw ~** (*inf*) to knock sb/sth (*inf*), to pull sb/sth to pieces (*inf*)

her|zig ['hɛrtsɪç] ADJ delightful, sweet

Herz-: Herz|in|farkt M heart attack, cardiac infarction (*spec*); **Herz|in|suf|fi|zi|enz** F cardiac insufficiency; **Herz|ja|gen** NT -s, *no pl* palpitations *pl*; **Herz-Je|su-Bild** NT Sacred Heart painting; **Herz|kam|mer** F ventricle; **Herz|kir|sche** F (bigarreau) cherry; **Herz|klap|pe** F cardiac or heart valve; **Herz|klap|pen|ent|zün|dung** F endocarditis; **Herz|klap|pen|feh|ler** M valvular heart defect; **Herz|klop|fen** NT -s, *no pl* **ich hatte/bekam ~** my heart was/started pounding; (*durch Kaffee*) I had/got palpitations; **mit ~** with a pounding heart, with one's heart in one's mouth; **Herz|krampf** M heart spasm; **herz|krank** ADJ suf-

fering from a heart condition; **~ sein/werden** to have/get a heart condition; **Herz|krank|heit** F heart condition; **Herz|kranz|ge|fäß** NT *usu pl* coronary (blood) vessel; **Herz-Kreis|lauf-Er|kran|kung** F cardiovascular disease or condition; **Herz|lei|den** NT heart condition; **herz|lei|dend** ADJ with a heart condition

herz|lich ['hɛrtslɪç] 🕂 48.2, 49, 50.6, 51.1, 51.2, 51.3, 52 ADJ *Empfang, Freundschaft, Atmosphäre* warm; *Wesen, Mensch* warm(-hearted); *Lachen* hearty; *Bitte* sincere; **~e Grüße an Ihre Frau** kind(est) regards to your wife, remember me to your wife; **mit ~en Grüßen** kind regards; **~en Dank!** many thanks, thank you very much indeed; **~es Beileid!** you have my sincere or heartfelt sympathy or condolences *pl*; **zu jdm ~ sein** to be kind to sb; **eine ~e Bitte an jdn richten** to make a cordial request to sb → **Glückwunsch**
ADV (= *freundlich*) warmly; *sich bedanken, Glück wünschen* sincerely; (= *ziemlich*) *langweilig, uninteressant* totally; **jdm ~ gratulieren** to congratulate and wish sb all the best; **~ schlecht** pretty awful; **~ wenig** precious little; **verbleibe ich als Ihr ~ grüßender...** I remain with best regards your...; **~ gern!** with the greatest of pleasure!; **ich würde ~ gern einmal wieder die Stätten meiner Kindheit besuchen** I should so much like to visit my childhood haunts again; **ich habe es ~ satt** I am thoroughly or utterly sick of it, I'm sick and tired of it

Herz|lich|keit F -, *no pl* (*von Empfang, Freundschaft*) warmth; (*von Wesen, Mensch*) warm(-hearted)ness

Herz-: Herz|lieb|chen NT (*old*) sweetheart, dearest; **Herz|liebs|te(r)** [hɛrts'li:pstə] MF *decl as adj* (*old*) darling, dearest; **Herz|li|nie** F heart line; **herz|los** ADJ heartless, unfeeling; **Herz|lo|sig|keit** F -, *no pl* heartlessness *no pl*; **Herz-Lun|gen-Ma|schi|ne** F heart-lung machine; **Herz|mas|sa|ge** F heart massage; **Herz|mit|tel** NT cardiac drug; **Herz|mu|schel** F (*Zool*) cockle; **Herz|mus|kel** M heart or cardiac muscle

Her|zog ['hɛrtso:k] M -s, ⸗e or (*rare*) -e ['hɛrsø:gə, -tso:gə] duke; **Otto ~ von Stein** Otto Duke of Stein, Otto Duke of Stein

Her|zo|gin ['hɛrtso:gɪn] F -, -nen duchess

her|zog|lich ['hɛrtso:klɪç] ADJ *attr* ducal

Her|zogs|wür|de F (= *Rang*) dignity or rank of a duke; (= *Titel*) dukedom; **der König verlieh ihm die ~** the king bestowed a dukedom or the rank of duke upon him

Her|zog|tum ['hɛrtso:ktu:m] NT -s, Herzogtümer [-ty:mə] dukedom, duchy

Herz-: Herz|pa|ti|ent(in) M(F) heart or cardiac patient; **Herz|rhyth|mus** M heart or cardiac rhythm; **Herz|rhyth|mus|stö|rung** F palpitations *pl*, cardiac disrhythmia (*spec*); **Herz|schei|de|wand** F (*Anat*) heart septum, septum of the heart; **Herz|schlag** M **a** (*einzelner*) heartbeat; **einen ~ lang** (*liter*) for one fleeting second; **mit jedem ~** (*liter*) with every beat of my/his *etc* heart **b** (= *Herztätigkeit*) heart or pulse rate; (*fig liter*) throbbing or pulsating life **c** (= *Herzstillstand*) heart attack, heart failure *no indef art, no pl*; **Herz|schmerz** M stabbing pain in the chest

Herz-Schmerz- *in cpds* (*inf*) schmaltzy (*inf*); **Herz-Schmerz-Ro|man** M (*inf*) schmaltzy novel (*inf*)

Herz-: Herz|schritt|ma|cher M pacemaker; **Herz|schwä|che** F heart failure; **wegen einer vorübergehenden ~** because my/his *etc* heart faltered for a moment; **an ~ leiden** to have a weak heart; **herz|stär|kend** ADJ cardiotonic (*spec*); **ein ~es Mittel** a cardiac stimulant, a cardiotonic (*spec*) ADV **~ wirken** to stimulate the heart; **Herz|stich** M *usu pl* stabbing pain in the chest; **Herz|still|stand** M cardiac arrest; **Herz|stol|pern** NT -s, *no pl* irregular heartbeat; **Herz|stück** NT (*fig geh*) heart, core; **Herz|tä|tig|keit** F heart or cardiac activity; **Herz|tod** M death from heart disease; **Herz|töne** PL (Med) cardiac sounds

her|zu- [hɛɐˈtsuː] in cpds = **herbei-**

Her|zug M (inf) **a** (Rail) down train **b** no pl (= Umzug) **seit meinem ~** since I came here, since coming here

Herz-: **Herz|ver|fet|tung** F fatty degeneration of the heart; **Herz|ver|sa|gen** NT heart failure; **Herz|vier ▲** F **die ~** the four of hearts; **herz|zer|rei|ßend** ADJ heartbreaking, heart-rending ADV **~ weinen** to weep distressingly

He|se|ki|el [heˈzeːkieːl, -kiːl] M -' Ezekiel

Hes|se [ˈhɛsə] M -n, -n, **Hes|sin** [ˈhɛsɪn] F -, -nen Hessian

Hes|sen [ˈhɛsn] NT -s Hesse

hes|sisch [ˈhɛsɪʃ] ADJ Hessian

He|tä|re [heˈtɛːrə] F -, -n (Hist) hetaira; (fig geh: = Dirne) courtesan

He|te [ˈheːtə] F -, -n usu pl (pej sl: = Heterosexuelle(r)) hetty (sl)

He|te|ra [ˈheːtera, ˈhɛtera, heˈteːra] F -, -s (inf) heterosexual female

he|te|ro [ˈheːtero, ˈhɛtero, heˈteːro] ADJ pred (inf) hetero (inf), straight (inf)

He|te|ro [ˈheːtero, ˈhɛtero, heˈteːro] M -s, -s (inf) hetero (inf)

He|te|ro-: **he|te|ro|dox** [heteroˈdɔks] ADJ (geh) heterodox; **He|te|ro|do|xie** [heterodɔˈksiː] F -, -n [-ˈksiːən] (geh) heterodoxy; **he|te|ro|gen** [heteroˈgeːn] ADJ (geh) heterogeneous; **He|te|ro|ge|ni|tät** [heterogeniˈtɛːt] F -, no pl (geh) heterogeneity; **he|te|ro|nom** [heteroˈnoːm] ADJ (geh) heteronomous; **He|te|ro|no|mie** [heteronoˈmiː] F -, no pl (geh) heteronomy; **He|te|ro|se|xu|a|li|tät** [hetero-] F heterosexuality; **he|te|ro|se|xu|ell** [hetero-] ADJ heterosexual; **He|te|ro|se|xu|el|le(r)** [heteroseˈksuɛla] MF decl as adj heterosexual

He|thi|ter [heˈtiːtə] M -s, -, **He|thi|te|rin** [-ərɪn] F -, -nen Hittite

he|thi|tisch [heˈtiːtɪʃ] ADJ Hittite

Hetz [hɛts] F -, (rare) -en (Aus inf) laugh (inf); **aus** or **zur ~** for a laugh

Hetz- (pej) in cpds inflammatory, rabble-rousing (pej); **Hetz|ar|ti|kel** M (pej; Press) inflammatory article; **Hetz|blatt** NT (pej; Press) smearsheet, scandal rag

Het|ze [ˈhɛtsə] F -, -n **a** no pl (= Hast) (mad) rush, hurry, (= Getriebensein) hustle and bustle, (mad) rush **b** no pl (pej: = Aufreizung) rabble-rousing propaganda **c** (Hunt) hounding (auf +acc of)

het|zen [ˈhɛtsn] VT **a** (lit, fig: = jagen) to hound; **die Hunde auf jdn/etw ~** to set the dogs on(to) sb/sth → **Hund a**
b (inf: = antreiben) to rush, to hurry
VR to hurry oneself, to rush oneself
VI **a** (= sich beeilen) to rush; **hetz nicht so** don't be in such a rush
b aux sein (= eilen) to tear, to race, to dash; **ich bin ganz schön gehetzt, um ...** I rushed like mad to ... (inf), I had an awful rush to ...; **hetz nicht so** don't go so fast
c (pej: = Hass schüren) to agitate, to stir up hatred; (inf: = lästern) to say malicious things; **gegen jdn/etw ~** to stir up hatred against sb/sth; **er hetzt immer gegen seinen Onkel** he's always running his uncle down, he's always saying malicious things about his uncle; **sie hat so lange gehetzt, bis er ...** she kept on being nasty until he finally ...; **zum Krieg ~** to agitate for war; **gegen Minderheiten ~** to stir up hatred against minorities; **bei jdm gegen jdn ~** to try to turn or set sb against sb → **auch gehetzt**

Het|zer [ˈhɛtsə] M -s, -, **Het|ze|rin** [-ərɪn] F -, -nen rabble-rouser, malicious agitator

Het|ze|rei [hɛtsəˈrai] F -, -en **a** no pl (= Hast) (mad) rush, hurry **b** (= das Hassschüren) rabble-rousing, malicious agitation, mischief-making; **~ zum Krieg** warmongering **c** (= hetzerische Äußerung) rabble-rousing attack (gegen on)

het|ze|risch [ˈhɛtsərɪʃ] ADJ rabble-rousing attr, virulent

Hetz-: **hetz|hal|ber** ADV (Aus inf) for a laugh (inf); **Hetz|hund** M hound, hunting dog; **Hetz|jagd** F **a** (lit, fig) hounding (auf +acc of) **b** (fig: = Hast) rush, hurry; **es war die reinste ~** it was one mad rush; **Hetz|kam|pag|ne** F malicious campaign; **Hetz|re|de** F inflammatory speech

Heu [hɔy] NT -(e)s, no pl hay; **Geld wie ~ haben** (inf) to have pots or oodles of money (inf)

Heu-: **Heu|bo|den** M , (Sw) **Heu|büh|ne** F hayloft; **Heu|bün|del** NT bundle or bale of hay

Heu|che|lei [hɔyçəˈlai] F -, -en hypocrisy; **spar dir deine ~en** cut out the hypocrisy or cant

heu|cheln [ˈhɔyçln] VI to be a hypocrite VT Zuneigung, Mitleid etc to feign, to simulate

Heuch|ler [ˈhɔyçlə] M -s, -, **Heuch|le|rin** [-ərɪn] F -, -nen hypocrite

heuch|le|risch [ˈhɔyçlərɪʃ] ADJ hypocritical; **~es Gerede** hypocritical talk, cant

heu|en [ˈhɔyən] VI (dial) to make hay; **das Heu|en** haymaking

heu|er [ˈhɔyə] ADV (S Ger, Aus, Sw) this year

Heu|er [ˈhɔyə] F -, -n (Naut) pay

Heu|er-: **Heu|er|bü|ro** NT (seamen's) employment office; **Heu|er|lohn** M pay

heu|ern [ˈhɔyɐn] VT to sign on, to engage, to hire

Heu|ern|te F hay harvest; (= Ertrag) hay crop

Heu|er|ver|trag M contract of employment (of seaman)

Heu-: **Heu|fie|ber** NT hay fever; **Heu|for|ke** F (N Ger), **Heu|ga|bel** F pitchfork, hayfork; **Heu|hau|fen** M haystack, hayrick

Heul|bo|je F (Naut) whistling buoy

heu|len [ˈhɔylən] VI **a** (inf: = weinen) to howl, to bawl (inf), to wail; (vor Schmerz) to scream; (vor Wut) to howl; **ich hätte ~ können** I could have cried; **es ist einfach zum Heulen** it's enough to make you weep → **Elend b** (Flugzeug, Motor) to roar; (Wind, Tiere) to howl; (Sirene) to wail

Heu|len NT -s, no pl **a** (= das Weinen) howling, bawling, wailing; **~ und Zähneklappern** (Bibl) wailing and gnashing of teeth **b** (von Flugzeug, Motor) roaring; (von Wind, Tier) howling; (von Sirene) wailing

Heu|ler [ˈhɔylə] M -s, - **a** (von Motor) roar **b** (= Feuerwerkskörper) screamer **c** (= Seehundsbaby) seal pup

Heu|le|rei [hɔyləˈrai] F -, -en (inf) constant bawling (inf)

Heul- (inf): **Heul|krampf** M fit of blubbering (inf); **Heul|pe|ter** [ˈhɔylpeːtə] M -s, -, **Heul|su|se** [ˈhɔylzuːzə] F -, -n crybaby (inf); **Heul|ton** M pl -töne (von Sirene) wail

Heu-: **Heu|ma|chen** NT -s, no pl, **Heu|mahd** F haymaking; **Heu|mond** M (old liter), **Heu|mo|nat** M (old) July; **Heu|rei|ter** M , **Heu|reu|ter** [-ərɐ] M -s, - rickstand

heu|rig [ˈhɔyrɪç] ADJ attr (S Ger, Aus) this year's; **der -e Wein** this year's wine

Heu|ri|ge [ˈhɔyrɪgə] PL decl as adj (esp Aus) early potatoes pl

Heu|ri|ge(r) [ˈhɔyrɪgə] M decl as adj (esp Aus) new wine

HEURIGER

Heuriger is the name given in Austria to wine from the most recent harvest, drunk from Martinmas (November 11th) onwards. Bars where the wine is drunk are also called **Heurige**. The **Heurige** bars in the area around Vienna are especially well known.

Heu|ris|tik [hɔyˈrɪstɪk] F -, no pl heuristics sing

heu|ris|tisch [hɔyˈrɪstɪʃ] ADJ heuristic

Heu-: **Heu|schnup|fen** M hay fever; **Heu|scho|ber** M barn; **Heu|schre|cke** [ˈhɔyʃrɛkə] F -, -n grasshopper; (in heißen Ländern) locust; **Heu|schre|cken|pla|ge** F plague of locusts; **Heu|spei|cher** M (S Ger), **Heu|sta|del** M (Aus, Sw) barn

heu|te [ˈhɔytə], **heut** [hɔyt] (inf) ADV **a** (= an diesem Tag) today; **~ Morgen** this morning; **~ Abend** this evening, tonight; **~ früh** this morning; **~ Nacht** tonight; **„heute geschlossen"** "closed today"; **~ noch** (= heutzutage) still ... today, even today; **ich muss ~ noch zur Bank** I must go to the bank today; **bis ~** (= bisher, heute immer noch) to this day; **bis ~ nicht** (= noch nicht) not ... to this day; **von ~ ab** or **an, ab ~** from today (on), from this day (forth) (liter); **~ in einer Woche** a week today or from now, today week; **~ vor acht Tagen** a week ago today; **~ in einem Jahr** a year from today or now, a year hence (geh); **Milch/die Zeitung von ~** today's milk/paper; **~ mir, morgen dir** (Prov) (it's my turn today,) your turn may come tomorrow; **lieber ~ als morgen** the sooner the better; **etw von ~ auf morgen verschieben** to put sth off until tomorrow; **von ~ auf morgen** (fig: = rasch, plötzlich) overnight, from one day to the next
b (= in der gegenwärtigen Zeit) nowadays, these days, today; **das Heute** the present, today; **das Italien/der Mensch von ~** present-day or contemporary or modern Italy/man; **der Bauer/die Frau/die Stadt von ~** the farmer/woman/town of today, today's farmers/women/towns; **die Jugend von ~** the young people of today, modern youth

heu|tig [ˈhɔytɪç] ADJ attr today's; (= von heute auch) the day's; (= gegenwärtig) modern, contemporary; **der ~e Tag** today; **am ~en Abend** this evening; **anlässlich Ihres ~en Geburtstags** to mark your birthday today; **unser ~es Schreiben** (Comm) our letter of today('s date); **die ~e Zeitung** today's paper; **bis zum ~en Tage** to date, to this day; **aus ~er Sicht** from today's standpoint, from a modern or contemporary point of view; **wir Heutigen** (geh) we people of today, we modern men and women

heu|ti|gen|tags [ˈhɔytɪgnˈtaːks, ˈhɔytɪgntaːks] ADV (dated) = **heute b**

heut|zu|ta|ge [ˈhɔyttsutaːgə] ADV nowadays, these days, today

Heu-: **Heu|wa|gen** M haycart, haywagon; **Heu|wen|der** [-vɛndə] M -s, - tedder

He|xa- [hɛksa] in cpds hexa-; **he|xa|de|zi|mal** [hɛksadetsiˈmaːl] ADJ (Comput) hexadecimal, hex; **He|xa|de|zi|mal|zahl** F (Comput) hexadecimal number; **He|xa|e|der** [hɛksaˈleːdə] NT -s, - hexahedron; **He|xa|gon** [hɛksaˈgoːn] NT -s, -e hexagon; **he|xa|go|nal** [hɛksagoˈnaːl] ADJ hexagonal; **He|xa|gramm** [hɛksaˈgram] NT pl -gramme hexagram; **He|xa|me|ter** [hɛˈksaːmetə] M hexameter

He|xe [ˈhɛksə] F -, -n witch; (inf: = altes Weib) old hag or crone; **diese kleine ~!** that little minx or hussy!

he|xen [ˈhɛksn] VI to practise (Brit) or practice (US) witchcraft; **er kann ~** he knows (how to work) black magic; **ich kann doch nicht ~** (inf) I can't work miracles, I'm not a magician VT to conjure up; **~, dass ...** to cast a (magic) spell so that ...

He|xen-: **He|xen|ein|mal|eins** NT magic square; **He|xen|glau|be** M belief in witches; **He|xen|haus** NT enchanted house; **He|xen|häus|chen** [-hɔyscən] NT gingerbread house; **He|xen|jagd** F (Hist, fig) witch-hunt; **He|xen|kes|sel** M (fig) pandemonium no art, bedlam no art; **im wahrer ~** absolute pandemonium or bedlam; **He|xen|kü|che** F (fig) witches' kitchen; **He|xen|kunst** F witchcraft, sorcery, witchery; **He|xen|meis|ter** M sorcerer; **He|xen|pro|be** F (Hist) witches' ordeal; **He|xen|pro|zess ▲** M witch trial; **He|xen|ring** M fairy ring; **He|xen|sab|bat** M witches' sabbath; (fig) bedlam no art, pandemonium no art; **es war ein wahrer ~** it was sheer pandemonium; **He|xen|schuss** ▲ M (Med) lumbago; **He|xen|ver|bren|nung** F burning of a witch/witches; **He|xen|ver|fol|gung** F witch-hunt; **He|xen|wahn** M obsessive belief in witches; **He|xen|werk** NT sorcery, witchcraft, witchery

He|xer ['hɛksɐ] M **-s, -** sorcerer

He|xe|rei [hɛksə'rai] F **-, -en** witchcraft no pl, sorcery, witchery no pl; (von Zaubertricks) magic no pl

HG F - abbr von **Handelsgesellschaft**

hg. abbr von **herausgegeben** ed.

Hi|a|tus ['hia:tʊs] M **-, -** ['hia:tu:s] hiatus

hib|be|lig ['hɪbəlɪç] ADJ (dial) jittery

Hi|bis|kus [hi'bɪskʊs] M **-, Hibisken** [-kn] hibiscus

hick [hɪk] INTERJ hic

Hick|hack ['hɪkhak] M OR NT **-s, -s** squabbling no pl

hie [hi:] ADV (old) here; **~ und da** (= manchmal) (every) now and then, every so often, (every) once in a while; (= stellenweise) here and there; **~ ... ~** or **da** on the one side ... on the other (side)

hieb (geh) pret von **hauen**

Hieb [hi:p] M **-(e)s, -e** [-bə] **a** (= Schlag) stroke, blow; (= Fausthieb) blow; (= Peitschenhieb) lash, crack; (Fechten) cut; **auf den ersten ~ fällt kein Baum** (prov) Rome wasn't built in a day (Prov); **auf einen ~** (inf) in one go; **ein Glas auf einen ~ leer trinken** (inf) to down a glass in one (inf) **b** (= Hiebwunde) gash, slash **c Hiebe** PL (dated: = Prügel) hiding, thrashing, beating; **~e bekommen** to get a hiding or thrashing or beating; **gleich gibt es or setzt es ~e!** you'll get a (good) hiding in a minute **d** (fig) dig, cutting remark; **der ~ saß** that (dig) went or struck home; **~e bekommen** to be on the receiving end of some cutting remarks

Hieb-: **hieb|fest** ADJ hieb- und stichfest (fig) watertight; **Hieb|waf|fe** F cutting weapon; **Hieb|wun|de** F gash, slash

hielt pret von **halten**

hie|nie|den ['hi:'ni:dn, hi'ni:dn, (emph) 'hi:-ni:dn] ADV (old liter) here below

hier [hi:ɐ] ADV **a** (räumlich) here; (= in diesem Land) here, (here) in this country; (= hier am Ort) here, locally; **~ zu Lande** in these parts; **das Haus ~** this house; **dieser ~** this one (here); **~!** (beim Appell) present!, here!; **~ und da** here and there; **Herr Direktor ~, Herr Direktor da** (iro) yes sir, yes sir, three bags full, sir; **~ drau-ßen/drinnen** out/in here; **~ entlang** along here; **~ herum** hereabouts, (a)round here; **~ hinein** in here; **~ oben/unten** up/down here; **~ vorn/hin-ten** in front/at the back here, here in front/at the back; **er ist von ~** he's a local (man), he comes from (a)round here; **er ist nicht von ~** he's a stranger here, he's not a local; **Tag Klaus, ~ (spricht) Hans** (Telec) hello, Klaus, Hans here; **~ spricht Dr. Müller** (Telec) this is Dr Müller (speaking); **von ~ ab** from here (on or onwards); **von ~ aus** from here; **~ sehen Sie ...** here you (can) see ...; **~ und heute** (geh) here and now; **das Hier und Heute** (geh) the here and now; **~ ist ein bisschen ~ oben** (inf) he's got a screw loose (inf) **b** (zeitlich) now; **~ und da** (every) now and then, every so often; **von ~ ab** or **an** from now on, henceforth (form) **c** (fig) here; **das steht mir bis ~** (inf) I'm fed up to here (inf) or to the back teeth (inf) (with it), I've had it up to here (inf); **~ versagte ihm die Stimme** here or at this point or at this juncture his voice failed him

hie|ran ['hi:'ran, hi'ran, (emph) 'hi:ran] ADV **a** (lit) here **b** (fig) **wenn ich ~ denke** when I think of or about this; **er erinnert sich ~** he remembers this; **~ erkenne ich es** I recognize it

by this; **~ kann es keinen Zweifel geben** there can be no doubt about that

Hie|rarch [hie'rarç] M **-en, -en a** (Hist) high priest (in ancient Greece) **b** (fig: = Machtha-ber) top man

Hie|rar|chie [hierar'çi:] F **-, -n** [-'çi:ən] hierarchy

hie|rar|chisch [hie'rarçɪʃ] ADJ hierarchic(al) ADV hierarchically; **aufbauen, gliedern** with a hi-erarchical structure

hier-: **hie|rauf** ['hi:'rauf, hi:'rauf, (emph) 'hi:rauf] ADV **a** (lit) (on) here, on this **b** (fig) on this; (= daraufhin) hereupon; **er setzte sich, und ~** he sat down and then ...; **hie|rauf|hin** ['hi:-rauf'hɪn, hi:rauf'hɪn, (emph) 'hi:rauf hɪn] ADV hereupon; **und ~ ...** and then ...; **hie|raus** ['hi:'raus, hi:'raus, (emph) 'hi:raus] ADV **a** (lit) out of this, from here; **~ ist das Geld gestohlen worden** the money was stolen from here **b** (fig) from this; **~ folgt, dass ...,** **~ geht hervor, dass ...** from this it follows that ..., hence (it follows that) ...; **hier be|hal|ten** ▲ VT irreg **jdn/etw ~** to keep sb/sth here; **hier|bei** ['hi:ɐ-'bai, hi:ɐ'bai, (emph) 'hi:ɐbai] ADV **a** (= während-dessen) doing this **b** (fig) (= bei dieser Gele-genheit) on this occasion; (= in diesem Zusam-menhang) in this connection; **hier blei|ben** ▲ VI irreg aux sein to stay here; **hier geblieben!** stop!; **hier|durch** ['hi:ɐ'dʊrç, hi:ɐ'dʊrç, (emph) 'hi:ɐdʊrç] ADV **a** (lit) through here **b** (fig) through this; **ich lasse mich ~ nicht ärgern** I won't let this annoy me; **~ teilen wir Ihnen mit, dass ...** we hereby inform you that ...; **hier|rein** ['hi:'rain, hi:'rain, (emph) 'hi:rain] ADV (lit) in (-to) this, in here; **hier|für** ['hi:ɐ'fy:ɐ, hi:ɐ'fy:ɐ, (emph) 'hi:ɐfy:ɐ] ADV for this; **hier|ge|gen** ['hi:ɐ'ge:gn, hi:ɐ'ge:gn, (emph) 'hi:ɐge:gn] ADV (lit, fig) against this; **hier|her** ['hi:ɐ'he:ɐ, hi:ɐ-'he:ɐ, (emph) 'hi:ɐhe:ɐ] ADV here; **(komm) ~!** come here or hither (liter, old); **bis ~** (örtlich) up to here; (zeitlich) up to now, so far; **mir stehts bis ~** (inf) I'm fed up to here or to the back teeth (inf) → **bis ²**; **hier|her|rauf** ['hi:ɐ-'rauf, hi:ɐ'rauf, (emph) 'hi:ɐherauf] ADV up here; **bis ~** up to here

hier|her: **hier|her be|mü|hen** ▲ (geh) VT jdn to ask or trouble to come (here) VR to take the trouble to come (here); **hier|her bit|ten** ▲ VT irreg to ask to come (here); **hier|her bli|cken** ▲ VI to look this way, to look over here; **hier|her brin|gen** ▲ VT irreg to bring (over) here; **hier|her fah|ren** ▲ irreg VI aux sein to come here VT etw to drive here; jdn to drive (here), to give a lift or ride here; **hier|her füh|ren** ▲ VI (Weg etc) to lead here, to come this way; **hier|her ge|hören** ▲ VI to belong here; (fig: = relevant sein) to be relevant; **~de Bemerkungen** irrelevant remarks; **hier|her ho|len** ▲ VT to bring here; **hier|her kom|men** ▲ VI irreg aux sein to come here; **hier|her lau|fen** ▲ VI irreg aux sein to run here; **hierher gelaufen kommen** to come running up; **hier|her le|gen** ▲ VT to lay (down) here VR to lie (down) here, to lay one-self (down) here; **hier|her lo|cken** ▲ VT to entice or lure here; **hier|her schaf|fen** ▲ VT to bring here; **hier|her schi|cken** ▲ VT to send here; **hier|her set|zen** ▲ VT to put here VR to sit (down) here; **hier|her stel|len** ▲ VT to put here VR to stand here; **hier|her tra|gen** ▲ VT irreg to carry here

hier|he|rum ['hi:ɐhe'rʊm, hi:ɐhe'rʊm, (emph) 'hi:ɐherʊm] ADV (a)round here; (= in diese Rich-tung) this way (a)round; (inf: = ungefähr hier) hereabouts, (a)round here (somewhere)

hier|her: **hier|her wa|gen** ▲ VR to dare to come here; **hier|her zie|hen** ▲ irreg VT (fig) to bring here VI aux sein to come here; (= um-ziehen) to move here

hier-: **hier|hin** ['hi:ɐ'hɪn, hi:ɐ'hɪn, (emph) 'hi:ɐ-hɪn] ADV here; **~ und dorthin** here and there, hither and thither (liter); **bis ~** up to here; **hier|hi|nab** ['hi:ɐ'hɪnap, hi:ɐ'hɪnap, (emph) 'hi:ɐ-hɪnap] ADV down here; **hier|hi|nauf** ['hi:ɐhɪ-

'nauf, hi:ɐhɪ'nauf, (emph) 'hi:ɐhɪnauf] ADV up here; **hier|hi|naus** ['hi:ɐhɪ'naus, hi:ɐhɪ'naus, (emph) 'hi:ɐhɪnaus] ADV out here; **hier|hi|nein** ['hi:ɐhɪ'nain, hi:ɐhɪ'nain, (emph) 'hi:ɐhɪnain] ADV in here; **hier|hin|ter** ['hi:ɐ'hɪntɐ, hi:ɐ-'hɪntɐ, (emph) 'hi:ɐhɪntɐ] ADV behind here; **hier|hi|nun|ter** ['hi:ɐhɪ'nʊntɐ, hi:ɐhɪ'nʊntɐ, (emph) 'hi:ɐhɪnʊntɐ] ADV down here; **hier|rin** ['hi:'rɪn, hi:'rɪn, (emph) 'hi:rɪn] ADV (lit, fig) in this; **hier las|sen** ▲ VT irreg to leave here; **hier|mit** ['hi:ɐ'mɪt, hi:ɐ'mɪt, (emph) 'hi:ɐmɪt] ADV with this, herewith (obs, form); **~ ist der Fall erledigt** this settles the matter; **~ bin ich einverstanden** I agree to this; **~ erkläre ich ...** (form) I hereby declare ... (form); **~ bestätigen wir den Eingang Ihres Briefes** we herewith or hereby acknowledge receipt of your letter; **~ wird bescheinigt, dass ...** this is to certify that ...; **hier|nach** ['hi:ɐ'na:x, hi:ɐ'na:x, (emph) 'hi:ɐ-na:x] ADV after this, afterwards; (= daraus fol-gend) according to this; **hier|ne|ben** ['hi:ɐ-'ne:bn, hi:ɐ'ne:bn, (emph) 'hi:ɐne:bn] ADV be-side this, next to this

Hie|ro|gly|phe [hiero'gly:fə] F **-, -n** hiero-glyph(ic); (fig hum) hieroglyphic

Hie|ro|gly|phen|schrift F hieroglyphic script or writing

hier-: **hier|orts** ['hi:ɐ'lɔrts, hi:ɐ'lɔrts, (emph) 'hi:ɐ-lɔrts] ADV (geh) here; **hier sein** ▲ VI irreg aux sein to be here; **Hier|sein** NT **während meines ~s** during my stay; **was ist der Zweck seines ~s?** what is the purpose of his being here or of his presence?; **hier|selbst** ['hi:ɐ'zɛlpst, hi:ɐ-'zɛlpst, (emph) 'hi:ɐzɛlpst] ADV in this very place, even here (old); **hie|rü|ber** ['hi:'ry:bɐ, hi:'ry:bɐ, (emph) 'hi:ry:bɐ] ADV **a** (lit) over this or here; (= oberhalb dieser Stelle) over it **b** (fig) about this; (geh: = währenddessen) in the midst of it; **~ ärgere ich mich** this makes me angry; **hie|rum** ['hi:'rʊm, hi:'rʊm, (emph) 'hi:rʊm] ADV **a** (lit) (a)round this or here **b** (fig) about or concerning this; **~ handelt es sich nicht** this isn't the issue; **hie|run|ter** ['hi:'rʊntɐ, hi:'rʊntɐ, (emph) 'hi:rʊntɐ] ADV **a** (lit) under or beneath this or here **b** (fig) by this or that; (= in dieser Kategorie) among these; **~ fallen auch die Sonn-tage** this includes Sundays; **hier|von** ['hi:ɐ'fɔn, hi:ɐ'fɔn, (emph) 'hi:ɐfɔn] ADV **a** (lit) (örtlich) from here or this; (= von diesem etc) from this; (= aus diesem Material) out of this **b** **~ habe ich nichts gewusst** I knew nothing of or about this; **~ abgesehen** apart from this; **~ kannst du nichts haben** you can't have any of this; **hier|vor** ['hi:ɐ'fo:ɐ, hi:ɐ'fo:ɐ, (emph) 'hi:ɐfo:ɐ] ADV **a** (lit) in front of this or here **b** (fig) **~ ekele/fürchte ich mich** it revolts/frightens me; **~ mö-ge uns Gott bewahren** may God preserve us from this; **~ hat er großen Respekt** he has a great respect for this; **hier|zu** ['hi:ɐ'tsu:, hi:ɐ-'tsu:, (emph) 'hi:ɐtsu:] ADV **a** (= dafür) to this; (= dazu) with this **b** (= außerdem) in addition to this, moreover **c** (= zu diesem Punkt) about this; **~ gehören auch die Katzen** this also in-cludes the cats; **~ habe ich etwas Wichtiges zu sagen** I have something important to say on or about or to this; **~ wünsche ich Ihnen viel Glück** I wish you luck in this; **vgl. ~ S.370** cf p 370; **hier|zu|lan|de** ['hi:ɐtsu'landə, (emph) 'hi:-ɐtsu'landə] ADV in these parts → auch **hier** a; **hier|zwi|schen** ['hi:ɐ'tsvɪʃn, hi:ɐ'tsvɪʃn, (emph) 'hi:ɐtsvɪʃn] ADV between these

hie|sig ['hi:zɪç] ADJ attr local; **die ~en Verhält-nisse** local conditions, conditions here; **meine ~en Verwandten** my relatives here; **er ist kein Hiesiger** he is not a local (man), he's not from these parts

hieß pret von **heißen**

hie|ven ['hi:fn, 'hi:vn] VT (esp Naut) to heave

Hi-Fi-An|la|ge ['haifi-] F hi-fi set or system

Hift|horn ['hɪfthɔrn] NT (Hunt) hunting horn

high [hai] ADJ pred (inf) high (inf)

high|ja|cken ['haidʒɛkn] VT insep to hi(gh)jack

High|ja|cker [ˈhaidʒɛkɐ] M **-s, -, High|ja|cke|rin** [-ərɪn] F **-, -nen** hi(gh)jacker

High|life [ˈhailaif] NT **-s,** no pl high life; **~ machen** (inf) to live it up (inf)

High|light [ˈhailait] NT **-s, -s** highlight

high|lighten [ˈhailaitn] VT insep (Comput) Textpassagen etc to highlight

High|sno|bie|ty ▲, **High Sno|bie|ty** [ˈhaisnoˈbaiiti] F **-,** no pl (hum) snob class, snobby social circles pl

High|so|cie|ty ▲, **High So|cie|ty** [ˈhaisoˈsaiiti] F **-,** no pl high society

High|tech ▲ [haiˈtɛk] NT **-,** no pl high tech, hi tech

High|tech- ▲ [haiˈtɛk] in cpds high-tech; **High|tech|in|dus|trie** ▲ F high-tech industry; **High|tech|pro|dukt** ▲ NT high-tech product; **High|tech|un|ter|neh|men** ▲ NT high-tech company

hi|hi [hiˈhiː] INTERJ heehee, teehee

hi|ja|cken [ˈhaidʒɛkn] VT insep to hi(gh)jack

Hi|ja|cker [ˈhaidʒɛkɐ] M **-s, -, Hi|ja|cke|rin** [-ərɪn] F **-, -nen** hi(gh)jacker

hilb [hɪlp] ADJ (Sw) sheltered, protected from the wind

Hil|de|brands|lied [ˈhɪldəbrants-] NT , no pl (Liter) Lay of Hildebrand

hilf [hɪlf] imper sing von **helfen**

Hil|fe [ˈhɪlfə] F **-, -n** a no pl help; (finanzielle) aid, assistance, help; (für Notleidende) aid, relief; **zu ~!** help!; **um ~ rufen/schreien** to call/shout for help; **jdm zu ~ kommen** to come to sb's aid or assistance or rescue; **jdn um ~ bitten** to ask sb for help or assistance; **jdm ~ leisten** to help sb; **bei jdm ~ suchen** to seek sb's help or assistance; **~ suchend** (Mensch) seeking help; **Blick** imploring, beseeching; **die ~ Suchenden** those seeking help; **sich ~ suchend umsehen** or **umblicken** to look (a)round for help; **täglich wenden sich Hunderte** or **hunderte ~ suchend an diese Organisation** hundreds turn every day to this organization seeking help; **mit ~** with the help or aid (gen of); **ohne ~** without help or assistance; (= selbständig) unaided; **etw zu ~ nehmen** to use sth; **ohne fremde ~ gehen** to walk unaided; **jds Gedächtnis** (dat) **zu ~ kommen** to jog sb's memory → **erste(r, s), mithilfe** **b** (= Hilfsmittel, Hilfestellung) aid; (= Haushaltshilfe) (domestic) help; **~n geben** (beim Turnen) to give support; (beim Reiten) to give aids; **du bist mir eine schöne ~!** (iro) a fine help YOU are (to me)! (iro) **c** (Comput) help; **Online-Hilfe** on-line help

Hil|fe-: hil|fe|be|dürf|tig ADJ = hilfsbedürftig; **Hil|fe|be|dürf|tig|keit** F = Hilfsbedürftigkeit; **hil|fe|fle|hend** ADJ imploring, beseeching; **Hil|fe|funk|ti|on** F (Comput; in Software) help function; **Hil|fe|ge|such** NT request for help; **Hil|fe|leis|tung** F aid, assistance; **unterlassene ~** (Jur) denial of assistance; **Hil|fe|me|nü** NT (Comput; in Software) help menu; **Hil|fe|ruf** M call for help; **Hil|fe|schrei** M cry or shout for help, cry of "help"; **Hil|fe|stel|lung** F (Sport, fig) support; **jdm ~ geben** to give sb support; (fig auch) to back sb up; **Hil|fe|su|chen|de(r)** △ ADJ, ADV → Hilfe a; **Hil|fe|su|chen|de(r)** MF decl as adj person seeking help, person in need of help; **die ~n** pl those seeking help, those in need of help → auch **Hilfe a; Hil|fetas|te** F (Comput) help key

Hilf-: hilf|los ADJ helpless; (= schutzlos auch) defenceless (Brit), defenseless (US); (= ratlos auch) clueless (inf) ADV helplessly; **meinen, stammeln** uncertainly; **einer Sache** (dat) **~ ausgeliefert sein** to be completely at the mercy of sth; **Hilf|lo|sig|keit** F **-,** no pl helplessness; (= Schutzlosigkeit auch) defencelessness (Brit), defenselessness (US); (= Ratlosigkeit auch) cluelessness (inf); **hilf|reich** ADJ helpful; (= nützlich auch) useful; **eine ~e Hand** a helping hand; **er reichte ihr ~ seine Hand** he held out a helping hand to her

Hilfs-: Hilfs|ak|ti|on F relief action; **Hilfs|arbei|ter(in)** M(F) labourer (Brit), laborer (US); (in Fabrik) unskilled worker; **Hilfs|as|sistent(in)** M(F) (Univ) ≈ tutorial assistant; **hilfs|be|dürf|tig** ADJ in need of help; (= Not leidend) needy, in need pred; **die Hilfsbedürftigen** the needy, those in need; **Hilfs|be|dürftig|keit** F need(iness); **hilfs|be|reit** ADJ helpful, ready to help pred; **Hilfs|be|reitschaft** F helpfulness, readiness to help; **Hilfs|dienst** M emergency service; (bei Katastrophenfall) (emergency) relief service; (= Kfz-Hilfsdienst) (emergency) breakdown service; **Hilfs|feu|er|wehr** F auxiliary fire service; **Hilfs|fonds** M relief fund; **Hilfs|geist|liche(r)** MF decl as adj curate; **Hilfs|gel|der** PL back-up funds pl; **Hilfs|gü|ter** PL relief aid sing; **Hilfs|ko|mi|tee** NT relief action committee; **Hilfs|kon|struk|ti|on** F (Math) rough diagram; (fig) temporary measure; **Hilfs|kraft** F assistant, helper; (= Aushilfe) temporary worker; **wissenschaftliche/fachliche ~** research/technical assistant; **Hilfs|leh|rer(in)** M(F) supply teacher; **Hilfs|li|nie** F (Math) auxiliary line; **Hilfs|maß|nah|me** F relief action no pl; (zur Rettung) rescue action no pl; **Hilfs|me|nü** NT (Comput; in Software) help menu; **Hilfs|mit|tel** NT aid; **Hilfs|mo|tor** M (Aut) auxiliary engine; **Fahrrad mit ~** moped, motor-assisted bicycle; **Hilfs|or|ga|ni|sa|ti|on** F relief organization; **Hilfs|pa|ket** NT aid package; **Hilfs|perso|nal** NT auxiliary staff; (= Aushilfspersonal) temporary staff or help; **Hilfs|po|li|zei** F auxiliary police; **Hilfs|po|li|zist(in)** M(F) auxiliary policeman/-woman; **Hilfs|pre|di|ger(in)** M(F), **Hilfs|pries|ter** M curate; **Hilfs|programm** NT a (zur Hungerhilfe etc) relief or aid programme (Brit) or program (US) b (Comput) utility program; **Hilfs|quel|le** F a (= Geldquelle) source of money, pecuniary or financial (re)sources pl b (für wissenschaftliche Arbeit) source; **Hilfs|ru|der** NT (Aviat) auxiliary rudder; **Hilfs|schiff** NT auxiliary vessel; **Hilfs|schu|le** F (dated) special school; **Hilfs|schüler(in)** M(F) (dated) pupil at/from a special school; **Hilfs|schul|leh|rer(in)** M(F) (dated) teacher at a special school; **Hilfs|schwes|ter** F auxiliary (nurse); **Hilfs|she|riff** M assistant or deputy sheriff; **Hilfs|spra|che** F auxiliary language; **Hilfs|trans|port** M transport of relief aid; **Hilfs|trieb|werk** NT auxiliary engine; **Hilfs|trupp** M group of helpers; **Hilfs|truppe** F (Mil) auxiliary troops pl; (= Verstärkung) reinforcements pl; (Pol pej) back-up army or boys pl; **Hilfs|verb** NT auxiliary or helping (US) verb; **Hilfs|werk** NT relief organization; **hilfs|wil|lig** ADJ willing to help pred; **Hilfswil|li|ge(r)** [-vɪlɪɡə] MF decl as adj voluntary helper; **Hilfs|wis|sen|schaft** F (+gen to) complementary science; (= Geisteswissenschaft) complementary subject; **Hilfs|zeit|wort** NT auxiliary or helping (US) verb

hilft [hɪlft] 3. pers sing pres von **helfen**

Hi|ma|la|ja [hiˈmaːlaja, himaˈlaːja] M **-(s) der ~** the Himalayas pl

Him|bee|re [ˈhɪmbeːrə] F raspberry

Himbeer-: Him|beer|eis NT raspberry ice (cream); **Him|beer|geist** M , no pl (white) raspberry brandy; **him|beer|rot** ADJ raspberry-coloured (Brit), raspberry-colored (US); **Him|beer|saft** M raspberry juice; **Him|beerstrauch** M raspberry bush

Him|mel [ˈhɪml] M **-s,** (poet) - a sky; **am ~** in the sky; **unter dem ~ Spaniens, unter spanischem ~** under or beneath a Spanish sky; **zwischen ~ und Erde** in midair; **~ und Erde** (Cook) mashed potato and apple with black pudding and fried liver sausage **in den ~ ragen** to tower (up) into the sky; **jdn/etw in den ~ (er-) heben** or **loben** or **rühmen** to praise sb/sth to the skies; **jdm hängt der ~ voller Geigen** everything in the garden is lovely for sb; **gute Lehrer fallen nicht vom ~** good teachers don't grow on trees; **der Frieden fällt nicht einfach vom ~,**

sondern ... peace doesn't just fall out of the blue, but ...; **eher stürzt der ~ ein, als dass ...** (geh) the skies will fall before ... (liter) **b** (Rel: = Himmelreich) heaven; **im ~** in heaven; **den Blick gen ~ richten** (liter) to look heavenward(s), to raise one's eyes toward(s) heaven; **in den ~ kommen** to go to heaven; **zum** or **in den ~ auffahren, gen ~ fahren** (liter) to ascend to heaven; **der Sohn des ~s** (Kaiser von China) the Celestial Emperor; **der ~ auf Erden** heaven on earth; **dem ~ sei Dank** (old) thank God or Heaven(s); **der ~ ist** or **sei mein Zeuge** (old) as Heaven or God is my witness; **(das) weiß der ~!** (inf) God or Heaven (only) knows; **der ~ bewahre mich davor!** (old) may Heaven or God preserve me; **das schreit zum ~** it's a scandal; **es stinkt zum ~** (inf) it stinks to high heaven (inf); **der ~ verhüte** (old) Heaven or God forbid; **(ach) du lieber ~!** (inf) good Heavens!, good (-ness) gracious!; **~ (noch mal)!** (inf) good God!, hang it all! (inf); **um(s) ~s willen** (inf) for Heaven's or goodness' sake (inf); **~, Arsch und Zwirn** (dated inf) or **Wolkenbruch** (dated inf) bloody hell! (Brit inf), Christ Almighty! (inf); **~ und Hölle** (= Kinderspiel) hopscotch; **~ und Hölle** or **Erde in Bewegung setzen** to move heaven and earth **c** (= Betthimmel etc) canopy; (im Auto) roof

Him|mel-: him|mel|an [hɪmlˈlan] ADV (poet) heavenward(s); **him|mel|angst** [ˈhɪmlˈlaŋst] ADJ pred **mir wurde ~** I was scared to death; **Him|mel|bett** NT four-poster (bed); **himmel|blau** ADJ sky-blue, azure (liter); **Himmel|don|ner|wet|ter** [ˈhɪmlˈdɔnɐˈvɛtɐ] INTERJ (inf) damn it (inf); **~ noch (ein)mal!** damn and blast it! (inf)

Him|mel|fahrt F a (Rel) **Christi ~** the Ascension of Christ; **Mariä ~** the Assumption of the Virgin Mary **b** (no art: = Feiertag) Ascension Day

HIMMELFAHRT

Himmelfahrt (Ascension Day) is a public holiday in Germany and celebrates the Ascension of Christ into heaven forty days after Easter. It is also popularly called **Vatertag** (Father's Day) or **Männertag**: fathers, like mothers on Mother's Day, receive a small present from their children. Men often take advantage of the opportunity to leave their wives and children at home on this day and go out drinking with their friends.

Him|mel|fahrts-: Him|mel|fahrts|kom|mando NT (Mil inf) suicide squad or (= Unternehmung) mission; **Him|mel|fahrts|na|se** F (hum inf) turned-up or snub nose; **Him|melfahrts|tag** M **der ~** Ascension Day; **am ~** on Ascension Day

Him|mel-: Him|mel|herr|gott [ˈhɪmlˈhɛrgɔt] INTERJ (inf) damn it (inf), bloody hell (Brit inf); **~ noch (ein)mal!** damn and blast it! (inf); **Him|mel|herr|gott|sak|ra** [ˈhɪmlˈhɛrgɔtˈzaːkra] INTERJ (S Ger, Aus) damn it (inf), bloody hell (Brit inf); **him|mel|hoch** ADJ sky-high ADV high into the sky; **~ jauchzend, zu Tode betrübt** one up minute and down the next; **Himmel|reich** NT , no pl (Rel) Kingdom of Heaven; **ins ~ eingehen** or **kommen** to enter the Kingdom of Heaven; **ein ~ für ...** I'd give anything or my right arm for ...

Him|mels-: Him|mels|ach|se F celestial axis; **Him|mels|äqua|tor** M celestial equator, equinoctial line or circle; **Him|mels|bahn** F (liter) celestial path or orbit; **Him|mels|blau** NT (liter) sky blue; **Him|mels|braut** F (liter) bride of Christ (liter)

Him|mel-: Him|mel|schlüs|sel M OR NT (Bot) cowslip; **him|mel|schrei|end** ADJ **Unrecht** outrageous, scandalous; **Unkenntnis, Verhältnisse** appalling; **Unsinn** utter attr; **Schande** crying attr

Him|mels-: Him|mels|er|schei|nung F celestial phenomenon; **Him|mels|fes|te** F (liter)

firmament (*liter*); **Him|mels|fürst** M (*Rel, liter*) King of Heaven; **Him|mels|ga|be** F (*geh*) gift from heaven; **Him|mels|ge|wöl|be** NT (*liter*) vault of heaven (*liter*), firmament (*liter*); **Him|mels|kar|te** F star map *or* chart; **Him|mels|kö|ni|gin** F (*Rel*) Queen of Heaven; **Him|mels|kör|per** M heavenly *or* celestial body; **Him|mels|ku|gel** F (*liter*) celestial globe (*liter*) *or* sphere (*liter*); **Him|mels|kun|de** F astronomy; **Him|mels|kup|pel** F (*liter*) vault of heaven (*liter*), firmament (*liter*); **Him|mels|lei|ter** F (*Bot*) Jacob's Ladder; **Him|mels|macht** F **die Liebe ist eine ~** love is a power of heaven; **Him|mels|pfor|te** F (*liter*) gate of heaven; **Him|mels|pol** M celestial pole; **Him|mels|rich|tung** F direction; **die vier ~en** the four points of the compass; **Him|mels|schlüs|sel** M OR NT (*Bot*) cowslip; **Him|mels|schrift** F skywriting; **Him|mels|spi|on** M (*inf*) spy satellite; **Him|mels|stür|mer(in)** M(F) (*liter*) (romantic) idealist; **Him|mels|tor** NT , **Him|mels|tür** **F** (*geh*) gate of heaven

him|mel|stür|mend ADJ *attr* (*liter*) boundless; *Projekt, Vision* highly ambitious

Him|mels-: Him|mels|wa|gen M (*Astron*) Great Bear; **Him|mels|zelt** NT (*poet*) canopy of heaven (*poet*), firmament (*liter*)

him|mel-: him|mel|wärts ['hɪmlvɛrts] ADV (*liter*) heavenward(s); **him|mel|weit** (*fig inf*) **ADJ** tremendous, fantastic (*inf*); **zwischen uns besteht ein ~er Unterschied** there's a world of difference between us **ADV** ~ **voneinander entfernt** (*fig*) ~ **verschieden** (*fig*) poles apart; **sich ~ unterscheiden** to be worlds apart from each other, to be totally different from each other; **wir sind noch ~ davon entfernt** we're still nowhere near it

himm|lisch ['hɪmlɪʃ] **ADJ** **a** *attr* (= *göttlich*) heavenly, celestial (*liter*); **eine ~e Fügung** divine providence; **der ~e Vater** our Heavenly Father; **die Himmlischen** (*old poet*) the gods; **das ~e Jerusalem** the new Jerusalem **b** (*fig*) (= *wunderbar*) heavenly, divine; (= *unerschöpflich*) *Geduld* infinite **ADV** (= *wunderbar*) **schmecken** heavenly; ~ **passen** to fit perfectly; ~ **singen** to sing exquisitely *or* divinely; ~ **schön** just heavenly, perfectly beautiful; ~ **warm** wonderfully warm; ~ **bequem** beautifully *or* wonderfully comfortable

hin [hɪn] ADV **a** (*räumlich*) **bis zum Haus ~** up to the house, as far as the house; **geh doch ~ zu ihr!** go to her; (= *besuche sie auch*) go and see her; **nach Süden/Stuttgart ~** towards (*Brit*) *or* toward (*US*) the south/Stuttgart; **über die ganze Welt ~** all over the world, throughout the world; **die Wüste erstreckt sich über 2000 km ~** the desert stretches for 2000 km; **nach außen ~** (*fig*) outwardly; **das Boot glitt über die Wellen ~** the boat glided along over the waves; ~ **fahre ich mit dem Zug, zurück ...** on the way out I'll take the train, coming back ...; **die Fähre ist heute Abend nur noch (zur Insel) ~** the ferry's only making the outward trip *or* is only going out (to the island) this evening; **zur anderen Seite ~ sind es 2 km** it's 2 kms to the other side; **bis zu diesem Punkt ~** up to this point; **die Straße verläuft nach rechts ~** the road goes off to the right; **dreht euch/seht mal alle zur Tafel ~** face the/look at the blackboard **b** (*als Teil eines Wortpaares*) ~ **und her** (*räumlich*) to and fro, back and forth; (= *hin und zurück*) there and back; ~ **und her fahren** to travel to and fro, to travel back and forth; **jdn/etw ~ und her fahren** to drive sb/sth to and fro, to drive sb/sth back and forth; **etw ~ und her überlegen** to weigh sth up; **etw ~ und her diskutieren** to discuss sth over and over, to discuss sth a lot; **das Hin und Her** the comings and goings *pl*, the to-ings and fro-ings *pl*; **nach langem Hin und Her** eventually; **das reicht nicht ~ und her** (*inf*) that won't go very far at all, that's nothing like enough (*inf*); **Regen/Skandal ~,** Regen/Skandal her rain/scandal or

no rain/scandal, whether it rains/whether it's a scandal or not; **Mörder/Sohn ~, Mörder/Sohn her** murderer/son or not, I don't care whether he is a murderer/his *etc* son; ~ **und zurück** there and back; **eine Fahrkarte ~ und zurück** a return (ticket), a round trip ticket (*esp US*); **einmal London ~ und zurück** a return *or* round trip ticket (*esp US*) to London; ~ **und zurück? – nein, nur ~ bitte** return *or* round trip ticket (*esp US*) ? – no, just a single (*Brit*) or one way please; **der Flug von X nach Y ~ und zurück kostet ...** the return flight *or* round trip ticket (*esp US*) from X to Y costs ...; ~ **und wieder** (every) now and then, (every) now and again **c** (*zeitlich*) **es sind nur noch drei Tage ~** it's only three days (from) now; **bis zu den Wahlen sind es noch drei Wochen ~** it's (still) three weeks till *or* until the elections; **noch weit ~** a long way off *or* away; **lange Zeit ~** for a long time, over a long period; **zum Sommer ~** toward(s) summer, as summer draws nearer *or* approaches; **gegen Mittag ~** toward(s) midday; **über die Jahre ~** over the years, as (the) years go by; **die Kälte zog sich bis in den Juni ~** the cold lasted up until (and during) June **d** (*fig*) **auf meine Bitte/meinen Vorschlag ~** at my request/suggestion; **auf meinen Brief/Anruf ~** on account of my letter/phone call; **auf die Gefahr ~, ... zu werden** at the risk of being ...; **auf sein Versprechen ~** on the basis of his promise; **auf seinen Rat ~** on his advice; **etw auf etw** (*acc*) ~ **untersuchen/prüfen** to inspect/check sth for sth; **etw auf etw** (*acc*) ~ **planen/anlegen** to plan/design sth with sth in mind; **vor sich ~ sprechen** *etc* to talk *etc* to oneself; **vor sich ~ stieren** to stare straight ahead, to stare into space; **vor sich ~ dösen** to doze **e** (*inf*: *als trennbarer Bestandteil von Adverbien*) **da will ich nicht ~** I don't want to go (there); **wo geht ihr ~?** where are you going? **f** (*elliptisch*) **nichts wie ~** (*inf*) let's go (then)!, what are we waiting for? (*inf*); **wo ist es/sie ~?** where has it/she gone? → **hin sein, nach, zu** *etc*

hi|nab [hɪ'nap] ADV, PREF = **hinunter**

hi|nan [hɪ'nan] ADV (*liter*) upwards

hi|nan- PREF (*liter*) = **hinauf-**

hin+ar|bei|ten VI *sep* **auf etw** (*acc*) ~ (*auf ein Ziel*) to work toward(s) sth, to aim at sth; *auf eine Prüfung* to work for sth

hi|nauf [hɪ'nauf] ADV up; **den Berg/die Straße ~** up the mountain/street; **den Fluss ~** up the river; **die Treppe ~** up the stairs, upstairs; **dort ~** up there; **bis ~ zu** up to

hi|nauf- PREF → *auch* **herauf-, rauf-** up; **hi|nauf+ar|bei|ten** VR *sep* (*lit, fig*) to work one's way up; **hi|nauf+be|ge|ben** *ptp* **hinaufbegeben** VR *sep irreg* (*geh*) to go up(stairs); **hi|nauf+be|glei|ten** *ptp* **hinaufbegleitet** VT *sep* to take up(stairs); **hi|nauf+be|mü|hen** *ptp* **hinaufbemüht** *sep* (*geh*) **VT** to trouble to go/come up(stairs) **VR** to take the trouble *or* to trouble to go/come up(stairs); **hi|nauf+bit|ten** VT *sep irreg* to ask to come up(stairs); **hi|nauf+bli|cken** VI *sep* to look up; **hi|nauf+brin|gen** VT *sep irreg* to take up; **hi|nauf+fah|ren** *sep irreg* **VI** *aux sein* to go up; (*in Auto auch*) to drive up **VT** *jdn* to take up; (*in Auto auch*) to drive up; *Aufzug* to take up; **hi|nauf+fal|len** VI *sep irreg aux sein* **die Treppe ~** (*hum*) to fall up the stairs; **hi|nauf+füh|ren** VTI *sep* to lead up; **hi|nauf+ge|hen** VI *sep irreg aux sein* to go up; (*Preise, Fieber auch*) to rise; **die Treppe ~** to go *or* walk up the stairs; **einen Berg ~** to climb *or* go up a mountain; **mit dem Preis ~** to put up the price; **hi|nauf+ge|lan|gen** *ptp* **hinaufgelangt** VI *sep aux sein* (*geh*) to (manage to) get up; **hi|nauf+klet|tern** VI *sep aux sein* to climb up; **auf einen Baum ~** to climb up a tree; **hi|nauf+kom|men** VI *sep irreg aux sein* to come up; (= *schaffen*) to (manage to) get up; **hi|nauf+lau|fen** VI *sep irreg aux sein* to run up; **die Treppe ~** to run up the stairs; (*im Haus auch*) to run upstairs; **hi|nauf+rei|chen** *sep* **VI** to reach up **VT** to hand *or* pass up; **hi|-**

nauf+schau|en VI *sep* (*dial*) to look up; **hi|nauf+schi|cken** VT *sep* to send up; **hi|nauf+schie|ben** VT *sep irreg* to push up; **hi|nauf+schrau|ben** VT *sep* to screw up; (*fig*) *Preise* to put *or* push (*esp US*); *Produktion, Forderungen* to step up; **hi|nauf+se|hen** VI *sep irreg* to look up; **hi|nauf+set|zen** VT *sep* (*fig*) *Preis etc* to raise, to increase, to put *or* push (*esp US*) up; **hi|nauf+stei|gen** VI *sep irreg aux sein* to climb up; **hi|nauf+tra|gen** VT *sep irreg* to carry *or* take up; **hi|nauf+trei|ben** VT *sep irreg* **a** *Vieh etc* to drive up; **das Vieh den Berg ~** to drive the cattle up the mountain **b** (*fig*) *Kurs, Preis* to push up, to force up; **hi|nauf+zie|hen** *sep irreg* **VT** to pull up **VI** *aux sein* to move up **VR** to pull oneself up; **sich an einem Seil ~** to pull oneself up with a rope

hi|naus [hɪ'naus] ADV **a** (*räumlich*) out; ~ **(mit dir)!** (get) out!, out you go!; **über** (+*acc*) ~ beyond, over; **aus dem** *or* **zum Fenster ~** out of the window; **hier/dort ~** this/that way out; **nach hinten/vorn ~** at the back *or* rear/front; **nach hinten/vorn ~ wohnen** to live towards (*Brit*) *or* toward (*US*) *or* facing the back/the front; **zur Straße ~** facing the street; **durch die Tür ~** out of *or* out through the door **b** (*zeitlich*) **auf Jahre/Monate ~** for years/months to come; **bis weit über die siebzig ~** until well over *or* after *or* past seventy; **wir werden damit über Mittwoch ~ beschäftigt sein** we'll be busy with that until after Wednesday **c** (*fig*) **über** (+*acc*) ~ over and above; (*über Gehalt, Summe auch*) on top of; **über das Grab ~** beyond the grave; **darüber ~** over and above this, on top of this, in addition to this → **hinaus sein, hinauswollen** *etc*

hi|naus- PREF → *auch* **heraus-, raus-**: **hi|naus+be|för|dern** *ptp* **hinausbefördert** VT *sep jdn* to kick out (*inf*), to chuck out (*inf*) (*aus of*); **hi|naus+be|ge|ben** *ptp* **hinausbegeben** VR *sep irreg* (*geh*) to go out (*aus of*); **hi|naus+be|glei|ten** *ptp* **hinausbegleitet** VT *sep* to see out (*aus of*); **hi|naus+beu|gen** VR *sep* to lean out (*aus of*); **sich zum Fenster ~** to lean out of the window; **hi|naus+bli|cken** VI *sep* to look out (*aus of*); **zum Fenster ~** to look out of the window; **hi|naus+brin|gen** VT *sep irreg* to take out (*aus of*); **hi|naus+bug|sie|ren** *ptp* **hinausbugsiert** VT *sep* (*inf*) to ease *or* hustle out (*aus of*); **hi|naus+drän|gen** *sep* **VT** to force out (*aus of*); (*eilig*) to hustle out (*aus of*); (*fig*) to oust (*aus from*), to force out (*aus of*) **VI** *aux sein* to push *or* force one's way out (*aus of*); **hi|naus+dür|fen** VI *sep irreg* to be allowed (to go) out (*aus of*); **darf ich hinaus?** may I go out?; **über einen Punkt nicht ~** not to be allowed (to go) beyond a point; **hi|naus+ei|len** VI *sep aux sein* (*geh*) to hurry out (*aus of*); **hi|naus+ekeln** VT *sep* (*inf*) to drive out (*aus of*); **hi|naus+fah|ren** *sep irreg* **VI** *aux sein* **a** *aus etw* ~ to go out of sth, to leave sth; (*in Fahrzeug auch*) to drive out of sth **b** (= *reisen*) to go out; **aufs Meer ~** to sail out across the sea **c** *über etw* (*acc*) ~ to go beyond sth **VT** *Wagen* to drive out (*aus of*); **hi|naus+fal|len** VI *sep irreg aux sein* (*aus of*) to fall out; (*Licht*) to come out; **hi|naus+fin|den** *sep irreg* to find one's *or* the way out (*aus of*); **ich finde schon allein hinaus** I can find my own way out, I can see myself out; **hi|naus+flie|gen** *sep irreg* **VI** *aux sein* (*aus of*) **a** (= *fortfliegen*) to fly out; (*über +acc ~*: = *hinausfallen*) to go flying out (*inf*); **über ein Ziel ~** to fly past *or* go flying past a target **b** (*inf*: = *hinausgeworfen werden*) to get kicked *or* chucked out (*inf*) **VT** to fly out (*aus of*); **hi|naus+füh|ren** *sep* **a** (= *nach draußen führen*) to lead out (*aus of*) **b** (= *weiter führen als*) **über etw** (*acc*) ~ (*lit, fig*) to go beyond sth **VT** to lead out (*aus of*); (*Weg, Reise*) to take (*über +acc beyond*); **hi|naus+ge|hen** *sep irreg aux sein* **VI a** (= *nach draußen gehen*) to go out(side); **aus dem Zimmer/auf die Straße ~** to go *or* walk out of the room/onto the street **b** (= *gesandt werden*) to go (out), to be sent out **c** **auf etw** (*acc*) ~ (*Tür, Zimmer*) to open onto sth; (*Fenster*) to look (out) onto sth, to open onto sth; **das Fenster geht nach Osten hinaus** the window looks *or* faces east; **das Fenster geht zum Hof hinaus** the window looks out onto the courtyard; **zu** *or* **nach etw ~** (*Straße, Weg*) to go out to **d** (*fig: = überschreiten*) **über etw** (*acc*) **~** to go beyond sth; **das geht über meine Kräfte hinaus** it's too much for me to bear, I (just) can't take any more; **über seine Befugnisse ~** to overstep one's authority, to exceed one's powers **VI** *impers* **wo geht es hinaus?** where's the way out?; **hi|naus+ge|lan|gen** *ptp* **hinausgelangt** VI *sep aux sein* (*geh*) (*lit*) to get out; **über etw** (*acc*) **~** (*fig*) to get beyond sth; **hi|naus+ge|lei|ten** *ptp* **hinausgeleitet** VT *sep* (*geh*) to show out (*aus of*); **hi|naus+grau|len** VT *sep* (*inf*) to drive out (*aus of*); **hi|naus+grei|fen** VT *sep irreg* (*fig*) **über etw** (*acc*) **~** to reach beyond sth; **hi|naus+hal|ten** VT *sep irreg* to hold out; **den Kopf zum Fenster ~** to stick *or* put one's head out of the window; **hi|naus+hän|gen** VTI *sep irreg* to hang out; **eine Fahne zum Fenster ~** to hang a flag out of the window; **hi|naus+he|ben** VT *sep irreg* **etw über etw** (*acc*) **~** to raise *or* lift sth above sth, to put sth on a higher *or* different level from sth; **hi|naus+ja|gen** *sep* (*aus of*) **VT** (*lit: aus dem Zimmer, nach draußen*) to drive *or* chase out; (*fig: aus dem Haus*) to turn *or* drive out **VI** *aux sein* to bolt *or* dive out; **hi|naus+ka|ta|pul|tie|ren** *ptp* **hinauskatapultiert** VT *sep* (*Pol sl*) to throw out, to chuck out (*inf*) (*aus of*); **hi|naus+klet|tern** VI *sep aux sein* to climb out (*aus of*); **hi|naus+kom|men** VI *sep irreg aux sein* **a** (*= nach außen kommen*) to come out(side); **ich bin den ganzen Tag noch nicht hinausgekommen** I haven't been out(side) yet today; **zu jdm aufs Land ~** to come out to see sb in the country **b** **über etw** (*acc*) **~** to go beyond sth; (*fig*) to get beyond sth **c** (*fig: = hinauslaufen*) **das kommt auf dasselbe** *or* **auf eins** *or* **aufs Gleiche hinaus** it boils *or* comes down to the same thing, it amounts *or* comes to the same thing; **hi|naus+kom|pli|men|tie|ren** [hɪ'naʊskɔmpli-mɛnti:rən] *ptp* **hinauskomplimentiert** VT *sep* (*hum*) to usher out (*aus of*); **hi|naus+kön|nen** VI *sep irreg* (*inf*) to be able to get out; **hi|naus+las|sen** VT *sep irreg* (*aus of*) to leave out; (*= hinausbegleiten*) to show out; **hi|naus+lau|fen** VI *sep irreg aux sein* (*aus of*) **a** (*lit*) to run out **b** (*fig*) **auf etw** (*acc*) **~** to amount to sth; **es läuft auf dasselbe** *or* **auf eins** *or* **aufs Gleiche hinaus** it boils *or* comes down to the same thing, it amounts *or* comes to the same thing; **wo(rauf) soll das ~?** how's it all going to end?, what are things coming to?; **hi|naus+leh|nen** VR *sep* to lean out (*aus of*); **sich zum Fenster ~** to lean out of the window; **hi|naus+ma|növ|rie|ren** *ptp* **hinausmanövriert** VT *sep* (*aus of*) **jdn aus etw ~** to manoeuvre (*Brit*) *or* maneuver (*US*) oneself/sb out of sth; **hi|naus+müs|sen** VI *sep irreg* to have to go out (*aus of*); **hi|naus+neh|men** VT *sep irreg* to take out (*aus of*); **hi|naus+po|sau|nen** *ptp* **hinausposaunt** VT *sep* (*inf*) to broadcast (*inf*); **hi|naus+ra|gen** VI *sep aux sein* **a** (*horizontal*) to project, to jut out (*über +acc beyond*); (*vertikal*) to tower up (*über +acc above, over*) **b** (*fig*) **über jdn/etw ~** to tower above sb/sth; **hi|naus+re|den** VR *sep* (*dial*) to talk one's way out of it (*inf*); **hi|naus+rei|chen** *sep* **VT** to hand *or* pass out (*aus of*); **jdm etw zum Fenster ~** to hand *or* pass sb sth out of the window **VI** **a** (*= bis nach draußen reichen*) to reach, to stretch (*bis as far as*) **b** **über etw** (*acc*) **~** (*lit*) to stretch beyond sth; (*fig*) to go beyond sth; **hi|naus+ren|nen** VI *sep irreg aux sein* to run out (*aus of*); **hi|naus+rü|cken** VI *sep aux sein* (*lit*) to move out (*aus of*); **die Soldaten rückten zur Stadt hinaus** the soldiers marched *or* moved out of (the) town; **hi|naus+schaf|fen** VT *sep* to take out (*aus of*); **hi|naus+schau|en** VI *sep* (*dial*) = **hi**nausblicken; **hi|naus+sche|ren** VR *sep* to get out (*aus of*); **hi|naus+schi|cken** VT *sep* to

send out (*aus of*); **hi|naus+schie|ben** VT *sep irreg* **a** *Gegenstand* to push out (*aus of*) **b** (*fig*) to put off, to postpone; **hi|naus+schie|ßen** VI *sep irreg* **a** **er hat zum Fenster hinausgeschossen** he fired out of the window **b** *aux sein* (*= hinausrennen*) to shoot *or* dart out (*aus of*); **hi|naus+schmei|ßen** VT *sep irreg* (*inf*) to kick *or* chuck out (*inf*) (*aus of*); **Hi|naus-schmiss** ▲ M (*inf*) **man drohte ihm mit ~ (aus dem Restaurant)** they threatened to kick *or* chuck him out (of the restaurant) (*inf*); **das war ein regelrechter ~** he was simply kicked *or* chucked out (*inf*); **hi|naus+schmug|geln** VT *sep* to smuggle out (*aus of*); **hi|naus+schrei|en** *sep irreg* **VI** to shout out (*aus of*); **zum Fenster ~** to shout out of the window **VT** (*geh*) *Schmerz, Hass* to proclaim (*geh*); **hi|naus+schwim|men** VI *sep irreg aux sein* (*aus of*) (*über +acc beyond, past*) to swim out; (*Gegenstände*) to float out; **hi|naus+se|hen** VI *sep irreg* = **hi**nausblicken; **hi|naus sein** ▲ VI *irreg aux sein* **a** (*lit inf: = hinausgegangen sein*) to be out, to have gone out **b** (*fig: = hinter sich haben*) **über etw** (*acc*) **~** (*über Kindereien, Dummheiten*) to be past *or* beyond sth; *über ein Alter* to be past sth; **hi|naus+set|zen** *sep* **VT** to put out(side); **jdn ~** (*inf*) to chuck *or* kick sb out (*inf*) (*um* (*inf*) to go and) sit outside; **hi|naus+sprin|gen** VI *sep irreg aux sein* to jump out (*aus, zu of*); **hi|naus+steh|len** VR *sep irreg* (*geh*) to steal out (*geh*); **hi|naus+stei|gen** VI *sep irreg aux sein* to climb out (*aus of*); **zum Fenster ~** to climb out of the window; **hi|naus+stel|len** VT *sep* to put *or* take out(side); *Sportler* to send off; **hi|naus+stre|cken** VT *sep* to stick *or* put out (*aus of*); **hi|naus+strö|men** VI *sep aux sein* to pour out (*aus of*); (*geh: Menschenmassen auch*) to come milling out (*aus of*); **hi|naus+stür|men** VI *sep aux sein* to storm out (*aus of*); **hi|naus+stür|zen** *sep* (*aus of*) **VI** *aux sein* **a** (*= hinausfallen*) to fall out **b** (*= hinauseilen*) to rush *or* dash out **VR** to throw oneself out, to dive out **VT** to throw out; **hi|naus+tra|gen** VT *sep irreg* **a** (*= nach außen tragen*) to carry out (*aus of*) **b** (*geh*) **etw in alle Welt ~** to spread sth abroad **c** (*= weiter tragen als*) **etw über etw** (*acc*) **~** to carry sth over *or* beyond sth; **hi|naus+trei|ben** VT *sep irreg* to drive out (*aus of*); **hi|naus+tre|ten** VI *sep irreg aux sein* to step out(side); **ins Leben ~** (*geh*) to go out into the world; **hi|naus+trom|pe|ten** *ptp* **hinaustrompetet** VT *sep* (*inf*) to broadcast (*inf*); **hi|naus+wach|sen** VI *sep irreg aux sein* **über etw** (*acc*) **~** (*lit*) to grow taller than sth; (*fig: durch zunehmende Reife, Fortschritte etc*) to outgrow sth; **er wuchs über sich selbst hinaus** he surpassed himself; **hi|naus+wa|gen** VR *sep* to venture out (*aus of*); **hi|naus+wei|sen** *sep irreg* **VT** **jdn ~** to show sb the door, to ask sb to leave **VI** to point out(wards); **über eine Frage/Sache ~** (*fig*) to reach *or* point beyond a question/matter; **hi|naus+wer|fen** VT *sep irreg* (*aus of*) **a** (*= nach außen werfen, wegwerfen*) to throw *or* cast (*liter*) out; **einen Blick ~** to glance *or* look out(side), to take a glance *or* look out(side); **das ist hinausgeworfenes Geld** it's money down the drain; **Geld zum Fenster ~** to throw money out of the window *or* down the drain **b** (*inf*) (*= entfernen*) to chuck *or* kick out (*inf*); **hi|naus+wol|len** VI *sep* to want to go *or* get out (*aus of*); **worauf willst du hinaus?** (*fig*) what are you getting *or* driving at?; **hoch ~** to aim high, to set one's sights high

Hi|naus|wurf M (*inf*) **einen ~ riskieren** to risk getting thrown *or* kicked out; **jdm mit dem ~ drohen** to threaten to throw *or* kick sb out

hi|naus- PREF → *auch* **heraus-, raus-**: **hi|naus+zie|hen** *sep irreg* **VT** **a** (*= nach draußen ziehen*) to pull out (*aus of*) **b** (*fig*) *Verhandlungen etc* to protract, to drag out; *Urlaub etc* to prolong **VI** *aux sein* to go out (*aus of*); **in die Welt ~** to go out into the world; **aufs Land/vor die Stadt ~** to move out into the country/out of town; **den Dampf/Rauch ~ lassen** to let the

steam/smoke out **VR** (*Verhandlungen etc*) to drag on; (*Abfahrt etc*) to be delayed, to be put off **VT** *impers* **es zog ihn hinaus in die weite Welt** he felt the urge to go out into the big wide world; **mich zieht's wieder hinaus in die Ferne** I feel the urge to travel again; **bei diesem schönen Wetter zieht's mich hinaus** I want to be out-of-doors with the weather like this; **hi|naus+zö|gern** *sep* **VT** to delay, to put off **VR** to be delayed, to be put off

hin-: **hin+be|ge|ben** *ptp* **hinbegeben** VR *sep irreg* (*geh*) **sich zu jdm ~** (*form*) to go to sb, to betake oneself to sb (*old, form*); **hin+be|kom|men** *ptp* **hinbekommen** VT *sep irreg* (*inf*) = **hin**kriegen; **hin+be|mü|hen** *ptp* **hinbemüht** *sep* (*geh*) **jdn ~** to trouble sb to go, to give sb the trouble of going **VR** to take the trouble to go; **hin+be|or|dern** *ptp* **hinbeordert** VT *sep* to summon, to send for; **hin+be|stel|len** *ptp* **hinbestellt** VT *sep* to tell sb to go/come; **hin+bie|gen** VT *sep irreg* (*fig inf*) (*= in Ordnung bringen*) to arrange, to sort out; (*= deichseln*) to wangle (*inf*); (*= interpretieren*) *Text, Wortlaut* to twist; **die Sache** *or* **das werden wir schon ~** we'll sort it out somehow; **hin+blät|tern** VT *sep* (*inf*) to fork *or* shell out (*inf*), to cough up (*inf*); **Hin|blick** M *im* *or* *in* (*+acc*) (*= angesichts*) in view of; (*= mit Bezug auf*) with regard to; **im ~ darauf, dass ...** in view of the fact that ...; **hin+bli|cken** VI *sep* to look *or* glance (*auf +acc, nach* at, towards); **hin+brin|gen** VT *sep irreg* **a** *etw* to take there; (*= begleiten*) *jdn* to take there; (*in Auto*) to drive *or* take there **b** (*fig*) *Zeit* to spend, to pass; (*in Muße*) to idle *or* while away; **sein Leben kümmerlich ~** to eke out an existence **c** = **hin**kriegen; **hin+deich|seln** VT *sep* (*inf*) *etw* to arrange, to sort out; **hin+den|ken** VI *sep irreg* **wo denkst du hin?** whatever are you thinking of!

hin|der|lich ['hɪndɛlɪç] **ADJ** **~ sein** to be in the way, to be a nuisance; (*Kleidungsstück auch*) to be restricting; **ein ~er Gipsverband** a restricting (plaster) cast, a (plaster) cast that gets in the way *or* that is a nuisance; **einer Sache** (*dat*) **~ sein** to be a hindrance *or* obstacle to sth; **eher ~ als nützlich sein** to be more of a hindrance than a help; **jdm ~ sein** to get in sb's way **ADV** **sich ~ auswirken** to prove to be a hindrance

hin|dern ['hɪndɐn] **VT** **a** *Fortschritte, Wachstum* to impede, to hamper; *jdn* to hinder (*bei in*) **b** (*= abhalten von*) to prevent (*an +dat* from), to stop; **ja bitte, ich will Sie nicht ~** please do, I won't stand in your way; **machen Sie, was Sie wollen, ich kann Sie nicht ~** do what you like, I can't stop *or* prevent you; **was hindert dich (daran), hinzugehen?** what prevents *or* keeps you from going (there)?, what stops you going (there)? **VI** (*= stören*) to be a hindrance (*bei to*)

Hin|der|nis ['hɪndɐnɪs] **NT -ses, -se a** (*lit, fig*) obstacle; (*= Erschwernis, Behinderung*) hindrance; (*beim Sprechen*) handicap, impediment; **sie empfand das Kind als ~/als ~ für ihre Karriere** she saw the child as a hindrance/as a hindrance to *or* an obstacle for her career; **gesetzliches ~** (*form*) legal impediment *or* obstacle; **jdm ~se in den Weg legen** (*fig*) to put obstacles in sb's path *or* way; **eine Reise mit ~sen** a journey full of hitches **b** (*Sport: = Hürde*) hurdle; (*beim Pferderennen*) fence, jump; (*Golf*) hazard

Hin|der|nis-: **Hin|der|nis|lauf** M steeplechase (*in athletics*); **Hin|der|nis|läu|fer(in)** M(F) steeplechaser (*in athletics*); **Hin|der|nis|ren|nen** NT steeplechase

Hin|de|rung F **-, -en a** (*= Behinderung*) hindrance; **ohne ~** without let *or* hindrance (*Jur*) **b** (*= Störung*) obstruction

Hin|de|rungs|grund M obstacle; **etw als ~ angeben** to give sth as an excuse

hin+deu|ten VI *sep* to point (*auf +acc, zu* at); **es deutet alles darauf hin, dass ...** everything indicates that ..., everything points to the fact that ...

| + separable verbs | German spelling reform (see supplement): ▲ new spelling △ old spelling |

Hin|di ['hɪndi] NT - Hindi

Hin|din ['hɪndɪn] F **-, -nen** (old, liter) hind

hin-: hin+drän|gen sep **VT** jdn zum Ausgang ~ to push sb toward(s) the exit **VR** sich zu etw ~ to push one's way toward(s) sth **VI** zum Ausgang ~ to push one's way toward(s) the exit; auf eine Änderung ~ to agitate for a change; alles in ihrem Innern drängte zum Künstlerberuf hin everything within her urged her toward(s) an artistic profession; **hin+dre|hen** VT sep (fig inf) to arrange

Hin|du ['hɪndu] M **-(s), -(s)** Hindu

Hin|du|is|mus [hɪndu'ɪsmʊs] M **-**, no pl Hinduism

hin|du|is|tisch [hɪndu'ɪstɪʃ] **ADJ** Hindu **ADV** ~ denken to have Hindu beliefs; ~ beeinflusst influenced by Hinduism; ~ erzogen werden to be brought up (as) a Hindu

hin|durch [hɪn'dʊrç] ADV **a** (räumlich) through; dort ~ through there; **mitten** ~ straight through; **quer** ~ straight across; **durch den Wald** ~ through the wood **b** (zeitlich) through(out); **das ganze Jahr** ~ throughout the year, all (the) year round; **die ganze Nacht** ~ all (through) the night, throughout the night, all night long; **die ganze Zeit** ~ all the time; **Jahre** ~ for years (and years); **den ganzen Tag** ~ all day (long); **durch etw** ~ through sth

hin|durch+ge|hen VI sep irreg aux sein (lit, fig) to go through (durch etw sth)

hin+dür|fen VI sep irreg to be allowed to go (zu to); **da darfst du nicht mehr hin** you are not to go or you mustn't go there any more

Hin|dus|tan ['hɪndʊstaːn, -tan] NT **-s** Hindustan

Hin|dus|ta|ni [hɪndʊs'taːni] NT **-(s)**, no pl Hindustani

hin+ei|len VI sep aux sein (geh) to rush or hurry (zu to); **ich eilte sofort hin** I rushed there at once

hi|nein [hɪ'naɪn] ADV **a** (räumlich) in; **da** ~ in there; **nur** ~! (inf) go right in!; ~ **mit dir!** (inf) in you go!; **in etw** (acc) ~ into sth; **bis in etw** (acc) ~ right inside sth; **mitten** ~ **in etw** (acc) right into the middle of sth; **leg es oben/unten** ~ put it in the top/bottom → **Blaue²** **b** (zeitlich) into; **bis tief in die Nacht** ~ well or far into the night

hi|nein- PREF → auch **ein-, herein-, rein-** in; **hi|nein+be|ge|ben** ptp **hineinbegeben** VR sep irreg (geh) to enter (in etw (acc) sth); **hi|nein+bei|ßen** VI sep irreg = rein in (in etw (acc) to), to take a bite of; **hi|nein+be|kom|men** ptp **hineinbekommen** VT sep irreg (inf) to get in (in +acc -to); **hi|nein+be|mü|hen** ptp **hineinbemüht** sep (geh) **VT** to trouble to get in (in +acc -to); **hi|nein+bli|cken** VI sep = hineinsehen; **hi|nein+boh|ren** sep (in +acc -to) to dig in **VR** to bore one's way in; **hi|nein+brin|gen** VT sep irreg **a** (= hineintragen) to take in (in +acc -to) **b** (inf: = hineinbekommen) to get in (in +acc -to); **hi|nein+bug|sie|ren** ptp **hineinbugsiert** VT sep (inf) to manoeuvre (Brit) or maneuver (US) in (in +acc -to); **hi|nein+den|ken** VR sep irreg sich in ein Problem ~ to think oneself into a problem, sich in jdn ~ to put oneself in sb's position; **hi|nein+deu|ten** VT sep etw in einen Satz ~ to read sth into a sentence; **etw in die Natur** ~ to attribute nature with sth; **hi|nein+drän|gen** sep (in +acc -to) **VT** to push in **VR** (vi: aux sein) to push one's way in; **hi|nein+dür|fen** VI sep irreg (inf) to be allowed in (in +acc -to); **Kinder dürfen in den Film nicht hinein** children are not allowed to see the film or movie (US); **hi|nein+fal|len** VI sep irreg aux sein to fall in (in +acc -to); **hi|nein+fin|den** VR sep irreg (fig: = sich vertraut machen) to find one's feet; (= sich abfinden) to come to terms with it; **sich ~ in etw** (acc) to get familiar with sth; (= to come to terms with sth); **hi|nein+fres|sen** VT sep irreg (inf) **etw in sich** (acc) ~ (lit) to wolf sth (down) (inf), to gobble

sth down or up; (fig) Kummer etc to suppress sth; **hi|nein+ge|heim|nis|sen** [hɪ'naɪngəhaɪmnɪsn] ptp **hineingeheimnisst** VT sep (inf) **etw in etw** (acc) ~ to read sth into sth; **hi|nein+ge|hen** VI sep irreg aux sein **a** (= betreten) to go in; **in etw** (acc) ~ to go into sth, to enter sth **b** (= hineinpassen) to go in (in +acc -to); **in den Bus gehen 50 Leute hinein** the bus holds 50 people, there is room for 50 people in the bus; **hi|nein+ge|lan|gen** ptp **hineingelangt** VI sep aux sein (geh) to get in (in +acc -to); **hi|nein+ge|ra|ten** ptp **hineingeraten** VI sep irreg aux sein in etw (acc) ~ to get involved in sth, to get into sth; **in ein Unwetter** ~ to be caught in a thunderstorm; **in eine Schlägerei** ~ to get into a brawl, to get involved in a brawl; ~ **nein+gie|ßen** VT sep irreg to pour in (in +acc -to); **etw in sich** ~ (inf) to pour sth down one's throat (inf), to down sth; **hi|nein+grei|fen** VI sep irreg to reach inside; **in etw** (acc) ~ to reach into sth; **hi|nein+gu|cken** VI sep (inf, in Zimmer, Kiste) to look or take a look in (in +acc -to); (in Buch) to take a look in (in etw (acc) sth); **hi|nein+hal|ten** sep irreg **VT** to put in (in etw (acc) sth) **VI** (inf: mit Gewehr etc) to aim (in +acc at); **mitten in die Menge** ~ to aim into the crowd; **hi|nein+hei|ra|ten** VI sep = einheiraten; **hi|nein+in|ter|pre|tie|ren** ptp **hineininterpretiert** VT sep = hineindeuten; **hi|nein+klet|tern** VI sep aux sein to climb in (in +acc -to); **hi|nein+knien** VR sep sich in etw (acc) ~ to get into sth (inf); **hi|nein+kom|men** VI sep irreg aux sein (in +acc -to) **a** (= betreten) to come in **b** (lit, fig: = hineingelangen können) to get in; **nach 21 Uhr kommt man nicht mehr hinein** you can't get in after 9 o'clock **c** = hineingeraten; **hi|nein+kom|pli|men|tie|ren** [hɪ'naɪnkɔmplimɛn'tiːrən] ptp **hineinkomplimentiert** VT sep to usher in (in +acc -to); **hi|nein+krie|chen** VI sep irreg aux sein to creep or slip in (in +acc -to) → auch **reinkriechen**; **hi|nein+krie|gen** VT sep (inf) to get in (in +acc -to); **hi|nein+la|chen** VI sep in sich ~ to laugh to oneself; **hi|nein+las|sen** VT sep irreg to let in (in +acc -to); **hi|nein+lau|fen** VI sep irreg aux sein to run in (in +acc -to); **in sein eigenes Unglück** ~ to be heading for misfortune; **etw in sich** ~ **lassen** (inf) to knock sth back (inf); **hi|nein+le|gen** VT sep **a** (lit, fig) Gefühl etc to put in (in +acc -to); **b** (= hineindeuten) **etw in jds Worte** ~ to put sth in sb's mouth; **hi|nein+le|sen** VT sep irreg **etw in etw** (acc) ~ to read sth into sth; **hi|nein+leuch|ten** VI sep to shine in (in +acc -to); **mit einer Lampe in eine Höhle** ~ to shine a light into a cave; **hi|nein+ma|növ|rie|ren** ptp **hineinmanövriert** VT sep to manoeuvre (Brit) or maneuver (US) in (in +acc -to); **hi|nein+pas|sen** sep **VI in etw** (acc) ~ to fit into sth; (fig) to fit in with sth **VT** to fit in (in +acc -to); **hi|nein+pfu|schen** VI sep (inf) jdm in seine Arbeit/Angelegenheiten ~ to meddle or interfere in sb's work/affairs; **hi|nein+plat|zen** VI sep aux sein (fig inf) to burst in (in +acc -to); **hi|nein+pres|sen** VT sep **a** Gegenstand to press in (in +acc -to) **b** (fig) **etw in ein Schema** ~ to force sth into a mould (Brit) or mold (US); **er lässt sich in kein Schema** ~ he won't be pigeonholed (inf); **hi|nein+pro|ji|zie|ren** ptp **hineinprojiziert** VT sep to project (in +acc into); **sich in jdn** ~ to project one's ideas/feelings etc into or onto sb; **hi|nein+pum|pen** VT sep to pump in (in +acc -to); Geld auch to pour in; **hi|nein+quet|schen** VT sep Gegenstand to squeeze or press in (in etw (+acc) ~ to squeeze into sth; **sie konnte sich gerade noch ~** (in Bus etc) she just about managed to squeeze in; **hi|nein+ra|gen** VI sep aux sein (lit, fig) to project (in +acc into); **hi|nein+re|den** VI sep **a** (lit: = unterbrechen) to interrupt (in jdm sb); jdm ~ (fig: = sich einmischen) to meddle or interfere in sb's affairs; jdm in seine Angelegenheiten/Entscheidungen/in alles ~ to meddle or interfere in all sb's affairs **b** ins Leere ~ to talk into a vacuum, to talk to

oneself; **sich in (seine) Wut** ~ to work oneself up into a rage; **hi|nein+reg|nen** VI impers sep es regnet (ins Zimmer) hinein (the) rain is coming in(to) the room; **hi|nein+rei|chen** sep **VT** to hand or pass in; (jdm) etw zum or durchs Fenster ~ to hand or pass sth in (to sb) through the window **VI** (= lang genug sein) to reach in (in +acc -to); (= sich erstrecken) to extend (in +acc as far as); **in etw** (acc) ~ (zeitlich) to go over into sth; **Bräuche, die bis ins 21. Jahrhundert** ~ customs that persist into the 21st century; **hi|nein+rei|ßen** VT sep irreg (fig inf) to drag in (in +acc -to); **hi|nein+rei|ten** sep irreg **VI** aux sein to ride in (in +acc -to) **VT** (inf) = reinreiten; **hi|nein+ren|nen** VI sep irreg aux sein to run in (in +acc -to); **in sein Unglück/Verderben** ~ to be heading for misfortune/disaster; **hi|nein+ru|fen** VT sep irreg to call or shout in (in +acc -to); **hi|nein+rut|schen** VI sep aux sein **a** (lit) to slide (in +acc -to) **b** (fig) → hineinschliddern; **hi|nein+schaf|fen** VT sep to bring/take in (in +acc -to); **hi|nein+schau|en** VI sep (dial) = hineinsehen; **hi|nein+schau|feln** VT sep to shovel in (in +acc -to); **Essen in sich** ~ (inf) to shovel food into oneself or down one's gullet (inf); **hi|nein+schie|ßen** VI sep irreg **a** (aux sein: Wasser etc) to rush or gush in (in +acc -to); (**hineingeschossen kommen** (Wasser) to come gushing or rushing in; (inf: Mensch) to shoot in (inf), to come shooting in (inf) **b** in eine Menschenmenge ~ to shoot into a crowd; **hi|nein+schla|gen** VT sep irreg (in +acc -to) Nagel to knock in; Eier to break in; Krallen to sink in; **ein Loch ins Eis** ~ to knock a hole in the ice; **hi|nein+schlei|chen** VIR sep irreg (vi: aux sein) to creep or sneak in (in +acc -to); **hi|nein+schlid|dern** VI sep aux sein (inf) in etw (acc) ~ to get involved in sth, to get mixed up with sth; **hi|nein+schlin|gen** VT sep irreg **etw (gierig) in sich** (acc) ~ to devour sth (greedily); **hi|nein+schlit|tern** VI sep aux sein (inf) = hineinschliddern; **hi|nein+schlüp|fen** VI sep aux sein to slip in (in +acc -to); **hi|nein+schmug|geln** VT sep to smuggle in (in +acc -to); **hi|nein+schnei|en** sep **VI** impers es schneit (ins Zimmer) hinein the snow is coming in(to the room) **VI** aux sein (inf) to drop in (inf); **hi|nein+schnup|pern** VI sep (fig inf) in etw (+acc) ~ (= ausprobieren) to give sth a try; (in Firma etc) to take a look at sth; (in eine Arbeit) to have a go at sth, to get a taste of sth; (in Buch) to dip into sth; **hi|nein+schrei|ben** VT sep irreg to write in (in etw (acc) sth); **hi|nein+schüt|ten** VT sep to pour in (in +acc -to); **etw in sich** ~ (inf) to knock sth back (inf); **hi|nein+se|hen** VI sep irreg to look in; **ins Zimmer/Fenster** ~ to look into the room/in at the window; **eben mal** ~ (inf) to look or pop in (inf); **sich** (dat) **in etw** (acc) **nicht ~ lassen** to keep sth to oneself; **hi|nein+set|zen** sep **VT** to put in (in +acc -to) **VR** (in Fahrzeug) to get into (in etw (acc) sth); (in Sessel) to sit (oneself) down (in +acc in(to)); (in Sessellift, Kettenkarussell etc) to sit oneself in (in +acc sth); **sich wieder ~/ins Zimmer** ~ to go back and sit inside/in the room; **hi|nein+spa|zie|ren** ptp **hineinspaziert** VI sep aux sein to walk in (in +acc -to); **nur hineinspaziert!** please go in; **hi|nein+spie|len** sep **VI** (= beeinflussen) to have a part to play (in +acc in); **in etw** (acc) ~ (= grenzen an) to verge on sth; **da spielen noch andere Gesichtspunkte hinein** other factors enter into it **VT** (Sport) **den Ball in den Strafraum** etc ~ to play the ball into the penalty area etc; **hi|nein+spre|chen** VI sep irreg **ins Mikrofon** ~ to speak or talk into the microphone; **hi|nein+sprin|gen** VI sep irreg aux sein (in +acc -to) **a** (= hineinhüpfen) to jump or leap or spring in **b** (inf: = hineinlaufen) to pop in (inf); **hi|nein+ste|cken** VT sep (in +acc -to) to put in; Nadel etc auch to stick in; **den Kopf zum Fenster** ~ to put or stick one's head in at or in through the window; **Geld/Arbeit** etc **in etw** (acc) ~ to put money/some work etc into sth; **viel Mühe in etw** (acc) ~ to put a lot of effort into sth; **hi|nein+stei|gern** VR sep to get into a state, to work oneself up into a state, to get worked up; **sich in seine Wut/Hysterie/seinen Ärger ~** to work oneself up into a rage/hysterics/a temper; **sich in seinen Kummer ~** to let oneself be completely taken up with one's worries; **sich in seinen Schmerz ~** to let the pain take one over completely; **sie hat sich in die Vorstellung hineingesteigert, dass ...** she has managed to convince herself that ..., she has talked herself into believing that ...; **sich in eine Rolle ~** to become completely caught up in a role; **hi|nein+stop|fen** VT sep to stuff or cram in (in +acc -to); **Essen in sich** (acc) **~** to stuff oneself (with food) (inf); **hi|nein+sto|ßen** sep irreg **VT** Schwert etc to thrust in (in +acc -to); **jdn in etw ~** (fig) to push sb into sth; (fig) to plunge sb into sth **VI** aux sein **in eine Lücke ~** to steer into a space; **in ein Gebiet ~** to enter a district; **hi|nein+strö|men** VI sep aux sein to stream or flood in (in +acc -to); (geh: Menschenmassen) to pour in (in +acc -to); **hi|nein+stür|men** VI sep aux sein to storm in (in +acc -to), to come storming in; **hi|nein+stür|zen** sep **VI** aux sein to plunge in (in +acc -to); (= hineineilen) to rush in (in +acc -to); **zur Tür ~** to rush in through the door **VT** to throw or hurl in (in +acc -to); **jdn ins Elend ~** to plunge sb into misery **VR** (in +acc -to) to throw or hurl oneself in, to plunge in; **sich in die Arbeit ~** to throw oneself into one's work; **sich ins Vergnügen ~** to plunge in and start enjoying oneself, to let it all hang out (inf); **hi|nein+tap|pen** VI sep aux sein (fig inf) to walk right into it (inf); **in eine Falle ~** to walk into a trap; **hi|nein+tra|gen** VT sep irreg (in +acc -to) to carry in; (fig) to bring in; **hi|nein+trei|ben** VT sep irreg to drive in (in +acc -to); **hi|nein+tun** VT sep irreg to put in (in +acc -to); **einen Blick in etw** (acc) **~** to take a look in sth; (ins Buch etc) to take a look at sth; **hi|nein+ver|set|zen** ptp hineinversetzt VR sich in jdn or in jds Lage to put oneself in sb's position; **sich in etw** (acc) **hineinversetzt fühlen** to imagine oneself in sth; **sich in eine Rolle ~** to empathize with a part; **hi|nein+wach|sen** VI sep irreg aux sein in etw (acc) **~** (lit, fig) to grow into sth; **hi|nein+wa|gen** VR sep to venture in (in +acc -to); **hi|nein+we|hen** VI sep in etw (acc) **~** (Wind, fig) to blow into sth; Brise to waft into sth; **hi|nein+zer|ren** VT sep (lit, fig) to drag in (in +acc -to); **hi|nein+zie|hen** sep irreg **VT** to pull or drag in (in +acc -to); **jdn in eine Angelegenheit/einen Streit ~** to drag sb into an affair/a quarrel **VI** aux sein (in +acc -to) to go in; (in ein Haus) to move in; **hi|nein+zwän|gen** sep (in +acc -to) **VT** to force or squeeze in **VR** to squeeze (oneself) in; **hi|nein+zwin|gen** VT sep irreg to force in (in +acc -to)

hin-: hin|fah|ren sep irreg **VI** aux sein to go there; (mit Fahrzeug auch) to drive there; (mit Schiff auch) to sail there; **mit der Hand über etw** (acc) **~** (fig) to run one's hand over sth; **fahre hin!** (old, poet) farewell! (old), fare-thee-well! (old, poet) **VT** to drive or take there; **Hin|fahrt** F journey there; (Naut) voyage out; (Rail) outward journey; **auf der ~** on the journey or way there etc; **hin+fal|len** VI sep irreg aux sein to fall (down)

hin|fäl|lig ADJ **a** Mensch frail **b** (fig: = ungültig) invalid; Argument untenable, invalid; **etw ~ machen** to render sth invalid, to invalidate sth

Hin|fäl|lig|keit F , no pl frailness; (von Argument) invalidity

hin-: hin+fin|den VIR sep irreg (inf) to find one's way there; **hin+flä|zen, hin|fle|geln** VR sep (inf) to loll about (Brit) or around; **hin+flie|gen** VI sep irreg aux sein to fly there; (inf: =

fallen) to come a cropper (Brit inf), to fall flat on one's face (inf); **der Ball flog über die Köpfe hin** the ball flew over their heads; **Hin|flug** M outward flight

hin|fort [hɪnˈfɔrt] ADV (old) henceforth (old)

hin|füh|ren sep **VT** to lead there; **jdn zu etw ~** (fig) to lead sb to sth **VI** to lead or go there; **zu/zwischen etw** (dat) **~** to lead to/between sth; **wo soll das ~?** (fig) where is this leading to?

hing pret von **hängen**

Hin|ga|be F , no pl (fig) (= Begeisterung) dedication; (= Selbstlosigkeit) devotion; (= völliges Aufgehen) (self-)abandon; **mit ~ tanzen/singen** etc to dance/sing etc with abandon; **unter ~ seines Lebens** (geh) by laying down one's life

hin|ga|be|fä|hig ADJ (= begeisterungsfähig) capable of dedication; (= selbstlos) capable of devotion

Hin|gang M , no pl (old, form) decease, demise (form)

hin+ge|ben sep irreg **VT** to give up; Ruf, Zeit, Geld auch to sacrifice; Leben to lay down, to sacrifice **VR a sich einer Sache** (dat) **~** (der Arbeit) to devote or dedicate oneself to sth; dem Laster, Genuss, der Verzweiflung to abandon oneself to sth; **sich Hoffnungen ~** to cherish hopes; **sich einer Illusion ~** to labour (Brit) or labor (US) under an illusion **b sie gab sich ihm hin** she gave herself or surrendered to him; **sich Gott ~** to give oneself to God

hin|ge|bend ADJ devoted

Hin|ge|bung [ˈhɪŋeːbʊŋ] F -, no pl = **Hingabe**

hin|ge|bungs|voll ADJ (= selbstlos) devoted; (= begeistert) abandoned ADV (= selbstlos) devotedly; (= begeistert) with abandon; **lauschen** raptly

hin|ge|gen [hɪnˈgeːgn̩] CONJ (geh) however; (= andererseits auch) on the other hand

hin-: hin|ge|gos|sen [ˈhɪŋɡəɡɔsn̩] ADJ (fig inf) **sie lag/saß wie ~ auf dem Bett** she had draped herself artistically on the bed; **hin+ge|hen** VI sep irreg aux sein **a** (= dorthin gehen) to go (there); **gehst du auch hin?** are you going too?; **wo gehst du hin?** where are you going?; **wo geht es hier hin?** where does this go? **b** (Zeit) to pass, to go by **c** (fig: = tragbar sein) **das geht gerade noch hin** that will just about do or pass; **diesmal mag es noch ~** I'll let it go or pass this once; **(jdm) etw ~ lassen** to let sth pass, to let sb get away with sth; **hin+ge|hö|ren** ptp hingehört VI sep to belong; **wo gehört das hin?** where does this belong or go?; **wo gehören die Gabeln hin?** where do the forks live (Brit inf) or belong?; **hin+ge|lan|gen** ptp hingelangt VI sep aux sein (geh) to get there; **hin+ge|ra|ten** ptp hingeraten VI sep irreg aux sein **irgendwo ~** to get somewhere; **wo bin ich denn da ~?** (inf) what kind of place is this then?; **hin|ge|ris|sen** ADJ enraptured, enchanted; **hin- und hergerissen sein** to be torn (zwischen between); **ich bin ganz hin- und hergerissen** (iro) absolutely great or fantastic! (iro) ADV with rapt attention; **~ lauschen** to listen with rapt attention → auch **hinreißen**; **Hin|ge|schie|de|ne(r)** MF decl as adj (geh euph) **der/die ~** the deceased also pl, the departed also pl; **hin+glei|ten** VI sep irreg aux sein to glide; (geh: Zeit) to slip away; **Hin|gu|cker** M (inf) (= Mensch) looker (inf); (= Sache) eye-catcher (inf); **hin+ha|ben** VT sep irreg (inf) **wo willst du dies ~?** where do you want this (to go)?; **hin+hal|ten** VT sep irreg **a** (= entgegenstrecken) to hold out (jdm to sb) **b** (fig) jdn to put off, to stall; (Mil) to stave off

Hin|hal|te-: Hin|hal|te|po|li|tik F stalling or delaying policy; **Hin|hal|te|tak|tik** F stalling or delaying tactics pl

hin-: hin+hän|gen sep irreg (inf) VT **a** (= aufhängen) to hang up **b** (fig inf: = melden, verpetzen, verleumden) jdn (bei jdm) **~** to blacken somebody's name (with sb); **hin+hau|en** sep irreg (inf) VT **a** (= nachlässig machen) to knock

off (inf) **b** (= hinwerfen) to slam or plonk (inf) or bang down; (fig: = aufgeben) Arbeit, Studium, Ausbildung to chuck in (inf) **VI a** (= zuschlagen) to hit hard; **(mit der Faust) ~** to thump or clobber (inf) it/sth (with one's fist) **b** (= gut gehen) **es hat hingehauen** I/we etc just managed it; **das wird schon ~** it will be OK (inf) or all right **c** (= klappen, in Ordnung sein) to work; **ich habe das so lange geübt, bis es hinhaute** I practised (Brit) or practiced (US) it till I could do it **VR** (inf: = sich schlafen legen) to crash out (inf) **VT** impers **es hat ihn hingehauen** he fell over; **hin+ho|cken** VR sep to squat (down); **hock dich hin!** (inf) plonk yourself down; **hin+hö|ren** VI sep to listen; **hin+kau|ern** VR sep to cower (down)

Hin|ke|bein [ˈhɪŋkəbain] NT , **Hin|ke|fuß** [ˈhɪŋkəfuːs] M (inf: = verletztes Bein) gammy leg (inf)

Hin|kel|stein [ˈhɪŋkl̩-] M (inf) menhir

hin|ken [ˈhɪŋkn̩] VI **a** (= gehbehindert sein) to limp, to walk with a limp; **mit** or **auf dem rechten Bein ~** to have a limp in one's right leg **b** aux sein (= sich fortbewegen) to limp **c** (fig) (Beispiel) to be inappropriate; (Vergleich) to be misleading; (Vers, Reim) to be clumsy

hin-: hin+klot|zen VT sep (inf) Hochhäuser etc to throw up; **hin+knal|len** sep (inf) **VT** to slam or bang down **VI** aux sein to fall flat; **hin+knien** VIR sep (vi: aux sein) to kneel (down); **hin+kom|men** VI sep irreg aux sein **a** (= an einen Ort hinkommen) **(da) ~** to get there; **nach X ~** to get to X; **kommst du mit hin?** are you coming too?; **wie komme ich zu dir hin?** how do I get to your place?; **könnt ihr alle zu ihm ~?** can you all go to his place? **b** (= an bestimmten Platz gehören) to go; **wo ist das Buch hingekommen?** where has the book got to (Brit) or gone?; **wo kämen wir denn hin, wenn ...** (inf) where would we be if ...; **wo kämen wir denn da hin?** (inf) where would we be then? **c** (inf: = in Ordnung kommen) **das kommt schon hin** that will turn out OK (inf) **d** (inf: = auskommen) to manage; **wir kommen (damit) hin** we will manage **e** (inf: = ausreichen, stimmen) to be right; **hin+krie|gen** VT sep (inf) **a** (= fertig bringen) to do, to manage; **wie er es nur immer hinkriegt, dass die anderen alles für ihn machen** I don't know how he manages to get the others to do everything for him; **das hast du gut hingekriegt** you've made a nice job of it; **wie kriegt sie das bloß immer hin?** I don't know how she does it **b** (= in Ordnung bringen) to mend, to fix; (gesundheitlich) to cure; **hin+krit|zeln** VT sep to scribble down; **hastig hingekritzelte Zeilen** hastily scribbled lines

Hin|kunft F (Aus) **in ~** in (the) future

hin|künf|tig (Aus) ADJ future ADV in (the) future

hin+lan|gen VI sep (inf) **a** (= zupacken) to grab him/her/it etc; (= ziehen/schieben) to pull/push hard; (dial: = anfassen) to touch; (= zuschlagen) to take a (good) swipe (inf); (= foulen) to play rough → **Gras b** (= sich bedienen) to help oneself to a lot; (= viel Geld verlangen) to overcharge **c** (= ausreichen) to do; (Geld) to stretch; **mein Geld langt dafür nicht hin** my money won't stretch to that (esp Brit) or that far **d** (= auskommen) to manage

hin|läng|lich [ˈhɪnlɛŋlɪç] ADJ (= ausreichend) adequate; **keine ~e Anzahl** an insufficient number ADV (= ausreichend) adequately; (= zu Genüge) sufficiently; **~ bekannt sein** to be common knowledge

hin+las|sen VT sep irreg jdn (da) **~** to let sb go (there)

hin+lau|fen VI sep irreg aux sein **a** (= zu bestimmter Stelle laufen) to run there; (= vorbei-, entlang-, dahinlaufen) to run; (inf: zu Veranstaltung, Amt, Rechtsanwalt etc) to rush **b** (dial inf: = nicht fahren) to walk **c** (= verlaufen: mit Ortsangabe, in bestimmte Richtung) to run

hin+le|gen sep **VT a** (= hintun) to put down; Zettel to leave (jdm for sb); (= flach legen) Verletzten etc to lay down; (ins Bett, zum Schlafen) to put to bed; (inf: = bezahlen müssen) to fork out (inf) **b** (inf: = glänzend darbieten) to perform; Rede, Vortrag to give effortlessly and brilliantly; **er hat einen tollen Stepptanz hingelegt** he did a neat bit of tap-dancing **VR** to lie down; **~!** (Mil) down!; **sich lang ~, sich der Länge nach ~** (inf) to fall flat; **da legst du dich (lang) hin!** (inf) it's unbelievable

hin+len|ken VT sep etw auf etw (acc) ~ (Fahrzeug, Pferd) to steer sth toward(s) sth; Fluss, Wasser, Blicke, jds Aufmerksamkeit to direct sth to sth; Schritte, Gespräch to turn sth to sth

hin+lüm|meln VR sep (inf) to loll or lounge about (Brit) or around (auf +acc on)

hin+ma|chen sep **VT a** (= anbringen) to put on; Bild to put up **b** (= kaputtmachen) to wreck, to ruin **VI a** (inf: = Notdurft verrichten) to do one's/its etc business (euph) **b** (inf: = sich beeilen) to get a move on (inf) **c** aux sein (dial inf: = an bestimmten Ort gehen) to go there

Hin-: **Hin|marsch** M way or (Mil) march there; **hin+mor|den** VT sep (geh) to massacre; **hin+müs|sen** VI sep irreg to have to go; **Hin|nah|me** ['hɪnnaːmə] F -, no pl acceptance; **hin+neh|men** VT sep irreg **a** (= ertragen) to take, to accept; Beleidigung to swallow; **etw als selbstverständlich ~** to take sth for granted **b** (inf: = mitnehmen) to take; **hin+nei|gen** sep **VT** Kopf, Körper to incline **VR** (zu towards) (Mensch) to lean; (fig) to incline, to have leanings; (Zweige, Baum) to lean; (Landschaft) to incline **VI** (fig) **zu etw ~** to incline toward(s) sth; **zu Vorbild** to tend to follow sth

hin|nen ['hɪnən] ADV (old, liter) **von ~** hence; **von ~ gehen** or **scheiden** (fig) to depart (from) this life (form), to pass on

hin-: **hin+pas|sen** VI sep (= Platz haben) to fit (in); (= gut aussehen) to go (well); (Mensch: = am Platz sein) to fit in; **hin+pfef|fern** VT sep (inf) Gegenstand to bang or slam down (inf); (fig) Antwort, Kritik (mündlich) to rap out; (schriftlich) to scribble down; **hin+pfu|schen** VT sep (inf) to dash off; **hin+plap|pern** VT sep to say; Unsinn to talk; **das hat sie nur so hingeplappert** she said that without thinking; **hin+plump|sen** VI sep aux sein (inf) to fall down (with a thud); **etw ~ lassen** to dump or plump (inf) sth down; **sich ~ lassen** to plump oneself down (inf), to flop down; **hin+raf|fen** VT sep (liter) to carry off; **hin+rei|ßen** VT sep (S Ger inf) **jdm etw ~** to rub sb's nose in sth; **hin+rei|chen** sep **VT jdm etw ~** to hand or pass sb sth or sth to sb; Hand to hold out sth to sb **VI a** (= ausreichen) to be enough, to suffice (form) **b** (= sich erstrecken) **bis zu etw ~** to stretch to sth; **hin|rei|chend** **ADJ** (= ausreichend) adequate; (= genug) sufficient; (= reichlich) ample; **keine ~en Beweise** insufficient evidence; **gegen ihn besteht ~er Tatverdacht** there is sufficient suspicion against him **ADV** lange, oft enough; aufklären, informieren adequately; **es ist noch ~ Zeit** there is ample time; **Hin|rei|se** F journey there or out, outward journey; (mit Schiff) voyage out, outward voyage; **die Hin- und Rückreise** journey there and back; **die ~ nach London** the journey to London; **auf der ~** on the way there; **hin+rei|ßen** VT sep irreg (fig) **a** (= begeistern) to thrill, to enrapture → auch **hingerissen b** (= überwältigen) jdn zu etw ~ to force sb into sth; **die Zuschauer zu Beifallsstürmen ~** to elicit thunderous applause from the audience; **sich ~ lassen** to let oneself be or get carried away; **sich zu einer Entscheidung ~ lassen** to let oneself be carried away into making a decision; **hin|rei|ßend** **ADJ** fantastic; Landschaft, Anblick enchanting; Schönheit, Mensch captivating; Redner thrilling, fantastic **ADV** **~ (schön) aussehen** to look quite enchanting; **~ (schön) Klavier spielen** to play the piano quite enchantingly or delightfully; **~ tanzen** to dance enchantingly or delightfully; **hin+ren|nen** VI sep irreg aux sein =

hinlaufen a; **hin|rich|ten** VT sep to execute; **jdn durch den Strang ~** to hang sb; **jdn durch den elektrischen Stuhl ~** to execute sb on the electric chair

Hin|rich|tung F execution

Hin|rich|tungs-: **Hin|rich|tungs|kom|man|do** NT execution or (bei Erschießen) firing squad; **Hin|rich|tungs|stät|te** F place of execution

hin-: **hin+rot|zen** VT sep (inf) to spew out (inf); **hin+rü|cken** VT sep Gegenstand to push over; **Hin|run|de** F (Sport) first half of the season; (= Hinspiel) ≈ corresponding match (Brit) or game (US) in the first half of the season; **hin+sa|gen** VT sep to say without thinking; **hin+schaf|fen** VT sep to get there; **hin+schau|en** VI sep (dial) = hinsehen; **hin+schei|den** VI sep irreg aux sein (liter) to pass away, to depart (from) this life (form); **der Hingeschiedene** the deceased, the (dear (Brit) or dearly) departed; **Hin|schei|den** NT -s, no pl (liter) demise; **hin+schei|ßen** VI sep irreg (vulg) to crap (sl); **hin+schi|cken** VT sep to send; **hin+schie|ben** VT sep irreg to push over; **Hin|schied** ['hɪnʃiːt] M -(e)s [-dəs] no pl (Sw liter) demise; **hin+schie|len** VI sep to glance (zu at); **hin+schlach|ten** VT sep to slaughter, to butcher; **hin+schla|gen** VI sep irreg **a** (= dageschlagen) to strike, to hit **b** aux sein (= hinfallen) to fall over; **der Länge nach** or **längelang** or **lang ~** (inf) to fall flat (on one's face); **hin+schlei|chen** VIR sep irreg (vi: aux sein) to creep or steal or sneak up; **hin+schlep|pen** sep **VT** to carry, to lug (inf); (inf: = mitnehmen) to drag along **VR** (Mensch) to drag oneself along; (fig) to drag on; **hin+schlu|dern** VT sep (inf) Arbeit to dash off; **hin+schmei|ßen** VT sep irreg (inf) = hinwerfen) to fling or chuck down (inf); (fig: = aufgeben) Arbeit etc to chuck or pack in (inf); **hin+schmel|zen** VI sep irreg aux sein (hum, inf) (Mensch) to swoon, (Wut) to melt away; **hin+schmie|ren** VT sep (inf) Schmutz to spread, to smear; (pej: = malen) to daub; (= flüchtig schreiben) to scribble; **hin+schrei|ben** sep irreg **VT** to write; (= flüchtig niederschreiben) to scribble down (inf); Aufsatz to dash off **VI** (inf) to write (there); **hin+schwin|den** VI sep irreg aux sein = dahinschwinden; **hin+se|hen** VI sep irreg to look; **ich kann (gar) nicht ~** I can't bear to look; **ohne hinzusehen** without looking; **bei genauerem Hinsehen** on looking more carefully; **vor sich ~** to look or stare straight ahead

hin sein ▲ VI irreg aux sein (inf) **a** (= kaputt sein) to have had it; **hin ist hin** what's done is done **b** (= erschöpft sein) to be shattered (Brit inf) or exhausted **c** (= verloren sein) to be lost; (Ruhe) to have disappeared; (= ruiniert sein) to be in ruins **d** (= tot sein) to have kicked the bucket (inf) **e** (= begeistert sein) **(von etw) hin (und weg) sein** to be mad about sth **f** **bis dahin ist es noch lange hin** it's a long time till then

hin+set|zen sep **VT** to put or set down; jdn to seat, to put; Kind to sit **VR** (lit) to sit down; **sich gerade ~** to sit up straight **VR** (inf: = sich bemühen) to buckle down to it, to set to

Hin|sicht ✪ 32.3 F -, no pl **in dieser ~** in this respect or regard; **in mancher** or **gewisser ~** in some or many respects or ways; **in jeder ~** in every respect; **in finanzieller ~** financially; **in wirtschaftlicher ~** economically; **in beruflicher ~** with regard to my/his etc job; **in ~ auf** (+acc) (= bezüglich) with regard to; (= in Anbetracht) in view of

hin|sicht|lich ['hɪnzɪçtlɪç] PREP +gen (= bezüglich) with regard to; (= in Anbetracht) in view of

hin-: **hin+sie|chen** VI sep aux sein (geh) = dahinsiechen; **hin+sin|ken** VI sep irreg aux sein (geh) to sink (down); (= ohnmächtig werden) to faint, to swoon; (tot) to drop down dead; **hin+sol|len** VI sep (inf) **wo soll ich/das Buch hin?** where do I/does the book go?; **wo soll ich mit dem Brief hin?** what should I do with this letter?;

eigentlich sollte ich ja zur Party hin I really ought to go to the party; **Hin|spiel** NT (Sport) first leg; **hin+star|ren** VI sep to stare; **hin+stel|len** sep **VT a** (= niederstellen) Gebäude to put down; (an bestimmte Stelle) to put; (inf) Gebäude to put up; (= abstellen) Fahrzeug to put, to park; **er tut seine Pflicht, wo man ihn auch hinstellt** he does his duty wherever he is **b** (= auslegen) Vorfall, Angelegenheit, Sachlage to describe; **jdn/etw als jdn/etw ~** (= bezeichnen) to make sb/sth out to be sb/sth **VR** to stand; (Fahrer) to park; **sich gerade ~** to stand up straight; **sich vor jdn** or **jdm ~** to stand in front of sb; **sie hat sich vor mich/ihn hingestellt** she came and stood in front of me/went and stood in front of him; **sich als etw ~** (fig) to make oneself out to be sth; **hin+steu|ern** sep **VI a** aux sein to steer; **wo steuert sie hin?** where is she going? **b** (fig) **in der Diskussion auf etw** (acc) ~ to steer the discussion toward(s) sth; **auf ein Ziel ~** (fig) to aim at a goal **VT** to steer; **hin+stre|cken** sep **VT a** Hand, Gegenstand to hold out **b** (liter) jdn to fell **VR** to stretch (oneself) out, to lie down; **hin+strö|men** VI sep aux sein (Fluss, Wasser) to flow; (geh: Menschen) to flock there; **sie strömten zur Ausstellung hin** they flocked to the exhibition; **hin+stür|zen** VI sep aux sein **a** (= hinfallen) to fall down heavily **b** (= hineinen) **zu jdm/etw ~** to rush or dash toward(s) sb/sth

Hint|an-: **hint|an+set|zen** [hɪnt'lan-] VT sep (= zurückstellen) to put last; (= vernachlässigen) to neglect; **Hint|an|set|zung** [hɪnt'lanzetsʊŋ] F -, no pl disregard; (= Vernachlässigung) neglect; **un- ter ~ einer Sache** (gen) (form) regardless of sth, without regard for sth; **hint|an|stel|len** [hɪnt'lan-] VT sep (= zurückstellen) to put last; (= vernachlässigen) to neglect

hin|ten ['hɪntn̩] ADV **a** behind; **von ~** from the back; (bei Menschen auch) from behind; **nach ~** to the back; **von weit ~** from the very back; **~ im Buch/in der Schlange** at the back of the book/queue (Brit) or line (US); **~ auf der Liste** at the end of the list; **sich ~ anstellen** to join the end of the queue (Brit) or line (US); **~ im Bild** in the back of the picture; **nach ~ abgehen** (Theat) to exit at the back of the stage; **nach ~ laufen** to run to the back; **von ~ anfangen** to begin from the end; **das Alphabet von ~ aufsagen** to say the alphabet backwards; **etw ~ anfügen** to add sth at the end; **~ bleiben** (lit) to stay behind, to stay at the back; (fig) to lag behind **b** (= am rückwärtigen Ende) at the back; (Naut) aft; (= am Gesäß) on one's behind; **von ~ sehen** from behind; **jdn erkennen auch** from the back; **~ im Auto/Bus** in the back of the car/bus; **der Blinker ~** the rear indicator (esp Brit) or blinker (US); **~ und vorn nichts haben** (inf) to be as flat as a pancake (esp Brit inf) or board (US inf); **nach ~** to the back; fallen, ziehen backwards; **jdn am liebsten von ~ sehen** (inf) to be glad to see the back of sb; **~ ausschlagen** (Pferd) to kick out → **Auge** **c** (= auf der Rückseite) at the back; (von Gebäude) at the back or rear; **das Buch ist ~ schmutzig** the back (cover) of the book is dirty; **auf der Medaille** on the back or the reverse side of the medal; **ein nach ~ gelegenes Zimmer** a room facing the back; **ein Blick nach ~** a look behind; **etw von ~ und vorn betrachten** (fig) to consider sth from all angles **d** (= weit entfernt) **das Auto da** ~ the car back there; **sie waren ziemlich weit** ~ they were quite far back; **~ im Walde** deep in the forest; **~ in der Mongolei** far away in Mongolia **e** (fig) **~ und vorn** (betrügen) left, right and centre (Brit) or center (US); bedienen hand and foot; verwöhnen rotten (inf); egal sein absolutely, utterly; **das stimmt ~ und vorn nicht, das stimmt weder ~ noch vorn** that is absolutely untrue; **das reicht** or **langt ~ und vorn nicht** or **weder ~ noch vorn** that's nowhere near enough; **dann heißt es Frau Schmidt ~ und Frau Schmidt vorn** then it's Mrs Schmidt this and Mrs Schmidt that; **ich weiß nicht mehr, wo ~**

und vorn ist I don't know whether I'm coming or going

hin|ten-: hin|ten|dran ['hɪntn'dran] ADV (inf) (= am hinteren Ende) at the back; (fig: = im Hintertreffen) behind; **hin|ten|drauf** ['hɪntn'drauf] ADV (inf) on the back; (von LKW) in the back; (= auf Gesäß) on one's behind; **hin|ten|drein** ['hɪntn'drain] ADV = hinterher; **hin|ten|he|rum** ['hɪntnhe'rʊm] ADV a (= von der hinteren Seite) from the back; **kommen Sie ~** come (a)round the back b (fig inf) (= auf Umwegen) in a roundabout way; (= illegal) under the counter; **er hat mir ~ erzählt, dass sie ...** he told me behind her back that she ...; **hin|ten|nach** ['hɪntn'na:x] ADV (Aus, S Ger) = hinterher; **hin|ten|rum** ['hɪntn'rʊm] ADV (inf) = hintenherum; **hin|ten|über** ['hɪntn'|y:bɐ] ADV backwards; **er fiel/kippte ~** he fell over backwards; **hin|ten|über|kip|pen** VI sep aux sein to topple or fall over backwards

hin|ter ['hɪntɐ] PREP +dat or (mit Bewegungsverben) +acc a (räumlich) behind; **~ dem Haus** behind the house, at the back or rear of the house; **~ jdm/etw her** behind sb/sth; **~ etw** (acc) **kommen** (fig: = herausfinden) to get to the bottom of sth; **~ die Wahrheit kommen** to get to the truth; **sich ~ jdn stellen** (lit) to stand behind sb; (fig) to support sb, to get behind sb; **~ jdm/etw stehen** (lit, fig) to be behind sb/sth; **jdn ~ sich** (dat) **haben** (lit, fig) to have sb behind one; **~ dem Hügel/der Tür hervor** (out) from behind the hill/door; **jdn weit ~ sich** (dat) **lassen** to leave sb far behind; (im Rennen auch) to outdistance sb; **~ etw** (dat) **stecken, sich ~ etw** (dat) **verbergen** to be or lie behind sth; **~ seinen Reden steckt nicht viel** there's not much in his speeches **b** +dat (= nach) after; **vier Kilometer ~ Glasgow/~ der Grenze** four kilometres (Brit) or kilometers (US) outside Glasgow/beyond the border; **~ diesem Satz steht ein Fragezeichen** there is a question mark at the end of this sentence; **er ist ~ mir dran** it's his turn after me **c** +dat (in Rangfolge) after; (in Bedeutung) behind; **an Talent nicht ~ jdm zurückstehen** to be just as talented as sb; **sie stand nicht ~ ihm zurück** she did not lag behind him; **ich stelle das Privatleben ~ der Arbeit zurück** I put my work before my private life **d** etw ~ sich (dat) **haben** (= zurückgelegt haben) to have got through sth; Strecke to have covered sth; Land to have left sth; (= überstanden haben) to have got sth over (and done) with; Krankheit, Zeit to have been through sth; anstrengende Tage to have had sth; Studium to have completed or finished sth; **sie hat viel ~ sich** she has been through a lot; **das Schlimmste haben wir ~ uns** we're past the worst, we are over the worst; **etw ~ sich** (acc) **bringen** to get sth over (and done) with; Strecke to cover sth; Arbeit to get sth done; **das liegt ~ ihr** that is behind her; **sich ~ etw** (acc) **machen** to get down to sth → **her sein c** **e** (inf) = dahinter

Hin|ter-: Hin|ter|achs|an|trieb M (Mot) rear wheel drive; **Hin|ter|achse** F rear or back axle; **Hin|ter|an|sicht** F rear or back view; **Hin|ter|aus|gang** M back or rear exit; **Hin|ter|ba|cke** F usu pl buttock; (von Tier) hindquarter; **sich auf die ~n setzen** (fig inf) to get down to it; **Hin|ter|bänk|ler** [-bɛŋklɐ] M -s, -, **Hin|ter|bänk|le|rin** [-ərɪn] F -, -nen (Pol pej) backbencher; **Hin|ter|bein** NT hind leg; **sich auf die ~e stellen** or **setzen** (lit) to rear up (on one's hind legs); (fig inf) (= sich widersetzen) to kick up a fuss (inf); (= sich anstrengen) to pull one's socks up (inf)

Hin|ter|blie|be|nen-: Hin|ter|blie|be|nen|für|sor|ge F welfare service for surviving dependents; **Hin|ter|blie|be|nen|ren|te** F surviving dependents' pension

Hin|ter|blie|be|ne(r) [hɪntɐ'bli:b(ə)nə] MF decl as adj surviving dependent; **die ~n** the bereaved family

hin|ter-: hin|ter|brin|gen ptp **hinterbracht** VT insep irreg jdm etw ~ to mention sth to sb; **Hin|ter|deck** NT (Naut) afterdeck; **hin|ter|drein** [hɪntɐ'drain] ADV = hinterher

hin|te|re ADJ = hintere(r, s)

hin|ter|ei|nan|der [hɪntɐai'nandɐ] ADV (räumlich) one behind the other, behind each other; (= in einer Reihe nebeneinander) next to one another; (= in Reihenfolge, nicht gleichzeitig, ohne Unterbrechung) one after the other; **~ hereinkommen** to come in one by one, to come in one at a time; **dicht ~** (räumlich) close behind one another; (zeitlich) close one after another; **zwei Tage ~** two days running; **dreimal ~** three times in a row; **es hat monatelang ~ geregnet** it has rained for months on end; **etw ~ tun** (= nicht gleichzeitig) to do sth one after the other; (= der Reihe nach) to do sth in turn; (= ohne Unterbrechung) to do sth in one go

hin|ter|ei|nan|der-: hin|ter|ei|nan|der fah|ren ▲ VI irreg aux sein (mit Auto/Fahrrad) to drive/ride one behind the other; **hin|ter|ei|nan|der ge|hen** ▲ VI irreg aux sein to walk one behind the other; **hin|ter|ei|nan|der|her** ADV behind one another; **hin|ter|ei|nan|der schal|ten** ▲ VT (Elec) to connect in series; **Hin|ter|ei|nan|der|schal|tung** F (Elec) series connection; **hin|ter|ei|nan|der ste|hen** ▲ VI irreg aux haben or (S Ger) sein to stand one behind the other; **hin|ter|ei|nan|der|weg** [hɪntɐlainandɐ'vɛk] ADV (zeitlich) running; (= nacheinander) one after the other

Hin|ter|ein|gang M rear entrance

Hin|te|re(r) ['hɪntərə] MF decl as adj person/man/woman etc at the back

hin|te|re(r, s) ['hɪntərə] ADJ back; (von Tier, Gebäude, Zug auch) rear; **der/die/das Hintere** the one at the back; **das ~ Ende des Saals** the back or rear of the room; **die Hinteren** those at the back, those behind; **am ~n Ende** at the far end → **hinterste(r, s)**

Hin|ter-: hin|ter|fot|zig [hɪntɐfɔtsɪç] ADJ (dial inf) underhand(ed); **Hin|ter|fot|zig|keit** F -, -en (dial inf) underhandedness; (= Bemerkung) underhand(ed) remark; **hin|ter|fra|gen** ptp **hinterfragt** VT insep to question; **etw kritisch ~** to examine sth critically; **Hin|ter|fuß** M hind foot; **Hin|ter|gau|men|laut** M velar (sound); **Hin|ter|ge|bäu|de** NT = Hinterhaus; **Hin|ter|ge|dan|ke** M ulterior motive; **ohne ~n** without any ulterior motive(s); **hin|ter|ge|hen¹** ptp **hintergangen** VT insep irreg (= betrügen) to deceive; Ehepartner etc auch to be unfaithful to; (= umgehen) Verordnung, Gesetze, Prinzip to circumvent; **hin|ter|ge|hen²** VI sep irreg aux sein (dial inf) to go to the back or rear (in +acc of); **Hin|ter|ge|stell** NT (hum inf) (= Beine) hind legs pl (inf), pins pl (inf); (= Po) rump (inf), backside (inf); **Hin|ter|glas|ma|le|rei** F (= Bild) verre églomisé picture; (= Technik) verre églomisé technique

Hin|ter|grund M (von Bild, Raum) background; (von Bühne, Saal) back; (Theat: = Kulisse) backdrop, backcloth; (fig: = verborgene Zusammenhänge) background no pl (+gen to); **im ~** in the background; **~ der Bühne** at the back of the stage; **vor dem ~** (lit, fig) against the background; **der musikalische/akustische ~** the background music/sounds pl; **im ~ bleiben/stehen** (lit, fig) to stay/be in the background; **in den ~ treten** or **rücken** (fig) to be pushed into the background; **jdn/etw in den ~ drängen** to push sb/sth into the background

Hin|ter|grund|be|richt M background report

Hin|ter|grund|ge|spräch NT (Pol) briefing

hin|ter|grün|dig ['hɪntɐgryndɪç] ADJ cryptic, enigmatic ADV cryptically, enigmatically

Hin|ter|grün|dig|keit F -, -en crypticness, enigmaticness; (= Bemerkung) cryptic or enigmatic remark

Hin|ter|grund|in|for|ma|ti|on F background information no pl (über +acc about, on); **eine ~** (a piece of or some) background information

Hin|ter|grund|mu|sik F background music

Hin|ter|grund|pro|gramm NT (Comput) background program

Hin|ter-: hin|ter+ha|ken VI sep (inf) to follow that/it etc up; **Hin|ter|halt** M a ambush; **jdn aus dem ~ überfallen** to ambush or waylay sb; **jdm/etw aus dem ~ angreifen** (esp Mil) to ambush sb/sth; (Sport, fig) to make a surprise attack on sb/sth; **im ~ sein** or **liegen** to lie in wait or (esp Mil) ambush b (inf) **etw im ~ haben** to have sth in reserve; **ohne ~** unreservedly; **hin|ter|häl|tig** ['hɪntɐhɛltɪç] ADJ underhand(ed), devious; Lächeln devious ADV in an underhand way, deviously; **Hin|ter|häl|tig|keit** F -, -en underhandedness, deviousness; (= Handlung) underhand(ed) or devious act; **Hin|ter|hand** F (von Pferd, Hund) hindquarters pl; **etw in der ~ haben** (fig: = in Reserve) to have sth up one's sleeve; **Hin|ter|haupt** NT back of one's/the head; **Hin|ter|haus** NT part of a tenement house accessible only through a courtyard and thus considered inferior

hin|ter|her [hɪntɐ'he:ɐ, 'hɪntɐhe:ɐ] ADV (räumlich) behind, after; (zeitlich) afterwards

hin|ter|her-: hin|ter|her+fah|ren VI sep irreg aux sein to drive behind (jdm sb); **hin|ter|her+ge|hen** VI sep irreg aux sein to follow (jdm sb); **hin|ter|her+hin|ken** VI sep aux sein to limp behind (jdm sb); (fig) to lag behind (hinter etw (dat) sth, mit with, in); **hin|ter|her+kom|men** VI sep irreg aux sein a (= danach kommen) (räumlich) to follow (behind or after); (zeitlich) to come after b (= als Letzter kommen) to bring up the rear; **hin|ter|her+lau|fen** VI sep irreg aux sein to run behind (jdm sb); **jdm ~** (fig inf: = sich bemühen um) to run after sb, to run (a)round after sb; **einem Mädchen ~** (inf) to run after a girl; **hin|ter|her+ru|fen** VI sep irreg **jdm (etw) ~** to call (sth) after sb; **hin|ter|her+schi|cken** VT sep to send on (jdm to sb); jdn to send after (jdm sb); **hin|ter|her sein** ▲ VI sep irreg aux sein (inf) (lit: = verfolgen) to be after (jdm sb); (fig: = zurückgeblieben sein) to lag behind; **~, dass ...** to see to it that ...

Hin|ter-: Hin|ter|hof M back yard; (zwischen Vorder- und Hinterhaus) courtyard; **Hin|ter|in|di|en** NT South-East Asia; **Hin|ter|kan|te** F rear edge; (Aerodynamics) trailing edge; **Hin|ter|kopf** M back of one's/the head; **etw im ~ haben/behalten** (inf) to have/keep sth in the back of one's mind; **Hin|ter|la|der** ['hɪntɐla:dɐ] M -s, - breech-loader; (inf: = Homosexueller) fag (pej); **Hin|ter|la|ge** F (Sw) security; **Hin|ter|land** NT hinterland; (Mil) back-up area; **hin|ter|las|sen¹** ptp **hinterlassen** VT insep irreg to leave; (testamentarisch auch) to bequeath (jdm etw sb sth, sth to sb); **~e Werke/Schriften** posthumous works; **hin|ter+las|sen²** VT sep irreg (dial inf) **jdn ~** to let sb go behind, to allow sb to go behind; **Hin|ter|las|sen|schaft** [hɪntɐ'lasnʃaft] F -, -en estate; (literarisch, fig) legacy; **die ~ seines Vorgängers aufarbeiten** to finish (off) somebody else's (unfinished) work; **jds ~ antreten** (= beerben) to inherit sb's estate; (= jdm nachfolgen) to follow sb; **Hin|ter|las|sung** [hɪntɐ'lasʊŋ] F -, no pl (form) **unter ~ von Schulden** leaving (unsettled or unpaid) debts; **hin|ter|las|tig** [-lastɪç] ADJ (Aviat) tail-heavy; (Naut) sternheavy; **Hin|ter|lauf** M (Hunt) hind leg; **hin|ter|le|gen** ptp **hinterlegt** VT insep a (= verwahren lassen) to deposit b (= als Pfand hinterlegen) to leave

Hin|ter|le|gung [hɪntɐ'le:gʊŋ] F -, -en deposit

Hin|ter|le|gungs-: Hin|ter|le|gungs|schein M deposit receipt; **Hin|ter|le|gungs|sum|me** F sum deposited

Hin|ter|leib M (Zool) hindquarters pl; (von Insekten) abdomen

Hin|ter|list F **a** (= *Tücke*) craftiness, cunning; (= *Verrat*) treachery; (= *Betrug*) deceitfulness **b** (= *Trick, List*) ruse, trick

hin|ter|lis|tig ADJ (= *tückisch*) crafty, cunning; (= *verräterisch*) treacherous; (= *betrügerisch*) deceitful ADV (= *tückisch*) cunningly; (= *betrügerisch*) deceitfully

hin|term ['hɪntəm] = hinter dem

Hin|ter|mann M *pl* -männer **a** person behind; (= *Auto*) car behind; **mein ~** the person/car behind me **b** (*inf*) (= *Gewährsmann*) contact; **die Hintermänner des Skandals** the men behind the scandal **c** (*Fin*: *von Wechsel*) subsequent endorser

Hin|ter|mann|schaft F (*Sport*) defence (*Brit*), defense (*US*)

hin|tern ['hɪntən] = hinter den

Hin|tern ['hɪntən] M **-s, -** (*inf*) bottom (*inf*), backside (*inf*), behind; **ein Tritt in den ~** a kick up the backside (*inf*), a kick in the pants (*inf*); **jdm den ~ versohlen** to tan sb's hide; **ein paar auf den ~ bekommen, den ~ voll bekommen** to get one's bottom smacked (*inf*); **sich auf den ~ setzen** (= *hinfallen*) to fall on one's bottom *etc*; (= *eifrig arbeiten*) to buckle down to work; **jdm in den ~ kriechen** to lick sb's boots, to suck up to sb; **mit dem Zeugnis kann er sich** (*dat*) **den ~ (ab)wischen** he might as well use that certificate for toilet paper; **ich könnte mir** or **mich in den ~ beißen** I could kick myself

Hin|ter-: Hin|ter|pfo|te F hind paw; **Hin|ter|pfuil|teu|fel** ['hɪntəpfuɪ'tɔʏfl] NT **-s**, *no pl* (*pej inf*) the back of beyond (*esp Brit*), the middle of nowhere

Hin|ter|rad NT rear or back wheel

Hin|ter|rad-: Hin|ter|rad|an|trieb M rear wheel drive; **Hin|ter|rad|brem|se** F rear (wheel) brake

hin|ter|rücks ['hɪntərʏks] ADV from behind; (*fig*: = *heimtückisch*) behind sb's back; **jdn ~ er-morden** to murder sb treacherously

hin|ters ['hɪntəs] = hinter das

Hin|ter-: Hin|ter|schiff NT stern; **Hin|ter|sei|te** F back; (*von Münze*) reverse side; (*inf* = *Hintern*) backside (*inf*); **Hin|ter|sinn** M , *no pl* underlying or deeper meaning (+*gen* behind); **hin|ter|sin|nig** ADJ cryptic

Hin|ters|te(r) ['hɪntəstə] M *decl as adj* (*inf*) bottom (*inf*), backside (*inf*), behind

hin|ters|te(r, s) ['hɪntəstə] ADJ *superl von* **hin-tere(r, s)** very back, backmost; (= *entlegenste*) remotest; **die Hintersten** those at the very back; **das ~ Ende** the very end or (*von Saal*) back; **in der ~n Reihe** in the very back row; **das Hinterste zuvorderst kehren** (*inf*) to turn everything upside down

Hin|ter-: Hin|ter|ste|ven M (*Naut*) sternpost; (*hum inf*: = *Gesäß*) backside (*inf*); **Hin|ter|stüb|chen** NT **etw im ~ haben** (*fig*) to have sth at the back of one's mind; **Hin|ter|teil** NT **a** (*inf*) backside (*inf*); (*von Tier*) hindquarters *pl* **b** *auch* M back or rear part; **Hin|ter|tref|fen** NT **im ~ sein** to be at a disadvantage; **ins ~ ge-raten** or **kommen** to fall behind; **hin|ter|trei-ben** *ptp* **hintertrieben** VT *insep irreg* (*fig*) to foil, to thwart; *Gesetz* to block; **Hin|ter|trei-bung** ['-traɪbʊŋ] F **-, -en** foiling, thwarting; (*von Ge-setz*) blocking; **Hin|ter|trep|pe** F back stairs *pl*; **Hin|ter|trep|pen|ro|man** M (*pej*) cheap or trashy novel, penny dreadful (*dated Brit*), dime novel (*US*); **Hin|ter|tup|fin|gen** [hɪnt-'tʊpfɪŋən] NT **-s**, *no pl* (*inf*) the back of be-yond (*esp Brit*), the middle of nowhere; **Hin|ter|tür** F , (*Aus*) **Hin|ter|türl** [-ty:əl] NT **-s, -n** back door; (*fig inf*: = *Ausweg, Umweg*) loophole; **durch die ~** (*inf*) through the back door; **sich** (*dat*) **eine ~** or **ein ~chen offen halten** or **offen lassen** (*fig*) to leave oneself a way out or a loophole; **Hin|ter|wäld|ler** [-vɛltlɐ] M **-s, -,** **Hin|ter|wäld|le|rin** [-ərɪn] F **-, -nen** (*inf*) back-woodsman, hillbilly (*esp US*); **hin|ter|wäld-le|risch** [-vɛltlərɪʃ] ADJ (*inf*) backwoods *attr*

Ansichten, Benehmen, Methoden auch hick *attr*; **ein ~er Mensch** a backwoodsman, a hillbilly (*esp US*); **hin|ter|zie|hen** *ptp* **hinterzogen** VT *insep irreg Steuern* to evade; *Material* to appropri-ate; **Hin|ter|zie|hung** F (*von Steuern*) evasion; (*von Material*) appropriation; **Hin|ter|zim|mer** NT back room

hin-: hin+tra|gen VT *sep irreg* to take or carry there; **hin+trei|ben** *sep irreg* VT (*Wind*) to blow; (*Strömung*) to wash VT *impers* **es trieb ihn immer wieder hin** something always drove him back there; **hin+tre|ten** VI *sep irreg* **a** *aux sein* **vor jdn** to go up to sb; *vor Gott* to step before sb; **zu jdm/etw ~** to step over to sb/sth **b** (= *mit Fuß stoßen*) to kick; **hin+tun** VT *sep irreg* (*inf*) to put; **ich weiß nicht, wo ich ihn ~ soll** (*fig*) I can't (quite) place him

hi|nü|ber [hɪ'ny:bɐ] ADV over; (*über Grenze, Stra-ße, Fluss auch*) across; **da ~** over there; **~ und herüber** back and forth; **quer ~** right across; **bis zum anderen Ufer ~** over or across to the other bank → **hinüber sein**

hi|nü|ber- PREF → *auch* **herüber-, rüber-: hi|nü-ber+be|för|dern** *ptp* **hinüberbefördert** VT *sep* to transport across (*über etw* (*acc*)) sth); **hi|nü-ber+bli|cken** VI *sep* to look across (*zu jdm* to sb); **hi|nü|ber+brin|gen** VT *sep irreg* to take a-cross (*über etw* (*acc*)) sth); **hi|nü|ber+däm-mern** VI *sep aux sein* (= *einschlafen*) to doze off; (= *sterben*) to pass away in one's sleep; **hi|nü-ber+fah|ren** *sep irreg* VT (*über etw* (*acc*)) sth) *jdn* to take across; *Gepäck etc auch* to carry a-cross; *Auto* to drive across VI *aux sein* to travel or go across; **nach Frankreich ~** to cross or go across to France; **über den Fluss ~** to cross the river; **hi|nü|ber+füh|ren** VT *jdn* (**über die Straße/dort/in das andere Zimmer**) to take sb across (the street)/over (there)/over (into the other room) VI (= *verlaufen*: *Straße, Brücke*) to go across (*über etw* (*acc*)) sth); **hi|nü|ber+ge-hen** VI *sep irreg aux sein* **a** (= *hingehen*) to go or walk across; (*zu anderem Haus, zu jdm*) to go or walk over (*über etw* (*acc*)) sth) **b** (*euph*: = *sterben*) to pass away; **hi|nü|ber+ge|lan|gen** *ptp* **hinübergelangt** VI *sep aux sein* (*geh*) to get across (*über etw* (*acc*)) sth); **hi|nü|ber+hel|fen** VI *sep irreg* **jdm ~** to help sb across (*über etw* (*acc*)) sth); (*fig*: *über Schwierigkeiten*) to help sb out (*über* +*acc* of); **jdm (ins Jenseits) ~** (= *leich-ten Tod verschaffen*) to help sb to die; (= *töten*) to bump sb off (*inf*); **hi|nü|ber+kom|men** VI *sep irreg aux sein* (*über etw* (*acc*)) sth) to come across; (*über Brücke, Fluss auch, über Hindernis, zu Besuch*) to come over; (= *hinüberkönnen*) to get across/over; **hi|nü|ber+las|sen** VT *sep irreg* to let or allow across; (*über Kreuzung, Brücke auch, zu Be-such*) to let or allow over (*über etw* (*acc*)) sth); **hi|nü|ber+rei|chen** *sep* VT to pass across; (*über Zaun etc*) to pass over (*jdm* to sb, *über etw* (*acc*)) sth); (*fig*) to extend (*in* +*acc* into); **hi|nü-ber+ret|ten** VT *sep* to bring to safety; (*fig*) *Hu-mor, Tradition* to keep alive; **etw in die Gegen-wart ~** to keep sth alive; (*fig*: *Brauch*) to be kept alive; **hi|nü|ber+ru|fen** *sep irreg* VT to call out VI to call over (*über etw* (*acc*)) sth); **hi|nü-ber+schaf|fen** VT *sep* to get across (*über etw* (*acc*)) sth); **hi|nü|ber+schi|cken** VT *sep* to send across or (*zu Besuch*) over (*über etw* (*acc*)) sth); **hi|nü|ber+schlum|mern** VI *sep aux sein* (*euph*: = *sterben*) to pass away; **hi|nü-ber+schwim|men** VI *sep irreg aux sein* to swim across (*über etw* (*acc*)) sth); **hinüber sein** ▲ VI *irreg aux sein* (*inf*) **a** (= *verdorben sein*) to be off or bad; (= *kaputt, unbrauchbar, tot sein*) to have had it (*inf*); (= *ruiniert sein*: *Firma, Politiker*) to be done for (*inf*) **b** (= *betrunken sein*) to be well away (*inf*); (= *betäubt sein*) to be (knocked) out (*inf*); **hi|nü|ber+spie|len** *sep* VI (*geh*) **die-ses Rot spielt leicht ins Violett hinüber** this red has a slight purple tinge or tinge of purple VT *Ball* to pass (*jdm* to sb); **hi|nü|ber+stei|gen** VI *sep irreg aux sein* to climb over (*über etw* (*acc*)

sth); **hi|nü|ber+tra|gen** VT *sep irreg* to carry a-cross (*über etw* (*acc*)) sth); **hi|nü|ber+wech-seln** VI *sep aux haben* or *sein* to change over (*zu, in* +*acc* to); **zu einer anderen Partei ~** to go over to another party; **hi|nü|ber+wer|fen** VT *sep irreg* to throw over (*über etw* (*acc*)) sth); **ei-nen Blick ~** to glance over; **hi|nü|ber+zie|hen** *sep irreg* VT to pull across (*über etw* (*acc*)) sth); (*fig*: = *umstimmen*) to win over (*auf* +*acc* to) VI *aux sein* **a** (= *marschieren*) to move or march a-cross **b** (= *sich bewegen*: *Rauch, Wolken*) to move across (*über etw* (*acc*)) sth) VR (= *sich er-strecken*) to stretch over (*nach, zu* to)

hin und her → **hin**

hin- und her|be|we|gen VTR *sep* to move back and forward or forth

Hin|und|her|ge|re|de NT (*inf*) **das ewige ~** this continual argy-bargy (*Brit inf*) or carrying-on (*inf*)

hin- und her|ge|ris|sen ADJ *pred* **~ sein** to be in a terrible dilemma, to be torn (*zwischen* +*dat* between)

Hin- und Rück-: Hin- und Rück|fahrt F re-turn journey, round trip (*US*); **Hin- und Rück|flug** M return flight; **Hin- und Rück|rei|se** F journey or trip (*esp US*) there and back, round trip; **Hin- und Rück|weg** M round trip

hi|nun|ter [hɪ'nʊntɐ] ADV down; **bis ~ zu** down to; **ins Tal ~** down into the valley; **am Hügel ~** down the hill; **dort** or **da ~** down there; **~ mit ihm!** down with him; **~ mit der Arznei** get this medicine down PREP +*acc* (*nachgestellt*) down

hi|nun|ter- PREF → *auch* **herunter-, runter-** down; **hi|nun|ter+bli|cken** VI *sep* to look down; **hi|nun|ter+brin|gen** VT *sep irreg* to take down; (*inf*: = *schlucken können*) to be able to get down; **hi|nun|ter+fah|ren** *sep irreg* VI *aux sein* to go down; (*Fahrstuhl, Bergbahn auch*) to descend; **in etw** (*acc*)/**nach etw ~** to go down into sth/to sth VT *jdn* to take down; *Fahrzeug* to drive down; **hi|nun|ter+fal|len** VI *sep irreg aux sein* to fall down; **hi|nun|ter+flie|ßen** VI *sep irreg aux sein* to flow down; **hi|nun|ter+ge-hen** VI *sep irreg aux sein* to go down; (*zu Fuß auch*) to walk down; (*Flugzeug*) to descend (*auf* +*acc* to); **hi|nun|ter+gie|ßen** VT *sep irreg* to pour down; *Getränke* to knock back (*inf*); **hi|-nun|ter+kip|pen** VT *sep* to tip down; (*inf*) *Ge-tränke* to knock back (*inf*); **hi|nun|ter+klet-tern** VI *sep aux sein* to climb down; **hi|nun-ter+las|sen** VT *sep irreg* to lower, to let down; **er lässt mich nicht hinunter** (*inf*) he won't let me get down; **hi|nun|ter+lau|fen** VI *sep irreg aux sein* to run down; **es lief ihm eiskalt den Rücken hinunter** a shiver ran down his spine; **hi|nun|ter+rei|chen** *sep* VT to hand or pass down VI to reach down; (*fig*: *in Rangfolge*) to apply (*bis zu* down to); **hi|nun|ter+rei|ßen** VT *sep irreg* to pull or drag down; **hi|nun-ter+schal|ten** VI *sep* (*Aut*) to change or shift (*US*) down; **hi|nun|ter+schau|en** VI *sep* (*dial*) to look down; **hi|nun|ter+schlin|gen** VT *sep irreg* (*inf*) to gulp down; *Essen* to gobble down; **hi|nun|ter+schlu|cken** VT *sep* to swallow (down); (*fig*) *Beleidigung* to swallow; *Kritik* to take; *Ärger, Tränen* to choke back; **hi|nun-ter+schmei|ßen** VT *sep irreg* (*inf*) to throw or chuck (*inf*) down; **hi|nun|ter+schüt|ten** VT *sep* = **hinuntergießen**; **hi|nun|ter+se|hen** VI *sep irreg* to look down; **hi|nun|ter+spü|len** VT *sep* **a** (*in Toilette, Ausguss*) to flush away; **etw die Toilette/den Ausguss ~** to flush sth down the toilet/drain **b** *Essen, Tablette* to wash down; (*fig*) *Ärger* to soothe; **hi|nun|ter+stür-zen** VI *sep* *aux sein* **a** (= *hinunterfallen*) to tum-ble or fall down **b** (= *eilig hinunterlaufen*) to rush or dash down; *Getränk* to gulp down VR to throw or fling oneself down; **hi|nun|ter+wer|fen** VT *sep irreg* to throw down; (*inf*: = *fallen lassen*) to drop; **einen Blick ~** to glance down; **hi|nun-ter+wür|gen** VT *sep Essen etc* to choke down;

(fig) Wut, Tränen to choke back; **hi|nun|ter+zie|hen** sep irreg **VT** to pull down **VI** aux sein to move down

hin|wa|gen VR sep to dare to go there

hin|wärts ['hɪnvɛrts] ADV on the way there; **die Strecke ~** the way there

hin|weg [hɪn'vɛk] ADV **a** (old: = fort) away; **~ mit der Unterdrückung** down with oppression **b** über jdn/etw ~ over sb or sb's head/sth; über alle Hindernisse etc ~ (fig) despite all the difficulties etc **c** (zeitlich) über eine Zeit ~ over a period of time; über zwei Jahre ~ over (a period of) two years

Hin|weg M way there; **auf dem ~** on the way there

hin|weg- PREF → auch weg- away; **hin|weg+brin|gen** VT sep irreg (fig) jdn über etw (acc) ~ to help sb get over sth; **hin|weg+ge|hen** VI sep irreg aux sein über etw (acc) ~ to pass over or across sth; (= nicht beachten) to pass over or disregard sth; **hin|weg+hel|fen** VI sep irreg (fig) jdm über etw (acc) ~ to help sb get over sth; **hin|weg+kom|men** VI sep irreg aux sein (fig) über etw (acc) ~ (= überstehen, verwinden) to get over sth; (= sich hinwegsetzen können) to dismiss sth; **ich komme nicht darüber hinweg, dass ...** (inf) I can't get over the fact that ...; **hin|weg+raf|fen** VT sep (geh) to carry off; **hin|weg+se|hen** VI sep irreg über jdn/etw ~ (lit) to see over sb or sb's head/sth; (fig) (= ignorieren) to ignore sb/sth; (= unbeachtet lassen) to overlook sb/sth; **darüber ~, dass ...** to overlook the fact that ...; **hin|weg+set|zen** sep irreg (fig) **VI** aux haben or sein über etw (acc) ~ to jump or leap over sth **VR** (fig) sich über etw (acc) ~ (= nicht beachten) to disregard or dismiss sth; (= überwinden) to overcome sth; **hin|weg+täu|schen** VT sep jdn über etw (acc) ~ to mislead or deceive sb about sth; **darüber ~, dass ...** to hide the fact that ...; **sich nicht darüber ~ lassen, dass ...** not to blind oneself to the fact that ...; **hin|weg+trös|ten** VT sep jdn über etw (acc) ~ to console sb about sth; **deine Entschuldigung tröstet mich nicht darüber hinweg, dass ...** your apology does not make up for the fact that ...

Hin|weis ['hɪnvais] M **-es, -e** [-zə] **a** (= Rat) tip, piece of advice; (= Bemerkung) comment; (amtlich) notice; **darf ich mir den ~ erlauben, dass ...** may I point out that ..., may I draw your attention to the fact that ...; **~e für den Benutzer** notes for the user **b** (= Verweis) reference; **unter ~ auf** (+acc) with reference to **c** (= Anhaltspunkt, Anzeichen) indication; (esp von Polizei) clue **d** (= Anspielung) allusion (auf +acc to)

hin+wei|sen sep irreg **VT** jdn auf etw (acc) ~ to point sth out to sb **VI** auf jdn/etw ~ to point to sb/sth; (= verweisen) to refer to sb/sth; **darauf ~, dass ...** to point out that ...; (nachdrücklich) to stress or emphasize that ...; (= anzeigen) to indicate that ...

hin|wei|send ADJ (Gram) demonstrative

Hin|weis|schild NT pl **-schilder**, **Hin|weis|ta|fel** F sign

hin+wen|den sep irreg **VT** to turn (zu, nach towards) **VR** (lit) to turn (zu, nach towards, to); (fig: Mensch) to turn (zu to); **Hin|wen|dung** F (fig) turning (zu to); **eine ~ zum Besseren** a turn for the better

hin+wer|fen sep irreg **VT a** (= wegwerfen, zu Boden werfen) to throw down; **jdm etw ~** to throw sth to sb **b** (= flüchtig machen) Bemerkung to drop casually; Wort to say casually; Zeilen, Roman, Zeichnung to dash off; **einen Blick ~** to glance at it/them; **eine hingeworfene Bemerkung** a casual remark **c** (inf: = aufgeben) Arbeit, Stelle to give up, to chuck (in) (inf) **VR** to throw or fling oneself down; (auf die Knie) to go down or throw oneself down on one's knees

hin|wie|der [hɪn'viːdɐ], **hin|wie|de|rum** [hɪn'viːdərʊm] (old) ADV (= dagegen) on the other hand; (= dann wieder) in turn

hin-: hin+wir|k|en VI sep auf etw (acc) ~ to work toward(s) sth; **kannst du (nicht) (bei ihm) darauf ~, dass er mich empfängt?** couldn't you use your influence to get him to see me or to make him see me?; **hin+wol|len** VI sep (inf) to want to go

Hinz [hɪnts] M **~ und Kunz** (inf) every Tom, Dick and Harry; **von ~ zu Kunz** from pillar to post (Brit), from one place to another

hin-: hin+zäh|len VT sep to count out (jdm to sb); **hin+zau|bern** VT sep (fig) to rustle or whip up (inf); **hin+zie|hen** sep irreg **VT a** (= zu sich ziehen) to draw or pull (zu towards); (fig: = anziehen) to attract (zu to); **es zieht sie zur Kunst hin** she feels attracted to art **b** (fig: = in die Länge ziehen) to draw or drag out **VI** aux sein **a** (= sich in bestimmte Richtung bewegen) to move (über +acc across, zu towards); (= weggehen, -marschieren) to move or go away **b** (Liter: Wolken, Rauch etc) to drift, to move (an +dat across) **c** (= umziehen) to move there **VR a** (= lange dauern) to drag on; (= sich verzögern) to be delayed **b** (= sich erstrecken) to stretch, to extend; **hin+zie|len** VI sep auf etw (acc) ~ to aim at sth; (Pläne etc) to be aimed at sth; (Bemerkung) to refer to sth

hin|zu [hɪn'tsuː] ADV (räumlich) there, thither (obs); (= überdies, obendrein) besides, in addition; **~ kommt noch, dass ich ...** moreover I ...

hin|zu-: hin|zu+be|kom|men ptp hinzubekommen VT sep irreg to get in addition; **hin|zu+den|ken** VT sep irreg to add in one's mind or imagination; **hin|zu+dich|ten** VT sep = hinzuerfinden; **hin|zu+er|fin|den** ptp hinzuerfunden VT sep irreg to make up and add sth (zu to); **hin|zu+fü|gen** VT sep to add (+dat to); (= beilegen) to enclose; **Hin|zu|fü|gung** F addition; **unter ~ von etw** (form) by adding sth; (als Beilage) enclosing sth; **hin|zu+ge|sel|len** ptp hinzugesellt VR sep (geh) to join (jdm sb); **hin|zu+ge|win|nen** ptp hinzugewonnen VT sep irreg to get in addition; **neue Mitglieder ~** to gain; **hin|zu+kau|fen** VTI sep to buy in addition (zu to); **Karten ~** to buy more or additional tickets; **hin|zu+kom|men** VI sep irreg aux sein **a** (= hinkommen, eintreffen) to arrive; **sie kam gerade hinzu, als ...** she happened to come on the scene when ...; **es werden später noch mehrere ~** more people will join us later or will come along later; (zu etw) (= sich anschließen) to join sth **b** (= zusätzlich eintreten) to supervene, to ensue; (= beigefügt werden) to be added; **zu etw ~** to be added to sth; **es kommt noch hinzu, dass ...** there is also the fact that ...; **kommt sonst noch etwas hinzu?** will there be anything else?; **hin|zu+neh|men** VT sep irreg to include; **etw zu etw ~** to add sth to sth; **hin|zu+rech|nen** VT sep to add on; **hin|zu+set|zen** VT sep to add; **hin|zu+sto|ßen** VI sep irreg aux sein (geh = hinzukommen) to arrive, to join up with; **hin|zu+tre|ten** VI sep irreg aux sein **a** (= herantreten) to come up; **zu den anderen ~** to join the others **b** (zusätzlich) = hinzukommen b; **hin|zu+tun** VT sep irreg (inf) to add; **Hin|zu|tun** NT (= Hinzutun) to add; **hin|zu+zäh|len** VT sep to add; **hin|zu+zie|hen** VT sep irreg to consult; **Hin|zu|zie|hung** F, no pl consultation (+gen with); **unter ~ eines Lexikons** by consulting an encyclop(a)edia

Hiob ['hiːɔp] M **-s** Job; **das Buch ~** the Book of Job

Hiobs|bot|schaft F, **Hiobs|post** F (old) bad news no pl or tidings pl

hip [hɪp] ADJ (sl) hip (inf)

Hip-Hop ['hɪphɔp] M **-(s)**, no pl, **Hip|hop** ▲ M **-(s)**, no pl (Mus) hip-hop

Hip|pe ['hɪpə] F **-, -n** (= Messer) pruning knife; (= Sense des Todes) scythe

hipp, hipp, hur|ra ['hɪp 'hɪp hʊ'raː] INTERJ hip, hip, hurrah or hurray

Hipp|hipp|hur|ra ['hɪp'hɪphʊ'raː] NT **-s, -s** cheer; **ein dreifaches ~** three cheers

Hip|pie ['hɪpi] M **-s, -s** hippie

Hip|po|drom [hɪpo'droːm] NT OR M **-s, -e** hippodrome

hip|po|kra|tisch [hɪpo'kraːtɪʃ] ADJ Hippocratic; **~er Eid** Hippocratic oath

Hirn [hɪrn] NT **-(e)s, -e a** (Anat) brain **b** (inf) (= Kopf) head; (= Verstand) brains pl, mind; **sich** (dat) **das ~ zermartern** to rack one's brain(s); **diese Idee ist doch nicht deinem ~ entsprungen?** that's not your own idea or your brainwave, is it? **c** (Cook) brains pl

Hirn- → auch Gehirn-: **Hirn|an|hang** M, **Hirn|an|hang(s)|drü|se** F (Anat) pituitary gland; **Hirn|funk|ti|on** F (= Funktion) brain function, function of the brain; (= Funktionieren) functioning of the brain; **hirn|ge|schä|digt** ADJ brain-damaged; **Hirn|ge|spinst** NT fantasy; **Hirn|haut** F (Anat) meninges pl; **Hirn|haut|ent|zün|dung** F (Med) meningitis; **hirn|los** ADJ brainless; **Hirn|lo|sig|keit** F (fig pej) brainlessness; (Handlung) crazy thing to do; **Hirn|mas|se** F cerebral matter; **Hirn|rin|de** F (Anat) cerebral cortex; **hirn|ris|sig** ADJ hare-brained; **Hirn|scha|den** M brain damage; **Hirn|scha|le** F (Anat) cranium; **Hirn|stamm** M (Anat) brainstem; **Hirn|sub|stanz** F (Anat) cerebral matter; **Hirn|tod** M (Med) brain death; **hirn|tot** ADJ braindead; **Hirn|to|te(r)** MF decl as adj braindead person/man/woman; **die ~n** the braindead; **Hirn|tu|mor** M brain tumour (Brit) or tumor (US); **hirn|ver|brannt** ADJ hare-brained; **Hirn|win|dung** F (Anat) convolution of the brain; **Hirn|zent|rum** NT brain centre (Brit) or center (US)

Hirsch [hɪrʃ] M **-es, -e a** (= Paarhufer) deer; (= Rothirsch) red deer; (= männlicher Rothirsch) stag; (Cook) venison **b** (inf: Schimpfwort) clod (Brit inf), clod (US inf)

Hirsch-: Hirsch|art F kind or species sing of deer; **Hirsch|bock** M stag; **Hirsch|bra|ten** M (Cook) roast of venison; (= Gericht) roast venison; **Hirsch|brunft** F, **Hirsch|brunst** F rut; **zur Zeit der ~** during the rutting season; **Hirsch|fän|ger** M hunting knife; **Hirsch|ge|weih** NT antlers pl

Hirsch|horn NT horn

Hirsch|horn-: Hirsch|horn|knopf M horn button; **Hirsch|horn|salz** NT (Chem) ammonium carbonate

Hirsch-: Hirsch|jagd F stag hunt; **Hirsch|kä|fer** M stag beetle; **Hirsch|kalb** NT (male) fawn, (male) deer calf; **Hirsch|keu|le** F haunch of venison; **Hirsch|kuh** F hind; **Hirsch|le|der** NT buckskin, deerskin; **hirsch|le|dern** ADJ buckskin, deerskin; **Hirsch|le|der|ne** [-leːdənə] F decl as adj (esp Aus) buckskin breeches pl, buckskins pl (US)

Hir|se ['hɪrzə] F **-, -n** millet

Hir|se-: Hir|se|brei M millet gruel; **Hir|se|korn** NT pl **-körner** millet seed

Hirt [hɪrt] M **-en, -en** (dated) herdsman; (= Schafhirt) shepherd; **wie der ~, so die Herde** (Prov) like master, like man (prov) → auch Hirtin

Hir|te ['hɪrtə] M **-n, -n a** = Hirt **b** (Eccl: = Seelsorger) shepherd; **der Gute ~** the Good Shepherd

Hir|ten-: Hir|ten|amt NT (Eccl) pastorate, pastorship; **Hir|ten|brief** M (Eccl) pastoral; **Hir|ten|dich|tung** F (Liter) pastoral poetry; **Hir|ten|flö|te** F shepherd's pipe; **Hir|ten|ge|dicht** NT pastoral; **Hir|ten|gott** M god of shepherds; **Hir|ten|hund** M sheepdog; **Hir|ten|jun|ge** M, **Hir|ten|kna|be** M (liter) shepherd boy; **Hir|ten|lied** NT shepherd's song; **hir|ten|los** ADJ (lit, fig) shepherdless; **Hir|ten|mäd|chen** NT young shepherdess; **Hir|ten|spiel** NT pastoral (play); **Hir|ten|stab** M shepherd's crook; (Eccl) crosier; **Hir|ten|tä|schel|(kraut)** NT ['hɪrtntɛʃl-] **-s, -** shepherd's-purse; **Hir|ten|volk** NT pastoral people

Hir|tin ['hɪrtɪn] F **-, -nen** herdswoman; (= Schafhirtin) shepherdess → auch Hirt

His [hɪs] NT **-, -**, **his** NT **-, -** (Mus) B sharp

Hisb Allah [hɪsˈbɔlaː] F -, *no pl*, **His|bol|lah** [hɪsˈbɔla] F -, *no pl* Hizbollah

His|pa|nis|mus [hɪspaˈnɪsmʊs] M -, **Hispanis-men** [-mən] (*Ling*) Hispanicism

His|pa|nist [hɪspaˈnɪst] M -en, -en, **His|pa|nis|tin** [-ˈnɪstɪn] F -, -nen Spanish specialist, Hispanist; (= *Student*) Spanish student; (= *Professor etc*) Spanish lecturer/professor

His|pa|nis|tik [hɪspaˈnɪstɪk] F -, *no pl* Spanish (language and literature)

his|sen [ˈhɪsn] VT to hoist

His|ta|min [hɪstaˈmiːn] NT -s, *no pl* histamine

His|to|lo|ge [hɪstoˈloːgə] M -n, -n, **His|to|lo|gin** [-ˈloːgɪn] F -, -nen histologist

His|to|lo|gie [hɪstoloˈgiː] F -, *no pl* histology

his|to|lo|gisch [hɪstoˈloːgɪʃ] ADJ histological

His|tör|chen [hɪsˈtøːɐ̯çən] NT -s, - anecdote; (= *Klatschgeschichte*) little tale or story

His|to|rie [hɪsˈtoːriə] F -, -n **a** *no pl* (*old:* = *Weltgeschichte*) history **b** (= *Erzählung*) story, tale; **Shakespeares ~** Shakespeare's history plays or histories

His|to|ri|en-: His|to|ri|en|ma|ler(in) M(F) historical painter; **His|to|ri|en|ma|le|rei** F historical painting

His|to|rik [hɪsˈtoːrɪk] F -, *no pl* history

His|to|ri|ker [hɪsˈtoːrɪkə] M -s, -, **His|to|ri|ke|rin** [-ərɪn] F -, -nen historian

His|to|ri|o|graf ▲ [hɪstorioˈgraːf] M -en, -en, **His|to|ri|o|gra|fin** ▲ [-ˈgraːfɪn] F -, -nen historiographer

his|to|risch [hɪsˈtoːrɪʃ] ADJ historical; *Verständnis, Kenntnisse auch* of history; (= *geschichtlich bedeutsam*) *Gestalt, Ereignis, Gebäude* historic ADV historically; **das ist ~ belegt** there is historical evidence for this, that is historically documented; **~ denken** to think in historical terms; **~ betrachtet** seen in the light of history, looked at or considered from a historical perspective

his|to|risch-kri|tisch ADJ *Ausgabe* historico-critical

His|to|ris|mus [hɪstoˈrɪsmʊs] M -, *no pl* historicism

Hit [hɪt] M -s, -s (*Mus, fig inf*) hit

Hit|ler [ˈhɪtlə] M -s Hitler

Hit|ler|bärt|chen M Hitler or toothbrush moustache

Hit|le|rei [hɪtləˈrai] F -, *no pl* (*pej inf*) (= *Hitlerfaschismus*) Hitlerite fascism; (= *Hitlerkult*) Hitlerite cult

Hit|ler-: Hit|ler|gruß M Hitler salute; **Hit|ler|ju|gend** F Hitler Youth (organization); **Hit|ler|jun|ge** M member of the Hitler Youth; **Hit|ler|reich** NT -, *no pl* (Third) Reich; **Hit|ler|zeit** F Hitler era

Hit-: Hit|lis|te F (*Mus*) charts *pl → auch* **Hitparade**; **Hit|pa|ra|de** F hit parade; **in der ~** (*Mus*) in the charts *pl*; **hit|ver|däch|tig** ADJ **ein ~es** Lied a potential hit; **der Song ist ~** the song could hit the charts

Hit|ze [ˈhɪtsə] F -, -n **a** heat; (= *Hitzewelle*) heat wave; **~ abweisend** heat-repellent; **vor ~ umkommen** to be sweltering (in the heat); **eine ~ ist das!** the heat (is incredible)!; **die fliegende ~ bekommen** (*Med*) to get hot flushes (*Brit*) or flashes (*US*); (*inf*) to get all hot and bothered; **bei starker/mittlerer/mäßiger ~ backen** (*Cook*) bake in a hot/medium/moderate oven **b** (*fig*) passion; **in ~ geraten** to get heated; **leicht in ~ geraten** to get worked up easily; **jdn in ~ bringen** to get sb all worked up; **sich in ~ reden** to get oneself all worked up; **in der ~ des Gefecht(e)s** (*fig*) in the heat of the moment **c** (*Zool*) heat

Hit|ze-: hit|ze|ab|wei|send △ ADJ → Hitze a; **Hit|ze|aus|schlag** M heat rash, prickly heat *no art*; **hit|ze|be|stän|dig** ADJ heat-resistant; **Hit|ze|be|stän|dig|keit** F heat resistance; **Hit|ze|bläs|chen** [-ˌblɛːsçən] PL heat spots *pl* (*Brit*), heat rash *sing*; **Hit|ze|ein|wir|kung** F

effect of (the) heat; **hit|ze|emp|find|lich** ADJ sensitive to heat; **Hit|ze|fe|ri|en** PL (*Sch*) time off from school on account of excessively hot weather; **hit|ze|fest** ADJ heat-resistant, heatproof; **hit|ze|frei** ADJ ~ **haben** to have time off from school on account of excessively hot weather

---

HITZEFREI

Since German school holidays are spread out through the summer, lessons take place in July and August when it can be very hot. If at noon the temperature is above 30°C in the shade, the day is declared **hitzefrei** and pupils and teachers are sent home.

Hit|ze-: Hit|ze|pe|ri|o|de F hot spell; **Hit|ze|pi|ckel** PL (*inf*) heat spots *pl* (*Brit*), heat rash *sing*; **Hit|ze|(schutz)|schild** M heat shield; **Hit|ze|stau** M heat accumulation, accumulation of heat, build-up of heat; **Hit|ze|wal|lung** F *usu pl* (*Med*) hot flush (*Brit*) or flash (*US*); **Hit|ze|wel|le** F heat wave

hit|zig [ˈhɪtsɪç] ADJ **a** (= *aufbrausend*) *Mensch* hot-headed; *Antwort, Reaktion, Atmosphäre, Debatte* heated; (= *leidenschaftlich*) *Temperament, Typ, Diskussionsteilnehmer* passionate; *Blut* hot; **~ werden** (*Mensch*) to flare up; (*Debatte*) to grow heated; **nicht so ~!** don't get so excited!, hold your horses! (*inf*); **ein ~er Kopf** (*geh*) a hothead **b** (*dated Med:* = *fiebrig*) *Kopf, Gesichtsfarbe* fevered; *Fieber* high **c** (*Zool*) on (*esp Brit*) or in heat ADV (= *heftig*) heatedly; **eine Debatte ~ führen** to lead a heated debate; **es ging ~ zu** things got heated

Hit|zig|keit F -, *no pl* (*von Mensch*) hot-headedness; (*von Antwort, Reaktion, Debatte*) heatedness; (*von Temperament, Typ, Diskussionsteilnehmer*) passion

Hitz-: Hitz|kopf M hothead; **hitz|köp|fig** ADJ hot-headed; **Hitz|schlag** M (*Med*) heat-stroke

HIV [haːiːˈfau] NT -(s), (*rare*) -(s) *abbr von* **Human Immunodeficiency Virus** HIV

HIV- [haːiːˈfau] *in cpds* HIV-; **HIV-in|fi|ziert** [haːiːˈfau-] ADJ HIV-infected; **HIV-ne|ga|tiv** [-ˈneːgatiːf] ADJ HIV-negative; **HIV-Ne|ga|ti|ve(r)** [-ˈneːgatiːvə] MF *decl as adj* person who is HIV-negative; **HIV-po|si|tiv** [-ˈpoːzitiːf] ADJ HIV-positive; **HIV-Po|si|ti|ve(r)** [-ˈpoːzitiːvə] MF *decl as adj* person who is HIV-positive; **HIV-Test** M HIV test; **HIV-Vi|rus** NT HIV-virus

Hi|wi [ˈhiːvi] M -s, -s **a** *abbr von* Hilfswillige(r) **b** (*Univ sl*) helper **c** (*pej inf:* = *Hilfskraft*) dogsbody (*Brit inf*), drudge (*US*)

hj. *abbr von* **halbjährlich**

Hj. *abbr von* **Halbjahr**

hl. *abbr von* **heilig**

Hl. *abbr von* **Heilige(r)** St

hm [hm] INTERJ hm

H-Milch [ˈhaː-] F long-life milk

h-Moll [ˈhaː-] NT -, *no pl* B-minor

HNO-Arzt [haːɛnˈʔoː-] M , **HNO-Ärz|tin** F ENT specialist

hob *pret von* **heben**

Hob|by [ˈhɔbi] NT -s, -s hobby

Hob|by-: Hob|by|fe|ri|en PL activity holiday *sing* (*Brit*), golfing/climbing/painting *etc* vacation (*US*); **Hob|by|fo|to|graf(in)** M(F) amateur photographer; **Hob|by|gärt|ner(in)** M(F) amateur or keen gardener; **sie ist ~in** gardening is her hobby; **Hob|by|koch** M , **Hob|by|kö|chin** F *erl as* ~ cooking is his hobby; **Hob|by|raum** M hobby room, workroom

Ho|bel [ˈhoːbl] M -s, - (*Tech*) plane; (*Cook*) slicer

Ho|bel-: Ho|bel|bank F *pl* -bänke carpenter's or joiner's bench; **Ho|bel|ei|sen** NT plane iron; **Ho|bel|ma|schi|ne** F planer, planing machine; **Ho|bel|mes|ser** NT plane iron

ho|beln [ˈhoːbln] VT **a** *auch vi* (*Tech*) to plane (*an etw* (*dat*) sth); (= *glätten*) *Brett* to plane down; **wo gehobelt wird, da fallen Späne** (*Prov*) you can't make an omelette without breaking eggs (*Prov*) **b** (*Cook*) to slice

Ho|bel|span M , (*Aus*) **Ho|bel|schar|te** F shaving

Ho|boe [hoˈboːə] F -, -n (*old*) oboe

---

hoch [hoːx]

1 ADJEKTIV	2 ADVERB

1 – ADJEKTIV
attr **hohe(r, s)** [ˈhoːə], *comp* **höher** [ˈhøːɐ], *superl* **≈ste(r, s)** [ˈhøːçstə]

a längenmäßig high; *Wuchs, Baum, Mast* tall; *Leiter* tall, long; **ein hohes, geräumiges Zimmer** a spacious room with a high ceiling, a spacious, high-ceilinged room; **der Schnee lag/das Wasser stand zwei Meter hoch** the snow/water was two metres (*Brit*) or meters (*US*) deep; **der Eiffelturm ist 321 m hoch** the Eiffel tower is 321 metres (*Brit*) or meters (*US*) high; **das ist mir zu hoch** (*fig inf*) that's (well) above (*esp Brit*) or over my head

b mengenmäßig *Preis, Verdienst, Temperatur, Druck etc* high; *Betrag, Summe* large; *Strafe, Gewicht* heavy; *Schaden* extensive; *Lotteriegewinn* big; *Profit* high, big; **die britische Armee musste hohe Verluste hinnehmen** the British Army suffered heavy losses; **in hohem Maße verdächtig** highly suspicious; **in hohem Maße gefährdet** in grave danger; **das ist in hohem Maße abhängig von ...** this is heavily dependent on ...; **mit hoher Wahrscheinlichkeit** in all probability

c Alter great, advanced; **ein hohes Alter erreichen** to live to a great or an advanced age; **er ist hoch an Jahren** he has reached a great or an advanced age

d Mus high; **das hohe C** top C

e = bedeutend *Stellung, Position, Rang, Amt, Adel, Meinung, Lebensstandard, Ansprüche* high; *Offizier* high, noble; *Ehre, Bedeutung, Genuss, Gut, Glück* great; *Fest, Besuch, Feiertag, Jubiläum* important; *Offizier* high-ranking; **er/sie ist hoher** or **der hohe Favorit** he/she is the hot favourite (*Brit*) or favorite (*US*); **ein hohes Tier** (*fig inf*) a big fish (*inf*); **hohe Herrschaften** (*form: als Anrede*) ladies and gentlemen; **hohe Persönlichkeiten aus Politik und Wirtschaft** important or top (*inf*) politicians and businesspeople; **ein Mann von hohem Ansehen/hoher Bildung** a man of high standing/of great culture; **das hohe Haus** (*Parl*) the House → **Gewalt**

f feste Wendungen **in hoher Blüte stehen** to be in full bloom; (*Mensch*) to be in one's prime; (*Kultur*) to be at its zenith; **hohe Flut** spring tide; **die hohe Jagd** deer hunting; **das Hohe Lied** (*Bibl*) the Song of Songs; **ein hohes Lied auf jdn/etw singen** to sing sb's/sth's praises; **der hohe Norden** the far North; **die hohe Schule** (*beim Reiten*) haute école; (*old geh:* = *Hochschule*) university; **die hohe Schule des Lebens** the school of life; **im hohen Sommer** at the height of summer; **es ist hohe Zeit** (*geh*) it's high time → **höchste(r, s)**, **bestimmen**, **Welle** a, **Kopf** a, **Tasse**, **Bogen** a, **Kante**

2 – ADVERB
comp **höher**, *superl* **am ≈sten**

a = oben high; **hoch oben** high up; **ein hoch gelegener Ort in den Alpen** a place situated high up in the Alps; **hoch am Himmel** high in the sky; (*Flugzeug, Vogel*) high up in the sky; **die Sonne steht hoch** the sun is high in the sky; **10.000 Fuß hoch fliegen** to fly at a height of 10,000 feet; **zwei Treppen hoch wohnen** to live two floors up; **hoch sitzen** to sit up high; **die See geht hoch** the sea is running high; **wie hoch steht das Thermometer?** what's the temperature?; **der Alkoholgehalt liegt sehr hoch** the alcohol level is very high; **wie hoch kalku-**

lieren Sie seine Chancen? how high would you put *or* how would you rate his chances? **b** = nach oben up; **er sah zu uns hoch** (*inf*) he looked up to us; **hoch emporragend** towering (up); **hoch werfen** to throw high; **hoch gewachsen** tall; **ein hoch aufgeschossener Mann** a very tall man; **den Kopf hoch tragen** to hold one's head high; **die Nase hoch tragen** (*inf*) to be stuck-up (*inf*) *or* toffee-nosed (*Brit inf*); **nach Hamburg hoch** up to Hamburg **c** Mus high; **die Sopranistin sang etwas zu hoch** the soprano sang a bit sharp **d** Math **3 hoch 2** 3 squared, 3 (raised) to the power (of) 2; **7 hoch 3** 7 cubed, 7 to the power of 3; **3 hoch 4/5** 3 raised to the power of 4/5 **e** im übertragenen Sinn

◆ **hoch + Adjektiv hoch begabt** highly gifted *or* talented; **er ist hoch betagt** he has reached a great *or* an advanced age; **hoch empfindlich** (*Tech, Material, Gerät, Instrumente*) highly sensitive; *Film* fast; *Stoff* very delicate; **diese Farbe/dieser Teppich ist hoch empfindlich** this colour (*Brit*) *or* color (*US*)/carpet shows up everything; **hoch verzinslich** high interest-bearing; **sie sind uns als Gäste hoch willkommen** we are delighted to welcome them as our guests; **hoch zufrieden** very satisfied

◆ **hoch + Verb**

Die in Verbindung mit **hoch** verwendeten Verben sind alphabetisch angeordnet.

das rechne ich ihm hoch an (I think) that is very much to his credit; **hoch angesehen** highly regarded; **hoch auflösend** (*Comput, TV*) high-resolution; **hoch beansprucht** (*Tech*) highly stressed; **hoch beglückt** highly delighted; **ein hoch beladener Lastwagen** a lorry with a high load; **hoch besteuert** heavily taxed; **hoch bezahlt** highly paid; **hoch dotiert** (*Mensch*) highly remunerated; *Arbeit* highly remunerative; **hoch geehrt** highly honoured (*Brit*) *or* honored (*US*); **hoch geehrter Herr** (*old: im Brief*) esteemed Sir (*old*); **hoch einschätzen** to estimate generously; **zu hoch einschätzen** to overestimate; **hoch entwickelt** (*Kultur, Volk, Land*) highly developed; (= *verfeinert*) *Geräte, Maschinen, Methoden* highly sophisticated; **hoch erfreut** very pleased; **hoch favorisiert sein** to be the hot favourite (*Brit*) *or* favorite (*US*); **hoch gewinnen** to win handsomely; **es ging hoch her** (*inf*) there were lively goings-on (*inf*); **hoch hinauswollen** to be ambitious; **hoch industrialisiert** highly industrialized; **wie hoch kommt das?** how much is that?; **wenn es hoch kommt** (*inf*) at (the) most, at the outside; **hoch lebe der König!** long live the King!; **hoch qualifiziert** highly qualified; *Arbeitsplätze* for the highly qualified; **hoch schätzen** to estimate generously; **zu hoch schätzen** to overestimate; **hoch geschätzt** (*Mensch*) highly esteemed; *Organisation, Preis* highly prestigious; **in Japan ist dieses Gericht eine hoch geschätzte Delikatesse** in Japan, this dish is considered a great delicacy; **hoch setzen** *or* **spielen** to play for high stakes; **hoch spezialisiert** highly specialized; **hoch gesteckt** (*fig, Ziele*) ambitious; *Ansprüche, Erwartungen* considerable; **hoch stehend** (*gesellschaftlich*) of high standing; (*kulturell*) highly advanced; (*geistig*) highly intellectual; (*entwicklungsmäßig, qualitativ*) superior; **hoch gestellte Persönlichkeiten aus Politik und Wirtschaft** important *or* top (*inf*) politicians and businesspeople; **in der Rangordnung sehr hoch stehen** to be very high up in the hierarchy; **hoch verlieren** to lose heavily; **hoch verschuldet** deep in debt; **dieses Gemälde ist hoch versichert** this picture is heavily insured, this picture is insured for a large sum; **hoch wetten** to place high bets → **Kurs b, hochleben**

f andere Wendungen **die Polizei rückte an, 50 Mann hoch** (*inf*) the police arrived, 50 strong; **hoch!** cheers!; **die Menge rief hoch!** the crowd cheered

◆ **hoch in hoch in den Bergen** high in the mountains; **hoch in der Luft** high in the air; **hoch in den Siebzigern** in one's late seventies; **bis hoch ins 13. Jahrhundert** until well into the 13th century

◆ **hoch und heilig hoch und heilig versprechen** to promise faithfully; **hoch und heilig schwören** (*inf*) to swear blind (*inf*)

Hoch [hoːx] NT **-s, -s a** (= *Ruf*) **ein (dreifaches) ~ für** *or* **auf jdn ausbringen** to give three cheers for sb; **ein ~ dem Brautpaar** a toast to the bride and groom **b** (*Met, fig*) high

Hoch-: **hoch|acht|bar** ADJ *attr* (*dated*) highly respectable; **hoch ach|ten** ▲ VT to respect highly; **Hoch|ach|tung** F deep respect; **jdm seine ~ für seine Leistung zollen** to be full of admiration for sb's achievement; **bei aller ~ vor jdm/etw** with the (greatest) respect for sb/sth; **meine ~!** well done!; **mit vorzüglicher ~** (*form: Briefschluss*) yours faithfully; **hoch|ach|tungs|voll** ADV (*Briefschluss*) (*bei Anrede mit Sir/Madam*) yours faithfully (*Brit*), sincerely yours (*US*); (*bei Anrede mit Namen*) yours sincerely (*Brit*), sincerely yours (*US*); **Hoch|adel** M high nobility; **hoch|ak|tiv** ADJ *Atommüll etc* high-level; **hoch|ak|tu|ell** ADJ highly topical; **hoch|al|pin** ADJ (high) alpine; *Ausrüstung* high-altitude; **Hoch|al|pi|nist(in)** M(F) high-altitude climber; **Hoch|al|tar** M high altar; **Hoch|amt** NT (*Eccl*) High Mass; **hoch|an|ge|se|hen** △ ADJ *attr* → **hoch 2 e**; **hoch|an|stän|dig** ADJ very decent; **Hoch|an|ten|ne** F roof aerial (*Brit*) *or* antenna (*US*); **hoch|ar|bei|ten** VR *sep* to work one's way up; **hoch|auf|lö|send** △ ADJ → **hoch 2 e**; **Hoch|bahn** F elevated railway (*Brit*) *or* railroad (*US*), el (*US inf*); **Hoch|ba|rock** M OR NT high baroque; **Hoch|bau** M , *no pl* structural engineering → **Hoch-und-Tiefbau**; **hoch+bäu|men** [-bɔymən] VR *sep* (*Tier*) to rear; **hoch|be|an|sprucht** △ [-bəlanʃprʊxt] ADJ *attr* → **hoch 2 e**; **hoch|be|gabt** △ ADJ *attr* → **hoch 2 e**; **Hoch|be|gab|ten|för|de|rung** F bursary (*Brit*) *or* scholarship for gifted students; **Hoch|be|gab|te(r)** MF *decl as adj* gifted person *or* child; **hoch|be|glückt** [-bəɡlʏkt] ADJ *attr* supremely *or* blissfully happy; **hoch|bei|nig** ADJ long-legged; *Auto* high on the road; **hoch+be|kom|men** ptp **hochbekommen** VT *sep irreg Stein, Motorhaube etc* to (manage to) lift *or* get up; *Reißverschluss* to (manage to) get *or* do up; **er bekommt keinen hoch** (*inf: Erektion*) he can't get it up (*inf*); **hoch|be|la|den** △ ADJ *attr* → **hoch 2 e**; **hoch|be|rühmt** ADJ very famous; **hoch|be|tagt** ADJ aged *attr*, advanced in years; **Hoch|be|trieb** M (*in Geschäft, Fabrik etc*) peak period; (*im Verkehr*) rush hour; (= *Hochsaison*) high season; **~ haben** to be at one's/its busiest; **hoch+bie|gen** VTR *sep irreg* to bend up *or* upward(s); **hoch+bin|den** VT *sep irreg Haare, Pflanze* to tie up; **hoch+bli|cken** VI *sep* to look up; **Hoch|blü|te** F (*fig*) (*von Geschichte, Literatur*) golden age; **seine ~ haben** to be at its zenith; **hoch+bo|cken** VT *sep* to jack up; **hoch+brin|gen** VT *sep irreg* (*inf*) **a** (= *nach oben bringen*) to bring *or* take up **b** (*inf: hochheben, hochdrücken können*) to (manage to) get up; **einen/keinen ~** (*inf*) to be able/not to be able to get it up (*inf*) **c** (*fig*) (= *leistungsfähig machen*) to get going; *Kranken* to get back on his *etc* feet; *Schüler* to get up to scratch **d** (*fig inf:* = *ärgern*) **jdn ~** to get sb's back up (*inf*); **Hoch|burg** F (*fig*) stronghold; **Hoch|de|cker** [-dɛkɐ] M **-s, -** (*Aviat*) high-wing monoplane; **hoch|deutsch** ADJ standard *or* High German; **die ~e Lautverschiebung** the High German sound shift; **Hoch|deutsch(e)** NT standard *or* High German, the standard *or* High German language → *auch* **Deutsch(e)**; **hoch+die|nen** VR *sep* to work one's way up; **hoch|do|tiert** △ [-dotiːɐt] ADJ *attr* → **hoch 2 e**; **hoch+dre|hen** VT *sep Fenster* to wind up; *Motor* to rev

Hoch|druck M **a** *no pl* (*Met*) high pressure **b** *no pl* (*Typ:* = *Verfahren*) surface *or* relief printing **c** *pl* **-drucke** (*Typ:* = *Gedrucktes*) relief print **d** *no pl* (*Phys*) high pressure **e** *no pl* (*Med:* = *Blutdruck*) high blood pressure **f** *no pl* (*fig*) **mit ~ arbeiten** to work at full stretch

Hoch|druck-: **Hoch|druck|ge|biet** NT (*Met*) high-pressure area, anticyclone; **Hoch|druck|ver|fah|ren** NT (*Typ*) relief printing method

Hoch|druck|zo|ne F (*Met*) high-pressure area, anticyclone

Hoch-: **Hoch|ebe|ne** F plateau; **hoch|emp|find|lich** △ ADJ → **hoch 2 e**; **Hoch|ener|gie-La|ser** M high-energy laser; **hoch|ent|wi|ckelt** △ [-lɛntvɪklt] ADJ *attr* → **hoch 2 e**; **hoch|er|freut** [-ɛɐˈfrɔyt] ADJ delighted (*über +acc* at); **hoch|er|ho|ben** [-lɛɐˈhoːbn] ADJ raised high; **~en Hauptes** (*fig*) with (one's) head held high; **hoch|ex|plo|siv** ADJ (*lit, fig*) highly explosive; **hoch+fah|ren** *sep irreg* **VI** *aux sein* **a** (= *nach oben fahren*) to go up; (*in Auto*) to drive *or* go up **b** (*erschreckt*) to start (up); **aus dem Schlaf ~** to wake up with a start **c** (= *aufbrausen*) to flare up **VT** to take up; (*in Auto auch*) to drive up; (*fig*) *Produktion* to raise, to increase; *Reaktor* (= *in Betrieb nehmen*) to start up; (= *Leistung erhöhen*) to ramp up; *Computer* to boot up; **hoch|fah|rend** ADJ **a** (= *überheblich*) arrogant **b** = *hochfliegend*; **hoch|fein** ADJ (= *qualitativ hochwertig*) high quality; (= *auserlesen*) highly select; **hoch|fest** ADJ *Kunststoff* reinforced; **Hoch|fi|nanz** F high finance; **Hoch|flä|che** F plateau; **hoch flie|gen** ▲ VI *irreg aux sein* to fly up; (*Vogel auch*) to soar; (= *in die Luft geschleudert werden*) to be thrown up; **hoch|flie|gend** ADJ *Pläne, Ideen etc* ambitious; (= *übertrieben*) high-flown; **hoch|flo|rig** [-floːrɪç] ADJ *Samt, Teppich* deep-pile *attr*; **Hoch|form** F top form; **Hoch|for|mat** NT vertical format; **hoch|fre|quent** ADJ high frequency

Hoch|fre|quenz F (*Elec*) high frequency, radio frequency

Hoch|fre|quenz-: **Hoch|fre|quenz|strom** M high-frequency current; **Hoch|fre|quenz|tech|nik** F radio-frequency engineering

Hoch-: **Hoch|fri|sur** F upswept hairstyle; **sie hat eine ~** she wears her hair up; **Hoch|ga|ra|ge** F multistorey car park (*Brit*), multistory parking garage (*US*); **hoch|ge|be|ne|deit** [-ɡəbenedait] ADJ (*old, Eccl*) most blessed; **Hoch|ge|bir|ge** NT high mountains *pl*, high mountain region *or* area; **Hoch|ge|birgs|pflan|ze** F alpine plant; **hoch|ge|bo|ren** ADJ (*dated*) high-born; **(Eure** *or* **Euer) Hochgeboren** (*Anrede*) your Honour (*Brit*) *or* Honor (*US*); **seine Hochgeboren** his Honour (*Brit*) *or* Honor (*US*); **Hoch|ge|fühl** NT elation; **ein ~ haben** to have a feeling of elation, to feel elated; **im ~ des Sieges** elated by the victory; **hoch gehen** ▲ VI *irreg aux sein* (= *sich nach oben bewegen*) to rise; (*Preise*) to go up, to rise; (*Ballon*) to ascend, to rise; (*Wellen*) to surge; **hoch+ge|hen** VI *sep irreg aux sein* **a** (*inf:* = *hinaufgehen*) to go up **b** (*inf:* = *explodieren*) to blow up; (*Bombe*) to go off; **etw ~ lassen** to blow sth up **c** (*inf:* = *wütend werden*) to go through the roof; **da geht einem der Hut hoch** (*inf*) it's enough to make you blow your top (*inf*) **d** (*inf:* = *gefasst werden*) to get nabbed (*inf*); **jdn ~ lassen** to bust sb (*inf*); **hoch|geis|tig** ADJ highly intellectual; *Lektüre, Mensch* high-brow *no adv*; **hoch|ge|le|gen** △ ADJ *attr* → **hoch 2 a**; **hoch|ge|lehrt** ADJ erudite, very learned; **hoch|ge|mut** [-ɡəmuːt] ADJ (*geh*) cheerful, in good spirits; **Hoch|ge|nuss** ▲ M great *or* special treat; (= *großes Vergnügen*) great pleasure; **jdm ein ~ sein** to be a real treat for sb; **Hoch|ge|richt** NT (*Hist*) (= *Gericht*) criminal court; (= *Richtstätte*) scaffold; **hoch|ge|rüs|tet** [-ɡərʏstət] ADJ *Land* with a full military arsenal; *Technik, System* highly sophisticated; **eine ~e Supermacht** a military superpower; **hoch|ge|schätzt** △ ADJ *attr* → **hoch 2 e**; **hoch|ge|schlos|sen** ADJ *Kleid etc* high-necked

Hoch|ge|schwin|dig|keits- in cpds high-speed; **Hoch|ge|schwin|dig|keits|ka|me|ra** F high-speed camera; **Hoch|ge|schwin|dig|keits|stre|cke** F (Rail) high-speed rail link; **Hoch|ge|schwin|dig|keits|zug** M **a** (Rail) high-speed train **b** (= Rennstrecke) high-speed track; (Abschnitt) high-speed section

hoch-: hoch|ge|spannt ADJ (fig) Erwartungen extreme; **hoch|ge|steckt** △ [-gəʃtɛkt] ADJ → **hoch 2 e; hoch|ge|stellt** [-gəʃtɛlt] ADJ attr Ziffer superscript, superior → auch **hoch 2 e; hoch|ge|sto|chen** ADJ (pej inf) highbrow; Reden highfaluting; Stil pompous; (= eingebildet) stuck-up (inf); **hoch|ge|wach|sen** △ ADJ → **hoch 2 b; hoch|ge|züch|tet** [-gətsʏçtət] ADJ (usu pej) Motor souped-up (inf); Geräte fancy (inf); Tiere, Pflanzen overbred; System, Wohlfahrtsstaat etc over-developed

Hoch|glanz M high polish or shine; (Phot) gloss; **etw auf ~ polieren** or **bringen** to polish sth until it gleams; (fig) to make sth spick and span

Hoch|glanz- in cpds glossy; **Hoch|glanz|ab|zug** M (Phot) glossy print; **Hoch|glanz|blatt** NT (Press) glossy (inf)

hoch|glän|zend ADJ Stoff, Oberfläche very shiny; Papier, Fotoabzug very glossy; Möbel highly polished

Hoch|glanz-: Hoch|glanz|ma|ga|zin NT (Press) glossy magazine, glossy (inf); **Hoch|glanz|pa|pier** NT high gloss paper; **Hoch|glanz|po|li|tur** F (= Oberfläche) mirror polish or finish; (= Poliermittel) (furniture) polish

Hoch-: Hoch|go|tik F high gothic period; **hoch|gra|dig** [-graːdɪç] ADJ no pred extreme; (inf) Unsinn etc absolute, utter ADV extremely; **hoch+gu|cken** VI sep to look up; **hoch|ha|ckig** [-hakɪç] ADJ Schuhe high-heeled; **hoch+hal|ten** VT sep irreg **a** (= in die Höhe halten) to hold up **b** (= in Ehren halten) to uphold; **Hoch|haus** NT high-rise building, multistorey (Brit) or multistory (US) building; (= Wolkenkratzer) sky-scraper; **hoch+he|ben** VT sep irreg Hand, Arm to lift, to raise, to hold up; Kind, Last to lift up; **durch Hochheben der Hände abstimmen** to vote by (a) show of hands; **hoch|herr|schaft|lich** ADJ very elegant or grand; Wohnung auch palatial; **hoch|her|zig** ADJ generous, magnanimous; Mensch auch big-hearted; **Hoch|her|zig|keit** F [-hɛrtsɪçkaɪt] F ~, no pl generosity, magnanimity; (von Mensch auch) big-heartedness; **hoch|in|dust|ri|a|li|siert** △ [-ɪndustrializiːɐt] ADJ attr → **hoch 2 e; hoch|in|tel|li|gent** ADJ highly intelligent; **hoch|in|te|res|sant** ADJ very or most interesting; **hoch+ja|gen** VT sep (inf) **a** (= aufscheuchen) Vögel to scare up; Menschen to get up **b** (= sprengen) Motor to rev up; **hoch+ju|beln** VT sep (inf) Künstler, Film, Politiker etc to build up, to hype (inf); **hoch+käm|men** VT sep Haar to put up; **hoch|kant** F [hoːxkant] ADV **a** (lit) on end; **~ stellen** to up-end, to put on end **b** (fig inf: auch hochkantig) **~ hinauswerfen/hinausfliegen** to chuck/be chucked out (inf); **hoch|ka|rä|tig** ADJ Diamanten, Gold high-carat **b** (fig) top-class ADV ein **~ besetzter Film** a film with a top-class cast; **Hoch|kir|che** F High Church; **hoch|klapp|bar** ADJ Tisch, Stuhl folding; Sitz tip-up; **hoch+klap|pen** sep VT Tisch, Stuhl to fold up; Sitz to tip up; Kühlerhaube, Deckel to raise, to lift up; Mantelkragen to turn up VI aux sein (Tisch, Stuhl) to fold up; (Sitz) to tip up; **hoch+klet|tern** VI sep aux sein (lit, fig) to climb up; **hoch+ko|chen** sep VT Thema to stir up VI aux sein (Emotionen) to run high; **hoch+kom|men** VI sep irreg aux sein **a** (= hinauf-, heraufkommen) to come up **b** (inf) **das Essen ist ihm hochgekommen** he threw up (his meal) (inf); **es kommt mir hoch** it makes me sick **c** (= aufstehen können) to (manage to) get up; (fig: = sich aufraffen, gesund werden) to get back on one's feet **d** (inf: beruflich, gesellschaftlich) to come up in the world; **niemanden (neben sich dat) ~ lassen** not to toler-

ate competition; **hoch|kom|pli|ziert** ADJ highly complicated or complex; **Hoch|kon|junk|tur** F boom; **hoch+kön|nen** VI sep irreg (inf) (= aufstehen können) to be able to get up; (= hinaufsteigen können) to be able to get up (auf etw (acc) onto sth, auf Berg the mountain); **hinten nicht mehr ~** (inf) to be more dead than alive; **hoch|kon|zent|riert** ADJ **a** (Chem) highly concentrated **b** Mensch very focused; Gesichtsausdruck of great concentration; **hoch+krem|peln** VT sep Ärmel, Hosenbeine to roll up; **hoch+krie|gen** VT sep (inf) = hochbekommen; **hoch|kul|ti|viert** ADJ highly sophisticated; Lebensart highly civilized; **Hoch|kul|tur** F (very) advanced civilization; **hoch+kur|beln** VT sep Fenster to wind up; **Hoch|la|den** VT sep irreg (Comput) to upload; **Hoch|land** NT highland; **das schottische ~** the Scottish Highlands pl; **Hoch|län|der** [ˈhoːxlɛndɐ] M -s, -, **Hoch|län|de|rin** [-ərɪn] F -, -nen highlander; **Hoch|land|kaf|fee** M high-grown coffee; **Hoch|lau|tung** F (Ling) Standard German pronunciation; **hoch+le|ben** VI sep jdn ~ lassen to give three cheers for sb; **er lebe hoch!** three cheers (for him)!; **hoch lebe der König!** long live the King!; **hoch+le|gen** VT sep **a** Beine etc to put up **b** (inf: = nach oben legen) to put high up

Hoch|leis|tung F first-class performance

Hoch|leis|tungs- in cpds high-performance; **Hoch|leis|tungs|mo|tor** M high-performance engine; **Hoch|leis|tungs|öl** NT heavy-duty oil; **Hoch|leis|tungs|sor|te** F (Agr) high-yield variety; **Hoch|leis|tungs|sport** M top-class sport; **Hoch|leis|tungs|sport|ler(in)** M(F) top athlete; **Hoch|leis|tungs|trai|ning** NT intensive training

höch|lich(st) [ˈhøːçlɪçst] ADV (dated) highly, greatly, most

Hoch-: hoch|löb|lich ADJ (dated) very or highly praiseworthy; (iro) most appreciated; **Hoch|lohn|land** NT country with high wage costs; **Hoch|mit|tel|al|ter** NT high Middle Ages pl; **hoch|mo|dern** [-modɛrn] ADJ very modern, ultra-modern ADV in a very modern way, show in an ultra-modern way; **hoch|mo|disch** ADJ highly or very fashionable, the height of fashion pred; **hoch|mö|gend** ADJ influential; **Hoch|moor** NT moor; **Hoch|mut** M arrogance; **~ kommt vor dem Fall** (Prov) pride comes before a fall (Prov); **hoch|mü|tig** [ˈhoːxmyːtɪç] ADJ arrogant; **Hoch|mü|tig|keit** F ~, no pl arrogance; **hoch|nä|sig** [ˈhoːxnɛːzɪç] (inf) ADJ snooty (inf) ADV snootily (inf), haughtily, snobbishly; **Hoch|nä|sig|keit** F -, no pl (inf) snootiness (inf); **Hoch|ne|bel** M (low) stratus; **hoch+neh|men** VT sep irreg **a** (= heben) to lift; Kind, Hund to pick or lift up **b** (dial: in oberes Stockwerk) to take up **c** (inf: = necken) **jdn ~** to pull sb's leg **d** (inf: = verhaften) to pick up (inf); **Hoch|ofen** M blast furnace; **hoch|of|fi|zi|ell** ADJ highly or extremely formal; **hoch+päp|peln** VT sep (inf) Tier, Kind, Kranken to feed up; (fig) to nurse back to health; **Hoch|par|ter|re** NT raised ground floor; **Hoch|pla|teau** NT plateau; **hoch|po|ly|mer** [-polymeːɐ] ADJ (Chem) high-polymeric; **hoch|prei|sig** [-praizɪç] ADJ high-priced; **Hoch|preis|po|li|tik** F policy of high pricing; **hoch|pro|zen|tig** ADJ alkoholische Getränke high-proof; Lösung highly concentrated; Gewinnzuwächse, Rabatte high-percentage; Wertpapiere high-interest; **hoch+pu|schen** VT sep Problem to play up, to make a lot of; **er wurde zur literarischen Sensation hochgepuscht** he was built up to be a literary sensation; **hoch|qua|li|fi|ziert** △ ADJ attr → **hoch 2 e; Hoch|rad** NT penny-farthing (Brit) or ordinary (US) (bicycle); **hoch|räd|rig** ADJ with high wheels; **hoch+ra|gen** VI sep aux sein or haben (Bäume) to rise (up); (Berge, Türme, Häuser) to tower (up), to rise (up); **hoch+ran|ken** VIR sep (vi: aux sein) to creep (up), to climb (up); **hoch+rech|nen** sep VT to project VI to make a projec-

tion; **Hoch|rech|nung** F projection; **Hoch|reck** NT high or horizontal bar; **hoch+re|cken** sep VT Arme, Hände to raise or stretch up; **den Hals** or **Kopf ~** to crane one's neck VR to draw oneself up; **hoch|rein** ADJ high-purity; **hoch+rei|ßen** VT sep irreg Arme to bring up; Kamera, Waffe to lift quickly; (Aviat) to put into a steep climb, to hoick (spec); **Hoch|re|li|ef** NT high relief; **Hoch|re|nais|sance** F high renaissance; **hoch|rot** ADJ bright red; **mit ~em Gesicht** with one's face as red as a beetroot (Brit) or beet (US); **Hoch|ruf** M cheer; **hoch+rüs|ten** VT sep **ein Land ~** to increase the weaponry of a country; **Hoch|rüs|tung** F , no pl arms build-up; **hoch+rut|schen** VI sep aux sein (Kleidungsstück) to ride up; (inf: = aufrücken) to move up; **Hoch|sai|son** F high season; **hoch schät|zen** ▲ VT to respect highly; **hoch+schau|keln** VT sep Problem, Angelegenheit to blow up VR to work oneself up; **hoch+scheu|chen** VT sep (inf) = aufscheuchen; **hoch+schie|ßen** sep irreg VI aux sein to shoot up VT Feuerwerksrakete, Leuchtkugel to send up; **hoch+schla|gen** sep irreg VT Kragen to turn up VI (aux sein) (Wellen) to surge up; (Flammen) to leap up; **hoch+schnel|len** VI sep aux sein (Lachse) to leap up; (Feder, Mensch, Preise auch) to shoot up; **Hoch|schrank** M tall cupboard; **hoch schrau|ben** ▲ VT (lit) to raise; (fig) Preise to force up; Erwartungen to raise; Forderungen, Ansprüche to increase; **hoch+schre|cken** VTI sep (vi: irreg aux sein) = aufschrecken

Hoch|schul-: Hoch|schul|ab|schluss ▲ M degree; **mit ~ with a degree; Hoch|schul|ab|sol|vent(in)** M(F) graduate; **Hoch|schul(-aus)|bil|dung** F (= Ausbildung) college training; (an Universität) university training; (= Bildung) university education

Hoch|schu|le F college; (= Universität) university; **Technische ~** technical college, college of technology

Hoch|schü|ler(in) M(F) student; (Univ auch) undergraduate

Hoch|schul-: Hoch|schul|leh|rer(in) M(F) → Hochschule college/university teacher, lecturer (Brit); **Hoch|schul|po|li|tik** F higher education policy; **Hoch|schul|re|form** F university reform; **Hoch|schul|rei|fe** F academic standard required for university entrance **er hat (die) ~** he's got his A-levels (Brit), ≈ he's graduated from high school (US); **Hoch|schul|stu|di|um** NT higher education, university education; **Hoch|schul|we|sen** NT , no pl system of higher education, university system; **Hoch|schul|zu|gang** M university entrance or admission

hoch|schwan|ger ADJ well advanced in pregnancy, very pregnant

Hoch|see F high sea; **auf ~** on the high seas or open sea

Hoch|see-: Hoch|see|fi|sche|rei F deep-sea fishing; **Hoch|see|jacht** F ocean(-going) yacht; **Hoch|see|kut|ter** M deep-sea cutter; **Hoch|see|schiff|fahrt** ▲ F deep-sea shipping; **hoch|see|tüch|tig** ADJ ocean-going

Hoch-: hoch+se|hen VI sep irreg to look up; **Hoch|seil** NT high wire, tightrope; **Hoch|seil|akt** M (von Artisten) high-wire or tightrope act; (fig) tightrope walk; **hoch|sen|si|bel** ADJ Apparat, Angelegenheit, Gespräch, Daten, Patient highly sensitive; **Hoch|si|cher|heits|ge|fäng|nis** NT high-security prison; **Hoch|si|cher|heits|trakt** M high-security wing; **Hoch|sitz** M (Hunt) (raised) hide; **Hoch|som|mer** M height of the summer; (= Zeitabschnitt) midsummer no art; **hoch|som|mer|lich** ADJ very summery

Hoch|span|nung F (Elec) high voltage, high tension; (fig) high tension; „**Vorsicht ~**" "danger - high voltage"

Hoch|span|nungs-: Hoch|span|nungs|lei|tung F high-tension line, power line; **Hoch|-**

span|nungs|mast M pylon; **Hoch|span|nungs|tech|nik** F high-voltage engineering

hoch|spe|zi|a|li|siert △ [-ʃpetsiali'si:ɐt] ADJ → hoch 2 e

Hoch-: hoch+spie|len VT sep (fig) to blow up, to play up; **etw (künstlich) ~** to blow sth (up) out of all proportion; **Hoch|spra|che** F standard language; **hoch|sprach|lich** ADJ standard; **~ Prosa** prose in standard German/English etc ADV **~ heißt es ...** in standard German/English etc that's ...; **hoch+sprin|gen** VI sep irreg aux sein **a** (inf: = aufspringen) to jump up (an jdm on sb); **auf etw** (acc) **~** to jump (up) on sth **b** (inf: = schnell hinauflaufen) to run up **c** infin, ptp only (Sport) to do the high jump; **Hoch|sprin|ger(in)** M(F) high jumper; **Hoch|sprung** M (= Disziplin) high jump; (= Sprung) jump

höchst [høːçst] ADJ → höchste(r, s) ADV (= überaus) highly, extremely, most

Höchst|al|ter [høːçst-] NT maximum age

Hoch-: hoch|stäm|mig ADJ Baum tall; Rosen long-stemmed; **Hoch|stand** M (Hunt) (raised) hide; **Hoch|sta|pe|lei** [hoːxʃtaːpə'lai] F -, -(Jur) fraud; (einzelner Fall) swindle, con trick; (fig: = Aufschneiderei) boasting no pl; **hoch+sta|peln** [hoːxʃtaːpl̩n] VI sep to be fraudulent, to practise fraud (form); (fig) to put one over (inf); **Hoch|stap|ler** [hoːxʃtaːplɐ] M -s, -, **Hoch|stap|le|rin** [-ərɪn] F -, -nen confidence trickster; (Mann auch) con man (inf); (fig) fraud; **Hoch|start** M (Sport) standing start

Höchst-: Höchst|be|trag [høːçst-] M maximum amount; **Höchst|bie|ten|de(r)** [høːçstbiːtndə] MF decl as adj highest bidder

höchs|te ADJ = höchste(r, s)

Höchs|te = Höchste(r), Höchste(s)

hoch-: hoch+ste|cken VT sep to pin up; Haare auch to put up; **hoch|ste|hend** ADJ a △ → hoch 2 e **b** Kragen turned-up; **hoch+stei|gen** VI sep irreg aux sein = **hinaufsteigen, heraufsteigen a, aufsteigen a**

höchst|ei|gen [høːçst'aign] ADJ, ADV (dated, hum) in person; **in ~er Person** (dated, hum) in person; **in ~em Interesse** in one's own interest

hoch-: hoch+stel|len VT sep **a** (an höhere Stelle) Stühle etc to put up; (außer Reichweite) to put or place high up; **hochgestellte Zahlen** superior numbers **b** (inf: = höher einstellen) Heizung, Ventilator etc to turn up **c** Kragen to turn up; **Hoch|stell|tas|te** F (Comput) shift key; **hoch+stem|men** sep VR to lift or raise up (with great effort) VR to raise oneself up

höchs|ten|falls [høːçstnfals] ADV at (the) most, at the outside

höchs|tens [høːçstns] ADV **a** (= nicht mehr, länger als) not more than; (= bestenfalls) at the most, at best **b** (= außer) except

Höchs|te(r) [høːçstə] M decl as adj **der ~** the Lord, the Supreme Being

höchs|te(r, s) [høːçstə] ADJ superl von hoch **a** (räumliche Ausdehnung) highest; Wuchs, Zimmer, Baum, Mast tallest; Leiter tallest, longest **b** Preis, Verdienst, Temperatur, Druck etc highest; Betrag, Summe largest; Strafe, Gewicht heaviest; Profit highest, biggest; Lotteriegewinn biggest; Verlust most severe; Schaden most expensive; (= maximal) Verdienst, Temperatur, Geschwindigkeit etc maximum attr; **im ~n Grade/Maße** extremely; **im ~n Fall(e)** at the most **c** (im Rang) highest; Ehre greatest; Fest most important; Offizier highest-ranking; **das ~ We-sen** the Supreme Being; **die ~ Instanz** the supreme court of appeal; **sich an ~r Stelle be-schweren** to complain to the highest authority **d** attr (qualitativ, äußerst) Ansprüche highest; Bedeutung, Genuss, Glück greatest, supreme; Gut, Freude greatest; Not, Gefahr, Wichtigkeit utmost, greatest; Konzentration extreme; **zu meiner ~n Zufriedenheit** to my great satisfaction **e** Alter greatest; (Mus) highest

---

f (in Wendungen) **~ Zeit** or **Eisenbahn** (inf) high time; **der ~ Norden** the extreme North; **das ist das ~ der Gefühle** that is the highest or most sublime feeling or of feelings; **aufs Höchste** or **erfreut** etc highly or greatly or tremendously (inf) pleased etc; **das ist das Höchste, was ich bezahlen/tun kann** that is the most I can pay/do

am ~n ADV **a** (= in größter Höhe) highest; **mittags steht die Sonne am ~n** the sun is highest at noon **b** (= in größtem Ausmaß) verehren, schätzen most (of all); versichern, begabt most; besteuert, verlieren (the) most heavily; verschuldet (the) most deeply; **in der Rangordnung am ~n stehen** to be the highest up in the hierarchy; **er ist am ~n qualifiziert** he is the most (highly) qualified; **am ~n stehen** (Kurse, Temperatur) to be at its highest

Höchs|te(s) [høːçstə] NT decl as adj (fig) highest good; **nach dem ~n streben** to aspire to the ideal or to perfection

Höchst- [høːçst-]: **Höchst|fall** M **im ~** (= nicht mehr, länger als) not more than; (= bestenfalls) at the most, at best; **Höchst|form** F (Sport) top form; **Höchst|fre|quenz|wel|le** F microwave; **Höchst|ge|bot** NT highest bid; **Höchst|ge-schwin|dig|keit** F top or maximum speed; **zulässige ~** speed limit; **Höchst|gren|ze** F upper limit

Hoch-: hoch|stie|lig [-ʃtiːlɪç] ADJ long-stemmed; **hoch+sti|li|sie|ren** ptp hochstilisiert VT sep to build up (zu into); **Hoch|stim|mung** F high spirits pl

Höchst-: Höchst|leis|tung F best performance; (bei Produktion) maximum output; **Höchst|mar|ke** F (von Wasserstand etc) highest level or mark; **Höchst|maß** NT maximum amount (an +dat of); **höchst|per|sön|lich** [høːçstpɛr'zøːnlɪç] ADV personally; **es ist der Prinz ~** it's the prince in person; **Höchst|preis** M top or maximum price

Hoch-: Hoch|stra|ße F fly-over; **hoch+stre-ben** VI sep aux sein (geh) **a** (= aufragen) to soar, to tower **b** (fig: = nach Höherem streben) to aspire (nach to, after); **hoch+strei|fen** VT sep Ärmel to push up

Höchst-: höchst|rich|ter|lich [høːçst'rɪçtəlɪç] ADJ of the supreme court; **Höchst|satz** M (beim Glücksspiel) maximum stake; (bei Versicherungen) maximum rate; **Höchst|stand** M highest level; **Höchst|stra|fe** F maximum penalty; **höchst|wahr|schein|lich** [høːçstvaːɐ-ʃainlɪç] ⊗ 42.2 ADV in all probability, most probably or likely; **Höchst|wert** M maximum value

hoch+sty|len VT sep to give style to; (pej) Person to hype (inf); Auto to soup up (inf); Laden etc to tart up (Brit inf), to dress up (esp US); **ein hochgestyltes Produkt** a stylish product

höchst|zu|läs|sig ADJ attr maximum (permissible)

Hoch-: Hoch|tal NT high-lying valley; **Hoch-tech|no|lo|gie** F high technology; **Hoch-tem|pe|ra|tur|re|ak|tor** M high temperature reactor; **hoch|tö|nend** ADJ Worte, Reden high-sounding; **Hoch|tö|ner** M (= Hochtonlautspre-cher) tweeter; **Hoch|tour** F **auf ~en laufen/ar-beiten** (Maschinen) to run at full speed; (fig: Mensch, Fabrik etc) to run/work at full steam; **etw auf ~en bringen** (Motor) to rev sth up to full speed; Maschine, Produktion, Kampagne to get sth into full swing; **jdn auf ~en bringen** (inf) to get sb really going (inf); **hoch|tou|rig** [-tuːrɪç] ADJ Motor high-revving ADV **~ fahren** to drive at high revs; **hoch|tra|bend** (pej) ADJ pompous, turgid ADV pompously; **hoch trei|ben ▲** VT irreg **a** (= hinauftreiben) to drive up **b** (fig) Preise, Löhne, Kosten to force up; **Hoch- und Tief|bau** M , no pl structural and civil engineering; **hoch|ver|dient** ADJ attr Mensch of great merit; Lob, Sieg much-deserved; **hoch|ver|ehrt** ADJ attr highly respected or esteemed;

(in Brief) esteemed (old); **~er Herr Vorsitzender ...** Mr Chairman ...; **~er Herr Präsident!** Mr President, Sir!; (in Brief) Dear Sir; **Hoch|ver|rat** M high treason; **Hoch|ver|rä|ter(in)** M(F) person guilty of high treason, traitor; **hoch|ver|rä|te|risch** ADJ treasonable; **hoch|ver-schul|det** △ [-fɛɐ̯ʃʊldət] ADJ attr → hoch 2 e; **hoch|ver|zins|lich** △ ADJ → hoch 2 e; **Hoch|wald** M timber forest

Hoch|was|ser NT pl -wasser **a** (= Höchststand von Flut) high tide **b** (= überhoher Wasserstand in Flüssen, Seen) high water; (= Überschwemmung) flood; **~ haben** (Fluss) to be in flood; **er hat ~** (hum inf) his trousers are at half-mast (esp Brit inf), he has (on) floods (US inf)

Hoch|was|ser-: Hoch|was|ser|ge|fahr F danger of flooding; **Hoch|was|ser|ho|sen** PL (hum inf) trousers pl at half-mast (Brit inf), floods pl (US inf); **Hoch|was|ser|ka|ta|stro-phe** F flood disaster; **Hoch|was|ser|mar|ke** F high-water mark; **Hoch|was|ser|scha|den** M flood damage; **Hoch|was|ser|stand** M high-water level

Hoch-: hoch+wer|fen VT sep irreg to throw up; **hoch|wer|tig** ADJ high-quality attr, of high quality; Nahrungsmittel highly nutritious; Stahl high-grade; (Chem) high-valency attr, of high valency; **Hoch|wild** NT big game (including bigger game birds); **hoch|will|kom|men** ADJ attr most or very welcome; **hoch|wirk|sam** ADJ highly effective; **hoch+wöl|ben** sep VT **etw ~** to make sth bulge up or up; **hoch+wol|len** VI sep (inf) to want up (inf); (= aufstehen wollen auch) to want to get up; (= die Höhe wollen, nach Norden wollen) to want to go up; **Hoch|wür|den** M -s, no pl (dated: Anrede) Reverend Father; **hoch|wür|dig** ADJ (dated) Reverend; **Hoch|zahl** F exponent

Hoch|zeit[1] [hɔxtsait] ⊗ 51.3, 52.1 F -, -en wedding; (= Eheschließung auch) marriage; **~ ma-chen** or **haben** to get married; **~ halten** or **feiern** to have a wedding; **etw zur ~ geschenkt be-kommen/schenken** to get/give sth as a wedding present; **grüne ~** wedding day; **silberne/gol-dene/diamantene ~** silver/golden/diamond wedding (anniversary); **man kann nicht auf zwei ~en tanzen** (prov) you can't have your cake and eat it (prov)

Hoch|zeit[2] [hoːxtsait] F -, -en (= Blütezeit) golden age

hoch|zei|ten [hɔxtsaitn] VI insep (dated, Aus, S Ger) to marry

Hoch|zei|ter [hɔxtsaitɐ] M -s, - (dated, Aus, Sw, S Ger) bridegroom; **die ~** the bride and groom

Hoch|zei|te|rin [hɔxtsaitərɪn] F -, -nen (dated, Aus, Sw, S Ger) bride

hoch|zeit|lich [hɔxtsaitlɪç] ADJ bridal attr, wedding attr ADV **die Braut war ~ gekleidet** the bride was in her wedding dress; **der Bräuti-gam war ~ gekleidet** the groom was in his wedding attire; **~ geschmückt** decorated for a/the wedding

Hoch|zeits- in cpds wedding; **Hoch|zeits|an-zei|ge** F wedding announcement; **Hoch-zeits|fei|er** F wedding celebration; (= Emp-fang) reception, wedding breakfast; **Hoch-zeits|fest** NT wedding celebration; **Hoch-zeits|flug** M (Zool) nuptial flight; **Hoch-zeits|gast** M wedding guest; **Hoch|zeits-ge|sell|schaft** F wedding party; **Hoch|zeits-kleid** NT wedding dress, bridal dress or gown; **Hoch|zeits|nacht** F wedding night; **Hoch-zeits|rei|se** F honeymoon; **wohin geht die ~?** where are you going on (your) honeymoon?; **Hoch|zeits|rei|sen|de** PL decl as adj honey-moon couple, honeymooners pl; **Hoch|zeits-tag** M wedding day; (= Jahrestag) wedding an-niversary; **Hoch|zeits|zug** M wedding pro-cession

Hoch-: hoch+zie|hen sep irreg VT **a** Gegen-stand to pull up; Hosen etc auch to hitch up; Fah-ne to run up; Augenbrauen to raise, to lift; **die Maschine ~** (Aviat) to put the aircraft into a steep climb **b** (*inf*: = *bauen*) to throw up (*inf*) **VR** to pull oneself up; **sich an etw** (*dat*) ~ to climb up sth; (*fig inf*) to get a kick out of sth (*inf*); **Hoch|ziel** NT (*geh*) ultimate goal

Hoch|zins-: Hoch|zins|pha|se F (*Fin*) period of high interest rates, high interest rate policy; **Hoch|zins|po|li|tik** F (*Fin*) high interest rate policy

Hock [hɔk] M **-s, ¨-e** ['hœkə] (*Sw, dial*) get-together

Ho|cke¹ ['hɔkə] F **-, -n** squatting position; (= *Übung*) squat; (*beim Turnen*) squat vault; (*beim Skilaufen*) crouch; (*beim Ringen*) mat position; **in die ~ gehen** to squat (down); **in der ~ sitzen** to squat

Ho|cke² F **-, -n** stook, shock

ho|cken ['hɔkn] **VI** (*S Ger*: *aux sein*) **a** (= *in der Hocke sitzen*) to squat, to crouch **b** (*inf*: = *sitzen*) to sit; (*auf Hocker*) to perch **c** (*pej inf*) to sit around **d** (*Sport*) **übers Pferd ~** to squat-vault over the horse **VR a** (= *in Hockstellung gehen*) to squat **b** (*inf*: = *sich setzen*) to sit down, to plonk oneself down (*inf*)

ho|cken blei|ben ▲ VI *irreg aux sein* (*dial inf*) = **sitzen bleiben**

Ho|cker ['hɔkɐ] M **-s, -** **a** (= *Stuhl*) stool; **jdn vom ~ reißen** *or* **hauen** (*fig inf*) to bowl sb over (*inf*) **b** (*Archeol*) seated burial

Hö|cker ['hœkɐ] M **-s, -** **a** (*von Kamel, inf*: = *Buckel*) hump; (*auf Schnabel*) knob **b** (= *Erhebung*) bump; (*in Gelände*) hump; (= *kleiner Hügel*) hummock, hump

Ho|cker|grab NT seated burial

hö|cke|rig ['hœkərɪç] ADJ (= *uneben*) bumpy; (= *buckelig*) hunch-backed; **Nase** with a bump; **Schnabel** with a knob

Ho|ckey ['hɔki, 'hɔke] NT **-s**, *no pl* hockey (*Brit*), field hockey (*US*)

Ho|ckey-: Ho|ckey|ball M (field *US*) hockey ball; **Ho|ckey|schlä|ger** M (field *US*) hockey stick; **Ho|ckey|spie|ler(in)** M(F) (field *US*) hockey player; **Ho|ckey|stock** M (field *US*) hockey stick

höck|rig ['hœkrɪç] ADJ = **höckerig**

Hock-: Hock|sitz M squat; **Hock|sprung** M (*Sport*) (*über Gerät*) squat vault; (*beim Bodenturnen*) crouch jump; **Hock|stel|lung** F crouched *or* squatting position; (*Archeol*) seated position

Ho|de ['ho:də] M **-n, -n** *or* f **-, -n**, **Ho|den** ['ho:dn] M **-s, -** testicle

Ho|den-: Ho|den|bruch M scrotal hernia; **Ho|den|ent|zün|dung** F inflammation of the testicles, orchitis (*spec*); **Ho|den|sack** M scrotum

Hof [ho:f] M **-(e)s, ¨-e** ['hø:fə] **a** (= *Platz*) yard; (= *Innenhof*) courtyard; (= *Schulhof*) schoolyard, playground; (= *Kasernenhof*) square **b** (= *Bauernhof*) farm; (= *Gebäudekomplex*) farm(yard) **c** (= *Fürstenhof*) court; **bei** *or* **am ~** at court; **am ~e Ludwig XIV.** at the court of Louis XIV; **~ halten** (*lit, fig*) to hold court **d** **einem Mädchen den ~ machen** (*dated, hum*) to court a girl (*dated*), to pay court to a girl (*form*) **e** (*um Sonne, Mond*) halo **f** (*in Namen:* = *Gasthof, Hotel*) hotel, inn

Hof-: Hof|amt NT court appointment; **Hof|arzt** M , **Hof|ärz|tin** F court physician; **Hof|ball** M court ball; **Hof|da|me** F lady-in-waiting; **Hof|dich|ter(in)** M(F) court poet; (*in GB*) poet laureate; **Hof|ein|fahrt** F courtyard entrance

hö|feln ['hø:fln] VI (*Sw*) to flatter (*jdm sb*)

Hof-: Hof|er|be M , **Hof|er|bin** F heir to a/the farm; **Hof|eti|ket|te** F court etiquette; **hof|fä|hig** ['hɔfːɛːɪç] ADJ acceptable at court; (= *gesellschaftsfähig*) presentable; **jdn/etw ~ machen** (*fig*) to make sb/sth (socially) acceptable; **Hof|fä|hig|keit** F (*fig*) (social) acceptability

Hof|fart ['hɔfart] F **-**, *no pl* (*dated*) pride, arrogance, haughtiness

hof|fär|tig ['hɔfɛrtɪç] ADJ (*dated*) proud, arrogant, haughty

hof|fen ['hɔfn] ✪ 30, 31, 48.2 **VI a** (= *von Hoffnung erfüllt sein*) to hope; **auf Gott ~** to trust in God; **auf jdn ~** to set one's hopes on sb; **auf etw ~** (*acc*) to hope for sth; **da bleibt nur zu ~** one can only hope; **sie hofften auf ihre Verbündeten** (*auf Erscheinen*) they were waiting for their allies; (*auf Hilfe*) they set their hopes on their allies; **der Mensch hofft, solange er lebt** (*Prov*) hope springs eternal (*prov*); **Hoffen und Harren macht manchen zum Narren** (*Prov*) some people never give up hoping **b** (= *wünschen und erwarten*) to hope; **~, dass ...** to hope that ...; **ich will nicht ~, dass er das macht** I hope he doesn't do that; **ich will/wir wollen ~, dass ...** we can only hope that ..., it is to be hoped that ... **VT** to hope for; **~ wir das Beste!** let's hope for the best!; **es ist zu ~** it is to be hoped; **ich hoffe es** I hope so; **das will ich (doch wohl) ~** I should (jolly well (*Brit inf*)) hope so; **das wollen wir ~** let's hope so; **ich will es nicht ~** I hope not; **sie hatten nichts mehr zu ~** they had nothing left to hope for

hof|fent|lich ['hɔfntlɪç] ADV hopefully; **~!** I hope so, let us hope so; **~ nicht** I/we hope not; **~ ist das bald vorbei** I/we *etc* hope that it will be over soon, hopefully it will be over soon; **du bist mir doch ~ nicht böse** I (do) hope (that) you're not angry with me

-höf|fig [hœfɪç] ADJ *suf* (*Min*) promising a rich yield of; **ein erdölhöffiges Gebiet** an area which promises a rich yield of oil

höff|lich ['hœflɪç] ADJ (*Min*) promising a rich yield

Hoff|nung ['hɔfnʊŋ] F **-, -en** hope; (*auf Gott*) trust (*auf +acc* in); **sich** (*dat*) **~en machen** to have hopes; **sich** (*dat*) **keine ~en machen** not to hold out any hopes; **er macht sich ~en bei ihr** (*inf*) he fancies his chances with her (*Brit inf*), he thinks his chances with her are quite good (*esp US*); **mach dir keine ~(en)!** I wouldn't even think about it; **jdm ~en machen** to raise sb's hopes; **jdm ~en machen, dass ...** to lead sb to hope that ...; **jdm ~en** (*acc*) **machen** to lead sb to expect sth; **jdm keine ~en machen** not to hold out any hopes for sb; **seine ~en auf jdn/etw setzen** to place one's hopes on sb/sth, to pin one's hopes on sb/sth; **die ~ aufgeben/verlieren** to abandon/lose hope; **eine ~ begraben** *or* **zu Grabe tragen** to abandon a hope; **eine ~ zerstören/enttäuschen** to dash/disappoint sb's hopes; **in der ~, bald von Ihnen zu hören** hoping to hear from you soon, in the hope of hearing from you soon; **sich einer ~/unbegründeten/falschen ~en hingeben** to cherish hopes/unfounded hopes/false hopes; **zu schönen** *or* **zu den schönsten ~en berechtigen** to give rise to great hopes; **~ auf etw** (*acc*) **haben** to have hopes of getting sth; **guter ~ sein** (*euph*: = *schwanger*) to be expecting

Hoff|nungs-: hoff|nungs|freu|dig, hoff|nungs|froh ADJ hopeful ADV in happy anticipation; **Hoff|nungs|fun|ke(n)** M glimmer of hope; **Hoff|nungs|lauf** M (*Sport*) repechage; **hoff|nungs|los** ADJ hopeless ADV hopelessly; **Hoff|nungs|lo|sig|keit** F **-**, *no pl* hopelessness; (= *Verzweiflung*) despair; **Hoff|nungs|schim|mer** M glimmer of hope; **Hoff|nungs|strahl** M ray of hope; **Hoff|nungs|trä|ger(in)** M(F) person on whom hopes are pinned; **er war der ~ der Partei** he carried the hopes of the party; **hoff|nungs|voll** ADJ hopeful; (= *viel versprechend*) promising ADV full of hope

Hof-: Hof|gang M *pl* **-gänge** yard exercise; **Hof|geist|li|che(r)** MF *decl as adj* court chaplain; **Hof|ge|sell|schaft** F court society; **Hof|ge|sin|de** NT **a** (*auf Bauernhof*) farm workers *pl* **b** (*am Fürstenhof*) servants *pl* at (the/a) court; **hof+hal|ten** △ VI *sep irreg* → **Hof c**; **Hof|hal|tung** F (holding of) court;

Hof|herr(in) M(F) (= *Gutsherr*) estate owner; (*in England*) squire; **Hof|hund** M watchdog

ho|fie|ren [ho'fi:rən] *ptp* **hofiert** VT (*dated*) to court

hö|fisch ['hø:fɪʃ] ADJ **a** (= *eines Fürstenhofs*) Leben, Sitten, Vergnügen courtly *no adv* **b** (*Liter*) Dichtung *etc* courtly *no adv* **c** (*old:* = *kultiviert*) Benehmen, Kleidung sophisticated

Hof-: Hof|ka|pel|le F **a** (= *Kirche am Hof*) court chapel **b** (*Mus*) court orchestra; **Hof|knicks** M court or formal curtsey (*Brit*) or curtsy (*US*); **Hof|la|ger** NT temporary residence; **~ halten** to hold court; **Hof|le|ben** NT court life

höf|lich ['hø:flɪç] ADJ polite; (= *zuvorkommend*) courteous ADV politely; **ich bitte Sie ~** I (would) respectfully ask you; **wir teilen Ihnen ~(st) mit** we would inform you, we would like to inform you

Höf|lich|keit F **-, -en** **a** *no pl* politeness; (= *Zuvorkommenheit*) courteousness; **jdm etw mit aller ~ sagen** to tell sb sth very politely, to tell sb sth with the utmost politeness **b** (= *höfliche Bemerkung*) compliment; **jdm ~en sagen** to compliment sb

Höf|lich|keits-: Höf|lich|keits|be|such M courtesy visit; **Höf|lich|keits|be|zei|gung** [-bətsaigʊŋ] F **-, -en** act *or* mark of courtesy; **Höf|lich|keits|flos|kel** F (*pej*), **Höf|lich|keits|for|mel** F polite phrase; **höf|lich|keits|hal|ber** ADV out of courtesy

Hof|lie|fe|rant(in) M(F) purveyor to the court

Höf|ling ['hø:flɪŋ] M **-s, -e** courtier; (*pej:* = *Schmeichler*) sycophant

Hof-: Hof|mar|schall M (*Hist*) major-domo; (*in GB*) Lord Chamberlain; **Hof|meis|ter** M (*Hist*) **a** (= *Gutsverwalter*) steward, bailiff **b** (= *Erzieher*) (private) tutor; **Hof|narr** M (*Hist*) court jester; **Hof|pre|di|ger** M (*Hist*) court chaplain; **Hof|rat¹** M (*Hist*) Court Counsellor (*Brit*) or Counselor (*US*); **Hof|rat²** M , **Hof|rä|tin** F **a** (*in GB*) Privy Councillor (*Brit*) or Councilor (*US*) **b** (*Aus: Ehrentitel*) Hofrat, ≈ Councillor (*Brit*), ≈ Councilor (*US*); **Hof|sän|ger** M (*Hist*) minstrel; **Hof|schran|ze** [-ʃrantsə] F **-, -n** *or* (*rare*) m **-n, -n** (*Hist pej*) fawning courtier; **Hof|sei|te** F courtyard side (*of building*); **Hof|staat** M ['ho:fʃtaːt] M (*royal etc*) household; **Hof|statt** ['ho:fʃtat] F **-, -en** *or* **Hofstätten** [-ʃtɛtn] farmstead; **Hof|the|a|ter** NT (*Hist*) court or royal theatre (*Brit*) or theater (*US*); **Hof|tor** NT yard gate; **Hof|trau|er** F court mourning; **Hof|tür** F yard gate

HO-Ge|schäft [ha:ˈo:-] NT (*DDR*) state retail shop

ho|he ADJ → **hoch**

Höhe ['hø:ə] F **-, -n** **a** (= *Ausdehnung nach oben*) height; (= *Flughöhe, Berghöhe, über Meeresspiegel*) height, altitude; (*Astron, Math*) altitude; (*von Schnee, Wasser*) depth; **in die/der ~** (up) into/in the air; **aus der ~** from above; **Ehre sei Gott in der ~** glory to God in the highest *or* on high; **an ~ gewinnen** (*Aviat*) to gain height, to climb; **in einer ~ von** at a height/an altitude of; **in die ~ gehen/treiben** (fig: Preise etc) to go up/force up; **einen Betrieb wieder in die ~ bringen** to put a business back on its feet again; **in die ~ gehen** (fig inf) to hit the roof (*inf*) **b** (= *Anhöhe*) hill; (= *Gipfel*) top, summit; (fig: = *Höhepunkt, Blütezeit etc*) height; **auf der ~ sein** (fig inf) (*leistungsfähig*) to be at one's best; (*gesund*) to be fighting fit (*Brit inf*), to be (as) fit as a fiddle; **die sanften ~n** the gentle slopes; **sich nicht auf der ~ fühlen, nicht auf der ~ sein** (*leistungsmäßig*) to feel below par; (*gesundheitlich*) not to be up to scratch; **auf der ~ des Lebens** in the prime of (one's) life; **die ~n und Tiefen des Lebens** the ups and downs of life; **auf der ~ der Zeit** up-to-date; **das ist doch die ~!** (fig inf) that's the limit! **c** (= *Ausmaß, Größe*) (von Mieten, Preisen, Unkosten, Temperatur, Geschwindigkeit, Strafe, Phys: von Stromspannung) level; (von Summe, Gewinn, Verlust, Gewicht, Geldstrafe) size, amount; (von Wert,

Druck) amount; (*von Einkommen*) size; (*von Schaden*) extent; **ein Zuwachs/Betrag in ~ von** an increase/amount of; **Zinsen in ~ von** interest at the rate of; **bis zu einer ~ von** up to a maximum of

d (*fig*: = *Größe: von Lebensstandard, Ansprüchen etc*) level

e (*Tonhöhe*) (*Mus: von Stimme*) pitch; (*Rad*) treble *no pl*; **die ~n einstellen** (*Rad*) to adjust the treble

f (*Naut, Geog*: = *Breitenlage*) latitude; **auf der ~ von** at the level of; **auf der ~ von Dover** (*Naut*) off Dover; **auf gleicher ~** level with each other

Ho|heit ['ho:hait] F -, -en **a** *no pl* (= *Staatshoheit*) sovereignty (*über +acc* over) **b** (= *Mitglied einer fürstlichen Familie*) member of a/the royal family; (*als Anrede*) Highness; **Seine/Ihre Königliche ~** His/Her Royal Highness

ho|heit|lich ['ho:haitlɪç] ADJ (*von Staatsgewalt ausgehend*) *Befehl, Handlung, Aufgabe, Behörde* sovereign; (*von einem Fürsten*) *Gemächer* royal; *Auftreten, Geste* majestic

Ho|heits-: Ho|heits|ab|zei|chen NT nationality marking; **Ho|heits|akt** M act of sovereignty; **Ho|heits|be|reich** M **a** (= *Hoheitsgebiet*) sovereign territory **b** (= *Rechtsbereich*) jurisdiction; **Ho|heits|ge|biet** NT sovereign territory; **Ho|heits|ge|walt** F (national) jurisdiction; **Ho|heits|ge|wäs|ser** PL territorial waters *pl*; **Ho|heits|recht** NT *usu pl* sovereign jurisdiction *or* rights *pl*; **ho|heits|voll** ADJ majestic; **Ho|heits|zei|chen** NT national emblem

Ho|he|lied [ho:ə'li:t] NT **Hohen Liedes** [ho:ən 'li:dəs] *no pl* Song of Songs; (*fig geh*) song

Hö|hen-: Hö|hen|an|ga|be F altitude reading; (*auf Karte*) altitude mark; **Hö|hen|angst** F fear of heights; **Hö|hen|flos|se** F (*Aviat*) tailplane; **Hö|hen|flug** M high-altitude flight; **geistiger/ künstlerischer ~** intellectual/artistic flight (of fancy); **Hö|hen|gleich** ADJ level ADV on a level; **Hö|hen|kli|ma** NT mountain climate; **Hö|hen|krank|heit** F (*Med*) altitude sickness; (*im Gebirge auch*) mountain sickness; (*beim Fliegen auch*) aeroembolism (*spec*); **Hö|hen|kur|ort** M mountain (health) resort; **Hö|hen|la|ge** F altitude; **Hö|hen|leit|werk** NT (*Aviat*) elevators *pl*; **Hö|hen|li|nie** F contour (line); **Hö|hen|luft** F mountain air; **Hö|hen|mar|ke** F benchmark; **Hö|hen|mes|ser** M -s, - (*Aviat*) altimeter, altitude meter; **Hö|hen|mes|sung** F **a** (*Aviat*) measuring altitude **b** (*Tech*) levelling (*Brit*), leveling (*US*); **Hö|hen|me|ter** M (*nach oben*) elevation gain; (*nach unten*) elevation descent; **die letzten 50 ~** the last 50 metres (*Brit*) *or* meters (*US*) in height; **Hö|hen|re|kord** M (*Aviat*) altitude record; **Hö|hen|rü|cken** M (mountain) crest *or* ridge; **Hö|hen|ru|der** NT (*Aviat*) elevator; **Hö|hen|schicht** F contour level; **Hö|hen|schrei|ber** M (*Aviat*) altigraph; **Hö|hen|son|ne** F (*im Gebirge*) mountain sun; (= *Lampe*) sunray lamp; (= *Behandlung*) sunray treatment; **Hö|hen|steu|er** NT (*Aviat*) elevator; **Hö|hen|strah|lung** F cosmic radiation; **Hö|hen|trai|ning** NT (*Sport*) (high-)altitude training; **Hö|hen|un|ter|schied** M difference in altitude; **Hö|hen|ver|lust** M loss of height *or* altitude; **hö|hen|ver|stell|bar** ADJ height-adjustable; **Hö|hen|weg** M (*am Gebirgskamm*) ridgeway, ridge path; (*an Höhenzug entlang*) path running along a/the mountain range; **Hö|hen|wind** M high-altitude wind; **Hö|hen|zahl** F (*auf Landkarten*) height above sea level; **Hö|hen|zug** M range of hills, mountain range

Ho|he|pries|ter [ho:ə'pri:stɐ] M **Hohen Priesters**, - high priest

ho|he|pries|ter|lich [ho:ə'pri:stɐlɪç] ADJ *Gewänder, Amt* high priest's *attr*

Hö|he|punkt M highest point; (*von Abend, Tag, Leben*) high point, high spot; (*von Veranstaltung*) high spot, highlight; (*von Karriere, des Ruhms, der Macht*) pinnacle, peak, height; (*des Glücks etc*) height, peak; (*von Entwicklung*) peak, summit, a-

---

pex; (*von Kurve*) vertex; (*eines Stücks,* = *Orgasmus*) climax; **auf den ~ bringen** to bring to a climax; **den ~ erreichen** to reach a *or* its/one's climax; (*Krankheit*) to reach *or* come to a crisis; **den ~ überschreiten** to pass the peak

hö|her ['hø:ɐ] ADJ *comp von* **hoch** (*lit, fig*) higher; *Macht* superior; *Klasse* upper; *Auflage* bigger; (*Comput*) *Programmiersprache* high-level; **~e Berufsstände** the professions; **~e Bildung** higher education; **~es Lehramt** ≈ graduate teachership; **~e Schule** secondary school, high school (*esp US*); **~e Töchterschule** (*old, hum*) school for young ladies; **~e Tochter** (*dated, hum*) young lady; **~e Gewalt** an act of God; **in ~em Maße** to a greater extent; **~er Blödsinn** (*iro*) utter nonsense; **in ~en Regionen** *or* **Sphären schweben** to have one's head in the clouds; **sich zu Höherem berufen fühlen** to feel (oneself) called to higher *or* greater things

ADV **a** (= *weiter nach oben*) *wachsen, steigen, fliegen* higher; **~ liegen** to be higher up; **~ liegend** higher; **ihre Herzen schlugen ~** their hearts beat faster

b (= *mit höherem Wert*) *bewertet, versichert* more highly; **etw ~ bewerten** to rate sth higher *or* more highly; **sich ~ versichern** to increase one's insurance (cover); **~ gestellt** higher, more senior; **~ stehend** higher

ho|he(r, s) ADJ → **hoch**

hö|her-: hö|her|ge|stellt △ ADJ *attr* → **höher** ADV **b**; **hö|her|klas|sig** ADJ (*Sport*) *Verein, Mannschaft, Fußball* higher-division *attr*; **hö|her|lie|gend** △ ADJ *attr* → **höher** ADV **a**; **hö|her schrau|ben** ▲ VT (*fig*) *Anforderungen* to increase, to step up; *Ansprüche* to increase; *Preise* to force *or* push up; **hö|her|ste|hend** △ ADJ *attr* → **höher** ADV **b**; **hö|her stu|fen** ▲ VT *Person* to upgrade; **hö|her|wer|tig** ADJ of higher quality; *Qualität* higher; (*Chem*) of higher valency

hohl [ho:l] ADJ **a** (*lit, fig*: = *leer*) hollow; *Geschwätz etc* empty, shallow; *Blick* empty, vacant **b** (= *konkav*) hollow; *Augen, Wangen* hollow, sunken; **ein ~es Kreuz** a hollow back; **in der ~en Hand** in the hollow of one's hand; **aus der ~en Hand trinken** to drink with cupped hands; **eine ~e Hand machen** (*lit*) to cup one's hand; (*fig auch*) to hold one's hand out (*for money, a tip etc*); **~e Gasse** narrow pass *or* defile **c** *Klang, Stimme, Husten* hollow ADV **~ klingen** to sound hollow; **~ scheinen** to appear *or* seem hollow

Hohl-: hohl|äu|gig ADJ hollow-eyed, sunken-eyed; **Hohl|block** M *pl* **-blöcke, Hohl|block|stein** M , **Hohl|block|zie|gel** M cavity block

Höh|le ['hø:lə] F -, -n cave, cavern; (*in Baum*) hole, hollow bit; (= *Tierbehausung*) cave, den; (= *Augenhöhle*) socket; (*fig*: = *schlechte Wohnung*) hovel, hole (*inf*)

Höh|len- *in cpds* cave; **Höh|len|bär** M cave-bear; **Höh|len|be|woh|ner(in)** M(F) cave dweller, troglodyte; (*männlich auch*) caveman; **Höh|len|for|scher(in)** M(F) cave explorer; (*unter der Erde auch*) potholer; **Höh|len|for|schung** F , **Höh|len|kun|de** F speleology; **Höh|len|gleich|nis** NT (*Philos*) Allegory of the Cave; **Höh|len|ma|le|rei** F cave painting; **Höh|len|mensch** M caveman; **Höh|len|tier** NT cave-animal; **Höh|len|zeich|nung** F (*Hist*) cave drawing

Hohl-: Hohl|heit F -, *no pl* (*lit, fig*: = *Leere*) hollowness; (*von Geschwätz*) emptiness, shallowness; (*von Kopf*) (*pej*) blockhead (*inf*), numskull (*inf*), dunce; **hohl|köp|fig** ADJ (*pej*) empty-headed, brainless, foolish; **Hohl|kör|per** M hollow body; **Hohl|kreuz** NT (*Med*) hollow back; **Hohl|ku|gel** F hollow sphere; **Hohl|maß** NT measure of capacity; (*für Getreide etc auch*) dry measure; **Hohl|na|del** F (*Med*) cannula

Hohl|raum M hollow space; (*Build auch*) cavity

Hohl|raum-: Hohl|raum|ver|sie|ge|lung F (*Aut*) cavity seal; **Hohl|raum|zie|gel** M cavity block

Hohl-: Hohl|saum M (*Sew*) hemstitch; **Hohl|saum|ar|beit** F drawn-thread work; **Hohl|schliff** M hollow grinding; **ein Messer mit ~** a hollow-ground knife; **Hohl|spie|gel** M concave mirror; **Hohl|tie|re** PL coelenterata (*spec*)

Höh|lung ['hø:lʊŋ] F -, -en hollow

Hohl-: hohl|wan|gig [-vaŋɪç] ADJ hollow-cheeked; **Hohl|weg** M narrow pass *or* defile; **Hohl|wür|mer** PL aschelminthes *pl* (*spec*); **Hohl|zie|gel** M **a** (= *Hohlstein*) cavity brick **b** (= *Dachziegel*) hollow tile

Hohn [ho:n] M -(e)s, *no pl* scorn, derision, mockery; **jdn mit ~ und Spott überschütten** to heap *or* pour scorn on sb; **nur ~ und Spott ernten** to get nothing but scorn and derision; **das hat er mir zum ~ getan** he did it just to show his contempt for me; **ein ~ auf etw** (*acc*) a mockery of sth; **das ist der reine** *or* **reinste ~** it's a sheer *or* utter mockery; **den Tatsachen zum ~** in defiance of the facts; **~ lachen** to laugh scornfully *or* derisively; **ich höre ihn schon ~ lachen** I can hear his sneers already; **~ sprechen** to make a mockery (+*dat* of); **jdm ~ sprechen** to mock (at) sb, to deride sb; **das spricht jeder Vernunft ~** that flies right in the face of all reason

höh|nen ['hø:nən] VT (*geh*) *jdn* to mock VI to jeer, to scoff, to sneer (*über +acc* at)

Hohn|ge|läch|ter NT scornful *or* derisive *or* sneering laughter

höh|nisch ['hø:nɪʃ] ADJ scornful, mocking, sneering ADV scornfully, mockingly; **~ grinsen** to sneer, to smirk, to grin scornfully; **jdn ~ ver|spotten** to jeer at sb, to deride sb

Hohn-: Hohn|la|chen NT scornful *or* derisive *or* sneering laughter; **hohn+la|chen** VI *sep* → **Hohn**; **hohn+spre|chen** VI *sep irreg* → **Hohn**

ho|ho [ho'ho:] INTERJ oho

hoi [hɔy] INTERJ (*Sw*) hello

Hö|ker ['hø:kɐ] M -s, -, **Hö|ker|frau** F , **Hö|ke|rin** [-ərɪn] F -, -nen, **Hö|ker|weib** NT (*old, pej*) street trader, pedlar (*Brit*), peddler (*US*)

hö|kern ['hø:kɐn] VI (*old*) to peddle; **mit etw ~** to peddle sth

Ho|kus|po|kus [ho:kʊs'po:kʊs] M -, *no pl* (= *Zauberformel*) hey presto; (= *Zauberstück*) (conjuring) trick(s *pl*); (*fig*) (= *Täuschung*) hocus-pocus (*inf*), jiggery-pokery (*Brit inf*); (= *Drumherum*) palaver (*esp Brit inf*), fuss; **die veranstalten immer einen ~, wenn Besuch kommt** they always make such a palaver (*esp Brit inf*) *or* fuss when they have visitors

hold [hɔlt] ADJ **a** (*poet, dated*) fair, sweet; (*hum*) dear, beloved, fair; **~er Friede** sweet *or* blessed peace; **die ~e Weiblichkeit** (*hum*) the fair sex; **mein ~er Gatte** (*hum*) my dear *or* beloved husband; **meine Holde** (*hum*) my sweet **b** *pred* (*geh*: = *gewogen*) **jdm ~ sein** to be fond of *or* well-disposed to(wards) sb; **das Glück war ihm ~** fortune smiled upon him

Hol|der ['hɔldɐ] M -s, - (*dial*) elder; (= *Früchte*) elderberries *pl*

Hol|ding ['ho:ldɪŋ] F -, -s, **Hol|ding|ge|sell|schaft** F (*Comm*) holding company

Hold|rio ['hɔldrio] NT -s, -s (shout of) halloo

hold|se|lig ADJ (*liter*) sweet, lovely, fair

ho|len ['ho:lən] VT **a** (= *holen gehen*) to fetch, to get; (= *herunternehmen*) to get *or* take *or* fetch down; (= *herausnehmen*) to get *or* take out; **Luft** *or* **Atem ~** to draw breath; **jdn aus dem Bett ~** to get *or* drag (*inf*) sb out of bed; **das Kind musste geholt werden** the baby had to be pulled out → **Teufel b** **b** (= *abholen*) to fetch, to pick up; *Verbrecher, Patienten* to take away **c** (= *kaufen*) to get, to pick up (*inf*) **d** (= *herbeirufen, holen lassen*) *Polizei, Hilfe* to

---

fetch, to get; **jdn ~ lassen** to send for sb; **einen Moment, ich lasse ihn schnell ans Telefon ~** just a moment, I'll have someone fetch or get him to the phone; **der Professor hat seinen Assistenten an die neue Uni geholt** the professor brought his assistant to the new university **e** (= erringen, gewinnen) Sieg, Preis to win, to get **f** (= sich zuziehen) Krankheit to catch, to get; elektrischen Schlag to get; **sich** (dat) **Schläge ~** to get a beating; **sonst wirst du dir etwas ~** or you'll catch something; **sich** (dat) **eine Erkältung/den Tod** (inf) **~** to catch a cold/one's death (inf) **g** (= bekommen, erwerben) to get; **sich** (dat) **etw ~** to get (oneself) sth; **dabei ist nichts zu ~** (inf) there's nothing in it; **bei ihm ist nichts zu ~** (inf) you etc won't get anything out of him **h** (Naut) Anker to raise, to hoist; Segel, Taue to take in

ho|lis|tisch [hoˈlɪstɪʃ] **ADJ** holistic **ADV** holistically

hol|la [ˈhɔla] **INTERJ** hullo, hallo, hello, hey; (überrascht) hey; (= hoppla) whoops

Hol|land [ˈhɔlant] **NT -s** Holland, the Netherlands pl

Hol|län|der¹ [ˈhɔlɛndɐ] **M -s,** no pl (= Käse) Dutch cheese

Hol|län|der² [ˈhɔlɛndɐ] **M -s, -** (bei Papierherstellung) hollander

Hol|län|der³ [ˈhɔlɛndɐ] **M -s, -** (= Mensch) Dutchman; **die ~** the Dutch (people); **er ist ~** he is Dutch or a Dutchman → fliegend

Hol|län|de|rin [ˈhɔlɛndərɪn] **F -, -nen** Dutchwoman, Dutch girl → auch **Holländer³**

hol|län|disch [ˈhɔlɛndɪʃ] **ADJ** Dutch

Hol|län|disch(e) [ˈhɔlɛndɪʃ] **NT** Dutch, the Dutch language → auch **Deutsch(e)**

Hol|le [ˈhɔla] **F - Frau ~ schüttelt die Betten aus** it is snowing

Höl|le [ˈhœla] **F -,** (rare) **-n** hell; **in der ~** in hell; **die ~ auf Erden** hell on earth; **fahr zur ~!** (liter) go to the devil!; **zur ~ mit...** to hell with ... (inf); **in die ~ kommen** to go to hell; **ich werde ihm die ~ heiß machen** (inf) I'll give him hell (inf); **sie machte ihm das Leben zur ~** she made his life (a) hell (inf); **es war die (reinste) ~** (inf) it was (pure) hell (inf); **die ~ ist los** (inf) all hell has broken loose (inf)

Höl|len- in cpds (= der Hölle) of hell, infernal; (inf: = groß) hellish (inf), infernal (inf); **Höl|len|angst** F (inf) terrible fear; **eine ~ haben** to be scared stiff (inf); **Höl|len|brand** M (liter) hellfire; **Höl|len|brut** F (pej liter) diabolical or fiendish mob or rabble; **Höl|len|fahrt** F Descent into Hell; **Höl|len|fürst** M (liter) Prince of Darkness; **Höl|len|ge|stank** M (inf) diabolical smell or stench; **Höl|len|hund** M (Myth) hound of hell, hellhound; **Höl|len|lärm** M (inf) hellish or infernal noise (inf); **Höl|len|mäch|te** PL (liter) powers of darkness pl; **Höl|len|ma|schi|ne** F (dated) infernal machine (dated), time bomb; **Höl|len|pein** F (liter), **Höl|len|qual** F (liter) torments pl of hell; (fig inf) agony; **eine Höllenqual/Höllenqualen ausstehen** to suffer agony; **Höl|len|ra|chen** M (liter), **Höl|len|schlund** M (liter) jaws pl of hell; **Höl|len|spek|ta|kel** M (inf) hellish or infernal noise (inf); **Höl|len|stein** M (Chem) silver nitrate, lunar caustic

Hol|ler [ˈhɔla] **M -s, -** (dial) elder; (= Früchte) elderberries pl

Hol|le|rith|ma|schi|ne [ˈhɔlərɪt-, ˈhɔlərɪt-] **F** Hollerith machine

höl|lisch [ˈhœlɪʃ] **ADJ a** attr (= die Hölle betreffend) infernal, of hell **b** (inf: = außerordentlich) dreadful, frightful, hellish (inf); **eine ~e Angst haben** to be scared stiff (inf) **ADV** (inf) like hell (inf), hellishly (inf); **~ fluchen** to swear like a trooper; **es tut ~ weh** it hurts like hell (inf), it's hellish(ly) painful (inf); **die Prüfung war ~ schwer** the exam was hellish(ly) difficult (inf)

Hol|ly|wood|schau|kel [ˈhɔliwʊd-] **F** swing hammock

Holm¹ [hɔlm] **M -(e)s, -e a** (von Barren) bar; (von Geländer) rail; (von Leiter) side rail **b** (Aviat) (längs) longeron; (quer) spar **c** (= Stiel, Griff) (= Axtholm) shaft, handle; (= Ruderholm) shaft

Holm² **M -(e)s, -e** islet, small island

Hol|mi|um [ˈhɔlmiʊm] **NT -s,** no pl (abbr **Ho**) holmium

Ho|lo|caust [ˈhoːlokaʊst, holoˈkaʊst, ˈhɔlɔkɔːst] **M -(s), -(s)** holocaust

Ho|lo|caust- [ˈhoːlokaʊst, holoˈkaʊst, ˈhɔlɔkɔːst] in cpds holocaust; **Ho|lo|caust-Ge|denk|stät|te** F holocaust memorial

Ho|lo|gra|fie ▲ [hologra'fiː] **F -, -n** [-'fiːən] holography

Ho|lo|gramm [holoˈgram] **NT** pl **-gramme** hologram

hol|pe|rig [ˈhɔlpərɪç] **ADJ a** Weg, Pflaster bumpy **b** (= schwerfällig) Rede, Verse clumsy, jerky **ADV ~ lesen** to read jerkily or haltingly

hol|pern [ˈhɔlpɐn] **VI** to bump, to jolt; **beim Lesen holpert er noch** he still stumbles (over his words) when reading, he still reads haltingly; **~de Verse** rough or stumbling or halting verse

Hol|per|schwel|le [ˈhɔlpɐ-] **F** (Mot) speed bump or hump, sleeping policeman (inf Brit)

holp|rig [ˈhɔlprɪç] **ADJ** = holperig

Hol|schuld [ˈhoːl-] **F** (Comm) debt to be collected from the debtor at his residence

hol|ter|die|pol|ter [hɔltɐdiˈpɔltɐ] **ADV** helter-skelter; **der Wagen fuhr ~ den Berg hinunter** the cart went careering down the mountainside; **die Blechdose fiel ~ die Treppe hinunter** the tin went crash bang wallop down the stairs (inf)

hol|über [hoːlˈyːbɐ] **INTERJ** (old) Fährmann **~!** ahoy there, ferryman or boatman!

Ho|lun|der [hoˈlʊndɐ] **M -s, -** elder; (= Früchte) elderberries pl; **Spanischer** or **Blauer ~** lilac

Ho|lun|der- in cpds elder; **Ho|lun|der|bee|re** F elderberry; **Ho|lun|der|busch** M, **Ho|lun|der|strauch** M elder bush; **Ho|lun|der|wein** M elderberry wine

Holz [hɔlts] **NT -es, ⸚er** [ˈhœltsə] **a** wood; (esp zum Bauen, Schreinern) timber, lumber (esp US); (= Streichholz) match; **ein ~** a piece of wood or timber or lumber (esp US); (= Holzart) a wood; **lange Hölzer** long, untrimmed logs or timbers; **runde Hölzer** short, untrimmed logs or timbers; **flüssiges ~** (Tech) plastic wood; **aus ~** made of wood, wooden; **~ fällen** to fell trees, to cut down trees; **~ sägen** (lit) to saw wood; (inf: = schnarchen) to snore, to saw wood (US inf); **~ verarbeitend** wood-processing; **aus einem anderen ~ (geschnitzt) sein** (fig) to be cast in a different mould (Brit) or mold (US); **aus grobem ~ geschnitzt sein** (fig) to be insensitive; **aus hartem** or **härterem ~ geschnitzt sein** (fig) to be made of stern or sterner stuff; **aus demselben ~ geschnitzt sein** (fig) to be cast in the same mould (Brit) or mold (US); **er saß da wie ein Stück ~** he sat there like a block of wood; **ich bin nicht aus ~!** I'm not made of stone, I am made of flesh and blood; **~ vor der Hütte** or **Tür haben** (inf) to be well-endowed or well-stacked (inf), to have big boobs (inf); **~!** (Tennis etc) wood!; **Dummheit und Stolz wachsen auf einem ~** (Prov) stupidity and pride grow on the same tree (prov) **b** (= Kegel) skittle, ninepin; **~ schieben** to play skittles or ninepins; **gut ~!** have a good game! **c** (dated: = Wald, Gehölz) wood, woods pl

Holz- in cpds wood; (= aus Holz auch) wooden; (Build, Comm etc) timber, lumber (esp US); **Holz|ap|fel** M crab apple; **Holz|ar|bei|ter(in)** M(F) woodworker; (im Wald) woodcutter, lumberjack (esp US); **holz|arm** ADJ Gegend sparsely wooded or timbered; Papier with (a) low wood content; **Holz|art** F kind of wood or timber; **holz|ar|tig** ADJ woody,

wood-like; **Holz|asche** F wood ashes pl; **Holz|au|ge** **NT ~ sei wachsam** (inf) be careful; **Holz|bau** M **a** no pl wood-frame or timber-frame construction **b** pl **-bauten** wooden building; **Holz|bau|wei|se** F, no pl timber or wood-frame construction; **Holz|be|ar|bei|tung** F woodworking; (im Sägewerk) timber processing; **Holz|bein** NT wooden leg; **Holz|be|stand** M stock of wood or timber, wood or timber stock; (im Wald) stand of timber; **Holz|bild|hau|er(in)** M(F) wood carver; **Holz|blä|ser(in)** M(F) woodwind player; **wo sitzen die ~?** where do the woodwind sit?, where does the woodwind section sit?; **Holz|blas|in|stru|ment** NT woodwind instrument; **Holz|block** M pl **-blöcke** block of wood; **Holz|bock** M **a** (= Stützgestell) wooden stand or trestle **b** (= Insekt) wood tick, dog tick; **Holz|bo|den** M **a** (= Fußboden) wooden floor **b** (für Holz) wood loft, timber loft **c** (von Truhe etc) wooden bottom **d** (Forest) wooded or timbered ground; **Holz|boh|rer** M **a** (Tech) wood drill **b** (Zool) goat moth, leopard moth; **Holz|brand|ma|le|rei** F (Art) pokerwork, pyrography (form); **Holz|brei** M wood pulp; **Holz|bün|del** NT bundle of wood, faggot

Hölz|chen [ˈhœltsçən] **NT -s, -** small piece of wood; (= Streichholz) match

Holz-: **Holz|druck** M pl **-drucke** (Art) wood engraving; **Holz|dü|bel** M wooden dowel; **Holz|ein|schlag** M tree-felling, cutting-down of trees, timber harvesting (inf)

hol|zen [ˈhɔltsn] **VI a** (= Bäume fällen) to cut down or fell timber, to lumber (esp US); (fig inf: = abbauen, reduzieren) to cut back **b** (esp Ftbl) to hack; (inf: = sich schlagen) to fight; (Mus) to play badly **c** (inf: = schimpfen) to moan or grumble (gegen about) **VT** (rare) Wald to clear

Hol|zer [ˈhɔltsɐ] **M -s, -, Hol|ze|rin** [-ərɪn] **F -, -nen** (esp Ftbl) hacker, rough player

Hol|ze|rei [hɔltsəˈraɪ] **F -, -en** (inf) (= Rauferei) roughhouse (inf); (Ftbl auch) rough game or match; (Mus) third- or fourth-rate playing

höl|zern [ˈhœltsɐn] **ADJ** (lit, fig) wooden; **so ein ~er Kerl** such a wooden sort of chap **ADV** (fig) woodenly, stiffly

Holz-: **Holz|fäl|len** NT **-s,** no pl tree-felling, lumbering; **Holz|fäl|ler** [-fɛlɐ] **M -s, -, Holz|fäl|le|rin** [-fɛlərɪn] **F -, -nen** woodcutter, lumberjack (esp US); **Holz|fa|ser** F wood fibre (Brit) or fiber (US); **Holz|fa|ser|plat|te** F (wood) fibreboard (Brit) or fiberboard (US); **Holz|fäu|le** F wood rot; **holz|frei** ADJ Papier wood-free; **Holz|fre|vel** M (Jur) offence (Brit) or offense (US) against forest laws, infringement of forest regulations; **Holz|ha|cken** NT **-s,** no pl cutting or chopping wood; **Holz|ha|cker(in)** M(F) (Aus, old) woodcutter; **holz|hal|tig** ADJ Papier woody; **Holz|ham|mer** M mallet; **jdm etw mit dem ~ beibringen** to hammer sth into sb (inf); **Holz|ham|mer|me|tho|de** F (inf) sledgehammer method (inf); **Holz|han|del** M timber or lumber (esp US) trade; **Holz|hau|fen** M woodpile, pile or stack of wood; **Holz|haus** NT wooden or timber house

hol|zig [ˈhɔltsɪç] **ADJ** woody; Spargel, Rettich auch stringy, tough

Holz-: **Holz|kitt** M plastic wood; **Holz|klotz** M wood block, block of wood, log; (= Spielzeug) wooden brick; **er saß da wie ein ~** (inf) he sat there like a block or lump of wood; **Holz|koh|le** F charcoal; **Holz|kopf** M (fig inf) blockhead (inf); **Holz|la|ger** NT timberyard; **Holz|na|gel** M wooden nail or peg; **Holz|ofen** M wood-burning oven; **Holz|pan|ti|ne** F, **Holz|pan|tof|fel** M clog; **Holz|pflas|ter** NT wood-block paving; **Holz|pflock** M (wooden) peg; **holz|reich** ADJ well-wooded; **ein ~es Land** a country rich in timber; **Holz|reich|tum** M abundance of timber; **Holz|schäd|ling** M wood pest; **Holz|scheit** NT piece of (fire)wood, log; **Holz|schlag** M (= Vorgang) tree-felling, lumbering;

(= *Ort*) felling *or* lumbering area; **Holz|schliff** M mechanical wood pulp; **Holz|schnei-der(in)** M(F) wood engraver; **Holz|schnitt** M (*Art*) **a** (= *Kunst*) (art of) wood engraving **b** (= *Gegenstand*) wood engraving, woodcut; **holz|schnitt|ar|tig** (*fig*) **ADJ** simplistic; **ADV** simplistically; **Holz|schnit|zer(in)** M(F) wood carver; **Holz|schnit|ze|rei** F (art *or* craft of) wood carving; **Holz|schuh** M wooden shoe, clog, sabot; **Holz|schuh|tanz** M clog dance; **Holz|schutz|mit|tel** NT wood preservative; **Holz|schwamm** M wood fungus, dry rot; **Holz|span** M chip (of wood); (*beim Hobeln*) wood shaving; **Holz|split|ter** M splinter *or* sliver of wood; **Holz|sta|pel** M pile of wood, woodpile; **Holz|stich** M wood engraving; **Holz|stift** M small wooden nail *or* pin; **Holz|stock** M (engraved) wood block; **Holz|stoß** M pile of wood, woodpile; **Holz|ta|fel** F wooden panel; (*Sch*) wooden blackboard; **Holz|tä|fe|lung** F wood(en) panelling (*Brit*) *or* paneling (*US*); **Holz|tau|be** F wood pigeon; **holz|ver|ar|bei|tend** △ ADJ attr → Holz **a**; **Holz|ver|ar|bei|tung** F woodworking; (= *Holzveredelung*) wood processing; **Holz|ver|e|de|lung** F wood processing; **Holz|ver|koh|lung** F carbonization, wood distillation; **Holz|ver|schlag** M **a** (= *Schuppen*) wooden shed **b** (= *Verpackung*) wooden crate; **Holz|wa|ren** PL wooden articles, articles made of wood; **Holz|weg** M logging-path; **auf dem ~ sein** (*fig inf*) to be on the wrong track (*inf*); **wenn du meinst, ich gebe dir das, dann bist du auf dem ~** if you think I'm going to give it to you, you've got another think (*Brit*) *or* thought (*US*) coming (*inf*); **Holz|wirt|schaft** F timber *or* lumber (*esp US*) industry; **Holz|wol|le** F wood-wool; **Holz|wurm** M woodworm

Home- ['hom-]: **Home|ban|king** ['ho:mbɛŋkɪŋ] NT -, *no pl* home banking; **Home|page** ['ho:mpeːdʒ] F -, -s (*Comput, im Internet*) home page

ho|me|risch [ho'meːrɪʃ] ADJ Homeric

Home- ['ho:m-]: **Home|sit|ter** ['ho:mzɪtɐ] M -s, -, **Home|sit|te|rin** [-ərɪn] F -, -nen housesitter; **Home|trai|ner** ['ho:mtreːnɐ] M -s, - = **Heim-trainer**

Hom|mage [ɔ'maːʒ] F -, -n homage

Ho|mo ['ho:mo] M -s, -s (*dated inf*) homo (*dated inf*), queer (*inf*)

ho|mo-, **Homo-** *in cpds* homo; **ho|mo|gen** [homo'geːn] ADJ homogeneous; **ho|mo|ge|ni|sie|ren** [homogeni'ziːrən] *ptp* **homogenisiert** VT to homogenize; **Ho|mo|ge|ni|tät** [homogeni'tɛːt] F -, *no pl* homogeneity; **Ho|mo|graf** ▲ [homo'graːf] NT -s, -e (*Ling*) homograph; **Ho|mo|gra|fie** ▲ [homogra'fiː] F -, *no pl* (*Ling*) homography; **ho|mo|nym** [homo'nyːm] ADJ homonymous; **Ho|mo|nym** [homo'nyːm] NT -(e)s, -e homonym; **Ho|mo|ny|mie** [homony'miː] F -, *no pl* homonymy

Ho|mö|o|path [homøo'paːt] M -en, -en, **Ho|mö|o|pa|thin** [-'paːtɪn] F -, -nen homoeopath

Ho|mö|o|pa|thie [homøopa'tiː] F -, *no pl* homoeopathy

ho|mö|o|pa|thisch [homøo'paːtɪʃ] ADJ homoeopathic

Ho|mo-: **ho|mo|phil** [homo'fiːl] ADJ (*geh*) homophile; **ho|mo|phob** [homo'foːp] ADJ (*geh*) homophobic; **ho|mo|phon** [homo'foːn], **ho|mo|fon** ▲ ADJ (*Mus*) homophonic; (*Ling*) homophonous; **Ho|mo|phon** [homo'foːn] NT -s, -e, **Ho|mo|fon** ▲ NT -s, -e (*Ling*) homophone; **Ho|mo|pho|nie** ▲ [homofo'niː] F -, *no pl*, **Ho|mo|fo|nie** ▲ F - (*Mus, Ling*) homophony; **Ho|mo|se|xu|a|li|tät** [homozɛksuali'tɛːt] F homosexuality; **ho|mo|se|xu|ell** [homozɛ'ksuɛl] ADJ homosexual; **Ho|mo|se|xu|el|le(r)** [homozɛ'ksuɛlə] MF *decl as adj* homosexual

Ho|mun|ku|lus [ho'mʊŋkulʊs] M -, -se *or* **Ho|munkuli** [-li] homunculus

Hon|du|ras [hɔn'duːras] NT - Honduras

---

ho|nett [hɔ'nɛt] ADJ (*dated, geh*) honest, upright, respectable

Hong|kong ['hɔŋkɔŋ] NT -s Hong Kong

Ho|nig ['ho:nɪç] M -s, *no pl* honey; **türkischer ~** halva(h), = nougat; **sie schmierte ihm ~ ums Maul** *or* **um den Bart** *or* **um den Mund** (*fig inf*) she buttered him up (*inf*); **~ aus etw saugen** (*fig inf*) to capitalize on sth

Ho|nig-: **Ho|nig|bie|ne** F honeybee; **Ho|nig|brot** NT **a** (= *Kuchen*) honey cake **b** (= *Brot mit Honig*) bread and honey; **ho|nig|far|ben** ADJ honey-coloured (*Brit*), honey-colored (*US*), honey-yellow; **ho|nig|gelb** ADJ honey-yellow; **Ho|nig|klee** M (*Bot*) melitot; **Ho|nig|ku|chen** M honey cake; **Ho|nig|ku|chen|pferd** NT (*fig inf*) simpleton; **grinsen wie ein ~** to grin like a Cheshire cat; **Ho|nig|le|cken** NT -s, *no pl* (*fig*) **das ist kein ~** it's no picnic; **Ho|nig|me|lo|ne** F honeydew melon; **Ho|nig|mond** M (*rare*) honeymoon; **Ho|nig|schle|cken** NT -s, *no pl* **das ist kein ~** it's no picnic; **Ho|nig|schleu|der** F honey extractor; **ho|nig|süß** ADV as sweet as honey; (*fig*) Worte, Ton honeyed; *Lächeln* sickly sweet **ADV er lächelte ~** he smiled a sickly sweet smile; **Ho|nig|tau** M (*pflanzlich, tierisch*) honeydew; **Ho|nig|wa|be** F honeycomb; **Ho|nig|wein** M mead; **Ho|nig|zel|le** F honeycomb cell

Hon|neurs [(h)ɔ'nøːɐs] PL **die ~ machen** (*geh, iro*) to do the honours (*Brit*) *or* honors (*US*), to welcome the guests

Ho|no|rar [hono'raːɐ] NT -s, -e fee; (= *Autorenhonorar*) royalty

Ho|no|rar-: **Ho|no|rar|ab|rech|nung** F statement of account; (*von Schriftsteller*) royalties account; **Ho|no|rar|ba|sis** F **auf ~** on a fee-paying basis; **ho|no|rar|frei** ADJ free of charge; **Ho|no|rar|kon|sul(in)** M(F) honorary consul; **Ho|no|rar|pro|fes|sor(in)** M(F) honorary professor (*with no say in faculty matters*)

Ho|no|ra|ti|o|ren [honora'tsioːrən] PL dignitaries *pl*, notabilities *pl*

ho|no|rie|ren [hono'riːrən] *ptp* **honoriert** VT **a** (= *bezahlen*) to pay; (*Fin*) Wechsel, Scheck to honour (*Brit*), to honor (*US*), to meet; **jdm etw ~** to pay sb (a fee) for sth, to remunerate sb for sth; **meine Arbeit wird schlecht honoriert** my work is poorly remunerated **b** (= *zu würdigen wissen*) Vorschläge to acknowledge; (= *belohnen*) Bemühungen to reward

Ho|no|rie|rung F -, -en (*einer Rechnung*) payment (of a fee); (= *Bezahlung*) remuneration; (*Comm: von Wechsel, Scheck*) acceptance

ho|no|rig [ho'noːrɪç] ADJ (*dated*) (= *ehrenhaft*) honourable (*Brit*), honorable (*US*); (= *anständig*) decent

Ho|no|rig|keit F -, *no pl* (*dated*) (= *Ehrenhaftigkeit*) honourableness (*Brit*), honorableness (*US*); (= *Anständigkeit*) decency

ho|no|ris cau|sa [ho'noːrɪs 'kauza] ADV Dr. ~ - honorary doctor

hop|fen ['hɔpfn] VT Bier to hop

Hop|fen ['hɔpfn] M -s, - (*Bot*) hop; (*beim Brauen*) hops *pl*; **bei** *or* **an ihm ist ~ und Malz verloren** (*inf*) he's a hopeless case, he's a dead loss (*Brit inf*)

Hop|fen- *in cpds* hop; **Hop|fen|(an)|bau** M , *no pl* hop cultivation, hop-growing; **Hop|fen|dar|re** F hop drier *or* kiln; **Hop|fen|stan|ge** F hop-pole

Hop|lit [hɔ'pliːt] M -en, -en (*Hist*) hoplite

hopp [hɔp] INTERJ quick; **bei ihr muss alles ~ ~ gehen** she insists on doing everything doublequick *or* at the double (*inf*); **mach mal ein bisschen ~!** (*inf*) chop, chop! (*inf*); **~e ~e Reiter machen** (*baby-talk*) to ride a cock-horse (*on sb's knee, Brit*), to ride the horsy (*US*)

hop|peln ['hɔpln] VI *aux sein* (Hase) to lollop

Hop|pel|pop|pel ['hɔpl'pɔpl] NT -s, - (*dial*) **a** *breakfast made from scrambled egg with ham and fried potatoes* **b** (= *Getränk*) eggnog

---

hopp|la ['hɔpla] INTERJ (*beim Stolpern, Zusammenstoßen, Fangen etc*) whoops, oops; (*beim Zuwerfen*) catch; **~, jetzt habe ich die richtige Idee!** aha *or* Eureka, now I've got it!; **~, wer kommt denn da?** oh look, who's that coming there?; **~, jetzt komm ich!** look out, here I come!

hopp+neh|men VT *sep* (*inf*: = *verhaften*) to catch, to nick (*inf*)

hops¹ [hɔps] INTERJ jump; **~ waren sie über den Graben weg** with a jump they were over the ditch

hops² ADJ *pred* (*inf*) **~ sein** (= *verloren*) to be lost; (*Geld*) to be down the drain (*inf*); (= *entzwei*) to be broken *or* kaputt (*inf*) → **hopsgehen, hopsnehmen**

Hops [hɔps] M -es, -e (*inf*) hop, jump; **einen ~ über etw** (*acc*) **machen** to hop *or* jump over sth

hop|sa ['hɔpsa] INTERJ = **hoppla**

hop|sa|la ['hɔpsala] INTERJ upsadaisy

hop|sa|sa ['hɔpsasa] INTERJ up we go

hop|sen ['hɔpsn] VI *aux sein* (*inf*) (= *hüpfen*) to hop; (= *springen*) to jump

Hop|ser ['hɔpsɐ] M -s, - **a** (*inf*: = *kleiner Sprung*) (little) jump *or* leap; **sein Herz tat vor Freude einen ~** his heart gave a little leap for joy **b** (= *Tanz*) ecossaise

Hop|se|rei [hɔpsə'rai] F -, -en (*inf*) (= *Hüpferei*) jumping about, jumping up and down; (*pej*: = *Tanzen*) hopping about (*Brit*) *or* around

hops+ge|hen VI *sep irreg aux sein* (*inf*: = *verloren gehen*) to get lost; (*inf*: = *entzweigehen*) to get broken; (*inf*: = *sterben*) to kick the bucket (*inf*), to croak (*inf*)

hops+neh|men VT *sep irreg* **jdn ~** (*inf*: = *verhaften*) to nab sb (*inf*)

Hör-: **Hör|ap|pa|rat** M hearing aid; **hör|bar** ADJ audible; **sich ~ machen** (*inf*) to speak up; **hör|be|hin|dert** ADJ hard of hearing *pred*, partially deaf, with impaired hearing *pred*; **Hör|be|hin|der|te(r)** MF *decl as adj* person who is hard of hearing, hearing-impaired person; **Hör|be|reich** M (*des Ohrs*) hearing range; (*eines Senders*) transmission area; **Hör|bild** NT (*Rad*) feature broadcast, radio feature; **Hör|bril|le** F hearing-aid glasses *pl or* spectacles *pl*; **Hör|buch** NT talking book

hor|chen ['hɔrçn] VI to listen (+*dat, auf* +*acc* to); (*heimlich*) to eavesdrop; **horch!** (*liter*) hark! (*old, liter*)

Hor|cher ['hɔrçɐ] M -s, -, **Hor|che|rin** [-ərɪn] F -, -nen eavesdropper; **der ~ an der Wand hört seine eigne Schand** (*Prov*) eavesdroppers never hear any good about themselves

Horch-: **Horch|ge|rät** NT (*Mil*) sound detector *or* locator; (*Naut*) hydrophone; **Horch|pos|ten** M (*Mil*) listening post; **auf ~ sein** to be listening out for sth

Hor|de¹ ['hɔrdə] F -, -n (*lit, fig*) horde

Hor|de² F -, -n rack

hor|den|wei|se ['hɔrdnvaizə] ADV in hordes

hö|ren ['høːrən] VTI **a** (= *wahrnehmen*) to hear; **ich höre dich nicht** I can't hear you; **ich hörte ihn kommen** I heard him coming; **sei mal still, ich will das ~** be quiet, I want to hear this *or* listen to this; **er hat an der Wand gehört** he was listening at the wall; **gut/schlecht ~** to have good/bad hearing, to hear/not to hear well; **schwer ~** to be hard of hearing; **du hörst wohl schwer** *or* **schlecht!** (*inf*) you must be deaf!, are you hard of hearing?; **hört, hört!** (*Zustimmung*) hear! hear!; (*Missfallen*) come, come!; **etw an etw** (*dat*) **~** to hear sth from sth; **das lässt sich ~** (*fig*) that doesn't sound bad; **das lässt sich schon eher ~** (*inf*) that sounds (a bit) more like it; **das werde ich noch lange ~ müssen** *or* **zu ~ bekommen** I shall never hear the end *or* last of it; **ich will gar nichts ~!** I don't want to hear it; **ich habe sagen ~** I've heard it said *or* tell; **ich habe es sagen ~** I've heard it said; **er hört sich gern reden** he likes the sound

---

of his own voice; **hör mal!**, **~ Sie mal!** listen; **na hör mal!**, **na ~ Sie mal!** wait a minute!, look here!, listen here!

b (= *anhören*) *Hörspiel, Vortrag, Radio* to listen to; *Berichte, Sänger* to hear; (= *zu Wort kommen lassen*) to listen to, to hear; (*Rad*: = *empfangen*) to get; **ich will auch gehört werden** I want to be heard too; **bei wem ~ Sie in diesem Semester?** whose lectures are you going to this term?; **eine französische Vorlesung bei Professor X ~** to go to a French lecture by Professor X

c (= *sich nach etw richten*) to listen, to pay attention; (*dial*: = *gehorchen*) to obey, to listen; **auf jdn/etw ~** to listen to *or* heed sb/sth; **wer nicht ~ will, muss fühlen** (*Prov*) what did I tell you?; **der Hund hört auf den Namen Tobias** the dog answers to the name of Tobias

d (= *erfahren*) to hear; **von etw ~** to hear about *or* of sth; **von jdm gehört haben** to have heard of sb; **von jdm ~** (= *Nachricht bekommen*) to hear from sb; **Sie werden noch von mir ~** *or* **zu ~ kriegen** (*inf*: = *Drohung*) you'll be hearing from me, you haven't heard the last of this; **man hörte nie mehr etwas von ihm** he was never heard of again; **nie gehört!** (*inf*) never heard of him/it *etc*; **etwas/nichts von sich ~ lassen** to get/not to get in touch; **lassen Sie von sich ~** keep in touch; **ich lasse von mir ~** I'll be in touch; **er ließ nichts von sich ~** I *etc* haven't heard from him; **nach allem, was ich (über ihn/darüber) höre** from what I've heard *or* I hear (about him/it); **soviel man hört** from what I hear/one hears; **er kommt, wie ich höre** I hear he's coming; **man höre und staune!** would you believe it!; **so etwas** *or* **das habe ich ja noch nie gehört!** I've never heard anything like it (in all my life)!; **er wollte nichts** *or* **von uns gehört haben** he pretended not to have heard anything about it; **ich will davon** *or* **von der Sache nichts gehört haben** I don't want to know anything about it; **ich will mal nichts gehört haben** (*inf*) I haven't heard a thing, right? (*inf*)

Hö|ren NT -s, *no pl* hearing; (= *Radiohören*) listening; **das ~ von Musik** listening to music; **es verging ihm ~ und Sehen** he didn't know whether he was coming or going (*inf*); **er fuhr so schnell, dass mir ~ und Sehen verging** he drove so fast I almost passed out

Hö|ren|sa|gen NT **vom ~** from *or* by hearsay

hö|rens|wert ADJ **~ sein** to be worth hearing, to be worth listening to

Hö|rer¹ ['høːɐ] M -s, - (*Telec*) receiver; (= *Kopfhörer*) headphone, earphone

Hö|rer² ['høːɐ] M -s, -, **Hö|re|rin** [-ərɪn] F -, -nen (*Rad*) listener; (*Univ*) student (attending lectures); **sich als ~ einschreiben** to enrol (*Brit*) *or* enroll (*US*) for a lecture course

Hö|rer|brief M listener's letter

Hö|rer|schaft ['høːrəʃaft] F -, (*rare*) -en (*Rad*) listeners *pl*, audience; (*Univ*) number of students (attending a lecture)

Hör-: Hör|feh|ler M (*Med*) hearing defect; **diese falsche Information beruht auf einem ~** the wrong information was relayed because something was misheard; **das war ein ~ I/he** *etc* misheard it; **Hör|fol|ge** F (*Rad*) radio series; (= *Geschichte in Fortsetzungen*) radio serial; **Hör|funk** M sound radio; **Hör|ge|rät** NT, **Hör|hil|fe** F hearing aid; **hör|ge|schä|digt** ADJ hard of hearing *pred*, partially deaf, with impaired hearing *pred*; **Hör|gren|ze** F auditory threshold, limit of hearing

hö|rig ['høːrɪç] ADJ dependent (+*dat* on); (*Hist*) in bondage; **jdm (sexuell) ~ sein** to be (sexually) dependent on sb; **sich** (*dat*) **jdn ~ machen** to make sb sexually dependent on one; **er ist ihr ~** she has sexual power over him

Hö|ri|ge(r) ['høːrɪgə] MF *decl as adj* (*Hist*) bondsman/-woman, serf; (*fig*: = *sexuell Hörige*) person who is sexually dependent on sb

Hö|rig|keit F -, *no pl* dependence; (*Hist*) bondage, serfdom (*sexuell*) sexual dependence

Ho|ri|zont [hori'tsɔnt] M -(e)s, -e (*lit, fig*) horizon; (*Geol auch*) zone; **am ~** on the horizon; **das geht über meinen ~** (*fig*) that is beyond me or my comprehension; **er hat einen begrenzten** *or* **beschränkten ~** he has limited horizons; **künstlicher ~** (*Aviat*) artificial horizon

ho|ri|zon|tal [horitsɔn'taːl] ADJ horizontal; **das ~e Gewerbe** (*inf*) the oldest profession in the world (*inf*) ADV horizontally

Ho|ri|zon|ta|le [horitsɔn'taːlə] F -(n), -n (*Math*) horizontal (line); **er befindet sich in der ~n** (*inf*) he is lying down (in bed); **sich in die ~ begeben** (*inf*) to adopt the horizontal (*hum*)

Hor|mon [hɔr'moːn] NT -s, -e hormone

hor|mo|nal [hɔrmo'naːl], **hor|mo|nell** [hɔrmo'nɛl] ADJ hormone *attr*, hormonal ADV behandeln, beeinflussen with hormones; **beeinflusst, gesteuert** by hormones; **~ bedingt sein** to be caused by hormones; (*Störung*) to be caused by a hormonal imbalance; **jdn/etw ~ behandeln** to treat sb/sth with hormones, to give sb hormone treatment

Hor|mon-: Hor|mon|be|hand|lung F hormone treatment; **Hor|mon|cock|tail** M hormone cocktail; **Hor|mon|drü|se** F endocrine gland; **Hor|mon|haus|halt** M hormone *or* hormonal balance; **Hor|mon|prä|pa|rat** NT hormone preparation; **Hor|mon|skan|dal** M (growth) hormone scandal; **Hor|mon|spie|gel** M hormone level; **Hor|mon|sprit|ze** F hormone injection, shot of hormones (*inf*)

Hör|mu|schel F (*Telec*) earpiece

Horn [hɔrn] NT -(e)s, ⸚er ['hœrnə] **a** (*von Tieren*, = *Trinkhorn*) horn; (*fig inf*: = *Beule*) bump, lump; **jdn mit den Hörnern aufspießen** to gore sb; **sich** (*dat*) **die Hörner ablaufen** *or* **abschleifen** (*inf*) to sow one's wild oats; **jdm Hörner aufsetzen** (*inf*) to cuckold sb, to give sb horns (*old*); **Hörner tragen** (*fig*) to be a cuckold; **das ~ von Afrika** (*Geog*) the Horn of Africa → **Stier**

b (*Mus*) (*Mil*) bugle; (*von Auto etc*) horn, hooter; **die Hörner** (*im Orchester*) the horns *pl*, the horn section; **ins ~ stoßen** to blow *or* sound the horn; **ins gleiche ~ blasen** *or* **stoßen** *or* **tuten** (*fig*) to sing the same tune; **kräftig ins ~ stoßen** (*fig inf*: = *angeben*) to blow one's own trumpet

c (*bei Schnecke*) horn, feeler

Horn-: horn|ar|tig ADJ horn-like; **Horn|ber|ger Schie|ßen** ['hɔrnbɛrgə] NT **wie das ~ ausgehen** *or* **enden** to come to nothing; **Horn|blä|ser(in)** M(F) (*Mus*) horn player; **Horn|blen|de** F (*Geol*) hornblende; **Horn|bril|le** F horn-rimmed glasses *pl or* spectacles *pl*

Hörn|chen ['hœrnçən] NT -s, - **a** (= *kleines Horn*) little horn **b** (= *Gebäck*) croissant **c** (*Zool*) squirrel; (= *Backenhörnchen*) chipmunk, ground squirrel; (= *Flughörnchen*) flying squirrel

Hör|ner|klang M sound of horns *or* bugles

hör|nern ['hœrnən] ADJ (made of) horn

Hör|nerv M auditory nerve

Horn-: horn|för|mig ADJ horn-shaped; **Horn|ge|stell** NT **eine Brille mit ~** horn-rimmed glasses *pl*; **Horn|haut** F (patch of) hard *or* horny skin, callous; (*des Auges*) cornea; **Horn|haut|ent|zün|dung** F (*Med*) inflammation of the cornea, keratitis (*spec*); **Horn|haut|trü|bung** F (*Med*) corneal opacity

hor|nig ['hɔrnɪç] ADJ horny, like horn

Hor|nis|se [hɔr'nɪsə] F -, -n hornet

Hor|nis|sen|nest NT hornet's nest

Hor|nist [hɔr'nɪst] M -en, -en, **Hor|nis|tin** [-'nɪstɪn] F -, -nen horn player; (*Mil*) bugler

Horn-: Horn|kamm M horn comb; **Horn|ochs** M, **Horn|och|se** M (*fig inf*) blockhead (*inf*), idiot; **Horn|sig|nal** NT (*Mil*) bugle call; (*Rail*) horn signal; (*von Auto*) honk, hoot

Hor|nung ['hɔrnʊŋ] M -s, -e (*obs*) February

Horn|vieh NT horned cattle *pl*; (*fig inf*: = *Idiot*) blockhead (*inf*), idiot

Hör|or|gan NT organ of hearing

Ho|ro|skop [horo'skoːp] NT -s, -e horoscope; **jdm das ~ stellen** to cast sb's horoscope

Hör|pro|be F **jetzt eine ~ aus seiner letzten CD** now here's a sample from his latest CD

hor|rend [hɔ'rɛnt] ADJ horrendous ADV *teuer* horrendously

hor|ri|bi|le dic|tu [hɔ'riːbile 'dɪktu] ADV (*geh*) terrible to relate

hor|ri|do [hɔri'doː] INTERJ (*Hunt*) halloo

Hor|ri|do [hɔri'doː] NT -s, -s halloo(ing)

Hör|rohr NT **a** ear trumpet **b** (*Med*) stethoscope

Hor|ror ['hɔrɔːɐ] M -s, *no pl* horror (*vor* +*dat* of); **ein unbeschreiblicher ~ überfiel mich** I was seized by an indescribable feeling of horror

Hor|ror- *in cpds* horror; **Hor|ror|film** M horror film; **Hor|ror|scho|cker** M (*Press sl*) (= *Film*) horror film; (= *Roman*) horror novel; (= *Buch*) horror book; **Hor|ror|sze|na|rio** NT nightmare scenario; **Hor|ror|sze|ne** F scene of horror, horrific scene; **Hor|ror|trip** M (*inf*) horror trip (*inf*); **Hor|ror|vi|si|on** M nightmare vision

Hör-: Hör|saal M (*Univ*) lecture room *or* hall, lecture theatre (*Brit*) *or* theater (*US*); **Hör|schwel|le** F auditory threshold

Hors d'oeuv|re [(h)ɔr'dœːvrə, (h)ɔːrə'dœːvrə] NT -s, -s hors d'oeuvre

Hör|spiel NT (*Rad*) radio play

Horst [hɔrst] M -(e)s, -e **a** (= *Nest*) nest; (= *Adlerhorst*) eyrie **b** (= *Gehölz*) thicket, shrubbery **c** (*Bot*) (*von Blumen*) cluster; (*von Bambus, Gras*) tuft **d** (*Geol*) horst **e** (= *Fliegerhorst*) military airfield, military aerodrome (*Brit*)

Hör|sturz M hearing loss

Hort [hɔrt] M -(e)s, -e **a** (*old, poet*: = *Schatz*) hoard, treasure **b** (*geh*: = *Zufluchtsstätte*) refuge, shelter; **ein ~ der Freiheit** a stronghold of liberty; **der Herr sei mein ~** (*Bibl*) the Lord be my refuge (*Bibl*) **c** (= *Kinderhort*) ≈ after-school care club (*Brit*), ≈ after-school daycare (*US*)

hor|ten ['hɔrtn] VT *Geld, Vorräte etc* to hoard; *Rohstoffe etc* to stockpile

Hor|ten|sie [hɔr'tɛnziə] F -, -n hydrangea

Hort|platz M (= *Platz in Kinderhort*) place in an after-school care club *or* centre (*Brit*) *or* center (*US*)

Hor|tung F -, -en hoarding; (*von Rohstoffen*) stockpiling

Hör-: Hör|ver|mö|gen NT hearing (capacity); **Hör|wei|te** F hearing range; **in/außer ~** within/out of hearing *or* earshot; **Hör|zent|rum** NT (*Anat*) auditory *or* acoustic centre (*Brit*) *or* center (*US*)

Hös|chen ['høːsçən] NT -s, - **a** (= *Kinderhose*) (pair of) trousers *pl* (*esp Brit*) *or* pants *pl* (*esp US*); (= *Strampelhöschen*) (pair of) rompers *pl*; **kurze(s) ~** (= *Unterhose*) (pair of) shorts *pl* **b** (= *Unterhose*) (pair of) panties *pl or* knickers *pl* (*Brit*); (*für Kinder*) (pair of) underpants *pl or* pants *pl* (*Brit*) **c** (*Zool*: *einer Biene*) pollen load *or* pellet

Hös|chen|win|del F disposable nappy (*Brit*) *or* diaper (*US*)

Ho|se ['hoːzə] F -, -n trousers *pl* (*esp Brit*), pants *pl* (*esp US*); (= *Damenhose auch*) slacks *pl*; (= *Bundhose*) breeches *pl*; (= *Reithose*) jodhpurs *pl*, (riding) breeches *pl*; (= *Badehose*) swimming trunks *pl*; (= *Unterhose*) underpants *pl*, pants *pl* (*Brit*); (*von Vogel*) leg feathers *pl*; **ich brauche eine neue ~** I need a new pair of trousers *etc*, I need some new trousers *etc*; **zwei ~n** two pairs of trousers *etc*; **die ~n anhaben** (*fig inf*) to wear the trousers (*Brit*) *or* pants (*inf*); **das Herz fiel** *or* **rutschte ihm in die ~** (*inf*) his heart was in his mouth; **die ~n voll haben** (*lit*) to have dirtied oneself, to have made a mess in one's pants (*Brit*); (*fig inf*) to be scared shitless (*sl*), to be wetting oneself (*inf*); **sich** (*dat*) **in die ~n machen** (*lit*) to dirty oneself, to make a mess in one's pants (*Brit*); (*fig inf*) to shit (*sl*) *or* wet (*inf*) oneself; **in die ~ gehen** (*inf*) to be a complete flop (*inf*); **tote ~** (*inf*) nothing doing (*inf*); **der Film war tote ~** (*inf*) the film was a dead loss (*Brit inf*) *or* a waste of time

Ho|sen-: Ho|sen|an|zug M trouser suit (*Brit*), pantsuit (*US*); **Ho|sen|auf|schlag** M turn-up (*Brit*), cuff (*US*); **Ho|sen|band** [-bant] NT *pl* **-bänder** knee-band; **Ho|sen|band|or|den** M Order of the Garter; **Ho|sen|bein** NT trouser (*esp Brit*) *or* pant (*esp US*) leg; **Ho|sen|bo-den** M seat (of trousers *esp Brit*) *or* pants (*esp US*); **den ~ voll kriegen** (*inf*) to get a smacked bottom; **sich auf den ~ setzen** (*inf*) (= *arbeiten*) to get stuck in (*inf*), to knuckle down; (= *stillsitzen*) to sit down and stay sitting down; **Ho|sen|bo|je** F (*Naut*) breeches buoy; **Ho-sen|bü|gel** M trouser (*esp Brit*) *or* pant (*esp US*) hanger; **Ho|sen|bund** M *pl* **-bünde** waistband; **Ho|sen|klam|mer** F trouser clip (*esp Brit*), cycle clip; **Ho|sen|klap|pe** F flap; **Ho-sen|knopf** M trouser (*esp Brit*) *or* pant (*esp US*) button; **Ho|sen|latz** M (= *Verschluss*) flies *pl*, fly; (*von Latzhose*) bib; **Ho|sen|matz** M (*inf*) (= *kleines Kind*) **du (kleiner) ~** my little darling; **Ho|sen|naht** F trouser (*esp Brit*) *or* pant (*esp US*) seam; **mit den Händen an der ~** (*Mil*) (stand to attention,) thumbs on (your) trouser (*esp Brit*) *or* pant (*esp US*) seams; **Ho|sen-rock** M divided skirt, culottes *pl*; **Ho|sen|schei|ßer(in)** M(F) **a** (*inf*: = *Kind*) mucky pup (*Brit inf*), pig (*inf*); **du kleiner ~** you mucky little pup (*Brit inf*), you little pig (*inf*) **b** (*sl*: = *Feigling*) chicken (*inf*); (= *Junge*) scaredy-pants (*inf*); **Ho|sen|schlitz** M flies *pl*, fly; **Ho|sen-span|ner** M trouser (*esp Brit*) *or* pant (*esp US*) hanger; **Ho|sen|stall** M (*inf*: = *Schlitz*) flies *pl*, fly; **Ho|sen|ta|sche** F trouser pocket (*Brit*), pant(s) *or* trousers pocket (*US*); **Ho-sen|trä|ger** PL (pair of) braces *pl* (*Brit*) *or* suspenders *pl* (*US*)

ho|si|an|na [ho'ziana] INTERJ hosanna

Ho|si|an|na [ho'ziana] NT **-s, -s** hosanna

Hos|pi|tal [hɔspi'ta:l] NT **-s, -e** *or* **Hospitäler** [-'tɛ:lɐ] (*dated*) **a** (= *Krankenhaus*) hospital **b** (= *Pflegeheim*) (old people's) home

Hos|pi|ta|lis|mus [hɔspita'lɪsmʊs] M **-**, *no pl* (*Med*) hospitalism

Hos|pi|tant [hɔspi'tant] M **-en, -en**, **Hos|pi-tan|tin** [-'tantɪn] F **-, -nen** (*Univ*) someone sitting in on lectures *or* (*Sch*) classes, auditor (*US*)

Hos|pi|ta|ti|on [hɔspita'tsio:n] F **-, -en** (*Univ*) sitting in on lectures *or* (*Sch*) classes (*bei jdm* with sb)

hos|pi|tie|ren [hɔspi'ti:rən] *ptp* **hospitiert** VI (*Univ*) to sit in on lectures *or* (*Sch*) classes (*bei jdm* with sb)

Hos|piz [hɔs'pi:ts] NT **-es, -e** hospice; (= *christliches Hospiz*) *private hotel under religious management*

Host [hoːst] M **-s, -s** (*Comput*) host

Host|com|pu|ter [hoːst-] M (*Comput*) host (computer)

Hos|tess ▲ ['hɔstɛs, hɔs'tɛs] F **-, -en** hostess

Hos|tie ['hɔstiə] F **-, -n** (*Eccl*) host, consecrated wafer

Hos|ti|en-: Hos|ti|en|ge|fäß NT pyx, ciborium; **Hos|ti|en|kelch** M chalice; **Hos|ti|en|schach|tel** F box for communion wafers; **Hos|ti|en|schrein** M tabernacle; **Hos|ti|en|tel|ler** M paten

Hot|dog ▲ ['hɔt'dɔk] NT OR M **-s, -s**, **Hot Dog** ▲ NT OR M **-s, -s** (*Cook*) hot dog

Ho|tel [ho'tɛl] NT **-s, -s** hotel

Ho|tel|boy M page (boy), bellboy (*US*), bellhop (*US*)

Ho|tel|fach NT , *no pl* hotel management

Ho|tel|fach-: Ho|tel|fach|frau F hotel manageress; **Ho|tel|fach|mann** M hotel manager; **Ho|tel|fach|schu|le** F college of hotel management

Ho|tel|füh|rer M hotel guide

Ho|tel gar|ni [ho'tɛl gar'ni:] NT **- -, -s -s** bed and breakfast hotel

Ho|tel-: Ho|tel|ge|wer|be NT hotel business; **Ho|tel|hal|le** F (hotel) lobby

Ho|te|li|er [hotɛ'lie:] M **-s, -s** hotelier

Ho|tel|le|rie [hotɛlə'ri:] F **-**, *no pl* (*Sw*) hotel business

Ho|tel-: Ho|tel|nach|weis M hotel register; **Ho|tel|pa|ge** M page (boy), bellboy (*US*), bellhop (*US*); **Ho|tel|per|so|nal** NT hotel staff; **Ho|tel|por|ti|er** M hotel *or* hall porter; **Ho|tel|rech|nung** F hotel bill (*Brit*) *or* check (*US*); **Ho|tel|sil|ber** NT hotel cutlery; **Ho|tel-und Gast|stät|ten|ge|wer|be** NT hotel and restaurant trade, catering industry; **Ho|tel|ver|zeich|nis** NT hotel register; **Ho|tel|zim-mer** NT hotel room

Hot|key ['hɔtki:] M **-s, -s** (*Comput*) hot key

Hot|line ['hɔtlaɪn] F **-, -s** (*Telec*: = *Informationsdienst, Sorgentelefon*) helpline; **eine ~ einrichten** to set up a helpline

Hot|spot ['hɔtspɔt] M **-s, -s** (*Geol, Comput*) hot spot

hott [hɔt] INTERJ (= *vorwärts*) gee up; (= *nach rechts*) gee

Hot|ten|tot|te [hɔtn̩'tɔtə] M **-n, -n**, **Hot|ten-tot|tin** [-'tɔtɪn] F **-, -nen** Hottentot; **sie benehmen sich wie die ~n** (*inf*) they behave like savages

hpts. *abbr von* **hauptsächlich**

Hptst. *abbr von* **Hauptstadt**

Hr. *abbr von* **Herr** Mr

Hrn. *abbr von* **Herrn**

hrsg. *abbr von* **herausgegeben** edited, ed.

Hrsg. *abbr von* **Herausgeber** ed.

HTML [ha:te:ɛm'ɛl] *abbr* (*Comput, Internet*) *von* **HyperText Markup Language** HTML

http [ha:te:te:'pe:] *abbr* (*Comput, Internet*) *von* **hypertext transfer** *or* **transport protocol** http

hu [hu:] INTERJ (*Schaudern*) ugh; (*Schrecken, Kälte etc*) whew

hü [hy:] INTERJ (= *vorwärts*) gee up; (= *nach links*) wo hi; **einmal sagt er hü, einmal hott** (*inf*) first he says one thing and then another, he's always chopping and changing (*Brit inf*)

Hub [hu:p] M **-(e)s, ⸚e** ['hy:bə] (*Tech*) **a** (*bei Maschinen*: = *Kolbenhub*) (piston) stroke **b** (*bei Kränen*: = *Leistung*) lifting *or* hoisting capacity, lift

Hub|bel ['hʊbl] M **-s, -** (*inf*) bump

hub|be|lig ['hʊbəlɪç] ADJ (*inf*) bumpy

Hub|ble-Te|le|skop ['habl-] NT , **Hub|ble-te|le|skop** NT Hubble telescope

hubb|lig ['hʊblɪç] ADJ (*inf*) bumpy

Hub|brü|cke F lift bridge

Hu|bel ['hu:bl] M **-s, -** (*inf*) bump

hü|ben ['hy:bn̩] ADV over here, (on) this side; **~ und** *or* **wie drüben** on both sides

Hu|ber|tus|jagd [hu'bɛrtʊs-] F St Hubert's Day hunt

Hub-: Hub|in|sel F drilling rig *or* platform; **Hub|kar|ren** M lift(ing) truck; **Hub|kraft** F lifting *or* hoisting capacity; **Hub|mag|net** M solenoid; **Hub|raum** M (*Aut*) cubic capacity

hübsch [hypʃ] ADJ **a** (= *gut aussehend*) pretty; (= *reizvoll*) *Ausflug, Geschenk* lovely, delightful, nice; (*inf*: = *nett*) lovely, nice; **sich ~ machen** to make oneself look pretty; **das wäre doch ~, wenn ...** it would be lovely if ...; **ihr (beiden) Hübschen** (*inf*) you two
b (*iro inf*: = *unangenehm*) fine, pretty, nice; **eine ~e Geschichte/Bescherung** a pretty kettle of fish, a fine how-d'ye-do; **das kann ja ~ werden** that'll be just great; **da hast du dir etwas Hübsches eingebrockt!** now you've got yourself into a fine *or* pretty mess!
c (*inf*: = *beträchtlich*) tidy, pretty, nice; **ein ~es Vermögen** a pretty penny (*inf*); **ein ~es Summchen** a tidy sum
ADV **a** (= *nett*) *einrichten, dekorieren, gestalten*,

sich kleiden nicely; **~ aussehen** to look pretty; **er macht das schon ganz ~** he's doing it very nicely *or* well
b (= *ziemlich*) pretty; *fluchen, dazulernen, reinlegen* really; **da musste ich aber ganz ~ arbeiten** I really had to work pretty hard; **ganz ~ viel bezahlen** to pay quite a bit
c (*inf*: = *wie es sein soll*) **~ artig/leise** nice and good/quiet; **das werde ich ~ bleiben lassen** I'm going to leave well alone; **das wirst du ~ bleiben lassen!** don't you dare; **das wirst du ~ sein lassen** you're going to do nothing of the kind; **sei ~ artig!** be a good boy/girl; **immer ~ langsam!** nice and easy does it, (take it) nice and slowly

Hub|schrau|ber ['hu:pʃraubɐ] M **-s, -** helicopter

Hub|schrau|ber-: Hub|schrau|ber|dienst M helicopter service; **Hub|schrau|ber|flug-platz** M , **Hub|schrau|ber|lan|de|platz** M heliport; **Hub|schrau|ber|trä|ger** M (*Naut*) helicopter-carrier

Hub-: Hub|stap|ler [-ʃta:plɐ] M **-s, -** stacking truck; **Hub|vo|lu|men** NT (*Tech*) cubic capacity

huch [hʊx] INTERJ ooh

Hu|cke ['hʊkə] F **-, -n** (*obs*) (= *Last*) load; (= *Korb*) pannier; **jdm die ~ voll hauen** (*inf*) to give sb a good thrashing (*inf*) *or* hiding (*inf*); **die ~ voll kriegen** (*inf*) to get a thrashing (*inf*) *or* hiding; **jdm die ~ voll lügen** (*inf*) to tell sb a pack of lies; **sich** (*dat*) **die ~ voll saufen** (*inf*) to have a skinful (*Brit inf*), to have a few (too many)

hu|cke|pack ['hʊkəpak] ADV piggy-back (*auch Comput*), pick-a-back; **ein Kind ~ nehmen/tra-gen** to give a child a piggy-back (ride), to carry a child piggy-back *or* pick-a-back

Hu|cke|pack- ['hʊkəpak-]: **Hu|cke|pack|ver-fah|ren** NT (*Space, Rail*) piggy-back system; (*Chem*) piggy-back process; **Hu|cke|pack|ver-kehr** M (*Rail*) piggy-back transport (*US*), motorail service; **im ~** by motorail

Hu|de|lei [hu:də'lai] F **-, -en** (*esp S Ger, Aus*: *inf*) slipshod *or* sloppy (*inf*) work

hu|deln ['hu:dln̩] VI (*esp S Ger, Aus*: *inf*) to work sloppily, to do slipshod work

Hud|ler ['hu:dlɐ] M **-s, -**, **Hud|le|rin** [-ərɪn] F **-, -nen** (*esp S Ger, Aus*: *inf*) slipshod *or* sloppy worker, bungler (*inf*)

hud|lig ['hu:dlɪç] (*esp S Ger, Aus*: *inf*) ADJ slipshod, sloppy (*inf*) ADV sloppily, carelessly; **~ arbeiten** to work sloppily, to do sloppy *or* slipshod work

Hud|ri|wud|ri ['hu:dri'vu:dri] M **-s, -s**, **Hud|ri-Wud|ri** M **-s, -s** (*Aus, inf*: = *unruhiger Mensch*) bag *or* bundle of nerves

Huf [hu:f] M **-(e)s, -e** hoof; **einem Pferd die ~e beschlagen** to shoe a horse

Huf|be|schlag M (horse)shoeing

Huf|ei|sen NT horseshoe

Huf|ei|sen-: huf|ei|sen|för|mig ADJ horseshoe-shaped, (in) the shape of a horseshoe ADV in the shape of a horseshoe; **Huf|ei|sen-mag|net** M horseshoe magnet

Hu|fen|dorf NT *village arranged in a straight line with strips of farmland extending behind each house*

Huf-: Huf|lat|tich M (*Bot*) coltsfoot; **Huf|na-gel** M horseshoe nail; **Huf|schlag** M (= *Getrappel*) hoofbeats *pl*; (= *Stoß*) kick (from a horse); **dabei hat er einen ~ abbekommen** the horse kicked him; **Huf|schmied(in)** M(F) blacksmith, farrier; **Huf|schmie|de** F smithy, blacksmith's *or* farrier's (workshop)

Hüft-: Hüft|bein NT hipbone; **hüft|be|tont** ADJ **ein ~es Kleid** a dress that emphasizes the hips; **Hüft|bruch** M fractured hip, hip fracture

Hüf|te ['hʏftə] F **-, -n** hip; (*von Tieren*) haunch; **bis an die ~n reichen** to come up to the waist; **wir standen bis an die ~n in Brennnesseln/im**

Wasser we stood waist-high *or* up to the waist in (stinging) nettles/waist-deep *or* up to the waist in water; **aus der ~ schießen** to shoot from the hip; **mit wiegenden ~n** with hips swaying; **die Arme in die ~n stützen** to put one's hands on one's hips; **er stand mit den Armen in die ~n gestützt da** he stood there hands on hips, he stood there with arms akimbo

Hüft-: Hüft|ge|gend F hip region; **Hüft|ge|lenk** NT hip joint; **Hüft|gür|tel** M , **Hüft|hal|ter** M girdle; **hüft|hoch** ADJ *Pflanzen etc* waist-high; *Wasser etc* waist-deep; **hüft|hohe Gummistiefel** rubber waders ADV **wir standen ~ im Farnkraut/Schlamm** we stood waist-high *or* up to the waist in ferns/waist-deep *or* up to the waist in mud

Huf|tier NT hoofed animal, ungulate *(form)*

Hüft-: Hüft|kno|chen M hipbone; **Hüft|lei|den** NT hip trouble; **Hüft|schmerz** M pain in the hip; **Hüft|um|fang** M hip measurement; **Hüft|ver|ren|kung** F dislocation of the hip

Hü|gel ['hy:gl] M **-s, -** hill; (= *Grab-, Erdhaufen*) mound; **ein kleiner ~** a hillock

Hü|gel-: hü|gel|ab [hy:gl'lap] ADV downhill; **hü|gel|an** [hy:gl'lan], **hü|gel|auf** [hy:gl'lauf] ADV uphill; **Hü|gel|beet** NT raised bed; **Hü|gel|grab** NT (*Archeol*) barrow, tumulus

hü|ge|lig ['hy:gəlɪç] ADJ hilly, undulating, rolling *attr*

Hü|gel-: Hü|gel|ket|te F range *or* chain of hills; **Hü|gel|land** NT hilly country

Hu|ge|not|te [hugə'nɔtə] M **-n, -n, Hu|ge|not|tin** [-'nɔtɪn] F **-, -nen** Huguenot

hüg|lig ['hy:glɪç] ADJ = hügelig

huh [hu:] INTERJ = hu

hüh [hy:] INTERJ = hü

Huhn [hu:n] NT **-(e)s, ⸚er** ['hy:nɐ] **a** chicken (*auch Cook*); (= *Henne*) hen, chicken; (*Gattung*) fowl, gallinaceous bird *(form)*; **mit den Hühnern aufstehen** (*inf*) to get up with the lark; **mit den Hühnern zu Bett gehen** (*inf*) to go to bed early; **da lachen ja die Hühner** (*inf*) what a joke, it's enough to make a cat laugh (*inf*); **ich sehe aus wie ein gerupftes ~** (*inf*) my hair looks like a haystack (*Brit inf*) *or* a rat's nest (*US inf*) → **blind a**
b (*inf*) **du krankes ~** you poor old thing; **ein verrücktes** *or* **komisches** *or* **ulkiges ~** a queer bird *or* fish (*Brit inf*), a strange *or* odd character; **ein dummes ~** a silly goose; **ein versoffenes ~** a tippler (*inf*)

Hühn|chen ['hy:nçən] NT **-s, -** (young) chicken, pullet; (= *Brathühnchen*) (roast) chicken; **mit jdm ein ~ zu rupfen haben** (*inf*) to have a bone to pick with sb (*inf*)

Hüh|ner-: Hüh|ner|au|ge NT (*Med*) corn; **jdm auf die ~n treten** (*hum*) to tread on sb's corns (*Brit inf*) *or* feet (*US inf*); **Hüh|ner|au|gen|pflas|ter** NT corn plaster; **Hüh|ner|bouil|lon** F , **Hüh|ner|brü|he** F (clear) chicken broth; **Hüh|ner|brust** F (*Cook*) chicken breast; (*Med inf*) pigeon breast (*Brit*), chicken breast (*US*); (*sl*: = *flacher Busen*) **eine ~ haben** to be as flat as a pancake (*esp Brit inf*) *or* a board (*US inf*); **Hüh|ner|dieb(in)** M(F) chicken thief; **er musste sich wie ein ~ wegschleichen** he had to slink off with his tail between his legs; **Hüh|ner|draht** M chicken wire; **Hüh|ner|ei** [-lai] NT hen's egg; **Hüh|ner|farm** F chicken farm; **Hüh|ner|fleisch** NT chicken (meat); **Hüh|ner|fri|kas|see** NT chicken fricassee; **Hüh|ner|fut|ter** NT chicken feed; **Hüh|ner|gott** M (*Miner*) holystone; **Hüh|ner|ha|bicht** M goshawk; **Hüh|ner|haus** NT henhouse, chicken coop; **Hüh|ner|hof** M chicken run; **Hüh|ner|hund** M pointer; **Hüh|ner|klein** [-klain] NT **-s, no pl** (*Cook*) chicken trimmings *pl*; **Hüh|ner|lei|ter** F chicken ladder; **Hüh|ner|mist** M chicken droppings *pl*; (*zum Düngen*) chicken manure; **Hüh|ner|pas|te|te** F chicken pie;

Hüh|ner|pest F (*Vet*) fowl pest; **Hüh|ner|stall** M henhouse, chicken coop; **Hüh|ner|stan|ge** F perch, (chicken) roost; **Hüh|ner|sup|pe** F chicken soup; **Hüh|ner|vö|gel** PL (*Orn*) gallinaceans *pl* (*form*), gallinaceous birds *pl* (*form*); **Hüh|ner|zucht** F chicken breeding *or* farming

hui [hui] INTERJ whoosh; **~, das war aber schnell!** wow, that was quick!; **außen ~, innen pfui** (*prov inf*) he/she/it is fine on the outside, but inside it's a different story (*inf*)

Hu|la-Hoop [hu:la'hʊp] M OR NT **-s, no pl** Hula Hoop®

Hu|la-Hoop-Rei|fen [hu:la'hʊp-] M Hula Hoop®

Huld [hʊlt] F **-, no pl** (*old liter*) (= *Güte*) grace, graciousness; (= *Gunst*) favour (*Brit*), favor (*US*); **jdm seine ~ schenken** to bestow one's favour (*Brit*) *or* favor (*US*) upon sb (*liter*); **sie stand in seiner ~** she was in his good graces

hul|di|gen ['hʊldɪgn] VI +*dat* (*liter*) **a** *einem König, Papst etc* to render *or* do *or* pay homage to; *einem Künstler, Lehrmeister etc* to pay homage to; *einer Dame* to pay one's attentions *or* addresses to (*liter*) **b** *einer Ansicht* to subscribe to; *einer Sitte, einem Glauben etc* to embrace; *einem Laster* to indulge in

Hul|di|gung F **-, -en** (*old, liter*) **a** (*Hist:* = *Treueid*) homage, oath of allegiance **b** (= *Verehrung*) homage; (*einer Dame*) attentions *pl* (*liter*), addresses *pl* (*liter*); (= *Beifall*) homage; **jdm seine ~ darbringen** to pay homage to sb

huld|reich, huld|voll ADJ (*old, liter*) gracious ADV (*geh*) graciously; **~ lächelnd** with a gracious smile; **~ tun** (*iro*) to act gallantly

Hül|fe ['hʏlfə] F **-, -n** (*obs*) = **Hilfe a**

Hül|le ['hʏlə] F **-, -n a** cover; (*für Ausweiskarten etc*) holder, case; (= *Cellophanhülle*) wrapping; (*liter, hum:* = *Kleidung*) clothes *pl*, piece of clothing; (*liter: eines Menschen*) exterior; (= *abgestreifte Schlangenhaut*) skin; **die ~n fallen lassen** to peel *or* strip off; **die letzten ~n fallen lassen** to shed the last layer; **der Körper als ~ der Seele** the body as the temple of the soul; **die sterbliche ~** the mortal remains *pl*
b (*Anat*) integument **c** (*Bot*) involucre (*form*) **d** (*Phys:* = *Atomhülle*) shell **e** **in ~ und Fülle** in abundance; **Äpfel/Whisky/Frauen/Sorgen etc in ~ und Fülle** apples/whisky/women/worries etc galore; **es gab alles in ~ und Fülle** there was plenty *or* an abundance of everything

hül|len ['hʏlən] VT (*geh*) to wrap; **in Dunkel gehüllt** shrouded in darkness; **in Flammen gehüllt** enveloped in flames; **in Wolken gehüllt** covered *or* enveloped *or* veiled (*liter*) in clouds; **sich fest in seinen Mantel ~** to wrap oneself up tight in one's coat; **sich (über etw acc) in Schweigen ~** to remain silent (on *or* about sth)

hül|len|los ADJ unclothed

Hüll|wort NT *pl* **-wörter** (*Ling*) euphemism

Hül|se ['hʏlzə] F **-, -n a** (= *Schale*) hull, husk; (= *Schote*) pod; (*Bot:* = *Frucht*) involucre (*form*) **b** (= *Etui, Kapsel*) case; (*für Film*) cartridge; (*Phys: für gefährliche Stoffe*) capsule; (*von Geschoss*) case; (*von Patronen*) (cartridge) case; **er ist nur noch eine leere ~** he is now just an empty shell

Hül|sen|frucht F *usu pl* peas and beans *pl*, pulse (*form*)

hu|man [hu'ma:n] ADJ humane; (= *verständnisvoll auch*) considerate ADV (= *menschenfreundlich*) humanely; **die Abschiebung ~er gestalten** to carry out deportations in a more humane way

Human-: Hu|man|ge|ne|tik F human genetics *sing*; **Hu|man|ge|ne|ti|ker(in)** M(F) human geneticist; **hu|man|ge|ne|tisch** ADJ human genetic *attr*

Hu|ma|ni|sie|rung [humani'zi:rʊŋ] F **-, no pl** humanization

Hu|ma|nis|mus [huma'nɪsmʊs] M **-, no pl** humanism; (*Hist*) Humanism

Hu|ma|nist [huma'nɪst] M **-en, -en, Hu|ma|nis|tin** [-'nɪstɪn] F **-, -nen** humanist; (*Hist*) Humanist; (= *Altsprachler*) classicist

hu|ma|nis|tisch [huma'nɪstɪʃ] ADJ humanist(ic); (*Hist*) Humanist; (= *altsprachlich*) classical; **~e Bildung** classical education, education in the classics *or* the humanities; **~es Gymnasium** *secondary school with bias on Latin and Greek*, ≈ grammar school (*Brit*) ADV **jdn ~ bilden** to provide sb with a humanistic *or* classical education; **~ gebildet** educated in the classics *or* humanities; **~ erzogen werden** to receive a classical *or* humanistic education

hu|ma|ni|tär [humani'tɛ:ɐ] ADJ humanitarian

Hu|ma|ni|tät [humani'tɛ:t] F **-, no pl** humaneness, humanity; (*als Bildungsideal*) humanitarianism

Hu|ma|ni|täts|du|se|lei [-duzəlai] F **-, -en** (*pej*) sentimental humanitarianism

Human-: Hu|man|me|di|zin F (human) medicine; **Hu|man|me|di|zi|ner(in)** M(F) (= *Student*) medical student; (= *Arzt*) doctor of medicine; **hu|man|me|di|zi|nisch** ADJ human medicine *attr*; **hu|man|öko|lo|gisch** ADJ human ecological *attr*

Hum|bug ['hʊmbʊk] M **-s, no pl** (*inf*) (= *Schwindel*) humbug (*inf*); (= *Unsinn auch*) stuff and nonsense (*inf*)

Hum|mel ['hʊml] F **-, -n** bumblebee; **~n im** *or* **unterm Hintern haben** (*dated inf*) to have ants in one's pants (*inf*)

Hum|mer ['hʊmɐ] M **-s, -** lobster

Hum|mer-: Hum|mer|cock|tail M lobster cocktail; **Hum|mer|fleisch** NT lobster (meat); **Hum|mer|krab|ben** PL king prawns *pl*; **Hum|mer|reu|se** F lobster pot; **Hum|mer|sche|re** F lobster claw

Hu|mor [hu'mo:ɐ] M **-s, (rare) -e** humour (*Brit*), humor (*US*); (= *Sinn für Humor*) sense of humo(u)r; **er hat keinen (Sinn für) ~** he has no sense of humo(u)r; **etw mit ~ nehmen/tragen** to take/bear sth cheerfully *or* with a sense of humo(u)r; **er nahm die Bemerkung mit ~ auf** he took the remark good-humo(u)redly *or* in good humo(u)r; **er hat einen eigenartigen ~** he has a strange sense of humo(u)r; **er verliert nie den ~** he never loses his sense of humo(u)r; **langsam verliere ich den ~** it's getting beyond a joke; **da hat selbst er den ~ verloren** it was going too far even for him, even he didn't think it funny any more; **~ ist, wenn man trotzdem lacht** (*prov*) having a sense of humo(u)r means looking on the bright side

Hu|mo|res|ke [humo'rɛskə] F **-, -n** (*Liter*) humorous story; (= *Sketch*) humorous sketch; (*Mus*) humoresque

hu|mo|rig [hu'mo:rɪç] ADJ (*geh*) humorous, genial

Hu|mo|rist [humo'rɪst] M **-en, -en, Hu|mo|ris|tin** [-'rɪstɪn] F **-, -nen a** humorist **b** (= *Komiker*) comedian; (*Frau auch*) comedienne

hu|mo|ris|tisch [humo'rɪstɪʃ] ADJ humorous; **er ist** *or* **hat ein großes ~es Talent** he is a very funny *or* amusing person

Humor-: hu|mor|los ADJ humourless (*Brit*), humorless (*US*); *Buch etc auch* lacking in *or* devoid of humour (*Brit*) *or* humor (*US*); *Mensch auch* lacking a sense of humour (*Brit*) *or* humor (*US*) ADV humourlessly (*Brit*), humorlessly (*US*); **sich ~ verhalten** to have no sense of humour (*Brit*) *or* humor (*US*); **er hat recht ~ auf unsere Scherze reagiert** he didn't find our jokes funny at all; **Hu|mor|lo|sig|keit** F **-, no pl** humourlessness (*Brit*), humorlessness (*US*); (*von Mensch auch*) lack of humour (*Brit*) *or* humor (*US*); **mit der für ihn typischen ~** with his usual lack of humour (*Brit*) *or* humor (*US*); **hu|mor|voll** ADJ humorous, amusing ADV humorously, amusingly, wittily; **~ über etw** (*acc*) **hinweggehen** to make light of sth; **er kann sehr**

~ erzählen he is a very amusing or humorous talker

hu|mos [huˈmoːs] ADJ Boden humus attr

Hum|pe|lei [hʊmpəˈlai] F -, no pl (inf) hobbling

hum|peln [ˈhʊmpln] VI **a** aux sein to hobble **b** (inf: = ständig hinken) to limp, to walk with a limp, to have a limp

Hum|pen [ˈhʊmpn] M -s, - tankard, mug; (aus Ton) stein

Hu|mus [ˈhuːmʊs] M -, no pl humus

Hu|mus|bo|den M , **Hu|mus|er|de** F humus soil

Hund [hʊnt] M -(e)s, -e [-də] **a** dog; (esp Jagdhund) hound; (inf: = Schurke) swine (inf), bastard (sl); **der Große/Kleine ~** (Astron) Great (-er)/Little or Lesser Dog; **junger ~** puppy, pup; **die Familie der ~e** the dog or canine family; **~e, die (viel) bellen, beißen nicht** (Prov) empty vessels make most noise (Prov); **getroffene ~e bellen** (inf) if the cap fits, wear it; **viele ~e sind des Hasen Tod** (Prov) there is not much one person can do against many; **wie ~ und Katze leben** to live like cat and dog, to lead a cat-and-dog life; **ich würde bei diesem Wetter keinen ~ auf die Straße jagen** I wouldn't send a dog out in this weather; **damit kann man keinen ~ hinterm Ofen hervorlocken** (inf) that's not going to tempt anybody; **müde wie ein ~ sein** (inf) to be dog-tired; **er ist bekannt wie ein bunter ~** (inf) everybody knows him; **kein ~ nimmt ein Stück Brot von ihm** everyone avoids him like the plague; **das ist (ja) zum Junge-Hunde-Kriegen** (inf) it's enough to give you kittens; **da wird der ~ in der Pfanne verrückt** (inf) it's enough to drive you crazy (inf) or round the twist (Brit inf); **da liegt der ~ begraben** (inf) (so) that's what is/was behind it all; (Haken, Problem etc) that's the problem; **er ist mit allen ~en gehetzt** (inf) he knows all the tricks, there are no flies on him (Brit inf); **er ist ein armer ~** he's a poor soul or devil (inf); **er ist völlig auf dem ~** (inf) he's really gone to the dogs (inf); **auf den ~ kommen** (inf) to go to the dogs (inf); **jdn auf den ~ bringen** (inf) to ruin sb; (gesundheitlich) to ruin sb's health; **die Weiber haben/der Suff hat ihn auf den ~ gebracht** (inf) women have/drink has been his ruin or downfall; **vor die ~e gehen** (inf) to go to the dogs (inf); (= sterben) to die, to perish; (= getötet werden) to cop it (Brit inf), to be killed; **du blöder ~** (inf) you silly or stupid bastard (sl); **du gemeiner ~** (inf) you rotten bastard (sl); **du schlauer or gerissener ~** (inf) you sly or crafty devil or old fox; **schlafende ~e soll man nicht wecken** (prov) let sleeping dogs lie (Prov) **b** (Min: = Förderwagen) truck, tub

Hünd|chen [ˈhʏntçən] NT -s, - dim von Hund doggy (baby-talk), little dog; (= kleiner Hund) small or little dog; (= junger Hund) puppy, pup, puppy dog (inf)

Hun|de-: Hun|de|ar|beit F (fig inf) **eine ~** an awful job, the devil's own job (inf); **Hun|de|art** F breed (of dog); **Hun|de|biss** ▲ M dog bite; **er hat einen ~ abbekommen** he has been bitten by a dog; **Hun|de|blick** M jdn mit **~ ansehen** to give sb a hangdog look; **Hun|de|dreck** M dog dirt (Brit) or mess (inf); **hun|de|elend** ADJ (inf) **mir ist ~** I feel lousy (inf); **Hun|de|fän|ger(in)** M(F) dog-catcher; **Hun|de|floh** M dog flea; **Hun|de|fraß** M (pej inf) (pig)swill (pej inf); **Hun|de|füh|rer(in)** M(F) dog handler; **Hun|de|fut|ter** NT dog food; **Hun|de|ge|bell** NT barking (of dogs); **Hun|de|ge|kläff** NT (pej) yapping (of dogs); **Hun|de|ge|spann** NT team of dogs; **Hun|de|hals|band** NT dog collar; **Hun|de|hal|ter(in)** M(F) (form) dog owner; **Hun|de|hal|tung** F owning dogs; **Hun|de|hüt|te** F (lit, fig) (dog) kennel; **hun|de|kalt** ADJ (inf) freezing cold; **Hun|de|käl|te** F (inf) freezing cold; **Hun|de|kot** M dog dirt (Brit) or mess (inf); **Hun|de|köt|tel** [-kœtl] M -s, - (inf) dog dirt (Brit) or mess (inf); **Hun|de|ku|chen** M dog biscuit;

Hun|de|le|ben NT (inf) dog's life (inf); **Hun|de|lei|ne** F dog lead (Brit) or leash; **Hun|de|lieb|ha|ber(in)** M(F) dog lover; **Hun|de|lohn** M (pej inf) miserable or rotten (inf) wage(s pl); **Hun|de|mar|ke** F dog licence (Brit) or license (US) disc, dog tag (US); (hum inf: = Erkennungsmarke) identity disc, dog tag (US inf); **hun|de|mü|de** ADJ pred ADV (inf) dog-tired; **Hun|de|narr** M , **Hun|de|när|rin** F (inf) fanatical dog lover, dog freak (inf); **Hun|de|ras|se** F breed (of dog); **Hun|de|ren|nen** NT greyhound or dog racing no art, dogs (inf); (= Wettkampf) greyhound race

hun|dert [ˈhʊndɐt] NUM a or one hundred; **ei|nige ~** or **Hundert Menschen** a few hundred people; **einer unter ~** one in a hundred; **in ~ Jahren** in a hundred years (from now); **ich wette ~ gegen eins** (inf) I'll bet or lay a hundred to one, I'll bet you anything (inf)

Hun|dert¹ [ˈhʊndɐt] F -, -en (= Zahl) hundred

Hun|dert² NT -s, -e hundred; **es geht in die ~e** or **hunderte** it runs into the hundreds; **~e** or **hunderte von Menschen** hundreds of people; **einer unter ~en** or **hunderten** one out of hundreds; **zehn vom ~** ten per cent (Brit) or percent (US); **zu ~en** or **hunderten** by the hundred, in (their) hundreds; **einige ~** or **hundert (Stecknadeln)** a few hundred (pins)

hun|dert|eins [ˈhʊndɐtˈlains] NUM a or one hundred and one

Hun|der|ter [ˈhʊndɐtɐ] M -s, - **a** (von Zahl) (the) hundred **b** (= Geldschein) hundred(-euro/-pound/-dollar etc note (Brit) or bill (US))

hun|der|ter|lei [ˈhʊndɐtɐˈlai] ADJ inv a hundred and one

Hun|dert-: Hun|dert|eu|ro|schein M (one-)hundred euro note (Brit) or bill (US); **hun|dert|fach, hun|dert|fäl|tig** (geh) ADJ hundredfold; **die ~e Menge** a hundred times the amount ADV a hundred times; **jdm etw ~ zu|rückgeben** (fig) to repay sb a hundredfold for sth, to repay sb a hundred times over for sth; **hun|dert|fünf|zig|pro|zen|tig** (iro) fanatical; **er ist ein Hundertfünfzigprozentiger** he's a fanatic ADV **sich/etw ~ beweisen** to prove oneself/sth twice over; **Hun|dert|jahr|fei|er** F centenary, centennial (US); (= Festlichkeiten auch) centenary or centennial celebrations pl; **hun|dert|jäh|rig** ADJ attr (one-)hundred-year-old; **der Hundertjährige Kalender** the Hundred Years' Calendar (for weather prediction); **der Hundertjährige Krieg** (Hist) the Hundred Years' War; **das Ergebnis einer ~en Entwicklung/Arbeit** the result of a hundred years of development/work; **Hun|dert|jäh|ri|ge(r)** [-jɛːrɪgə] MF decl as adj centenarian; **hun|dert|jäh|rlich** ADJ every hundred years; **hun|dert|mal** ADV a hundred times; **ich hab dir schon ~ gesagt ...** if I've told you once I've told you a hundred times ...; **Hun|dert|me|ter|lauf** M (Sport) der/ein ~ the/a 100 metres (Brit) or meters (US) sing; **hun|dert|pro|zen|tig** ADJ (a or one) hundred per cent (Brit) or percent (US); Alkohol pure; **ein ~er Konservativer** etc an out-and-out conservative etc ADV sicher sein, einer Meinung sein one hundred per cent (Brit) or percent (US); **er ist ~ Amerikaner** etc he's one hundred per cent (Brit) or percent (US) American etc; **Sie haben ~ Recht** you're absolutely right; **das weiß ich ~** that's a fact; **ich werde ihn ~ im Krankenhaus besuchen** I'll definitely visit him in hospital; **~?** (inf) are you absolutely sure?; **Hun|dert|satz** M (form) percentage; **Hun|dert|schaft** [ˈhʊndɐtʃaft] F -, -en (Mil) group of a or one hundred; (Hist: bei den Römern) century

hun|derts|te(r, s) [ˈhʊndɐtstə] ADJ hundredth; **vom Hundertsten ins Tausendste kommen** (fig) to get carried away

hun|derts|tel [ˈhʊndɐtstl] ADJ hundredth; **eine ~ Sekunde** a hundredth of a second

Hun|derts|tel [ˈhʊndɐtstl] NT -s, - hundredth; **sie hat zwei ~ Vorsprung** (Sport) she leads by two hundredths of a second

Hun|derts|tel|se|kun|de F hundredth of a second

Hun|dert-: hun|dert|tau|send NUM a or one hundred thousand; **~e** or **Hunderttausende von Menschen** hundreds of thousands of people; **Hun|dert|tau|sends|tel** NT hundred thousandth; **hun|dert|und|eins** [ˈhʊndɐtʊntˈlains] NUM a or one hundred and one; **hun|dert|wei|se** ADV by the hundred, in hundreds

Hun|de-: Hun|de|sa|lon M dog parlour (Brit) or parlor (US); **Hun|de|schei|ße** F (inf) dog shit (sl), dog mess (inf); **Hun|de|schlit|ten** M dog sled(ge) or sleigh; **Hun|de|schnau|ze** F nose, snout; **kalt wie eine ~** (fig inf) cold (-blooded); **Hun|de|sohn** M (pej liter) cur; **Hun|de|sper|re** F ban on (bringing in) dogs; **Hun|de|staf|fel** F dog branch; **Hun|de|stau|pe** F (Vet) distemper; **Hun|de|steu|er** F dog licence (Brit) or license (US) fee; **Hun|de|wa|che** F (Naut) middle watch; **Hun|de|wet|ter** NT (inf) foul or filthy weather; **Hun|de|zucht** F dog breeding; **Hun|de|züch|ter(in)** M(F) dog breeder; **Hun|de|zwin|ger** M (dog) compound; (städtisch) dog pound

Hün|din [ˈhʏndɪn] F -, -nen bitch

hün|disch [ˈhʏndɪʃ] ADJ (fig) fawning attr, sycophantic; **~e Ergebenheit** dog-like devotion

Hünd|lein [ˈhʏntlain] NT -s, - dim von Hund doggy (baby-talk), little dog; (= kleiner Hund) little or small dog

Hunds-: Hunds|fott [ˈhʊntsfɔt] M -s, **Hundsfötter** [-fœtə] (obs, dial) (miserable) cur; **hunds|föt|tisch** [ˈhʊntsfœtɪʃ] ADJ (obs, dial) dastardly (old); **hunds|ge|mein** [ˈhʊntsgəˈmain] (inf) ADJ shabby, mean; (= schwierig) fiendishly difficult; Schmerz etc terrible; **er kann ~ werden** he can get really nasty ADV **es tut ~ weh** it hurts like hell (inf); **hunds|mi|se|ra|bel** [ˈhʊntsmizəˈraːbl] (inf) ADJ abominable, abysmal (inf), lousy (inf) ADV abominably; **~ arbeiten** to do abysmal or pitiful work; **mir geht es ~, ich fühle mich ~** I feel rotten (inf) or lousy (inf); **Hunds|stern** [ˈhʊnts-] M Dog Star; **Hunds|ta|ge** [ˈhʊnts-] PL dog days pl; **Hunds|veil|chen** [ˈhʊnts-] NT (heath) dog violet

Hü|ne [ˈhyːnə] M -n, -n giant, colossus; **ein ~ von Mensch** (inf) a giant of a man

Hü|nen-: Hü|nen|ge|stalt F (geh) Titanic or colossal figure or frame; **Hü|nen|grab** NT megalithic grave; **hü|nen|haft** ADJ (geh) gigantic, colossal

Hun|ger [ˈhʊŋɐ] M -s, no pl (lit, fig) hunger (nach for); (= Hungersnot) famine; (nach Bildung) thirst, hunger; (nach fernen Ländern, Sonne etc) yearning; (nach Literatur) appetite; **~ bekommen/haben** to get/be hungry; **ich habe keinen richtigen ~** I'm not really hungry; **~ auf etw** (acc) **haben** to feel like (eating) sth; **den ~ bekämpfen** to combat hunger; **~ leiden** (geh) to go hungry, to starve; **ich habe ~ wie ein Wolf** or **Bär** I could eat a horse (inf); **~s** (liter) or **vor ~ sterben** to die of hunger or starvation, to starve to death; **ich sterbe vor ~** (inf) I'm starving (inf), I'm dying of hunger (inf); **~ ist der beste Koch** (Prov) hunger is the best cook (Prov)

Hun|ger-: Hun|ger|blo|cka|de F hunger or starvation blockade; **Hun|ger|da|sein** NT existence at starvation level; **Hun|ger|ge|fühl** NT hungry feeling; **Hun|ger|jahr** NT hungry year, year of hunger; **Hun|ger|künst|ler(in)** M(F) (professional) faster, person who, for pay, goes without nourishment for prolonged periods **ich bin doch kein ~** I'm not on a starvation diet; **Hun|ger|kur** F starvation diet; **Hun|ger|land** NT famine-stricken country; **Hun|ger|le|ben** NT existence at starvation level; **Hun|ger|lei|der** [-laidə] M -s, -, **Hun|ger|lei|de|rin** [-ərɪn] F -, -nen (dated) starving wretch, starveling; **Hun|ger|lohn** M starvation wages pl; (fig auch) pittance

hun|gern ['hʊŋɐn] **VI** **a** (= Hunger leiden) to go hungry, to starve; **jdn ~ lassen** to let sb go hungry; (zur Strafe auch) to make sb starve; **ich hungere schon seit fünf Tagen** I haven't eaten a thing for five days **b** (= fasten) to go without food **c** (fig geh: = verlangen) to hunger (nach for) **VT impers** (geh) **mich hungert** I am or feel hungry; **ihn hungert nach Macht** he hungers or is hungry for power **VR sich zu Tode ~** to starve oneself to death; **sich schlank ~** to go on a starvation diet; **er hat sich durch die Studentenzeit gehungert** he starved his way through university

hun|gernd ADJ no comp hungry, starving

Hun|ger|ödem NT (Med) famine oedema (spec)

Hun|gers|not F famine

Hunger-: Hun|ger|streik M hunger strike; **Hun|ger|tag** M (inf) fast day; **Hun|ger|tod** M death from starvation; **den ~ erleiden** or **sterben** to die of hunger or starvation; **Hun|ger|tuch** NT pl **-tücher** (Eccl) Lenten veil; **am ~ nagen** (fig) to be starving, to be on the breadline (inf); **Hun|ger|turm** M (Hist) dungeon, oubliette

hung|rig ['hʊŋrɪç] ADJ (lit, fig) hungry (nach for); **Arbeit macht ~** work makes you hungry, work gives you an appetite; **Gartenarbeit macht ~** gardening is hungry work; **ich bin ~ wie ein Wolf** (I'm so hungry) I could eat a horse; **~ nach etw** or **auf etw** (acc) **sein** to feel like (eating) sth; **~ nach Luft** gasping for air; **~ nach Literatur** hungry for good literature

Hun|ne ['hʊnə] M -n -n, **Hun|nin** ['hʊnɪn] F -, -nen (Hist) Hun

Hun|ni ['hʊni] M -s, -s (hum inf: = Hunderteuroschein) hundred (inf)

Hu|pe ['huːpə] F -, -n horn; **auf die ~ drücken** to sound the horn

hu|pen ['huːpn] VI to sound or hoot or honk (Aut inf) the horn, to hoot; „hupen" "sound your horn"

Hüpf|burg ['hʏpf-] F bouncy castle®

hup|fen ['hʊpfn] VI (esp S Ger) aux sein = **hüpfen das ist gehupft wie gesprungen** (inf) it doesn't make any difference, it's six of one and half a dozen of the other (inf)

hüp|fen ['hʏpfn] VI aux sein to hop; (Lämmer, Zicklein etc) to frisk, to gambol; (Ball) to bounce; **vor Freude ~** to jump for joy; **die Kinder hüpften vor Freude im Zimmer herum** the children went skipping round the room in sheer delight; **sein Herz hüpfte vor Freude** his heart leapt for joy; **Hüpfen spielen** to play (at) hopscotch

Hüp|fer ['hʏpfɐ] M -s, -, (esp S Ger) **Hup|fer** ['hʊpfɐ] M -s, - hop, skip, bounce; **mein Herz machte einen ~** my heart leapt

Hüpf|spiel NT hopscotch

Hup-: Hup|kon|zert NT (inf) chorus of hooting or horns; **Hup|sig|nal** NT (Aut) hoot; „Hupsignal geben" "sound your horn"; **Hup|ton** M (= Ton) sound of a horn; **Hup|ver|bot** NT (Hinweis) no horns to be sounded; **Hup|zei|chen** NT (Aut) hoot; „Hupzeichen geben" "sound your horn"

Hür|de ['hʏrdə] F -, -n **a** (Sport, fig) hurdle; **eine ~ nehmen** to take or clear a hurdle **b** (= Viehzaun) fold, pen

Hürden-: Hür|den|lauf M (= Sportart) hurdling; (= Wettkampf) hurdles pl or sing; **Hür|den|läu|fer(in)** M(F) hurdler; **Hür|den|ren|nen** NT (Pferdesport) steeplechase

Hu|re ['huːrə] F -, -n whore

hu|ren ['huːrən] VI (inf) to whore, to go whoring

Huren-: Hu|ren|bock M (vulg) whoremonger; **hu|ren|haft** ADJ (pej) whorish; **Hu|ren|haus** NT (dated) whorehouse (inf), broth-

el; **Hu|ren|kind** NT (old) child of a whore; (Typ) widow; **Hu|ren|sohn** M (vulg) bastard (sl), son of a bitch (sl)

Hu|re|rei [huːrəˈraɪ] F -, no pl (inf) whoring

hur|ra [hʊˈraː, ˈhʊra] INTERJ hurray, hurrah

Hur|ra [hʊˈraː, ˈhʊra] NT -s, -s cheers pl; **ein dreifaches ~** three cheers

Hurra-: Hur|ra|ge|schrei NT cheering; **Hur|ra|pat|ri|ot(in)** M(F) flag-waving patriot, jingoist, chauvinist; **Hur|ra|pat|ri|o|tis|mus** M flag-waving, jingoism, chauvinism; **Hur|ra|ruf** M cheer

Hur|ri|kan ['hʊrikan, 'harɪkən] M -s, -e or (bei engl. Aussprache) -s hurricane

hur|tig ['hʊrtɪç] ADJ (old, dial) nimble; (= schnell) quick

Hur|tig|keit F -, no pl (old, dial) nimbleness; (= Schnelligkeit) quickness, speed

Hu|sar [huˈzaːɐ] M -en, -en (Hist) hussar

Hu|sa|ren|streich M , **Hu|sa|ren|stück** NT (fig) (daring) escapade or exploit

husch [hʊʃ] INTERJ **a** (aufscheuchend) shoo **b** (antreibend) come on **c** (= schnell) quick, quickly now; **er macht seine Arbeit immer ~ ~** (inf) he always whizzes through his work (inf); **und ~, weg war er** and whoosh! he was gone

Husch [hʊʃ] M -(e)s, -e (inf) **im ~** in a flash (inf) or jiffy (inf); **er kam auf einen ~ vorbei** he dropped in on me or dropped by for a minute

hu|schen ['hʊʃn] VI aux sein to dart, to flit; (Mäuse etc auch) to scurry; (Lächeln) to flash, to flit; (Licht) to flash

Hus|ky ['haski] M -s, -s husky

hus|sa(sa) ['hʊsa(sa)] INTERJ (old liter) tally-ho; (= hü) gee up

hüs|teln ['hyːstln] VI to give a slight cough, to cough slightly; **er hüstelt noch** he still has a slight cough; **anstatt zu antworten, hüstelte er nur spöttisch** instead of answering he just cleared his throat sarcastically

hus|ten ['huːstn] **VI** to cough; **auf etw** (acc) **~** (inf) not to give a damn for sth (inf); **der Motor hustet** (inf) the engine is coughing (and spluttering) **VT** to cough; **Blut** to cough (up); **denen werde ich was** or **eins ~** (inf) I'll tell them where they can get off (inf)

Hus|ten ['huːstn] M -s, no pl cough; **~ haben** to have a cough

Husten-: Hus|ten|an|fall M coughing fit; **Hus|ten|bon|bon** M OR NT cough drop, cough sweet (Brit); **Hus|ten|mit|tel** NT cough medicine; (= Bonbon) cough drop, cough sweet (Brit); **Hus|ten|reiz** M tickle in or irritation of the throat; **seinen ~ unterdrücken** to suppress the need or urge to cough; **Hus|ten|saft** M cough syrup or mixture; **hus|ten|stil|lend** ADJ cough-relieving ADV **das wirkt ~** it relieves coughing or one's cough; **Hus|ten|tee** M tea which is good for coughs; **Hus|ten|trop|fen** PL cough drops pl

Hut¹ [huːt] M -(e)s, ⁼e ['hyːtə] hat; (von Pilz) cap; **den ~ aufsetzen/abnehmen/lüften** (geh) to put on/take off/raise one's hat; **den** or **mit dem ~ in der Hand** with one's hat in one's hand; **vor jdm den ~ abnehmen** or **ziehen** (fig) to take off one's hat to sb; **vor etw** (dat) **den ~ ziehen** (fig) to take off one's hat to sth; **~ ab!** I take my hat off to him/you etc; **~ ab vor solcher Leistung!** I take my hat off to you/that; **mit dem ⁼e in der Hand kommt man durch das ganze Land** (Prov) politeness will serve you well in life; **das kannst du dir an den ~ stecken!** (inf) you can stick (inf) or keep (inf) it; **unter einen ~ bringen** or **kriegen** (inf) to reconcile, to accommodate, to cater for; Verpflichtungen, Termine to fit in; **da geht einem der ~ hoch** (inf, vor Zorn) it's enough to make you blow your top (inf); (vor Spaß, Überraschung) it is amazing, it beats everything; **den** or **seinen ~ nehmen (müssen)** (inf) to (have to) go, to (have to) pack one's bags (inf); **das ist doch ein alter ~!** (inf) that's old hat!

(inf); **jdm eine auf den ~ geben** (inf) to give sb a rocket (Brit inf), to give sb an earful (inf); **eins auf den ~ kriegen** (inf) to get a rocket (Brit inf), to get an earful (inf); **damit/mit ihm habe ich nichts am ~** (inf) I don't want to have anything to do with that/him

Hut² F -, no pl **a** (geh) protection, keeping; **unter** or **in meiner ~** in my keeping; (Kinder) in my care; **in guter** or **sicherer ~** in safe keeping, in good or safe hands **b** **auf der ~ sein** to be on one's guard (vor +dat against)

Hut-: Hut|ab|la|ge F hat rack; **Hut|band** [-bant] NT pl **-bänder** hatband; (von Damenhut) hat ribbon

Hüt|chen ['hyːtçən] NT -s, - dim von Hut¹ little hat

Hüt|chen|spiel NT thimblerig

Hüt|chen|spie|ler(in) M(F) thimblerigger

Hü|te|jun|ge M (liter) shepherd boy

hü|ten ['hyːtn] ⊘ 28.1, 29.2 **VT** to look after, to mind; Vieh etc auch to tend, to keep watch over (liter); (geh) Geheimnisse to guard, to keep; (geh) Briefe, Gegenstände to keep; **das Bett/Haus ~** to stay in bed/indoors; **hüte deine Zunge!** (liter) guard your tongue! (liter) **VR** to guard (vor +dat against), to be on one's guard (vor +dat against), to beware (vor +dat of); **ich werde mich ~!** not fear!, not likely!, I'll do nothing of the kind!; **du wirst dich schwer ~!** you'll do nothing of the kind!; **ich werde mich ~, ihm das zu erzählen** there's no chance of me telling him that; **sich ~, etwas zu tun** to take care not to do sth; **hüte dich, etwas zu verraten** take care not to give anything away, mind you don't give anything away; **~ Sie sich vor ihm** be on your guard against him

Hü|ter ['hyːtɐ] M -s, -, **Hü|te|rin** [-ərɪn] F -, -nen guardian, keeper, custodian; (= Viehhüter) herdsman; **die ~ der Ordnung** (hum) the custodians of the law; **soll ich meines Bruders ~ sein?** (Bibl) am I my brother's keeper?

Hut-: Hut|fe|der F (hat) feather; (größere, bei Tracht) plume; **Hut|filz** M (hat) felt; **Hut|ge|schäft** M hat shop, hatter's (shop); (für Damen auch) milliner's (shop); **Hut|grö|ße** F hat size, size of hat; **Hut|krem|pe** F brim (of a hat); **Hut|la|den** M = Hutgeschäft; **Hut|ma|cher(in)** M(F) hatter, hat maker; (von Damenhüten auch) milliner; **Hut|na|del** F hatpin; **Hut|schach|tel** F hatbox

Hut|sche ['hʊtʃə] F -, -n (Aus) swing

hut|schen ['hʊtʃn] (Aus) **VI** = schaukeln **VR** (inf) to go away

Hut-: Hut|schlei|fe F hat bow; **Hut|schnur** F hat string or cord; **das geht mir über die ~** (inf) that's going too far

Hutsch|pferd ['hʊtʃ-] NT (Aus) rocking horse

Hut|stän|der M hat stand

Hüt|te ['hytə] F -, -n **a** hut; (= schäbiges Häuschen) shack, hut; (hum: = Haus) humble abode; (= Jagdhütte) (hunting) lodge; (= Holzhütte, Blockhütte) cabin; (= Wochenendhäuschen) cottage; (= Schutzhütte) hut, bothy (Scot); (= Hundehütte) kennel; (Bibl) Tabernacle; (Naut) poop; **hier lasst uns eine ~ bauen** let's stay here → Glanz **b** (Tech: = Hüttenwerk) iron and steel works pl or sing; (= Glashütte) glassworks pl or sing; (= Ziegelhütte) brickworks pl or sing

Hütten-: Hüt|ten|ar|bei|ter(in) M(F) worker in an iron and steel works; **Hüt|ten|in|dust|rie** F iron and steel industry; **Hüt|ten|kä|se** M cottage cheese; **Hüt|ten|kom|bi|nat** NT (DDR) iron and steel combine; **Hüt|ten|kun|de** F metallurgy; **Hüt|ten|rauch** M (Chem) flaky arsenic; (Metal) waste gases pl; **Hüt|ten|ru|he** F **um zehn ist ~** lights out at ten; **Hüt|ten|schuh** M slipper-sock; **Hüt|ten|tech|nik** F metallurgical engineering; **Hüt|ten|werk** NT = Hütte b; **Hüt|ten|we|sen** NT , no pl iron and steel industry; **Hüt|ten|zau|ber** M après-ski party

Hut|zel ['hʊtsl] F -, -n (S Ger) a dried pear b (inf) wizened or wrinkled old woman

Hut|zel|brot NT (S Ger) fruit bread; **ein ~ a** fruit loaf

hut|ze|lig ['hʊtsəlɪç] ADJ Obst dried; Mensch wizened

Hut|zel-: Hut|zel|männ|chen NT , **Hut|zel-männ|lein** NT gnome; **Hut|zel|weib|lein** NT (inf) wizened or wrinkled old woman

hutz|lig ['hʊtslɪç] ADJ = hutzelig

HwG [haːveːˈgeː] (Admin sl) abbr von **häufig wech-selnder Geschlechtsverkehr** frequent changing of sexual partners

HwG-Mäd|chen [haːveːˈgeː-] NT (Admin sl) girl listed by police or medical authorities as being promiscuous

Hy|ä|ne ['hyɛːnə] F -, -n hyena; (fig) wildcat

Hy|a|zin|the [hyaˈtsɪntə] F -, -n hyacinth

hyb|rid [hyˈbriːt] ADJ a (Biol, Ling) hybrid b (liter: = hochmütig) arrogant, hubristic (liter)

Hyb|rid|an|trieb [hyˈbriːt-] M hybrid drive

Hyb|ri|de [hyˈbriːdə] F -, -n or m -n, -n (Biol) hybrid

Hyb|ris ['hyːbrɪs] F -, no pl (liter) hubris (liter)

Hyd|ra ['hyːdra] F - (Zool, Myth, fig liter) hydra

Hyd|rant [hyˈdrant] M -en, -en hydrant

Hyd|rat [hyˈdraːt] NT -(e)s, -e hydrate

Hyd|rau|lik [hyˈdraʊlɪk] F -, no pl hydraulics sing; (= Antrieb, Anlage) hydraulic system, hydraulics pl

hyd|rau|lisch [hyˈdraʊlɪʃ] ADJ hydraulic ADV hydraulically

Hyd|rid [hyˈdriːt] NT -(e)s, -e [-də] hydride

hyd|rie|ren [hyˈdriːrən] ptp **hydriert** VT (Chem) to hydrogenate

Hydro- [hydro-]: **Hyd|ro|bi|o|lo|gie** F hydrobiology; **Hyd|ro|dy|na|mik** F hydrodynamics sing; **hyd|ro|dy|na|misch** ADJ hydrodynamic; **hyd|ro|ge|o|lo|gisch** ADJ hydrogeological; **Hyd|ro|gra|fie** ▲ [hydrograˈfiː] F -, no pl hydrography; **hyd|ro|gra|fisch** ▲ [hydroˈgraːfɪʃ] ADJ hydrographic(al); **Hyd|ro|kul|tur** [hydro-, ˈhyːdro-] F (Bot) hydroponics sing; **Hyd|ro|ly-se** [hydroˈlyːzə] F -, -n (Chem) hydrolysis; **hyd|ro|nuk|le|ar** ADJ hydronuclear; **hyd|ro|phil** [hydroˈfiːl] ADJ hydrophilic; **hyd|ro|phob** [hydroˈfoːp] ADJ hydrophobic; **Hyd|ro|sta|tik** F (Phys) hydrostatics sing; **Hyd|ro|the|ra|pie** F (Med) hydrotherapy

Hy|gi|e|ne [hyˈgieːnə] F -, no pl hygiene; **politische ~** political expediency

Hy|gi|e|ne- [hyˈgieːnə]: **Hy|gi|e|ne|ar|ti|kel** PL toiletries pl; **Hy|gi|e|ne|pa|pier** NT (toilet) tissue

hy|gi|e|nisch [hyˈgieːnɪʃ] ADJ hygienic ADV hygienically; **das ist ~ nicht zu vertreten** that's not at all hygienic

Hygro- [hygro-]: **Hyg|ro|me|ter** [hygroˈmeːtɐ] NT (Met) hygrometer; **Hyg|ro|skop** [hygro-ˈskoːp] NT -s, -e (Met) hygroscope

Hy|men ['hyːmən] NT -s, - (Anat) hymen, maidenhead

Hym|ne ['hʏmnə] F -, -n hymn; (= Nationalhymne) (national) anthem

hym|nisch ['hʏmnɪʃ] ADJ hymnal; **~e Worte** (liter) paean (liter); **jdn/etw in ~en Worten loben** (liter) to sing paeans to sb/sth (liter)

Hym|nus ['hʏmnʊs] M -, **Hymnen** [-nən] (liter) hymn

hy|per|ak|tiv [hypɐˈakˈtiːf] ADJ hyperactive

Hy|per|ak|ti|vi|tät F hyperactivity

Hy|per|bel [hyˈpɐbl] F -, -n (Math) hyperbola; (Rhetorik) hyperbole

hy|per|bo|lisch [hypɐˈboːlɪʃ] ADJ hyperbolic

hy|per|kor|rekt [hyːpɐ-] ADJ hypercorrect

hy|per|kri|tisch [hypɐ-, ˈhyːpɐ-] ADJ hypercritical

Hy|per|link ['haipɐlɪŋk] M OR NT -s, -s (Comput) hyperlink

Hy|per|me|dia [hyːpɐ-] NT no art (Comput) hypermedia sing

Hy|per|me|di|um [hyːpɐ-] NT -s, -**me**dien [-diən] (Comput) hypermedium

hy|per|mo|dern [hyːpɐ-] (inf) ADJ ultramodern ADV in an ultramodern way

hy|per|sen|si|bel [hypɐ-] ADJ hypersensitive

hy|per|sen|si|bi|li|sie|ren [hypɐzɛnzibiliˈziː-rən] ptp **hypersensibilisiert** VT insep (esp Phot) to hypersensitize

Hy|per|text ['haipɐ-] M , no pl (Comput) hypertext

Hy|per|to|nie [hypɐtoˈniː] F -, -n [-ˈniːən] (Med) hypertonia

hy|per|troph [hypɐˈtroːf] ADJ (Med) hypertrophic; (fig liter) hypertrophied (liter)

Hy|per|tro|phie [hypɐtroˈfiː] F -, -n (Med) hypertrophy

Hy|per|ven|ti|la|ti|on [hypɐ-] F (Med) hyperventilation

Hyp|no|se [hʏpˈnoːzə] F -, -n hypnosis; **unter ~ stehen** to be under hypnosis; **jdn in ~ verset-zen** to put sb under hypnosis

Hyp|no|se|be|hand|lung F hypnotherapy

Hyp|no|ti|kum [hʏpˈnoːtikʊm] NT -s, **Hypno**ti-ka [-ka] (Pharm) hypnotic

hyp|no|tisch [hʏpˈnoːtɪʃ] ADJ hypnotic

Hyp|no|ti|seur [hʏpnotiˈzøːɐ] M -s, -e, **Hyp|-no|ti|seu|rin** [-ˈzøːrɪn] F -, -nen hypnotist

hyp|no|ti|sier|bar ADJ hypnotizable

hyp|no|ti|sie|ren [hʏpnotiˈziːrən] ptp **hypnoti-siert** VT to hypnotize

Hyp|no|tis|mus [hʏpnoˈtɪsmʊs] M -, no pl hypnotism

Hy|po|chon|der [hypoˈxɔndɐ, hypɔ-] M -s, - hypochondriac

Hy|po|chond|rie [hypoxɔnˈdriː, hypɔ-] F -, (rare) -n [-ˈdriːən] hypochondria

hy|po|chond|risch [hypoˈxɔndrɪʃ, hypɔ-] ADJ hypochondriac(al)

Hy|po|krit [hypoˈkriːt] M -en, -en, **Hy|po|kri-tin** [-ˈkriːtɪn] F -, -nen (liter) hypocrite

hy|po|kri|tisch [hypoˈkriːtɪʃ] ADJ (liter) hypocritical

Hy|po|phy|se [hypoˈfyːzə] F -, -n (Anat) hypophysis (spec), pituitary gland

Hy|po|sen|si|bi|li|sie|rung [hypozɛnzibiliˈziː-rʊŋ] F (Med) hyposensitization, desensitization

Hy|pos|ta|se [hypoˈstaːzə] F -, -n (liter, Philos) hypostasis

hy|pos|ta|sie|ren [hypostaˈziːrən] ptp **hyposta-siert** VTI (liter, Philos) to hypostatize

Hy|pos|ta|sie|rung F -, -en (liter, Philos) hypostatization

hy|po|tak|tisch [hypoˈtaktɪʃ] ADJ (Gram) hypotactic

Hy|po|ta|xe [hypoˈtaksə] F (Gram) hypotaxis

Hy|po|te|nu|se [hypoteˈnuːzə] F -, -n (Math) hypotenuse

Hy|po|thek [hypoˈteːk] F -, -en mortgage; (fig) (= Belastung) burden of guilt; (= Handikap) handicap; **eine ~ aufnehmen** to raise a mortgage; **etw mit einer ~ belasten** to mortgage sth

hy|po|the|ka|risch [hypoteˈkaːrɪʃ] ADJ **~er Gläubiger** mortgagee; **~er Kredit** mortgage credit; **~e Sicherheit** mortgage security ADV **das Haus ist ~ belastet** the house is mortgaged

Hy|po|the|ken-: Hy|po|the|ken|bank F pl -banken bank specializing in mortgages; **Hy|-po|the|ken|brief** M mortgage deed or certificate; **Hy|po|the|ken|dar|le|hen** NT mortgage (loan); **hy|po|the|ken|frei** ADJ unmortgaged; **Hy|po|the|ken|gläu|bi|ger(in)** M(F) mortgagee; **Hy|po|the|ken|pfand|brief** M mortgage bond; **Hy|po|the|ken|schuld** F mortgage debt; **Hy|po|the|ken|schuld|ner(in)** M(F) mortgagor, mortgager; **Hy|po|the|ken|ur-kun|de** F mortgage deed or certificate; **Hy|-po|the|ken|zin|sen** PL mortgage interest

Hy|po|the|se [hypoˈteːzə] F hypothesis

hy|po|the|tisch [hypoˈteːtɪʃ] ADJ hypothetical ADV hypothetically

Hys|te|rek|to|mie [hʏsterɛktoˈmiː] F -, -n [-ˈmiːən] hysterectomy

Hys|te|rie [hʏsteˈriː] F -, -n [-ˈriːən] hysteria

Hys|te|ri|ker [hʏsˈteːrikɐ] M -s, -, **Hys|te|ri-ke|rin** [-ərɪn] F -, -nen hysteric, hysterical person

hys|te|risch [hʏsˈteːrɪʃ] ADJ hysterical; **einen ~en Anfall bekommen** (fig) to go into or have hysterics ADV hysterically

I

I, i [iː] NT I, i; **der Punkt** or **das Tüpfelchen auf dem i** (lit) the dot on the i; (fig) the final touch

i [iː] INTERJ (inf) ugh (inf); **i bewahre!** (dated) not on your life! (inf); **i wo!** not a bit of it! (inf), (good) heavens no!

i. A. abbr von **im Auftrag** pp

IAA [iːaˈʔaː] F -, -s abbr von **Internationale Automobil-Ausstellung** International Car Show

IAEA [iːaˈeˈʔaː] F - abbr von **Internationale Atomenergie-Agentur** IAEA

i|ah [iˈʔaː, iˈʔaː] INTERJ heehaw

i|a|hen [iˈʔaːən, iˈʔaːən] ptp **iaht** VI to heehaw (inf), to bray

i. allg. abbr von **im Allgemeinen**

Iam|bus [ˈiambʊs] M -, **Iamben** [-bn] (Poet) iamb(us), iambic foot

I|be|rer [iˈbeːrɐ] M -s, -, **I|be|re|rin** [-ərɪn] F -, -nen Iberian

i|be|risch [iˈbeːrɪʃ] ADJ Iberian; **die Iberische Halbinsel** the Iberian Peninsula

I|be|ro|ame|ri|ka [iˈbeːroʔameˈriːka] NT Ibero-America

i|be|ro|ame|ri|ka|nisch [iˈbeːroʔameˈrikaːnɪʃ] ADJ Ibero-American

IBFG [iːbeːʔɛfˈgeː] M -s abbr von **Internationaler Bund Freier Gewerkschaften** ICFTU

i|bi|dem [iˈbiːdɛm, ˈiːbidɛm] ADV ibid

I|bi|za [iˈbitsa] NT -s Ibiza

IC® [iːˈtseː] M -(s), -s abbr von **Intercityzug**

IC- [iːˈtseː] in cpds intercity; **IC-Be|treu|er(in)** M(F) intercity steward

ICE® [iːtseːˈʔeː] M -(s), -s abbr von **Intercity-Expresszug**

ICE

The **ICE** – or **Intercityexpresszug** – is a high-speed train running every two hours on various routes in Germany. As well as a sometimes drastically reduced journey time, the **ICE** offers increased comfort, with telephone, laptop points and video screens for first-class passengers. Accordingly, fares for the **ICE** are considerably higher than for other trains.

---

ich [ɪç] PERS PRON gen **meiner**, dat **mir**, acc **mich** I; **immer ~!** (it's) always me!; **immer ~ soll an allem schuld sein** it's always my fault; **~ Idiot!** what an idiot I am!; **und ~ Idiot habe es gemacht** and I, like a fool, did it, and idiot that I am, I did it; **~ nicht!** not me!, not I!; **ihr könnt ja hingehen, aber ~ nicht!** you're welcome to go, but I won't; **wer hat den Schlüssel? – ~ nicht!** who's got the key? – not me!; **~ selbst** I myself; **könnte ~ bitte den Chef sprechen? – das bin ~ (selbst)** could I speak to the boss? – I am the boss or that's me; **~ (selbst) war es** it was me or I (form); **wer hat gerufen? – ~!** who called? – (it was) me, I!; **kennst du mich nicht mehr? – ~ bins!** don't you remember me? it's me!; **~, der immer so gutmütig ist, ~, der ~ immer so gutmütig bin** I, who am always so good-natured

Ich [ɪç] NT -(s), -(s) self; (Psych) ego; **das eigene ~** one's (own) self/ego; **das eigene ~ verleug-**

---

nen to deny the self; **mein anderes** or **zweites ~** (= selbst) my other self; (= andere Person) my alter ego

Ich-: **Ich|be|wusst|sein** ▲ NT awareness of the self; **ich|be|zo|gen** ADJ self-centred (Brit), self-centered (US), egocentric; **Ich|be|zo|gen-heit** F -, no pl self-centredness (Brit), self-centeredness (US), egocentricity; **Ich|er|zäh-ler(in)** ▲ M(F) first-person narrator; **Ich|er-zäh|lung** F story in the first person, first-person narrative; **Ich|form** F first person; **Ich-ge|fühl** NT (Psych) consciousness or perception of the self; **Ich|laut** ▲ M (Phon) ch sound as in ich; **Ich|ro|man** ▲ M novel in the first person, first-person novel; **Ich|stär|ke** F (Psych) ego strength; **Ich|sucht** F , no pl egoism; **ich|süch|tig** ADJ egoistic(al)

Icon [ˈaikn, ˈaikɔn] NT -s, -s (Comput) icon

IC-Zu|schlag [iːˈtseː-] M intercity supplement

i|de|al [ideˈaːl] ADJ ideal ADV ideally; **da wohnt ihr ~** where you live is ideally located

I|de|al [ideˈaːl] NT -s, -e ideal; **sie ist das ~ einer Lehrerin** she's the ideal or perfect teacher

I|de|al- in cpds ideal; **I|de|al|be|set|zung** F (von Rolle) ideal casting; (von Team, Firma etc) ideal person, perfect choice; (zwei oder mehr Personen) dream team, ideal line-up; **I|de|al|bild** NT ideal

i|de|a|ler|wei|se [ideˈalɐˈvaizə] ADV ideally

I|de|al-: **I|de|al|fall** M ideal case; **im ~** ideally; **I|de|al|fi|gur** F ideal figure; **I|de|al|ge|wicht** NT ideal or optimum weight

i|de|a|li|sie|ren [ideaˈliˈziːrən] ptp **idealisiert** VT to idealize

I|de|a|li|sie|rung F -, -en idealization

I|de|a|lis|mus [ideaˈlɪsmʊs] M -, no pl idealism

I|de|a|list [ideaˈlɪst] M -en, -en, **I|de|a|lis|tin** [-ˈlɪstɪn] F -, -nen idealist

i|de|a|lis|tisch [ideaˈlɪstɪʃ] ADJ idealistic

I|de|al-: **I|de|al|kon|kur|renz** F (Jur) commission of two or more crimes in one and the same act; **I|de|al|li|nie** F (Sport) ideal or racing line; **I|de|al|ty|pus** M (Sociol) ideal type; **I|de|al|vor|stel|lung** F ideal; **I|de|al|zu-stand** M ideal state of affairs

I|dee [ideˈeː] ⊙ 38.1, 38.2, 40.3, 53.1, 53.3 F -, -n [iˈdeːən] **a** (= Einfall, Philos) idea; **die ~ zu etw** the idea for sth; **überhaupt keine ~n haben** to have not a single idea in one's head, to have no ideas at all; **wie kommst du denn auf DIE ~?** whatever gave you that idea?; **ich kam auf die ~, sie zu fragen** I hit on the idea of asking her; **jdn auf die ~ bringen, etw zu tun** to give sb the idea of doing sth; **jdn auf andere ~n bringen** to make sb think about something else; **~n müsste man haben!** what it is to have ideas! **b** (= ein wenig) shade, trifle; **eine ~ Salz** a touch or hint of salt; **keine ~ besser** not a whit better

i|de|ell [ideˈɛl] ADJ ideational (form, Philos); Wert, Anteil, Gesichtspunkt, Ziele non-material; Bedürfnisse, Unterstützung spiritual

I|de|en- [ideˈeːn-]: **i|de|en|arm** ADJ (= einfallsarm) lacking in ideas; (= fantasiearm) unimaginative, lacking in imagination; **I|de|en|ar|mut**

F (= Einfallsarmut) lack of ideas; (= Fantasiearmut) unimaginativeness, lack of imagination; **I|de|en|aus|tausch** M exchange of ideas; **I|de|en|gut** NT , no pl ideas pl, intellectual goods pl; **i|de|en|los** ADJ (= einfallslos) devoid of ideas; (= fantasielos) unimaginative, devoid of imagination; **I|de|en|lo|sig|keit** F -, no pl lack of ideas; (= Fantasielosigkeit) unimaginativeness, lack of imagination; **i|de|en|reich** ADJ (= einfallsreich) full of ideas; (= fantasiereich) imaginative, full of imagination; **I|de|en|reich|tum** M inventiveness; (= Fantasie) imaginativeness; **I|de|en|welt** F world of ideas or forms

I|den [ˈiːdn] PL **die ~ des März** the Ides of March

I|den|ti|fi|ka|ti|on [idɛntifikaˈtsioːn] F -, -en identification

I|den|ti|fi|ka|ti|ons|fi|gur F role model

i|den|ti|fi|zie|ren [idɛntifiˈtsiːrən] ptp **identifiziert** VT to identify VR **sich ~ mit** to identify (oneself) with

I|den|ti|fi|zie|rung F -, -en identification

i|den|tisch [iˈdɛntɪʃ] ADJ identical (mit with)

I|den|ti|tät [idɛntiˈtɛːt] F -, -en identity

I|den|ti|täts-: **I|den|ti|täts|kar|te** F (Sw) identity or ID card, ID (inf); **I|den|ti|täts|kri-se** F identity crisis; **I|den|ti|täts|nach|weis** M proof of identity

I|deo|gramm [ideoˈgram] NT pl **-gramme** (Ling) ideogram

I|deo|lo|ge [ideoˈloːgə] M -n, -n, **I|deo|lo|gin** [-ˈloːgɪn] F -, -nen ideologist

I|deo|lo|gie [ideoloˈgiː] F -, -n [-ˈgiːən] ideology

i|deo|lo|gie|frei ADJ free from ideology pred, ideologically unencumbered or unbiased

i|deo|lo|gisch [ideoˈloːgɪʃ] ADJ ideological ADV ideologically

i|deo|lo|gi|sie|ren [ideoloˈgiˈziːrən] ptp **ideologisiert** VT to ideologize

I|deo|lo|gi|sie|rung F -, -en ideologization

I|di|om [iˈdioːm] NT -s, -e idiom

I|di|o|ma|tik [idioˈmaːtɪk] F -, no pl idiomaticalness; (= Redewendungen) idioms pl

i|di|o|ma|tisch [idioˈmaːtɪʃ] ADJ idiomatic ADV idiomatically; **~ völlig einwandfreie/richtige Übersetzungen** perfect/correct idiomatic translations

I|di|o|plas|ma [idioˈplasma] NT (Biol) germ plasm, idioplasm

I|di|ot [iˈdioːt] M -en, -en, **I|di|o|tin** [iˈdioːtɪn] F -, -nen idiot; (auch inf) fool

I|di|o|ten-: **I|di|o|ten|ar|beit** F (pej inf) donkeywork (inf), drudgery, mindless work or job; **I|di|o|ten|hü|gel** M (hum inf) nursery or beginners' slope; **i|di|o|ten|si|cher** (inf) ADJ foolproof no adv ADV **etw ~ erklären** to explain sth so that even a fool or an idiot could understand it; **~ gestaltet** or **konzipiert sein** to be designed to be foolproof; **~ zu bedienen** extremely easy or simple to operate

I|di|o|tie [idioˈtiː] F -, -n [-ˈtiːən] idiocy; (inf) lunacy, madness, craziness

---

I|di|o|tin F -, -nen idiot; (*auch inf*) fool

i|di|o|tisch [i'dio:tɪʃ] ADJ idiotic

I|di|o|tis|mus [idio'tɪsmʊs] M -, **Idiotismen** [-mən] idiotism; (*inf*) lunacy, madness, craziness

I|dol [i'do:l] NT -s, -e idol

I|dyll [i'dʏl] NT -s, -e idyll; (= *Gegend*) idyllic place *or* spot

I|dyl|le [i'dʏlə] F -, -n idyll

i|dyl|lisch [i'dʏlɪʃ] ADJ idyllic ADV idyllically; **hier wohnt ihr wirklich ~** it is really idyllic where you live

IG [i:'ge:] F -, -s *abbr von* **Industriegewerkschaft** ≈ TU (*Brit*)

I|gel ['i:gl] M -s, - **a** (*Zool*) hedgehog; (= *Blumenigel*) pin holder **b** (*Mil*: = *Igelstellung*) position of all-round defence (*Brit*) *or* defense (*US*)

i|gitt|(i|gitt) [i'gɪt(i'gɪt)] INTERJ (*inf*) ugh! (*inf*)

Ig|lu ['i:glu] M OR NT -s, -s igloo

ig|no|rant [ɪgno'rant] ADJ ignorant

Ig|no|rant [ɪgno'rant] M -en, -en, **Ig|no|ran|tin** [-'rantɪn] F -, -nen ignoramus

Ig|no|ranz [ɪgno'rants] F -, *no pl* ignorance

ig|no|rie|ren [ɪgno'ri:rən] *ptp* **ignoriert** VT to ignore

IHK [i:ha:'ka:] F -, -s *abbr von* **Industrie- und Handelskammer**

ihm [i:m] PERS PRON *dat von* **er** *von* **es** [1] (*bei Personen*) to him; (*bei Tieren und Dingen*) to it; (*nach Präpositionen*) him/it; **ich gab es ~** I gave it (to) him; **ich gab ~ den Brief** I gave him the letter, I gave the letter to him; **ich sagte ~, dass ...** I told him that ..., I said to him that ...; **ich wer-de es ~ sagen** I'll tell him; **es war ~, als ob er träumte** he felt as though he were dreaming; **es ist ~ nicht gut** he doesn't feel well; **sie schnitt ~ die Haare** she cut his hair (for him); **ein Freund von ~** a friend of his, one of his friends; **wir gingen zu ~** (= *haben ihn aufgesucht*) we went to see him; (= *mit zu ihm nach Hause*) we went to his place; **ich habe ~ das gemacht** I did it for him; **sie hat ~ einen Pulli gestrickt** she knitted him a sweater, she knitted a sweater for him

ihn [i:n] PERS PRON *acc von* **er** him; (*bei Tieren und Dingen*) it

ih|nen ['i:nən] PERS PRON *dat von* **sie** **b** to them; (*nach Präpositionen*) them → *auch* **ihm**

Ih|nen ['i:nən] PERS PRON *dat von* **Sie** to you; (*nach Präpositionen*) you → *auch* **ihm**

ihr [i:ɐ] PERS PRON **a** *gen* **euer**, *dat* **euch**, *acc* **euch** 2. *pers pl nom* you; **Ihr** (*obs, dial*: *als Anrede eines Erwachsenen*) thou (*obs, dial*) **b** *dat von* **sie a** (*bei Personen*) to her; (*bei Tieren und Dingen*) to it; (*nach Präpositionen*) her/it; **Ihr** (*obs*: *in der Anrede eines weiblichen Wesens*) to thee (*obs, dial*) → *auch* **ihm** POSS PRON **a** (*einer Person*) her; (*eines Tiers, Dinges, Abstraktum*) its **b** (*von mehreren*) their

Ihr [i:ɐ] PERS PRON → **ihr** PERS PRON a, b POSS PRON *sing and pl* your; **~ Franz Müller** (*Briefschluss*) yours, Franz Müller

ih|rer ['i:rɐ] PERS PRON (*geh*) **a** *gen von* **sie a** (*bei Personen*) of her; **wir werden ~ gedenken** we will remember her **b** *gen von* **sie b** of them; **es waren ~ zehn** there were ten of them, they were ten; **wir werden ~ gedenken** we will remember them

Ih|rer ['i:rɐ] PERS PRON *gen von* **Sie** (*geh*) of you; **wir werden ~ gedenken** we will remember you

ih|re(r, s) ['i:rə] POSS PRON (*substantivisch*) **a** (*einer Person*) hers; (*eines Tiers*) its; **der/die/das ~** *or* **Ihre** (*geh*) hers/its; **sie** did *her part*; **Ihre Majestät** Her Majesty; **sie und die ~n** *or* **Ihren** (*geh*: = *Familie*) she and hers; **das ~** *or* **Ihre** (*geh*: = *Besitz*) what is hers **b** (*von mehreren*) theirs; **der/die/das ~** *or* **Ihre** (*geh*) theirs; **sie taten das ~** *or* **Ihre** (*geh*) they did their part

Ih|re(r, s) ['i:rə] POSS PRON *sing and pl* (*substantivisch*) yours; **der/die/das ~** (*geh*) yours; **stets** *or* **ganz der ~** (*old*) yours ever; **schöne Grüße an Sie und die ~n** (*geh*) best wishes to you and your family; **tun Sie das ~** (*geh*) you do your bit

ih|rer|seits ['i:rɐ'zaits] ADV (*bei einer Person*) for her part; (*bei mehreren*) for their part; (*von ihrer Seite*) on her/their part

Ih|rer|seits ['i:rɐ'zaits] ADV for your part; (*von Ihrer Seite*) on your part

ih|res|glei|chen ['i:rəs'glaiçn] PRON *inv* (*von einer Person*) people like her; (*von mehreren*) people like them; (*von Dingen*) others like it, similar ones; (*pej*) people like her/them, her/their sort, the likes of her/them; **sie fühlt sich unter ~ am wohlsten** she feels most at home among her own kind *or* among people like her(self); **eine Frechheit, die ~ sucht!** incredible impudence!

Ih|res|glei|chen ['i:rəs'glaiçn] PRON *inv* people like you; (*pej auch*) your sort, the likes of you; **Sie sollten Kontakt mit ~ pflegen** you should keep in contact with your own kind (of people) *or* with people like yourself *or* you

ih|ret|hal|ben ['i:rət'halbn] (*dated*), **ih|ret|we-gen** ['i:rət've:gn], **ih|ret|wil|len** ['i:rət'vilən] ADV (*bei Personen*) (= *wegen ihr/ihnen*) (*sing*) because of her; (*pl*) because of them; (= *ihr/ihnen zuliebe auch*) for her sake/their sake(s); (= *um sie*) about her/them; (= *für sie*) on her/their behalf; (*bei Dingen und Tieren*) (*sing*) because of it; (*pl*) because of them; **sie sagte, ihretwegen könnten wir gehen** she said that, as far as she was concerned, we could go

Ih|ret|hal|ben ['i:rət'halbn] (*dated*), **Ih|ret|we-gen** ['i:rət've:gn], **Ih|ret|wil|len** ['i:rət'vilən] ADV because of you; (= *Ihnen zuliebe*) (*sing auch*) for your sake; (*pl auch*) for your sake(s); (= *um Sie*) about you; (= *für Sie*) on your behalf

ih|ri|ge ['i:rɪgə] POSS PRON (*old, geh*) **der/die/das ~** *or* **Ihrige** (*von einer Person*) hers; (*von mehreren*) theirs → *auch* **ihre(r, s)**

Ih|ri|ge ['i:rɪgə] POSS PRON **der/die/das ~** yours → *auch* **Ihre(r, s)**

Ih|ro ['i:ro] POSS PRON (*obs*) your

i. J. *abbr von* **im Jahre**

I|ke|ba|na [ike'ba:na] NT -s, *no pl* ikebana

I|kon ['aikɔn] NT -s, -e (*Comput*) icon

I|ko|ne [i'ko:nə] F -, -n (*auch fig*) icon

I|ko|nen|ma|le|rei F icon painting; (*Bild*) icon

I|lex ['i:lɛks] F OR M -, - holly

I|li|as ['i:lias] F - Iliad

ill. *abbr von* **illustriert**

il|le|gal [ɪle'ga:l, 'ɪl-] ADJ illegal ADV illegally; **sich ~ betätigen** to engage in illegal activities

Il|le|ga|li|tät [ɪlegali'tɛ:t, 'ɪl-] F -, -en illegality

il|le|gi|tim [ɪlegi'ti:m, 'ɪl-] ADJ illegitimate

Il|le|gi|ti|mi|tät [ɪlegitimi'tɛ:t, 'ɪl-] F -, *no pl* illegitimacy

il|li|quid [ɪli'kvi:t, 'ɪl-] ADJ (*Comm*) illiquid

Il|li|qui|di|tät [ɪlikvidi'tɛ:t, 'ɪl-] F -, *no pl* (*Comm*) illiquidity

il|lo|yal [ɪloa'ja:l, 'ɪl-] ADJ disloyal ADV *sich verhalten* disloyally

Il|lo|ya|li|tät [ɪloajali'tɛ:t, 'ɪl-] F -, *no pl* disloyalty

Il|lu|mi|na|ti|on [ɪlumina'tsio:n] F -, -en illumination

il|lu|mi|nie|ren [ɪlumi'ni:rən] *ptp* **illuminiert** VT to illuminate

Il|lu|si|on [ɪlu'zio:n] F -, -en illusion; **jdm alle ~en nehmen** *or* **rauben** to rob sb of all his/her etc illusions; **sich (dat) ~en machen** to delude oneself; **darüber macht er sich keine ~en** he doesn't have any illusions about it; **sich der ~ hingeben, dass ...** to be under the illusion that ..., to labour (*Brit*) *or* labor (*US*) under the misapprehension that ...

il|lu|si|o|när [ɪluzio'nɛ:ɐ] ADJ illusionary

Il|lu|si|o|nis|mus [ɪluzio'nɪsmʊs] M -, *no pl* illusionism

Il|lu|si|o|nist [ɪluzio'nɪst] M -en, -en, **Il|lu|si|o|nis|tin** [-'nɪstɪn] F -, -nen illusionist

il|lu|si|o|nis|tisch [ɪluzio'nɪstɪʃ] ADJ (*Art*) illusionistic

il|lu|si|ons|los ADJ **ein ~er Mensch** a person with no illusions; **~ sein** to have no illusions; **~ werden** to lose one's illusions

Il|lu|si|ons|lo|sig|keit F -, *no pl* lack of illusions

il|lu|so|risch [ɪlu'zo:rɪʃ] ADJ illusory; **es ist völlig ~, zu glauben ...** it's a complete illusion to believe ...

il|lus|ter [ɪ'lʊstɐ] ADJ (*geh*) illustrious

Il|lust|ra|ti|on [ɪlʊstra'tsio:n] F -, -en illustration; **zur ~ von etw** to illustrate sth, as an illustration of sth

il|lust|ra|tiv [ɪlʊstra'ti:f] ADJ **a** (*mit Anschauungsmaterial*) illustrated **b** (= *anschaulich*) illustrative ADV **a** = *mit Anschauungsmaterial*) with illustrations; **etw ~ aufzeigen** to show sth with illustrations **b** (= *anschaulich*) vividly; **er hat sehr ~ geschildert, wie ...** he described very vividly how ...

Il|lust|ra|tor [ɪlʊs'tra:to:ɐ] M -s, **Illustratoren**, **Il|lust|ra|to|rin** [-'to:rɪn] F -, -nen illustrator

il|lust|rie|ren [ɪlʊs'tri:rən] *ptp* **illustriert** VT to illustrate (*jdm etw* sth for sb)

Il|lust|rier|te [ɪlʊs'tri:ɐtə] F *decl as adj* magazine, mag (*inf*)

Il|lust|rie|rung F -, -en illustration

Il|tis ['ɪltɪs] M -ses, -se polecat

im [ɪm] PREP *contr von* **in dem a** (*räumlich*) in the; **im zweiten Stock** on the second floor; **im Theater** at the theatre (*Brit*) *or* theater (*US*); **die Beleuchtung im Theater** the lighting in the theatre (*Brit*) *or* theater (*US*); **Freiburg im Breisgau** Freiburg in Breisgau; **im Bett** in bed; **im „Faust"** in "Faust"
b (*zeitlich*) in the; **im Mai** in May; **im Jahre 1866** in (the year) 1866; **im Alter von 91 Jahren** at the age of 91; **im letzten/nächsten Jahr** last/next year; **im letzten Jahr des Krieges** in the last year of the war; **im nächsten Jahr ging er (in) the next year he went
c *+superl* **nicht im Geringsten** not in the slightest
d (*als Verlaufsform*) **im Kommen/Gehen** *etc* **sein** to be coming/going *etc*; **etw im Liegen/Stehen** *etc* **tun** to do sth lying down/standing up *etc*
e **im Trab/Laufschritt** *etc* at a trot/run *etc*

IM [i:'ɛm] *abbr von* **inoffizieller Mitarbeiter (der Stasi)** (Stasi) collaborator

---

IM

IM is an abbreviation of **inoffizieller Mitarbeiter**, meaning an unofficial collaborator of the Stasi in the former East Germany. These were members of the public who – sometimes voluntarily, so as to receive financial and other perks, sometimes because of external pressures – spied on their colleagues and friends and even their own families on behalf of the Stasi. The number of **IM**s is estimated at 500,000 → STASI

I|mage ['ɪmɪtʃ] NT -(s), -s image

I|mage-: i|mage|bil|dend ADJ image-building; **I|mage|bro|schü|re** F (*esp Comm*) promotional pamphlet *or* brochure; **I|mage|kam|pag|ne** F (*Pol, Comm*) image-building *or* image-rebuilding campaign; **I|mage|pfle|ge** F image building; **I|mage|ver|fall** M loss of prestige; **I|mage|ver|lust** M damage to one's image; **I|mage|wer|bung** F image promotion; **~ (für sich) betreiben** to promote one's image

i|ma|gi|när [imagi'nɛ:ɐ] ADJ imaginary

I|ma|gi|na|ti|on [imagina'tsio:n] F -, -en (*geh*) imagination

---

I|ma|go [i'ma:go] F -, Imagines [i'ma:gine:s] (*Biol*, *Psych*) imago; (*Art*) image

I|mam [i'ma:m] M -s, -s or -e imam

Im|biss ▲ ['ɪmbɪs] M -es, -e snack

Im|biss-: **Im|biss|bu|de** ▲ F = Imbissstand; **Im|biss|hal|le** ▲ F snack bar; **Im|biss|stand** ▲ M ≈ hot-dog stall or stand; **Im|biss|stu|be** ▲ F café; (*in Kaufhaus etc*) cafeteria

I|mi|ta|ti|on [imita'tsio:n] F -, -en imitation

I|mi|ta|tor [imi'ta:to:ɐ] M -s, Imitatoren, **I|mi|ta|to|rin** [-'to:rɪn] F -, -nen imitator; (*von Schmuck, einem Bild*) copyist

i|mi|tie|ren [imi'ti:rən] ptp **imitiert** VT to imitate; **imitierter Schmuck** imitation jewellery (*Brit*) or jewelry (*US*)

Im|ker ['ɪmkɐ] M -s, -, **Im|ke|rin** [-ərɪn] F -, -nen beekeeper, apiarist (*form*)

Im|ke|rei [ɪmkə'rai] F -, no pl beekeeping, apiculture (*form*)

im|kern ['ɪmkɐn] VI to keep bees

im|ma|nent [ɪma'nɛnt] ADJ inherent, intrinsic; *Kriterien* internal; (*Philos*) immanent; **einer Sache** (*dat*) **~ sein** to be inherent in sth; **~e Wiederholung** incorporative repetition

Im|ma|nenz [ɪma'nɛnts] F -, no pl (*Philos*) immanence

im|ma|te|ri|ell [ɪmate'riɛl, 'ɪm-] ADJ *Vermögenswerte* incorporeal, immaterial

Im|mat|ri|ku|la|ti|on [ɪmatrikula'tsio:n] F -, -en matriculation (*form*), registration (*at university*)

im|mat|ri|ku|lie|ren [ɪmatriku'li:rən] ptp **immatrikuliert** VT to register (*at university*) (*an* +dat at) to matriculate (*form*), to register (*at university*)

Im|me ['ɪmə] F -, -n (*poet*) bee

im|mens [ɪ'mɛns] ADJ immense, huge, enormous ADV immensely, enormously; **~ groß sein** to be huge

im|mer ['ɪmɐ] ADV **a** (= *häufig, ständig*) always; **schon ~** always; **auf** or **für ~** for ever, for always; **~ diese Aufregung/Nörgelei** this continual excitement/grumbling; **~ diese Probleme!** all these problems!; **~ diese Studenten** these wretched students (*inf*); **~ das Telefon** that wretched phone (*inf*); **~, wenn ...** whenever ..., every time that ...; **~ mal** (*inf*) from time to time, now and again; **~ geradeaus gehen** to keep going straight on; **~ während** perpetual, eternal; *Kalender* perpetual; **~ und ewig** (*liter*) for ever and ever; **~ langsam voran!** (*inf*) (nur) **~ langsam!** (*inf*) take your time (about it), take it slowly; **~ (schön) mit der Ruhe** (*inf*) take it easy; **(nur) ~ her damit!** (*inf*) (just) hand it over!; **noch ~, ~ noch** still; **~ noch nicht** still not (yet); **bist du denn ~ noch nicht fertig?** are you still not ready?, aren't you ready yet?; **nur ~ zu!** keep it up!, keep up the good work!; **~ wieder** again and again, time after time, time and (time) again; **etw ~ wieder tun** to keep on doing sth; **wie ~** as usual, as always → **Sprung a, Nase a**

b +comp **~ besser** better and better; **~ häufiger** more and more often; **~ mehr** more and more; **es nimmt ~ mehr zu** it increases all the time, it increases continually, it keeps on increasing; **größer werdende Schulden** constantly increasing debts; **sein Verhältnis zu ihr wird ~ schlechter** his relationship with her gets worse and worse, his relationship with her goes from bad to worse; **nicht ~, aber ~ öfter** not always, but more and more often

c **wer (auch) ~** whoever; **wie (auch) ~** however; **wann (auch) ~** whenever; **wo (auch) ~** wherever; **was (auch) ~** whatever

d (inf: = jeweils) **gib mir ~ drei Bücher auf einmal** give me three books at a time; **stellt euch in einer Reihe auf, ~ zwei zusammen** line up in twos; **~ am dritten Tag** every third day

im|mer-: im|mer|dar ['ɪmɐ'da:ɐ] ADV (*liter*) forever, evermore; **im|mer|fort** ['ɪmɐ'fɔrt] ADV =

immerzu; **im|mer|grün** ['ɪmɐgry:n] ADJ attr (*lit*, *fig*) evergreen; **Im|mer|grün** ['ɪmɐgry:n] NT evergreen; **im|mer|hin** ['ɪmɐ'hɪn] ADV all the same, anyhow, at any rate; (= *wenigstens*) at least; (= *schließlich*) after all; **im|mer|wäh|rend** △ ['ɪmɐ'vɛ:rənt] ADJ attr → immer a; **im|mer|zu** ['ɪmɐ'tsu:] ADV all the time, the whole time, constantly

Im|mig|rant [ɪmi'grant] M -en, -en, **Im|mig|ran|tin** [-'grantɪn] F -, -nen immigrant

Im|mig|ra|ti|on [ɪmigra'tsio:n] F -, -en immigration

im|mig|rie|ren [ɪmi'gri:rən] ptp **immigriert** VI aux sein to immigrate

Im|mis|si|on [ɪmi'sio:n] F (*Jur*) effect on nearby property of gases, smoke, noise, smells etc

Im|mis|si|ons-: **Im|mis|si|ons|scha|den** M pollution damage; **Im|mis|si|ons|schutz** M air pollution control; **Im|mis|si|ons|schutz|ge|setz** NT air pollution laws pl

im|mo|bil [ɪmo'bi:l, 'ɪm-] ADJ immobile, immoveable; *Vermögen, Besitz* real, immoveable

Im|mo|bi|lie [ɪmo'bi:liə] F -, -n **eine ~** a property **b** **Immobilien** PL real estate sing, real or immoveable property sing (*form*), immoveables pl (*form*); (*in Zeitungsannoncen*) property sing

Im|mo|bi|li|en-: **Im|mo|bi|li|en|fonds** M (*Fin*) real estate fund; **Im|mo|bi|li|en|händ|ler(in)** M(F), **Im|mo|bi|li|en|mak|ler(in)** M(F) (real) estate agent (*Brit*), realtor (*US*); **Im|mo|bi|li|en|markt** M (*Comm*) property market

Im|mo|ra|li|tät [ɪmorali'tɛ:t, 'ɪm-] F immorality

Im|mor|ta|li|tät [ɪmortali'tɛ:t, 'ɪm-] F immortality

Im|mor|tel|le [ɪmɔr'tɛlə] F -, -n (*Bot*) everlasting (flower), immortelle

im|mun [ɪ'mu:n] ADJ immune (*gegen* to)

Im|mun- in cpds (*Med*) immune; **Im|mun|ab|wehr** [ɪ'mu:n-] F (*Med*) immune defence (*Brit*) or defense (*US*); **Im|mun|glo|bu|lin** [ɪ'mu:nglobuli:n] NT -s, -e (*Med*) immunoglobulin

im|mu|ni|sie|ren [ɪmuni'zi:rən] ptp **immunisiert** VT (*form*) to immunize (*gegen* against)

Im|mu|ni|sie|rung F -, -en (*form*) immunization (*gegen* against)

Im|mu|ni|tät [ɪmuni'tɛ:t] F -, (*rare*) -en immunity

im|mu|no|gen ADJ immunogenic

Im|mu|no|ge|ni|tät [ɪmunogeni'tɛ:t] F -, no pl immunogenicity

Im|mu|no|lo|ge [ɪmuno'lo:gə] M -n, -n, **Im|mu|no|lo|gin** [-'lo:gɪn] F -, -nen immunologist

Im|mu|no|lo|gie [ɪmunolo'gi:] F -, no pl immunology

im|mu|no|lo|gisch [ɪmuno'lo:gɪʃ] ADJ immunological

Im|mun-: **Im|mun|re|ak|ti|on** F (*Med*) immunological reaction, immunoreaction; **Im|mun|schwä|che|krank|heit** F immune deficiency disease or syndrome; **Im|mun|sys|tem** NT immune system; **Im|mun|the|ra|pie** F (*Med*) immunotherapy

Im|pe|danz F -, -en (*Phys*, *Elec*: = *Scheinwiderstand*) impedance

Im|pe|ra|tiv ['ɪmperati:f] M -s, -e [-və] (*Gram*) imperative (form); (*Philos*) imperative

im|pe|ra|ti|visch [ɪmpera'ti:vɪʃ] ADJ (*Gram*) imperative

Im|pe|ra|tor [ɪmpe'ra:to:ɐ] M -s, Imperatoren (*Hist*) emperor; (*Mil*) general

im|pe|ra|to|risch [ɪmpera'to:rɪʃ] ADJ imperial; (*fig*) imperious

Im|per|fekt ['ɪmpɛrfɛkt] NT , **Im|per|fek|tum** [ɪmpɛr'fɛktʊm, 'ɪm-] NT (*Gram*) imperfect (tense)

Im|pe|ri|a|lis|mus [ɪmperia'lɪsmʊs] M -, no pl imperialism

Im|pe|ri|a|list [ɪmperia'lɪst] M -en, -en, **Im|pe|ri|a|lis|tin** [-'lɪstɪn] F -, -nen imperialist

im|pe|ri|a|lis|tisch [ɪmperia'lɪstɪʃ] ADJ imperialistic

Im|pe|ri|um [ɪm'pe:riʊm] NT -s, Imperien [-riən] (= *Gebiet*) empire; (= *Herrschaft*) imperium

im|per|ti|nent [ɪmpɛrti'nɛnt] ADJ (*geh*) impertinent, impudent

Im|per|ti|nenz [ɪmpɛrti'nɛnts] F -, -en (*geh*) impertinence, impudence

Im|pe|tus ['ɪmpetʊs] M -, no pl (*geh*) impetus, momentum; (= *Tatkraft*) drive

Impf-: **Impf|ak|ti|on** F vaccination or inoculation programme (*Brit*) or program (*US*); **Impf|arzt** M , **Impf|ärz|tin** F vaccinator, inoculator; **Impf|aus|weis** M vaccination card

imp|fen ['ɪmpfn] VT to vaccinate, to inoculate

Impf|ling ['ɪmpflɪŋ] M -s, -e person who has just been or is to be vaccinated

Impf-: **Impf|pass** ▲ M vaccination card, record of the vaccinations one has been given; **Impf|pflicht** F compulsory vaccination or inoculation, requirement to be vaccinated or inoculated; **Impf|pis|to|le** F vaccination gun; **Impf|scha|den** M vaccine damage; **Impf|schein** M certificate of vaccination or inoculation; **Impf|schutz** M protection given by vaccination; **Impf|stoff** M vaccine, serum

Impf|ung F -, -en vaccination, inoculation

Impf|zwang M = Impfpflicht

Im|plan|tat [ɪmplan'ta:t] NT -(e)s, -e implant

Im|plan|ta|ti|on [ɪmplanta'tsio:n] F -, -en (*Med*) implantation

im|ple|men|tie|ren [ɪmplemɛn'ti:rən] ptp **implementiert** VT to implement

im|pli|zie|ren [ɪmpli'tsi:rən] ptp **impliziert** VT to imply

im|pli|zit [ɪmpli'tsi:t], **im|pli|zi|te** [ɪm'pli:tsite] (*geh*) ADV by implication, implicitly; **etw ~ sagen** to imply sth, to say sth by implication

im|plo|die|ren [ɪmplo'di:rən] ptp **implodiert** VI aux sein to implode

Im|plo|si|on [ɪmplo'zio:n] F -, -en implosion

Im|pon|de|ra|bi|li|en [ɪmpɔndera'bi:liən] PL (*geh*) imponderables pl

im|po|nie|ren [ɪmpo'ni:rən] ptp **imponiert** VI to make an impression (*jdm* on sb), to impress (*jdm* sb); **dadurch hat er imponiert** he made an impression by that; **es imponiert mir, wie sie das schafft** it impresses me how she manages it, I'm impressed by the way she manages it

im|po|nie|rend ADJ impressive; *Gebäude auch* imposing

Im|po|nier|ge|ha|be NT (*Zool*) display pattern; (*fig pej*) exhibitionism

Im|port [ɪm'pɔrt] M -(e)s, -e **a** (= *Handel*) import; **der ~ sollte den Export nicht übersteigen** imports should not exceed exports; **der ~ von Obst und Gemüse ist gestiegen** the import or importation of fruit and vegetables has increased, fruit and vegetable imports have increased **b** (= *Importware*) import; **der Salat ist holländischer ~** the lettuce was imported from Holland

Import- in cpds import

Im|por|te [ɪm'pɔrtə] F -, -n usu pl imported cigar

Im|por|teur [ɪmpɔr'tø:ɐ] M -s, -e, **Im|por|teu|rin** [-'tø:rɪn] F -, -nen importer

Import|fir|ma F import business, importer(s pl)

Import|ge|schäft NT (= *Handel*) import trade; (= *Firma*) import business

im|por|tie|ren [ɪmpɔr'ti:rən] ptp **importiert** VT (auch Comput) to import

Import|land NT importing country

im|po|sant [ɪmpo'zant] ADJ *Gebäude, Kunstwerk, Figur* imposing; *Leistung* impressive; *Stimme* commanding

im|po|tent ['ɪmpotɛnt, ɪmpo'tɛnt] ADJ impotent

Im|po|tenz [ˈɪmpotɛnts, ɪmpoˈtɛnts] F -, no pl impotence

im|präg|nie|ren [ɪmprɛˈgniːrən] ptp **imprägniert** VT to impregnate; (= wasserdicht machen) to (water)proof

Im|präg|nie|rung F -, -en impregnation; (von Geweben) (water)proofing; (nach der Reinigung) reproofing

im|prak|ti|ka|bel [ˈɪmpraktikaːbl, ɪmprakti-ˈkaːbl] ADJ impracticable

Im|pre|sa|rio [ɪmprɛˈzaːrio] M -s, -s or **Impresari** [-ri] impresario

Im|pres|si|on [ɪmprɛˈsioːn] F impression (über +acc of)

Im|pres|si|o|nis|mus [ɪmprɛsioˈnɪsmʊs] M -, no pl impressionism

Im|pres|si|o|nist [ɪmprɛsioˈnɪst] M -en, -en, **Im|pres|si|o|nis|tin** [-ˈnɪstɪn] F -, -nen impressionist

im|pres|si|o|nis|tisch [ɪmprɛsioˈnɪstɪʃ] ADJ impressionistic

Im|pres|sum [ɪmˈprɛsʊm] NT -s, **Impressen** [-sn] imprint; (von Zeitung) masthead

Im|pri|ma|tur [ɪmpriˈmaːtʊr] NT -s, no pl (Typ) imprimatur

Im|pro|vi|sa|ti|on [ɪmproviˈzaːtsioːn] F -, -en improvisation; (von Rede, Gedicht, Musik auch) extemporization

Im|pro|vi|sa|ti|ons|ta|lent NT talent for improvisation; (= Mensch) (great) improviser

im|pro|vi|sie|ren [ɪmproviˈziːrən] ptp **improvisiert** VTI to improvise; (Mus auch) to extemporize; eine Rede auch to ad-lib (inf), to extemporize

Im|puls [ɪmˈpʊls] M -es, -e impulse; etw aus einem ~ heraus tun to do sth on the spur of the moment, to do sth on impulse; einer Sache (dat) neue ~e geben to give sth new impetus or momentum; äußere ~e veranlassten ihn dazu external factors made him do it

im|pul|siv [ɪmpʊlˈziːf] ADJ impulsive; ~e Äußerungen/Entschlüsse spur of the moment or impulsive remarks/decisions ADV impulsively; ~ handeln to act impulsively or on impulse

Im|pul|si|vi|tät [ɪmpʊlziviˈtɛːt] F -, no pl impulsiveness

im|stan|de [ɪmˈʃtandə] ♥ 43.4 ADJ pred ~ sein, etw zu tun (= fähig) to be able to do sth, to be capable of doing sth; (= in der Lage) to be in a position to do sth; er ist zu allem ~ he's capable of anything; er ist ~ und erzählt es meiner Mutter he's (quite) capable of telling my mother

in [ɪn] PREP → auch im, ins a (räumlich) (wo? +dat) in; (innen) in(side); (wohin? +acc) in, into; sind Sie schon in Deutschland gewesen? have you ever been to Germany?; in der Schweiz in Switzerland; in die Schweiz to Switzerland; er ist Professor in St. Andrews he is a professor at St. Andrews (University); in die Schule/Kirche gehen to go to school/church; er ist in der Schule/Kirche he's at or in school/church; die Heizung in der Schule/Kirche the heating in the school/church; er ging ins Konzert he went to the concert b (zeitlich: wann? +dat) in; in diesem Jahr (laufendes Jahr) this year; (jenes Jahr) in that year; heute/morgen in acht Tagen/zwei Wochen a week/two weeks today/tomorrow; bis ins 18. Jahrhundert into or up to the 18th century; vom 16. bis ins 18. Jahrhundert from the 16th to the 18th century; bis ins 18. Jahrhundert zurück back to the 18th century c in Englisch steht er sehr schwach he's very weak in or at English; das ist in Englisch it's in English; ins Englische übersetzen to translate into English; in Geschichte haben wir einen neuen Lehrer we've a new teacher in or for history; in die hunderte or Hunderte gehen to run into (the) hundreds; er macht jetzt in Gebrauchtwagen (inf) he's in the second-hand car

business now; sie hat es in sich (dat) (inf) she's quite a girl; der Text/die Rechenarbeit hat es in sich (dat) (inf) the text/the arithmetic test is a tough one; dieser Whisky hat es in sich (dat) (inf) this whisky packs quite a punch (inf), this whisky has quite a kick (inf) ADJ pred (inf) in sein to be in (inf)

in|ad|ä|quat ADJ inadequate

in|ak|ku|rat ADJ inaccurate

in|ak|tiv ADJ inactive; Mitglied non-active; (Mil) inactive, on the reserve list

In|ak|ti|vi|tät F inactivity; (von Mitglied) non-activity

in|ak|zep|ta|bel ADJ unacceptable

In|an|griff|nah|me [ɪnˈʔangrɪfnaːmə] F -, -n (form) starting, commencement (form)

In|an|spruch|nah|me [ɪnˈʔanʃprʊxnaːmə] F -, -n (form) a (= Beanspruchung) demands pl, claims pl (+gen on); seine ~ durch diese Nebenbeschäftigung the demands or claims made on him by this second job; im Falle einer ~ von Arbeitslosenunterstützung where unemployment benefit has been sought (form); bei ~ des Versicherungsschutzes entfällt der Rabatt the discount is forfeited should an insurance claim be submitted b (= Auslastung: von Einrichtungen, Verkehrssystem etc) utilization; wegen zu geringer ~ der Cafeteria as a result of under-utilization of the cafeteria

in|ar|ti|ku|liert [ˈɪnʔartikuliːt, ɪnʔartikuˈliːt] ADJ inarticulate

In|au|gen|schein|nah|me [ɪnˈʔaugnʃainnaːmə] F -, -n (form) inspection

inbegr. abbr von **inbegriffen**

In|be|griff [ˈɪnbəgrɪf] M , no pl perfect example; (der Schönheit, Güte, des Bösen etc) epitome, embodiment; sie war der ~ der Schönheit/Tugend she was beauty/virtue personified or incarnate; diese neue Kirche ist der ~ der modernen Architektur this new church epitomizes modern architecture

in|be|grif|fen [ˈɪnbəgrɪfn] ADJ pred included; die Mehrwertsteuer ist im Preis ~ the price includes VAT, the price is inclusive of VAT, VAT is included in the price

In|be|sitz|nah|me [ɪnbəˈzɪtsnaːmə] F -, -n (form) taking possession

In|be|trieb|nah|me [ɪnbəˈtriːpnaːmə] F -, -n commissioning; (von Gebäude, U-Bahn etc) inauguration; die ~ des Geräts erfolgt in zwei Wochen the appliance will be put into operation in two weeks

In|brunst [ˈɪnbrʊnst] F , no pl fervour (Brit), fervor (US), ardour (Brit), ardor (US)

in|brüns|tig [ˈɪnbrʏnstɪç] ADJ fervent, ardent ADV fervently, ardently

In|bus|schlüs|sel® [ˈɪnbʊs-] M (Tech) Allen key®

In|cen|tive|rei|se [ɪnˈsɛntɪv-] F incentive holiday

In|danth|ren® [ɪndanˈtreːn] NT -s, -e colour-fast dye

In|de|fi|nit|pro|no|men [ˈɪndefiˈniːt-, ˈɪndefi-niːt-] NT indefinite pronoun

in|de|kli|na|bel [ˈɪndeklinaːbl] ADJ (Ling) indeclinable

in|dem [ɪnˈdeːm] CONJ a (= während der ganzen Zeit) while, whilst (Brit liter); (= in dem Augenblick) as; ~ er sich hinsetzte, sagte er ... sitting down, he said ..., as he sat down he said ... b (= dadurch, dass) ~ man etw macht by doing sth ADV (old) meanwhile, (in the) meantime

In|der [ˈɪndɐ] M -s, -, **In|de|rin** [-ərɪn] F -, -nen Indian; zum ~ gehen to go to a/the Indian restaurant

in|des [ɪnˈdɛs], **in|des|sen** [ɪnˈdɛsn] ADV a (zeitlich) meanwhile, (in the) meantime b (adversativ) however CONJ a (geh) (zeitlich) while b (adversativ) ~ (liter) however; (= andererseits) whereas

In|dex [ˈɪndɛks] M -(es), -e or **Indizes** [ˈɪnditseːs] index (auch Comput); (Eccl) Index

In|dex|an|lei|he F (Fin) index-linked loan, index loan

in|de|xie|ren [ɪndɛˈksiːrən] ptp **indexiert** VTI (Comput) to index

in|de|zent [ˈɪndetsɛnt] ADJ (geh) indecent

In|di|a|ner [ɪnˈdiaːnɐ] M -s, -, **In|di|a|ne|rin** [-ərɪn] F -, -nen American Indian, Native American; (in Western) (Red) Indian

In|di|a|ner|re|ser|vat NT Native American reservation, Indian reservation

in|di|a|nisch [ɪnˈdiaːnɪʃ] ADJ American Indian, Native American; (in Western) (Red) Indian

In|di|a|nis|tik [ɪndiaˈnɪstɪk] F -, no pl American Indian studies pl, Native American studies pl

In|di|en [ˈɪndiən] NT -s India

In|dienst|nah|me [ɪnˈdiːnstnaːmə] F (geh) commissioning, taking into service

in|dif|fe|rent [ˈɪndɪfərɛnt, ɪndɪfəˈrɛnt] ADJ a (geh) indifferent (gegenüber to) b (Chem, Phys) inert; Gas inert, rare, inactive

In|dif|fe|renz [ˈɪndɪfərɛnts, ɪndɪfəˈrɛnts] F (geh) indifference (gegenüber to, towards)

In|di|gna|ti|on [ɪndɪgnaˈtsioːn] F -, no pl (geh) indignation (über +acc at)

in|di|gniert [ɪndɪˈgniːt] ADJ (geh) indignant

In|di|gni|tät [ɪndɪgniˈtɛːt] F -, no pl (Jur) incapability of inheriting

In|di|go [ˈɪndigo] NT OR M -s, -s indigo

in|di|go|blau ADJ indigo-blue

In|di|ka|ti|on [ɪndikaˈtsioːn] F -, -en (Med) indication; ethische/eugenische/medizinische/soziale ~ ethical/eugenic/medical/social grounds for the termination of pregnancy

In|di|ka|tiv [ˈɪndikatiːf] M -s, -e [-və] (Gram) indicative

in|di|ka|ti|visch [ɪndikaˈtiːvɪʃ, ˈɪn-] ADJ (Gram) indicative

In|di|ka|tor [ɪndiˈkaːtoːɐ] M -s, **Indikatoren** indicator

In|dio [ˈɪndio] M -s, -s (Central/South American) Indian

in|di|rekt [ˈɪndirɛkt, ɪndiˈrɛkt] ADJ indirect; ~e Rede indirect or reported speech ADV indirectly; ~ beleuchtet sein to have indirect lighting

in|disch [ˈɪndɪʃ] ADJ Indian; der Indische Ozean the Indian Ocean

In|dis|kret [ɪndɪsˈkreːt, ˈɪn-] ADJ indiscreet ADV indiscreetly

In|dis|kre|ti|on [ɪndɪskreˈtsioːn, ˈɪn-] F indiscretion

in|dis|ku|ta|bel [ɪndɪskuˈtaːbl, ˈɪn-] ADJ out of the question; (= sehr schlecht) indescribably bad

in|dis|po|niert [ɪndɪspoˈniːt, ˈɪn-] ADJ (geh) indisposed

In|dis|po|si|ti|on [ɪndɪspoziˈtsioːn, ˈɪn-] F (geh) indisposition

In|di|um [ˈɪndiʊm] NT -s, no pl (abbr **In**) indium

in|di|vi|du|a|li|sie|ren [ɪndividualiˈziːrən] ptp **individualisiert** VT to individualize

In|di|vi|du|a|li|sie|rung F -, -en individualization

In|di|vi|du|a|lis|mus [ɪndividuaˈlɪsmʊs] M -, no pl individualism

In|di|vi|du|a|list [ɪndividuaˈlɪst] M -en, -en, **In|di|vi|du|a|lis|tin** [-ˈlɪstɪn] F -, -nen individualist

in|di|vi|du|a|lis|tisch [ɪndividuaˈlɪstɪʃ] ADJ individualistic

In|di|vi|du|a|li|tät [ɪndividualiˈtɛːt] F -, -en a no pl individuality b (= Charakterzüge) individual characteristic

In|di|vi|du|al|ver|kehr [ɪndividuˈaːl-] M (Mot) private transport

in|di|vi|du|ell [ɪndiviˈduɛl] ADJ individual ADV individually; etw ~ gestalten to give sth a personal note; **es ist ~ verschieden** it differs from person to person *or* from case to case, it's different for each person

In|di|vi|du|um [ɪndiˈviːduʊm] NT **-s, Individuen** [-duən] individual

In|diz [ɪnˈdiːts] NT **-es, -ien** [-tsiən] **a** *(Jur)* clue; *(als Beweismittel)* piece of circumstantial evidence; **alles beruht nur auf ~ien** everything rests only on circumstantial evidence **b** *(= Anzeichen)* sign, indication *(für of)*

In|di|zes pl von **Index**

In|di|zi|en|be|weis M circumstantial evidence *no pl*, piece of circumstantial evidence

in|di|zie|ren [ɪndiˈtsiːrən] ptp **indiziert** VT *(Med)* to indicate; *(Eccl)* to put on the Index; *(Comput)* to index

In|do|chi|na [ˈɪndoˈçiːna] NT Indochina

In|do|eu|ro|pä|er(in) [ˈɪndoˌɔyroˈpɛːɐ] M(F) Indo-European

in|do|eu|ro|pä|isch [ˈɪndoˌɔyroˈpɛːɪʃ] ADJ Indo-European

in|do|ger|ma|nisch [ˈɪndoɡɛrˈmaːnɪʃ] ADJ Indo-Germanic, Indo-European

In|dok|tri|na|ti|on [ɪndɔktrinaˈtsioːn] F **-, -en** indoctrination

in|dok|tri|nie|ren [ɪndɔktriˈniːrən] ptp **indoktriniert** VT to indoctrinate

In|do|ne|si|en [ɪndoˈneːziən] NT **-s** Indonesia

In|do|ne|si|er [ɪndoˈneːziɐ] M **-s, -, In|do|ne|si|e|rin** [-iərɪn] F **-, -nen** Indonesian

in|do|ne|sisch [ɪndoˈneːzɪʃ] ADJ Indonesian

In|dos|sa|ment [ɪndɔsaˈmɛnt] NT **-(e)s, -e** *(Comm)* endorsement

In|dos|sant [ɪndɔˈsant] M **-en, -en, In|dos|san|tin** [-ˈsantɪn] F **-, -nen** *(Comm)* endorser

In|dos|sat [ɪndɔˈsaːt] M **-en, -en, In|dos|sa|tin** [-ˈsaːtɪn] F **-, -nen** *(Comm)* endorsee

in|dos|sie|ren [ɪndɔˈsiːrən] ptp **indossiert** VT *(Comm)* to endorse

In|duk|ti|on [ɪndʊkˈtsioːn] F **-, -en** induction

In|duk|ti|ons-: **in|duk|ti|ons|ge|här|tet** [-ɡəhɛrtət] ADJ induction-hardened; **In|duk|ti|ons|schlei|fe** F induction loop; **In|duk|ti|ons|strom** M induced current

in|duk|tiv [ɪndʊkˈtiːf, ˈ--] ADJ inductive

in|dust|ri|a|li|sie|ren [ɪndʊstrialiˈziːrən] ptp **industrialisiert** VT to industrialize

in|dust|ri|a|li|siert [ɪndʊstrialiˈziːɐt] ptp von **industrialisieren** ADJ industrialized

In|dust|ri|a|li|sie|rung F **-, -en** industrialization

In|dust|rie [ɪndʊsˈtriː] F **-, -n** [-ˈtriːən] industry; **in der ~ arbeiten** to be *or* work in industry

In|dust|rie- *in cpds* industrial; **In|dust|rie|ab|fäl|le** PL industrial waste; **In|dust|rie|ab|wäs|ser** PL industrial sewage *sing or* wastewater *sing*, industrial effluents *pl*; **In|dust|rie|an|la|ge** F industrial plant *or* works *pl*; **In|dust|rie|be|trieb** M industrial firm *or* company; **In|dust|rie|bra|che** F industrial wasteland, brownfield site; **In|dust|rie|er|zeug|nis** NT industrial product; **In|dust|rie|ge|biet** NT , **In|dust|rie|ge|län|de** NT industrial area; *(= Gewerbegebiet)* industrial estate; **In|dust|rie|ge|werk|schaft** F industrial (trade) union; **~ Druck und Papier** printers' union; **In|dust|rie|ka|pi|tän(in)** M(F) *(inf)* captain of industry; **In|dust|rie|kauf|mann** M , **In|dust|rie|kauf|frau** F industrial clerk; **In|dust|rie|kom|bi|nat** NT *(DDR)* industrial combine; **In|dust|rie|land** NT industrialized country; **In|dust|rie|land|schaft** F industrial landscape

in|dust|ri|ell [ɪndʊstriˈɛl] ADJ industrial ADV industrially; **Japan hat nach dem zweiten Weltkrieg ~ enorm expandiert** Japan experienced a period of enormous industrial expansion *or* development after World War II

In|dust|ri|el|le(r) [ɪndʊstriˈɛlə] MF *decl as adj* industrialist

In|dust|rie-: **In|dust|rie|müll** M industrial waste; **In|dust|rie|na|ti|on** F industrial nation; **In|dust|rie|park** M industrial estate *(Brit) or* park *(US)*; **In|dust|rie|ro|bo|ter** M industrial robot; **In|dust|rie|spi|o|na|ge** F industrial espionage; **In|dust|rie|staat** M industrial nation; **In|dust|rie|stand|ort** M site of major industries, (heavily) industrialized area; **In|dust|rie|stadt** F industrial town; **In|dust|rie- und Han|dels|kam|mer** F chamber of commerce; **In|dust|rie|zweig** M branch of industry

in|du|zie|ren [ɪnduˈtsiːrən] ptp **induziert** VT *(Phys)* to induce

in|ef|fek|tiv [ɪnˈɛfɛkˈtiːf, ˈɪn-] ADJ ineffective, ineffectual; *(= unproduktiv auch)* inefficient ADV ineffectively; *(= unproduktiv auch)* inefficiently

In|ef|fek|ti|vi|tät [ɪnˈɛfɛktiviˈtɛːt, ˈɪn-] F ineffectiveness, ineffectualness; *(= Unproduktivität auch)* inefficiency

in|ei|nan|der [ɪnˌaiˈnandɐ] ADV *sein, liegen etc* in(side) one another *or* each other; *legen, hängen etc* into one another *or* each other; **~ übergehen** to merge (into one another *or* each other); **die Fäden haben sich alle ~ verwickelt** the threads have got all tangled up in each other *or* in one another; **sich ~ verlieben** to fall in love with each other

in|ei|nan|der: **in|ei|nan|der flie|ßen** ▲ VI *irreg aux sein* to merge; *(Farben, Flüsse auch)* to flow into each other *or* one another; **in|ei|nan|der fü|gen** ▲ VT to fit into each other *or* one another; **in|ei|nan|der grei|fen** ▲ VI *irreg (lit)* to interlock; *(Zahnräder, Zinken auch)* to mesh *or* engage (with each other *or* one another); *(fig: Ereignisse, Ressorts etc)* to overlap; **in|ei|nan|der pas|sen** ▲ VI to fit into each other *or* one another, to fit together; **in|ei|nan|der schie|ben** ▲ VTR *irreg* to telescope; **sich ~ lassen** to be telescopic

in|fam [ɪnˈfaːm] ADJ infamous

In|fa|mie [ɪnfaˈmiː] F **-, -n** [-ˈmiːən] *(geh)* infamy; **das ist eine ~** that's infamous *or* outrageous

In|fan|te|rie [ɪnfantəˈriː, ˈɪn-] F **-, -n** [-ˈriːən] infantry

In|fan|te|rie|re|gi|ment NT infantry *or* foot regiment

In|fan|te|rist [ɪnfantəˈrɪst, ˈɪn-] M **-en, -en, In|fan|te|ris|tin** [-ˈrɪstɪn] F **-, -nen** infantryman/-woman, foot soldier

in|fan|til [ɪnfanˈtiːl] ADJ infantile

In|fan|ti|lis|mus [ɪnfantiˈlɪsmʊs] M **-, Infantilismen** infantilism

In|fan|ti|li|tät [ɪnfantiliˈtɛːt] F **-, no pl** childishness, puerility *(pej)*

In|farkt [ɪnˈfarkt] M **-(e)s, -e** *(Med)* infarct *(spec)*; *(= Herzinfarkt)* coronary (thrombosis)

in|farkt|ge|fähr|det ADJ *Patient* coronary-risk *attr*

In|fekt [ɪnˈfɛkt] M **-(e)s, -e, In|fek|ti|on** [ɪnfɛkˈtsioːn] F **-, -en** infection

In|fek|ti|ons-: **In|fek|ti|ons|ge|fahr** F danger of infection; **In|fek|ti|ons|herd** M focus of infection; **In|fek|ti|ons|ket|te** F chain of infection; **In|fek|ti|ons|krank|heit** F infectious disease; **In|fek|ti|ons|ri|si|ko** NT risk of infection, infection risk

in|fek|ti|ös [ɪnfɛkˈtsiøːs] ADJ infectious

in|fer|na|lisch [ɪnfɛrˈnaːlɪʃ] ADJ *(geh)* infernal

In|fer|no [ɪnˈfɛrno] NT **-s, no pl** *(lit, fig)* inferno

In|filt|ra|ti|on F infiltration

in|filt|rie|ren [ɪnfɪlˈtriːrən] ptp **infiltriert** VT to infiltrate

in|fi|nit [ɪnfiˈniːt, ˈɪn-] ADJ *(Gram)* non-finite

in|fi|ni|te|si|mal [ɪnfiniteziˈmaːl] ADJ *(Math)* infinitesimal

In|fi|ni|tiv [ˈɪnfinitiːf] M **-s, -e** [-və] infinitive

In|fi|ni|tiv-: **In|fi|ni|tiv|kon|struk|ti|on** F infinitive construction; **In|fi|ni|tiv|satz** M infinitive clause

in|fi|zie|ren [ɪnfiˈtsiːrən] ptp **infiziert** VT to infect VR to be *or* get infected *(bei* by)

in flag|ran|ti [ɪn flaˈɡranti] ADV in the act, red-handed, in flagrante delicto *(form)*

In|fla|ti|on [ɪnflaˈtsioːn] F **-, -en** inflation

in|fla|ti|o|när [ɪnflatsioˈnɛːɐ] ADJ inflationary; *(fig)* over-extensive ADV **sich ~ entwickeln** to develop in an inflationary way

in|fla|ti|o|nis|tisch [ɪnflatsioˈnɪstɪʃ] ADJ inflationary

In|fla|ti|ons-: **In|fla|ti|ons|angst** F fear of inflation; **in|fla|ti|ons|hem|mend** ADJ anti-inflationary ADV **~ wirken** to be anti-inflationary; **In|fla|ti|ons|ra|te** F rate of inflation; **in|fla|ti|ons|si|cher** ADJ inflation-proof ADV **Geld ~ anlegen** to put money into inflation-proof investments

in|fla|to|risch [ɪnflaˈtoːrɪʃ] ADJ inflationary

in|fle|xi|bel [ɪnflɛˈksiːbl, ˈɪn-] ADJ *(lit, fig)* inflexible

In|fle|xi|bi|li|tät [ɪnflɛksibiliˈtɛːt, ˈɪn-] F *(lit, fig)* inflexibility

In|flu|enz [ɪnfluˈɛnts] F **-, -en** *(Phys)* electrostatic induction

In|fo [ˈɪnfo] NT **-, -s** *(inf)* **a** *(= Information)* info *(inf)* **b** *(Sch inf: = Informatik)* computer studies *pl*

in|fol|ge [ɪnˈfɔlɡə] ✪ 44.1 PREP *+gen or von* as a result of, owing to, because of

in|fol|ge|des|sen [ɪnfɔlɡəˈdɛsn] ADV consequently, as a result (of that), because of that

In|for|mant [ɪnfɔrˈmant] M **-en, -en, In|for|man|tin** [-tɪn] F **-, -nen** **a** *(= Informationsquelle)* source (of information); *(in Forschung, für Regierung)* informant **b** *(= Denunziant)* informer

In|for|ma|tik [ɪnfɔrˈmaːtɪk] F **-, no pl** information technology, informatics *sing*; *(= Schulfach)* computer studies *pl*

In|for|ma|ti|ker [ɪnfɔrˈmaːtikɐ] M **-s, -, In|for|ma|ti|ke|rin** [-ərɪn] F **-, -nen** computer *or* information scientist

In|for|ma|ti|on [ɪnfɔrmaˈtsioːn] ✪ 46.1, 46.4, 47.1, 48.3 F **a** information *no pl (über +acc* about, on); **eine ~** (a piece of) information; **-en weitergeben** to pass on information; **zu Ihrer ~** for your information **b** *(= Stelle)* information desk

in|for|ma|ti|o|nell [ɪnfɔrmatsioˈnɛl] ADJ informational; **~e Selbstbestimmung** control over one's personal data

In|for|ma|ti|ons-: **In|for|ma|ti|ons|aus|tausch** M exchange of information; **In|for|ma|ti|ons|bü|ro** NT information bureau; **In|for|ma|ti|ons|de|fi|zit** NT information lag, lack of information; **In|for|ma|ti|ons|fluss** ▲ M flow of information; **In|for|ma|ti|ons|ge|halt** M information content; **In|for|ma|ti|ons|ge|sell|schaft** F information society; **In|for|ma|ti|ons|ge|win|nung** F information gathering; **In|for|ma|ti|ons|lü|cke** F information gap; **In|for|ma|ti|ons|ma|te|ri|al** NT information (material); *(= Prospekte etc)* literature; **In|for|ma|ti|ons|quel|le** F source of information; **In|for|ma|ti|ons|stand** M **a** information stand **b** *no pl (= Wissensstand)* level of information; **In|for|ma|ti|ons|tech|nik** F information technology; **In|for|ma|ti|ons|the|o|rie** F information theory; **In|for|ma|ti|ons|trä|ger** M *(Comput)* (data) storage medium; **In|for|ma|ti|ons|ver|ar|bei|tung** F information processing; **In|for|ma|ti|ons|vor|sprung** M **einen ~ haben** to be better informed; **In|for|ma|ti|ons|wis|sen|schaft** F information science; **In|for|ma|ti|ons|zent|rum** NT information centre *(Brit) or* center *(US)*

in|for|ma|tiv [ɪnfɔrmaˈtiːf] ADJ informative ADV informatively; **~ beschreiben** to describe informatively *or* in great detail; **~ berichten** to give an informative report

in|for|ma|to|risch [ɪnfɔrmaˈtoːrɪʃ] ADJ informational

in|for|mell [ɪnfɔr'mɛl, 'ɪn-] **ADJ** informal **ADV** informally; **die EU-Minister trafen sich ~** EU ministers met informally

in|for|mie|ren [ɪnfɔr'miːrən] *ptp* **informiert VT** to inform (*über +acc, von* about, of); **da bist du falsch** or **nicht richtig informiert** you've been misinformed, you've been wrongly informed; **jdn nur unvollständig/einseitig ~** to give sb only part of/one side of the information; **informierte Kreise** informed circles **VR** to find out, to inform oneself (*über +acc* about); **sich ständig über den neuesten Stand der Medizin ~** to keep oneself informed about the latest developments in medicine

In|for|miert|heit F -, *no pl* knowledge; **wegen der zunehmenden ~ der Jugendlichen** since young people are becoming increasingly well-informed; **die mangelnde ~ der Bevölkerung** the population's lack of information

Info|stand ['ɪnfo-] M (*inf*) information stand

In|fo|tain|ment [ɪnfo'teːnmənt] NT -s, *no pl* infotainment

Info-Tele|fon ['ɪnfo-] NT , **In|fo|te|le|fon** NT information line

in|fra|ge [ɪn'fraːgə], **in Fra|ge** ADV **~ kommen** to be possible; **~ kommend** possible; *Bewerber* worth considering; **sollte er für diese Stelle ~ kommen, ...** if he should be considered for this position ...; **für jdn/etw nicht ~ kommen** to be out of the question for sb/sth; **das kommt (überhaupt) nicht ~!** that's (quite) out of the question!; **etw ~ stellen** to question sth, to query sth, to call sth into question

Infra- ['ɪnfra-] **infra|rot** ADJ infrared; **Infra|rot|strah|ler** M infrared lamp; **Infra|rot|strah|lung** F infrared radiation; **Infra|schall** M infrasonic or subsonic waves *pl*; **Infra|struk|tur** F infrastructure

In|fu|si|on [ɪnfu'ziːoːn] F infusion

In|fu|si|ons|schlauch M drip tube, IV or intravenous tube

Ing. *abbr von* **Ingenieur**

In|ge|ni|eur [ɪnʒe'niøːɐ] M -s -e, **In|ge|ni|eu|rin** [-'niøːrɪn] F -, -nen engineer

In|ge|ni|eur- [ɪnʒe'niøːɐ-]: **In|ge|ni|eur|bü|ro** NT engineer's office; **In|ge|ni|eur|schu|le** F school of engineering

In|gre|di|enz [ɪngre'diɛnts] F -, -en (= *Zutat, Bestandteil*) **a** (*Cook*) ingredient **b** (*Pharm etc*) constituent (part), component

In|grimm M (*liter*) wrath, ire (*liter*)

in|grim|mig ADJ (*liter*) wrathful (*liter*), ireful (*liter*)

Ing|wer ['ɪŋvɐ] M -s, - ginger

Inh. **a** *abbr von* **Inhaber** prop. **b** *abbr von* **Inhalt**

In|ha|ber ['ɪnhaːbɐ] M -s, -, **In|ha|be|rin** [-ərɪn] F -, -nen (*von Geschäft, Firma*) owner; (*von Hotel, Restaurant auch*) proprietor/proprietress; (*von Konto, Aktie, Lizenz, Patent, Rekord, Orden*) holder; (*von Scheck, Pass*) bearer

In|ha|ber|pa|pier NT (*Fin*) bearer security

In|ha|ber|schuld|ver|schrei|bung F (*Fin*) bearer bond

in|haf|tie|ren [ɪnhaf'tiːrən] *ptp* **inhaftiert VT** *insep* to take into custody

In|haf|tie|rung F -, -en (= *das Inhaftieren*) arrest; (= *Haft*) imprisonment

In|ha|la|ti|on [ɪnhala'tsioːn] F -, -en (*Med*) inhalation

in|ha|lie|ren [ɪnha'liːrən] *ptp* **inhaliert VTI** *insep* (*Med, inf*) to inhale

In|halt M **a** (*von Behälter, Paket*) contents *pl* **b** (*von Buch, Brief, Begriff*) content, contents *pl*; (*des Lebens*) meaning; **welchen ~ hatte der Film/das Gespräch?, was hatte der Film/das Gespräch zum ~?** what was the subject matter or content of the film/discussion?; **über ~ e diskutieren** to discuss the real issues; **im Brief des ~ s, dass ...** (*form*) a letter to the effect that ... **c** (*Math*) (= *Flächeninhalt*) area; (= *Rauminhalt*) volume; **der ~**

der Flasche beträgt zwei Liter the bottle has a volume of two litres (*Brit*) or liters (*US*), the bottle holds two litres (*Brit*) or liters (*US*)

in|halt|lich ['ɪnhaltlɪç] ADJ, ADV as regards content

Inhalts-: In|halts|an|ga|be F summary, précis (*esp Sch*); **in|halts|arm, in|halts|leer** ADJ (*geh*) lacking (in) content; *Leben* meaningless; **in|halts|be|zo|gen** ADJ (*Ling*) content-oriented; **in|halts|gleich** ADJ **a** (*Math*) equal **b** *Buch etc* **... ist ~ mit ...** ... has the same content(s) as ..., ... is identical in content to ...; **in|halts|los** ADJ empty; (*geh*) *Leben auch* meaningless; *Buch, Vortrag* lacking in content; **in|halts|reich** ADJ *Leben, Tag* full; *Ausstellung, Text* substantial; *Beziehung* meaningful; **in|halts|schwer** ADJ (*geh*: = *bedeutungsvoll*) significant, of consequence; **In|halts|stoff** M constituent, ingredient; **In|halts|über|sicht** F summary of the contents; **In|halts|ver|zeich|nis** NT list or table of contents; (*Comput*) directory; „**Inhaltsverzeichnis**" "contents"

in|hä|rent [ɪnhɛ'rɛnt] ADJ (*geh*) inherent

in|hu|man [ɪnhu'maːn, 'ɪn-] **ADJ** (= *unmenschlich, brutal*) inhumane; (= *unbarmherzig*) inhumane **ADV** inhumanly

In|hu|ma|ni|tät [ɪnhumani'tɛːt, 'ɪn-] F inhumanity

I|ni|ti|a|le [ini'tsiaːlə] F -, -n (*geh*) initial

i|ni|ti|a|li|sie|ren [initsiali'ziːrən] *ptp* **initialisiert VT** (*Comput*) to initialize

I|ni|ti|a|li|sie|rung F -, -en (*Comput*) initialization

I|ni|ti|a|ti|on [initsia'tsioːn] F -, -en initiation

I|ni|ti|a|ti|ons|ri|tus M initiation rite

i|ni|ti|a|tiv [initsia'tiːf] ADJ **~ werden** to take the initiative

I|ni|ti|a|ti|ve [initsia'tiːvə] F -, -n **a** initiative; **aus eigener ~** on one's own initiative; **die ~ ergreifen** to take the initiative; **auf jds ~** (*acc*) **hin** on sb's initiative **b** (*Sw Pol*) petition for a referendum

I|ni|ti|a|tor [ini'tsiaːtoːɐ] M -s, **Initiatoren**, **I|ni|ti|a|to|rin** [-'toːrɪn] F -, -nen (*geh*) initiator

i|ni|ti|ie|ren [initsi'iːrən] *ptp* **initiiert VT** (*geh*) initiate

In|jek|ti|on [ɪnjɛk'tsioːn] F -, -en injection

In|jek|ti|ons|sprit|ze F hypodermic (syringe)

in|ji|zie|ren [ɪnji'tsiːrən] *ptp* **injiziert VT** (*form*) to inject (*jdm etw* sb with sth)

In|ka ['ɪŋka] M -(s), -s Inca

In|kar|na|ti|on [ɪnkarna'tsioːn] F -, -en incarnation

In|kas|so [ɪn'kaso] NT -s, -s or (*Aus*) **Inkassi** [-si] (*Fin*) collection

In|kas|so-: In|kas|so|bü|ro NT , **In|kas|so|fir|ma** F (*Fin*) collection agency; **In|kas|so|stel|le** F (*Fin*) collection point

In|kauf|nah|me [ɪn'kaufnaːmə] F -, *no pl* (*form*) acceptance; **unter ~ finanzieller Verluste** accepting the inevitable financial losses

inkl. *abbr von* **inklusive**

in|klu|si|ve [ɪnklu'ziːvə] **PREP** *+gen* inclusive of, including; **~ Heizung** heating included, inclusive of or including heating **ADV** inclusive

in|kog|ni|to [ɪn'kɔgnito] ADV incognito

In|kog|ni|to [ɪn'kɔgnito] NT -s, -s incognito

in|kom|pa|ti|bel [ɪnkɔmpa'tiːbl, 'ɪn-] ADJ incompatible

In|kom|pa|ti|bi|li|tät F incompatibility

in|kom|pe|tent [ɪnkɔmpe'tɛnt, 'ɪn-] ADJ incompetent

In|kom|pe|tenz [ɪnkɔmpe'tɛnts, 'ɪn-] F incompetence

in|kon|gru|ent [ɪnkɔŋgru'ɛnt, 'ɪn-] ADJ (*Math*) non-congruent

In|kon|gru|enz [ɪnkɔŋgru'ɛnts, 'ɪn-] F (*Math*) non-congruence

in|kon|se|quent [ɪnkɔnze'kvɛnt, 'ɪn-] **ADJ** inconsistent **ADV** inconsistently

In|kon|se|quenz [ɪnkɔnze'kvɛnts, 'ɪn-] F inconsistency

in|kons|tant [ɪnkɔn'stant, 'ɪn-] ADJ inconstant

In|kons|tanz [ɪnkɔn'stants, 'ɪn-] F inconstancy

in|kon|ti|nent ['ɪnkɔntinɛnt] ADJ (*Med*) incontinent

In|kon|ti|nenz ['ɪnkɔntinɛnts] F -, -en (*Med*) incontinence

In|kor|po|ra|ti|on F (*geh*) incorporation

in|kor|po|rie|ren [ɪnkɔrpo'riːrən] *ptp* **inkorporiert VT** (*geh*) to incorporate (*in +acc* in, into)

in|kor|rekt [ɪnkɔ'rɛkt, 'ɪn-] **ADJ** incorrect **ADV** incorrectly; *gekleidet* inappropriately

In|kor|rekt|heit F **a** *no pl* (*des Benehmens*) incorrectness, impropriety; (*der Arbeit etc*) incorrectness, inaccuracy **b** (= *Formfehler*) impropriety, breach of propriety; (= *Ungenauigkeit*) inaccuracy

In-Kraft-Tre|ten ▲ [ɪn'krafttreːtn] NT -s, *no pl* coming into effect or force; **das ~ von etw verhindern** to prevent sth from coming into effect or force; **bei ~ von etw** when sth comes/came *etc* into effect or force

in|kri|mi|nie|ren [ɪnkrimi'niːrən] *ptp* **inkriminiert VT** to incriminate

In|ku|ba|ti|on [ɪnkuba'tsioːn] F -, -en incubation

In|ku|ba|ti|ons|zeit F incubation period

In|ku|ba|tor [ɪnku'baːtoːɐ] M -s, **Inkubatoren** incubator

In|ku|bus ['ɪnkubus] M -, **Inkuben** [-bn] incubus

In|ku|lanz [ɪnku'lants, 'ɪn-] F disobligingness

In|ku|na|bel [ɪnku'naːbl] F -, -n incunabulum

In|land NT , *no pl* **a** (*als Staatsgebiet*) home; **im ~ hergestellte Waren** home-produced goods, goods produced at home; **im In- und Ausland** at home and abroad; **die Gebühren für einen Brief im ~** inland or domestic letter rates **b** (= *Inneres eines Landes*) inland; **im ~** inland; **ins ~ ziehen** to move inland

In|land- *in cpds* (*Comm*) home, domestic; (*Geog*) inland; **In|land|be|darf** M home or domestic requirements *pl*; **In|land|eis** NT ice sheet; **In|land|flug** M domestic or internal flight

in|län|disch ['ɪnlɛndɪʃ] ADJ domestic; (*Geog*) inland

Inlands-: In|lands|ge|schäft NT (*Comm*) domestic trade; **In|lands|ge|spräch** NT (*Telec*) inland call; **In|lands|markt** M home or domestic market; **In|lands|por|to** NT inland postage; **In|lands|ver|kehr** M domestic traffic; (= *Handel*) home trade; **Briefe im ~** letters within the country, inland or domestic letters; **er ist Fernfahrer, aber nur im ~** he's a long-distance driver, but only on inland or domestic routes

In|laut M **im ~ vorkommen** to occur (word) medially, to occur in (word) medial position

In|lett ['ɪnlɛt] NT -(e)s, -e (= *Hülle*) cambric case; (= *Inlettstoff*) cambric

in|lie|gend ADJ, ADV (*form, Aus*) enclosed

In|li|ner ['ɪnlaɪnɐ] M -s, - (= *Rollschuh*) in-line skate, Rollerblade®

in|line|ska|ten ['ɪnlaɪnskeːtn] VI *only infinitive* to go or to be in-line skating or roller-blading, to blade (*inf*)

In|line-Ska|ter¹ ['ɪnlaɪnskeːtɐ] M -s, -, **In|line|ska|ter¹** M -s, - (= *Rollschuh*) in-line skate, Rollerblade®

In|line-Ska|ter² ['ɪnlaɪnskeːtɐ] M -s, -, **In|line|ska|ter²** M -s, -, **In|line-Ska|te|rin** ['ɪnlaɪnskeːtərɪn] F -, -nen, **In|line|ska|te|rin** F -, -nen rollerblader

In|line-Skates ['ɪnlaɪnskeːts] *pl*, **In|line|skates** *pl* in-line skates, Rollerblades® *pl*

in|mit|ten [ɪn'mɪtn] **PREP** *+gen* in the middle or midst of **ADV ~ von** amongst, surrounded by

in|ne+ha|ben ['ɪnəhaːbn] VT *sep irreg* (*form*) to hold

in|ne+hal|ten ['ɪnəhaltn] *sep irreg* **VI** to pause, to stop; **er hielt im Satz inne** he paused in mid-sentence; **er hielt im Sprechen inne** he stopped speaking in mid-flow; **mit der Rede ~** to pause, to stop speaking; **mit der Rede ~, um Luft zu holen** to pause for breath **VT** (*old*) = **einhalten**

in|nen ['ɪnən] ADV **a** inside; (= *auf der Innenseite*) on the inside; (*in Haus*) indoors, inside; **~ und außen** inside and out(side); **der Mantel hat ~ Pelz und außen Leder** the coat has fur (on the) inside and leather (on the) outside; **nach ~ inwards**; **tief ~ tut es doch weh** deep down inside it really hurts; **die Tür geht nach ~ auf** the door opens inwards; **die Truppen drangen nach ~ vor** the troops pushed inland; **die Haare nach ~ tragen** to have one's hair curled under; **nach ~ laufen** to be pigeon-toed; **von ~** from (the) inside; **wie sieht das Haus von ~ aus?** what does the house look like inside?, what does the inside of the house look like?; **sich von ~ her aufwärmen** to warm oneself from (the) inside, to get warm inside
b (*esp Aus*) = **drinnen**

In|nen-: In|nen|an|ten|ne F indoor aerial (*Brit*) or antenna (*US*); **In|nen|ar|bei|ten** PL work on the interior; **In|nen|ar|chi|tekt(in)** M(F) interior designer; **In|nen|ar|chi|tek|tur** F interior design; **In|nen|auf|nah|me** F indoor photo(graph); (*Film*) indoor shot or take; **In|nen|aus|stat|tung** F interior décor *no pl*; (= *das Ausstatten*) interior decoration and furnishing; (*von Auto*) interior fittings *pl* (*Brit*) or fixtures *pl*; **In|nen|bahn** F (*Sport*) inside lane; **In|nen|be|leuch|tung** F interior lighting; **In|nen|de|ko|ra|ti|on** F interior decoration; **In|nen|dienst** M office duty; **im ~ sein** to work in the office; **~ machen** or **haben** to work in the office, to be on office duty; **in|nen|drin** ['ɪnən'drɪn] ADV (*inf*) inside; **In|nen|ein|rich|tung** F (interior) furnishings *pl*; (= *das Einrichten*) interior furnishing *no pl*; **In|nen|flä|che** F **a** (= *innere Fläche*) inside, inside or interior surface; (*der Hand*) palm **b** (= *Flächeninhalt*) internal surface area; **In|nen|hof** M inner courtyard; (*bei Universitäten, Klöstern*) quadrangle, quad (*inf*); **In|nen|kur|ve** F inside bend; **In|nen|le|ben** NT , *no pl* (*inf: seelisch*) inner or emotional life; **sein ~ offenbaren** to reveal one's innermost thoughts or feelings **b** (*inf: körperlich*) insides *pl*; **In|nen|leuch|te** F (*Aut*) courtesy or interior light; **In|nen|mi|nis|ter(in)** M(F) minister of the interior; (*in GB*) Home Secretary; (*in den USA*) Secretary of the Interior; **In|nen|mi|nis|te|ri|um** NT ministry of the interior; (*in GB*) Home Office; (*in den USA*) Department of the Interior; **In|nen|po|li|tik** F domestic policy; (= *innere Angelegenheiten*) home or domestic affairs *pl*; **In|nen|po|li|ti|ker(in)** M(F) domestic politician; **in|nen|po|li|tisch** ADJ domestic, internal; *Sprecher* on domestic policy; **auf ~em Gebiet** in the field of home affairs; **aus ~er Sicht** (seen) from the point of view of domestic policy ADV **~ gesehen** from the point of view of domestic policy; **~ bewandert sein** to be well-versed in or familiar with domestic policy; **~ unverantwortlich/bedenklich** irresponsible/questionable as far as domestic policy is concerned; **~ hat die Regierung versagt** the government has failed with its domestic policy; **In|nen|raum** M **a** Innenräume inner rooms *pl*; **die prächtigen Innenräume des alten Schlosses** the magnificent interior or rooms of the old castle **b** *no pl* room inside; (*von Wagen*) interior; **einen kleinen ~ haben** to be small inside, not to have much room inside; (*Wagen auch*) to have a small interior; **mit großem** with a lot of room inside; (*Wagen auch*) with a large interior; **In|nen|rol|le** F , *no pl* **eine ~ tragen** to have one's hair turned or curled under at the ends; **In|nen|sei|te** F inside; **die ~ von etw nach außen kehren** to turn sth inside out; **In|nen|spie|gel** M (*Aut*) interior mirror;

In|nen|stadt F town centre (*Brit*) or center (*US*), centre (*Brit*) or center (*US*) of the town; (*einer Großstadt*) city centre (*Brit*) or center (*US*), centre (*Brit*) or center (*US*) of the city; **In|nen|ta|sche** F inside pocket; **In|nen|tem|pe|ra|tur** F inside temperature; (*in einem Gebäude*) indoor temperature; **wir haben 20° ~** the temperature indoors is 20°; **bei 20° ~** when the temperature indoors or the indoor temperature is 20°, when it's 20° indoors; **In|nen|toi|let|te** F inside toilet; **In|nen|welt** F , *no pl* inner world; **er hat sich völlig in seine ~ zurückgezogen** he has withdrawn completely into his own private world; **In|nen|win|kel** M (*Math*) interior angle

in|ner-: in|ner|be|trieb|lich ADJ in-house ADV in-house, within the company or corporation; **das wird ~ geregelt werden** that will be settled in-house; **in|ner|deutsch** ADJ **der ~e Handel** the domestic German trade; **die ~e Grenze** (*Hist*) the inner-German border; **Ministerium für ~e Beziehungen** (*Hist*) Ministry (*Brit*) or Department of Intra-German Relations; **in|ner|dienst|lich** ADJ internal, in-house

In|ne|rei|en [ɪnəˈraɪən] PL innards *pl*; (*von Geflügel auch*) giblets *pl*

In|ne|re(r, s) ['ɪnərə] ADJ **a** (*örtlich*) inner; (= *im Körper befindlich, inländisch*) internal; **Facharzt für ~ Krankheiten** internist; **das ~ Ohr** the inner ear; **die ~n Angelegenheiten eines Landes** the internal or home or domestic affairs of a country; **der Whisky sorgte für die ~ Wärme** (*hum*) the whisky warmed our/their *etc* insides (*inf*); **Innere Mission** Home Mission; (= *Diakonisches Werk*) church social welfare programme (*Brit*) or program (*US*); **~r Monolog** (*Liter*) interior monologue; **im innersten Herzen** deep in one's heart, in one's heart of hearts; **eine ~ Uhr** (*inf*) an internal or a biological clock; **~ Emigration** inner emigration, *withdrawal into private life of artists and intellectuals who remained in Germany through the Nazi period but did not support the Third Reich; any similar withdrawal*
b (= *geistig, seelisch*) inner; **~ Werte** *pl* inner worth *no pl*; **eine ~ Stimme** an inner voice, a voice within; **vor meinem ~n Auge** in my mind's eye; **~ Führung** (*Mil*) moral leadership

In|ne|re(s) ['ɪnərə] NT *decl as adj* **a** inside; (*von Kirche, Wagen, Schloss*) interior, inside; (= *Mitte*) middle, centre (*Brit*), center (*US*); **Minister des Inner(e)n** minister of the interior; (*in GB*) Home Secretary; (*in den USA*) Secretary of the Interior; **das ~ nach außen kehren** to turn something inside out; **ins ~ des Landes** into the heart of the country **b** (*fig: Gemüt, Geist*) heart; **ich wusste, was in seinem ~ vorging** I knew what was going on inside him; **sein ~s rebellierte dagegen** his inner self rebelled against it; **im tiefsten ~n** (deep) in one's heart, in one's heart of hearts

in|ner|halb ['ɪnəhalp] PREP *+gen* **a** (*örtlich*) inside, within; **~ dieser Regelung** within this ruling **b** (*zeitlich*) within; **~ (von) zehn Minuten** within ten minutes, in ten minutes, inside (of) ten minutes ADV inside; (*eines Landes*) inland; **weiter ~** further in; **weiter ~ im Lande** further inland

in|ner|lich ['ɪnɛlɪç] ADJ **a** (= *körperlich*) internal **b** (*geistig, seelisch*) inward, inner *no adv*; (*Gedicht, Mensch*) inward; **Hemmung** inner ADV **a** (= *im Körper*) internally; **dieses Medikament ist ~ anzuwenden** this medicine is to be taken internally **b** (= *gemütsmäßig*) inwardly; **~ gefestigt sein** to have inner strength; **jdm ~ verbunden sein** to have very deep feelings for sb; **ein ~ gefestigter Mensch** a person of inner strength; **~ schäumte er vor Wut** inwardly or inside he was boiling with rage; **~ lachen** to laugh inwardly or to oneself

In|ner|lich|keit F , *no pl* (*liter*) inwardness

in|ner|par|tei|lich ADJ within the party; **~e Schwierigkeiten** internal difficulties in the party, difficulties within the party; **eine ~e Diskussion** a party discussion; **~e Demokratie** democracy (with)in the party structure ADV (with)in the party; **in|ner|staat|lich** ADJ domestic, internal

in|ners|te(r, s) ['ɪnɛstə] ADJ *superl von* innere(r, s) innermost, inmost; (*fig auch*) deepest

In|ners|te(s) ['ɪnɛstə] NT *decl as adj* (*lit*) innermost part, heart; (*fig*) heart; **tief im ~n liebe sie ihn** in her heart of hearts she loved him, deep in her heart she loved him; **bis ins ~ getroffen** hurt to the quick, deeply or profoundly hurt

in|nert ['ɪnɛt] PREP *+gen or dat* (*Aus, Sw*) within, in, inside (of); **~ nützlicher Frist** (= *in der vorgeschriebenen Zeit*) within the allotted time, within the time allowed; (= *in absehbarer Zeit*) in the foreseeable future

in|ne+wer|den ['ɪnə-] VI *sep irreg aux sein* (**sich** *dat*) **einer Sache** (*gen*) **~** to become aware or cognizant (*form*) of sth

in|ne+woh|nen ['ɪnə-] VI *sep +dat* to be inherent in

in|nig ['ɪnɪç] ADJ **a** *Glückwünsche, Grüße* heartfelt *no adv*, hearty; *Beileid* heartfelt, deep, profound; *Vergnügen* deep, profound; *Freundschaft, Kontakte* close, intimate; *Beziehung* intimate; **mein ~ster Wunsch** my dearest wish **b** (*Chem*) *Verbindung* intimate ADV deeply, profoundly; **etw aufs ~ste** or **Innigste erhoffen/wünschen** to hope/wish for sth most fervently or ardently; **jdn ~ lieben** to love sb dearly or deeply, to love sb with all one's heart

In|nig|keit F , *no pl* (*von Glückwünschen, Grüßen*) warmth, sincerity; (*von Empfindung*) depth; (*von Liebe*) intensity; (*von Freundschaft, Kontakten, Beziehung*) closeness; **mit ~ beten/hoffen** to pray/hope fervently

in|nig|lich ['ɪnɪklɪç] ADV (*poet*) (= *herzlich*) sincerely, warmly; (= *tief*) deeply, profoundly; *lieben* deeply, dearly; (= *eng*) intimately, closely

In|no|va|ti|on [ɪnovaˈtsioːn] F -, -en innovation

in|no|va|ti|ons-: in|no|va|ti|ons|feind|lich ADJ hostile to (any form of) innovation, unwilling to adapt (to the times), Luddite; **in|no|va|ti|ons|freu|dig** ADJ innovative

In|nung ['ɪnʊŋ] F -, -en (trade) guild; **du blamierst die ganze ~** (*hum inf*) you're letting the (whole) side down (*inf*)

in|of|fi|zi|ell [ɪnɔfiˈtsiɛl, 'ɪn-] ADJ unofficial ADV unofficially; **jdm etw ~ mitteilen** to tell sb sth unofficially or off the record

In|oku|la|ti|on [ɪnʔokulaˈtsioːn] F -, -en inoculation

in|oku|lie|ren [ɪnʔokuˈliːrən] *ptp* inokuliert VT to inoculate

in|ope|ra|bel [ɪnʔopeˈraːbl, 'ɪn-] ADJ (*Med*) inoperable

in|op|por|tun [ɪnʔɔpɔrˈtuːn, 'ɪn-] ADJ inopportune

in pet|to [ɪn 'pɛto] → **petto**

in punc|to [ɪn 'pʊŋkto] → **punkto**

In|put ['ɪnpʊt] M OR NT -s, -s input

In|qui|si|ti|on [ɪnkviziˈtsioːn] F -, -en Inquisition

In|qui|si|ti|ons-: In|qui|si|ti|ons|ge|richt NT Court of the Inquisition, inquisitional court; **In|qui|si|ti|ons|me|tho|de** F inquisitional method

In|qui|si|tor [ɪnkviˈziːtoːɐ] M -s, Inquisitoren inquisitor

in|qui|si|to|risch [ɪnkviziˈtoːrɪʃ] ADJ inquisitorial ADV inquisitorially

ins [ɪns] *contr von* in das **~ Rollen/Rutschen geraten** or **kommen** to start rolling/sliding

In|sas|se ['ɪnsasə] M -n, -n, **In|sas|sin** ['ɪnsasɪn] F -, -nen (*von Fahrzeug*) passenger; (*von Auto auch*) occupant; (*von Anstalt*) inmate

In|sas|sen|ver|si|che|rung F passenger insurance

ins|be|son|de|re [ɪnsbəˈzɔndərə] ADV particularly, (e)specially, in particular

In|schrift F inscription, legend (form)

In|sekt [ɪnˈzɛkt] NT -(e)s, -e insect; ~en fressend insect-eating, insectivorous (form)

In|sek|ten-: In|sek|ten|be|kämp|fung F insect control; **In|sek|ten|be|kämp|fungs|mit|tel** NT insecticide; **in|sek|ten|fres|send** △ ADJ attr → **Insekt**; **In|sek|ten|fres|ser** M insect eater, insectivore (form); **In|sek|ten|gift** NT insecticide; **In|sek|ten|kun|de** F entomology; **In|sek|ten|pla|ge** F plague of insects; **In|sek|ten|pul|ver** NT insect powder, (powder) insecticide; **In|sek|ten|schutz|mit|tel** NT insect repellent; **In|sek|ten|spray** NT insect spray, bug (US inf) spray; **In|sek|ten|stich** M (von Ameisen, Mücken, Flöhen) insect bite; (von Bienen, Wespen) (insect) sting; **In|sek|ten|ver|til|gungs|mit|tel** NT insecticide

In|sek|ti|zid [ɪnzɛktiˈtsiːt] NT -s, -e [-də] (form) insecticide

In|sel [ˈɪnzl] F -, -n (lit, fig) island, isle (poet); **die Britischen ~n** the British Isles; **die ~ Man** the Isle of Man; **reif für die ~ sein** (inf) to be ready to get away from it all

In|sel|be|woh|ner(in) M(F) islander, inhabitant of an/the island

In|sel|chen [ˈɪnzlçən] NT -s, - little island, islet (poet)

In|sel-: In|sel|grup|pe F archipelago, group of islands; **In|sel|ket|te** F chain or string of islands, island chain; **In|sel|la|ge** F island position; **Großbritannien, infolge seiner ~ ...** Great Britain, because it is an island ...; **In|sel|men|ta|li|tät** F insular mentality; **in|sel|reich** ADJ with a lot of islands; **In|sel|reich** NT island kingdom; **In|sel|staat** M island state; **In|sel|volk** NT island nation or race or people; **In|sel|welt** F island world; **die ~ Mittelamerikas** the world of the Central American islands

In|se|rat [ɪnzeˈraːt] NT -(e)s, -e advert (inf), ad (inf), advertisement

In|se|ra|ten|teil M advertisement section, adverts pl (inf), ads pl (inf)

In|se|rent [ɪnzeˈrɛnt] M -en, -en, **In|se|ren|tin** [-ˈrɛntɪn] F -, -nen advertiser

in|se|rie|ren [ɪnzeˈriːrən] ptp **inseriert** VTI to advertise; **etw in der Zeitung ~** to advertise sth in the paper, to insert or put an advertisement in the paper for sth

ins|ge|heim [ɪnsɡəˈhaɪm, ˈɪns-] ADV secretly, in secret

ins|ge|mein [ɪnsɡəˈmaɪn, ˈɪns-] ADV (old) in general, on the whole, by and large

ins|ge|samt [ɪnsɡəˈzamt, ˈɪns-] ADV (= alles zusammen) altogether, (= im Großen und Ganzen) all in all, on the whole, by and large; **die Kosten belaufen sich auf ~ 1.000 EUR** the costs amount to a total of EUR 1,000; **ein Verdienst von ~ 2.000 EUR** earnings totalling (Brit) or totaling (US) EUR 2,000

In|si|der [ˈɪnsaɪdɐ] M -s, -, **In|si|de|rin** [-ərɪn] F -, -nen insider; **der Witz war nur für ~ verständlich** that was an in-joke (Brit) or inside joke (esp US), that joke was just for the in-crowd; **~ der Jazzszene** those in on the jazz scene, those in the know about the jazz scene

In|si|der-: In|si|der|ge|schäft NT insider deal; **In|si|der|han|del** M insider trading or dealing; **In|si|der|krei|se** PL insider circles pl, (the) inner circle sing (iro); **In|si|der|wis|sen** NT inside knowledge

In|sig|ni|en [ɪnˈzɪɡniən] PL insignia pl

in|sig|ni|fi|kant [ɪnzɪɡnifiˈkant, ˈɪn-] ADJ (geh) insignificant, of no consequence

in|sis|tie|ren [ɪnzɪsˈtiːrən] ptp **insistiert** VI (geh) to insist (auf +dat on)

In|skrip|ti|on [ɪnskrɪpˈtsioːn] F -, -en inscription

ins|künf|tig [ˈɪnskʏnftɪç] ADJ, ADV (Sw) = **zukünftig**

in|so|fern [ɪnzoˈfɛrn, ɪnˈzoːfɛrn, ˈɪn-] ADV in this respect; **~ als** in so far as, inasmuch as, in that; **er hat ~ Recht, als ...** he's right in so far as or inasmuch as or in that ... CONJ [ɪnzoˈfɛrn, ɪnˈzoːfɛrn, ˈɪn-] (= wenn) if

in|sol|vent [ɪnzɔlˈvɛnt, ˈɪn-] ADJ (Comm) insolvent

In|sol|venz [ɪnzɔlˈvɛnts, ˈɪn-] F -, -en (Comm) insolvency

in|so|weit [ɪnˈzoːvait, ɪnzoˈvait, ˈɪn-] ADV, CONJ = **insofern**

Insp. abbr von **Inspektor**

in spe [ɪn ˈspeː] ADJ (inf) to be, future; **unser Schwiegersohn ~** our son-in-law-to-be, our future son-in-law

In|spek|teur [ɪnspɛkˈtøːɐ] M -s, -e, **In|spek|teu|rin** [-ˈtøːrɪn] F -, -nen (Mil) Chief of Staff

In|spek|ti|on [ɪnspɛkˈtsioːn] F -, -en a inspection; (Aut) service; **ich habe mein Auto zur ~ gebracht** I've taken my car in for a service or to be serviced b (= Behörde) inspectorate

In|spek|ti|ons|rei|se F tour of inspection

In|spek|tor [ɪnˈspɛktoːɐ] M -s, **Inspektoren, In|spek|to|rin** [-ˈtoːrɪn] F -, -nen inspector; (= Verwalter, Aufseher) superintendent

In|spi|ra|ti|on [ɪnspiraˈtsioːn] F -, -en inspiration

in|spi|rie|ren [ɪnspiˈriːrən] ptp **inspiriert** VT to inspire; **sich von etw ~ lassen** to get one's inspiration from sth

In|spi|zi|ent [ɪnspiˈtsiɛnt] M -en, -en, **In|spi|zi|en|tin** [-ˈtsiɛntɪn] F -, -nen (Theat) stage manager; (= Aufseher) inspector

in|spi|zie|ren [ɪnspiˈtsiːrən] ptp **inspiziert** VT to inspect

In|spi|zie|rung F -, -en inspection

in|sta|bil [ɪnstaˈbiːl, ˈɪn-] ADJ unstable

In|sta|bi|li|tät F instability

In|stal|la|teur [ɪnstalaˈtøːɐ] M -s, -e, **In|stal|la|teu|rin** [-ˈtøːrɪn] F -, -nen plumber; (= Elektroinstallateur) electrician, electrical fitter; (= Gasinstallateur) gas fitter

In|stal|la|ti|on [ɪnstalaˈtsioːn] F -, -en a (no pl: = das Installieren) installation; (Tech) installation, fitting b (= Anlage) installation; (in Bauten) fittings pl, installations pl; (= Wasserinstallation) plumbing no pl c (old, Sw: = Amtseinsetzung) installation

in|stal|lie|ren [ɪnstaˈliːrən] ptp **installiert** VT to install (auch fig, Comput), to put in VR to install oneself

in|stand [ɪnˈʃtant] ADJ in good condition or repair; (= funktionsfähig) in working order, working; **etw ~ halten** to maintain sth, to keep sth in good condition or repair/in working order; **etw ~ setzen** to get sth into good condition or repair/into working order; (= reparieren auch) to repair sth

In|stand-: In|stand be|set|zen ▲ VT **ein Haus ~** to squat in a house (and do it up); **In|stand|hal|tung** F (von Gerät) maintenance, servicing; (von Gebäude) maintenance, upkeep; **In|stand|hal|tungs|kos|ten** PL maintenance costs pl; (von Gebäude auch) upkeep costs pl

in|stän|dig [ˈɪnʃtɛndɪç] ADJ urgent ADV ~ bitten to beg, to implore, to beseech; **~ hoffen** to hope fervently

In|stand-: In|stand|set|zung F -, -en (von Gerät) overhaul; (von Gebäude) restoration; (= Reparatur) repair; **In|stand|set|zungs|ar|bei|ten** PL repairs pl, repair work

In|stanz [ɪnˈstants] F -, -en a (= Behörde) authority; **er ging von einer ~ zur nächsten** he went from one office or department to the next b (Jur) court; (= Verhandlungsstadium) (court) case; **Verhandlung in erster/letzter ~** first/final court case; **Verhandlung in zweiter ~** second

court case, hearing at the court of second instance (form); **Berufung in erster/zweiter ~** first/second appeal; **ein Urteil letzter ~** (lit, fig) a final judgement; **er ging durch alle ~en** he went through all the courts

In|stan|zen|weg M, **In|stan|zen|zug** M (Aus) official or prescribed channels pl; (Jur) stages pl of appeal; **auf dem ~** through (the official or prescribed) channels/the various stages of appeal

In|stinkt [ɪnˈstɪŋkt] M -(e)s, -e (lit, fig) instinct; **aus ~** instinctively, by instinct

ins|tinkt|haft ADJ instinctive

Ins|tinkt|hand|lung F instinctive act; **das ist eine reine ~** it's purely instinctive (behaviour (Brit) or behavior (US))

ins|tink|tiv [ɪnstɪŋkˈtiːf] ADJ instinctive ADV instinctively

ins|tinkt|los ADJ Art, Bemerkung insensitive

ins|tinkt|mä|ßig ADJ instinctive ADV instinctively, by instinct; (= Instinkte betreffend) as far as instinct is concerned

ins|tinkt|si|cher ADJ ~ sein to have a good or unerring instinct, to have a good nose (inf) ADV ~ handeln to rely on one's instincts; **er hat wieder einmal ~ gehandelt** his instinct proved him right again

In|sti|tut [ɪnstiˈtuːt] NT -(e)s, -e institute; (Jur: = Institution) institution

In|sti|tu|ti|on [ɪnstituˈtsioːn] F -, -en institution

in|sti|tu|ti|o|na|li|sie|ren [ɪnstitutsionaliˈziːrən] ptp **institutionalisiert** VT to institutionalize

in|sti|tu|ti|o|nell [ɪnstitutsioˈnɛl] ADJ institutional

In|sti|tuts|lei|ter(in) M(F) director of an/the institute

in|stru|ie|ren [ɪnstruˈiːrən] ptp **instruiert** VT to instruct; (über Unternehmen, Plan etc) to brief; **Anwalt** to brief

In|struk|teur [ɪnstrʊkˈtøːɐ] M -s, -e, **In|struk|teu|rin** [-ˈtøːrɪn] F -, -nen instructor

In|struk|ti|on [ɪnstrʊkˈtsioːn] F -, -en instruction; **laut ~** according to instructions

in|struk|tiv [ɪnstrʊkˈtiːf] ADJ instructive

In|stru|ment [ɪnstruˈmɛnt] NT -(e)s, -e instrument; (= Hammer etc auch) tool, implement; **er ist ~ des ...** he is the instrument of ...

in|stru|men|tal [ɪnstrumɛnˈtaːl] (Mus) ADJ instrumental ADV ~ begleiten to provide the instrumental accompaniment for sb; **~ musizieren** to play musical instruments

In|stru|men|tal- in cpds instrumental; **In|stru|men|tal|be|glei|tung** F instrumental accompaniment; **ohne ~ singen** to sing unaccompanied

in|stru|men|ta|li|sie|ren [ɪnstrumɛntaliˈziːrən] ptp **instrumentalisiert** VT a (Mus) to arrange for instruments b (fig) instrumentalize; Theorie, Plan etc to harness; (= ausnutzen) to exploit

In|stru|men|ta|li|sie|rung F (Mus) instrumental arrangement; (fig) instrumentalization

In|stru|men|tal-: In|stru|men|tal|satz M (Gram) instrumental clause; (Mus) (= Bearbeitung) instrumental version; (= Teilstück) instrumental section; **In|stru|men|tal|stück** NT instrumental piece

In|stru|men|ta|ri|um [ɪnstrumɛnˈtaːriʊm] NT -s, **Instrumentarien** (lit) equipment, instruments pl; (Mus) instruments pl; (fig) apparatus

in|stru|men|tell [ɪnstrumɛnˈtɛl] ADJ a (= mit Instrumenten) with instruments; Analytik instrumental b (= als Mittel dienend) Vernunft, Intelligenz used as an instrument

In|stru|men|ten-: In|stru|men|ten|brett NT instrument panel; **In|stru|men|ten|flug** M instrument flight; (= das Fliegen auch) instrument flying, flying on instruments; **In|stru|men|ten|ta|fel** F control or instrument panel

in|stru|men|tie|ren [ɪnstrʊmɛnˈtiːrən] *ptp* **instrumentiert** VT *(Mus)* to arrange for instruments; *(für Orchester)* to orchestrate; *(Tech)* to fit out *or* equip with instruments

In|stru|men|tie|rung F -, -en instrumentation

In|suf|fi|zi|enz [ˈɪnzʊfitsiɛnts] F -, -en *(Med, geh)* insufficiency

In|su|la|ner [ɪnzuˈlaːnɐ] M -s, -, **In|su|la|ne|rin** [-ərɪn] F -, -en *(usu hum)* islander

in|su|lar [ɪnzuˈlaːɐ] ADJ insular

In|su|lin [ɪnzuˈliːn] NT -s, *no pl* insulin

Insu|lin- *in cpds* insulin; **In|su|lin|schock** M insulin *or* hypoglycaemic *(Brit spec) or* hypoglycemic *(US spec)* shock; **In|su|lin|sprit|ze** F insulin injection *or* jab *(inf)*, insulin shot *(US)*; **In|su|lin|stoß** M insulin boost

In|sze|na|tor [ɪnstseˈnaːtoːɐ] M -s, Inszenatoren, **In|sze|na|to|rin** [-ˈtoːrɪn] F -, -nen *(Theat)* director; *(fig)* stage manager

in|sze|na|to|risch [ɪnstsenaˈtoːrɪʃ] ADJ directing *attr*, directorial; **Anforderungen** directorial; **eine ~e Glanzleistung** a brilliant piece of directing *or (fig)* stage management

in|sze|nie|ren [ɪnstseˈniːrən] *ptp* **inszeniert** VT **a** *(Theat)* to direct; *(Rad, TV)* to produce **b** *(fig)* to stage-manage; **einen Streit ~** to start an argument; **ein Theater ~** to kick up a fuss *(inf)*

In|sze|nie|rung F -, -en production; **ein Stück in neuer ~ aufführen** to put on a new production of a play

in|takt [ɪnˈtakt] ADJ intact; **ich bin nach meiner Grippe noch nicht ganz ~** *(inf)* I'm still feeling a bit fragile after my flu

In|takt|heit F -, *no pl* intactness

In|tar|sia [ɪnˈtarzia] F -, Intarsien [-ziən], **In|tar|sie** [ɪnˈtarziə] F -, -n *usu pl* marquetry *no pl*, inlay, inlaid work *no pl*

in|te|ger [ɪnˈteːgɐ] *(geh)* ADJ **~ sein** to be full of integrity; **ein integrer Mensch** a person of integrity ADV **sich ~ verhalten** to behave with integrity

in|te|gral [ɪnteˈgraːl] ADJ *attr* integral

In|te|gral [ɪnteˈgraːl] NT -s, -e integral

Integral-: **In|te|gral|helm** M full-face helmet; **In|te|gral|rech|nung** F integral calculus

In|te|gra|ti|on [ɪntegraˈtsioːn] F -, -en integration

Integrations-: **In|te|gra|ti|ons|fi|gur** F unifying figure; **In|te|gra|ti|ons|klas|se** F *(Sch)* integrated class; **In|te|gra|ti|ons|kraft** F unifying force

---

INTEGRATIONSKLASSEN

Integrationsklassen are classes designed to enable physically and mentally disabled children and young people to attend a conventional school instead of a special school. This is regarded as having benefits for both the disabled and able-bodied children.

---

in|te|gra|tiv [ɪntegraˈtiːf] ADJ **Erziehung, Zusammenarbeit etc** integrated; **Weltanschauung etc** holistic

in|te|grier|bar ADJ integrable *(auch Math)*

in|te|grie|ren [ɪnteˈgriːrən] *ptp* **integriert** VT to integrate *(auch Math)*

in|te|griert [ɪnteˈgriːɐt] ADJ integrated *(in into)*; **Sicherheitsvorrichtung auch** integral, in-built; **~e Schaltung** integrated circuit; **~e Gesamtschule** ≈ comprehensive (school) *(Brit)*, ≈ high school *(US)*

In|te|grie|rung F -, -en integration *no pl*

In|te|gri|tät [ɪntegriˈtɛːt] F -, *no pl (geh)* integrity

In|tel|lekt [ɪntɛˈlɛkt] M -(e)s, *no pl* intellect

In|tel|lek|tu|a|lis|mus [ɪntɛlɛktuaˈlɪsmʊs] M -, *no pl* intellectualism

in|tel|lek|tu|ell [ɪntɛlɛkˈtuɛl] ADJ intellectual

In|tel|lek|tu|el|le(r) [ɪntɛlɛkˈtuɛlə] MF *decl as adj* intellectual

---

In|tel|lel|le(r) [ɪntɛˈlɛlə] MF *decl as adj* (*hum inf*) intellectual, egghead *(inf)*

in|tel|li|gent [ɪntɛliˈgɛnt] ADJ intelligent ADV cleverly, ingeniously; **sich verhalten** intelligently; **~ ausgedacht** well thought out

In|tel|li|genz [ɪntɛliˈgɛnts] F -, -en intelligence; *(= Personengruppe)* intelligentsia *pl*; **Elefanten haben eine hoch entwickelte ~** elephants are highly intelligent; **künstliche ~** artificial intelligence

Intelligenz-: **In|tel|li|genz|bes|tie** F *(pej inf)* egghead *(inf)*; **In|tel|li|genz|grad** M intelligence level, level of intelligence

In|tel|li|gen|zi|ja [ɪntɛliˈgɛntsija] F -, *no pl* intelligentsia *pl*

In|tel|li|genz|leis|tung F display of intelligence; **eine ~ von jdm** a display of sb's intelligence; **das war wieder eine ~ von dir!** *(iro)* that was intelligent *or* bright of you *(iro)*

In|tel|li|genz|ler [ɪntɛliˈgɛntslɐ] M -s, -, **In|tel|li|genz|le|rin** [-ərɪn] F -, -nen *(inf)* egghead *(inf)*

Intelligenz-: **In|tel|li|genz|quo|ti|ent** M intelligence quotient, IQ; **In|tel|li|genz|test** M intelligence test; **einen ~ mit jdm machen** to give sb an intelligence test, to test sb's IQ

In|ten|dant [ɪntɛnˈdant] M -en, -en, **In|ten|dan|tin** [-ˈdantɪn] F -, -nen director; *(Theat)* theatre *(Brit) or* theater *(US)* manager

In|ten|dan|tur [ɪntɛndanˈtuːɐ] F -, -en *(= Amtszeit)* period of directorship; *(= Amtssitz)* director's office; *(Theat)* theatre *(Brit) or* theater *(US)* manager's office; **während seiner ~** while he was director/theatre *(Brit) or* theater *(US)* manager, during his directorship

In|ten|danz [ɪntɛnˈdants] F -, -en *(= Amt)* directorship; *(= Büro)* director's office; *(Theat)* theatre *(Brit) or* theater *(US)* manager's office

in|ten|die|ren [ɪntɛnˈdiːrən] *ptp* **intendiert** VT *(geh)* to intend; **eine Beleidigung hatte ich damit nicht intendiert** I didn't intend that as an insult

In|ten|si|tät [ɪntɛnziˈtɛːt] F -, *(rare)* -en intensity

in|ten|siv [ɪntɛnˈziːf] ADJ **Arbeit, Forschung, Diskussion, Kontakte, Landwirtschaft** intensive; **Beziehungen** deep, very close; **Farbe, Gefühl, Geschmack** intense; **Geruch** intense, powerful, strong; **Blick** intent, intense ADV **jdn ~ beobachten** to watch sb intently; *(Polizei)* to put sb under close surveillance; **sich ~ bemühen** to try hard; **~ bestrebt sein** to make an intense effort; **~ duftend** with an intense *or* powerful scent; **~ nach etw schmecken** to taste strongly of sth

in|ten|si|vie|ren [ɪntɛnziˈviːrən] *ptp* **intensiviert** VT to intensify

In|ten|si|vie|rung F -, -en intensification

Intensiv-: **In|ten|siv|kurs** M intensive course; **In|ten|siv|me|di|zin** F intensive care (medicine); **In|ten|siv|sta|ti|on** F intensive care unit

In|ten|ti|on [ɪntɛnˈtsioːn] F -, -en intention, intent

in|ten|ti|o|nal [ɪntɛntsioˈnaːl] ADJ *(auch Philos)* intentional

in|ter- [ɪntɐ], **In|ter-** *in cpds* inter-; **In|ter|ak|ti|on** F interaction; **in|ter|agie|ren** *ptp* **interagiert** VI to interact; **in|ter|ak|tiv** ADJ interactive ADV interactively; **~ gestaltet** designed for interactive use

In|ter|ci|ty [ɪntɐˈsɪti] M -(s), -s intercity (train)

Intercity-: **In|ter|ci|ty|ex|press** ▲ M high-speed intercity (train); **In|ter|ci|ty|ver|kehr** M *(Rail)* intercity traffic, express traffic; **In|ter|ci|ty|zug** M intercity (train)

Inter-: **in|ter|de|pen|dent** [ɪntɐdepənˈdɛnt] ADJ interdependent; **In|ter|de|pen|denz** F interdependence; **in|ter|dis|zi|pli|när** [ɪntɐdɪstsipliˈnɛːɐ] ADJ interdisciplinary ADV **diese Probleme müssen ~ gelöst werden** interdisciplinary solutions are required here; **~ ausgerichtet/angelegt/zusammengesetzt** interdisciplinary

---

in|te|res|sant [ɪntərɛˈsant] ADJ interesting; **zu diesem Preis ist das nicht ~ für uns** *(Comm)* we are not interested at that price; **das ist ja ~!** (that's) very interesting!; **sich ~ machen** to attract attention (to oneself); **sich bei jdm ~ machen** to attract sb's attention ADV **sich ~ anhören, ~ klingen** to sound interesting; **sich ~ lesen** to be interesting; **diese Autorin schreibt sehr ~** this author's writing is very interesting; **~ erzählen** to tell interesting stories; **~ erzählen können** to be a good storyteller

in|te|res|san|ter|wei|se [ɪntərɛˈsantɐvaizə] ADV interestingly enough

In|te|res|se [ɪntəˈrɛsə] ⊘ 28.1, 29.2, 47.1 NT -s, -n interest; **~ an jdm/etw** *or* **für jdn/etw haben** to be interested in sb/sth; **aus ~** out of interest, for interest; **mit (großem) ~** with (great) interest; **im ~ +gen** in the interests of; **es liegt in Ihrem eigenen ~** it's in your own interest(s); **die ~n eines Staates wahrnehmen** to look after the interests of a state; **sein ~ gilt ...** his interest is *or* lies in ..., he's interested in ...; **das ist für uns nicht von ~** that's of no interest to us, we're not interested in that; **er tat es** *or* **handelte in meinem ~** he did it for my good *or* in my interest

Interesse-: **in|te|res|se|hal|ber** ADV for *or* out of interest; **in|te|res|se|los** ADJ indifferent; **In|te|res|se|lo|sig|keit** F -, *no pl* indifference

Interessen-: **In|te|res|sen|be|reich** M , **In|te|res|sen|ge|biet** NT field of interest; **das gehört nicht zu meinem ~** that isn't one of my interests, that's outside my field of interests; **In|te|res|sen|gen|satz** M clash of interests; **In|te|res|sen|ge|mein|schaft** F **a** community of interests; *(= Menschen)* group of people sharing interests **b** *(Econ)* syndicate; **In|te|res|sen|grup|pe** F interest group; *(= Lobby)* lobby; **In|te|res|sen|kol|li|si|on** F conflict of interests; **In|te|res|sen|schwer|punkt** M focus of interest; **In|te|res|sen|sphä|re** F *(Pol)* sphere of influence

In|te|res|sent [ɪntərɛˈsɛnt] M -en, -en, **In|te|res|sen|tin** [-ˈsɛntɪn] F -, -nen interested person *or* party *(form)*; *(= Bewerber auch)* applicant; *(Comm: = Kauflustiger auch)* prospective customer; **~en werden gebeten ...** those interested are requested ...; **es haben sich mehrere ~en gemeldet** several people have shown interest

In|te|res|sen|ten|kreis M market

Interessen-: **In|te|res|sen|ver|band** M syndicate; *(= Lobby)* lobby; **In|te|res|sen|ver|tre|tung** F representation of interests; *(= Personen)* group representing one's interests

in|te|res|sie|ren [ɪntərɛˈsiːrən] *ptp* **interessiert** VT to interest *(für, an +dat* in); **es würde mich doch sehr ~, was du damit machen willst** it would interest me very much to know *or* I'd be very interested to know what you want to do with it; **das interessiert mich (gar) nicht!** I'm not (the least *or* slightest bit) interested; **ich liege im Sterben, aber das interessiert dich gar nicht** here I am on my deathbed, but you don't care; **das hat dich nicht zu ~!** that's none of your business!, don't be so nosey! *(inf)*
VR to be interested *(für* in); *(= mit Interesse verfolgen auch)* to take an interest *(für* in); **er begann schon mit acht Jahren, sich für Musik zu ~** he started to be interested in music when he was eight, he started to take *or* show an interest in music when he was eight

in|te|res|siert [ɪntərɛˈsiːɐt] ADJ interested *(an +dat* in); **vielseitig ~ sein** to have a wide range of interests; **politisch ~** interested in politics; **ein ~er Mensch** a person with a number of interests ADV with interest; **sich ~ zeigen** to act interested; **sich an etw** *(dat)* **~ zeigen** to show an interest in sth; **~ zuhören** *etc* to listen *etc* with interest

In|ter|face [ˈɪntɐfeːs] NT -, -s *(Comput)* interface

In|ter|fe|renz [ɪntɐfeˈrɛnts] F -, -en *(Phys, Ling)* interference *no pl*

In|ter|fe|ron [ɪntɐfeˈroːn] NT **-s, -e** interferon
In|ter|ho|tel [ˈɪntɐ-] NT *(DDR)* international hotel
In|te|ri|eur [ɛ̃teˈriøːɐ] NT **-s, -s** or **-e** *(geh)* interior
In|te|rim [ˈɪntɐɪm] NT **-s, -s** interim
In|te|rims- in cpds interim; **In|te|rims|ab|kom|men** NT interim agreement; **In|te|rims|lö|sung** F interim or stopgap solution; **In|te|rims|re|gie|rung** F caretaker or provisional government; **In|te|rims|schein** M *(Fin)* scrip
In|ter|jek|ti|on [ɪntɐjɛkˈtsioːn] F **-, -en** interjection
In|ter-: **in|ter|kon|fes|si|o|nell** [ɪntɐkɔnfesɪoˈnɛl] ADJ interdenominational; **in|ter|kon|ti|nen|tal** [ɪntɐkɔntinɛnˈtaːl] ADJ intercontinental; **In|ter|kon|ti|nen|tal|ra|ke|te** [ɪntɐkɔntinɛnˈtaːl-] F intercontinental missile; **In|ter|leu|kin** [ɪntɐlɔyˈkiːn] NT **-s, -e** interleukin; **in|ter|li|ne|ar** [ɪntɐlineˈaːɐ] ADJ interlinear
In|ter|mez|zo [ɪntɐˈmɛtso] NT **-s, -s** or **Inter|mezzi** [-tsi] *(Mus)* intermezzo; *(fig auch)* interlude; *(ärgerlich)* contretemps sing
in|ter|mit|tie|rend [ɪntɐmɪˈtiːrənt] ADJ intermittent
in|tern [ɪnˈtɛrn] ADJ internal; **~er Schüler** boarder; **diese Maßnahmen müssen vorläufig ~ blei-ben** for the time being these measures must be kept private; **die ~en Schwierigkeiten des Lan-des** the country's internal or domestic difficul-ties ADV internally
-in|tern suf **schulinterne/ausschussinterne Angelegenheiten** internal school/committee matters; **etw schulintern regeln** to settle sth in-ternally within the school/schools
in|ter|na|li|sie|ren [ɪntɐnaliˈziːrən] ptp **interna-lisiert** VT *(spec)* to internalize
In|ter|nat [ɪntɐˈnaːt] NT **-(e)s, -e** boarding school
in|ter|na|tio|nal [ɪntɐnatsioˈnaːl] ADJ interna-tional ADV internationally; **~ von Interesse** of international interest; **~ operierende Organisa-tionen** international organizations; **~ kochen** to cook foreign dishes
In|ter|na|tio|na|le [ɪntɐnatsioˈnaːlə] F **-, -n** In-ternationale
in|ter|na|tio|na|li|sie|ren [ɪntɐnatsionali-ˈziːrən] ptp **internationalisiert** VT to interna-tionalize
In|ter|na|tio|na|lis|mus [ɪntɐnatsionaˈlɪsmʊs] M **-,** no pl internationalism
In|ter|nats|schu|le F boarding school
In|ter|nats|schü|ler(in) M(F) boarder, board-ing (school) pupil
In|ter|net [ˈɪntɐnɛt] NT **-,** no pl *(Comput)* Inter-net; **Anschluss ans ~ haben** to be connected to the Internet; **im ~ surfen** to surf the Internet
In|ter|net-: **In|ter|net|a|dres|se** F Internet address; **In|ter|net|auf|tritt** M web presence; (= *Homepage*) website; **In|ter|net|be|nut-zer(in)** M(F) Internet user; **In|ter|net|brow-ser** M Internet browser; **In|ter|net|ca|fé** NT Internet café; **In|ter|net|kno|ten** M point of presence, pop; **In|ter|net|nut|zer(in)** M(F) Internet user; **In|ter|net|pro|vi|der** M Inter-net provider
in|ter|nie|ren [ɪntɐˈniːrən] ptp **interniert** VT to intern
In|ter|nier|te(r) [ɪntɐˈniːɐtə] MF decl as adj in-ternee
In|ter|nie|rung F **-, -en** internment
In|ter|nie|rungs|la|ger NT internment camp
In|ter|nist [ɪntɐˈnɪst] M **-en, -en**, **In|ter|nis|tin** [-ˈnɪstɪn] F **-, -nen** internist
In|tern|spei|cher [ɪnˈtɛrn-] M *(Comput)* mem-ory
In|ter|num [ɪnˈtɛrnʊm] NT **-s, Interna** [-na] usu pl *(geh)* internal matter; *(geheim)* restricted in-formation

in|ter|par|la|men|ta|risch [ɪntɐparlamɛnˈtaːrɪʃ] ADJ interparliamentary
In|ter|pel|la|ti|on [ɪntɐpɛlaˈtsioːn] F **-, -en** (par-liamentary) question
in|ter|pel|lie|ren [ɪntɐpɛˈliːrən] VI to ask a (parliamentary) question
in|ter|pla|ne|tar [ɪntɐplaneˈtaːr], **in|ter|pla-ne|ta|risch** [ɪntɐplaneˈtaːrɪʃ] ADJ interplanetary no adv
In|ter|pol [ˈɪntɐpoːl] F - Interpol
In|ter|po|la|ti|on [ɪntɐpolaˈtsioːn] F **-, -en** in-terpolation
in|ter|po|lie|ren [ɪntɐpoˈliːrən] VT to interpolate
In|ter|pret [ɪntɐˈpreːt] M **-en, -en**, **In|ter|pre-tin** [-ˈpreːtɪn] F **-, -nen** interpreter *(of music, art etc)*; **Lieder verschiedener ~en** songs by var-ious singers
In|ter|pre|ta|ti|on [ɪntɐpretaˈtsioːn] F **-, -en** in-terpretation; *(eines Liedes auch)* version
In|ter|pre|ter [ɪnˈtøːɐpretɐ, ɪnˈtœr-] M **-s, -** *(Comput)* interpreter
in|ter|pre|tie|ren [ɪntɐpreˈtiːrən] ptp **interpre-tiert** VT to interpret; **etw falsch ~** to misinter-pret sth
In|ter|pre|tin F → **Interpret**
in|ter|punk|tie|ren [ɪntɐpʊŋkˈtiːrən] ptp **inter-punktiert** VT to punctuate
In|ter|punk|ti|on F punctuation
In|ter|punk|ti|ons-: **In|ter|punk|ti|ons|re|gel** F rule of punctuation, punctuation rule; **In|ter|punk|ti|ons|zei|chen** NT punctuation mark
In|ter|rail|kar|te [ˈɪntɐreɪl-] F inter-rail ticket
In|ter|re|gio [ɪntɐˈreːgio] M **-s, -s**, **In|ter|re|gi-o|zug** M fast train running at regular inter-vals
In|ter|reg|num [ɪntɐˈreːgnʊm] NT **-s, Interreg-nen** or **Interregna** [-nən, -na] interregnum
in|ter|ro|ga|tiv [ɪntɐrogaˈtiːf, ˈɪntɐ-] ADJ inter-rogative
In|ter|ro|ga|tiv-: **In|ter|ro|ga|tiv|pro|no|men** [ɪntɐrogaˈtiːf-] NT interrogative pronoun; **In|ter|ro|ga|tiv|satz** [ɪntɐrogaˈtiːf-] M interroga-tive clause
In|ter|rupt [ɪntɐˈrʊpt] M **-s, -s** *(Comput)* inter-rupt
In|ter|rup|tus [ɪntɐˈrʊptʊs] M **,** no pl *(inf)* coitus interruptus
In|ter|shop [ˈɪntɐʃɔp] M **-s, -s** *(DDR)* interna-tional shop
in|ter|stel|lar [ɪntɐstɛˈlaːɐ] ADJ interstellar
In|ter|vall [ɪntɐˈval] NT **-s, -e** interval *(auch Mus)*; **sich in längeren ~en sehen** to see each other at infrequent intervals
In|ter|vall-: **In|ter|vall|schal|tung** F interval switch; **In|ter|vall|trai|ning** NT interval train-ing
in|ter|ve|nie|ren [ɪntɐveˈniːrən] ptp **interveniert** VI to intervene
In|ter|ven|ti|on [ɪntɐvɛnˈtsioːn] F **-, -en** in-tervention
In|ter|view [ˈɪntɐvjuː, ɪntɐˈvjuː] NT **-s, -s** inter-view
in|ter|vie|wen [ɪntɐˈvjuːən, ˈɪntɐ-] ptp **interviewt** VT to interview *(jdn zu etw sb on or about sth)*
In|ter|vie|wer [ɪntɐˈvjuːɐ, ˈɪntɐ-] M **-s, -**, **In|ter-vie|we|rin** [-ərɪn] F **-, -nen** interviewer
In|ter|vi|si|on [ɪntɐviˈzioːn] F Intervision
In|ter|zo|nen- in cpds *(Hist)* interzonal; **In|ter-zo|nen|zug** [ɪntɐˈtsoːnən-] M *(Hist)* train for traffic between West Germany and the GDR
In|thro|ni|sa|ti|on [ɪntroniːzaˈtsioːn] F **-, -en** enthronement
in|thro|ni|sie|ren [ɪntroniˈziːrən] ptp **inthroni-siert** VT to enthrone
In|ti|fa|da [ɪntiˈfaːda] F **-,** no pl intifada

in|tim [ɪnˈtiːm] ADJ intimate; **ein ~er Kenner von etw sein** to have an intimate knowledge of sth; **etw im ~en Kreis feiern** to celebrate sth with one's closest or most intimate friends; **meine ~en Angelegenheiten** my intimate personal af-fairs
In|tim-: **In|tim|be|reich** M **a** *(Anat)* genital ar-ea **b** *(fig)* = **Intimsphäre**; **In|tim|feind(in)** M(F) favourite *(Brit)* or favorite *(US)* enemy; **In|tim|hy|gie|ne** F personal hygiene
In|ti|mi|tät [ɪntimiˈtɛːt] F **-, -en** intimacy; **jdm allerlei ~en erzählen** to tell sb all kinds of inti-mate details or intimacies; **bitte keine ~en!** please don't go into intimate details; **zwischen den beiden kam es zu ~en** they became inti-mate with each other; **~en austauschen** to kiss and pet; **bitte keine ~en in meinem Haus!** I'll have none of that sort of thing going on in my house!; **er hat sich einige ~en erlaubt** he be-came rather familiar
In|tim-: **In|tim|ken|ner(in)** M(F) *(form)* expert *(von, +gen* on or in*)*, authority *(von, +gen* on*)*, connoisseur *(von, +gen* of*)*; **er ist ein ~ von ...** he has an intimate knowledge of ...; **In|tim|kon|takt** M *(form)* intimate contact; **In|tim|le|ben** NT sex or love life; **In|tim|lo|ti|on** F vaginal lotion; **In|tim|part|ner(in)** M(F) *(form)* sexual partner; **In|tim|pfle|ge** F inti-mate hygiene; *(von Frauen meist)* feminine hy-giene; **In|tim|schmuck** M body jewellery *(Brit)* or jewelry *(US)*; **In|tim|sphä|re** F pri-vate life; **jds ~ verletzen** to invade sb's privacy; **diese Frage greift in die ~ ein** that question is an invasion of my/your etc privacy; **In|tim|spray** NT intimate deodorant spray
In|ti|mus [ˈɪntimʊs] M **-, Intimi** [-mi] *(hum)* con-fidant
In|tim|ver|kehr M intimacy; **~ mit jdm haben** to be intimate with sb
in|to|le|rant [ɪntoleˈrant, ˈɪn-] ADJ intolerant *(ei-ner Sache gegenüber* of sth, *jdm gegenüber* of or towards sb*)* ADV intolerantly; **in solchen Din-gen zeigt er sich absolut ~** he is completely intolerant about such things
In|to|le|ranz [ɪntoleˈrants, ˈɪn-] F intolerance
In|to|na|ti|on [ɪntonaˈtsioːn] F **-, -en** intonation
in|to|nie|ren [ɪntoˈniːrən] ptp **intoniert** VT **a** **einen Satz falsch/anders ~** to give a sentence the wrong/a different intonation **b** *(Mus)* Me-lodie to sing; *(Kapelle)* to play; *Ton* to give; **wer kann das Lied ~?** who can start the song off?, who can show us how the song goes?
In|tra|net [ˈɪntranɛt] NT **-s, -s** *(Comput)* Intranet
in|tran|si|gent [ɪntranziˈgɛnt] ADJ *(liter)* intransigent
in|tran|si|tiv [ˈɪntranziˌtiːf] ADJ intransitive ADV intransi-tively
in|tra|ve|nös [ɪntraveˈnøːs] ADJ intravenous ADV intravenously
int|ri|gant [ɪntriˈgant] ADJ *(geh)* scheming, designing
Int|ri|gant [ɪntriˈgant] M **-en, -en**, **Int|ri|gan|tin** [-ˈgantɪn] F **-, -nen** schemer, intriguer
Int|ri|ge [ɪnˈtriːgə] F **-, -n** intrigue, conspiracy, scheme
Int|ri|gen-: **Int|ri|gen|spiel** NT intriguing, plotting; **Int|ri|gen|wirt|schaft** F **,** no pl hive of intrigue
int|ri|gie|ren [ɪntriˈgiːrən] ptp **intrigiert** VI to in-trigue, to scheme, to plot
In|tro|i|tus [ɪnˈtroːitʊs] M **-, -** (= *Gesang*) introit; *(Anat)* introitus
int|ro|ver|tiert [ɪntrovɛrˈtiːɐt] ADJ introverted
In|tro|ver|tiert|heit F **-,** no pl introversion
in|tu|bie|ren [ɪntuˈbiːrən] ptp **intubiert** VT *(Med)* to intubate
In|tu|i|ti|on [ɪntuiˈtsioːn] F **-, -en** intuition
in|tu|i|tiv [ɪntuiˈtiːf] ADJ intuitive ADV intui-tively

in|tus ['ɪntʊs] ADJ *(inf)* **etw ~ haben** (= *wissen*) to get *or* have got *(Brit)* sth into one's head *(inf)*; *Essen, Alkohol* to have sth down *(inf)* or inside one *(inf)*; **er hat schon etwas** *or* **einiges ~** he's had a few

in|valid [ɪnva'liːt], **in|va|li|de** [ɪnva'liːdə] ADJ *(rare)* disabled, invalid *attr*

In|va|li|de [ɪnva'liːdə] M **-n, -n**, **In|va|li|din** [-'liːdɪn] F **-, -nen** disabled person, invalid; **er ist ~** he's disabled, he's an invalid; **der Krieg hat ihn zum ~n gemacht** he was disabled in the war; **ich mache dich zum ~n!** *(inf)* I'll cripple you! *(Brit inf)* I'll kill you!

In|va|li|den-: In|va|li|den|heim NT home for disabled persons *or* people, home for the disabled; **In|va|li|den|ren|te** F disability pension; **In|va|li|den|ver|si|che|rung** F disability insurance

In|va|li|din F → **Invalide**

In|va|li|di|tät [ɪnvalidi'tɛːt] F **-,** *no pl* disability

in|va|ri|a|bel [ɪnva'riaːbl, 'ɪn-] ADJ invariable

in|va|ri|ant [ɪnva'riant, 'ɪn-] ADJ invariant

In|va|ri|an|te F **-, -n** *(Math)* invariant, invariable

In|va|ri|anz [ɪnva'riants, 'ɪn-] F **-, -en** invariance

In|va|si|on [ɪnva'zioːn] F **-, -en** *(lit, fig)* invasion

In|va|sor [ɪn'vaːzoːɐ] M **-s, Invasoren**, **In|va|so|rin** [-'zoːrɪn] F **-, -nen** *usu pl* invader

In|vek|ti|ve [ɪnvɛk'tiːvə] F **-, -n** *(geh)* invective *no pl*

In|ven|tar [ɪnvɛn'taːɐ] NT **-s, -e** **a** (= *Verzeichnis*) inventory; *(Comm)* assets and liabilities *pl*; **das ~ aufnehmen** to do the inventory; **etw ins ~ aufnehmen** to put sth on the inventory **b** (= *Einrichtung*) fittings *pl (Brit)*, equipment; (= *Maschinen*) equipment *no pl*, plant *no pl*; **leben-des ~** livestock; **totes ~** fixtures and fittings *pl (Brit)*, fixtures and equipment *(US)*; **er gehört schon zum ~** *(fig)* he's part of the furniture

In|ven|ta|ri|sa|ti|on [ɪnvɛntariza'tsioːn] F **-, -en** compilation of an inventory

in|ven|ta|ri|sie|ren [ɪnvɛntari'ziːrən] *ptp* **inventarisiert** VT to take *or* make an inventory of

In|ven|ta|ri|sie|rung F **-, -en** compilation of an inventory

In|ven|tur [ɪnvɛn'tuːɐ] F **-, -en** stocktaking; **~ machen** to stocktake

In|ver|si|on [ɪnvɛr'zioːn] F **-, -en** *(Gram)* inversion

In|ver|si|ons-: In|ver|si|ons|la|ge F *(Met)* temperature inversion, inverted atmospheric conditions *pl*; **In|ver|si|ons|tem|pe|ra|tur** F temperature inversion; **In|ver|si|ons|wet|ter|la|ge** F *(Met)* inverted atmospheric conditions *pl*, temperature inversion

in|ver|tiert [ɪnvɛr'tiːɐt] ADJ inverted

in|ves|tie|ren [ɪnvɛs'tiːrən] *ptp* **investiert** VT *(Comm)* to invest; *(fig auch)* to put; **Geld in sei-ne Freundin ~** *(inf)* to invest money in one's girlfriend *(hum)*; **Gefühle in jdn ~** *(inf)* to become (emotionally) involved with sb VI to invest

In|ves|tie|rung F **-, -en**, **In|ves|ti|ti|on** [ɪnvɛs-ti'tsioːn] F **-, -en** *(Gram)* inversion

In|ves|ti|ti|ons- *in cpds* investment; **In|ves|ti|ti|ons|an|reiz** M investment incentive; **In|ves|ti|ti|ons|gut** NT *usu pl* item of capital expenditure; **In|ves|ti|ti|ons|hil|fe** F investment aid; **In|ves|ti|ti|ons|kos|ten** PL investment costs *pl*, cost *(sing)* of investment

In|ves|ti|tur [ɪnvɛsti'tuːɐ] F **-, -en** *(Eccl)* investiture

in|ves|tiv [ɪnvɛs'tiːf] ADJ investment *attr*

In|vest|ment [ɪn'vɛstmənt] NT **-s, -s** investment

In|vest|ment-: In|vest|ment|ban|ker(in) M(F) investment banker; **In|vest|ment|ban|king** NT **-s,** *no pl* investment banking; **In|vest|ment|fonds** M investment fund; **In|vest|ment|ge|sell|schaft** F investment trust; **In|vest|ment|pa|pier** NT , **In|vest|ment-**

zer|ti|fi|kat NT investment fund certificate; **In|vest|ment|spa|ren** NT saving through an investment trust

In|ves|tor [ɪn'vɛstoːɐ] M **-s, -en** [ɪnvɛs'toːrən], **In|ves|to|rin** [ɪnvɛs'toːrɪn] F **-, -nen** *(Econ)* investor

In-vit|ro-Fer|ti|li|sa|ti|on [ɪn'viːtrofɛrtilizatsi-oːn] F **-, -en** in vitro fertilization

in|wärts ['ɪnvɛrts] ADV = **einwärts**

in|wen|dig ['ɪnvɛndɪç] ADJ **a** *(inf)* jdn/etw in- und auswendig kennen to know sb/sth inside out **b** (= *innen*) inside; **die Pflaume war ~ schlecht** the plum was rotten inside

in|wie|fern [ɪnvi'fɛrn], **in|wie|weit** [ɪnvi'vait] ADV *(im Satz)* to what extent, how far; *(allein stehend)* in what way

In|zah|lung|nah|me [ɪn'tsaːlʊŋnaːmə] F **-, -n** *(Comm)* **die ~ von etw** the acceptance of sth in part payment *or* as a trade-in; **bei ~ des alten Wagens** when the old car is traded in *or* is taken as a trade-in

In|zest ['ɪntsɛst] M **-(e)s, -e** incest *no pl*

in|zes|tu|ös [ɪntsɛstu'øːs] ADJ incestuous ADV **er lebte jahrelang ~ mit seiner Tochter** he lived for years in an incestuous relationship with his daughter

In|zucht F inbreeding

inzw. *abbr von* **inzwischen**

in|zwi|schen [ɪn'tsvɪʃn] ADV (in the) meantime, meanwhile; **ich gehe ~ zur Bank** I'll go to the bank in the meantime; **sie hatte ~ davon erfah-ren** meanwhile *or* in the meantime she'd learned of this; **er hat sich ~ verändert** he's changed since (then); **er ist ~ 18 geworden** he's now 18

IOK [iːʔoː'kaː] NT **-s** *abbr von* **Internationales Olympisches Komitee** IOC

Ion [ioːn, 'iːɔn] NT **-s, -en** ['ioːnən] ion

Io|nen|(aus)tau|scher [-(ʔaus)taʊʃɐ] M **-s, -** ion exchanger

Io|ni|sa|ti|on [ioniza'tsioːn] F **-, -en** ionization

io|nisch ['ioːnɪʃ] ADJ *(Archit, Poet)* ionic; *(Mus)* i-onian; **Ionisches Meer** Ionian Sea; **die Ioni-schen Inseln** the Ionian Islands

io|ni|sie|ren [ioni'ziːrən] *ptp* **ionisiert** VT to i-onize

Io|no|sphä|re [iono'sfɛːrə] F ionosphere

I-Punkt ['iː-] M dot on the i; **~e setzen** *or* **ma-chen** to dot one's *or* the i's, to put the dots on the i's

IQ [iː'kuː] M **-s, -s** *abbr von* **Intelligenzquotient** IQ

IR [iː'ɛr] M **-(s), -s** *abbr (Rail) von* **Interregiozug** ≈ fast train running at regular intervals

i. R. [iː'ɛr] *abbr von* **im Ruhestand** retd

IRA [iː'ɛr'aː] *abbr -, no pl von* **Irisch-Republikani-sche Armee** IRA

Irak [i'raːk, 'iːraːk] M **-s (der) ~** Iraq

Ira|ker [i'raːkɐ] M **-s, -**, **Ira|ke|rin** [-ərɪn] F **-, -nen** Iraqi

ira|kisch [i'raːkɪʃ] ADJ Iraqi

Iran [i'raːn] M **-s (der) ~** Iran

Ira|ner [i'raːnɐ] M **-s, -**, **Ira|ne|rin** [-ərɪn] F **-, -nen** Iranian

ira|nisch [i'raːnɪʃ] ADJ Iranian

ir|den ['ɪrdn] ADJ earthenware, earthen; **~e Wa-ren** earthenware

ir|disch ['ɪrdɪʃ] ADJ earthly *no adv*; **den Weg al-les Irdischen gehen** to go the way of all flesh

Ire ['iːrə] M **-n, -n** Irishman; Irish boy; **die ~n** the Irish; **er ist ~** he is Irish → *auch* **Irin**

ir|gend ['ɪrgnt] ADV at all; **wenn ~ möglich** if it's at all possible; **was ich ~ kann ...** whatever I can ...; **wer (es) ~ kann, wer ~ es kann** whoever can; **so sanft wie ~ möglich** as gently as possible, as gently as I/you *etc* possibly can; **so lange ich ~ kann** as long as I possibly can; **wo es ~ geht, wo ~ es geht** where

it's at all possible, wherever (it's) possible *mit indef pron* **~ so ein Tier** some animal; **ein Fuchs oder ~ so ein Tier** a fox or some such animal → **irgendetwas, irgendjemand**

ir|gend|ein ['ɪrgnt'ʔain] INDEF PRON some; *(fra-gend, verneinend, bedingend)* any; **er hat so ~ Schimpfwort verwendet** he used some swear-word or other; **ich will nicht ~ Buch** I don't want just any *(old (inf))* book; **haben Sie noch ~en Wunsch?** is there anything else you would like?; **das kann ~ anderer machen** somebody *or* someone else can do it

ir|gend|ei|ne(r, s) ['ɪrgnt'ʔainə] INDEF PRON *(nominal) (bei Personen)* somebody, someone; *(bei Dingen)* something; *(fragend, verneinend, be-dingend)* anybody, anyone; anything; **welchen wollen Sie? – ~n** which one do you want? – any one *or* any old one *(inf)*

ir|gend|ein|mal ['ɪrgnt'ʔain'maːl] ADV some time or other, sometime; *(fragend, bedingend)* ever

ir|gend|et|was ▲ ['ɪrgnt'ʔɛtvas] INDEF PRON something; *(fragend, verneinend, bedingend)* any-thing; **was zieh ich an? – ~** what shall I wear? – anything *or* any old thing *(inf)*

ir|gend|je|mand ▲ ['ɪrgnt'jeːmant] INDEF PRON somebody; *(fragend, verneinend, bedingend)* anybody; **ich bin nicht ~** I'm not just an-ybody

ir|gend|wann ['ɪrgnt'van] ADV some time; **~ werde ich wohl kommen** I'll come some time; **~ einmal** some time; *(fragend, bedingend)* ever

ir|gend|was ['ɪrgnt'vas] INDEF PRON *(inf)* some-thing; *(fragend, verneinend, bedingend)* anything; **er murmelte so ~** he murmured something or other; **was soll ich sagen? – ~** what shall I say? – anything *or* any old thing *(inf)*

ir|gend|wel|che(r, s) ['ɪrgnt'vɛlçə] INDEF PRON some; *(fragend, verneinend, bedingend)* any; (= *je-de beliebige*) any; **sind noch ~ Reste da?** is there still something left?, is there anything left?

ir|gend|wer ['ɪrgnt'veːɐ] INDEF PRON *(inf)* somebody; *(fragend, verneinend, bedingend)* an-ybody; **ich bin nicht ~** I'm not just anybody

ir|gend|wie ['ɪrgnt'viː] ADV somehow (or oth-er); **ist es ~ möglich?** is it at all possible?; **kannst du dir das ~ vorstellen?** can you possi-bly imagine it?; **ich hab das ~ schon mal gese-hen** I've just got a feeling I've seen it before

ir|gend|wo ['ɪrgnt'voː] ADV somewhere (or oth-er), someplace *(esp US inf)*; *(fragend, vernei-nend, bedingend)* anywhere, any place *(esp US inf)*

ir|gend|wo|her ['ɪrgntvoː'heːɐ] ADV from some-where (or other), from someplace *(esp US inf)*; *(fragend, verneinend, bedingend)* from anywhere or any place *(esp US inf)*

ir|gend|wo|hin ['ɪrgntvoː'hɪn] ADV somewhere (or other), someplace *(esp US inf)*; *(fragend, verneinend, bedingend)* anywhere, any place *(esp US inf)*

Iri|di|um [i'riːdiʊm] NT **-s,** *no pl (abbr* **Ir***)* iridi-um

Irin ['iːrɪn] F **-, -nen** Irishwoman; Irish girl; **sie ist ~** she is Irish → *auch* **Irin**

Iris ['iːrɪs] F **-, -** *or (Opt auch)* **Iriden** [i'riːdn] iris

irisch ['iːrɪʃ] ADJ Irish; **~-römisches Bad** Turkish bath; **Irische See** Irish Sea

Iris-: Iris|di|ag|nos|tik F iridology; **Iris|di-ag|nos|ti|ker(in)** M(F) iridologist

iri|sie|ren [iri'ziːrən] *ptp* **irisiert** VI to iridesce; **~d** iridescent

IRK [iː'ɛr'kaː] *abbr -(s), no pl von* **Internationales Rotes Kreuz** IRC

Ir|land ['ɪrlant] NT **-s** Ireland; (= *Republik Irland*) Eire

ir|län|disch ['ɪrlɛndɪʃ] ADJ Irish; **Irländisches Moos** Irish moss

Iro|ke|sen|(haar)schnitt [iro'keːzn-] M mo-hican (haircut) *(Brit)*, mohawk *(US)*

I|ro|nie [iro'niː] F **-**, *(rare)* **-n** [-'niːən] irony

i|ro|nisch [i'roːnɪʃ] ADJ ironic, ironical ADV ironically

i|ro|ni|sie|ren [ironi'ziːrən] *ptp* **ironisiert** VT to treat ironically

irr [ɪr] ADJ, ADV = **irre**

ir|ra|ti|o|nal [ɪratsio'naːl, 'ɪr-] ADJ irrational *(auch Math)* ADV irrationally

Ir|ra|ti|o|na|lis|mus M irrationalism

Ir|ra|ti|o|na|li|tät [ɪratsionali'tɛːt, 'ɪr-] F irrationality

ir|re ['ɪrə] ADJ **a** (= *geistesgestört*) mad, crazy, insane; **das macht mich ganz ~** it's driving me mad *or* crazy *or* insane; **jdn für ~ halten** *(inf)* to think sb is mad *or* crazy; **jdn für ~ erklären** *(inf)* to tell sb he/she *etc* is mad *or* crazy; **~s Zeug reden** *(fig)* to say crazy things, to babble away **b** *pred* (= *verwirrt, unsicher*) muddled, confused → **irrewerden**
c *(dated inf)* Party, Hut wild *(inf)*, crazy *(inf)* ADV **a** (= *verrückt*) insanely, in a mad *or* insane way; **wie ~** *(fig inf)* like mad *(inf)* or crazy *(inf)* **b** *(dated inf)* **er war ~ angezogen** he was wearing outrageous *or* wild *(inf)* clothes **c** *(dated inf.* = *sehr)* incredibly *(inf)*; **~ gut** brilliant *(inf)*; **~ hübsch** *(sl)* dead *(Brit inf)* or real *(esp US inf)* pretty

Ir|re ['ɪrə] F **-**, *no pl* **jdn in die ~ führen** *(lit, fig)* to lead sb astray; **sich in die ~ führen lassen** *(lit, fig)* to be led astray, to be misled

ir|re|al ['ɪreaːl, ɪre'aːl] ADJ unreal

Ir|re|a|li|tät [ɪreali'tɛːt, 'ɪr-] F unreality

ir|re-: **ir|re+füh|ren** VT *sep* to mislead; *(lit auch)* **sich ~ lassen** to be misled, to be led astray; **ir|re|füh|rend** ADJ misleading ADV **sie hat sich ~ ausgedrückt** the way she said it was very misleading; **die Strecke ist ~ ausgeschildert** the signs are very misleading; **Ir|re|füh|rung** F misleading; **durch bewusste ~ der Öffentlichkeit** by deliberately misleading the public; **ir|re+ge|hen** VI *sep irreg aux sein* **a** *(lit geh)* (= *sich verirren*) to go astray, to lose one's way; (= *umherirren*) to wander astray **b** *(fig)* to be mistaken

ir|re|gu|lär [ɪregu'lɛːɐ, 'ɪr-] ADJ *(auch Mil)* irregular

Ir|re|gu|la|ri|tät [ɪregulari'tɛːt, 'ɪr-] F **-**, **-en** irregularity

ir|re+lei|ten VT *sep* to mislead, to lead astray; **irregeleitete Jugendliche** misguided youth; **~de Informationen** misleading information

ir|re|le|vant [ɪrele'vant, 'ɪr-] ADJ irrelevant *(für for, to)*

Ir|re|le|vanz [ɪrele'vants, 'ɪr-] F irrelevance *(für for, to)*

ir|re|li|gi|ös [ɪreli'giøːs, 'ɪr-] ADJ irreligious

Ir|re|li|gi|o|si|tät [ɪreligiozi'tɛːt, 'ɪr-] F irreligion

ir|re+ma|chen VT *sep* to confuse, to muddle

ir|ren ['ɪrən] ☼ 39.1 VI **a** (= *sich täuschen*) to be mistaken *or* wrong; **Irren ist menschlich** *(Prov)* to err is human *(Prov)* **b** *aux sein* (= *ziellos umherschweifen*) to wander, to stray, to roam VR **a** to be mistaken *or* wrong; **jeder kann sich mal ~** anyone can make a mistake, everyone makes mistakes; **sich in jdm/etw ~** to be mistaken in *or* about sb/about sth, to be wrong about sb/sth; **wenn ich mich nicht irre ...** if I'm not mistaken ..., unless I'm very much mistaken ...; **ich irre mich nie!** I'm never wrong *or* mistaken!, I never make mistakes!

Ir|ren-: **Ir|ren|an|stalt** F *(dated)* lunatic asylum *(dated)*, loony bin *(inf)*; **Ir|ren|arzt** M , **Ir|ren|ärz|tin** F *(old, pej)* psychiatrist; **Ir|ren|haus** NT *(dated, pej)* lunatic asylum *(dated)*, loony bin *(inf)*; **hier geht es zu wie im ~** *(inf)* this place is an absolute madhouse; **ir|ren|haus|reif** ADJ *(inf)* **~ sein** to be cracking up *(inf)*

ir|re|pa|ra|bel [ɪrepa'raːbl, 'ɪr-] ADJ irreparable ADV **beschädigen** irreparably; **das Organ/Gewebe**

ist ~ geschädigt the organ/tissue has suffered irreversible damage

Ir|re(r) ['ɪrə] MF *decl as adj* lunatic; *(fig auch)* madman/-woman; **ein armer ~r** *(hum inf)* a poor fool *or* idiot

ir|re+re|den VI *sep* to rave, to rant, to talk dementedly

Ir|re|sein NT insanity; **manisch-depressives ~** manic depression, manic-depressive psychosis

ir|re|ver|si|bel [ɪrever'ziːbl, 'ɪr-] ADJ *(Phys, Biol)* irreversible

Ir|re|ver|si|bi|li|tät [ɪreverzibili'tɛːt, 'ɪr-] F **-**, *no pl (Phys, Biol)* irreversibility

ir|re+wer|den ▲ VI *sep irreg aux sein* **an jdm/etw ~** *(liter)* to lose one's faith in sb/sth

Irr-: **Irr|fahrt** F wandering, odyssey *(liter)*; **nach langer ~** after a long period of wandering *(auch fig)*, **Irr|gang** M *pl* **-gänge** *(lit)* blind alley *(in maze, pyramid)*; *(fig: usu pl)* maze, labyrinth; **die Irrgänge des Gebäudes** the maze *or* labyrinth of corridors in the building; **Irr|gar|ten** M maze, labyrinth; **Irr|glau|be(n)** M *(Rel)* heretical belief, heresy *(auch fig)*; (= *irrige Ansicht*) mistaken belief; **irr|gläu|big** ADJ heretical; **die Irrgläubigen** the heretics

ir|rig ['ɪrɪç] ADJ incorrect, wrong, false

ir|ri|ger|wei|se ['ɪrɪgɐvaizə] ADV wrongly, incorrectly; **etw ~ glauben** to believe sth mistakenly *or* wrongly

Ir|ri|ta|ti|on [ɪrita'tsioːn] F **-**, **-en** irritation

ir|ri|tie|ren [ɪri'tiːrən] *ptp* **irritiert** VT (= *verwirren*) to confuse, to muddle; (= *ärgern*) to irritate

Irr-: **Irr|läu|fer** M **a** *stray letter, document etc delivered to the wrong address* **b** *(Mil)* stray bullet/grenade *etc*; **Irr|leh|re** F heresy, heretical *or* false doctrine; **Irr|licht** M jack-o'-lantern, will-o'-the-wisp; **irr|lich|tern** ['ɪrlɪçtɐn] VI *insep* to flit about; **der ~de Künstler** the erratic artist

Irr|sinn M , *no pl* madness, insanity; **das ist ja ~!** *(inf)* that's (sheer *or* absolute) madness *or* lunacy!; **auf den ~ verfallen, etw zu tun** to have the mad *or* crazy idea of doing sth

irr|sin|nig ADJ mad, crazy, insane; *(inf:* = *stark)* terrific, tremendous; **wie ein Irrsinniger** like a madman; **ein ~er Verkehr** *(inf)* a terrific *or* crazy *(inf)* amount of traffic ADV like crazy; (= *äußerst*) terribly, dreadfully, incredibly; **sich freuen** so much; **das Kind schrie wie ~** the child yelled like mad *(inf)* or like crazy *(inf)*; **~ viel** an insane amount, an incredible amount, a hell of a lot *(inf)*; **~ viele Leute** *(inf)* a tremendous *or* terrific number of people

Irr|sin|nig|keit ['ɪrzɪnɪçkait] F **-**, *no pl* madness, craziness, insanity

Irr|sinns- *in cpds (inf)* terrific, tremendous; **Irr|sinns|hit|ze** F *(inf)* **da ist eine ~** the heat there is absolutely incredible; **Irr|sinns|tat** F insanity; **Irr|sinns|ver|kehr** M *(inf)* **da ist ein ~** there's a crazy *(inf)* or terrific amount of traffic there

Irr|tum ['ɪrtuːm] M **-s**, **-̈er** mistake, error; **ein ~ von ihm** a mistake on his part; **im ~ sein, sich im ~ befinden** to be wrong *or* mistaken, to be in error; **~! wrong!, you're wrong there!; ~, ich war es gar nicht!** that's where you're wrong *or* you're wrong there, it wasn't me!; **~ vorbehalten!** *(Comm)* errors excepted; **einen ~ zugeben** to admit to (having made) a mistake *or* an error; **jdm einen ~ nachweisen** to show that sb has made a mistake

irr|tüm|lich ['ɪrtyːmlɪç] ADJ *attr* incorrect, erroneous ADV incorrectly, erroneously; (= *aus Versehen*) by mistake

irr|tüm|li|cher|wei|se ['ɪrtyːmlɪçɐvaizə] ADV mistakenly, erroneously; (= *aus Versehen*) by mistake

Ir|rung ['ɪrʊŋ] F **-**, **-en** *(liter)* **die ~en und Wirrungen meines Lebens** the aberrations of my life → **Irrtum**

Irr-: **Irr|weg** M **a** wandering *or* tortuous path; (= *Irrfahrt*) wandering **b** *(fig)* **auf dem ~ sein** to be on the wrong track; **zu studieren erwies sich für ihn als ~** going to university turned out to be a mistake for him; **auf ~e geraten** to go astray, to leave the straight and narrow; **irr+wer|den** ▲ VI *sep irreg aux sein* **an jdm/etw ~** *(liter)* to lose one's faith in sb/sth; **Irr|wisch** ['ɪrvɪʃ] M **-es**, **-e** **a** (= *Irrlicht*) jack-o'-lantern, will-o'-the-wisp **b** (= *lebhafter Mensch*) imp; **Irr|witz** M madness; **irr|wit|zig** ADJ mad

ISBN [iːɛsbeː'ɛn] F **-**, **-s** *abbr* **a** *von* **Internationale Standard-Buchnummer** ISBN **b** *(Comput) von* **Industrial Standard Business Network** ISBN

ISBN-Num|mer [iːɛsbeː'ɛn-] F *(von Büchern)* ISBN (number)

Is|chi|as ['ɪʃias, 'ɪsçias] M OR NT **-**, *no pl* sciatica

Is|chi|as|nerv M sciatic nerve

ISDN [iːɛsdeː'ɛn] *abbr von* **Integrated Services Digital Network** *(Telec)* ISDN

ISDN- [iːɛsdeː'ɛn]: **ISDN-An|schluss** ▲ [iːlɛsdeː'ɛn-] M *(Telec)* ISDN connection; **ISDN-Netz** [iːlɛsdeː'ɛn-] NT *(Telec)* ISDN network

I|se|grim ['iːzəgrɪm] M **-s**, **-e** *(Liter)* the big bad wolf

Is|lam [ɪs'laːm, 'ɪslam] M **-s**, *no pl* Islam

is|la|misch [ɪs'laːmɪʃ] ADJ Islamic ADV **~ den|ken** to have Islamic beliefs; **~ heiraten** to have a Muslim wedding; **~ beeinflusst** influenced by Islam; **seine Kinder ~ erziehen** to raise one's children as Muslims

Is|la|mi|sie|rung [ɪslami'ziːrʊŋ] F **-**, **-en** Islamization

Is|land ['iːslant] NT **-s** Iceland

Is|län|der ['iːslɛndɐ] M **-s**, **-**, **Is|län|de|rin** [-ərɪn] F **-**, **-nen** Icelander

is|län|disch ['iːslɛndɪʃ] ADJ Icelandic; **Isländisches Moos** Iceland moss

Is|län|disch(e) ['iːslɛndɪʃ] NT Icelandic → *auch* **Deutsch(e)**

Is|mus ['ɪsmʊs] M **-**, **Ismen** [-mən] *(pej)* ism

I|so|ba|re [izo'baːrə] F **-**, **-n** isobar

i|so|chron [izo'kroːn] ADJ isochronous, isochronal

I|so|chro|nis|mus [izokro'nɪsmʊs] M **-**, *no pl* isochronism

I|so-Drink ['iːzo-] M **-s**, **-s**, **I|so|drink** M **-s**, **-s** isotonic drink

I|so|la|ti|on [izola'tsioːn] F **-**, **-en** **a** (= *das Absondern, Isolieren*) isolation *(auch Med, Biol)*; *(von Häftlingen)* isolation, putting in solitary confinement; (= *das Isoliertsein*) isolation *(auch Med, Biol)*; *(von Häftlingen)* solitary confinement; **die Studenten protestierten gegen die ~ politischer Häftlinge** the students protested against political prisoners' being put in solitary confinement **b** *(Elec, gegen Lärm, Kälte etc)* insulation

I|so|la|ti|o|nis|mus [izolatsio'nɪsmʊs] M **-**, *no pl* isolationism

i|so|la|ti|o|nis|tisch [izolatsio'nɪstɪʃ] ADJ isolationist

I|so|la|ti|ons|fol|ter F *(pej)*, **I|so|la|ti|ons|haft** F solitary confinement

I|so|la|tor [izo'laːtoːɐ] M **-s**, **Isolatoren** insulator

I|so|lier- [izo'liːɐ-]: **I|so|lier|band** [-bant] NT *pl* **-bänder** insulating tape, friction tape *(US)*; **i|so|lier|bar** ADJ isolable; *(Tech)* insulable; **I|so|lier|box** F *(für Imbiss, Getränke etc)* cooler (box)

i|so|lie|ren [izo'liːrən] *ptp* **isoliert** VT **a** (= *absondern*) to isolate *(auch Med, Biol)*; Häftlinge to isolate, to put in(to) solitary confinement; **jdn isoliert halten** to keep sb in isolation *or* isolated/in solitary confinement; **völlig isoliert leben** to live in complete isolation, to live isolated from the world; **ein Problem isoliert betrachten** to look at a problem in isolation **b** *elektrische Leitungen, Häuser, Fenster* to insulate

VR to isolate oneself *or* to cut oneself off (from the world)

I|so|lier-: I|so|lier|fens|ter NT double-glazed window; **I|so|lier|haft** F solitary confinement; **I|so|lier|kan|ne** F Thermos® flask, vacuum flask; **I|so|lier|mas|se** F insulating compound; **I|so|lier|ma|te|ri|al** NT insulating material; **I|so|lier|schicht** F insulating layer; **I|so|lier|sta|ti|on** F isolation ward

I|so|liert|heit [izo'li:ɐthait] F -, -en isolatedness

I|so|lie|rung F -, -en = **Isolation**

Iso-Mat|te ['i:zo-] F , **I|so|mat|te** F foam mattress, Karrimat®

I|so|mer [izo'me:ɐ] NT -s, -e (*Chem*) isomer

I|so|me|rie [izome'ri:] F -, *no pl* isomerism

I|so|met|rie [izome'tri:] F -, *no pl* isometry

i|so|met|risch [izo'me:trɪʃ] ADJ isometric

i|so|morph [izo'mɔrf] ADJ isomorphic; *Kristalle auch* isomorphous

I|so|ther|me [izo'tɛrmə] F isotherm

i|so|to|nisch ADJ isotonic

I|so|top [izo'to:p] NT -s, -e isotope

Is|ra|el ['ɪsraeːl, 'ɪsraɛl] NT -s Israel; **das Volk ~** the people of Israel

Is|ra|e|li[1] [ɪsra'e:li] M -(s), -(s) Israeli

Is|ra|e|li[2] [ɪsra'e:li] F -, -(s), **Is|ra|e|lin** [ɪsra'e:lɪn] F -, -nen Israeli

is|ra|e|lisch [ɪsra'e:lɪʃ] ADJ Israeli

Is|ra|e|lit [ɪsrae'li:t] M -en, -en, **Is|ra|e|li|tin** [-'li:tɪn] F -, -nen Israelite

is|ra|e|li|tisch [ɪsrae'li:tɪʃ] ADJ Israelite

isst ▲ [ɪst] *3. pers sing pres von* **essen**

ist [ɪst] *3. pers sing pres von* **sein**[1]

Is|tan|bul ['ɪstambu:l] NT -s Istanbul

Ist|be|stand ▲ ['ɪst-] M (= *Geld*) cash in hand; (= *Waren*) actual stock

Ist|gleich|zei|chen [ɪst'glaiç-] NT equals sign

Isth|mus ['ɪstmʊs] M -, **Isthmen** [-mən] isthmus

Ist|leis|tung F actual output

Is|tri|en ['ɪstriən] NT -s Istria

Ist- ['ɪst-]: **Ist|stär|ke** F (*Mil*) actual *or* effective strength; **Ist|wert** M actual value; **Ist|zu|stand** M actual state *or* status

I|ta|ker ['i:takɐ] M -s, -, **I|ta|ke|rin** [-ərɪn] F -, -nen (*pej dated inf*) dago (*pej*), Eyetie (*Brit pej*)

I|ta|li|en [i'ta:liən] NT -s Italy

I|ta|li|e|ner [ita'lie:nɐ] M -s, -, **I|ta|li|e|ne|rin** [-ərɪn] F -, -nen Italian; **zum ~ gehen** to go to an/the Italian restaurant

i|ta|li|e|nisch [ita'lie:nɪʃ] ADJ Italian; **die ~e Schweiz** Italian-speaking Switzerland

I|ta|li|e|nisch(e) [ita'lie:nɪʃ] NT Italian → *auch* **Deutsch(e)**

I|ta|lo|wes|tern ['i:talo-, i'ta:lo-] M spaghetti western

ITB [i:te:'be:] F *abbr von* **Internationale Tourismusbörse** *travel and tourism fair in Berlin*

i|te|ra|tiv [itera'ti:f, 'i:t-] ADJ (*Gram*) iterative

i-Tüp|fel|chen ▲ ['i:-] NT dot (on the/an i); **bis aufs ~** (*fig*) (right) down to the last (little) detail

It|zig ['ɪtsɪç] M -(e)s, -e [-gə] (*dated pej*) Yid (*pej*), Jewboy (*pej*)

i. V. [i:'fau] *abbr von* **in Vertretung**, **von im Vorjahre**, **von in Vorbereitung**

I|wan [i'va:n] M -s, *no pl* (*inf*) **der ~** (= *Volk*) the Russkies *pl* (*inf*); (= *Mensch*) the Russky (*inf*)

IWF [i:ve:'ɛf] M - *abbr von* **Internationaler Währungsfonds** IMF

J

J, j [jɔt, (*Aus*) jeː] NT J, j

ja [jaː] ADV **a** (*zustimmend*) yes; (*bei Trauung*) I do; **kommst du morgen? – ja** are you coming tomorrow? – yes(, I am); **haben Sie das gesehen? – ja** did you see it? – yes(, I did); **ich glaube ja** (yes), I think so; **sagen Sie doch Ja** *or* **ja** please say yes; **zu etw Ja** *or* **ja sagen** to say yes to sth; **Ja und Amen** *or* **ja und amen zu etw sagen** (*inf*) to agree (slavishly) with sth; **wenn ja** if so; **ja! ja!, riefen die Zuschauer** go on! go on!, shouted the crowd

b (*fragend*) really?; **er war gestern da – ja?** he was there yesterday – really? *or* was he?; **ich habe gekündigt – ja?** I've quit – really? *or* have you?; **ja, bitte?** yes?, hello?

c (*feststellend*) **aber ja!** yes, of course, but of course; **ach ja!** oh yes; **nun ja** oh well; **kann ich reinkommen? – ja bitte** can I come in? – yes, do; **ja doch** *or* **freilich** *or* **gewiss** yes, of course; **ja so!** I see

d (*zweifelnd, ungläubig*) really?; **ich esse gern rohen Fisch – ja?** I like raw fish – really? *or* do you?; **er braucht keinen Urlaub, er arbeitet lieber – ja?** he doesn't need a holiday (*esp Brit*) *or* vacation (*US*), he'd rather work – really? *or* would he?

e (*unbedingt*) **komm ja pünktlich!** be punctual; **sei ja vorsichtig!** be careful; **vergessen Sie es JA nicht!** don't forget, whatever you do!; **tu das JA nicht, ich warne dich!** just don't do that, I'm warning you

f (*einräumend, schließlich*) **es ist ja noch früh** it's still early (after all); **sie ist ja erst fünf** (after all) she's only five; **es ist ja nicht so schlimm** it's not really as bad as all that, (after all) it's not that bad; **das ist ja richtig, aber ...** that's (certainly) right, but ...; **ich kann es ja mal versuchen, aber ...** I could always try it, but ...

g (*als Steigerung*) even, nay (*liter*); **das ist gut, ja sogar sehr gut** it's good, in fact it's very good; **das ist es ja** that's just it; **hier IST ja Herr Meier** this is Mr Meier himself; **ja, was haben wir denn hier?** well, what have we here?; **das sag ich ja!** that's just what I say; **das wissen wir ja alle** we all know that (anyway); **Sie wissen ja, dass ...** you (already) know that ..., as you know ...; **Sie wissen ja, wie das so ist** you know how it is(, don't you?)

i (*verstärkend = wirklich*) just; **das ist ja fürchterlich** that's (just) terrible, terrible, that's what it is!; **das weiß man ja eben nie vorher** you just never know in advance

j (*= aber*) **ja, sagen Sie mal** now look here; **ja, was du nicht sagst!** you don't say!

k (*vergewissernd*) right?, OK?; **du kommst doch morgen, ja?** you're coming tomorrow, right? *or* aren't you?; **du rufst mich doch an, ja?** you'll give me a call, OK? *or* won't you?; **das ist also abgemacht, ja?** that's agreed then, right? *or* OK?

Ja [jaː] NT -s, -(s) yes; **mit Ja antworten/stimmen** to answer/vote yes; **ein Ja zum Kind/Frieden** a vote in favour (*Brit*) *or* favor (*US*) of children/peace; **das Ja vor dem Traualtar sprechen** to say "I do" at the altar

---

Ja|bo ['jaːbo] M -s, -s *abbr von* **Jagdbomber**

Jacht [jaxt] F -, -en yacht

Jacht-: Jacht|ha|fen M marina; **Jacht|klub** M yacht club; **Jacht|sport** M yachting, sailing

jäck [jɛk] ADJ (*dial*) crazy

Jäck|chen ['jɛkçən] NT -s, - **a** *dim von* **Jacke** little jacket **b** (= *Babyjäckchen*) matinée jacket (*Brit*), knitted cardigan

Ja|cke ['jakə] F -, -n jacket, coat (*esp US*); (= *Wolljacke*) cardigan; (*Comm: = Unterhemd*) vest (*Brit*), undershirt (*US*); **das ist ~ wie Hose** (*inf*) it doesn't make any difference (either way), it's six of one and half a dozen of the other (*inf*); **jdm die ~ voll hauen** (*inf*) to give sb a thrashing; **wem die ~ passt ...** (*fig inf*) if the cap (*Brit*) *or* shoe (*US*) fits ...

Ja|cken-: Ja|cken|kleid NT (= *Kostüm*) costume, suit, two-piece; (= *Kleid und Jacke*) two-piece, dress and jacket; **Ja|cken|ta|sche** F jacket *or* coat (*esp US*) pocket

Ja|cket|kro|ne ['dʒɛkt-] F (*Zahnmedizin*) jacket crown

Ja|ckett [ʒaˈkɛt] NT -s, -s jacket, coat (*esp US*)

Ja|ckett|ta|sche ▲ F jacket *or* coat (*esp US*) pocket

Jack|pot ['dʒɛkpɔt] M -s, -s (*im Lotto etc*) rollover jackpot; **den ~ knacken** to hit the jackpot

Jac|quard|mus|ter [ʒaˈkaːr-] NT Jacquard weave

Ja|de ['jaːdə] M OR F -, *no pl* jade

ja|de|grün ADJ jade green

Jagd [jaːkt] F -, -en [-dn] **a** hunt; (= *das Jagen*) hunting; (*fig: = Verfolgung*) chase (*nach* after); (= *Wettlauf*) race; **die ~ auf Rotwild/Fasanen** deer-hunting/pheasant-hunting; **hohe/niedere ~** big/small game-hunting; **auf der ~ (nach etw) sein** (*lit*) to be hunting (for sth); (*fig auch*) to be on the hunt (for sth); **auf die ~ (nach etw) gehen** (*lit, fig*) to go hunting (for sth); **auf jdn/etw ~ machen** (*lit, fig*) to hunt for sb/sth; **von der ~ leben** to live by hunting; **ein Buch über die ~** a book about hunting; **die ~ nach Geld/Glück** the pursuit of *or* quest for money/fortune; **in wilder ~ sprengten sie über die Brücke** in their wild chase they charged over the bridge

b (= *Jagdrevier*) preserve, shoot

c (= *Wildbestand*) game

d (= *Jagdgesellschaft*) hunt, hunting *or* shooting party

Jagd-: Jagd|auf|se|her(in) M(F) (= *Angestellter*) gamekeeper; (= *Beamter*) game warden; **jagd|bar** ADJ **... sind ~ ...** may be hunted; **Jagd|beu|te** F bag; **Jagd|bom|ber** M (*Mil*) fighter-bomber; **Jagd|fie|ber** NT hunting fever; **Jagd|flin|te** F hunting rifle, sporting gun *or* rifle, shotgun; **Jagd|flug|zeug** NT (*Mil*) fighter plane *or* aircraft; **Jagd|fre|vel** M (*form*) poaching; **Jagd|frev|ler(in)** M(F) (*form*) poacher; **Jagd|ge|biet** NT hunting ground; **Jagd|ge|schwa|der** NT (*Mil*) fighter squadron; **Jagd|ge|sell|schaft** F hunt, hunting *or* shooting party; **Jagd|ge|wehr** NT hunting rifle, sporting gun *or* rifle, shotgun; **Jagd|glück** NT good luck *or* fortune in hunting; **wir hatten**

---

kein ~ we didn't bag anything; **Jagd|göt|tin** F goddess of hunting *or* the hunt *or* the chase (*liter*); **Jagd|grün|de** PL **in die ewigen ~ eingehen** to go to the happy hunting grounds; **Jagd|haus** NT hunting lodge; **Jagd|herr(in)** M(F) owner of a/the hunting ground; **Jagd|horn** NT hunting horn; **Jagd|hund** M hunting dog; **Jagd|hüt|te** F hunting lodge; **Jagd|mes|ser** NT hunting knife; **Jagd|päch|ter(in)** M(F) game tenant; **Jagd|recht** NT **a** hunting *or* shooting rights *pl* **b** (= *Jagdbestimmungen*) game laws *pl*; **Jagd|ren|nen** NT steeplechase; **Jagd|re|vier** NT shoot; (*von Indianern etc*) preserve; **Jagd|scha|den** M damage caused by hunting; **Jagd|schein** M hunting licence (*Brit*) *or* license (*US*); (*für Jagd mit Gewehr auch*) shooting licence (*Brit*) *or* license (*US*); **einen ~ haben** (*hum*) to be certified (*inf*); **Jagd|schloss** ▲ NT hunting lodge; **Jagd|schutz** M **a** (*Hunt*) game protection **b** (*Mil*) fighter cover; **Jagd|staf|fel** F (*Mil*) fighter squadron; **Jagd|sze|ne** F (*Art*) hunting scene; **Jagd|ta|sche** F game bag; **Jagd|ver|bot** NT ban on hunting; (*als Strafe*) ban from hunting; **Jagd|we|sen** NT , *no pl* hunting; **Jagd|wild** NT game; **Jagd|wurst** F smoked sausage; **Jagd|zeit** F hunting *or* shooting season

ja|gen ['jaːgn] VT **a** *Tier, Menschen* to hunt **b** (= *hetzen*) to chase, to drive; (= *treiben*) *Wild* to drive; **jdn in die Flucht ~** to put sb to flight; **jdn zu Tode ~** to hound sb to death; **jdn aus dem Bett ~** (*inf*) to chase sb out of bed; **jdn aus dem Haus ~** to drive *or* chase sb out of the house; **jdm eine Spritze in den Arm ~** (*inf*) to stick a needle in sb's arm; **ein Unglück jagte das andere** one misfortune followed hard on (the heels of) the other; **Geld/Benzin durch den Auspuff ~** (*inf*) to burn money/a lot of juice (*inf*); **sein ganzes Geld durch die Kehle ~** to booze (*esp Brit inf*) *or* drink all one's money away; **mit diesem Essen kannst du mich ~** (*inf*) I wouldn't eat this if you paid me

c (= *erlegen*) to bag

VI **a** (= *auf die Jagd gehen*) to hunt, to go hunting

b *aux sein* (= *rasen*) to race; **nach etw ~** to chase after sth; **in ~der Eile** in great haste

VR (*Geschennisse etc*) to follow one on the heels of the other

Jä|ger ['jɛːgɐ] M -s, - **a** hunter, huntsman; **~ und Sammler** hunters and gatherers **b** (*Mil*) (= *Gebirgsjäger*) rifleman; (= *Jagdflieger*) fighter pilot **c** (= *Jagdflugzeug*) fighter (plane)

Jä|ger|ba|tail|lon NT rifle battalion

Jä|ge|rei [jɛgəˈraɪ] F -, *no pl* hunting

Jä|ger|hut M Tyrolean hat

Jä|ge|rin ['jɛːgərɪn] F -, -nen huntress, huntswoman → *auch* Jäger a, b

Jä|ger-: Jä|ger|la|tein NT (*inf*) hunters' yarns *pl*; **jdm ~ auftischen** to tell sb tall stories about one's hunting exploits; **Jä|ger|schnit|zel** NT veal *or* pork cutlet with mushrooms and peppers

Jä|gers|mann M *pl* -leute (*dated, liter*) hunter, huntsman

Jäger-: Jä|ger|spra|che F hunter's jargon; **Jä|ger|zaun** M rustic fence

Ja|gu|ar ['ja:gua:ɐ] M **-s, -e** jaguar

jäh [jɛː], **jä|he** ['jɛːə] (geh) **ADJ** **a** (= plötzlich) sudden; Schmerz sudden, sharp; (= unvermittelt) Wechsel, Ende, Bewegung sudden, abrupt; Flucht sudden, headlong, precipitous **b** (= steil) sheer **ADV** **a** (= plötzlich) suddenly, just; enden, wechseln, sich bewegen abruptly; **eine grandiose Idee schoss ihr ~ durch den Kopf** a grandiose idea just popped (right) into her head **b** (= steil) steeply, sharply; **der Abhang steigt ~ an/fällt ~ ab** the slope rises/falls sharply or steeply

jäh|lings ['jɛːlɪŋs] ADV (liter) **a** (= plötzlich) suddenly; aufhören, abbrechen suddenly, abruptly; fliehen headlong **b** (= steil) steeply, precipitously; hinabfallen headlong

Jahr [jaːɐ] NT **-(e)s, -e** **a** year; **ein halbes ~** six months sing or pl; **ein drei viertel ~** nine months sing or pl; **anderthalb ~e** one and a half years sing, eighteen months sing or pl; **zwei ~e Garantie** a two-year guarantee; **im ~(e) 1066** in (the year) 1066; **die sechziger ~e** the sixties sing or pl; **alle ~e** every year; **alle zehn ~e** every ten years; **alle ~e wieder** year after year; **ein ~ ums andere** year after year; **auf ~e hinaus** for years ahead; **auf ~ und Tag** to the very day; **einmal im ~(e)** once a year; **das ganze ~** all year (round or through); **pro ~** a year, per annum; **das Buch des ~es** the book of the year; **noch nach ~en** years later; **nach ~ und Tag** (many) years; **vor ~ und Tag** (many) years ago; **seit ~ und Tag** for years; **mit den ~en** as (the) years go by, over the years; **zwischen den ~en** (inf) between Christmas and New Year; **(freiwilliges) soziales/ökologisches ~** year of voluntary work in the social services/environmental sector **b** (= Alter, Lebensjahr) **er ist zehn ~e (alt)** he is ten years old; **mit dreißig ~en, in seinem dreißigsten ~** (liter) at the age of thirty, in his thirtieth year (liter); **Personen über 18 ~e/unter 18 ~en** people over/under (the age of) 18; **in die ~e kommen** (inf) to be getting on (in years); **man sieht ihm seine ~e nicht an** his age doesn't show; **in den besten ~en sein** or **stehen** to be in the prime of one's life; **mit den ~en** as one gets older

jahr|aus [jaːɐ'|aus] ADV **~, jahrein** year in, year out

Jahr|buch NT yearbook; (= Ausgabe einer Sammlung etc) annual; (= Kalender) almanac

Jähr|chen ['jɛːçən] NT **-s, -** (hum inf) year

jah|re|lang ['jaːrəlaŋ] **ADJ** attr years of; **~es Warten** years of waiting; **~e Planung/Forschung** years of planning/research **ADV** for years; **und dann dauerte es noch ~, bevor ...** and then it took years until ...; **schon ~ verspricht man uns ...** they've been promising us ... for years

jäh|ren ['jɛːrən] VR **heute jährt sich der Tag, dass ...** or **an dem ...** it's a year ago today that ...; **der Tag jährt sich zum dritten Mal, dass ...** or **an dem ...** it's three years ago that ...

Jah|res- in cpds annual, yearly; **Jah|res|ab|rech|nung** F (Comm) → **Jahresabschluss a**; **Jah|res|ab|schluss ▲** M **a** (Comm) annual accounts pl **b** (= Jahresende) end of the year; **Jah|res|an|fang** M beginning of the year; **Jah|res|ar|beits|zeit** F working year; **meine ~ beträgt 1500 Stunden** my working year consists of 1500 hours, I work 1500 hours per year; **Jah|res|aus|gleich** M (Fin) = **Lohnsteuerjahresausgleich**; **Jah|res|aus|klang** M (geh) **zum ~** to see the old year out; **Jah|res|be|ginn** M beginning of the year; **Jah|res|bei|trag** M annual or yearly subscription; **Jah|res|be|richt** M annual or yearly report; **Jah|res|best|leis|tung** F (Sport) year's best performance or time (in races), best performance of or for the year; **Jah|res|best|zeit** F (Sport) best time of or for the year; **Jah|res|bi|lanz** F (Comm) annual balance sheet; **Jah|res|durch|schnitt** M annual or yearly average; **Jah|res|-**

ein|kom|men NT annual income; **Jah|res|en|de** NT end of the year; **Jah|res|fei|er** F anniversary; (= Feierlichkeiten) anniversary celebrations pl; **Jah|res|frist** F binnen/nach ~ within/after (a period of) one year; **Jah|res|ge|halt** NT annual salary; **Jah|res|haupt|ver|samm|lung** F (Comm) annual general meeting, AGM; **Jah|res|kar|te** F annual season ticket; **Jah|res|mit|te** F middle of the year; **Jah|res|mit|tel** NT (Met) average annual temperature; **Jah|res|netz|kar|te** F annual season ticket; **Jah|res|ring** M (eines Baumes) annual ring; **Jah|res|rück|blick** M review of or (a) look back at the year's events; **Jah|res|tag** M anniversary; **Jah|res|um|satz** M (Comm) annual or yearly turnover; **Jah|res|ur|laub** M annual holiday (esp Brit) or vacation (US), annual leave; **Jah|res|ver|dienst** M annual income, annual earnings pl; **Jah|res|wa|gen** M one-year-old car; **Jah|res|wech|sel** M , **Jah|res|wen|de** F new year; **jdm zum ~ Glück wünschen** to wish sb a happy New Year; **Jah|res|zahl** F date, year; **Jah|res|zeit** F season; **für die ~ zu kalt** cold for the time of year

Jahr|fünft [jaːɐ'fʏnft] NT **-(e)s, -e** five years pl, quinquennium (form)

Jahr|gang M pl **-gänge** **a** (Sch, Univ) year; **er ist ~ 1980** he was born in 1980; **die Jahrgänge 1980-83** the 1980-83 age group; **er ist mein ~, wir sind ein ~** we were born in the same year; (als Schulabgänger etc) we were in the same year **b** (= alle Zeitschriften etc von einem Jahr) year's issues pl; (einer Fachzeitschrift) volume; **Nr. 20, ~ 31** No. 20, 31st year; **Spiegel, ~ 1980** Spiegel of the year 1980 or for 1980 **c** (von Wein) vintage, year

Jahr|hun|dert [jaːɐ'hʊndɛt] NT century; **das ~ der Aufklärung** the Age of Enlightenment; **~e haben die Menschen ...** for centuries men have ...

jahr|hun|der|te- [jaːɐ'hʊndɐtə-]: **jahr|hun|der|te|alt** ADJ centuries-old; **jahr|hun|der|te|lang** **ADJ** centuries of; **eine ~e Entwicklung** a development lasting centuries **ADV** for centuries

Jahr|hun|dert-: Jahr|hun|dert|fei|er F centenary; (= Feierlichkeiten) centenary celebrations pl; **Jahr|hun|dert|hoch|was|ser** NT (dieses Jahrhunderts) flood of the century; (nur alle hundert Jahre vorkommend) once-in-a-century flood; **Jahr|hun|dert|wein** M (der ganze Jahrgang) vintage of the century; (einzelne Sorte) rare vintage; **Jahr|hun|dert|wen|de** F turn of the century

Jahr|hun|dert|wen|de F turn of the century

-jäh|rig [jɛːrɪç] ADJ suf **a** (= ... Jahre alt) -year-old; **ein Fünfjähriger** a five-year-old **b** (= Jahre dauernd) years of; **nach elfjährigen Verhandlungen** after eleven years of negotiations; **nach dreijähriger Verspätung** after a three-year delay **c** (Ordinalzahl) **das 70-jährige Jubiläum** the 70th anniversary; **das zehnjährige Bestehen von etw** the tenth anniversary of sth

jähr|lich ['jɛːrlɪç] **ADJ** annual, yearly **ADV** every year, annually, yearly; (Comm) per annum; **einmal/zweimal ~** once/twice a year or yearly

Jähr|ling ['jɛːrlɪŋ] M **-s, -e** yearling

Jahr|markt M (fun-)fair; **~ der Eitelkeiten** (liter) vanity fair

Jahr|markts-: Jahr|markts|bu|de F booth or stall (at a fairground); (= Schaubude) sideshow; **Jahr|markts|künst|ler(in)** M(F) fairground artiste

Jahr-: Jahr|mil|lio|nen [jaːɐmɪˈlioːnən] PL millions of years; **jahr|mil|lio|nen|lang** [jaːɐmɪ'lioːnən-] **ADJ** millions of years of; **eine ~e Entwicklung** a development lasting millions of years **ADV** for millions of years; **Jahr|tau|send** [jaːɐ'tauznt] NT millennium, a thousand years; **in unserem ~** in our millennium; **~e tausends of years; jahr|tau|sen|de|lang** [jaːɐ'tauzndə-] **ADJ** thousands of years of; **eine ~e Entwicklung** a development lasting thousands of years **ADV**

for millennia or thousands of years; **Jahr|tau|send|fei|er** [jaːɐ'tauznt-] F millennium; (= Feierlichkeiten) millennium celebrations pl; **Jahr|tau|send|wen|de** F millennium; **Jahr|zehnt** [jaːɐ'tseːnt] NT **-(e)s, -e** decade; **jahr|zehn|te|lang** [jaːɐ'tseːntə-] **ADJ** decades of; **eine ~e Entwicklung** a development lasting decades **ADV** for decades

Jah|ve ['jaːvə] M **-s, Jah|we** ['jaːvə] M **-s** Jehovah, Yahweh (rare)

Jäh|zorn M violent temper; (plötzlicher Ausbruch) outburst of temper or rage, violent outburst; **im ~** in a violent temper or rage; **zum ~ neigen** to be prone to violent outbursts (of temper)

jäh|zor|nig ADJ violent-tempered, irascible; (= erregt) furious, in a violent temper; **er ist manchmal so ~, dass ...** he sometimes becomes so furious that ..., he sometimes gets into such a violent temper that ...

Jak [jak] M **-s, -s** yak

Ja|kob ['jaːkɔp] M **-s** James; (Bibl) Jacob → **wahr**

Ja|ko|bi|ner [jakoˈbiːnɐ] M **-s, -, Ja|ko|bi|ne|rin** [-ərɪn] F **-, -nen** (Hist) Jacobin; (Rel auch) Dominican

Ja|ko|bi|ner|müt|ze F liberty cap

Ja|kobs|lei|ter F (Bibl, Bot) Jacob's ladder; (Naut auch) rope ladder

Ja|kobs|mu|schel F scallop

Ja|ko|bus [jaˈkoːbʊs] M **-'** James

Ja|lou|sie [ʒaluˈziː] F **-, -n** [-ˈziːən] venetian blind

Ja|mai|ka [jaˈmaika] NT **-s** Jamaica

Ja|mai|ka|ner [jamaiˈkaːnɐ] M **-s, -, Ja|mai|ka|ne|rin** [-ərɪn] F **-, -nen** Jamaican

ja|mai|ka|nisch [jamaiˈkaːnɪʃ] ADJ Jamaican

Jam|ben|dich|tung F iambic poetry

jam|bisch ['jambɪʃ] ADJ (Poet) iambic

Jam|bus ['jambʊs] M **-, Jamben** [-bn] (Poet) iamb(us), iambic foot

Jam|mer ['jamɐ] M **-s, no pl** **a** (= Elend) misery, wretchedness; **ein Bild des ~s bieten** or **sein** to be the picture of misery; **der ~ überkam ihn** a feeling of misery came over him; **es ist ein ~, diesen Verfall mit ansehen zu müssen** it is a wretched thing or it is heartbreaking to have to watch this decay; **es wäre ein ~, wenn ...** (inf) it would be a crying shame if ... (inf) **b** (= Klage) wailing

Jam|mer-: Jam|mer|bild NT (geh) picture of misery, piteous or wretched sight; **Jam|mer|ge|schrei** NT (inf) wailing; **Jam|mer|ge|stalt** F wretched figure; **Jam|mer|lap|pen** M (sl) wet (inf), sissy (inf)

jäm|mer|lich ['jɛmɐlɪç] ADJ wretched, pitiful; (= beklagenswert auch) lamentable, deplorable; (inf) Erklärung, Bericht, Entschuldigung etc pitiful, pathetic (inf); Feigling appalling, terrible **ADV** sterben etc pitifully, miserably; versagen miserably; (inf: = sehr) terribly (inf); (inf: = schlecht) pathetically

Jäm|mer|lich|keit F **-, no pl** wretchedness

jam|mern ['jamɐn] **VI** to wail (über +acc over); (= sich beklagen auch) to moan, to yammer (inf); **nach jdm/etw ~** to whine or yammer (inf) for sb/sth; **der Gefangene jammerte um Wasser** the prisoner begged pitifully or moaned for water **VT** (old) to move to pity; **er jammert mich** I feel sorry for him, I pity him

Jam|mer-: jam|mer|scha|de ADJ **es ist ~** (inf) it's a terrible pity, it's a crying shame (inf); **Jam|mer|tal** NT (Bibl, liter) vale of tears (liter); **jam|mer|voll** ADJ, ADV = **jämmerlich**

Jan|ker ['jaŋkɐ] M **-s, -** (S Ger, Aus) Tyrolean jacket; (= Strickjacke) cardigan

Jän|ner ['jɛnɐ] M **-s, -** (Aus, Sw, S Ger) January

Ja|nu|ar ['januaːɐ] M **-(s), -e** January → auch **März**

Ja|nus- ['jaːnʊs-] (Myth, liter): **Ja|nus|ge|sicht** NT , **Ja|nus|kopf** M Janus face; **ja|nus|ge|sich|tig, ja|nus|köp|fig** ADJ Janus-faced; **Ja|-**

nus|köp|fig|keit F -, *no pl* Janus-faced character

Ja|pan ['jaːpan] NT **-s** Japan

Ja|pa|ner [ja'paːnɐ] M **-s, -**, **Ja|pa|ne|rin** [-ərɪn] F **-, -nen** Japanese

ja|pa|nisch [ja'paːnɪʃ] ADJ Japanese

Ja|pa|nisch(e) [ja'paːnɪʃ] NT Japanese → *auch* **Deutsch(e)**

Ja|pa|no|lo|ge [japano'loːgə] M **-n, -n**, **Ja|pa|no|lo|gin** [-'loːgɪn] F **-, -nen** Japanese specialist; (= *Student*) student of Japanese (studies)

Ja|pa|no|lo|gie [japanolo'giː] F **-, *no pl*** Japanese studies

jap|pen ['japn] VI (*N Ger inf*: = *japsen*) to pant

Japs [japs] M **-es, -e** (*pej inf*: = *Japaner*) Jap (*pej inf*)

jap|sen VI (*inf*) to pant

Jar|gon [ʒar'gõː] M **-s, -s** jargon, slang, lingo (*inf*)

Ja|sa|ger ['jaːzaːgɐ] M **-s, -** yes man

Ja|sa|ge|rin ['jaːzaːgərɪn] F **-, -nen** yes woman

Jas|min [jas'miːn] M **-s, -e** jasmine

Jas|pis ['jaspɪs] M **-(ses), -e** jasper

Ja|stim|me ['jaː-] F vote in favour (*Brit*) or favor (*US*) (of), vote for; (*Parl auch*) aye (*Brit*), yea (*US*)

jä|ten ['jeːtn] VTI to weed

Jau|che ['jauxə] F **-, *no pl*** liquid manure; (*Med*) sanies (*form*), ichor (*form*); (= *Abwasser*) sewage; **das stinkt wie ~** it stinks like nobody's business (*inf*), it stinks to high heaven

Jau|che|gru|be F cesspool, cesspit; (*Agr*) liquid manure pit

jau|chen ['jauxn] **Ⅵ** to manure; (*Med*) to discharge (sanies (*form*) or ichor (*form*)) **Ⅶ** to manure

Jau|chen|gru|be F = **Jauchegrube**

Jau|che|wa|gen M liquid manure transporter or (= *Karren*) cart

jauch|zen ['jauxtsn] VI (*geh*) to rejoice (*liter*), to exult (*liter*); (*Publikum*) to cheer; (*Kinder*) to shout and cheer; (*Säugling*) to chuckle, to laugh

Jauch|zer ['jauxtsɐ] M **-s, -** jubilant cheer or shout; **sie stieß einen lauten, begeisterten ~ aus** she gave a loud yippee (*inf*), she cheered

jau|len ['jaulən] VI (*lit, fig*) to howl; (*lit*) to yowl

Jau|se ['jauzə] F **-, -n** (*Aus*) break (for a snack); (= *Proviant*) snack; **eine ~ halten** or **machen** to stop for a snack

jau|sen ['jauzn] VI (*Aus*) = **jausnen**

Jau|sen|sta|ti|on F (*Aus*) snack bar

jaus|nen ['jauznən] VI (*Aus*) to stop for a bite to eat or a snack; (*auf Arbeit*) to have a tea (*Brit*) or coffee (*esp US*) break

Ja|va ['jaːva] NT **-s** Java

Ja|va|ner [ja'vaːnɐ] M **-s, -**, **Ja|va|ne|rin** [-ərɪn] F **-, -nen** Javanese

ja|va|nisch [ja'vaːnɪʃ] ADJ Javanese

ja|wohl [ja'voːl] ADV , **ja|woll** [ja'vɔl] (*hum, inf*) ADV yes; (*Mil*) yes, sir; (*Naut*) aye, aye, sir; **stimmt das wirklich? – ~** is that really right? – yes, it is or yes, indeed; **haben Sie 50 euro gesagt? – ~** did you say 50 euros? – right or correct or I did or I did indeed

Ja|wort ['jaː-] NT *pl* **-worte** **jdm das ~ geben** to consent to marry sb, to say yes to sb; (*bei Trauung*) to say "I do"; **sich** or **einander das ~ geben** to get married

Jazz [dʒɛs, jats] M **-, *no pl*** jazz

Jazz- *in cpds* jazz; **Jazz|band** ['dʒɛs-, 'jats-] F jazz band

Jaz|zer ['dʒɛsɐ, 'jatsɐ] M **-s, -**, **Jaz|ze|rin** [-ərɪn] F **-, -nen** (*inf*) jazz musician; (*Mann auch*) jazzman (*inf*)

Jazz-: Jazz|gym|nas|tik ['dʒɛs-, 'jats-] F jazz gymnastics *sing*, popmobility, jazzercise (*US*); **Jazz|kel|ler** ['dʒɛs-, 'jats-] M jazz club

---

je¹ [jeː] **ADV** **a** (= *jemals*) ever

b (= *jeweils*) every, each; **für je drei Stück zahlst du einen Euro** you pay one euro for (every) three; **je zwei Schüler aus jeder Klasse** two children from each class; **ich gebe euch je zwei Äpfel** I'll give you two apples each, I'll give each of you two apples; **sie zahlten je einen Euro** they paid one euro each, each (of them) paid one euro

PREP +*acc* (= *pro*) per; **je Person zwei Stück** two per person; **je zehn Exemplare ein Freiexemplar** one free copy for every ten copies

CONJ **a** **je eher, desto** or **umso besser** the sooner the better; **je länger, je lieber** the longer the better

b **je nach** according to, depending on; **je nach Wunsch** just as one wishes; **je nachdem** it all depends; **je nachdem, wie gut man arbeitet ...** depending on how well you work ...

je² INTERJ **ach** or **o je!** oh dear!; **o je!** (*old*) alas! (*old*); **je nun** (*dated*) oh, well

Jeans [dʒiːnz] PL jeans *pl*

Jeans- [dʒiːnz] *in cpds* denim; **Jeans|an|zug** ['dʒiːnz-] M denim suit; **jeans|far|ben** ['dʒiːnz-] ADJ denim-coloured (*Brit*), denim-colored (*US*); **Jeans|ho|se** ['dʒiːnz-] F = **Jeans**; **Jeans|ja|cke** ['dʒiːnz-] F denim jacket; **Jeans|stoff** ['dʒiːnz-] M denim

Jeck [jɛk] M **-en, -en** (*dial*) fool; (*zu Fasching*) carnival reveller (*Brit*) or reveler (*US*)

je|den|falls ['jeːdn'fals] ADV anyhow, in any case; (= *zumindest*) at least, at any rate; **~ ist es schon zu spät** it's too late now anyhow or in any case; **er ist nicht gekommen, aber er hat sich ~ entschuldigt** he didn't come but at least he apologized or he did at least apologize; **ob er krank ist, weiß ich nicht, ~ ist er nicht gekommen** I don't know whether he's ill or not, at any rate or in any case or anyhow he didn't come; **er sagte nichts über den Mord, ~ nichts Neues** he said nothing about the murder, or at any rate or at least nothing new; **er ist noch reif zum Studieren, ~ jetzt noch nicht** he's not mature enough to study, at least or at any rate not yet; **ich weiß nicht, ob das nötig ist, ~ ist es hier so üblich** I don't know if it's necessary, but it's what we do here (anyhow or at any rate)

je|de(r, s) ['jeːdə] INDEF PRON **a** (*adjektivisch*) (= *einzeln*) each; (*esp von zweien*) either; (= *jeder von allen*) every; (= *jeder beliebige*) any; **~ von beiden kann sich verspäten** either of them could be late; **ohne ~ Anstrengung/Vorstellung** *etc* without any effort/idea *etc*, with no effort/idea *etc*; **~s Mal** every or each time; **~s Mal, wenn sie ...** each or every time she ..., whenever she ...; **~s Mal ist es so(, dass ...)** it happens every or each time (that ...); **zu ~r Stunde** at all times; **es kann ~n Augenblick passieren** it might happen any minute or at any moment; **fern von ~r Kultur** far from all civilization → **Kind**

b (*substantivisch*) (= *einzeln*) each (one); (= *jeder von allen*) everyone, everybody; (= *jeder Beliebige*) anyone, anybody; **~r von uns** each (one)/every one/any one of us; **ein ~r** (*liter*) each (one); **~r von uns beiden** each (one) of us; **er gab ~m von beiden ein Buch** he gave each or both of them a book; **~r Zweite** every other or second one; **~r für sich** everyone for himself; **~r/~/~s für sich ist ganz nett, aber beide zusammen ...** each one by himself/herself/itself or each one alone is quite nice, but together ...; **geht jetzt ~r in sein Bett!** go to bed now, both/all of you; **das kann ~r** anyone or anybody can do that; **das kann nicht ~r** not everyone or everybody can do that; **er spricht nicht mit ~m** he doesn't speak to just anybody or anyone

je|der|mann ['jeːdɐman] INDEF PRON everyone, everybody; (= *jeder Beliebige auch*) anyone, anybody; **Jedermann** (*Theat*) Everyman; **das ist nicht ~s Sache** it's not everyone's cup of tea (*inf*); **Herr/Frau Jedermann** Mr/Mrs Average (Citizen)

---

je|der|zeit ['jeːdɐ'tsait] ADV at any time; **du kannst ~ kommen** you can come any time (you like); **ja, ~** sure, any time

je|des|mal △ ['jeːdəs'maːl] ADV → **jede(r, s) a**

je|doch [je'dɔx] CONJ, ADV however; **er verlor ~ die Nerven** he lost his nerve however or though

jed|we|de(r, s) ['jeːt've:də] INDEF PRON (*old*) = **jede(r, s)**

Jeep® [dʒiːp] M **-s, -s** Jeep®

jeg|li|che(r, s) ['jeːklɪçə] INDEF PRON (*adjektivisch*) any; (*substantivisch*: *old, liter*: *auch* **ein jeglicher**) each (one)

je|her ['jeːheːɐ, 'jeːheːɐ] ADV **von** or **seit ~** always; **das ist schon seit ~ so** it has always been like that

Je|ho|va [je'hoːva] M **-s** Jehovah; **die Zeugen ~s** Jehovah's Witnesses

jein [jain] ADV (*hum*) yes and no

Je|län|ger|je|lie|ber [je'lɛŋɐje'liːbɐ] NT **-s, -** honeysuckle

je|mals ['jeːmaːls] ADV ever

je|mand ['jeːmant] INDEF PRON somebody, someone; (*bei Fragen, bedingenden Sätzen auch, Negation*) anybody, anyone; **ist da ~?** is anybody or somebody there?; **du lachst so, hat dir ~ ein Kompliment gemacht?** why are you smiling? has somebody or someone paid you a compliment?; **ohne ~en zu fragen** without asking anybody or anyone; **ich brauche ~en, der mir den Fernseher repariert** I need somebody or someone to repair my television set; **~ Fremdes** a stranger; **~ Neues** somebody or someone new; **~ anders** somebody or someone else

Je|men ['jeːmən] M **-s der ~** Yemen

je|mi|ne ['jeːmine] INTERJ (*old*) = **ojemine, herrjemine**

Je|na|er Glas® ['jeːnaɐ] NT Pyrex®, heatproof glass

je|ne(r, s) ['jeːnə] DEM PRON (*geh*) **a** (*adjektivisch*) that; (*pl*) those; (= *der Vorherige, die Vorherigen*) the former; **in ~m Leben, in ~r Welt** in the next life or world; **in ~n Tagen** in those days; (*zukünftig*) in those days ahead, in those days to come; **in ~r Zeit** at that time, in those times

b (*substantivisch*) that one; (*pl*) those (ones); (= *der Vorherige, die Vorherigen*) the former; **bald dieser, bald ~r** first one then the other; **von diesem und ~m sprechen** to talk about this and that

jen|sei|tig ['jeːnzaitɪç, 'jɛn-] ADJ *attr* opposite, other; **die ~en Vororte** the suburbs on the other side; **das ~e Leben** the life hereafter, the life after death

jen|seits ['jeːnzaits, 'jɛn-] PREP +*gen* on the other side of; **2 km ~ der Grenze** 2 kms beyond the border, 2 kms the other side of the border

ADV ~ von on the other side of; **~ von Gut und Böse** beyond good and evil, over and above good and evil; (*hum inf*) past it (*inf*)

Jen|seits ['jeːnzaits, 'jɛn-] NT **-, *no pl*** hereafter, next world; **jdn ins ~ befördern** (*inf*) to send sb to kingdom come (*inf*)

Jen|seits|glau|be M belief in life after death, belief in the afterlife

Je|re|mi|as [jere'miːas] M **-'** (*Bibl*) Jeremiah

Jer|sey ['dʒɔːɐzi] NT **-s** (*Geog*) Jersey

Je|sa|ja [je'zaːja] M **-s** (*Bibl*) Isaiah

Jes|ses ['jɛsəs] INTERJ (*inf*) Jesus (*inf*)

Je|su|it [je'zuːit] M **-en, -en** Jesuit

Je|su|iten-: Je|su|i|ten|or|den M Jesuit Order; **Je|su|i|ten|schu|le** F Jesuit school

je|su|i|tisch [je'zuːitɪʃ] ADJ Jesuit

Je|sus ['jeːzʊs] M *gen* **Jesu**, *dat* - or **Jesu** ['jeːzu], *acc* - or **Jesum** ['jeːzʊm] Jesus; **~ Christus** Jesus Christ; **~, Maria (und Josef)!** (*dial inf*) holy Mary mother of God! (*dial inf*)

Je|sus-: Je|sus|kind NT das **~** the Infant Jesus, the Christ Child; **Je|sus|kna|be** M der **~** the

---

Infant Jesus, the boy Jesus; **Je|sus|lat|schen** PL (inf) Jesus sandals pl

Jet [dʒɛt] M -(s), -s (inf) jet

Jet|lag ['ʤɛtlɛg] M -s, -s jetlag; **unter ~ leiden** to suffer from jetlag, to be jetlagged

Je|ton [ʒə'tõː] M -s, -s chip

Jet|set ▲ ['dʒɛtsɛt] M -s, (rare) -s (inf) jet set

jet|ten ['dʒɛtn] VI aux sein (inf) to jet (inf), to fly

Jet-Zeit|al|ter NT (inf) jet age

jet|zig ['jɛtsɪç] ADJ attr present attr, current; **in der ~en Zeit** in our or present times; **im ~en Augenblick** at the present moment (in time)

jet|zo ['jɛtso] ADV (obs) = jetzt

jetzt [jɛtst] ADV now; (= heutzutage auch) nowadays; **sie ist ~ in der Schweiz** she's in Switzerland now, she's now in Switzerland; **bis ~** so far; **ich bin ~ (schon) fünf Tage hier** I have been here five days now; **für ~** for now, for the present; **gleich ~, ~ gleich** right now, straight away; **schon ~** already; **~ schon?** already?; **~ noch?** (what) now?; **das ist noch ~ der Fall** it's still the case today; **~ oder nie!** (it's) now or never!; **habe ich ~ das Bügeleisen herausgezogen?** now did I unplug the iron?, did I unplug the iron now?

Jetzt [jɛtst] NT -, no pl (geh) present

Jetzt|zeit F , no pl (geh) present (time), modern times pl or age

jew. abbr von jeweils

je|wei|lig ['je:vaɪlɪç] ADJ attr respective; (= vorherrschend) Verhältnisse, Bedingungen prevailing; **die ~e Regierung** the government of the day

je|weils ['je:vaɪls] ADV at a time, at any one time; (= jedes Mal) each time; (= jeder Einzelne) each; **~ am Monatsletzten** on the last day of each month; **die ~ betroffenen Landesregierungen müssen ...** each of the governments concerned must ...; **die ~ durch Schiebetüren abgetrennten Räume** the rooms, each (of which are) separated (off) by sliding doors; **die ~ Größten aus einer Gruppe** the biggest from each group

Jg. abbr von Jahrgang

JH abbr von Jugendherberge YH

Jh. abbr von Jahrhundert

jhrl. abbr von jährlich

jid|disch ['jɪdɪʃ] ADJ Yiddish

Jid|disch(e) ['jɪdɪʃ] NT Yiddish → auch Deutsch(e)

Jiu-Jit|su ['dʒiːuˈdʒɪtsu] NT -s, no pl j(i)u-jitsu

Job [dʒɔp] M -s, -s (inf) job

job|ben ['dʒɔbn] VI (inf) to work, to have a job

Job|ber ['dʒɔbɐ] M -s, -, **Job|be|rin** [-ərɪn] F -, -nen (inf) jobber

Job- [dʒɔp]

Job|kil|ler ['dʒɔpkɪlɐ] M (inf) job killer

Job|sha|ring ▲ ['dʒɔpʃɛːrɪŋ] NT -s, no pl job sharing

Job|su|che ['dʒɔp-] F , no pl job hunting; **auf ~ sein** to be looking for a job

Joch [jɔx] NT -(e)s, -e **a** (lit, fig) yoke; **Ochsen ins ~ spannen** to yoke or harness oxen; **sich einem ~** or **unter ein ~ beugen** (fig) to submit to or bend under the yoke; **das ~ abwerfen** or **abschütteln** (fig) to shake or throw off the yoke **b** (dated: = Gespann Ochsen) yoke **c** (Archit) truss; (= Kirchenjoch) bay; (= Brückenjoch) span **d** (= Bergjoch) ridge **e** (= Feldmaß) acre

Joch-: **Joch|bein** NT cheekbone, malar bone (form); **Joch|bo|gen** M **a** (Anat) zygomatic arch (spec), zygoma (spec) **b** (Archit) bay

Jo|ckei ['dʒɔke, 'dʒɔkaɪ] M -s, -s, **Jo|ckey** ['dʒɔ-ki] M -s, -s jockey

Jo|ckey|müt|ze F jockey cap

Jod [joːt] NT -(e)s [-dəs] no pl (abbr **J**) iodine

jo|deln ['joːdln] VTI to yodel

jod|hal|tig ADJ containing iodine, iodic (form)

jo|diert [jo'diːɐt] ADJ ~**es Speisesalz** iodized table salt

Jod|ler¹ ['joːdlɐ] M -s, - (= Ruf) yodel

Jod|ler² ['joːdlɐ] M -s, -, **Jod|le|rin** [-ərɪn] F -, -nen yodeller (Brit), yodeler (US)

Jod-: **Jod|man|gel** M iodine deficiency; **Jod|prä|pa|rat** NT iodine preparation; **Jod|quel|le** F iodine(-containing) spring; **Jod|sal|be** F iodine ointment; **Jod|salz** NT iodized salt; **Jod|tink|tur** F iodine tincture

Jo|ga ['joːga] M OR NT -(s), no pl yoga

Jo|ga|sitz M , no pl lotus position

jog|gen ['dʒɔgn] VI to jog

Jog|ger ['dʒɔgɐ] M -s, -, **Jog|ge|rin** [-ərɪn] F -, -nen jogger

Jog|ging ['dʒɔgɪŋ] NT -, no pl jogging

Jog|ging- in cpds jogging; **Jog|ging|an|zug** M jogging suit, tracksuit

Jo|ghurt ['joːgʊrt] M OR NT -(s), -(s) yog(h)urt

Jo|ghurt|be|rei|ter [-bəraitɐ] M -s, -s yog(h)urt maker

Jo|gi ['joːgi] M -s, -s yogi

Jo|gurt ▲ ['joːgʊrt] M OR NT -(s), -(s) → **Joghurt**

Jo|gurt|be|rei|ter ▲ [-bəraitɐ] M -s, -s → **Joghurtbereiter**

Jo|hann [jo'han, 'joːhan] M -s John

Jo|han|na [jo'hana] F -s Joanna; **(die heilige) ~ von Orléans** (Saint) Joan of Arc

Jo|han|nes [jo'hanəs, jo'hanɛs] M -' or (ohne Artikel) **Johannis** [-nɪs] **a** (Bibl) John **b** (sl: = Penis) John Thomas (Brit hum inf), Johnnie (US hum inf)

Jo|han|nes|evan|ge|li|um NT St John's Gospel, Gospel according to St. John

Jo|han|ni(s) [jo'hani, jo'hanɪs] NT - Midsummer's Day

Jo|han|nis-: **Jo|han|nis|bee|re** F **Rote ~** redcurrant; **Schwarze ~** blackcurrant; **Jo|han|nis|beer|strauch** M (roter) redcurrant bush; (schwarzer) blackcurrant bush; **Jo|han|nis|brot** NT (Bot) carob; **Jo|han|nis|brot|baum** M carob tree; **Jo|han|nis|fest** NT Midsummer's Day; **Jo|han|nis|feu|er** NT Midsummer's Eve bonfire; **Jo|han|nis|kä|fer** M (= Glühwürmchen) glow-worm; (= Junikäfer) summer chafer; **Jo|han|nis|kraut** NT , no pl St. John's wort; **Jo|han|nis|nacht** F Midsummer's Eve; **Jo|han|nis|tag** M Midsummer's Day; **Jo|han|nis|trieb** M (Bot) lammas shoot; (fig) late romantic stirrings pl; **Jo|han|nis|würm|chen** NT = **Johanniskäfer**

Jo|han|ni|ter [joha'niːtɐ] M -s, - Knight of St. John of Jerusalem; **~ Unfallhilfe** St. John's Ambulance (Brigade)

Jo|han|ni|ter|or|den M Order of St. John of Jerusalem

joh|len ['joːlən] VI to howl

Joint [dʒɔynt] M -s, -s (inf) joint (inf)

Joint|ven|ture ▲ [dʒɔynt 'vɛntʃə] NT -s, -s, **Joint Ven|ture** ▲ NT -s, -s (Comm) joint venture

Jo|jo [jo'jo, 'joːjo] NT -s, -s yo-yo

Jo|jo-Ef|fekt M yo-yo effect

Jo|ker ['joːkɐ, 'dʒoːkɐ] M -s, - (Cards) joker; (fig) trump card

Jo|kus ['joːkʊs] M -, -se (dated, inf) jape (dated), joke, prank; **da hat sich jemand einen ~ gemacht** someone's been playing a prank

Jol|le ['jɔlə] F -, -n (Naut) jolly boat, dinghy

Jol|len|kreu|zer M cabin yacht

Jo|na ['joːna] M -s, **Jo|nas** ['joːnas] M -' (Bibl) Jonah

Jong|leur [ʒõ'gløːɐ, ʒɔŋ'løːɐ] M -s, -e, **Jong|leu|rin** F -, -nen juggler

jong|lie|ren [ʒõ'gliːrən, ʒɔŋ'liːrən] ptp **jongliert** VI (lit, fig) to juggle

Jop|pe ['jɔpə] F -, -n (dial) jacket

Jor|dan ['jɔrdan] M -s Jordan; **über den ~ gehen** (inf) to cross the great divide (inf)

Jor|da|ni|en [jɔr'daːniən] NT -s Jordan

Jor|da|ni|er [jɔr'daːniɐ] M -s, -, **Jor|da|ni|e|rin** [-iərɪn] F -, -nen Jordanian

jor|da|nisch [jɔr'daːnɪʃ] ADJ Jordanian

Jo|sef ['joːzɛf] M -s, **Jo|seph** M -s Joseph

Jot [jɔt] NT -, - (the letter) J/j

Jo|ta ['joːta] NT -(s), -s iota; **kein ~, nicht ein ~** not a jot, not one iota

Joule [dʒuːl] NT -(s), - (abbr **J**) joule

Jour fixe [ʒuːrˈfɪks] M -s -, - s regular meeting

Jour|nail|le [ʒʊr'naljə, ʒʊr'naːjə] F -, no pl (pej) yellow press; (= Presse im Allgemeinen) press; (= Journalisten) hacks pl (pej)

Jour|nal [ʒʊr'naːl] NT -s, -e **a** (dated: = Tagebuch) journal (old), diary; (Comm) daybook; (Naut) log(book) **b** (dated: = Zeitschrift) magazine, periodical; (old: = Zeitung) journal (old); (= Fachjournal) journal

Jour|nal|dienst M (Aus) = **Bereitschaftsdienst**

Jour|na|lis|mus [ʒʊrna'lɪsmʊs] M -, no pl journalism

Jour|na|list [ʒʊrna'lɪst] M -en, -en, **Jour|na|lis|tin** [-'lɪstɪn] F -, -nen journalist

Jour|na|lis|tik [ʒʊrna'lɪstɪk] F -, no pl journalism

jour|na|lis|tisch [ʒʊrna'lɪstɪʃ] ADJ journalistic ADV **~ arbeiten** to work as a journalist; **jdn ~ ausbilden** to train sb to be a journalist; **etw ~ aufbereiten** to edit sth for journalistic purposes; **~ geschrieben** written in a journalistic style

jo|vial [jo'viaːl] ADJ jovial ADV jovially

Jo|via|li|tät [joviali'tɛːt] F -, no pl joviality

Joy|stick ['dʒɔystɪk] M -s, -s (Comput) joystick

jr. abbr von junior jnr, jr

Ju|bel ['juːbl] M -s, no pl (von Volk, Menge etc) jubilation; (= Jubelrufe auch) cheering; **~, Trubel, Heiterkeit** laughter and merriment

Ju|bel-: **Ju|bel|fei|er** F , **Ju|bel|fest** NT jubilee; (= Feierlichkeiten) jubilee celebration; **Ju|bel|ge|schrei** NT (pej) shouting and cheering; **Ju|bel|greis(in)** M(F) old person celebrating a jubilee or anniversary (fig inf) cheerful old soul (inf); **Ju|bel|hoch|zeit** F special wedding anniversary (silver, golden etc anniversary); **Ju|bel|jahr** NT jubilee year; **nur alle ~e (einmal)** (inf) once in a blue moon (inf)

ju|beln ['juːbln] VI to cheer, to shout with joy, to rejoice (liter); **jubelt nicht zu früh** don't start celebrating too early

Ju|bel-: **Ju|bel|paar** NT happy couple (celebrating a special e.g. silver or golden wedding anniversary); **Ju|bel|ruf** M (triumphant) cheer; **Ju|bel|tag** M (silver, golden etc) wedding anniversary

Ju|bi|lar [jubi'laːɐ] M -s, -e, **Ju|bi|la|rin** [-'laːrɪn] F -, -nen person celebrating an anniversary

Ju|bi|la|te [jubi'laːtə] no art (Eccl) Jubilate (Sunday)

Ju|bi|lä|um [jubi'lɛːʊm] NT -s, **Jubiläen** [-'lɛːən] jubilee; (= Jahrestag) anniversary

Ju|bi|lä|ums- in cpds jubilee; **Ju|bi|lä|ums|jahr** NT jubilee year

ju|bi|lie|ren [jubi'liːrən] ptp **jubiliert** VI (liter) to rejoice (liter); (Vögel) to sing joyfully

juch|he(i) [jʊx'heː, jʊx'hai], **juch|hei|ßa** [jʊx'haisa], **juch|hu** [jʊx'huː] INTERJ hurrah, hooray

Juch|ten ['jʊxtn] NT OR M -s, no pl **a** (= Juchtenleder) Russia leather or calf, Russia **b** (= Parfüm) Russian leather

Juch|ten|le|der NT Russia leather or calf, Russia

juch|zen ['jʊxtsn] VI to shriek with delight

ju|ckeln ['jʊkln] VI aux sein (inf: Auto, Zug) to jog or chug along; **er ist durch die Stadt/über Land**

gejuckelt he's been jogging around town/across country

ju|cken ['jʊkn] **VTI** to itch; **es juckt mich am Rücken, der Rücken juckt mir** or **mich** my back itches; **der Stoff juckt mich** this material makes me itch; **es juckt mich, das zu tun** (inf) I'm itching to do it (inf); **ihn juckt das Geld dabei** (inf) he finds the money attractive; **das juckt mich doch nicht** (inf) I don't care; **lass ~** (sl) let your hair down (inf); **ihn** or **ihm juckt das Fell** (inf) or **der Buckel** (inf) he's asking for a good hiding; **wens juckt, der kratze sich** (prov) if you don't like it you know what you can do (inf) **VT** (= kratzen) to scratch

Juck-: Juck|pul|ver NT itching powder; **Juck|reiz** M itching; **einen ~ in der Nase haben** to have an itch in one's nose

Ju|däa [ju'dɛ:a] NT **-s** Jud(a)ea

Ju|da|is|mus [juda'ɪsmʊs] M **-**, no pl Judaism

Ju|das¹ ['ju:das] M **-'** (Bibl) Judas

Ju|das² M **-'**, **-se** (fig liter) Judas

Ju|das-: Ju|das|kuss ▲ M (liter) Judas kiss; **der ~** (Bibl) the Betrayal; **Ju|das|lohn** M (liter) blood money, thirty pieces pl of silver

Ju|de ['ju:də] M **-n**, **-n** Jew; **er ist ~** he is a Jew → **ewig** ADJ → auch **Jüdin**

Juden-: Ju|den|christ(in) M(F) Judaeo-Christian; **Ju|den|feind(in)** M(F) anti-Semite; **ju|den|feind|lich** ADJ anti-Semitic **sich ~ verhalten** to be anti-Semitic; **sich ~ äußern** to make anti-Semitic remarks; **Ju|den|geg|ner(in)** M(F) anti-Semite; **Ju|den|hass** ▲ M anti-Semitism; **Ju|den|heit** F **-**, no pl Jewry; **Ju|den|stern** M star of David; **Ju|den|tum** ['ju:dntu:m] NT **-s**, no pl **a** (= Judaismus) Judaism **b** (= Gesamtheit der Juden) Jews pl, Jewry **c** (= jüdisches Wesen) Jewishness; **Ju|den|ver|fol|gung** F persecution of (the) Jews; **Ju|den|vier|tel** NT Jewish quarter

Jü|din ['jy:dɪn] F **-**, **-nen** Jew, Jewish woman

jü|disch ['jy:dɪʃ] ADJ Jewish ADV **~ denken** to have Jewish beliefs; **~ heiraten** to have a Jewish wedding; **~ beeinflusst** influenced by Judaism; **seine Kinder ~ erziehen** to raise one's children as Jews

ju|di|zie|ren [judi'tsi:rən] ptp **judiziert** VI (old, Jur) = **urteilen**

Ju|do¹ ['ju:do] M **-s**, **-s** (Pol inf) Young Democrat

Ju|do² NT **-s**, no pl judo

Ju|do|an|zug M judo outfit or uniform

Ju|do|ka [ju'do:ka] M **-(s)**, **-(s)** judoka

Ju|gend ['ju:gnt] F **-**, no pl **a** (= Jugendzeit) youth; (= das Jungsein, Jugendlichkeit) youth, youthfulness; **frühe ~** early youth, adolescence; **früheste ~** early adolescence; **in ihrer ~ waren sie ...** in their youth they were ...; **von ~ an** or **auf** from one's youth **b** (= junge Menschen) youth, young people pl; **die heutige ~**, **die ~ von heute** young people or the youth of today, modern youth; **die weibliche/männliche ~** young women/men; **die studentische ~** student youth; **~ hat keine Tugend** (Prov) young people are all the same; **Haus der ~** youth centre (Brit) or center (US) **c** (Sport) youth team

Ju|gend-: Ju|gend|al|ter NT adolescence; **Ju|gend|amt** NT youth welfare department; **Ju|gend|ar|beit** F, no pl **a** (= Arbeit Jugendlicher) youth employment **b** (= Jugendfürsorge) youth work; **Ju|gend|ar|beits|lo|sig|keit** F youth unemployment; **Ju|gend|ar|rest** M (Jur) detention; **Ju|gend|ban|de** F gang of youths; **Ju|gend|be|kannt|schaft** F friend of one's youth; **Ju|gend|be|treu|er(in)** M(F) youth leader, ≈ adult supervisor who looks after young people; **Ju|gend|be|we|gung** F **a** youth movement **b** (Hist) German Youth Movement (of the early 1920s); **Ju|gend|bild** NT picture or photo taken when one was young; **~er Churchills** pictures of the young Churchill; **Ju|gend|bild|nis** NT (Art, fig) **~ von X** portrait of X as a young man/woman;

Ju|gend|bri|ga|de F (DDR) youth brigade (work team consisting of young people); **Ju|gend|buch** NT book for the younger reader or for young people; **Ju|gend|bü|che|rei** F library for the younger reader; **Ju|gend|buch|ver|lag** M publishing house specializing in literature for young people; **Ju|gend|elf** F youth team; **Ju|gend|er|in|ne|rung** F youthful memory; **meine ~en** memories of my youth; **ju|gend|frei** ADJ suitable for young people; Film U(-certificate) (Brit), G (US); **Ju|gend|freund** M(F) friend of one's youth; **Ju|gend|funk** M (Rad) broadcasting or radio for young people; (= Sendung) broadcast or programme (Brit) or program (US) for young people; **Ju|gend|für|sor|ge** F youth welfare; (für Schulkinder) child guidance; **Ju|gend|ge|dicht** NT youthful poem; **ju|gend|ge|fähr|dend** ADJ liable to corrupt the young; **Ju|gend|ge|richt** NT juvenile court; **Ju|gend|ge|spie|le** M , **Ju|gend|ge|spie|lin** F (hum) young playmate; **Ju|gend|grup|pe** F youth group; **Ju|gend|heim** NT **a** youth club **b** (= Wohnheim) young people's home

Ju|gend|her|ber|ge F youth hostel

Ju|gend|her|bergs-: Ju|gend|her|bergs|aus|weis M youth hostelling card (Brit), youth hostel ID (US), YHA card (Brit); **Ju|gend|her|bergs|mut|ter** F , **Ju|gend|her|bergs|va|ter** M youth hostel warden; **Ju|gend|her|bergs|ver|band** M ≈ Youth Hostel Association (Brit), youth hostelling association

Ju|gend-: Ju|gend|hil|fe F (Admin) help for young people; **Ju|gend|ir|re|sein** NT (Med) juvenile schizophrenia; **Ju|gend|jah|re** PL days pl of one's youth; **Ju|gend|kri|mi|na|li|tät** F juvenile delinquency

ju|gend|lich ['ju:gntlɪç] ADJ (= jung) young; (= von Jugend, jung wirkend) youthful; **eine ~e Erscheinung** a young-looking or youthful-looking person; **~e Banden** gangs of youths; **ein ~er Täter** a young offender, a juvenile delinquent; **~er Leichtsinn** youthful frivolity; **das sagst du so in deinem ~en Leichtsinn** (hum) I admire your confidence ADV youthfully; **sich ~ geben** to appear youthful; **~ wirken** to seem youthful; **er kleidet sich immer sehr ~** he always wears very youthful or young-looking clothes

Ju|gend|li|che(r) ['ju:gntlɪçə] MF decl as adj (männlich auch) youth

Ju|gend|lich|keit F, no pl youthfulness

Ju|gend-: Ju|gend|lie|be F **a** young love **b** (= Geliebter) love or sweetheart of one's youth; **Ju|gend|li|te|ra|tur** F literature for younger readers or young people; **Ju|gend|mann|schaft** F youth team; **Ju|gend|meis|ter(in)** M(F) (Sport) youth champion; **Ju|gend|meis|ter|schaft** F (Sport) youth championships pl; **Ju|gend|or|ga|ni|sa|ti|on** F youth organization; **Ju|gend|pfle|ge** F youth welfare; **Ju|gend|pfle|ger(in)** M(F) youth (welfare) worker; **Ju|gend|psy|cho|lo|gie** F adolescent psychology; **Ju|gend|recht** NT law relating to young persons; **Ju|gend|rich|ter(in)** M(F) (Jur) magistrate (in a juvenile court); **Ju|gend|schrif|ten** PL publications pl for young people; (= junge Autors) youthful writings pl; **Ju|gend|schrift|stel|ler(in)** M(F) writer of books for young people; **Ju|gend|schutz** M protection of children and young people; **Ju|gend|sek|te** F youth sect; **Ju|gend|sen|dung** F (Rad) programme (Brit) or program (US) for younger listeners; (TV) programme (Brit) or program (US) for younger viewers; **Ju|gend|spie|le** PL youth games pl; **Ju|gend|stil** M , no pl (Art) Art Nouveau; **Ju|gend|straf|an|stalt** F (form) young offenders' institution (Brit), juvenile correction institution or facility (US); **Ju|gend|stra|fe** F detention no art in a young offenders' (Brit) or juvenile correction (US) institution; **Ju|gend|streich** M youthful exploit or escapade; **Ju|gend|sün|de** F youthful misdeed; **Ju|gend-**

the|a|ter NT youth theatre (Brit) or theater (US); **Ju|gend|tor|heit** F youthful folly, folly of one's youth; **Ju|gend|traum** M youthful dream; **Ju|gend|ver|band** M youth organization; **Ju|gend|ver|bot** NT **für einen Film ~ aussprechen** to ban a film for young people; **Ju|gend|ver|tre|tung** F youth representatives pl; **Ju|gend|vor|stel|lung** F performance for young people; **Ju|gend|wei|he** F (Rel) initiation; (in Eastern Germany) ceremony in which 14-year-olds are given adult social status; **Ju|gend|zeit** F youth, younger days pl; **Ju|gend|zent|rum** NT youth centre (Brit) or center (US)

Ju|go|sla|we [jugo'sla:və] M **-n**, **-n**, **Ju|go|sla|win** [-'sla:vɪn] F **-**, **-nen** Yugoslav

Ju|go|sla|wi|en [jugo'sla:viən] NT **-s** Yugoslavia

ju|go|sla|wisch [jugo'sla:vɪʃ] ADJ Yugoslav(ian)

Ju|lei [ju'lai, 'ju:lai] M **-(s)**, **-s** (esp Comm) July

Ju|li¹ ['ju:li] M **-(s)**, **-s** July → auch **März**

Ju|li² M **-s**, **-s** (Pol inf) Young Liberal

ju|li|a|nisch [ju'lia:nɪʃ] ADJ **der ~e Kalender** the Julian calendar

Jum|bo ['jʊmbo] M **-s**, **-s**, **Jum|bo|jet** ['jʊmbodʒɛt] M **-s**, **-s** jumbo (jet)

Jum|per ['jʊmpɐ, 'dʒampɐ] M **-s**, **-** jumper (Brit), sweater

Jum|per|kleid ['jʊmpɐ, 'dʒampɐ] NT jumper dress

jun. abbr von junior jun

jung [jʊŋ] ADJ comp **=er** ['jʏŋɐ], superl **=ste(r, s)** ['jʏŋstɐ] (lit, fig) young; Aktien new; **Jung und Alt** (both) young and old; **von ~ auf** from one's youth; **der ~e Meyer** young Meyer; (= Sohn) Meyer junior; **sie ist 18 Jahre ~** (hum) she's 18 years young (hum); **sich** (dat) **ein ~es Herz bewahren** to stay young at heart; **wie ein ~er Gott** divinely; **er sieht aus wie ein ~er Gott** he looks divine (inf) → **jünger**, **jüngste(r, s)**, Blut, Gemüse, Wein, Pferd

ADV comp **=er**, superl **am =sten ~ aussehen** to look young; **~ heiraten/sterben** to marry/die young; **jünger heiraten** to marry earlier; **sie starb jünger als ihr Mann** she died before her husband; **~ gefreit, nie gereut** (Prov) if you marry young you won't regret it; **so ~ kommen wir nicht mehr zusammen** (hum) you're only young once

Jung- in cpds young; **Jung|aka|de|mi|ker(in)** M(F) graduate; **Jung|ar|bei|ter(in)** M(F) juvenile employee or worker; **Jung|bau|er** M pl **-bäuer**, **Jung|bäu|e|rin** F young farmer; **Jung|brun|nen** M fountain of youth; **Jung|bür|ger(in)** M(F) junior citizen

Jung|chen ['jʊŋçən] NT **-s**, **-** (inf) lad (inf), laddie (Scot inf)

Jung|de|mo|krat(in) M(F) Young Democrat

Jun|ge ['jʊŋə] M **-n**, **-n** or (dated inf) **-ns** or (inf) **Jungs** [jʊŋs] boy; (= Laufjunge) errand boy; (Cards) jack, knave; **~, ~!** (inf) boy oh boy (inf); **sie ist ein richtiger ~** she's a real tomboy; **alter ~** (inf) my old mate (Brit inf) or pal (inf); **mein lieber ~!** my dear boy; (in Brief) my dear son; **ein schwerer ~** (inf) a (big-time) crook (inf); **unsere Jungs haben gewonnen** our boys or lads (Brit inf) won

Jün|gel|chen ['jʏŋlçən] NT **-s**, **-** (pej) young lad (Brit inf) or boy

jun|gen ['jʊŋən] VI to have young; (Hündin auch) to have pups; (Katze auch) to have kittens

Jun|gen-: Jun|gen|ge|sicht NT boy's or boyish face; **jun|gen|haft** ADJ boyish; **sie ist ein ~es Mädchen** she's a bit of a tomboy; **Jun|gen|klas|se** F (Sch) boys' class; **Jun|gen|schu|le** F boys' school; **Jun|gen|streich** M boyish prank or trick

Jun|ge(r) MF decl as adj (inf) **der/die ~** Mr/Miss X junior, the young Mr/Miss X; **die ~n** the young ones

jün|ger ['jʏŋɐ] ADJ **a** comp von **jung** younger; **Holbein der Jüngere** Holbein the Younger, the younger Holbein **b** *Geschichte, Entwicklung etc* recent; **die ~e Steinzeit** the later *or* New Stone Age ADV **sie sieht ~ aus, als sie ist** she looks younger than she is, she doesn't look her age → *auch* **jung**

Jün|ger ['jʏŋɐ] M **-s, -** (*Bibl, fig*) disciple

Jün|ge|rin ['jʏŋərɪn] F **-, -nen** (*fig*) disciple

Jün|ger|schaft ['jʏŋɐʃaft] F **-,** *no pl* disciples *pl*; (= *Jüngertum*) discipleship

Jun|ge(s) ['jʊŋə] NT *decl as adj* (*Zool*) young one; (*von Hund*) pup(py); (*von Katze*) kitten; (*von Wolf, Löwe, Bär*) cub; (*von Vogel*) young bird, nestling; **die ~n** the young

Jung|fer ['jʊŋfɐ] F **-, -n** **a** (*old, hum*) (= *ledige Frau*) spinster; **eine alte ~** an old maid **b** (*old:* = *Jungfrau*) virgin, maiden (*old*); (*als Anrede*) mistress (*old*) **c** (= *Kammerjungfer*) maid

jüng|fer|lich ['jʏŋfɐlɪç] ADJ old-maidish

Jung|fern-: Jung|fern|fahrt F maiden voyage; **Jung|fern|flug** M maiden flight; **Jung|fern|häut|chen** NT (*Anat*) hymen (*Anat*), maidenhead; **Jung|fern|in|seln** PL Virgin Islands *pl*; **Jung|fern|kranz** M (*old*) (bridal) bouquet; **Jung|fern|re|de** F (*Parl*) maiden speech; **Jung|fern|rei|se** F maiden voyage; **Jung|fern|schaft** ['jʊŋfɐnʃaft] F **-,** *no pl* virginity; **Jung|fern|stand** M (*old*) spinsterhood; **Jung|fern|zeu|gung** F (*Biol*) parthenogenesis

Jung|fil|mer(in) M(F) young film maker; **die deutschen ~** the young German film makers

Jung|frau F virgin; (*Astron, Astrol*) Virgo *no art*; **ich bin ~** I am a virgin; (*Astrol*) I am (a) Virgo; **die ~ Maria** the Virgin Mary; **die Heilige ~** the Blessed *or* Holy Virgin; **die ~ von Orléans** Joan of Arc, the Maid of Orleans; **dazu bin ich gekommen wie die ~ zum Kind(e)** it just fell into my hands → **eisern** ADJ **a**

jung|fräu|lich ['jʊŋfrɔylɪç] ADJ *Mädchen, Schnee* virgin; (*liter*) *Seele* pure, innocent

Jung|fräu|lich|keit F **-,** *no pl* (*von Mädchen, Schnee*) virginity; (*liter: von Seele*) purity, innocence

Jung|ge|sel|le M bachelor

Jung|ge|sel|len-: Jung|ge|sel|len|bu|de F (*inf*) bachelor pad (*inf*); **Jung|ge|sel|len|da|sein** NT bachelor's life; **Jung|ge|sel|len|haus|halt** M bachelor('s) household *or* pad; **Jung|ge|sel|len|le|ben** NT bachelor's life; **Jung|ge|sel|len|tum** ['jʊŋɡəzɛləntuːm] NT **-s,** *no pl* bachelorhood, bachelordom; **Jung|ge|sel|len|wirt|schaft** F **,** *no pl* (*inf*) bachelor squalor; **Jung|ge|sel|len|woh|nung** F bachelor flat (*Brit*) *or* apartment; **Jung|ge|sel|len|zeit** F bachelor days *pl*

Jung|ge|sel|lin F single woman

Jung|leh|rer(in) M(F) student teacher

Jüng|ling ['jʏŋlɪŋ] M **-s, -e** (*liter, hum*) youth

Jüng|lings-: Jüng|lings|al|ter NT (*liter*) youth; **jüng|lings|haft** ADJ (*geh*) youthful, boyish

Jung-: Jung|mä|del NT (*dated*) young girl; **Jung|mann** M *pl* **-männer** (*dated*) young man; **Jung|pflan|ze** F young plant, seedling; **Jung|so|zi|a|list(in)** M(F) Young Socialist

jüngst [jʏŋst] ADV (*geh*) recently, lately; **der ~ verstorbene ...** the late ...; **der ~ erlassene Befehl** the recent decree

Jung|stein|zeit F Neolithic age, New Stone Age

jüngs|tens ['jʏŋstns] ADV (*old, liter*) = **jüngst**

jüngs|te(r, s) ['jʏŋstə] ADJ **a** *superl von* **jung** youngest **b** *Werk, Schöpfung, Ereignis* latest, (most) recent; *Zeit, Vergangenheit* recent; **in der ~n Zeit** recently; **ein Ausdruck aus der ~n Zeit** a recent expression; **das Jüngste Gericht** the Last Judgement; **der Jüngste Tag** Doomsday, the Day of Judgement; **man merkt, dass er/sie nicht mehr der/die Jüngste ist** you can tell that

he/she is not as young as he/she used to be; **sie ist auch nicht mehr die Jüngste** she's no (spring) chicken (*inf*)

Jung-: Jung|stier M young steer; **Jung|tier** NT young animal; **Jung|un|ter|neh|mer(in)** M(F) young entrepreneur, young businessman/-woman; **Jung|ver|hei|ra|te|te(r)** [-fɛɐ-hairatətə] MF *decl as adj* newly-wed; **jung|ver|mählt** [-fɛɛmɛːlt] ADJ (*geh*) newly-wed, recently married; **die Jungvermählten** the newly-weds; **Jung|ver|mähl|te(r)** MF *decl as adj* (*form*) **die (beiden) ~n** the newly-weds *pl*, the young couple *sing*; **Jung|vieh** NT young cattle *pl*; **Jung|wäh|ler(in)** M(F) young voter; **Jung|wild** NT young game

Ju|ni ['juːni] M **-(s), -s** June → *auch* **März**

Ju|ni|kä|fer M chafer

ju|ni|or ['juːnioːɐ] ADJ **Franz Schulz ~** Franz Schulz, Junior

Ju|ni|or ['juːnioːɐ] M **-s, Junioren** [juːˈnioːrən] **a** (*usu hum:* = *Sohn*) junior; **wie gehts dem ~?** how's junior? **b** (*auch* **Juniorchef**) son of the boss; (= *Sohn des Vorsitzenden*) son of the chair (-man); **kann ich mal den ~(chef) sprechen?** can I speak to Mr X junior? **c** *usu pl* (*Sport*) junior

Ju|ni|or|chef M boss's son, son of the boss

Ju|ni|or|che|fin F boss's daughter, daughter of the boss

Ju|ni|o|rin [juːˈnioːrɪn] F **-, -nen** → **Junior c**

Ju|ni|or-: Ju|ni|or|part|ner(in) M(F) junior partner; **Ju|ni|or|pass** ▲ M (*Rail*) ≈ young person's railcard (*Brit*), ≈ youth railroad pass (*US*)

Junk-Bond ['dʒaŋkbɔnd] M **-s, -s, Junk|bond** M **-s, -s** (*Fin*) junk bond

Jun|ker ['jʊŋkɐ] M **-s, -** (*Hist*) squire; (*preußisch*) Junker

Jun|ker|tum ['jʊŋkɐtuːm] NT **-s,** *no pl* squirarchy; (*in Preußen*) Junkerdom

Junk|food ['dʒaŋkfuːd] NT **-s, -s, Junk Food** NT **-s, -s** (*inf*) junk food

Jun|kie ['dʒaŋki] M **-s, -s** (*inf*) junkie (*inf*)

Junk|tim ['jʊŋktɪm] NT **-s, -s** (*Pol:* = *Paket*) package (deal); **zwischen X und Y besteht ein ~** X is dependent on Y

Ju|no ['juːno] M **-(s), -s** (*esp Comm*) June

Jun|ta ['xʊnta, 'jʊnta] F **-, Junten** [-tn] (*Pol*) junta

Jupe [ʒyːp] M **-s, -s** (*Sw*) skirt

Ju|pi|ter ['juːpitɐ] M **-s** Jupiter

Ju|pi|ter|lam|pe® F klieg light

jur. *abbr von* **juristisch**

Ju|ra¹ ['juːra] M **-s,** *no pl* (*Geol, Geog*) Jura (Mountains) *pl*

Ju|ra² *no art* (*Univ*) law

Ju|ras|si|er [juˈrasiɐ] M **-s, -, Ju|ras|si|e|rin** [-iərɪn] F **-, -nen** person from the Canton of Jura

ju|ras|sisch [juˈrasɪʃ] ADJ (*Geol*) Jurassic; (= *aus Kanton Jura*) of the Canton of Jura

Ju|ra|stu|di|um NT study of law; **das ~ dauert acht Semester** the law degree (course) takes four years

ju|ri|disch [juˈriːdɪʃ] ADJ, ADV (*old, Aus*) = **juristisch**

Ju|ris|dik|ti|on [jurɪsdɪkˈtsioːn] F **-,** *no pl* (*geh*) administration of justice; (*rare:* = *Gerichtshoheit*) jurisdiction

Ju|ris|pru|denz [jurɪspruˈdɛnts] F **-,** *no pl* (*geh*) jurisprudence

Ju|rist [juˈrɪst] M **-en, -en, Ju|ris|tin** [-ˈrɪstɪn] F **-, -nen** jurist, legal eagle (*hum inf*); (= *Student*) law student

Ju|ris|ten|deutsch NT , **Ju|ris|ten|spra|che** F , *no pl* legalese (*pej*), legal jargon *or* language

Ju|ris|te|rei [jurɪstəˈrai] F **-,** *no pl* (*inf*) law

ju|ris|tisch [juˈrɪstɪʃ] ADJ legal; *Problem etc auch* juridical (*form*); *Studium auch* law *attr*; **die ~e Fakultät** the Faculty of Law; **eine ~e Person** a legal entity, a corporation, a corporate body ADV legally; **~ denken** to think in legal terms; **etw ~ betrachten** to consider the legal aspects of sth; **etw ~ bewerten** to assess sth from a legal point of view

Ju|ror ['juːroːɐ] M **-s, Juroren** [-ˈroːrən], **Ju|ro|rin** [-ˈroːrɪn] F **-, -nen** juror, member of the jury; (*bei Wettbewerb*) member of the jury, judge, adjudicator

Jur|te ['jʊrtə] F **-, -n** yurt

Ju|ry [ʒyˈriː, ˈʒyːri] F **-, -s** jury *sing or pl*; (*bei Wettbewerb auch*) judges *pl*, adjudicators *pl*

Jus¹ [ʒyː] F OR M OR NT **-,** *no pl* **a** (= *Bratensaft*) gravy; (*geliert*) dripping **b** (*Sw:* = *Fruchtsaft*) juice

Jus² [juːs] NT **-, Jura** ['juːra] (*Aus, Sw:* = *Univ*) law

just [jʊst] ADV (*old*) precisely, exactly, just; **~ gekommen** just come

jus|tier|bar [jʊsˈtiːɐbaːɐ] ADJ (*Tech*) adjustable

jus|tie|ren [jʊsˈtiːrən] *ptp* **justiert** VT to adjust; *Gewehr, Zielfernrohr etc auch* to collimate (*form*); *Münzen auch* to weight; (*Typ, Comput*) to justify

Jus|tier|schrau|be F (*Tech*) adjusting screw

Jus|tie|rung F **-, -en** adjustment; (*von Gewehr, Zielfernrohr auch*) collimation (*form*); (*von Münzen auch*) weighting; (*Typ, Comput*) justification

Jus|tier|waa|ge F adjusting balance

Jus|ti|tia [jʊsˈtiːtsia] F **-s** Justice; (*fig*) the law

jus|ti|ti|a|bel [jʊstiˈtsiaːbl] ADJ (*geh*) litigable

Jus|ti|ti|ar [jʊstiˈtsiaːɐ] M **-s, -e, Jus|ti|ti|a|rin** [-ˈtsiaːrɪn] F **-, -nen** lawyer, legal adviser

Jus|tiz [jʊsˈtiːts] F **-,** *no pl* (*als Prinzip*) justice; (*als Institution*) judiciary; (= *die Gerichte*) courts *pl*

Jus|tiz-: Jus|tiz|be|am|te(r) M *decl as adj*, **Jus|tiz|be|am|tin** F judicial officer; **Jus|tiz|be|hör|de** F legal *or* judicial authority; **Jus|tiz|ge|walt** F judiciary (power); **Jus|tiz|ho|heit** F legal sovereignty; **Jus|tiz|irr|tum** M miscarriage of justice, judicial error (*esp US*); **Jus|tiz|mi|nis|ter(in)** M(F) minister of justice, justice minister; **Jus|tiz|mi|nis|te|ri|um** NT ministry of justice, ≈ Department of Justice (*US*); **Jus|tiz|mord** M judicial murder; **Jus|tiz|pa|last** M palace of justice; **Jus|tiz|ver|wal|tung** F administration of justice; **Jus|tiz|voll|zugs|an|stalt** F (*form*) place of detention

Ju|te ['juːtə] F **-,** *no pl* jute

Ju|te|ta|sche ['juːtə-] F jute *or* burlap bag

Jüt|land ['jyːtlant] NT **-s** (*Geog*) Jutland

ju|ve|nil [juveˈniːl] ADJ (*geh*) juvenile

Ju|wel¹ [juˈveːl] M OR NT **-s, -en** jewel, gem; **~en** (= *Schmuck*) jewellery (*Brit*), jewelry (*US*)

Ju|wel² NT **-s, -e** (*fig*) jewel, gem

Ju|we|lier [juveˈliːɐ] M **-s, -e, Ju|we|lie|rin** [-ˈliːrɪn] F **-, -nen** jeweller (*Brit*), jeweler (*US*); (= *Geschäft*) jewel(l)er's (shop)

Ju|we|lier-: Ju|we|lier|ge|schäft NT jeweller's (*Brit*) *or* jeweler's (*US*) (shop); **Ju|we|lier|wa|ren** PL jewellery (*Brit*), jewelry (*US*)

Jux [jʊks] M **-es, -e** (*inf*) **etw aus ~ tun/sagen** to do/say sth as a joke *or* in fun; **etw aus lauter ~ und Tollerei tun** to do sth out of sheer high spirits *or* for sheer fun; **sich** (*dat*) **einen ~ aus etw machen** to make a joke (out) of sth

ju|xen ['jʊksn] VI (*inf*) to joke

ju|xig ['jʊksɪç] ADJ (*inf*) funny

jwd [jɔtveːˈdeː] ADV (*hum*) in the back of beyond (*Brit*), in the middle of nowhere; (= *weit entfernt*) miles out (*inf*)

K

K, k [kaː] NT -, - K, k

Ka|a|ba ['kaːaba] F -, *no pl* Kaaba, Caaba

Ka|ba|le [ka'baːlə] F -, -**n** (*old*) cabal (*old*)

Ka|ba|rett [kaba'rɛt, 'kabarɛt, -rɛ] NT -s, -e *or* -s **a** cabaret; (= *Darbietung*) cabaret (show); **ein politisches ~** a satirical political revue, a political satire **b** (= *Servierplatte*) serving dish (*divided into sections*)

Ka|ba|rett|ist [kabarɛ'tɪst] M -en, -en, **Ka|ba|rett|is|tin** [-'tɪstɪn] F -, -**nen** cabaret artist

ka|ba|rett|is|tisch [kabarɛ'tɪstɪʃ] ADJ cabaret *attr*; (*politisch-satirisch*) political revue *attr*

Ka|bäus|chen [ka'bɔysçən] NT -s, - (*inf*) (= *Zimmer*) cubbyhole (*inf*); (= *Laube*) hut, cabin

Kab|ba|la ['kabala] F - (*Rel*) cabbala

Kab|be|lei [kabə'laɪ] F -, -en (*inf*) bickering, squabbling

kab|be|lig ['kabəlɪç] ADJ *Meer* choppy

kab|beln ['kabln] VIR (*inf*) to bicker, to squabble

Ka|bel ['kaːbl] NT -s, - **a** (*Elec*) wire; (*von Elektrogeräten*) wire, flex (*Brit*); (= *Telefonkabel*) flex (*Brit*), cord; (= *Strom- oder Telegrafenleitung*) cable **b** (*old Naut*: = *Tau*) rope; (= *Drahtseil*) cable **c** (*old*: = *Telegramm*) cable(gram)

Kabel-: Ka|bel|an|schluss ▲ M (*TV*) cable connection; **~ bekommen** to get cable (TV); **Ka|bel|baum** M (*Elec*) harness; **Ka|bel|be|richt** M cabled report; **Ka|bel|fern|se|hen** NT cable television

Ka|bel|jau ['kaːbljaʊ] M -s, -e *or* -s cod

Ka|bel-: Ka|bel|klem|me F (*Tech*) cable clip *or* clamp; **Ka|bel|län|ge** F (*Naut*) cable, cable's length; **Ka|bel|le|ger** [-leːgɐ] M -s, - (*Naut*) cable layer; **Ka|bel|man|tel** M cable covering

ka|beln ['kaːbln] VTI to cable

Ka|bel-: Ka|bel|netz NT (*TV*) cable network; **Ka|bel|trom|mel** F cable drum *or* reel; **Ka|bel|tu|ner** M (*TV*) cable decoder *or* tuner

Ka|bi|ne [ka'biːnə] F -, -**n** (= *Umkleidekabine*, *Anprobierkabine*, *Duschkabine*) cubicle; (*Naut*, *Aviat*, *von Kran*) cabin; (= *Vorführkabine*) projection room; (= *Seilbahnkabine*) car

Ka|bi|nen-: Ka|bi|nen|bahn F cable railway; **Ka|bi|nen|kof|fer** M cabin trunk; **Ka|bi|nen|per|so|nal** NT (*Aviat*) cabin crew; **Ka|bi|nen|rol|ler** M bubble car

Ka|bi|nett¹ [kabi'nɛt] NT -s, -e **a** (*Pol*) cabinet **b** (*für Kunstsammlungen*) gallery; (= *Schrank*) cabinet **c** (= *Zimmer*) (*Aus*: = *kleines Zimmer*) closet; (*old*: = *Arbeitszimmer*) cabinet

Ka|bi|nett² M -s, -e (= *Wein*) high-quality German white wine

Ka|bi|netts-: Ka|bi|netts|be|schluss ▲ M cabinet decision; **Ka|bi|netts|bil|dung** F formation of a/the cabinet; **Ka|bi|netts|fra|ge** F (*rare*) = **Vertrauensfrage**; **Ka|bi|netts|jus|tiz** F interference in the course of justice by a sovereign; **Ka|bi|netts|mit|glied** NT cabinet member, member of the cabinet

Ka|bi|nett|stück NT **a** (*old*: *einer Sammlung*) showpiece, pièce de résistance **b** (*fig*) masterstroke

Ka|bi|netts|um|bil|dung F cabinet reshuffle

Ka|bi|nett|wein M high-quality German white wine

Ka|bis ['kaːbɪs] M -, *no pl* (*Sw*, *S Ger*) = **Weißkohl**

Kab|rio ['kaːbrio] NT -(s), -s (*inf*) convertible

Kab|ri|o|lett [kabrio'lɛt, (*Aus*, *S Ger*) kabrio'leː] NT -s, -s **a** (*Aut*) convertible **b** (*Hist*) cabriolet

Ka|buff [ka'bʊf] NT -s, -e *or* -s (*inf*) (poky) little corner

Ka|chel ['kaxl] F -, -**n** (glazed) tile; **etw mit ~n auslegen** to tile sth, to cover sth with *or* in tiles

ka|cheln ['kaxln] VT to tile

Ka|chel|ofen M tiled stove

kack|braun ADJ (*sl*) dirty brown

Ka|cke ['kakə] F -, *no pl* **a** (*vulg*) crap (*sl*), shit (*sl*); **dann ist aber die ~ am Dampfen** (*sl*) then the shit really will hit the fan (*sl*) **b** (*sl*: = *Mist*) crap (*inf*); **so 'ne ~** shit (*sl*)

ka|cken ['kakn] VI (*vulg*) to crap (*sl*), to shit (*sl*)

ka|ckig ['kakɪç] ADJ (*sl*) *Farbe* shitty (*inf*)

Ka|da|ver [ka'daːvɐ] M -s, - carcass

Ka|da|ver|ge|hor|sam M (*pej*) blind or slavish obedience

Ka|denz [ka'dɛnts] F -, -en cadence; (= *Improvisation*) cadenza

Ka|der ['kaːdɐ] M -s, - (*Mil*, *Pol*) cadre; (*Sport*) squad; (= *Fachleute*) group of specialists; (= *Fachmann*) specialist; (*Sw*: = *Vorgesetzte*) management

Ka|der-: Ka|der|lei|ter(in) M(F) (*Hist*) personnel officer; **Ka|der|schmie|de** F , *no pl* (*pej*) élite school

Ka|dett [ka'dɛt] M -en, -en, **Ka|det|tin** [-'dɛtɪn] F -, -**nen** (*Mil*) cadet

Ka|det|ten-: Ka|det|ten|an|stalt F cadet school; **Ka|det|ten|schul|schiff** NT naval (cadet) training ship

Ka|di ['kaːdi] M -s, -s (*dated inf*) beak (*inf*); **jdn vor den ~ schleppen** to take sb to court; **zum ~ laufen** to go to court

Kad|mi|um ['katmiʊm] NT -s, *no pl* cadmium

Kä|fer ['kɛːfɐ] M -s, - **a** beetle (*auch inf*: *VW*) **b** (*dated inf*: = *Mädchen*) bird (*esp Brit inf*), chick (*esp US inf*), babe (*inf*); **ein flotter ~** a nice bit of skirt (*Brit inf*), a real babe (*inf*)

Kaff [kaf] NT -s, -s *or* -e (*inf*) dump (*inf*), hole (*inf*)

Kaf|fee¹ ['kafe, ka'feː] M -s, -s **a** coffee; **zwei ~, bitte!** two coffees, please; **~ mit Milch** white coffee (*Brit*), coffee with milk; **schwarzer ~** black coffee; **~ verkehrt** (*dated*) white coffee (*Brit*) (*made with hot milk*), coffee with hot milk; **~ kochen** to make coffee; **das ist kalter ~** (*inf*) that's old hat (*inf*) **b** *no pl* (= *Nachmittagskaffee*) ≈ (afternoon) tea (*Brit*), (afternoon) coffee and cake; **~ und Kuchen** coffee and cakes, ≈ afternoon tea (*Brit*); **jdn zu ~ und Kuchen einladen** to invite sb for *or* to coffee and cakes or (afternoon) tea (*Brit*)

Kaf|fee² NT -s, -s (*old*: = *Café*) café

Kaffee-: Kaf|fee|au|to|mat M coffee machine *or* dispenser; **Kaf|fee|boh|ne** F coffee bean; **kaf|fee|braun** ADJ coffee-coloured (*Brit*), coffee-colored (*US*); **Kaf|fee-Er|satz** M coffee substitute; **Kaf|fee-Ex|trakt** M coffee essence; **Kaf|fee|fahrt** F day trip; (= *Verkaufsfahrt*) promotional trip (*during which passengers are served coffee and offered goods to buy*); **Kaf|fee|fil|ter** M coffee filter; (*inf*: = *Filterpapier*) filter (paper); **Kaf|fee|ge|schirr** NT coffee set; **Kaf|fee|haus** NT café; **Kaf|fee|haus|mu|sik** F (*pej*) palm court music; **Kaf|fee|kan|ne** F coffeepot; **Kaf|fee|klatsch** M , *no pl* (*inf*), **Kaf|fee|kränz|chen** NT coffee klatsch (*US*), ≈ coffee morning (*Brit*); **ich treffe mich mit meinen Freundinnen zu einem ~** I'm meeting some friends for a chat over (a cup of) coffee *or* tea; **Kaf|fee|löf|fel** M coffee spoon; **Kaf|fee|ma|schi|ne** F coffee machine; **Kaf|fee|mi|schung** F blended coffee; **Kaf|fee|müh|le** F coffee grinder; **Kaf|fee|müt|ze** F cosy (*Brit*) or cozy (*US*, *for coffeepot*); **Kaf|fee|pau|se** F coffee break; **Kaf|fee|rös|ter** [-røːstɐ, -rœstɐ] M -s, - coffee roaster; **Kaf|fee|sah|ne** F (coffee) cream; **Kaf|fee|satz** M coffee grounds *pl*; **aus dem ~ wahrsagen** *or* **lesen** to read (the) tea leaves; **Kaf|fee|ser|vice** [-zɛrviːs] NT coffee set; **Kaf|fee|sor|te** F type *or* sort of coffee; **Kaf|fee|strauch** M coffee tree; **Kaf|fee|stu|be** F coffee shop; **Kaf|fee|tan|te** F (*hum*) coffee addict; (*in Café*) old biddy; **Kaf|fee|tas|se** F coffee cup; **Kaf|fee|tisch** M (= *Frühstückstisch*) breakfast table; (*nachmittags*) (afternoon) tea table (*Brit*), serving table (*US*); **Kaf|fee|wär|mer** [-vɛrmɐ] M -s, - cosy (*Brit*) or cozy (*US*, *for coffeepot*); **Kaf|fee|was|ser** NT , *no pl* water for coffee, coffee water; **ich habe das ~ schon aufgesetzt** I've just put the kettle on; **Kaf|fee|wei|ßer** [-vaisə] M , *no pl* coffee whitener (*Brit*) or creamer (*US*)

Kaf|fer¹ ['kafe] M -s, - (*pej inf*: = *dummer Kerl*) thickhead (*inf*), duffer (*inf*)

Kaf|fer² ['kafe] M -n, -n, **Kaf|fe|rin** [-ərɪn] F -, -**nen** kaffir; (*pej inf*) nigger (*pej*)

Kä|fig ['kɛːfɪç] M -s, -e [-gə] cage; **sie sitzt in einem goldenen ~** (*fig*) she is just a bird in a gilded cage

Kä|fig-: Kä|fig|hal|tung F caging; **Kä|fig|vo|gel** M cage bird

kaf|ka|esk [kafka'ɛsk] ADJ Kafkaesque

Kaf|tan ['kaftan] M -s, -e caftan

kahl [kaːl] ADJ *Mensch*, *Kopf* bald; (= *kahl geschoren*) shaved, shorn; *Vogel* bald, featherless; *Wand*, *Raum* bare; *Pflanze*, *Baum* bare, leafless; *Landschaft*, *Berge* barren, bleak; **eine ~e Stelle** a bald patch; **~ werden** (*Mensch*) to go bald; (*Baum*) to lose its leaves; **~ geschoren** (*Kopf*) shaven, shorn

Kahl-: Kahl|fraß M defoliation; **kahl fres|sen** ▲ VT *irreg* to strip bare; *Ernte* to destroy completely; **Kahl|frost** M black frost; **kahl|ge|scho|ren** △ ADJ = **kahl**; **Kahl|heit** F -, *no pl* (*von Mensch*, *Kopf*, *Vogel*) baldness; (*von Wand*, *Raum*) bareness; (*von Pflanze*, *Baum*) bareness, leaflessness; (*von Landschaft*, *Berg*) barrenness; **Kahl|kopf** M bald head; (= *Mensch*) bald person; **ein ~ sein** to be bald; **kahl|köp|fig** ADJ baldheaded; **Kahl|köp|fig|keit** [-kœpfɪçkait] F

-, *no pl* baldness; **kahl sche|ren** ▲ VT *irreg Schafe* to shear; *Hecken* to cut right back; **jdn ~** to shave sb's head; **Kahl|schlag** M **a** (= *abgeholzte Fläche*) clearing **b** (= *Tätigkeit*) deforestation **c** (*inf*) (**Aktion**) ~ (= *Entlassungen*) axing; (= *Abriss*) demolition; **kahl schla|gen** ▲ VT *irreg* to deforest, to clear; **Kahl|wild** NT (= *geweihlose, weibliche Tiere*) does *pl*; (= *geweihlose Kälber*) fawns *pl*

Kahm [kaːm] M -(e)s, *no pl* mould (*Brit*), mold (*US*)

kah|mig ['kaːmɪç] ADJ mouldy (*Brit*), moldy (*US*)

Kahn [kaːn] M -(e)s, ⸚e ['kɛːnə] **a** (small) boat; (= *Stechkahn*) punt; ~ **fahren** to go boating/punting **b** (= *Lastschiff*) barge; **ein alter ~** (*inf*) an old tub (*inf*) **c** (*inf*) (= *Bett*) bed, pit (*inf*); (*dated*: = *Gefängnis*) jug (*dated inf*); (*Ftbl*: = *Tor*) net **d Kähne** PL (= *große Schuhe*) clodhoppers *pl* (*inf*)

Kahn|fahrt F row; (*in Stechkahn*) punt

Kai [kai] M -s, -e *or* -s quay; (= *Uferdamm auch*) waterfront

Kai|an|la|ge F quayside

Kai|man ['kaiman] M -s, -e (*Zool*) cayman

Kai|mau|er F quay wall

Kains|mal ['kains-] NT *pl* -**male, Kains|zei|chen** NT (= *Stigma*) mark of Cain

Kai|ro ['kairo] NT -s Cairo

Kai|ser ['kaizɐ] M -s, - emperor; **der deutsche ~** the German Emperor, the Kaiser; **des ~s neue Kleider** (*fig*) the emperor's new clothes; **wo nichts ist, hat der ~ sein Recht verloren** (*Prov*) you can't get blood from a stone; **gebt dem ~, was des ~s ist!** (*Bibl*) render unto Caesar the things which are Caesar's; (**da,**) **wo selbst der ~ zu Fuß hingeht** (*dated hum*) the smallest room (in the house) (*hum*); **das ist ein Streit um des ~s Bart** that's just splitting hairs; **er kommt sich vor wie der ~ von China** (*inf*) he thinks he's the king of the castle, he thinks he's God → *auch* **Kaiserin**

Kai|ser-: Kai|ser|ad|ler M imperial eagle; **Kai|ser|haus** NT imperial family

Kai|se|rin ['kaizərɪn] F -, -**nen** empress → *auch* **Kaiser**

Kai|se|rin|mut|ter F *pl* -**mütter** dowager empress

Kai|ser|kro|ne F **a** imperial crown **b** (*Bot*) crown imperial

kai|ser|lich ['kaizɐlɪç] ADJ imperial; **diese Besitzungen waren früher ~** these possessions used to belong to the Emperor; **Seine Kaiserliche Majestät/Hoheit** His Imperial Majesty/Highness ADV ~ **gesinnt** monarchistic, imperialistic

Kai|ser|li|che(r) ['kaizɐlɪçɐ] MF *decl as adj* Imperialist

kai|ser|lich-kö|nig|lich ['kaizɐlɪçˈkøːnɪklɪç] ADJ imperial and royal (*pertaining to the Dual Monarchy of Austro-Hungary*)

Kai|ser-: Kai|ser|pfalz F imperial palace; **Kai|ser|reich** NT empire; **Kai|ser|schmar|ren** M , **Kai|ser|schmarrn** M (*Aus*) sugared, cut-up pancake with raisins; **Kai|ser|schnitt** M Caesarean (section); **Kai|ser|sem|mel** M (*S Ger, Aus*) bread roll (*with a raised pattern on top*), kaiser roll (*US*); **Kai|ser|stadt** F imperial city

Kai|ser|tum ['kaizɐtuːm] NT -s, **Kaisertümer** [-tyːmɐ] **a** (= *Regierungsform, Reich*) Empire **b** (= *Amt*) emperorship

Kai|ser-: Kai|ser|wet|ter NT (*dated*) magnificent sunshine; **Kai|ser|wür|de** F **a** (= *Ehre*) honour (*Brit*) *or* honor (*US*) *or* dignity of an emperor **b** (= *Amt*) emperorship

Ka|jak ['kaːjak] M OR NT -s, -s kayak

Ka|jal [ka'jaːl] M -, *no pl* kohl

Ka|jal|stift M kohl eye pencil

Ka|je ['kaːjə] F -, -n (*N Ger*) quay; (= *Uferdamm auch*) waterfront

---

Ka|jüt|boot NT cabin boat

Ka|jü|te [ka'jyːtə] F -, -n cabin; (*größer auch*) stateroom

Ka|ka|du ['kakadu] M -s, -s cockatoo

Ka|kao [ka'kaːo, ka'kau] M -s, -s cocoa; **jdn durch den ~ ziehen** (*inf*) (= *veralbern*) to make fun of sb, to take the mickey out of sb (*Brit inf*); (= *boshaft reden*) to run *or* do sb down (*Brit*), to put sb down

Ka|kao-: Ka|kao|boh|ne F cocoa bean; **Ka|kao|pul|ver** NT cocoa powder; **Ka|kao|strauch** M cacao palm

ka|keln ['kaːkln] VI (*inf*) to chat, to blether (*Brit inf*), to blather

Ka|ker|lak ['kaːkɛlak] M -s *or* -en, -en cockroach

Ka|ki ['kaːki] F -, -s (= *Frucht*) kaki; (= *Baum auch*) Japanese persimmon

Ka|ko|pho|nie [kakofo'niː] F -, -n [-'niːən], **Ka|ko|fo|nie** ▲ F -, -n [-'niːən] (*geh*) cacophony

Kak|tee [kak'teː] F -, -n [-'teːən], **Kak|tus** ['kaktʊs] M -, **Kakteen** [-'teːən] *or* (*inf*) -**se** cactus

Ka|lab|re|ser [kala'breːzɐ] M -s, - slouch hat

Ka|lab|ri|en [ka'laːbriən] NT -s Calabria

Ka|la|mi|tät [kalami'tɛːt] F -, -en (*geh*) calamity; (= *heikle Lage*) predicament

Ka|lan|der [ka'landɐ] M -s, - (*Tech*) calender

ka|lan|dern [ka'landɐn] *ptp* **kalandert** VT (*Tech*) to calender

Ka|lasch|ni|kow [ka'laʃnikɔf] F -, -s kalashnikov

Ka|lau|er ['kaːlauɐ] M -s, - corny joke; (= *Wortspiel*) corny pun; (= *alter Witz*) old chestnut

ka|lau|ern ['kaːlauɐn] VI (*inf*) to joke; (= *Wortspiele machen*) to pun

Kalb [kalp] NT -(e)s, ⸚er ['kɛlbɐ] **a** calf; (*von Rehwild auch*) fawn ~ **golden ADJ b** (*inf*: = *Mädchen*) silly young girl *or* thing

Kälb|chen ['kɛlpçən] NT -s, - *dim von* Kalb

kal|ben ['kalbn] VI (*Kuh, Gletscher*) to calve

Käl|ber|mast ['kɛlbɐ-] F (*Agr*) calf-fattening

kal|bern ['kalbɛn], **käl|bern** ['kɛlbɐn] VI (*inf*) to fool *or* mess about *or* around (*inf*)

Käl|ber|ne(s) ['kɛlbɛnə] NT *decl as adj* (*S Ger, Aus*) veal

Kalb-: Kalb|fell NT = **Kalbsfell; Kalb|fleisch** NT veal; **Kalb|le|der** NT calfskin

Kälb|lein ['kɛlplain] NT -s, - *dim von* Kalb

Kalbs-: Kalbs|bra|ten M roast veal; **Kalbs|brust** F (*Cook*) breast of veal; **Kalbs|fell** NT **a** (= *Fell*) calfskin **b** (*old*: = *Trommel*) drum; **Kalbs|hach|se** F , **Kalbs|ha|xe** F (*Cook*) knuckle of veal; **Kalbs|keu|le** F leg of veal; **Kalbs|le|ber** F calves' liver; **Kalbs|le|der** NT calfskin; **Kalbs|schnit|zel** NT veal cutlet

Kal|dau|ne [kal'daunə] F -, -n entrails *pl*

Ka|le|bas|se [kale'basə] F -, -n calabash

Ka|le|do|ni|en [kale'doːniən] NT -s (*liter*) Caledonia

Ka|lei|do|skop [kalaido'skoːp] NT -s, -e kaleidoscope

ka|lei|do|sko|pisch [kalaido'skoːpɪʃ] ADJ kaleidoscopic

ka|len|da|risch [kalɛn'daːrɪʃ] ADJ according to the calendar, calendrical (*spec*)

Ka|len|da|ri|um [kalɛn'daːriʊm] NT -s, **Kalendarien** [-riən] (*geh, Eccl*) calendar

Ka|len|der [ka'lɛndɐ] M -s, - calendar; (= *Taschenkalender*) diary; **etw im ~ rot anstreichen** to make sth a red-letter day

Ka|len|der-: Ka|len|der|blatt NT page of a/the calendar; **Ka|len|der|block** M *pl* -**blöcke** *or* -**blocks** day-by-day calendar; **Ka|len|der|jahr** NT calendar year; **Ka|len|der|mo|nat** M calendar month; **Ka|len|der|spruch** M calendar motto; **Ka|len|der|tag** M calendar day; **Ka|len|der|wo|che** F calendar week

---

Ka|le|sche [ka'lɛʃə] F -, -n (*Hist*) barouche

Kal|fak|ter [kal'faktɐ] M -s, -, **Kal|fak|tor** [kal'faktoːɐ] M -s, **Kalfaktoren a** (*old*: = *Heizer*) boilerman, stoker **b** (= *allgemeiner Gehilfe*) odd-jobman

kal|fa|tern [kal'faːtɐn] *ptp* **kalfatert** VTI (*Naut*) to caulk

Ka|li ['kaːli] NT -s, -s potash

Ka|li|ber [ka'liːbɐ] NT -s, - (*lit, fig*) calibre (*Brit*), caliber (*US*); (*zum Messen*) calibrator

Ka|li-: Ka|li|berg|werk NT potash mine; **Ka|li|dün|ger** M potash fertilizer

Ka|lif [ka'liːf] M -en, -en caliph

Ka|li|fat [kali'faːt] NT -(e)s, -e caliphate

Ka|li|for|ni|en [kali'fɔrniən] NT -s California

ka|li|for|nisch [kali'fɔrnɪʃ] ADJ Californian

ka|li|hal|tig ADJ containing potassium

Ka|li|ko ['kaliko] M -s, -s calico; (*für Buchbinderei*) cloth

Ka|li-: Ka|li|sal|pe|ter M saltpetre (*Brit*), saltpeter (*US*); **Ka|li|salz** NT potassium salt

Ka|li|um ['kaːliʊm] NT -s, *no pl* (*abbr* **K**) potassium

Ka|li|um|per|man|ga|nat ['kaːliʊmpermaŋga'naːt] NT -s, *no pl* (*Chem*) potassium permanganate

Kalk [kalk] M -(e)s, -e lime; (*zum Tünchen*) whitewash; (*Anat*) calcium; **gebrannter ~** quicklime; **gelöschter ~** slaked lime; **Wände/Decken mit ~ bewerfen** to whitewash walls/ceilings; **bei ihm rieselt schon der ~** (*inf*) he's going a bit gaga (*Brit inf*), he's losing his marbles (*inf*)

Kalk-: kalk|ar|tig ADJ chalky, calcareous (*form*); **Kalk|bo|den** M chalky soil; **Kalk|bren|ne|rei** F lime works *sing or pl*

kal|ken ['kalkn] VT **a** (= *tünchen*) to whitewash **b** (*Agr*) to lime

Kalk-: Kalk|er|de F chalky soil; **Kalk|gru|be** F lime pit; **kalk|hal|tig** ADJ *Boden* chalky; *Wasser* hard; **Kalk|man|gel** M (*Med*) calcium deficiency; (*von Boden*) lime deficiency; **Kalk|ofen** M limekiln; **Kalk|schie|fer** M calcareous slate; (*Typ*) lithostone; **Kalk|stein** M limestone; **Kalk|stein|bruch** M limestone quarry

Kal|kül [kal'kyːl] M OR NT -s, -e **a** calculation *usu pl* **b** (*Math*) calculus

Kal|ku|la|ti|on [kalkula'tsioːn] F -, -en calculation; (= *Kostenberechnung*) costing

Kal|ku|la|tor [kalku'laːtoːɐ] M -s, **Kalkulatoren** [-'toːrən], **Kal|ku|la|to|rin** [-'toːrɪn] F -, -**nen a** (*als Beruf*) cost estimator **b** (= *berechnender Mensch*) calculator, calculating person

kal|ku|la|to|risch [kalkula'toːrɪʃ] ADJ arithmetical; (*Fin*) *Kosten* imputed; **~ Methoden** methods of calculation ADV **das ist ~ einwandfrei, aber ...** the figures are perfect, but ...; **eine ~ notwendige Bedingung** a necessary premise for the calculations

kal|ku|lier|bar ADJ calculable

Kal|ku|lier|bar|keit F -, *no pl* calculability

kal|ku|lie|ren [kalku'liːrən] *ptp* **kalkuliert** VT to calculate

Kal|kut|ta [kal'kʊta] NT -s Calcutta

Kal|li|gra|fie ▲ [kaligra'fiː] F -, *no pl* calligraphy

kal|lös [ka'løːs] ADJ (*Med*) callous

Kal|lus ['kalʊs] M -, -se (*Biol, Med*) callus

Kal|me ['kalmə] F -, -n (*Naut*) calm

Kal|men|gür|tel M , **Kal|men|zo|ne** F calm belt *or* zones *pl*

Kal|mück [kal'mʏk] M -en, -en, **Kal|mü|cke** [kal'mʏkə] M -n, -n, **Kal|mü|ckin** F -, -**nen** Kalmu(c)k (*member of Mongol tribe*)

Ka|lo|rie [kalo'riː] F -, -n [-'riːən] calorie

Ka|lo|ri|en-: ka|lo|ri|en|arm ADJ low-calorie ADV **sich ~ ernähren** to have *or* be on a low-calorie diet; **~ essen** to eat low-calorie food; **~ süßen** to use low-calorie sweeteners; **Ka|lo|ri|-**

---

en|be|darf M calorie requirement; **ka|lo|ri-
en|be|wusst ▲** ADJ *Ernährungsweise etc* calorie-
-conscious ADV **sich ~ ernähren** to (only) eat
low-calorie foods, to count one's calories (*inf*);
Ka|lo|ri|en|bom|be F (*inf*) **das ist eine echte
~** it's got about sixty million calories (*inf*); **Ka-
lo|ri|en|ge|halt** M calorie content; **ka|lo|ri|-
en|re|du|ziert** [-redutsiːɐt] ADJ *Mahlzeit* re-
duced-calorie; **~e Kost** reduced calorie food;
ka|lo|ri|en|reich ADJ high-calorie ADV **~ es-
sen** to eat high-calorie food; **sich ~ ernähren** to
have or be on a high-calorie diet, to eat high-
-calorie foods

Ka|lo|ri|me|ter [kalori'meːtɐ] M calorimeter

kalt [kalt] ADJ *comp* **=er** ['kɛltɐ], *superl* **=este(r, s)**
['kɛltəstə] cold; **mir ist/wird ~** I am/I'm getting
cold; **im Kalten** in the cold; **~e Platte** *plate of
cold meats, cheeses, salad etc* **jdm die ~e
Schulter zeigen** to give sb the cold shoulder, to
cold-shoulder sb; **den Sprung ins ~e Wasser
wagen** (*fig*) to jump in at the deep end; **~es
Grausen** or **Entsetzen überkam mich** my blood
ran cold; **der Kalte Krieg** the Cold War; **~er
Krieger** cold warrior; **ein ~er Staatsstreich** a
bloodless coup → **Hundeschnauze, Fuß a, heiß
a, Kaffee a**
ADV *comp* **=er**, *superl* **am =esten ~ schlafen** to
sleep in an unheated room; **~ baden/duschen**
to have a cold bath/to take a cold shower; **etw
~ waschen** to wash sth in cold water; **abends
essen wir ~** we eat a cold meal in the evening;
etw ~ stellen to put sth to chill; **etw ~ lagern**
to store sth cold; **etw ~ bearbeiten** (*Tech*) to
work sth cold; **die Wohnung kostet ~ 500 EUR**
the flat (*Brit*) or apartment costs 500 euros
without heating; **~ rauchen** (*hum*) to have an
unlit cigarette in one's mouth; **da kann ich nur
~ lächeln** (*inf*) that makes me laugh; **~ lächelnd**
(*iro*) cool as you please; **es überlief** or **überrie-
selte ihn ~** cold shivers ran through him; **jdn ~
erwischen** to shock sb

Kalt-: kalt blei|ben ▲ VI *irreg aux sein* (*fig*) to
remain unmoved or impassive; **Kalt|blut** NT
carthorse; **Kalt|blü|ter** [-blyːtɐ] M -s, - (*Zool*)
cold-blooded animal; **kalt|blü|tig** ADJ **a** (*fig*)
Mensch, Mord cold-blooded; (= *gelassen*) *Handlung* cool; *Mensch* cool, cool-headed, calm **b**
(*Zool*) cold-blooded ADV cold-bloodedly; *ermor-
den* in cold blood, cold-bloodedly; **Kalt|blü-
tig|keit** [-blyːtɪçkait] F -, *no pl* (*fig*) (*von Mensch,
Verbrechen*) cold-bloodedness; (= *Gelassenheit*)
(*von Handlung*) cool(ness); (*von Mensch*) cool
(-ness), cool-headedness

Käl|te ['kɛltə] F -, *no pl* **a** (*von Wetter, Material
etc*) cold; (= *Kälteperiode*) cold spell; **die ~ des
Stahls/Steins** *etc* the coldness or cold of the
steel/stone *etc*; **fünf Grad ~** five degrees of frost
or below freezing; **vor ~ zittern** to shiver with
cold; **bei dieser ~** in this cold; **hier ist eine solche ~, dass ...** it is so cold here that ... **b** (*fig*)
coldness, coolness

Käl|te-: Käl|te|an|la|ge F refrigeration plant;
käl|te|be|stän|dig ADJ cold-resistant, resis-
tant to cold; **Käl|te|brü|cke** F (*Build*) trans-
mitter of cold; **die Fugen wirken als ~n** the gaps
introduce cold air; **Käl|te|ein|bruch** M (sud-
den) cold spell; (*für kurze Zeit*) cold snap; **käl|-
te|emp|find|lich** ADJ sensitive to cold;
Mensch auch chilly; **Käl|te|er|zeu|gung** F re-
frigeration; **käl|te|fest** ADJ cold-resistant,
resistant to cold; **Käl|te|ge|fühl** NT feeling of
cold(ness); **Käl|te|grad** M degree of frost;
Käl|te|ma|schi|ne F refrigeration machine;
Käl|te|pe|ri|o|de F cold spell; **Käl|te|pol** M
(*Geog*) cold pole, pole of cold; **käl|te|re|sis|-
tent** ADJ cold-resistant, resistant to cold;
Käl|te|re|sis|tenz F cold resistance, resist-
ance to cold; **Käl|te|schutz** M protection a-
gainst (the) cold; **käl|te|sen|si|bel** ADJ sensi-
tive to cold; *Mensch auch* chilly; **Käl|te|star|re**
F (*Zool*) (cold-induced) torpor; **Käl|te|sturz**
M cold spell; **Käl|te|tech|nik** F refrigeration
technology; **Käl|te|the|ra|pie** F (*Med*) cryo-
therapy; **Käl|te|tod** M **den ~ sterben** to freeze

to death, to die of exposure; (*Erde*) to freeze o-
ver completely; **käl|te|to|le|rant** ADJ tolerant
of cold; **käl|te|un|emp|find|lich** ADJ insensi-
tive to cold; **Käl|te|wel|le** F cold spell

Kalt-: Kalt|front F (*Met*) cold front; **kalt|ge|-
presst ▲** [-gəprest] ADJ *Öl* cold-pressed; **Kalt|-
haus** NT refrigerated glasshouse; **kalt|her|zig**
ADJ cold-hearted; **Kalt|her|zig|keit** [-hertsɪk-
kait] F -, *no pl* cold-heartedness; **kalt|lä-
chelnd** △ ADV → **kalt** ADV; **kalt las|sen ▲**
VT *irreg* (*fig*) **jdn ~** to leave sb cold; **Kalt|leim**
M wood glue; **Kalt|luft** F (*Met*) cold air;
Kalt|luft|front F (*Met*) cold front; **Kalt|luft|-
mas|sen** PL (*Met*) cold air mass(es *pl*);
kalt+ma|chen VT *sep* (*sl*) to do in (*inf*); **Kalt|-
mie|te** F rent exclusive of heating; **Kalt|-
scha|le** F (*Cook*) *cold sweet soup*; **kalt|-
schnäu|zig** [-ʃnɔytsɪç] (*inf*) ADJ **a** (= *gefühllos*)
cold, unfeeling, callous; (= *unverschämt*) insolent; *Kritiker* sarky (*Brit inf*), sarcastic ADV **a** (=
gefühllos) coldly, unfeelingly, callously; (= *unverschämt*) insolently; **~ sagte sie ...** as cool as you
please she said ...; **Kalt|schnäu|zig|keit** F -,
no pl (*inf*) (= *Gefühllosigkeit*) coldness, callousness; (= *Unverschämtheit*) insolence; (*von Kriti-
kern*) sarcasm; **Kalt|schwei|ßen** NT -s, *no pl*
cold weld; **Kalt|start** M (*Aut, Comput*) cold
start; **Kalt|start|au|to|ma|tik** F automatic
choke; **kalt+stel|len** VT *sep* (*inf*) **jdn ~** to de-
mote, to put out of harm's way (*inf*); **Kalt|-
was|ser|kur** F = Kneippkur; **Kalt|wel|le** F (=
Frisur) cold perm or wave

Kal|va|ri|en|berg [kal'vaːriən-] M Calvary

kal|vi|nisch [kal'viːnɪʃ] ADJ Calvinistic

Kal|vi|nis|mus [kalvi'nɪsmʊs] M -, *no pl* Calvin-
ism

Kal|vi|nist [kalvi'nɪst] M -en, -en, **Kal|vi|nis|tin**
[-'nɪstɪn] F -, -nen Calvinist

kal|vi|nis|tisch [kalvi'nɪstɪʃ] ADJ Calvinist(ic)

Kal|zi|um ['kaltsiʊm] NT -s, *no pl* (*abbr* **Ca**) cal-
cium

Kal|zi|um|kar|bo|nat NT (*Chem*) calcium car-
bonate

kam *pret von* **kommen**

Ka|ma|ril|la [kama'rɪlja, kama'rɪla] F -, **Kamaril|-
len** [-'rɪljən, -'rɪlan] (*geh*) political clique

Kam|bod|scha [kam'bɔdʒa] NT -s Cambodia

Kam|bod|scha|ner [kambɔ'dʒaːnɐ] M -s, -,
Kam|bod|scha|ne|rin [-ərɪn] F -, -nen Cam-
bodian

kam|bod|scha|nisch [kambɔ'dʒaːnɪʃ] ADJ
Cambodian

Ka|mee [ka'meː] F -, -n [-'meːən] cameo

Ka|mel [ka'meːl] NT -(e)s, -e **a** camel; **eher
geht ein ~ durchs Nadelöhr ...** (*prov*) it is easier
for a camel to go through the eye of a needle
... (*prov*) **b** (*inf*) clot (*Brit inf*), clown (*inf*); **ich
~!** silly or stupid me!

Ka|mel-: Ka|mel|foh|len NT, **Ka|mel|fül|len**
NT camel foal; **Ka|mel|haar** NT (*Tex*) camel
hair

Ka|me|lie [ka'meːliə] F -, -n camellia

Ka|mel|le [ka'mɛlə] F -, -n *usu pl* (*inf*) **das sind
doch alte** or **olle ~n** that's old hat (*inf*); **er hat
nichts als alte** or **olle ~n erzählt** he just said
the same old things

Ka|mel|trei|ber(in) M(F) camel driver, camel-
eer

Ka|me|ra ['kamera, 'kaːmərə] F -, -s camera

Ka|me|rad [kama'raːt] M -en, -en [-dn], **Ka|me|-
ra|din** [-'raːdɪn] F -, -nen (*Mil etc*) comrade; (=
Gefährte, Lebenskamerad) companion, friend;
(*dated:* = *Arbeitskamerad*) workmate; (*dated:* =
Freund) friend, buddy (*inf*), chum (*inf*)

Ka|me|ra|den|schwein NT (*sl pej*) backstab-
ber

Ka|me|ra|de|rie [kamaradə'riː] F -, *no pl* (*pej*)
bonhomie

Ka|me|rad|schaft [kama'raːtʃaft] F -, -en com-
radeship, camaraderie

ka|me|rad|schaft|lich [kama'raːtʃaftlɪç] ADJ
comradely; **eine ~e Ehe** a companionate marriage ADV **rein ~ zusammenleben** to live together purely as friends; **sich ~ verhalten** to act
or behave loyally; **~ miteinander umgehen** to be
very friendly to each other

Ka|me|rad|schaft|lich|keit F -, *no pl* com-
radeship

**Ka|me|rad|schafts-: Ka|me|rad|schafts|-
abend** M reunion; **Ka|me|rad|schafts|ehe**
F companionate marriage; **Ka|me|rad|-
schafts|geist** M , *no pl* spirit of comradeship,
esprit de corps

Ka|me|ra-: Ka|me|ra|ein|stel|lung F shot;
Ka|me|ra|fahrt F camera movement; **Ka|me|-
ra|frau** F camerawoman; **Ka|me|ra|füh|rung**
F camera work; **ka|me|ra|ge|recht** ADJ suita-
ble for the cameras ADV **sie stellte sich ~ in
Pose** she posed for the cameras

Ka|me|ra|lis|tik [kamera'lɪstɪk] F -, *no pl* **a** (*old:*
= *Finanzwirtschaft*) finance **b** (= *Buchführung*)
governmental accounting

ka|me|ra|lis|tisch [kamera'lɪstɪʃ] ADJ *Rechnungs-
wesen, Buchhaltungsverfahren* governmental

Ka|me|ra-: Ka|me|ra|mann M *pl* -**männer** cam-
eraman; **ka|me|ra|scheu** ADJ camera-shy;
Ka|me|ra|schwenk M pan; **ka|me|ra|über|-
wacht** ADJ *Gebäude, Platz* under video surveillance *pred*

Ka|me|run ['kaməruːn] NT -s the Cameroons *pl*

Ka|mi|ka|ze [kami'kaːtsə, kami'kaːzə] M -, - ka-
mikaze

Ka|mi|ka|ze- *in cpds* kamikaze; **Ka|mi|ka|ze|-
an|griff** M kamikaze attack; **Ka|mi|ka|ze|-
flie|ger(in)** M(F) kamikaze pilot

Ka|mil|le [ka'mɪlə] F -, -n camomile

Ka|mil|len|tee M camomile tea

Ka|min [ka'miːn] M OR (*dial*) NT -s, -e **a** (=
Schornstein) chimney; (= *Abzugsschacht*) flue; **etw
in den ~ schreiben** to write sth off **b** (= *offene
Feuerstelle*) fireplace; **eine Plauderei am ~** a fireside chat; **wir saßen am** or **vor dem ~** we sat by
or in front of the fire **c** (*Geol:* = *Felskamin*)
chimney

Ka|min-: Ka|min|be|steck NT fireside com-
panion set; **Ka|min|feu|er** NT open fire, fire in
the grate; **Ka|min|gar|ni|tur** F fireside com-
panion set; **Ka|min|keh|rer** [-keːrɐ] M -s, -,
Ka|min|keh|re|rin [-ərɪn] F -, -nen (*dial*) chim-
ney sweep; **Ka|min|sims** M OR NT mantel-
piece

Kamm [kam] M -(e)s, **=e** ['kɛmə] **a** (*für Haar, =
Webekamm*) comb; **sich** (*dat*) **mit dem ~ durch
die Haare fahren** to run a comb through one's
hair; **alle/alles über einen ~ scheren** (*fig*) to
lump everyone/everything together **b** (*von Vogel, Eidechse etc*) comb → **schwellen** VI **c** (*von
Pferd*) crest **d** (*Cook*) (*Hammelfleisch*) (middle)
neck; (*Schweinefleisch*) shoulder; (*Rindfleisch*)
neck **e** (*von Trauben*) stalk **f** (= *Gebirgskamm*)
crest, ridge; (= *Wellenkamm*) crest

käm|men ['kɛmən] VT *Haar, Baumwolle* to comb;
Wolle auch to card, to tease; **sie kämmte ihm die
Haare** she combed his hair VR to comb one's
hair

Kam|mer ['kamɐ] F -, -n **a** (*allgemein*) chamber;
(*Parl*) chamber, house; (= *Ärztekammer, Anwalts-
kammer*) professional association; (= *Herzkam-
mer*) ventricle; (*Mil*) store *usu pl*; **erste/zweite ~**
Upper/Lower House **b** (= *Zimmer*) (small)
room, boxroom (*Brit*); (*dial:* = *Schlafzimmer*)
bedroom

Kam|mer-: Kam|mer|bul|le M (*Mil sl*) quar-
termaster; **Kam|mer|die|ner** M valet

Käm|me|rei [kɛmə'rai] F -, -en **a** (*Hist:* = *Finanz-
verwaltung*) treasury (*old*); finance department
b (*Tex*) combing works *sing or pl*

Käm|me|rer ['kɛmərɐ] M -s, - **a** (= *Beamter*) fi-
nance officer → *auch* **Kämmrerin b** (*Hist, Eccl*)
chamberlain

Kam|mer-: Kam|mer|frau F (*Hist*) lady-in--waiting; **Kam|mer|ge|richt** NT ≈ Supreme Court; **Kam|mer|herr** M (*Hist*) chamberlain; **Kam|mer|jä|ger(in)** M(F) (= *Schädlingsbekämpfer*) pest controller (*Brit*), exterminator (*US*); (= *Leibjäger*) (head) gamekeeper; **Kam|mer|jung|fer** F lady-in-waiting; **Kam|mer|kon|zert** NT chamber concert

Käm|mer|lein ['kɛmɐlain] NT -s, - chamber; **im stillen ~** in private

Kam|mer-: Kam|mer|mäd|chen NT lady-in--waiting; **Kam|mer|mu|sik** F chamber music; **Kam|mer|or|ches|ter** NT chamber orchestra; **Kam|mer|sän|ger(in)** M(F) , **Kam|mer|schau|spie|ler(in)** M(F) (*Titel*) title formerly given by Duke etc, now by authorities, to singer/actor for excellence; **Kam|mer|spiel** NT a (= *Schauspiel*) play for a studio theatre (*Brit*) or theater (*US*) b (= *Theater*) studio theatre (*Brit*) or theater (*US*); **Kam|mer|ton** M , no pl concert pitch; **Kam|mer|zo|fe** F chambermaid

Kamm-: Kamm|garn NT worsted; **Kamm|mu|schel** ▲ F scallop; **Kamm|rad** NT cogwheel

Käm|re|rin ['kɛmrərɪn] F -, -nen (= *Beamtin*) finance officer

Kamm|stück NT (*Cook*) shoulder

Kammuschel △ F → **Kammmuschel**

Kamp [kamp] M -(e)s, ⁻e ['kɛmpə] (*N Ger*) plot (of land), field

Kam|pag|ne [kam'panjə] F -, -n a campaign b (*bei Ausgrabungen*) stage

Käm|pe ['kɛmpə] M -n, -n (*obs, iro*) (old) campaigner or soldier

Kampf [kampf] M -(e)s, ⁻e ['kɛmpfə] fight, struggle (*um* for); (*Mil auch*) combat; (*Mil:* = *Gefecht*) battle; (*Mil:* = *Feindbegegnung*) engagement, encounter; (*= Boxkampf*) fight, bout, contest; **jdm/einer Sache den ~ ansagen** (*fig*) to declare war on sb/sth; **den ~ (gegen jdn/etw) aufnehmen** to commence battle (against sb/sth); (*fig*) to take up the fight or struggle (against sb/sth); **den ~/die Kämpfe einstellen** to stop fighting; **den ~ um etw verloren geben** to abandon the struggle for sth; **den ~ aufgeben** to give up the struggle; **den ~ abbrechen** (*Sport*) to stop the fight; **es kam zum ~** clashes occurred, fighting broke out; **auf in den ~!** (*hum*) once more unto the breach! (*hum*); **er ist im ~ gefallen** he fell in action or battle; **im ~ für die Freiheit** in the fight or struggle for freedom; **im ~ für Frankreich** in the battle for France; **der ~ ums Dasein** the struggle for existence; **der ~ der Geschlechter** or **zwischen den Geschlechtern** the battle of the sexes; **der ~ um die Macht** the battle or struggle for power; **ein ~ auf Leben und Tod** a fight to the death; **dem Atomtod!** fight the nuclear menace!; **innere Kämpfe** inner conflicts

Kampf-: Kampf|ab|schnitt M combat zone or sector; **Kampf|ab|stim|mung** F vote; **es kam zur ~** they put it to the vote; **Kampf|ab|zei|chen** NT campaign medal; **Kampf|an|sa|ge** F declaration of war; (*Sport*) announcement; **Kampf|an|zug** M (*Mil etc*) battle dress no art, battle uniform; **Kampf|aus|bil|dung** F (*Mil*) combat training; **Kampf|bahn** F sports stadium, arena; **Kampf|be|gier|de** F (*liter*) bellicosity (*liter*); **kampf|be|reit** ADJ ready for battle; **Kampf|be|reit|schaft** F readiness for battle; **kampf|be|tont** ADJ (*Sport*) Spiel, Partie tough, hard, attacking attr; **Kampf|bom|ber** M fighter-bomber; **Kampf|ein|heit** F (*Mil*) combat mission; **Kampf|ein|satz** M (*Mil*) combat mission

kämp|fen ['kɛmpfn] VI to fight, to struggle (*um*, *für* for); (*Sport:* = angreifen) to attack; **gegen etw ~** to fight (against) sth; **die Rangers-Elf kämpft morgen gegen Celtic** Rangers are playing (against) Celtic tomorrow; **mit dem Tode ~** to fight for one's life; **mit den Tränen ~** to fight back one's tears; **gegen die Wellen ~** to battle against the waves; **ich hatte mit schweren Problemen zu ~** I had difficulty problems to con-

tend with; **ich habe lange mit mir ~ müssen, ehe ...** I had a long battle with myself before ... **VT** (*usu fig*) *Kampf* to fight

Kampf|fer ['kampfɐ] M -s, no pl camphor

Kämp|fer¹ ['kɛmpfɐ] M -s, - (*Archit*) impost

Kämp|fer² ['kɛmpfɐ] M -s, -, **Kämp|fe|rin** [-ərɪn] F -, -nen fighter; (= *Krieger auch*) warrior

kämp|fe|risch ['kɛmpfərɪʃ] ADJ aggressive; Spiel auch attacking ADV aggressively; **sich ~ einsetzen** to fight hard; **sich ~ bewähren** to fight well

Käm|pfer|na|tur F born fighter

kampf|er|probt [-ɛɐpro:pt] ADJ battle-tried

Kampf|fes|lust F pugnacity

kampf|fes|lus|tig ADJ belligerent, pugnacious

Kampf-: kampf|fä|hig ADJ (*Mil*) fit for action; *Boxer* fit to fight; *Gewerkschaft etc* able to fight; **Männer im ~en Alter** men of fighting age; **Kampf|fä|hig|keit** F (*Mil*) fitness for action; (*von Boxer*) fitness to fight; (*von Gewerkschaft etc*) ability to fight; **Kampf|flug|zeug** NT fighter (plane); **Kampf|gas** NT poison gas; **Kampf|geist** M , no pl fighting spirit; **Kampf|ge|mein|schaft** F (*Pol*) action group; **Kampf|ge|sche|hen** NT , no pl fighting, action; **ins ~ eingreifen** (*lit, fig*) to enter the fray; **Kampf|grup|pe** F task force; (*Mil auch*) combat group; **Kampf|hahn** M (*lit, fig*) fighting cock; **Kampf|hand|lung** F usu pl clash usu pl; **Kampf|hub|schrau|ber** M helicopter gunship; **Kampf|hund** M fighting dog; **Kampf|kraft** F fighting strength; **kampf|los** ADJ peaceful; *Sieg* uncontested, unopposed ADV peacefully, without a fight; **sich ~ ergeben**, **~ aufgeben** to surrender without a fight; **kampf|lus|tig** ADJ belligerent, pugnacious; **Kampf|maß|nah|me** F offensive measure; **~ ergreifen** to go onto the offensive; **Kampf|pan|zer** M combat tank; **Kampf|pau|se** F lull in the fighting or battle; **Kampf|platz** M battlefield; (*Sport*) arena, stadium; **Kampf|preis** M a (*in Wettkampf*) prize b (*Comm*) cut-throat price; **Kampf|rich|ter(in)** M(F) (*Sport*) referee; (*Tennis*) umpire; (*Schwimmen, Skilaufen*) judge; **Kampf|schrift** F broadsheet; **Kampf|sport** M martial art; **kampf|stark** ADJ *Heer, Sportler, Hunderasse* powerful; **Kampf|stär|ke** F (*Mil*) combat strength; **Kampf|stoff** M weapon, warfare agent; **Kampf|tag** M ~ **der Arbeiterklasse** (*DDR*) May Day; **Kampf|trin|ker** M (*sl*) pisshead (*inf*); **kampf|un|fä|hig** ADJ (*Mil*) unfit for action; *Boxer* unfit to fight; **einen Panzer/ein Schiff ~ machen** to put a tank/ship out of action, to cripple a tank/ship; **~ schlagen** (*Boxen*) to put out of the fight; **Kampf|un|fä|hig|keit** F (*Mil*) unfitness for action; (*von Boxer*) unfitness to fight; **Kampf|wa|gen** M chariot

kam|pie|ren [kam'pi:rən] ptp **kampiert** VI to camp (out); **im Wohnzimmer ~** (*inf*) to doss down (*Brit*) or camp out (*US*) in the sitting room (*inf*)

Ka|na|an ['ka:naan] NT -s (*Bibl*) Canaan

Ka|na|da ['kanada] NT -s Canada

Ka|na|di|er [ka'na:diɐ] M -s, - a Canadian b (*Sport*) Canadian canoe

Ka|na|di|e|rin [ka'na:diərɪn] F -, -nen Canadian (woman/girl)

ka|na|disch [ka'na:dɪʃ] ADJ Canadian

Ka|nail|le [ka'naljə] F -, -n (*dated pej*) (= *gemeiner Mensch*) scoundrel, rascal; (= *Pöbel, Mob*) rabble, canaille

Ka|na|ke [ka'na:kə] M -n, -n, **Ka|na|kin** [-'na:kɪn] F -, -nen (= *Südseeinsulaner*) Kanaka; (*pej sl:* = *Ausländer, Südländer*) wop (*pej*), dago (*pej*)

Ka|nal [ka'na:l] M -s, **Kanäle** [ka'nɛ:lə] a (= *Schifffahrtsweg*) canal; (= *Wasserlauf*) channel; (*zur Bewässerung*) ditch, canal; (*zur Entwässerung*) drain; (*für Abwässer*) sewer; **der (Ärmel)kanal** the (English) Channel b (*Rad, TV, fig:* = *Weg*) channel; **etw durch die richtigen Kanäle weiter-**

leiten to pass sth on through the proper channels; **dunkle Kanäle** dubious channels

Ka|nal-: Ka|nal|ar|bei|ter(in) M(F) a sewerage worker b PL (*Pol fig*) pressure group; **Ka|nal|bau** M pl -bauten canal building or construction; **Ka|nal|de|ckel** M drain cover

Ka|nal|in|seln PL die ~ (*im Ärmelkanal*) the Channel Islands pl

Ka|na|li|sa|ti|on [kanaliza'tsio:n] F -, -en a (*für Abwässer*) sewerage system, sewers pl; (= *das Kanalisieren*) sewerage installation b (= *Begradigung eines Flusslaufes*) canalization

Ka|na|li|sa|ti|ons|sys|tem NT (*für Abwässer*) sewerage system, sewers pl

ka|na|li|sie|ren [kanali'zi:rən] ptp **kanalisiert** VT *Fluss* to canalize; (*fig*) *Energie, Emotionen, Informationen* to channel; *Gebiet* to install or lay sewers in

Ka|nal-: Ka|nal|rohr NT sewage pipe; **Ka|nal|tun|nel** M Channel Tunnel; **Ka|nal|zo|ne** F canal zone

Ka|na|pee ['kanape] NT -s, -s (*old, hum*) sofa, couch, settee

Ka|na|ren [ka'na:rən] PL (*form*) Canaries pl, Canary Islands pl

Ka|na|ri|en|vo|gel [ka'na:riən-] M canary

Ka|na|ri|sche In|seln [ka'na:rɪʃə] PL Canaries pl, Canary Islands pl

Kan|da|re [kan'da:rə] F -, -n (curb) bit; **jdn an die ~ nehmen** (*fig*) to take sb in hand

Kan|de|la|ber [kande'la:bɐ] M -s, - candelabra

Kan|di|dat [kandi'da:t] M -en, -en, **Kan|di|da|tin** [-'da:tɪn] F -, -nen candidate; (*bei Bewerbung auch*) applicant; **jdn als ~en aufstellen** to nominate sb, to put sb forward as a candidate

Kan|di|da|ten|lis|te F list of candidates

Kan|di|da|tur [kandida'tu:ɐ] F -, -en candidature, candidacy

kan|di|die|ren [kandi'di:rən] ptp **kandidiert** VI (*Pol*) to stand, to run (*für* for); **für das Amt des Präsidenten ~** to stand or run for president

kan|diert [kan'di:ɐt] ADJ *Frucht* candied

Kan|dis|(zu|cker) ['kandɪs-] M -, no pl rock candy

Kän|gu|ru ▲ ['kɛŋguru] NT -s, -s, **Kän|gu|ruh** △ NT -s, -s kangaroo

Ka|nin [ka'ni:n] NT -s, -e rabbit (fur)

Ka|nin|chen [ka'ni:nçan] NT -s, - rabbit; **sich wie ~ vermehren** (*inf*) to breed like rabbits

Ka|nin|chen-: Ka|nin|chen|bau M pl -baue rabbit warren; **Ka|nin|chen|stall** M rabbit hutch

Ka|nis|ter [ka'nɪstɐ] M -s, - can; (= *Blechkanister*) jerry can

kann [kan] 3. pers sing pres von **können**

Kann|be|stim|mung ▲ ['kan-] F (*Jur*) discretionary provision

Känn|chen ['kɛnçən] NT -s, - (*für Milch*) jug; (*für Kaffee*) pot; **ein ~ Kaffee** a pot of coffee

Kan|ne ['kanə] F -, -n can; (= *Teekanne, Kaffeekanne*) pot; (= *Milchkanne*) churn; (= *Ölkanne*) can, tin; (= *Weinkanne*) ≈ tankard; (= *Gießkanne*) watering can; **sich die ~ geben** (*sl:* = *sich betrinken*) to get pissed (*Brit inf, inf*) or plastered

kan|ne|liert [kanə'li:ɐt] ADJ (*Archit*) fluted

Kan|ni|ba|le [kani'ba:lə] M -n, -n, **Kan|ni|ba|lin** [-'ba:lɪn] F -, -nen cannibal

kan|ni|ba|lisch [kani'ba:lɪʃ] ADJ cannibalistic; (= *brutal*) rough; **ich habe ~en Hunger** (*hum inf*) I could eat a horse (*inf*)

Kan|ni|ba|lis|mus [kaniba'lɪsmʊs] M -, no pl cannibalism

kann|te pret von **kennen**

Ka|non ['ka:nɔn] M -s, -s canon

Ka|no|na|de [kano'na:də] F -, -n (*Mil*) barrage; (*fig auch*) tirade

Ka|no|ne [ka'no:nə] F -, -n a gun; (*Hist*) cannon; (*sl:* = *Pistole*) rod (*US sl*), gat (*sl*), shooter (*inf*); **~n auffahren** (*lit, fig*) to bring up the big guns; **mit ~n auf Spatzen schießen** (*inf*) to take a sledgehammer to crack a nut **b** (*fig inf:* = *Könner*) ace (*inf*) **c** (*inf*) **das ist unter aller ~** that defies description

Ka|no|nen-: Ka|no|nen|boot NT gunboat; **Ka|no|nen|boot|dip|lo|ma|tie** F , **Ka|no|nen|boot|po|li|tik** F gunboat diplomacy; **Ka|no|nen|don|ner** M rumbling of guns; **Ka|no|nen|fut|ter** NT (*inf*) cannon fodder; **Ka|no|nen|ku|gel** F cannon ball; **Ka|no|nen|ofen** M cylindrical iron stove; **Ka|no|nen|rohr** NT gun barrel; **heiliges ~!** (*inf*) good grief! (*inf*); **Ka|no|nen|schlag** M (= *Feuerwerkskörper*) (fire)cracker

Ka|no|nier [kano'niːɐ] M -s, -e, **Ka|no|nie|rin** [-'niːrɪn] F -, -nen (*Mil*) gunner

Ka|no|ni|ker [ka'noːnɪkɐ] M -s, -, **Ka|no|ni|kus** [ka'noːnɪkʊs] M -, **Kanoniker** (*Eccl*) canon

Ka|no|ni|sa|ti|on [kanoniza'tsioːn] F -, -en (*Eccl*) canonization

ka|no|nisch [ka'noːnɪʃ] ADJ (*Eccl*) canonical; **~es Recht** canon law

ka|no|ni|sie|ren [kanoni'ziːrən] *ptp* **kanonisiert** VT (*Eccl*) to canonize

Ka|no|nis|se [kano'nɪsə] F -, -n, **Ka|no|nis|sin** [kano'nɪsɪn] F -, -nen canoness

Ka|nos|sa [ka'nɔsa] NT -s (*fig*) humiliation → **Gang**

Ka|nos|sa|gang M *pl* -gänge **einen ~ machen** *or* **antreten müssen** to eat humble pie

kan|ta|bel [kan'taːbl] ADJ (*Mus*) cantabile; *Musikstück* songlike; (= *sangbar*) singable

Kan|ta|te¹ [kan'taːtə] F -, -n (*Mus*) cantata

Kan|ta|te² *no art* (*Eccl*) *fourth Sunday after Easter*

Kan|te ['kantə] F -, -n (*eines Gegenstandes, einer Fläche*) edge; (= *Rand, Borte*) border; (= *Webkante*) selvage; **wir legten die Steine ~ an ~** we laid the stones end to end; **etw auf ~ kleben** to stick up sth with the edges flush; **Geld auf die hohe ~ legen** (*inf*) to put money by (*Brit inf*) *or* a-way; **Geld auf der hohen ~ haben** (*inf*) to have (some) money put by (*Brit inf*) *or* away → **abstoßen** VT a, **fehlen** VI *impers*

kan|ten ['kantn] VT **a** (= *auf die Kante stellen*) to tilt; **nicht ~!** (*bei Kisten etc*) do not tilt!, this way up! **b** (= *mit Kanten versehen*) to trim, to edge **c** *auch vi* (*Ski*) to edge

Kan|ten ['kantn] M -s, - (*N Ger*) crust, heel (*dial*)

Kan|ter ['kantɐ] M -s, - canter

Kan|ter|sieg M (*Sport*) runaway victory, walkover, walkaway (*US*)

Kant-: Kant|ha|ken M **jdn beim ~ nehmen** (*inf*) **jdn beim ~ zu fassen kriegen** (*inf*) to haul (*Brit*) *or* rake sb over the coals (*inf*); **Kant|holz** NT (piece of) squared timber

kan|tig ['kantɪç] ADJ *Holz* edged, squared; *Gesicht* angular; *Charakter* awkward

Kan|ti|le|ne [kanti'leːnə] F -, -n (*Mus*) cantilena

Kan|ti|ne [kan'tiːnə] F -, -n canteen

Kan|ti|nen|es|sen NT **a** (= *einzelnes Gericht*) canteen meal **b** (= *in einer Kantine angebotene Gerichte*) canteen food, canteen meals *pl*

kan|tisch ['kantɪʃ] ADJ Kantian

Kan|ton [kan'toːn] M -s, -e canton

KANTON

Switzerland is a democratic federal state made up of individual states called cantons. There are 26 cantons, of which six are so-called demi-cantons formed by splitting single cantons in two. The cantons are autonomous within the limits set by the Federal Constitution. They are thus responsible for the organization of their own government by means of a cantonal constitution. The result is that state authorities differ from canton to canton both in name and structure.

---

kan|to|nal [kanto'naːl] ADJ cantonal ADV **~ anerkannt** recognized *or* accepted throughout the canton; **~ finanziert** financed by the canton; **~ geregelt** regulated by the cantons *or* at cantonal level; **~ unterschiedliche Praxis** practices that differ from one canton to the other

Kan|to|nal|wahl F (*Sw*) cantonal election

Kan|to|nist [kanto'nɪst] M -en, -en **ein unsicherer ~** sein to be unreliable

Kan|tons-: Kan|tons|rat M (*Sw*) **a** (= *Kantonsparlament*) cantonal council **b** (= *Mitglied des Kantonsrats*) member of a/the cantonal council; **Kan|tons|rä|tin** F (*Sw*, = *Mitglied des Kantonsrats*) member of a/the cantonal council

Kan|tor ['kantoːɐ] M -s, **Kantoren** choirmaster; (*in Synagoge*) cantor

Kan|to|rei [kanto'rai] F -, -en (church) choir

Kan|to|rin [kan'toːrɪn] F -, -nen choirmistress

Ka|nu ['kaːnu] NT -s, -s canoe

Ka|nü|le [ka'nyːlə] F -, -n (*Med*) cannula

Ka|nu|te [ka'nuːtə] M -n, -n, **Ka|nu|tin** [-'nuːtɪn] F -, -nen canoeist

Kan|zel ['kantsl] F -, -n **a** pulpit; **auf der ~** in the pulpit; **die ~ besteigen** to get into the pulpit; **von der ~ herab** from the pulpit **b** (*Aviat*) cockpit **c** (*eines Berges*) promontory, spur **d** (*Hunt*) (look-out) platform

Kan|zel-: Kan|zel|dach NT canopy; **Kan|zel|red|ner(in)** M(F) orator

kan|ze|ro|gen [kantsero'geːn] ADJ (*Med*) *Stoff etc* carcinogenic, cancer-causing

Kanz|lei [kants'lai] F -, -en **a** (= *Dienststelle*) office; (= *Büro eines Rechtsanwalts, Notars etc*) chambers *pl* **b** (*Hist, Pol*) chancellery

Kanz|lei-: Kanz|lei|spra|che F official language; **Kanz|lei|stil** M (*pej*) officialese

Kanz|ler ['kantslɐ] M -s, -, **Kanz|le|rin** [-ərɪn] F -, -nen **a** (= *Regierungschef*) chancellor → **Bundeskanzler(in), Reichskanzler b** (= *diplomatischer Beamter*) chancellor, chief secretary **c** (*Univ*) vice chancellor

Kanz|ler-: Kanz|ler|amt NT (= *Gebäude*) chancellery; (= *Posten*) chancellorship; **Kanz|ler|amts|chef(in)** M(F) head of the chancellory; **Kanz|ler|be|ra|ter(in)** M(F) adviser to the chancellor; **Kanz|ler|bo|nus** M advantage of being the chancellor in power

Kanz|le|rin F → **Kanzler**

Kanz|ler|kan|di|dat(in) M(F) candidate for the post (*esp Brit*) *or* position of chancellor

Kanz|list [kants'lɪst] M -en, -en (*old*) clerk

Ka|o|lin [kao'liːn] M OR NT -s, -e kaolin

Kap [kap] NT -s, -s cape, headland; **~ der Guten Hoffnung** Cape of Good Hope; **~ Hoorn** Cape Horn

Ka|paun [ka'paun] M -s, -e capon

Ka|pa|zi|tät [kapatsi'tɛːt] F -, -en capacity; (*fig:* = *Experte*) expert, authority

Ka|pa|zi|täts|gren|ze F limit of capacity, capacity limit, maximum capacity

Ka|pee [ka'peː] NT **schwer von ~ sein** (*inf*) to be slow on the uptake (*inf*)

Ka|pel|le [ka'pɛlə] F -, -n **a** (= *kleine Kirche etc*) chapel **b** (*Mus*) band, orchestra

Ka|pell|meis|ter(in) M(F) (*Mus*) director of music; (*Mil, von Tanzkapelle etc*) bandmaster, bandleader

Ka|per¹ ['kaːpɐ] F -, -n (*Bot, Cook*) caper

Ka|per² M -s, - (*Naut*) privateer

Ka|per|brief M letter of marque

ka|pern ['kaːpɐn] VT (*Naut*) *Schiff* to seize, to capture; (*fig*) *Ding* to commandeer (*inf*), to grab; *jdn* to grab; (= *mit Beschlag belegen*) to buttonhole, to collar (*inf*)

Ka|per|schiff NT privateer

ka|pie|ren [ka'piːrən] *ptp* **kapiert** (*inf*) VT to get (*inf*), to understand VI to get it (*inf*), to understand; **kapiert?** got it? (*inf*); **kapierst du (denn)**

jetzt? do you get it now? (*inf*); **er hat schnell kapiert** he caught on quick (*inf*)

ka|pil|lar [kapi'laːr] ADJ *Blutgefäße, Durchblutung* capillary

Ka|pil|lar|ge|fäß [kapɪ'laːɐ-] NT (*Anat*) capillary

ka|pi|tal [kapi'taːl] ADJ **a** (*Hunt*) *Hirsch* royal; **einen ~en Bock schießen** (*fig*) to make a real bloomer (*Brit inf*) *or* blooper (*US inf*) **b** (= *grundlegend*) *Missverständnis etc* major

Ka|pi|tal [kapi'taːl] NT -s, -e *or* -ien [-liən] **a** (*Fin*) capital *no pl*; (= *angelegtes Kapital*) capital investments *pl*; **flüssiges** *or* **verfügbares ~** ready *or* available capital; **genehmigtes ~** authorized capital; **er ist mit 35% am ~ dieser Firma beteiligt** he has a 35% stake in this firm **b** (*fig*) asset; **aus etw ~ schlagen** (*pej*) (*lit, fig*) to make capital out of sth; (*fig auch*) to capitalize on sth

Ka|pi|tal-: Ka|pi|tal|ab|fluss ▲ M , *no pl* capital outflow; **Ka|pi|tal|ab|wan|de|rung** F exodus of capital, investment of capital; **Ka|pi|tal|an|la|ge** F capital investment, investment of capital; **Ka|pi|tal|an|la|ge|ge|sell|schaft** F investment fund; **Ka|pi|tal|auf|sto|ckung** F capital increase; **Ka|pi|tal|be|darf** M capital requirements *pl*; **Ka|pi|tal|be|tei|li|gungs|ge|sell|schaft** F capital investment company; **Ka|pi|tal|de|cke** F capital resources *pl*; **Ka|pi|tal|ein|la|ge** F capital contribution; **Ka|pi|tal|er|hö|hung** F capital increase; **Ka|pi|tal|er|trags|steu|er** F capital gains tax; **Ka|pi|tal|flucht** F flight of capital; **Ka|pi|tal|ge|sell|schaft** F (*Comm*) joint-stock company; **ka|pi|tal|in|ten|siv** ADJ capital-intensive

ka|pi|ta|li|sie|ren [kapitali'ziːrən] *ptp* **kapitalisiert** VT to capitalize

Ka|pi|ta|lis|mus [kapita'lɪsmʊs] M -, *no pl* capitalism

Ka|pi|ta|list [kapita'lɪst] M -en, -en, **Ka|pi|ta|lis|tin** [-'lɪstɪn] F -, -nen capitalist

ka|pi|ta|lis|tisch [kapita'lɪstɪʃ] ADJ capitalist

Ka|pi|tal-: ka|pi|tal|kräf|tig ADJ financially strong; **~ sein** to have plenty of capital; **Ka|pi|tal|le|bens|ver|si|che|rung** F capital sum life insurance, endowment insurance; **Ka|pi|tal|markt** M money market; **Ka|pi|tal|sam|mel|stel|le** F institutional investor; **ka|pi|tal|schwach** ADJ financially weak; **kapitalschwache Länder** countries which are short of capital *or* financially weak; **~ sein** to be short of capital; **ka|pi|tal|stark** ADJ = **kapitalkräftig**; **Ka|pi|tal|stück|kos|ten** PL (*Econ*) unit production costs *pl*; **Ka|pi|tal|ver|bre|chen** NT serious crime; (*mit Todesstrafe*) capital crime, capital offence (*Brit*) *or* offense (*US*); **Ka|pi|tal|ver|mö|gen** NT (*Fin*) capital assets *pl*; **Ka|pi|tal|ver|si|che|rung** F (*Insur*) capital insurance

Ka|pi|tän [kapi'tɛːn] M -s, -e, **Ka|pi|tä|nin** [-'tɛːnɪn] F -, -nen **a** (*Naut, Mil*) captain; (*esp auf kleinerem Schiff*) skipper (*inf*); **~ zur See** (*Mil*) captain **b** (*Sport*) captain **c** (*Aviat*) captain

Ka|pi|tän|leut|nant M lieutenant commander

Ka|pi|täns|pa|tent NT master's certificate

Ka|pi|tel [ka'pɪtl] M -s, - **a** chapter; (*fig*) period, chapter; (= *Angelegenheit*) chapter of events, story; **ein dunkles ~ in seinem Leben** a dark chapter in his life; **das ist ein anderes ~** that's another story; **das ist ein ~ für sich** that's a story all to itself; **für mich ist dieses ~ erledigt** as far as I'm concerned the matter is closed **b** (*Eccl:* = *Domkapitel*) chapter

Ka|pi|tell [kapi'tɛl] NT -s, -e capital

Ka|pi|tel-: Ka|pi|tel|saal M (*Eccl*) chapter house; **Ka|pi|tel|über|schrift** F chapter heading

Ka|pi|tu|la|ti|on [kapitula'tsioːn] F -, -en (*von Armee, Land*) surrender, capitulation (*auch fig*) (*vor +dat* to, in the face of); **bedingungslose ~** unconditional surrender; **das ist eine ~ vor deinen Pflichten** that's refusing to face up to your responsibilities; **das ist eine ~ vor deinen Kindern** that's capitulating to your children

ka|pi|tu|lie|ren [kapitu'li:rən] *ptp* **kapituliert** VI (= *sich ergeben*) to surrender, to capitulate; (*fig*: = *aufgeben*) to give up, to capitulate (*vor +dat* in the face of)

Kap|lan [ka'pla:n] M **-s, Kapläne** [ka'plɛ:nə] (*in Pfarrei*) curate; (*mit besonderen Aufgaben*) chaplain

Ka|po ['kapo] M **-s, -s a** (= *Aufseher*) overseer; (*S Ger inf*: = *Vorarbeiter*) gaffer (*Brit inf*), foreman **b** (*Mil sl*) (= *Unteroffizier*) NCO; (= *Feldwebel*) sarge (*sl*); (= *Obergefreiter*) corp (*sl*)

Ka|po|das|ter [kapo'dastɐ] M **-s, -** capo

Ka|pok ['kapɔk, 'ka:pɔk] M **-s, no pl** (*Tex*) kapok

Ka|po|si [ka'po:zi] NT **-(s), -s, Ka|po|si|sar|kom** NT (*Med*) Kaposi's sarcoma

Kap|pe ['kapə] F **-, -n** cap; (= *Fliegerkappe, Motorradmütze*) helmet; (= *Narrenmütze*) jester's cap; (*von Jude*) skullcap; (*von Füllfederhalter, Saftflaschen*) top, cap; (= *Schuhkappe*) (*vorne*) toe(cap); (*hinten*) heelpiece; (*Archit*) coping; **eine ~ aus Schnee** a snowcap; **das nehme ich auf meine ~** (*fig inf*) I'll take the responsibility for that, on my head be it; **das geht auf meine ~** (*inf*) (= *ich bezahle*) that's on me; (= *ich übernehme die Verantwortung*) that's my responsibility; **jdm die ~ waschen** (*Sw inf*: = *tadeln*) to give sb a piece of one's mind

kap|pen ['kapn] VT **a** (*Naut*) Tau, Leine to cut; Ast to cut back, to trim; (*Med*) Mandeln to clip (off); (*fig inf*) Finanzmittel to cut (back) **b** (= *kastrieren*) Hähne to caponize

Kap|pen|abend M carnival fancy-dress party (*where fancy-dress hats are worn*)

Kap|pes ['kapəs] M **-, -** (*dial*: = *Kohl*) cabbage; **~ reden** (*inf*) to talk (a load of) rubbish *or* baloney (*inf*)

Käp|pi ['kɛpi] NT **-s, -s** cap

Kapp|naht F French seam

Kap|pungs|gren|ze ['kapʊŋs-] F (*für Mieten, Kosten etc*) cap

Kap|ri|ce [ka'pri:sə] F **-, -n** caprice

Kap|ri|o|le [kapri'o:lə] F **-, -n** capriole; (*fig*) caper; **~n machen** to cut capers

Kap|ri|ze [ka'pri:tsə] F **-, -n** (*Aus*) caprice

kap|ri|zie|ren [kapri'tsi:rən] *ptp* **kapriziert** VR (*geh*) to insist (*auf +acc* on)

kap|ri|zi|ös [kapri'tsiø:s] ADJ (*geh*) capricious

Kap|sel ['kapsl] F **-, -n** (= *Etui*) container; (*Anat, Bot, Pharm, Space etc*) capsule; (*an einer Flasche*) cap, top; (= *Sprengkapsel*) detonator

Kap|sel|he|ber M **-s, -** bottle-opener

ka|putt [ka'pʊt] ADJ (*inf*) broken; *esp Maschine, Glühbirne etc* kaput (*inf*); (= *erschöpft*) *Mensch* shattered (*Brit inf*), done in (*inf*), knackered (*Brit inf*); Ehe broken; Beziehungen, Gesundheit ruined; Nerven shattered; Firma bust *pred* (*inf*); **das alte Auto/das Dach/ihre Ehe ist ~** (= *irreparabel*) the old car/the roof/her marriage has had it (*inf*); **irgendetwas muss an deinem Auto ~ sein** something must be wrong with your car; **der Fernseher ist ~** (*zeitweilig*) the TV is on the blink (*inf*); **mein ~es Bein** my gammy (*Brit inf*) or bad leg; (*gebrochen*) my broken leg; **mein ~es Auge** my bad eye (*inf*); **meine Jacke ist ~** (= *nicht mehr tragbar*) my jacket has had it (*inf*); (= *zerrissen*) my jacket is torn or ripped; (*am Saum*) my jacket is coming apart; **das ~e Deutschland** the (war-)shattered Germany; **die ~e Welt** this mess of a world; **ein ~er Typ** a wreck (*inf*)

ka|putt-: ka|putt+ar|bei|ten VR *sep* (*inf*) to work oneself to death; **ka|putt+är|gern** VR *sep* (*inf*) **ich hab mich kaputtgeärgert** (*über jdn/ etw*) I was furious; (*über mich selbst*) I could have kicked myself; **ka|putt+fah|ren** VT *sep irreg* (*inf*) to run over; Auto to drive or run into the ground, to knacker (*Brit inf*); (*durch Unfall*) to smash (up), to write off; **ka|putt+ge|hen** VI *sep irreg aux sein* (*inf*) to break; (*esp Maschine*)

to go kaput (*inf*); (*esp Glühbirne, Elektronenröhre etc*) to go kaput (*inf*), to go phut (*inf*); (*Ehe*) to break up, to go on the rocks (*Brit inf*) (*an +dat* because of); (*Beziehungen, Gesundheit, Nerven*) to be ruined, to go to pot (*inf*); (*Firma*) to go bust (*inf*), to fold (up); (*Waschmaschine, Auto*) to break down, to pack up (*Brit inf*); (*Kleidung*) to come to pieces; (= *zerrissen werden*) to tear; (*Blumen*) to die off; **der Fernseher ist schon wieder kaputtgegangen** (*zeitweilig*) the TV has gone on the blink again (*inf*); **in dem Büro/an diesem Job gehe ich noch kaputt** this office/ job will be the death of me (*inf*); **ka|putt+krie|gen** VT *sep* (*inf*) Zerbrechliches to break; Auto to ruin; jdn to wear out; **das Auto/der Hans ist nicht kaputtzukriegen** this car/ Hans just goes on for ever; **ka|putt+la|chen** VR *sep* (*inf*) to die laughing (*inf*); **ich lach mich kaputt!** what a laugh!; **ich hätte mich ~ können** I nearly killed myself laughing (*inf*); **ka|putt+ma|chen** *sep* (*inf*) VT to ruin; Zerbrechliches to break, to smash; Brücke, Sandburg to knock down; (= *erschöpfen*) jdn to wear out, to knacker (*Brit inf*); **diese ewigen Sorgen/die Kinder machen mich kaputt** these never-ending worries/the children will be the death of me (*inf*) VR (= *sich überanstrengen*) to wear oneself out, to run oneself into the ground (*inf*), to knacker oneself (*Brit inf*); **ka|putt+schla|gen** VT *sep irreg* (*inf*) to break, to smash

Ka|pu|ze [ka'pu:tsə] F **-, -n** hood; (= *Mönchskapuze*) cowl

Ka|pu|zi|ner¹ [kapu'tsi:nɐ] M **-s, -** (*Bot: auch* **Kapuzinerkresse**) nasturtium

Ka|pu|zi|ner² [kapu'tsi:nɐ] M **-s, -, Ka|pu|zi|ne|rin** [-ərɪn] F **-, -nen** (*Eccl*) Capuchin

Kar [ka:ɐ] NT **-(e)s, -e** corrie, cwm, cirque

Ka|ra|bi|ner [kara'bi:nɐ] M **-s, - a** (= *Gewehr*) carbine **b** (= *Karabinerhaken*) karabiner, snap link, crab (*inf*)

Ka|ra|cho [ka'raxo] NT **-s, no pl mit** *or* **im ~** (*inf*) at full tilt, hell for leather (*esp Brit inf*); **er rannte/fuhr mit ~ gegen die Wand** he ran/drove smack into the wall (*inf*)

Ka|raf|fe [ka'rafə] F **-, -n** carafe; (*mit Stöpsel*) decanter

Ka|ram|bo|la|ge [karambo'la:ʒə] F **-, -n** (*Aut*) collision, crash; (*Billard*) cannon

Ka|ram|bo|le [karam'bo:lə] F **-, -n** (*Billard*) red (ball)

ka|ram|bo|lie|ren [karambo'li:rən] *ptp* **karamboliert** VI *aux sein* (*Billard*) to cannon; (*Autos*) to crash (*mit into*), to collide (*mit with*)

Ka|ra|mell ▲ [kara'mɛl] M **-s, no pl** caramel *no pl*

Ka|ra|mel|le [kara'mɛlə] F **-, -n** caramel (toffee)

Ka|ra|o|ke [kara'o:ke] NT **-, no pl** karaoke

Ka|rat [ka'ra:t] NT **-(e)s, -e** *or* (*bei Zahlenangabe*) **-** (*Measure*) carat; **das Gold dieses Ringes hat 9 ~** this ring is made of 9-carat gold

Ka|ra|te NT **-(s), no pl** karate

Ka|ra|te|hieb M karate chop

-ka|rä|ter [kara:tɐ] M *suf in cpds* **-s, - Zehnkarä|ter** ten-carat stone; (= *Diamant*) ten-carat diamond

-ka|rä|tig [kara:tɪç] ADJ *suf* carat; **zehnkarätig** ten-carat

Ka|ra|vel|le [kara'vɛlə] F **-, -n** caravel

Ka|ra|wa|ne [kara'va:nə] F **-, -n** caravan

Ka|ra|wa|nen|stra|ße F caravan route

Kar|bid [kar'bi:t] NT **-(e)s, -e** [-də] carbide

Kar|bid|lam|pe F Davy lamp

Kar|bol [kar'bo:l] NT **-s, no pl, Kar|bol|säu|re** F carbolic acid

Kar|bo|nat [karbo'na:t] NT **-(e)s, -e** carbonate

kar|bo|ni|sie|ren [karboni'zi:rən] *ptp* **karbonisiert** VT to carbonize; Getränke to carbonate

Kar|bun|kel [kar'bʊŋkl] M **-s, -** (*Med*) carbuncle

Kar|da|mom [karda'mo:m] M **-s, -e(n)** cardamom

Kar|dan- [karda:n-]: **Kar|dan|ge|lenk** NT universal joint; **Kar|dan|tun|nel** M transmission tunnel; **Kar|dan|wel|le** F prop(eller) shaft

Kar|di|nal [kardi'na:l] M **-s, Kardinäle** [-'nɛ:lə] **a** (*Eccl*) cardinal **b** (*Orn*) cardinal (bird)

Kar|di|nal-: Kar|di|nal|feh|ler M cardinal error; **Kar|di|nal|fra|ge** F (*geh*) cardinal or crucial question

Kar|di|nals|kol|le|gi|um NT (*Rel*) College of Cardinals, Sacred College

Kar|di|nal-: Kar|di|nal|tu|gend F (*Philos, Rel*) cardinal virtue; **Kar|di|nal|zahl** F cardinal (number)

Kar|di|o|gramm [kardio'gram] NT *pl* **-gramme** cardiogram

Kar|di|o|lo|ge [kardio'lo:gə] M **-n, -n, Kar|di|o|lo|gin** [-'lo:gɪn] F **-, -nen** cardiologist

Kar|di|o|lo|gie [kardiolo'gi:] F **-, no pl** cardiology

kar|di|o|lo|gisch [kardio'lo:gɪʃ] ADJ cardiological

Ka|renz- [ka'rɛnts-]: **Ka|renz|tag** M unpaid day of sick leave; **Ka|renz|zeit** F waiting period

Kar|fi|ol [kar'fio:l] M **-s, no pl** (*Aus*) cauliflower; **zwei (Rosen) ~** two cauliflowers

Kar|frei|tag [ka:ɐ'fraita:k] M Good Friday

Kar|fun|kel [kar'fʊŋkl] M **-s, - a** (*Med*) carbuncle **b** = **Karfunkelstein**

Kar|fun|kel|stein M *red precious stone such as ruby or garnet*, carbuncle (stone)

karg [kark] ADJ **a** (= *spärlich*) Vorrat meagre (*Brit*), meager (*US*), sparse; (= *unfruchtbar*) Boden barren; (= *dürftig*) Gehalt, Einkommen meagre (*Brit*), meager (*US*)
b (= *geizig*) mean, sparing ADV **a** (= *spärlich*) **~ ausgestattet sein** (*Mensch*) to have few possessions; **seine Bibliothek ist noch ziemlich ~ ausgestattet** there aren't many books in his library yet; **möbliert** sparsely furnished; **~ leben** to lead a meagre (*Brit*) or meager (*US*) existence **b** (= *knapp*) **~ ausfallen/bemessen sein** to be meagre (*Brit*) or meager (*US*); **etw ~ bemessen** to be mean (*Brit*) or stingy (*inf*) with sth; **die Portionen sind sehr ~ bemessen** they are very mean (*Brit*) or stingy (*inf*) with the helpings

kar|gen ['kargn] VI (= *sparsam sein*) to stint (*mit* on), to scrimp and save (*mit* with); (= *knausern*) to be mean (*Brit*) or stingy (*inf*) (*mit* with); (*mit Lob*) to be grudging

Karg|heit ['karkhait] F **-, no pl** (*von Vorrat*) meagreness (*Brit*), meagerness (*US*); (*von Möblierung*) sparseness; (*von Boden*) barrenness; (*von Gehalt, Einkommen*) meagreness (*Brit*), meagerness (*US*)

kärg|lich ['kɛrklɪç] ADJ Vorrat meagre (*Brit*), meager (*US*), sparse; Mahl frugal; (= *dürftig*) Gehalt, Einkommen meagre (*Brit*), meager (*US*); **un|ter ~en Bedingungen leben** to live in impoverished conditions ADV **sie leben ~** they lead a meagre (*Brit*) or meager (*US*) existence

Kärg|lich|keit F **-, no pl** (*von Vorrat, Menge*) meagreness (*Brit*), meagerness (*US*), sparseness; (*von Mahlzeit*) frugality

Kar|go ['kargo] M **-s, -s** cargo

Ka|ri|be [ka'ri:bə] M **-n, -n, Ka|ri|bin** [-'ri:bɪn] F **-, -nen** Carib

Ka|ri|bik [ka'ri:bɪk] F **- die ~** the Caribbean

ka|ri|bisch [ka'ri:bɪʃ] ADJ Caribbean; **das Karibische Meer** the Caribbean Sea; **die Karibischen Inseln** the Caribbean Islands

ka|riert [ka'ri:ɐt] ADJ Stoff, Muster checked, checkered (*esp US*); Papier squared ADV (*inf*) **red nicht so ~!** don't talk such rubbish; **~ gu|cken** to look puzzled

Ka|ri|es ['ka:ries] F **-, no pl** caries

Ka|ri|ka|tur [karika'tu:ɐ] F **-, -en** caricature; **eine ~ von jdm/etw zeichnen** (*lit*) to draw a caricature of sb/sth; (*lit, fig*) to caricature sb/sth

Ka|ri|ka|tu|rist [karikatuˈrɪst] M **-en, -en, Ka|ri|-ka|tu|ris|tin** [-ˈrɪstɪn] F **-, -nen** cartoonist; (= *Personenzeichner auch*) caricaturist

ka|ri|ka|tu|ris|tisch [karikatuˈrɪstɪʃ] **ADJ** caricatural (*form*), caricature; **dieser Artikel ist ~** this article is a caricature **ADV** **~ wirken** to seem like a caricature; **~ geprägt** caricature-like; **in ~ überspitztem Stil geschrieben** written in a style exaggerated to the point of caricature

ka|ri|kie|ren [kariˈkiːrən] *ptp* **karikiert** VT to caricature

ka|ri|ös [kaˈriøːs] ADJ *Zahn* carious, decayed

Ka|ri|tas [ˈkaːritas] F **-**, *no pl* (= *Nächstenliebe*) charity

ka|ri|ta|tiv [karitaˈtiːf] **ADJ** charitable **ADV** **sich ~ betätigen, ~ tätig sein** to do charitable work

Kar|kas|se [karˈkasə] F **-, -n** **a** (*Cook*) carcass **b** (*Aut: von Reifen*) casing

Karl [karl] M **-s** Charles; **~ der Große** Charlemagne

Kar|ma [ˈkarma] NT **-s**, *no pl* karma

Kar|me|li|ter [karmeˈliːtɐ] M **-s, -, Kar|me|li|-te|rin** [-ərɪn] F **-, -nen** Carmelite

Kar|me|sin [karmeˈziːn] NT **-s**, *no pl* crimson

kar|me|sin(rot) [karmeˈziːn-] ADJ crimson

kar|min(rot) [karˈmiːn-] ADJ carmine (red)

Kar|ne|val [ˈkarnəval] M **-s, -e** *or* **-s** carnival

KARNEVAL

Karneval is the period of celebration between Epiphany and Ash Wednesday, also colloquially known as the **fünfte Jahreszeit** (fifth season). Celebrations take a variety of forms: there are meetings at which humorous speeches are made and carnival songs are sung; masked balls for young and old; and on the so-called **tolle Tage** (literally, "crazy days") normal life in many regions is turned completely upside down. During the **tolle Tage** power is symbolically assumed in many towns by a carnival prince and princess. This is especially so in Rheinland, where **Karneval** has been celebrated in its present form since 1823. **Rosenmontag** is generally a holiday in this region, allowing people to watch the processions and join in the celebrations. In Southern Germany and Austria the carnival period is called **Fasching** and the processions take place on the Tuesday before Ash Wednesday → Fastnacht, Rosenmontag

---

Kar|ne|vals-: Kar|ne|vals|prinz M carnival prince; **Kar|ne|vals|prin|zes|sin** F carnival princess; **Kar|ne|vals|zug** M carnival procession

Kar|ni|ckel [karˈnɪkl] NT **-s, -** (*inf*) **a** bunny (rabbit) (*inf*), rabbit; **sich wie die ~ vermehren** (*inf*) to breed like rabbits **b** (*hum:* = *Schuldiger*) scapegoat

Kar|ni|ckel-: Kar|ni|ckel|bock M buck rabbit; **Kar|ni|ckel|stall** M rabbit hutch

kar|ni|vor [karniˈvoːɐ] ADJ (*Biol*) carnivorous

Kar|ni|vo|re [karniˈvoːrə] M **-n,** *usu pl* (*Biol*) carnivore

Kärn|ten [ˈkɛrntn] NT **-s** Carinthia

Ka|ro [ˈkaːro] NT **-s, -s a** (= *Quadrat*) square; (*auf der Spitze stehend*) diamond, lozenge; (*Muster*) check; (*diagonal*) diamond **b** *no pl* (*Cards*) diamonds *pl*

Ka|ro|lin|ger [ˈkaːrolɪŋɐ] M **-s, -, Ka|ro|lin|ge|-rin** [-ərɪn] F **-, -nen** Carolingian

ka|ro|lin|gisch [ˈkaːrolɪŋɪʃ] ADJ Carolingian; **~e Minuskeln** Caroline minuscule

Ka|ro|mus|ter NT checked *or* checkered (*esp US*) pattern

Ka|ros|se [kaˈrɔsə] F **-, -n** (= *Prachtkutsche*) (state) coach; (*fig:* = *großes Auto*) limousine

Ka|ros|se|rie [karɔsəˈriː] F **-, -n** [-ˈriːən] bodywork

Ka|ros|se|rie-: Ka|ros|se|rie|bau|er(in) M(F) *pl* **-bauer(innen)** coach-builder; **Ka|ros|se|rie|-scha|den** M damage to the bodywork; **Ka|ros|se|rie|schlos|ser(in)** M(F) panel beater; **Ka|ros|se|rie|werk|statt** F body (repair) shop

Ka|ro|tin [karoˈtiːn] NT **-s, -e** carotene, carotin

Ka|rot|te [kaˈrɔtə] F **-, -n** (small) carrot

Ka|rot|ten|saft M carrot juice

Kar|pa|ten [karˈpaːtn] PL Carpathian Mountains *pl*, Carpathians *pl*

Kar|pell [karˈpɛl] NT **-s, -e** *or* **-a** [-ˈpɛla] (*Bot*) carpel

Karp|fen [ˈkarpfn] M **-s, -** carp

Karp|fen-: karp|fen|ar|tig ADJ (*lit*) carp-like; (*fig*) *Gesicht, Aussehen* fish-like; **Karp|fen|teich** M carp pond → **Hecht**

Kar|re [ˈkarə] F **-, -n a** = **Karren b** (*inf:* = *klappriges Auto*) (old) crate (*inf*) *or* heap (*inf*)

Kar|ree [kaˈreː] NT **-s, -s a** (= *Viereck*) rectangle; (= *Rhombus*) rhombus; (= *Quadrat*) square; (= *Formation: esp Mil*) square **b** (= *Häuserblock*) block; **einmal ums ~ gehen** to walk round the block **c** (*esp Aus:* Cook) loin

kar|ren [ˈkarən] VT to cart; **jdn ~** (*inf: mit Auto*) to give sb a lift, to drive sb VI *aux sein* (*inf: mit dem Auto*) to drive (around)

Kar|ren [ˈkarən] M **-s, - a** (= *Wagen*) cart; (*esp für Garten, Baustelle*) (wheel)barrow; (*für Gepäck etc*) trolley; **ein ~ voll Obst** a cartload of fruit **b** (*fig inf*) **jdm an den ~ fahren** *or* **pinkeln** to take sb to task; **den ~ einfach laufen lassen** to let things go *or* slide; **den ~ in den Dreck fahren** to ruin things, to get things in a mess; **der ~ ist hoffnungslos verfahren, der ~ steckt im Dreck** we/they *etc* are really in a mess; **den ~ aus dem Dreck ziehen, den ~ wieder flottmachen** to put things back on the rails, to get things sorted out

Kar|ren|gaul M (*pej*) (old) nag

Kar|ret|te [kaˈrɛtə] F **-, -n** (*Sw.* = *Schubkarre*) (hand)cart, trolley

Kar|rie|re [kaˈriːrə] F **-, -n a** (= *Laufbahn*) career; **~ machen** to make a career for oneself **b** (= *voller Galopp*) (full) gallop; **~ reiten** to gallop, to ride at a gallop

Kar|rie|re-: kar|rie|re|be|wusst ▲ ADJ career-conscious; **kar|rie|re|dien|lich** ADJ career-enhancing; **Kar|rie|re|frau** F career woman; **kar|rie|re|geil** ADJ (*pej*) career-mad, career-obsessed; **Kar|rie|re|knick** M **es kam zu einem ~** his/her career took a downturn; **Kar|rie|re|lei|ter** F ladder of success, career ladder; **die ~ erklimmen** to rise up the ladder; **ganz oben auf der ~ stehen** to be at the top of the ladder *or* tree; **Kar|rie|re|ma|cher(in)** M(F) careerist; **kar|rie|re|süch|tig** ADJ career-driven; **Kar|rie|re|typ** M careerist

Kar|rie|rist [karieˈrɪst] M **-en, -en, Kar|rie|ris|-tin** [-ˈrɪstɪn] F **-, -nen** careerist

kar|ri|o|len [kaˈrioːlən] *ptp* **karriolt** VI *aux sein* (*dated inf*) to gallivant (around)

Kärr|ner [ˈkɛrnɐ] M **-s, -** (= *Fuhrmann*) carter

Kärr|ner|ar|beit F hard labour (*Brit*) *or* labor (*US*), hard toil

Kar|sams|tag [kaːɐˈzamstaːk] M Easter Saturday, Holy Saturday

Karst¹ [karst] M **-(e)s, -e** (= *Hacke*) two-pronged mattock *or* hoe

Karst² [karst] M **-(e)s, -e** (*Geog, Geol*) karst

kars|tig [ˈkarstɪç] ADJ karstic

Karst|land|schaft F (area of) karst; (*größeres Gebiet*) karst country *no art*

Kar|tät|sche [karˈtɛtʃə] F **-, -n a** (*Mil*) case shot **b** (*Build*) plasterer's float, darby

Kar|tau|se [karˈtauzə] F **-, -n** chartreuse, Carthusian monastery

Kar|täu|ser¹ [karˈtɔyzɐ] M **-s, -** (= *Likör*) chartreuse

Kar|täu|ser² [karˈtɔyzɐ] M **-s, -**, **Kar|täu|se|rin** [-ərɪn] F **-, -nen** Carthusian

Kar|te [ˈkartə] F **-, -n** (*auch Comput*) card **b** (= *Fahrkarte, Eintrittskarte*) ticket; (= *Einladungskarte*) invitation (card); (= *Bezugsschein*) coupon; (= *Essenskarte*) luncheon voucher, meal ticket (*US*); (= *Mitgliedskarte*) (membership) card; **die ~n, bitte!** tickets, please! **c** (= *Landkarte*) map; (= *Seekarte*) chart; **~n le|sen** to mapread **d** (= *Speisekarte*) menu; (= *Weinkarte*) wine list; **nach der ~** à la carte **e** (= *Spielkarte*) (playing) card; **jdm die ~ lesen** to tell sb's fortune from the cards; **mit offenen ~n spielen** (*lit*) to play with one's cards on the table; (*fig*) to put one's cards on the table; **er spielt mit verdeckten ~n** (*fig*) he's playing his cards *or* it very close to his chest; **du solltest deine ~n aufdecken** (*fig*) you ought to show your hand, you ought to put your cards on the table; **alle ~n in der Hand halten** (*fig*) to hold all the cards; **er lässt sich nicht in die ~n sehen** *or* **gucken** (*fig*) he's playing it close to his chest; **jdm in die ~n sehen** (*lit*) to look *or* take a look at sb's cards; **alles auf eine ~ setzen** (*lit*) to stake everything on one card; (*fig*) to stake everything on one chance; (= *andere Möglichkeiten ausschließen*) to put all one's eggs in one basket (*prov*); **du hast auf die falsche ~ gesetzt** (*fig*) you backed the wrong horse; **schlechte/gute ~n haben** to have a bad/good hand; (*fig*) to be in a difficult/strong position

Kar|tei [karˈtai] F **-, -en** card file, card index

Kar|tei-: Kar|tei|kar|te F file *or* index card; **Kar|tei|kas|ten** M file-card box; **Kar|tei|lei|-che** F (*inf*) sleeping *or* non-active member; **die meisten Mitglieder sind bloß ~n** most of the members are just names on the files; **Kar|tei|schrank** M filing cabinet

Kar|tell [karˈtɛl] NT **-s, -e a** (*Comm*) cartel **b** (= *Interessenvereinigung*) alliance; (*pej*) cartel

Kar|tell-: Kar|tell|amt NT , **Kar|tell|be|hör|de** F ≈ Monopolies and Mergers Commission (*Brit*), anti-trust commission (*esp US*); **Kar|tell|ge|setz** NT monopolies *or* (*esp US*) anti-trust law; **Kar|tell|ge|setz|ge|bung** F legislation against monopolies, anti-trust legislation (*esp US*); **Kar|tell|recht** NT (= *Kartellgesetz*) monopolies *or* (*esp US*) anti-trust law; (= *Kartellgesetzgebung*) legislation against monopolies, anti-trust legislation (*esp US*)

Kar|ten-: Kar|ten|be|stel|lung F ticket reservation(s *pl*); **Kar|ten|blatt** NT map, (map) sheet; **Kar|ten|haus** NT **a** house of cards; **wie ein ~ zusammenstürzen** *or* **in sich zusammenfallen** to collapse like a house of cards **b** (*Naut*) chart room; **Kar|ten|kunst|stück** NT card trick; **Kar|ten|le|gen** NT **-s**, *no pl* **a** = **Kartenlesen b** (= *Patience*) patience; **Kar|ten|le|ger** [-leːgɐ] M **-s, -, Kar|ten|le|ge|rin** [-ərɪn] F **-, -nen** fortune-teller (*who reads cards*); **Kar|ten|le|se|lam|pe** F (*Aut*) mapreading lamp; **Kar|ten|le|sen** NT **-s**, *no pl* **a** (*von Landkarten etc*) mapreading **b** (= *Wahrsagen*) fortune-telling (*using cards*), reading the cards, cartomancy (*form*); **Kar|ten|le|ser(in)** M(F) (*von Landkarten*) mapreader; **Kar|ten|or|-ga|ni|sa|ti|on** F credit card company; **Kar|ten|spiel** NT **a** (= *das Spielen*) card-playing; (= *ein Spiel*) card game; **beim ~** when playing cards **b** (= *Karten*) pack *or* deck (of cards); **Kar|ten|te|le|fon** NT cardphone; **Kar|ten|vor|ver|kauf** M advance sale of tickets; (= *Stelle*) advance booking office; **Kar|ten|werk** NT map book, book of maps; **Kar|ten|zei|chen** NT (map) symbol; **Kar|ten|zeich|ner(in)** M(F) cartographer, mapmaker

kar|te|si|a|nisch [karteˈziaːnɪʃ], **kar|te|sisch** [karˈteːzɪʃ] ADJ Cartesian

Kar|tha|ger [karˈtaːgɐ] M **-s, -, Kar|tha|ge|rin** [-ərɪn] F **-, -nen** Carthaginian

Kar|tha|go [karˈtaːgo] NT **-s** Carthage

---

kar|tie|ren [kar'tiːrən] *ptp* **kartiert** VT *Gebiet* to map out; (= *in Kartei einordnen*) to file

Kar|tof|fel [kar'tɔfl] F -, -n **a** potato; **rin in die ~n, raus aus den ~n** (*inf*) first it's one thing, then (it's) another, you're/he's *etc* always chopping and changing; **etw/jdn fallen lassen wie eine heiße ~** (*inf*) to drop sth/sb like a hot potato → **Bauer** 1 a **b** (*inf*) (= *Nase*) hooter (*Brit inf*), conk (*inf*); (= *Loch*) (gaping) hole

Kar|tof|fel- *in cpds* potato; **Kar|tof|fel|brei** M mashed potatoes *pl*; **Kar|tof|fel|chips** PL potato crisps *pl* (*Brit*), potato chips *pl* (*US*); **Kar|tof|fel|fe|ri|en** PL (*inf*) autumn holiday(s *pl*) or fall holiday (*US, originally in celebration of the potato harvest*); **Kar|tof|fel|feu|er** NT *fire made from dried potato leaves etc with general celebration after potato harvest*; **Kar|tof|fel|gra|tin** [-gra'tɛ̃ː] NT (*Cook*) gratiné(e) potatoes *pl*; **Kar|tof|fel|kä|fer** M Colorado beetle; **Kar|tof|fel|kloß** M , **Kar|tof|fel|knö|del** M (*esp S Ger, Aus; Cook*) potato dumpling; **Kar|tof|fel|kraut** NT potato foliage or leaves *pl*; **Kar|tof|fel|mehl** NT potato flour; **Kar|tof|fel|mie|te** F (*Agr*) potato clamp; **Kar|tof|fel|puf|fer** M *fried grated potato cakes*; **Kar|tof|fel|pü|ree** NT mashed potatoes *pl*; **Kar|tof|fel|sa|lat** M potato salad; **Kar|tof|fel|scha|len** PL potato skin *sing*; (*abgeschält*) potato peel *sing* or peelings *pl*; **Kar|tof|fel|schä|ler** [-ʃɛːlɐ] M -s, - potato peeler; **Kar|tof|fel|stamp|fer** M potato masher

Kar|to|graf ▲ [karto'graːf] M -en, -en, **Kar|to|gra|fin** ▲ [-'graːfɪn] F -, -nen cartographer

Kar|to|gra|fie ▲ [kartogra'fiː] F -, *no pl* cartography

kar|to|gra|fisch ▲ [karto'graːfɪʃ] ADJ cartographic(al) **ADV** **diese Gegend ist noch nicht besonders gut ~ erfasst** this area hasn't been mapped very well yet

Kar|ton [kar'tɔŋ, kar'tõː, kar'tɔːn] M -s, -s **a** (= *steifes Papier, Pappe*) card, cardboard; **ein ~** a piece of card or cardboard **b** (= *Schachtel*) cardboard box **c** (*Art*) cartoon **d** (= *Leerblatt*) blank page for one's own notes

Kar|to|na|ge [karto'naːʒə] F -, -n (= *Verpackung*) cardboard packaging

kar|to|nie|ren [karto'niːrən] *ptp* **kartoniert** VT *Bücher* to bind in board; **kartoniert** paperback

Kar|to|thek [karto'teːk] F -, -en card file, card index

Kar|tu|sche [kar'tuʃə] F -, -n **a** (= *Behälter*) cartridge; (*Hist Mil*: = *Patronentasche*) ammunition pouch **b** (*Archit, Her*) cartouche

Ka|rus|sell [karʊ'sɛl] NT -s, -s or -e merry-go-round, roundabout (*Brit*), carousel; **~ fahren** to have a ride on the merry-go-round *etc*

Kar|wo|che ['kaːrɛ-] F (*Eccl*) Holy Week

Ka|ry|a|ti|de [karya'tiːdə] F -, -n (*Archit*) caryatid

Kar|zer ['kartsɐ] M -s, - (*Hist*) **a** (= *Zelle*) detention cell (*in school or university*) **b** (= *Strafe*) detention

kar|zi|no|gen [kartsino'geːn] (*Med*) **ADJ** carcinogenic **ADV** **~ wirken** to act as a carcinogen

Kar|zi|no|gen [kartsino'geːn] NT -s, -e carcinogen

Kar|zi|no|lo|gie [kartsinolo'giː] F -, *no pl* (*Med*) oncology

Kar|zi|nom [kartsi'noːm] NT -s, -e (*Med*) carcinoma, malignant growth

Ka|sack ['kaːzak] M -s, -s tunic

Ka|schem|me [ka'ʃɛmə] F -, -n low dive

ka|schen ['kaʃn] VT (*inf*) to catch; (= *verhaften*) to nab (*inf*)

ka|schie|ren [ka'ʃiːrən] *ptp* **kaschiert** VT **a** (*fig*: = *überdecken*) to conceal **b** *Bucheinband* to laminate

Kasch|mir[1] ['kaʃmiːɐ] NT -s (*Geog*) Kashmir

Kasch|mir[2] M -s, -e (*Tex*) cashmere

Ka|schu|be [ka'ʃuːbə] M -n, -n, **Ka|schu|bin** [-'ʃuːbɪn] F -, -nen Kashub(e)

Kä|se ['kɛːzə] M -s, - a cheese; **weißer ~** curd cheese; **~ schließt den Magen** cheese rounds off a meal nicely **b** (*inf*: = *Unsinn*) rubbish (*Brit*), twaddle (*inf*)

Kä|se- *in cpds* cheese; **Kä|se|auf|lauf** M (*Cook*) cheese soufflé; **Kä|se|blatt** NT , **Kä|se|blätt|chen** NT (*inf*) local rag (*inf*); **Kä|se|brot** NT bread and cheese; **Kä|se|ecke** F cheese triangle; **Kä|se|fon|due** NT cheese fondue; **Kä|se|fü|ße** PL (*inf*) smelly or cheesy feet *pl*; **Kä|se|ge|bäck** NT cheese savouries *pl* or savories *pl* (*US*); **Kä|se|glo|cke** F cheese cover; (*fig*) dome; **Kä|se|ho|bel** M cheese slice

Ka|se|in [kaze'iːn] NT -s, -e casein

Ka|se|ku|chen M cheesecake

Ka|sel ['kaːzl] F -, -n (*Eccl*) chasuble

Ka|se|mat|te [kazə'matə] F -, -n casemate

kä|sen ['kɛːzn] VI (*rare*) to make cheese

Kä|se|plat|te F cheeseboard

Kä|se|rei [kɛːzə'rai] F -, -en **a** (= *Betrieb*) cheese dairy **b** *no pl* (= *Käseherstellung*) cheese-making

Ka|ser|ne [ka'zɛrnə] F -, -n barracks *pl*

Ka|ser|nen-: Ka|ser|nen|ar|rest M confinement to barracks; **Ka|ser|nen|hof** M barrack square; **Ka|ser|nen|hof|ton** M *pl* -**töne es herrscht ein richtiger ~** it's like being on the parade ground

ka|ser|nie|ren [kazɛr'niːrən] *ptp* **kaserniert** VT *Truppen* to quarter in barracks; *Flüchtlinge, Obdachlose etc* to quarter, to billet

Kä|se-: Kä|se|stan|ge F cheese straw (*Brit*), cheese stick (*US*); **Kä|se|tor|te** F cheesecake; **kä|se|weiß** ADJ (*inf*) white or pale (as a ghost)

kä|sig ['kɛːzɪç] ADJ **a** (*fig inf*) *Gesicht, Haut* pasty, pale; (*vor Schreck*) white, pale **b** (*lit*) cheesy

Ka|si|no [ka'ziːno] NT -s, -s **a** (= *Spielbank*) casino **b** (= *Offizierskasino*) (officers') mess or club; (= *Speiseraum*) dining room, cafeteria

Kas|ka|de [kas'kaːdə] F -, -n **a** (= *Wasserfall*) waterfall, cascade (*poet*); (*in Feuerwerk*) cascade; **die Wasser stürzen in ~n hinab** the waters cascade down **b** (= *Zirkussprung*) acrobatic leap

kas|ko|ver|si|chern ['kasko-] *ptp* **kaskoversichert** VT insep, only infin and ptp (*Aut*) to insure against own damage; ≈ to insure comprehensively; **kaskoversichert sein** ≈ to have comprehensive insurance

Kas|ko|ver|si|che|rung ['kasko-] F (*Aut*) (= *Teilkaskoversicherung*) ≈ third party, fire and theft insurance; (= *Vollkaskoversicherung*) fully comprehensive insurance; (*Naut*) hull insurance

Kas|per ['kaspɐ] M -s, -, (*Aus, S Ger*) **Kas|perl** ['kaspɐl] M OR NT -s, -(n), (*S Ger*) **Kas|per|le** ['kaspɐlə] M OR NT -s, - **a** (*im Puppenspiel*) Punch (*esp Brit*) **b** (*inf*) clown (*inf*), fool

Kas|per|le-: Kas|per|le|fi|gur F Punch glove (*Brit*) or hand (*US*) puppet; **Kas|per|le|the|a|ter** NT Punch and Judy (show) (*esp Brit*), puppet show; (= *Gestell*) Punch and Judy theatre (*esp Brit*), puppet theater (*US*)

kas|pern ['kaspɐn] VI (*inf*) to clown (*inf*) or fool around

Kas|pi|sches Meer ['kaspɪʃəs] NT Caspian Sea

Kas|sa ['kasa] F -, **Kas|sen** ['kasn] (*esp Aus*) = **Kasse a**

Kas|sa- (*esp Aus*): **Kas|sa|ge|schäft** NT (*Comm*) cash transaction; (*St Ex*) spot transaction; **Kas|sa|kurs** M spot rate; **Kas|sa|markt** M spot market

Kas|sand|ra|ruf [ka'sandra-] M prophecy of doom, gloomy prediction

Kas|sa|ti|on [kasa'tsioːn] F -, -en (*Jur*) quashing, reversal; (*von Urkunde*) annulment

Kas|sa|ti|ons-: Kas|sa|ti|ons|ge|richt NT (*Jur*) court of appeal; **Kas|sa|ti|ons|hof** M (*Jur*) Supreme Court of Appeal; (*in der Schweiz*) *court of appeal in matters of state versus cantonal law*

Kas|se ['kasə] F -, -n **a** (= *Zahlstelle*) cash desk (*Brit*) or point, till (*Brit*), cash register (*US*), counter (*esp US*); (= *Zahlraum*) cashier's office; (*Theat etc*) box office; (*in Bank*) bank counter; (*in Supermarkt*) checkout; **an der ~** (*in Geschäft*) at the desk (*esp Brit*), at the (checkout) counter (*esp US*)
b (= *Geldkasten*) cash box; (*in Läden*) cash register, till (*Brit*); (= *Geldmittel*) coffers *pl*; (*bei Spielen*) kitty; (*in einer Spielbank*) bank; **in die ~ greifen** (*inf*) to dip into the till (*Brit*) or cashbox; **der Film hat volle ~n gemacht** the film was a big box-office success; **die ~n klingeln** the tills are ringing (*Brit*), the money is really rolling in
c (= *Bargeld*) cash; **ein Verkauf per ~** (*form*) a cash sale; **netto ~** net payment; **gegen ~** for cash; **bei ~ sein** (*inf*) to be flush (*inf*), to be in the money (*inf*); **knapp bei ~ sein** (*inf*) to be short of cash, to be out of pocket (*Brit*); **gut/schlecht bei ~ sein** (*inf*) to be well-off/badly-off; **~ machen** to check one's finances; (*in Geschäft*) to cash up (*Brit*), to count up the earnings (*US*); **die ~ führen** to be in charge of the money; **die ~ stimmt!** (*inf*) the money's OK (*inf*); **ein Loch in die ~ reißen** (*fig*) to make a dent or hole in one's finances; **zur ~ bitten** to ask for money; **jdn zur ~ bitten** to ask sb to pay up
d (*inf*: = *Sparkasse*) (savings) bank
e (= *Krankenkasse*)

Kas|se|ler ['kasələ] NT -s, - *lightly smoked pork loin*

Kas|sen-: Kas|sen|ab|schluss ▲ M cashing up; **~ machen** to cash up (*Brit*), to count up the earnings (*US*); **Kas|sen|arzt** M , **Kas|sen|ärz|tin** F *doctor who treats members of medical insurance schemes*; ≈ National Health general practitioner (*Brit*), ≈ preferred provider (*US*); **kas|sen|ärzt|lich** ADJ **~e Behandlung** treatment by a health scheme doctor (*Brit*) or preferred provider (*US*); **Kas|sen|au|to|mat** M cash dispenser (*Brit*), automatic teller, money machine (*US*); **Kas|sen|be|leg** M sales receipt or check (*US*); **Kas|sen|be|richt** M financial report; (*in Verein etc auch*) treasurer's report; **Kas|sen|be|stand** M cash balance, cash in hand; **Kas|sen|bon** M sales slip or receipt; **Kas|sen|bril|le** F (*pej inf*) NHS specs *pl* (*Brit inf*), standard-issue glasses *pl*; **Kas|sen|buch** NT cashbook; **Kas|sen|er|folg** M (*Theat etc*) box-office hit; **Kas|sen|füh|rer(in)** M(F) treasurer; **Kas|sen|fül|ler** M box-office hit; **Kas|sen|la|ge** F (*inf*) state of one's finances, cash flow situation; **die ~ überprüfen** to check how much cash one has; **Kas|sen|ob|li|ga|ti|on** F (*St Ex*) medium-term bond; **Kas|sen|pa|ti|ent(in)** M(F) *patient belonging to medical insurance scheme*; ≈ National Health patient (*Brit*); **Kas|sen|preis** M cash price, sales price; **Kas|sen|prü|fung** F audit; **Kas|sen|re|kord** M record takings *pl*; **Kas|sen|schal|ter** M = **Kasse a**; **Kas|sen|schla|ger** M (*inf*) (*Theat etc*) box-office hit; (*Ware*) big seller; **Kas|sen|stand** M (*Comm*) cash in till (*Brit*) or register (*US*); **Kas|sen|stun|den** PL hours of business (*of cashier's office etc*); **Kas|sen|sturz** M (*Comm*) cashing up (*Brit*), counting up the earnings (*US*); **~ machen** to check one's finances; (*Comm*) to cash up (*Brit*), to count up the earnings (*US*); **Kas|sen|wart** [-vart] M -s, -e, **Kas|sen|war|tin** [-vartɪn] F -, -nen treasurer; **Kas|sen|zet|tel** M sales slip

Kas|se|rol|le [kasə'rɔlə] F -, -n saucepan; (*mit Henkeln*) casserole

Kas|set|te [ka'sɛtə] F -, -n **a** (= *Kästchen*) case, box **b** (*für Bücher*) slipcase; (= *Bücher in Kassette*) set, pack (*Comm*); (= *Geschenkkassette*) gift case/set; (*für Schallplatten*) box; set; (= *Tonbandkassette, Filmbehälter*) cassette; (= *Aufbewahrungskassette*) container; (*für Bücher*) library case; (*für Film*) can **c** (*Archit*) coffer

Kas|set|ten-: Kas|set|ten|deck NT cassette deck; **Kas|set|ten|de|cke** F coffered ceiling; **Kas|set|ten|film** M (*Phot*) cartridge film; **Kas|set|ten|re|kor|der** M cassette recorder

Kas|si|ber [ka'siːbɐ] M **-s, -** secret message, stiff (*US inf*)

Kas|sie|r [ka'siːɐ] M **-s, -e, Kas|sie|rin** [ka'siːrɪn] F **-, -nen** (*S Ger, Aus, Sw*) = **Kassierer**

kas|sie|ren [ka'siːrən] *ptp* **kassiert** **VT** **a** *Gelder etc* to collect (up), to take in; (*inf*) *Abfindung, Finderlohn* to pick up (*inf*); **nach seinem Tode kassierte sie 50.000 Euro** (*inf*) after his death she collected 50,000 euros; **bei jedem Verkauf kassiert er eine Menge Geld** (*inf*) he makes a packet (*Brit*) or bundle on every sale (*inf*) **b** (*inf: = wegnehmen*) to take away, to confiscate **c** (*inf: = verhaften*) to nab (*inf*) **d** (*Jur*) *Urteil* to quash **VI** (= *abrechnen*) to take the money; **bei jdm ~** to collect or get money from sb; **Sie haben bei mir schon kassiert** I've paid already; **darf ich ~, bitte?** would you like to pay now?

Kas|sie|rer [ka'siːrɐ] M **-s, -, Kas|sie|re|rin** [-ərɪn] F **-, -nen** cashier; (= *Bankkassierer*) clerk, teller; (= *Einnehmer*) collector; (*eines Klubs*) treasurer

Kas|tag|net|te [kastan'jɛtə] F **-, -n** castanet

Kas|ta|nie [kas'taːniə] F **-, -n** chestnut; (= *Rosskastanie*) (horse) chestnut; (= *Edelkastanie*) (sweet) chestnut; (*Holz*) chestnut (wood); **gla-sierte ~n** marrons glacés; **für jdn die ~n aus dem Feuer holen** (*fig*) to pull sb's chestnuts out of the fire

Kas|ta|ni|en-: Kas|ta|ni|en|baum M chestnut tree; **kas|ta|ni|en|braun** ADJ maroon; *Pferd, Haar* chestnut; **Kas|ta|ni|en|holz** NT chestnut (wood)

Käst|chen ['kɛstçən] NT **-s, -** **a** (= *kleiner Kasten*) small box; (*für Schmuck*) case, casket **b** (*auf kariertem Papier*) square

Kas|te ['kastə] F **-, -n** caste

kas|tei|en [kas'taiən] *ptp* **kasteit** VR (*als Bußübung*) to castigate or chastise oneself, to mortify the flesh (*liter*); (= *sich Entbehrungen auferlegen*) to deny oneself

Kas|tei|ung F **-, -en** castigation

Kas|tell [kas'tɛl] NT **-s, -e** (small) fort; (*Naut, Hist*) castle

Kas|tel|lan [kastɛ'laːn] M **-s, -e** (= *Aufsichtsbeamter, Hausmeister*) steward; (*old dial: in Schulen etc*) janitor, caretaker; (*Hist:* = *Schlossvogt*) castellan

Kas|ten ['kastn] M **-s, ≈** ['kɛstn] **a** box; (= *Kiste*) crate, case; (= *Truhe*) chest; (*Aus:* = *Schrank*) cupboard; (*N Ger:* = *Schublade*) drawer; (= *Briefkasten*) postbox (*Brit*), letter box (*Brit*), mailbox (*US*); (= *Schaukasten*) showcase, display case; (= *Brotkasten*) breadbin (*Brit*), breadbox (*US*); (*Sport:* = *Gerät*) box **b** (*inf:* = *altes Schiff*) tub (*inf*); (= *alter Wagen, Flugzeug*) crate (*inf*); (= *altes großes Haus*) barn (of a place) (*inf*); (= *Radio, Fernsehapparat etc*) box (*inf*) **c** (*inf:* = *großer, breiter Mann*) heavyweight (*inf*), big bloke (*Brit inf*) **d** (*inf*) **er hat viel auf dem ~** he's brainy (*inf*) **e** (*inf:* = *Fußballtor*) goal; **sie müssen noch ein Tor in den ~ bringen** they need to put another one in the back of the net (*inf*); **wer geht in den ~?** who's going in goal?

Kas|ten-: Kas|ten|form F (*Cook*) (square) baking tin (*Brit*) or pan (*US*); **kas|ten|för|mig** [-fœrmɪç] ADJ box-shaped; **Kas|ten|geist** M , *no pl* (*Sociol, Rel*) caste spirit; (*von Cliquen*) clannishness, cliquishness; (= *Klassenbewusstsein*) class spirit or outlook; **Kas|ten|wa|gen** M (*Aut*) van, truck, panel truck (*US*); (*auf Bauernhof*) box cart; **Kas|ten|we|sen** NT , *no pl* caste system

Kas|ti|li|en [kas'tiːliən] NT **-s** Castille

Kast|rat [kas'traːt] M **-en, -en** eunuch; (*Mus Hist*) castrato

Kast|ra|ti|on [kastra'tsioːn] F **-, -en** castration; **chemische ~** chemical castration

Kast|ra|ti|ons-: Kast|ra|ti|ons|angst F fear of castration; **Kast|ra|ti|ons|kom|plex** M castration complex

kast|rie|ren [kas'triːrən] *ptp* **kastriert** VT (*lit, fig*) to castrate; *Tiere auch* to geld

Ka|su|is|tik [kazu'ɪstɪk] F **-,** *no pl* casuistry

ka|su|is|tisch [kazu'ɪstɪʃ] ADJ casuistic

Ka|sus ['kaːzʊs] M **-, -** ['kaːzuːs] (*Gram*) case

Ka|sus-: Ka|sus|bil|dung F case formation, declension; **Ka|sus|en|dung** F (case) ending

Kat [kat] M **-s, -s** (*Aut*) *abbr von* **Katalysator** cat

Ka|ta- [kata] *in cpds* cata-; **Ka|ta|falk** [kata'falk] M **-s, -e** catafalque; **Ka|ta|kom|be** [kata-'kɔmbə] F **-, -n** catacomb

Ka|ta|la|ne [kata'laːnə] M **-n, -n, Ka|ta|la|nin** [-'laːnɪn] F **-, -nen** Catalan

Ka|ta|la|ni|en [kata'laːniən] NT **-s** Catalonia

ka|ta|la|nisch [kata'laːnɪʃ] ADJ Catalan

Ka|ta|la|nisch(e) [kata'laːnɪʃ] NT Catalan → *auch* **Deutsch(e)**

Ka|ta|log [kata'loːk] M **-(e)s, -e** [-gə] catalogue (*Brit*), catalog (*US*)

ka|ta|lo|gi|sie|ren [katalogi'ziːrən] *ptp* **katalogisiert** VT to catalogue (*Brit*), to catalog (*US*)

Ka|ta|lo|gi|sie|rung F **-, -en** cataloguing (*Brit*), cataloging (*US*)

ka|ta|log|mä|ßig ADJ *Liste* catalogued (*Brit*), cataloged (*US*) ADV **er erfasste seine Funde ~** he made a catalogue (*Brit*) or catalog (*US*) of his finds, he catalogued (*Brit*) or cataloged (*US*) his finds

Ka|ta|lo|ni|en [kata'loːniən] NT **-s** Catalonia

Ka|ta|ly|sa|tor [kataly'zaːtor] M **-s, Katalysa-toren** (*lit, fig*) catalyst; (*Aut*) catalytic converter

Ka|ta|ly|sa|tor-: Ka|ta|ly|sa|tor|au|to NT car fitted with a catalytic converter; **Ka|ta|ly|sa-tor-Mo|dell** NT model with a catalytic converter

Ka|ta|ly|se [kata'lyːzə] F **-, -n** (*Chem*) catalysis

ka|ta|ly|tisch [kata'lyːtɪʃ] ADJ catalytic

Ka|ta|ma|ran [katama'raːn] M **-s, -e** catamaran

Ka|ta|pult [kata'pʊlt] NT OR M **-(e)s, -e** catapult

ka|ta|pul|tie|ren [katapʊl'tiːrən] *ptp* **katapul-tiert** VT to catapult VR to catapult oneself; (*Pilot*) to eject

Ka|ta|pult|sitz M ejector or ejection seat

Ka|ta|rakt [kata'rakt] M **-(e)s, -e** cataract

Ka|tarr ▲ [ka'tar] M **-s, -e, Ka|tarrh** M **-s, -e** catarrh

Ka|tas|ter [ka'tastɐ] M OR NT **-s, -** land register, cadaster (*spec*)

Ka|tas|ter|amt NT land registry

ka|tas|trie|ren [katas'triːrən] *ptp* **katastriert** VT *Grundstücke* to register, to enter in the land register

ka|ta|stro|phal [katastro'faːl] ADJ disastrous; *Auswirkungen etc auch* catastrophic; (= *haarsträubend schlecht auch*) atrocious; **der Mangel an Brot ist ~ geworden** the bread shortage has become catastrophic ADV **sich ~ auswirken** to have catastrophic effects; **~ geschwächt** disastrously weakened; **jds Gesundheit ~ beein-trächtigen** to ruin sb's health; **~ unterernährt sein** to be disastrously undernourished; **das Zimmer sieht ja ~ aus** the room looks absolutely disastrous

Ka|ta|stro|phe [katas'troːfə] F **-, -n** disaster, catastrophe; (*Theat, Liter*) catastrophe, (*tragic*) dénouement; **der ist eine ~** (*inf*) he's a real disaster (area) (*inf*) or catastrophe (*inf*)

Ka|ta|stro|phen-: Ka|ta|stro|phen|ab|wehr F disaster prevention; **Ka|ta|stro|phen|alarm** M emergency alert; **Ka|ta|stro|phen|dienst** M emergency service; **Ka|ta|stro|phen|ein-satz** M duty or use in case of disaster; **für den ~** for use in case of disaster; **Ka|ta|stro|phen|-**

ge|biet NT disaster area; **Ka|ta|stro|phen-op|fer** NT disaster victim; **Ka|ta|stro|phen-schutz** M disaster control; (*im Voraus*); **Ka|ta-stro|phen|stim|mung** F doomsday atmosphere or mood; **Ka|ta|stro|phen|tou|ris|mus** M disaster tourism

Ka|ta|to|nie [katato'niː] F **-, -n** [-'niːən] (*Psych*) catatonia

Kat|au|to ['kat-] NT (*Mot inf*) cat car

Ka|te ['kaːtə] F **-, -n** (*N Ger*) cottage, croft (*Scot*)

Ka|te|che|se [kate'çeːzə] F **-, -n** catechesis

Ka|te|chet [kate'çeːt] M **-en, -en, Ka|te|che|tin** [-'çeːtɪn] F **-, -nen** catechist

Ka|te|chis|mus [kate'çɪsmʊs] M **-, Katechismen** [-mən] catechism

Ka|te|chist [kate'çɪst] M **-en, -en, Ka|te|chis-tin** [-'çɪstɪn] F **-, -nen** catechist

ka|te|go|ri|al [katego'riaːl] ADJ categorical

Ka|te|go|rie [katego'riː] F **-, -n** [-'riːən] category; **er gehört auch zur ~ derer, die ...** he's one of those who ..., he's the sort or type who ...

ka|te|go|risch [kate'goːrɪʃ] ADJ categorical, absolute; *Ablehnung auch* flat; **der ~e Imperativ** the categorical imperative ADV categorically, absolutely; *ablehnen* categorically, flatly; *behaupten, formulieren* categorically; **ich weigerte mich ~** I refused outright, I absolutely refused; **... er-klärte er ~ ...** he declared emphatically

ka|te|go|ri|sie|ren [kategori'ziːrən] *ptp* **katego-risiert** VT to categorize

Ka|ter ['kaːtɐ] M **-s, -** **a** tom(cat); **wie ein ver-liebter ~** like an amorous tomcat → **gestiefelt** **a** **b** (*nach Alkoholgenuss*) hangover

Ka|ter-: Ka|ter|früh|stück NT *breakfast (of pickled herring etc)* to cure a hangover; **Ka-ter|stim|mung** F depression, the blues *pl* (*inf*)

kat|e|xo|chen [katɛksɔ'xeːn] ADV (*liter*) **Demo-kratie ~** the epitome of democracy

kath. *abbr von* **katholisch**

Ka|thar|sis ['kaːtarzɪs, ka'tarzɪs] F **-,** *no pl* (*Liter, fig*) catharsis

ka|thar|tisch [ka'tartɪʃ] ADJ (*Liter, fig*) cathartic

Ka|the|der [ka'teːdɐ] M OR NT **-s, -** (*in Schule*) teacher's desk; (*in Universität*) lectern; **etw vom ~ herab erklären** to declare sth ex cathedra (*hum, form*)

Ka|thed|ra|le [kate'draːlə] F **-, -n** cathedral

Ka|the|ter [ka'teːtɐ] M **-s, -** (*Med*) catheter

Ka|tho|de [ka'toːdə] F **-, -n** (*Phys*) cathode

Ka|tho|den-: Ka|tho|den|strah|len PL (*Phys*) cathode rays *pl*; **Ka|tho|den|strahl|röh|re** F (*TV etc*) cathode-ray tube

Ka|tho|le [ka'toːlə] M **-n, -n, Ka|tho|lin** [-'toː-lɪn] F **-, -nen** (*inf*) Catholic, Papist (*pej*)

Ka|tho|lik [kato'liːk] M **-en, -en, Ka|tho|li|kin** [-'liːkɪn] F **-, -nen** (Roman) Catholic

ka|tho|lisch [ka'toːlɪʃ] ADJ (Roman) Catholic; **sie ist streng ~** she's a strict Catholic ADV **~ denken** to have Catholic views; **~ heiraten** to have a Catholic wedding; **~ beerdigt werden** to have a Catholic burial; **~ beeinflusst** influenced by Catholicism; **seine Kinder ~ erziehen** to raise one's children (as) Catholics

Ka|tho|li|zis|mus [katoli'tsɪsmʊs] M **-,** *no pl* (Roman) Catholicism

Kat-Mo|dell NT (*Aut*) *abbr von* **Katalysator-Mo-dell**

Katt|an|ker ['kat|aŋkɐ] M (*Naut*) kedge

Kat|te|gatt ['katəgat] NT **-s** Kattegat

Kat|tun [ka'tuːn] M **-s, -e** (*old*) cotton, calico

katz|bal|gen ['katsbalgn] VR to romp around

Katz|bal|ge|rei [katsbalgə'rai] F romping

katz|bu|ckeln ['katsbʊkln] VI (*pej inf*) to bow and scrape, to grovel

Kätz|chen ['kɛtsçən] NT **-s, -** **a** (= *junge Katze, inf:* = *Mädchen*) kitten; (= *Katze*) pussy (*inf*) **b** (*Bot*) catkin

Kat|ze ['katsə] F -, -n cat; **meine Arbeit war für die Katz** (fig) my work was a waste of time; **das hat die ~ gefressen** (fig) the fairies took it (hum inf); **Katz und Maus mit jdm spielen** to play cat and mouse with sb; **wie die ~ um den heißen Brei herumschleichen** to beat about the bush; **die ~ aus dem Sack lassen** (inf) to let the cat out of the bag; **die ~ im Sack kaufen** to buy a pig in a poke (prov); **die ~ lässt das Mausen nicht** (Prov) the leopard cannot change its spots (Prov); **bei Nacht sind alle ~n grau** all cats are grey (Brit) or gray (US) at night; **wenn die ~ aus dem Haus ist, tanzen die Mäuse (auf dem Tisch)** (Prov) when the cat's away the mice will play (Prov)

Kat|zel|ma|cher(in) M(F) (S Ger, Aus: pej: = Italiener) dago (pej), Eyetie (Brit pej)

Kat|zen-: Kat|zen|au|ge NT a (= Straßenmarkierung) Catseye®; (= Rückstrahler) reflector b (Min) cat's-eye; **Kat|zen|bu|ckel** M arched back (of a cat); **einen ~ machen** to arch one's back; **kat|zen|freund|lich** ADJ (pej) overfriendly; **Kat|zen|fut|ter** NT cat food; **kat|zen|haft** ADJ cat-like, feline; **Kat|zen|hai** M dogfish; **Kat|zen|jam|mer** M (inf) a (= Kater) hangover b (= jämmerliche Stimmung) depression, the blues pl (inf); **ich habe ~** I feel down (in the dumps) (inf), I've got the blues (inf); **Kat|zen|klo** NT (inf) cat litter tray (Brit) or box (US); **Kat|zen|kopf** M (fig) a (= Kopfstein) cobble(stone) b (Sch: = Schlag) cuff (on the head), box round the ears; **Kat|zen|kraut** NT catnip; **Kat|zen|mu|sik** F (fig) caterwauling, din, racket (inf); **Kat|zen|mut|ter** F (doting) cat owner; **Kat|zen|sprung** M (inf) stone's throw; **Kat|zen|streu** F cat litter; **Kat|zen|tisch** M (hum) children's table; **die Kinder essen am ~** the children are eating at their own table; **Kat|zen|tür** F cat flap; **Kat|zen|wä|sche** F (hum inf) a lick and a promise (inf), a cat's lick (Brit inf); **~ machen** to give oneself a lick and a promise; **Kat|zen|zun|ge** F (= Schokolade) chocolate langue de chat

Katz-und-Maus-Spiel NT cat-and-mouse game

Kau- [kau-]: **Kau|ap|pa|rat** M masticatory apparatus; **Kau|be|we|gung** F chewing movement

Kau|der|welsch ['kaudəvɛlʃ] NT -(s), no pl (pej) (= Fach- oder Geheimsprache) lingo (inf), jargon; (= Gemisch aus mehreren Sprachen/Dialekten) hotchpotch (Brit) or hodgepodge or mishmash (of different languages/dialects); (= unverständliche Sprache) double Dutch, gibberish

kau|der|wel|schen ['kaudəvɛlʃn] VI (unverständlich) to talk double Dutch, to talk gibberish; (in Fachsprache) to talk jargon; (in Gemisch aus mehreren Sprachen/Dialekten) to talk a hotchpotch (Brit) or hodgepodge or mishmash of languages/dialects

kau|en ['kauən] VT to chew; Nägel to bite, to chew; Wein to taste VI to chew; **an etw** (dat) **~** to chew (on) sth; **an den Nägeln ~** to bite or chew one's nails; **daran hatte ich lange zu ~** (fig) it took me a long time to get over it; **daran wird er zu ~ haben** (fig) that will really give him food for thought or something to think about; **gut gekaut ist halb verdaut** (Prov) you should chew your food properly; **das Kauen** chewing

kau|ern ['kauən] VIR (vi auch sein) to crouch (down); (ängstlich) to cower; (Schutz suchend) to be huddled (up)

Kauf [kauf] M -(e)s, Käufe ['kɔyfə] (= das Kaufen) buying no pl, purchase (esp form), purchasing no pl (esp form); (= das Gekaufte) purchase (esp form), buy; **das war ein günstiger ~** that was a good buy; **diese Käufe haben sich gelohnt** it was worth buying these; **mit diesem Anzug machen Sie bestimmt einen guten ~** this suit is definitely a good buy; **ein ~ auf Kredit** a credit purchase; **etw zum ~ anbieten** to offer sth for sale; **einen ~ abschließen** or **tätigen** (form) to complete a purchase; **etw durch ~ erwerben**

(form) to purchase sth; **etw in ~ nehmen** (lit) to accept sth in part exchange; (fig) to accept sth

Kauf-: Kauf|ab|sicht F intention to buy; **Kauf|auf|trag** M purchasing or buying order; **Kauf|be|reit|schaft** F willingness to buy; **Kauf|brief** M deed of purchase; (esp für Grundstücke) title deed

kau|fen ['kaufn] VT a (auch **sich** (dat) **kaufen**) to buy, to purchase (esp form); **ich kauf dir ein Geschenk** I'll buy you a present, I'll buy a present for you; **ich habe (mir) einen neuen Anzug gekauft** I bought (myself) a new suit; **diese Zigaretten werden viel gekauft** we sell a lot of these cigarettes; **diese Zigaretten werden nicht gekauft** nobody buys these cigarettes; **jetzt wird nicht schon wieder eine neue Jacke gekauft!** you're not going to buy another jacket!; **dafür kann ich mir nichts ~** (iro), **was kann man sich** (dat) **dafür (schon) ~** (iro) what use is that to me!, that's a fat lot of use! (inf) b (= bestechen) jdn to bribe, to buy off; Spiel to fix; Stimmen to buy; **der Sieg war gekauft** it was fixed c **sich** (dat) **jdn ~** (inf) to give sb a piece of one's mind (inf); (tätlich) to fix sb (inf) d auch vi (Cards) to buy VI to buy; (= Einkäufe machen) to shop; **auf dem Markt kauft man billiger** it is cheaper to shop at the market, you can buy things cheaper at the market; **das Kaufen** buying, purchasing (esp form)

Käu|fer ['kɔyfɐ] M -s, -, **Käu|fe|rin** [-ərɪn] F -, -nen buyer, purchaser (esp form); (= Kunde) customer, shopper

Käu|fer-: Käu|fer|kreis M group of customers or buyers; **Käu|fer|schicht** F class of customer(s)

Kauf-: Kauf|fah|rer M (old) merchant ship, merchantman; **Kauf|frau** F businesswoman; **Kauf|hal|le** F department store; (esp DDR) small supermarket; **Kauf|haus** NT department store; **Kauf|haus|de|tek|tiv(in)** M(F) store detective; **Kauf|in|te|res|sent(in)** M(F) prospective purchaser or buyer, prospect; **Kauf|kraft** F (von Geld) buying or purchasing power; (vom Käufer) spending power; **Kunden mit ~** customers with money to spend; **kauf|kräf|tig** ADJ **eine ~e Währung** a currency with good purchasing power; **~e Kunden** customers with money to spend; **ein ~er Markt** a market with strong purchasing power

Kaufkraft-: Kauf|kraft|len|kung F control of (consumer) spending; **Kauf|kraft|schwund** M drop in purchasing power; **Kauf|kraft|über|hang** M excess or surplus (consumer) spending power; **Kauf|kraft|ver|lust** M loss of purchasing power

Kauf-: Kauf|la|den M a (rare: = Ladengeschäft) (small) shop b (= Spielzeug) toy shop; **Kauf|leu|te** pl von **Kaufmann**

käuf|lich ['kɔyflɪç] ADJ a (= zu kaufen) for sale, purchasable (form); **etwas, was nicht ~ ist** something which cannot be bought b (fig) venal; **~e Liebe** prostitution; **ein ~es Mädchen** (geh) a woman of easy virtue; **Freundschaft ist nicht ~** friendship cannot be bought c (fig: = bestechlich) venal; **~ sein** to be easily bought; **ich bin nicht ~** you cannot buy me! ADV **etw ~ erwerben** (form) to purchase sth

Käuf|lich|keit F -, no pl a **Kennzeichen des Kapitalismus ist die ~ aller Dinge** it is a characteristic of capitalism that everything can be bought or is for sale b (fig: = Bestechlichkeit) corruptibility, venality

Kauf-: Kauf|lust F desire to buy (things); (St Ex) buying; **die ~ hat plötzlich zugenommen** people have suddenly gone on a spending spree; **kauf|lus|tig** ADJ inclined to buy, in a buying mood; **in den Straßen drängten sich die Kauflustigen** the streets were thronged with shoppers

Kauf|mann M pl -leute a (= Geschäftsmann) businessman; (= Händler) trader; (= Tabakkaufmann, Gewürzkaufmann, Wollkaufmann etc) mer-

chant; **gelernter ~** person with qualifications in business or commerce; **jeder ~ lobt seine Ware** (Prov) a salesman will always praise his own wares b (= Einzelhandelskaufmann) small shopkeeper, grocer; **zum ~ gehen** to go to the grocer's

kauf|män|nisch [-mɛnɪʃ] ADJ commercial, business attr; **~er Angestellter** office worker; **~e Buchführung** commercial book-keeping; **er wollte einen ~en Beruf ergreifen** he wanted to make a career in business or commerce; **er übt einen ~en Beruf aus** he is in business or commerce; **Fachschule für ~e Berufe** commercial college, business school; **alles Kaufmännische** everything commercial, everything to do with business; **alles Kaufmännische macht seine Frau für ihn** his wife looks after the business side of things for him ADV **sie ist ~ tätig** she is in business, she is a businesswoman; **~ denken** to think in commercial or business terms; **nicht sehr ~ gedacht** not very businesslike; **~ handeln** to act businesslike or like a businessman/-woman

Kauf|mann|schaft ['kaufmanʃaft] F -, no pl (geh) merchants pl

Kauf|manns-: Kauf|manns|ge|hil|fe M , **Kauf|manns|ge|hil|fin** F assistant, clerk; (im Laden) sales assistant, clerk (US); **Kauf|manns|la|den** M a (dated) grocer's; (= Gemischtwarenhandlung) general store b (= Spielzeug) toy grocer's shop, miniature grocery store (US); **Kauf|manns|lehr|ling** M management trainee; **Kauf|manns|stand** M merchant class

Kauf-: Kauf|op|ti|on F (St Ex) call option; (Comm) option to buy; **Kauf|preis** M purchase price; **Kauf|rausch** M spending spree; **im ~ sein** to be on a spending spree; **Kauf|sucht** F compulsive shopping; **ihre ~** her shopping addiction; **kauf|süch|tig** ADJ addicted to shopping; **~ sein** to be a compulsive shopper or a shopaholic (inf), to be addicted to shopping; **Kauf|sum|me** F money; **Kauf|un|lust** F consumer resistance; **Kauf|ver|trag** M bill of sale; **Kauf|wert** M market value; **Kauf|zwang** M obligation to buy; **kein/ohne ~** no/without obligation

Kau|gum|mi M OR NT chewing gum

Kau|ka|si|en [kau'ka:ziən] NT -s Caucasia

Kau|ka|si|er [kau'ka:ziɐ] M -s, -, **Kau|ka|si|e|rin** [-iərɪn] F -, -nen Caucasian

kau|ka|sisch [kau'ka:zɪʃ] ADJ Caucasian

Kau|ka|sus ['kaukazʊs] M - der ~ (the) Caucasus

Kaul|quap|pe ['kaul-] F tadpole

kaum [kaum] ADV a (= noch nicht einmal) hardly, scarcely, barely; **er verdient ~ 1500 Euro** he earns barely 1500 euros; **ich habe ~ noch 10 Liter** I've barely 10 litres (Brit) or liters (US) left; **das kostet ~ 100 Euro** it doesn't even cost 100 euros; **man braucht ~ 10 Liter** you'll need less than 10 litres (Brit) or liters (US); **sie war ~ hereingekommen, als ...** hardly or scarcely or no sooner had she come in when ..., she had hardly etc come in when ...; **jemand/jemals ~** hardly or scarcely anyone/ever; **es ist ~ möglich, dass ...** it is hardly or scarcely possible that ...; **es ist ~ zu glauben, wie ...** it's hardly or scarcely believable or to be believed how ...; **wir hatten ~ noch Vorräte** we had hardly or scarcely any supplies left, we hardly had any supplies left; **er kann ~ noch sprechen/laufen** he can hardly etc speak/walk any more; **ich hatte ~ noch damit gerechnet, dass ...** I hardly or scarcely thought that ... any more b (= wahrscheinlich nicht) hardly, scarcely; **~!** hardly, scarcely; **wohl ~, ich glaube ~** I hardly or scarcely think so; **ich glaube ~, dass ...** I hardly or scarcely think that ...; **das wird wohl ~ stimmen** (= richtig sein) that can hardly be right, surely that can't be right; (= wahr sein) that can hardly be true, surely that can't be true; **das wird ~ passieren** that's hardly or scarcely likely to happen

CONJ hardly, scarcely; **~ dass wir das Meer erreicht hatten ...** hardly or scarcely had we reached the sea when ..., no sooner had we reached the sea than ...; **~ gerufen, eilte der Diener herbei** no sooner summoned, the servant hurried in; **er verdient äußerst wenig, ~ dass er davon satt wird** he earns extremely little and can hardly even buy enough to eat

Kau|mus|kel M jaw muscle, masseter (spec)

Kau|ri|mu|schel ['kauri-] F cowrie shell

kau|sal [kau'zaːl] ADJ causal; **~e Therapie** (Med) causal therapy; **~ für etw sein** to be the cause of sth ADV causally

Kau|sal|be|zie|hung F causal connection

Kau|sal|ge|setz NT law of causality

Kau|sa|li|tät [kauzali'tɛːt] F -, -en causality

Kau|sa|li|täts|prin|zip NT principle of causality

Kau|sal-: Kau|sal|ket|te F causal chain, chain of cause and effect; **Kau|sal|ne|xus** [-nɛksʊs] M -, - [-nɛksuːs] (geh) causal connection; **Kau|sal|satz** M causal clause; **Kau|sal|zu|sam|men|hang** M causal connection

kau|sa|tiv ['kauzatiːf] ADJ (Gram) causative

Kau|sa|tiv ['kauzatiːf] NT -s, -e [-və] (Gram) causative

kaus|tisch ['kaustɪʃ] ADJ (Chem, fig) caustic ADV **~ wirken** (lit) to have a caustic effect; **seine Worte wirkten ~** his words were caustic; **sich ~ äußern** to make a caustic remark

Kau|ta|bak M chewing tobacco

Kau|tel [kau'teːl] F -, -en (geh) proviso

Kau|ti|on [kau'tsioːn] F -, -en a (Jur) bail; **~ stellen** to stand bail; **er stellte 1000 Euro ~** he put up 1000 euros (as) bail; **gegen ~** on bail; **jdn gegen ~ freilassen** to release sb on bail; **gegen ~ freikommen** to get out on bail; **jdn gegen ~ freibekommen** to bail sb out b (Comm) security c (für Miete) deposit; **zwei Monatsmieten ~** two months' deposit

Kau|ti|ons|sum|me F a (Jur) (amount of) bail b (Comm, Jur) (amount of) security

Kaut|schuk ['kautʃʊk] M -s, -e (India) rubber

Kaut|schuk|milch F latex

Kau|werk|zeu|ge PL masticatory organs pl

Kauz [kauts] M -es, Käuze ['kɔytsə] a screech owl b (= Sonderling) odd or strange fellow, oddball (inf); **ein komischer ~** an odd bird; **ein wunderlicher alter ~** a strange old bird

Käuz|chen ['kɔytsçən] NT -s, - dim von **Kauz** a

kau|zig ['kautsɪç] ADJ odd ADV oddly

Kau|zig|keit F -, no pl oddness

Ka|va|lier [kava'liːɐ] M -s, -e a (= galanter Mann) gentleman; **er ist immer ~** he's always a gentleman, he's always chivalrous; **der ~ genießt und schweigt** one does not boast about one's conquests b (dated: = Begleiter einer Dame) beau (old), young man (dated)

Ka|va|liers|de|likt NT trivial offence (Brit) or offense (US), (mere) peccadillo

Ka|va|lier(s)-: Ka|va|lier(s)|start M (Aut) racing start; **Ka|va|lier(s)|tuch** NT (dated) handkerchief in one's top pocket

Ka|val|ka|de [kaval'kaːdə] F -, -n cavalcade

Ka|val|le|rie [kavalə'riː] F -, -n [-'riːən] (Mil) cavalry

Ka|val|le|rie|pferd NT cavalry horse

Ka|val|le|rist [kavalə'rɪst] M -en, -en (Mil Hist) cavalryman

Ka|vents|mann [ka'vɛnts-] M pl -männer (N Ger inf) whopper (inf)

Ka|ver|ne [ka'vɛrnə] F -, -n cavern

Ka|vi|ar ['kaːviar] M -s, -e caviar

Ka|vi|ar|brot NT French loaf

KB [kaː'beː] NT -(s), -(s), **KByte** [kaː'bait] NT -(s), -(s) abbr von **Kilobyte** k, kbyte

kcal abbr von **Kilokalorie**

Ke|bab [ke'baːp, ke'bap] M -(s), -s kebab

Keb|se ['keːpsə] F -, -n, **Kebs|weib** NT (old, Bibl) concubine

keck [kɛk] ADJ a (= frech) cheeky (Brit), saucy, fresh (US) b (= flott) Mädchen pert; Kleidungsstück jaunty, saucy c (old: = tapfer) bold ADV cheekily (Brit), saucily; **sie trug den Hut ~ auf einem Ohr** she wore her hat at a jaunty or saucy angle over one ear

ke|ckern ['kɛkərn] VI to snarl, to growl

Keck|heit F -, -en a (= Frechheit) cheekiness (Brit), impudence b (old: = Tapferkeit) boldness

Kee|per ['kiːpɐ] M -s, -, **Kee|pe|rin** ['kiːpərɪn] F -, -nen (Aus Sport) (goal)keeper

Keep smi|ling [kiːp'smailɪŋ] NT -(s), no pl fixed smile

Ke|fir ['keːfɪr, 'keːfiːɐ] M -s, no pl kefir (a milk product similar to yoghurt, of Turkish origin)

Ke|gel ['keːgl] M -s, - a (= Spielfigur) skittle, ninepin; (bei Bowling) pin; **~ schieben** or (Aus) **scheiben** to play skittles or ninepins; (bei Bowling) to play bowls; **~ aufsetzen** to set the skittles/pins up → **Kind** b (Geometrie) cone; (= Bergkegel) peak c (= Lichtkegel, Scheinwerferkegel) beam (of light) d (Typ) body, shank

Ke|gel-: Ke|gel|bahn F (bowling) lane; (= Anlage) skittle alley; (automatisch) bowling alley; **Ke|gel|bru|der** M (inf) → **kegeln** member of a skittle/bowling club; **ke|gel|för|mig** ADJ conical ADV conically; **Ke|gel|ku|gel** F bowl; **Ke|gel|man|tel** M surface of a cone

ke|geln ['keːgln] VI to play skittles or ninepins; (bei Bowling) to play bowls; **~ gehen** to play skittles; to go bowling

Ke|geln ['keːgln] M (playing) skittles sing or ninepins sing; (= Bowling auf Gras) (playing) bowls sing; (auf Kegelbahn) bowling

Ke|gel-: Ke|gel|rad NT (Tech) bevelled or mitre wheel (Brit), beveled or miter wheel (US); **ke|gel|schei|ben** [-ʃaibn] (Aus), **Ke|gel|schie|ben** VI sep irreg → **Kegel** a; **Ke|gel|schnitt** M conic section; **Ke|gel|schwes|ter** F (inf) → **kegeln** member of a skittle/bowling club; **Ke|gel|sport** M bowling; **Ke|gel|stumpf** M frustum

Keg|ler ['keːglɐ] M -s, -, **Keg|le|rin** [-ərɪn] F -, -nen skittle-player; (bei Bowling) bowler

Keh|le ['keːlə] F -, -n a (= Gurgel) throat; **das ist ihm in die falsche ~ gekommen, er hat das in die falsche ~ bekommen** (lit) it went down the wrong way, it got stuck in his throat; (fig) he took it the wrong way; **eine raue ~ haben** to be hoarse; **aus voller ~** at the top of one's voice or one's lungs; **er hat eine trockene ~** (inf) he needs a drink; (gewohnheitsmäßig) he likes his or a drink (inf); **(sich dat) die ~ schmieren** (inf) or **anfeuchten** (inf) to wet one's whistle (inf); **jdm die ~ durchschneiden** to cut or slit sb's throat; **jetzt geht es ihm an die ~** (fig) now things have turned nasty for him → **schreien** VR, **zuschnüren**

b (= ausgerundeter Winkel) moulding (Brit), molding (US); (= Rille) groove

keh|lig ['keːlɪç] ADJ throaty; Stimme auch guttural ADV **~ lachen** to give a throaty laugh; **eine ~ klingende Stimme** a throaty voice

Kehl|kopf M larynx

Kehl|kopf-: Kehl|kopf|ent|zün|dung F , **Kehl|kopf|ka|tarr(h)** ▲ M laryngitis; **Kehl|kopf|krebs** M cancer of the throat; **Kehl|kopf|mi|kro|fon** ▲ NT throat microphone; **Kehl|kopf|spie|gel** M laryngoscope

Kehl|laut M guttural (sound)

Kehl|lung ['keːlʊŋ] F -, -en (Archit) groove, flute

Kehl|ver|schluss|laut ▲ M (Phon) glottal stop

Kehr-: Kehr|aus ['keːrʔaus] M -, no pl last dance; (fig = Abschiedsfeier) farewell celebration; **den ~ machen** (fig) to have a farewell celebration; **Kehr|be|sen** M broom; **Kehr|blech** NT (S Ger) shovel

---

Keh|re ['keːrə] F -, -n a (sharp) turn or bend; (= Haarnadelkurve) hairpin bend b (= Turnübung) rear or back vault

keh|ren¹ ['keːrən] VT a (= drehen) to turn; **die Augen** or **den Blick zum Himmel ~** (liter) to turn one's eyes heavenwards, to gaze heavenwards; **die Augen** or **den Blick zu Boden ~** (liter) to cast one's eyes to the ground (liter); **in sich** (acc) **gekehrt** (= versunken) pensive, wrapped in thought; (= verschlossen) introspective, introverted → **Rücken**

b (= kümmern) to bother; **was kehrt mich das?** what do I care about that?; **das kehrt mich einen Dreck!** (inf) I don't give a damn about that! (inf)

VR a (= sich drehen) to turn; **eines Tages wird sich sein Hochmut gegen ihn ~** one day his arrogance will rebound against him

b **er kehrt sich nicht daran, was die Leute sagen** he doesn't mind or care what people say VI to turn (round); (Wind) to turn

keh|ren² VTI (esp S Ger: = fegen) to sweep; **ich muss noch ~** I've still got to do the sweeping; **jeder kehre vor seiner (eigenen) Tür!** (prov) everyone should first put his own house in order → **Besen**

Keh|richt ['keːrɪçt] M OR NT -s, no pl a (old, form) sweepings pl; **den ~ zusammenfegen** to sweep up the rubbish → **feucht** b (Sw: = Müll) rubbish (Brit), trash (US)

Keh|richt|sack M (Sw: = Müllsack) rubbish or refuse bag

Keh|richt|schau|fel F dustpan

Keh|richt|ver|bren|nungs|an|la|ge F (Sw) incineration plant

Kehr-: Kehr|ma|schi|ne F (= Straßenkehrmaschine) road-sweeper, road sweeping machine; (= Teppichkehrmaschine) carpet-sweeper; **Kehr|platz** M (Sw) turning area; **Kehr|reim** M chorus, refrain; **Kehr|schau|fel** F shovel; **Kehr|sei|te** F a (von Münze) reverse b (inf: = Rücken) back; (hum: = Gesäß) backside (inf), behind; (fig: = Nachteil) drawback; **jdm seine ~ zuwenden** to turn one's back on sb c (fig: = Schattenseite) other side; **die ~ der Medaille** the other side of the coin

kehrt [keːrt] INTERJ (Mil) **ganze Abteilung ~!** company, about turn!

Kehrt-: kehrt|ma|chen VI sep to turn round, to do an about-turn; (= zurückgehen) to turn back; (Mil) to about-turn; **Kehrt|wen|de** F , **Kehrt|wen|dung** F about-turn; **diese plötzliche Kehrtwendung wurde scharf kritisiert** this sudden about-turn or volte-face was sharply criticized

Kehr|wert M reciprocal value

> **KEHRWOCHE**
>
> The **Kehrwoche** is the week when a tenant living in a building containing several flats is responsible for keeping the staircase and/or pavement clean. The **Kehrwoche** is observed especially strictly in Swabia.

kei|fen ['kaifn] VI to bicker

Kei|fe|rei [kaifə'rai] F -, -en (inf) bickering

Keil [kail] M -(e)s, -e wedge (auch Mil); (als Hemmvorrichtung auch) chock; (= Faustkeil) hand-axe (Brit), hand-ax (US); (Sew: = Zwickel) gusset; (= Kopfkeil) headrest; **einen ~ in etw** (acc) **treiben** to put a wedge in sth; (zum Befestigen auch) to wedge sth; **einen ~ zwischen zwei Freunde treiben** (fig) to drive a wedge between two friends → **grob**

Keil-: Keil|ab|satz M wedge heel, wedge; **Keil|bein** NT sphenoid (bone)

Kei|le ['kailə] PL (inf) thrashing, hiding; **~ bekommen** or **kriegen** or **beziehen** to get or to be given a thrashing or hiding; **dahinten gibts gleich ~** there's going to be a fight over there

kei|len [ˈkailən] **VT a** (*mit Keil*) to wedge **b** (*dated sl*: = *anwerben*) Mitglieder to rope in (*inf*) **VR** (*dial inf*: = *sich prügeln*) to fight

Kei|ler [ˈkailɐ] M **-s, -** wild boar

Kei|le|rei [kailəˈrai] F **-, -en** (*inf*) punch-up (*inf*), brawl, fight

Keil-: keil|för|mig **ADJ** wedge-shaped **ADV** sich ~ zuspitzen to form a wedge; (*Turmspitze*) to form a point; **ein Auto mit ~ gestylter Karosserie** a car with a wedge-shaped body; **Keil|haue** F (*Min*) pick(axe) (*Brit*), pick(ax) (*US*); **Keil|ho|se** F, **Keil|ho|sen** PL slacks *pl*, ski pants *pl*; **Keil|kis|sen** NT , (*Aus*) **Keil|pols|ter** NT wedge-shaped pillow (*used as a headrest*); **Keil|rah|men** M stretcher (*for artist's canvas*); **Keil|rie|men** M drive belt; (*Aut*) fan belt; **Keil|schrift** F cuneiform script

Keim [kaim] M **-(e)s, -e a** (= *kleiner Trieb*) shoot, sprout; **die ersten ~e ihrer jungen Liebe** (*liter*) the first blossomings or burgeoning of their young love (*liter*) **b** (= *Embryo, fig*) embryo, germ; (= *Krankheitskeim*) germ; **im ~e** (*fig*) in embryo, in embryonic form; **etw im ~ ersticken** to nip sth in the bud **c** (*fig*: *des Hasses, der Liebe etc*) seed *usu pl*; **den ~ zu etw legen** to sow the seeds of sth; **den ~ zu etw in sich** (*dat*) **tragen** to carry the seeds of sth

Keim-: Keim|blatt NT **a** (*Bot*) cotyledon **b** (*Zool*) blastema; **Keim|drü|se** F gonad; **Keim|drü|sen|hor|mon** NT sex hormone

kei|men [ˈkaimən] VI **a** (*Saat*) to germinate; (*Pflanzen*) to put out shoots, to shoot; (*Knollen*) to sprout **b** (*Verdacht*) to be aroused; (*Hoffnung*) to stir (*in one's breast* (*liter*)); **das ~de Leben** (*geh*) the seeds of a new life

Keim-: keim|frei ADJ germ-free, free of germs *pred*; (*Med, auch fig*) sterile; **~ machen** to sterilize; **keim|haft** ADJ (*geh*) embryonic, seminal; **~ vorhanden sein** to be present in embryo or in embryonic form or in seminal form; **Keim|ling** [ˈkaimlɪŋ] M **-s, -e a** (= *Embryo*) embryo **b** (= *Keimpflanze*) sprout, shoot; **Keim|öl** NT wheat germ oil, seed oil; **Keim|plas|ma** NT germ plasma; **keim|tö|tend** ADJ germicidal; **~es Mittel** germicide; **Keim|trä|ger(in)** M(F) carrier

Kei|mung [ˈkaimʊŋ] F **-, -en** germination

Keim|zel|le F germ cell; (*fig*) nucleus

kein [kain], **kei|ne** [ˈkainə], **kein** INDEF PRON **a** (*adjektivisch*) no; (*mit sing n*) no, not a; (*mit pl n, bei Sammelbegriffen, bei Abstrakten*) no, not any; **~ Mann/~ Häuser/~ Whisky ...** no man/ houses/whisky ...; **hast du ~ Herz?** have you no heart? (*esp Brit*), don't you have a heart?; **hast du ~ Gefühl?** have you no feeling? (*esp Brit*), haven't you got (*esp Brit*) or don't you have any feeling?; **hast du ~en Bleistift?** haven't you got (*esp Brit*) or don't you have a pencil?, have you no pencil? (*esp Brit*); **hast du ~e Vorschläge/Geschwister?** haven't you got any or have you no suggestions/brothers and sisters? (*esp Brit*), don't you have any suggestions/brothers and sisters?; **ich sehe da ~en Unterschied** I see no difference, I don't see any or a difference; **da sind ~e Häuser** there are no houses there, there aren't any houses there; **er hatte ~e Chance** he had no chance, he didn't have a or any chance; **er ist ~ echter Schotte** he is no true Scot, he is not a true Scot; **er ist ~ Lehrer** he is not a teacher; (= *kein guter auch*) he's no teacher; **~e Widerrede/Ahnung!** no arguing/idea!; **~e schlechte Idee** not a bad idea; **~e Lust!** don't want to; **~e Angst!** don't worry; **das ist ~e Antwort auf unsere Frage** that's not an or the answer to our question; **er ist noch ~ erfahrener Lehrer** he is not yet an experienced teacher; **~ bisschen** not a bit; **ich habe ~ bisschen Lust/Zeit** I've absolutely no desire to/ time; **ich bin doch ~ Kind mehr!** I am not a child any longer, I am no longer a child; **~ anderer als er ...** only he ..., no-one else but he ...; **das habe ich ~em anderen als dir gesagt** I have told nobody else apart from you, I

haven't told anybody else apart from you; **~ Einziger** (= *niemand*) not a single one or person; **~ einziges Mal** not a single time; **in ~ster Weise** (*strictly incorrect*) not in the least **b** (= *nicht einmal*) less than; **~e Stunde/drei Monate** less than an hour/three months; **~e 5 Euro** under 5 euros

kei|ne(r, s) [ˈkainə] INDEF PRON (*substantivisch*) **a** (= *niemand*) nobody (*auch subj*), no-one (*auch subj*), not anybody, not anyone; (*von Gegenstand*) not one, none; (*bei Abstraktum*) none; (*obj*) not any, none; (*von Gegenständen, bei Abstrakta*) none; (*obj*) not any, none; **~r liebt mich** nobody or no-one loves me; **es war ~r da** there was nobody *etc* there, there wasn't anybody *etc* there; (*Gegenstand*) there wasn't one there; **es waren ~ da** there wasn't anybody *etc* there; (*Gegenstände*) there weren't any there, there were none there; **ich habe ~s** I haven't got one; **von diesen Platten ist ~ ...** none or not one of these records is ...; **haben Sie Avocados? – nein, leider haben wir ~** have you (*esp Brit*) or do you have any avocados? – no, I'm afraid we haven't (*any*); **hast du schon ein Glas? – nein, ich habe (noch) kein(e)s** have you a glass? – no, I haven't (*got one*) or no, I don't (*US*); **~r von uns/von uns beiden** none/neither of us; (*betont*) not one of us; **er hat ~n von beiden angetroffen** he didn't meet either of them, he met neither of them; **~s der (beiden) Kinder/Bücher** neither of the children/books; **~s der sechs Kinder/Bücher** none of the six children/books; (*betont*) not one of the six children/books; **er kannte ~s der (fünf) Kinder** he didn't know any of the (five) children, he knew none of the (five) children; **ist Bier da? – nein, ich habe kein(e)s gekauft** is there any beer? – no, I didn't buy any

kei|ner|lei [ˈkainɐˈlai] ADJ *attr inv* no ... what(so)ever or at all; **dafür gibt es ~ Beweise** there is no proof of it what(so)ever or at all

kei|ner|seits [ˈkainɐˈzaits] ADV **sein Vorschlag fand ~ Zustimmung** his suggestion met with no support anywhere or from any side; **ich möchte mich ~ festlegen** I wouldn't like to commit myself in any direction

kei|nes|falls [ˈkainəsˈfals] ADV under no circumstances, not ... under any circumstances; **~ darfst du ...** under no circumstances or on no account must you ...; **das bedeutet jedoch ~, dass ...** however, in no way does this mean that ...

kei|nes|wegs [ˈkainəsˈveːks] ADV not at all, by no means; (*als Antwort*) not in the least, not at all; **ich fühle mich ~ schuldig** I do not feel in the least guilty or in any way guilty

kein|mal [ˈkainmaːl] ADV never once, not once; **ich bin ihr noch ~ begegnet** I've never met her → **einmal**

keins [kains] = **keines**

Keks [keːks] M **-es, -e** or (*Aus*) nt **-, -** biscuit (*Brit*), cookie (*US*); **jdm auf den ~ gehen** (*inf*) to get on sb's nerves

Kelch [kɛlç] M **-(e)s, -e a** (= *Trinkglas*) goblet; (*Eccl*) chalice, communion cup; **den (bitteren) ~ (des Leidens) bis zur Neige leeren** (*fig*) to drain the (bitter) cup of sorrow (to the last); **möge dieser ~ an mir vorübergehen** (*Bibl*) let this cup pass from me; **dieser ~ ist noch einmal an mir vorübergegangen** I have been spared again, the Good Lord has spared me again **b** (*Bot*) calyx

Kelch-: Kelch|blatt NT sepal; **kelch|för|mig** ADJ cup-shaped, bell-shaped; **Kelch|glas** NT goblet, goblet-shaped glass

Ke|lim [ˈkeːlɪm] M **-(s), -(s)** kilim (*Eastern carpet*)

Kel|le [ˈkɛlə] F **-, -n a** (= *Suppenkelle etc*) ladle; (= *Schaumlöffel*) strainer, straining spoon **b** (= *Maurerkelle*) trowel **c** (= *Signalstab*) signalling (*Brit*) or signaling (*US*) disc

Kel|ler [ˈkɛlɐ] M **-s, -** cellar; (= *Geschoss*) basement; (= *Esslokal*) (cellar) restaurant; (= *Kneipe*) (cellar) bar; **im ~ sein** (*fig*) to be at rock-bottom; **in den ~ rutschen** or **fallen** (*fig*) to reach rock-bottom; (*Preise etc auch*) to go or fall through the floor; **im ~ sitzen** (*inf*: *beim Kartenspiel*) to have minus points

Keller-: Kel|ler|as|sel F woodlouse; **Kel|ler|bar** F cellar or basement bar

Kel|le|rei [kɛləˈrai] F **-, -en** (= *Weinkellerei*) wine producer's; (= *Sektkellerei*) champagne producer's; (= *Lagerraum*) cellar(s *pl*); **Wein direkt von der ~ kaufen** to buy wine direct from the producer's

Keller-: Kel|ler|ge|schoss ▲ NT basement; **Kel|ler|ge|wöl|be** NT vaulted cellar roof; (= *Keller*) cellars *pl*; (= *Verlies*) dungeon; **Kel|ler|kind** NT unhealthy slum kid; **Kel|ler|knei|pe** F (*inf*), **Kel|ler|lo|kal** NT cellar bar; **Kel|ler|meis|ter(in)** M(F) vintner; (*in Kloster*) cellarer; **Kel|ler|woh|nung** F basement flat (*Brit*) or apartment

Kell|ner [ˈkɛlnɐ] M **-s, -** waiter

Kell|ne|rin [ˈkɛlnərɪn] F **-, -nen** waitress

kell|nern [ˈkɛlnɐn] VI (*inf*) to work as a waiter/ waitress, to wait on tables (*US*)

Kel|te [ˈkɛltə] M **-n, -n**, **Kel|tin** [ˈkɛltɪn] F **-, -nen** Celt

Kel|ter [ˈkɛltɐ] F **-, -n** winepress; (= *Obstkelter*) press

kel|tern [ˈkɛltɐn] VT Trauben, Wein to press

kel|tisch [ˈkɛltɪʃ] ADJ Celtic

Kel|vin [ˈkɛlvɪn] NT **-s, no pl** (*Phys*) Kelvin

Ke|me|na|te [keməˈnaːtə] F **-, -n** lady's heated apartment(s *pl*) (*in a castle*); (*fig*) boudoir

Ke|nia [ˈkeːnia] NT **-s** Kenya

Ke|ni|a|ner [keˈniaːnɐ] M **-s, -**, **Ke|ni|a|ne|rin** [-ərɪn] F **-, -nen** Kenyan

ke|ni|a|nisch [keˈniaːnɪʃ] ADJ Kenyan

ken|nen [ˈkɛnən] pret **kannte** [ˈkantə], ptp **gekannt** [gəˈkant] VT to know; (= *kennen gelernt haben auch*) to be acquainted with; (*geh*: = *erkennen*) to recognize; **er kennt das Leben** he knows the ways of the world, he knows about life; **er kennt den Hunger nicht** he has never known hunger, he doesn't know what hunger is; **er kennt keine Müdigkeit** he never gets tired, he doesn't know what tiredness means; **kein Erbarmen/Mitleid ~** to know no mercy/ pity *etc*; **ich habe mich nicht mehr gekannt vor Wut** I was beside myself with anger; **so was ~ wir hier nicht!** we don't have that sort of thing here; **jdn als etw ~** to know sb to be sth; **~ Sie sich schon?** do you know each other (already)?; **~ Sie den (schon)?** (*Witz*) have you heard this one?; **das ~ wir (schon)** (*iro*) we know all about that; **kennst du mich noch?** do you remember me?; **wie ich ihn kenne ...** if I know him (at all) ...; **du kennst dich doch!** you know what you're like; **so kenne ich dich ja (noch) gar nicht!** I've never known you like this before; **da kennst du mich aber schlecht** you don't know me, that just shows how little you know me; **da kennt er gar nichts** (*inf*) = (*hat keine Hemmungen*) he has no scruples whatsoever; (= *ihm ist alles egal*) he doesn't give a damn (*inf*)

ken|nen ler|nen ▲ VT to get to know, to become acquainted with (*form*); (= *zum ersten Mal treffen*) to meet; **sich ~** to get to know each other; to meet each other; **jdn/etw näher ~** to get to know sb/sth better, to become better acquainted with sb/sth; **ich freue mich, Sie kennen zu lernen** (*form*) (I am) pleased to meet you or to make your acquaintance (*form*); **ich habe ihn als einen zuverlässigen Mitarbeiter kennen gelernt** I came to know him as a reliable colleague; **der soll** or **wird mich noch ~** (*inf*) he'll have me to reckon with (*inf*); **bei näherem Kennenlernen erwies er sich als ...** on closer acquaintance he proved to be ...

Ken|ner ['kɛnɐ] M **-s, -, Ken|ne|rin** [-ərɪn] F **-, -nen** a (= *Sachverständiger*) expert (*von, +gen* on *or* in), authority (*von, +gen* on); **~ der internen Vorgänge** those who know about the internal procedures; **da zeigt sich der ~, da merkt man den ~** there you (can) see the (touch of the) expert b (= *Weinkenner etc*) connoisseur, co(g)noscente (*esp Art*)

Ken|ner|blick M expert's eye

ken|ner|haft ADJ like a connoisseur; **mit ~em Blick/Griff** with the eye/touch of an expert ADV expertly; **lächeln, nicken** knowingly

ken|ne|risch ['kɛnərɪʃ] ADJ = **kennerhaft**

Ken|ner-: Ken|ner|mie|ne F connoisseur's expression; **mit ~ betrachtete er...** he looked at ... like a connoisseur; **er versuchte, eine ~ aufzusetzen** he tried to look like a connoisseur; (*bei Erklärung etc*) he tried to look knowledgeable; **Ken|ner|schaft** ['kɛnɐʃaft] F **-, no pl** connoisseurship (*rare*); (= *Fachkenntnis*) expertise

Kenn-: Kenn|kar|te F (*dated*) identity card; **Kenn|mar|ke** F identity tag

kennt|lich ['kɛntlɪç] ADJ (= *zu erkennen*) recognizable, distinguishable (*an +dat* by); (= *deutlich*) clear; **etw ~ machen** to identify *or* indicate sth (clearly); **etw für jdn ~ machen** to make sth clear to sb, to indicate sth to sb; **bei Dunkelheit gut ~ sein** to be easily visible *or* distinguishable in the dark

Kennt|nis ['kɛntnɪs] ✪ 46.2, 46.3 F **-, -se** a (= *Wissen*) knowledge *no pl*; **über ~ von etw verfügen** to be knowledgeable about sth, to know about sth; **gute ~se in Mathematik haben** to have a good knowledge of mathematics; **ohne ~ des Englischen** without any *or* a knowledge of English, without knowing English b *no pl* (*form*) **etw zur ~ nehmen, von etw ~ nehmen** to note sth, to take note of sth; **ich nehme zur ~, dass ...** I note that ...; **jdn von etw in ~ setzen** to inform *or* advise (*Comm, form*) sb about sth; **von etw ~ erhalten** to learn *or* hear about sth; **das entzieht sich meiner ~** I have no knowledge of it; **bei voller ~ der Sachlage** in full knowledge of the situation; **ohne ~ der Umstände** without any knowledge of the circumstances

Kennt|nis-: Kennt|nis|nah|me [-na:mə] F **-, no pl** (*form*) **zur ~ an ...** for the attention of ...; **nach ~** after perusal (*form*); **kennt|nis|reich** (*geh*) knowledgeable ADV knowledgeably; **Kennt|nis|reich|tum** M (*geh*) knowledgeableness; **ihr ~** her breadth *or* wealth of knowledge, her knowledgeableness

-kennt|nis|se [-knɪsə] PL *suf in cpds* knowledge of ...; **Sprach-/Englischkenntnisse** knowledge of languages/English

Kennt|nis|stand M , *no pl* **nach dem neuesten ~** according to the latest information

Ken|nung ['kɛnʊŋ] F **-, -en** (*Telec*) call sign; (*von Leuchtfeuern*) signal; (*Comput*) password

Kenn-: Kenn|wort NT *pl* **-wörter** (= *Chiffre*) code name; (= *Losungswort*) password, code word; (*Comm*) reference; **Kenn|zahl** F code *or* identification number; (*Telec auch*) code

Kenn|zei|chen NT a (*Aut*) number plate (*Brit*), license plate (*US*); (*Aviat*) markings *pl*; **amtliches** *or* **polizeiliches ~** registration number (*Brit*), license number (*US*); **ein Hamburger/Berliner ~** a Hamburg/Berlin registration (number) (*Brit*) *or* license number (*US*) b (= *Markierung*) mark, sign; (*bei Tier*) marking(s *pl*); (*in Personenbeschreibung*) **unveränderliche ~** distinguishing marks *or* features; **besondere ~** particular characteristics c (= *Eigenart, Charakteristikum*) (typical) characteristic (*für, +gen* of); (*für Qualität*) hallmark; (= *Erkennungszeichen*) mark, sign; **ein typisches ~ des Intellektuellen** a typical mark *or* sign of the intellectual; **als ~ eine Nelke im Knopfloch vereinbaren** to agree on a carnation in one's buttonhole as a means of identification; **ein ~**

des Genies a mark *or* sign *or* hallmark of genius d (= *Anzeichen*) symptom (*für* of)

kenn|zeich|nen insep VT a (= *markieren*) to mark, to indicate; (*durch Etikett*) to label; **Weg etc** to mark, to signpost; (*Logik*) to denote; **etw als zerbrechlich ~** to mark *or* label sth fragile b (= *charakterisieren*) to characterize; **jdn als etw ~** to show sb to be sth, to mark sb out as sth VR to be characterized

kenn|zeich|nend ADJ (= *charakteristisch*) typical, characteristic (*für* of)

kenn|zeich|nungs|pflich|tig ADJ **Waren** subject to the accurate labelling (*Brit*) *or* labeling (*US*) of products

Kenn|zif|fer F (*code*) number; (*Math*) characteristic; (*Comm*) reference number; (*bei Zeitungsinserat*) box number

Ke|no|taph [keno'ta:f] NT **-s, -e** cenotaph

Ken|taur [kɛn'tauɐ] M **-en, -en** centaur

ken|tern ['kɛntɐn] VI *aux sein* a (*Schiff*) to capsize b **die Ebbe/Flut kentert** the tide is turning

kep|ler|sche Ge|set|ze ▲ ['kɛplɐʃə] PL Kepler's laws *pl*

kep|peln ['kɛpln] VI (*Aus inf*: = *keifen*) to bicker

Ke|ra|mik [ke'ra:mɪk] F **-, -en** a *no pl* (*Art*) ceramics *pl*; (*als Gebrauchsgegenstände*) pottery, ceramics *pl*; (= *Arbeitszweig*) ceramics *sing* b (= *Kunstgegenstand*) ceramic; (= *Gebrauchsgegenstand*) piece of pottery, ceramic; **~en** ceramics/pottery

ke|ra|misch [ke'ra:mɪʃ] ADJ ceramic; **Gebrauchsgegenstand auch** pottery

Ker|be ['kɛrbə] F **-, -n** notch; (*kleiner*) nick; **in die gleiche** *or* **dieselbe ~ hauen** *or* **schlagen** (*fig inf*) to take the same line

Ker|bel ['kɛrbl] M **-s, no pl** chervil

ker|ben ['kɛrbn] VT **Holz** to cut *or* carve a notch/notches in, to notch; **Inschrift, Namen** to carve

Kerb|holz NT (*fig inf*) **etwas auf dem ~ haben** to have done something wrong *or* bad; **er hat so manches auf dem ~** he has quite a record; **er hat Ladendiebstahl auf dem ~** he has a record for shoplifting; **es gab fast keinen, der nichts auf dem ~ hatte** there was hardly anybody who had a completely clean record

Kerb|tier NT insect

Ker|bung ['kɛrbʊŋ] F **-, -en** (= *das Kerben*) notching; (= *die Kerben*) notches *pl*; (*kleiner*) nicks *pl*

Ker|ker ['kɛrkə] M **-s, -** a (*Hist, geh*) dungeon (*esp Hist*), prison; (= *Strafe*) imprisonment b (*Aus*) = **Zuchthaus**

Ker|ker-: Ker|ker|haft F a (*Hist*) imprisonment in the dungeons; **drei Jahre ~** three years in the dungeons b (*Aus*: = *Zuchthausstrafe*) imprisonment; **Ker|ker|meis|ter(in)** M(F) (*Hist, geh*) gaoler, jailer; **Ker|ker|stra|fe** F (*Hist*) imprisonment in the dungeons b (*Aus*: = *Zuchthausstrafe*) prison sentence

Kerl [kɛrl] M **-s, -e** *or* **-s** (*inf*) chap, fellow, guy, bloke (*Brit, all inf*); (*pej*) character; (= *Mädchen*) girl, lass (*Brit inf*); **du gemeiner ~!** you mean thing (*inf*), you swine (*inf*); **ein ganzer** *or* **richtiger ~** a real man; **er ist nicht ~ genug dazu** he is not man enough to do that; **sie hat schon wieder einen neuen ~** she's already got another guy (*inf*) *or* bloke (*Brit inf*); **die langen ~s** (*Hist*) (soldiers of) the bodyguard of the King of Prussia

Kern [kɛrn] M **-(e)s, -e** (*von Obst*) pip, seed; (*von Steinobst*) stone; (= *Nusskern*) kernel; (*Phys, Biol*) nucleus; (= *Holzkern*) heartwood; (*fig*) (*von Problem, Sache*) heart, crux, core; (*von Stadt*) centre (*Brit*), center (*US*); (*von Gruppe*) core; **jede Legende hat einen wahren ~** at the heart of every legend there is a core of truth; **in ihr steckt ein guter ~** there's some good in her somewhere; **bis zum ~ einer Sache vordringen** to get to the

heart *or* the bottom of a matter; **der harte ~** (*fig*) the hard core

Kern-: Kern|ar|beits|zeit F core time; **Kern|bei|ßer** [-baisɐ] M **-s, -** (*Orn*) hawfinch; **Kern|brenn|stab** M nuclear fuel rod; **Kern|brenn|stoff** M nuclear fuel; **Kern|che|mie** F nuclear chemistry; **Kern|ener|gie** F nuclear energy; **Kern|ener|gie|geg|ner(in)** M(F) opponent of nuclear energy; **Kern|ex|plo|si|on** F nuclear explosion; **Kern|fach** NT (*Sch*) core subject; **Kern|fa|mi|lie** F (*Sociol*) nuclear family; **Kern|for|scher(in)** M(F) nuclear scientist *or* researcher; **Kern|for|schung** F nuclear research; **Kern|for|schungs|an|la|ge** F nuclear research facility; **Kern|for|schungs|zent|rum** NT nuclear research centre (*Brit*) *or* center (*US*); **Kern|fra|ge** F central issue, central question; **Kern|frucht** F malaceous fruit (*form*), pome (*form*); **Kern|fu|si|on** F nuclear fusion; **Kern|ge|biet** NT heartland; **Kern|ge|dan|ke** M central idea; **Kern|ge|häu|se** NT core; **Kern|ge|schäft** NT (*Econ*) core (business) activity; **kern|ge|sund** ADJ as fit as a fiddle, completely fit; (*fig*) **Staatshaushalt, Firma, Land** very healthy; **Kern|grup|pe** F nucleus; **Kern|holz** NT heartwood

ker|nig ['kɛrnɪç] ADJ a (*fig*) **Ausspruch** pithy; (= *urwüchsig*) earthy; (= *kraftvoll*) robust, powerful; (*sl*: = *gut*) great (*inf*) b (*lit*) **Frucht** full of pips ADV pithily

Kern|ket|ten|re|ak|ti|on F nuclear chain reaction

Kern|kraft F **-, no pl** nuclear power

Kern|kraft- *in cpds* nuclear power; **Kern|kraft|be|für|wor|ter(in)** M(F) supporter of nuclear power

Kern|kräf|te PL forces *pl* in the nucleus, nuclear forces *pl*

Kern|kraft-: Kern|kraft|geg|ner(in) M(F) opponent of nuclear power; **Kern|kraft|werk** NT nuclear power station, nuke (*US inf*)

Kern-: Kern|la|dungs|zahl F atomic number; **Kern|land** NT heartland; **kern|los** ADJ seedless; (*Biol*) **Bakterium, Blutkörperchen** containing no nucleus; **Kern|mann|schaft** F (*Sport, fig*) core *or* nucleus of a/the team; (*von Partei*) central caucus; (*von Regierung*) inner cabinet; **Kern|mo|dell** NT model of the nucleus; **Kern|obst** NT pomes *pl* (*spec*); **Kern|phy|sik** F nuclear physics *sing*; **Kern|phy|si|ker(in)** M(F) nuclear physicist; **Kern|plas|ma** NT nucleoplasm; **Kern|prob|lem** NT central problem; **Kern|punkt** M central point, crux; **Kern|re|ak|ti|on** F nuclear reaction; **Kern|re|ak|tor** M nuclear reactor; **Kern|satz** M a key sentence, key phrase b (*Ling*) kernel sentence; (*Satzform*) simple sentence; **Kern|schat|ten** M complete shadow; (*Astron*) umbra; **Kern|schmel|ze** F meltdown; **Kern|sei|fe** F washing soap; **Kern|spal|tung** F nuclear fission; **die erste ~** the first splitting of the atom; **Kern|spei|cher** M core memory; **Kern|spin-To|mo|graf** ['kɛrnspɪn-] M MRI scanner; **Kern|spin-To|mo|gra|fie** F magnetic resonance imaging; **Kern|spreng|kopf** M nuclear warhead; **Kern|spruch** M pithy saying; **Kern|stück** NT (*fig*) main item, centrepiece (*Brit*), centerpiece (*US*); (*von Theorie etc*) crucial *or* central element, crucial *or* central part, core; (*von Roman etc*) crucial *or* key passage; **Kern|tech|nik** F nuclear technology, nucleonics *sing*; **kern|tech|nisch** ADJ **~e Anlage** nuclear plant; **~e Entwicklung** development of nuclear technology; **Kern|teil|chen** NT nuclear particle; **Kern|tei|lung** F nuclear division; **Kern|trup|pe** F (*Mil*) core unit *or* division; (*fig*) core team; **Kern|un|ter|richt** M (*Sch*) core curriculum; **Kern|ver|schmel|zung** F a (*Phys*) nuclear fusion b (*Biol*) cell union

Kern|waf|fe F nuclear weapon

Kern|waf|fen-: kern|waf|fen|frei ADJ nuclear-free; **Kern|waf|fen|sperr|ver|trag** M Nuclear Nonproliferation Treaty; **Kern|waf|fen|ver|such** M nuclear (weapons) test

Kern|zeit F core time

Ke|ro|sin [kero'ziːn] NT **-s, -e** kerosene

Ke|rub ['keːrʊp] M **-s, -im** or **-e** [-rubiːm, -bə] cherub

Ker|ze ['kɛrtsə] F **-, -n** a (= *Wachskerze*) candle; (= *Blüte der Kastanie*) candle, thyrus (*form*) b (*Aut*) plug c (*Turnen*) shoulder-stand d (*Ftbl*) skyer

Ker|zen-: Ker|zen|be|leuch|tung F candle-light; **Ker|zen|bir|ne** F (*Elec*) candle bulb; **Ker|zen|docht** M candle wick; **Ker|zen|form** F (*einer Glühbirne*) candle shape; **ker|zen|för|mig** ADJ candle-shaped; **ker|zen|ge|ra|de** ADJ (*lit*) totally or perfectly straight; (*fig*) Mensch (as) straight as a die (*Brit*) or an arrow (*US*); **Ker|zen|ge|sicht** NT (*Tech*) appearance or look of a/the (spark) plug; **Ker|zen|hal|ter** M candlestick; (*am Weihnachtsbaum, auf Kuchen etc*) candle holder; **Ker|zen|leuch|ter** M candlestick; **Ker|zen|licht** NT , *no pl* candlelight; **Ker|zen|schein** M candlelight; **im ~ des Weihnachtsbaumes** in the light of the Christ-mas-tree candles, in the candle-lit glow of the Christmas-tree; **Ker|zen|schlüs|sel** M (spark) plug spanner (*Brit*), (spark) plug wrench (*US*); **Ker|zen|stän|der** M (*für mehrere Kerzen*) candelabra; (*für eine einzige Kerze*) candlestick; **Ker|zen|stum|mel** M , **Ker|zen|stumpf** M candle stump

Ke|scher ['kɛʃɐ] M **-s, -** fishing net; (= *Hamen*) landing net

kess ▲ [kɛs] ADJ (= *flott*) saucy; *Kleid, Hut etc* jaunty; (= *vorwitzig*) cheeky (*Brit*), fresh (*US*); (= *frech*) fresh (*US*), impudent; **eine ~e Lippe riskieren** to be cheeky (*Brit*) or fresh (*US*) ADV saucily

Kes|sel ['kɛsl] M **-s, -** a (= *Teekessel*) kettle; (= *Waschkessel*) copper; (= *Kochkessel*) pot; (*für offenes Feuer*) cauldron; (*esp in Brauerei*) vat; (= *Dampfkessel*) boiler; (*Behälter für Flüssigkeiten etc*) tank b (= *Mulde*) basin, basin-shaped valley; (*Hunt*) semi-circular ring of hunters; (*Mil*) encircled area

Kes|sel-: Kes|sel|fleisch NT (*Cook*) boiled pork belly; **Kes|sel|fli|cker** [-flɪkɐ] M **-s, -**, **Kes|sel|fli|cke|rin** [-ərɪn] F **-, -nen** tinker; **Kes|sel|haus** NT boiler house; **Kes|sel|jagd** F = Kesseltreiben; **Kes|sel|pau|ke** F kettle drum; **Kes|sel|raum** M boiler room; **Kes|sel|schlacht** F (*Mil*) battle of encirclement; **Kes|sel|stein** M scale, fur; **Kes|sel|trei|ben** NT (*Hunt*) hunt using a circle of beaters (*fig: in Zeitung etc*) witch-hunt; **Kes|sel|wa|gen** M (*Rail*) tank wagon or car

Kess|heit ▲ F **-, -en** sauciness; (= *Vorwitzigkeit*) cheekiness (*Brit*), impudence

Ket|chup △ ['kɛtʃap] M OR NT → Ketschup

Ketsch [kɛtʃ] F **-, -en** (*Naut*) ketch

Ket|schup ▲ ['kɛtʃap] M OR NT **-(s), -s** ketchup

Ket|te ['kɛtə] F **-, -n** a chain; (*von Kettenfahrzeug*) chain track; **einen Hund an die ~ legen** to put a dog on the chain, to chain up a dog; **jdn in ~n legen** or **schlagen** (*liter*) to put sb in chains; **jdn an die ~ legen** (*fig*) to keep sb on a tight leash or rein; **in ~n liegen** (*fig geh*) to be in chains or bondage; **seine ~n zerreißen** or **sprengen** (*fig geh*) to throw off one's chains or shackles or fetters b (*fig*) (= *ununterbrochene Reihe*) chain; (*von Menschen*) line, chain; (*von Fahrzeugen*) line, string; (*von Unfällen, Erfahrungen etc*) series, string; **eine ~ von Ereignissen** a chain of events c (= *Bergkette, Seenkette*) chain d (*Hunt*) (*von Rebhühnern*) covey; (*von Wildenten*) skein e (*Aviat, Mil*) flight f (*Comm*) (*von Läden etc*) chain g (*Tex*) warp

Ket|tel ['kɛtl] M **-s, -** or f **-, -n** (*dial*: = *Krampe*) staple

ket|ten ['kɛtn] VT to chain (*an +acc* to); **jdn an sich ~** (*fig*) to bind sb to oneself; **sich an jdn/etw ~** (*fig*) to tie or bind oneself to sb/sth

Ket|ten-: Ket|ten|an|trieb M chain drive; **mit ~** chain-driven; **Ket|ten|arm|band** NT chain bracelet; **Ket|ten|brief** M chain letter; **Ket|ten|brü|cke** F chain bridge; **Ket|ten|fahr|zeug** NT tracked vehicle, track-laying vehicle; **Ket|ten|ge|bir|ge** NT mountain chain; **Ket|ten|glied** NT (chain-)link; **Ket|ten|hemd** NT (*Hist*) coat of (chain) mail; **Ket|ten|hund** M guard dog, watchdog; **Ket|ten|ka|rus|sell** NT merry-go-round (*with gondolas or seats suspended on chains*); **Ket|ten|rad** NT sprocket (wheel); **Ket|ten|rau|chen** NT chain-smoking; **Ket|ten|rau|cher(in)** M(F) chain-smoker; **Ket|ten|re|ak|ti|on** F chain reaction; **Ket|ten|reim** M (*Poet*) interlaced rhyme; **Ket|ten|sä|ge** F chain saw; **Ket|ten|schal|tung** F dérailleur gear; **Ket|ten|schluss** ▲ M (*Logik*) sorites; **Ket|ten|schutz** M chain guard; **Ket|ten|span|ner** M (*bei Fahrrad etc*) chain adjuster; **Ket|ten|stich** M (*Sew*) chain stitch

Ket|zer ['kɛtsɐ] M **-s, -**, **Ket|ze|rin** [-ərɪn] F **-, -nen** (*Eccl, fig*) heretic

Ket|ze|rei [kɛtsə'rai] F **-,** *no pl* heresy

Ket|zer|ge|richt NT (*Hist*) (court of) inquisition

ket|ze|risch ['kɛtsərɪʃ] ADJ (*Eccl, fig*) heretical ADV heretically; **~ klingen** to sound like heresy

Ket|zer|tau|fe F (*Hist*) heretical baptism

keu|chen ['kɔyçn] VI a (= *schwer atmen*) to pant, to gasp (for breath); (*Asthmatiker etc*) to wheeze; **mit ~dem Atem** panting, puffing; wheezing b *aux sein* (= *sich schwer atmend fortbewegen*) to pant, to puff; (*Zug*) to puff, to chug

Keuch|hus|ten M whooping cough

Keu|le ['kɔylə] F **-, -n** a club, cudgel; (*Sport*) (Indian) club b (*Cook*) leg; (*von Wild*) leg, haunch c **chemische ~** (*bei Polizeieinsatz*) Chemical Mace®; **die chemische ~ einsetzen** (*Agr. zur Insektenvernichtung etc*) to use chemical agents

keu|len ['kɔylən] VT (*Vet*) to cull; **das massenhafte Keulen von Schafen** the mass cull of sheep

Keu|len-: Keu|len|hieb M , **Keu|len|schlag** M blow with a club or cudgel; **er bekam einen ~ auf den Kopf** he was hit on the head with a club or cudgel; **es traf ihn wie ein Keulenschlag** (*fig*) it hit him like a thunderbolt; **Keu|len|schwin|gen** NT **-s,** *no pl* (*Sport*) (Indian) club swinging

Keu|per M **-s,** *no pl* (*Geol*) Keuper

keusch [kɔyʃ] ADJ (*lit, fig*) chaste; **~ und züchtig** pure and chaste ADV chastely

Keu|sche ['kɔyʃə] F **-, -n** (*Aus inf*) cottage; (*pej*: = *baufälliges Haus*) hovel

Keusch|heit F , *no pl* chastity

Keusch|heits-: Keusch|heits|ge|lüb|de NT vow of chastity; **Keusch|heits|gür|tel** M chastity belt

Key|board ['kiːbɔːɐd] NT **-s, -s** (*Comput, Mus*) keyboard; **sie spielt ~** she plays keyboards

Key|board|spie|ler(in) ['kiːbɔːɐd-] M(F) (*Mus*) keyboards player

kfm. *abbr von* **kaufmännisch**

Kfz [kaɛf'tsɛt] NT **-(s), -(s)** (*form*) *abbr von* **Kraftfahrzeug** motor vehicle

Kfz- *in cpds* = **Kraftfahrzeug-**

KFZ-KENNZEICHEN

German **Kfz-Kennzeichen** are vehicle number plates which provide information about where a particular vehicle is registered. The first letters before the hyphen are an abbreviation for the administrative district: a single letter for a city, eg "M" for **München** or "K"

for **Köln**, and two or three letters for towns or districts. The number plate also bears the stamp of the licensing authority and a disc indicating when the next **TÜV** test and test of emission levels are due → TÜV

---

kg *abbr von* **Kilogramm** kg

KG [kaːˈgeː] F **-, -s** *abbr von* **Kommanditgesellschaft** ≈ limited partnership

KGB [kaːgeːˈbeː] M **-(s),** *no pl* KGB

KGB-Chef(in) [kaːgeːˈbeː-] M(F) head of the KGB

kgl. *abbr von* **königlich** royal

K-Grup|pe ['kaː-] F (*Pol*) Communist splinter group

k.g.V., kgV *abbr von* **kleinstes gemeinsames Vielfaches** lowest common multiple, lcm

kha|ki ['kaːki] ADJ *pred* khaki

Kha|ki¹ ['kaːki] M **-s,** *no pl* (= *Stoff*) khaki

Kha|ki² NT **-s,** *no pl* (= *Farbe*) khaki

kha|ki|far|ben [-farbn] ADJ khaki(-coloured (*Brit*), khaki(-colored (*US*))

Khar|tum ['kartʊm, kar'tuːm] NT **-s** Khartoum

Khmer¹ [kmeːɐ] M **-s, -** (= *Volksstamm in Kambodscha*) Khmer; **die ~ pl** the Khmer

Khmer² NT **-s,** *no pl* (*Ling*) Khmer

KHz, kHz *abbr von* **Kilohertz** kHz

kib|beln ['kɪbln] VIR (*dial*) to bicker, to squabble

Kib|buz [kɪˈbuːts] M **-, Kibbuzim** or **-e** [kɪbuˈtsiːm] kibbutz

Ki|be|rer ['kiːbərɐ] M **-s, -** (*Aus inf*: = *Polizist*) copper, rozzer (*Brit sl*), pig (*US sl*)

Ki|che|rei [kɪçəˈrai] F **-, -en** giggling

Ki|cher|erb|se F chickpea

ki|chern ['kɪçɐn] VI to giggle

Kick [kɪk] M **-(s), -s** (*inf*: = *Stoß*) kick; (*sl*: = *Spiel*) kick-about, kick-around; (*fig inf*: = *Nervenkitzel*) kick (*inf*)

Kick-: Kick|bo|xen NT kick boxing; **Kick|bo|xer(in)** M(F) kick boxer, **Kick-down** ▲ [kɪkˈdaun] NT **-s,** *no pl*, **Kick|down** NT **-s,** *no pl* (*Aut*) kickdown

ki|cken ['kɪkn] (*Ftbl inf*) VT to kick, to boot (*inf*) VI to play football (*Brit*) or soccer; (= *den Ball kicken*) to kick; **für eine Mannschaft ~** to play for a team

Ki|cker ['kɪkɐ] M **-s, -**, **Ki|cke|rin** [-ərɪn] F **-, -nen** (*Ftbl inf*) player

Kick-off [kɪkˈɔf] M **-s, -s**, **Kick|off** ▲ M **-s, -s** (*Ftbl: esp Sw*) kick-off

Kick|star|ter M (*bei Motorrad*) kick-starter

Kid [kɪt] NT **-s, -s** a *usu pl* (*inf*: = *Jugendlicher*) kid (*inf*) b (*Leder*) kid (leather) c *usu pl* (*Handschuh*) kid glove

kid|nap|pen ['kɪtnɛpn] VT *insep* to kidnap

Kid|nap|per ['kɪtnɛpɐ] M **-s, -**, **Kid|nap|pe|rin** [-ərɪn] F **-, -nen** kidnapper

Kid|nap|ping ['kɪtnɛpɪŋ] NT **-s, -s** kidnapping

kie|big ['kiːbɪç] ADJ (*inf*) (= *vorlaut, frech*) cheeky (*Brit*), fresh (*US*); (= *gereizt*) tetchy

Kie|bitz ['kiːbɪts] M **-es, -e** (*Orn*) lapwing, peewit, green plover; (*Cards inf*) kibitzer

kie|bit|zen ['kiːbɪtsn] VI (*inf*) to spy; (*Cards*) to kibitz

Kie|fer¹ ['kiːfɐ] F **-, -n** pine (tree); (= *Holz*) pine(-wood)

Kie|fer² M **-s, -** jaw; (= *Kieferknochen*) jawbone

Kie|fer-: Kie|fer|ano|ma|lie F malformation of the jaw; **Kie|fer|bruch** M broken or fractured jaw; **Kie|fer|chi|rurg(in)** M(F) oral surgeon; **Kie|fer|chi|rur|gie** F oral surgery

Kie|fer|höh|le F (*Anat*) maxillary sinus

Kie|fer|höh|len-: Kie|fer|höh|len|ent|zün|dung F sinusitis; **Kie|fer|höh|len|ver|ei|te|rung** F sinus infection

Kie|fer|kno|chen M (*Anat*) jawbone

Kie|fern-: Kie|fern|holz NT pine(wood); **Kie|fern|na|del** F pine needle; **Kie|fern|scho|nung** F pinery, pine plantation; **Kie|fern|wald** M pine wood; (*größer*) pine forest; **Kie|fern|zap|fen** M pine cone

Kie|fer-: Kie|fer|or|tho|pä|de M , **Kie|fer|or|tho|pä|din** F orthodontist; **Kie|fer|or|tho|pä|die** F orthodontics *sing*; **kie|fer|or|tho|pä|disch** ADJ orthodontic

kie|ken ['ki:kn] VI (*dial*) = **gucken**

Kie|ker ['ki:kɐ] M -s, - **a** (*N Ger inf*) binoculars *pl* **b** jdn auf dem ~ haben (*inf*) to have it in for sb (*inf*)

Kiel [ki:l] M -(e)s, -e **a** (= *Schiffskiel*) keel; **ein Schiff auf ~ legen** to lay down a ship **b** (= *Federkiel*) quill

Kiel-: Kiel|boot NT keel boat; **Kiel|fe|der** F quill pen; **kiel|ho|len** VT *insep* (*Naut*) **a** Schiff to careen **b** Matrosen to keelhaul; **Kiel|li|nie** F line ahead; **kiel|oben** ADV bottom up; **Kiel|raum** M bilge; **Kiel|was|ser** NT wake, wash; **in jds ~** (*dat*) **segeln** or **schwimmen** (*fig*) to follow in sb's wake

Kie|me ['ki:mə] F -, -n gill

Kie|men- (*Zool*): **Kie|men|at|mer** [-ʔa:tmɐ] M -s, - gill-breather; **Kie|men|at|mung** F gill-breathing

Kien [ki:n] M -(e)s, *no pl* pine

Kien-: Kien|ap|fel M pine cone; **Kien|holz** NT pine(wood); **Kien|span** M pinewood spill; **Kien|zap|fen** M pine cone

Kie|pe ['ki:pə] F -, -n (*dial*) pannier, dosser

Kie|pen|hut M poke bonnet

Kies [ki:s] M -es, -e **a** gravel; (*am Strand*) shingle **b** *no pl* (*inf*: = *Geld*) dough (*inf*), lolly (*inf*)

Kie|sel ['ki:zl] M -s, - pebble

Kie|sel|er|de F silica

kie|seln ['ki:zln] VT to gravel

Kie|sel-: kie|sel|sau|er ADJ (*Chem*) silicic; **kieselsaures Natrium** silicate of sodium; **Kie|sel|säu|re** F (*Chem*) **a** silicic acid **b** (= *Siliziumdioxyd*) silica; **Kie|sel|stein** M pebble; **Kie|sel|strand** M pebble beach, shingle beach

Kies|gru|be F gravel pit

kie|sig ['ki:zɪç] ADJ gravelly; *Strand* shingly

Kies-: Kies|strand M shingle beach; **Kies|weg** M gravel path

Kiez [ki:ts] M -es, -e (*dial*) **a** (= *Stadtgegend*) district, area **b** (*inf*: = *Bordellgegend*) red-light district

kif|fen ['kɪfn] VI (*inf*) to smoke pot (*inf*) or grass (*inf*), to smoke (*inf*)

Kif|fer ['kɪfɐ] M -s, -, **Kif|fe|rin** [-ərɪn] F -, -nen (*inf*) pot-smoker (*inf*)

ki|ke|ri|ki [kikəri'ki:] INTERJ cock-a-doodle-doo

Ki|ke|ri|ki [kikəri'ki:] NT -s, -s (= *Hahnenschrei*) cock-a-doodle-doo

Kil|bi ['kɪlbi] F -, **Kilbenen** ['kɪlbənən] (*Sw*) fair, kermis (*US*)

kil|le|kil|le ['kɪlə'kɪlə] INTERJ (*baby-talk*) tickle, tickle, kitchie, kitchie; (**bei jdm**) **~ machen** to tickle sb

kil|len¹ ['kɪlən] (*sl*) VT to bump off (*inf*), to do in (*inf*), to kill; (*esp mit Auftrag*) to hit (*inf*) VI to kill, to murder

kil|len² VI (*Naut*) to shake, to shiver

Kil|ler ['kɪlɐ] M -s, -, **Kil|le|rin** [-ərɪn] F -, -nen (*inf*) killer, murderer; (*gedungener*) hit man/woman

Kil|ler- *in cpds* killer; **Kil|ler|ins|tinkt** M (*inf*) killer instinct; **Kil|ler|kom|man|do** NT death squad; **Kil|ler|wal** M killer whale, orca; **Kil|ler|zel|le** F (*Physiol*) killer cell

Ki|lo ['ki:lo] NT -s, -(s) kilo

Ki|lo- [ki:lo] *in cpds* kilo-; **Ki|lo|byte** NT kilobyte; **Ki|lo|gramm** [kilo'gram] NT kilogram(me); **Ki|lo|hertz** [kilo'hɛrts, 'kilo-] NT kilohertz; **Ki|lo|joule** NT kilojoule; **Ki|lo|ka|lo|rie** F kilocalorie

Ki|lo|me|ter [kilo'me:tɐ] M kilometre (*Brit*), kilometer (*US*); (*inf*: = *Stundenkilometer*) k (*inf*); **bei ~ 547** (= *Kilometerstein*) at kilometre (*Brit*) or kilometer (*US*) 547; **wir konnten nur 80 ~ fahren** we could only do 80

Ki|lo|me|ter-: Ki|lo|me|ter|fres|ser(in) M(F) (*inf*) long-haul driver; **er ist ein richtiger ~** he really eats up the miles (*inf*); **Ki|lo|me|ter|geld** NT mileage (allowance); **ki|lo|me|ter|lang** ADJ miles long; **-e Strände** miles and miles of beaches; **ein ~er Stau** a traffic jam several miles/kilometres (*Brit*) or kilometers (*US*) long ADV for miles (and miles), for miles on end; **Ki|lo|me|ter|pau|scha|le** F mileage allowance (against tax); **Ki|lo|me|ter|stand** M mileage; **der ~ des Autos ist ...** the car has done ..., the car has ... on the clock (*Brit inf*), the mileage on the car is ...; **Ki|lo|me|ter|stein** M milestone; **ki|lo|me|ter|weit** ADJ miles long; **in ~er Entfernung** miles away in the distance; **ein ~er Marsch** a march of several miles/kilometres (*Brit*) or kilometers (*US*) ADV for miles (and miles); **man konnte ~ sehen** you could see for miles (and miles); **Ki|lo|me|ter|zäh|ler** M mileage indicator or counter, mileometer (*Brit*), odometer (*esp US*)

Ki|lo-: Ki|lo|watt [kilo'wat, 'kilo-] NT kilowatt; **Ki|lo|watt|stun|de** F kilowatt hour

ki|lo|wei|se [-vaizə] ADV by the kilo

Kim|bern ['kɪmbɐn] PL (*Hist*) Cimbri *pl*

Kimm [kɪm] F -, *no pl* (*Naut*) **a** (= *Horizont*) apparent or visual horizon **b** (*am Schiffskörper*) bilge

Kim|me ['kɪmə] F -, -n **a** (*von Gewehr*) back sight **b** (*inf*: = *Gesäßfalte*) cleft between the buttocks, great divide (*hum*) **c** (*rare*) = **Kerbe**

Kim|mung ['kɪmʊŋ] F -, -en (*Naut*) **a** (= *Horizont*) visual horizon **b** (= *Luftspiegelung*) mirage

Ki|mo|no ['ki:mono, ki'mo:no, 'kɪmono] M -s, -s kimono

Kind [kɪnt] NT -(e)s, -er [-dɐ] child, kid (*inf*); (= *Kleinkind*) baby; (*esp Psych, Med*) infant; **ein ~ erwarten** to be expecting a baby; **ein ~ bekommen** or **kriegen** to have a baby or child; **sie kriegt ein ~** she's going to have a baby or child; **von ~ an** or **auf hat er ...** since he was a child or from childhood he has ...; **von ~ an** or **auf haben wir ...** since we were children or from childhood we have ...; **einem Mädchen ein ~ machen** (*inf*) to knock a girl up (*inf*), to put a girl in the club (*Brit inf*); **aber ~!** child, child; **schönes ~!** (*old*: *als Anrede*) my pretty maid (*old*); **die ~er Gottes** (*geh*) the children of the Lord; **ein echtes Wiener ~** (*dated*) a true son/daughter of Vienna; **ein ~ seiner Zeit sein** to be a child of one's times; **sie ist kein ~ von Traurigkeit** (*hum*) she enjoys life; **er ist ein großes ~** he's a big baby; **sich freuen wie ein ~** to be as pleased as Punch; **er kann sich wie ein ~ freuen** he takes a childlike pleasure in (simple) things; **das weiß doch jedes ~!** any five-year-old would tell you that!; **du bist aber ein kluges ~!** (*iro*) clever kid!; **da kommt das ~ im Manne durch** all men are boys at heart; **wie sag ichs meinem ~e?** (*hum*) I don't know how to put it; (*bei Aufklärung*) what to tell your children; **das ist nichts für kleine ~er** (*fig inf*) that's not for your innocent or your young ears/eyes; **aus ~ern werden Leute** (*prov*) children grow up quickly, don't they?; **~er und Narren** or **Betrunkene sagen die Wahrheit** (*fig*) children and fools speak the truth; **ein ~ des Todes sein** (*dated*) to be a goner (*inf*); **mit ~ und Kegel** (*hum inf*) with the whole family; **das ~ muss einen Namen haben** (*fig*) you/we *etc* have to call it something; **das ~ mit dem Bade ausschütten** (*prov*) to throw out the baby with the bathwater (*prov*); **wir werden das ~ schon schaukeln** (*inf*) we'll soon have that or everything sorted out; **los, ~er!** let's go, kids!; **hört mal alle her, ~er!** listen, kids; **~er, ~er!** dear, dear!, goodness me!, good heavens!

Kind-: Kind|bett NT (*old*) childbed (*old*); **im ~ in confinement**; **Kind|bett|fie|ber** NT childbed fever

Kind|chen ['kɪntçən] NT -s, - *dim von* **Kind** child; (*zu Erwachsenen*) kid(do) (*inf*)

Kin|del ['kɪndl] NT -s, -(n) (*dial*) *dim von* **Kind** kiddy

Kin|der-: Kin|der|ar|beit F child labour (*Brit*) or labor (*US*); **kin|der|arm** ADJ with few children; *Familie* small; **ein ~es Land** a country with a low birth rate; **Kin|der|ar|mut** F **a** (= *Bedürftigkeit*) child poverty **b** (= *Mangel an Kindern*) small number of children; **Kin|der|art** F the way children are; **Kin|der|arzt** M , **Kin|der|ärz|tin** F paediatrician (*Brit*), pediatrician (*US*); **Kin|der|au|gen** PL children's eyes *pl*; **etw mit ~ anschauen** to gaze wide-eyed at sth; **vor Erstaunen ~ machen/bekommen** to be wide-eyed with astonishment; **Kin|der|bei|hil|fe** F (*Aus*) child benefit (*Brit*), benefit paid for having children; **Kin|der|bei|la|ge** F children's supplement, children's page; **Kin|der|be|klei|dung** F children's wear; **Kin|der|be|steck** NT child's cutlery; **Kin|der|bett** NT cot; **Kin|der|bild** NT childhood photograph; **das ist ein ~ (von) meiner Mutter** that's a photograph of my mother as a child or when she was a child; **Kin|der|buch** NT children's book; **Kin|der|bü|ro** NT children's advice bureau (*for complaints, suggestions etc*)

Kin|der|chen ['kɪndɐçən] PL children *pl*

Kin|der-: Kin|der|chor M children's choir; **Kin|der|dorf** NT children's village

Kin|de|rei [kɪndə'rai] F -, -en childishness *no pl*; **~en** childishness, childish nonsense

Kin|der-: Kin|der|er|zie|hung F bringing up of children; (*durch Schule*) education of children; **sie versteht nichts von ~** she knows nothing about bringing up/educating children; **Kin|der|fahr|kar|te** F child's ticket; **Kin|der|fahr|rad** NT child's or children's bicycle; **Kin|der|feind(in)** M(F) child-hater; **kin|der|feind|lich** ADJ hostile to children, anti-child; *Architektur, Planung* not catering for children; **~e Steuerpolitik** tax policies which penalize having children; **eine ~e Gesellschaft** a society hostile to children ADV without regard to children; **sich ~ verhalten** to be hostile to children; **Kin|der|feind|lich|keit** F hostility to children, anti-child attitude; (*von Architektur*) failure to cater for children; **Kin|der|fern|se|hen** NT children's television; **Kin|der|fest** NT children's party or (*von Stadt etc*) fête; **Kin|der|film** M children's film; **Kin|der|frau** F , **Kin|der|fräu|lein** NT (*dated*) nanny, children's nurse; **Kin|der|geld|be|trag** M child allowance; **Kin|der|freund(in)** M(F) **~ sein** to be fond of children; **kin|der|freund|lich** ADJ *Mensch* fond of children; *Gesellschaft* child-orientated; *Möbel, Architektur etc* child-friendly; **ei|ne ~e Steuerpolitik** a tax policy which encourages one to have children ADV with children in mind; **sich ~ äußern** to say one is fond of children; **sich ~ verhalten** to be tolerant of children; **sich ~ geben** to show a fondness for children; (*heucheln*) to pretend to be fond of children; **Kin|der|freund|lich|keit** F (*von Mensch*) fondness for children; (*von Möbeln, Architektur etc*) child-friendliness; **der Autor beklagt die mangelnde ~ in Deutschland** the author laments the fact that German society is not child-orientated; **Kin|der|freund|schaft** F friendship between children; **Kin|der|funk** M children's radio or programmes *pl* (*Brit*) or programs *pl* (*US*); **Kin|der|gar|ten** M ≈ nursery school, ≈ kindergarten

KINDERGARTEN/KIGA

A **Kindergarten**, or **KiGa** for short, is an establishment for preschool children between the ages of three and five. On the educational side it concentrates on games, singing and group activities rather than the three Rs. This is designed to encourage children to develop their capabilities and powers of concentration at their own pace and without the usual pressure to succeed. Most **Kindergärten** are run by churches or local authorities. Attendance is voluntary and a fee is payable.

Kin|der-: **Kin|der|gärt|ner(in)** M(F) ≈ nursery-school *or* kindergarten teacher; **Kin|der-ge|burts|tag** M (= *Feier*) children's birthday party; **Kin|der|geld** NT child benefit (*Brit*), *benefit paid for having children*; **Kin|der|ge-schrei** NT screams pl of children; **er kann ~ nicht vertragen** he can't stand children screaming; **dieses ~ ...!** these children *or* kids (*inf*) screaming; **Kin|der|ge|sicht** NT baby face; **Kin|der|glau|be** M child-like faith; **Kin|der-got|tes|dienst** M children's service; **Kin-der|heil|kun|de** F paediatrics sing (*Brit*), pediatrics sing (*US*); **Facharzt für ~** paediatrician (*Brit*), pediatrician (*US*); **Kin|der|heim** NT children's home; **Kin|der|hort** M day-nursery (*Brit*), crèche (*Brit*), daycare centre (*Brit*) *or* center (*US*); **Kin|der|jah|re** PL childhood years pl; **Kin|der|ka|nal** M (*TV*) children's channel; **Kin|der|klei|dung** F children's clothes pl; **Kin|der|kli|nik** F children's clinic, paediatric (*Brit*) *or* pediatric (*US*) clinic; **Kin-der|kram** M (*inf*) kids' stuff (*inf*); **Kin|der-kran|ken|haus** NT children's hospital; **Kin|der|kran|ken|schwes|ter** F (*sick*) children's nurse, paediatric (*Brit*) *or* pediatric (*US*) nurse; **Kin|der|krank|heit** F childhood illness *or* disease; (*fig*) teething troubles pl; **Kin|der|kreuz-zug** M (*Eccl Hist*) Children's Crusade; **Kin|der|krie|gen** NT **-s,** *no pl* **sie hat keine Lust zum ~** she doesn't want to have children; **Kin|der|krip|pe** F day-nursery (*Brit*), crèche (*Brit*), daycare centre (*Brit*) *or* center (*US*); **Kin|der|la|den** M (left-wing) playgroup; **Kin-der|läh|mung** F poliomyelitis, polio; **Kin|der|läh|mungs|imp|fung** F polio vaccination *or* inoculation; **kin|der|leicht** [ADJ] childishly simple, dead easy (*inf*); **es ist ~** it's child's play *or* kid's stuff (*inf*) [ADV] easily

Kin|der|lein ['kɪndɐlaɪn] PL children pl

Kin|der-: **kin|der|lieb** ADJ fond of children; **Kin|der|lie|be** F (= *Liebe zwischen Kindern*) children's love, children's affection; (= *Liebe zu Kindern*) love of *or* for children; **Kin|der|lied** NT nursery rhyme; **kin|der|los** ADJ childless; **Kin|der|lo|sig|keit** F -, *no pl* childlessness; **Kin|der|mäd|chen** F nanny; **Kin|der|mär-chen** NT (children's) fairy tale, fairy story; **Kin|der|mo|den** PL children's fashions pl; **Kin|der|mord** M child murder; (*Jur*) infanticide; **der bethlehemitische ~** (*Bibl*) **der ~ zu Bethlehem** (*Bibl*) the massacre of the innocents; **Kin|der|mör|der** M child-murderer; **Kin|der|mör|de|rin** F child-murderess; **Kin|der|mund** M (*fig*) children's talk, child's way of talking; **das wirkt spaßig, weil es aus ~ kommt** that sounds funny coming from a child; **~ tut Wahr-heit kund** (*Prov*) out of the mouths of babes and sucklings (*prov*); **Kin|der|narr** M , **Kin|der|när|rin** F great lover of children; **er ist ein ~** he adores children; **Kin|der|pa|ra|dies** NT children's paradise; **Kin|der|pfle|ger** M paediatric (*Brit*) *or* pediatric (*US*) nurse; **Kin|der|pfle|ge|rin** F paediatric (*Brit*) *or* pediatric (*US*) nurse; (= *Kindermädchen*) nanny; **Kin|der|po|po** M (*inf*) baby's bottom (*inf*); **glatt wie ein ~** smooth as a baby's bottom (*inf*); **Kin|der|por|no|gra|fie** ▲ F child pornography; **Kin|der|pros|ti|tu|ti|on** F child prostitution; **Kin|der|psy|cho|lo|gie** F child psychology; **Kin|der|raub** M baby-snatching; (= *Entfüh-rung*) kidnapping (of a child/children); **kin|der|reich** ADJ with many children; **Familie** large; **Kin|der|reich|tum** M an abundance of children; **der ~ Kenias** the abundance of children in Kenya; **Kin|der|reim** M nursery rhyme; **Kin|der|rei|se|bett** NT travel cot; **Kin|der|sa|chen** PL (= *Kleidung*) children's

clothes pl; (= *Gegenstände*) children's things pl; (= *Spielsachen*) toys pl; **Kin|der|schän|der** [-ʃɛndɐ] M **-s, -,** **Kin|der|schän|de|rin** [-ərɪn] F **-, -nen** child molester; **Kin|der|schar** F swarm of children; **Kin|der|schreck** M bo-g(e)yman; **Kin|der|schuh** M child's shoe; **~e sind teuer** children's shoes are dear; **etw steckt noch in den ~en** (*fig*) sth is still in its infancy; **Kin|der|schutz** M protection of children; **Kin|der|schutz|bund** M *pl* **-bünde** child protection agency, ≈ NSPCC (*Brit*); **Kin|der-schwes|ter** F paediatric (*Brit*) *or* pediatric (*US*) nurse; **Kin|der|se|gen** M (*dated*) children pl; **es war ihnen kein ~ beschert** they were not blessed with children; **kin|der|si-cher** [ADJ] childproof [ADV] *aufbewahren* out of reach of children; **die Autotür lässt sich ~ ver-schließen** the car door has a child lock; **die Flasche lässt sich ~ verschließen** the bottle has a childproof cap; **Kin|der|si|che|rung** F (*Aut*) childproof safety catch; (*an Flasche*) childproof cap; **Kin|der|sitz** M child's seat; (*im Auto*) child seat; **Kin|der|spiel** NT children's game; (*fig*) child's play *no art*; **Kin|der|spiel|platz** M children's playground; **Kin|der|spiel|zeug** NT (children's) toys pl; **Kin|der|spra|che** F (*von Kindern*) children's language; (*verniedlichend von Erwachsenen*) baby talk *no art*; **Kin|der-sta|ti|on** F children's ward; **Kin|der|sterb-lich|keit** F infant mortality; **Kin|der|stim|me** F child's voice; **Kin|der|streich** M childish prank; **Kin|der|stu|be** F (*fig*) upbringing; **Kin|der|stuhl** M child's chair; (= *Hochstuhl*) high chair; **Kin|der|stun|de** F children's hour; **Kin|der|ta|ges|heim** NT , **Kin|der|ta-ges|stät|te** F day nursery (*Brit*), crèche (*Brit*), daycare centre (*Brit*) *or* center (*US*)

KINDERTAGESSTÄTTE/KITA

Kindertagesstätten, or **KiTas** for short, are daycare centres for children whose parents are in full-time employment. They range from crèches for babies to playgroups for children between the ages of one and three and day centres for children of school age.

Kin|der-: **Kin|der|tau|fe** F infant baptism; **Kin|der|tel|ler** M (*in Restaurant*) children's portion; **Kin|der|the|a|ter** NT children's theatre (*Brit*) *or* theater (*US*); (= *Jugendtheater*) youth theatre (*Brit*) *or* theater (*US*); **Kin|der|trom|mel** F toy drum; **Kin|der|vers** M nursery rhyme; **Kin|der|vor|stel|lung** F (*Theater, Kino etc*) children's performance *or* show; **Kin|der|wa|gen** M pram (*Brit*), baby carriage (*US*), perambulator (*form*); (= *Sportwagen*) pushchair (*Brit*), (baby-)stroller (*esp US*); **Kin|der|welt** F world of children; **Kin|der|wunsch** M (*von Frau, Paar*) desire for *or* to have children/a child; **ihr ~ blieb unerfüllt** she wanted to have children (but couldn't); **Kin|der|zahl** F number of children; **Kin|der|zim-mer** NT child's/children's room; (*esp für Klein-kinder*) nursery; **Kin|der|zu|la|ge** F , **Kin|der|zu|schlag** M child benefit (*Brit*), *benefit paid for having children*

Kin|des-: **Kin|des|ab|trei|bung** F abortion; **Kin|des|al|ter** NT childhood; **im ~ at an early age; **Kin|des|aus|set|zung** F abandoning of children; **~en** cases of children being abandoned; **Kin|des|bei|ne** PL **von ~n an** from childhood, from an early age; **Kin|des|ent-füh|rung** F kidnapping (of a child/children); **Kin|des|ent|zie|hung** F (*Jur*) child abduction; **Kin|des|kind** NT grandchild; **Kin|des-lie|be** F child's/children's love; **Kin|des-miss|brauch** ▲ M child abuse; **Kin|des-miss|hand|lung** ▲ F child abuse; **Kin|des-mord** M child-murder, murder of a child; **Kin|des|mör|der** M child-murderer; **Kin|des|mör|de|rin** F child-murderess; **Kin-des|nö|te** PL (*old*) travail (*old*); **Kin|des|raub** M = **Kinderraub**; **Kin|des|tö|tung** F (*Jur: von ei-*

genem Säugling) infanticide; **Kin|des|ver-wechs|lung** F confusion of children's identity

Kind-: **Kind|frau** F Lolita; **kind|ge|mäß** [ADJ] suitable for children/a child [ADV] appropriately for children/a child; (*ausdrücken, formulieren* in children's terms; **kind|ge|recht** [ADJ] suitable for children/a child [ADV] *entwickeln, ausrichten* to suit children/a child; **kind|haft** ADJ child-like

Kind|heit F **-, -en** childhood; (= *früheste Kind-heit*) infancy

Kind|heits-: **Kind|heits|er|in|ne|rung** F childhood memory; **Kind|heits|traum** M childhood dream

Kin|di ['kɪndi] M **-s, -** (*inf:* = *Kindergarten*) nursery

kin|disch ['kɪndɪʃ] (*pej*) [ADJ] childish [ADV] child-ishly; **sich ~ über etw** (*acc*) **freuen** to be as pleased as Punch about sth; **er kann sich ~ freuen** he takes a childlike pleasure in (simple) things

Kindl ['kɪndl] NT **-s, -(n)** (*dial*) dim von **Kind**

kind|lich ['kɪndlɪç] [ADJ] childlike [ADV] like a child; **~ wirken** to seem childlike

Kind|lich|keit F **-,** *no pl* childlikeness

Kinds- in cpds = **Kindes-:** **Kinds|be|we|gun-gen** PL (*Med*) foetal (*Brit*) *or* fetal (*US*) movements pl; **Kinds|kopf** M (*inf*) big kid (*inf*); **sei kein ~** don't be so childish; **Kinds|la|ge** F (*Med*) presentation of the foetus (*Brit*) *or* fetus (*US*); **Kinds|tod** M **plötzlicher ~** cot death (*Brit*), crib death (*US*)

Kind|tau|fe F (*old*) christening

Ki|ne|ma|thek [kinema'te:k] F **-, -en** film libra-ry *or* archive

Ki|ne|ma|to|gra|phie [kinematogra'fi:] F **-,** *no pl* cinematography

Ki|ne|tik [ki'ne:tɪk] F **-,** *no pl* kinetics sing

ki|ne|tisch [ki'ne:tɪʃ] ADJ kinetic

King [kɪŋ] M **-s, -s** (*inf*) king

Ki|ni|gel|ha|se ['kɪnɪgl-] M (*Aus, dial:* = *Kanin-chen*) rabbit

Kin|ker|litz|chen ['kɪŋkɛlɪtsçən] PL (*inf*) knick-knacks pl (*inf*); (= *dumme Streiche*) horse-play sing

Kinn [kɪn] NT **-(e)s, -e** chin

Kinn-: **Kinn|ba|cke** F (*S Ger*) jaw; **Kinn|bart** M goatee (beard); **Kinn|ha|ken** M hook to the chin; **Kinn|la|de** F jaw(-bone); **Kinn|rie-men** M (*am Helm*) chinstrap; **Kinn|schutz** M (*Hockey*) chin-guard

Ki|no [ki:no] NT **-s, -s** cinema; (= *Gebäude*) cine-ma, movie theater (*US*); **ins ~ gehen** to go to the cinema *or* pictures (*Brit*) *or* movies (*esp US*)

Ki|no- in cpds cinema, movie (*esp US*); **Ki|no-be|such** M visit to the cinema; (= *Besucherrate*) cinema attendances pl; **Ki|no|be|su|cher(in)** M(F) cinemagoer (*Brit*), moviegoer (*US*); **Ki|no|er|folg** M screen hit *or* success; **Ki|no-film** M cinema film; **ki|no|freu|dig** ADJ cine-ma-loving; **Ki|no|gän|ger** [-gɛŋɐ] M **-s, -,** **Ki|no|gän|ge|rin** [-ərɪn] F **-, -nen** cinemagoer (*Brit*), moviegoer (*US*); **Ki|no|hit** M block-buster; **Ki|no|kar|te** F cinema ticket; **Ki|no|kas|se** F cinema box office; **Ki|no|pro-gramm** NT film programme (*Brit*) *or* program (*US*); (= *Übersicht*) film guide; **Ki|no|pub|li-kum** NT cinema (*Brit*) *or* movie (*US*) audi-ence(s pl), cinemagoers pl (*Brit*), moviegoers pl (*US*); **Ki|no|re|kla|me** F (= *Werbespot*) cin-ema advertisement; (= *Werbung*) cinema adver-tising; **Ki|no|vor|stel|lung** F performance, programme (*Brit*), program (*US*); **Ki|no|wer-bung** F cinema advertising

Kin|topp ['kɪ:ntɔp] M OR NT **-s, -s** *or* ⸚e [-tœpə] (*dated*) **a** pictures pl (*Brit*), movies pl (*US*); **im ~ sein** to be at the pictures (*Brit*) *or* movies (*US*) **b** (*als Kulturphänomen*) cinema

Ki|osk ['ki:ɔsk, kiɔsk] M **-(e)s, -e** kiosk

Ki|pa ['kɪpa] F **-, -s** kippa

Kipf [kɪpf] M -(e)s, -e (S Ger) (stick) loaf

Kip|fe(r)l ['kɪpfl̩, 'kɪpfɐl] NT -s, -(n) (Aus) croissant

Kipf|ler ['kɪpflɐ] PL (Aus) salad potatoes pl

Kip|pe ['kɪpə] F -, -n **a** (Sport) spring **b** auf der ~ stehen (Gegenstand) to be balanced precariously; **sie steht auf der ~** (fig) it's touch and go with her; **es steht auf der ~, ob ...** (fig) it's touch and go whether ...; **zwei Schüler stehen auf der ~** two pupils might have to repeat the year **c** (inf) (= Zigarettenstummel) cigarette stub, fag-end (Brit inf), dog-end (Brit inf); (= Zigarette) fag (Brit inf), butt (US inf) **d** (= Müllkippe, Min) tip

kip|pe|lig ['kɪpəlɪç] (inf) ADJ (= wackelig) wobbly; Möbel auch rickety; Angelegenheit shaky **ADV** der Tisch steht ~ the table's wobbly; **in Mathe siehts ~ bei mir aus** I'm a little shaky in maths

kip|peln ['kɪpl̩n] VI (inf) to wobble, to be wobbly or rickety; **(mit dem Stuhl) ~** to tilt (on one's chair)

kip|pen ['kɪpn̩] **VT a** Behälter, Fenster to tilt; Ladefläche, Tisch to tip or tilt (up); (fig: = umstoßen) Urteil to overturn; Regierung, Minister to topple; **etw aus dem Gleichgewicht ~** to tilt sth; **„bitte nicht ~"** "please do not tilt"; **einen ~** (inf: = trinken) to have a drink; **ein paar or einen hinter die Birne or hinter den Latz ~** (inf) to have a couple (inf) **b** (= schütten) to tip **VI** aux sein to tip over; (esp höhere Gegenstände) to topple (over); (Fahrzeug, Schiff) to overturn; (Mensch) to topple, to fall; (Wechselkurse, Gewinne) to plummet; **aus den Latschen or Pantinen ~** (fig inf) (= überrascht sein) to fall through the floor (inf); (= ohnmächtig werden) to pass out

Kip|per ['kɪpɐ] M -s, - (Aut) tipper, dump(er) truck; (Rail) (tipper) wagon

Kipp|fens|ter NT tilt window

kipp|lig ['kɪplɪç] ADJ = **kippelig**

Kipp-: Kipp|lo|re F tipper wagon; **Kipp|schal|ter** M toggle switch; **Kipp|wa|gen** M = **Kipper**

Kir [kiːɐ] M -s, -s kir

Kir|che ['kɪrçə] F -, -n (= Gebäude, Organisation) church; (= bestimmte Glaubensgemeinschaft) Church; (= Gottesdienst) church no art; **zur ~ gehen** to go to church; **die ~ im Dorf lassen** (fig) not to get carried away

Kir|chen- in cpds church; **Kir|chen|äl|tes|te(r)** MF decl as adj church elder; **Kir|chen|amt** NT **a** ecclesiastical office **b** (= Verwaltungsstelle) church offices pl; **Kir|chen|aus|tritt** M leaving the Church no art; **-e** (cases of) people leaving the Church; **Kir|chen|bank** F pl -bänke (church) pew; **Kir|chen|bann** M anathema; (= Interdikt) interdict; **den ~ über jdn verhängen** to excommunicate sb; (= Interdikt verhängen) to interdict sb; **Kir|chen|be|su|cher(in)** M(F) churchgoer; **Kir|chen|blatt** NT parish magazine; **Kir|chen|buch** NT church register; **Kir|chen|chor** M church choir; **Kir|chen|die|stahl** M theft from a/the church; **Kir|chen|die|ner(in)** M(F) sexton; **kir|chen|feind|lich** ADJ anticlerical ADV **sich ~ äußern** to make anticlerical remarks; **~ eingestellt sein** to be opposed to the Church; **Kir|chen|fens|ter** NT church window; **Kir|chen|fest** NT religious or church festival; **Kir|chen|frau** F churchwoman; **Kir|chen|fürst** M high dignitary of the Church; (katholisch) prince of the Church; **Kir|chen|ge|mein|de** F parish; **Kir|chen|ge|schich|te** F church or ecclesiastical history; **Kir|chen|glo|cke** F church bell; **Kir|chen|gut** NT church property; **Kir|chen|jahr** NT church or ecclesiastical year; **Kir|chen|kampf** M struggle between Church and state; **Kir|chen|la|tein** NT Church Latin; **Kir|chen|leh|rer(in)** M(F) Doctor of the Church; **Kir|**

chen|lei|tung F government of the Church; (= Gremium) governing body of the Church; **Kir|chen|licht** NT kein (großes) ~ sein (fig inf) to be not very bright; **Kir|chen|lied** NT hymn; **Kir|chen|mann** M pl -männer churchman; **Kir|chen|maus** F arm wie eine ~ poor as a church mouse; **Kir|chen|mu|sik** F church or sacred music; **Kir|chen|pa|tron(in)** M(F) (church's) patron saint; **Kir|chen|po|li|tik** F church policy; **kir|chen|po|li|tisch** ADJ relating to church policy ADV in relation to church policy; **Kir|chen|rat¹** M (= Gremium) Church Council; **Kir|chen|rat²** M , **Kir|chen|rä|tin** F member of the Church Council; **Kir|chen|raub** M theft from a/the church; (von geweihtem Gegenstand) sacrilege; **Kir|chen|räu|ber(in)** M(F) church-robber; **Kir|chen|recht** NT canon law; **kir|chen|recht|lich** ADJ canonical; **Kir|chen|schän|der** [-ʃɛndɐ] M -s, -, **Kir|chen|schän|de|rin** [-ərɪn] F -, -nen desecrator, profaner; **Kir|chen|schiff** NT (= Längsschiff) nave; (= Querschiff) transept; **Kir|chen|spal|tung** F schism; **Kir|chen|staat** M (Hist) Papal States pl; (= Vatikanstaat) Vatican City; **Kir|chen|steu|er** F church tax; **Kir|chen|stra|fe** F ecclesiastical punishment; **Kir|chen|tag** M Church congress; **Kir|chen|ton|art** F church or ecclesiastical mode; **Kir|chen|va|ter** M Father of the Church, Church Father; **Kir|chen|ver|fol|gung** F persecution of the Church; **Kir|chen|vor|stand** M parish council

Kirch-: Kirch|gang M pl -gänge going to church no art; **der sonntägliche ~** going to church on Sunday; **Kirch|gän|ger** [-gɛŋɐ] M -s, -, **Kirch|gän|ge|rin** [-ərɪn] F -, -nen churchgoer; **Kirch|hof** M churchyard; (= Friedhof) graveyard

kirch|lich ['kɪrçlɪç] ADJ church attr; Zustimmung, Missbilligung by the church; Amt church attr, ecclesiastical; Gebot, Gericht ecclesiastical; Musik church attr, sacred, religious; Feiertag church attr, religious; Land, Mensch religious, devout; Recht canon ADV **sich ~ trauen lassen** to get married in church, to have a church wedding; **~ bestattet werden** to have a Christian funeral

Kirch-: Kirch|spiel NT , **Kirch|spren|gel** M parish; **Kirch|tag** M (Aus, S Ger) fair, kermis (US)

Kirch|turm M church steeple

Kirch|turm|spit|ze F church spire

Kirch|weih [-vai] F -, -en fair, kermis (US)

Kirch|wei|he F consecration of a/the church

Kir|gi|se [kɪr'giːzə] M -n, -n, **Kir|gi|sin** [-'giːzɪn] F -, -nen Kirghiz

Kir|gi|si|en [kɪr'giːziən] NT -s Kirghizia

kir|gi|sisch [kɪr'giːzɪʃ] ADJ Kirghiz, Kirghizian

Kir|gis|tan ['kɪrgɪstaːn] NT -s, **Kir|gi|sis|tan** [kɪr'giːzɪstaːn] NT -s Kirghizia

Kir|mes ['kɪrmɛs, 'kɪrməs] F -, -sen (dial) fair, kermis (US)

kir|re ['kɪrə] ADJ pred (inf) Tier tame; Mensch compliant; **jdn ~ machen** to soften sb up (inf)

Kirsch [kɪrʃ] M -(e)s, - kirsch

Kirsch- in cpds cherry; **Kirsch|baum** M cherry tree; (= Holz) cherry (wood); **Kirsch|blü|te** F cherry blossom; (= Zeit) cherry blossom time

Kir|sche ['kɪrʃə] F -, -n cherry; (= Holz) cherry(-wood); **mit ihm ist nicht gut ~ essen** (fig) it's best not to tangle with him

Kir|schen|mund M (poet) cherry (red) lips pl

Kirsch-: Kirsch|ent|ker|ner [-ɛntkɛrnɐ] M -s, -, **Kirsch|ent|stei|ner** [-ɛntʃtainɐ] M -s, - cherry-stoner; **Kirsch|kern** M cherry stone; **Kirsch|ku|chen** M cherry cake; **Kirsch|li|kör** M cherry brandy; **kirsch|rot** ADJ cherry(-red); **Kirsch|stein** M cherry stone; **Kirsch|to|ma|te** F cherry tomato; **Kirsch|tor|te** F cherry gateau (Brit) or cake; **Schwarzwälder ~** Black Forest gateau (Brit) or cake (US); **Kirsch|was|ser** NT kirsch

Kis|met ['kɪsmɛt] M -s, no pl kismet no pl, fate, destiny

Kis|sen ['kɪsn̩] NT -s, - cushion; (= Kopfkissen) pillow; (= Stempelkissen, an Heftpflaster) pad; (= Duftkissen, Haarshampookissen) sachet

Kis|sen-: Kis|sen|be|zug M cushion cover; (von Kopfkissen) pillow case; **Kis|sen|schlacht** F pillow fight; **Kis|sen|über|zug** M cushion cover; (von Kopfkissen) pillowcase

Kis|te ['kɪstə] F -, -n **a** (= Behälter) box; (für Obst) box, case; (für Wein etc) case; (= Lattenkiste) crate; (= Truhe) chest; (sl: = Bett) sack (inf); **eine ~ Wein** a case of wine; **eine ~ Zigarren** a box of cigars; **(mit jdm) in die ~ springen** (sl: = ins Bett gehen) to jump into the sack (with sb) (inf) **b** (inf) (= Auto, Flugzeug) crate (inf); (= Schiff) tub (inf); (= Fernsehen) box (inf); (= Computer) computer **c** (inf) (= Angelegenheit) affair; (= Beziehungskiste) relationship; **fertig ist die ~!** that's that (done)!; **das ist eine faule ~!** that's a fishy business! (inf); **immer dieselbe ~** always the same old thing; **eine schwere ~** a big problem; **eine alte ~** an old chestnut; **sie hat die (ganze) ~ allein geschmissen** (inf) she did everything herself

kis|ten|wei|se ['kɪstn̩vaizə] ADV → Kiste a by the box/case etc

Kit|che|nette [kɪtʃə'nɛt] F -, -s kitchenette

Kitsch [kɪtʃ] M -es, no pl kitsch

kit|schig ['kɪtʃɪç] ADJ kitschy ADV in a kitschy way

Kitt [kɪt] M -(e)s, -e (Fensterkitt) putty; (für Porzellan, Stein etc) cement; (fig) bond; **der ganze ~** (inf) the whole (kit and) caboodle (inf)

Kitt|chen ['kɪtçən] NT -s, - (inf) clink (inf)

Kit|tel ['kɪtl̩] M -s, - **a** (= Arbeitskittel) overall; (von Arzt, Laborant etc) (white) coat **b** (= blusenartiges Kleidungsstück) smock **c** (Aus: = Damenrock) skirt

Kit|tel-: Kit|tel|kleid NT frock; **Kit|tel|schür|ze** F overall

kit|ten ['kɪtn̩] VT to cement, to stick together with cement; Fenster to putty; (= füllen) to fill; (fig) to patch up

Kitz [kɪts] NT -es, -e (= Rehkitz) fawn; (= Ziegenkitz, Gämsenkitz) kid

Kit|zel ['kɪtsl̩] M -s, - tickle; (= Kitzelgefühl) tickling feeling; (fig) thrill

Kit|zel|ge|fühl NT tickling feeling

kit|ze|lig ['kɪtsəlɪç] ADJ (lit, fig) ticklish

Kit|ze|lig|keit F -, -en (lit, fig) ticklishness

kit|zeln ['kɪtsl̩n] VT (lit, fig) to tickle; **jdn unter den Armen/am Bauch ~** to tickle sb under the arms/sb's stomach; **jdn ~** (inf) (= reizen) to tickle; **jdn bis zum Zwerchfell ~** (fig) to make sb laugh; **ihn kitzelt der Reiz des Neuen** he cannot resist the challenge of something new VI to tickle VT impers **es kitzelt mich** I've got a tickle; **es kitzelt mich, das zu tun** I'm itching to do it

Kit|zeln NT -s, no pl tickling; **er findet das ~ angenehm** he likes being tickled; **ein angenehmes ~** a nice tickle

Kitz|ler ['kɪtslɐ] M -s, - (Anat) clitoris

kitz|lig ['kɪtslɪç] ADJ (lit, fig) ticklish

Ki|wi¹ ['kiːvi] F -, -s (= Frucht) kiwi

Ki|wi² M -s, -s (Orn) kiwi; (inf: = Neuseeländer) Kiwi

KKW [kaːkaːˈveː] NT -s, -s abbr von **Kernkraftwerk**

kla|bas|tern [klaˈbastn] ptp **klabạstert** VI aux sein (N Ger) to plod, to clump, to stump

Kla|bau|ter|mann [klaˈbautə-] M pl **-männer** (Naut) ship's kobold

klạck [klak] INTERJ click; (platschend) splosh

klạ|cken [ˈklakn] VI (inf) to click; (bei Aufprall) to crash; (= klappern) to rattle

klạ|ckern [ˈklakɐn] VTI (dial) = **kleckern**

klạcks [klaks] INTERJ splosh

Klạcks [klaks] M **-es, -e** (inf) **a** (= Geräusch) splosh **b** (von Kartoffelbrei, Sahne etc) dollop (inf); (von Senf, Farbe etc) blob (inf), dollop (inf) **c** (fig) **das ist ein ~** = (= einfach) that's a piece of cake (inf); (= wenig) that's nothing (inf); **die 500 Euro sind für ihn ein ~** the 500 euros are peanuts or chicken feed to him (inf)

klạck|sen [ˈklaksn] (inf) VT Sahne, Kartoffelbrei etc to dollop (inf); Farbe to splash; **die Sahne/den Kartoffelbrei** etc **auf etw** (acc) ~ to put a dollop of cream/mashed potato on sth (inf) VI (Brei, Sahne) to go smack; (Farbe) to splash

Klạd|de [ˈkladə] F -, -n (Sch) rough book; (= Notizbuch) notebook; (= Block) scribbling pad; (= Hilfsmittel) crib (inf); **in** ~ (inf) in rough; ~ **führen** to take notes

klad|de|ra|dạtsch [kladəraˈdatʃ] INTERJ crash-bang-wallop

Klad|de|ra|dạtsch [kladəraˈdatʃ] M **-(e)s, -e** (inf) **a** (Geräusch) crash-bang-wallop (inf) **b** (fig) (= Kram, Durcheinander) mess; (= Streit) bust-up (inf); (= Skandal) scandal; **da haben wir den ~!** what a mess!

klạf|fen [ˈklafn] VI to gape; (Spalte, Abgrund auch) to yawn; **da klafft eine Wunde/ein Loch** there is a gaping wound/hole; **zwischen uns beiden klafft ein Abgrund** (fig) we are poles apart

kläf|fen [ˈklɛfn] VI (pej, fig) to yap

klạf|fend ADJ gaping; Spalte, Abgrund auch yawning; (fig) irreconcilable; Widerspruch blatant

Kläf|fer [ˈklɛfɐ] M **-s, -**, **Kläf|fe|rin** [-ərɪn] F **-, -nen** (lit, fig: pej) yapper

Klạf|ter [ˈklaftɐ] M OR NT **-s, -** or (rare) f **-, -n** fathom

klạf|ter|wei|se ADV (fig) by the ton

klạg|bar ADJ (Jur) Sache actionable; Anspruch, Forderung enforceable

Klạ|ge [ˈklaːgə] F **-, -n** **a** (= Beschwerde) complaint; **(bei jdm) über jdn/etw ~ führen** to lodge a complaint (with sb) about sb/sth; **~n (über jdn/etw) vorbringen** to make complaints (about sb/sth); **Grund zu ~n** or **zur ~** reason for complaint or to complain; **dass mir keine ~n kommen!** (inf) don't let me hear any complaints **b** (= Äußerung von Schmerz) complaint; (= Äußerung von Trauer) lament(ation) (um, über +acc for); (= Klagelaut) plaintive cry **c** (Jur) (im Zivilrecht) action, suit; (im Strafrecht) charge, action; (= Scheidungsklage) petition, action; (= Klageschrift, Wortlaut) (im Strafrecht) charge; (im Zivilrecht) charge, plaint; **eine ~ gegen jdn einreichen** or **erheben** to institute proceedings against sb; **eine ~ abweisen** to reject a charge; **über eine ~ entscheiden** to reach a decision on a charge; **eine ~ auf etw** (acc) an action for sth; **öffentliche ~** = criminal charge

Klạge-: Klạ|ge|ab|wei|sung F (Jur) dismissal of an action; **Klạ|ge|er|he|bung** F (Jur) institution of proceedings; **Klạ|ge|frist** F (Jur) period for instituting proceedings; **klạ|ge|füh|rend** ADJ (Jur) suing; **die ~e Partei** the plaintiff; **Klạ|ge|ge|sang** M lament; **Klạ|ge|ge|schrei** NT wailing; **Klạ|ge|grund** M (Jur) cause of action; **Klạ|ge|laut** M plaintive cry; (schmerzerfüllt) cry of pain; **Klạ|ge|lied** NT lament; **ein ~ über jdn/etw anstimmen** (fig) to

complain about sb/sth; **Klạ|ge|mau|er** F **die ~** the Wailing Wall

kla|gen [ˈklaːgn] VI **a** (= jammern) to moan, to wail; (Tiere) to cry **b** (= trauern, Trauer äußern) to lament (um jdn/etw sb/sth), to wail **c** (= sich beklagen) to complain; **über etw** (acc) ~ to complain about sth; **über Rückenschmerzen/Schlaflosigkeit ~** to complain of backache/insomnia; **ohne zu ~** without complaining; **ich kann nicht ~** (inf) mustn't grumble (inf) **d** (Jur) to sue (auf +acc for) VT **a** jdm sein Leid/seine Not/seinen Kummer ~ to pour out one's sorrow/distress/grief to sb; **Gott** or **dem Himmel seis geklagt** alas, alack **b** (Aus) = **verklagen**

kla|gend ADJ (= trauererfüllt) Mensch lamenting; Blick, Ton, Schrei plaintive; Gesicht sorrowful; (= schmerzerfüllt) pained; (= jammernd, sich beklagend) complaining; **der ~e Teil, die ~e Partei** (Jur) the plaintiff ADV singen mournfully; klingen plaintively; **jdn laut ~ beweinen** to loudly lament the loss of sb

Klạge-: Klạ|ge|par|tei F (Jur) plaintiff; **Klạ|ge|punkt** M usu pl → **Klage c** particular of a charge/petition/plaint

Klä|ger [ˈklɛːgɐ] M **-s, -**, **Klä|ge|rin** [-ərɪn] F **-, -nen** (Jur) (im Zivilrecht) plaintiff; (im Strafrecht auch) prosecuting party; (in Scheidungssachen) petitioner; **wo kein ~ ist, ist auch kein Richter** (Prov) well, if no-one complains ...

Klạge-: Klạ|ge|ruf M plaintive cry; (= Schmerzensschrei) cry of pain; **Klạ|ge|schrift** F (Jur) charge; (bei Scheidung) petition; **Klạ|ge|ton** M plaintive sound; (pej) whine; **Klạ|ge|weg** M (Jur) **auf dem ~** or **im ~(e)** by (taking or bringing) legal action; **den ~ beschreiten** to take legal action; **Klạ|ge|weib** NT wailer, mourner

kläg|lich [ˈklɛːklɪç] ADJ pitiful; Ende auch wretched; Leistung auch, Einwand pathetic; Rest miserable; Niederlage pathetic, miserable; Verhalten despicable ADV fehlschlagen, scheitern, misslingen miserably; miauen, blöken, wimmern, betteln pitifully; **~ versagen** to fail miserably

Kläg|lich|keit F **-, no pl die ~ des Angebots** the pathetic choice

klag|los ADJ (Jur) Schuld, Forderung non-actionable ADV (= ohne Klagen) uncomplainingly; **etw ~ hinnehmen** (ohne zu klagen) to accept sth without complaint; (ohne zu widersprechen) to accept sth without objection

Kla|mauk [klaˈmauk] M **-s, no pl** (inf) (= Alberei) horseplay; (im Theater etc) slapstick; (= Lärm) racket (inf); (= Reklamewirbel) hullabaloo; (= Aufheben) fuss, to-do; **~ machen** (= albern) to fool about; **lass den ~** stop fooling about/making this racket/making such a fuss

klamm [klam] ADJ **a** (= steif vor Kälte) numb **b** (= feucht) damp **c** (inf: finanziell) hard up (inf)

Klamm [klam] F **-, -en** gorge

Klạm|mer [ˈklamɐ] F **-, -n** **a** (= Wäscheklammer) peg; (= Hosenklammer) clip; (= Büroklammer) paperclip; (= Heftklammer) staple **b** (= Haarklammer) (hair)grip **c** (Med) (= Wundklammer) clip; (= Zahnklammer) brace **d** (in Text, Math, = Klammerausdruck) bracket; (Mus) brace; **~ auf/zu** open/close brackets or parentheses (esp US); **in ~n** in brackets or parentheses (esp US); **runde ~n** round brackets, parentheses (esp US); **eckige ~n** square brackets, (square) brackets (US); **geschweifte** or **geschwungene ~n** braces; **spitze ~n** pointed or angle brackets; **eine ~ auflösen** (Math) to eliminate the brackets or parentheses (esp US) **e** (= Bauklammer) clamp, cramp; (zur Verpackung) cramp

Klạm|mer-: Klạm|mer|af|fe M **a** (Zool) spider monkey; **er ist ein richtiger ~** (fig inf) he's always clinging on to you; **sie saß wie ein ~ auf dem Motorrad** (inf) she sat on the motorcycle clinging on for dear life **b** (Typ) at-sign, "@"; **Klạm|mer|beu|tel** M peg bag; **dich haben sie wohl als Kind zu heiß gebadet** (inf) you must be off

your rocker (Brit inf), you must be crazy; **Klạm|mer|griff** M tight grip, clinch; **Klạm|mer|hef|ter** M stapler

klạm|mern [ˈklamɐn] VT (an +acc to) Wäsche to peg; Papier etc to staple; (Tech) to clamp; (Med) Wunde to clip; Zähne to brace VR **sich an jdn/etw ~** (lit, fig) to cling to sb/sth VI (Sport) to clinch

klamm|heim|lich (inf) ADJ clandestine, on the quiet; **eine ~e Freude empfinden** to be secretly delighted ADV on the quiet; **~ aus dem Haus gehen** to sneak out of the house

Kla|mọt|te [klaˈmɔtə] F **-, -n** **a** Klamotten PL (inf) (= Kleider) gear sing (inf) **b** (pej: = Theaterstück, Film) rubbishy old play/film etc; **das ist doch eine alte ~** (inf) **das sind doch alte ~n** (inf) that's old hat (inf)

Kla|mọt|ten|kis|te F aus der ~ hervorholen (pej inf) to dig up again

Klạmp|fe [ˈklampfə] F **-, -n** (inf) guitar

kla|mü|sern [klaˈmyːzɐn] ptp **klamüsert** VT (N Ger inf) to puzzle over

Klan [klaːn] M **-s, -e** (lit, fig) clan

klạng pret von **klingen**

Klạng [klaŋ] M **-(e)s, ⸚e** [ˈklɛŋə] sound; (= Tonqualität) tone; (= Melodie) tune; **der ~ von Glocken** the chiming of bells; **der ~ von Glöckchen** the tinkling of small bells; **der ~ von Gläsern** the clinking of glasses; **Klänge** pl (= Musik) sounds, tones; **unter den Klängen** (+gen) to the sound of; **der Name hat einen guten ~** the name has a good ring to it; (= guten Ruf) the name has a good reputation → **Sang**

Klạng-: Klạng|bild NT sound; (Phys) sound pattern; **Klạng|bo|den** M sounding board; **Klạng|ef|fekt** M sound effect; **Klạng|far|be** F tone colour (Brit) or color (US); **Klạng|fol|ge** F tonal sequence; **Klạng|fül|le** F richness of tone; (von Stimme, Gedicht) sonority; **Klạng|kör|per** M (von Musikinstrument) body; (= Orchester) orchestra; (= Klangbild) body of sound

klạng|lich [ˈklaŋlɪç] ADJ Qualität tonal; ~e Unterschiede differences in sound; (von Tonqualität) sound difference ADV tonally; **~ gut sein** (Musik, Lied, Gedicht, Stimme) to sound good; (Instrument, Gerät) to have a good tone or sound; **~ ähnlich** similar as far as tone is concerned; **die Flöte könnte ~ reiner sein** the tone of the flute could be purer

klạng|los ADJ toneless → **sang- und klanglos**

Klạng-: Klạng|reg|ler M (Rad etc) tone control; **klạng|rein** ADJ pure; **~ sein** to have a pure tone; **Klạng|rein|heit** F purity of tone; **klạng|schön** ADJ beautiful-sounding; **Klạng|schön|heit** F (von Stimme) beautiful sound; **Klạng|spek|trum** NT range of sound(s), tonal palette; **klạng|treu** ADJ Wiedergabe faithful; Empfänger high-fidelity; Ton true; **~ sein** to have high fidelity; **Klạng|treue** F fidelity; **klạng|voll** ADJ Stimme, Sprache sonorous, euphonic (liter); Wiedergabe full; Melodie tuneful; (fig) Titel, Name fine-sounding; **Klạng|wort** NT pl **-wörter** onomatopoeia

klạpp [klap] INTERJ snap; (beim Türschließen) click → **klipp**

Klạpp-: Klạpp|bett NT folding bed; **Klạpp|brü|cke** F bascule bridge; **Klạpp|de|ckel** M hinged lid

Klạp|pe [ˈklapə] F **-, -n** **a** flap; (an Lastwagen) tailgate; (seitlich) side-gate; (an Kombiwagen) back; (von Tisch) leaf; (von Ofen) shutter, flap; (= Klappdeckel) (hinged) lid; (an Oboe etc) key; (= Falltür) trapdoor; (Film) clapperboard; **die ~ fällt** (es ist Schluss) it's over **b** (= Schulterklappe) strap; (= Hosenklappe, an Tasche) flap; (= Augenklappe) patch; (von Visier) shutter; **wenn er schon das Wort Überstunden hört, geht bei ihm die ~ runter** (inf) as soon as he hears the word overtime, the shutters come down (inf) **c** (= Fliegenklappe) (fly) swat **d** (= Herzklappe) valve

---

c (*inf: = Mund*) trap (*inf*); **die ~ halten** to shut one's trap (*inf*); **eine große ~ haben** to have a big mouth (*inf*)

f (*Aus Telec*) extension

g (*sl: von Homosexuellen*) pick-up spot, cottage (*sl*)

klap|pen ['klapn] **VT** etw nach oben/unten ~ (*Sitz, Bett*) to fold sth up/down; *Kragen* to turn sth up/down; *Deckel* to lift sth up/to put sth down, to raise/lower sth; **etw nach vorn/hinten ~** (*Sitz*) to tip sth forward/back; *Deckel* to lift sth forward/back

VI **a** (*fig inf*) (*= gelingen*) to work; (*= gut gehen*) to work (out); (*= reibungslos stattfinden: Aufführung, Abend*) to go smoothly; **wenn das mal klappt** if that works out; **hat es mit den Karten/dem Job geklappt?** did you get the tickets/job all right *or* OK (*inf*)?; **mit dem Flug hat alles geklappt** the flight went all right, there was no problem with the flight

b (*geräuschvoll, = schlagen*) to bang

Klap|pen-: Klap|pen|feh|ler M (*Med*) valvular defect; **Klap|pen|text** M (*Typ*) blurb

Klap|per ['klapɐ] F **-, -n** rattle

Klap|per-: klap|per|dürr ADJ (*inf*) thin as a rake (*Brit*) *or* rail (*US*); **Klap|per|ge|stell** NT (*hum inf*) (*= Mensch*) bag of bones; (*= Fahrzeug*) boneshaker (*Brit inf*), jalopy (*inf*)

klap|pe|rig ['klapərɪç] ADJ = klapprig

Klap|per|kas|ten M , **Klap|per|kis|te** F (*pej*) boneshaker (*Brit inf*), jalopy (*inf*)

klap|pern ['klapɐn] VI **a** (*= Geräusch machen*) to clatter; (*Klapperschlange, Fenster, Baby*) to rattle; (*Lider*) to bat; (*Mühle*) to clack; (*auf der Schreibmaschine*) to clatter away; (*mit Stricknadeln*) to click; **er klapperte vor Kälte/Angst mit den Zähnen** his teeth were chattering with cold/fear; **Klappern gehört zum Handwerk** (*prov*) making a big noise is part of the business **b** *aux sein* (*= sich klappernd fortbewegen*) to clatter along; (*Auto etc auch*) to rattle along

klap|pernd ADJ clattering; *Auto* rattling; *Zähne* chattering

Klap|per-: Klap|per|schlan|ge F (*Zool*) rattlesnake; (*fig*) rattletrap; **Klap|per|storch** M (*baby-talk*) stork; **er glaubt noch immer an den ~** he still thinks babies are found under the gooseberry bush (*Brit*), he still believes in the stork

Klapp-: Klapp|fahr|rad NT folding bicycle *or* bike (*inf*); **Klapp|fens|ter** NT top-hung window; **Klapp|hut** M crush-hat; **Klapp|la|den** M folding shutter; **Klapp|mes|ser** NT flick knife (*Brit*), switchblade (*US*); **Klapp|rad** NT folding bicycle *or* bike (*inf*)

klapp|rig ['klaprɪç] ADJ rickety, shaky, (*fig inf*) *Mensch* shaky, tottery

Klapp-: Klapp|sitz M folding seat; **Klapp|stuhl** M folding chair; **Klapp|stul|le** F (*N Ger*) sandwich; **Klapp|tisch** M folding table; **Klapp|tür** F trapdoor; **Klapp|ver|deck** NT folding *or* collapsible hood; **Klapp|zy|lin|der** M opera hat

Klaps [klaps] M **-es, -e** **a** (*inf*) **einen ~ haben** to have a screw loose (*inf*), to be off one's rocker (*inf*) **b** (*= Schlag*) smack, slap

Klaps|müh|le F (*pej inf*), **Klap|se** F (*pej inf*) loony bin (*inf*), nut house (*inf*)

klar [klaːɐ] ✪ 42.1, 53.6 **ADJ** clear; (*= fertig*) ready; **~ zum Gefecht** *or* **Einsatz** (*Mil*) ready for action; **~ zum Start** (*Sport*) ready (for the start); **~ Schiff machen** (*lit, fig, Naut*) to clear the decks; **ein ~er Fall** (*inf*) sure thing (*inf*); **ein ~er Fall von ...** (*inf*) a clear case of ...; **das ist doch ~!** (*inf*) of course; **alles ~?** everything all right *or* OK? (*inf*); **jetzt ist** *or* **wird mir alles ~!** now I understand; **einen ~en Augenblick haben** to have a lucid moment; **geistig ~ sein, bei ~em Verstand sein** to be in full possession of one's faculties; (*inf*) to be in one's right mind; **~ wie Kloßbrühe** *or* **dicke Tinte** (*inf*) clear as mud (*inf*); **sich** (*dat*) **über etw** (*acc*) **im Klaren sein** to

be aware of sth; **sich** (*dat*) **darüber im Klaren sein, dass ...** to realize that ...; **ins Klare kommen** to get things straight; **mit jdm ins Klare kommen** to straighten things out with sb; **mit seinem Privatleben ins Klare kommen** to sort out one's private life

ADV clearly; **~ denkend** clear-thinking; **immer ~er hervortreten** to become more and more apparent; **habe ich mich ~ genug ausgedrückt?** have I made myself perfectly clear?; **na ~!** (*inf*) of course!, sure! (*inf*); **etw ~ und deutlich sagen** to spell sth out; **jdm etw ~ und deutlich sagen** to tell sb sth straight (*inf*); **etw tritt ~ zutage** sth becomes apparent *or* obvious *or* clear; **~ auf der Hand liegen** to be perfectly obvious *or* clear → **klipp**

Klar [klaːɐ] NT **-(e)s, -(e)** (*Aus: = Eiweiß*) (egg) white, white of an egg

Klär-: Klär|an|la|ge F sewage plant; (*von Fabrik*) purification plant; **Klär|be|cken** NT (*von Klär-anlage*) clearing tank

Klar-: Klar|ap|fel M early dessert apple; **Klar|blick** M (*fig*) clear-sightedness; **klar|den|kend** △ ADJ → klar ADV

klä|ren ['klɛːrən] **VT** to clear; *Wasser, Luft* to purify; *Abwasser* to treat; *Bier, Wein* to fine; *Fall, Sachlage* to clarify, to clear up; *Frage* to settle **VR** (*Sport*) to clear (the ball) **VR** (*Wasser, Himmel*) to clear; (*Wetter*) to clear up; (*Meinungen, Sachlage*) to become clear; (*Streitpunkte*) to be clarified; (*Frage*) to be settled

Kla|re(r) ['klaːrə] M decl as adj (*inf*) schnapps

klar+ge|hen VI sep irreg aux sein (*inf*) to be all right *or* OK (*inf*); **ist es mit dem Examen klargegangen?** did the exam go all right *or* OK? (*inf*)

Klär|gru|be F cesspit

Klar|heit F **-, -en** **a** (*fig*) (*= Deutlichkeit*) clarity; (*= geistige Klarheit*) lucidity; **sich** (*dat*) **~ über etw** (*acc*) **verschaffen** to find out about sth, to get clear about sth; *über Sachlage* to clarify sth; **~ über etw** (*acc*) **haben** to be clear about sth; **darüber besteht** (*völlige*) **~** that is (completely) clear; **an ~ nichts zu wünschen übrig lassen** to be completely clear; **jdm etw in aller ~ sagen** to tell sb sth in plain language; **in dieser Frage müssen wir für ~ sorgen** we must clarify the issue; **alle ~en** (*restlos*) **beseitigt!** (*hum*) (it's as) clear as mud! (*inf*) **b** (*von Wasser, Fluss*) clarity, clearness

kla|rie|ren [kla'riːrən] ptp **klariert** VT **a** (*Naut*) to make ready **b** (*Zoll*) to clear (through customs)

Kla|ri|net|te [klari'nɛtə] F **-, -n** clarinet

Kla|ri|net|tist [klarinɛ'tɪst] M **-en, -en**, **Kla|ri|net|tis|tin** [-'tɪstɪn] F **-, -nen** clarinettist

Kla|ris|se [kla'rɪsə] F **-, -n**, **Kla|ris|sin** [kla'rɪsɪn] F **-, -nen** nun of the order of St Clare

Klar-: klar+kom|men VI sep irreg aux sein (*inf*) to manage, to get by (*inf*); **mit etw ~** to be able to cope with sth; **mit jdm ~** to be able to deal *or* cope with sb; **klar+krie|gen** VT sep (*inf*) to sort out; **ein Problem ~** to sort out *or* crack (*inf*) a problem; **Klar|lack** M clear varnish; **klar|lack|be|han|delt** ADJ varnished; **klar+le|gen** VT sep to make clear, to explain; **Klar|luft|tur|bu|lenz** F (*Aviat*) clear air turbulence

klar+ma|chen sep **VT** to make clear, to explain; *Schiff* to make ready, to get ready; *Flugzeug* to clear; **jdm etw ~** to make sth clear to sb; **sich** (*dat*) **etw ~** to realize sth; **sich** (*dat*) **die Unterschiede ~** to get the differences clear in one's own mind; **sich** (*dat*) **ein Thema ~** to get a subject sorted out in one's mind **VI** (*Naut*) to make ready, to get ready; **zum Gefecht ~** to clear the decks for action

Klar|na|me M (*von Agent*) real name

Klär|schlamm M sludge

Klar|schrift|le|ser M (*optischer*) ~ optical character reader

klar se|hen ▲ VI irreg to see clearly; **in etw** (*dat*) **~** to have understood sth

Klar|sicht- ['klaːɐzɪçt] in cpds transparent; **Klar|sicht|fo|lie** F clear film; **Klar|sicht|hül|le** F clear plastic folder; **Klar|sicht|pa|ckung** F see-through pack; **Klar|sicht|schei|be** F (*Aut*) anti-mist panel

Klar-: klar+spü|len VTI sep to rinse; **klar+stel|len** VT sep (*= klären*) to clear up, to clarify; (*= klarmachen*) to make clear; **ich möchte ~, dass ...** I would like to make it clear that ...; **Klar|stel|lung** F clarification; **Klar|text** M uncoded text, text in clear; **im ~** in clear; (*fig inf*) in plain English; **wir sollten endlich ~ reden** (*fig inf*) let's not beat about the bush anymore (*inf*); **mit jdm ~ reden** (*fig inf*) to give sb a piece of one's mind

Klä|rung ['klɛːrʊŋ] F **-, -en** **a** purification **b** (*fig*) clarification

klar wer|den ▲ irreg aux sein **VR** sich (*dat*) (**über etw** *acc*) ~ to get (sth) clear in one's mind **VI** jdm wird etw klar sth becomes clear to sb; **es muss ~, dass ...** it must be made clear that ...; **ist dir das noch immer nicht klar geworden?** do you still not understand?

klass ▲ [klas] ADJ (*Aus inf*) = klasse

klas|se ['klasə] (*inf*) **ADJ** great (*inf*), brilliant; **das finde ich ~** I think that's great (*inf*) *or* brilliant **ADV** brilliantly → *auch* Klasse a

Klas|se ['klasə] F **-, -n** **a** class; (*= Steuerklasse auch*) bracket; (*= Wertklasse auch*) rate; (*= Spielklasse*) league; (*= Güteklasse*) grade; (*= Führerscheinklasse, Gewinnklasse*) category; **ein Maler erster ~** a first-class *or* first-rate painter; **ein Fahrschein zweiter ~** a second-class ticket; **das ist (große) ~!** (*inf*) that's great *or* tremendous *or* marvellous (*Brit*) *or* marvelous (*US*)! (*all inf*) **b** (*Sch*) class, form; (*= Raum*) classroom

Klas|se- in cpds (*inf*) top-class; **eine Klassemannschaft** a top-class team; **Petra ist eine Klassefrau** Petra is a great *or* wonderful woman; (*= gut aussehen*) Petra is a gorgeous woman

Klas|se|frau F (*inf*) **das ist eine ~** she's a wonderful person; (*= eine Schönheit*) she's a real looker, she's quite stunning

Klas|se|ment [klasə'mãː] NT **-s, -s** (*Sport*) (list of) rankings *pl*

Klas|sen-: Klas|sen|äl|tes|te(r) MF decl as adj oldest pupil (in the class); **Klas|sen|ar|beit** F (written) class test; **Klas|sen|auf|satz** M essay written in class; **Klas|sen|aus|flug** M class outing (*esp Brit*), field trip; **Klas|sen|bes|te(r)** MF decl as adj best pupil (in the class); **wer ist ~(r)?** who is top of the class?; **klas|sen|be|wusst** ▲ ADJ class-conscious; **Klas|sen|be|wusst|sein** ▲ NT class consciousness; **Klas|sen|bild** NT class photograph; **Klas|sen|buch** NT (class-)register; **Klas|sen|buch|füh|rer(in)** M(F) pupil in charge of the class-register; **Klas|sen|dün|kel** M snobbishness, snobbery; **Klas|sen|durch|schnitt** M class average; **Klas|sen|er|halt** M (*Sport*) staying up; **um den ~ kämpfen** to fight to stay up, to fight against relegation; **Klas|sen|ers|te(r)** MF decl as adj = Klassenbeste(r); **Klas|sen|fahrt** F (*Sch*) class trip; **Klas|sen|feind(in)** M(F) (*Pol*) class enemy; **Klas|sen|fo|to** NT class photograph; **Klas|sen|fre|quenz** F size of a/the class; **Klas|sen|ge|gen|satz** M usu pl (*Sociol*) class difference; **Klas|sen|geist** M (*Sch dated, Sociol*) class spirit; **Klas|sen|ge|sell|schaft** F class society; **Klas|sen|hass** ▲ M (*Sociol*) class hatred; **Klas|sen|herr|schaft** F class rule; **Klas|sen|in|ter|es|se** NT (*Sociol*) class interest; **Klas|sen|jus|tiz** F (*Pol*) legal system with class bias; **Klas|sen|ka|me|rad(in)** M(F) classmate; **Klas|sen|kampf** M class struggle; **Klas|sen|kei|le** F (*Sch dated*) a thrashing from the rest of the class, a thrashing from one's classmates; **Klas|sen|krieg** M class warfare; **Klas|sen|la|ge** F (*Sociol*) class position; **Klas|sen|leh|rer** M , **Klas|sen|lei|ter** M class teacher, form teacher *or* master (*Brit*), homeroom teacher (*US Highschool*); **Klas|sen|leh|re|rin** F , **Klas|sen|lei|te|rin** F class teacher, form teacher *or* mistress (*Brit*); **Klas|sen|lek|tü|re** F class reading; **klas|sen|los** ADJ *Gesellschaft* classless; *Krankenhaus* one-class; **Klas|sen|los** NT *draw ticket in a Klassen-lotterie*; **Klas|sen|lot|te|rie** F *lottery in which draws are made on a number of different days and in which tickets can be bought for each individual draw*; **Klas|sen|raum** M classroom; **Klas|sen|schrank** M classroom cupboard; **Klas|sen|schran|ke** F class barrier; **Klas|sen|spie|gel** M (*Sch*) seating plan of the class; **Klas|sen|spre|cher(in)** M(F) (*Sch*) class representative, ≈ form captain (*Brit*); **Klas|sen|staat** M (*Pol*) state governed by one class; **Klas|sen|stär|ke** F (*Sch*) size of a/the class/the classes; **Klas|sen|tref|fen** NT (*Sch*) class reunion; **Klas|sen|un|ter|schied** M class difference; **Klas|sen|ver|band** M im ~ as a class; **Klas|sen|vor|stand** M (*esp Aus*) = Klassenlehrer(in); **Klas|sen|wahl|recht** NT , **Klas|sen|wahl|sys|tem** NT electoral system based on class, class system of franchise; **klas|sen|wei|se** ADJ by class; **~r Aufbau** arrangement by class ADV *sitzen, aufstellen* in classes; *erscheinen* as a class; **Klas|sen|ziel** NT (*Sch*) required standard; **das ~ nicht errei-chen** not to reach the required standard; (*fig*) not to make the grade; (*fig*) **Klas|sen|zim|mer** NT classroom

Klas|se|spiel NT (*inf: Sport*) great *or* brilliant game

Klas|si|fi|ka|ti|on [klasifika'tsio:n] F -, -en clas-sification

klas|si|fi|zier|bar ADJ classifiable

klas|si|fi|zie|ren [klasifi'tsi:rən] ptp **klassifiziert** VT to classify; **~d** classificatory

Klas|si|fi|zie|rung F -, -en classification

-klas|sig [klasıç] ADJ suf -class; **erst-/zweitklas-sig** first-/second-class

Klas|sik ['klasık] F -, no pl classical period; (*inf:* = *klassische Musik, Literatur*) classical music/lite-rature; **die antike ~** Classical Antiquity

Klas|si|ker ['klasıkɐ] M -s, -, **Klas|si|ke|rin** [-ərın] F -, -nen classic; **ein ~ des Jazz** a jazz classic; **ein ~ der modernen Musik** a classic of modern music; **die antiken ~** the classics

klas|sisch ['klasıʃ] ADJ **a** (= *die Klassik betreffend, antik, traditionell*) classical **b** (= *typisch, vorbildlich, zeitlos*) classic **c** (*iro inf:* = *prächtig*) classic ADV classically

Klas|si|zis|mus [klasi'tsısmʊs] M -, no pl classi-cism

klas|si|zis|tisch [klasi'tsıstıʃ] ADJ classical

Klass|leh|rer M (*S Ger, Aus*) = Klassenlehrer

Klass|leh|re|rin F (*S Ger, Aus*) = Klassenlehre-rin

-kläss|ler ▲ [klɛslɐ] M -s, -, **-kläss|le|rin** ▲ [-ərın] F -, -nen in cpds (*Sch*) -former; **Erst-/Zweitklässler(in)** first-/second-former

klatsch [klatʃ] INTERJ splash, splosh; (*bei Schlag, Aufprall*) smack

Klatsch [klatʃ] M -(e)s, -e **a** splosh, splash; (*bei Schlag, Aufprall*) smack **b** no pl (*pej inf:* = *Tratsch*) gossip, scandal

Klatsch|ba|se F (*pej inf*) (*tratschend*) scan-dalmonger, gossip; (*redselig*) chatterbox (*inf*)

Klat|sche ['klatʃə] F -, -n (*inf*) **a** (*pej:* = *Klatsch-base*) gossip **b** (*Sch*) (= *Denunziant*) sneak, tell-tale (*inf*); (= *Hilfsmittel*) crib (*Brit inf*), cheat sheet (*US inf*) **c** (= *Fliegenklappe*) fly swatter

klat|schen ['klatʃn] VI **a** (= *Geräusch machen*) to clap; **in die Hände ~** to clap one's hands **b** (= *einen Klaps geben*) to slap; **jdm auf die Schenkel/sich** (*dat*) **gegen die Stirn ~** to slap sb's thighs/one's forehead **c** *aux sein* (= *aufschlagen*) (*harte Gegenstände*) to go smack; (*Flüssigkeiten*) to splash; **der Regen klatschte gegen die Fenster** the rain beat a-

gainst the windows
d (*pej inf*) (= *tratschen*) to gossip; (*dial:* = *petzen*) to sneak, to tell tales (*bei* to); **über jdn/etw ~** to gossip *or* spread gossip about sb/sth VT **a** (= *geräuschvoll schlagen*) to clap; **Takt zu clap out**; **jdm Beifall ~** to applaud *or* clap sb; **den Rhythmus ~** (*Mus*) to clap (out) the rhythm; (*mitklatschen*) to clap along **b** (= *knallen*) to smack, to slap; (= *werfen*) to throw; *Fliegen* to swat; (*sl:* = *zusammenschlagen*) to beat up (*inf*), to bash up (*Brit inf*); **jdm eine ~** (*inf*) to give sb a clip round the ear (*inf*)

Klat|schen NT -s, no pl **a** (= *Beifallklatschen*) ap-plause **b** (*inf:* = *Tratschen*) gossiping

klat|sche|nass ▲ ADJ (*inf*) = klatschnass

Klat|scher ['klatʃɐ] M -s, -, **Klat|sche|rin** [-ərın] F -, -nen **a** (*pej:* = *Klatschmaul*) gossip **b** (= *Beifallklatscher*) applauder

Klat|sche|rei [klatʃə'rai] F -, -en (*pej inf*) **a** (= *Beifallklatscherei*) clapping **b** (= *Tratscherei*) gos-siping, gossipmongering

Klatsch-: **Klatsch|ge|schich|te** F (*pej*) gossip no pl; **eine ~** a piece of gossip; **klatsch|haft** ADJ gossipy; **Klatsch|ko|lum|nist(in)** M(F) (*inf*) gossip columnist; **Klatsch|maul** NT (*pej inf*) **a** big mouth **b** (= *Mensch*) gossip (mer-chant), scandalmonger; **Klatsch|mohn** M (corn) poppy; **klatsch|nass** ▲ ADJ (*inf*) sop-ping wet (*inf*); **Klatsch|spal|te** F (*Press inf*) gossip column; **klatsch|süch|tig** ADJ extremely gossipy; **Klatsch|tan|te** F , **Klatsch|weib** NT (*pej inf*) gossip(monger), scandalmonger

klau|ben ['klaubn] VT **a** (*S Ger, Aus, Sw*) (= *auf-lesen*) to pick up; (= *auslesen*) to pick out; **etw in einen Korb ~** to pick sth up and put it in a bas-ket; **etw aus etw ~** to pick sth out from sth **b** (*Aus:* = *sammeln*) to collect; *Holz, Pilze, Kräuter* to gather, to collect; *Beeren* to pick **c** (*Sw:* = *knei-fen*) to pinch; **Worte ~** (*dial*) to split hairs

Klaue ['klauə] F -, -n claw; (= *Huf*) hoof; (*pej inf* = *Hand*) talons *or* paw (*pej inf*); (= *Schrift*) scrawl (*pej*); **in den ~n der Verbrecher** *etc* in the clutches of the criminals *etc*; **den ~n des Todes entkommen** to escape from the jaws of death

klau|en ['klauən] *VT* (*inf*) to nick (*Brit inf*), to pinch (*inf*) (*jdm etw* sth from sb); *Ideen auch* to crib (*jdm etw* sth from sb) *VI* to steal, to nick (*Brit inf*) or pinch things (*inf*)

Klau|en|seu|che F → Maul- und Klauenseuche

Klau|se ['klauzə] F -, -n **a** (*von Mönch, Einsiedler*) hermitage; (= *Klosterzelle*) cell; (*fig hum*) den **b** (mountain) defile

Klau|sel ['klauzl] F -, -n clause; (= *Vorbehalt*) proviso; (= *Bedingung*) condition, stipulation

Klaus|ner ['klausnɐ] M -s, -, **Klaus|ne|rin** [-ərın] F hermit

Klaust|ro|pho|bie [klaustrofo'bi:] F -, -n [-'bi:ən] (*Psych*) claustrophobia

klaust|ro|pho|bisch [klaustro'fo:bıʃ] ADJ (*Psych*) claustrophobic

klau|su|lie|ren [klauzu'li:rən] ptp **klausuliert** VT = verklausulieren

Klau|sur [klau'zu:ɐ] F -, -en **a** (*Univ auch* **Klau-surarbeit**) exam, paper; **~n korrigieren** to mark exam papers **b** no pl (= *Abgeschlossenheit*) seclusion; **eine Arbeit unter** *or* **in ~ schreiben** to write an essay under examination condi-tions **c** (*Eccl:* = *Räume*) enclosure, cloister

Klau|sur|ta|gung F convention, conference

Kla|vi|a|tur [klavia'tu:ɐ] F -, -en keyboard

Kla|vi|chord [klavi'kɔrt] NT -(e)s, -e [-də] clavi-chord

Kla|vier [kla'vi:ɐ] NT -s, -e piano; **~ spielen** to play the piano

Kla|vier- in cpds piano; **Kla|vier|aus|zug** M pi-ano score; **Kla|vier|a|bend** M piano recital; **Kla|vier|bau|er** M -s, -, **Kla|vier|bau|e|rin** F -, -nen piano-maker; **Kla|vier|be|ar|bei|tung** F piano arrangement; **Kla|vier|be|glei|tung** F piano accompaniment; **Kla|vier|de|ckel** M

piano lid; **Kla|vier|ho|cker** M piano stool; **Kla|vier|kon|zert** NT **a** (= *Musik*) piano con-certo **b** (= *Vorstellung*) piano recital; **Kla|vier-schu|le** F (= *Lehrbuch*) piano tutor; **Kla|vier-so|na|te** F piano sonata; **Kla|vier|spiel** NT piano playing; **Kla|vier|spie|ler(in)** M(F) pi-anist, piano player; **Kla|vier|stim|mer(in)** M(F) piano tuner; **Kla|vier|stück** NT piano piece, piece of piano music; **Kla|vier|stun|de** F piano lesson; **~n nehmen** to have *or* to take piano lessons

Kle|be-: **Kle|be|band** [-bant] NT pl -bänder adhesive tape, sticky tape; **Kle|be|bin|dung** F (*Typ*) adhesive binding; **Kle|be|falz** M (gummed) stamp hinge *or* mount; **Kle|be|fo|lie** F = Klebfolie; **Kle|be|mit|tel** NT adhesive

kle|ben ['kle:bn] VI **a** (= *festkleben*) to stick; **an etw** (*dat*) **~** (*lit*) to stick to sth; **am Vordermann ~** (*Aut inf*) to tailgate the person in front; **an den Traditionen ~** to cling *or* stick to tradition; **an seinen Händen klebt Blut** (*fig*) he has blood on his hands; **sein schlechter Ruf klebte an ihm** his bad reputation stuck; **klebt nicht so am Text** don't stick so much *or* so close to the text
b (*inf: für Sozialversicherung*) to pay stamps VT to stick; (*mit Klebstoff auch*) to glue; (*mit Leim auch*) to paste; *Film, Tonband* to splice; **Marken ~** (*Insur inf*) to pay stamps; **jdm eine ~** (*inf*) to belt sb (one) (*inf*)

kle|ben blei|ben ▲ VI *irreg aux sein* to stick (*an* +*dat* to); (*Sch inf*) to stay down a year (*Brit*), to repeat a year; (*fig inf:* = *nicht wegkom-men*) to get stuck

Kle|be-: **Kle|be|pflas|ter** NT sticking plaster (*Brit*), adhesive tape (*US*); **Kle|be|pres|se** F splicer

Kle|ber ['kle:bɐ] M -s, - **a** (*inf:* = *Klebstoff*) glue **b** (*im Mehl*) gluten

Kle|be-: **Kle|be|stel|le** F join; (*an Film*) splice; **Kle|be|stift** M glue stick; **Kle|be|stoff** M adhesive; **Kle|be|strei|fen** M = Klebstreifen; **Kle|be|ver|band** M adhesive dressing; **Kle|be|zet|tel** M gummed label

Kleb-: **Kleb|fes|tig|keit** F adhesiveness; **Kleb|flä|che** F surface to be stuck; **Kleb|fo|lie** F adhesive film; (= *d-c-fix®*) Fablon®; (*für Lebensmittel*) clingfilm; **Kleb|kraft** F adhesive strength; **Kleb|mit|tel** NT adhesive

kleb|rig ['kle:brıç] ADJ sticky; *Farbe* tacky; (*Geld*)*geschäfte* shady; (= *klebfähig*) adhesive

Kleb|rig|keit F -, no pl stickiness; (*von Farbe*) tackiness

Kleb-: **Kleb|stoff** M adhesive; **Kleb|strei|fen** M adhesive tape; (*selbstklebend auch*) sticky tape; (*zum Befeuchten*) gummed tape; (*durchschei-nend*) Sellotape® (*esp Brit*)

Kle|bung ['kle:bʊŋ] F -, -en bond

Kle|cke|rei [klɛkə'rai] F -, -en mess; **ohne ~ gehts nicht** you can't do it without making a mess

Kle|cker|kram ['klɛkɐ-] M -s, no pl (*inf, pej*) dribs and drabs pl (*inf*)

kle|ckern ['klɛkɐn] *VT* to spill; *Farbe auch* to splash VI **a** (= *Kleckse machen*) to make a mess **b** (= *tropfen*) to spill; (*Farbe*) to spill, to splash **c** (*inf:* = *stückchenweise arbeiten*) to fiddle a-round; **nicht ~, sondern klotzen** (*inf*) to do things in a big way (*inf*), to think big (*inf*); **ge-kleckert kommen** to come in dribs and drabs

kle|cker|wei|se ['klɛkɐvaizə] ADV in dribs and drabs

Klecks [klɛks] M -es, -e (= *Tintenklecks*) (ink)blot; (= *Farbklecks*) blob; (= *Fleck*) stain

kleck|sen ['klɛksn] VI (*mit Tinte*) to make blots/a blot; (*Kugelschreiber etc auch*) to blot; (*pej inf:* = *malen*) to daub

Kleck|se|rei [klɛksə'rai] F -, -en (*pej inf*) daub-ing; (*von Schüler, Kugelschreiber*) making blots

Klee [kle:] M -s, no pl clover; **jdn/etw über den grünen ~ loben** to praise sb/sth to the skies

Klee|blatt NT cloverleaf; (*Mot*) cloverleaf (intersection); (*fig*: = *Menschen*) threesome, trio; **vierblättriges ~** four-leaf clover; **das irische ~** the (Irish) shamrock

Klei|ber ['klaɪbɐ] M **-s, -** (*Orn*) nuthatch

Kleid [klaɪt] NT **-(e)s, -er** [-dɐ] **a** (= *Damenkleid*) dress; **ein zweiteiliges ~** a two-piece (suit) **b** **Kleider** PL (= *Kleidung*) clothes *pl*, clothing *sing* (*esp Comm*), garments *pl* (*Comm*); **warme ~er mitbringen** to bring warm clothes or clothing; **jdm die ~er vom Leib reißen** to tear sb's clothes off; **~er machen Leute** (*Prov*) fine feathers make fine birds (*Prov*); **ich bin zwei Tage nicht aus den ~ern gekommen** I haven't been to bed for two days **c** (*old*: = *Gewand*) garment; (*old, Sw, S Ger*: = *Herrenanzug*) suit; (*liter*: = *Uniform*) uniform **d** (*liter*) (= *Federkleid*) plumage; (= *Pelz*) coat, fur; (*fig*: *von Natur, Bäumen etc*) mantle (*liter*), cloak (*liter*); **der Winter hatte der Erde ein weißes ~ angezogen** winter had clad the earth in white (*liter*)

-kleid NT *suf in cpds* **Sommerkleid** summer dress; **Ordenskleid** monastic robe; **Herbstkleid** autumn cloak or mantle (*liter*)

Kleid|chen ['klaɪtçən] NT **-s, -** *dim von* **Kleid** little dress; (*leicht*) flimsy dress

klei|den ['klaɪdn] VR to dress; (*geh*: = *Kleider anziehen auch*) to dress oneself, to clothe oneself (*liter, form*); **sie kleidet sich sportlich** she dresses casually; **gut/schlecht gekleidet sein** to be well/badly dressed; **weiß/schwarz gekleidet** dressed in white/black; **die Natur kleidet sich in Weiß** (*liter*) nature dons a cloak or mantle of white (*liter*)

▮VT▮ (*geh*) **a** (= *mit Kleidern versehen*) to clothe, to dress; (*fig*) *Gedanken, Ideen* to clothe, to couch; **die Armen ~** to clothe the poor; **etw in schöne Worte ~** to dress sth up or to couch sth in fancy words; **ich kann meine Gefühle nicht in Worte ~** I cannot put my feelings into words **b** **jdn ~** (= *jdm stehen*) to suit sb

Klei|der-: **Klei|der|ab|la|ge** F (= *Raum*) cloakroom; (= *Garderobenablage*) coat rack; (= *Ständer*) hat stand, coat stand; **Klei|der|bü|gel** M coat hanger; **Klei|der|bürs|te** F clothes brush; **Klei|der|ha|ken** M coat hook; **Klei|der|kam|mer** F (*Mil etc*) uniform store; **Klei|der|kas|ten** M (*Aus, Sw*) wardrobe (*esp Brit*), closet (*US*); **Klei|der|ma|cher(in)** M(F) (*Aus*) tailor; (= *Damenschneiderin auch*) dressmaker; **Klei|der|ord|nung** F dress regulations *pl*; **Klei|der|sack** M suit bag; **Klei|der|schrank** M **a** wardrobe **b** (*inf*: *Mensch*) great hulk (of a man) (*inf*)

kleid|sam ['klaɪtzaːm] ADJ flattering

Klei|dung ['klaɪdʊŋ] F **-, *no pl*** clothes *pl*, clothing *sing* (*esp Comm*); **warme ~** warm clothing or clothes; **für jds (Nahrung und) ~ sorgen** to (feed and) clothe sb

Klei|dungs|stück NT garment; **~e** *pl* clothes *pl*; **ein warmes ~ mitnehmen** to bring something warm (to wear)

Kleie ['klaɪə] F **-, *no pl*** bran

klein [klaɪn] ▮ADJ▮ **a** little, small; *Finger* little; *Format, Gehalt, Rente, Zahl, Abstand, Buchstabe* small; (*Mus*) *Terz* minor; **die Kleinen Antillen** *etc* the lesser Antilles *etc*; **Klein Paris** little or miniature Paris; **der Kleine Bär** or **Wagen** the Little Bear, Ursa Minor; **die Kleine Strafkammer** (*Jur*) the lower criminal court; **x ist ~ er als 10** (*Math*) x is less than ten; **haben Sie es nicht ~er?** don't you have anything smaller?; **ein ~ bisschen** or **wenig** a little (bit); **ein ~ bisschen** or **wenig Salat** a little (bit of) salad; **ein ~es Bier, ein Kleines** (*inf*) a small beer, ≈ half a pint (*Brit*), ≈ a half (*Brit*); **~es Geld** small change; **Klein Roland** little Roland; **du ~er Teufel!** you little devil!; **ein süßes ~es Püppchen** a sweet little thing; **hallo, ~er Mann!** hello, little man; **ein schönes ~es Auto** a nice little car; **er fährt ein ~es Auto** he drives a small car; **mit seiner ~en Frau** with his little wife; **ich wusste nicht, dass seine Frau**

so ~ ist I didn't know his wife was so small or little; **eine ~e, hübsche Wohnung** a small, pretty flat (*Brit*) or apartment; **eine hübsche ~e Wohnung** a nice little flat (*Brit*) or apartment; **mein ~er Bruder** my little brother; **er ist ~er als sein Bruder** he's smaller than his brother; **als ich (noch) ~ war** when I was little; **~ für sein Alter** small or little for his age; **sich ~ machen** (= *sich bücken*) to bend down low; (= *sich zusammenrollen*) to curl up tight; **um durch die enge Tür zu kommen, muss man sich ~ machen** to get through this narrow door you have to squeeze yourself in; **macht euch ein bisschen ~er!** squeeze up closer; **den mach ich SO ~ (mit Hut)!** (*hum*) I'll cut him down to size, I'll make him look THAT big; **~ aber oho** (*inf*) small but impressive; **jdn ~ und hässlich machen** (*inf*) to make sb feel small; **ganz ~ (und hässlich) werden** (*inf*) to look humiliated or deflated; **im Kleinen** in miniature; **bis ins Kleinste** in every possible detail, in minute detail, right down to the smallest detail; **von ~ an** or **auf** (= *von Kindheit an*) from his childhood or early days; (= *von Anfang an*) from the very beginning, from scratch; **~e Kinder ~e Sorgen, große Kinder große Sorgen** (*prov*) bigger children just mean bigger problems; **um ein Kleines zu ...** (*geh*) a little or a trifle too ... → **Finger, Geschenk**
b (= *kurz*) *Wuchs, Schritt* little, small, short; *Weile, Pause* little, short; *Vortrag* short; **~en Augenblick, bitte!** just one moment, please; **einen Kopf ~er als jd sein** to be a head shorter than sb
c (= *geringfügig*) little, small, slight; *Betrag, Summe* little, small; **beim ~sten Schreck** at the slightest or smallest shock; **das ~ere Übel** the lesser evil; **ein paar ~ere Fehler** a few minor mistakes; **eine ~ere Unpässlichkeit** a minor ailment
d (= *unbedeutend*) petty (*pej*); *Leute* ordinary; **er ist ein ~er Geist** he is small-minded; **der ~e Mann** the ordinary citizen, the man in the street; **ein ~er Ganove** a small-time or petty crook; **die Kleinen fängt man** or **werden gehängt, die Großen lässt man laufen** (*prov*) it's always the big fish that get away; **sein Vater war (ein) ~er Beamter** his father was a minor civil servant; **~e Leute übersieht man** (*hum*) I'm *etc* so small and insignificant → **Fisch a**
e (= *armselig*) *Verhältnisse* humble, lowly, modest
f *Prüfung* intermediate

▮ADV▮ **a** (= *in kleiner Schrift*) small; **er schreibt sehr ~** he writes very small, his writing is very small; **ein Wort ~ drucken** to print a word without a capital; **~ gedruckt** in small print; **~ gemustert** small-patterned; **~ kariert** (*Stoff*) finely checked or chequered (*Brit*) or checkered (*US*) → **kleinkariert, kleinschreiben**
b (*auf kleine Hitze*) **etw ~ stellen** or **drehen** to put sth on low or on a low heat; **etw ~er stellen** or **drehen** to turn sth down
c (*in Wendungen*) **~ anfangen** to start off in a small way; **~ beigeben** (*inf*) to give in; **~ geraten sein** (*Gegenstand*) to have come out a little (too) small; (*Mensch*) to be a bit small; **etw ~ halten** (*Anzahl, Kosten*) to keep sth down; *Party, Feier* to keep sth small

-klein NT *suf in cpds* **-s**, *no pl* → **Gänseklein, Hasenklein** *etc*

Klein-: **Klein|ak|ti|o|när(in)** M(F) small shareholder; **Klein|an|le|ger(in)** M(F) (*Fin*) small investor; **Klein|an|zei|ge** F classified advertisement, small ad (*inf*); **Klein|ar|beit** F detailed work; **in zäher/mühseliger ~** with rigorous/painstaking attention to detail; **Klein|asi|en** NT Asia Minor; **klein|asi|a|tisch** ADJ of or from Asia Minor; **im ~en Raum** in Asia Minor; **Klein|au|to** NT small car; **Klein|bahn** F narrow-gauge railway (*Brit*) or railroad (*US*); **Klein|bau|er** M *pl* **-bauern**, **Klein|bäu|e|rin** F **-, -nen** small farmer, smallholder; **klein+be|kom|men** VT *sep irreg* = **kleinkriegen**; **Klein|be|trieb** M small business; **bäuer-**

licher ~ smallholding; **handwerklicher ~** (small) workshop; **industrieller ~** small factory; **Klein|bild|ka|me|ra** F 35mm camera; **Klein|buch|sta|be** M small letter; **Klein|bür|ger(in)** M(F) petty bourgeois; **klein|bür|ger|lich** ADJ lower middle-class, petty bourgeois (*pej*); **er reagierte typisch ~** his reaction was typically lower middle-class or typically petty bourgeois; **Klein|bür|ger|tum** NT (*Sociol*) lower middle class, petty bourgeoisie; **Klein|bus** M minibus

Klei|ne|leu|te|mi|li|eu NT world of ordinary people

Klei|ne(r) ['klaɪnə] MF *decl as adj* **a** little one or child; (= *Junge*) little boy; (= *Mädchen*) little girl; (= *Säugling*) baby; **unser ~r** (= *Jüngster*) our youngest (child); **die lieben ~n** (*iro*) the dear or sweet little things; **eine hübsche ~** a pretty little girl or thing; **die Katze mit ihren ~n** the cat with its kittens or babies (*inf*) **b** (*inf*: *auch* **Kleines:** = *Schatz, Liebling*) baby (*inf*); **na ~/~r!** (*zu einem Kind*) hello little girl/boy!; **na ~r!** (*Prostituierte zu einem Passanten*) hello, love (*esp Brit*) or dear

Klei|ne(s) ['klaɪnə] NT *decl as adj* **etwas ~s** (*inf*) a little baby or stranger (*hum*)

Klein-: **Klein|fa|mi|lie** F (*Sociol*) nuclear family; **Klein|for|mat** NT small format; **ein Buch/ Bild im ~** a small-format book/picture; **klein|for|ma|tig** ADJ small-format; **Klein|gar|ten** M allotment (*Brit*), garden plot; **Klein|gärt|ner(in)** M(F) allotment holder (*Brit*), garden plot holder; **Klein|ge|bäck** NT biscuits *pl* (*Brit*), cookies *pl* (*US*); **klein|ge|druckt** △ ADJ *attr* = **klein** ADV a; **Klein|ge|druck|te(s)** [-gədrʊktə] NT *decl as adj* small print; **Klein|geist** M (*pej*) small-minded person; **klein|geis|tig** ADJ (*pej*) small-minded, petty; **Klein|geis|tig|keit** F (*pej*) small-mindedness, pettiness; **Klein|geld** NT (small) change; **das nötige ~ haben** (*fig*) to have the necessary wherewithal (*inf*); **klein|ge|mus|tert** △ ADJ → **klein** ADV a; **klein|ge|wach|sen** ADJ short, small; *Baum* small; **klein|gläu|big** ADJ **a** (*Rel*) doubting, sceptical (*Brit*), skeptical (*US*); **der ~e Thomas** doubting Thomas; **ihr Kleingläubigen!** (*Bibl*) o ye of little faith **b** (= *zweiflerisch*) timid; **~ sein** to lack conviction; **sei doch nicht so ~!** don't be so timid; **Klein|grup|pe** F (*Sociol*) small group; **klein ha|cken** ▲ VT to chop up small; **Klein|häus|ler** [-hɔʏslɐ] M **-s, -**, **Klein|häus|le|rin** [-ərɪn] F **-, -nen** (*Aus*) small farmer; **Klein|heit** F **-**, *no pl* smallness, small size; **klein|her|zig** ▮ADJ▮ fainthearted ▮ADV▮ faintheartedly; *sich verhalten* timidly; **Klein|hirn** NT (*Anat*) cerebellum; **Klein|holz** NT , *no pl* firewood, kindling; **~ aus jdm machen** (*inf*) to make mincemeat out of sb (*inf*)

Klei|nig|keit ['klaɪnɪçkaɪt] F **-, -en** **a** little or small thing; (= *Bagatelle*) small or trifling or trivial matter or thing, trifle; (= *Einzelheit*) minor detail or point, small point; **ich habe noch ein paar ~en in der Stadt zu erledigen** I still have a few little things to attend to in town; **es war nur eine ~ zu reparieren** there was only something minor to be repaired; **die Reparatur/Prüfung war eine ~** the repair job/exam was no trouble at all; **eine ~ essen** to have a bite to eat, to eat a little something; **jdm eine ~ schenken/bezahlen** to give/pay sb a little something; **die ~ von 1.000 Euro** (*iro*) the small matter of 1,000 euros; **das kostet eine ~** (*iro*) that'll cost a pretty penny (*esp Brit*); **wegen** or **bei jeder ~** for the slightest reason; **sich um jede ~ selbst kümmern müssen** to have to take care of every little detail personally; **das war doch (nur) eine ~!** it was nothing; **das ist doch eine ~!** that isn't (asking) much; **das ist für mich keine ~** that is no small matter for me; **wir haben noch ein paar ~en geändert** we've changed one or two details, we've made one or two small changes; **großen Wert auf ~en legen** to be a stickler for detail(s); **bis auf die letzten ~en ist alles fertig** everything is ready apart from the last-minute odds and ends; **sich nicht mit ~en abgeben** or

befassen not to bother over details

b (= *ein bisschen*) **eine ~** a little (bit), a trifle, a shade; **eine ~ zu groß/nach rechts** a little (bit) *etc* too big/to the right; **das wird eine ~ dauern** it will take a little while

Kleinigkeits-: Kleinigkeitskrämer(in) M(F) (*pej*) stickler for detail, pedant; **Kleinigkeitskrämerei** F -, **-en** [-krɛːməˈraɪ] (*pej*) pernicketiness, pedantry

Klein-: Kleinkaliber NT small bore; **Kleinkalibergewehr** NT small-bore rifle; **kleinkalibrig** [-kaliːbrɪç] ADJ *Waffe* small-bore *attr*; **kleinkariert** ADJ (*fig*) tuppenny-ha'penny *attr* (*Brit inf*), small-time (*inf*); **~ sein** (*fig*) to be small-minded *or* petty-minded ADV *reagieren* narrow-mindedly; **~ denken** to think small; **~ handeln, sich ~ verhalten** to be narrow-minded → *auch* klein ADV a; **Kleinkariertheit** F, *no pl* (*fig*) small-mindedness, petty-mindedness; **Kleinkind** NT small child, toddler (*inf*), infant (*Psych*); **Kleinklima** NT (*Met*) microclimate; **Kleinkram** M (*inf*) odds and ends *pl*; (= *kleinere Arbeiten*) odd jobs *pl*; (= *Trivialitäten*) trivialities *pl*, trivia *pl*; **Kleinkrämer(in)** M(F) (*pej*) small-minded person; **kleinkrämerisch** ADJ *Person* small-minded; *Vorbehalte* petty, trivial; **Kleinkredit** M personal loan; **Kleinkrieg** M (*fig*) battle; **einen ~ mit jdm führen** to be fighting a running battle with sb

klein+kriegen VT *sep* **a** (*lit*) *Holz* to chop (up); *Nuss* to break; **er kann das Fleisch mit dem Messer nicht ~** he can't cut up the meat with his knife

b (*inf*: = *kaputtmachen*) to smash, to break **c** (*inf*) (= *gefügig machen*) to bring into line (*inf*); (= *unterkriegen, müde machen*) to get down; (*körperlich*) to tire out; **er ist einfach nicht kleinzukriegen** he just won't be beaten; **unser altes Auto ist einfach nicht kleinzukriegen** our old car just goes on for ever; **er ließ sich auch trotz erpresserischer Drohungen nicht ~** in spite of being blackmailed he was not to be intimidated **d** (*inf*) *Geld* to blow (*inf*), to get through

Kleinkriminelle(r) MF *decl as adj* petty criminal

Kleinkunst F cabaret

Kleinkunstbühne F cabaret

Kleinlaster M pickup truck

kleinlaut ADJ abashed, subdued, meek; **dann wurde er ganz ~** it took the wind out of his sails, that made him shut up ADV *fragen* meekly; **etw ~ zugeben** to admit sth shamefacedly; **~ um Verzeihung bitten** to apologize rather sheepishly

kleinlich [ˈklaɪnlɪç] ADJ petty, (= *knauserig*) mean (*esp Brit*), stingy (*inf*); (= *engstirnig*) narrow-minded ADV (= *knauserig*) stingily; (= *engstirnig*) narrow-mindedly

Kleinlichkeit F -, *no pl* pettiness; (= *Knauserigkeit*) meanness (*esp Brit*), stinginess (*inf*); (= *Engstirnigkeit*) narrow-mindedness

klein machen ▲ VT **a** (= *zerkleinern*) to chop up, to cut up **b** (*inf*) *Geld* (= *wechseln*) to change; (= *ausgeben*) to blow (*inf*) **c** (*inf*: = *erniedrigen*) **jdn ~** to make sb look small

Klein-: Kleinmöbel PL smaller items *pl* of furniture; **Kleinmut** M faintheartedness, timidity; **kleinmütig** [-myːtɪç] ADJ fainthearted, timid ADV timidly

Kleinod [ˈklaɪnoːt] NT -(e)s, -ien *or* -e [-ˈloːdiən, -də] (*lit, fig*) jewel, gem; **sie war sein ~** (*liter*) she was his treasure *or* his pride and joy

Klein-: Kleinräumig ADJ *Gebiet, Wohnung* small; **Kleinrentner(in)** M(F) *person living on small pension*; **klein schneiden** ▲ VT *irreg* to cut up small, to cut up into small pieces; **klein schreiben** ▲ VT *irreg* (*fig*) to set little store by; **klein geschrieben werden** to count for (very) little; **klein+schreiben** VT *sep irreg* (*mit kleinem Anfangsbuchstaben*) to write without a capital; **ein Wort ~** to write a word without a capital; **Kleinschreibung** F use of small ini-

tial letters; **Kleinsparer(in)** M(F) small saver; **Kleinstaat** M small state; **Kleinstadt** F small town; **Kleinstädter(in)** M(F) small-town dweller, provincial (*pej*); **kleinstädtisch** ADJ provincial (*pej*), small-town *attr*

Kleinstbetrag [ˈklaɪnst-] M small sum; (*bei Wetten*) minimum stake; **Kleinstbeträge unter EUR 1 sind unzulässig** sums below the minimum of 1 euro are not acceptable

kleinste(r, s) [ˈklaɪnstə] *superl von* klein

Kleinst-: Kleinstformat NT **ein Radio im ~** a tiny *or* miniature radio; **kleinstmöglich** ADJ smallest possible; **Kleinstwagen** M (*Aut*) minicar; **Kleinstwohnung** F one-room flatlet (*Brit*) *or* apartment

Klein-: kleinteilig ADJ *Struktur* divided into small sections; **~es Denken** excessive concern with small details ADV **ein ~ angelegter Park** a park laid out in small sections; **~ denken** to be excessively concerned with small details; **Kleintier** NT small animal; **Kleintierhaltung** F keeping of small livestock; **Kleintierpraxis** F small animal (veterinary) practice; **Kleintransporter** M (*Aut*) pickup (truck); **Kleinvieh** NT **~ macht auch Mist** (*prov*) many a mickle makes a muckle (*Scot*), every little helps; **Kleinwagen** M small car; **kleinweis** [ˈklaɪnvaɪs] ADV (*Aus*) gradually; **Kleinwild** NT small game; **Kleinwohnung** F flatlet (*Brit*), small apartment; **kleinwüchsig** [-vyːksɪç] ADJ (*geh*) small; *Volk auch* small in stature; **Kleinwüchsigkeit** F (*Med*) restricted growth; **Kleinzeug** NT , *no pl* (*inf*) small odds and ends *pl*

Kleister [ˈklaɪstə] M -s, - (= *Klebstoff*) paste; (*pej*: *dicke Speise*) goo (*inf*)

kleisterig [ˈklaɪstərɪç] ADJ (*pej inf*) gooey (*inf*)

kleistern [ˈklaɪstən] VT **a** (= *zusammenkleben*) to paste **b** (*dated inf*) **jdm eine ~** to slap sb in the face, to slap sb's face

kleistrig [ˈklaɪstrɪç] ADJ (*pej inf*) gooey (*inf*)

Klematis [kleˈmaːtɪs, ˈkleːmatɪs] F -, - (*Bot*) clematis

Klementine [klemɛnˈtiːnə] F -, -n clementine

Klemmappe △ F → **Klemmmappe**

Klemmbrett NT clipboard

Klemme [ˈklɛmə] F -, -n **a** (= *Haarklemme, für Papiere etc*) clip; (*Elec*) crocodile clamp *or* clip; (*Med*) clamp **b** (*fig inf*) **in der ~ sitzen** *or* **sein** to be in a fix *or* tight spot *or* jam (*all inf*); **jdm aus der ~ helfen** to help sb out of a fix *or* tight spot *or* jam (*all inf*)

klemmen [ˈklɛmən] VT *Draht etc* to clamp, to clip; (*in Spalt*) to wedge, to jam; **sich** (*dat*) **den Finger in etw** (*dat*) **~** to catch *or* trap one's finger in sth; **sich** (*dat*) **etw unter den Arm ~** to stick *or* tuck sth under one's arm; **sich** (*dat*) **eine Zigarette zwischen die Lippen ~** (*inf*) to stick a cigarette in one's mouth VR to catch oneself (*in +dat*); **sich hinter etw** (*acc*) **~** (*inf*) to get stuck into sth (*inf*); **sich hinter jdn ~** (*inf*) to get on to sb VI (*Tür, Schloss etc*) to stick, to jam

Klemmer [ˈklɛmə] M -s, - pince-nez

Klemm-: Klemmlampe F clamp-on lamp; **Klemmmappe** ▲ F spring folder *or* binder

Klempner [ˈklɛmpnə] M -s, -, **Klempnerin** [-ərɪn] F -, -nen plumber

Klempnerei [klɛmpnəˈraɪ] F -, -en **a** *no pl* plumbing **b** (= *Werkstatt*) plumber's workshop

Klempnerladen M plumber's (shop); **der General trägt** *or* **hat einen ganzen ~ auf der Brust** (*hum*) the general has a whole load of ironmongery on his breast (*Brit hum inf*), the general is covered in medals

klempnern [ˈklɛmpnən] VI to do plumbing

Kleopatra [kleˈoːpatra] F -s Cleopatra

Klepper [ˈklɛpə] M -s, - nag, hack

Klepper-®: Klepperboot NT faltboat, foldboat, folding boat; **Kleppermantel** M mackintosh (*Brit*), mac (*Brit inf*), trench coat

Kleptomane [klɛptoˈmaːnə] M -n, -n, **Kleptomanin** [-ˈmaːnɪn] F -, -nen kleptomaniac

Kleptomanie [klɛptomaˈniː] F -, *no pl* kleptomania

klerikal [kleriˈkaːl] ADJ (*pej*) clerical ADV *gesinnt, eingestellt* clerically

Klerikalismus [klerikaˈlɪsmʊs] M -, *no pl* (*pej*) clericalism

Kleriker [ˈkleːrɪkə] M -s, -, **Klerikerin** [-ərɪn] F -, -nen cleric

Klerus [ˈkleːrʊs] M -, *no pl* clergy

Klettband [ˈklɛtbant] NT *pl* **-bänder** Velcro® (strip)

Klette [ˈklɛtə] F -, -n (*Bot*) burdock; (= *Blütenkopf*) bur(r); (*pej*: = *lästiger Mensch*) nuisance, bind (*inf*); **sich wie eine ~ an jdn hängen** to cling to sb like a bur *or* like a limpet *or* barnacle (*Brit*); **wie die ~n zusammenhalten** to stick together

Kletter-: Kletteraffe M (*inf*) **er ist ein richtiger ~** he can climb like a monkey; **Kletterbaum** M climbing tree

Kletterer [ˈklɛtərə] M -s, -, **Kletterin** [-ərɪn] F -, -nen climber

Klettergerüst NT climbing frame

Klettermax [ˈklɛtəmaks] M -es, -e, **Klettermaxe** [-maksə] M -n, -n (*inf*) steeplejack

klettern [ˈklɛtən] VI *aux sein* to climb; (*mühsam*) to clamber; **auf Bäume ~** to climb trees

Kletter-: Kletterpartie F climbing trip *or* outing; **Kletterpflanze** F climbing plant, climber; **Kletterrose** F climbing rose; **Kletterstange** F climbing pole; **Klettertour** F climbing trip

Klettverschluss ▲ [ˈklɛt-] M Velcro® fastener

Kletze [ˈklɛtsə] F -, -n (*S Ger, Aus*) dried pear

Kletzenbrot NT (*S Ger, Aus*) fruit bread

Klick [klɪk] M -s, -s (*Comput*) click

klicken [ˈklɪkn] VI to click

Klicker [ˈklɪkə] M -s, - marble; (= *Spiel*) marbles *sing*

klickern [ˈklɪkən] VI to play marbles

Klient [kliˈɛnt] M -en, -en, **Klientin** [-ˈɛntɪn] F -, -nen client

Klientel [kliɛnˈteːl] F -, -en clients *pl*, clientele

klieren [ˈkliːrən] VI (*dial*) to scrawl

Kliff [klɪf] NT -(e)s, -e cliff

Kliffküste F cliffs *pl*

Klima [ˈkliːma] NT -s, -s *or* Klimate [kliˈmaːtə] (*lit, fig*) climate; (*fig auch*) atmosphere

Klima-: Klimaänderung F climatic change; **Klimaanlage** F air conditioning (system); **mit ~** air-conditioned; **Klimaforscher(in)** M(F) climatologist; **Klimagipfel** M (*inf*) climate conference *or* summit; **Klimakammer** F climatic chamber; **Klimakatastrophe** F climatic disaster; **Klimakollaps** M climatic breakdown

Klimakterium [klimakˈteːriʊm] NT -s, *no pl* climacteric, menopause

Klima-: Klimakunde F climatology; **Klimaschwankung** F climatic variation

klimatisch [kliˈmaːtɪʃ] ADJ *no pred* climatic ADV **~ günstige Verhältnisse** a favourable (*Brit*) *or* favorable (*US*) climate; **~ ungünstiger Ort** a location with an unfavourable (*Brit*) *or* unfavorable (*US*) climate; **eine ~ angenehme Gegend** an area with a pleasant climate; **~ bedingt sein** (*Wachstum*) to be dependent on the climate; (*Krankheit*) to be caused by climatic conditions

klimatisieren [klimatiˈziːrən] *ptp* **klimatisiert** VT to air-condition

Klimatologie [klimatoloˈgiː] F -, *no pl* climatology

Kli|ma|ver|än|de|rung F , **Kli|ma|wech|sel** M (*lit, fig*) climate change, change in (the) climate

Kli|max ['kliːmaks] F -, (*rare*) -**e** (*geh*: = *Höhepunkt*) climax

Kli|ma|zo|ne F (climatic) zone

Klim|bim [klɪm'bɪm] M -s, *no pl* (*inf*) odds and ends *pl*; (= *Umstände*) fuss (and bother)

klim|men ['klɪmən] *pret* **klomm** *or* **klimmte** [klɔm, 'klɪmtə], *ptp* **geklommen** *or* **geklimmt** [gə'klɔmən, gə'klɪmt] VI *aux sein* (*geh*) to clamber, to scramble

Klimm|zug M (*Sport*) pull-up; **geistige Klimmzüge machen** (*fig*) to do intellectual *or* mental acrobatics

Klim|pe|rei [klɪmpə'raɪ] F -, -**en** (*inf*) tinkling; (*stümperhaft*) plonking (*inf*); (*auf Banjo etc*) twanging

Klim|per|kas|ten M (*inf*) piano, joanna (*inf*)

klim|pern ['klɪmpɐn] VI to tinkle; (= *stümperhaft klimpern*) to plonk away (*inf*); (*auf Banjo*) to twang; **mit Geld ~** to jingle coins; **mit den Wimpern ~** (*inf*) to flutter one's eyelashes

kling [klɪŋ] INTERJ clink, ting, ding; **~ machen** (*Metall, Glas etc*) to clink; **mit Kling und Klang** (*old*) to the sound of music

Klin|ge ['klɪŋə] F -, -**n** blade; (*liter*: = *Schwert*) sword, blade (*liter*); **eine gute ~ schlagen** (*Fechten*) to be a good swordsman; **mit blanker ~** (*liter*) with drawn sword; **er führt eine scharfe ~** (*fig*) he is a dangerous opponent; **mit jdm die ~(n) kreuzen** (*lit, fig*) to cross swords with sb; **jdn über die ~ springen lassen** (*inf*) (= *umbringen*) to bump sb off (*inf*), to rub sb out (*inf*); (= *opfern*) to leave sb to be killed

Klin|gel ['klɪŋl] F -, -**n** bell

Klin|gel-: Klin|gel|an|la|ge F bell system; **Klin|gel|beu|tel** M collection bag; **Klin|gel|draht** M bell wire

klin|ge|ling [klɪŋə'lɪŋ] INTERJ ding-a-ling

Klin|gel|knopf M bell button *or* push

klin|geln ['klɪŋln] VI to ring (*nach* for); (*Motor*) to pink, to knock; **es hat schon zum ersten/zweiten/dritten Mal geklingelt** (*in Konzert, Theater*) the three-/two-/one-minute bell has already gone; **es hat schon geklingelt** (*in Schule*) the bell has already gone; **es hat geklingelt** (*Telefon*) the phone just rang; (*an Tür*) somebody just rang the doorbell; **es klingelt an der Tür** (*als Bühnenanweisung*) there is a ring at the door; **hat es jetzt endlich (bei dir) geklingelt?** (*fig inf*) has the penny finally dropped? (*inf*); **Klingeln** ringing

Klin|gel-: Klin|gel|schnur F bell pull; **Klin|gel|zei|chen** NT ring; **auf ein ~ hin** at the ring of a bell; **auf ein besonderes ~ hin** in response to a special ring; **Klin|gel|zug** M bell pull

klin|gen ['klɪŋən] ✪ 38 *pret* **klang** [klaŋ], *ptp* **geklungen** [gə'kluŋən] VI to sound; (*Glocke, Ohr*) to ring; (*Glas*) to clink; (*Metall*) to clang; **nach etw ~** to sound like sth; **mein linkes Ohr klingt** I have a ringing (sound) in my left ear; **das klingt mir wie Musik in den Ohren** that is music to my ears; **die Gläser ~ lassen** to clink glasses; **die Glocke klingt dumpf/hell** the bell has a dull/clear ring → **Münze**

klin|gend ADJ **mit ~em Spiel** (*old Mil*) with fife and drum; **in** *or* **mit ~er Münze** (*old, liter*) in coin of the realm; **~e Register** (*Mus*) (sounding) stops *pl*; **~er Reim** (*Poet*) feminine rhyme

Kli|nik ['kliːnɪk] F -, -**en** clinic; (= *Universitätsklinik*) (university) hospital

Kli|ni|ka, Kli|ni|ken *pl von* **Klinikum**

Kli|ni|ker ['kliːnɪkɐ] M -s, -, **Kli|ni|ke|rin** [-ərɪn] F -, -**nen** (*Med*) clinician; (*Univ*) medical student attached to a hospital

Kli|ni|kum ['kliːnɪkʊm] NT -s, **Klinika** *or* **Kliniken** [-ka, -kn] (*Univ*) **a** medical centre (*Brit*) *or* center (*US*) **b** (= *Ausbildung*) internship

kli|nisch ['kliːnɪʃ] ADJ clinical; **~er Blick** cold glance ADV clinically; **~ tot** clinically dead

Klin|ke ['klɪŋkə] F -, -**n** (= *Türklinke*) (door) handle; (= *Sperrklinke*) catch, ratchet, pawl; (*Telec*) jack; **~n putzen** (*inf*) to go *or* canvass from door to door, to go *or* do door-to-door canvassing; (*um Ware zu verkaufen*) to sell from door to door, to go *or* do door-to-door selling; **die Interessenten geben sich** (*dat*) **die ~ in die Hand** there's a constant stream of interested parties

Klin|ken|put|zer [-pʊtsɐ] M -s, -, **Klin|ken-put|ze|rin** [-ərɪn] F -, -**nen** (*inf*) (= *Hausierer*) hawker; (= *Vertreter*) door-to-door salesman/saleswoman; (= *Wahlkandidat*) door-to-door canvasser; (= *Bettler*) beggar

Klin|ker ['klɪŋkɐ] M -s, - **a** (= *Ziegelstein*) clinker brick, (Dutch) clinker **b** (*Naut*) clinker

Klin|ker-: Klin|ker|bau M *pl* -**bauten** clinker building; **Klin|ker|boot** NT clinker(-built) boat; **Klin|ker|stein** M clinker brick, (Dutch) clinker

Kli|no|mo|bil [klinomo'biːl] NT -s, -**e** mobile clinic

klipp [klɪp] INTERJ **~, klapp** click, clack; (*Schuhe, Hufe*) clip, clop ADV **~ und klar** clearly, plainly; (= *offen*) frankly, openly

Klipp [klɪp] M -s, -s clip

Klip|pe ['klɪpə] F -, -**n** (= *Felsklippe*) cliff; (*im Meer*) rock; (*fig*) hurdle, obstacle; **~n umschiffen** (*lit, fig*) to negotiate obstacles

Klip|pen-: Klip|pen|küs|te F rocky coast; **klip|pen|reich** ADJ rocky

Klipp-: Klipp|fisch M dried, salted cod; **Klipp|schu|le** F (*pej*) second-rate school

Klips [klɪps] M -es, -e = **Clip**

klir|ren ['kliːrən] VI to clink; (*Glas auch*) to tinkle; (*Fensterscheiben*) to rattle; (*Waffen*) to clash; (*Ketten, Sporen*) to jangle; (*Lautsprecher, Mikrofon*) to crackle; (*Eis*) to crunch; **~de Kälte** crisp cold; **~der Frost** sharp frost; **~de Töne** tinny sounds

Klirr|fak|tor M distortion (factor)

Kli|schee [kli'ʃeː] NT -s, -s (*Typ*) plate, block; (*fig*: = *Ausdruck, Phrase*) cliché

Kli|schee-: Kli|schee|an|stalt F (*Typ*) platemaker's; **kli|schee|haft** ADJ (*fig*) stereotyped, hackneyed ADV stereotypically; **Kli|schee-vor|stel|lung** F cliché, stereotype

kli|schie|ren [kli'ʃiːrən] *ptp* **klischiert** VT (*Typ*) to make plates for, to stereotype

Klis|tier [klɪs'tiːɐ] NT -s, -**e** enema, clyster (*spec*)

Klis|tier|sprit|ze F enema (syringe)

Kli|to|ris ['kliːtɔrɪs] F -, - *or* **Klitorides** [kli'toːriːdeːs] clitoris

klitsch [klɪtʃ] INTERJ **~, klatsch** slip, slop

Klitsch [klɪtʃ] M -(**e**)**s**, -**e** (*dial*) **a** (= *Schlag*) slap, smack **b** (= *Brei*) doughy *or* soggy mass

Klit|sche ['klɪtʃə] F -, -**n** (*pej inf*) dilapidated building; (*Theat*) small-time theatre (*Brit*) *or* theater (*US*); (= *Kleinbetrieb*) tiny outfit (*inf*)

klit|schig ['klɪtʃɪç] ADJ (*dial*) doughy, soggy

klitsch|nass ▲ ADJ (*inf*) drenched, soaking *or* sopping (*inf*) wet

klit|tern ['klɪtɐn] VT *Geschichte* to concoct

Klit|te|rung F -, -**en** → **Geschichtsklitterung**

klit|ze|klein ['klɪtsə'klaɪn] ADJ (*inf*) tiny, teeny-weeny (*inf*); very small ADV *schneiden, schreiben, kopieren* very small

Kli|vie ['kliːviə] F -, -**n** (*Bot*) clivia

Klo [kloː] NT -s, -s (*inf*) loo (*Brit inf*), john (*US inf*); **aufs ~ gehen** to go to the loo (*Brit inf*) *or* john (*US inf*)

Klo|a|ke [klo'aːkə] F -, -**n** sewer; (*fig auch*) cesspool; (*Zool*) cloaca

Klo|a|ken-: Klo|a|ken|jour|na|lis|mus M gutter journalism; **Klo|a|ken|tie|re** PL the monotremes *pl* (*form*)

Klo|ben ['kloːbn] M -s, - **a** (= *Holzklotz*) log **b** (= *Eisenhaken*) hook

klo|big ['kloːbɪç] ADJ hefty (*inf*), bulky; *Mensch* hulking great (*inf*); *Schuhe* clumpy; *Benehmen* boorish; *Hände* massive, hefty (*inf*) ADV *aussehen* bulky; *bauen, sich abheben* massively; **~ wirken** (*Gebäude*) to look big and clumsy; (*Schuhe*) to seem clumpy

Klo-: Klo|bril|le F (*inf*) toilet *or* loo (*Brit inf*) seat; **Klo|bürs|te** F (*inf*) toilet *or* loo (*Brit inf*) brush; **Klo|frau** F , **Klo|mann** M *pl* -**männer** (*inf*) toilet *or* loo (*Brit inf*) attendant

klomm *pret von* **klimmen**

Klon [kloːn] M -s, -**e** clone

klo|nen ['kloːnən] VTI to clone

Klo|nen NT -s, *no pl* cloning; **das ~ von Menschen** human cloning; **therapeutisches ~** therapeutic cloning

klö|nen ['kløːnən] VI (*inf*) to (have a) natter (*Brit inf*) *or* chat

Klön|schnack M (*N Ger inf*) natter (*Brit inf*), chat

Klo|pa|pier NT (*inf*) toilet *or* loo (*Brit inf*) paper, bumf (*dated Brit inf*)

Klöp|fel ['klœpfl] M -s, - **a** (= *Holzhammer*) square mallet; (= *Steinmetzwerkzeug*) stonemason's maul **b** (*old*: = *Glockenklöpfel*) tongue, clapper

klop|fen ['klɔpfn] VT to knock; *Fleisch, Teppich* to beat; *Steine* to knock down; **den Takt ~** to beat time

VI to knock; (*leicht auch*) to tap; (*Herz*) to beat; (*vor Aufregung, Anstrengung*) to pound; (*Puls, Schläfe*) to throb; (*Specht*) to tap, to hammer; (*Motor*) to knock, to pink; (*beim Kartenspiel*) to pass; **klopf doch noch mal!** give another knock, knock again; **sie klopften wiederholt heftig an die Tür** they kept pounding away at the door; **der Winter klopft an die Tür** winter is approaching; **es klopft** (*Theat*) there is a knock at the door; **es hat geklopft** there's someone knocking at the door; **„bitte laut ~"** "please knock loudly"; **jdm auf die Schulter ~** to tap sb on the shoulder; **jdm auf den Rücken/den Hintern ~** to tap sb on the back/the bottom; **jdm auf die Finger ~** (*lit, fig*) to give sb a rap on the knuckles, to rap sb on the knuckles; **mit ~dem Herzen** with beating *or* pounding heart; **ein ~der Schmerz** a throbbing pain → **Busch**

Klop|fen ['klɔpfn] M -s, *no pl* knock(ing); (*leise*) tap(ping); (*von Motor*) knock(ing)

Klop|fer ['klɔpfɐ] M -s, - (= *Türklopfer*) (door) knocker; (= *Fleischklopfer*) (meat) mallet; (= *Teppichklopfer*) carpet beater

Klopf-: klopf|fest ADJ antiknock; **Klopf|fes-tig|keit** F antiknock quality; **Klopf|zei|chen** NT knock

Klop|pe ['klɔpə] PL (*dial inf*) **~ kriegen** to be given a hiding *or* thrashing

Klöp|pel ['klœpl] M -s, - (= *Glockenklöppel*) tongue, clapper; (= *Spitzenklöppel*) bobbin; (= *Trommelklöppel*) stick

Klöp|pel|ar|beit F pillow lace

Klöp|pe|lei [klœpə'laɪ] F -, -**en** (pillow) lace making

klöp|peln ['klœpln] VI to make (pillow) lace; **eine Tischdecke ~** to make a lace tablecloth

Klöp|pel|spit|ze F pillow lace

klop|pen ['klɔpn] (*N Ger inf*) VT to hit → **Griff, Skat** VR to fight, to scrap (*inf*), to brawl

Klop|pe|rei [klɔpə'raɪ] F -, -**en** (*N Ger inf*) fight, brawl

Klöpp|ler ['klœplɐ] M -s, -, **Klöpp|le|rin** [-ərɪn] F -, -**nen** (pillow) lace maker

Klops [klɔps] M -es, -**e** (*Cook*) meatball; (*dated inf*: = *schwerer Fehler*) howler (*inf*), clanger (*Brit inf*)

Klo|schüs|sel F (*inf*) loo (*Brit inf*) *or* toilet bowl, lavatory pan (*Brit*)

Klo|sett [klo'zɛt] NT -s, -**e** *or* -**s** lavatory, toilet

Klo|sett-: Klo|sett|be|cken NT lavatory (*esp Brit*) *or* toilet bowl, lavatory pan (*Brit*); **Klo-**

sẹtt|bril|le F toilet seat; **Klo|sẹtt|bürs|te** F lavatory (*esp Brit*) or toilet brush; **Klo|sẹtt-|de|ckel** M lavatory (*esp Brit*) or toilet seat lid; **Klo|sẹtt|frau** F , **Klo|sẹtt|mann** M *pl* **-männer** lavatory (*esp Brit*) or toilet attendant; **Klo|sẹtt|pa|pier** NT lavatory (*esp Brit*) or toilet paper

Kloß [klo:s] M **-es, ⸚e** [ˈkløːsə] dumpling; (= *Fleischkloß*) meatball; (= *Bulette*) rissole; **einen ~ im Hals haben** (*fig*) to have a lump in one's throat

Kloß|brü|he F **klar wie ~** (*inf*) (= *völlig klar*) as clear as day; (*iro:* = *unklar*) as clear as mud

Klos|ter [ˈkloːstɐ] NT **-s, ⸚** [ˈkløːstɐ] cloister; (= *Mönchskloster auch*) monastery; (= *Nonnenkloster auch*) convent, nunnery (*old*); **ins ~ gehen** to enter a monastery/convent, to become a monk/nun

Klos|ter-: Klos|ter|bru|der M (*old*) monk; **Klos|ter|frau** F (*old*) nun; **Klos|ter|kir|che** F monastery/convent church; **Klos|ter|le|ben** NT monastic/convent life

klös|ter|lich [ˈkløːstɐlɪç] ADJ *Leben* monastic/convent; *Stille, Abgeschiedenheit* cloistered

Klos|ter|schu|le F monastic/convent school

Klos|ter|schwes|ter F (*old*) nun

Klö|ten [ˈkløːtn] PL (*sl*) balls *pl* (*sl*)

Klotz [klɔts] M **-es, ⸚e** [ˈklœtsə] or (*inf*) **-er** (= *Holzklotz*) block (of wood); (*pej:* = *Betonklotz*) concrete block or monstrosity; (*inf:* = *Person*) great lump (*inf*) or clod (*inf*); **sich** (*dat*) **einen ~ ans Bein binden** (*inf*) to tie a millstone around one's neck; **jdm ein ~ am Bein sein** to be a hindrance to sb, to be a millstone around sb's neck; **schlafen wie ein ~** (*inf*) to sleep like a log; **auf die Klötzer treten** (*Aut inf*) to slam on the brakes

Klötz|chen [ˈklœtsçən] NT **-s, ** - (building) block; **etw aus ~ bauen** to build sth with blocks

klot|zen [ˈklɔtsn] VT (*inf*) *Hochhäuser in die Stadt ~* to throw up skyscrapers in the town ◼ VI (*sl*) (= *hart arbeiten*) to slog (away) (*inf*) → **kleckern**

klot|zig [ˈklɔtsɪç] (*inf*) ADJ huge, massive ◼ ADV ◼a *werben* like crazy (*inf*); **~ verdienen/absahnen** to rake it in (*inf*) ◼b (= *klobig*) massively; **~ wirken** to seem bulky

Klub [klʊb] M **-s, -s** ◼a club ◼b (*Aus:* = *Parlamentsfraktion*) (parliamentary) party

Klub-: Klub|abend M club night; **Klub|gar|ni|tur** F club-style (three-piece) suite; **Klub|haus** NT clubhouse; **Klub|ja|cke** F blazer; **Klub|le|ben** NT club life; **Klub|lo|kal** NT club bar; **Klub|ob|frau** F **-, -en** (*Aus*) (parliamentary) party leader, floor leader (*US*); **Klub|ob|mann** M (*Aus*) (parliamentary) party leader, floor leader (*US*); **Klub|ses|sel** M club chair

klu|ckern [ˈklʊkɐn] VI = **gluckern**

Kluft [klʊft] F **-, ⸚e** [ˈklʏftə] ◼a (= *Erdspalte*) cleft; (*zwischen Felsenrändern*) ravine; (*in Bergen*) crevasse; (= *Abgrund*) chasm ◼b (*fig*) gulf, gap; **in der Partei tat sich eine tiefe ~ auf** a deep rift opened up in the party ◼c *no pl* (= *Kleidung, Kleidung*) uniform; (*inf:* = *Kleidung*) gear (*inf*), garb (*hum*); **sich in seine gute** or **beste ~ werfen** (*inf*) to put on one's Sunday best or to put on one's glad rags (*hum*)

klug [kluːk] ADJ *comp* **-er** [ˈkluːgɐ], *superl* **-ste(r, s)** [ˈkluːkstə] clever, intelligent; *Augen* intelligent; *Humor* witty, sophisticated; (= *vernünftig*) *Entscheidung, Rat* wise, sound; *Überlegung* prudent; (= *geschickt*) *Antwort, Analyse, Geschäftsmann* shrewd, clever; **es wird am klügsten sein, wenn ...** it would be most sensible if ..., it would be the best idea if ...; **es wäre politisch/geschäftlich ~ ...** it would make good political/business sense ...; **ein ~er Philosoph** an astute philosopher; **ein ~er Kopf** a capable person; **ein ~er Kopf, der Kleine** he's a bright boy; **in ~er Voraussicht** with shrewd foresight; **ich werde da-**

raus nicht ~, da soll einer draus ~ werden I cannot make head or tail (*Brit*) or heads or tails (*US*) of it, I can't make it out; **aus ihm wer-de ich nicht ~** I don't know what to make of him, I can't make him out; **im Nachhinein ist man immer klüger** one learns by experience; **~e Reden halten** or **führen** (*iro*) to make fine-sounding speeches; **~e Bemerkungen/Ratschlä-ge** (*iro*) clever or helpful remarks/advice (*iro*); **wer war denn so ~ ...** (*iro*) who was the bright or clever one ...; **so ~ bin ich auch** (*iro*) you don't say!; **nun bin ich genauso ~ wie zuvor** or **vorher** I am still none the wiser; **der Klügere gibt nach** (*Prov*) discretion is the better part of valour (*Brit*) or valor (*US, Prov*); **der ~e Mann baut vor** (*Prov*) the wise man takes precautions; **wer ~ ist, fährt mit der Bahn** it makes more sense to go by train; **wenn du ~ bist, haust du sofort ab** if you're smart you'll beat it (*inf*)

◼ADV *comp* **-er**, *superl* **am ⸚sten** ◼a (= *gescheit*) cleverly; **~ geschrieben/durchdacht** cleverly or intelligently written/thought out; **~ reden** or **tun kann jeder ...** anyone can talk ...

◼b (*iro:* = *dumm*) cleverly

klü|geln [ˈklyːgln] VI to puzzle (*wie/was* as to how/what); **wieder etwas zum Klügeln für un-sere Rätselfreunde** another brain-teaser for our puzzle fans

klu|ger|wei|se [ˈkluːgɐˈvaizə] ADV (very) cleverly, (very) wisely

Klug|heit F **-,** *no pl* cleverness, intelligence; (= *Vernünftigkeit: von Entscheidung, Rat*) wisdom, soundness; (= *Geschicktheit: von Antwort, Ge-schäftsmann*) shrewdness; **aus ~** (= very) wisely; **die ~ eines Sokrates** the astuteness of a Socra-tes; **deine ~en kannst du dir sparen** (*iro*) you can save your clever remarks

Klüg|ler [ˈkyːglɐ] M **-s, -**, **Klüg|le|rin** [-ərɪn] F **-, -nen** fiddle, fiddly person

Klug-: klug re|den ▲ VI to talk big, to make fine-sounding speeches; **Klug|red|ner(in)** M(F) know-all (*Brit*), know-it-all (*US*); **klug+schei|ßen** VI *sep irreg* (*inf*) to shoot one's mouth off (*inf*); **Klug|schei|ßer(in)** M(F) big mouth (*inf*), smart aleck (*inf*), smart-ass (*esp US sl*); **klug schna|cken** ▲ VI (*N Ger inf*) = klug reden; **Klug|schna|cker** [-ˈʃnakɐ] M **-s, -**, **Klug|schna|cke|rin** [-ərɪn] F **-, -nen** (*N Ger inf*) = Klugredner

Klump [klʊmp] *no art* (*inf*) **ein Auto zu ~ fahren** to smash up a car; **jdn zu ~ hauen** to beat sb to a pulp (*inf*)

Klum|patsch [ˈklʊmpatʃ] M **-s,** *no pl* (*inf*) **der ganze ~** the whole (kit and) caboodle (*inf*)

Klümp|chen [ˈklʏmpçən] NT **-s, -** *dim von* **Klum-pen**

klüm|pen [ˈklʏmpn] VI (*Sauce*) to go lumpy

Klum|pen [ˈklʊmpn] M **-s, -** lump; (= *Erdklumpen auch*) clod; (= *Goldklumpen*) nugget; (= *Blutklum-pen*) clot; **~ bilden** (*Mehl etc*) to go lumpy; (*Blut*) to clot; **steht doch nicht alle auf einem ~!** don't all stand in a huddle

Klum|pert [ˈklʊmpɐt] NT **-s,** *no pl* (*Aus*) = **Klum-patsch**

Klump-: Klump|fuß M club foot; **klump|fü-ßig** ADJ club-footed

klum|pig [ˈklʊmpɪç] ADJ lumpy

Klün|gel [ˈklʏŋl] M **-s, -** (*inf:* = *Clique*) clique; (*dial:* = *Kram*) mess

Klün|gel|wirt|schaft F (*inf*) nepotism *no pl*

Klun|ker [ˈklʊŋkɐ] M **-s, -** (*inf:* = *Edelstein*) rock (*inf*); (= *großer Modeschmuck*) chunky jewellery (*Brit*) or jewelry (*US*)

Klup|perl [ˈklʊpɐl] NT **-s, -(n)** (*Aus:* = *Wäsche-klammer*) clothes peg, clothes pin (*US*)

Klü|se [ˈkyːzə] F **-, -n** ◼a (*Naut*) hawsehole ◼b **Klüsen** PL (*N Ger inf*) eyes *pl*

Klü|ver [ˈkyːvɐ] M **-s, -** (*Naut*) jib

Klü|ver|baum M (*Naut*) jib boom

km *abbr von* **Kilometer** km

km/h *abbr von* **Kilometer pro Stunde** kph

kn (*Naut*) *abbr von* **Knoten** kt

knab|bern [ˈknabɐn] VTI to nibble; **etwas zum Knabbern holen** to get something to nibble on (*inf*) or something to eat; **nichts zu ~ haben** (*inf*) to have nothing to eat; **im Nachhinein ist daran wirst du noch zu ~ haben** (*fig inf*) it will really give you something to think about or to get your teeth into; **an dieser Aufgabe habe ich lange zu ~ ge-habt** (*fig inf*) I spent ages puzzling over this ex-ercise

Kna|be [ˈknaːbə] M **-n, -n** (*liter*) boy, lad (*esp Brit inf*); **na alter ~!** (*inf*) well old boy (*inf*) or chap (*inf*)

Kna|ben-: Kna|ben|al|ter NT boyhood; **im ~** in his boyhood; **Kna|ben|chor** M boys' choir; **kna|ben|haft** ADJ boyish; **Kna|ben|kraut** NT (wild) orchid; **Kna|ben|lie|be** F (*liter*) paederasty (*Brit*), pederasty (*US*); **Kna|ben-|schu|le** F (*old*) boys' school; **Kna|ben|stim-me** F boy's voice; (*Mus auch*) treble voice

knack [knak] INTERJ crack; **~ machen** to crack, to go crack

Knack [knak] M **-(e)s, -e** crack

Knä|cke|brot [ˈknɛkə-] NT crispbread

kna|cken [ˈknakn] ◼**VT** ◼a *Nüsse* to crack; *Läuse* to squash, to crush

◼b (*inf*) *Auto* to break into, to burgle; *Geld-schrank* to crack; (*Mil sl*) *Panzer* to knock out

◼c (*fig inf:* = *bezwingen*) *Rätsel, Kode, Organisation* to crack; *Tabu* to break

◼**VI** ◼a (= *brechen*) to crack, to snap; (*Glas etc*) to crack; (*Dielen, Stuhl*) to creak; (*Holz:* = *knistern*) to crackle; **mit den Fingern ~** to crack one's fingers; **es knackt im Radio** the radio is crack-ling; **die Leitung knackt** (*Telec*) the line is crackly; **es knackt im Gebälk** the beams are creaking; **an etw** (*dat*) **zu ~ haben** (*inf*) to have sth to think about or to chew on (*inf*); (= *darü-ber hinwegkommen*) to have a rough time getting over sth; **an dieser Aufgabe hatte ich ganz schön zu ~** (*inf*) I really had to sweat over this exercise

◼b (*inf:* = *schlafen*) to kip (*Brit inf*), to sleep

Kna|cker [ˈknakɐ] M **-s, -** ◼a = Knackwurst ◼b (*pej inf*) *alter ~* old fog(e)y (*inf*)

knack|frisch ADJ (*inf*) (nice and) crisp, crunchy

Kna|cki [ˈknaki] M **-s, -s** (*inf:* = *Knastbruder*) jail-bird (*inf*); (*sl:* = *alter Mann*) old bloke (*Brit inf*) or guy (*inf*)

kna|ckig [ˈknakɪç] ADJ crisp; *Apfel auch, Salat, Gemüse* crunchy; (*inf*) *Mädchen* tasty (*inf*); *Figur, Rock, Hose* sexy; *Musik* hot; *Tonfall, Sprüche* snap-py (*inf*) ◼ADV (*inf*) ◼a (= *mit Schwung*) **~ range-hen** (*bei Arbeit*) to get a move on (*inf*); (*beim an-deren Geschlecht*) to move in fast (*inf*) ◼b (= *or-dentlich*) **~ braun sein** to have a fantastic tan

Knack-: Knack|laut M glottal stop; **Knack|-man|del** F almond in the shell; **Knack|-punkt** M (*inf*) crunch (*inf*)

knacks [knaks] INTERJ crack, crash

Knacks [knaks] M **-es, -e** ◼a (= *Sprung, Ge-räusch*) crack ◼b (*inf:* = *Schaden*) **das Radio/der Fernseher hat einen ~** there is something wrong with the radio/television; **die Ehe der beiden hat schon lange einen ~** their marriage has been breaking up for a long time; **er hat ei-nen ~ (weg)bekommen** he or (*gesundheitlich*) his health or (*psychisch*) his nerves took a knock; **er hat einen ~ weg** he's a bit screwy (*inf*); (*gesundheitlich*) his health isn't so good

knacksen [ˈknaksn] VI (*inf*) to crack

Knack|wurst F type of frankfurter, the skin of which makes a cracking sound when bitten

Knall [knal] M **-(e)s, -e** bang; (*mit Peitsche*) crack; (*bei Tür*) bang, slam; (*von Korken*) pop; (*inf:* = *Krach*) trouble; **der ~ eines Schusses** a shot; **~ auf Fall** (*inf*) all of a sudden; **jdn ~ auf Fall entlassen** (*inf*) to dismiss sb completely out of the blue (*inf*); **einen ~ haben** (*inf*) to be crazy (*inf*) or crackers (*Brit inf*); **der große ~ kommt noch** (*inf*) there's big trouble coming

Knall-: Knall|bon|bon NT (Christmas) cracker; **knall|bunt** ADJ (inf) brightly coloured (Brit) or colored (US); **Knall|ef|fekt** M (inf) bombshell (inf); **einen ~ haben** to come as a real bombshell; **ein ~ sein** to be a real bombshell

knal|len ['knalən] **VI a** (= krachen) to bang; (= explodieren) to explode; (Schuss) to ring out; (Feuerwerk) to (go) bang; (Korken) to (go) pop; (Peitsche) to crack; (Tür etc) to bang, to slam; (Auspuff) to misfire; (aux sein: = auftreffen) to bang; **mit der Tür ~** to bang or slam the door; **mit den Absätzen ~** (Soldaten etc) to click one's heels; **die Korken ~ lassen** (fig) to pop a cork; **die Sektkorken knallten** (fig) the champagne was flowing; **draußen knallte es** there was a shot/were shots outside; **bleib stehen, sonst knallts** (inf: = es wird geschossen) freeze or I'll shoot; **sei nicht so frech, sonst knallts** (inf: = es gibt Prügel) don't be so cheeky (Brit) or fresh (US), or there'll be trouble; **der Fahrer ist gegen die Windschutzscheibe geknallt** the driver hit the windscreen (Brit) or windshield (US); **der Ball knallte gegen den Pfosten** (inf) the ball banged or slammed against the post
b (inf: Sonne) to blaze or beat down
VT to bang; Tür, Buch auch to slam; Ball auch to belt (inf), to slam; Peitsche to crack; **den Hörer auf die Gabel ~** (inf) to slam or bang down the receiver; **jdm eine ~** (inf) to clout sb (one) (Brit inf), to belt sb (one) (inf); **jdm ein paar vor den Latz ~** (inf) to clout sb one (Brit inf), to stick one on sb (Brit inf), to belt sb (one) (inf)

knal|lend ADJ Farbe bright, loud, gaudy; Sonne scorching, blazing

knall|eng ADJ (inf) skintight

Knal|ler ['knalɐ] M -s, - (inf) **a** (= Knallkörper) banger (Brit), firecracker (esp US) **b** (fig, = Sensation) sensation **c** (= Sonderpreis) fantastic or incredible price

Knall|erb|se F toy torpedo

Knall|le|rei [knalə'rai] F -, -en (inf) (= Schießerei) shooting; (Feuerwerk) banging of fireworks

Knall-: Knall|frosch M jumping jack; **Knall|gas** NT oxyhydrogen; **knall|gelb** ADJ (inf) bright yellow; **knall|grün** ADJ (inf) bright green; **knall|hart** (inf) **ADJ** Film brutal; Porno hardcore; Job, Geschäft, Wettbewerb really tough; Truppen, Mensch really tough, as hard as nails; Schuss, Schlag really hard; Methode brutal; Forderung uncompromising; **ein ~er Schuss/Schlag** a real humdinger (of a shot/punch) (inf) **ADV** brutally; **der Film zeigt ~, wie ...** the film shows brutally or without pulling any punches how ...; **~ verhandeln** to drive a hard bargain; **knall|heiß** ADJ (inf) blazing or boiling hot; **Knall|hit|ze** F (inf) blazing heat, heat wave

knall|lig ['knalıç] (inf) **ADJ** Farben loud, gaudy **ADV** **~ gelb** gaudy yellow; **~ bunt** gaudy

Knall-: Knall|kopf M (inf), **Knall|kopp** [-kɔp] (inf) M -s, -köppe [-kœpə] fathead (inf), blockhead (inf); **Knall|kör|per** M firecracker; **knall|rot** ADJ (inf) bright red, scarlet; Gesicht as red as a beetroot (Brit inf) or beet (US inf); **Knall|schlep|pe** F (Aviat) sonic boom; **knall|voll** ADJ (inf) **a** (= total gefüllt) jam-packed (inf), chock-a-block (inf) **b** (= völlig betrunken) completely plastered, paralytic (Brit inf), pissed (Brit inf) or drunk (US) out of one's mind

knapp [knap] **ADJ a** (= nicht ausreichend vorhanden) Vorräte, Arbeitsstellen scarce, in short supply; Geld tight, scarce; Taschengeld meagre (Brit), meager (US); Gehalt low, meagre (Brit), meager (US); **mein Geld ist ~** I'm short of money; **mein Geld wird ~** I am running short of or out of money; **das Essen wird ~** we/they etc are running short of or out of food; **~ mit (dem) Geld sein** (inf) to be short of money → **Kasse**
b (= gerade noch ausreichend) Zeit, Geld, Miete just or barely sufficient, just or barely enough; Mehrheit narrow, small, bare; Sieg narrow; Klei-

dungsstück etc (= eng) tight; (= kurz) short; Bikini scanty
c (= nicht ganz) almost; **ein ~es Pfund Mehl** just under a pound of flour; **seit einem ~en** or **~ einem Jahr wohne ich hier** I have been living here for almost a year
d (= kurz und präzis) Stil, Worte concise; Geste terse; (= lakonisch) Antwort pithy
e (= gerade so eben) just; **mit ~er Not** only just, by the skin of one's teeth
ADV a (= nicht reichlich) rechnen, kalkulieren conservatively; bemessen too closely; **mein Geld/meine Zeit ist ~ bemessen** I am short of money/time; **er hat ihr das Taschengeld ~ bemessen** he was mean (Brit) or stingy (inf) with her pocket money
b (= haarscharf) **wir haben ~ verloren/gewonnen** we only just lost/won; **er ist ~ an mir vorbeigefahren** he just got or scraped past me; **der Rock endete ~ über dem Knie** the skirt came to just above the knee; **es war ~ daneben** it was a near miss; **~ vorbei ist auch daneben** (inf) a miss is as good as a mile (prov); **ich verprügele dich, aber nicht zu ~** I'll give you a thrashing, and how!
c (= nicht ganz) not quite; **~ zwei Wochen** not quite two weeks

Knap|pe ['knapə] M -n, -n **a** (Hist: eines Ritters) squire **b** (Min) qualified miner

knapp hal|ten ▲ VT irreg **jdn ~** to keep sb short (mit of)

Knapp|heit F -, no pl (= Lebensmittelknappheit) scarcity, shortage; (von Zeit, Geld, Produkt) shortage; (fig: des Ausdrucks) conciseness, concision; **wegen der ~ der uns zur Verfügung stehenden Zeit** because of the shortness of the time at our disposal

Knapp|schaft ['knapʃaft] F -, -en (Min) miners' guild

knap|sen ['knapsn] VI (inf) to scrimp (mit, an +dat on), to be stingy (mit, an +dat with) (inf); **an etw** (dat) **zu ~ haben** to have a rough time getting over sth

Knar|re ['knarə] F -, -n **a** (sl: = Gewehr) shooter (inf) **b** (= Rassel) rattle

knar|ren ['knarən] VI to creak; **eine ~de Stimme** a rasping or grating voice

Knast M -(e)s, ̈-e or -e (inf) clink (inf), can (US sl); **in den ~ wandern** to be put behind bars

Knast|bru|der M (inf) jailbird (inf)

Knas|ter ['knastɐ] M -s, - (dated inf) baccy (Brit inf), tobacco; **was rauchst du denn für einen ~!** what's that foul-smelling stuff you're smoking!

Knas|ti ['knasti] M -s, -s (hum inf: = Gefangener) jailbird (inf)

Knas|to|lo|ge [knasto'lo:gə] M -n, -n, **Knas|to|lo|gin** [-'lo:gın] F -, -nen (hum) jailbird (inf)

Knast|schwes|ter F (inf) jailbird (inf)

Knatsch [knatʃ] M -es, no pl (inf) trouble; **das gibt ~** that means trouble

knat|schig ['kna:tʃıç] ADJ (inf) (= verärgert) miffed (inf); (= schlecht gelaunt) grumpy (inf)

knat|tern ['knatɐn] VI (Motorrad) to roar; (Presslufthammer) to hammer; (Maschinengewehr) to rattle, to chatter; (Schüsse) to rattle out; (Fahne im Wind) to flap

Knäu|el ['knɔyəl] M OR NT -s, - ball; (wirres) tangle; (fig: = Durcheinander) muddle; (von Menschen) group, knot; (in Problemen) knot, tangle; (hum: Hund) bundle of fluff (inf)

Knauf [knauf] M -(e)s, **Knäufe** ['knɔyfə] (= Türknauf) knob; (von Schwert etc) pommel

Knau|ser ['knauzɐ] M -s, -, **Knau|se|rin** [-ərın] F -, -nen (inf) scrooge (inf)

Knau|se|rei [knauzə'rai] F -, no pl (inf) meanness (esp Brit), stinginess (inf)

knau|se|rig ['knauzərıç] ADJ (inf) mean (esp Brit), stingy (inf)

Knau|se|rig|keit F -, no pl (inf) meanness (esp Brit), stinginess (inf)

Knau|se|rin F -, -nen (inf) scrooge (inf)

knau|sern ['knauzɐn] VI (inf) to be mean (esp Brit) or stingy (inf) (mit with)

Knaus-O|gi|no-Me|tho|de ['knaus|o'gi:no-] F (Med) rhythm method

knau|srig ADJ (inf) mean (esp Brit), stingy (inf)

Knaus|rig|keit F -, no pl (inf) meanness (esp Brit), stinginess (inf)

knaut|schen ['knautʃn] VTI (inf) to crumple (up); Kleid etc auch to crease

knaut|schig ['knautʃıç] ADJ (inf) Anzug, Kleid crumpled-up, crumply (inf)

Knautsch-: Knautsch|lack M , **Knautsch-(lack)|le|der** NT wet-look leather; **Knautsch|zo|ne** F (Aut) crumple zone

Kne|bel ['kne:bl] M -s, - (= Mundknebel) gag; (= Paketknebel) (wooden) handle; (an Mänteln) toggle; (= Fensterknebel) (handle of) window catch

Knebel-: Kne|bel|bart M Van Dyke (beard); **Kne|bel|knopf** M toggle fastening

kne|beln ['kne:bln] VT jdn, Presse to gag

Kne|be|lung ['kne:bəlʊŋ] F -, no pl (lit, fig) gagging

Kne|bel|ver|trag M oppressive contract; **jdn durch einen ~ binden** to screw sb down with a tight contract (inf)

Knecht [knɛçt] M -(e)s, -e **a** servant; (beim Bauern) (farm) labourer (Brit) or laborer (US), farm worker; (= Stallknecht) stableboy **b** (fig: = Sklave) slave (+gen to) **c** **~ Ruprecht** helper to St Nicholas (Santa Claus)

knech|ten ['knɛçtn] VT (geh) to subjugate, to oppress; **alle unterdrückten und geknechteten Völker ...** all oppressed and enslaved peoples ...; **sie wollten sich nicht mehr von ihm ~ lassen** they refused to be his slaves any longer

knech|tisch ['knɛçtıʃ] **ADJ** (geh) Charakter subservient, submissive; Unterwürfigkeit, Verhalten auch servile, slavish **ADV** **sich ~ verhalten** to be servile; **jdm/einer Sache ~ ergeben sein** to be a complete slave or to be totally enslaved to sb/sth

Knecht|schaft ['knɛçtʃaft] F -, -en slavery, servitude, bondage

Knech|tung ['knɛçtʊŋ] F -, no pl (geh) enslavement, subjugation

knei|fen ['knaifn] pret **kniff** [knıf], ptp **gekniffen** [gə'knıfn] **VT** to pinch; **jdn ~** to pinch sb; **jdn** or **jdm in den Arm ~** to pinch sb's arm; **der Hund kniff den Schwanz zwischen die Beine** the dog put his tail between his legs **VI a** (= zwicken) to pinch; **die Bluse kneift** the blouse is too tight **b** (inf) (= ausweichen) to chicken out (inf), to get or back out (vor +dat of); (vor Arbeit) to duck or back out (vor +dat of); (vor Auseinandersetzung) to back out **c** (Univ sl) to fail to remain motionless during a student duel

Knei|fer ['knaifɐ] M -s, -a (= Brille) pince-nez

Kneif|zan|ge F pliers pl; (kleine) pincers pl; **eine ~** (a pair of) pliers/pincers

Knei|pe ['knaipə] F -, -n (inf: = Lokal) pub (Brit), bar, saloon (US)

Kneipen-: Knei|pen|bum|mel M pub crawl (Brit), bar hop (US); **Knei|pen|wirt(in)** M(F) (inf) publican (Brit), pub owner (Brit), (pub) landlord/landlady (Brit), barkeeper, saloonkeeper (US)

Knei|per ['knaipɐ] M -s, -, **Knei|pe|rin** [-ərın] F -, -nen, **Knei|pier** [knai'pie:] M -s, -s (inf) = Kneipenwirt(in)

kneip|pen ['knaipn] VI to undergo a Kneipp cure

Kneipp|kur F Kneipp cure (type of hydropathic treatment combined with diet, rest etc)

knei|sen ['knaizn] VT (Aus inf) to notice

Knes|set(h) ['knɛsɛt] F -, no pl Knesset

Knet [kne:t] M -s, no pl modelling (Brit) or modeling (US) clay; (= Plastilin) Plasticine®

knet|bar ADJ workable; *Teig auch* kneadable

Kne|te ['kneːtə] F -, *no pl* (*dated sl*: = *Geld*) dough (*inf*)

kne|ten ['kneːtn] VT *Teig* to knead; *Plastilin, Ton* to work; *Figuren* to model; (= *formen*) to form, to shape; *Muskeln, Rücken* to knead, to work VI (= *mit Plastilin spielen*) to play with Plasticine® or modelling (*Brit*) or modeling (*US*) clay

Knet-: **Knet|gum|mi** M OR NT Plasticine®; **Knet|ma|schi|ne** F kneading machine; **Knet|mas|se** F modelling (*Brit*) or modeling (*US*) clay

Knick [knɪk] M -(e)s, -e *or* -s **a** (= *leichter Sprung*) crack **b** (= *Kniff, Falte*) crease, crinkle; (= *Eselsohr*) dog-ear; (= *Biegung*) (sharp) bend; (*bei Draht, auf Oberfläche*) kink; **einen ~ machen** to bend sharply → **Optik c** (*fig: in Karriere etc*) downturn **d** -s (*N Ger*: = *Hecke*) hedgerow

Kni|cke|bein ['knɪkə-] M -s, *no pl* advocaat

kni|cken ['knɪkn] VI *aux* sein to snap VT to snap; *Papier* to fold, to crease; **„nicht ~!"** "do not bend *or* fold" → *auch* **geknickt**

Kni|cker ['knɪkɐ] M -s, -, **Kni|cke|rin** [-ərɪn] F -, -nen (*inf*) scrooge (*inf*)

Kni|cker|bo|cker ['knɪkɛbɔkɐ] PL knickerbockers *pl* (*old*), plus fours *pl*

kni|cke|rig ['knɪkarɪç] ADJ (*inf*) stingy (*inf*), mean (*esp Brit*)

Kni|cke|rig|keit F -, *no pl* (*inf*) stinginess (*inf*), meanness (*esp Brit*)

Kni|cke|rin F -, -nen (*inf*) scrooge (*inf*)

kni|ckern ['knɪkɐn] VI (*inf*) to be stingy (*inf*) (*mit* with)

Knick|fuß M (*Med*) (type of) club foot

knick|rig ['knɪkrɪç] ADJ (*inf*) stingy (*inf*), mean (*esp Brit*)

Knick|rig|keit F -, *no pl* (*inf*) stinginess (*inf*), meanness (*esp Brit*)

Knicks [knɪks] M -es, -e **a** bob; (*tiefer*) curts(e)y; **einen ~ machen** to drop a curts(e)y, to curts(e)y (*vor* +*dat* to) **b** (= *heller Knacks*) crack, click

knick|sen ['knɪksn] VI to curts(e)y, to drop a curts(e)y (*vor* +*dat* to)

Knie [kniː] NT -s, - **a** knee; **auf ~n** on one's knees, on bended knee; (**vor jdm**) **auf die ~ fal- len** *or* **in die ~ sinken** to fall on *or* drop to one's knees (before sb); **sich vor jdm auf die ~ werfen** to throw oneself on one's knees in front of (sb); **jdn auf ~n bitten** to go down on bended knees to sb (and beg); **jdm auf ~n danken** to go down on one's knees and thank sb; **bis zu den ~n im Sumpf stecken** (*lit*) to be up to one's knees in mud; **in die ~ gehen** to kneel, to fall on one's knees; (*fig*) to be brought to one's knees; **jdn in** *or* **auf die ~ zwingen** (*esp fig*) to bring sb to his/ her knees; **jdn übers ~ legen** (*inf*) to put sb a- cross one's knee; **etw übers ~ brechen** (*fig*) to rush (at) sth; **die ~ beugen** to bend one's knees; (*vor dem Altar*) to bow, to genuflect (*form*); (*fig*) to give in, to bend the knee **b** (= *Flussknie*) sharp bend; (*in Rohr*) elbow **c** (*Tech*: = *Winkelstück*) elbow

Knie-: **Knie|beu|ge** F (*Sport*) knee bend; **in die ~ gehen** to bend one's knees; **Knie|bund- hose** F knee breeches *pl*; **Knie|fall** M genu- flection (*form*); **einen ~ vor jdm tun** (*geh*) *or* **ma- chen** (*lit, fig*) to kneel before sb; (*fig auch*) to bow before sb; **knie|fäl|lig** ADJ *Verehrung* humble, lowly ADV on one's knees, on bended knee; **knie|frei** ADJ *Rock* above the knee; **Knie|ge|lenk** NT knee joint; **knie|hoch** ADJ *Schnee, Wasser* knee-deep; *Gras* knee-high; **Knie|ho|se** F knee breeches *pl*; **Knie|keh|le** F back *or* hollow of the knee; **Knie|kis|sen** NT (*Eccl*) hassock; **knie|lang** ADJ knee-length

knien [kniːn, 'kniːən] VI to kneel; **im Knien** on one's knees, kneeling VR to kneel (down); **sich in die Arbeit ~** (*fig*) to get down to *or* to get stuck into (*inf*) one's work

Knie|rohr NT elbow (pipe)

Knies [kniːs] M -, *no pl* (*dial inf*) row, argument

Knie-: **Knie|schei|be** F kneecap; **Knie|schei- ben|re|flex** M , **Knie|seh|nen|re|flex** M knee *or* patellar (*spec*) reflex; **Knie|schnack- ler** [-ʃnaklɐ] M -s, - (*dial inf*) wobbly knees *pl*; **Knie|scho|ner** M = Knieschützer; **Knie- schüt|zer** [-ʃʏtsɐ] M -s, - kneepad, kneeguard; **Knie|strumpf** M knee sock, knee-length sock; **Knie|stück** NT elbow joint; **knie|tief** ADJ knee-deep; **Knie|wel|le** F knee circle

kniff pret von **kneifen**

Kniff [knɪf] M -(e)s, -e **a** (*inf*) trick; **den ~ bei etw heraushaben** to have the knack of sth (*inf*); **es ist ein ~ dabei** there is a (special) knack to it (*inf*) **b** (= *Falte*) crease, fold **c** (= *Kneifen*) pinch

Kniff|e|lei [knɪfə'lai] F -, -en (*inf*) fiddly job

kniff|e|lig ['knɪfəlɪç], **kniff|lig** ['knɪflɪç] ADJ (*inf*) fiddly; (= *heikel*) tricky

Knig|ge ['knɪgə] M -(s), - etiquette manual

Knilch [knɪlç] M -, -e (*pej inf*) twit (*Brit inf*), clown (*inf*)

knips [knɪps] INTERJ click

knip|sen ['knɪpsn] VT **a** *Fahrschein* to punch, to clip **b** (*Phot inf*) to snap (*inf*) VI **a** (*Phot inf*) to take pictures **b** (= *klicken*) to click; **mit den Fingern ~** to snap one's fingers

Knip|ser ['knɪpsɐ] M -s, - (*inf*), **Knips|schal|ter** M shutter

Knirps [knɪrps] M -es, -e **a** (= *Junge*) whip- persnapper; (*pej*) squirt **b** ® ~® folding *or* tele- scopic umbrella

knir|schen ['knɪrʃn] VI (*Sand, Schnee*) to crunch; (*Getriebe*) to grind; **mit den Zähnen ~** to grind one's teeth; (*vor Wut auch*) to gnash one's teeth

knis|tern ['knɪstɐn] VI (*Feuer*) to crackle; (*Pa- pier, Seide*) to rustle; **mit Papier etc ~** to rustle paper *etc*; **es knistert im Gebälk** (*fig*) there is trouble brewing *or* afoot (+*gen* in)

Knit|tel ['knɪtl] M -s, - (*dial*) = **Knüppel a**

Knit|tel|vers M rhyming couplets (using a four-stress line)

knit|ter-: **knit|ter|arm** ADJ crease-resistant; **Knit|ter|fal|te** F crease, wrinkle (*esp US*); **knit|ter|fest** ADJ = knitterfrei; **knit|ter|frei** ADJ *Stoff, Kleid* non-crease

knit|te|rig ADJ creased

knit|tern ['knɪtɐn] VTI to crease, to crush

knitt|rig ADJ creased

Kno|bel|be|cher M **a** dice cup **b** (*Mil sl*) ar- my boot

kno|beln ['knoːbln] VI **a** (= *würfeln*) to play dice; (*um eine Entscheidung*) to toss for it (*inf*); **sie knobelten darum, wer bezahlen sollte** they tossed (for it) to decide who should pay **b** (= *nachdenken*) to puzzle (*an* +*dat* over)

Knob|lauch ['knoːplaux, 'knoːblaux, 'knɔplaux, 'knɔblaux] M , *no pl* garlic

Knob|lauch-: **Knob|lauch|brot** NT garlic bread; **Knob|lauch|but|ter** F garlic butter; **Knob|lauch|ge|ruch** M smell of garlic; **Knob|lauch|pres|se** F garlic press; **Knob- lauch|ze|he** F clove of garlic

Knö|chel ['knœçl] M -s, - **a** (= *Fußknöchel*) an- kle; **bis über die ~** up to the ankles, ankle- deep **b** (= *Fingerknöchel*) knuckle

Knö|chel-: **Knö|chel|bruch** M broken ankle; **knö|chel|lang** ADJ ankle-length; **knö|chel- tief** ADJ ankle-deep

Kno|chen ['knɔxn] M -s, - **a** bone; **Fleisch mit/ ohne ~** meat on/off the bone; **die Wunde geht bis auf den ~** the wound has penetrated to the bone; **mir tun alle ~ weh** (*inf*) every bone in my body is aching; **er ist bis auf die ~ abgemagert** he is just a (bag of) skin and bones; **brich dir nicht die ~!** (*inf*) don't break anything *or* your neck!; **dem breche ich alle ~ einzeln** (*inf*) I'll break every bone in his body; **das geht auf die ~** (*inf*) it knackers you (*Brit inf*), it breaks your

back; **ihm steckt** *or* **sitzt die Grippe in den ~** (*inf*) he's got flu; **ihm steckt** *or* **sitzt die Angst in den ~** (*inf*) he's scared stiff (*inf*); **die Angst ist ihm in die ~ gefahren** it gave him a real fright; **der Schreck fuhr ihm in die ~** he was paralyzed with shock; **nass bis auf die ~** (*inf*) soaked to the skin; **kein Mark** *or* **keinen Mumm in den ~ haben** (*inf*) to have no guts *or* spunk (*inf*); **sich bis auf die ~ blamieren** (*inf*) to make a proper fool of oneself (*inf*); **er ist konservativ bis in** *or* **auf die ~** (*inf*) he is conservative through and through, he is a dyed-in-the-wool conservative **b** (*sl*: = *Kerl*) chap (*inf*), bloke (*Brit inf*); **du fauler/müder ~** you lazy/indolent so-and-so (*inf*)

Kno|chen-: **Kno|chen|ar|beit** F hard graft (*inf*); **Kno|chen|bau** M , *no pl* bone structure; **Kno|chen|bruch** M fracture; **Kno|chen|er- wei|chung** [-lɛvaiçʊŋ] F -, -en (*Med*) softening of the bones, osteomalacia (*spec*); **Kno|chen- ge|rüst** NT skeleton; **kno|chen|hart** (*inf*) ADJ rock-hard; (*fig*) *Job, Kerl* really tough ADV *vorge- hen* ruthlessly; *trainieren, fordern, verhandeln* rig- orously; **Kno|chen|haut** F periosteum (*spec*); **Kno|chen|haut|ent|zün|dung** F periostitis (*spec*); **Kno|chen|leim** M bone glue; **Kno- chen|mann** M , *no pl* (*liter*) Death; **Kno- chen|mark** NT bone marrow; **Kno|chen- mark|ent|zün|dung** F osteomyelitis; **Kno- chen|mehl** NT bone meal; **Kno|chen|naht** F (*Anat*) bone suture; **Kno|chen|schin|ken** M ham on the bone; **Kno|chen|schwund** M bone atrophy, atrophy of the bone; **kno- chen|tro|cken** (*inf*) bone-dry (*inf*); (*fig*) *Humor etc* very dry ADV very dryly; **Kno|chen- tu|ber|ku|lo|se** F bone tuberculosis, tubercu- losis of the bone

knö|che|rig ['knœçərɪç] ADJ **a** (= *knochenartig*) bony, bone-like, osseous (*form*) **b** = **knöchern**

knö|chern ['knœçɐn] ADJ *Gerät etc* bone attr, of bone; *Material auch* bony, osseous (*form*); (*inf*: = *großknochig*) *Mensch, Körperbau* bony; (*pej inf*: = *nicht anpassungsfähig*) set in one's ways

kno|chig ['knɔxɪç] ADJ bony

knöch|rig ['knœçrɪç] ADJ = **knöcherig**

Knock-down ▲ [nɔk'daun] M -(s), -s, **Knock- down** M -(s), -s knockdown

Knock-out ▲ [nɔk'aut] M -(s), -s, **Knock|out** M -(s), -s knockout

Knö|del ['knøːdl] M -s, - dumpling

knö|deln ['knøːdln] VI to sing in a strangled voice

Kno|fel ['knoːfl] M -s, *no pl* (*inf*) garlic

Knöll|chen ['knœlçən] NT -s, - **a** *dim von* Knol- le **b** (*inf*: = *Strafzettel*) (parking) ticket

Knöll|chen|bak|te|rien PL rhizobin *pl*

Knol|le ['knɔlə] F -, -n (*Bot*) nodule, tubercule; (*von Kartoffel, Dahlie*) tuber; (= *Kartoffel*) potato; (*inf*: = *Nase*) conk (*Brit inf*), honker (*US inf*)

Knol|len ['knɔlən] M -s, - **a** = Knolle **b** (= *Klumpen*) lump

Knol|len-: **Knol|len|blät|ter|pilz** M , **Knol- len|blät|ter|schwamm** M amanita; **grüner ~** deadly amanita, death cap, death angel; **weißer ~** destroying angel; **Knol|len|na|se** F (*Med*) rhinophyma (*spec*), (nodular) swelling of the nose; (*inf*) conk (*Brit inf*), honker (*US inf*)

knol|lig ['knɔlɪç] ADJ *Wurzel* tuberous; *Auswuchs* knobbly, knotty; *Nase* bulbous; (*inf*: = *klumpig*) lumpy

Knopf [knɔpf] M -(e)s, -e ['knœpfə] **a** (*an Klei- dungsstück etc*) button; **etw an den Knöpfen ab- zählen** to decide sth by counting off one's but- tons **b** (*an Gerät, elektrischer Anlage etc*) (push) button; (*an Akkordeon*) button **c** (*an Tür, Stock*) knob; (= *Sattelknopf, Degenknopf*) pommel **d** (*S Ger, Aus*: = *Knoten*) knob **e** (*inf*: = *Junge*) lit- tle chap *or* fellow; (= *Mädchen*) little lass (*Brit*) *or* lassie (*esp Scot*), little girl; (= *Kerl*) chap, fel- low; **ein fieser ~** a nasty so-and-so

Knopf-: Knopf|au|gen PL big round eyes *pl*; **Knopf|druck** M , *no pl* **auf ~, mit einem ~** at the touch *or* press of a button, at the flick of a switch (*fig*)

knöp|fen ['knœpfn], (*Aus*) **knöp|feln** ['knœpfln] (*inf*) VT to button (up); **einen Kragen auf ein Kleid ~** to button a collar to a dress; **ein Kleid zum Knöpfen** a dress that buttons up

Knopf-: Knopf|leis|te F button tape *or* facing; **Mantel mit verdeckter ~** coat with a fly *or* button-down (*esp US*) front; **Knopf|loch** NT buttonhole; **aus allen Knopflöchern platzen** (*inf*) to be bursting at the seams; **Knopf|zel|le** F round cell battery

Knopp [knɔp] M **-s, ⸚e** ['knœpə] (*dial*) = **Knopf**

knor|ke ['knɔrkə] (*dated sl*) ADJ smashing (*Brit inf*), swell (*esp US inf*) ADV terrifically

Knor|pel ['knɔrpl] M **-s, -** (*Anat, Zool*) cartilage; (*Cook*) gristle

knor|pe|lig ['knɔrpəlɪç] ADJ (*Anat*) cartilaginous; *Fleisch* gristly

Knor|ren ['knɔrən] M **-s, -** (*im Holz*) knot; (*an Weide*) burl, burr; (= *Baumstumpf*) (tree) stump; (= *Aststumpf*) snag

knor|rig ['knɔrɪç] ADJ *Baum* gnarled; *Holz, Klotz* knotty; (*fig*) *alter Mann* rugged; (= *eigenwillig*) *Mensch, Charakter* surly, gruff

Knos|pe ['knɔspə] F **-, -n** bud; **~n ansetzen** *or* **treiben** to bud; **die zarte ~ ihrer Liebe** (*liter*) the tender bud of their love

knos|pen ['knɔspən] VI to bud; **~d** (*lit, fig*: *liter*) budding

Knöt|chen ['knøːtçən] NT **-s, -** *dim von* **Knoten**

kno|ten ['knoːtn] VT *Seil etc* to (tie into a) knot, to tie a knot in

Kno|ten ['knoːtn] M **-s, - a** knot; (*Med*) (= *Geschwulst*) lump; (= *Gichtknoten*) tophus (*spec*); (*Phys, Bot, Math, Astron*) node; (*fig*: = *Verwicklung*) plot; **sich** (*dat*) **einen ~ ins Taschentuch machen** (*inf*) to tie a knot in one's handkerchief **b** (*Naut*) knot **c** (= *Haarknoten*) bun, knot **d** = **Knotenpunkt**

Knoten-: Kno|ten|bahn|hof M junction; **Kno|ten|punkt** M (*Mot*) (road) junction, (road) intersection; (*Rail*) junction; (*fig*) centre (*Brit*), center (*US*); (*von Argumentation, Handlung etc*) nodal point

Knö|te|rich ['knøːtərɪç] M **-s, -e** knotgrass

kno|tig ['knoːtɪç] ADJ knotty, knotted, full of knots; *Äste, Finger, Hände* gnarled; *Geschwulst* nodular

Know-how ['noːhau, noːˈhau] NT **-s**, *no pl* know-how

Knub|bel ['knʊbl] M **-s, -** (*inf*) lump

knud|de|lig ['knʊdəlɪç] ADJ (*inf*: = *niedlich*) cuddly

knud|deln ['knʊdln] VT (*dial*) to kiss and cuddle

Knuff [knʊf] M **-(e)s, ⸚e** ['knʏfə] (*inf*) poke; (*mit Ellbogen*) nudge

knuf|fen ['knʊfn] VTI (*inf*) to poke (*inf*); (*mit Ellbogen*) to nudge

knül|le ['knʏlə] ADJ *pred* (*dial inf*) tight (*inf*)

knül|len ['knʏlən] VT to crumple, to crease (up)

Knül|ler ['knʏlɐ] M **-s, -** (*inf*) sensation; (*Press*) scoop

knüp|fen ['knʏpfn] VT *Knoten* to tie; *Band* to knot, to tie (up); *Teppich* to knot; *Netz* to mesh; *Freundschaft* to form, to strike up; **jdn an den nächsten Baum/Galgen ~** (*inf*) to hang sb from the nearest tree/the gallows, to string sb up (*inf*); **etw an etw** (*acc*) **~** (*lit*) to tie *or* knot sth to sth; (*fig*) *Bedingungen* to attach sth to sth; *Hoffnungen* to pin sth on sth; **große Erwartungen an etw** (*acc*) **~** to have great expectations of sth; **Kontakte ~ (zu** *or* **mit)** to establish contact (with); **Freundschaftsbande enger ~** to strengthen *or* tighten the bonds of friendship → **Band²**

VR **sich an etw** (*acc*) **~** to be linked to *or* connected with sth; **an diese Bemerkung knüpften sich einige Fragen** this remark raised several questions; **an diese Zeit ~ sich für mich viele Erinnerungen** I have many memories of this time; **an diese Erfindung ~ sich viele technische Möglichkeiten** this discovery has many technical possibilities

Knüp|pel ['knʏpl] M **-s, - a** stick; (= *Waffe*) cudgel, club; (= *Polizeiknüppel*) truncheon; (*Metal*) billet; **Politik des großen ~s** big stick policy; **den ~ aus dem Sack holen** (*fig inf*) to wield a big stick (*inf*); **man sollte mit dem ~ dreinschlagen** (*fig*) someone ought to get tough *or* to wave the big stick; **jdm (einen) ~ zwischen die Beine werfen** (*fig*) to put a spoke in sb's wheel (*Brit*), to throw a spanner (*Brit*) *or* (monkey) wrench (*US*) in the works **b** (*Aviat*) control stick, joystick; (*Aut*) gear stick (*Brit*), gearshift (*US*) **c** (*dial*: = *Brötchen*) ≈ crusty bridge roll

Knüp|pel-: Knüp|pel|damm M log road; **knüp|pel|dick** ADJ (*inf*) *Steak, Schicht* very thick, good and thick *pred*; **knüp|pel|hart** (*inf*) ADJ rock-hard; (*fig*) *Job, Kerl* really tough ADV ruthlessly

knüp|peln ['knʏpln] VI to use one's truncheon; (*Sport sl*) to hack, to kick wildly VT to club, to beat with a club *or* stick; (*Polizei*) to use one's truncheon on, to beat with one's truncheon → *auch* **geknüppelt**

Knüp|pel-: Knüp|pel|schal|tung F (*Aut*) floor-mounted gear change (*Brit*), floor shift (*US*); **knüp|pel|voll** ADJ (*inf*) jam-packed, packed solid

knur|ren ['knʊrən] VI (*Hund etc*) to growl; (*wütend*) to snarl; (*Magen*) to rumble; (*fig*: = *sich beklagen*) to moan, to groan (*über +acc* about) VTI (= *mürrisch sagen*) to growl

Knur|ren NT **-s**, *no pl* (*von Hund*) growl(ing); (*wütend*) snarl(ing); (*von Magen*) rumble, rumbling; (= *Klagen*) moan(ing)

Knurr|hahn M gurnard

knur|rig ['knʊrɪç] ADJ grumpy; *Angestellte etc* disgruntled

Knus|per|häus|chen [-hɔysçən] NT gingerbread house

knus|pe|rig ['knʊspərɪç] ADJ = **knusprig**

knus|pern ['knʊspɐn] VTI to crunch; **etwas zum Knuspern** something to nibble; **an etw** (*dat*) **~** to crunch away at sth

knus|prig ['knʊsprɪç] ADJ *Braten* crisp; *Gebäck auch* crunchy; *Brötchen auch* crusty; (*fig*) *Mädchen* scrumptious (*inf*) ADV *gebacken, gebraten* crisply; **~ braun** (*Hähnchen*) crispy brown; *Mensch* with a super tan; **etw ~ grillen** to grill sth until it is crispy

Knust [knuːst] M **-(e)s, -e** *or* **⸚e** ['knyːstə] (*N Ger*) (end) crust, heel

Knu|te ['knuːtə] F **-, -n** (*old*) knout (*old*), lash; **jds ~ zu spüren bekommen** to feel sb's lash; **unter jds ~** (*dat*) **stehen/leben** to be completely dominated by sb; **jdn unter seine ~ bringen** to get sb in one's clutches

knut|schen ['knuːtʃn] (*inf*) VT to pet with, to smooch with (*inf*), to neck with (*inf*) VIR to pet, to smooch (*inf*), to neck (*inf*)

Knut|sche|rei [knuːtʃəˈrai] F **-, -en** petting, smooching (*inf*), necking (*inf*)

Knutsch|fleck M (*inf*) lovebite (*inf*)

Knüt|tel ['knʏtl] M **-s, -** = **Knüppel a**

Knüt|tel|vers M = **Knittelvers**

k. o. [kaːˈʔoː] ADJ *pred* (*Sport*) knocked out; (*fig inf*) whacked (*inf*), all in (*inf*); **jdn ~ schlagen** to knock sb out

K. O. [kaːˈʔoː] M **-(s), -s** knockout, K.O.; **Sieg durch ~** victory by a knockout

ko|a|gu|lie|ren [koaguˈliːrən] *ptp* **koaguliert** VTI (*Med, Chem*) to coagulate, to clot

Ko|a|la [koˈaːla] M **-s, -s**, **Ko|a|la|bär** M koala (bear)

ko|a|lie|ren [koaˈliːrən] *ptp* **koaliert** VI (*esp Pol*) to form a coalition (*mit* with)

Ko|a|li|ti|on [koaliˈtsioːn] F **-, -en** (*esp Pol*) coalition; **kleine/große ~** little/grand coalition

---

KOALITION

There are various names for the groupings of political parties which form governments. A **große Koalition** is an alliance between the two large parties **CDU/CSU** and **SPD**, something which seldom happens on account of the incompatibility of their policies. A **kleine Koalition** is an alliance between a large and a small party. Recently there has also been an **Ampelkoalition** – red for **SPD**, yellow for **FDP** and green for **Bündnis 90/Die Grünen** → Bündnis 90/Die Grünen, CDU/CSU, FDP, SPD

Ko|a|li|ti|o|när [koalitsioˈnɛːɐ] M **-s, -e**, **Ko|a|li|ti|o|nä|rin** ['-nɛrɪn] F **-, -nen** (*Pol*) (= *Abgeordneter*) coalition member; (= *Partei auch*) coalition party

Ko|a|li|ti|ons- *in cpds* coalition; **Ko|a|li|ti|ons|ab|spra|che** F coalition agreement; **Ko|a|li|ti|ons|aus|sa|ge** F statement of willingness to form a coalition; **ko|a|li|ti|ons|fä|hig** ADJ **~ sein** to be suitable as a coalition partner; **Ko|a|li|ti|ons|fä|hig|keit** F suitability as a coalition partner; **Ko|a|li|ti|ons|frei|heit** F freedom to form a coalition; **Ko|a|li|ti|ons|ge|spräch** NT coalition talks *pl*; **Ko|a|li|ti|ons|krieg** M (*Hist*) coalition war; **Ko|a|li|ti|ons|kri|se** F crisis within a/the coalition; **Ko|a|li|ti|ons|part|ner(in)** M(F) coalition partner; **Ko|a|li|ti|ons|recht** NT right of combination; **Ko|a|li|ti|ons|re|gie|rung** F coalition government; **Ko|a|li|ti|ons|ver|ein|ba|rung** F coalition agreement, agreement on a coalition

Ko|au|tor(in) ['koː-] M(F) co-author

ko|a|xi|al [koaˈksiaːl] ADJ (*Tech*) coaxial

Ko|a|xi|al|ka|bel NT (*Tech*) coaxial cable

Ko|balt ['koːbalt] NT **-s**, *no pl* (*abbr* **Co**) cobalt

ko|balt|blau ADJ cobalt blue

Ko|bel ['koːbl] M **-s, -** (*S Ger, Aus*), **Ko|ben** ['koːbn] M **-s, - a** = **Schuppen a b** = **Stall a**

Ko|bold ['koːbɔlt] M **-(e)s, -e** [-də] goblin, imp

Ko|bolz ['koːbɔlts] M **~ schießen** to turn or do somersaults

Kob|ra ['koːbra] F **-, -s** cobra

Koch¹ [kɔx] M **-s, ⸚e** ['kœçə], **Kö|chin** ['kœçɪn] F **-, -nen** cook; (*von Restaurant etc*) chef, cook; **viele Köche verderben den Brei** (*Prov*) too many cooks spoil the broth (*Prov*)

Koch² NT **-s**, *no pl* (*Aus*) (= *Brei*) ≈ (*Apfelmus etc*) purée; (= *Griesbrei etc*) pudding

Koch-: Koch|an|lei|tung F cooking instructions *pl*; **Koch|ap|fel** M cooking apple, cooker; **koch|bar** ADJ suitable for boiling, that may be boiled; **Koch|beu|tel** M **Reis im ~** boil-in-the-bag rice; **Koch|buch** NT cookery book, cookbook; **koch|echt** ADJ (*Tex*) *Farbe* fast at 100°, fast even in boiling water; *Wäsche etc* suitable for boiling, that may be boiled; **Koch|e|cke** F kitchen *or* cooking area

kö|cheln ['kœçln] VI (*lit, fig*) to simmer

Kö|chel|ver|zeich|nis ['kœçl-] NT (*Mus*) Köchel index; **~ 25** Köchel *or* K. (number) 25

ko|chen ['kɔxn] VI **a** (*Flüssigkeit, Speise*) to boil; **etw langsam** *or* **auf kleiner Flamme ~ lassen** let sth simmer *or* to simmer sth (over a low heat); **etw zum Kochen bringen** to bring sth to the boil; **jdn zum Kochen bringen** (*fig inf*) to make sb's blood boil; **der Kühler/das Auto kocht** (*inf*) the cooling system/car is overheating; **er kochte vor Wut** (*inf*) he was boiling *or* seething with rage

b (= *Speisen zubereiten*) to cook; (= *als Koch fungieren*) to do the cooking; (= *als Koch arbeiten*) to work as a cook; **er kocht gut** he's a good cook, he is good at cooking; **er kocht pikant** his cooking is (always) highly seasoned

VT **a** *Flüssigkeit, Teer, Nahrungsmittel, Wäsche* to boil; **etw langsam** or **auf kleiner Flamme ~** to simmer sth over a low heat

b (= *zubereiten*) *Essen* to cook; *Kakao* to make; (= *aufgießen*) *Kaffee, Tee* to make, to brew; **etw gar/weich ~** to cook sth through/until (it is) soft; **Eier weich/hart ~** to soft-boil/hard-boil eggs

VI *impers* (*fig*) to be boiling; **es kocht in ihm** he is boiling or seething with rage; **im Stadion kochte es wie in einem Hexenkessel** the atmosphere in the stadium was electric

VR **sich gut/schlecht ~** to cook/not to cook well

ko|chend **ADJ** (*lit, fig*) boiling; (*liter*) *See* raging
ADV **~ heiß sein** to be boiling hot; (*Suppe etc*) to be piping hot

ko|chend|heiß △ ADJ *attr* → **kochend ADV**

Ko|cher ['kɔxɐ] M **-s, -** (= *Herd*) cooker, stove; (= *Campingkocher*) (Primus®) stove; (= *Kochplatte*) hotplate; (= *Wasserkocher*) ≈ (electric) kettle

Kö|cher ['kœçɐ] M **-s, -** (*für Pfeile*) quiver; (*für Golfschläger*) golf bag; (*für Kameraobjektiv etc*) case

Ko|che|rei [kɔxə'rai] F **-, no pl** (*inf*) cooking

Koch-: Koch|feld NT ceramic hob; **koch|fer|tig** ADJ ready-to-cook *attr*, ready to cook *pred*; **koch|fest** ADJ (*Tex*) = **kochecht**; **Koch|fleisch** NT stewing or braising meat; **Koch|ge|le|gen|heit** F cooking facilities *pl*; **Koch|ge|schirr** NT (*esp Mil*) billy(can), mess tin (*Mil*); **Koch|herd** M cooker, stove

Kö|chin F → **Koch**[1]

Koch-: Koch|kä|se M (type of) soft cheese; **Koch|kunst** F culinary art, art of cooking; **seine ~** or **Kochkünste** his cooking (ability); **Koch|künst|ler(in)** M(F) cookery expert, expert cook; **Koch|kurs** M cookery course; **Koch|löf|fel** M cooking spoon; **Koch|ni|sche** F kitchenette; **Koch|plat|te** F **a** (= *Herdplatte*) hotplate **b** (= *Kocher*) cooker; **Koch|re|zept** NT recipe; **Koch|salz** NT common salt; (*Chem auch*) sodium chloride; (*Cook*) cooking salt; **Koch|salz|in|fu|si|on** F (*Med*) saline infusion; **Koch|schin|ken** M boiled ham; **Koch|stel|le** F **a** (*im Freien*) campfire hearth **b** (= *Kochplatte*) hotplate; **Koch|topf** M (cooking) pot; (*mit Stiel*) saucepan; **Koch|wä|sche** F washing that can be boiled; **Koch|was|ser** NT *, no pl* cooking water, water in which (the) vegetables have been boiled; **Koch|zeit** F cooking time

kod|de|rig ['kɔdərɪç], **kodd|rig** ['kɔdrɪç] ADJ (*N Ger inf*) **a** (= *unwohl*) sick, queasy; **mir ist ganz ~** I feel sick or queasy **b** (= *frech*) insolent, impudent

Ko|de [ko:t, 'ko:də] M **-s, -s** code

Ko|de|in [kode'i:n] NT **-s, no pl** codeine

Kö|der ['kø:dɐ] M **-s, -** bait; (*fig auch*) lure

Kö|der|fisch M bait fish

kö|dern ['kø:dɐn] VT (*lit*) to lure; (*fig*) to tempt, to entice; **er will dich mit diesen Versprechungen nur ~** these promises of his are only a bait (to lure you); **jdn zu ~ versuchen** to woo sb; **jdn für etw ~** to rope sb into sth (*inf*); **sich von jdm/etw nicht ~ lassen** not to be tempted by sb/sth; **sie köderte ihn mit ihrem Charme** she seduced him with her charms; **sie köderte ihn mit ihrem Geld** she lured him with her money

Ko|dex ['ko:dɛks] M **-** or **-es, -e** or **Kodices** or **Kodizes** ['ko:ditsɛːs] (= *Gesetzbuch*) codex, code; (= *Handschrift*) codex, manuscript; (*fig*) (moral) code

ko|die|ren [ko'di:rən] *ptp* **kodiert** VT to (en)code

Ko|die|rung F **-, -en** coding, encoding

Ko|di|fi|ka|ti|on [kodifika'tsio:n] F **-, -en** codification

ko|di|fi|zie|ren [kodifi'tsi:rən] *ptp* **kodifiziert** VT to codify; (*fig geh*) to write down; **kodifiziertes Recht** codified or statute law

---

Ko|edu|ka|ti|on ['ko:|edukatsio:n, ko|eduka'tsi-o:n] F **-, no pl** coeducation

Ko|ef|fi|zi|ent [ko|efi'tsiɛnt] M **-en, -en** coefficient

Ko|exis|tenz ['ko:|ɛksɪstɛnts, ko|ɛksɪs'tɛnts] F *, no pl* coexistence

Ko|fel ['ko:fl] M **-s, -** (*Aus, S Ger*) rounded or dome-shaped mountain top

Kof|fe|in [kɔfe'i:n] NT **-s, no pl** caffeine

kof|fe|in|frei ADJ decaffeinated

kof|fe|in|hal|tig ADJ caffeinated, containing caffeine *pred*

Kof|fer ['kɔfɐ] M **-s, -** **a** (suit)case, bag; (= *Überseekoffer, Schrankkoffer*) trunk; (= *Arztkoffer*) bag; (*für Schreibmaschine, Kosmetika etc*) (carrying) case; **die ~ packen** (*lit, fig*) to pack one's bags; **aus dem ~ leben** to live out of a suitcase **b** (*Mil sl*) heavy shell

Kof|fer|an|hän|ger M luggage or baggage label or tag

Köf|fer|chen ['kœfɐçən] NT **-s, -** *dim von* **Koffer**

Kof|fer-: Kof|fer|ge|rät NT portable (set); **Kof|fer|ku|li** M (luggage) trolley (*Brit*), cart (*US*); **Kof|fer|ra|dio** NT portable radio; **Kof|fer|raum** M (*Aut*) boot (*Brit*), trunk (*US*); (= *Volumen*) luggage or baggage space; **Kof|fer|schreib|ma|schi|ne** F portable (typewriter); **Kof|fer|trä|ger(in)** M(F) porter

Ko|gel ['ko:gl] M **-s, -** (*Aus, S Ger*) = **Kofel**

Kog|ge ['kɔgə] F **-, -n** (*Naut*) cog

Kog|nak ['kɔnjak] M **-s, -s** or **-e** brandy

Kog|nak-: Kog|nak|glas NT brandy glass; **Kog|nak|schwen|ker** [-ʃvɛnkɐ] M **-s, -** brandy glass or balloon, balloon glass

kog|ni|tiv [kɔgni'ti:f] ADJ (*Philos, Psych*) cognitive

Ko|ha|bi|ta|ti|on [kohabita'tsio:n] F **-, -en** (*form*) cohabitation

Ko|hä|si|on [kohɛ'zio:n] F **-, no pl** (*Phys, geh*) cohesion

Ko|hä|si|ons|kraft F (*Phys, geh*) cohesive force

Kohl [ko:l] M **-(e)s, -e** **a** cabbage; **das macht den ~ auch nicht fett** (*inf*) that's not much help **b** (*inf*: = *Unsinn*) rubbish (*Brit inf*), nonsense; **aufgewärmter ~** old stuff or story

Kohl|dampf M *, no pl* (*inf*) **~ haben** or **schieben** to be starving or famished

Koh|le ['ko:lə] F **-, -n** **a** (= *Brennstoff*) coal; (= *Stück Kohle*) (lump of) coal; (*dial*: = *Brikett*) briquette; **wir haben keine ~n mehr** we have no coal left; **weiße ~** white coal, water power, hydroelectric power; **glühende ~n** (*lit*) (glowing) embers; **glühende** or **feurige ~n auf jds Haupt sammeln** (*geh*) to heap coals of fire on sb's head; **(wie) auf (glühenden** or **heißen) ~n sitzen** to be like a cat on hot bricks (*Brit*) or on a hot tin roof, to be on tenterhooks (*esp Brit*); **die ~n aus dem Feuer holen** (*fig*) to pull the chestnuts out of the fire

b (= *Verkohltes, Holzkohle*) charcoal; **(tierische** or **medizinische) ~** animal charcoal

c (*Art*: = *Kohlestift*) (stick of) charcoal; **mit ~ zeichnen** to draw with or in charcoal

d (*Tech*) carbon

e (*inf*: = *Geld*) dough (*inf*), cash (*inf*); **die ~ stimmt** the money's right; **gut** or **fett ~ machen** (*sl*: = *gut verdienen*) to make a packet (*Brit inf*), to make a lot of money

Kohle-: Koh|le|fil|ter M charcoal filter; **Koh|le|hydrat** NT carbohydrate; **Koh|le|hyd|rie|rung** [-hydri:rʊŋ] F *, no pl* (*Tech*) hydrogenation of coal; **Koh|le|kraft|werk** NT coal-fired power station

koh|len[1] ['ko:lən] VI **a** (*Naut, Rail*) to take on coal **b** (= *verkohlen*) to char, to carbonize **c** (= *Ruß erzeugen*) to smoke

koh|len[2] VTI (*inf*) to talk a load of rubbish (*Brit inf*) or nonsense; (= *lügen*) to lie, to tell lies; **unglaublich, was der wieder kohlt** it's in-

---

credible the nonsense he's been talking again/ the lies he's been telling again

Koh|len- *in cpds* coal; **Koh|len|berg|bau** M coal-mining; **Koh|len|berg|werk** NT coal mine, pit, colliery; **Koh|len|bun|ker** M coal bunker; **Koh|len|di|oxid** NT carbon dioxide; **Koh|len|gas** NT coal gas; **Koh|len|ge|biet** NT coal-mining area; **Koh|len|gru|be** F coal mine, pit; **Koh|len|grus** M (coal) slack; **Koh|len|hal|de** F pile of coal; **Koh|len|hal|den** PL coal stocks *pl*; **Koh|len|hei|zung** F coal heating; (= *Anlage*) coal heating system; **Koh|len|herd** M range; **Koh|len|hydrat** NT = **Kohlehydrat**; **Koh|len|in|dust|rie** F coal industry; **Koh|len|kas|ten** M coal box; **Koh|len|kel|ler** M coal cellar; **Koh|len|la|ger** NT **a** (= *Vorrat*) coal depot **b** (*im Stollen, Berg*) coal seam or bed; **Koh|len|mo|no|xid** NT carbon monoxide; **Koh|len|ofen** M (coal-burning) stove; **Koh|len|pott** M **a** coal-mining area **b** (*inf*: = *Ruhrgebiet*) Ruhr (basin or valley); **Koh|len|re|vier** NT coal-mining area; **Koh|len|sack** M coal sack; **koh|len|sau|er** ADJ **kohlensaurer Kalk** calcium carbonate; **kohlensaures Natrium** sodium carbonate; **Koh|len|säu|re** F **a** (*Chem*) carbonic acid **b** (*inf*: in *Getränken*) fizz (*inf*); **koh|len|säu|re|hal|tig** ADJ *Getränke* carbonated; **Koh|len|schau|fel** F coal shovel; **Koh|len|staub** M coal dust; **Koh|len|staub|lun|ge** F anthracosis

Koh|len|stoff M (*abbr* **C**) carbon

Koh|len|stoff-Da|tie|rung [-dati:rʊŋ] F **-, -en** (radio)carbon dating

Koh|len-: Koh|len|trim|mer [-trɪmɐ] M **-s, -** (coal) trimmer; **Koh|len|wa|gen** M **a** (*Rail*) (= *Tender*) tender; (= *Waggon*) coal truck **b** (= *LKW*) coal lorry (*Brit*) or truck; **Koh|len|was|ser|stoff** M hydrocarbon; **Koh|len|zan|ge** F (pair of) fire or coal tongs *pl*; **Koh|len|ze|che** F coal mine, pit, colliery

Kohle-: Koh|le|ofen M coal(-burning) stove; **Koh|le|pa|pier** NT carbon paper; **Koh|le|pfen|nig** M *, no pl* (*Hist*) special tax paid on electricity to subsidize the coal industry

Köh|ler ['kø:lɐ] M **-s, -**, **Köh|le|rin** [-ərɪn] F **-, -nen** charcoal burner

Köh|le|rei [kølə'rai] F **-, no pl** charcoal burning

Kohle-: Koh|le|stab M (*Tech*) carbon rod; **Koh|le|stift** M (*Art*) piece or stick of charcoal; **Koh|le|tab|let|te** F (*Med*) charcoal tablet; **Koh|le|vor|kom|men** NT coal deposit(s *pl*); **Koh|le|zeich|nung** F charcoal drawing

Kohl-: Kohl|kopf M cabbage; **Kohl|mei|se** F great tit; **kohl|(pech)|ra|ben|schwarz** ADJ **a** *Haar* jet black, raven *attr*, raven-black; *Nacht* pitch-black **b** (*inf*: = *sehr schmutzig*) as black as coal; **Kohl|ra|bi** [ko:l'ra:bi] M **-(s), -** kohlrabi; **Kohl|rou|la|de** F (*Cook*) stuffed cabbage leaves *pl*; **Kohl|rü|be** F (*Bot*) swede (*Brit*), rutabaga (*US*); **Kohl|sa|lat** M coleslaw; **kohl|schwarz** ADJ *Haare, Augen* jet black; *Gesicht, Hände* black as coal; **Kohl|spros|se** F (*Aus*) (Brussels) sprout; **Kohl|weiß|ling** [-vaislɪŋ] M **-s, -e** cabbage white (butterfly)

Ko|hor|te [ko'hɔrtə] F **-, -n** (*Hist*) cohort

ko|i|tie|ren [ko|i'ti:rən] *ptp* **koitiert** VI (*esp Med*) to engage in coitus or sexual intercourse

Ko|i|tus ['ko:itʊs] M **-, -se** or **-** ['ko:itu:s] (*esp Med*) coitus, coition

Ko|je ['ko:jə] F **-, -n** **a** (*esp Naut*) bunk, berth; (*inf*: = *Bett*) bed; **sich in die ~ hauen** (*inf*) to hit the sack (*inf*) or the hay (*inf*) **b** (= *Ausstellungskoje*) stand

Ko|jo|te [ko'jo:tə] M **-n, -n** coyote

Ko|ka ['ko:ka] F **-, -** (*Bot*) coca

Ko|ka|in [koka'i:n] NT **-s, no pl** cocaine

ko|ka|in|süch|tig ADJ addicted to cocaine; **ein Kokainsüchtiger** a cocaine addict

Ko|kar|de [ko'kardə] F **-, -n** cockade

---

ko|keln ['ko:kln] VI (inf) to play with fire; **mit Kerzen/Streichhölzern ~** to play with (lighted) candles/matches

Ko|ke|rei [ko:kə'rai] F -, -en (= Tätigkeit) coking; (= Anlage) coking plant

ko|kett [ko'kɛt] ADJ coquettish, flirtatious ADV coquettishly

Ko|ket|te|rie [kokɛtə'ri:] F -, -n [-'ri:ən] a no pl (= Eigenschaft) coquettishness, coquetry, flirtatiousness b (= Bemerkung) coquettish or flirtatious remark, coquetry

ko|ket|tie|ren [kokɛ'ti:rən] ptp **kokettiert** VI to flirt; **mit seinem Alter ~** to play up or upon one's age; **mit einem Gedanken/System** etc **~** to toy with an idea/method etc

Ko|ko|lo|res [koko'lo:rɛs] M -, no pl (inf) a (= Unsinn) rubbish (Brit inf), nonsense, twaddle (Brit inf) b (= Umstände) palaver (inf), fuss; **mach doch nicht solchen ~** don't make such a palaver (inf) or fuss

Ko|kon [ko'kõ:] M -s, -s (Zool) cocoon

Ko|kos¹ ['ko:kɔs] F -, - (= Palme) coconut palm or tree

Ko|kos² NT -, no pl coconut

Ko|kos- in cpds coconut; **Ko|kos|fa|ser** F coconut fibre (Brit) or fiber (US); **Ko|kos|fett** NT coconut oil; **Ko|kos|flo|cken** PL desiccated coconut; **Ko|kos|läu|fer** M coconut matting; **Ko|kos|mat|te** F coconut mat(ting), coir mat(ting); **Ko|kos|milch** F coconut milk; **Ko|kos|nuss** ▲ F coconut; **Ko|kos|öl** NT coconut oil; **Ko|kos|pal|me** F coconut palm or tree; **Ko|kos|ras|peln** PL desiccated coconut

Ko|kot|te [ko'kɔtə] F -, -n (old) cocotte

Koks¹ [ko:ks] M -es, -e coke; (inf) (= Unsinn) rubbish (Brit inf), nonsense; (= Geld) dough (inf), cash (inf)

Koks² M OR NT -es, no pl (inf: = Kokain) coke (inf)

kok|sen ['ko:ksn] VI (inf: = Kokain nehmen) to take coke (inf)

Kok|ser ['ko:ksɐ] M -s, -, **Kok|se|rin** [-ərɪn] F -, -nen (inf) cocaine or coke (inf) addict

Ko|la¹ ['ko:la] F -, no pl (Nuss) cola or kola nut

Ko|la² pl von **Kolon**

Ko|la-: Ko|la|baum M cola or kola tree; **Ko|la|nuss** ▲ F cola or kola nut

Kol|ben ['kɔlbn] M -s, - a (= dickes Ende, Gewehrkolben) butt; (Tech: = Motorkolben, Pumpenkolben) piston; (Chem: = Destillierkolben) retort; (von Glühlampe) bulb; (von Lötapparat) bit; (sl: = Penis) prick (sl), cock (sl), tool (sl) b (Bot) spadix; (= Maiskolben) cob

Kol|ben-: kol|ben|för|mig ADJ club-shaped ADV **etw verdickt sich ~** sth widens into a club shape; **Kol|ben|fres|ser** M (inf) piston seizure; **(den) ~ haben** to have piston seizure; **Kol|ben|hal|ter** M plunger refill (fountain) pen; **Kol|ben|hub** M (von Pumpe) plunger stroke; (Aut) piston stroke; **Kol|ben|ring** M piston ring

Kol|chos ['kɔlçɔs] M OR NT -, Kolchose [-'ço:zə], **Kol|cho|se** [kɔl'ço:zə] F -, -n collective farm, kolkhoz

Kol|chos|bau|er M pl -bauern, **Kol|chos|bäu|e|rin** F -, -nen worker on a collective farm

Ko|li|bak|te|ri|en ['ko:li-] PL E.coli pl

Ko|li|bri ['ko:libri] M -s, -s humming bird, colibri (spec)

Ko|lik ['ko:lɪk] F -, -en colic

ko|lik|ar|tig ADJ colicky

Kol|ra|be ['kɔl-] M raven

kol|la|bie|ren [kɔla'bi:rən] ptp **kollabiert** VI aux sein (Med, fig) to collapse

Kol|la|bo|ra|teur [kɔlabora'tø:ɐ] M -s, -e, **Kol|la|bo|ra|teu|rin** [-'tø:rɪn] F -, -nen (Pol) collaborator

Kol|la|bo|ra|ti|on [kɔlabora'tsio:n] F -, -en collaboration

kol|la|bo|rie|ren ptp **kollaboriert** VI to collaborate

Kol|lage [kɔ'la:ʒə] F -, -n = **Collage**

Kol|laps ['kɔlaps, kɔ'laps] M -es, -e (Med, fig) collapse; **einen ~ erleiden** to collapse

Kol|la|te|ral|scha|den [kɔlate'ra:l-] M (Mil; euph) collateral damage

Kol|la|ti|on [kɔla'tsio:n] F -, -en (Liter) collation, comparison; (Typ) collation

kol|la|ti|o|nie|ren [kɔlatsio'ni:rən] ptp **kollationiert** VT (Liter) to collate, to compare; (Typ) to collate

Kol|leg [kɔ'le:k] NT -s, -s or -ien [-giən] a (Univ) (= Vorlesung) lecture; (= Vorlesungsreihe) (course of) lectures pl b (Sch) college c (Eccl) theological college

Kol|le|ge [kɔ'le:gə] M -n, -n, **Kol|le|gin** [-'le:gɪn] F -, -nen colleague; (Arbeiter auch) workmate; **seine ~n vom Fach** his professional colleagues; **meine ~n** the people I work with, my colleagues; **seine ~n in der Ärzteschaft** his fellow doctors; **~ kommt gleich!** somebody will be with you right away; **Herr ~!** Mr X; **der (Herr) ~ (Müller)** (Parl) the honourable (Brit) or honorable (US) member

Kol|le|gen-: Kol|le|gen|kreis M **im ~** among colleagues; **Kol|le|gen|ra|batt** M trade discount; **Kol|le|gen|schaft** [kɔ'le:gnʃaft] F -, -en colleagues pl

Kol|leg-: Kol|leg|geld NT lecture fee; **Kol|leg|heft** NT (student's) notebook

kol|le|gi|al [kɔle'gia:l] ADJ **das war nicht sehr ~ von ihm** that wasn't what you would expect from a colleague; **mit ~en Grüßen** ~ yours sincerely (Brit), sincerely yours (US) ADV loyally; **sich ~ verhalten** to be a good colleague; **~ eingestellt sein** to be cooperative

Kol|le|gi|a|li|tät [kɔlegiali'tɛ:t] F -, no pl loyalty (to one's colleagues)

Kol|le|gi|at [kɔle'gia:t] M -n, -n, **Kol|le|gi|a|tin** [kɔle'gia:tɪn] F -, -nen a (Univ) college student on a course for university entrance qualification b (Sch: = Schüler der Kollegstufe) ≈ sixth form college (Brit) or junior college (US) student

Kol|le|gin F → **Kollege**

Kol|le|gi|um [kɔ'le:giʊm] NT -s, Kollegien [-giən] a (Lehrerkollegium etc) staff; (= Ausschuss) working party b = **Kolleg**

Kol|leg|map|pe F document case

KOLLEGSTUFE

The **Kollegstufe**, or **reformierte gymnasiale Oberstufe**, refers to the final two school years in a **Gymnasium** (two and a half years in some **Länder**). Pupils have the opportunity to choose which subjects to study, thereby taking account of their abilities and interests, and to follow courses for one semester only. This system, devised in the 1970s, is designed to prepare pupils for university → GYMNASIUM.

Kol|lek|te [kɔ'lɛktə] F -, -n (Eccl) offering, collection, offertory

Kol|lek|ti|on [kɔlɛk'tsio:n] F -, -en collection; (= Sortiment) range; (Fashion) collection; **~ (an Mustern)** (set of) samples

kol|lek|tiv [kɔlɛk'ti:f] ADJ collective ADV collectively

Kol|lek|tiv [kɔlɛk'ti:f] NT -s, -e [-və] collective

Kol|lek|tiv-: Kol|lek|tiv|ar|beit F (= Tätigkeit) collective work, collaboration; (= Ergebnis) collective piece of work; **Kol|lek|tiv|be|griff** M (Ling) collective (term); **Kol|lek|tiv|geist** M corporate or collective spirit

kol|lek|ti|vie|ren [kɔlɛkti'vi:rən] ptp **kollektiviert** VT to collectivize

Kol|lek|ti|vis|mus [kɔlɛkti'vɪsmʊs] M -, no pl collectivism

Kol|lek|ti|vist [kɔlɛkti'vɪst] M -en, -en, **Kol|lek|ti|vis|tin** [-'vɪstɪn] F -, -nen collectivist

Kol|lek|tiv-: Kol|lek|tiv|schuld F collective guilt; **Kol|lek|tiv|stra|fe** F collective punishment

Kol|lek|ti|vum [kɔlɛk'ti:vʊm] NT -s, Kollektiva or Kollektiven [-va, -vn] (Ling) collective (noun)

Kol|lek|tiv-: Kol|lek|tiv|ver|trag M collective agreement; **Kol|lek|tiv|wirt|schaft** F (Econ) collective economy

Kol|lek|tor [kɔ'lɛkto:ɐ] M -s, Kollektoren [-'to:rən] (Elec) collector; (= Sonnenkollektor) solar collector or panel

Kol|ler ['kɔlɐ] M -s, - a (inf) (= Anfall) silly or funny mood; (= Wutanfall) rage; (= Tropenkoller) tropical madness; (= Gefängniskoller) prison madness; **seinen ~ bekommen/haben** to get into/to be in one of one's silly or funny moods; **einen ~ haben/bekommen** to be in/fly into a rage b (Vet: bei Pferden) staggers sing

kol|lern ['kɔlɐn] VI a (Truthahn etc) to gobble; (Magen, Darm) to rumble b aux sein (dial: = kullern) to roll VI impers **es kollert in seinem Bauch** his stomach is rumbling

kol|li|die|ren [kɔli'di:rən] ptp **kollidiert** VI (geh) a aux sein (Fahrzeuge) to collide, to be in collision b aux sein or haben (fig) to conflict, to be in conflict, to clash; (Termine) to clash; **mit|einander ~** to conflict, to clash, to be in conflict (with each other); **er ist mit dem Gesetz kollidiert** he has collided with the law

Kol|li|er [kɔ'lie:] NT -s, -s necklet, necklace

Kol|li|si|on [kɔli'zio:n] F -, -en (geh) (= Zusammenstoß) collision; (= Streit) conflict, clash; (von Terminen) clash; **mit dem Gesetz in ~ geraten** or **kommen** to come into conflict with the law, to collide with the law

Kol|li|si|ons|kurs M (Naut, Aviat) collision course; **auf ~ gehen, einen ~ ansteuern** (fig) to be heading for trouble

Kol|lo|id [kɔlo'i:t] NT -s, -e [-də] (Chem) colloid

Kol|lo|ka|ti|on [kɔloka'tsio:n] F -, -en (Ling) collocation

Kol|lo|qui|um [kɔ'lo:kviʊm, kɔ'lɔkviʊm] NT -s, Kolloquien [-kviən] colloquium; (Aus Univ: = Prüfung) examination

Köln [kœln] NT -s Cologne

Köl|ner¹ ['kœlnɐ] ADJ attr Cologne; **der ~ Dom** Cologne Cathedral

Köl|ner² ['kœlnɐ] M -s, -, **Köl|ne|rin** [-ərɪn] F -, -nen inhabitant or (gebürtiger) native of Cologne; **er ist ~** (wohnhaft) he lives in Cologne; (kommt aus Köln) he comes from Cologne

köl|nisch ['kœlnɪʃ] ADJ Cologne attr; **er spricht Kölnisch** he speaks (the) Cologne dialect

Köl|nisch|was|ser NT -, no pl, **köl|nisch Was|ser** ▲ NT -, no pl eau de Cologne, cologne

Ko|lo|fo|ni|um [kolo'fo:niʊm] ▲ NT -s, no pl = **Kolophonium**

Ko|lom|bi|ne [kolɔm'bi:nə] F -, -n (Theat) Columbine

Ko|lon ['ko:lɔn] NT -s, -s or **Kola** [-la] (Typ, Anat) colon

Ko|lo|ni|a|kü|bel [ko'lo:nia-] M (Aus) dustbin (Brit), trash or garbage can (US)

ko|lo|ni|al [kolo'nia:l] ADJ (rare) colonial

Ko|lo|ni|al- [kolo'nia:l] in cpds colonial; **Ko|lo|ni|al|be|sitz** M colonial possessions pl; **das Land ist in ~** that country is a colony; **Ko|lo|ni|al|herr** M colonial master; (= Herrscher) colonial ruler; **Ko|lo|ni|al|herr|schaft** F colonial rule

ko|lo|ni|a|li|sie|ren [koloniali'zi:rən] ptp **kolonialisiert** VT to colonize

Ko|lo|ni|a|lis|mus [kolonia'lɪsmʊs] M -, no pl colonialism

Ko|lo|ni|al-: Ko|lo|ni|al|macht F colonial power; **Ko|lo|ni|al|reich** NT colonial empire;

Ko|lo|ni|al|stil M Colonial (style); **Ko|lo|ni-|al|wa|ren** PL groceries pl; (= Erzeugnisse der Kolonien) colonial produce; **Ko|lo|ni|al|wa|ren-|händ|ler(in)** M(F) (dated) grocer; **Ko|lo|ni-|al|wa|ren|hand|lung** F , **Ko|lo|ni|al|wa|ren-|ge|schäft** NT (dated) grocer's (shop); **Ko|lo-|ni|al|zeit** F colonial times pl; **ein Relikt aus der ~** a relic of the colonial past or of colonial times

Ko|lo|ni|a|wa|gen [ko:lo:nia-] M (Aus) refuse lorry (Brit) or truck

Ko|lo|nie [kolo'ni:] F **-, -n** [-'ni:ən] (alle Bedeutungen) colony; (= Ansiedlung auch) settlement; (= Ferienkolonie) camp

Ko|lo|ni|sa|ti|on [koloniza'tsio:n] F **-,** no pl a (= Erschließung: von Gebiet) settlement b (= Kolonisieren: von Land) colonization

ko|lo|ni|sie|ren [koloni'zi:rən] ptp **kolonisiert** VT a (= erschließen) Gebiet to settle in b (= zur Kolonie machen) Land to colonize

Ko|lo|nist [kolo'nɪst] M **-en, -en**, **Ko|lo|nis|tin** [-'nɪstɪn] F **-, -nen** colonist; (= Siedler) settler

Ko|lon|na|de [kɔlɔ'na:də] F **-, -n** colonnade

Ko|lon|ne [ko'lɔnə] F **-, -n** column; (= Autoschlange, fig: = Menge) queue (Brit), line; (zur Begleitung esp Mil) convoy; (= Arbeitskolonne) gang; „Achtung ~!" "convoy"; **~ fahren** to drive in (a) convoy; **fünfte ~** fifth column

Ko|lon|nen-: Ko|lon|nen|fah|ren NT **-s,** no pl driving in (a) convoy; **Ko|lon|nen|sprin|gen** NT jumping the (traffic) queue (Brit) or line (US); **Ko|lon|nen|sprin|ger(in)** M(F) queue--jumper (Brit), line-jumper (US); **Ko|lon|nen-|ver|kehr** M a queue/queues of traffic (Brit), a line/lines of traffic, a tailback (Brit)

Ko|lo|pho|ni|um [kolo'fo:niʊm] NT **-s,** no pl rosin, resin, colophony (spec)

Ko|lo|ra|tur [kolora'tu:ɐ] F **-, -en** coloratura

ko|lo|rie|ren [kolo'ri:rən] ptp **koloriert** VT to colour (Brit), to color (US)

Ko|lo|rit [kolo'ri:t] NT **-(e)s, -e** (Art) colouring (Brit), coloring (US); (Mus) (tone) colour (Brit) or color (US); (Liter, fig) atmosphere, colour (Brit), color (US)

Ko|lo|sko|pie [kolosko'pi:] F **-, -n** [-'pi:ən] (Med) colonoscopy

Ko|loss ▲ [ko'lɔs] M **-es, -e** colossus; (fig auch) giant; **der ~ von Rhodos** the Colossus of Rhodes

ko|los|sal [kɔlɔ'sa:l] ADJ Gebäude, Figur colossal, enormous; Glück, Gefühl tremendous; Dummheit crass ADV (inf) tremendously, enormously; **sich ~ verschätzen** to make a colossal mistake

Ko|los|sal-: Ko|los|sal|film M epic film, (film) epic; **Ko|los|sal|ge|mäl|de** NT (inf) spectacular painting; **Ko|los|sal|schin|ken** M (pej geh) spectacular

Ko|los|ser [ko'lɔsɐ] M **-s,** , **Ko|los|se|rin** [-ərɪn] F **-, -nen** a (Hist) Colossian b (Bibl) = **Kolosserbrief**

Ko|los|ser|brief M Epistle to the Colossians, Colossians sing, no def art

Ko|los|se|um [kɔlɔ'se:ʊm] NT **-s,** no pl **das ~** the Colosseum

Kol|por|ta|ge [kɔlpɔr'ta:ʒə] F **-, -n** a (Press) cheap sensationalism b (= minderwertige Literatur) trash, rubbish (esp Brit inf) c (old: = Wandergewerbe) peddling

Kol|por|ta|ge-: Kol|por|ta|ge|li|te|ra|tur F trashy literature; **Kol|por|ta|ge|ro|man** M trashy novel

kol|por|tie|ren [kɔlpɔr'ti:rən] ptp **kolportiert** VT a Nachricht to spread, to circulate; **Gerüchte** to spread, to peddle; **die Zeitung kolportierte, dass ...** the paper spread the story that ... b (old) Bücher etc to peddle

kölsch [kœlʃ] ADJ = **kölnisch**

Kölsch [kœlʃ] NT **-,** a (= Bier) ≈ (strong) lager b (= Dialekt) **er spricht ~** he speaks (the) Cologne dialect

Ko|lum|bi|a|ner [kolʊm'bia:nɐ] M **-s, -, Ko|-|lum|bi|a|ne|rin** [-ərɪn] F **-, -nen** Colombian

ko|lum|bi|a|nisch [kolʊm'bia:nɪʃ] ADJ Colombian

Ko|lum|bi|en [ko'lʊmbiən] NT **-s** Colombia

Ko|lum|bi|er [kolʊm'bɪɐ] M **-s, -, Ko|lum|bi|e|-|rin** [-iərɪn] F **-, -nen** Colombian

Ko|lum|bi|ne [kolʊm'bi:nə] F **-, -n** (Theat) Columbine

ko|lum|bisch [ko'lʊmbɪʃ] ADJ Colombian

Ko|lum|bus [ko'lʊmbʊs] M **-'** **Christoph ~** Christopher Columbus → **Ei**

Ko|lum|ne [ko'lʊmnə] F **-, -n** (Typ, Press) column

Ko|lum|nen|ti|tel M (Typ) headline, running head; **toter ~** folio, page number; **lebender ~** running head

Ko|lum|nist [kolʊm'nɪst] M **-en, -en**, **Ko|lum-|nis|tin** [-'nɪstɪn] F **-, -nen** columnist

Ko|ma ['ko:ma] NT **-s, -s** or **-ta** [-ta] (Med) coma; **im ~ liegen** to be in a coma; **ins ~ fallen** to go or fall into a coma

Kom|bat|tant [kɔmba'tant] M **-en, -en**, **Kom-|bat|tan|tin** [-'tantɪn] F **-, -nen** (geh) combatant

Kom|bi ['kɔmbi] M **-s, -s** (Aut) estate (car) (Brit), station wagon (esp US)

Kom|bi|kar|te F (= Fahr- und Eintrittskarte) combined ticket (for travel and admission)

Kom|bi|lohn M wage subsidized by the state

Kom|bi|nat [kɔmbi'na:t] NT **-s, -e** (Econ) combine

Kom|bi|na|ti|on [kɔmbina'tsio:n] F **-, -en** a (= Verbindung, Zusammenstellung, Zahlenkombination) combination; (Sport: = Zusammenspiel) concerted move, (piece of) teamwork; **alpine/nordische ~** (Ski) Alpine/Nordic combination b (= Schlussfolgerung) deduction, reasoning; (= Vermutung) conjecture c (= Kleidung) suit, ensemble; (= Hemdhose) combinations pl, combs pl (inf); (= Arbeitsanzug) overalls pl, boiler suit; (= Fliegerkombination) flying suit

Kom|bi|na|ti|ons-: Kom|bi|na|ti|ons|ga|be F powers pl of deduction or reasoning; **Kom-|bi|na|ti|ons|mög|lich|keit** F possible combination; **Kom|bi|na|ti|ons|prä|pa|rat** NT (Pharm) compound preparation; **Kom|bi|na|ti-|ons|schloss** ▲ NT combination lock; **Kom-|bi|na|ti|ons|ver|mö|gen** NT powers pl of deduction

Kom|bi|na|to|rik [kɔmbina'to:rɪk] F **-,** no pl (Math) combination theory, theory of combinations

kom|bi|na|to|risch [kɔmbina'to:rɪʃ] ADJ a Fähigkeiten deductive; Problem, Logik combinatory b (Ling) **~er Lautwandel** conditioned sound change

kom|bi|nier|bar [-ba:ɐ] ADJ combinable; Kleidungsstücke mix-and-match attr

kom|bi|nie|ren [kɔmbi'ni:rən] ptp **kombiniert** VT to combine; Kleidungsstücke auch to wear together; **Möbel zum Kombinieren** unit furniture; **zum beliebigen Kombinieren** to mix and match VI a (= folgern) to deduce; (= vermuten) to suppose; **gut ~** to be good at deducing or deduction; **ich kombiniere: ...** I conclude: ...; **du hast richtig kombiniert** your conclusion is right, you have come to the right conclusion b (Sport) to make a concerted move

Kom|bi|nie|rer M **-s, -, Kom|bi|nie|re|rin** F **-, -nen** (Ski) competitor in the combination (event)

Kom|bi-: Kom|bi|wa|gen M estate (car) (Brit), station wagon (esp US); **Kom|bi|zan|-|ge** F combination pliers pl

Kom|bü|se [kɔm'by:zə] F **-, -n** (Naut) galley

Ko|met [ko'me:t] M **-en, -en** comet; (fig) meteor

ko|me|ten-: ko|me|ten|ar|tig ADJ a (Astron) comet-like b (fig) = **kometenhaft**; **ko|me-|ten|haft** ADJ (fig) Aufstieg, Karriere meteoric; Aufschwung rapid

Kom|fort [kɔm'fo:ɐ] M **-s,** no pl (von Hotel etc) luxury; (von Möbel etc) comfort; (von Auto) luxury features pl; (von Gerät) extras pl; (von Wohnung) amenities pl, mod cons pl (Brit inf); **ein Auto mit allem ~** a luxury car, a car with many luxury features

-kom|fort M suf in cpds comfort; **Fahrkomfort** (motoring) comfort; **ein Fernsehgerät mit großem Bedienungskomfort** a television set with easy-to-use controls

kom|for|ta|bel [kɔmfɐ'ta:bl] ADJ (= mit Komfort ausgestattet) luxurious, luxury attr; Haus, Wohnung well-appointed; (= bequem) Sessel, Bett comfortable; (= praktisch) Bedienung convenient ADV (= bequem) comfortably; (= mit viel Komfort) luxuriously

Kom|fort|woh|nung [kɔm'fo:ɐ-] F luxury flat (Brit) or apartment

Ko|mik ['ko:mɪk] F **-,** no pl (= das Komische) comic; (= komische Wirkung) comic effect; (= lustiges Element: von Situation) comic element; **tragische ~** tragicomedy; **ein Sinn für ~** a sense of the comic

Ko|mi|ker ['ko:mɪkɐ] M **-s, -, Ko|mi|ke|rin** [-ərɪn] F **-, -nen** comedian, comic; (fig auch) joker (inf); **Sie ~** you must be joking

Kom|in|form [kɔmɪn'fɔrm] NT **-s,** no pl (Hist) **das ~** the Cominform

Kom|in|tern [kɔmɪn'tɛrn] F **-,** no pl (Hist) **die ~** the Comintern

ko|misch ['ko:mɪʃ] ADJ a (= spaßhaft, ulkig) funny, comical; (Theat) Rolle, Person, Oper comic; **der ~e Alte** (Theat) the comic old man; **das Komische** (Liter) the comic; **das Komische daran** the funny thing about it b (= seltsam, verdächtig) funny, strange, odd; **das Komische daran ist ...** the funny or strange or odd thing about it is ...; **~, ich hab schon wieder Hunger** funny, I'm hungry again already; **~, dass ich das übersehen habe** it's funny or odd that I should have missed that; **mir ist/wird so ~** (inf) I feel funny or strange or odd; **er war so ~ zu mir** he acted so strangely towards (Brit) or toward (US) me ADV strangely; riechen, schmecken, sich fühlen strange; **jdm ~ vorkommen** to seem strange to sb

ko|mi|scher|wei|se ['ko:mɪʃɐ'vaizə] ADV funnily enough

Ko|mi|tee [komi'te:] NT **-s, -s** committee

Kom|ma ['kɔma] NT **-s, -s** or **-ta** [-ta] comma; (Math) decimal point; **fünf/null ~ drei** five/nought point three

Kom|man|dant [kɔman'dant] M **-en, -en**, **Kom|man|dan|tin** [-'dantɪn] F **-, -nen** (Mil) commanding officer; (von Festung auch) commander; (Naut) captain; (von Stadt) commandant

Kom|man|dan|tur [kɔmandan'tu:ɐ] F **-, -en** (= Funktion) command; (= Gebäude auch) headquarters sing

Kom|man|deur [kɔman'dø:ɐ] M **-s, -e, Kom-|man|deu|rin** [-'dø:rɪn] F **-, -nen** commander

kom|man|die|ren [kɔman'di:rən] ptp **kommandiert** VT a (= befehligen) to command, to be in command of b (= befehlen) jdn an einen Ort ~ to order sb to a place; **ich kommandierte ihn zu mir** I ordered him to appear before me; **sich von jdm ~ lassen** to let oneself be ordered about by sb VI a (= Befehlsgewalt haben) to be in command; **~der General/Offizier** commanding general/officer b (= Befehle geben) to command, to give (the) orders; **er kommandiert gern** he likes to be the one to give (the) orders, he likes ordering people about

Kom|man|dit|ge|sell|schaft [kɔman'di:t-] F (Comm) ≈ limited partnership

Kom|man|di|tist [kɔmandi'tɪst] M **-en, -en**, **Kom|man|di|tis|tin** [-'tɪstɪn] F **-, -nen** ≈ limited partner

---

Kom|man|do [kɔ'mando] NT **-s, -s** **a** (= *Befehl*) command, order; **das ~ zum Schießen geben** to give the command *or* order to fire; **auf ~ schreit ihr alle …** (up)on the command (you) all shout …; **ich mache nichts auf ~** I don't do things to order *or* on command; **wie auf ~ stehen bleiben** to stand still as if by command; **der Hund gehorcht auf ~** the dog obeys on command

b (= *Befehlsgewalt*) command; **wer hat das ~?** who is in command?; **das ~ haben** *or* **führen/übernehmen** to be in *or* have/take command (*über +acc* of); **dem ~ von … unterstehen** to be under the command of …

c (*Mil*) (= *Behörde*) command; (= *Abteilung*) commando

Kom|man|do-: **Kom|man|do|brü|cke** F (*Naut*) bridge; **Kom|man|do|kap|sel** F (*Space*) command module; **Kom|man|do|raum** M control room; **Kom|man|do|stab** M command (staff); **Kom|man|do|stand** M , **Kom|man|do|turm** M (*Naut*) conning tower; **Kom|man|do|un|ter|neh|men** NT commando operation; **Kom|man|do|wirt|schaft** F controlled economy; **Kom|man|do|zent|ra|le** F control centre (*Brit*) *or* center (*US*); (*Mil etc*) command headquarters *sing or pl*

Kom|ma|set|zung F **a** (= *Regeln der Kommasetzung*) comma rules *pl*, rules *pl* for the use of commas **b** (*persönlicher Gebrauch*) use of commas

---

kom|men ['kɔmən] *aux sein*
pret **kam** [kaːm], *ptp* **gekommen** [ɡə'kɔmən]

1 INTRANSITIVES VERB	3 TRANSITIVES VERB
2 UNPERSÖNLICHES VERB	

1 – INTRANSITIVES VERB

a allgemein to come; **komm sofort her!** come here at once!; **wenn meine Eltern kommen, gibt es immer Erbsensuppe** when my parents come (over) they always get pea soup; **wenn ich zu meinen Eltern komme, gibt es immer Erbsensuppe** when I go over to my parents I always get pea soup; **ich komme (schon)** I'm (just) coming; **er wird gleich kommen** he'll be here right away; **da kommt er ja!** here he comes!; **ich habe zwei Stunden gewartet, aber sie kam und kam nicht** I waited two hours but she just didn't come; **der Nachtisch kommt gleich** the dessert is coming right now *or* is just coming; **er schießt auf alles, was ihm vor die Flinte kommt** he shoots at everything he gets in his sights; **da kann** *or* **könnte ja jeder kommen und sagen …** anybody could come along and say …; **wann soll das Baby kommen?** when's the baby due?; **wann kommt Ihr Baby?** when is your baby due?; **das Baby kam zu früh/an Heiligabend** the baby arrived early/on Christmas Eve; **das Kind ist gestern Nacht gekommen** the baby arrived last night; **bei Schmidts kommt ein Baby** the Schmidts are going to have a baby; **komm ich heut nicht, komm ich morgen** (*prov*) you'll see me when you see me; **kommt Zeit, kommt Rat** (*Prov*) things have a way of working themselves out; **wer zuerst kommt, mahlt zuerst** (*Prov*) first come first served (*prov*); **Torwart zu sein ist langweilig, wenn nie ein Ball kommt** being goalkeeper is boring if the ball never comes your way; **wann kommt der Bus endlich?** when is the bus going to come?; **wann soll der Zug kommen?** when's the train due?; **der Winter ist dieses Jahr sehr früh gekommen** winter has come very early this year; **der Winter kommt mit großen Schritten** winter is fast approaching; **der Mai ist gekommen** May is here; **ich glaube, es kommt ein Unwetter** I think there's some bad weather on the way; **nach dem Krieg kam noch die Hungersnot** after the war came the famine; **der Motor kommt nicht in Gang** the car is difficult to get started, the car won't start; **das Feuer kommt nicht richtig in Gang** it's difficult to get the fire going properly

◆ **(nach Hause) kommen** (= *ankommen*) to get home; (= *zurückkehren*) to come home; **ich komme oft erst um 6 Uhr nach Hause** I often don't get home until 6 o'clock; **wann kommst du nach Hause?** when will you get *or* be home today?; **ich komme heute etwas später nach Hause** I'll get *or* be home a bit later today; **bitte komm nach Hause!** please come home!; **wann kommst du endlich nach Hause?** when are you going to come home?; **mein Mann kommt alle drei Wochen nach Hause** my husband comes home every three weeks; **wann kommt er von der Arbeit?** when does he get home from work?; **ich komme manchmal erst spät von der Arbeit** I sometimes get home from work really late; **zum Essen kommen** to come home for lunch/dinner *etc*

◆ **komm!** come on!; **komm, wir gehen** come on, we're going; **komm, sag schon** come on, tell me; **komm, sei nicht so stur** come on don't be so obstinate; **ach komm!** come on!; **komm, fang bloß nicht wieder damit an** come on, don't start that again

◆ **komm, komm!** come on!; **komm, komm, wir müssen uns beeilen!** come on, we must hurry!; **komm, komm, werd nicht frech!** now now, don't be cheeky (*Brit*) *or* fresh (*US*)!

b = aufgenommen werden to go; **ins Gefängnis kommen** to go to prison; **auf die Universität kommen** to go to university; **ins Altersheim/Krankenhaus kommen** to go into an old people's home (*esp Brit*) *or* senior citizens' home (*US*)/into hospital; **in die** *or* **zur Schule kommen** to start school

c = hingehören to go; **das Buch kommt ins oberste Fach** the book goes on the top shelf; **der Kühlschrank kommt hier in die Ecke** the fridge is going in this corner; **das kommt unter "Sonstiges"** that comes under "miscellaneous"; **da kommt ein Deckel drauf** it has to have a lid on it

d = erscheinen, folgen to come; (*Zähne*) to come (through); **das Zitat/Lied kommt gleich** that line/song is coming now; **das Zitat/Lied kommt erst später** that line/song doesn't come till later; **das Lied kommt als Nächstes** that song is next; **ich komme zuerst an die Reihe** I'm first; **bohren, bis Öl/Grundwasser kommt** to bore until one strikes oil/finds water; **pass auf, ob hier ein Tankstelle kommt** watch out for a filling station; **jetzt muss bald die Grenze/Hannover kommen** we should soon be at the border/in Hanover; **die Kreuzung/das Zitat muss noch kommen** we haven't come to the crossing/that line yet; **das Schlimmste kommt noch** the worst is yet to come; **warte, das kommt noch** wait, that comes later; **jetzt kommts!** wait for it! (*inf*); **wie sie (gerade) kommen** just as they come

e = gelangen, erreichen können to get; (= *mit Hand etc erreichen können*) to reach; **wie komme ich nach London?** how do I get to London?; **ich komme zur Zeit nicht an die frische Luft/aus dem Haus** at the moment I never get out into the fresh air/out of the house; **durch den Zoll/die Prüfung kommen** to get through customs/the exam; **ich komme mit meiner Hand bis an die Decke** I can reach *or* touch the ceiling with my hand; **in das Alter kommen, wo …** to reach the age when …; **die Entwicklung kam zu ihrem Höhepunkt** developments reached their climax

f = aufgeführt oder gesendet werden (*TV, Rad, Theat etc*) to be on; **was kommt im Fernsehen?** what's on TV?; **was kommt diese Woche im Kino/Theater?** what's on at the cinema/theatre (*Brit*) *or* theater (*US*) this week?; **Kobra 13, bitte kommen!** come in Kobra 13!

g = geschehen, sich zutragen to happen; **egal, was kommt, ich fahre morgen nach Paris** whatever happens, I'm going to Paris tomorrow; **komme, was da wolle** come what may; **seine Hochzeit kam für alle überraschend** his wedding came as a surprise to everyone; **das musste ja so kommen, so musste es ja kommen** it had to happen; **das hätte nicht kommen dürfen** that shouldn't have happened → *auch* **2**

◆ **davon** *oder* **daher kommen** **daher kommt es, dass …** that's why …; **das kommt davon, dass …** that's because …; **das kommt davon** *or* **daher, dass es so viel geregnet hat** it's because of all the rain we've had; **das kommt davon, wenn man nicht zuhört** that comes of (*Brit*) *or* from not listening; **das kommt davon!** see what happens?

h = geraten **ins Wackeln kommen** to start shaking *or* to shake; **in Bewegung kommen** to start moving; **jetzt müssen wir mit dem Gerede aufhören und endlich in Bewegung kommen** now we must stop gossiping and get moving; **ins Reden kommen** to start talking; **ins Erzählen kommen** to start telling a story; **zum Blühen kommen** to start flowering *or* to flower; **zum Wachsen kommen** to start growing *or* to grow; **zum Stehen** *or* **Stillstand kommen** to come to a halt *or* standstill

i = sich entwickeln (*Samen, Pflanzen*) to come on; **der Schnittlauch kommt schön** the chives are coming on well; **schau mal, da kommen die Sonnenblumen!** look how the sunflowers are coming on!; **die Petersilie will dieses Jahr gar nicht kommen** the parsley won't come this year

j = einen Orgasmus haben (*inf*) to come (*sl*); **es kommt ihm** he's coming (*inf*)

k mit Dativ

> Wenn **kommen** mit dem Dativ und einem Substantiv oder Adjektiv verwendet wird, siehe auch unter dem Eintrag für das entsprechende Substantiv oder Adjektiv.

ihm kamen Zweifel he started to have doubts; **jdm kommen die Tränen** tears come to sb's eyes; **mir kommen die Tränen!** you're going to make me cry!; **ihm kam das Grausen** he was seized by terror; **mir kommt ein Gedanke** *or* **eine Idee** I've just had a thought; **langsam kam ihm das Verständnis** understanding slowly came to him; **es kommt mir gerade, dass …** it has just occurred to me that …; **das Wort/sein Name kommt mir im Moment nicht** the word/his name escapes me for the moment; **du kommst mir gerade recht** (*iro*) you're just what I need; **das kommt mir gerade recht** that's just fine; **jdm frech kommen** to be cheeky (*Brit*) *or* fresh (*US*) to sb; **jdm dumm kommen** to act stupid; **komm mir nur nicht so!** don't take that attitude with me!; **wie kommst du mir denn?** what kind of attitude is that?; **so darfst du mir nicht kommen!** you'd better not take that attitude with me!

l mit Verb

> Wenn **kommen** mit einem Verb verbunden ist, siehe auch unter dem Eintrag für das jeweilige Verb.

wir standen an der Ecke, und der kleine Johannes kam angelaufen we were standing on the corner and little Johannes came running up to us; **bei einem Unfall kommen immer Schaulustige herbeigelaufen** whenever there's an accident curious spectators come running; **da kommt ein Vogel geflogen** there's a bird; **ich komme dann zu dir gefahren** I'll drive over to your place then; **kommt essen!** come and eat!; **jdn besuchen kommen** to come and see sb; **wann kommt ihr mich mal besuchen?** when are you going to come and see me?; **auf dem Sessel/neben jdm zu sitzen kommen** to get to sit in the armchair/next to sb; **jdm kommen sehen** to see sb coming; **ich habe es ja kommen sehen** I saw it coming

◆ **jdn kommen lassen** to send for sb

◆ **etw kommen lassen** *Mahlzeit, Taxi* to order sth; *Seil* to let sth come; **den Motor kommen lassen** to rev the engine; **und jetzt müssen Sie die Kupplung langsam kommen lassen** and now let the clutch in gently *or* slowly

m mit Präposition

Wenn **kommen** mit einer Präposition verwendet wird, siehe auch unter dem Eintrag für die entsprechende Präposition.

♦ **an etw** *(acc)* **kommen** (= *sich verschaffen*) to get hold of sth; **ich bin mit der Hand an die Kochplatte gekommen** I touched the hotplate; **er ist an das Glasregal gekommen und hat es umgeworfen** he brushed against the glass shelf and knocked it over

♦ **auf etw** *(acc)* **kommen** (= *kosten, sich belaufen, sprechen über*) to come to; (= *sich erinnern, sich ausdenken*) to think of; **und dann kamen wir auf das leidige Thema Überstunden** then we came onto the vexed question of overtime; **auf eine Idee kommen** to get an idea; **auf einen Gedanken kommen** to get an idea; **wie kommst du darauf?** what makes you think that?; **darauf bin ich nicht gekommen** I didn't think of that; **der Wagen kommt in 16 Sekunden auf 100 km/h** the car reaches 100 km/h in 16 seconds; **auf jeden Haushalt kommen 100 Liter Wasser pro Tag** each household gets 100 litres (*Brit*) or liters (*US*) of water per day; **das kommt auf die Rechnung/auf mein Konto** that goes onto the bill/into my account; **ich komme im Moment nicht auf seinen Namen** his name escapes me for the moment; **auf ihn/darauf lasse ich nichts kommen** (*inf*) I won't hear a word against him/it

♦ **hinter etw** *(acc)* **kommen** (= *herausfinden*) to find sth out, to find out sth

♦ **mit etw/jdm kommen** da kommt sie mit ihrem kleinen Bruder here she comes *or* there she is with her little brother; **mit einer Frage/einem Anliegen kommen** to have a question/a request; **komm mir nicht wieder damit!** don't start that all over again!; **komm (mir) bloß nicht mit DER Entschuldigung** don't come to me with THAT excuse; **damit kann ich ihm nicht kommen** (*mit Entschuldigung*) I can't give him that; (*mit Bitte*) I can't ask him that; **komm mir nicht schon wieder mit deinem Vater!** don't start going on about your father again!

♦ **um etw kommen** (= *verlieren*) um Geld, Besitz, Leben to lose sth; um Essen, Schlaf to go without sth

♦ **zu etw kommen** (= *Zeit finden für*) to get round to sth; (= *erhalten*) to come by sth; zu Ehre to receive sth; (= *erben*) to come into sth; **wie komme ich zu der Ehre?** to what do I owe this honour (*Brit*) or honor (*US*)?; **wie bin ich zu der Ehre/zu einer Einladung, bei Ihnen eingeladen zu werden?** how come I've had the honour (*Brit*) or honor (*US*) of an invitation from you?; **zu einem Entschluss/einer Entscheidung/einer Einigung kommen** to come *or* get to a conclusion/a decision/an agreement

♦ **zu nichts kommen** (*zeitlich*) not to get (a)round to anything; (= *erreichen*) to achieve nothing

♦ **zu sich kommen** (= *Bewusstsein wiedererlangen*) to come round; (= *aufwachen*) to come to one's senses; (= *sich fassen*) to get over it; (= *sich finden*) to find oneself

2 – UNPERSÖNLICHES VERB

a **es kommen jetzt die Clowns** and now the clowns; **es kommen jetzt die Nachrichten** and now the news

b *im übertragenen Sinn* **es ist weit gekommen!** it has come to that!; **es kommt noch einmal so weit** *or* **dahin, dass** ... it will get to the point where ...; **so weit kommt es (noch)** that'll be the day (*inf*); **ich wusste, dass es so kommen würde** I knew that would happen; **wie kommt es, dass du ...?** how is it that you ...?, how come you ...? (*inf*); **dazu kam es gar nicht mehr** it didn't come to that; **wir wollten noch eine Reise nach Italien machen, aber es kam nicht mehr dazu** we would have liked to have gone to Italy, but it wasn't to be; **es kam zum Streit** there was a quarrel; **es kam eins zum anderen** one thing led to another; **und so kam es, dass ...** and that is how it came about *or* happened

that ...; **es kam, wie es kommen musste** the inevitable happened; **es kommt immer anders, als man denkt** (*prov*), **erstens kommt es anders und zweitens als man denkt** (*hum inf*) things never turn out the way you expect; **es mag kommen, wie es kommen will** come what may; **vielleicht gehe ich ins Kino oder einen trinken, wie es (gerade) kommt** (*inf*) maybe I'll go to the cinema, or for a drink, whatever (*inf*)

3 – TRANSITIVES VERB

(*inf.* = *kosten*) to cost; **das kommt Sie auf 200 Euro** that'll cost you 200 euros; **das kommt mich auf die Dauer teurer** that'll cost me more in the long term

Kom|men NT -s, *no pl* coming; **ein einziges ~ und Gehen** a constant coming and going; **etw ist im ~** sth is coming in, sth is on the way in; **jd ist im ~** sb is on his/her way up

kom|mend ADJ Jahr, Woche, Generation coming; Ereignisse, Mode future; **die nach uns Kommenden** (*geh*) the coming generations, generations to come; **(am) ~en Montag** next Monday; **~e Weihnachten** next Christmas; **in den ~en Jahren** in the coming years, in the years to come; **der ~e Meister** the future champion; **er ist der ~e Mann in der Partei** he is the rising star in the party

kom|men|su|ra|bel [kɔmɛnzuˈraːbl] ADJ (*Math, fig geh*) commensurable

Kom|ment [kɔˈmɑ̃ː] M -s, -s (*Univ*) code of conduct (*of student fraternity*)

Kom|men|tar [kɔmɛnˈtaːɐ] M -s, -e (= *Bemerkung, Stellungnahme*) comment; (*Press, Jur, Liter*) commentary; **jeden (weiteren) ~ ablehnen** to decline to comment (further) *or* to make any (further) comment; **kein ~!** no comment; **~ überflüssig!** no comment (necessary)!; **einen ~ (zu etw) abgeben** to (make a) comment (on sth); **musst du zu allem deinen ~ abgeben?** (*inf*) do you have a comment to make about everything?

kom|men|tar|los [-loːs] ADV without comment

Kom|men|ta|tor [kɔmɛnˈtaːtoɐ] M -s, **Kommentatoren** [-ˈtoːrən], **Kom|men|ta|to|rin** [-ˈtoːrɪn] F -, -nen commentator

kom|men|tie|ren [kɔmɛnˈtiːrən] ptp **kommentiert** VT (*Press etc*) to comment on; (*Jur, Liter*) to write a commentary on; **kommentierte Ausgabe** (*Liter*) annotated edition

Kom|mers [kɔˈmɛrs] M -es, -e evening meeting of student fraternity with drinking ceremony

Kom|merz [kɔˈmɛrts] M -es, *no pl* (*pej*) commercialism; **reiner ~** pure commercialism; **nur auf ~ aus sein** to have purely commercial interests, to be out for profit

kom|mer|zi|a|li|sie|ren [kɔmɛrtsialiˈziːrən] ptp **kommerzialisiert** VT **a** (= *vermarkten*) to commercialize **b** (= *Schulden umwandeln*) **eine öffentliche Schuld ~** to convert a public debt into a private loan

Kom|mer|zi|a|li|sie|rung F -, -en **a** (= *Vermarktung*) commercialization **b** (= *Schuldenumwandlung*) **die ~ einer öffentlichen Schuld** the conversion of a public debt into a private loan

Kom|mer|zi|al|rat [kɔmɛrˈtsiaː-l-] M (*Aus*) = **Kommerzienrat**

kom|mer|zi|ell [kɔmɛrˈtsiɛl] ADJ commercial **ADV** commercially; **rein ~ denken** to think purely in commercial terms *or* purely commercially

Kom|mer|zi|en|rat [kɔˈmɛrtsiən-] M (*old*) title conferred on distinguished businessman

Kom|mi|li|to|ne [kɔmiliˈtoːnə] M -n, -n, **Kom|mi|li|to|nin** [-ˈtoːnɪn] F -, -nen fellow student; **wir brauchen noch drei ~n, die Flugblätter verteilen** we need three more people *or* students to hand out leaflets

Kom|miss ▲ [kɔˈmɪs] M -es, *no pl* (*dated inf*) army; **beim ~ sein** to be in the army; **zum ~ müssen** to have to go into the army

Kom|mis|sar [kɔmɪˈsaːɐ] M -s, -e, **Kom|mis|sa|rin** [-ˈsaːrɪn] F -, -nen, (*esp Aus*) **Kom|mis|sär** [kɔmɪˈsɛːɐ] M -s, -e, **Kom|mis|sä|rin** [-ˈsɛːrɪn] F -, -nen (*Admin*) commissioner; (= *Polizeikommissar*) inspector; (*ranghöher*) (police) superintendent

Kom|mis|sa|ri|at [kɔmɪsaˈriaːt] NT -(e)s, -e **a** (*Admin*) (= *Amt*) commissionership; (= *Dienststelle, Amtsbereich*) commissioner's department **b** (*Polizei*) (= *Amt*) office of inspector; office of superintendent; (= *Dienststelle, Amtsbereich*) superintendent's department; (*Aus: = Polizeidienststelle*) police station

Kom|mis|sa|rin F , **Kom|mis|sä|rin** F → Kommissar

kom|mis|sa|risch [kɔmɪˈsaːrɪʃ] ADJ temporary ADV temporarily

Kom|miss|brot ▲ NT rye bread; (= *Armeebrot*) army bread

Kom|mis|si|on [kɔmɪˈsioːn] F -, -en **a** (= *Ausschuss*) committee; (*zur Untersuchung*) commission **b** (*Comm*) commission; **etw in ~ geben** to give sth (to a dealer) for sale on commission; **etw in ~ nehmen/haben** to take/have sth on commission

Kom|mis|si|o|när [kɔmɪsioˈnɛːɐ] M -s, -e, **Kom|mis|si|o|nä|rin** [-ˈnɛːrɪn] F -, -nen commission agent; (*im Verlagswesen*) wholesale bookseller, wholesaler

kom|mis|si|o|nie|ren [kɔmɪsioˈniːrən] ptp **kommissioniert** VT (*Aus*) to commission

Kom|mis|si|ons-: **Kom|mis|si|ons|buch|han|del** M wholesale book trade; **Kom|mis|si|ons|ge|bühr** F commission; **Kom|mis|si|ons|ge|schäft** NT commission *or* agency business

Kom|miss|stie|fel ▲ M army boot; (*fig pej*) jackboot

kom|mod [kɔˈmoːt] ADJ (*old, dial*) comfortable ADV comfortably

Kom|mo|de [kɔˈmoːdə] F -, -n chest of drawers; (*hohe*) tallboy, highboy (*US*)

Kom|mo|di|tät [kɔmodiˈtɛːt] F -, -en (*old*) comfort

Kom|mo|do|re [kɔmoˈdoːrə] M -s, -n or -s, **Kom|mo|do|rin** [-ˈdoːrɪn] F -, -nen (*Naut*) commodore; (*Aviat*) wing commander (*Brit*), lieutenant colonel (*US*)

kom|mu|nal [kɔmuˈnaːl] ADJ local; (= *städtisch auch*) municipal; **~es Wahlrecht** right to vote in local elections ADV locally; (= *städtisch auch*) municipally

Kom|mu|nal-: Kom|mu|nal|ab|ga|ben PL local rates and taxes *pl*; **Kom|mu|nal|an|lei|he** F municipal loan

kom|mu|na|li|sie|ren [kɔmunaliˈziːrən] ptp **kommunalisiert** VT to put under the control of the local authorities

Kom|mu|nal-: Kom|mu|nal|ob|li|ga|ti|on F municipal bond; **Kom|mu|nal|po|li|tik** F local government politics *sing or pl*; **Kom|mu|nal|ver|wal|tung** F local government; **Kom|mu|nal|wah|len** PL local (government) elections *pl*

Kom|mu|nar|de [kɔmuˈnardə] M -n, -n, **Kom|mu|nar|din** [-ˈnardɪn] F -, -nen (*Hist*) Communard **b** (*dated: = Mitglied einer Wohngemeinschaft*) member of a commune, commune-dweller, communard; **er ist ein ~** he lives in a commune

Kom|mu|ne [kɔˈmuːnə] F -, -n **a** local authority district **b** (= *Wohngemeinschaft*) commune **c** (*Hist: = Pariser Kommune*) (Paris) Commune

Kom|mu|ni|kant [kɔmuniˈkant] M -en, -en, **Kom|mu|ni|kan|tin** [-ˈkantɪn] F -, -nen (*Eccl*) communicant; (= *Erstkommunikant*) first communicant

Kom|mu|ni|ka|ti|on [kɔmunika'tsioːn] F **-, -en** communication; **die ~ ist unmöglich geworden** communication has become impossible

Kom|mu|ni|ka|ti|ons-: Kom|mu|ni|ka|ti|ons|mit|tel NT means *sing* of communication; **Kom|mu|ni|ka|ti|ons|sa|tel|lit** M communications satellite; **Kom|mu|ni|ka|ti|ons|schwie|rig|kei|ten** PL communication difficulties *pl*; **Kom|mu|ni|ka|ti|ons|wis|sen|schaf|ten** PL communication studies *pl*

kom|mu|ni|ka|tiv [kɔmunika'tiːf] ADJ communicative; *Brief etc auch* informative

Kom|mu|ni|kee ▲ [kɔmuni'keː] NT **-s, -s** communiqué

Kom|mu|ni|on [kɔmu'nioːn] F **-, -en** (*Eccl*) (Holy) Communion; (= *Erstkommunion*) first Communion

Kom|mu|ni|on-: Kom|mu|ni|on|bank F *pl* **-bänke** Communion rail; **Kom|mu|ni|on|kind** NT first communicant; **Kom|mu|ni|on|kleid** NT first communicant's (white) dress

Kom|mu|ni|qué [kɔmyni'keː, kɔmuni'keː] NT **-s, -s** communiqué

Kom|mu|nis|mus [kɔmu'nɪsmʊs] M **-**, *no pl* communism

Kom|mu|nist [kɔmu'nɪst] M **-en, -en, Kom|mu|nis|tin** [-'nɪstɪn] F **-, -nen** Communist

Kom|mu|nis|ten|fres|ser(in) M(F) (*pej inf*) Commie basher (*inf*)

kom|mu|nis|tisch [kɔmu'nɪstɪʃ] ADJ communist; **das Kommunistische Manifest** the Communist Manifesto

kom|mu|ni|zie|ren [kɔmuni'tsiːrən] *ptp* **kom|muni|ziert** VI **a** (= *in Kommunikation sein*) to communicate; **~de Röhren** (*Phys*) communicating tubes **b** (*Eccl*) to receive (Holy) Communion

Ko|mö|di|ant [komø'diant] M **-en, -en, Ko|mö|di|an|tin** [-'diantɪn] F **-, -nen a** (*old*) actor/actress, player (*old*) **b** (*fig*) play-actor

Ko|mö|di|an|ten-: ko|mö|di|an|ten|haft ADJ *Gebaren* theatrical; (*pej*) histrionic ADV *sich benehmen* theatrically; (*pej*) histrionically; **Ko|mö|di|an|ten|tum** [komø'diantntuːm] NT **-s**, *no pl* (*pej*) histrionics *pl*

Ko|mö|di|an|tin F → Komödiant

ko|mö|di|an|tisch [komø'diantɪʃ] ADJ (= *schauspielerisch*) acting; (*pej*) theatrical, histrionic ADV comically

Ko|mö|die [ko'møːdiə] F **-, -n** comedy; (*fig*) (= *heiteres Ereignis*) farce; (= *Täuschung*) play-acting; **die Stuttgarter ~** the Stuttgart Comedy Theatre (*Brit*) or Theater (*US*); **~ spielen** (*fig*) to put on an act

Kom|pag|non [kɔmpaŋ'jõː, 'kɔmpanjõ] M **-s, -s** (*Comm*) partner, associate; (*iro*) pal (*inf*), chum (*inf*), buddy (*inf*)

kom|pakt [kɔm'pakt] ADJ compact; *Gestein, Schicht, Brot, Masse* solid; (*inf*: = *gedrungen*) *Mensch* stocky ADV compactly

Kom|pakt-: Kom|pakt|an|la|ge F (*Rad*) audio system; **Kom|pakt|au|to** NT compact (*US*), medium-sized family saloon; **Kom|pakt|bau|wei|se** F compact functional style; **Kom|pakt|ka|me|ra** F compact camera; **Kom|pakt|ski** M compact ski; **Kom|pakt|wa|gen** M (*Aut*) small family car, subcompact (*US*)

Kom|pa|nie [kɔmpa'niː] F **-, -n** [-'niːən] (*Mil*) company; (*old Comm*) trading company; (= *Firma*) firm; **damit kann man ja eine ganze ~ füttern** that's enough to feed a whole army

Kom|pa|nie|chef(in) M(F), **Kom|pa|nie|füh|rer(in)** M(F) (*Mil*) company commander

Kom|pa|ra|ti|on [kɔmpara'tsioːn] F **-, -en** (*Gram*) comparison

Kom|pa|ra|tis|tik [kɔmpara'tɪstɪk] F **-**, *no pl* comparative literature

Kom|pa|ra|tiv ['kɔmparatiːf] M **-s, -e** [-və] (*Gram*) comparative

Kom|par|se [kɔm'parzə] M **-n, -n, Kom|par|sin** [-'parzɪn] F **-, -nen** (*Film*) extra; (*Theat*) supernumerary; **er war nur ein ~** he only had a walk-on part

Kom|par|se|rie [kɔmparzə'riː] F **-, -n** [-'riːən] extras *pl*; supernumeraries *pl*; **die ganze ~ ...** all those with walk-on parts ...

Kom|pass ▲ ['kɔmpas] M **-es, -e** compass; **nach dem ~** by the compass

Kom|pass-: Kom|pass|häus|chen ▲ [-hɔysçən] NT (*Naut*) binnacle; **Kom|pass|na|del** ▲ F compass needle

kom|pa|ti|bel [kɔmpa'tiːbl] ADJ (*liter, Tech*) compatible

Kom|pa|ti|bi|li|tät [kɔmpatibili'tɛːt] F **-, -en** (*liter, Tech*) compatibility

Kom|pen|di|um [kɔm'pɛndiʊm] NT **-s, Kompendien** [-diən] **a** (= *Abriss*) compendium **b** (*Phot*) lens hood (with bellows extension)

Kom|pen|sa|ti|on [kɔmpɛnza'tsioːn] F **-, -en** compensation

Kom|pen|sa|ti|ons|ge|schäft NT barter (transaction)

Kom|pen|sa|tor [kɔmpɛn'zaːtoːɐ] M **-s, Kompensatoren** [-'toːrən] (*Tech*) compensator

kom|pen|sie|ren [kɔmpɛn'ziːrən] *ptp* **kompensiert** VT to compensate for, to offset

kom|pe|tent [kɔmpe'tɛnt] ADJ competent; (= *befugt auch*) authorized; **für solche Fälle ist dieses Gericht nicht ~** this court has no jurisdiction in such cases, this court is not competent to decide such cases; **der dafür ~e Kollege** the man responsible for that; **dafür bin ich nicht ~** I'm not responsible for that ADV competently; **der Minister hat sich zu dieser Frage nicht besonders ~ geäußert** the minister did not speak very competently on the issue; **jdm ~ Auskunft geben** to inform sb knowledgeably

Kom|pe|tenz [kɔmpe'tɛnts] F **-, -en a** (*area of*) authority *or* competence; (*eines Gerichts*) jurisdiction, competence; **da hat er ganz eindeutig seine ~en überschritten** he has quite clearly exceeded his authority *or* powers here; **er hat die alleinige ~**, hierüber zu entscheiden he alone has the authority *or* competence *or* is competent to decide on this issue; **ich will dir nicht deine ~(en) streitig machen** I don't want to infringe on your field; **das fällt in die ~ dieses Amtes** that's the responsibility of this office; **seine mangelnde ~ in dieser Frage** his lack of competence in this issue **b** (*Ling*) competence

Kom|pe|tenz-: Kom|pe|tenz|be|reich M area of competence; **Kom|pe|tenz|ge|ran|gel** NT bickering over responsibilities; **Kom|pe|tenz|strei|tig|kei|ten** PL dispute over respective areas of responsibility; **Kom|pe|tenz|wirr|warr** M confusion about areas of responsibilities

Kom|pi|la|ti|on [kɔmpila'tsioːn] F **-, -en** (*geh*) compilation

kom|pi|lie|ren [kɔmpi'liːrən] *ptp* **kompiliert** VT (*geh*) to compile

kompl. *abbr von* **komplett** complete

Kom|ple|ment [kɔmple'mɛnt] NT **-(e)s, -e** (*Math*) complement

kom|ple|men|tär [kɔmplemɛn'tɛːɐ] ADJ complementary

Kom|ple|men|tär [kɔmplemɛn'tɛːɐ] M **-s, -e**, **Kom|ple|men|tä|rin** [-'tɛːrɪn] F **-, -nen** *fully liable partner in a limited partnership*

Kom|ple|men|tär|far|be F complementary colour (*Brit*) or color (*US*)

kom|ple|men|tie|ren [kɔmplemɛn'tiːrən] *ptp* **komplementiert** VT (*geh*) to complement

Kom|plet¹ [kõ'pleː, kɔm'pleː] NT **-(s), -s** (*Fashion*) matching dress/skirt and coat

Kom|plet² [kɔm'pleːt] F **-, -e** (*Eccl*) complin(e)

kom|plett [kɔm'plɛt] ADJ complete; **ein ~es Frühstück** a full breakfast; **ein ~es Menü** a (full) three course meal ADV completely

kom|plet|tie|ren [kɔmple'tiːrən] *ptp* **komplettiert** VT (*geh*) to complete

Kom|plett-: Kom|plett|lö|sung F complete solution; **Kom|plett|preis** M all-inclusive *or* all-in (*Brit*) price; **kom|plex** [kɔm'plɛks] ADJ complex ADV complexly; **die Situation stellt sich ~ dar** the situation appears to be complex; **~ aufgebaut** complex in structure; **Kom|plex** [kɔm'plɛks] M **-es, -e a** (= *Gebäudekomplex*) complex; (= *Fragen-/Themenkomplex*) group *or* set of questions/issues **b** (*Psych*) complex; **er steckt voller ~e** he has so many complexes *or* hang-ups (*inf*); **Kom|ple|xi|tät** [kɔmplɛksi'tɛːt] F **-**, *no pl* complexity; **Kom|pli|ce** [kɔm'pliːtsə] M **-n, -n** accomplice; **Kom|pli|ka|ti|on** [kɔmplika'tsioːn] F **-, -en** complication; **Kom|pli|ment** [kɔmpli'mɛnt] NT **-(e)s, -e** compliment; **jdm ~e machen** to pay sb compliments, to compliment sb (*wegen* on); **mein ~!** my compliments!; **Kom|pli|ze** [kɔm'pliːtsə] M **-n, -n, Kom|pli|zin** [-'pliːtsɪn] F **-, -nen** accomplice; **kom|pli|zie|ren** [kɔmpli'tsiːrən] *ptp* **kompliziert** VT to complicate; **kom|pli|ziert** [kɔm'pliːtsiːɐt] ADJ complicated, involved; (*Med*) *Bruch* compound; **sei doch nicht so ~** don't be so complicated ADV *aufgebaut* in a complicated way; **sich ~ ausdrücken** to express oneself in a complicated *or* an involved way; **das ist sehr ~ dargestellt** the presentation is quite complicated; **die Angelegenheit hat sich ~ entwickelt** the matter has become very complicated; **Kom|pli|ziert|heit** F **-**, *no pl* complexity; **Kom|pli|zin** F **-, -nen** accomplice; **Kom|plott** [kɔm'plɔt] NT **-(e)s, -e** plot, conspiracy; **ein ~ schmieden** to hatch a plot; **ein ~ zur Ermordung ...** a plot or conspiracy to murder ...; **Kom|po|nen|te** [kɔmpo'nɛntə] F **-, -n** component; **kom|po|nie|ren** [kɔmpo'niːrən] *ptp* **komponiert** VTI to compose; (*Liter auch*) to construct; **Kom|po|nist** [kɔmpo'nɪst] M **-en, -en, Kom|po|nis|tin** [-'nɪstɪn] F **-, -nen** composer; **Kom|po|si|ta** *pl von* Kompositum; **Kom|po|si|ti|on** [kɔmpozi'tsioːn] F **-, -en** composition; (*Liter auch*) construction; **kom|po|si|to|risch** [kɔmpozi'toːrɪʃ] ADJ compositional; **Kom|po|si|tum** [kɔm'poːzitʊm] NT **-s, Komposita** [-ta] (*Gram, Pharm*) compound; **Kom|post** [kɔm'pɔst, 'kɔmpɔst] M **-(e)s, -e** compost; **Kom|pos|ter** [kɔm'pɔstɐ] M **-s, -** compost maker

Kom|post-: Kom|post|er|de F compost; **Kom|post|hau|fen** M compost heap

Kom|pos|tier|an|la|ge F composting facility *or* station

kom|pos|tier|bar ADJ *Abfälle, Kunststoffe* compostible

kom|pos|tie|ren [kɔmpɔs'tiːrən] *ptp* **kompostiert** VT to compost VI to make compost

Kom|pott [kɔm'pɔt] NT **-(e)s, -e** stewed fruit, compote

kom|press ▲ [kɔm'prɛs] ADV (*Typ*) solid

Kom|pres|se [kɔm'prɛsə] F **-, -n** compress

Kom|pres|si|on [kɔmprɛ'sioːn] F **-, -en** (*Tech*) compression

Kom|pres|si|ons-: Kom|pres|si|ons|pro|gramm NT (*Comput*) compression program; **Kom|pres|si|ons|pum|pe** F pressure pump; **Kom|pres|si|ons|ver|band** M compression *or* pressure bandage

Kom|pres|sor [kɔm'prɛsoːɐ] M **-s, Kompresso|ren** [-'soːrən] compressor

kom|pri|mie|ren [kɔmpri'miːrən] *ptp* **kompri|miert** VT to compress; (*fig*) to condense

Kom|pro|miss ▲ [kɔmpro'mɪs] M **-es, -e** compromise; **einen ~ schließen** to (make) a compromise; **sie sind zu keinem ~ bereit** they are not prepared to compromise

Kom|pro|miss-: kom|pro|miss|be|reit ▲ ADJ prepared *or* willing to compromise *pred*; **Kom|pro|miss|be|reit|schaft** ▲ F willingness to compromise; **kom|pro|miss|fä|hig** ▲ ADJ able to compromise *pred*, capable of compromise *pred*; **kom|pro|miss|los** ▲ ADJ uncompromising; **Kom|pro|miss|lo|sig|keit** ▲ F -, *no pl* (*von Mensch*) uncompromising attitude; (*von Haltung, Politik*) uncompromising nature; **Kom|pro|miss|lö|sung** ▲ F compromise solution; **Kom|pro|miss|vor|schlag** ▲ M compromise proposal

kom|pro|mit|tie|ren [kɔmprɔmɪˈtiːrən] *ptp* **kompromittiert** VT to compromise VR to compromise oneself

Kom|so|mol [ˈkɔmzoˈmɔl] M -, *no pl* Comsomol

Kom|so|mol|ze [ˈkɔmzoˈmɔltsə] M -n, -n, **Kom|so|mol|zin** [-ˈmɔltsɪn] F -, -nen member of the Comsomol

Kom|tess [kɔmˈtɛs, kõˈtɛs] F - *or* -e, -en countess

Kom|tur [kɔmˈtuːɐ] M -s, -e commander (of a knightly order)

Kon|den|sat [kɔndɛnˈzaːt] NT -(e)s, -e condensate; (*fig*) distillation, condensation

Kon|den|sa|ti|on [kɔndɛnzaˈtsioːn] F -, -en (*Chem, Phys*) condensation

Kon|den|sa|tor [kɔndɛnˈzaːtoːɐ] M -s, **Kondensatoren** [-ˈtoːrən] (*Aut, Chem*) condenser; (*Elec auch*) capacitor

kon|den|sie|ren [kɔndɛnˈziːrən] *ptp* **kondensiert** VTI (*vi: aux haben or sein*) (*lit, fig*) to condense; (*fig auch*) to distil (*Brit*), to distill (*US*)

Kon|dens- [kɔnˈdɛns-]: **Kon|dens|milch** F evaporated milk; **Kon|dens|strei|fen** M (*Aviat*) vapour (*Brit*) *or* vapor (*US*) trail; **Kon|dens|was|ser** NT condensation

Kon|di|ti|on [kɔndiˈtsioːn] F -, -en a condition, shape, form; (= *Durchhaltevermögen*) stamina; **wie ist seine ~?** what sort of condition *etc* is he in?; **er hat überhaupt keine ~** he is completely unfit; (*fig*) he has absolutely no stamina; **er zeigte heute eine ausgezeichnete ~** he was in top form today b *usu pl* (*Comm: = Bedingung*) condition; **zu den üblichen ~en** under the usual terms

kon|di|ti|o|nal [kɔnditsioˈnaːl] ADJ conditional

Kon|di|ti|o|nal|satz M conditional clause

kon|di|ti|o|nie|ren [kɔnditsioˈniːrən] *ptp* **konditioniert** VT (*Biol, Psych*) to condition

Kon|di|ti|ons-: **kon|di|ti|ons|schwach** ADJ (*very*) unfit; **Kon|di|ti|ons|schwä|che** F lack *no pl* of fitness; **kon|di|ti|ons|stark** ADJ very fit; **Kon|di|ti|ons|trai|ning** NT fitness training

Kon|di|tor [kɔnˈdiːtoːɐ] M -s, **Konditoren** [-ˈtoːrən], **Kon|di|to|rin** [-ˈtoːrɪn] F -, -nen pastry cook (*Brit*), confectioner (*US*)

Kon|di|to|rei F -, -en cake shop (*Brit*), confectioner's shop (*US*); (*mit Café*) café

Kon|di|tor|wa|ren PL cakes and pastries *pl*

Kon|do|lenz- [kɔndoˈlɛnts] *in cpds* of condolence; **Kon|do|lenz|be|such** M visit of condolence; **Kon|do|lenz|buch** NT book of condolence; **Kon|do|lenz|schrei|ben** NT (= *Kondolenzbrief*) letter of condolence

kon|do|lie|ren [kɔndoˈliːrən] *ptp* **kondoliert** VI (*jdm*) **~** to offer one's condolences (to sb), to condole with sb; **schriftlich ~** to write a letter of condolence

Kon|dom [kɔnˈdoːm] M OR NT -s, -e condom, contraceptive sheath

Kon|do|me|rie [kɔndoməˈriː] F -, -n [-ˈriːən] (*inf*) condom shop (*esp Brit*) *or* store (*US*)

Kon|do|mi|ni|um [kɔndoˈmiːniʊm] NT -s, **Kondominien** [-niən] condominium

Kon|dor [ˈkɔndoːɐ] M -s, -e condor

Kon|duk|teur [kɔndʊkˈtøːɐ] M -s, -e (*Aus, Sw*) conductor

Kon|duk|teu|rin [kɔndʊkˈtøːrɪn] F -, -nen (*Aus, Sw*) conductress

Ko|nen *pl von* **Konus**

Kon|fekt [kɔnˈfɛkt] NT -(e)s, -e confectionery

Kon|fek|ti|on [kɔnfɛkˈtsioːn] F -, -en (= *Herstellung*) manufacture of off-the-peg (*Brit*) *or* ready-made *or* ready-to-wear clothing; (= *Industrie*) clothing industry, rag trade (*inf*); (= *Bekleidung*) off-the-peg (*Brit*) *or* ready-made *or* ready-to-wear clothes *pl or* clothing

Kon|fek|ti|o|när [kɔnfɛktsioˈnɛːɐ] M -s, -e, **Kon|fek|ti|o|nä|rin** [-ˈnɛːrɪn] F -, -nen clothing manufacturer

kon|fek|ti|o|nie|ren [kɔnfɛktsioˈniːrən] *ptp* **konfektioniert** VT *Kleidung* to make

Kon|fek|ti|o|nie|rung [kɔnfɛktsioˈniːrʊŋ] F -, -en (= *serienmäßiges Herstellen*) manufacture, (assembly-line) production

Kon|fek|ti|ons- *in cpds* off-the-peg (*Brit*), ready-made, ready-to-wear; **Kon|fek|ti|ons|an|zug** M off-the-peg *etc* suit; **Kon|fek|ti|ons|ge|schäft** NT (off-the-peg *etc*) clothes shop *or* store; **Kon|fek|ti|ons|grö|ße** F (*clothing*) size; **welche ~ haben Sie?** what size are you?; **Kon|fek|ti|ons|wa|re** F off-the-peg *etc* clothing

Kon|fe|renz [kɔnfeˈrɛnts] F -, -en conference; (= *Besprechung*) meeting; (= *Ausschuss*) committee

Kon|fe|renz- *in cpds* conference; **Kon|fe|renz|raum** M conference room; **Kon|fe|renz|schal|tung** F (*Telec*) conference circuit; (*Rad, TV*) (television/radio) linkup; **Kon|fe|renz|teil|neh|mer(in)** M(F) → **Konferenz** person attending a conference/meeting; **Kon|fe|renz|zim|mer** NT conference room

kon|fe|rie|ren [kɔnfeˈriːrən] *ptp* **konferiert** VI to confer, to have *or* hold a conference *or* discussion (*über +acc* on *or* about)

Kon|fes|si|on [kɔnfɛˈsioːn] F -, -en (religious) denomination; **welche ~ haben Sie?** what denomination are you?; **die Augsburger ~** the Augsburg Confession

kon|fes|si|o|nell [kɔnfɛsioˈnɛl] ADJ denominational ADV **~ gebundene Schulen** schools which are affiliated with a specific denomination; **~ verschiedene Ehen** marriages between different religions

Kon|fes|si|ons-: **kon|fes|si|ons|los** ADJ nondenominational, undenominational; **Kon|fes|si|ons|schu|le** F denominational school

Kon|fet|ti [kɔnˈfɛti] NT -s, *no pl* confetti

Kon|fet|ti-: **Kon|fet|ti|re|gen** M shower of confetti; (*in US: bei Empfängen*) shower of ticker tape; **Kon|fet|ti|schlacht** F confetti battle

Kon|fi|dent [kɔnfiˈdɛnt] M -en, -en (*old*) confidant; (*Aus*) police informer

Kon|fi|den|tin [kɔnfiˈdɛntɪn] F -, -nen (*old*) confidante; (*Aus*) police informer

Kon|fi|gu|ra|ti|on [kɔnfigʊraˈtsioːn] F -, -en configuration

kon|fi|gu|rie|ren [kɔnfigʊˈriːrən] *ptp* **konfiguriert** VT *Computer, Software* to configure

Kon|fir|mand [kɔnfɪrˈmant] M -en, -en [-dn], **Kon|fir|man|din** [-ˈmandɪn] F -, -nen (*Eccl*) candidate for confirmation, confirmand

Kon|fir|man|den|bla|se F (*inf*) weak *or* Chinese (*hum sl*) bladder

Kon|fir|man|den|un|ter|richt M confirmation classes *pl*

Kon|fir|ma|ti|on [kɔnfɪrmaˈtsioːn] F -, -en (*Eccl*) confirmation

Kon|fir|ma|ti|ons- *in cpds* confirmation; **Kon|fir|ma|ti|ons|spruch** M confirmation text (*chosen by confirmand as motto*)

kon|fir|mie|ren [kɔnfɪrˈmiːrən] *ptp* **konfirmiert** VT (*Eccl*) to confirm

Kon|fi|se|rie [kõfizəˈriː] F -, -n [-ˈriːən] (*Sw*) a (= *Konditorei*) cake shop (*Brit*), confectioner's (*shop*) (*US*); (*mit Café*) café b (= *Konfekt*) confectionery

Kon|fis|ka|ti|on [kɔnfɪskaˈtsioːn] F -, -en confiscation

kon|fis|zie|ren [kɔnfɪsˈtsiːrən] *ptp* **konfisziert** VT to confiscate

Kon|fi|tü|re [kɔnfiˈtyːrə] F -, -n jam

Kon|flikt [kɔnˈflɪkt] M -s, -e conflict; **bewaffneter ~** armed conflict; **mit etw in ~ geraten** to come into conflict with sth; **kommst du da nicht mit deinem Gewissen in ~?** how can you reconcile that with your conscience?; **er befindet sich in einem ~** he is in a state of inner conflict

Kon|flikt-: **Kon|flikt|be|ra|tung** F (*vor Abtreibung*) abortion counselling (*Brit*) *or* counseling (*US*); **kon|flikt|fä|hig** ADJ **~ sein** to be able to deal with conflict; **wir benötigen einen ~en Manager** we need a manager who is able to deal with conflict; **er ist nicht ~** he isn't good at dealing with conflict; **Kon|flikt|fall** M conflict; **im ~** in case of conflict; **Kon|flikt|feld** NT area of conflict; **Kon|flikt|for|scher(in)** M(F) researcher into conflict; **Kon|flikt|for|schung** F conflict studies *pl*, research into the subject of conflict; **kon|flikt|frei** ADV conflict-free ADV without conflict; **kon|flikt|freu|dig** ADJ combative; **er ist sehr ~** he is very combative, he thrives on conflict; **kon|flikt|ge|la|den** ADJ conflict-ridden; *Situation* explosive; **Kon|flikt|herd** M (*esp Pol*) centre (*Brit*) *or* center (*US*) of conflict; **kon|flikt|los** ADJ, ADV without conflict; **kon|flikt|reich** ADJ full of conflict; **kon|flikt|scheu** ADJ **~ sein** to be afraid of conflict; **ein ~er Mensch** someone who is afraid of dealing with conflict; **Kon|flikt|si|tu|a|ti|on** F conflict situation; **Kon|flikt|stoff** M cause for conflict; **kon|flikt|träch|tig** ADJ *Situation* likely to lead to conflict

Kon|fö|de|ra|ti|on [kɔnfødɛraˈtsioːn] F -, -en confederacy

kon|fö|de|rie|ren [kɔnfødeˈriːrən] *ptp* **konföderiert** VR (*liter*) to confederate

Kon|fö|de|rier|te(r) [kɔnfødeˈriːɐtə] MF *decl as adj* confederate

kon|form [kɔnˈfɔrm] ADJ *Ansichten etc* concurring; **in etw** (*dat*) **~ sein** to agree on sth ADV **mit jdm/etw ~ gehen** to agree with sb/sth (*in +dat* about), to be in agreement with sb/sth (*in +dat* about)

-kon|form ADJ SUF in conformity with; **CSU-konforme Kandidaten** candidates adhering to the CSU line

Kon|for|mis|mus [kɔnfɔrˈmɪsmʊs] M -, *no pl* conformism

Kon|for|mist [kɔnfɔrˈmɪst] M -en, -en, **Kon|for|mis|tin** [-ˈmɪstɪn] F -, -nen (*pej*) conformist

kon|for|mis|tisch [kɔnfɔrˈmɪstɪʃ] ADJ conformist, conforming ADV **~ eingestellt sein** to tend to conform with everything; **sich ~ verhalten** to be a conformist

Kon|for|mi|tät [kɔnfɔrmiˈtɛːt] F -, -en conformity

Kon|fra|ter [kɔnˈfraːtɐ] M (*Eccl*) fellow clergyman; fellow monk

Kon|fron|ta|ti|on [kɔnfrɔntaˈtsioːn] F -, -en confrontation

Kon|fron|ta|ti|ons|kurs M **auf ~ gehen, ~ steuern** to be heading for a confrontation

kon|fron|tie|ren [kɔnfrɔnˈtiːrən] *ptp* **konfrontiert** VT to confront (*mit* with); **zwei Parteien ~** to bring two parties face to face, to confront two parties with one another

Kon|fron|tie|rung F -, -en confrontation

kon|fus [kɔnˈfuːs] ADJ confused, muddled ADV confusedly; **~ klingen** to sound confused; **ein ~ geschriebener Bericht** a report written in a confused style

Kon|fu|si|on F -, -en confusion

kon|fu|zi|a|nisch [kɔnfuˈtsiaːnɪʃ] ADJ Confucian

Kon|fu|zi|a|nis|mus M -, *no pl* Confucianism

Kon|fu|zi|us [kɔnˈfuːtsiʊs] M -' Confucius

kon|ge|ni|al [kɔŋge'nia:l] ADJ *(geh)* sympathetic; **~e Geister** kindred *or* congenial spirits

Kon|glo|me|rat [kɔŋglome'ra:t, kɔŋ-] NT **-(e)s, -e** **a** *(Geol)* conglomerate **b** *(= Ansammlung)* conglomeration

Kon|go ['kɔŋgo] M **-(s)** **a** *(auch* **Demokratische Republik Kongo)** (Democratic Republic of the) Congo; *(auch* **Kongo-Brazzaville)** (Republic of the) Congo **b** *(= Fluss)* Congo

Kon|go|le|se [kɔŋgo'le:zə] M **-n, -n, Kon|go|le|sin** [-'le:zɪn] F **-, -nen** Congolese

kon|go|le|sisch [kɔŋgo'le:zɪʃ] ADJ Congolese

Kon|gress ▲ [kɔn'grɛs, kɔŋ-] M **-es, -e** **a** *(Pol)* congress; *(fachlich)* convention, conference; **der Wiener ~** the Congress of Vienna **b** *(in USA)* Congress

Kon|gress-: Kon|gress|hal|le F congress *or* conference hall, convention hall *(esp US)*; **Kon|gress|mit|glied** ▲ NT **a** → **Kongress a** person attending a congress/conference *or* convention **b** *(in USA)* congressman/-woman; **Kon|gress|teil|neh|mer(in)** ▲ M(F) → **Kongress a** person attending a congress/conference *or* convention; **Kon|gress|zent|rum** ▲ NT → **Kongress a** congress/conference centre *(Brit)* or center *(US)*

kon|gru|ent [kɔngru'ɛnt, kɔŋ-] ADJ *(Math)* congruent; *(Gram)* concordant, congruent; *(geh)* Ansichten concurring

Kon|gru|enz [kɔngru'ɛnts, kɔŋ-] F **-, -en** *(Math)* congruence; *(Gram)* concord, agreement, congruence; *(geh: von Ansichten)* concurrence

kon|gru|ie|ren [kɔngru'i:rən, kɔŋ-] ptp **kongruiert** VI to be congruent; *(geh: Ansichten)* to concur, to correspond

K.-o.-Nie|der|la|ge [ka:'|o:-] F KO defeat

Ko|ni|fe|re [koni'fe:rə] F **-, -n** conifer

Kö|nig ['kø:nɪç] M **-s, -e** [-gə] king; **des ~s Rock** *(old, liter)* the king's uniform; **die Heiligen Drei ~e** The Three Kings *or* Magi; **der ~ der Tiere** the king of the beasts; **der ~ der Lüfte** the lord of the skies; **während der Weltmeisterschaft regierte in Deutschland ~ Fußball** during the World Cup Germany went football mad *(Brit)* or soccer crazy *(US)*; **der Kunde ist ~** the customer is always right

Kö|ni|gin ['kø:nɪgɪn] F **-, -nen** *(auch Zool)* queen; **~ der Nacht** *(Bot)* queen of the night, night-flowering cereus

Kö|ni|gin-: Kö|ni|gin|mut|ter F *pl* **-mütter** queen mother; **Kö|ni|gin|pas|te|te** F vol-au-vent; **Kö|ni|gin|wit|we** F dowager queen

kö|nig|lich ['kø:nɪklɪç] ADJ royal; *Auftreten, Stolz etc auch* regal; *Geschenk, Gehalt* princely; **das ~e Spiel** chess, the royal game, the game of kings; **Seine/Ihre Königliche Hoheit** His/Her Royal Highness; **~-preußisch/bayrisch** Royal Prussian/Bavarian ADV **a** *(inf: = köstlich, ungeheuer)* **sich ~ freuen** to be as pleased as Punch *(inf)*; **sich ~ amüsieren** to have the time of one's life *(inf)* **b** *(= fürstlich)* bewirten like royalty; *belohnen* richly

Kö|nig|reich NT kingdom, realm *(poet)*

Kö|nigs-: kö|nigs|blau ADJ royal blue; **Kö|nigs|hof** M royal *or* king's court; **Kö|nigs|ker|ze** F *(Bot)* mullein; **Kö|nigs|kind** NT *(liter)* royal son/daughter; **Kö|nigs|kro|ne** F royal crown; **Kö|nigs|paar** NT royal couple; **Kö|nigs|mord** M regicide; **Kö|nigs|ma|cher(in)** M(F) *(lit, fig)* kingmaker; **Kö|nigs|sohn** M *(liter)* king's son, prince; **Kö|nigs|ti|ger** M Bengal tiger; **Kö|nigs|toch|ter** F *(liter)* king's daughter, princess; **kö|nigs|treu** ADJ royalist; **Kö|nigs|was|ser** NT , *no pl* *(Chem)* aqua regia; **Kö|nigs|weg** M *(fig: = idealer Weg)* ideal way; **Kö|nigs|wür|de** F royal dignity

Kö|nig|tum ['kø:nɪçtu:m] NT **-s, Königtümer** [-ty:mə] **a** *no pl* kingship **b** *(= Reich)* kingdom

ko|nisch ['ko:nɪʃ] ADJ conical ADV conically

Kon|jek|tur [kɔnjɛk'tu:ɐ] F **-, -en** *(= Vermutung)* conjecture; *(Liter: = Lesart)* conjectured version

Kon|ju|ga|ti|on [kɔnjuga'tsio:n] F **-, -en** conjugation

kon|ju|gie|ren [kɔnju'gi:rən] ptp **konjugiert** VT to conjugate

Kon|junk|ti|on [kɔnjʊŋk'tsio:n] F **-, -en** *(Astron, Gram)* conjunction

Kon|junk|ti|o|nal|satz [kɔnjʊŋktsio'na:l-] M *(Gram)* conjunctional clause

Kon|junk|tiv ['kɔnjʊŋktɪf] M **-s, -e** [-və] *(Gram)* subjunctive

kon|junk|ti|visch ['kɔnjʊŋkti:vɪʃ] ADJ subjunctive

Kon|junk|tur [kɔnjʊŋk'tu:ɐ] F **-, -en** economic situation, economy; *(= Hochkonjunktur)* boom; **steigende/fallende** *or* **rückläufige ~** upward/downward economic trend, increasing/decreasing economic activity

Kon|junk|tur-: kon|junk|tur|ab|hän|gig ADJ dependent on economic factors; **Kon|junk|tur|ab|hän|gig|keit** F dependence on economic factors; **Kon|junk|tur|ab|schwung** M economic downturn; **Kon|junk|tur|auf|schwung** M economic upturn; **kon|junk|tur|be|dingt** ADJ influenced by *or* due to economic factors; **Kon|junk|tur|be|le|bung** F business revival; *(= aktives Beleben der Konjunktur)* stimulation of the economy

kon|junk|tu|rell [kɔnjʊŋktu'rɛl] ADJ economic; *Arbeitslosigkeit* resulting from the economic situation, due to economic factors ADV economically; **~ bedingt** caused by economic factors

Kon|junk|tur-: Kon|junk|tur|flau|te F economic slowdown; *(= ernsthafte Krise)* slump, recession; **Kon|junk|tur|kli|ma** NT economic *or* business climate; **Kon|junk|tur|po|li|tik** F measures *or* policies aimed at preventing economic fluctuation; **Kon|junk|tur|rück|gang** M slowdown in the economy; **Kon|junk|tur|schwä|che** F weakness in the economy; **Kon|junk|tur|zu|schlag** M refundable increase in taxation paid into the Bundesbank to help the national economy

kon|kav [kɔn'ka:f, kɔŋ-] ADJ concave ADV concavely

Kon|kav|spie|gel M concave mirror

Kon|kla|ve [kɔn'kla:və, kɔŋ-] NT **-s, -n** *(Eccl)* conclave

Kon|klu|si|on [kɔnklu'zio:n, kɔŋ-] F **-, -en** *(geh, Philos)* conclusion

Kon|kor|danz [kɔnkɔr'dants, kɔŋ-] F **-, -en** concordance

Kon|kor|dat [kɔnkɔr'da:t, kɔŋ-] NT **-(e)s, -e** concordat

kon|kret [kɔn'kre:t, kɔŋ-] ADJ concrete; **ich kann dir nichts Konkretes sagen** I can't tell you anything definite *or* concrete ADV **drück dich etwas ~er aus** would you put that in rather more concrete terms; **ich kann mir ~ vorstellen, wie ...** I can very clearly imagine how ...; **ich kann es dir noch nicht ~ sagen** I can't tell you definitely

kon|kre|ti|sie|ren [kɔnkreti'zi:rən, kɔŋ-] ptp **konkretisiert** VT to put in concrete form *or* terms

Kon|ku|bi|nat [kɔnkubi'na:t, kɔŋ-] **-(e)s, -e** NT concubinage

Kon|ku|bi|ne [kɔnku'bi:nə, kɔŋ-] F **-, -n** concubine

Kon|kur|rent [kɔnkʊ'rɛnt, kɔŋ-] M **-en, -en, Kon|kur|ren|tin** [-'rɛntɪn] F **-, -nen** rival; *(Comm auch)* competitor

Kon|kur|renz [kɔnkʊ'rɛnts, kɔŋ-] F **-, -en** *(= Wettbewerb)* competition, rivalry; *(= Konkurrenzbetrieb)* competitors *pl*; *(= Gesamtheit der Konkurrenten)* competition, competitors *pl*; **die ~ in diesem Sport/auf diesem Gebiet ist größer geworden** the competition in this sport/field has increased; **jdm ~ machen** *(Comm, fig)* to compete with sb; *(Comm auch)* to be in competition

---

with sb; **zur ~ (über)gehen** to go over to the competition; **als ~ zu etw** as competition for sth; **außer ~ sein** to have no competition; **dieser Film läuft außer ~** *(bei Festival etc)* the film is running outside of the main competition

Kon|kur|renz-: Kon|kur|renz|druck M , *no pl* pressure of competition; **kon|kur|renz|fä|hig** ADJ competitive; **Kon|kur|renz|fä|hig|keit** F competitiveness; **Kon|kur|renz|kampf** M competition; *(zwischen zwei Menschen auch)* rivalry; **wir müssen mit einem sehr harten ~ rechnen** we have to reckon with some very tough competition; **ein ~, bei dem wir uns durchgesetzt haben** a competitive situation in which we won out; **Kon|kur|renz|klau|sel** F *(in Vertrag)* noncompetition clause; **kon|kur|renz|los** ADJ without competition ADV **das Angebot ist ~ günstig** you won't find a better offer anywhere else; **~ billig** undoubtedly the cheapest; **Kon|kur|renz|neid** M , *no pl* professional jealousy; **Kon|kur|renz|pro|dukt** NT rival product; **Kon|kur|renz|ver|bot** NT (agreement on) restraint of trade

kon|kur|rie|ren [kɔnkʊ'ri:rən, kɔŋ-] ptp **konkurriert** VI to compete; *(Comm auch)* to be in competition

Kon|kurs [kɔn'kʊrs, kɔŋ-] M **-es, -e** bankruptcy; **in ~ gehen** to go bankrupt, to go into receivership *(esp form)*; **~ machen** *(inf)* to go bankrupt *or* bust *(inf)* → **anmelden**

Kon|kurs-: Kon|kurs|er|öff|nung F opening of bankruptcy proceedings; **Kon|kurs|mas|se** F bankrupt's estate; **Kon|kurs|ver|fah|ren** NT bankruptcy proceedings *pl*; **Kon|kurs|ver|wal|ter(in)** M(F) receiver; *(von Gläubigern bevollmächtigt)* trustee

kön|nen ['kœnən] ✪ 36, 37.4, 42.3, 42.4, 43.3, 43.4, 52.2 pret **konnte** ['kɔntə], ptp **gekonnt** *or* *(bei modal aux vb)* **können** [gə'kɔnt, 'kœnən] VTI, MODAL AUX VB **a** *(= vermögen)* to be able to; **ich kann es/das machen** I can do it, I am able to do it; **ich kann es/das nicht machen** I cannot *or* can't do it, I am not able to do it; **man konnte ihn retten** they were able to save him, they managed to save him; **man konnte ihn nicht retten** they couldn't save him, they were unable to save him; **ich konnte es nicht verstehen** I could not *or* couldn't understand it, I was unable to understand it; **ich habe es sehen ~** I could see it, I was able to see it; **es ist furchtbar, nicht schlafen zu ~** it's terrible not to be able to sleep; **er hat es gekonnt** he could do it, he was able to do it; **morgen kann ich nicht** I can't (manage) tomorrow; **das hättest du gleich sagen ~** you could *or* might have said that straight away; **das hätte ich dir gleich sagen ~** I could have told you that straight away; **ich kann das nicht mehr sehen** I can't stand the sight of it any more; **ich kann das nicht mehr hören** I don't want to hear that again; **ich kann nicht mehr** I can't go on; *(ertragen)* I can't take any more; *(essen)* I can't manage *or* eat any more; **kannst du noch?** can you go on?; *(essen)* can you manage some more?; **mir kann keiner!** *(inf)* I'm all right, Jack *(Brit inf)*, it's not my problem; **ich habe das alles schriftlich, mir kann keiner!** I've got it all in writing, they can't touch me; **so schnell er konnte** as fast as he could *or* was able to; **~ vor Lachen!** *(inf)* I wish I could, chance would be a fine thing *(inf)*; **man kann alles, wenn man (nur) will** where there's a will there's a way *(Prov)*

b *(= beherrschen)* Sprache to (be able to) speak; *Schach* to be able to play; *Klavier spielen, lesen, schwimmen, Ski laufen etc* to be able to, to know how to; **er kann seine Schulaufgabe wieder nicht** he can't do his homework again; *(= nicht gemacht)* he hasn't done his homework again; **was ~ Sie?** what can you do?; **was du alles kannst!** the things you can do!; **er kann was** he's very capable *or* able; **unser Chef kann viel** our boss is a very capable *or* able man; **unser Chef kann nichts** our boss is incapable *or* useless; **er kann gut Englisch** he speaks English

---

well; **er kann kein Französisch** he doesn't speak French; **er kann/er kann nicht schwimmen** he can/can't swim → *auch* **gekonnt**

c (= *dürfen*) to be allowed to, to be permitted to; **kann ich jetzt gehen?** can I go now?; **könnte ich ...?** could I ...?; **er kann sich nicht beklagen** he can't complain; **man kann wohl sagen, dass ...** one could well say that ...; **du kannst mich (gern haben)!** (*inf*) get lost! (*inf*); **er kann mich (mal)** (*inf*) he can get stuffed (*Brit inf*), he can go to hell (*inf*)

d (= *möglich sein*) **Sie könnten Recht haben** you could *or* might *or* may be right; **er kann jeden Augenblick kommen** he could *or* might *or* may come any minute; **das kann nur er gewesen sein** it can only have been him; **das kann nicht sein** that can't be true; **das kann fast nicht sein** that can't be true, it's almost unbelievable; **es kann sein, dass er dabei war** he could *or* might *or* may have been there; **es kann nicht sein, dass er dabei war** he couldn't *or* can't possibly have been there; **kann sein** maybe, could be

e (*mit Partikel*) **für etw ~** to be responsible for sth, to be to blame for sth; **ich kann nichts dafür** it's not my fault; **ich kann nichts dazu** I can't do anything about it

Kön|nen NT **-s**, *no pl* ability, skill

Kön|ner ['kœnɐ] M **-s, -**, **Kön|ne|rin** [-ərɪn] F **-, -nen** expert

Kon|nex [kɔ'nɛks] M **-es, -e** (*geh*) connection; (= *Verbindung auch*) contact

Kon|nos|se|ment [kɔnɔsə'mɛnt] NT **-s, -s** (*Comm*) bill of lading

kon|nte *pret von* **können**

Kon|rek|tor ['kɔn-] M , **Kon|rek|to|rin** F (*an Schule*) deputy head teacher (*Brit*), assistant principal; (*an Universität*) deputy vice chancellor (*Brit*), vice president (*US*)

Kon|sek|ra|ti|on [kɔnzekra'tsio:n] F **-, -en** (*Eccl*) consecration

kon|sek|rie|ren [kɔnze'kri:rən] *ptp* **konsekriert** VT (*Eccl*) to consecrate

kon|se|ku|tiv ['kɔnzekuti:f, kɔnzeku'ti:f] ADJ consecutive

Kon|se|ku|tiv|satz M consecutive clause

Kon|sens [kɔn'zɛns] M **-es, -e** [-zə] agreement, assent, consent

kon|se|quent [kɔnze'kvɛnt] ADJ consistent; (*Sport*) Deckung close, tight; **~e Weiterentwicklung eines Stils** logically consistent development of a style
ADV *sich weigern, einhalten, befolgen* strictly; *ablehnen* emphatically; *verfechten, eintreten für* rigorously; *behandeln, argumentieren, verbieten* consistently; **~ handeln** to be consistent; **er hat ~ "Nein" gesagt** he stuck to his answer of "no"; **wir werden ~ durchgreifen** we will take rigorous action; **wenn du das ~ durchdenkst** if you follow it through to its logical conclusion; **eine Spur ~ verfolgen** to follow up a clue rigorously; **ein Ziel ~ verfolgen** to pursue an objective single-mindedly; **einen Fall ~ untersuchen** to investigate a case rigorously *or* thoroughly

Kon|se|quenz [kɔnze'kvɛnts] F **-, -en a** (= *Schlussfolgerung*) consequence; **die ~en tragen** to take the consequences; **(aus etw) die ~en ziehen** to come to the obvious conclusion, to take the appropriate *or* logical step; **wenn es dir hier nicht gefällt, solltest du die entsprechenden ~en ziehen und gehen** if you don't like it here, you should do something about it and go; **ich werde meine ~en ziehen** there's only one thing for me to do **b** (= *Beharrlichkeit*) consistency; (*bei Maßnahmen*) rigorousness, strictness; **die ~, mit der er sein Ziel verfolgte** the single-mindedness with which he pursued his aim

Kon|ser|va|tis|mus [kɔnzerva'tɪsmʊs] M **-**, *no pl* conservatism

kon|ser|va|tiv [kɔnzerva'ti:f, 'kɔnzervati:f] ADJ conservative; (*Brit Pol*) Conservative, Tory ADV

conservatively; **das ist ~ gerechnet** that's a conservative estimate

Kon|ser|va|ti|ve(r) [kɔnzerva'ti:və] MF *decl as adj* conservative; (*Brit Pol*) Conservative, Tory

Kon|ser|va|ti|vis|mus [kɔnzervati'vɪsmʊs] M **-**, *no pl* conservatism

Kon|ser|va|tor [kɔnzer'va:tɔr] M **-s, Konservatoren** [-'to:rən], **Kon|ser|va|to|rin** [-'to:rɪn] F **-, -nen** curator, keeper

Kon|ser|va|to|ri|um [kɔnzerva'to:riʊm] NT **-s, Konservatorien** [-riən] conservatory

Kon|ser|ve [kɔn'zervə] F **-, -n** preserved food; (*in Dosen*) tinned (*Brit*) or canned food; (= *Konservendose*) tin (*Brit*), can; (*Med*: = *Blutkonserve etc*) stored blood *etc*; blood bottle; (*Rad, TV*) prerecorded *or* canned (*inf*) material; (= *Tonkonserve*) recorded music; (*auf Band*) taped music; **sich aus** *or* **von ~n ernähren** to live out of tins (*Brit*) or cans

Kon|ser|ven|büch|se F , **Kon|ser|ven|do|se** F tin (*Brit*), can

kon|ser|vie|ren [kɔnzer'vi:rən] *ptp* **konserviert** VT to preserve, to conserve; *Leichen* to preserve; *Auto* to wax

Kon|ser|vie|rung F **-**, *no pl* preservation, conservation; (*der Umwelt*) conservation; (*von Leichen*) preservation

Kon|ser|vie|rungs|mit|tel NT , **Kon|ser|vie|rungs|stoff** M preservative

kon|sis|tent [kɔnzɪs'tɛnt] ADJ **a** (*fest*) *Masse* solid **b** (*konsequent*) *Politik, Antwort* consistent **c** (*Comput*) *Daten, Oberfläche* consistent ADV *durchführen, behaupten* consistently

Kon|sis|tenz [kɔnzɪs'tɛnts] F **-, -en** consistency; (*von Gewebe*) texture

Kon|so|le [kɔn'zo:lə] F **-, -n** (*Archit*: = *Kragstein*) console, corbel; (*old*: *an Möbeln*) bracket

kon|so|li|die|ren [kɔnzoli'di:rən] *ptp* **konsolidiert** VT (*also Fin, Econ*) to consolidate VR to consolidate

Kon|so|li|die|rung F **-, -en** consolidation

Kon|so|li|die|rungs|pha|se F consolidation phase

Kon|so|nant [kɔnzo'nant] M **-en, -en** consonant

kon|so|nan|tisch [kɔnzo'nantɪʃ] ADJ consonant(al)

Kon|so|nanz [kɔnzo'nants] F **-, -en** (*Mus*) consonance

Kon|sor|ten [kɔn'zɔrtn] PL (*pej inf*) gang (*inf*), mob (*inf*), crowd (*inf*); **X und ~** X and his gang *etc* (*inf*)

Kon|sor|ti|al|bank [kɔnzɔr'tsia:l-] F *pl* **-banken** (*Comm*) consortium bank

Kon|sor|ti|um [kɔn'zɔrtsiʊm] NT **-s, Konsortien** [-tsiən] (*Comm*) consortium, syndicate, group

Kon|spi|ra|ti|on [kɔnspira'tsio:n] F **-, -en** conspiracy, plot

kon|spi|ra|tiv [kɔnspira'ti:f] ADJ conspiratorial; **~er Treff** meeting place (*for terrorists etc*), meet; **~e Wohnung** safe house

kon|spi|rie|ren [kɔnspi'ri:rən] *ptp* **konspiriert** VI to conspire, to plot

kon|stant [kɔn'stant] ADJ constant ADV *gut, schlecht, niedrig, hoch* consistently

Kon|stan|te [kɔn'stantə] F **-(n), -n** constant

Kon|stan|ten|spei|cher M (*Comput*) macro

Kon|stan|tin ['kɔnstanti:n] M **-s** Constantine

Kon|stan|ti|no|pel [kɔnstanti'no:pl] NT **-s** (*old*) Constantinople

Kon|stanz[1] [kɔn'stants] F **-**, *no pl* (*geh*) constancy

Kon|stanz[2] ['kɔnstants] NT (*Geog*) - Constance

kon|sta|tie|ren [kɔnsta'ti:rən] *ptp* **konstatiert** VT to see, to notice; **ich konstatiere, Sie haben schon wieder Ihre Hausaufgaben nicht gemacht** I see *or* notice you haven't done your homework once again; **in ihrer Rede konstatierte**

sie, dass ... in her speech she made the point that ...

Kons|tel|la|ti|on [kɔnstela'tsio:n] F **-, -en a** constellation **b** (*fig*) line-up; (*von Umständen, Faktoren etc*) combination; **diese wirtschaftliche/politische ~** this economic/political situation; **die neue ~ in der Partei** the new line-up in the party; **die ~ in dem Gremium** the make-up of the committee

kons|ter|nie|ren [kɔnster'ni:rən] *ptp* **konsterniert** VT to scandalize

kon|sti|tu|ie|ren [kɔnstitu'i:rən] *ptp* **konstituiert** VT to constitute, to set up; **~de Versammlung** constituent assembly VR to be constituted, to be set up

Kon|sti|tu|ie|rung [kɔnstitu'i:rʊŋ] F **-, -en** (= *Gründung*) constitution

Kon|sti|tu|ti|on [kɔnstitu'tsio:n] F **-, -en** (*Pol, Med*) constitution; (*Phys auch*) structure

kon|sti|tu|ti|o|nell [kɔnstitutsio'nel] ADJ constitutional ADV **a** (*Pol*: = *verfassungsmäßig*) constitutionally **b** (*Med*: = *körperlich*) **er war ~ im Vorteil** he had a better constitution; **für etw ~ anfällig sein** to be intrinsically susceptible to sth

kon|sti|tu|tiv [kɔnstitu'ti:f] ADJ constitutive

kon|stru|ie|ren [kɔnstru'i:rən] *ptp* **konstruiert** VT to construct (*auch Math*); (*Gram auch*) to construe; **ein konstruierter Fall** a hypothetical case; **ein konstruiertes Wort** a made-up word; **der Satz klingt sehr konstruiert** the sentence sounds very artificial

Kon|strukt [kɔn'strʊkt] NT **-(e)s, -e** (*Ling*) construct

Kon|struk|teur [kɔnstrʊk'tø:ɐ] M **-s, -e**, **Kon|struk|teu|rin** [-'tø:rɪn] F **-nen** designer

Kon|struk|ti|on [kɔnstrʊk'tsio:n] F **-, -en** construction; (= *Entwurf, Bauart auch*) design; (*gedanklich, philosophisch auch*) construct; **erlauben Sie mir die ~ des folgenden Falles** allow me to make up *or* construct the following case; **es bieten sich folgende ~en des Handlungsvorganges an** there are several possible reconstructions of the event

Kon|struk|ti|ons-: **Kon|struk|ti|ons|bü|ro** NT drawing office; **Kon|struk|ti|ons|feh|ler** M (*im Entwurf*) design fault; (*im Aufbau*) structural defect; **Kon|struk|ti|ons|plan** M structural plan

kon|struk|tiv [kɔnstrʊk'ti:f] ADJ constructive ADV constructively

Kon|struk|ti|vis|mus [kɔnstrʊkti'vɪsmʊs] M **-**, *no pl* (*Art*) constructivism

Kon|sul ['kɔnzʊl] M **-s, -n**, **Kon|su|lin** [-lɪn] F **-, -nen** consul

kon|su|la|risch [kɔnzu'la:rɪʃ] ADJ consular

Kon|su|lat [kɔnzu'la:t] NT **-(e)s, -e** consulate

Kon|sul|ta|ti|on [kɔnzʊlta'tsio:n] F **-, -en** (*form*) consultation; **jdn zur ~ hinzuziehen** to consult sb

kon|sul|tie|ren [kɔnzʊl'ti:rən] *ptp* **konsultiert** VT (*form*) to consult

Kon|sum M **-s, -s a** [kɔn'zu:m] *no pl* (= *Verbrauch*) consumption **b** ['kɔnzu:m, 'kɔnzʊm] (= *Genossenschaft*) cooperative society; (= *Laden*) cooperative store, co-op (*inf*)

Kon|sum|ar|ti|kel [kɔn'zu:m-] M consumer item; **~** *pl* consumer goods *pl*

Kon|su|ma|ti|on [kɔnzuma'tsio:n] F **-, -en** (*Aus, Sw*) food and drink consumed in a restaurant

Kon|su|ment [kɔnzu'mɛnt] M **-en, -en**, **Kon|su|men|tin** [-'mɛntɪn] F **-, -nen** consumer

Kon|su|men|ten|hal|tung F (*pej*) passive *or* nonparticipating attitude

Kon|sum-: **Kon|sum|ge|nos|sen|schaft** [kɔn'zu:m-] F co-operative society; **Kon|sum|ge|sell|schaft** F consumer society; **Kon|sum|gut** NT *usu pl* consumer item; **Konsumgüter** *pl* consumer goods *pl*; **kon|sum|hung|rig** ADJ consumption-oriented; *Gesellschaft auch* consumerist

kon|su|mie|ren [kɔnzu'miːrən] *ptp* **konsumiert** VT to consume

Kon|su|mis|mus [kɔnzu'mɪsmʊs] M -, *no pl* consumerism

Kon|sum-: Kon|sum|kli|ma NT consumer demand *or* confidence; **das ~ ist gut/schlecht** consumer *or* buyer demand is up/down; **Kon|sum|müll** M (*pej*) consumer waste; **Kon|sum|tem|pel** [kɔn'zuːm-] M shrine to consumerism; **Kon|sum|ter|ror** M (*pej*) pressures *pl* of a materialistic society; **Kon|sum|ver|zicht** M non-consumption; **~ üben** to practise (*Brit*) *or* practice (*US*) non-consumption; **Kon|sum|zwang** M (*Sociol*) compulsion to buy

Kon|takt [kɔn'takt] M -(e)s, -e contact (*auch Elec*); **~e** *pl* (*Aut*) contact breakers *pl*; **mit jdm/ etw in ~ kommen** to come into contact with sb/sth; **mit jdm ~ bekommen, zu jdm ~ finden** to get to know sb; **ich bekomme mit ihm keinen ~** I don't feel I really know him; **mit jdm ~ aufnehmen** to get in contact *or* touch with sb, to contact sb; **mit jdm in ~ stehen** to be in contact *or* touch with sb; **~ herstellen** to make *or* establish contact; **den ~ unterbrechen** to break contact; **keinen ~ mehr haben, den ~ verloren haben** to have lost contact *or* touch, to be out of touch; **sie hat keinen ~ zu ihrer Familie** she has no contact with her family

Kon|takt-: Kon|takt|ab|zug M (*Phot*) contact print; **Kon|takt|ad|res|se** F accommodation address; **er hinterließ eine ~** he left behind an address where he could be contacted; **Kon|takt|an|zei|ge** F lonely hearts ad (*Brit*), personal ad; **Kon|takt|an|zei|gen** PL personal column; **Kon|takt|arm** ADJ **er ist ~** he lacks contact with other people; **Kon|takt|ar|mut** F lack of human contact; **Kon|takt|bild|schirm** M touch-sensitive screen; **Kon|takt|frau** F (= *Agentin*) contact; **Kon|takt|freu|de** F sociability; **kon|takt|freu|dig** ADJ sociable, outgoing; **sie ist ~** she makes friends easily; **Kon|takt|freu|dig|keit** F sociability; **Kon|takt|lin|se** F contact lens; **Kon|takt|man|gel** M lack of contact; **Kon|takt|mann** M *pl* **-männer** (= *Agent*) contact; **Kon|takt|nah|me** [-naːmə] F -, -n (*form*) contacting; **Kon|takt|per|son** F contact; **Kon|takt|pfle|ge** F staying in contact, keeping in touch; **kon|takt|scheu** ADJ shy; **sie ist ~** she doesn't like socializing

Kon|ta|mi|na|ti|on [kɔntamina'tsioːn] F -, -en (*auch Kerntechnik*) contamination; (*Gram*) blend(ing); **die ~ der Luft durch gefährliche Stoffe** the contamination of the air by dangerous substances

kon|ta|mi|nie|ren [kɔntami'niːrən] *ptp* **kontaminiert** VI to contaminate, to pollute; (*Gram*) to blend

Kon|temp|la|ti|on [kɔntɛmpla'tsioːn] F -, -en contemplation

kon|temp|la|tiv [kɔntɛmpla'tiːf] ADJ contemplative

Kon|ten *pl von* Konto

Kon|te|nan|ce [kɔntə'nãːs] F -, *no pl* (*geh*) composure; **die ~ bewahren** to keep one's composure *or* countenance

Kon|ter ['kɔntɐ] M -s, - **a** (*Boxen*) counter (-punch); (*Ballspiele*) counterattack, break; **sich** (*dat*) **einen ~ einfangen** to be caught by a counterpunch **b** (*fig*: = *Handlung*) countermove; (= *Äußerung*) rejoinder, parry

Kon|ter- ['kɔntɐ] *in cpds* counter-; **Kon|ter|ad|mi|ral(in)** M(F) rear admiral; **Kon|ter|an|griff** M counterattack; **Kon|ter|ban|de** F -, *no pl* contraband

Kon|ter|fei ['kɔntɐfai, kɔntɐ'fai] NT -s, -s *or* -e (*old, hum*) likeness, portrait

kon|ter|fei|en [kɔntɐ'faiən, 'kɔntɐfaiən] *ptp* **konterfeit** VT to portray

kon|ter|ka|rie|ren [kɔntɐka'riːrən] *ptp* **konterkariert** VT to counteract; *Aussage* to contradict

kon|tern ['kɔntɐn] **VT** *Angriff, Vorwurf* to counter **VI** to counter; (*Sport*) to counterattack

kon|ter-: kon|ter|pro|duk|tiv ADJ = **kontraproduktiv; Kon|ter|re|vo|lu|ti|on** F counter-revolution; **kon|ter|re|vo|lu|ti|o|när** ADJ counter-revolutionary; **Kon|ter|schlag** M (*Sport, fig*) counterattack; (*Boxen*) counter(-blow), counterpunch

Kon|text ['kɔntɛkst] M context

Kon|ti *pl von* Konto

Kon|ti|nent ['kɔntinɛnt, kɔnti'nɛnt] M -(e)s, -e continent

kon|ti|nen|tal [kɔntinɛn'taːl] ADJ continental

Kon|ti|nen|tal-Drift F continental drift; **Kon|ti|nen|tal|eu|ro|pa** NT the Continent; **kon|ti|nen|tal|eu|ro|pä|isch** ADJ Continental; **Kon|ti|nen|tal|kli|ma** NT continental climate; **Kon|ti|nen|tal|so|ckel** M continental shelf; **Kon|ti|nen|tal|sper|re** F (*Hist*) Continental System; **Kon|ti|nen|tal|ver|schie|bung** F (*Geol*) continental drift

Kon|tin|gent [kɔntɪŋ'gɛnt] NT -(e)s, -e (*Mil*: = *Truppenkontingent*) contingent; (*Comm*) quota, share; (= *Zuteilung*) allotment, allocation

kon|tin|gen|tie|ren [kɔntɪŋgɛn'tiːrən] *ptp* **kontingentiert** VT (*Comm*) to allocate, to apportion; **den Import ~** to fix *or* impose import quotas

Kon|tin|genz [kɔntɪŋ'gɛnts] F -, -en (*Philos*) contingency

Kon|ti|nua *pl von* Kontinuum

kon|ti|nu|ier|lich [kɔntinu'iːɐlɪç] ADJ continuous **ADV** continuously

Kon|ti|nu|i|tät [kɔntinui'tɛːt] F -, *no pl* continuity

Kon|ti|nu|um [kɔn'tiːnuʊm] NT -s, Kontinua [-ua] continuum

Kon|to ['kɔnto] NT -s, Konten *or* Konti ['kɔntn, 'kɔnti] account; **auf meinem/mein ~** in my/into my account; **das geht auf mein ~** (*inf*) (= *ich bin schuldig*) I am responsible *or* to blame for this; (= *ich zahle*) this is on me (*inf*)

Kon|to-: Kon|to|aus|zug M (bank) statement, statement (of account); **Kon|to|aus|zugs|dru|cker** M *bank statement machine*; **Kon|to|be|we|gung** F transaction; **kon|to|füh|rend** ADJ *Bank* where an account is held; **Kon|to|füh|rung** F running of an account; **Kon|to|füh|rungs|ge|bühr** F bank charge; **Kon|to|in|ha|ber(in)** M(F) account holder; **Kon|to|num|mer** F account number

Kon|tor [kɔn'toːɐ] NT -s, -e **a** (= *Büro*) office → **Schlag b** (= *Handelsniederlassung*) branch office

Kon|to|rist [kɔnto'rɪst] M -en, -en clerk

Kon|to|ris|tin F -, -nen clerkess

Kon|to|stand M balance, state of an account

kont|ra ['kɔntra] PREP +*acc* against; (*Jur*) versus

Kont|ra ['kɔntra] NT -s, -s (*Cards*) double; **~ ge|ben** (*Cards*) to double; **jdm ~ geben** (*fig*) to contradict sb

Kont|ra-: Kont|ra|bass ▲ M double bass; **kont|ra|dik|to|risch** [kɔntradɪk'toːrɪʃ] **ADJ** contradictory **ADV** **sich ~ äußern/ausdrücken** to contradict oneself

Kont|ra|hent [kɔntra'hɛnt] M -en, -en, **Kont|ra|hen|tin** [-'hɛntɪn] F -, -nen (= *Vertragsschließender*) contracting party; (= *Gegner*) opponent, adversary

kon|tra|hie|ren [kɔntra'hiːrən] *ptp* **kontrahiert** VT (*Ling, Med*) to contract

Kont|ra|in|di|ka|ti|on [kɔntra-, 'kɔntra-] F (*Med*) contraindication

Kon|trakt [kɔn'trakt] M -(e)s, -e contract

Kon|trak|ti|on [kɔntrak'tsioːn] F -, -en (*Med*) contraction

Kont|ra-: Kont|ra|post [kɔntra'pɔst] M -(e)s, -e (*Art*) contrapposto; **kont|ra|pro|duk|tiv**

ADJ counterproductive; **Kont|ra|punkt** M (*Mus*) counterpoint; **kont|ra|punk|tisch** [kɔntra'pʊŋktɪʃ] ADJ (*Mus*) contrapuntal

kont|rär [kɔn'trɛːɐ] ADJ (*geh*) *Meinungen* contrary, opposite

Kont|rast [kɔn'trast] M -(e)s, -e contrast

Kont|rast-: kon|trast|arm ADJ **~ sein** to be lacking in contrast; (*Programm, Landschaft*) to be monotonous; **Kon|trast|brei** M (*Med*) barium meal; **Kon|trast|far|be** F contrasting colour (*Brit*) *or* color (*US*); **Kon|trast|fil|ter** M (*Phot*) yellow filter

kon|tras|tie|ren [kɔntras'tiːrən] *ptp* **kontrastiert** VI to contrast

kon|tras|tiv [kɔntras'tiːf] ADJ (*Ling*) contrastive

Kont|rast-: Kont|rast|mit|tel NT (*Med*) contrast medium; **Kont|rast|pro|gramm** NT alternative programme (*Brit*) *or* program (*US*); **Kont|rast|re|ge|lung** F contrast control; **Kont|rast|reg|ler** M contrast (control); **kon|trast|reich** ADJ **~ sein** to be full of contrast

Kont|ra|te|nor [-tenoːɐ] M countertenor

Kont|ra|zep|ti|on [kɔntratsɛp'tsioːn] F -, *no pl* (*form*) contraception

kon|tri|bu|ie|ren [kɔntribu'iːrən] *ptp* **kontribuiert** VT (*old*) to contribute

Kon|tri|bu|ti|on [kɔntribu'tsioːn] F -, -en (*old*) contribution

Kon|troll-: Kon|troll|ab|schnitt M (*Comm*) counterfoil, stub; **Kontrolllampe** △ F → **trolllampe; Kon|troll|be|am|te(r)** M *decl as adj*, **Kon|troll|be|am|tin** F -, -nen inspector; (*an der Grenze*) frontier guard; (*zur Passkontrolle*) passport officer; (*zur Zollkontrolle*) customs officer; (*zur Überwachung*) security officer; **Kon|troll|be|hör|de** F supervisory body

Kon|trol|le [kɔn'trɔlə] F -, -n **a** (= *Beherrschung, Regulierung*) control; **über jdn/etw die ~ verlie|ren** to lose control of sb/sth; **jdn/etw unter ~ haben/halten** to have/keep sb/sth under control; **der Brand geriet außer ~** the fire got out of control **b** (= *Nachprüfung*) check (+*gen* on); (= *Aufsicht*) supervision; (= *Schutz*) safeguard; (= *Passkontrolle*) passport control; (= *Zollkontrolle*) customs examination; **jdn/etw einer ~ unterziehen** to check sb/sth; **zur ~ haben wir noch einmal alles nachgerechnet** we went over all the figures again to check; **~ durchführen** to carry out *or* make checks; **der Luftverkehr ist unter ständiger ~** air traffic is kept under constant surveillance, a constant check is kept on air traffic; **die ~n an der Grenze wurden verschärft** the border controls were tightened; **nach einer sorgfältigen ~ der Waren** after a careful inspection of the goods, after a careful check on *or* of the goods; **die ~ von Lebensmitteln** the inspection of foodstuffs **c** (= *Stelle*) (*für Überprüfung, Verkehr*) checkpoint; (= *Pass-/Zollkontrolle*) passport control/customs; (*vor Fabrik*) gatehouse; (*an der Grenze*) border post; (*in Bibliothek etc*) checkout desk **d** (= *Person*) inspector; (= *Pass-/Zollkontrolle*) passport/customs officer; (*in Fabrik*) security officer; (= *Polizist*) (*im Verkehr*) traffic police; (*an der Grenze*) frontier guard; (*in Bibliotheken etc*) person at the checkout desk

Kon|trol|leur [kɔntrɔ'løːɐ] M -s, -e, **Kon|trol|leu|rin** [-'løːrɪn] F -, -nen inspector

Kon|troll-: Kon|troll|funk|ti|on F controlling function; **Kon|troll|gang** M *pl* **-gänge** (inspection) round; **Kon|troll|grup|pe** F **a** (*Med, Psych*) control group **b** (= *Aufsichtsorgan*) surveillance group

kon|troll|ier|bar ADJ controllable; *Behauptung* checkable, verifiable

kon|trol|lie|ren [kɔntrɔ'liːrən] *ptp* **kontrolliert** VT **a** (= *regulieren, beherrschen*) to control **b** (= *nachprüfen, überwachen*) to check; *Pass, Fahrkarte etc* to inspect, to check; (= *Aufsicht haben über*) to supervise; **die Qualität der Waren muss streng kontrolliert werden** a strict check must be kept on the quality of the goods; **jdn/etw nach etw** or **auf etw** (*acc*) ~ to check sb/sth for sth; **Gemüse aus kontrolliert biologischem Anbau** organically grown vegetables; **kontrollierte Drogenabgabe** medical prescription of narcotics; **staatlich kontrolliert** state-controlled

Kontrollliste △ F → **Kontrollliste**

Kon|troll-: Kon|troll|kom|mis|si|on F control commission; **Kon|troll|lam|pe** ▲ F , **Kon|troll|leuch|te** ▲ F pilot lamp; (*Aut: für Ölstand*) warning light or lamp; **Kon|troll|lis|te** ▲ F check list; **Kon|troll|or|gan** NT monitoring body; **Kon|troll|pflicht** F control; **seine ~ vernachlässigen** to neglect one's supervisory responsibilities; **Kon|troll|punkt** M checkpoint; **Kon|troll|rat** M **Alliierter ~** Allied Control Council; **Kon|troll|stel|le** F checkpoint; **Kon|troll|stem|pel** M inspection stamp; **Kon|troll|sys|tem** NT control system; **Kon|troll|turm** M control tower; **Kon|troll|uhr** F time clock; **Kon|troll|un|ter|su|chung** F control test; **Kon|troll|waa|ge** F (*in Verpackungs-, Pharmaindustrie*) checkweigher; **Kon|troll|zent|rum** NT control centre (*Brit*) or center (*US*); (*Space also*) mission control

kont|ro|vers [kɔntro'vɛrs] **ADJ** controversial **ADV (etw) ~ diskutieren** to have a controversial discussion (on sth)

Kont|ro|ver|se [kɔntro'vɛrzə] F **-, -n** controversy

Kon|tur [kɔn'tuːɐ] F **-, -en** outline, contour; **~en annehmen** to take shape

Kon|tu|ren|stift M liner

kon|tu|rie|ren [kɔntu'riːrən] *ptp* **konturiert** VT (*lit, fig*) to outline

kon|tur|los ADJ shapeless, flat; *Person, Politiker* faceless

Kon|tur|sitz M contoured seat

Ko|nus ['koːnʊs] M **-, -se** or (*Tech*) **Konen** ['koːnən] (*Math*) cone; (*Tech*) taper; (*Typ*) body

Kon|va|les|zenz [kɔnvalɛs'tsɛnts] **-,** (*rare*) **-en** F (*Med*) convalescence

Kon|vek|tor [kɔn'vɛktɔr] **-s, Konvektoren** [-'toːrən] M convector (heater)

Kon|ve|ni|enz [kɔnve'niɛnts] F **-, -en** (*geh*) propriety; (*= Bequemlichkeit*) convenience

Kon|vent [kɔn'vɛnt] M **-(e)s, -e** **a** (*= Versammlung*) convention **b** (*= Kloster*) convent; (*= Mönchskonvent*) monastery

Kon|ven|ti|on [kɔnvɛn'tsioːn] F **-, -en** **a** (*= Herkommen*) convention; **sich über die ~en hinwegsetzen** to sweep aside or ignore (social) conventions **b** (*im Völkerrecht*) convention

Kon|ven|ti|o|nal|stra|fe [kɔnvɛntsionaː'l-] F penalty or fine (for breach of contract)

kon|ven|ti|o|nell [kɔnvɛntsio'nɛl] ADJ conventional **ADV** conventionally

kon|ver|gent [kɔnvɛr'gɛnt] ADJ convergent, converging

Kon|ver|genz [kɔnvɛr'gɛnts] F **-, -en** convergence

Kon|ver|genz-: Kon|ver|genz|kri|te|rien PL convergence criteria *pl*; **Kon|ver|genz|the|o|rie** F theory of convergence

kon|ver|gie|ren [kɔnvɛr'giːrən] *ptp* **konvergiert** VI to converge

Kon|ver|sa|ti|on [kɔnvɛrza'tsioːn] F **-, -en** conversation; **~ machen** to make conversation or small talk (*inf*)

Kon|ver|sa|ti|ons|le|xi|kon NT encyclopaedia (*Brit*), encyclopedia (*US*)

Kon|ver|si|on [kɔnvɛr'zioːn] F **-, -en** conversion

Kon|ver|ter [kɔn'vɛrtɐ] M **-s, -** converter

kon|ver|ti|bel [kɔnvɛr'tiːbl] ADJ (*Fin*) convertible

Kon|ver|ti|bi|li|tät [kɔnvɛrtibili'tɛːt] F **-, no pl** (*Fin*) convertibility

kon|ver|tier|bar [kɔn'vɛrtiːɐbaːɐ] ADJ (*Fin*) convertible

Kon|ver|tier|bar|keit F **-, no pl** (*Fin*) convertibility

kon|ver|tie|ren [kɔnvɛr'tiːrən] *ptp* **konvertiert** VT to convert (*in +acc* to) VI *aux* haben or sein to be converted

Kon|ver|tit [kɔnvɛr'tiːt] M **-en, -en, Kon|ver|ti|tin** [-'tiːtɪn] F **-, -nen** convert

kon|vex [kɔn'vɛks] ADJ convex **ADV** convexly

Kon|vex-: kon|vex|kon|kav ADJ convexoconcave; **Kon|vex|lin|se** F convex lens; **Kon|vex|spie|gel** M convex mirror

Kon|vikt [kɔn'vɪkt] NT **-(e)s, -e** seminary

Kon|voi ['kɔnvɔy, kɔn'vɔy] M **-s, -s** convoy; **im ~ fahren** to drive in convoy

Kon|vo|lut [kɔnvo'luːt] NT **-(e)s, -e** (*geh*) bundle (of papers)

Kon|vul|si|on [kɔnvʊl'zioːn] F **-, -en** *usu pl* (*Med*) convulsion

kon|vul|si|visch [kɔnvʊl'ziːvɪʃ] (*Med*) ADJ convulsive **ADV** convulsively

kon|ze|die|ren [kɔntse'diːrən] *ptp* **konzediert** VT (*geh*) to concede, to grant (*jdm etw* sb sth)

Kon|zent|rat [kɔntsɛn'traːt] NT **-(e)s, -e** concentrate; (*fig: eines Buches etc*) condensed version

Kon|zent|ra|ti|on [kɔntsɛntra'tsioːn] F **-, -en** concentration (*auf +acc* on)

Kon|zent|ra|ti|ons-: Kon|zent|ra|ti|ons|fä|hig|keit F powers *pl* of concentration; **Kon|zent|ra|ti|ons|la|ger** NT concentration camp; **Kon|zent|ra|ti|ons|man|gel** M lack of concentration; **Kon|zent|ra|ti|ons|schwä|che** F weak or poor concentration; **Kon|zent|ra|ti|ons|ver|mö|gen** NT powers *pl* of concentration

kon|zent|rie|ren [kɔntsɛn'triːrən] *ptp* **konzentriert** VT to concentrate (*auf +acc* on); *Truppen auch* to mass VR to concentrate (*auf +acc* on); (*Untersuchung, Arbeit etc*) to be concentrated (*auf +acc* on)

kon|zent|riert [kɔntsɛn'triːɐt] ADJ **a** (*Chem*) concentrated **b** **mit ~er Aufmerksamkeit** with all one's concentration **ADV** *arbeiten, zuhören* intently; *nachdenken, spielen* intensely; *rechnen* carefully

kon|zent|risch [kɔn'tsɛntrɪʃ] (*Math, Mil*) ADJ concentric **ADV** concentrically

Kon|zept [kɔn'tsɛpt] NT **-(e)s, -e** (*= Rohentwurf*) draft, notes *pl*; (*für Aufsatz etc auch*) rough copy; (*= Plan, Programm*) plan, programme (*Brit*), program (*US*); (*= Begriff, Vorstellung*) concept; **es ist jetzt wenigstens als** or **im ~ fertig** at least the draft *etc* is ready now; **jdn aus dem ~ bringen** to put sb off (*esp Brit*), to break sb's train of thought; (*inf: aus dem Gleichgewicht*) to upset sb; **aus dem ~ geraten** to lose one's thread; (*inf: aus dem Gleichgewicht*) to get upset; **das passt mir nicht ins ~** that doesn't fit in with my plans or doesn't suit my plans; (*= gefällt mir nicht*) I don't like the idea; **jdm das ~ verderben** to spoil sb's plans

Kon|zep|ti|on [kɔntsɛp'tsioːn] F **-, -en** **a** (*Med*) conception **b** (*geh*) (*= Gedankengang*) idea; (*= Entwurf*) conception; **seine ~ der Außenpolitik** his idea or conception of foreign policy; **ein schon in der ~ verfehltes Gedicht** a poem which in its (very) conception was a failure

kon|zep|ti|o|nell [kɔntsɛptsio'nɛl] (*geh*) ADJ conceptional **ADV** conceptionally

Kon|zep|ti|ons-: Kon|zep|ti|ons|furcht F (*Psych*) conception phobia, fear of conceiving; **kon|zep|ti|ons|los** ADJ without a definite line; **das Programm wirkt auf mich recht ~** the programme (*Brit*) or program (*US*) strikes me as lacking any definite line; **Kon|zep|ti|ons|lo|sig|keit** F **-, no pl** lack of any definite line

Kon|zept-: Kon|zept|kunst F conceptual art; **Kon|zept|pa|pier** NT rough paper

Kon|zern [kɔn'tsɛrn] M **-s, -e** combine, group (of companies); **die ~e haben zu viel Macht** the big companies have too much power

Kon|zern-: Kon|zern|bil|dung F formation of combines; **Kon|zern|lei|tung** F **, no pl** **a** (*= Leitung als Aufgabengebiet*) (central) management of a group of companies **b** (*= leitende Personen*) group management; **Kon|zern|spit|ze** F top management (*of a/the group of companies*), (a/the) group's top management

Kon|zert [kɔn'tsɛrt] NT **-(e)s, -e** concert; (*von klassischen Solisten auch*) recital; (*= Komposition*) concerto; **die Kinder heulten im ~** the children cried in unison

Kon|zert-: Kon|zert|abend M concert evening; **Kon|zert|agen|tur** F concert artists' agency

kon|zer|tant [kɔntsɛr'tant] ADJ (*Mus*) in concerto form; *Sinfonie concertante*

Kon|zert-: Kon|zert|be|su|cher(in) M(F) concertgoer; **Kon|zert|flü|gel** M concert grand (*Brit*), grand piano; **Kon|zert|gi|tar|re** F classical guitar; **Kon|zert|hal|le** F concert hall or auditorium

kon|zer|tie|ren [kɔntsɛr'tiːrən] *ptp* **konzertiert** VI to give a concert; (*= als Solist mitwirken*) to play in a concert VT (*geh: = abstimmen*) to concert

kon|zer|tiert [kɔntsɛr'tiːɐt] ADJ **~e Aktion** (*Fin, Pol*) concerted action

Kon|zer|ti|na [kɔntsɛr'tiːna] F **-, Konzertinen** [-'tiːnən] concertina

Kon|zert-: Kon|zert|meis|ter(in) M(F) leader (*Brit*), concertmaster (*US*); **Kon|zert|pa|vil|lon** M bandstand; **Kon|zert|pia|nist(in)** M(F) concert pianist; **Kon|zert|rei|he** F series of concerts, concert series; **Kon|zert|saal** M concert hall, auditorium; **Kon|zert|sän|ger(in)** M(F) concert singer

Kon|zes|si|on [kɔntse'sioːn] F **-, -en** **a** (*= Gewerbeerlaubnis*) concession, licence (*Brit*), license (*US*), franchise **b** (*= Zugeständnis*) concession (*an +acc* to)

Kon|zes|si|o|när [kɔntsesio'nɛːɐ] M **-s, -e, Kon|zes|si|o|nä|rin** [-'nɛːrɪn] F **-, -nen** concessionaire, licensee

Kon|zes|si|ons-: kon|zes|si|ons|be|reit ADJ ready or willing to make concessions; **Kon|zes|si|ons|be|reit|schaft** F readiness to make concessions; **kon|zes|si|ons|pflich|tig** ADJ requiring a licence (*Brit*) or license (*US*) *pred*

kon|zes|siv [kɔntse'siːf] ADJ (*Gram*) concessive

Kon|zes|siv|satz M (*Gram*) concessive clause

Kon|zil [kɔn'tsiːl] NT **-s, -e** or **-ien** [-liən] (*Eccl, Univ*) council

kon|zi|li|ant [kɔntsi'liant] ADJ (*= versöhnlich*) conciliatory; (*= entgegenkommend*) generous **ADV** **sich ~ geben** to be conciliatory; **~ gestimmt sein** to be inclined to be conciliatory

Kon|zi|pi|ent [kɔntsi'piɛnt] M **-en, -en, Kon|zi|pi|en|tin** [-'piɛntɪn] F **-, -nen** (*Aus*) articled clerk

kon|zi|pie|ren [kɔntsi'piːrən] *ptp* **konzipiert** VT to conceive; (*= entwerfen auch*) to design VI (*Med*) to conceive

kon|zis [kɔn'tsiːs] (*liter*) ADJ concise **ADV** concisely

Koof|mich ['koːfmɪç] M **-s, -s** or **-e** (*pej inf*) businessman type

Koog [koːk] M **-es, Köge** ['køːgə] (*N Ger*) polder

Ko|ope|ra|ti|on [koʔopera'tsioːn] F **-, -en** cooperation

Ko|ope|ra|ti|ons|part|ner(in) M(F) cooperative partner, joint venture partner

ko|ope|ra|tiv [koʔopera'tiːf] ADJ cooperative **ADV** cooperatively

Ko|ope|ra|ti|ve [koʔopera'tiːvə] F **-, -n** (*Econ*) cooperative

Ko|ope|ra|tor [koʔope'raːtɔɐ] M **-s, Kooperatoren** [-'toːrən], **Ko|ope|ra|to|rin** [-'toːrɪn] F **-, -nen** **a** (*Aus*) curate **b** (*rare*) cooperator

ko|ope|rie|ren [koˌopeˈriːrən] *ptp* **kooperiert**
VI to cooperate

Ko|op|ta|ti|on [koˌɔptaˈtsi̯oːn] F -, -en coopting, cooption

Ko|or|di|na|te [koˌɔrdiˈnaːtə] F -, -n (*Math*) coordinate

Ko|or|di|na|ten- (*Math*): **Ko|or|di|na|ten-ach|se** F coordinate axis; **Ko|or|di|na|ten-kreuz** NT , **Ko|or|di|na|ten|sys|tem** NT coordinate system

Ko|or|di|na|ti|on [koˌɔrdinaˈtsi̯oːn] F -, -en co-ordination

Ko|or|di|na|tor [koˌɔrdiˈnaːtoːɐ] M -s, **Koordinatoren** [-ˈtoːrən], **Ko|or|di|na|to|rin** [-ˈtoːrɪn] F -, -nen coordinator

ko|or|di|nie|ren [koˌɔrdiˈniːrən] *ptp* **koordiniert**
VT to coordinate

ko|or|di|nie|rend ADJ (*auch Gram*) coordinating

Ko|pe|ke [koˈpeːkə] F -, -n copeck, kopeck

Ko|pen|ha|gen [koːpnˈhaːgn] NT -s Copenhagen

Ko|pen|ha|ge|ner[1] [koːpnˈhaːgənɐ] ADJ Copenhagen *attr*

Ko|pen|ha|ge|ner[2] [koːpnˈhaːgənɐ] M -s, -, **Ko|pen|ha|ge|ne|rin** [-ərɪn] F -, -nen person from Copenhagen

Kö|pe|ni|cki|a|de [køːpənɪˈki̯aːdə] F -, -n hoax involving impersonation

Kö|per [ˈkøːpɐ] M -s, *no pl* (*Tex*) twill

ko|per|ni|ka|nisch [kopɛrniˈkanɪʃ] ADJ Copernican

Kopf [kɔpf] -(e)s, ⸚e [ˈkœpfə]

SUBSTANTIV (M)

a allgemein head; **eine zehn Köpfe starke Gruppe** a group of ten people; **Kopf hoch!** chin up!; **sie sprang Kopf voraus ins Wasser** she jumped into the water headfirst; **sie stürzte sich Kopf voraus in ihr Unglück** she rushed headlong into disaster; **Kopf weg!** (*inf*) mind your head!; **Kopf runter** *or* **ab!** off with his/her head!; **von Kopf bis Fuß** from head to foot; **einen schweren** *or* **dicken Kopf haben** to be groggy; (*von Alkohol*) to have a hangover → **Schlinge**, **Sand** → *auch* **d**, **e**

b = Teil (*von Plattenspieler, Zug, Nagel, Stecknadel, Münze, Blume*) head; (= *Zeitungskopf*) head; (= *Nachrichtenüberschrift*) heading; (= *Briefkopf*) (letter)head; (= *Pfeifenkopf*) bowl; (= *Sprengkopf, Gefechtskopf*) warhead; **Salatkopf** head of lettuce; **Kohlkopf** head of cabbage; **Kopf oder Zahl?** heads or tails?; **am Kopf der Tafel sitzen** to sit at the head of the table

c im übertragenen Sinn (= *Verstand*) head; (= *Sinn*) head, mind; (= *Denker*) thinker; (= *leitende Persönlichkeit*) leader; (= *Bandenführer*) brains *sing*; **ein kluger/findiger Kopf** an intelligent/ingenious person; **er ist ein fähiger Kopf** he's a very capable person; **in seinem Team sitzen einige hervorragende Köpfe** there are some outstanding people in his team; **die besten Köpfe** the best brains; **ich habe den Kopf voll genug** (*inf*) I've got enough on my mind; **seinen eigenen Kopf haben** (*inf*) to have a mind of one's own; **der Kopf der Gruppe ist Herr Meier** Herr Meier is the leader of the group; **sie war der Kopf der Bande** she was the brains of the gang → *auch* **d**, **e**

d mit Präposition

♦ **an + Kopf Kopf an Kopf** shoulder to shoulder; (*Sport, Pferderennen*) neck and neck; **jdm etw an den Kopf werfen** *or* **schmeißen** (*inf*) to chuck (*inf*) *or* sling (*inf*) sth at sb; **jdm Beschimpfungen** *or* **Beleidigungen an den Kopf werfen** (*inf*) to hurl insults at sb; **sich** (*dat*) **an den Kopf fassen** *or* **schlagen** (*verständnislos*) to be left speechless

♦ **auf + Kopf auf dem Kopf stehen** to stand on one's head; **die ganze Gesellschaftsordnung**

steht auf dem Kopf the whole social system is stood on its head; **er hat bei seiner Sauftour sein ganzes Gehalt auf den Kopf gehauen** (*inf*) he blew all his wages on his drinking spree; **jdm auf den Kopf spucken können** (*inf*) to tower above sb; **jdm auf dem Kopf herumtrampeln** (*inf*) to walk all over sb (*inf*); **er ist nicht auf den Kopf gefallen** he's no fool; **etw auf den Kopf stellen** to turn sth upside down; **Tatsachen auf den Kopf stellen** to stand facts on their heads, to turn facts upside down; **du kannst dich auf den Kopf stellen, du wirst ihn nicht umstimmen** (*inf*) you can talk till you're blue in the face, you won't get him to change his mind (*inf*); **jdm etw auf den Kopf zusagen** to say sth straight out to sb (*esp Brit*), to tell sb sth to his/her face; **auf jds Kopf** (*acc*) **20.000 EUR aussetzen** to put 20,000 euros on sb's head

♦ **aus dem Kopf der Gedanke will mir nicht aus dem Kopf** I can't get the thought out of my head *or* mind; **diese Melodie geht mit einfach nicht mehr aus dem Kopf** I just can't get this tune out of my head; **sich** (*dat*) **etw aus dem Kopf schlagen** to put sth out of one's mind

♦ **durch den Kopf sich** (*dat*) **etw durch den Kopf gehen lassen** to think about sth

♦ **im Kopf** in one's head; **etw im Kopf haben** to have sth in one's head; **ich habe die Melodie genau im Kopf** I know the tune exactly; **was man nicht im Kopf hat, muss man in den Beinen haben** (*inf*) a bit of thought would save a lot of legwork; **im Kopf muss mans haben** (*inf*) you need brains; **nichts als Tanzen/Fußball im Kopf haben** to think of nothing but dancing/football; **andere Dinge im Kopf haben** to have other things on one's mind; **der Gedanke geht mir im Kopf herum** I can't get the thought out of my head *or* mind; **etw im Kopf rechnen** to work sth out in one's head; **er ist nicht ganz richtig** *or* **klar im Kopf** (*inf*) he is not quite right in the head (*inf*); **das hältst du** *or* **hält man ja im Kopf nicht aus!** (*inf*) it's absolutely incredible! (*inf*)

♦ **in den Kopf mir ist neulich in den Kopf gekommen, dass ...** the other day it *or* the idea crossed my mind that ...; **es will mir nicht in den Kopf** I can't figure it out; **sie hat es sich** (*dat*) **in den Kopf gesetzt, das zu tun** she's dead set on doing it

♦ **mit + Kopf mit bloßem Kopf** bareheaded; **mit besoffenem Kopf** (*inf*) drunk out of one's mind (*inf*); **mit dem Kopf durch die Wand wollen** (*inf*) to be hell-bent on getting one's own way(, regardless)

♦ **nach + Kopf es muss ja nicht immer alles nach deinem Kopf gehen** you can't have things your own way all the time; **immer muss alles nach deinem Kopf gehen!** you always want things your own way!

♦ **pro Kopf also 20 Euro, das gibt dann 5 Euro pro Kopf** so 20 euros, that means 5 euros each; **das Einkommen pro Kopf** the per capita income

♦ **über + Kopf jdm über den Kopf wachsen** (*lit*) to outgrow sb; (*fig*) (*Sorgen etc*) to be more than sb can cope with; (*Konkurrent etc*) to outstrip sb; **das könnt ihr nicht einfach über ihren Kopf hinweg entscheiden** you can't just decide without consulting her; **er ist bis über den Kopf in Schulden** he's up to his neck *or* ears in debt

♦ **um + Kopf sich um seinen Kopf reden** to sign one's own death warrant

♦ **vor den Kopf ich war wie vor den Kopf geschlagen** I was dumbfounded; **musst du den Chef immer so vor den Kopf stoßen?** must you always antagonize the boss?; **da hat er mit einem einzigen Satz die Gewerkschaften vor den Kopf gestoßen** with a single phrase he alienated the unions

♦ **zu Kopf(e) (jdm) zu Kopf(e) steigen** to go to sb's head

e mit Verb

Die in Verbindung mit **Kopf** verwendeten Verben sind alphabetisch angeordnet (siehe auch unter dem Eintrag für das jeweilige Verb).

er wird uns nicht gleich den Kopf abschlagen *or* **abreißen, wenn wir fünf Minuten zu spät kommen** he won't kill us if we're five minutes late; **den Kopf oben behalten** to keep one's chin up; **einen kühlen Kopf behalten** *or* **bewahren** to keep a cool head; **seinen Kopf durchsetzen** to get one's own way; **jds Kopf fordern** (*fig*) to bay for sb's blood; **dafür halte ich meinen Kopf nicht hin** (*inf*) I'm not putting my head on the block for that; **den Kopf hängen lassen** (*lit*) to hang one's head; (*fig*) to be despondent; **die Rosen lassen schon den Kopf hängen** the roses are drooping already; **den Kopf für jdn/etw hinhalten** (*inf*) to take the blame *or* rap (*inf*) for sb/sth; **jdn den Kopf kosten** (*fig*) to cost sb his career *or* job; **das hat ihn den Kopf gekostet** (*fig*) that was the end of the road for him; **sich einen/keinen Kopf um** *or* **über etw** (*acc*) **machen** to think/not think about sth; **mach dir keinen Kopf!** (*inf: = keine Sorgen*) don't worry yourself (*inf*); **jdn einen Kopf kürzer machen** (*inf*) to cut *or* chop sb's head off; **für etw Kopf und Kragen riskieren** to risk one's neck for sth; **es werden Köpfe rollen** heads will roll; **Kopf stehen** (*lit*) to stand on one's head; (*fig*) (*vor Ausgelassenheit*) to go wild (with excitement); (*vor Aufregung*) to be in a state of excitement; (*vor Empörung*) to be in a (state of) turmoil; (*durcheinander sein: Haus etc*) to be upside down; **ich weiß schon gar nicht mehr** *or* **kaum mehr, wo mir der Kopf steht** I don't know if I'm coming or going; **mir steht der Kopf nach Tanzen** I'm in the mood for dancing; **jdm den Kopf verdrehen** to turn sb's head; **den Kopf verlieren** to lose one's head; **den Kopf nicht verlieren** to keep one's head, not to lose one's head; **nur nicht den Kopf verlieren!** don't lose your head!; **Kopf und Kragen wagen** (*inf*) (*körperlich*) to risk life and limb; (*beruflich etc*) to risk one's neck; **jdm den Kopf waschen** (*lit*) to wash sb's hair; (*fig inf*) to give sb a telling-off; **sich** (*dat*) **den Kopf waschen** to wash one's hair; **den Kopf in den Nacken werfen** to throw one's head back; **sich** (*dat*) **über etw** (*acc*) **den Kopf zerbrechen** to rack one's brains over sth; **jdm den Kopf zurechtsetzen** *or* **zurechtrücken** to bring sb to his/her senses, to give sb a talking-to; **die Köpfe zusammenstecken** to go into a huddle (*inf*); **sich** (*dat*) **den Kopf zuschütten** to get tanked up (*inf*) → *auch* **d**

Kopf-: **Kopf-an-Kopf-Ren|nen** NT neck-and-neck race; **Kopf|ar|beit** F brainwork; **Kopf|ar|bei|ter(in)** M(F) brainworker; **Kopf|bahn|hof** M terminus (station) (*Brit*), terminal (station)

Kopf|ball M (*Ftbl*) header

Kopf|ball-: **kopf|ball|stark** ADJ (*Ftbl*) strong in the air *pred*; **ein ~er Spieler** a good header of the ball; **Kopf|ball|tor** NT (*Ftbl*) headed goal

Kopf-: **Kopf|be|de|ckung** F headgear; **als ~ trug er ...** on his head he wore ...; **ohne ~** without a hat; **Kopf|be|trag** M per capita sum, sum per head; **Kopf|be|we|gung** F movement of the head, head movement; **Kopf|bild** NT (portrait of sb's) head

Köpf|chen [ˈkœpfçən] NT -s, - *dim von* Kopf little head; (*fig hum*) brains *pl*; **~, ~!** clever stuff!; **~ haben** to have brains, to be brainy (*inf*); **du bist aber ein kluges ~** (*iro*) clever *or* smart cookie, eh! (*inf*)

köp|feln [ˈkœpfln] (*Aus*) VI (= *einen Kopfsprung machen*) to dive (headfirst), to take a header VT (*Ftbl*) to head; **ins Tor ~** to head a goal, to head the ball in

köp|fen [ˈkœpfn] VT **a** *jdn* to behead, to decapitate; (*hum*) *Flasche Wein* to crack (open); **ein Ei ~** to cut the top off an egg **b** (*Ftbl*) to head

VI **a** (als Todesstrafe) **in Saudi-Arabien wird immer noch geköpft** they still behead or decapitate people in Saudi Arabia; **das Köpfen** beheading, decapitation **b** (Ftbl) **ins Tor ~** to head a goal, to head the ball in

Kopf-: Kopf|en|de NT head; **Kopf|form** F shape of (the) head; **Kopf|fü|ßer** [-fy:sɐ] M **-s, -** (Zool) cephalopod (spec); **Kopf|ge|burt** F (fig) intellectual creation; **Kopf|geld** NT bounty (on sb's head); **Kopf|geld|jä|ger** M bounty hunter; **kopf|ge|steu|ert** ADJ Person, Handeln etc rational; **Kopf|griff** M (Rettungsschwimmen) chinhold; (Ringen) headlock; **Kopf|grip|pe** F flu (and headache); (epidemic) encephalitis (spec); **Kopf|haar** NT hair on one's head; (einzelnes) hair from the head; **Kopf|hal|tung** F **eine gerade ~ haben** to hold one's head straight; **Kopf|haut** F scalp; **Kopf|hö|rer** M headphone

-köp|fig [kœpfɪç] ADJ suf -headed; **eine fünf köpfige Familie** a family of five

Kopf-: Kopf|jä|ger(in) M(F) head-hunter; **Kopf|ju|cken** NT **-s,** no pl itching of the scalp; **Kopf|keil** M (wedge-shaped) bolster; **Kopf|kis|sen** NT pillow; **Kopf|kis|sen|be|zug** M pillow case or slip; **Kopf|la|ge** F (Med) head presentation; **Kopf|län|ge** F **um eine ~** by a head; **kopf|las|tig** [-lastɪç] ADJ (lit, fig) top-heavy; Flugzeug nose-heavy; **Kopf|las|tig|keit** F **-,** no pl (von Flugzeug) nose-heaviness; **Kopf|laus** F head louse; **Kopf|leis|te** F (Typ) head rule; **kopf|los** ADJ (fig) in a panic, panicky, in a flap (Brit inf); (lit) headless; **~ werden** to lose one's head, to get into a flap (Brit inf) ADV **~ handeln** to lose one's head; **~ reagieren** to lose one's head; **~ durch die Gegend laufen** to run about like a headless chicken (Brit), to run around like a chicken with its head cut off (US); **Kopf|lo|sig|keit** F **-,** no pl (= Panik) panic; **Kopf|ni|cken** NT **-s,** no pl nod (of the head); **Kopf|nuss** ▲ F (inf) clip (round the earhole) (inf); **Kopf|prä|mie** F reward; **Kopf|putz** [-pʊts] M **-es, -e** headdress; **kopf|rech|nen** VI infin only to do mental arithmetic; **Kopf|rech|nen** NT mental arithmetic; **Kopf|sa|lat** M lettuce; **kopf|scheu** ADJ timid, nervous, shy; **jdn ~ machen** to intimidate sb; **Kopf|schmer|zen** PL headache; **~ haben** to have a headache; **sich** (dat) **über** or **um etw** (acc) **or wegen etw ~ machen** (fig) to worry about sth; **Kopf|schmerz|tab|let|te** F aspirin, headache tablet; **Kopf|schup|pe** F flake of dandruff; **er hat ~n** he's got dandruff sing; **Kopf|schmuck** M headgear; (bei Tracht) headdress; **Kopf|schuss** ▲ M shot in the head; **Kopf|schüt|teln** NT **-s,** no pl shaking the head; **mit einem ~** with a shake of the or one's head; **sein ~ zeigte mir, dass er ...** the way he shook his head told me that he ...; **kopf|schüt|telnd** ADJ shaking one's head ADV with a shake of one's head, shaking one's head; **Kopf|schutz** M protection for the head; (= Kopfschützer) headguard; **Kopf|schüt|zer** [-ʃʏtsɐ] M **-s, -** headguard; **Kopf|sei|te** F (von Münze) heads, face side; (von Zeitung) front page; **Kopf|spiel** NT (Ftbl) heading; **Kopf|sprung** M header, dive; **einen ~ machen** to take a header, to dive (headfirst); **Kopf|stand** M headstand; **einen ~ machen** to stand on one's head; **kopf+ste|hen** △ VI sep irreg aux sein → **Kopf** e; **Kopf|stein** = Kopfsteinpflaster, cobblestone; **Kopf|stein|pflas|ter** NT cobblestones pl; **eine Gasse mit ~** a cobbled street; **Kopf|steu|er** F poll tax; **Kopf|stim|me** F (Mus) falsetto; (Phon) head voice; **Kopf|stoß** M (Billard) massé; **Kopf|stück** NT (Cook) head end; **Kopf|stüt|ze** F headrest; (Aut) head restraint; **Kopf|tuch** NT pl **-tücher** (head)scarf; **Kopf|über** ADV (lit, fig) headfirst, headlong; **Kopf|ver|band** M (Med) head bandage; **Kopf|ver|let|zung** F head injury; **Kopf|wä|sche** F hair wash; **Kopf|weh** NT headache; **~ haben** to have a headache; **Kopf|wei|de** F (Bot) pollarded willow; **Kopf|wun|de** F head wound;

Kopf|zahl F number of persons; **Kopf|zei|le** F (Comput) header; **Kopf|zer|bre|chen** NT **-s,** no pl **jdm ~ machen** to be a worry to sb, to be a headache for sb (inf); **sich** (dat) **über etw** (acc) **~ machen** to worry about sth

Ko|pie [ko'pi:, (Aus) 'ko:piə] F **-, -n** [-'pi:ən, (Aus) -piən] copy; (= Durchschlag auch) carbon (copy); (= Ablichtung) photocopy; (Phot) print; (Film) print, copy; (von Statue) copy, replica, (fig) carbon copy; **das ist nicht das Original sondern eine ~** it's not the original but a copy or imitation

Kopier-: Ko|pier|an|stalt F (Film) printing laboratory, print lab (inf); **Ko|pier|ap|pa|rat** M photocopier; **Ko|pier|be|fehl** M (Comput) copy command

ko|pie|ren [ko'pi:rən] ptp **kopiert** VT to copy; (= nachahmen) to imitate; (= ablichten) to photocopy; (= durchpausen) to trace; (Phot) Film to print; **eine Datei auf die Festplatte ~** to copy a file onto the hard disk; **oft kopiert, nie erreicht** often imitated but never equalled (Brit) or equaled (US) VI to copy; (= fotokopieren) to photocopy

Ko|pie|rer [ko'pi:rɐ] M **-s, -** copier

Kopier-: Ko|pier|funk|ti|on F (Comput) copy function; **Ko|pier|ge|rät** NT photocopier; **ko|pier|ge|schützt** ADJ (Comput, HiFi) copy-protected; **Ko|pier|pa|pier** NT photocopy paper; **Ko|pier|rad** NT (Sew) tracing wheel; **Ko|pier|rah|men** M printing frame; **Ko|pier|schutz** M (Comput, HiFi) copy protection; **mit ~ protected**; **Ko|pier|sper|re** F anti-copy device; **Ko|pier|stift** M indelible pencil; **Ko|pier|ver|fah|ren** NT photocopying process

Ko|pi|lot(in) ['ko:-] M(F) copilot

Ko|pist [ko'pɪst] M **-en, -en, Ko|pis|tin** [-'pɪstɪn] F **-, -nen** (= Nachahmer) imitator; (Art) copyist

Kop|pe ['kɔpə] F **-, -n** (rounded) hilltop

Kop|pel¹ [kɔpl] NT **-s, -** or (Aus) f **-, -n** (Mil) belt

Kop|pel² F **-, -n** **a** (= Weide) paddock, enclosure; **auf** or **in der ~** in the paddock etc **b** (= Hundekoppel) pack; (= Pferdekoppel) string **c** (Mus = Registerzug) coupler

Kop|pel|ge|schäft NT tie-in deal

kop|peln ['kɔpln] VT **a** (= zusammenbinden) Tiere to tie together **b** (= verbinden) to couple, to join (etw an etw acc sth to sth); zwei Dinge to couple together, to join together; Raumschiffe to link up; (fig) to link, to couple; (als Bedingung) to tie; Ziele, Zwecke to conjoin, to combine; **eine Dienstreise mit einem Urlaub ~** to combine a business trip with a holiday (esp Brit) or vacation (US); **einen Vertrag mit einer Klausel ~** to attach a clause to a contract **c** (Elec) couple **d** (Typ) Wort to hyphenate

Kop|pel-: Kop|pel|rick [-rɪk] NT **-s, -e** (Pferderennen) fence; **Kop|pel|schloss** ▲ NT (Mil) belt buckle

Kop|pe|lung ['kɔpəlʊŋ] F **-, -en** **a** (Elec) coupling **b** (= Verbindung) (lit) coupling, joining; (fig, von Raumschiffen) linkup **c** (Mus) coupler

Kop|pe|lungs|ma|nö|ver NT (Space) docking manoeuvre (Brit) or maneuver (US); **ein ~ durchführen** to link up

Köp|per ['kœpɐ] M **-s, -** (N Ger inf) header; **einen ~ machen** to take a header, to dive headfirst

kopp|heis|ter [kɔp'haistɐ] ADV (N Ger) headfirst, headlong; **~ schießen** to do a somersault

Kopp|lung ['kɔplʊŋ] F = Koppelung

Kopp|lungs|ge|schäft F (Econ) package or tie-in (US) deal

Ko|pra ['ko:pra] F **-,** no pl copra

Ko|pro|duk|ti|on ['ko:-] F coproduction

Ko|pro|du|zent(in) ['ko:-] M(F) coproducer

Ko|pro|pha|gie [koprofa'gi:] F **-,** no pl (Psych) coprophagy

Kop|te ['kɔptə] M **-n, -n, Kop|tin** [-tɪn] F **-, -nen** Copt

kop|tisch ['kɔptɪʃ] ADJ Coptic

Ko|pu|la ['ko:pula] F **-, -s** or **-e** [-lɛ:] (Gram) copula

Ko|pu|la|ti|on [kopula'tsio:n] F **-, -en** (Biol) copulation, coupling; (Hort) splice grafting; (old Jur. = Trauung) union

ko|pu|la|tiv [kopula'ti:f] ADJ (Gram) copulative

ko|pu|lie|ren [kopu'li:rən] ptp **kopuliert** VT (Hort) to splice-graft; (old Jur. = trauen) to unite VI (= koitieren) to copulate

kor pret von **küren**

Ko|ral|le [ko'ralə] F **-, -n** coral

Ko|ral|len-: Ko|ral|len|bank F pl **-bänke** coral reef; **Ko|ral|len|fi|scher(in)** M(F) coral fisherman; **Ko|ral|len|pilz** M goatsbeard; **Ko|ral|len|riff** NT coral reef; **ko|ral|len|rot** ADJ coral(-red); **Ko|ral|len|tie|re** PL coral

Ko|ran [ko'ra:n, 'ko:ra(:)n] M **-s,** no pl Koran

Ko|ran|schu|le F Koranic school

Korb [kɔrp] M **-(e)s, ⸚e** ['kœrbə] **a** basket (auch Econ, Fin); (= Tragkorb für Lasttiere auch) pannier; (= Fischkorb auch) creel; (= Bienenkorb) hive; (= Förderkorb) cage; (= Degenkorb, Säbelkorb) basket hilt; **ein ~ Äpfel** a basket of apples; **ein ~ ausländischer Währungen** a basket of foreign currencies **b** (= Korbgeflecht) wicker; **ein Sessel aus ~** a wicker(work) chair, a basket(work) chair **c** (inf: = Abweisung) refusal, rebuff; **einen ~ bekommen/kriegen, sich** (dat) **einen ~ holen** to get a refusal, to be turned down; **jdm einen ~ geben** to turn sb down

Korb-: Korb|ar|beit F wickerwork no pl; **Korb|ball** M basketball; **Korb|blüt|ler** [-bly:tlɐ] M **-s, -** (Bot) composite (flower)

Körb|chen ['kœrpçən] NT **-s, -** **a** dim von **Korb** (von Hund) basket; **ins ~!** (baby-talk) off to or time for beddy-bye(s) (baby-talk) **b** (von Biene) (pollen) basket; (von Büstenhalter) cup

Korb-: Korb|fla|sche F demijohn; **Korb|flech|ter** [-flɛçtɐ] M **-s, -, Korb|flech|te|rin** [-ərɪn] F **-, -nen** basket maker; **Korb|flech|te|rei** [-flɛçtə'rai] F **-,** no pl basket-making; **Korb|ge|flecht** NT basketwork, wickerwork; **Korb|ma|cher(in)** M(F) basket maker; **Korb|mö|bel** PL wicker(work) furniture; **Korb|ses|sel** M , **Korb|stuhl** M wicker(work) chair; **Korb|wa|gen** M bassinet; **Korb|wa|ren** PL wickerwork (articles pl); **Korb|wei|de** F osier; **korb|wei|se** ADV by the basketful

Kord [kɔrt] M **-(e)s, -e** [-də] (Tex) cord, corduroy

Kor|del ['kɔrdl] F **-, -n** cord

Kord|ho|se F corduroy trousers pl (esp Brit), corduroy pants pl (esp US), cords pl (inf); **eine ~** (a pair of) corduroy trousers pl (esp Brit) or pants pl (esp US)

Kor|dil|le|ren [kɔrdɪl'je:rən] PL (Geog) Cordilleras pl

Kord-

Kord|ja|cke F cord(uroy) jacket

Kord|jeans F OR PL cord(uroy) jeans pl; **eine ~** (a pair of) cord(uroy) jeans pl

Kor|don [kɔr'dõ:, (Aus) kɔr'do:n] M **-s, -s** or (Aus) **-e** [-'do:nə] (Mil, Bot) cordon; (= Ordensband auch) ribbon

Kord|samt M cord velvet

Ko|re ['ko:rə] F **-, -n** (Archit) caryatid

Ko|rea [ko're:a] NT **-s** Korea

Ko|re|a|ner [kore'a:nɐ] M **-s, -, Ko|re|a|ne|rin** [-ərɪn] F **-, -nen** Korean

ko|re|a|nisch [kore'a:nɪʃ] ADJ Korean

Ko|re|a|nisch(e) [kore'a:nɪʃ] NT Korean → auch **Deutsch(e)**

Ko|re|a|stra|ße F **die ~** the Korea Strait

Ko|re|fe|rat ['ko:-] NT = **Korreferat**

Ko|re|fe|rent(in) ['ko:-] M(F) = **Korreferent(in)**

kö|ren ['kø:rən] VT to select for breeding purposes

Kor|fi|ot [kɔrˈfioːt] M **-en, -en, Kor|fi|o|tin** [-ˈfioːtɪn] F **-, -nen** Corfuan, Corfiote

Kor|fu [ˈkɔrfu, kɔrˈfuː] NT **-s** Corfu

Kör|hengst M stud

Ko|ri|an|der [koˈriandɐ] M **-s,** no pl coriander

Ko|rinth [koˈrɪnt] NT **-s** Corinth

Ko|rin|the [koˈrɪntə] F **-, -n** currant

Ko|rin|then|ka|cker [-kakɐ] M **-s, -, Ko|rin-then|ka|cke|rin** [-ərɪn] F **-, -nen** (inf) fusspot (Brit inf), fussbudget (US inf)

Ko|rin|ther [koˈrɪntɐ] M **-s, -** Corinthian

Ko|rin|ther|brief M Epistle to the Corinthians, Corinthians sing, no def art

ko|rin|thisch [koˈrɪntɪʃ] ADJ Corinthian

Kork [kɔrk] M **-(e)s, -e** **a** (Bot) cork **b** (= Korken) cork; (aus Plastik) stopper

Kork|ei|che F cork oak or tree

Kor|ken [ˈkɔrkn] M **-s, -** cork; (aus Plastik) stopper

Kor|ken-: Kor|ken|zie|her [-tsiːɐ] M **-s, -** corkscrew; **Kor|ken|zie|her|lo|cken** PL corkscrew curls pl

kor|kig [ˈkɔrkɪç] ADJ corky ADV **~ schmecken** (Wein) to be corked

Kork|mund|stück NT cork filter

Kor|mo|ran [kɔrmoˈraːn] M **-s, -e** cormorant

Korn¹ [kɔrn] NT **-(e)s, -er** [ˈkœrnɐ] **a** (= Samenkorn) seed, grain; (= Pfefferkorn) corn; (= Salzkorn, Sandkorn, Tech, Phot, Typ) grain; (= Hagelkorn) stone; (= Staubkorn) speck **b** no pl (= Getreide) grain, corn (Brit); **das ~ steht gut** the grain or corn (Brit) looks promising

Korn² M **-(e)s, -** or **-s** (= Kornbranntwein) corn schnapps

Korn³ NT **-(e)s, -e** (am Gewehr) front sight, bead; **jdn/etw aufs ~ nehmen** (lit) to draw a bead on sb/sth; (fig) to hit out at sth; **jdn aufs ~ nehmen** (fig) to start keeping tabs on sb

Korn-: Korn|äh|re F ear of corn (Brit) or grain; **Korn|blu|me** F cornflower; **korn|blu|men|blau** ADJ cornflower blue; (hum: = volltrunken) as drunk as a lord (Brit) or sailor (US); **Korn|brannt|wein** M (form) corn schnapps

Körn|chen [ˈkœrnçən] NT **-s, -** dim von **Korn¹** small grain, granule; **ein ~ Wahrheit** a grain of truth

Körndl|bau|er [ˈkœrndl-] M pl **-bauern, Körndl|bäu|e|rin** F (Aus) corn-growing (Brit) or grain-growing farmer

kör|nen [ˈkœrnən] VT to granulate, to grain; (= aufrauen) to roughen

Kör|ner [ˈkœrnɐ] M **-s, -** centre (Brit) or center (US) punch

Kör|ner-: Kör|ner|fres|ser M (Zool) grain-eating bird, granivore (form); **Kör|ner|fres|ser(in)** M(F) (inf) health food freak (inf); **Kör|ner|fut|ter** NT grain or corn (Brit) (for animal feeding)

Kor|nett¹ [kɔrˈnɛt] NT **-s, -e** or **-s** (Mus) cornet

Kor|nett² M **-(e)s, -e** or **-s** (old Mil) cornet (old)

Korn|feld NT cornfield (Brit), grain field

kör|nig [ˈkœrnɪç] ADJ granular, grainy

-kör|nig ADJ suf -grained; **grob-/feinkörnig** coarse-/fine-grained

kor|nisch [ˈkɔrnɪʃ] ADJ Cornish

Korn-: Korn|kä|fer M corn weevil; **Korn|kam|mer** F (lit, fig) granary; **Korn|ra|de** F (Bot) corncockle; **Korn|spei|cher** M granary

Kör|nung [ˈkœrnʊŋ] F **-, -en** (Tech) grain size; (Phot) granularity; (Hunt) decoy place; **Schmirgelpapier mit feiner ~** fine-grain sandpaper

Ko|ro|na [koˈroːna] F **-, Koronen** [-nən] corona; (inf) crowd (inf), gang (inf)

Ko|ro|nar- [koroˈnaːr-] (Anat, Med) in cpds coronary; **Ko|ro|nar|ar|te|rie** F coronary artery; **Ko|ro|nar|ge|fäß** NT coronary vessel

Kör|per [ˈkœrpɐ] M **-s, -** (alle Bedeutungen) body; (= Schiffskörper) hull; **~ und Geist** mind and

---

body; **das braucht der ~** it's good for you; **am ganzen ~ beben** or **zittern/frieren** to tremble/to be cold all over

Kör|per-: Kör|per|bau M , no pl physique, build; **Kör|per|bau|typ** M physical type; **Kör|per|be|herr|schung** F physical control; **kör|per|be|hin|dert** [-bəhɪndɐt] ADJ physically handicapped or disabled; **Kör|per|be|hin|der|te(r)** MF decl as adj physically handicapped or disabled person; **die ~n** the disabled, the physically handicapped; **kör|per|be|tont** ADJ (Sport) (very) physical; (Fashion) Kleid etc figure-hugging ADV **~ geschnitten** (Kleid etc) cut to emphasize the figure; **kör|per|ei|gen** ADJ produced or occurring naturally in the body; **Kör|per|er|tüch|ti|gung** F physical training, keep-fit exercises pl; **das dient der ~** it helps keep you fit; **Kör|per|fül|le** F (euph) corpulence; **Kör|per|ge|ruch** M body odour (Brit) or odor (US), BO (inf); **Kör|per|ge|wicht** NT weight; **Kör|per|grö|ße** F height; **Kör|per|hal|tung** F posture, bearing; **Kör|per|kon|takt** M physical or bodily contact; **Kör|per|kraft** F physical or bodily strength; **Kör|per|län|ge** F height; (von Schlange etc) (body) length

kör|per|lich [ˈkœrpɐlɪç] ADJ physical; (= stofflich) material, corporeal; **~e Arbeit** manual work; **~e Züchtigung** corporal punishment; **~e Vereinigung** (geh) physical union ADV physically; **sich ~ ertüchtigen** to keep oneself physically fit

Kör|per-: kör|per|los ADJ bodiless, incorporeal; **Kör|per|lo|ti|on** F body lotion; **Kör|per|ma|ße** PL measurements pl; **Kör|per|öff|nung** F (Anat) orifice of the body; **Kör|per|pfle|ge** F personal hygiene; **Kör|per|pu|der** M OR NT body powder; **kör|per|reich** ADJ Wein full-bodied; **Kör|per|säf|te** PL (liter) blood sing; (= Körperflüssigkeit) body or bodily fluids pl

Kör|per|schaft [ˈkœrpɐʃaft] F **-, -en** corporation, (corporate) body; **gesetzgebende ~** legislative body

Kör|per|schaft(s)|steu|er F corporation tax

Kör|per-: Kör|per|schwä|che F physical weakness; **Kör|per|spra|che** F body language; **Kör|per|spray** M OR NT body spray; **Kör|per|teil** M part of the body; **Kör|per|tem|pe|ra|tur** F body temperature; **Kör|per|ver|let|zung** F (Jur) bodily or physical injury; **fahrlässige ~** physical injury resulting from negligence; **einfache ~** actual bodily harm; **schwere ~** grievous bodily harm; **~ im Amt** injury caused by a policeman/public official – **mit tödlichem Ausgang** manslaughter; **Kör|per|wär|me** F body heat; **Kör|per|zel|le** F body cell

Kor|po|ral [kɔrpoˈraːl] M **-s, -e** or **Korporäle** [-ˈrɛːlə], **Kor|po|ra|lin** [-ˈraːlɪn] F **-, -nen** corporal

Kor|po|ra|ti|on [kɔrporaˈtsioːn] F **-, -en** **a** (= Studentenverbindung) student society, fraternity (US) **b** (= Körperschaft) corporation

kor|po|ra|tiv [kɔrporaˈtiːf] ADJ Staat corporate

kor|po|riert [kɔrpoˈriːɐt] ADJ pred **~ sein** to be a member of a students' society (which fights duels)

Korps [koːɐ] NT **-, -** [koːɐ(s), koːɐs] (Mil) corps; (Univ) (duelling (Brit) or dueling (US)) corps

Korps-: Korps|bru|der M fellow member of a student (duelling (Brit) or dueling (US)) society; **Korps|geist** M esprit de corps; **Korps|stu|dent** M student belonging to a (duelling (Brit) or dueling (US)) society

kor|pu|lent [kɔrpuˈlɛnt] ADJ corpulent

Kor|pu|lenz [kɔrpuˈlɛnts] F **-,** no pl corpulence

Kor|pus¹ [ˈkɔrpʊs] M **-, -se** (Art) body of Christ; (hum inf: = Körper) body

Kor|pus² NT **-, Korpora** [ˈkɔrpora] **a** (Ling) corpus **b** (Mus) resonance box

kor|pus|ba|siert ADJ (Ling) Lexikografie corpus-based

Kor|pus|kel [kɔrˈpʊskl] NT **-s, -n** or f **-, -n** (Phys) particle, corpuscle

Kor|pus|lin|gu|is|tik F (Ling) corpus linguistics sing

Kor|re|fe|rat [ˈkɔ-] NT **a** (= Vortrag) supplementary paper or report **b** (= Prüfung) second marking or assessment

Kor|re|fe|rent(in) [ˈkɔ-] M(F) **a** (= Redner) reader of a supplementary paper **b** (= Prüfer) second examiner

kor|rekt [kɔˈrɛkt] ADJ **a** (= richtig, anständig) correct; Frage civil; **politisch ~** politically correct **b** (sl: = toll) shit-hot (Brit sl), wicked (sl) ADV correctly; gekleidet appropriately; darstellen accurately

kor|rekt|er|wei|se [kɔˈrɛktɐˈvaizə] ADV to be correct, by rights

Kor|rekt|heit F **-,** no pl correctness; **politische ~** political correctness

Kor|rek|tiv [kɔrɛkˈtiːf] NT **-s, -e** [-və] corrective

Kor|rek|tor [kɔˈrɛktoːɐ] M **-s,** **Korrektoren** [-ˈtoːrən], **Kor|rek|to|rin** [-ˈtoːrɪn] F **-, -nen** (Typ) proofreader

Kor|rek|tur [kɔrɛkˈtuːɐ] F **-, -en** correction; (Typ) (= Vorgang) proofreading; (= Verbesserung) proof correction; (= Korrekturfahne) proof; **~ lesen** to read or correct (the) proofs, to do (the) proofreading (bei etw for sth), to proofread (bei etw sth); **kann er ~ lesen?** can he proofread?

Kor|rek|tur-: Kor|rek|tur|ab|zug M galley (proof); **Kor|rek|tur|band** [-bant] NT pl **-bänder** correction tape; **Kor|rek|tur|bo|gen** M page proof; **Kor|rek|tur|fah|ne** F galley (proof); **Kor|rek|tur|flüs|sig|keit** F correction fluid, White-Out® (US); **Kor|rek|tur|le|sen** NT proofreading; **Kor|rek|tur|spei|cher** M correction memory; **Kor|rek|tur|tas|te** F correction key; **Kor|rek|tur|zei|chen** NT proofreader's mark

Kor|re|lat [kɔreˈlaːt] NT **-(e)s, -e** correlate

kor|re|lie|ren [kɔreˈliːrən] ptp **korreliert** VI to correlate

kor|re|pe|tie|ren [kɔrepeˈtiːrən] ptp **korrepetiert** VI to act as a repetitor, to coach opera singers

Kor|re|pe|ti|tor [kɔrepeˈtiːtoːɐ] M **-s, Korrepetitoren** [-ˈtoːrən] (Mus) répétiteur, coach

Kor|re|pe|ti|to|rin [kɔrepetiˈtoːrɪn] F **-, -nen** (Mus) répétiteuse, coach

Kor|res|pon|dent [kɔrɛspɔnˈdɛnt] M **-en, -en, Kor|res|pon|den|tin** [-ˈdɛntɪn] F **-, -nen** correspondent

Kor|res|pon|denz [kɔrɛspɔnˈdɛnts] F **-, -en** correspondence; **mit jdm in ~ stehen** to be in correspondence with sb

Kor|res|pon|denz-: Kor|res|pon|denz|bü|ro NT news or press agency; **Kor|res|pon|denz|schrift** F (Comput) letter quality

kor|res|pon|die|ren [kɔrɛspɔnˈdiːrən] ptp **korrespondiert** VI **a** (in Briefwechsel stehen) to correspond; **~des Mitglied** corresponding member **b** (= entsprechen) to correspond (mit to, with); **~der Winkel** corresponding angle

Kor|ri|dor [ˈkɔridoːɐ] M **-s, -e** (= auch Luftkorridor etc) corridor; (= Flur) hall; **der (Polnische) ~** (Hist) the Polish Corridor

kor|ri|gier|bar ADJ able to be corrected, corrigible (form); **ein nicht so leicht ~er Sprachfehler** a speech defect which is not so easy to put right or to correct

kor|ri|gie|ren [kɔriˈgiːrən] ptp **korrigiert** VT (= berichtigen) to correct; Aufsätze etc auch to mark; Meinung, Einstellung to alter, to change; **nach oben ~** to adjust upwards; Gehaltsangebot etc auch to top up; **nach unten ~** to adjust downwards; Gehaltsforderung etc auch to trim down

kor|ro|die|ren [kɔroˈdiːrən] ptp **korrodiert** VTI (vi: aux sein) to corrode

Kor|ro|si|on [kɔroˈzioːn] F **-, -en** corrosion

Kor|ro|si|ons-: kor|ro|si|ons|an|fäl|lig ADJ corrosion-prone; **kor|ro|si|ons|be|stän|dig, kor|ro|si|ons|fest** ADJ corrosion-resistant; **kor|ro|si|ons|frei** ADJ noncorrosive, non-corroding; **Kor|ro|si|ons|schutz** M corrosion prevention

kor|ro|siv [kɔro'ziːf] ADJ corrosive

kor|rum|pie|ren [kɔrʊm'piːrən] ptp **korrumpiert** VT to corrupt

kor|rum|piert [kɔrʊm'piːɐt] ADJ corrupt

kor|rupt [kɔ'rʊpt] ADJ corrupt ADV handeln corruptly; **als ~ gelten** to be considered corrupt

Kor|rupt|heit F -, *no pl* corruptness

Kor|rup|ti|on [kɔrʊp'tsioːn] F -, *no pl* corruption

Kor|rup|ti|ons|af|fä|re F corruption scandal

Kor|sa|ge [kɔr'zaːʒə] F -, -n corsage

Kor|sar [kɔr'zaːɐ] M -en, -en (*Hist*) corsair

Kor|se ['kɔrzə] M -n, -n, **Kor|sin** ['kɔrzɪn] F -, -nen Corsican

Kor|se|lett [kɔrzə'lɛt] NT -(e)s, -e *or* -s corselet

Kor|sett [kɔr'zɛt] NT -s, -s *or* -e corset, corsets *pl*

Kor|sett|stan|ge F stay

Kor|si|ka ['kɔrzika] NT -s Corsica

Kor|sin F -, -nen Corsican

kor|sisch ['kɔrzɪʃ] ADJ Corsican

Kor|sisch(e) NT Corsican → *auch* **Deutsch(e)**

Kor|so ['kɔrso] M -s, -s (= *Umzug*) parade, procession; (= *breite Straße*) avenue; (*old:* = *Pferderennen*) horse race

Kor|tex ['kɔrtɛks] M -(es), **Kortizes** [kɔr'titseːs] (*Anat*) cortex

kor|ti|kal [kɔrti'kaːl] ADJ (*Anat*) cortical

Kor|ti|son [kɔrti'zoːn] NT -s, -e (*Med*) cortisone

Ko|rund [ko'rʊnt] M -(e)s, -e [-də] (*Geol*) corundum

Kö|rung ['køːrʊŋ] F -, -en selection for breeding purposes

Kor|vet|te [kɔr'vɛtə] F -, -n (*Naut*) corvette; (*Sport*) jump to handstand

Kor|vet|ten|ka|pi|tän(in) M(F) lieutenant commander

Ko|ry|phäe [kory'fɛːə] F -, -n genius; (*auf einem Gebiet*) eminent authority

Ko|sak [ko'zak] M -en, -en Cossack

Ko|sa|ken|müt|ze F cossack hat

Ko|sche|nil|le [kɔʃə'nɪljə] F -, *no pl* cochineal

ko|scher ['koːʃɐ] ADJ (*Rel, fig inf*) kosher ADV a ~ **kochen/schlachten** to cook/slaughter according to kosher requirements b (*fig inf*) **dabei ist es nicht ganz ~ zugegangen** that wasn't quite kosher (*inf*)

K.-o.-Schlag [kaː'oː-] M knockout blow; **durch ~ siegen** to win by a knockout

ko|sen ['koːzn] VTI (*dated, geh*) **jdn ~, mit jdm ~** to fondle *or* caress sb; **~d** caressingly; **miteinander ~** to bill and coo

Ko|se|form F affectionate *or* familiar form (*of proper name*)

Ko|se|na|me M pet name; **Ko|se|wort** NT *pl* **-wörter** *or* **-worte** term of endearment *or* affection

K.-o.-Sieg [kaː'oː-] M knockout victory

Ko|si|nus ['koːzinʊs] M (*Math*) cosine

Kos|me|tik [kɔs'meːtɪk] F -, *no pl* beauty culture; (= *Kosmetika, fig*) cosmetics *pl*; **eine Reform, die sich nicht nur auf ~ beschränkt** a reform which is not merely cosmetic

Kos|me|ti|ker [kɔs'meːtɪkɐ] M -s, -, **Kos|me|ti|ke|rin** [-ərɪn] F -, -nen beautician, cosmetician

Kos|me|tik-: Kos|me|tik|in|sti|tut NT beauty parlour (*Brit*) *or* parlor (*US*); **Kos|me|tik|kof|fer** M vanity case; **Kos|me|tik|sa|lon** beauty parlour (*Brit*), beauty parlor (*US*); **Kos|me|tik|tuch** NT *pl* **-tücher** paper tissue

Kos|me|ti|kum [kɔs'meːtɪkʊm] NT -s, **Kosmetika** [-ka] cosmetic

kos|me|tisch [kɔs'meːtɪʃ] ADJ cosmetic; **ein ~es Mittel** a cosmetic ADV behandeln cosmetically

kos|misch ['kɔsmɪʃ] ADJ cosmic; **~ beeinflusst werden** to be influenced by the stars *or* the cosmos

Kos|mo- [kɔsmo-]: **Kos|mo|bio|lo|gie** F space *or* cosmic biology; **Kos|mo|go|nie** [kɔsmogo-'niː] F -, -n [-'niːən] cosmogony; **Kos|mo|lo|ge** [kɔsmo'loːgə] M -n, -n, **Kos|mo|lo|gin** [-'loːgɪn] F -, -nen cosmologist; **Kos|mo|lo|gie** [kɔsmolo'giː] F -, -n [-'giːən] cosmology; **Kos|mo|naut** [kɔsmo'naut] M -en, -en, **Kos|mo|nau|tin** [-'nautɪn] F -, -nen cosmonaut; **Kos|mo|po|lit** [kɔsmopo'liːt] M -en, -en, **Kos|mo|po|li|tin** [-'liːtɪn] F -, -nen cosmopolitan; **kos|mo|po|li|tisch** [kɔsmopo'liːtɪʃ] ADJ cosmopolitan

Kos|mos ['kɔsmɔs] M -, *no pl* cosmos

Ko|so|va|re [kɔso'vaːrə] M -n, -n Kosovar, **Ko|so|va|rin** [kɔso'vaːrɪn] F -, -nen Kosovar woman *or* girl

Ko|so|vo ['kɔsovo] M -s (*Geog*) (**der**) ~ Kosovo

Ko|so|vo-Al|ba|ner(in) M(F) Kosovo Albanian

Kost [kɔst] F -, *no pl* a (= *Nahrung, Essen*) food, fare; **vegetarische/fleischlose ~** vegetarian/meatless diet; **geistige ~** (*fig*) intellectual fare; **leichte/schwere ~** (*fig*) easy/heavy going, heavy stuff (*inf*) b (*dated:* = *Beköstigung*) board; **jdn in ~ nehmen** to take sb as a boarder; **(freie) ~ und Logis** *or* **Wohnung** (free) board and lodging

kost|bar ADJ (= *wertvoll*) valuable, precious; (= *luxuriös*) luxurious, sumptuous ADV verziert, geschmückt, geschnitzt, gearbeitet sumptuously; *sich kleiden* luxuriously

Kost|bar|keit ['kɔstbaːɐkait] F -, -en (= *Gegenstand*) treasure, precious object; (= *Leckerbissen*) delicacy

kos|ten¹ ['kɔstn] VT a (*lit, fig*) to cost; **was kostet das?** how much *or* what does it cost?, how much is it?; **was soll das ~?** what's it going to cost?; **das kostet nicht die Welt** it doesn't cost the earth; **koste es, was es wolle** whatever the cost; **das/die lasse ich mich etwas ~** I don't mind spending a bit of money on it/them; **jdn sein Leben/den Sieg ~** to cost sb his life/the victory; **was kostet die Welt?** (*inf*) the world's your/their *etc* oyster b (= *in Anspruch nehmen*) Zeit, Geduld *etc* to take VI to cost; **das kostet** (*inf*) it costs something *or* a bit; **das hat gekostet** (*inf*) it cost something *or* a bit

kos|ten² VT (= *probieren*) to taste, to try, to sample; (*fig*) to taste; Freuden *etc* to taste, to taste of (*liter*) VI to taste; **willst du mal ~?** would you like a taste?; **von etw ~** to taste *or* try *or* sample sth

Kos|ten ['kɔstn] PL cost(s); (*Jur*) costs *pl*; (= *Unkosten*) expenses *pl*; **die ~ tragen** to bear the cost(s); **auf ~ von** *or* +*gen* at the expense of; **auf ~ des Steuerzahlers** at the expense of the taxpayer, at the taxpayer's expense; **auf meine ~** (*lit, fig*) at my expense; **auf seine ~ kommen** to cover one's expenses, (*fig*) to get one's money's worth, to have a very good time; **~ spielen keine Rolle** money's no object; **~ sparend** cost-saving; **etw ~ sparend herstellen** to produce sth at low cost; **~ sparender arbeiten** to reduce costs

Kos|ten-: Kos|ten|auf|stel|lung F statement of costs; **Kos|ten|auf|wand** M expense; **mit einem ~ von 50.000 EUR** at a cost of 50,000 euros; **kos|ten|be|wusst** ▲ ADJ cost-conscious; **Kos|ten|be|wusst|sein** ▲ NT cost-consciousness, cost-awareness; **Kos|ten|bin|dung** F cost controls *pl*; **Kos|ten|brem|se** F (*inf*) **auf die ~ treten, die ~ anziehen** to curb costs; **Kos|ten|dämp|fung** F curbing cost expansion; **kos|ten|de|ckend** ADJ **~e Preise** prices that cover one's costs ADV without a

loss, cost-effectively; **~ arbeiten** to cover one's costs, to break even; **~ wirtschaften** to avoid a deficit; **Kos|ten|de|ckung** F cost-effectiveness; **Kos|ten|de|ckungs|grad** M level of cost-effectiveness; **Kos|ten|er|spar|nis** F cost saving; **Kos|ten|er|stat|tung** F reimbursement of costs *or* expenses; **Kos|ten|ex|plo|si|on** F (*inf*) costs explosion; **Kos|ten|fak|tor** M cost factor; **Kos|ten|fra|ge** F question of cost(s); **kos|ten|frei** ADJ cost-free, free of cost ADV free of cost; **kos|ten|güns|tig** ADJ economical ADV arbeiten, produzieren economically; **kos|ten|in|ten|siv** ADJ (*Econ*) cost-intensive; **Kos|ten|la|wi|ne** F spiralling (*Brit*) *or* spiraling (*US*) costs *pl*; **eine ~ auslösen** *or* **lostreten** to cause costs to spiral; **kos|ten|los** ADJ, ADV free (of charge); **kos|ten|mie|te** F rent which covers costs; **kos|ten|neu|tral** ADJ self-financing; **Kos|ten-Nut|zen-Ana|ly|se** F, **Kos|ten-Nut|zen-Rechnung** F cost-benefit analysis; **kos|ten|pflich|tig** [-pflɪçtɪç] ADJ liable to pay costs, with costs ADV **eine Klage ~ abweisen** to dismiss a case with costs; **~ verwarnt werden** to be fined; **~ verurteilt werden** to have costs awarded against one, to have to pay costs; **ein Kfz ~ abschleppen** to tow away a car at the owner's expense, to impound a car; **Kos|ten|pla|nung** F costing; **Kos|ten|punkt** M cost question; **~?** (*inf*) what'll it cost?, how much?; **~: 100 EUR** (*inf*) cost, 100 euros; **Kos|ten|rech|nung** F calculation of costs; **Kos|ten|satz** M rate; **Kos|ten|schrau|be** F cost spiral; **an der ~ drehen** to (try to) cut down on costs; **Kos|ten|spa|rend** △ ADJ → **Kosten**; **Kos|ten|stei|ge|rung** F increase in costs; **Kos|ten|stel|le** F cost centre (*Brit*) *or* center (*US*); **Kos|ten|trä|ger(in)** M(F) (*der*) ~ **sein** to bear the cost; **Kos|ten|vor|an|schlag** M (costs) estimate; **Kos|ten|vor|schuss** ▲ M advance

Kost-: Kost|gän|ger [-gɛŋɐ] M -s, -, **Kost|gän|ge|rin** [-ərɪn] F -, -nen (*dated*) boarder; **Kost|geld** NT board

köst|lich ['kœstlɪç] ADJ a Wein, Speise exquisite; Luft magnificent b (= *amüsant*) priceless; **~, wie er darauf reagiert hat** it was priceless the way he reacted; **du bist ja ~** you're priceless ADV a (= *gut*) schmecken delicious b **sich ~ amüsieren/unterhalten** to have a great time

Köst|lich|keit F -, -en a (= *köstliche Sache*) treat, delight; **eine kulinarische ~** a culinary delicacy; **eine literarische ~** a literary gem b *no pl* (*von Speise, Getränk*) **ein Wein von einmaliger ~** a uniquely exquisite wine

Kost-: Kost|pro|be F (*von Wein, Käse etc*) taste; (*fig*) sample; **bei der ~** while tasting; **warst du auch bei der ~?** were you at the tasting too?; **kost|spie|lig** [-ʃpiːlɪç] ADJ costly, expensive

Kos|tüm [kɔs'tyːm] NT -s, -e a (*Theat:* = *Tracht*) costume b (= *Maskenkostüm*) fancy dress c (= *Damenkostüm*) suit

Kos|tüm-: Kos|tüm|ball M fancy-dress ball; **Kos|tüm|bild|ner(in)** M(F) costume designer; **Kos|tüm|fest** NT fancy-dress ball; **Kos|tüm|film** M period film *or* picture

kos|tü|mie|ren [kɔsty'miːrən] ptp **kostümiert** VR to dress up

Kos|tüm-: Kos|tüm|pro|be F (*Theat*) dress rehearsal; **Kos|tüm|ver|leih** M (theatrical) costume agency

Kost|ver|äch|ter(in) M(F) **kein ~/keine ~in sein** (*hum*) (= *Feinschmecker sein*) to be fond of one's food, to enjoy one's food; **bei Frauen ist er kein ~** he's one for the ladies (*Brit*), he's a bit of a lad (*Brit inf*) *or* a womanizer

Kot [koːt] M -(e)s, *no pl* (*form*) excrement, faeces *pl* (*Brit form*), feces *pl* (*US form*); (*liter:* = *Schmutz, Dreck*) mire, filth

Ko|tan|gens ['koː-] M (*Math*) cotangent

Ko|tau ['koːtau] M -s, -s **(einen)** ~ **machen** (*pej*) to kowtow (*vor jdm* to sb)

Ko|te¹ ['koːtə] F -, -n (Surv) spot height

Ko|te² F -, -n (= Lappenzelt) tent

Ko|te|lett ['kɔtlɛt, kɔt'lɛt] NT -(e)s, -s or (rare) -e chop, cutlet

Ko|te|let|te [kotə'lɛtə] F -, -n usu pl (side) whisker, sideboard (Brit), sideburn

ko|ten ['koːtn] VI (form) to defecate (form)

Kö|ter ['koːtɐ] M -s, - (pej) damn dog (inf)

Kot|flü|gel M (Aut) wing

ko|tig ['koːtɪç] ADJ filthy

K.-o.-Trop|fen [kaː'oː-] PL (inf) knockout drops pl (inf)

Kotz|bro|cken M (inf) mean bastard (Brit sl), son of a bitch (esp US sl)

Kot|ze¹ ['kɔtsə] F -, no pl (vulg = Erbrochenes) vomit, puke (sl); **dabei krieg ich die ~** it makes me want to puke (sl); **da kommt einem die ~ hoch** it makes you want to puke (sl)

Kot|ze² F -, -n (S Ger, Aus, = Umhang aus Wolle) woollen (Brit) or woolen (US) cape

kot|zen ['kɔtsn] VI (sl) to throw up (inf), to puke (sl); **das ist zum Kotzen** it makes you sick; **du bist zum Kotzen** you make me sick, you make me want to throw up (inf) or puke (sl); **da kann man das große Kotzen kriegen** it makes you want to throw up (inf) or puke (sl)

kotz|übel ADJ (inf) **mir ist ~** I feel like throwing up (inf)

KP [kaː'peː] F -, -s abbr von **Kommunistische Partei**

KPD [kaːpeː'deː] F - abbr von **Kommunistische Partei Deutschlands**

KPdSU [kaːpeːdeːɛs'uː] F - (Hist) abbr von **Kommunistische Partei der Sowjetunion** Communist Party of the Soviet Union

Kraal [kraːl] M -s, -e kraal

Krab|be ['krabə] F -, -n a (Zool) (klein) shrimp; (größer) prawn b (dated inf: = Kind) tot (inf), mite (inf); **eine süße kleine ~** a sweet little thing c (Archit) crocket

Krab|bel-: Krab|bel|al|ter NT crawling stage (of a baby); **Krab|bel|grup|pe** F playgroup

krab|beln ['krabln] VI aux sein to crawl VT (= kitzeln) to tickle VTI impers (= kitzeln) to tickle; (= jucken) to itch → **kribbeln**

Krab|ben|cock|tail M prawn cocktail

krach [krax] INTERJ crash, bang

Krach [krax] M -(e)s, ⸚e ['krɛçə] a no pl (= Lärm) noise, din, racket (inf); (= Schlag) crash, bang; **~ machen** to make a noise etc b (inf: = Zank, Streit) row, quarrel, fight (um about); **mit jdm ~ haben** to have a row etc with sb, to row or quarrel or fight with sb; **mit jdm ~ kriegen** to get into trouble with sb, to have a row with sb; **~ schlagen** to make a fuss c (= Börsenkrach) crash

kra|chen ['kraxn] VI a (= Lärm machen) to crash, to bang; (Holz) to creak; (Schuss) to ring out; (Donner) to crash; **~d fallen** etc to fall etc with a crash or bang; **..., dass es nur so krachte** (lit) ... with a bang or crash; (fig) ... with a vengeance; **sonst krachts!** (inf) or there'll be trouble; **gleich krachts** (inf) there's going to be trouble; **es hat gekracht** (inf: Zusammenstoß) there's been a crash b aux sein (inf) (= aufplatzen) to rip (open), to split; (= brechen) to break; (Eis) to crack; (Betrieb) to crash c aux sein (inf: = aufprallen) to crash VR (inf) to have a row or fight or quarrel

Kra|cher ['kraxɐ] M -s, - banger (Brit), firecracker (US)

Kra|cherl ['kraxɐl] NT -s, -(n) (Aus inf) fizzy pop (Brit inf) or drink

Krach-: krach|le|dern ['kraxleːdɐn] ADJ (fig hum) rustic; **Krach|le|der|ne** ['kraxleːdɐnə] F decl as adj leather shorts pl, lederhosen pl; **Krach|ma|cher(in)** M(F) (inf) (lit) noisy person or character; (fig) troublemaker; **hör auf, du ~!** must you make so much noise!

kräch|zen ['krɛçtsn] VI to croak; (Vogel) to caw; **eine ~de Stimme** a croaky voice

Kräch|zen NT -s, no pl croak(ing); (von Vogel) caw(ing)

kra|cken ['krakn, 'krɛkn] VT (Chem) to crack

Krä|cker ['krɛkɐ] M -s, - (Cook) cracker

Krad [kraːt] NT -(e)s, ⸚er ['krɛːdɐ] (Mil, dated) motorcycle

Krad-: Krad|fah|rer(in) M(F) (dated) motor cyclist; **Krad|mel|der(in)** M(F) (Mil) motorcycle despatch rider

kraft [kraft] PREP +gen (form) by virtue of; (= mittels) by use of; **~ meines Amtes** by virtue of my office; **~ meiner Befugnisse** on the strength of or by virtue of my authority

Kraft [kraft] F -, ⸚e ['krɛftə] a (körperlich, sittlich) strength no pl; (geistig, schöpferisch) powers pl; (militärisch, wirtschaftlich) strength, power; (von Prosa, Stimme) strength, power, force; (= Energie) energy, energies pl; **er weiß nicht wohin mit seiner ~** (inf) he's just bubbling over with energy; **er kann vor ~ nicht mehr laufen** (hum) he's so muscle-bound he can hardly move; **die Kräfte (mit jdm) messen** to try or pit one's strength (against sb); (fig) to pit oneself against sb; **wenn man alle Kräfte anspannt** or **zusammennimmt** if you summon up all your strength; **seine Kräfte sammeln** to build up or recover one's strength; **mit frischer ~** with renewed strength; **mit letzter ~** with one's last ounce of strength; **die ~ aufbringen, etw zu tun** to find the strength to do sth; **mit vereinten Kräften werden wir ...** if we combine our efforts or if we join forces we will ...; **die ~ der Verzweiflung** the strength born of desperation; **das geht über meine Kräfte, das übersteigt meine Kräfte** it's more than I can take, it's too much for me; **ich bin am Ende meiner ~** I can't take any more; **mit aller ~** or **voller ~** with all one's might or strength; **er will mit aller ~ durchsetzen, dass ...** he will do his utmost to ensure that ...; **aus eigener ~** by oneself; (fig auch) by one's own efforts, single-handedly; **nach (besten) Kräften** to the best of one's ability; **er tat, was in seinen Kräften stand** he did everything (with)in his power; **nicht bei Kräften sein** not to be in very good shape; **wieder bei Kräften sein** to have (got) one's strength back; **wieder zu Kräften kommen** to regain one's strength → **messen** VTI b (Phys: einer Reaktion etc) force; (einer Wirkung) strength, power; (no pl: = Wirksamkeit, liter, Bibl: = Macht) power; **die treibende ~** (fig) the driving force; **das Gleichgewicht der Kräfte** (Pol) the balance of power; **das Parallelogramm der Kräfte** (Phys) the parallelogram of forces; **die heilende ~ der Sonne** the healing power of the sun; **die tröstende ~ der Musik** the comforting power of music c (usu pl: in Wirtschaft, Politik etc) force d no pl (Jur: = Geltung) force; **in ~ sein/treten/setzen** to be in/come into/bring into force; **außer ~ sein** to have ceased to be in force, to be no longer in force; **außer ~ treten** to cease to be in force; **außer ~ setzen** to cancel, to annul e no pl (Naut: = Geschwindigkeit) **halbe/volle ~ voraus!** half/full speed ahead f (= Arbeitskraft) employee, worker; (= Haushaltskraft) domestic help; (= Lehrkraft) teacher

Kraft-: Kraft|akt M strongman act; (fig) show of strength; **Kraft|an|stren|gung** F exertion; **Kraft|an|trieb** M power drive; **mit ~** power-driven; **Kraft|arm** M (Phys) lever arm to which force is applied; **Kraft|auf|wand** M effort; **unnützer ~** wasted effort, waste of energy; **Kraft|aus|druck** M pl -ausdrücke swearword; **Kraftausdrücke** strong language; **Kraft|brü|he** F beef tea; **Kraft|drosch|ke** F (form) hackney carriage (form), taxicab; **Kraft|ein|heit** F (Phys) unit of force

Kräf|te|pa|ral|le|lo|gramm NT parallelogram of forces

Kraft|er|spar|nis F saving of energy or effort

Kräf|te-: Kräf|te|spiel NT power play; **Kräf|te|ver|fall** M loss of strength; **Kräf|te|ver|hält|nis** NT (Pol) balance of power; (von Mannschaften etc) relative strength; **Kräf|te|ver|la|ge|rung** F (Pol) power shift; **Kräf|te|ver|schleiß** M waste of energy

Kraft|fah|rer(in) M(F) (form) motorist, driver; (als Beruf) driver

Kraft|fahr-: Kraft|fahr|park M fleet of motor vehicles; **kraft|fahr|tech|nisch** ADJ attr mechanical; **~e Ausbildung** training in motor mechanics ADV mechanically; **Kraft|fahr|trup|pe** F (Mil) motorized unit

Kraft|fahr|zeug NT motor vehicle

Kraft|fahr|zeug-: Kraft|fahr|zeug|brief M (vehicle) registration document, logbook (Brit); **Kraft|fahr|zeug|kenn|zei|chen** NT (vehicle) registration; **Kraft|fahr|zeug|me|cha|ni|ker(in)** M(F) motor mechanic; **Kraft|fahr|zeug|schein** M (vehicle) registration document; **Kraft|fahr|zeug|steu|er** F motor vehicle tax, road tax (Brit); **Kraft|fahr|zeug|ver|si|che|rung** F car insurance

Kraft-: Kraft|feld NT (Phys) force field; **Kraft|fut|ter** NT concentrated feed(stuff)

kräf|tig ['krɛftɪç] ADJ strong; Mann, Geschmack, Muskel, Stimme auch powerful; Ausdrucksweise auch powerful, forceful; Haarwuchs healthy, strong; Pflanze healthy; Farbe rich, strong; Schlag hard, powerful, hefty (inf); Händedruck firm, powerful; Fluch violent; Suppe, Essen nourishing; (= groß) Portion, Preiserhöhung big, massive; Beifall loud; **~e Ausdrücke** strong language; **einen ~en Schluck nehmen** to take a good or big swig; **eine ~e Tracht Prügel** a good or sound or thorough beating ADV a gebaut strongly, powerfully; zuschlagen, treten, pressen, drücken, blasen hard; klatschen loudly; lachen, mitsingen heartily; fluchen, niesen violently; **etw ~ schütteln/polieren/umrühren** to shake/polish/stir sth vigorously, to give sth a good shake/polish/stir; **jdn ~ verprügeln** to give sb a sound or good or thorough beating; **~ essen** to eat well; **~ trinken** to drink a lot; **husten Sie mal ~** have a good cough; **er hat sich ~ dagegen gewehrt** he objected most strongly; (körperlich) he put up a strong resistance; **sich für etw ~ einsetzen** to support sth strongly or energetically b (zur Verstärkung) really; **es hat ~ geregnet/geschneit** it really rained/snowed, it rained/snowed heavily; **die Preise sind ~ gestiegen** prices have gone up a lot, prices have really gone up; **jdn ~ ausschimpfen** to give sb a good bawling out (inf), to really give sb a bawling out (inf); **sich ~ täuschen** (inf) to be really or very much or greatly mistaken; **jdn ~ belügen** (inf) to tell sb a pack of lies; **sich ~ ausweinen** (inf) to have a good cry; **sich ~ ärgern** to get really or mighty (inf) annoyed

kräf|ti|gen ['krɛftɪɡn] VT (geh) Körper, Muskeln to strengthen; **jdn ~** to build up sb's strength; (Luft, Bad etc) to invigorate sb; (Essen, Mittel etc) to fortify sb

Kräf|ti|gung ['krɛftɪɡʊŋ] F -, no pl (geh) strengthening; (durch Luft, Bad) invigoration; (durch Essen, Mittel) fortification

Kräf|ti|gungs|mit|tel NT tonic

Kräf|ti|ni|en PL (Phys) lines pl of force

kraft|los ADJ (= schwach) feeble, weak; (= schlaff) limp; (= machtlos) powerless; (Jur) invalid ADV weakly; **~ zur Seite fallen** to fall limply to one side; **~ sank er zurück** he fell feebly back

Kraft|los|er|klä|rung F (Jur) invalidation, annulment

Kraft|lo|sig|keit F -, no pl feebleness, weakness

Kraft-: Kraft|mei|er [-maɪɐ] M -s, - (inf) muscle man (inf); (fig) strongman; **Kraft|mei|e|rei** [-maɪə'raɪ] F -, no pl strong-arm tactics pl; **ver|bale ~** tough talking; **Kraft|mensch** M strong-man, muscle man (inf); **Kraft|mes|ser** M -s, -

dynamometer (*form*); (*auf Jahrmarkt*) test-your-strength machine; **Kraft|pa|ket** NT (= *Mensch*) powerhouse; (= *Auto, Maschine*) powerful machine; **Kraft|post** F post(al) bus service; **Kraft|pro|be** F test of strength; (*zwischen zwei Gruppen, Menschen*) trial of strength; **Kraft|protz** M (*inf*) muscle man (*inf*); **Kraft|rad** NT motorcycle, motorbike; **Kraft|raum** M power training gym; **Kraft|re|ser|ven** PL energy reserves *pl*, reserves *pl* of strength; **Kraft|sport** M sport(s *pl*) involving strength; **Kraft|sport|ler(in)** M(F) power athlete; **Kraft|spruch** M strong words *pl*

Kraft|stoff M fuel

Kraft|stoff-: Kraft|stoff|an|zei|ge F, **Kraft|stoff|an|zei|ger** M fuel gauge; **Kraft|stoff|ver|brauch** M fuel consumption

Kraft-: kraft|strot|zend ADJ exuding vitality, vigorous; *Pflanze* healthy-looking, vigorous; (= *muskulös*) with bulging muscles; **ein ~es Baby** a big strong bouncing baby; **Kraft|trai|ning** NT power training; **Kraft|über|tra|gung** F power transmission; **Kraft|ver|geu|dung** F waste of energy *or* effort; **Kraft|ver|kehr** M motor traffic; **Kraft|ver|schwen|dung** F waste of energy *or* effort; **kraft|voll** ADJ (*geh*) *Stimme* powerful ADV powerfully; **bei etw ~ zubeißen können** to be able to sink one's teeth into sth; **Kraft|wa|gen** M motor vehicle; **Kraft|werk** NT power station; **Kraft|wort** NT *pl* -wörter swearword; **Kraftwörter** strong language

Krag|dach ['kra:g-] NT overhanging roof

Kra|gen ['kra:gn̩] M **-s,** - *or* (*S Ger, Sw auch*) = ['krɛ:gn̩] collar; **jdn am** *or* **beim ~ packen** to grab sb by the collar; (*fig inf*) to collar sb; **mir platzte der ~** (*inf*) I blew my top (*inf*); **jetzt platzt mir aber der ~!** this is the last straw!; **jetzt gehts ihm an den ~** (*inf*) he's in for it now (*inf*) → **Kopf e**

Kra|gen-: Kra|gen|knopf M collar stud; **Kra|gen|num|mer** F collar size; **Kra|gen|spie|gel** M (*Mil*) collar patch; **Kra|gen|wei|te** F (*lit*) collar size; **eine ~ zu groß für jdn sein** (*fig inf*) to be too much for sb (to handle); **das ist nicht meine ~** (*fig inf*) that's not my cup of tea (*inf*)

Krag|stein ['kra:g-] M (*Archit*) console

Krä|he ['krɛ:ə] F -, -n crow; **eine ~ hackt der anderen kein Auge aus** (*Prov*) birds of a feather stick *or* flock together (*Prov*)

krä|hen ['krɛ:ən] VI to crow → **Hahn a**

Krä|hen-: Krä|hen|fuß M (= *Eisenkralle*) crowbar; **Krä|hen|fü|ße** PL (*an den Augen*) crow's-feet *pl*; (= *Schriftkrakel*) scrawl *sing*; **Krä|hen|nest** NT (*Naut*) crow's-nest

Kräh|win|kel M (*pej*) cultural backwater

Kra|kau ['kra:kau] NT **-s** Cracow

Kra|kau|er[1] ['krakauɐ] F -, - (*Cook*) spicy smoked sausage with garlic

Kra|kau|er[2] ['krakauɐ] M **-s,** -, **Kra|kau|e|rin** [-ərɪn] F -, -nen Cracovian

Kra|ke ['kra:kə] M **-n,** -n octopus; (*Myth*) Kraken

Kra|keel [kra'ke:l] M **-s,** *no pl* (*inf*) row; **~ ma|chen** (*inf*) to kick up a row *or* racket (*inf*)

kra|kee|len [kra'ke:lən] *ptp* **krakeelt** VI (*inf*) to make *or* kick up a row *or* racket (*inf*)

Kra|kee|ler [kra'ke:lɐ] M **-s,** -, **Kra|kee|le|rin** [-ərɪn] F -, -nen rowdy (*inf*), rowdy type (*inf*)

Kra|kel ['kra:kl̩] M **-s,** - (*inf*) scrawl, scribble

Kra|ke|lei [krakə'lai] F -, -en (*inf*) scrawl, scribble

kra|ke|lig ['kra:kəlɪç] ADJ scrawly ADV **~ schrei|ben** to scrawl, to scribble; **~ unterschreiben** to scrawl one's signature; **meine Kinder malen ~** my children do scribbly drawings

kra|keln ['kra:kl̩n] VTI to scrawl, to scribble

Kra|kel|schrift ['kra:kl̩-] F (*inf pej*) spidery handwriting *or* scrawl

Kral [kra:l] M **-s,** -e kraal

Kral|le ['kralə] F -, -n claw; (*von Raubvogel auch*) talon; (*pej*: = *Fingernagel*) claw, talon; (= *Parkkralle*) wheel clamp (*Brit*), Denver boot (*US*); **jdn/etw in seinen ~n haben** (*fig inf*) to have sb/sth in one's clutches; (**jdm**) **~n zeigen** (*fig*) to show (sb) one's claws; **die ~ einziehen** (*fig*) to put one's claws away; **jdn aus den ~n des Todes retten** to rescue sb from the jaws of death; (**bar**) **auf die ~** (*inf*) (cash) on the nail (*Brit inf*) *or* on the barrelhead (*US inf*)

kral|len ['kralən] VR **sich an jdn/etw ~** (*lit, fig*) to cling to sb/sth; (*Tier*) to dig its claws into sb/sth; **sich in etw** (*acc*) **~** to sink its claws into sth; (*mit Fingern*) to dig one's fingers into sth VT **a die Finger in etw** (*acc*) **~** to dig one's fingers into sth; **die Finger um etw ~** to clutch sth; **er krallte vor Schmerz die Finger in die Stuhllehne** he clawed (at) the back of the chair in pain **b** (*sl*) to pinch (*Brit inf*), to swipe (*inf*); **sich** (*dat*) **etw ~** to pinch (*Brit*) *or* swipe sth (*inf*); **den haben sich die Bullen gekrallt** the cops nicked (*Brit*) *or* nabbed him (*inf*) **c** (*Aut*) to clamp (*Brit*), to (Denver) boot (*US*) VI to claw (*an* +*dat* at)

Kram [kra:m] M **-(e)s,** *no pl* (*inf*) (= *Gerümpel*) junk; (= *Zeug*) things *pl*, stuff (*inf*); (= *Angelegenheit*) business; **den ~ satt haben/hinschmeißen** to be fed up with/to chuck the whole thing *or* business (*inf*); **das passt mir nicht in den ~** it's a confounded nuisance; **mach doch deinen ~ allein!** do it yourself!; **lass mich meinen ~ alleine machen** don't tell me what to do

kra|men ['kra:mən] VI **a** (= *wühlen*) to rummage about (*in* +*dat* in, *nach* for) **b** (*Sw inf*) to do a bit of shopping VT **etw aus etw ~** to fish sth out of sth

Krä|mer ['krɛ:mɐ] M **-s,** -, **Krä|me|rin** [-ərɪn] F -, -nen small shopkeeper, grocer; (= *Laden*) small general store, grocer's; **ein Volk von ~n** a nation of shopkeepers

Krä|mer|geist M, **Krä|mer|see|le** F small-minded *or* petty-minded person; **ein ~** *or* **eine Krämerseele sein** to be small-minded *or* petty-minded; **einen ~** *or* **eine Krämerseele haben** to have a small *or* petty mind

Kram|la|den M (*pej inf*) tatty little shop (*inf*); (= *Trödelladen*) junk shop

Kram|pe ['krampə] F -, -n staple

Kram|pen ['krampn̩] M **-s,** - staple; (*Aus*: = *Spitzhacke*) pick(axe) (*Brit*), pick(ax) (*US*)

Krampf [krampf] M **-(e)s,** **-e** ['krɛmpfə] **a** (= *Zustand*) cramp; (= *Verkrampfung, Zuckung*) spasm; (*wiederholt*) convulsion(s *pl*); (= *Anfall, Lachkrampf*) fit; **einen ~ haben/bekommen** to have/get (a) cramp **b** *no pl* (*inf*) (= *Getue*) palaver (*inf*); (= *Unsinn*) nonsense, rubbish **c** (*esp Sw inf*: = *krampfhaftes Tun, Bemühen*) strain; **einen ~ drehen** to do a job (*inf*)

Krampf-: Krampf|ader F varicose vein; **krampf|ar|tig** ADJ convulsive ADV convulsively

kramp|fen ['krampfn̩] VT *Finger, Hand* to clench (*um etw* around sth); **die Finger in etw** (*acc*) **~** to dig one's fingers into sth VR **sich um etw ~** to clench sth VI **a** (= *Krämpfe haben*) to have a convulsion/convulsions **b** (*Sw inf*: = *hart arbeiten*) to slave away (*inf*)

Krampfer ['krampfɐ] M **-s,** -, **Krampfe|rin** [-ərɪn] F -, -nen (*sl*) grafter (*Brit inf*), hard worker

Krampf-: krampf|haft ADJ *Zuckung* convulsive; (*inf*: = *angestrengt, verzweifelt*) frantic, desperate; *Lachen* forced *no adv* ADV **sich ~ bemühen** to try desperately hard; **~ nachdenken** to rack one's brains; **sich ~ an etw** (*dat*) **festhalten** (*lit, fig inf*) to cling desperately to sth; **Krampf|hus|ten** M (*Aus inf*) whooping cough; **krampf|lin|dernd** ADJ antispasmodic (*spec*); **krampf|lö|send** ADJ antispasmodic (*spec*)

Kram|pus ['krampʊs] M **-, -se** (*Aus*) companion of St Nicholas

Kran [kra:n] M **-(e)s,** **-e** ['krɛ:nə] *or* **-e** **a** crane **b** (*dial*: = *Hahn*) tap (*esp Brit*), faucet (*US*)

Kran|füh|rer(in) M(F) crane driver *or* operator

krän|gen ['krɛŋən] VI (*Naut*) to heel (over)

Kra|nich ['kra:nɪç] M **-s,** -e (*Orn*) crane

krank [kraŋk] ADJ *comp* **=er** ['krɛŋkɐ], *superl* **=ste(r, s)** ['krɛŋksta] **a** (= *nicht gesund*) ill *usu pred*, sick (*auch fig*), not well; (= *leidend*) invalid; *Pflanze, Organ* diseased; *Zahn, Bein* bad; *Wirtschaft, Firma* ailing; (*Hunt*) *Wild* wounded; **~ werden** to fall ill *or* sick, to be taken ill *or* sick; **schwer ~** seriously ill; **~ am Herzen** *or* **an der Seele** (*liter*) sick at heart (*liter*); **vor Aufregung/Angst ~** sick with excitement/fear; **vor Heimweh ~** homesick; **vor Liebe ~** lovesick; **du bist wohl ~!** (*inf iro*) there must be something wrong with you!; **der ~e Mann am Bosporus** the Sick Man of Europe **b** (*sl*: = *verrückt*) off one's head (*inf*) ADV *comp* **=er,** *superl* **am =sten sich ~ stellen** to pretend to be ill *or* sick, to malinger; **das macht/du machst mich ~!** (*inf*) it gets/you get on my nerves! (*inf*), it drives/you drive me crazy *or* (a)round the bend! (*inf*)

krän|keln ['krɛŋkl̩n] VI to be ailing (*auch Wirtschaft, Firma*), to be sickly, to be in bad *or* poor health; **sie ~ leicht** they're often poorly (*Brit*) *or* sick

kran|ken ['kraŋkn̩] VI to suffer (*an* +*dat* from); **das krankt daran, dass …** (*fig*) it suffers from the fact that …

krän|ken ['krɛŋkn̩] VT **jdn ~** to hurt sb('s feelings), to wound sb; **sie war sehr gekränkt** she was very hurt; **es kränkt mich, dass …** it hurts *or* grieves me that …; **jdn in seiner Ehre ~** to offend sb's pride; **~d** hurtful VR **sich über etw** (*acc*) **~** (*dated, dial*) to feel upset about sth

Kran|ken-: Kran|ken|ak|te F medical file; **Kran|ken|an|stalt** F *usu pl* hospital; **Kran|ken|au|to** NT ambulance; **Kran|ken|be|richt** M medical report; **Kran|ken|be|such** M visit (to a sick person); (*von Arzt*) (sick) call; **Kran|ken|bett** NT sickbed; **Kran|ken|blatt** NT medical report, doctor's notes *pl*; **Kran|ken|geld** NT sickness benefit; (*von Firma*) sick pay; **Kran|ken|ge|schich|te** F medical history; **Kran|ken|gym|nast** [-gʏmnast] M **-en,** -en, **Kran|ken|gym|nas|tin** [-gʏmnastɪn] F -, -nen physiotherapist; **Kran|ken|gym|nas|tik** F physiotherapy

Kran|ken|haus NT hospital; **ins ~ gehen** (*als Patient*) to go into the (*US*) hospital; **im ~ liegen** to be in (the *US*) hospital; **jdn in einem ~ unterbringen** to put sb in a hospital, to hospitalize sb; **an einem ~ sein** (*Arzt, Schwester etc*) to work in a hospital

Kran|ken|haus- *in cpds* hospital; **Kran|ken|haus|arzt** M, **Kran|ken|haus|ärz|tin** F hospital doctor; **Kran|ken|haus|auf|ent|halt** M stay in hospital; **Kran|ken|haus|kos|ten** PL hospital charges *pl or* costs *pl*; **Kran|ken|haus|rech|nung** F bill for hospital treatment; **kran|ken|haus|reif** ADJ in need of hospital treatment; **jdn ~ schlagen** to make a stretcher-case out of sb (*Brit inf*), to beat the hell out of sb (*inf*); **Kran|ken|haus|seel|sor|ger(in)** M(F) hospital chaplain; **Kran|ken|haus|ta|ge|geld** NT (hospital) daily benefit

Kran|ken-: Kran|ken|kas|se F (= *Versicherung*) medical *or* health insurance; (= *Gesellschaft*) medical *or* health insurance company; **ich bin in einer privaten ~** I am in a private medical insurance scheme, I'm privately insured; **er ist in keiner ~** he has no medical insurance; **Kran|ken|kas|sen|bei|trag** M health insurance contribution, contribution to a/the medical insurance scheme; **Kran|ken|la|ger** NT (= *Krankenbett*) sickbed; (= *Kranksein*) illness; **das Fieber warf ihn aufs ~** (*geh*) the fever confined him to his sickbed; **Kran|ken|pfle|ge** F nursing; **Kran|ken|pfle|ge|hel|fer(in)** M(F) nursing auxiliary (*Brit*), auxiliary nurse; **Kran|ken|pfle|ger** M orderly; (*mit Schwesternausbildung*) male nurse; **Kran|ken|pfle|ge|rin** F nurse; **Kran|ken|pfle|ge|schü|ler(in)** M(F) student nurse; **Kran|ken|saal** M ward; **Kran|ken|sal|bung** F (Eccl) anointing of the sick; **Kran|ken|schein** M medical insurance record card; **Kran|ken|schwes|ter** F nurse; **Kran|ken|stand** M **a** (von Firma) level of sickness, number of employees sick **b** **im ~ sein** to be sick or ill; **Kran|ken|stuhl** M invalid chair, Bath chair; (= Nachtstuhl) commode; **Kran|ken|trans|port** M transportation of sick people; (mittels Krankenwagen) ambulance service; (die Kranken selbst) shipload/busload etc of sick people; **kran|ken|ver|si|chern** ptp krankenversichert VT to take out medical or health insurance (jdn for); **sich ~** to take out medical or health insurance; **krankenversichert** medically insured; **sind Sie krankenversichert?** do you have medical or health insurance or cover?; **Kran|ken|ver|si|che|rung** F medical or health insurance; **soziale/private ~** state or national/private health insurance; **Kran|ken|ver|si|che|rungs|aus|weis** M health insurance card, medical card (Brit); **Kran|ken|wa|gen** M ambulance; **Kran|ken|wär|ter** M orderly; **Kran|ken|wär|te|rin** F nurse; **Kran|ken|zim|mer** NT sickroom; (im Krankenhaus) hospital room

Kran|ke(r) ['kraŋkə] MF decl as adj sick person, invalid; (= Patient) patient; **die ~n** the sick

krank+fei|ern VI sep (inf) to be off sick, to skive off work (Brit inf); **das Krankfeiern ist ein großes Problem** absenteeism is a great problem; **geh doch heute nicht ins Büro, feier doch krank** don't go in to the office today, say you're not feeling well; **ich glaube, ich muss morgen ~** I think I'll have to be off sick tomorrow

krank|haft ADJ **a** Stelle, Zelle diseased; Vergrößerung, Zustand morbid; Aussehen sickly; Augen ill-looking; **die Untersuchungen haben keinen ~en Befund ergeben** the examinations revealed no sign(s) of disease; **~er Befund der Leber** affected or diseased liver; **~e Veränderung** affection; **der ~e Zustand der britischen Wirtschaft** the ailing condition of the British economy; **das Krankhafte an unserer Gesellschaft** the sickness affecting our society **b** (seelisch) pathological; Misstrauen, Eifersucht etc chronic, pathological; **sein Geiz/diese Vorstellung ist schon ~** his meanness/this idea is almost pathological or has reached almost pathological proportions **ADV a** (Med) abnormally; **sich ~ verändern** to show pathological changes **b** (auf seelische Zustände bezogen) pathologically

Krank|heit F -, -en (lit, fig) illness, sickness; (eine bestimmte Krankheit wie Krebs, Masern etc auch) disease; (von Pflanzen) disease; **wegen ~** due to illness; **eine ~ durchmachen, an einer ~ leiden** to suffer from or have a disease or an illness; **einer ~ vorbeugen** to take preventive measures against an illness or a disease; **(eine) ~ vorschützen, eine ~ vortäuschen** to pretend to be ill, to fake an illness; **sich (dat) eine ~ zuziehen** to catch or contract (form) an illness or a disease; **von einer ~ befallen werden** to catch or contract (form) an illness or a disease; (Pflanze, Organ) to become diseased; **von einer ~ genesen** to recuperate from an illness; **nach langer/schwerer ~** after a long/serious illness; **während/seit meiner ~** during/since my illness; **das soll ein Auto sein? das ist eine ~!** (fig inf) call that a car? that's just an apology or excuse for one!

-krank|heit F suf in cpds disease; **Lungenkrankheit** lung disease; **Blutkrankheit** disease of the blood

Krank|heits-: **krank|heits|be|dingt** ADJ due to illness or sickness pred ADV due to illness or sickness; **Krank|heits|bild** NT symptoms pl, syndrome (spec); **Krank|heits|er|re|ger** M pathogen, disease-causing agent; **krank|heits|hal|ber** ADV due to illness; **Krank|-**

heits|herd M focus of a/the disease; **Krank|heits|keim** M germ (of a/the disease); **Krank|heits|tag** M day of illness or sickness

krank+la|chen VR (inf) to kill oneself (laughing) (inf); **ich hab mich bei dem Film krankgelacht** he just about killed himself (laughing) (inf) or died laughing when he saw the film

kränk|lich ['krɛŋklɪç] ADJ sickly, in poor or bad health

Krank-: **krank+ma|chen** VI sep (inf) = krankfeiern; **krank+mel|den** ▲ VR sep to let sb/one's boss etc know that one is sick or ill; (telefonisch) to phone in sick; (esp Mil) to report sick; **sie hat sich krankgemeldet** she is off sick; **Krank|mel|dung** F notification of illness or sickness; **krank+schrei|ben** ▲ VT sep irreg to give sb a medical certificate; (esp Mil) to put sb on the sick list; **er ist schon seit einem halben Jahr krankgeschrieben** he's been off sick for six months; **Krank|schrei|bung** F medical certificate, doctor's certificate (US), sick note (inf)

Krän|kung ['krɛŋkʊŋ] F -, -en **a** insult; **etw als ~ empfinden** to take offence (Brit) or offense (US) at sth, to be hurt by sth; **jdm eine (tiefe) ~ zufügen** to hurt sb (deeply) **b** (= Kränken) offending, insulting; **das war eine ~ seiner Gefühle** that hurt his feelings

Kranz [krants] M -es, ⸚e ['krɛntsə] **a** wreath; (= Siegerkranz, Dichterkranz, Brautkranz auch) garland; (fig: von Geschichten, Anekdoten etc) cycle; **da kannst du dir gleich einen ~ schicken lassen** (inf) you'll be signing your own death warrant **b** (= kreisförmig Angeordnetes) ring, circle; (= Haarkranz) plaits pl round one's head (Brit), braids pl around one's head (US); (obs: von Mädchen) bevy **c** (Tech: = Radkranz) rim; (von Glocke auch) lip **d** (dial Cook) ring

Kranz|ar|te|rie F coronary artery

Kränz|chen ['krɛntsçən] NT -s, - **a** → Kranz a small wreath/garland **b** (fig: = Kaffeekränzchen) coffee circle

krän|zen ['krɛntsn] VT (liter) to garland, to a-dorn (with garlands)

Kranz-: **Kranz|ge|fäß** NT (Anat) coronary artery; **Kranz|geld** NT (Jur) money paid by a man to a woman as a fine for having sexual intercourse with her after pretending to make her an offer of marriage; **Kranz|ge|sims** NT (Archit) cornice; **Kranz|jung|fer** F (dial) bridesmaid; **Kranz|nie|der|le|gung** F wreath laying

Krap|fen ['krapfn] M -s, - (dial Cook) ≈ doughnut (Brit), ≈ donut (US)

Krapp M -(e)s, no pl madder

Kräp|pel ['krɛpl] M -s, - (dial Cook) ≈ doughnut (Brit), ≈ donut (US)

Krapp-: **Krapp|lack** M madder paint; **Krapp|rot** NT madder red

krass ▲ [kras] ADJ **a** (= auffallend) Beispiel glaring; Widerspruch, Gegensatz glaring, stark; Farben garish, gaudy; Dissonanz harsh, jarring; Unterschied extreme; (= unerhört) Ungerechtigkeit, Lüge blatant, gross; (= extrem) Fall, Haltung, Lage extreme; Materialist, Egoist out-and-out, blatant; Außenseiter rank, complete; (= unverblümt) Schilderung, Worte, Stil stark; **etw ~ finden** (inf) to find sth gross **b** (sl: = unmöglich) gross (inf); **das ist echt ~** that's a real bummer (inf) or pisser (Brit sl) **c** (sl: = toll) wicked (sl) ADV **sich ausdrücken** crudely; schildern garishly; widersprechen, kontrastieren sharply; **sich ~ von etw abheben** to contrast sharply with sth; **das war ~ gelogen** that was a blatant lie; **um es ~ zu sagen, ~ gesagt** to put it bluntly

Kra|ter ['kra:tɐ] M -s, - crater

Kra|ter-: **Kra|ter|land|schaft** F crater(ed) landscape; **Kra|ter|see** M (Geol) crater lake

Krät|ten ['krɛtn] M -s, - (S Ger, Sw) (small) basket

Kratz-: **Kratz|bee|re** F (dial: = Brombeere) blackberry, bramble; **Kratz|bürs|te** F wire brush; (inf) prickly character; **kratz|bürs|tig** [-bʏrstɪç] ADJ (inf) prickly

Krätz|chen ['krɛtsçən] NT -s, - (Mil sl) forage cap

Krat|ze ['kratsə] F -, -n scraper; (Tex) carding machine

Krät|ze¹ ['krɛtsə] F -, no pl **a** (Med) scabies; **da kriegt man doch die ~** (fig inf) it drives you up the wall (inf) **b** (Tech) scrapings pl, (metal) waste

Krät|ze² F -, -n (S Ger) basket

krat|zen ['kratsn] VT **a** (mit Nägeln, Werkzeug) to scratch; (= abkratzen) to scrape (von off); **seinen Namen in die Wand ~** to scratch one's name on the wall; **der Rauch kratzt (mich) im Hals** the smoke irritates my throat; **es kratzt (mich) im Hals** my throat feels rough **b** (inf: = stören) to bother; **das kratzt mich nicht** (inf) **das soll** or **kann mich nicht ~** (inf) I couldn't care less (about that), I don't give a damn (about that) (inf); **was kratzt mich das?** what do I care about that?; **das braucht dich (doch) nicht (zu) ~** it's nothing to do with you **c** (Tex) to card, to tease VI to scratch; **der Pulli kratzt fürchterlich** the pullover scratches terribly or is terribly scratchy (inf); **es kratzt (mir) im Hals** my throat feels rough; **an etw** (acc) **~** (fig) to scratch away at sth; **diese Sache hat an seinem guten Ruf gekratzt** this business has tarnished his reputation VR to scratch oneself

Krat|zer ['kratsɐ] M -s, - (= Schramme) scratch

Krät|zer ['krɛtsɐ] M -s, - (inf) rough or vinegary wine, plonk no pl (Brit inf); (Aus) sweet young Tirolean wine

kratz|fest ADJ non-scratch attr, scratchproof

Kratz|fuß M (dated inf) (low) bow (with one foot drawn backwards); **einen ~ machen** to bow low

krat|zig ['kratsɪç] ADJ (inf) scratchy (inf)

krät|zig ['krɛtsɪç] ADJ scabious

Krätz|mil|be F (Zool) itch mite

Kratz-: **Kratz|putz** M sgraffito; **Kratz|spur** F scratch (mark); **Kratz|wun|de** F scratch

krau|chen ['krauxn] VI aux sein (dial) to crawl

krau|eln ['krauəln], **krau|en** ['krauən] VT = kraulen²

Kraul [kraul] NT -(s), no pl (Schwimmen) crawl; **(im) ~ schwimmen** to do the crawl

krau|len¹ ['kraulən] VI aux haben or sein (Schwimmen) to do or swim the crawl VT **er hat** or **ist die Strecke gekrault** he swam the stretch front crawl; **er hat** or **ist 100 m gekrault** he did a 100m crawl

krau|len² VT to fondle; **jdn am Kinn ~** to chuck (Brit) or tickle sb under the chin; **jdn in den Haaren ~** to run one's fingers through sb's hair

kraus [kraus] ADJ crinkly; Haar, Kopf frizzy; Stirn wrinkled, furrowed; (= zerknittert) crumpled, wrinkled; (fig: = verworren) muddled, confused; **die Stirn ~ ziehen** to wrinkle up or knit one's brow; (missbilligend) to frown; **die Nase ~ ziehen** to screw up one's nose

Krau|se ['krauzə] F -, -n **a** (= Halskrause) ruff; (an Ärmeln etc) ruffle, frill **b** (inf) (= Krausheit) crinkliness; (von Haar, Kopf) frizziness; (= Frisur) frizzy hair; **im Regen bekomme ich eine ~** my hair goes frizzy in the rain

Kräu|sel-: **Kräu|sel|band** [-bant] NT pl -bänder decorative ribbon; **Kräu|sel|krepp** M (Tex) crepe; (= Streifenkrepp) seersucker

kräu|seln ['krɔyzln] VT **a** Haar to make frizzy; (Sew) to gather; (Tex) to crimp; Stirn to knit, to wrinkle; Nase to screw up **b** Lippen, Mund to pucker; Wasseroberfläche to ruffle VR **a** (Haare) to go frizzy; (Stoff) to go crinkly; (Stirn, Nase) to wrinkle up; **gekräuselte Haare** frizzy hair **b**

(*Lippen*) to pucker; (*Wasser*) to ripple; (*Rauch*) to curl (up)

krau|sen ['krauzn] VTR = **kräuseln** VT a VR a

Kraus-: **kraus|haa|rig** ADJ frizzy-haired; **Kraus|kopf** M frizzy head; (= *Frisur*) frizzy hair/hairstyle; (= *Mensch*) curly-head

Kraut [kraut] NT -(e)s, **Kräuter** ['krɔytɐ] a (*Pflanze:* = esp *Heilkraut, Würzkraut*) herb; **dagegen ist kein ~ gewachsen** (*fig*) there is no remedy for that, there's nothing anyone can do about that b no pl (= grüne Teile von Pflanzen) foliage, stems and leaves pl, herbage; (von Gemüse) tops pl; (= Kartoffelkraut) potato foliage; (= Spargelkraut) asparagus leaves pl; **wie ~ und Rüben durcheinander liegen** (*inf*) to lie (about (*Brit*) or around) all over the place (*inf*); **ins ~ schießen** (*lit*) to go to seed; (*fig*) to get out of control, to run wild c no pl (= Rotkraut, Weißkraut) cabbage; (= Sauerkraut) sauerkraut d (pej: = Tabak) tobacco

Krau|ter M -s, - (*pej*) small-timer (*inf*)

Kräuter-: **Kräu|ter|but|ter** F herb butter; **Kräu|ter|frau** F herb woman; **Kräu|ter|gar|ten** M herb garden; (am Fensterbrett) potted herbs pl; **Kräu|ter|he|xe** F (*pej*) herb woman; (fig) old hag (pej); **Kräu|ter|kä|se** M herb cheese; **Kräu|ter|li|kör** M herbal liqueur; **Kräu|ter|müh|le** F herb mill; **Kräu|ter|samm|ler(in)** M(F) herbalist; **Kräu|ter|tee** M herb(al) tea; **Kräu|ter|weib|lein** NT herb woman

Kraut-: **Kraut|jun|ker** M (*pej*) country squire; **Kraut|kopf** M (*S Ger, Aus*) (head of) cabbage; **Kraut|sa|lat** M = coleslaw; **Kraut|wi|ckel** M (*S Ger, Aus: Cook*) stuffed cabbage leaves pl

Kra|wall [kra'val] M -s, -e (= Aufruhr) riot; (*inf:* = Rauferei) brawl; (= Lärm) racket (*inf*), din (*inf*); **~ machen** (*inf*) to kick up a row; (= randalieren) to go on the rampage; (*auch* **Krawall schlagen:** = sich beschweren) to kick up a fuss

Kra|wall|bru|der M , **Kra|wall|ma|cher(in)** M(F) (*inf*) hooligan; (= Krakeeler) rowdy (*inf*)

Kra|wal|lo [kra'valo] M -s, -s (*inf*) hooligan

Kra|wat|te [kra'vatə] F -, -n tie, necktie (*esp US*); (= kleiner Pelzkragen) tippet; (Ringkampf) headlock

Krawatten-: **Kra|wat|ten|hal|ter** M , **Kra|wat|ten|klem|me** F tie clip; **Kra|wat|ten|kno|ten** M tie knot; **Kra|wat|ten|na|del** F tiepin; **Kra|wat|ten|zwang** M **da ist ~** you have to wear a tie there; **der ~ ...** the fact that you have to wear a tie ...

kra|xeln ['kraksln] VI aux sein (*S Ger*) to clamber (up)

Kre|a|ti|on [krea'tsioːn] F -, -en (*Fashion etc*) creation

kre|a|tiv [krea'tiːf] ADJ creative ADV creatively; **~ veranlagt** creatively inclined; **~ begabt** creative

Kre|a|ti|ve(r) [krea'tiːvə] MF decl as adj (*inf*) creative person; **er ist einer der ~n** he's one of the creators

Kre|a|ti|vi|tät [kreativi'tɛːt] F -, no pl creativity

Kre|a|tur [krea'tuːɐ] F -, -en a (lit, fig, pej) creature; (= abhängiger Mensch) minion, creature (*liter*) b no pl (= alle Lebewesen) creation; **die ~** all creation

kre|a|tür|lich [krea'tyːɐlɪç] ADJ (= naturhaft) natural; *Angst etc* animal attr

Krebs [kreːps] M -es, -e a (= Taschenkrebs, Einsiedlerkrebs) crab; (= Flusskrebs) crayfish, crawfish (*US*); **rot wie ein ~** red as a lobster b (Gattung) crustacean; (= Hummer, Krabbe etc) crayfish, crawfish (*US*) c (Astrol) Cancer; **der ~** (*Astron*) Cancer, the Crab d (Med) cancer; (Bot) canker; **~ erregend** or **auslösend** carcinogenic e (Typ inf) return

krebs-: **krebs|ar|tig** ADJ (*Zool*) crablike; crayfish-like; crustaceous; (*Med*) cancerous ADV (*Med*) **~ wuchern** to spread like cancer; **sich ~**

verändern to become cancerous; **krebs|aus|lö|send** ADJ carcinogenic ADV **~ wirken** to cause cancer, to be carcinogenic

kreb|sen ['kreːpsn] VI a (*inf:* = sich abmühen) to struggle; (*Umsatz, Industrie*) to languish; **in den Umfragen krebst die Partei bei 6 Prozent** the party is languishing at 6 per cent in the polls; **er hat schwer zu ~** he really has to struggle, he finds it really hard going b (= Krebse fangen) to go crabbing, to catch crabs

Krebs-: **krebs|er|re|gend**, **krebs|er|zeu|gend** ADJ, ADV = krebsauslösend; **krebs|för|dernd** ADJ cancer-inducing; **eine ~ Wirkung haben** to increase the risk of cancer ADV **~ wirken** to increase the risk of (getting) cancer; **Krebs|for|schung** F cancer research; **Krebs|früh|er|ken|nung** F early detection of cancer; **Krebs|gang** [-gaŋ] M , no pl (fig) retrogression; **im ~ gehen** to regress, to go backwards; **Krebs|ge|schwulst** F (*Med*) cancer, cancerous tumour (*Brit*) or tumor (*US*), cancerous growth; **Krebs|ge|schwür** NT (*Med*) cancerous ulcer; (fig) cancer, cancerous growth; **krebs|hem|mend** ADJ cancer-inhibiting; **eine ~e Wirkung haben** to reduce the risk of cancer ADV **~ wirken** to reduce the risk of (getting) cancer; **Krebs|kli|nik** F cancer clinic; **krebs|krank** ADJ suffering from cancer; **~ sein** to have cancer; **Krebs|kran|ke(r)** MF decl as adj cancer victim; (= Patient) cancer patient; **Krebs|krank|heit** F cancer; **krebs|rot** ADJ red as a lobster; **Krebs|sche|re** F **Krebs a** claws pl or pincers pl of the crab/crayfish; **Krebs|tie|re** PL crustaceans pl, crustacea pl; **Krebs|vor|sor|ge** F , **Krebs|vor|sor|ge|un|ter|su|chung** F cancer checkup; **Krebs|zel|le** F (*Med*) cancer cell

Kre|denz [kre'dɛnts] F -, -en (dated, Aus) sideboard

kre|den|zen [kre'dɛntsn] ptp **kredenzt** VT (liter) **jdm etw ~** to proffer sb sth (liter)

Kre|dit[1] [kre'diːt] M -(e)s, -e (= Darlehen auch) loan; (fig auch) standing, (good) repute; **auf ~** on credit; **jdm einen ~ gewähren** to grant sb credit/a loan; **einen ~ kündigen** to withdraw credit facilities or a credit; **er hat bei uns/der Bank ~** his credit is good with us/the bank; **in seiner Stammkneipe hat er ~** he gets credit at his local; **~ haben** (fig) to have standing or a good reputation

Kre|dit[2] ['kreːdɪt] NT -s, -s (= Habenseite) credit (side)

Kre|dit-: **Kre|dit|an|stalt** F credit institution, credit or loan bank; **Kre|dit|auf|nah|me** F borrowing; **sich zu einer ~ entschließen** to decide to obtain a loan; **Kre|dit|bank** M pl -banken credit bank; **Kre|dit|be|darf** M borrowing requirement(s pl), credit demand; **Kre|dit|be|din|gun|gen** PL credit terms pl; **Kre|dit|brief** M letter of credit; **kre|dit|fä|hig** ADJ credit-worthy; **Kre|dit|fä|hig|keit** F credit-worthiness; **Kre|dit|ge|ber(in)** M(F) creditor; **Kre|dit|hai** M (*inf*) loan shark (*inf*)

kre|di|tie|ren [kredi'tiːrən] ptp **kreditiert** VT **jdm einen Betrag ~**, **jdn für einen Betrag ~** to advance sb an amount, to credit sb with an amount

Kredit-: **Kre|dit|in|sti|tut** [kre'diːt-] NT bank; **Kre|dit|kar|te** F credit card; **Kre|dit|kar|ten|or|ga|ni|sa|ti|on** F credit card company; **Kre|dit|kauf** M credit sale; **Kre|dit|lauf|zeit** F credit period; **Kre|dit|li|mit** NT credit limit; (für Bankkonto) overdraft limit; **Kre|dit|li|nie** F line of credit; **Kre|dit|neh|mer(in)** M(F) borrower; **Kre|dit|po|li|tik** F lending policy; **kre|dit|po|li|tisch** ADJ Maßnahme, Beschluss on lending ADV **~ in terms of lending policy; **~ sinnvoll sein** to be good lending policy; **Kre|dit|rah|men** M credit range; **den ~ ausschöpfen/sprengen** to use up/exceed the credit range; **Kre|dit|sper|re** F credit freeze; **Kre|dit|sprit|ze** F (fig inf) credit injection; **Kre|**

dit|ver|ein|ba|rung F usu pl credit agreement; **Kre|dit|vo|lu|men** NT lending volume, total lending; **Kre|dit|wirt|schaft** F , no pl banking industry; **kre|dit|wür|dig** ADJ creditworthy; **Kre|dit|wür|dig|keit** F creditworthiness; **Kre|dit|zins** M lending rate

Kre|do ['kreːdo] NT -s, -s (lit, fig) creed, credo

kre|gel ['kreːgl] (dial) ADJ lively ADV in a lively manner

Krei|de ['kraidə] F -, -n chalk; (Geol: = Kreidezeit) Cretaceous (period); **eine ~** a piece of chalk; **bei jdm (tief) in der ~ sein** or **stehen** to be (deep) in debt to sb, to owe sb (a lot of) money

Krei|de-: **krei|de|bleich** ADJ (as) white as chalk or a sheet; **Krei|de|fel|sen** M chalk cliff; **Krei|de|for|ma|ti|on** F (Geol) Cretaceous (formation); **krei|de|hal|tig** ADJ chalky, cretaceous (spec); **Krei|de|stift** M chalk; **krei|de|weiß** ADJ = kreidebleich; **Krei|de|zeich|nung** F chalk drawing; **Krei|de|zeit** F , no pl (Geol) Cretaceous period

krei|dig ['kraidɪç] ADJ chalky

kre|ie|ren [kre'iːrən] ptp **kreiert** VT (Fashion, Theat etc, Eccl) to create; **jdn zum Kardinal ~** (form) to create or appoint sb (a) cardinal

Kreis [krais] M -es, -e [-zə] a circle; **einen ~ beschreiben** or **schlagen** or **ziehen** to describe a circle; **einen ~ um jdn bilden** or **schließen** to form or make a circle around sb, to encircle sb; **im ~ (gehen/sitzen)** (to go (a)round/sit) in a circle; **~ ziehen** (lit) to circle; **(weite) ~e ziehen** (fig) to have (wide) repercussions; **sich im ~ bewegen** or **drehen** (lit) to go or turn (a)round in a circle; (fig) to go (a)round in circles; **mir dreht sich alles im ~e** everything's going (a)round and (a)round, my head is reeling or spinning; **der ~ schließt sich** (fig) we etc come full circle, the wheel turns full circle; **störe meine ~e nicht!** (fig) leave me in peace! b (Elec: = Stromkreis) circuit c (= Stadtkreis, Landkreis) district; (= Gemeindewahlkreis) ward; (= Landeswahlkreis) constituency; **~ Leipzig** Leipzig District, the District of Leipzig d (fig: von Menschen) circle; **der ~ seiner Leser** his readership, his readers pl; **weite ~e der Bevölkerung** wide sections of the population; **im ~e von Freunden/seiner Familie** among or with friends/his family, in the family circle; **eine Feier im engen** or **kleinen ~e** a celebration for a few close friends and relatives; **in seinen/ihren etc ~en** in the circles in which he/she etc moves; **das kommt (auch) in den besten ~en vor** that happens even in the best society or the best of circles e (= Bereich: von Interessen, Tätigkeit etc) sphere; (= Ideenkreis) body of ideas; (= Sagenkreis) cycle; **im ~ des Scheinwerferlichtes** in the arc or pool of light thrown by the headlamps

Kreis-: **Kreis|ab|schnitt** M segment; **Kreis|aus|schnitt** M sector; **Kreis|bahn** F (Astron, Space) orbit; **Kreis|be|we|gung** F rotation, circular motion; **Kreis|bo|gen** M arc (of a circle)

krei|schen ['kraiʃn] VI pret **kreischte** or (old, hum) **krisch** [krɪʃ], ptp **gekreischt** or (old, hum) **gekrischen** [gə'krɪʃn] to screech; (Vogel auch) to squawk; (Reifen, Bremsen auch) to squeal; (Mensch auch) to shriek, to squeal

Kreis-: **Kreis|di|a|gramm** NT pie or circular chart; **Kreis|durch|mes|ser** M diameter (of a/the circle)

Krei|sel ['kraizl] M -s, - (Tech) gyroscope; (= Spielzeug) (spinning) top; (inf: im Verkehr) roundabout (Brit), traffic circle (US), rotary (US); **den ~ schlagen** to spin the top

Kreisel-: **Krei|sel|be|we|gung** F gyration; **Krei|sel|kom|pass** ▲ M gyroscopic compass, gyrocompass

krei|seln ['kraɪzln] VI **a** aux sein or haben (= sich drehen) to spin around, to gyrate **b** (= mit Kreisel spielen) to play with a top, to spin a top

krei|sen ['kraɪzn] VI aux sein or haben to circle (um a)round, über +dat over); (um eine Achse) to revolve (um around), (Satellit, Planet) to orbit (um etw sth), to circle (um etw (a)round sth); (Blut, Öl etc) to circulate (in +dat through); (fig: Gedanken, Wünsche, Gespräch) to revolve (um a-round); **die Arme ~ lassen** to swing one's arms around (in a circle); **den Becher ~ lassen** to hand the cup (a)round

Kreis-: Kreis|flä|che F circle; (= Kreisinhalt) are-a of a/the circle; **kreis|för|mig** ADJ circular **ADV sich ~ bewegen** to move in a circle; **~ an-gelegt** arranged in a circle; **sich ~ aufstellen** to form a circle; **kreis|frei** ADJ **-e Stadt** town which is an administrative district in its own right; **Kreis|in|halt** M area of a/the circle; **Kreis|kol|ben|mo|tor** M rotary piston en-gine; **Kreis|kran|ken|haus** NT district hospi-tal

Kreis|lauf M (= Blutkreislauf, Ölkreislauf, von Geld) circulation; (der Natur, des Wassers) cycle

Kreis-: Kreis|lauf|kol|laps M circulatory collapse; **Kreis|lauf|mit|tel** NT cardiac stimu-lant; **Kreis|lauf|stö|run|gen** PL circulation or circulatory trouble sing or disorders pl

Kreis-: Kreis|li|nie F circle; **vom Mittelpunkt durch die ~** from the centre (Brit) or center (US) through the circumference (of a/the cir-cle); **kreis|rund** ADJ (perfectly) circular; **Kreis|sä|ge** F circular saw; (inf: = Hut) boater; **Kreis|seg|ment** NT segment of a/the circle)

krei|ßen ['kraɪsn] VI (old) to be in labour (Brit) or labor (US); **der Berg kreißt und gebiert eine Maus** (prov) the mountain laboured (Brit) or la-bored (US) and brought forth a mouse

Kreiß|saal M delivery room

Kreis-: Kreis|stadt F chief town of a district, district town, ≈ county town (Brit); **Kreis|tag** M district assembly, ≈ county council (Brit); **Kreis|um|fang** M circumference (of a/the cir-cle); **Kreis|ver|kehr** M roundabout (Brit) or rotary (US) traffic; (= Kreisel) roundabout (Brit), traffic circle (US), rotary (US); **im ~ muss man ...** on a roundabout etc one must ...; **dort gibt es viel ~** there are a lot of roundabouts etc there; **Kreis|ver|wal|tung** F district adminis-tration; (= Behörde) district or local (esp Brit) authority; **Kreis|wehr|er|satz|amt** NT district recruiting office; **Kreis|zahl** F , no pl (Math) pi

Kre|ma|to|ri|um [krema'to:riʊm] NT **-s, Krema-torien** [-riən] crematorium

kre|mig ['kre:mɪç] ADJ creamy **ADV rühren, schla-gen** until creamy; **~ schmecken** to taste creamy

Kreml ['kre:ml, 'krɛml] M **-s der ~** the Kremlin

Kreml-: Kreml-Astro|lo|ge M , **Kreml-Ast-ro|lo|gin** F (Pol sl) Kremlin watcher; **Kreml-chef(in)** M(F) Kremlin chief

Krem|pe ['krɛmpə] F **-, -n** (= Hutkrempe) brim; **ein Hut mit breiter ~** a broad-brimmed hat

Krem|pel¹ ['krɛmpl] M **-s**, no pl (inf) (= Sachen) stuff (inf), things pl; (= wertloses Zeug) junk, rubbish; **ich werfe den ganzen ~ hin** I'm chuck-ing the whole lot or business in (inf); **dann kannst du deinen ~ allein machen** then you can (damn well (inf)) do it yourself

Krem|pel² F **-, -n** carding machine

Krem|pel|arm M (Fashion) rolled sleeve

krem|peln ['krɛmpln] VT **a** (Tex) to card **b** → **hochkrempeln, umkrempeln** etc

Kren [kre:n] M **-s**, no pl (Aus) horseradish

Kre|o|le [kre'o:lə] M **-n, -n, Kre|o|lin** [-'o:lɪn] F **-, -nen** Creole

kre|o|lisch [kre'o:lɪʃ] ADJ Creole

Kre|o|lisch(e) NT Creole → auch **Deutsch(e)**

kre|pie|ren [kre'pi:rən] ptp **krepiert** VI aux sein **a** (= platzen) to explode, to go off **b** (inf: = sterben) to croak (it) (inf), to snuff it (Brit inf), to kick the bucket (inf); (= elend sterben) to die

a wretched death; **das Tier ist ihm krepiert** the animal died on him (inf)

Krepp [krɛp] M **-s, -e** or **-s** crepe

Krepp|pa|pier ▲ NT crepe paper

Krepp|soh|le F crepe sole

Kres|se ['krɛsə] F **-**, no pl cress

Kre|ta ['kre:ta] NT **-s** Crete

Kre|ter ['kre:tə] M **-s, -, Kre|te|rin** [-ərɪn] F **-, -nen** Cretan

Kre|thi und Ple|thi ['kre:ti ʊnt 'ple:ti] PL no art (inf) every Tom, Dick and Harry

Kre|tin [kre'tɛ̃:] M **-s, -s** (Med, pej) cretin

Kre|ti|nis|mus [kreti'nɪsmʊs] M **-**, no pl (Med) cretinism

kre|tisch ['kre:tɪʃ] ADJ Cretan

Kre|ton [kre'tɔ:n] M **-s, -e** (Aus), **Kre|ton|ne** [kre'tɔn] M OR F **-, -s** (Tex) cretonne

kreucht [krɔʏçt] (obs, poet) 3. pers sing pres von **kriechen alles was da ~ und fleucht** all living creatures, all things that do creep and fly (po-et)

kreuz [krɔʏts] ADV **~ und quer** all over; **~ und quer durch die Gegend fahren** to travel or (im Auto) drive all over the place

Kreuz¹ [krɔʏts] NT **-es, -e a** cross; (als Anhänger etc) crucifix; **das ~ des Südens** (Astron) the Southern Cross; **jdn ans ~ schlagen** or **nageln** to nail sb to the cross; **ein ~ schlagen** or **ma-chen** to make the sign of the cross; (= sich be-kreuzigen auch) to cross oneself; **zwei Gegen-stände über ~ legen** to put two objects cross-wise one on top of the other; **mit jdm über ~ sein** or **stehen** (fig) to be on bad terms with sb; **sein ~ auf sich nehmen** (fig) to take up one's cross; **es ist ein** or **ich habe mein ~ mit ihm/da-mit** he's/it's an awful problem; **ich mache drei ~e, wenn er geht** (inf) it'll be such a relief when he has gone; **er machte ein ~ (als Unterschrift/am Rand)** he put a cross (for his signature/in the margin); **zu ~e kriechen** (fig) to eat humble pie, to eat crow (US)
b (Anat) small of the back; (von Tier) back; **ich habe Schmerzen im ~** I've got (a) backache; **ich habs im ~** (inf) I have back trouble; **aufs ~ fal-len** to fall on one's back; (fig inf) to be stag-gered (inf), to fall through the floor (inf); **jdn aufs ~ legen** to throw sb on his back; (fig inf) to take sb for a ride (inf) → **leiern**
c (Archit: = Fensterkreuz) mullion and transom
d (Mus) sharp
e (= Autobahnkreuz) intersection
f (Cards) (= Farbe) clubs pl; (= Karte) club; **die ~dame** the Queen of Clubs
g (Typ) dagger, obelisk

Kreuz² F **in die ~ und in die Quer** this way and that

Kreuz-: Kreuz|ab|nah|me F Descent from the Cross; **Kreuz|band** [-bant] NT pl **-bänder a** (Anat) cruciate ligament **b** (Post: = Streifband) wrapper; **Kreuz|bar** ADJ (Biol) crossable; **Kreuz|bein** NT (Anat) sacrum; (von Tieren) rump-bone; **Kreuz|blu|me** F (Bot) milkwort; (Archit) finial; **Kreuz|blüt|ler** [-bly:tlə] M **-s, -** cruciferous plant; **kreuz|brav** ADJ Kind terribly good or well-behaved, as good as gold; Beneh-men, Karriere faultless; Film, Theaterstück etc conventional **ADV** inszenieren, aufführen conven-tionally; **sich ~ benehmen** to be terribly well-behaved

kreu|zen ['krɔʏtsn] VT to cross (auch Biol); **die Degen** or **Klingen** or **Schwerter mit jdm ~** (lit, fig) to cross swords with sb; **die Arme ~** to fold or cross one's arms; **die Beine ~** to cross one's legs; **jds Weg ~** to cross sb's path VR to cross; (Meinungen, Interessen) to clash; (Biol) to in-terbreed; **unsere Wege haben sich nie wieder gekreuzt** our paths have never crossed again; **die Briefe haben sich gekreuzt** the letters crossed in the post (Brit) or mail VI aux haben or sein (Naut) to cruise; (= Zickzack fahren) to tack

Kreu|zer ['krɔʏtsə] M **-s, - a** (Naut) cruiser **b** (Hist: = Münze) kreutzer

Kreu|zes-: Kreu|zes|tod ['krɔʏtsəs-] M (death by) crucifixion; **den ~ erleiden** to die on the cross; **Kreu|zes|zei|chen** NT sign of the cross

Kreuz-: Kreuz|fah|rer M (Hist) crusader; **Kreuz|fahrt** F **a** (Naut) cruise; **eine ~ machen** to go on a cruise **b** (Hist) crusade; **Kreuz-feu|er** NT (Mil, fig) crossfire; **im ~ (der Kritik) stehen** to be under fire (from all sides); **im ~ (der Kritik) geraten** (fig) to come under fire (from all sides); **kreuz|fi|del** ADJ (inf) happy as a sandboy (Brit inf) or lark; **kreuz|för|mig** ADJ cross-shaped, cruciform (form) **ADV** in the shape of a cross; **etw ~ anordnen** to arrange sth crossways or crosswise; **Kreuz|gang** M pl **-gänge** cloister; **Kreuz|ge|lenk** NT (Tech) uni-versal joint; **Kreuz|ge|wöl|be** NT (Archit) cross or groin vault

kreu|zi|gen ['krɔʏtsɪgn] VT to crucify

Kreu|zi|gung ['krɔʏtsɪgʊŋ] F **-, -en** crucifixion

Kreuz-: Kreuz|kno|ten M reef knot; **Kreuz-küm|mel** M cumin; **kreuz|lahm** ADJ Pferd broken-backed; (inf) Mensch exhausted; **Kreuz|läh|me** [-lɛːmə] **-, -n** F (Vet) paralysis of the hindquarters; **Kreuz|mast** M (Naut) mizzen mast; **Kreuz|ot|ter** F (Zool) adder, vi-per; **Kreuz|reim** M (Liter) alternate rhyme; **Kreuz|rip|pen|ge|wöl|be** NT (Archit) ribbed vault; **Kreuz|rit|ter** M (Hist) crusader; (vom deutschen Ritterorden) knight of the Teutonic Or-der; **Kreuz|schiff** NT **a** (Naut) cruise ship; (größer) cruise liner **b** (Archit: in Kirche) tran-sept; **Kreuz|schlitz|schrau|be** F Phillips® screw; **Kreuz|schlitz|schrau|ben|zie|her** M Phillips® screwdriver; **Kreuz|schlüs|sel** M wheel brace; **Kreuz|schmer|zen** PL backache sing, pains pl in the small of the back; **Kreuz-schna|bel** M (Orn) crossbill; **Kreuz|spin|ne** F (Zool) garden or cross spider; **kreuz|stän-dig** ADJ (Bot) decussate; **Kreuz|stich** M (Sew) cross-stitch

Kreu|zung ['krɔʏtsʊŋ] F **-, -en a** (= Straßenkreu-zung) crossroads sing, intersection (esp US) **b** (= das Kreuzen) crossing; (von Tieren) crossing, cross-breeding, interbreeding **c** (= Rasse) hy-brid; (= Tiere) cross, cross-breed

kreuz|un|glück|lich ADJ absolutely miserable

kreu|zungs|frei ADJ Strecke, Ausbau without crossroads

Kreuz-: Kreuz|ver|band M (Med) crossed bandage; (Build) cross bond; **Kreuz|ver|hör** NT cross-examination; **jdn ins ~ nehmen** to cross-examine sb; **Kreuz|weg** M **a** (= Weg-kreuzung, fig) crossroads sing **b** (Rel: = Christi Leidensweg) way of the cross; **den ~ beten** to do the stations of the cross; **Kreuz|weh** NT (inf) backache; **kreuz|wei|se** ADV crosswise, crossways; **du kannst mich ~!** (inf) (you can) get stuffed! (Brit inf), you can kiss my ass! (US sl); **Kreuz|wort|rät|sel** NT crossword puzzle; **Kreuz|zei|chen** NT sign of the cross; **Kreuz-zug** M (lit, fig) crusade

Kre|vet|te [kre'vɛtə] F **-, -n** shrimp

krib|be|lig ['krɪbəlɪç] ADJ (inf) fidgety, edgy (inf); (= kribbelnd) tingly (inf)

krib|beln ['krɪbln] VT (= kitzeln) to tickle; (= ju-cken) to make itch; (= prickeln) to make tingle VI **a** (= jucken) to itch, to tickle; (= prickeln) to prickle, to tingle; **auf der Haut ~** to cause a prickling sensation; (angenehm) to make the skin tingle; **es kribbelt mir im Fuß** (lit) I have pins and needles in my foot; **es kribbelt mir in den Fingern, etw zu tun** (inf) I'm itching to do sth; **ein Kribbeln im Bauch haben** to have a feeling of anticipation in one's stomach
b aux sein (Insekten) **~ (und krabbeln)** to scurry or swarm (around); **es kribbelt von Ameisen** the place is crawling or swarming or teeming with ants; **es kribbelt und krabbelt wie in ei-nem Ameisenhaufen** it's like an ant hill

kribb|lig ['krɪblɪç] ADJ = **kribbelig**

kri|cke|lig [ˈkrɪkəlɪç] ADJ, ADV (inf) = **krakelig**

Kri|ckel|kra|kel [ˈkrɪklˈkraːkl] NT **-s, -** (inf) scrawl, scribble; (= Krakeln) scrawling, scribbling

kri|ckeln [ˈkrɪkln] VI (inf) to scrawl, to scribble

Kri|cket [ˈkrɪkət] NT **-s, -s** (Sport) cricket

Kri|da [ˈkriːda] F **-**, no pl faked bankruptcy

krie|chen [ˈkriːçn] pret **kroch** [krɔx], ptp **gekrochen** [gəˈkrɔxn] VI aux sein to crawl (auch Pflanze, Tech); (= langsam fahren) to creep or crawl (along); (fig: Zeit) to creep by; (fig: = unterwürfig sein) to grovel (vor +dat before), to crawl (vor +dat to); **aus dem Ei ~** to hatch (out); **ins Bett ~** (inf) to go to bed; (sehr müde, erschöpft) to crawl into bed; **auf allen vieren ~** to crawl on all fours; **unter die Bettdecke ~** to slip under the covers or blankets; **die Kälte kroch mir in die Knochen** the cold seeped into my bones → **Arsch, Kreuz**[1] **a, Leim**

Krie|cher [ˈkriːçɐ] M **-s, -**, **Krie|che|rin** [-ərɪn] F **-, -nen** (inf) groveller (Brit), groveler (US), bootlicker (inf), crawler (Brit inf)

krie|che|risch [ˈkriːçərɪʃ] (inf) **ADJ** grovelling (Brit), groveling (US), servile, bootlicking attr (inf) **ADV sich ~ benehmen/verhalten** to grovel

Kriech-: **Kriech|gang** [-gaŋ] M , no pl crawling gear; **Kriech|spur** F crawler lane; **Kriech|strom** F (Elec) leakage current; **Kriech|tier** NT (Zool) reptile

Krieg [kriːk] M **-(e)s, -e** [-gə] war; (= Art der Kriegsführung) warfare; **~ der Sterne** (Pol) Star Wars; **~ anfangen mit** to start a war with; **einer Partei** etc **den ~ erklären** (fig) to declare war on a party etc; **~ führen (mit** or **gegen)** to wage war (on); **~ führend** belligerent, warring; **in ~ und Frieden** in war and peace; **im ~(e)** in war; (als Soldat) away in the war, away fighting; **im ~ sein** or **stehen (mit)**, **~ haben (mit)**, **sich im ~ befinden (mit)** to be at war (with); **im ~ fallen, im ~ bleiben** to be killed in the war or in action; **in den ~ ziehen** to go to war; **in einem ständigen ~ leben** (fig) to be constantly feuding

krie|gen [ˈkriːgn] VT (inf) to get; Zug, Bus, Schnupfen, Weglaufenden auch to catch; Schlaganfall, eine Spritze, Besuch auch to have; **Junge, ein Kind** to have; **sie kriegt ein Kind** she's going to have a baby; **graue Haare ~** to get grey (Brit) or gray (US) hairs, to go grey (Brit) or gray (US); **eine Glatze ~** to go bald; **es mit jdm zu tun ~** to be in trouble with sb; **wenn ich dich kriege!** just you wait till I catch you!; **sie ~ sich** (in Kitschroman) boy gets girl; **dann kriege ich zu viel** then it gets too much for me; **was kriegt der Herr?** yes sir, what will you have?; **ich kriege ein Steak** I'll have a steak; **~ Sie schon?** are you being or have you been served?; **wenn du nicht sofort aufhörst, kriegst du ein paar!** (inf) if you don't stop that right now, I'll belt you! (inf); **ich kriegs im Kopf** (inf) I'm about to go nuts (inf); **jdn dazu ~, etw zu tun** to get sb to do sth; **etw gemacht ~** to get sth done; **das kriege ich einfach nicht übersetzt** I just can't get it translated; **kann ich das bestätigt ~?** can I have or get that confirmed? → **Kurve**

Krie|gen NT **-s**, no pl (game of) tag

Krie|ger [ˈkriːgɐ] M **-s, -**, **Krie|ge|rin** [-ərɪn] F **-, -nen** warrior; (= Indianerkrieger) brave; **alter ~** veteran (soldier), old campaigner or warhorse; **ein müder ~ sein** (fig inf) to have no go left in one

Krie|ger|denk|mal NT war memorial

krie|ge|risch [ˈkriːgərɪʃ] **ADJ** warlike no adv; Haltung auch belligerent; Einsatz military; **eine ~e Auseinandersetzung** fighting no pl, military conflict **ADV** auftreten, eingestellt sein belligerently; **sich ~ auseinander setzen** to engage in military conflict; **einen Konflikt ~ austragen** to resolve a conflict by military means

Krie|ger|wit|we F war widow

Krieg-: **krieg|füh|rend** △ ADJ → Krieg; **Krieg|füh|ren|de(r)** MF decl as adj **die ~n** the bellig-

erents; **Krieg|füh|rung** F warfare no art; (eines Feldherrn) conduct of the war

Kriegs-: **Kriegs|an|lei|he** F war loan; **Kriegs|aus|bruch** M outbreak of war; **es kam zum ~** war broke out; **kriegs|be|dingt** ADJ resulting from or caused by (the) war; **Kriegs|be|ginn** M start of the war; **Kriegs|beil** NT tomahawk; **das ~ begraben** (fig) to bury the hatchet; **das ~ ausgraben** (fig) to start a fight; **Kriegs|be|ma|lung** F (lit, hum) war paint; **Kriegs|be|richt|er|stat|ter(in)** M(F) war correspondent; **kriegs|be|schä|digt** [-bəfɛːdɪçt] ADJ war-disabled; **Kriegs|be|schä|dig|te(r)** MF decl as adj war-disabled person; **die ~n** the war disabled; **Kriegs|blin|de(r)** MF decl as adj **die ~n** the war-blind

Kriegs|dienst M (old, form) military service; **den ~ verweigern** to be a conscientious objector

Kriegs|dienst-: **Kriegs|dienst|ver|wei|ge|rer** [-fɛvaɪgəʁɐ] M **-s, -**, **Kriegs|dienst|ver|wei|ge|rin** [-ərɪn] F **-, -nen** conscientious objector; **Kriegs|dienst|ver|wei|ge|rung** F refusal to fight in a war

Kriegs-: **Kriegs|ein|wir|kung** F effects pl or aftermath no pl of war; **Kriegs|en|de** NT end of the war; **Kriegs|ent|schä|di|gun|gen** PL reparations pl; **Kriegs|er|klä|rung** F declaration of war; **Kriegs|er|leb|nis** NT wartime experience; **Kriegs|fall** M (eventuality of a) war; **dann träte der ~ ein** then war would break out; **Kriegs|film** M war film; **Kriegs|flag|ge** F naval ensign; **Kriegs|flot|te** F navy, fleet; **Kriegs|fol|ge** F consequence of (a/the) war; **Kriegs|frei|wil|li|ge(r)** MF decl as adj (wartime) volunteer; **Kriegs|fuß** M (inf) **mit jdm auf ~ stehen** to be at loggerheads with sb (esp Brit), to be at odds with sb; **Kriegs|ge|biet** NT war zone; **Kriegs|ge|fahr** F danger of war; **~ zieht herauf** (geh) the war clouds are gathering; **Kriegs|ge|fan|ge|ne(r)** MF decl as adj prisoner of war, P.O.W.; **Kriegs|ge|fan|gen|schaft** F captivity; **in ~ sein** to be a prisoner of war; **aus der ~ kommen** to return or be released from captivity; **Kriegs|geg|ner(in)** M(F) **a** opponent of a/the war; (= Pazifist) pacifist, opponent of war **b** (= Gegner im Krieg) wartime enemy; **Kriegs|ge|rät** M military equipment; **Kriegs|ge|richt** NT (wartime) court martial; **jdn vor ein ~ stellen** to court-martial sb; **kriegs|ge|schä|digt** [-gəfɛːdɪçt] ADJ war-damaged; **Kriegs|ge|schrei** NT war cry; **Kriegs|ge|winn|ler** [-gəvɪnlɐ] M **-s, -**, **Kriegs|ge|winn|le|rin** [-ərɪn] F **-, -nen** (pej) war-profiteer; **Kriegs|glück** NT (liter) fortunes pl of war; **dann verließ Hannibal sein ~** then the fortunes of war turned against or deserted Hannibal; **Kriegs|gott** M god of war; **Kriegs|göt|tin** F goddess of war; **Kriegs|grä|ber|für|sor|ge** F War Graves Commission; **Kriegs|gräu|el** ▲ PL war atrocities pl; **Kriegs|grund** M reason for war; **Kriegs|ha|fen** M naval port, naval harbour (Brit) or harbor (US); **Kriegs|hand|werk** NT (old) soldiering; **Kriegs|held** M great warrior; (in moderner Zeit) military hero; **Kriegs|hel|din** F great warrior; (in moderner Zeit) military heroine; **Kriegs|herr(in)** M(F) warlord; **oberster ~** (Hist) commander-in-chief; **Kriegs|het|ze** F war-mongering; **Kriegs|in|va|li|de** M , **Kriegs|in|va|li|din** F decl as adj war-disabled person; **Kriegs|jahr** NT year of war; **die ~e** the war years; **im ~ 1945** (during the war) in 1945; **im dritten ~** in the third year of the war; **Kriegs|ka|me|rad(in)** M(F) fellow soldier, war(time) comrade; **Kriegs|kas|se** F war chest; **Kriegs|kind** NT war baby; **Kriegs|kos|ten** PL cost of the war sing; **Kriegs|kunst** F art of war(fare); **Kriegs|list** F (old, liter) ruse of war, stratagem; **Kriegs|ma|ri|ne** F navy; **Kriegs|ma|schi|ne|rie** F machinery of war; **kriegs|mä|ßig** ▲ for war; Kleidung, Bemalung war- **ADV ~ gekleidet/ausgerüstet** dressed/equipped for war; **die Indianer waren ~**

bemalt the Indians wore war paint; **ein ~ vorbereitetes Land** a country prepared for war; **~ klingende Musik** martial music; **Kriegs|mi|nis|ter(in)** M(F) (Hist, Pol pej) minister of war; **Kriegs|mi|nis|te|ri|um** NT (Hist) War Office (Brit), War Department (US); **kriegs|müde** ADJ war-weary; **Kriegs|op|fer** NT war victim; **Kriegs|pfad** M (liter) **auf dem ~** on the warpath; **Kriegs|rat** M council of war; **~ halten** (fig) to have a pow-wow (inf); **Kriegs|recht** NT conventions of war pl; (Mil) martial law; **Kriegs|schä|den** PL war damage; **Kriegs|schau|platz** M theatre (Brit) or theater (US) of war; **Kriegs|schiff** NT warship, man-of-war; **Kriegs|schuld** F war guilt; **Kriegs|schul|den** PL war debts pl; **Kriegs|spiel** NT war game; **Kriegs|spiel|zeug** NT war toy; **Kriegs|stär|ke** F war establishment; **die Armee auf ~ bringen** to make the army ready for war; **Kriegs|teil|neh|mer** M combatant; (= Staat) combatant nation, belligerent; (= ehemaliger Soldat) ex-serviceman; **Kriegs|teil|neh|me|rin** F combatant; (= ehemalige Soldatin) ex-servicewoman; **Kriegs|to|te(r)** MF decl as adj war dead; **30.000 ~** 30,000 killed in action; **Kriegs|trau|ung** F war wedding; **Kriegs|trei|ber** M **-s, -**, **Kriegs|trei|be|rin** F **-, -nen** (pej) warmonger; **kriegs|tüch|tig** ADJ (old) fit for active service; **kriegs|un|taug|lich** ADJ unfit for active service; **Kriegs|ver|bre|chen** NT war crime; **Kriegs|ver|bre|cher(in)** M(F) war criminal; **Kriegs|ver|let|zung** F war wound; **kriegs|ver|sehrt** ADJ war-disabled; **Kriegs|ver|sehr|te(r)** MF decl as adj war-disabled person; **die Kriegsversehrten** the war-disabled; **kriegs|ver|wen|dungs|fä|hig** ADJ (form) fit for active service; **Kriegs|wir|ren** PL (geh) chaos of war sing; **Kriegs|wirt|schaft** F war economy; **Kriegs|zeit** F wartime; **in ~en** in times of war; **sie erzählten von ihrer ~** they told about their wartime experiences; **kriegs|zer|stört** ADJ destroyed in (the) war pred; **Kriegs|zug** M (old) campaign, military expedition; **Kriegs|zu|stand** M state of war; **im ~** at war

Kriek|en|te [ˈkriːk-] F (green-winged) teal

Krill [krɪl] M **-(s)**, no pl (Biol) krill

Krim [krɪm] F **- die ~** the Crimea

Kri|mi [ˈkriːmi] M **-s, -s** (inf) (crime) thriller; (rätselhaft) murder mystery, whodunnit (inf); (= Buch: mit Detektiv als Held) detective novel

Kri|mi|nal|be|am|te(r) [krimiˈnaːl-] M decl as adj, **Kri|mi|nal|be|am|tin** F detective, CID officer (Brit)

Kri|mi|na|le(r) [krimiˈnaːlə] M decl as adj (sl) plain-clothes man, detective, CID officer (Brit)

Kri|mi|nal-: **Kri|mi|nal|film** M crime thriller or film or movie (esp US); (rätselhaft) murder mystery, whodunnit (inf); **Kri|mi|nal|ge|richt** NT criminal court; **Kri|mi|nal|gro|tes|ke** F black comedy; **Kri|mi|nal|hör|spiel** NT radio thriller; (rätselhaft) murder mystery, whodunnit (inf)

kri|mi|na|li|sie|ren ptp **kriminalisiert** VT to criminalize

Kri|mi|na|list M **-en, -en**, **Kri|mi|na|lis|tin** F **-, -nen** criminologist

Kri|mi|na|lis|tik F **-**, no pl criminology

kri|mi|na|lis|tisch **ADJ** criminological; **~er Spürsinn besitzen** to have a nose for solving crimes **ADV ~ begabt sein** to have a talent for solving crimes

Kri|mi|na|li|tät F **-**, no pl crime; (= Ziffer) crime rate; **organisierte ~** organized crime

Kri|mi|nal-: **Kri|mi|nal|kom|mis|sar(in)** M(F) detective superintendent; **Kri|mi|nal|ko|mö|die** F comedy thriller; **Kri|mi|nal|li|te|ra|tur** F crime literature; **Kri|mi|nal|mu|se|um** NT crime museum; **Kri|mi|nal|po|li|zei** F criminal investigation department; **Kri|mi|nal|po|li|zist(in)** M(F) detective, CID officer (Brit); **Kri|mi|nal|ro|man** M → **Krimi** (crime) thriller; detective novel; murder mystery, whodunnit (inf); **Kri|mi|nal|stück** NT → **Krimi** thriller; detective play; murder mystery, whodunnit (inf); **kri|mi|nal|tech|nisch** ADJ forensic **ADV** forensically

kri|mi|nell [krimi'nɛl] **ADJ** (lit, fig inf) criminal; **~ werden** to turn to crime, to become a criminal; (junger Mensch auch) to become delinquent; **~e Energie** criminal resolve **ADV** **a** fährlässig criminally; (inf: = gefährlich) glatt, schlüpfrig, schnell dangerously

Kri|mi|nel|le(r) [krimi'nɛlə] MF decl as adj criminal

Kri|mi|no|lo|ge [krimino'lo:gə] M -n, -n, **Kri|mi|no|lo|gin** [-'lo:gɪn] F -, -nen criminologist

Kri|mi|no|lo|gie [kriminolo'gi:] F -, no pl criminology

kri|mi|no|lo|gisch [krimino'lo:gɪʃ] ADJ criminological

Krim|krieg M Crimean War

Krims|krams ['krɪmskrams] M -es, no pl (inf) odds and ends pl, bits and pieces pl, rubbish

Krin|gel ['krɪŋl] M -s, - (der Schrift) squiggle; (Cook: = Zuckerkringel etc) ring

krin|ge|lig ['krɪŋəlɪç] ADJ crinkly; **sich ~ lachen** (inf) to laugh oneself silly (inf), to kill oneself (laughing) (inf)

krin|geln ['krɪŋln] VR to go frizzy, to curl; **sich ~ vor Lachen** (inf) to kill oneself (laughing) (inf)

Kri|no|li|ne [krino'li:nə] F -, -n (Hist) crinoline

Kri|po ['kri:po, 'krɪpo] F -, -s (inf) abbr von **Kriminalpolizei die ~** the cops pl (inf), the CID (Brit)

Kri|po- in cpds (inf) police; **Kri|po|be|am|te(r)** M decl as adj, **Kri|po|be|am|tin** **F** police detective

Krip|pe ['krɪpə] F -, -n **a** (= Futterkrippe) (hay)-rack, (hay)box; **sich an die ~ drängen** (fig) to start jockeying for position; **an der ~ sitzen** (fig) to live a life of ease, to live in comfort **b** (= Kinderkrippe, Weihnachtskrippe) crib; (Bibl) crib, manger **c** (= Kinderhort) crèche (Brit), daycare centre (Brit) or center (US) **d** (Astron) Manger

Krip|pen-: Krip|pen|spiel NT nativity play; **Krip|pen|tod** M cot death (Brit), crib death (US)

krisch (old, hum) pret von **kreischen**

Kri|se ['kri:zə] F -, -n crisis; **in eine ~ geraten** to enter a state of crisis; **er hatte eine schwere ~** he was going through a difficult crisis; **die ~ kriegen** (inf) to do one's nut (Brit inf), to go crazy (inf)

kri|seln ['kri:zln] VI impers (inf) **es kriselt** there is a crisis looming, trouble is brewing; **in seiner Ehe kriselt es** trouble's brewing in his marriage

Kri|sen-: kri|sen|an|fäl|lig ADJ crisis-prone; **Kri|sen|an|fäl|lig|keit** F wegen der **~ dieser Gegend** as this area is so crisis-prone; **kri|sen|fest** **ADJ** stable, crisis-proof **ADV** **Geld ~ in Grundbesitz anlegen** to invest money in property to secure it against or to hedge against economic crises; **Kri|sen|fes|tig|keit** F stability (in the face of a crisis); **Kri|sen|ge|biet** NT crisis area; **kri|sen|ge|schüt|telt** [-gəʃʏtlt] ADJ crisis-ridden; **kri|sen|haft** ADJ Situation, Entwicklung critical **ADV** critically; **Kri|sen|herd** M flash point, trouble spot; **Kri|sen|ma|nage|ment** NT crisis management; **Kri|sen|ma|na|ger(in)** M(F) crisis manager; **Kri|sen|plan** M contingency plan; **Kri|sen|re|gi|on** F trouble spot; **kri|sen|si|cher** **ADJ** stable, crisis-proof **ADV** **Geld ~ in Grundbesitz anlegen** to invest money in property to secure it against or to hedge against economic crises; **Kri|sen|si|tu|a|ti|on** F crisis (situation); **Kri|sen|sit|zung** F emergency session; **Kri|sen|stab** M (special) action or crisis committee; **Kri|sen|stim|mung** F crisis mood, mood of crisis

Kri|sis ['kri:zɪs] F -, Krisen ['kri:zn] (liter) crisis

Kris|tall¹ ['krɪs'tal] M -s, -e crystal; **~e bilden** to crystallize, to form crystals

---

Kris|tall² NT -s, no pl (= Kristallglas) crystal (glass); (= Kristallwaren) crystalware, crystal goods pl

Kris|tall|bil|dung F crystallization

kris|tal|len [krɪs'talən] ADJ (made of) crystal; Stimme crystal-clear

Kristalleuchter △ M → **Kristallleuchter**

Kris|tall-: kris|tall|git|ter NT crystal lattice; **Kris|tall|glas** NT crystal glass

kris|tal|lin [krɪsta'li:n], **kris|tal|li|nisch** [krɪsta-'li:nɪʃ] ADJ crystalline

Kris|tal|li|sa|ti|on [krɪstaliza'tsio:n] F -, -en crystallization

Kris|tal|li|sa|ti|ons|punkt M (fig) focal point

kris|tal|li|sie|ren [krɪstali'zi:rən] ptp **kristallisiert** VIR (lit, fig) to crystallize

Kris|tall-: kris|tall|klar ADJ crystal-clear; **Kris|tall|leuch|ter** ▲ M , **Kris|tall|lüs|ter** ▲ M (geh) crystal chandelier; **Kris|tall|nacht** F (Hist) Crystal night, night of 9th/10th November 1938, during which the Nazis organized a pogrom throughout Germany, burning synagogues and breaking windows of Jewish shops

Kristallüster △ M → **Kristalllüster**

Kris|tall-: Kris|tall|wa|ren PL crystalware sing, crystal goods pl; **Kris|tall|zu|cker** M refined sugar (in) crystals

Kri|te|ri|um [kri'te:riʊm] NT -s, Kriterien [-riən] **a** criterion **b** (Radfahren) circuit race

Kri|tik [kri'ti:k] F -, -en **a** no pl criticism (an +dat of); **an jdm/etw ~ üben** to criticize sb/sth; **auf (heftige) ~ stoßen** to come in for or to come under (severe) criticism; **Gesellschafts-/ Literaturkritik** social/literary criticism; **unter aller** or **jeder ~ sein** (inf) to be beneath contempt **b** (= Rezensieren) criticism; (= Rezension) review, notice, crit (inf); **eine gute ~ haben** to get good reviews etc; **der Film bekam schlechte ~en** the film got bad reviews etc **c** no pl (= die Kritiker) critics pl **d** no pl (= Urteilsfähigkeit) discrimination; **ohne jede ~** uncritically **e** (Philos: = kritische Analyse) critique

Kri|ti|kas|ter [kriti'kaste] M -s, -, **Kri|ti|kas|te|rin** [-ərɪn] F -, -nen (dated pej) caviller (Brit), caviler (US), fault-finder, criticaster (rare)

Kri|ti|ker ['kri:tike] M -s, -, **Kri|ti|ke|rin** [-ərɪn] F -, -nen critic

Kri|tik-: kri|tik|fä|hig ADJ able to criticize; **Kri|tik|fä|hig|keit** F critical faculty; **kri|tik|los** **ADJ** uncritical **ADV** uncritically; **etw ~ hin|nehmen** to accept sth without criticism or protest; **Kri|tik|punkt** M point of criticism; **es gibt noch einen weiteren ~** and there's another point which is open to criticism; **kri|tik|wür|dig** ADJ reprehensible

kri|tisch ['kri:tɪʃ] **ADJ** (alle Bedeutungen) critical; **wenn dieser Mitarbeiter auch noch ausfällt, dann wird es ~** if we lose this worker too things will become critical **ADV** kommentieren, bewerten, sich äußern critically; **~ eingestellt sein** to be critical; **sich jdm gegenüber ~ verhalten** to be critical of sb; **die Lage ~ beurteilen** to make a critical appraisal of the situation; **jdm/ einer Sache ~ gegenüberstehen** to be critical of sb/sth, to regard or consider sb/sth critically

kri|ti|sie|ren [kriti'zi:rən] ptp **kritisiert** VTI to criticize; **er hat** or **findet an allem etwas zu ~** he always has or finds something to criticize

Kri|ti|zis|mus [kriti'tsɪsmʊs] M -, no pl (Philos) critical philosophy

Krit|te|lei [krɪtə'lai] F -, -en fault-finding no pl, cavilling no pl (Brit), caviling no pl (US)

krit|teln ['krɪtln] VI to find fault (an +dat, über +acc with), to cavil (an +dat, über +acc at)

Krit|ze|lei [krɪtsə'lai] F -, -en scribble; (= das Kritzeln) scribbling; (= Männchenmalen etc) doodle, doodling; (an Wänden) graffiti

---

krit|zeln ['krɪtsln] VTI to scribble, to scrawl; (= Männchen malen etc) to doodle

Kro|a|te [kro'a:tə] M -n, -n, **Kro|a|tin** [-'a:tɪn] F -, -nen Croat, Croatian

Kro|a|ti|en [kro'a:tsiən] NT -s Croatia

kro|a|tisch [kro'a:tɪʃ] ADJ Croat, Croatian

Kro|a|tisch(e) [kro'a:tɪʃ] NT Croatian → auch **Deutsch(e)**

Kro|atz|bee|re [kro'ats-] F (esp S Ger: = Brombeere) blackberry, bramble

kroch pret von **kriechen**

Kro|cket|(spiel) ['krɔkət-, krɔ'ket-] NT -s, no pl croquet

Kro|kant [kro'kant] M -s, no pl (Cook) cracknel

Kro|ket|te [kro'ketə] F -, -n (Cook) croquette

Kro|ko ['kroko] NT -s, no pl crocodile leather

Kro|ko|dil [kroko'di:l] NT -s, -e crocodile

Kro|ko|dil|le|der NT crocodile leather or skin

Kro|ko|dils|trä|nen PL crocodile tears pl

Kro|kus ['kro:kʊs] M -, - or -se crocus

krö|nen ['krø:nçən] NT -s, - dim von **Krone**

Kro|ne ['kro:nə] F -, -n **a** crown; (eines Grafen etc) coronet; **die ~** (fig) the Crown **b** (= Mauerkrone) coping; (= Schaumkrone) cap, crest; (= Zahnkrone) crown, cap; (an Uhr) winder; (= Geweihkrone) surroyal (antler); (= Baumkrone) top; (= Erntekrone) harvest wreath or crown; **die ~ der Schöpfung** the pride of creation, creation's crowning glory; **die ~ des Lebens** (Bibl) (a) crown of life; **die ~ des Ganzen war, dass ...** (fig) (but) what crowned or capped it all was that ...; **das setzt doch allem die ~ auf** (inf) that beats everything; **das setzt der Dummheit die ~ auf** (inf) that beats everything for stupidity; **einen in der ~ haben** (inf) to be tipsy, to have had a drop too much; **dabei fällt dir keine Perle** or **kein Stein** or **Zacken aus der ~** (inf) it won't hurt you **c** (= Währungseinheit) (in Tschechien, Slowakei) crown; (in Dänemark, Norwegen) krone; (in Schweden, Island) krona

krö|nen ['krø:nən] VT (lit, fig) to crown; Bauwerk to crown, to top, to cap; **jdn zum König ~** to crown sb king; **von Erfolg gekrönt sein/werden** to be crowned with success; **gekrönte Häupter** crowned heads; **damit wurde ihre glänzende Laufbahn gekrönt** this was the crowning achievement in or the culmination of her career; **der ~de Abschluss** the culmination

Kro|nen-: Kro|nen|kor|ken M crown cap; **Kro|nen|mut|ter** F pl -muttern (Tech) castle nut

Kron-: Kron|er|be M heir to the crown or throne; **Kron|er|bin** F heiress to the crown or throne; **Kron|gut** NT crown estate; **Kron|ju|we|len** PL crown jewels pl; **Kron|ko|lo|nie** F crown colony; **Kron|kor|ken** M crown cap; **Kron|land** NT crown land

Krön|lein ['krø:nlain] NT -s, - dim von **Krone**

Kron-: Kron|leuch|ter M chandelier; **Kron|prä|ten|dent(in)** M(F) pretender (to the crown); **Kron|prinz** M crown prince; (in Großbritannien auch) Prince of Wales; (fig) heir apparent; **Kron|prin|zes|sin** F crown princess; (fig) heir apparent; **Kron|rat** M crown council

Krons|bee|re ['kro:ns-] F (N Ger: = Preiselbeere) cranberry

Krö|nung ['krø:nʊŋ] F -, -en coronation; (fig) culmination; (von Veranstaltung) high point, culmination; (Archit) coping stone

Kron|zeu|ge ['kro:n-] M , **Kron|zeu|gin** F (Jur) person who gives or turns King's/Queen's evidence (Brit) or State's evidence (US); (= Hauptzeuge) principal witness; (fig) main authority; **~ sein**, **als ~ auftreten** to turn King's/ Queen's evidence (Brit) or State's evidence (US); to appear as principal witness

Kron|zeu|gen|re|ge|lung ['kro:n-] F (Jur) regulation guaranteeing a state witness from a

---

terrorist background immunity from prosecution or a lenient sentence

Kropf [krɔpf] M -(e)s, ⸚e ['krœpfə] **a** (von Vogel) crop **b** (Med) goitre (Brit), goiter (US); **überflüssig wie ein ~** totally superfluous

Kröpf|chen ['krœpfçən] NT -s, - dim von Kropf a

kröp|fen ['krœpfn] **VT** (= füttern, nudeln) to cram **VI** (= fressen: Raubvögel) to gorge

Kropf|tau|be F pouter (pigeon)

Kropp|zeug ['krɔp-] NT , no pl (pej inf: = Gesindel) scum; **dieses ganze ~** all this junk (inf)

kross ▲ [krɔs] (N Ger) **ADJ** crisp; Brötchen auch crusty **ADV** backen, braten until crisp

Krö|sus ['krø:zʊs] M -, -se Croesus; **ich bin doch kein ~** (inf) I'm not made of money (inf)

Krö|te ['krø:tə] F -, -n **a** (Zool) toad; **eine freche (kleine) ~** (inf) a cheeky (little) minx (Brit inf), a little devil (esp US inf); **eine giftige ~** (inf) a spiteful creature; **eine ~ schlucken** (fig inf) to bite the bullet **b Kröten** PL (inf) pennies (inf); **die paar ~n** the few pounds

Krö|ten|test M (Med) Hogben (pregnancy) test

Krü|cke ['krykə] F -, -n **a** crutch; (fig) prop, stay; **auf** or **an ~n gehen** (dat) to walk on crutches **b** (= Schirmkrücke) crook **c** (zum Harken etc) rake **d** (inf) (= Nichtskönner) dead loss (inf), washout (inf); (= altes Fahrrad) unfashionable bike

Krück|stock M walking stick → Blinde(r)

krud [kru:t], **krude** ['kru:də] (geh) **ADJ** crude **ADV** sich ausdrücken crudely

Krug [kru:k] M -(e)s, ⸚e ['kry:gə] **a** (= Milchkrug etc) jug, pitcher (old); (= Weinkrug) jug; (= Bierkrug) (beer) mug, stein, tankard; (= Maßkrug) litre (Brit) or liter (US) mug; (= Kruke) jar; **der ~ geht so lange zum Brunnen, bis er bricht** (Prov) one day you/they etc will come unstuck or come to grief **b** (N Ger: = Wirtshaus) inn, pub (Brit)

Krü|gel ['kry:gl] NT -s, - (Aus) half-litre (Brit) or half-liter (US) mug

Kru|ke ['kru:kə] F -, -n stone jar; (= Wärmkruke) bed-warmer, earthenware or stone hot-water bottle

Kru|me ['kru:mə] F -, -n (geh) **a** (= Brotkrume) crumb **b** (liter: = Ackerkrume) (top)soil

Krü|mel ['kry:ml] M -s, - **a** (= Brotkrümel etc) crumb **b** (inf: = Kind) little one, tiny tot (inf)

krü|me|lig ['kry:məlɪç] ADJ crumbly

krü|meln ['kry:mln] VTI to crumble; (beim Essen) to make crumbs

krumm [krʊm] **ADJ** **a** crooked; (= verbogen) bent, crooked; (= hakenförmig) hooked; Beine bandy; Rücken hunched; **~e Nase** hook(ed) nose; **etw ~ biegen** to bend sth; **~ und schief** askew, skewwhiff (Brit inf); **sich ~ und schief lachen** (inf) to fall about laughing (inf); **jdn ~ und lahm schlagen** to beat sb black and blue; **eine ~e Hand machen** (inf) to hold one's hand out; **einen ~en Rücken machen** to stoop; (fig) to bow and scrape; **mach nicht solchen ~en Rücken!** straighten your shoulders, hold yourself straight **b** (inf: = unehrlich) crooked (inf); **~er Hund** (pej) crooked swine; **ein ~es Ding drehen** (sl) to do something crooked, **er hat während seiner Zeit als Buchhalter viele ~e Dinger gedreht** (sl) while he was a book-keeper he got up to all sorts of crooked tricks (inf); **etw auf die ~e Tour versuchen** to try to fiddle (inf) or wangle (inf) sth; **er hat sie auf die ~e Tour herumgekriegt** he conned her (inf); **~e Wege gehen** to err from the straight and narrow **ADV** (= nicht gerade) **~ stehen/sitzen** to slouch; **steh/sitz nicht so ~ da!** stand/sit up straight, don't slouch; **~ gehen** to walk with a stoop; **~ wachsen** to grow crooked; **~ gewachsen** crooked; **keinen Finger ~ machen** (inf) not to lift a finger

krumm|bei|nig ADJ bow-legged, bandy (-legged)

Krumm|dolch M curved dagger, jhambaia (spec)

krüm|men ['krymən] **VT** to bend; **die Katze krümmte den Buckel** the cat arched its back; **gekrümmte Oberfläche** curved surface → Haar c **VR** to bend; (Fluss) to wind; (Straße) to bend, to curve; (Wurm) to writhe; (Mensch) to double up; **sich vor Lachen ~** to double up with laughter, to crease up (inf); **sich vor Schmerzen** (dat) **~** to double up or writhe with pain

Krumm-: Krumm|horn NT crumhorn, krummhorn; **krumm+la|chen** VR sep (inf) to double up laughing or with laughter, to fall about laughing or with laughter; **krumm le|gen** ▲ VR (inf) to pinch and scrape (inf); **krumm|na|sig** ADJ (pej) hook-nosed; **krumm neh|men** ▲ VT irreg (inf) **(jdm) etw ~** to take offence (Brit) or offense (US) at sth, to take sth amiss (esp Brit); **Krumm|sä|bel** M scimitar; **Krumm|schwert** NT scimitar; **Krumm|stab** M crook, crozier

Krüm|mung ['krymʊŋ] F -, -en **a** (= das Krümmen) bending **b** (= Biegung) (von Weg, Fluss) bend, turn; (Math, Med, von Fläche) curvature; (Opt: von Linse) curve, curvature, figure

krum|pe|lig ['krʊmpəlɪç], **krump|lig** ['krʊmplɪç] ADJ (dial) creased, crumpled

Krup|pe ['krʊpə] F -, -n (Zool) croup, crupper

Krüp|pel ['krypl] M -s, - cripple; **ein seelischer/ geistiger ~ sein** to be an emotional/intellectual cripple, to be emotionally/intellectually stunted; **zum ~ werden** to be crippled; **jdn zum ~ machen** to cripple sb; **jdn zum ~ schlagen** to (beat and) cripple sb

krüp|pe|lig ['krypəlɪç], **krüpp|lig** ['kryplɪç] **ADJ** Mensch crippled, deformed; Baum, Wuchs stunted **ADV** **~ gewachsen** misshapen

Krupp|hus|ten ['krʊp-] M (Med) croupy cough

Krus|ta|ze|en [krʊsta'tse:ən] PL (spec) crustacea pl

Krus|te ['krʊstə] F -, -n crust; (von Schweinebraten) crackling; (von Braten) crisped outside

Krus|ten|tie|re PL crustaceans pl, crustacea pl (spec)

krus|tig ['krʊstɪç] ADJ crusty; Topf etc encrusted

Krux [krʊks] F -, no pl = Crux

Kru|zi|fix ['kru:tsifɪks, krutsi'fɪks] NT -es, -e crucifix; **~!** (inf) Christ almighty! (sl)

Kru|zi|tür|ken [krutsi'tyrkn] INTERJ (S Ger inf) confound it, curse it

kry|o|kon|ser|vie|ren [kryokɔnzɛr'vi:rən] ptp **kryokonserviert** VT to preserve cryogenically

Kryp|ta ['krypta] F -, Krypten ['kryptn] crypt

kryp|tisch ['kryptɪʃ] ADJ Bemerkung cryptic; **sich ~ ausdrücken** to express oneself cryptically

Krypto- [krypto], **kryp|to-** in cpds crypto-; **Kryp|to|fa|schist(in)** M(F) crypto-fascist; **Kryp|to|gramm** NT cryptogram; **Kryp|to|gra|fie** ▲ [kryptogra'fi:] F **a** (= Geheimschrift) cryptography **b** (Psych: = Kritzelzeichnung) doodle (used in psychoanalysis); **Kryp|to|lo|ge** [krypto'lo:gə] M -n, -n, **Kryp|to|lo|gin** [-'lo:gɪn] **F** -, -nen cryptologist

Kryp|ton ['kryptɔn, kryp'to:n] NT -s, no pl (abbr **Kr**) krypton

KSZE [ka:ɛstsɛt'ʔe:] F - (Hist) abbr von Konferenz über Sicherheit und Zusammenarbeit in Europa CSCE

Ku|ba ['ku:ba] NT -s Cuba

Ku|ba|ner [ku'ba:nɐ] M -s, -, **Ku|ba|ne|rin** [-ərɪn] F -s, - Cuban

ku|ba|nisch [ku'ba:nɪʃ] ADJ Cuban

Kü|bel ['ky:bl] M -s, - bucket, pail; (für Jauche etc) container; (inf: im Gefängnis) latrine or toilet bucket, crapper (inf); (für Bäume) tub; **es regnet (wie) aus** or **mit ~n** it's bucketing down (Brit),

it's coming down in buckets (US); **~ von Schmutz** or Unrat (fig geh) torrents of abuse

kü|beln ['ky:bln] VI (sl: = sich übergeben) to puke (inf)

Kü|bel|pflan|ze F tub plant

Ku|ben pl von Kubus

Ku|bik [ku'bi:k] NT -, - (Aut inf: = Hubraum) cc

Kubik-: Ku|bik|me|ter M OR NT cubic metre (Brit) or meter (US); **Ku|bik|wur|zel** F cube root; **Ku|bik|zahl** F cube number; **Ku|bik|zen|ti|me|ter** M OR NT cubic centimetre (Brit) or centimeter (US)

ku|bisch ['ku:bɪʃ] ADJ cubic(al); Gleichung cubic; Lampen cube-shaped

Ku|bis|mus [ku'bɪsmʊs] M -, no pl (Art) cubism

Ku|bist [ku'bɪst] M -en, -en, **Ku|bis|tin** [-'bɪstɪn] F -, -nen (Art) cubist

ku|bis|tisch [ku'bɪstɪʃ] ADJ (Art) cubist(ic)

Ku|bus ['ku:bʊs] M -, Kuben ['ku:bn] or - cube

Kü|che ['kyçə] F -, -n **a** kitchen; (klein) kitchenette; **es wurde alles aufgetischt, was ~ und Keller zu bieten hatten** he/they etc served up a meal fit for a king **b** (= Kochkunst) gutbürgerliche ~ good home cooking; **chinesische ~** Chinese cooking **c** (= Speisen) meals pl, dishes pl, food; **warme/kalte ~** hot/cold food

Ku|chen ['ku:xn] M -s, - cake; (= Torte) cake, gateau (Brit); (mit Obst gedeckt) (fruit) flan, gateau (Brit)

Küchen-: Kü|chen|ab|fäl|le PL kitchen scraps pl; **Kü|chen|ab|zugs|hau|be** F extractor hood (Brit), fan hood (US); **Kü|chen|be|nut|zung** F use of kitchen

Ku|chen|blech NT baking sheet or tin (Brit) or pan (US)

Küchen-: Kü|chen|bul|le M (Mil sl) cookhouse wallah (Mil sl); **Kü|chen|chef(in)** M(F) chef; **Kü|chen|ein|rich|tung** F (fitted) kitchen; **Kü|chen|fee** F (hum inf) (lady) cook

Küchen-: Kü|chen|form F cake tin (Brit) or pan (US); **Kü|chen|ga|bel** F pastry fork

Küchen-: Kü|chen|ge|rät NT kitchen utensil; (kollektiv) kitchen utensils pl; (elektrisch) kitchen appliance; **Kü|chen|ge|schirr** NT kitchenware no pl; **Kü|chen|hand|tuch** NT kitchen towel; **Kü|chen|herd** M cooker (Brit), range (US); **Kü|chen|hil|fe** F kitchen help; **Kü|chen|ho|bel** M slicer, cutter; **Kü|chen|jun|ge** M (dated) apprentice cook or chef; **Kü|chen|ka|bi|nett** NT (Pol) inner circle, kitchen cabinet (inf); **Kü|chen|la|tein** NT dog Latin; **Kü|chen|ma|schi|ne** F food processor; **Kü|chen|meis|ter(in)** M(F) chef; **Kü|chen|mes|ser** NT kitchen knife; **Kü|chen|per|so|nal** NT kitchen staff; **Kü|chen|rol|le** F kitchen roll; **Kü|chen|scha|be** F (Zool) cockroach; **Kü|chen|schel|le** F (Bot) pasqueflower; **Kü|chen|schrank** M (kitchen) cupboard

Ku|chen|teig M cake mixture; (= Hefeteig) dough

Küchen-: Kü|chen|tisch M kitchen table; **Kü|chen|tuch** NT pl -tücher kitchen towel; **Kü|chen|uhr** F kitchen clock; **Kü|chen|waa|ge** F kitchen scales pl; **Kü|chen|wa|gen** M (Mil) mobile field-kitchen; **Kü|chen|zei|le** F kitchen units pl; **Kü|chen|zet|tel** M menu

Küch|lein ['ky:çlain] NT -s, - **a** small cake **b** (= Küken) chick

ku|cken ['kʊkn] VI (N Ger, inf) = gucken

Kü|cken ['kykn] NT -s, - (Aus) = Küken a

ku|ckuck ['kʊkʊk] INTERJ cuckoo

Ku|ckuck ['kʊkʊk] M -s, -e **a** cuckoo **b** (inf: = Siegel des Gerichtsvollziehers) bailiff's seal (for distraint of goods) **c** (euph inf: = Teufel) devil; **zum ~ (noch mal)!** hell's bells! (inf), darn it! (esp US inf); **hols der ~!** botheration! (inf); **geh zum ~, scher dich zum ~** go to blazes (inf); **(das) weiß der ~** heaven (only) knows (inf)

Kuckucks-: Ku|ckucks|ei NT cuckoo's egg; (inf: = außerehelich gezeugtes Kind) illegitimate child; **man hat uns ein ~ untergeschoben** (*inf*) we've been left holding the baby (*inf*); **jdm ein ~ ins Nest legen** (*inf*) to foist something on sb; **Ku|ckucks|uhr** F cuckoo clock

Kud|del|mud|del ['kʊdlmʊdl] M OR NT **-s**, *no pl* (*inf*) muddle, mess, confusion; (= *Aufsatz etc auch*) hotchpotch (*Brit inf*), hodgepodge (*US inf*)

Ku|fe ['kuːfə] F **-**, **-n** **a** (*von Schlitten, Schlittschuh etc*) runner; (*von Flugzeug*) skid **b** (*Holzbottich*) tub

Kü|fer ['kyːfɐ] M **-s**, **-** cellarman; (*S Ger: = Böttcher*) cooper

Kü|fe|rin ['kyːfərɪn] F **-**, **-nen** cellarwoman; (*S Ger: = Böttcherin*) cooper

Ku|gel ['kuːɡl] F **-**, **-n** **a** ball; (*geometrische Figur*) sphere; (= *Erdkugel*) sphere, globe; (*Sport sl: = Ball*) ball; (= *Kegelkugel*) bowl; (= *Gewehrkugel*) bullet; (*für Luftgewehr*) (= *Kanonenkugel*) (cannon)ball; (*Sport: = Stoßkugel*) shot; (= *Murmel*) marble; (= *Papierkugel*) ball; (*kleine*) pellet; (= *Christbaumkugel*) glitter ball; **sich** (*dat*) **eine ~ durch den Kopf jagen or schießen** to blow one's brains out; **ich geb mir die ~** (*sl: = erschieße mich*) I'll shoot myself (*inf*); **eine ruhige ~ schieben** (*inf*) to have a cushy number or job (*inf*); (*aus Faulheit*) to swing the lead (*Brit inf*), to play hookey (*US inf*); **rund wie eine ~** (*inf*) like a barrel; **die ~ rollt** (*fig*) the roulette wheels are spinning **b** (= *Gelenkkugel*) head (of a bone)

Ku|gel-: Ku|gel|ab|schnitt M (*Math*) spherical segment; **Ku|gel|aus|schnitt** M (*Math*) spherical sector; **Ku|gel|bauch** M pot belly, paunch; **Ku|gel|blitz** M (*Met*) ball lightning

Kü|gel|chen ['kyːɡlçən] NT **-s**, **-** *dim von* **Kugel** small ball; (*aus Schrot, Papier etc*) pellet

Ku|gel-: Ku|gel|fang M butt; **die Leibwächter sollen als ~ dienen** the bodyguards are meant to act as a bullet-screen; **ku|gel|fest** ADJ = **kugelsicher**; **Ku|gel|fisch** M globefish, puffer; **Ku|gel|flä|che** F (*Math*) spherical surface; **ku|gel|för|mig** ADJ spherical ADV spherically; **Ku|gel|ge|lenk** NT (*Anat, Tech*) ball-and-socket joint; **Ku|gel|ha|gel** M hail of bullets

ku|ge|lig ['kuːɡəlɪç] ADJ (= *kugelförmig*) spherical; (*inf*) *Person* tubby, dumpy; *Bauch* plump ADV **a** spherically **b** **sich ~ lachen** to double up (laughing)

Ku|gel-: Ku|gel|kopf M golf ball; **Ku|gel|kopf|schreib|ma|schi|ne** F golf-ball typewriter; **Ku|gel|la|ger** NT ball bearing

ku|geln ['kuːɡln] VI *aux sein* (= *rollen, fallen*) to roll VR to roll (about); **sich (vor Lachen) ~** (*inf*) to double up (laughing); **ich könnte mich ~** (*inf*) it's killingly funny (*inf*)

Ku|gel-: Ku|gel|re|gen M hail of bullets; **ku|gel|rund** ADJ as round as a ball; (*inf*) *Mensch* tubby, barrel-shaped (*inf*); **Ku|gel|schrei|ber** M ballpoint (pen), Biro® (*Brit*); **Ku|gel|schrei|ber|mi|ne** F refill (for a ballpoint pen); **ku|gel|si|cher** ADJ bullet-proof; **Ku|gel|sto|ßen** NT **-s**, *no pl* shot-putting, putting the shot; **Sieger im ~** winner in the shot(-put); **Ku|gel|sto|ßer** [-ʃtoːsɐ] M **-s**, **-**, **Ku|gel|sto|ße|rin** [-ərɪn] F **-**, **-nen** shot-putter; **Ku|gel|ven|til** NT (*Tech*) ball valve; **Ku|gel|wech|sel** M exchange of shots

Kuh [kuː] F **-**, **¨e** ['kyːə] cow; (*pej inf: = Mädchen, Frau*) cow (*inf*); **wie die ~ vorm neuen Tor da|stehen** (*inf*) to be completely bewildered; **die ~ vom Eis bringen** (*fig inf*) to save the situation; **heilige ~** (*lit, fig*) sacred cow

Kuh-: Kuh|au|gen PL (*pej inf*) goggle eyes *pl* (*inf*); **Kuh|dorf** NT (*pej inf*) one-horse town (*inf*); **Kuh|fla|den** M cowpat; **Kuh|fuß** M (*Tech*) crowbar; **Kuh|glo|cke** F cowbell; **Kuh|han|del** M (*pej inf*) horse-trading (*inf*) *no pl*; **ein ~** a bit of horse-trading; **kuh|han|deln** VI *insep* (*inf*) to do horse-trading; **Kuh|haut** F cowhide; **das geht auf keine ~** (*inf*) that is ab-

solutely staggering *or* incredible; **Kuh|her|de** F herd of cows; **Kuh|hirt** M , **Kuh|hir|te** M , **Kuh|hir|tin** F cowhand, cowherd

kühl [kyːl] ADJ (*lit, fig*) cool; (= *abweisend*) cold; **mir wird etwas ~** I'm getting rather chilly; **abends wurde es ~** in the evenings it got cool; **ein ~er Kopf** (*fig*) a cool-headed person; **einen ~en Kopf bewahren** to keep a cool head, to keep cool; **ein ~er Rechner** a cool, calculating person ADV coolly; (= *nüchtern*) coolly, calmly; **etw ~ lagern** to store sth in a cool place; „**kühl servieren**" "serve chilled"

Kühl-: Kühl|ag|gre|gat NT refrigeration unit; **Kühl|an|la|ge** F refrigeration plant, cold storage plant; **Kühl|be|cken** NT (*für Brennelemente*) cooling pond; **Kühl|box** F cold box (*Brit*), cooler

Kuh|le ['kuːlə] F **-**, **-n** (*N Ger*) hollow; (= *Grube*) pit

Küh|le ['kyːlə] F **-**, *no pl* (*lit*) cool(ness); (*fig*) coolness; (= *Abweisung*) coldness

küh|len ['kyːlən] VT to cool; (*auf Eis*) to chill → **Mütchen** → *auch* **gekühlt** VI to be cooling, to have a cooling effect; **bei großer Hitze kühlt Tee am besten** in very hot weather tea cools you down best

Küh|ler ['kyːlɐ] M **-s**, **-** (*Tech*) cooler; (*Aut*) radiator; (*inf: = Kühlerhaube*) bonnet (*Brit*), hood (*US*); (= *Sektkühler*) ice bucket; **ich hätte die al|te Frau beinahe auf den ~ genommen** (*inf*) the old lady almost ended up on my bonnet (*Brit*) *or* car hood (*US*); **jdm vor den ~ rennen** (*inf*) to run (out) right in front of sb *or* right under sb's front wheels

Küh|ler-: Küh|ler|fi|gur F (*Aut*) radiator mascot (*Brit*), hood ornament (*US*); **Küh|ler|grill** M radiator grill; **Küh|ler|hau|be** F (*Aut*) bonnet (*Brit*), hood (*US*)

Kühl-: Kühl|fach NT freezer *or* ice compartment (*Brit*), deep freeze; **Kühl|flüs|sig|keit** F coolant; **Kühl|haus** NT cold storage depot; **Kühl|ket|te** F chain of cold storage units; **Kühl|la|ge|rung** F cold storage; **Kühl|mit|tel** NT (*Tech*) coolant, cooling agent; **Kühl|ofen** M (*Tech*) annealing oven; **Kühl|raum** M cold store *or* storage room; **Kühl|rip|pe** F (*Aut*) cooling fin; **Kühl|schiff** NT refrigerator ship; **Kühl|schrank** M refrigerator, fridge, icebox (*US*); **Kühl|ta|sche** F cold bag; **Kühl|tru|he** F (chest) freezer, deep freeze; (*in Lebensmittelgeschäft*) freezer (cabinet); **Kühl|turm** M (*Tech*) cooling tower

Kühl-: Kühl|vit|ri|ne F refrigerated counter *or* cabinet; **Kühl|wa|gen** M (*Rail*) refrigerator *or* refrigerated wagon, cold storage wagon **b** (= *Lastwagen*) refrigerator *or* refrigerated truck, cold storage truck; **Kühl|was|ser** NT coolant; (*Aut*) radiator water; **Kühl|was|ser|turm** M cooling tower; **Kühl|wir|kung** F cooling effect

Kuh-: Kuh|magd F (*dated*) milkmaid, dairymaid; **Kuh|milch** F cow's milk; **Kuh|mist** M cow dung

kühn [kyːn] ADJ (*lit, fig*) bold; **das übertrifft meine ~sten Erwartungen** it's beyond *or* it surpasses my wildest hopes *or* dreams ADV (*lit, fig*) boldly; **~ formuliert** radically stated; **eine ~ geschwungene Nase** an aquiline nose

Kühn|heit F **-**, **-en** **a** *no pl* boldness **b** (*Handlung*) bold act

Kuh-: Kuh|po|cken PL cowpox *sing*; **Kuh|schei|ße** F (*inf*) cowshit (*sl*); **Kuh|schel|le** F (*Bot*) pasqueflower; **Kuh|stall** M cowshed, byre; **Kuh|stall|wär|me** F (*fig*) cosy camara-

derie; **kuh|warm** ADJ *Milch* warm *or* fresh from the cow; **Kuh|wei|de** F pasture

ku|jo|nie|ren [kujoˈniːrən] *ptp* **kujoniert** VT (*old*) to bully, to harass

k. u. k. ['kaːʊntˈkaː] *abbr von* **kaiserlich und kö|niglich** imperial and royal

Kü|ken ['kyːkn] NT **-s**, **-** **a** (= *Huhn*) chick; (*inf*) (= *junges Mädchen*) young goose (*inf*); (= *Nesthäkchen*) youngest child, baby of the family (*inf*); (= *jüngste Person*) baby **b** (*Tech*) plug

Ku-Klux-Klan [kuklʊksˈklaːn] M **-s** Ku Klux Klan

Ku|ku|ruz ['kukurʊts, 'kuːkurʊts] M **-(es)**, *no pl* (*Aus*) maize, corn

ku|lant [kuˈlant] ADJ obliging, accommodating; *Bedingungen* fair ADV accommodatingly

Ku|lanz [kuˈlants] F **-**, *no pl* **auf** *or* **aus ~** as a courtesy; **kann ich auf Ihre ~ zählen?** I wonder if you could oblige me in this

Ku|lanz|leis|tung F gesture of goodwill

Ku|li ['kuːli] M **-s**, **-s** **a** (= *Lastträger*) coolie; (*fig*) slave; **wie ein ~ arbeiten** (*inf*) to work like a slave (*inf*) **b** (*inf: = Kugelschreiber*) ballpoint (pen), Biro® (*Brit*)

ku|li|na|risch [kuliˈnaːrɪʃ] ADJ culinary; (*fig*) entertainment-orientated

Ku|lis|se [kuˈlɪsə] F **-**, **-n** scenery *no pl*; (= *Teilstück*) flat, piece of scenery; (*hinten auf Bühne*) backdrop; (*an den Seiten*) wing; (*fig: = Hintergrund*) background, backdrop, backcloth; (*St Ex*) unofficial market; **die ~n für das Stück** the scenery for the play; **vor der ~ der Schweizer Alpen** against the backdrop of the Swiss Alps; **das ist alles nur ~** (*fig*) that is only a façade; **hinter den ~n** (*fig*) behind the scenes; **jdm/einer Sache als ~ dienen** (*fig*) to serve as a backdrop for sb/to sth; **die ~ für etw bilden** (*lit, fig*) to provide the backdrop for *or* to sth

Ku|lis|sen-: Ku|lis|sen|ma|ler(in) M(F) scene-painter; **Ku|lis|sen|schie|ber** [-ʃiːbɐ] M **-s**, **-**, **Ku|lis|sen|schie|be|rin** [-ərɪn] F **-**, **-nen** scene-shifter

Kul|ler-: Kul|ler|au|gen PL (*inf*) big wide eyes *pl*; **Kul|ler|ball** M (*baby-talk*) little ball

kul|lern ['kʊlɐn] VTI (*vi: aux sein*) (*inf*) to roll

Kul|mi|na|ti|on [kʊlminaˈtsioːn] F **-**, **-en** culmination; (*fig auch*) apex; **obere/untere ~** highest/lowest point

Kul|mi|na|ti|ons|punkt M (*Astron*) point of culmination; (*fig*) culmination, apex

kul|mi|nie|ren [kʊlmiˈniːrən] *ptp* **kulminiert** VI to culminate; (*fig auch*) to reach its peak

Kult [kʊlt] M **-(e)s**, **-e** cult; (= *Verehrung*) worship; **einen ~ mit jdm/etw treiben** to make a cult out of sb/sth, to idolize sb; **mit denen wird jetzt so ein ~ getrieben** they have become such cult figures

Kult- *in cpds* cult-; **Kult|bild** NT religious symbol; **Kult|buch** NT cult book; **Kult|fi|gur** F cult figure; **Kult|film** M cult film; **Kult|ge|mein|schaft** F cult; **Kult|hand|lung** F ritual(istic) act

kul|tig ['kʊltɪç] ADJ (*sl*) cult; **voll ~: die neue CD von XY** a real cult object: XY's new CD

kul|tisch ['kʊltɪʃ] ADJ ritual(istic), cultic (*rare*) ADV ritualistically; **er wird geradezu ~ verehrt** they almost make a god out of him

kul|ti|vier|bar ADJ *Land, Mikroorganismen* cultiv(at)able; **dieser Boden ist nur schwer ~** the soil is very hard to cultivate

kul|ti|vie|ren [kʊltiˈviːrən] *ptp* **kultiviert** VT (*lit, fig*) to cultivate

kul|ti|viert [kʊltiˈviːɐt] ADJ cultivated, cultured, refined; **Kerzen beim Essen, das ist sehr ~** meals by candlelight, very civilized ADV *speisen, sich einrichten* stylishly; *sich ausdrücken* in a refined manner; **könnt ihr euch nicht etwas ~er unterhalten?** couldn't you make your language just a little more refined?; **in dieser Familie musst du dich ein bisschen ~er benehmen als**

sonst in this family you'll have to behave with a little more refinement *or* class (*inf*) than usual; **wenn Sie ~ reisen wollen** if you want to travel in style; **wenn man mal ~ essen will** if you want a civilized meal

Kul|ti|viert|heit F -, *no pl* refinement

Kul|ti|vie|rung F -, -en (*lit*, *fig*) cultivation

Kult-: Kult|spra|che F language of worship; **Kult|stät|te** F place of worship; **Kult|sym|bol** NT ritual symbol

Kul|tur F -, -en **a** (*no pl*: = *Kunst und Wissenschaft*) culture; **ein Volk von hoher ~ a** highly cultured *or* civilized people; **er hat keine ~** he is uncultured; **politische ~** political culture **b** (= *Lebensform*) civilization; **dort leben verschiedene ~en harmonisch zusammen** different cultures live harmoniously together there **c** (= *Bakterienkultur, Pilzkultur etc*) culture **d** *no pl* (*von Mikroben etc*) culture; (*des Bodens*) culture, cultivation **e** (= *Bestand angebauter Pflanzen*) plantation

Kul|tur-: Kul|tur|ab|kom|men NT cultural agreement; **Kul|tur|an|ge|bot** NT programme (*Brit*) *or* program (*US*) of cultural events, cultural scene; **Münchens vielfältiges ~** Munich's rich and varied cultural life; **Kul|tur|an|thro|po|lo|gie** F cultural anthropology; **Kul|tur|ar|beit** F cultural activities *pl*; **Kul|tur|at|ta|ché** M cultural attaché; **Kul|tur|aus|tausch** M cultural exchange; **Kul|tur|au|to|no|mie** F independence in cultural (and educational) matters; **Kul|tur|ba|nau|se** M, **Kul|tur|ba|nau|sin** F (*inf*) philistine; **kul|tur|be|flis|sen** ADJ (*geh*) (very) culturally-minded; **sie ist sehr ~** she's a real culture vulture (*inf*); **Kul|tur|bei|la|ge** F cultural *or* arts supplement *or* review; **Kul|tur|be|trieb** M (*inf*) culture industry; **Kul|tur|beu|tel** M sponge *or* toilet bag (*Brit*), washbag, cosmetic case (*US*); **Kul|tur|bo|den** M cultivated *or* arable land; **Kul|tur|denk|mal** NT cultural monument

kul|tu|rell [kʊltu'rɛl] ADJ cultural ADV culturally

Kul|tur-: Kul|tur|er|be NT cultural heritage; **Kul|tur|film** M documentary film; **Kul|tur|fö|de|ra|lis|mus** M (*Pol*) cultural and educational devolution; **Kul|tur|geo|gra|fie** ▲ F human geography; **Kul|tur|ge|schich|te** F history of civilization; **Sozial- und ~ der Etrusker** social and cultural history of the Etruscans; **kul|tur|ge|schicht|lich** ADJ historico-cultural, concerning the history of civilization ADV **eine ~ interessante Ära** an era interesting from a cultural and historical point of view; **Kul|tur|gut** NT cultural possessions *pl* *or* assets *pl*; **Kul|tur|haupt|stadt** F cultural capital; **~ Europas, Europäische ~** European City of Culture; **kul|tur|his|to|risch** ADJ, ADV = **kulturgeschichtlich**; **Kul|tur|ho|heit** F independence in matters of education and culture; **Kul|tur|in|dust|rie** F culture industry; **Kul|tur|kampf** M, *no pl* cultural war; (*Hist*) Kulturkampf (*struggle between Church and State 1872-1887*); **Kul|tur|kon|sum** [-kɔnzuːm] M (*inf*) consumption of culture, cultural consumption; **Kul|tur|kreis** M culture group *or* area; **Kul|tur|kri|tik** F critique of (our) civilization *or* culture; **Kul|tur|land** NT cultivated *or* arable land; **Kul|tur|land|schaft** F land developed and cultivated by man; (*fig*) cultural landscape; **Kul|tur|le|ben** NT cultural life; **kul|tur|los** ADJ lacking culture; *Mensch auch* uncultured; **Kul|tur|lo|sig|keit** F -, *no pl* lack of culture; **Kul|tur|mi|nis|ter(in)** M(F) minister of education and the arts; **Kul|tur|mi|nis|te|ri|um** NT ministry of education and the arts; **Kul|tur|na|ti|on** F cultural nation; **Kul|tur|pa|last** M (*esp DDR*) palace of culture *or* the arts; (*pej*) cultured extravagance; **Kul|tur|pes|si|mis|mus** M despair of civilization; **Kul|tur|pflan|ze** F cultivated plant; **Kul|tur|po|li|tik** F cultural and educational policy; **Kul|tur|po|li|ti|ker(in)** M(F) politician who concerns himself

mainly with cultural and educational policies; **kul|tur|po|li|tisch** ADJ politico-cultural; **~e Fragen** matters with both a cultural and a political aspect ADV from a politico-cultural point of view; **~ bedeutsame Vorschläge** propositions that are significant from both a cultural and a political point of view; **Kul|tur|psy|cho|lo|gie** F psychology of culture; **Kul|tur|raum** M cultural area; **im südostasiatischen ~** in the Southeast Asian cultural area; **Kul|tur|re|fe|rat** NT (*einer Gemeinde, Stadt etc*) cultural affairs department; **Kul|tur|re|vo|lu|ti|on** F cultural revolution; **Kul|tur|schaf|fen|de(r)** [-ʃafndə] MF *decl as adj* creative artist; **Kul|tur|scha|le** F Petri dish; **Kul|tur|schan|de** F crime against civilization, cultural outrage; (*fig inf*) insult to good taste, offence (*Brit*) *or* offense (*US*) against good taste; **Kul|tur|schock** M culture shock; **Kul|tur|so|zi|o|lo|gie** F cultural sociology, sociology of culture; **kul|tur|so|zi|o|lo|gisch** ADJ socio-cultural ADV *betrachten* from a sociological and cultural *or* socio-cultural viewpoint; **Kul|tur|spra|che** F language of the civilized world; **Kul|tur|stät|te** F place of cultural interest; **Kul|tur|step|pe** F (*Geog*) cultivated steppe; **Kul|tur|stu|fe** F stage *or* level of civilization; **Kul|tur|teil** M (*von Zeitung*) arts section; **Kul|tur|trä|ger(in)** M(F) vehicle of culture *or* civilization; **Kul|tur|volk** NT civilized people *sing or* nation; **Kul|tur|wan|del** M cultural change; **Kul|tur|wis|sen|schaft** F study of civilization; **~en** cultural studies; **Kul|tur|zent|rum** NT **a** (= *Stadt*) centre (*Brit*) *or* center (*US*) of cultural life, cultural centre (*Brit*) *or* center (*US*) **b** (= *Anlage*) arts centre (*Brit*) *or* center (*US*)

Kul|tus- [kʊltʊs-]: **Kul|tus|frei|heit** F religious freedom, freedom of worship; **Kul|tus|ge|mein|de** F religious community; **Kul|tus|mi|nis|ter(in)** M(F) minister of education and the arts; **Kul|tus|mi|nis|te|ri|um** NT ministry of education and the arts

Kum|me ['kʊmə] F -, -n (*N Ger*) bowl

Küm|mel ['kʏml] M -s, - **a** *no pl* (= *Gewürz*) caraway (seed) **b** (*inf*: = *Schnaps*) kümmel

Küm|mel-: Küm|mel|brannt|wein M (*form*) kümmel; **Küm|mel|öl** NT caraway oil; **Küm|mel|tür|ke** M, **Küm|mel|tür|kin** F (*pej inf*: = *Türke*) Turk, wog (*pej sl*)

Kum|mer ['kʊmə] M -s, *no pl* (= *Gram, Betrübtheit*) grief, sorrow; (= *Unannehmlichkeit, Ärger*) trouble, problems *pl*; **hast du ~?** is something wrong?, have you got problems? (*esp Brit*); **aus** *or* **vor ~ sterben** to die of sorrow *or* grief; **vor ~ vergehen** to be pining away with sorrow *or* grief; **aus** *or* **vor ~ nahm er sich** (*dat*) **das Leben** grief-stricken *or* in his grief he took his life; **er fand vor ~ keinen Schlaf mehr** such was his grief *or* sorrow that he was unable to sleep; **jdm ~ machen** *or* **bereiten** to cause sb worry; **zu jds ~** to sb's dismay; **wenn das dein einziger ~ ist** if that's your only problem *or* worry; **wir sind (an) ~ gewöhnt** (*inf*) it happens all the time, nothing's ever perfect

Kum|mer|bund M -(e)s, -e cummerbund

Kum|mer|fal|ten PL wrinkles *pl*; **das sind ~** that's the worry

Kum|mer|kas|ten M (*inf*: *in Zeitung, Zeitschrift*) agony column (*Brit*), advice column

Kum|mer|kas|ten|on|kel M (*inf*) agony uncle (*Brit inf*), advice columnist

Kum|mer|kas|ten|tan|te F (*inf*) agony aunt (*Brit inf*), advice columnist

küm|mer|lich ['kʏmɐlɪç] ADJ **a** (= *karg, armselig*) wretched, miserable; *Reste, Ausbeute, Rente* miserable, meagre (*Brit*), meager (*US*), paltry; *Lohn, Mahlzeit* paltry, measly (*inf*); *Aufsatz* scanty **b** (= *schwächlich*) puny; *Vegetation, Baum* stunted ADV *leben, wachsen, sich entwickeln* poorly; **sich ~ ernähren** to live on a meagre (*Brit*) *or* meager (*US*) diet

Küm|mer|ling ['kʏmɐlɪŋ] M -s, -e **a** (*Zool*) stunted person/plant/animal; **die Pflanze war**

von Anfang an ein ~ the plant always was a sickly thing **b** (*inf*: = *Schwächling*) weakling, weed (*pej inf*)

küm|mern[1] ['kʏmɐn] VI (*Hunt, Zool*) to become *or* grow stunted; (*fig*) to shrivel

küm|mern[2] VT to concern; **was kümmert mich die Firma?** why should I worry about the firm?, what do I care about the firm?; **was kümmert Sie das?** what business *or* concern is that of yours?; **was kümmert mich das?** what's that to me?

VR **sich um jdn/etw ~** to look after sb/sth; **sich um einen Kranken/jds Kinder ~** to look after *or* take care of a sick person/sb's children; **sich um die Karten/das Essen ~** to look after *or* take care of *or* see to the tickets/the food; **sich darum ~, dass ...** to see to it that ...; **aber darum kümmert sich im Stadtrat ja keiner** but nobody on the council does anything about it; **kümmere dich nicht um Sachen, die dich nichts angehen** don't worry about things that don't concern you; **kümmere dich gefälligst um deine eigenen Angelegenheiten!** mind your own business!; **er kümmert sich nicht darum, was die Leute denken** he doesn't mind *or* isn't worried about *or* doesn't care (about) what people think → **Dreck b**

Küm|mer|nis ['kʏmɐnɪs] F -, -se (*liter*) troubles *pl*, worries *pl*

Küm|mer-: Küm|mer|speck M (*inf*) *flab caused by overeating because of emotional problems* **sie hat ganz schön ~ angesetzt** she's been putting on weight through comfort eating; **küm|mer|voll** ADJ sorrowful, sad, woebegone *no adv*

Küm|mer|wuchs M stunted growth

Kum|met ['kʊmət] NT -s, -e horse collar

Kü|mo ['kyːmo] NT -s, -s *abbr von* **Küstenmotorschiff** coaster

Kum|pan [kʊm'paːn] M -s, -e, **Kum|pa|nin** [-'paːnɪn] F -, -nen (*dated inf*) pal (*inf*), chum (*inf*), mate (*Brit inf*), buddy (*esp US inf*)

Kum|pa|nei [kʊmpa'nai] F -, *no pl* (*pej*) chumminess

Kum|pel ['kʊmpl] M -s, - *or* (*inf*) -s *or* (*Aus*) -n **a** (*Min*: = *Bergmann*) pitman, miner **b** (*inf*: = *Arbeitskollege, Kamerad*) pal (*inf*), chum (*inf*), mate (*Brit inf*), buddy (*esp US inf*)

kum|pel|haft [-haft] ADJ (*inf*) pally (*inf*), chummy (*inf*)

Kumt NT -(e)s, -e horse collar

Ku|mu|la|ti|on [kumula'tsioːn] F -, -en **a** (*von Ämtern*) plurality **b** (*von Wahlstimmen*) accumulation

ku|mu|la|tiv [kumula'tiːf] ADJ cumulative ADV cumulatively

ku|mu|lie|ren [kumu'liːrən] *ptp* **kumuliert** VT to accumulate; **~de Bibliografie** cumulative bibliography

Ku|mu|lie|rung F -, -en cumulative voting; (*von Wahlstimmen*) accumulation

Ku|mu|lus ['kuːmulʊs] M -, **Kumuli** ['kuːmuli], **Ku|mu|lus|wol|ke** F cumulus (cloud)

kund [kʊnt] ADJ *inv* (*obs*) **jdm etw ~ und zu wissen tun** to make sth known to sb

künd|bar ADJ *Vertrag* terminable; *Anleihe* redeemable; **Beamte sind nicht ohne weiteres ~** civil servants cannot be given (their) notice *or* cannot be dismissed just like that; **die Mitgliedschaft ist sehr schwer ~** it is very difficult to terminate *or* cancel one's membership

Künd|bar|keit ['kʏntbaːɐkait] F -, *no pl* **die ~ von Verträgen ist gesetzlich geregelt** the termination of contracts is controlled by law

Kun|de[1] ['kʊndə] F -, *no pl* (*geh*) news *sing*, tidings *pl* (*old*); **der Welt von etw ~ geben** to proclaim sth to the world; **von etw ~ geben** *or* **ablegen** to bear witness to sth

Kun|de[2] ['kʊndə] M -n, -n, **Kun|din** [-dɪn] F -, -nen customer; (*pej inf*) customer (*inf*), character

-kun|de ['kʊndə] F *suf in cpds* study of; **Denkmalskunde** study of historical monuments; **Erdkunde** geography; **Pflanzenkunde** botany

kün|den ['kʏndn] **VT** (*geh*) to announce, to herald **VI** (*geh*) **von etw ~** to tell of sth, to bear witness to sth

Kun|den-: Kun|den|be|ra|tung F customer advisory service; **Kun|den|dienst** M customer *or* after-sales service; (= *Abteilung*) service department; **Kun|den|fang** M (*pej*) touting *or* looking for customers; **auf ~ sein** to be touting *or* looking for customers; **Kun|den|kar|te** F (*von Firma, Organisation*) charge card; (*von Kaufhaus etc*) (department (US)) store card; (*von Bank*) bank card; **Kun|den|kar|tei** F customer file; **Kun|den|kreis** M customers *pl*, clientele; **Kun|den|num|mer** F customer number; **Kun|den|park|platz** M customer car park, customer parking lot (US); **Kun|den|spra|che** F thieves' cant (Brit), argot, slang; **Kun|den|stamm** M , (*Aus*) (regular) customers *pl*, clientèle; **Kun|den|wer|bung** F publicity aimed at attracting custom (Brit) *or* customers

Kün|der ['kʏndɐ] M **-s, -**, **Kün|de|rin** [-ərɪn] F **-, -nen** (*rare*) messenger, harbinger (*obs, liter*)

kund+ge|ben ['kʊntgeːbn] *sep irreg* **VT** (*dated*) to make known, to announce; *Meinung, Gefühle* to express, to declare; **etw ~** to announce sth (*jdm* to sb), to make sth known (*jdm* to sb) **VR** to be revealed

Kund|ge|bung ['kʊntgeːbʊŋ] F **-, -en** **a** (*Pol*) rally **b** (= *Bekanntgabe*) declaration, demonstration

kun|dig ['kʊndɪç] ADJ (*geh*) well-informed, knowledgeable; (= *sachkundig*) expert; **einer Sache** (*gen*) **~ sein** to have a knowledge of sth; **sich ~ machen** to inform oneself

-kun|dig ADJ *suf* with a good knowledge of; **fachkundig** with a good knowledge of the subject; **gesetzkundig** well-versed in the law

kün|di|gen ['kʏndɪgn] **VT** *Stellung* to hand in one's notice for; *Abonnement, Mitgliedschaft, Kredite* to cancel, to discontinue; *Vertrag* to terminate; *Tarife* to discontinue; *Hypothek* (*Bank*) to foreclose (on); (*Hausbesitzer*) to terminate; (*Aus*) *Person* to sack (*inf*), to fire (*inf*), to dismiss; **jdm die Wohnung ~**, **jdn aus einer Wohnung ~** (*Aus*) to give sb notice to quit his/her flat (Brit) *or* to vacate his/her apartment (US); **ich habe meine Wohnung gekündigt** I've given in (my) notice that I'm leaving my flat (Brit) *or* apartment, I've given in my notice for my flat (Brit) *or* apartment; **die Stellung ~** to hand *or* give in one's notice; **jdm die Stellung ~** to give sb his/her notice; **ihm wurde sein Kredit gekündigt** his credit was cancelled (Brit) *or* canceled (US) *or* withdrawn; **Beträge über ... muss man ~** for sums in excess of ... notification must be given in advance; **jdm die Freundschaft ~** to break off a friendship with sb **VI** (*Arbeitnehmer*) to hand *or* give in one's notice; (*Mieter*) to give in one's notice; **jdm ~** (*Arbeitgeber*) to give sb his/her notice, to dismiss sb; (*Arbeitnehmer*) to hand *or* give in one's notice to sb; (*Vermieter*) to give sb notice to quit (Brit) *or* to vacate his apartment (US); (*Mieter*) to give in one's notice to sb; **zum 1. April ~** to give *or* hand in one's notice for April 1st; (*Mieter*) to give notice for *or* give in one's notice for April 1st; (*bei Mitgliedschaft*) to cancel one's membership as of April 1st; **ihm ist zum 1. Februar gekündigt worden** he's been given his notice for February 1st *or* as from February 1st; (*bei Wohnung*) he's been given notice to quit (Brit) *or* to vacate his apartment (US) for February 1st; **ich kann nur mit Monatsfrist ~** I have to give a clear (Brit) *or* one month's notice; **bei jdm/einer Firma ~** to give *or* hand in one's notice to sb/a firm

Kün|di|gung ['kʏndɪgʊŋ] F **-, -en** **a** (= *Mitteilung*) (*von Vermieter*) notice to quit (Brit) *or* to vacate one's apartment (US); (*von Mieter*) no-

tice; (*von Stellung*) notice; (*von Vertrag*) termination; (*von Hypothek*) notice of foreclosure; (*von Anleihe*) notice of withdrawal; (*von Mitgliedschaft, Abonnement*) (letter of) cancellation

b (= *das Kündigen*) (*von Mieter, Vermieter*) giving notice; (*von Arbeitgeber*) dismissal; (*von Arbeitnehmer*) handing *or* giving in one's notice; (*von Vertrag*) termination; (*von Hypothek*) foreclosure; (*von Anleihe*) withdrawal; (*von Tarifen*) discontinuation; (*von Mitgliedschaft, Abonnement*) cancellation; **wegen schlechten Betragens des Mieters entschloss sich der Vermieter zur ~** the landlord decided to give the tenant his notice (to quit (Brit) *or* to vacate his apartment (US)) because of his unruly conduct; **ich drohte (dem Chef) mit der ~** I threatened to give *or* hand in my notice (to my boss), I threatened to quit; **ihm wurde gestern die ~ ausgesprochen** he was given his notice yesterday; **ich erwäge eine ~ meiner Stelle** I'm considering handing *or* giving in my notice; **Vertrag mit vierteljährlicher ~** contract with three months' notice on either side; **vierteljährliche ~ haben** to have (to give) three months' notice

Kün|di|gungs-: Kün|di|gungs|frist F period of notice; **Kün|di|gungs|geld** NT (*Fin*) deposits *pl* at notice; **Kün|di|gungs|grund** M reason *or* grounds *pl* for giving notice; (*von Arbeitgeber auch*) grounds *pl* for dismissal; **Kün|di|gungs|schrei|ben** NT written notice; (*des Arbeitgebers*) letter of dismissal; **Kün|di|gungs|schutz** M protection against wrongful dismissal

Kun|din F **-, -nen** customer; (*pej inf*) customer (*inf*), character

kund+ma|chen ['kʊntmaxn] VT *sep* (*old, liter*) = **kundgeben VT**

Kund|ma|chung ['kʊntmaxʊŋ] F **-, -en** (*Aus, Sw, S Ger*) = **Bekanntmachung**

Kund|schaft ['kʊntʃaft] F **-, -en** **a** customers *pl*; **~! shop!**, service!; **es ist ~ im Geschäft** there are customers in the shop; **die ~ bleibt neuerdings aus** customers have been staying away recently **b** (= *Erkundung*) reconnaissance; **jdn auf ~ ausschicken** *or* **senden** (*Mil*) to send sb out to reconnoitre (Brit) *or* reconnoiter (US) *or* on reconnaissance; **auf ~ (aus)gehen** (*Mil*) to go out on reconnaissance **c** (*old:* = *Nachricht*) news *sing*, tidings *pl* (*old*)

kund|schaf|ten ['kʊntʃaftn] VI *insep* (*Mil*) to reconnoitre (Brit), to reconnoiter (US)

Kund|schaf|ter ['kʊntʃaftɐ] M **-s, -**, **Kund|schaf|te|rin** [-ərɪn] F **-, -nen** spy; (*Mil*) scout

kund+tun ['kʊnttuːn] VT *sep irreg* (*geh*) to make known, to proclaim

kund+wer|den ['kʊntverdn] VI *sep irreg aux sein* (*liter*) to become known

künf|tig ['kʏnftɪç] ADJ future; **das ~e Leben** the next life, the life to come; **meine ~e Frau** my future wife, my wife-to-be; **mein ~er Schwager** my future brother-in-law, my brother-in-law to be ADV in future

Kun|ge|lei [kʊŋə'lai] F **-, -en** (*inf*) scheming, wheeling and dealing

kun|geln ['kʊŋln] VI (*inf*) to scheme; **mit denen hat er viel gekungelt** he did a lot of wheeling and dealing with them

Kung-Fu [kʊŋ'fuː] NT **-, no pl** kung fu

Kunst [kʊnst] F **-, ⁻e** ['kʏnstə] **a** art; **die schönen Künste** fine art *sing*, the fine arts → **bildend, darstellen** VT a, **schwarz** a

b (= *Können, Fertigkeit*) art, skill; **seine ~ an jdm versuchen** to try *or* practise (Brit) *or* practice (US) one's skills on sb; **seine ~ zeigen** to show what one can do; **mit seiner ~ am** *or* **zu Ende sein** to be at one's wits' end; **die ~ besteht darin, ...** the art *or* knack is in ...; **ärztliche ~** medical skill → **Regel** a

c (= *Kunststück*) trick; **er wandte alle Künste der Rhetorik an** he used all the arts *or* tricks of rhetoric; **sie versuchte all ihre Künste an ihm** she used all her charms and wiles on him; **das**

ist keine ~! it's like taking candy from a baby (*inf*); (= *ein Kinderspiel*) it's a piece of cake (*inf*); **so einfach ist das, das ist die ganze ~** it's that easy, that's all there is to it

d (*inf*) **das ist eine brotlose ~** there's no money in that; **was macht die ~?** how are things?, how's tricks? (Brit *inf*)

Kunst- *in cpds* (*Art*) art; (= *künstlich*) artificial; **Kunst|aka|de|mie** F college of art, art college; **Kunst|aus|stel|lung** F art exhibition; **Kunst|ba|nau|se** M , **Kunst|ba|nau|sin** F (*pej*) philistine; **kunst|be|flis|sen** ADJ (*hum*) **~ sein** to be keen on art; **~e Menschen/Museumsbesucher** people who are keen on art/ visiting museums; **Kunst|darm** M artificial sausage skin; **Kunst|denk|mal** NT work of art (*from an older culture*); **Kunst|druck** M *pl* **-drucke** art print; **Kunst|druck|pa|pier** NT art paper; **Kunst|dün|ger** M chemical *or* artificial fertilizer

Küns|te|lei [kʏnstə'lai] F **-, -en** affectation

Kunst-: kunst|emp|fäng|lich ADJ artistic, appreciative of art; **Kunst|er|zie|her(in)** M(F) art teacher; **Kunst|er|zie|hung** F (*Sch*) art; **Kunst|fa|ser** F man-made *or* synthetic fibre (Brit) *or* fiber (US); **Kunst|feh|ler** M professional error; (*weniger ernst*) slip; **wegen eines ärztlichen ~s** because of medical malpractice; **kunst|fer|tig** (*geh*) ADJ skilful (Brit), skillful (US) ADV skilfully (Brit), skillfully (US); **Kunst|fer|tig|keit** F skill, skilfulness (Brit), skillfulness (US); **Kunst|fi|gur** F fictional character; **Kunst|flie|ger(in)** M(F) stunt *or* aerobatic pilot, stunt flyer; **Kunst|flug** M aerobatics *sing*, aerobatic *or* stunt flying; **ein ~** a piece of aerobatic *or* stunt flying; **Kunst|freund(in)** M(F) art lover, patron *or* lover of the arts; **Kunst|ge|gen|stand** M objet d'art, art object; (*Gemälde*) work of art; **kunst|ge|mäß**, **kunst|ge|recht** ADJ (= *fachmännisch*) proficient, skilful (Brit), skillful (US) ADV proficiently, skilfully (Brit), skillfully (US); **Kunst|ge|nuss** ▲ M (= *Freude an der Kunst*) enjoyment of art; (= *Konzert, Theateraufführung etc*) aesthetic treat; **Kunst|ge|schich|te** F history of art, art history; **kunst|ge|schicht|lich** ADJ, ADV = kunsthistorisch; **Kunst|ge|wer|be** NT arts and crafts *pl*; **im Fachgeschäft für ~** an arts and crafts shop, a craft shop; **Kunst|ge|werb|ler** [-gəverplɐ] M **-s, -**, **Kunst|ge|werb|le|rin** [-ərɪn] F **-, -nen** artisan, craftsman/-woman; **kunst|ge|werb|lich** ADJ **~e Gegenstände** craft objects; **~er Zweig** arts and crafts department; **Kunst|griff** M trick, dodge (*inf*); **Kunst|han|del** M art trade; **Kunst|händ|ler(in)** M(F) art dealer; **Kunst|hand|werk** NT craft industry; **Kunst|harz** NT synthetic resin; **Kunst|herz** NT artificial heart; **kunst|his|to|risch** ADJ art-historical, relating to art history; **~es Museum** art history museum; **~es Interesse** interest in art history ADV from the point of view of art history; **Kunst|hoch|schu|le** F college of art, art college; **Kunst|ho|nig** M artificial *or* synthetic honey; **Kunst|ken|ner(in)** M(F) art connoisseur; **Kunst|kri|tik** F , *no pl* art criticism; (= *die Kritiker*) art critics *pl*; (= *Rezension*) art review; **Kunst|kri|ti|ker(in)** M(F) art critic; **Kunst|le|der** NT artificial *or* imitation leather

Künst|ler ['kʏnstlɐ] M **-s, -**, **Künst|le|rin** [-ərɪn] F **-, -nen** **a** artist; (= *Unterhaltungskünstler*) artiste; **bildender ~** visual artist **b** (= *Könner*) genius (*in +dat* at)

Künst|ler|ein|gang M stage door

künst|le|risch ['kʏnstlərɪʃ] ADJ artistic ADV artistically; **~ wertvoll** of *or* having artistic value

Künst|ler-: Künst|ler|knei|pe F bar popular with *or* frequented by artists; **Künst|ler|ko|lo|nie** F artists' colony, colony of artists; **Künst|ler|le|ben** NT life of an artist; **ein ~** an artist's life; **Künst|ler|mäh|ne** F (*inf*) mane of hair; **Künst|ler|na|me** M pseudonym; (*von Schriftsteller auch*) pen name, nom de plume; (*von*

Schauspieler auch) stage name; **Künst|ler|pech** NT (*inf*) hard luck; **Künst|ler|tum** ['kʏnstlə-tuːm] NT **-s**, *no pl* artistry, artistic genius; **Künst|ler|ver|band** M artists' association

künst|lich ['kʏnstlɪç] ADJ artificial; *Auge auch* glass; *Zähne, Wimpern, Fingernägel* false; *Faserstoffe* synthetic, man-made; *Diamanten* imitation, fake (*inf*); **~e Intelligenz** artificial intelligence → **Befruchtung** ADV **a** *fertigen, herstellen* artificially, synthetically **b** (*mit Apparaten*) **jdm ~ Insulin zuführen** to administer insulin to sb; **jdn ~ ernähren** (*Med*) to feed sb artificially → **beatmen c** (*inf: = übertrieben*) **sich ~ aufregen** to get all worked up (*inf*) or excited about nothing

Künst|lich|keit F **-**, *no pl* artificiality

Kunst-: **Kunst|licht** NT (*Phot*) artificial light; **Kunst|lied** NT composed or art song, kunstlied; **kunst|los** ADJ unsophisticated, simple ADV simply; **Kunst|lo|sig|keit** F **-**, *no pl* simplicity; **Kunst|maler(in)** M(F) artist, painter; **Kunst|mär|chen** NT literary fairy tale; **Kunst|ob|jekt** NT art object, objet d'art; **Kunst|pau|se** F (*als Spannungsmoment*) dramatic pause, pause for effect; (*iro: beim Stocken*) awkward pause, hesitation; **eine ~ machen** to pause for effect; to pause awkwardly; **Kunst|ra|sen** M artificial turf; **Kunst|raub** M art theft; **kunst|reich** ADJ, ADV (*geh*) = **kunstvoll**; **Kunst|rei|se** F art tour; **Kunst|rei|ter(in)** M(F) trick or circus rider; **Kunst|samm|lung** F art collection; **Kunst|schät|ze** PL art treasures *pl*; **Kunst|schnee** M artificial snow; **Kunst|schnee|pis|te** F artificial snow piste; **Kunst|schwim|men** NT exhibition swimming; **Kunst|sei|de** F artificial silk; **Kunst|sinn** M artistic sense or taste, appreciation of art, feeling for art; **kunst|sin|nig** ADJ artistic, appreciative of art; **Kunst|spra|che** F artificial or invented language; **Kunst|sprin|gen** NT diving

Kunst|stoff M man-made or synthetic material or substance

Kunst|stoff-: **kunst|stoff|be|schich|tet** ADJ synthetic-coated; **Kunst|stoff|flasche** F plastic bottle; **Kunst|stoff|ka|ros|se|rie** F fibreglass (*Brit*) or fiberglass (*US*) body

Kunst-: **kunst+stop|fen** *sep infin and ptp only* VT to repair by invisible mending, to mend invisibly VI to do invisible mending; **Kunst|stück** NT trick; **~!** (*iro*) hardly surprising!, no wonder!; **das ist kein ~** (*fig*) there's nothing to it; (= *keine große Leistung*) that's nothing to write home about; **Kunst|sze|ne** F art scene; **Kunst|tisch|ler(in)** M(F) cabinet-maker; **Kunst|tur|nen** NT gymnastics *sing*; **Kunst|ver|stand** M feeling for art, appreciation of art, artistic taste or sense; **kunst|ver|stän|dig** ADJ appreciative of art, having artistic sense or taste ADV **er äußerte sich ~** he showed his appreciation of art; **Kunst|ver|ständ|nis** NT feeling for art, appreciation of art, artistic taste or sense; **kunst|voll** ADJ artistic; (= *kompliziert*) elaborate ADV elaborately; **Kunst|werk** NT work of art; **Kunst|wis|sen|schaft** F aesthetics *sing*, art; **Kunst|wort** NT *pl* **-wörter** artificial or made-up word

kun|ter|bunt ADJ *Sammlung, Gruppe etc* motley *attr*; (= *vielfarbig auch*) multi-coloured (*Brit*), multi-colored (*US*), many-coloured (*Brit*), many-colored (*US*); *Programm* varied; *Leben* chequered (*Brit*), checkered (*US*) ADV chaotically; **eine ~ zusammengewürfelte Gruppe** a motley assortment; **~ durcheinander** all jumbled up, higgledy-piggledy (*inf*); **hier geht es ~ zu** it's pretty chaotic here

Kunz [kʊnts] M → **Hinz**

Ku|pee ▲ [ku'peː] NT **-s, -s** coupé

Kup|fer ['kʊpfɐ] NT **-s**, *no pl* (*abbr* **Cu**) **a** *no pl* (*Chem*) copper; **etw in ~ stechen** to do a copper engraving of sth, to engrave or etch sth on copper **b** *no pl* (= *Gegenstände aus Kupfer*) copper; (= *Kupfergeld*) coppers *pl* **c** (= *Kupferstich*) copperplate

Kupfer- *in cpds* copper; **Kup|fer|blech** NT sheet copper; **Kup|fer|draht** M copper wire; **Kup|fer|druck** M *pl* **-drucke** copperplate engraving or etching; **Kup|fer|geld** NT coppers *pl*, copper coins *pl*; **kup|fer|hal|tig** ADJ containing copper, cupriferous (*form*)

kup|fe|rig ['kʊpfərɪç] ADJ coppery

kup|fern ['kʊpfɐn] ADJ copper; **~e Hochzeit** 7th wedding anniversary

Kupfer-: **kup|fer|rot** ADJ copper-red, copper-coloured (*Brit*), copper-colored (*US*); **Kup|fer|schmied(in)** M(F) coppersmith; **Kup|fer|ste|cher** [-ʃtɛçɐ] M **-s, -**, **Kup|fer|ste|che|rin** [-ərɪn] F **-**, **-nen** copper(plate) engraver; **mein lieber Freund und ~** (*inf*) now then my dear old chap; **Kup|fer|stich** M **a** copperplate (engraving or etching) **b** (*Kunst*) copper(plate) engraving or etching; **Kup|fer|vit|ri|ol** NT blue vitriol; (*dated Chem*) copper sulphate

kupf|rig ['kʊpfrɪç] ADJ = **kupferig**

ku|pie|ren [ku'piːrən] *ptp* **kupiert** VT *Schwanz, Ohren* to crop, to dock; *Karten* to cut; (*form*) *Wein* to blend; (*Med*) *Krankheit* to check, to arrest

Ku|pon [ku'põː] M **-s, -s** coupon → *auch* **Coupon**

Kupon- [ku'põː-]: **Ku|pon|steu|er** F (*Fin*) coupon tax; **Ku|pon|ter|min** M (*Fin*) coupon date

Kup|pe ['kʊpə] F **-**, **-n** (= *Bergkuppe*) (rounded) hilltop; (*von Straße*) hump; (= *Fingerkuppe*) tip

Kup|pel ['kʊpl] F **-**, **-n** dome, cupola

Kup|pel|dach NT domed or dome-shaped roof

Kup|pe|lei [kʊpə'lai] F **-**, *no pl* (*Jur*) procuring, procuration

Kup|pel|mut|ter F *pl* **-mütter** procuress, bawd

kup|peln ['kʊpln] VT **a** = **koppeln a, b b** (*Tech*) to couple VI **a** (*Aut*) to operate or use the clutch **b** (*inf: = Paare zusammenführen*) to match-make

Kup|pel|pelz M **sich** (*dat*) **einen ~ verdienen** (*fig*) to arrange or make a match

Kup|pe|lung ['kʊpəlʊŋ] F **-**, **-en** coupling

Kupp|ler ['kʊplɐ] M **-s, -**, **Kupp|le|rin** [-ərɪn] F **-**, **-nen** matchmaker (+*gen* for); (*Jur*) procurer/procuress

Kupp|lung ['kʊplʊŋ] F **-**, **-en a** (*Tech*) coupling; (*Aut etc*) clutch; **die ~ (durch)treten** to disengage the clutch; **die ~ kommen lassen** (*Aut*) to let the clutch up or in **b** (= *das Koppeln*) coupling

Kupplungs- *in cpds* (*Aut*) clutch; **Kupp|lungs|be|lag** M clutch lining; **Kupp|lungs|pe|dal** NT clutch pedal; **Kupp|lungs|schei|be** F clutch plate; **Kupp|lungs|seil** NT, **Kupp|lungs|zug** M clutch cable

Kur [kuːɐ] F **-**, **-en** (*in Badeort*) (health) cure; (= *Haarkur etc*) treatment *no pl*; (= *Schlankheitskur, Diätkur*) diet; **er ist zur ~ in Baden-Baden** he's on a health cure or he is taking a cure or he is taking the waters in Baden-Baden; **in or zur ~ fahren** to go to a health resort or spa; **jdm eine ~ verordnen** to prescribe a stay in a health resort or a spa for sb; **jdn zur ~ schicken** to send sb to a health resort or to a spa; **eine ~ machen** to take or undergo a cure; (= *Schlankheitskur*) to diet; **ich mache zur Zeit eine ~ gegen meinen Ausschlag** (*mit Cremes etc*) I'm taking a course of treatment for my rash

Kür [kyːɐ] F **-**, **-en a** (*Sport*) free section; **eine ~ laufen** to do the free skating; **eine ~ tanzen/turnen** to do the free section **b** (*old: = Wahl*) election

Ku|rant [ku'rant] M **-en, -en**, **Ku|ran|tin** [-'ran-tɪn] F **-**, **-nen** (*Sw*) = **Kurgast**

Kü|rass ▲ ['kyːras] M **-es, -e** cuirass

Kü|ras|sier [kyra'siːɐ] M **-s, -e** (*Mil Hist*) cuirassier

Ku|rat [ku'raːt] M **-en, -en** curate

Ku|ra|tel [kura'teːl] F **-**, **-en** (*old*) (= *Pflegschaft*) trusteeship; (= *Vormundschaft*) guardianship; **unter** (*jds*) (*dat*) **~ stehen** (*fig dated*) to be under sb's thumb; **jdn unter ~ stellen** (*old*) to keep a watch on sb

ku|ra|tiv [kura'tiːf] ADJ (*Med*) curative

Ku|ra|tor [ku'raːtoːɐ] M **-s, Kuratoren** [-'toːrən], **Ku|ra|to|rin** [-'toːrɪn] F **-**, **-nen a** (= *Vormund*) guardian **b** (= *Verwalter einer Geldstiftung*) trustee **c** (*von Museum*) curator **d** (*Univ*) ≈ registrar

Ku|ra|to|ri|um [kura'toːriʊm] NT **-s, Kuratorien** [-riən] **a** (*Vereinigung*) committee **b** (*Amt*) curatorship

Kur-: **Kur|auf|ent|halt** M stay at a health resort or spa; **Kur|bad** NT spa, watering place (*old*)

Kur|bel ['kʊrbl] F **-**, **-n** crank; (*an Fenstern, Rollläden etc*) winder

kur|beln VTI to turn, to wind; (*inf: = filmen*) to film, to shoot; **wenn du daran kurbelst ...** if you turn or wind it ...; **die Markise vors Fenster ~** to wind up the awning in front of the window

Kur|bel-: **Kur|bel|stan|ge** F connecting rod; **Kur|bel|wel|le** F crankshaft

Kür|bis ['kʏrbɪs] M **-ses, -se** pumpkin; (*inf: = Kopf*) nut (*inf*)

Kür|bis|fla|sche F gourd

Kur|de ['kʊrdə] M **-n, -n**, **Kur|din** [-dɪn] F **-**, **-nen** Kurd

Kur|dis|tan ['kʊrdɪstaːn, ˌkʊrdɪstan] NT **-s** Kurdistan

ku|ren ['kuːrən] VI (*Sw, inf*) to take a cure; (*in Mineralbad*) to take the waters

kü|ren ['kyːrən] *pret* **kürte** or (*rare*) **kor** ['kyːɐtə, koːɐ], *ptp* **gekürt** or **gekoren** [gə'kyːɐt, gə'koːrən] VT (*old, geh*) to choose, to elect (*zu* as)

Kur|fürst M Elector, electoral prince

Kur|fürs|ten|tum NT electorate

kur|fürst|lich ADJ electoral

Kur-: **Kur|gast** M (*Patient*) patient at a spa or health resort; (*Tourist*) visitor to a spa or health resort; **Kur|haus** NT assembly rooms *pl* (at a spa or health resort), spa rooms *pl*

Ku|rie ['kuːriə] F **-**, *no pl* **a** (*Eccl*) Curia **b** (*Hist*) curia

Ku|rier [ku'riːɐ] M **-s, -e**, **Ku|rie|rin** F **-**, **-nen** courier; (*Hist*) messenger

Ku|rier|dienst M courier service

ku|rie|ren [ku'riːrən] *ptp* **kuriert** VT (*lit, fig*) to cure (*von* of); **von dieser Stadt/Idee/ihm bin ich kuriert** I've gone right off (*Brit*) or I've had enough of this town/this idea/him

Ku|rier|post F mail sent by courier

ku|ri|os [ku'riːoːs] ADJ (= *merkwürdig*) strange, odd, curious ADV strangely, oddly, curiously

Ku|ri|o|sa *pl von* **Kuriosum**

Ku|ri|o|si|tät [kuriozi'tɛːt] F **-**, **-en a** (*Gegenstand*) curio(sity) **b** (= *Eigenart*) peculiarity, oddity

Ku|ri|o|si|tä|ten|ka|bi|nett NT collection of curios; (*fig*) collection of odd people

Ku|ri|o|sum [ku'rioːzʊm] NT **-s, Kuriosa** [-za] (*geh*) curious or strange or odd thing

Kur|kon|zert NT concert (at a spa or health resort), spa concert

Kur|ku|ma ['kʊrkuma] F **-**, **Kurkumen** [-'kuːmən] turmeric

Kur|laub ['kuːɐlaup] M **-(e)s, -e** health spa holiday (*Brit*) or vacation (*US*)

Kür|lauf M free skating

Kur|ort M spa, health resort

KURORT

A **Kurort** is an area specializing in natural health remedies such as springs, mud and salt water. When patients are sent by their doctors to a **Kurort**, the insurance companies pay most of the cost. **Kurorte** also levy

---

a **Kurtaxe** on every visitor. This is a special charge to help cover the cost of the many recreational and leisure facilities available in the resort.

Kur-: Kur|pa|ckung F (*für Haare*) hair repair kit; **Kur|park** M spa gardens *pl*; **Kur|pfalz** F Palatinate, Palatine electorate; **kur|pfäl|zisch** ADJ Palatine; **kur|pfu|schen** ['kuːɐpfʊʃn] VI *insep* to play the quack; **Kur|pfu|scher(in)** M(F) (*pej inf*) quack (doctor); **Kur|pfu|sche|rei** [kuːɐpfʊʃə'raɪ] F (*pej inf*) quackery; **Kur|prinz** M heir of an Elector; **Kur|pro|me|na|de** F promenade (at a spa *or* health resort)

Kur|re ['kʊrə] F -, -n (*Naut*) trawl (net)

kur|rent [kʊ'rɛnt] ADJ, ADV (*Aus*) in gothic handwriting

Kur|rent|schrift [kʊ'rɛnt-] F **a** cursive writing *or* script **b** (*Aus*) gothic handwriting

Kur|ri|ku|lum [kʊ'riːkulʊm] NT -s, Kurrikula [-la] **a** (= *Lehrplan*) curriculum **b** (*obs*: = *Lebenslauf*) curriculum vitae (*Brit*), résumé (*US*)

Kurs [kʊrs] M -es, -e [-zə] **a** (*Naut, Aviat, fig*) course; (*Pol,* = *Richtung*) line, course; **den ~ hal|ten** to hold (the) course; **vom ~ ab|kommen** to deviate from one's/its course; **~ nehmen auf** (+*acc*) to set course for, to head for; **auf (südwestlichen) ~ gehen** to set a (southwesterly) course; **auf (südwestlichem) ~ sein** to be on a (southwesterly) course; **~ haben auf** (+*acc*) to be heading for; **harter/weicher ~** (*Pol*) hard/soft line; **den ~ ändern** (*lit, fig*) to change *or* alter (one's) course; **einen neuen ~ einschlagen** (*lit, fig*) to go in a new direction, to follow a new course; **den ~ beibehalten** (*lit, fig*) to stick to *or* hold (one's) course; **jdn/etw wieder auf ~ bringen** (*fig*) to bring sb/sth back on course **b** (*Fin*) (= *Wechselkurs*) rate of exchange, exchange rate; (= *Börsenkurs, Aktienkurs*) price, (going) rate; (= *Marktpreis*) market value *or* price, going rate; **zum ~ von** at the rate of; **der amtliche ~ des Dollars** the official dollar exchange rate; **die ~e fallen/steigen** prices *or* rates are falling/rising; **hoch im ~ stehen** (*Aktien*) to be high; (*fig*) to be popular (*bei* with); **etw außer ~ setzen** to withdraw sth from circulation **c** (= *Lehrgang*) course (*in* +*dat, für* in); **einen ~ belegen** to do a course; **einen ~ besuchen** *or* **mitmachen** to attend a course

Kurs-: Kurs|ab|schlag M (*Fin*) markdown, backwardation (*Brit*); **Kurs|än|de|rung** F (*lit, fig*) change of course; **Kurs|an|stieg** M (*St Ex*) rise in (market) prices; **Kurs|auf|schlag** M (*Fin*) markup, contango (*Brit*); **Kurs|be|richt** M (*Fin*) stock market report; **Kurs|be|we|gung** F (*Fin*) price movement; **Kurs|bil|dung** F formation of rates; **Kurs|blatt** NT (*Fin*) stock-exchange (price) list, list of quotations; **Kurs|buch** NT (*Rail*) (railway) timetable, Bradshaw (*dated Brit*)

Kur|schat|ten M -s, - (*hum inf*) lady/gentleman friend (*met during a stay at a spa*); **sie war zuerst nur sein ~** he first met her at a spa

Kürsch|ner ['kyrʃnɐ] M -s, -, **Kürsch|ne|rin** [-ərɪn] F -, -nen furrier

Kürsch|ne|rei [kyrʃnə'raɪ] F -, -en **a** (= *Handwerk*) furrier's trade **b** (= *Werkstatt*) furrier's workshop

Kur|se *pl von* **Kursus**

Kurs-: Kurs|ein|bruch M (*Fin*) sudden fall in prices; **Kurs|ein|bu|ße** F decrease *or* fall in value; **das Pfund hat weitere ~n hinnehmen müssen** the pound suffered further losses (on the exchange market); **Kurs|ent|wick|lung** F (*Fin*) price trend; **Kurs|er|ho|lung** F (*Fin*) rally in prices, price rally; **Kurs|fest|set|zung** F (*Fin*) exchange rate fixing; **Kurs|ge|winn** M profit (on the stock exchange *or* (*bei Wechsel*) foreign exchange market); **der jüngste ~ des Pfundes** the recent increase in the value of the pound; **einen ~ haben** to make a profit

kur|sie|ren [kʊr'ziːrən] *ptp* **kursiert** VI *aux haben or sein* to be in circulation, to circulate; (*fig*) to circulate, to go (a)round

kur|siv [kʊr'ziːf] ADJ italic; **Anmerkungen sind ~** notes are in italics ADV **in** italics; **etw ~ drucken** to print sth in italics, to italicize sth

Kur|si|ve [kʊr'ziːvə] F -, -n, **Kur|siv|schrift** F italics *pl*; **in ~ gesetzt** printed in italics, italicized

Kurs-: Kurs|kor|rek|tur F (*lit, fig*) course correction *or* adjustment; (*St Ex*) corrective price adjustment, corrective rate adjustment; **Kurs|lei|ter(in)** M(F) course tutor (*esp Brit*); **Kurs|mak|ler(in)** M(F) (*St Ex*) market maker; **Kurs|no|tie|rung** F (market) quotation, quotation (of stock exchange prices)

kur|so|risch [kʊr'zoːrɪʃ] ADJ *Behandlung, Lektüre* cursory ADV **etw ~ lesen/überfliegen** to skim through sth

Kurs-: Kurs|pfle|ge F price support; **Kurs|ri|si|ko** NT price risk; **Kurs|rück|gang** M fall in prices; **Kurs|schwan|kung** F fluctuation in rates of exchange *or* exchange rates; (*St Ex*) fluctuation in market rates *or* prices; **Kurs|si|che|rung** F price support; **Kurs|sicherungs|ge|schäft** NT price support operation; **Kurs|stei|ge|rung** F (*Fin*) price increase; **Kurs|sturz** M sharp fall in prices; **Kurs|system** NT (*St, Univ*) course system

Kur|sus ['kʊrzʊs] M -, Kurse ['kʊrzə] (*geh*: = *Lehrgang*) course

Kurs-: Kurs|ver|lust M (*Fin*) loss (on the stock exchange *or* foreign exchange market); **das Pfund musste ~e hinnehmen** the pound suffered losses on the foreign exchange market; **Kurs|wa|gen** M (*Rail*) through coach; **Kurs|wech|sel** M (*Fin*) change of direction; **Kurs|wert** M (*Fin*) market value *or* price; **Kurs|zet|tel** (*Fin*) stock exchange (price) list, list of quotations; **Kurs|zu|satz** M excess supply and demand indicator

Kur|ta|xe F visitors' tax (at spa *or* health resort) → *auch* **Kurort**

Kur|ti|sa|ne [kʊrti'zaːnə] F -, -n courtesan

Kurt|scha|to|vi|um [kʊrtʃa'toːviʊm] NT -s, *no pl* abbr **Ku** rutherfordium, kurchatovium

Kür|übung F (*Sport*) free section

Kur|ve ['kʊrvə, 'kʊrfə] F -, -n (*Math, inf*: = *Körperrundung*) curve; (= *Biegung, Straßenkurve*) bend; (*an Kreuzung*) corner; (*von Geschoss*) trajectory; (*statistisch,* = *Fieberkurve etc*) graph; **die Straße macht eine ~** the road bends; **eine ~ fliegen** (*Aviat*) to bank, to do a banking turn; **die ~ kratzen** (*inf*) to scrape through (*inf*); (= *schnell weggehen*) to make tracks (*inf*); **die ~ kriegen** (*inf*) (*mit Auto etc*) to make the corner; (*fig*) to make it, to manage it; **die ~ nicht kriegen** (*inf*) (*mit Auto etc*) not to make the corner; (*fig*) not to get round to it

kur|ven ['kʊrvn, 'kʊrfn] VI *aux sein* (*inf*) (*Aviat*) to circle; **durch Italien ~** to drive around Italy

Kur|ven-: Kur|ven|dia|gramm NT graph; **Kur|ven|la|ge** F (*Mot*) roadholding (in bends *or* curves (*US*)), cornering (ability); **eine gute ~ haben** to hold the road well (in bends *or* curves (*US*)), to corner well; **Kur|ven|li|ne|al** NT curve template *or* templet, French curve; **kur|ven|reich** ADJ *Straße, Strecke* bendy, winding; (*inf*) *Frau* curvaceous, shapely; „*kurvenreiche Strecke*" "(series of) bends"; **Kur|ventech|nik** F (*Sport*) cornering technique

Kur|ver|wal|tung F spa authorities *pl*

kur|vig ['kʊrvɪç] ADJ winding, twisting ADV **die Straße verläuft sehr ~** the street bends sharply; **eine ~ geschwungene Treppe** a winding staircase; **ihr ~ geformter Körper** her curvy build

kurz [kʊrts] ADJ *comp* **⸚er** ['kʏrtsɐ], *superl* **⸚este(r, s)** ['kʏrtsəstə] short; *Zeit, Aufenthalt, Besuch, Bericht, Antwort etc auch* brief; *Gedächtnis auch* short-lived; *Blick, Folge* quick; (= *klein und stämmig*) stocky, squat; **etw kürzer machen** to make sth shorter, to shorten sth; **ich will es ~ machen**

I'll make it brief, I'll be brief; **machs ~!** make it brief *or* quick, be brief, keep it short; **~e Hosen** short trousers; (= *Shorts*) shorts; **~e See** (*Naut*) choppy sea; **den Kürzeren ziehen** (*fig inf*) to come off worst, to get the worst of it; **~ verliert, lang gewinnt** whoever draws the shortest (straw) loses; **in** *or* **mit ein paar ~en Worten** in a few brief words, briefly; **in kürzester Frist** before very long; **Pippin der Kurze** Pippin the Short → **Prozess a**

ADV *comp* **⸚er** ['kʏrtsɐ], *superl* **am ⸚esten a** ~ **atmen** to take short breaths; **X hat ~ abgespielt** (*Sport*) X's pass was short; (**zu**) ~ **schießen/werfen** *etc* to shoot/throw *etc* (too) short; **die Hundeleine ~ halten** to keep the dog on a short lead (*Brit*) *or* line (*US*); **eine Sache ~ abtun** to dismiss sth out of hand; **zu ~ kommen** to come off badly, to get a raw deal (*inf*); **zu ~ greifen** not to go far enough; **zu ~ denken** to see things too simply; ~ **entschlossen** without a moment's hesitation, without the slightest hesitation; ~ **fassen** to be brief; ~ **gefasst** concise; ~ **geschnitten** cropped; ~ **und bündig** concisely, tersely (*pej*); ~ **und gut** in short, in a word; ~ **und schmerzlos** (*inf*) short and sweet; **jdn ~ und klein hauen** *or* **schlagen** to beat sb up; **etw ~ und klein hauen** *or* **schlagen** to smash sth to pieces

b (= *für eine kurze Zeit*) briefly; **ich bleibe nur ~** I'll only stay for a short while; **darf ich mal ~ stören?** could I just interrupt for a moment *or* second?; **ich muss mal ~ weg** I'll just have to go for a moment *or* second; **darf ich mal ~ fragen ...?** could I just quickly ask ...?; **ich werde ~ mal gucken** I'll have a quick look

c (*zeitlich, räumlich*: = *nicht lang, nicht weit*) shortly, just; ~ **bevor/nachdem** shortly *or* just before/after; ~ **vor Köln/Ostern** shortly *or* just before Cologne/Easter; **binnen ~em** (*form*) shortly, before long; **er hat den Wagen erst seit ~em** he's only had the car for a short *or* little while; **seit ~em gibt es Bier in der Kantine** recently there's been beer in the canteen; **über ~ oder lang** sooner *or* later; **(bis) vor ~em** (until) recently; ~ **nacheinander** shortly after each other

Kurz-: Kurz|ar|beit F short time; **kurz+arbei|ten** VI *sep* to be on short time, to work short time; **Kurz|ar|bei|ter(in)** M(F) shorttime worker; **Kurz|ar|bei|ter|geld** NT shorttime allowance

Kurz-: kurz|är|me|lig, kurz|ärm|lig ADJ short-sleeved; **kurz|at|mig** [-laːtmɪç] ADJ (*Med*) short of breath; (*fig*) short-winded; **Kurz|atmig|keit** F -, *no pl* (*Med*) shortness of breath; (*fig*) short-windedness; **Kurz|aus|bil|dung** F short training course; **Kurz|au|to** NT short-wheelbase car; **Kurz|be|richt** M brief report; (= *Zusammenfassung*) summary; **Kurz|be|such** M brief *or* flying visit; **Kurz|brief** M memo

Kür|ze ['kʏrtsə] F -, -n **a** *no pl* shortness; (*von Besuch, Bericht etc*) brevity, briefness, shortness; (*fig*) (= *Bündigkeit*) brevity, conciseness; (= *Barschheit*) abruptness, curtness, bluntness; **in ~** (= *bald*) shortly, soon; (= *kurz umrissen*) briefly *or* in brief; **in aller ~** very briefly; **der ~ halber** for the sake of brevity; **in der ~ liegt die Würze**

(*Prov*) brevity is the soul of wit **b** (*Poet*: = *Silbe*) short (syllable)

Kür|zel ['kʏrtsl] NT **-s, -** (= *stenografisches Zeichen*) shorthand symbol; (*Ling*: = *Kurzwort*) contraction; (= *Abkürzung*) abbreviation

kür|zen ['kʏrtsn] VT *Kleid, Rede etc* to shorten; *Buch auch* to abridge; (*Math*) *Bruch* to cancel (down); *Gehalt, Etat, Ausgaben, Produktion* to cut (back)

Kurz|ent|schlos|se|ne(r) [-ɛntʃlɔsənə] MF *decl as adj* last-minute decision-maker **ein Schnäppchen für ~** (*bei Urlaubsbuchung*) last-minute deals *pl*

Kur|ze(r)[1] ['kʊrtsə] M *decl as adj* (*inf*) **a** (= *Schnaps*) short **b** (= *Kurzschluss*) short (circuit)

Kur|ze(r)[2] MF *decl as adj* (*inf*: = *Kind*) kid (*inf*)

kur|zer|hand ['kʊrtsə'hant] ADV without further ado; *entlassen* on the spot; **etw ~ ablehnen** to reject sth out of hand

Kurz-: **Kurz|fas|sung** F abridged version; **Kurz|film** M short (film); **Kurz|form** F shortened form (*von, zu* of, for); **kurz|fris|tig** [-frɪstɪç] ADJ short-term; *Wettervorhersage* short--range ADV (= *auf kurze Sicht*) for the short term; (= *für kurze Zeit*) for a short time; **etw ~ erledigen** to do sth without delay; **~ seine Pläne ändern** to change one's plans at short notice; **~ gesehen** looked at in the short term; **kurz|ge|faßt** △ ADJ → **kurz** ADV a; **Kurz|ge|schich|te** F short story; **kurz|ge|schnit|ten** △ ADJ *attr* → **kurz** ADV a; **Kurz|haar|da|ckel** M short-haired dachshund; **kurz|haa|rig** ADJ short-haired; **Kurz|haar|schnitt** M short haircut, crop; **kurz|hal|sig** ADJ short-necked; **kurz hal|ten** △ VT *irreg* **jdn ~** to keep sb short; **Kurz|han|tel** F dumbbell; **Kurz|in|for|ma|ti|on** F information summary; (= *Blatt*) information sheet; **Kurz|läu|fer** M (*Fin*) short, short-dated bond; **kurz|le|big** [-le:bɪç] ADJ short-lived; (*Konsumgut*) with a short lifespan; **Kurz|le|big|keit** F -, *no pl* (*von Mensch, Tier*) short lifespan; **ich bin von der ~ dieser Mode überzeugt** I'm convinced this fashion won't last; **aufgrund der ~ dieser Maschine ...** since this machine is not built to last ...

kürz|lich ['kʏrtslɪç] ADV recently, lately; **erst** *or* **gerade ~** only *or* just recently, only a short time ago ADJ recent

Kurz-: **Kurz|mel|dung** F newsflash; **Kurz|nach|richt** F **a** (= *Information*) **~en** *pl* the news headlines *pl*; (*in Zeitung auch*) the news *sing* in brief, news brief **b** (= *SMS*) text message; **Kurz|par|ker** [-parkɐ] M **-s, -** *„nur für ~ "* "short-stay (*Brit*) *or* short-term parking only"; **Kurz|park|zo|ne** F short-stay (*Brit*) *or* short--term parking zone; **Kurz|rei|se** F short trip; **Kurz|rei|se|kof|fer** M overnight bag; **kurz+schal|ten** VR *sep* to get in contact (*mit* with); **kurz+schlie|ßen** *sep irreg* VT to short--circuit VR (*mit with*) to get in contact (*mit with*); **Kurz|schluss** △ M **a** (*Elec*) short circuit; **einen ~ haben** to be short-circuited; **einen ~ bekommen** to short-circuit **b** (*fig: auch* **Kurzschlusshandlung**) rash action; **das war ein ~** *or* **eine ~handlung** something just went snap; **Kurz|schluss|re|ak|ti|on** △ F knee-jerk *or* rash reaction; **Kurz|schrift** F shorthand; **kurz|schrift|lich** ADJ shorthand ADV in shorthand; **kurz|sich|tig** [-zɪçtɪç] (*lit, fig*) ADJ short-sighted ADV short-sightedly; **Kurz|sich|tig|keit** F -, *no pl* (*lit, fig*) short--sightedness

Kurz|stre|cken-: **Kurz|stre|cken|flug|zeug** NT short-haul *or* short-range aircraft; **Kurz|-**

stre|cken|jet M short-range jet; **Kurz|stre|cken|läu|fer(in)** M(F) (*Sport*) sprinter, short distance runner; **Kurz|stre|cken|ra|ke|te** F short-range missile; **Kurz|stre|cken|waf|fe** F short-range weapon

kurz-: **kurz tre|ten** △ VI *irreg* (*Mil*) to march with short steps; (*fig inf*) to go easy; **Kurz|trip** M (*inf*) short holiday; **kurz|um** [kʊrts'lʊm, 'kʊrts'ʊm] ADV in short, in a word

Kür|zung ['kʏrtsʊŋ] F -, **-en** shortening; (*eines Berichts, Buchs etc*) abridgement; (*von Gehältern, von Etat, der Produktion*) cut (+*gen* in)

Kurz-: **Kurz|ur|laub** M short holiday (*esp Brit*) *or* vacation (*US*); (*Mil*) short leave; **Kurz|wahl** F one-touch dialling (*Brit*) *or* dialing (*US*), quick *or* speed (*US*) dial; **Kurz|wahl|spei|cher** M quick-dial number memory; **Kurz|wa|ren** PL haberdashery (*Brit*), notions *pl* (*US*); **Kurz|weil** [-vail] F -, *no pl* (*old*) pastime, diversion; **allerlei ~ treiben** to amuse oneself; **zur ~** as a pastime; **kurz|wei|lig** [-vailɪç] ADJ entertaining; **Kurz|wel|le** F (*Rad*) short wave; **Kurz|wel|len|sen|der** M short-wave transmitter; **Kurz|wort** NT *pl* **-wörter** abbreviation, abbreviated word

Kurz|zeit- *in cpds* short-term; **Kurz|zeit|ef|fekt** M short-term effect; **Kurz|zeit|ge|dächt|nis** NT short-term memory

kurz|zei|tig ADJ (= *für kurze Zeit*) short, brief; (= *kurzlebig*) short-lived *attr* ADV for a short time, briefly

Kurz|zeit-: **Kurz|zeit|mes|ser** M **-s, -** timer; **Kurz|zeit|spei|cher** M short-term memory

kusch [kʊʃ] INTERJ (*an Hund*) down

ku|sche|lig ['kʊʃəlɪç] (*inf*) ADJ cosy (*Brit*), cozy (*US*), snug ADV **~ weich** soft and cosy (*Brit*) *or* cozy (*US*); **~ warm** snug and warm

ku|scheln ['kʊʃln] VI to cuddle (*mit* with) VR **sich an jdn ~** to snuggle up to sb, to cuddle up to sb; **sich in etw** (*acc*) **~** to snuggle up in sth, to cuddle up in sth

Kuschel-: **Ku|schel|rock** M (*Mus inf*) soft rock; **Ku|schel|sex** M loving sex; **wir machen nur ~** we don't have full sex, we just cuddle up together in bed; **Ku|schel|tier** NT cuddly toy

ku|schen ['kʊʃn] VI (*Hund etc*) to get down; (*fig*) to knuckle under

Ku|si|ne [ku'zi:nə] F -, **-n** (female) cousin

Kuss △ [kʊs] M **-es,** ⁔**e** ['kʏsə] kiss; **Gruß und ~ dein X** (*hum inf*) love and kisses, yours X

Küss|chen △ ['kʏsçən] NT **-s, -** little kiss, peck (*inf*); **gib ~** give us a kiss

küss|die|hand △ ['kʏsdi:'hant], **küss die Hand** △ INTERJ (*Aus*) your servant (*old*); (= *guten Tag*) your servant (*old*), how do you do? (*Brit*); (= *auf Wiedersehen auch*) good day (*form*)

kuss|echt △ ADJ *Lippenstift* kiss-proof

küs|sen ['kʏsn] VTI to kiss; **jdm die Hand ~** to kiss sb's hand; **küss die Hand** (*S Ger, Aus*) = **küssdiehand** VR to kiss (each other)

Kuss-: **kuss|fest** △ ADJ = **kussecht**; **Kuss|hand** △ F **jdm eine ~ zuwerfen** to blow sb a kiss; **mit ~!** with (the greatest) pleasure!, gladly!; **jdn/etw mit ~ nehmen** (*inf*) to be only too glad to take sb/sth; **Kuss|mund** △ M puckered lips *pl*

Küs|te ['kʏstə] F -, **-n** coast; (= *Ufer*) shore; **die zerklüftete ~ Schottlands** the jagged coastline *or* coast of Scotland

Küs|ten- *in cpds* coastal; **Küs|ten|be|woh|ner(in)** M(F) coast-dweller; **die ~ Englands** people who live on the English coast; **Küs|-**

ten|fi|sche|rei F inshore fishing *or* fishery (*form*); **Küs|ten|ge|biet** NT coastal area; **Küs|ten|ge|wäs|ser** PL , **Küs|ten|meer** NT coastal waters *pl*; **Küs|ten|mo|tor|schiff** NT coaster; **Küs|ten|nä|he** F **in ~** near the coast; **Küs|ten|re|gi|on** F coastal area; **Küs|ten|schiff|fahrt** F coastal shipping; **Küs|ten|strich** M stretch of coast; **Küs|ten|wa|che** F , **Küs|ten|wacht** F coastguard(s *pl*)

Küs|ter ['kʏstɐ] M **-s, -**, **Küs|te|rin** [-ərɪn] F -, **-nen** verger, sexton

Küs|te|rei [kʏstə'rai] F -, **-en** verger's *or* sexton's house

Kus|to|de [kʊs'to:də] M **-n, -n**, **Kus|to|din** [-'to:dɪn] F -, **-nen**, **Kus|tos** ['kʊstɔs] M -, **Kus|to|den** [-'to:dn] (*in Museum*) curator

Ku|ti|ku|la [ku'ti:kula] F -, **-s** (*spec*) cuticle, cuticula (*spec*)

Kutsch|bock M coach box

Kut|sche ['kʊtʃə] F -, **-n** coach, carriage; (*inf*: = *Auto*) jalopy (*inf*)

kut|schen ['kʊtʃn] VTI (*old*) = **kutschieren**

Kut|scher ['kʊtʃɐ] M **-s, -** coachman, driver

Kut|sche|rin ['kʊtʃərɪn] F -, **-nen** driver

Kutscher-: **Kut|scher|ma|nie|ren** PL (*pej*) manners *pl* like a navvy; **Kut|scher|sitz** M coach box

kut|schie|ren [kʊ'tʃi:rən] *ptp* **kutschiert** VI *aux sein* to drive, to ride; **durch die Gegend ~** (*inf*) to drive *or* ride around VT to drive; **jdn im Auto durch die Gegend ~** to drive sb around

Kutsch|kas|ten M luggage compartment on a coach

Kut|te ['kʊtə] F -, **-n** habit

Kut|tel ['kʊtl] F -, **-n** *usu pl* (*S Ger, Aus, Sw*) entrails *pl*

Kut|ter ['kʊtɐ] M **-s, -** (*Naut*) cutter

Ku|vert [ku've:ɐ, ku've:ɐ̯, ku'vɛrt] NT **-s, -s** *or* (*bei dt. Aussprache*) **-(e)s, -e** **a** (= *Briefkuvert*) envelope **b** (= *Gedeck*) cover

ku|ver|tie|ren [kuvɛr'ti:rən] *ptp* **kuvertiert** VT (*form*) to put into an envelope

Ku|ver|tü|re [kuvɛr'ty:rə] F -, **-n** (*Cook*) (chocolate) coating

Ku|wait [ku'vait, 'ku:vait] NT **-s** Kuwait

Ku|wai|ter [ku'vaitɐ, 'ku:vaitɐ] M **-s, -**, **Ku|wai|te|rin** [-ərɪn] F -, **-nen** Kuwaiti

ku|wai|ti [ku'vaiti] M **-s, -s** Kuwaiti

ku|wai|tisch [ku'vaitɪʃ, 'ku:vaitɪʃ] ADJ Kuwaiti

KV *abbr von* **Köchelverzeichnis**

kW *abbr von* **Kilowatt**

KW *abbr von* **Kalenderwoche**

kWh *abbr* = **Kilowattstunde**

Ky|ber|ne|tik [kybɐ'ne:tɪk] F -, *no pl* cybernetics *sing*

Ky|ber|ne|ti|ker [kybɐ'ne:tikɐ] M **-s, -**, **Ky|ber|ne|ti|ke|rin** [-ərɪn] F -, **-nen** cybernetician

ky|ber|ne|tisch [kybɐ'ne:tɪʃ] ADJ cybernetic

Kyk|la|den [ky'kla:dn] PL Cyclades *pl*

kym|risch ['kʏmrɪʃ] ADJ Cymric, Welsh

Ky|rie ['ky:rie] NT -, **-s**, **Ky|rie|elei|son** ['ky:rie'laizɔn, -le'le:izɔn] NT **-s, -s** Kyrie (eleison)

ky|ril|lisch [ky'rɪlɪʃ] ADJ Cyrillic

KZ [ka:'tsɛt] NT **-s, -s** *abbr von* **Konzentrationslager**

KZler [ka:'tsɛtlɐ] M **-s, -**, **KZle|rin** [-ərɪn] F -, **-nen** (*inf*) concentration camp prisoner

---

L

L, l [ɛl] NT **-, - L, l**

l *abbr von* **Liter**

Lab [laːp] NT **-(e)s, -e** [-bə] rennin

lab|be|rig ['labərɪç], **labb|rig** ['labrɪç] ADJ *(dial) Bier, Suppe* watery; *Kaffee, Tee auch* weak; *Essen* mushy; *Stoff etc* floppy, limp; *Hose* flappy

La|bel ['leːbl] NT **-s, -** label

la|ben ['laːbn] *(liter)* VR to feast (oneself) (*an +dat* on); *(an einer Quelle etc)* to refresh oneself (*mit, an +dat* with); **wir labten uns an dem An-blick** we drank in the view, we feasted our eyes on the view VT *(Mensch)* to feast; *(Quelle)* to refresh

la|bern ['laːbɐn] *(inf)* VI to prattle (on *or* away) *(inf)*, to jabber (on *or* away) *(inf)* VT to talk; **was laberst du denn da?** what are you prattling *etc* on about? *(inf)*

la|bi|al [la'biaːl] ADJ *(Ling)* labial

La|bi|al(laut) [la'biaːl-] M **-s, -e** labial

la|bil [la'biːl] ADJ *Gesundheitszustand, Gleichgewicht, Lage, Markt* unstable; *Gesundheit* delicate; *Kreislauf* poor; *Patient* frail; *(psychisch) Mensch* with no strength of character; *Charakter* weak ADV **die Situation wird als ~ eingeschätzt** the situation is considered to be unstable; **jdn als psychisch ~ einstufen** to consider sb emotionally unstable

La|bi|li|tät [labili'tɛːt] F **-, no pl** instability; *(von Patient)* frailness; **wegen der ~ seiner Gesundheit** because of his unstable state of health; **die ~ seines Kreislaufs/Charakters** his poor circulation/weak character; **er ist von einer großen ~** he has no strength of character at all

la|bi|o|den|tal [labioden'taːl] ADJ *(Ling)* labiodental

Lab-: Lab|kraut NT *(Bot)* bedstraw; **Lab|ma-gen** M *(Zool)* abomasum *(spec)*, fourth stomach

La|bor [la'boːɐ] NT **-s, -s** *or* **-e** laboratory, lab *(inf)*

La|bo|rant [labo'rant] M **-en, -en, La|bo|ran-tin** [-'rantɪn] F **-, -nen** lab(oratory) technician

La|bo|ra|to|ri|um [labora'toːriʊm] NT **-s, Labo-ratorien** [-riən] laboratory

La|bor|be|fund M laboratory findings *pl*

la|bo|rie|ren [labo'riːrən] *ptp* **laboriert** VI to labour *(Brit)*, to labor *(US)* (*an +dat* at); *(= leiden)* to be plagued (*an +dat* by)

La|bor-: La|bor|schiff NT laboratory ship; **La-bor|ver|such** M laboratory experiment; **La-bor|wer|te** PL laboratory results *pl*

La|bra|dor [labra'doːɐ] M **-s, -e, La|bra|dor-hund** M *(Zool)* labrador

Lab|sal ['laːpzaːl] NT **-(e)s, -e** (*or Aus auch*) F **-, -e** *(old, liter)* refreshment

Labs|kaus ['lapskaus] NT **-, no pl** *(N Ger) stew made of meat, fish and mashed potato*

La|bung ['laːbʊŋ] F **-, -en** *(liter)* refreshment

La|by|rinth [laby'rɪnt] NT **-(e)s, -e** *(lit, Med)* labyrinth; *(fig auch)* maze

la|by|rin|thisch ADJ labyrinthine, maze-like ADV **der Weg verläuft ~** the road follows a maze-like path

---

Lach|an|fall M laughing fit

La|che¹ ['laxə, 'laːxə] F **-, -n** puddle; *(von Benzin, Blut etc auch)* pool

La|che² ['laxə] F **-, -n** *(inf)* laugh

lä|cheln ['lɛçln] VI to smile; **verlegen/freundlich ~** to give an embarrassed/a friendly smile

Lä|cheln NT **-s,** *no pl* smile

la|chen ['laxn] VI to laugh (*über +acc* at); **jdn zum Lachen bringen, jdn ~ machen** to make sb laugh; **zum Lachen sein** (= *lustig*) to be hilarious; (= *lächerlich*) to be laughable; **mir ist nicht zum Lachen (zumute)** I'm in no laughing mood; **dass ich nicht lache!** *(inf)* don't make me laugh! *(inf)*; **da kann ich doch nur ~** I can't help laughing (at that); **du hast gut ~!** it's all right for you to laugh! *(inf)*; **lach du nur!** you can laugh!; **gezwungen/verlegen/herzlich ~** to give a forced/an embarrassed/a hearty laugh; **wer zuletzt lacht, lacht am besten** *(Prov)* he who laughs last, laughs longest *(Prov)*; **die ~den Er-ben** *(hum)* the joyful heirs; **die Sonne** *or* **der Himmel lacht** the sun is shining brightly; **ihm lachte das Glück/der Erfolg** fortune/success smiled on him *or* favoured *(Brit) or* favored *(US)* him → **Dritte(r)**

VT **da gibt es gar nichts zu ~** that's nothing to laugh about; (= *es ist etwas Ernstes auch*) that's no laughing matter, that's not funny; **was gibt es denn da zu ~?** what's so funny about that?; **er hat bei seiner Frau nichts zu ~** *(inf)* he has a hard time of it with his wife; **wenn dieses Ver-sehen herauskommt, hast du nichts zu ~** *(inf)* you won't have anything to laugh about *or* it won't be funny if that mistake comes to light; **das wäre doch gelacht** it would be ridiculous; **sich scheckig ~** *(inf)* **sich** *(dat)* **einen Ast** *or* **Bruch ~** *(inf)* to split one's sides (laughing) *(inf)*, to kill oneself laughing, to laugh oneself silly *(inf)*; **sich** *(dat)* **eins (ins Fäustchen) ~** *(inf)* to have a little snigger → **Träne**

La|chen NT **-s,** *no pl* laughter, laughing; (= *Art des Lachens*) laugh; **vor ~ schreien** to shriek with laughter; **dir wird das ~ schon noch verge-hen!** you'll soon be laughing on the other side of your face *(Brit) or* out of the other side of your mouth *(US)*

La|cher ['laxɐ] M **-s, -** lougher; **die ~ auf sei-ner Seite haben** to have the last laugh; (= *einen Lacherfolg verbuchen*) to get a laugh **b** *(inf: = La-che)* laugh

Lach|er|folg M **ein ~ sein, einen ~ haben** *or* **er-zielen** to make everybody laugh

lä|cher|lich ['lɛçɐlɪç] ADJ **a** ridiculous, absurd, ludicrous; (= *komisch*) comical, funny; **jdn/etw ~ machen** to make sb/sth look silly *or* stupid *(vor jdm* in front of sb); **jdn/sich ~ machen** to make a fool of sb/oneself *(vor jdm* in front of sb); **etw ins Lächerliche ziehen** to make fun of sth **b** (= *geringfügig*) *Kleinigkeit, Anlass* trivial, petty; *Preis* ridiculously *or* absurdly low ADV ridiculously, absurdly

lä|cher|li|cher|wei|se ['lɛçɐlɪçɐ'vaizə] ADV ridiculously enough

Lä|cher|lich|keit F **-, -en** **a** *no pl* (*von Argu-ment etc*) absurdity; **die ~ seiner Bemerkung/ih-rer Verkleidung** his ridiculous comment/her ri-

---

diculous get-up *(inf)*; **jdn der ~ preisgeben** to make a laughing stock of sb **b** (= *Geringfügig-keit*) triviality

Lach-: Lach|fal|ten PL laughter lines *pl*, laugh lines *pl* *(US)*; **Lach|gas** NT laughing gas; **lach|haft** ADJ ridiculous, ludicrous; *Ansichten, Argument auch* laughable; **Lach|krampf** M par-oxysm (of laughter); **einen ~ bekommen** to go (off) into fits of laughter; **Lach|mö|we** F black-headed gull; **Lach|mus|kel** M *(Anat)* ri-sorius; **das ist was für Ihre ~n** this will really make you laugh; **Lach|num|mer** F *(inf: = Witz, Mensch)* joke *(inf)*

Lachs [laks] M **-es, -e** salmon

Lach|sal|ve F burst *or* roar of laughter

Lachs-: lachs|far|ben [-farbn], **lachs|far|big** ADJ salmon pink, salmon(-coloured) *(Brit)*, salmon(-colored) *(US)*; **Lachs|fo|rel|le** F salmon *or* sea trout; **Lachs|schin|ken** M *smoked, rolled fillet of ham*

Lach|tau|be F ringdove, Barbary dove

Lack [lak] M **-(e)s, -e** (= *Holzlack, Nagellack*) var-nish; (= *Autolack*) paint; *(für Lackarbeiten)* lacquer → **fertig a**

Lack-: Lack|af|fe M *(pej inf)* flash Harry *(Brit inf)*, real flashy dude *(US inf)*; **Lack|ar|beit** F lacquerwork

La|cke ['lakə] F **-, -n** *(Aus)* puddle

La|ckel ['lakl] M **-s, -** *(S Ger, Aus)* oaf

la|cken ['lakn] VT *(Tech)* to lacquer

Lack|far|be F gloss paint

La|ckier|ar|bei|ten PL *(von Möbeln etc)* var-nishing; *(von Autos)* spraying

la|ckie|ren [la'kiːrən] *ptp* **lackiert** VTI *Holz* to varnish; *Fingernägel auch* to paint; *Auto* to spray; **am Ende war ich der Lackierte** *(inf)* I ended up looking a fool

La|ckie|rer [la'kiːrɐ] M **-s, -, La|ckie|re|rin** [-ərɪn] F **-, -nen** varnisher; *(von Autos)* sprayer

La|ckie|re|rei [laki:rə'rai] F **-, -en** **a** (= *Autolak-kiererei*) paint shop; (= *Möbellackiererei*) var-nisher's **b** *(Handwerk)* lacquerwork

La|ckie|rung F **-, -en** **a** (= *das Lackieren*) *(von Autos)* spraying; *(von Möbeln)* varnishing **b** (= *der Lack)* paint(work); (= *Holzlackierung*) varnish; *(für Lackarbeiten)* lacquer

La|ckier|werk|statt F, **La|ckier|werk|stät-te** F *(für Autos)* paint shop; *(für Möbel)* var-nisher's

Lack|le|der NT patent leather

lack|mei|ern ['lakmaiɐn] VT → **gelackmeiert**

Lack|mus ['lakmʊs] NT OR M **-,** *no pl* litmus

Lack|mus|pa|pier NT litmus paper

Lack-: Lack|scha|den M damage to the paint-work; **Lack|schuh** M patent-leather shoe

lad|bar ADJ *(Comput)* loadable

La|de [la'daːə] F **-, -n** chest; *(inf: = Schublade)* drawer

La|de-: La|de|baum M derrick; **La|de|brü-cke** F loading bridge; **La|de|bucht** F *(Space)* loading bay; **La|de|büh|ne** F loading ramp; **La|de|flä|che** F load area; **La|de|ge|rät** NT battery charger; **La|de|ge|wicht** NT load

---

capacity; **La|de|gut** NT (= *Ladung*) load; (= *Fracht*) freight *no pl*; **La|de|hem|mung** F das Gewehr hat ~ the gun is jammed; **er hatte plötzlich ~** (*inf*) he had a sudden mental block; **La|de|höhe** F Lkw mit einer ~ bis zu ... Meter loads not exceeding ... metres (*Brit*) or meters (*US*) (in height); **La|de|klap|pe** F tailboard, tailgate; **La|de|kon|trol|le** F (*Aut*) (generator) charge indicator; **La|de|lu|ke** F cargo or loading hatch

la|den[1] ['laːdn] *pret* **lud** [luːt], *ptp* **geladen** [ɡəˈlaːdn] **VT** **a** (= *beladen*) to load; **einen Sack Mehl auf den Rücken ~** to load or hump a sack of flour on one's back; **das Schiff hat Autos geladen** the ship has a cargo of cars; **der Lkw hat zu viel geladen** the lorry is overloaded; **Verantwortung/Schulden auf sich** (*acc*) ~ to saddle or load oneself with responsibility/debts; **eine schwere Schuld auf sich** (*acc*) ~ to place oneself under a heavy burden of guilt; **da habe ich ja etwas auf mich geladen** I've taken on more than I'd bargained for → *auch* **geladen**
  b *Schusswaffe* to load; (= *wieder aufladen*) *Batterie, Akku* to recharge; (*Phys*) to charge
  c (*Comput*) to load
  VI **a** (*auch Comput*) to load (up)
  b (*Phys*) to charge

la|den[2] *pret* **lud** [luːt], *ptp* **geladen** [ɡəˈlaːdn] VT
  a (*liter*: = *einladen*) to invite; **nur für geladene Gäste** by invitation only **b** (*form*: *vor Gericht*) to summon

La|den[1] ['laːdn] M -s, ¨ [ˈlɛːdn] **a** (= *Geschäft*) shop (*esp Brit*), store (*US*); (*inf*: = *Betrieb, Unternehmung*) outfit (*inf*); **der ~ läuft** (*inf*) business is good; **es wird eine Zeit dauern, bis der ~ läuft** (*inf*) it will be some time before the business gets going or gets off the ground; **dann kann er den ~ zumachen** or **dichtmachen** (*inf*) he might as well shut up shop (and go home) (*inf*); **den ~ schmeißen** (*inf*) to run the show; (= *zurechtkommen*) to manage; **den (ganzen) ~ hinschmeißen** (*inf*) to chuck the whole thing in (*inf*)

La|den[2] M -s, ¨ *or* - (= *Fensterladen*) shutter

La|den-: **La|den|be|sit|zer(in)** M(F) shop-owner (*esp Brit*), shopkeeper (*esp Brit*), storekeeper (*US*); **La|den|de|tek|tiv(in)** M(F) store detective; **La|den|dieb(in)** M(F) shoplifter; **La|den|dieb|stahl** M shoplifting; **La|den|ein|rich|tung** F shop fittings *pl*, store fixtures *pl*; **La|den|ge|schäft** NT retail business; **La|den|hü|ter** M non-seller; **La|den|kas|se** F cash desk, till; **La|den|ket|te** F chain of shops (*esp Brit*) or stores; **La|den|lo|kal** NT shop or store (*US*) premises *pl*; **La|den|öff|nungs|zeit** F *usu pl* shop (*esp Brit*) or store (*US*) opening hours *pl*; **La|den|preis** M shop (*esp Brit*) or store (*US*) price; **La|den|schild** NT shop (*esp Brit*) or store (*US*) sign

La|den|schluss ▲ M nach/vor ~ after/before the shops (*esp Brit*) or stores (*US*) shut; **kurz vor ~** (*lit, fig*) just before we/they shut up shop; **um fünf Uhr ist ~** the shops (*esp Brit*) or stores (*US*) shut at five o'clock

---

LADENSCHLUSS

In Germany and Austria **Ladenschluss** - the time when a shop has to close - is controlled by law. In Germany shops are allowed to stay open until 8pm on weekdays and until 4pm on Saturdays. Generally they are not permitted to open on Sundays and holidays, although bakers may open for three hours to sell fresh bread rolls. However, apart from in the large commercial towns, most shops close at between 6pm and 7pm and on Saturdays at 1pm. Petrol stations are not subject to these regulations and they often stay open selling goods until late at night. In Austria shops must close on weekdays by 7.30pm. In Switzerland regulations vary from canton to canton.

La|den|schluss-: **La|den|schluss|ge|setz** ▲ NT *law governing the hours of trading*; **La|den|schluss|zeit** ▲ F (shop (*esp Brit*) or store (*US*)) closing time

La|den-: **La|den|stra|ße** F shopping street; **La|den|tisch** M shop counter; **über den/unter dem ~** over/under the counter; **La|den|toch|ter** F (*Sw*) shop (*esp Brit*) or sales assistant, salesgirl

Lade-: **La|de|platz** M loading bay or area; **La|de|ram|pe** F loading ramp; **La|de|raum** M load room; (*Aviat, Naut*) hold; **La|de|stock** M ramrod; **La|de|zo|ne** F loading bay or area

lä|die|ren [lɛˈdiːrən] *ptp* **lädiert** VT *Kunstwerk, Briefmarke* to damage; *Körperteil* to injure; **lädiert sein/aussehen** (*hum*) to be/look the worse for wear; **sein lädiertes Image** his tarnished image

Lad|ne|rin ['laːdnərɪn] F -, -nen (*old: S Ger, Aus*) shop assistant

lädt [lɛːt] *3. pers sing pres von* **laden**

La|dung ['laːdʊŋ] F -, -en **a** load; (*von Schnee, Steinen, Unflätigkeit etc*) whole load (*inf*); (*von Sprengstoff*) charge; **eine geballte ~ Schnee/Dreck** (*inf*) a handful of snow/mud; **eine geballte ~ von Schimpfwörtern** a whole torrent of abuse **b** (= *Vorladung*) summons *sing*

La|dy ['leːdi] F -, -s lady; (*Adlige*) Lady

La|fet|te [laˈfɛtə] F -, -n (*Mil*) (gun) carriage

Laf|fe [laf] M -n, -n (*pej*) flash Harry (*Brit inf*), real flashy dude (*US inf*)

lag *pret von* **liegen**

La|ge ['laːɡə] ✪ 39.2, 42.4, 43.4 F -, -n **a** (= *geografische Lage*) situation, location; **in günstiger ~** well-situated; **eine gute/ruhige ~ haben** to be in a good/quiet location; **in höheren ~n Schneefall** snow on higher ground
  b (= *Art des Liegens*) position; **eine bequeme ~ haben, sich in einer bequemen ~ befinden** to be lying comfortably, to be (lying) in a comfortable position
  c (= *Situation*) situation; **in der ~ sein, etw zu tun** (*befähigt sein*) to be able to do sth, to be capable of doing sth; **dazu bin ich nicht in der ~** I'm not in a position to do that; **er wird wohl nie in die ~ kommen, das zu tun** he'll never be in a position to do it; **in der glücklichen/beneidenswerten ~ sein, etw zu tun** to be in the happy/enviable position of doing sth; **Herr der ~ sein/bleiben** to be/remain master of or in control of the situation; **nach ~ der Dinge** as things stand; **die ~ der Dinge erfordert es, dass ... the situation requires that ... →** **peilen**
  d (= *Schicht*) layer
  e (*Mus*) (= *Stimmlage*) register; (= *Tonlage*) pitch; (*auf Instrument*) position; **enge/weite ~** close/open harmony
  f (= *Runde*) round

Lage-: **La|ge|be|richt** M report; (*Mil*) situation report; **La|ge|be|spre|chung** F discussion of the situation; **eine ~ abhalten** to discuss the situation

Lagen-: **La|gen|schwim|men** NT , *no pl* (*Sport*) individual medley; **La|gen|staf|fel** F (*Sport*) (*Schwimmen*) medley relay; (= *Mannschaft*) medley relay team

la|gen|wei|se ['laːɡnvaizə] ADV in layers

La|ge|plan M ground plan

La|ger ['laːɡə] NT -s, - **a** (= *Unterkunft*) camp; **sein ~ aufschlagen** to set up camp
  b (*liter*: = *Schlafstätte*) bed; **die Krankheit fesselte ihn wochenlang ans ~** the illness kept him abed (*old*) or in bed for weeks; **sie wachten an ~ des Königs** they kept watch at the King's bedside
  c (*fig*) (= *Partei*) camp; (*von Staaten*) bloc; **ins andere ~ überwechseln** to change camps or sides
  d *pl auch* **Läger** ['lɛːɡə] (= *Vorratsraum*) store (-room); (*von Laden*) stockroom; (= *Lagerhalle*) warehouse; (= *Vorrat*) stock; **am ~ sein** to be in stock; **etw auf ~ legen** (*Comm*) to store sth; **etw auf ~ haben** to have sth in stock; (*fig*) *Witz etc*

to have sth on tap (*inf*), to have sth (at the) ready
  e (*Tech*) bearing
  f (*Geol*) bed; (= *Lagerstätte*) deposit

Lager-: **La|ger|be|stand** M stock, inventory (*US*); **den ~ aufnehmen** to do the stocktaking (*Brit*) or inventory (*US*); **La|ger|den|ken** NT (*Pol*) stereotype thinking, thinking in stereotypes; **la|ger|fä|hig** ADJ storable; **La|ger|feu|er** NT campfire; **La|ger|flä|che** F storage area; (*gemessen*) storage or floor space; **La|ger|ge|bühr** F , **La|ger|geld** NT storage charge; **La|ger|haft** F detention in a (prison) camp; **nach sieben Jahren ~** after seven years in a prison camp; **La|ger|hal|le** F warehouse; **La|ger|hal|tung** F storekeeping; **~ rentiert sich bei uns nicht** it doesn't pay us to keep a large stock; **La|ger|haus** NT warehouse

La|ge|rist [laɡəˈrɪst] M -en, -en storeman

La|ge|ris|tin [laɡəˈrɪstɪn] F -, -nen storewoman

Lager-: **La|ger|kol|ler** M (*inf*) **das hat einen ~ gekriegt** life in the camp turned his mind; **La|ger|kos|ten** PL storage charges *pl*, storage *sing*; **La|ger|le|ben** NT camp life; **La|ger|lei|ter(in)** M(F) camp commander; (*in Ferienlager etc*) camp leader

la|gern ['laːɡən] **VT** **a** (= *aufbewahren*) to store; **kühl ~!** keep or store in a cool place **b** (= *hinlegen*) *jdn* to lay down; *Bein etc* to rest; **den Kopf/einen Kranken weich ~** to rest one's head/lay an invalid on something soft; **das Bein hoch ~** to put one's leg up; **die Patienten müssen gelagert werden** the patients must be bedded down or must lie comfortably → *auch* **gelagert VI a** (*Vorräte, Waren, Abfall etc*) to be stored or kept **b** (= *liegen*) to lie; **vor der Küste lagert Erdöl** there are deposits of oil lying off the coast **c** (*Truppen etc*) to camp, to be encamped **VR** (*geh*) to settle oneself (down)

Lager-: **La|ger|platz** M **a** (*über Nacht*) place to spend the night **b** (*Econ*: = *Warenlager*) storage place; **La|ger|raum** M storeroom; (*in Geschäft*) stockroom; **La|ger|statt** F *pl* -stätten [-ʃtɛtn] (*old liter*) bed, couch (*liter*); **La|ger|stät|te** F **a** (*old liter*: = *Bett*) bed, couch (*liter*) **b** (*Geol*) deposit; **La|ger|the|o|rie** F (*Pol*) theory of political stereotypes

La|ge|rung ['laːɡərʊŋ] F -, -en storage; (= *das Lagern auch*) storing

Lager-: **La|ger|ver|wal|ter(in)** M(F) stores supervisor; **La|ger|vor|rat** M stock, supply

La|ge|skiz|ze F sketch-map

La|gu|ne [laˈɡuːnə] F -, -n lagoon

La|gu|nen|stadt F town built on a lagoon; **die ~** (*Venedig*) Venice

lahm [laːm] **ADJ** **a** (= *gelähmt*) *Bein, Mensch, Tier* lame; (*inf*: = *steif*) stiff; **er ist auf dem linken Bein ~** he is lame in his or the left leg; **er hat ein ~es Bein** he is lame in one leg, he has a gammy (*Brit*) or gimpy (*US*) leg (*inf*) **b** (*inf*: = *langsam, langweilig*) dreary, dull; *Ausrede, Entschuldigung* lame; *Geschäftsgang* slow, sluggish; **eine ~e Ente sein** (*inf*) to have no zip (*inf*) **ADV** (*inf*: = *langsam*) slowly; (= *wenig überzeugend*) lamely; **eine ~ verfilmte Story** a dully filmed story

Lahm-: **Lahm|arsch** M (*inf*) slowcoach (*Brit inf*), slowpoke (*US inf*); **lahm|ar|schig** [-larʃɪç] (*inf*) **ADJ** bloody (*Brit inf*) or damn (*inf*) slow **ADV** bloody (*Brit inf*) or damn (*inf*) slowly

lah|men ['laːmən] VI to be lame (*auf +dat* in)

läh|men ['lɛːmən] VT to paralyze; (*fig*) *Industrie, Regierung auch* to cripple; *Verhandlungen, Verkehr* to hold up; **er ist durch einen Unfall gelähmt** he was paralyzed in an accident; **des Entsetzen befiel die Zuschauer** the onlookers were paralyzed with horror → *auch* **gelähmt**

Lah|me(r) ['laːmə] MF *decl as adj* (*old*) cripple

Lahm|heit F -, *no pl* **a** (*von Mensch, Tier, Bein*) lameness **b** (*inf*: = *Langsamkeit, Langeweile*) dreariness, dullness; (*von Geschäft, Konjunktur*) slowness, sluggishness

lahm le|gen ▲ VT *Verkehr, Produktion* to bring to a standstill *or* halt; *Industrie auch, Stromversorgung* to paralyze; **einen Flughafen ~** to bring an airport to a standstill

Läh|mung ['lɛːmʊŋ] F **-, -en** *(lit)* paralysis; *(fig)* immobilization

Läh|mungs|er|schei|nun|gen PL signs *pl* of paralysis

Lahn [laːn] F **-, -en** *(Aus)* avalanche

Laib [laip] M **-(e)s, -e** [-bə] *(esp S Ger)* loaf

Laich [laiç] M **-(e)s, -e** spawn

lai|chen ['laiçn] VI to spawn

Laich-: Laich|platz M spawning ground; **Laich|zeit** F spawning season

Laie ['laiə] M **-n, -n** *(lit, fig)* layman, layperson; **er ist ein ökonomischer ~** he is no expert in economics; **~n** the lay public; *auch* **~n** *pl (Eccl)* the laity; **da staunt der ~, der Fachmann wundert sich** *(hum inf)* that's a real turn-up for the book(s) *(Brit inf)*, that's a real unexpected surprise

Laien-: Lai|en|apos|to|lat [-lapɔstolaːt] NT **-(e)s, -e** lay apostolate; **Lai|en|bru|der** M lay brother; **Lai|en|büh|ne** F amateur dramatic society; *(Gebäude)* amateur theatre *(Brit)* or theater *(US)*; **Lai|en|dar|stel|ler(in)** M(F) amateur actor/actress; **lai|en|haft** ADJ *Arbeit* amateurish, unprofessional; *Urteil, Meinung* lay *attr* ADV *spielen* amateurishly, unprofessionally; **etw ~ ausdrücken** to put sth in simple terms; **etw ~ übersetzen** to do an amateurish translation of sth; **ich benutze den Computer ~** I am an amateur when it comes to computers; **Lai|en|pre|di|ger(in)** M(F), **Lai|en|pries|ter(in)** M(F) lay preacher; **Lai|en|rich|ter(in)** M(F) lay judge; **Lai|en|schwes|ter** F lay sister; **Lai|en|spiel** NT amateur play; **Lai|en|spiel|grup|pe** F amateur theatre *(Brit)* or theater *(US)* group; **Lai|en|stand** M laity; **Lai|en|the|a|ter** NT amateur theatre *(Brit)* or theater *(US)*; *(Ensemble)* amateur theatre *(Brit)* or theater *(US)* group; **Lai|en|tum** ['laiəntuːm] NT **-s,** *no pl* laity; **er musste sich zwischen Priestertum und entscheiden** he had to decide whether to become a priest or remain a layman; **Lai|en|ver|stand** M lay mind, layman's *or* layperson's knowledge

lai|si|e|ren [lai'ziːrən] ptp **laisiert** VT to unfrock

Lais|ser-faire [lɛse'fɛːr] NT **-,** *no pl (Econ, fig)* laisser-faire, laissez-faire

La|i|zis|mus [lai'tsɪsmʊs] M **-,** *no pl* laicism

la|i|zis|tisch [lai'tsɪstɪʃ] ADJ laicist

La|kai [la'kai] M **-en, -en** *(lit, fig)* lackey

la|kai|en|haft ADJ servile ADV **sich benehmen** in a servile way

La|ke ['laːkə] F **-, -n** brine

La|ken ['laːkn] NT **-s,** - sheet

la|ko|nisch [la'koːnɪʃ] ADJ laconic ADV laconically

Lak|ritz [la'krɪts] M **-es, -e** *(dial)*, **Lak|rit|ze** [la'krɪtsə] F **-, -n** liquorice *(Brit)*, licorice

Lak|to|se [lak'toːzə] F **-,** *no pl* lactose

la|la ['la'la] ADV *(inf)* **so ~** so-so *(inf)*, not too bad *(inf)*

lal|len ['lalən] VTI to babble; *(Betrunkener)* to mumble

La|ma¹ ['la:ma] NT **-s, -s** *(Zool)* llama

La|ma² M **-(s), -s** *(Rel)* lama

La|ma|is|mus [lama'ɪsmʊs] M **-,** *no pl* Lamaism

La|ma|klos|ter NT lamasery

La|mäng [la'mɛŋ] F **aus der (kalten) ~** *(sl)* just like that

Lamb|da-Son|de ['lampda-] F *(Aut)* Lambda probe

La|mé [la'meː] M **-s, -s** *(Tex)* lamé

La|mel|le [la'mɛlə] F **-, -n** a *(Biol)* lamella b *(Tech)* commutator bar *or* segment; *(von Jalousien)* slat

la|mel|len|för|mig ADJ lamellate, lamellar

La|mel|len|pilz M agaric

la|men|tie|ren [lamɛn'tiːrən] ptp **lamentiert** VI to moan, to complain

La|men|to [la'mɛnto] NT **-s, -s** *(Mus)* lament; **wegen etw ein ~ anstimmen** *(fig)* to bewail sth

La|met|ta [la'mɛta] NT **-s,** *no pl* lametta; *(hum: = Orden)* gongs *pl (inf)*

La|mi|nat [lami'naːt] NT **-s, -e** laminate

la|mi|nie|ren [lami'niːrən] ptp **laminiert** VT *(Tex)* to draw; *(Typ)* to laminate

Lamm [lam] NT **-(e)s, ⸚er** ['lɛmɐ] lamb; **das ~ Gottes** the Lamb of God

Lamm|bra|ten M roast lamb

Läm|mer|wölk|chen PL fleecy *or* cotton-wool clouds *pl (inf)*

Lamm|es|ge|duld F patience of a saint

Lamm-: Lamm|fell NT lambskin; **Lamm|fleisch** NT lamb; **lamm|fromm** ADJ *Gesicht, Miene* innocent; **~ sein** to be like a (little) lamb ADV **like a little lamb/little lambs; sie saßen ~ auf ihren Plätzen** they were sitting in their seats like little lambs *or* as good as gold; **Lamm|ko|te|lett** NT lamb chop; **Lamm|rü|cken** M *(Cook)* saddle of lamb

Lamms|ge|duld F patience of a saint

Lamm|wol|le F lambswool

Lam|pe ['lampə] F **-, -n** light; *(= Öllampe, Stehlampe, Tischlampe)* lamp; *(= Glühlampe)* bulb; **die ~n auf der Straße** the street lights; **einen auf die ~ gießen** *(inf)* to wet one's whistle *(inf)* → **Meister** c

Lampen-: Lam|pen|fie|ber NT stage fright; **Lam|pen|licht** NT artificial light; **Lam|pen|schirm** M lampshade

Lam|pi|on [lam'piõː, lam'piɔŋ] M **-s, -s** Chinese lantern

LAN [lan] NT **-s, -s** *(Comput)* LAN

lan|cie|ren [lãː'siːrən] ptp **lanciert** VT *Produkt, Künstler, Initiative* to launch; *Meldung, Nachricht* to put out; **jdn/etw in etw** *(acc)* **~** to get sb/sth into sth; **sein Onkel hat ihn in diese hohe Stellung lanciert** his uncle got him (into) that high position; **etw an die Presse ~** to leak sth to the press

Land [lant] NT **-(e)s, ⸚er** ['lɛndɐ] a *(= Gelände, Festland)* land; *(= Landschaft)* country, landscape; **ein Stück ~** a plot of land *or* ground; **~ bestellen** to till the soil *or* land; **~ bebauen** to cultivate the land; **~ gewinnen** *(lit)* *(am Meer)* to reclaim land; *(Agr)* to cultivate land; *(fig)* to gain ground; **an ~ gehen** to go ashore; **jdn an ~ setzen** to put sb ashore; **an ~ schwimmen** to swim to the shore; **~ sehen** *(lit)* to see *or* sight land; **endlich können wir ~ sehen/sehe ich ~** *(fig)* at last we/I can see the light at the end of the tunnel; **kein ~ mehr sehen (können)** *(fig)* to be completely muddled, to be in a complete muddle; **etw an ~ ziehen** to pull sth ashore; **ein Boot an ~ ziehen** to beach a boat; **einen Fisch an ~ ziehen** to land a fish; **einen Millionär/einen Auftrag an ~ ziehen** *(inf)* to land a millionaire/an order; **~ in Sicht!** land ahoy!; **~ unter!** land submerged!; **bei uns/euch zu ~e** back home, where we/you come from *or* live, in our/your country

b *(= ländliches Gebiet)* country; **aufs ~** (in)to the country; **auf dem ~(e)** in the country; **vom ~(e)** from the country; **über ~ fahren** *(mit Auto etc)* to drive/travel across country; *(Fahrschüler)* to drive on country roads; *(old: = reisen)* to travel

c *(= Staat)* country, land *(esp liter)*; *(= Bundesland)* *(in BRD)* Land, state; *(in Österreich)* province; **das ~ Hessen** the state of Hesse; **das ~ Tirol** the province of Tyrol, Tyrol province; **außer ~es gehen** to be out of/leave the country; **~ und Leute kennen lernen** to get to know the country and its inhabitants; **das ~ der unbegrenzten Möglichkeiten** the new world, the land of limitless opportunity; **das ~ der aufgehenden Sonne** the land of the rising sun; **aus**

aller Herren Länder(n) from all over the world, from the four corners of the earth; **der Frühling war ins ~ gezogen** *(liter)* spring had arrived; **seitdem waren viele Jahre ins ~ gegangen** *or* **gezogen** *(liter)* many years had passed since then; **bleibe im ~e und nähre dich redlich** *(prov)* stay put and prosper → **Milch**

d **Lande** PL *(poet)* lands *pl*; **in fernen ~en** *(liter)* in distant lands, in faraway lands; **durch die ~e ziehen** *(liter)* to roam abroad

---

LAND

Germany is a federal republic made up of 16 **Länder**: Baden-Württemberg, Bavaria, Berlin, Bremen, Hamburg, Hesse, Lower Saxony, North Rhine-Westphalia, Rhineland-Palatinate, Saarland, Schleswig-Holstein and the so-called **neue Länder** which acceded to the constitution after re-unification on 3rd October 1990 (Brandenburg, Saxony, Saxony-Anhalt, Mecklenburg-West Pomerania and Thuringia). The **Länder** have their own state authorities and their own legislation. However, the rule that "Federal law takes precedence over **Land** law" means that in many cases **Land** legislation is no longer observed. The **Länder** are responsible for education and policing. In addition they shoulder the main burden of administrative work, since they are generally in charge of implementing Federal laws.

Austria is also a federal state, consisting of nine **Länder**: Burgenland, Carinthia, Lower Austria, Upper Austria, Salzburg, Styria, Tyrol, Vorarlberg and Vienna.

Land-: land|ab [lant'|ap] ADV → **landauf**; **Land|adel** M landed gentry; **Land|am|mann** M *(Sw)* **highest official in a Swiss canton**; **Land|ar|beit** F agricultural work; **Land|ar|bei|ter(in)** M(F) agricultural worker; **Land|aris|to|kra|tie** F landed aristocracy; **Land|arzt** M, **Land|ärz|tin** F country doctor

Lan|dau|er ['landaue] M **-s,** - landau

Land-: land|auf [lant'|auf] ADV **~, landab** all over the country, the length and breadth of the country; **land|aus** [lant'|aus] ADV **~, landein** all over the world; **Land|bau** M , *no pl* **= Ackerbau**; **Land|be|sitz** M landholding; **~ haben** to be a landowner, to own land; **Land|be|sit|zer(in)** M(F) landowner; **Land|be|völ|ke|rung** F rural population; **Land|be|woh|ner(in)** M(F) country dweller; **~ sind ...** people who live in the country are ...; **Land|brot** NT *brown bread usually made from rye flour*; **Land|brü|cke** F land bridge; **Land|but|ter** F farm butter

Län|de ['lɛndə] F **-, -n** *(dial)* landing stage

Lan|de-: Lan|de|an|flug M approach; **Lan|de|bahn** F runway; **Lan|de|brü|cke** F jetty, landing stage; **Lan|de|er|laub|nis** F landing permission, permission to land; **Lan|de|fäh|re** F *(Space)* landing module

Land-: Land|ei NT farm egg; *(pej sl)* country bumpkin *(inf)*; **land|ein** [lant'|ain] ADV → **landaus**; **land|ein|wärts** [lant'|ainverts] ADV inland

Lan|de-: Lan|de|klap|pe F landing flap; **Lan|de|kopf** M *(Mil)* beachhead; **Lan|de|kor|ri|dor** M *(Space)* re-entry corridor *or* window; **Lan|de|ma|nö|ver** NT landing manoeuvre *(Brit)* or maneuver *(US)*

lan|den ['landn] VI aux sein to land; *(inf)* *(= enden)* to land up; *(= Eindruck machen)* to get somewhere; **weich ~** to make a soft landing; **alle anonymen Briefe ~ sofort im Papierkorb** all anonymous letters go straight into the wastepaper basket; **mit deinen Komplimenten kannst du bei mir nicht ~** your compliments won't get you anywhere *or* very far with me VT *(lit, fig)* to land → **Coup**

län|den ['lɛndn] VT *(dial)* *Leiche* to recover *(aus* from*)*

Land|en|ge F isthmus

Lan|de-: Lan|de|pis|te F landing strip; **Lan|de|platz** M (für Flugzeuge) place to land; (ausgebaut) landing strip; (für Schiffe) landing place; **Lan|de|recht** NT (Aviat) landing rights pl

Län|de|rei|en [lɛndəˈraiən] PL estates pl

Län|der-: Län|der|fi|nanz|aus|gleich M , no pl balancing of federal budgets; **Län|der|kampf** M (Sport) international contest; (= Länderspiel) international (match); **Län|der|kun|de** F regional studies pl; **Län|der|na|me** M name of a/the country; **Län|der|spiel** NT international (match)

Lan|des-: Lan|des|bank F pl -banken regional bank; **Lan|des|be|am|te(r)** M decl as adj, **Lan|des|be|am|tin** F civil servant employed by a Land rather than the nation; **Lan|des|be|hör|de** F regional authorities pl; **Lan|des|bo|den|brief** M land mortgage certificate; **Lan|des|brauch** M national custom, custom of the country; **nach ~ ist es hier üblich ...** in this country it is customary ...; **Lan|des|ebe|ne** F **auf ~** at state level; **lan|des|ei|gen** ADJ **→ Land c** owned by the country/state or Land/province; **Lan|des|far|ben** PL (von Staat) national colours pl (Brit) or colors pl (US); (von Bundesland) state colours pl (Brit) or colors pl (US); (in Österreich) colours pl (Brit) or colors pl (US) of the province; **Lan|des|fürst(in)** M(F) prince/princess; (inf: = Ministerpräsident) state boss; **Lan|des|ge|richt** NT district court; **Lan|des|gren|ze** F (von Staat) national boundary; (von Bundesland) state or (Aus) provincial boundary; **Lan|des|haupt|mann** M (Aus) head of the government of a province; **Lan|des|haupt|stadt** F capital of a Land; (Aus) capital of a province, provincial capital; **Lan|des|herr(in)** M(F) (Hist) sovereign, ruler; **Lan|des|ho|heit** F sovereignty; **Lan|des|in|ne|re(s)** NT decl as adj interior; **Lan|des|kind** NT (von Staat) native of a/the country; (von Bundesland) native of a/the Land or (Aus) province; **Lan|des|kir|che** F national church; (in Deutschland) established Protestant church in some Länder; **Lan|des|kun|de** F knowledge of the/a country; (Univ) regional and cultural studies pl; **lan|des|kun|dig** ADJ **~er Reiseleiter** courier who knows the country; **lan|des|kund|lich** [-kʊntlɪç] ADJ Kenntnisse, Aspekte of a/the country's geography and culture ADV in geography and culture; **Lan|des|lis|te** F (Parl) regional list of parliamentary candidates for election to Federal parliament; **Lan|des|me|di|en|ge|setz** NT law relating to the running and content of regional media; **Lan|des|meis|ter(in)** M(F) (Sport) regional champion; **Lan|des|mut|ter** F pl -**müt|ter** (liter) mother of the people (liter); **die britische ~** the mother of the British nation (liter); **Lan|des|par|tei|tag** M regional party conference; **Lan|des|rat** , **Lan|des|rä|tin** F (Aus) highest official of an administrative district; **Lan|des|recht** NT law of a Land or (Aus) province; **Lan|des|re|gie|rung** F government of a Land; (Aus) provincial government; **Lan|des|spra|che** F national language; **der ~ un|kundig sein** not to know the language

Lan|de|steg M landing stage

Lan|des-: Lan|des|teil M region, area; **Lan|des|tracht** F national dress or costume; **lan|des|üb|lich** ADJ customary; **das ist dort ~** that's the custom there; **Lan|des|va|ter** M (liter) father of the people (liter); **Lan|des|ver|rat** M treason; **Lan|des|ver|rä|ter(in)** M(F) traitor; **Lan|des|ver|si|che|rungs|an|stalt** F regional pensions office (for waged employees); **Lan|des|ver|tei|di|gung** F national defence (Brit) or defense (US); **lan|des|ver|wie|sen** M (rare) expelled, banished (old); (= exiliert) exiled; **Lan|des|wäh|rung** F national or local currency; **Lan|des|zent|ral|bank** F pl -banken State Central Bank

Lan|de-: Lan|de|übung F landing exercise; **Lan|de|ver|bot** NT refusal of landing permission; **~ erhalten** to be refused landing permission or permission to land

Land-: Land|fah|rer(in) M(F) (form) vagrant; **land|fein** ADJ (dated) spruced up; **Land|flucht** F migration from the land, emigration to the cities; **Land|frau** F countrywoman; **Land|frie|de(n)** M (Hist) King's/Queen's Peace; **Land|frie|dens|bruch** M (Jur) breach of the peace; **Land|funk** M farming (radio) programme (Brit) or program (US); **Land|gang** M pl -**gänge** shore leave; **Land|ge|mein|de** F country community; **Land|ge|richt** NT district court; **land|ge|stützt** [-gəʃtʏtst] ADJ Raketen land-based; **Land|ge|win|nung** F land reclamation; **Land|graf** M landgrave; **Land|gut** NT estate; **Land|haus** NT country house; **Land|heer** NT army; **Land|heim** M = Schullandheim, **Land|jä|ger** M **a** (Hist) country policeman **b** (= Wurst) pressed smoked sausage; **Land|kar|te** F map; **Land|kli|ma** NT continental climate; **Land|kreis** M administrative district; **Land|krieg** M land warfare; **Luft- und ~ war** in the air and on the ground; **See- und ~ war** at sea and on land; **Land|kriegs|ord|nung** F **Haager ~** Hague Land Warfare Convention; **land|läu|fig** ADJ popular, common; **entgegen ~er** or **der ~en Meinung** contrary to popular opinion ADV commonly

Länd|le [ˈlɛntlə] NT -s, no pl **das ~** (inf) Baden-Württemberg

Länd|le|ben NT country life

Länd|ler [ˈlɛntlɐ] M -s, - (S Ger) country dance

Land|leu|te PL country people pl or folk pl

länd|lich [ˈlɛntlɪç] ADJ rural; Tracht country attr; Tanz country attr, folk attr; Idylle pastoral; Stille, Frieden of the countryside, rural ADV **eine ~ ge|prägte Region** a rural area; **eine ~ wirkende Stadt** a town which gives a rural impression

Land-: land|lie|bend ADJ country-loving attr; **Land|luft** F country air; **Land|macht** F land power; **Land|mann** M pl -**männer** (old, liter) husbandman (old, liter); **Land|ma|schi|nen** PL agricultural machinery sing or machines pl; **Land|mes|ser** [-mɛsɐ] M -s, -, **Land|mes|se|rin** [-ərɪn] F -, -nen land surveyor; **Land|mi|ne** F landmine; **Land|nah|me** [-naːmə] F -, -n (Hist) acquisition of land; **Land|par|tie** F (old) country outing; **Land|pfar|rer(in)** M(F) country parson; **Land|pfle|ger** M (Bibl) governor; **Land|pla|ge** F plague; (fig inf) pest; **Land|pol|me|ran|ze** F (dated pej) country cousin; **Land|pra|xis** F (Med) country practice; **Land|rat**[1] M (Sw) cantonal parliament; **Land|rat**[2] M , **Land|rä|tin** F (Ger) head of the administration of a Landkreis; **Land|rat|te** F (hum) landlubber; **Land|re|form** F land reform; **Land|re|gen** M steady rain; **Land|rü|cken** M ridge of land; **Land|sas|se** [ˈlantzasə] M -n, -n (Hist) freeholder

Land|schaft [ˈlantʃaft] F -, -en scenery no pl; (Gemälde) landscape; (= ländliche Gegend) countryside; (fig) landscape, scene; **eine öde ~** a barren landscape or region; **die ~ um London** the countryside around London; **die ~en Italiens** the types of countryside in Italy; **wir sahen eine reizvolle ~** we saw some delightful scenery; **vor uns tat sich eine liebliche ~ auf** (geh) a lovely view appeared before us; **in der ~ herumstehen** (inf) to stand around; **da stand einsam ein Hochhaus in der ~ (herum)** (inf) there was one solitary skyscraper to be seen; **die politische ~** the political scene or landscape; **die kulinarische/kulturelle ~** the culinary/cultural scene

land|schaft|lich [ˈlantʃaftlɪç] ADJ Schönheiten etc scenic; Besonderheiten regional ADV abwechslungsreich, eintönig scenically; **das Dorf liegt ~ einmalig** (inf) the village is surrounded by the most fantastic scenery; **diese Gegend ist ~ ausgesprochen reizvoll** the scenery in this area is particularly delightful; **das ist ~ unterschiedlich**

it differs from one part of the country to another, it differs in various parts of the country; **„Klempner" heißt ~ auch „Spengler"** in some areas the word "Spengler" is used for "Klempner"

Land|schafts-: Land|schafts|bild NT view; (Gemälde) landscape (painting); (Fotografie) landscape (photograph); **Land|schafts|form** F land form; **Land|schafts|gärt|ner(in)** M(F) landscape gardener; **Land|schafts|ma|ler(in)** M(F) landscape painter; **Land|schafts|pfle|ge** F , **Land|schafts|schutz** M protection of the countryside; **Land|schafts|schutz|ge|biet** NT nature reserve; **Land|schafts|ver|brauch** M encroachment on the countryside

Land|schul|heim NT = Schullandheim

Land|ser [ˈlantsɐ] M -s, - (dated inf) private

Lands|frau F (= Landsmännin) compatriot, fellow countrywoman

Land|sitz M country seat

Lands-: Lands|knecht M (Hist) lansquenet; **fluchen wie ein ~** to swear like a trooper; **Lands|mann** M pl -**leute** compatriot, fellow countryman; **Lands|män|nin** [-mɛnɪn] F -, -nen compatriot, fellow countrywoman; **Lands|mann|schaft** F welfare and cultural association for Germans born in the eastern areas of the former Reich

Land-: Land|spit|ze F point, promontory, headland; **Land|stän|de** PL (Hist) body of representatives of various classes in medieval provincial politics; **Land|stra|ße** F country road; (= Straße zweiter Ordnung) secondary or B (Brit) road; (im Gegensatz zur Autobahn) ordinary road; **Land|strei|cher** M -s, -, **Land|strei|che|rin** [-ərɪn] F -, -nen (pej) tramp, hobo (US); **Land|strei|che|rei** [lantʃtraiçəˈrai] F -, no pl vagrancy; **Land|streit|kräf|te** PL land forces pl; **Land|strich** M area; **ein flacher ~** a flat belt of land; **Land|sturm** M conscripted militia in times of war, ≈ Home Guard (Brit); **Land|tag** M Landtag (state parliament); **Land|tags|wah|len** PL (West) German regional elections pl; **Land|trup|pen** PL land forces pl

Lan|dung [ˈlandʊŋ] F -, -en (von Flugzeug, Truppen etc) landing; **zur ~ gezwungen werden** to be forced to land, to be forced down

Lan|dungs-: Lan|dungs|boot NT landing craft; **Lan|dungs|brü|cke** F jetty, landing stage; **Lan|dungs|platz** M landing place; **Lan|dungs|steg** M landing stage; **Lan|dungs|trup|pen** PL land assault forces pl

Land-: Land|ur|laub M shore leave; **Land|ver|mes|ser** [-fɛɛmɛsɐ] M -s, -, **Land|ver|mes|se|rin** [-ərɪn] F -, -nen land surveyor; **Land|ver|mes|sung** F land surveying; **Land|vogt** M (Hist) landvogt (governor of a royal province); **Land|volk** NT country people pl or folk pl

landw. abbr von landwirtschaftlich

Land-: land|wärts [ˈlantvɛrts] ADV landwards; **Land|weg** M **auf dem ~** by land; **Land|wein** M vin ordinaire (Brit), homegrown wine; **Land|wind** M offshore wind; **Land|wirt(in)** M(F) farmer

Land|wirt|schaft F agriculture, farming; (Betrieb) farm; (= Landwirte) farmers pl; **~ betreiben** to farm; **~ haben** (inf) to have a farm

land|wirt|schaft|lich ADJ agricultural; **~e Geräte** agricultural or farm implements ADV **tätig sein** agriculturally; **geprägt sein** by agriculture; **~ genutzt** used for agricultural purposes

Land|wirt|schafts- in cpds agricultural; **Land|wirt|schafts|be|ra|ter(in)** M(F) agricultural adviser; **Land|wirt|schafts|brief** M (Fin) agricultural bond; **Land|wirt|schafts|mi|nis|te|ri|um** NT ministry of agriculture, ≈ Department of Agriculture (US); **Land|wirt|schafts|schu|le** F agricultural college (Brit) or school (US)

Land|zun|ge F spit (of land), promontory

lang [laŋ] **ADJ** *comp* **⁼er** ['lɛŋə], *superl* **⁼ste(r, s)** ['lɛŋstə] **a** long; *Film, Roman, Aufenthalt, Rede* long, lengthy; **das ist seit ~em geplant** that has been planned (for) a long time; **das war seit ~em geplant** it was planned a long time ago; **vor ~er Zeit** a long time ago; **in nicht allzu ~er Zeit** before too *or* very long, in the not too distant future; **das hat die längste Zeit gedauert!** that's gone on long enough!; **hier wird mir der Tag** *or* **die Zeit nicht ~** I won't get bored here; **etw länger machen** to make sth longer, to lengthen sth; **es ist eine ~e Strecke bis Bristol, jedenfalls länger, als ich gedacht hatte** it's a long way to Bristol, at least, further than I thought; **die Tage werden wieder länger** the days are drawing out, the days are getting longer; **er machte ein ~es Gesicht** his face fell; **man sah überall nur ~e Gesichter** you saw nothing but long faces; **von ~er Hand vorbereiten** to prepare sth carefully; **des Langen und Breiten** at great length; **einen ~en Hals machen** (*inf*) to crane one's neck → **Leine, Sicht a, Bank¹ a, Leitung d, Rede a**

b (*inf*: = groß gewachsen) *Mensch* tall; **eine ~e Latte sein, ein ~er Lulatsch sein, ein ~es Elend** *or* **Ende sein** to be a (real) beanpole (*inf*); **er ist so ~ wie er dumm ist** he's as thick as two short planks (*inf*)

ADV *comp* **⁼er** ['lɛŋə], *superl* **am ⁼sten der ~ erwartete Regen** the long-awaited rain; **der ~ ersehnte Tag/Urlaub** the longed-for day/holiday (*esp Brit*) *or* vacation (*US*); **~ anhaltender Beifall** prolonged *or* long applause; **~ gehegt** (*Wunsch*) long-cherished; **~ gestreckt** long; *Dorf* auch strung-out; **~ gezogen** (*Ton, Schrei*) long-drawn-out; *Kurve* long; **nur einen Augenblick ~** only for a moment *or* second; **zwei Stunden ~** for two hours; **mein ganzes Leben ~** all my life, my whole life; **~ und breit** at great length → *auch* **lange, entlang**

lang-: lang|är|me|lig ADJ long-sleeved; **lang|ar|mig** ADJ long-armed; **lang|ärm|lig** ADJ long-sleeved; **lang|at|mig** [-la:tmɪç] ADJ long-winded **ADV** in a long-winded way; **er schreibt ~** his style of writing is long-winded; **Lang|at|mig|keit** F -, *no pl* long-windedness; **lang|bei|nig** ADJ long-legged

lan|ge ['laŋə], (*S Ger*) **lang**, (*Aus*) ADV *comp* **⁼er** ['lɛŋə], *superl* **am längsten** ['lɛŋstn] **a** (*zeitlich*) a long time; (*in Fragen, Negativsätzen*) long; **die Sitzung hat heute ~/nicht ~ gedauert** the meeting went on (for) a long time/didn't go on (for) long today; **wie ~ lernst du schon Deutsch/bist du schon hier?** how long have you been learning German (for)/been here (for)?; **es ist noch gar nicht ~ her, dass wir diese Frage diskutiert haben** we discussed this question not long ago, it's not long since we discussed this question; **er wird nicht mehr ~ machen** (*inf*) he won't last long, he's not got long to go; **bis Weihnachten ist es ja noch ~ hin** it's still a long time till Christmas, we're a long way from Christmas; **je länger, je lieber** the more the better; (*zeitlich*) the longer the better

b (*inf*: = längst) **noch ~ nicht** not by any means, not by a long chalk (*Brit inf*) *or* shot; **~ nicht so ...** nowhere near as ..., not nearly as ...; **er verdient ~ nicht so viel** he doesn't earn nearly as much, he doesn't earn anywhere near as much; **wenn er das schafft, kannst du das schon ~** if he can do it, you can do it easily

Län|ge ['lɛŋə] F -, -n **a** (*zeitlich, räumlich*) length; (*inf: von Mensch*) height; **eine ~ von 10 Metern haben** to be 10 metres (*Brit*) *or* meters (*US*) long *or* in length; **ein Seil von 10 Meter ~** a rope 10 metres (*Brit*) *or* meters (*US*) long; **ein Vortrag von einer Stunde ~** an hour-long lecture; **eine Fahrt von einer Stunde ~** an hour's journey; **Bauarbeiten auf 5 km ~** roadworks (*Brit*) *or* road construction (*US*) for 5 kms; **etw der ~ nach falten** to fold sth lengthways *or* lengthwise; **der ~ nach hinfallen** to fall flat, to

go sprawling; **in die ~ gehen** (*Kleidungsstücke*) to stretch; **in die ~ schießen** *or* **wachsen** to shoot up; **etw in die ~ ziehen** to protract sth, to drag sth out (*inf*); **sich in die ~ ziehen** to go on and on; **einen Artikel in seiner vollen ~ abdrucken** to print an article in its entirety

b (*Sport*) length; **mit einer ~ gewinnen** to win by a length; **die anderen Wagen kamen mit einigen ~n Abstand** the other cars came in several lengths behind; **(jdm/etw) um ~n voraus sein** (*fig*) to be streets ahead (of sb/sth); **um ~n geschlagen werden** (*fig*) to be well beaten **c** (*Geog*) longitude; **der Ort liegt auf** *or* **unter 20 Grad östlicher ~** the town has a longitude of 20 degrees east **d** (*in Buch*) long-drawn-out passage; (*in Film*) long-drawn-out scene

lan|gen ['laŋən] (*dial inf*) **VI a** (= *sich erstrecken, greifen*) to reach (*nach* for, *in* +*acc* in, into); **bis an etw** (*acc*) **~** to reach sth **b** (= *fassen*) to touch (*an etw* (*acc*) sth) **c** (= *ausreichen*) to be enough; (= *auskommen*) to get by, to manage; **mir** *or* **für mich langt es** I've had enough; **das Geld langt nicht** there isn't *or* we *etc* haven't enough money; **jetzt langts mir aber!** I've had just about enough! → **hinten e** **VT** (= *reichen*) **jdm etw ~** to give *or* pass *or* hand sb sth; **jdm eine ~** to give sb a clip on the ear (*inf*); **sich** (*dat*) **etw ~** to take sth

Län|gen-: Län|gen|grad M **a** degree of longitude **b** (*auch* **Längenkreis**) meridian; **Län|gen|maß** NT measure of length, linear measure (*form*)

län|ger *comp von* **lang** *von* **lange**

län|ger|fris|tig [-frɪstɪç] ADJ longer-term **ADV** in the longer term; *planen* for the longer term

lan|ger|hans|sche In|seln ▲ ['laŋəhansʃə] PL (*Med*) islets *pl* of Langerhans

lan|ger|sehnt △ ADJ *attr* → **lang** ADV

Lan|ge|wei|le ['laŋəvailə, laŋə'vailə] F *gen* - *or* **Langenweile** ['laŋənvailə], *dat* - *or* **Langerweile** ['laŋəvailə] *no pl* boredom; **~ haben** to be bored

Lang-: lang|fä|dig [-fɛ:dɪç] (*Sw*) ADJ long-winded **ADV** in a long-winded way; **er schreibt sehr ~** his style of writing is very long-winded; **Lang|fin|ger** M (*hum*) pickpocket; **lang|fin|ge|rig** [-fɪŋərɪç], **lang|fing|rig** [-fɪŋrɪç] ADJ long-fingered; (*hum*) light-fingered; **Lang|for|mat** NT Briefumschläge im ~ long envelopes; Zigaretten im ~ long(-length) cigarettes; **lang|fris|tig** [-frɪstɪç] ADJ long-term **ADV** in the long term; *planen* for the long term; **lang|ge|hegt** △ ADJ *attr* → **lang** ADV; **lang|ge|hen** *sep irreg* **VI a** (*Weg etc*) **wo gehts hier lang?** where does this (road *etc*) go? **b** **sie weiß, wo es langgeht** she knows what's what; **hier bestimme ich, wo es langgeht** I decide what's what here **VT** to go along; **lang|ge|streckt** △ ADJ → **lang** ADV; **lang|ge|zo|gen** △ ADJ → **lang** ADV; **lang|glie|de|rig** [-gli:dərɪç], **lang|glied|rig** [-gli:drɪç] ADJ long-limbed; **lang|haa|rig** ADJ long-haired; **Lang|haa|ri|ge(r)** [-ha:rɪgə] MF *decl as adj* long-haired man/woman *etc*; **so ein ~ some long-haired type; diese dreckigen ~n** (*pej*) these long-haired layabouts (*Brit*) *or* good-for-nothings; **Lang|haar|pe|rü|cke** F long wig; **Lang|han|tel** F barbell; **Lang|haus** NT nave; **Lang|holz** NT uncut timber; **Lang|holz|wa|gen** M timber lorry (*Brit*) *or* truck; **lang|jäh|rig** ADJ *Freundschaft, Bekannter, Gewohnheit* long-standing; *Erfahrung, Verhandlungen, Recherchen* many years of; *Mitarbeiter* of many years' standing **ADV** for many years; **Lang|lauf** M (*Ski*) cross-country (skiing); **Sieger im ~** winner of the cross-country (event); **Lang|läu|fer** M (*Fin*) long(-dated) security; **Lang|läu|fer(in)** M(F) (*Ski*) cross-country skier; **Lang|lauf|ski** M cross-country ski; **lang|le|big** [-le:bɪç] ADJ long-lasting; *Stoff, Waren etc* auch durable; *Gerücht* persistent; *Melodie* enduring; *Mensch, Tier* long-lived; **~ sein** to last a long time; to have a long life, to be durable; to be persistent; to live to an old age; **Lang|le|big-**

keit F -, *no pl* (*von Stoff, Waren*) durability; (*von Gerücht*) persistence; (*von Mensch, Tier*) longevity; **die ~ dieser giftigen Substanzen** the fact that these toxic substances last so long; **lang+le|gen** VR *sep* to have a lie-down

läng|lich ['lɛŋlɪç] ADJ long, elongated

Lang-: lang+lie|gen VI *sep irreg* (*inf*) to be in bed; **lang+ma|chen** VR *sep* (*inf, = sich ausruhen*) to have a lie-down *or* a rest (*US*), to stretch out (on the bed/sofa *etc*); **lang|mäh|nig** [-mɛ:nɪç] ADJ with a long mane, long-maned; (*inf*) *Mensch* long-haired; **Lang|mut** ['laŋmu:t] F -, *no pl* patience, forbearance; **lang|mü|tig** ['laŋmy:tɪç] ADJ patient, forbearing; **Lang|mü|tig|keit** F -, *no pl* forbearance; **Lang|ohr** NT (*hum*) rabbit, bunny (*inf*); (= *Häschen*) hare; **Meister ~** Master Longears; **Lang|pferd** NT (*Sport*) (long) horse

längs [lɛŋs] ADV lengthways, lengthwise; **~ gestreift** (*Stoff*) with lengthways stripes; *Kleid, Vorhang etc auch* with vertical stripes **PREP** +*gen* along; **~ der Straße stehen Kastanien** chestnut trees line the road, there are chestnut trees along the road; **die Bäume ~ des Flusses** the trees along (the banks of) the river

Längs|ach|se F longitudinal axis

lang|sam ['laŋza:m] ADJ slow **ADV a** slowly; **geh/fahr/sprich ~er!** slow down!, walk/drive/speak (a bit) more slowly *or* (a bit) slower! (*inf*); **~, ~!, immer schön ~!** (*inf*) (take it) easy!, easy does it!; **~, aber sicher** slowly but surely

b (= *allmählich, endlich*) **es wird ~ Zeit, dass ...** it's about time that ..., it's high time that ...; **~ müsstest du das aber wissen** it's about time you knew that, it's high time you knew that; **ich muss jetzt ~ gehen** I must be getting on my way, I'd better be thinking about going; **kannst du dich ~ mal entscheiden?** could you start making up your mind?; **~ (aber sicher) reicht es mir** I've just about had enough; **ist das ~ fertig?** is it ready yet?

Lang|sam|keit F -, *no pl* slowness

lang|sam tre|ten ▲ VI *irreg* (*inf*) to go easy (*inf*); (*gesundheitlich auch*) to take things easy

Lang-: Lang|schaft|ter ['laŋʃɛftə] M -s, - high boot; (*aus Gummi*) wader; **lang|schäf|tig** ['laŋʃɛftɪç] ADJ *Stiefel* high; **Lang|schiff** NT nave; **Lang|schlä|fer(in)** M(F) late-riser; **Lang|schrift** F longhand; **Lang|sei|te** F long side

Längs-: Längs|fal|den M warp; **Längs|fal|te** F lengthways fold; **längs|ge|streift** △ ADJ → **längs** ADV; **Längs|li|nie** F vertical line, line down

Lang|spiel-: Lang|spiel|band [-bant] NT *pl* -bänder long-playing tape; **Lang|spiel|plat|te** F long-playing record

Längs-: Längs|rich|tung F longitudinal direction; **in ~ zu etw verlaufen** to run longitudinally along sth; **längs|schiffs** ['lɛŋsʃɪfs] ADV broadside on; **Längs|schnitt** M longitudinal section; **Längs|sei|te** F long side; (*Naut*) broadside; **längs|seit(s)** ['lɛŋszait(s)] ADV, PREP +*gen* alongside; **die beiden Boote lagen längs|seits** the boats were lying alongside one another; **Längs|strei|fen** PL lengthways stripes *pl*; (*von Kleid, Vorhängen auch*) vertical stripes *pl*

längst [lɛŋst] ADV **a** (= *seit langem, schon lange*) for a long time; (= *vor langer Zeit*) a long time ago, long ago; **er ist inzwischen ~ gestorben** he has been dead (for) a long time now; **als wir ankamen, war der Zug ~ weg** when we arrived the train had long since gone **b** → **lange b**

Längs|tal NT longitudinal valley

längs|tens ['lɛŋstns] ADV **a** (= *höchstens*) at the most **b** (= *spätestens*) at the latest

längs|te(r, s) ['lɛŋstə] *superl von* **lang**

lang|stie|lig [-ʃti:lɪç] ADJ long-stemmed

Lang|stre|cken-: Lang|stre|cken|flug M long-distance flight; **Lang|stre|cken|flug|zeug** NT long-range *or* long-haul aircraft; **Lang|stre|cken|lauf** M (*Disziplin*) long-distance running; (*Wettkampf*) long-distance race; **Lang|stre|cken|läu|fer(in)** M(F) long-distance runner; **Lang|stre|cken|ra|ke|te** F long-range missile; **Lang|stre|cken|waf|fe** F long-range weapon

Lang|streck|ler [-ʃtrɛklɐ] M -s, -, **Lang|streck|le|rin** [-ərɪn] F -, -nen (*inf*) long-distance runner

Längs|wand F long wall

Lan|gus|te [laŋˈgʊstə] F -, -n crayfish, crawfish (*US*)

lang|wei|len [ˈlaŋvailən] insep VT to bore VT to be boring VR to be bored; **sich tödlich** or **zu Tode ~** to be bored to death or to tears → auch **gelangweilt**

Lang|wei|ler [ˈlaŋvailɐ] M -s, -, **Lang|wei|le|rin** [-ərɪn] F -, -nen bore; (= *langsamer Mensch*) slowcoach (*Brit inf*), slowpoke (*US inf*)

lang|wei|lig [ˈlaŋvailɪç] ADJ a boring b (*inf*: = *langsam*) slow; **er ist so ~ mit allem** he's so slow or such a slowcoach (*Brit inf*) or such a slowpoke (*US inf*) at everything ADV boringly

Lang|wei|lig|keit F -, no pl **aufgrund der ~ ihres Unterrichts/des Buches** because her teaching/the book is so boring; **seine Geschichten sind von einer extremen ~** his stories are so incredibly boring

Lang-: Lang|wel|le F long wave; **lang|wel|lig** ADJ long-wave; **lang|wie|rig** [ˈlaŋviːrɪç] ADJ long, lengthy; *Verhandlungen, Behandlung, Krankheit auch* prolonged ADV over a long period; **~ planen** to plan long-term; **eine ~ verlaufende Krankheit** a long-term illness; **über etw** (*acc*) **beraten** to have lengthy or prolonged discussions about sth; **Lang|wie|rig|keit** F -, no pl lengthiness

Lang|zeit- [ˈlaŋtsait] in cpds long-term; **Lang|zeit|ar|beits|lo|se(r)** MF decl as adj **ein ~r** someone who is long-term unemployed; **die ~n** the long-term unemployed; **Lang|zeit|ge|dächt|nis** NT long-term memory; **Lang|zeit|pro|gramm** NT long-term programme (*Brit*) or program (*US*); **Lang|zeit|ri|si|ko** NT long-term risk; **Lang|zeit|stu|die** F long-range study; **Lang|zeit|ver|such** M long-term trial; **Lang|zeit|wert** M , no pl long-term result; **Lang|zeit|wir|kung** F long-term effect

lang zie|hen ▲ VT irreg to stretch → Ohr, Hammelbeine

La|no|lin [lanoˈliːn] NT -s, no pl lanolin

Lan|than [lanˈtaːn] NT -s, no pl (*abbr* **La**) lanthanum

Lan|ze [ˈlantsə] F -, -n a (= *Waffe*) lance; (*zum Werfen*) spear; **für jdn eine ~ brechen** (*fig*) to take up the cudgels for sb (*Brit*), to go to bat for sb (*esp US*) b (*sl*: = *Penis*) tool (*sl*)

Lan|zen-: Lan|zen|spit|ze F tip of a lance; (*von Wurfwaffe*) tip of a spear; **Lan|zen|stich** M (*von Wurfwaffe*) lance thrust; (*Wunde*) lance/spear wound; **er wurde von einem ~ getroffen** he was hit by a lance/spear; **Lan|zen|stoß** M lance thrust; (*von Wurfwaffe*) spear thrust

Lan|zet|te [lanˈtsɛtə] F -, -n (*Med*) lancet

Lan|zett-: Lan|zett|fisch M , **Lan|zett|fisch|chen** [lanˈtsɛtfɪʃçən] NT -s, - lancelet; **lan|zett|för|mig** ADJ (*Bot*) lanceolate (*spec*)

La|os [ˈlaːɔs] NT -' Laos

La|o|te [laˈoːtə] M -n, -n, **La|o|tin** [laˈoːtɪn] F -, -nen Laotian

la|o|tisch [laˈoːtɪʃ] ADJ Laotian

La|ot|se [laˈoːtsə, ˈlaʊtsə] M -s Lao-Tse

La|pa|ro|sko|pie [laparoskoˈpiː] F -, -n [-ˈpiːən] (*Med*) laparoscopy

la|pa|ro|sko|pisch [laparoˈskoːpɪʃ] ADJ (*Med*) laparoscopic

la|pi|dar [lapiˈdaːɐ] ADJ succinct ADV succinctly

La|pis|la|zu|li [lapɪsˈlaːtsuli] M -, - lapis lazuli

Lap|pa|lie [laˈpaːliə] F -, -n trifle, petty little matter

Läpp|chen [ˈlɛpçən] NT -s, - (small) cloth

Lap|pe [ˈlapə] M -n, -n, **Lap|pin** [ˈlapɪn] F -, -nen Lapp, Lapplander

Lap|pen [ˈlapn] M -s, - a (= *Stück Stoff*) cloth; (= *Waschlappen*) face cloth, flannel (*Brit*), washcloth (*US*) b (*inf*: = *Geldschein*) note, bill (*US*); **die paar ~** ≈ a couple of quid (*Brit inf*) or dollars (*US*) c (*sl*: = *Führerschein*) licence (*Brit*), license (*US*) d (= *Hautstück*) fold of skin e (*inf*) **jdm durch die ~ gehen** to slip through sb's fingers; **die Sendung ist mir durch die ~ gegangen** I missed the programme (*Brit*) or program (*US*)

läp|pern [ˈlɛpɐn] VR impers (*inf*) **es läppert sich** it (all) mounts up

lap|pig [ˈlapɪç] ADJ (*inf*) limp

Lap|pin F -, -nen Lapp, Lapplander

läp|pisch [ˈlɛpɪʃ] ADJ silly; **wegen ~en zwei Euro macht er so ein Theater** (*inf*) he makes such a fuss about a mere two euros ADV **sich verhalten** foolishly

Lapp|land [ˈlaplant] NT -s Lapland

Lapp|län|der [ˈlaplɛndɐ] M -s, -, **Lapp|län|de|rin** [-ərɪn] F -, -nen Lapp, Lapplander

lapp|län|disch [ˈlaplɛndɪʃ] ADJ Lapp

Lap|sus [ˈlapsʊs] M -, - [ˈlapsuːs] mistake, slip; (*gesellschaftlich, diplomatisch*) faux pas; **~ Linguae** slip of the tongue; **mir ist ein ~ unterlaufen** or **passiert, ich habe einen ~ begangen** I've made a mistake/faux pas

Lap|top [ˈlɛptɔp] M -s, -s (*Comput*) laptop

Lär|che [ˈlɛrçə] F -, -n larch

large [larʒ] ADJ (*Sw*) generous

Lär|ge [ˈlɛrgə] F -, -n (*dial, pej*) Silesian

Lar|go [ˈlargo] NT -s, -s or **Larghi** [ˈlargi] (*Mus*) largo

la|ri|fa|ri [lariˈfaːri] INTERJ nonsense, fiddlesticks, fiddle-de-dee ADJ inv airy-fairy

La|ri|fa|ri [lariˈfaːri] NT -s, no pl (*inf*) nonsense

Lärm [lɛrm] M -(e)s, no pl noise; (= *Geräuschbelästigung auch*) din, row, racket; (= *Aufsehen*) fuss; **~ schlagen** (*lit*) to raise the alarm; (*fig*) to kick up a fuss, to raise a commotion; **„Viel ~ um nichts"** "Much Ado about Nothing"; **viel ~ um nichts machen** to make a lot of fuss or a lot of ado or a big to-do (*inf*) about nothing; **viel ~ um jdn/etw machen** to make a big fuss about sb/sth

Lärm-: Lärm|be|kämp|fung F noise abatement; **Lärm|be|läs|ti|gung** F noise pollution; **sie beschwerten sich wegen der unzumutbaren ~** they complained about the unacceptable noise level; **lärm|emp|find|lich** ADJ sensitive to noise; **Lärm|emp|find|lich|keit** F sensitivity to noise

lär|men [ˈlɛrmən] VI to make a noise; **~d** noisy

Lärm-: lärm|ge|plagt [-gəplaːkt] ADJ plagued with noise; **lärm|ge|schä|digt** [-gəʃeːdɪçt] ADJ suffering physical damage as a result of exposure to noise

lär|mig ADJ (*esp Sw*) noisy

Lärm-: Lärm|mess|ge|rät ▲ NT noise meter; **lärm|min|dernd** ADJ *Straßenbelag, Maßnahmen* noise-reducing

lar|mo|yant [larmoaˈjant] (*geh*) ADJ lachrymose (*liter*) ADV lachrymosely (*liter*)

Lar|mo|yanz [larmoaˈjants] F -, no pl (*geh*) sentimentality

Lärm-: Lärm|pe|gel M noise level; **Lärm|quel|le** F source of noise/the noise; **Lärm|schä|den** PL , **Lärm|schä|di|gun|gen** PL injuries pl caused by excessive noise

Lärm|schutz M noise prevention

Lärm|schutz-: Lärm|schutz|maß|nah|men PL noise prevention measures pl; **Lärm|schutz|wall** M , **Lärm|schutz|wand** F sound or noise barrier

Lärv|chen [ˈlɛrfçən] NT -s, - a dim von Larve b (*dated inf*: = *Gesicht*) baby-doll face

Lar|ve [ˈlarfə] F -, -n a (= *Tierlarve*) larva b (= *Maske*) mask

las pret von **lesen**

La|sag|ne [laˈzanjə] PL lasagne sing

lasch [laʃ] ADJ a *Erziehung, Gesetz, Kontrolle, Polizei, Eltern* lax; *Vorgehen* feeble b (= *schlaff*) *Bewegungen* feeble; *Händedruck* limp c *Speisen* insipid, wishy-washy (*inf*) ADV a (= *nicht streng*) in a lax way; (= *schlaff*) *bewegen* feebly b (= *schlaff*) *bewegen* feebly; *die Hände drücken* limply

La|sche [ˈlaʃə] F -, -n (= *Schlaufe*) loop; (= *Schuhlasche*) tongue; (*als Schmuck, Verschluss*) tab, flap; (*Tech*) splicing plate; (*von Kette*) sideplate; (*Rail*) fishplate

Lasch|heit F -, no pl a (*von Erziehung, Gesetz, Kontrolle etc*) laxity; (*von Vorgehen*) feebleness b (= *Schlaffheit*) (*von Bewegungen*) feebleness; (*von Händedruck*) limpness

La|ser [ˈleːzɐ] M -s, - laser

La|ser- [ˈleːzɐ] in cpds laser; **La|ser|chi|rur|gie** F laser surgery; **La|ser|dru|cker** M (*Typ*) laser (printer); **La|ser|ka|no|ne** ▲ F laser gun

la|sern [ˈleːzɐn] VTI (*Med*) to treat with laser

La|ser-: La|ser|pis|to|le F laser gun; (*bei Geschwindigkeitskontrollen*) radar gun; **La|ser|strahl** M laser beam; **La|ser|tech|nik** F , no pl laser technology; **La|ser|waf|fe** ▲ F laser weapon

la|sie|ren [laˈziːrən] ptp **lasiert** VT *Bild, Holz* to varnish; *Glas* to glaze

Las|sa|fie|ber [ˈlasa-] NT , no pl Lassa fever

---

las|sen [ˈlasn]
pret **ließ** [liːs], *ptp* **gelassen** [gəˈlasn]

1 MODALVERB	3 INTRANSITIVES VERB
2 TRANSITIVES VERB	4 REFLEXIVES VERB

1 – MODALVERB ptp lassen

Die Übersetzung hängt oft vom Vollverb ab, siehe auch dort.

a = **veranlassen etw tun lassen** to have or get sth done; **ich muss mich mal untersuchen lassen** I'll have to have a checkup; **sich** (*dat*) **einen Zahn ziehen lassen** to have a tooth out; **jdm mitteilen lassen, dass ...** to let sb know that ...; **jdn etw wissen lassen** to let sb know sth; **jdm ausrichten lassen, dass ...** to leave a message for sb that ...; **er lässt Ihnen mitteilen, dass ...** he wants or wishes (*form*) you to know that ...; **jdn rufen** or **kommen lassen** to send for sb; **sich** (*dat*) **etw kommen lassen** to have sth delivered; **eine Versammlung einberufen lassen** to have a meeting called; **mein Vater wollte mich studieren lassen** my father wanted me to study; **Goethe lässt Faust sagen ...** Goethe has Faust say ...

b = **zulassen**

Bei absichtlichen Handlungen wird **lassen** mit **to let** übersetzt, bei versehentlichen Handlungen mit **to leave**.

die Bohnen fünf Minuten kochen lassen let the beans boil for five minutes; **Wasser in die Badewanne laufen lassen** to run water into the bath; **sich** (*dat*) **einen Bart/die Haare wachsen lassen** to grow a beard/one's hair, to let one's beard/hair grow; **warum hast du das Licht brennen lassen?** why did you leave the light on?; **hast du den Motor absichtlich laufen lassen?** have you left the engine running on purpose?; **jdn warten lassen** to keep sb waiting; **den Tee ziehen lassen** to let the tea draw (*Brit*) or steep (*US*); **etw kochen lassen** to bring sth to the boil

c = **erlauben** to let, to allow; **er hat mich nicht ausreden lassen** he didn't allow me to finish speaking, he didn't let me finish speaking; **jdn etw sehen/hören lassen** to let sb see/hear sth; **er hat sich überreden lassen** he let himself be persuaded, he allowed himself to be persuaded; **er hat sich nicht überreden lassen** he couldn't be persuaded; **ich lasse mich nicht belügen/zwingen** I won't be lied to/coerced; **ich lasse gern mit mir handeln** I'm quite willing to

---

negotiate; **lass mich machen!** let me do it!; **lass das sein!** don't (do it)!; (= *hör auf*) stop it!; **lass doch die Arbeit Arbeit sein** forget about work (*inf*)

d = Möglichkeit bieten **das Fenster lässt sich leicht öffnen** the window opens easily; **das Fenster lässt sich nicht öffnen** (*grundsätzlich nicht*) the window doesn't open; (*momentan nicht*) the window won't open; **das Wort lässt sich schwer/nicht übersetzen** the word is hard to translate/can't be translated *or* is untranslatable; **das lässt sich machen** that's possible, that can be done; **es lässt sich essen/trinken** it's edible/drinkable; **hier lässt es sich bequem sitzen** it's nice sitting here; **das lässt sich zehn Jahre später nicht mehr feststellen** ten years on this can no longer be established, ten years on it is too late to establish this; **das lässt sich nicht mehr ändern** it's too late to do anything about it now; **daraus lässt sich schließen** *or* **folgern, dass ...** one can conclude from this that ...

e im Imperativ **lass uns gehen!** let's go!; **lass uns all das vergessen!** let's forget all this!; **lass es dir gut gehen!** take care of yourself!; **lass dir das gesagt sein!** let me tell you this!; **lass ihn nur kommen!** just let him show his face!, just let him come!; **lasset uns beten** let us pray; **lasset die Kindlein zu mir kommen** (*Bibl*) suffer the little children to come unto me (*Bibl*)

2 – TRANSITIVES VERB

a = unterlassen to stop; (= *momentan aufhören*) to leave; **das lassen wir fürs erste** let's leave this for the moment; **lass das!** don't do it!; (= *hör auf*) stop that!; **lass das Jammern** stop your moaning; **lass diese Bemerkungen!** that's enough of that kind of remark!; **lassen wir das!** let's leave it!; **er kann das Rauchen/Trinken nicht lassen** he can't stop smoking/drinking; **tu was du nicht lassen kannst!** if you must, you must!

♦ **es lassen er kann es nicht lassen!** he will keep on doing it!; **er hat es versucht, aber er kann es nicht lassen** he's tried, but he can't help it *or* himself; **dann lassen wir eben** let's drop the whole idea; **ich will aber nicht! – dann lassen wir es eben** but I don't want to! – let's not bother then; **wenn du nicht willst, dann lass es doch** if you don't want to, then don't; **ich habe es dann doch gelassen** in the end I didn't

b = zurücklassen, loslassen to leave; **jdn allein lassen** to leave sb alone; **er hat dort viel Geld gelassen** he left with his pockets a lot lighter; **lass mich (los)!** let me go!; **lass mich (in Ruhe)!** leave me alone!

c = überlassen **jdm etw lassen** to let sb have sth; (= *behalten lassen*) to let sb keep sth; **Peter will mir meinen Ball nicht lassen** (= *nicht geben*) Peter won't let go of my ball; **lass ihr schon den Ball, sonst weint sie wieder** let her keep the ball otherwise she'll start crying again; **das muss man ihr lassen** (= *zugestehen*) you've got to give *or* grant her that

d = hineinlassen, hinauslassen to let (*in +acc* into, *aus* out of); **er ließ mich nicht aus dem Haus** he wouldn't let me out of the house; **Wasser in die Badewanne lassen** to run water into the bath; **lass bloß den Hund nicht auf das Sofa!** don't let the dog get on the sofa!; **einen (Furz) lassen** (*inf*) to let off (*inf*)

e = belassen to leave; **etw lassen, wie es ist** to leave sth (just) as it is; **etw ungesagt/ungetan lassen** (*geh*) to leave sth unsaid/undone

3 – INTRANSITIVES VERB

♦ **von jdm/etw lassen** (= *ablassen*) to give sb/ sth up; **sie konnte vom Gin nicht lassen** she couldn't give up the gin (*inf*); **wir wollen von unserem Anspruch nicht lassen** we're determined not to give up our claim

♦ **lass mal lass mal,** ich mach das schon leave it, I'll do it; **lass mal,** ich zahle das schon no, that's all right, I'll pay

+ separable verbs

4 – REFLEXIVES VERB

♦ **sich lassen sich vor Freude nicht zu lassen wissen** *or* **nicht lassen können** to be beside oneself with joy

läs|sig ['lɛsɪç] **ADJ** (= *ungezwungen*) casual; (= *nachlässig*) careless; (*inf*: = *gekonnt*) cool **ADV** (= *ungezwungen*) casually; (= *nachlässig*) carelessly; (*inf*: = *leicht*) easily; **die heutigen Kinder bedienen den Computer ganz ~** using a computer seems to come naturally to today's children; **das hat er ganz ~ hingekriegt** pretty cool, the way he did that (*inf*)

Läs|sig|keit F -, *no pl* (= *Ungezwungenheit*) casualness; (= *Nachlässigkeit*) carelessness; (*inf*: = *Gekonntheit*) coolness (*inf*)

läss|lich ▲ ['lɛslɪç] ADJ (*Eccl*) *Sünde* venial, pardonable

Läss|lich|keit ▲ F -, -en (= *Fehlverhalten*) misdemeanour (*Brit*), misdemeanor (*US*)

Las|so ['laso] M OR NT -s, -s lasso

lässt [lɛst] 3. *pers sing pres von* **lassen**

Last [last] F -, -en a load; (= *Traglast*) load, burden; (*lit, fig*: = *Gewicht*) weight; **Aufzug nur für ~en** goods lift *or* hoist; **des Lebens ~ und Mühe** (*liter*) the trials and tribulations of life b (*fig*: = *Bürde*) burden; **eine ~ für jdn sein** to be a burden on sb; **jdm zur ~ fallen/werden** to be/become a burden on sb; **die ~ der Verantwortung** the burden of responsibility; **die ~ des Amtes** the weight of office; **sich** (*dat*) **selbst eine ~ sein** to be a burden to oneself; **damit war uns eine schwere ~ vom Herzen** *or* **von der Seele genommen** that took a load off our minds; **jdm eine ~ abnehmen** to take a load off sb's shoulders; **jdm etw zur ~ legen** to accuse sb of sth; **der neuerliche Überfall geht zulasten** *or* **zu ~en der Rebellen** the rebels are being held responsible for the recent attack; **das geht zulasten** *or* **zu ~en der Sicherheit im Lande** that is detrimental to national security c **Lasten** PL (= *Kosten*) costs; (*des Steuerzahlers*) charges; **soziale ~en** welfare costs *or* charges; **die steuerlichen ~en für die kleinen Unternehmen** the tax burden for small concerns; **zu jds ~en gehen** to be chargeable to sb

Last-: Last|arm M (*Phys*) load arm; **Last|au|to** NT van, truck

las|ten ['lastn] VI to weigh heavily (*auf +dat* on); **eine schwere Sorge hat auf ihr gelastet** a terrible worry weighed her down; **eine lähmende Schwüle lastete über der Stadt** (*geh*) an oppressive heat hung heavily over the town; **auf dem Haus lastet noch eine Hypothek** the house is still encumbered (with a mortgage) (*form*); **auf ihm lastet die ganze Verantwortung** all the responsibility rests on him; **auf ihm lastet die ganze Arbeit** all the work falls on him

Las|ten-: Las|ten|auf|zug M hoist, goods lift (*Brit*) *or* elevator (*US*); **Las|ten|aus|gleich** M *system of financial compensation for losses suffered in the Second World War*

las|tend ADJ (*geh*) *Stille, Schwüle* oppressive

Las|ten-: las|ten|frei ADJ *Grundstück* unencumbered; **Las|ten|ta|xi** NT *van plus driver to rent*

Las|ter¹ ['lastɐ] M -s, - (*inf*: = *Lastwagen*) lorry (*Brit*), truck

Las|ter² NT -s, - (= *Untugend*) vice → **Müßiggang**

Läs|te|rei [lɛstə'raɪ] F -, -en (*inf*) a *no pl* (= *das Lästern*) running down (*über +acc* of), nasty comments *pl* b (= *Lästerwort*) nasty remark

Läs|te|rer ['lɛstərɐ] M -s, -, **Läs|te|rin** [-ərɪn] F -, -nen a (= *jd, der lästert*) to have a vicious tongue (in one's head) b (= *Gotteslästerer*) blasphemer

las|ter|haft ['lastɐhaft] ADJ depraved ADV ~ **leben** to lead a depraved life *or* a life of depravity

Las|ter|haf|tig|keit ['lastɐhaftɪçkaɪt] F - depravity

Las|ter|höh|le F den of vice *or* iniquity

Läs|te|rin F -, -nen → **Lästerer**

Las|ter|le|ben NT (*old, iro*) life of sin and depravity

läs|ter|lich ['lɛstɐlɪç] ADJ malicious; (= *gotteslästerlich*) blasphemous; **~e Bemerkung** gibe (*über +acc* at)

Läs|ter|maul NT (*inf*) = **Lästerer** a

läs|tern ['lɛstɐn] VI to bitch (*inf*); **über jdn/etw ~** to bitch about sb/sth (*inf*), to run sb/sth down; **wir haben gerade über dich gelästert** (*hum*) we were just talking about you, we were just taking your name in vain (*hum*) VT *Gott* to blaspheme against, to curse

Läs|ter-: Läs|ter|wort NT *pl* -worte a gibe b (*gegen Gott*) blasphemy; **~e** blasphemous words; **Läs|ter|zun|ge** F vicious tongue

Last|esel M pack mule

Las|tex® ['lastɛks] NT -, *no pl* stretch fabric

Las|tex-® *in cpds* stretch; **Las|tex|ho|se** F stretch fabric trousers *pl* (*Brit*), stretch pants *pl*

Last-: Last|fahr|zeug NT goods vehicle; **Last|fuh|re** F **mit dem Mietwagen dürfen keine ~n unternommen werden** the hired car is not to be used for the carriage of goods

läs|tig ['lɛstɪç] ADJ tiresome; (= *ärgerlich auch*) annoying, irksome, aggravating; *Husten, Kopfschuppen etc* troublesome; **wie ~!** what a nuisance!; **jdm ~ sein** to bother sb; **der Regenschirm ist mir ~** the umbrella is a nuisance to me; **dieser Verband ist mir ~** this bandage is bothering me; **jdm ~ fallen** to be a nuisance to sb; **jdm ~ werden** to become a nuisance (to sb); (= *zum Ärgernis werden*) to get annoying (to sb); **etw als ~ empfinden** to think sth is annoying *or* a pain (*inf*)

Last-: Last|kahn M barge; **Last|kraft|wa|gen** M (*form*) heavy goods vehicle

Last-Minute- [laːstˈmɪnɪt-]: **Last-Mi|nute-Flug** M late availability flight (*Brit*), standby flight; **Last-Mi|nute-Rei|se** F late availability holiday (*esp Brit*) *or* vacation (*US*); **Last-Mi|nute-Ti|cket** NT standby ticket

Last-: Last|schiff NT freighter, cargo ship; **Last|schrift** F debit; (*Eintrag*) debit entry; **Last|tier** NT beast of burden, pack animal; **Last|trä|ger(in)** M(F) carrier, porter; **Last|wa|gen** M lorry (*Brit*), truck; **Last|wa|gen|fah|rer(in)** M(F) lorry (*Brit*) *or* truck driver; **Last|zug** M truck-trailer (*US*), juggernaut (*Brit inf*)

La|sur [laˈzuːɐ] F -, -en (*auf Holz, Bild*) varnish; (*auf Glas, Email*) glaze

La|sur|stein M lapis lazuli

las|ziv [lasˈtsiːf] (*geh*) ADJ lascivious ADV lasciviously

Las|zi|vi|tät [lastsiviˈtɛːt] F -, *no pl* (*geh*) lasciviousness

Lä|ta|re [lɛˈtaːrə] *no art* (*Eccl*) Laetare Sunday, 3rd Sunday before Easter

La|tein [laˈtaɪn] NT -s Latin; **mit seinem ~ am Ende sein** to be stumped (*inf*)

Latein-: La|tein|ame|ri|ka NT Latin America; **La|tein|ame|ri|ka|ner(in)** M(F) Latin American; **la|tein|ame|ri|ka|nisch** ADJ Latin-American

La|tei|ner [laˈtaɪnɐ] M -s, -, **La|tei|ne|rin** [-ərɪn] F -, -nen Latin scholar; (*Sch*) Latin pupil

la|tei|nisch [laˈtaɪnɪʃ] ADJ Latin

La|tein|schu|le F (*Hist*) grammar school

la|tent [laˈtɛnt] ADJ latent; *Selbstmörder* potential ADV latently; **~ vorhanden sein** to be latent

La|tenz [laˈtɛnts] F -, *no pl* latency

La|tenz-: La|tenz|pe|ri|o|de F latency period; **La|tenz|zeit** F latent period

la|te|ral [lateˈraːl] ADJ (*Sci*) lateral

La|ter|na ma|gi|ca [laˈtɛrna ˈmaːgika] F -, La|ter|nae magicae [laˈtɛrnɛ ˈmaːgitsɛ] magic lantern

La|ter|ne [laˈtɛrnə] F -, -n (= *Leuchte, Archit*) lantern; (= *Straßenlaterne*) streetlight, streetlamp

La|ter|nen-: La|ter|nen|licht NT light of the street lamp(s); **La|ter|nen|par|ker(in)** M(F) (inf) kerbside (Brit) or curbside (US) parker; **La|ter|nen|pfahl** M lamppost

La|tex ['la:tɛks] M -, **Latizes** [la'titse:s] latex

La|ti|fun|di|um [lati'fʊndiʊm] NT -s, **Latifundien** [-diən] usu pl latifundium

la|ti|ni|sie|ren [latini'zi:rən] ptp **latinisiert** VT to latinize

La|ti|nist [lati'nɪst] M -en, -en, **La|ti|nis|tin** [-'nɪstɪn] F -, -nen Latinist, Latin scholar

La|ti|no [la'ti:no] M -s, -s Latino (esp US)

La|ti|num [la'ti:nʊm] NT -s, no pl **kleines/großes ~** ≈ Latin O-level/A-level (exam) (Brit), basic/advanced Latin exam

La|ti|um ['la:tsiʊm] NT -s Latium

La|tri|ne [la'tri:nə] F -, -n latrine

Lat|sche ['la:tʃə] F -, -n (Bot) mountain pine

lat|schen ['la:tʃn] VI aux sein (inf) to wander; (durch die Stadt etc) to traipse; (schlurfend) to slouch along → **Bremse**[1]

Lat|schen ['la:tʃn] M -s, - (inf) (= Hausschuh) slipper; (pej: = Schuh) worn-out shoe

Lat|schen|kie|fer F mountain pine

lat|schig ['la:tʃɪç] (inf) ADJ slovenly, sloppy (inf) ADV slovenly, sloppily (inf)

Lat|te ['latə] F -, -n a (= schmales Brett) slat b (Sport) bar; (Ftbl) cross)bar c (inf: = Liste) string (ganze) **~ von Wünschen/Vorstrafen** a whole string of things that he etc wants/of previous convictions → **lang** ADJ b d (sl) **eine ~ haben** to have a hard-on (sl)

Lat|ten-: Lat|ten|holz NT lath wood; **Lat|ten|kis|te** F crate; **Lat|ten|kreuz** NT corner of the goalpost; **Lat|ten|rost** M duckboards pl, lath floor; (in Bett) slatted frame; **Lat|ten|schuss** ▲ M (Ftbl) shot against the bar; **nach dem ~ von Matthäus** after Matthäus hit the crossbar; **Lat|ten|ver|schlag** M crate; (abgeteilte Fläche) enclosure; (für Hühner etc) run; **Lat|ten|zaun** M wooden fence, paling

Lat|tich ['latɪç] M -s, -e (Bot) lettuce

La|tüch|te [la'tʏçtə] F -, -n (hum) = Laterne

Latz [lats] M -es, ~e ['lɛtsə] or (Aus) -e (bei Kleidung = Lätzchen) bib; (= Hosenlatz) (front) flap; **jdm eins vor den ~ knallen** (inf) or **ballern** (inf) to sock sb one (inf)

Lätz|chen ['lɛtsçən] NT -s, - bib

Latz|ho|se F (pair of) dungarees pl (Brit) or overalls pl (US)

lau [lau] ADJ a (= mild) Wind, Abend mild b (= lauwarm) Flüssigkeit tepid, lukewarm; (fig) Freundschaft, Begeisterung, Haltung lukewarm, half-hearted ADV a (= mild) wehen gently b (fig) empfangen, behandeln half-heartedly

Laub [laup] NT -(e)s [-bəs] no pl leaves pl; (von Bäumen etc auch) foliage; **~ tragend** deciduous

Laub-: Laub|baum M deciduous tree; **Laub|blatt** NT (fallen) leaf; **Laub|dach** NT leafy canopy (liter)

Lau|be ['laubə] F -, -n a (= Gartenhäuschen) summerhouse b (= Gang) arbour (Brit), arbor (US), pergola; (= Arkade) arcade → **fertig a**

Lau|ben-: Lau|ben|gang M pl -gänge arbour (Brit), arbor (US), pergola; **Lau|ben|ko|lo|nie** F area of allotments (Brit) or garden plots; **Lau|ben|pie|per** [-pi:pɐ] M -s, -, **Lau|ben|pie|pe|rin** [-ərɪn] F -, -nen (dial) allotment gardener (Brit), plot gardener

Laub-: Laub|fall M **vor dem ~** before the leaves fall; **Laub|fär|bung** F colouring (Brit) or coloring (US) of the leaves; **Laub|frosch** M (European) tree frog; **Laub|höl|zer** PL deciduous trees pl; **Laub|hüt|ten|fest** NT Feast of Tabernacles, Sukkoth; **Laub|kro|ne** F treetop; **Laub|sä|ge** F fret saw; **Laub|sä|ge|ar|beit** F fretwork; **laub|tra|gend** ADJ = **Laub** tragend; **Laub|wald** M deciduous wood or (größer) forest; **Laub|werk** NT foliage (auch Art)

Lauch [laux] M -(e)s, -e allium (form); (esp S Ger. = Porree) leek

Lauch|zwie|bel F spring onion (Brit), scallion (US)

Lau|da|tio [lau'da:tsio] F -, **Laudationes** [lauda-'tsio:ne:s] encomium, eulogy

Laue ['lauə] F -, -nen, **Lau|e|ne** ['lauənə] F -, -n (esp Sw) avalanche

Lau|er ['lauɐ] F -, no pl **auf der ~ sein** or **liegen** to lie in wait; **sich auf die ~ legen** to settle down to lie in wait

lau|ern ['lauɐn] VI (lit, fig) to lurk, to lie in wait (auf +acc for); (inf) to wait (auf +acc for); **ein ~der Blick** a furtive glance

Lauf [lauf] M -(e)s, **Läufe** ['lɔyfə] a (= schneller Schritt) run; (Sport: = Wettlauf, -fahrt) race; (= Durchgang) run, race, heat; **sein ~ wurde immer schneller** he ran faster and faster; **im ~ innehalten** to stop running for a moment b (= Verlauf) course; **im ~e der Jahre** in the course of the years, over or through the years; **im ~e der Zeit** in the course of time; **im ~e des Gesprächs** in the course of the conversation, during the conversation; **einer Entwicklung** (dat) **freien ~ lassen** to allow a development to take its (own) course; **seiner Fantasie freien ~ lassen** to give free rein to one's imagination; **sie ließ ihren Gefühlen freien ~** she gave way to her feelings; **seinen ~ nehmen** to take its course; **den Dingen ihren ~ lassen** to let matters or things take their course; **das ist der ~ der Dinge** or **der Welt** that's the way of the world, that's the way things go c (= Gang, Arbeit) running, operation; (Comput) run d (= Flusslauf, auch Astron) course; **der obere/untere ~ der Donau** the upper/lower reaches of the Danube e (= Gewehrlauf) barrel; **ein Tier vor den ~ bekommen** to get an animal in one's sights f (Hunt: = Bein) leg g (Mus) run

Lauf-: Lauf|bahn F career; **die ~ des Beamten einschlagen** to embark or enter on a career as a civil servant; **Lauf|band** [-bant] NT pl -bänder (= Förderband) conveyor belt; (in Flughafen etc) travelator (Brit), moving sidewalk (US); (= Sportgerät) treadmill; **Lauf|bur|sche** M errand boy, messenger boy

lau|fen ['laufn] pret **lief** [li:f], ptp **gelaufen** [gə'laufn] VI a (= rennen) to run; **lauf doch!** get a move on! (inf) b (inf) (= gehen) to go; (= seine Notdurft verrichten) to run (to the toilet) (inf); **er läuft dauernd ins Kino/auf die Polizei** he's always off to the cinema/always running to the police c (= zu Fuß gehen) to walk; **das Kind läuft schon** the child can already walk or is already walking; **das Laufen lernen** to learn to walk; **er läuft sehr unsicher** he's very unsteady on his feet; **es sind noch/nur 10 Minuten zu ~** it's another/only 10 minutes' walk d (= fließen) to run; (= schmelzen: Käse, Butter) to melt; **in Strömen ~** to stream or pour (in/out/down etc); **Wasser in einen Eimer/die Badewanne ~ lassen** to run water into a bucket/the bath; **das Bier muss ~** the beer must be kept flowing e (= undicht sein) Gefäß, Wasserhahn to leak; (Wunde) to weep; **seine Nase läuft, ihm läuft die Nase** his nose is running, he's got a runny nose f (= in Betrieb sein) to run, to go; (Uhr) to go; (Gerät, Maschine) (= eingeschaltet sein) to be on; (= funktionieren) to work; **wir haben jetzt drei neue Maschinen ~** (inf) we've got three new machines going (inf); **er hat vier Mädchen ~** (sl) he's got four girls out on the game (inf), he's got four girls hustling for him (inf) g (Comput) to run; **ein Programm ~ lassen** to run a program h (fig: = im Gange sein) Prozess, Verhandlung to go on, to be in progress; (Bewerbung, Antrag) to be

---

under consideration; (= gezeigt werden) (Film) to be on, to be showing; (Stück) to be on, to be playing; **der Film lief schon, als wir ankamen** the film had already started when we arrived; **der Film läuft über drei Stunden** the film goes on for three hours; **etw läuft gut/schlecht** sth is going well/badly; **die Sache/das Geschäft läuft jetzt** it/the shop is going well now; **sehen wie die Sache läuft** to see how things go; **alles/die Dinge ~ lassen** to let everything/things slide; **die Sache ist gelaufen** (inf) it's in the bag (inf), it's all wrapped up (inf); **jdm zeigen, wie es läuft** (inf) to show sb the ropes (inf) i (= gültig sein) Vertrag, Abkommen) to run; **der Kredit läuft über zwei Jahre** the loan is repayable over two years j (= bezeichnet werden) **das Auto läuft unter meinem Namen** or **auf meinen Namen** the car is in my name; **das Konto läuft unter der Nummer ...** the number of the account is ...; **der Agent läuft unter dem Decknamen „Spinne"** the agent goes by the cover name of "Spider"; **das läuft unter „Sonderausgaben"** that comes under "special expenses" k (= sich bewegen) to run; **auf eine Mine ~** to hit a mine; **auf Grund ~** to run aground; **in den Hafen ~** to enter port; **es lief mir eiskalt über den Rücken** a chill ran or went up my spine → **Geld a, Stapel c** l (= verlaufen) (Fluss etc) to run; (Weg) to go, to run

VT a aux haben or sein (Sport) Rekordzeit to run; Rekord to set; **Rennen ~** to run (in races); **Ski ~** to ski; **Schlittschuh ~** to skate; **Rollschuh ~** to roller-skate → **Gefahr b** b aux sein (= fahren: Auto etc) Strecke to do c aux sein (= zu Fuß gehen) to walk; (schnell) to run d **sich** (dat) **eine Blase ~** to give oneself a blister; **sich** (dat) **ein Loch in die Sohlen ~** to wear a hole in one's soles

VR **sich warm ~** to warm up; **sich müde ~** to tire oneself out; **in den Schuhen läuft es sich gut/schlecht** these shoes are good/bad for walking/running in; **zu zweit läuft es sich besser** it's better walking/running in twos

lau|fend ADJ attr (= ständig) Arbeiten, Ausgaben regular; Kredit outstanding; (= regelmäßig) Wartung routine; Monat, Jahr, Konto (form) current; **15 EUR der ~e Meter** EUR 15 per metre (Brit) or meter (US); **~e Nummer** serial number; (von Konto) number; **auf dem Laufenden bleiben/sein** to keep (oneself)/be in the picture or up-to-date or informed; **jdn auf dem Laufenden halten** to keep sb posted or up-to-date or informed; **mit etw auf dem Laufenden sein** to be up-to-date on sth → **Band**[1] ADV continually, constantly

lau|fen las|sen ▲ ptp **laufen lassen** or (rare) **laufen gelassen** VT irreg (inf) jdn **~** to let sb go

Läu|fer[1] ['lɔyfɐ] M -s, - a (Chess) bishop b (Teppich) rug; (= Treppenläufer, Tischläufer) runner c (Tech) (= Laufkatze) crab; (= Laufgewicht) sliding weight d (Build) stretcher e (= junges Schwein) young pig

Läu|fer[2] ['lɔyfɐ] M -s, -, **Läu|fe|rin** [-ərɪn] F -, -nen (Sport) runner; (= Hürdenläufer) hurdler; (Ftbl) halfback; (dated: = Laufbursche) messenger; **rechter/linker ~** (Ftbl) right/left half

Lau|fe|rei [laufə'rai] F -, -en (inf) running about no pl

Läu|fer|stan|ge F stair rod

Lauf-: lauf|fä|hig ADJ (Comput) das Programm **ist unter Windows ~** the program can be run under Windows; **lauf|faul** ADJ lazy; **das Kind ist ~** the child isn't keen on running; **er war während des Spiels ~** he didn't run around very much during the game; **Lauf|feu|er** NT **sich wie ein ~ verbreiten** to spread like wildfire; **Lauf|flä|che** F (von Reifen) tread; **lauf|freu|dig** ADJ Fußballer etc keen on running; (= wanderfreudig) keen on walking; **Lauf|ge|wicht** NT

---

sliding weight; Lauf|git|ter NT playpen; **Lauf|gra|ben** M approach trench

läu|fig ['lɔyfɪç] ADJ on (Brit) or in heat

Lauf-: Lauf|jun|ge M errand boy; **Lauf|kat|ze** F (Tech) crab; **Lauf|kran** M (overhead) travelling (Brit) or traveling (US) crane; **Lauf|kun|de** M , **Lauf|kun|din** F occasional customer; **Lauf|kund|schaft** F occasional customers pl; **Lauf|leis|tung** F (Mot, von Reifen, Fahrzeug) mileage; ~en von mehr als 500.000 km haben (Motor) to cover more than 300,000 miles (without overhaul); **Lauf|ma|sche** F ladder (Brit), run; ~n aufnehmen to mend ladders (Brit) or runs; **Lauf|pass** ▲ M jdm den ~ ge-ben (inf) to give sb his marching orders (inf); Freundin etc auch to chuck sb (inf); **Lauf|plan|ke** F (Naut) gangplank; **Lauf|rad** NT traversing wheel; (ohne Antrieb) trailing wheel; (in Turbine) rotor; **Lauf|rich|tung** F (Mech) direction of travel; **Lauf|rol|le** F roller; (unter Möbeln) castor; **Lauf|rost** M duckboards pl (Brit), lath floor; **lauf|ru|hig** ADJ Motor quiet; **Lauf-schritt** M trot; (Mil) double-quick, double time; **im ~** (Mil) at the double; **er näherte sich im ~** he came trotting up; **Lauf|schuh** M (inf) walking shoe; **Lauf|sport** M running; **Lauf-stall** M a playpen b (für Tiere) pen; **Lauf-stark** ADJ Sportler good at running pred; **er ist sehr ~** he's a strong runner; **Lauf|steg** M cat-walk

läuft [lɔyft] 3. pers sing pres von **laufen**

Lauf-: Lauf|werk NT running gear; (Comput) drive; **Lauf|zeit** F a (von Wechsel, Vertrag) term, period of validity; (von Kredit) period b (von Maschine = Lebensdauer) (operational) life; (= Betriebszeit) running time c (von Brief, Post-sendung) delivery time d (Comput: von Pro-gramm) run-time e (Sport) time f (Zool: = Brunstzeit) **während der ~** while on (Brit) or in heat; **Lauf|zet|tel** M (an Akten, Maschinen) docket

Lau|ge ['laugə] F -, -n (Chem) lye, leach; (= Sei-fenlauge) soapy water; (= Salzlauge) salt solution

Lau|gen|bre|zel F pretzel stick

Lau|heit F -, no pl (von Wind, Abend) mildness; (von Haltung) half-heartedness

Lau|ne ['launə] F -, -n a (= Stimmung) mood; (je) nach (Lust und) ~ just as the mood or fancy takes one; **gute/schlechte ~ haben, (bei or in) guter/schlechter ~ sein** to be in a good/bad mood or temper; **jdn bei guter ~ or bei ~** (inf) **halten** to keep sb happy or in a good mood; **was hat er für ~?** what sort of (a) mood is he in?; **seine ~ an jdm auslassen** to take one's temper out on sb; **~ machen** to be fun b (= Grille, Einfall) whim, caprice; **die ~n des Glücks** the vagaries of fortune; **eine ~ der Natur** a whim or caprice of nature; **etw aus einer ~ he-raus tun** to do sth on a whim

lau|nen|haft ADJ moody; (= unberechenbar) capricious; Wetter changeable ADV moodily; (= unberechenbar) capriciously

Lau|nen|haf|tig|keit ['launənhaftɪçkaɪt] F -, no pl moodiness; (= Unberechenbarkeit) capricious-ness; (von Wetter) changeability

lau|nig ['launɪç] (dated) ADJ witty ADV ~ ge-stimmt sein to be witty or in a witty mood; **eine ~ formulierte Rede** a witty speech

Lau|nig|keit F -, no pl wittiness

lau|nisch ['launɪʃ] ADJ, ADV = launenhaft

Lau|re|at [laure'aːt] M -en, -en, **Lau|re|a|tin** [-'aːtɪn] F -, -nen (geh) laureate

Laus [laus] F -, Läuse ['lɔyzə] louse; (= Blattlaus) greenfly, blackfly; **jdm/sich eine ~ in den Pelz setzen** (inf) to land sb/oneself in it (Brit inf), to let sb/oneself in for it (inf); **ihm ist (wohl) ei-ne ~ über die Leber gelaufen** or **gekrochen** (inf) something's eating at him (inf)

Laus|bub M (dated) rascal, scamp, scallywag; (= jungenhaftes Mädchen) tomboy

Laus|bu|ben|ge|sicht NT (dated) scampish or roguish face

Laus|bü|be|rei [lausbyːbə'rai] F -, -en (dated) devilry, prank(s pl)

laus|bü|bisch ['lausbyːbɪʃ] (dated) ADJ roguish, scampish, rascally; Mädchen tomboyish ADV sich ~ benehmen (Junge) to behave like a ras-cal; (Mädchen) to behave like a tomboy

Lausch|an|griff M bugging operation (gegen on)

lau|schen ['lauʃn] VI a (geh) to listen (+dat, auf +acc to) b (= heimlich zuhören) to eaves-drop

Läus|chen ['lɔysçən] NT -s, - dim von Laus

Lau|scher[1] ['lauʃɐ] M -s, - (Hunt: = Ohr) ear

Lau|scher[2] ['lauʃɐ] M -s, -, **Lau|sche|rin** [-ərɪn] F -, -nen eavesdropper; **der ~ an der Wand hört seine eigene Schand** (Prov) people who listen at doors never hear any good of themselves

lau|schig ['lauʃɪç] ADJ Plätzchen cosy (Brit), co-zy (US), snug; (im Freien) secluded

Lau|se-: Lau|se|ben|gel M (inf), **Lau|se|jun-ge** M (inf) blighter (Brit inf), little devil (inf); (wohlwollend) scamp, rascal; **lau|se|kalt** ADJ (inf) perishing (inf), freezing (cold); **Lau|se-käl|te** F (inf) freezing or perishing (inf) cold

lau|sen ['lauzn] VT to delouse; **jdn ~** (inf: = über-vorteilen) to fleece sb (inf); **ich glaub, mich laust der Affe!** (inf) well blow me down! (inf), well I'll be blowed! (Brit inf)

Lau|ser ['lauzɐ] M -s, - (S Ger: = Lausbub) rascal, scamp, scallywag

lau|sig ['lauzɪç] (inf) ADJ lousy (inf), awful; Kälte freezing, perishing ADV awfully; (vor Adjektiv auch) damn(ed) (inf), bloody (Brit inf)

Lau|sitz ['lauzɪts] F - die ~ Lusatia

laut[1] [laut] ADJ a (= nicht leise) loud b (= lärmend, voll Lärm) noisy; (= auffällig, auf-dringlich) Mensch loudmouthed; Farbe etc loud; **er wird immer gleich/wird niemals ~** he always/never gets obstreperous c (= hörbar) out loud pred, adv, aloud pred, adv; **~ werden** (= bekannt) to become known; **etw ~ werden lassen** to make sth known, to let sth be known d (Hunt: = windstill) still ADV loudly; **~er sprechen** to speak louder or more loudly, to speak up; **etw ~(er) stellen** to turn sth up (loud); **~ auflachen** to burst out laughing, to laugh out loud; **~ nachdenken** to think aloud; **etw ~ sagen** (lit) to say sth out loud; (fig) to shout sth from the rooftops, to tell sth to the whole world; **das kannst du aber ~ sagen** (fig inf) you can say that again

laut[2] PREP +gen or dat (geh) according to

Laut [laut] M -(e)s, -e sound; **heimatliche ~e** sounds of home; **wir hörten bayerische ~e** we heard Bavarian accents; **keinen ~ von sich** (dat) **geben** not to make a sound; **~ geben** (Hund) to give tongue; (fig inf) to give a shout

laut|bar ADJ ~ werden to become known

Laut|bil|dung F articulation

Lau|te ['lautə] F -, -n lute

lau|ten ['lautn] VI to be; (Rede, Argumentation) to go; (Schriftstück) to read, to go; (= sich belaufen) to amount (auf +acc to); **dieser Erlass lautet wörtlich ...** the exact text of this decree is ...; **auf den Namen ... ~** (Pass) to be in the name of ...; (Scheck) to be payable to ..., to be made out to ...; **die Anklage lautet auf Mord** the charge is (one of) murder

läu|ten ['lɔytn] VTI a (Glocke, Mensch) to ring; (Wecker) to go (off); **es hat geläutet** the bell rang or went; **es läutet zur Stunde** (Sch) the bell is ringing or going for the next lesson; **jdn zu Grabe ~** (liter) to sound sb's funeral knell, to toll the bells for sb's funeral; **(nach) jdm ~** to ring for sb ➤ **Sturm** b **er hat davon (etwas) ~ hören** he has heard something about it

Lau|te|nist [lautə'nɪst] M -en, -en, **Lau|te|nis-tin** [-'nɪstɪn] F -, -nen, **Lau|ten|spie|ler(in)** M(F) lute player, lutenist

lau|ter[1] ['lautɐ] ADJ inv (= nur) nothing but; **~ Unsinn/Freude** etc pure or sheer nonsense/joy etc; **das sind ~ Lügen** that's nothing but lies, that's all a pack of lies; **vor ~ Rauch/Autos kann man nichts sehen** you can't see anything for all the smoke/cars; **das sind ~ Idioten** they are nothing but idiots

lau|ter[2] ['lautɐ] a (liter. = rein) Gold, Wein pure b (geh: = aufrichtig) Mensch, Absichten honourable (Brit), honorable (US); Wahrheit honest; **~er Wettbewerb** fair competition

Lau|ter|keit F -, no pl (geh: = Aufrichtigkeit) in-tegrity

läu|tern ['lɔytɐn] VT (liter) to purify; (fig) to re-form

Läu|te|rung ['lɔytərʊŋ] F -, -en (liter) purifica-tion; (fig) reformation

Läu|te|werk NT (Rail) signal bell

Laut-: laut|ge|treu ADJ phonetic; **laut|hals** ['lauthals] ADV at the top of one's voice; **Laut-leh|re** F phonetics sing, phonology; **laut|lich** ['lautlɪç] ADJ ADV phonetically; **laut|los** ADJ silent; Schritt, Bewegung auch soundless, noiseless; Stille utter, complete ADV silently; fal-len, sich bewegen auch soundlessly, noiselessly; **laut|ma|lend** ADJ onomatopoeic; **Laut|ma-le|rei** F onomatopoeia; (Ausdruck auch) ono-matopoeic word; **laut|ma|le|risch** ADJ ono-matopoeic; **laut|schrift** F phonetics pl; (Sys-tem auch) phonetic alphabet or script

Laut|spre|cher M (loud)speaker; **über ~** over the loudspeaker(s)

Laut|spre|cher-: Laut|spre|cher|an|la|ge F öffentliche ~ public address or PA system, Tan-noy® (Brit); **Laut|spre|cher|box** F speaker; **Laut|spre|cher|durch|sa|ge** F announce-ment over the public address, PA announce-ment; **Laut|spre|cher|wa|gen** M loudspeaker car or (größer) van

Laut-: Laut|stand M (Ling) stage of develop-ment of the sound system; **laut|stark** ADJ loud; (Rad, TV etc) high-volume; Partei, Protest vociferous ADV loudly; protestieren auch vocifer-ously; **Laut|stär|ke** F a loudness; (von Protest etc) vociferousness b (Rad, TV etc) volume; **das Radio auf volle ~ einstellen** to turn the radio right up, to turn the radio up to full volume; **Laut|stär|ke|reg|ler** M (Rad, TV) volume control; **laut|treu** ADJ phonetic

Lau|tung ['lautʊŋ] F -, -en (geh) articulation

Laut-: Laut|ver|schie|bung F sound shift; **Laut|wan|del** M sound change

Läut|werk NT (Rail) signal bell

Laut|zei|chen NT phonetic symbol

lau|warm ADJ slightly warm; Flüssigkeit luke-warm; (fig) lukewarm, half-hearted ADV (fig) half-heartedly

La|va ['laːva] F -, Laven ['laːvn] lava

La|va|bo NT -(s), -s a [la'vaːbo] (Rel) lavabo b ['laːvabo] (Sw) washbasin, sink

Lava-: La|va|mas|se F mass of (molten) lava; **La|va|strom** M stream or flow of (molten) la-va

La|ven|del [la'vɛndl] M -s, - lavender

la|vie|ren[1] [la'viːrən] ptp laviert VI a (Naut) to tack b (fig) to manoeuvre (Brit), to maneuver (US)

la|vie|ren[2] ptp laviert VT (Art) to wash; **lavierte Zeichnung** wash drawing

La|voir [la'voaːʀ] NT -s, -s (old, Aus) washbasin, washbowl, sink

Law and or|der [lɔːˈəndˈɔːdə] no art law and order

Law-and-or|der- [lɔːˈəndˈɔːdə] in cpds law-and--order; **Law-and-or|der-Kurs** M law-and-or-der campaign; **Law-and-or|der-Pro|gramm** NT law-and-order policy

La|wi|ne [la'viːnə] F -, -n (lit, fig) avalanche

La|wi|nen-: la|wi|nen|ar|tig ADJ like an ava-lanche ADV like an avalanche; **~ anwachsen** to snowball; **La|wi|nen|ge|fahr** F danger of avalanches; **La|wi|nen|op|fer** NT avalanche victim; **La|wi|nen|schutz|wald** M barrier forest; **la|wi|nen|si|cher** ADJ Ort secure from avalanches ADV gebaut to withstand avalanches; **La|wi|nen|ver|bau|ung** [-fɛbauʊŋ] F -, -en avalanche barrier; **La|wi|nen|war|nung** F avalanche warning

Law|ren|ci|um [loˈrɛntsiʊm] NT -s, no pl (abbr **Lr**) lawrencium

lax [laks] ADJ lax ADV laxly

Lax|heit F -, no pl laxity, laxness

Lay-out ▲ [ˈleˑaut] NT -s, -s, **Lay|out** NT -s, -s layout

Lay|ou|ter [ˈleˑautɐ] M -s, -, **Lay|ou|te|rin** [-ərɪn] F -, -nen designer

La|za|rett [latsaˈrɛt] NT -(e)s, -e (Mil) (in Kaserne etc) sickbay; (selbstständiges Krankenhaus) hospital

La|za|rett-: La|za|rett|schiff NT hospital ship; **La|za|rett|zug** M hospital train

La|za|rus [ˈlaːtsarʊs] M -, -se (Bibl) Lazarus; **armer ~!** poor beggar (Brit) or devil!

LCD- [ɛltseˈdeː-] in cpds LCD; **LCD-An|zei|ge** F LCD display

Lead|sän|ger(in) [ˈliːd-] M(F) lead singer

lea|sen [ˈliːzn] VT (Comm) to lease

Lea|sing [ˈliːzɪŋ] NT -s, -s (Comm) leasing; **etw im ~ bekommen** to lease sth

Leasing- [ˈliːzɪŋ-]: **Lea|sing|ge|ber(in)** M(F) lessor; **Lea|sing|neh|mer(in)** M(F) lessee; **Lea|sing|ra|te** F leasing payment; **Lea|sing-Ver|trag** M lease

Le|be|da|me [ˈleːbə-] F courtesan

Le|be|hoch [leːbəˈhoːx] NT -(s), -(s) ≈ three cheers; **~ rufen** ≈ to give three cheers; **ein (drei|faches) ~ auf jdn ausbringen** ≈ to give sb three cheers

Le|be|mann [ˈleːbə-] M pl **-männer** roué, rake, playboy

le|ben [ˈleːbn] VI to live; (= am Leben sein) to be alive; (= weiterleben) to live on; **er lebt noch** he is still alive; **er lebt nicht mehr** he is no longer alive; **er hat nicht lange gelebt** he didn't live (for) long; **ich möchte nicht mehr ~** I don't want to go on living; **er wird nicht mehr lange zu ~ haben** he won't have much longer; **von etw ~** to live on sth; **es lebe** or **lang lebe der König!** long live the King!; **so wahr ich lebe!** (obs) 'pon my life! (obs); **wie geht es dir?** – **man lebt (so)** (inf) how are you? – surviving; **lebst du noch?** (hum inf) are you still in the land of the living? (hum); **genug zu ~ haben** to have enough to live on; **~ und ~ lassen** to live and let live; **so was lebt, und Schiller musste sterben!** (hum inf) some mothers do have 'em (inf), it's a sad case (inf); **zum Leben zu wenig, zum Sterben zu viel**, **davon kann man nicht ~ und nicht sterben** it's barely enough to keep body and soul together; **man lebt nur einmal!** you only live once; **einsam/christlich/gesund ~** to live or lead a lonely/Christian/healthy life; **allein/glücklich ~** to live alone/happily; **ganz für sich ~** to live a secluded life; **für etw ~**, **einer Sache (dat) ~** (geh) to live for sth; **leb(e) wohl!** (liter) farewell! (liter); **hier lebt es sich gut, hier lässt es sich (gut) ~** it's a good life here; **mit etw (gut) ~ können** to be able to live with sth → **hoch 2 g**

VT to live; **jeder muss sein eigenes Leben ~** we've all got our own lives to live or lead

Le|ben [ˈleːbn] NT -s, - a life; **das ~** life; **das ~ des Menschen/der Tiere** etc the life of man/animals etc; **am ~ sein/bleiben** to be/stay alive; **das ~ als Milchmann** life as a milkman, a milkman's life; **das ~ Hemingways** Hemingway's life, the life of Hemingway; **das ~ vor/hinter sich (dat) haben** to have one's life ahead of or in front of or before/behind one; **solange ich am ~ bin** as long as I live; **sich des ~s freuen, das** or **sein ~ genießen** to enjoy life; **das** or **sein ~ verlieren** to lose one's life; **jdm das ~ retten** to

save sb's life; **es geht um ~ und Tod, es ist eine Sache auf ~ und Tod** it's a matter of life and death; **wenn dir dein ~ lieb ist** if you value your life; **ein glückliches** etc **~ führen** to lead a happy etc life; **mit dem ~ davonkommen** to escape with one's life; **mit dem ~ spielen, sein ~ aufs Spiel setzen** to take one's life in one's hands, to dice with death; **mit dem ~ abschließen** to prepare for death; **seinem ~ ein Ende machen** or **bereiten** to put an end to one's life; **einer Sache (dat) zu neuem ~ verhelfen** to breathe new life into sth, to revitalize sth; **etw ins ~ rufen** to bring sth into being; **jdn vom ~ zum Tode bringen** (form) or **befördern** (inf) to kill sb, to take sb's life, to take care of sb (inf) (bei Hinrichtung auch) to put sb to death; **seines ~s nicht mehr sicher sein** to fear for one's life; **ums ~ kommen** to die, to lose one's life; **sein ~ lassen (müssen)** to lose one's life; **jdn am ~ lassen** to spare sb's life; **um sein ~ laufen** or **rennen** to run for one's life or for dear life; **sich (dat) das ~ nehmen** to take one's (own) life; **jdn wieder ins ~ zurückrufen** to bring sb back to life; **Bewusstlosen zu neuem ~ verhelfen** (Brit) or **around** (US); **was ist das für ein ~?** what kind of (a) life is that?; **der Mann/die Frau meines ~s** my ideal man/woman; **etw für sein ~ gern tun** to love doing sth, to be mad about doing sth (inf); **etw für sein ~ gern essen/trinken** to be mad about sth (inf), to love sth; **jdn künstlich am ~ erhalten** to keep sb alive artificially; **ein ~ in Frieden/in Armut** etc a life of peace/poverty etc; **er hat es nie leicht gehabt im ~** he has never had an easy life; **ein ~ lang** one's whole life (long); **zum ersten Mal** or **das erste Mal im ~** for the first time in one's life; **ich habe noch nie im** or **in meinem ~ geraucht** I have never smoked (in) all my life or in my whole life; **nie im ~!** never!; **sich durchs ~ schlagen** to struggle through (life); **ins ~ treten** to go out into the world; **im ~ stehen** to have some standing in the world; (= nicht weltfremd sein) to know what life is all about; (draußen) **im ~ ist das ganz anders** in real life it's very different; **ein Roman, den das ~ schrieb** a novel of real life; **ein Film nach dem ~** a film from real life; **das ~ geht weiter** life goes on; **unser ~ währet siebenzig Jahr ...** (Bibl) the days of our years are three score years and ten (Bibl); **so ist das ~ (eben)** that's life, such is life, that's the way the cookie crumbles (inf)

b (= Betriebsamkeit) life; **auf dem Markt herrscht reges ~** the market is a hive of activity; **in dieser Stadt ist wenigstens ~** at least there is some life in this town; **jdn** or **etw (acc) bringen** (inf) to liven or brighten sth up; **voller ~ stecken** to be full of life; **es war überhaupt kein ~ in seinem Vortrag** there wasn't a spark of life in his lecture → **Bude c**

le|bend ADJ live attr, alive pred; Wesen, Seele, Beispiel, Sprache living; **„Vorsicht, ~e Tiere"** "attention or with care, live animals"; **ein noch ~er Zeuge** a witness who is still alive or living today; **~es Inventar** livestock; **die Lebenden** the living; **~es Bild** tableau ADV alive; **ein Tier ~ fangen** to catch an animal alive; **~ gebärend** viviparous, live-bearing

Le|bend-: le|bend|ge|bä|rend △ ADJ → **lebend** ADV, **Le|bend|ge|burt** F live birth; **Le|bend|ge|wicht** NT live weight; (von Rindern auch) weight on the hoof

le|ben|dig [leˈbɛndɪç] ADJ a (= nicht tot) live attr, alive pred; Wesen living; **~e Junge** live young; **~e Junge gebären** to bear one's young live; **die Lebendigen und die Toten** (Bibl) the Quick and the Dead (Bibl); **jdn bei ~em Leibe verbrennen, jdn ~en Leibes verbrennen** (liter) to burn sb alive; **wieder ~ werden** to come back to life; **er nimmts von den Lebendigen** (hum inf) he'll have the shirt off your back (inf), it's daylight robbery (Brit) or highway robbery what he charges (inf)

b (fig: = lebhaft) lively no adv; Darstellung, Bild, Erinnerung lively, vivid; Glaube fervent

ADV a (= lebend) alive; **er ist dort ~ begraben** (fig inf) it's a living death for him there

b (fig: = lebhaft) vividly

Le|ben|dig|keit F -, no pl (fig: = Lebhaftigkeit) liveliness; (von Darstellung, Bild, Erinnerung auch) vividness

Le|bend|spen|der(in) M(F) (Med) living donor

Lebens-: Le|bens|abend M old age, autumn (Brit) or twilight of one's life (liter); **Le|bens|ab|schnitt** M phase in or of one's life; **Le|bens|ab|schnitts|part|ner(in)** M(F) (inf, usu hum) companion for a while; **ihr aktueller ~** her present companion or cohabitee; **Le|bens|ader** F (fig) lifeline; **Le|bens|al|ter** NT age; **ein hohes ~ erreichen** to have a long life; (Mensch auch) to reach a ripe old age (inf); **Le|bens|angst** F angst; **Le|bens|an|schau|ung** F philosophy of life; **Le|bens|ar|beits|zeit** F working life; **Le|bens|ar|beits|zeit|ver|kür|zung** F shortening of one's working life; **Le|bens|art** F , no pl a (= Lebensweise) way of life
b (= Manieren) manners pl; (= Stil) style, savoir-vivre; **eine feine ~ haben** to have exquisite manners/style; **eine kultivierte ~ haben** to be cultivated; **Le|bens|auf|fas|sung** F attitude to life; **Le|bens|auf|ga|be** F life's work; **Le|bens|äu|ße|rung** F sign of life; **Le|bens|baum** M (Bot) arbor vitae; (fig, Art) tree of life; **Le|bens|be|din|gun|gen** PL living conditions pl; **le|bens|be|dro|hend, le|bens|be|droh|lich** ADJ life-threatening ADV krank, verletzt critically; **Le|bens|be|ja|hend** ADJ positive; **eine ~e Einstellung** a positive approach to life; **Le|bens|be|ja|hung** F positive attitude to life; **Le|bens|be|rech|ti|gung** F right to exist; (von Menschen, Tieren auch) right to live; **Le|bens|be|reich** M area of life; **Le|bens|be|schrei|bung** F biography; **Le|bens|bild** NT (fig) picture of sb's life; **Le|bens|dau|er** F life (-span); (von Maschine) life; **le|bens|echt** ADJ true-to-life ADV realistically, authentically; **Le|bens|ein|stel|lung** F attitude or approach to life; **Le|bens|eli|xier** NT elixir of life; **Le|bens|en|de** NT end (of sb's/one's life); **sie lebte bis an ihr ~ in Armut** she lived in poverty till the day she died; **Le|bens|ener|gie** F , no pl vitality; **Le|bens|ent|wurf** M life plan; **Le|bens|er|fah|rung** F experience of life; **le|bens|er|hal|tend** ADJ life-preserving; Geräte life-support attr; **Le|bens|er|hal|tungs|sys|tem** NT life-support system; **Le|bens|er|in|ne|run|gen** PL memoirs pl; **Le|bens|er|war|tung** F life expectancy; **le|bens|fä|hig** ADJ (Med) capable of life or of living, viable; (fig) capable of surviving, viable; **Le|bens|fä|hig|keit** F (Med, fig) viability; **Le|bens|form** F (Biol) life form; (Psych, Philos) form of life, type of man; (= Form menschlichen Zusammenlebens) way of life; **Le|bens|fra|ge** F vital matter; **le|bens|fremd** ADJ remote from life, out of touch with life; **Le|bens|freu|de** F joie de vivre, zest for life; **le|bens|freu|dig** ADJ **~ sein** to enjoy life; **le|bens|froh** ADJ merry, full of the joys of life; **Le|bens|füh|rung** F lifestyle; **Le|bens|ge|fahr** F (mortal) danger; **„Lebensgefahr!"** "danger!"; **es besteht (akute) ~** there is danger (to life); **er ist** or **schwebt in (akuter) ~** his life is in danger, he is in danger of his life; (Patient) he is in a critical condition; **außer ~ sein** to be out of danger; **etw unter ~ (dat) tun** to risk one's life doing sth; **der Film wurde unter ~ gedreht** the film was made at great personal risk to the crew; **le|bens|ge|fähr|lich** ADJ highly dangerous; Krankheit, Verletzung critical ADV verletzt critically; (inf) glatt, schnell dangerously; **Le|bens|ge|fähr|te** M , **Le|bens|ge|fähr|tin** F partner; **Le|bens|ge|fühl** NT , no pl awareness of life, feeling of being alive; **ein ganz neues ~ haben** to feel (like) a different person; (= neuen Auftrieb bekommen) to have a new lease of life (Brit) or on life; **Le|bens|geis|ter** PL (hum inf) **jds/seine ~ auffrischen** or **wecken** to pep sb/oneself up (inf), to put some life into

sb/oneself; **Le|bens|ge|mein|schaft** F long-term relationship; (*Biol, Zool*) symbiosis; **Le|bens|ge|nuss** ▲ M enjoyment of life; **Le|bens|ge|schich|te** F life story, life history; **Le|bens|ge|wohn|heit** F habit; **Le|bens|glück** NT happiness; **le|bens|groß** ADJ, ADV life-size; **Le|bens|grö|ße** F life-size; **eine Figur in** ~ a life-size figure; **etw in** ~ **malen** to paint sth life-size; **da stand er in voller** ~ (*hum*) there he was (as) large as life (and twice as ugly) (*inf*); **er erhob sich zu seiner vollen** ~ (*hum*) he drew himself up to his full height; **Le|bens|grund|la|ge** F (basis for one's livelihood)

Le|bens|hal|tung F **a** (= *Unterhaltskosten*) cost of living **b** (= *Lebensführung*) lifestyle

Le|bens|hal|tungs-: **Le|bens|hal|tungs|in|dex** M cost-of-living index; **Le|bens|hal|tungs|kos|ten** PL cost of living *sing*

Le|bens-: **Le|bens|hauch** M (*liter*) breath of life; **Le|bens|hil|fe** F counselling (*Brit*), counseling (*US*); **er missversteht Literatur als** ~ he makes the mistake of thinking that literature can help him with the problems of life; **Le|bens|hun|ger** M thirst for life; **le|bens|hun|grig** ADJ eager or thirsty for life; **Le|bens|in|halt** M purpose in life, raison d'être; **etw zu seinem** ~ **machen** to devote oneself to sth, to make sth one's mission in life; **das ist sein gan-zer** ~ his whole life revolves (a)round it, it's the be-all and end-all of his existence; **Le|bens|jahr** NT year of (one's) life; **in seinem fünften** ~ in the fifth year of his life; **nach Voll-endung des 18. ~es** on attaining the age of 18; **Le|bens|ka|me|rad(in)** M(F) longtime companion; **Le|bens|kampf** M struggle for life or existence; **le|bens|klug** ADJ experienced; **Le|bens|klug|heit** F experience of life; **Le|bens|kraft** F vitality; **Le|bens|kreis** M (= *Lebensbereich*) sphere of life; **Le|bens|künst|ler(in)** M(F) **er ist ein echter** ~ he really knows how to live or how to enjoy life; **Le|bens|la|ge** F situation; **in jeder** ~ in any situation; **le|bens|lang** ADJ *Freundschaft, Siechtum* lifelong; *Haft, Gefangenschaft* life *attr*, for life; ADV for the rest of one's life; **mit jdm verbunden sein** for one's entire life; **Le|bens|lang** NT -, *no pl* life (sentence); **le|bens|läng|lich** ADJ *Rente, Strafe* for life; *Gefangenschaft auch* life *attr*; **ein Lebenslänglicher** (*inf*) a lifer (*inf*); **sie hat „le-benslänglich“ or Lebenslänglich bekommen** (*inf*) she got life (*inf*) ADV for life; ~ **im Zuchthaus or hinter Gittern sitzen** (*inf*) to be inside for life (*inf*), to be behind bars for life (*inf*); **Le|bens|lauf** M 46.2 M life; (*bei Bewerbungen*) curriculum vitae (*Brit*), résumé (*US*); **Le|bens|licht** NT **a** (*fig*) flame of life (*liter*); **jdm das** ~ **aus-blasen or auslöschen** (*liter*) to snuff out sb's life **b** (= *Geburtstagskerze*) candle; **Le|bens|li|nie** F lifeline; **Le|bens|lü|ge** F sham existence; **mit einer** ~ **leben** to live a lie; **Le|bens|lust** F zest for life, joie de vivre; **le|bens|lus|tig** ADJ in love with life; **Le|bens|mit|te** F middle years *pl*; **die Krise in der** ~ the midlife crisis

Le|bens|mit|tel PL food *sing*, food(stuff)s *pl* (*form*); (*als Kaufware auch*) groceries *pl*

Le|bens|mit|tel-: **Le|bens|mit|tel|che|mie** F food chemistry; **le|bens|mit|tel|ge|recht** ADJ suitable for putting food in ADV *verpacken* suitably for food; **Le|bens|mit|tel|ge|schäft** NT grocer's (shop); **Le|bens|mit|tel|ge|setz** M food law; **Le|bens|mit|tel|kar|te** F food ration card; **Le|bens|mit|tel|ver|gif|tung** F food poisoning; **Le|bens|mit|tel|vor|rat** M food supplies *pl*, provisions *pl*

Le|bens-: **Le|bens|mo|nat** M **in den ersten ~en** in or during the first few months of life; **le|bens|mü|de** ADJ weary or tired of life; **ein Lebensmüder** a potential suicide; **ich bin doch nicht** ~**!** (*inf*: = *verrückt*) I'm not completely mad! (*inf*); **Le|bens|mü|dig|keit** F weariness of life; **Le|bens|mut** M courage to face life; **le|bens|nah** ADJ true-to-life ADV realistically; **Le|bens|nerv** M (*fig*) **eine Industrie/eine Stadt an ihrem** ~ **treffen** to cripple an indus-

try/a town; **der Tourismus ist der** ~ **Mallorcas** tourism is Majorca's lifeblood; **le|bens|not|wen|dig** ADJ essential, vitally necessary; *Organ, Sauerstoff etc* vital (for life), essential for life; **Le|bens|not|wen|dig|keit** F necessity of life, essential; **Le|bens|ord|nung** F way of life; (*Eccl*) canons and ordinances *pl* (*of the German Protestant Church*); **Le|bens|pfad** M , *no pl* (*liter*) journey through life; **Le|bens|phi|lo|so|phie** F philosophy of life; **Le|bens|qua|li|tät** F quality of life; **Le|bens|raum** M (*Pol*) lebensraum; (*Biol*) habitat; **Le|bens|re|gel** F rule (of life); **Le|bens|rei|se** F , *no pl* (*liter*) journey through life; **le|bens|ret|tend** ADJ lifesaving; **Le|bens|ret|ter(in)** M(F) rescuer; **du bist mein** ~ you've saved my life; **Le|bens|ret|tungs|me|dail|le** F lifesaving medal; **Le|bens|rhyth|mus** M rhythm of life; **Le|bens|span|ne** F lifespan; **Le|bens|stan|dard** M standard of living; **Le|bens|stel|lung** F job for life; **Le|bens|stil** M lifestyle, style of life; **le|bens|tüch|tig** ADJ able to cope with life; **Le|bens|über|druss** ▲ M weariness with life, world-weariness; **Le|bens|um|stän|de** PL circumstances *pl*; **da-mals waren die** ~ **schwierig** conditions made life difficult in those days; **le|bens|un|fä|hig** ADJ *Lebewesen, System* nonviable; **Le|bens|un|ter|halt** M **a** **seinen** ~ **verdienen** to earn one's living; **seinen** ~ **bestreiten** to make one's living, to support oneself; **sie verdient den** ~ **für die Familie** she is the breadwinner of the family, she supports the family; **für jds** ~ **sor-gen** to support sb; **etw zu seinem** ~ **tun** to do sth for a living or livelihood; **nur das Nötigste zum** ~ **haben** to have just enough to live on **b** (= *Unterhaltskosten*) cost of living; **le|bens|un|tüch|tig** ADJ unable to cope with life; **le|bens|ver|län|gernd** ADJ *Maßnahme* life-prolonging; **le|bens|ver|nei|nend** ADJ negative; **eine ~e Einstellung** a negative approach to life; **Le|bens|ver|si|che|rung** F life assurance (*Brit*) or insurance; **eine** ~ **abschließen** to take out a life assurance (*Brit*) or insurance policy; **Le|bens|wan|del** M way of life; **einen einwandfreien/zweifelhaften** *etc* ~ **führen** to lead an irreproachable/a dubious *etc* life; **Le|bens|weg** M journey through life; **den ge-meinsamen** ~ **antreten** to begin one's life to-gether; **alles Gute für den weiteren** or **ferneren** ~ all the best for the future; **Le|bens|wei|se** F way of life; **Le|bens|weis|heit** F maxim; (= *Lebenserfahrung*) wisdom; **Le|bens|wen|de** F (*geh*) turning point in (one's/sb's) life; **Le|bens|werk** NT life's work, lifework; **le|bens|wert** ADJ worth living; **le|bens|wich|tig** ADJ essential, vital; *Organ, Bedürfnisse, Entscheidung* vital; *Nährstoffe* essential; **~e Verbindungslinie** vital link, lifeline; **Le|bens|wil|le** M will to live; **le|bens|zei|chen** NT sign of life; **kein** ~ **mehr von sich geben** to show no sign(s) of life; **Le|bens|zeit** F life(time); **auf** ~ for life; **Beam-ter auf** ~ permanent (*Brit*) or tenured (*US*) civil servant; **Mitglied auf** ~ life member; **Le|bens|ziel** NT goal or aim in life; **Le|bens|zweck** M purpose in life

Le|ber ['le:be] F -, -n liver; **ich habe es mit der** ~ **zu tun** (*inf*) **ich habe es an der** ~ (*inf*) I've got liver trouble; **frei** or **frisch von der** ~ **weg reden** (*inf*) to speak out, to speak frankly; **sich** (*dat*) **etw von der** ~ **reden** (*inf*) to get sth off one's chest → **Laus**

Le|ber-: **Le|ber|blüm|chen** NT liverleaf; **Le|ber|ent|zün|dung** F hepatitis, inflammation of the liver; **Le|ber|fleck** M mole; (*Hautfär-bung*) liver spot; **Le|ber|ha|ken** M (*Sport*) hook to the liver; **Le|ber|kä|se** M , *no pl* = meat loaf; **Le|ber|knö|del** M liver dumpling; **le|ber|krank** ADJ suffering from a liver disor-der; **Le|ber|krebs** M cancer of the liver; **Le|ber|lei|den** NT liver disorder; **Le|ber|pas|te|te** F liver pâté; **Le|ber|scha|den** M damaged liver, liver damage; **Le|ber|tran** M cod-liver oil; **Le|ber|wert** M liver function read-

ing; **Le|ber|wurst** F liver sausage → **beleidigt**; **Le|ber|zir|rho|se** [-tsɪro:zə] F -, -n (*Med*) cir-rhosis of the liver, hepatocirrhosis (*spec*)

Le|be|we|sen NT living thing; **kleinste** ~ mi-croorganisms

Le|be|wohl [le:bə'vo:l] NT -s, *no pl* (*liter*) fare-well (*liter*); **die Stunde des** ~**s** the hour of fare-well; **jdm** ~ **sagen** to bid sb farewell or adieu

leb|haft ADJ **a** (= *voll Leben, rege*) lively *no adv*; *alter Mensch* sprightly, lively; *Temperament* vivacious, lively; *Gespräch, Streit* animated; (*Comm*) *Geschäfte, Verkehr, Nachfrage* brisk **b** (= *deutlich*) *Erinnerung, Eindruck, Vorstellungsver-mögen* vivid; (= *einfallsreich*) *Fantasie* lively; **in ~er Erinnerung bleiben** to remain a vivid mem-ory; **etw in ~er Erinnerung haben** to remember sth vividly **c** (= *kräftig*) *Muster, Interesse, Beifall* lively; *Farbe* bright, lively ADV **a** (= *rege*) *reagieren, strampeln* strongly; ~ **diskutieren** to have a lively discussion; **es geht** ~ **zu** it is lively, things are lively; **das Geschäft geht** ~ business is brisk or lively; **die Börse schloss** ~ business was brisk or lively on the Stock Exchange at the close of the day **b** (= *deutlich*) vividly, clearly; **ich kann mir** ~ **vorstellen, dass …** I can (very) well imagine that … **c** (= *intensiv*) intensely; **eine ~ geführte Debat-te** a lively debate; ~ **bedauern** to regret deeply, to be really sorry about

Leb|haf|tig|keit ['le:phaftɪçkait] F -, *no pl* liveli-ness; (*Comm: von Geschäften*) briskness; (= *Deut-lichkeit: von Erinnerung, Eindruck*) vividness; (*von Farbe*) brightness

Leb|ku|chen M gingerbread

LEBKUCHEN

Lebkuchen are a sort of Christmas ginger-bread. They are generally round and made with syrup or honey and lots of spices, including cinnamon, cardamom and allspice. They are often coated with chocolate or sugar icing.

Leb-: **leb|los** ADJ *Körper, Augen, Stadt, Text* life-less; *Pracht* empty; ~**er Gegenstand** inanimate object; **Leb|lo|sig|keit** F -, *no pl* lifelessness; **Leb|tag** M (*inf*) **mein/dein** *etc* ~ all my/your *etc* life, all my/your *etc* born days; **das habe ich mein ~ noch nicht gesehen** I've never seen the like (of it) in all my life or in all my born days; **das werde ich mein ~ nicht vergessen** I'll never forget that as long as I live; **Leb|zei|ten** PL zu jds ~ (= *Leben*) while sb is/was alive, in sb's lifetime; (= *Zeit*) in sb's day; **sie war schon zu ~ eine Legende** she was a legend in her own life-time

lech|zen ['leçtsn] VI to pant; (*Hund auch*) to have its tongue hanging out; **nach etw** ~ to thirst for sth, to crave sth, to long for sth; **mit ~der Zunge** with one's tongue hanging out → **Blut**

Le|ci|thin [letsi'ti:n] NT -s, *no pl* lecithin

leck [lɛk] ADJ leaky; ~ **sein** to leak

Leck [lɛk] NT -(e)s, -s leak

Le|cka|ge [lɛ'ka:ʒə] F -, -n **a** (= *Gewichtsverlust*) leakage **b** (= *Leck*) leak

Le|cke ['lɛkə] F -, -n (*Hunt*) salt lick

le|cken¹ ['lɛkn] VI (= *undicht sein*) to leak

le|cken² VTI to lick; **an jdm/etw** ~ to lick sb/sth; **sich** (*dat*) **die Wunden** ~ to lick one's wounds → *auch* **geleckt, Arsch a, Finger**

le|cker ['lɛkɐ] ADJ *Speisen* delicious, lovely, yum-my (*inf*); (*inf*) *Mädchen* lovely, delectable ADV *zubereitet* deliciously; ~ **schmecken/aussehen** to taste/look delicious

Le|cker|bis|sen M **a** (*Speise*) delicacy, titbit (*Brit*), tidbit (*US*) **b** (*fig*) gem

Le|cke|rei F -, -en **a** (= *Leckerbissen*) delicacy, titbit (*Brit*), tidbit (*US*) **b** (= *Süßigkeit*) dainty

Le|cker|maul NT , **Le|cker|mäul|chen** [-mɔylçən] NT **-s, -** (*inf*) sweet-toothed child/ person *etc*; **ein ~ sein** to have a sweet tooth

leck+schla|gen VTI *sep irreg* to hole

Leck|stein M licking stone

LED [ɛl|eː'deː] F **-, -s** LED

led. *abbr von* **ledig**

Le|der ['leːdɐ] NT **-s, -** a leather; (= *Fensterleder*) chamois, chammy; (= *Wildleder*) suede; **in ~ ge-bunden** leather-bound; **zäh wie ~** as tough as old boots (*Brit inf*), as tough as shoe leather (*US*); **vom ~ ziehen** (*inf*) to let rip (*inf*) *or* fly (*inf*); **was das ~ hält** (*inf, kämpfen, lügen*) like mad, like crazy b (*dated inf*: = *Haut*) hide (*inf*); **jdm das ~ gerben** *or* **versohlen** to tan sb's hide; **jdm ans ~ wollen** to want to get one's hands on sb c (*inf*: = *Fußball*) ball; **am ~ bleiben** to stick with the ball

Le|der- *in cpds* leather; **le|der|ar|tig** ADJ *Stoff* leatherlike; **Le|der|band** [-bant] M *pl* **-bände** (*Buch*) leather-bound volume; **Le|der|fett** NT dubbin; **Le|der|gar|ni|tur** F leather-uphol-stered suite; **Le|der|haut** F (*Anat*) dermis (*spec*), derma (*spec*); (*um den Augapfel*) sclera (*spec*); **Le|der|ho|se** F leather trousers *pl* (*esp Brit*) *or* pants *pl* (*esp US*); (*aus Wildleder*) suede trousers *pl* (*esp Brit*) *or* pants *pl* (*esp US*); (*kurz*) lederhosen *pl*; (*von Tracht*) leather shorts *pl*; (*Bundhose*) leather breeches *pl*

LEDERHOSE

Contrary to popular belief outside the coun-try, **Lederhose** is not the traditional costume for the whole of Germany. Only in Bavaria and Austria are leather knee-breeches and the **Gamsbart** hat the traditional male cos-tume. The women in these areas wear a **Dirndl**: a dress with a bodice and apron. Other parts of Germany have different cos-tumes – for example, in the Black Forest the traditional costume for women includes a wide black hat with three large red bobbles on top.

Le|der-: **Le|der|ja|cke** F leather jacket; (*aus Wildleder*) suede jacket; **Le|der|man|tel** M leather coat; (*aus Wildleder*) suede coat

le|dern ['leːdɐn] ADJ a (*aus Leder*) leather b (= *zäh*) *Fleisch, Haut* leathery; (*fig*) *Vortrag etc* dry (as dust) ▶ VT a (= *gerben*) to tan b (= *putzen*) to leather

Le|der-: **Le|der|na|cken** PL leathernecks *pl*; **Le|der|rü|cken** M (*von Buch*) leather spine; **Le|der|schurz** M leather apron; **Le|der|wa-ren** PL leather goods *pl*; **Le|der|zeug** NT , *no pl* leather gear; (*Mil*) leathers *pl*

le|dig ['leːdɪç] ADJ a (= *unverheiratet*) single; (*inf*) *Mutter* unmarried; (*S Ger*) *Kind* illegitimate b (*geh*: = *unabhängig*) free; (**los und**) **~ sein** to be footloose and fancy free; **aller Pflichten** (*gen*) (**los und**) **~ sein** to be free of all commit-ments

Le|di|ge(r) ['leːdɪɡə] MF *decl as adj* single per-son

le|dig|lich ['leːdɪklɪç] ADV merely, simply

Lee [leː] F **-,** *no pl* (*Naut*) lee; **in ~ liegen** to be on the lee side; **nach ~ drehen** to turn to lee-ward

leer [leːɐ] ADJ empty; *Blätter, Seite auch* blank; *Ge-sichtsausdruck, Blick* blank, vacant; (*geh*) *der Kosmos* the cosmos; **eine ~e Stelle** an empty space; **vor einem ~en Haus** *or* **vor ~en Bänken spielen** (*Theat*) to play to an empty house; **ins Leere starren/treten** to stare/step into space; **ins Leere greifen** to clutch at thin air; **ins Leere laufen** (*fig*) to come to nothing, to get nowhere; **mit ~en Händen** (*fig*) empty-handed ▶ ADV **eine Zeile ~ lassen** to leave a line (blank *or* free); **etw ~ machen** to empty sth; **den Teller ~ essen** to eat everything on the plate; (**wie**) **~ gefegt** (*Straßen, Stadt etc*) deserted; **etw ~ trin-ken** to empty sth; **etw ~ pumpen** to pump sth

dry; **~ stehen** to stand empty; **~ stehend** emp-ty; **einen Laden ~ kaufen** to buy a shop (*esp Brit*) *or* store (*US*) out → **leer laufen**

Lee|re ['leːrə] F **-,** *no pl* (*lit, fig*) emptiness; (**eine**) **geistige ~** a mental vacuum; (**eine**) **gähnende ~** a gaping *or* yawning void

lee|ren ['leːrən] VT to empty; *Briefkasten auch* to clear; **jdm die Taschen ~** (*inf*) to clean sb out (*inf*) ▶ VR to empty

Leer-: **Leer|fahrt** F (*von Bus, Lkw*) empty trip; **Leer|for|mel** F empty phrase; **leer|ge|fegt** △ [-ɡəfeːkt] ADJ (*fig*) → **leer** ADV; **Leer|ge|wicht** NT unladen weight, tare; (*von Behälter*) empty weight; **Leer|gut** NT empties *pl*; **Leer|lauf** M a (*Aut*) neutral; (*von Fahrrad*) freewheel; **im ~ fahren** to coast; **das Auto ist im ~** the engine is in neutral; (= *stehend mit laufendem Motor*) the engine is idling b (*fig*) slack; **leer lau|fen** ▲ VI *irreg aux sein* a (*Fass etc*) to run dry; **~ lassen** to empty, to drain b (*Motor*) to idle; (*Maschine*) to run idle; (*Betrieb etc*) to be idle; **Leer|pa-ckung** F (*empty*) display package, dummy; **Leer|po|si|ti|on** F (*St Ex*) short position; **leer|ste|hend** △ ADJ → **leer** ADV; **Leer|stel-le** F blank (space); **Leer|tas|te** F (*bei Schreib-maschine*) space-bar

Lee|rung ['leːrʊŋ] F **-, -en** emptying; **die ~ der Mülltonnen erfolgt wöchentlich** the dustbins (*Brit*) *or* garbage cans (*US*) are emptied once a week; **nächste ~ 18 Uhr** (*an Briefkasten*) next col-lection (*Brit*) *or* pickup (*US*) 6 p.m.

Leer-

Leer|ver|kauf M (*St Ex*) short sale

Leer|zei|chen NT (*Comput*) blank (character), space (character)

Leer|zei|le F (*Typ*) blank line; **zwei ~n lassen** to leave two lines free *or* blank, to leave two empty lines

Lef|ze ['lɛftsə] F **-, -n** *usu pl* chaps *pl*; (*von Pferd*) lip

le|gal [le'ɡaːl] ADJ legal, lawful ADV legally

le|ga|li|sie|ren [leɡali'ziːrən] *ptp* **legalisiert** VT to legalize

le|ga|lis|tisch [leɡa'lɪstɪʃ] ADJ legalistic ADV le-galistically

Le|ga|li|tät [leɡali'tɛːt] F **-,** *no pl* legality; (**etwas**) **außerhalb der ~** (*euph*) (slightly) outside the law

Le|gas|the|nie [leɡaste'niː] F **-, -n** [-'niːən] dys-lexia

Le|gas|the|ni|ker [leɡas'teːnikɐ] M **-s, -,** **Le|-gas|the|ni|ke|rin** [-ərɪn] F **-, -nen** dyslexic

le|gas|the|nisch [leɡas'teːnɪʃ] ADJ dyslexic

Le|gat¹ [le'ɡaːt] NT **-(e)s, -e** (*Jur*) legacy

Le|gat² M **-en, -en** (*Eccl, Hist*) legate

Le|ga|ti|on [leɡa'tsioːn] F **-, -en** legation

Le|ga|ti|ons|rat M , **Le|ga|ti|ons|rä|tin** F counsellor to a legation (*Brit*), legation coun-selor (*US*)

Le|ga|to [le'ɡaːto] NT **-(s), -s** *or* **Legati** [-ti] (*Mus*) legato

Le|ge|bat|te|rie F hen battery

Le|ge|hen|ne F , **Le|ge|huhn** NT layer, laying hen

Le|gel ['leːɡl] M **-s, -** (*Naut*) cringle, grummet

le|gen ['leːɡn] VT a (= *lagern*) to lay down; (*mit adv*) to lay; *Flasche etc* to lay on its side; (= *zu-sammenlegen*) *Wäsche* to fold; (*dial*) *Kartoffeln etc* to plant, to put in; (*Sport*) to bring down b (*mit Raumangabe*) to put, to place; **wir müs-sen uns ein paar Flaschen Wein in den Keller ~** we must lay down a few bottles of wine; **etw beiseite ~** to put sth aside *or* (*weglegen*) away; **etw in Essig** *etc* **~** to preserve sth in vinegar *etc*; **ein Tier an die Kette ~** to chain an animal (up); **jdn in Ketten** *or* **Fesseln ~** to put sb in chains, to chain sb; (*fig hum*) to (en)snare sb c (*mit Angabe des Zustandes*) **etw in Falten ~** to fold sth; **er legte die Stirn in Falten** he frowned, he creased his brow; **eine Stadt in**

Schutt und Asche ~ to reduce a town to rubble d (= *verlegen*) *Fliesen, Leitungen, Schienen, Minen etc* to lay, to put down; *Bomben* to plant; **Feuer** *or* **einen Brand ~** to start a fire; **sich** (*dat*) **die Haare ~ lassen** to have one's hair set; **sich** (*dat*) **Dauerwellen** *etc* **~ lassen** to have a perm *etc*, to have one's hair permed *etc* e (*Huhn*) *Eier* to lay ▶ VI (*Huhn*) to lay ▶ VR a (= *hinlegen*) to lie down (*auf +acc* on); **sich ins** *or* (*geh*) **zu Bett ~** to go to bed, to retire (*form*); **sich in die Sonne ~** to lie in the sun; **leg dich!** (*zum Hund*) lie down! → **schlafen** VI b (*mit Ortsangabe*) (= *niederlegen*: *Nebel, Rauch*) to settle (*auf +acc* on); **sich auf die Seite ~** to lie on one's side; (*Boot*) to heel over, to go over onto its side; **sich in die Kurve ~** to lean into the corner; **sich auf ein Spezialgebiet ~** to con-centrate on *or* specialize in a particular field c (= *abnehmen*) (*Lärm*) to die down, to abate; (*Sturm, Wind auch, Kälte*) to let up; (*Rauch, Nebel*) to clear; (*Zorn, Begeisterung auch, Arroganz, Ner-vosität*) to wear off; (*Anfangsschwierigkeiten*) to sort themselves out; **das Fieber legt sich bald** his/her *etc* temperature will come down soon

le|gen|där [leɡen'dɛːɐ] ADJ legendary; (= *obskur*) apocryphal; **er/das ist schon fast ~** he/it has al-ready become almost legendary

Le|gen|de [le'ɡɛndə] F **-, -n** (*alle Bedeutungen*) legend; **sich** (*dat*) **eine ~ zulegen** to assume a false identity

le|gen|den|um|wo|ben [-ʊmvoːbn] ADJ fa-bled, surrounded by legends

le|ger [le'ʒeːɐ, le'ʒɛːɐ] ADJ a (= *bequem*) *Kleidung* casual; *Sitz* comfortable b (= *ungezwungen*) *Be-nehmen, Ausdrucksweise* casual; *Typ* casual, infor-mal; *Atmosphäre* relaxed, informal ADV a (= *bequem*) *sich kleiden* casually; **etw sitzt ~** sth is comfortable; **etw fällt ~** sth is comfortably fit-ting b (= *ungezwungen*) casually; *sich ausdrü-cken* informally

Le|ge|zeit F laying season *or* time

Leg|föh|re ['leːk-] F mountain pine

Leg|gings ['leɡɪŋs] PL , **Leg|gins** ['leɡɪns] PL leggings *pl*

Leg|hen|ne ['leːk-] F layer, laying hen

le|gie|ren [le'ɡiːrən] *ptp* **legiert** VT a *Metall* to alloy b (*Cook*) *Suppe etc* to thicken

Le|gie|rung [le'ɡiːrʊŋ] F **-, -en** alloy; (*Verfahren*) alloying

Le|gi|on [le'ɡioːn] F **-, -en** legion; **die Zahl der Toten war ~** (*geh*) the number of the dead was legion (*liter*)

Le|gi|o|när [leɡio'nɛːɐ] M **-s, -e** legionary, le-gionnaire

Le|gi|o|närs|krank|heit F legionnaire's dis-ease

le|gis|la|tiv [leɡisla'tiːf] ADJ legislative ADV **~ handeln** to take legislative action; **eine Reform ~ absichern** to validate a reform through legis-lation

Le|gis|la|ti|ve [leɡisla'tiːvə] F **-, -n** legislature, legislative assembly *or* body

Le|gis|la|tur [leɡisla'tuːɐ] F **-, -en** a (*rare*: = *Ge-setzgebung*) legislation; (*obs*: = *gesetzgebende Ge-walt*) legislature b (*inf*: = *Legislaturperiode*) par-liamentary term (*Brit*), legislative period (*US*)

Le|gis|la|tur|pe|ri|o|de F parliamentary term (*Brit*), legislative period (*US*)

le|gi|tim [leɡi'tiːm] ADJ legitimate; **als ~ aner-kannt** recognized as legitimate; **etw als ~ be-trachten** to consider sth legitimate; **ich finde seine Kritik ~** I find his criticism legitimate; **deine Vorwürfe erscheinen mir ~** I think your accusations are justified ADV legitimately; **der Zusammenschluss ist nicht ganz ~ zustande ge-kommen** the merger wasn't set up in a strictly legal way

Le|gi|ti|ma|ti|on [leɡitima'tsioːn] F **-, -en** iden-tification; (= *Berechtigung*) authorization; (*eines Kindes*) legitimation

---

le|gi|ti|mie|ren [legiti'mi:rən] *ptp* **legitimiert** **VT** *Beziehung, Kind* to legitimize; (= *berechtigen*) to entitle; (= *berechtigt erscheinen lassen*) to justify, to warrant; (= *Erlaubnis geben*) to authorize; **die demokratisch legitimierte Regierung** the democratically elected government **VR** to show (proof of) authorization; (= *sich ausweisen*) to identify oneself, to show proof of one's identity

Le|gi|ti|mie|rung [legiti'mi:rʊŋ] F legitimizing, legitimization; (= *Berechtigung*) justification

Le|gi|ti|mi|tät [legitimi'tɛ:t] F -, *no pl* legitimacy

Le|go|stein® ['le:go-] M Lego® brick

Le|gu|an [le:gu'a:n, 'le:gua:n] M -s, -e iguana

Le|hen ['le:ən] NT -s, - (*Hist*) fief, feoff, feu (*Scot*); **jdm ein Gut zu ~ geben** to enfeoff sb

Le|hens- *in cpds* = **Lehns-**

Lehm [le:m] M -(e)s, -e loam; (= *Ton*) clay

Lehm-: Lehm|bau M *pl* -bauten, **Lehm|bau|wei|se** F clay building; **lehm|far|ben** [-farbn], **lehm|far|big** ADJ clay-coloured (*Brit*), clay-colored (*US*); **Lehm|hüt|te** F mud hut

lehm|mig ['le:mıç] ADJ loamy; (= *tonartig*) claylike, clayey

Lehm-: Lehm|pa|ckung F mudpack; **Lehm|zie|gel** M clay brick

Lehn [le:n] NT -s, - = **Lehen**

Lehn|bil|dung F (*Ling*) loan formation

Leh|ne ['le:nə] F -, -n **a** (= *Armlehne*) arm(rest); (= *Rückenlehne*) back (rest) **b** (*old, S Ger.* = *Berghang*) slope

leh|nen ['le:nən] **VT** to lean (*an +acc* against) **VI** to be leaning (*an +dat* against) **VR** to lean (*an +acc* against, *auf +acc* on); **„nicht aus dem Fenster ~!"** (*Rail*) "do not lean out of the window"

Lehns|dienst ['le:ns-] M (*Hist*) vassalage

Lehn|ses|sel M easy chair

Lehns- ['le:ns-]: **Lehns|herr** M (*Hist*) feudal lord; **Lehns|mann** M *pl* -männer *or* -leute (*Hist*) vassal; **Lehns|pflicht** F (*Hist*) feudal duty

Lehn|stuhl M easy chair

Lehns|wesen ['le:ns-] NT (*Hist*) feudal system, feudalism

Lehn-: Lehn|über|set|zung F (*Ling*) loan translation; **Lehn|wort** NT *pl* -wörter (*Ling*) loan word, borrowing

Lehr|amt NT **das ~** the teaching profession; (= *Lehrerposten*) teaching post (*esp Brit*) *or* position; **ein ~ ausüben** to hold a teaching post (*esp Brit*) *or* position; **Prüfung für das höhere ~** examination for secondary school teachers; **das ~ an Gymnasien** ≈ grammar school teaching (*Brit*), ≈ high school teaching (*US*); **sie studiert ~ für Französisch und Englisch** she's studying to be a teacher of French and English; **sein ~ ernst nehmen** (*Univ*) to take one's teaching responsibilities seriously

Lehr|amts-: Lehr|amts|an|wär|ter(in) M(F), **Lehr|amts|kan|di|dat(in)** M(F) prospective teacher; **Lehr|amts|stu|di|um** NT teacher training

Lehr-: Lehr|an|stalt F (*form*) educational establishment; **höhere ~** establishment of secondary education; **Lehr|auf|trag** M (*als Sonderlehrer*) special teaching post (*esp Brit*) *or* position; **einen ~ für etw haben** (*Univ*) to give lectures on sth; **lehr|bar** ADJ teachable; **Lehr|be|auf|trag|te(r)** MF *decl as adj* (*Univ*) **~(r) für etw sein** to give lectures on sth; **Lehr|be|fä|hi|gung** F teaching qualification; **Lehr|be|halt** [-bəhalt] M -s, -e (*Aus*) teaching aid; (*pl auch*) teaching materials *pl*; **Lehr|be|rech|ti|gung** F *jdm* **die ~ erteilen** to register sb as a teacher; **ihm wurde die ~ entzogen** he was struck off the register of teachers; **für Latein hat er keine ~** he isn't qualified to teach Latin; **Lehr|be|ruf** M **a** (*als Lehrer*) teaching profession; **den ~ ergreifen** to go into teaching **b** (=

Beruf mit Lehrzeit) trade requiring an apprenticeship, skilled trade; **Lehr|be|trieb** M (*Univ*) teaching; **Lehr|brief** M **a** (= *Zeugnis*) apprenticeship certificate **b** (= *Lektion*) correspondence lesson; **Lehr|bub** M apprentice; **Lehr|buch** NT textbook; **lehr|buch|ge|recht** ADJ **a** **die ~e Bearbeitung eines Textes** the editing of a text for a school edition **b** (= *gut ausgeführt*) textbook *attr*, perfect; **Lehr|bur|sche** M (*dial*) apprentice; **Lehr|dich|tung** F didactic poetry

Leh|re ['le:rə] F -, -n **a** (= *das Lehren*) teaching **b** (*von Christus, Buddha, Marx etc*) teachings *pl*; (= *Lehrmeinung*) doctrine; (*von Galilei, Kant, Freud etc*) theory; (*von Erdaufbau, Leben etc*) science; **die christliche ~** Christian doctrine/teaching **c** (= *negative Erfahrung*) lesson; (= *Ratschlag*) (piece of) advice; (*einer Fabel*) moral; **jdm eine ~ erteilen** to teach sb a lesson; **seine ~(n) aus etw ziehen** to learn a lesson from sth; (*aus einer Fabel etc*) to draw a moral from sth; **lass dir das eine ~ sein, lass es dir zur ~ dienen!** (*geh*) let that be a lesson to you! **d** (= *Berufslehre*) apprenticeship; (*in nicht handwerklichem Beruf*) training; **eine ~ machen** to train; (*in Handwerk*) to do an apprenticeship; **bei jdm die ~ (durch)machen, bei jdm in die ~ gehen** to serve one's apprenticeship with *or* under sb; **sie machte eine ~ als** *or* **zur Bürokauffrau** she trained as an office administrator; **du kannst bei ihm noch in die ~ gehen** (*fig*) he could teach you a thing or two **e** (*Tech*) gauge; (= *Muster*) template

---

LEHRE

Lehre is the name for vocational training in trade and industry. It is strictly regulated and usually lasts three years, although those who have their **Abitur** are often allowed to reduce this by one year. The trainees, so-called **Auszubildende** or **Azubis** for short, work in a company and become familiar with all the different areas of their future profession. In addition, they receive instruction at a vocational college for two days a week or in blocks of seminars. At the end of the training period they take their **Gesellenprüfung** → ABITUR

---

leh|ren ['le:rən] VTI to teach; (*Univ auch*) to lecture (*ein Fach* in a subject); **die Wissenschaft lehrt, dass ...** science tells us that ...; **jdn** *or* **jdm** (*inf*) **lesen** *etc* **~** to teach sb to read *etc*; **die Zukunft wird es ~** time (alone) will tell; **ich werde dich ~, so frech zu antworten!** I'll teach you to answer back! (*inf*) → *auch* **gelehrt**

Leh|rer ['le:rɐ] M -s, -, **Leh|re|rin** [-ərın] F -, -nen teacher; (= *Privatlehrer, Nachhilfelehrer auch*) tutor; (= *Fluglehrer, Fahrlehrer etc*) instructor/ instructress; **er ist ~** he's a (school)teacher; **~(in) für Philosophie/Naturwissenschaften** teacher of philosophy/science; (*in der Schule*) philosophy/science teacher

Leh|rer-: Leh|rer|aus|bil|dung F teacher training; **Leh|rer|be|ruf** M teaching profession, career as a teacher; **Leh|rer|hand|rei|chung|en** PL teacher's notes *pl*; **Leh|rer|kol|le|gi|um** NT (*teaching*) staff; **in diesem ~** amongst the teaching staff of this school; **Leh|rer|kon|fe|renz** F (*Sch*) staff meeting

Leh|rer|laub|nis F → **Lehrberechtigung**

Leh|rer-: Leh|rer|man|gel M teacher shortage; **Leh|rer|schaft** ['le:rəʃaft] F -, -en (*form*) (teaching) staff; **Leh|rer|schwem|me** F surplus of teachers; **Leh|rer|se|mi|nar** NT (*für Referendare, inf:* = *Pädagogische Hochschule*) teacher training college; (*Kurs*) in-service course for teachers; **Leh|rer|zim|mer** NT staff (*esp Brit*) *or* teachers' room

Lehr-: Lehr|fach NT subject; **Lehr|film** M educational film; **Lehr|frei|heit** F freedom to teach as one sees fit; **Lehr|gang** M *pl* -gänge course (*für* in); **Lehr|ge|bäu|de** NT (*fig*) sys-

tem of theories; (*Eccl*) doctrinal system; **Lehr|ge|gen|stand** M subject; **Lehr|geld** NT (*Hist*) (apprenticeship) premium; **(teures) ~ für etw zahlen müssen** (*fig*) to pay dearly for sth; **lass dir dein ~ zurückgeben!** (*hum inf*) go to the bottom of the class! (*hum inf*); **Lehr|ge|rüst** NT centring (*Brit*), centering (*US*); **lehr|haft** ADJ didactic; **Lehr|herr(in)** M(F) master (of an apprentice); **Lehr|jahr** NT year as an apprentice; **~e sind keine Herrenjahre** (*Prov*) life's not easy at the bottom; **Lehr|jun|ge** M (*dated*) apprentice; **Lehr|kan|zel** F (*Aus*) = **Lehrstuhl**; **Lehr|kör|per** M (*form*) teaching staff; (*Univ auch*) academic staff; **Lehr|kraft** F (*form*) teacher

Lehr|ling ['le:rlıŋ] M -s, -e apprentice; (*in nicht handwerklichem Beruf*) trainee

Lehr-: Lehr|mäd|chen NT (*dated*) apprentice; **Lehr|mei|nung** F opinion; (*von einer bestimmten Gruppe vertreten*) school of thought; (*Eccl*) doctrine; **Lehr|meis|ter(in)** M(F) master; **seinen ~ finden** to meet one's master; **du bist mir ein schöner ~** you're a fine example; **Lehr|me|tho|de** F teaching method; **Lehr|mit|tel** NT teaching aid; (*pl auch*) teaching materials *pl*; **Lehr|plan** M (*teaching*) curriculum; (*für ein Schuljahr*) syllabus; **Lehr|pro|be** F demonstration lesson, crit (*Brit inf*); **Lehr|pro|gramm** NT teaching programme (*Brit*) *or* program (*US*); **lehr|reich** ADJ (= *informativ*) instructive; *Erfahrung* educational; **Lehr|satz** M (*Math, Philos*) theorem; (*Eccl*) dogma; **Lehr|schwimm|be|cken** NT beginners' *or* teaching pool; **Lehr|stel|le** F position for an apprentice; (*in nicht handwerklichem Beruf*) position for a trainee; (*aus Sicht des Auszubildenden*) position as an apprentice/a trainee; **wir haben zwei ~n zu vergeben** we have vacancies for two apprentices/ trainees; **Lehr|stoff** M subject; (*eines Jahres*) syllabus; **das ist ~ der dritten Klasse** that's on the syllabus for the third year; **Lehr|stuhl** M (*Univ*) chair (*für* of); **jdn auf einen ~ berufen** to offer sb a chair; **Lehr|tä|tig|keit** F (*Univ*) (= *Unterrichten*) teaching; (= *Stelle*) teaching post *or* job; **eine ~ ausüben** to teach; **Lehr|toch|ter** F (*Sw*) apprentice; (*in nicht handwerklichem Beruf*) trainee; **Lehr|ver|an|stal|tung** F (*Univ*) (= *Vorlesung*) lecture; (= *Seminar*) seminar; **Lehr|ver|hält|nis** NT contractual relationship (*between apprentice and master/trainee and employer*); **in einem ~ stehen** (*form*) to be apprenticed (*bei* to); **Lehr|ver|trag** M indentures *pl*; (*in nicht handwerklichem Beruf*) contract as a trainee; **Lehr|werk** NT (*form*) textbook; (*Buchreihe*) series *sing* of textbooks; **Lehr|werk|statt** F training workshop; **Lehr|zeit** F apprenticeship

Leib [laip] M -(e)s, -er [-bə] **a** (= *Körper*) body; **der ~ des Herrn** (*Eccl*) the Body of Christ; **Gefahr für ~ und Leben** (*geh*) danger to life and limb; **~ und Leben wagen** (*geh*) to risk life and limb; **mit ~ und Seele** heart and soul; *wünschen* with all one's heart; **mit ~ und Seele singen** to sing one's heart out; **mit ~ und Seele dabei sein** to put one's heart and soul *or* one's whole heart into it; **etw am eigenen ~(e) erfahren** *or* **(ver)spüren** to experience sth for oneself; **kein Hemd mehr am ~ haben** to be completely destitute; **keinen trockenen Faden am ~ haben** (*inf*) to be soaked to the skin (*inf*); **der hat vielleicht einen Ton am ~!** (*inf*) talk about rude!; **am ganzen ~(e) zittern/frieren/schwitzen** to be shaking/freezing/sweating all over; **sich** (*dat*) **alles an den ~ hängen** (*inf*) to spend everything on clothes; **die Rolle ist ihr wie auf den ~ geschrieben** the part is tailor-made for her; **der Beruf ist ihr wie auf den ~ geschnitten** that job is tailor-made for her, that job suits her to a T (*esp Brit inf*); **kein Herz im ~e haben** to have no heart at all, to be completely heartless; **sich** (*dat*) **jdn/etw vom ~e halten** to keep *or* hold sb/ sth at bay; **halt ihn mir vom ~** keep him away from me; **jdm vom ~ bleiben** to keep away from sb; **geh mir vom ~!** get away (from me)!;

(= *lass mich in Ruhe*) get off my back! (*inf*); **bleib mir damit vom ~e!** (*inf*) stop pestering me with it (*inf*) → **rücken** VI

b (*old, dial*: = *Bauch*) stomach; (= *Mutterleib*) womb; **ich habe noch nichts im ~(e)** I haven't eaten yet; **gut bei ~e sein** (*iro*) to be well-upholstered (*iro*)

Leib-: Leib|arzt M , **Leib|ärz|tin** F personal physician; **Leib|bin|de** F truss; (*nach Geburt*) abdominal binder (*Brit*) or belt (*US*)

Leib|chen ['laɪpçən] NT **-s, -** **a** (*old*) bodice **b** (= *Unterhemd*) vest (*Brit*), undershirt (*US*); (= *Hemdchen*) top

Leib-: leib|ei|gen ADJ unfree, in bondage; (*im Mittelalter*) serf *attr*; **~ sein** not to be a free man/woman; (*im Mittelalter*) to be a serf; **Leib|ei|ge|ne(r)** ['laɪplaɪgənə] MF *decl as adj* bond(s)man/-woman; (*im Mittelalter*) serf; **er behandelt seine Frau wie eine ~** he treats his wife as though she were one of his possessions; **Leib|ei|gen|schaft** F bondage; (*im Mittelalter*) serfdom

lei|ben ['laɪbn] VI **wie er leibt und lebt** to the life, to a T (*esp Brit inf*)

Leibes-: Lei|bes|er|zie|hung F physical education; **Lei|bes|frucht** F (*geh*) unborn child, fruit of one's/sb's womb (*poet*); **Lei|bes|fül|le** F , *no pl* (*geh*) corpulence (*form*); (*von Mann*) portliness (*geh*); **Lei|bes|kraft** F **aus Leibeskräften schreien** *etc* to shout *etc* with all one's might (and main); **Lei|bes|übung** F (*physical*) exercise; **~en** (*Schulfach*) physical education *no pl*; **Lei|bes|vi|si|ta|ti|on** F body search; (*Mil*) physical inspection, medical

Leib-: Leib|gar|de F (*Mil*) bodyguard; **die ~ der englischen Königin** the Queen's Guards *pl*; **Leib|gar|dist** M soldier in a bodyguard; **Leib|ge|richt** NT favourite (*Brit*) or favorite (*US*) meal

leib|haft ADJ (*rare*) = **leibhaftig**

leib|haf|tig [laɪp'haftɪç, 'laɪphaftɪç] ADJ personified, incarnate; **die ~e Güte** *etc* goodness *etc* personified or incarnate; **(wie) der ~e Teufel**, **(wie) der Leibhaftige** (as) the devil himself ADV in person, in the flesh

Leib|koch M , **Leib|kö|chin** F personal chef

leib|lich ['laɪplɪç] ADJ **a** (= *körperlich*) physical, bodily; **die ~e Genüsse** the pleasures of the flesh; **die ~e Hülle** (*geh*) the mortal remains *pl*; **für das ~e Wohl sorgen** to take care of our/ their *etc* bodily needs **b** *Mutter, Vater* natural; *Kind* by birth; *Bruder, Schwester* full; *Verwandte* blood; (*emph*: = *eigen*) (very) own

Leib-: Leib|pacht F (*old*) life tenancy, lease for life; **Leib|ren|te** F life annuity; **Leib|rie|men** PL (*old*) belt; **Leib|schmer|zen** PL (*old, dial*) stomach pains *pl*; **Leib|spei|se** F favourite (*Brit*) or favorite (*US*) food; **Leib|wa|che** F bodyguard; **Leib|wäch|ter(in)** M(F) bodyguard; **Leib|wä|sche** F underwear, underclothes *pl*; **Leib|weh** NT (*old*) stomachache

Leich [laɪç] M **-(e)s, -e** (*Liter*) lay

Lei|che ['laɪçə] F **-, -n** **a** body, corpse; (*inf*: = *Bierleiche, Schnapsleiche*) drunken body (*inf*); **die Insassen konnten nur noch als ~n geborgen werden** the passengers were dead when the rescuers arrived; **eine lebende** or **wandelnde ~** (*inf*) a corpse; **wie eine lebende** or **wandelnde ~ aussehen** to look like death (warmed up (*Brit inf*) or over (*US inf*)); **er geht über ~n** (*inf*) he'd stop at nothing, he'd sell his own grandmother (*inf*); **nur über meine ~!** (*inf*) over my dead body!; **eine ~ im Keller haben** (*fig*) to have a skeleton in the cupboard (*Brit*) or closet

b (*S Ger*) (= *Beerdigung*) funeral; (= *Leichenschmaus*) funeral meal; **die ~ begießen** (*inf*) to drink the dead man's health

c (*Typ*) omission

Lei|chen-: Lei|chen|be|gäng|nis [-bəgɛŋnɪs] NT **-ses, -se** (*form*), **Lei|chen|be|gräb|nis** NT funeral; **Lei|chen|be|schau|er** [-bəʃaʊɐ] M **-s, -**, **Lei|chen|be|schau|e|rin** [-ərɪn] F **-, -nen**

doctor conducting a postmortem; **Lei|chen|bit|ter|mie|ne** F (*inf*) mournful or doleful expression; **lei|chen|blass** ▲ ADJ deathly pale, as pale as death; **Lei|chen|fled|de|rei** [-fledəraɪ] F **-, -en** robbing of dead people; **das ist die reinste ~** (*fig*) what vultures!; **Lei|chen|fled|de|rer** M , **Lei|chen|fled|de|rin** F person who robs dead people; (*fig*) vulture; **Lei|chen|frau** F layer-out; **Lei|chen|hal|le** F , **Lei|chen|haus** NT mortuary; **Lei|chen|hemd** NT shroud; **Lei|chen|kon|ser|vie|rung** F preservation of corpses; **Lei|chen|öff|nung** F autopsy; **Lei|chen|re|de** F funeral oration (*liter*) or address; **Lei|chen|schän|dung** F desecration of corpses; (*sexuell*) necrophilia; **Lei|chen|schau** F postmortem (examination); **Lei|chen|schau|haus** NT morgue; **Lei|chen|schmaus** M funeral meal; **Lei|chen|star|re** F rigor mortis *no art*; **Lei|chen|tuch** NT *pl* **-tücher** shroud; **Lei|chen|ver|bren|nung** F cremation; **Lei|chen|wa|gen** M hearse; **Lei|chen|zug** M funeral procession

Leich|nam ['laɪçnaːm] M **-s, -e** (*form*) body

leicht [laɪçt] ADJ **a** (= *von geringem Gewicht, nicht schwerfällig, Mil*) light; (= *aus leichtem Material*) *Koffer, Kleidung* lightweight; **einen ~en Gang haben** to have an easy walk; **mit ~er Hand** lightly; (*fig*) effortlessly; **eine ~e Hand mit jdm/ für etw haben** to have a way with sb/sth; **~en Fußes** (*liter*) with a spring in one's step; **gewogen und zu ~ befunden** (*fig*) tried and found wanting; **jdn um einiges ~er machen** to relieve sb of some of his money → **Feder**

b (= *schwach, geringfügig, nicht wichtig*) slight; *Regen, Wind, Frost, Schläge, Schlaf, Berührung, Atmen* light; (*Jur*) *Diebstahl, Vergehen etc* minor, petty

c (*von geringem Gehalt*) *Essen, Musik, Lektüre etc* light

d (= *ohne Schwierigkeiten, einfach*) easy; **~er Absatz** (*Comm*) quick turnover (*von inf*); **mit dem werden wir (ein) ~es Spiel haben** he'll be a pushover (*inf*) or walkover (*inf*), he'll be no problem; **keinen ~en Stand haben** not to have an easy time of it (*bei, mit* with); **das ist ihr ein Leichtes** (*geh*) that will present no problem to or for her; **nichts ~er als das!** nothing (could be) easier or simpler

e (= *moralisch locker*) *Lebenswandel* loose; **~es Mädchen** tart (*Brit inf*), floozy (*inf*)

f (= *unbeschwert*) *Herz, Gefühl* light; **etw ~en Herzens** or **Sinnes tun** to do sth with a light heart → **Schulter**

ADV **a** (= *einfach*) easily; **jdm etw ~ machen** to make it easy for sb; **es sich** (*dat*) **(bei etw) ~ machen** not to make much of an effort (with sth); **sie hat es immer ~ gehabt (im Leben)** she's always had it easy, she's always had an easy time of it; **man hats nicht ~** (*inf*) it's a hard life; **das ist gar nicht so ~** it's quite easy or simple; **die Aufgabe ist ~ zu lösen** or **lässt sich ~ lösen** the exercise is easy to do; **mach es dir nicht zu ~** (= *bequem*) don't make things too easy for yourself; (= *sei gewissenhaft auch*) don't take the easy way out; (= *vereinfache es nicht*) don't oversimplify things; **das ist ~er gesagt als getan** that's easier said than done; **du hast ~ reden/ lachen** it's all very well for you or it's all right for you to talk/laugh

b (= *problemlos*) easily; **~ zu beantworten/verstehen** easily answered/understood, easy to answer/understand; **~ verständlich** readily or easily understood; **er ist ~ herumzukriegen/zu überzeugen** he's easy to win round/convince, he's easily won round/convinced; **~ begreifen** to understand quickly or readily; **das kann ich mir ~ vorstellen** or **denken** I can easily or well imagine (it); **~ verdaulich** (*Speisen, Informationen*) easily digestible; *Kunst, Musik etc* not too demanding

c (= *unbekümmert*) **das Leben ~ nehmen** not to take things too seriously; **das Leben nicht ~ nehmen** to take everything too seriously; **~ beschwingt** (*Musik*) light; **~beschwingte Melodien**

melodies for easy listening; **sich ~ und beschwingt fühlen** to be walking on air, to be up in the clouds; **mir ist so ~ ums Herz** my heart is so light; **mir ist jetzt viel ~er** I feel a lot easier now; **nimm das nicht zu ~** don't take it too lightly

d (= *schnell, unversehens*) easily; **er wird ~ böse/ ist ~ beleidigt** *etc* he is quick to get angry/take offence (*Brit*) or offense (*US*) *etc*, he gets angry/takes offence (*Brit*) or offense (*US*) *etc* easily; **~ zerbrechlich** very fragile; **~ verderblich** highly perishable; **man kann einen Fehler ~ übersehen** it's easy to miss a mistake, mistakes are easily missed; **das ist ~ möglich** that's quite possible; **~ entzündlich** (*Brennstoff etc*) highly (in)flammable; **~ entzündliche Haut** skin which easily becomes inflamed; **~ entzündlich sein** (*Gas, Brennstoff*) to be highly inflammable; (*Haut*) to become easily inflamed; **man hat ~ etwas gesagt, was man nachher bereut** it's easy to say something (without thinking) that you regret later; **das passiert mir so ~ nicht wieder** I won't let that happen again in a hurry (*inf*); **das passiert mir so ~ nicht wieder, dass ich dir Geld borge** I won't lend you money again in a hurry (*inf*)

e (= *geringfügig, nicht schwer*) gewebt finely; *bewaffnet* not heavily, lightly; **das Haus ist ~ gebaut** the house is built of light materials; **ein zu ~ gebautes Haus/Auto** a flimsily built house/car; **~ bekleidet sein** to be scantily clad or dressed; **~ gekleidet sein** to be (dressed) in light clothes; **~ geschürzt** (*hum*) scantily clad or dressed

f (= *schwach*) *regnen* not hard; **es hat ~ gefroren** there was a light frost; **~ gewürzt/gesalzen** lightly seasoned/salted; **zu ~ gewürzt/gesalzen** not seasoned/salted enough; **~ waschen** to wash gently

g (= *nicht ernsthaft*) *beschädigt* slightly; *gekränkt auch* a little; **~ verletzt** slightly injured; (*in Gefecht, Schlägerei etc auch*) slightly wounded; **~er verletzt** not as seriously injured; **~ verwundet** slightly wounded

Leicht-: Leicht|ath|let(in) M(F) (track and field) athlete; **Leicht|ath|le|tik** F (track and field) athletics *sing*; **leicht|ath|le|tisch** ADJ athletic *attr* ADV as regards (track and field) athletics; **Leicht|bau|stoff** M lightweight building material; **Leicht|bau** M *pl* **-bauten**, **Leicht|bau|wei|se** F lightweight construction; **in ~ using lightweight materials; **Leicht|ben|zin** NT benzine; **leicht|be|schwingt** △ ADJ → **leicht** ADV **c**; **Leicht|be|ton** M lightweight concrete; **leicht|be|waff|net** △ ADJ *attr* → **leicht** ADV **e**; **leicht|ent|zünd|lich** △ ADJ *attr* → **leicht** ADV **d**

Leich|ter ['laɪçtɐ] M **-s, -** (*Naut*) lighter

leich|tern ['laɪçtɐn] VT (*Naut*) to lighten (*form*)

Leicht-: leicht fal|len ▲ VI *irreg aux sein* to be easy (*jdm* for sb); **Sprachen sind mir schon immer leicht gefallen** I've always found languages easy; **leicht|fer|tig** ADJ thoughtless; (*moralisch*) of easy virtue ADV thoughtlessly; **~ handeln** to act without thinking; **etw ~ aufs Spiel setzen** to risk sth without giving it a thought; **Leicht|fer|tig|keit** F thoughtlessness; (*moralisch*) loose morals *pl*; **leicht|flüs|sig** ADJ *attr* (easily) fusible; **Leicht|fuß** M (*old*) (*Bruder*) ~ adventurer; **leicht|fü|ßig** (*liter*) ADJ light-footed ADV light-footedly; **leicht|gän|gig** ADJ *Getriebe* smooth; *Motor auch* smooth-running; **leicht|ge|schürzt** △ [-gəʃʏrtst] ADJ *attr* → **leicht** ADV **e**; **Leicht|ge|wicht** NT (*Sport, fig*) lightweight; **Weltmeister im ~** world lightweight champion; **leicht|ge|wich|tig** ADJ (*lit, fig*) lightweight; **Leicht|ge|wicht|ler** [-gəvɪçtlɐ] M **-s, -**, **Leicht|ge|wicht|le|rin** [-ərɪn] F **-, -nen** (*Sport*) lightweight; **Leicht|ge|wichts|klas|se** F lightweight class; **leicht|gläu|big** ADJ credulous; (= *leicht zu täuschen*) gullible; **Leicht|gläu|big|keit** F credulity; (= *Arglosigkeit*) gullibility

---

Leicht|heit F -, no pl lightness; (= Geringfügigkeit) slightness; (= Einfachheit: von Aufgabe etc) easiness

leicht|her|zig ADJ light-hearted ADV naively, light-heartedly

leicht|hin ['laiçthin] ADV lightly

Leich|tig|keit ['laiçtiçkait] F -, no pl **a** (= Mühelosigkeit) ease; **mit ~** easily, with no trouble (at all) **b** (= Unbekümmertheit) light-heartedness

Leicht-: Leicht|in|dust|rie F light industry; **Leicht|kraft|rad** NT moped; **leicht|le|big** [-le:bıç] ADJ happy-go-lucky, easygoing; **Leicht|le|big|keit** F -, no pl happy-go-lucky or easygoing nature; **Leicht|lohn|grup|pe** F group of (usually female) workers paid less than workers in comparable jobs; **leicht ma|chen** ▲ VT (jdm) **etw ~** to make sth easy (for sb); **sich** (dat) **etw ~, sich** (dat) **es mit etw ~** (= es sich bequem machen) to make things easy for oneself with sth; (= nicht gewissenhaft sein) to take it easy with sth; (= vereinfachen) to oversimplify sth; **er machte es sich** (dat) **leicht und vermied eine Entscheidung** he took the easy way out and avoided making a decision; **Leicht|mat|ro|se** M , **Leicht|mat|ro|sin** F ordinary seaman; **Leicht|me|tall** NT light metal; **leicht neh|men** ▲ VT irreg **etw ~** (= nicht ernsthaft behandeln) to take sth lightly; (= sich keine Sorgen machen) not to worry about sth → auch leicht ADV c; **Leicht|öl** NT light oil

Leicht|sinn M (= unvorsichtige Haltung) foolishness; (= Unbesorgtheit, Sorglosigkeit) thoughtlessness; **sträflicher ~** criminal negligence; **unverzeihlicher ~** unforgivable stupidity; **das ist (ein) ~** that's foolish or silly; **so ein ~!** how silly (can you get)!

leicht|sin|nig ADJ foolish; (= unüberlegt) thoughtless ADV handeln, mit etw umgehen thoughtlessly, carelessly; **~ schnell fahren** to drive recklessly; **~ mit etw umgehen** to be careless with sth

Leicht|sin|nig|keit F -, -en foolishness; (= Unüberlegtheit) thoughtlessness

Leicht|sinns|feh|ler M careless mistake, slip

Leicht-: leicht|ver|dau|lich △ ADJ attr → **leicht** ADV b; **leicht|ver|derb|lich** △ ADJ attr → **leicht** ADV d; **leicht|ver|letzt** △ [-fɛɛlɛtst] ADJ attr → **leicht** ADV g; **Leicht|ver|letz|te(r)** MF decl as adj **die ~n** the slightly injured; (in Gefecht, Schlägerei auch) the slightly wounded; **leicht|ver|ständ|lich** △ ADJ attr → **leicht** ADV b; **leicht|ver|wun|det** △ ADJ attr → **leicht** ADV g; **Leicht|ver|wun|de|te(r)** MF decl as adj slightly wounded soldier/man etc; **die ~n** the walking wounded; **Leicht|was|ser|re|ak|tor** M light water reactor

leid [lait] ADJ pred (= überdrüssig) **jdn/etw ~ sein** to be tired of sb/sth; **das lange Warten bin ich ~ geworden** I'm tired of all this waiting → **Leid** b

Leid [lait] ✪ 39.3, 45.1, 45.3, 48.1 NT -(e)s [-dəs] no indef art **a** (= Unglück) misfortune; (= Böses, Schaden) harm; **jdm in seinem tiefen ~ beistehen** to stand by sb in his/her (hour of) affliction or sorrow; **um jdn ~ tragen** (geh) to mourn sb; **ihm ist großes ~ widerfahren** he has suffered great misfortune; **viel ~ erfahren/ertragen (müssen)** to suffer/have to suffer a great deal; **es soll dir kein ~ zugefügt werden** or **geschehen** you will come to no harm, no harm will come to you; **jdm ein ~ antun** (liter) to harm sb; (moralisch) to wrong sb, to do sb wrong; **sich** (dat) **ein ~ antun** (liter) to injure oneself; **jdm sein ~ klagen** to tell sb one's troubles, to cry on sb's shoulder; **zu ~e = zuleide**

b **etw tut jdm ~** sb is sorry about or for sth; **es tut jdm ~, dass ...** sb is sorry that ...; **tut mir ~!** (I'm) sorry!; **es tut mir ~, dass ich so spät gekommen bin** I'm sorry for coming so late or (that) I came so late; **es tut mir nur ~, dass ...** I'm only sorry that ..., my only regret is that ...,

I only regret that ...; **es tut uns ~, Ihnen mitteilen zu müssen ...** we regret to have to inform you ...; **es tut einem ~, zu sehen, wie ...** it makes you feel sorry when you see how ...; **er/ sie tut mir ~** I'm sorry for him/her, I pity him/ her; **er/sie kann einem ~ tun** you can't help feeling sorry for him/her, you can't (help) but feel sorry for him/her; **du kannst einem ~ tun** you really are to be pitied; **es kann einem ~ tun, wenn ...** you can't help feeling sorry when ...; **es tut mir um ihn/darum ~** I'm sorry about him/that; **das wird dir noch ~ tun** you'll regret it, you'll be sorry

c (Sw: = Begräbnis) funeral

d (Sw: = Trauerkleidung) mourning; **(um jdn) ~ tragen, im ~ sein** to wear mourning (for sb), to be in mourning (for sb)

Lei|de|form ['laidə-] F (Gram) passive (voice)

lei|den ['laidn] pret **litt** [lıt], ptp **gelitten** [gə'lıtn] VT **a** (= ertragen müssen) Schaden, Hunger, Schmerz, Unrecht etc to suffer; **viel zu ~ haben** to have a great deal to bear or endure **b** **ich kann** or **mag ihn/es (gut) ~** I like him/it (very much); **ich kann** or **mag ihn/es nicht (gut) ~** I don't like him/it very much, I'm not very fond of him/it **c** (geh: = zulassen, dulden) to allow, to permit, to suffer (old); **er ist bei allen wohl gelitten** everybody holds him in high regard or great esteem VI to suffer (an +dat, unter +dat from); **die Farbe hat durch die grelle Sonne sehr gelitten** the harsh sun hasn't done the paint any good → **leidend**

Lei|den ['laidn] NT -s, - **a** suffering; **das sind (nun mal) die Freuden und ~ des Lebens!** ah, the ups and downs or the trials and tribulations of life!; **du siehst aus wie das ~ Christi** (inf) you look like death warmed up (Brit inf) or over (US inf) **b** (= Krankheit) illness; (= Beschwerden) complaint; **das ist ja eben das ~!** (inf) that's just the trouble **c** (hum inf: Mensch) **ein langes ~** a beanpole (inf)

-lei|den NT suf in cpds complaint, condition; **Augen-/Leberleiden** eye/liver complaint or condition

lei|dend ADJ (= kränklich) ailing; (inf) Miene long-suffering; **~ aussehen** to look ill; **sich ~ fühlen** (form) to feel ill

Lei|den|de(r) ['laidndə] MF decl as adj sufferer; **die ~n** the afflicted pl

Lei|den|schaft ['laidnʃaft] F -, -en passion; **seine ~ für etw entdecken** to develop a passion for sth; **etw mit ~ tun** to do sth with passionate enthusiasm; **ich koche mit großer ~** cooking is a great passion of mine; **er ist Lehrer aus ~** he teaches for the love of it

lei|den|schaft|lich ['laidnʃaftlıç] ADJ passionate; Liebhaber auch ardent; Rede auch impassioned ADV passionately; **etw ~ gern tun** to be mad about doing sth (inf), to be passionately fond of doing sth

Lei|den|schaft|lich|keit F -, no pl passion; (von Mensch) passionate nature; (im Beruf) dedication; (bei Hobby) burning enthusiasm

lei|den|schafts|los ADJ dispassionate ADV dispassionately

Leidens-: Lei|dens|druck M , no pl mental trauma; **lei|dens|fä|hig** ADJ **wir sind nicht unbegrenzt ~** we do not have an unlimited capacity for suffering; **Lei|dens|fä|hig|keit** F capacity for suffering; **Lei|dens|ge|fähr|te** M , **Lei|dens|ge|fähr|tin** F , **Lei|dens|ge|nosse** M , **Lei|dens|ge|nos|sin** F fellow-sufferer; **Lei|dens|ge|schich|te** F tale of woe; **die ~ (Christi)** (Bibl) Christ's Passion; **Lei|dens|mie|ne** F (hum inf) (long-)suffering expression; **Lei|dens|weg** M life of suffering; **Christi ~** Christ's suffering; **seinen ~ gehen** to bear one's cross

lei|der ['laidɐ] ✪ 36.3, 39, 45.3, 47.2, 47.4, 48.3, 52.4, 52.5 ADV unfortunately; **~ (Gottes) ja!, ja ~!** (yes,) more's the pity (inf), I'm afraid so,

yes, unfortunately; **~ (Gottes) nein/nicht!** unfortunately not, I'm afraid not, no, worse luck (inf); **ich kann ~ nicht kommen** unfortunately I can't come, I'm afraid I can't come

leid-: leid|ge|beugt [-gəbɔykt] ADJ bowed down with sorrow; **leid|ge|prüft** [-gəpry:ft] ADJ sorely afflicted

lei|dig ['laidıç] ADJ attr tiresome; **wenn bloß das ~e Geld nicht wäre** if only we didn't have to worry about money

leid|lich ['laitlıç] ADJ reasonable, fair ADV reasonably; **wie gehts? – danke, ~!** how are you? – not too bad or all right, thanks; **sie ist noch so ~ davongekommen** she didn't come out of it too badly

Leid|tra|gen|de(r) ['laittragndə] MF decl as adj **a** (= Hinterbliebener eines Verstorbenen) **ein ~r** a bereaved man; **eine ~** a bereaved woman; **die ~n** the bereaved **b** (= Benachteiligter) **der/die ~** the sufferer, the one to suffer

leid|voll ADJ (geh) Miene sorrowful; Erfahrung painful

Leid|we|sen ['laitve:zn] NT **zu jds ~** (much) to sb's disappointment or chagrin

Lei|er ['laiɐ] F -, -n **a** (Mus) lyre; (= Drehleier) hurdy-gurdy; **es ist immer dieselbe** or **die alte** or **die gleiche ~** (inf) it's always the same old story **b** (Astron) Lyra

Lei|er|kas|ten M barrel organ, hurdy-gurdy

Lei|er|kas|ten|frau F , **Lei|er|kas|ten|mann** M pl -männer organ-grinder

lei|ern ['laiɐn] VT Drehorgel to grind, to play; (inf: = kurbeln) to wind; (inf) Gedicht, Gebete etc to drone (out); **jdm etw aus dem Kreuz** or **den Rippen ~** to squeeze sth out of sb (inf) VI (= Drehorgel spielen) to grind or play a barrel organ; (inf: = drehen) to crank (an etw (dat) sth); (inf: beim Beten, Gedichtaufsagen etc) to drone

Lei|er|schwanz M lyrebird

Leih-: Leih|ar|beit F , no pl subcontracted work; **Leih|ar|bei|ter(in)** M(F) subcontracted worker; **Leih|au|to** NT hire(d) car (Brit), rental (car) (US); **Leih|bib|li|o|thek** F , **Leih|büche|rei** F lending library

Lei|he ['laiə] F -, -n (= das Verleihen) lending; (= das Vermieten) hiring; (= das Verpfänden) pawning; (inf: = Leihhaus) pawnshop; **etw in ~** or **in die ~ geben** to pawn or pop (inf) sth; **etw in ~ nehmen** to take sth in pawn

lei|hen ['laiən] pret **lieh** [li:], ptp **geliehen** [gə'li:ən] VT (= verleihen) Geld to lend; Sachen auch to loan; (= entleihen) to borrow; (= mieten, ausleihen) to hire; **ich habe es (mir) geliehen** I've borrowed or (gemietet) hired it, I've got it on loan or (gemietet) hire; **jdm seinen Beistand/sein Ohr/seine Aufmerksamkeit ~** (geh) to lend sb one's support/one's ear/one's attention; **jdm seine Stimme ~** (Synchronsprecher) to lend one's voice to sb

Leih-: Leih|fla|sche F returnable bottle; **Leih|ga|be** F loan; **dieses Bild ist eine ~ der Tate Gallery** this picture is on loan from the Tate Gallery; **Leih|ge|bühr** F hire or rental charge; (für Buch) lending charge; **Leih|haus** NT pawnshop; **Leih|mut|ter** F pl -mütter surrogate mother; **Leih|mut|ter|schaft** F surrogate motherhood, surrogacy; **Leih|schein** M (in der Bibliothek) borrowing slip; (im Leihhaus) pawn ticket; **Leih|schwan|ger|schaft** F surrogate pregnancy; **Leih|stim|me** F (Pol) tactical vote; **Leih|ver|kehr** M **ein Buch über den auswärtigen ~ bestellen** to order a book on interlibrary loan; **im ~ erhältlich** available on loan; **Leih|wa|gen** M hire(d) car (Brit), rental (car) (US); **leih|wei|se** ADV on loan

Leim [laim] M -(e)s, -e glue; (zum Vogelfangen) (bird)lime; **jdm auf den ~ führen** or **locken** (inf) to take sb in; **jdm auf den ~ gehen** or **kriechen** (inf) to be taken in by sb; **aus dem ~ gehen** (inf) (Sache) to fall apart or to pieces; (Mensch) to lose one's figure

lei|men ['laimən] VT (= *zusammenkleben*) to glue (together); (= *mit Leim bestreichen*) to spread with glue; (*zum Vogelfangen*) to lime; (*inf*) *Ehe* to patch up (*inf*); **jdn ~** (*inf*) to take sb for a ride (*inf*); **der Geleimte** the mug (*inf*)

Leim|far|be F distemper

lei|mig ['laimɪç] ADJ sticky, gluey

Leim|ru|te F lime twig

Lei|mung ['laimʊŋ] F -, *no pl* sizing

Lein [lain] M -(e)s, -e flax

Lei|ne ['lainə] F -, -n cord; (= *Tau, Zeltleine*) rope; (= *Schnur*) string; (= *Angelleine, Wäscheleine, Naut*) line; (= *Hundeleine*) lead (*Brit*), leash; **Hunde bitte an der ~ führen!** dogs should or must be kept on a leash; **den Hund an die ~ nehmen** to put the dog on the lead (*Brit*) or leash; **jdn an der ~ halten** or **haben** (*inf*) to keep sb on a tight rein; **jdn an die ~ nehmen** (*inf*), to hook sb (*inf*), to drag sb to the altar (*inf*); **jdn an die kurze ~ nehmen** or **legen** (*inf*) to keep sb on a short leash; **jdn an die lange ~ legen** to give sb his/ her head; **~ ziehen** (*inf*) to clear out (*inf*), to push off (*inf*); **~n los!** cast off!

lei|nen ['lainən] ADJ linen; (*grob*) canvas; *Bucheinband* cloth

Lei|nen ['lainən] NT -s, - linen; (*grob, segeltuchartig*) canvas; (*als Bucheinband*) cloth

Lei|nen-: Lei|nen|band [-bant] M *pl* -**bände** cloth(bound) volume; **ein Buch als ~ haben** to have the clothbound edition of a book; **Lei|nen|schlaf|sack** M sheet sleeping bag; **Lei|nen|ta|sche** F canvas bag; **Lei|nen|tuch** NT *pl* -**tücher** linen (cloth); (*grob, segeltuchartig*) canvas; **Lei|nen|zeug** NT linen

Lei|ne|we|ber(in) M(F) linen weaver

Lei|ne|we|be|rei F (*Fabrik*) linen mill; (*Herstellung*) linen weaving

Lein-: Lein|kraut NT toadflax; **Lein|öl** NT linseed oil; **Lein|pfad** M towpath; **Lein|sa|men** M linseed; **Lein|tuch** NT *pl* -**tücher** (*S Ger, Aus, Sw*) sheet

Lein|wand F -, *no pl* canvas; (*für Dias*) screen; **wenn der Film über die ~ läuft** when the film is being shown or screened; **Dias auf die ~ werfen** to show or project slides

lei|se ['laizə] ADJ **a** quiet; *Stimme, Schritt, Klopfen* soft, quiet; *Radio* low; (*aus der Ferne*) faint; **auf ~n Sohlen** treading softly; **... sagte er mit ~r Stimme** ... he said in a low voice, ... he said quietly

b (= *gering, schwach*) slight, faint; *Schlaf, Regen, Berührung* light; *Wind, Wellenschlag* light, gentle; **nicht die ~ste Ahnung haben** not to have the slightest or faintest or foggiest (*inf*) (idea); **ich habe nicht die ~ste Veranlassung, ...** there isn't the slightest or faintest reason why I ...

c (= *sanft, zart*) soft, gentle; *Musik* soft

ADV (= *nicht laut*) quietly, softly; **~r singen** to sing more quietly; **ein ~ geführtes Gespräch** a quiet talk; **das Radio (etwas) ~r stellen** to turn the radio down (slightly); **sprich doch ~r!** keep your voice down a bit

Lei|se|tre|ter [-tre:tɐ] M -s, -, **Lei|se|tre|te|rin** [-ərɪn] F -, -**nen** (*pej inf*) pussyfoot(er) (*pej inf*); (= *Duckmäuser*) creep (*pej inf*)

Leis|te ['laistə] F -, -n **a** (= *Holzleiste etc*) strip (of wood etc); (= *Zierleiste*) trim; (= *Umrandung*) border; (*zur Bilderaufhängung, zur Führung von Arbeitsstücken etc*) rail; (= *Scheuerleiste*) skirting (board) (*Brit*), baseboard (*US*) **b** (*Anat*) groin

leis|ten ['laistn] VT **a** (= *erringen, erreichen*) to achieve; *Arbeit, Überstunden* to do; (*Maschine*) to manage; (= *ableisten*) *Wehrdienst etc* to complete; **etwas/viel/nichts ~** (*Mensch*) (= *arbeiten*) to do something/a lot/nothing; (= *schaffen auch*) to get something/a lot/nothing done; (= *vollbringen*) to achieve something/a great deal/nothing; (*Maschine*) to be quite good/very good/no good at all; (*Auto, Motor etc*) to be quite powerful/very powerful/to have no power; **der Motor des Autos leistet 150 PS** the car has a 150-hp engine; **Großartiges/Erstaunliches/Überragen-**

des *etc* ~ to do or achieve something really great/amazing/excellent *etc*; **gute/ganze Arbeit ~** to do a good/thorough job; **in meiner Position muss ich schon etwas ~** in my position I have to do my work and do it well; **er leistet genauso viel wie ich** he's just as efficient as I am; **was eine Mutter alles ~ muss** the things that a mother has to cope with; **er hat immer das Gefühl, nichts zu ~** he always has the feeling that he isn't doing a good job; **seine Arbeit ~** to do one's work well; **ich muss genauso meine Arbeit ~ wie jeder andere auch** I've got my job to do like everybody else

b (*in festen Verbindungen mit n siehe auch dort*) (*jdm*) *Beistand ~* to lend (sb) one's support; **jdm Hilfe ~** to give sb some help; **jdm gute Dienste ~** (*Gegenstand*) to serve sb well; (*Mensch*) to be useful to sb; *Folge ~* to comply (+*dat* with); *Zahlungen ~* to make payments; **jdm eine Garantie ~** to give sb a guarantee (*auf etw (acc)* on sth); **jdm Gewähr ~** to give sb a guarantee (*für etw* for sth, *dafür, dass ... that ...*)

c *sich (dat) etw ~* to allow oneself sth; (= *sich gönnen*) to treat oneself to sth; (= *kaufen*) to buy sth; **sich (dat) etw ~ können** (*finanziell*) to be able to afford sth; **sich (dat) eine Frechheit/Frechheiten ~** to be cheeky (*Brit*) or impudent; **er leistete sich die Frechheit, ungebeten zu erscheinen** he had the cheek (*Brit*) or gall to turn up uninvited; **da hast du dir ja was (Schönes or Nettes) geleistet** (*iro*) you've really done it now; **er hat sich tolle Sachen/Streiche geleistet** he got up to the craziest things/pranks

Leis|ten ['laistn] M -s, - (= *Schuhleisten*) last; **al|le/alles über einen ~ schlagen** (*fig*) to measure everyone/everything by the same yardstick → **Schuster**

Leis|ten-: Leis|ten|bruch M (*Med*) hernia, rupture; **Leis|ten|ge|gend** F inguinal region (*form*), groin

Leis|tung ['laistʊŋ] F -, -en **a** (= *Geleistetes*) performance; (*großartige, gute, Sociol*) achievement; (= *Ergebnis*) result(s); (= *geleistete Arbeit*) work *no pl*; **eine große ~** a great achievement; **das ist eine ~!** that's quite or really something (*inf*), that's quite an achievement or quite a feat; **das ist keine besondere ~** that's nothing special; **nach ~ bezahlt werden** to be paid on results; **nicht das Geschlecht, nur die ~ zählt** your sex isn't important, it's how you do the job that counts; **das liegt weit unter der üblichen ~** that is well below the usual standard; **die ~en sind besser geworden** the levels of performance have improved; (*in Fabrik, Schule auch*) the standard of work has improved; **seine schulischen/sportlichen ~en haben nachgelassen** his school work/athletic ability has deteriorated; **er ist auf seine sportlichen ~en stolz** he's proud of his athletic achievement(s); **eine ~ der Technik** a feat of engineering; **schwache ~!** poor show! (*dated inf*) that's not very good

b (= *Leistungsfähigkeit*) capacity (*auch Comput*); (*von Motor, Energiequelle*) power; (*von Fabrik, Firma*) potential output

c (*Jur*) (= *Übernahme einer Verpflichtung*) obligation; (= *Zahlung*) payment; **die ~en des Reiseveranstalters** what the travel company offers; **~ eines Ersatzes** obligation to provide a replacement

d (= *Aufwendungen*: *einer Versicherung, Krankenkasse, sozial*) benefit; (= *Dienstleistung*) service; (= *Zahlungsleistung*) payment

e (= *Ableistung*) completion; **die ~ des Wehrdienstes ist Pflicht** completion of national service is obligatory

Leis|tungs-: Leis|tungs|ab|fall M (*in Bezug auf Qualität*) drop in performance; (*in Bezug auf Quantität*) drop in productivity; **Leis|tungs|aus|fall** M loss of productivity; **leis|tungs|be|zo|gen** ADJ performance-related; **Leis|tungs|bi|lanz** F (*einer Firma*) current balance including investments; (*eines Landes*) balance of payments including invisible trade; **Leis|-**

tungs|druck M , *no pl* pressure (to do well); **Leis|tungs|emp|fän|ger(in)** M(F) beneficiary; **Leis|tungs|fach** NT (*Sch*) special subject; **leis|tungs|fä|hig** ADJ (= *konkurrenzfähig*) competitive; (= *produktiv*) efficient, productive; *Motor* powerful; *Maschine* productive; (*Fin*) able to pay, solvent; *Mensch* able, capable; *Arbeiter* efficient; *Organ, Verdauungssystem etc* functioning properly; **Leis|tungs|fä|hig|keit** F (= *Konkurrenzfähigkeit*) competitiveness; (= *Produktivität*) efficiency, productivity; (*von Motor*) power(fulness); (*von Maschine, Körperorgan etc*) capacity; (*Fin*) ability to pay, solvency; (*von Mensch*) ability, capability; (*von Arbeiter*) efficiency; **das übersteigt meine ~** that's beyond my capabilities; **leis|tungs|feind|lich** ADJ **hohe Steuern sind ~** high taxes inhibit productivity; **leis|tungs|för|dernd** ADJ conducive to efficiency; (*in Schule, Universität etc*) conducive to learning; *Substanz* performance-enhancing ADV to improve performance; **leis|tungs|ge|recht** ADJ *Bezahlung* preformance-related; **Leis|tungs|ge|sell|schaft** F meritocracy, achievement-orientated society (*pej*); **Leis|tungs|gren|ze** F upper limit; **Leis|tungs|kla|ge** F (*Jur*) suit for fulfilment (*Brit*) or fulfillment (*US*) of obligations; **Leis|tungs|klas|se** F (*Sport*) class; **Leis|tungs|kon|trol|le** F (*Sch, Univ*) assessment; (*in der Fabrik*) productivity check; **zur ~** (in order) to assess progress/check productivity; **Leis|tungs|kraft** F power; **eine hohe ~ haben** to be very powerful; **Leis|tungs|kurs** M *advanced course in specialist subjects*

LEISTUNGSKURS

Leistungskurse are the two specialist subjects chosen by pupils in the upper classes of a **Gymnasium**, during the **Kollegstufe**. Six hours a week are devoted to each of these subjects, allowing more time for special projects and the pupils' own work. Those taking the **Abitur** have to write a **Facharbeit** – similar to a short university seminar paper – in one of the subjects. Together with examinations in both specialist subjects, this makes up a third of the overall mark for the **Abitur**. In a **Gesamtschule**, *Leistungskurse* are more advanced courses → ABITUR, GESAMTSCHULE, GYMNASIUM, KOLLEGSTUFE

Leis|tungs-: Leis|tungs|kur|ve F productivity curve; **Leis|tungs|lohn** M piece rates *pl*; **Leis|tungs|merk|mal** NT performance feature; **Leis|tungs|mes|ser** M -s, - (*Phys*) power output meter; (*Elec*) wattmeter; **Leis|tungs|mes|sung** F assessment of achievement; (*in Fabrik*) measuring or assessment of productivity; (*Phys, Elec*) measurement of power; **Leis|tungs|mo|ti|va|ti|on** F achievement motivation; **Leis|tungs|nach|weis** M certificate (*of academic achievement*); **leis|tungs|ori|en|tiert** ADJ *Gesellschaft* competitive; *Lohn* performance-related; **Leis|tungs|prä|mie** F productivity bonus; **Leis|tungs|prin|zip** NT achievement principle; **Leis|tungs|prü|fung** F (*Sch*) achievement test; (*Tech*) performance test; **Leis|tungs|schau** F exhibition, show; **Leis|tungs|sport** M competitive sport; **leis|tungs|stark** ADJ (= *konkurrenzfähig*) highly competitive; (= *produktiv*) highly efficient or productive; *Motor* very powerful; *Maschine* highly productive; **Leis|tungs|stei|ge|rung** F → *Leistung* a, b increase in performance/achievement *etc*; **Leis|tungs|stu|fe** F (*Sch*) special subject class; **Leis|tungs|test** M (*Sch*) achievement test; (*Tech*) performance test; **Leis|tungs|trä|ger(in)** M(F) **a** (*esp Sport*) key player **b** (*von Sozialleistungen*) (health care *etc*) service provider; **Leis|tungs|ver|mö|gen** NT capabilities *pl*; **Leis|tungs|wett|kampf** M competition; **Leis|tungs|wil|le** M motivation; **Leis|tungs|zu|la|ge** F , **Leis|tungs|zu-**

---

schlag M productivity bonus; **Leis|tungs|-zwang** M pressure to do well

Leit- ['lait-]: **Leit|ar|ti|kel** M leader (Brit), editorial; **leit|ar|ti|keln** [-larti:kln, -lartɪkln] ptp **leitartikelt** VTI insep (inf) to lead; **Leit|ar|tik|ler** [-larti:klɐ, -lartɪklɐ] M -s, -, **Leit|ar|tik|le|rin** [-ərɪn] F -, -nen leader writer (Brit), editorial writer; **Leit|bild** NT model; **Leit|bün|del** NT (Bot) vascular bundle

lei|ten ['laitn] VT **a** (= in bestimmte Richtung lenken) to lead; (= begleiten, führen) to conduct, to lead; (fig) Leser, Schüler etc to guide; Verkehr to route; Gas, Wasser to conduct; (= umleiten) to divert; **etw an die zuständige Stelle ~** to pass sth on to the proper authority; **sich von jdm/etw ~ lassen** (lit, fig) to (let oneself) be guided by sb/sth; von Vorstellung, Idee, Emotion to be governed by sth; **das Öl wird (durch Rohre) zum Hafen geleitet** the oil is piped to the port

b (= verantwortlich sein für) to be in charge of; (administrativ) to run, to be in charge of; Expedition, Partei, Regierung, Bewegung etc to lead, to head; Betrieb to manage, to be in charge of; Theater to run; Orchester, Theatergruppe etc to direct, to run; Sitzung, Diskussion, Gespräch, Verhandlungen to lead; (als Vorsitzender) to chair; Geschick(e) to determine, to guide

c (Phys) Wärme, Strom, Licht to conduct; **(etw) gut/schlecht ~** to be a good/bad conductor (of sth)

lei|tend ADJ leading; Gedanke, Idee central, dominant; Stellung, Position managerial; Ingenieur, Beamter in charge; (Phys) conductive; **nicht ~** (Phys) nonconductive; **~e(r) Angestellte(r)** executive; **~er Beamter, ~e Beamtin** senior official; **die ~e Hand** (fig) the guiding hand

Lei|ter¹ ['laitɐ] F -, -n (lit, fig) ladder; (= Stehleiter) steps pl, stepladder; (Sport) wall bars pl; **an der ~ turnen** to work on the wall bars

Lei|ter² M -s, - **a** leader; (von Hotel, Restaurant, Geschäft) manager; (= Abteilungsleiter, in Firma) head; (von Schule) head (esp Brit), principal (esp US); (von Orchester, Chor, Theatergruppe etc) director; (von Kirchenchor) choirmaster; **kaufmännischer/künstlerischer** = sales/artistic director → auch **Leiterin b** (Phys) conductor

Lei|ter|bahn F (Comput) strip conductor

Lei|te|rin ['laitərɪn] F -, -nen leader; (von Hotel, Restaurant) manager; (von Geschäft) manageress; (= Abteilungsleiterin, in Firma) head; (von Schule) head (esp Brit), principal (esp US); (von Orchester, Chor, Theatergruppe etc) director; (von Kirchenchor) choirmaster; **kaufmännische/künstlerische** = sales/artistic director

Lei|ter-: **Lei|ter|plat|te** F (Comput) circuit board; **Lei|ter|spros|se** F rung; **eine ~ des Erfolgs höher kommen** t; **Lei|ter|wa|gen** M handcart

Leit-: **Leit|fa|den** M (fig) main connecting thread or theme; (Fachbuch) introduction; (= Gebrauchsanleitung) manual; **leit|fä|hig** ADJ (Phys) conductive; **Leit|fä|hig|keit** F (Phys) conductivity; **Leit|feu|er** NT beacon; **Leit|fos|sil** NT index fossil; **Leit|ge|dan|ke** M central idea; **er machte diesen Spruch zum ~n seines Lebens** he made this saying his motto in life; **Leit|ge|ra|de** F (Math) directrix; **Leit|ge|we|be** NT (Biol) vascular tissue; **Leit|ham|mel** M bellwether; (fig inf) leader, bellwether (liter); **Leit|hund** M (Hunt) leader of the pack; **Leit|idee** F central idea; **Leit|li|nie** F (im Verkehr) broken (white) line; (fig) broad outline; (= Bestimmung) guideline; (Math) directrix; **Leit|mo|tiv** NT (Mus, Liter, fig) leitmotif; **Leit|pfos|ten** M reflector post; **Leit|plan|ke** F crash barrier; **Leit|preis** M guide price; **Leit|satz** M basic principle; **Leit|schie|ne** F guide rail; **Leit|spin|del** F (Tech) lead screw; **Leit|spruch** M motto; **Leit|stel|le** F regional headquarters pl; (= Funkleitstelle) control centre (Brit) or center (US); **Leit|stern** M (lit) lodestar; (fig auch) guiding star; **Leit|strahl** M (Aviat, Mil, Space) control beam;

(Math) radius vector; **Leit|tier** NT leader (of a herd etc); **Leit|ton** M pl -töne (Mus) leading note; **Leit|trieb** M (Bot) leader

Lei|tung ['laitʊŋ] F -, -en **a** no pl (= das Leiten) leading; (= Begleitung, Führung) conducting; (von Verkehr) routing; (von Gas, Wasser) conducting **b** no pl (von Menschen, Organisationen) running; (von Partei, Regierung) leadership; (von Betrieb) management; (von Schule) headship (esp Brit), principalship (esp US); **die ~ einer Sache** (gen) **haben** to be in charge of sth; **unter der ~ von jdm** (Mus) conducted by sb; **die ~ des Gesprächs hat Horst Bauer** Horst Bauer is leading the discussion

c (= die Leitenden) leaders pl; (eines Betriebes etc) management sing or pl; (einer Schule) head teachers pl

d (für Gas, Wasser, Elektrizität etc bis zum Haus) main; (für Gas, Wasser im Haus) pipe; (für Elektrizität im Haus) wire; (dicker) cable; (= Überlandleitung für Elektrizität) line; (= Telefonleitung) line; (= Draht) wire; (dicker) cable; (= Verbindung) line; **die ~ ist ganz fürchterlich gestört** (Telec) it's a terrible line, there's a lot of interference on the line; **gehen Sie aus der ~!** (inf) get off the line; **da ist jemand in der ~** (inf) there's somebody else on the line; **eine lange ~ haben** (hum inf) to be slow on the uptake, to be slow to catch on; **bei dir steht wohl jemand** or **du stehst wohl auf der ~** (hum inf) you're slow on the uptake, you're slow to catch on

Lei|tungs-: **Lei|tungs|anäs|the|sie** F (Med) nerve-block or conduction anaesthesia (Brit) or anesthesia (US); **Lei|tungs|draht** M wire; **Lei|tungs|mast** M (Elec) (electricity) pylon; **Lei|tungs|netz** NT (Elec) (electricity) grid; (für Wasser, Gas) mains system; (Telec) (telephone) network; **Lei|tungs|rohr** NT main; (im Haus) (supply) pipe; **Lei|tungs|was|ser** NT tap water, mains water; **Lei|tungs|wi|der|stand** M (Elec) resistance

Leit-: **Leit|ver|mö|gen** NT (Phys) conductivity; **Leit|wäh|rung** F reserve currency; **Leit|werk** NT (Aviat) tail unit, empennage (spec); **Leit|wert** M conductance; **Leit|wolf** M (Zool, fig) leader of the pack, alpha male; **Leit|wort** NT pl -wörter motto

Leit|zins M base rate, (central bank) discount rate, prime rate (US)

Leit|zins-: **Leit|zins|er|hö|hung** F increase in the base rate; **Leit|zins|satz** M bank rate

Leitz-Ord|ner® [laits-] M lever-arch file

lei|wand ['laivant] ADJ (Aus inf) brilliant, fantastic

Lek|ti|on [lɛk'tsio:n] F -, -en lesson; **jdm eine ~ erteilen** (fig) to teach sb a lesson

Lek|tor ['lɛkto:ɐ] M -s, Lektoren [-'to:rən], **Lek|to|rin** [-'to:rɪn] F -, -nen (Univ) foreign language assistant, lector; (= Verlagslektor) editor

Lek|to|rat [lɛkto'ra:t] NT -(e)s, -e (im Verlag) editorial office; (Gutachten) editorial report

lek|to|rie|ren [lɛkto'ri:rən] ptp **lektoriert** VT etw = sth, to prepare sth for press VI to work as an editor

Lek|tü|re [lɛk'ty:rə] F -, -n (no pl: = das Lesen) reading; (= Lesestoff) reading matter; **das wird zur ~ empfohlen** that is recommended reading; **das ist eine gute/interessante** etc ~ it makes good/interesting etc reading, it's a good/an interesting etc read; **das ist eine schlechte ~** it doesn't make good reading, it's not a good read; **das ist keine (passende) ~ für dich/Kinder** that's not suitable reading for you/children, that's not suitable for you/children to read; **ich muss noch (etwas) leichte ~ besorgen** I've still got to get something light to read

Lem|ma ['lema] NT -s, -ta [-ta] lemma

Lem|ming ['lɛmɪŋ] M -s, -e lemming

Len|de ['lɛndə] F -, -n (Anat, Cook) loin

Len|den-: **Len|den|bra|ten** M loin roast (Brit), porterhouse (steak); **Len|den|ge|gend** F lumbar region; **len|den|lahm** ADJ **a** (dated)

Pferd broken-backed; **er ist ~** his back is crippling him **b** (inf: = impotent) **er ist ~** he can't get it up (inf); **Len|den|schurz** M loincloth; **Len|den|stück** NT piece of loin; **Len|den|wir|bel** M lumbar vertebra

Le|ni|nis|mus [leni'nɪsmʊs] M -, no pl Leninism

Le|ni|nist [leni'nɪst] M -en, -en, **Le|ni|nis|tin** [-'nɪstɪn] F -, -nen Leninist

le|ni|nis|tisch [leni'nɪstɪʃ] ADJ Leninist ADV **~ klingend** Leninist-sounding; **~ gesinnt** Leninist; **~ beeinflusst** influenced by (the teachings of) Lenin

Lenk-: **Lenk|ach|se** F pivoted axle; **lenk|bar** ADJ (Tech) steerable; Kind tractable; Rakete guided; **leicht/schwer ~ sein** to be easy/difficult to steer, to have light/heavy steering; **das Kind ist leicht/schwer ~** the child can be easily guided/won't be guided; **Lenk|bar|keit** F -, no pl (Tech) steerability; **die schwere ~ des Fahrzeugs** the vehicle's heavy steering; **Lenk|com|pu|ter** M guide computer

len|ken ['lɛŋkn] VT **a** (= führen, leiten) to direct, to guide; (fig: = beeinflussen) Sprache, Presse etc to influence; Kind to guide; **gelenkte Wirtschaft** planned economy; **staatlich gelenkte Medien** state-controlled media

b (= steuern) Auto, Flugzeug, Schiff etc to steer; Pferde to drive; **sich leicht ~ lassen** to be easy to steer/drive

c (fig) Schritte, Gedanken, seine Aufmerksamkeit, Blick to direct (auf +acc to); jds Aufmerksamkeit, Blicke to draw (auf +acc to); Verdacht to throw, to draw (auf +acc onto); Gespräch to lead, to steer; Schicksal to guide; **das Gespräch in eine andere Richtung ~** to steer the conversation in another direction; **die Geschicke des Landes/der Partei ~** to control the future of the country/party; **seine Schritte heimwärts ~** (liter, hum inf) to wend one's way homewards (liter, hum), to turn one's steps to home (liter, hum) VI (= steuern) to steer

Len|ker¹ ['lɛŋkɐ] M -s, - **a** (= Fahrradlenker etc) handlebars pl **b** (Tech) guide; (= Lenkung) steering gear

Len|ker² ['lɛŋkɐ] M -s, -, **Len|ke|rin** [-ərɪn] F -, -nen driver; (fig) guide

Lenk|ge|trie|be NT steering gear

Lenk|rad NT (steering) wheel; **jdm ins ~ greifen** to grab the (steering) wheel from sb

Lenk|rad- (Aut): **Lenk|rad|schal|tung** F column(-mounted) (gear) change (Brit) or shift (US), **Lenk|rad|schloss** ▲ NT steering (wheel) lock; **Lenk|rad|sper|re** F steering wheel lock

Lenk|säu|le F steering column

Lenk|stan|ge F (von Fahrrad etc) handlebars pl

Len|kung ['lɛŋkʊŋ] F -, -en **a** (= das Lenken) direction, guidance; (fig: = Beeinflussung) influencing; (= das Steuern) steering **b** (Tech: = Lenkeinrichtung) steering

Len|kungs|aus|schuss ▲ M (Pol) steering committee

Lenk-: **Lenk|ver|hal|ten** NT (von Auto) steering no indef art; **Lenk|waf|fe** F guided missile

Len|ti|vi|rus [lɛnti'vi:rʊs] NT OR M lentivirus

len|to ['lento] ADV (Mus) lento

Lenz [lɛnts] M -es, -e (liter: = Frühling) spring (-time), springtide (liter); **der ~ des Lebens** the springtime of one's life (liter); **sie zählt 20 ~e** (hum) she has seen 20 summers (liter, hum); **einen ~ schieben** or **haben** (inf) to have a good time (inf); **sich** (dat) **einen (faulen** or **schönen) ~ machen** (inf) to laze about (Brit) or around, to swing the lead (Brit inf)

len|zen ['lɛntsn] (Naut) VT (= leer pumpen) to pump out VI (= vor dem Wind segeln) to scud

Lenz-: **Lenz|pum|pe** F (Naut) bilge pump; **Lenz|tag** M (liter) spring day

Le|o|pard [leo'part] M -en, -en [-dn] leopard

Le|o|par|din [leo'pardɪn] F -, -nen leopardess

Le|po|rel|lo [lepo'rɛlo] NT OR M **-s, -s** concertina folder

Lep|ra ['le:pra] F **-,** no pl leprosy

Lep|rom [le'pro:m] NT **-s, -e** leprous lesion

lep|ros [le'pro:s], **lep|rös** [le'prø:s] ADJ leprous

Lep|rö|se(r) [le'prø:zə] MF decl as adj leper

Lep|ro|so|ri|um [lepro'zo:riʊm] NT **-s,** Leprosorien [-riən] leprosarium

lep|to|som [lɛpto'zo:m] ADJ (form) asthenic (form), leptosome (form)

Ler|che ['lɛrçə] F **-, -n** lark

Lern-: **lern|bar** ADJ learnable; **Lern|be|gier (-de)** F eagerness to learn; **lern|be|gie|rig** ADJ eager to learn; **lern|be|hin|dert** [-bəhɪndət] ADJ with learning difficulties; **Lern|be|hin|der|te(r)** MF decl as adj child/person etc with learning difficulties; **Lern|dis|ket|te** F tutorial disk or diskette; **Lern|ei|fer** M eagerness to learn; **lern|ei|frig** ADJ eager to learn

ler|nen ['lɛrnən] **VT** **a** (= Fertigkeit erwerben in) to learn; **lesen/schwimmen** etc ~ to learn to read/swim etc; **Stenografie/Schreibmaschine ~** to learn shorthand/typing or to type; **~, etw zu tun** to learn to do sth; (= sich Fähigkeit, Können aneignen auch) to learn how to do sth; **etw von/bei jdm ~** to learn sth from sb; **jdn lieben/schätzen ~** to come or learn to love/appreciate sb; **er lernts nie** he never learns; **er wirds nie ~** he'll never learn → **Hänschen**

b Beruf to learn; Bäcker, Schlosser etc to train as, to learn the trade of; **er hat zwei Jahre gelernt** he trained for two years, he did two years' training; (in Handwerk) he did a two-year apprenticeship; **das will gelernt sein** it's a question of practice; **gelernt ist gelernt** (Prov) once you've learned something ...; **lerne was, so kannst/bist du was** (prov) it never hurt anyone to learn anything → auch **gelernt**

VI **a** (= Kenntnisse erwerben) to learn; (= arbeiten) to study; (= Schulaufgaben machen) to do (one's) homework; **die Mutter lernte drei Stunden mit ihm** his mother spent three hours helping him with his homework; **lerne fleißig in der Schule** work hard at school; **von ihm kannst du noch (was) ~!** he could teach you a thing or two; **nicht für die Schule, sondern für das Leben ~ wir** (prov) learning is not just for school but for life

b (= sich in der Ausbildung befinden) to go to school; (in Universität) to study; (in Beruf) to train; **er lernt bei der Firma Braun** he's training at Braun's, Braun's are training him

VR **der Text/die Rolle lernt sich leicht/schwer/schnell** the text/part is easy/hard to learn/doesn't take long to learn

Ler|ner ['lɛrnɐ] M **-s, -,** **Ler|ne|rin** [-ərɪn] F **-, -nen** learner

Lern|er|folg M learning success; **den ~ messen** to measure the success of the learning process

Lern-: **lern|fä|hig** ADJ capable of learning pred; **Lern|hil|fe** F educational aid; **Lern|kur|ve** F (Psych) learning curve; **Lern|ma|schi|ne** F teaching machine; **Lern|mit|tel** PL schoolbooks and equipment pl; **Lern|mit|tel|frei|heit** F free provision of schoolbooks and equipment; **Lern|pro|gramm** NT (Comput) (für Software) tutorial program; (didaktisches Programm) learning program; **Lern|pro|zess** ▲ M learning process; **Lern|psy|cho|lo|gie** F psychology of learning; **Lern|schwes|ter** F student nurse; **lern|wil|lig** ADJ willing to learn pred; **Lern|ziel** NT learning goal

Les-: **Les|art** F (lit, fig) version; **les|bar** ADJ **a** (= leserlich) legible; (Comput) readable **b** (= verständlich) Buch readable ADV **a** (= leserlich) legibly; **gut ~ angebracht** very visible **b** (= verständlich) readably

Les|be ['lɛsbə] F **-, -n** (inf) lesbian

Les|bie|rin ['lɛsbiərɪn] F **-, -nen** lesbian

les|bisch ['lɛsbɪʃ] ADJ lesbian

Le|se ['le:zə] F **-, -n** (= Ernte) harvest; (= Weinart) vintage; (= Beerenlese) picking

Lese-: **Le|se|abend** M evening of readings; **Le|se|bril|le** F reading glasses pl; **Le|se|buch** NT reader; **Le|se|ecke** F reading or readers' corner; **Le|se|ge|rät** NT (Comput) reading device, reader; **Le|se|ge|schwin|dig|keit** F (auch Comput) reading speed; **Le|se|ge|wohn|hei|ten** PL reading habits pl; **Le|se|kar|te** F reader's ticket; **Le|se|kopf** M (Comput) read head; **Le|se|kreis** M reading circle; **Le|se|lam|pe** F reading lamp; **Le|se|lis|te** F reading list; **Le|se|map|pe** F (= Zeitschrift) magazine in a folder

le|sen¹ ['le:zn] pret **las** [la:s], ptp **ge|le|sen** [gə'le:zn] **VTI** **a** Geschriebenes to read (auch Comput); (Eccl) Messe to say; **hier/in der Zeitung steht** or **ist zu ~, dass ...** it says here/in the paper that ...; **die Schrift ist kaum zu ~** the writing is scarcely legible → **Leviten**

b (= deuten) Gedanken to read; **jdm (sein Schicksal) aus der Hand ~** to read sb's palm; **in den Sternen ~** to read or see in the stars; **aus ihren Zeilen habe ich einen Vorwurf/eine gewisse Unsicherheit gelesen** I could tell from what she had written that she was reproaching me/felt a certain amount of uncertainty; **etw in jds Augen/Miene** (dat) **~** to see sth in sb's eyes/from sb's manner; **es war in ihrem Gesicht zu ~** it was written all over her face, you could see it in her face

c (Univ) to lecture; **er liest Englisch an der Universität** he lectures in English at the university **VR** (Buch, Bericht etc) to read; **bei diesem Licht liest es sich nicht gut** this light isn't good for reading (in); **sich in den Schlaf ~** to read oneself to sleep

le|sen² pret **las** [la:s], ptp **ge|le|sen** [gə'le:zn] VT **a** (= sammeln) Trauben, Beeren to pick; (nach der Ernte) Ähren to glean **b** (= verlesen) Erbsen, Linsen etc to sort; Salat to clean

le|sens|wert ADJ worth reading

Lese-: **Le|se|pro|be** F **a** (Theat) reading **b** (= Ausschnitt aus Buch) extract, excerpt; **Le|se|pult** NT lectern

Le|ser ['le:zɐ] M **-s, -,** **Le|se|rin** [-ərɪn] F **-, -nen** reader; **seine Romane haben viele ~ gefunden** his novels have gained a large readership

Le|se|rat|te F (inf) bookworm (inf)

Le|ser|brief M (reader's) letter; **einen ~ an eine Zeitung schreiben** to write a letter to a newspaper; **„Leserbriefe"** "letters to the editor", "readers' letters"

Le|se|rei [le:zə'raɪ] F **-,** no pl (inf) reading; **kannst du jetzt nicht endlich mit der ~ aufhören?** can't you take your nose out of your books? (inf)

le|ser|freund|lich ADJ easy-to-read attr, easy to read pred; **wenig ~** difficult to read, hard on the eyes; **~e Gestaltung** reader-friendly layout ADV **~ gestaltet** designed to be easy to read; Nachschlagewerk designed for easy reference

Le|se|rin F → **Leser**

Le|se|ring® M book club

Leser-: **Le|ser|kreis** M readership; **le|ser|lich** ['le:zɐlɪç] ADJ legible ADV legibly; **Le|ser|lich|keit** F **-,** no pl legibility; **Le|ser|schaft** ['le:zɐʃaft] F **-, -en** readership; **Le|ser|stamm** M regular readers; **Le|ser|wunsch** M wish(es) of the readers; **auf vielfachen ~** at the request of many readers; **Le|ser|zu|schrift** F = Leserbrief

Lese-: **Le|se|saal** M reading room; **Le|se|spei|cher** M (Comput) read-only memory, ROM; **Le|se|stift** M (für Barcodes) barcode scanner; **Le|se|stoff** M reading material; **ich brauche noch ~** I need something to read; **Le|se|stück** NT reading passage; **Le|se|wut** F craze for reading; **von (der) ~ gepackt sein** to have caught the reading bug (inf); **Le|se|zei|chen** NT bookmark(er); **Le|se|zim|mer** NT reading room; **Le|se|zir|kel** M magazine subscription club

Le|sung ['le:zʊŋ] F **-, -en** (= Dichterlesung, Parl) reading; (Eccl auch) lesson

le|tal [le'ta:l] ADJ (Med) lethal

Le|thar|gie [letar'gi:] F **-, -n** [-'gi:ən] (Med, fig) lethargy

le|thar|gisch [le'targɪʃ] (Med, fig) ADJ lethargic ADV lethargically

Le|the ['le:tə] F **-** (Myth) Lethe; (poet: = Vergessenheit) waters pl of oblivion

Let|te ['lɛtə] M **-n, -n,** **Let|tin** ['lɛtɪn] F **-, -nen** Lett, Latvian

Let|ten ['lɛtn] M **-s, -** (potter's) clay

Let|ter ['lɛtɐ] F **-, -n** character

let|tisch ['lɛtɪʃ] ADJ Lettish, Latvian

Let|tisch(e) ['lɛtɪʃ] NT Latvian → auch **Deutsch(e)**

Lett|land ['lɛtlant] NT **-s** Latvia

Lett|ner ['lɛtnɐ] M **-s, -** (Archit) choir screen

Let|ze|bur|gisch(e) NT (Ling) Letzeburgesch → auch **Deutsch(e)**

Letzt [lɛtst] F **zu guter ~** finally, in the end

letzt|emal △ ADV → **letzte(r, s) a**

letzt|end|lich ['lɛtst|ɛntlɪç] ADV at (long) last; (= letzten Endes) at the end of the day

letz|tens ['lɛtstns] ADV recently; **erst ~, ~ erst** just or only recently

Letz|te(r) ['lɛtstə] MF decl as adj **der ~ seines Stammes** the last of his line; **der ~ des Monats** the last (day) of the month; **der/die ~ in der Klasse sein** to be bottom (Brit) or at the bottom of the class; **die ~n werden die Ersten sein** (Bibl) the last shall be first (Bibl); **~(r) werden** to be last; **als ~(r) (an)kommen/(weg)gehen/fertig sein** to arrive/leave/finish last, to be the last to arrive/leave/finish; **als ~(r) gehen** to be the last to go; (in Reihenfolge auch) to go last; (in Prozession etc) to bring up the rear; **er wäre der ~, dem ich ...** he would be the last person I'd ...; **den ~n beißen die Hunde** (Prov) (the) devil take the hindmost (prov)

letz|te(r, s) ['lɛtstə] ADJ **a** (örtlich, zeitlich) last; (= endgültig, allerletzte) final, last; (= restlich) last (remaining); **auf dem ~n Platz** or **an ~r Stelle liegen** to be (lying) last; (in Tabelle, Liga auch) to be (lying) bottom (Brit), to be (lying) at the bottom; **mein ~s Geld** the last of my money; **das ~ Mal** (the) last time; **zum ~n Mal** (for) the last time; **die ~n zwei Tage/Jahre** the last two days/years; (vor heute/diesem Jahr auch) the past two days/years; **in ~r Zeit** recently; **jdm die ~ Ehre erweisen, jdm das ~ Geleit geben** to pay one's last respects to sb; **die ~n Dinge** death and the life to come; **die Lehre der ~n Dinge** eschatology; **das ~ und höchste Ziel meines Lebens/des Werkes** the ultimate aim of my life/of the work; **der Letzte Wille** the last will and testament

b (= neueste) Mode, Nachricht, Neuigkeit etc latest

c (= schlechtester) most terrible; **das ist der ~ Schund** or **Dreck** that's absolute trash; **er ist der ~ Mensch** (inf) he's a terrible person; **jdn wie den ~n Dreck/Sklaven** etc **behandeln** to treat sb like dirt/a slave etc

letz|te|re(r, s) ['lɛtstərə] ADJ the latter

Letz|te(s) ['lɛtstə] NT decl as adj **a** (= Äußerste) last thing; **es geht ums ~** everything is at stake; **sein ~s (her)geben** to give one's all, to do one's utmost; **bis zum ~n gehen** to do all that one possibly can; **das ist das ~, was ich tun würde** that's the last thing I'd do; **das ist ja das ~!** (inf) that really is the limit → **bis 2 b**

b **zum Dritten und zum ~n** (bei Auktion) for the (third and) last time of asking; **bis aufs ~** completely, totally; **bis ins ~** (right) down to the last detail; **etw bis ins ~ kennen** to know sth like the back of one's hand; **bis zum ~n** to the utmost; **am** or **zum ~n** last; **fürs ~** lastly

Letzt-: **letzt|ge|nannt** ADJ last-named; **letzt|hin** ['lɛtst'hɪn] ADV → letztens; **letzt|in|stanz|lich** ['lɛtstɪnstantslɪç] ADJ Urteil in the court of last instance; (fig) in the last instance ADV by the court of last instance; **etw ~ entscheiden** (fig) to have the final decision on sth; **letzt|-**

jäh|rig ['lɛtstjeːrɪç] ADJ attr last year's no art; **letzt|lich** ['lɛtstlɪç] ADV in the end; **das ist ~ egal** it comes down to the same thing in the end; **letzt|ma|lig** ['lɛtstmaːlɪç] ADJ attr last **ADV** for the last time; **letzt|mals** ['lɛtstmaːls] ADV for the last time; **letzt|mög|lich** ADJ attr last possible; **Letzt|num|mern|spei|cher** M last number redial; **letzt|wil|lig** (form) **ADJ** **~e Verfügung** last will and testament **ADV** ~ verfügen, dass ... to state in one's last will and testament that ...

Leu [lɔy] M **-en, -en** (obs, poet) lion

Leucht-: **Leucht|an|zei|ge** F illuminated display; **Leucht|bo|je** F light buoy; **Leucht|di|o|de** F light-emitting diode; **Leucht|di|o|den|an|zei|ge** F LED display

Leuch|te ['lɔyçtə] F **-, -n** (= Leuchtkörper) light; (old: = Laterne) lamp, lantern; (inf: Mensch) genius; **auf einem Gebiet/in einem Fach eine ~ sein** to shine in a particular field/subject

leuch|ten ['lɔyçtn] VI **a** (Licht) to shine; (Flammen, Feuer, Lava, Zifferblatt) to glow; (= aufleuchten) to flash **b** (Mensch) **mit einer Lampe in/auf etw** (acc) **~** to shine a lamp into/onto sth; **musst du mir direkt in die Augen ~?** do you have to shine that thing straight into my eyes?; **kannst du (mir) nicht mal ~?** can you point or shine the lamp or (mit Taschenlampe) the torch (Brit) or flashlight (for me)?; **leuchte mal hierher!** shine some light over here

leuch|tend **ADJ** (lit, fig) shining; Farbe bright, radiant; **etw in den ~sten Farben schildern/preisen** to paint sth/speak of sth in glowing colours (Brit) or colors (US); **ein ~es Vorbild** a shining example **ADV** rot, gelb radiant, bright; **etw ~ gelb malen** to paint sth a radiant or bright yellow; **der Nachthimmel war ~ hell** the night sky was brightly lit

Leuch|ter ['lɔyçtɐ] M **-s, -** (= Kerzenleuchter) candlestick; (= Armleuchter) candelabra; (= Kronleuchter) chandelier; (= Wandleuchter) sconce

Leucht-: **Leucht|far|be** F fluorescent colour (Brit) or color (US); (= Anstrichfarbe) fluorescent paint; (für Farbbad) fluorescent dye; (= Druckfarbe) fluorescent ink; **Leucht|feu|er** NT navigational light; **Leucht|gas** NT town gas; **Leucht|ge|schoss** ▲ NT flare; **Leucht|kä|fer** M glow-worm; **Leucht|kraft** F brightness; (von Birne etc auch) luminous power (form); (von Stern auch) luminosity (form); **Leucht|ku|gel** F flare; **Leucht|pat|ro|ne** F flare; **Leucht|pis|to|le** F flare pistol; **Leucht|pult** NT light box; **Leucht|ra|ke|te** F signal rocket; **Leucht|rek|la|me** F neon sign; **Leucht|röh|re** F fluorescent tube; **Leucht|schirm** M fluorescent screen; **Leucht|schrift** F neon writing; **eine ~** a neon sign

Leucht|spur F trail of light

Leucht|spur-: **Leucht|spur|ge|schoss** ▲ NT (Mil) tracer bullet; **Leucht|spur|mu|ni|ti|on** F (Mil) tracer bullets pl

Leucht-: **Leucht|stift** M highlighter; **Leucht|ton|ne** F light buoy; **Leucht|turm** M lighthouse; **Leucht|zei|ger** M luminous hand; **Leucht|zif|fer|blatt** NT luminous face or dial

leug|nen ['lɔygnən] ✪ 42.1 **VT** to deny; **~, etw getan zu haben** to deny having done sth; **es ist nicht zu ~, dass ...** it cannot be denied that ...; **der Angeklagte leugnete die Tat** the defendant denied the offence (Brit) or offense (US); (vor Gericht) the defendant pleaded not guilty **VI** to deny everything

Leug|nung ['lɔygnʊŋ] F **-, -en** denial

Leu|kä|mie [lɔykɛ'miː] F **-, -n** [-'miːən] leukaemia (Brit), leukemia (US)

Leu|kä|mie|kran|ke(r) MF decl as adj leukaemia (Brit) or leukemia (US) sufferer

leu|kä|misch [lɔy'kɛːmɪʃ] ADJ leukaemic (Brit), leukemic (US)

Leu|ko|plast® [lɔyko'plast] NT **-(e)s, -e** sticking plaster (Brit), Elastoplast® (Brit), Bandaid® (US)

Leu|ko|zy|t [lɔyko'tsyːt] M **-en, -en** leucocyte (spec), white corpuscle

Leu|ko|zy|ten|zäh|lung F blood count (of the white corpuscles)

Leu|mund ['lɔymʊnt] M **-(e)s** [-dəs] no pl reputation, name

Leu|munds|zeug|nis NT character reference

Leut|chen ['lɔytçən] PL (inf) people pl, folk pl (inf); **kommt, ~!** come on everyone or folks (inf)

Leu|te ['lɔytə] PL **a** people pl; (inf: = Eltern) folks pl (inf), people pl; (inf: = Verwandte) people pl; **arme/reiche/alte/junge ~** poor/rich/old/young folk(s) (inf) or people; **alle ~** everybody; **vor allen ~n** in front of everybody; **kleine ~** (fig) ordinary folk (inf) or people; **die kleinen ~** (hum, inf: Kinder) the little ones; **die ~ waren von dem Stück begeistert** people were enthusiastic about the play; **was sollen denn die ~ davon denken?** what will people think?; **aber liebe ~!** come on now! (inf); **~, ~!** (inf) dear me, (dear) oh dear; **kommt, ~!** come on folks; **aber die Sache ist doch in aller ~ Mund!** but everybody's talking about it!; **es ist noch nicht wie bei armen ~n** (hum inf) we're not on the breadline yet (hum inf); **ich kenne meine ~!** (inf) I know them/him etc; **etw unter die ~ bringen** (inf, Gerücht, Geschichte) to spread sth around, to put sth about; (Geld to spend sth; **unter die ~ kommen** (inf) (Mensch) to meet people; (Gerüchte etc) to go around, to go or do the rounds (inf); **das sind wohl nicht die richtigen ~** they're not the right kind of people

b (= Mannschaft, Arbeiter etc) **der Offizier ließ seine ~ antreten** the officer ordered his men to fall in; **dafür brauchen wir mehr ~** we need more people or (Personal) staff for that

Leu|te|schin|der [-ʃɪndɐ] M **-s, -**, **Leu|te|schin|de|rin** [-ərɪn] F **-, -nen** slave driver

Leut|nant ['lɔytnant] M **-s, -s** or **-e** (second) lieutenant; (bei der Luftwaffe) pilot officer (Brit), second lieutenant (US); **~ zur See** sublieutenant (Brit), lieutenant junior grade (US); **jawohl, Herr ~!** yes, sir; (Naut) aye aye, sir

leut|se|lig ['lɔytzeːlɪç] **ADJ** affable, genial **ADV** affably, genially

Leut|se|lig|keit F **-, no pl** (= Umgänglichkeit) affability

Le|van|te [le'vantə] F **-, no pl** Levant

le|van|ti|nisch [levan'tiːnɪʃ] ADJ Levantine

Le|vi|a|than [le'viːatan] M **-s** (Myth) leviathan

Le|vit [le'viːt] M **-en, -en** (Bibl) Levite; (Eccl) deacon

Le|vi|ten [le'viːtn] PL **jdm die ~ lesen** (inf) to haul sb over the coals (inf), to read sb the riot act (inf)

Lev|ko|je [lɛf'koːjə] F **-, -n** (Bot) stock

Lex [lɛks] F **-, Leges** ['leːgəs] (parliamentary) bill; **~ Smythe/Braun** etc Smythe's/Braun's etc bill

Le|xem [lɛ'kseːm] NT **-s, -e** (Ling) lexeme

Le|xik ['lɛksɪk] F **-, no pl** (Ling) lexis

le|xi|ka|lisch [lɛksi'kaːlɪʃ] ADJ lexical **ADV** lexically

Le|xi|ko|graf ▲ [lɛksiko'graːf] M **-en, -en**, **Le|xi|ko|gra|fin** ▲ [-'graːfɪn] F **-, -nen** lexicographer

Le|xi|ko|gra|fie ▲ [lɛksikogra'fiː] F **-, -n** [-'fiːən] lexicography

le|xi|ko|gra|fisch ▲ [lɛksiko'graːfɪʃ] **ADJ** lexicographic(al) **ADV** lexicographically

Le|xi|ko|lo|ge [lɛksiko'loːgə] M **-n, -n**, **Le|xi|ko|lo|gin** F **-, -nen** lexicologist

Le|xi|ko|lo|gie [lɛksikolo'giː] F **-, no pl** lexicology

le|xi|ko|lo|gisch [lɛksiko'loːgɪʃ] **ADJ** lexicological **ADV** lexicologically

Le|xi|kon ['lɛksikɔn] NT **-s, Lexika** [-ka] encyclopedia; (= Wörterbuch) dictionary, lexicon

lfd. abbr von **laufend**

Li|ai|son [liɛ'zõː] F **-, -s** liaison

Li|a|ne ['liːanə] F **-, -n** liana

Li|ba|ne|se [liba'neːzə] M **-n, -n**, **Li|ba|ne|sin** [-'neːzɪn] F **-, -nen** Lebanese

li|ba|ne|sisch [liba'neːzɪʃ] ADJ Lebanese

Li|ba|non ['liːbanɔn] M **-(s) der ~** (Land) the Lebanon; (Gebirge) the Lebanon Mountains pl

Li|ba|non|ze|der F cedar of Lebanon

Li|bel|le [li'bɛlə] F **-, -n** (Zool) dragonfly; (in Wasserwaage) spirit level

li|be|ral [libe'raːl] **ADJ** liberal **ADV** liberally; **~ eingestellt sein** to be liberal

Li|be|ra|le(r) [libe'raːlə] MF decl as adj (Pol) Liberal

li|be|ra|li|sie|ren [liberali'ziːrən] ptp **liberalisiert** VT to liberalize

Li|be|ra|li|sie|rung F **-, -en** liberalization

Li|be|ra|lis|mus [libera'lɪsmʊs] M **-, no pl** liberalism

li|be|ra|lis|tisch [libera'lɪstɪʃ] ADJ liberalist

Li|be|ra|li|tät [liberali'tɛːt] F **-, no pl** liberality

Li|be|ro ['liːbero] M **-s, -s** (Ftbl) sweeper

Li|ber|tin [libɛr'tɛ̃ː] M **-s, -s** (old, geh) libertine (old)

li|bi|di|nös [libidi'nøːs] ADJ (Psych) libidinous, libidinal

Li|bi|do [li'biːdo, 'liːbido] F **-, no pl** (Psych) libido

Lib|ret|tist [librɛ'tɪst] M **-en, -en**, **Lib|ret|tis|tin** [-'tɪstɪn] F **-, -nen** librettist

Lib|ret|to [li'brɛto] NT **-s, -s** or **Libretti** [-ti] libretto

Li|by|en ['liːbyən] NT **-s** Libya

Li|by|er ['liːbyɐ] M **-s, -**, **Li|by|e|rin** [-ərɪn] F **-, -nen** Libyan

li|bysch ['liːbyʃ] ADJ Libyan

licht [lɪçt] ADJ **a** (= hell) light; (liter) Morgen bright; **am ~en Tag** in broad daylight; **es wird schon ~** (geh) it is getting light, (the) day is dawning (liter); **einen ~en Augenblick** or **Moment haben** to have a lucid moment, (fig inf) to have a brainwave (inf); **auch ich habe ~e Augenblicke** even I have my lucid moments **b** Wald sparse; Haar thin, sparse; **eine ~e Stelle im Wald** a sparsely-wooded spot in the forest **c** (Tech) **~e Höhe** headroom; **~e Weite** (internal) width; **~er Durchmesser** internal diameter

Licht [lɪçt] NT **-(e)s, -er** or (rare) **-e** **a** no pl light; **~ machen** (= anschalten) to turn or switch or put on a light; (= anzünden) to light a candle/lantern etc; **das ~ brennt** or **ist an** the light is on or is burning; (Kerze) the candle is burning; **das ~ des Tages/der Sonne** the light of day/the sun; **ich möchte es noch bei ~ fertig bekommen** I'd like to get it finished in daylight or while it's still light; **~ ins Zimmer lassen** to let light into the room; **in der ganzen Stadt fiel das ~ aus** all the lights in the town went out; **hier gehen bald die ~er aus** (fig) we're about to hit troubled waters; **etw gegen das ~ halten** to hold sth up to the light; **gegen das ~ fotografieren** to take a photograph into the light; **bei ~e besehen** or **betrachtet** (lit) in the daylight; (fig) in the cold light of day; **das ist nicht das richtige ~** that's not the right sort of light; **das Bild hängt hier nicht im richtigen ~** the light is wrong for the picture here; **du nimmst mir das ganze ~ weg** you're in the or my light; **jdm im ~ stehen** (lit) to stand in sb's light; **(jdm) aus dem ~ gehen** to move or get out of the or sb's light; **~ und Schatten** light and shade (auch Art); **wo ~ ist, ist auch Schatten** (Prov) there's no joy without sorrow (prov); **das ~ der Welt erblicken** (geh) to (first) see the light of day; **das ~ scheuen** (lit) to shun the light (of day); **Geschäfte, die das ~ scheuen** shady deals; **grünes ~ (für etw) geben** to give the green light (to or for sth); **~ am Ende des Tunnels sehen** (fig) to see a light at the end of the tunnel; **sein ~ leuchten lassen** (fig) to shine → **Scheffel** **b** (fig) light; (= Könner) genius; **das ~ der Wahr-**

heit/Erkenntnis *etc* the light of truth/knowledge *etc*; **~ in eine (dunkle) Sache bringen** to cast *or* shed some light on a matter; **im ~(e) unserer Erfahrungen** in the light of our experiences; **etw ans ~ bringen/zerren** to bring/drag sth out into the open; **ans ~ kommen** to come *or* get out, to come to light; **jdn hinters ~ führen** to pull the wool over sb's eyes, to lead sb up (*Brit*) *or* down (*US*) the garden path; **mir geht ein ~ auf(, warum ...)** now it's dawned on me (why ...), now I see (why ...); **etw in milderem ~ sehen** to see sth in a more favourable (*Brit*) *or* favorable (*US*) light; **ein schiefes/schlechtes** *or* **kein gutes ~ auf jdn/etw werfen** to show sb/sth in the wrong/a bad light; **das wirft ein bezeichnendes ~ auf seinen Charakter** that shows him for what he really is; **in ein schiefes** *or* **falsches ~ geraten** to be seen in the wrong light; **etw ins rechte ~ rücken** *or* **setzen** to show sth in a favourable (*Brit*) *or* favorable (*US*) light; (= *richtig stellen*) to show sth in its true light; **etw ins falsche ~ rücken** *or* **setzen** to show sth in an unfavourable (*Brit*) *or* unfavorable (*US*) light; (= *falsch darstellen*) to put a wrong complexion on sth, to misrepresent sth

c (= *Lichtquelle*) light; (= *Kerze*) candle; **die ~er der Großstadt** the bright lights of the big city; **~er führen** (*Naut*) to display *or* show lights; **jdm ein ~ aufstecken** *or* **aufsetzen** (*fig inf*) to put sb wise (*inf*)

d (*Hunt*) eye (*of deer etc*)

Licht-: Licht|an|la|ge F lights *pl*; **er hat sich** (*dat*) **eine ganze ~ gebastelt** he put together a whole lighting system; **Licht|be|hand|lung** F (*Med*) phototherapy; **licht|be|stän|dig** ADJ lightproof; *Farben, Stoff* non-fade; **Licht|bild** NT (= *Dia*) transparency, slide; (*form*: = *Foto*) photograph; **Licht|bil|der|vor|trag** M illustrated talk *or* lecture; **Licht|blick** M (*fig*) ray of hope; **Licht|bo|gen** M arc; **licht|bre|chend** ADJ (*Opt*) refractive; **Licht|bre|chung** F refraction; **Licht|brü|cke** F lighting rig; **Licht|bün|del** NT pencil (of rays); **Licht-druck** M *pl* **-drucke** (*Typ*) collotype; (*Phys*) light pressure; **licht|durch|flu|tet** ADJ flooded with light, bathed in light; **licht|durch|läs|sig** ADJ pervious to light, light-transmissive (*form*); *Stoff* that lets the light through; **dieser Stoff ist ~er/zu ~** this material lets more/too much light through; **Licht|durch|läs|sig|keit** F perviousness to light

Lich|te ['lıçtə] F -, *no pl* (internal) width

Licht-: licht|echt ADJ non-fade; **Licht|echt-heit** F non-fade properties *pl*; **Licht|ef|fekt** M lighting effect; **Licht|ein|fall** M incidence of light; **Licht|ein|wir|kung** F action of light; **licht|elek|trisch** ADJ photoelectric; **licht-emp|find|lich** ADJ sensitive to light, photosensitive (*Tech*); **Licht|emp|find|lich|keit** F sensitivity to light, photosensitivity (*Tech*); (*Phot*) film speed

lich|ten[1] ['lıçtn] VT *Wald* to thin (out); **den Steuerdschungel ~** (*fig*) to cut through the jungle of tax regulations VR (*Reihen, Wald, Dickicht, Haare*) to thin (out); (*Nebel*) to clear, to lift; (*Wolken, Dunkel*) to lift; (*Bestände*) to go down, to dwindle; (*fig: Angelegenheit*) to be cleared up

lich|ten[2] VT *Anker* to weigh

Lichter-: Lich|ter|baum M Christmas tree; **Lich|ter|fest** NT **a** (*liter*: = *Weihnachten*) Yule (*old*), Christmas **b** (*jüdisches Fest*) Festival of Lights, Hanuk(k)ah; **Lich|ter|glanz** M blaze of lights; **in festlichem ~ erstrahlen** to be a blaze of festive lights; **Lich|ter|ket|te** F (*an Weihnachtsbaum*) fairy lights *pl*; (*von Menschen*) *long line of demonstrators carrying lights*; **lich|ter|loh** ['lıçtɐ'loː] ADV **~ brennen** (*lit*) to be ablaze; (*fig: Herz*) to be aflame; **Lich|ter-meer** NT (*liter*) sea of light; **das ~ von New York** the sea of light that is New York

Licht-: Licht|fil|ter NT OR M (light) filter; **Licht|ge|schwin|dig|keit** F the speed of

---

light; **Licht|ge|stalt** F (*fig*) shining light; **Licht|grif|fel** M (*Comput*) light pen; **Licht-hof** M **a** (*Archit*) air well **b** (*Phot*) halation (*spec*) **c** (*des Mondes*) halo; **Licht|hu|pe** F (*Aut*) flash (of the headlights); **jdn durch ~ war-nen** to warn sb by flashing one's lights; **Licht-jahr** NT light year; **~e entfernt sein** (*fig*) to be light years away (*von* from); **jdm um ~e voraus sein** to be light years ahead of sb; **etw um ~e zurückwerfen** to set sth back a long way; **Licht|ke|gel** M (*Phys*) cone of light; (*von Scheinwerfer*) beam (of light); **er stand im ~** he stood in the spotlight; (*von Autoscheinwerfer*) he stood in the beam of the headlights; **Licht-kreis** M circle *or* pool of light; **Licht|lei|tung** F lighting wire; **licht|los** ADJ dark; **ein ~es Zimmer** a room which doesn't get any light; **Licht|man|gel** M lack of light; **Licht|ma-schi|ne** F (*für Gleichstrom*) dynamo; (*für Drehstrom*) alternator; **Licht|mast** M lamppost; **Licht|mess** ▲ ['lıçtmɛs] *no art* **Mariä ~** Candlemas; **Licht|mes|ser** M light meter; **Licht|mess|ver|fah|ren** ▲ NT (*Mil*) flash ranging; **Licht|nel|ke** F catchfly, lychnis (*form*); **Licht|or|gel** F clavilux, colour (*Brit*) *or* color (*US*) organ; **Licht|pau|se** F photocopy; (*bei Blaupausverfahren*) blueprint; **Licht|punkt** M point of light; **Licht|quant** NT photon; **Licht|quel|le** F source of light; **Licht|rek|la-me** F neon sign; **Licht|satz** M (*Typ*) filmsetting, photocomposition; **in ~ hergestellt** filmset; **Licht|schacht** M air shaft; **Licht|schal-ter** M light switch; **Licht|schein** M gleam of light; **licht|scheu** ADJ averse to light; (*fig*) *Gesindel* shady; **Licht|schim|mer** M gleam of light; **Licht|schran|ke** F photoelectric barrier

Licht|schutz-: Licht|schutz|fak|tor M protection factor; **Licht|schutz|fil|ter** M light filter

Licht-: Licht|setz|ma|schi|ne F (*Typ*) photosetting machine; **Licht|sig|nal** NT light signal; **Licht|spiel|haus** NT , **Licht|spiel|the|a|ter** NT (*dated*) cinema, picture palace (*Brit old*); **licht|stark** ADJ (*Opt*) intense; (*Phot*) fast; **Licht|stär|ke** F (*Opt*) luminous intensity; (*Phot*) speed; **Licht|stift** M (*Comput*) light pen; **Licht|stock** M (= *Kerze*) wax taper; **Licht|strahl** M beam *or* ray of light; (*fig*) ray of sunshine; **Licht|strom** M (*Opt*) luminous *or* light flux; **Licht|the|ra|pie** F (*Med*) light therapy; **licht|un|durch|läs|sig** ADJ opaque

Lich|tung ['lıçtʊŋ] F -, **-en** clearing, glade

Licht-: Licht|ver|hält|nis|se PL lighting conditions *pl*; **Licht|ver|schmut|zung** F light pollution; **Licht|wech|sel** M change of light; (*Astron*) light variation; **Licht|weg** M light path; **licht|wen|dig** ADJ (*Bot*) phototropic

Lid [liːt] NT **-(e)s, -er** [-də] eyelid

Lid-: Lid|schat|ten M eye shadow; **Lid|schlag** M blink; **Lid|strich** M eyeliner

lieb [liːp] ADJ **a** (= *liebenswürdig, hilfsbereit*) kind; (= *nett, reizend*) nice; (= *niedlich*) *Kerl(chen), Ding* sweet, lovely, cute (*inf*); (= *artig*) *Kind, Schulklasse* good; **(es sendet dir) (viele) ~e Grüße deine Silvia** love Silvia; **~e Grüße an deine Eltern** give my best wishes to your parents; **würdest du (bitte) so ~ sein und das Fenster aufmachen** *or* **das Fenster aufzumachen?, sei bitte so ~ und mache das Fenster auf** would you do me a favour (*Brit*) *or* favor (*US*) *or* (would you) be an angel (*inf*) and open the window?; **willst du wohl (endlich) ~ sein?!** are you going to be good *or* to behave now?; **bei jdm ~ Kind sein** (*pej*) to be sb's (little) darling *or* pet; **beim Leh-rer ~ Kind sein** (*pej*) to be teacher's pet; **sich bei jdm ~ Kind machen** (*pej*) to suck up to sb, to worm one's way into sb's good books

b *Gast, Besuch* (= *angenehm*) pleasant; (= *willkommen*) welcome; **bei uns bist du jederzeit ein ~er Gast** you're always welcome, we're always pleased to see you

c (= *angenehm*) **etw ist jdm ~** sb likes sth; **es wäre mir ~, wenn ...** I'd be glad if ..., I'd like it

---

if ...; **es ist mir ~, dass ...** I'm glad that ...; **es wäre ihm ~er** he would prefer it → *auch* **lieber** ADV, **liebste(r, s)** ADV

d (= *geliebt, geschätzt*) dear, beloved (*iro, form*); (*in Briefanrede*) dear; **~e Monika, das geht doch nicht** (my) dear Monika, that's just not on; **~e Brüder und Schwestern** (*Rel*) dearly beloved; **der ~e Gott** the Good Lord; **~er Gott** (*Anrede*) dear God *or* Lord; **unsere Liebe Frau** (*Eccl*) Our Lady; **Liebe Anna, ~er Klaus! ...** Dear Anna and Klaus, ... **(mein) Liebes** (my) love *or* pet, honey (*esp US*); **er ist mir ~ und wert** *or* **teuer** he's very dear to me; **~ geworden** well-loved; *Klischee* much-loved; **eine mir ~ gewor-dene Gewohnheit** a habit of which I've grown very fond; **den ~en langen Tag** (*inf*) the whole livelong day; **das ~e Geld!** the money, the money!; **(ach) du ~er Himmel/~der Gü-te/~e Zeit/~es Lieschen** *or* **Lottchen/~es biss-chen** (*inf*) good heavens *or* Lord!, goodness me! → **Not**

e **~ste(r, s)** favourite (*Brit*), favorite (*US*); **sie ist mir die Liebste von allen** she is my favourite (*Brit*) *or* favorite (*US*)

ADV a (= *liebenswürdig*) *danken, grüßen* sweetly, nicely; **jdm ~ schreiben** to write a sweet letter to sb; **jdn ~ beschenken** to give sb a sweet present; **sich ~ um jdn kümmern** to be very kind to sb; **er hat mir wirklich ~ geholfen** it was really sweet the way he helped me; **jdn ~ be-halten** to stay fond of sb

b (= *artig*) nicely; **geh jetzt ~ nach Hause** be a sweetie, go home

lieb|äu|geln ['liːpɔygln] VI *insep* **mit etw ~** to have one's eye on sth; **mit einem neuen Auto ~** to be toying with the idea of getting a new car; **mit dem Gedanken ~, etw zu tun** to be toying *or* flirting with the idea of doing sth

Lieb|chen ['liːpçən] NT **-s, -** (*old*) sweetheart

Lie|be ['liːbə] F -, **-n a** love (*zu jdm, für jdn* for *or* of sb, *zu etw* of sth); **die große ~** the love of one's life, the real thing (*inf*); **Heirat aus ~** love match; **aus ~ zu jdm/einer Sache** for the love of sb/sth; **ein Kind der ~** (*liter*) a love child; **etw mit viel ~ tun** to do sth with loving care; **bei aller ~** with the best will in the world; **in ~ with love; in ~ dein Theobald** with all my love, Theobald; **~ macht blind** (*Prov*) love is blind (*Prov*); **wo die ~ hinfällt!** love is a funny thing

b (= *Sex*) sex; **eine Nacht der ~** a night of love; **von der ~ leben** (*Prostituierte etc*) to live off sex, to live off one's favours (*Brit*) *or* favors (*US, euph*); **ein Meister der ~** an expert at lovemaking, an expert in love; **sie/er ist gut in der ~** (*inf*) she/he is good at making love

c (*inf*: = *Gefälligkeit*) favour (*Brit*), favor (*US*); **tu mir doch bitte die ~ und ...** would you do me a favour (*Brit*) *or* favor (*US*) and ...

d (= *Geliebte(r)*) love, darling; **sie ist eine alte ~ von mir** she is an old flame of mine

Lie|be-: lie|be|be|dürf|tig ADJ **~ sein, ein ~es Wesen haben** *or* **sein** to need a lot of love *or* affection; **Lie|be|die|ne|rei** F -, *no pl* (*pej*) subservience, fawning (*gegenüber* to); **lie|be|die|nern** [-diːnɐn] VI *insep* (*pej*) to fawn (*jdm* to sb); **lie|be|leer** ADJ *Leben, Dasein* loveless

Lie|be|lei [liːbə'lai] F -, **-en** (*inf*) flirtation, affair

lie|ben ['liːbn] VT to love; (*als Liebesakt*) to make love (*jdn* to sb); **etw nicht ~** not to like sth; **ich liebe es nicht, wenn man mich unterbricht** I do not like being interrupted; **das liebe ich (gera-de)!** (*iro*) marvellous (*Brit*) *or* marvelous (*US*), isn't it? (*iro*); **sich ~ einander ~** to love one another *or* each other; (*euph*) to make love → *auch* **geliebt** VI to love; **etw ~d gern tun** to love to do sth

Lie|ben|de(r) ['liːbndə] MF *decl as adj* lover

lie|ben ler|nen ▲ VT to come to love

lie|bens|wert ADJ lovable, endearing

lie|bens|wür|dig ADJ kind; (= *liebenswert*) charming; **würden Sie so ~ sein und die Tür**

schließen? would you be so kind as to shut the door? **ADV** kindly

lie|bens|wür|di|ger|wei|se [ˈliːbnsvʏrdɪgɐˈvaɪzə] **ADV** kindly

Lie|bens|wür|dig|keit F -, -en **a** (= Höflichkeit) politeness; (= Freundlichkeit) kindness; **würden Sie die ~ haben, das zu tun or und das tun?** (form) would you be kind or good enough to do that?, would you have the goodness to do that? **b** (iro: = giftige Bemerkung) charming remark (iro)

lie|ber [ˈliːbɐ] ✪ 31, 33.3, 34, 35.5, 36.3 **ADJ** comp von **lieb**
ADV comp von **gern** **a** (= vorzugsweise) rather, sooner; **das tue ich ~** (im Augenblick) I would or I'd rather or I'd sooner do that; (grundsätzlich auch) I prefer doing that; **das würde ich ~ tun** I would or I'd rather or I'd sooner do that, I would prefer to do that; **ich trinke ~ Wein als Bier** I prefer wine to beer; **(das möchte ich) ~ nicht!** I would or I'd sooner or rather not, I would or I'd prefer not to; **er sieht es ~, wenn du das nicht tust** he would or he'd prefer you not to do that, he would or he'd prefer it if you didn't do that, he would or he'd sooner or he'd rather you didn't do that; (grundsätzlich) he prefers you not to do that, he prefers it if you don't do that
b (= besser, vernünftigerweise) better; **bleibe im Bett** you had or you'd better stay in bed, I would or I'd stay in bed if I were you; **ich hätte ~ nachgeben sollen** I would have done better or I'd have done better to have given in; **sollen wir gehen? – ~ nicht!** should we go? – better not; **nichts ~ als das** there's nothing I'd rather do/have etc

Lie|be(r) [ˈliːbə] **MF** decl as adj dear; **meine ~n** my dears

Lie|bes- in cpds love; **Lie|bes|aben|teu|er** NT amorous adventure; **Lie|bes|akt** M love or sex act; **Lie|bes|af|fä|re** F (love) affair; **Lie|bes|ap|fel** M (obs) tomato; **Lie|bes|ban|de** PL (liter) bonds pl of love; **Lie|bes|be|zie|hung** F romantic attachment, (sexual) relationship; **Lie|bes|bo|te** M , **Lie|bes|bo|tin** F messenger of love; **Lie|bes|brief** M love letter; **Lie|bes|die|ne|rin** F (inf) lady of the night (euph); **Lie|bes|dienst** M labour (Brit) or labor (US) of love; (fig: = Gefallen) favour (Brit), favor (US); **jdm einen ~ erweisen** to do sb a service of love/a favour (Brit) or favor (US); **Lie|bes|ent|zug** M , no pl withdrawal of affection; **Lie|bes|er|klä|rung** F declaration of love; **jdm eine ~ machen** to declare one's love to sb; **Lie|bes|film** M love film; **Lie|bes|ge|dicht** NT love poem; **Lie|bes|ge|schich|te** F **a** (Liter) love story **b** (inf: = Liebschaft) love affair; **Lie|bes|glück** NT joy(s pl) of love; (= glückliche Liebe) happy love affair; **Lie|bes|gott** M god of love; **Lie|bes|göt|tin** F goddess of love; **Lie|bes|han|del** M , **Lie|bes|hän|del** [-hɛndl] M -s, - (obs) love affair; **Lie|bes|hei|rat** F love match; **Lie|bes|kum|mer** M lovesickness; **~ haben** to be lovesick; **vor ~ konnte sie nicht mehr essen** she was so lovesick that she couldn't eat; **Lie|bes|kunst** F art of love; **Lie|bes|lau|be** F (hum) love nest; **Lie|bes|le|ben** NT love life; **Lie|bes|lied** NT love song; **Lie|bes|müh** F **das ist vergebliche or verlorene ~** that is futile; **Lie|bes|nacht** F night of love; **Lie|bes|nest** NT (inf) love nest; **Lie|bes|paar** NT lovers pl; **Lie|bes|per|len** PL hundreds and thousands pl (Brit); **Lie|bes|ro|man** M romantic novel; **Lie|bes|scha|tul|le** F (hum sl: = Vagina) love hole (sl); **Lie|bes|spiel** NT love play; **Lie|bes|schwur** M lover's oath; **Lie|bes|sze|ne** F love scene; **Lie|bes|toll** ADJ love-stricken, lovelorn; **Lie|bes|tö|ter** [-tøːtɐ] PL (hum) long johns pl, passion killers pl (Brit hum); **Lie|bes|trank** M (liter) love potion; **lie|bes|trun|ken** ADJ (geh) in an ecstasy of love; **Lie|bes|ver|hält|nis** NT (sexual) relationship, liaison

lie|be|voll ADJ loving; Umarmung affectionate ADV lovingly; umarmen affectionately; **sie sah ihn ~ an** she looked at him lovingly or with affection; **alle nannten ihn ~ Blacky** he was affectionately known to all as Blacky

lieb-: **lieb ge|win|nen** ▲ VT irreg to get or grow fond of; **liebge|wor|den** △ ADJ attr → **lieb ha|ben** d; **lieb ha|ben** ▲ VT irreg to love; (weniger stark) to be (very) fond of

Lieb|ha|ber [-haːbɐ] M -s, -, **Lieb|ha|be|rin** [-ərɪn] F -, -nen **a** lover **b** (= Interessent, Freund) enthusiast; (= Sammler) collector; **ein ~ von etw** a lover of sth; **das ist nur etwas für ~** it's an acquired taste; **das ist ein Wein/Auto für ~** that is a wine/car for connoisseurs

Lieb|ha|be|rei [-haːbəˈraɪ] F -, -en (fig: = Steckenpferd, Hobby) hobby; **etw aus ~ tun** to do sth as a hobby

Lieb|ha|ber-: **Lieb|ha|ber|preis** M collector's price; **Lieb|ha|ber|stück** NT collector's item; **Lieb|ha|ber|wert** M collector's value

lieb|ko|sen [lɪpˈkoːzn̩] ptp **liebkost** VT insep (liter) to caress, to fondle

Lieb|ko|sung F -, -en (liter) caress

lieb|lich [ˈliːplɪç] ADJ charming, lovely, delightful; Landschaft lovely, delightful; Duft, Geschmack, Wein sweet ADV singen delightfully; ~ **klingen** to sound delightful; ~ **aussehen** to look sweet or lovely; ~ **duften/schmecken** to smell/taste sweet

Lieb|lich|keit F -, -en loveliness, delightfulness; (von Duft, Geschmack, Wein) sweetness; **Ihre ~, Prinzessin Sylvia** (im Fasching) Her Sweetness Princess Sylvia (title of carnival princess)

Lieb|ling [ˈliːplɪŋ] M -s, -e darling; (= bevorzugter Mensch) favourite (Brit), favorite (US)

Lieblings- ✪ 34.1, 34.3 in cpds favourite (Brit), favorite (US); **mein Lieblingsgericht** my favo(u)rite meal

Lieb-: **lieb|los** ADJ Ehemann, Eltern unloving; Bemerkung, Behandlung unkind; Benehmen inconsiderate ADV unkindly; (= ohne Sorgfalt) carelessly, thoughtlessly; ~ **gekocht/zubereitet** etc cooked/prepared etc any old how (Brit inf) or any old way (inf); **Lieb|lo|sig|keit** F -, -en **a** no pl (= liebloser Charakter) (von Ehemann, Eltern) unloving nature; (von Bemerkung, Behandlung) unkindness; (von Benehmen) inconsiderateness **b** (Äußerung) unkind remark; (Tat) unkind act; **~en** (Benehmen) unkind behaviour sing (Brit) or behavior sing (US); **Lieb|reiz** M (liter) charm; **lieb|rei|zend** (liter) ADJ charming ADV charmingly; **Lieb|schaft** [ˈliːpʃaft] F -, -en affair

liebs|ten [ˈliːpstn̩] ADV am ~ → **liebste(r, s)** ADV

Liebs|te(r) [ˈliːpstə] MF decl as adj sweetheart

liebs|te(r, s) [ˈliːpstə] ADJ superl von **lieb** ADV superl von **gern** am ~n best; **am ~n hätte ich ...** what I'd like most would be (to have) ..., most of all or best of all I'd like (to have) ...; **am ~n würde ich ...** what I'd like most would be to ..., most of all or best of all I'd like to ...; **am ~n lese ich Kriminalromane/esse ich scharfe Speisen/gehe ich ins Kino** most or best of all I like detective novels/spicy food/going to the cinema; **am ~n hätte ich ihm eine geklebt!** (inf) I could have belted him (one) (inf); **das würde ich am ~n tun** that's what I'd like to do best, that's what I'd prefer to do

Lieb|stö|ckel [ˈliːpʃtœkl] M OR NT -s, - (Bot) lovage

Liech|ten|stein [ˈlɪçtn̩ʃtaɪn] NT -s Liechtenstein

Liech|ten|stei|ner [ˈlɪçtn̩ʃtaɪnɐ] M -s, -, **Liech|ten|stei|ne|rin** [-ərɪn] F -, -nen Liechtensteiner

liech|ten|stei|nisch [ˈlɪçtn̩ʃtaɪnɪʃ] ADJ Liechtenstein, of Liechtenstein

Lied [liːt] M -(e)s, -er [-dəs, -dɐ] song; (= Kirchenlied) hymn; (= Weihnachtslied) carol; (Mus) lied (spec); **das Ende vom ~** (fig inf) the upshot

or outcome (of all this); **das ist dann immer das Ende vom ~** it always ends like that; **es ist immer dasselbe** or **das alte** or **gleiche ~** (inf) it's always the same old story (inf); **davon kann ich ein ~ singen, davon weiß ich ein ~ zu singen** I could tell you a thing or two about that (inf)

Lie|der-: **Lie|der|abend** M evening of songs; (von Sänger) song recital; **Lie|der|buch** NT → **Lied** songbook; hymn book; book of carols; **Lie|der|dich|ter(in)** M(F) lyrical poet; (des Mittelalters) minstrel; **Lie|der|hand|schrift** F collection of ballads

Lie|der|jan [ˈliːdɐjaːn] M -(e)s, -e (dated inf) wastrel

lie|der|lich [ˈliːdɐlɪç] ADJ (= schlampig) slovenly attr, pred; (= nachlässig auch) sloppy; (= unmoralisch) Leben, Mann dissolute, dissipated; Frau, Mädchen loose; **ein ~es Frauenzimmer** (pej) a slut (pej); **Bruder Liederlich** (old) wastrel ADV (= schlampig) sloppily; (= unmoralisch) dissolutely

Lie|der|lich|keit F -, no pl (= Schlampigkeit) slovenliness; (= Nachlässigkeit auch) sloppiness

Lie|der-: **Lie|der|ma|cher(in)** M(F) singersongwriter; **Lie|der|zyk|lus** M song cycle

Lied-: **Lied|gut** NT , no pl song literature, body of song; **deutsches ~** German song; **Lied|text** M lyrics pl, words pl

lief pret von **laufen**

Lie|fe|rant [lifəˈrant] M -en, -en, **Lie|fe|ran|tin** [-ˈrantɪn] F -, -nen supplier; (= Auslieferer) deliveryman/-woman

Lie|fe|ran|ten|ein|gang M tradesmen's entrance; (von Warenhaus etc) goods entrance

Lie|fer-: **Lie|fer|auf|trag** M order; **Lie|fer|au|to** NT van, delivery van or truck (US); **lie|fer|bar** ADJ (= vorrätig) available; (= zustellbar) deliverable (rare); **die Ware ist sofort ~** the article can be supplied/delivered at once; **diese Sachen sind auch kurzfristig ~** these goods can be supplied/delivered at short notice; **Lie|fer|be|din|gun|gen** PL conditions pl or terms pl of supply or (für Zustellung) delivery; **Lie|fer|fir|ma** F supplier; (= Zusteller) delivery firm; **Lie|fer|frist** F delivery period; **die ~ einhalten** to meet the delivery date; **Lie|fer|kos|ten** PL delivery charges pl, shipping costs pl; **Lie|fer|land** NT supplier country; **Lie|fer|men|ge** F quantity delivered or ordered; **Lie|fer|mo|nat** M (Comm) contract month, delivery month

lie|fern [ˈliːfɐn] VT **a** Waren to supply; (= zustellen) to deliver (an +acc to); **jdm etw ~** to supply sb with sth/deliver sth to sb
b (= zur Verfügung stellen) to supply; Beweise, Gesprächsstoff, Informationen, Sensationen to provide, to furnish, to supply; Ertrag to yield; (= hervorbringen) Ergebnis to produce; (inf: = stellen) to provide; **jdm eine Schlacht/ein Wortgefecht ~** to do battle/verbal battle with sb; **sie lieferten sich eine regelrechte Schlacht** they had a real battle; (Sport) they put up a real fight; **ein spannendes Spiel ~** (Sport) to put on an exciting game; **jdm eine gute/schlechte Partie ~** to give/not to give sb a good game; **jdm einen Vorwand ~** to give sb an excuse → auch **geliefert**
VI to supply; (= zustellen) to deliver; **wir ~ nicht ins Ausland/nach Frankreich** we don't supply the foreign market/(to) France; **eine Firma, die wegen eines Streiks nicht mehr ~ kann** a firm which is no longer able to deliver because of a strike

Lie|fer-: **Lie|fer|schein** M delivery note; **Lie|fer|schwie|rig|kei|ten** PL delivery problems pl; **Lie|fer|ter|min** M delivery date

Lie|fe|rung [ˈliːfərʊŋ] F -, -en **a** (= Versand, Versandgut) delivery; (= Versorgung) supply; **bei ~ zu bezahlen** payable on delivery; **Zahlung bis 14 Tage nach ~** account payable within 14 days of delivery **b** (von Buch) instalment (Brit), installment (US)

Lie|fe|rungs|be|din|gun|gen PL = Lieferbedingungen

Lie|fer-: Lie|fer|ver|kehr M delivery traffic; „Lieferverkehr frei" "delivery vehicles only"; **Lie|fer|ver|trag** M contract of sale, sale contract; **ein ~ über 5.000 Autos** a contract to supply or (für Zustellung) deliver 5,000 cars; **Lie|fer|wa|gen** M van, delivery van or truck (US); (offen) pick-up; **Lie|fer|zeit** F delivery period, lead time (Comm); **Lie|fer|zet|tel** M delivery order

Lie|ge ['li:gə] F -, -n couch; (= Campingliege) camp bed (Brit), cot (US); (für Garten) lounger (Brit), lounge chair (US)

Lie|ge-: Lie|ge|deck NT (Naut) sun deck; **Lie|ge|geld** NT (Naut) demurrage; **Lie|ge|kar|te** F (Rail) couchette ticket; **Lie|ge|kur** F rest-cure

---

lie|gen ['li:gn]
pret **lag** [la:g], ptp **gelegen** [gə'le:gn] aux haben or (S Ger) sein

INTRANSITIVES VERB

Siehe auch **liegen bleiben, liegen lassen, gelegen**.

a = flach liegen: Mensch to lie; (inf: = krank sein) to be laid up (inf); **vom stundenlangen Liegen auf dem harten Boden war mir ganz steif** I was stiff after lying for hours on the hard ground; **ich liege nicht gerne weich** I don't like sleeping on a soft mattress; **ich liege lieber hart** I prefer (to sleep on) a hard mattress; **unbequem liegen** to lie uncomfortably or in an uncomfortable position; **in diesem Bett liegt es sich** or **liegt man hart/weich** this bed is hard/soft; **im Bett/Krankenhaus liegen** to be in bed/hospital; **zu Bett liegen** (form) to have retired (form); (= krank sein) to have taken to one's bed (form); **der Kranke muss unbedingt liegen** the patient really must stay or keep lying down; **das lange Liegen** (von Patient etc) being in bed a long time; **in diesem Grab liegen meine Eltern** my parents are in this grave; **auf welchem Friedhof liegt dein Vater?** which cemetery is your father buried in?; **auf den Knien liegen** to be on one's knees

b = flach liegen: Gegenstand to lie; (Flasche etc) to lie on its side; (Schnee) to be; (Hitze, Nebel) to hang; **auf dem Boden haben sie teure Teppiche liegen** they have expensive carpets on the floor; **ich habe noch einen guten Wein im Keller liegen** I've got a good wine in the cellar; **die Stadt lag in dichtem Nebel** the town was enveloped in thick fog, thick fog hung over the town; **über dem Tal lag Nebel** fog hung over the valley; **der Schnee lag 4 m hoch** the snow was 4m deep; **der Schnee bleibt nicht liegen** the snow isn't lying (esp Brit) or sticking (US); **auf den Bergen lag schon Schnee** there was already snow on the mountains; **der Kopf muss hoch/tief liegen** the head must be higher/lower than the rest of the body; **etw liegen lassen** to leave sth (there); **meine Haare liegen heute nicht richtig** my hair doesn't look right today; **wenn ich Ihre Haare so schneide, liegen sie viel besser** if I cut your hair in this style it'll look much better; **der Stoff liegt 90 cm breit** the material is 90 cm wide; **der Vogel/das Flugzeug lag ganz ruhig in der Luft** the bird/plane was gliding through the air; **in der Kurve liegen** (Auto) to hold the corner; (Rennfahrer) to corner; **der Wagen liegt gut auf der Straße** the car holds the road well

c = sich befinden to be; **das Schiff liegt am Kai** the ship is (lying) alongside the quay; **das Schiff liegt vor Anker** the ship is lying at anchor; **die Betonung liegt auf der zweiten Silbe** the stress is on the second syllable; **ein Lächeln lag auf ihrem Gesicht** there was a smile on her face; **die Preise liegen zwischen 60 und 80 Eu-**

---

ro the prices are between 60 and 80 euros; **seine Fähigkeiten liegen auf einem anderen Gebiet** his abilities lie in a different direction; **in jds Absicht** (dat) **liegen** to be sb's intention; **so, wie die Dinge jetzt liegen** as things are or stand at the moment; **damit liegst du (gold)richtig** (inf) you're (dead (inf) or absolutely) right there; **bei mir liegen Sie richtig (damit)** (inf) you've come to the right person (for that)

d = eine bestimmte Lage haben to be; (Haus, Stadt etc) to be (situated or located); **verstreut liegen** to be scattered; **nach Süden/der Straße liegen** to face south/the road; **das Haus liegt ganz ruhig** the house is in a very quiet position or location; **das liegt doch ganz in der Nähe** it's quite close; **das liegt doch auf dem Weg** it's on the way; **einen Ort links/rechts liegen lassen** to pass by a place

e = einen bestimmten Rang haben to be; **auf den hintersten Plätzen/in Führung/an der Spitze liegen** to be at the bottom/in the lead/right out in front; **der zweite Läufer liegt weit hinter dem ersten** the second runner is a long way behind the first

f = lasten **auf dieser Familie scheint ein Fluch zu liegen** there seems to be a curse on this family; **die Verantwortung/Schuld dafür liegt bei ihm** the responsibility/blame for that lies or rests with him; **die Schuld liegt schwer auf mir** my guilt weighs heavily on me; **damit liegt die ganze Arbeit auf mir** that means all the work falls on me; **die Entscheidung liegt beim Volk/bei Ihnen** the decision rests with the people/with you; **das liegt ganz bei dir** that is completely up to you; **es liegt in seiner Gewalt, das zu tun** it is or lies within his power to do that

g = geeignet sein, passen **das liegt mir/ihm nicht** it doesn't suit me/him; (Beruf) it doesn't appeal to me/him; (jds Art) I don't/he doesn't like it; (Mathematik etc) I have/he has no aptitude for it; **Krankenschwester liegt mir nicht** (inf) nursing doesn't appeal to me; **diese Rolle liegt ihr** this part is perfect for her

h Redewendungen

♦ **liegen an es liegt mir viel daran** (= ist mir wichtig) that matters a lot to me, that is important to me; **es liegt mir wenig/nichts daran** that doesn't matter much/at all to me, that isn't very important/isn't at all important to me; **es liegt mir viel an ihm/an meinem Beruf** he/my job is very important to me or matters a lot to me; **mir liegt an einer schnellen Fertigstellung des Hauses** I am concerned that the house should be finished quickly; **was liegt (dir) schon daran?** what does it matter (to you)?; **an jdm/etw liegen** (= als Grund haben) to be because of sb/sth; **woran liegt es?** why is that?; **das liegt daran, dass ...** that is because...; **an mir soll es nicht liegen!** I'll go along with that; **an mir soll es nicht liegen, dass** or **wenn die Sache schiefgeht** it won't be my fault if things go wrong

---

lie|gen blei|ben ▲ VI irreg aux sein **a** (= nicht aufstehen) to remain lying (down); (im Bett) ~ to stay in bed; **er blieb bewusstlos auf dem Boden liegen** he lay unconscious on the floor; **bleib liegen!** don't get up!, stay down! **b** (= vergessen werden) to get or be left behind; **mein Schirm muss irgendwo liegen geblieben sein** I must have left my umbrella somewhere **c** (= nicht verkauft werden) not to sell, to be left unsold; **wenn uns diese Sachen ~** if we are left with these things (on our hands) **d** (= nicht ausgeführt werden) to get or be left (undone), not to get done **e** (= auf einer Stelle bleiben) to lie about; (Schnee) to lie **f** (Auto) to conk out (inf)

lie|gend ADJ (Art) reclining; **~e Güter** immovable property sing (form), real estate ADV **a** (= flach) ~ **aufbewahren** to store flat; Flasche etc to

---

store on its side **b** (= im Liegen) while lying down

Lie|gen|de(r) ['li:gndə] MF decl as adj (Art) reclining figure

lie|gen las|sen ▲ ptp **liegen lassen** or (rare) **liegen gelassen** VT irreg (= nicht erledigen) to leave; (= vergessen) to leave (behind); (= herumliegen lassen) to leave lying about or around; **sie hat alles liegen gelassen, um dem Kind zu helfen** she dropped everything to (go and) help the child → **links** ADV a, **stehen lassen**

Lie|gen|schaft ['li:gnʃaft] F -, -en, **Lie|gen|schaf|ten** PL real estate sing, property sing

Lie|ge-: Lie|ge|platz M place to lie; (auf Schiff, in Zug etc) berth; (= Ankerplatz) moorings pl; (von großem Schiff) berth; **Lie|ge|sitz** M reclining seat; (auf Boot) couchette; **Lie|ge|statt** F pl **-stätten** [-ʃtɛtn] (old, dial) bed; **Lie|ge|stuhl** M (mit Holzgestell) deck chair; (mit Metallgestell) lounger (Brit), lounge chair (US); **Lie|ge|stütz** [-ʃtyts] M **-es, -e** (Sport) press-up (Brit), push-up (US); **~e machen** to do press-ups (Brit) or push-ups (US); **in den ~!** press-ups! (Brit), push-ups! (US); **Lie|ge|wa|gen** M (Rail) couchette coach or car (esp US); **~ buchen** to book a couchette; **Lie|ge|wie|se** F lawn (for sunbathing); **Lie|ge|zeit** F **a** (Naut) lay days pl (form) **b** rest period

lieh pret von **leihen**

Liek [li:k] NT **-(e)s, -en** (Naut) boltrope

lies [li:s] IMPER sing von **lesen**

Lies|chen ['li:sçən] NT **-s, -** Liz(zie); **~ Müller** (inf) the average woman in the street → **fleißig** a, **lieb** d

ließ pret von **lassen**

liest [li:st] 3. pers sing pres von **lesen**

Life|style ['laɪfstaɪl] M **-s, -s** lifestyle

Lift [lɪft] M **-(e)s, -e** or **-s** (= Personenlift) lift (Brit), elevator (esp US); (= Güterlift) lift (Brit), hoist; (= Skilift) ski lift

Lift|boy ['lɪftbɔy] M liftboy (Brit), elevator boy (US)

lif|ten ['lɪftn] VT to lift; **sich** (dat) **das Gesicht ~ lassen** to have a face-lift

Lift-off [lɪft'ɔf] M **-(s), -s** liftoff

Li|ga ['li:ga] F -, **Ligen** [-gn] league

Li|ga|tur [liga'tu:ɐ] F -, **-en** ligature; (Mus: = Verbindung zweier Noten) tie

light [laɪt] ADJ pred inv **a** light; Limo ~ diet lemonade, low calorie lemonade **b** (iro: = seicht) lightweight

Light- [laɪt] in cpds light, lite; (= kalorienarm auch) low-calorie, diet attr

Lightpen ▲ ['laɪtpɛn] M **-s, -s** light pen

Lig|nin [lɪ'gni:n] NT **-s, -e** lignin(e)

Li|gus|ter [li'gʊstɐ] M **-s, -** privet

li|ie|ren [li'i:rən] ptp **liiert** VT to bring or get together; Firmen etc to get to work together; **liiert sein** to have joined forces; (Firmen etc) to be working together; (Pol) to be allied; (= ein Verhältnis haben) to have a relationship VR to join forces; (Firmen etc) to work together; (Pol) to enter into an alliance; (= ein Verhältnis eingehen) to get together, to form a liaison

Li|kör [li'kø:ɐ] M **-s, -e** liqueur

li|la ['li:la] ADJ inv purple

Li|la ['li:la] NT **-s** (inf) **-s** purple

Li|lie ['li:liə] F -, -n lily; **keusch wie eine ~** as pure as the driven snow

Li|li|put- ['li:lipʊt] in cpds miniature; **eine Liliputeisenbahn** a miniature railway; **im Liliputformat** in miniature

Li|li|pu|ta|ner [lilipu'ta:nɐ] M **-s, -**, **Li|li|pu|ta|ne|rin** [-ərɪn] F -, **-nen** dwarf, midget; (= Bewohner von Liliput) Liliputian

Lim|bo ['lɪmbo] M **-s, -s** limbo

Lim|bur|ger (Käse) ['lɪmbʊrgɐ] M **-s, -** Limburger, Limburg cheese

Li|me|rick ['lɪmərɪk] M **-(s), -s** limerick

Li|mes ['liːmɛs] M **-, -** a no pl (Hist) limes b (Math) limit

Li|met|te [li'mɛtə] F **-, -n** sweet lime

Li|mit ['lɪmɪt] NT **-s, -s** or **-e** limit; (Fin) ceiling; **jdm ein ~ setzen** to set sb a limit

li|mi|tie|ren [limi'tiːrən] ptp **limitiert** VT (form) to limit; (Fin) to put a ceiling on; **nicht limitiert** unlimited, open-ended; **eine streng limitierte Auflage** a strictly limited edition

Li|mo ['lɪmo, 'liːmo] F **-, -s** (inf) = **Limonade**

Li|mo|na|de [limo'naːdə] F **-, -n** lemonade; (in weiterem Sinn) soft drink

Li|mo|ne [li'moːnə] F **-, -n** lime

Li|mou|si|ne [limu'ziːnə] F **-, -n** saloon (Brit), sedan (US)

lind [lɪnt] ADJ (liter) balmy; Regen gentle ADV a (liter: = mild) gently b (Sw) **~ (gewürzt)** lightly spiced; **~ gewürzter Käse** mild cheese

Lin|dan [lɪn'daːn] NT **-** lindane

Lin|de ['lɪndə] F **-, -n** (= Baum) linden or lime (tree); (= Holz) limewood

Lin|den|blü|ten|tee M lime blossom tea

lin|dern ['lɪndɐn] VT to ease, to relieve, to alleviate; Hustenreiz, Sonnenbrand etc auch to soothe

Lin|de|rung ['lɪndərʊŋ] F **-, -en** easing, relief, alleviation; (von Hustenreiz, Sonnenbrand etc auch) soothing

Lin|de|rungs|mit|tel NT pain reliever, analgesic

Lind-: **lind|grün** ADJ lime green; **Lind|wurm** M (Myth) lindworm (type of wingless dragon)

Li|ne|al [line'aːl] NT **-s, -e** ruler; **einen Strich mit dem ~ ziehen** to rule a line (esp Brit), to draw a line with a ruler; **er geht, als ob er ein ~ verschluckt hätte** (inf) he walks with his back as stiff as a ramrod

li|ne|ar [line'aːɐ] ADJ linear; **~e Abschreibung** (Fin) straight-line depreciation ADV linearly

Li|ne|ar|be|schleu|ni|ger M (Phys) linear accelerator

Li|ne|ar|schrift F linear script; **~ B** Linear B

Li|ne|a|tur [linea'tuːɐ] F **-, -en** ruling, lines pl

Li|ner ['laɪnɐ] M **-s, -** (Naut) liner

Lin|ge|rie [lɛ̃ʒə'riː] F **-, -n** (Sw) lingerie

lin|gu|al [lɪŋ'gua:l] ADJ (form) lingual

Lin|gu|ist [lɪŋ'gʊɪst] M **-en, -en**, **Lin|gu|is|tin** [-'gʊɪstɪn] F **-, -nen** linguist

Lin|gu|is|tik [lɪŋ'gʊɪstɪk] F **-,** no pl linguistics sing

lin|gu|is|tisch [lɪŋ'gʊɪstɪʃ] ADJ linguistic ADV linguistically; **~ interessiert** interested in linguistics

Li|ni|a|tur [linia'tuːɐ] F **-, -en** ruling, lines pl

Li|nie ['liːniə] ✪ 53.5 F **-, -n** a line (auch Sport, Pol, Naut); (= Umriss) (out)line; **ein Schreibblock mit ~n** a ruled (esp Brit) or lined notepad; **die ~n (in) seiner Hand** the lines of or on his hand; **in einer ~ stehen** to be in a line; **sich in einer ~ aufstellen** to line up; **die Buchstaben halten nicht ~** (Typ) the letters are not in line; **auf der gleichen ~** along the same lines; **einer Sache** (dat) **fehlt die klare ~** there's no clear line to sth; **eine klare ~ für sein Leben finden**, **seinem Leben eine klare ~ geben** to give one's life a clear sense of direction; **eine ~ ziehen zwischen ...** (+dat) (fig) to draw a distinction between ...; **auf der ganzen ~** (fig) all along the line; **auf ~ bleiben** (fig) to toe the line; **sie hat ein Gesicht mit klaren/verschwommenen ~n** she has clear-cut/ill-defined features; **auf die (schlanke) ~ achten** to watch one's figure; **in direkter ~ von jdm abstammen** to be a direct descendant of sb; **die männliche/weibliche ~ eines Geschlechts** the male/female line of a family; **in erster/zweiter ~ kommen** (fig) to come first/second, to take first/second place; **in erster ~ muss die Arbeitslosigkeit bekämpft werden** the fight against unemployment must come first or must take priority → **erste(r, s) a** b (Mil = Stellung) line; (= Formation) rank; **in ~**

antreten! fall in!; **in ~ zu drei Gliedern** in ranks three deep; **die feindliche/vorderste ~** the enemy lines pl/front line

c (= Verkehrsverbindung, -strecke) route; (= Buslinie, Eisenbahnlinie) line, route; **fahren Sie mit der ~ 2** take or the (number) 2; **auf einer ~ verkehren** to work a route; **die ~ Köln-Bonn** the Cologne-Bonn line

Li|ni|en-: **Li|ni|en|ball** M (Tennis) ball (right) on the line; **Li|ni|en|blatt** NT ruled (esp Brit) or lined sheet (placed under writing paper), line guide; **Li|ni|en|bus** M public service bus, regular bus; **Li|ni|en|damp|fer** M regular service steamer; **Li|ni|en|dienst** M regular service; (Aviat) scheduled service; **Li|ni|en|flug** M scheduled flight; **Li|ni|en|flug|zeug** NT scheduled (service) plane; **Li|ni|en|füh|rung** F a (Art etc) lines pl b (von Bus etc) route; **Li|ni|en|ma|schi|ne** F scheduled flight; **mit einer ~** on a scheduled flight; **Li|ni|en|netz** NT network of routes; **das ~ der U-Bahn** the underground (Brit) or subway (US) (system); **das ~ der Straßenbahnen** the tram (esp Brit) or streetcar (US) system; **Li|ni|en|pa|pier** NT ruled (esp Brit) or lined paper; **Li|ni|en|rich|ter** M (Sport) linesman; (Tennis) line judge; **Li|ni|en|rich|te|rin** F (Sport) lineswoman; (Tennis) line judge; **Li|ni|en|schiff** NT regular service ship; **li|ni|en|treu** ADJ loyal to the party line; **~ sein** to follow or toe the party line; **Li|ni|en|treue** F loyalty to the party line; **Li|ni|en|ver|kehr** M regular traffic; (Aviat) scheduled traffic; **im ~ fliegen** to fly on scheduled services; **im ~ fahren** to operate on regular services

li|ni|e|ren [li'niːrən] ptp **liniert**, **li|ni|ie|ren** [lini-'iːrən] ptp **liniiert** VT to rule, to rule (esp Brit) or draw lines on; **lini(i)ert** lined, feint (spec)

Li|nie|rung F **-, -en**, **Li|ni|ie|rung** F **-, -en** ruling

link [lɪŋk] (inf) ADJ Typ underhanded, double-crossing; Masche, Tour dirty, low-down (US inf); **ein ganz ~er Hund** (pej) a nasty piece of work (pej inf); **ein ganz ~es Ding drehen** to get up to a bit of no good (inf) ADV **jdn ~ behandeln**, **sich jdm gegenüber ~ verhalten** to mess (Brit) or jerk (esp US) sb around (inf); **komm mir nicht so ~** stop messing (Brit) or jerking (esp US) me around (inf)

Lin|ke ['lɪŋkə] F decl as adj a (Hand) left hand; (Seite) left(-hand) side; (Boxen) left; **zur ~n (des Königs)** to the left (of the king) or on the (king's) left sat ... b (Pol) **die ~** the Left

lin|ken ['lɪŋkn] VT (inf: = hereinlegen) to con (inf)

Lin|ke(r) ['lɪŋkə] MF decl as adj (Pol) left-winger, leftist (pej), lefty (pej inf)

lin|ke(r, s) ['lɪŋkə] ADJ attr a left; Rand, Spur etc left(-hand); **die ~ Seite** the left(-hand) side; (von Stoff) the wrong side, the reverse (side); **auf der ~n Seite** on the left-hand side, on the left; **~r Hand, zur ~n Hand** to the left, on the left, on one's left; **~ Masche** (Stricken) purl (stitch); **eine ~ Masche stricken** to purl one; **zwei ~ Maschen haben** (inf) to have two left hands (inf); **das mache ich mit der ~n Hand** (inf) I can do that with my eyes shut (inf); **er ist heute mit dem ~n Bein** or **Fuß zuerst aufgestanden** (inf) he got out of bed on the wrong side this morning (inf) b (Pol) left-wing, leftist (pej), lefty (pej inf); Flügel left

lin|ker|seits ['lɪŋkɐzaɪts] ADV to the left, on the left-hand side

lin|kisch ['lɪŋkɪʃ] ADJ clumsy, awkward ADV clumsily, awkwardly; tanzen, begrüßen awkwardly

links [lɪŋks] ADV a on the left; schauen, abbiegen (to the) left; **nach ~** (to the) left; **von ~** from the left; **~ von etw** (to the or on the) left of sth; **von jdm** (to the or on sb's left); **sich ~ halten** to keep to the left; **weiter ~** further to the left; **sich ~ einordnen** to move into or take the

left-hand lane; **jdn ~ liegen lassen** (fig inf) to ignore sb; **weder ~ noch rechts schauen** (lit) to look neither left nor right; (fig) not to let oneself be distracted; **~ von der Mitte** (Pol) (to the) left of centre (Brit) or center (US); **stehen** or **sein** (Pol) to be left-wing or on the left or a left-winger; **mit ~** (inf) just like that, without any trouble; **das mache ich mit ~** (inf) I can do that with my eyes shut (inf); **Augen ~!** (Mil) eyes left!; **~ um!** (Mil) left about turn; **~ schwenkt, marsch!** (Mil) left wheel! b (= verkehrt) bügeln on the reverse or wrong side; tragen reverse or wrong side out; liegen reverse or wrong side up; **~ stricken** to purl; **eine (Masche) ~, drei (Maschen) rechts** purl one, knit three; **der Pullover ist nur ~ gestrickt** the pullover is knitted all in purl PREP +gen on or to the left of

Links-: **Links|ab|bie|ger¹** [-ˈapbiːgɐ] M **-s, -** (= Spur) left-hand turn-off lane; **Links|ab|bie|ger²** [-ˈapbiːgɐ] M **-s, -**, **Links|ab|bie|ge|rin** [-ərɪn] F **-, -nen** motorist/cyclist/car etc turning left; **Links|ab|bie|ger|spur** F left-hand turn-off lane; **Links|ab|weich|ler(in)** M(F) (Pol inf) left-wing dissenter; **Links|au|ßen** [-ˈlausn] M **-, -** (Ftbl) outside left; (Pol) extreme left-winger; **links|bün|dig** ADJ (Typ) ranged or flush left ADV flush left; **links|drall** M (lit) (im Gewehrlauf) anticlockwise rifling (Brit), counterclockwise rifling (US); (von Geschoss, Billardball) swerve to the left; (von Auto, Pferd) pull to the left; (fig) leaning to the left; **einen ~ haben** to swerve/pull/lean to the left; **links|dre|hend** ADJ (Chem) laevorotatory (Brit spec), levorotatory (US spec); **Links|dre|hung** F anticlockwise rotation, counter-rotation (US); **Links|ext|re|mist(in)** M(F) left-wing extremist; **Links|gang** M pl **-gänge** (Tech) left-handed thread; **links|gän|gig** ADJ (Tech) left-handed; **links|ge|rich|tet** [-ˈgərɪçtət] ADJ (Pol) left-wing; **Links|ge|win|de** NT left-handed thread; **Links|ha|ken** M left hook; **Links|hän|der** [-hɛndɐ] M **-s, -**, **Links|hän|de|rin** [-ərɪn] F **-, -nen** left-hander, left-handed person; **~ sein** to be left-handed; **links|hän|dig** ADJ, ADV left-handed; **Links|hän|dig|keit** F **-,** no pl left-handedness; **links|her** ['lɪŋksheːɐ] ADV (old) from the left; **links|he|ran** ['lɪŋksheran] ADV over to the left; **links|he|rum** ['lɪŋksherʊm] ADV (round) to the left; sich drehen etc anticlockwise (Brit), counterclockwise (US); **links|hin** ['lɪŋkshɪn] ADV (old) (to the) left; **Links|in|tel|lek|tu|el|le(r)** MF decl as adj (Pol) left-wing intellectual; **Links|kur|ve** F (von Straße) left-hand bend; (von Bahn auch) left-hand curve; **links|las|tig** [-lastɪç] ADJ (lit) Boot listing to the left; Auto down at the left; (fig) leftist (pej), leaning to the left; **links|läu|fig** ADJ Gewinde left-handed; Schrift right-to-left; **Links|par|tei** F left-wing party; **links|ra|di|kal** ADJ (Pol) radically left-wing; **die Linksradikalen** the left-wing radicals ADV **~ eingestellt sein** to be a left-wing radical; **~ klingen** to sound radically left-wing; **Links|ra|di|ka|lis|mus** M (Pol) left-wing radicalism; **links|rhei|nisch** ADJ, ADV to or on the left of the Rhine; **Links|ruck** M , **Links|rutsch** M , **Links|schwenk** M (Pol) shift to the left; **links|rum** ['lɪŋksrʊm] ADV (inf) = linksherum; **links|sei|tig** [-zaɪtç] ADJ, ADV on the left(-hand) side; **~ gelähmt** paralyzed on the left side; **~ blind** blind in the left eye; **er war ~ amputiert** his left arm/leg was amputated; **Links|steu|e|rung** F (Mot) left-hand drive; **links|um** [lɪŋksˈʊm, 'lɪŋksʊm] ADV (Mil) to the left; **~ machen** (inf) to do a left turn; **~ kehrt!** to the left about turn!; **Links|ver|kehr** M , no pl driving on the left no def art; **in Großbritannien ist ~** they drive on the left in Britain; **im ~ muss man ...** when driving on the left one must ...

Lin|nen ['lɪnən] ADJ (liter) = **leinen**

Lin|nen ['lɪnən] NT **-s, -** (liter) linen

Li|no|le|um [li'noːleʊm] NT **-s,** no pl linoleum, lino

Li|nol- [li'no:l-]: **Li|nol|säu|re** F linoleic acid; **Li|nol|schnitt** M (Art) linocut

Li|non [li:'nõ:] M **-(s), -s** (Tex) lawn

Lin|se ['lɪnzə] F **-, -n a** (Bot, Cook) lentil **b** (Opt) lens

lin|sen ['lɪnzn] VI (inf) to peep, to peek (inf); (Sch) to copy (bei off, from)

Lin|sen-: Lin|sen|ge|richt NT lentil dish; (Bibl, fig) mess of potage; **Lin|sen|sup|pe** F lentil soup; **Lin|sen|trü|bung** F (Med) cataract

Lip|gloss ['lɪpglɔs] NT **-, -** lip gloss

Lip|pe ['lɪpə] F **-, -n** lip; (Bot auch) labium; **eine (große** or **dicke) ~ riskieren** (inf) to be brazen; **das bringe ich nicht über die ~n** I can't bring myself to say it; **es wird** or **soll kein Wort über meine ~n kommen** not a word shall cross or pass my lips; **er brachte kein Wort über die ~n** he couldn't say or utter a word; **das Wort erstarb ihm auf den ~n** (liter) the word froze on his lips; **von den ~n lesen** to read lips → **hängen 1 k, beißen** VR

Lip|pen-: Lip|pen|bal|sam M lip balm; **Lip|pen|be|kennt|nis** NT lip service; **ein ~ ablegen** to pay lip service (to one's ideals etc); **Lip|pen|blüt|ler** [-bly:tlɐ] M **-s, -** (Bot) labiate; **Lip|pen|laut** M (Ling) labial; **Lip|pen|pfle|ge|stift** M lip salve (stick) (Brit), chapstick®; **Lip|pen|stift** M lipstick

li|quid [li'kvi:t] ADJ = **liquide**

Li|qui|da ['li:kvida] F **-, Liquidä** or **Liquiden** [-dɛ:, li'kvi:dn] (Ling) liquid

Li|qui|da|ti|on [likvida'tsio:n] F **-, -en** (form) **a** (= Auflösung) liquidation; **in ~ treten** to go into liquidation; **sie haben die ~ beschlossen** they decided to go into liquidation **b** (= Rechnung) account

Li|qui|da|ti|ons|wert M (Fin) net asset value, break-up value

Li|qui|da|tor [likvi'da:tɔɐ] M **-s, Liquidatoren** [-'to:rən], **Li|qui|da|to|rin** [-'to:rɪn] F **-, -nen** (Fin) liquidator

li|qui|de [li'kvi:də] ADJ (Econ) Geld, Mittel liquid; Firma, Geschäftsmann solvent; **ich bin nicht ~** (inf) I'm out of funds (inf), I'm short of the readies (Brit inf)

li|qui|die|ren [likvi'di:rən] ptp **liquidiert** VT **a** Geschäft to put into liquidation, to wind up; Betrag to charge; **einen Kontrakt in bar ~** to settle a contract in cash **b** Firma to liquidate; jdn to eliminate

Li|qui|die|rung F **-, -en** (von Firma) liquidation; (von Person) elimination

Li|qui|di|tät [likvidi'tɛ:t] F **-, no pl** (Econ) liquidity

lis|men ['lɪsmən] VTI (Sw) to knit

lis|peln ['lɪspln] VTI to lisp; (= flüstern) to whisper

Lis|sa|bon ['lɪsabɔn, lɪsa'bɔn] NT **-s** Lisbon

Lis|sa|bon|ner¹ ['lɪsabɔnɐ, lɪsa'bɔnɐ] ADJ attr Lisbon

Lis|sa|bon|ner² ['lɪsabɔnɐ, lɪsa'bɔnɐ] M **-s, -**, **Lis|sa|bon|ne|rin** [-ərɪn] F **-, -nen** native of Lisbon; (Einwohner) inhabitant of Lisbon

List [lɪst] F **-, -en** (= Täuschung) cunning, artfulness; (= trickreicher Plan) trick, ruse; **mit ~ und Tücke** (inf) with a lot of coaxing; **zu einer ~ greifen, (eine) ~ anwenden** to use a bit of cunning, to resort to a ruse

Lis|te ['lɪstə] F **-, -n** (= Aufstellung) list; (= Wählerliste) register; (von Parteien) (party) list (of candidates under the proportional representation system); **sich in eine ~ eintragen** or **(ein)schreiben** to put oneself or one's name (down) on a list

Lis|ten-: Lis|ten|füh|rer(in) M(F) list keeper; **Lis|ten|platz** M (Pol) place on the party list (of candidates under the proportional representation system); **Lis|ten|preis** M list price; **Lis|ten|wahl** F electoral system in which a

vote is cast for a party rather than a specific candidate

lis|tig ['lɪstɪç] ADJ cunning, crafty, wily no adv ADV cunningly

lis|ti|ger|wei|se ['lɪstɪgɐ'vaizə] ADV cunningly, craftily

Li|ta|nei [lita'nai] F **-, -en** (Eccl, fig) litany; **eine ~ von Klagen/Beschwerden** etc a long list or catalogue (Brit) or catalog (US) of complaints; **immer dieselbe ~ beten** to go on about the same old things all the time (inf)

Li|tau|en ['li:tauən, 'lɪtauən] NT **-s** Lithuania

Li|tau|er ['li:tauɐ, 'lɪtauɐ] M **-s, -**, **Li|tau|e|rin** [-ərɪn] F **-, -nen** Lithuanian

li|tau|isch ['li:tauɪʃ, 'lɪtauɪʃ] ADJ Lithuanian

Li|tau|isch(e) NT (Ling) Lithuanian → auch **Deutsch(e)**

Li|ter ['li:tɐ, 'lɪtɐ] M OR NT **-s, -** litre (Brit), liter (US)

li|te|rar|his|to|risch [lɪtɐ'ra:ɐ-] ADJ literary historical attr; Buch, Artikel auch relating to literary history ADV from a literary historical point of view; **~ interessant** of interest to literary history

li|te|ra|risch [lɪtɐ'ra:rɪʃ] ADJ literary ADV **~ gebildet/informiert sein** to be knowledgeable in literature; **~ interessiert** interested in literature

Li|te|rat [lɪtɐ'ra:t] M **-en, -en** man of letters; (= Schriftsteller) literary figure; **die ~en** the literati (form)

Li|te|ra|tin [lɪtɐ'ra:tɪn] F **-, -nen** woman of letters; (= Schriftstellerin) literary figure

Li|te|ra|tur [lɪtɐra'tu:ɐ] F **-, -en** literature

Li|te|ra|tur-: Li|te|ra|tur|an|ga|be F bibliographical reference; (Zusammenfassung) bibliography; **Li|te|ra|tur|be|trieb** M, no pl literary scene; **Li|te|ra|tur|denk|mal** NT literary monument; **Li|te|ra|tur|gat|tung** F literary genre; **Li|te|ra|tur|ge|schich|te** F history of literature; **Li|te|ra|tur|ge|schicht|lich** ADJ, ADV = literarhistorisch; **Li|te|ra|tur|hin|weis** M literary reference (auf +acc to); **Li|te|ra|tur|kri|tik** F literary criticism; (= Kritikerschaft) literary critics pl; **Li|te|ra|tur|kri|ti|ker(in)** M(F) literary critic; **Li|te|ra|tur|nach|weis** M bibliographical reference; (Zusammenfassung) bibliography; **Li|te|ra|tur|papst** M, **Li|te|ra|tur|päps|tin** F literary pundit; **Li|te|ra|tur|preis** M prize or award for literature, literary prize or award; **Li|te|ra|tur|ver|zeich|nis** NT bibliography; **Li|te|ra|tur|wis|sen|schaft** F literary studies pl; **vergleichende ~** comparative literature; **Li|te|ra|tur|wis|sen|schaft|ler(in)** M(F) literary or literature specialist

Li|ter-: Li|ter|fla|sche F litre (Brit) or liter (US) bottle; **Li|ter|leis|tung** F power output per litre (Brit) or liter (US); **Li|ter|maß** NT litre (Brit) or liter (US) measure; **li|ter|wei|se** ADV (lit) by the litre (Brit) or liter (US); (fig) by the gallon

Lit|faß|säu|le ['lɪtfas-] F advertisement pillar

Li|thi|um ['li:tiʊm] NT **-s, no pl** (abbr **Li**) lithium

Li|tho ['li:to] NT **-s, -s** (inf) abbr von **Lithografie**

Li|tho-: Li|tho|graf ▲ [lito'gra:f] M **-en, -en**, **Li|tho|gra|fin** ▲ [-'gra:fɪn] F **-, -nen** lithographer; **Li|tho|gra|fie** ▲ [litogra'fi:] F **-, -n** [-'fi:ən] **a** (Verfahren) lithography **b** (Druck) lithograph; **li|tho|gra|fie|ren** ▲ [litogra'fi:rən] ptp **lithografiert** VT to lithograph; **li|tho|gra|fisch** ▲ [lito'gra:fɪʃ] ADJ lithographic(al)

Li|to|tes [li'to:tɛs] F **-, -** (Liter) litotes

Lit|schi ['lɪtʃi] F **-, -s** lychee, litchi

litt ptp von **leiden**

Li|tur|gie [litʊr'gi:] F **-, -n** [-'gi:ən] liturgy

li|tur|gisch [li'tɔrgɪʃ] ADJ liturgical

Lit|ze ['lɪtsə] F **-, -n** braid; (Elec) flex

live [laif] ADJ pred ADV (Rad, TV) live; **wir konnten ~ dabei sein** we were able to see everything live; **„live im ZDF"** "live on ZDF"

Live-: Live|be|richt [laif-] M (Sport) live commentary; (= Reportage) on-the-spot report; **das war ein Livebreicht von X in Basra** that was X reporting live from Basra; **Live|mitt|schnitt** ['laifmɪtʃnɪt] M live recording; **Live|mu|sik** [laif-] F live music; **Live-Sen|dung** [laif-] F live programme (Brit) or program (US), live broadcast; **Live|über|tra|gung** [laif-] F live transmission

Liv|ree [li'vre:] F **-, -n** [-'re:ən] livery

liv|riert [li'vri:ɐt] ADJ liveried

Li|zenz [li'tsɛnts] F **-, -en** licence (Brit), license (US); **eine ~ dafür haben, etw zu tun** to have a licence (Brit) or license (US) to do sth, to be licensed to do sth; **etw in ~ herstellen** to manufacture sth under licence (Brit) or license (US)

Li|zenz-: Li|zenz|ab|ga|be F licence (Brit) or license (US) fee; (im Verlagswesen) royalty; **Li|zenz|ab|kom|men** NT licensing agreement; **Li|zenz|aus|ga|be** F licensed edition; **Li|zenz|ge|ber(in)** M(F) licenser; (Behörde) licensing authority; **Li|zenz|ge|bühr** F licence (Brit) or license (US) fee; (im Verlagswesen) royalty

li|zen|zie|ren [litsɛn'tsi:rən] ptp **lizenziert** VT (form) to license

Li|zenz-: Li|zenz|in|ha|ber(in) M(F) licensee, licence (Brit) or license (US) holder; **er ist ~** he has a licence (Brit) or license (US), he is licensed; **Li|zenz|neh|mer(in)** M(F) licensee; **Li|zenz|pres|se** F (Pol) licensed press; **Li|zenz|spie|ler(in)** M(F) (Ftbl) professional player; **Li|zenz|trä|ger(in)** M(F) licensee

Lkw M, **LKW** ['ɛlka:ve:, ɛlka:'ve:] M **-(s), -(s)** abbr von **Lastkraftwagen**

Lob¹ [lo:p] M **-(e)s** [-bəs] no pl praise; (= Belobigung) commendation; **~ verdienen** to deserve praise, to deserve to be praised; **(viel) ~ für etw bekommen** to come in for (a lot of) praise for sth, to be (highly) praised for sth; **(über jdn/etw) des ~es voll sein** (geh) to be full of praise (for sb/sth); **ein ~ der Köchin** (my/our) compliments to the chef!; **den Schülern wurde für ihre hervorragenden Leistungen ein ~ erteilt** the pupils were commended for their outstanding achievements; **Gott sei ~ und Dank** praise be to God, God be praised; **zum ~e Gottes** in praise of the Lord; **über jedes ~ erhaben sein** to be beyond praise; **sein eigenes ~ singen** (inf) to sing one's own praises, to blow one's own trumpet (inf); **jdm ~ spenden** or **zollen** to praise sb

Lob² [lɔp] M **-(s), -s** (Tennis, Volleyball) lob

lob|ben ['lɔbn] VTI (Tennis, Volleyball) to lob

Lob|by ['lɔbi] F **-, -s** lobby

Lob|by|is|mus [lɔbi'ɪsmʊs] M **-, no pl** lobbyism

Lob|by|ist [lɔbi'ɪst] M **-en, -en**, **Lob|by|is|tin** [-'ɪstɪn] F **-, -nen** lobbyist

Lo|be|lie [lo'be:liə] F **-, -n** (Bot) lobelia

lo|ben [lo:bn] ✪ 40.4 VT to praise; **sein neues Werk wurde allgemein sehr gelobt** his new work was universally acclaimed; **jdn/etw ~d erwähnen** to commend sb/sth; **das lob ich mir** that's what I like (to see/hear etc); **seinen Fleiß lob ich mir** his diligence is most laudable; **da lob ich mir doch ein gutes Glas Wein** I always say you can't beat a good glass of wine → **Abend a, Klee**

lo|bens|wert ADJ praiseworthy, laudable ADV praiseworthily, laudably

lo|be|sam ['lo:bəza:m] (obs) ADJ virtuous ADV virtuously

Lo|bes|hym|ne F (fig) hymn of praise, panegyric

Lob-: Lob|ge|sang M song or hymn of praise; **einen ~ auf jdn/etw anstimmen** (fig) to sing sb's praises/the praises of sth; **Lob|hu|de|lei** [lo:phu:də'lai] F **-, -en** (pej) gushing; **lob|hu|deln** ['lo:phu:dln] VI insep jdm ~ (pej) to gush over sb (inf)

---

löb|lich ['løːplɪç] ADJ (also iro) commendable, laudable; **die ~e Ausnahme sein** to be the notable exception

Lob-: Lob|lied NT song or hymn of praise; **ein ~ auf jdn/etw anstimmen** or **singen** (fig) to sing sb's praises/the praises of sth; **Lob|preis** M (liter) praise no art; **lob|prei|sen** ptp **lob(ge)-priesen** VT insep (liter) to praise; **Gott auch** to glorify; **Lob|re|de** F eulogy, panegyric; **eine ~ auf jdn halten** (lit) to make a speech in sb's honour (Brit) or honor (US); (fig) to eulogize or extol sb; **sich in ~n über jdn/etw ergehen** to eulogize or extol sb/sth; **Lob|red|ner(in)** M(F) (lit) speaker; (fig) eulogist; **lob|sin|gen** ptp **lobgesungen** VI sep irreg +dat **Gott** to praise; (fig) to sing the praises of; **Lob|spruch** M eulogy (über +acc of), encomium (form); (Gedicht) panegyric

Lo|cal-Bus ['loːkəlbas] M (Comput) local bus

Loch [lɔx] NT **-(e)s, ¨er** ['lœçə] (= Öffnung, Lücke, Defizit) hole; (in Zahn auch) cavity; (in Reifen) puncture; (= Luftloch) gap; (Billard) pocket; (fig inf: = elende Wohnung, Raum) dump (inf), hole (inf); (inf: = Kneipe) dive (inf); (inf: = Gefängnis) jug (inf), clink (inf), can (esp US inf); (vulg: = Vagina) cunt (vulg), hole (sl); **sich** (dat) **ein ~ in den Kopf/ins Knie etc schlagen** to gash one's head/knee etc, to cut one's head/knee etc open; **jdm ein ~** or **Löcher in den Bauch fragen** (inf) to pester the living daylights out of sb (with all one's questions) (inf); **sie redet einem ein ~** or **Löcher in den Bauch** (inf) she could talk the hind legs off a donkey (inf); **ein ~** or **Löcher in die Luft gucken** or **starren** or **in die Wand stieren** (inf) to gaze into space or thin air; **in ein ~ fallen** (fig) to come off the rails; **ein großes ~ in jds (Geld)beutel** (acc) or **Tasche** (acc) **reißen** (inf) to make a big hole in sb's pocket; **jdn ins ~ stecken** (inf: = ins Gefängnis) to put sb in the clink (inf) → **pfeifen**

Loch|ei|sen NT punch

lo|chen ['lɔxn] VT to punch holes/a hole in; (= perforieren) to perforate; **Fahrkarte** to punch, to clip; **gelochter Schreibblock** tear-off file pad

Lo|cher¹ ['lɔxɐ] M **-s, -** (= Gerät)

Lo|cher² ['lɔxɐ] M **-s, -**, **Lo|che|rin** [-ərɪn] F **-, -nen** punch card operator

lö|che|rig ['lœçərɪç] ADJ (lit, fig) full of holes; **ganz ~ sein** to be full of holes

lö|chern ['lœçɐn] VT (inf) to pester (to death) with questions (inf); **er löchert mich seit Wochen, wann ...** he's been pestering me for weeks wanting to know when ...

Loch-: Loch|ka|me|ra F pinhole camera; **Loch|kar|te** F punch card; **Loch|kar|ten|ma|schi|ne** F punch card machine

löch|rig ['lœçrɪç] ADJ = löcherig

Loch-: Loch|sä|ge F keyhole saw; **Loch|sti|cke|rei** F broderie anglaise; **Loch|strei|fen** M (punched) paper tape

Lo|chung ['lɔxʊŋ] F **-, -en** punching; (= Perforation) perforation

Loch-: Loch|ver|stär|ker M paper reinforcement ring; **Loch|zan|ge** F punch; **Loch|zie|gel** M airbrick (esp Brit)

Lo|cke¹ ['lɔkə] F **-, -n** (Haar) curl; **~n haben** to have curly hair

Lo|cke² F **-, -n** (Pfeife) (bird) call

lo|cken¹ ['lɔkn] VTR **Haar** to curl; **gelockt** (Haar) curly; **Mensch** curly-haired, curly-headed

lo|cken² VT **a** **Tier** to lure; **die Henne lockte ihre Küken** the hen called to its chicks **b** **jdn** to tempt; (mit Ortsangabe) to lure; **es lockt mich in den Süden** I can feel the call of the south; **jdn in einen Hinterhalt ~** to lead or lure sb into a trap; **das Angebot lockt mich sehr** I'm very tempted by the offer → **Falle a, Tasche b**

lö|cken ['lœkn] VI **wider den Stachel ~** (geh) to kick against the pricks (Brit liter), to oppose authority

lo|ckend ADJ tempting, enticing, alluring

Lo|cken-: Lo|cken|kopf M curly hairstyle; (Mensch) curly-head; **Lo|cken|pracht** F (magnificent) head of curls; **Lo|cken|sche|re** F curling tongs pl (Brit), curling iron (US); **Lo|cken|stab** M (electric) curling tongs pl (Brit), (electric) curling iron (US); **Lo|cken|wi|ckel** M , **Lo|cken|wick|ler** [-vɪklɐ] M **-s, -** (hair) curler; **das Haar auf ~ drehen** to put one's hair in curlers

lo|cker ['lɔkɐ] ADJ (lit, fig) loose; **Schnee, Erdreich** auch loose-packed; **Kuchen, Schaum** light; (= nicht gespannt) slack; **Haltung, Sitzweise, Muskulatur** relaxed; (inf: = liberal, unkompliziert) laid-back (inf); **~ werden** (lit, fig) to get loose; (Muskeln, Mensch) to loosen up; (Seil) to get or go slack; (Verhältnis) to get more relaxed; (Kuchen) to be light; **eine ~e Hand haben** (fig = schnell zuschlagen) to be quick to hit out; (beim Schreiben) to have a flowing hand; **ein ~er Vogel** (inf) or **Zeisig** (dated inf) a bit of a lad (inf) or rake (dated), a gay dog (dated) → **Mundwerk, Schraube a** **ADV** **a** (= nicht stramm) loosely; **etw ~ machen** to loosen sth; **Seil etc** to slacken sth; **etw ~ lassen** to slacken sth off; **Bremse** to let sth off; **~ sitzen** (Ziegel, Schraube etc) to be loose; **bei ihm sitzt das Geld ~** he is free with money; **bei ihr sitzt die Hand ziemlich ~** she's quick to lash out (inf); **bei ihm sitzt der Revolver ~** he's trigger-happy; **bei ihm sitzt das Messer ~** he'd pull a knife at the slightest excuse **b** (= nicht verkrampft) laufen loosely; schreiben naturally; **etw ~ sehen** to be relaxed about sth; **jdn ~ machen** to relax sb; **~ sitzen** (Mensch) to relax, to sit in a relaxed position; **~ drauf sein** (inf) to be laid-back (inf) **c** (= oberflächlich) kennen, bekannt sein casually **d** (inf: = leicht) easily; **~ vom Hocker** (sl) just like that (inf); **das mache ich ganz ~** I can do it just like that (inf)

lo|cker-flo|ckig ADJ (inf) easy-going, laid-back

Lo|cker|heit F **-, no pl** looseness; (von Kuchen etc) lightness; (von Seil etc) slackness; (= Entspanntheit) relaxed state; **etw in aller ~ tun** to do sth in a relaxed way

lo|cker-: lo|cker+las|sen VI sep irreg (inf) **nicht ~** not to give up, not to let up; **lo|cker+ma|chen** VT sep (inf) **Geld** to shell out (inf), to part with; **bei jdm 100 Euro ~** to get sb to shell out (inf) or part with 100 euros

lo|ckern ['lɔkɐn] VT **a** (= locker machen) to loosen; **Boden** to break up; **Griff** to relax, to loosen; **Seil** to slacken; (lit, fig) **Zügel** to slacken **b** (= entspannen) **Arme, Beine, Muskeln** to loosen up; (fig) **Vorschriften, Atmosphäre** to relax VR to work itself loose; (Moral) to become loose or lax; (Sport) to loosen up; (zum Warmwerden) to limber up, to warm up; (Verkrampfung, Spannung) to ease off; (Atmosphäre, Beziehungen, Mensch) to get more relaxed

Lo|cke|rung ['lɔkərʊŋ] F **-, -en** **a** loosening; (von Griff) relaxation, loosening; (von Seil) slackening **b** (von Armen, Beinen, Muskeln) loosening up; (von Beziehungen) easing, relaxation

Lo|cke|rungs-: Lo|cke|rungs|mit|tel NT raising agent; **Lo|cke|rungs|übung** F loosening-up exercise; (zum Warmwerden) limbering-up exercise, warm-up exercise

lo|ckig ['lɔkɪç] ADJ **Haar** curly; **Mensch** curly-headed

Lock-: Lock|mit|tel NT lure; **Lock|pfei|fe** F (bird) call; (für Hund) whistle; **Lock|ruf** M (fig) call; **Lock|spit|zel** M agent provocateur; **Lock|stoff-Fal|le** F pheromone-baited insect trap

Lo|ckung ['lɔkʊŋ] F **-, -en** lure; (= Versuchung) temptation

Lock|vo|gel M decoy (bird); (fig) lure, decoy

Lock|vo|gel|an|ge|bot NT inducement

Lod|del ['lɔdl] M **-s, -** (inf) ponce (esp Brit inf), pimp

Lo|den ['loːdn] M **-s, -** loden (cloth)

Lo|den|man|tel M loden (coat)

lo|dern ['loːdɐn] VI (lit, fig) to blaze; (= emporlodern) to blaze up; **in seinen Augen loderte Hass/Gier** his eyes blazed with hatred/greed

Löf|fel ['lœfl] M **-s, -** **a** (als Besteck) spoon; (als Maßangabe) spoonful; (von Bagger) bucket; **den ~ abgeben** (inf) to kick the bucket (inf); **mit einem silbernen** or **goldenen ~ im Mund geboren sein** to be born with a silver spoon in one's mouth → **balbieren** **b** (Hunt) ear; (inf: von Mensch) ear, lug (Brit inf); **jdm ein paar hinter die ~ hauen** (inf) jdm **eins hinter die ~ geben** (inf) to give sb a clip (a)round the ear; **ein paar hinter die ~ kriegen** (inf) to get a clip (a)round the ear; **sich** (dat) **etw hinter die ~ schreiben** (inf) to get sth into one's head (inf); **sperr doch deine ~ auf** (inf) pin back your lugholes (Brit inf), listen properly; **die ~ spitzen** (inf) to prick up one's ears

Löf|fel|bag|ger M excavator, mechanical shovel

Löf|fel|bis|kuit M OR NT sponge finger, ladyfinger (US)

löf|feln ['lœfln] VT to spoon; (mit der Kelle) to ladle

Löf|fel-: Löf|fel|stiel M spoon handle; **löf|fel|wei|se** ADV by the spoonful

Löff|ler ['lœflɐ] M **-s, -** (Zool) spoonbill

Loft [lɔft] NT **-s, -s** (Build) luxury attic flat (Brit) or apartment

log¹ pret von **lügen**

log² abbr von **Logarithmus**

Log [lɔk] NT **-s, -e** [-gə] (Naut) log

Lo|ga|rith|men|ta|fel F log table

lo|ga|rith|mie|ren [logarɪtˈmiːrən] ptp **logarithmiert** VT to find the log(arithm) of VI to find the log(arithm)

lo|ga|rith|misch [logaˈrɪtmɪʃ] ADJ logarithmic

Lo|ga|rith|mus [logaˈrɪtmʊs] **-, Logarithmen** [-mən] M logarithm, log

Log|buch NT log(book)

Lo|ge ['loːʒə] F **-, -n** **a** (Theat) box **b** (= Freimaurerloge) lodge **c** (= Pförtnerloge) lodge

Lo|gen-: Lo|gen|bru|der M lodge brother; **Lo|gen|meis|ter** M master of a/the lodge; **Lo|gen|platz** M (Theat) seat in a box

Log|ger ['lɔgɐ] M **-s, -** (Naut) lugger

Log|gia ['lɔdʒa] F **-, Loggien** [-dʒiən] (= Bogenhalle) loggia; (= Balkon auch) balcony

Log|glas NT log glass

Lo|gier|be|such M (dated) house guest(s pl)

lo|gie|ren [loˈʒiːrən] ptp **logiert** (dated) VI to stay; (als Zimmerherr) to lodge VT **jdn ~** to put sb up

Lo|gier|gast M (dated) (= Besuch) house guest; (= Untermieter) lodger

Lo|gik ['loːgɪk] F **-, no pl** logic; **in der ~** in logic; **du hast vielleicht eine ~!** your logic is a bit quaint; **dieser Aussage fehlt die ~** this statement is illogical or is lacking in logic

Lo|gi|ker ['loːgikɐ] M **-s, -**, **Lo|gi|ke|rin** [-ərɪn] F **-, -nen** logician

Lo|gis [loˈʒiː] NT **-, -** (dated) lodgings pl, rooms pl; (Naut) forecastle, crew's quarters pl; **Kost und ~** board and lodging; **bei jdm in** or **zu ~ wohnen** to lodge with sb

lo|gisch ['loːgɪʃ] ADJ logical; (inf: = selbstverständlich) natural; **gehst du auch hin? – ~** are you going too? – of course ADV logically; **~ denken** to think logically; **~ folgern** to come to a logical conclusion

lo|gi|scher|wei|se ['loːgɪʃəˈvaizə] ADV logically

Lo|gis|tik [loˈgɪstɪk] F **-, no pl** **a** (Math) logic **b** (Mil, Econ) logistics sing

lo|gis|tisch [loˈgɪstɪʃ] ADJ logistic ADV logistically

Log|lei|ne F (Naut) log line

lo|go ['loːgo] INTERJ (inf) you bet (inf)

Lo|go ['loːgo] NT **-(s), -s** (= Firmenlogo) logo

Lo|go|pä|de [logo'pɛ:də] M **-n, -n, Lo|go|pä|din** [-'pɛːdɪn] F **-, -nen** speech therapist

Lo|go|pä|die [logopɛ'diː] F **-, no pl** speech therapy

Lo|gos ['lɔgɔs] M **-, Logoi** ['lɔgɔy] (Philos) logos; (Rel) Logos

Lo|go|ty|pe [logo'tyːpə] F **-, -n** logotype

Lo|he¹ ['loːə] F **-, -n** (liter) raging flames pl

Lo|he² F **-, -n** (= Gerbrinde) tan

lo|hen¹ ['loːən] VI (liter) to blaze

lo|hen² VT Felle to tan

Loh-: Loh|ger|ber(in) M(F) tanner; **Loh|ger|bung** F tanning

Lohn [loːn] M **-(e)s, ⸚e** ['løːnə] a (= Arbeitsentgelt) wage(s), pay no pl, no indef art; **wie viel ~ bekommst du?** how much do you get (paid)?, what are your wages?; **2% mehr ~ verlangen** to demand a 2% pay rise (Brit) or pay raise (US); **gleicher ~ für gleiche Arbeit** equal pay for equal work; **bei jdm in ~ und Brot stehen** (old) to be in sb's employ (old); **jdn um ~ und Brot bringen** (old) to deprive sb of a living or livelihood; **jdn in ~ und Brot nehmen** (old) to take sb into one's employ (old) b (fig) (= Belohnung/Vergeltung) reward; (= Strafe) punishment; **als** or **zum ~ für …** as a reward/punishment for …; **sein verdienter ~** one's just reward; **das ist nun der ~ für meine Mühe!** (iro) **das ist ein schlechter ~ für all die Mühe** that's what I get for my trouble, that's all the thanks I get for my trouble

Lohn-: Lohn|ab|bau M reduction of earnings; **lohn|ab|hän|gig** ADJ Arbeiter wage-earning; Leistungen, Rente wage-linked; **Lohn|ab|hän|gi|ge(r)** MF decl as adj wage earner; **Lohn|ab|kom|men** NT wages or pay agreement; **Lohn|ab|rech|nung** F wages slip (Brit), pay slip; **Lohn|ab|schluss** ▲ M wage or pay agreement; **Lohn|ab|zug** M deduction from one's wages; **Lohn|ar|beit** F labour (Brit), labor (US); **Lohn|auf|trag** M etw im ~ herstellen or fertigen to manufacture sth under a contracting-out agreement; **Lohn|aus|fall** M loss of earnings; **Lohn|aus|gleich** M wage adjustment; **bei vollem ~** with full pay; **Lohn|aus|zah|lung** F payment of wages; **Lohn|buch|hal|ter(in)** M(F) wages clerk (Brit), pay clerk; **Lohn|buch|hal|tung** F wages accounting; (= Büro) wages office (Brit), pay(roll) office; **Lohn|bü|ro** NT wages office (Brit), pay(roll) office; **Lohn|dum|ping** NT reduction in wage levels (due to an influx of cheap labour); **Lohn|emp|fän|ger(in)** M(F) wage earner

loh|nen ['loːnən] VIR (with sich) to be worth it; **es lohnt (sich), etw zu tun** it is worth or worthwhile doing sth; **die Mühe lohnt sich** it is worth the effort, the effort is worthwhile; **der Film lohnt sich wirklich** the film is really worth seeing; **Fleiß lohnt sich immer** hard work always pays (off) or is always worthwhile; **das lohnt sich nicht für mich** it's not worth my while VT a (= es wert sein) to be worth; **das Ergebnis lohnt die Mühe** the result makes all the effort worthwhile, the result amply repays all the effort b (= danken) jdm etw ~ to reward sb for sth; **er hat mir meine Hilfe mit Undank gelohnt** he repaid my help with ingratitude

loh|nend ADJ rewarding; (= nutzbringend) worthwhile; (= einträglich) profitable; (= sehens-/hörenswert) worth seeing/hearing

loh|nens|wert ADJ worthwhile; **es ist ~, etw zu tun** it is worthwhile or worth doing sth

Lohn-: Lohn|er|hö|hung F (wage or pay) rise (Brit), (wage or pay) raise (US); **Lohn|for|de|rung** F wage demand or claim; **Lohn|fort|zah|lung** F continued payment of wages;

Lohn|ge|fäl|le NT pay differential; **Lohn|grup|pe** F wage group; **Lohn|herr(in)** M(F) (old) employer; **lohn|in|ten|siv** ADJ Arbeit, Betrieb wage-intensive; **Lohn|kos|ten** PL wage costs pl (Brit), labor costs pl (US); **Lohn|kür|zung** F wage or pay cut; **Lohn|lis|te** F payroll; **Lohn|ne|ben|kos|ten** PL additional wage costs pl (Brit) or labor costs pl (US); **Lohn|ni|veau** NT wage level; **Lohn|po|ker** NT (fig) wages haggling; **Lohn|po|li|tik** F pay policy; **Lohn-Preis-Spi|ra|le** F (Econ) wage-price spiral; **Lohn|run|de** F pay round; **Lohn|sen|kung** F cut in wages or pay; **Lohn|ska|la** F pay or wages scale

Lohn|steu|er F income tax (paid on earned income)

Lohn|steu|er-: Lohn|steu|er|jah|res|aus|gleich M annual adjustment of income tax; **beim letzten ~ habe ich 500 Euro zurückbekommen** at the end of the last tax year I got back 500 euros; **Lohn|steu|er|kar|te** F (income) tax card

---

LOHNSTEUERKARTE

The **Lohnsteuerkarte** is a card showing the income tax and social security contributions paid by an employee in a particular year. If the employee changes jobs, this card and their **Sozialversicherungsausweis** must be handed over to their new employer. At the end of the year the **Lohnsteuerkarte** is returned to the employee. They can then present it to the tax office together with their income tax return and so claim any tax rebates to which they may be entitled → SOZIALVERSICHERUNGSAUSWEIS

Lohn-: Lohn|stopp M wages or pay freeze; **Lohn|strei|fen** M pay slip; **Lohn|stück|kos|ten** PL (Comm) unit wage costs pl (Brit) or labor costs pl (US); **Lohn|ta|rif** M wage rate; **Lohn|tü|te** F pay packet

Löh|nung ['løːnʊŋ] F **-, -en** a (= Auszahlung) payment; (auch **Löhnungstag**) pay day b (= Lohn) pay

Lohn-: Lohn|ver|hand|lung F pay or wage negotiations pl; **Lohn|ver|zicht** M ~ üben to take a cut in wages or pay; **wir mussten einen ~ hinnehmen** we had to accept a cut in wages or pay; **Lohn|zah|lung** F payment of wages; **Lohn|zet|tel** M pay slip

Loi|pe ['lɔypə] F **-, -n** cross-country ski run

Lok [lɔk] F **-, -s** abbr von **Lokomotive** engine

lo|kal [lo'kaːl] ADJ a (= örtlich) local; **~es Rechnernetz** (Comput) local area network b (Gram) of place ADV locally; **jdn ~ betäuben** to give sb a local anaesthetic (Brit) or anesthetic (US); **ein ~ wirkendes Schmerzmittel** a local painkiller

Lo|kal [lo'kaːl] NT **-s, -e** a (= Gaststätte) pub (esp Brit), bar; (= auf dem Land) inn (esp Brit), restaurant (esp US); (= Restaurant) restaurant b (= Versammlungsraum) meeting place

Lo|kal- in cpds local; **Lo|kal|anäs|the|sie** F (Med) local anaesthesia (Brit) or anesthetic (US); **Lo|kal|au|gen|schein** M (Aus Jur) visit to the scene of the crime; **Lo|kal|aus|ga|be** F (von Zeitung) local edition; **Lo|kal|blatt** NT local paper; **Lo|kal|der|by** NT local derby

Lo|ka|le(s) [lo'kaːlə] NT decl as adj local news sing

Lo|kal|fern|se|hen NT local television

Lo|ka|li|sa|ti|on [lokaliza'tsioːn] F **-, -en** a (= Ortsfeststellung) location b (Med) localization; (= Beschränkung auf einen Ort) limiting c (Comput) localization

lo|ka|li|sie|ren [lokali'ziːrən] ptp **lokalisiert** VT a (= Ort feststellen) to locate b (Med) to localize; (auf einen Ort) to limit (auf +acc to)

Lo|ka|li|sie|rung F = Lokalisation

Lo|ka|li|tät [lokali'tɛːt] F **-, -en** a (= örtliche Beschaffenheit) locality; (= Raum) facilities pl; **sich mit den ~en auskennen** to know the district; **die ~en verlassen** to leave the premises b (hum inf: = Lokal) pub (esp Brit), bar c (hum inf: = WC) cloakroom (euph), washroom, bathroom (esp US)

Lo|kal-: Lo|kal|ko|lo|rit NT local colour (Brit) or color (US); **Lo|kal|ma|ta|dor(in)** M(F) local hero/heroine; **Lo|kal|nach|rich|ten** PL local news sing; **Lo|kal|pat|ri|o|tis|mus** M local patriotism; **Lo|kal|re|dak|ti|on** F local newsroom; **Lo|kal|re|por|ter(in)** M(F) local reporter; **Lo|kal|run|de** F eine ~ ausgeben or schmeißen to buy drinks or a round for everyone (in the house); **Lo|kal|satz** M (Gram) (adverbial) clause of place; **Lo|kal|teil** M local section; **Lo|kal|ter|min** M (Jur) visit to the scene of the crime; **Lo|kal|ver|bot** NT ban; **~ haben** to be barred or banned from a pub (esp Brit) or bar; **Lo|kal|zei|tung** F local newspaper

Lo|ka|tiv ['loːkatiːf] M **-s, -e** [-və] (Gram) locative (case)

Lok|füh|rer(in) M(F) engine driver, engineer (US)

Lo|ko|ge|schäft ['loːko-] NT (St Ex) spot deal

Lo|ko|mo|ti|ve [lokomo'tiːvə, lokomi'tiːfə] F **-, -n** locomotive, (railway) engine

Lo|ko|mo|tiv-: Lo|ko|mo|tiv|füh|rer(in) M(F) engine driver, engineer (US); **Lo|ko|mo|tiv|schup|pen** M engine shed

Lo|ko|preis ['loːko-] M (St Ex) spot price

Lo|ko|wa|re ['loːko-] F (Comm, St Ex) spot goods pl

Lo|kus ['loːkʊs] M **- or -ses, - or -se** (inf) toilet, bathroom (esp US)

Lol|li ['lɔli] M **-(s), -s** (inf) lollipop, lolly (esp Brit)

Lom|bard ['lɔmbart] M OR NT **-(e)s, -e** [-də] (Fin) loan on security

Lom|bard|ge|schäft NT loan on security

lom|bar|die|ren [lɔmbar'diːrən] ptp **lombardiert** VT (Fin) to accept as collateral

Lombard-: Lom|bard|kas|se F guaranty authority; **Lom|bard|kre|dit** [-kreˈdiːt] M collateral loan; **Lom|bard|satz** M rate for loans on security

Lon|don ['lɔndən] NT **-s** London

Lon|do|ner¹ ['lɔndənɐ] ADJ attr London

Lon|do|ner² ['lɔndənɐ] M **-s, -, Lon|do|ne|rin** [-ərɪn] F **-, -nen** Londoner

Long|drink ['lɔŋdrɪŋk] M long drink

Lon|ge ['lõːʒə] F **-, -n** (für Pferde) lunge; (für Akrobaten) harness

lon|gie|ren [lõ'ʒiːrən] ptp **longiert** VT Pferd to lunge

Look [lʊk] M **-s, -s** (Fashion) look

Loo|ping ['luːpɪŋ] M OR NT **-s, -s** (Aviat) looping the loop; **einen ~ machen** to loop the loop

Lor|bass ▲ ['lɔrbas] M **-es, -e** (dial inf) sly devil (inf), sharp one (inf)

Lor|beer ['lɔrbeːɐ] M **-s, -en** a (lit: Gewächs) laurel; (als Gewürz) bay leaf; (= Lorbeerkranz) laurel wreath b **Lorbeeren** PL (fig: = Erfolg) laurels pl; **sich auf seinen ~en ausruhen** (inf) to rest on one's laurels; **seine ersten ~en ernten** to win one's first laurels; **damit kannst du keine ~en ernten** that's no great achievement

Lor|beer-: Lor|beer|baum M laurel (tree); **Lor|beer|blatt** NT bay leaf; **Lor|beer|kranz** M laurel wreath

Lor|do|se [lɔr'doːzə] F **-, -n** (Med) lordosis (spec)

Lo|re ['loːrə] F **-, -n** a (Rail) truck, wagon; (= Kipplore) tipper, dumper b (Kohlenmaß: = 200 Zentner) 10,000 kilos (of coal)

Lorg|net|te [lɔrn'jɛtə] F **-, -n** lorgnette

Lorg|non [lɔrn'jõː] NT **-s, -s** lorgnon

---

los [loːs] **ADJ** *pred* **a** (= *nicht befestigt*) loose; **der Hund ist von der Leine ~** the dog is off the lead (*Brit*) *or* leash

b (= *frei*) **jdn/etw ~ sein** (*inf*) to be rid *or* shot (*Brit inf*) of sb/sth, to have got *or* gotten (*US*) rid of sb/sth; **ich bin mein ganzes Geld ~** (*inf*) I'm cleaned out (*inf*)

c (*inf*) **etwas ist ~/es ist nichts ~** (= *geschieht*) there's something/nothing going on *or* happening; (= *nicht in/in Ordnung*) there's something/ nothing wrong *or* the matter, something's/nothing's up; **mit jdm/etw ist etwas/ nichts ~** there's something/nothing wrong *or* the matter with sb/sth; **mit jdm/etw ist nichts (mehr) ~** (*inf*) sb/sth isn't up to much (any more), sb/sth is a dead loss (now) (*inf*); **was ist denn hier/da ~?** what's going on here/there (then)?, what's up here/there (then)?; **was ist ~?** what's up?, what's wrong?, what's the matter?; **was ist da abends ~?** what is there going on there in the evenings?; **wo ist denn hier was ~?** where's the action here (*inf*)?; **als mein Vater das hörte, da war was ~!** when my father heard about it all hell broke loose (*inf*)

ADV **a** (*Aufforderung*) **~!** come on!; (= *geh/lauf schon*) go on!, get going!; **nun aber ~!** let's get going; (*zu andern*) get going *or* moving (*inf*); **nichts wie ~!** let's get going; (*na*) **~, mach schon!** (come on,) get on with it; **~, schreib/ fahr** *etc* **doch endlich** come on, start writing/ driving *etc*; **auf die Plätze ~ Achtung, fertig, ~** on your marks, get set, go!, ready, steady, go!

b (= *weg*) **sie wollen ~ vom Reich/Kapitalismus** they want to break away from the Reich/from capitalism; **wir wollen früh ~** we want to leave early, we want to be off early

Los [loːs] **NT -es, -e** [-zə] **a** (*für Entscheidung*) lot; (*in der Lotterie, auf Jahrmarkt etc*) ticket; **das große ~ ziehen** (*lit, fig*) to hit the jackpot; **etw durch das ~ entscheiden** *or* **bestimmen** *or* **ermitteln** to decide sth by drawing *or* casting lots; **jdn durch das ~ bestimmen** to pick sb by drawing lots; **etw durch das ~ gewinnen** to win sth in a lottery *or* (*bei Tombola*) raffle *or* (*auf Jahrmarkt*) tombola; **auf dieses ~ entfiel der Hauptgewinn** this ticket won first prize; **das ~ hat mich getroffen** it fell to my lot

b *no pl* (= *Schicksal*) lot; **er hat ein hartes** *or* **schweres ~** his is a hard *or* not an easy lot; **das gleiche ~ erfahren** to share the same lot; **jds ~ teilen** to share sb's lot

c (*Comm*) lot

-los **ADJ** *suf* -less; **vater-/mutterlos** father-/mother-erless; **richtungslos** without direction

los+bal|lern **VI** *sep* (*inf*) to start banging away (*inf*); (*stärker*) to start blazing away

lös|bar **ADJ** soluble

los-: **los+bel|len** **VI** *sep* (*Hund*) to start barking; (*Mensch*) to start yelling; **los+bin|den** **VT** *sep irreg* to untie (*von* from); **los+bre|chen** *sep irreg* **VT** to break off **VI** *aux sein* (*Gelächter etc*) to break out; (*Sturm, Gewitter*) to break

Lösch-: **Lösch|ar|beit** **F** *usu pl* firefighting operations *pl*; **lösch|bar** **ADJ** **a** *Feuer, Flammen* extinguishable; *Kalk* slakable; *Durst* quenchable; *Schrift, Daten, Tonband* erasable; **die Hypothek/ Schuld ist ~** the mortgage/debt can be paid off; **die Eintragung ist ~** the entry can be deleted; **das Konto ist ~** the account can be closed **b** (*Naut*) unloadable; **Lösch|blatt** **NT** sheet *or* piece of blotting paper; **Lösch|ei|mer** **M** fire bucket

lö|schen [ˈlœʃn] **VT** **a** *Feuer, Brand, Flammen, Kerze* to put out, to extinguish; *Licht* to switch out *or* off, to turn out *or* off; *Kalk, Durst* to slake; *Durst* to quench; *Schrift (an Tafel), Tonband etc* to wipe *or* rub off, to erase; *Tafel* to wipe; *Schuld* to cancel; *Eintragung, Zeile* to delete; *Konto* to close; *Firma, Name* to strike (*Brit*) *or* cross off; (= *aufsaugen*) *Tinte* to blot; (*Comput*) *Speicher, Bildschirm* to clear; *Festplatte* to wipe; *Daten, Information* to erase, to delete **b** (*Naut*) *Ladung* to unload **VI** **a** (*Feuerwehr etc*) to put out a/the

fire **b** (= *aufsaugen*) to blot **c** (*Naut*) to unload

Lö|scher [ˈlœʃɐ] **M -s, -** (fire-)extinguisher; (= *Tintenlöscher*) blotter

Lösch-: **Lösch|fahr|zeug** **NT** fire engine; **Lösch|flug|zeug** **NT** firefighting plane; **Lösch|kalk** **M** slaked lime; **Lösch|mann|schaft** **F** team of firemen *or* firefighters; **Lösch|mit|tel** **NT** (fire-)extinguishing agent; **Lösch|pa|pier** **NT** (piece of) blotting paper; **Lösch|schaum** **M** extinguishant foam; **Lösch|tas|te** **F** (*Comput*) delete key; **Lösch|trupp** **M** fire-fighting team *or* squad

Lö|schung [ˈlœʃʊŋ] **F -, -en** **a** (*von Schuld, Hypothek*) paying off; (*von Eintragung*) deletion; (*von Konto*) closing; (*von Firma, Namen*) striking (*Brit*) *or* crossing off; (*Comput: von Daten*) erasing, deletion **b** (*Naut: von Ladung*) unloading

Lösch-: **Lösch|was|ser** **NT** , *no pl* water for firefighting; **Lösch|zug** **M** convoy of fire engines, set of appliances (*form*)

los+don|nern **VI** *sep* (*lit, fig*) to start to thunder

lo|se [ˈloːzə] **ADJ** (*lit, fig*) loose; (= *nicht gespannt*) *Seil* slack; (= *schelmisch*) *Streich* mischievous; **etw ~ verkaufen** to sell sth loose → **Maul, Zunge ADV** loosely; **~ sitzen** to be loose

Lo|se|blatt|aus|ga|be **F** loose-leaf edition

Lö|se|geld **NT** ransom (money)

los+ei|sen *sep* (*inf*) **VT** to get *or* prise away (*bei* from); **jdn von einer Verpflichtung ~** to get sb out of an obligation **VR** to get away (*bei* from); (*von Verpflichtung etc*) to get out (*von* of)

lo|sen [ˈloːzn] **VI** to draw lots (*um* for); **wir ~, wer …** we'll draw lots to decide who …

lö|sen [ˈløːzn] **VT** **a** (= *losmachen, abtrennen, entfernen*) to remove (*von* from); *Boot* to cast off (*von* from); (= *ablösen*) *Fleisch, Briefmarken, Tapete etc* to get off (*von etw* sth), to remove (*von* from); (= *herauslösen*) to get out (*aus* of), to remove (*aus* from); (= *aufbinden*) *Knoten, Fesseln, Gürtel, Haare* to undo; *Arme* to unfold; *Hände* to unclasp; *Handbremse* to take *or* let off; *Husten, Krampf* to ease; *Muskeln* to loosen up; (*lit, fig: = lockern*) to loosen; **sie löste ihre Hand aus der seinen** she slipped her hand out of his → *auch* **gelöst**

b (= *klären, Lösung finden für*) *Aufgabe, Problem* to solve; *Konflikt, Schwierigkeiten* to resolve

c (= *annullieren*) *Vertrag* to cancel; *Verlobung* to break off; *Verbindung, Verhältnis* to sever; *Ehe* to dissolve

d (= *zergehen lassen*) to dissolve (*auch Chem*)

e (= *kaufen*) *Karte* to buy, to get

VR **a** (= *sich losmachen*) to detach oneself (*von* from); (= *sich ablösen*) to come off (*von etw* sth); (*Knoten, Haare*) to come undone; (*Schuss*) to go off; (*Husten, Krampf, Spannung*) to ease; (*Schleim, Schmutz*) to loosen; (*Atmosphäre*) to relax; (*Muskeln*) to loosen up; (*lit, fig: = sich lockern*) to (be)come loose; (*Lawine*) to break away; **sich von jdm ~** to break away from sb (*auch Sport*); **sich von etw ~** (*von Verpflichtungen*) to free oneself of sth; *von Vorstellung, Vorurteilen, Gedanken* to rid oneself of sth; *von Partnern, Vaterland, Vergangenheit* to break with sth, to break away from sth; **das Boot hat sich aus der Verankerung gelöst** the boat has broken (away from) its moorings; **eine Gestalt löste sich aus der Dunkelheit** (*liter*) a figure detached itself *or* emerged from the darkness

b (= *sich aufklären*) to be solved; **sich von selbst ~** (*Verbrechen*) to solve itself; (*Problem auch*) to clear itself up, to resolve itself

c (= *zergehen*) to dissolve (*in +dat* in) (*auch Chem*); **die Tablette löst sich gut/schlecht** the tablet dissolves easily/doesn't dissolve easily; **ihre Anspannung/ihr Schmerz löste sich in Tränen** her tension/pain found relief in tears

Los|ent|scheid **M** drawing (of) lots; **die Gewinner werden durch Lostentscheid ermittelt** the winners are established by drawing lots

Lo|ser [ˈluːzɐ] **M -s, -** (*inf: = Verlierer*) loser

los-: **los+fah|ren** **VI** *sep irreg aux sein* **a** (= *abfahren*) to set off; (*Fahrzeug*) to move off; (*Auto*) to drive off **b** (*inf: = schimpfen, anfallen*) **auf jdn ~** to lay into sb (*inf*), to attack sb; **los+ge|hen** **VI** *sep irreg aux sein* **a** (= *weggehen*) to set off; (*Schuss, Bombe etc*) to go off; (**mit dem Messer**) **auf jdn ~** to go for sb (with a knife) **b** (*inf: = anfangen*) to start; (*Geschrei der Menge*) to go up; **gleich gehts los** it's just about to start; (*bei Streit*) any minute now; **jetzt gehts los!** here we go!; (*Vorstellung*) it's starting!; (*Rennen*) they're off!; (*Reise, Bewegung*) we're/you're etc off!; **jetzt gehts wieder los (mit ihren Klagen)** here we go again (with all her moans); **gehts bald los?** will it start soon?; (*Reise etc*) are we off soon?; **bei drei gehts los** you/they etc start on the count of three; **jetzt gehts aber los!** (*inf*) you're kidding! (*inf*); (*bei Frechheit*) do you mind! **c** (*inf: = abgehen*) to come off; **los+ha|ben** **VI** *sep irreg* (*inf*) **etwas/nichts ~** to be pretty clever (*inf*)/pretty stupid (*inf*); **los+heu|len** **VI** *sep* to burst out crying

-lo|sig|keit *suf* **-, -en** -lessness; **Hoffnungslosigkeit** hopelessness

los-: **los+kau|fen** *sep* **VT** to buy out; *Entführten* to ransom **VR** to buy oneself out (*aus* of); **los+knüp|fen** **VT** *sep* to untie, to undo; **los+kom|men** **VI** *sep irreg aux sein* (*Mensch*) to get away (*von* from); (= *sich befreien*) to free oneself, to get free (*von* of); **das Boot kam von der Sandbank los/nicht los** the boat came off/ wouldn't come off the sandbank; **von Schulden ~** to get out of debt; **von einer Sucht ~** to get free of an addiction; **los+kön|nen** **VI** *sep irreg* (*inf*) to be able to get away; **los+krie|gen** **VT** *sep* (*inf*) to undo; (= *losreißen*) to get rid *or* shot (*Brit inf*) of; **los+la|chen** **VI** *sep* to burst out laughing; **laut ~** to laugh out loud; **los+las|sen** **VT** *sep irreg* **a** (= *nicht mehr festhalten*) to let go of; (*fig: = nicht fesseln*) *Mensch* to let go; **der Gedanke/die Frage** *etc* **lässt mich nicht mehr los** the thought/problem haunts me *or* won't go out of my mind; **das Buch lässt mich nicht mehr los** I can't put the book down **b** (*inf: = abfeuern*) *Feuerwerk, Bombe* to let off; (*fig*) *Rede, Witze, Geschichte* to come out with; *Beschwerden, Schimpfkanonade* to launch into; *Schrift* to launch; *Brief* to send off **c** **jdn (auf jdn) ~** (*fig inf*) to let sb loose (on sb); **die Hunde auf jdn ~** to put *or* set the dogs on(to) sb; **und so was lässt man nun auf die Menschheit los!** (*hum inf*) what a thing to unleash on an unsuspecting world; **wehe, wenn sie losgelassen …** (*hum inf*) once you're off the leash …; **los+lau|fen** **VI** *sep irreg aux sein* (= *zu laufen anfangen*) to start to run; (= *weggehen*) to run out; **los+le|gen** **VI** *sep* (*inf*) to get going *or* started; (*mit Schimpfen*) to let fly (*inf*) *or* rip (*inf*); **er legte gleich mit seinen Ideen los** he started on about his ideas; **nun leg mal los und erzähle …** now come on and tell me/us …

lös|lich [ˈløːslɪç] **ADJ** soluble; **leicht/schwer ~** readily/not readily soluble; **~er Kaffee** instant coffee

Lös|lich|keit **F -**, *no pl* (*Chem*) solubility

los-: **los+lö|sen** *sep* **VT** to remove (*von* from); (= *ablösen auch*) to take off (*von etw* sth); (= *herauslösen auch*) to take out (*aus* of); (= *lockern*) to loosen **VR** to detach oneself (*von* from); (= *sich ablösen auch*) to come off (*von etw* sth); (= *lockern auch*) to become loose; **sich von jdm ~** to break away from sb; **los+ma|chen** *sep* **VT** (= *befreien*) to free; (= *losbinden*) to untie; *Handbremse* to let *or* take off; **jdn von einer Kette ~** to unchain sb **VI** **a** (*Naut*) to cast off **b** (*inf: = sich beeilen*) to step on it (*inf*), to get a move on (*inf*) **VR** to get away (*von* from); **der Hund hat sich losgemacht** the dog has got loose; **los+müs|sen** **VI** *sep irreg* (*inf*) to have to go

Los|num|mer **F** ticket number

los-: **los+plat|zen** **VI** *sep aux sein* (*inf*) (= *lachen*) to burst out laughing; (*spontan, vorzeitig äußern*) to start yapping (*inf*); **mit etw ~** to burst out with sth; **platz nicht immer gleich los** think before you speak; **los+prus|ten** VI *sep* (*inf*) to explode (with laughter); **los+quat|schen** [-kvatʃn] VI *sep* (*inf*) to prattle away (*inf*); **los+ra|sen** VI *sep aux sein* (*inf*) to race or tear off; **los+rei|ßen** *sep irreg* **VT** (= *abreißen*) to tear or rip off (*von etw* sth); (= *herunterreißen*) to tear or rip down (*von etw* from sth); (= *herausreißen*) to tear or rip out (*aus* of); **jdn ~** to tear sb away **VR** **sich (von etw) ~** (*Hund etc*) to break free or loose (from sth); (*fig*) to tear oneself away (from sth); **los+ren|nen** VI *sep irreg aux sein* (*inf*) to run off; (= *anfangen zu laufen*) to start to run

Löss ▲ [lœs] M **-es, -e**, **Löß** [løːs] M **-es, -e** (*Geol*) loess

los+sa|gen VR *sep* **sich von etw ~** to renounce sth; **sich von jdm/seiner Vergangenheit ~** to dissociate oneself from or break with sb/the or one's past

Los|sa|gung ['loːszaːɡʊŋ] F **-, no pl** renunciation (*von* of); dissociation (*von* from)

Löss|bo|den ▲ M , **Löß|bo|den** M loess soil

los-: los+schi|cken VT *sep* to send off; **los+schie|ßen** VI *sep irreg* **a** (= *zu schießen anfangen*) to open fire; **schieß los!** (*fig inf*) fire away! (*inf*) **b** *aux sein* (= *schnell starten*) to shoot or race off; **auf jdn ~** to race toward(s) sb; **los+schla|gen** *sep irreg* **VI** to hit out; (*Mil*) to (launch one's) attack; **auf jdn/aufeinander ~** to go for sb/one another or each other **VT a** (= *abschlagen*) to knock off **b** (*inf*: = *verkaufen*) to get rid of; **los+schnal|len** VT *sep* to unbuckle; **los+schrau|ben** VT *sep* to unscrew; (= *lockern auch*) to loosen; **los+sprin|gen** VI *sep irreg aux sein* to jump; **auf jdn/etw ~** to leap for sb/sth; **los+steu|ern** VI *sep aux sein auf jdn/etw ~** to head or make for sb/sth; **los+stür|zen** VI *sep aux sein* to rush off; **auf jdn/etw ~** to pounce on sb/sth

Lost [lɔst] M **-(e)s, no pl** (*Chem*) mustard gas

los-: los+ti|gern VI *sep aux sein* (*inf*) to toddle off (*inf*); **los+tren|nen** VT *sep* = **abtrennen a**; **los+tre|ten** VT *sep irreg* to kick off

Los|trom|mel F drum (*containing lottery tickets*)

Lo|sung¹ ['loːzʊŋ] F **-, -en a** (= *Devise, Parole*) motto **b** (= *Kennwort*) password

Lo|sung² F **-, -en** (*Hunt*) droppings *pl*

Lö|sung ['løːzʊŋ] F **-, -en a** solution (+*gen* to); (= *das Lösen*) solution (+*gen* of); (*eines Konfliktes, von Schwierigkeiten*) resolving; **zur ~ dieser Schwierigkeiten** to resolve these problems **b** (= *Annullierung*) (*eines Vertrages*) cancellation; (*von Beziehungen, einer Verlobung*) breaking off; (*einer Verbindung, eines Verhältnisses*) severing, severance; (*einer Ehe*) dissolving **c** (*Chem*) solution

Lö|sungs-: Lö|sungs|mit|tel NT solvent; **Lö|sungs|vor|schlag** M suggested solution; (*bei Frage, Rätsel etc*) suggested answer; **Lö|sungs|weg** M path towards a solution

Lö|sungs|wort NT *pl* **-worte** password

Lö|sungs|wort NT *pl* **-wörter** answer

Los-: Los|ver|fahren NT decision by lot; **etw im ~ entscheiden** to decide sth by drawing lots; **Los|ver|käu|fer(in)** M(F) ticket seller (*for lottery, raffle etc*); **los+wer|den** VT *sep irreg aux sein* to get rid of; *Angst etc auch* to rid oneself of; *Hemmungen auch* to lose; *Gedanken* to get away from, to get out of one's mind; *Geld (beim Spiel etc), Hab und Gut* to lose; *Geld* (= *ausgeben*) to spend; **er wird eine Erkältung einfach nicht los** he can't shake off or get rid of his cold; **los+zie|hen** VI *sep irreg aux sein* **a** (= *aufbrechen*) to set out or off (*in +acc, nach* for) **b** **gegen jdn/etw ~** (*inf*) to lay into sb/sth (*inf*)

Lot¹ [loːt] NT **-(e)s, -e a** (= *Senkblei*) plumb line; (*Naut*) sounding line, plumb line; **im ~ sein** to be in plumb **b** (*Math*) perpendicular; **das ~ fällen** to drop a perpendicular; **seine Finanzen wieder ins ~ bringen** to put one's fi-

nances back on an even keel; **die Sache ist wieder im ~** things have been straightened out; **die Sache wieder ins (rechte) ~ bringen** to put things right, to put the record straight (*inf*); **aus dem ~ geraten** to be thrown out of kilter **c** (*old*) old unit of weight varying between 14 and 18 grams **d** (= *Lötmetall*) solder; **Lot²** M **-s** (*Bibl*) Lot; **Löt|ap|pa|rat** M soldering appliance; **löt|bar** ADJ solderable; **lo|ten** ['loːtn] VT to plumb; **lö|ten** ['løːtn] VTI to solder; **Loth|rin|gen** ['loːtrɪŋən] NT **-s** Lorraine; **Loth|rin|ger** ['loːtrɪŋɐ] M **-s, -**, **Loth|rin|ge|rin** [-ərɪn] F **-, -nen** Lorrainer; **loth|rin|gisch** ['loːtrɪŋɪʃ] ADJ of Lorraine, Lorrainese; **Lo|ti|on** [loˈtsioːn] F **-, -en** lotion

Löt-: Löt|kol|ben M soldering iron; **Löt|lam|pe** F blowlamp

Löt|lei|ne F plumb line

Löt|me|tall NT solder

Lo|to|pha|ge [lotoˈfaːɡə] M **-n, -n**, **Lo|to|pha|gin** [-ˈfaːɡɪn] F **-, -nen** (*Myth*) lotus-eater

Lo|tos ['loːtɔs] M **-, -** lotus

Lo|tos-: Lo|tos|blu|me F lotus (flower); **Lo|tos|sitz** M lotus position

lot|recht ADJ perpendicular **ADV** perpendicularly

Lot|rech|te F *decl as adj* (*Math*) perpendicular

Löt|rohr NT blowpipe

Lot|se ['loːtsə] M **-n, -n**, **Lot|sin** [-tsɪn] F **-, -nen** (*Naut*) pilot; (= *Fluglotse*) air-traffic or flight controller; (*Aut*) navigator; (*fig*) guide

lot|sen ['loːtsn] VT to guide; *Schiff auch* to pilot; **jdn irgendwohin ~** (*inf*) to drag sb somewhere (*inf*) → **Geld a**

Lot|sen-: Lot|sen|boot NT pilot boat; **Lot|sen|dienst** M pilot service; (*Aut*) driver-guide service; **Lot|sen|fisch** M pilot fish; **Lot|sen|geld** NT pilotage; **Lot|sen|zwang** M compulsory pilotage

Lot|sin F → **Lotse**

Löt-: Löt|stein M sal ammoniac block; **Löt|stel|le** F soldered point

Lot|te ['lɔtə] F - *contr von* **Charlotte**

Lot|ter|bett ['lɔtɐ-] NT (*old, hum*) old bed

Lot|te|rie [lɔtəˈriː] F **-, -n** [-ˈriːən] lottery; (= *Tombola*) raffle

Lot|te|rie-: Lot|te|rie|ge|winn M → **Lotterie** lottery/raffle prize or (*Geld*) winnings *pl*; **Lot|te|rie|los** NT → **Lotterie** lottery/raffle ticket; **Lot|te|rie|spiel** NT (*lit*) lottery; (*fig*) gamble

lot|te|rig ['lɔtərɪç] (*inf*) ADJ slovenly *no adv*; *Mensch, Arbeit auch* sloppy (*inf*) **ADV herum|laufen** to go around looking a mess (*inf*)

Lot|ter|le|ben NT (*inf*) dissolute life

lot|tern ['lɔtɐn] VI (*S Ger, Sw:* = *lose sein*) to wobble

Lot|ter|wirt|schaft F (*inf*) muddle, slovenly mess

Lot|to ['lɔto] NT **-s, -s a** lottery, ≈ National Lottery (*Brit*); **(im) ~ spielen** to do (*Brit*) or play the lottery; **du hast wohl im ~ gewonnen** you must have won the pools (*Brit*) or the lottery **b** (= *Gesellschaftsspiel*) lotto

Lot|to-: Lot|to|ge|schäft NT , **Lot|to|la|den** M (*inf*) lottery agency; **Lot|to|ge|winn** M lottery win; (*Geld*) lottery winnings *pl*; **Lot|to|kö|nig(in)** M(F) (*inf*) jackpot winner; **Lot|to|schein** M lottery coupon; **Lot|to|spie|ler(in)** M(F) lottery player or participant; **Lot|to- und Toto|an|nah|me|stel|le** F lottery and football pools agency; **Lot|to|zah|len** PL winning lottery numbers *pl*

lott|rig ['lɔtrɪç] ADJ, ADV (*inf*) = **lotterig**

Lö|tung ['løːtʊŋ] F **-, -en** (= *das Löten*) soldering; (= *Lötstelle*) soldered joint

Lo|tus ['loːtʊs] M **-, -** (*Bot*) (= *Hornklee*) bird's-foot trefoil **b** = **Lotos**

Löt|zinn M solder

Louis|dor [luiˈdoːɐ̯] M **-s, -e** or (*bei Zahlenangaben*) **-** (*Hist*) louis (d'or)

Lo|ver ['lavɐ] M **-s, -** (*inf*: = *Liebhaber*) lover

Low-Bud|get- [loʊˈbadʒət] *in cpds* low-budget; **Low-Bud|get-Pro|duk|ti|on** F low-budget production; **Low-Bud|get-Sen|dung** F low-budget programme (*Brit*) or program (*US*)

Lö|we ['løːvə] M **-n, -n** lion; **der ~** (*Astron*) Leo, the Lion; (*Astrol*) Leo; **im Zeichen des ~n geboren sein** to be born under the sign of) Leo; **~ sein** to be (a) Leo; **sich in die Höhle des ~n begeben** (*inf*) to beard the lion in his den (*Brit prov*), to go into the lion's den

Löwen-: Löwen|an|teil M (*inf*) lion's share; **Löwen|bän|di|ger(in)** M(F) lion tamer; **Löwen|gru|be** F (*Bibl*) lions' den; **Löwen|herz** NT **Richard ~** m Richard (the) Lionheart; **Löwen|jagd** F lion hunt; **Löwen|mäh|ne** F (*lit*) lion's mane; (*fig*) flowing mane; **Löwen|maul** NT , **Löwen|mäul|chen** [-mɔylçən] NT **-s, -** snapdragon, antirrhinum; **Löwen|mut** M (*liter*) leonine courage (*liter*); **mit ~** as brave as a lion; **Löwen|zahn** M dandelion

Lö|win ['løːvɪn] F **-, -nen** lioness

lo|yal [loaˈjaːl] ADJ loyal **ADV** loyally; **sich jdm gegenüber ~ verhalten** to be loyal to(wards) sb

Lo|ya|li|tät [loajaliˈtɛːt] F **-, -en** loyalty (*jdm gegenüber* to sb)

LP [ɛlˈpeː] F **-, -s** LP

LPG [ɛlpeːˈɡeː] F **-, -s** (*DDR*) *abbr von* **Landwirtschaftliche Produktionsgenossenschaft**

LSD [ɛlɛsˈdeː] NT **-(s)** LSD

lt. *abbr von* **laut²**

Luch [luːx] F **-, ⁼e** ['lyːçə] or *nt* **-(e)s, -e** (*dial*) marsh

Luchs [lʊks] M **-es, -e** lynx; **Augen wie ein ~ haben** (*inf*) to have eyes like a hawk, to be eagle-eyed

Luchs|au|gen PL (*inf*) eagle eyes *pl*

luch|sen ['lʊksn] VI (*inf*) to peep

Lü|cke ['lʏkə] F **-, -n** (*lit, fig*) gap; (*zwischen Wörtern auch, auf Formularen etc*) space; (= *Ungereimtheit, Unvollständigkeit etc*) hole; (= *Gesetzeslücke*) loophole; (*in Versorgung*) break; **~n (im Wissen) haben** to have gaps in one's knowledge; **sein Tod hinterließ eine schmerzliche ~** (*geh*) his death has left a void in our lives

Lücken-: Lücken|bü|ßer(in) M(F) (*inf*) stopgap; **~ spielen** to be used as a stopgap; **lücken|haft** ADJ full of gaps; *Bericht, Sammlung, Beweis etc auch* incomplete; *Kenntnisse auch* sketchy; *Versorgung* deficient; *Gesetz, Alibi* full of holes; **sein Wissen ist sehr ~** there are great gaps in his knowledge **ADV** *erinnern* vaguely; *informieren, zusammenstellen* sketchily; *ausbilden, versorgen* deficiently; **Lücken|haf|tig|keit** ['lʏknhaftɪçkaɪt] F **-, -en** incompleteness; (*von Kenntnissen auch*) sketchiness; (*von Versorgung*) deficiency; **wegen der ~ des Berichts/des Gesetzes** because of all the gaps in the report/all the loopholes in the law; **lücken|los** ADJ complete; *Kontrolle auch, Überwachung* thorough; *Kenntnisse* perfect; (*Mil*) *Abwehr* perfect; *Aufklärung* full **ADV** completely; **Lücken|test** M (*Sch*) completion test (*Brit*), fill-in-the-gaps test; **Lücken|text** M (*Sch*) completion exercise

lud *pret von* **laden¹** *von* **laden²**

Lu|de ['luːdə] M **-n, -n** (*sl*) ponce (*Brit inf*), pimp

Lu|der ['luːdɐ] NT **-s, - a** (*Hunt:* = *Aas*) bait **b** (*inf*) minx; **armes/dummes ~** poor/stupid creature; **so ein ordinäres ~!** what a common little hussy!

Lu|der|jan ['luːdɐjaːn] M **-(e)s, -e** (*inf*) wastrel

Lud|wig ['luːdvɪç] M **-s** Ludwig; (= *französischer Königsname*) Louis

Lu|es ['luːɛs] F *no pl* (*Med*) syphilis, lues (*spec*)

lu|e|tisch [luˈeːtɪʃ] ADJ (*Med*) syphilitic, luetic (*spec*)

Luft [lʊft] F **-**, (liter) **ⁿe** ['lʏftə] **a** air no pl; **die Lüfte** pl (liter) the skies, the air sing; **frische ~ hereinlassen** to let some fresh air in; **im Zimmer ist schlechte ~** the room is stuffy, the air or it is stuffy in the room; **bei schlechter ~ kann ich nicht schlafen** I can't sleep when it's stuffy; **dicke ~** (inf) a bad atmosphere; **~ an etw** (acc) **kommen lassen** to let the air get to sth; **an der/die/den (frischen) ~** in the fresh air; **an die (frische) ~ gehen/kommen** to get out in the fresh air; **(frische) ~ schnappen** (inf) or **schöpfen** (geh) to get some fresh air; **die ~ ist rein** (inf) the coast is clear; **die ~ reinigen** (lit, fig) to clear the air; **jetzt ist das Flugzeug in der ~** the plane is now airborne or in the air; **aus der ~** from the air; **die ~ aus etw lassen** to let the air out of sth; **die ~ ist raus** (fig inf) the fizz has gone; **jdn an die (frische) ~ setzen** (inf) to show sb the door; (Sch) to send sb out; (= entlassen) to give sb the push (inf); **in die ~ fliegen** (inf) to explode, to go up; **etw in die ~ jagen** (inf) or **sprengen** to blow sth up; **leicht** or **schnell in die ~ gehen** (fig) to be quick to blow one's top (inf), to be very quick-tempered; **er geht gleich in die ~** (fig) he's about to blow his top; **es liegt ein Gewitter in der ~** there's a storm brewing; **es liegt etwas in der ~** there's something in the air; **in die ~ starren** or **gucken** to stare into space or thin air; **in die ~ gucken** (fig inf: = leer ausgehen) to come away empty-handed (inf); **jdn/etw in der ~ zerreißen** (inf) to tear sb/sth to pieces; **das kann sich doch nicht in ~ aufgelöst haben** it can't have vanished into thin air; **in der ~ hängen** (Sache) to be (very much) up in the air; (Mensch) to be in (a state of) limbo, to be dangling; **die Behauptung ist aus der ~ gegriffen** this statement is (a) pure invention; **vor Freude in die ~ springen** to jump for or with joy; **von ~ und Liebe/von ~ leben** to live on love/air; **jdn wie ~ behandeln** to treat sb as though he/she just didn't exist; **er ist ~ für mich** I'm not speaking to him

b (= Atem) breath; **der Kragen schnürt mir die ~ ab** this collar is choking me, I can't breathe in this collar; **nach ~ schnappen** to gasp for breath or air; **die ~ anhalten** (lit) to hold one's breath; **nun halt mal die ~ an!** (inf) (= rede nicht) hold your tongue!, put a sock in it! (inf); (= übertreibe nicht) come off it! (inf), come on! (inf); **keine ~ mehr kriegen** not to be able to breathe; **nach ~ ringen** to struggle for breath; **tief ~ holen** (lit, fig) to take a deep breath; **... da musste ich erst mal tief ~ holen** (fig: = war perplex) it really made me gasp; **mir blieb vor Schreck/Schmerz die ~ weg** I was breathless with shock/pain; **wieder ~ bekommen** or **kriegen/haben** (nach Sport etc) to get/have got one's breath back; (nach Schnupfen etc) to be able to breathe again; (fig) to get/have a chance to catch one's breath

c (= Wind) breeze; **linde/laue Lüfte** (liter) gentle/warm breezes; **sich** (dat) **~ machen** (= fächeln) to fan oneself; **sich** (dat) **~ machen** (fig) **seinem Herzen ~ machen** (fig) to get everything off one's chest; **seinem Ärger/Zorn** etc **~ machen** to give vent to one's annoyance/anger etc

d (fig: = Spielraum, Platz) space, room; **zwischen Wand und Regal etwas ~ lassen** to leave a space between the wall and the bookcase

Luft-: Luft|ab|wehr F (Mil) anti-aircraft defence (Brit) or defense (US); **Luft|ab|wehr|ra|ke|te** F anti-aircraft missile; **Luft|ab|zug** M air vent; **Luft|alarm** M air-raid alarm; **Luft|an|griff** M air raid (auf +acc on); **einen ~ auf eine Stadt fliegen** to bomb a town, to carry out an air raid on a town; **Luft|auf|klä|rung** F aerial or air reconnaissance; **Luft|auf|nah|me** F aerial photo(graph); **Luft|auf|sicht** F (Aviat) air traffic control; **Luft|bal|lon** M balloon; **Luft|be|feuch|ter** [-bəfɔʏçtɐ] M **-s, -** humidifier; **Luft|be|las|tung** F, no pl atmospheric pollution; **Luft|be|tan|kung** [-bətaŋkʊŋ] F **-, -en** (Aviat) in-flight refuelling (Brit) or refueling (US); **Luft|be|we|gung** F movement of the air; **Luft|bild** NT aerial picture; **Luft|bläs-**

chen [-blɛːsçən] NT (Anat) air sac; **Luft|bla|se** F air bubble, bubble of air; **Luft-Bo|den-Flug|kör|per** M air-to-surface ballistic missile; **Luft|brem|se** F air brake; **Luft|brü|cke** F airlift; **über eine ~** by airlift

Lüft|chen ['lʏftçən] NT **-s, -** breeze

Luft-: luft|dicht ADJ airtight no adv ADV **die Ware ist ~ verpackt** the article is in airtight packaging; **ein ~ verschlossener Behälter** an airtight container, a container with an airtight seal; **Luft|druck** M, no pl air pressure; **Luft|druck|wel|le** F (Met) pressure wave; (= Knallwelle) blast; **luft|durch|läs|sig** ADJ pervious to air; Pflaster, Binde breathable; **Luft|durch|läs|sig|keit** F perviousness to air; **ein Pflaster von größerer ~** a more breathable plaster

lüf|ten ['lʏftn] VT **a** Raum, Kleidung, Bett to air; (ständig, systematisch) to ventilate **b** (= hochheben) Hut, Schleier to raise, to lift; **das Geheimnis war gelüftet** the secret was out VI (= Luft hereinlassen) to let some air in; (Betten, Kleider etc) to air

Lüf|ter ['lʏftɐ] M **-s, -** fan

Luft|fahrt F aeronautics sing; (mit Flugzeugen) aviation no art

Luft|fahrt-: Luft|fahrt|ge|sell|schaft F airline (company); **Luft|fahrt|in|ge|nieur(in)** M(F) aviation engineer; **Luft|fahrt|kar|te** F aviation chart; **Luft|fahrt|me|di|zin** F aeromedicine; **Luft|fahrt|schau** F air show

Luft-: Luft|fahr|zeug NT aircraft; **Luft|feuch|tig|keit** F (atmospheric) humidity; **Luft|fil|ter** NT OR M air filter; **Luft|flot|te** F air fleet; **Luft|fracht** F air freight; **Luft|geist** M (Myth) spirit of the air; **luft|ge|kühlt** ADJ air-cooled; **luft|ge|schützt** ADJ sheltered ADV **etw ~ auf|bewahren** to keep sth in an airtight container; **luft|ge|stützt** [-gəʃtʏtst] ADJ Flugkörper air-launched; **luft|ge|trock|net** [-gətrɔknət] ADJ air-dried; **Luft|ge|wehr** NT air rifle, air gun; **Luft|hauch** M (geh) gentle breeze; **Luft|herr|schaft** F air supremacy; **Luft|ho|heit** F air sovereignty; **Luft|ho|len** NT **-s**, no pl breathing; **zum ~ an die Oberfläche kommen** to come up for air; **Luft|hül|le** F mantle of air; **luft|hung|rig** ADJ longing for fresh air; **ein ~er Mensch** a fresh-air fiend

luf|tig ['lʊftɪç] ADJ Zimmer airy; Plätzchen breezy; Kleidung light; **in ~er Höhe** (liter) at a dizzy height ADV **~ gekleidet** lightly dressed; **das Restaurant war hell und ~ eingerichtet** the restaurant's furnishings lent it a light, airy feeling

Luf|ti|kus ['lʊftikʊs] M **-(ses), -se** (inf) happy-go-lucky sort of fellow

Luft-: Luft|kampf M air or aerial battle; **Luft|kis|sen** NT air cushion; (von Luftkissenboot) cushion of air; **Luft|kis|sen|boot** NT, **Luft|kis|sen|fahr|zeug** NT hovercraft; **Luft|klap|pe** F ventilation flap; **Luft|kor|ri|dor** M air corridor; **luft|krank** ADJ airsick; **Luft|krank|heit** F airsickness; **Luft|kreuz** NT, **Luft|kreu|zung** F centre (Brit) or center (US) of air routes; **Luft|krieg** M aerial warfare; **Luft- und Seekrieg** warfare at sea and in the air; **Luft|küh|lung** F air-cooling; **Luft|kur|ort** M (climatic) health resort; **Luft|lan|de|trup|pe** F airborne troops pl; **luft|leer** ADJ (völlig) **~ sein** to be a vacuum; **~er Raum** vacuum; **etw im ~en Raum diskutieren** (fig) to discuss sth in a vacuum or in the abstract; **Luft|li|nie** F **200 km etc ~** 200 km etc as the crow flies

Lüftl|ma|le|rei ['lʏftl-] F (Art) (Gemälde) (outdoor) wall or mural painting(s pl); façade painting(s pl), outdoor mural(s pl); (Kunstart) (oudoor) wall or mural painting, façade painting

Luft-: Luft|loch NT air hole; (Aviat) air pocket; **Luft|man|gel** M lack of air; **Luft|ma|sche** F (Sew) chain stitch; **Luft|mas|sen** PL air masses pl; **Luft|mat|rat|ze** F air bed (Brit), Lilo® (Brit), air mattress (esp US); **Luft|pi|rat(in)** M(F) (aircraft) hijacker, skyjacker (esp US); **Luft|pols|ter** NT air cushion

Luft|post F airmail; **mit ~** by airmail

Luft|post-: Luft|post|leicht|brief M aerogramme, air letter (Brit); **Luft|post|pa|pier** NT airmail paper

Luft-: Luft|pum|pe F air or pneumatic pump; (für Fahrrad) (bicycle) pump; **Luft|qua|li|tät** F air quality; **Luft|raum** M airspace; **Luft|raum|über|wa|chung** F air traffic control; **Luft|recht** NT air traffic law; **Luft|rei|fen** M pneumatic tyre (Brit) or tire (US); **Luft|rein|hal|tung** F prevention of air pollution; **Luft|rei|ni|ger** M air purifier; **Luft|ret|tungs|dienst** M air rescue service; **Luft|röh|re** F (Anat) windpipe, trachea; **Luft|röh|ren|schnitt** M tracheotomy; **Luft|sack** M (Aut) air bag; (Orn) air sac; **Luft|schacht** M ventilation shaft; **Luft|schau|kel** F swingboat; **Luft|schicht** F (Met) layer of air; **Luft|schiff** NT airship; **Luft|schiff|fahrt** ▲ F aeronautics sing; **Luft|schlacht** F air battle; **die ~ um England** the Battle of Britain; **Luft|schlan|ge** F (paper) streamer; **Luft|schlitz** M (Aut) ventilation slit; **Luft|schloss** ▲ NT (fig) castle in the air, pipe dream; **Luftschlösser bauen** to build castles in the air; **Luft|schnei|se** F air lane; **Luft|schrau|be** F propeller, airscrew

Luft|schutz M anti-aircraft defence (Brit) or defense (US)

Luft|schutz-: Luft|schutz|bun|ker M, **Luft|schutz|kel|ler** M, **Luft|schutz|raum** M air-raid shelter; **Luft|schutz|übung** F air-raid drill

Luft-: Luft|sieg M air victory; **Luft|sper|re** F (Mil) aerial barrage; **Luft|spie|ge|lung** F mirage; **Luft|sprung** M jump in the air; **vor Freude einen ~** or **Luftsprünge machen** to jump for or with joy; **Luft|stoß** M gust (of wind); **Luft|stra|ße** F air route; **Luft|stre|cke** F air route; **Luft|streit|kräf|te** PL air force sing; **Luft|strom** M stream of air; **Luft|strö|mung** F current of air; **Luft|stütz|punkt** M air base; **Luft|tan|ken** NT **-s**, no pl in-flight refuelling (Brit) or refueling (US); **Luft|ta|xi** NT air taxi; **Luft|tem|pe|ra|tur** F air temperature; **Luft|tor|pe|do** M aerial torpedo; **luft|tro|cken** ADJ air-dry; **luft|tüch|tig** ADJ Flugzeug airworthy; **Luft|über|wa|chung** F air surveillance; **Luft|über|wa|chungs|flug|kör|per** M airborne warning and control system; **Luft- und Raum|fahrt|in|dust|rie** F aerospace industry; **Luft- und Raum|fahrt|tech|nik** F aerospace technology

Lüf|tung ['lʏftʊŋ] F **-, -en** airing; (ständig, systematisch) ventilation

Lüf|tungs-: Lüf|tungs|an|la|ge F ventilation (system); **Lüf|tungs|klap|pe** F ventilation flap; **Lüf|tungs|rohr** NT ventilation pipe; **Lüf|tungs|schacht** M ventilation shaft

Luft-: Luft|un|ter|stüt|zung F (Mil) air support; **Luft|ver|än|de|rung** F change of air; **Luft|ver|flüs|si|gung** F liquefaction of air; **Luft|ver|kehr** M air traffic; **Luft|ver|kehrs|ge|sell|schaft** F airline; **Luft|ver|kehrs|li|nie** F air route; **Luft|ver|pes|tung** F (pej), **Luft|ver|schmut|zung** F air pollution; **Luft|ver|sor|gung** F air supplies pl; **Luft|ver|tei|di|gung** F air defence (Brit) or defense (US); **Luft|waf|fe** F (Mil) air force; **die (deutsche) ~** the Luftwaffe; **Luft|waf|fen|stütz|punkt** M air-force base; **Luft|weg** M (= Flugweg) air route; (= Atemweg) respiratory tract; **etw auf dem ~ befördern** to transport by air; **Luft|wi|der|stand** M air resistance; **Luft|wi|der|stands|bei|wert** M drag coefficient; **Luft|zu|fuhr** F air supply; **Luft|zug** M wind, (mild) breeze; (in Gebäude) draught (Brit), draft (US)

Lug [luːk] M **- und Trug** lies pl (and deception)

Lü|ge ['lyːgə] F **-, -n** lie, falsehood; **jdn einer ~ beschuldigen** or **bezichtigen** to accuse sb of lying; **jdn der ~ überführen** to catch sb (out) lying; **das ist alles ~** that's all lies; **jdn/etw ~n strafen** to give the lie to sb/sth, to belie sth; **~n**

haben kurze Beine (*prov*) truth will out (*esp Brit prov*), truth will prevail

lu|gen ['lu:gn] VI (*dial*) to peep, to peek

lü|gen ['ly:gn] *pret* **log** [lo:k], *ptp* **gelogen** [gə'lo:gn] **VI** to lie; **ich müsste ~, wenn ... I** would be lying if ...; **sie lügt, wenn sie nur den Mund aufmacht** she's a born liar; **wie gedruckt ~** (*inf*) to lie like mad (*inf*); **wer einmal lügt, dem glaubt man nicht, und wenn er auch die Wahrheit spricht** (*Prov*) remember the boy who cried "wolf" (*prov*) **VT das ist gelogen!, das lügst du doch!** (*inf*) that's a lie!, you're lying! → **Blaue(s) a**

Lü|gen-: Lü|gen|be|richt M fabrication; **Lü|gen|bold** [-bɔlt] M **-(e)s, -e** [-də] (*dated inf*) (inveterate) liar; **Lü|gen|de|tek|tor** M lie detector; **Lü|gen|dich|tung** F (*lit, fig*) wildly improbable story, tall tale (*lit, Liter*); **Lü|gen|ge|bäu|de** NT, **Lü|gen|ge|spinst** NT (*geh*) **Lü|gen|ge|we|be** NT (*liter*) tissue or web of lies; **Lü|gen|ge|schich|te** F pack of lies; **lü|gen|haft** ADJ *Erzählung* made-up, mendacious (*form*); *Bericht auch* false; **seine ~en Geschichten** his tall stories; **Lü|gen|kam|pag|ne** F campaign of lies; **Lü|gen|mär|chen** NT tall story, cock-and-bull story; **Lü|gen|maul** NT (*pej inf*) liar; **Lü|gen|pro|pa|gan|da** F propagandist lies *pl*, mendacious propaganda

Lü|ge|rei [ly:gə'rai] F **-, -en** lying *no pl*, fibbing *no pl*

Lüg|ner ['ly:gnɐ] M **-s, -**, **Lüg|ne|rin** [-ərɪn] F **-, -nen** liar

lüg|ne|risch ['ly:gnərɪʃ] ADJ *Mensch, Worte* lying *attr*, untruthful, mendacious (*form*)

Lu|kas ['lu:kas] M **-'** Luke

Lu|kas|evan|ge|li|um NT Gospel according to St. Luke, St. Luke's Gospel

Lu|ke ['lu:kə] F **-, -n** hatch; (= *Dachluke*) skylight

luk|ra|tiv [lukra'ti:f] ADJ lucrative **ADV** lucratively

lu|kul|lisch [lu'kʊlɪʃ] **ADJ** epicurean **ADV** exquisitely

Lu|kul|lus [lu'kʊlʊs] M **-, -se** (*fig*) epicure, gourmet, gastronome

Lu|latsch ['lu:la(:)tʃ] M **-(es), -e** (*hum inf*) **langer ~** beanpole (*inf*)

lul|len ['lʊlən] VT (*dated*) **ein Kind in den Schlaf ~** to lull a child to sleep

Lum|ba|go [lʊm'ba:go] F **-**, *no pl* lumbago

lum|be|cken ['lʊmbɛkn] VT (*Typ*) to adhesive-bind

Lum|ber|jack ['lambɐdʒɛk] M **-s, -s** (*dated*) lumber jacket

Lum|me ['lʊmə] F **-, -n** guillemot

Lüm|mel ['lyml] M **-s, -** **a** (*pej*) lout, oaf; **du ~, du** you rascal or rogue you **b** (*hum inf*: = *Penis*) willie (*Brit inf*), weenie (*US inf*)

Lüm|me|lei [lymə'lai] F **-, -en** (*inf*) sprawling about; (= *Flegelei*) rudeness *no pl*

lüm|mel|haft (*pej*) **ADJ** ill-mannered **ADV** ill-mannered

lüm|meln ['lymln] VR (*inf*) to sprawl; (= *sich hinlümmeln*) to flop down

Lüm|mel|tü|te F (*hum inf*: = *Kondom*) French letter (*Brit inf*), rubber (*US inf*)

Lüm|mer ['lymɐ] M **-s, -** (*S Ger: Cook*) roast loin; (*vom Rind*) sirloin

Lump [lʊmp] M **-en, -en** (*pej*) rogue, blackguard (*dated*)

lum|pen ['lʊmpn] VT (*inf*) **sich nicht ~ lassen** to splash out (*inf*) **VI** (*old, dial*) to go out on the tiles (*inf*)

Lum|pen ['lʊmpn] M **-s, -** **a** rag **b** (*S Ger.*: = *Lappen*) cloth

Lum|pen-: Lum|pen|ge|sin|del NT (*pej*) rabble *pl* (*pej*), riffraff *pl* (*pej*); **Lum|pen|händ|ler** M rag-and-bone man; **Lum|pen|pack** NT (*pej inf*) rabble *pl* (*pej*), riffraff *pl* (*pej*); **Lum|pen|pro|le|ta|ri|at** NT (*Sociol*) lumpenproletariat; **Lum|pen|samm|ler** M **a** (= *Lumpen-*

händler) rag-and-bone man **b** (*hum.*: = *Bus/ Bahn/Zug*) last bus/tram/train, drunks' special (*hum*)

Lum|pe|rei [lʊmpə'rai] F **-, -en** (*inf*) mean or dirty trick

lum|pig ['lʊmpɪç] **ADJ** **a** *Kleidung* ragged, tattered **b** *Gesinnung, Tat* shabby, mean **c** *attr* (*inf*: = *geringfügig*) paltry, measly (*inf*); **~e 10 Euro** 10 paltry or measly (*inf*) euros **ADV** **a** (= *zerlumpt*) raggedly; **~ aussehen** to look tattered; **~ herumlaufen** to go around in rags; **sich ~ anziehen** to be dressed in rags **b** (= *gemein*) shabbily

Lu|na|tis|mus [luna'tɪsmʊs] M **-**, *no pl* (*Psych*) sleepwalking, somnambulism (*form*)

Lunch [lanʃ, lantʃ] M **-(es)** or **-s, -e(s)** or **-s** lunch, luncheon (*form*)

lun|chen ['lanʃn, 'lantʃn] VI (*geh*) to lunch (*form*)

Lunch|pa|ket ['lanʃ-, 'lantʃ-] NT packed lunch, lunchbox, box lunch (*US*)

Lü|ne|bur|ger Hei|de ['ly:nəbʊrgɐ] F Lüneburg Heath

Lun|ge ['lʊŋə] F **-, -n** lungs *pl*; (= *Lungenflügel*) lung; **(auf) ~ rauchen** to inhale; **sich** (*dat*) **die ~ aus dem Hals** or **Leib schreien** (*inf*) to yell till one is blue in the face (*inf*); **sich** (*dat*) **die ~ aus dem Leib husten** (*inf*) to cough one's lungs up (*Brit inf*) or out (*esp US inf*); **die (grünen) ~n einer Großstadt** the lungs of a city → **eisern a**

Lun|gen-: Lun|gen|bläs|chen [-blɛːsçən] NT pulmonary alveolus (*spec*); **Lun|gen|bra|ten** M (*Aus*) loin roast (*Brit*), porterhouse (steak); **Lun|gen|em|bo|lie** F pulmonary embolism (*spec*); **Lun|gen|em|phy|sem** [-lɛmfyze:m] NT **-s, -e** pulmonary emphysema; **Lun|gen|ent|zün|dung** F pneumonia; **Lun|gen|fisch** M lungfish; **Lun|gen|flü|gel** M lung; **Lun|gen|ha|sche** NT (*Cook*) hash made with calf's *lights*; **Lun|gen|heil|stät|te** F TB or tuberculosis sanitarium (*US*) or sanatorium; **lun|gen|krank** ADJ **~ sein** to have a lung or pulmonary (*form*) disease; **Lun|gen|kran|ke(r)** MF *decl as adj* person suffering from a lung or pulmonary (*form*) disease; **Lun|gen|krank|heit** F lung or pulmonary (*form*) disease; **Lun|gen|kraut** NT (*Bot*) lungwort; **Lun|gen|krebs** M lung cancer; **Lun|gen|sa|na|to|ri|um** NT tuberculosis sanitarium (*US*) or sanatorium; **Lun|gen|tuber|ku|lo|se** F tuberculosis (of the lung), TB; **Lun|gen|tu|mor** M lung tumour (*Brit*) or tumor (*US*); **Lun|gen|zug** M deep drag (*inf*); **ei|nen ~ machen** to inhale deeply, to take a deep drag (*inf*)

lun|gern ['lʊŋɐn] VI (*inf*) to loaf or hang about (*Brit inf*) or around

Lun|te ['lʊntə] F **-, -n** **a** (*Hist*) fuse; **~ riechen** (= *Verdacht schöpfen*) to smell a rat (*inf*); (= *Gefahr wittern*) to smell (*inf*) or sense danger **b** (*Hunt*: = *Fuchsschwanz*) brush

Lu|pe ['lu:pə] F **-, -n** magnifying glass; **so etwas/ solche Leute kannst du mit der ~ suchen** things/people like that are few and far between; **jdn/etw unter die ~ nehmen** (*inf*) (= *beobachten*) to keep a close eye on sb/sth; (= *prüfen*) to examine sb/sth closely

lu|pen|rein **ADJ** (*lit*) *Edelstein* flawless; *Diamant auch* of the first water; (*fig*) *Vergangenheit etc auch* unimpeachable, unblemished; *Englisch, Bayrisch auch* perfect; *Gentleman, Intellektueller, Demokrat* through and through *pred*; **das Geschäft war nicht ganz ~** the deal wouldn't stand close scrutiny or wasn't quite all above board **ADV** *trennen* absolutely; *darstellen* flawlessly

lup|fen ['lʊpfn], **lüp|fen** ['lʏpfn] VT (*S Ger, Aus, Sw*) to lift, to raise

Lu|pi|ne [lu'pi:nə] F **-, -n** lupin

Lurch [lʊrç] M **-(e)s, -e** amphibian

Lu|re ['lu:rə] F **-, -n** lur

Lu|rex® ['lu:rɛks] NT **-**, *no pl* Lurex®

Lu|sche ['lʊʃə] F **-, -n** (*Cards*) low card; (*fig*) cipher

Lust [lʊst] F **-**, **=e** ['lʏstə] **a** *no pl* (= *Freude*) pleasure, joy; **er hat die ~ daran verloren, die ~ daran ist ihm vergangen** he has lost all interest in it; **da kann einem die (ganze)** or **alle ~ vergehen, da vergeht einem die ganze ~** it puts you off; **jdm die ~ an etw** (*dat*) **nehmen** to take all the fun out of sth for sb; **ich habe immer mit und Liebe gekocht** I've always enjoyed cooking; **sie ging mit/ohne ~ an die Arbeit** she set to work enthusiastically/without enthusiasm **b** *no pl* (= *Neigung*) inclination; **zu etw ~ (und Liebe) haben** to feel like sth; **ich habe keine ~, das zu tun** I don't really want to do that; (= *bin nicht dazu aufgelegt*) I don't feel like doing that; **ich habe keine ~ zu arbeiten** I'm not in the mood to work or for working, I don't feel like work or working; **ich habe ~, das zu tun** I'd like to do that; (= *bin dazu aufgelegt*) I feel like doing that; **ich habe jetzt keine ~** I'm not in the mood just now; **ich hätte ~ dazu** I'd like to; **das mache ich erst, wenn ich ~ dazu habe** I'll do that when I feel like it or when I'm in the mood; **hast du ~?** how about it?; **auf etw** (*acc*) **~ haben** to feel like sth, to fancy sth; **jdm ~ zu etw** or **auf etw** (*acc*) **machen** to put sb in the mood for sth; **mach, wie du ~ hast** (*inf*) do as you like; **er kann bleiben, solange er ~ hat** he can stay as long as he likes; **~ kriegen, etw zu tun** to feel like doing sth; **ich habe nicht übel ~, zu ... zu ...** I've a good or half a mind to ...; **ganz** or **je nach ~ und Laune** (*inf*) just depending on how I/you *etc* feel, just depending on my/your *etc* mood **c** (= *sinnliche Begierde*) desire; (*sexuell*) desire, lust (*usu pej*); **~ haben** to feel desire; **er/sie hat ~** (*inf*) he's/she's in the mood (*inf*); **seinen Lüsten leben** or **frönen** to indulge one's desires/lusts (*pej*)

Lust|aus|ter F (*hum sl*: = *Vagina*) love hole (*sl*)

Lust|bar|keit ['lʊstba:ɐkait] F **-, -en** (*dated*) jollity

lust|be|tont **ADJ** pleasure-orientated, governed by the pleasure principle; *Beziehung, Mensch* sensual **ADV** sensually; **~ unterrichten** to teach in such a way that learning is fun; **sein Leben so ~ wie möglich gestalten** to live one's life as enjoyably as possible

Lus|ter ['lʊstɐ] M **-s, -** (*Aus*: = *Leuchter*) chandelier

Lüs|ter ['lʏstɐ] M **-s, -** **a** (= *Leuchter*) chandelier **b** (= *Stoff, Glanzüberzug*) lustre (*Brit*), luster (*US*)

Lüs|ter|klem|me F (*Elec*) connector

lüs|tern ['lʏstɐn] **ADJ** lascivious; *Mann auch* lecherous; **nach etw ~ sein** to lust after or for sth **ADV** lecherously; lasciviously

Lüs|tern|heit F **-**, *no pl* lasciviousness; (*von Mann auch*) lecherousness

Lust-: lust|feind|lich ADJ (*geh*) opposed to carnal pleasures; **Lust|film** M (*dated*) comedy film; **Lust|gar|ten** M (*old*) pleasance; **Lust|ge|fühl** NT feeling of pleasure; (*sexuell auch*) desire; **Lust|ge|winn** M pleasure; **Lust|greis** M (*inf*) dirty old man (*inf*), old lecher; **Lust|haus** NT (*dated*) summer house, garden pavilion; **Lust|höh|le** F (*hum sl*: = *Vagina*) love hole (*sl*)

lus|tig ['lʊstɪç] **ADJ** (= *munter*) merry, jolly; *Mensch auch* jovial; (= *humorvoll*) funny, amusing; (= *emsig*) happy, merry, cheerful; **es wurde ~** things got quite merry; **seid ~!** liven up and have a bit of fun; **Lustige Person** (*Theat*) clown, fool, buffoon; **Die Lustige Witwe** the Merry Widow; **Bruder Lustig** (*old*) jolly or merry fellow (*dated*); **das ist ja ~!** (*iro*) **das finde ich aber ~!** (*iro*) (that's) very or most amusing (*iro*); **das kann ja ~ werden!** (*iro*) that's going to be fun (*iro*); **das kannst du tun, solange du ~ bist** (*inf*) you can do that as long as you like or please; **sich über jdn/etw ~ machen** to make fun of sb/sth

ADV a (= *fröhlich*) **sich ~ unterhalten** to have a lot of fun; **auf ihren Partys geht es ~ zu** her parties are always a lot of fun; **schau doch ein bisschen ~er** come on, cheer up **b** (= *humorvoll*) amusingly **c** (*inf:* = *unbekümmert*) happily

Lus|tig|keit F -, *no pl* (= *Munterkeit*) merriness (*dated*); (*von Mensch auch*) joviality; (*von Geschichte*) funniness

Lust|kna|be M (*old, hum*) catamite

Lüst|ling ['lʏstlɪŋ] M **-s, -e** debauchee, lecher; **ein alter ~** an old lecher, a debauched old man

Lust-: **lust|los ADJ** unenthusiastic; (*Fin*) *Börse* slack, dull **ADV** unenthusiastically; **Lust|lo|sig|keit** F -, *no pl* lack of enthusiasm; (*Fin: von Börse*) slackness; **Lust|molch** M (*hum inf*) sex maniac (*inf*); (*bewundernd*) sexy beast (*inf*), sexpot (*inf*); **Lust|mord** M sex murder; **Lust|mör|der(in)** M(F) sex killer *or* murderer; **Lust|objekt** NT sex object; **Lust|prin|zip** NT (*Psych*) pleasure principle; **Lust|schloss ▲** NT summer residence; **Lust|spiel** NT comedy; **Lust|spiel|dich|ter(in)** M(F) comedy writer, writer of comedies; **Lust|ver|lust** M , *no pl* **un|ter ~ leiden** to have lost one's zest for life; **lust|voll ADJ** full of relish **ADV** with relish; **lust|wan|deln** VI *insep aux sein or haben* (*liter*) to (take a) stroll, to promenade (*old*)

Lu|te|tium [lu'teːtsiʊm] NT **-s,** *no pl* (*abbr* **Lu**) lutecium

luth. *abbr von* **lutherisch**

Lu|the|ra|ner [lutəˈraːnɐ] M **-s, -, Lu|the|ra|ne|rin** [-ərɪn] F **-, -nen** Lutheran

Lu|ther|bi|bel F Lutheran translation (*of the Bible*)

lu|the|risch ['lʊtərɪʃ], **lu|thersch** ['lʊtɐʃ] ADJ Lutheran

lut|schen ['lʊtʃn] VTI to suck (*an etw* (*dat*) sth)

Lut|scher ['lʊtʃɐ] M **-s, -** lollipop

Lutsch|tab|let|te F (*Med*) lozenge

lütt [lʏt] ADJ (*N Ger inf*) little, wee (*esp Scot*); **die Lütten** (= *Kinder*) the kids

Lüt|tich ['lʏtɪç] NT **-s** Liège

Luv [luːf] F -, *no pl* (*Naut*) windward *or* weather side; **nach ~** to windward

lu|ven ['luːvn, 'luːfn] VI (*Naut*) to luff (up)

Luv|sei|te F windward side

Lux [lʊks] NT **-, -** (*Phys*) lux

Lu|xa|ti|on [lʊksa'tsioːn] F **-, -en** (*Med*) dislocation

Lu|xem|burg ['lʊksmbʊrk] NT **-s** Luxembourg

Lu|xem|bur|ger ['lʊksmbʊrgɐ] M **-s, -, Lu|xem|bur|ge|rin** [-ərɪn] F **-, -nen** Luxembourger

lu|xem|bur|gisch ['lʊksmbʊrgɪʃ] ADJ Luxembourgian

lu|xu|ri|ös [lʊksu'riøːs] **ADJ** luxurious; **ein ~es Leben** a life of luxury **ADV** luxuriously; **~ Urlaub machen** to take a luxurious holiday (*esp Brit*) *or* vacation (*US*)

Lu|xus ['lʊksʊs] M -, *no pl* luxury; (*pej:* = *Verschwendung, Überfluss*) extravagance; **im ~ leben/schwelgen** to live in (the lap of) luxury; **den ~ lieben** to love luxury; **mit etw ~ treiben** to be extravagant with sth, to lash out on sth (*inf*); **ich leiste mir den ~ und ...** I'll treat myself to the luxury of ...

Lu|xus- *in cpds* luxury; **Lu|xus|ar|ti|kel** M luxury article; **~** *pl* luxury goods *pl*; **Lu|xus|aus|füh|rung** F de luxe model; **Lu|xus|aus|ga|be** F de luxe edition; **Lu|xus|damp|fer** M luxury cruise ship; **Lu|xus|frau** F (*inf*) piece of class (*inf*), classy woman; **Lu|xus|gü|ter** PL luxury goods *pl*; **Lu|xus|ho|tel** NT luxury hotel; **Lu|xus|klas|se** F , *no pl* **der ~** (*nachgestellt*) de luxe *attr*, luxury-class *attr*, deluxe *attr* (*US*), luxury *attr*; **Lu|xus|kör|per** M (*hum*) beautiful body; **Lu|xus|li|mou|si|ne** F limousine; **Lu|xus|res|tau|rant** NT first-class restaurant; **Lu|xus|schlit|ten** M (*inf*) classy car (*inf*) *or* job (*inf*); **Lu|xus|weib|chen** NT (*pej*) classy piece (*inf*); **Lu|xus|zug** M Pullman (train)

Lu|zern [lu'tsɛrn] NT **-s** Lucerne

Lu|zer|ne [lu'tsɛrnə] F **-, -n** (*Bot*) lucerne

lu|zid [lu'tsiːt] ADJ (*liter*) lucid; (= *durchsichtig*) translucent

Lu|zi|fer ['luːtsifɐ] M **-s** Lucifer

lu|zi|fe|risch [lutsi'feːrɪʃ] ADJ diabolical, satanic

LVA [ɛlfau'aː] F **-, -s** *abbr von* **Landesversicherungsanstalt**

LW [ɛl've:] *abbr von* **Langwelle** LW

Ly|chee ['lɪtʃi] F **-, -s** lychee, litchi

Lymph- ['lʏmf-]: **Lymph|bahn** F lymph vessel; **Lymph|drä|na|ge** F lymphatic drainage; **Lymph|drü|se** F lymph(atic) gland

Lym|phe ['lʏmfə] F **-, -n** lymph

Lymph|kno|ten ['lʏmf-] M lymph node, lymph(atic) gland

Lymph|kno|ten- ['lʏmf-]: **Lymph|kno|ten|ent|zün|dung** F inflammation of the lymph node; **Lymph|kno|ten|schwel|lung** F swelling of the lymph node

Lym|pho|zyt [lʏmfo'tsyːt] M **-en, -en** lymphocyte

lyn|chen ['lʏnʧn, 'lɪnʧn] VT (*lit*) to lynch; (*fig*) to kill

Lynch- ['lʏnʧ-]: **Lynch|jus|tiz** F lynch law; **Lynch|mord** M lynching

Ly|o|ner ['lioːnɐ] F **-, -** (= *Wurst*) type of pork *or* veal sausage

Ly|ra ['lyːra] F **-, Lyren** [-rən] (*Mus*) lyre; **die ~** (*Astron*) Lyra, the Lyre

Ly|rik ['lyːrɪk] F **-,** *no pl* lyric poetry *or* verse

Ly|ri|ker ['lyːrikɐ] M **-s, -, Ly|ri|ke|rin** [-ərɪn] F **-, -nen** lyric poet, lyricist

ly|risch ['lyːrɪʃ] **ADJ** (*lit, fig*) lyrical; *Dichtung, Dichter* lyric **ADV** lyrically

Ly|ze|um [ly'tseːʊm] NT **-s, Lyzeen** [ly'tseːən] **a** (= *Gymnasium*) girls' grammar school (*Brit*), girls' high school **b** (*Sw.* = *Oberstufe*) upper school

M

M, **m** [ɛm] NT -, - M, m

m abbr von **Meter**

MA. abbr von **Mittelalter**

M.A. [ɛm'ˈaː] (Univ) abbr von **Magister Artium** MA, M.A. (US)

Mä|an|der [mɛ'andɐ] M -s, - (Geog, Art) meander

mä|an|dern [mɛ'andɐn] ptp **mäandert** [VI] (Geog) to meander [VT] (Art) to decorate with meanders

mä|and|risch [mɛ'andrɪʃ] [ADJ] meandering [ADV] sich ~ schlängeln to meander; ~ verziert (Art) decorated with meanders

Maar [maːɐ] NT -(e)s, -e (Geol) maar (spec), volcanic lake

Maas [maːs] F - Meuse, Maas

Maas|tricht-Ver|trag [maːsˈtrɪçt] M Maastricht Treaty

Maat [maːt] M -(e)s, -e or -en (Naut) (ship's) mate

Mac|chi|a ['makia] F -, **Macchien**, **Mac|chi|e** ['makiə] F -, **Macchien** (Bot) maquis, macchia

Mach [max] NT -(s), - (Phys) Mach

Ma|chan|del [maˈxandl] M -s, -, **Ma|chan|del|baum** M (N Ger) juniper (tree)

Mach|art F make; (= Muster) design; (lit, fig: = Stil) style

mach|bar ADJ feasible, possible

Mach|bar|keit ['maxbaːɐkait] F -, no pl feasibility

Mach|bar|keits|stu|die F feasibility study

Ma|che ['maxə] F -, -n (inf) **a** (= Technik) structure **b** (= Vortäuschung) sham; **reine** or **pure ~ sein** to be (a) sham **c** **etw in der ~ haben** (inf) to be working on sth, to have sth on the stocks; **in der ~ sein** (inf) to be in the making; **der Film war noch in der ~** (inf) the film was still being made

ma|chen ['maxn]

1 TRANSITIVES VERB	3 REFLEXIVES VERB
2 INTRANSITIVES VERB	

1 – TRANSITIVES VERB

Wenn **machen** sich auf eine nicht näher gekennzeichnete Aktivität bezieht oder stellvertretend für ein anderes Verb steht, wird es in den meisten Fällen mit **to do** übersetzt.

a = tun | to do; **was machst du heute Abend?** what are you doing this evening?; **was machen wir mit dem restlichen Brot?** what shall we do with the rest of the bread?; **die Hausarbeit/den Garten machen** to do the housework/the garden; **er machte sich (dat) Zucker in den Kaffee** (inf) he put sugar in his coffee; **ich muss noch so viel machen** I still have so much to do; **ich mache dir das schon** I'll do that for you; **ich mache das schon** (= bringe das in Ordnung) I'll see to that; (= erledige das) I'll do that; **gut, wird gemacht** right, will do (inf); **gut, mache ich** right, will do (inf) or I'll do that; **wie mans macht, ists verkehrt** whatever you do is wrong; **was habe ich nur falsch gemacht?** what have I

done wrong?; **er macht, was er will** he does what he likes; **soll ich ihn nach seinem Gehalt fragen? – so etwas macht man nicht!** shall I ask how much he earns? – you don't ask that (question)!; **wie machen Sie das nur?** how do you do it?; **das lässt sich machen/nicht machen** that can/can't be done; **das ist zu/nicht zu machen** that can/can't be done; **(da ist) nichts zu machen** (= geht nicht) (there's) nothing to be done; (= kommt nicht infrage) nothing doing; **ich kann da auch nichts machen** I can't do anything about it either; **ich mache es wohl am besten so, dass ich etwas früher komme** I would do best to come a bit earlier; **es ist schon gut gemacht, wie sie die Rolle der Ophelia mit echtem Leben erfüllt** it's wonderful how she brings the role of Ophelia to life; **damit/mit ihr kann man etwas machen** you could do something with it/her; **das lässt er nicht mit sich machen** he won't stand for that → auch **gemacht**

◆ **was macht jd/etw?** **was machst du da?** what are you doing (there)?; **was hast du denn nun wieder gemacht?** what have you done now?; **was machst du denn hier?** what (on earth) are you doing here?; **was macht denn das Fahrrad hier im Hausflur?** what's this bicycle doing in the hall?; **was macht die Arbeit?** how's the work going?; **was macht dein Bruder (beruflich)?** what does your brother do (for a living)?; **was macht dein Bruder?** (= wie geht es ihm?) how's your brother doing?

◆ **es machen machs kurz!** make it short!; **machs gut!** all the best!; **er wirds nicht mehr lange machen** (inf) he won't last long; **es mit jdm machen** (inf: = Sex haben) to make or do it with sb (inf); **es jdm machen** (sl: = befriedigen) to bring sb off (sl); **es sich (dat) selber machen** (sl) to bring oneself off (inf); **mit mir kann mans ja machen!** (inf) the things I put up with! (inf)

b = anfertigen, zubereiten | to make; **Bier wird aus Gerste gemacht** beer is made from barley; **aus Holz gemacht** made of wood; **sich/jdm etw machen lassen** to have sth made for oneself/sb; **er ist für den Beruf wie gemacht** he's made for the job; **das Essen machen** to make the meal; **jdm einen Drink machen** (Cocktail) to make or mix sb a drink

c = verursachen, bewirken | Schwierigkeiten, Arbeit to make (jdm for sb), Mühe, Schmerzen to cause (jdm for sb); **jdm Angst/Sorgen/Freude machen** to make sb afraid/worried/happy; **jdm Hoffnung/Mut/Kopfschmerzen machen** to give sb hope/courage/a headache; **das macht Appetit** that gives you an appetite; **das macht Hunger** that makes you hungry; **das macht die Kälte** it's the cold that does that; **jdn lachen/weinen/etw vergessen machen** to make sb laugh/cry/forget sth; **machen, dass etw geschieht** to make sth happen; **mach, dass er gesund wird!** make him better!; **es sind all die vielen Zigaretten, dass du hustest** it's all those cigarettes that make you cough; **(viel) von sich reden machen** to be much talked about → **schaffen** [2]

d = hervorbringen | Laut, Geräusch to make; **mäh/miau machen** to baa/miaow; **brumm machen** to go "brumm"; **wie macht das Kindchen?** say

please!; **wie macht das feine Hündchen?** be a clever dog!

e = bilden | Kreuzzeichen, Kreis to make; **die Straße macht einen Knick** the road bends

f machen + Substantiv

Siehe auch unter dem Eintrag für das jeweilige Substantiv.

einen Ausflug machen to go on an outing; **Bilder machen** to take photos; **ein Defizit machen** to make a loss; **ein Diplom machen** to do a diploma; **einen Doktor machen** to do a doctorate; **ein Fest machen** to have a party; **Fotos machen** to take photos; **das Geschirr machen** to do the dishes; **einen Gewinn machen** to make a profit; **Grimassen machen** to make a face; **Halt machen** to call a halt; **einen Handstand machen** to do a handstand; **auf jdn/etw Jagd machen** to hunt sb/sth; **einen Kopfsprung machen** to take a header (Brit), to dive (headfirst); **einen Kurs machen** (= teilnehmen) to do a course; **Nachtdienst machen** to do night duty; **eine Party machen** to have a party; **Pause machen** to have a break; **mach mir mal einen (guten) Preis!** make me an offer!; **eine Prüfung machen** to do (esp Brit) or take an exam; **Punkte machen** to get points; **jdm die Rechnung machen** to make up sb's bill; **Schicht machen** to work shifts; **einen Spaziergang machen** to go for a walk; **ein Spiel machen** to play a game

g machen + Adjektiv

Siehe auch unter dem Eintrag für das jeweilige Adjektiv.

to make; **jdn nervös/unglücklich machen** to make sb nervous/unhappy; **etw größer/kleiner machen** to make sth bigger/smaller; **etw sauber/schmutzig machen** to get sth clean/dirty; **etw leer machen** to empty sth; **etw kürzer machen** to shorten sth; **einen Stuhl frei machen** to vacate a chair; **jdn alt/jung machen** (= aussehen lassen) to make sb look old/young; **jdn wieder sehend machen** to make sb see again; **machs dir doch bequem/gemütlich** make yourself comfortable/at home; **mach es ihm nicht noch schwerer** don't make it harder for him; **er macht es sich (dat) nicht leicht** he doesn't make it easy for himself

h = ergeben | (inf) to make; Summe, Preis to be; **das macht (zusammen) 23** that makes 23 altogether; **drei und fünf macht** three and five makes or is eight; **fünf mal vier macht** or **machen zwanzig** five fours are twenty, five times four is twenty; **was macht die Rechnung?** how much is the bill?, what does the bill come to?; **was** or **wie viel macht sechs geteilt durch zwei?** what is six divided by two?; **100 cm machen einen Meter** 100 cm make a metre (Brit) or meter (US); **was** or **wie viel macht das (alles zusammen)?** how much is that altogether?

i = spielen | (inf, Theat) to play; Dolmetscher, Schiedsrichter etc to be; **den Weihnachtsmann machen** to play Santa Claus; **den Ghostwriter für jdn machen** to be sb's ghostwriter

j = Notdurft verrichten | (inf) **einen Haufen** or **sein Geschäft machen** (euph:) (Hund) to do its business (euph) → **Aa**, **Pipi** etc

k = ordnen, reparieren, säubern to do; **die Küche muss mal wieder gemacht werden** (= *gereinigt, gestrichen*) the kitchen needs doing again; **das Auto machen lassen** to have the car seen to *or* done; **er macht mir die Haare** (*inf*) he does my hair; **das Bett machen** to make the bed; **ich muss noch die Betten machen** I've still got the beds to make; **mach den Fleck aus der Bluse, ehe du sie wäschst** get the stain out of the blouse before you wash it

l andere Wendungen

♦ **machen + aus** etw aus jdm/etw machen (= *verwandeln in*) to turn sb/sth into sth; (= *darstellen, interpretieren als*) to make sth of sb/sth; **aus dem Haus könnte man schon etwas machen** you could really make something of that house; **eine große Sache aus etw machen** to make a big thing of sth; **etwas aus sich** (*dat*) **machen** to make something of oneself; **was soll ich aus dieser Sache machen?** (= *verstehen, interpretieren*) what am I to make of this?

♦ **machen + zu** jdn/etw zu etw machen (= *verwandeln in*) to turn sb/sth into sth; **jdn zum Star/Helden machen** to turn sb into a star/hero; **jdn zum Wortführer/Sklaven/zu seiner Frau machen** to make sb spokesman/a slave/one's wife; **jdm etw zur Hölle/Qual machen** to make sth hell/a misery for sb

♦ **nichts/etwas machen** (= *ausmachen, schaden*) **macht nichts!** it doesn't matter!; **macht das was?** does that matter?; **das macht durchaus etwas** it does indeed matter; **das macht mir doch nichts!** that doesn't matter to me!; **der Regen/die Kälte macht mir nichts** I don't mind the rain/cold; **die Kälte macht dem Motor nichts** the cold doesn't hurt the engine; **es macht mir nichts, durch den Regen zu gehen** I don't mind walking in the rain

♦ **sich etw machen** sich (*dat*) **viel aus jdm/etw machen** to like sb/sth; **sich** (*dat*) **wenig aus jdm/etw machen** not to be very keen on (*esp Brit*) or thrilled with (*esp US*) sb/sth; **sich** (*dat*) **nichts aus etw machen** (= *keinen Wert legen auf*) not to be very keen on (*esp Brit*) or thrilled with (*esp US*) sth; (= *sich nicht ärgern*) not to let sth bother one; **mach dir nichts draus!** don't let it bother you!; **sich** (*dat*) **einen schönen Abend/ein paar gemütliche Stunden machen** to have a nice evening/a few pleasant hours; **sich** (*dat*) **ein Vergnügen aus etw machen** to take delight in sth; **sich** (*dat*) **Umstände/Mühe machen** to go to a lot of bother/trouble; **machen Sie sich keine Umstände** don't go to any trouble; **sich** (*dat*) **Sorgen machen** to worry; **sich** (*dat*) **(auf etw** *acc*) **Hoffnungen machen** to have hopes (of sth); **sich** (*dat*) **jdn zum Freund/Feind machen** to make sb one's friend/enemy; **sich** (*dat*) **etw zur Aufgabe/zum Grundsatz/Motto machen** to make sth one's job/a principle/one's watchword

2 – INTRANSITIVES VERB

a = tun **lass ihn nur machen** (= *hindre ihn nicht*) just let him do it; (= *verlass dich auf ihn*) just leave it to him; **lass mich mal machen** let me do it; (= *ich bringe das in Ordnung*) let me see to that

b machen + Adjektiv **das macht müde/gesund/ schlank** that makes you tired/healthy/slim; **das Kleid macht alt/schlank** that dress makes you look old/slim

c = sich beeilen (*inf*) to get a move on (*inf*), to hurry up; **mach schon!, mach schnell** *or* **schneller!** get a move on! (*inf*), hurry up!; **ich mach ja schon!** I'm being as quick as I can!; **sie machten, dass sie nach Hause kamen** they hurried home; **mach, dass du hier wegkommst** *or* **verschwindest!** (you just) get out of here!

d = Notdurft verrichten (*inf*) to go to the toilet (*esp Brit*) or bathroom (*esp US*) or restroom (*US*); (*Hund etc*) to do its business (*euph*); **(sich) in die Hosen machen** (*lit, fig*) to wet oneself; **ins Bett machen** to wet the bed; **groß/**

klein machen (*baby-talk*) to do a poo/wee (*baby-talk*)

e = reisen (*dial*) to go; **nach Amerika machen** to go to America; **über die (grüne) Grenze machen** to go over the border

f Redewendungen

♦ **machen auf etw** (*acc*) (*inf*) **jetzt macht sie auf große Dame** she's playing the grand lady now; **er macht auf Staatsmann** he's playing the statesman; **sie macht auf verständnisvoll/gebildet** she's doing her understanding/cultured bit (*inf*); **jetzt macht sie auf beleidigt** now she's acting the injured innocent (*Brit*), now she's acting insulted (*esp US*); **er macht auf Schau** he's out for effect (*inf*)

♦ **machen in etw** (*dat*) (*inf, beruflich*) to be in sth; **er macht in Politik** he's in politics; **er macht in Nächstenliebe/Großzügigkeit** he puts on a show of compassion/generosity

3 – REFLEXIVES VERB

♦ **sich machen**

a = sich entwickeln to come on; **wie macht sich der Garten?** how is the garden coming on?

b = aussehen to look; **der Schal macht sich sehr hübsch zu dem Kleid** the scarf looks very pretty with that dress

c andere Wendungen **sich an etw** (*acc*) **machen** to get down to sth; **sich auf den Weg machen** to get going; **sich über das Essen machen** (*inf*) to get stuck in (*inf*); **sich zum Fürsprecher/Anwalt machen** to make oneself spokesman/advocate; **sich verständlich machen** to make oneself understood; **sie will sich doch nur wichtig machen** she's trying to make herself seem important; **sich bei jdm beliebt/verhasst machen** (*inf*) to make oneself popular with/hated by sb

---

Ma|chen|schaf|ten ['maxnʃaftn] PL wheelings and dealings *pl*, machinations *pl*

Ma|cher ['maxɐ] M **-s, -**, **Ma|che|rin** [-ərɪn] F **-, -nen** (*inf*) doer, man/woman of action

-ma|cher(in) M(F) *suf in cpds* -maker; **Kleider-/Möbelmacher(in)** clothes/furniture-maker

Ma|cher|lohn M labour (*Brit*) *or* labor (*US*) charge; (*bei Kleidung*) making-up charge

Ma|che|te [ma'xe:tə, ma'tʃe:tə] F **-, -n** machete

Ma|chi|a|vel|lis|mus M Machiavellianism

ma|chi|a|vel|lis|tisch [makiave'lɪstɪʃ] ADJ Machiavellian ADV like a true Machiavellian

Ma|chis|mo [ma'tʃɪsmo] M **-s**, *no pl* machismo

Ma|cho ['matʃo] M **-s, -s** macho (*inf*)

Macht [maxt] F **-, ⸚e** [ˈmɛçtə] **a** *no pl* (= *Einfluss, Kraft*) power; (= *Stärke*) might, power; **die ~ der Gewohnheit/Verhältnisse/des Schicksals** the force of habit/circumstance(s)/destiny; **alles, was in unserer ~ steht, alles in unserer ~ Stehende** everything (with)in our power; **es stand nicht in seiner ~, zu ...** it was not *or* did not lie within his power to ...; **mit ~** with a vengeance; **mit aller ~** with might and main, with all one's might; **~ geht vor Recht** (*Prov*) might is right (*Prov*)

no pl (= *Herrschaft, Befehlsgewalt*) power; **die ~ ergreifen/erringen** to seize/gain power; **an die ~ gelangen** (*form*) *or* **kommen** to come to power; **jdn an die ~ bringen** to bring sb to power; **an der ~ sein/bleiben** to be/remain in power; **seine ~ behaupten** to maintain control, to continue to hold sway; **die ~ übernehmen** to assume power, to take over

c (= *außerirdische Kraft, Großmacht*) power; **die Mächte der Finsternis** (*old, liter*) the Powers of Darkness (*old, liter*)

d (*dated* = *Heeresmacht*) forces *pl*

Macht-: Macht|an|spruch M claim to power; **Macht|ap|pa|rat** M (*Pol*) machinery of power; **der an der ~ hindern** to prevent sb from exercising his power; **Macht|be|fug|nis** F power, authority *no pl*; **Macht|be|reich** M sphere of

influence *or* control; **macht|be|ses|sen** ADJ power-crazed; **Macht|block** M *pl* **-blöcke** power bloc

Mäch|te|grup|pie|rung F grouping of the powers

Macht-: Macht|ent|fal|tung F display of power; **zur Zeit der größten ~** at the height *or* peak of its power; **Macht|er|grei|fung** F seizure of power; **Macht|erhalt** M retention of power; **der Regierungspartei geht es nur um den ~** the ruling party is only interested in staying in power; **Macht|fül|le** F power *no indef art*; **Macht|ge|fü|ge** NT power structure; **Macht|gier** F lust for power; **Macht|ha|ber** [-ha:bɐ] M **-s, -**, **Macht|ha|be|rin** [-ərɪn] F **-, -nen** ruler; (*pej*) dictator; **die ~ in Ruritanien** the rulers of *or* powers-that-be in Ruritania; **Macht|hun|ger** M (*liter*) craving *or* hunger for power; **macht|hung|rig** ADJ (*liter*) power-hungry; **~ sein** to crave power

mäch|tig ADJ **a** (= *einflussreich*) powerful; **die Mächtigen (dieser Erde)** the powerful (of this world)

b (= *sehr groß*) mighty; *Baum, Felsen* massive, mighty; *Körper* massive; *Stimme, Wirkung, Schlag, Schultern* powerful, mighty; *Essen* heavy; (*inf*: = *enorm*) *Hunger, Durst, Glück* terrific (*inf*), tremendous; **~e Angst** *or* **einen ~en Bammel haben** (*inf*) to be scared stiff

c (*liter*) **seiner selbst** (*gen*) *or* **seiner Sinne** (*gen*) **nicht ~ sein** not to be in control of oneself; **einer Sprache** (*gen*) **~ sein** to have a good command of a language

ADV (*inf*: = *sehr*) terrifically (*inf*), tremendously; *schneien, brüllen, sich beeilen* like mad (*inf*); **sich ~ anstrengen** to make a terrific (*inf*) *or* tremendous effort; **da hast du dich ~ getäuscht** you've made a big mistake there; **darüber hat sie sich ~ geärgert** she got really angry about it

Mäch|tig|keit F **-**, *no pl* powerfulness, power; (*von Felsen, Körper*) massiveness

Macht-: Macht|kampf M power struggle, struggle for power; **macht|los** ADJ powerless, (= *hilflos*) helpless; **gegen diese Argumente war ich ~** I was powerless against these arguments ADV powerlessly; (= *hilflos*) helplessly; **Macht|lo|sig|keit** F **-**, *no pl* powerlessness; (= *Hilflosigkeit*) helplessness; **Macht|mensch** M power-seeker; **Macht|miss|brauch** ▲ M abuse *or* misuse of power; **Macht|mit|tel** NT instrument of power; **Macht|mo|no|pol** NT monopoly of power; **Macht|po|li|tik** F power politics *pl*; **Macht|po|si|ti|on** F position of power; **Macht|pro|be** F trial of strength; **Macht|stel|lung** F position of power; (= *einflussreiche Stellung auch*) powerful position; **Macht|stre|ben** NT striving for power; **Macht|struk|tur** F power structure; **Macht|tech|ni|ker(in)** M(F) powermonger; **Macht|über|nah|me** F takeover (*durch* by); **Macht|va|ku|um** NT power vacuum; **Macht|ver|hält|nis|se** PL balance *sing* of power; **Macht|ver|lust** M loss of power; **Macht|ver|schie|bung** F shift of power; **macht|voll** ADJ powerful ADV powerfully; *eingreifen* decisively; **~ auftrumpfen** to flex one's muscles; **Macht|voll|kom|men|heit** F absolute power; **Macht|wech|sel** M changeover of power; **Macht|wort** NT *pl* **-worte** word (+*gen* from); **ein ~ sprechen** to exercise one's authority

Mach|werk NT (*pej*) sorry effort; **das ist ein ~ des Teufels** that is the work of the devil

Mach|zahl ▲ F (*Phys*) Mach number

Ma|cke ['makə] F **-, -n** (*inf*) **a** (= *Tick, Knall*) quirk; **eine ~ haben** (*inf*) to be cracked (*inf*), to have a screw loose (*inf*) **b** (= *Fehler, Schadstelle*) fault; (*bei Maschinen*) defect, fault; (*bei Kartoffeln etc*) bad patch

Ma|cker ['makɐ] M **-s, -** (*inf*) fellow (*inf*), bloke (*Brit inf*), guy (*inf*); **spiel hier nicht den ~** don't come (*Brit*) *or* play the tough guy here (*inf*)

MAD [ɛmlaːˈdeː] M - *abbr von* **Militärischer Abschirmdienst** ≈ MI5 (*Brit*), ≈ CIA (*US*)

Ma|da|gas|kar [madaˈgaskar] NT -s Madagascar; (*Pol: heutzutage*) Malagasy Republic

Ma|da|gas|se [madaˈgasə] M -n, -n, **Ma|da|gas|sin** [-ˈgasɪn] F -, -nen Madagascan; Malagasy

ma|da|gas|sisch [madaˈgasɪʃ] ADJ Madagascan; Malagasy

Ma|dam [maˈdam] F -, -s *or* -en **a** (*hum dated*) lady; **meine ~** my old woman *or* lady (*inf*) **b** (*in Bordell*) madam

Mäd|chen [ˈmɛːtçən] NT -s, - girl; (= *Tochter auch*) daughter; (*dated*: = *Freundin*) girl(friend); (= *Dienstmädchen*) maid; **ein unberührtes ~** a virgin; **ein ~ für alles** (*inf*) a dogsbody (*Brit*), a gofer; (*im Haushalt auch*) a maid-of-all-work → **spät** ADJ, **leicht** ADJ **e**

Mäd|chen-: **Mäd|chen|buch** NT book for girls; **mäd|chen|haft** ADJ girlish ADV *sich bewegen, aussehen* like a (young) girl; *kichern auch* girlishly (*pej*); **sich ~ kleiden** to dress like a girl; **Mäd|chen|han|del** M white slave trade; **Mäd|chen|händ|ler(in)** M(F) white-slaver; **Mäd|chen|klas|se** F girls' class, girls' form (*Brit*); **Mäd|chen|klei|dung** F girls' clothing *or* clothes *pl*; **Mäd|chen|na|me** M **a** (*Vorname*) girl's name; **~n** girls' names **b** (*von verheirateter Frau*) maiden name; **Mäd|chen|pen|si|o|nat** NT girls' boarding school; **diese Kaserne ist kein ~!** (*hum*) these barracks aren't a finishing school; **Mäd|chen|schu|le** F girls' school; **Mäd|chen|zim|mer** NT (*dated*) maid's room; (*für Tochter*) girl's room

Ma|de [ˈmaːdə] F -, -n maggot; **wie die ~ im Speck leben** (*inf*) to live *or* be in clover, to live in (the lap of) luxury

Ma|dei|ra [maˈdeːra] M -s, -s (= *Wein*) Madeira

Mä|del [ˈmɛːdl] NT -s, -(s) (*dial*), **Ma|del** [ˈmaːdl] NT -s, -n (*Aus*) lass (*dial*), girl → *auch* **Mädchen**

Ma|den|wurm M threadworm

Mä|derl [ˈmɛːdɛl] NT -s, -n (*Aus*) little lass (*dial*) *or* girl

ma|dig [ˈmaːdɪç] ADJ maggoty; *Obst auch* wormeaten; **jdn/etw ~ machen** (*inf*) to run sb/sth down; **jdm etw ~ machen** (*inf*) to put sb off sth

Mad|jar [maˈdjaːɐ] M -en, -en Magyar

Madl [ˈmaːdl] NT -s, -n (*Aus*), **Mäd|le** [ˈmɛːdlə] NT -s, - (*S Ger*) lass (*dial*), girl → *auch* **Mädchen**

Ma|don|na [maˈdɔna] F -, **Madonnen** [-ˈdɔnən] Madonna

Ma|don|nen-: **Ma|don|nen|bild** NT (picture of the) Madonna; **ma|don|nen|haft** ADJ madonna-like ADV *schön, unschuldig* as a madonna

Mad|rid [maˈdrɪt] NT -s Madrid

Mad|ri|der¹ [maˈdrɪdɐ] ADJ *attr* Madrid

Mad|ri|der² [maˈdrɪdɐ] M -s, -, **Mad|ri|de|rin** [-ərɪn] F -, -nen native of Madrid; (*Einwohner*) inhabitant of Madrid

Mad|ri|gal [madriˈgaːl] NT -s, -e madrigal

Ma|est|ro [maˈɛstro] M -s, -s *or* **Maestri** [-tri] maestro

Ma|fia [ˈmafia] F , **Maf|fia** [ˈmafia] F -, *no pl* Mafia

Mafia-Boss ▲ M , **Maf|fia-Boss** ▲ M Mafia boss

Ma|fia|me|tho|den PL Mafia(-type) methods *pl*

ma|fi|os [maˈfioːs] ADJ Mafia *attr*; *Zustände* Mafia-like

Ma|fi|o|so [maˈfioːzo] M -, **Mafiosi** [-zi] mafioso

mag [maːk] 3. *pers sing pres von* **mögen**

Ma|ga|zin [magaˈtsiːn] NT -s, -e **a** (= *Lager*) storeroom; (*esp für Sprengstoff, Waffen, old*: = *Speicher*) magazine; (= *Bibliotheksmagazin*) stockroom **b** (*am Gewehr*) magazine **c** (= *Zeitschrift*) magazine, journal; (*TV, Rad*) magazine programme (*Brit*) *or* program (*US*)

Ma|ga|zi|ner [magaˈtsiːnɐ] M -s, - (*Sw*), **Ma|ga|zi|neur** [magatsiˈnøːɐ] M -s, -e (*Aus*) storeman

Ma|ga|zi|ne|rin [magaˈtsiːnərɪn] F -, -nen (*Sw*), **Ma|ga|zi|neu|rin** [magatsiˈnøːrɪn] F -, -nen (*Aus*) storewoman

Ma|ga|zin|sen|dung F (*Rad, TV*) magazine programme (*Brit*) *or* program (*US*)

Magd [maːkt] F -, ⸚e [ˈmɛːkdə] **a** (*old*) (= *Dienstmagd*) maid; (= *Landarbeiterin*) farm lass (*dial*) *or* girl; (= *Kuhmagd*) milkmaid **b** (*liter*: = *Mädchen, Jungfrau*) maid(en) (*old, liter*); **Maria, die reine ~** Mary, the holy virgin; **Maria, die ~ des Herrn** Mary, the handmaid of the Lord

Mäg|de|lein [ˈmɛːkdəlain] NT -s, -, **Mägd|lein** [ˈmɛːktlain] NT -s, - (*obs, poet*) maid(en) (*old, liter*)

Ma|gen [ˈmaːgn] M -s, ⸚ [ˈmɛːgn] *or* - stomach, tummy (*inf*); **mit leerem ~, auf nüchternen ~** on an empty stomach; **mein ~ rebelliert** (= *mir ist schlecht*) I feel sick; **(die) Liebe geht durch den ~** (*Prov*) the way to a man's heart is through his stomach (*prov*); **etw liegt jdm** (**schwer** *or* **wie Blei** *or* **bleiern**) **im ~** (*inf*) sth lies heavily on *or* in sb's stomach; (*fig*) sth preys on sb's mind; **jdm auf den ~ schlagen** (*inf*) to upset sb's stomach, to give sb an upset stomach; (*fig*) to upset sb; **sich** (*dat*) **den ~ verderben** *or* **verkorksen** (*inf*) to get an upset stomach, to upset one's stomach → **umdrehen** VR, **verrenken** VT

Magen-: **Ma|gen|aus|gang** M (*Anat*) pyloric orifice (*spec*); **Ma|gen|be|schwer|den** PL stomach *or* tummy (*inf*) trouble *sing*; **Ma|gen|bit|ter** M bitters *pl*; **Ma|gen|blu|tung** F stomach bleeding, stomach haemorrhaging (*Brit*) *or* hemorrhaging (*US*); **Ma|gen-Darm-Ka|tarr(h)** ▲ M gastroenteritis; **Ma|gen-Darm-Trakt** M gastrointestinal tract; **Ma|gen|drü|cken** NT -s, - stomachache; **Ma|gen|ge|gend** F stomach region; **Ma|gen|ge|schwür** NT stomach ulcer; **Ma|gen|gru|be** F pit of the stomach; **ein Schlag in die ~** a blow in the solar plexus; **Ma|gen|knur|ren** NT -s, *no pl* tummy (*inf*) *or* stomach rumbles *pl*; **Ma|gen|krampf** M stomach cramp; **ma|gen|krank** ADJ with stomach trouble; **~ sein** to have stomach trouble; **jdn ~ machen** to give sb stomach trouble; **Ma|gen|krebs** M stomach cancer, cancer of the stomach; **Ma|gen|lei|den** NT stomach disorder *or* complaint; **ma|gen|lei|dend** ADJ = **magenkrank**; **Ma|gen|mit|tel** NT stomachic (*spec*); **jdm ein ~ verschreiben** to give sb something for his stomach; **Ma|gen|saft** M gastric juice; **Ma|gen|säu|re** F gastric acid; **Ma|gen|schleim|haut** F stomach lining; **Ma|gen|schleim|haut|ent|zün|dung** F gastritis; **Ma|gen|schmer|zen** PL stomachache *sing*, tummy-ache *sing* (*inf*); (= *Krämpfe auch*) stomach pains *pl*; **Ma|gen|son|de** F stomach probe; **Ma|gen|spie|ge|lung** F gastroscopy (*spec*); **Ma|gen|spü|lung** F irrigation of the stomach

Ma|gen|ta [maˈdʒɛnta] NT -, *no pl* magenta

Ma|gen-: **Ma|gen|ver|stim|mung** F upset stomach, stomach upset; **Ma|gen|weh** NT = **Magenschmerzen**

ma|ger [ˈmaːgɐ] ADJ **a** (= *fettarm*) *Fleisch* lean; *Kost* low-fat, low in fat **b** (= *dünn*) thin, skinny (*inf*); (= *abgemagert*) emaciated; (*Typ*) *Druck* roman **c** (= *unfruchtbar*) *Boden, Felder* poor, infertile **d** (= *dürftig*) meagre (*Brit*), meager (*US*); *Ernte, Ertrag* lean, meagre (*Brit*), meager (*US*); (*Tech*) *Mischung* weak; *Ergebnis* poor; **die sieben ~en Jahre** the seven lean years ADV **a** (= *fettarm*) **~ essen** to be on a low-fat diet; **~ kochen** to cook low-fat meals; **etw ist ~ zubereitet** sth is low-fat **b** (= *dürftig*) meagrely (*Brit*), meagerly (*US*); **~ ausfallen** to be meagre (*Brit*) *or* meager (*US*) **c** (*Typ*) **~ drucken/setzen** to print/typeset in roman

Ma|ger|keit F -, *no pl* **a** (= *Fettarmut*) (*von Fleisch*) leanness; (*von Kost*) low fat content **b** (*von Mensch*) thinness; (= *Abgemagertheit*) emaciation

Ma|ger-: **Ma|ger|milch** F skimmed milk; **Ma|ger|quark** [-kvark] M low-fat cottage cheese (*US*) *or* curd cheese; **Ma|ger|sucht** F (*Med*) anorexia; **ma|ger|süch|tig** ADJ (*Med*) anorexic; **~ sein** to be anorexic

Ma|gie [maˈgiː] F -, *no pl* magic

Ma|gier [ˈmaːgiɐ] M -s, -, **Ma|gie|rin** [-iərɪn] F -, -nen magician; **die drei ~** the three Magi

Ma|gi|not-Li|nie F , **Ma|gi|not|linie** [maʒiˈnoː-] F Maginot Line

ma|gisch [ˈmaːgɪʃ] ADJ magic(al); *Quadrat*, (*Tech*) *Auge*, (*Econ*) *Dreieck*, (*Phys*) *Zahlen* magic; **nach ~en Vorstellungen** according to various concepts of magic; **mit ~er Gewalt** with magical force; (*fig*) as if by magic ADV magically; **von jdm/etw ~ angezogen werden** to be attracted to sb/sth as if by magic

Ma|gis|ter [maˈgɪstɐ] M -s, - ~ (*Artium*) (*Univ*) M.A., Master of Arts; ~ (**Pharmaciae**) (*Aus*) MSc *or* Master of Science in pharmacology

---

MAGISTER

In Germany **Magister** is an academic degree awarded in the arts. Students must study for at least eight semesters, write a **Magisterarbeit** and take an examination in one principal subject and two subsidiary subjects.

Ma|gis|tra|le [magɪsˈtraːlə] F -, -n (*Mot*) main thoroughfare

Ma|gist|rat [magɪsˈtraːt] M -(e)s, -e municipal authorities *pl*

Mag|ma [ˈmagma] NT -s, **Magmen** [-mən] (*Geol*) magma

mag|na cum lau|de [ˈmagna ˈkʊm ˈlaudə] ADV (*Univ*) magna cum laude

Mag|nat [maˈgnaːt] M -en, -en, **Mag|na|tin** [maˈgnaːtɪn] F -, -nen magnate (*auch Hist*)

Mag|ne|sia [maˈgneːzia] F -, *no pl* (*Chem*) magnesia; (*Sport*) chalk

Mag|ne|si|um [maˈgneːziʊm] NT -s, *no pl* (*abbr* **Mg**) magnesium

Mag|net [maˈgneːt] M -s *or* -en, -e(n) (*lit, fig*) magnet

Magnet- *in cpds* magnetic; **Mag|net|auf|zeich|nung** F magnetic recording; **Mag|net|bahn** F magnetic railway; **Mag|net|band** [-bant] NT *pl* **-bänder** magnetic tape; **Mag|net|berg** M (*liter*) mountain believed to draw ships to their doom by its magnetic properties; **Mag|net|bild|ver|fah|ren** NT video recording; **Mag|net|ei|sen|stein** M lodestone, magnetite; **Mag|net|feld** NT magnetic field

mag|ne|tisch [maˈgneːtɪʃ] ADJ (*lit, fig*) magnetic; **eine ~e Anziehungskraft auf jdn ausüben** (*fig*) to have a magnetic attraction for sb ADV magnetically; **von etw ~ angezogen werden** (*fig*) to be drawn to sth like a magnet

mag|ne|ti|sie|ren [magnetiˈziːrən] *ptp* **magnetisiert** VT *Metall* to magnetize; *jdn* to use animal magnetism on

Mag|ne|tis|mus [magneˈtɪsmʊs] M -, *no pl* magnetism; (= *Mesmerismus*) animal magnetism; (*heutzutage*) form of healing where the illness is supposedly drawn out by the magnetic power of the healer

Mag|net-: **Mag|net|kar|te** F magnetic card; (*von Bank etc auch*) cashpoint card (*Brit*), ATM card (*US*); **Mag|net|kar|ten|le|ser** M magnetic card reader; **Mag|net|kern** M (*magnet*) core; **Mag|net|kom|pass** ▲ M magnetic compass; **Mag|net|na|del** F magnetic needle

Mag|ne|to- [magneto-]: **Mag|ne|to|phon®** [magneˈtoːfoːn] NT -(e)s, -e steel tape recorder, Magnetophone®; **Mag|ne|to|phon|band®** [-bant] NT *pl* **-bänder** steel recording tape; **Mag|ne|to|sphä|re** F magnetosphere

---

Magnet-: Magnet|plat|te F (Comput) magnetic disk; **Magnet|pol** M magnetic pole; **Magnet|schal|ter** M (Aut) solenoid switch; **Magnet|schwe|be|bahn** F magnetic levitation railway; **Magnet|spu|le** F coil; **Magnet|strei|fen** M magnetic strip; **Magnet|strei|fen|kar|te** F magnetic strip card; **Magnet|ton|band** NT magnetic tape; **Magnet|ton|ge|rät** NT magnetic (sound) recorder; **Magnet|ton|ver|fah|ren** NT magnetic (sound) recording; **Magnet|zün|dung** F (Aut) magneto ignition

Mag|ni|fi|kat [ma'gni:fikat] NT -(s), no pl Magnificat

Mag|ni|fi|zenz [magnifi'tsɛnts] F -, -en (Univ) (**Euer** or **Eure**)**/Seine ~** Your/His Magnificence (title given to German university rectors)

Mag|no|lie [mag'no:liə] F -, -n magnolia

Mag|num|fla|sche ['magnʊm-] F magnum (bottle)

Mag|yar [ma'dja:ɐ] M -en, -en, **Mag|ya|rin** [ma'dja:rɪn] F -, -nen (Aus, liter) Magyar

mag|ya|risch [ma'dja:rɪʃ] ADJ (Aus, liter) Magyar

mäh [mɛ:] INTERJ baa

Ma|ha|go|ni [maha'go:ni] NT -s, no pl mahogany

Ma|ha|rad|scha [maha'ra:dʒa] M -s, -s maharaja(h)

Ma|ha|ra|ni [maha'ra:ni] F -, -s maharani

Mäh|bin|der M reaper-binder, reaping-and-binding machine

Mahd¹ [ma:t] F -, -en [-dn] (dial) reaping; (= das Abgemähte) cut grass

Mahd² NT -(e)s, ⸚er ['mɛ:də] (Sw, Aus) mountain pasture

Mäh|der ['mɛ:dɐ] M -s, -, **Mäh|de|rin** [-ərɪn] F -, -nen (dial: = Mäher) mower; (von Getreide) reaper

Mäh|dre|scher M combine (harvester)

mä|hen¹ ['mɛ:ən] VT Gras to cut; Getreide auch to reap; Rasen to mow VI to reap; (= Rasen mähen) to mow

mä|hen² VI (Schaf) to bleat

Mä|her ['mɛ:ɐ] M -s, -, **Mä|he|rin** [-ərɪn] F -, -nen mower; (von Getreide) reaper

Mahl [ma:l] NT -(e)s, -e or ⸚er ['mɛ:lə] (liter) meal, repast (form); (= Gastmahl) banquet; **beim ~e sitzen** (liter) to be at table

mah|len ['ma:lən] pret **mahlte** ['ma:ltə], ptp **gemahlen** [gə'ma:lən] VT to grind VI to grind; (Räder) to spin

Mahl-: Mahl|gang M pl **-gänge** (Tech) pair of millstones; **Mahl|gut** NT material to be ground; (= Getreide) grain (to be ground), grist; **Mahl|werk** NT mill, milling device

mäh|lich ['mɛ:lɪç] ADJ, ADV (poet) = **allmählich**

Mahl-: Mahl|statt F pl **-stätte** [-ʃtɛtə], **Mahl|stät|te** F (Hist) meeting place of the Teutons; **Mahl|stein** M millstone; (prähistorisch) quern; **Mahl|strom** M = **Malstrom**; **Mahl|zahn** M grinder

Mahl|zeit F meal; **~!** (inf) greeting used around mealtimes (= guten Appetit) enjoy your meal; (**prost**) **~!** (iro inf) that's just great (inf) or swell (esp US inf)

Mäh|ma|schi|ne F mower; (= Rasenmähmaschine auch) mowing machine; (= Getreidemähmaschine) reaper

Mahn|be|scheid M , **Mahn|brief** M reminder

Mäh|ne ['mɛ:nə] F -, -n (lit, fig) mane; **du hast wieder eine ~!** (inf) you're looking rather wild and woolly again (inf)

mah|nen ['ma:nən] VT a (= erinnern) to remind (wegen, an +acc of); (warnend, missbilligend) to admonish (wegen, an +acc on account of); **Schuldner** to send a reminder to; **jdn schriftlich/brieflich ~** to remind sb in writing/by letter; **gemahnt werden** (Schuldner) to receive a

reminder; **eine ~de Stimme** (liter) an admonishing or admonitory voice

b (= auffordern) **jdn zur Eile/Geduld/Ruhe** etc **~** to urge or (warnend, missbilligend) admonish sb to hurry/be patient/be quiet etc; **jdn zur Mäßigkeit ~** to urge sb to be moderate, to urge moderation on sb

VI a (wegen Schulden etc) to send a reminder **b zur Eile/Geduld/Vorsicht ~** to urge haste/patience/caution; **der Lehrer mahnte zur Ruhe** the teacher called for quiet; **die Uhr mahnte zur Eile** the clock indicated that haste was called for

Mah|ner ['ma:nɐ] M -s, -, **Mah|ne|rin** ['ma:nərɪn] F -, -nen (geh) admonisher (geh)

Mahn-: Mahn|ge|bühr F reminder fee; **Mahn|mal** NT memorial; **Mahn|ruf** M (liter) exhortation; **Mahn|schrei|ben** NT reminder

Mah|nung ['ma:nʊŋ] F -, -en a (= Ermahnung) exhortation; (warnend, missbilligend) admonition **b** (geh: = warnende Erinnerung) reminder; **zur ~ an** (+acc) in memory of **c** (= Mahnbrief) reminder

Mahn-: Mahn|ver|fah|ren NT collection proceedings pl; **Mahn|wa|che** F (Pol) picket; **eine demonstrative ~** a protest picket; **jdn als institutionelle ~ einstellen** to appoint sb as an official watchdog

Mäh|re ['mɛ:rə] F -, -n (old, pej) nag, jade

Mäh|ren ['mɛ:rən] NT -s Moravia

mäh|risch ['mɛ:rɪʃ] ADJ Moravian

Mai [mai] M -(e)s or - or (poet) **-en**, **-e** May; **der Erste ~** May Day; **des Lebens ~** (poet) the springtime of one's life (poet); **wie einst im ~** (as if) in the first flush of youth, as if young again → auch **März**

Mai- in cpds May; (Pol) May Day; **Mai|an|dacht** F May devotions pl; **Mai|baum** M maypole; **Mai|bow|le** F white wine punch (flavoured with woodruff)

Maid [mait] F -, -en [-dn] (old, liter) maid(en) (old, liter); (hum) wench (old, hum)

Mai-: Mai|fei|er F May Day celebrations pl; **Mai|fei|er|tag** M (form) May Day (no art); **Mai|glöck|chen** NT lily of the valley; **Mai|kä|fer** M cockchafer; **Mai|kö|ni|gin** F Queen of (the) May; **Mai|kund|ge|bung** F May Day rally

Mail [me:l] F -, -s (Comput) e-mail, mail

Mai|land ['mailant] NT -s Milan

Mai|län|der¹ ['mailɛndɐ] ADJ attr Milan; **die ~ Scala** La Scala (in Milan)

Mai|län|der² ['mailɛndɐ] M -s, -, **Mai|län|de|rin** F -, -nen Milanese

mai|län|disch ['mailɛndɪʃ] ADJ Milanese

Mail|box ['me:lbɔks] F (Comput) mailbox

mai|len ['me:ln] VTI (Comput) to e-mail

Mai|ling ['me:lɪŋ, 'meilɪŋ] NT -s, -s mailing, mailshot (Brit); **etw per ~ erhalten** to receive sth in a mailing; **ein ~ an alle Kunden durchführen** to send a mailing or mailshot (Brit) to all customers

Main [main] M -s Main

Main|li|nie F line formed by the River Main roughly dividing North and South Germany

Mais [mais] M -es, no pl maize, (Indian) corn (esp US)

Mais-: Mais|brei M thick maize porridge; **Mais|brot** NT corn bread

Maisch|bot|tich M mash tub; (für Wein) fermenting vat

Mai|sche ['maiʃə] F -, -n (= Biermaische) mash; (= Weinmaische) must; (= Schnapsmaische) wort

mai|schen ['maiʃn] VT to mash; Trauben to ferment

Mais-: Mais|flo|cken PL cornflakes pl; **mais|gelb** ADJ corn-coloured (Brit), corn-colored (US); **Mais|kol|ben** M corn cob; (Gericht) corn on the cob; **Mais|korn** NT pl **-körner** grain of maize or corn (esp US); (als Sammel-

griff) maize or corn (esp US) grain; **Mais|mehl** NT maize or corn (esp US) meal

Mai|so|net|te [mɛzo'nɛt] F -, -n, **Mai|so|net-te-Woh|nung** F maisonette

Mais|stär|ke F cornflour (Brit), cornstarch (US)

Maî|tre de plai|sir [mɛtrə(də)plɛ'zi:r] M - - -, -s - - (old, hum) Master of Ceremonies

Maî|tre d'hô|tel [mɛtrədo'tɛl] M - -, -s - maître d'hôtel

Ma|jes|tät [majɛs'tɛ:t] F -, -en a (Titel) Majesty; **Seine/Ihre/Eure** or **Eure)/Seine ~** His/Her/Your Majesty; **die (kaiserlichen** etc) **~en ...** their (Imperial etc) Majesties ... **b** (liter) majesty, grandeur

ma|jes|tä|tisch [majɛs'tɛ:tɪʃ] ADJ majestic ADV majestically

Ma|jes|täts-: Ma|jes|täts|be|lei|di|gung F lèse-majesté; **Ma|jes|täts|ver|bre|chen** NT (Jur) crime against the crown

Ma|jo ['ma:jo] F -, -s (inf: = Majonäse) mayo (inf)

Ma|jo|li|ka [ma'jo:lika] F -, -s or **Majoliken** [-kn] majolica

Ma|jo|nä|se [majo'nɛ:zə] F -, -n mayonnaise

Ma|jor [ma'jo:ɐ] M -s, -e, **Ma|jo|rin** [ma'jo:rɪn] F -, -nen (Mil) major; (in Luftwaffe) squadron leader (Brit), major (US)

Ma|jo|ran ['majora:n, 'ma:joran] M -s, -e marjoram

Ma|jo|rat [majo'ra:t] NT -(e)s, -e (old) a (Jur) primogeniture **b** (= Erbgut) estate to which the eldest son is entitled

Ma|jo|ret|te [majo'rɛtə] F -, -n or -s majorette

Ma|jo|rin F → **Major**

ma|jo|ri|sie|ren [majori'zi:rən] ptp **majorisiert** VT to outvote

Ma|jo|ri|tät [majori'tɛ:t] F -, -en majority; **die ~ haben** to have a majority

Ma|jo|ri|täts-: Ma|jo|ri|täts|be|schluss ▲ M majority decision; **Ma|jo|ri|täts|prin|zip** NT principle of majority rule; **Ma|jo|ri|täts|wahl** F election by a simple majority, first-past-the-post election (Brit)

Ma|jors|rang M (Mil) rank of major; **im ~ sein** to hold the rank of major

Ma|jorz [ma'jɔrts] M -es, no pl (Sw) first-past-the-post system; (= Mehrheit) majority

Ma|jus|kel [ma'jʊskl] F -, -n (geh) majuscule (spec), capital (letter)

MAK [ɛm|a:'ka:] abbr von **Maximale Arbeitsplatzkonzentration** maximum permitted exposure level of pollution at the place of work **~-Liste** list of products or materials which are harmful to health

ma|ka|ber [ma'ka:bɐ] ADJ macabre; Witz, Geschichte sick

Ma|kak [ma'ka:k, 'ma:kak] M -s or -en, -e, (Zool) macaque

Ma|ke|do|ni|en [make'do:niən] NT -s Macedonia

Ma|ke|do|ni|er [make'do:niɐ] M -s, -, **Ma|ke|do|ni|e|rin** [-iərɪn] F -, -nen Macedonian

ma|ke|do|nisch [make'do:nɪʃ] ADJ Macedonian

Ma|kel ['ma:kl] M -s, - a (= Schandfleck) stigma; **ohne ~** without a stain on one's reputation; (Rel) unblemished; **ein ~ auf seiner blütenreinen Weste** a blot on his escutcheon (Brit), a stain on his reputation; **mit einem ~ behaftet sein** (liter) to be stigmatized **b** (= Fehler) blemish; (von Waren) flaw, defect; **ohne ~** without blemish, flawless

Mä|ke|lei [mɛkə'lai] F -, -en carping no pl, fault-finding no pl (an +dat, über +acc about, over)

mä|ke|lig ['mɛ:kəlɪç] ADJ (inf) finicky (inf)

ma|kel|los ADJ Reinheit, Frische spotless; Charakter, Lebenswandel, Gesinnung unimpeachable; Figur, Haut, Frisur perfect, flawless; Kleidung, Haare immaculate; Alibi watertight; Vortrag, Spiel flawless; *Klang (von Instrument)* perfect; *Englisch, Deutsch* flawless, perfect **ADV** *rein* spotlessly; ~ **gekleidet sein** to be impeccably dressed; ~ **weiß** spotless white

Ma|kel|lo|sig|keit F -, no pl (= *Reinheit*) spotlessness; *(moralisch)* unimpeachability; *(von Haut, Vortrag, Spiel)* flawlessness

ma|keln ['ma:kln] **VI** **a** *(St Ex, Fin)* to act as a broker **b** *(Telec)* to make a conference call **VT** *(St Ex, Fin)* to be a broker for

mä|keln ['mɛːkln] VI *(inf)* (= *nörgeln)* to carp, to cavil *(an +dat* at); (= *zu wählerisch sein)* to be finicky *(inf) (an +dat* about, over)

Make-up [meːkˈʔap] NT -s, -s make-up; *(flüssig)* foundation, liquid make-up; **sie braucht zwei Stunden fürs** ~ she needs two hours for her make-up *or* to put on her make-up

Mak|ka|bä|er [makaˈbɛːɐ] PL Maccabees *pl*

Mak|ka|ro|ni [makaˈroːni] PL macaroni *sing*

Mak|ler ['maːklɐ] M -s, -, **Mak|le|rin** [-ərɪn] F -, -nen broker; (= *Grundstücksmakler)* estate agent *(Brit)*, real-estate agent *(US)*; *(fig)* middleman; **der ehrliche** ~ *(fig)* the honest broker

Mäk|ler M -s, -, **Mäk|le|rin** F -, -nen **a** *(inf)* *(nörglerisch)* fault-finder, carper; *(wählerisch)* fusspot *(inf)* **b** (= *Makler)* broker; (= *Grundstücksmakler)* estate agent *(Brit)*, real-estate agent *(US)*

Mak|ler-: **Mak|ler|bü|ro** NT *(St Ex)* broker's office; *(für Immobilien)* estate agent's office *(Brit)*, realtor's office *(US)*; **Mak|ler|ge|bühr** F *(St Ex)* broker's commission, brokerage; *(für Immobilie)* estate agent's fee *(Brit)*, realtor's fee *(US)*

mäk|lig ['mɛːklɪç] ADJ *(inf)* finicky *(inf)*

Ma|ko ['maːko] M OR F OR NT -(s), -s *(Tex)* Egyptian cotton

Mak|re|le [maˈkreːlə] F -, -n mackerel

Mak|ro ['makro] NT -s, -s *(Comput)* macro

Makro-, **makro-** [makro] *in cpds* macro-; **Mak|ro|be|fehl** M *(Comput)* macro command; **mak|ro|bio|tisch** [-ˈbioːtɪʃ] **ADJ** macrobiotic **ADV** **sich** ~ **ernähren** to be on a macrobiotic diet; **Mak|ro|kli|ma** NT macroclimate; **Mak|ro|kos|mos** M macrocosm

Mak|ro|ne [maˈkroːnə] F -, -n macaroon

Makro-: **Mak|ro|öko|no|mie** F macroeconomics *sing;* **Mak|ro|pha|ge** [makroˈfaːgə] F -, -n *(Med* = *Fresszelle)* macrophage; **mak|ro|ze|phal** [-tseˈfaːl] ADJ megacephalic

Ma|ku|la|tur [makulaˈtuːɐ] F -, -en *(Typ)* wastepaper; *(fig pej)* rubbish; ~ **reden** *(inf)* to talk rubbish *(Brit inf)* or trash *(inf)*

Ma|ku|la|tur|bo|gen M *pl* -bogen *(Typ)* waste *or* spoiled sheet

ma|ku|lie|ren [makuˈliːrən] *ptp* **makuliert** VT to pulp

mal¹ [maːl] ADV *(Math)* times; *(bei Maßangaben)* by; **ein** ~ **eins ist eins** one times one is one; **zwei** ~ **zwei** *(Math)* two times two, two twos, twice two *(Brit);* **zwei** ~ **drei ist (gleich) sechs** two times *or* twice *(Brit)* three is *or* equals or are six

mal² ADV *(inf)* = **einmal**

-mal ADV *suf* times; **drei-/fünfmal** three/five times

Mal¹ [maːl] NT -(e)s, -e *or (poet)* =er ['mɛːlɐ] **a** (= *Fleck)* mark; *(fig liter:* = *Kennzeichen)* brand, mark, sign **b** *(liter:* = *Ehrenmal)* memorial, monument **c** *(Sport) (Schlagball)* base; *(Rugby)* posts *pl;* (= *Malfeld)* touch

Mal² NT -(e)s, -e time; **das eine** ~ once; **erinnerst du dich an das eine** ~ **in Düsseldorf?** do you remember that time in Düsseldorf?; **nur das eine** ~ just (the) once; **(nur) dieses eine** ~ (just) this once; **das eine oder andere** ~ now and then *or* again, from time to time; **ein/kein einziges** ~ once/not once; **wenn du bloß ein einziges** ~ **auf mich hören würdest** if you would only listen to me for once; **manch liebes** ~ *(dat-*

ed) **manches liebe** ~ *(dated)* many a time; **ein für alle** ~**(e)** once and for all; **ein über das andere** ~, **ein ums andere** ~, **ein** ~ **über das** *or* **ums andere** ~ time after time; **voriges** *or* **das vorige** ~ the time before; **das soundsovielte** *or* **x-te** ~ *(inf)* the umpteenth *(inf)* or nth time; **ein erstes** ~ *(liter)* for the first time ever; **ein letztes** ~ *(liter)* one last time; **als ich letztes** *or* **das letzte** ~ **in London war** (the) last time I was in London; **beim ersten** ~**(e)** the first time; **beim zweiten/letzten** etc ~ the second/last *etc* time; **zum ersten/letzten** etc ~ for the first/last *etc* time; **zu verschiedenen** ~**en** at various times; **zu wiederholten** ~**en** repeatedly, time and again; **von** ~ **zu** ~ each *or* every time; **er wird von** ~ **zu** ~ **besser/dümmer** he gets better and better/more and more stupid, he gets better/more stupid each *or* every time; **für dieses** ~ for the time being, for now; **mit einem** ~**(e)** all at once, all of a sudden, suddenly

Ma|la|chit [malaˈxiːt] M -s, -e malachite

ma|lad [maˈlaːt]

ma|la|de [maˈlaːdə] ADJ *(dial)* ill, sick *(esp US)*

Ma|la|ga(wein) ['ma(ː)laga-] M -s, -s Malaga

Ma|la|ie [maˈlaɪə] M -n, -n, **Ma|lai|in** [maˈlaɪɪn] F -, -nen Malay

ma|lai|isch [maˈlaɪɪʃ] ADJ Malayan, Malay *attr;* **der Malaiische Archipel** the Malay Archipelago; **Malaiischer Bund** *(Hist)* Federation of Malaya

Ma|lai|isch(e) [maˈlaɪɪʃ] NT Malay → *auch* **Deutsch(e)**

Ma|lai|se [maˈlɛːzə] F -, -n *or (Sw)* nt -s, - *(geh)* malaise

Ma|la|ria [maˈlaːria] F -, no pl malaria

Ma|la|ria|pro|phy|la|xe F (= *Vorsorge)* malaria prophylaxis; (= *Medikament)* malaria tablets *pl;* (= *Therapie)* course of malaria tablets

Ma|la|wi [maˈlaːvi] NT -s Malawi

Ma|la|wi|er [maˈlaːviɐ] M -s, -, **Ma|la|wi|e|rin** [-iərɪn] F -, -nen Malawian

ma|la|wisch [maˈlaːvɪʃ] ADJ Malawian, Malawi *attr*

Ma|lay|sia [maˈlaɪzia] NT -s Malaysia

Ma|lay|si|er [maˈlaɪzɪɐ] M -s, -, **Ma|lay|si|e|rin** [-iərɪn] F -, -nen Malaysian

ma|lay|sisch [maˈlaɪzɪʃ] ADJ Malaysian

Mal|buch NT colouring *(Brit)* or coloring *(US)* book

Ma|le|di|ven [maleˈdiːvn] PL Maldives *pl,* Maldive Islands *pl*

ma|len ['maːlən] **VTI** **a** *(mit Pinsel und Farbe)* to paint; (= *zeichnen)* to draw; (= *langsam schreiben)* to write with painstaking care; **sich/jdn** ~ **lassen** to have one's/sb's portrait painted; **etw rosig/schwarz** ~ to paint a rosy/black *etc* picture of sth; **er hat während des Vortrags (Männchen) gemalt** he was doodling during the talk; **er malt** *(als Beruf)* he's a painter or an artist → **Teufel b** **b** *(inf:* = *streichen)* to paint **VR** **a** (= *Selbstbildnis machen)* to paint or do a self-portrait, to paint a picture of oneself **b** *(fig liter)* to show itself, to be reflected

Ma|ler ['maːlɐ] M -s, -, **Ma|le|rin** [-ərɪn] F -, -nen painter; (= *Kunstmaler auch)* artist

Ma|le|rei [maləˈraɪ] F -, -en **a** *(no pl* = *Malkunst)* art **b** (= *Bild)* painting; (= *Zeichnung)* drawing

Ma|ler|far|be F paint

Ma|le|rin F -, -nen (woman) painter; (= *Kunstmalerin auch)* artist

ma|le|risch ['maːlərɪʃ] **ADJ** **a** (= *bildnerisch)* in painting; *Talent, Können* as a painter; **das** ~**e Schaffen Leonardos** Leonardo's painting; **seine** ~**en Mittel** his technique as a painter **b** (= *pittoresk)* picturesque, scenic **ADV** (= *pittoresk)* picturesquely

Maler-: **Ma|ler|lein|wand** F artist's canvas; **Ma|ler|meis|ter(in)** M(F) *(master)* painter; **Ma|ler|schu|le** F school of painting

Mal|heur [maˈløːɐ] NT -s, -s *or* -e mishap; **ihm ist ein kleines** ~ **passiert** *(inf)* he's had a little

accident *(auch euph)* or a mishap; **das ist doch kein** ~! it's not serious

Ma|li ['maːli] NT -s Mali

Ma|li|er ['maːlɪɐ] M -s, -, **Ma|li|e|rin** [-iərɪn] F -, -nen Malian

ma|lig|ne [maˈlɪgnə] ADJ *(Med)* malignant

ma|li|zi|ös [mali'tsiøːs] **ADJ** malicious **ADV** maliciously

Mal-: **Mal|kas|ten** M paintbox; **Mal|krei|de** F artist's chalk

mall [mal] ADJ *(Naut)* variable; *(N Ger inf)* barmy *(Brit inf)*, batty *(inf)*

Mal|lor|ca [maˈjɔrka, maˈlɔrka] NT -s Majorca, Mallorca

mal|lor|qui|nisch [malɔrˈkiːnɪʃ] ADJ Majorcan

mal+neh|men VTI *sep irreg* to multiply *(mit* by)

Ma|lo|che [maˈlɔxə, maˈloːxə] F -, no pl *(inf)* graft *(Brit inf)*, hard work; **auf** ~ **sein** to be grafting *(Brit inf)* or working hard; **du musst zur** ~ you've got to go to work

ma|lo|chen [maˈlɔxn, maˈloːxn] *ptp* **malocht** VI *(inf)* to graft *(Brit inf)*, to sweat away *(inf)*

Ma|lo|cher [maˈlɔxɐ, maˈloːxɐ] M -s, -, **Ma|lo|che|rin** [-ərɪn] F -, -nen *(inf)* grafter *(Brit inf)*, hard worker

Mal|stift M crayon

Mal|strom M Maelstrom; *(fig liter)* maelstrom

Mal|ta ['malta] NT -s Malta

Mal|tech|nik F painting technique

Mal|te|ser [malˈteːzɐ] M -s, -, **Mal|te|se|rin** [-ˈteːzərɪn] F -, -nen Maltese

Malteser-: **Mal|te|ser|kreuz** NT Maltese cross *(auch Tech)*; **Mal|te|ser|or|den** M (Order of the) Knights *pl* of Malta *or* of St John; **Mal|te|ser|rit|ter** M Knight of Malta, (Knight) Hospitaller

mal|te|sisch [malˈteːzɪʃ] ADJ Maltese

Mal|to|se [malˈtoːzə] F -, no pl maltose

mal|trä|tie|ren [maltrɛˈtiːrən] *ptp* **malträtiert** VT to ill-treat, to maltreat

Ma|lus ['maːlʊs] M -ses, - [-luːs] *or* -se *(Insur)* supplementary (high-risk) premium; *(Univ)* minus point; **sein** ~ **ist ihr Bonus** his loss is her gain

Mal|ve ['malvə] F -, -n *(Bot)* mallow; (= *Stockrose)* hollyhock

mal|ven|far|ben [-farbn], **mal|ven|far|big** ADJ mauve

Mal|vi|nen [malˈviːnən] PL Falklands *pl,* Malvinas *pl*

Malz [malts] NT -es, no pl malt → **Hopfen**

Malz-: **Malz|bier** NT malt beer, ≈ stout *(Brit);* **Malz|bon|bon** NT OR M malt lozenge

Mal|zei|chen NT multiplication sign

mäl|zen ['mɛltsn] VTI to malt

Mäl|zer ['mɛltsɐ] M -s, -, **Mäl|ze|rin** [-ərɪn] F -, -nen maltster

Mäl|ze|rei [mɛltsəˈraɪ] F -, -en malt house, malting

Malz-: **Malz|ex|trakt** M malt extract; **Malz|kaf|fee** M *coffee substitute made from barley malt;* **Malz|zu|cker** M maltose, malt sugar

Ma|ma¹ ['mama] F -, -s *(inf)* mummy *(Brit)*, mommy *(US)*

Ma|ma² [maˈmaː] F -, -s *(dated)* mama *(dated)*

Mama-: **Ma|ma-** ['mama-] **Ma|ma|kind** NT *(pej)* mummy's boy/girl *(Brit)*, mommy's boy/girl *(US);* **Ma|ma|söhn|chen** NT *(pej)* mummy's darling *(Brit)*, mommy's darling *(US)*

Mam|ba ['mamba] F -, -s *(Zool)* mamba; **Schwarze** ~ black mamba; **Grüne** ~ West African mamba

Ma|me|luck [maməˈlʊk] M -en, -en *(Hist)* Mameluke

Ma|mi ['mami] F -, -s *(inf)* mummy, mommy *(US)*

Mam|mo|gra|fie ▲ [mamograˈfiː] F -, -n [-ˈfiːən] mammography

Mam|mon ['mamɔn] M **-s**, *no pl* Mammon; **der schnöde ~** Mammon, filthy lucre; **dem ~ dienen** to serve Mammon

Mam|mons|die|ner(in) M(F) (*pej*) servant of Mammon

Mam|mut ['mamʊt, 'mamuːt] NT **-s, -s** *or* **-e** mammoth

Mam|mut- *in cpds* (*lit, fig*) mammoth; (= *lange dauernd*) marathon; **Mam|mut|baum** M sequoia, giant redwood; **Mam|mut|pro|gramm** NT huge programme (*Brit*) *or* program (*US*); (*lange dauernd*) marathon programme (*Brit*) *or* program (*US*); **Mam|mut|pro|zess** ▲ M marathon trial; **Mam|mut|sit|zung** F marathon meeting

mamp|fen ['mampfn] VTI (*inf*) to munch, to chomp (*inf*); **ich brauche was zu ~** I want something to eat

Mam|sell [mam'zɛl] F **-, -en** *or* **-s** (*dated hum*) lady; (*old*: = *Wirtschafterin*) housekeeper

man¹ [man] INDEF PRON *dat* **einem**, *acc* **einen**
a you, one; (= *ich*) one; (= *wir*) we; **~ kann nie wissen** you *or* one can never tell, there's no knowing; **das tut ~ nicht** that's not done; **~ wird doch wohl noch fragen dürfen** there's no law against asking

b (= *jemand*) somebody, someone; **~ hat mir gesagt ...** I was told ..., somebody told me ...; **~ hat mir erklärt, dass ...** it was explained *or* somebody explained to me that ...; **~ hat festgestellt, dass ...** it has been established that ...

c (= *die Leute*) they *pl*, people *pl*; **früher glaubte ~, dass ...** they *or* people used to believe that ...; **~ will die alten Häuser niederreißen** they want to pull down the old houses; **diese Hemden trägt ~ nicht mehr** people don't wear these shirts any more; **~ hat öfters versucht, ...** many attempts have been made ...

d **~ wende sich an ...** apply to ... → **nehmen c**

man² ADV (*N Ger inf*) just; **denn ~ los!** let's go then!; **~ sachte!** (just) take it easy!; **jetzt ~ schnell!** we'd/you'd *etc* better hurry

Ma|na|ge|ment ['mɛnɛdʒmənt] NT **-s, -s** management

Ma|nage|ment-Buy-out ▲ ['mɛnɛdʒməntbaiaʊt] NT **-s, -s** (*Ind*) management buyout

ma|na|gen ['mɛnɛdʒn] VT (*inf*) to manage; (= *hinkriegen auch*) to fix; **ich manage das schon!** I'll manage *or* fix it somehow!

Ma|na|ger ['mɛnɛdʒɐ] M **-s, -**, **Ma|na|ge|rin** [-ərɪn] F **-, -nen** manager

Ma|na|ger-: Ma|na|ger|krank|heit F (*inf*) executivitis (*hum*); **Ma|na|ger|typ** M management *or* executive type

manch [manç] INDEF PRON **a** *inv* (*in Zusammensetzung mit ein, eine(r, s), substantiviertem Adjektiv und (geh) Substantiv*) many a; **~ eine(r)**, **~ ein Mensch** many a person, (a good) many people, quite a few people; **~ einem kann man nie Vernunft beibringen** you can never teach sense to some people; **~ anderer** many another; **~ Schönes** (*geh*) many a beautiful thing; **~ Erlebnis/ schöne Geschichte/Kind** (*all liter*) many an experience/a lovely story/a child

b (*adjektivisch*) **~e(r, s)** a good many +*pl*, a fair number +*pl*, quite a few +*pl*, many a +*sing*; (*pl*: = *einige*) some +*pl*; **~er, der ...** many a person who ..., many *pl* who ..., a good many people *pl* who ..., some (people) *pl* who ...; **~e hundert Euro** some *or* several hundreds of euros; **~es Schöne** a number of beautiful things, quite a few beautiful things

c (*substantivisch*) **~e(r)** a good many people *pl*, many a person/man/woman *etc*; (*pl*: = *einige*) some (people); **~er lernts nie** some people never learn; **~es** (= *vieles*) a good many things *pl*, a number of things *pl*, quite a few things *pl*; (= *einiges*) some things *pl*; **in ~em hat er Recht** he's right about a lot of/some things; **so** *or* **gar** (*old*) **~es** a good many things *pl*, quite a few things *pl*

man|chen|orts ['mançn'ɔrts] ADV = **mancherorts**

man|cher|lei ['mançɐ'lai] ADJ *inv* (*adjektivisch mit pl n*) various, a number of; (*substantivisch*) various things *pl*, a number of things

man|cher|orts ['mançɐ'ɔrts], **man|cher|or|ten** ['mançɐ'ɔrtn] ADV in a number of places, in many a place

Man|ches|ter [man'fɛstɐ] M **-s**, *no pl* (*Tex*) broad-ribbed cord(uroy)

manch|mal ['mançmaːl] ADV sometimes

Man|dant [man'dant] M **-en, -en**, **Man|dan|tin** [-'dantɪn] F **-, -nen** (*Jur*) client

Man|da|rin [manda'riːn] M **-s, -e** (*Hist*) mandarin

Man|da|ri|ne [manda'riːnə] F **-, -n** mandarin (orange), tangerine

Man|dat [man'daːt] NT **-(e)s, -e** **a** (= *Auftrag, Vollmacht*) mandate (*auch Pol*), authorization (+*gen* from); (*von Anwalt*) brief; (*Parl*: = *Abgeordnetensitz*) seat; **sein ~ niederlegen** (*Parl*) to resign one's seat; **imperatives ~** (*Pol*) fixed mandate **b** (= *Gebiet*) mandated territory, mandate

Man|da|tar [manda'taːɐ] M **-s, -e** **a** (*rare*: = *Beauftragter*) mandatary (*form*), agent **b** (*Aus*) member of parliament, representative

Man|da|tar|staat M mandatary

Man|dats-: Man|dats|ge|biet NT mandated territory, mandate; **Man|dats|macht** F mandatory power; **Man|dats|trä|ger(in)** M(F) mandate holder; **Man|dats|ver|lust** M loss of a seat

Man|del ['mandl] F **-, -n** **a** almond **b** (*Anat*) tonsil **c** (*obs*: *Measure*) fifteen

Man|del-: Man|del|au|gen PL (*poet*) almond eyes *pl*; **man|del|äu|gig** ADJ (*poet*) almond-eyed; **Man|del|baum** M almond tree; **Mandel|ent|zün|dung** F tonsillitis; **man|del|förmig** ADJ almond-shaped; **Man|del|kern** M almond (kernel); **Man|del|kleie** F almond meal; **Man|del|öl** NT almond oil

Man|derl ['mandɐl] NT **-s, -n** (*Aus*), **Mandl** ['mandl] NT **-s, -n** (*S Ger, inf*) **a** (= *Männchen*) little man **b** (= *Vogelscheuche*) scarecrow

Man|do|li|ne [mando'liːnə] F **-, -n** mandolin

Mand|ra|go|ra [man'draːgora] F **-, Mandragoren** [-'goːrən] (*Bot*) mandrake

Mand|rill [man'drɪl] M **-s, -e** (*Zool*) mandrill

Mand|schu ['mandʒu, 'mantʃu] NT **-(s)**, *no pl* (*Ling*) Manchu

Mand|schu|rei [mandʒu'rai, mantʃu'rai] F **- die ~** Manchuria

mand|schu|risch [man'dʒuːrɪʃ, man'tʃuːrɪʃ] ADJ Manchurian

Ma|ne|ge [ma'neːʒə] F **-, -n** ring, arena

mang [maŋ] PREP +*dat* *or acc* (*N Ger inf*) among(st)

Man|gan [maŋ'gaːn] NT **-s**, *no pl* (*abbr* **Mn**) manganese

Man|ga|nat [maŋga'naːt] NT **-s, -e** (*Chem*) manganate

Man|gan-: Man|gan|ei|sen NT ferro-manganese; **Man|gan|erz** NT manganese ore; **Mangan|stahl** M manganese steel

-man|gel M *suf in cpds* shortage of ...; (*Med*) ... deficiency; **Ärztemangel** shortage of doctors; **Vitaminmangel** vitamin deficiency

Man|gel¹ ['maŋəl] F **-, -n** mangle; (= *Heißmangel*) rotary iron; **durch die ~ drehen** to put through the mangle; (*fig inf*) to put through it (*inf*); *Prüfling etc* to put through the mill; **jdn in die ~ nehmen/in der ~ haben** (*fig inf*) to give sb a going-over (*inf*); (= *ausfragen auch*) to give sb a grilling (*inf*)

Man|gel² M **-s, ⸚** ['mɛŋl] **a** (= *Fehler*) fault; (*bei Maschine*) defect, fault; (= *Unzulänglichkeit*) fault, shortcoming; (= *Charaktermangel*) flaw

b *no pl* (= *das Fehlen*) lack (*an* +*dat* of); (= *Knappheit*) shortage (*an* +*dat* of); (*Med*) deficiency (*an* +*dat* of); **aus ~** *or* **wegen ~s an** (+*dat*) for lack of, due to a lack of; **wegen ~s an Beweisen** for lack of evidence; **~ an Vitamin C** lack of vitamin C, vitamin C deficiency; **es besteht** *or* **herrscht ~ an etw** (*dat*) there is a lack/shortage of sth; **~ an etw** (*dat*) **haben** *or* **leiden** (*liter*) to be short of sth, to lack sth, to have a lack of sth

c *no pl* (= *Entbehrung*) privation, need, want; **~ leiden** (*liter*) to go short, to suffer hardship *or* privation; **keinen ~ leiden** to want for nothing

Män|gel-: Män|gel|an|zei|ge F notification of defects; **Män|gel|be|richt** M list of faults

Man|gel-: Man|gel|be|ruf M undersubscribed *or* understaffed profession; **Man|gel|er|nährung** F malnutrition; **Man|gel|er|schei|nung** F (*Med*) deficiency symptom; **eine ~ sein** (*fig*) to be in short supply (*bei* with)

man|gel|frei, **män|gel|frei** ADJ free of faults *or* defects

man|gel|haft ADJ (= *unzulänglich, schlecht*) poor; *Beleuchtung, Ausrüstung auch* inadequate; *Informationen, Interesse* insufficient; (= *fehlerhaft*) *Sprachkenntnisse, Ware* faulty; (*Schulnote*) unsatisfactory, poor ADV poorly, inadequately; **sich in der Stadt nur ~ auskennen** not to know one's way around town very well; **er spricht nur ~ Englisch** he doesn't speak English very well

Män|gel|haf|tung F (*Jur*) liability for faults *or* defects

Man|gel|krank|heit F deficiency disease

Män|gel|lis|te F list of faults *or* defects

man|geln¹ ['maŋln] VT *Wäsche* to (put through the) mangle; (= *heiß mangeln*) to iron, to press VI to use the mangle; (*mit Heißmangel*) to use the rotary iron

man|geln² VI *impers* **es mangelt an etw** (*dat*) there is a lack of sth; (= *unzureichend vorhanden auch*) there is a shortage of sth; **er ließ es an nichts ~** he made sure that he/they *etc* lacked nothing, he made sure that nothing was lacking; **es mangelt jdm an etw** (*dat*) sb lacks sth; **es mangelt ihm an Selbstvertrauen/Erfahrung** he is lacking in *or* he lacks self-confidence/experience; **~des Selbstvertrauen/Verständnis** *etc* a lack of self-confidence/understanding *etc*; **wegen ~der Aufmerksamkeit** through not paying attention; **das Kino wurde wegen ~der Sicherheit geschlossen** the cinema was closed because of inadequate safety precautions

VI **etw mangelt jdm/einer Sache** sb/sth lacks sth; (*Verständnis, Selbstvertrauen, Erfahrung auch*) sb is lacking in sth

Män|gel|rü|ge F (*Admin*) (letter of) complaint

man|gels ['maŋls] PREP +*gen* (*form*) for lack of

Man|gel-: Man|gel|wa|re F scarce commodity, commodity in short supply; **~ sein** (*fig*) to be a rare thing; (*Ärzte, gute Lehrer etc*) not to grow on trees; **Man|gel|wä|sche** F ironing (*to be done in a rotary iron*); **Man|gel|wirt|schaft** F , *no pl* economy of scarcity

Man|go ['maŋgo] F **-, -s** *or* **-nen** [-'goːnən] (*auch* **Mangopflaume**) mango

Man|go|baum M mango tree

Man|gold ['maŋgɔlt] M **-(e)s, -e** [-də] mangel (-wurzel)

Mang|ro|ve [maŋ'groːvə] F **-, -n** mangrove

Mang|ro|ven|sumpf M mangrove swamp

Ma|nie [ma'niː] F **-, -n** [-'niːən] (*Med, fig*) mania; (*fig auch*) obsession

Ma|nier [ma'niːɐ] F **-, -en** **a** *no pl* (= *Art und Weise*) manner; (*eines Künstlers etc*) style; **in überzeugender ~** in a most convincing manner **b Manieren** PL (= *Umgangsformen*) manners; **jdm ~en beibringen** to teach sb (some) manners; **~en lernen** to learn (some) manners, to learn (how) to behave; **was sind das für ~en?** (*inf*) that's no way to behave **c** (= *Angewohnheit*) affectation

ma|nie|riert [mani'riːɐt] ADJ affected; *Benehmen auch* mannered

Ma|nie|riert|heit F -, -en affectation

Ma|nie|ris|mus [mani'rɪsmʊs] M -, no pl (Liter, Art) mannerism

ma|nie|ris|tisch [mani'rɪstɪʃ] ADJ (Liter, Art, fig) mannerist, manneristic

ma|nier|lich [ma'niːɐlɪç] **ADJ a** Kind well-mannered, well-behaved; Benehmen good **b** (inf: = einigermaßen gut) decent, reasonable; Aussehen, Frisur, Kleidung respectable **ADV** essen politely; sich benehmen properly; sich kleiden respectably

ma|ni|fest [mani'fɛst] ADJ (liter) manifest

Ma|ni|fest [mani'fɛst] NT -(e)s, -e **a** manifesto **b** (Naut) manifest

Ma|ni|fes|tant [manifes'tant] M -en, -en, **Ma|ni|fes|tan|tin** [-'tantɪn] F -, -nen (Sw) demonstrator

Ma|ni|fes|ta|ti|on [manifesta'tsioːn] F -, -en manifestation; (= offenkundiger Beweis) demonstration; (Sw: = Kundgebung) demonstration

ma|ni|fes|tie|ren [manifɛs'tiːrən] ptp **manifes|tiert** (geh) **VT** to demonstrate, to manifest **VR** (Sw) to demonstrate **VR** to manifest oneself

Ma|ni|kü|re [mani'kyːrə] F -, -n **a** (= Handpflege) manicure **b** (= Handpflegerin) manicurist

ma|ni|kü|ren [mani'kyːrən] ptp **manikürt** VT to manicure

Ma|ni|la [ma'niːla] NT -s Manil(l)a

Ma|ni|la-: Ma|ni|la|hanf M Manil(l)a (hemp); **Ma|ni|la|zi|gar|re** F Manil(l)a (cigar)

Ma|ni|ok [ma'nioːk] M -s, -s (Bot) cassava

Ma|ni|ok|wur|zel F cassava root

Ma|ni|pu|lant [manipu'lant] M -en, -en, **Ma|ni|pu|lan|tin** [-'lantɪn] F -, -nen manipulator; (Aus: = Amtshelfer) assistant

Ma|ni|pu|la|ti|on [manipula'tsioːn] F -, -en manipulation; (= Trick) manoeuvre (Brit), maneuver (US)

Ma|ni|pu|la|tor¹ [manipu'laːtoːɐ] M -s, **Manipu|latoren** [-'toːrən] (Tech) manipulator

Ma|ni|pu|la|tor² [manipu'laːtoːɐ] M -s, **Manipu|latoren** [-'toːrəm], **Ma|ni|pu|la|to|rin** [-'toːrɪn] F -, -nen (fig) conjurer, magician

ma|ni|pu|lier|bar ADJ manipulable; **leicht ~** easily manipulated; **schwer ~** difficult to manipulate; **beliebig ~** manipulable at will

Ma|ni|pu|lier|bar|keit [manipu'liːɐbaːɐkaɪt] F -, no pl manipulability

ma|ni|pu|lie|ren [manipu'liːrən] ptp **manipuliert** VT to manipulate

Ma|ni|pu|lie|rung F -, -en manipulation

ma|nisch [ˈmaːnɪʃ] ADJ manic; **~~depressiv**, **~~melancholisch** manic-depressive; **~~melancholische Krankheit** manic depression

Ma|ni|tu [ˈmaːnitu] M -s Manitou

Man|ko [ˈmaŋko] NT -s, -s **a** (Comm: = Fehlbetrag) deficit; **~ haben** (inf) or **machen** (inf) to be short (inf); **~ machen** (inf: bei Verkauf) to make a loss **b** (fig: = Nachteil) shortcoming

Mann [man] M -(e)s, **ˮer** [ˈmɛnɐ] **a** man; **ein Überschuss an Männern** a surplus of males or men; **der böse** or **schwarze ~** the bogeyman; **ein feiner ~** a (perfect) gentleman; **ein ~ aus dem Volk(e)** a man of the people; **der erste ~ sein** (fig) to be in charge; **der ~ im Mond(e)** the man in the moon; **ein ~ der Feder/Wissenschaft** a man of letters/science; **ein ~ des Todes** a dead man, a man marked for death; **ein ~ von Wort** a man of his word; **wo Männer noch Männer sind** where men are men; **er ist unser ~** he's the man for us, he's our man; **er ist nicht der ~ dafür** he's not the man for that; (= nicht seine Art) he's not the sort; **drei ~ hoch** (inf) three of them together; **wie ein ~** as a or one man; **auf den ~ dressiert sein** to be trained to go for people; **etw an den ~ bringen** (inf) to get rid of sth; **seinen ~ stehen** to hold one's own; (= auf eigenen Füßen stehen) to stand on one's own two feet; **einen kleinen ~ im Ohr haben** (hum) to be crazy (inf); **und ein ~, ein Wort, er hats auch gemacht** and, as good as his

word, he did it; **~ an ~** close together, next to one another; **~ für ~** (= einzeln hintereinander) one after the other; (= allesamt) every single one; **~ gegen ~** man against man; **pro ~** per head; **ein Gespräch unter Männern** or **von ~ zu ~** a man-to-man talk → **Mannen, Not a, tot a**

b (= Ehemann) husband; **jdn an den ~ bringen** (inf) to marry sb off (inf), to find sb a husband; **~ und Frau werden** to become man and wife

c pl **Leute** (= Besatzungsmitglied) hand, man; **20 ~** 20 hands or men; **mit ~ und Maus untergehen** to go down with all hands; (Passagierschiff) to go down with no survivors → **Bord¹**

d pl **Leute** (= Teilnehmer, Sport, Cards) player, man; **auf den ~ spielen** to play the ball at one's opponent; (beim Zuspielen) to pass accurately; **den dritten ~ spielen** (Cards) to play or take the third hand

e (inf: als Interjektion) (my) God (inf); (auffordernd, bewundernd, erstaunt) (my) God (inf), hey, (hey) man (inf); **~, das kannst du doch nicht machen!** hey, you can't do that!; **mach schnell, ~!** hurry up, man!; **~, oh ~!** oh boy! (inf); **(mein) lieber ~!** my God! (inf); (erstaunt, bewundernd auch) wow! (inf)

Man|na [ˈmana] NT -(s), no pl F -, no pl (Bibl, fig) manna (from heaven)

mann|bar ADJ **a** Junge sexually mature; (= mutig) brave **b** Mädchen marriageable

Männ|chen [ˈmɛnçən] NT -s, - dim von **Mann** **a** little man; (= Zwerg) man(n)ikin; **~ malen** to draw (little) matchstick men (Brit) or stickmen (US), ≈ to doodle **b** (Biol) male; (= Vogelmännchen) male, cock **c** **~ machen** (Tier) to sit up on its hind legs; (Hund) to (sit up and) beg; (pej inf) (Mensch) to grovel; (hum: Soldat) to jump smartly to attention

Mann|de|ckung F (Sport) man-to-man marking, one-on-one defense (US); **einen Spieler in ~ nehmen** to mark or guard (US) a player man-to-man or closely

Män|ne [ˈmɛnə] M -, no pl **a** (dial) dim von **Hermann** **b** (inf: = Ehemann) hubby (inf)

Man|nen [ˈmanən] PL (Hist: = Gefolgsleute) men pl

Man|ne|quin [manə'kɛ̃ː, ˈmanəkɛ̃ː] NT -s, -s (fashion) model

Män|ner pl von **Mann**

Män|ner- in cpds men's; (= eines bestimmten Mannes) man's; **Män|ner|be|kannt|schaft** F usu pl man friend, boyfriend; **von ~en leben** to earn one's living from prostitution; **Män|ner|be|ruf** M male profession; **Män|ner|bund** M pl -bünde male organization; **Män|ner|chor** M male-voice choir; **Män|ner|do|mä|ne** F male domain; **technische Berufe waren früher ~** technical professions used to be a male preserve or domain; **Män|ner|fang** M auf ~ aus|gehen/sein to go/be looking for a man/men; (zwecks Heirat) to go/be husband-hunting; **Män|ner|freund|schaft** F friendship between men; **er hat immer ~en vorgezogen** he has always preferred friendship with other men; **Män|ner|ge|fäng|nis** NT men's prison; **Män|ner|ge|sang|ver|ein** M male choral society, men's glee club (US); **Män|ner|ge|schich|te** F affair with a man; (= Erlebnisse) sexploits (hum inf), experiences with men; **Män|ner|ge|sell|schaft** F (Sociol) male-dominated society; (= Gesellschaft von Männern) all-male company; **Män|ner|grup|pe** F men's group; **Män|ner|hass** ▲ M hatred of men; **Män|ner|haus** NT men's house; **Män|ner|herr|schaft** F male domination; **Män|ner|klos|ter** NT monastery; **Män|ner|ma|ga|zin** NT magazine for men; **män|ner|mor|dend** ADJ man-eating; **Män|ner|sa|che** F (Angelegenheit) man's business; (Arbeit) job for a man, man's job; **~n** men's affairs; **Fußball war früher ~** football used to be a male preserve or domain; **Män|ner|sport** M men's sport; **Män|ner|stim|me** F man's voice; (Mus) male voice; **Män|ner|treu** [-trɔy] F -, - (Bot) speedwell; **Män|ner|über|**

schuss ▲ M surplus of men; **Män|ner|welt** F (dated hum) **die ~** men pl

Man|nes-: Man|nes|al|ter NT manhood no art; **im besten ~ sein** to be in one's prime, to be in the prime of (one's) life; **Man|nes|jah|re** PL years pl of manhood; **in die ~ kommen** to reach manhood; **Man|nes|kraft** F (dated, hum) virility

Man|nes|mann|rohr® NT seamless metal tube, Mannesmann tube

Man|nes-: Man|nes|stolz M masculine pride; **Man|nes|wür|de** F (old) accoutrements pl (Brit) or accouterments pl (US) of manhood; (hum) dignity as a man

mann|haft **ADJ** manly no adv; (= tapfer) manful, valiant; (= entschlossen) resolute; Widerstand stout **ADV** (= tapfer) valiantly; (= entschlossen) resolutely

man|nig|fach [ˈmanɪçfax] ADJ attr manifold, multifarious

man|nig|fal|tig [ˈmanɪçfaltɪç] ADJ diverse, varied

Mann|jahr NT (Ind) man-year

Männ|lein [ˈmɛnlaɪn] NT -s, - dim von **Mann** little man; (= Zwerg) man(n)ikin; **~ und Weiblein** (hum inf) boys and girls

männ|lich [ˈmɛnlɪç] **ADJ a** male; Reim, Wort masculine **b** (fig: = mannhaft) Stärke, Mut, Entschluss, Wesen manly; Stimme masculine, manly; Auftreten masculine; Frau masculine, mannish **ADV ~ dominiert** male-dominated; **~ geprägt** masculine

Männ|lich|keit F -, no pl (fig) manliness; (von Stimme auch) masculinity; (von Auftreten) masculinity; (von Frau) masculinity, mannishness

Männ|lich|keits|wahn M machismo

Mann|loch NT (Tech) manhole

man|no [ˈmano], **man|no|mann** [ˈmanoman] INTERJ (inf) boy, boy oh boy

Manns|bild NT (dated pej) fellow, male

Mann|schaft F -, -en (Sport, fig) team; (Naut, Aviat) crew; **~(en)** (Mil) men pl

mann|schaft|lich ADJ as a team pred; **Schalkes Stärke ist die ~e Geschlossenheit** Schalke's strength is that they play together as a team

Mann|schafts- in cpds (Sport) team; **Mann|schafts|auf|stel|lung** F team line-up; (das Aufstellen) selection of the team; **Mann|schafts|dienst|grad** M (Mil) other rank usu pl; **Mann|schafts|füh|rer(in)** M(F) (Sport) (team) captain; **Mann|schafts|geist** M team spirit; **Mann|schafts|kampf** M (Sport) team event; **Mann|schafts|ka|pi|tän** M (Sport) (team) captain, skipper (inf); **Mann|schafts|kost** F (Sport) team fare; (Mil) troops' rations pl; (Naut, Aviat) crew's rations pl; **Mann|schafts|raum** M (Sport) team quarters pl; (Mil) men's quarters pl; (Naut) crew's quarters pl; (= Umkleideraum) changing rooms pl, locker rooms pl; **Mann|schafts|sie|ger** M (Sport) winning team; **Mann|schafts|spiel** M , **Mann|schafts|sport** M team sport; **Mann|schafts|ver|pfle|gung** F = Mannschaftskost; **Mann|schafts|wa|gen** M police van; (Mil) troop carrier; **Mann|schafts|wer|tung** F (Sport) team score

Manns- [ˈmans-]: **manns|hoch** ADJ as high as a man; **der Schnee liegt ~** the snow is six feet deep; **Manns|leu|te** PL (dated inf) men pl; **Manns|per|son** F (dated pej) fellow, male; **manns|toll** ADJ man-mad (esp Brit inf), mad about men; **Manns|toll|heit** F nymphomania; **Manns|volk** NT (dated inf) men pl

Mann|weib NT (pej) masculine or mannish woman

Ma|no|me|ter [mano'meːtɐ] NT -s, - (Tech) pressure gauge; **~!** (inf) wow! (inf), boy oh boy! (inf)

Ma|nö|ver [ma'nøːvɐ] NT -s, - (lit, fig) manoeuvre (Brit), maneuver (US); **ins ~ gehen** or

ziehen to go on manoeuvres (*Brit*) or maneuvers (*US*); **nach größeren ~n ...** (*Mot, fig etc*) after a lot of manoeuvring (*Brit*) or maneuvering (*US*) ...

Ma|nö|ver-: Ma|nö|ver|ge|län|de NT exercise area; (*ständig*) ranges *pl*; **Ma|nö|ver|kri|tik** F (*fig*) inquest, postmortem; **Ma|nö|ver|scha|den** M damage resulting from military manoeuvres (*Brit*) or maneuvers (*US*)

ma|növ|rie|ren [manøˈvriːrən] *ptp* **manövriert** VTI (*lit, fig*) to manoeuvre (*Brit*), to maneuver (*US*)

Ma|növ|rier-: ma|növ|rier|fä|hig ADJ manoeuvrable (*Brit*), maneuverable (*US*); (*fig*) flexible; **Ma|növ|rier|fä|hig|keit** F manoeuvrability (*Brit*), maneuverability (*US*); (*fig*) flexibility; **Ma|növ|rier|mas|se** F (= *Geldsumme*) transferable sum; (*fig*: = *Menschen*) pawns *pl* who can be pushed around; **ma|növ|rier|un|fä|hig** ADJ disabled

Man|sar|de [manˈzardə] F -, -n garret; (*Boden*) attic

Man|sar|den- *in cpds* attic; **Man|sar|den|woh|nung** F attic flat (*Brit*) or apartment; **Man|sar|den|zim|mer** NT attic room

Mansch [manʃ] M -es, *no pl* (*inf*) (= *Brei*) mush; (= *Schlamm*) mud

man|schen [ˈmanʃn] VI (*inf*) to mess around (*inf*)

Man|schet|te [manˈʃɛtə] F -, -n **a** (= *Ärmelaufschlag*) cuff; (*zur Blutdruckmessung*) blood pressure cuff **b** (= *Umhüllung*) frill **c** (*Tech*: = *Dichtung*) seal **d** (*Sport*: = *Würgegriff*) stranglehold; **~n haben** (*inf*) to be scared stupid (*inf*); **vor seinem Vater/der Prüfung hat er mächtige ~n** (*inf*) his father/the thought of the exam scares him stupid (*inf*); **~n kriegen** (*inf*) to get cold feet

Man|schet|ten|knopf M cufflink

Man|tel [ˈmantl] M -s, ⸗ [ˈmɛntl] **a** coat; (= *Umhang*) cloak → **Wind a** **b** (*Tech*) (= *Glockenmantel*) cope; (= *Rohrmantel*) jacket; (= *Geschossmantel*) jacket, casing; (= *Kabelmantel*) casing; (= *Reifenmantel*) outer tyre (*Brit*) or tire (*US*), casing **c** (*fig*) cloak, mantle; **etw mit dem ~ der christlichen Nächstenliebe zudecken** to forgive and forget sth **d** (*Fin*) share certificate **e** (*Comm*: = *Firmenmantel*) form **f** (*Zool*) mantle, pallium **g** (*Math*) curved surface

Män|tel|chen [ˈmɛntlçən] NT -s, - *dim von* **Mantel einer Sache** (*dat*) **ein ~ umhängen** to cover sth up → **Wind a**

Man|tel- *in cpds* (*Tex*) coat; **Man|tel|fut|ter** NT coat lining; **Man|tel|ge|schoss** ▲ NT jacketed bullet; **Man|tel|ge|setz** NT *general outline of a law providing guidelines for specific elaboration*; **Man|tel|pa|vi|an** M sacred or hamadryas baboon; **Man|tel|stoff** M coating, coat fabric; **Man|tel|ta|rif|ver|trag** M (*Ind*) general agreement on conditions of employment; **Man|tel|tie|re** PL tunicates *pl* (*spec*)

Man|tel-und-De|gen- *in cpds* swashbuckling

Man|tel-und-De|gen-Film M swashbuckling film

Man|tra [ˈmantra] NT -(s), -s mantra

Mantsch [mantʃ] M -es, *no pl* (*inf*) (= *Brei*) mush; (= *Schlamm*) mud

mant|schen [ˈmantʃn] VI (*inf*) to mess around (*inf*)

Ma|nu|al [maˈnuaːl] NT -s, -e **a** (*Mus*) manual **b** (*old Comm*) daily ledger

ma|nu|ell [maˈnuɛl] ADJ *Arbeit, Bedienung* manual (*adv*) manually, by hand

Ma|nu|fak|tur [manufakˈtuːɐ] F -, -en (*old, Soziol*) **a** *no pl* manufacture **b** (= *Fabrik*) factory, manufactory (*old*)

Ma|nu|fak|tur|wa|ren PL manufactured goods *pl*; (= *Textilien*) textiles *pl*

Ma|nu|skript [manuˈskrɪpt] NT -(e)s, -e manuscript; (*Rad, Film, TV*) script

Ma|o|is|mus [maoˈɪsmʊs] M -, *no pl* Maoism

Ma|o|ist [maoˈɪst] M -en, -en, **Ma|o|is|tin** [-ˈɪstɪn] F -, -nen Maoist

ma|o|is|tisch [maoˈɪstɪʃ] ADJ Maoist ADV **~ ge|sinnt** Maoist; **~ beeinflusst** influenced by (the teachings) of Mao; **~ klingend** Maoist-sounding

Ma|o|ri [ˈmauri, maˈoːri] M -(s), -(s) or f -, -(s) Maori

Map|pe [ˈmapə] F -, -n (= *Aktenhefter*) folder, file; (= *Aktentasche*) briefcase; (= *Schulmappe*) (school) bag; (= *Federmappe, Bleistiftmappe*) pencil case

Mär [mɛːɐ] F -, -en (*old*) (= *Nachricht*) tidings *pl*, news *sing*; (= *Märchen*) (fairy) tale; (*hum inf*) fairy story

Ma|ra|bu [ˈmaːrabu] M -s, -s (*Orn*) marabou

Ma|ra|but [maraˈbuːt] M -(s), -(s) (*Rel*) marabout

Ma|ra|cu|ja [maraˈkuːja] F -, -s passion fruit

Ma|ra|thon¹ [ˈmaːratɔn, ˈmaratɔn] M -s, -s marathon

Ma|ra|thon² NT -s, -s (*fig*) marathon

Ma|ra|thon- *in cpds* marathon; **Ma|ra|thon|lauf** M marathon; **Ma|ra|thon|läu|fer(in)** M(F) marathon runner; **Ma|ra|thon|sit|zung** F marathon meeting or session

Mär|chen [ˈmɛːɐçən] NT -s, - fairy tale, fairy story; (*inf*) tall story

Mär|chen- *in cpds* fairy-tale; **Mär|chen|buch** NT book of fairy tales; **Mär|chen|er|zäh|ler(in)** M(F) teller of fairy tales; (*fig*) storyteller; **Mär|chen|film** M film of a fairy tale; **mär|chen|haft** ADJ fairy-tale *attr*, fabulous; (*fig*) fabulous, fantastic ADV *reich* fabulously; *singen, malen* beautifully; **~ schön** incredibly beautiful; **Mär|chen|land** NT fairyland; **Mär|chen|prinz** M Prince Charming; (*fig auch*) fairy-tale prince; **Mär|chen|prin|zes|sin** F (*fig*) fairy-tale princess; **Mär|chen|stun|de** F story time

Mar|der [ˈmardɐ] M -s, - marten

Mar|der|fell NT , **Mar|der|pelz** M marten (fur)

Mä|re [ˈmɛːrə] F -, -n (*old*) (= *Nachricht*) tidings *pl*, news *sing*; (= *Märchen*) (fairy) tale; (*hum inf*) fairy story

Mar|ga|re|te [margaˈreːtə] F - Margaret

Mar|ga|ri|ne [margaˈriːnə, (*Aus*) -ˈriːn] F -, -n margarine

Mar|ge [ˈmarʒə] F -, -n (*Comm*) margin

Mar|ge|ri|te [margəˈriːtə] F -, -n daisy, marguerite

mar|gi|nal [margiˈnaːl] ADJ marginal ADV marginally; *betreffen, interessieren* slightly

Mar|gi|na|lie [margiˈnaːliə] F -, -n *usu pl* marginalia *pl*

Ma|ria [maˈriːa] F -s Mary; **die Mutter ~** the Virgin Mary, Our (Blessed) Lady

Ma|riä- [maˈriːɛ-]: **Ma|riä Emp|fäng|nis** F the Immaculate Conception; **Ma|riä Ge|burt** F (the) Nativity of Mary; **Ma|riä Him|mel|fahrt** F Assumption

Ma|ria|the|re|si|en|ta|ler M , **Ma|ria-The|re|si|en-Ta|ler** [-teˈreːziən-] M Maria Theresa thaler, Levant dollar

Ma|ri|en- [maˈriːən-]: **Ma|ri|en|al|tar** M Lady altar; **Ma|ri|en|bild** NT picture of the Virgin Mary; **Ma|ri|en|dich|tung** F hymns *pl* and poems *pl* in praise of the Virgin Mary; **Ma|ri|en|fest** NT Lady Day; **Ma|ri|en|kä|fer** M ladybird (*Brit*), ladybug (*US*); **Ma|ri|en|kult** M Mariolatry (= cult of the Virgin Mary); **Ma|ri|en|le|ben** NT (*Art, Liter*) Life of the Virgin Mary; **Ma|ri|en|ver|eh|rung** F adoration or veneration of the Virgin Mary

Ma|ri|hua|na [mariˈhuaːna] NT -s, *no pl* marijuana

Ma|ril|le [maˈrɪlə] F -, -n (*Aus*) apricot

Ma|ri|na [maˈriːna] F -, -s marina

Ma|ri|na|de [mariˈnaːdə] F -, -n **a** (*Cook*) marinade; (= *Soße*) mayonnaise-based sauce **b** **Marinaden** PL (= *Fischkonserven*) canned or tinned (*Brit*) fish

Ma|ri|ne [maˈriːnə] F -, -n navy

Ma|ri|ne- *in cpds* naval; **ma|ri|ne|blau** ADJ navy-blue; **Ma|ri|ne|flie|ger(in)** M(F) naval pilot; **Ma|ri|ne|flug|zeug** NT naval aircraft or plane; **Ma|ri|ne|in|fan|te|rie** F marines *pl*; **Ma|ri|ne|in|fan|te|rist(in)** M(F) marine; **Ma|ri|ne|ma|ler(in)** M(F) marine or seascape painter; **Ma|ri|ne|mi|nis|ter(in)** M(F) minister of naval affairs, ≈ Secretary of the Navy (*US*); **Ma|ri|ne|mi|nis|te|ri|um** NT ministry of naval affairs, ≈ Navy Department (*US*); **Ma|ri|ne|of|fi|zier** M naval officer

Ma|ri|ner [maˈriːnɐ] M -s, - (*inf*) sailor

Ma|ri|ne-: Ma|ri|ne|sol|dat(in) M(F) marine; **Ma|ri|ne|stütz|punkt** M naval base; **Ma|ri|ne|trup|pen** PL marines *pl*; **Ma|ri|ne|we|sen** NT navy; **ein Begriff aus dem ~** a nautical term

ma|ri|nie|ren [mariˈniːrən] *ptp* **mariniert** VT *Fisch, Fleisch* to marinate, to marinade; **marinierter Hering** pickled herring

Ma|ri|o|net|te [marioˈnɛtə] F -, -n marionette, puppet; (*fig*) puppet

Ma|ri|o|net|ten- *in cpds* puppet; **Ma|ri|o|net|ten|re|gie|rung** F puppet government; **Ma|ri|o|net|ten|spie|ler(in)** M(F) puppeteer; **Ma|ri|o|net|ten|the|a|ter** NT puppet theatre (*Brit*) or theater (*US*)

ma|ri|tim [mariˈtiːm] ADJ maritime

Mark¹ [mark] NT -(e)s, *no pl* (= *Knochenmark*) marrow; (*Bot*: = *Gewebemark*) medulla, pith; (= *Fruchtfleisch*) purée; **Brühe mit ~** (*Cook*) consommé or broth with beef marrow; **bis ins ~** (*fig*) to the core; **jdn bis ins ~ treffen** (*fig*) to cut sb to the quick; **es geht mir durch ~ und Bein** (*inf*) it goes right through me; **kein ~ in den Knochen haben** (*fig*) to have no guts or backbone; **jdm das ~ aus den Knochen saugen** (*liter*) to bleed sb dry

Mark² F -, -en **a** (= *Grenzland*) borderland, march (*arch*); **die ~ Brandenburg, die ~** (*inf*) the Mark Brandenburg, the Brandenburg Marches; **die ~en** (*Hist*) the Marches **b** (*Rugby*) touch

Mark³ F -, - or (*hum*) ⸗er [ˈmɛrkɐ] (*Hist*) mark; **Deutsche ~** German mark, Deutschmark; **vier ~ zwanzig** four marks twenty (pfennigs); **mit je|der ~ rechnen, die** or **jede ~ umdrehen** to think twice before spending anything; **mit jeder ~ rechnen müssen** to have to count every penny

mar|kant [marˈkant] ADJ (= *ausgeprägt*) clear-cut; *Schriftzüge* clearly defined; (= *hervorstechend*) *Kinn etc* prominent; (= *auffallend*) *Erscheinung, Persönlichkeit* striking ADV (= *auffallend*) strikingly; **sich ~ unterscheiden** to be strikingly different

Mark Au|rel [ˈmark auˈreːl] M - -s Marcus Aurelius

mark|durch|drin|gend (*geh*) ADJ bloodcurdling ADV **er schrie ~** his screams were bloodcurdling

Mar|ke [ˈmarkə] F -, -n **a** (*bei Lebens- und Genussmitteln*) brand; (*bei Industriegütern*) make; **du bist (vielleicht) eine ~!** (*inf*) you're a right one or fine one (*inf*); **eine komische ~** (*fig inf*) a queer or rum (*dated*) customer or character (*Brit*), an odd or a strange customer or character **b** (= *Briefmarke*) stamp; **zehn ~n à** or **zu fünfzig** ten fifty-cent stamps **c** (= *Essenmarke*) voucher; (= *Rabattmarke*) (trading) stamp; (= *Lebensmittelmarke*) coupon; (*old*: = *Rentenmarke*) stamp; **~n kleben** (*inf*) to buy one's stamps **d** (= *Erkennungsmarke*) disc, tag; (= *Hundemarke*) dog licence disc (*Brit*), dog tag (*US*); (= *Garderobenmarke*) cloakroom counter; (*Zettel*) cloakroom ticket or check (*US*); (= *Polizeimarke*) badge; (= *Spielmarke*) chip; (= *Pfandmarke etc*) token

e (= *Rekordmarke*) record; (= *Wasserstandsmarke*) watermark; (= *Stand, Niveau*) level

mär|ken ['mɛrkn] VT (*Aus*) *Wäsche* to mark

Mar|ken-: Mar|ken|al|bum NT (*inf*) stamp album; **Mar|ken|ar|ti|kel** M proprietary article; **Mar|ken|be|wusst|sein** ▲ NT brand awareness; **Mar|ken|but|ter** F nonblended butter, best quality butter; **Mar|ken|er|zeug|nis** NT , **Mar|ken|fab|ri|kat** NT proprietary article; **mar|ken|frei** ADJ **a** (= *ohne Lebensmittelmarken etc*) unrationed, not on coupons **b** (= *ohne Warenzeichen*) nonbranded (*Brit*), generic (*US*); **Mar|ken|her|stel|ler(in)** M(F) manufacturer of proprietary goods; **Mar|ken|name** M brand *or* proprietary name; **Mar|ken|pi|ra|te|rie** F brand name piracy; **Mar|ken|schutz** M protection of trademarks; **Mar|ken|treue** F brand loyalty; **Mar|ken|wa|re** F proprietary goods *pl*; **Mar|ken|zei|chen** NT (*lit, fig*) trademark

Mar|ker ['markɐ] M -s, -(s) **a** (*Med*) marker **b** (= *Markierstift*) highlighter

mark|er|schüt|ternd ADJ = **markdurchdringend**

Mar|ke|ten|der [markə'tɛndɐ] M -s, -, **Mar|ke|ten|de|rin** [-ərɪn] F -, -nen (*Hist*) sutler

Mar|ke|ten|der|wa|re F (*Mil*) goods *pl or* (*einzelner Artikel*) article sold at army stores

Mar|ke|ting ['markətɪŋ] NT -s, *no pl* marketing

Mark- (*Hist*): **Mark|graf** M margrave; **Mark|grä|fin** F margravine; **mark|gräf|lich** ADJ margravial; **Mark|graf|schaft** F margravate

mar|kie|ren [mar'kiːrən] *ptp* **markiert** VT (*lit, fig, Sport*) to mark; (*Comput auch*) to highlight; (*inf*: = *vortäuschen*) to play, to fake; **den starken Mann ~** to come (*Brit*) *or* play the strong man; **den Dummen** *or* **Dusseligen ~** (*inf*) to act daft (*Brit*) *or* dumb (*inf*) VI (*inf*: = *so tun, als ob*) to put it on (*inf*); **markier doch nicht!** stop putting it on (*inf*)

Mar|kier|stift M highlighter

Mar|kie|rung F -, -en marking; (= *Zeichen*) mark

Mar|kie|rungs-: Mar|kie|rungs|li|nie F (marking) line; **Mar|kie|rungs|punkt** M marker; **Mar|kie|rungs|zei|chen** NT (*Comput*) marker

mar|kig ['markɪç] ADJ (= *kraftvoll, kernig*) *Spruch, Worte* pithy; *Drohung* strong; (*iro*: = *großsprecherisch*) grandiloquent, bombastic ADV (*iro*: = *großsprecherisch*) bombastically; **sich ~ ausdrücken** to be fond of strong expressions; **~ schallen** to ring out sharply

mär|kisch ['mɛrkɪʃ] ADJ of the Mark Brandenburg

Mar|ki|se [mar'kiːzə] F -, -n awning, (sun) blind

Mark|klöß|chen NT (*Cook*) bone marrow dumpling

Mark|kno|chen M (*Cook*) marrowbone

Mark|schei|de F (*Min*) boundary line

Mark|schei|de|kun|de F , **Mark|schei|de|kunst** F mine surveying

Mark|schei|der [-ʃaidɐ] M -s, -, **Mark|schei|de|rin** [-ərɪn] F -, -nen mine surveyor

Mark-: Mark|stein M (*lit, fig*) milestone; (*an Feldern etc*) boundary stone; **Mark|stück** NT (*Hist*) (one-)mark piece; **mark|stück|groß** ADJ (*fig*) the size of a one-mark piece

Markt [markt] M -(e)s, -̈e ['mɛrktə] **a** market; (= *Jahrmarkt*) fair; **zum** *or* **auf den ~ gehen** to go to (the) market/to the fair; **~ abhalten** to hold *or* have a market; **dienstags/jede Woche einmal ist ~** *or* **wird ~ abgehalten** there is a market every Tuesday/week **b** (*Comm*) market; (= *Warenverkehr*) trade; **auf dem** *or* **am ~** on the market; **auf den ~ bringen** to put on the market; **neue Märkte erschließen** to develop new markets; **etw in großen Mengen auf den ~ werfen** to flood the market with sth; **auf den ~ kommen** *or* **gebracht werden** to come on the market; **etw vom ~ nehmen** to

withdraw sth from the market **c** (= *Marktplatz*) marketplace, market square; **am ~** in the marketplace; **am ~ wohnen** to live on the marketplace **d** (*geh*: = *Marktflecken*) small market town

Markt- *in cpds* market; **Markt|ab|spra|che** F marketing agreement; **Markt|ana|ly|se** F market analysis; **Markt|an|teil** M market share, share of the market; **markt|be|herr|schend** ADJ **~ sein, eine ~e Stellung einnehmen** to control *or* dominate the market; **Markt|be|rei|ni|gung** F market adjustment, shakeout (*inf*); **Markt|be|richt** M (*Fin*) stock market report; **Markt|bu|de** F market stall; **Markt|chan|ce** F *usu pl* sales opportunity; **Markt|er|folg** M sales success, success on the market; **markt|fä|hig** ADJ *Produkt, Unternehmen* marketable; **Markt|fä|hig|keit** F marketability; **Markt|fah|rer(in)** M(F) (*Aus*) (travelling (*Brit*) *or* traveling (*US*)) market trader; **Markt|fle|cken** M small market town; **Markt|for|scher(in)** M(F) market researcher; **Markt|for|schung** F market research; **Markt|frau** F market woman, (*woman*) stallholder; **Markt|füh|rer(in)** M(F) market leader; **markt|gän|gig** ADJ (= *marktfähig*) marketable; (= *marktüblich*) current; **markt|ge|recht** ADJ in line with market requirements, geared to market requirements ADV **etw ~ einführen/präsentieren** to introduce/present sth in line with market requirements; **das Produkt war nicht ~ verpackt** the packaging of the product was not in line with market requirements; **Markt|hal|le** F covered market; **Markt|hel|fer(in)** M(F) market hand; **Markt|la|ge** F state of the market; **Markt|lü|cke** F gap in the market; **in eine ~ stoßen** to fill a gap in the market; **Markt|macht** F , *no pl* market power; **Markt|ni|sche** F (market) niche; **Markt|ord|nung** F market regulations *pl*; **Markt|ort** M (small) market town; **Markt|platz** M marketplace, market square; **am/auf dem ~** on/in the marketplace; **Markt|preis** M market price; **Markt|psy|cho|lo|gie** F marketing psychology; **Markt|recht** NT (*Hist*) market rights *pl*; **markt|reif** ADJ *Produkt* ready for the market; **Markt|rei|fe** F **ein Produkt zur ~ entwickeln** to develop a product into a marketable commodity; **Markt|schrei|er(in)** M(F) barker, market crier; **markt|schrei|e|risch** [-ʃraiəriʃ] ADJ loud and vociferous; (*fig*) blatant ADV loudly and vociferously; (*fig*) blatantly; **Markt|seg|ment** NT market segment *or* sector; **Markt|stand** M market stall *or* stand; **Markt|stu|die** F market survey; **markt|üb|lich** ADJ *Preis, Konditionen* current; **zu ~en Konditionen** at usual market terms; **Markt|weib** NT (*pej*) market woman; (*fig*) fishwife; **Markt|wert** M market value; **Markt|wirt|schaft** F market economy → **frei b**; **markt|wirt|schaft|lich** ADJ *attr* market-economy ADV **~ orientiert** market-economy-based; **~ organisiert** with a market-based economy; **eine ~ sinnvolle Änderung** an economically worthwhile change; **~ arbeiten** to work economically

Mar|kus ['markʊs] M -' Mark

Mar|kus|evan|ge|li|um NT St Mark's Gospel, Gospel according to St Mark

Mar|ma|ra|meer ['marmara-] NT Sea of Marmara

Mar|mel ['marml] F -, -n marble

Mar|me|la|de [marmə'laːdə] F -, -n jam (*Brit*), jelly (*US*); (= *Orangenmarmelade*) marmalade

Mar|me|la|den-: Mar|me|la|den|brot NT jam (*Brit*) *or* jelly (*US*) sandwich; (*Scheibe*) slice of bread and jam (*Brit*) *or* bread and jelly (*US*); **Mar|me|la|den|glas** NT jam jar (*Brit*), jelly jar (*US*)

mar|meln ['marmln] VI to play marbles

Mar|mor ['marmɔr] M -s, -e marble

Mar|mor- *in cpds* marble; **Mar|mor|bild** NT (*liter*) marble statue; **Mar|mor|bruch** M marble quarry

mar|mo|rie|ren [marmo'riːrən] *ptp* **marmoriert** VT to marble; **mit marmoriertem Schnitt** with marbled edges, marbled

Mar|mor|ku|chen M marble cake

mar|morn ['marmɔrn, 'marmoːɐn] ADJ marble

ma|ro|de [ma'roːdə] ADJ (*inf*) washed-out (*inf*); *Gebäude, Anlagen* ramshackle; *Wirtschaft etc* ailing

ma|ro|deur [maro'døːɐ] M -s, -e marauder

ma|ro|die|ren [maro'diːrən] *ptp* **marodiert** VI to maraud

Ma|rok|ka|ner [marɔ'kaːnɐ] M -s, -, **Ma|rok|ka|ne|rin** [-ərɪn] F -, -nen Moroccan

ma|rok|ka|nisch [marɔ'kaːnɪʃ] ADJ Moroccan

Ma|rok|ko [ma'rɔko] NT -s Morocco

Ma|ro|ne¹ [ma'roːnə] F -, -n, **Ma|ro|ni** [ma'roː-ni] F -, - (*sweet or* Spanish) chestnut

Ma|ro|ne² F -, -n, **Ma|ro|nen|pilz** M , **Ma|ro|nen|röhr|ling** M chestnut boletus, boletus badius (*spec*)

Ma|ro|ni|bra|ter [-braːtɐ] M -s, -, **Ma|ro|ni|bra|te|rin** [-ərɪn] F -, -nen (*Aus*) chestnut vendor

Ma|ro|nit [maro'niːt] M -en, -en, **Ma|ro|ni|tin** [-'niːtɪn] F -, -nen Maronite

Ma|rot|te [ma'rɔtə] F -, -n quirk; **das ist ihre ~** that's one of her little quirks

Mar|quis [mar'kiː] M -, - marquis, marquess

Mar|qui|se [mar'kiːzə] F -, -n marquise, marchioness

Mars¹ [mars] M -, *no pl* (*Myth, Astron*) Mars

Mars² M -, -e (*Naut*) top

Mars|be|woh|ner(in) M(F) Martian

marsch [marʃ] INTERJ **a** (*Mil*) march; **vorwärts ~!** forward march!; (*im Laufschritt,*) **~! ~!** (at the double,) quick march! **b** (*inf*) off with you; **~ ins Bett!** off to bed with you at the double! (*inf*); **raus hier, ~! ~!** get out of here at the double! (*inf*)

Marsch¹ [marʃ] M -(e)s, -̈e ['mɛrʃə] **a** (= *das Marschieren*) march; (= *Wanderung*) hike; **einen ~ machen** to go on a march/hike; **sich in ~ setzen** to move off **b** (= *Marschmusik*) march; **jdm den ~ blasen** (*inf*) to give sb a rocket (*inf*)

Marsch² F -, -en marsh, fen

Mar|schall ['marʃal] M -s, **Marschälle** [-ʃɛlə] (*field*) marshal

Mar|schall|stab M (*field*) marshal's baton; **den ~ im Tornister haben** (*fig*) to be a potential leader of men

Marsch-: Marsch|be|fehl M (*Mil*) (*für Truppen*) marching orders *pl*; (*für Einzelnen*) travel orders *pl*; **marsch|be|reit** ADJ ready to move; **Marsch|bo|den** M marshy soil

Mar|schen|dorf NT fenland village

Marsch-: marsch|fer|tig ADJ = **marschbereit**; **Marsch|flug|kör|per** M cruise missile; **Marsch|ge|päck** NT pack

mar|schie|ren [mar'ʃiːrən] *ptp* **marschiert** VI *aux sein* to march; (*fig*) to march off, to take oneself off; **getrennt ~, vereint schlagen** to unite for the attack

Marsch-: Marsch|ko|lon|ne F column; **Marsch|kom|pass** ▲ M compass; **Marsch|land** NT marsh(land), fen; **marsch|mä|ßig** ADJ *Ausrüstung etc* marching *attr*; (*für Wanderung*) hiking *attr* ADV **~ angezogen** dressed for marching/hiking; **Marsch|mu|sik** F military marches *pl*; **Marsch|or|der** F (*Mil*) marching orders *pl*; (*fig*) go-ahead; **Marsch|ord|nung** F marching order; **Marsch|pau|se** F halt; **Marsch|rich|tung** F , **Marsch|rou|te** F (*lit*) route of march; (*fig*) line of approach; **Marsch|tem|po** NT marching time; (*Mus*) march time *or* tempo; **Marsch|ver|pfle|gung** F rations *pl*; (*Mil*) field rations *pl*; **Marsch|ziel** NT destination

Mar|seil|lai|se [marzɛjɛːzə, marsɛ'jɛːz] F -, *no pl* **die ~** the Marseillaise

Mar|seille [mar'zɛ:j, mar'sɛ:j] NT **-s** Marseilles

Mars|feld NT (in Rom) Campus Martius; (in Paris) Champs de Mars

Mar|shall|plan ['marʃal-] M (Pol) Marshall Plan

Mars|mensch M Martian

Mars|se|gel M (Naut) topsail

Mar|stall ['marʃtal] M **-(e)s, Marställe** [-ʃtɛlə] (Hist) royal stables pl

Mar|ter ['martɐ] F **-, -n** (liter) torment; **das kann zur ~ werden** it can be a painful ordeal

Mar|ter|ge|rät NT , **Mar|ter|in|stru|ment** NT instrument of torture

Mar|terl ['martɛl] NT **-s, -n** (S Ger, Aus) wayside shrine with a crucifix

mar|tern ['martɐn] (liter) **VT** to torture, to torment; **jdn zu Tode ~** to torture sb to death **VR** to torment or torture oneself

Mar|ter-: Mar|ter|pfahl M stake; **Mar|ter|tod** M (liter) = **Märtyrertod**

Mar|te|rung ['martərʊŋ] F **-, -en** (liter) torment

mar|ti|a|lisch [mar'tsia:lɪʃ] (geh) **ADJ** martial, warlike **ADV** brüllen, aussehen in a warlike manner

Mar|tin-Horn® ['marti:n-] NT = **Martinshorn**

Mar|ti|ni [mar'ti:ni] NT **-, no pl** (Eccl) Martinmas

Mar|tins|fest NT , **Mar|tins|tag** M Martinmas

MARTINSTAG

November 11th is **Martinstag** (Martinmas), which is celebrated throughout Germany in a variety of ways. Processions are common: as soon as darkness falls, groups of young children with lanterns go singing through the streets. Sometimes the story of St Martin of Tours is acted out, describing how he tore his cloak in two and shared it with a beggar. A special meal of roast goose – the **Martinsgans** – is often eaten.

Mar|tins-: Mar|tins|gans F Martinmas goose; **Mar|tins|horn** NT (von Polizei und Feuerwehr) siren; mit ~ with its siren blaring or going

Mär|ty|rer ['mɛrtyrɐ] M **-s, -, Mär|ty|re|rin** [-ərɪn] F **-, -nen** (Eccl, fig) martyr; **jdn zum ~ machen** to make a martyr of sb; **sich als ~ aufspielen** (pej) to make a martyr of oneself

Mär|ty|rer-: Mär|ty|rer|kro|ne F martyr's crown; **Mär|ty|rer|tod** M martyr's death; **den ~ sterben** to die a martyr's death; **Mär|ty|rer|tum** ['mɛrtyrɐtu:m] NT **-s, no pl** martyrdom

Mar|ty|ri|um [mar'ty:riʊm] NT **-s, Martyrien** [-riən] **a** (= Opfertod) martyrdom; (fig) ordeal **b** (= Grabkirche) martyry

Mar|xis|mus [mar'ksɪsmʊs] M **-, no pl** Marxism

Mar|xis|mus-Le|ni|nis|mus M Marxism-Leninism

Mar|xist [mar'ksɪst] M **-en, -en, Mar|xis|tin** [-'ksɪstɪn] F **-, -nen** Marxist

mar|xis|tisch [mar'ksɪstɪʃ] **ADJ** Marxist **ADV** klingen etc Marxist; **~ gesinnte Kreise** Marxist groups; **seine Lehre ist ~ beeinflusst** he is influenced by (the teachings of) Marx

marxsch ▲ [marksʃ] ADJ attr Marxian; **die ~e Dialektik** Marx's or Marxian dialectic

März [mɛrts] M **-(es)** or (poet) **-en, -e** March; **im ~** in March; **im ~ 2001** (in Brief) Berlin, March, im ~ 2001 (in Brief) Berlin, March 2001; **im Monat ~** in the month of March; **heute ist der zweite ~** today is the second of March, today is March the second or March second (US); (geschrieben) today is 2nd March or March 2nd; (in Brief) **Berlin, den 4. ~ 2001** Berlin, March 4th, 2001, Berlin, 4th March 2001; **am Mittwoch, dem or den 4. ~** on Wednesday the 4th of March; **am ersten ~ fahren wir nach ...** on the first of March we are going to ...; **in diesem ~** this March; **im Laufe des ~** during March; **der ~ war sehr warm** March was very warm; **Anfang/Ende/Mitte ~** at the

beginning/at the end/in the middle of March → **Iden**

März|be|cher M (Bot) snowflake; (inf: = Narzisse) narcissus

März|bier NT , **Mär|zen** ['mɛrtsn] NT **-(s), -** strong light beer

Mär|zen|be|cher M (Bot) snowflake; (inf: = Narzisse) narcissus

Mär|zen|bier NT strong light beer

Mar|zi|pan [martsi'pa:n, 'martsipa:n] NT **-s, -e** marzipan

März-: März|re|vo|lu|ti|on F (Hist) Revolution of March 1848; **März|veil|chen** NT sweet violet

Ma|sche ['maʃə] F **-, -n a** (= Strickmasche, Häkelmasche) stitch; (von Netz) hole; (von Kettenhemd) link; (= Laufmasche) ladder (Brit), run; **die ~n eines Netzes** the mesh sing of a net; **eine ~ aufnehmen/fallen lassen** to pick up/drop a stitch; **rechte/linke ~n** (beim Stricken) plain/purl stitches; **jdm durch die ~n schlüpfen** to slip through sb's net; (fig auch) to slip through sb's fingers; **durch die ~n des Gesetzes schlüpfen** to slip through a loophole in the law **b** (S Ger, Aus: = Schleife) bow **c** (inf) (= Trick) trick, dodge (inf); (= Eigenart) fad, craze; **die ~ raushaben** to know how to do it; **er versucht es immer noch auf die alte ~** he's still trying the same old trick; **das ist seine neueste ~, das ist die neueste ~ von ihm** that's his latest (fad or craze); **eine ~ abziehen** to pull a stunt/trick

Ma|schen-: Ma|schen|draht M wire netting; **Ma|schen|draht|zaun** M wire-netting fence; **ma|schen|fest** ADJ Strümpfe non-run; **Ma|schen|netz** NT mesh, net; **Ma|schen|werk** NT (fig) **sich im ~ von etw verfangen** to become enmeshed in sth

Ma|scherl ['maʃɛl] NT **-s, -n** (Aus inf: = Fliege, Zierschleife) bow tie

Ma|schin- [ma'ʃi:n] (Aus) in cpds = **Maschine(n)-**

Ma|schi|ne [ma'ʃi:nə] F **-, -n** machine (auch Comput); (= Motor) engine; (= Flugzeug) plane; (= Schreibmaschine) typewriter; (inf: = Motorrad) bike; **eine bloße ~ sein** (fig) to be no more than a machine; **zur ~ werden** (fig) to become a machine; **Kaffee mit der ~ machen** to make coffee in the coffee-maker; **etw in der ~ waschen** to machine-wash sth; **etw auf or mit der ~ schreiben, etw in die ~ tippen** or schreiben to type sth; **~ schreiben** to type; **sie schreibt ~** she types

ma|schi|ne|ge|schrie|ben ADJ typewritten, typed

ma|schi|nell [maʃi'nɛl] **ADJ** Herstellung, Bearbeitung mechanical, machine attr; Anlage, Übersetzung machine attr; **~e Ausstattung** machines pl **ADV** mechanically, by machine; **die Produktion erfolgt weitgehend ~** production is predominantly mechanized

Ma|schi|nen-: Ma|schi|nen|an|trieb M machine drive; **mit ~** machine-driven, mechanically driven; **Ma|schi|nen|ar|beit** F machine work; **Ma|schi|nen|bau** M mechanical engineering; **Ma|schi|nen|bau|er(in)** M(F) pl -bauer(innen) mechanical engineer; **Ma|schi|nen|bau|in|ge|ni|eur(in)** M(F) mechanical engineer; **Ma|schi|nen|de|fekt** M mechanical fault; **Ma|schi|nen|dik|tat** NT typing directly from dictation; **Ma|schi|nen|ele|ment** NT machine component; **Ma|schi|nen|fab|rik** F engineering works sing or pl; **Ma|schi|nen|garn** NT machine thread; **ma|schi|nen|ge|schrie|ben** ADJ typewritten, typed; **Ma|schi|nen|ge|schütz** NT machine gun; **ma|schi|nen|ge|strickt** [-gəʃtrɪkt] ADJ machine-knitted; **Ma|schi|nen|ge|wehr** NT machine gun; **mit ~(en) beschießen** to machine-gun; **Ma|schi|nen|ge|wehr-Schüt|ze** M , **Ma|schi|nen|ge|wehr-Schüt|zin** F machine-gunner; **Ma|schi|nen|haus** NT machine room; **Ma|schi|nen|in|dust|rie** F engineering industry;

Ma|schi|nen|kraft F mechanical power; **Ma|schi|nen|lauf|zeit** F machine running time; **ma|schi|nen|les|bar** ADJ machine-readable; **Ma|schi|nen|les|bar|keit** [-le:sba:ɐkait] F **-, no pl** machine-readability; **ma|schi|nen|mä|ßig** ADJ in terms of machinery; **~e Ausstattung** machinery; **Ma|schi|nen|meis|ter(in)** M(F) (= Aufseher) machine minder; (Theat) stage technician; (Typ) pressman; **Ma|schi|nen|öl** NT lubricating oil; **Ma|schi|nen|park** M plant; **Ma|schi|nen|pis|to|le** F submachine gun; **Ma|schi|nen|raum** M plant room; (Naut) engine room; **Ma|schi|nen|re|vi|si|on** F (Typ) press proof; **Ma|schi|nen|saal** M machine room; (Typ) pressroom; (in Setzerei) caseroom; **Ma|schi|nen|satz** M **a** machine unit **b** (Typ) machine setting or composition; **Ma|schi|nen|scha|den** M mechanical fault; (Aviat etc) engine fault; **Ma|schi|nen|schlos|ser(in)** M(F) machine fitter

Ma|schi|ne(n)-: ma|schi|ne(n)+schrei|ben △ VI sep irreg → **Maschine**; **Ma|schi|ne(n)|schrei|ben** NT typing, typewriting; **Ma|schi|ne(n)|schrei|ber(in)** M(F) typist

Ma|schi|nen-: Ma|schi|nen|schrift F typescript, typing; (Schriftart) typeface; **in ~** typed, typewritten; **ma|schi|nen|schrift|lich** **ADJ** typewritten no adv **ADV** **sich ~ bewerben** to submit a typewritten application; **ein ~ präsentierter Text** a typewritten text; **Ma|schi|nen|set|zer(in)** M(F) machine compositor or typesetter; **Ma|schi|nen|spra|che** F machine language; **Ma|schi|nen|stür|mer** M (Hist, fig) Luddite; **Ma|schi|nen|stür|me|rei** [-ʃtyrmə'rai] F **-, no pl** Luddism; **Ma|schi|nen|teil** NT machine part; **Ma|schi|nen|wär|ter(in)** M(F) machine minder; **Ma|schi|nen|wä|sche** F (= Wäsche) machine-washed clothes pl or laundry; (= das Waschen) machine washing; (Etikett) machine-wash; **Ma|schi|nen|zeit|al|ter** NT machine age

Ma|schi|ne|rie [maʃinə'ri:] F **-, -n** [-'ri:ən] **a** (dated: = Mechanismus) piece of machinery **b** (= Bühnenmaschinerie) stage machinery **c** (fig: = Getriebe) machinery

Ma|schi|nist [maʃi'nɪst] M **-en, -en, Ma|schi|nis|tin** [-'nɪstɪn] F **-, -nen** (= Schiffsmaschinist) engineer; (= Eisenbahnmaschinist) engine driver, engineer (US)

Ma|ser¹ ['ma:zɐ] F **-, -n** vein; **Holz mit feinen ~n** wood with a fine grain

Ma|ser² ['me:zɐ, 'ma:zɐ] M **-s, -** (Phys) maser

Ma|ser|holz NT grained wood

ma|se|rig ['ma:zərɪç] ADJ grained

ma|sern ['ma:zɐn] **VT** to grain → auch gemasert **VI** to become grained

Ma|sern ['ma:zɐn] PL measles sing; **die ~ haben** to have (the) measles

Ma|se|rung ['ma:zərʊŋ] F **-, -en** grain

Mas|ke ['maskə] F **-, -n a** (lit, fig, Sport, Med) mask; **sein Gesicht wurde** or **erstarrte zur ~** his face froze (into a mask); **eine ~ aufsetzen** (lit, fig) to put on a mask; **die ~ abnehmen** or **ablegen** to take off one's mask, to unmask; (fig) to drop all pretence (Brit) or pretense (US), to let fall one's mask; **die ~ fallen lassen** or **abwerfen** (fig) to throw off one's mask; **jdm die ~ herunterreißen** or **vom Gesicht reißen** (fig) to unmask sb; **ohne ~** (fig) undisguised; **unter der ~ von etw** (fig) under the guise of sth; **das ist alles nur ~** that's all just pretence (Brit) or pretense (US) **b** (Theat: = Aufmachung) make-up; **~ machen** to make up **c** (Typ, Comput) mask **d** (= maskierte Person) mask, domino (old); (fig) phony (inf) **e** (Tech) frame

Mas|ken-: Mas|ken|ball M masked ball; **Mas|ken|bild|ner(in)** M(F) make-up artist; **mas|ken|haft** ADJ, ADV mask-like, like a mask; **Mas|ken|kleid** NT , **Mas|ken|kos|tüm** NT fancy-dress costume; **Mas|ken|spie-**

le PL (*Liter*) masques *pl*; **Mas|ken|ver|leih** M fancy-dress hire, costume shop (*US*); **Mas|ken|zug** M carnival procession; **Mas|ken|zwang** M , *no pl* requirement to wear masks; (*auf Einladungsschreiben*) masks will be worn

Mas|ke|ra|de [maskə'ra:də] F **-, -n** (= *Verkleidung*) costume; (*old:* = *Kostümfest*) masquerade

mas|kie|ren [mas'ki:rən] *ptp* **maskiert** VT **a** (= *verkleiden*) to dress up; (= *unkenntlich machen*) to disguise **b** (= *verbergen*) to mask, to disguise VR to dress up; (= *sich unkenntlich machen*) to disguise oneself; **sich als jd/etw ~** (*fig*) to masquerade as sb/sth

mas|kiert [mas'ki:ɐt] ADJ masked

Mas|kie|rung F **-, -en** **a** (= *das Verkleiden*) dressing up; (= *Sich-Unkenntlichmachen*) disguising oneself **b** (= *Verkleidung*) fancy-dress costume; (*von Spion etc*) disguise **c** (= *Verhüllung*) masking

Mas|kott|chen [mas'kɔtçən] NT **-s, -** (lucky) mascot

mas|ku|lin [masku'li:n] ADJ **a** (*Gram, Poet*) masculine **b** (= *betont männlich*) masculine

Mas|ku|li|num ['maskuli:nʊm] NT **-s, Maskulina** [-na] masculine noun

Ma|so ['ma:zo] M **-s**, *no pl* (*inf*) *abbr von* **Masochismus**

Ma|so|chis|mus [mazo'xɪsmʊs] M **-**, *no pl* masochism

Ma|so|chist [mazo'xɪst] M **-en, -en**, **Ma|so|chis|tin** [-'xɪstɪn] F **-, -nen** masochist

ma|so|chis|tisch [mazo'xɪstɪʃ] ADJ masochistic ADV **~ veranlagt sein** to be a masochist, to have masochistic inclinations

maß *pret von* **messen**

Maß¹ [ma:s] NT **-es, -e** **a** (= *Maßeinheit*) measure (*für* of); (= *Zollstock*) rule; (= *Bandmaß*) tape measure; **~e und Gewichte** weights and measures; **das ~ aller Dinge** (*fig*) the measure of all things; **das richtige** *or* **rechte ~ halten** (*fig*) to strike the right balance; **mit zweierlei** *or* **verschiedenem ~ messen** (*fig*) to operate a double standard; **das ~ ist voll** (*fig*) that's enough (of that), enough's enough; **das macht das ~ voll** (*fig*) that's the last straw, enough's enough; **und, um das ~ voll zu machen ...** (*fig*) and to cap it all ... (*esp Brit*), and to top it all off ... (*esp US*); **in reichem ~(e)** abundantly; **in reichem ~(e) vorhanden sein** to be abundant; (*Energie, Zeit etc*) to be plentiful; **das (übliche) ~ überschreiten** to overstep the mark; **ihr Engagement im Beruf geht weit über das übliche ~ hinaus** her commitment to the job far exceeds the norm; **die edlen ~e dieser Plastik** (*geh*) the noble proportions of this statue **b** (= *Abmessung*) measurement; (*von Zimmer, Möbelstück*) dimension, measurement; **ihre ~e sind: ...** her measurements are ..., her vital statistics are ... (*inf*); **sich** (*dat*) **etw nach ~ anfertigen lassen** to have sth made to measure *or* order; **~ nehmen** to measure up; **bei jdm ~ nehmen** to measure sb, to take sb's measurements; **Schuhe/Hemden nach ~** shoes/shirts made to measure *or* order, custom-made shoes/shirts **c** (= *Ausmaß*) extent, degree; **ein solches/gewisses ~ an** *or* **von ...** such a degree/a certain degree of ...; **in hohem ~(e)** to a high degree; **in solchem ~(e) dass ..., in einem ~(e), dass ...** to such an extent that ...; **in nicht geringem ~(e)** in no small measure; **in geringem ~(e)** to a small extent; **in großem ~e** to a great extent; **in vollem ~e** fully; **in demselben** *or* **gleichem ~e wie die Produktion steigt auch der Verbrauch** when production increases, consumption increases accordingly; **die Drucker verlangen eine Lohnerhöhung in demselben** *or* **in gleichem ~e wie die Metaller** the print workers are demanding a pay rise comparable to *or* with that of the metal workers; **in besonderem ~e** especially; **in gewissem/höherem** *or* **stärkerem/beschränktem/erheblichem ~** to a certain/greater/limited/considerable degree *or* extent; **in höchstem ~e**

extremely; **über alle ~en** (*liter*) beyond (all) measure

d (= *Mäßigung*) moderation; **~ halten** to be moderate, to practise (*Brit*) *or* practice (*US*) moderation; **in** *or* **mit ~en** in moderation; **weder ~ noch Ziel kennen** to know no bounds; **ohne ~ und Ziel** immoderately

Maß² F **-, -** (*S Ger, Aus*) litre (*Brit*) *or* liter (*US*) (tankard) of beer; **zwei ~ Bier** two litres (*Brit*) *or* liters (*US*) of beer

Mas|sa|ge [ma'sa:ʒə] F **-, -n** massage; **~n nehmen** to have massage treatment

Mas|sa|ge-: Mas|sa|ge|in|sti|tut NT (*euph*) massage parlour (*Brit*) *or* parlor (*US*); **Mas|sa|ge|öl** NT massage oil; **Mas|sa|ge|pra|xis** F physiotherapy centre (*Brit*) *or* center (*US*); **Mas|sa|ge|sa|lon** M (*euph*) massage parlour (*Brit*) *or* parlor (*US*); **Mas|sa|ge|stab** M vibrator

Mas|sa|ker [ma'sa:kɐ] NT **-s, -** massacre

mas|sak|rie|ren [masa'kri:rən] *ptp* **massakriert** VT (*dated inf*) to massacre

Maß-: Maß|ana|ly|se F (*Chem*) volumetric analysis; **Maß|an|fer|ti|gung** F **a** *no pl* (*von Kleidung*) (custom *or* bespoke) tailoring; (*von Möbeln*) custom building; **das Hemd ist ~** the shirt is made to measure *or* custom-made **b** (= *Kleidungstück*) made-to-measure item, tailor-made item, bespoke item (*geh*); (= *Möbelstück*) specially made item, custom-made *or* custom-built item; **Maß|an|ga|be** F measurement; (*bei Hohlmaßen*) volume *no pl*; **Gläser in Restaurants müssen eine ~ haben** glasses in restaurants must show how much they hold; **Maß|an|zug** M made-to-measure *or* bespoke *or* made-to-order (*US*) suit, custom-made suit; **Maß|ar|beit** F (*inf*) **das war ~** that was a neat bit of work

Mas|se ['masə] F **-, -n** **a** (= *Stoff*) mass; (*Cook*) mixture; (= *für den Guss der Glocke* the molten metal for casting the bell **b** (= *große Menge*) heaps *pl* (*inf*), stacks *pl* (*inf*); (*von Besuchern etc*) host; **die (breite) ~ der Bevölkerung** the bulk of the population; **eine ganze ~** (*inf*) a lot, a great deal; **sie kamen in wahren ~n** they came in droves, they came in their thousands; **die ~ muss es bringen** (*Comm*) the profit only comes with quantity; **die wenigen guten Bücher gehen in der ~ der Neuerscheinungen unter** the few good books are lost in the mass of new titles **c** (= *Menschenmenge*) crowd; **in der ~ untertauchen** to disappear into the crowd **d** (= *Bevölkerungsmasse*) masses *pl* (*auch pej*); **die namenlose** *or* **graue** *or* **breite ~** the masses *pl*; **der Geschmack der ~** the taste of the masses **e** (= *Konkursmasse*) assets *pl*; (= *Erbmasse*) estate **f** (*Phys*) mass

Mas|se|gläu|bi|ger(in) M(F) (*Jur*) preferential creditor

Maß-: Maß|ein|heit F unit of measurement; **Maß|ein|tei|lung** F (measuring) scale

Mas|se|ka|bel NT ground cable

Mas|sen- *in cpds* mass; **Mas|sen|ab|fer|ti|gung** F (*usu pej*) mass *or* wholesale processing; **Mas|sen|ab|füt|te|rung** F (*inf pej*) feeding of the masses; **Mas|sen|ab|satz** M bulk selling; **das ist kein Artikel für den ~** that isn't intended for the mass market; **Mas|sen|an|drang** M crush; **Mas|sen|an|ge|bot** NT glut; **sie waren im ~ auf dem Markt** there was a glut of them on the market; **Mas|sen|an|zie|hung** F (*Phys*) gravitation; **Mas|sen|ar|beits|lo|sig|keit** F mass unemployment; **Mas|sen|ar|ti|kel** M mass-produced article; **Mas|sen|auf|ge|bot** NT large body; **in einem ~ erscheinen** to turn up in force; **Mas|sen|auf|lauf** M , *no pl* crowds *pl* of people; **es gab einen ~ am Unfallort** huge crowds of people gathered at the scene of the accident; **Mas|sen|be|darf** M requirements *pl* of the masses; (*Comm*) requirements *pl* of the mass market; **Mas|sen|be-**

darfs|gü|ter PL basic consumer goods *pl*; **Mas|sen|be|ein|flus|sung** F mass propaganda; **Mas|sen|be|för|de|rungs|mit|tel** NT means *sing* of mass transportation; **Mas|sen|druck|sa|che** F bulk printed matter; „Massendrucksache" "(bulk) printed matter"; **Mas|sen|ent|las|sung** F mass redundancy; **Mas|sen|fab|ri|ka|ti|on** F , **Mas|sen|fer|ti|gung** F mass production; **Mas|sen|flucht** F mass exodus; (*panikartig*) mass stampede; **Mas|sen|ge|sell|schaft** F faceless society; **Mas|sen|grab** NT mass grave; **Mas|sen|gü|ter** PL bulk goods *pl*; **mas|sen|haft** ADJ on a huge *or* massive scale; **~ Fanbriefe/Sekt** *etc* (*inf*) masses of fan letters/champagne *etc* (*inf*) ADV on a huge *or* massive scale; **kommen, erscheinen, eingehen, austreten** in droves; **Mas|sen|her|stel|lung** F mass production; **Mas|sen|hys|te|rie** F mass hysteria; **Mas|sen|ka|ram|bo|la|ge** F multiple (car) crash, pile-up (*inf*); **Mas|sen|kom|mu|ni|ka|ti|ons|mit|tel** NT mass medium *usu pl*; **Mas|sen|me|di|en** PL mass media *pl*; **Mas|sen|mord** M mass murder; **Mas|sen|mör|der(in)** M(F) mass murderer; **Mas|sen|par|tei** F party of the masses; **Mas|sen|pres|se** F popular press; **Mas|sen|pro|duk|ti|on** F mass production; **Mas|sen|psy|cho|lo|gie** F crowd psychology; **Mas|sen|psy|cho|se** F mass hysteria; **Mas|sen|quar|tier** NT camp; **Mas|sen|spei|cher** M (*Comput*) mass storage (device); **Mas|sen|ster|ben** NT mass of deaths; **Mas|sen|sze|ne** F crowd scene; **Mas|sen|ter|ror** M mass terror; **Mas|sen|tier|hal|tung** F intensive livestock farming; **Mas|sen|ver|an|stal|tung** F huge event; **Mas|sen|ver|kehrs|mit|tel** NT means *sing* of mass transportation

Mas|sen|ver|nich|tung F mass extermination

Mas|sen|ver|nich|tungs-: Mas|sen|ver|nich|tungs|la|ger NT extermination camp; **Mas|sen|ver|nich|tungs|mit|tel** PL means *sing* of mass extermination; **Mas|sen|ver|nich|tungs|waf|fe** F weapon of mass destruction

Mas|sen-: Mas|sen|ver|samm|lung F mass meeting; **Mas|sen|wahn** M mass hysteria; **Mas|sen|wa|re** F mass-produced article; **mas|sen|wei|se** ADJ, ADV = **massenhaft**; **Mas|sen|wir|kung** F mass effect

Mas|seur [ma'søːɐ] M **-s, -e** masseur

Mas|seu|rin [ma'søːrɪn] F **-, -nen** (*Berufsbezeichnung*) masseuse

Mas|seu|se [ma'søːzə] F **-, -n** (*in Eros-Center etc*) masseuse

Maß|ga|be F (*form*) stipulation; **mit der ~, dass ...** with the proviso that ..., on (the) condition that ...; **nach ~** (+*gen*) according to

maß|ge|bend ADJ (= *ausschlaggebend*) *Einfluss* decisive; *Meinung, Ansicht* definitive; *Text* definitive, authoritative; *Fachmann* authoritative; (= *wichtig*) *Persönlichkeit* leading; (= *zuständig*) competent; **das Verhalten des Chefs ist ~ für die Mitarbeiter** the boss's behaviour (*Brit*) *or* behavior (*US*) sets the standard for his employees; **das ist hier nicht ~** that doesn't weigh *or* signify here; **das war für mich nicht ~** that didn't weigh with me ADV **er hat ~ dazu beigetragen** he made a significant contribution to it

maß|geb|lich ADJ (= *entscheidend*) *Einfluss* decisive; *Faktor* deciding, decisive; (= *führend*) *Person, Firma, Rolle* leading; *Beteiligung* substantial; **~en Anteil an etw** (*dat*) **haben** to make a major contribution to sth ADV decisively; **~ an etw** (*dat*) **beteiligt sein** to play a substantial role in sth

maß|ge|schnei|dert [-gəʃnaidɐt] ADJ *Anzug* made-to-measure, made-to-order (*US*), custom-made; (*fig*) *Lösung, Produkte* tailor-made

Maß|hal|te|ap|pell M , **Maß|hal|te|pa|ro|le** F appeal for moderation

maß+hal|ten △ VI *sep irreg* → **Maß¹ d**

mas|sie|ren¹ [ma'si:rən] *ptp* **massiert** VT *Körper, Haut* to massage VI to give (a) massage

mas|sie|ren² ptp **massiert** VT *Truppen* to mass VR to amass; (*Truppen*) to mass

mas|sig ['masɪç] ADJ massive, huge ADV (inf: = sehr viel) **~ Arbeit/Geld** etc masses or stacks of work/money etc (inf)

mä|ßig ['mɛːsɪç] ADJ **a** (= bescheiden) moderate; *Preise* moderate, reasonable; **in etw** (dat) **~ sein** to be moderate in sth **b** (= unterdurchschnittlich) *Leistung, Schulnote* etc mediocre, indifferent; *Begabung, Beifall, Erfolg* moderate; *Gesundheit* middling, indifferent ADV **a** (= nicht viel) moderately; **etw ~ tun** to do sth in moderation; **~ essen** to eat with moderation; **~ rauchen** to be a moderate smoker, to smoke in moderation; **~, aber regelmäßig** in moderation but regularly **b** (= nicht besonders) moderately; *groß* reasonably; **sich nur ~ anstrengen** not to make much of an effort

-mä|ßig ADJ, ADV suf **a** (in einer bestimmten Art) -like; **geschäftsmäßiges Verhalten** businesslike behaviour (Brit) or behavior (US) **b** (bezüglich einer Sache) -wise; **geldmäßig haben wir Probleme** we are having problems moneywise

mä|ßi|gen ['mɛːsɪɡn] VT (= mildern) *Anforderungen* to moderate; *Sprache* auch to tone down; *Zorn, Ungeduld* to curb, to check; **sein Tempo ~** to slacken one's pace, to slow down → auch **gemäßigt** VR (im Essen, Trinken, Temperament) to restrain or control oneself; (*Sturm*) to abate, to die down; **~ Sie sich!** control yourself!; **sich in seinem Temperament ~** to control or restrain oneself; **sich im Ton ~** to moderate one's tone; **~ Sie sich in Ihren Worten!** tone down your language!

Mas|sig|keit F -, no pl massiveness, hugeness

Mä|ßig|keit F -, no pl **a** (beim Essen, Trinken) moderation, restraint; (von Forderungen, Preisen etc) moderateness; **~ üben** to exercise or show moderation or restraint **b** (= Mittelmäßigkeit) mediocrity; (von Begabung, Beifall) moderateness

Mä|ßi|gung F -, no pl restraint; (beim Essen etc auch) moderation

mas|siv [ma'siːf] ADJ **a** (= pur, nicht hohl, stabil) solid **b** (= heftig) *Beleidigung* gross; *Drohung, Kritik* serious; *Anschuldigung* severe; *Protest, Forderung, Unterstützung* strong; **~ werden** (inf) to turn nasty ADV **a** (= wuchtig) *gebaut* massively **b** (= heftig) severely; *protestieren, fördern, unterstützen* strongly; **jdm ~ drohen** to issue a serious threat to sb; **jdn ~ kritisieren** to severely criticize sb **c** (= stark) *zunehmen, verstärken* greatly; *erhöhen* massively; *steigen* strongly; *einschränken, behindern* severely; **sich ~ verschlechtern** to deteriorate or worsen sharply

Mas|siv [ma'siːf] NT -s, -e [-və] (Geol) massif

Mas|siv|bau|wei|se F masonry construction

Mas|si|vi|tät [masivi'tɛːt] F -, no pl **a** (= Stabilität) solidness **b** (= Heftigkeit) **die ~ seiner Kritik** his serious criticism

Maß-: Maß|klei|dung F made-to-measure or made-to-order (US) or custom-made clothing; **Maß|krug** M litre (Brit) or liter (US) beer mug; (= Steinkrug) stein; **Maß|lieb** ['maːsliːp] NT -(e)s, -e **Maß|lieb|chen** ['maːsliːpçən] NT -s, - daisy, marguerite

maß|los ADJ extreme; (= übermäßig) *Forderungen* auch excessive; (= grenzenlos) *Trauer, Freude, Ehrgeiz* auch boundless; *Mensch* (in Forderungen etc auch, im Essen etc) immoderate; **er war ~ in seiner Wut/Freude** etc his rage/joy etc knew no bounds ADV (= äußerst) extremely; *übertreiben* grossly, hugely; **es ist alles ~ traurig** (inf) it's all very or terribly (inf) sad; **er raucht/trinkt ~** he smokes/drinks to excess

Maß|lo|sig|keit F -, -en extremeness; (= Übermäßigkeit) excessiveness; (= Grenzenlosigkeit) boundlessness; (im Essen etc) lack of moderation; **die ~ seiner Forderungen** his excessive demands

Maß|nah|me [-naːmə] F -, -n measure; **~n treffen** or **ergreifen, um etw zu tun** to take steps or measures to do sth; **~n gegen jdn/etw treffen** or **ergreifen** to take measures against sb/sth; **vor ~n zurückschrecken** to shrink from taking action; **sich zu ~n gezwungen sehen** to be forced to take action

Maß|nah|men|ka|ta|log M catalogue (Brit) or catalog (US) of measures

Maß|nah|men|pa|ket NT package of measures

Maß|re|gel F rule

maß|re|geln VT insep (= zurechtweisen) to reprimand, to rebuke, to reprove; (= bestrafen) to discipline; (Sport) to penalize

Maß|re|ge|lung F **a** no pl (= Zurechtweisung) reprimanding, rebuking, reproval; (= Bestrafung) disciplining; (Sport) penalizing **b** (= Rüge) reprimand, rebuke; (von Beamten) disciplinary action; (Sport) penalty

Maß|schnei|der(in) M(F) (= Lineal) bespoke or custom (US) tailor

Maß|stab M **a** (= Lineal) ruler; (= Zollstock) rule **b** (= Kartenmaßstab, Modell) scale; (= Ausmaß) scale; **die Karte hat einen kleinen/großen ~** it's a small-scale/large-scale map, the map is on a small/large scale; **im ~ 1:1000** on a scale of 1:1000; **im ~ 1:25000 gezeichnet** drawn to a scale of 1:25000; **etw in verkleinertem ~ darstellen** to scale sth down; **Klimaverschiebungen im großen ~** large-scale climate changes **c** (fig: = Richtlinie, Kriterium) standard; **einen hohen/strengen ~ anlegen** to apply a high/strict standard (an +acc to); **für jdn als** or **zum ~ dienen, für jdn einen ~ abgeben** to serve as a model for sb; **sich** (dat) **jdn/etw zum** or **als ~ nehmen** to take sb/sth as a yardstick, to take sth as a benchmark; **das ist für mich kein ~** I don't take that as my yardstick or benchmark

maß|stäb|lich [-ʃtɛːplɪç] ADJ scale attr, to scale

maß|stab(s)|ge|recht, maß|stab(s)|ge|treu ADJ, ADV (true) to scale; **eine ~e Karte** an accurate scale map

Maß-: Maß|sys|tem NT system of measures; **maß|voll** ADJ moderate ADV moderately; **Maß|vor|la|ge** F (Ftbl) spot-on (inf) or accurate pass; **Maß|werk** NT (Archit) tracery

Mast¹ [mast] M -(e)s, -en or -e (Naut, Rad, TV) mast; (= Stange) pole; (Elec) pylon

Mast² F -, -en (= das Mästen) fattening; (= Futter) feed; (= Schweinemast) mast

Mast-: Mast|baum M mast; **Mast|darm** M rectum

mäs|ten ['mɛstn] VT to fatten VR (inf) to gorge or stuff (inf) oneself

Mäs|te|rei [mɛstə'raɪ] F -, -en (= Schweinemästerei) pig fattening unit

Mast|fut|ter NT (fattening) feed; (für Schweine) mast

Mas|ti|no [mas'tiːno] M -s, **Mastini** [-ni] mastiff

Mast-: Mast|korb M (Naut) top; **Mast|kur** F (hum inf) fattening diet; **Mast|schwein** NT (zu mästen) porker; (gemästet) fattened pig; **er sieht wie ein ~ aus** he looks like a little (fat) piggy

Mäs|tung F -, -en, **Mas|tung** ['mastʊn] F -, -en fattening

Mas|tur|ba|ti|on [mastʊrba'tsioːn] F -, -en masturbation

mas|tur|bie|ren [mastʊr'biːrən] ptp **masturbiert** VTI to masturbate

Mast|vieh NT fat stock; (zu mästendes Vieh) fattening stock

Ma|sur|ka [ma'zʊrka] F -, -s mazurka

Ma|ta|dor [mata'doːɐ] M -s, -e, **Ma|ta|do|rin** [-'doːrɪn] F -, -nen (= Stierkämpfer, fig) matador; (fig) kingpin

Match [mɛtʃ] NT OR M -(e)s, -e(s) match

Match- [mɛtʃ-]: **Match|ball** M (Tennis) match point; **Match|beutel** M , **Match|sack** M duffel bag

Ma|te ['maːtə] M -, no pl maté, Paraguay tea

Ma|ter ['maːtə] F -, -n (Typ) matrix, mould (Brit), mold (US)

Ma|te|ri|al [mate'riaːl] NT -s, -ien [-liən] material; (= Baumaterial, Utensilien, Gerät) materials pl; (= Beweismaterial, Belastungsmaterial) evidence; **rollendes ~** (Rail) rolling stock

Ma|te|ri|al-: Ma|te|ri|al|aus|ga|be F **a** (Raum) stores pl **b** (Vorgang) issue of stores and equipment; **Ma|te|ri|al|be|darf** M material requirements pl; **Ma|te|ri|al|er|mü|dung** F (von Metall) metal fatigue; **Ma|te|ri|al|feh|ler** M material defect, defect in the material

Ma|te|ri|a|li|sa|ti|on [materializa'tsioːn] F -, -en materialization

ma|te|ri|a|li|sie|ren [materiali'ziːrən] ptp **materialisiert** VTR to materialize

Ma|te|ri|a|lis|mus [materia'lɪsmʊs] M - materialism

Ma|te|ri|a|list [materia'lɪst] M -en, -en, **Ma|te|ri|a|lis|tin** [-'lɪstɪn] F -, -nen materialist

ma|te|ri|a|lis|tisch [materia'lɪstɪʃ] ADJ materialist(ic); (pej) materialistic ADV materialistically

Ma|te|ri|al-: Ma|te|ri|al|kos|ten PL cost of materials pl; **Ma|te|ri|al|la|ger** NT stores pl, inventory (US); **Ma|te|ri|al|prü|fung** F testing of materials; **Ma|te|ri|al|samm|lung** F collection of material; **ich habe jetzt die ~ abgeschlossen** I have now finished collecting or gathering the material; **Ma|te|ri|al|scha|den** M material defect, defect in the material; **Ma|te|ri|al|schlacht** F (Mil) matériel battle; **Ma|te|ri|al|wert** M material value; (von Münzen) intrinsic value

Ma|te|rie [ma'teːriə] F -, -n **a** no pl (Phys, Philos) matter no art **b** (= Stoff, Thema) subject matter no indef art; **die ~ beherrschen** to know one's stuff

ma|te|ri|ell [mate'riɛl] ADJ **a** (Philos) material, physical; *Recht* substantive **b** (= wirtschaftlich) *Not, Versorgung, Vorteile* material, financial; (= gewinnsüchtig) materialistic; **nur ~e Interessen haben** to be only interested in material things ADV **a** (= finanziell) financially; (pej: = materialistisch) materialistically; **~ eingestellt sein** (pej) to be materialistic **b** (= das Material betreffend) materially; **die Behörde war ~ und personell umfangreich ausgestattet** the authority was fully provided for with resources and staff

ma|tern ['maːtɐn] VT (Typ) to make a plate for

Ma|te|tee ['maːtə-] M maté, Paraguay tea

Math. abbr von **Mathematik**

Ma|the ['matə] F -, no pl (Sch inf) maths sing (Brit inf), math (US inf)

Ma|the|ma|tik [matema'tiːk] F -, no pl mathematics sing, no art

Ma|the|ma|ti|ker [mate'maːtikɐ] M -s, -, **Ma|the|ma|ti|ke|rin** [-ərɪn] F -, -nen mathematician

ma|the|ma|tisch [mate'maːtɪʃ] ADJ mathematical ADV mathematically

Ma|ti|nee [mati'neː] F -, -n [-'neːən] matinée

Mat|jes ['matjəs] M -, -, **Mat|jes|he|ring** M young herring

Mat|rat|ze [ma'tratsə] F -, -n mattress

Mat|rat|zen|la|ger NT **für die Kinder ein ~ herrichten** to put down a mattress for the children

Mät|res|se [mɛ'trɛsə] F -, -n mistress

mat|ri|ar|cha|lisch [matriar'çaːlɪʃ] ADJ matriarchal ADV **eine ~ orientierte Bewegung** a matriarchal movement; **sie regiert die Familie ~** she rules the family like a matriarch

Mat|ri|ar|chat [matriar'çaːt] NT -(e)s, -e matriarchy, matriarchate

Ma|tri|kel [ma'triːkl] F -, -n (old, Aus) register; (Univ: = Aufnahmeverzeichnis) matriculation register (Brit), registration list (US); **Student mit kleiner/großer ~** occasional/full-time student

Ma|tri|kel|num|mer F (Univ) registration or matriculation number

Mat|rix ['maːtrɪks] F -, **Matrizen** or **Matrizes** [maˈtriːtsn̩, maˈtriːtsəs] (*Math, Med, Biol*) matrix

Mat|rix|dru|cker M dot-matrix (printer)

Mat|ri|ze [maˈtriːtsə, maˈtrɪtsə] F -, -n (*Typ*) matrix, mould (*Brit*), mold (*US*); (*für Schreibmaschine*) stencil; **etw auf ~ schreiben** to stencil sth

Mat|ro|ne [maˈtroːnə] F -, -n matron

mat|ro|nen|haft ADJ matronly ADV in a matronly way

Mat|ro|se [maˈtroːzə] M -n, -n, **Mat|ro|sin** [-ˈtroːzɪn] F sailor; (*als Rang*) rating (*Brit*), ordinary seaman

Mat|ro|sen- in cpds sailor; **Mat|ro|sen|an|zug** M sailor suit; **Mat|ro|sen|müt|ze** F sailor's cap; **Mat|ro|sen|uni|form** F sailor's uniform

Mat|ro|sin F → **Matrose**

matsch [matʃ] ADJ pred (*dial*) **a** Obst rotten, bad **b** (*Cards*) beaten; **~ werden** to be beaten **c** **sich ~ fühlen** to feel whacked (*Brit inf*) or beat (*esp US inf*)

Matsch [matʃ] M -(e)s, no pl (*inf*) (= breiige Masse) mush; (= Schlamm) mud, sludge; (= Schneematsch) slush; **~ aus jdm machen** (*sl*) to beat sb to a pulp (*inf*)

Matsch|bir|ne F (*inf*) bad head (*inf*)

mat|schen ['matʃn̩] VI (*inf*) to splash (about or around)

mat|schig ['matʃɪç] ADJ (*inf*) (= breiig) Obst mushy; (= schlammig) Straße, Weg muddy, sludgy; Schnee slushy

Matsch|wet|ter NT (*inf*) muddy or (*mit Schneematsch*) slushy weather

matt [mat] ADJ **a** (= schwach) Kranker weak; Stimme, Lächeln weak, faint; Glieder weary; **sich ~ fühlen** to have no energy **b** (= glanzlos) Augen, Metall, Farbe dull; (= nicht glänzend) Farbe, Papier, Foto mat(t); (= trübe) Licht dim, subdued; Glühbirne opal, pearl; Spiegel cloudy, dull **c** (= undurchsichtig) Glas frosted, opaque **d** (*fig*) Entschuldigung, Widerspruch, Entgegnung feeble; Echo faint; (*St Ex: = flau*) slack **e** (*Chess*) check(mate); **jdn ~ setzen** to checkmate sb (*auch fig*), to mate sb ADV **a** (= schwach) weakly; lächeln faintly, weakly **b** (= nicht hell) dimly; **~ glänzend** dull **c** (= ohne Nachdruck) lamely

Matt [mat] NT -s, -s (*Chess*) (check)mate

matt|blau ADJ pale blue

Mat|te[1] ['matə] F -, -n mat; **auf der ~ stehen** (*inf: = bereit sein*) to be there and ready for action; **du musst um sechs bei mir auf der ~ stehen** you must be at my place at six; **jdn auf die ~ legen** (= niederschlagen) to floor sb; (*fig inf*) to make mincemeat of sb (*inf*); (= übervorteilen) to put one over on sb (*inf*)

Mat|te[2] F -, -n (*liter, Sw, Aus*) alpine meadow

Mat|ter|horn ['matɐhɔrn] NT -s das ~ the Matterhorn

Matt-: Matt|glanz M mat(t) finish; **Matt|glas** NT frosted or ground glass; **Matt|gold** NT dull gold; (*Farbe*) pale gold

Mat|thäi [maˈtɛːiː] gen von **Matthäus bei ihm ist ~ am letzten** he's had it (*inf*)

Mat|thä|us [maˈtɛːʊs] M **Matthäi** [maˈtɛːiː] Matthew

Mat|thä|us|evan|ge|li|um NT St Matthew's Gospel, Gospel according to St Matthew

Matt|heit F -, no pl **a** (= Schwäche) weakness; (*von Stimme*) weakness, faintness; (*von Gliedern*) weariness; (= Energielosigkeit) lack of energy **b** (= Glanzlosigkeit: von Augen, Farbe) dullness; (= Trübheit: von Licht) dimness

mat|tie|ren [maˈtiːrən] ptp **mattiert** VT to give a mat(t) finish to; **mattiert sein** to have a mat(t) finish; **mattierte Gläser** frosted glasses

Mat|tig|keit ['matɪçkaɪt] F -, no pl weariness; (*von Kranken*) weakness

Matt-: Matt|lack M dull or mat(t) lacquer or varnish; **Matt|pa|pier** NT mat(t) or unglazed paper

Matt|schei|be F **a** (*Phot*) focus(s)ing screen; (*inf: = Fernseher*) telly (*Brit inf*), (goggle)box (*Brit inf*), tube (*US inf*) **b** (*inf*) **eine ~ haben/kriegen** (= dumm sein) to be soft/go soft in the head (*inf*); (= nicht klar denken können) to have/get a mental block; **als ich das gesagt habe, muss ich wohl eine ~ gehabt haben** I can't have been really with it when I said that (*inf*)

Ma|tur [maˈtuːɐ] NT -s, no pl, **Ma|tu|rum** [maˈtuːrʊm] NT -s, no pl (old), **Ma|tu|ra** [maˈtuːra] F -, no pl (*Aus, Sw*) → **Abitur**

Ma|tu|rand [matuˈrant] M -en, -en [-dn̩], **Ma|tu|ran|din** [-ˈrandɪn] F -, -nen (old, Sw), **Ma|tu|rant** [matuˈrant] M -en, -en [-tn̩], **Ma|tu|ran|tin** [-ˈrantɪn] F -, -nen (*Aus*) → **Abiturient(in)**

ma|tu|rie|ren [matuˈriːrən] ptp **maturiert** VI (*Aus: = Abitur machen*) to take one's school-leaving exam (*Brit*), to graduate (from high school) (*US*)

Ma|tu|ri|tät [maturiˈtɛːt] F -, no pl (*Sw: = Hochschulreife*) matriculation exam(ination) (*Brit*), high school diploma (*US*)

Ma|tu|ri|täts- in cpds = **Reife-**

Matz [mats] M -es, ⸚e ['mɛtsə] (*dated inf*) laddie (*Scot inf*), guy (*inf*)

Mätz|chen ['mɛtsçən] NT -s, - (*inf*) **a** antic; **~ machen** to play or fool around (*inf*); **mach keine ~, schmeiß die Pistole weg!** don't try anything funny, just drop the gun! **b** dim von **Matz**

Mat|ze ['matsə] F -, -n, **Mat|zen** ['matsn̩] M -s, - (*Cook*) matzo

mau [mau] ADJ pred (*inf*) poor, bad; **mir ist ~** I feel poorly (*Brit inf*) or sick ADV **die Geschäfte gehen ~** business is slack

Mau|er ['mauɐ] F -, -n **a** wall; **etw mit einer ~ umgeben** to wall sth in; **in den ~n der Stadt** (*fig*) in the city; **die (Berliner) ~** (*Hist*) the (Berlin) Wall **b** (*fig*) wall; **gegen eine ~ des Schweigens anrennen** (*fig*) to run up against a wall of silence; **die ~n einreißen** to tear down the barriers

Mauer-: Mau|er|ab|satz M ledge; **Mau|er|ar|beit** F bricklaying (work) no pl; **Mau|er|as|sel** F woodlouse; **Mau|er|bau** M , no pl (*Hist*) building of the Berlin Wall; **Mau|er|blüm|chen** NT (*fig inf*) (*beim Tanzen*) wallflower; (= schüchternes Mädchen) shy young thing; **Mau|er|bre|cher** M (*Mil*) battering ram; **Mau|er|durch|bruch** M (= das Durchbrechen) breaching of a/the wall; (= Stelle) breach in a/the wall; **Mau|er|fall** M , no pl (*Hist*) fall of the Berlin Wall; **beim ~** when the Berlin Wall came down or fell; **Mau|er|ha|ken** M (*Bergsteigen*) piton, peg; **Mau|er|kel|le** F (bricklayer's) trowel; **Mau|er|kro|ne** F wall coping

mau|ern ['mauɐn] VI **a** (= Maurerarbeit machen) to build, to lay bricks **b** (*Cards*) to hold back; (*Ftbl sl*) to stonewall, to play defensively; (*fig*) to stall, to stonewall (*esp Parl*) VT **a** to build; (= mit Zement verfugen) to build with mortar; **der Beckenrand muss gemauert werden** the edge of the pool must be bedded in mortar

Mau|er-: Mau|er|schau F , no pl (*Liter*) reporting of offstage events (by a character on stage); **Mau|er|schüt|ze** M East German border guard who shot people fleeing west; **Mau|er|schwal|be** F , **Mau|er|seg|ler** M swift; **Mau|er|speis** [-ʃpaɪs] M -es, no pl, **Mau|er|spei|se** F (*esp S Ger: = Mörtel*) mortar; **Mau|er|stein** M building stone; **Mau|er|ver|band** M bond; **Mau|er|vor|sprung** M projection on a/the wall; **Mau|er|werk** NT **a** (= Steinmauer) stonework, masonry; (= Ziegelmauer) brickwork; **ein mittelalterliches ~** a medieval stone structure **b** (= die Mauern) walls pl; **Mau|er|zie|gel** M (building) brick

Mau|ke ['maukə] F -, no pl (*Vet*) malanders pl

Mau|ken ['maukn̩] PL (*dial inf*) hooves pl (*hum*)

Maul [maul] NT -(e)s, **Mäuler** ['mɔylɐ] mouth; (*von Löwe etc, von Zange*) jaws pl; (*inf: von Menschen*) gob (*Brit inf*), trap (*esp US sl*); (*von Schraubenschlüssel*) head; **ein böses** or **ungewaschenes** or **gottloses ~** (*inf*) an evil or a wicked or a malicious tongue; **jdm übers ~ fahren** (*inf*) to choke sb off (*inf*); **das ~ zu weit aufreißen** (*sl*) das ~ zu voll nehmen (*sl*) to be too cocksure (*inf*); **ein großes ~ haben** (*inf*) to have a big mouth, to be a bigmouth (*inf*); **(hungrige) Mäuler stopfen** (*inf*) to feed or fill (hungry) mouths; **darüber werden sich die Leute das ~ zerreißen** (*inf*) that will start people's tongues wagging; **dem Volk** or **den Leuten aufs ~ schauen** (*inf*) to listen to what people really say; (= Meinung ermitteln) to sound out public opinion, to listen to the man in the street; **halt's ~!** (*vulg*) **~ halten!** (*vulg*) shut your face (*sl*) or trap (*sl*) or gob (*Brit inf*); **halt dein ungewaschenes ~** (*sl*) keep your dirty mouth shut (*inf*); **sich** (*dat*) **das ~ verbrennen** (*inf*) to talk one's way or oneself into trouble

Maul-: Maul|af|fen PL **~ feilhalten** to stand gawping or gaping; **Maul|beer|baum** M mulberry (tree); **Maul|bee|re** F mulberry

mau|len ['maulən] VI (*inf*) to moan

Maul-: Maul|esel M mule, hinny; **maul|faul** ADJ (*inf*) uncommunicative; **Maul|held(in)** M(F) (*pej*) loudmouth (*inf*), show-off; **Maul|hu|re|rei** F (*geh*) foul-mouthedness

Maul|korb M (*lit, fig*) muzzle; **einem Hund/jdm einen ~ umhängen** to put a muzzle on a dog/sb, to muzzle a dog/sb

Maul|korb- (*fig inf*): **Maul|korb|er|lass** ▲ M decree muzzling freedom of speech; **Maul|korb|ge|setz** NT law muzzling freedom of speech

Maul-: Maul|schel|le F (*dated inf*) slap in the face; **Maul|sper|re** F **er kriegte die ~** (*inf*) his mouth dropped open; **Maul|ta|schen** PL (*Cook*) pasta squares pl; **Maul|tier** NT mule; **Maul|trom|mel** F Jew's harp; **Maul- und Klau|en|seu|che** F (*Vet*) foot-and-mouth disease (*Brit*), hoof-and-mouth disease (*US*)

Maul|wurf ['maulvʊrf] M -(e)s, **Maulwürfe** [-vʏrfə] (*auch fig*) mole

Maul|wurfs|hau|fen M , **Maul|wurfs|hü|gel** M molehill

maun|zen ['mauntsn̩] VI (*S Ger*) (= winseln) to whine; (*Katze*) to mew

Mau|re ['maurə] M -n, -n, **Mau|rin** ['maurɪn] F -, -nen (*Hist*) Moor

Mau|rer ['maurɐ] M -s, -, **Mau|re|rin** [-ərɪn] F -, -nen bricklayer, brickie (*Brit inf*); **~ lernen** to learn bricklaying, to learn to be a bricklayer; **pünktlich wie die ~** (*hum*) super-punctual; **pünktlich wie die ~ ließ er seinen Kugelschreiber fallen** bang on the dot he put down his pen

Maurer-: Mau|rer|ar|beit F bricklaying (work) no pl; **Mau|rer|ge|sel|le** M , **Mau|rer|ge|sel|lin** F journeyman bricklayer; **Mau|rer|ham|mer** M bricklayer's hammer; **Mau|rer|hand|werk** NT bricklaying

Mau|re|rin F → **Maurer**

Maurer-: Mau|rer|kel|le F (bricklayer's) trowel; **Mau|rer|ko|lon|ne** F bricklaying gang; **Mau|rer|meis|ter(in)** M(F) master builder; **Mau|rer|po|lier(in)** M(F) foreman/-woman (bricklayer)

Mau|re|ta|ni|en [maureˈtaːniən] NT -s Mauritania, Mauretania

Mau|re|ta|ni|er [maureˈtaːniɐ] M -s, -, **Mau|re|ta|ni|e|rin** [-iərɪn] F -, -nen Mauritanian

mau|re|ta|nisch [maureˈtaːnɪʃ] ADJ Mauritanian

Mau|rin F -, -nen (*Hist*) Moor

mau|risch ['maurɪʃ] ADJ Moorish

Mau|ri|ti|er [mauˈriːtsɪɐ] M **-s, -**, **Mau|ri|ti|e|rin** [-ɪərɪn] F **-, -nen** Mauritian

Mau|ri|ti|us [mauˈriːtsɪʊs] NT -ʼ Mauritius

Maus [maus] F **-, Mäuse** [ˈmɔyzə] **a** mouse; **wei|ße ~** (*fig inf*) traffic cop (*inf*); **weiße Mäuse sehen** (*fig inf*) to see pink elephants (*inf*); **da beißt die ~ keinen Faden ab** (*inf: = nicht zu ändern*) there's no changing that **b** (*inf*) (*= Frau*) woman; (*= Mädchen, Freundin*) bird (*esp Brit inf*), chick (*esp US inf*); **eine süße ~** (*= Kind*) a sweet little thing (*inf*); **eine graue ~** (*inf*) a mouse (*inf*) **c** (*Comput*) mouse **d Mäuse** PL (*dated sl: = Geld*) bread (*inf*), dough (*inf*)

Mau|sche|lei [mauʃəˈlai] F **-, -en** (*inf: = Korruption*) fiddle (*Brit inf*), swindle; **das war bestimmt ~** it was definitely a fiddle (*Brit inf*) or a swindle

mau|scheln [ˈmauʃln] **VI** (*= Jiddisch sprechen*) to talk Yiddish **VTI** (*= manipulieren*) to fiddle (*inf*)

Mau|scheln NT **-s** (*Cards*) cheat

Mäus|chen [ˈmɔysçən] NT **-s, -** **a** little mouse; **da möchte ich mal ~ sein** or **spielen** (*inf*) I'd like to be a fly on the wall **b** (*fig*) sweetheart (*inf*), love (*Brit inf*), honey (*esp US inf*) **c** (*= Musikantenknochen*) funny bone (*Brit inf*), crazy bone (*US inf*)

mäus|chen|still [ˈmɔysçənˈʃtɪl] ADJ dead quiet; *Mensch auch* (as) quiet as a mouse; (*= reglos*) stock-still ADV quiet as a mouse

Mäu|se|bus|sard M (common) buzzard

Mau|se|fal|le F , **Mäu|se|fal|le** F (*rare*) mousetrap; (*fig*) police roadblock; **in eine ~ kommen** or **geraten** to get caught in a police roadblock

Mäu|se|gift NT mouse poison

Mau|se|loch NT , **Mäu|se|loch** NT (*rare*) mousehole; **sich in ein ~ verkriechen** (*fig*) to crawl into a hole in the ground

Mäu|se|mel|ken NT **-s**, *no pl* **das/es ist zum ~** (*dated inf*) it's enough to drive you up the wall (*inf*)

mau|sen [ˈmauzn] **VI** to catch mice; **diese Katze maust gut** the cat is a good mouser **VT** (*dated inf*) to pinch (*inf*), to nick (*Brit inf*)

Mau|ser¹ [ˈmauzɐ] F **-**, *no pl* (*Orn*) moult (*Brit*), molt (*US*); **in der ~ sein** to be moulting (*Brit*) or molting (*US*)

Mau|ser²® F **-, -** (*= Pistole*) Mauser

Mau|ser|ge|wehr NT Mauser (rifle)

Mäu|se|rich [ˈmɔyzərɪç] M **-s, -e** (*hum*) Mr Mouse (*hum*)

mau|sern [ˈmauzɐn] VR **a** (*Orn*) to moult (*Brit*), to molt (*US*) **b** (*inf*) to blossom out (*inf*)

Mau|ser|pis|to|le F **-, -n** Mauser

mau|se|tot [ˈmauzəˈtoːt] ADJ (*inf*) stone-dead, as dead as a doornail

maus|ge|steu|ert [-ɡəʃtɔyɐt] ADJ (*Comput*) mouse-driven, mouse-controlled

maus|grau ADJ **a** (*= mausfarben*) mouse-grey (*Brit*), mouse-gray (*US*) **b** (*= unauffällig*) mousy

mau|sig [ˈmauzɪç] ADJ **sich ~ machen** (*inf*) to get uppity (*inf*)

Maus-: Maus|klick [-klɪk] M **-s, -s** (*Comput*) mouse click; **etw per ~ steuern/aktivieren** to control/activate sth by clicking the mouse; **Maus|loch** NT = Mauseloch; **Maus|mat|te** F (*Comput*) mouse pad

Mau|so|le|um [mauzoˈleːʊm] NT **-s, Mausoleen** [-ˈleːən] mausoleum

Maus-: Maus|pad [-pɛt] NT (*Comput*) mouse pad; **Maus|steu|e|rung** F (*Comput*) mouse control; **Maus|tas|te** F (*Comput*) mouse button; **Maus|zei|ger** M (*Comput*) mouse pointer

Maut [maut] F **-, -en** toll

Maut-: Maut|ge|bühr F toll (charge); **maut|pflich|tig** ADJ toll *attr*, subject to a toll *pred*; **Maut|schran|ke** F toll barrier (*Brit*), turnpike

(*US*); **Maut|stel|le** F tollgate; **Maut|stra|ße** F toll road, turnpike (*US*)

max. *abbr von* **maximal**

ma|xi [ˈmaksi] ADJ *pred* (*Fashion*) maxi; **Maxi tragen** to wear maxi *or* ankle-length skirts/dresses

Ma|xi- [ˈmaksi] *in cpds* maxi- **a** (*= Riesen-*) giant-sized; **eine Maxiflasche** a giant-sized bottle **b** (*Fashion*) (really) long; **ein Maxikleid** a long dress

ma|xi|mal [maksiˈmaːl] ADJ maximum ADV (*= höchstens*) at most; **bis zu ~ £ 100** up to a maximum of £100

Ma|xi|mal- [maksiˈmaːl] *in cpds* maximum; **Ma|xi|mal|ge|schwin|dig|keit** F maximum *or* top speed; **zulässige ~** maximum permitted speed; **Ma|xi|mal|ge|wicht** NT maximum weight

ma|xi|me [maˈksiːmə] F **-, -n** (*Liter, Philos*) maxim

ma|xi|mie|ren [maksiˈmiːrən] *ptp* **maximiert** VT (*Econ*) to maximize

Ma|xi|mie|rung F **-, -en** (*Econ*) maximization

Ma|xi|mum [ˈmaksimʊm] NT **-s, Maxima** [-ma] maximum (*an +dat* of)

Ma|xi-Sin|gle [-sɪŋgl] F twelve-inch single

Ma|ya [ˈmaːja] M **-(s), -(s)** *or f* **-, -(s)** Maya

Ma|yo [ˈmaːjo] F **-, -s** (*inf*) mayonnaise, mayo (*inf*)

Ma|yon|nai|se [majoˈnɛːzə] F **-, -n** mayonnaise

Ma|ze|do|ni|en [matseˈdoːniən] NT **-s** Macedonia

Mä|zen [mɛˈtseːn] M **-s, -e**, **Mä|ze|nin** [-ˈtseːnɪn] F **-, -nen** patron

Mä|ze|na|tentum [mɛtseˈnaːtntuːm] NT **-s**, *no pl* **a** (*= Kunstförderung*) patronage (of the arts) **b** (*= Wesen eines Mäzens*) spirit of patronage

Ma|zur|ka [maˈzʊrka] F **-, -s** mazurka

MB [ɛmˈbeː] *abbr von* **Megabyte** Mb

MByte, Mbyte [ˈɛmbait] *abbr von* **Megabyte** mbyte

Mc-Job [ˈmɛkdʒɔp] M (*sl*) McJob

MdB M , **M. d. B.** [ɛmdeːˈbeː] M **-s, -s** *abbr von* **Mitglied des Bundestages** Member of the Bundestag

MdE [ɛmdeːˈeː] M **-s, -s**, **MdEP** [ɛmdeːˈeːˈpeː] M **-s, -s** *abbr von* **Mitglied des Europäischen Parlaments** MEP

MdL M , **M. d. L.** [ɛmdeːˈlel] M **-s, -s** *abbr von* **Mitglied des Landtages** Member of the Landtag

MDR [ɛmdeːˈɛr] M - *abbr von* **Mitteldeutscher Rundfunk**

m. E. *abbr von* **meines Erachtens** in my opinion

mech. *abbr von* **mechanisch**

Me|cha|nik [meˈçaːnɪk] F **-, -en** **a** *no pl* (*Phys*) mechanics *sing* **b** (*rare: = Mechanismus*) mechanism

Me|cha|ni|ker [meˈçaːnikɐ] M **-s, -**, **Me|cha|ni|ke|rin** [-ərɪn] F **-, -nen** mechanic

me|cha|nisch [meˈçaːnɪʃ] ADJ (*alle Bedeutungen*) mechanical; **~er Webstuhl** power loom ADV mechanically

me|cha|ni|sie|ren [meçaniˈziːrən] *ptp* **mechanisiert** VT to mechanize

Me|cha|ni|sie|rung F **-, -en** mechanization

Me|cha|ni|sie|rungs|pro|zeß M process of mechanization

Me|cha|nis|mus [meçaˈnɪsmʊs] M **-, Mechanismen** [-mən] mechanism; (*= Methode, Arbeitsablauf*) machinery

me|cha|nis|tisch [meçaˈnɪstɪʃ] ADJ (*Philos, Psych*) mechanistic

meck [mɛk] INTERJ (*Ziege*) **~, ~!** meh, meh!

Me|cke|re|cke F (*inf, in Zeitung, Zeitschrift*) complaints column

Me|cke|rei [mɛkəˈrai] F **-, -en** (*inf*) moaning, grumbling, griping (*inf*)

Me|cke|rer [ˈmɛkərɐ] M **-s, -**, **Me|cke|rin** [-ərɪn] F (*inf*) moaner, grumbler, griper (*inf*)

Me|cker-: Me|cker|frit|ze M (*inf*) bellyacher (*inf*), wailing Willie (*Brit inf*); **Me|cker|lie|se** [-liːzə] F **-, -n** (*inf*) moaning minnie (*Brit inf*), moaner (*inf*)

me|ckern [ˈmɛkɐn] **VI** (*Ziege*) to bleat; (*inf: Mensch*) to moan, to bleat (*inf*), to gripe (*inf*); **über jdn/etw** (*acc*) **~** (*inf*) to moan or bleat (*inf*) about sb/sth

Me|cker|zie|ge F (*inf*) sourpuss (*inf*), ratbag (*Brit inf*)

Meck|len|burg-Vor|pom|mern [ˈmeːklənbʊrkfoːɐpɔmɐn, ˈmɛklənbʊrk-] NT Mecklenburg-West Pomerania

med. *abbr von* **medizinisch**

Me|dail|le [meˈdaljə] F **-, -n** (*= Gedenkmünze*) medallion; (*bei Wettbewerben*) medal

Me|dail|len- [meˈdaljən-]: **Me|dail|len|ge|win|ner(in)** M(F) medallist, medal winner; **Me|dail|len|spie|gel** M medals table

Me|dail|lon [medalˈjõː] NT **-s, -s** **a** (*= Bildchen*) medallion; (*= Schmuckkapsel*) locket **b** (*Cook*) médaillon

me|di|al [meˈdiaːl] ADJ **a** (*= die Medien betreffend*) media *attr* **b** (*Gram*) middle **c** (*Med*) medial, median; (*Psych*) mediumistic ADV **wir leben in einer ~ vernetzten Welt** we live in a world interconnected through the media; **ein Ereignis ~ ausschlachten** to exploit an event in the media

Me|di|a|thek [mediaˈteːk] F **-, -en** multimedia centre (*Brit*) or center (*US*)

Me|di|a|ti|on [mediaˈtsioːn] F **-, -en** mediation

Me|di|ä|vist [mediˈɛvɪst] M **-en, -en**, **Me|di|ä|vis|tin** F [-ˈvɪstɪn] **-, -nen** medievalist

Me|di|ä|vis|tik [mediˈɛvɪstɪk] F **-**, *no pl* medieval studies *sing or pl*

Me|di|en [ˈmeːdiən] PL media *pl*

Me|di|en-: Me|di|en|be|ra|ter(in) M(F) press adviser; **Me|di|en|er|eig|nis** NT media event; **Me|di|en|for|schung** F media research; **me|di|en|ge|recht** ADJ suited to the media ADV in a manner or way suited to the media; **Me|di|en|ge|setz** NT media law; **Me|di|en|gi|gant** M media giant; **Me|di|en|kon|zern** M media group or concern; **Me|di|en|land|schaft** F , *no pl* media landscape; **Me|di|en|mo|gul** M media mogul; **Me|di|en|po|li|tik** F (mass) media policy; **Me|di|en|prä|senz** F , *no pl* media presence; **Me|di|en|re|fe|rent(in)** M(F) press officer; **Me|di|en|re|so|nanz** F media response or resonance; **Me|di|en|rum|mel** M media excitement; **Me|di|en|schel|te** F media-bashing (*inf*); **~ betreiben** to knock the media; **Me|di|en|spek|ta|kel** NT media circus; **Me|di|en|ver|bund** M **etw im ~ lernen** to learn sth using the multimedia system; **me|di|en|wirk|sam** ADJ **eine ~e Kampagne** a campaign geared toward(s) the media ADV **etw ~ präsentieren** to gear sth toward(s) the media

Me|di|ka|ment [medikaˈmɛnt] NT **-(e)s, -e** medicine

Me|di|ka|men|ten-: me|di|ka|men|ten|ab|hän|gig ADJ **~ sein** to be addicted to medical drugs; **Me|di|ka|men|ten|ab|hän|gig|keit** F addiction to medical drugs; **Me|di|ka|men|ten|miss|brauch** ▲ M drug abuse; **Me|di|ka|men|ten|sucht** F , *no pl* drug dependency

me|di|ka|men|tös [medikamɛnˈtøːs] ADJ *Behandlung, Therapie* medicinal ADV **behandeln** medicinally

Me|di|kus [ˈmeːdikʊs] M **-, Medizi** [-tsi] *or* **-se** (*hum*) quack (*hum inf*), doc (*inf*); (*esp Student*) medic (*inf*)

Me|di|o [ˈmeːdio] M **-(s), -s** (*Fin*) middle of the month, mid-month

me|di|o|ker [meˈdioːkɐ] (*geh*) ADJ mediocre ADV **der Schüler hat ~ abgeschnitten** the pupil got mediocre marks (*Brit*) or grades (*US*)

Me|di|o|kri|tät F **-, -en** (*geh*) mediocrity

Me|di|o|thek [medioˈteːk] F **-, -en** multimedia centre (*Brit*) or center (*US*)

Me|di|o|wech|sel M (*Fin*) bill for payment mid-month

Me|di|sance [medi'zã:sə] F -, -n (*geh*) malicious remark

Me|di|ta|ti|on [medita'tsio:n] F -, -en meditation

me|di|ta|tiv [medita'ti:f] ADJ meditative; **in ~er Versunkenheit** lost in meditation ADV meditatively

me|di|ter|ran [medite'ra:n] ADJ Mediterranean

me|di|tie|ren [medi'ti:rən] ptp **meditiert** VI to meditate

Me|di|um ['me:diʊm] NT -s, **Medien** [-diən] medium; (*Gram*) middle (voice)

Me|di|zin [medi'tsi:n] F -, -en **a** no pl (= *Heilkunde*) medicine **b** (*inf*: = *Heilmittel*) medicine; **das ist ~ für ihn** that's his medicine; (*fig*: *Lektion, Denkzettel*) that'll teach him a lesson

Me|di|zi|nal- [meditsina:l-]: **Me|di|zi|nal|as|sis|tent(in)** M(F) houseman (*Brit*), intern (*US*); **Me|di|zi|nal|rat** M , **Me|di|zi|nal|rä|tin** F medical officer of health; **Me|di|zi|nal|sta|tis|tik** F medical statistics *pl*

Me|di|zin|ball M (*Sport*) medicine ball

Me|di|zi|ner [medi'tsi:nɐ] M -s, -, **Me|di|zi|ne|rin** [-ərɪn] F -, -nen **a** doctor **b** (*Univ*) medic (*inf*)

me|di|zi|nisch [medi'tsi:nɪʃ] ADJ **a** (= *ärztlich*) medical; **~e Fakultät** school or faculty of medicine; **~e Klinik** clinic for internal medicine; **~-technische Assistentin, ~-technischer Assistent** medical technician **b** (= *heilend*) Kräuter, Bäder medicinal; Shampoo medicated ADV **a** (*von einem Arzt*) medically; **sich ~ beraten lassen** to get medical advice; **jdn ~ behandeln** to treat sb (medically); **~ betreut werden** to be in medical care, to be treated; **~ beobachtet werden** to be under (medical) observation **b** (= *heilkundlich*) ausbilden medically; **~ wirksame Kräuter** medicinal herbs

Me|di|zin-: Me|di|zin|mann M *pl* -männer medicine man, witch doctor; (*hum*: = *Arzt*) quack (*inf*), medico (*US inf*); **Me|di|zin|schränk|chen** NT medicine cabinet or cupboard; **Me|di|zin|stu|dent(in)** M(F) medical student; **Me|di|zin|stu|di|um** NT study of medicine

Med|ley ['mɛdli] NT -s, -s (*Mus*) medley

Me|du|se [me'du:zə] F -, -n **a** (*Myth*) Medusa **b** (*Zool*) medusa (*spec*), jellyfish

Me|du|sen|haupt NT **a** (*Liter*) head of Medusa **b** (*Med*) caput medusae (*spec*)

Meer [me:ɐ] NT -(e)s, -e **a** sea; (= *Weltmeer*) ocean; **am ~(e)** by the sea; **diesseits des ~es** at home; **jenseits des ~es** across the sea; **übers ~ fahren** to travel (across) the seas; **ans ~ fahren** to go to the sea(side); **über dem ~** above sea level **b** (*fig*: = *riesige Menge*) sea

Meer-: Meer|bu|sen M gulf, bay; **Bottnischer ~** Gulf of Bothnia; **Meer|en|ge** F straits *pl*, strait

Mee|res-: Mee|res|al|gen PL seaweed, marine algae *pl* (*spec*); **Mee|res|arm** M arm of the sea, inlet; **Mee|res|bio|lo|ge** M , **Mee|res|bio|lo|gin** F marine biologist; **Mee|res|bo|den** M seabed, sea bottom, bottom of the sea; **Mee|res|fau|na** F marine fauna; **Mee|res|fisch** M saltwater fish; **Mee|res|flo|ra** F marine flora; **Mee|res|for|schung** F oceanography; **Mee|res|frei|heit** F (*Jur*) freedom of the seas; **Mee|res|früch|te** PL seafood *sing*; **Mee|res|grund** M seabed, sea bottom, bottom of the sea; **Mee|res|hö|he** F sea level; **Mee|res|kli|ma** NT maritime climate; **Mee|res|kun|de** F oceanography; **mee|res|kund|lich** [-kʊntlɪç] ADJ oceanographic(al); **Mee|res|leuch|ten** NT -s, no pl marine phosphorescence; **Mee|res|ober|flä|che** F surface of the sea; **Mee|res|schild|krö|te** F turtle; **Mee|res|spie|gel** M sea level; **über/unter dem ~** above/below sea level; **Mee|res|stil|le**

F calm (at sea); **Mee|res|strand** M (*liter*) seashore, strand (*poet*); **Mee|res|stra|ße** F waterway; **Mee|res|strö|mung** F ocean current; **Mee|res|tie|fe** F depth (of the sea or ocean); **Mee|res|tier** NT marine creature; **Mee|res|ufer** NT seashore, coast

Meer-: Meer|gott M (*Myth*) sea god; **Meer|göt|tin** F sea goddess; **meer|grün** ADJ sea-green; **Meer|jung|fer** F , **Meer|jung|frau** F mermaid; **Meer|kat|ze** F long-tailed monkey, guenon; **Meer|ret|tich** M horseradish; **Meer|salz** NT sea salt; **Meer|schaum** M (*Miner*) meerschaum; **Meer|schaum|pfei|fe** F meerschaum (pipe); **Meer|schwein|chen** NT guinea pig, cavy (*spec*); **meer|um|schlun|gen** ADJ (*poet*) seagirt (*poet*), seabound; **Meer|un|ge|heu|er** NT sea monster; **meer|wärts** ['me:ɐverts] ADV seawards

Meer|was|ser NT sea water

Meer|was|ser-: Meer|was|ser|auf|be|rei|tung F treatment of sea water; **Meer|was|ser|ent|sal|zung** F desalination of sea water; **Meer|was|ser|ent|sal|zungs|an|la|ge** F desalination plant

Mee|ting ['mi:tɪŋ] NT -s, -s meeting

Me|ga-, me|ga- ['me:ga] *in cpds* **a** (*eine Million*) mega- **b** (*inf*: = *Super-*) mega- (*inf*); **Me|ga|bit** NT megabit; **Me|ga|bit-Chip** M megabit chip; **Me|ga|byte** [-'baɪt] NT megabyte; **Me|ga|fon** ▲ [mega'fo:n] NT -s, -e = Megaphon; **me|ga|geil** ADJ (*sl*) mega (*inf*); **Me|ga|hertz** NT megahertz; **me|ga|in** ADJ pred (*inf*) mega cool (*inf*)

Me|ga|lith [mega'li:t] M -en, -en (*Archeol*) megalith

Me|ga|lith-: Me|ga|lith|grab NT (*Archeol*) dolmen, megalithic tomb; **Me|ga|lith|kul|tur** F (*Hist*) megalithic culture

Me|ga|lo-: me|ga|lo|man [megalo'ma:n] ADJ (*geh*) megalomanic; **Me|ga|lo|ma|nie** [megalo-ma'ni:] F (*geh*) megalomania; **Me|ga|lo|po|lis** [mega'lo:polɪs] F -, **Megalopolen** [megalo-'po:lən] megalopolis

Me|ga-: me|ga-out ['me:ga'laʊt] ADJ pred (*inf*) mega uncool (*inf*); **Me|ga|phon** [mega'fo:n] NT -s, -e megaphone; **Me|gä|re** [me'gɛ:rə] F -, -n **a** (*Myth*) Megaera **b** (*fig liter*) shrew, termagant (*liter*)

Me|ga-: Me|ga|star M (*inf*) megastar; **Me|ga|ton|ne** F megaton; **Me|ga|ton|nen|bom|be** F megaton bomb; **Me|ga|watt** NT -s, - megawatt

Mehl [me:l] NT -(e)s, -e flour; (*gröber*) meal; (= *Knochenmehl*) bone meal; (= *Pulver, Zementmehl*) powder

Mehl-: mehl|ar|tig ADJ floury, mealy; **Mehl|bee|re** F berry of the whitebeam; **Mehl|brei** M pap, flummery

meh|lig ['me:lɪç] ADJ Äpfel, Kartoffeln mealy ADV **~ schmecken** to taste mealy; **~ kochend** mealy

Mehl-: Mehl|kleis|ter M flour paste; **Mehl|kloß** M dumpling; **Mehl|papp** M (*inf*) mush (*inf*); **Mehl|sack** M flour bag; **wie ein ~** (*inf*) like a sack of potatoes; **Mehl|schwal|be** F (*Orn*) house martin; **Mehl|schwit|ze** F (*Cook*) roux; **Mehl|spei|se** F **a** (= *Gericht*) flummery **b** (*Aus*) (= *Nachspeise*) sweet, dessert; (= *Kuchen*) pastry; **Mehl|sup|pe** F gruel; **Mehl|tau** M (*Bot*) mildew; **Mehl|wurm** M (*Zool*) mealworm

mehr [me:ɐ] INDEF PRON INV *comp von* **viel** *von* **sehr** more; **was wollen Sie ~?** what more do you want?; **zu ~ hat es nicht gelangt** or **gereicht** that was all I/you etc could manage; **~ will er nicht bezahlen** he doesn't want to pay (any) more; **ist das alles, ~ kostet das nicht?** is that all it costs?; **je ~ er hat, je ~ er will** (*Prov*) the more he has, the more he wants; **sich für ~ halten** (*inf*) to think one is something more; **mit ~ oder weniger Erfolg** with a greater or lesser degree of success ADV **a** (= *in höherem Maße*) more; **immer ~** more and more; **~ oder weniger** or **minder** (*geh*)

more or less; **~ lang als breit** more long than wide, longer than it is/they are wide; **~ ein juristisches Problem** more (of) a legal problem; **war er brav/sind Sie beleidigt/hat es Ihnen geschmeckt? – ~ als das** was he good/are you insulted/did you like it? – "good/insulted/like" is not the word for it; **würden Sie das gerne tun? – ja, nichts ~ als das** would you like to? – there's nothing I'd rather do **b** (+*neg*: = *sonst, länger*) **ich habe kein Geld ~** I have no more money, I haven't or I don't have any more money; **du bist doch kein Kind ~!** you're not a child any longer or any more!, you're no longer a child!; **es hat sich keiner ~ beworben** nobody else has applied; **es besteht keine Hoffnung ~** there's no hope left; **kein Wort ~!** not another word!; **es war niemand ~ da** there was no-one left, everyone had gone; **daran erinnert sich niemand ~** nobody can remember that any more; **wenn niemand ~ einsteigt, ...** if nobody else gets in ...; **nicht ~** not any longer, not any more, no more, no longer; **nicht ~ lange** not much longer; **das benutzt man nicht ~** that's not used any more or any longer, it's no longer used; **er lebt nicht ~** he is dead; **das darf nicht ~ vorkommen** that must not or never happen again; **wenn unser Opa nicht ~ ist** (*euph*) when Grandpa is no longer with us; **nichts ~** nothing more; **ich kann nichts ~ sagen** I can say nothing more, I can't say anything more; **nie ~** never again, nevermore (*liter*); **ich will dich nie ~ wiedersehen** I never want to see you again, I don't ever want to see you again

Mehr [me:ɐ] NT -, no pl **a** (*esp Sw*: = *Mehrheit*) majority **b** (= *Zuwachs*) increase; **mit einem ~ an Mühe** with more effort; **auf das ~ oder Weniger an Erfahrung kommt es nicht an** it's not a question of having more or less experience

Mehr-: Mehr|ar|beit F overtime, extra time or work; **Mehr|auf|wand** M (= *Kosten*) additional expenditure; (= *Mühe*) additional effort; **Mehr|aus|ga|be** F extra or additional expense(s *pl*); **mehr|bän|dig** ADJ in several volumes, multi-volume; **Mehr|be|darf** M greater need (*an +dat* of, for); (*Comm*) increased demand, increase in demand (*an +dat* for); **Mehr|be|las|tung** F excess load; (*fig*) extra or additional burden; **Mehr|be|nut|zer-** *in cpds* (*Comput*) = Mehrplatz-; **Mehr|be|reichs|öl** NT (*Aut*) multigrade oil; **Mehr|be|trag** M **a** (= *zusätzliche Zahlung*) extra or additional amount **b** (= *Überschuss*) surplus; **mehr|deu|tig** [-dɔytɪç] ADJ ambiguous, equivocal ADV ambiguously; **Mehr|deu|tig|keit** F -, -en ambiguity, equivocalness; **mehr|di|men|si|o|nal** ADJ multidimensional ADV darstellen multi-dimensionally; **eine ~ arbeitendes Programm** a multi-dimensional program; **Mehr|ein|nah|me** F additional revenue

meh|ren ['me:rən] VT (*liter*) (= *vergrößern*) to augment, to increase; (= *fördern*) to further VR (*geh*: = *sich vermehren*) to multiply; **seid fruchtbar und mehret Euch!** (*Bibl*) be fruitful and multiply!

Meh|rer ['me:rɐ] M -s, -, **Meh|re|rin** [-ərɪn] F -, -nen (*liter*) augmenter (*form*)

meh|re|re ['me:rərə] INDEF PRON several; (= *verschiedene auch*) various

meh|re|res ['me:rərəs] INDEF PRON several or various things *pl*

meh|rer|lei ['me:rɐ'lai] INDEF PRON inv **a** (*substantivisch*) several things *pl* **b** (*adjektivisch*) several kinds of

Mehr-: Mehr|er|lös M additional revenue; **Mehr|er|trag** M additional yield, increase in yield

mehrf. abbr von **mehrfach**

mehr|fach ['me:ɐfax] ADJ multiple; (= *zahlreich*) numerous; (= *wiederholt*) repeated; **ein ~er Millionär** a multimillionaire; **der ~e Meister im Weitsprung** the man who has been the long jump champion several times; **die Unterlagen**

in ~er Ausfertigung einsenden to send in several copies of the documents **ADV** (= *öfter*) many or several times; (= *wiederholt*) repeatedly

Mehr|fach-: Mehr|fach|be|hin|der|te(r) MF *decl as adj* person with multiple disabilities; **Mehr|fach|be|steu|e|rung** F multiple taxation

Mehr|fa|che(s) ['meːɐfaxə] NT *decl as adj* **das ~** *or* **ein ~s des Kostenvoranschlags** several times the estimated cost; **verdient er wirklich mehr? – ja, das ~** *or* **ein ~s** does he earn more? – yes, several times as much

Mehr|fach-: Mehr|fach|fahr|schein M multi-journey ticket; **Mehr|fach|steck|do|se** F (*Elec*) multiple socket; **Mehr|fach|ste|cker** M (*Elec*) multiple adaptor; **Mehr|fach|tä|ter(in)** M(F) multiple offender

Mehr-: Mehr|fahr|ten|kar|te F multi-journey ticket; **Mehr|fa|mi|li|en|haus** NT multiple dwelling (*form*), house for several families; **Mehr|far|ben|druck** M *pl* **-drucke** **a** *no pl* (= *Verfahren*) colour (*Brit*) *or* color (*US*) *or* polychromatic (*form*) printing **b** (= *Druck*) colour (*Brit*) *or* color (*US*) *or* polychromatic (*form*) print; **mehr|far|big** ADJ multicoloured (*Brit*), multicolored (*US*), polychromatic (*form*); **Mehr|ge|päck** NT excess baggage; **Mehr|ge|wicht** NT additional *or* excess weight; (= *Übergewicht*) excess weight; **Mehr|ge|winn** M additional *or* surplus profits *pl*

Mehr|heit F **-, -en** **a** *no pl* (= *größerer Teil*) majority (*with sing or pl vb*); **weitaus in der ~** decidedly in the majority **b** (= *Stimmenmehrheit*) majority; **die absolute/einfache** *or* **relative ~** an absolute/a simple *or* relative majority; **die ~ haben** *or* **besitzen/gewinnen** *or* **erringen** to have/win *or* gain a majority; **die ~ der Stimmen auf sich vereinigen** to secure a majority of votes; **die ~ verlieren** to lose one's majority; **mit zwei Stimmen ~** with a majority of two (votes)

mehr|heit|lich [-haitlɪç] ADV **wir sind ~ der Ansicht, dass ...** the majority of us think(s) that ...; **der Stadtrat hat ~ beschlossen ...** the town council has reached a majority decision ...; **an einer Gesellschaft ~ beteiligt sein** to be the majority shareholder *or* to have the majority holding in a company; **eine Gesellschaft ~ übernehmen** to become the majority shareholder in a company

Mehr|heits-: Mehr|heits|be|schaf|fer M **-s, -, Mehr|heits|be|schaf|fe|rin** F **-, -nen** (*Pol*) junior coalition partner (*securing majority*); **Mehr|heits|be|schluss** ▲ M majority decision; **Mehr|heits|be|tei|li|gung** F (*Econ*) majority holding; **Mehr|heits|ent|schei|dung** F majority decision; **mehr|heits|fä|hig** ADJ capable of winning a majority; **Mehr|heits|füh|rer(in)** M(F) leader of the majority faction; **Mehr|heits|grund|satz** M principle of majority rule; **Mehr|heits|par|tei|en** PL majority parties *pl*; **Mehr|heits|prin|zip** NT principle of majority rule; **Mehr|heits|ver|hält|nis** NT majority; **~se** *pl* distribution of power; **Mehr|heits|wahl** F first-past-the-post election; **Mehr|heits|wahl|recht** NT first-past-the-post system, majority vote system

Mehr-: mehr|jäh|rig ADJ *attr* of several years; **~e Klinikerfahrung** several years of clinical experience; **Mehr|kampf** M (*Sport*) multidiscipline event; **Mehr|kämp|fer(in)** M(F) (*Sport*) all-round (*Brit*) *or* all-around (*US*) athlete, all-rounder (*Brit*); **mehr|köpf|ig** ADJ *attr* **eine ~e Familie** a multi-member family; **Mehr|kos|ten** PL additional costs *pl*; (*in Hotel etc*) additional expenses *pl*; **Mehr|la|de|ge|wehr** NT , **Mehr|la|der** [-laːdɐ] M **-s, -** repeater, repeater rifle; **mehr|ma|lig** ['meːɐmaːlɪç] ADJ *attr* repeated; **mehr|mals** ['meːɐmaːls] ADV several times, repeatedly; **Mehr|par|tei|en|sys|tem** NT multiparty system; **Mehr|pha|sen|strom** M (*Elec*) multiphase *or* polyphase current

Mehr|platz- ['meːɐplats] *in cpds* (*Comput*) multi-user; **mehr|platz|fä|hig** ADJ (*Comput*) capable of supporting multi-user operation; **Mehr|platz|rech|ner** M (*Comput*) multi-user system

Mehr-: Mehr|rumpf|boot NT multihull (boat); **mehr|schich|tig** [-ʃɪçtɪç] ADJ (*lit, fig*) multilayered; **mehr|sil|big** ADJ polysyllabic, multisyllabic; **mehr|spra|chig** ADJ *Person, Wörterbuch* multilingual, polyglot (*form*); *Brief, Fragebogen etc* in several languages **ADV** in more than one language, in several languages; **~ aufwachsen** to grow up multilingual, to grow up speaking several languages; **Mehr|spra|chig|keit** F **-,** *no pl* multilingualism; **mehr|stel|lig** ADJ *attr Zahl, Betrag* multidigit; **mehr|stim|mig** ADJ (*Mus*) for several voices; **~es Lied** part-song **ADV** *spielen* in more than one voice; **~ singen** to sing in harmony; **Mehr|stim|mig|keit** F (*Mus*) polyphony; **mehr|stö|ckig** ADJ multistorey (*Brit*), multistory (*US*) **ADV ~ bau|en** to build *or* erect multistorey (*Brit*) *or* multistory (*US*) buildings; **~ planen** to plan a multistorey (*Brit*) *or* multistory (*US*) building; **Mehr|stu|fen|ra|ke|te** F multistage rocket; **mehr|stu|fig** ADJ multistage; **mehr|stün|dig** ADJ *attr Verhandlungen* lasting several hours; **mit ~er Verspätung eintreffen** to arrive several hours late; **mehr|tä|gig** ADJ *attr Konferenz* lasting several days; **nach ~er Abwesenheit** after an absence of several days, after several days' absence; **Mehr|tei|ler** M **a** (= *Kleidungsstück*) combination; (= *Anzug*) suit **b** (*TV*) (= *Serie*) series; (= *Film*) serial; **mehr|tei|lig** ADJ in several parts

Meh|rung ['meːrʊŋ] F **-,** *no pl* (*liter*) increase

Mehr|ver|brauch M additional consumption

Mehr|weg- ['meːɐveːk] *in cpds* reusable; **Mehr|weg|fla|sche** F returnable bottle; **Mehr|weg|sys|tem** NT (bottle *or* packaging) return system; **Mehr|weg|ver|pa|ckung** F reusable packaging

Mehr-: Mehr|wert M (*Econ*) added value; **mehr|wer|tig** ADJ (*Chem*) polyvalent, multivalent; **Mehr|wert|steu|er** F value added tax, VAT; **mehr|wö|chig** [-vœçɪç] ADJ *attr* lasting several weeks; *Abwesenheit* of several weeks; **Mehr|zahl** F **,** *no pl* **a** (*Gram*) plural **b** (= *Mehrheit*) majority; **mehr|zei|lig** ADJ of several lines; **mehr|zel|lig** [-tsɛlɪç] ADJ multicellular

Mehr|zweck- ['meːɐtsvɛk] *in cpds* multipurpose; **Mehr|zweck|ge|rät** NT multipurpose gadget; **Mehr|zweck|hal|le** F multipurpose room

mei|den ['maidn] *pret* **mied** [miːt], *ptp* **gemieden** [ɡəˈmiːdn] VT to avoid

Mei|e|rei [maiəˈrai] F **-, -en** **a** (*dial*: = *Molkerei*) dairy (farm) **b** (*old*: = *Pachtgut*) leasehold farm

Mei|le ['mailə] F **-, -n** mile; (= *4,8 km*) league; **das riecht man drei ~n gegen den Wind** (*inf*) you can smell *or* tell that a mile off (*Brit*) *or* away (*inf*)

Mei|len-: mei|len|lang ADJ mile-long **ADV** for miles; **Mei|len|stein** M (*lit, fig*) milestone; **Mei|len|stie|fel** PL seven-league boots *pl*; **mei|len|weit** ADJ of many miles; **~e Sandstrände** miles and miles of sandy beaches **ADV** for miles; **~ auseinander/entfernt** (*lit, fig*) miles apart/away; **Mei|len|zahl** F mileage; **Mei|len|zäh|ler** M mileometer (*Brit*), clock (*Brit inf*), odometer

Mei|ler ['mailɐ] M **-s, -** (= *Kohlenmeiler*) charcoal kiln *or* pile; (= *Atommeiler*) (atomic) pile

mein [main] POSS PRON **a** (*adjektivisch*) my; **~ verdammtes Auto** (*inf*) this damn car of mine (*inf*); **ich trinke so ~e fünf Flaschen Bier pro Tag** I drink my five bottles of beer a day **b** (*old: substantivisch*) mine; **Mein und Dein verwechseln** (*euph*) to take what doesn't belong to one PERS PRON *gen von* **ich** (*old, poet*) of me

Mein|eid ['mainait] M perjury *no indef art*; **ei|nen ~ leisten** *or* **ablegen** to perjure oneself, to commit perjury

mein|ei|dig ['mainaidɪç] ADJ perjured; **~ wer|den** to commit perjury, to perjure oneself

Mein|ei|di|ge(r) ['mainaidɪɡə] MF *decl as adj* perjurer

mei|nen ['mainən] ✪ **29.1, 53.2** VI (= *denken, glauben*) to think; **ich würde/man möchte ~** I/one would think; **ich meine, ...** I think ..., I reckon ... (*inf*); **~ Sie?** (do) you think so?, do you reckon? (*inf*); **wie ~ Sie?** I beg your pardon?; **ich meine nur so** (*inf*) it was just a thought; **wie Sie ~!** as you wish; (*drohend auch*) have it your own way; **wenn du meinst!** if you like, I don't mind; **man sollte ~** one would have thought

VT **a** (= *der Ansicht sein*) to think; **was ~ Sie da|zu?** what do you think *or* say?; **~ Sie das im Ernst?** are you serious about that?; **das will ich ~!** I quite agree!; **das sollte man ~!** one would think so

b (= *sagen wollen*) to mean; (*inf:* = *sagen*) to say; **was ~ Sie damit?**, **wie ~ Sie das?** what *or* how do you mean?; (*drohend*) (just) what do you mean by that?

c (*geh:* = *bedeuten*) to mean

d (= *bezeichnen wollen*) to mean; **damit bin ich gemeint** that's meant for me, they mean/he means *etc* me

e (= *beabsichtigen*) to mean, to intend; **so war es nicht gemeint** it wasn't meant like that; **sie meint es gut** she means well; **sie meint es nicht böse** she means no harm, she doesn't mean any harm; **die Sonne hat es aber heute wieder gut (mit uns) gemeint!** the sun's done its best for us again today

mei|ner ['mainɐ] PERS PRON *gen von* **ich** of me

mei|ne(r, s) ['mainə] POSS PRON (*substantivisch*) mine; **der/die/das Meine** (*geh*) mine; **ich tu das Meine** (*geh*) I'll do my bit; **das Meine** (*geh:* = *Besitz*) what is mine; **die Meinen** (*geh:* = *Familie*) my people, my family

mei|ner|seits ['mainɐzaits] ADV as far as I'm concerned, for my part; **ich ~** I personally, I myself, I for my part; **Vorschläge/Einwände ~** suggestions/objections from me; **ganz ~!** the pleasure's (all) mine

mei|nes-: mei|nes|glei|chen ['mainəsˈɡlaiçn] PRON *inv* (= *meiner Art*) people such as I *or* me, people like me *or* myself; (= *gleichrangig*) my own kind, my equals; **Leute** *or* **Menschen ~** (= *meiner Art*) people like me *or* myself; (= *gleichrangig*) people of my own kind, my equals; **mei|nes|teils** ['mainəsˈtails] ADV for my part

mei|net-: mei|net|hal|ben ['mainətˈhalbn] (*dated*), **mei|net|we|gen** ['mainətˈveːɡn] ADV **a** (= *wegen mir*) because of me, on account of me, on my account; (= *mir zuliebe*) for my sake; (= *um mich*) for me; (= *für mich*) on my behalf **b** (= *von mir aus*) as far as I'm concerned; **mei|netwegen!** if you like; **wenn Ihr das tun wollt, meinetwegen, aber ...** if you want to do that, fair enough (*inf*), but ...; **mei|net|wil|len** ['mainətˈvilən] ADV **um ~** (= *mir zuliebe*) for my sake; (= *wegen mir*) on my account

mei|ni|ge ['mainɪɡə] POSS PRON **der/die/das Meinige** *or* (*form, old*) mine; **die Meinigen** (*geh*) my family, my people

meins [mains] POSS PRON mine

Mei|nung ['mainʊŋ] ✪ **29.2, 33, 34.5, 38.1, 39.1, 40.1, 40.4, 41, 53.3, 53.5** F **-, -en** opinion; (= *Anschauung auch*) view; (= *Urteil*) judgement, estimation; **eine vorgefasste ~** a preconceived idea; **nach meiner ~, meiner ~ nach** in my opinion *or* view; **ich bin der ~, dass ...** I'm of the opinion that ..., I take the view that ...; **eine/keine hohe ~ von jdm/etw haben** to think/not to think highly of sb/sth, to have a high/low opinion of sb/sth; **seine ~ ändern** to change one's opinion *or* mind; **einer ~ sein** to share the same opinion, to think the same; **geteilter ~ sein** to have different opinions; **was ist Ihre ~ dazu?** what's your opinion *or* view (about *or* on that)?; **von seiner ~ eingenommen sein** to be opinionated; **ganz meine ~!** I completely agree!, hear, hear!; **das ist auch meine ~!** that's just what I think; **jdm (kräftig** or **vernünftig) die ~ sagen** (*inf*) to give sb a piece of one's mind (*inf*)

Meinungs-: Meinungsänderung F change of opinion; **Meinungsäußerung** F (expression of) opinion; **Meinungsaustausch** M exchange of views (*über +acc* on, about); **meinungsbildend** ADJ opinion-forming; **Meinungsbildung** ~ wirken to shape public opinion; **Meinungsbildung** F formation of opinion; **der Prozess der ~ ist noch nicht abgeschlossen** we have not yet formed an opinion; **Meinungsforscher(in)** M(F) (opinion) pollster; **Meinungsforschung** F (public) opinion polling or research; **Meinungsforschungsinstitut** NT opinion research institute; **Meinungsfreiheit** F freedom of speech; **Meinungsführer(in)** M(F) opinion leader; **die Rolle als ~ verlieren** (*Pol*) to no longer set the (political) agenda; **Meinungsklima** NT climate of public opinion; **meinungslos** ADJ without opinions, viewless; **~ sein** to have no opinions; **Meinungsmache** F (*pej inf*) propaganda; **Meinungsmacher(in)** M(F) (*inf*) opinion-maker, opinion-leader; **Meinungsmanipulation** F manipulation of (public) opinion; **Meinungsmonopol** NT monopoly of opinion; **Meinungsstreit** M conflict of views or opinions, controversy, dispute; **Meinungsumfrage** F (public) opinion poll; **Meinungsumschwung** M swing of opinion; **Meinungsunterschied** M *usu pl* difference of opinion; **da gibt es ~e** opinions are divided on that; **zwischen Herrn Meier und mir gibt es erhebliche ~e, was … angeht** where … is or are concerned, Mr Meier and I have considerable differences of opinion or think quite differently; **Meinungsverschiedenheit** F difference of opinion

Meise ['maɪzə] F -, -n titmouse; **eine ~ haben** (*inf*) to be crackers (*Brit*) or crazy (*inf*)

Meisenring M bird-feeding ring

Meißel ['maɪsl] M -s, - chisel

meißeln ['maɪsln] VTI to chisel

Meißener ['maɪsənə], **Meißner** ['maɪsnɐ] ADJ **Meiß(e)ner Porzellan** Dresden or Meissen china

meist [maɪst] ADV = **meistens**

Meist-: meistbegünstigt [-bəgʏnstɪçt] ADJ (*Econ*) most-favoured (*Brit*), most-favored (*US*); **Meistbegünstigung** F (*Econ, Pol*) most-favoured-nation (*Brit*) or most-favored-nation (*US*) treatment; **Meistbegünstigungsklausel** F (*Econ, Pol*) most-favoured-nation (*Brit*) or most-favored-nation (*US*) clause; **meistbietend** ADJ highest bidding; **Meistbietender** highest bidder; **~ or an den Meistbietenden versteigern** to sell or auction (off) to the highest bidder

meisten ['maɪstn] **am ~** ADV **a** *superl von* **viel** the most **b** *superl von* **sehr** most of all; **am ~ bekannt** best known

meistens ['maɪstns] ADV mostly, more often than not; (= *zum größten Teil*) for the most part

meistenteils ['maɪstn'taɪls] ADV = **meistens**

Meister ['maɪstɐ] M -s, - **a** (= *Handwerksmeister*) master (craftsman); (*in Laden*) boss (*inf*); (*in Fabrik*) foreman, boss (*inf*); (*sl: als Anrede*) guv (*Brit inf*), chief (*Brit inf*), mac (*US inf*); (*Sport*) champion; (*Mannschaft*) champions *pl*; **seinen ~ machen** to take one's master craftsman's diploma

b (= *Lehrmeister, Künstler*) master (*auch fig*); **alter ~** (*Art*) (old) master; **~ vom Stuhl** (*Freimaurer*) Master of the Lodge; **er hat seinen ~ gefunden** (*fig*) he's met his match; **~ einer Sache** (*gen*) or **in etw** (*dat*) past master at sth; **ein ~ seines Faches sein** to be a master of one's craft; **es ist noch kein ~ vom Himmel gefallen** (*Prov*) no-one is born a master

c (*old liter*) master; **~ Zwirn** Snip, the tailor; **~ Knieriem** or **Pfriem/Lampe** Master Cobbler/Hare; **~ Urian** Old Nick

meiste(r, s) ['maɪstə] INDEF PRON *superl von* **viel a** (*adjektivisch*) **die ~n Leute** most people; **die ~n Leute, die …** most people who …, most of the people who …; **du hast die ~ Zeit** you have (the) most time **b** (*substantivisch*) **die ~n** most people; **die ~n (von ihnen)** most (of them), the majority (of them); **das ~ von dir** most of it; **du hast das ~** you have (the) most

Meister- *in cpds* master; **Meisterbrief** M master craftsman's diploma or certificate; **Meistergesang** M (*Liter*) poetry of the Meistersingers; **meisterhaft** ADJ masterly, brilliantly; **er versteht es ~ zu lügen** he is brilliant at lying; **Meisterhand** F **von ~** by a master hand

Meisterin ['maɪstərɪn] F -, -nen (= *Handwerksmeisterin*) master craftswoman; (= *Frau von Handwerksmeister*) master craftsman's wife; (*in Fabrik*) forewoman; (*Sport*) champion; **Frau ~!** madam!

Meister-: Meisterklasse F master class; **Meisterleistung** F masterly performance; (*iro*) brilliant achievement

meisterlich ['maɪstɐlɪç] ADJ, ADV = **meisterhaft**

meistern ['maɪstɐn] VT to master; *Schwierigkeiten* to overcome; **sein Leben ~** to come to grips with one's life

Meisterprüfung F examination for master craftsman's diploma or certificate

Meisterschaft ['maɪstɐʃaft] F -, -en **a** (*Sport*) championship; (*Veranstaltung*) championships *pl* **b** *no pl* (= *Können*) mastery; **es zu wahrer ~ bringen** (*als Künstler etc*) to become really proficient or expert, to achieve real mastery or proficiency; (*als Dieb etc*) to get it down to a fine art

Meisterschafts-: Meisterschaftsfeier F (*Sport*) title-winners' celebration; **Meisterschaftsspiel** NT (*Sport*) league match

Meister-: Meisterschule F school for master craftspeople; **Meisterschüler(in)** M(F) (*Art, Mus*) pupil (*in a master class*); **Meisterschuss** ▲ M brilliant shot; **Meisterschütze** M marksman, crack shot; **Meisterschützin** F markswoman, crack shot; **Meistersinger** [-zɪŋɐ] M -s, - (*Hist*) meistersinger, mastersinger; **Meisterstück** NT (*von Handwerker*) work done to qualify as master craftsman (*fig*) masterpiece; (= *geniale Tat*) master stroke; **Meistertitel** M (*im Handwerk*) title of master craftsman; (*Sport*) championship title

Meisterung ['maɪstərʊŋ] F -, *no pl* mastery

Meisterwerk NT masterpiece

Meist-: Meistgebot NT highest bid, best offer; **meistgebräuchlich** ADJ *attr* commonest; **meistgefragt** ADJ *attr* most popular, most in demand; *Wohngegend auch* most sought-after; **meistgekauft** [-gəkauft] ADJ *attr* best-selling; **meistgelesen** ADJ *attr* most widely read; **meistgenannt** ADJ *attr* most frequently mentioned; **meistverkauft** [-fɛɐkauft] ADJ *attr* best-selling

Meitnerium [maɪt'neːriʊm] NT -s, *no pl* (*abbr* **Mt**) meitnerium

Mekka ['mɛka] NT -s (*Geog, fig*) Mecca

Melancholie [melaŋko'liː] F -, -n [-'liːən] melancholy

Melancholiker [melaŋ'koːlikɐ] M -s, -, **Melancholikerin** [-ərɪn] F -, -nen melancholic

melancholisch [melaŋ'koːlɪʃ] ADJ melancholy; ~ **sagen** in a melancholy voice; **er schreibt ~** his writing is melancholy; **sie sann ~ vor sich hin** she was thinking melancholy thoughts

Melanesien [mela'neːziən] NT -s Melanesia

Melanesier [mela'neːziɐ] M -s, -, **Melanesierin** [-ərɪn] F -, -nen Melanesian

melanesisch [mela'neːzɪʃ] ADJ Melanesian

Melange [me'lãːʒə] F -, -n **a** (*rare*: = *Mischung*) blend **b** (*Aus*: = *Milchkaffee*) white coffee (*Brit*), coffee with milk

Melanin [mela'niːn] NT -s, -e (*Chem*) melanin

Melanom [mela'noːm] NT -s, -e (*Med*) melanoma

Melanzani [melan'tsaːni] F -, - (*Aus*) aubergine, eggplant (*esp US*)

Melasse [me'lasə] F -, -n molasses

Melde-: Meldeamt NT , **Meldebüro** (*inf*) NT registration office; **Meldebehörde** F registration authorities *pl*; **Meldefahrer(in)** M(F) (*Mil*) dispatch rider; **Meldefrist** F registration period

melden ['mɛldn] ⊗ 27.5, 27.7 VT **a** (= *anzeigen*) *Unfall, Verlust, ansteckende Erkrankungen* to report; (= *berichten*) to report; (= *registrieren lassen*) to register; (= *denunzieren*) to report; **eine Geburt/Änderungen (der Behörde** *dat*) ~ to notify the authorities of a birth/changes; **wie soeben gemeldet wird** (*Rad, TV*) according to reports just coming in; **das wird gemeldet!** (*Sch*) I'll tell on you (*Sch inf*); **(bei jdm) nichts zu ~ haben** (*inf*) to have no say; **er hat hier nichts zu ~** (*inf*) he has no say in this; **melde gehorsamst** (*old Mil*) beg to report; **(als) arbeitslos gemeldet sein** to be registered unemployed

b (= *ankündigen*) to announce; **ich ging zur Sekretärin und ließ mich beim Direktor ~** I went to the secretary and asked her to tell the director that I was there; **wen darf ich ~?** who(m) shall I say (is here)?, who(m) shall I announce?

VR **a** (= *antreten*) to report (*zu* for); **sich zum Dienst ~** to report for work; **sich freiwillig ~** to volunteer; **sich zu** or **für etw ~** (*esp Mil*) to sign up for sth, to volunteer for sth; (*für Arbeitsplatz*) to apply for sth; (*für Lehrgang*) to enrol (*Brit*) or enroll (*US*) for sth, to sign on for sth; **sich auf eine Anzeige ~** to answer an advertisement; **sich polizeilich** or **bei der Polizei ~** to register with the police; **sich arbeitslos ~** to register as unemployed, to sign on → **krankmelden**

b (*fig: = sich ankündigen*) to announce one's presence; (*Alter, Hunger*) to make itself or its presence felt; (*Winter, Dunkelheit*) to draw or set in; (*Sport, zur Prüfung*) to enter (one's name) (*zu* for); (*durch Handaufheben*) to put one's hand up, to hold up one's hand; (*Rad, TV*) to come on the air → **Wort c**

c (*esp Telec*: = *antworten*) to answer; **bitte ~!** (*Telec*) come in, please; **es meldet sich niemand** there's no answer

d (= *von sich hören lassen*) to get in touch (*bei* with); **melde dich wieder** keep in touch; **seitdem hat er sich nicht mehr gemeldet** he hasn't been heard of since; **wenn du was brauchst, melde dich** if you need anything give (me) a shout (*inf*)

Melde-: Meldepflicht F **a** (*beim Ordnungsamt*) compulsory registration, obligation to register (*when moving house*); **polizeiliche ~** obligation to register with the police **b** **des Arztes** the doctor's obligation to notify the authorities (*of people with certain contagious diseases*); **meldepflichtig** [-pflɪçtɪç] ADJ **a** *Mensch* obliged to register **b** *Krankheit* notifiable; *Unfall, Schadensfall* that must be reported

---

MELDEPFLICHT

A **Meldepflicht** is a regulation requiring an individual to notify the authorities of certain things such as a change of address or a birth. Everyone who takes up residence in Germany is obliged to register with the **Einwohnermeldeamt** within a week (three days in Austria). If you move to a different address, you must first of all inform the authorities in your previous place of residence. In Switzerland regulations vary from canton to canton.

Melder ['mɛldɐ] M -s, -, **Melderin** [-ərɪn] F -, -nen dispatch rider

Melde-: Melderegister NT register (of residents); **Meldeschein** M registration form; **Meldeschluss** ▲ M closing date; **Meldestelle** F place of registration; **Meldewe-**

sen NT , *no pl* registration system; **Mel|de|zet|tel** M (*Aus*) certificate of registration

Mel|dung ['mɛldʊŋ] F -, -en **a** (= *Mitteilung*) announcement **b** (*Press, Rad, TV*) report (*über +acc* on, about); **~en in Kürze** news headlines *pl*; **~en vom Sport** sports news *sing* **c** (*dienstlich*) report; (**eine**) **~ machen** to make a report **d** (*bei der Polizei*) report **e** (*Sport, = Examensmeldung*) entry; **seine ~ zurückziehen** to withdraw **f** (*Comput*) (on-screen) message

me|liert [me'liːɛt] ADJ *Haar* greying (*Brit*), graying (*US*), streaked with grey (*Brit*) or gray (*US*); *Wolle* flecked; **sein Haar war grau ~** his hair was streaked with grey (*Brit*) or gray (*US*)

Me|lio|ra|ti|on [meliora'tsioːn] F -, -en (*Agr*) soil improvement

Me|lis|se [me'lɪsə] F -, -n balm

Me|lis|sen|geist® M medicinal spirit

Melk- *in cpds* milking; **Melk|an|la|ge** F milking plant

mel|ken ['mɛlkn] *pres* **melkt** or (*old*) **milkt** [mɛlkt, mɪlkt], *pret* **melkte** or (*old*) **molk** ['mɛlktə, mɔlk], *ptp* **gemolken** or (*rare*) **gemelkt** [gə'mɔlkn, gə'mɛlkt] VT **a** *Kuh, Ziege etc* to milk; **frisch gemolkene Milch** milk fresh from the cow **b** (*fig inf*) to milk (*inf*), to fleece (*inf*) VI to milk

Mel|ker ['mɛlkɐ] M -s, - milker

Mel|ke|rei [mɛlkə'rai] F -, -en (= *Milchwirtschaft*) dairy (farm)

Mel|ke|rin ['mɛlkərɪn] F -, -en milkmaid

Me|lo|die [melo'diː] F -, -n [-'diːən] melody; (= *Weise auch*) tune; **nach der ~ von ...** to the tune of ...

Me|lo|die|ins|tru|ment NT melodic instrument

Me|lo|di|en|fol|ge [-'diːən-] F , **Me|lo|di|en|rei|gen** [-'diːən-] M (*Rad*) medley of tunes

Me|lo|dik [me'loːdɪk] F -, *no pl* **a** (*Theorie*) melodics *sing* **b** (= *musikalische Eigenart*) musical idiom

me|lo|di|ös [melo'diøːs] (*geh*) ADJ melodious ADV melodiously; **~ klingen** to sound melodious

me|lo|disch [me'loːdɪʃ] ADJ *Musik* melodic, tuneful; *Sprache, Wort* melodic ADV **~ klingen** to sound melodic

Me|lo|dram [melo'draːm] NT -s, **Melo|dra|men** (*liter*), **Me|lo|dra|ma** NT melodrama (*auch fig*)

me|lo|dra|ma|tisch [melodra'maːtɪʃ] ADJ melodramatic (*auch fig*) ADV melodramatically; **~ klingen** to sound melodramatic

Me|lo|ne [me'loːnə] F -, -n **a** melon **b** (*Hut*) bowler (*Brit*), derby (*US*)

Memb|ran [mɛm'braːn] F -, -en, **Memb|ra|ne** [mɛm'braːnə] F -, -n **a** (*Anat*) membrane **b** (*Phys, Tech*) diaphragm

Me|men|to [me'mɛnto] NT -s, -s (*liter*) admonition, warning

Mem|me ['mɛmə] F -, -n (*inf*) sissy (*inf*), yellow-belly (*inf*)

mem|men|haft (*inf*) ADJ lily-livered (*inf*), yellow-bellied (*inf*) ADV like a yellow-belly (*inf*)

Me|mo ['meːmo] NT -s, -s memo

Me|moire [me'moaːr(ə)] NT -s, -s (*Pol*) memorandum

Me|moi|ren [me'moaːrən] PL memoirs *pl*

Me|mo|ran|dum [memo'randʊm] NT -s, **Memoranden** or **Memoranda** [-dn, -da] (*Pol*) memorandum

me|mo|rie|ren [memo'riːrən] *ptp* **memoriert** VT (*old*) **a** (= *sich einprägen*) to memorize, to commit to memory **b** (= *aufsagen*) to recite (from memory)

Me|na|ge [me'naːʒə] F -, -n **a** (= *Gewürzständer*) cruet (set) **b** (*Aus = Verpflegung*) rations *pl*

Me|na|ge|rie [menaʒə'riː] F -, -n [-'riːən] menagerie

Me|nar|che [me'narçə] F -, *no pl* (*Med*) menarche (*spec*), first menstruation

---

Men|de|le|vi|um [mɛnde'leːviʊm] NT -s, *no pl* (*abbr* **Md**) mendelevium

men|deln ['mɛndln] VI (*Biol*) to mendelize (*spec*), to conform to Mendel's laws

men|del|sche Re|geln ▲ ['mɛndlʃə] PL (*Biol*) Mendel's laws *pl*

Me|ne|te|kel [mene'teːkl] NT -s, - (*liter*) warning sign, portent; **das ~ an der Wand** the writing on the wall

Men|ge ['mɛŋə] F -, -n **a** (= *Quantum*) amount, quantity; **in ~n zu** in quantities of **b** (*inf*) (= *große Anzahl*) lot, load (*inf*); (= *Haufen*) pile (*inf*), heap (*inf*); **eine ~** a lot, lots (*inf*); **eine ~ Zeit/Häuser** a lot or lots (*inf*) of time/ houses; **jede ~ masses** *pl* (*inf*), loads *pl* (*inf*); **jede ~ Zeit/Geld** masses (*inf*) or loads (*inf*) of time/money; **wir haben jede ~ getrunken** we drank an enormous amount, we drank a hell of a lot (*inf*); **es gab Wein jede ~** or **jede ~ Wein** there was masses or loads of wine (*inf*); **eine ganze ~** quite a lot; **sie bildet sich eine ~ auf ihre Schönheit ein** she's incredibly conceited about her looks; **Bücher in ~n** any amount of books → **rau e**

c (= *Menschenmenge*) crowd; (*geh*) (= *Masse*) mass; (= *das Volk*) people; (*pej*: = *Pöbel*) mob; **in der ~ untertauchen** to disappear into the crowd

d (*Math*) set

men|gen ['mɛŋən] VT (*geh*) to mix (*unter +acc* with) VR to mingle (*unter +acc* with); (*fig*: = *sich einmischen*) to meddle, to interfere (*in +acc* with, in)

Men|gen-: Men|gen|an|ga|be F quantity, indication of quantity; **Men|gen|be|griff** M uncountable noun; (*Math*) concept of the set; **Men|gen|be|zeich|nung** F unit of quantity; **Men|gen|leh|re** F (*Math*) set theory; **men|gen|mä|ßig** ADJ as far as quantity is concerned, quantitative ADV as far as quantity is concerned; **Men|gen|preis** M bulk price; **Men|gen|ra|batt** M bulk or quantity discount; **Men|gen|ver|hält|nis** NT relative proportions *pl* (*zwischen +dat* of), quantitative ratio (*form*) (*zwischen +dat* between)

Meng|sel ['mɛŋzl] NT -s, - (*dial*) mixture

Men|hir ['mɛnhiːɐ] M -s, -e (*Archeol*) standing stone, menhir

Me|nin|gi|tis [menɪŋ'giːtɪs] F -, **Meningitiden** [menɪŋgi'tiːdn] (*Med*) meningitis

Me|nis|kus [me'nɪskʊs] M -, **Menisken** [-kn] (*Anat, Phys*) meniscus; (*Phot auch*) meniscal lens

Me|nis|kus|riss ▲ M torn meniscus

Men|jou|bärt|chen ['mɛnʒu-] NT pencil moustache (*Brit*) or mustache (*US*)

Men|ken|ke [mɛn'kɛŋkə] F -, -s or -n (*dial*) fuss

Men|ni|ge ['mɛnɪɡə] F -, *no pl* minium, red lead

Men|no|nit [meno'niːt] M -en, -en, **Men|no|ni|tin** [-'niːtɪn] F -, -nen Mennonite

Me|no|pau|se [meno'pauzə] F (*Med*) menopause

Me|no|sta|se [meno'staːzə] F -, -n (*Med*) menostasis

Men|sa ['mɛnza] F -, **Mensen** [-zn] (*Univ*) canteen, refectory (*Brit*), dining hall

Men|sa|es|sen NT (*Univ*) (= *Mahlzeit*) college meal; (= *Kost*) college food

Mensch¹ [mɛnʃ] M -en, -en **a** (= *Person*) person, man/woman; **ein anderer ~ werden** to become a different person or man/woman; **ein neuer ~ werden** to become a new person or man/woman; **von ~ zu** ~ man-to-man/woman-to-woman; **es war kein ~ da** there was nobody there, there was not a soul there; **als ~** as a person; **des ~en Wille ist sein Himmelreich** (*Prov*) do what you want if it makes you happy (*inf*); **das konnte kein ~ ahnen!** no-one (on earth) could have foreseen that!; **viel unter (die) ~en kommen** to meet a lot of people, to get around (a lot); **man muss die ~en nehmen, wie sie sind** you have to take people as they

---

are or come; **Aktion ~** *charity for people with disabilities*

b (*als Gattung*) **der ~** man; **die ~en** man *sing*, human beings *pl*, people *pl*; **die Ruritanier sind gutmütige ~en** the Ruritanians are a good-natured race or a good-natured people; **ein Tier, das keine ~en mag** an animal that doesn't like people or humans; **~ bleiben** (*inf*) to stay human; **ich bin auch nur ein ~!** I'm only human; **wer so etwas macht, ist kein ~ mehr** somebody who does something like that is not human; **wie die ersten** or **letzten ~en** (*inf*) like animals; **~ und Tier** man and beast; **alle ~en müssen sterben** we are all mortal; **alle ~en haben tierische Gelüste** all human beings have animal cravings

c (= *die Menschheit*) **die ~en** mankind, man, humankind (*esp US*); **des ~en Sohn** (*Bibl*) the Son of Man; **Jesus ist gekommen, um die ~en zu retten** Jesus came to save mankind or humankind (*esp US*); **alle ~en** everyone; **so sind die ~en** that's human nature

d (*inf: als Interjektion*) hey; (*erstaunt*) hey, wow, blimey (*Brit sl*); **~, hat die Beine!** hey or wow! has she got a pair of legs! (*inf*); **~, das habe ich ganz vergessen** damn, I completely forgot (*inf*); **~, da habe ich mich aber getäuscht** boy, was I wrong! (*inf*); **~, habe ich mich beeilt/geärgert!** boy, did I rush/was I angry! (*inf*); **~ Meier!** golly! (*dated inf*), gosh! (*dated inf*)

Mensch² NT -(e)s, -er (*sl*) cow (*inf*); (*gemein*) bitch (*sl*)

Mensch är|ge|re dich nicht [mɛnʃ 'ɛrɡərə dɪç nɪçt] NT - - - -, *no pl* (= *Spiel*) ludo (*Brit*), aggravation (*US*)

men|scheln ['mɛnʃln] VI *impers* **a** **es menschelt** there's no escaping (from) one's humanity **b** (*in Märchen*) **es menschelt** I smell or sense a human

Men|schen- *in cpds* human; **Men|schen|af|fe** M ape, anthropoid (ape); **men|schen|ähn|lich** ADJ manlike, humanlike (*esp US*), like a human being/human beings; **Men|schen|al|ter** NT **a** (= *30 Jahre*) generation **b** (= *Lebensdauer*) lifetime; **Men|schen|an|samm|lung** F gathering (of people); **Men|schen|art** F **a** *nach* ~ like human beings/a human being **b** (= *menschliche Schwäche*) human nature; **Men|schen|auf|lauf** M crowd (of people); **Men|schen|feind(in)** M(F) misanthropist; **men|schen|feind|lich** ADJ *Mensch* misanthropic; *Landschaft etc* hostile to man, inhospitable; *Politik, Gesellschaft* inhumane; **Men|schen|fleisch** NT human flesh; **Men|schen|fres|ser(in)** M(F) **a** (*inf*) (= *Kannibale*) cannibal; (= *Raubtier*) man-eater; **ich bin doch kein ~!** I won't eat you! **b** (*Myth*) ogre; **Men|schen|fres|se|rei** F (*inf*) cannibalism; **Men|schen|freund(in)** M(F) philanthropist; **men|schen|freund|lich** ADJ *Mensch* philanthropic, benevolent; *Gegend* hospitable; *Politik, Gesellschaft* humane; **diese Affenart ist nicht sehr ~** this species of ape does not like humans ADV **sich ~ geben** to like to give the impression of being a philanthropist; **Men|schen|freund|lich|keit** F philanthropy, benevolence; **aus reiner ~** out of the sheer goodness of one's heart; **Men|schen|füh|rung** F leadership; **Men|schen|ge|den|ken** NT *der kälteste Winter seit* ~ the coldest winter in living memory; **hier hat sich seit ~ nichts geändert** nothing has changed here from time immemorial; **Men|schen|ge|stalt** F human form; **ein Teufel** or **Satan in ~** a devil in disguise; **Men|schen|ge|wühl** NT milling crowd; **Men|schen|hai** M man-eating shark, man-eater; **Men|schen|hand** F human hand; **von ~ geschaffen** fashioned by the hand of man; **das liegt nicht in ~** that is beyond man's control; **Men|schen|han|del** M slave trade; (*Jur*) trafficking (in human beings); **Men|schen|händ|ler(in)** M(F) slave-trader; (*Jur*) trafficker (in human beings); **Men|schen|hass** ▲ M misanthropy, hatred of people; **Men|schen|has|ser** [-hasɐ] M -s, -, **Men|schen-**

has|se|rin [-ərɪn] F -, -nen misanthropist; **Men|schen|jagd** F manhunts *pl*, manhunting; **eine ~** a manhunt; **Men|schen|jä|ger(in)** M(F) manhunter; **Men|schen|ken|ner(in)** M(F) judge of character, connoisseur of human nature; **Men|schen|kennt|nis** F , *no pl* knowledge of human nature; **~ haben** to know human nature; **Men|schen|ket|te** F human chain; **Men|schen|kind** NT creature, soul; **Men|schen|kun|de** F anthropology; **Men|schen|le|ben** NT human life; **ein ~ lang** a whole lifetime; **~ beklagen** to report fatalities; **~ waren nicht zu beklagen** there was no loss of life, no fatalities were reported; **Verluste an ~** loss of human life; **das Unglück hat zwei ~ gefordert** the accident claimed two lives; **men|schen|leer** ADJ deserted; **Men|schen|lie|be** F **a** (*Bibl*) human love **b** (= *Nächstenliebe*) love of mankind or humanity, philanthropy; **aus reiner ~** from the sheer goodness of one's heart; **tätige ~** concrete humanitarianism, active philanthropy; **Men|schen|mas|se** F crowd or mass (of people); **Men|schen|ma|te|ri|al** NT manpower; **Men|schen|men|ge** F crowd (of people); **men|schen|mög|lich** ADJ humanly possible; **das Menschenmögliche tun** to do all that is humanly possible; **Men|schen|op|fer** NT **a** human sacrifice **b** (= *Menschenleben*) **es waren ~ zu beklagen** there were (some) fatalities; **Men|schen|raub** M (*Jur*) kidnapping; **Men|schen|räu|ber(in)** M(F) (*Jur*) kidnapper

Men|schen|recht NT human right; **die Allgemeine Erklärung** or **Deklaration der ~e** the Universal Declaration of Human Rights

Men|schen|rechts-: **Men|schen|rechts|kom|mis|si|on** F Commission on Human Rights; **Men|schen|rechts|kon|ven|ti|on** F Human Rights Convention; **Men|schen|rechts|or|ga|ni|sa|ti|on** F human rights organization; **Men|schen|rechts|ver|let|zung** F violation of human rights

Men|schen-: **men|schen|scheu** ADJ afraid of people; **Men|schen|scheu** F fear of people; **krankhafte ~** anthropophobia (*spec*); **Men|schen|schin|der(in)** M(F) slave-driver; **Men|schen|schlag** M (*inf*) kind of people, breed (*inf*); **Men|schen|schlan|ge** F queue (of people) (*Brit*), line (of people) (*US*); **Men|schen|see|le** F human soul; **keine ~** (*fig*) not a (living) soul

Men|schens|kind INTERJ good heavens, heavens above

Men|schen-: **Men|schen|sohn** M (*Bibl*) Son of Man; **Men|schen|strom** M stream or flood of people; **Men|schen|trau|be** F cluster of people; **men|schen|un|mög|lich** ADJ absolutely impossible; **das Menschenunmögliche versuchen/vollbringen** to attempt/achieve the impossible; **men|schen|un|wür|dig** beneath human dignity; *Behandlung* inhumane; *Behausung* unfit for human habitation **ADV** *behandeln* inhumanely; *hausen, unterbringen* under inhuman conditions; **Men|schen|ver|ach|tend** inhuman **ADV** inhumanely; **Men|schen|ver|äch|ter(in)** M(F) despiser of mankind or humanity; **Men|schen|ver|ach|tung** F contempt for mankind or humanity; **Men|schen|ver|stand** M human understanding *no art*; **gesunder ~** common sense; **Men|schen|ver|such** M human experiment; **Men|schen|werk** NT (*old, liter*) work of man or humans (*esp US*); **alles ~ ist vergänglich** all works of men or humans (*esp US*) are transient; **Men|schen|wür|de** F human dignity *no art*; **men|schen|wür|dig** ADJ *Behandlung* humane; *Leben, Tod* dignified; *Lebensbedingungen* fit for human beings; *Unterkunft* fit for human habitation; **~e Entlohnung** decent living wage **ADV** *behandeln* humanely; *unterbringen, wohnen* in decent conditions; **~ leben** to live in conditions fit for human beings

Men|sche|wik [mɛnʃe'vɪk] M -en, -en or -i [-ki], **Men|sche|wi|kin** [-'vɪkɪn] F -, -nen (*Hist*) Menshevik

Men|sche|wis|mus [mɛnʃe'vɪsmʊs] M -, *no pl* (*Hist*) Menshevism

Mensch|heit F, *no pl* **die ~** mankind, humanity; **zum Wohle der ~** for the benefit of mankind or humanity; **eine Geißel der ~** the scourge of humanity; **Verdienste um die ~** services to humanity; **Verdienste im Namen der ~** services in the name of humanity; **Verbrechen gegen die ~** crimes against humanity

Mensch|heits-: **Mensch|heits|ent|wick|lung** F development of mankind or humanity; **Mensch|heits|ge|schich|te** F history of the human race or of mankind

mensch|lich ['mɛnʃlɪç] **a** human; **das ~e Leben** human life; **der ~e Körper/Geist** the human body/mind; **die ~e Gesellschaft** the society of man; **die ~e Gemeinschaft** the human community; **jede ~e Hilfe kam zu spät für sie** she was beyond human help **b** (*inf*: = *zivilisiert*) human **c** (= *human*) *Behandlung etc* humane; **eine ~e Seite haben** to have a human side to one **ADV a** (= *human*) humanely **b** (*inf*: = *zivilisiert*) decently; (*einigermaßen*) ~ **aussehen** (*inf*) to look more or less human; **sich wieder ~ fühlen** to feel more human (again) **c** (= *als Mensch*) personally, as a person; **sie ist mir ~ sympathisch** I like her as a person

Mensch|lich|keit F -, *no pl* humanity *no art*; **aus reiner ~** on purely humanitarian grounds; **Verbrechen gegen die ~** crimes against humanity

Mensch|wer|dung [-veːdʊŋ] F -, *no pl* **a** (*Bibl*) incarnation **b** (*Biol*) anthropogenesis

Men|ses ['mɛnzeːs] PL (*geh euph*: = *Menstruation*) menstruation

Menst|ru|a|ti|on [mɛnstrua'tsioːn] F -, -en menstruation

menst|ru|ie|ren [mɛnstru'iːrən] *ptp* **menstruiert** VI to menstruate

Men|sur [mɛn'zuːɐ] F -, -en (*Univ*) (students') fencing bout; **eine ~ schlagen** or **fechten** to fight a duel

men|tal [mɛn'taːl] ADJ *Einstellung, Reaktion* mental; **~es Training** mental training, mind training **ADV** mentally; **körperlich und ~** physically and mentally

Men|ta|li|tät [mɛntali'tɛːt] F -, -en mentality

Men|thol [mɛn'toːl] NT -s, -e menthol

Men|tor ['mɛntoːɐ] M -s, **Mentoren** [-'toːrən], **Men|to|rin** [-'toːrɪn] F -, -nen **a** (*dated, geh*) mentor **b** (*Sch*) ≈ tutor

Me|nü [me'nyː] NT -s, -s **a** (= *Tagesmenü*) set meal or menu, table d'hôte (*form*); **~ essen** to have one of the set meals, to have the set menu; **~ des Tages** (set) meal of the day (*Brit*), (daily) special **b** (*Comput*) menu

Me|nü- *in cpds* (*Comput*) menu; **Me|nü|an|zei|ge** F menu display

Me|nu|ett [me'nʊɛt] NT -s, -e (*Tanz, Kunstmusik*) minuet

Me|nü- (*Comput*): **Me|nü|füh|rung** F menu-driven operation; **me|nü|ge|steu|ert** [-gəʃtɔyɐt] ADJ menu-driven; **Me|nü|leis|te** F menu strip; **Me|nü|steu|e|rung** F menu-driven operation; **Me|nü|zei|le** F menu line

me|phis|to|phe|lisch [mefɪsto'feːlɪʃ] (*liter*) ADJ Mephistophelian **ADV** *lachen, grinsen* devilishly

Mer|chan|di|sing ['mœːtʃəndaɪzɪŋ] NT -s, *no pl* merchandising

Mer|gel ['mɛrɡl] M -s, - (*Geol*) marl

Mer|gel|bo|den M (*Geol*) marly or marlacious (*spec*) soil

mer|ge|lig ['mɛrɡəlɪç], **merg|lig** ['mɛrɡlɪç] ADJ marly, marlacious (*spec*)

Me|ri|di|an [meri'diaːn] M -s, -e (*Astron, Geog*) meridian

Me|ri|di|an|kreis M (*Astron*) meridian circle

Me|rin|ge [me'rɪŋə] F -, -n, **Me|ring|el** [me'rɪŋl] NT -s, -, **Me|rin|gue** [me'rɛ̃ːk] F -, -s (*Sw*) meringue

Me|ri|no [me'riːno] M -s, -s, **Me|ri|no|schaf** NT merino (sheep)

Me|ri|no|wol|le F merino wool

Me|ri|ten [me'riːtn] PL (*geh*) merits *pl*; **sich** (*dat*) **~ um etw erwerben** to receive plaudits for sth; **auf seinen alten ~ ruhen** to rest on one's laurels, to rest on one's past merits

mer|kan|til [mɛrkan'tiːl] ADJ (*Hist, geh*) mercantile

Mer|kan|ti|lis|mus [mɛrkanti'lɪsmʊs] M -, *no pl* (*Hist*) mercantilism

mer|kan|ti|lis|tisch [mɛrkanti'lɪstɪʃ] ADJ (*Hist*) mercantilist(ic)

Merk-: **merk|bar** ADJ **a** (= *wahrnehmbar*) noticeable **b** (= *im Gedächtnis zu behalten*) retainable; **leicht/schwer ~** easy/difficult to remember or retain **ADV** noticeably; **Merk|blatt** NT leaflet; (*mit Anweisungen auch*) instructions *pl*; **Merk|buch** NT notebook

mer|ken ['mɛrkn] VT **a** (= *wahrnehmen, entdecken*) to notice; (= *spüren*) to feel; (= *erkennen*) to realize; **ich merke nichts!** I can't feel anything!; **davon habe ich nichts gemerkt** I didn't notice anything; **das kann man leicht ~** that's easy to see; **jdn ~ lassen** to make sb feel sth; **seine Gefühle ~ lassen** to let one's feelings show; **hat er dich etwas ~ lassen?** did you notice anything in the way he behaved?; **woran hast du das gemerkt?** how could you tell that?; **wie soll ich das ~?** how am I supposed to tell (that)?; **du merkst auch alles!** (*iro*) nothing escapes you, does it?, you ARE observant(, aren't you?); **das merkt jeder/keiner!** everyone/no-one will notice!; **das ist kaum zu ~, davon merkt man kaum etwas** it's hardly noticeable; **das ist zu ~** you can tell; **ich merke keinen Unterschied** I can't tell the difference; (*weil es keinen gibt*) I can't see a difference **b** (= *im Gedächtnis behalten*) to remember, to retain; **merke: ...** NB or note: ...; **sich** (*dat*) **jdn/etw ~** to remember sb/sth; **sich** (*dat*) **eine Autonummer ~** to make a (mental) note of a licence (*Brit*) or license (*US*) or registration number; **das werde ich mir ~!, ich werds mir ~!** (*inf*) I'll remember that, I won't forget that; **das hat er sich gemerkt** he's taken it to heart; **merk dir das!** mark my words! **c** (= *im Auge behalten*) **sich** (*dat*) **etw ~** to remember sth, to make a note of sth; **~ Sie sich** (*dat*) **den Mann!** keep an eye on that man; **diesen Schriftsteller wird man sich** (*dat*) **~ müssen** this author is someone to take note of

Merk-: **Merk|fä|hig|keit** F memory capacity; **Merk|heft** NT notebook; **Merk|hil|fe** F mnemonic (aid)

merk|lich ['mɛrklɪç] ADJ noticeable, marked, distinct; **kein ~er Unterschied** no noticeable difference **ADV** noticeably; **kaum ~** almost imperceptibly

Merk|mal ['mɛrkmaːl] NT -s, -e characteristic, feature; (*Biol, Zool*) distinctive mark or marking; **„besondere ~e ...“** "distinguishing marks ..."

Merk- (*Sch*): **Merk|satz** M mnemonic (sentence); **Merk|spruch** M mnemonic (*form*), memory aid

Mer|kur [mɛr'kuːɐ] M -s, *no pl* (*Myth, Astron*) Mercury; (*obs*: = *Quecksilber*) quicksilver, mercury

Merk-: **Merk|vers** M (*Sch*) jingle, mnemonic (rhyme) (*form*); **Merk|wort** NT (*Theat*) cue; **merk|wür|dig** ['mɛrkvʏrdɪç] ADJ strange, odd, curious **ADV** strangely, oddly; **~ riechen** to have a strange smell; **er hat sich ganz ~ verändert** he has undergone a strange change; **merk|wür|di|ger|wei|se** ['mɛrkvʏrdɪɡɐ'vaɪzə] ADV strangely or oddly or curiously enough; **Merk|wür|dig|keit** F -, -en **a** *no pl* (= *Seltsam-*

keit) strangeness, oddness **b** (= *Eigentümlichkeit*) peculiarity; **Merk|zet|tel** M (reminder) note

Mer|le ['mɛrlə] F -, -n (*dial: Orn*) blackbird

Me|sal|li|ance [meza'liãːs] F -, -n (*liter*) misalliance, mésalliance (*liter*)

me|schug|ge [me'ʃʊgə] ADJ (*inf*) nuts (*inf*), barmy (*Brit inf*)

Mes|ka|lin [mɛska'liːn] NT -s, *no pl* mescalin(e)

Mes|me|ris|mus [mɛsmə'rɪsmʊs] M -, *no pl* mesmerism

Mes|ner ['mɛsnɐ] M -s, -, **Mes|ne|rin** [-ərɪn] F -, -nen (*dial*) verger, sexton

Me|so|karp [mezo'karp] NT -s, -e (*Bot*) mesocarp

Me|so|li|thi|kum [mezo'liːtikʊm] NT -s, *no pl* (*Geol*) Mesolithic period

me|so|li|thisch [mezo'liːtɪʃ] ADJ (*Geol*) Mesolithic

Me|son ['meːzɔn] NT -s, -en [-'zoːnən] (*Phys*) meson, mesotron

Me|so|po|ta|mi|en [mezopo'taːmiən] NT -s Mesopotamia

Me|so|po|ta|mi|er [mezopo'taːmiɐ] M -s, -, **Me|so|po|ta|mi|e|rin** [-iərɪn] F -, -nen Mesopotamian

me|so|po|ta|misch [mezopo'taːmɪʃ] ADJ Mesopotamian

Me|so|ze|pha|le(r) [mezotse'faːlə] MF *decl as adj* mesocephalic

Me|so|zo|i|kum [mezo'tsoːikʊm] NT -s, *no pl* (*Geol*) Mesozoic

Mess-: Mess|band ▲ [-bant] NT *pl* -bänder tape measure; **mess|bar** ▲ **ADJ** measurable **ADV** measurably; **er hat ~ an Zustimmung verloren** he has lost a measurable amount of support; **Mess|be|cher** ▲ M (*Cook*) measuring jug; **Mess|be|reich** ▲ M measuring range; **Mess|buch** ▲ NT (*Eccl*) missal, Mass book; **Mess|da|ten** ▲ PL readings *pl*; **Mess|die|ner(in)** ▲ M(F) (*Eccl*) server, acolyte (*form*)

Mes|se¹ ['mɛsə] F -, -n (*Eccl, Mus*) mass; **in die** *or* **zur ~ gehen** to go to mass; **die ~ lesen** *or* **halten** to say mass; **für jdn eine ~ lesen lassen** to have a mass said for sb; **die hohe ~** High Mass

Mes|se² F -, -n (trade) fair; **auf der ~** at the fair

Mes|se³ F -, -n (*Naut, Mil*) mess

Mes|se- *in cpds* fair; **Mes|se|an|ge|bot** NT exhibits *pl* (at a/the fair), fair exhibits *pl*; **Mes|se|gast** M visitor to a/the fair, fair visitor; **Mes|se|ge|län|de** NT exhibition centre (*Brit*) *or* center (*US*); **Mes|se|hal|le** F fair pavilion

mes|sen ['mɛsn̩] *pret* **maß** [maːs], *ptp* **gemessen** [gə'mɛsn̩] **VT** to measure; (*Tech*: = *anzeigen auch*) to gauge; *Verlauf* to time; (= *abschätzen*) *Entfernung etc* to judge, to gauge; **jds Blutdruck/Temperatur ~** (*Arzt*) to take sb's blood pressure/temperature; (*Instrument*) to measure sb's blood pressure/temperature; **während ich lief, maß er die Zeit** I ran and he timed me or he took the time; **er misst 1,90 m** he is 1.90 m tall; **seine Kräfte/Fähigkeiten mit jdm ~** to match one's strength/skills against sb's, to try or measure one's strength/skills with sb; **seine Kräfte/Fähigkeiten an etw** (*dat*) **~** to test one's strength/skills on sth; **etw an etw** (*dat*) **~** (= *ausprobieren*) to try sth out on sth; (= *vergleichen*) to compare sth with sth; **jdn mit den Blicken ~** (*geh*) to look sb up and down → *auch* **gemessen** **VI** to measure

VR **a** **sich mit jdm ~** (*geh: im Wettkampf*) to compete with sb; (*in geistigem Wettstreit*) to pit oneself against sb

b **sich mit jdm/etw nicht ~ können** to be no match for sb/sth

Mes|se|neu|heit F new product (*shown at a trade fair*)

Mes|ser ['mɛsɐ] NT -s, - knife; (*Tech auch*) cutter, blade; (= *Rasiermesser*) (cut-throat) razor; **jdm ein ~ in den Leib stoßen**, **jdm ein ~ in den Bauch jagen** (*inf*) to stick a knife into sb; **unters**

~ kommen (*Med inf*) to go under the knife; **jdn unters ~ nehmen** (*Med inf*) to put sb under the knife; **jdm das ~ an die Kehle setzen** (*lit, fig*) to hold a knife to sb's throat; **die ~ wetzen** (*fig*) to get ready *or* to prepare for the kill; **damit würden wir ihn ans ~ liefern** (*fig*) that would be putting his head on the block; **jdn der Mafia ans ~ liefern** to shop sb to the Mafia (*Brit inf*), to rat on sb to the Mafia (*sl*); **ins (offene) ~ laufen** to walk straight into the trap; **ein Kampf/sich bekämpfen bis aufs ~** (*fig*) a fight/to fight to the finish; **ihm ging das ~ in der Tasche auf** (*inf*) he lost the place; **auf des ~s Schneide stehen** (*fig*) to be *or* hang (very much) in the balance, to be on a razor-edge *or* razor's edge; **es steht auf des ~s Schneide, ob ...** it's touch and go whether ..., it's very much in the balance whether ...; **es wird eine Nacht der langen ~ geben** (*fig*) heads will roll → **locker**

Mes|ser- *in cpds* knife; **Mes|ser|griff** M , **Mes|ser|heft** NT knife handle; **Mes|ser|held(in)** M(F) (*inf*) knifer (*inf*); **Mes|ser|rü|cken** M back of a/the knife; **mes|ser|scharf** **ADJ** (*lit, fig*) razor-sharp; *Folgerung* clear-cut **ADV** *argumentieren* shrewdly; **~ schließen** (*iro*) to conclude shrewdly (*iro*); **Mes|ser|schmied(in)** M(F) cutler; **Mes|ser|schnei|de** F knife edge; **Mes|ser|spit|ze** F knife point; **eine ~ (voll)** (*Cook*) a pinch; **Mes|ser|ste|cher** [-ʃtɛçɐ] M -s, -, **Mes|ser|ste|che|rin** [-ərɪn] F -, -nen knifer (*inf*); **Mes|ser|ste|che|rei** [-ʃtɛçə'rai] F -, -en knife fight; **in eine** *or* **zur ~ ausarten** to end up in a knife fight; **Mes|ser|stich** M knife thrust; (*Wunde*) stab wound; **Mes|ser|wer|fer(in)** M(F) knife-thrower

Mes|se-: Mes|se|stadt F (town with an) exhibition centre (*Brit*) or center (*US*); **Mes|se|stand** M stand (at the/a fair)

Mess-: Mess|füh|ler ▲ M probe, detector; (*Met*) gauge; **Mess|ge|rät** ▲ NT **a** (*für Öl, Druck etc*) measuring instrument, gauge **b** (*Eccl*) Mass requisites *pl*; **Mess|ge|wand** ▲ NT chasuble; **Mess|glas** ▲ NT graduated measure

mes|si|a|nisch [mɛ'sia:nɪʃ] ADJ (*Rel, Philos*) Messianic

Mes|si|as [mɛ'siːas] M -, -se (*Rel, fig*) Messiah

Mes|sie ['mɛsi] M -s, -s (*inf*: = *krankhaft unordentlicher Mensch*) messy person

Mes|sing ['mɛsɪŋ] NT -s, *no pl* brass; **mit ~ beschlagen** brass-bound

Mes|sing- *in cpds* brass; **Mes|sing|blech** NT sheet brass; **Mes|sing|schild** NT brass plate

Mess-: Mess|in|stru|ment ▲ NT gauge; **Mess|lat|te** ▲ F measuring stick; (*fig*: = *Maßstab*) threshold; **die ~ hoch legen** (*fig*) to set a high standard; **Mess|op|fer** ▲ NT (*Eccl*) Sacrifice of the Mass; **Mess|ord|nung** ▲ F (*Eccl*) ordinary (of the Mass); **Mess|plat|te** ▲ M (*Surv*) surveyor's staff *or* rod; **Mess|stab** ▲ M **a** (*Surv*) surveyor's staff **b** (*Aut*: = *Ölmessstab etc*) dipstick; **Mess|tech|nik** ▲ F measurement technology, metrology; **Mess|tisch** ▲ M (*Surv*) surveyor's table; **Mess|tisch|blatt** ▲ NT ordnance survey map; **Mess|uhr** ▲ F (*Tech*) meter, gauge

Mes|sung ['mɛsʊŋ] F -, -en **a** (= *das Messen*) measuring; (= *das Ablesen*) reading; (*von Blutdruck*) taking; (*Tech*: = *das Anzeigen*) gauging **b** (= *Messergebnis*) measurement; (= *Ableseergebnis*) reading

Mess-: Mess|wein ▲ M (*Eccl*) Communion wine; **Mess|wert** ▲ M measurement; (= *Ableseergebnis*) reading; **Mess|zahl** ▲ F measurement; **Mess|zy|lin|der** ▲ M measuring cylinder, graduated measure

Mes|ti|ze [mɛs'tiːtsə] M -n, -n mestizo

Mes|ti|zin [mɛs'tiːtsɪn] F -, -nen mestiza

MESZ *abbr von* **mitteleuropäische Sommerzeit**

Met [meːt] M -(e)s, *no pl* mead

Me|ta|bo|lis|mus [metabo'lɪsmʊs] M -, **Metabolismen** (*Physiol*) metabolism

Me|tall [me'tal] NT -s, -e **a** metal; **~ verarbeitend** (*Industrie, Unternehmen*) metal-processing *attr*, metal-working *attr* **b** (*geh: der Stimme*) metallic ring, metallic timbre (*Brit*) or timber (*US*)

Me|tall- *in cpds* metal-; **Me|tall|ar|bei|ter(in)** M(F) metalworker; **me|tall|ar|tig** **ADJ** metallic **ADV** metallically; **~ aussehen** to look metallic; **sich ~ anfühlen** to feel like metal; **Me|tall|be|ar|bei|tung** F metal processing, metalworking

me|tal|len [me'talən] ADJ metal; (*geh*) *Klang, Stimme* metallic **ADV** *glänzen* metallically; **~ klingen** to sound tinny

Me|tall|er [me'talɐ] M -s, -, **Me|tall|e|rin** [-ərɪn] F -, -nen (*inf*) metalworker

Me|tall-: Me|tall|er|mü|dung F metal fatigue; **Me|tall|geld** NT specie, metallic currency; **me|tall|hal|tig** ADJ metalliferous, metalline

me|tal|lic [me'talɪk] ADJ metallic; **~-blau** metallic blue

Me|tal|lic- [me'talɪk] *in cpds* metallic; **Me|tal|lic|lack** M metallic paint

Me|tall|in|dus|trie F , *no pl* metal industry

me|tal|lisch [me'talɪʃ] **ADJ** (= *aus Metall*) metal; (*fig*: = *metallartig*) *Stimme, Klang* metallic **ADV** metallically; **~ glänzen** to gleam like metal; **~ schmecken** to have a metallic taste; **zu ~ klingen** to sound too tinny

Me|tall-: Me|tall|kun|de F metallurgy; **Me|tall|sä|ge** F hacksaw; **Me|tall|stift** M metal pin

Me|tall|urg [meta'lʊrk] M -en, -en [-gn], **Me|tall|ur|ge** [meta'lʊrgə] M -n, -n, **Me|tall|ur|gin** [-'lʊrgɪn] F -, -nen metallurgist

Me|tall|ur|gie [metalʊr'giː] F -, *no pl* metallurgy

me|tall|ur|gisch [meta'lʊrgɪʃ] **ADJ** metallurgical **ADV** metallurgically

Me|tall-: me|tall|ver|ar|bei|tend △ ADJ → **Metall** a; **Me|tall|ver|ar|bei|tung** F metal processing; **Me|tall|wa|ren** PL hardware *sing*

Me|ta|mor|pho|se [metamɔr'foːzə] F -, -n metamorphosis

Me|ta|pher [me'tafɐ] F -, -n (*Liter, Poet*) metaphor

Me|ta|pho|rik [meta'foːrɪk] F -, *no pl* (*Liter, Poet*) imagery

me|ta|pho|risch [meta'foːrɪʃ] (*Liter, Poet*) **ADJ** metaphoric(al) **ADV** metaphorically; **ein ~ reicher Text** a text full of metaphors; **ein ~ überladener Roman** a novel with too many metaphors

Me|ta|phy|sik [meta-] F metaphysics *sing*

me|ta|phy|sisch ADJ metaphysical

Me|ta|psy|cho|lo|gie F metapsychology

Me|ta|spra|che F metalanguage

Me|ta|sta|se [meta'staːzə] F -, -n (*Med*) metastasis

Me|ta|the|se [meta'teːzə] F , **Me|ta|the|sis** [me'taːtezɪs] F -, **Metathesen** [-'teːzn̩] (*Ling*) metathesis

Me|te|or [mete'oːɐ, 'meːteoɐ] M OR NT -s, -e [-'oːrə] meteor

Me|te|or|ei|sen NT meteoric iron

Me|te|o|rit [meteo'riːt] M -en, -en meteorite

Me|te|o|ro|lo|ge [meteoro'loːgə] M -n, -n, **Me|te|o|ro|lo|gin** [-'loːgɪn] F -, -nen meteorologist; (*im Wetterdienst*) weather forecaster, weatherman/-woman (*inf*)

Me|te|o|ro|lo|gie [meteorolo'giː] F -, *no pl* meteorology

me|te|o|ro|lo|gisch [meteoro'loːgɪʃ] **ADJ** meteorological **ADV** meteorologically; **sich ~ auswirken** to have a meteorological effect

Me|te|or|stein M meteorite

Me|ter ['meːtɐ] M OR NT -s, - **a** metre (*Brit*), meter (*US*); **in einer Entfernung von 40 ~(n)** at a distance of 40 metres (*Brit*) or meters (*US*); **in/auf 500 ~(n) Höhe** at a height of 500 metres (*Brit*) or meters (*US*); **nach ~n** by the metre

---

(*Brit*) or meter (*US*) **b** (= *Meterstab*) metric measure **c** (*inf*) = **Metermaß**

Me|ter-: me|ter|dick ADJ metres (*Brit*) or meters (*US*) thick ADV **Schlammmassen bedeckten die Straßen ~** layers of mud several metres (*Brit*) or meters (*US*) thick covered the streets; **der Betonbelag war ~ aufgetragen** the cement covering was several metres (*Brit*) or meters (*US*) thick; **er hat seine Botschaft ~ aufgetragen** (*pej*) he laid it on too thick (*inf*); **me|ter-hoch** ADJ *Wellen, Mauer, Pflanze* metres (*Brit*) or meters (*US*) high; *Schnee* metres (*Brit*) or meters (*US*) deep ADV **das Grundstück war ~ eingezäunt** the estate was bordered by a very high fence; **der Schnee lag ~** the snow was very deep; **die Akten türmten sich ~ auf seinem Schreibtisch** the files were piled three feet high on his desk; **me|ter|lang** ADJ metres (*Brit*) or meters (*US*) long; **~e Lochstreifen** yards and yards of punch tape; **Me|ter|maß** NT **a** (= *Bandmaß*) tape measure, measuring tape **b** (= *Stab*) (metre (*Brit*) or meter (*US*)) rule; **Me|ter-wa|re** F (*Tex*) piece goods; **me|ter|wei|se** ADV by the metre (*Brit*) or meter (*US*); **me|ter|weit** ADJ (*breit*) metres (*Brit*) or meters (*US*) wide; (*lang*) metres (*Brit*) or meters (*US*) long ADV for yards; **er schoss ~ vorbei** his shot was yards or miles (*inf*) off target

Me|tha|don [meta'do:n] NT **-s**, *no pl* methadone

Me|than [me'ta:n] NT **-s**, *no pl*, **Me|than|gas** NT methane

Me|tha|nol [meta'no:l] NT **-s**, *no pl* methyl *or* wood alcohol

Me|tho|de [me'to:də] ✪ 39.2 F **-, -n** **a** method; **etw mit ~ machen** to do sth methodically *or* systematically; **das hat ~** (*inf*) there's (a) method behind it; **er hat ~ in den Laden gebracht** (*inf*) he knocked things into shape; **er hat (so) seine ~n** (*inf*) he's got his methods **b** **Metho-den** (= *Sitten*) behaviour (*Brit*), behavior (*US*); **was sind denn das für ~n?** what sort of way is that to behave?

Me|tho|den|leh|re F methodology
Me|tho|dik [me'to:dɪk] F **-, -en** methodology
Me|tho|di|ker [me'to:dikɐ] M **-s, -**, **Me|tho|di|ke|rin** F **-, -nen** methodologist
me|tho|disch [me'to:dɪʃ] ADJ methodical ADV methodically
Me|tho|dist [meto'dɪst] M **-en, -en**, **Me|tho|dis|tin** [-'dɪstɪn] F **-, -nen** Methodist
me|tho|dis|tisch [meto'dɪstɪʃ] ADJ Methodist
Me|tho|do|lo|gie [metodolo'gi:] F **-, -n** [-'gi:ən] methodology
me|tho|do|lo|gisch [metodo'lo:gɪʃ] ADJ methodological
Me|thu|sa|lem [me'tu:zalɛm] M **-s** Methuselah; **alt wie ~** as old as Methuselah
Me|thyl|al|ko|hol [me'ty:l-] M methyl *or* wood alcohol
Me|ti|er [me'tie:] NT **-s, -s** job, profession; **sich auf sein ~ verstehen** to be good at one's job
Me|to|ny|mie [metony'mi:] F **-, -n** [-'mi:ən] (*Liter*) metonymy
me|to|ny|misch [meto'ny:mɪʃ] ADJ (*Liter*) metonymical
Met|rik ['me:trɪk] F **-, -en** (*Poet, Mus*) metrics *sing*
met|risch ['me:trɪʃ] ADJ (*Sci*) *Maß* metric; (*Poet, Mus auch*) metrical ADV metrically, in metres (*Brit*) or meters (*US*)
Met|ro ['me:tro, 'metro] F **-, -s** metro
Met|ro|nom [metro'no:m] NT **-s, -e** (*Mus*) metronome
Met|ro|po|le [metro'po:lə] F **-, -n** **a** (= *größte Stadt*) metropolis **b** (= *Zentrum*) capital, centre (*Brit*), center (*US*) **c** (*Pol*: = *Mutterland*) home country
Met|ro|po|lit [metropo'li:t] M **-en, -en** metropolitan

Met|rum ['me:trʊm] NT **-s, Metren** ['me:trən] metre (*Brit*), meter (*US*)
Mett [mɛt] NT **-(e)s**, *no pl* (*Cook*) (lean) minced (*Brit*) or ground (*US*) pork/beef
Met|ta|ge [mɛ'ta:ʒə] F **-, -n** (*Typ*) make-up; (*Arbeitsort*) make-up room
Met|te ['mɛtə] F **-, -n** (*Eccl*) matins *sing*; (= *Abendmette*) vespers *sing*
Met|teur [mɛ'tø:ɐ] M **-s, -e**, **Met|teu|rin** [-'tø:rɪn] F **-, -nen** (*Typ*) make-up man/woman
Mett|wurst F (smoked) pork/beef sausage
Met|ze ['mɛtsə] F **-, -n** (*obs*: = *Hure*) strumpet (*old*)
Met|ze|lei [mɛtsə'lai] F **-, -en** butchery, slaughter
met|zeln ['mɛtsln] VT to slaughter, to butcher; (*S Ger*: = *schlachten*) to slaughter
Met|zel|sup|pe ['mɛtsl-] F (*S Ger*) meat broth
Metz|ger ['mɛtsgɐ] M **-s, -**, **Metz|ge|rin** [-ərɪn] F **-, -nen** butcher
Metz|ger- *in cpds* → **Fleischer-**
Metz|ge|rei [mɛtsgə'rai] F **-, -en** butcher's (shop)
Meu|chel- ['mɔʏçl-]: **Meu|chel|mord** M (treacherous) murder; **Meu|chel|mör|der(in)** M(F) (treacherous) assassin
meu|cheln ['mɔʏçln] VT (*old*) to assassinate
meuch|le|risch ['mɔʏçlərɪʃ] ADJ (*old*) murderous; *Mörder* treacherous
meuch|lings ['mɔʏçlɪŋs] ADV treacherously
Meu|te ['mɔʏtə] F **-, -n** pack (of hounds); (*fig pej*) mob; **die ~ loslassen** *or* **loskoppeln** to release the hounds
Meu|te|rei [mɔʏtə'rai] F **-, -en** mutiny; (*fig auch*) rebellion
meu|tern ['mɔʏtɐn] VI to mutiny; (*inf auch*) to rebel; (*dial inf*: = *meckern*) to moan, to grouch (*inf*); **die ~den Soldaten** the mutinous soldiers
Me|xi|ka|ner [mɛksi'ka:nɐ] M **-s, -**, **Me|xi|ka|ne|rin** [-ərɪn] F **-, -nen** Mexican
me|xi|ka|nisch [mɛksi'ka:nɪʃ] ADJ Mexican
Me|xi|ko ['mɛksiko] NT **-s** Mexico; **~ City**, **~-Stadt** Mexico City
MEZ *abbr von* **mitteleuropäische Zeit**
Mez|za|nin [mɛtsa'ni:n] M OR NT **-s, -e** (*Archit*) mezzanine; (*unter dem Dach*) attic
mez|zo|for|te ['mɛtso-] ADJ (*Mus*) mezzo forte
mez|zo|pia|no ['mɛtso-] ADJ (*Mus*) mezzo piano
Mez|zo|sop|ran ['mɛtso-] M mezzo-soprano
mg *abbr von* **Milligramm** mg
MG [ɛm'ge:] NT **-(e)s, -(s)** *abbr von* **Maschinengewehr**
mhd *abbr von* **mittelhochdeutsch**
MHz *abbr von* **Megahertz**
mi|au [mi'au] INTERJ miaow (*Brit*), meow
mi|au|en [mi'auən] *ptp* **miaut** VI to miaow (*Brit*), to meow
mich [mɪç] PERS PRON *acc von* **ich** me REFL PRON myself; **ich fühle ~ wohl** I feel fine
Mi|cha|el ['mɪçae:l, 'mɪçaɛl] M **-s** Michael
Mi|cha|e|li(s) [mɪça'e:li, mɪça'e:lɪs] NT **-**, *no pl* Michaelmas
Mi|chel ['mɪçl] M **-s** Mike, Mick; **der deutsche ~** (*fig*) the plain honest German
Mi|chi|gan|see ['mɪʃɪgən-] M Lake Michigan
mi|cke|rig ['mɪkərɪç], **mick|rig** ['mɪkrɪç] (*inf*) ADJ pathetic; *Betrag auch* paltry; *altes Männchen* puny ADV pathetically
Mi|cky|maus ['mɪki-] F Mickey Mouse
mi|di ['mɪdi] ADJ *pred* (*Fashion*) midi; **Midi tragen** to wear midi *or* mid-length skirts/dresses
Mi|di- ['mɪdi] *in cpds* midi; **Mi|di-An|la|ge** F, **Mi|di-Sys|tem** NT midi (system)
mied *pret von* **meiden**
Mie|der ['mi:dɐ] NT **-s, -** **a** (= *Leibchen*) bodice **b** (= *Korsage*) girdle

Mie|der-: Mie|der|hös|chen [-hø:sçən] NT panty girdle; **Mie|der|wa|ren** PL corsetry *sing*
Mief [mi:f] M **-s**, *no pl* (*inf*) fug; (*muffig*) stale air; (= *Gestank*) stink, pong (*Brit inf*); **der ~ der Provinz/des Kleinbürgertums** (*fig*) the oppressive claustrophobic atmosphere of the provinces/petty bourgeoisie
mie|fen ['mi:fn] VI (*inf*) to stink, to pong (*Brit inf*); (= *furzen*) to make a smell; **hier mieft es** there's a pong (*Brit inf*) or smell in here; (*muffig*) the air in here is so stale; **was mieft denn hier so?** what's this awful pong (*Brit inf*) or smell?
Mief|quirl M (*inf, hum*) fan
Mie|ne ['mi:nə] F **-, -n** (= *Gesichtsausdruck*) expression, face, mien (*liter*); **eine finstere ~ machen** to look grim; **gute ~ zum bösen Spiel machen** to grin and bear it; **~ machen, etw zu tun** to make a move to do sth; **seine ~ verfinsterte** *or* **verdüsterte sich** his face darkened; **sich** (*dat*) **etw mit eisiger ~ anhören** to listen to sth in stony silence → **verziehen** VT a
Mie|nen|spiel NT facial expressions *pl*; **ein lebhaftes ~ haben** to express a lot with one's face
mies [mi:s] (*inf*) ADJ rotten (*inf*), lousy (*inf*); *Lokal auch* crummy (*inf*); *Laune auch* foul; *Qualität* poor; **mir ist ~** I feel lousy (*inf*) or rotten (*inf*) ADV badly; **er hat sich ihr gegenüber ~ verhalten** he was rotten to her (*inf*); **er hat das ~ übersetzt** his translation was lousy (*inf*) or crummy (*inf*)
Mie|se ['mi:zə] PL (*inf*) **in den ~n sein** (*bei der Bank*) to be in the red; (*beim Kartenspiel*) to be down on points; **in die ~n kommen** (*bei der Bank*) to get into the red; (*beim Kartenspiel*) to get minus points
Mie|se|pe|ter ['mi:zəpe:tɐ] M **-s, -** (*inf*) misery-guts (*Brit inf*), grouch (*inf*)
mie|se|pe|te|rig ['mi:zəpe:tərɪç], **mie|se|pet-rig** ['mi:zəpe:trɪç] ADJ (*inf*) miserable, grouchy (*inf*)
Mie|se|pet|rig|keit F **-**, *no pl* (*inf*) grouchiness (*inf*)
mies machen ▲ VT (*inf*) to run down
Mies|ma|cher(in) M(F) (*inf*) killjoy
Mies|ma|che|rei [mi:smaxə'rai] F **-, -en** (*inf*) belly-aching (*inf*)
Mies|mu|schel F mussel
Miet-: Miet|aus|fall M loss of rent; **Miet|au|to** NT hire(d) car; **Miet|bei|hil|fe** F rent allowance *or* subsidy
Mie|te¹ ['mi:tə] F **-, -n** (*für Wohnung*) rent; (*für Gegenstände*) rental; (*für Dienstleistungen*) charge; **rückständige ~** (rent) arrears; **zur ~ wohnen** to live in rented accommodation; **das ist die halbe ~** (*fig inf*) that's half the battle
Mie|te² ['mi:tə] F **-, -n** (= *Kartoffelmiete*) clamp (*Brit*), pit (*US*); (= *Schober*) stack
Miet|ein|nah|me F *usu pl* rental income *sing*
mie|ten ['mi:tn] VT to rent; *Boot, Auto* to rent, to hire (*esp Brit*)
Mie|ter ['mi:tɐ] M **-s, -**, **Mie|te|rin** [-ərɪn] F **-, -nen** tenant; (= *Untermieter*) lodger
Mie|ter|hö|hung F rent increase
Mie|ter-: Mie|ter|schaft ['mi:tɐʃaft] F **-, -en** tenants *pl*; **Mie|ter|schutz** M rent control; **Mie|ter|schutz|bund** M tenants' (rights) association; **Mie|ter|schutz|ge|setz** NT Rent Act
Miet-: Mie|ter|trag M rent(al) (income); **miet|frei** ADJ, ADV rent-free; **Miet|ga|ran|tie** F proof of ability to pay rent; **Miet|kauf** M (*Comm*) lease-purchase agreement (*with option to buy at the end of the lease period*), hire purchase (*Brit*); **Miet|kau|ti|on** F deposit; **Miet|par|tei** F tenant (and family); **Miet-preis** M rent; (*für Sachen*) rental (fee *or* rate (*US*)), hire charge (*Brit*); **Miet|recht** NT rent

law; **Miet|rück|stän|de** PL rent arrears pl; **Miet|schuld** F back rent; **~en** rent arrears pl

Miets-: Miets|haus NT block of (rented) flats (Brit), apartment house (US); **Miets|ka|ser|ne** F (pej) tenement house

Miet-: Miet|spie|gel M rent level; **Miet|stei|ge|rung** F rent increase; **Miet|ver|hält|nis** NT tenancy; **Miet|ver|trag** M lease; (von Auto) rental agreement; **Miet|wa|gen** M hire(d) car (Brit), rental (car) (US); **Miet|wert** M letting or rental value; **Miet|woh|nung** F rented flat (Brit) or apartment; **Miet|wu|cher** M exorbitant rent; **~ ist strafbar** charging exorbitant rent(s) is a punishable offence (Brit) or offense (US); **Miet|zah|lung** F payment of the rent; **Miet|zins** M (S Ger, Aus) rent

Mie|ze ['miːtsə] F -, -n (inf) **a** (= Katze) pussy (-cat) (inf) **b** (Mädchen) chick (inf), bird (Brit inf); (als Anrede) baby (inf), honey (inf)

Mie|ze-: Mie|ze|kätz|chen NT (baby-talk) (little) pussy(-cat); **Mie|ze|kat|ze** F (baby-talk) pussy(-cat)

MiG [mɪɡ] F -s, -s (Mil) MiG

Mig|rä|ne [miˈɡrɛːnə] F -, no pl migraine

Mig|rä|ne|an|fall M attack of migraine

Mig|ra|ti|on [miɡraˈtsioːn] F -, -en (Sociol, Comput, Biol) migration

Mi|ka|do¹ [miˈkaːdo] NT -s, -s (= Spiel) pick-a-stick

Mi|ka|do² M -s, -s (old: = Kaiser von Japan) mikado

Mik|ro ['miːkro] NT -s, -s (inf) abbr von **Mikrofon** mike (inf)

Mik|ro|be [miˈkroːbə] F -, -n microbe

Mik|ro- in cpds micro-; **Mik|ro|bi|o|lo|gie** F microbiology; **Mik|ro|chip** M microchip; **Mik|ro|com|pu|ter** M microcomputer, micro; **Mik|ro|elekt|ro|nik** F microelectronics sing; **Mik|ro|fa|ser** F microfibre (Brit), microfiber (US); **Mik|ro|fiche** ['miːkrofiʃ] M OR NT -s, -s microfiche

Mik|ro|fon [mikroˈfoːn, ˈmiːkrofoːn] NT -s, -e microphone

Mik|ro|gramm NT microgram(me)

Mik|ro|kos|mos M microcosm

Mik|ro|me|ter NT micron; (Gerät) micrometer

Mik|ron ['miːkrɔn] NT -s, - micron

Mik|ro|or|ga|nis|mus M microorganism

Mik|ro|phon [mikroˈfoːn, ˈmiːkrofoːn] NT -s, -e microphone

Mik|ro-: Mik|ro|pille F (Med) ≈ mini-pill; **Mik|ro|pro|zes|sor** M microprocessor; **Mik|ro|se|kun|de** F microsecond; **Mik|ro|sen|der** M microtransmitter

Mik|ro|skop [mikroˈskoːp] NT -s, -e microscope

Mik|ro|sko|pie [mikroskoˈpiː] F -, no pl microscopy

mik|ro|sko|pie|ren [mikroskoˈpiːrən] ptp **mik-roskopiert** VT (rare) to examine under or with the microscope VI to work with a/the microscope

mik|ro|sko|pisch [mikroˈskoːpɪʃ] ADJ microscopic ADV microscopically; **etw ~ untersu-chen** to examine sth under the microscope; **~ klein** (fig) microscopically small

Mik|ro|struk|tur F microstructure

Mik|ro|wel|le F microwave

Mik|ro|wel|len|herd M microwave (oven)

Mik|ro|zen|sus M sample census

Mik|ro|ze|pha|le(r) [mikrotseˈfaːlə] MF decl as adj microcephalic

Mi|lan ['miːlan, miˈlaːn] M -s, -e (Orn) kite

Mil|be ['mɪlbə] F -, -n mite

Milch [mɪlç] F -, no pl (alle Bedeutungen) milk; (= Fischsamen) milt, soft roe; **dicke ~** curd(s); **~ ge-ben** (Kuh) to yield milk; **das Land, wo ~ und Ho-nig fließt** the land of or flowing with milk and

honey; **aussehen wie ~ und Blut** to have a pea-ches-and-cream complexion

Milch- in cpds milk; **milch|ar|tig** ADJ milky; **Milch|bar** F milk bar; (sl: = Busen) tits pl (sl); **Milch|bart** M (inf) downy or fluffy beard, bum-fluff (Brit inf), peach fuzz (US inf); (fig pej: = Jüngling) milksop; **Milch|brei** M ≈ milk pudding; **Milch|bröt|chen** NT roll made with milk and sugar; **Milch|drü|se** F mammary gland; **Milch|eis** NT milk-based ice cream; **Milch|ei|weiß** NT lactoprotein; **Milch|fett** NT milk fat; **Milch|fla|sche** F milk bottle; **Milch|fluss** ▲ M (Med) galactorrhoea (Brit), galactorrhea (US); **Milch|frau** F (inf) dairy-woman; **Milch|ge|biss** ▲ NT milk teeth pl; **Milch|ge|schäft** NT dairy; **Milch|ge|sicht** NT (inf) baby-face; **Milch|glas** NT frosted glass; **Milch|han|del** M dairy business; **Milch|händ|ler** M dairyman; **Milch|händ|le-rin** F dairywoman

Milch-: Milch|kaf|fee M milky coffee; **Milch|kalb** NT sucking calf; **Milch|kan|ne** F milk can; (größer) (milk) churn; **Milch|kuh** F milk or milch (spec) cow; (fig inf) milch cow (Brit inf), source of easy income; **Milch|la|den** M dairy; **Milch|mäd|chen** NT (= Milchverkäufe-rin) dairy girl; (= Milchkassiererin) milk girl; **Milch|mäd|chen|rech|nung** F (inf) naïve fal-lacy; **Milch|mann** M pl **-männer** milkman; **Milch|mix|ge|tränk** NT milk shake

Milch|ner ['mɪlçnɐ] M -s, - milter

Milch-: Milch|pro|dukt NT milk product; **Milch|pul|ver** NT dried or powdered milk; **Milch|pum|pe** F breast pump; **Milch|quo|te** F (in der EU) milk quota; **Milch|reis** M round-grain rice; (als Gericht) rice pudding; **Milch|saft** M (Bot) latex; **Milch|säu|re** F lactic acid; **Milch|scho|ko|la|de** F milk chocolate; **Milch|schorf** M cradle cap; **Milch|see** M (in der EU) milk lake; **Milch|spei|se** F milky or milk-based food; **Milch|stra|ße** F Milky Way; **Milch|stra|ßen|sys|tem** M Milky Way sys-tem or galaxy; **Milch|sup|pe** F **a** ≈ warm blancmange (Brit), milk soup (US) **b** (dated inf: = Nebel) peasouper (Brit inf), thick fog; **Milch|tü|te** F milk carton; **Milch|vieh** NT dairy cattle pl; **Milch|wirt|schaft** F dairy farming; **Milch|zahn** M milk tooth; **Milch|zu|cker** M lactose

mild [mɪlt], **mil|de** ['mɪldə] ADJ **a** (= sanft, lind) Wetter, Abend mild; Luft gentle, mild **b** (= nach-sichtig, barmherzig) Behandlung, Beurteilung, Strafe, Richter lenient; Worte mild; **eine ~e Gabe** alms pl **c** Käse, Zigaretten mild; Seife gentle, mild; Speisen light ADV **a** (= sanft) mildly, gently **b** (= nachsichtig) leniently; **das Urteil fiel ~/-er aus** the sentence was lenient/more lenient; **jdn ~ stimmen** to put sb in a generous mood; **~e ge-sagt** or **ausgedrückt** to put it mildly **c** (= nicht stark) gewürzt mildly; **~ schmecken** to taste mild; **die Seife riecht ~** the soap is mildly scented

Mil|de ['mɪldə] F -, no pl **a** (= Sanftheit, Lindheit) mildness, gentleness **b** (= Nachsichtigkeit, Barm-herzigkeit) leniency; **~ walten lassen** to be leni-ent

mil|dern ['mɪldɐn] VT (geh) Schmerz to ease, to soothe, to alleviate; Kälte to alleviate; Angst to calm; Strafe, Urteil to moderate, to mitigate; Ge-gensätze to reduce, to make less crass or severe; Schärfe, Konflikt, Problem, Härte, Druck to reduce; Ausdrucksweise, Zorn to moderate; Sanktionen to relax; Folgen to make less severe; **~de Umstän-de** (Jur) mitigating or extenuating circumstances VR (Wetter) to become milder; (Gegensätze) to become less crass; (Zorn) to abate; (Schmerz) to ease

Mil|de|rung ['mɪldərʊŋ] F -, no pl (von Schmerz) easing, soothing, alleviation; (von Ausdruck, des Klimas) moderation; (von Strafe) moderation,

mitigation; **spüren Sie schon eine ~?** can you feel any easing (of the pain)?

Mil|de|rungs|grund M mitigating cause or cir-cumstance

Mild-: mild|her|zig ADJ (old) = barmherzig; **mild|tä|tig** ADJ (geh) charitable; **er war sein ganzes Leben lang ~** he performed charitable deeds throughout his life; **für ~e Zwecke** for charity; **Mild|tä|tig|keit** F (geh) charity

Mi|li|eu [miˈliøː] NT -s, -s (= Umwelt) environ-ment, milieu; (= Lokalkolorit) atmosphere; (= Ver-brechermilieu) underworld; (von Prostitution) world of prostitutes

Mi|li|eu- [miˈliøː-]: **mi|li|eu|ge|schä|digt** [-ɡəʃɛːdɪçt], **mi|li|eu|ge|stört** ADJ maladjusted (due to adverse social factors); **Mi|li|eu-scha|den** M effects pl of adverse social fac-tors; **Mi|li|eu|schil|de|rung** F background de-scription; **Mi|li|eu|stu|di|en** PL **~ treiben** (usu hum) to study the locals (hum); **Mi|li|eu|the-o|rie** F (Sociol) environmentalism no art; **Mi|li|eu|wech|sel** F change of environment; (= Abwechslung) change of scene

mi|li|tant [miliˈtant] ADJ militant ADV **~ kom-munistisch/antikommunistisch sein** to be a mili-tant communist/anticommunist; **der ~ auftre-tende Präsident** the militant president

Mi|li|tanz [miliˈtants] F -, no pl militancy

Mi|li|tär¹ [miliˈtɛːɐ] NT -s, no pl military, armed forces pl; **beim ~ sein** (inf) to be in the forces; **zum ~ einberufen werden** to be called up (Brit) or drafted (US); **zum ~ müssen** (inf) to have to join up (Brit) or join the army; **zum ~ gehen** to join up (Brit), to join the army; **vom ~ entlas-sen werden** to be discharged from the armed forces; **(gegen jdn) ~ einsetzen** to use the mili-tary (against sb); **wir sind doch hier nicht beim ~!** we're not in the army, you know!; **da geht es zu wie beim ~** the place is run like an army (Brit) or military camp

Mi|li|tär² M -s, -s (army) officer

Mi|li|tär- in cpds military; **Mi|li|tär|a|ka|de|mie** F military academy; **Mi|li|tär|ak|ti|on** F mili-tary action; **Mi|li|tär|arzt** M , **Mi|li|tär|ärz|tin** F army doctor; (= Offizier) medical officer; **Mi|li|tär|dienst** M military service; **(seinen) ~ ab-leisten** to do national service; **Mi|li|tär|dik|ta-tur** F military dictatorship; **Mi|li|tär|ein|satz** M (= Einsatz von Militär) deployment of troops; (= Kampfhandlung) military action; **Mi|li|tär-geist|li|che(r)** MF decl as adj (army) chaplain; **Mi|li|tär|ge|län|de** NT military property; **Mi|li|tär|ge|richt** NT military court, court mar-tial; **Internationales ~** International Military Tribunal; **vor ein ~ gestellt werden** to be tried by a court martial; **wenn Sie das machen, wer-den Sie vor ein ~ gestellt** if you do that you'll be court-martialled (Brit) or court-martialed (US); **Mi|li|tär|hil|fe** F military aid

Mi|li|ta|ria [miliˈtaːria] PL things pl military

mi|li|tä|risch [miliˈtɛːrɪʃ] ADJ military; **jdm ~e** or **die ~en Ehren erweisen** to give sb military hon-ours (Brit) or honors (US); **mit allen ~en Ehren** with full military honours (Brit) or honors (US); **einen Konflikt mit ~en Mitteln lösen** to resolve a conflict with the use of troops ADV militarily; **~ grüßen** to salute; **es geht dort streng ~ zu** it's very regimented there; **sich ~ geben** to behave in a military fashion

mi|li|ta|ri|sie|ren [militariˈziːrən] ptp **militari-siert** VT to militarize

Mi|li|ta|ris|mus [militaˈrɪsmʊs] M -, no pl mili-tarism

Mi|li|ta|rist [militaˈrɪst] M -en, -en, **Mi|li|ta|ris-tin** [-ˈrɪstɪn] F -, -nen militarist

mi|li|ta|ris|tisch [militaˈrɪstɪʃ] ADJ militaristic

Mi|li|tär-: Mi|li|tär|macht F military power; **Mi|li|tär|mu|sik** F military marches pl, milita-ry music; **Mi|li|tär|pa|ra|de** F military parade; **Mi|li|tär|putsch** M military putsch; **Mi|li|tär-re|gime** NT military regime; **Mi|li|tär|schlag** M military strike or action; **Mi|li|tär|seel|sor-**

ge F spiritual welfare of the armed forces; **Mi|li|tär|we|sen** NT military affairs pl; **Mi|li|tär|wis|sen|schaft** F military science

Mi|li|ta|ry [ˈmɪlɪtəri] F -, -s (Sport) three-day event

Mi|li|tär|zeit F army days pl, days pl as a soldier

Mi|liz [miˈliːts] F -, -en militia; (in Osteuropa: = Polizei) police

Mi|li|zio|när [militsioˈnɛːɐ] M -s, -e, **Mi|li|zi|o|nä|rin** [-ˈnɛːrɪn] F -, -nen militiaman/-woman; (in Osteuropa: = Polizist) policeman/-woman

Mi|liz|sol|dat M (old) militiaman

milkt [mɪlkt] (old) 3. pers sing pres von **melken**

Mill. abbr von **Million(en)**

mil|le [ˈmɪlə] pro ~ = Promille

Mil|le [ˈmɪlə] F -, - (inf) grand (inf); **5** ~ 5 grand (inf)

Mil|len|ni|um [mɪˈlɛniʊm] NT -s, **Mil|len|nien** [-niən] (geh) millennium

Mil|li|ar|där [mɪliarˈdɛːɐ] M -s, -e, **Mil|li|ar|dä|rin** [-ˈdɛːrɪn] F -, -nen multi-millionaire, billionaire

Mil|li|ar|de [mɪˈliardə] F -, -n thousand millions (Brit), billion (US); **zwei ~n Euro** two thousand million euros (Brit), two billion euros (US); **~n (von) Menschen** thousands of millions of people, billions of people

Mil|li|ar|den-: Mil|li|ar|den|be|trag M (amount of) thousands of millions pl (Brit), billions pl (US); **Mil|li|ar|den|de|fi|zit** NT (multi)billion dollar/euro etc deficit; **Mil|li|ar|den|grab** NT (inf) expensive white elephant; **dieses neue Projekt ist ein ~** this new project is gobbling up vast amounts of money; **Mil|li|ar|den|hö|he** F in ~ amounting to a billion/billions

mil|li|ards|tel [mrˈliartstl] ADJ thousand millionth (Brit), billionth (US); **ein ~ Meter** a or one thousand millionth of a metre (Brit), a or one billionth of a meter (US), a or one bicron (US)

Mil|li|ards|tel [mrˈliartstl] NT -s, - thousand millionth part (Brit), billionth part (US)

mil|li|ards|te(r, s) [mrˈliartstə] ADJ thousand millionth (Brit), billionth (US)

Mil|li- [ˈmɪli] in cpds milli-; **Mil|li|bar** NT millibar; **Mil|li|gramm** NT milligram(me); **Mil|li|me|ter** M OR NT millimetre (Brit), millimeter (US); **mil|li|me|ter|ge|nau** ADJ Berechnung, Planung extremely precise ADV to the millimetre (Brit) or millimeter (US); **Mil|li|me|ter|pa|pier** NT graph paper

Mil|li|on [mrˈlioːn] F -, -en million; **eine ~ Londoner ist** or **sind unterwegs** a million Londoners are on their way; **zwei ~en** two millions; **zwei ~en Einwohner** two million inhabitants; **~en begeisterter Zuschauer** or **von begeisterten Zuschauern** millions of enthusiastic viewers; **~en Mal** a million times

Mil|li|o|när [mɪlioˈnɛːɐ] M -s, -e millionaire; **vom Tellerwäscher zum ~** from rags to riches; **es zum ~ bringen** to make a million

Mil|li|o|nä|rin [mɪlioˈnɛːrɪn] F -, -nen millionairess

Mil|li|o|nen-: Mil|li|o|nen|auf|la|ge F million copies pl; millions of copies pl; **Mil|li|o|nen|auf|trag** M contract worth millions; **Mil|li|o|nen|er|be** M , **Mil|li|o|nen|er|bin** F inheritor of millions; **mil|li|o|nen|fach** ADJ millionfold; **der ~e Mord an den Juden** the murder of millions of Jews ADV a million times; **Mil|li|o|nen|ge|schäft** NT multi-million-pound/dollar etc industry; **ein ~ abschließen** to conclude a (business) deal worth millions; **Mil|li|o|nen|ge|winn** M **a** (= Ertrag) profit of millions; **manche Firmen haben ~e gemacht** some firms have made profits running into millions **b** (= Lotteriegewinn) prize of a million; **Mil|li|o|nen|heer** NT army of millions; **Mil|li|o|nen|hö|he**

F in ~ amounting to a million/millions; **die Explosion verursachte einen Schaden in ~** the explosion caused damage running into millions of dollars etc; **mil|li|o|nen|mal** △ ADV → Million; **Mil|li|o|nen|scha|den** M damage no pl amounting to millions, damage no pl running into millions; **mil|li|o|nen|schwer** ADJ (inf) Person worth a few million; Verlust, Schuld of a few million; Maßnahme costing a few million; **Mil|li|o|nen|stadt** F town with over a million inhabitants

Mil|li|ons|tel [mrˈlioːnstl] ADJ millionth

Mil|li|ons|tel [mrˈlioːnstl] NT -s, - millionth part

mil|li|ons|te(r, s) [mrˈlioːnstə] ADJ millionth

Mil|li|rem NT millirem

Milz [mɪlts] F -, -en spleen

Milz|brand M (Med, Vet) anthrax

Mi|me [ˈmiːmə] M -n, -n, **Mi|min** [ˈmiːmɪn] F -, -nen (old, liter) mime (old), Thespian

mi|men [ˈmiːmən] VT to mime; **er mimt den Unschuldigen** (inf) he's acting innocent or the innocent (Brit); **er mimt den Kranken** (inf) he's pretending to be sick VI to play-act

Mi|me|sis [ˈmiːmezɪs] F -, **Mimesen** [miˈmeːzn] (Liter, Philos) mimesis

mi|me|tisch [miˈmeːtɪʃ] ADJ (Liter, Philos) mimetic

Mi|mik [ˈmiːmɪk] F -, no pl facial expression; **etw durch ~ ausdrücken** to express sth facially

Mi|mi|ker [ˈmiːmikɐ] M -s, -, **Mi|mi|ke|rin** [-ərɪn] F -, -nen mime(r)

Mi|mi|kry [ˈmiːmikri] F -, no pl (Zool, fig) mimicry

Mi|min F → Mime

mi|misch [ˈmiːmɪʃ] ADJ mimic ADV darstellen using mime; sich verständigen, zum Ausdruck bringen by using mime, by miming

Mi|mo|se [miˈmoːzə] F -, -n mimosa; **empfindlich wie eine ~ sein** to be oversensitive

mi|mo|sen|haft ADJ (fig) oversensitive ADV (fig) reagieren oversensitively

mims|en [ˈmɪmzn] VTI (Telec: inf) to send an MMS (message)

min.¹ abbr von minimal

Min., min.² abbr von Minute(n)

Mi|na|rett [minaˈrɛt] NT -s, -e or -s minaret

min|der [ˈmɪndɐ] ADV less; **mehr oder ~** more or less; **nicht mehr und nicht ~** neither more nor less, no more and no less; **nicht ~ wichtig als** no less important than; **und das nicht ~** and no less so

Min|der-: Min|der|aus|ga|ben PL reduced expenditure sing; **min|der|be|gabt** ADJ less gifted; **Min|der|be|gab|te** PL decl as adj less gifted people pl; **min|der|be|gü|tert** ADJ less well-off; **Min|der|be|gü|ter|te** [-bəɡyːtəta] PL decl as adj people pl in the lower income brackets; **Min|der|be|las|te|te(r)** [-balastətə] MF decl as adj (Jur) less incriminated person; **min|der|be|mit|telt** ADJ less well-off; **geistig ~** (iro) mentally less gifted; **Min|der|be|mit|tel|te** [-bəmɪtltə] PL decl as adj (dated) people pl with a limited income; (iro) not very bright people pl; **Min|der|ein|nah|men** PL decrease sing in receipts

min|de|re(r, s) ADJ attr lesser; Güte, Qualität inferior

Min|der|ge|wicht NT short weight

Min|der|heit F -, -en minority

Min|der|hei|ten- (Pol): **Min|der|hei|ten|fra|ge** F minorities problem; **Min|der|hei|ten|schutz** M protection of minorities

Min|der|heits- (Pol): **Min|der|heits|rech|te** PL rights pl of minorities; **Min|der|heits|re|gie|rung** F minority government

min|der|jäh|rig [-jɛːrɪç] ADJ who is (still) a minor; **Min|der|jäh|ri|ge(r)** [-jɛːrɪɡə] MF decl as adj minor; **Min|der|jäh|rig|keit** [-jɛːrɪçkait] F -, no pl minority

min|dern [ˈmɪndɐn] VT (= herabsetzen) Ansehen to diminish; (= verringern) Wert, Qualität to reduce, to diminish, to erode; Rechte to erode; Freude, Vergnügen to detract from, to lessen; Risiko, Chancen to reduce VR (Ansehen, Wert, Qualität) to diminish; (Freude, Vergnügen) to lessen

Min|de|rung [ˈmɪndərʊŋ] F -, -en (= Herabsetzung) diminishing (von Wert, Qualität) reduction (+gen in); (von Rechten) erosion; (von Freude, Vergnügen) lessening

Min|der|wert M (Jur) decrease in value

min|der|wer|tig ADJ inferior; Waren, Material auch poor-quality, low-quality; Arbeit auch poor(-quality); Qualität auch low; Charakter low, base

Min|der|wer|tig|keit F inferiority; **die ~ der Qualität** the low quality

Min|der|wer|tig|keits-: Min|der|wer|tig|keits|ge|fühl NT feeling of inferiority; **~e haben** to feel inferior; **Min|der|wer|tig|keits|kom|plex** M inferiority complex

Min|der|zahl F minority; **in der ~ sein** to be in the minority

Min|dest- [ˈmɪndəst] in cpds minimum; **Min|dest|ab|stand** M minimum distance; **Min|dest|al|ter** NT minimum age; **Min|dest|be|steu|e|rung** F lowest or minimum tax rate; **Min|dest|be|trag** M minimum amount; **Waren für einen ~ von EUR 100** goods to a minimum value of 100 euros; **Min|dest|ein|kom|men** NT minimum income

min|des|tens [ˈmɪndəstns] ADV at least

min|des|te(r, s) [ˈmɪndəstə] superl von **wenig** ADJ attr least, slightest; Ahnung auch faintest, foggiest (inf); **nicht die ~ Angst** not the slightest or least trace of fear; **er hat nicht das ~ bisschen Arbeit geleistet** he didn't do a single stroke (of work); **das Mindeste** (the very) least; **ich verstehe nicht das Mindeste von (der) Kunst** I don't know the slightest thing about art; **das wäre das Mindeste gewesen** that's the least he/she etc could have done

ADV **zum Mindesten** at least, at the very least; **(nicht) im Mindesten** (not) in the least; **das bezweifle ich nicht im Mindesten** I don't doubt that at all, I don't doubt that in the slightest

Min|dest-: Min|dest|for|de|rung F minimum demand; **Min|dest|ge|bot** NT (bei Auktionen) reserve or knockdown price; **Min|dest|ge|schwin|dig|keit** F minimum speed; **Min|dest|grö|ße** F minimum size; (von Menschen) minimum height; **Min|dest|halt|bar|keits|da|tum** NT best-before date; **Min|dest|lohn** M minimum wage; **Min|dest|maß** NT minimum, minimum amount (an +dat of); **sich auf das ~ beschränken** to limit oneself to the (absolute) minimum; **Min|dest|preis** M minimum price; **Min|dest|re|ser|ve** F (Fin) minimum reserves pl; **Min|dest|re|ser|ve|satz** M (Fin) minimum reserve ratio; **Min|dest|stra|fe** F minimum penalty; **Min|dest|um|tausch** M minimum obligatory exchange; **Min|dest|ur|laub** M minimum holiday (esp Brit) or vacation (US) entitlement; **Min|dest|wert** M minimum value; **im ~ von** to a minimum value of; **Min|dest|zins|satz** M minimum lending rate, MLR

Mi|ne [ˈmiːnə] F -, -n **a** (Min) mine; **in den ~n arbeiten** to work down or in the mines **b** (Mil) mine; **auf eine ~ fahren/treten/laufen** to drive over/to step on/to strike or hit a mine; **~ legen** to lay mines **c** (= Bleistiftmine) lead; (= Kugelschreibermine, Filzstiftmine) reservoir; (= Farbmine) cartridge; (austauschbar) refill; **die ~ ist leer/läuft aus** (von Kugelschreiber) the Biro® (Brit) or pen has run out/is leaking; (von Filzstift) the felt-tip has run out/is leaking; **eine neue ~** a refill; (für Bleistift) a new lead

Mi|nen-: Mi|nen|feld NT (Mil) minefield; **Mi|nen|le|ger** [-leːɡɐ] M -s, - (Mil, Naut) minelayer; **Mi|nen|räum|boot** NT minesweeper; **Mi|nen|sper|re** F (Mil) mine barrage; **Mi|nen|such|boot** NT , **Mi|nen|su|cher** M (inf)

minesweeper; **Mi|nen|such|ge|rät** NT mine detector; **Mi|nen|wer|fer** M (old Mil) mortar

Mi|ne|ral [mineˈraːl] NT **-s, -e** or **-ien** [-liən] mineral

Mi|ne|ral-: Mi|ne|ral|bad NT mineral bath; (= Ort) spa; (= Schwimmbad) swimming pool fed from a mineral spring; **Mi|ne|ral|brun|nen** M mineral spring; **Mi|ne|ral|dün|ger** M inorganic fertilizer

Mi|ne|ra|li|en|samm|lung [-liən-] F collection of minerals

mi|ne|ra|lisch [mineˈraːlɪʃ] ADJ mineral

Mi|ne|ra|lo|ge [mineraˈloːɡə] M **-n, -n, Mi|ne|ra|lo|gin** [-ˈloːɡɪn] F **-, -nen** mineralogist

Mi|ne|ra|lo|gie [mineraloˈɡiː] F **-, no pl** mineralogy

mi|ne|ra|lo|gisch [mineraˈloːɡɪʃ] ADJ mineralogical

Mi|ne|ral-: Mi|ne|ral|öl NT (mineral) oil; **Mi|ne|ral|öl|ge|sell|schaft** F oil company; **Mi|ne|ral|öl|steu|er** F tax on oil; **Mi|ne|ral|quel|le** F mineral spring; **Mi|ne|ral|salz** NT mineral salt; **Mi|ne|ral|was|ser** NT mineral water

mi|ni [ˈmɪni] ADJ **inv** (Fashion) mini; **Mini tragen** to wear a mini

Mi|ni [ˈmɪni] M **-s, -s** (inf: = Minirock) mini

Mi|ni- in cpds mini-; **Mi|ni-An|la|ge** F mini hi-fi

Mi|ni|a|tur [miniaˈtuːɐ] F **-, -en** (Art) miniature; (fig, Liter) thumbnail sketch

Mi|ni|a|tur- in cpds miniature; **Mi|ni|a|tur|aus|ga|be** F miniature version; (Buch) miniature edition; **Mi|ni|a|tur|bild** NT miniature; **Mi|ni|a|tur|bild|nis** NT miniature portrait; **Mi|ni|a|tur|for|mat** NT miniature format; **eine Bibel in ~** a miniature Bible; **Mi|ni|a|tur|ge|mäl|de** NT miniature; **Mi|ni|a|tur|ma|ler(in)** M(F) miniaturist; **Mi|ni|a|tur|ma|le|rei** F miniature painting; **Mi|ni|a|tur|staat** M tiny state or country

Mi|ni-: Mi|ni|bar F (im Hotel etc) minibar; **Mi|ni|bi|ki|ni** M scanty bikini; **Mi|ni|bus** M minibus; **Mi|ni|car** M minicab; **Mi|ni|com|pu|ter** M minicomputer; **Mi|ni|disk, Mi|ni|disc** [-dɪsk] F **-, -s** (= Tonträger) Minidisc®; (Comput) minidisk; **Mi|ni|golf** NT crazy golf (Brit), putt-putt golf (US); **Mi|ni|kas|set|te** F mini-cassette

mi|ni|mal [miniˈmaːl] ADJ Unterschied, Aufwand minimal; Verlust, Verbesserung, Steigerung marginal; Gewinn, Chance very small; Preise, Benzinverbrauch, Gehalt very low; **mit ~er Anstrengung** with a minimum of effort ADV (= wenigstens) at least; (= geringfügig) minimally, marginally

Mi|ni|mal- in cpds minimum; **Mi|ni|mal|be|trag** M minimum amount; **Mi|ni|mal|for|de|rung** F minimum demand; **mi|ni|mal-in|va|siv** [-ɪnvaˈziːf] ADJ minimally invasive; **~e Chirurgie** minimally invasive surgery; **Mi|ni|mal|kon|sen|sus** M basic area of agreement; **Mi|ni|mal|lö|sung** F minimal solution; **Mi|ni|mal|pro|gramm** NT basic programme (Brit) or program (US)

mi|ni|mie|ren [miniˈmiːrən] ptp **minimiert** VT to minimize

Mi|ni|mie|rung F **-, -en** minimization

Mi|ni|mum [ˈmiːnimʊm] NT **-s, Minima** [-ma] minimum (an +dat of); **barometrisches ~** (Met) barometric low

Mi|ni-: Mi|ni|pil|le F minipill; **Mi|ni|rock** M miniskirt; **Mi|ni|spi|on** M miniaturized bugging device

Mi|nis|ter [miˈnɪstɐ] M **-s, -, Mi|nis|te|rin** [-tərɪn] F **-, -nen** (Pol) minister (Brit) (für of), secretary (für for)

Mi|nis|ter-: Mi|nis|ter|amt NT ministerial office; **Mi|nis|ter|bank** F pl **-bänke** government front bench

Mi|nis|te|ri|al- [minɪsteriˈaːl-]: **Mi|nis|te|ri|al|be|am|te(r)** M decl as adj, **Mi|nis|te|ri|al|be-**

am|tin F ministry official; **Mi|nis|te|ri|al|di|rek|tor(in)** M(F) head of a government department, permanent secretary (Brit); **Mi|nis|te|ri|al|di|ri|gent(in)** M(F) , **Mi|nis|te|ri|al|rat** M , **Mi|nis|te|ri|al|rä|tin** F assistant head of a government department, assistant secretary (Brit)

mi|nis|te|ri|ell [minɪsteˈriɛl] ADJ **attr** ministerial

Mi|nis|te|rin F → **Minister**

Mi|nis|te|ri|um [minɪsˈteːriʊm] NT **-s, Minis|te|rien** [-riən] ministry (Brit), department

Mi|nis|ter-: Mi|nis|ter|kon|fe|renz F conference of ministers, ministerial conference; **Mi|nis|ter|prä|si|dent(in)** M(F) prime minister; (eines Bundeslandes) leader of a Federal German state; **Mi|nis|ter|rat** M council of ministers; (von EG) Council of Ministers; **Mi|nis|ter|ses|sel** M ministerial post (esp Brit) or position

mi|nist|ra|bel [minɪsˈtraːbl] ADJ (Pol inf) suitable for ministerial office

Mi|nist|rant [minɪsˈtrant] M **-en, -en, Mi|nist|ran|tin** [-ˈtrantɪn] F **-, -nen** (Eccl) server

mi|nist|rie|ren [minɪsˈtriːrən] ptp **ministriert** VI (Eccl) to serve, to act as server

Min|na [ˈmɪna] F **-, no pl** (dated: = Hausangestellte) maid; (fig inf) skivvy (Brit inf), maid; **jdn zur ~ machen** (inf) to give sb a piece of one's mind, to tear a strip off sb (Brit inf) → **grün**

Min|ne [ˈmɪna] F **-, no pl** (Liter, Hist) courtly love

Min|ne-: Min|ne|dienst M homage rendered by a knight to his lady; **Min|ne|ge|sang** M minnesong; **Min|ne|lied** NT minnelied; **Min|ne|o|la** F **-, -s** minneola; **Min|ne|sang** M minnesong; **Min|ne|sän|ger** M , **Min|ne|sin|ger** M **-, -** minnesinger

mi|no|isch [miˈnoːɪʃ] ADJ Minoan

Mi|no|ri|tät [minoriˈtɛːt] F **-, -en** minority

Mi|nu|end [miˈnuɛnt] M **-en, -en** [-dn] (Math) minuend

mi|nus [ˈmiːnʊs] PREP +gen minus, less; (Math) minus ADV minus; (Elec) negative; **~ 10 Grad, 10 Grad ~** minus 10 degrees, 10 degrees below (zero); **~ machen** (inf) to make a loss

Mi|nus [ˈmiːnʊs] NT **-, -** a (= Fehlbetrag) deficit; (auf Konto) overdraft; (fig: = Nachteil) bad point; (in Beruf etc) disadvantage b (= Minuszeichen) minus (sign)

Mi|nus|kel [miˈnʊskl] F **-, -n** (geh) minuscule (spec), small or lower-case letter

Mi|nus-: Mi|nus|pol M negative pole; **Mi|nus|punkt** M minus or penalty point; (fig) minus point; **ein ~ für jdn sein** to count against sb, to be a point against sb; **Mi|nus|tem|pe|ra|tur** F temperature below freezing or zero; **Mi|nus|zei|chen** NT minus sign

Mi|nu|te [miˈnuːtə] F **-, -n** minute; (fig: = Augenblick auch) moment; **es ist 10 Uhr und 21 ~n** (form) it is 21 minutes past 10 o'clock; **auf die ~ (genau** or **pünktlich)** (right) on the dot; **in letzter ~** at the last moment or minute; **~ auf** or **um ~ verging** or **verstrich** or **verrann** (liter) the minutes ticked by or went by; **auf die ~ kommt es nicht an** a few minutes one way or another don't matter; **es vergeht keine ~, ohne dass ...** not a moment goes by without ...

Mi|nu|ten-: mi|nu|ten|lang ADJ **attr** several minutes of; **~es Schweigen** several minutes' silence, silence for several minutes ADV for several minutes; **Mi|nu|ten|schnel|le** F **in ~** in minutes, in a matter of minutes; **Mi|nu|ten|takt** M **im ~** (Telefongebühren) (charged) per minute or by the minute; (fig: = schnell, häufig) one a minute; **die Tore fielen jetzt im ~** the goals came thick and fast; **Mi|nu|ten|zei|ger** M minute hand

mi|nu|ti|ös [minuˈtsiøːs], **mi|nu|zi|ös** [minuˈtsiøːs] (geh) ADJ Nachbildung, Mensch meticulous; Schilderung auch, Fragen detailed ADV meticulously; **erklären** in great detail

Min|ze [ˈmɪntsə] F **-, -n** (Bot) mint

Mio. abbr von **Million(en)** m

mir [miːɐ] PERS PRON dat von **ich** to me; (nach Präpositionen) me; **ein Freund von ~** a friend of mine; **von ~ aus!** (inf) I don't mind, fair enough; **~ nichts, dir nichts** (inf: unhöflich) without so much as a by-your-leave; **es war ~ nichts, dir nichts weg** the next thing I knew it had gone; **wie du ~, so ich dir** (prov) tit for tat (inf); (als Drohung) I'll get my own back (on you); **und das ~!** why me (of all people)?; **dass ihr ~ nicht an die Bücher geht!** (inf) don't you touch those books!; **du bist ~ vielleicht einer!** (inf) you're a right one, you are! (inf) → **auch ihm**

Mi|ra|bel|le [miraˈbɛlə] F **-, -n** mirabelle, small yellow plum

Mi|ra|kel [miˈraːkl] NT **-s, -** (old, liter) miracle

Mi|san|throp [mizanˈtroːp] M **-en, -en, Mi|san|thro|pin** [-ˈtroːpɪn] F **-, -nen** (geh) misanthropist

Mi|san|thro|pie [mizantroˈpiː] F **-, no pl** (geh) misanthropy

Misch-: Misch|ar|beits|platz M (Comput) mixed work station; **misch|bar** ADJ mixable, miscible (form); **~ sein** to mix; **Misch|bat|te|rie** F mixer tap; **Misch|brot** NT bread made from more than one kind of flour; **Misch|ehe** F mixed marriage

mi|schen [ˈmɪʃn] VT to mix; Tabak-, Tee-, Kaffeesorten auch to blend; Karten to shuffle; (Comput) Dateien to merge; **sie mischt Realität und Einbildung** she mixes up reality and fantasy; **die Karten neu ~** (fig) to reshuffle the pack → **auch gemischt** VR (= sich vermengen) to mix; **sich unter jdn ~** to mix or mingle with sb; **sich unter etw** (acc) **~** to mix with sth; **sich in etw** (acc) **~** to meddle or interfere in sth; **sich in das Gespräch ~** to butt or cut into the conversation VI (Cards) to shuffle; **wer mischt?** whose turn is it to shuffle?

Mi|scher [ˈmɪʃɐ] M **-s, -** (inf) a (= Mischpult) mixing desk or panel; (von Band) sound mixer b (= Zementmischer) cement-mixer

Misch-: misch|er|big ADJ (Biol) heterozygous (spec); **Misch|far|be** F mixed or blended colour (Brit) or color (US); (Phys) secondary colour (Brit) or color (US); **Misch|fi|nan|zie|rung** F mixed financing; **Misch|form** F mixture; (von zwei Elementen auch) hybrid (form); **Misch|fut|ter** NT (Agr) compound feed; **Misch|gas** NT mixture of coal gas and water gas; **Misch|ge|mü|se** NT mixed vegetables pl; **Misch|ge|we|be** NT mixed fibres (Brit) or fibers (US) pl; **Misch|haut** F combination skin; **Misch|kal|ku|la|ti|on** F mixed calculation; **Misch|kon|zern** M conglomerate; **Misch|kost** F mixed diet; **Misch|kul|tur** F a (Agr) mixed cultivation; **~en anbauen** to grow different crops side by side or in the same field b (Sociol) mixed culture

Misch|ling [ˈmɪʃlɪŋ] M **-s, -e** a (Mensch) half-caste, half-breed b (Zool) half-breed

Misch|lings|kind NT half-caste child

Misch-: Misch|masch [ˈmɪʃmaʃ] M **-(e)s, -e** (inf) (aus of) hotchpotch (Brit), hodgepodge (US), mishmash; (Essen auch) concoction; **sie redet einen fürchterlichen ~** she speaks a horrible jumble or hotchpotch (Brit) or hodgepodge (US) of different languages; **Misch|ma|schi|ne** F cement-mixer; **Misch|po|ke** [ˈmɪʃpoːkə] F **-, no pl, Misch|po|che** [ˈmɪʃpɔxa] F **-, no pl** (sl) clan (inf), mob (inf); **Misch|pult** NT (Rad, TV) mixing desk or panel; (von Band) sound mixer; **Misch|ras|se** F a (Tiere) crossbreed b (Menschen) mixed race; **Misch|trom|mel** F (drum in) cement-mixer

Mi|schung [ˈmɪʃʊŋ] F **-, -en** a (= das Mischen) mixing; (von Tee-, Kaffee-, Tabaksorten) blending, mixing b (lit, fig: = Gemischtes) mixture; (von Tee etc) blend, mixture; (von Süßigkeiten etc) assortment, mixture; (fig) mixture, combination (aus of) c (Chem) mixture

Mi|schungs|ver|hält|nis NT ratio (of a mixture)

Misch-: Misch|volk NT mixed race; **Misch|-wald** M mixed (deciduous and coniferous) woodland; **Misch|wort** NT pl **-wörter** hybrid word

mi|se|ra|bel [mizə'ra:bl] (inf) ADJ lousy (inf); Leistungen auch pathetic; Gesundheit miserable, wretched; Gefühl ghastly; Benehmen dreadful; Qualität poor; Ruf terrible; (= gemein) Kerl etc nasty ADV dreadfully; ~ schmecken to taste lousy (inf); man isst dort ~ the food there is just lousy (inf); ~ riechen to smell horrible; er hat ~ abgeschnitten he got lousy marks (Brit inf) or grades (US inf)

Mi|se|re [mi'ze:rə] F -, -n (von Leuten, Wirtschaft etc) plight; (von Hunger, Krieg etc) misery, miseries pl; in einer ~ stecken to be in a terrible or dreadful state; (Mensch) to be in a mess, to have run into trouble; jdn aus einer ~ heraus-holen to get sb out of trouble or a mess; das war eine einzige ~ that was a real disaster; es ist eine ~, wie/dass ... it is dreadful how/that ...; es ist die ~ des Alltags, dass ... it is one of life's hardships that ...

Mi|se|re|re [mize're:rə] NT -(s), no pl **a** (Eccl) miserere **b** (Med) faecal (Brit) or fecal (US) vomiting

Mi|so|gyn [mizo'gy:n] M -s or -en, -en (liter) misogynist

Mis|pel ['mɪspl] F -, -n medlar (tree)

miss ▲ imper sing von **messen**

Miss ▲ [mɪs] F -, -es ['mɪsɪz] Miss

miss|ach|ten ▲ [mɪs'|axtn, 'mɪs-] ptp **missachtet** VT insep **a** (= ignorieren) Warnung, Ratschlag to ignore, to disregard; Gesetz, Verbot to flout **b** (= gering schätzen) jdn to despise; Hilfe, Angebot to disdain

Miss|ach|tung ▲ F **a** (= Ignorieren) disregard (gen for); (von Gesetz, Verbot) flouting (gen of) **b** (= Geringschätzung) disrespect (+gen for); disdain (+gen of, for)

miss|be|ha|gen ▲ [mɪs'bəha:gn] ptp **missbe-hagt** VI insep +dat das missbehagt ihm that was not to his liking; es missbehagte mir, schon wieder umziehen zu müssen it ill suits me to have to move again

Miss|be|ha|gen ▲ NT (geh) (= Unbehagen) uneasiness; (= Missfallen) discontent(ment); jdm ~ bereiten to cause sb uneasiness/discontent (-ment)

miss|bil|den ▲ ['mɪsbɪldn] VT to deform

Miss|bil|dung ▲ F deformity, malformation

miss|bil|li|gen ▲ [mɪs'bɪlɪgn] ptp **missbilligt** VT insep to disapprove of, to object to

miss|bil|li|gend ▲ ADJ disapproving ADV disapprovingly

Miss|bil|li|gung ▲ F disapproval

Miss|brauch ▲ ['mɪsbraux] M abuse; (= falsche Anwendung) misuse; (von Notbremse, Feuerlöscher, Kreditkarte) improper use; (geh: einer Person) sexual assault (+gen, von on); ~ mit etw betreiben to abuse or misuse sth; ~ zur Unzucht (Jur) sexual offence committed by person in position of authority over victim vor ~ wird gewarnt use only as directed; (an Notbremse etc) do not misuse; unter ~ seines Amtes in abuse of his office; „Missbrauch strafbar!" "penalty for misuse"

miss|brau|chen ▲ [mɪs'brauxn] ptp **miss-braucht** VT insep Vertrauen to abuse; (geh: = vergewaltigen) to assault; den Namen Gottes ~ (liter) to take the Lord's name in vain; jdn für or zu etw ~ to use sb for sth, to use sb to do sth; etw für politische Zwecke ~ to abuse sth for political purposes; jdn zu allem Möglichen ~ to impose on sb; sexuell missbraucht sexually abused

miss|bräuch|lich ▲ ['mɪsbrɔyçlɪç] ADJ incorrect; (= unerlaubt) improper ADV incorrectly; (= unerlaubterweise) improperly

miss|deu|ten ▲ [mɪs'dɔytn] ptp **missdeutet** VT insep to misinterpret

Miss|deu|tung ▲ F misinterpretation

mis|sen ['mɪsn] VT (geh) to go or do without; Erfahrung to miss; das möchte ich nicht ~ I wouldn't do without it/miss it (for the world); ich möchte meine Kinder nicht ~ I could not do without my children

Miss|er|folg ▲ M failure; (Theat, Buch etc auch) flop

Miss|ern|te ▲ F crop failure

Mis|se|tat ['mɪsəta:t] F (old, liter) misdeed, misdemeanour (Brit), misdemeanor (US)

Mis|se|tä|ter(in) M(F) (old, liter) culprit; (= Verbrecher auch) wrongdoer

miss|fal|len ▲ [mɪs'falən] ptp **missfallen** VI insep irreg +dat to displease; es missfällt mir, wie er ... I dislike the way he ...

Miss|fal|len ▲ NT -s, no pl displeasure (über +acc at), disapproval (über +acc of); jds ~ erre-gen to incur sb's displeasure

Miss|fal|lens-: Miss|fal|lens|äu|ße|rung ▲ F expression of disapproval or displeasure; **Miss|fal|lens|be|kun|dung** ▲ F, **Miss|fal|lens|kund|ge|bung** ▲ F expression or demonstration of disapproval or displeasure

miss|fäl|lig ▲ ['mɪsfɛlɪç] ADJ Bemerkung disparaging, deprecatory ADV disparagingly

miss|ge|bil|det ▲ [mɪsgəbɪldət] ADJ deformed

Miss|ge|burt ▲ F deformed person/animal; (fig inf) failure; das Kind ist eine ~ the child was born deformed; du ~! (sl) you spastic! (Brit pej sl), you psycho! (pej sl)

miss|ge|launt ▲ ['mɪsgəlaunt] ADJ (geh) bad--tempered, ill-humoured (Brit), ill-humored (US)

Miss|ge|schick ▲ NT mishap; (= Pech, Unglück) misfortune; ein kleines ~ a slight mishap; vom ~ verfolgt werden (geh) to be dogged by misfortune

miss|ge|stalt ▲ ['mɪsgəʃtalt] (liter), **miss|ge|stal|tet** ▲ ['mɪsgəʃtaltət] (geh) ADJ misshapen

Miss|ge|stalt ▲ F (liter) misshapen figure

miss|ge|stimmt ▲ ['mɪsgəʃtɪmt] ADJ (geh) ill--humoured (Brit), ill-humored (US); ~ sein to be in an ill humour (Brit) or humor (US)

miss|glü|cken ▲ [mɪs'glʏkn] ptp **missglückt** VI insep aux sein to fail, to be unsuccessful; der Versuch ist missglückt the attempt failed; der Versuch ist ihm missglückt his attempt failed; das ist ihr missglückt she failed; der Kuchen ist (mir) missglückt the cake didn't turn out; ihm missglückt alles everything he does goes wrong; ein missglückter Versuch an unsuccessful attempt

miss|gön|nen ▲ [mɪs'gœnən] ptp **missgönnt** VT insep jdm etw ~ to (be)grudge sb sth; sie miss-gönnt es ihm, dass er erfolgreich ist she (be-)grudges him his success, she resents his success

Miss|griff ▲ M mistake

Miss|gunst ▲ F enviousness (gegenüber of)

miss|güns|tig ▲ ADJ envious (auf +acc of) ADV enviously

miss|han|deln ▲ [mɪs'handln] ptp **misshandelt** VT insep to ill-treat, to maltreat

Miss|hand|lung ▲ F ill-treatment, maltreatment; (= Kindesmisshandlung) cruelty (to children)

Miss|hel|lig|keit ▲ ['mɪshɛlɪçkait] F -, -en (geh) difference, disagreement

Miss|singsch ['mɪsɪŋʃ] NT -, no pl mixture of High and Low German

Mis|si|on [mɪ'sio:n] F -, -en (Eccl, Pol, fig) mission; (= diplomatische Vertretung) legation, mission (US); (= Gruppe) delegation; ~ treiben to do missionary work; in der ~ tätig sein to be a missionary

Mis|si|o|nar [mɪsio'na:ɐ] M -s, -e, **Mis|si|o|na|rin** [-'na:rɪn] F -, -nen, (Aus) **Mis|si|o|när** [mɪ-sio'nɛ:ɐ] M -s, -e, **Mis|si|o|nä|rin** [-'nɛ:rɪn] F -, -nen missionary

mis|si|o|na|risch [mɪsio'na:rɪʃ] ADJ missionary; mit ~em Eifer with missionary zeal ADV with missionary zeal

Mis|si|o|nars|stel|lung F (fig) missionary position

mis|si|o|nie|ren [mɪsio'ni:rən] ptp **missioniert** VI to do missionary work, to proselytize; (fig) to preach, to proselytize VT Land, Mensch to (work to) convert, to proselytize; (fig) to convert, to proselytize

Mis|si|o|nie|rung F -, no pl conversion, proselytization

Mis|si|ons-: Mis|si|ons|chef(in) M(F) (Pol) head of a legation; (einer Gruppe) leader of a delegation; **Mis|si|ons|ge|sell|schaft** F missionary society; **Mis|si|ons|schu|le** F mission school; **Mis|si|ons|schwes|ter** F nun working at a mission

Miss|klang ▲ M discord (auch Mus), dissonance; (= Misston) discordant note; ein ~ (fig) a note of discord, a discordant note

Miss|kre|dit ▲ [-kre'di:t] M -, no pl discredit; jdn/etw in ~ bringen to bring sb/sth into discredit, to discredit sb/sth; in ~ geraten or kommen to be discredited

miss|lang ▲ pret von **misslingen**

miss|lau|nig ▲ ['mɪslaunɪç] ADJ bad-tempered, ill-humoured (Brit), ill-humored (US)

miss|lich ▲ ['mɪslɪç] ADJ (geh) Lage awkward, difficult; Umstand auch, Verzögerung unfortunate, regrettable; das ist ja eine ~ Sache that is a bit awkward/unfortunate; es steht ~ um dieses Vorhaben the outlook for this plan is not good

Miss|lich|keit ▲ F -, -en (Umstand) unfortunate or regrettable situation; tägliche ~en everyday difficulties

miss|lie|big ▲ ['mɪsli:bɪç] ADJ unpopular; sich (bei jdm) ~ machen to make oneself unpopular (with sb); politisch ~e Personen people who have fallen out of favour (Brit) or favor (US) with the government

miss|lin|gen ▲ [mɪs'lɪŋən] pret **misslang** [mɪs-'laŋ], ptp **misslungen** [mɪs'lʊŋən] VI insep aux sein = **missglücken**

Miss|lin|gen ▲ NT -s, no pl failure

miss|lun|gen ▲ ptp von **misslingen**

Miss|ma|nage|ment ▲ NT mismanagement

Miss|mut ▲ M sullenness, moroseness; (= Unzufriedenheit) displeasure, discontent; seinen ~ über etw (acc) zeigen/äußern to show/express one's displeasure or discontent at sth

miss|mu|tig ▲ ['mɪsmu:tɪç] ADJ sullen, morose; (= unzufrieden) discontented; Äußerung, Aussehen disgruntled; mach nicht so ein ~es Gesicht don't look so morose ADV sullenly, morosely; (= unzufrieden) discontentedly; sagen, sich äußern disgruntledly

miss|ra|ten¹ ▲ [mɪs'ra:tn] ptp **missraten** VI insep irreg aux sein to go wrong; (Kind) to become wayward; der Kuchen ist (mir) ~ the cake didn't turn out

miss|ra|ten² ▲ [mɪs'ra:tn] ADJ Kind wayward; der ~e Kuchen the cake which went wrong

Miss|stand ▲ M disgrace no pl, outrage; (allgemeiner Zustand) bad or deplorable state of affairs no pl; (= Ungerechtigkeit) abuse; (= Mangel) defect; einen ~/Missstände beseitigen to remedy something which is wrong/things which are wrong; Missstände in der Regierung/im Management anprangern to denounce misgovernment/ mismanagement

Miss|stim|mung ▲ F **a** (= Uneinigkeit) friction, discord; eine ~ a note of discord, a discordant note **b** (= Missmut) ill feeling no indef art

misst ▲ [mɪst] 3. pers sing pres von **messen**

Miss|ton ▲ M pl **-töne** (Mus, fig) discordant note; (fig auch) note of discord; **Misstöne** (Klang) discordant sound; (fig) discord

miss|tö|nend ▲ ['mɪstøːnənd], **miss|tö|nig** (*rare*) ▲ ['mɪstøːnɪç] ADJ discordant; *Stimme, Instrument* unpleasant(-sounding)

miss|trau|en ▲ [mɪs'trauən] *ptp* **misstraut** VI *insep* +*dat* to mistrust, to be suspicious or wary of

Miss|trau|en ▲ ['mɪstrauən] NT **-s**, *no pl* mistrust, distrust (*gegenüber* of); (*esp einer Sache, Handlung gegenüber*) suspiciousness (*gegenüber* of); **~ gegen jdn/etw haben** *or* **hegen** (*liter*), **jdm/ einer Sache ~ entgegenbringen** to mistrust sb/ sth, to be suspicious of sth

Miss|trau|ens- (*Parl*): **Miss|trau|ens|an|trag** ▲ M motion of no confidence; **Miss|trau|ens|vo|tum** ▲ NT vote of no confidence

miss|trau|isch ▲ ['mɪstrauɪʃ] ADJ mistrustful, distrustful; (= *argwöhnisch*) suspicious ADV sceptically (*Brit*), skeptically (*US*)

Miss|ver|gnü|gen ▲ NT (*geh*) displeasure, disgruntlement

miss|ver|gnügt ▲ ['mɪsfɛɐgnyːkt] ADJ (*geh*) disgruntled, displeased

Miss|ver|hält|nis ▲ NT discrepancy, disparity; (*in Proportionen*) imbalance; **seine Leistung steht im ~ zu seiner Bezahlung** there is a discrepancy or disparity between the work he does and his salary

miss|ver|ständ|lich ▲ ['mɪsfɛɐʃtɛntlɪç] ADJ unclear; **~e Ausdrücke** expressions which could be misunderstood or misleading ADV unclearly; **ich habe mich ~ ausgedrückt** I didn't express myself clearly

Miss|ver|ständ|nis ▲ NT **a** misunderstanding; (= *falsche Vorstellung*) misconception **b** *usu pl* (= *Meinungsverschiedenheit*) misunderstanding, disagreement

miss|ver|ste|hen ▲ ['mɪsfɛɐʃteːən] *ptp* **missverstanden** VT *insep irreg* to misunderstand; **Sie dürfen mich nicht ~** please do not misunderstand me; **in nicht misszuverstehender Weise** unequivocally

Miss|wahl ▲ F beauty contest

Miss|wei|sung ▲ F (*form*) (*von Kompass*) magnetic declination or variation; (*von Radar*) indication error

Miss|wirt|schaft ▲ F maladministration, mismanagement

Miss|wuchs ▲ M malformed growth, malformation

Mist [mɪst] M **-es**, *no pl* **a** (= *Tierkot*) droppings *pl*; (= *Pferdemist, Kuhmist etc*) dung; (= *Misthaufen*) manure or muck heap; **~ streuen** *or* **fahren** to spread manure or muck; **das ist nicht auf seinem ~ gewachsen** (*inf*) he didn't think that up himself

b (*inf*) (= *Unsinn*) rubbish (*esp Brit*), nonsense; (= *Schund*) rubbish, trash; **~!** blow!, blast! (*inf*); **so ein ~!** what a darned or blasted nuisance (*inf*); **was soll der ~?** what's all this rubbish (*esp Brit*) or nonsense?; **er hat einen ~ geredet** he talked a load of rubbish (*esp Brit*) or nonsense; **da hat er ~ gemacht** *or* **gebaut** he really messed that up (*inf*); **~ verzapfen** (= *dummes Zeug reden*) to talk rubbish (*Brit inf*) or nonsense; **allerlei ~ machen** to do all sorts of stupid things; **mach keinen ~!** don't be a fool!

Mist|beet NT (*Hort*) hotbed

Mis|tel ['mɪstl] F **-, -n** mistletoe *no pl*

Mis|tel|zweig M sprig of mistletoe; **ein Kuss unterm ~** a kiss under the mistletoe

mis|ten¹ ['mɪstn] VT **a** *Stall* to muck out; *Acker* to manure **b** (*inf*) *Schrank etc* to tidy out; *Zimmer* to clean out VI (*im Stall*) to do the mucking out; (= *düngen*) to do the manuring

mis|ten² VI *impers* (*Naut*) **es mistet** it is misting over

Mist-: Mist|ga|bel F pitchfork (*used for shifting manure*); **Mist|gru|be** F manure pit; **Mist|hau|fen** M manure heap; **Mist|kä|fer** M dung beetle; **Mist|kerl** M (*inf*) dirty swine (*Brit inf*), dirty or rotten pig (*inf*); **Mist|stück** NT (*inf*), **Mist|vieh** NT (*inf*) (= *Mann*) bastard

---

(*sl*); (= *Frau auch*) bitch (*sl*); **Mist|wa|gen** M dung cart; **Mist|wet|ter** NT (*inf*) lousy weather

Mis|zel|len [mɪs'tselən] PL (*liter*) short articles or items *pl*; **das fällt unter ~** that comes under miscellaneous

mit [mɪt] PREP +*dat* **a** with; **Tee ~ Zitrone** lemon tea, tea with lemon; **~ dem Hut in der Hand** (with) his hat in his hand; **ein Topf ~ Suppe** a pot of soup; **ein Kleid ~ Jacke** a dress and jacket; **wie wärs ~ einem Bier?** (*inf*) how about a beer?

b (= *mit Hilfe von*) with; **~ einer Zange** with or using a pair of pliers; **~ der Bahn/dem Bus/dem Auto** by train/bus/car; **ich fahre ~ meinem eigenen Auto zur Arbeit** I drive to work in my own car; **~ der Post** by post (*Brit*) or mail; **~ Gewalt** by force; **~ Bleistift/Tinte/dem Kugelschreiber schreiben** to write in pencil/ink/ballpoint; **~ dem nächsten Flugzeug/Bus kommen** to come on the next plane/bus; **~ etwas Liebe/ Verständnis** with a little love/understanding; **~ einem Wort** in a word

c (*zeitlich*) **~ achtzehn Jahren** at (the age of) eighteen; **~ einem Mal** all at once, suddenly, all of a sudden; **~ heutigem Tage** (*form*) as from today; **~ beginnendem Sommer** at the start of summer; **~ der Zeit** in time

d (*bei Maß-, Mengenangaben*) **~ 1 Sekunde Vorsprung gewinnen** to win by 1 second; **etw ~ 50.000 EUR versichern** to insure sth for EUR 50,000; **~ 80 km/h** at 80 km/h; **~ 4:2 gewinnen** to win 4-2

e (= *einschließlich*) with, including; **~ mir waren es 5** there were 5 with or including or counting me

f (*Begleitumstand, Art und Weise, Eigenschaft*) with; **er ~ seinem Herzfehler kann das nicht** he can't do that with his heart condition; **du ~ deinen dummen Ideen** (*inf*) you and your stupid ideas; **~ Muße** at (one's) leisure; **ein junger Dichter, Rosenholz ~ Namen** (*old*) a young poet, Rosenholz by name or called Rosenholz; **~ einem Schlage** in a flash; **~ lauter Stimme** in a loud voice; **~ Verlust** at a loss

g (= *betreffend*) **was ist ~ ihr los?** what's the matter with her?, what's up with her?; **was geht** *or* **steht es ~ deiner Arbeit?** how is your work going?, how are you getting on with your work?; **~ meiner Reise wird es nichts** my trip is off

ADV **er war ~ dabei** he went or came too; **er ist ~ der Beste der Gruppe/Mannschaft** he is one of or among the best in the group/the team; **das gehört ~ dazu** that's part and parcel of it; **etw ~ in Betracht ziehen** to consider sth as well

Mit|an|ge|klag|te(r) MF *decl as adj* co-defendant

Mit|ar|beit F cooperation, collaboration; (= *Hilfe auch*) assistance; (= *Teilnahme*) participation (*auch Sch*); **~ bei** *or* **an etw** (*dat*) work on sth; **er ist an einer ~ bei diesem Projekt interessiert** he is interested in working on this project; **unter ~ von** in collaboration with

mit+ar|bei|ten VI *sep* (= *mithelfen*) to cooperate (*bei* on); (*bei Projekt etc*) to collaborate; **an** *or* **bei etw ~** to work on sth; **er hat beim Bau des Hauses mitgearbeitet** he helped build the house; **im Unterricht ~** to take an active part in lessons; **seine Frau arbeitet mit** (*inf*) his wife works too

Mit|ar|bei|ter(in) M(F) (= *Betriebsangehöriger*) employee; (= *Kollege*) colleague; (*an Projekt etc*) collaborator; **die ~ an diesem Projekt/bei dieser Firma** those who work on this project/for this firm; **freier ~** freelance; **inoffizieller ~** (*DDR: von Stasi*) unofficial collaborator

Mit|ar|bei|ter|stab M staff

Mit|be|grün|der(in) M(F) co-founder

mit+be|kom|men *ptp* **mitbekommen** VT *sep irreg* **a** **etw ~** to get or be given sth to take with one; *Rat, Ausbildung* to get or be given sth; (*als*

Mitgift) to be given sth as a dowry **b** (*inf*) (= *verstehen*) to get (*inf*); (= *bemerken*) to realize; **hast du das noch nicht ~?** (= *erfahren*) you mean you didn't know that?

mit+be|nut|zen *ptp* **mitbenutzt**, (*esp S Ger, Aus, Sw*) **mit+be|nüt|zen** *ptp* **mitbenützt** VT *sep* to share (the use of)

Mit|be|nut|zung F , (*esp S Ger, Aus, Sw*) **Mit|be|nüt|zung** F -, -en joint use

Mit|be|sitz M co-ownership, joint ownership; **~ an etw** (*dat*) **haben** to have a share in the ownership of sth

Mit|be|sit|zer(in) M(F) joint owner, co-owner

mit+be|stim|men *ptp* **mitbestimmt** *sep* VI to have a say (*bei* in); **~d sein** *or* **wirken** to have an influence (*bei, für* on) VT to have an influence on

Mit|be|stim|mung F co-determination, participation (*bei* in); **~ der Arbeiter** *or* **am Arbeitsplatz** worker participation

Mit|be|stim|mungs-: Mit|be|stim|mungs|ge|setz NT worker participation law; **Mit|be|stim|mungs|recht** NT right of participation (*in decision-making etc*)

Mit|be|wer|ber(in) M(F) (fellow) competitor; (*für Stelle*) (fellow) applicant

Mit|be|woh|ner(in) M(F) (fellow) occupant; **die ~ in unserem Haus** the other occupants of the house

mit+brin|gen VT *sep irreg* **a** *Geschenk etc* to bring; *Freund, Begleiter* to bring along; (*beim Zurückkommen*) to bring back; **jdm etw ~** to bring sth for sb, to bring sb sth; **jdm etw von** *or* **aus der Stadt ~** to bring (sb) sth back from town; **jdm etw vom Bäcker ~** to get (sb) sth from the baker's; **was sollen wir der Gastgeberin ~?** what should we take to our hostess?; **die richtige Einstellung ~** to have the right attitude; **bring gute Laune mit** come ready to enjoy yourself; **Sie haben schönes Wetter mitgebracht!** lovely weather you've brought with you!

b *Mitgift, Kinder, Kapital* to bring with one; **etw in die Ehe ~** to have sth when one gets married; **sie hat ein ansehnliches Vermögen in die Ehe mitgebracht** she brought a considerable fortune with her when she got married; **meine Frau hat den Hund in die Ehe mitgebracht** my wife had the dog before our marriage; **sie hat zwei Kinder aus der ersten Ehe mitgebracht** she has two children from her first marriage

c (*fig*) *Befähigung, Voraussetzung etc* to have, to possess

Mit|bring|sel ['mɪtbrɪŋzl] NT **-s, -** (*Geschenk*) small present; (*Andenken*) souvenir

Mit|bür|ger(in) M(F) fellow citizen; **meine Stuttgarter ~** my fellow citizens from Stuttgart; (*in Anrede*) fellow citizens of Stuttgart; **die älteren ~** senior citizens

mit+den|ken VI *sep irreg* (= *Gedankengänge/Beweisführung mitvollziehen*) to follow sb's train of thought/line of argument; (= *Ideen einbringen*) to make a contribution; **zum Glück hat er mitgedacht** luckily he did not let me/us etc forget; **du denkst ja mit!** good thinking; **denk mal mit** help me/us etc think

mit+dür|fen VI *sep irreg* **wir durften nicht mit** we weren't allowed to go along

Mit|ei|gen|tum NT = Mitbesitz

Mit|ei|gen|tü|mer(in) M(F) joint owner, co-owner

mit|ei|nan|der [mɪtai'nandɐ] ADV with each other, with one another; (= *gemeinsam*) together; **alle ~!** all together; **wir haben lange ~ geredet** we had a long talk; **sie reden nicht mehr ~** they are not talking (to each other or to one another) any more; **guten Tag ~** (*esp S Ger*) hello everybody or all

Mit|ei|nan|der [mɪtai'nandɐ] NT **-s**, *no pl* cooperation; **ein ~ ist besser als ein Gegeneinander** it is better to work with each other than against each other

---

mit+emp|fin|den *ptp* **mitempfunden** *sep irreg* **VT** to feel too, to share **VI** **mit jdm ~** to feel for sb, to sympathize with sb

Mit|emp|fin|den NT sympathy

Mit|er|be M , **Mit|er|bin** F joint heir; **außer ihm sind es noch 4 ~n** there are 4 other heirs apart from him

mit+er|le|ben VT *sep* to experience; *Krieg auch* to live through; *(im Fernsehen)* to watch

mit+es|sen *sep irreg* **VT** *Schale etc* to eat as well; *Mahlzeit* to share **VI** **(bei jdm) ~** to eat with sb, to have a meal with sb; **willst du nicht ~?** why don't you have something to eat too?

Mit|es|ser M blackhead

mit+fah|ren VI *sep irreg aux sein* to go (with sb); **sie fährt mit** she is going too; *(mit mir/uns zusammen)* she is going with me/us; **(mit jdm) ~** to go with sb; *(auf Reise auch)* to travel with sb; *(= mitgenommen werden)* to get a lift *or* ride *(esp US)* with sb, to be given a lift *or* ride *(esp US)* by sb; **jdn ~ lassen** to allow sb to go; *(= jdn mitnehmen)* to give sb a lift *or* ride *(esp US)*; **kann ich (mit Ihnen) ~?** can you give me a lift *or* a ride *(esp US)*; **ich fahre jeden Morgen mit mir im Auto mit** I give him a lift *or* ride *(esp US)* in my car every morning; **wie viel Leute können bei dir ~?** how many people can you take (with you)?; **ich fahre nicht gern mit ihr im Auto mit** I don't like going in her car; **auf der Lokomotive ~** to ride with the driver

Mit|fah|rer(in) M(F) fellow passenger; *(vom Fahrer aus gesehen)* passenger

Mit|fahr-: Mit|fahr|ge|le|gen|heit F lift; **~en nach Rom** lifts *or* rides *(esp US)* offered to Rome; **Mit|fahr|zen|tra|le** F agency for arranging lifts *or* rides *(esp US)*

mit+füh|len VI *sep* **mit jdm ~** to feel for sb

mit|füh|lend ADJ sympathetic, compassionate ADV sympathetically, compassionately

mit+füh|ren VT *sep Papiere, Ware, Waffen etc* to carry (with one); *(Fluss)* to carry along

mit+ge|ben VT *sep irreg* **jdn jdm ~** to send sb along with sb; **jdm etw ~** to give sb sth to take with them; *Rat, Erziehung* to give sb sth; **das gebe ich dir noch mit** take that (with you) too

Mit|ge|fan|ge|ne(r) MF *decl as adj* fellow prisoner

Mit|ge|fühl NT sympathy

mit+ge|hen VI *sep irreg aux sein* **a** *(= mit anderen gehen)* to go too *or* along; **mit jdm ~** to go with sb; *(= begleiten auch)* to accompany sb; **gehen Sie mit?** are you going (too)?; **ich gehe bis zur Ecke mit** I'll go to the corner with you/him *etc*; **er ging bis 25.000 Euro mit** *(bei Auktion)* he went with the bidding until it reached 25,000 euros; **mit der Zeit ~** to move with the times; **mit der Mode ~** to keep up with fashion; **mitgegangen, (mitgefangen,) mitgehangen** *(Prov)* fly with the crows, get shot with the crows *(prov)*
b *(fig: Publikum etc)* to respond (favourably *(Brit)* *or* favorably *(US)*) *(mit* to); **man merkt, wie die Zuhörer richtig (mit ihm) ~** you can see that the audience is really with him
c *(inf)* **etw ~ lassen** to lift *or* pinch sth *(Brit inf)*, to steal sth

Mit|gift ['mɪtɡɪft] F **-, -en** dowry

Mit|gift|jä|ger M *(inf)* dowry-hunter *(Brit)*, fortune-hunter

Mit|glied ['mɪtɡliːt] NT member *(+gen, bei, in +dat* of); **~ eines Komitees sein** to sit on a committee, to be a member of a committee

Mit|glie|der-: Mit|glie|der|lis|te F list of members; **Mit|glie|der|schwund** M dwindling membership (numbers *pl*); **Mit|glie|der|ver|samm|lung** F general meeting; **Mit|glie|der|zahl** F membership, number of members; **Mit|glie|der|zu|wachs** M increase *or* growth in membership

Mit|glieds-: Mit|glieds|aus|weis M membership card; **Mit|glieds|bei|trag** M membership subscription *or* fee, membership dues *pl*

Mit|glied|schaft ['mɪtɡliːtʃaft] F **-, -en** membership

Mit|glieds|staat M member state *or* country

mit+ha|ben VT *sep irreg* **etw ~** to have sth (with one); **jdn ~** to have brought sb with one; **hast du alles mit?** have you got everything?

Mit|häft|ling M fellow prisoner; **die ~e** *pl* the other prisoners

Mit|haf|tung F *(Jur)* joint liability

mit+hal|ten ✪ 32.3 VI *sep irreg* *(= sich beteiligen)* to join in *(mit* with); *(= bei Leistung, Tempo etc nachkommen)* *(mit* with) to keep up, to keep pace; *(bei Versteigerung)* to stay in the bidding; **beim Trinken hat er immer feste mitgehalten** he would always drink as much as the rest; **bei einer Diskussion ~ können** to be able to hold one's own in a discussion; **er kann so erstklassig Englisch, da kann keiner ~** he speaks such excellent English, no-one can touch him *(inf)*; **ich halte mit** *(= mitmachen)* count me in (on that)

mit+hel|fen VI *sep irreg* to help; **beim Bau des Hauses ~** to help build the house; **hilf doch ein bisschen mit** give us *or* lend us a hand

Mit|he|raus|ge|ber(in) M(F) co-editor, joint editor; *(Verlag)* co-publisher

mit|hil|fe ▲ [mɪt'hɪlfə] PREP +gen with the help *or* aid (+gen of)

Mit|hil|fe F assistance, aid; **unter ~ der Kollegen** with the aid *or* assistance of colleagues

mit|hin [mɪt'hɪn] ADV *(dated)* therefore, consequently

mit+hö|ren *sep* **VT** to listen to (too); *Gespräch* to overhear; *(heimlich)* to listen in on; *Vorlesung* to attend, to go to; **ich habe alles mitgehört** I heard everything **VI** *(zusammen mit jdm)* to listen (too); *(= Radio hören, Gespräch belauschen)* to listen in *(bei* on); *(zufällig)* to overhear; **Feind hört mit** *(Mil prov)* careless talk costs lives; *(fig hum)* someone may be listening **VI** *impers* **es hört jd mit** sb is listening

Mit|in|ha|ber(in) M(F) *(von Haus etc)* joint owner, co-owner; *(von Firma auch)* joint proprietor

mit+kämp|fen VI *sep* to fight; **mit jdm ~** to fight alongside sb

Mit|kämp|fer(in) M(F) *(im Krieg)* comrade-in-arms; *(Sport)* *(= Teamkollege)* team-mate; *(= Partner)* partner

mit+klin|gen VI *sep irreg* *(Ton, Saite)* to sound, to resonate; **bei dem ersten Lied klangen eigenartige Töne mit** there were some odd notes in the first song; **in ihrer Äußerung klang Traurigkeit/ein leichter Vorwurf mit** there was sadness/a slight note of reproach in her remark; **Assoziationen, die bei diesem Wort ~** associations contained in this word

mit+kom|men VI *sep irreg aux sein* **a** *(= mit anderen kommen)* to come along *(mit* with); *(Sendung, Brief etc)* to come, to arrive; **kommst du auch mit?** are you coming too?; **ich kann nicht ~** I can't come; **komm doch mit!** (do) come with us/me *etc!*, why don't you come too?; **kommst du mit ins Kino?** are you coming to the cinema (with me/us)?; **bis zum Bahnhof ~** to come as far as the station; **ich bin gerade noch mit dem Zug mitgekommen** I just caught the train
b *(inf)* *(= mithalten)* to keep up; *(= verstehen)* to follow; **da komme ich nicht mit** that's beyond me; **sie kommt in der Schule/in Französisch gut mit** she is getting on well at school/with French

mit+kön|nen VI *sep irreg (inf)* **a** *(= mitkommen können)* to be able to come *(mit* with); *(= mitgehen können)* to be able to go *(mit* with) **b** *(usu neg)* *(= verstehen)* to be able to follow; **da kann ich nicht mehr mit** I can't follow that

mit+krie|gen VT *sep (inf)* = **mitbekommen**

mit+lau|fen VI *sep irreg aux sein* to run *(mit* with); *(Rad, Zeiger etc)* to turn; *(Kamera, Tonband)* to run; **er läuft beim 100-Meter-Lauf mit** he's running in the 100 metres *(Brit)* *or* meters *(US)*

Mit|läu|fer(in) M(F) *(Pol, pej)* fellow traveller *(Brit)* *or* traveler *(US)*

Mit|laut M consonant

Mit|leid NT , *no pl* pity, compassion *(mit* for); *(= Mitgefühl)* sympathy *(mit* with, for); **~ erregend** pitiable, pitiful

Mit|lei|den|schaft F **jdn/etw in ~ ziehen** to affect sb/sth (detrimentally)

mit|lei|dig ['mɪtlaɪdɪç] ADJ pitying; *(= mitfühlend)* sympathetic; *Mensch* compassionate, sympathetic ADV pityingly; *(= mitfühlend)* compassionately

Mit|leid(s)-: mit|leid(s)|los ADJ pitiless, heartless ADV pitilessly, heartlessly; **mit|leid(s)|voll** ADJ sympathetic, compassionate ADV sympathetically, compassionately

mit+ler|nen VTI *sep* to learn too; *(= durch jdn lernen)* to learn *(mit* from)

mit+le|sen VTI *sep irreg* to read too; *Text* to follow; **etw (mit jdm) ~** to read sth at the same time (as sb)

mit+ma|chen VTI *sep* **a** *(= teilnehmen)* *Spiel, Singen etc* to join in; *Reise, Expedition, Ausflug so* to go on; *Kurs* to do; *Mode* to follow; *Wettbewerb* to take part in; **(bei) etw ~** to join in sth; **er hat schon viele Partys mitgemacht** he has been to lots of parties; **er macht alles mit** he always joins in (all the fun); **jede Mode ~** to follow every fashion; **da mache ich nicht mit** *(= ist nicht mein Fall)* that's not my scene; *(= ohne mich)* count me out!; **wenn das Wetter mitmacht** if the weather cooperates
b *(inf: = einverstanden sein)* **da kann ich nicht ~** I can't go along with that; **da macht mein Chef nicht mit** my boss won't go along with that; **das mache ich nicht mehr mit** I've had quite enough (of that); **ich mache das nicht lange mit** I won't take that much longer
c *(= erleben)* to live through; *(= erleiden)* to go through; **sie hat viel mitgemacht** she has been through a lot in her time

Mit|mensch M fellow man *or* creature, neighbour *(Brit)*, neighbor *(US)*; **wir müssen in jedem den ~en sehen** we must see people as neighbours *(Brit)* *or* neighbors *(US)*

mit|mensch|lich ADJ *Kontakte, Probleme etc* human; *Verhalten* considerate

Mit|mensch|lich|keit F humanity

mit+mi|schen VI *sep (inf)* *(= sich beteiligen)* to be involved *(in* +dat, *bei* in)

mit+müs|sen VI *sep irreg* *(= mitkommen müssen)* to have to come too; *(= mitgehen müssen)* to have to go too

Mit|nah|me [-naːmə] F , *no pl* **(jdm) die ~ von etw empfehlen** to recommend sb to take sth with them

Mit|nah|me-: Mit|nah|me|ar|ti|kel M impulse buy; **Mit|nah|me|markt** M cash-and-carry

mit+neh|men VT *sep irreg* **a** *(= mit sich nehmen)* to take (with one); *(= ausleihen)* to borrow; *(= kaufen)* to take; **jdn (im Auto) ~** to give sb a lift *or* ride *(esp US)*; **der Bus konnte nicht alle ~** the bus couldn't take everyone; **sie nimmt alles mit, was sich bietet** she makes the most of everything life has to offer; **(das ist) zum Mitnehmen** please take one; **einmal Pommes frites zum Mitnehmen** a bag of chips to take away *(Brit)*, French fries to go *(US)*; **Gewinne ~** *(St Ex)* to take profits
b *(= erschöpfen)* *jdn* to exhaust, to weaken; *(= beschädigen)* to be bad for; **mitgenommen aussehen** to look the worse for wear
c *(= stehlen)* to walk off with
d *(inf)* *Sehenswürdigkeit, Veranstaltung* to take in

mit|nich|ten [mɪtˈnɪçtn̩] ADV (old) not at all, by no means, in no way

Mit|ra [ˈmiːtra] F -, **Mitren** [-trən] (Eccl) mitre (Brit), miter (US)

Mit|rau|chen NT -s, no pl passive smoking

Mit|rau|cher(in) M(F) passive smoker

mit+rech|nen VT sep to count; Betrag to count in; **Feiertage nicht mitgerechnet** excluding public holidays

mit+re|den sep **VI** (= Meinung äußern) to join in (bei etw sth); (= mitbestimmen) to have a say (bei in); **da kann er nicht ~** he wouldn't know anything about that; **da kann ich ~** I should know; **da kann ich aus Erfahrung ~** I know from my own experience; **sie will überall ~** (inf) she always has to have her say **VT** **da möchte ich auch ein Wörtchen ~** I'd like to have some say (in this) too; **Sie haben hier nichts mitzure- den** this is none of your concern

mit+rei|sen VI sep aux sein to travel (too) (mit with)

Mit|rei|sen|de(r) MF decl as adj fellow passenger

mit+rei|ßen VT sep irreg (Fluss, Lawine) to sweep or carry away; (Fahrzeug) to carry along; **sich ~ lassen** (fig) to allow oneself to be carried away; **der Schauspieler/seine Rede hat alle mitgerissen** everyone was carried away by the actor's performance/his speech

mit|rei|ßend ADJ Rhythmus, Enthusiasmus infectious; Reden, Musik rousing; Film, Fußballspiel thrilling, exciting ADV vortragen infectiously; **er redete ~** he gave a rousing speech

mit|samt [mɪtˈzamt] PREP +dat together with

mit+schi|cken VT sep (in Brief etc) to enclose

mit+schlei|fen VT sep to drag along

mit+schlep|pen VT sep jdn/etw ~ to drag or cart (inf) sb/sth along

mit+schnei|den VT sep irreg to record

Mit|schnitt M recording

mit+schrei|ben sep irreg **VT** etw ~ to write or take sth down; (Sekretärin) to take sth down; **er hat ein Stück Zeitgeschichte mitgeschrieben** he helped shape recent history **VI** to take notes; **nicht so schnell, ich kann nicht mehr ~** not so fast, I can't keep up

Mit|schrift F record; (von Vorlesung etc) notes pl; **für the record; nicht zur ~ bestimmt** or **gedacht** off the record

Mit|schuld F share of the blame or responsibility (an +dat for); (an einem Verbrechen) complicity (an +dat in); **ihn trifft eine ~** a share of the blame falls on him or must be taken by him; (an Verbrechen) he is implicated (an +dat in)

mit|schul|dig ADJ (an Verbrechen) implicated (an +dat in); (an Unfall) partly responsible or to blame (an +dat for); **sich ~ machen** to incur (some) blame (an +dat for); (an Verbrechen) to become implicated (an +dat in)

Mit|schul|di|ge(r) MF decl as adj accomplice; (= Helfershelfer) accessory

Mit|schü|ler(in) M(F) school-friend; (in dersel- ben Klasse) classmate

mit+schwin|gen VI sep irreg (lit) to resonate too; **was bei** or **in diesem Wort mitschwingt** the overtones or associations contained in or con- jured up by this word; **in seiner Stimme schwang ein Ton von Enttäuschung mit** there was a note of disappointment in his voice

mit+sin|gen sep irreg **VT** to join in (singing) **VI** to join in the singing, to sing along; **in einer Oper/einem Chor** etc ~ to sing in an opera/ choir etc

mit+spie|len VI sep **a** (= auch spielen) to play too; (in Mannschaft etc) to play (bei in); **in einem Film/bei einem Theaterstück ~** to be in a film/ play; **bei einem Orchester ~** to play in an or- chestra; **wer spielt mit?** who wants to play?; (in Mannschaft) who's playing?; (Theat etc) who's in it?

b (fig inf) (= mitmachen) to play along (inf); (= sich beteiligen) to be involved in; **wenn das Wet- ter mitspielt** if the weather's OK (inf)

c (Gründe, Motive) to play a part or role (bei in), to be involved (bei in)

d (= Schaden zufügen) **er hat ihr übel** or **schlimm** or **arg** or **hart mitgespielt** he has treat- ed her badly; **das Leben hat ihr übel** etc **mitge- spielt** she has had a hard life, life has been hard to her

Mit|spie|ler(in) M(F) (Sport) player; (Theat) member of the cast; **seine ~** (Sport) his team- mates; (Theat) the other members of the cast

Mit|spra|che F a say

Mit|spra|che|recht NT right to a say in a mat- ter; **jdm ein ~ einräumen** or **gewähren** to allow or grant sb a say (bei in); **bei dieser Entschei- dung möchte ich ein ~** I want to have a say in this matter

mit+spre|chen sep irreg **VT** Gebet etc to join in (saying); **etw (mit jdm) ~** to say sth with sb, to say sth at the same time as sb **VI** to join in; **bei etw ~** to join in sth; (= mitbestimmen) to have a say in sth; **sie will überall ~** she always wants to have her say

Mit|strei|ter(in) M(F) (geh) comrade-in-arms

mit|tag △ [ˈmɪtaːk] ADV → **Mittag** a

Mit|tag¹ [ˈmɪtaːk] M -(e)s, -e **a** midday; **gegen ~** around or about midday or noon; **über ~** at midday, at lunchtime(s); **am ~** at midday, at lunchtime; **jeden ~** every day at midday, every lunchtime; **jeden ~ gegen halb eins** every day at half past twelve; **gestern/heute/morgen ~** at midday yesterday/today/tomorrow, yesterday/ today/tomorrow lunchtime; **Dienstag ~** midday Tuesday, Tuesday (at) midday, Tuesday lunch- time; **kurz vor/nach ~** shortly before/after mid- day; **des ~s** (geh) around noon or midday; **ei- nes ~s** (geh) one day around noon or midday; **zu ~ essen** to have lunch or dinner, to have one's midday meal; **etwas Warmes zu ~ essen** to have a cooked lunch (Brit) or warm lunch (US)

b (inf: Pause) lunch hour, lunch-break; **~ ma- chen/haben** to take/have one's lunch hour or lunch-break; **sie macht gerade ~** she's (off) at lunch

c (old, liter: = Süden) south

Mit|tag² NT -s, no pl (inf: = Mittagessen) lunch

Mit|tag|es|sen NT lunch, midday meal; **er kam zum ~** he came to lunch; **sie saßen beim ~** they were having lunch, they were having their midday meal

mit|tä|gig ADJ attr midday

mit|täg|lich ADJ attr midday, lunchtime; Schläf- chen afternoon ADV at lunchtimes

mit|tags ADV at lunchtime; **die Deutschen es- sen ~ warm** the Germans have a hot meal at midday; **~ (um) 12 Uhr, (um) 12 Uhr ~** at 12 noon, at 12 o'clock midday; **sonnabends ~** Saturday lunchtime

Mit|tags-: **Mit|tags|aus|ga|be** F midday or lunchtime edition; **Mit|tags|brot** NT (dial) lunch; **Mit|tags|glut** F (liter), **Mit|tags|hit- ze** F midday or noonday heat, heat of midday; **Mit|tags|mahl** NT (liter), **Mit|tags|mahl|zeit** F midday meal; **Mit|tags|pau|se** F lunch hour, lunch-break; **~ machen/haben** to take/ have one's lunch hour or lunch-break; (Geschäft etc) to close at lunchtime; **Mit|tags|ru|he** F period of quiet (after lunch); (in Geschäft) mid- day-closing; **~ halten** to have a period of quiet after lunch; (Geschäft) to close for lunch; **Mit- tags|schlaf** M afternoon nap; **Mit|tags|son- ne** F midday sun; **Mit|tags|stun|de** F mid- day, noon; **um die** or **zur** (geh) ~ around mid- day or noon; **Mit|tags|tisch** M **a** dinner ta- ble; **den ~ decken** to lay (esp Brit) or set the table for lunch; **am ~ sitzen** to be sitting (at the table) having lunch **b** (im Restaurant) busi- nessman's lunch; **Mit|tags|zeit** F lunchtime; **während** or **in der ~ lunchtime; um die ~ a-

round midday or lunchtime; **zur ~** (geh) at mid- day

Mit|tä|ter(in) M(F) accomplice

Mit|tä|ter|schaft F complicity; **die ~ leugnen** or **abstreiten** to deny complicity

Mitt|drei|ßi|ger ['mɪtdraisɪɡɐ] M -s, -, **Mitt- drei|ßi|ge|rin** [-ərɪn] F -, **-nen** man/woman in his/her mid-thirties

Mit|te [ˈmɪtə] F -, -n **a** (= Mittelpunkt, mittlerer Teil) middle; (von Kreis, Kugel, Stadt) centre (Brit), center (US); (von Straße) centre (Brit), center (US); **ein Buch bis zur ~ lesen** to read half of a book; **~ August** in the middle of August; **~ des Jahres/des Monats** halfway through the year/ month; **~ der siebziger Jahre** in the mid-seven- ties; **er ist ~ vierzig** or **der Vierziger** he's in his mid-forties; **die goldene ~** the golden mean; **die rechte ~** a happy medium; **in der ~** in the middle; (zwischen zwei Menschen) in between (them/us etc); (zwischen Ortschaften) halfway, midway; **sie nahmen sie in die ~** they took her between them → **ab** ADV, **Reich a**

b (Pol) centre (Brit), center (US); **die linke/ rechte ~** centre-left/-right (Brit), center-left/ -right (US); **in der ~ stehen** to be moderate; **in der ~ zwischen** midway between; **rechts/links von der ~** right/left of centre (Brit) or center (US)

c (von Gruppe, Gesellschaft) **einer aus unserer ~** one of us, one of our number; **ich bin gern in eurer ~** I like being with you; **in unserer ~** with us, in our midst, among(st) us; **wir haben ihn in unserer ~ willkommen geheißen** we welcomed him into our midst; **er wurde aus unserer ~ ge- rissen** he was taken from our midst or from a- mongst us

mit+teil|bar ADJ communicable

mit+tei|len sep ✪ 31, 45.3, 46.5, 48.3, 51.4 **VT** **jdm etw ~** to tell sb sth; (= benachrichtigen) to inform sb of or about sth, to communicate sth to sb (form); (= bekannt geben) to announce sth to sb; (Comm, Admin) to inform or notify sb of sth; **hiermit teilen wir Ihnen mit, dass ...** we hereby inform you that ...; **teile ihm die Nach- richt schonend mit** break the news to him gently; **es wurde mitgeteilt, dass ...** it was an- nounced that ...; **wie die Polizei mitteilt, ...** as announced by the police ...

VR **a** (= kommunizieren) to communicate (jdm with sb); **er kann sich gut/schlecht ~** he finds it easy/difficult to communicate

b (geh: Stimmung) to communicate itself (jdm to sb)

mit+teil|sam [ˈmɪttailzaːm] ADJ communicative; (pej) talkative, garrulous

Mit|tei|lung F (= Bekanntgabe) announcement; (= Erklärung) statement; (= Benachrichtigung) no- tification; (Comm, Admin) communication; (an Mitarbeiter etc) memo; (von Korrespondenten, Re- porter etc) report; **jdm (eine) ~ (von etw) machen** (form) to inform sb (of sth), to report (sth) to sb; (= bekannt geben) to announce sth to sb; (= Erklärung abgeben) to make a statement (about sth) to sb; (= benachrichtigen) to inform or notify sb (of sth); **eine ~ bekommen, dass ...** to hear that ...

Mit|tei|lungs|be|dürf|nis NT need to talk to other people

mit|tel [ˈmɪtl] ADJ = **mittlere(r, s) b**

Mit|tel [ˈmɪtl] **NT** -s, - **a** (Math: = Durchschnitt) average; **im ~** on average; **arithmetisches/geo- metrisches ~** arithmetical/geometrical mean

b (= Mittel zum Zweck, Transportmittel etc) means sing; (= Maßnahme, Methode) way, method; (= Werbemittel, Propagandamittel, zur Verkehrsbeein- flussung) device; (= Lehrmittel) aid; **~ und Wege finden** to find ways and means; **~ zum Zweck** a means to an end; **kein ~ unversucht lassen** to try everything; **~ gegen die Inflation** ways of beating inflation; **als letztes** or **äußerstes ~** as a last resort; **zu anderen ~n greifen, andere ~ anwenden** to use or employ other means or methods; **ihm ist jedes ~ recht** he will do anything (to achieve his ends); **ihm war jedes ~ recht, dazu war ihm jedes ~ recht** he did not care how he did it *or* what means he used to a-chieve his ends; **er ist in der Wahl seiner ~ nicht zimperlich** he is not fussy about what methods he chooses; **etw mit allen ~n verhin-dern/bekämpfen** to do one's utmost *or* to do everything one can to prevent/oppose sth; **etw mit allen ~n versuchen** to try one's utmost to do sth; **sie hat mit allen ~n gekämpft, um ...** she fought tooth and nail to ...

c PL (= *Geldmittel*) funds *pl*, resources *pl*; (= *Privatmittel*) means *pl*, resources *pl*

d (= *Medikament, kosmetisch*) preparation; (*Med*) drug, preparation; (= *Medizin*) medicine; (= *Putzmittel*) cleaning agent; (= *Fleckenmittel*) spot *or* stain remover; (= *Waschmittel*) detergent; (= *Haarwaschmittel*) shampoo; **welches ~ nimmst du?** what do you use?; (*Med:* = *einnehmen*) what do you take?; **ein ~ zum Einreiben** (*flüssig*) something *or* a lotion to be rubbed in; (*Salbe*) an ointment to be rubbed in; (*Creme*) a cream to be rubbed in; **das ist ein ~ gegen meine Er-kältung/Schuppen** that is for my cold/dandruff; **~ zum Putzen** cleaning things *pl or* stuff; **sich** (*dat*) **ein ~ (gegen Kopfschmerzen/Husten** *etc*) **verschreiben lassen** to get the doctor to pre-scribe something (for headaches/a cough *etc*); **welches ~ hat der Arzt dir verschrieben?** what did the doctor give you?; **es gibt kein ~ gegen Schnupfen** there is no cure for the common cold; **das beste ~ für** *or* **gegen etw** the best cure *or* remedy for sth

e (*Phys, Chem:* = *Medium*) medium

Mịt|tel-: Mịt|tel|ach|se F (*von Fläche, Körper*) central axis; (*von Auto*) central axle; **mịt|tel-ak|tiv** ADJ *Atommüll etc* intermediate-level; **Mịt|tel|al|ter** NT Middle Ages *pl*; **da herr-schen Zustände wie im ~!** (*inf*) it is positively medieval there; **mịt|tel|al|ter|lich** [-laltəlɪç] ADJ medieval ADV **eine ~ anmutende Stadt** a medieval-looking town; **~ geprägt sein** to show a medieval influence; **Mịt|tel|ame|ri|ka** NT Central America (and the Caribbean); **mịt|tel|ame|ri|ka|nisch** ADJ Central Ameri-can; **mịt|tel|bar** ADJ indirect (*auch Jur*); *Scha-den* consequential ADV indirectly; **Mịt|tel|bau** M *pl* **-bauten a** (*Gebäude*) central block **b** *no pl* (*Univ*) non-professorial teaching staff; **mịt|tel|deutsch** ADJ (*Geog, Ling*) Central Ger-man; (*dated Pol*) East German; **Mịt|tel-deutsch** NT Central German dialects *pl*; **Mịt|tel|deutsch|land** NT *Germany east of the Harz Mountains excluding Pomerania etc* (*dated Pol:* = *DDR*) East Germany; **Mịt|tel-ding** NT (= *Mischung*) cross (*zwischen +dat, aus* between); **Mịt|tel|eu|ro|pa** NT Central Europe; **Mịt|tel|eu|ro|pä|er(in)** M(F) Central European; **ich als normaler ~** (*inf*) any average person like myself; **mịt|tel|eu|ro|pä|isch** ADJ Central European; **~e Zeit** Central European Time; **mịt|tel|fein** ADJ *Erbsen etc* medium-sized; *Kaffee, Mehl etc* medium-ground ADV **den Kaffee/das Mehl ~ mahlen** to grind the coffee/flour medium-fine; **Mịt|tel|feld** NT (*Sport*) midfield; (*die Spieler auch*) midfield players *pl*; **Mịt|tel|fin|ger** M middle finger; **Mịt|tel-fran|ken** [-fraŋkn] NT **-s** Central Franconia; **mịt|tel|fris|tig** [-frɪstɪç] ADJ *Finanzplanung, Kre-dite* medium-term; *Voraussage* medium-range ADV in the medium term; **Mịt|tel|gang** M centre aisle (*Brit*), center aisle (*US*); **Mịt|tel-ge|bir|ge** NT low mountain range; **Mịt|tel-ge|wicht** NT middleweight; **Meister im ~** mid-dleweight champion; **mịt|tel|groß** ADJ medi-um-sized; **mịt|tel|hoch|deutsch** ADJ Middle High German; **Mịt|tel|hoch|deutsch(e)** NT Middle High German; **Mịt|tel|klas|se** F **a** (*Comm*) middle of the market; **ein Wagen der ~** a mid-range car **b** (*Sociol*) middle classes *pl*; **Mịt|tel|klas|se|wa|gen** M mid-range car, middle of the range car; **mịt|tel|län|disch** [-lɛndɪç] ADJ Mediterranean; **das Mittelländi-sche Meer** (*form*) the Mediterranean Sea; **Mịt-tel|lauf** M (*eines Flusses*) middle reaches *pl*;

Mịt|tel|läu|fer(in) M(F) (*Sport*) centre-half (*Brit*), center-half (*US*); **Mịt|tel|li|nie** F centre (*Brit*) *or* center (*US*) line; **mịt|tel|los** ADJ without means; (= *arm*) impoverished; **Mịt|tel-lo|sig|keit** F **-, -en** lack of means; **Mịt|tel-maß** NT mediocrity *no art*; **das (gesunde) ~** the happy medium; **~ sein** to be average; **seine Leistungen bewegen sich im ~**, **seine Leistun-gen gehen nicht über das ~ hinaus** his perform-ance is mediocre; **mịt|tel|mä|ßig** ADJ medio-cre; *Schriftsteller, Spieler etc auch* indifferent; **als Redner gibt er eine recht ~e Figur ab** he's a pretty mediocre *or* indifferent speaker ADV in-differently; *begabt, gebildet* moderately; *ausge-stattet* modestly; **~ ausgebildet** moderately well-trained; **wie gefällt es dir hier? – so ~** how do you like it here? – so-so (*inf*); **Mịt|tel|mä-ßig|keit** F mediocrity

Mịt|tel|meer NT Mediterranean (Sea), Med (*inf*)

Mịt|tel|meer- *in cpds* Mediterranean; **Mịt|tel-meer|raum** M Mediterranean (region), Med (*inf*)

Mịt|tel|ohr|ent|zün|dung F , **Mịt|tel|ohr-ver|ei|te|rung** F inflammation of the middle ear, otitis (media) (*spec*)

Mịt|tel-: mịt|tel|präch|tig (*hum inf*) ADJ rea-sonable, not bad *pred*, so-so *pred* (*inf*); (= *ziemlich schlecht*) pretty awful (*inf*) ADV not bad; **sich ~ fühlen** to feel not too bad; **Mịt|tel-punkt** M (*Math, räumlich*) centre (*Brit*), center (*US*); (*fig: visuell*) focal point; **er muss immer ~ sein** *or* **im ~ stehen** he always has to be the centre (*Brit*) *or* center (*US*) of attention; **er steht im ~ des Interesses** he is the centre (*Brit*) *or* center (*US*) of attention; **Mịt|tel|punkt-schu|le** F *school at the centre of a rural catchment area or rural service area*

mịt|tels [mɪtls] PREP *+gen or dat* (*geh*) by means of

Mịt|tel-: Mịt|tel|schei|tel M centre parting (*Brit*), center part (*US*); **Mịt|tel|schicht** F (*Sociol*) middle class; **Mịt|tel|schiff** NT (*Archit*) nave; **Mịt|tel|schu|le** F **a** (*inf:* = *Realschule*) secondary modern school (*dated Brit*), ≈ juni-or high (*US*) **b** (*Sw, Aus:* = *Oberschule*) second-ary school, high school (*US*); **mịt|tel|schwer** ADJ *Text etc* of medium difficulty *pred*; *Verlet-zungen* moderately severe; *Unfall, Katastrophe* fairly serious ADV *verletzt* seriously; **etw als ~ einstufen** to classify sth as intermediate

Mịt|tels|mann M *pl* **-männer** *or* **-leute**, **Mịt|-tels|per|son** F intermediary

mịt|telst PREP (*old*) by means of

Mịt|tel-: Mịt|tel|stand M middle classes *pl*; **mịt|tel|stän|dig** ADJ (*Bot*) perigynous (*spec*); **mịt|tel|stän|disch** ADJ a middle-class *Betrieb* medium-sized **c** (*Pol*) centrist; **Mịt|tel-ständ|ler** [-ʃtɛndlə] M **-s, -**, **Mịt|tel|ständ|le-rin** [-ərɪn] F **-, -nen** a middle-class person **b** (*Pol*) centrist; **Mịt|tel|stein|zeit** F Mesolithic period; **Mịt|tel|stel|lung** F medium setting; (*fig*) intermediate position; **Mịt|tel|stim|me** F (*Mus*) middle voice

Mịt|tel|stre|cke F (*Sport*) middle-distance e-vent; (*Aviat*) medium haul; (*von Rakete etc*) medi-um range

Mịt|tel|stre|cken-: Mịt|tel|stre|cken|flug-zeug NT medium-haul aircraft; **Mịt|tel|stre-cken|lauf** M middle-distance race; (*Disziplin*) middle-distance running; **Mịt|tel|stre|cken-läu|fer(in)** M(F) middle-distance runner; **Mịt|tel|stre|cken|ra|ke|te** F intermediate-range *or* medium-range missile; **Mịt|tel|stre-cken|waf|fe** F intermediate-range weapon

Mịt|tel-: Mịt|tel|strei|fen M central reservation (*Brit*), median (strip) (*US*); **Mịt|tel|stück** NT middle part, centre (*Brit*) *or* center (*US*) part; (*von Braten etc*) middle; **Mịt|tel|stu|fe** F (*Sch*) middle school (*Brit*), junior high (*US*); **Mịt|tel|stür|mer(in)** M(F) (*Sport*) centre-for-ward (*Brit*), center-forward (*US*); **Mịt|tel|teil** M OR NT middle section; **Mịt|tel|weg** M mid-

dle course; **der goldene ~** the happy medium, the golden mean; **einen ~ gehen** *or* **einschlagen** to steer a middle course; **einen ~ suchen** to try to find a happy medium; **Mịt|tel|wel|le** F (*Rad*) medium wave(band); **auf ~ senden** to broadcast on the medium waveband *or* on (the) medium wave; **Mịt|tel|wert** M mean; **Mịt|tel|wort** NT *pl* **-wörter** (*Gram*) participle; **~ der Gegenwart/Vergangenheit** present/past par-ticiple

mịt|ten [mɪtn] ADV **~ an etw** (*dat*)**/auf etw** (*dat*)**/in etw** (*dat*)**/bei etw** (right) in the middle of sth; **~ aus etw** (right) from the middle of sth; (*aus Gedränge etc auch*) from the midst of sth; **~ durch etw** (right) through the middle of sth; **~ darin/darein** (right) in the middle of it; **~ darun-ter** (*räumlich*) right under it/them; (= *dabei*) right amongst it/them, right in the middle of it/them; **~ (hin)durch** right through the middle; **~ im Urwald** in the middle *or* depths of the jun-gle; **~ in der Luft/im Atlantik** in mid-air/mid-At-lantic; **~ ins Gesicht** right in the face; **es ist noch ~ in der Nacht** it's still the middle of the night; **~ im Leben** in the middle of life; **~ in** *or* **bei der Arbeit** in the middle of working; **~ beim Frühstück/Essen sein** to be in the middle of (one's) breakfast/of eating; **~ unter uns** (right) in our midst; **der Stock brach ~ entzwei** the stick broke clean in two

mịt|ten-: mịt|ten|drin [mɪtn'drɪn] ADV (right) in the middle of it; **~ in der Stadt/der Arbeit** (right) in the middle of the town/one's work; **~, etw zu tun** (right) in the middle of doing sth; **mịt|ten|durch** [mɪtn'dʊrç] ADV (right) through the middle; **mịt|ten|mạng** [mɪtn'maŋ] (*dial reg*) PREP *+dat or* (*sl*) *acc* among ADV (right) in the middle of it/them

Mịt|ter|nacht F midnight *no art*

mịt|ter|näch|tig [-nɛçtɪç], **mịt|ter|nächt|lich** ADJ *attr* midnight; **zu ~er Stunde** (*geh*) at the midnight hour

Mịt|ter|nachts-: Mịt|ter|nachts|son|ne F midnight sun; **Mịt|ter|nachts|stun|de** F witching hour; **Mịt|ter|nachts|va|se** F (*hum*) chamber pot

Mịtt|fünf|zi|ger [mɪtfʏnftsɪgə] M **-s, -**, **Mịtt-fünf|zi|ge|rin** [-ərɪn] F **-, -nen** man/woman in his/her mid-fifties

Mịtt|ler [mɪtlə] M **-s, -**, **Mịtt|le|rin** [-ərɪn] F **-, -nen** mediator; (*liter: Ideen, Sprache etc*) medium

Mịtt|ler|amt NT mediatory position

mịtt|le|re(r, s) [mɪtlərə] ADJ *attr* **a** (= *dazwi-schenliegend*) middle; **der/die/das ~** the middle one; **der Mittlere Osten** the Middle East; **der ~ Weg** (*fig*) the middle course

b (= *den Mittelwert bildend*) medium; (= *mittel-schwer*) *Kursus, Aufgabe* intermediate; (= *durch-schnittlich*) average; (*Math*) mean; (= *von mittlerer Größe*) *Betrieb* medium-sized; **von ~m Wert** of medium value; **~r Beamter** *person in the sec-tion of the civil service for which the entry requirement is the Abitur*, ≈ civil servant of the administrative class (*Brit*); **~n Alters** mid-dle-aged; **~ Reife** (*Sch*) first public examina-tion in secondary school, ≈ O-levels (*Brit*)

MITTLERE REIFE

mittlere Reife is the term still generally used for the intermediate school certificate. This is normally gained after successful completion of the six years (four in many **Länder**) in a **Realschule**. All pupils who complete their tenth year at a **Gymnasium** also automatically receive their **mittlere Reife**. If pupils from a **Realschule** achieve good examination results, they can move up to the eleventh year of a **Gymnasium** and try for the **Abitur**. The **mitt-lere Reife** entitles a pupil to attend a **Fach-oberschule** and take the **Fachabitur** there af-ter two years → ABITUR, GYMNASIUM, REALSCHULE

Mitt|ler-: Mitt|ler|funk|ti|on F mediating role, role as (a) mediator; **Mitt|ler|rol|le** F role of mediator, mediatory role

mitt|ler|wei|le ['mɪtlɐ'vailə] ADV in the meantime; **ich habe mich ~ daran gewöhnt** I've got used to it in the meantime

mit-: mit+tra|gen VT sep irreg Last to help (to) carry; Kosten, Verantwortung, Schuld to share; Entscheidung, Planung to share responsibility for; Politik, Programm, Vorschlag to lend one's support to; **mit+trin|ken** sep irreg **VT** to drink with us/ them etc; **er wollte nichts ~** he didn't want to join us/them etc in a drink **VI** to have a drink with us/them etc

Mitt-: mitt|schiffs ['mɪtʃɪfs] ADV (Naut) (a)midships; **Mitt|sech|zi|ger** ['mɪtzɛçtsɪgɐ] M **-s, -, Mitt|sech|zi|ge|rin** [-ərɪn] F **-, -nen** man/woman in his/her mid-sixties; **Mitt|sieb|zi|ger** ['mɪtzi:ptsɪgɐ] M **-s, -, Mitt|sieb|zi|ge|rin** [-ərɪn] F **-, -nen** man/woman in his/ her mid-seventies; **Mitt|som|mer** ['mɪtzɔmɐ] M midsummer; **Mitt|som|mer|nacht** F Midsummer's Night

mit+tun VI sep irreg (inf) to join in

Mitt-: Mitt|vier|zi|ger ['mɪtfɪrtsɪgɐ] M **-s, -, Mitt|vier|zi|ge|rin** [-ərɪn] F **-, -nen** man/woman in his/her mid-forties; **mitt|wegs** ['mɪtve:ks] ADV (old) midway; **Mitt|woch** ['mɪtvɔx] M **-s, -e** Wednesday → auch Dienstag; **mitt|wochs** ['mɪtvɔxs] ADV on Wednesdays → auch dienstags; **Mitt|zwan|zi|ger** ['mɪttsvantsɪgɐ] M **-s, -, Mitt|zwan|zi|ge|rin** [-ərɪn] F **-, -nen** man/woman in his/her mid-twenties

mit|un|ter [mɪt'ʊntɐ] ADV from time to time, now and then or again, (every) once in a while

mit+un|ter|schrei|ben ptp **mitunterschrieben** VTI sep irreg to sign too

Mit|ver|an|stal|ter(in) M(F) co-organizer; (von Konzert etc) co-promoter

mit|ver|ant|wort|lich ADJ jointly responsible pred

Mit|ver|ant|wort|lich|keit F joint responsibility

Mit|ver|ant|wor|tung F share of the responsibility; **~ haben** to have or bear a share of the responsibility; **die ~ ablehnen** to abnegate (all) responsibility

mit+ver|die|nen ptp **mitverdient** VI sep to (go out to) work as well

Mit|ver|fas|ser(in) M(F) co-author

Mit|ver|schul|den NT ihm wurde ein **~ nachgewiesen** he was shown to have been partially or partly to blame; **ihn trifft ein ~ an diesem Vorfall** he was partially or partly to blame for this incident

Mit|ver|schwo|re|ne(r) [-fæʃvo:rənə] MF decl as adj crony (hum inf); (pej, bei Verbrechen) conspirator

Mit|ver|schwö|rer(in) M(F) conspirator

mit+ver|si|chern ptp **mitversichert** VT sep to include in the insurance; **bei seinen Eltern mitversichert sein** to be included on one's parents' insurance (policy)

Mit|ver|si|cher|te(r) MF decl as adj jointly insured (party)

Mit|welt F die **~** the people or those about one; **es dauerte lange, bis die ~ seine Leistungen würdigte** it was a long time before his contemporaries learned to appreciate his achievements (Brit)

mit+wir|ken VI sep to play a part (an +dat, bei in); (Fakten, Faktoren etc auch) to contribute (an +dat, bei to); (= beteiligt sein) to be involved (an +dat, bei in); (= mitspielen) (Schauspieler, Diskussionsteilnehmer) to take part (an +dat, bei in); (in Film) to appear (an +dat in); (in Chor, Orchester etc) to perform (in +dat in); (Tänzer, Orchester, Chor) to perform (an +dat, bei in); **ohne sein Mitwirken wäre das unmöglich gewe-**

sen it would have been impossible without his involvement

Mit|wir|ken|de(r) [-vɪrkndə] MF decl as adj participant (an +dat, bei in); (= Mitspieler) performer (an +dat, bei in); (= Schauspieler) actor (an +dat, bei in); **die ~n** (Theat) the cast pl

Mit|wir|kung F (= Beteiligung, Mitarbeit) involvement (an +dat, bei in); (= Zusammenarbeit) cooperation (an +dat, bei in); (an Buch, Film) collaboration (an +dat, bei on); (= Teilnahme) (an Diskussion, Projekt) participation (an +dat, bei in); (von Tänzer, Orchester, Chor) appearance (an +dat, bei in); (von Tänzer, Orchester, Chor) performance (an +dat, bei in); **unter ~ von** with the assistance or aid or help of

Mit|wir|kungs-: Mit|wir|kungs|pflicht F , no pl (Jur) duty to cooperate; **Mit|wir|kungs|recht** NT , no pl (Jur) right of participation

Mit|wis|ser [-vɪsɐ] M **-s, -, Mit|wis|se|rin** [-ərɪn] F **-, -nen** (Jur) accessory (+gen to); **~ sein** to know about it; **~ einer Sache** (gen) **sein** to know about sth; **jdn zum ~ machen** to tell sb (all) about it; (Jur) to make sb an accessory; **er wollte nicht so viele ~ haben** he didn't want so many people to know about it

Mit|wis|ser|schaft [-vɪsɐʃaft] F **-, no pl er wurde wegen ~ angeklagt** he was charged with being an accessory (to the crime); **an seiner ~ kann kein Zweifel bestehen** there can be no doubt that he was an accessory (to it) (Jur), there can be no doubt that he knew about it

Mit|wohn|zent|ra|le F agency for arranging shared accommodation

mit+wol|len VI sep (= mitgehen wollen) to want to go along; (= mitkommen wollen) to want to come along

mit+zäh|len VTI sep (= count; Betrag to count in

mit+zie|hen VI sep irreg aux sein (fig inf) to go along with it

Mix [mɪks] M **-, -e** mixture

Mix|be|cher M (cocktail) shaker

Mixed [mɪkst] NT **-(s), -(s)** (Sport) (= Spiel) mixed doubles sing; (= Mannschaft) mixed doubles pair

mi|xen ['mɪksn] VT Getränke to mix; (Rad, TV) to mix

Mi|xer¹ ['mɪksɐ] M **-s, -** (= Küchenmixer) blender; (= Rührmaschine) mixer

Mi|xer² ['mɪksɐ] M **-s, -, Mi|xe|rin** [-ərɪn] F **-, -nen** a (= Barmixer) cocktail waiter/waitress b (Film, Rad, TV) mixer

Mix|ge|tränk NT mixed drink; (alkoholisch) cocktail; (= Milchmixgetränk) milk shake

Mix|tur [mɪks'tu:ɐ] F **-, -en** (Pharm, Mus, fig) mixture

MKS abbr von **Maul- und Klauenseuche** FMD, foot and mouth disease

ml abbr von **Milliliter** millilitre (Brit), milliliter (US)

mm abbr von **Millimeter** millimetre (Brit), millimeter (US)

MMS [ɛmɛm'ɛs] F **-, -** abbr von **Multimedia Messaging Service** MMS; **jdm eine ~ schicken** to send sb an MMS (message)

Mne|mo- [mnemo-]: **Mne|mo|tech|nik** F mnemonics sing; **mne|mo|tech|nisch** ADJ mnemonic ADV mnemonically

Mob [mɔp] M **-s, no pl** (pej) mob

mob|ben ['mɔbn] VT to harass or bully (at work)

Mob|bing ['mɔbɪŋ] NT **-s, no pl** workplace bullying

Mö|bel ['mø:bl] NT **-s, -** (= Möbelstück) piece of furniture; **~ pl** furniture sing; **~ rücken** to shift the furniture

Mö|bel- in cpds furniture; **Mö|bel|haus** NT furniture shop (Brit) or store (US); **Mö|bel|la|ger** NT furniture showroom; **Mö|bel|pa|cker(in)** M(F) furniture packer; **Mö|bel|schrei|ner(in)**

M(F) cabinet-maker; **Mö|bel|spe|di|ti|on** F removal firm (Brit), moving company (US); **Mö|bel|stoff** M furnishing fabric; **Mö|bel|stück** NT piece of furniture; **Mö|bel|tisch|ler(in)** M(F) cabinet-maker; **Mö|bel|wa|gen** M removal van (Brit), moving van or truck (US), pantechnicon (Brit)

mo|bil [mo'bi:l] ADJ a mobile; (Comm, Jur) Vermögen, Kapital movable; (= mitnehmbar) Drucker portable; **~es Vermögen** movables pl; **~ machen** (Mil) to mobilize b (inf: = flink, munter) lively; **jdn ~ machen** to liven sb up ADV **mit jdm ~ telefonieren** to call sb on one's mobile (phone)

Mo|bi|le ['mo:bilə] NT **-s, -s** mobile

Mo|bil|funk M cellular radio

Mo|bil|funk|netz NT cellular network

Mo|bi|li|ar [mobi'lia:ɐ] NT **-s, no pl** furnishings pl

Mo|bi|li|en [mo'bi:liən] PL (old) furnishings pl; (Jur) chattels pl, movables pl

mo|bi|li|sie|ren [mobili'zi:rən] ptp **mobilisiert** VT (Mil, fig) to mobilize; (Comm) Kapital to make liquid; **die Straße** or **den Mob ~** to rouse the mob

Mo|bi|li|sie|rung F mobilization; (Econ) realization

Mo|bi|li|tät [mobili'tɛ:t] F **-, no pl** mobility (auch Sociol); (geistig) agility

Mo|bil-: Mo|bil|ma|chung [mo'bi:lmaxʊŋ] F **-, -en** (Mil) mobilization; **die ~ ausrufen/beschließen** to mobilize/decide to mobilize; **Mo|bil|te|le|fon** NT mobile phone

möbl. abbr von **möbliert** furnished

möb|lie|ren [mø'bli:rən] ptp **möbliert** VT to furnish; **neu ~** to refurnish; **ein möbliertes Zimmer** a furnished room; **ein möblierter Herr** (hum inf) a lodger; **möbliert wohnen** to live in furnished accommodation

Moc|ca ['mɔka] M **-s, -s** mocha

moch|te pret von **mögen**

Möch|te|gern- ['mœçtəgɛrn] in cpds (iro) would-be; **ein ~Schauspieler** a would-be actor

mod. abbr von **modern**

mo|dal [mo'da:l] ADJ (Gram) modal

Mo|da|li|tät [modali'tɛ:t] F **-, -en** a usu pl (von Plan, Vertrag etc) arrangement; (von Verfahren, Arbeit) procedure b (Philos) modality

Mo|dal- (Gram): **Mo|dal|satz** M (adverbial) clause of manner; **Mo|dal|verb** NT modal verb

Mod|der ['mɔdɐ] M **-s, no pl** (N Ger) mud

mod|de|rig ['mɔdərɪç], **modd|rig** ['mɔdrɪç] ADJ (N Ger) muddy

Mo|de ['mo:də] F **-, -n** fashion; (= Sitte) custom; **~n** (= Kleider) fashions, fashionwear sing, apparel sing (esp US); **~ sein** to be fashionable, to be the fashion, to be in vogue; (Sitte) to be the custom; **das ist jetzt ~** that's the latest fashion; **Radfahren/Alaska wird jetzt große ~** cycling/Alaska is becoming very fashionable nowadays; **in ~/aus der ~ kommen** to come into/go out of fashion; **die ~ alle ~n mitmachen, mit** or **nach der ~ gehen, sich nach der ~ richten** to keep up with the latest fashions; **sich nach der (neuesten) ~ kleiden** to wear the latest fashions; **wir wollen keine neuen ~n einführen** (inf) we don't want any new-fangled ideas

Mo|de-: Mo|de|ar|ti|kel M a fashion accessory b (in Zeitung) fashion article; **Mo|de|arzt** M , **Mo|de|ärz|tin** F fashionable doctor; **Mo|de|aus|druck** M pl **-ausdrücke** in-phrase, trendy expression (inf); (Wort) in-word, vogue or trendy (inf) word, buzz word; **mo|de|be|wusst** ▲ ADJ fashion-conscious; **Mo|de|be|wusst|sein** ▲ F fashion-consciousness; **Mo|de|de|si|gner(in)** M(F) fashion designer; **Mo|de|dro|ge** F recreational drug; **Mo|de|er|schei|nung** F vogue, (passing) fashion; **Mo|de|far|be** F fashionable colour (Brit) or color (*US*), in-colour (*Brit inf*), in-color (*US inf*); **mo|de|ge|recht** ADJ fashionable; **Mo|de|ge|schäft** NT fashion shop; **Mo|de|haus** NT fashion house; **Mo|de|heft** NT , **Mo|de|jour|nal** NT fashion magazine; **Mo|de|krank|heit** F fashionable complaint

Mo|del¹ ['mɔdl] NT -s, -s (*Fashion*) model

Mo|del² ['mo:dl] NT -s, - (*Cook*) wooden mould (*Brit*) or mold (*US*)

Mo|dell [mo'dɛl] NT -s, -e **a** model; (= *naturgetreue Nachbildung*) mock-up, model **b** (*Art*: = *Fotomodell*) model; **zu etw ~ stehen** to be the model for sth; **jdm ~ stehen/sitzen** to sit for sb

Mo|dell-: **Mo|dell|cha|rak|ter** M , *no pl* = **haben** to serve as a model; **Mo|dell|ei|sen|bahn** F model railway (*esp Brit*) or railroad (*US*); (*als Spielzeug*) train set; **Mo|dell|flug|zeug** NT model aeroplane (*Brit*) or airplane (*US*)

mo|del|lie|ren [mode'li:rən] *ptp* **modelliert** VTI to model

Mo|del|lier|mas|se F modelling (*Brit*) or modeling (*US*) clay

Mo|dell-: **Mo|dell|kleid** NT model (dress); **Mo|dell|ver|such** M (*esp Sch*) experiment; **Mo|dell|zeich|nung** F drawing of a model; (*Art*) drawing from a model

mo|deln¹ ['mɔdln] VI (*Fashion*) to model

mo|deln² ['mo:dln] VT to model

Mo|dem ['mo:dɛm] NT -s, -e modem

Mo|de|ma|cher(in) M(F) (*inf*) fashion designer

Mo|den-: **Mo|den|schau** F fashion show; **Mo|den|zei|tung** F fashion magazine

Mo|de|pup|pe F , **Mo|de|püpp|chen** NT model type (*inf*)

Mo|der ['mo:dɐ] M -s, *no pl* mustiness; (*geh*: = *Verwesung*) decay; (= *Schimmel*) mildew; **es riecht nach ~** it smells musty; **in ~ übergehen** to decay; (*Grabstein etc*) to become mildewed

mo|de|rat [mode'ra:t] ADJ moderate, reasonable; **nach außen hin gibt sich der Parteichef ~** outwardly the party leader gives the impression of being a moderate **ADV** moderately; **die Krankenkassenbeiträge sollen ~ erhöht werden** there are to be moderate increases in health insurance contributions

Mo|de|ra|ti|on [modera'tsio:n] F -, -en (*Rad, TV*) presentation; **die ~ heute Abend hat: ...** tonight's presenter is ...

Mo|de|ra|to [mode'ra:to] NT -s, -s or Moderati (*Mus*) moderato

Mo|de|ra|tor [mode'ra:tɐ] M -s, Moderatoren [-'to:rən], **Mo|de|ra|to|rin** [-'to:rɪn] F -, -nen presenter

Mo|der|ge|ruch M musty odour (*Brit*) or odor (*US*)

mo|de|rie|ren [mode'ri:rən] *ptp* **moderiert** VTI (*Rad, TV*) to present; **das Moderieren** the presentation

mo|de|rig ['mo:dərɪç] ADJ Geruch musty **ADV** ~ **riechen** to smell musty; **~ schmecken** to taste mouldy (*Brit*) or moldy (*US*)

mo|dern¹ ['mo:dɐn] VI aux sein or haben to rot

mo|dern² [mo'dɛrn] ADJ modern *no adv*; (= *zeitgemäß*) Maschine, Vorrichtung auch up-to-date *no adv*; (= *modisch*) fashionable; Politik, Ansichten, Eltern, Lehrer progressive; **~ sein** (*Kleidung, Möbel*) to be fashionable; **~ werden** to come into fashion, to become fashionable; **der ~e Mensch** modern man **ADV** bauen, ausstatten in a modern style; **sich kleiden** fashionably; **denken** open-mindedly; **~ wohnen** to live in modern housing; **eine ~ eingerichtete Wohnung** an apartment furnished in a modern style; **~ eingestellt sein** to be modern

Mo|der|ne [mo'dɛrnə] F -, *no pl* (*geh*) modern age; **das Zeitalter der ~** the modern age

mo|der|ni|sie|ren [modɛrni'zi:rən] *ptp* **modernisiert** VT Gebäude to modernize; Gesetz, Arbeitsmethoden, Wirtschaft, Unternehmen auch to

bring up to date; *Kleidung* to revamp, to make more fashionable **VI** to get up to date

Mo|der|nis|mus [modɛr'nɪsmʊs] M -, *no pl* modernism

mo|der|nis|tisch [modɛr'nɪstɪʃ] ADJ modernistic **ADV** modernistically

Mo|der|ni|tät [modɛrni'tɛ:t] F -, *no pl* (*geh*) modernity

Mo|de-: **Mo|de|sa|che** F das ist reine ~ it's just the fashion; **Mo|de|sa|lon** M fashion house; **Mo|de|schmuck** M costume jewellery (*Brit*) or jewelry (*US*); **Mo|de|schöp|fer** M fashion designer, couturier; **Mo|de|schöp|fe|rin** F fashion designer, couturière; **Mo|de|schrei** der letzte ~ the latest fashion; **Mo|de|schrift|stel|ler(in)** M(F) popular writer; **Mo|de|tanz** M popular dance; **Mo|de|tor|heit** F fashion fad; **Mo|de|trend** M fashion(able) trend; **Mo|de|wort** NT pl -wörter in-word, vogue or trendy (*inf*) word, buzz word; **Mo|de|zeich|ner(in)** M(F) fashion illustrator; **Mo|de|zeit|schrift** F fashion magazine

Mo|di pl von **Modus**

Mo|di|fi|ka|ti|on [modifika'tsio:n] F -, -en modification

mo|di|fi|zie|ren [modifi'tsi:rən] *ptp* **modifiziert** VT to modify

Mo|di|fi|zie|rung F -, -en modification

mo|disch ['mo:dɪʃ] ADJ stylish, fashionable, modish **ADV** fashionably, stylishly, modishly

Mo|dis|tin [mo'dɪstɪn] F -, -nen milliner

mod|rig ['mo:drɪç] ADJ, ADV = **moderig**

Mo|dul¹ ['mo:dʊl] M -s, -n (*Archit*) module; (*Math*) modulus

Mo|dul² [mo'du:l] NT -s, -e (*Comput*) module

mo|du|lar [modu'la:ɐ] ADJ modular **ADV** of modules

Mo|du|la|ti|on [modula'tsio:n] F -, -en modulation

mo|du|lie|ren [modu'li:rən] *ptp* **moduliert** VT to modulate

Mo|dus ['mo:dʊs, 'mɔdʊs] M -, Modi ['mo:di, 'mɔdi] **a** way; **~ Vivendi** (*geh*) modus vivendi **b** (*Gram*) mood **c** (*Comput*) mode

Mo|fa ['mo:fa] NT -s, -s small moped, motor-assisted bicycle (*form*)

Mo|ge|lei [mogə'lai] F -, -en cheating *no pl*

mo|geln ['mo:gln] VI to cheat; **beim Kartenspiel/bei der Prüfung ~** to cheat at cards/in an exam; **nicht ~!** no cheating!

Mo|gel-: **Mo|gel|pa|ckung** F misleading packaging; (*fig*) sham, fraud; **den Wählern eine ~ verkaufen** (*fig*) to sell the electorate false promises; **Mo|gel|zet|tel** M (*Sch*) crib (*Brit*), cheat sheet (*US inf*)

mö|gen ['mø:gn] ◊ 34, 35, 36.3 *pret* **mochte** ['mɔxtə], *ptp* **gemocht** [gə'mɔxt] VT to like; **~ Sie ihn/Operettenmusik?** do you like him/operetta?; **ich mag ihn/Operettenmusik nicht** I don't like him/operetta, I don't care for him/operetta; **sie mag das (gern)** she (really) likes that; **sie mag kein Sauerkraut** she doesn't like sauerkraut; **was möchten Sie, bitte?** what would you like? (*Verkäufer*) what can I do for you?; **~ Sie eine Praline/etwas Wein?** (*form*) would you like a chocolate/some wine?, would you care for a chocolate/some wine?; **nein danke, ich möchte lieber Tee** no thank you, I would prefer tea or would rather have tea **VI a** (= *wollen*) (*eine Praline/etwas Wein etc mögen*) to like one/some; (= *etw tun mögen*) to like to; **ich mag nicht mehr** I've had enough; (= *bin am Ende*) I can't take any more; **kommen Sie mit? – ich möchte schon, aber ...** are you coming too? – I'd like to, but ... **b** (= *gehen/fahren wollen*) to want to go; **ich möchte (gern) nach Hause** I want to go home; **ich möchte lieber in die Stadt** I would prefer to go or I would rather go into town *ptp*

mögen

MODAL AUX VB a (*im Konjunktiv: Wunsch*) to like to +*infin*; **möchten Sie etwas essen?** would you like something to eat?, would you care for something to eat?; **wir möchten (gern) etwas trinken** we would like something to drink; **ich möchte gern Herrn Schmidt sprechen** I would like to speak to Mr Schmidt; **hier möchte ich nicht wohnen** (= *würde nicht gern*) I wouldn't like to live here; (= *will nicht*) I don't want to live here; **ich möchte dazu nichts sagen** I don't want to say anything about that, no comment; **ich hätte gern dabei sein ~** I would like or have liked to have been there; **ich hätte lieber dabei sein ~** I would prefer or have preferred to have been there; **das möchte ich auch wissen** I'd like to know that too; **möge er/mögest du Erfolg haben** (*old*) may he/you be successful **b** (*im Konjunktiv: einschränkend*) **man möchte meinen, dass ...** you would think that ...; **ich möchte fast sagen ...** I would almost say ... **c** (*geh: Einräumung*) **es mag wohl sein, dass er Recht hat, aber ...** he may well be right, but ...; **wie dem auch sein mag** however that may be; **was sie auch sagen mag** whatever she says; **oder wie er auch heißen mag** or whatever he is or might be or may be called; **es mag dieses Mal gehen** it's all right this time; **mag kommen was da will** come what may; **mag es schneien, so viel es will** it can snow as much as it likes, let it snow as much as it likes; **von mir aus mag er warten** as far as I'm concerned he can wait; **man mag es tun, wie man will, aber ...** you can do it how you like, but ... **d** (*Vermutung*) **es mochten etwa fünf Stunden vergangen sein** about five hours must or would have passed; **sie mag/mochte etwa zwanzig sein** she must or would be/have been about twenty; **wie alt mag sie sein?** how old might or would she be?, how old is she, I wonder?; **wo mag sie das gehört haben?** where could or might she have heard that?; **was mag das wohl heißen?** what might that mean? **e** (= *wollen*) to want; **sie mag nicht bleiben** she doesn't want to stay **f** (*Aufforderung, indirekte Rede*) **(sagen Sie ihm,) er möchte zu mir kommen** would you tell him to come and see me; **Sie möchten zu Hause anrufen** you should call home; **du möchtest dich brieflich melden** you should write

Mog|ler ['mo:glɐ] M -s, -, **Mog|le|rin** [-ərɪn] F -, -nen cheat

mög|lich ['mø:klɪç] ◊ 36.1, 39.2, 42.3, 43.3, 46.6 ADJ **a** possible; **alles Mögliche** everything you or one can think of; **alles Mögliche tun** to do everything possible, to do everything one can; **er tat sein Möglichstes** he did his utmost, he did all he could; **aus allen ~en Richtungen** from all directions; **er hat allen ~en Blödsinn gemacht** he did all sorts of stupid things; **so viel/bald wie ~** as much/soon as possible; **das ist schon** or **wohl** or **durchaus ~** that's quite possible; **wenn es irgend ~ ist** if (it's) at all possible; **können Sie es ~ machen, dass Sie schon morgen kommen** or **schon morgen zu kommen?** could you manage to come tomorrow?; **es war mir nicht ~ mitzukommen** I couldn't manage to come, it wasn't possible for me to come; **das ist doch nicht ~!** that's impossible!; **nicht ~!** never!, impossible!; **das wäre woanders nicht ~** that couldn't happen anywhere else; **ist denn so was ~?** would you credit it? (*inf*); **im Bereich** or **Rahmen des Möglichen** within the realms of possibility **b** (*attr*: = *eventuell*) Kunden, Interessenten, Nachfolger potential, possible; **alle ~en Fälle** every eventuality; **alles Mögliche bedenken** to consider everything **ADV** = **möglichst**

mög|li|cher|wei|se ['mø:klɪçɐ'vaizə] ADV possibly; **~ kommt er morgen** he may or might (possibly) come tomorrow; **da liegt ~ ein Missverständnis vor** it's possible that there is a misunderstanding, there is possibly a misunderstanding

Mög|lich|keit ✪ 39.2, 42.3, 43.3, 46.1 **F -, -en a** possibility; **es besteht die ~, dass ...** there is a possibility that ..., it is possible that ...; **es besteht die ~ zu kündigen** it would (always) be possible to hand in your notice; **alle ~en in Betracht ziehen** to take all the possibilities into account; **nach ~** if possible; **ist denn das die ~?** (*inf*) **ist es die ~!** (*inf*) it's impossible!, I don't believe it!

b (= *Aussicht*) chance; (= *Gelegenheit*) opportunity, chance; **die ~ haben, etw zu tun** to have the chance/opportunity to do sth *or* of doing sth; **er hatte keine andere ~** he had no other choice *or* alternative; **das Land der unbegrenzten ~en** the land of unlimited opportunity; **ungeahnte ~en eröffnen** to open up undreamed-of opportunities (*Brit*)

c *usu pl* (= *Fähigkeiten*) capabilities; **der Mietpreis übersteigt meine finanziellen ~en** the rent is beyond my means

mög|lichst ['møːklɪçst] ADV **~ genau/schnell/oft** as accurately/quickly/often as possible; **in ~ kurzer Zeit** as quickly as possible

Mo|gul ['moːgʊl, moˈguːl] M **-s, -n** *or* **-e** (*Hist, fig*) mogul

Mo|hair [moˈhɛːɐ] M **-s, -e, Mo|här** [moˈhɛːɐ] M **-s, -e** (*Tex*) mohair

Mo|ham|me|da|ner [mohameˈdaːnɐ] M **-s, -, Mo|ham|me|da|ne|rin** [-ərɪn] F **-, -nen** Mohammedan (*dated*)

mo|ham|me|da|nisch [mohameˈdaːnɪʃ] ADJ Mohammedan (*dated*) ADV **erziehen** as a Mohammedan (*dated*); **aufwachsen** Mohammedan (*dated*)

Mo|hi|ka|ner [mohiˈkaːnɐ] M **-s, -, Mo|hi|ka|ne|rin** [-ərɪn] F **-, -nen** Mohican; **der letzte ~** (*fig*) the very last one

Mohn [moːn] M **-(e)s, -e a** poppy **b** (= *Mohnsamen*) poppy seed

Mohn- *in cpds* poppy; (*Cook*) (poppy-)seed; **Mohn|blu|me** F poppy; **Mohn|bröt|chen** NT poppy, *roll sprinkled with poppy seeds*; **Mohn|ku|chen** M poppy-seed cake

Mohr [moːɐ] M **-en, -en, Moh|rin** [-rɪn] F **-, -nen** (*old*) (blacka)moor (*old*); **Othello, der ~ von Venedig** Othello, the Moor of Venice; **schwarz** *or* **braun gebrannt wie ein ~** (*dated inf*) as brown as a berry; **der ~ hat seine Schuldigkeit getan, der ~ kann gehen** (*prov*) as soon as you've served your purpose they've no further interest in you

Möh|re ['møːrə] F **-, -n** carrot

Moh|ren|kopf M *small chocolate-covered cream cake* (= *Negerkuss*) *chocolate marshmallow with biscuit base*

Mohr|rü|be F carrot

moin [mɔyn] INTERJ (*N Ger, inf*) **~(, ~)!** morning (*inf*); (= *hallo*) hi (*inf*)

Moi|ré [moaˈreː] M OR NT **-s, -s** (*Tex*) moiré

mo|kant [moˈkant] (*geh*) ADJ sardonic, mocking ADV sardonically

Mo|kas|sin [mokaˈsiːn, ˈmɔkasiːn] M **-s, -s** moccasin

Mo|kick ['moːkɪk] NT **-s, -s** moped with a kick-starter

mo|kie|ren [moˈkiːrən] *ptp* **mokiert** VR to sneer (*über +acc* at)

Mok|ka ['mɔka] M **-s, -s** mocha

Mok|ka-: Mok|ka|löf|fel M coffee spoon; **Mok|ka|tas|se** F, **Mok|ka|täss|chen** ▲ NT coffee cup

Mol [moːl] NT **-s, -e** (*Chem*) mole

Mo|lar(zahn) [moˈlaːɐ-] M **-s, -en** molar (tooth)

Molch [mɔlç] M **-(e)s, -e** salamander

Mol|dau ['mɔldau] F **- a** (*Fluss*) Vltava **b** (*Republik*) = **Moldawien**

Mol|da|wi|en [mɔlˈdaːviən] NT **-s** Moldavia

Mo|le ['moːlə] F **-, -n** (*Naut*) mole

Mo|le|kül [moleˈkyːl] NT **-s, -e, Mo|le|kel** [moˈleːkl] (*old*) NT **-s, -** *or* f **-, -n** molecule

mo|le|ku|lar [moleku'laːɐ] ADJ molecular

Mo|le|ku|lar-: Mo|le|ku|lar|bi|o|lo|ge M, **Mo|le|ku|lar|bi|o|lo|gin** F molecular biologist; **Mo|le|ku|lar|bi|o|lo|gie** F molecular biology

molk *pret von* **melken**

Mol|ke ['mɔlkə] F **-, no pl, Mol|ken** ['mɔlkn] M **-s, no pl** (*dial*) whey

Mol|ke|rei [mɔlkəˈrai] F **-, -en** dairy

Mol|ke|rei-: Mol|ke|rei|but|ter F blended butter; **Mol|ke|rei|ge|nos|sen|schaft** F dairy cooperative; **Mol|ke|rei|pro|dukt** NT dairy product

Moll [mɔl] NT **-, -** (*Mus*) minor (key); **in ~ übergehen** to go into the minor; **a-Moll** A minor; **a-Moll-Tonleiter** scale of A minor; **Violinkonzert Nummer 4 a-Moll** violin concerto Number 4 in A minor; **alles in ~ sehen** to see only the gloomy side of things

Mol|le ['mɔlə] F **-, -n** (*dial*) beer; **eine ~ mit Korn** a beer and a (glass of) schnapps

mol|lert ['mɔlɐt] ADJ (*Aus inf*) plump

mol|lig ['mɔlɪç] (*inf*) ADJ **a** cosy (*Brit*), cozy (*US*); (= *warm, behaglich*) snug, cosy (*Brit*), cozy (*US*) **b** (= *rundlich*) plump ADV **~ warm** warm and cosy (*Brit*) *or* cozy (*US*)

Moll-: Moll|ton|art F minor key; **Moll|ton|lei|ter** F minor scale

Mol|lus|ke [mɔˈlʊskə] F **-, -n** (*spec*) mollusc

Mo|loch ['moːlɔx] M **-s, -e** Moloch

Mo|lo|tow|cock|tail ['moːlotɔf-] M Molotov cocktail

Mo|luk|ken [moˈlʊkn] PL (*Geog*) Moluccas *pl*, Spice Islands *pl*

Mo|lyb|dän [mɔlypˈdɛːn] NT **-s, no pl** (*abbr* **Mo**) molybdenum

Mo|ment¹ [moˈmɛnt] M **-(e)s, -e** moment; **einen ~ lang** for a moment; **jeden ~** any time *or* minute *or* moment; **einen ~, bitte** one minute *or* moment please; **kleinen ~!** just a tick (*Brit inf*) *or* a second!; **~ mal!** just a minute!; **im ~** at the moment; **im letzten/richtigen** *etc* **~** at the last/right *etc* moment; **im ersten ~** for a moment

Mo|ment² NT **-(e)s, -e a** (= *Bestandteil*) element **b** (= *Umstand*) fact; (= *Faktor*) factor **c** (*Phys*) moment; (= *Kraftwirkung*) momentum

mo|men|tan [momɛnˈtaːn] ADJ **a** (= *vorübergehend*) momentary **b** (= *augenblicklich*) present *attr* ADV **a** (= *vorübergehend*) for a moment, momentarily **b** (= *augenblicklich*) at the moment, at present

Mo|ment|auf|nah|me F (*Phot*) photo(graph)

Mo|na|co ['moːnako, moˈnako] NT **-s** Monaco

Mo|na|de [moˈnaːdə] F **-, -n** (*Philos*) monad

Mo|na|den|leh|re F, **Mo|na|do|lo|gie** [monadoloˈgiː] F **-, no pl** (*Philos*) monadology

Mo|narch [moˈnarç] M **-en, -en, Mo|nar|chin** [-ˈnarçɪn] F **-, -nen** monarch

Mo|nar|chie [monarˈçiː] F **-, -n** [-ˈçiːən] monarchy

mo|nar|chisch [moˈnarçɪʃ] ADJ monarchic(al)

Mo|nar|chist [monarˈçɪst] M **-en, -en, Mo|nar|chis|tin** [-ˈçɪstɪn] F **-, -nen** monarchist

mo|nar|chis|tisch [monarˈçɪstɪʃ] ADJ pro-monarchist ADV **eine ~ orientierte Partei** a pro-monarchist party

Mo|nat ['moːnat] M **-(e)s, -e** month; **der ~ Mai** the month of May; **im ~ Mai** in the month of May; **sie ist im sechsten ~ (schwanger)** she's over five months pregnant *or* gone (*inf*), she's in the sixth month; **was verdient er im ~?** how much does he earn a month?; **am 12. dieses ~s** *or* **des laufenden ~s** on the 12th (of this month); **auf ~e hinaus** months ahead; **jdn zu drei ~en (Haft) verurteilen** to sentence sb to

three months' imprisonment, to send sb down for three months (*inf*); **von ~ zu ~** month by month

mo|na|te|lang ADJ *attr* Verhandlungen, Kämpfe which go on for months; **seine ~e Abwesenheit** his months of absence; **nach ~em Warten** after waiting for months, after months of waiting; **mit ~er Verspätung** months late ADV for months

-mo|na|tig [moːnatɪç] ADJ *suf* -month; **ein dreimonatiger Urlaub** a three-month holiday (*esp Brit*) *or* vacation (*US*)

mo|nat|lich ['moːnatlɪç] ADJ monthly ADV every month, monthly; **er zahlt ~ 500 Euro** he pays 500 euros a month

-mo|nat|lich ADJ *suf* **zwei-/dreimonatlich** every two/three months; **allmonatlich** every month

Mo|nats-: Mo|nats|an|fang M beginning of the month; **Mo|nats|bei|trag** M monthly contribution; (*bei Abonnement*) monthly subscription; **Mo|nats|bin|de** F sanitary towel (*Brit*), sanitary napkin (*US*); **Mo|nats|blu|tung** F menstrual period; **Mo|nats|ein|kom|men** NT monthly income; **Mo|nats|en|de** NT end of the month; **Mo|nats|ers|te(r)** M *decl as adj* first (day) of the month; **Mo|nats|frist** F *innerhalb* *or* *binnen* **~** within a month; **Mo|nats|ge|halt** NT monthly salary; **ein ~** one month's salary; **Mo|nats|hälf|te** F half of the month; **Mo|nats|heft** NT monthly (journal *or* periodical); **Mo|nats|kar|te** F monthly season ticket; **Mo|nats|lohn** M monthly wage; **~ bekommen** to be paid monthly; **Mo|nats|mie|te** F monthly rent; **zwei ~n als Kaution** two months' rent in advance (as a deposit); **Mo|nats|mit|te** F middle of the month; **Mo|nats|mit|tel** NT monthly average; **im ~** on average for a month; **Mo|nats|na|me** M name of the/a month; **Mo|nats|ra|te** F monthly instalment (*Brit*) *or* installment (*US*); **Mo|nats|schrift** F monthly (journal *or* periodical); **Mo|nats|wech|sel** M monthly allowance

mo|nat(s)|wei|se ADV every month, monthly ADJ monthly

Mönch [mœnç] M **-(e)s, -e** monk; (= *Bettelmönch auch*) friar; **wie ein ~ leben** to live like a monk

mön|chisch ['mœnçɪʃ] ADJ Geduld, Fleiß monastic; **ein ~es Leben führen** (*fig*) to live like a monk ADV **~ enthaltsam/zurückgezogen leben** to live like a monk/hermit

Mönchs-: Mönchs|ka|pu|ze F cowl; **Mönchs|klos|ter** NT monastery; (*von Bettelmönchen*) friary; **Mönchs|kut|te** F → **Mönch** monk's/friar's habit; **Mönchs|le|ben** NT monastic life; **Mönchs|or|den** M monastic order

Mönchs|tum ['mœnçstuːm] NT **-s, no pl** monasticism

Mönchs-: Mönchs|we|sen NT monasticism; **Mönchs|zel|le** F monastic cell

Mönch|tum ['mœnçtuːm] NT **-s, no pl** monasticism

Mond [moːnt] M **-(e)s, -e** [-də] **a** moon; **den ~ anbellen** (*fig*) to bay at the moon; **auf** *or* **hinter dem ~ leben** (*inf*) to be *or* live behind the times; **du lebst wohl auf dem ~!** (*inf*) where have you been?; **drei Meilen hinter dem ~** (*inf*) in the Stone Age (*hum*); **in den ~ gucken** (*inf*) to go empty-handed; **deine Armbanduhr geht nach dem ~** (*inf*) your watch is way out (*inf*); **ich hätte ihn auf den ~ schießen können** (*inf*) I could have killed him (*inf*); **das Geld können wir in den ~ schreiben** (*inf*) we can write the money off **b** (*old*: = *Monat*) moon (*old*), month

mon|dän [mɔnˈdɛːn] ADJ chic; **dort geht es mir zu ~ zu** it's too chic for me there

Mond-: Mond|auf|gang M moonrise; **Mond|au|to** NT moon buggy *or* rover; **Mond|bahn** F moon's orbit, orbit of the moon; (*Space*) lunar orbit; **mond|be|schie|nen** [-bəʃiːnən] ADJ (*geh*) bathed in moonlight, moonlit

Mon|den|schein M (*geh*), **Mon|des|glanz** M (*poet*) moonlight

Mond-: Mond|fäh|re F (*Space*) lunar module; **Mond|fins|ter|nis** F eclipse of the moon, lunar eclipse; **Mond|ge|bir|ge** NT mountains *pl* of the moon; **Mond|ge|sicht** NT moonface; (*gemalt*) *simple representation of a face*; **Mond|ge|stein** NT moon rocks *pl*; **Mond|göt|tin** F moon goddess; **mond|hell** ADJ moonlit; **~ erleuchtet** lit by the moon, moonlit; **Mond|jahr** NT lunar year; **Mond|kalb** NT (*dated inf*: = *Dummkopf*) mooncalf; **Mond|kra|ter** M lunar crater; **Mond|lan|de|fäh|re** F (*Space*) lunar module; **Mond|land|schaft** F lunar landscape; **Mond|lan|dung** F lunar or moon landing; **Mond|licht** NT moonlight; **mond|los** ADJ (*geh*) moonless; **Mond|nacht** F (*geh*) moonlit night; **Mond|ober|flä|che** F surface of the moon; **Mond|pha|sen** PL phases of the moon; **Mond|preis** M (*inf*) astronomical price (*inf*); **Mond|schein** M moonlight; **Mond|si|chel** F crescent moon; **Mond|son|de** F (*Space*) lunar probe; **Mond|stein** M moonstone; **mond|süch|tig** ADJ **~ sein** to sleepwalk; **Mond|süch|tig|keit** F sleepwalking, somnambulism (*form*); **Mond|um|lauf|bahn** F (*Space*) lunar orbit; **Mond|un|ter|gang** F moonset

Mo|ne|gas|se [mone'gasə] M **-s, -n**, **Mo|ne|gas|sin** F [-'gasɪn] F **-, -nen** Monegasque

mo|ne|gas|sisch [mone'gasɪʃ] ADJ Monegasque

mo|ne|tär [mone'tɛːɐ] ADJ monetary ADV **ihre Politik ist ~ geprägt** her policy is monetary; **ei|ne ~ orientierte Denkweise** monetary thinking

Mo|ne|ta|ris|mus [moneta'rɪsmʊs] M **-**, *no pl* (*Econ*) monetarism

Mo|ne|ta|rist [moneta'rɪst] M **-en, -en**, **Mo|ne|ta|ris|tin** F [-'rɪstɪn] F **-, -nen** (*Econ*) monetarist

Mo|ne|ten [mo'neːtn] PL (*inf*) bread *sing* (*inf*), dough *sing* (*inf*); **~ machen** to make some bread (*inf*) or dough (*inf*)

Mon|go|le [mɔŋ'goːlə] M **-n, -n**, **Mon|go|lin** F [-'goːlɪn] F **-, -nen** Mongolian, Mongol

Mon|go|lei [mɔŋgo'laɪ] F **- die ~** Mongolia; **die Innere/Äußere ~** Inner/Outer Mongolia

Mon|go|len-: Mon|go|len|fal|te F epicanthus; **Mon|go|len|fleck** M Mongolian spot

mon|go|lid [mɔŋgo'liːt] ADJ Mongoloid

Mon|go|li|de(r) [mɔŋgo'liːdə] MF *decl as adj* Mongoloid

Mon|go|lin F **-, -nen** Mongolian, Mongol

mon|go|lisch [mɔŋ'goːlɪʃ] ADJ Mongolian

Mon|go|lisch(e) NT Mongolian → *auch* **Deutsch(e)**

Mon|go|lis|mus [mɔŋgo'lɪsmʊs] M **-**, *no pl* (*Med*) mongolism

mon|go|lo|id [mɔŋgolo'iːt] ADJ Mongol; (*Med*) mongoloid

Mon|go|lo|i|de(r) [mɔŋgolo'iːdə] MF *decl as adj* Mongol; (*Med*) mongol

mo|nie|ren [mo'niːrən] *ptp* **moniert** VT to complain about; **sie hat moniert, dass ...** she complained that ... VI to complain

Mo|nis|mus [mo'nɪsmʊs] M **-**, *no pl* (*Philos*) monism

Mo|ni|tor ['moːnitoːɐ] M **-s, -e** or **Monitoren** [-'toːrən] (*TV, Phys*) monitor

Mo|no-, mo|no- ['moːno, 'mɔno] *in cpds* mono-; **mo|no|chrom** [mono'kroːm] ADJ monochrome; **mo|no|color** [mono'loːɐ] ADJ (*Aus*) **eine ~e Regierung** a single-party government; **mo|no|gam** [mono'gaːm] ADJ monogamous ADV **leben** monogamously; **Mo|no|ga|mie** [monoga'miː] F **-**, *no pl* monogamy; **mo|no|gra|fie** ▲ [monogra'fiː] F **-, -n** [-'fiːən] monograph; **Mo|no|gramm** [mono'gram] NT *pl* **-gramme** monogram; **mo|no|kau|sal** [monokau'zaːl] ADJ *Erklärung* monocausal ADV **ein Problem ~ sehen** to see only one aspect of a

problem; **ein Problem ~ erklären** to attribute a problem to a single cause

Mo|no|kel [mo'nɔkl] NT **-s, -** monocle

mo|no|klo|nal [monoklo'naːl] ADJ **~e Antikörper** monoclonal antibodies

Mo|no|kul|tur F (*Agr*) monoculture

Mo|no|lith [mono'liːt] M **-en, -e(n)** monolith

mo|no|li|thisch [mono'liːtɪʃ] (*lit, fig*) ADJ monolithic ADV monolithically

Mo|no|log [mono'loːk] M **-(e)s, -e** [-gə] (*Liter, fig*) monologue; (= *Selbstgespräch*) soliloquy; **ei|nen ~ sprechen** to hold a monologue/give a soliloquy; **einen ~ halten** (*fig*) to hold a monologue, to talk on and on

mo|no|lo|gisch [mono'loːgɪʃ] ADJ monologic(al) ADV **etw ~ erzählen** to give a monologue about sth

mo|no|lo|gi|sie|ren [monologi'ziːrən] *ptp* **monologisiert** VI to hold a monologue; (= *ein Selbstgespräch führen*) to soliloquize

mo|no|man [mono'maːn] ADJ (*geh*) monomaniacal

Mo|no|ma|ne [mono'maːnə] M **-n, -n**, **Mo|no|ma|nin** [-'maːnɪn] F **-, -nen** (*geh*) monomaniac

Mo|no|ma|nie [monoma'niː] F **-, -n** [-'niːən] (*geh*) monomania; (*fig*) obsession

mo|no|ma|nisch ADJ (*geh*) monomaniacal

Mo|noph|thong [mono'ftɔŋ] M **-s, -e** (*Ling*) monophthong

Mo|no|pol [mono'poːl] NT **-s, -e** monopoly (*auf* +*acc, für* on)

Mo|no|pol- *in cpds* monopoly; **Mo|no|pol|bil|dung** F monopolization *no pl*

mo|no|po|li|sie|ren [monopoli'ziːrən] *ptp* **monopolisiert** VT (*lit, fig*) to monopolize

Mo|no|po|li|sie|rung F **-, -en** monopolization

Mo|no|po|list [monopo'lɪst] M **-en, -en**, **Mo|no|po|lis|tin** [-'lɪstɪn] F **-, -nen** monopolist

Mo|no|pol-: Mo|no|pol|ka|pi|tal NT (*Kapital*) monopoly capital; (*Kapitalisten*) monopoly capitalism; **Mo|no|pol|ka|pi|ta|lis|mus** M monopoly capitalism; **Mo|no|pol|ka|pi|ta|list(in)** M(F) monopolist; **mo|no|pol|ka|pi|ta|lis|tisch** ADJ monopolistic; **Mo|no|pol|kom|mis|si|on** F monopolies commission; **Mo|no|pol|stel|lung** F monopoly

Mo|no|po|ly® [mo'noːpoli] NT **-**, *no pl* Monopoly®

Mo|no|se|mie [monoze'miː] F **-**, *no pl* (*Ling*) monosemy

Mo|no|the|is|mus [monote'ɪsmʊs] M monotheism

mo|no|ton [mono'toːn] ADJ monotonous ADV monotonously

Mo|no|to|nie [monoto'niː] F **-, -n** [-'niːən] monotony

Mo|no|xid ['moːnɔksiːt, 'mɔnɔksiːt, mono'ksiːt] NT (*spec*), **Mo|no|xyd** ['moːnɔksyːt, 'mɔnɔksyːt, mono'ksyːt] NT monoxide

Mons|ter ['mɔnstɐ] NT **-s, -** (*inf*) = **Monstrum**

Mons|ter- *in cpds* (*usu pej*) mammoth, monster; **Mons|ter|film** M mammoth (film) production

Monst|ranz [mɔn'strants] F **-, -en** (*Eccl*) monstrance

Monst|ren *pl von* **Monstrum**

monst|rös [mɔn'strøːs] ADJ monstrous; (= *riesig groß*) monster ADV **sich benehmen** monstrously; **~ aussehen** to look monstrous; **~ aussehende Kreaturen** monstrous-looking creatures

Monst|ro|si|tät [mɔnstrozi'tɛːt] F **-, -en** monstrosity; (= *riesige Größe*) monstrous size; (= *Ungeheuer*) monster

Monst|rum ['mɔnstrʊm] NT **-s, Monstren** or (*geh*) **Monstra** [-trən, -tra] (= *Ungeheuer*) monster; (*fig*: = *Missbildung*) monstrosity; (*inf*: = *schweres Möbel*) hulking great piece of furniture (*inf*)

Mon|sun [mɔn'zuːn] M **-s, -e** monsoon

Mon|sun|re|gen M monsoon rain

Mon|tag ['moːntaːk] M Monday → **blau** c, **Dienstag**

Mon|ta|ge [mɔn'taːʒə] F **-, -n** a (*Tech*) (= *Aufstellung*) installation; (*von Gerüst*) erection; (= *Zusammenbau*) assembly; (*Typ*) stripping; **auf ~** (*dat*) **sein** to be away on a job b (*Art, Liter*) montage; (*Film*) editing

Mon|ta|ge-: Mon|ta|ge|band [-bant] NT *pl* **-bänder** assembly line; **Mon|ta|ge|hal|le** F assembly shop; **Mon|ta|ge|werk** NT assembly plant

mon|tags ['moːntaːks] ADV on Mondays → *auch* **dienstags**

Mon|tags|au|to NT (*hum*) problem car, Friday-afternoon car (*Brit hum*)

Mon|tan- [mɔn'taːn-]: **Mon|tan|in|dust|rie** F coal and steel industry; **Mon|tan|uni|on** F European Coal and Steel Community

Mon|te Car|lo ['mɔntə 'karlo] NT **- -s** Monte Carlo

Mon|teur [mɔn'tøːɐ] M **-s, -e**, **Mon|teu|rin** [-'tøːrɪn] F **-, -nen** (*Tech*) fitter; (*Aut*) mechanic; (= *Heizungsmonteur, Fernmeldemonteur, Elektromonteur*) engineer; (*Elec*) electrician

Mon|teur|an|zug [-'tøːɐ-] M boiler suit (*Brit*), overalls *pl*

mon|tie|ren [mɔn'tiːrən] *ptp* **montiert** VT a (*Tech*) to install; (= *zusammenbauen*) to assemble; (= *befestigen*) *Bauteil* to fit (*auf* +*acc, an* +*acc* to); *Dachantenne* to put up; (= *aufstellen*) *Gerüst* to erect; **etw an die Wand ~** to fix sth to the wall b (*Art, Film, Liter*) *Einzelteile* to create a montage from; **aus etw montiert sein** to be a montage of sth

Mon|tur [mɔn'tuːɐ] F **-, -en** (*inf*) (*hum*: = *Arbeitskleidung*) gear (*inf*), rig-out (*Brit inf*); (*Aus*: = *Uniform*) uniform

Mo|nu|ment [monu'mɛnt] NT **-(e)s, -e** monument

mo|nu|men|tal [monumɛn'taːl] ADJ *Gebäude, Gemälde, Roman* monumental ADV monumentally; **~ anmutende Architektur** monumental architecture

Mo|nu|men|tal- [monumɛn'taːl-] *in cpds* monumental; **Mo|nu|men|tal|bau** M monumental building; **Mo|nu|men|tal|film** M (*screen*) epic, (*Hollywood*) spectacular; **Mo|nu|men|tal|werk** NT monumental work; (*Literatur auch*) epic work

Moon|boots ['muːnbuːts] PL moon boots *pl*

Moor [moːɐ] NT **-(e)s, -e** bog; (= *Hochmoor*) moor

Moor-: Moor|bad NT mud bath; **Moor|bo|den** M marshy soil; **Moor|huhn** NT grouse; **Moor|huhn|jagd** F a (= *Jagd*) grouse shoot, grouse hunt (*US*); (= *das Jagen*) grouse shooting b (= *Computerspiel*) moorhen-chicken chase

moo|rig ['moːrɪç] ADJ boggy

Moor-: Moor|ko|lo|nie F fen community; **Moor|kul|tur** F cultivation of peat bogs; **Moor|land** NT marshland; (= *Hochmoorland*) moorland; **Moor|pa|ckung** F mudpack; **Moor|sied|lung** F fen community

Moos [moːs] NT **-es, -e** moss; **von ~ überzogen** overgrown with moss, moss-grown; **~ ansetzen** to become covered with moss, to become moss-grown; (*fig*) to become hoary with age

moos-: moos|be|deckt ADJ moss-covered; **moos|grün** ADJ moss-green

moo|sig ['moːzɪç] ADJ mossy

Moos|ro|se F , **Moos|rös|chen** [-røːsçən] NT moss rose

Mop △ [mɔp] M **-s, -s** → **Mopp**

Möp △ [mœp] M **-s, -s** or f **-, -s** → **Möpp**

Mo|ped ['moːpɛt, 'moːpeːt] NT **-s, -s** moped

Mo|ped|fah|rer(in) M(F) moped rider

Mopp ▲ [mɔp] M **-s, -s** mop

Möpp ▲ [mœp] M **-s, -s** or f **-, -s ein fieser** or **eine fiese ~** (dial inf) a nasty piece of work (inf)

Mop|pel ['mɔpl] M **-s, -** (inf) tubby (inf)

mop|pen ['mɔpn] VT to mop

Mops [mɔps] M **-es, ⸚e** ['mœpsə] **a** (Hund) pug (dog) **b** (= Dickwanst) roly-poly (inf), dumpling (inf) **c Möpse** PL (sl: = Busen) tits pl (sl)

möp|seln ['mœpsln] VI (dial) to be smelly

mop|sen ['mɔpsn] VT (dated inf) to nick (Brit inf), to pinch (inf)

Mops-: mops|fi|del ADJ (dated inf) chirpy (inf); **Mops|ge|sicht** NT (inf) pug-face, puggy face (inf)

mop|sig ['mɔpsɪç] ADJ (inf) **a** Kerl, Gesicht podgy (inf) **b** (= frech) **sich ~ machen, ~ werden** to get cheeky (Brit) or fresh (US) **c** (= langweilig) boring

Mo|ral [mo'ra:l] F **-, no pl a** (= Sittlichkeit) morals pl; (= gesellschaftliche Norm) morality, morals pl; **eine hohe/keine ~ haben** to have high moral standards/no morals; **private ~** personal morals; **die ~ sinkt/steigt** moral standards are declining/rising; **die bürgerliche/sozialistische ~** bourgeois/socialist morality; **gegen die (geltende) ~ verstoßen** to violate the (accepted) moral code; **eine doppelte ~** double standards pl, a double standard; **~ predigen** to moralize (jdm to sb) **b** (= Lehre, Nutzanwendung) moral; **und die ~ von der Geschicht': ...** and the moral of this story is ... **c** (= Ethik) ethics pl, moral code; **nach christlicher ~** according to Christian ethics, according to the Christian (moral) code **d** (= Disziplin: von Volk, Soldaten) morale; **die ~ sinkt** morale is falling, morale is getting lower

Mo|ral- in cpds moral; **Mo|ral|apos|tel** M (pej) upholder of moral standards

Mo|ra|lin [mora'li:n] NT **-s, no pl** (hum) priggishness

mo|ra|lin|sau|er (hum) ADJ priggish ADV priggishly; **~ reden** to talk like a prig; **~ klingen** to sound priggish

mo|ra|lisch [mo'ra:lɪʃ] ADJ moral; **das war eine ~e Ohrfeige für die Regierung** that was one in the eye (Brit) or that was a black eye (US) for the government (inf); **einen or seinen Moralischen haben** (inf) to have (a fit of) the blues (inf), to be down in the dumps (inf) ADV bedenklich, verpflichtet morally; **ein ~ hoch stehender Mensch** a person of high moral standing

mo|ra|li|sie|ren [morali'zi:rən] ptp **moralisiert** VI to moralize

Mo|ra|lis|mus [mora'lɪsmʊs] M **-, no pl** (geh) morality; **einem unbestechlichen ~ leben** to live a life of incorruptible morality

Mo|ra|list [mora'lɪst] M **-en, -en, Mo|ra|lis|tin** [-'lɪstɪn] F **-, -nen** moralist

mo|ra|lis|tisch [mora'lɪstɪʃ] ADJ moralistic

Mo|ra|li|tät [morali'tɛːt] F **-, -en** morality; (Theat) morality play

Mo|ral-: Mo|ral|ko|dex M moral code; **Mo|ral|phi|lo|so|phie** F moral philosophy; **Mo|ral|pre|di|ger(in)** M(F) moralizer; **Mo|ral|pre|digt** F homily, sermon; **~en halten** to moralize; **jdm eine ~ halten** to give sb a homily or sermon; **Mo|ral|theo|lo|gie** F moral theology; **Mo|ral|vor|stel|lung** F moral or ethical standards pl

Mo|räne [mo'rɛːnə] F **-, -n** (Geol) moraine

Mo|rast [mo'rast] M **-(e)s, -e** or **Moräste** [mo'rɛstə] (lit, fig) mire, quagmire; (= Sumpf auch) morass

mo|ras|tig [mo'rastɪç] ADJ marshy; (= schlammig) muddy

Mo|ra|to|ri|um [mora'to:riʊm] NT **-s, Moratorien** [-riən] moratorium

mor|bid [mɔr'bi:t] ADJ (Med) morbid; (fig geh) degenerate

Mor|bi|di|tät [mɔrbidi'tɛːt] F **-, no pl** (Med) morbidity; (fig geh) degeneracy

Mor|bus-Down-Syn|drom ['mɔrbʊs'daun-] NT Down's syndrome

Mor|chel ['mɔrçl] F **-, -n** (Bot) morel

Mord [mɔrt] M **-(e)s, -e** [-də] murder, homicide (US) (an +dat of); (an Politiker etc) assassination (an +dat of); **wegen ~es** for murder or homicide (US); **„Mord an altem Mann"** "old man slain or murdered"; **politischer ~** political killing; **auf ~ sinnen** (old, liter) to devise murderous schemes; **das ist ja ~!** (inf) it's (sheer) murder! (inf); **dann gibt es ~ und Totschlag** (inf) all hell will be let loose (Brit inf) or will break out (inf), there'll be hell to pay (inf); **von ~ und Totschlag handeln** to be full of violence

Mord-: Mord|an|kla|ge F murder charge, charge of homicide (US); **~ erheben** to file a murder charge, to file a charge of murder (US); **unter ~ stehen** to be on a murder charge, to be on a charge of homicide (US); **Mord|an|schlag** M assassination (auf +acc of); (erfolglos) assassination attempt (auf +acc on), attempted assassination (auf +acc of); **einen ~ verüben** to carry out an assassination attempt; **einen ~ auf jdn verüben** to try to assassinate sb; (erfolgreich) to assassinate sb; **Mord|bren|ner(in)** M(F) (old, liter) arsonist, incendiary; **Mord|bu|be** M (obs) murderer; **Mord|dro|hung** F threat on one's life, murder or death threat

mor|den ['mɔrdn] VTI (liter) to murder, to kill, to slay (liter); **das sinnlose Morden** senseless killing

Mör|der ['mœrdɐ] M **-s, -, Mör|de|rin** [-ərɪn] F **-, -nen** murderer (auch Jur), killer; (Frau auch) murderess; (= Attentäter) assassin

Mör|der-: Mör|der|ban|de F gang or bunch of murderers or killers; **Mör|der|gru|be** F **aus seinem Herzen keine ~ machen** to speak frankly; **Mör|der|hand** F (old, liter) **durch ~ fallen** or **sterben** to die or perish (old) at the hands of a murderer

Mör|de|rin F → **Mörder**

mör|de|risch ['mœrdərɪʃ] ADJ (lit) Anschlag murderous; (fig) (= schrecklich) dreadful, terrible; Tempo breakneck attr; Preise iniquitous; Konkurrenzkampf cutthroat attr; (inf) (= entsetzlich) dreadfully, terribly; stinken like hell (inf); wehtun like crazy (inf); **~ fluchen** to curse like blazes (inf); **~ schreien** to scream blue murder (Brit) or bloody murder (inf)

Mord-: Mord|fall M murder or homicide (US) (case); **der ~ Dr. Praun** the Dr Praun murder or homicide (US) (case); **Mord|gier** F (geh) desire to kill; **mord|gie|rig** ADJ (geh) bloodthirsty; **Mord|in|stru|ment** NT murder weapon

mor|dio ['mɔrdio] INTERJ (old) → **zetermordio, Zeter**

Mord-: Mord|kom|mis|si|on F murder squad, homicide squad or division (US); **Mord|lust** F desire to kill; **Mord|pro|zess** ▲ M murder trial

Mords- ['mɔrts] in cpds (inf) incredible, terrible, awful; (= toll, prima) hell of a (inf); **Mords|ding** NT (inf) whopper (inf); **Mords|du|sel** M (inf) tremendous stroke of luck; **einen ~ haben** to be dead (Brit inf) or completely lucky; **Mords|gau|di** F (S Ger inf) whale of a time (inf); **Mords|geld** NT (inf) fantastic amount of money; **Mords|glück** NT (inf) = **Mordsdusel**; **Mords|hit|ze** F (inf) scorching heat; **es ist eine ~ heute!** it's a real scorcher today (inf); **Mords|hun|ger** M (inf) **einen ~ haben** to be famished or ravenous, to be dying of hunger; **Mords|kerl** M (inf) **a** (= verwegener Mensch) hell of a guy (inf) **b** (= starker Mann) enormous fellow or guy (inf); **Mords|krach** M (inf) hell of a din (inf), fearful or terrible din; (= Streit) hell of a row (inf); **Mords|lärm** M (inf) hell of a noise (inf), fearful or terrible noise; **mords|-**

mä|ßig (inf) ADJ incredible; **ich habe einen ~en Hunger** I could eat a horse (inf) ADV (= sehr) incredibly; (= furchtbar) dreadfully, terribly; **Mords|spaß** M (inf) **einen ~ haben** to have a great time; **etw macht ~** sth is great fun; **Mords|wut** F (inf) terrible temper or rage; **eine ~ im Bauch haben** to be in a hell of a (inf) or in a terrible temper or rage

Mord-: Mord|tat F (liter) murderous deed; **Mord|ver|dacht** M suspicion of murder; **unter ~** (dat) **stehen** to be suspected of murder; **Mord|waf|fe** F murder weapon

Mo|rel|le [mo'rɛlə] F **-, -n** (Bot) morello cherry

Mo|res [mo're:s] PL **jdn ~ lehren** (dated inf) to teach sb some manners

mor|gen ['mɔrgn] ADV tomorrow; **~ früh/Mittag/Abend** tomorrow morning/lunchtime/evening; **~ in acht Tagen** tomorrow week, a week (from) tomorrow; **~ um diese** or **dieselbe Zeit** this time tomorrow; **bis ~/~ früh!** see you tomorrow/in the morning; **Kartoffeln gibt es erst wieder ~** we/they etc won't have any potatoes till tomorrow; **hast du ~ Zeit?** are you free tomorrow?; **~, ~, nur nicht heute, sagen alle faulen Leute** (Prov) tomorrow never comes (Prov); **~ ist auch (noch) ein Tag!** (Prov) tomorrow is another day (prov); **die Technik von ~** the technology of tomorrow → **heute** a, **Morgen¹** a

Mor|gen¹ ['mɔrgn] M **-s, - a** (= Tagesanfang) morning; **am ~, des ~s** (geh) in the morning; **gegen ~** toward(s) (the) morning; **gestern ~** yesterday morning; **heute ~** this morning; **bis in den ~ (hinein)** into the wee small hours (Brit), into the early hours; **am nächsten** or **den nächsten ~** the next morning; **früh/spät am ~** early/late in the morning; **eines ~s** one morning; **den ganzen ~ (über)** the whole morning; **es wird ~** day is breaking; **der ~ dämmert** or **bricht an** (liter) **der ~ graut** or **zieht herauf** (liter) dawn is breaking; **guten ~!** good morning; **~!** (inf) morning, hello, hi (inf); **(jdm) guten ~ sagen** to say good morning (to sb); (= morgens kurz besuchen) to say hello (to sb); **schön frisch wie der junge ~** (liter) fresh as a daisy **b** no pl (old, liter: = Osten) East **c** (liter: = Zukunft) dawn; **der ~ einer neuen Zeit bricht an** a new age is dawning

Mor|gen² M **-s, -** (Measure) ≈ acre; **drei ~ Land** ≈ three acres of land

Mor|gen- in cpds morning; **Mor|gen|aus|gabe** F morning edition; **Mor|gen|däm|me|rung** F dawn, daybreak; **in der ~** at first light, at the first light of dawn

mor|gend|lich ['mɔrgntlɪç] ADJ morning attr; (= frühmorgendlich) early morning attr; **die ~e Stille** the quiet of the early morning ADV **es war ~ kühl** or **frisch** it was cool as it often is in the morning; **~ frisch aussehen** to look as fresh as a daisy

Mor|gen-: Mor|gen|dunst M early morning mist; **Mor|gen|es|sen** NT (Sw: = Frühstück) breakfast; **Mor|gen|frü|he** F early morning; **sie brachen in aller ~ auf** they left at the break of dawn; **Mor|gen|ga|be** F (Hist) gift given to a bride by her husband after the wedding night; **Mor|gen|grau|en** [-grauən] NT **-s, -** dawn, daybreak; **im** or **beim ~** in the first light of dawn; **Mor|gen|gym|nas|tik** F morning exercises pl; **~ machen** to do one's morning exercises; **Mor|gen|land** NT (old, liter) Orient, East; **die Weisen aus dem ~** the Wise Men from the East; **Mor|gen|län|der** [-lɛndɐ] M **-s, -, Mor|gen|län|de|rin** [-ərɪn] F **-, -nen** (old, iro) Oriental; **mor|gen|län|disch** [-lɛndɪʃ] ADJ (old, iro) Oriental, Eastern; **Mor|gen|lat|te** F (sl) early-morning hard-on (sl); **Mor|gen|licht** NT early morning light; **Mor|gen|luft** F early morning air; **~ wittern** (fig inf) to see one's chance; **Mor|gen|man|tel** M dressing gown; (für Damen auch) housecoat; **Mor|gen|muf|fel** M (inf) **sie ist ein schrecklicher ~** she's terribly grumpy in the mornings (inf); **Mor|gen|ne|bel** M early morning mist;

Mor|gen|post F morning post (*Brit*) or mail; **Mor|gen|rock** M housecoat; **Mor|gen|rot** NT **-s**, *no pl*, **Mor|gen|röte** F **-**, **-n** sunrise; (*fig*) dawn(ing); **~ deutet auf schlechtes Wetter hin** red sky in the morning, shepherd's warning (*prov*)

mor|gens ['mɔrgns] ADV in the morning; **(um) drei Uhr ~**, **~ (um) drei Uhr** at three o'clock in the morning, at three a.m.; **~ und abends** morning and evening; (*fig: = dauernd*) morning, noon and night; **von ~ bis mittags** in the morning; **von ~ bis abends** from morning to night; **nur ~** mornings only; **Freitag ~** on Friday morning

Mor|gen-: Mor|gen|son|ne F morning sun; **~ haben** to get or catch the morning sun; **Mor|gen|stern** M morning star; (*Schlagwaffe auch*) flail; **Mor|gen|stun|de** F morning hour; **zu früher ~** early in the morning; **bis in die frühen ~n** into the early hours, into the wee small hours (*Brit*); **Morgenstund(e) hat Gold im Mund(e)** (*Prov*) the early bird catches the worm (*Prov*); **Mor|gen|toi|let|te** F , *no pl* (*geh*) morning ablutions *pl*; **Mor|gen|zug** M early (morning) train

mor|gig ['mɔrgɪç] ADJ *attr* tomorrow's; **die ~e Veranstaltung/Zeitung** tomorrow's event/paper; **der ~e Tag** tomorrow; **sein ~er Besuch** his visit tomorrow

mo|ri|bund [mori'bʊnt] ADJ (*Med, fig*) moribund

Mo|ri|tat ['mo:rita:t] F **-**, **-en** a (= *Vortrag*) street ballad b (= *Geschehen*) murderous deed

Mor|mo|ne [mɔr'mo:nə] M **-n**, **-n**, **Mor|mo|nin** [-'mo:nɪn] F **-**, **-nen** Mormon

mor|mo|nisch [mɔr'mo:nɪʃ] ADJ Mormon ADV erziehen as a Mormon; aufwachsen Mormon

Mor|phem [mɔr'fe:m] NT **-s**, **-e** morpheme

Mor|pheus ['mɔrfɔys] M **-'** Morpheus; **in ~' Armen ruhen** (*liter*) to be in the arms of Morpheus (*liter*)

Mor|phin [mɔr'fi:n] NT **-s**, *no pl* (*Chem*) morphine, morphia

Mor|phi|nis|mus [mɔrfi'nɪsmʊs] M **-**, *no pl* morphine addiction

Mor|phi|nist [mɔrfi'nɪst] M **-en**, **-en**, **Mor|phi|nis|tin** [-'nɪstɪn] F **-**, **-nen** morphine addict

Mor|phi|um ['mɔrfiʊm] NT **-s**, *no pl* morphine, morphia

mor|phi|um|süch|tig ADJ addicted to morphine

Mor|pho|lo|gie [mɔrfolo'gi:] F **-**, *no pl* morphology

mor|pho|lo|gisch [mɔrfo'lo:gɪʃ] ADJ morphological

morsch [mɔrʃ] ADJ (*lit, fig*) rotten; *Knochen* brittle; *Gebäude* ramshackle

Morse- ['mɔrzə-]: **Mor|se|al|pha|bet** NT Morse (code); **im ~** in Morse (code); **Mor|se|ap|pa|rat** M Morse telegraph

mor|sen ['mɔrzn] VI to send a message in Morse (code) VT to send in Morse (code)

Mör|ser ['mœrzə] M **-s**, **-** mortar (*auch Mil*); **etw im ~ zerstoßen** to crush sth with a pestle and mortar

Mor|se|zei|chen ['mɔrzə-] NT Morse signal

Mor|ta|del|la [mɔrta'dɛla] F **-**, *no pl* mortadella, baloney (*US*)

Mor|ta|li|tät [mɔrtali'tɛ:t] F **-**, *no pl* mortality rate

Mör|tel ['mœrtl] M **-s**, **-** (*zum Mauern*) mortar; (= *Putz*) stucco

Mo|sa|ik [moza'i:k] NT **-s**, **-e(n)** (*lit, fig*) mosaic

Mo|sa|ik- *in cpds* mosaic; **mo|sa|ik|ar|tig** ADJ like a mosaic, tessellated *no adv* ADV like a mosaic; **Mo|sa|ik|fuß|bo|den** M mosaic or tessellated floor; **Mo|sa|ik|stein** M tessera

mo|sa|isch [mo'za:ɪʃ] ADJ Mosaic

Mo|sam|bik [mozam'bɪk, -'bi:k] NT **-s** Mozambique

Mo|schee [mɔ'ʃe:] F **-**, **-n** [-'ʃe:ən] mosque

Mo|schus ['mɔʃʊs] M **-**, *no pl* musk

Mo|schus|och|se M musk ox

Mo|se ['mo:zə, 'mo:zɛ] M = **Moses → Buch a**

Mö|se ['mø:zə] F **-**, **-n** (*vulg*) cunt (*vulg*)

Mo|sel¹ ['mo:zl] F **-** (*Geog*) Moselle

Mo|sel² M **-s**, **-**, **Mo|sel|wein** M Moselle (wine)

mo|sern ['mo:zɛn] VI (*dial inf*) to gripe (*inf*), to bellyache (*inf*); **er hat immer was zu ~** he always has something to gripe or bellyache about (*inf*)

Mo|ses¹ ['mo:zəs, 'mo:zɛs] M **-'** or (*liter*) **Mosis** ['mo:zɪs] Moses; **bin ich ~?** (*hum inf*) don't ask me

Mo|ses² M **-**, **-** (*Naut inf*) ship's boy

Mos|kau ['mɔskau] NT **-s** Moscow

Mos|kau|er¹ ['mɔskauɐ] ADJ *attr* Moscow *attr*

Mos|kau|er² ['mɔskauɐ] M **-s**, **-**, **Mos|kau|e|rin** [-ərɪn] F **-**, **-nen** Muscovite

Mos|ki|to [mɔs'ki:to] M **-s**, **-s** mosquito

Mos|ki|to|netz NT mosquito net

Mos|ko|wi|ter¹ [mɔsko'vi:tɐ] ADJ *attr* Muscovite

Mos|ko|wi|ter² [mɔsko'vi:tɐ] M **-s**, **-**, **Mos|ko|wi|te|rin** [-ərɪn] F **-**, **-nen** Muscovite

Mos|lem ['mɔslɛm] M **-s**, **-s**, **Mos|le|min** [mɔs-'le:mɪn] F **-**, **-nen** Moslem

mos|le|misch [mɔs'le:mɪʃ] ADJ *attr* Moslem ADV erziehen as a Moslem; aufwachsen Moslem

Mos|li|me [mɔs'li:mə] F **-**, **-n** Moslem

Most [mɔst] M **-(e)s**, *no pl* a (unfermented) fruit juice; (*für Wein*) must b (*S Ger, Sw*) (= *Obstwein*) fruit wine; (= *Birnenmost*) perry; (= *Apfelmost*) cider

Most|ap|fel M cider apple

Most|ge|wicht NT specific gravity of the must

Most|rich ['mɔstrɪç] M **-s**, *no pl* (*dial*) mustard

Mo|tel [mo'tɛl] NT **-s**, **-s** motel

Mo|tet|te [mo'tɛta] F **-**, **-n** (*Mus*) motet

Mo|ti|on [mo'tsio:n] F **-**, **-en** a (*Sw: = Antrag*) motion b (*Gram: = Abwandlung*) inflection (for gender)

Mo|tiv [mo'ti:f] NT **-s**, **-e** [-və] a (*Psych, Jur, fig*) motive; **das ~ einer Tat** the motive for a deed; **aus welchem ~ heraus?** for what motive?, what are your/his etc motives?; **er wurde aus politischen ~en umgebracht** his murder was politically motivated; **ohne erkennbares ~** without any apparent motive b (*Art, Liter*) subject; (= *Leitmotiv, Topos, Mus*) motif

Mo|ti|va|ti|on [motiva'tsio:n] F **-**, **-en** motivation

Mo|tiv-: Mo|tiv|for|schung F motivation research; **mo|tiv|gleich** ADJ with the same theme or motif; **~ sein** to have the same motif

mo|ti|vie|ren [moti'vi:rən] *ptp* **motiviert** VT a *Mitarbeiter* (= *anregen*) to motivate; **politisch motiviert** politically motivated b (= *begründen*) *etw* (*jdm gegenüber*) **~** to give (sb) reasons for sth; (*rechtfertigend*) to justify sth (to sb); *Verhalten, Abwesenheit* to account for sth (to sb)

Mo|ti|vie|rung F **-**, **-en** motivation; (= *erklärende Rechtfertigung*) explanation

Mo|ti|vik [mo'ti:vɪk] F **-**, *no pl* motifs *pl*

Mo|to-Cross ['mo:tokrɔs] NT **-**, **-e**, **Mo|to|cross** ▲ NT **-**, **-e** motocross

Mo|tor ['mo:tor, mo'to:ɐ] M **-s**, **-en** [-'to:rən] motor; (*von Fahrzeug*) engine; (*fig*) driving force (+*gen* in)

Mo|tor-: Mo|tor|an|trieb M motor drive; **mit ~** motor-driven; **Mo|tor|block** M *pl* **-blöcke** engine block; **Mo|tor|boot** NT motorboat

Mo|to|ren-: Mo|to|ren|ge|räusch NT sound of the/an engine/engines; **Mo|to|ren|lärm** M noise or roar of (the) engines; **Mo|to|ren|öl** NT engine oil

Mo|tor|hau|be F bonnet (*Brit*), hood (*US*); (*Aviat*) engine cowling

-mo|to|rig [moto:rɪç] ADJ *suf* -engined; **einmotorig** one-engined, single-engined; **zweimotorig** twin-engined

Mo|to|rik [mo'to:rɪk] F **-**, *no pl* (*Physiol*) motor activity; (= *Lehre*) study of motor activity

Mo|to|ri|ker [mo'to:rikɐ] M **-s**, **-**, **Mo|to|ri|ke|rin** [-ərɪn] F **-**, **-nen** (*Psych*) motor type

mo|to|risch [mo'to:rɪʃ] ADJ (*Physiol*) *Nerv, Störung* motor *attr* ADV **sie ist ~ gestört** she suffers from an impairment of the motor nerves; **~ geschickt** well coordinated

mo|to|ri|sie|ren [motori'zi:rən] *ptp* **motorisiert** VT to motorize; *Landwirtschaft* to mechanize; (= *mit Motor ausstatten*) to fit with an engine; **sich ~** to get motorized; **motorisiertes Zweirad** motorized bike

Mo|to|ri|sie|rung F **-**, *no pl* motorization; (*der Landwirtschaft*) mechanization; (= *Ausstattung mit Motor*) fitting with an engine

Mo|tor-: Mo|tor|jacht F motor yacht; **Mo|tor|küh|lung** F engine cooling system; **Mo|tor|lärm** M noise or roar of the engine; **Mo|tor|leis|tung** F engine performance; **Mo|tor|öl** NT engine oil

Mo|tor|rad ['mo:tɔrra:t, mo'to:ɐra:t] NT motorbike, motorcycle; **fahren Sie (ein) ~?** do you ride a motorbike?

Mo|tor|rad-: Mo|tor|rad|fah|rer(in) M(F) motorcyclist; **Mo|tor|rad|helm** M (motorcylce or motorcyclist's) crash helmet; **Mo|tor|rad|ren|nen** NT motorcycle race; (= *Sportart*) motorcycle racing; **Mo|tor|rad|renn|fah|rer(in)** M(F) motorcycle racer; **Mo|tor|rad|sport** M motorcycle racing

Mo|tor-: Mo|tor|raum M engine compartment; **Mo|tor|rol|ler** M (motor) scooter; **Mo|tor|sä|ge** F power saw; **Mo|tor|scha|den** M engine trouble *no pl*; **Mo|tor|schiff** NT motor vessel or ship; **Mo|tor|schlit|ten** M motorized sleigh; **Mo|tor|sport** M motor sport

Mot|te ['mɔtə] F **-**, **-n** moth; **von ~n zerfressen** moth-eaten; **angezogen wie die ~n vom Licht** attracted like moths to a flame; **du kriegst die ~n!** (*inf*) blow me! (*inf*)

Mot|ten-: mot|ten|fest ADJ mothproof; **Mot|ten|kis|te** F (*fig*) **etw aus der ~ hervorholen** to dig sth out; **aus der ~ des 19. Jahrhunderts stammen** (*inf*) to be a relic of the 19th century; **Mot|ten|ku|gel** F mothball; **Mot|ten|pul|ver** NT moth powder; **mot|ten|zer|fres|sen** ADJ moth-eaten

Mot|to ['mɔto] NT **-s**, **-s** a (= *Wahlspruch*) motto; **unter dem ~ ... stehen** to have ... as a or one's motto b (*in Buch*) epigraph c (= *Kennwort*) password

mot|zen ['mɔtsn] VI (*inf*) to beef (*inf*), to gripe (*inf*); **was hast du jetzt zu ~?** what are you beefing or griping about now? (*inf*)

mouil|lie|ren [mu'ji:rən] *ptp* **mouilliert** VT (*Ling*) to palatalize

Moun|tain|bike ['mauntınbaik] NT **-s**, **-s** mountain bike

mous|sie|ren [mu'si:rən] *ptp* **moussiert** VI to effervesce; **~d** (*Wein*) sparkling

Mö|we ['mø:və] F **-**, **-n** seagull, gull

Mo|zart- ['mo:tsart-]: **Mo|zart|ku|gel** F chocolate truffle with marzipan soaked in liqueur; **Mo|zart|schlei|fe** F Mozart cravat

MP F **-**, **-s** a [ɛm'pe:] *abbr von* **Militärpolizei** Military Police b [ɛm'pi:] *abbr von* **Maschinenpistole**

Mrd. *abbr von* **Milliarde**

MS [ɛm'ɛs] *abbr von* **Multiple Sklerose** MS

Ms., Mskr. *abbr von* **Manuskript** ms

MS- [ɛm'ɛs]: **MS-krank** ADJ suffering from MS; **MS-Kran|ke(r)** MF *decl as adj* MS sufferer, person with MS

MTA[1] [ɛmteːˈʔaː] M **-s, -s** *abbr von* **medizinisch-
-technischer Assistent**

MTA[2] [ɛmteːˈʔaː] F **-, -s** *abbr von* **medizinisch-
-technische Assistentin**

mtl. *abbr von* **monatlich**

Mü|cke ['mʏkə] F **-, -n** (= *Insekt*) mosquito,
midge (*Brit*), gnat; **aus einer ~ einen Elefanten
machen** (*inf*) to make a mountain out of a
molehill

Mü|cke|fuck ['mʏkəfʊk] M **-s,** *no pl* (*inf*) coffee
substitute, ersatz coffee

mu|cken ['mʊkn] **VI** (*inf*) to mutter; **ohne zu ~**
without a murmur **VR** to make a sound

Mu|cken ['mʊkn] PL (*inf*) moods *pl*; **(seine) ~
haben** to be moody; (*Sache*) to be temperamental; (*zu diesem Zeitpunkt*) (*Mensch*) to be in one
of one's moods; (*Sache*) to play up; **jdm die ~
austreiben** to sort sb out (*inf*)

Mü|cken|pla|ge F plague of mosquitoes *or*
midges (*Brit*)

Mü|cken|stich M mosquito *or* gnat bite, midge
bite (*Brit*)

Mu|cki|bu|de F (*inf:* = *Fitnesscenter*) muscle
factory (*inf*)

Mu|ckis PL (*inf hum:* = *Muskeln*) (bulging) mus-
cles *pl*; (= *Bauch- und Brustmuskeln*) abs *pl* and
pecs *pl* (*hum*)

mu|ckisch ['mʊkɪʃ], **muksch** [mʊkʃ] ADJ (*dial*)
peeved

Mucks [mʊks] M **-es, -e** (*inf*) sound; **einen/kei-
nen ~ sagen** to make/not to make a sound;
(*widersprechend*) to say/not to say a word; **ohne
einen ~** (= *widerspruchslos*) without a murmur

muck|sen ['mʊksn] VR (*inf*) **sich nicht ~** not to
budge (*inf*), not to move (a muscle); (= *sich
nicht äußern*) not to make a sound; (*Mensch*) not
to say a dickybird (*Brit inf*), not to make a
peep

mucks|mäus|chen|still [-mɔʏsɡən-] ADJ, ADV
(*inf*) (as) quiet as a mouse

Mud [mʊt] M **-s,** *no pl*, **Mudd** [mʊt] M **-s,** *no pl*
(*Naut*) mud

mü|de ['myːdə] **ADJ** **a** tired; (= *erschöpft*) weary,
tired; *Haupt* weary
　b (= *überdrüssig*) tired, weary; **einer Sache**
(*gen*) **~ werden** to tire *or* weary of sth, to grow
tired *or* weary of sth; **einer Sache** (*gen*) **~ sein**
to be tired *or* weary of sth; **ich bin es ~, das zu tun**
I'm tired *or* weary of doing that; **sie wird nicht
~, das zu tun** she never tires *or* wearies of doing that; **keine ~ Mark** (*inf*) not a single penny
ADV **a** (= *erschöpft*) **sich ~ reden/kämpfen** to
tire oneself out talking/fighting; **sich ~ laufen**
to tire oneself out running about
　b (= *gelangweilt*) **~ lächeln** to give a weary
smile; **~ lächelnd** with a weary smile; **~ abwinken** to make a weary gesture (with one's hand)

-mü|de ADJ *suf* tired *or* weary of ...; **amtsmüde**
tired of office; **kampfmüde** tired *or* weary of
fighting

Mü|dig|keit ['myːdɪçkait] F **-,** *no pl* (= *Schlafbe-
dürfnis*) tiredness; (= *Schläfrigkeit*) sleepiness; (=
Erschöpfung) weariness, fatigue, tiredness; **die ~
überwinden** to overcome one's tiredness; **sich**
(*dat*) **~ vertreiben, gegen die ~ ankämpfen**
to fight one's tiredness; **vor ~** (*dat*) **umfallen** to
drop from exhaustion; **alle ~ fiel von ihm ab** all
of his tiredness melted away; **nur keine ~ vorschützen!** (*inf*) don't (you) tell me you're tired

Mud|scha|hed|din [mʊdʒahɛˈdiːn] M **-(s), -**,
Mud|scha|hi|din [mʊdʒahˈdiːn] M **-(s), -** Mu-
jaheddin

Mü|es|li ['myːɛsli] NT **-s, -s** (*Sw*) muesli

Mu|ez|zin [muˈɛtsiːn] M **-s, -s** muezzin

Muff[1] [mʊf] M **-s,** *no pl* (*N Ger*) **a** (= *Modergeruch*) musty smell, mustiness; (*fig:* = *Rückständigkeit*) fustiness **b** (= *Schimmel, Moder*) mildew

Muff[2] M **-(e)s, -e** muff

Muf|fe ['mʊfə] F **-, -n** **a** (*Tech*) sleeve **b** (*inf*) ~
kriegen/haben to be scared stiff (*inf*), to get/
have the shits (*sl*); **ihm geht die ~ (eins zu hun-
derttausend)** he's scared stiff (*inf*)

Muf|fel[1] ['mʊfl] M **-s, -** (*Hunt:* = *Maul*) muzzle
b (*inf:* = *Murrkopf*) grouch (*inf*), griper (*inf*)

-muf|fel M *suf in cpds* (*inf*) **ein Mode-/Computer-
muffel sein** to have no time for fashion/com-
puters; **er ist ein fürchterlicher Krawattenmuffel**
he hates wearing ties

muf|fe|lig ['mʊfəlɪç] (*inf*) **ADJ** grumpy **ADV**
grumpily; **~ aussehen** to look grumpy; **~ an die
Arbeit herangehen** to start work with a grumpy
attitude

muf|feln ['mʊfln] (*inf*) **VI** **a** (= *mürrisch sein*) to
be grumpy **b** (*dial inf*) = **müffeln** **VTI** (= *mürrisch reden*) to mutter

müf|feln ['mʏfln] VI (*dial inf*) to smell musty;
es müffelt there's a musty smell

Muf|fen|sau|sen ['mʊfnzauzn] NT (*inf*) **~ krie-
gen/haben** to get/be scared stiff (*inf*)

muf|fig ['mʊfɪç] **ADJ** **a** *Geruch, Zimmer* musty;
(*fig*) *Tradition, Institution* stuffy **b** (*inf*) *Gesicht*
grumpy **ADV** **a** *riechen* musty **b** (*inf:* = *lustlos*)
grumpily; **~ dreinsehen** to look grumpy

müf|fig ['mʏfɪç] (*dial*) **ADJ** musty **ADV** *riechen*
musty

muff|lig ['mʊflɪç] ADJ, ADV (*inf*) = **muffelig**

Muff|lon ['mʊflɔn] M **-s, -s** (*Zool*) mouflon,
moufflon

Muf|ti ['mʊfti] M **-s, -s** mufti

Mu|gel ['muːɡl] M **-s, -n**, **Mugl** ['muɡl] M **-s,
-(n)** (*Aus inf*) hillock, hummock

Mug|ge ['mʊɡə] F **-, -n** *abbr von* **musikalisches
Gelegenheitsgeschäft** (*inf*) gig (*inf*)

muh [muː] INTERJ moo

Mü|he ['myːə] F **-, -n** trouble; (= *Anstrengung
auch*) effort; (= *Arbeitsaufwand auch*) bother; **ohne ~** without any trouble *or* bother; **nur mit ~**
only just; **mit Müh und Not** (*inf*) with great difficulty; **unter (großen) ~n** with a great deal of effort; **er kann mit Müh und Not seinen Namen
schreiben** he can just about write his
name; **alle/viel ~ haben** to have a tremendous
amount of/a great deal of trouble *or* bother
(*etw zu tun* doing sth); **wenig/keine ~ haben** not
to have much trouble *or* bother (*etw zu tun* doing sth); **das ist mit einigen ~n** *or* **einiger ~ verbunden** that involves considerable effort; **mit
jdm/etw seine ~ haben** to have a great deal of
trouble *or* bother with sb/sth; **es ist der** (*gen*)
~ wert, es lohnt die ~ it's worth the trouble *or* bother (*etw zu tun* of doing sth); **die kleine ~ hat sich gelohnt** it was worth the little bit
of trouble; **sich** (*dat*) **etwas/mehr/keine ~ geben**
to take some/more/no trouble; **er hat sich** (*dat*)
große ~ gegeben he has taken great pains, he
has taken a lot of trouble; **gib dir keine ~!** (=
sei still) save your breath; (= *hör auf*) don't bother, save yourself the trouble; **sich** (*dat*) **die ~
machen, etw zu tun** to take the trouble to do
sth, to go to the trouble *or* bother of doing sth;
sich (*dat*) **nicht die ~ machen, etw zu tun** not to
take the trouble to do sth, not to bother to do
sth; **machen Sie sich** (*dat*) **keine ~!** (*please*)
don't go to any trouble *or* bother; **ihre ganze
Müh ~ umsonst gemacht** her efforts were
wasted; **jdm ~ machen** to give sb some trouble
or bother; **wenn es Ihnen keine ~ macht** if it is-
n't too much *or* any trouble *or* bother; **viel ~
auf etw** (*acc*) **verwenden** to take a lot of trouble
or bother with sth; **es hat viel ~ gekostet** it
took a great deal of trouble; **verlorene ~** a
waste of effort

mü|he|los ['myːə-] **ADJ** effortless; *Sieg, Aufstieg auch* easy
ADV effortlessly

Mü|he|lo|sig|keit F **-,** *no pl* effortlessness; (*von
Sieg, Aufstieg auch*) ease

mu|hen ['muːən] VI to moo, to low

mü|hen ['myːən] VR to strive (*um* for); **sosehr er
sich auch mühte ...** strive as he might ...

mü|he|voll **ADJ** laborious, arduous; *Leben* ardu-
ous **ADV** with difficulty; **~ verdientes Geld**
hard-earned money

Muh|kuh F (*baby-talk*) moo-cow (*baby-talk*)

Mühl|bach M mill stream

Müh|le ['myːlə] F **-, -n** **a** mill; (= *Kaffeemühle*)
grinder **b** (*fig:* = *Routine*) treadmill; (= *Bürokratie*) wheels *pl* of bureaucracy; **die ~n der Justiz
mahlen langsam** the wheels of justice grind
slowly **c** (= *Mühlespiel*) nine men's morris (*esp
Brit*) **d** (*inf*) (*Auto*) banger (*Brit inf*), jalopy
(*inf*); (*Fahrrad*) boneshaker (*Brit inf*); (*Flugzeug*)
crate (*inf*)

Müh|len- *in cpds* = **Mühl-**

Müh|le|spiel NT *das* = nine men's morris (*esp
Brit*)

Mühl- ['myːl] *in cpds* mill; **Mühl|gra|ben** M mill
race; **Mühl|rad** NT millwheel; **Mühl|stein** M
millstone

Muh|me ['muːmə] F **-, -n** (*obs*) aunt

Müh|sal ['myːzaːl] F **-, -e** (*geh*) tribulation; (=
Strapaze) toil; **die ~e des Lebens** the trials and
tribulations of life

müh|sam ['myːzaːm] **ADJ** *Aufstieg, Weg, Leben* ar-
duous; *Aufgabe, Amt auch* laborious; **ein ~es Geschäft sein** to be a painstaking business **ADV**
with difficulty; **nur ~ vorwärts kommen** to make
painfully slow progress; **~ verdientes Geld**
hard-earned money

müh|se|lig ['myːzeːlɪç] **ADJ** arduous, toilsome
(*liter*); **Ihr Mühseligen und Beladenen** (*Bibl*) ye
that labour (*Brit*) *or* labor (*US*) and are heavy
laden **ADV** **sich ~ ernähren** *or* **durchschlagen** to
toil for one's living

mu|kös [muˈkøːs] ADJ (*Med*) mucous

Mu|ko|vis|zi|do|se [mukovɪstsiˈdoːzə] F **-,** *no pl*
(*Med*) mucoviscidosis (*spec*), cystic fibrosis

Mu|lat|te [muˈlatə] M **-n, -n**, **Mu|lat|tin** [-ˈlatɪn]
F **-, -nen** mulatto

Mulch [mʊlç] M **-(e)s, -e** (*Agr*) mulch

Mul|de ['mʊldə] F **-, -n** **a** (= *Geländesenkung*)
hollow **b** (= *Trog*) trough **c** (*für Bauschutt*)
skip

Mu|li ['muːli] NT OR M **-s, -(s)** **a** (= *Maultier*)
mule **b** (*Ind inf:* = *Gabelstapler*) fork-lift (*inf*)

Mull [mʊl] M **-(e)s, -e** **a** (= *Torfmull*) garden
peat **b** (= *Gewebe*) muslin; (*Med*) gauze

Müll [mʏl] M **-(e)s, -e** **a** (= *Haushaltsmüll*) rubbish, garbage (*esp US*), trash (*US*), refuse
(*form*); (= *Gerümpel*) rubbish, junk, garbage
(*esp US*); (= *Industriemüll*) waste; (*inf:* = *Unsinn*)
rubbish (*Brit inf*), trash (*inf*); **etw in den ~ werfen** to throw sth out; **„Müll abladen verboten“**
"dumping prohibited", "no tipping" (*Brit*)

Müll-: **Müll|ab|fuhr** F (= *Müllabholung*) refuse
or garbage (*US*) *or* trash (*US*) collection; (=
Stadtreinigung) refuse *etc* collection department;
Müll|ab|la|de|platz M rubbish dump *or* tip
(*Brit*), garbage dump (*US*), dump

Mul|lah ['mʊla] M **-s, -s** Mullah

Müll-: **Müll|berg** M rubbish heap (*Brit*), gar-
bage dump (*US*); **Müll|beu|tel** M bin liner
(*Brit*), garbage bag (*US*)

Mull|bin|de F gauze bandage

Müll-: **Müll|con|tai|ner** M rubbish *or* garbage
(*US*) skip, dumpster (*US*); **Müll|de|po|nie** F
waste disposal site (*form*), sanitary (land)fill
(*US form*); **Müll|ei|mer** M rubbish bin (*Brit*),
garbage can (*US*)

Müll|er ['mʏlɐ] M **-s, -** miller

Mül|le|rin ['mʏlərɪn] F **-, -nen** miller; (*obs:* = *Frau
des Müllers*) miller's wife; **~ Art** (*Cook*) meunière;
Forelle (nach) ~ Art trout meunière

Müll|er-Thur|gau [-ˈtuːrɡau] M **-, -** (= *Rebe,* =
Weinsorte) Müller-Thurgau

Müll-: **Müll|fah|rer(in)** M(F) dustman (*Brit*),
garbage man (*US*), trash collector (*US*), refuse
collector (*esp US*); **Müll|gru|be** F rubbish tip
(*Brit*) *or* refuse pit (*US*); **Müll|hal|de** F rubbish
heap (*Brit*), garbage dump (*US*); **Müll|hau|fen**

M rubbish or garbage (US) or trash (US) heap; **Müll|heiz|kraft|werk** NT *power station using refuse-derived fuel;* **Müll|kas|ten** M (dial) dustbin (Brit), ashcan (US), trash can (US); **Müll|kip|pe** F rubbish or garbage (US) dump; **Müll|kut|scher** M (N Ger), **Müll|mann** M pl **-männer** or **-leute** (inf) dustman (Brit), garbage man (US), trash collector (US), refuse collector (esp US); **Müll|schau|fel** F , **Müll|schip|pe** F dustpan; **Müll|schlu|cker** M refuse chute; **Müll|sor|tier|an|la|ge** F refuse sorting plant; **Müll|sor|tie|rung** F -, no pl sifting of waste; **Müll|ton|ne** F dustbin (Brit), ashcan (US), trash can (US); **Müll|tou|ris|mus** M , no pl shipment of waste to other countries; **Müll|tren|nung** F waste separation; **Müll|tü|te** F bin liner (Brit), trash-can liner (US)

Müll|ver|bren|nungs-: **Müll|ver|bren|nungs|an|la|ge** F incinerating plant; **Müll|ver|bren|nungs|ofen** M incinerator

Müll-: **Müll|ver|fül|lung** [-veefylʊŋ] F -, no pl waste relocation; **Müll|ver|mei|dung** F waste prevention or avoidance; **Müll|ver|wer|tung** F refuse utilization; **Müll|ver|wer|tungs|werk** NT waste reprocessing plant; **Müll|wa|gen** M dust-cart (Brit), garbage truck (US)

Mull|win|del F gauze nappy (Brit) or diaper (US)

mul|mig ['mʊlmɪç] ADJ a (= morsch) Holz etc rotten b (inf: = bedenklich) uncomfortable; **es wird ~** things are getting (a bit) uncomfortable; **ich hatte ein ~es Gefühl im Magen, mir war ~ zumute** or **zu Mute** (lit) I felt queasy; (fig) I had butterflies (in my tummy) (inf)

Mul|ti ['mʊlti] M -s, -s (inf) multinational (organization)

Mul|ti-, mul|ti- [mʊlti] in cpds multi-; **mul|ti|funk|tio|nal** ADJ multi-function(al); **Mul|ti|funk|ti|ons|tas|ta|tur** F (Comput) multi-functional keyboard; **mul|ti|kau|sal** ADJ ~ sein to have multiple causes; **Mul|ti|kul|ti** ['mʊltikʊlti] NT -s, no pl (inf) multiculturalism; **die ~-Gesellschaft** the multicultural society; **mul|ti|kul|tu|rell** ADJ multicultural; **~e Gesellschaft** multicultural society; **mul|ti|la|te|ral** ADJ multilateral ADV multilaterally

Mul|ti|me|dia [mʊlti'me:dia] PL multimedia pl

Mul|ti|me|dia- in cpds multimedia; **mul|ti|me|dia|fä|hig** ADJ PC capable of multimedia

Mul|ti-: **mul|ti|me|di|al** [mʊltime'dia:l] ADJ multimedia attr; **das ~e Zeitalter** the age of multimedia ADV **eine ~ geprägte Welt** a world dominated by multimedia; **der Computer kann ~ genutzt werden** the computer is equipped for multimedia use; **Mul|ti|mil|lio|när(in)** M(F) multimillionaire; **mul|ti|na|tio|nal** ADJ multinational ADV multinationally

mul|ti|pel [mʊl'ti:pl] ADJ multiple; **multiple Sklerose** multiple sclerosis

Mul|ti|ple-choice-Ver|fah|ren [ˈmaltɪpl-ˈtʃɔys-] NT , **Mul|ti|ple|choice|ver|fah|ren** ▲ NT multiple choice (method)

Mul|ti|plex-Ki|no NT , **Mul|ti|plex|ki|no** ['mʊltipleks-] NT multiplex (cinema)

Mul|ti|pli|kand [mʊltipli'kant] M -en, -en [-dn] (Math) multiplicand

Mul|ti|pli|ka|ti|on [mʊltiplika'tsio:n] F -, -en multiplication

Mul|ti|pli|ka|ti|ons-: **Mul|ti|pli|ka|ti|ons|punkt** M multiplication point; **Mul|ti|pli|ka|ti|ons|zei|chen** NT multiplication sign

Mul|ti|pli|ka|tor[1] [mʊltipli'ka:tɔɐ] M -s, **Multiplikatoren** [-'to:rən] (Math) multiplier

Mul|ti|pli|ka|tor[2] [mʊltipli'ka:tɔɐ] M -s, **Multiplikatoren** [-'to:rən], **Mul|ti|pli|ka|to|rin** [-'to:rɪn] F -, -nen (fig) disseminator

mul|ti|pli|zier|bar ADJ multipliable

mul|ti|pli|zie|ren [mʊltipli'tsi:rən] ptp **multipliziert** VT (lit, fig) to multiply (mit by) VR (fig) to multiply

Mul|ti|ta|lent NT all-rounder (Brit), multi-talent (US)

Mu|mie ['mu:miə] F -, -n mummy; **wie eine wandelnde ~** (inf) like death warmed up (inf)

mu|mi|en|haft [-iən-] ADJ like a mummy

mu|mi|fi|zie|ren [mumifi'tsi:rən] ptp **mumifiziert** VT to mummify

Mumm [mʊm] M -s, no pl (inf) a (= Kraft) strength b (= Mut) spunk (dated inf), guts pl (inf)

Mum|mel|greis(in) ['mʊml-] M(F) (inf) old fogey (inf)

Müm|mel|mann ['mʏml-] M pl **-männer** (hum) hare

mum|meln ['mʊmln] VTI a (= undeutlich reden) to mumble b (= behaglich kauen) to chew slowly, to munch VTR a (= einhüllen) jdn/sich in etw (acc) ~ to wrap or muffle sb/oneself up in sth; **sich ins Bett ~** to huddle up in bed

müm|meln ['mʏmln] VI to nibble

Mum|men|schanz ['mʊmənʃants] M -es, no pl masquerade

Mum|pitz ['mʊmpɪts] M -es, no pl (inf) balderdash (dated inf)

Mumps [mʊmps] M OR (INF) F -, no pl (the) mumps sing

Mün|chen ['mʏnçən] NT -s Munich

Mün|che|ner[1] ['mʏnçənɐ] ADJ attr Munich; **das ~ Abkommen** (Hist) the Munich Agreement

Mün|che|ner[2] ['mʏnçənɐ] M -s, -, **Mün|che|ne|rin** [-ərɪn] F -, -nen native of Munich; (Einwohner) inhabitant of Munich

Münch|hau|sen ['mʏnçhauzn] M -s, -(s) (fig) yarn-spinner

Münch|hau|se|ni|a|de [mʏnçhauzə'nia:də] F -, -n, **Münch|hau|si|a|de** [mʏnçhau'zia:də] F -, -n cock-and-bull story, tall story

Münch|ner ['mʏnçnɐ] = **Münchener**

Mund [mʊnt] M -(e)s, ⁺er or (rare) -e or ⁺e ['mʏndə, -da, 'mʏnda] mouth; (inf: = Mundwerk) tongue; **ein Glas an den ~ setzen** to raise a glass to one's mouth or lips; **~ und Nase aufsperren** to gape (with astonishment or amazement); **etw in den ~ nehmen** to put sth in one's mouth; **dieses Wort nehme ich nicht in den ~ I** never use that word; **den ~ aufmachen** or **auftun** (lit, fig) to open one's mouth; (fig: = seine Meinung sagen) to speak up; **einen großen ~ haben** (fig) (= aufschneiden) to talk big (inf); (= frech sein) to be cheeky (Brit) or fresh (US); **jdm den ~ verbieten** to order sb to be quiet; **halt den ~!** shut up! (inf), hold your tongue!; **er kann den ~ einfach nicht halten** (inf) he can't keep his big mouth shut (inf); **jdm über den ~ fahren** to cut sb short; **jdm den ~ stopfen** (inf) to shut sb up (inf); **Sie haben mir das in den ~ gelegt** you're putting words into my mouth; **in aller ~e sein** to be on everyone's lips; **wie aus einem ~e** with one voice; **von ~ zu ~ gehen** to be passed on from person to person; **und das** or **so etwas aus deinem/seinem** etc ~(e)! and (that) coming from you/him etc too!; **an jds ~(e)** (dat) **hängen** (fig) to hang on sb's every word; **Sie nehmen mir das Wort aus dem ~(e)** you've taken the (very) words out of my mouth; **jdm nach dem ~(e) reden** (inf) to say what sb wants to hear; **sie ist nicht auf den ~ gefallen** (inf) she's never at a loss for words; **den ~ (zu/reichlich) voll nehmen** (inf) to talk (too/pretty) big (inf); **den ~ aufreißen** (inf) to talk big (inf); **ein ~ voll** a mouthful; **ein paar ~ voll** a few mouthfuls

Mund|art F dialect; **~ sprechen** to speak dialect

Mund|art-: **Mund|art|dich|ter(in)** M(F) dialect poet; **Mund|art|dich|tung** F dialect poetry

Mund|ar|ten|for|schung F , **Mund|art|for|schung** F dialect research

mund|art|lich ['mʊntla:etlɪç] ADJ dialect(al) ADV in dialect; **das Wort wird ~ gebraucht** it's a dialect word, the word is used in dialect

Mund|art-: **Mund|art|spre|cher(in)** M(F) dialect speaker; **Mund|art|wör|ter|buch** NT dialect dictionary

Mund-: **Mund|at|mung** F oral breathing; **Mund|du|sche** F water jet

Mün|del ['mʏndl] NT OR (JUR) M -s, - ward

mün|del|si|cher (St Ex) ADJ ≈ gilt-edged no adv ADV **anlegen** in secure gilt-edged investments

mun|den ['mʊndn] VI (liter) jdm trefflich/köstlich ~ to taste excellent/delicious to sb; **südländisch ~** to have a Mediterranean flavour (Brit) or flavor (US); **sich** (dat) **etw ~ lassen** to savour (Brit) or savour (US) sth; **es mundete ihm nicht, es wollte ihm nicht ~** he found it unpalatable

mün|den ['mʏndn] VI aux sein or haben (Bach, Fluss) to flow (in +acc into); (Straße, Gang) to lead (in +acc, auf +acc into); (fig: Fragen, Probleme) to lead (in +acc or dat to); **die B 3 mündet bei Celle in die B 1** the B3 joins the B1 at Celle

Mund-: **mund|faul** ADJ (inf) too lazy to say much; **sei doch nicht so ~!** make an effort and say something!; **Mund|fäu|le** F (Med) stomatitis; **Mund|flo|ra** F (Med) (bacterial) flora of the oral cavity or of the mouth; **mund|ge|bla|sen** ADJ Glas (mouth-)blown; **mund|ge|recht** ADJ bite-sized; **jdm etw ~ machen** (fig) to make sth attractive or palatable to sb ADV zubereiten, schneiden in bite-sized pieces; **Mund|ge|ruch** M bad breath, halitosis; **etwas gegen ~ tun** to do something about one's (bad) breath; **Mund|har|mo|ni|ka** F mouth organ, harmonica; **Mund|höh|le** F oral cavity; **Mund|hy|gi|e|ne** F oral hygiene

mun|dig ['mʊndɪç] ADJ (geh) appetizing, savoury (Brit), savory (US); Wein full-bodied

mün|dig ['mʏndɪç] ADJ of age; (fig) mature, responsible; **~ werden** to come of age, to reach or attain one's majority; **jdn (für) ~ erklären** to declare sb of age; **der ~e Bürger** the politically mature citizen

Mün|dig|keit F -, no pl majority; (fig) maturity, responsibility

Mün|dig-: **mün|dig spre|chen** ▲ VT irreg to declare of age; **Mün|dig|spre|chung** [-ʃpre-çʊŋ] F -, no pl declaration of majority

münd|lich ['mʏntlɪç] ADJ verbal; Prüfung, Leistung oral; **~e Verhandlung** (Jur) hearing; **etw durch ~e Überlieferung weitergeben** to pass sth on by word of mouth; **das Mündliche** (inf: Sch, Univ) (in Fremdsprache) the oral; (bei Doktorprüfung etc) the oral, the viva (voce) (Brit) ADV testen orally; informieren, besprechen personally; **jdn ~ prüfen** to submit sb to an oral examination; **etw ~ abmachen** to have a verbal agreement; **etw ~ überliefern** to pass sth on by word of mouth; **einen Fall ~ verhandeln** (Jur) to hear a case; **alles andere** or **Weitere ~!** I'll tell you the rest when I see you

Mund-: **Mund|or|gel** F cheng; **Mund|pfle|ge** F oral hygiene no art; **Mund|pro|pa|gan|da** F verbal propaganda; **Mund|raub** M (Jur) theft of comestibles for personal consumption; **Mund|schenk** ['mʊntʃɛŋk] M -en, -en (Hist) cupbearer; (fig) wine-waiter; **Mund|schleim|haut** F mucous membrane of the oral cavity or of the mouth; **Mund|schutz** M mask (over one's mouth); **Mund|spal|te** F oral fissure

M-und-S-Rei|fen ['ɛmʊnt'ʔɛs-] M winter tyre (Brit) or tire (US)

Mund-: **Mund|stel|lung** F position of the mouth, embouchure; **Mund|stück** NT (von Pfeife, Blasinstrument) mouthpiece; (von Zigarette) tip; **ohne ~** untipped; **mit ~** tipped; **mund|tot** ADJ (inf) **jdn ~ machen** to silence sb; **Mund|tuch** NT pl **-tücher** serviette (Brit), napkin

Mün|dung ['mʏndʊŋ] F -, -en (von Fluss) mouth; (= Trichtermündung) estuary; (von Rohr) mouth;

(*von Straße*) end; (= *Gewehrmündung, Kanonen-mündung*) muzzle; **die ~ des Missouri in den Mississippi** the confluence of the Missouri and the Mississippi, the point where the Missouri flows into the Mississippi; **die ~ der Straße auf die B 11** the point where the road joins the B11

Mün|dungs-: Mün|dungs|feu|er NT flash from the muzzle; **Mün|dungs|ge|biet** NT (*eines Flusses*) estuary (area)

Mund-: Mund|ver|kehr M oral intercourse; **Mund|voll** △ M → **Mund**; **Mund|vor|rat** M provisions *pl*; **Mund|was|ser** NT mouthwash; **Mund|werk** NT (*inf*) **ein gutes** *or* **flinkes ~ haben** to be a fast talker (*inf*); **ein böses ~ haben** to have a vicious tongue (in one's head); **ein freches ~ haben** to be cheeky (*Brit*) *or* fresh (*US*); **ein loses** *or* **lockeres ~ haben** to have a big mouth (*inf*); **ein großes ~ haben** to talk big (*inf*); **der mit seinem großen ~!** him with all his big talk (*inf*); **ihr ~ steht nie still** her tongue never stops wagging (*inf*); **Mund|werk|zeu|ge** PL (*Zool*) mouth parts *pl*; **Mund|win|kel** M corner of one's mouth; **Mund-zu-Mund-Be-at|mung** F mouth-to-mouth resuscitation

Mun|go¹ ['mʊŋgo] M **-(s), -s** (*Zool*) mongoose

Mun|go² M **-(s), -s** (*Tex*) mungo

Mu|ni|ti|on [muni'tsioːn] F **-, -en** ammunition; (*Mil: als Sammelbegriff*) munitions *pl*; **~ fassen** (*Mil*) to be supplied with ammunition/munitions; **keine ~ mehr haben** (*lit, fig*) to have run out of ammunition; **seine ~ verschießen** (*lit*) to use up one's ammunition; (*fig*) to shoot one's bolt; **jdm ~ liefern** (*fig*) to provide sb with ammunition

mu|ni|ti|o|nie|ren [munitsio'niːrən] *ptp* **munitioniert** VT to provide with ammunition

Mu|ni|ti|ons-: Mu|ni|ti|ons|de|pot NT munitions *or* ammunition dump *or* store; **Mu|ni|ti|ons|fab|rik** F munitions *or* ordnance factory; **Mu|ni|ti|ons|la|ger** NT munitions *or* ammunition dump *or* store; **Mu|ni|ti|ons|zug** M (*Rail*) ammunition train

mun|keln ['mʊŋkln] VTI **man munkelt** *or* **es wird gemunkelt, dass ...** it's rumoured (*Brit*) *or* rumored (*US*) that ..., there's a rumour (*Brit*) *or* rumor (*US*) that ...; **ich habe ~ hören, dass ...** I've heard it rumoured (*Brit*) *or* rumored (*US*) that ...; **man munkelt allerlei, allerlei wird ge-munkelt** you hear all kinds of rumours (*Brit*) *or* rumors (*US*); **im Dunkeln ist gut ~** darkness is the friend of thieves/lovers

Mun-Sek|te ['muːn-] F Moonies *pl*

Müns|ter¹ ['mʏnstɐ] NT **-s, -** minster, cathedral

Müns|ter² ['mʏnstɐ] NT **-s, -**, **Müns|ter|kä|se** M Münster cheese

mun|ter ['mʊntɐ] ADJ **a** (= *lebhaft*) lively *no adv*; *Farben* bright, gay; (= *fröhlich*) cheerful, merry; **~ werden** to liven up; **~ und vergnügt** bright and cheery → **Fisch a b** (= *wach*) awake; (= *aufgestanden*) up and about; **jdn ~ machen** to wake sb up; **jdn wieder ~ machen** to wake sb up (again) ADV (= *unbekümmert*) blithely; **~ drauflosreden** to prattle away merrily; **~ drauf-losgehen** to go at it with a will; **sie redete ~ weiter** she just kept on talking regardless

Mun|ter|keit F **-, no pl** (= *Lebhaftigkeit*) liveliness; (*von Farben*) brightness; (= *Fröhlichkeit*) cheerfulness

Mun|ter|ma|cher M (*Med inf*) stimulant, pick-me-up (*inf*)

Münz-: Münz|an|stalt F mint; **Münz|au|to|mat** M slot machine

Mün|ze ['mʏntsə] F **-, -n a** (= *Geldstück*) coin; (= *Münzsystem*) coinage; **jdm etw mit** *or* **in gleicher ~ heimzahlen** (*fig*) to pay sb back in his own coin for sth → **bar a b** (= *Münzanstalt*) mint

Münz|ein|wurf M (coin) slot

mün|zen ['mʏntsn] VT to mint, to coin; **das war auf ihn gemünzt** (*fig*) that was aimed at him, that was meant for him

Mün|zen|samm|lung F coin *or* numismatic (*form*) collection

Münz-: Münz|fäl|scher(in) M(F) (*Jur*) counterfeiter (*of coins*); **Münz|fäl|schung** F (*Jur*) counterfeiting of coins; **Münz|fern|spre|cher** M (*form*) pay phone; (= *Telefonzelle*) pay phone, call box (*Brit*); **Münz|fund** M find of coins; **Münz|gas|zäh|ler** M slot gas meter; **Münz-geld** NT coin; **Münz|ge|wicht** NT coin weight; **Münz|ho|heit** F prerogative of coinage; **Münz|kun|de** F numismatics *sing*; **Münz|samm|lung** F coin *or* numismatic (*form*) collection; **Münz|schacht** M coin slot; **Münz|spiel|au|to|mat** M , **Münz|spiel|ge-rät** NT (*form*) coin-operated gaming machine (*form*), slot machine; **Münz|sys|tem** NT coinage; **Münz|tank** M coin-operated petrol (*Brit*) *or* gas(oline) (*US*) pump; **Münz|te|le|fon** NT pay phone; (= *Telefonzelle*) pay phone, call box (*Brit*); **Münz|wechs|ler** M change machine; **Münz|we|sen** NT coinage

Mur [muːɐ] F **-, -en** (*Aus*) mud

Mu|rä|ne [mu'rɛːnə] F **-, -n** moray

mür|be ['mʏrbə], (*esp Aus, S Ger*) **mürb** [mʏrp] ADJ **a** crumbly; (= *zerbröckelnd*) crumbling; *Stoff, Gewebe* worn through; *Holz* rotten **b** *Fleisch* tender; (= *abgehangen*) well-hung; **~ klopfen** to tenderize, to hammer **c** *Obst* soft; **etw ~ werden lassen** to let sth ripen **d** (*fig*: = *zermürbt*) **jdn ~ machen** to wear sb down; **~ werden/sein** to be worn down; **jdn ~ kriegen** to break sb

Mür|be|teig M short(-crust) pastry

Mu|re ['muːrə] F **-, -n** (*Geol*) mudflow

Mur|kel ['mʊrkl] M **-s, -** (*dial inf*) squirt (*inf*), shrimp (*inf*)

mur|ke|lig ['mʊrkəlɪç], **murk|lig** ['mʊrklɪç] ADJ (*dial inf*) tiny, wee (*esp Scot*)

Murks [mʊrks] M **-es, no pl** (*inf*) **~ machen** *or* **bauen** to bungle things (*inf*), to botch things up (*inf*); **das ist ~!** that's a botch-up (*inf*); **so ein ~!** what a botch-up!

murk|sen ['mʊrksn] VI (*inf*) to fiddle around; (= *vermurksen*) to bungle things (*inf*), to botch things up (*inf*)

Murk|se|rei [mʊrksə'rai] F **-, -en** (*inf*) botching things up (*inf*); **eine ~** a botch-up (*inf*)

Mur|mel ['mʊrml] F **-, -n** marble

mur|meln ['mʊrmln] VTI to murmur; (*undeutlich*) to mumble; (= *brummeln*) to mutter; **etw vor sich** (*acc*) **hin ~** to mutter sth to oneself VI (= *mit Murmeln spielen*) to play marbles

Mur|mel|tier NT marmot → **schlafen VI**

mur|ren ['mʊrən] VI to grumble (*über +acc* about); **etw ohne Murren** *or* **ohne zu ~ ertragen** to put up with sth without grumbling

mür|risch ['mʏrɪʃ] ADJ (= *abweisend*) sullen, morose, surly; (= *schlecht gelaunt*) grumpy ADV (= *abweisend*) sullenly, morosely, surlily; (= *schlecht gelaunt*) grumpily

Mus [muːs] NT OR M **-es, -e** mush; (= *Apfelmus, Kartoffelmus*) puree; (= *Pflaumenmus*) jam (*Brit*), jelly (*US*); **~ aus Kartoffeln machen** to cream *or* mash potatoes; **sie wurden fast zu ~ zerdrückt** *or* **zerquetscht** (*inf*) they were (nearly) squeezed to death; **jdn zu ~ schlagen** (*inf*) to make mincemeat of sb (*inf*)

Mu|schel ['mʊʃl] F **-, -n a** mussel (*auch Cook*), bivalve; (*Schale*) shell **b** (= *Ohrmuschel*) external ear, pinna **c** (*Telec*) (= *Sprechmuschel*) mouthpiece; (= *Hörmuschel*) ear piece

Mu|schel-: Mu|schel|bank F *pl* **-bänke** mussel bed; **Mu|schel|kalk** M Muschelkalk (*spec*)

Mu|schi ['mʊʃi] F **-, -s** (*inf*) pussy (*sl*)

Musch|ko|te [mʊʃ'koːtə] M **-n, -n** (*Mil sl*) private

Mu|se ['muːzə] F **-, -n** (*Myth*) Muse; **die heitere** *or* **leichte ~** (*fig*) light entertainment; **von der ~ geküsst werden** (*fig*) to be inspired

mu|se|al [muze'aːl] ADJ **a** (*geh*) museum *attr*; **das Haus sieht zu ~ aus** the house looks too much like a museum **b** (*fig*) out-of-date; *Gerät, Auto etc* antiquated, ancient

Mu|sel|man ['muːzlman] M **-en, -en**, **Mu|sel-ma|nin** [-'maːnɪn] F **-, -nen**, **Mu|sel|mann** ['muːzlman] M *pl* **-männer** (*dated*), **Mu|sel-män|nin** [-mɛnɪn] F **-, -nen** (*dated*) Moslem

Mu|sen-: Mu|sen|al|ma|nach M (*old*) poetry periodical published in the 17th and 18th centuries; **Mu|sen|tem|pel** M (*old, liter*) theatre (*Brit*), theater (*US*)

Mu|se|um [mu'zeːʊm] NT **-s, Museen** [-'zeːən] museum

Mu|se|ums-: Mu|se|ums|die|ner(in) M(F) (*dated*) museum attendant; **Mu|se|ums|füh-rer(in)** M(F) museum guide; **mu|se|ums|reif** ADJ (*hum*) antique; **~ sein** to be almost a museum piece; **Mu|se|ums|stück** NT museum piece

Mu|si|cal ['mjuːzikl] NT **-s, -s** musical

Mu|sic|box ['mjuːzik-] F jukebox

Mu|sik [mu'ziːk] F **-, -en a** music; **die ~ lieben** to love music; **etw in ~ setzen** (*geh*) to set *or* put sth to music; **~ machen** to play some music; **das ist ~ in meinen Ohren** (*fig*) that's music to my ears **b** (*inf*) **hier ist** *or* **spielt die ~!** (*fig inf*) this is where it's at (*inf*)

Mu|sik|aka|de|mie F musical academy, academy of music

Mu|si|ka|li|en [muzi'kaːliən] PL music *sing*

Mu|si|ka|li|en|hand|lung F music shop (*Brit*) *or* store

mu|si|ka|lisch [muzi'kaːlɪʃ] ADJ musical ADV begabt musically; **jdn ~ ausbilden** to give sb a musical training, to give sb a training in music

Mu|si|ka|li|tät [muzikali'tɛːt] F **-, no pl** musicality

Mu|si|kant [muzi'kant] M **-en, -en**, **Mu|si|kan-tin** [-'kantɪn] F **-, -nen** musician, minstrel (*old*)

Mu|si|kan|ten|kno|chen M funny bone, crazy bone (*US*)

Mu|sik-: Mu|sik|au|to|mat M musical box (*Brit*), music box; (= *Musikbox*) jukebox; **mu-sik|be|geis|tert** ADJ fond of music, music-loving *attr*; **Mu|sik|be|glei|tung** F musical accompaniment; **unter ~** accompanied by music, to the accompaniment of music; **Mu|sik-be|rie|se|lung** F (*inf*) constant background music; **Mu|sik|be|trieb** M music industry; **Mu|sik|box** F jukebox; **Mu|sik|dra|ma** NT music drama

Mu|si|ker ['muːzikɐ] M **-s, -**, **Mu|si|ke|rin** [-ərɪn] F **-, -nen** musician

Mu|sik-: Mu|sik|er|zie|hung F (*form*) musical education; **Mu|sik|freund(in)** M(F) music-lover; **Mu|sik|ge|schich|te** F history of music; **Mu|sik|hoch|schu|le** F college of music; **Mu|sik|in|stru|ment** NT musical instrument; **Mu|sik|ka|pel|le** F band; **Mu|sik|kas|set|te** F music cassette; **Mu|sik|kon|ser|ve** F (*inf*) canned music *no pl*; **Mu|sik|korps** NT music corps *sing*; **Mu|sik|kri|tik** F music criticism; (= *Rezension*) music criticism, music crit (*Brit*); (= *Kritikerschaft*) music critics *pl*; **Mu|sik|kri|ti-ker(in)** M(F) music critic; **Mu|sik|leh|rer(in)** M(F) music teacher; **Mu|sik|le|xi|kon** NT encyclopaedia of music; (*Wörterbuch*) dictionary of music; **Mu|sik|lieb|ha|ber(in)** M(F) music-lover; **Mu|sik|pro|gramm** NT music station; (*Sendung*) music programme (*Brit*) *or* program (*US*); **Mu|sik|saal** M music room; **Mu|sik-schu|le** F music school; **Mu|sik|sen|dung** F music programme (*Brit*) *or* program (*US*); **Mu-sik|stück** NT piece of music; **Mu|sik|stun|de** F music lesson; **Mu|sik|thea|ter** NT music theatre (*Brit*) *or* theater (*US*); **Mu|sik|truhe** F radiogram, radio-phonograph (*US*); **Mu|sik-**

un|ter|richt M music lessons pl; (Sch) music; **Mu|sik|wunsch** M (Rad) listener's request (for a piece of music)

Mu|si|kus ['mu:zikʊs] M -, **Musizi** [-tsi] (hum) musician

Mu|sik-: Mu|sik|werk NT (geh) musical composition or work; **Mu|sik|wis|sen|schaft** F musicology; **Mu|sik|wis|sen|schaft|ler(in)** M(F) musicologist; **Mu|sik|zim|mer** NT music room

mu|sisch ['mu:zɪʃ] ADJ Fächer, Gymnasium (fine) arts attr; Begabung for the arts; Erziehung in the (fine) arts; Veranlagung, Mensch artistic **ADV** ~ begabt/interessiert gifted/interested in the (fine) arts; ~ talentiert sein to have artistic talent; ~ veranlagt artistically inclined

Mu|si|zi pl von Musikus

mu|si|zie|ren [muzi'tsi:rən] ptp musiziert VI to play a musical instrument; sie saßen auf dem Marktplatz und musizierten they sat in the market place playing their instruments; sonntags abends wird bei uns immer musiziert we always have a musical evening on Sundays

Mus|kat [mʊs'ka:t, 'mʊskat] M -(e)s, -e nutmeg

Mus|kat|blü|te F mace

Mus|ka|tel|ler(wein) [mʊska'tɛlɐ-] M -s, - muscatel

Mus|kat|nuss ▲ F nutmeg

Mus|kat|rei|be F nutmeg grater

Mus|kel ['mʊskl] M -s, -n muscle; (viele) ~n haben to be muscular; seine ~n spielen lassen (lit, fig) to flex one's muscles

Mus|kel-: mus|kel|be|packt ADJ (inf) muscly, with bulging muscles (nachgestellt), musclebound (pej); **Mus|kel|dys|tro|phie** [-dystrofi:] F -, -n [-'fi:ən] muscular dystrophy; **Mus|kel|fa|ser** F muscle fibre (Brit) or fiber (US); **Mus|kel|fa|ser|riss** ▲ M torn muscle fibre (Brit) or fiber (US); **Mus|kel|fleisch** NT flesh; **Mus|kel|ka|ter** M aching muscles pl; ~ haben to be stiff; er hatte (einen) ~ in den Beinen his legs were stiff; **Mus|kel|kraft** F physical strength; **Mus|kel|krampf** M muscle cramp no indef art; **Mus|kel|mann** M pl -männer, **Mus|kel|pa|ket** NT, **Mus|kel|protz** M (inf) muscleman (inf); **Mus|kel|riss** ▲ M torn muscle; sich (dat) einen ~ zuziehen to tear a muscle; **Mus|kel|schmer|zen** PL muscle pains pl; **Mus|kel|schwä|che** F (Med) myasthenia (spec), muscle weakness; **Mus|kel|schwund** M muscular atrophy or wasting; **Mus|kel|spiel** NT muscle play; **Mus|kel|star|re** F muscular rigidity; **Mus|kel|zer|rung** F pulled muscle

Mus|ke|te [mʊs'ke:tə] F -, -n musket

Mus|ke|tier [mʊske'ti:ɐ] M -s, -e musketeer

Mus|ku|la|tur [mʊskula'tu:ɐ] F -, -en muscular system, musculature (spec)

mus|ku|lös [mʊsku'lø:s] ADJ muscular **ADV** ~ gebaut sein to have a muscular build

Müs|li ['my:sli] NT -(s), -s muesli

Müs|li|rie|gel M cereal bar

Mus|lim ['mʊslɪm] M -s, -s Moslem

Mus|li|me [mʊs'li:mə] F -, -n Moslem

muss [mʊs] 3. pers sing pres von müssen

Muss ▲ [mʊs] NT -, no pl es ist ein/kein ~ it's/it's not a must

Muss|be|stim|mung ▲ F fixed regulation

Mu|ße ['mu:sə] F -, no pl leisure; (die) ~ für or zu etw finden to find the time and leisure for sth; dafür fehlt mir die ~ I don't have the time or leisure; sich (dat) ~ gönnen to allow oneself some (time for) leisure; etw mit ~ tun to do sth in a leisurely way

Muss|ehe ▲ F (inf) shotgun wedding (inf)

müs|sen ['mysn] ⟳ 27.7, 37, 39.3, 42, 45.1, 48.1, 48.3 **MODAL AUX VB** pret musste ['mʊstə], ptp müssen **a** (Zwang) to have to; (Notwendigkeit) to need to, to have to; **ich muss** (Zwang) I have to, I must only pres, I've got to (esp

Brit); (Notwendigkeit auch) I need to; **ich muss nicht** (Zwang) I don't have to, I haven't got to (esp Brit); (Notwendigkeit auch) I don't need to, I needn't; **muss er?** must he?, does he have to?, has he got to? (esp Brit); **musstest du?** did you have to?; **das hat er tun/nicht tun ~** had to/didn't have to do it; **er hatte es tun ~** he had had to do it; **es musste ins Haus gebracht werden** it had to be brought inside; **das muss irgendwann mal gemacht werden** it will have to be done some time; **er sagte, er müsse bald gehen** he said he would have to go soon; **ich hätte es sonst allein tun ~** otherwise I would have had to do it alone; **dafür ~/müssten Sie einen Polizisten fragen** you'll/you'd have or need to ask a policeman about that; **ich muss jeden Tag um sechs Uhr aufstehen** I have to get up at six every day; **ich muss jetzt gehen** or **weg** (inf) I must be going now or be off now, I've got to go now, I'll have to go now; **man musste lachen/weinen** etc you couldn't help laughing/crying etc, you had to laugh/cry etc; **wir ~ Ihnen leider mitteilen, dass ...** we regret to (have to) inform you (that) ...; **muss das (denn) sein?** is that (really) necessary?; **must you/he?**, do you/does he have to?; **das muss sein** it's necessary, I do/he does have to; **das musste (ja so) kommen** that had to happen, that was bound to happen; **das muss man sich** (dat) **mal vorstellen!** (just) imagine that!, think of it!; **jetzt muss ich dir mal was sagen** now let me tell you something; **was habe ich da hören ~?** what's this I hear?

b (= sollen) **das müsste ich/müsstest du eigentlich wissen** I/you ought to know that, I/you should know that; **ich hätte es gestern tun ~** I ought to or should have done it yesterday; **das musst du nicht tun!** you oughtn't to do that, you shouldn't do that

c (Vermutung, Wahrscheinlichkeit) **es muss geregnet haben** it must have rained; **es muss wahr sein** it must be true, it's got to be true; **es muss nicht wahr sein** it needn't be true; **er muss es gewesen sein** it must have been him, it has to have been him, it's got to have been him; **es müssten zehntausend Zuschauer im Stadion gewesen sein** there must have been ten thousand spectators in the stadium; **er müsste schon da sein** he should be there by now; **so muss es gewesen sein** that's how it must have been; **was ~ bloß die Leute (von uns) denken!** what must people think (of us); **was muss bloß in ihm vorgehen?** what goes on in his mind?

d (Wunsch) **(viel) Geld müsste man haben!** if only I were rich!; **man müsste noch mal von vorn anfangen können!** if only one could begin again!; **man müsste noch mal zwanzig sein!** oh, to be twenty again!

VI pret musste ['mʊstə], ptp gemusst [gə'mʊst] **a** (= weggehen, -fahren müssen) to have to go; **ich muss jetzt zur Schule** I must go to school now, I've got to go (esp Brit) or I have to go to school now; **wann müsst ihr zur Schule?** when do you have to go to school?; **der Brief muss heute noch zur Post** the letter must be or has to be posted (Brit) or mailed (esp US) today

b (inf: = austreten müssen) **ich muss mal** I need to go to the loo (Brit inf) or bathroom (esp US)

c (= gezwungen sein) to have to; **hast du gewollt? – nein, gemusst** did you want to? – no, I had to; **kein Mensch muss ~** (hum) there's no such thing as `must'

Mu|ße|stun|de F hour of leisure; **seine ~n** one's leisure hours

Muss|hei|rat ▲ F (inf) shotgun wedding (inf)

mü|ßig ['my:sɪç] **ADJ** (= untätig) idle; Leben, Tage, Stunden of leisure; (= überflüssig, unnütz) futile, pointless **ADV** (= untätig) idly

Mü|ßig-: Mü|ßig|gang [-gaŋ] M , no pl (liter. = Untätigkeit) idleness; **sich dem ~ hingeben** to lead a life of idleness, to lead an idle life; **~ ist aller Laster Anfang** (Prov) the devil finds work

for idle hands (Prov); **Mü|ßig|gän|ger** [-gɛŋɐ] M -s, -, **Mü|ßig|gän|ge|rin** [-ərɪn] F -, -nen (liter) idler

Mü|ßig|keit F -, no pl (= Überflüssigkeit) futility, pointlessness

muss|te ▲ pret von müssen

Muss|vor|schrift ▲ F fixed regulation

Mus|tang ['mʊstaŋ] M -s, -s mustang

Mus|ter ['mʊstɐ] NT -s, - **a** (= Vorlage, Dessin) pattern; (für Brief, Bewerbung etc) specimen; **nach einem ~ stricken** etc to knit etc from a pattern; **die Parade läuft immer nach demselben ~ ab** the parade always takes the same form

b (= Probestück) sample; (Buch, Korrekturfahne etc) specimen; **~ ohne Wert** sample of no commercial value

c (fig: = Vorbild) model (an +dat of); (= Verhaltensmuster) pattern; **als ~ dienen** to serve as a model; **sich** (dat) **ein ~ an jdm nehmen** to take sb as an example; **er ist ein ~ von einem Schüler/Ehemann/Staatsbürger** he is a model student/husband/citizen; **ein ~ an Tugend** a paragon of virtue

Mus|ter- in cpds model; **Mus|ter|bei|spiel** NT classic or prime example; **Mus|ter|be|trieb** M model business; **Mus|ter|brief** M specimen letter; **Mus|ter|buch** NT pattern book; **Mus|ter|dorf** NT model village; **Mus|ter|ehe** F perfect marriage; **Mus|ter|exem|plar** NT fine specimen; **ein ~ von einer Frau** a model wife; **ein ~ von einem Idioten** a perfect idiot; **Mus|ter|fall** M model case; (positiv) perfect or classic example; **Mus|ter|gat|te** M model husband; **Mus|ter|gat|tin** F model wife; **mus|ter|gül|tig** **ADJ** exemplary **ADV** **sich ~ benehmen** to be a model of good behaviour (Brit) or behavior (US); **Mus|ter|gül|tig|keit** F **die ~ seines Benehmens** his exemplary behaviour (Brit) or behavior (US); **Mus|ter|gut** NT model farm; **mus|ter|haft** **ADJ** exemplary **ADV** exemplarily; **er hat sich ~ verhalten** his conduct was exemplary; **Mus|ter|haus** NT show house (Brit), model house (US); **Mus|ter|kna|be** M (iro) paragon; **Mus|ter|kof|fer** M sample case; **Mus|ter|kol|lek|ti|on** F collection of samples; (Fashion) collection of models; **Mus|ter|länd|le** NT (inf) das ~ Baden-Württemberg; **Mus|ter|mes|se** F trade fair

mus|tern ['mʊstɐn] VT **a** (= betrachten) to scrutinize, to look over, to survey; **jdn kühl/skeptisch ~** to survey or eye sb coolly/sceptically (Brit) or skeptically (US); **jdn von oben bis unten ~** or **von Kopf bis Fuß ~** to look sb up and down, to scrutinize sb from head to toe **b** (Mil: = inspizieren) to inspect, to review **c** (Mil: für Wehrdienst) **jdn ~** to give sb his/her medical **d** (Tex) ⟳ gemustert

Mus|ter-: Mus|ter|pa|ckung F sample pack; (= Attrappe) display pack; **Mus|ter|pro|zess** ▲ M test case; **Mus|ter|schü|ler(in)** M(F) model pupil; (fig) star pupil; **Mus|ter|schutz** M protection of patterns and designs; **Mus|ter|sen|dung** F selection of samples; **Mus|ter|stadt** F model town; **Mus|ter|stück** NT (usu iro) = Musterexemplar

Mus|te|rung F -, -en **a** (= Muster) pattern **b** (Mil) (von Truppen) inspection, review; (von Rekruten) medical examination for military service **c** (durch Blicke) scrutiny

Mus|te|rungs-: Mus|te|rungs|aus|schuss ▲ M recruiting or draft (US) board; **Mus|te|rungs|be|scheid** M notification of the recruiting or draft (US) board's decision; **Mus|te|rungs|kom|mis|si|on** F recruiting or draft (US) board

Mut [mu:t] M -(e)s, no pl **a** courage, pluck (inf) (zu +dat for); (= Zuversicht) heart; (wieder) ~ fassen to pluck up courage (again); ~ haben to have (a lot of) courage; keinen ~ haben not to have any courage; mit frischem ~ with new heart; nur ~! (= Zuversicht) heart!, cheer up!, keep your pecker up! (Brit inf); jdm den ~ nehmen to discourage sb, to make sb lose heart; den ~

verlieren to lose heart; **~ bekommen** to gain confidence; **wieder ~ bekommen** to take heart; **den ~ aufbringen, etw zu tun** to find the courage to do sth; **jdm ~ zusprechen** or **machen** to encourage sb; **sich gegenseitig ~ machen** to keep each other's spirits up; **das gab ihr wieder neuen ~** that gave her new heart; **ihm sank der ~** his heart sank; **mit dem ~ der Verzweiflung** with the courage born of desperation or despair; **der ~ zum Leben** the will to live; **der ~ zur Lücke** (hum) the courage to admit when one doesn't know something; **zu ~e** = **zumute** **b** (old: = Laune, Stimmung) spirits pl; **frohen** or **guten ~es sein** to be of good cheer (old), to be in good spirits; **mit frohem ~** with good cheer (old)

Mu|tant [mu'tant] M **-en, -en, Mu|tan|te** [mu-'tantə] F **-, -n** (Biol) mutant, mutation; **du ~!** (sl) you spastic! (Brit pej sl), you psycho! (pej sl)

Mu|ta|ti|on [muta'tsioːn] F **-, -en a** mutation **b** (Med) breaking of the voice; **er hat die ~ gerade hinter sich** his voice has just broken

Mut|be|weis M proof of his etc courage

Müt|chen ['myːtçən] NT **-s, no pl sein ~ an jdm kühlen** (inf) to take it out on sb (inf)

mu|ten ['muːtn] VI (Min) to divine

Mu|ter ['muːtɐ] M **-s, -, Mu|te|rin** [-ərɪn] F **-, -nen** (Min) diviner

mu|tie|ren [mu'tiːrən] ptp **mutiert** VI **a** (= sich erblich ändern) to mutate **b** (Med, Aus) **er hat schon mutiert** his voice has already broken

mu|tig ['muːtɪç] ADJ courageous, brave; **dem Mutigen gehört die Welt** (Prov) fortune favours (Brit) or favors (US) the brave (Prov) ADV courageously, bravely

Mut-: mut|los ADJ (= niedergeschlagen) discouraged no adv, disheartened no adv; (= bedrückt) despondent, dejected; **jdn ~ machen** to discourage sb, to make sb lose heart ADV dejectedly; **~ wirken** to seem discouraged; **~ dastehen** (vor Aufgabe) to stand there discouraged; **Mut|lo|sig|keit** F **-, no pl** (= Niedergeschlagenheit) discouragement; (= Bedrücktheit) despondency, dejection

mut|ma|ßen ['muːtmaːsn] VTI insep to conjecture; **es wurde viel über seine Abwesenheit gemutmaßt** there was a lot of conjecture as to the reason for his absence

mut|maß|lich ['muːtmaːslɪç] ADJ attr Vater presumed; Täter, Terrorist suspected ADV **alle Fahrgäste sind ~ ums Leben gekommen** it is presumed that all the passengers were killed; **~ soll er der Vater sein** he is presumed to be the father

Mut|ma|ßung ['muːtmaːsʊŋ] F **-, -en** conjecture; **wir müssen uns auf ~en stützen** we can only conjecture

Mut|pro|be F test of courage

Mutt|chen ['mʊtçən] NT **-s, -** (inf) **a** (= Mutter) mummy (Brit inf), mommy (US inf) **b** (= biedere Hausfrau) little housewife **c** (= alte Frau) grandma

Mut|ter¹ ['mʊtɐ] F **-, ¨** ['mʏtɐ] mother; **sie ist jetzt ~** she's a mother now; **~ werden** to have a baby; **sie ist ~ von drei Kindern** she's a mother of three; **als Frau und ~** as a wife and a mother; **~ Natur/Erde** (liter) Mother Nature/Earth; **die ~ der Kompanie** (Mil hum) the sergeant major; **wie bei ~n** (dial) just like (at) home; (Essen) just like mother makes; **die ~ aller ...** (fig) the mother of all ...

Mut|ter² F **-, -n** (Tech) nut

Müt|ter|be|ra|tungs|stel|le F child welfare clinic

Mut|ter-: Mut|ter|bin|dung F (Psych) mother fixation; **Mut|ter|bo|den** M topsoil; **Mut|ter|brust** F mother's breast; (Ernährung) mother's milk; **an der ~** at one's mother's breast; **da war ich ja noch an der ~!** I was just a babe-in-arms then

Müt|ter|chen ['mʏtçən] NT **-s, -** **a** (= Mutter) mummy (Brit inf), mommy (US inf) **b** (= alte Frau) grandma **c ~ Russland** Mother Russia

Mut|ter-: Mut|ter|er|de F topsoil; (liter: = Heimaterde) native soil; **Mut|ter|fahr|zeug** NT (Space) mother or parent ship; **Mut|ter|fi|gur** F mother figure; **Mut|ter|freu|den** PL the joys pl of motherhood

Müt|ter|ge|ne|sungs-: Müt|ter|ge|ne|sungs|heim NT rest centre for mothers, especially of large families; **Müt|ter|ge|ne|sungs|werk** NT organization providing rest for mothers

Mut|ter-: Mut|ter|ge|sell|schaft F (Comm) parent company; **Mut|ter|ge|win|de** NT (Tech) female thread; **Mut|ter|glück** NT das ~ the joy of motherhood; **Mut|ter|got|tes** [mʊtɐ'gɔtəs] F **-, no pl** Mother of God; (Abbild) Madonna; **Mut|ter|got|tes|bild** NT (image of the) Madonna; **Mut|ter|haus** NT (Rel) training centre (Brit) or center (US); (von Kloster) mother house; **Mut|ter|herz** NT maternal heart; **Mut|ter|ins|tinkt** M maternal instinct; **Mut|ter|kir|che** F mother church; **Mut|ter|kom|plex** M mother complex; **Mut|ter|korn** NT pl **-korne** (Bot) ergot; **Mut|ter|ku|chen** M (Anat) placenta; **Mut|ter|kult** M mother cult; **Mut|ter|land** NT mother country; **Mut|ter|leib** M womb

Müt|ter|lein ['mʏtɐlain] NT **-s, - =** Mütterchen a, b

müt|ter|lich ['mʏtɐlɪç] ADJ **a** maternal; Seite, Linie maternal, distaff; (für ~en Pflichten one's duties as a mother; **auf ~er Seite** on his/her etc mother's side, on the distaff side **b** (= liebevoll besorgt) motherly no adv ADV like a mother; **jdn ~ umsorgen** to mother sb

müt|ter|li|cher|seits ADV on his/her etc mother's side, on the distaff side; **sein Großvater ~** his maternal grandfather

Müt|ter|lich|keit F **-, no pl** motherliness

Mut|ter-: Mut|ter|lie|be F motherly love; **mut|ter|los** ADJ motherless; **Mut|ter|mal** NT pl **-male** birthmark, mole; **Mut|ter|milch** F mother's milk; **etw mit der ~ einsaugen** (fig) to learn sth from the cradle; **Mut|ter|mord** M matricide; **Mut|ter|mund** M (Anat) cervix, neck of the uterus or womb

Mut|tern|schlüs|sel M (Tech) spanner (Brit), wrench (US)

Mut|ter-: Mut|ter|pass ▲ M document held by expectant mothers in which the details of the pregnancy are entered, ≈ antenatal card (Brit); **Mut|ter|pferd** NT dam; **Mut|ter|pflan|ze** F parent (plant); **Mut|ter|pla|ti|ne** F (Comput) motherboard; **Mut|ter|recht** NT (Sociol) matriarchy; **mut|ter|recht|lich** ADJ (Sociol) matriarch(al); **Mut|ter|schaf** NT ewe

Mut|ter|schaft F **-, no pl** motherhood; (nach Entbindung) maternity

Mut|ter|schafts-: Mut|ter|schafts|geld NT maternity pay (esp Brit); **Mut|ter|schafts|hil|fe** F maternity benefit (esp Brit); **Mut|ter|schafts|ur|laub** M maternity leave; **Mut|ter|schafts|ver|tre|tung** F maternity cover

Mut|ter-: Mut|ter|schiff NT (Space) mother or parent ship; **Mut|ter|schutz** M legal protection of expectant and nursing mothers; **Mut|ter|schutz|ge|setz** NT law for the protection of expectant and nursing mothers; **Mut|ter|schwein** NT sow; **mut|ter|see|len|al|lein** ADJ, ADV all alone, all on one's own; **Mut|ter|söhn|chen** NT (pej) mummy's boy (Brit), mommy's boy (US); **Mut|ter|spra|che** F native language, mother tongue; **Gälisch ist seine ~** Gaelic is his native language, he's a native speaker of Gaelic; **Mut|ter|sprach|ler** [-ʃpraːxlɐ] M **-s, -, Mut|ter|sprach|le|rin** [-ərɪn] F **-, -nen** native speaker; **mut|ter|sprach|lich** ADJ native-language attr; **~er Unterricht für Ausländer** language lessons for foreigners in their mother tongue; **Mut|ter|stel|-**

le F **bei jdm ~ vertreten** to be like a mother to sb; (Jur) to stand in loco parentis to sb

Müt|ter|sterb|lich|keit F mortality in childbirth

Mut|ter-: Mut|ter|stu|te F dam; **Mut|ter|tag** M Mother's Day; **Mut|ter|tier** NT mother (animal); (= Zuchttier) brood animal; **Mut|ter|witz** M (= Schläue) mother wit; (= Humor) natural wit

Mut|ti ['mʊti] F **-, -s** (inf) mummy (Brit inf), mum (Brit inf), mommy (US inf)

Mut|wil|le ['muːtvɪlə] M **-ns, no pl a** (geh: = Übermut) mischief; **aus bloßem** or **reinem ~n** out of pure mischief **b** (= böse Absicht) malice; **etw mit** or **aus ~n tun** to do sth out of malice

mut|wil|lig ['muːtvɪlɪç] ADJ **a** (geh: = übermütig) Streiche, Dummheiten mischievous **b** (= böswillig) malicious; Beschädigung, Zerstörung wilful, malicious ADV (= absichtlich) zerstören etc wilfully

Mut|wil|lig|keit F = Mutwille

Müt|ze ['mʏtsə] F **-, -n** cap; (= Pudelmütze, Pelzmütze) hat; **die ~ ziehen** to doff one's cap (dated); (fig) to take one's hat off (vor jdm to sb); **was** or **eins auf die ~ kriegen** (inf) to get a ticking-off (Brit inf) or telling-off (inf); (= verprügelt werden) to get thumped (Brit inf) or bashed (inf); **eine ~ voll Schlaf** (inf) a good kip (Brit inf), a long nap

Müt|zen|schirm M peak

MW abbr von **Megawatt**

MwSt., MWSt. abbr von **Mehrwertsteuer** VAT

My|an|mar [myːˈanmaːɐ] NT **-s** Myanmar

My|ke|nä [myːˈkeːnɛ] NT **-s, My|ke|ne** [myː-ˈkeːnə] NT **-s** Mycenae

my|ke|nisch [myːˈkeːnɪʃ] ADJ Mycenaean

My|om [myˈoːm] NT **-s, -e** (Med) myoma

My|ri|a|de [myˈriaːdə] F **-, -n** (lit, fig) myriad

Myr|re ▲ ['mʏrə] F **-, -en, Myr|rhe** ['mʏrə] F **-, -n** myrrh

Myr|ren|öl ▲ NT , **Myr|rhen|öl** NT oil of myrrh

Myr|te ['mʏrtə] F **-, -n** myrtle

Myr|ten|kranz M myrtle wreath

Mys|te|ri|en- [mʏsˈteːriən-] (Hist): **Mys|te|ri|en|kult** M mystery cult; **Mys|te|ri|en|spiel** NT (Theat) mystery play

mys|te|ri|ös [mʏsteˈriøːs] ADJ mysterious ADV (= unter mysteriösen Umständen) sterben mysteriously; **~ verschwundene Gelder** money that disappeared mysteriously

Mys|te|ri|um [mʏsˈteːriʊm] NT **-s, Mysterien** [-riən] (alle Bedeutungen) mystery

mys|ti|fi|ka|ti|on [mʏstifikaˈtsioːn] F **-, -en** mystification

mys|ti|fi|zie|ren [mʏstifiˈtsiːrən] ptp **mystifiziert** VT to mysticize

Mys|ti|fi|zie|rung F **-, -en** mystification

Mys|tik ['mʏstɪk] F **-, no pl** mysticism no art

Mys|ti|ker ['mʏstikɐ] M **-s, -, Mys|ti|ke|rin** [-ərɪn] F **-, -nen** mystic

mys|tisch ['mʏstɪʃ] ADJ mystic(al); (fig: = geheimnisvoll) mysterious

Mys|ti|zis|mus [mʏstiˈtsɪsmʊs] M **-, no pl** mysticism

My|then-: My|then|bil|dung F zur ~ beitragen to help to create a myth; **my|then|haft** ADJ mythical

my|thisch ['myːtɪʃ] ADJ mythical

My|tho|lo|gie [mytoloˈgiː] F **-, -n** [-ˈgiːən] mythology

my|tho|lo|gisch [mytoˈloːgɪʃ] ADJ mythologic(al)

My|thos ['myːtɔs] M **-, Mythen** ['myːtn], **My|thus** ['myːtʊs] M **-, Mythen** ['myːtn] (lit, fig) myth; **er war zeitlebens von einem ~ umgeben** he was a legend in his time

N

N, n [ɛn] NT **-, -** N, n; **n-te** nth

N *abbr von* **Norden**

'n [n] (*inf*) *abbr von* **ein** *von* **einen**

na¹ [na] INTERJ (*inf*) **a** (*Frage, Anrede*) well; (*Aufforderung*) then; **na, kommst du mit?** well, are you coming?, are you coming then?; **na du?** hey, you!

b (*zögernde Zustimmung, Resignation*) well; **na ja** well; **na ja, aber nur noch zehn Minuten** well yes *or* I suppose so, but only another ten minutes; **na gut, na schön** all right, OK (*inf*)

c (*Bestätigung, Erleichterung*) well; **na also!, na eben!** (well,) there you are (then)!; **na, endlich!** about time!, at last!; **na und ob!** (= *auf jeden Fall*) you bet! (*inf*), not half! (*Brit inf*); (= *und wie*) and how! (*inf*)

d (*Beschwichtigung*) come (on) (now)

e (*Ermahnung*) now; (*Zurückweisung*) well; **na (na)!** now, now!, now then!; **na warte!** just you wait!; **na so was** *or* **so etwas!** well, I never!; **na und?** so what?; **na ich danke!** no thank you!; **na, wirds bald?** come on, aren't you ready yet?

f (*Zweifel*) well; **na, wenn das mal klappt!** well, if it comes off

na² [naː] ADV (*S Ger, Aus inf*) = **nein**

Na̲|be ['naːbə] F **-, -n** hub

Na̲|bel ['naːbl] M **-s, -** (*Anat*) navel, umbilicus (*spec*); (*Bot*) hilum; **der ~ der Welt** (*fig*) the hub of the universe, the centre (*Brit*) *or* center (*US*) of the world

Na̲|bel-: Na̲|bel|bin|de F umbilical bandage; **Na̲|bel|bruch** M umbilical hernia; **na̲|bel|frei** ADJ **~es T-Shirt** crop top ADV **~ gehen** to wear a crop top, to bare one's navel; **Na̲|bel|schau** F **~ betreiben** to be bound up in oneself; **Na̲|bel|schnur** F , **Na̲|bel|strang** M (*Anat*) umbilical cord

Na̲|ben|schal|tung F (*beim Fahrrad*) hub gear

Na̲|bob ['naːbɔp] M **-s, -s** nabob

nach [naːx] PREP +dat **a** (*örtlich*) to; **ich nahm den Zug ~ Mailand** (= *bis*) I took the train to Milan; (= *in Richtung*) I took the Milan train, I took the train for Milan; **das Schiff/der Zug fährt ~ Kiel** the boat/train is bound for Kiel, the boat/train is going to Kiel; **er ist schon ~ London abgefahren** he has already left for London; **~ Osten** eastward(s), to the east; **~ Westen** westward(s), to the west; **von Osten ~ Westen** from (the) east to (the) west; **~ links/rechts** (to the) left/right; **von links ~ rechts** from (the) left to (the) right; **~ jeder Richtung, ~ allen Richtungen** (*lit*) in all directions; (*fig*) on all sides; **~ hinten/vorn** to the back/front; (*in Wagen/Zug etc auch*) to the rear/front; **... ~ zu** towards ... (*Brit*), toward ... (*US*); **~ Norden zu** *or* **hin** to(wards) the north

b (*in Verbindung mit vb siehe auch dort*) **~ jdm/etw suchen** to look for sb/sth; **sich ~ etw sehnen** to long for sth; **~ etw schmecken/riechen** to taste/smell of sth

c (*zeitlich*) after; **fünf (Minuten) ~ drei** five (minutes) past *or* after (*US*) three; **~ Christi Geburt, ~ unserer Zeitrechnung** AD, anno Domini (*form*); **sie kam ~ zehn Minuten** she came ten minutes later, she came after ten minutes; **~ zehn Minuten war sie wieder da** she was back

in ten minutes, she was back ten minutes later; **~ zehn Minuten wurde ich schon unruhig** after ten minutes I was getting worried; **was wird man ~ zehn Jahren über ihn sagen?** what will people be saying about him in ten years *or* in ten years' time?; **~ Empfang** *or* **Erhalt** *or* **Eingang** on receipt; **drei Tage ~ Empfang** three days after receipt; **~ allem, was geschehen ist** after all that has happened

d (*Reihenfolge*) after; **eine(r, s) ~ dem/der anderen** one after another *or* the other; **die dritte Straße ~ dem Rathaus** the third road after *or* past the town hall; **ich komme ~ Ihnen!** I'm *or* I come after you; **(bitte) ~ Ihnen!** after you!; **der Leutnant kommt ~ dem Major** (*inf*) a lieutenant comes after a major; **~ „mit" steht der Dativ** "mit" is followed by *or* takes the dative

e (*laut, entsprechend*) according to; (= *im Einklang mit*) in accordance with; **~ dem Gesetz, dem Gesetz ~** according to the law; **~ römischem Gesetz** according to *or* under Roman law; **~ Artikel 142c** under article 142c; **manche Arbeiter werden ~ Zeit, andere ~ Leistung bezahlt** some workers are paid by the hour, others according to productivity; **etw ~ Gewicht kaufen** to buy sth by weight; **~ Verfassern/Gedichtanfängen** in order of *or* according to authors/first lines; **die Uhr ~ dem Radio stellen** to put a clock right by the radio; **seinem Wesen** *or* **seiner Natur ~ ist er sehr sanft** he's very gentle by nature; **seiner Veranlagung ~ hätte er Musiker werden sollen** with his temperament he should have been a musician; **ihrer Sprache ~ (zu urteilen)** from her language, judging by her language; **~ dem, was er gesagt hat** from what he's said, according to what he's said; **~ allem, was ich gehört habe** from what I've heard; **~ allem, was ich weiß** as far as I know; **Knödel ~ schwäbischer Art** Swabian dumplings

f (= *angelehnt an*) after; **~ dem Russischen** after the Russian; **~ einem Gedicht von Schiller** after a poem by Schiller

g **er wurde ~ seinem Großvater genannt** he was named after (*Brit*) *or* for (*US*) his grandfather

ADV **a** (*räumlich*) **mir ~!** (*old, liter*) follow me! **b** (*zeitlich*) **~ und ~** little by little, gradually; **~ wie vor** still; **wir treffen uns ~ wie vor im „Goldenen Handschuh"** we still meet in the "Golden Glove" as always

nach+äf|fen VT *sep* (*pej*) *Moden, Ideen, Stil* to ape; *jdn* to take off (*Brit*), to mimic; (= *imitieren*) to copy

Nach|äf|fe|rei [naːxɛfə'raɪ] F **-, no pl** (*pej*) (*von Mode, Ideen*) aping; (*von Menschen*) mimicry; (= *das Imitieren*) copying

nach+ah|men ['naːxʔaːmən] VT *sep* to imitate; (= *nacheifern auch*) to emulate; (= *karikieren*) to take off (*Brit*), to mimic; (= *kopieren*) to copy

nach|ah|mens|wert ADJ exemplarily; **~ leben** to lead an exemplary life

Nach|ah|mer ['naːxʔaːmɐ] M **-s, -** , **Nach|ah|me|rin** [-ərɪn] F **-, -nen** imitator; (*eines großen Vorbilds*) emulator; (*pej: Art, Liter*) copyist

Nach|ah|mer|me|di|ka|ment NT , **Nach|ah|mer|prä|pa|rat** NT generic drug

Nach|ah|mung ['naːxʔaːmʊŋ] F **-, -en** **a** (= *das Imitieren*) imitation; (= *das Nacheifern*) emulation; (= *das Karikieren*) taking off (*Brit*), mimicking; (= *das Kopieren*) copying; **etw zur ~ anraten** *or* **empfehlen** to recommend sth as an example **b** (= *die Imitation*) imitation; (= *Karikatur*) take-off (*Brit*), impression; (= *Kopie*) copy

Nach|ah|mungs-: Nach|ah|mungs|tä|ter(in) M(F) copy-cat criminal; **Nach|ah|mungs|trieb** M imitative instinct

nach+ar|bei|ten *sep* VT **a** (= *aufholen*) to make up **b** (= *überarbeiten*) to work over; (*Art etc*) to touch up **c** (= *nachbilden*) to copy, to reproduce VI **wir müssen morgen ~** we'll have to make up the work tomorrow

Nach|bar ['naxbaːɐ] M **-n** *or* **-s, -n**, **Nach|ba|rin** [-rɪn] F **-, -nen** neighbour (*Brit*), neighbor (*US*); (*in Nachbarwohnung, Nachbarhaus auch*) next-door neighbo(u)r; (= *Nachbarland auch*) neighbo(u)ring country; **Herr X war beim Konzert mein ~** Mr X sat next to me at the concert; **ich war eben bei ~s** (*inf*) I've just been round to the neighbo(u)rs'; **~s Garten** the next-door garden; **die lieben ~n** (*iro*) the neighbo(u)rs

Nach|bar-: Nach|bar|dorf NT neighbouring (*Brit*) *or* neighboring (*US*) village; **Nach|bar|grund|stück** NT property next door, neighbouring (*Brit*) *or* neighboring (*US*) property; **Nach|bar|haus** NT house next door, neighbouring (*Brit*) *or* neighboring (*US*) house; **in unserem ~, bei uns im ~** in the house next door (to us)

Nach|ba|rin F **-, -nen** → **Nachbar**

Nach|bar|land NT neighbouring (*Brit*) *or* neighboring (*US*) country

nach|bar|lich ['naxbaːɐlɪç] ADJ (= *freundlich*) neighbourly *no adv* (*Brit*), neighborly *no adv* (*US*); (= *benachbart*) neighbo(u)ring *no adv*; **~e Freundlichkeit** neighbo(u)rliness

Nach|bar|schaft ['naxbaːɐʃaft] F **-, no pl** (= *Gegend*) neighbourhood (*Brit*), neighborhood (*US*); (= *Nachbarn*) neighbo(u)rs *pl*; (= *Nähe*) vicinity; **gute ~ halten** *or* **pflegen** to keep on good terms with the neighbo(u)rs

Nach|bar|schafts|hil|fe F neighbourly (*Brit*) *or* neighborly (*US*) help; **man ist ja wohl zu ein bisschen ~ verpflichtet** you have to help your neighbo(u)rs a bit

Nach|bars-: Nach|bars|fa|mi|lie F next-door family, family next door; **Nach|bars|frau** F lady next door; **Nach|bars|kind** NT child next door; **Nach|bars|leu|te** PL neighbours *pl* (*Brit*), neighbors *pl* (*US*); (*von nebenan auch*) people *pl* next door

Nach|bar-: Nach|bar|stadt F neighbouring (*Brit*) *or* neighboring (*US*) town; **Nach|bar|tisch** M next table; **am ~** at the next table

Nach|be|ben NT aftershock

nach+be|han|deln *ptp* **nachbehandelt** VT *sep* (*Med*) *jdn/etw ~* to give sb aftercare, to give sb/sth follow-up treatment

Nach|be|hand|lung F (*Med*) follow-up treatment *no indef art*

nach+be|rei|ten *ptp* **nachbereitet** VT *sep* (*Sch*) to assess *or* evaluate afterwards

nach+bes|sern *sep* **VT** *Lackierung* to retouch; *Gesetz, Vertrag* to amend; *Angebot* to improve **VI** to make improvements

Nach|bes|se|rung F -, -en *(von Gesetz, Beschluss)* amendment; **~en vornehmen/fordern** to make/demand improvements

Nach|bes|se|rungs|klau|sel F clause improving the terms of a/the contract

nach+be|stel|len *ptp* **nachbestellt** VT *sep* to order some more; *(Comm)* to reorder, to put in a repeat order for; *(nachträglich)* to put in or make a late order for; **ich habe gerade noch Sekt/noch zwei Flaschen Sekt nachbestellt** I've just ordered some more champagne/another two bottles of champagne

Nach|be|stel|lung F repeat order *(gen* for); (= *nachträgliche Bestellung)* late order *(gen* for)

nach+be|ten VT *sep (inf)* to repeat parrot-fashion, to parrot

Nach|be|ter ['na:xbe:tɐ] M -s, -, **Nach|be|te|rin** [-ərɪn] F -, -nen *(inf)* echoer, parrot *(inf)*

nach+be|zah|len *ptp* **nachbezahlt** *sep* **VT** to pay; *(später)* to pay later; **Steuern ~** to pay back-tax **VI** to pay the rest

Nach|bild NT *(Opt)* afterimage

nach+bil|den VT *sep* to copy; *(exakt)* to reproduce; **einer Sache** *(dat)* **nachgebildet sein** to be modelled *(Brit)* or modeled *(US)* on sth, to be a copy/reproduction of sth

Nach|bil|dung F copy; *(exakt)* reproduction

nach+blät|tern VI *sep* to have a quick look; **in etw** *(dat)* **~** to flick through sth again

nach+blei|ben VI *sep irreg aux sein (dial)* to stay behind

nach+bli|cken VI *sep* = **nachsehen** VI a

Nach|blu|tung F *(Med)* secondary haemorrhage *(Brit)* or hemorrhage *(US)*; *(nach Operation)* postoperative h(a)emorrhage; *(nach Geburt)* postpartum h(a)emorrhage

nach+boh|ren *sep* **VT** *Öffnung* to drill out **VI** *(lit)* to drill out some more; **(bei jdm) ~** *(fig inf)* to probe

Nach|bör|se F *(St Ex)* after-hours market, kerb market

nach|börs|lich ADJ *(St Ex)* **~e Kurse** after-hours prices; **~e Notierung** after-hours quotation

Nach|bren|ner M *(Aviat)* afterburner

nach+brin|gen VT *sep irreg* (= *hinterherbringen*) to bring afterwards; (= *zusätzlich servieren*) to bring some more; **er brachte mir den Schirm nach** he came after me with my umbrella

nach|christ|lich ADJ **in den ersten ~en Jahrhunderten** in the first centuries AD

nach+da|tie|ren *ptp* **nachdatiert** VT *sep* to postdate

nach|dem [na:x'de:m] CONJ **a** *(zeitlich)* after **b** *(modal)* → **je ¹ CONJ b c** *(S Ger: = da, weil)* since

nach+den|ken VI *sep irreg* to think *(über +acc* about); **darüber darf man gar nicht ~** it doesn't bear thinking about; **laut ~** to think aloud, to think out loud; **denk doch mal nach!** think about it!; **denk mal gut** or **scharf nach!** think carefully!

Nach|den|ken NT thought, reflection; **nach langem ~** after (giving the matter) considerable thought; **gib mir ein bisschen Zeit zum ~** give me a bit of time to think (about it)

nach|denk|lich ['na:xdɛŋklɪç] ADJ *Mensch, Miene* thoughtful, pensive; *Geschichte, Worte* thought-provoking; **jdn ~ stimmen** or **machen** to set sb thinking; **~ gestimmt sein** to be in a thoughtful mood

Nach|denk|lich|keit F -, *no pl* thoughtfulness

nach+dich|ten VT *sep (Liter)* to give a free rendering of

Nach|dich|tung F *(Liter)* free rendering

nach+drän|gen VI *sep aux sein* to push from behind; **jdm ~** to throng after sb *(liter)*

Nach|druck M *pl* **-drucke** **a** *no pl* (= *Betonung*) stress, emphasis; (= *Tatkraft*) vigour *(Brit)*, vigor *(US)*, energy; **einer Sache** *(dat)* **~ verleihen** to lend weight to sth; **besonderen ~ darauf legen, dass ...** to put special emphasis on the fact that ..., to stress or emphasize particularly that ...; **mit ~** vigorously, emphatically; **etw mit ~ be-treiben** to pursue sth with vigo(u)r; **etw mit ~ sagen** to say sth emphatically **b** (= *das Nach-drucken*) reprinting; (= *das Nachgedruckte*) reprint; **„Nachdruck verboten"** "no part of this publication may be reproduced without the prior permission of the publishers"

nach+dru|cken VT *sep* to reprint

nach|drück|lich ['na:xdrʏklɪç] ADJ emphatic; *Warnung auch* firm; **jdm den ~en Rat geben, etw zu tun** to advise sb strongly or urge sb to do sth **ADV** firmly; **sich ~ für/gegen etw ausspre-chen** to come out firmly in favour *(Brit)* or favor *(US)* of sth/against sth; **jdm ~ raten, etw zu tun** to advise sb strongly or urge sb to do sth; **jdn ~ warnen** to give sb a firm warning

Nach|drück|lich|keit F -, *no pl* insistence

nach|drucks|voll ADJ emphatic **ADV** emphatically

nach+dun|keln VI *sep aux sein* to get or grow darker; *(Bild)* to darken

Nach|durst M *(nach Alkoholgenuss)* dehydration; **~ haben** to be dehydrated

nach+ei|fern VI *sep* **jdm/einer Sache ~** to emulate sb/sth

nach|ei|ferns|wert ADJ worth emulating, worthy of emulation

nach+ei|len VI *sep aux sein (geh)* **jdm/einer Sa-che ~** to run or hurry after sb/sth

nach+ei|nan|der [na:x|ai'nandɐ] ADV *(räum-lich)* one after another, one after the other; *(zeitlich auch)* in succession; **zweimal ~** twice running, twice in a row; **kurz/unmittelbar ~** shortly/immediately after each other

nach+emp|fin|den *ptp* **nachempfunden** VT *sep irreg* **a** *Stimmung* to feel; *Text, Musik* to relate to; (= *nachvollziehen*) to understand; **niemand kann solchen Schmerz ~** no-one can really feel such grief; **ich kann (Ihnen) Ihre Entrüstung ~** I can understand how horrified you must be; **das kann ich ihr ~** I can understand her feel-ings or how she feels **b** (= *nachgestalten*) to a-dapt *(+dat* from); **etw jdm ~** (= *nachahmen*) to base sth on sb; **etw einer Sache ~** to model sth on sth

Na|chen ['naxn] M -s, - *(liter)* barque *(poet)*

Nach|ern|te F second harvest; (= *Ährennach-ernte*) gleaning; (= *Ertrag*) gleanings *pl*; **~ halten** to glean the remains of the harvest

nach+er|zäh|len *ptp* **nacherzählt** VT *sep* to re-tell; **dem Türkischen nacherzählt** *(geh)* adapted from the Turkish

Nach|er|zäh|lung F retelling; *(Sch)* (story) re-production

nach+exer|zie|ren *ptp* **nachexerziert** VI *sep (Mil)* to do extra drill

Nachf. *abbr von* **Nachfolger**

Nach|fahr ['na:xfa:ɐ] M -s, -en, **Nach|fah|rin** [-rɪn] F -, -nen *(liter)* descendant

nach+fah|ren VI *sep irreg aux sein* to follow (on); **jdm ~** to follow sb

Nach|fass|ak|ti|on ▲ F *(in der Werbung)* fol-low-up campaign

nach+fas|sen *sep* **VI** **a** (= *nachgreifen*) to get a firmer grip; (= *noch einmal zufassen*) to regain one's grip **b** *(inf:* = *nachforschen)* to probe a bit deeper **c** *(inf:* = *Essen nachfassen)* to have a sec-ond helping **VT** *(inf:* = *nachholen)* to have a second helping of; **Essen ~** to have a second helping

Nach|fei|er F continuation of the party; *(spä-ter)* celebration *(held some time after the e-vent)*

nach+fei|ern VI *sep* **a** *auch vt* (= *später feiern)* to celebrate later **b** (= *weiterfeiern)* to carry on celebrating

nach+fei|len VT *sep* to file off

nach+fi|nan|zie|ren *ptp* **nachfinanziert** VT *sep* to find additional finance for

Nach|fi|nan|zie|rung F additional financing

Nach|fol|ge F , *no pl* **a** succession; **jds ~ an-treten** to succeed sb, to be sb's successor **b** (= *Nacheiferung*) emulation; **in jds ~ stehen** to em-ulate sb; **in der ~ seines Lehrmeisters** in emula-tion of his master; **die ~ Christi** the imitation of Christ

Nach|fol|ge- *in cpds* follow-up; **Nach|fol|ge-mo|dell** NT *(von Produkt, Auto)* successor, fol-low-up model *(+gen* to)

nach+fol|gen VI *sep aux sein* **a** (= *hinterherkom-men*) to follow (on); **jdm ~** to follow sb; **jdm im Amt ~** to succeed sb in office; **sie ist ihrem Gat-ten nachgefolgt** *(euph)* she has gone to join her husband *(euph)* **b** *+dat* (= *Anhänger sein*) to follow

nach|fol|gend ADJ following; **wie im Nachfol-genden ausgeführt** as detailed below; **Nachfol-gendes, das Nachfolgende** the following

Nach|fol|ge|or|ga|ni|sa|ti|on F successor or-ganization

Nach|fol|ger ['na:xfɔlgɐ] M -s, -, **Nach|fol|ge|rin** [-ərɪn] F -, -nen *(im Amt etc)* successor; **Friedrich Reißnagel ~** successors to Friedrich Reißnagel

Nach|fol|ge|re|ge|lung F regulations *pl* gov-erning the succession; *(in einer Firma, Partei etc)* succession planning

Nach|fol|ge|staat M succession state

nach+for|dern VT *sep* to put in another de-mand for

Nach|for|de|rung F subsequent demand

nach+for|schen VI *sep* to try to find out; *(poli-zeilich etc)* to carry out an investigation *(+dat* into); *(amtlich etc)* to make inquiries *(+dat* into)

Nach|for|schung F enquiry; *(polizeilich etc)* in-vestigation; **~en anstellen** to make inquiries

Nach|fra|ge F **a** *(Comm)* demand *(nach, in +dat* for); **danach besteht eine rege/keine ~** there is a great/no demand for it **b** (= *Erkundi-gung)* inquiry; **danke der ~** *(form)* thank you for your concern; *(inf)* nice of you to ask

nach+fra|gen ✪ 46.1, 48.1 VI *sep* to ask, to in-quire

Nach|fra|ge-: **Nach|fra|ge|rück|gang** M drop or fall in demand; **Nach|fra|ge|schub** M surge in demand; **Nach|fra|ge|schwä|che** F weak demand; **Nach|fra|ge|über|hang** M surplus demand

Nach|frist F extension; **jdm eine ~ setzen** to extend sb's deadline, to give or grant sb an ex-tension

nach+füh|len VT *sep* = **nachempfinden** a

nach+fül|len VT *sep leeres Glas etc* to refill; *halb-leeres Glas, Batterie etc* to top up *(Brit)* or off *(US)*; **Öl ~** to top up *(Brit)* or off *(US)* with oil; **darf ich (Ihr Glas) ~?** can I fill/top you up *(Brit)* or off *(US)* ?, would you like a refill?

Nach|füll|pack M , **Nach|füll|pa|ckung** F refill pack; **etw im ~ kaufen** to buy the refill pack of sth

nach+gä|ren VI *sep irreg aux haben or sein* to be lagered

Nach|gä|rung F lagering

nach+ge|ben *sep irreg* **VI** **a** *(Boden, Untergrund)* to give way *(+dat* to); (= *federn)* to give; *(fig)* *(Mensch)* to give in or way *(+dat* to); (= *aufge-ben)* to give up or in **b** *(Comm: Preise, Kurse)* to drop, to fall **VT** (= *noch mehr geben)* **darf ich Ihnen noch etwas Gemüse ~?** may I give you a few more vegetables?; **er ließ sich** (dat) **Fleisch ~** he had another helping of meat

nach|ge|bo|ren ADJ **a** (mit großem Altersunterschied) late(r)-born; **die Nachgeborenen** (geh) future generations **b** (= nach Tod des Vaters geboren) posthumous

Nach|ge|bühr F excess (postage)

Nach|ge|burt F (= Gewebe) afterbirth; (= Vorgang) expulsion of the afterbirth

Nach|ge|fühl NT feeling

nach+ge|hen VI sep irreg aux sein **a** +dat (= hinterhergehen) to follow; jdm to go after, to follow **b** (Uhr) to be slow; **deine Uhr geht fünf Minuten nach** your clock is five minutes slow **c** +dat (= ausüben) Beruf to practise (Brit), to practice (US); Studium, Vergnügungen, Interesse etc to pursue; Geschäften to go about; **welcher Tätigkeit gehen Sie nach?** what is your occupation?; **seiner Arbeit ~** to do one's job **d** +dat (= erforschen) to investigate, to look into **e** +dat (= zu denken geben) to haunt

nach|ge|las|sen ADJ Werke, Briefe, Papiere posthumously published; **seine ~en, bis heute nicht veröffentlichten Fragmente** the fragments he left which remain unpublished to this day → auch **nachlassen**

nach|ge|macht ADJ Gold, Leder etc imitation; Geld counterfeit → auch **nachmachen**

nach|ge|ord|net ADJ (form) Behörde, Dienststelle subordinate

nach|ge|ra|de ['naːxɡəˈraːdə] ADV (= geradezu) practically, virtually; (= nach wie vor) still

nach|ge|ra|ten ptp **nachgeraten** VI sep irreg aux sein jdm to take after sb; **sie ist ganz ihrer Mutter ~** she's just like her mother

Nach|ge|schmack M (lit, fig) aftertaste; **einen üblen ~ hinterlassen** (fig) to leave a bad or nasty taste in one's or the mouth

nach|ge|wie|se|ner|ma|ßen ['naːxɡəviːznɐˈmaːsn] ADV = **erwiesenermaßen**

nach|gie|big ['naːxɡiːbɪç] ADJ **a** Material pliable; Boden soft; **~ sein** to be pliable/soft **b** (fig) Mensch, Haltung soft; (= entgegenkommend) accommodating, compliant; **jdn ~ machen** to soften sb up ADV **sie behandelt die Kinder zu ~** she's too soft with the children

Nach|gie|big|keit F -, no pl **a** (von Material) pliability; (von Boden) softness **b** (fig) (von Mensch, Haltung) softness; (= Entgegenkommen) compliance; **~ zeigen** to be accommodating; **er tendiert zu ~** he tends to be soft; **es darf keine ~ gegenüber Schulschwänzern geben** we must stand firm against truancy

nach+gie|ßen sep irreg VT Wasser, Milch, Benzin to add; **darf ich Ihnen noch etwas Wein ~?** would you like some more wine? VI **er trinkt so schnell, dass man ständig ~ muss** he drinks so fast that you keep having to top up (Brit) or off (US) his glass; **darf ich (Ihnen) ~?** would you like some more?

nach+glü|hen VI sep to go on glowing

nach+grei|fen VI sep irreg = **nachfassen** VI a

nach+grü|beln VI sep to think (über +acc about); (= sich Gedanken machen) to ponder (über +acc on), to muse (über +acc about)

nach+gu|cken VTI sep = **nachsehen**

nach+ha|ken VI sep (inf) to dig deeper; **bei jdm ~** to pump sb (inf)

Nach|hall M reverberation; (= Nachklang) echo; (fig: = Anklang) response (auf +acc to); **künstlicher ~** echo effect, artificial echo; **das Echo hatte einen langen ~** the echo went on reverberating a long while

nach+hal|len VI sep to reverberate

nach|hal|tig ['naːxhaltɪç] ADJ lasting; Wachstum auch, Widerstand sustained; **~e Nutzung** (von Energie, Rohstoffen etc) sustainable use; **~es Wirtschaften** sustainable management ADV **a** (= mit langer Wirkung) with lasting effect; **ihre Gesundheit hat sich ~ gebessert** there has been a

lasting improvement in her health; **sich ~ verschlechtern** to continue to deteriorate; **etw ~ verändern** to change sth permanently; **~ beeindruckt** deeply impressed; **etw ~ beeinflussen** to have a profound effect on sth **b** (= ökologisch bewusst) with a view to sustainability

Nach|hal|tig|keit F -, no pl sustainability

nach+hän|gen VI sep irreg +dat to give oneself up to, to abandon oneself to; **seinen Erinnerungen ~** to lose oneself in one's memories

nach|hau|se ▲ [naːˈhauzə] ADV (Aus, Sw) home

Nach|hau|se|weg [naːˈhauzəveːk] M way home

nach+hel|fen VI sep irreg to help; **jdm ~** to help sb, to give sb a hand; **sie hat ihrer Schönheit etwas nachgeholfen** she has improved a little on Mother Nature, she has given nature a helping hand; **er hat dem Glück ein bisschen nachgeholfen** he engineered himself a little luck; **jds Gedächtnis ~** to jog sb's memory; **meine Güte, bist du braun! – na, ich hab auch ein bisschen nachgeholfen** good heavens, you're brown! – well, I did help it or things along a bit

nach|her [naːxˈheːɐ, 'naːx-] ADV **a** (= danach) afterwards; (= später) later; **bis ~** see you later! **b** (inf: = möglicherweise) **~ stimmt das gar nicht** that might not be true at all, (it) could be that's not true at all

Nach|hil|fe F help, assistance; (Sch) private coaching or tuition or tutoring (US)

Nach|hil|fe-: **Nach|hil|fe|leh|rer(in)** M(F) private tutor, crammer (Brit inf); **Nach|hil|fe|schü|ler(in)** M(F) private pupil; **Nach|hil|fe|stun|de** F private lesson; **Nach|hil|fe|un|ter|richt** M private coaching or tuition or tutoring (US)

Nach|hi|nein ▲ ['naːxhɪnain] ADV **im ~** afterwards; (rückblickend) in retrospect → **klug**

nach+hin|ken VI sep aux sein (fig inf) to lag behind; **hinter jdm/etw ~** to lag behind sb/sth

Nach|hol|be|darf M **einen ~ an etw** (dat) **haben** to have a lot of sth to catch up on

nach+ho|len VT sep **a** (= aufholen) Versäumtes to make up; **den Schulabschluss ~** to sit one's school exams as an adult **b** jdn ~ (= nachkommen lassen) to get sb to join one; (von Übersee) to bring sb over

Nach|hut ['naːxhuːt] F -, -en (Mil) rearguard; **bei der ~** in the rearguard

Nach|imp|fung F (= Zweitimpfung) reinoculation; (= Wiederholungsimpfung) booster

nach|in|dust|ri|ell ADJ (Sociol) post-industrial

nach+ja|gen VI sep aux sein +dat to chase (after); Vergnügungen, dem Glück auch to pursue

nach+kar|ten VI sep (inf) to reopen the subject

nach+kau|en VT sep (inf) to regurgitate

Nach|kauf M further purchase; **10 Jahre ~ garantiert** availability guaranteed for 10 years

nach+kau|fen VT sep to buy later; **kann man diese Knöpfe auch ~?** is it possible to buy replacements for these buttons?

Nach|kauf|ga|ran|tie F availability guarantee

Nach|klang M **der ~ der Mandolinen** the sound of the mandolins dying away; **ein ferner ~ von Mallarmé** a distant echo of Mallarmé

nach|klas|sisch ADJ post-classical

nach+klin|gen VI sep irreg aux sein (Ton, Echo) to go on sounding; (Worte, Erinnerung) to linger on, to linger; **die Melodie klang noch lange in mir nach** the tune stayed in my head for some time

Nach|kom|me ['naːxkɔmə] M -n, -n descendant; **ohne ~n** without issue (form)

nach+kom|men ↺ 39.3 VI sep irreg aux sein **a** (= später kommen) to follow later, to come (on) later; jdm ~ to follow sb; **wir kommen gleich nach** we'll follow or come in just a couple of minutes; **Sie können Ihre Familie/Ihr Gepäck ~**

lassen you can let your family join you later/ have your luggage or baggage sent on (after) **b** (= mitkommen, Schritt halten) to keep up; **ich komme nicht nach!** I can't keep up (with you/ them etc) **c** +dat (= erfüllen) seiner Pflicht to fulfil (Brit), to fulfill (US), to carry out; einer Anordnung, Forderung, einem Wunsch to comply with

Nach|kom|men|schaft ['naːxkɔmənʃaft] F -, -en descendants pl, issue (form); **seine zahlreiche ~** his numerous progeny pl or descendants

Nach|kömm|ling ['naːxkœmlɪŋ] M -s, -e **a** (= Nachzügler) late arrival, latecomer; (Kind) afterthought (hum) **b** (old: = Nachkomme) descendant

nach+kon|trol|lie|ren ptp **nachkontrolliert** VT sep to check (over)

Nach|kriegs- ['naːxkriːks-] in cpds post-war; **nach|kriegs|deutsch** ADJ post-war German; **Nach|kriegs|deutsch|land** NT post-war Germany; **Nach|kriegs|zeit** F postwar era, postwar years pl

Nach|kühl|strang ['naːxkyːl-] M (bei Kraftwerk) cooling phase

Nach|kur F follow-up cure

nach+la|den VTI sep irreg to reload

Nach|lass ▲ ['naːxlas] M -es, -e or -lässe [-lɛsə] **a** (= Preisnachlass) discount, reduction (auf +acc on) **b** (= Erbschaft) estate; **den ~ eröffnen** to read the will; **den ~ verwalten** to administer the estate; **literarischer ~** literary estate; **Gedichte aus dem ~** unpublished poems; **aus dem ~ des Dichters** from the poet's estate

nach+las|sen sep irreg VT **a** Preis, Summe to reduce; **10% vom Preis ~** to give a 10% discount or reduction **b** (= locker lassen) Zügel, Seil to slacken; Schraube to loosen **c** (old: = hinterlassen) to bequeath → auch **nachgelassen** VI to decrease, to diminish; (Interesse auch) to flag, to wane; (Sehvermögen, Gedächtnis, Gehör auch) to deteriorate; (Regen, Sturm, Nasenbluten) to ease off or up; (Hitze) to ease off; (Leistung, Geschäfte) to fall or drop off; (Preise) to fall, to drop; **nicht ~!** keep it up!; **bei der Suche nach etw nicht ~** not to let up in the search for sth; **er hat in letzter Zeit sehr nachgelassen** he hasn't been nearly as good recently; **er hat in** or **mit seinem Eifer sehr nachgelassen** he's lost a lot of his enthusiasm; **das hat nachgelassen** it's got better; **sobald die Kälte nachlässt** as soon as it gets a bit warmer

Nach|las|sen|schaft ['naːxlasnʃaft] F -, -en = **Hinterlassenschaft**

Nach|lass-: **Nach|lass|ge|richt** ▲ NT probate court; **Nach|lass|gläu|bi|ger(in)** ▲ M(F) (Jur) creditor of the estate

nach|läs|sig ['naːxlɛsɪç] ADJ careless, negligent; Arbeit auch slipshod; (= unachtsam) thoughtless ADV carelessly; (= unachtsam) thoughtlessly; **~ gekleidet** carelessly dressed

nach|läs|si|ger|wei|se ['naːxlɛsɪɡɐˈvaizə] ADV thoughtlessly

Nach|läs|sig|keit F carelessness; (= Unachtsamkeit) thoughtlessness

Nach|lass-: **Nach|lass|pfle|ger(in)** ▲ M(F), **Nach|lass|ver|wal|ter(in)** ▲ M(F) executor; **Nach|lass|steu|er** ▲ F inheritance tax, estate tax (US); **Nach|lass|ver|wal|tung** ▲ F administration of the estate

nach+lau|fen VI sep irreg aux sein +dat jdm/einer Sache ~ to run after sb/sth; (fig auch) to chase sb/sth; **den Mädchen ~** to chase girls

nach+le|ben VI sep jdm ~ to model one's life on sb's; **einem Ideal ~** to live according to an ideal

nach+le|gen sep VT **noch Kohlen/Holz ~** to put some more coal/wood on (the fire); **Geld/ein verbessertes Angebot ~** to come up with extra money/a better offer VI to make up the fire;

(fig) to come up with something better; **wir müssen ~** *(fig)* we have to do better

Nach|le|se F second harvest; (= *Ährennachlese*) gleaning; *(Ertrag)* gleanings *pl*; *(Liter)* further selection

nach+le|sen *sep irreg* **VT** **a** *(in einem Buch)* to read; (= *nachschlagen*) to look up; (= *nachprüfen*) to check up; **man kann das in der Bibel ~** it says so in the Bible; **das kannst du bei Goethe ~** you can find it in Goethe **b** **Ähren** to glean; **Beeren/Kartoffeln ~** to gather late berries/potatoes **VI** **a** (= *nachschlagen*) to look up; (= *nachprüfen*) to check up **b** *(Agr)* to have a second harvest; (= *Ähren nachlesen*) to glean

nach+lie|fern *sep* **VT** (= *später liefern*) to deliver at a later date; (= *zuzüglich liefern*) to make a further delivery of; *(inf: = später abgeben) Unterlagen* to hand in later; *(fig) Begründung etc* to give later; **könnten Sie noch 25 Stück ~?** could you deliver another 25? **VI** to make further deliveries

Nach|lie|fe|rung F delivery; **wir warten auf die ~** we're waiting for the rest to be delivered

nach+lö|sen *sep* **VI** to pay on the train; *(zur Weiterfahrt)* to pay the extra **VT** **Fahrkarte** to buy on the train; *(zur Weiterfahrt)* to buy another

nachm. *abbr von* **nachmittags** p.m.

nach+ma|chen **VT** *sep* **a** (= *nachahmen*) to copy; (= *nachäffen*) to take off *(Brit)*, to mimic; **sie macht mir alles nach** she copies everything I do; **das mach mir mal einer nach!, das macht mir so schnell keiner nach!, das soll erst mal einer ~!** I'd like to see anyone else do that! **b** (= *fälschen*) *Unterschrift* to forge; *Geld* to forge, to counterfeit; (= *imitieren*) to copy → *auch* **nachgemacht** **c** *(inf: = nachholen)* to make up; **er hat das Abitur in der Abendschule nachgemacht** ≈ he did A levels at night school *(Brit)*, ≈ he completed his high school diploma at night school *(US)*

nach+ma|len **VT** *sep* to copy; (= *übermalen*) to touch up

nach|ma|lig ['naːxmaːlɪç] ADJ *(old)* **der ~e Präsident** the future president; **der ~e Präsident X** President X, as he was to become

nach|mals ['naːxmaːls] ADV *(old)* later, subsequently

nach+mes|sen *sep irreg* **VT** to measure again; *Temperatur* to take again; (= *prüfend messen*) to check **VI** to check

Nach|mie|ter(in) M(F) next tenant; **unser ~** the tenant after us; **wir müssen einen ~ finden** we have to find someone to take over the apartment *etc*

Nach|mit|tag △ ['naːxmɪtaːk] ADV → **Nachmittag**

Nach|mit|tag ['naːxmɪtaːk] M afternoon; **am ~** in the afternoon; **gestern/morgen/Dienstag/heute ~** yesterday/tomorrow/Tuesday/this afternoon; **am heutigen ~** this afternoon; **am ~ des 14. Oktober** on the afternoon of October 14th; **den ganzen ~** (for) the whole afternoon; **im Laufe** *or* **während des ~s** during or in the course of the afternoon; *(heute)* some time this afternoon; **vom ~ an** from about two o'clock; **bis zum ~** till the afternoon; **des ~s** *(geh)* in the afternoon

nach|mit|tä|gig ['naːxmɪtɛːgɪç] ADJ *attr* afternoon

nach|mit|täg|lich ['naːxmɪtɛːglɪç] ADJ *no pred* afternoon *attr* **ADV** in the afternoon; **die ~ stattfindenden Kurse** the afternoon courses

nach|mit|tags ['naːxmɪtaːks] ADV in the afternoon; (= *jeden Nachmittag*) in the afternoon(s); **von ~ an** from about two o'clock; **Dienstag** *or* **dienstags ~** every Tuesday afternoon, on Tuesday afternoons; **er isst immer erst ~** he never eats till (the) afternoon

Nach|mit|tags-: **Nach|mit|tags|schlaf** M **~ halten** to have a sleep after lunch; **Nach|mit|tags|schläf|chen** NT *(inf)* **sein ~ halten** to

have one's afternoon nap, to have one's postprandial snooze *(Brit hum)*; **Nach|mit|tags|sen|dung** F *(TV)* afternoon programme *(Brit)* *or* program *(US)*, afternoon show *(esp US)*; **Nach|mit|tags|stun|de** F hour of the afternoon; **Nach|mit|tags|vor|stel|lung** F matinée (performance)

Nach|mus|te|rung F *(Mil)* medical re-examination

Nach|nah|me ['naːxnaːmə] F **-, -n** cash *or* collect *(US)* on delivery, COD; *(inf: = Nachnahmesendung)* COD parcel *(esp Brit)* *or* package; **etw als** *or* **per ~ schicken** to send sth COD

Nach|nah|me-: **Nach|nah|me|ge|bühr** F COD charge; **Nach|nah|me|sen|dung** F COD parcel *(esp Brit)* *or* package

Nach|na|me M surname, family *or* last name; **wie heißt du mit ~?** what is your surname?

nach+neh|men VTI *sep irreg* to take (some) more

nach+plap|pern VT *sep* to repeat parrot-fashion; **jdm alles ~** to repeat everything sb says parrot-fashion

Nach|por|to NT excess (postage)

nach+prä|gen VT *sep* (= *nachträglich prägen*) to mint *or* strike some more; (= *fälschen*) to forge; **es wurden 200 Stück nachgeprägt** a further 200 copies were struck

nach|prüf|bar ADJ verifiable; **die Ergebnisse sind jederzeit ~** the results can be verified *or* checked at any time **ADV** (= *nachweislich*) *wahr, falsch* demonstrably; **was er sagte, war ~ wahr** what he said could be proved *(Brit)* *or* proven to be true

Nach|prüf|bar|keit ['naːxpryːfbaːʁkait] F **-,** *no pl* verifiability

nach+prü|fen *sep* **VT** **a** *Aussagen, Tatsachen* to verify, to check **b** *Kandidaten* (= *nochmals prüfen*) to re-examine; (= *später prüfen*) to examine at a later date **VI** to check

Nach|prü|fung F **a** *(von Aussagen, Tatsachen)* check (+*gen* on); **bei der ~ der Meldungen** when the reports were checked **b** (= *nochmalige Prüfung*) re-examination; *(Termin)* resit; (= *spätere Prüfung*) later examination

nach+ra|sen VI *sep aux sein* +*dat* to race *or* chase after

nach+rech|nen VTI *sep* to check; **rechne noch einmal nach!** you'd better do your sums again, you'd better check your arithmetic

Nach|re|de F **a** (= *Verunglimpfung*) **üble ~** *(Jur)* defamation of character; **jdn in üble ~ bringen** to damage sb's reputation, to bring sb into ill repute; **üble ~ über jdn verbreiten** *or* **führen** to cast aspersions on sb's character; **in üble ~ geraten** *or* **kommen** to get a bad reputation **b** (= *Epilog*) epilogue *(Brit)*, epilog *(US)*

nach+re|den VT *sep* **a** (= *wiederholen*) to repeat; **er redet dir alles nach** he repeats everything you say **b** **jdm (etwas) Übles/Schlechtes ~** to speak ill/badly of sb

Nach|red|ner(in) M(F) later *or* subsequent speaker; **mein ~** the speaker after me

nach+rei|chen VT *sep* to hand in later

Nach|rei|fe F after-ripening

nach+rei|fen VI *sep aux sein* to after-ripen

nach+rei|sen VI *sep aux sein* **jdm ~** to follow sb

nach+rei|ten VI *sep irreg aux sein* +*dat* to ride after

nach+ren|nen VI *sep irreg aux sein (inf)* = **nachlaufen**

Nach|richt ['naːxrɪçt] ✪ 27.6, 51.3, 51.4 F **-, -en** **a** (= *Mitteilung, Botschaft*) message; (= *Meldung*) (piece of) news *sing*; **eine ~** a message; **some news** *sing,* a piece of news *sing*; **die ~en** the news *sing (auch Rad, TV)*; **~en aus Politik und Kultur** news from the world of politics and culture; **„die ~en"** to listen to the news; **„hier die ~en"** "this *or* here is the news"; **das sind aber schlechte ~en** that's bad news; **wer teilt**

ihm diese unangenehme ~ mit? who's going to break this unpleasant (piece of) news to him?; **die letzte ~ von ihm kam aus Indien** the last news of him was from India; **~ erhalten, dass ...** to receive (the) news that ...; **wir geben Ihnen ~** we'll let you know **b** (= *Bestätigung*) confirmation; **wir sind bezüglich unserer Bestellung immer noch ohne ~** we are still awaiting confirmation of our order

Nach|rich|ten-: **Nach|rich|ten|agen|tur** F news agency; **nach|rich|ten|arm** ADJ **in ~en Monaten** in the silly season *(Brit)* *or* off season *(US)*; **Nach|rich|ten|bü|ro** NT news agency; **Nach|rich|ten|dienst** M **a** *(Rad, TV)* news service **b** *(Pol, Mil)* intelligence (service); **nach|rich|ten|dienst|lich** ADJ *Erkenntnisse, Tätigkeit, Mittel etc* intelligence *attr*; *Vorschriften etc* intelligence service *attr* **ADV** **~ erfasst sein** to be on the files of the intelligence service; **~ beobachtet werden** to be under surveillance; **Nach|rich|ten|ma|ga|zin** NT news magazine; **Nach|rich|ten|re|dak|ti|on** F news department *or* room; **wie wir von der ~ erfahren, ...** as we hear from the news desk, ...; **Nach|rich|ten|sa|tel|lit** M (tele)communications satellite; news satellite; **Nach|rich|ten|sen|der** M *(Rad, TV)* news station; *(TV auch)* news channel; **Nach|rich|ten|sper|re** F news blackout *or* embargo; **Nach|rich|ten|spre|cher(in)** M(F) newsreader, newscaster; **Nach|rich|ten|tech|nik** F telecommunications *sing*; **Nach|rich|ten|über|mitt|lung** F communication; **Nach|rich|ten|ver|bin|dung** F line of communication (*zu* with, to); **Nach|rich|ten|we|sen** NT communications *pl*

nach|richt|lich ['naːxrɪçtlɪç] ADJ *Sendung etc* news *attr* **ADV** *(form)* **~ an** +*acc* copy to

nach+rü|cken VI *sep aux sein* to move up; *(auf Stelle, Posten)* to succeed (*auf* +*acc* to); *(Mil)* to advance; **dem Feind/nach Hanoi ~** to advance on the enemy/on Hanoi

Nach|rü|cker ['naːxrʏkɐ] M **-s, -, Nach|rü|cke|rin** [-ərɪn] F **-, -nen** successor, replacement

Nach|rü|cker|pha|se F period of succession, transition period

Nach|ruf M obituary

nach+ru|fen VTI *sep irreg* +*dat* to shout after

Nach|ruhm M fame after death

nach+rüh|men VT *sep* **jdm etw ~** to praise sb for sth

nach+rüs|ten *sep* **VI** *(Mil)* to deploy new arms; (= *modernisieren*) to modernize **VT** *Kraftwerk etc* to modernize; **ein Auto mit einem Airbag/einen Computer mit einer Soundkarte ~** to fit a car with an air bag/a computer with a sound card

Nach|rüst|satz M *(Aut)* additional components *pl*; *(von Spiel)* supplement

Nach|rüs|tung F **a** *(Mil)* deployment of new arms; (= *Modernisierung*) arms modernization **b** *(Tech) (von Kraftwerk etc)* modernization; *(von Auto etc)* refit

Nach|rüs|tungs-: **Nach|rüs|tungs|ab|kom|men** NT *(Mil)* agreement to deploy new arms; **Nach|rüs|tungs|be|schluss** ▲ M *(Mil)* decision to deploy new arms

nach+sa|gen VT *sep* **a** (= *wiederholen*) to repeat; **jdm alles ~** to repeat everything sb says; **das ist kein Grund für dich, es nachzusagen** that's no reason for you to say it too **b** **jdm etw ~** to attribute sth to sb; **jdm Schlechtes ~** to speak ill of sb; **man kann ihr nichts ~** you can't say anything against her; **ihm wird nachgesagt, dass ...** it's said that he ...; **das kannst du mir nicht ~** you can't accuse me of that; **das lasse ich mir nicht ~!** I'm not having that said of me!

Nach|sai|son F off season

nach+sal|zen *sep irreg* **VT** to add more salt to **VI** to add more salt

Nach|satz M **a** (= *Nachschrift*) postscript; (= *Nachtrag*) afterthought; **in einem ~ sagte er,**

dass ... he added, as an afterthought, that ... **b** (*Gram*) clause in sentence final position

nach+schaf|fen VT *sep irreg* to reproduce

nach+schau|en VTI *sep* (*esp dial*) = **nachsehen** VI VT a

nach+schen|ken VTI *sep jdm etw ~* to top sb up (*Brit*) or off (*US*) with sth; **darf ich Ihnen noch (etwas) ~?** may I top you up (*Brit*) or off (*US*)?, may I top up (*Brit*) or off (*US*) your glass/cup/mug?, may I give you a refill?; **darf ich (dir) noch etwas Wein ~?** can I give you a little or a drop more wine?

nach+schi|cken VT *sep* to send on, to forward; **bitte ~!** please forward

nach+schie|ben VT *sep irreg* (*inf*) *Erklärung, Begründung etc* to provide afterwards; **einer Sache** (*dat*) **etw ~** to follow sth up with sth; **nachgeschobene Gründe** rationalizations

nach+schie|ßen *sep irreg* VI a (*Ftbl*) to shoot again **b** (*inf*: = *Geld nachschießen*) to add something to it VT (*inf*) *Geld* to add (to it)

Nach|schlag M a (*inf*) second helping **b** (*Mus*) nachschlag (*spec, turn ending a trill*); **freier ~** *any grace note following the main note*

nach+schla|gen *sep irreg* VT *Stelle, Zitat, Wort* to look up VI a *aux sein* (= *ähneln*) **jdm ~** to take after sb **b** (*in Lexikon*) to look ~ (*Ftbl*) (= *sich revanchieren*) to retaliate; (*von hinten foulen*) to foul (one's opponent) from behind

Nach|schla|ge|werk NT reference book or work

nach+schlei|chen VI *sep irreg aux sein +dat* to creep after

nach+schlei|fen¹ VT *sep* (= *hinterherschleifen*) to drag along

nach+schlei|fen² VT *sep irreg eine Linse ~* to grind a lens a little more; **ein Messer ~** to sharpen up a knife

nach+schlep|pen VT *sep jdm etw ~* to lug sth after (*Brit*) or behind sb

nach+schleu|dern VT *sep* (*fig*) **jdm etw ~** to fling or hurl sth after sb (*Brit*) or at sb's back (*US*)

Nach|schlüs|sel M duplicate key; (= *Dietrich*) skeleton key

nach+schmei|ßen VT *sep irreg* (*inf*) **jdm etw ~** to fling sth after sb (*Brit*) or at sb's back (*US*); **das ist ja nachgeschmissen!** it's a real bargain

nach+schmin|ken VT *sep sich ~* to touch up one's make-up

nach+schnei|den VT *sep irreg Haare* to recut

nach+schnüf|feln VI *sep* (*inf*) to poke or sniff around (*inf*); **jdm ~** to spy on sb

nach+schrei|ben VT *sep irreg* (= *nachträglich schreiben*) to write later; (= *abschreiben*) to write out

Nach|schrift F (= *Protokoll*) transcript; (= *Zugefügtes*) (*abbr* **NS**) postscript, PS; **er hat eine ~ der Vorlesung angefertigt** he wrote up the lecture afterwards

Nach|schub M (*Mil*) supplies *pl* (*an +dat* of); (*Material*) reinforcements *pl*

Nach|schub- (*Mil*): **Nach|schub|ba|sis** F supply base; **Nach|schub|li|nie** F supply line; **Nach|schub|weg** M supply route

Nach|schu|lung F further training; (= *Kurs, Lehrgang*) further training course

Nach|schuss ▲ M a (*Comm*) additional payment; (*St Ex*) marginal call **b** (*Ftbl*) second shot

nach+schüt|ten VT *sep Kies, Sand* to pour in (some) more; *Kohlen* to put on (some) more; (*inf:* = *nachgießen*) to pour (some) more

nach+schwat|zen, (*S Ger, Aus*) **nach+schwät|zen** VT *sep* (*inf*) = **nachplappern**

nach+schwin|gen VI *sep irreg* = **nachklingen**

nach+se|hen *sep irreg* VI a **jdm/einer Sache** VT to follow sb/sth with one's eyes, to watch sb/

sth; (= *hinterherschauen*) to gaze after sb/sth **b** (= *gucken*) to have a look (and see), to look and see; (= *nachschlagen*) to (have a) look; **in der Schublade ~** to (have a) look in the drawer VT a to (have a) look at; (= *prüfen*) to check; *Schulaufgaben etc* (= *durchsehen*) to read through, to check; (= *korrigieren*) to mark; (= *nachschlagen*) to look up **b** (= *verzeihen*) **jdm etw ~** to forgive sb (for) sth

Nach|se|hen NT *das ~ haben* to be left standing; (= *keine Chance haben*) not to get a look-in (*inf*), not to get anywhere; (= *nichts bekommen*) to be left empty-handed

Nach|sen|de-: Nach|sen|de|an|schrift F forwarding address; **Nach|sen|de|an|trag** M *application to have one's mail forwarded*

nach+sen|den VT *sep irreg* to forward; **bitte ~!** please forward

nach+set|zen *sep* VT **jdm ~** to pursue sb VT a *Fuß* to drag **b** = **nachstellen** VT a

Nach|sicht ['naːxzɪçt] F -, *no pl* (= *Milde*) leniency, clemency; (= *Geduld*) forbearance; **er wurde ohne ~ bestraft** he was punished without mercy; **er kennt keine ~** he knows no mercy; **~ üben** to be lenient/forbearing; **mit jdm/etw (keine) ~ haben** to make (no) allowances for sb/sth; **jdn mit ~ behandeln** to show leniency or clemency to sb; (= *geduldig*) to be forbearing with sb; **jdn um ~ bitten** to ask sb to be lenient/forbearing

nach|sich|tig ['naːxzɪçtɪç], **nach|sichts|voll** ADJ (= *milde*) lenient; (= *geduldig*) forbearing (*gegen, mit* with) ADV leniently; **~ mit jdm umgehen** to be understanding with sb; **jdn ~ behandeln** to be lenient with sb

Nach|sich|tig|keit F -, *no pl* = **Nachsicht**

Nach|sil|be F suffix

nach+sin|gen VT *sep irreg* to sing

nach+sin|nen VI *sep irreg* to ponder (*über +acc* over, about)

nach+sit|zen VI *sep irreg* (*Sch*) **~ (müssen)** to be kept in, to have detention; **jdn ~ lassen** to keep sb in, to give sb detention

Nach|som|mer M Indian summer

Nach|sor|ge F (*Med*) aftercare

Nach|sor|ge|kli|nik F aftercare clinic

nach+spä|hen VI *sep jdm ~* to watch sb closely

Nach|spann ['naːxʃpan] M **-s, -e** credits *pl*

Nach|spei|se F dessert, sweet (*Brit*); **als ~** for dessert

Nach|spiel NT (*Theat*) epilogue (*Brit*), epilog (*US*); (*Mus*) closing section, postlude (*form*); (*fig*) sequel; **das geht nicht ohne ~ ab** that's bound to have repercussions; **das wird noch ein (unangenehmes) ~ haben** that will have (unpleasant) consequences; **ein gerichtliches ~ haben** to have legal repercussions

nach+spie|len *sep* VT to play VI (*Sport*) to play stoppage time (*Brit*) or overtime (*US*); (*wegen Verletzungen*) to play injury time (*Brit*) or injury overtime (*US*); **der Schiedsrichter ließ ~** the referee allowed stoppage time/injury time (*Brit*), the referee allowed (injury) overtime (*US*)

Nach|spiel|zeit F (*Sport*) (*wegen Unterbrechung*) stoppage time; (*wegen Verletzungen*) injury time

nach+spi|o|nie|ren *ptp* **nachspioniert** VI *sep* (*inf*) **jdm ~** to spy on sb

nach+spre|chen *sep irreg* VT to repeat; **jdm etw ~** to repeat sth after sb VI **wir mussten ihm ~** we had to repeat what he said

nach+spü|len VTI *sep* to rinse; **ein Bier zum Nachspülen** (*inf*) a beer to wash it down

nach+spü|ren VI *sep +dat* to track or hunt down; *einem Tier* to track; *einer Fährte* to follow; *einem Verbrechen, Fehler* to go or look into

nächst [nɛːçst] PREP *+dat* (*geh*) (*örtlich*) next to, beside; (= *außer*) apart or aside from

nach+star|ren VI *sep jdm ~* to stare after sb; **er starrte ihr einfach nach** he couldn't take his eyes off her

nächst|bes|te ['nɛːçst'bəstə] ADJ *attr* **der ~ Zug/Job** the first train/job that comes along; **der/die/das Nächstbeste** the first ... I/you *etc* see; **das Nächstbeste (zu tun) wäre ...** the first thing to do would be ...

nach+ste|hen VI *sep irreg* **jdm/etw ~** to take second place to sb/sth; **keinem ~** to be second to none (*in +dat* in); **jdm in nichts** (*dat*) **~** to be sb's equal in every way; **jdm an Intelligenz** (*dat*) **nicht ~** to be every bit as intelligent as sb

nach|ste|hend ADJ *attr Bemerkung, Ausführungen* following; (*Gram*) postpositive; **im Nachstehenden** below, in the following; **im Nachstehenden der Kläger genannt** here(in)after referred to as the plaintiff; **Nachstehendes müssen Sie beachten** you must take note of the following; **das ~e Adjektiv** the adjective which follows the noun ADV (= *weiter unten*) below

nach+stei|gen VI *sep irreg aux sein jdm ~* (*lit*) to climb up after sb; (*fig inf*) to run after or chase sb

nach+stel|len *sep* VT a (*Gram*) **nachgestellt** postpositive; **im Französischen wird das Adjektiv (dem Substantiv) nachgestellt** in French the adjective is put after the noun **b** (*Tech*) (= *neu einstellen*) to adjust; (= *zurückstellen*) to put back **c** *einen Vorfall/den Unfallhergang ~* to reconstruct an incident/the accident; **eine Szene ~** to recreate a scene; **etw in einem Roman ~** to reproduce sth in a novel VI **jdm ~** to follow sb; (= *aufdringlich umwerben*) to pester sb; **einem Tier ~** to hunt an animal

Nach|stel|lung F a (*Gram*) postposition (*form*) **b** (*Tech*) adjustment; (= *Zurückstellung*) putting back **c** *usu pl* (*old*) (= *Verfolgung*) pursuit *no pl*; (*= Aufdringlichkeit*) pestering *no pl*; (= *Versuchung*) temptation, snare

Nächs|ten|lie|be F brotherly love; (= *Barmherzigkeit*) compassion; **~ üben** to love one's neighbour (*Brit*) or neighbor (*US*) as oneself → **Mantel c**

nächs|tens ['nɛːçstns] ADV a (= *das nächste Mal*) (the) next time; (= *bald einmal*) some time soon, before long **b** (= *am Ende*) next

Nächs|te(r) ['nɛːçstə] MF *decl as adj* a the next one; **der ~, bitte** next please, first please (*US, Scot*) **b** (*fig:* = *Mitmensch*) neighbour (*Brit*), neighbor (*US*); **jeder ist sich selbst der ~** (*Prov*) charity begins at home (*Prov*); **du sollst deinen ~n lieben wie dich selbst** (*Bibl*) (thou shalt) love thy neighbo(u)r as thyself

nächs|te(r, s) ['nɛːçstə] ADJ *superl von nah(e)* a (= *nächstgelegen*) nearest; **der ~ Nachbar/das ~ Telefon** the nearest neighbour (*Brit*) or neighbor (*US*)/telephone; **ist dies der ~ Weg zum Bahnhof?** is this the shortest or quickest way to the station?; **in ~r Nähe** in the immediate vicinity; **in ~r Entfernung** not far away; **aus ~r Entfernung** or **Nähe** from close by; *sehen, betrachten* at close quarters; *schießen* at close range

b (= *unmittelbar folgend*) next; **im ~n Haus** next door

c (*zeitlich*) next; **~s Mal** next time; **bis zum ~n Mal!** till the next time!, see you (some time)!; **Dienstag ~r Woche** Tuesday next week; **Ende ~n Monats** at the end of next month; **am ~n Morgen/Tag(e)** (the) next morning/day; **~r Tage**, **in den ~n Tagen** in the next few days; **bei ~r** or **bei der ~n Gelegenheit** at the earliest opportunity; **in ~r Zukunft** in the near future; **in den ~n Jahren** in the next few years; **in ~r Zeit** some time soon

d *Angehörige, Freunde etc* closest; **die ~n Verwandten** the immediate family; **der ~ Angehörige** the next of kin

e (*in Adverbialkonstruktionen*) **am ~n** closest; (*räumlich auch*) nearest

Nächs|te(s) ['nɛːçstə] NT decl as adj das ~ the next thing; (= das erste) the first thing; **als ~s** next/first; **das ~ wäre, ...** the next/first thing or step would be ...; **fürs ~** for the time being

nächst-: nächst|fol|gend ADJ attr next; **nächst|ge|le|gen** ADJ attr nearest; **nächst|hö|her** ['nɛːçsthøːɐ] ADJ attr one higher; **die ~e Klasse** one class higher; **nächst|jäh|rig** ['nɛːçstjɛːrɪç] ADJ attr next year's; **nächst|lie|gend** ['nɛːçstliːgnt] ADJ attr (lit) nearest; (fig) most obvious; **das Nächstliegende** the most obvious thing (to do); **nächst|mög|lich** ['nɛːçstmøːklɪç] ADJ attr next possible; **zum ~en Zeitpunkt/Termin** at the earliest possible date

nach+stre|ben VI sep (geh) **jdm ~** to emulate sb; **einer Sache ~** to strive after sth

nach+stür|zen VI sep aux sein (Geröll) to cave in; **jdm ~** (fig) to dash or rush after sb

nach+su|chen VI sep a (= suchen) to look; **such mal nach, ob ...** (have a) look and see if ... b (form: = beantragen) **um etw ~** to request sth (bei jdm of sb), to apply for sth (bei jdm to sb)

Nach|su|chung ['naːxzuːxʊŋ] F -, -en (form) application (um for), request (um for)

nacht △ [naxt] ADV → **Nacht**

Nacht [naxt] F -, ¨e ['nɛçtə] night; **es wird/ist/war ~** it's getting/it is/it was dark; **heute ~** tonight; (= letzte Nacht) last night; **Dienstag ~** (on) Tuesday night; **12 Uhr ~** (Aus) midnight; **als die ~ hereinbrach** as night fell; **in der** or **bei ~** at night; **in der ~ vom 12. zum 13. April** during the night of April 12th to 13th; **in der ~ auf** or **zum Dienstag** during Monday night; **diese ~** tonight; **des ~s** (geh) at night; **spät in der ~** late in the or at night; **in tiefster ~** at dead of night; **bis tief in die ~ arbeiten, bis in die späte ~ arbeiten** to work late or far into the night; **vor der ~** (S Ger) before evening; **über ~** (lit, fig) overnight; **über ~ bleiben** to stay the night; **zu(r) ~ essen** (S Ger, Aus) to have supper; **sich** (dat) **die ~ um die Ohren schlagen** (inf) to make a night of it; **die ~ zum Tage machen** to stay up all night (working etc); **eines ~s** one night; **letzte** or **vergangene ~** last night; **ganze Nächte** for nights (on end); **die ganze ~ (lang)** all night long; **vier Nächte lang** for four nights; **gute ~!** good night!; **na, dann gute ~!** (inf) what a prospect!, what an outlook!; **bei ~ und Nebel** (inf) at dead of night; **die ~ des Wahnsinns/der Barbarei/des Krieges** (liter) the darkness of insanity/barbarism/war (liter); **es wurde ~ über Deutschland** (liter) the sun went down on Germany (liter); **die ~ hat (viele) Augen** (prov) the night has a thousand eyes

nach+tan|ken sep VI to get some more petrol (Brit) or gas (US) VT **fünf Liter ~** to put in another five litres (Brit) or liters (US)

Nacht- in cpds night; **nacht|ak|tiv** ADJ (Zool) nocturnal; **Nacht|ar|beit** F night-work; **Nacht|asyl** NT night shelter; **Nacht|aus|ga|be** F late final (edition); **nacht|blind** ADJ nightblind; **Nacht|blind|heit** F night blindness; **Nacht|bus** M night bus; **Nacht|dienst** M (von Person) night duty; (von Apotheke) all--night service; **~ haben** (Person) to be on night duty; (Apotheke) to be open all night

Nacht|teil ['naːxtail] ☉ 53.3, 53.4 M -(e)s, -e disadvantage; (= Schaden auch) detriment; **~ von** or **durch etw haben** to lose by sth; **jdm ~e bringen** to bring sb disadvantages, to be disadvantageous to sb; **im ~ sein, sich im ~ befinden** to be at a disadvantage (jdm gegenüber with sb); **daraus entstanden** or **erwuchsen ihm ~e** this brought its disadvantages for him; **der ~, allein zu leben** the disadvantage of living alone; **er hat sich zu seinem ~ verändert** he has changed for the worse; **das soll nicht Ihr ~ sein** you won't lose by it; **zu jds ~** to sb's disadvantage/detriment

nach|tei|lig ['naːxtailɪç] ADJ (= ungünstig) disadvantageous; (= schädlich) detrimental; **es ist**

nichts Nachteiliges über ihn bekannt nothing unfavourable (Brit) or unfavorable (US) is known about him ADV **behandeln** unfavourably (Brit), unfavorably (US); **er hat sich sehr ~ über mich geäußert** he spoke very unfavo(u)rably about me; **sich ~ auf etw** (acc) **auswirken** to have a detrimental effect on sth

näch|te|lang ['nɛçtəlaŋ] ADV night after night, for nights (on end)

nach|ten VI impers (Sw, poet) **es nachtet** it's growing dark, darkness or night is falling

Nacht-: Nacht|es|sen NT (S Ger, Aus) supper; **Nacht|eu|le** F (fig inf) night owl; **Nacht|fal|ter** M moth; **Nacht|flug** M night flight; **Nacht|flug|ver|bot** NT ban on night flights; **Nacht|frost** M night frost; **Nacht|ge|bet** NT evening prayer; **sein** or **das ~ sprechen** to say one's bedtime prayers; **Nacht|ge|schirr** NT (old, hum) chamber pot; **Nacht|ge|spenst** NT ghost (that walks at night); **Nacht|ge|wand** NT (geh) nightrobe; **Nacht|hemd** NT (für Damen) nightie, nightdress; (für Herren) nightshirt; **Nacht|him|mel** M night sky, sky at night

Nach|ti|gall ['naxtɪgal] F -, -en nightingale; **~, ick hör dir trapsen** (dial hum) I see it all now, now I see what you're/he's etc after

näch|ti|gen ['nɛçtɪgn] VI (geh) to spend the night

Nach|tisch M dessert, sweet (Brit); (zu Hause) dessert, sweet (Brit), pudding (Brit)

Nacht-: Nacht|käst|chen NT (S Ger, Aus) bedside table; **Nacht|klub** M night club; **Nacht|la|ger** NT (= Unterkunft) place for the night; (Mil auch) bivouac; **sein ~ aufschlagen** to settle down or to bed down for the night; (Mil) to bivouac; **Nacht|le|ben** NT night life

nächt|lich ['nɛçtlɪç] ADJ attr (= jede Nacht) nightly; (= in der Nacht) night; **die ~e Stadt** the town at night; **zu ~er Stunde** at a late hour; **~e Ausgangssperre** night-time curfew; **~e Ruhestörung** (Jur) breach of the peace during the night

Nacht-: Nacht|lo|kal NT night club; **Nacht|luft** F night air; **Nacht|mahl** NT (Aus) supper; **nacht|mah|len** ['naxtmaːlən] VI insep (Aus) to have supper; **Nacht|mahr** ['naxtmaːɐ] M -(e)s, -e (old, liter) nightmare; **Nacht|mensch** M night person; **Nacht|müt|ze** F nightcap (lit)

nach+tö|nen VI sep to resound

Nacht-: Nacht|por|tier M night porter; **Nacht|pro|gramm** NT late-night programme (Brit) or program (US); **Nacht|quar|tier** NT **ein ~** somewhere for the night, a place to sleep; **sein ~ aufschlagen** to bed down (for the night)

Nach|trag ['naːxtraːk] M -(e)s, **Nachträge** [-trɛːgə] postscript; (zu einem Buch) supplement

nach+tra|gen VT sep irreg a (= hinterhertragen) **jdm etw ~** (lit) to go after sb with sth, to take sth after sb; (fig) to hold sth against sb, to bear sb a grudge for sth b (= hinzufügen) to add; **Summe** to enter up

nach+tra|gend ADJ unforgiving; **er war nicht ~** he didn't bear a grudge

nach|träg|lich ['naːxtrɛːklɪç] ADJ (= zusätzlich) additional; (= später) later; (= verspätet) belated; (= nach dem Tod) posthumous ADV (= zusätzlich) additionally; (= später) later; (= verspätet) belatedly; (= nach dem Tod) posthumously

Nachtrags- in cpds supplementary; **Nachtrags|haus|halt** M (Pol) supplementary budget

nach+trau|ern VI sep +dat to mourn

Nacht|ru|he F night's rest or sleep; (in Anstalten) lights-out

nachts [naxts] ADV at night; **dienstags ~** (on) Tuesday nights

Nacht-: Nacht|schal|ter M night desk; **Nacht|schat|ten** M , no pl (Bot) nightshade; **Nacht|schat|ten|ge|wächs** NT (Bot) sola-

num (spec); (fig inf) night bird; **Nacht|schicht** F night shift; **~ haben** to be on night shift or on nights; **nacht|schla|fend** ADJ **bei** or **zu ~er Zeit** or **Stunde** in the middle of the night; **Nacht|schwär|mer** M (Zool) moth; **Nacht|schwär|mer(in)** M(F) (hum) night owl; **Nacht|schwes|ter** F night nurse; **Nacht|sicht|ge|rät** NT night vision aid; **Nacht|spei|cher|ofen** M storage heater; **Nacht|strom** M off-peak electricity; **Nacht|stuhl** M (old) commode

nachts|über ['naxtsyːbɐ] ADV by night

Nacht-: Nacht|ta|rif M (bei Verkehrsmitteln) night fares pl; (bei Strom etc) off-peak rate; **Nacht|tier** NT nocturnal animal; **Nacht|tisch** M bedside table; **Nacht|tisch|lam|pe** F , **Nacht|tisch|leuch|te** F bedside lamp; **Nacht|topf** M chamber pot

nach+tun VT sep irreg **es jdm ~** to copy or emulate sb

Nacht-: Nacht-und-Ne|bel-Ak|ti|on F cloak-and-dagger operation; **Nacht|vo|gel** M nocturnal or night bird; **Nacht|vor|stel|lung** F late-night performance; **Nacht|wa|che** F night watch; (im Krankenhaus) night duty; **bei einem Kranken ~ halten** to sit with a patient through the night; **~ haben** to be on night duty or on nights; **Nacht|wäch|ter(in)** M(F) (Hist) (night) watch; (in Betrieben etc) night watchman; (inf) dope (inf); **nacht|wan|deln** VI insep aux sein or haben to sleepwalk, to walk in one's sleep; **Nacht|wan|de|rung** F night ramble or walk; **Nacht|wand|ler** M -s, -, **Nacht|wand|le|rin** F -, -nen sleepwalker; **nacht|wand|le|risch** ['naxtvandlərɪʃ] ADJ **mit ~er Sicherheit** with instinctive assurance; **Nacht|zeit** F night-time; **Nacht|zeug** NT night things pl; **Nacht|zug** M night train; **Nacht|zu|schlag** M night supplement

Nach|un|ter|su|chung F (= weitere Untersuchung) further examination; (= spätere Untersuchung) check-up

nach+ver|an|la|gen ptp **nachveranlagt** VT sep (Fin) **jdn ~** to assess sb further

Nach|ver|an|la|gung F (Fin, von Steuern) supplementary assessment

Nach|ver|bren|nung F (Tech) after-burning no pl

nach+ver|lan|gen ptp **nachverlangt** VT sep **20 Euro ~** to demand an additional 20 euros

nach+ver|si|chern ptp **nachversichert** VT sep **Sie müssen neu erworbene Wertgegenstände ~** you must revise your insurance to cover newly-acquired valuables

nach+ver|steu|ern ptp **nachversteuert** VT sep (Fin) **etw ~** to pay supplementary tax on sth; **Steuerrückstände** to pay back tax on sth

nach+voll|zieh|bar ADJ comprehensible

nach+voll|zie|hen ptp **nachvollzogen** VT sep irreg to understand, to comprehend

nach+wach|sen VI sep irreg aux sein to grow again; **die neue Generation, die jetzt nachwächst** the young generation who are now taking their place in society

nach|wachs|end ADJ **Rohstoff** renewable; **Generation** up-and-coming, younger

Nach|wahl F (Pol) ≈ by-election

Nach|we|hen PL after-pains pl; (fig) painful aftermath sing

nach+wei|nen VI sep +dat to mourn; **dieser Sache weine ich nicht nach** or **keine Träne nach** I won't shed any tears over that

Nach|weis ['naːxvais] M -es, -e (= Beweis) proof (+gen, für, über +acc of); (= Zeugnis) certificate; (= Zahlungsnachweis) proof of payment (über +acc of); **als** or **zum ~** as proof; **den ~ für etw erbringen** or **führen** or **liefern** to furnish proof of sth; **der ~ seiner Bedürftigkeit ist ihm geglückt** he succeeded in proving his need

-nach|weis M suf in cpds a (= Vermittlungsstelle) agency; **Zimmernachweis** accommodation office; **Hotelnachweis** (*von Fremdenverkehrsbüro*) accommodation service **b** (= *Aufstellung*) directory, list; **Zimmernachweis** accommodation list; **Hotelnachweis** hotel directory, list of hotels

nach|weis|bar ADJ (= *beweisbar*) provable; *Fehler, Irrtum* demonstrable; (*Tech, Chem*) detectable; **dem Angeklagten ist keinerlei Schuld ~** it cannot be proved that the accused is in any way guilty ADV **ich war ~ 500 Kilometer entfernt** it can be proved that I was 500 kilometres (*Brit*) or kilometers (*US*) away; **Sie irren sich ~** it can be proved that you are wrong; **Radioaktivität ist ~ vorhanden** radioactivity is present in detectable amounts

Nach|weis|bar|keit ['na:xvaisbaːɐkait] F -, *no pl* (*Tech, Chem*) detectability

nach|wei|sen ['na:xvaizn] ✪ 53.4 VT *sep irreg* (= *beweisen, aufzeigen*) to prove; *Staatsangehörigkeit, Identität auch* to establish proof of; (*Tech, Med*) to detect; **die Polizei konnte ihm nichts ~** the police could not prove anything against him; **dem Angeklagten konnte seine Schuld nicht nachgewiesen werden** the accused's guilt could not be proved (*Brit*) or proven

nach|weis|lich ['na:xvaislɪç] ADJ provable; *Fehler, Irrtum* demonstrable ADV *falsch* demonstrably; **er war ~ in London** it can be proved (*Brit*) or proven that he was in London; **ich habe das ~ nicht gewusst** it can be proved (*Brit*) or proven that I knew nothing about it

Nach|welt F **die ~** posterity

nach+wer|fen VT *sep irreg* **jdm etw ~** (*lit*) to throw sth after (*Brit*) or at sb; **das ist nachgeworfen** (*inf*) that's dirt cheap (*inf*), that's a gift

nach+wie|gen *sep irreg* VT to weigh again VI to check the weight

nach+win|ken VI *sep* **jdm ~** to wave (goodbye) to sb

Nach|win|ter M late winter

nach+wir|ken VI *sep* to continue to have an effect

Nach|wir|kung F aftereffect; (*fig*) consequence

Nach|wort NT *pl* **-worte** epilogue (*Brit*), epilog (*US*)

Nach|wuchs M **a** (*fig*: = *junge Kräfte*) young people *pl*; **es mangelt an ~** there's a lack of young blood; **der wissenschaftliche ~** the new generation of academics, the up-and-coming academics **b** (*hum*: = *Nachkommen*) offspring *pl*

Nach|wuchs-: **Nach|wuchs|ar|beit** F (*esp Ftbl*) youth development; **Nach|wuchs|au|tor(in)** M(F) up-and-coming young author; **Nach|wuchs|kraft** F junior member of (the) staff; **Nach|wuchs|par|la|men|ta|ri|er(in)** M(F) junior parliamentarian; **Nach|wuchs|schau|spie|ler(in)** M(F) talented young actor/actress; **Nach|wuchs|sor|gen** PL recruitment problems *pl*; **Nach|wuchs|spie|ler(in)** M(F) (*Sport*) junior

nach+wür|zen VTI *sep* to season to taste

nach+zah|len VTI *sep* to pay extra; (= *später zahlen*) to pay later; **20 Euro ~** to pay 20 euros extra

nach+zäh|len VTI *sep* to check

Nach|zah|lung F (*nachträglich*) back-payment; (*zusätzlich*) additional payment

nach+zeich|nen VT *sep Linie, Umriss* to go over; (*fig*: = *wiedergeben*) to reproduce

Nach|zei|tig|keit ['na:xtsaitiçkait] F -, *no pl* (*Gram*) posteriority

nach+zie|hen *sep irreg* VT **a** (= *hinterherziehen*) **etw ~** to pull or drag sth behind one; **das rechte Bein ~** to drag one's right leg **b** *Linie, Umriss* to go over; **Lippen** to paint over or in; *Augenbrauen* to pencil over or in **c** *Schraube, Seil* to tighten (up) VI **a** *aux sein +dat* (= *folgen*) to follow **b** (*Schach etc*) to make the next move; (*inf*: = *gleichtun*) to follow suit

nach+zot|teln VI *sep aux sein* (*inf*) to lag behind

Nach|zug ['na:xtsu:k] M **a** (*Rail*) relief train **b** (*von Familie, Ehepartner*) joining one's family (*in country of immigration*); **der ~ wurde nur Kindern unter 10 gestattet** only children under 10 were allowed to join their families

Nach|züg|ler ['na:xtsy:klɐ] M **-s**, -, **Nach|züg|le|rin** [-ərɪn] F -, **-nen** latecomer, late arrival (*auch fig*)

Na|cke|dei ['nakədai] M **-(e)s**, **-e** or **-s** (*hum inf*) naked body or person; (*Kind*) little bare monkey (*hum inf*)

Na|cken ['nakn] M **-s**, - (nape of the) neck; **den ~ beugen** (*fig*) to submit; **jdm den ~ steifen** to encourage sb, to back sb up; **jdn im ~ haben** (*inf*) to have sb after one, to have sb on one's tail; **jdm im ~ sitzen** (*inf*) to breathe down sb's neck; **ihm sitzt die Furcht im ~** he's frightened out of his wits (*inf*); **ihm sitzt der Geiz im ~** he's a stingy so-and-so (*inf*); **den ~ steif halten** (*inf*) to stand one's ground, to stand fast; **er hat einen starren/störrischen/unbeugsamen ~** he's an obstinate/hard-headed/unbending character

na|ckend ['nakŋt] (*inf*) ADJ *Mensch* naked ADV in the nude

Na|cken-: **Na|cken|haar** NT hair at the nape of the neck; **Na|cken|he|bel** M (*Sport*) nelson; **Na|cken|rol|le** F bolster; **Na|cken|schlag** M rabbit punch; (*fig*) hard knock; **Na|cken|schutz** M neck guard; **Na|cken|star|re** F stiffness of the neck; **~ kriegen** to get a stiff neck; **Na|cken|stüt|ze** F (*Aut*) headrest, head restraint

na|ckig ['nakıç], (*Aus*) **na|ckert** ['nakɐt] (*inf*) ADJ bare; *Mensch* bare, starkers *pred* (*Brit inf*) ADV in the nude

nackt [nakt] ADJ **a** *Mensch* naked, nude (*esp Art*); *Arm, Kinn, Haut etc* bare; *neugeborenes Tier* naked; **einem ~en Mann in die Tasche greifen** (*fig inf*) to look for money where there is none **b** (= *unbewachsen, unbedeckt*) *Erde, Wand* bare; *Schwert* naked **c** (*fig*) (= *unverblümt*) naked; *Wahrheit* plain, naked; *Wirklichkeit* stark; *Tatsachen, Zahlen* bare; **mit ~en Worten** without mincing one's words; **die ~e Armut** naked or sheer poverty; **das ~e Leben retten** to escape with one's life ADV *baden, schlafen* in the nude; *tanzen, herumlaufen auch* naked; **er stand ganz ~ da** he was standing there absolutely starkers (*Brit inf*) or stark naked

Nackt-: **Nackt|ba|den** NT **-s**, *no pl* nude bathing, swimming in the nude; **Nackt|ba|de|strand** M nudist beach

Nack|te(r) ['naktə] MF *decl as adj* nude

Nackt-: **Nackt|heit** F -, *no pl* nakedness; (*von Mensch auch*) nudity; (= *Kahlheit*) bareness; (*von Landschaft*) starkness, bareness; **Nackt|kul|tur** F nudism, naturism; **Nackt|mo|dell** NT nude model; **Nackt|sa|mer** M **-s**, - (*Bot*) gymnosperm (*spec*); **Nackt|schne|cke** F slug; **Nackt|tän|zer(in)** M(F) nude dancer

Na|del ['na:dl] F -, **-n** **a** needle; (*von Plattenspieler*) stylus, needle; (= *Stecknadel, Comput: von Drucker*) pin; (= *Häkelnadel*) hook; (*inf*: = *Spritze*) needle; **mit ~ und Faden umgehen können** to be able to wield a needle and thread; **etw mit heißer ~ nähen** (*fig inf*) to cobble sth together quickly (*inf*); **nach einer ~ im Heuhaufen suchen** (*fig*) to look for a needle in a haystack; **er sitzt wie auf ~n** (*inf*) he's like a cat on hot bricks (*Brit inf*) or on a hot tin roof; **an der ~ hängen** (*inf*) to be hooked on heroin **b** (= *Haarnadel, Hutnadel, Krawattennadel*) pin; (= *Brosche*) brooch **c** (= *Blattnadel, Eisnadel, Kristallnadel*) needle

Na|del-: **Na|del|ab|wei|chung** F magnetic deviation or declination; **Na|del|ar|beit** F needlework *no pl*; **eine ~** a piece of needlework; **Na|del|baum** M conifer; **Na|del|brief** M packet of needles; **Na|del|büch|se** F pin tin; **Na|del|dru|cker** M dot-matrix printer; **Na|del|ein|fäd|ler** [-lainfɛːdlɐ] M **-s,** - needle

threader; **Na|del|filz** M needle felting; **na|del|för|mig** ADJ needlelike, needle-shaped; **Na|del|höl|zer** PL conifers *pl*; **Na|del|kis|sen** NT pincushion; **Na|del|kopf** M pinhead

na|deln ['na:dln] VI (*Baum*) to shed (its needles)

Na|del-: **Na|del|öhr** NT eye of a needle; (*fig*) narrow passage → **Kamel**; **Na|del|spit|ze** F point or tip (of a needle); (*Handarbeit*) needlepoint (lace); **Na|del|stär|ke** F size of needle; **Na|del|stich** M prick; (*beim Nähen, Med*) stitch; **jdm ~e versetzen** (*fig*) to needle sb; **eine Politik der ~e** a policy of pinpricks; **Na|del|strei|fen** PL pinstripes *pl*; **Na|del|strei|fen|an|zug** M pinstripe(d) suit; **Na|del|wald** M coniferous forest

Na|dir ['na:diːɐ, 'na:dɪr] M **-s**, *no pl* nadir

-Nad|ler ['na:dlɐ] M *suf* **-s**, - (*Comput inf*) **24-Nadler** 24-pin printer

Na|gel ['na:gl] M **-s**, - ['nɛːgl] nail (*auch Anat*); (= *Zwecke*) tack; (*aus Holz*) peg; (*an Schuhen*) hobnail, stud; (*Med*) pin; **sich** (*dat*) **etw unter den ~ reißen** or **ritzen** (*inf*) to pinch (*Brit*) or swipe sth (*inf*); **etw an den ~ hängen** (*fig*) to chuck sth in (*inf*); **den ~ auf den Kopf treffen** (*fig*) to hit the nail on the head; **Nägel mit Köpfen machen** (*inf*) to do the job or thing (*inf*) properly → **Sarg, brennen** VI

Na|gel-: **Na|gel|bett** NT (*Anat*) bed of the nail; **Na|gel|boh|rer** M gimlet; **Na|gel|brett** NT (*von Fakir*) bed of nails; **Na|gel|bürs|te** F nailbrush; **Na|gel|fei|le** F nailfile; **na|gel|fest** ADJ → **niet- und nagelfest**; **Na|gel|haut** F cuticle; **Na|gel|haut|ent|fer|ner** [-lɛntfɛrnɐ] M **-s**, - cuticle remover

Nä|gel|kau|en NT **-s**, *no pl* nail-biting

Na|gel-: **Na|gel|knip|ser** [-knɪpsɐ] M **-s**, - nail clippers *pl*; **Na|gel|kopf** M head (of a/the nail); **Na|gel|lack** M nail varnish or polish; **Na|gel|lack|ent|fer|ner** [-lɛntfɛrnɐ] M **-s**, - nail varnish remover

na|geln ['na:gln] VT to nail (*an +acc, auf +acc* (on)to); (*Med*) to pin; (= *mit Nägeln versehen*) to hobnail, to stud

Na|gel-: **na|gel|neu** ADJ (*inf*) brand new; **Na|gel|pfle|ge** F nail care; **~ machen** to give oneself a manicure; **Na|gel|pro|be** F (*fig*) acid test; **Na|gel|rei|ni|ger** M nail-cleaner; **Na|gel|sche|re** F (pair of) nail scissors *pl*; **Na|gel|schuh** M hobnailed boot; (= *Bergstiefel*) climbing boot; **Na|gel|zan|ge** F nail clippers *pl*; (*Tech*) (pair of) pincers *pl*

na|gen ['na:gn] VI (*lit, fig*) to gnaw (*an +dat* at); (= *knabbern*) to nibble (*an +dat* at); (*Rost, Wasser*) to eat (*an +dat* into); **an einem Knochen ~** to gnaw (on or at) a bone VT to gnaw; **wir haben nichts zu ~ noch zu beißen** (*old*) we've eaten our last crust

na|gend ADJ *Hunger* gnawing; *Zweifel, Gewissen* nagging

Na|ger ['na:gɐ] M **-s**, -, **Na|ge|tier** NT rodent

nah [na:] ADJ, ADV = **nahe**

Näh|ar|beit F sewing *no pl*; **eine ~** a piece of sewing

Nah|auf|nah|me F (*Phot*) close-up

Nah|be|reich M **a** (= *unmittelbare Nachbarschaft*) neighbourhood (*Brit*), neighborhood (*US*), vicinity; (= *Umgebung*) surroundings *pl*, environs *pl*; (= *Vorstädte*) suburbs *pl*, suburban areas *pl*; **der ~ von München** the Munich area; **Geschäfte/Züge im ~** nearby shops/local trains **b** (*Phot*) close-up range; **im ~** at close range

na|he ['na:ə] ADJ *comp* **näher** ['nɛːɐ], *superl* **nächs|te(r, s)** ['nɛːçstə] **a** (*örtlich*) near *pred*, close *pred*, nearby; **der Nahe Osten** the Middle East; **von ~m** from close to, at close quarters; **jdm nah sein** to be near (to) sb; **Gott ist uns nah** (*liter*) God is nigh; **Rettung** or **Hilfe ist nah** help is at hand **b** (*zeitlich*) near *pred*, approaching, nigh (*liter*) *pred*; **die ~ Zukunft** the near future

c (= *eng*) *Freund, Beziehung etc* close; **~ Verwandte** close relatives

ADV *comp* **näher** ['nɛːɐ], *superl* **am nächsten** **a** (*örtlich*) near, close; **~ an** near *or* close to; **nah(e) bei** close to *or* by, near; **nah beieinander** close together; **nah liegend** nearby; **~ liegend** (*Gedanke, Lösung*) which suggests itself; *Verdacht, Vermutung*) natural; **aus ~ liegenden Gründen** for obvious reasons; **~ vor** right in front of; **von nah und fern** from near and far; **jdm zu nah(e) treten** (*fig*) to offend sb; **jdm/einer Sache zu nah(e) kommen** to get too close to sb/sth → **daran**

b (*zeitlich*) **mein Prüfungstermin rückt allmählich nah(e)** my examination is getting close; **Weihnachten steht nah(e) bevor** Christmas is just (a)round the corner, Christmas is almost upon us; **nah(e) bevorstehend** approaching; **sie ist nah an die Achtzig** she's almost *or* nearing eighty

c (= *eng*) closely; **nah verwandt** closely-related; **mit jdm nah(e) verwandt sein** to be a near relative of sb's, to be closely related to sb

PREP +*dat* near (to), close to; **der Ohnmacht/dem Wahnsinn** *etc* **nah(e) sein** to be on the verge of fainting/madness *etc*

Nä|he ['nɛːə] F -, *no pl* **a** (*örtlich*) (= *Nahesein*) nearness, closeness, proximity; (= *Umgebung, Nachbarschaft*) vicinity, neighbourhood (*Brit*), neighborhood (*US*); **in meiner ~** near me; **in der ~ des Gebäudes** near the building, in the vicinity of the building; **in unmittelbarer ~** (+*gen*) right next to; **aus der ~** from close to, at close quarters **b** (*zeitlich*) closeness **c** (*emotional etc*) closeness

na|he|bei [naːə'bai] ADV nearby, close to *or* by

na|he brin|gen ▲ VT *irreg* +*dat* (*fig*) **jdm etw ~** to bring sth home to sb, to impress sth on sb; **jdn jdm ~** to bring sb close to sb

na|he ge|hen ▲ VI *irreg aux sein* +*dat* (*fig*) to upset

Nah|ein|stel|lung F (*Film*) close-up (shot)

na|he kom|men ▲ VI *irreg aux sein* +*dat* (*fig*) **jdm ~** (= *vertraut werden*) to get on close terms with sb, to get close to sb; **jdm/einer Sache ~** (= *fast gleichen*) to come close *or* near to sb/sth; **sich** *or* **einander ~** to become close; **das kommt der Wahrheit schon eher nahe** that is getting nearer the truth

na|he le|gen ▲ VT (*fig*) **jdm etw ~** to suggest sth to sb; **jdm ~, etw zu tun** to advise sb to do sth; **er legte es mir nahe, von mir aus zu kündigen** he put it to me that I should resign

na|he lie|gen ▲ VI *irreg* (*fig: Idee, Frage, Lösung*) to suggest itself; **die Vermutung/die Annahme/der Verdacht liegt nahe, dass …** it seems reasonable to suppose/assume/suspect that …; **der Gedanke lag nahe, ihn zum Teilhaber zu machen** the idea of making him a partner seemed to suggest itself

na|he|lie|gend △ ADJ → **nahe** ADV **a**

Na|he|lie|gen|de(s) NT *decl as adj* **das ~ wäre …** the obvious thing to do would be …

na|hen ['naːən] VIR *aux sein* (*liter*) to approach (*jdm/einer Sache* sb/sth), to draw near *or* nigh (*liter*) (*jdm/einer Sache* sb/sth)

nä|hen ['nɛːən] VT to sew; (= *mit Stichen befestigen auch*) to stitch; *Kleid* to make; *Wunde, Verletzten* to stitch (up), to suture (*spec*); **mit der Maschine/mit der** *or* **von Hand genäht** machine-/hand-sewn, sewn by machine/hand; **sich** (*dat*) **die Finger wund ~** to sew one's fingers to the bone; **er musste genäht werden** he had to have stitches → **doppelt** ADV **VI** to sew

nä|her ['nɛːɐ] *comp von* **nah** *etc* **ADJ** **a** (*örtlich*) closer, nearer; **jdm/einer Sache ~** closer to sb/sth, nearer (to) sb/sth; **dieser Weg ist ~** this road is shorter *or* quicker; **die ~e Umgebung** the immediate vicinity → **Hemd**

b (*zeitlich*) closer, sooner *pred*

c (= *genauer*) *Auskünfte, Einzelheiten* further *attr*,

more detailed *or* precise

d (= *enger*) *Verwandter, Bekannter, Beziehungen* closer; **die ~e Verwandtschaft** the immediate family

ADV **a** (*örtlich, zeitlich*) closer, nearer; **~ kommen** *or* **rücken** to come *or* draw nearer, to approach; **bitte treten Sie ~** just step up!; (*Beamter, Arzt*) please come over here

b (= *genauer*) more closely; *besprechen, erklären, ausführen* in more detail; **ich habe mir das Bild ~ angesehen** I had a closer look at the picture; **sich mit etw ~ befassen** *or* **beschäftigen** to go into sth; **jdn/etw ~ kennen lernen** to get to know sb/sth better; **ich kenne ihn nicht ~** I don't know him well; **der Sache** (*dat*) **~ kommen** to be nearer the mark

Nä|her ['nɛːɐ] M -s, -, **Nä|he|rin** [-ərɪn] F -, -nen sewing worker; (*Frau auch*) seamstress

nä|her brin|gen ▲ VT *irreg* +*dat* **jdm etw ~** to give sb an understanding of sth

Nä|he|rei [nɛːə'rai] F -, -en **a** (*no pl*: = *das Nähen*) sewing; (= *Näharbeit*) piece of sewing **b** (*Betrieb*) sewing works *sing or pl*; (*für Kleider*) garment factory

Nä|he|re(s) ['nɛːərə] NT *decl as adj* details *pl*; (*über Stellenangebote etc*) further details *pl*; **alles ~** all details; **~s erfahren Sie von …** further details from …; **ich kann mich des ~n nicht entsinnen** (*geh*) I can't remember the (precise) details

Nah|er|ho|lungs|ge|biet NT recreational area (*close to a town*)

Nä|he|rin F → **Näher**

nä|her kom|men ▲ VI *irreg aux sein* (*fig*) **jdm ~** to get closer to sb; **sie sind sich** *or* **einander näher gekommen** they've become closer

nä|her lie|gen ▲ VI *irreg* (*fig*) to be more obvious; (*Verdacht auch*) to be more natural; **was liegt näher, als …** what could be more obvious than …

Nä|her|lie|gen|de(s) NT *decl as adj* **das ~** the more obvious course

nä|hern ['nɛːɐn] **VR** **sich (jdm/einer Sache) ~** to approach (sb/sth), to get closer (to sb/sth), to draw nearer (to sb/sth); **der Abend näherte sich seinem Ende** the evening was drawing to a close **VT** to bring or draw closer

nä|her ste|hen ▲ VI *irreg* +*dat* (*fig*) to be closer to

nä|her tre|ten ▲ VI *irreg aux sein* +*dat* (*fig*) to get closer to; **ich werde Ihrem Vorschlag ~** (*form*) I shall give full consideration to your proposal

Nä|he|rung ['nɛːərʊŋ] F -, -en (*Math*) approximation

Nä|he|rungs|wert M (*Math*) approximate value

na|he ste|hen ▲ VI *irreg* +*dat* (*fig*) to be close to; (*Pol*) to sympathize with; **sich ~** (= *Menschen, Ideen*) to be close; **wir stehen uns (geistig) sehr nahe** our views are very close; **dem Präsidenten ~de Kreise** circles close to the president; **eine der Regierung ~de Zeitung** a pro-government newspaper

na|he|zu ['naːə'tsuː] ADV nearly, almost, virtually; **das ist ja ~ Wucher** that's little short of profiteering

Näh|fa|den M , **Näh|garn** NT (sewing) cotton (*Brit*) *or* thread

Näh|kampf M (*Mil*) close combat, hand-to-hand fighting

Nah|kampf|mit|tel PL , **Nah|kampf|waf|fen** PL close-range *or* short-range weapons *pl*

Näh-: Näh|käst|chen NT , **Näh|kas|ten** M workbox, sewing box; **aus dem ~ plaudern** (*inf*) to give away private details; **Näh|korb** M work basket, sewing basket

nahm *pret von* **nehmen**

Näh-: Näh|ma|schi|ne F sewing machine; **Näh|na|del** F needle

Nah|ost [naːˈʔɔst] M **in/aus ~** in/from the Middle East

Nah|ost|kon|flikt M , *no pl* (*Pol*) Middle East conflict

nah|öst|lich [naːˈʔœstlɪç] ADJ *attr* Middle East (-ern)

Nähr-: Nähr|bo|den M (*lit*) fertile soil; (*für Bakterien*) culture medium; (*fig*) breeding-ground; **ein guter ~** (*lit*) fertile *or* good soil *or* land; **diese Ideen fanden keinen guten ~** these ideas didn't take root; **Nähr|brü|he** F nutrient solution; **Nähr|cre|me** F skin food (*Brit*), skin-care product

näh|ren ['nɛːrən] (*geh*) **VT** to feed; (*fig*: = *steigern*) to increase, to feed; *Hoffnung* to build up; (= *haben*) *Hoffnungen, Zweifel, Verdacht* to nurture, to nurse; **er sieht gut genährt aus** he looks well-fed; **das Handwerk nährt seinen Mann** there's a good living to be made as a craftsman; **er nährt den Wunsch, berühmt zu werden** he has fond hopes of becoming famous **VR** to feed oneself; (*Tiere*) to feed; **sich von** *or* **mit etw ~** to live on sth → **bleiben b**, **Eichhörnchen** **VI** to be nourishing

nahr|haft ADJ *Kost* nourishing, nutritious; *Boden* fertile, rich; **ein ~es Essen** a square meal

Nähr-: Nähr|kraft F nutritional value; **Nähr|lö|sung** F nutrient solution; **Nähr|mit|tel** PL cereal products *pl*; **Nähr|salz** NT nutrient salt; **Nähr|stoff** M *usu pl* nutrient, nutriment; **nähr|stoff|arm** ADJ low-nutrient *attr*, low in nutrients *pred*; **Nähr|stoff|ge|halt** M nutrient content

Nah|rung ['naːrʊŋ] F -, *no pl* food; **flüssige ~** liquids *pl*; **feste ~** solids *pl*; **geistige ~** intellectual stimulation; **keine ~ zu sich** (*dat*) **nehmen** to take no nourishment; **sie verweigerten jegliche ~** they refused all nourishment; **einer Sache** (*dat*) **(neue) ~ geben** to help to nourish *or* feed sth; **dadurch fand** *or* **erhielt** *or* **bekam die ganze Sache neue ~** that just added fuel to the fire; **dem Feuer ~ geben** (*liter*) to build up the fire

Nah|rungs-: Nah|rungs|auf|nah|me F eating, ingestion (of food) (*form*); **die ~ verweigern** to refuse food *or* sustenance; **Nah|rungs|ket|te** F (*Biol*) food chain; **Nah|rungs|man|gel** M food shortage

Nah|rungs|mit|tel NT food(stuff)

Nah|rungs|mit|tel-: Nah|rungs|mit|tel|al|ler|gie F food allergy; **Nah|rungs|mit|tel|che|mie** F food chemistry; **Nah|rungs|mit|tel|che|mi|ker(in)** M(F) food chemist; **Nah|rungs|mit|tel|in|dust|rie** F , *no pl* food industry; **Nah|rungs|mit|tel|ver|gif|tung** F food poisoning

Nah|rungs-: Nah|rungs|quel|le F source of food; **Nah|rungs|su|che** F search for food; **Nah|rungs- und Ge|nuss|mit|tel|in|dust|rie** ▲ F food and allied industries *pl*; **Nah|rungs|ver|wei|ge|rung** F refusal of food, refusal to eat; **durch ~** by refusing food *or* to eat

Nähr|wert M nutritional value; **hat das einen praktischen ~?** (*inf*) does that have any practical value?; **das hat doch keinen (praktischen) ~** (*inf*) it's pretty pointless

Näh|sei|de F sewing-silk, silk thread

Naht [naːt] F -, ̈e ['nɛːtə] seam; (*Tech auch*) join; (*Med*) stitches *pl*, suture (*spec*); (*Anat*) suture; **aus allen Nähten platzen** to be bursting at the seams

Näh|tisch M , **Näh|tisch|chen** NT sewing table

naht|los ADJ (*lit*) *Teil, Anzug* seamless; (*fig*) *Übergang* smooth, imperceptible; *Bräune* perfect **ADV** **Vorlesung und Diskussion gingen ~ ineinander über** there was a smooth transition from the lecture to the discussion; **die Diskussion schloss (sich) ~ an den Vortrag an** the discussion followed on smoothly from the lecture; **sich ~ in etw** (*acc*) **einfügen** to fit right in with sth; **etw ~ fortsetzen** to carry sth on without interruption; **die Aussagen deckten sich ~**

the statements concurred exactly; **~ braun** tanned all over

Nah|tod|er|fah|rung F , **Nah|tod|er|leb|nis** NT near-death experience

Naht|stel|le F **a** (*Tech*) seam, joint **b** (*fig*) link

Nah|ver|kehr M local traffic; **der öffentliche ~** local public transport; **im ~** on local runs *or* journeys

Nah|ver|kehrs-: **Nah|ver|kehrs|mit|tel** PL means *pl* of local transport; **Nah|ver|kehrs|-zug** M local train

nah|ver|wandt △ ADJ attr → **nahe** ADV c

Näh|zeug NT *pl* **-zeuge** sewing kit, sewing things *pl*

Nah|ziel NT immediate aim *or* objective

na|iv [na'iːf] ADJ naive; **die Naive** (*Theat*) the Ingénue ADV naively; **sich ~ geben** to give the impression of being naive

Na|i|vi|tät [naivi'tɛːt] F -, *no pl* naivety

Na|iv|ling [na'iːflɪŋ] M **-s, -** (*inf*) simpleton; **wie kann man bloß so ein ~ sein!** how can anyone be so naive!

Na|ja|de [na'jaːdə] F **-, -n** naiad

Na|me ['naːmə] M **-ns, -n**, **Na|men** ['naːmən] M **-s, -** (= *Benennung*) name; (*fig*: = *Ruf*) name, reputation; **ein angenommener ~** an assumed name; (*von Autoren etc*) a pen name, a nom de plume, a pseudonym; **unter falschem ~n** under a false name; **der volle ~** his/her/their full name; **mit ~n, des ~ns** (*geh*) by the name of, called; **dem ~n nach** by name; **ich kenne das Stück nur dem ~n nach** I've heard of the play but that's all; **dem ~n nach müsste sie Schottin sein** judging by her name she must be Scottish; **auf jds ~n** (*acc*) in sb's name; **unter dem ~n** under the name of; **er war unter dem ~n Schmidt bekannt** he was known under *or* by the name of Schmidt, he was known as Schmidt; **er nannte seinen ~n** he gave his name; **ich möchte keine ~n nennen, aber ...** I don't want to mention any names but ...; **Ihr ~, bitte?** your *or* the name, please?; **wie war doch gleich Ihr ~?** what was the name?; **dazu gebe ich meinen ~n nicht her** I won't lend my name to that; **der ~ tut nichts zur Sache** his/my *etc* name's irrelevant; **einen ~n haben** (*fig*) to have a name; **sich** (*dat*) **(mit etw) einen ~n machen** to make a name for oneself (with sth); **etw beim ~n nennen** (*fig*) to call a spade a spade, to face facts; **im ~n** (+*gen*) on *or* in (*US*) behalf of; **im ~n des Volkes** in the name of the people; **im ~n des Gesetzes** in the name of the law; **in Gottes ~n!** (*inf*) for heaven's sake (*inf*)

Namen-: **Na|men|ge|bung** [-geːbʊŋ] F **-, -en** = **Namensgebung**; **Na|men|ge|dächt|nis** NT memory for names; **Na|men|kun|de** F science of names, onomastics (*spec*) *sing*; **Na|men|-lis|te** F list of names, name list

na|men|los ADJ **a** nameless (*auch fig*), unnamed; **Helfer** anonymous; **er will ~ bleiben** he wishes to remain anonymous; **die Millionen der Namenlosen** the nameless millions **b** (*geh*: = *unsäglich*) nameless, unspeakable, unutterable ADV (= *äußerst*) unspeakably, unutterably

na|mens ['naːməns] ADV (= *mit Namen*) by the name of, called, named PREP +*gen* (*form*: = *im Auftrag*) in the name of

Na|mens- *in cpds* name; **Na|mens|ak|tie** F (*St Ex*) registered *or* personal share; **Na|mens|än|de|rung** F change of name; **Na|mens|ge|bung** [-geːbʊŋ] F **-, -en** naming; **eine unglückliche ~ für eine Ware** an unfortunate choice of name for a product; **Na|mens|lis|te** F list of names, name list; **Na|mens|nen|nung** F naming names; **auf ~ wollen wir doch verzichten** we don't need to name names; **Na|mens|pa|pier** NT (*Fin*) registered security; **Na|mens|pat|-ron(in)** M(F) name saint; **Na|mens|recht** NT , *no pl* (*Jur*) *law relating to the use of names*; **Na|mens|re|gis|ter** NT list of names, name list; **Na|mens|schild** NT nameplate; **Na|-**

mens|schuld|ver|schrei|bung F (*Fin*) registered bond; **Na|mens|schwes|ter** F namesake; **Na|mens|tag** M name day, Saint's day

NAMENSTAG

In many regions of Germany, particularly in Catholic regions, a person's **Namenstag** is more important than their birthday. This is the day in the Church calendar dedicated to the saint after whom the person is named. On their name day people receive gifts and celebrate the occasion with family and friends.

Namens-: **Na|mens|ver|zeich|nis** NT list of names, name list; **Na|mens|vet|ter** M namesake; **Na|mens|zei|chen** NT initials *pl*; **Na|mens|zug** M signature; (= *Monogramm*) monogram

na|ment|lich ['naːməntlɪç] ADJ by name; **wir bitten, von einer ~en Aufführung der Spender abzusehen** we would request you to refrain from naming the donors; **~e Abstimmung** roll call vote; **~er Aufruf** roll call ADV **a** (= *insbesondere*) (e)specially, in particular, particularly **b** (= *mit Namen*) by name; **~ nicht genannt** not mentioned by name, not mentioned as such; **es wurde ~ abgestimmt** there was a roll call vote

Namen-: **Na|men|ver|zeich|nis** NT list of names, name list; **Na|men|wech|sel** M change of name

nam|haft ADJ **a** (= *bekannt*) famous, well-known; **~ machen** (*form*) to identify **b** (= *beträchtlich*) considerable, substantial ADV (= *beträchtlich*) considerably, substantially

Na|mi|bia [na'miːbia] NT **-s** Namibia

Na|mi|bi|er [na'miːbiɐ] M **-s, -**, **Na|mi|bi|e|rin** [-ərɪn] F **-, -nen** Namibian

na|mi|bisch [na'miːbɪʃ] ADJ Namibian

näm|lich ['nɛːmlɪç] ADV **a** (= *und zwar*) namely, to wit (*Jur, hum*); (*geschrieben*) viz; (= *genauer gesagt*) to be exact **b** (= *denn*) since; **..., es ist ~ sehr regnerisch** ... since it's very rainy; **es ging nicht schneller, wir haben ~ einen Umweg machen müssen** we couldn't be any quicker, we had to take a detour you see ADJ **der/die/das Nämliche** (*old*) the same

nann|te *pret von* **nennen**

Na|no- ['naːnoː-]: **Na|no|gramm** NT nanogram; **Na|no|me|ter** M OR NT nanometer; **Na|no|se|kun|de** F nanosecond

na|nu [na'nuː] INTERJ well I never; **~, wer ist das denn?** hello (hello), who's this?

Na|palm ['naːpalm] NT **-s**, *no pl* napalm

Na|palm|bom|be F napalm bomb

Napf [napf] M **-(e)s, =e** ['nɛpfə] bowl

Napf|ku|chen M ≈ ring-shaped pound cake

Naph|tha ['nafta] NT **-s** *or* f **-**, *no pl* naphtha

Naph|tha|lin [nafta'liːn] NT **-s**, *no pl* naphthalene

na|po|le|o|nisch [napole'oːnɪʃ] ADJ Napoleonic

Nap|pa(le|der) ['napa-] NT **-(s), -s** nappa leather

Nar|be ['narbə] F **-, -n a** (*lit, fig*) scar; (= *Pockennarbe*) pock(mark); **eine ~ hinterlassen** to leave a scar; **die ~ bleibt, auch wenn die Wunde heilt** (*Prov*) deep down, I/you *etc* still bear the scars **b** (*Bot*) stigma **c** (= *Grasnarbe*) turf **d** (= *Ledernarbe*) grain

Nar|ben ['narbn] M **-s, -** grain

Narben-: **Nar|ben|bil|dung** F scarring; **Nar|ben|ge|sicht** NT scarred face; (*als Name*) scarface

nar|big ['narbɪç] ADJ scarred

Nar|ko|se [nar'koːzə] F **-, -n** anaesthesia (*Brit*), anesthesia (*US*); **jdm eine ~ geben** to put sb under anaesthetic (*Brit*) *or* anesthetic (*US*); **in der ~ liegen** to be under an(a)esthetic; **ohne ~**

without an(a)esthetic; **unter ~** under an(a)esthetic; **aus der ~ aufwachen** to come out of the an(a)esthetic

Nar|ko|se-: **Nar|ko|se|ap|pa|rat** M anaesthetic (*Brit*) *or* anesthetic (*US*) apparatus *no indef art*; **Nar|ko|se|arzt** M , **Nar|ko|se|-ärz|tin** F anaesthetist (*Brit*), anesthesiologist (*US*); **Nar|ko|se|mas|ke** F anaesthetic (*Brit*) *or* anesthetic (*US*) mask; **Nar|ko|se|mit|tel** NT anaesthetic (*Brit*), anesthetic (*US*); **Nar|ko|se|zwi|schen|fall** M complication during anaesthesia (*Brit*) *or* anesthesia (*US*)

Nar|ko|ti|kum [nar'koːtikʊm] NT **-s, Narkotika** [-ka] (*Med*) narcotic

nar|ko|tisch [nar'koːtɪʃ] ADJ narcotic; *Düfte* overpowering ADV *duften* overpowering; **der süße Geruch wirkte ~ auf uns** the sweet smell had a druglike effect on us

nar|ko|ti|sie|ren [narkoti'ziːrən] *ptp* **narkotisiert** VT (*lit, fig*) to drug

Narr [nar] M **-en, -en**, **När|rin** [ˈnɛrɪn] F **-, -nen** fool; (= *Hofnarr auch*) jester; (= *Teilnehmer am Karneval*) carnival reveller (*Brit*) *or* reveler (*US*); **den ~en spielen** to act *or* play the fool; **die ~en werden nicht alle** (*Prov*) there's one born every minute (*inf*); **jdn zum ~en halten** to make a fool of sb; **er ist ein verliebter ~** he is love's dupe *or* fool; **dieser verliebte ~** this love--lorn fool → **fressen** VT b

nar|ra|tiv [nara'tiːf] ADJ narrative

nar|ren [ˈnarən] VT (*geh*) **jdn ~** (= *zum Besten haben*) to make a fool of sb, to fool sb; (= *täuschen*) to dupe sb, to fool sb

Narren-: **Nar|ren|frei|heit** F freedom to do whatever one wants; **sie hat bei ihm ~** he gives her (a) free rein; **nar|ren|haft** ADJ foolish ADV foolishly; **Nar|ren|hän|de** PL **~ beschmieren Tisch und Wände** (*Prov*) only fools go around defacing things; **Nar|ren|haus** NT madhouse; **du gehörst ins ~** you need locking up *or* putting away; **Nar|ren|kap|pe** F fool's *or* jester's cap; **nar|ren|si|cher** ADJ, ADV foolproof; **Nar|ren|streich** M (*old*) prank; (= *dumme Tat*) act of stupidity; **Nar|ren|zep|ter** NT fool's sceptre (*Brit*) *or* scepter (*US*), jester's bauble; **das ~ führen** to carry the fool's sceptre (*Brit*) *or* scepter (*US*)

Nar|re|tei [narə'tai] F **-, -en** (*geh*) folly

Narr|heit F **-, -en a** *no pl* folly, stupidity **b** (= *Streich*) prank; (= *dumme Tat*) act of stupidity, stupid thing to do

När|rin F **-, -nen** fool

när|risch [ˈnɛrɪʃ] ADJ foolish, silly; (= *verrückt*) mad; (*inf*: = *sehr*) madly; **die ~en Tage** Fasching and the period leading up to it **das ~e Treiben** Fasching celebrations **sich wie ~ gebärden** to act like a madman, to act crazy; **ganz ~ auf jdn/etw sein** (*inf*) to be crazy about sb/sth (*inf*), to be mad (keen) on sb/sth (*Brit inf*) ADV foolishly, silly; **es ~ treiben** to go wild; **sie hüpfte ganz ~ durchs Haus** she was bouncing around the house like crazy (*inf*)

Nar|ziss ▲ [nar'tsɪs] M **-es, -e** (*liter*) Narcissus

Nar|zis|se [nar'tsɪsə] F **-, -n** narcissus

Nar|ziss|mus ▲ [nar'tsɪsmʊs] M **-**, *no pl* narcissism

Nar|zisst ▲ [nar'tsɪst] M **-en, -en**, **Nar|ziss|tin** ▲ [-'tsɪstɪn] F **-, -nen** (*Psych*) narcissist

nar|ziss|tisch ▲ [nar'tsɪstɪʃ] ADJ narcissistic; **~e Persönlichkeitsstörung** (*Med*) narcissistic personality disorder

NASA F -, **Na|sa** ['naːza] F - NASA

na|sal [na'zaːl] ADJ nasal; **~er Ton** nasal twang ADV nasally; **~ klingen** to sound nasal

Na|sal [na'zaːl] M **-s, -e** nasal

na|sa|lie|ren [naza'liːrən] *ptp* **nasaliert** VT (*Ling*) to nasalize

Na|sal|laut M nasal (sound)

na|schen ['naʃn] VI to eat sweet things; (= *heimlich kosten*) to pinch (*Brit*) *or* snitch (*esp US*) a bit (*inf*); **darf ich mal ~?** can I try a bit?; **an etw** (*dat*) **~** to pinch (*Brit*) or snitch (*esp US*) a bit of sth (*inf*); (= *anknabbern*) to (have a) nibble at sth; **er hat von allem nur genascht** he had only a taste of everything; **die Kinder haben den ganzen Tag nur genascht** the children have been nibbling all day ⊡ **VT** to nibble; **sie nascht gern Süßigkeiten** she has a sweet tooth; **hast du was zum Naschen?** have you got something for my sweet tooth?

Näs|chen ['nɛːsçən] NT **-s, -** *dim von* **Nase**

Na|scher ['naʃɐ] M **-s, -**, **Na|sche|rin** [-ərɪn] F **-, -nen** nibbler; (*der Süßes mag*) sweet-eater

Na|sche|rei [naʃə'rai] F **-, -en** ⓐ *no pl* nibbling; (*von Süßigkeiten*) sweet-eating ⓑ **Naschereien** PL (= *Süßigkeiten*) sweets and biscuits *pl* (*Brit*), candy and cookies *pl* (*US*)

Nasch-: nasch|haft ADJ fond of sweet things; **die Kinder sind so ~** the children are always nibbling at things; **sei nicht so ~** you and your sweet tooth; **Nasch|haf|tig|keit** ['naʃhaftɪçkait] F **-**, *no pl* constant snacking; **Nasch|kat|ze** F (*inf*) guzzler (*inf*); **ich bin halt so eine alte ~** I've got such a sweet tooth; **Nasch|sucht** F craving for sweet things; **Nasch|werk** NT *, no pl* (*old*) dainties *pl*, sweetmeats *pl* (*old*)

Na|se ['naːzə] F **-, -n** ⓐ (*Organ, Sinn, fig*) nose; **durch die ~ reden** to talk through one's nose; **mir blutet die ~, meine ~ blutet** I've got a nosebleed, my nose is bleeding; **jdm die ~ put-zen** to wipe sb's nose; **sich** (*dat*) **die ~ putzen** (= *sich schnäuzen*) to blow one's nose; **pro ~** (*hum*) per head; **es liegt vor deiner ~** (*inf*) it's right in front of your nose or right under your nose (*inf*); **wir haben die Weinberge genau vor der ~** (*inf*) the vine slopes are right on our doorstep; (**immer**) **der ~ nachgehen** (*inf*) to follow one's nose; **eine gute ~ für etw haben** (*inf*) to have a good nose for sth; **die richtige ~ für etw haben** (*inf*) to have a nose for sth; **fass dich an deine eigene ~!** (*inf*) you can (*iro*) or can't talk!; **jdm etw/die Würmer aus der ~ ziehen** (*inf*) to drag sth/it all out of sb; **jdm etw unter die ~ reiben** (*inf*) to rub sb's nose or face in sth (*inf*); **die ~ rümpfen** to turn up one's nose (**über** +*acc* at); **jdm auf der ~ herumtanzen** (*inf*) to play sb up (*Brit inf*), to act up with sb (*inf*); **seine ~ gefällt mir nicht** (*inf*) I don't like his face; **es muss nicht immer nach deiner ~ gehen** (*inf*) you can't always have things your way; **ihm wurde ein Neuer vor die ~ gesetzt** (*inf*) they put a new man over him; **ich sah es ihm an der ~ an** (*inf*) I could see it on his face or written all over his face (*inf*); **auf der ~ liegen** (*inf*) (= *krank sein*) to be laid up; (= *hingefallen sein*) to be flat on one's face (*inf*); **steck deine ~ ins Buch!** (*inf*) get on with your book; **auf die ~ fallen** (*lit, fig*) or **fliegen** (*fig, inf*) to fall flat on one's face; **jdm etw vor der ~ wegschnappen** (*inf*) just to beat sb to sth; **die Katze hat dem Hund das Futter vor der ~ weggeschnappt** the cat took the dog's food away from right under its nose; **der Zug fuhr ihm vor der ~ weg** (*inf*) he missed the train by inches or seconds; **jdm eine (lange) ~ drehen** or **machen** (*inf*) to cock a snook at sb (*Brit*), to thumb one's nose at sb; **jdm etw unter die ~ halten** to shove sth right under sb's nose (*inf*); **jdn mit der ~ auf etw stoßen** (*inf*: = *überdeutlich werden*) to make it more than obvious to sb, to (really) spell it out to sb; **jdm eins auf die ~ geben** (*lit*) to punch sb on (*Brit*) or in (*US*) the nose; (*fig*) to tell sb what's what, to put sb in his place; **sich** (*dat*) **eine blutige ~ ho-len** (*lit, fig*) to get a bloody nose; **die ~ voll ha-ben** (*inf*) to be fed up (*inf*), to have had e-nough; **die ~ von jdm/etw voll haben** (*inf*) to be sick (to death) of sb/sth (*inf*), to be fed up to the back teeth with sth/sb (*Brit inf*); **jdn an der ~ herumführen** to give sb the runaround (*inf*); (*als Scherz*) to pull sb's leg; **an der ~ her-umgeführt werden** to get the runaround (*inf*); **jdm etw auf die ~ binden** (*inf*) to tell sb all a-bout sth; **jdm auf die ~ binden, dass ... ** (*inf*) to

tell sb that ...; **das werde ich ihm gerade auf die ~ binden** (*iro*) you think I'd tell him that!; **er steckt seine ~ in alles (hinein)** (*inf*) he sticks his nose into everything; **er sieht nicht weiter als seine ~** (*inf*) he can't see further than the end of his nose; **die ~ vorn haben** (*inf*) to be a-head by a nose; (*in Forschung etc auch*) to be one step ahead → **Mund, Tür, Wind a, hoch 2 a** ⓑ (*Mech*) handle, horn ⓒ (= *Farbtropfen*) run ⓓ (= *Halbinsel*) promontory, headland, naze; (= *Felsnase*) overhang

na|se|lang ADV **alle ~** all the time, again and again

nä|seln ['nɛːzln] VI to talk or speak through one's nose

nä|selnd ADJ *Stimme, Ton* nasal ⊡ ADV nasally; **~ sprechen** to talk through one's nose

Na|sen-: Na|sen|af|fe M proboscis monkey; **Na|sen|at|mung** F breathing through the nose; **Na|sen|bär** M coati; **Na|sen|bein** NT nose bone, nasal bone; **Na|sen|blu|ten** NT **-s**, *no pl* **~ haben** to have a nosebleed; **häufiges ~** frequent nosebleeds; **ich habe ~** my nose is bleeding, I have a nosebleed; **Na|sen|flü|gel** M side of the nose; **seine ~ fingen an zu zittern** his nose or nostrils began to twitch; **Na|sen|höh|le** F nasal cavity; **na|sen|lang** ADV = **naselang**; **Na|sen|län|ge** F (*fig*) **mit einer** or **um eine ~ gewinnen** to win by a nose; **jdm eine ~ voraus sein** to be a hair's breadth ahead of sb; **Na|sen|loch** NT nostril; **verliebte Nasenlö-cher machen** (*hum*) to make eyes; **Na|sen|ring** M (nose) ring; **Na|sen|rü|cken** M bridge of the nose; **Na|sen|schei|de|wand** F nasal sep-tum (*spec*); **Na|sen|schleim** M nasal mucus; **Na|sen|schleim|haut** F mucous membrane (of the nose); **Na|sen|schmuck** M nose orna-ment(s *pl*); **Na|sen|spit|ze** F tip of the/sb's nose; **ich seh es dir an der ~ an** I can tell by your face, I can see it written all over your face; **Na|sen|spray** M OR NT nasal or nose spray; **Na|sen|stü|ber** [-ʃtyːbɐ] M **-s, -** bump on the nose; **jdm einen ~ versetzen** (*lit*) to bash sb on the nose (*inf*); (*fig*) to tick (*Brit*) or tell sb off; **Na|sen|trop|fen** PL nose drops *pl*; **Na|sen|was|ser** NT **ein ~** (*inf*: = *so gut wie nichts*) next to nothing; **Na|sen|wur|zel** F bridge (of the nose)

Na|se-: Na|se|rümp|fen NT **-s**, *no pl* wrinkling (up) or screwing up (*Brit*) one's nose; **auf etw** (*acc*) **mit ~** reagieren to turn one's nose up at sth; **na|se|rümp|fend** ADV **er sagte ~ ...** screwing up (*Brit*) or wrinkling (up) his nose, he said ...; **die ~en Eltern** the disapproving par-ents; **na|se|weis** ['naːzəvais] ADJ cheeky (*Brit*), fresh (*US*), saucy; (= *vorlaut*) forward, preco-cious; (= *neugierig*) nosy (*inf*), inquisitive ADV (= *frech*) cheekily (*Brit*), impudently; (= *vorlaut*) precociously; (= *neugierig*) nosily; **Na|se|weis** ['naːzəvais] M **-es, -e** (= *Vorlauter*) cheeky (*Brit*) or precocious brat or monkey (*inf*); (= *Neugieri-ger*) nosy parker (*Brit inf*), curious George (*US inf*); (= *Überschlauer*) know-all (*Brit inf*), know--it-all (*US inf*), clever dick (*Brit inf*), wise guy (*inf*)

nas|füh|ren ['naːsfyːrən] VT *insep* **jdn ~** (*als Täu-schung*) to lead sb by the nose; (*als Scherz*) to pull sb's leg (*inf*); **ich war der/die Genasführte** I was the dupe

Nas|horn ['naːshɔrn] NT rhinoceros, rhino

-na|sig [nasɪç] ADJ *suf* **-nosed; platt|nasig** flat--nosed

nas|lang ['naːslaŋ] ADV = **naselang**

nass ▲ [nas] ADJ *comp* **nasser** or **nässer** ['nɛsɐ], *superl* **nasseste(r, s)** or **nässeste(r, s)** wet; **etw ~ machen** to make sth wet; (*für bestimmten Zweck*) to wet sth; *Bügelwäsche* to dampen sth; **sich ~ machen** (*inf*) to wet oneself; **das Bett ~ machen** to wet the bed; **nun mach dich bloß nicht ~!** (*inf*) keep your shirt (*inf*) or hair (*Brit inf*) on!; don't get your knick-ers in a twist! (*Brit inf*); **durch und durch ~** wet

through; **mit ~en Augen** with moist eyes, moist-eyed; **wie ein ~er Sack** (*inf*) like a wet rag (*inf*); **ein ~es Grab** (*fig*) a watery grave; **der ~e Tod** (*fig*) a watery death ADV *comp* **nasser** or **nässer**, *superl* **am nassesten** or **nässesten** *Staub wischen* with a damp cloth; **den Boden ~ wischen** to mop the floor

Nass ▲ [nas] NT **-es**, *no pl* (*liter, hum*) water; (*Ge-tränk*) liquid; **hinein ins kühle ~** (*hum*) into the foaming brine; **gierig trank er das erfrischende ~** (*liter*) eagerly he drank of the refreshing wa-ters (*liter*)

Nas|sauer ['nasaʊɐ] M **-s, -**, **Nas|saue|rin** [-ərɪn] F **-, -nen** (*inf*) sponger (*inf*), scrounger

nas|sau|ern ['nasaʊɐn] VI (*inf*) to sponge (*inf*), to scrounge (**bei** jdm on or off sb)

Näs|se ['nɛsə] F **-**, *no pl* wetness, damp(ness), moisture; **in der ~ stehen** to stand in the wet; **„vor ~ schützen"** "keep dry"; **vor ~ triefen** to be dripping or wringing wet

näs|sen ['nɛsn] VI (*Wunde*) to weep, to dis-charge ⊡ **VT** (*liter*: = *feucht machen*) to dampen, to wet, to moisten; *Bett* to wet

Nass-: nass|forsch ▲ (*inf*) ADJ brash ADV brashly; **nass|kalt** ▲ ADJ cold or chilly and damp, raw; **Nass|ra|sur** ▲ F **die ~** wet shav-ing; **eine ~** a wet shave; **Nass-Tro|cken-Ra-sie|rer** ▲ M wet/dry shaver; **Nass|wä|sche** ▲ F wet washing; **Nass|zel|le** ▲ F wet cell

Nas|tuch ['naːstuːx] NT *pl* **-tücher** (*S Ger, Aus, Sw*) handkerchief

Na|tal ['naːtal] NT **-s** Natal

Na|ti ['naːti] F (*Sw: inf*) **-, -s** (= *Nationalmann-schaft*) national team

Na|ti|on [naˈtsioːn] F **-, -en** nation; **Held der ~** national hero; **der Liebling der ~** the nation's favourite (*Brit*) or favorite (*US*); **die Vereinten ~en** the United Nations

na|ti|o|nal [natsioˈnaːl] ADJ national; (= *patrio-tisch*) nationalist, nationalistic (*usu pej*) ADV (= *auf nationaler Ebene*) nationwide; *regeln* na-tionally; (= *patriotisch*) nationalistically; **~ einge-stellt sein, ~ denken** to be nationalist or nationalistic (*usu pej*); **die Inflation muss ~ eingedämmt werden** inflation must be checked nationally or at the national level

Na|ti|o|nal- [natsioˈnaːl] *in cpds* national; **Na|ti|o|nal|bank** F *pl* **-banken** national bank; **na-ti|o|nal|be|wusst** ▲ ADJ nationally con-scious; **Na|ti|o|nal|be|wusst|sein** ▲ NT na-tional consciousness; **Na|ti|o|nal|bib|lio-thek** F national library; **Na|ti|o|nal|cha|rak-ter** M national character; **Na|ti|o|nal|china** NT Nationalist China; **na|ti|o|nal|chi|ne-sisch** ADJ Chinese Nationalist; **Na|ti|o|nal-ein|kom|men** NT national income; **Na|ti|o-nal|elf** F national (football) team; **die italieni-sche ~** the Italian (national) team, the Italian eleven; **er hat dreimal in der ~ gespielt** he's played for his country three times, he's been capped three times; **Na|ti|o|nal|epos** NT na-tional epic; **Na|ti|o|nal|far|ben** PL national colours *pl* (*Brit*) or colors *pl* (*US*); **Na|ti|o-nal|fei|er|tag** M national holiday; **Na|ti|o-nal|flag|ge** F national flag; **Na|ti|o|nal|gar-de** F National Guard; **Na|ti|o|nal|ge|fühl** NT national feeling or sentiment; **Na|ti|o|nal-ge|richt** NT national dish; **Na|ti|o|nal|ge-tränk** NT national drink; **Na|ti|o|nal|held** M national hero; **Na|ti|o|nal|hel|din** F national heroine; **Na|ti|o|nal|hym|ne** F national an-them

na|ti|o|na|li|sie|ren [natsionaliˈziːrən] *ptp* **na-tionalisiert** VT ⓐ (= *einbürgern*) to naturalize ⓑ (= *verstaatlichen*) to nationalize

Na|ti|o|na|li|sie|rung F **-, -en** ⓐ (= *Einbürge-rung*) naturalization ⓑ (= *Verstaatlichung*) na-tionalization

Na|ti|o|na|lis|mus [natsionaˈlɪsmʊs] M **-**, *no pl* nationalism

Na|ti|o|na|list [natsionaˈlɪst] M **-en, -en**, **Na-ti|o|na|lis|tin** F [-ˈlɪstɪn] **-, -nen** nationalist

na|ti|o|na|lis|tisch [natsiona'lɪstɪʃ] ADJ nationalist, nationalistic (*usu pej*) ADV nationalistically

Na|ti|o|na|li|tät [natsionali'tɛ:t] F -, **-en** nationality

Na|ti|o|na|li|tä|ten-: Na|ti|o|na|li|tä|ten|fra|ge F problem of different nationalities (within one state); **Na|ti|o|na|li|tä|ten|staat** M multinational state

Na|ti|o|na|li|täts|kenn|zei|chen NT nationality sticker *or* (*aus Metall*) plate

Na|ti|o|nal-: na|ti|o|nal|kon|ser|va|tiv ADJ conservative and nationalist *or* nationalistic (*usu pej*) ADV **~ eingestellt sein, ~ denken** to be conservative and nationalist *or* nationalistic (*usu pej*); **na|ti|o|nal|li|be|ral** ADJ liberal and nationalist *or* nationalistic (*usu pej*) ADV **~ eingestellt sein, ~ denken** to be liberal and nationalist *or* nationalistic (*usu pej*); **Na|ti|o|nal|mann|schaft** F national team; **er spielt in der schottischen ~** he plays for Scotland, he plays in (*Brit*) *or* on (*US*) the Scotland team; **die Fußball-Nationalmannschaft** the national football team; **er wurde mit der ~ Europameister** he played in (*Brit*) *or* on (*US*) the national team that won the European Championship; **Na|ti|o|nal|mu|se|um** NT national museum; **Na|ti|o|nal|öko|no|mie** F economics *sing*; **Na|ti|o|nal|park** M national park; **Na|ti|o|nal|rat**[1] M (*Gremium*) (*Sw*) National Council; (*Aus*) National Assembly; **Na|ti|o|nal|rat**[2] M , **Na|ti|o|nal|rä|tin** F (*Sw*) member of the National Council, ≈ MP; (*Aus*) deputy of *or* to the National Assembly, ≈ MP

NATIONALRAT

The Austrian **Nationalrat** is the representative body elected by the people for a period of four years. It is made up of 183 members whose main duties are to pass laws and to exercise political and financial control over the Federal government.

The Swiss **Nationalrat** is one of the two chambers of the **Bundesversammlung**. It consists of 200 members who are elected for four years by voters in the cantons and demi-cantons. Each canton has the right to at least one seat; the remaining seats are allocated in proportion to each canton's population → Bᴜɴᴅᴇsᴠᴇʀsᴀᴍᴍʟᴜɴɢ

Na|ti|o|nal-: Na|ti|o|nal|so|zia|lis|mus M National Socialism; **Na|ti|o|nal|so|zia|list(in)** M(F) National Socialist; **na|ti|o|nal|so|zia|lis|tisch** ADJ National Socialist ADV **~ denken** to be a follower of National Socialism; **Na|ti|o|nal|spie|ler(in)** M(F) international (footballer *etc*); **Na|ti|o|nal|staat** M nation-state; **na|ti|o|nal|staat|lich** ADJ of a nation-state/nation-states; **Ordnung** as a nation-state; **Na|ti|o|nal|stolz** M national pride; **Na|ti|o|nal|stra|ße** F (*Aus, Sw*) national highway; **Na|ti|o|nal|the|a|ter** NT national theatre (*Brit*) *or* theater (*US*); **Na|ti|o|nal|tracht** F national dress *or* costume; **Na|ti|o|nal|trai|ner(in)** M(F) manager of the national team; **Deutschlands ~ Meier** German manager Meier; **Na|ti|o|nal|ver|samm|lung** F National Assembly

NATO F -, **Na|to** ['na:to] F - **die ~** NATO

Na|to-: Na|to-Dop|pel|be|schluss ▲ M NATO twin-track policy; **Na|to|land** NT *usu pl* NATO country, NATO member, member of NATO; **Na|to|mit|glied** NT , **Na|to|mit|glied(s)staat** M NATO member, member of NATO; **Na|to-Ost|er|wei|te|rung** F NATO eastern *or* eastward expansion, NATO's expansion to the east; **Na|to-Stütz|punkt** M NATO base

Nat|ri|um ['na:triʊm] NT -s, *no pl* (*abbr* Na) sodium

Nat|ri|um|chlo|rid ['na:triʊmkloːriːt] NT (*abbr* NaCl) sodium chloride

Nat|ron ['na:trɔn] NT -s, *no pl* (*Chem*) bicarbonate of soda; (= *Backzutat*) bicarbonate of soda, baking soda, bicarb (*inf*); **kohlensaures ~** sodium carbonate; **doppeltkohlensaures ~** sodium bicarbonate, bicarbonate of soda

Nat|ron|lau|ge F caustic soda, sodium hydroxide

Nat|ter ['natɐ] F -, **-n** adder, viper; (*fig*) snake, serpent; **eine ~ am Busen nähren** (*liter*) to nurture a viper at one's breast *or* bosom

Nat|tern|brut F , **Nat|tern|ge|zücht** NT (*fig liter*) viper's brood

na|tur [na'tuːɐ] ADJ *inv* (*Cook*) **Schnitzel/Fisch ~** cutlet/fish not cooked in breadcrumbs **Zitrone ~** freshly-squeezed lemon juice

Na|tur [na'tuːɐ] F -, **-en** a *no pl* (= *Kosmos, Schöpfungsordnung*) nature; **die Giraffe ist ein Meisterwerk der ~** the giraffe is one of Nature's masterpieces; **die drei Reiche der ~** the three kingdoms of nature, the three natural kingdoms; **~ und Kultur** nature and civilization; **wider *or* gegen die ~ sein** to be unnatural, to be against nature; **wie sich dieses Tier in der freien ~ verhält** how this animal behaves in the wild

b *no pl* (= *freies Land*) countryside; **die freie ~, Gottes freie ~** (*liter*) the open country(side); **in der freien ~** in the open countryside

c *no pl* (= *Naturzustand*) nature; **ist ihr Haar gefärbt? – nein, das ist seine ~** is her hair dyed? – no, it's natural; **sie sind von ~ so gewachsen** they grew that way naturally; **ich bin von ~ (aus) schüchtern** I am shy by nature; **sein Haar ist von ~ aus blond** his hair is naturally blond; **zurück zur ~!** back to nature; **nach der ~ zeichnen/malen** to draw/paint from nature

d (= *Beschaffenheit, Wesensart*) nature; (*Mensch*) type; **die menschliche ~** human nature; **es liegt in der ~ der Sache *or* der Dinge** it is in the nature of things; **das geht gegen meine ~** it goes against the grain; **das entspricht nicht meiner ~, das ist meiner ~ zuwider** it's not in my nature; **eine Frage allgemeiner ~** a question of a general nature; **zurückhaltender ~ sein** to be of a retiring nature; **das ist ihm zur zweiten ~ geworden** it's become second nature to him; **eine eiserne ~ haben** to have a cast-iron constitution; **sie ist eine gutmütige ~** she's a good-natured type *or* soul; **das ist nichts für zarte ~en** that's not for sensitive types

Na|tu|ra|li|en [natu'ra:liən] PL a natural produce; **in ~ bezahlen** to pay in kind; **Handel mit ~ barter(ing) with goods** b (*Naturgeschichte*) natural history specimens *pl*

na|tu|ra|li|sie|ren [naturali'zi:rən] *ptp* **naturalisiert** VT a (*Jur*) to naturalize b (*Biol, Zool*) **naturalisiert werden, sich ~** to be naturalized, to naturalize

Na|tu|ra|li|sie|rung F -, *no pl* naturalization

Na|tu|ra|lis|mus [natura'lɪsmʊs] M -, *no pl* naturalism

Na|tu|ra|list [natura'lɪst] M **-en, -en, Na|tu|ra|lis|tin** [-'lɪstɪn] F -, **-nen** naturalist

na|tu|ra|lis|tisch [natura'lɪstɪʃ] ADJ naturalistic ADV naturalistically

Na|tu|ral|lohn M payment in kind

Na|tur-: Na|tur|apos|tel M (*hum*) health fiend (*inf*); **na|tur|be|las|sen** ADJ **Lebensmittel, Material** natural; **Na|tur|be|obach|tung** F observation of nature; **Na|tur|be|schrei|bung** F description of nature; **Na|tur|bur|sche** M (*dated*) nature-boy (*inf*); **Na|tur|denk|mal** NT natural monument

na|ture [na'tyːɐ] (*Sw*), **na|tu|rell** [naty'rɛl] (*geh*) ADJ *inv* (*Cook*) = natur

Na|tu|rell [naty'rɛl] NT -s, **-e** temperament, disposition

Na|tur-: Na|tur|er|eig|nis NT (impressive) natural phenomenon, phenomenon of nature; **Na|tur|er|schei|nung** F natural phenomenon; **Na|tur|er|zeug|nis** NT natural product; **Na|tur|far|be** F a natural colour (*Brit*) *or*

color (*US*) b (*auch* **Naturfarbstoff**) natural dye; **na|tur|far|ben** [-farbn] ADJ natural-coloured (*Brit*), natural-colored (*US*); **Na|tur|fa|ser** F natural fibre (*Brit*) *or* fiber (*US*); **Na|tur|for|scher(in)** M(F) natural scientist; **Na|tur|for|schung** F natural science; **Na|tur|freund(in)** M(F) nature-lover; **Na|tur|gas** NT (*S Ger, Sw*) natural gas; **Na|tur|ge|fühl** NT feeling for nature; **na|tur|ge|ge|ben** ADJ (*lit*) natural; (*fig auch*) normal; **na|tur|ge|mäß** ADJ **~e Waldwirtschaft** natural forestry methods ADV naturally; **Na|tur|ge|schich|te** F natural history; **na|tur|ge|schicht|lich** ADJ natural history *attr*; **Na|tur|ge|setz** NT law of nature; **na|tur|ge|treu** ADJ **Darstellung** lifelike, true to life; (= *in Lebensgröße*) life-size, full-scale ADV realistically; **etw ~ wiedergeben** to reproduce sth true to life; **Na|tur|ge|walt** F *usu pl* element; **na|tur|haft** (*geh*) ADJ natural ADV **~ gegebene Eigenschaften** natural characteristics; **Na|tur|haus|halt** M balance of nature, nature's balance, ecological balance; **Na|tur|heil|kun|de** F nature healing; **Na|tur|heil|ver|fah|ren** NT natural cure *or* remedy; **Na|tur|ka|ta|stro|phe** F natural disaster; **Na|tur|kind** NT child of nature; **Na|tur|kos|me|tik** F natural make-up; **Na|tur|kost** F health food(s *pl*); **Na|tur|kost|la|den** M health-food shop; **Na|tur|kraft** F natural energy *or* force; **Na|tur|kun|de** F natural history; **na|tur|kund|lich** [-kʊntlɪç] ADJ **Forschung, Zeitschrift, Museum** natural history *attr*; **Na|tur|land|schaft** F natural *or* virgin landscape; **Na|tur|leh|re** F (*Sch*) (physical) science; **Na|tur|lehr|pfad** M nature trail

na|tür|lich [na'tyːɐlɪç] ADJ (*alle Bedeutungen*) natural; **in seiner ~en Größe** life-size; **eines ~en Todes sterben** to die from *or* of natural causes, to die a natural death; **es ist doch (nur zu) ~, dass ...** it's (only) natural that ...; **~e Person** (*Jur*) natural person; **~e Zahl** natural number; **die ~ste Sache (von) der Welt** the most natural thing in the world; **es geht nicht mit ~en Dingen zu** there's something odd *or* fishy (*inf*) going on, I smell a rat (*inf*); **~e Grenze** natural frontier *or* boundary; **~e Auslese** (*Biol*) natural selection

ADV a naturally; **die Krankheit verlief ganz ~** the illness took its natural course

b (= *selbstverständlich*) naturally, of course; **~!** naturally!, of course!, certainly!

na|tür|li|cher|wei|se [na'tyːɐlɪçɐ'vaizə] ADV naturally, of course

Na|tür|lich|keit F -, *no pl* naturalness

Na|tur-: Na|tur|lo|cken PL natural curls *pl*; **Na|tur|mensch** M child of nature; **na|tur|nah** ADJ **Stoffe** natural; **~e Tierhaltung** keeping livestock in natural conditions; **~e Landwirtschaft** ≈ organic farming; **das ~e Wohnen ist ...** living close to nature is ... ADV **Tiere ~ halten** to keep animals in conditions close to their natural habitat *or* (*in der Landwirtschaft*) in natural conditions; **die Ferien ~ verbringen** to get close to nature on one's holidays (*esp Brit*) *or* vacation (*US*); **der Park sollte möglichst ~ gestaltet sein** the park should be laid out as naturally as possible; **Na|tur|park** M ≈ national park; **Na|tur|phi|lo|so|phie** F philosophy of nature; **Na|tur|pro|dukt** NT natural product; **~e pl** natural produce *sing*; **Na|tur|recht** NT natural right; **na|tur|recht|lich** ADJ **Wertvorstellungen, Begründungen** based on natural rights; **na|tur|rein** ADJ natural, pure, unadulterated; **Na|tur|schät|ze** PL natural resources *pl*; **Na|tur|schau|spiel** NT natural spectacle, spectacle of nature; **Na|tur|schutz** M conservation, nature conservancy; **unter (strengem) ~ stehen** (*Pflanze, Tier*) to be a protected species; **dieses Gebiet steht unter ~** this is a conservation *or* protected area; **etw unter ~ stellen** to classify sth as a protected species; **Na|tur|schüt|zer** [-ʃʏtsɐ] M **-s, -, Na|tur|schüt|ze|rin** [-ʃʏtsərɪn] F -, **-nen** conservationist; **Na|tur|schutz|ge|biet** NT conservation *or* protected area; **Na|tur|schutz|park** M ≈ national park; **Na|tur|sei|de** F natural silk; **Na|tur|stein** M natural stone; **Na|tur|ta|lent** NT (Person) naturally talented or gifted person; (Begabung) natural talent or gift; **sie ist ein ~** she is a natural; **Na|tur|the|a|ter** NT open-air theatre (Brit) or theater (US); **Na|tur|treue** F trueness to life, faithfulness, fidelity; **Na|tur|trieb** M (natural) instinct; **na|tur|trüb** ADJ Saft, Bier (naturally) cloudy; **na|tur|ver|bun|den** ADJ nature-loving, attached to nature; **Na|tur|ver|bun|den|heit** F love of nature; **Na|tur|ver|eh|rung** F nature worship; **na|tur|ver|träg|lich** ADJ compatible with the environment ADV **etw ~ bau|en** to build sth so that it is compatible with the environment; **etw ~ düngen** to use organic fertilizer on sth; **Na|tur|volk** NT primitive people

naturw. abbr von **naturwissenschaftlich**

Na|tur-: na|tur|wid|rig ADJ unnatural, against nature; (= nicht normal) abnormal; **Na|tur|wis|sen|schaft** F natural sciences pl; (Zweig) natural science; **Na|tur|wis|sen|schaft|ler(in)** M(F) (natural) scientist; **na|tur|wis|sen|schaft|lich** ADJ scientific ADV scientifically; **~ forschen/arbeiten** to do scientific research/ work; **~ interessiert sein** to be interested in science; **na|tur|wüch|sig** Entwicklung natural; Kunst native; **Na|tur|wun|der** NT miracle of nature, natural wonder; **Na|tur|zu|stand** M natural state

'nauf [nauf] ADV (dial) = **hinauf**

'naus [naus] ADV (dial) = **hinaus**

Nau|tik ['nautɪk] F -, no pl nautical science, navigation

nau|tisch ['nautɪʃ] ADJ navigational; Instrumente auch, Ausbildung, Ausdruck nautical; **~e Meile** nautical or sea mile

Na|vel|o|ran|ge F navel orange

Na|vi|ga|ti|on [naviga'tsio:n] F -, no pl navigation

Na|vi|ga|ti|ons-: Na|vi|ga|ti|ons|feh|ler M navigational error; **Na|vi|ga|ti|ons|ge|rät** NT navigation system; **Na|vi|ga|ti|ons|kar|te** F navigation chart; **Na|vi|ga|ti|ons|of|fi|zier(in)** M(F) navigation officer; **Na|vi|ga|ti|ons|raum** M charthouse, chartroom

Na|vi|ga|tor [navi'ga:tɐ] M -s, Navigatoren [-'to:rən], **Na|vi|ga|to|rin** [-'to:rɪn] F -, -nen (Aviat) navigator, navigation officer

na|vi|gie|ren [navi'gi:rən] ptp **navigiert** VTI to navigate

Na|za|re|ner [natsa're:nɐ] M -s, - Nazarene

Na|zi ['na:tsi] M -s, -s Nazi

Na|zi|re|gime NT Nazi regime

Na|zis|mus [na'tsɪsmʊs] M -, Nazismen [-mən] **a** (pej: = Nationalsozialismus) Nazism **b** (= Ausdruck) Nazi term or expression

na|zis|tisch [na'tsɪstɪʃ] (pej) ADJ Nazi ADV **~ orientierte Kreise** Nazi groups; **~ angehaucht sein** to be a Nazi sympathizer; **~ anmutende Parolen** Nazi-sounding slogans

Na|zi- in cpds Nazi; **Na|zi|ver|bre|chen** NT Nazi crime, Nazi atrocity; **Na|zi|zeit** F Nazi period

NB [ɛn'be:] abbr von **nota bene** NB

n. Br. abbr von **nördlicher Breite**

NC [ɛn'tse:] M -(s), -(s) (Univ) abbr von **Numerus clausus**

NC-Fach NT (Univ) subject with restricted entry

n. Chr. abbr von **nach Christus** AD

nd abbr von **niederdeutsch**

NDR [ɛnde:'ʔɛr] M -s abbr von **Norddeutscher Rundfunk**

ne [ne:] ADV (inf) = **nee**

'ne [nə] (inf) abbr von **eine**

Ne|an|der|ta|ler [ne'andɐta:lɐ] M -s, - Neanderthal man

Ne|a|pel [ne'a:pl] NT -s Naples

Ne|a|po|li|ta|ner[1] [neapoli'ta:nɐ] M -s, - (Aus: = Waffel) waffle

Ne|a|po|li|ta|ner[2] [neapoli'ta:nɐ] M -s, -, **Ne|a|po|li|ta|ne|rin** [-ərɪn] F -, -nen Neapolitan

Ne|bel ['ne:bl] M -s, - mist; (dichter) fog; (mit Abgasen) smog; (Mil: künstlich) smoke; (Astron) nebula; (fig) mist, haze; **bei (dichtem) ~** in thick mist/fog; **im ~ liegen** (lit) to be shrouded in mist/fog; (fig) to be shrouded in mystery; **im ~ verschwinden** (lit) to vanish into the mist/fog; (fig) to vanish into the mist; **im ~ stochern** (fig) to stumble or grope about in the dark → **Nacht**

Ne|bel-: Ne|bel|auf|lö|sung F nach ~ after the fog has lifted; **Ne|bel|bank** F pl -bänke fog bank; **Ne|bel|bil|dung** F fog; stellenweise ~ foggy patches; **Ne|bel|fleck** M **a** (Astron) nebula **b** (Zool) leucoma (spec), clouding (of the eye); **Ne|bel|gra|na|te** F smoke grenade or canister

ne|bel|haft ADJ (fig) Erklärung, Ausdrucksweise nebulous, vague; **es liegt in ~er Ferne** it's in the dim distance; (Vergangenes) it's in the distant past; (Zukünftiges) it's in the dim and distant future

Ne|bel|horn NT (Naut) foghorn

ne|be|lig ['ne:bəlɪç] ADJ misty; (bei dichterem Nebel) foggy

Ne|bel-: Ne|bel|kam|mer F (Phys) cloud chamber; **Ne|bel|krä|he** F hooded crow; **Ne|bel|leuch|te** F (Aut) rear fog light; **Ne|bel|meer** NT sea of mist; **Ne|bel|mo|nat** M (liter) November

ne|beln ['ne:bln] VI impers **es nebelt** it's misty/ foggy

Ne|bel-: Ne|bel|schein|wer|fer M (Aut) fog lamp; **Ne|bel|schlei|er** M (geh) veil of mist; **Ne|bel|schluss|leuch|te** ▲ F (Aut) rear fog light; **Ne|bel|schwa|den** M usu pl waft of mist

Ne|be|lung ['ne:bəlʊŋ] M -s, -e (obs) November

Ne|bel-: Ne|bel|wand F wall or bank of fog; (Mil) smokescreen; **Ne|bel|wer|fer** M (Mil) multiple rocket launcher; **Ne|bel|wet|ter** NT misty weather; (mit dichtem Nebel) foggy weather

ne|ben ['ne:bn] PREP **a** (örtlich: +dat or (mit Bewegungsverben) +acc) beside, next to; **er fuhr ~ dem Zug her** he kept level with the train; **er ging ~ ihr** he walked beside her; **ich stelle ihn ~ die größten Denker des 17. Jahrhunderts** I rank him among or with the greatest thinkers of the 17th century **b** (= außer +dat) apart from, besides, aside from (esp US); **du sollst keine anderen Götter haben ~ mir** (Bibl) thou shalt have no other gods before me (Bibl); **anderen Dingen** along with or as well as or amongst other things **c** (= verglichen mit: +dat) compared with or to

Ne|ben-: Ne|ben|ab|re|de F (Jur) supplementary agreement, sub-agreement; **Ne|ben|ab|sicht** F secondary aim or objective; **eine ~ haben** or **verfolgen** to have a secondary aim or objective; **Ne|ben|ak|zent** M (Ling) secondary stress; **Ne|ben|al|tar** M side altar; **Ne|ben|amt** **a** (= Nebenberuf) secondary or additional office **b** (Telec) branch or local exchange; **ne|ben|amt|lich** ADJ Tätigkeit secondary, additional ADV as a second job; **er unterrichtet ~** he also works as a teacher; **Ne|ben|aus|ga|ben** PL extras pl; (Econ) incidental expenses pl

ne|ben|an [ne:bn'ʔan] ADV next door; **die Tür ~** the next door

Ne|ben-: Ne|ben|an|schluss ▲ M (Telec) extension; **Ne|ben|ar|beit** F **a** (= Zusatzarbeit) extra work no indef art, no pl, extra job **b** (= Zweitberuf) second or extra job, sideline; **Ne|ben|arm** M (von Fluss) branch; **Ne|ben|aus|ga|be** F incidental expense; **~n** incidentals, incidental expenses; **Ne|ben|aus|gang** M

side exit; **Ne|ben|be|deu|tung** F secondary meaning or connotation

ne|ben|bei [ne:bn'bai] ADV **a** (= gleichzeitig) at the same time; **etw ~ machen** to do sth on the side **b** (= außerdem) additionally, in addition; **die ~ entstandenen Kosten** the additional expenses **c** (= beiläufig) incidentally; **~ bemerkt** or **gesagt** by the way, incidentally by the by(e); **das mache ich so ~** (inf) that's just a sideline; (= kein Problem) I'll do that with no bother (Brit inf) or without any problem

Ne|ben-: Ne|ben|be|mer|kung F aside; **Ne|ben|be|ruf** M second or extra job, sideline; **er ist im ~ Nachtwächter** he has a second job as a night watchman; **ne|ben|be|ruf|lich** ADJ extra, supplementary; **~e Arbeit/Tätigkeit** extra work/job, sideline, side job ADV as a second job, as a sideline (inf), as a side job (inf); **er verdient ~ mehr als hauptberuflich** he earns more from his second job than he does from his main job; **Ne|ben|blatt** NT (Bot) stipule (spec); **Ne|ben|be|schäf|ti|gung** F, **Ne|ben|be|tä|ti|gung** F **a** (= Zweitberuf) second or extra job, sideline **b** (= Ablenkung) **beim Fernsehen brauche ich immer eine kleine ~** I always need something else to do while I'm watching television; **Ne|ben|be|trieb** M **a** branch industry **b** (= Filiale) (Büro) branch (office); (Werk) subsidiary factory; **Ne|ben|buh|ler(in)** M(F) rival; **Ne|ben|buh|ler|schaft** ['ne:bnbu:lɐʃaft] F -, no pl rivalry; **Ne|ben|dar|stel|ler** M supporting actor; **die ~** the supporting cast sing; **Ne|ben|dar|stel|le|rin** F supporting actress; **Ne|ben|din|ge** PL secondary matters pl; **Ne|ben|ef|fekt** M side effect

ne|ben|ei|nan|der [ne:bn'ʔai'nandɐ] ADV **a** (räumlich) side by side; sitzen, liegen next to each other, side by side; (bei Rennen) neck and neck; **sie gingen ~ durchs Ziel** they were neck and neck at the finish; **drei ~, zu dritt ~** three abreast **b** (zeitlich) simultaneously, at the same time

Ne|ben|ei|nan|der [ne:bn'ʔai'nandɐ, 'ne:bn-] NT -s, no pl juxtaposition

ne|ben|ei|nan|der|her ADV side by side; **sie leben nur noch ~** (Ehepaar etc) they're just two people living in the same house

ne|ben|ei|nan|der-: ne|ben|ei|nan|der le|gen ▲ VT sep to lay side by side or next to each other; **ne|ben|ei|nan|der rei|hen** ▲ VT sep to place or put side by side, to place or put next to each other; **ne|ben|ei|nan|der schal|ten** ▲ VT sep (Elec) to put in parallel; **ne|ben|ei|nan|der set|zen** ▲ VT sep to place or put side by side, to place or put next to each other; **ne|ben|ei|nan|der sit|zen** ▲ VI sep irreg (S Ger: aux sein) to sit side by side or next to each other; **ne|ben|ei|nan|der stel|len** ▲ VT sep to place or put side by side, to place or put next to each other; (fig: = vergleichen) to compare

Ne|ben-: Ne|ben|ein|gang M side entrance; **Ne|ben|ein|künf|te** PL , **Ne|ben|ein|nah|men** PL additional or supplementary income, extra money; **Ne|ben|er|schei|nung** F concomitant; (von Krankheit) secondary symptom; (von Medikament) side effect; (von Tourismus etc) knock-on effect; **Ne|ben|er|werb** M second occupation; **Ne|ben|er|werbs|land|wirt(in)** M(F) part-time farmer; **Ne|ben|fach** NT (Sch, Univ) subsidiary (subject), minor (US); **Ne|ben|fi|gur** F minor character; **Ne|ben|flü|gel** M side wing; **Ne|ben|fluss** ▲ M tributary; **Ne|ben|form** F (Biol) variety; (Ling) variant; **Ne|ben|fra|ge** F side issue; **Ne|ben|frau** F concubine; **Ne|ben|ge|bäu|de** NT **a** (= Zusatzgebäude) annexe (Brit), annex, outbuilding **b** (= Nachbargebäude) neighbouring (Brit) or neighboring (US) building, adjacent building; **Ne|ben|ge|büh|ren** PL extra charges pl; **Ne|ben|ge|dan|ke** M ulterior motive; **Ne|ben|ge|räusch** NT (Rad, Telec) interference, noise; **Ne|ben|ge|schäft** NT sideline; **Ne|ben|ge|stein** NT (Min) country rock; **Ne|ben|ge|wer|be** NT second trade; **Ne|ben|gleis** NT (Rail) siding, sidetrack (US); **Ne|ben|hand|lung** F (Liter) subplot; **Ne|ben|haus** NT house next door, neighbouring (Brit) or neighboring (US) house

ne|ben|her [ne:bn'he:ɐ] ADV **a** (= zusätzlich) in addition, on the side **b** (= gleichzeitig) at the same time, simultaneously

ne|ben|her- [ne:bn'he:ɐ] PREF alongside, beside it/him etc; **neben etw nebenherfahren** (mit Auto) to drive alongside sth; (mit Fahrrad) to ride alongside sth; **nebenherlaufen** to run alongside

ne|ben|hin [ne:bn'hɪn] ADV (= beiläufig) in passing, by the way, casually

Ne|ben-: Ne|ben|höh|le F (Physiol) sinus (of the nose); **Ne|ben|höh|len|ent|zün|dung** F (Med) sinusitis; **Ne|ben|job** M (inf) second or extra job, sideline; **Ne|ben|kla|ge** F (Jur) incidental action; **Ne|ben|klä|ger(in)** M(F) (Jur) joint plaintiff; **Ne|ben|kos|ten** PL additional costs pl; **Ne|ben|kriegs|schau|platz** M secondary theatre (Brit) or theater (US) of war; (fig) secondary area of confrontation; **Ne|ben|li|nie** **a** (von Familie) collateral line **b** (Rail) branch line; **Ne|ben|mann** M pl **-männer** neighbour (Brit), neighbor (US); (Mann neben Ehemann) lover; **Ihr ~** the person next to you, your neighbour (Brit) or neighbor (US); **Ne|ben|nie|re** F suprarenal gland, adrenal body

ne|ben+ord|nen VT sep infin and ptp only (Gram) to coordinate

Ne|ben-: Ne|ben|ord|nung F (Gram) coordination; **Ne|ben|per|son** F minor character; **Ne|ben|platz** M (= Sitzplatz) next seat; (Ftbl) training ground; (Tennis) outside court; **auf meinem ~** in the seat next to me; **Ne|ben|pro|dukt** NT by-product; **Ne|ben|raum** M (benachbart) adjoining or next room; (weniger wichtig) side room; **Ne|ben|rech|te** PL (Jur) subsidiary rights pl; **Ne|ben|rol|le** F supporting role; (fig) minor role; **eine ~ spielen** (lit, fig) to play a supporting role; **das spielt für mich nur eine ~** that's only of minor concern to me; **Ne|ben|sa|che** F minor matter, trifle, triviality; **das ist (für mich) ~** that's irrelevant or that's not the point (as far as I'm concerned); **die schönste ~ der Welt** the greatest trivial pursuit in the world; **ne|ben|säch|lich** ADJ minor, trivial, of minor importance; **etw als ~ abtun** to dismiss sth as irrelevant or beside the point; **Nebensächliches** minor matters pl, trifles pl, trivia(lities) pl; **es ist doch völlig ~, wann er kommt** it doesn't matter a bit when he comes, it's quite irrelevant when he comes; **Ne|ben|säch|lich|keit** ['ne:bnzɛçlıçkaıt] F **-, -en** side issue; **Ne|ben|sai|son** F low season; **Ne|ben|satz** M (Gram) subordinate clause

ne|ben+schal|ten VT sep (Elec) to wire or connect in parallel

Ne|ben-: Ne|ben|schluss ▲ M (Tech) parallel connection, side (of a parallel circuit); **Ne|ben|son|ne** F mock sun, sundog, parhelion (spec); **ne|ben|ste|hend** ADJ **~e Erklärung/ Verbesserung** explanations/correction in the margin; **~e Abbildung** illustration opposite; **im Nebenstehenden wird erklärt ...** the marginal note explains ...; **Ne|ben|stel|le** F (Telec) extension; (Comm) branch; (Post) sub-post office; **Ne|ben|stel|len|an|la|ge** F (Telec) private branch exchange; **Ne|ben|stra|fe** F additional penalty; **Ne|ben|stra|ße** F (in der Stadt) side street; (= Landstraße) minor road, by-road; **Ne|ben|stre|cke** F (Rail) branch or local line; (Aut) minor road; **Ne|ben|the|ma** NT (Mus) minor theme; **Ne|ben|tisch** M adjacent table; **am ~** at the next table; **sie saßen an einem ~** they were sitting at a table near us; **Ne|ben|ton** M pl **-töne** (Ling) secondary stress; **Ne|ben|ur|sa|che** F secondary cause; **Ne|ben|ver|dienst** M secondary income; **Ne|ben|-**

weg M byway; **auf ~en** (lit, fig) by a roundabout route; **Ne|ben|win|kel** M (Math) adjacent angle; **Ne|ben|wir|kung** F side effect; **Ne|ben|woh|nung** F **a** next(-door) flat (Brit) or apartment, flat (Brit) or apartment next door; **in einer ~** in one of the flats (Brit) or apartments next door **b** (= Zweitwohnung) second flat (Brit) or apartment; **Ne|ben|zim|mer** NT (= benachbarter Raum) next or adjoining room; (= Nebengelass) side room; **in einem ~** in an adjoining room/a side room; **Ne|ben|zweck** M secondary aim

neb|lig ['ne:blɪç] ADJ = **nebelig**

nebst [ne:pst] PREP +dat together with; **viele Grüße, Onkel Otto ~ Familie** greetings from Uncle Otto and family

ne|bu|los [nebu'lo:s], **ne|bu|lös** [nebu'lø:s] ADJ nebulous, vague; **er redete so ~es Zeug** he was so vague ADV vaguely, nebulously

Ne|ces|saire [nesɛ'sɛːɐ] NT **-s, -s** (= Kulturbeutel) vanity bag or case; (zur Nagelpflege) manicure case; (= Nähzeug) sewing bag

ne|cken ['nɛkn] VT to tease; **jdn mit jdm/etw ~** to tease sb about sb/sth VR **sich** or **einander ~, sich mit jdm ~** to tease each other, to have a tease (inf); **was sich liebt, das neckt sich** (Prov) teasing is a sign of affection

Ne|cke|rei [nɛkə'raɪ] F **-, -en** teasing no pl

ne|ckisch ['nɛkɪʃ] ADJ **a** (= scherzhaft) merry, teasing; Einfall, Melodie amusing; Unterhaltung bantering; (inf: = kokett, kess) Kleid, Frisur coquettish, saucy; Spielchen mischievous, naughty ADV **a** (= scherzhaft) teasingly; (= kokett) coquettishly

nee [ne:] ADV (inf) no, nope (inf); **~, so was!** no, really!

Neer [ne:ɐ] F **-, -en** (N Ger) eddy

Nef|fe ['nɛfə] M **-n, -n** nephew

neg. ADJ abbr von **negativ** neg.

Ne|ga|ti|on [nega'tsio:n] F **-, -en** negation

ne|ga|tiv ['ne:gati:f, nega'ti:f] ADJ negative ADV **a** (= ablehnend) antworten negatively, in the negative; **jdm auf eine Frage ~ antworten** to answer sb's question in the negative; **sich ~ zu etw stellen** to adopt a negative attitude toward(s) sth; **sich ~ zu etw äußern** to speak negatively about sth; (ablehnen) to be against sth; **ich beurteile seine Arbeit sehr ~** I have a very negative view of his work; **die Untersuchung verlief ~** the examination proved negative; **die Antwort/Beurteilung fiel ~er aus als erwartet** the answer/assessment was less favourable (Brit) or favorable (US) than expected; **zu etw ~ eingestellt sein** to have reservations about sth; **alles ~ sehen** to be pessimistic **b** (= ungünstig) **sich ~ auf etw** (acc) **auswirken** to be detrimental to or for sth; **die Umsatzentwicklung wird ~ eingeschätzt** the prognosis for turnover is negative **c** (Elec) etw ~ **(auf)laden** to put a negative charge on sth

Ne|ga|tiv ['ne:gati:f, nega:ti:f] NT **-s, -e** [-və] (Phot) negative

Ne|ga|tiv-: Ne|ga|tiv|bei|spiel NT negative example; **Ne|ga|tiv|bi|lanz** F debit balance; **Ne|ga|tiv|bild** NT negative; **Ne|ga|tiv|druck** M pl **-drucke** etw im ~ **herstellen** to reverse sth out; **Ne|ga|tiv|film** M negative (film); **Ne|ga|tiv|image** [-ɪmɪtʃ] NT negative image

Ne|ga|ti|vi|tät [negativi'tɛːt] F **-, no pl** negativity

Ne|ga|tiv-: Ne|ga|tiv|ko|pie F (Typ) negative copy; **Ne|ga|tiv|lis|te** F (Med, Pharm) drug exclusion list **b** (allgemein: pej) black list

nei|ger ['ne:gɐ] ADJ pred (Aus inf: = pleite) broke (inf)

Ne|ger ['ne:gɐ] M **-s, -** **a** (usu pej) Negro (pej); **angeben wie ein nackte ~** (inf) to shoot one's big mouth off (inf); **~ schwarz a b** (TV sl) (= Gedächtnishilfe) idiot board (Brit inf), Teleprompter® (US); (= Verdunklungstafel) gobo

Ne|ge|rin ['ne:gərɪn] F **-, -nen** (usu pej) Negress (pej), Negro woman (pej)

Ne|ger-: Ne|ger|krau|se F (usu pej, dated) frizzy hair; **Ne|ger|kuss** ▲ M chocolate marshmallow with biscuit base; **Ne|ger|lein** ['ne:gəlaɪn] NT **-s, -** (usu pej) dim von **Neger** little Negro (pej); **Ne|ger|mu|sik** F (usu pej) Negro music (pej); **Ne|ger|skla|ve** M , **Ne|ger|skla|vin** F Negro slave

ne|gie|ren [ne'gi:rən] ptp **negiert** VT (= verneinen) Satz to negate; (= bestreiten) Tatsache, Behauptung to deny

Neg|li|gé [negli'ʒe:] NT **-s, -s**, **Neg|li|gee** ▲ NT **-s, -s** negligee, négligé

ne|grid [ne'gri:t] ADJ Rasse negro

ne|gro|id [negro'i:t] ADJ negroid

neh|men ['ne:mən] pret **nahm** [na:m], ptp **ge|nom|men** [gə'nɔmən] VTI **a** (= ergreifen) to take; **etw in die Hand ~** (lit) to pick sth up; (fig) to take sth in hand; **etw an sich** (acc) **~** (= aufbewahren) to take care or charge of sth, to look after sth; (= sich aneignen) to take sth (for oneself) **b** (= wegnehmen) to take; Schmerz to take away, to relieve; (= versperren) Blick, Sicht to block; **jdm etw ~** to take sth (away) from sb; **jdm die Hoffnung/den Glauben/die Freude ~** to take away sb's hope/faith/joy, to rob or deprive sb of his hope/faith/joy; **um ihm die Angst zu ~** to stop him being afraid; **ihm sind seine Illusionen genommen worden** his illusions were shattered; **er ließ es sich** (dat) **nicht ~, mich persönlich hinauszubegleiten** he insisted on showing me out himself; **diesen Erfolg lasse ich mir nicht ~** I won't be robbed of this success; **woher ~ und nicht stehlen?** (inf) where on earth am I going to find any/one etc?; **sie ~ sich** (dat) **nichts** (inf) there's nothing to choose between them, one's as good as the other; **sich** (dat) **vom Brot/Fleisch ~** to help oneself to bread/meat; **~ Sie sich doch bitte!** please help yourself **c** (= benutzen) Auto, Zug etc to take; Bürste, Zutaten, Farbe to use; **man nehme ...** (Cook) take ...; **sich** (dat) **etw ~** (Zimmer, Wohnung) to take sth; (= sich bedienen auch) to help oneself to sth; **sich** (dat) **einen Anwalt/eine Hilfe ~** to get a lawyer/ some help **d** (= annehmen) Geschenk, Stelle, Bewerber, Anwalt to take; (= berechnen) to charge; **was ~ Sie dafür?** how much will you take for it?; **jdn zu sich ~** to take sb in; **Gott hat ihn zu sich genommen** (euph) he has been called home to his maker; **etw ~, wie es kommt** to take sth as it comes; **jdn ~, wie er ist** to take sb as he is; **etw auf sich** (acc) **~** to take sth upon oneself; **er ist immer der Nehmende** he does all the taking, with him it's just take take take (inf); **die Nehmenden und die Gebenden** the takers and the givers **e** (= einnehmen) to take; Essen to have, to take; **sie nimmt Rauschgift/die Pille** she's on drugs/the pill, she takes drugs/the pill; **etw zu sich ~** to take sth, to partake of sth (liter); **der Patient hat nichts zu sich ~ können** the patient has been unable to take nourishment **f** (= auffassen) to take; (= behandeln) to handle, to treat; **wenn Sie das so ~ wollen** if you care or choose to take it that way; **etw für ein or als Zeichen ~** to take sth as a sign or an omen; **wie mans nimmt** (inf) depending on your point of view; **wissen, wie man jdn ~ muss** or **soll** to know how to take sb **g** (= auswählen) to take; Essen, Menü to have, to take; **sich** (dat) **einen Mann/eine Frau ~** to take a husband/wife **h** Hürde, Festung, Stadt, Frau to take; Schwierigkeiten to overcome; **das Auto nahm den Berg im dritten Gang** the car took the hill in third gear **i** (in festen Verbindungen mit n und adv siehe dort)

Neh|mer ['ne:mɐ] M **-s, -**, **Neh|me|rin** [-ərɪn] F **-, -nen** **a** recipient **b** (= Käufer) taker

Neh|rung ['ne:rʊŋ] F **-, -en** spit (of land)

Neid [naɪt] M -(e)s [-dəs] *no pl* envy, jealousy (*auf +acc* of); **aus ~** out of envy *or* jealousy; **der ~ der Besitzlosen** (*inf*) sour grapes (*inf*); **nur kein ~!** don't be envious *or* jealous!; **grün (und gelb) vor ~** (*inf*) green with envy; **das muss ihm der ~ lassen** (*inf*) you have to say that much for him, give the devil his due; **mit ~ auf etw** (*acc*) **blicken** to view sth with envy; **jds** (*acc*) *or* **bei jdm ~ erregen** *or* **(er)wecken** to make sb jealous *or* envious, to arouse sb's jealousy; **vor ~ platzen** (*inf*) *or* **vergehen** to die of envy → **erblassen**

nei|den ['naɪdn] VT **jdm etw ~** to envy sb (for) sth

Nei|der ['naɪdɐ] M -s, -, **Nei|de|rin** [-ərɪn] F -, -nen envious *or* jealous person; **reiche Leute haben viele ~** rich people are much envied; **ihre/seine** *etc* **~** those who envy her/him *etc*

Neid-: **neid|er|füllt** [-lɛɐfʏlt] ADJ *Blick* filled with *or* full of envy, envious ADV enviously; **~ auf jdn blicken** to look at sb enviously *or* jealously; **Neid|ham|mel** M (*inf*) jealous *or* envious person; **der alte/du alter ~!** he's/you're just jealous

nei|disch ['naɪdɪʃ], (*S Ger, Aus*) **nei|dig** ['naɪdɪç] ADJ jealous, envious; **auf jdn/etw ~ sein** to be jealous of sb/sth; **etw mit ~en Blicken betrachten** to look enviously at sth, to cast covetous glances at sth ADV jealously, enviously; **etw ~ kommentieren** to make envious comments about sth

neid|los ADJ ungrudging, without envy ADV graciously, gracefully; **das gebe ich ~ zu** I'm willing to admit it graciously; **etw ~ anerkennen** to acknowledge sth graciously

Nei|ge ['naɪgə] F -, -n **a** (= *Überrest*) remains *pl*; **das Glas bis zur ~ leeren** (*liter*) to drain the cup to the dregs; **den Kelch bis zur ~ leeren** *or* **trinken** (*fig liter*) to drain the bitter cup (*liter*); **etw bis zur ~ auskosten** (= *genießen*) to savour (*Brit*) *or* savor (*US*) sth to the full; **etw bis zur bitteren ~ auskosten** *or* **kennen lernen** to suffer sth to the full **b** *no pl* (*geh*: = *Ende*) **zur ~ gehen** to draw to an end *or* a close; **die Vorräte gehen zur ~** the provisions are fast becoming exhausted

nei|gen ['naɪgn] ⊙ 53.1 VT (= *beugen*) *Kopf, Körper* to bend; (*zum Gruß*) to bow; (= *kippen*) *Behälter, Glas* to tip, to tilt, to incline; **die Bäume ~ ihre Zweige bis zur Erde** (*geh*) the trees bow their branches to the ground; **geneigte Ebene** (*Math*) sloping surface

VR (*Ebene*) to slope, to incline; (*Mensch*) to bend; (*liter*: = *sich verneigen*) to bow; (*unter Last*: *Bäume etc*) to bow, to bend; (*Gebäude etc*) to lean; (= *kippen*) to tip (up), to tilt (up); (*Schiff*) to list; (*liter*: *Tag, Leben*) to draw to a close *or* an end; **sich nach vorne/nach hinten/zur Seite ~** (*Mensch*) to lean *or* bend forward/backwards/to one side; **ein leicht zur Seite geneigtes Gebäude** a building which is leaning *or* tilting over slightly; **mit seitwärts geneigtem Kopf** with his/her head held on *or* to one side; **die Waagschale neigt sich zu seinen Gunsten** (*geh*) the scales are tipping *or* the tide is turning in his favour (*Brit*) *or* favor (*US*)

VI **zu etw ~** to tend toward(s) sth, to have a tendency toward(s) sth; (= *für etw anfällig sein*) to be susceptible *or* prone to sth; **er neigt zum Alkohol** he has a tendency to drink; **er neigt zum Sozialismus** he tends *or* leans toward(s) socialism, he has socialist leanings; **zu der Ansicht** *or* **Annahme ~, dass ...** to tend *or* lean toward(s) the view that ..., to be inclined to take the view that ...; **ich neige eher zur klassischen Musik** I tend rather toward(s) classical music → *auch* **geneigt**

Neige-: **Nei|ge|tech|nik** F, *no pl* (*Rail*) tilting technology; **Nei|ge|tech|nik|zug** M , **Nei|ge|zug** M (*Rail*) tilting train

Nei|gung ['naɪgʊŋ] F -, -en **a** (= *das Neigen*) inclination; (= *Gefälle*) incline, slope; (*esp Rail*) gradient (*Brit*), grade (*US*); (= *Schräglage*) tilt;

(*von Schiff*) list; (*von Magnetnadel*) dip; (*Astron*) inclination

b (= *Tendenz*) tendency; (*Med*: = *Anfälligkeit*) proneness, tendency; (= *Hingezogensein, Veranlagung*) leaning *usu pl*; (= *Hang, Lust*) inclination; **er hat eine ~ zum Geiz/zum Trinken/zur Kritik** he has a tendency to be mean/to drink/to criticize, he inclines *or* tends to be mean/to drink/to criticize; **künstlerische/politische ~en** artistic/political leanings; **etw aus ~ tun** to do sth by inclination; **keine/geringe ~ verspüren, etw zu tun** to have *or* feel no/little inclination to do sth

c (= *Zuneigung*) affection, fondness; **zu jdm eine ~ fassen** to take a liking to sb; **jds ~ erwidern** to return sb's affection

Nei|gungs-: **Nei|gungs|ehe** F (*geh*) love match; **Nei|gungs|grup|pe** F (*Sch*) club; ~ **Fußball** (school) football club; **Nei|gungs|mes|ser** M -s, - inclinometer; **Nei|gungs|win|kel** M angle of inclination

nein [naɪn] ADV no; (*Überraschung*) no; **kommt er? – ~!** is he coming? – no(, he isn't); **ich sage nicht Nein** I wouldn't say no; **da sage ich nicht Nein** I wouldn't say no to that; **~, ~ und nochmals ~** for the last time, no!; **Hunderte, ~ Tausende, hunderte, ~ tausende** hundreds, no *or* nay (*liter*) thousands; **~, so was!** well I never!, you don't say!; **~ doch!** no!; **o ~!, aber ~!** certainly not!, of course not!; **~, dass du dich auch mal wieder sehen lässt!** fancy seeing you again; **~ wie nett, dass du mich mal besuchst!** well, how nice of you to visit me

Nein [naɪn] NT -s, *no pl* no; **bei seinem ~ bleiben** to stick to one's refusal, to remain adamant; **mit Ja oder ~ stimmen** to vote yes or no; (*Parl auch*) to vote yea or aye (*Brit*) or nay

Nein-: **Nein|sa|ger** [-za:gɐ] M -s, -, **Nein|sa|ge|rin** [-ərɪn] F -, -nen **er ist ein ewiger ~** he always says no; **Nein|stim|me** F (*Pol*) no (-vote), nay

Nekro-: **Nek|ro|log** [nekro'lo:k] M -(e)s, -e [-gə] (*liter*) obituary (notice), necrology (*form*); **Nek|ro|phi|lie** [nekrofi'li:] F -, *no pl* necrophilia; **Nek|ro|po|le** [nekro'po:lə] F -, -n necropolis

Nek|tar ['nɛktar] M -s, *no pl* (*Myth, Bot*: = *Fruchtnektar*) nectar

Nek|ta|ri|ne [nɛkta'ri:nə] F -, -n nectarine

Nel|ke ['nɛlkə] F -, -n **a** pink; (*gefüllt*) carnation **b** (*Gewürz*) clove

Nel|son ['nɛlzɔn] M -(s), -(s) (*Sport*) nelson

'nem [nɛm] *abbr von* **einem**

Ne|me|sis ['ne:mezɪs] F -, *no pl* nemesis

'nen [nɛn] *abbr von* **einen**

nenn|bar ADJ specifiable; *Gefühl, Phänomen, Gedanke etc* nam(e)able; **nicht ~** unspecifiable; unnam(e)able

Nenn|be|trag M (*Comm*) = **Nennwert**

nen|nen ['nɛnən] *pret* **nannte** ['nantə], *ptp* **genannt** [gə'nant] VT **a** (= *bezeichnen*) to call; (= *einen bestimmten Namen geben*) to name, to call; **jdn nach jdm ~** to name sb after (*Brit*) or for (*US*) sb; **Friedrich II., genannt „der Große"** Frederick II, known as Frederick the Great; **das nenne ich Mut!** that's what I call courage!; **das nennst du schön?** you call that beautiful? → **eigen, Name, so** ADV **b**

b (= *angeben, aufzählen*) to name; *Beispiel, Grund, Details* to give; **die genannten Namen** the names mentioned; **können Sie mir einen guten Anwalt ~?** could you give me the name of a good lawyer?

c (= *erwähnen*) to mention; **das (weiter oben) Genannte** the above; **das genannte Schloss** the above-mentioned castle, the castle referred to VR to call oneself; (= *heißen*) to be called, to call oneself; **er nennt sich nur so** that's just what he calls himself; **und so was nennt sich Liebe/modern** (*inf*) and they call that love/modern; **und so was (wie er) nennt sich modern/**

Dichter (*inf*) and he calls himself modern/a poet

nen|nens|wert ADJ considerable, not inconsiderable; **nicht ~** negligible, not worth mentioning; **keine ~en Schwierigkeiten** no great difficulties, no difficulties worth mentioning; **nichts Nennenswertes** nothing worth mentioning, nothing of any consequence; **die Demonstration verlief ohne ~e Zwischenfälle** the demonstration went off without major incident ADV significantly; **sich nicht ~ unterscheiden** not to be significantly different

Nen|ner ['nɛnɐ] M -s, - (*Math*) denominator; **kleinster gemeinsamer ~** (*lit, fig*) lowest common denominator; **etw auf einen (gemeinsamen) ~ bringen** (*lit, fig*) to reduce sth to a common denominator

Nenn-: **Nenn|fall** M nominative; **Nenn|form** F infinitive; **Nenn|on|kel** M **er ist nur ein ~** I just call him uncle; **ich bin nur ihr ~** she just calls me uncle; **Nenn|tan|te** F **sie ist nur eine ~** I just call her aunt; **ich bin nur seine ~** he just calls me aunt

Nen|nung ['nɛnʊŋ] F -, -en (= *das Nennen*) naming; (*Sport*) entry

Nenn-: **Nenn|wert** M (*Fin*) nominal *or* face *or* par value; **zum ~** at par; **über/unter dem ~** above/below par; **eine Aktie im** *or* **zum ~ von 50 EUR** a share with a nominal *or* face *or* par value of 50 euros; **nenn|wert|los** ADJ *Aktie* nonpar; **Nenn|wort** NT *pl* -wörter noun

neo-, Neo- [neo] *in cpds* neo-

Neo|dym [neo'dy:m] NT -s, *no pl* (*abbr* **Nd**) neodymium

Neo-: **Neo|fa|schis|mus** M neo-fascism; **Neo|klas|si|zis|mus** M neoclassicism; **Neo|li|be|ra|lis|mus** M neoliberalism

Neo|li|thi|kum [neo'li:tikʊm] NT -s, *no pl* Neolithic period

neo|li|thisch [neo'li:tɪʃ] ADJ *attr* Neolithic

Neo|lo|gis|mus [neolo'gɪsmʊs] M -, **Neologismen** [-mən] neologism

Ne|on ['ne:ɔn] NT -s, *no pl* (*abbr* **Ne**) neon

Neo-: **Neo|na|zi** ['neɔna:tsi] M neo-Nazi; **Neo|na|zis|mus** [neona'tsɪsmʊs, 'neɔ-] M neo-Nazism; **neo|na|zis|tisch** [neona'tsɪstɪç, 'neɔ-] ADJ neo-Nazi ADV **~ klingende Parolen** neo-Nazi sounding slogans; **~ ausgerichtete Kreise** neo-Nazi groups; **~ angehauchtes Denken** a mentality tainted by neo-Nazism

Neon-: **Neon|licht** NT neon light; **Neon|re|kla|me** F neon sign; **Neon|röh|re** F neon tube or strip

Neo|pren|an|zug [neo'pre:n-] M wet suit

Ne|pal ['ne:pal, ne'pa:l] NT -s Nepal

Ne|pa|le|se [nepa'le:zə] M -, -n, **Ne|pa|le|sin** [-'le:zɪn] F -, -nen Nepalese

ne|pa|le|sisch [nepa'le:zɪʃ] ADJ Nepalese

Ne|phri|tis [ne'fri:tɪs] F -, **Nephri|tiden** [nefri'ti:dn] (*Med*) nephritis

Ne|phrom [ne'fro:m] NT -s, -e (*Med*) nephroma

Ne|po|tis|mus [nepo'tɪsmʊs] M -, *no pl* (*geh*) nepotism

Nepp [nɛp] M -s, *no pl* (*inf*) **so ein ~!, das ist ja ~!** that's daylight (*Brit*) or highway robbery! (*inf*), it's a rip-off! (*inf*)

nep|pen ['nɛpn] VT (*inf*) to fleece (*inf*), to rip off (*inf*); **da bist du aber geneppt worden!** they must have seen you coming (*inf*)

Nepp|lo|kal NT (*inf*) clip joint (*inf*)

Nep|tun [nɛp'tu:n] M -s Neptune

Nep|tu|ni|um [nɛp'tu:niʊm] NT -s, *no pl* (*abbr* **Np**) neptunium

Nerv [nɛrf] M -s *or* -en, -en nerve; (*Bot auch*) vein; (*obs*: = *Sehne*) sinew; **(leicht) die ~en verlieren** to scare (easily), to get nervous (easily); **er hat trotz allem die ~en behalten** *or* **nicht verloren** in spite of everything he kept calm *or* kept his cool (*inf*); (*die Selbstbeherrschung nicht verloren*) in spite of everything he didn't lose control; **die ~en sind (mit) ihm durchgegangen** he lost control or his cool (inf), he snapped (inf); **gute/schlechte** or **schwache ~en haben** to have strong or good/bad or weak nerves; **sie kennt** or **hat keine ~en** she doesn't get nervous; **der hat (vielleicht) ~en!** (inf) he's got a nerve! (inf); **er hat ~e wie Drahtseile** or **Bindfäden** or **Stricke** he has nerves of steel; **es geht** or **fällt mir auf die ~en** (inf) it gets on my nerves; **jdm den (letzten) ~ töten** or **rauben** (inf) to get on sb's nerves or wick (inf); **bei ihm liegen die ~en blank** or **bloß** he's a bag of nerves (inf); **den ~ haben, etw zu tun** to have the nerve to do sth; **dafür fehlt mir der ~** I don't have the nerve for that; **jdn am ~ treffen** to touch a raw nerve; **den ~ von etw treffen** to touch or mention the essential part of sth; **jds ~ treffen** (inf, positiv) to be sb's kind of thing (inf); **das kostet ~en** it's a strain on the nerves; **das kostete ihn ~en** it was a strain on his nerves; **~en zeigen** to show nerves → **herunter sein**

ner|ven ['nɛrfn] (inf) **VT** jdn (mit etw) ~ to get on sb's nerves (with sth); **genervt sein** (= nervös sein) to be worked up; (= gereizt sein) to be irritated **VI das nervt** it gets on your nerves; **du nervst!** (inf) you're bugging me! (inf)

Ner|ven- ['nɛrfn-]: **Ner|ven|an|span|nung** F nervous tension; **Ner|ven|arzt** M , **Ner|ven|-ärz|tin** F neurologist; **ner|ven|auf|rei|bend** ADJ nerve-racking ADV **die Klasse ist ~ laut** the noise of the class plays on the nerves; **Ner|ven|bahn** F nerve; **Ner|ven|be|las|tung** F strain on the nerves; **Ner|ven|be|ru|hi|gungs|mit|tel** NT sedative, tranquillizer; **Ner|ven|bün|del** NT fascicle; (fig inf) bag or bundle of nerves (inf); **Ner|ven|chir|ur|gie** F neurosurgery; **Ner|ven|ent|zün|dung** F neuritis; **Ner|ven|fa|ser** F nerve fibre (Brit) or fiber (US); **Ner|ven|gas** NT (Mil) nerve gas; **Ner|ven|gift** NT neurotoxin; **Ner|ven|heil|an|stalt** F psychiatric or mental hospital; **Ner|ven|heil|kun|de** F neurology; **Ner|ven|kit|zel** M (fig) thrill; **etw als einen äußersten ~ empfinden** to get a big thrill or kick (inf) out of sth, to find sth really thrilling; **er liebt/sucht den ~** he gets a kick out of it (inf); **Ner|ven|kli|nik** F psychiatric clinic; **Ner|ven|kos|tüm** NT (hum) **ein starkes/schwaches ~ haben** to have strong/weak nerves; **Ner|ven|kraft** F strong nerves pl; **es erforderte einige ~** it took strong nerves; **meine ~ ist erschöpft** my nerves can't take any more; **ner|ven|krank** ADJ (geistig) mentally ill or disturbed; (körperlich) suffering from a nervous disease; **Ner|ven|krank|heit** F (geistig) mental illness or disorder; (körperlich) nervous disease or disorder; **Ner|ven|krieg** M (fig) war of nerves; **Ner|ven|läh|mung** F neuroparalysis; **Ner|ven|lei|den** NT nervous complaint or condition; **Ner|ven|mit|tel** NT sedative, tranquillizer (Brit), tranquilizer (US); **Ner|ven|nah|rung** F (fig) **das ist ~** it's good for my etc nerves; **Ner|ven|pro|be** F trial; **Ner|ven|sa|che** F (inf) question of nerves; **reine ~!** it's all a question of nerves; **Ner|ven|sä|ge** F (inf) pain (in the neck) (inf); **ner|ven|schä|di|gend** ADJ damaging to the nerves; **Ner|ven|schmerz** M neuralgia no pl; **Ner|ven|schock** M nervous shock; **ner|ven|schwach** ADJ with weak nerves, neurasthenic (spec); **er ist ~** he has weak nerves; **Ner|ven|schwä|che** F weak nerves pl, neurasthenia (spec); **ner|ven|stark** ADJ Mensch with strong nerves; Leistung determined; **er ist ~** he has strong nerves; **Ner|ven|stär|ke** F strong nerves pl; **es erforderte meine ganze ~** I needed nerves of steel to do it; **ner|ven|stär|kend** ADJ nerve-strengthening, tonic; **Ner|ven|strang** M nerve fibre (Brit) or fiber (US); **Ner|ven|sys|tem** NT nervous system; **Ner|ven|zel|le** F nerve cell; **Ner|ven|zent|rum** NT (Physiol, fig) nerve centre (Brit) or center (US); **Ner|ven|zu|sam|men|bruch** M nervous breakdown, crackup (inf)

ner|vig ['nɛrfɪç, 'nɛrvɪç] ADJ a (inf: = irritierend) Musik, Lärm, Mensch irritating; **Mensch, wie ~!** God, how irritating!; **der ist vielleicht ~** he gets on your nerves b Faust, Hand sinewy; Gestalt wiry

nerv|lich ['nɛrflɪç] ADJ Belastung, Anspannung nervous; **der ~e Zustand des Patienten** the state of the patient's nerves; **ein ~es Wrack** a nervous wreck ADV **er ist ~ erschöpft** he suffers from nervous exhaustion; **~ bedingt** nervous; **~ angespannt sein** to be suffering from nervous exhaustion; **~ überlastet** or **überanstrengt sein** to be under a great deal of stress

ner|vös [nɛr'vøːs] ADJ nervous; (= aufgeregt auch) jumpy (inf), jittery (inf), on edge; (Med) Magen nervous; **jdn ~ machen** to make sb nervous; (= ärgern) to get on sb's nerves ADV nervously; **er schreckt beim kleinsten Geräusch ~ zusammen** he jumps nervously at the slightest noise; **die Krankheit ist rein ~ bedingt** the illness is purely nervous in origin

Ner|vo|si|tät [nɛrvozi'tɛːt] F -, no pl nervousness; (Stimmung) tension

nerv|tö|tend ['nɛrf-] (inf) ADJ Geräusch, Gerede nerve-racking; Arbeit soul-destroying ADV langsam, langweilig, laut irritatingly

Nerz [nɛrts] M -es, -e mink

Nerz|man|tel M mink coat

Nes|sel¹ ['nɛsl] F -, -n a (Bot) nettle; **sich in die ~n setzen** (inf) to put oneself in a spot (inf) b **Nesseln** PL (= Quaddeln) nettle rash

Nes|sel² M -s, - (auch **Nesseltuch**, **Nessel-stoff**) (untreated) cotton

Nes|sel-: **Nes|sel|aus|schlag** M , **Nes|sel|-fie|ber** NT nettle rash; **Nes|sel|ge|wächs** NT urticaceae (spec); **Nes|sel|schlaf|sack** M sheet sleeping bag; **Nes|sel|tier** NT cnidarian (spec)

Nes|ses|sär ▲ NT -s, -s → **Necessaire**

Nest [nɛst] NT -(e)s, -er a (= Brutstätte) nest b (fig: = Schlupfwinkel) hideout, lair; **ein ~ von Dieben** a den of thieves; **das ~ leer finden** to find the bird has/the birds have flown c (fig: = Heim) nest, home; **sein eigenes ~ be-schmutzen** to foul one's own nest; **sich ins ge-machte** or **warme ~ setzen** (inf) (durch Heirat) to marry (into) money; (beruflich) to move straight into a good job; **da hat er sich ins gemachte** or **warme ~ gesetzt** (inf) he's got it made (inf) d (fig inf: = Bett) bed; **raus aus dem ~!** rise and shine! (inf), move a leg! (Brit inf) e (pej inf: Ort) (schäbig) dump (inf), hole (inf), one-horse town (inf); (klein) little place

Nest-: **Nest|bau** M , no pl nest-building; **Nest|be|schmut|zer** [-bəʃmʊtsɐ] M -s, -, **Nest|be|schmut|ze|rin** [-ərɪn] F -, -nen (pej) runner-down (inf) or denigrator of one's family/country; **Nest|be|schmut|zung** F (pej) running-down (inf) or denigration of one's family/country

nes|teln ['nɛstln] VI an etw (dat) ~ to fumble or fiddle (around) with sth VT (rare) to fasten

Nest-: **Nest|flüch|ter** [-flʏçtɐ] M -s, -, **Nest|-flüch|te|rin** [-ərɪn] F -, -nen bird that leaves the nest early (fig) person who leaves the family home at an early age; **Nest|häk|chen** NT baby of the family; **Nest|ho|cker** [-hɔkɐ] M -s, -, **Nest|ho|cke|rin** [-ərɪn] F -, -nen bird that stays a long time in the nest (fig) person who stays in the family home for a long time

Nes|tor ['nɛstoːɐ] M -s, Nestoren [-'toːrən] Nestor; (fig) doyen

Nes|to|rin [nɛsto'rɪn] F -, -nen (fig) doyenne

Nest-: **nest|warm** ADJ warm from the nest; **Nest|wär|me** F (fig) happy home life

Net-Sur|fer(in) ['nɛt-] M(F) (inf) Net-surfer (inf)

nett [nɛt] ADJ nice; (= hübsch auch) pretty, cute; **ein ganz ~es Sümmchen** a nice little sum; **eine ~e Stange Geld kosten** (inf) to cost a pretty penny (inf) or a tidy sum (inf); **das kann ja ~**

werden! (iro) that'll be nice or great (inf) (I don't think!); **sei so ~ und räum auf!** would you mind clearing up?, would you like to clear up?; **Oma war so ~ und hat schon abgewaschen** Grandma very nicely or kindly washed the dishes; **~, dass Sie gekommen sind!** nice or good of you to come; **das war ~/nicht ~ von ihm** that was nice/wasn't very nice of him; **was Netteres ist dir wohl nicht eingefallen?** (iro) you do say/do some nice things ADV nicely, nice; **wir haben uns ~ unterhalten** we had a nice chat; **hier werden die Gäste ~ bedient** the waiters are very friendly here; **~ aussehen** to be nice-looking; **die Geschenk war ~ gemeint** the gift was well-meant; **sie plaudert ~** she's nice to talk to

net|ter|wei|se ['nɛtɐˌvaizə] ADV kindly

Net|tig|keit ['nɛtɪçkait] F -, -en a no pl (= nette Art) kindness, goodness b **Nettigkeiten** PL (= nette Worte) kind words, nice things

Net|ti|ket|te [nɛti'ketə] F -, no pl, **Net|ti-quette** [nɛti'ket] F -, no pl (Comput: im Internet) netiquette

net|to ['nɛto] ADV (Comm) net; **ich verdiene ~ £ 1500** or **£ 1500 ~ im Monat** I earn £1500 net a month, I net £1500 a month

Net|to- in cpds net; **Net|to|ein|kom|men** NT , **Net|to|ein|künf|te** PL net income no pl; **Net|to|er|trag** M net profit; **Net|to|ge|halt** NT net salary; **mein ~ ist ...** (auch) I net ..., I take home ...; **Net|to|ge|wicht** NT net weight; **Net|to|ge|winn** M clear profit; **Net|to|kre|dit|auf|nah|me** [-ˈkreːdiːt-] F net borrowing; **Net|to|kurs** M net rate; **Net|to|lohn** M take-home pay; **Net|to|um|satz** M net turnover, net sales pl; **Net|to|ver|dienst** M net income sing

Netz [nɛts] NT -es, -e a net; (= Spinnennetz) web; (= Haarnetz) (hair)net; (= Einkaufsnetz) string bag, net bag; (= Gepäcknetz) (luggage) rack; (fig: von Lügen, Heuchelei) tissue, web; (= Maschenwerk) netting; **Fische mit dem ~ fangen** to catch fish with nets, to net fish; **ans ~ gehen** (Sport) to go up to the net; **ins ~ gehen** (Ftbl) to go into the (back of the) net; (Tennis) to hit the net; **ins ~ schlagen** to play into the net; **~!** (Sport) let!; **ohne ~ und doppelten Boden** without a safety net; **in jds ~ geraten** (fig) to fall into sb's clutches; **sich im eigenen ~ verstricken** to be caught in one's own trap, to be hoist with (Brit) or on (US) one's own petard (prov); **jdm ins ~ gehen** (fig) to fall into sb's trap; **jdm durchs ~ gehen** (fig) to give sb the slip b (= System) network; (= Stromnetz) mains sing or pl; (= Überlandnetz) (national) grid; (Comput) network; **das soziale ~** the social security net; **ans ~ gehen** (Kraftwerk) to be connected to the grid; **Strom geht ins ~** the grid is supplied with electricity; **das Kraftwerk musste vom ~ genommen werden** the power station had to be shut down c (= Internet) **das ~** the Net; **im ~ surfen** (inf) to surf the Net (inf) d (Math) net; (= Kartengitter) grid e (Anat) omentum (spec), caul (of the stomach)

Netz-: **Netz|an|bie|ter** [-anbiːtɐ] M -s, - (Telec) network provider; (Comput) Internet (service) provider; **Netz|an|schluss** ▲ M (Elec) mains connection; **netz|ar|tig** ADJ netlike, reticulate (form); **Netz|auf|schlag** M (Tennis) net let; **Netz|au|ge** NT compound eye; **Netz|ball** M (Tennis etc) net ball; **Netz|be|trei|ber** M (Telec) network operator; (Comput) Internet or Net operator; **Netz|com|pu|ter** M network computer

net|zen ['nɛtsn] VTI to moisten, to wet

Netz-: **Netz|flüg|ler** [-flyːglɐ] M -s, - neuropter (spec), lacewing; **die ~** die Neuroptera (spec); **Netz|fre|quenz** F mains frequency; **Netz|gar|di|ne** F net curtain; **Netz|garn** NT netting yarn; **Netz|ge|rät** NT mains receiver;

Nẹtz|ge|we|be NT gauze; **Nẹtz|ge|wöl|be** NT (Archit) fan vault

Nẹtz|haut F retina

Nẹtz|haut-: Nẹtz|haut|ab|lö|sung F detachment of the retina; **Nẹtz|haut|ent|zün|dung** F retinitis

Nẹtz-: Nẹtz|hemd NT string vest (Brit), mesh undershirt (US); **Nẹtz|kar|te** F (Rail) unlimited travel ticket, runabout ticket (Brit); **Nẹtz|ma|gen** M (Zool) second stomach; **Nẹtz|nut|zer(in)** M(F) Internet or Net user; **Nẹtz|plan** M critical path (diagram); **Nẹtz|plan|tech|nik** F critical path method; **Nẹtz|rol|ler** F (Tennis, Volleyball etc) net cord; **Nẹtz|span|nung** F mains voltage; **Nẹtz|spiel** NT net game; **Nẹtz|spie|ler(in)** M(F) (Volleyball) forward; (Tennis) net player; **Nẹtz|ste|cker** M mains plug, power or electrical (esp US) outlet; **Nẹtz|strümp|fe** PL fishnet stockings pl; **Nẹtz|sur|fer(in)** M(F) (inf) Net-surfer (inf); **Nẹtz|teil** NT mains adaptor

Nẹtz|werk NT (Elec, Comput, fig) network; (aus Draht) netting

Nẹtz|werk- (Comput): **Nẹtz|werk|kar|te** F network card; **Nẹtz|werk|ser|ver** M network server; **Nẹtz|werk|spiel** NT (Comput) Net or on-line game; **Nẹtz|werk|trei|ber** M network driver

Nẹtz|zu|gang M (Comput, Telec) network access; (zum Internet) Internet or Net access

neu [nɔy] ⓞ 50.2 **ADJ** new; Seite, Kräfte, Hoffnung, Truppen auch fresh; (= kürzlich entstanden auch) recent; (= frisch gewaschen) Hemd, Socken clean; Wein young; **das Neue Testament** the New Testament; **die Neue Welt** the New World; **jdm zum ~en Jahr Glück wünschen** to wish sb (a) Happy New Year; **ein ~er Anfang** a fresh or new start; **~eren Datums** of (more) recent date; **~e Hoffnung schöpfen** to take new or fresh hope; **eine ~e Mode** a new fashion; **ein ~er Tanz** a new dance; **die ~(e)ste Mode** the latest fashion; **der ~(e)ste Tanz** the latest dance; **die ~esten Nachrichten** the latest news; **die ~eren Sprachen** modern languages; **ein ganz ~er Wagen** a brand-new car; **das ist mir ~!** that's new(s) to me; **mir ist die Sache ~** this is all new to me; **schlechte Laune ist mir ~ an ihm** it's something new for me to see him in a bad mood; **sich wie ein ~er Mensch fühlen** to feel like a new person; **eine ~e Bearbeitung** a revised edition; (von Oper etc) a new version; **Geschichte der ~eren Zeit** recent or modern history; **in ~erer Zeit** in modern times; **erst in ~er Zeit** only recently; **viele alte Leute finden sich in der ~en Zeit nicht mehr zurecht** a lot of old people can't get on in the modern world; **seit ~(e)stem** recently, **seit ~(e)stem gibt es ...** since recently there has been ...; **aufs Neue** (geh) afresh, anew; **auf ein Neues!** (als Toast) (here's) to the New Year!; (Aufmunterung) let's try again; **der/die Neue** the newcomer, the new man/boy/woman/girl etc; **die Neuen** the newcomers, the new people; **Neue Welle** new wave; **was ist das Neue an dem Buch?** what's new about the book?; **das Neu(e)ste in der Mode/auf dem Gebiet der Weltraumforschung** the latest in fashion/in the field of space research; **weißt du schon das Neu(e)ste?** have you heard the latest (news)?; **was gibts Neues?** (inf) what's the latest?, what's new?; **das Neu(e)ste vom Tage** the latest news, up-to-the-minute news; **das Neu(e)ste vom Neuen** the very latest (things); **von ~em** (= von vorn) from the beginning, afresh, from scratch; (= wieder) again → Besen a, Weg a, alt a

ADV a (= von vorn) **~ anfangen** to start all over (again); **~ beginnen** to make a fresh start, to start again from scratch; **Vorhänge/ein Kleid ~ anfertigen lassen** to have new curtains/a new dress made; **~ entwickelt** newly developed; **sich/jdn ~ einkleiden** to buy oneself/sb a new set of clothes; **etw ~ anschaffen** to buy sth new; **~ bauen** to build a new house; **gescha-**

fen newly created

b (= zusätzlich) **~ hinzukommen zu etw** to join sth; **Mitarbeiter ~ einstellen** to hire new employees; **Tierarten ~ entdecken** to discover new species of animals; **~ entdeckt** newly or recently discovered

c (= erneut) **etw ~ auflegen** to publish a new edition of sth; **~ drucken** to reprint; **~ bearbeiten** to revise; **~ bearbeitet** revised; **ein Zimmer ~ einrichten** to refurnish a room; **frei werdende Stellen werden nicht ~ besetzt** vacant positions will not be filled; **ich hatte das Buch verloren und musste es ~ kaufen** I lost the book and had to buy another copy; **~ eröffnet** (= wieder eröffnet) reopened; **~ ordnen** to reorganize; **sich ~ verschulden** to borrow money again, to take out another loan; **die Rollen ~ besetzen** to recast the roles; **die Akten ~ ordnen** to reorganize the files

d (= seit kurzer Zeit) **ich habe mir das ganz ~ gekauft** I just bought it; **~ gebacken** fresh-baked, newly-baked; (fig) newly-fledged, brand-new; **das Buch ist ~ erschienen** the book is a recent publication or has just come out; **er ist ~ hinzugekommen** he's joined (him/them) recently; **~ gewählt** newly elected; **hier ist ein Supermarkt ~ entstanden/gebaut worden** a supermarket has just been opened/built here; **~ eröffnet** newly-opened; **wir sind ~ hierher gezogen** we have just moved here; **der Schüler ist ganz ~ in unserer Klasse** the pupil is new in our class, the pupil has just joined our class; **dieser Artikel ist ~ eingetroffen/~ im Sortiment** this article has just come in/has just been added to the range; **~ vermählt** newly married or wed

Neu-: Neu|an|fang M new beginning; **einen ~ machen** to start again from the scratch or from the beginning; **Neu|an|fer|ti|gung** F (= das Neuanfertigen) making (up), production (from scratch); (Produkt) newly-made article; **die ~ eines Anzugs dauert vier Wochen** it takes four weeks to make up a suit; **Neu|an|kömm|ling** M newcomer; **Neu|an|schaf|fung** F new purchase or acquisition; **eine ~ würde sich rentieren** it would be worth buying a new machine/part etc; **neu|apos|to|lisch** [ˈnɔylapɔˈstoːlɪʃ] **ADJ** New Apostolic **ADV jdn ~ erziehen** to raise sb as a member of the New Apostolic Church

neu|ar|tig ADJ new; **ein ~es Wörterbuch** a new type of dictionary; **es ist ganz ~** it is of a completely new type, it is a completely new departure

Neu|ar|tig|keit [ˈnɔylartɪçkait] F -, -en novelty

Neu-: Neu|auf|la|ge F reprint; (mit Verbesserungen) new edition; **Neu|aus|ga|be** F new edition

Neu|bau M pl -bauten new house/building

Neu|bau-: Neu|bau|ge|biet NT development area; **Neu|bau|sied|lung** F new housing estate; **Neu|bau|vier|tel** NT new district; **Neu|bau|woh|nung** F newly-built flat (Brit) or apartment

Neu-: neu|be|ar|bei|tet △ [-bəlarbaitət] ADJ attr → neu ADV c; **Neu|be|ar|bei|tung** F revised edition; (von Oper etc) new version; (= das Neubearbeiten) revision; **Neu|be|ginn** M new beginning(s pl); **Neu|be|le|bung** F revival; **Neu|be|set|zung** F replacement; (Theat) recasting; **in der ~** in the recast version; **eine ~ dieses Postens wurde nötig** it was necessary to find a replacement for this position; **Neu|bil|dung** F (= das Neubilden) forming, formation; (= neues Gebilde) new entity; (Ling) neologism; (Med) renewal, repair; **eine staatliche ~** a newly-formed state; **bei der ~ von Begriffen** in the formation of new concepts; **Neu|bür|ger(in)** M(F) new citizen; **Neu-Del|hi** [nɔyˈdɛːli] NT -s New Delhi; **neu|deutsch** (iro, pej) **ADJ** new German, neo-German **ADV** in the new German manner; **sprechen** in new German; **Neu|druck** M pl -drucke reprint; **Neu|ein|rich-**

tung F refurnishing; (= Möbel) new furnishings pl or furniture; **Neu|ein|stel|lung** F new appointment; **Neu|ein|stu|die|rung** F new production

Neu|en|burg [ˈnɔyənbʊrk] NT -s (Kanton) Neuchâtel

Neu-: Neu|eng|land NT New England; **neu|eng|lisch** ADJ **a** modern English **b** (= zu Neuengland gehörend) New England attr; **neu|ent|deckt** △ ADJ attr → neu ADV b; **Neu|ent|de|ckung** F rediscovery; (Mensch) new discovery; (Ort) newly discovered place; **neu|ent|wi|ckelt** △ [-lɛntvɪklt] ADJ attr → neu ADV a; **Neu|ent|wick|lung** F new development

neu|er|dings [ˈnɔyɐ'dɪŋs] ADV recently; (rare: = von neuem) again

Neu|e|rer [ˈnɔyɐrɐ] M -s, -, **Neu|e|rin** [-ərɪn] F -, -nen innovator

neu|er|lich [ˈnɔyɐlɪç] **ADV** lately, recently, of late; (= nochmals, wieder) again **ADJ** recent; (= wiederholt) further

Neu-: neu|er|öff|net △ [-lɛrlœfnət] ADJ attr → neu ADV c, d; **Neu|er|öff|nung** F (new) opening; (= Wiedereröffnung) reopening; **die ~ der Filiale** the opening of the new branch; **es gab zwanzig Geschäftsschließungen und nur zwei ~en** twenty shops (Brit) or stores were closed and only two new ones opened; **Neu|er|schei|nung** F (Buch) new or recent publication; (CD) new release; (= Neuheit) new or recent phenomenon

Neu|e|rung [ˈnɔyərʊŋ] F -, -en innovation; (= Reform) reform

neu|e|rungs|süch|tig ADJ over-anxious to carry out reforms, reform-mad (Brit inf), reform-crazy (inf)

Neu|er|wer|bung F new acquisition; (= Sportler) new signing; **die ~ von Büchern** the acquisition of new books

neu|es|tens [ˈnɔyəstns] ADV lately, recently

Neu-: Neu|fas|sung F new or revised version; **Neu|fest|set|zung** F reassessment; **Neu|fund|land** [nɔyˈfʊntlant] NT -s Newfoundland; **Neu|fund|län|der¹** M -s, - (Hund) Newfoundland (dog); **Neu|fund|län|der²** [nɔyˈfʊntlɛndɐ] M -s, -, **Neu|fund|län|de|rin** [-ərɪn] F -, -nen Newfoundlander; **neu|fund|län|disch** [nɔyˈfʊntlɛndɪʃ] ADJ Newfoundland; **neu|ge|ba|cken** ▲ ADJ attr → neu ADV d; **neu|ge|bo|ren** ADJ newborn; **sich wie ~ fühlen** to feel (like) a new man/woman; **Neu|ge|bo|re|ne(s)** NT decl as adj newborn child; **Neu|ge|burt** F (= Neugeborenes) newborn child/animal; (= Neuerscheinung) new phenomenon; (= Wiedergeburt) rebirth; **die ~en** the newborn; **neu|ge|schaf|fen** △ ADJ attr → neu ADV a; **neu|ge|stal|ten** ▲ VT to rearrange, to reorder; Beziehungen, Ordnung to reorganize; Platz, Stadion to redesign, to give a new layout; **Neu|ge|stal|tung** F rearrangement, reordering; (von Platz, Stadion) redesigning; (von Beziehungen, Ordnung) reorganization; **die ~ eines alten Themas** the reworking of an old theme; **neu|ge|wählt** △ [-gəvɛːlt] ADJ attr → neu ADV d

Neu|gier [ˈnɔygiːɐ] F -, no pl, **Neu|gier|de** [ˈnɔygiːɐdə] F -, no pl curiosity, inquisitiveness (auf +acc about); (pej auch) nosiness (inf); **aus (reiner) ~** out of (sheer) curiosity; **seine ~ befriedigen** to satisfy one's curiosity; **vor ~ platzen** to be bursting with curiosity

neu|gie|rig [ˈnɔygiːərɪç] **ADJ** inquisitive, curious (auf +acc about); (pej) prying, nosy (inf); (= gespannt) longing or curious to know; Blick, Fragen inquisitive; **ein Neugieriger** an inquisitive person; (pej auch) a nos(e)y parker (Brit inf), a curious George (US inf); **jdn ~ machen** to excite or arouse sb's curiosity; **ich bin ~, ob** I wonder if; **da bin ich aber ~!** this should be interesting, I can hardly wait (inf); **sei nicht so ~!** don't be so inquisitive or nosy (inf) or such a nos(e)y parker (Brit inf) or curious George (US inf)!

ADV full of curiosity; **etw ~ untersuchen** to study sth curiously; (*Tier*) to examine sth inquisitively; **er fragt zu ~** he's too curious

Neu-: Neu|glie|de|rung F reorganization, restructuring; **Neu|go|tik** F Gothic revival, neo-Gothic style; **neu|go|tisch** ADJ neo-Gothic; **neu|grie|chisch** ADJ Modern Greek; **Neu|grie|chisch(e)** NT Modern Greek → *auch* **Deutsch(e)**; **Neu|grün|dung** F (= *Wiederbegründung*) re-establishment, refoundation; **die ~ von Universitäten** the founding of new universities; **der Verein ist eine ~** the club was only recently founded; **Neu|grup|pie|rung** F regroupment, rearrangement; **Neu|gui|nea** [nɔygi'ne:a] NT New Guinea

Neu|heit ['nɔyhait] F -, -en **a** *no pl* (= *das Neusein*) novelty; **es wird bald den Reiz der ~ verlieren** the novelty will soon wear off **b** (= *neue Sache*) innovation, new thing/idea; **dieses Gerät ist eine ~ auf dem Markt** this item is new on the market

neu|hoch|deutsch ADJ New High German; **das Neuhochdeutsche** New High German

Neu|ig|keit ['nɔyiçkait] F -, -en **a** (piece of) news; **die ~en** the news *sing*; **die ~ des Tages** the (big) news of the day **b** (= *das Neusein*) novelty

Neu|in|sze|nie|rung F new production

Neu|jahr ['nɔyja:ɐ, nɔy'ja:ɐ] NT New Year; **an ~** on New Year's Day; **jdm zu(m) ~ gratulieren** to wish sb a Happy New Year; **~ begehen** *or* **feiern** to celebrate the New Year; **Pros(i)t ~!** (here's) to the New Year!

Neu|jahrs-: Neu|jahrs|abend M New Year's Eve, Hogmanay (*Scot*); **Neu|jahrs|ansprache** F New Year speech; **Neu|jahrs|empfang** M New Year reception; **Neu|jahrs|fest** NT New Year's Day; (= *Feier*) New Year celebrations *pl*; **Neu|jahrs|glück|wunsch** M New Year greeting; **Neu|jahrs|kar|te** F New Year card; **Neu|jahrs|kon|zert** NT New Year concert; **Neu|jahrs|tag** M New Year's Day

Neu-: Neu|ka|le|do|ni|en [nɔykale'do:niən] NT -s New Caledonia; **Neu|ka|le|do|ni|er** [nɔykale'do:niɐ] M -s, -, **Neu|ka|le|do|ni|e|rin** [-iərn] F -, -nen New Caledonian; **Neu|kun|de** M , **Neu|kun|din** F (*Comm*) new customer; **neu|ka|le|do|nisch** [nɔykale'do:nɪʃ] ADJ New Caledonian; **Neu|land** NT , *no pl* virgin land *or* territory, uncultivated land; (*fig*) new territory *or* ground; **~ gewinnen** (*lit*) to reclaim land; **~ betreten** *or* **beschreiten** to break new ground; **er betrat wissenschaftliches/geistiges ~** he broke new ground in science/intellectually; **neu|la|tei|nisch** ADJ neo-Latin, new Latin

neu|lich ['nɔylɪç] **ADV** recently, the other day; **~ Abend** *or* **abends** the other evening **ADJ** (*strictly incorrect*) recent

Neu|ling ['nɔylɪŋ] M -s, -e newcomer, new man/woman/boy/girl; (*pej auch*) beginner, greenhorn (*inf*)

neu|mo|disch (*pej*) **ADJ** new-fangled (*pej*), fashionable **ADV** **sich ~ anziehen** to dress in the latest fashions; **~ einrichten** to be furnished according to the latest style; **sich ~ ausdrücken** to use new-fangled words; **~ unterrichten** (*mit neuen Methoden*) to teach in a new-fangled way; (*modernes Wissen*) to teach new-fangled stuff

Neu|mond M new moon; **bei ~** at new moon; **heute ist ~** there's a new moon today

neun [nɔyn] NUM nine; **alle ~(e)!** (*beim Kegeln*) strike!; **er warf alle ~(e)** he got a strike → *auch* **vier**

Neun [nɔyn] F -, -en nine; **er hat die ~ ausgespielt** he played the nine; **ach du grüne ~e!** (*inf*) well I'm blowed (*Brit inf*) *or* I'll be damned! → *auch* **Vier**

Neun-: Neun|au|ge NT lamprey; **Neun|eck** NT nonagon; **neun|eckig** ADJ nonagonal

Neu|ner|pro|be ['nɔynɐ-] F (*Math*) casting out nines

Neun-: neun|hun|dert ['nɔyn'hʊndɐt] NUM nine hundred → *auch* **vierhundert**; **neun|mal** ['nɔynma:l] ADV nine times → *auch* **viermal**; **neun|mal|klug** (*iro*) **ADJ** smart-aleck *attr* (*inf*); **du bist ein ganz Neunmalkluger!** you're a real smart-aleck (*inf*), **ADV** like a smart-aleck (*inf*); **sie redet so ~ daher** she talks as if she knows it all; **neun|schwän|zig** [-ʃvɛntsɪç] **ADJ** **die ~e Katze** the cat-o'-nine-tails; **neun|tau|send** ['nɔyn'tauznt] NUM nine thousand → *auch* **viertausend**

Neun|tel ['nɔyntl] NT -s, - ninth → *auch* **Viertel** [1]

neun|tens ['nɔyntns] ADV ninth(ly), in the ninth place

neun|te(r, s) ['nɔyntə] ADJ ninth → *auch* **vierte(r, s)**

neun|zehn ['nɔyntse:n] NUM nineteen → *auch* **vierzehn**

neun|zehn|te(r, s) ['nɔyntse:ntə] ADJ nineteenth → *auch* **vierte(r, s)**

neun|zig ['nɔyntsɪç] NUM ninety; **auf ~ sein** (*inf*) to be in a blind fury *or* a filthy temper (*inf*) → *auch* **vierzig**

Neun|zi|ger ['nɔyntsɪgɐ] M -s, -, **Neun|zi|ge|rin** [-ərn] F -, -nen (*Mensch*) ninety-year-old, nonagenarian → *auch* **Vierziger** [2]

neun|zigs|te(r, s) ['nɔyntsɪçstə] ADJ ninetieth → *auch* **vierte(r, s)**

Neu-: Neu|ord|nung F reorganization, reordering; (= *Reform*) reform; **Neu|or|ga|ni|sa|ti|on** F reorganization; **Neu|ori|en|tie|rung** F reorientation; **Neu|phi|lo|lo|ge** M , **Neu|phi|lo|lo|gin** F modern linguist; **Neu|phi|lo|lo|gie** F modern languages *sing or pl*; **Neu|prä|gung** F (*Münze*) new minting; (*Begriff*) new coinage

Neu|ral|gie [nɔyral'gi:] F -, -n [-'gi:ən] neuralgia

neu|ral|gisch [nɔy'ralgɪʃ] ADJ neuralgic; **ein ~er Punkt** a trouble area; **diese Kreuzung/Zypern ist ein ~er Punkt** this crossroads/Cyprus is a trouble area *or* trouble spot

Neu|ral|the|ra|pie [nɔy'ral-] F neural therapy

Neu|ras|the|nie [nɔyraste'ni:] F -, -n [-'ni:ən] neurasthenia

Neu|ras|the|ni|ker [nɔyras'te:nikɐ] M -s, -, **Neu|ras|the|ni|ke|rin** [-ərn] F -, -nen neurasthenic

neu|ras|the|nisch [nɔyras'te:nɪʃ] ADJ neurasthenic

Neu-: Neu|re|ge|lung F adjustment, revision; **eine ~ des Verkehrs** a new traffic management scheme; **neu|reich** ADJ nouveau riche; **Neu|rei|che(r)** MF *decl as adj* nouveau riche; **die ~n** the nouveaux riches

Neu|ri|tis [nɔy'ri:tɪs] F -, Neuritiden [-ri'ti:dn] neuritis

Neu|ro-: Neu|ro- [nɔyro] *in cpds* neuro; **Neu|ro|chi|rur|gie** F neurosurgery; **Neu|ro|der|mi|tis** [nɔyroder'mi:tɪs] F -, **Neu|ro|der|mi|tiden** [nɔyroder'mi'ti:dn] (*Med*) neurodermatitis; **Neu|ro|lep|ti|kum** [nɔyro'lɛptikʊm] NT -s, Neuroleptika [-ka] (*Pharm*) neuroleptic (drug); **Neu|ro|lo|ge** [nɔyro'lo:gə] M -n, -n, **Neu|ro|lo|gin** [-'lo:gɪn] F -, -nen neurologist; **Neu|ro|lo|gie** [nɔyrolo'gi:] F -, -n [-'gi:ən] neurology; **neu|ro|lo|gisch** [nɔyro'lo:gɪʃ] **ADJ** neurological **ADV** neurologically; **~ erkrankt sein** to have a neurological disease

Neu|ron ['nɔyrɔn] NT -s, -e(n) [-'ro:nə(n)] neuron

Neu|ro-: Neu|ro|pa|thie [nɔyropa'ti:] F -, -n [-'ti:ən] neuropathy; **Neu|ro|pa|tho|lo|gie** F neuropathology

Neu|ro|se [nɔy'ro:zə] F -, -n neurosis

Neu|ro|ti|ker [nɔy'ro:tikɐ] M -s, -, **Neu|ro|ti|ke|rin** [-ərn] F -, -nen neurotic

neu|ro|tisch [nɔy'ro:tɪʃ] **ADJ** neurotic **ADV** neurotically; **~ klingen** to sound neurotic; **dein Misstrauen wirkt ~** you are neurotically suspicious

Neu|ro|trans|mit|ter [-transmɪtɐ] M -s, - (*Med*) neurotransmitter

Neu-: Neu|satz M (*Typ*) new setting; **Neu|schnee** M fresh snow; **über Nacht gab es bis zu 37 Zentimeter ~** up to 37 cm of fresh snow fell overnight; **Neu|schöp|fung** F new creation; (*Ausdruck*) invention; **Neu|see|land** [nɔy'ze:lant] NT -s New Zealand; **Neu|see|län|der** [nɔy'ze:lɛndɐ] [-ərn] F -, -nen New Zealander; **neu|see|län|disch** [nɔy'ze:lɛndɪʃ] ADJ New Zealand; **Neu|sil|ber** NT nickel silver; **Neu|sprach|ler** [-ʃpraxlɐ] M -s, -, **Neu|sprach|le|rin** [-ərn] F -, -nen modern linguist; **neu|sprach|lich** ADJ modern language *attr*; **~er Zweig** (*Sch*) modern language side; **~es Gymnasium** ≈ grammar school (*Brit*), ≈ high school (*esp US, Scot, stressing modern languages*); **Neu|stadt** F new town

neus|tens ['nɔystns] ADV = **neuestens**

Neu|struk|tu|rie|rung F restructuring

Neu|tö|ner [-tø:nɐ] M -s, -, **Neu|tö|ne|rin** [-ərn] F -, -nen (*Mus*) exponent of the New Music

neut|ral [nɔy'tra:l] **ADJ** neutral; (*rare: Gram*) neuter; **die Neutralen** (*Pol*) the neutrals **ADV** neutrally; **etw ~ bewerten** to give a neutral assessment of sth

Neut|ra|li|sa|ti|on [nɔytraliza'tsio:n] F -, -en neutralization; (*Sport: von Rennen*) suspension

neut|ra|li|sie|ren [nɔytrali'zi:rən] *ptp* **neutralisiert** VT to neutralize; (*Sport*) *Rennen* to suspend

Neut|ra|li|sie|rung F -, -en neutralization

Neut|ra|lis|mus [nɔytra'lɪsmʊs] M -, *no pl* (*Pol*) neutralism

Neut|ra|li|tät [nɔytrali'tɛ:t] F -, *no pl* neutrality

Neut|ra|li|täts-: Neut|ra|li|täts|ab|kom|men NT treaty of neutrality; **Neut|ra|li|täts|er|klä|rung** F declaration of neutrality; **Neut|ra|li|täts|po|li|tik** F policy of neutrality; **Neut|ra|li|täts|ver|let|zung** F violation of neutrality; **Neut|ra|li|täts|zei|chen** NT sign of neutrality

Neut|ri|no [nɔy'tri:no] NT -s, -s neutrino

Neut|ron ['nɔytrɔn] NT -s, -en [-'tro:nən] neutron

Neut|ro|nen-: Neut|ro|nen- *in cpds* neutron; **Neut|ro|nen|bom|be** F neutron bomb; **Neut|ro|nen|strah|len** PL neutron rays *pl*; **Neut|ro|nen|strah|lung** F neutron radiation

Neut|rum ['nɔytrʊm] NT -s, Neutra *or* Neutren [-tra, -trən] (*Gram, fig*) neuter; **ein ~** (*Gram*) a neuter noun; **sie wirkt auf mich wie ein ~** I don't think of her as a woman

Neu-: Neu|ver|an|la|gung F (*Fin*) reassessment; **Neu|ver|fil|mung** F remake; **Neu|ver|hand|lung** F *usu pl* renegotiation; **neu|ver|mählt** △ [-fɛɛme:lt] **ADJ** = **neu ADV d**; **Neu|ver|mähl|te(r)** [-fɛɛme:ltə] MF *decl as adj* **die ~n** the newly-weds; **Neu|ver|schul|dung** F new borrowings *pl*; **Neu|wa|gen** M new car; **Neu|wahl** F (*Pol*) new election, re-election; **die ~ des Präsidenten** the election of a new president; **es gab vorgezogene ~en** the elections were brought forward; **neu|welt|lich** ADJ (*geh*) new world; **Neu|wert** M value when new; **neu|wer|tig** ADJ as new; **Neu|wert|ver|si|che|rung** F new-for-old insurance (*Brit*), replacement value insurance; **Neu|zeit** F modern age *or* era, modern times *pl*; **Literatur/Gesellschaft der ~** modern literature/society; **die Olympischen Spiele der ~** the modern Olympics; **neu|zeit|lich** ADJ modern; **Neu|züch|tung** F (= *Tier*) new breed; (= *Pflanze*) new variety; **die ~ von Tieren** the breeding of new types of animal; **die ~ von Pflanzen** the cultivation of new types of plant; **Neu|zu|gang** M new entry; **Neu|zu|las|sung** F (*Aut*) ≈ registration of a new vehicle; (*von Arzneimittel*) licensing; **die meisten gestohlenen Autos waren ~en** most of the stolen cars were *or* had new registrations; **die Zahl der ~en steigt** the number of new vehicles being registered is increasing

New Age ['nju: 'e:dʒ] NT -, *no pl* new age

New|co|mer ['nju:kamɐ] M -(s), - newcomer

News|group ['nju:zgru:p] F -, -s (*Comput, Internet*) news group

News|let|ter ['nju:zlɛtɐ] M -s, -s (*Comput: im Internet*) newsletter

New Wave [nju:'we:v] F -, *no pl* new wave

New York ['nju:'jɔːk] NT -s New York

New Yor|ker[1] [nju:'jɔːkɐ] ADJ *attr* New York

New Yor|ker[2] [nju:'jɔːkɐ] M - -s, - -, **New Yor|ke|rin** [-ərɪn] F -, - -nen New Yorker

nhd. *abbr* (*Ling*) *von* **neuhochdeutsch**

Ni|be|lun|gen|treue [ni:bə'lʊŋən-] F unshakeable loyalty

nicht [nɪçt] ADV **a** (*Verneinung*) not; ~ **berufstätig** non-employed; ~ **leitend** non-conducting; ~ **organisiert** (*Arbeiter*) non-organized, non-union(ized); ~ **rostend** rustproof, non-rust; *Stahl* stainless; ~ **amtlich** unofficial; ~ **christlich** non-Christian; ~ **ehelich** = **nichtehelich**; ~ **geschäftsfähig** = **geschäftsunfähig**; ~ **metallisch** nonmetallic; ~ **öffentlich** = **nichtöffentlich er raucht** ~ (*augenblicklich*) he is not *or* isn't smoking; (*gewöhnlich*) he does not *or* doesn't smoke; **alle lachten, nur er** ~ everybody laughed except him, everybody laughed, only he didn't; **kommst du? – nein, ich komme** ~ are you coming? – no, I'm not (coming); **ich weiß auch** ~, **warum** I really don't know why; **ich kann das** ~ – **ich auch** ~ I can't do it – neither *or* nor can I; ~ **mehr** *or* **länger** not any longer; ~ **mehr als** no *or* not more than; ~ **mehr und** ~ **weniger als** no more and no less than; ~ **heute und** ~ **morgen** neither today nor tomorrow; ~ **ihn meinte ich, sondern sie** I didn't mean him, I meant her, it's not him I meant but her; **er** ~! not him, not he (*form*); ~ **(ein)mal** not even

b (*Bitte, Gebot, Verbot*) ~ **berühren!** do not touch; (*gesprochen*) don't touch; **ärgere dich** ~! don't be angry, do not be angry (*often liter*); ~ **rauchen!** no smoking; ~! don't!, no!; **tus** ~! don't do it!; ~ **doch!** stop it!, don't!; **bitte** ~! please don't!; **nur das** ~! anything but that!; **nun wein mal** ~ **gleich!** now don't start crying

c (*rhetorisch*) **er kommt,** ~ **(wahr)?** he's coming, isn't he *or* is he not (*esp Brit*)?; **sie kommen,** ~ **(wahr)?** they're coming, aren't they *or* are they not (*esp Brit*)?; **er kommt** ~, ~ **wahr?** he isn't coming, is he?; **ich darf kommen,** ~ **(wahr)?** I can come, can't I *or* can I?; **das ist schön,** ~ **(wahr)?** it's nice, isn't it?; **jetzt wollen wir Schluss machen,** ~? let's leave it now, right *or* OK?

d (*doppelte Verneinung*) ~ **uninteressant/unschön** *etc* not uninteresting/unattractive *etc*

e (*Verwunderung, Resignation etc*) **was die Kinder** ~ **alles wissen!** the things children know about!; **was ich** ~ **alles durchmachen muss!** the things I have to go through!

Nicht-, nicht- [nɪçt] PREF non-; **Nicht|ach|tung** F (+*gen* for) disregard, lack of regard; **jdn mit** ~ **strafen** to send sb to Coventry (*Brit*), to give sb the silent treatment; ~ **des Gerichts** contempt of court; **nicht|amt|lich** ADJ unofficial; **Nicht|an|er|ken|nung** F non-recognition; **Nicht|an|griffs|pakt** M non-aggression pact; **Nicht|ari|er(in)** M(F) non-Aryan; **Nicht|be|ach|tung** F, **Nicht|be|fol|gung** F non-observance; **Nicht|be|nut|zung** F (*form*) non-utilization (*form*); **bei** ~ **der Maschine** when the machine is not in use *or* being used; **nicht|be|rufs|tä|tig** △ ADJ *attr* → **nicht a**; **Nicht|be|zah|lung** F non-payment; **nicht|christ|lich** ADJ non-Christian

Nich|te ['nɪçtə] F -, -n niece

Nicht-: nicht|ehe|lich ADJ (*Jur*) *Kinder, Abstammung* illegitimate; *Mutter, Vater* unmarried; **in** ~ **er Lebensgemeinschaft leben** to cohabit; ~ **e Beziehungen zu jdm unterhalten** to cohabit with sb; **Kinder aus** ~ **en Beziehungen** children

---

born outside wedlock (*form*); **Nicht|ein|hal|tung** F non-compliance (+*gen* with), non-observance (+*gen* of); **Nicht|ein|mi|schung** F (*Pol*) non-intervention, non-interference; **Nicht|er|fül|lung** F (*Jur*) non-fulfilment (+*gen* of), default; **Nicht|er|schei|nen** NT non-appearance, failure to appear; **Nicht|fach|frau/Nicht|fach|mann** M non-specialist, non-expert; **nicht|flüch|tig** ADJ (*Chem, Comput*) non-volatile; **Nicht|ge|brauch** M = **Nichtbenutzung**; **Nicht|ge|fal|len** NT **bei** ~ (**zurück**) if not satisfied (return); **nicht|ge|schäfts|fä|hig** ADJ *attr* = **geschäftsunfähig**

nich|tig ['nɪçtɪç] ADJ **a** (*Jur: = ungültig*) invalid, void; **etw für** ~ **erklären** to declare sth invalid; *Ehe auch* to annul sth; **dadurch** *or* **hierdurch ist der Vertrag** ~ **geworden** the treaty has thereby become invalid → **null b** (= *unbedeutend*) trifling, trivial; *Versuch* vain; *Drohung* empty, vain; **die** ~ **en Dinge dieser Welt** (*liter*) the vain things *or* the vanities (*liter*) of this life

Nich|tig|keit F -, -en **a** (*Jur: = Ungültigkeit*) invalidity, nullity **b** *usu pl* (= *Kleinigkeit*) trifle, triviality, trivia *pl*

Nich|tig|keits-: Nich|tig|keits|er|klä|rung F (*Jur*) annulment; **Nich|tig|keits|kla|ge** F (*Jur*) nullity suit (*Brit*), filing for an annulment

Nicht-: Nicht|kom|bat|tant(in) M(F) (*form*) non-combatant; **nicht|lei|tend** △ ADJ (*Elec*) → **nicht a**; **Nicht|lei|ter** M (*Elec*) non-conductor; **Nicht|me|tall** NT nonmetal; **nicht|me|tal|lisch** ADJ nonmetallic; **Nicht|mit|glied** NT non-member; **nicht|öf|fent|lich** ADJ *attr* not open to the public, private; ~ **e Sitzung/Konferenz** meeting/conference in camera (*Jur*) *or* behind closed doors; **nicht|or|ga|ni|siert** △ ADJ *attr* → **nicht a**; **Nicht|rau|cher(in)** M(F) non-smoker; **ich bin** ~ I don't smoke, I'm a non-smoker; „**Nichtraucher**" (*Rail*) "no smoking" (*Brit*), "non-smoking car" (*US*); (*Aviat*) "non-smoking seats"; **Nicht|rau|cher|ab|teil** NT no-smoking compartment; **Nicht|rau|cher|zo|ne** F no-smoking area; **nicht|ros|tend** △ ADJ *attr* → **nicht a**

nichts [nɪçts] INDEF PRON *inv* nothing; (*fragend, bedingend auch*) not ... anything; **ich weiß** ~ I know nothing, I don't know anything; ~ **als** nothing but; ~ **anderes als** ... anything but or except; ~ **von Bedeutung** nothing of (any) importance; ~ **Besseres/Neues** *etc* nothing better/new *etc*; ~ **gegen Volksmusik, aber** ... (I've got) nothing against folk music, but ...; ~ **da!** (*inf*) (= *weg da*) no you don't!; (= *ausgeschlossen*) nothing doing (*inf*), no chance (*inf*); ~ **ahnend** (*adjektivisch*) unsuspecting; (*adverbial*) unsuspectingly; ~ **sagend** (*Buch, Rede, Worte*) empty, meaningless; *Vergnügen* trivial, trite, frivolous; *Mensch* insignificant; *Gesichtsausdruck* blank, vacant, expressionless; *Erklärung, Redensart* meaningless; *antworten* non-committally, vaguely; ~ **zu danken!** don't mention it, not at all; **für** *or* **um** ~ for nothing; **das ist** ~ **für mich** that's not (for) me, that's not my thing (*inf*), that's not my cup of tea (*Brit inf*); **für** ~ **und wieder** ~ (*inf*) for nothing at all, for damn all (*inf*); ~ **und niemand** nothing and nobody; ~ **zu machen** nothing doing (*inf*), nix (*inf*); (**es war**) ~ **mehr zu machen** there was nothing more that could be done; ~ **mehr** nothing more, not ... anything more; **ich weiß** ~ **Näheres** *or* **Genaueres** I don't know any details; **das war wohl** ~ (*inf*) you can't win them all (*inf*); ~ **wie raus/rein/hin** *etc* (*inf*) let's get out/in/over there *etc* (on the double); **aus** ~ **wird** ~ (*Prov*) **von** ~ **kommt** ~ (*Prov*) you can't make something out of nothing; **ich mag** *or* **will** ~ **mehr davon hören** I don't want to hear any more about it; **er ist zu** ~ **nutze** *or* **zu gebrauchen** he's useless *or* hopeless

Nichts[1] [nɪçts] NT -, *no pl* (*Philos*) nothingness; (= *Leere*) emptiness, void; (= *Kleinigkeit*) trifle, triviality, trivia *pl*; **etw aus dem** ~ **erschaffen** to create sth out of nothing(ness) *or* the void; **etw aus dem** ~ **aufbauen** to build sth up from nothing; **dieser Schriftsteller ist aus dem** ~ **aufge-**

---

taucht this author sprang up from nowhere; **vor dem** ~ **stehen** to be left with nothing; **alle seine Hoffnungen endeten im** ~ (*liter*) all his hopes came to nothing *or* nought

Nichts[2] NT -es, -e (= *Mensch*) nobody, nonentity, (mere) cipher

nichts|ah|nend △ ADJ → **nichts**

Nicht|schwim|mer(in) M(F) non-swimmer; **er ist** ~ he's a non-swimmer

Nicht|schwim|mer|be|cken NT pool for non-swimmers

nichts-: nichts|des|to|trotz [nɪçtsdɛsto'trɔts] ADV notwithstanding (*form*), nonetheless; **nichts|des|to|we|ni|ger** [nɪçtsdɛsto've:nɪgɐ] ADV nevertheless, nonetheless

Nicht|sein NT , **Nicht-Sein** ['nɪçtzaɪn] NT non-existence, non-being

Nicht|sess|haf|te(r) ▲ ['nɪçtzɛshaftə] MF *decl as adj* (*form*) person of no fixed abode (*form*)

Nichts-: Nichts|kön|ner(in) M(F) washout (*inf*), incompetent person; **er ist ein** ~ he's (worse than) useless; **Nichts|nutz** ['nɪçtsnʊts] M -es, -e good-for-nothing, useless bungler; **nichts|nut|zig** ['nɪçtsnʊtsɪç] ADJ useless, hopeless; (= *unartig*) good-for-nothing; **nichts|sa|gend** △ ADJ → **nichts**

nicht|staat|lich ADJ non-governmental; (= *privat*) private

Nichts-: Nichts|tu|er ['nɪçtstu:ɐ] M -s, -, **Nichts|tu|e|rin** [-ərɪn] F -, -nen idler, loafer; **Nichts|tun** ['nɪçtstu:n] NT idleness, inactivity; (= *Muße*) leisure; **das süße** ~ dolce far niente (*Brit*), idle bliss; **viel Zeit mit** ~ **verbringen** to spend a lot of time doing nothing; **nichts|wür|dig** ['nɪçtsvʏrdɪç] ADJ base, despicable; *Mensch auch* worthless; (**du**) **Nichtswürdiger!** (*old, liter*) vile *or* base wretch! (*old, liter*)

Nicht-: Nicht|tän|zer(in) M(F) non-dancer; **ich bin** ~ I don't dance; **Nicht|trin|ker(in)** M(F) non-drinker; **er ist** ~ he doesn't drink; **Nicht|über|ein|stim|mung** F discrepancy (+*gen* in, of, between); (= *Meinungsunterschied*) differences *pl*, disagreement; **Nicht|ver|an|la|gungs|be|scheid** M (*Fin*) non-assessment declaration; **Nicht|ver|an|la|gungs|be|schei|ni|gung** F (*Fin*) non-assessment note; **Nicht|ver|brei|tung** F (*von Kernwaffen etc*) non-proliferation; **Nicht|ver|fol|ger|land** NT , **Nicht|ver|fol|ger|staat** M (*Pol*) non-repressive country; **Nicht|vor|han|den|sein** NT absence; **Nicht|wähl|bar|keit** ['nɪçtvɛ:lba:ɐkaɪt] F -, *no pl* ineligibility (for office); **Nicht|wäh|ler(in)** M(F) non-voter; **Nicht|wei|ter|ver|brei|tung** F (*von Gefahrenstoffen, Atomwaffen*) non-proliferation; **Nicht|wis|sen** NT ignorance (*um* about); **sich mit** ~ **entschuldigen** to plead ignorance; **Nicht|zah|lung** F (*form*) non-payment; **im Falle der** ~, **bei** ~ in default of payment; **nicht|zie|lend** ADJ = **intransitiv**; **Nicht|zu|stan|de|kom|men** NT (*form*) non-completion; **Nicht|zu|tref|fen|de(s)** [-tsu:trɛfndə] NT *decl as adj* (**etwas**) ~ **s** something incorrect; ~ **s (bitte) streichen!** (please) delete as applicable

Ni|ckel ['nɪkl] NT -s, *no pl* (*abbr* **Ni**) nickel

Ni|ckel|bril|le F metal-rimmed glasses *pl*

ni|cken ['nɪkn] VI **a** (*lit, fig*) to nod; **mit dem Kopf** ~ to nod one's head; **ein leichtes Nicken** a slight nod **b** (*inf: = schlummern*) to snooze (*inf*), to doze, to nod

Ni|cker|chen ['nɪkɐçən] NT -s, - (*inf*) nap, snooze (*inf*), forty winks (*inf*); **ein** ~ **machen** *or* **halten** to take *or* have forty winks *or* a nap *or* a snooze (*inf*)

Ni|cki ['nɪki] M -s, -s velour(s) pullover

nid [ni:t] PREP +*dat* (*old*) beneath, under, 'neath (*poet*)

nie [ni:] ADV never; ~ **im Leben** never ever; **machst du das?** – ~ **im Leben!** will you do it? – not on your life!; ~ **und nimmer** never ever; ~

---

wieder or **mehr** never again; **ein ~ wieder gut zu machender Fehler** a mistake that can never be put right; **fast ~** hardly ever

nie|der ['niːdɐ] **ADJ** *attr* **a** *Triebe, Instinkt, Motiv* low, base; *Arbeit* menial **b** (= *primitiv*) *Kulturstufe* low, primitive; *Entwicklungsstufe* low, early **c** (= *weniger bedeutend*) lower; *Beamter* minor, lower; (= *geringer*) *Geburt, Herkunft* lowly; *Volk* common; *Klasse, Stand* lower; (*Comput*) *Programmiersprache* low(-level); (*Biol*) *Lebensformen, Organismen* lower; **der ~e Adel** the gentry, the lower or lesser aristocracy; **Hohe und Niedere** (*liter*), **Hoch und Nieder** (*liter*) (both) the high and the low **d** (*esp S Ger*: = *niedrig*) low; **die ~e Jagd** small game hunting
ADV down; **die Waffen ~!** lay down your arms; **auf und ~** up and down; **das Auf und Nieder** (*lit*) the bobbing up and down; (*fig*) the ups and (the) downs *pl*; **~ mit dem Kaiser!** down with the Kaiser!

Nie|der-, nie|der- ['niːdɐ] **PREF** (*Geog*) Lower, lower; **Niederbayern** Lower Bavaria; **niederbay(e)risch** lower Bavarian

nie|der+beu|gen *sep* **VT** (*lit, fig*) to bow down **VR** to bend down

nie|der+bren|nen **VTI** *sep irreg* (*vi: aux sein*) to burn down

nie|der+brin|gen **VT** *sep irreg Bohrung* to sink

nie|der+brül|len **VT** *sep Redner* to shout down

nie|der+bü|geln **VT** *sep* (*inf*) *Person, Einwand, Argument* to demolish; **jdn rhetorisch ~** to demolish sb with rhetoric

nie|der|deutsch **ADJ** **a** (*Geog*) North German **b** (*Ling*) Low German

Nie|der|deutsch(e) **NT** Low German → *auch* **Deutsch(e)**

nie|der+don|nern **VI** *sep aux sein* (*Lawine*) to thunder down

Nie|der|druck **M** , *no pl* (*Tech*) low pressure

nie|der+drü|cken **VT** *sep* **a** (*lit*) to press down; *Taste, Hebel* to press (down), to push, to depress (*form*) **b** (= *bedrücken*) **jdn ~** to depress sb, to get sb down (*inf*); **~d** depressing → **niedergedrückt**

nie|der+fah|ren **VI** *sep irreg aux sein* (*liter*) to descend

nie|der+fal|len **VI** *sep irreg aux sein* (*liter*) to fall or drop down

nie|der|fre|quent **ADJ** low-frequency *attr*

Nie|der|fre|quenz **F** low frequency; (*Akustik*) audio frequency

Nie|der|gang **M** *pl* **-gänge** **a** (*liter: der Sonne*) setting, going down (*poet*); (*fig*: = *Verfall*) decline, fall **b** (*Naut*) companionway

nie|der|ge|drückt **ADJ** depressed, dejected

nie|der+ge|hen **VI** *sep irreg aux sein* to descend; (*Aviat*) to descend, to come down; (*Bomben, Regen, Giftstoff, Komet*) to fall; (*Fallschirmspringer*) to drop; (*Vorhang*) to drop, to fall; (*Gewitter*) to break (*auch fig*); (*Boxer*) to go down

nie|der|ge|schla|gen **ADJ** dejected, despondent **ADV** dejectedly, despondently → *auch* **niederschlagen**

Nie|der|ge|schla|gen|heit **F** [-gəʃlaːgnhait] , *no pl* dejection, despondency

nie|der+hal|ten **VT** *sep irreg* to hold or keep down; *Volk* to oppress; (*Mil*) to pin or hold down

nie|der+hau|en **VT** *sep irreg Baum* to cut or chop down, to fell; *Gegner* to floor, to knock down, to fell

nie|der+ho|len **VT** *sep Segel, Flagge* to haul down, to lower; *Ballon* to bring down

Nie|der|holz **NT** , *no pl* underwood, underbrush

nie|der+kämp|fen **VT** *sep Feuer* to fight down or back; *Gegner* to overcome; *Tränen* to fight back; *Aufstand* to suppress

nie|der+kau|ern **VIR** (*vi: aux sein*) to crouch or cower down

nie|der+knal|len **VT** *sep* to shoot down

nie|der+kni|en **VI** *sep aux sein* to kneel down

nie|der+knüp|peln **VT** *sep* to club down

nie|der+kom|men **VI** *sep irreg aux sein* (*old*) to be delivered (*old*) (*mit* of)

Nie|der|kunft [-kʊnft] **F** **-, ⸚e** [-kʏnftə] (*old*) delivery

Nie|der|la|ge **F** **a** (*Mil, Sport, fig*) defeat (*gegen* by); (= *Misserfolg*) failure, defeat; **eine ~ einstecken müssen** or **hinnehmen müssen** or **erleiden** to suffer a defeat; **jdm eine ~ zufügen** or **beibringen** to defeat sb, to inflict a defeat on sb **b** (= *Lager*) warehouse, store, depot **c** (= *Filiale*) branch (office)

Nie|der|lan|de ['niːdɐlandə] **PL die ~** the Netherlands *sing* or *pl*, the Low Countries *pl*

Nie|der|län|der ['niːdɐlɛndɐ] **M -s, -** Dutchman; **die ~** the Dutch

Nie|der|län|de|rin ['niːdɐlɛndərɪn] **F -, -nen** Dutchwoman

nie|der|län|disch ['niːdɐlɛndɪʃ] **ADJ** Dutch, Netherlands

Nie|der|län|disch(e) ['niːdɐlɛndɪʃ] **NT** Dutch → *auch* **Deutsch(e)**

nie|der+las|sen **VR** *sep irreg* **a** (= *sich setzen*) to sit down; (= *sich niederlegen*) to lie down; (*Vögel*) to land, to alight (*form*) **b** (= *Wohnsitz nehmen*) to settle (down); (= *Praxis, Geschäft eröffnen*) to set up in business, to establish oneself, to set up shop (*inf*); **sich als Arzt/Rechtsanwalt ~** to set up (a practice) as a doctor/lawyer; **die niedergelassenen Ärzte** registered doctors/specialists with their own practices **die niedergelassenen Rechtsanwälte** lawyers in private practice

Nie|der|las|sung [-lasʊŋ] **F -, -en** **a** *no pl* (= *das Niederlassen*) settling, settlement; (*eines Arztes etc*) establishment, setting-up **b** (= *Siedlung*) settlement **c** (*Comm*) registered office; (= *Zweigstelle*) branch

Nie|der|las|sungs-: Nie|der|las|sungs|be|wil|li|gung **F** (*Sw*) residence permit; **Nie|der|las|sungs|frei|heit** **F** , *no pl* (*Jur*) freedom of establishment; **Nie|der|las|sungs|recht** **NT** , *no pl* (*Jur*) right of establishment

nie|der+le|gen *sep* **VT** **a** (= *hinlegen*) to lay or put or set down; *Kranz, Blumen* to lay; *Waffen* to lay down **b** (= *aufgeben*) *Dienst, Amt, Mandat* to resign (from), to give up; *Krone, Führung* to renounce, to give up; **die Arbeit ~** (= *aufhören*) to stop work(ing); (= *streiken*) to down tools **c** (= *schriftlich festlegen*) to write or set down **VR** to lie down; **da legst di nieder!** (*S Ger inf*) well I'm blowed (*Brit inf*) or I'll be damned!, by 'eck! (*N Engl inf*)

Nie|der|le|gung [-leːgʊŋ] **F -, -en** **a** (*von Kranz*) laying; (*von Waffen*) laying down **b** (*von Amt, Dienst, Mandat*) resignation (from); (*von Kommando*) resignation (of); (*der Krone*) abdication; **~ der Arbeit** walkout **c** (*schriftlich*) setting-out; **eine schriftliche ~ meiner Gedanken** setting out or putting down my thoughts in writing

nie|der+ma|chen **VT** *sep* **a** (= *töten*) to massacre, to butcher **b** (*fig*: = *heftig kritisieren*) to run down, to disparage (*form*)

nie|der+mä|hen **VT** *sep* (*lit, fig*) to mow down

nie|der+met|zeln **VT** *sep* to massacre, to butcher

Nie|der|ös|ter|reich **NT** Lower Austria

nie|der+pras|seln **VI** *sep aux sein* (*Regen, Hagel etc*) to beat down, to hammer down; (*fig: Beschimpfungen, Vorwürfe etc*) to rain or hail down

nie|der+rei|ßen **VT** *sep irreg jdn* to pull or drag down; *Gebäude* to pull or knock down; (*fig*) *Schranken* to tear down

Nie|der|rhein **M** Lower Rhine

nie|der|rhei|nisch **ADJ** lower Rhine

nie|der+rin|gen **VT** *sep irreg* to fight down; (*im Ringkampf auch*) to floor

Nie|der|sach|sen **NT** Lower Saxony

nie|der|säch|sisch **ADJ** of Lower Saxony

nie|der+sau|sen **VI** *sep aux sein* to rain or hail down

nie|der+schie|ßen *sep irreg* **VT** to shoot down **VI** *aux sein* (*Vogel etc*) to shoot or plummet down

Nie|der|schlag **M** **a** (*Met*) precipitation (*form*); (*Chem*) precipitate; (= *Bodensatz*) sediment, dregs *pl*; (*fig*: = *Ausdruck*) expression; **radioaktiver ~** (radioactive) fallout; **für morgen sind heftige Niederschläge gemeldet** tomorrow there will be heavy rain/hail/snow; **in diesem Gedicht haben seine eigenen Erfahrungen ihren ~ gefunden** his own experiences are reflected or find expression in this poem **b** (*Mus*) downbeat **c** (*Boxen*) knockdown blow; (*über 10 Sekunden*) knockout, KO; **~ bis 10** knockout, KO; **Sieg durch ~** win by a knockout

nie|der+schla|gen *sep irreg* **VT** **a** *jdn* to knock down, to fell; (*Regen, Hagel*) *Getreide* to beat down, to flatten; *Kragen, Hutkrempe* to turn down; *Aufstand, Revolte* to quell, to put down, to suppress; *Augen, Blick* to lower, to cast down (*liter*) → *auch* **niedergeschlagen b** (= *erlassen*) *Steuerschuld* to waive; **ein Verfahren ~** (*Jur*) to dismiss a case **c** (*Chem*) to precipitate **VR** (*Flüssigkeit*) to condense; (*Bodensatz*) to settle; (*Chem*) to precipitate; (*Met*) to fall; **die Untersuchung schlug sich in einer Reform nieder** the investigation resulted in a reform; **sich in etw** (*dat*) **~** (*Erfahrungen, Vorfälle etc*) to find expression in sth; **in Statistik** to be reflected in sth

Nie|der|schlags-: nie|der|schlags|arm **ADJ** *Wetter* not very rainy/snowy; **eine ~e Gegend** an area which gets little rain/snow; **die Südinsel ist niederschlagsärmer** the south island has a lower rainfall/gets less snow, the south island has a lower level of precipitation (*form*); **nie|der|schlags|frei** **ADJ** dry, without precipitation (*form*); **Nie|der|schlags|men|ge** **F** rainfall/snowfall, precipitation (*form*); **nie|der|schlags|reich** **ADJ** *Wetter* very rainy/snowy; **eine ~e Gegend** an area which gets a lot of rain/snow

Nie|der|schla|gung [-ʃlaːgʊŋ] **F -, -en** (*von Strafverfahren*) dismissal; (*von Steuerschuld*) waiving, writing-off; (*eines Aufstands*) suppression

nie|der+schmet|tern **VT** *sep* to smash or batter down; (*fig*) to shatter

nie|der+schmet|ternd **ADJ** *Nachricht, Ergebnis, Erlebnis* shattering

nie|der+schrei|ben **VT** *sep irreg* to write down

nie|der+schrei|en **VT** *sep irreg* to shout down

Nie|der|schrift **F** (= *das Niederschreiben*) writing down; (= *Niedergeschriebenes*) notes *pl*; (= *Schulaufsatz*) composition, essay; (= *Protokoll*) (*einer Sitzung*) minutes *pl*; (*Jur*) record; (*von Bandaufzeichnung*) transcript; **er brauchte viel Zeit für die ~ seiner Gedanken** he needed a lot of time to write down his thoughts; **die erste ~ eines Gedichts/Romans** the first draft of a poem/novel

nie|der+set|zen *sep* **VT** *Kind, Glas, Last* to put or set down **VR** to sit down; (*Vogel*) to perch, to settle, to alight

nie|der+sin|ken **VI** *sep irreg aux sein* (*geh*) to sink down

nie|der+sit|zen **VI** *sep irreg* (*S Ger, Aus, Sw*) to sit down

Nie|der|span|nung **F** (*Elec*) low voltage or tension

nie|der+ste|chen **VT** *sep irreg* to stab, to knife

nie|der+stei|gen **VI** *sep irreg aux sein* (*liter*) to descend

nie|der+stel|len **VT** *sep* to put down, to set down

nie|der+stim|men VT sep to vote down

nie|der+sto|ßen sep irreg **VT** to knock down **VI** aux sein (Raubvogel) to shoot or plummet down

nie|der+stre|cken sep (geh) **VT** to lay low **VR** to lie down, to stretch out

nie|der+stür|zen VI sep aux sein to crash down

nie|der|tou|rig [-tu:rɪç] **ADJ** Motor, Maschine low-revving **ADV** ~ fahren to drive with low revs

Nie|der|tracht ['ni:dɐtraxt] F -, no pl despicableness, vileness; (als Rache) malice, spite; (= niederträchtige Tat) vile or despicable act; **so viel ~ hätte ich ihm nicht zugetraut** I would not have suspected him of such a despicable or vile act; **die ~, mit der er bei seinen Betrügereien vorgegangen ist** the despicable way he went about his deceptions

nie|der|träch|tig ['ni:dɐtrɛçtɪç] **ADJ** despicable, vile; (= rachsüchtig) malicious, spiteful **ADV** despicably; verleumden maliciously; **jdn ~ verraten** to maliciously betray sb

Nie|der|träch|tig|keit F -, -en **a** no pl = **Niedertracht** **b** (Tat) despicable behaviour no pl (Brit) or behavior no pl (US); (rachsüchtig) malicious behaviour no pl (Brit) or behavior no pl (US); **das ist eine ~** that's despicable; **eine ~ begehen** to commit a vile or despicable act

nie|der+tram|peln VT sep to trample underfoot

nie|der+tre|ten VT sep irreg to trample down; Erde auch to stamp down; Teppich to wear (down)

Nie|de|rung ['ni:dərʊŋ] F -, -en (= Senke) depression; (= Mündungsgebiet) flats pl; (sumpfig) marsh; **die ~en des Alltags** the down side of everyday life; **in solche ~en begebe ich mich nicht** (fig) I will not sink to such depths

Nie|der|wald M (Forest) copse

nie|der+wal|zen VT sep to flatten

nie|der|wärts ['ni:dɐvɛrts] **ADV** (obs) down, downward(s)

nie|der+wer|fen sep irreg **VT** to throw or hurl or cast (liter) down; Aufstand to suppress, to put down; Gegner (lit) to throw down, to floor; (fig) to defeat, to overcome; **er wurde von einer Krankheit niedergeworfen** he was laid low with an illness **VR** to throw oneself down, to prostrate oneself

Nie|der|wer|fung [-vɛrfʊŋ] F -, no pl (von Aufstand) suppression; (von Gegner) defeat, overthrow

Nie|der|wild NT small game

nie|der+zwin|gen VT sep irreg (lit) to force down; (fig) to defeat, to vanquish; **er zwang seinen Gegner auf die Knie nieder** (lit, fig) he brought his enemy to his knees

nied|lich ['ni:tlɪç] **ADJ** sweet, cute, pretty little attr **ADV** cutely, sweetly; **~ aussehen** to look sweet; **sie hat das Lied ~ gesungen** she sang that song sweetly; **das Kätzchen lag so ~ auf meinem Bett** the kitten looked so sweet lying on my bed

Nied|na|gel ['ni:t-] M agnail, hangnail

nied|rig ['ni:drɪç] **ADJ** **a** (= tief) low **b** (= gering) low; Stand, Herkunft, Geburt low(ly), humble; **~ste Preise** lowest or rock-bottom prices **c** (= gemein) low no adv, base **ADV** **a** (= tief) fliegen, schießen low **b** (= gering) **etw ~er berechnen** to charge less for sth; **etw zu ~ veranschlagen** to underestimate sth; **etw ~ einstufen** to give sth a low classification; **jdn gehaltsmäßig ~er einstufen** to pay sb a lower salary; **ich schätze seine Chancen sehr ~ ein** I don't think much of his chances, I think his chances are very slim or small; **~ denken** to think base thoughts; **von jdm ~ denken, jdn ~ einschätzen** to have a low

or poor opinion of sb; **~ stehend** (Volk, Kultur) undeveloped, primitive

Nied|rig|ener|gie|haus NT low-energy house

Nied|rig|keit F -, no pl **a** lowness; **die ~ der Häuser** the low-built style of the houses **b** (von Gedanken, Beweggründen) baseness

Nied|rig-: Nied|rig|lohn M low wages pl; **Nied|rig|lohn|grup|pe** F low-wage bracket; **Nied|rig|lohn|land** NT low-wage country

nied|rig|ste|hend △ **ADJ** → **niedrig** ADV b

Nied|rig|strah|lung F low-level radiation

Nied|rig|was|ser NT pl -wasser (Naut) low tide, low water

nie|mals ['ni:ma:ls] **ADV** never

nie|mand ['ni:mant] **INDEF PRON** nobody, no-one; **es war ~ zu Hause** there was nobody or no-one at home, there wasn't anybody or anyone at home; **~ anders** or **anderer** (S Ger) **kam** nobody else came; **~ anders** or **anderer** (S Ger) **war da** there wasn't anybody else there, nobody else was there; **ich habe ~ anders** or **anderen** (S Ger) **gesehen** I didn't see anybody else; **herein kam ~ anders** or **anderer** (S Ger) **als der Kanzler selbst** in came the Chancellor himself, no less, in came none other than the Chancellor himself; **~ Fremdes** no strangers, not … any strangers; **er hat es ~(em) gesagt** he hasn't told anyone, he has told no-one; **sag das ~(em)!** don't tell anyone

Nie|mand ['ni:mant] M -s, no pl **er ist ein ~** he's a nobody

Nie|mands|land NT no-man's-land

Nie|re ['ni:rə] F -, -n kidney; **künstliche ~** kidney machine, artificial kidney; **es geht mir an die ~n** (inf) it gets me down (inf); **er hat es an der ~** or **den ~n** he has kidney problems

Nie|ren- in cpds (Anat) renal; **Nie|ren|be|cken** NT pelvis of the kidney; **Nie|ren|be|cken|ent|zün|dung** F pyelitis (spec); **Nie|ren|ent|zün|dung** F nephritis (spec); **nie|ren|för|mig** **ADJ** kidney-shaped; **Nie|ren|gurt** M (Aut) kidney belt; **Nie|ren|ko|lik** F renal colic; **nie|ren|krank** **ADJ** suffering from a kidney disease; **Nie|ren|krank|heit** F , **Nie|ren|lei|den** NT kidney disease; **Nie|ren|schale** F kidney dish; **Nie|ren|schüt|zer** M -s, - kidney belt; **Nie|ren|spen|der(in)** M(F) kidney donor; **Nie|ren|stein** M kidney stone, renal calculus (spec); **Nie|ren|stein|zer|trüm|me|rer** [-tsɛɐtrʏmərɐ] M -s, - lithotripter (spec); **Nie|ren|ta|sche** F bum bag (Brit), fanny pack (US); **Nie|ren|tisch** M kidney-shaped table; **Nie|ren|trans|plan|ta|ti|on** F kidney transplant; **Nie|ren|ver|sa|gen** NT kidney failure; **Nie|ren|wär|mer** [-vɛrmɐ] M -s, - kidney warmer

nie|seln ['ni:zln] VI impers to drizzle

Nie|sel|priem ['ni:zlpri:m] M -s, -e (inf) miseryguts (Brit inf), moaner

Nie|sel|re|gen M drizzle

nie|sen ['ni:zn] VI to sneeze

Nies|pul|ver NT sneezing powder

Nieß- ['ni:s-]: **Nieß|brauch** M (Jur) usufruct; **Nieß|brau|cher** [-brauxɐ] M -s, -, **Nieß|brau|che|rin** [-ərɪn] F -, -nen, **Nieß|nut|zer** [-nʊtsɐ] M -s, -, **Nieß|nut|ze|rin** [-ərɪn] F -, -nen (Jur) usufructuary

Nies|wurz ['ni:svʊrts] F -, no pl (Bot) hellebore

Niet [ni:t] M -(e)s, -e (spec), **Nie|te¹** ['ni:tə] F -, -n rivet; (auf Kleidung) stud

Nie|te² F -, -n (= Los) blank; (inf: = Mensch) dead loss (inf), washout (inf); **eine ~ ziehen** (lit) to draw a blank; **mit ihm haben wir eine ~ gezogen** he is a dead loss (inf); **~n in Nadelstreifen** (inf) incompetent managers

nie|ten ['ni:tn] VT to rivet

Nie|ten|ho|se F (pair of) studded jeans pl

niet- und na|gel|fest ['ni:tʔʊnt 'na:glfɛst] **ADJ** (inf) nailed or screwed down

ni|gel|na|gel|neu ['ni:gl'na:gl'nɔy] **ADJ** (inf) brand spanking new (inf)

Ni|ger¹ ['ni:gɐ] M -s (= Fluss) Niger

Ni|ger² NT -s (= Staat) Niger

Ni|ge|ria [ni'ge:ria] NT -s Nigeria

Ni|ge|ria|ner [nigeri'a:nɐ] M -s, -, **Ni|ge|ria|ne|rin** [-ərɪn] F -, -nen Nigerian

ni|ge|ria|nisch [nigeri'a:nɪʃ] **ADJ** Nigerian

Nig|ger ['nɪgɐ] M -s, - (pej) nigger (pej), coon (pej)

Nig|rer ['ni:grɐ] M -s, -, **Nig|re|rin** [-ərɪn] F -, -nen Nigerian

nig|risch ['ni:grɪʃ] **ADJ** Nigerian

Ni|hi|lis|mus [nihi'lɪsmʊs] M -, no pl nihilism

Ni|hi|list [nihi'lɪst] M -en, -en, **Ni|hi|lis|tin** [-'lɪstɪn] F -, -nen nihilist

ni|hi|lis|tisch [nihi'lɪstɪʃ] **ADJ** nihilistic

Nik|kei-In|dex ['nɪkei-] M -, no pl (St Ex) Nikkei Index

Ni|ko|laus ['nɪkolaus, 'ni:kolaus] M **a** -' (= Name) Nicholas **b** -, -e or (hum inf) **Nikoläuse** [-ɔyzə] St Nicholas; (= Nikolaustag) St Nicholas' Day

---

NIKOLAUS

Nikolaus (known as **Samichlaus** in Switzerland) is a saint, usually represented as wearing a tall hat, long gown and white bushy beard, who traditionally brings gifts for children on December 6th. He either places his presents in boots left outside the front door the night before, or he arrives in person. In many regions he is accompanied by **Knecht Ruprecht** or, particularly in Austria, by **Krampus**, who beats naughty children with a birch or carries them off in a sack. Increasingly, **Nikolaus** is presented as a benevolent character similar to the English and American Santa Claus.

Ni|ko|tin [niko'ti:n] NT -s, no pl nicotine

Ni|ko|tin-: ni|ko|tin|arm **ADJ** low-nicotine; **ni|ko|tin|frei** **ADJ** nicotine-free; **Ni|ko|tin|ge|halt** M nicotine content; **ni|ko|tin|hal|tig** **ADJ** containing nicotine; Zigarren sind **~er als** Zigaretten cigars contain more nicotine than cigarettes; **Ni|ko|tin|pflas|ter** NT nicotine patch; **ni|ko|tin|süch|tig** **ADJ** nicotine-addicted attr, addicted to nicotine pred; **Ni|ko|tin|ver|gif|tung** F nicotine poisoning

Nil [ni:l] M -s Nile

Nil-: Nil|del|ta NT Nile Delta; **Nil|pferd** NT hippopotamus, hippo

Nim|bus ['nɪmbʊs] M -, -se (= Heiligenschein) halo, aureole; (fig) aura; **sich mit dem ~ der Anständigkeit umgeben** to surround oneself with an aura of respectability; **im ~ der Heiligkeit stehen** to be thought of as a saint; **einen ~ zerstören** to shatter or destroy a myth

nimm [nɪm] imper sing von **nehmen**

nim|mer ['nɪmɐ] **ADV** **a** (liter: = niemals) never **b** (S Ger, Aus) = **nicht mehr**

Nim|mer|leins|tag ['nɪmɐlainsta:k] M = **Sankt-Nimmerleins-Tag**

nim|mer|mehr ['nɪmɐme:ɐ] **ADV** (liter) nevermore (liter), never again; **nie und ~** never ever

nim|mer|mü|de ['nɪmɐ'my:də] **ADJ** attr tireless, untiring

nim|mer|satt ['nɪmɐzat] **ADJ** gluttonous, insatiable

Nim|mer|satt ['nɪmɐzat] M -(e)s, -e glutton; **ein ~ sein** to be insatiable

Nim|mer|wie|der|se|hen NT (inf) **auf ~!** I don't or I never want to see you again; **ich habe meinen Koffer da stehen lassen – na dann, auf ~** I left my case there – well, you've seen the last of that; **auf ~ verschwinden** to disappear never to be seen again; **ich habe es ihm geborgt, hoffentlich nicht auf ~** I lent it to him, not permanently I hope *or* I hope not for ever

nimmt [nɪmt] *3. pers sing pres von* **nehmen**

Nim|rod ['nɪmrɔt] M **-s, -e** [-də] Nimrod

Ni|ob [nio:p] NT **-s,** *no pl,* **Ni|o|bi|um** ['nio:-biʊm] NT **-s,** *no pl (abbr* **Nb**) niobium

Nip|pel ['nɪpl] M **-s, -** **a** *(Tech)* nipple **b** *(inf: = Brustwarze)* nipple

nip|pen ['nɪpn] VTI to nip *(an +dat* at); *(an Glas etc)* to sip from; **am** *or* **vom Wein ~** to sip (at) the wine

Nip|pes ['nɪpəs] PL , **Nipp|sa|chen** ['nɪp-] PL ornaments *pl,* knick-knacks *pl,* bric-à-brac *sing*

Nipp|flut F , **Nipp|zeit** ['nɪp-] F neap tide

Nip|pon ['nɪpɔn] NT **-s** Japan

nir|gend|her ['nɪrgnt'he:ɐ] ADV = **nirgendsher**

nir|gend|hin ['nɪrgnt'hɪn] ADV = **nirgendwohin**

nir|gends ['nɪrgnts] ADV nowhere, not ... anywhere; **ihm gefällt es ~** he doesn't like it anywhere; **überall und ~** here, there and everywhere; **er ist überall und ~ zu Hause** he has no real home; **er fühlt sich ~ so wohl wie ...** there's nowhere *or* there isn't anywhere he feels so happy as ...; **~ sonst** nowhere else; **das sieht man fast ~ mehr** you hardly see that any more

nir|gends|her ['nɪrgnts'he:ɐ] ADV from nowhere, not ... from anywhere

nir|gends|hin ['nɪrgnts'hɪn] ADV = **nirgendwohin**

nir|gend|wo ['nɪrgnt'vo:] ADV = **nirgends**

nir|gend|wo|hin ['nɪrgntvo'hɪn] ADV nowhere, not ... anywhere; **wohin gehst du? – ~** where are you going? – nowhere; **wenn man ~ gehen kann, um zu übernachten** if you've got nowhere to spend the night, if you haven't got anywhere to spend the night

Ni|ros|ta® [ni'rɔsta] M **-,** *no pl* stainless steel

Nir|wa|na [nɪr'va:na] NT **-(s), Nir|va|na** [nɪr'va:-na] NT **-(s)** nirvana

Ni|sche ['ni:ʃə] F **-, -n** niche, alcove; *(= Kochnische etc)* recess; *(fig)* niche

Nis|se ['nɪsə] F **-, -n** nit

Nis|sen|hüt|te F Nissen hut *(Brit)*, Quonset hut *(US)*

nis|ten ['nɪstn] VI to nest; *(fig)* to take possession *(in +dat* of); **dieses Vorurteil nistete in seinem Hirn** this prejudice lodged in his mind; **in ihm nistete tiefes Misstrauen** he was filled with a deep mistrust VR **Hass nistete sich in ihr Herz** *(liter)* hatred gripped *or* filled her heart

Nist-: Nist|kas|ten M nest(ing) box; **Nist|platz** M nesting place; **Nist|zeit** F nesting time, (the) nesting season

Nit|rat [ni'tra:t] NT **-(e)s, -e** nitrate

Nit|rat|ge|halt M nitrate level; *(im Boden auch)* nitrate levels *pl*

nit|rie|ren [ni'tri:rən] *ptp* **nitriert** VT to nitrate

Nit|rit [ni'tri:t] NT **-s, -e** nitrite

Nit|ro- ['nitro] *in cpds* nitro; **Nit|ro|ben|zol** NT nitrobenzene; **Nit|ro|gly|ze|rin** NT nitroglycerine; **Nit|ro|lack** M nitrocellulose paint; **Nit|ro|ver|dün|nung** F cellulose thinner; **Nit|ro|ver|gif|tung** F nitrate poisoning

Ni|veau- [ni'vo:-]: **Ni|veau|li|nie** F contour line; **ni|veau|los** ADJ *Film etc* mediocre; *Unter-*

-haltung mindless ADV **sich ~ unterhalten** to have a mindless conversation; **sich ~ amüsieren** to amuse oneself with mindless things; **Ni|veau|un|ter|schied** M *(lit, fig)* difference of level; **ni|veau|voll** ADJ *Unterhaltung, Film etc* high-class ADV **sich ~ unterhalten** to have a quality conversation; **eine ~ inszenierte Komödie** a high-class comedy

ni|vel|lie|ren [nive'li:rən] *ptp* **nivelliert** VT *(lit, fig)* to level off *or* out VI *(Surv)* to level

Ni|vel|lie|rung F **-, -en** *(Surv)* levelling *(Brit)*, leveling *(US)*; *(= Ausgleichung)* level(l)ing out

nix [nɪks] INDEF PRON *(inf)* = **nichts**

Nix [nɪks] M **-es, -e** water sprite *(esp Brit)*, water pixie *(US)*; *(mit Fischschwanz)* merman

Ni|xe ['nɪksə] F **-, -n** water sprite *(esp Brit)*, water nymph, nix(ie); *(mit Fischschwanz)* mermaid; *(hum: = Badenixe)* bathing belle

Niz|za ['nɪtsa] NT **-s** Nice

NN *abbr von* **Normalnull**

N.N. *abbr von* **nomen nescio** N.N., name not known *or* unkown

NNO *abbr von* **Nordnordost** NNE

NNW *abbr von* **Nordnordwest** NNW

NO *abbr von* **Nordosten**

no|bel ['no:bl] ADJ *(= edelmütig)* noble; *(inf)* *(= großzügig)* generous, lavish; *(= kostspielig)* extravagant; *(= elegant)* posh *(inf)*; **ein nobler Kunde** *(iro inf)* a posh customer, a nice type of person ADV *(= edelmütig)* nobly; *(= großzügig)* generously; **~ wohnen** to live in posh surroundings; **das war ~ gedacht** that was a noble thought; **~ geht die Welt zugrunde** *(iro)* there's nothing like going out in style; **sich ~ zeigen** *(inf)* to be generous; **er zeigte sich sehr ~ und verzieh ihm** he nobly forgave him

No|bel|her|ber|ge F *(inf)* posh *or* classy hotel *(inf)*

No|be|li|um [no'be:liʊm] NT **-s,** *no pl (abbr* **No**) nobelium

No|bel|preis [no'bɛl-] M Nobel prize

No|bel|preis|trä|ger(in) M(F) Nobel prize-winner

No|bel|schup|pen M *(inf, usu iro)* posh place, classy joint *(inf)*

No|bel|vier|tel NT *(inf, usu iro)* posh *or* upmarket *(US)* area

Nob|les|se [no'blɛsə] F **-,** *no pl (geh)* noblesse; **dafür hat er zu viel ~** he's much too high-minded for that; **noblesse oblige** noblesse oblige *(form)*

No|bo|dy ['no:bɔdi] M **-(s), -s** *(usu pej)* nobody

noch [nɔx] ADV **a** *(= weiterhin, bis jetzt, wie zuvor)* still; **~ nicht** still not, not yet; **bist du fertig? – ~ nicht** are you ready? – not yet; **er ist ~ nicht da** he isn't here yet, he isn't here yet; **immer ~, ~ immer** still; **sie ist immer ~ nicht fertig** she still isn't ready (yet), she isn't ready yet; **er dachte ~ lange an sie** it was a long time before he stopped thinking of her; **du bist ~ zu klein** you're still too young; **er schläft ~** he's still asleep; **~ nie** never; **das habe ich ~ nie gehört** I've never known that (before); **ich gehe kaum ~ aus** I hardly go out any more; **ich möchte gerne ~ bleiben** I'd like to stay on longer

b *(= irgendwann)* some time, one day; **er wird sich (schon) ~ daran gewöhnen** he'll get used to it (some time *or* one day); **das kann ~ passieren** that just might happen, that might still happen; **er wird ~ kommen** he'll come (yet)

c *(= eben, nicht später als)* **das muss ~ vor Dienstag fertig sein** it has to be ready by Tuesday; **ich habe ihn ~ vor zwei Tagen gesehen** I saw him only two days ago; **er ist ~ am selben Tag gestorben** he died the very same day; **ich tue das ~ heute** *or* **heute ~** I'll do it today *or* this very day; **~ im 18. Jahrhundert** as late as the 18th century; **gerade ~** (only) just; **~ gestern war er frisch und munter** (only) yesterday he was still bright and cheerful; **~ keine drei Tage** not three days

d *(einschränkend)* (only) just; **(gerade) ~ gut genug** (only) just good enough

e *(= außerdem, zusätzlich)* **wer war ~ da?** who else was there?; **(gibt es) ~ etwas?** (is there) anything else?; **ich will ~ etwas sagen** there's something else *or* another thing I want to say; **~ etwas Fleisch** some more meat, a bit more meat; **~ einer** another (one); **~ ein Bier** another beer; **~ zwei Bier** two more beers, another two beers; **~ einmal** *or* **mal** (once) again, once more; **und es regnete auch ~ ~ dazu** and on top of that it was raining; **dumm und ~ dazu frech** stupid and impudent with it *(inf)*; **ich gebe Ihnen ~ zwei dazu** I'll give you two extra; **~ ein Wort!** (not) another word!

f *(bei Vergleichen)* even, still, yet; **~ größer** even *or* still *or* yet bigger; **er will ~ mehr haben** he wants even *or* still more; **das ist ~ besser** that's even better, that's better still *or* still better; **das ist ~ viel wichtiger als ...** that is far more important yet *or* still than ...; **(und) seien sie auch ~ so klein** however small they may *or* might be; **und wenn du auch ~ so bittest ...** however much you ask ...

g *(inf)* **wir fanden Fehler ~ und nöcher** *(hum inf)* we found tons *(inf)* or loads *(inf)* of mistakes; **Geld ~ und nöcher** *(hum inf)* heaps and heaps of money *(inf)*; **er kann ~ und nöcher erzählen** he can go on telling stories for ever; **ich kann Ihnen Beispiele ~ und nöcher geben** I can give you any number of examples; **sie hat ~ und nöcher versucht, ...** she tried again and again to ...

CONJ *(weder ... noch ...)* nor; **nicht X, ~ Y, ~ Z** not X nor Y nor Z

Noch|ge|schäft NT *(Fin)* option to double

noch|ma|lig ['nɔxma:lɪç] ADJ *attr* renewed; **eine ~e Überprüfung** another check

noch|mals ['nɔxma:ls] ADV again

No|cken|wel|le ['nɔkn-] F camshaft

No|ckerl ['nɔkɐl] NT **-s, -n** *usu pl (Aus Cook)* dumpling; **Salzburger ~n** *type of sweet whipped pudding eaten hot*

Noc|turne [nɔk'tyrn] NT **-s, -s** *or* f **-, -s** *(Mus)* nocturne

No-Fu|ture- ▲ [no'fju:tʃɐ], **No|fu|ture-** ▲ *in cpds* no-future; **No-Fu|ture-Ge|ne|ra|ti|on** ▲ F no-future generation

Noi|set|te [noa'zɛt] F **-, -s** noisette

NOK [ɛnʔo:'ka] NT **-s** *abbr von* **Nationales Olympisches Komitee**

nö|len ['nø:lən] VI *(inf)* to moan

no|lens vo|lens ['no:lɛns 'vo:lɛns] ADV *(geh)* like it or not *or* no, willy-nilly

No|li|me|tan|ge|re [no:lime'taŋgerə] NT **-, -** *(Bot)* touch-me-not

No|ma|de [no'ma:də] M **-n, -n, No|ma|din** [no'ma:dɪn] F **-, -nen** *(lit, fig)* nomad

No|ma|den- *in cpds* nomadic; **no|ma|den|haft** ADJ *(lit, fig)* nomadic; **No|ma|den|le|ben** NT nomadic life; **No|ma|den|tum** [no'ma:dntu:m] NT **-s,** *no pl* nomadism; **No|ma|den|volk** NT nomadic tribe *or* people; **No|ma|den|zelt** NT nomad('s) tent

No|ma|din F **-, -nen** *(lit, fig)* nomad

no|ma|disch [no'ma:dɪʃ] ADJ nomadic ADV **~ leben** to live a nomadic lifestyle

no|ma|di|sie|ren [nomadi'zi:rən] *ptp* **nomadisiert** VI to lead a nomadic existence; **~de Stämme** nomadic tribes

No|men ['no:mən] NT **-s, Nomina** ['no:mina] *(Gram)* noun; **nomen est omen** *(geh)* true to your/his *etc* name

No|men|kla|tur [nomɛnkla'tu:ɐ] F **-, -en** nomenclature

No|men|kla|tu|ra [nomɛnkla'tu:ra] F **-,** *no pl (= Führungsschicht)* top-ranking officials *pl*

No|mi|na *pl von* **Nomen**

no|mi|nal [nomi'na:l] *(Econ)* ADJ nominal ADV nominally

No|mi|nal- *in cpds* (*Gram, Fin*) nominal; **No|mi|nal|lohn** M nominal *or* money wages *pl*; **No|mi|nal|stil** M nominal style; **No|mi|nal|wert** M (*Fin*) nominal *or* face *or* par value; **No|mi|nal|zins** M (*Fin*) nominal interest rate

No|mi|na|ti|on [nomina'tsio:n] F -, -en (*Eccl*) nomination

No|mi|na|tiv ['nominati:f] M -s, -e [-və] nominative

no|mi|nell [nomi'nɛl] ADJ *Regierungschef, Unabhängigkeit* nominal, in name only ADV in name only

no|mi|nie|ren [nomi'ni:rən] *ptp* **nominiert** VT to nominate

No|mi|nie|rung [nomi'ni:rʊŋ] F nomination

No-Name-Pro|dukt ['no:ne:m-] NT (*Econ*) own-label *or* house-brand (*US*) product

Non|cha|lance [nõʃa'lã:s] F -, *no pl* (*geh*) nonchalance

non|cha|lant [nõʃa'lã:] (*geh*) ADJ nonchalant ADV nonchalantly; **sich ~ geben** to appear nonchalant

No|ne ['no:nə] F -, -n **a** (*Mus*) ninth **b** (*Eccl, Gebetsstunde*) nones *with sing vb*

Non-Food-Ab|tei|lung [nɔn'fu:d-] F non--food section

No|ni|us ['no:niʊs] M -, -se *or* **Nonien** [-niən] vernier (scale)

Non|kon|for|mist(in) M(F) nonconformist

non|kon|for|mis|tisch ADJ nonconformist ADV **sich ~ verhalten** to act unconventionally

Non|ne ['nɔnə] F -, -n **a** nun **b** (*Schmetterling*) nun moth **c** (*Dachziegel*) concave tile

Non|nen-: non|nen|haft ADJ nunlike ADV **sie lebte ~** she lived like a nun; **sie tut so ~** she pretends to be so chaste; **Non|nen|klos|ter** NT convent, nunnery (*old, hum*)

Non|plus|ul|tra [nɔnplʊs'ʊltra, no:nplʊs'ʊltra] NT -s, *no pl* (*geh*) ultimate, non plus ultra (*Brit*)

Non|sens ['nɔnzɛns] M -(es), *no pl* nonsense

non|stop [nɔn'ʃtɔp, -'stɔp] ADV non-stop

Non-Stop- ▲, Non|stop- *in cpds* non-stop; **Non|stop|be|trieb** M im ~ non-stop; **Non|stop|flug** M non-stop flight; **Non|stop|ki|no** NT cinema with a continuous programme (*Brit*) *or* program (*US*)

non|ver|bal [nɔnvɛr'ba:l] ADJ non-verbal ADV non-verbally

Nop|pe ['nɔpə] F -, -n (= *Gumminoppe*) nipple, knob; (*von Tischtennisschläger, Gummisohle auch*) pimple; (= *Knoten*) burl; (= *Schlinge*) loop; (= *Strickknoppe*) bobble; (*bei Blindenschrift*) braille dot; **Garn mit ~n** bouclé; **ein Teppich mit ~n** a loop pile carpet

nop|pen ['nɔpn] VT **a** (= *Noppen auszupfen*) *Rohgewebe* to burl **b** (= *mit Noppen versehen*) → *auch* **genoppt**

Nord [nɔrt] M -(e)s, (*rare*) -e [-də] **a** (*Naut, Met, liter*) north; **aus ~** *or* **von/nach ~** from the/to the north **b** (*liter. Wind*) north wind

Nord-, nord- *in cpds in Ländernamen*) (*politisch*) North; (*geografisch auch*) the North of ..., Northern; **Nord|afri|ka** NT North Africa; **Nord|ame|ri|ka** NT North America; **Nord|at|lan|tik** M North Atlantic; **Nord|at|lan|tik|pakt** M North Atlantic Treaty; **nord|at|lan|tisch** ADJ North Atlantic; **~es Verteidigungsbündnis, ~e Allianz** NATO Alliance; **nord|deutsch** ADJ North German; *Dialekt, Spezialität, Mentalität auch* Northern German; **die ~e Tiefebene** the North German lowlands *pl*; **die Norddeutschen** the North Germans; **Nord|deutsch|land** NT North(ern) Germany, the North of Germany

nor|den ['nɔrdn] VT *Karte* to orient(ate)

Nor|den ['nɔrdn] M -s, *no pl* north; (*von Land*) North; **aus dem ~, von ~ (her)** from the north; **gegen** *or* **gen** (*liter*) *or* **nach ~** north(wards), to the north; **der Balkon liegt nach ~** the balcony faces north(wards); **nach ~ hin** to the north; **im ~ der Stadt/des Landes** in the north of the town/country; **im/aus dem hohen ~** in/from the far north; **weiter** *or* **höher im ~** further north; **im Münchner ~** on the north side of Munich; **im ~ Frankreichs** in the north of France, in northern France

Nord-: Nord|eng|land NT the North of England; **Nord|eu|ro|pa** NT Northern Europe; **nord|frie|sisch** ADJ North Frisian; **Nord|halb|ku|gel** F northern hemisphere; **Nord|hang** M northern *or* north-facing slope; **nord|irisch** ADJ Northern Irish; **Nord|ir|land** NT Northern Ireland, Ulster; **Nord|ir|land|kon|flikt** M **der ~** the conflict in Northern Ireland, the Troubles *pl* (*euph*)

nor|disch ['nɔrdɪʃ] ADJ *Wälder* northern; *Völker, Sprache, Mythologie* Nordic; (*Ski*) nordic; **Ski ~** nordic skiing; **~e Kombination** (*Ski*) nordic combined

Nor|dist [nɔr'dɪst] M -en, -en, **Nor|dis|tin** [-'dɪstɪn] F -, -nen expert on Nordic languages; (*Student*) student of Nordic languages

Nor|dis|tik [nɔr'dɪstɪk] F -, *no pl* Nordic studies *sing*

Nord-: Nord|kap NT North Cape; **Nord|ko|rea** NT North Korea; **Nord|küs|te** F north (-ern) coast; **Nord|län|der** ['nɔrtlɛndɐ] M -s, -, **Nord|län|de|rin** [-ərɪn] F -, -nen northerner; (= *Skandinavier*) Scandinavian

nörd|lich ['nœrtlɪç] ADJ northern; *Kurs, Wind, Richtung* northerly; **der ~e Polarkreis** the Arctic Circle; **der ~e Wendekreis** the Tropic of Cancer; **52 Grad ~er Breite** 52 degrees north ADV (to the) north; **von Köln (gelegen)** north of Cologne; **es liegt ~er** *or* **weiter ~** it is further (to the) north PREP +*gen* (to the) north of

Nord|licht NT northern lights *pl*, aurora borealis; (*fig hum: Mensch*) Northerner

Nord|nord-: Nord|nord|ost M **a** (*Naut, Met, liter*) north-north-east, nor'-nor'-east (*Naut*) **b** (*liter. Wind*) nor'-nor'-easterly; **Nord|nord|os|ten** M north-north-east, nor'-nor'-east (*Naut*); **nord|nord|öst|lich** ADJ north-north-east(erly), nor'-nor'-east(erly) (*Naut*); **Nord|nord|west** M **a** (*Naut, Met, liter*) north-north--west, nor'-nor'-west (*Naut*) **b** (*liter. Wind*) nor'-nor'-westerly; **Nord|nord|wes|ten** M north-north-west, nor'-nor'-west (*Naut*); **nord|nord|west|lich** ADJ north-north-west (-erly), nor'-nor'-west(erly) (*Naut*)

Nord|ost M **a** (*Met, Naut, liter*) north-east, nor'-east (*Naut*); **aus ~** from the north-east **b** (*liter. Wind*) north-east(erly) wind, north-easter, nor'-easter (*Naut*)

Nord|ost- *in cpds* north-east; (*bei Namen*) North-East; **Nordostengland** North-East England

Nord|os|ten M north-east; (*von Land*) North East; **aus** *or* **von ~** from the north-east; **nach ~** to the north-east, north-east(wards); **im ~ Brasiliens** in the North East of Brazil, in north--east Brazil

nord|öst|lich ADJ *Gegend* north-eastern; *Wind* north-east(erly) ADV (to the) north-east; **~ von ... ** north-east of ... PREP +*gen* (to the) north--east of

Nord-Ost|see-Ka|nal M Kiel Canal

Nord|pol M North Pole

Nord|po|lar-: Nord|po|lar|ge|biet NT Arctic (Zone); **Nord|po|lar|meer** NT Arctic Ocean

Nord|rhein-West|fa|len ['nɔrtrainvɛst'fa:lən] NT North Rhine-Westphalia

nord|rhein-west|fä|lisch ['nɔrtrainvɛst'fɛ:lɪʃ] ADJ North Rhine-Westphalian

Nord-: Nord|see ['nɔrtze:] F North Sea; **Nord|see|insel** F island in the North Sea; **Nord|see|küs|te** F North Sea coast; **Nord|sei|te** F north side; (*von Berg*) north(ern) face; **Nord|staa|ten** PL (*Hist*) northern states *pl*, Union; **Nord|stern** M North Star, Polar Star; **Nord-Süd-Di|a|log** ['nɔrt'zy:t-] M north--south dialogue (*Brit*) *or* dialog (*US*); **Nord-Süd-Ge|fäl|le** ['nɔrt'zy:t-] NT north-south divide; **Nord|wand** F (*von Berg*) north face

nord|wärts ['nɔrtvɛrts] ADV north(wards); **der Wind dreht ~** the wind is moving round to the north

Nord|west M **a** (*Met, Naut, liter*) north-west; **aus ~** from the north-west **b** (*liter. Wind*) north-west(erly) wind, north-wester, nor'-wester (*Naut*)

Nord|west- *in cpds* north-west; (*bei Namen*) North-West; **Nordwestengland** North-West England

Nord|wes|ten M north-west; (*von Land*) North West; **aus** *or* **von ~** from the north-west; **nach ~** to the north-west, north-west(wards); **im ~ Englands** in the North West of England, in north-west England

nord|west|lich ADJ *Gegend* north-western; *Wind* north-west(erly) ADV (to the) north-west; **~ von** (to the) north-west of PREP +*gen* (to the) north-west of

Nord|wind M north wind

Nör|ge|lei [nœrgə'lai] F -, -en moaning, grumbling; (= *Krittelei*) carping, nit-picking (*inf*)

nör|ge|lig ['nœrgəlɪç] ADJ grumbly (*inf*), moaning; (= *krittelig*) carping, nit-picking (*inf*)

nör|geln ['nœrgln] VI to moan, to grumble; (= *kritteln*) to carp, to niggle (*an +dat, über +acc* about); **er hat immer an allem zu ~** he always finds something to moan about

Nörg|ler ['nœrglɐ] M -s, -, **Nörg|le|rin** [-ərɪn] F -, -nen grumbler, moaner; (= *Krittler*) carper, niggler, nit-picker (*inf*)

nörg|lig ['nœrglɪç] ADJ = nörgelig

Norm [nɔrm] F -, -en **a** norm; (= *Größenvorschrift*) standard (specification); **als ~ gelten, die ~ sein** to be (considered) normal, to be the usual thing; **gegen die ~ verstoßen** to be an exception to the norm; **der ~ entsprechen** to conform to the norm **b** (= *Leistungssoll*) quota, norm; **die ~ erfüllen/erreichen** to achieve one's quota, to meet one's target **c** (*Typ*) signature (*at foot of page*)

nor|mal [nɔr'ma:l] ADJ normal; *Format, Maß, Gewicht* standard; **bist du noch ~?** (*inf*) have you gone mad? ADV normally; **er ist ~ groß** his height is normal; **seine Nase ist nicht ~ lang** his nose is not normal length; **~ aussehen/riechen** to look/smell normal; **benimm dich ganz ~** act naturally; **benimm dich doch mal ~!** act like a normal human being, can't you?; **so hohe Trinkgelder sind ~ nicht üblich** such good tips aren't usual

Nor|mal- *in cpds* **a** (= *üblich*) normal **b** (= *genormt*) standard; **Nor|mal|ben|zin** NT regular (petrol (*Brit*) *or* gas (*US*)); **Nor|mal|bür|ger(in)** M(F) average citizen, man/woman in the street

Nor|ma|le F -(n), -n (*Math*) normal

nor|ma|ler|wei|se [nɔr'ma:lɐ'vaizə] ADV normally, usually

Nor|mal-: Nor|mal|fall M normal case; **im ~** normally, usually; **das ist der ~** that is the norm; **Nor|mal|film** M standard film; **Nor|mal|ge|wicht** NT normal weight; (*genormt*) standard weight

nor|ma|li|sie|ren [nɔrmali'zi:rən] *ptp* **normalisiert** VT to normalize VR to return to normal, to get back to normal

Nor|ma|li|sie|rung F -, -en normalization

Nor|ma|li|tät [nɔrmali'tɛːt] F -, -en normality, normalcy

Nor|mal-: Nor|mal|maß NT standard (measure); **Nor|mal|null** NT -s, *no pl* (*abbr* **NN**) ≙ sea level; **Nor|mal|spur** F (*Rail*) standard gauge; **Nor|mal|uhr** F (*old*) (synchronized) clock; **Nor|mal|ver|brau|cher(in)** M(F) average consumer; (*geistiger*) (~ *inf*) middlebrow; **Otto ~** (*inf*) Joe Bloggs (*Brit inf*), John Doe (*US inf*), the man in the street; **Nor|mal|zeit**

F standard time; **Nor|mal|zu|stand** M normal state; (= *normale Verhältnisse*) normal conditions *pl*; (*Chem, Phys*) natural state

Nor|man|die [nɔrman'diː, nɔrmãdiː] F - Normandy

Nor|man|ne [nɔr'manə] M **-n, -n, Nor|man|nin** [-'manɪn] F **-, -nen** Norman

nor|man|nisch [nɔr'manɪʃ] ADJ Norman

nor|ma|tiv [nɔrma'tiːf] **ADJ** normative **ADV Ar-beitszeiten ~ verbindlich regeln** to establish certain working hours as the norm

Nor|ma|tiv|be|stim|mun|gen PL (*Jur*) basic stipulations *pl*

Norm|blatt NT standard specifications sheet

nor|men ['nɔrmən] VT to standardize

Nor|men|kon|troll|kla|ge F (*Jur*) *legal proceedings brought to ask for judicial review*

nor|mie|ren [nɔr'miːrən] *ptp* **normiert** VT (*Tech, Jur*) to standardize

Nor|mie|rung F **-, -en** standardization

Norm|teil NT (*Tech*) standard part

Nor|mung ['nɔrmʊŋ] F **-, -en** (*Tech*) standardization

norm|wid|rig ADJ deviant; (*Tech*) non-standard

Nor|we|gen ['nɔrveːgn] NT **-s** Norway

Nor|we|ger ['nɔrveːgɐ] M **-s, -, Nor|we|ge|rin** [-ərɪn] F **-, -nen** Norwegian

Nor|we|ger|pul|lo|ver M Norwegian pullover

nor|we|gisch ['nɔrveːgɪʃ] ADJ Norwegian

Nor|we|gisch(e) ['nɔrveːgɪʃ] NT Norwegian → *auch* **Deutsch(e)**

Nos|tal|gie [nɔstal'giː] F **-, no pl** nostalgia

Nos|tal|gi|ker [nɔs'talgikɐ] M **-s, -, Nos|tal|gi|ke|rin** [-ərɪn] F **-, -nen** nostalgic person

nos|tal|gisch [nɔs'talgɪʃ] **ADJ** nostalgic **ADV** nostalgically; **~ anmutende Bilder** nostalgic pictures; **ein ~ gestimmtes Publikum** a nostalgic audience; **~ klingende Lieder** nostalgic(-sounding) songs

not △ [noːt] ADJ (*geh*) → **Not d**

Not [noːt] F **-, ~e** ['nøːtə] **a** *no pl* (= *Mangel, Elend*) need(iness), want, poverty; **hier herrscht große ~** there is great poverty here; **eine Zeit der ~** a time of need, a lean time; **aus ~** out of poverty; **~ leiden** to suffer deprivation; **~ lei-dend** (*Bevölkerung, Land*) impoverished; *Unter-nehmen, Wirtschaft* ailing; (*Comm*) *Wechsel, Wert-papier* dishonoured (*Brit*), dishonored (*US*); *Kredit* unsecured; **jds ~** (*acc*) **lindern** to improve sb's lot; **in ~ leben** to live in poverty; **~ macht erfinderisch** (*Prov*) necessity is the mother of invention (*Prov*); **in der ~ frisst der Teufel Flie-gen** (*Prov*) **in der ~ schmeckt jedes Brot** (*Prov*) beggars can't be choosers (*prov*); **~ kennt kein Gebot** (*Prov*) necessity knows no law (*Prov*) → **Geldnot, Zeitnot**

b (= *Bedrängnis*) distress *no pl*, affliction; (= *Problem*) problem; **die Nöte des Alltags** the problems of everyday living; **in seiner ~** in his hour of need; **in unserer ~ blieb uns nichts an-deres übrig** in this emergency we had no choice; **jdm seine ~ klagen** to tell sb one's trou-bles, to cry on sb's shoulder (*inf*); **in ~ sein** to be in distress; **in ~ geraten** to get into serious difficulties; **wenn ~ am Mann ist** if the need arises; (= *im Notfall*) in an emergency; **Freunde in der ~** (*gehen tausend auf ein Lot*) (*Prov*) a friend in need (is a friend indeed) (*Prov*); **der Retter in der ~** the knight in shining armour (*Brit*) or armor (*US*); **Hilfe in höchster ~** help in the nick of time; **in höchster ~ sein, sich in höchster ~ befinden** to be in dire straits; **in Ängsten und Nöten schweben** to be in fear and trembling; **jdm in der ~ beistehen** to help sb in or through times of trouble, to help sb in his need; **jetzt ist Holland in ~!** now we're in dire straits!

c *no pl* (= *Sorge, Mühe*) difficulty, trouble; **er hat seine liebe ~ mit ihr/damit** he really has problems with her/it, he really has his work

cut out with her/it (*inf*); **die Eltern hatten ~, ih-re fünf Kinder zu ernähren** the parents had dif-ficulty in feeding their five children; **es hat** or **damit hat's keine ~** (*old*) there's no rush → **knapp, Mühe**

d (= *Zwang, Notwendigkeit*) necessity; **der ~ ge-horchend** bowing to necessity; **etw nicht ohne ~ tun** not to do sth without having to; **ohne ~** without good cause; **zur ~** if necessary, if need(s) be; (= *gerade noch*) at a pinch, just a-bout; **aus der ~ geboren sein** to be born of necessity; **aus der ~ eine Tugend machen** to make a virtue (out) of necessity; **~ tun** or **sein** to be necessary; **ihm tat Hilfe ~** he needed help; **uns allen täte ein bisschen mehr Beschei-denheit ~** we could all benefit from a little more modesty

No|ta|beln [no'taːbln] PL (*geh*) notabilities *pl*

no|ta|be|ne [nota'beːnə] ADV (*geh*) please note, let it be noted

Not|an|ker M sheet anchor

No|tar [no'taːɐ] M **-s, -e, No|ta|rin** [-'taːrɪn] F **-, -nen** notary public

No|ta|ri|at [nota'riaːt] NT **-(e)s, -e** notary's of-fice

no|ta|ri|ell [nota'riɛl] (*Jur*) **ADJ** notarial **ADV** **beglaubigt** legally certified; **~ beurkunden** to notarize

Not-: Not|arzt M , **Not|ärz|tin** F emergency doctor; **Not|arzt|wa|gen** M emergency doc-tor's car; **den ~ rufen** to call the emergency doctor

No|ta|ti|on [nota'tsioːn] F **-, -en** (*Comput, Mus*) notation

Not-: Not|auf|nah|me F casualty (unit) (*Brit*), emergency room (*US*); **Not|auf|nah|me|la-ger** NT reception centre (*Brit*) or center (*US*), transit camp; **Not|aus|gang** M emergency ex-it; **Not|be|helf** M stopgap (measure), make-shift; **Not|be|leuch|tung** F emergency light-ing; **Not|brem|se** F emergency brake, com-munication cord (*Brit*); **die ~ ziehen** (*lit*) to pull the communication cord (*Brit*) or emer-gency brake; (*fig*) to put the brakes on; (*Ftbl sl:* = *foulen*) to commit a blatant foul; **Not|brem|-sung** F emergency stop; **Not|brü|cke** F tem-porary bridge; **Not|dienst** M **~ haben** (*Apothe-ke*) to be open 24 hours; (*Arzt, Elektriker etc*) to be on call

Not|durft ['noːtdʊrft] F **-, no pl a** (*euph geh*) call of nature (*euph*); **seine ~ verrichten** to re-lieve oneself, to answer the or a call of nature (*euph*) **b** (*old*) need; **des Lebens ~** the bare necessities of life; **des Leibes ~** enough to keep body and soul together

not|dürf|tig ['noːtdʏrftɪç] **ADJ** (= *kaum ausrei-chend*) meagre (*Brit*), meager (*US*), poor; (= *be-helfsmäßig*) makeshift *no adv*, rough and ready *no adv*; *Kleidung* scanty **ADV** *bekleidet* scantily; *reparieren* in a makeshift way; *versorgen* mea-grely (*Brit*), meagerly (*US*), poorly; **wir konnten uns mit den Einheimischen ~ verständigen** we could just about communicate with the na-tives; **damit Sie sich wenigstens ~ verständigen können** so that you can at least communicate to some extent; **nachdem wir das Netz ~ ge-flickt hatten** when we had patched up the net in a makeshift or rough-and-ready way

No|te ['noːtə] F **-, -n a** (*Mus*) note **b** **Noten** PL music; **~ lesen** to read music; **nach ~n spielen/singen** to play/sing from mu-sic; **nach ~n** (*fig inf*) thoroughly **c** (*Sch*) mark; **jdm einer Sache gute/schlechte ~n geben** to give sb/sth good/bad marks **d** (*Pol*) note **e** (= *Banknote*) (bank)note, bill (*US*) **f** *no pl* (= *Eigenart*) (*in Bezug auf Gespräch, Brief etc*) note; (*in Bezug auf Beziehungen, Atmosphäre*) tone, character; (*in Bezug auf Einrichtung, Klei-dung*) touch; **das ist meine persönliche ~** that's my trademark; **einer Sache** (*dat*) **eine persönli-che ~ verleihen** to give sth a personal touch; **ein Parfüm mit einer herben ~** a perfume with

something tangy about it or with a tangy quali-ty

g (*Sport*) mark

Note|book ['noːtbʊk] M OR NT **-s, -s** (*Comput*) notebook (computer)

Note|book|com|pu|ter ['noːtbʊk-] M note-book computer

No|ten-: No|ten|aus|tausch M (*Pol*) ex-change of notes; **No|ten|bank** F *pl* **-banken** issuing bank, bank of issue; **No|ten|blatt** NT sheet of music; **No|ten|de|ckung** F (*Fin*) (bank)note cover; **No|ten|durch|schnitt** M (*Sch*) average mark or grade (*esp US*); **No|ten|-ge|bung** F (*Sch:* = *das Benoten*) marking; **No|-ten|heft** NT (*mit Noten*) book of music; (*ohne Noten*) manuscript book; **No|ten|li|nie** F lines *pl* (of a stave); **Papier mit ~n** manuscript paper; **No|ten|pa|pier** NT manuscript paper; **No|-ten|pres|se** F money press; **No|ten|pult** NT music stand; **No|ten|schlüs|sel** M clef; **No|-ten|schrift** F musical notation; **No|ten|-stän|der** M music stand; **No|ten|um|lauf** M (*Fin*) circulation (of banknotes (*Brit*) or bills (*US*)); **No|ten|wech|sel** M (*Pol*) exchange of notes

Note|pad ['noːtpɛθ] NT **-s, -s** (*Comput*) notepad

Not|fall M emergency; **für den ~ nehme ich ei-nen Schirm mit** I'll take an umbrella (just) in case; **im ~** if necessary, if need(s) be; **bei einem ~ in case of emergency; **im äußersten ~** in an extreme emergency; **er ist ein ~** (*Kranker*) he is an emergency case

Not|fall|me|di|zin F , *no pl* (*Heilkunde*) emer-gency medicine

not|falls ['noːtfals] ADV if necessary, if need(s) be

Not|flag|ge F distress flag

not|ge|drun|gen ['noːtgədrʊŋən] **ADJ** enforced **ADV** of necessity, perforce (*form*); **ich muss mich ~ dazu bereit erklären** I'm forced to a-gree, I've no choice but to agree, I must per-force agree (*form*)

Not-: Not|geld NT emergency money; **Not|-ge|mein|schaft** F emergency organization; (= *Zwangsbündnis*) union of convenience; **im Kampf gegen die Schlammmassen waren wir alle eine ~** in the fight against the mud we all had to pull together; **Not|gro|schen** M nest egg; **sich** (*dat*) **einen ~** or **eine Summe als ~ zurückle-gen** to put some money away for a rainy day; **Not|ha|fen** M harbour (*Brit*) or harbor (*US*) of refuge; **wegen der Epidemie musste das Schiff einen ~ anlaufen** because of the epidem-ic the ship had to make an emergency stop; **Not|hel|fer(in)** M(F) (*Rel*) auxiliary saint; **Not|hil|fe** F assistance in an emergency

no|tie|ren [no'tiːrən] *ptp* **notiert** **VTI** **a** (= *Noti-zen machen*) to note down, to make a note of; (*schnell*) to jot down; (= *bemerken*) to note; **ich notiere (mir) den Namen** I'll make a note of the name; **Frau Becker, bitte ~ Sie!** please take a note/a letter *etc*, Ms Becker; **was möchten Sie bestellen? ich notiere** what would you like to order? I'll make a note of it or I'll take it down **b** (= *vormerken*) *Auftrag* to note, to book; **zu welchem Termin waren Sie notiert?** what time was your appointment?; **jdn (für etw) ~** to put sb's name or sb down (for sth) **c** (*St Ex:* = *festlegen*) to quote (*mit at*) **VI** (*St Ex:* = *wert sein*) to be quoted (*auf +acc* at); **an der Börse notiert sein** to be quoted or listed on the stock market

No|tie|rung F **-, -en a** (*Comm*) note **b** (*St Ex*) quotation **c** (*Mus*) notation

nö|tig ['nøːtɪç] ✪ 37.2 **ADJ** necessary; **das für die Reise ~e Geld** the necessary money for the journey, the money needed or necessary for the journey; **ist das unbedingt ~?** is that really or absolutely necessary?; **es ist nicht ~, zu sa-gen, wie …** it's not necessary or there's no need to say how …; **es ist nicht ~, dass er kommt** it's not necessary or there's no need for him to come, he doesn't need to come; **das war wirklich nicht ~** that really wasn't necessary, there was no need for that; (*nach spitzer Bemerkung auch*) that was uncalled for; **die ~en Unkosten** the unavoidable costs; **wenn ~** if necessary, if need(s) be; **etw ~ haben** to need sth; **etw bitter ~ haben** to need sth badly; **er hat das natürlich nicht ~** (*iro*) but, of course, he's different; **ich habe es nicht ~, mich von dir anschreien zu lassen** I don't need or I don't have to let you shout at me; **die habens gerade ~** (*inf*) that's the last thing they need; **du hast es gerade ~, so zu reden** (*inf*) you can or can't talk (*inf*), you're a fine one to talk (*inf*); **das habe ich nicht ~!** I can do without that, I don't need that; **etw ~ machen** to necessitate sth, to make sth necessary; **das Nötige** the necessary; **das Nötigste** the (bare) necessities or essentials; **alles zum Bergsteigen unbedingt Nötige** everything necessary or needed for mountaineering **ADV** (= *dringend*) **etwas ~ brauchen** to need something urgently; **ich muss mal ~** (*inf*) I'm dying to go (*inf*)

nö|ti|gen [ˈnøːtɪɡn̩] VT (*geh*: = *zwingen*) to force, to compel; (*Jur*) to coerce; (= *auffordern*) to urge, to press; **jdn ins Zimmer ~** to urge or press sb to go into a room; **sich ~ lassen** to need prompting or urging; **lassen Sie sich nicht (erst) ~!** don't wait to be asked → *auch* **genötigt**

nö|ti|gen|falls [ˈnøːtɪɡn̩fals] ADV (*form*) if necessary, if need(s) be

Nö|ti|gung [ˈnøːtɪɡʊŋ] F -, -en (= *Zwang*) compulsion; (*Jur*) coercion; **~ zum Diebstahl** coercion to commit theft; **sexuelle ~** sexual assault

No|tiz [noˈtiːts] F -, -en **a** (= *Vermerk*) note; (= *Zeitungsnotiz*) item; **sich** (*dat*) **~en machen** to make or take notes; **sich** (*dat*) **eine ~ von etw machen** to make a note of sth **b** **~ nehmen von** to pay attention to, to take notice of; **keine ~ nehmen von** to ignore; **kaum ~ nehmen von** to hardly take any notice of; **nimm keine ~!** take no notice, don't take any notice **c** (*St Ex*: = *Notierung*) quotation

No|tiz-: No|tiz|block M *pl* **-blöcke** notepad, jotter; **No|tiz|buch** NT notebook; **No|tiz|zet|tel** M piece of paper; **er hinterließ mir einen ~ mit seiner Adresse** he left me a note of his address on a piece of paper

Not-: Not|jahr NT year of need, difficult year; **Not|kühl|sys|tem** NT emergency cooling system; **Not|la|ge** F crisis; (= *Elend*) plight; **in ~n** in an emergency; **die wirtschaftliche ~ Mittelamerikas** Central America's economic plight; **jds ~** (*acc*) **ausnutzen** to exploit sb's situation; **in eine ~ geraten** to get into serious difficulties; **sich in einer (finanziellen** *etc*) **~ befinden** to find oneself in serious (financial *etc*) difficulties

not|lan|den [ˈnoːtlandn̩] *pret* **notlandete**, *ptp* **notgelandet** [ˈnoːtɡəlandət] VI *aux* **sein** to make a forced landing, to make an emergency landing

Not|lan|dung F forced or emergency landing

not|lei|dend △ ADJ → **Not a**

Not|lei|den|de(r) MF *decl as adj* **die ~n** the needy

Not-: Not|lei|ne F emergency cord; **Not|lö|sung** F compromise or less-than-ideal solution; (*provisorisch*) temporary solution; **Not|lü|ge** F white lie; **Not|maß|nah|me** F emergency measure; **Not|na|gel** M (*fig inf*) last resort; **Not|ope|ra|ti|on** F emergency operation; **Not|op|fer** NT emergency levy

no|to|risch [noˈtoːrɪʃ] **ADJ** **a** (= *gewohnheitsmäßig*) habitual **b** (= *allbekannt*) notorious **ADV** habitually

Not-: Not|rad NT (*Aut*) spare wheel; **Not|ruf** M (*Telec*) (*Gespräch*) emergency call; (*Nummer*) emergency number; **Not|ruf|säu|le** F emer-

gency telephone; **Not|rut|sche** F (*Aviat*) escape chute

not|schlach|ten [ˈnoːtʃlaxtn̩] *pret* **notschlachtete**, *ptp* **notgeschlachtet** [ˈnoːtɡəʃlaxtət] VT to destroy, to put down

Not-: Not|schlach|tung F putting down; **Not|schrei** M (*liter*) cry of distress, cry for help; **Not|sig|nal** NT distress signal; **Not|si|tu|a|ti|on** F emergency; **Not|sitz** M foldaway seat, tip-up seat

Not|stand M crisis; (*Pol*) state of emergency; (*Jur*) emergency; **innerer ~** domestic or internal state of emergency; **äußerer ~** threat of invasion or attack; **nationaler ~** national (state of) emergency; **ziviler ~** disaster; **übergesetzlicher ~** emergency situation in which a law no longer holds **den ~ ausrufen** to declare a state of emergency; **einen ~ beheben** to end or put an end to a crisis; **einen ~ abwenden** to avert a crisis/an emergency

Not|stands-: Not|stands|ge|biet NT (*wirtschaftlich*) depressed or deprived area; (*bei Katastrophen*) disaster area; **Not|stands|ge|set|ze** PL , **Not|stands|ver|fas|sung** F (*Pol*) emergency laws *pl*

Not-: Not|strom|ag|gre|gat NT emergency power generator; **Not|tau|fe** F emergency baptism; **not|tau|fen** [ˈnoːttaufn̩] *pret* **nottaufte**, *ptp* **notgetauft** [ˈnoːtɡətauft] VT **jdn ~** to administer an emergency baptism to sb

Not|tur|no [nɔˈturno] NT -s, -s or **Notturni** [-ni] nocturne

Not-: Not|un|ter|kunft F emergency accommodation; **Not|ver|band** M emergency or first-aid dressing; **Not|ver|ord|nung** F emergency decree

not|was|sern [ˈnoːtvasɐn] *pret* **notwasserte**, *ptp* **notgewassert** [ˈnoːtɡəvasɐt] VI to ditch (*Aviat sl*), to make a crash-landing in the sea

Not|wehr [ˈnoːtveːɐ] F , *no pl* self-defence (*Brit*), self-defense (*US*); **in** or **aus ~** in self-defence (*Brit*) or self-defense (*US*)

not|wen|dig [ˈnoːtvɛndɪç, noːtˈvɛndɪç] **ADJ** necessary; (= *unvermeidlich auch*) inevitable; **es ist ~, dass sie selbst kommt** it is necessary that she come(s) herself; **das Notwendige** the necessary, what is necessary; **ich habe alles Notwendige erledigt** I've done everything (that's) necessary; **das Notwendigste** the (bare) necessities or essentials; **sich auf das Notwendigste beschränken** to stick to essentials → **Übel b** **ADV** necessarily; **eine rationale Denkweise ist ~ geboten** rational thinking is strongly recommended; **~ brauchen** to need urgently; **es folgt ~** it necessarily follows; **es musste ~ zum Zusammenstoß kommen** the collision was inevitable

not|wen|di|ger|wei|se [ˈnoːtvɛndɪɡɐˈvaizə] ADV of necessity, necessarily, inevitably

Not|wen|dig|keit F -, -en **a** *no pl* necessity; **mit ~** of necessity; **die ~, etw zu tun** the necessity of doing sth; **die/keine ~ für etw sehen** to see the/no necessity for sth; **keine ~ sehen, etw zu tun** to see no necessity to do sth **b** (= *notwendige Sache*) necessity, essential

Not|zei|chen NT distress signal

Not|zucht F (*Jur*) rape; **~ begehen** or **verüben** to commit rape (**an** +*dat* on)

not|züch|ti|gen [ˈnoːttsʏçtɪɡn̩] *pret* **notzüchtigte**, *ptp* **genotzüchtigt** [ɡəˈnoːttsʏçtɪçt] VT (*Jur*) to rape, to ravish (*form*), to violate

Not|zucht|ver|bre|chen NT crime of rape

Nou|gat [ˈnuːɡat] M OR NT -s, -s nougat

No|va *pl von* **Novum**

No|vel|le [noˈvɛlə] F -, -n **a** novella **b** (*Pol*) amendment

no|vel|lie|ren [novɛˈliːrən] *ptp* **novelliert** VT (*Pol*) to amend

No|vel|lie|rung F -, *no pl* (*Pol*) amendment

No|vel|list [novɛˈlɪst] M -en, -en, **No|vel|lis|tin** [-ˈlɪstɪn] F -, -nen novella writer

no|vel|lis|tisch [novɛˈlɪstɪʃ] **ADJ** novella-like **ADV** **den Stoff ~ behandeln** to use the material for or in a novella; **eine ~ erzählte Geschichte** a novella-like story

No|vem|ber [noˈvɛmbɐ] M -(s), - November → *auch* **März**

no|vem|ber|lich [noˈvɛmbɐlɪç] ADJ November-like

No|ve|ne [noˈveːnə] F -, -n novena

No|vi|tät [noviˈtɛːt] F -, -en (*geh*) new product; (*Buch*) new publication; (*Theat*) new play; **das ist keine ~** that's nothing new

No|vi|ze [noˈviːtsə] **M** -n, -n **F** -, -n, **No|vi|zin** [-ˈviːtsɪn] F -, -nen novice

No|vi|zi|at [noviˈtsiaːt] NT -(e)s, -e novitiate

No|vum [ˈnoːvʊm] NT -s, **Nova** [-va] novelty

NPD [ɛnpeːˈdeː] F - *abbr von* **Nationaldemokratische Partei Deutschlands**

Nr. *abbr von* **Numero** *von* **Nummer** No.

NRW [ɛnɛrˈveː] *abbr von* **Nordrhein-Westfalen** North Rhine-Westphalia

NS [ɛnˈʔɛs] **a** *abbr von* **Nachschrift** PS **b** *abbr von* **nationalsozialistisch**

NS- *in cpds* Nazi; **NS-Dik|ta|tur** F Nazi dictatorship; **NS-Ver|bre|chen** NT Nazi crime or atrocity; **NS-Zeit** F Nazi era, (period of) Nazi rule

N. T. *abbr von* **Neues Testament** NT

nu [nuː] ADV (*dial inf*) = **nun**

Nu [nuː] M **im Nu** in no time, in a flash or trice

Nu|an|ce [ˈnyãːsə] F -, -n (= *kleiner Unterschied*) nuance; (= *Kleinigkeit*) shade; **um eine ~ zu laut** a shade too loud; **sie unterscheiden sich nur in ~n voneinander** they differ only very slightly

nu|an|cen|reich ADJ, ADV full of nuances

nu|an|cie|ren [nyãˈsiːrən] *ptp* **nuanciert** VT to nuance

'nü|ber [ˈnyːbɐ] ADV (*dial*) = **hinüber**

Nu|buk [ˈnʊbʊk, nuˈbʊk] NT -(s), *no pl*, **Nu|buk|le|der** NT nubuk

nüch|tern [ˈnʏçtɐn] **ADJ** **a** (*ohne Essen*) **der Patient muss ~ sein** the patient must have an empty stomach; **eine Medizin ~ einnehmen** to take a medicine on an empty stomach; **mit ~em/auf ~en Magen** with/on an empty stomach; **das war ein Schreck auf ~en Magen** (*hum*) my heart skipped a beat **b** (= *nicht betrunken*) sober; **wieder ~ werden** to sober up **c** (= *sachlich, vernünftig*) down-to-earth *no adv*, rational; **Zahlen, Tatsachen** bare, plain **d** (= *schmucklos*) sober **ADV** **a** (= *sachlich*) unemotionally, objectively **b** (= *schlicht*) **~ gestaltete Räume** soberly decorated rooms; **~ graue Wände** bare grey (*Brit*) or gray (*US*) walls; **~ schmucklose Häuser** plain unadorned buildings

Nüch|tern|heit F -, *no pl* **a** **überzeugen Sie sich von der ~ des Patienten** make sure that the patient's stomach is empty **b** (= *unbetrunkener Zustand*) soberness **c** (= *Sachlichkeit, Vernünftigkeit*) rationality **d** (= *Schmucklosigkeit*) soberness

Nu|ckel [ˈnʊkl] M -s, - (*inf*) (*auf Fläschchen*) teat (*Brit*), nipple (*US*); (= *Schnuller*) dummy (*Brit*), pacifier (*US*)

nu|ckeln [ˈnʊkln] VI (*inf*) (*Mensch*) to suck (*an* +*dat* at); (*Tier*) to suckle (*an* +*dat* from); **am Daumen ~** to suck one's thumb

Nu|ckel|pin|ne F (*inf*) old banger (*Brit inf*) or crate (*inf*)

Nu|cki [ˈnʊki] M -s, - (*Sw*) dummy (*Brit*), pacifier (*US*)

Nu|del [ˈnuːdl] F -, -n *usu pl* **a** (*als Beilage*) pasta *no pl*; (*als Suppeneinlage, chinesische*) noodle; (= *Fadennudel*) vermicelli *pl* **b** (*inf*: *Mensch*) (*dick*) dumpling (*inf*); (= *komisch*) character

Nu|del-: Nu|del|brett NT pastryboard; **nu|del|dick** ADJ (*inf*) podgy (*Brit inf*), pudgy (*US inf*); **Nu|del|holz** NT rolling pin

nu|deln ['nuːdln] VT *Gans* to force-feed; (*inf*) *Kind etc* to stuff (*inf*), to overfeed; **ich bin genudelt** (*inf*) I'm full to bursting (*inf*)

Nu|del-: **Nu|del|sa|lat** M pasta salad; **Nu|del|sup|pe** F noodle soup; **Nu|del|teig** M pasta dough; (*für Suppennudeln, chinesische Nudeln*) noodle dough

Nu|dis|mus [nuˈdɪsmʊs] M -, *no pl* nudism

Nu|dist [nuˈdɪst] M -en, -en, **Nu|dis|tin** [-ˈdɪstɪn] F -, -nen nudist

Nu|di|tät [nudiˈtɛːt] F -, -en *usu pl* (*geh: = Nacktbild*) nude (picture); (= *Nacktheit*) nudity

Nu|gat ['nuːgat] M OR NT -s, -s nougat

nuk|le|ar [nukleˈaːɐ] ADJ *attr* nuclear ADV with nuclear weapons; **jdn ~ bestrahlen** to expose sb to nuclear radiation

Nuk|le|ar- [nukleˈaːɐ] *in cpds* nuclear; **Nuk|le|ar|macht** F nuclear power; **Nuk|le|ar|me|di|zin** F nuclear medicine; **Nuk|le|ar|schlag** M nuclear strike; **Nuk|le|ar|test** M nuclear test; **Nuk|le|ar|waf|fe** F nuclear weapon

Nuk|le|in|säu|re F nucleic acid

Nuk|le|on ['nuːkleɔn] NT -s, **Nukleonen** [nukleˈoːnən] nucleon

Nuk|le|o|tid [nukleoˈtiːt] NT -s, -e [-ˈtiːdə] nucleotide

Nuk|le|us ['nuːkleʊs] M -, **Nuklei** [-klei] nucleus

Nuk|lid ['nuːkliːt] NT -s, -e [-də] nuclide

null [nʊl] NUM zero; (*inf: = kein*) zero (*inf*); (*Telec*) O (*Brit*), zero; (*Sport*) nil, nothing; (*Tennis*) love; **~ Komma eins** (nought) point one; **es ist ~ Uhr zehn** it's ten past twelve *or* midnight; **zwei Minuten ~ Sekunden** (*bei Zeitansagen*) two minutes precisely; (*bei Rennen*) two minutes dead *or* flat; **~ Grad** zero degrees; **~ Fehler** no *or* zero (*inf*) mistakes; **es steht ~ zu ~** there's no score; **das Spiel wurde ~ zu ~ beendet** the game was a goalless (*Brit*) *or* no-score draw; **eins zu ~** one-nil, one-nothing; **~ und nichtig** (*Jur*) null and void; **für ~ und nichtig erklären** (*Jur*) to declare null and void, to annul; **~ Ahnung haben** to have absolutely no idea; **das Thermometer steht auf ~** the thermometer is at *or* on zero; **Temperatur unter ~** sub-zero temperatures; **gleich ~ sein** to be absolutely nil *or* zero; **in ~ Komma nichts** (*inf*) in less than no time; **~ Komma - null** damn-all (*inf*), sweet Fanny Adams (*Brit inf*); **jdn auf ~ bringen** (*inf*) to fix sb for good (*inf*); **von ~ auf hundert in 20 Sekunden** (*Aut*) ≈ from nought (*esp Brit*) *or* zero to sixty in 20 seconds; **bei ~ anfangen** to start from scratch; **gegen ~ gehen** *or* **tendieren** to be virtually non-existent; (*Math*) to tend to zero; **seine Stimmung sank auf** *or* **unter ~** (*inf*) he sank into the depths of gloom; **im Jahre ~** in the year zero; **die Stunde ~** the new starting point → **Bock¹ h**

Null¹ [nʊl] F -, -en **a** (*Zahl*) nought, naught (*US*), zero; (= *Gefrierpunkt*) zero; **die** = the figure nought, zero; **eine schwarze ~ schreiben** (*Fin*) to break even **b** (*inf: Mensch*) dead loss (*inf*)

Null² M OR NT -(s), -s (*Cards*) nullo

null|acht|fünf|zehn [nʊlʔaxtˈfʏnftseːn], **null|acht|fuff|zehn** [nʊlʔaxtˈfʊftseːn] (*inf*) ADJ *inv* run-of-the-mill (*inf*) ADV in a run-of-the-mill way

Null|acht|fünf|zehn- [nʊlʔaxtˈfʏnftseːn-], **Null|acht|fuff|zehn-** [nʊlʔaxtˈfʊftseːn-] *in cpds* (*inf*) run-of-the-mill; **ein ~Restaurant** a run-of-the-mill restaurant; **er fährt ein ~Auto** he drives a pretty ordinary car

Null-Bock- [nʊlˈbɔk] (*inf*) *in cpds* apathetic; **~Generation** generation characterized by general apathy, "couldn't care less" generation, disaffected youth; **~Haltung** "couldn't care less" attitude

Null|di|ät F starvation diet

Null|lei|ter △ M → **Nullleiter**

Nul|li ['nʊli] M -s, -s (*sl*) loser (*inf*)

Null|li|nie △ F → **Nulllinie**

Null-: **Null|lei|ter** ▲ M (*Elec*) earth (wire) (*Brit*), ground (wire) (*US*); **Null|li|nie** ▲ F zero, nought, naught (*US*); **Null|lö|sung** ▲ F (*Pol*) zero option; **Null|men|ge** F (*Math*) empty set; **Null|me|ri|di|an** M Greenwich *or* prime Meridian; **Null-Null** ['nʊlˈnʊl] NT OR M -, *no pl* (*inf*) loo (*Brit inf*), restroom (*US*); **Null|num|mer** F **a** (*von Zeitung etc*) pilot **b** (= *Misserfolg*) flop (*inf*), washout (*inf*); (= *Nichtskönner*) no-hoper (*inf*)

Nullösung △ F → **Nulllösung**

Null-: **Null ou|vert** ['nʊl uˈvɛːɐ] M OR (RARE) NT -, - -s (*Cards*) null ouvert; **Null|punkt** M zero; **absoluter ~** absolute zero; **die Stimmung sank unter den ~** the atmosphere froze; **auf den ~ sinken, den ~ erreichen** to reach *or* hit rock-bottom; **auf dem ~ angekommen sein** *or* **am ~ angelangt sein** (*fig*) to have hit *or* reached rock-bottom; **Null|run|de** F in diesem Jahr gab es eine ~ für Beamte there has been no pay increase this year for civil servants; **ich bin gegen eine ~ bei den Renten** I am in favour (*Brit*) *or* favor (*US*) of an increase in pensions; **Null|spiel** NT (*Cards*) nullo; **Null|stel|lung** F zero position; **in der ~ sein** to be on zero; **Null|sum|men|spiel** NT zero-sum game; **Null|ta|rif** M (*für Verkehrsmittel*) free travel; (= *freier Eintritt*) free admission; **zum ~** (*hum*) free of charge; **Null|wachs|tum** NT (*Pol*) zero growth

Nul|pe ['nʊlpə] F -, -n (*inf*) clot (*Brit inf*), dope (*inf*), jerk (*inf*)

Nu|me|ra|le [numeˈraːlə] NT -s, **Numeralia** *or* **Numeralien** [-lia, -liən] (*Gram*) numeral

Nu|me|ri *pl von* **Numerus**

nu|me|rie|ren △ [numeˈriːrən] *ptp* **numeriert** VT → **nummerieren**

Nu|me|rie|rung △ F -, -en → **Nummerierung**

nu|me|risch [nuˈmeːrɪʃ] ADJ numeric(al); **~er Tastenblock** (*Comput*) numeric keypad ADV numerically; **~ überlegen/unterlegen sein** to be superior/inferior in number

Nu|me|ro ['nuːmero, 'nuːmero] NT -s, -s (*old, hum*) number; **eins/zwei** number one/two

Nu|me|rus ['nuːmerʊs, 'nuːmerʊs] M -, **Numeri** [-ri] (*Gram*) number; **~ clausus** (*Univ*) restricted entry; **sozialer ~ clausus** *restricted access to higher education on basis of financial means*

NUMERUS CLAUSUS

The **Numerus clausus**, or **NC** for short, controls admissions to certain over-subscribed university courses such as medicine, information technology and architecture. The main admission criterion is the mark obtained in the **Abitur**. Places are allocated by the Zentralstelle für die Vergabe von Studienplätzen, or ZVS → Abitur.

Nu|mis|ma|tik [numɪsˈmaːtɪk] F -, *no pl* numismatics *sing*

Num|mer ['nʊmɐ] ♥ 27 F -, -n (*Math, von Zeitschrift, in Varieté*) number; (= *Größe*) size; (*inf: Mensch*) character; (*inf: = Koitus*) screw (*sl*); (*mit Prostituierter*) trick (*inf*); **unser Haus hat die ~ 25** our house is number 25; **Bahnhofstraße ~ 15** number 15 Bahnhofstraße; **nur eine ~ unter vielen sein** (*fig*) to be a cog (in the machine); **er hat** *or* **schiebt eine ruhige ~** (*inf*) he's onto a cushy number (*inf*); **auf ~ Sicher gehen** (*inf*) to play (it) safe; **Gesprächsthema ~ eins** the number one talking point; **sie ist die ~ eins in Hollywood** she's number one *or* the number one star in Hollywood; **bei jdm eine gute ~ haben** (*inf*) to be well in with sb (*inf*); **eine ~ abziehen** (*inf*) to put on an act; **eine ~ machen** *or* **schieben** (*inf*) to have it off *or* away (*inf*); **dieses Geschäft ist eine ~/ein paar ~n zu groß für ihn** this business is out of/well out of his league; **der Pullover ist eine ~ zu klein** the jumper is one size too small

num|me|rie|ren ▲ [nʊmeˈriːrən] *ptp* **nummeriert** VT to number

Num|me|rie|rung ▲ F -, -en numbering

Num|mern-: **Num|mern|block** M (*Comput: auf Tastatur*) numeric keypad; **Num|mern|girl** [-gøːɐl] NT -s, -s ring card girl; **Num|mern|kon|to** NT (*Fin*) numbered account; **Num|mern|schei|be** F (*Telec*) dial; **Num|mern|schild** NT (*Aut*) number plate (*Brit*), registration plate (*Brit*), license plate (*US*); **Num|mern|spei|cher** M (*Telec*) memory; **Num|mern|zei|chen** NT (*Typ*) number sign

nun [nuːn] ADV **a** (= *jetzt*) now; **von ~ an** from now on, as of now, from here on in (*esp US*); **~ und nimmer(mehr)** (*liter*) nevermore (*liter*); **~, da er da ist, können wir anfangen** now that he's here we can get started; **~ erst, erst ~** only now; **~ ist aber genug!** now that's enough; **~ endlich** (now) at last; **was ~?** what now?; **was ~ (schon wieder)?** what (is it) now?

b (= *danach*) then; **~ erst ging er** only then did he go

c **ich bin ~ eben dumm** I'm just stupid, that's all; **er will ~ mal nicht** he simply doesn't want to; **wir hatten uns ~ eben entschlossen zu gehen ...** after all, we had decided to go ...; **dann muss ich das ~ wohl tun!** then I'll just have to do it; **~, wenns unbedingt sein muss** well, if I/you *etc* really must; **~, du hast ja Recht, wenn du das sagst, aber ...** well *or* OK (*inf*) or fair enough (*inf*) what you say is true but ...; **das ist ~ (ein)mal so** that's just the way things are; **~ ja** *or* **gut, aber ...** all right *or* OK (*inf*) but ...; **~ ja** well yes; **~ gut** (well) all right, (well) OK (*inf*); **~, meinetwegen** well, as far as I'm concerned; **er mag ~ wollen oder nicht** (*liter*) whether he wants to or not *or* no; **~ gerade erst!, ~ erst recht!** just for that (I'll do it)!; **~ taten wirs erst recht nicht** just because they/he/she *etc* said/ did that, we didn't do it

d (*Folge*) now; **das hast du ~ davon!** (it) serves you right

e (*Aufforderung*) come on, go on; **~ denn** (*geh*) well then; **~, wirds bald?** (*inf*) come on then, hurry up then

f (*bei Fragen*) well; **~?** well?

g (*beschwichtigend*) come on; **~, ~!** (*warnend*) come on now, come, come, now, now; (*tröstend*) there, there

CONJ (*obs*) since (that (*obs*), now that

nun|mehr ['nuːnˈmeːɐ] ADV (*geh*) (= *jetzt*) now, at this point; (= *von jetzt an*) henceforth (*form*), from now on, as of now; **die ~ herrschende Partei** the currently ruling party

nun|meh|rig ['nuːnmeːrɪç] ADJ *attr* (*form*) present, current

'nun|ter ['nʊntɐ] ADV (*dial*) *abbr von* **hinunter**

Nun|ti|us ['nʊntsiʊs] M -, **Nuntien** [-tsiən] nuncio

nur [nuːɐ] ADV **a** (*einschränkend*) only, just; **er ist ein sehr schneller Arbeiter, ~ müsste er etwas gründlicher sein** he is a very fast worker but *or* only he should be rather more thorough; **ich habe ~ ein Stück Brot gegessen** I've only eaten a piece of bread, I've eaten only *or* just a piece of bread; **alle, ~ ich nicht** everyone except *or* but me; **~ ich weiß** I'm the only one who knows, only I know; **~ schade, dass ...** it's just a pity that ...; **~ dass ...** it's just that ..., only ...; **~ noch zwei Minuten** only *or* just two minutes left *or* to go; **der Kranke isst fast ~ noch Obst** the sick man eats virtually nothing but fruit these days; **nicht ~ ..., sondern auch** not only *or* just ... but also; **alles, ~ das nicht!** anything but that!; **warum möchtest du das denn wissen? – ach, ~ so!** why do you want to know? – oh I just do *or* oh just because *or* oh no special reason; **ich hab das ~ so gesagt** I was just talking; **warum hast du das gemacht? – ~ so** why did you do that? – I just did; **~ kann man nie wissen, ob ...** only *or* but you never can *or* can never tell if ...

b (*verstärkend*) just; **wie schnell er ~ redet**

doesn't he speak fast!; **dass es ~ so krachte** making a terrible din *or* racket; **er fuhr, so schnell er ~ (fahren) konnte** he drove just as fast as he possibly could, he drove for all he was worth

c (*mit Fragepronomen*) -ever, on earth (*inf*); **was/wer/wie** *etc* **~?** but what/who/how *etc?*; **was hat er ~?** whatever is *or* what on earth (*inf*) is the matter with him?; **wie kannst du ~ (so etwas sagen)?** how could you (say such a thing)?; **sie bekommt alles, was sie ~ will** she gets whatever she wants

d (*Wunsch, Bedingung*) **wenn er ~ (erst) käme** if only he would come, if he would only come; **wüsste ich ~, wie** if only I knew how, if I only knew how; **es wird klappen, wenn er ~ nicht die Nerven verliert** it will be all right as long as *or* so long as (*inf*) *or* provided (that) he doesn't lose his nerve

e (*mit Negationen*) just, ... whatever you do; **lass das ~ niemand(en) wissen!** just don't let anyone find out, (but) don't let anyone find out whatever you do; **sagen Sie das ~ nicht Ihrer Frau!** just don't tell your wife (whatever you do)

f (*Aufforderung*) just; **geh ~!** just go, go on; **~ zu!** go on; **sieh ~** just look; **~ her damit!** (*inf*) let's have it; **sagen Sie es ~, Sie brauchen es ~ zu sagen** just say (the word), you only have to say (the word); **er soll ~ lachen!** let him laugh

g **~ mehr** (*dial, esp Aus*) only ... left; **ich habe ~ mehr einen Euro** I've only one euro left

Nur|haus|frau F full-time housewife

Nürn|berg ['nʏrnbɛrk] NT **-s** Nuremberg; **jdm etw mit dem ~er Trichter beibringen** (*inf*) to drum sth into sb; **die ~er Prozesse** the Nuremberg (war) trials

nu|scheln ['nʊʃln] VTI (*inf*) to mutter, to mumble

Nuss ▲ [nʊs] F **-, ~e** ['nʏsə] **a** nut; **eine harte ~ zu knacken haben** (*fig*) to have a tough nut to crack **b** (*inf: Mensch*) drip (*inf*), jerk (*inf*); **eine taube ~** a dead loss (*inf*), a washout (*inf*); **eine doofe ~** a stupid twit (*Brit inf*) or clown (*inf*) **c** (*inf: = Kopfnuss*) punch (in the head) **d** **Nüsse** (*sl: = Hoden*) nuts *pl* (*sl*)

Nuss-: Nuss|baum ▲ M (*Baum*) walnut tree; (*Holz*) walnut; **nuss|braun** ▲ ADJ nut-brown, hazel; **Nuss|kna|cker** ▲ M nutcracker, (pair of) nutcrackers *pl*; **Nuss|koh|le** ▲ F nut coal; **Nuss|scha|le** ▲ F nutshell; (*fig: Boot*) cockleshell, frail little boat

Nüs|ter ['nʏstɐ] F **-, -n** nostril

Nut [nuːt] F **-, -en** (*spec*), **Nu|te** ['nuːtə] F **-, -n** groove, flute, chase; (*zur Einfügung*) rabbet, slot; (*= Keilnut*) keyway, key seat; **~ und Feder** tongue and groove; **~ und Zapfen** mortise and tenon

nu|ten ['nuːtn] VT → **Nut** to groove, to flute; to rabbet, to slot; to cut a keyway in, to key seat

Nut|ria ['nuːtria] F **-, -s** (*Tier, Pelz*) coypu, nutria (*rare*)

Nut|te ['nʊtə] F **-, -n** (*inf*) tart (*inf*), pro (*inf*), hooker (*esp US inf*)

nut|tig ['nʊtɪç] ADJ (*inf*) tarty (*inf*)

Nut- und Fe|der|brett NT tongue and groove board

nutz [nʊts] ADJ (*S Ger, Aus*) = **nütze**

Nutz [nʊts] M **zu ~ und Frommen** +gen (*old liter*) for the greater good of (*form*); **sich** (*dat*) **etw zu ~e machen** → **zunutze**

Nutz|an|wen|dung F practical application; (*einer Geschichte*) moral

nutz|bar ADJ *Rohstoffe, Gebäude, Wasserstraßen* us(e)able; *Boden* productive; *Bodenschätze* exploitable; **~e Fläche** (*in Gebäude*) us(e)able floor space; **landwirtschaftlich ~e Fläche** agriculturally productive land; **~ machen** to make us(e)able *or* utilizable; *Sonnenenergie* to utilize, to harness, to turn to good use; *Sümpfe* to reclaim; *Bodenschätze* to exploit

Nutz|bar|keit ['nʊtsbaːɐkait] F **-**, *no pl* (*von Rohstoffen, Gebäude*) us(e)ability; **die ~ des Bodens lässt nach** the soil is becoming less and less productive

Nutz|bar|ma|chung ['nʊtsbaːɐmaxʊŋ] F **-**, *no pl* (*von Rohstoffen*); (*von Sümpfen*) reclamation; (*von Bodenschätzen*) exploitation

Nutz|bau M *pl* **-bauten** functional building

nutz|brin|gend ADJ profitable ADV profitably; **etw ~ anwenden** to use sth profitably *or* to good effect, to put sth to good use, to turn sth to good account

nüt|ze ['nʏtsə] ADJ *pred* **zu etw ~ sein** to be useful for sth; **zu nichts ~ sein** to be no use for anything

Nutz|ef|fekt M effectiveness, efficiency

nut|zen ['nʊtsn] VI to be of use, to be useful (*jdm zu etw* to sb for sth); **die Ermahnungen haben genutzt/nichts genutzt** the warnings had the desired effect/didn't do any good; **es nutzt nichts** it's no use *or* good, it's useless; **alle Anstrengungen haben nichts genutzt** all our efforts were useless *or* in vain; **da nutzt alles nichts** there's nothing to be done; **das nutzt (mir/dir) nichts** that won't help (me/you); **das nutzt niemandem** that's of no use to anybody; **es nutzt wenig** it isn't much use *or* good; **wozu soll das alles ~?** what's the use *or* point of that?

VT to make use of, to use; **Gelegenheit** to take advantage of; *Bodenschätze, Energien* to use, to exploit; **nutze den Tag!** gather ye rosebuds while ye may (*liter*)

Nut|zen ['nʊtsn] M **-s, -** **a** use; (*= Nützlichkeit*) usefulness; **es hat keinen ~, das zu tun** there's no use *or* point (in) doing that; **zum ~ der Öffentlichkeit** for the benefit of the public; **jdm von ~ sein** to be useful *or* of use to sb; (*einer anderen Person auch*) to be of service to sb; **von großem/geringem ~ sein** to be of great/little use

b (*= Vorteil*) advantage, benefit; (*= Gewinn*) profit; **jdm ~ bringen** (*Vorteil*) to be of advantage to sb; (*Gewinn*) to bring sb profit, to prove profitable to sb; **sich** (*dat*) **großen ~ von etw versprechen** to expect to benefit *or* profit greatly from sth; **von etw ~ haben** to gain *or* profit by sth; **aus etw ~ ziehen** to reap the benefits of sth

nüt|zen ['nʏtsn] VTI = **nutzen**

Nut|zer ['nʊtsɐ] M **-s, -**, **Nut|ze|rin** [-ərɪn] F **-, -nen** user

nut|zer|freund|lich, nut|zer|ge|recht ADJ user-friendly ADV **~ geschrieben** written in a user-friendly way/style; **~ gestaltet/eingerichtet sein** to be user-friendly

Nutz-: Nutz|fahr|zeug NT farm vehicle; military vehicle *etc*; (*Comm*) commercial vehicle, goods vehicle; (*= Straßenbahn etc*) public vehicle; **Nutz|flä|che** F utilizable *or* us(e)able floor space; (*landwirtschaftliche*) **~** (*Agr*) (agricultu-

rally) productive land; **Nutz|gar|ten** M vegetable *or* kitchen garden; **Nutz|ge|gen|stand** M article of purely practical value; **Nutz|holz** NT (utilizable) timber; **Nutz|last** F payload; **Nutz|leis|tung** F efficiency, effective capacity or output; (*Aut*) performance

nütz|lich ['nʏtslɪç] ADJ useful; *Hinweis, Wissen, Kenntnisse, Buch auch* helpful; **~ für die Gesundheit** beneficial for the health; **er könnte dir eines Tages sehr ~ werden** he might be very useful to you one day; **sich ~ machen** to make oneself useful; **kann ich Ihnen ~ sein?** may I be of service to you?

Nütz|lich|keit F **-**, *no pl* usefulness

Nütz|lich|keits-: Nütz|lich|keits|den|ken NT utilitarian thinking; **Nütz|lich|keits|prin|zip** NT utility principle

Nütz|ling ['nʏtslɪŋ] M **-s, -en** beneficial insect

nutz|los ADJ **a** useless; (*= unergiebig, vergeblich*) futile, vain *attr*, in vain *pred*; **es ist völlig ~, das zu tun** it's absolutely useless *or* pointless *or* futile doing that **b** (*= unnötig*) needless ADV **a** (*= ohne Nutzen*) uselessly; **ich fühle mich ~** I feel useless **b** (*= unnötig*) futilely, in vain; **er hat seine Zeit ~ mit Spielen zugebracht** he frittered away *or* wasted his time playing; **sein Leben ~ aufs Spiel setzen** to risk one's life needlessly *or* unnecessarily

Nutz|lo|sig|keit F **-**, *no pl* uselessness; (*= Uneinträglichkeit, Vergeblichkeit*) futility

Nutz|nie|ßer ['nʊtsniːsɐ] M **-s, -**, **Nutz|nie|ße|rin** [-ərɪn] F **-, -nen** beneficiary; (*Jur*) usufructuary

Nutz|nie|ßung ['nʊtsniːsʊŋ] F **-, -en** (*Jur*) usufruct

Nutz-: Nutz|pflan|ze F useful plant; **Nutz|tier** NT working animal

Nut|zung ['nʊtsʊŋ] F **-, -en** (*= Gebrauch*) use; (*das Ausnutzen*) exploitation; (*von Ressourcen, Technologie*) use; (*Jur: = Ertrag*) benefit; (*= Einkommen*) revenue (+*gen* from), return(s *pl*) (+*gen* on); **jdm etw zur ~ überlassen** to give sb *or* let sb have the use of sth; **die ~en aus etw ziehen** (*Jur*) to enjoy the benefit of sth

Nut|zungs-: Nut|zungs|dau|er F (useful) life; **Nut|zungs|recht** NT (*Jur*) usufruct; **Nut|zungs|ver|trag** M contract granting use (*im Verlagswesen*) rights contract

n. u. Z. *abbr von* **nach unserer Zeitrechnung** by our calendar

NVA [ɛnfaʊˈʔaː] **-**, *no pl* (*Hist*) *abbr von* **Nationale Volksarmee** National People's Army

NW *abbr von* **Nordwesten** NW

Ny|lon® ['nailɔn] NT **-(s)**, *no pl* nylon

Ny|lons ['nailɔns] PL nylons *pl*, nylon stockings *pl*

Ny|lon|strumpf ['nailɔn-] M nylon (stocking)

Nymph|chen ['nʏmfçən] NT **-s, -** nymphet

Nym|phe ['nʏmfə] F **-, -n** (*Myth*) nymph; (*fig*) sylph; (*Zool*) nymph(a); **die ~n** (*Anat*) the nymphae *pl*

Nym|pho|ma|nie [nʏmfomaˈniː] F **-**, *no pl* nymphomania

Nym|pho|ma|nin [nʏmfoˈmaːnɪn] F **-, -nen** nymphomaniac

nym|pho|ma|nisch [nʏmfoˈmaːnɪʃ] ADJ nymphomaniac

O

O, o [oː] NT **-, -** O, o

O INTERJ oh; **o Sünder!** (*liter*) O sinner; **O Gott!** O God!

O *abbr von* **Osten**

Olalse [oˈaːzə] F **-, -n** oasis; (*fig*) haven, oasis

ob [ɔp] **CONJ a** (*indirekte Frage*) if, whether; **wir gehen spazieren, ob es regnet oder nicht** we're going for a walk whether it rains or not; **Sie müssen kommen, ob Sie (nun) wollen oder nicht** like it or not, you have to come; **ob reich, ob arm** whether rich or poor; **ob er (wohl) morgen kommt?** I wonder if he'll come tomorrow?; **ob wir jetzt Pause machen?** shall we take a break now?; **ob ich nicht lieber gehe?** maybe I'd better go, hadn't I better go?; **ich muss mal nachsehen, ob sie nicht schon kommen** I must look and see if they're coming yet; **ob ich keine Angst gehabt hätte, fragte er** hadn't I been afraid, he asked; **er hat gefragt, ob dus geklaut hast – ob ich was?** (*inf*) he asked if you pinched (*Brit*) or swiped it – if I what? (*inf*); **kommst du mit? – was? – ob du mitkommen willst?** are you coming? – what? – are you coming?; **ob Sie mir wohl mal helfen können?** could you possibly help me?, I wonder if you could help me?

　b (*verstärkend*) **und ob** (*inf*) you bet (*inf*), of course; **und ob ich das gesehen habe!** you bet (*inf*) or of course I saw it!

　c (*vergleichend*) **als ob** as if; **(so) tun als ob** (*inf*) to pretend; **tu nicht so als ob!** stop pretending!

　d (*liter*) **ob ... auch, ob ... gleich** even though

　PREP *+gen* **a** (*old, liter*) on account of

　b (*in Ortsnamen*) (up)on

OB [oˈbeː] M **-s, -s** *abbr von* **Oberbürgermeister**

o. B. *abbr von* **ohne Befund**

Olbacht [ˈɔbaxt] F **-,** *no pl* (*esp S Ger*) **(aber) ~!** watch out!, look out!, careful!; **~ geben auf** (*+acc*) (= *aufmerken*) to pay attention to; (= *bewachen*) to keep an eye on; **du musst ~ geben, dass du keine Fehler machst** you must be careful not to make any mistakes; **gib** or **hab doch ~!** (*inf*) be careful!, watch it! (*inf*)

ÖBB *abbr von* **Österreichische Bundesbahnen**

Obldach NT **,** *no pl* (*geh*) shelter; **jdm (ein) ~ gewähren** or **geben** to give or offer sb shelter; **kein ~ haben** to be homeless; (*vorübergehend*) to have no shelter; **Menschen ohne ~** homeless people

obldachllos ADJ homeless; **~ werden** to be made homeless; **ADV die Flüchtlinge zogen ~ umher** the refugees wandered around with no home to go to

Obldachllolsen-: Obldachllolsenlasyl NT **, Obldachllolsenlheim** NT hostel for the homeless; **Obldachllolsenlsiedllung** F settlement for the homeless

Obldachllolse(r) [ˈɔpdaxloːzə] MF *decl as adj* homeless person; **die ~n** the homeless

Obldachllolsiglkeit F **-,** *no pl* homelessness

Obldukltilon [ɔpdʊkˈtsioːn] F **-, -en** postmortem (examination), autopsy

Obldukltilonslbelfund M postmortem findings *pl*, autopsy result

obldulzielren [ɔpduˈtsiːrən] *ptp* **obduziert** VT to carry out or do a postmortem or autopsy on

O-Beilne [ˈoː-] PL (*inf*) bow or bandy (*Brit*) legs *pl*

o-beilnig ▲ [ˈoː-], **O-beilnig** ADJ bow-legged, bandy-legged (*Brit*)

Obellisk [obəˈlɪsk] M **-en, -en** obelisk

olben [ˈoːbn] ADV **a** (= *am oberen Ende*) at the top; (= *an der Oberfläche*) on the surface; (*im Hause*) upstairs; (= *in der Höhe*) up; **(hier) ~!** (*auf Kisten etc*) this way up!, this side up!; **so ist das Leben, mal bist du ~, mal bist du unten** that's life, sometimes you're up, sometimes you're down; **~ und unten (von etw) verwechseln** to get sth upside down; **wo ist ~ (bei dem Bild)?** which is the top (of the picture)?, which is the right way up (for the picture)?; **die Leute, die ~ wohnen** the people on the floor above us/ you *etc*, the people (who live) upstairs; **wir möchten lieber ~ wohnen** we'd rather live high(er) up; **möchten Sie lieber ~ schlafen?** (*im oberen Bett*) would you like the top bunk?, would you like to sleep on top?; **wir wohnen rechts ~** or **~ rechts** we live on the top floor to the right; **~ rechts** or **rechts ~ (in der Ecke)** in the top right-hand corner; **die Abbildung ~ links** or **links ~ auf der Schautafel** the illustration on the top left corner or in the top left--hand corner of the diagram; **der ist ~ nicht ganz richtig** (*inf*) he's not quite right up top (*inf*); **~ ohne gehen** or **tragen** (*inf*) to be topless; **ganz ~** right at the top; **ganz ~ auf dem Stapel/ in der Rangordnung** right at the top of the pile/ of the hierarchy; **hier/dort ~** up here/there; **die ganze Sache steht mir bis hier ~** (*inf*) I'm sick to death of the whole thing (*inf*), I'm fed up to the back teeth with the whole thing (*Brit inf*); **bis ~ (hin)** to the top; **hoch ~** high (up) above; **beim Festessen saß er weiter ~ an der Tafel** at the banquet he sat nearer the top of the table; **~ auf dem Berg/der Leiter/dem Dach** on top of the mountain/ladder/roof; **~ am Himmel** up in the sky; **im Himmel** up in heaven, in heaven above (*liter*); **~ in Schottland** up in Scotland; **~ im Norden** up in (the) north; **~ herum** (a)round the top; (*von Frau*) up top; (*von Jacke*) (a)round the chest; **nach ~** up, upwards; (*im Hause*) upstairs; **der Fahrstuhl fährt nach ~** the lift (*Brit*) or elevator (*US*) is going up; **wir sind mit dem Fahrstuhl nach ~ gefahren** we went up in the lift (*Brit*) or elevator (*US*); **die Bergsteiger sind auf dem Weg nach ~** the climbers are on their way up; **der Weg nach ~** (*fig*) the road to the top; **endlich hat sie den Weg nach ~ geschafft** (*fig*) she finally got to the top or made it (to the top); **nach ~ zu** or **hin** towards (*Brit*) or toward (*US*) the top; **von ~ (her)** down; (*im Hause*) down(stairs); **ich komme gerade von ~** (*am Berg*) I've just come from the top; (*im Hause*) I've just been upstairs; **von ~ (aus) hat man eine schöne Aussicht** there's a nice view from the top; **von ~ bis unten** from top to bottom; (*von Mensch*) from top to toe; **jdn von ~ bis unten mustern** to look sb up and down; **jdn von ~ herab behandeln** to be condescending to sb, to treat sb condescendingly; **jdn von ~ herab ansehen** to look down on sb; **weiter ~** further

up; **das Gehöft liegt weiter ~ (am Berg/im Tal)** the farm is further or higher up (the mountain/ valley)

　b (*inf*: = *die Vorgesetzten*) **die da ~** the powers that be (*inf*), the top brass (*inf*); **das wird ~ entschieden** that's decided higher up; **er will sich nur ~ beliebt machen** he's just sucking up to the management (*inf*); **etw nach ~ (weiter-) melden/weitergeben** to report sth/to pass sth on to a superior; **der Befehl kommt von ~** it's orders from above

　c (= *vorher*) above; **siehe ~** see above; **~ erwähnt** *attr*, **~ genannt** *attr* above-mentioned; **wie ~ erwähnt** or **genannt** as mentioned above; **der ~ schon erwähnte Herr** the above-mentioned or aforementioned gentleman; **der weiter ~ erwähnte Fall** the case referred to before or above

olben-: olbenlan [ˈoːbnˈlan] ADV at the top, on (the) top; **sein Name steht ~ (auf der Liste)** his name is (at) the top (of the list); **an der Tafel saß er ~** he sat at the top of the table; **er will immer ~ sein** (*fig*) he always wants to be on top; **olbenlauf** [ˈoːbnˈlauf] ADV on (the) top; (= *an der Oberfläche*) on the top or surface; **gestern war er krank, aber heute ist er wieder ~** (*inf*) he wasn't well yesterday, but he's back on (*Brit*) or in (*US*) form today; **sie ist immer ~** (*inf*) she is always bright and cheery (*inf*); **olbenldrauf** [ˈoːbnˈdrauf] ADV (*inf*) on top; **olbenldrein** [ˈoːbnˈdrain] ADV (*inf*) on top of everything (*inf*); **olbenldrülber** [ˈoːbnˈdryːbə] ADV (*inf*, = *über*) above; (= *obendrauf*) on top; **olbenlerlwähnt** △ [ˈoːbnlɛvɛːnt] ADJ *attr* → **oben c**; **olbenlhelrum** [ˈoːbnhɛrʊm] ADV around the top; (*euph*: *am Körper*) around the chest

olbenlhin [ˈoːbnˈhɪn] ADV superficially; **etw nur so ~ sagen** to say sth lightly or casually or in an offhand way

Olben-ohlne- *in cpds* topless; **Olben-ohlne--Beldielnung** F topless waitress service

Olber [ˈoːbə] M **-s, -** **a** (= *Kellner*) waiter; **Herr ~!** waiter! **b** (*Cards*) ≈ Queen

olber- [ˈoːbə], **Olber-** *in cpds* (*Geog*) Upper; (*im Rang*) senior, chief; (*inf*: = *besonders*) really

Olberlarm M upper arm

Olberlarzt M **, Olberlärzltin** F senior physician

Olberlauflselher(in) M(F) (head) supervisor, superintendent; (*im Gefängnis*) head warder (*Brit*) or warden (*US*) or guard

Olberlauflsicht F supervision, superintendence; **die ~ haben** or **führen** to be in overall control (*über +acc* of); **unter (der) ~** (*+gen*) under the supervision or overall control (of)

Olberlbau M *pl* **-bauten** **a** (*von Brücke*) superstructure **b** (*Rail*) permanent way **c** **akademischer ~** academic teaching staff at professorial level

Olberlbelfehl M (*Mil*) supreme command; **den ~ haben** to be commander-in-chief or supreme commander, to be in supreme command (*über +acc* of)

O|ber|be|fehls|ha|ber(in) M(F) (*Mil*) commander-in-chief, supreme commander

O|ber|be|griff M generic term

O|ber|be|klei|dung F outer clothing, top clothes *pl*

O|ber|bett NT quilt

O|ber|bun|des|an|walt M , **O|ber|bun|des|an|wäl|tin** F chief public prosecutor

O|ber|bür|ger|meis|ter M Lord Mayor, Lord Provost (*Scot*)

O|ber|bür|ger|meis|te|rin F mayoress, Lord Provost (*Scot*)

O|ber|deck NT upper *or* top deck

o|ber|deutsch ADJ (*Ling*) Upper German

o|be|re(r, s) ['oːbərə] ADJ *attr Ende, Stockwerke, (Schul)klassen* upper, top; *Flusslauf* upper; **die Oberen** (*inf*) the top brass (*inf*), the bosses; (*Eccl*) the superiors; **die ~n Zehntausend** (*inf*) high society → **oberste(r, s)**

O|ber-: o|ber|faul ADJ (*inf*) very peculiar *or* odd *or* funny (*inf*); **O|ber|feld** M **-s, -s** (*Mil sl*) sarge (*inf*); **O|ber|feld|we|bel(in)** M(F) **a** (*Heer*) staff sergeant (*Brit*), first sergeant (*US*) **b** (*Luftwaffe*) flight sergeant (*Brit*), master sergeant (*US*)

O|ber|flä|che F surface (*auch fig*); (*Tech, Math*) surface area; (*Comput*) (user) interface; **an die ~ kommen** (*lit*) to come to the surface, to surface; (*fig*) to emerge; **an der ~ schwimmen** to float; **an der ~ bleiben** (*lit*) to remain on the surface; **das Buch bleibt an der ~** (*fig*) the book doesn't go very deep; **grafische ~** (*Comput*) graphical (user) interface

o|ber|fläch|lich [-flɛçlɪç] ADJ **a** (= *an der Oberfläche*) superficial; **~e Verletzung** surface wound

  b (= *flüchtig*) superficial; *Kenntnisse* superficial, shallow; **bei ~er Betrachtung** at a quick glance; **seine Englischkenntnisse sind nur ~** his knowledge of English is only superficial; **er ist sehr ~ in seiner Arbeit** his work is very superficial; **nach ~er Schätzung** at a rough estimate *or* guess

  c (= *seicht*) *Mensch, Unterhaltung* superficial, shallow

  ADV **a** (= *an der Oberfläche*) superficially, on the surface; **er ist nur ~ verletzt** he's only got superficial injuries

  b (= *flüchtig*) superficially, not thoroughly; **sie arbeitet ~** she doesn't do her work thoroughly; **er hat die Arbeit sehr ~ gemacht** he didn't do the work very thoroughly; **etw ~ lesen** to skim through sth; **jdn (nur) ~ kennen** to know sb (only) slightly, to have a nodding acquaintance with sb; **etw (nur) ~ kennen** to have (only) a shallow *or* superficial knowledge of sth

  c (= *seicht*) superficially; **sich ~ unterhalten** to have a superficial conversation; **~ leben** to lead a superficial life

O|ber|fläch|lich|keit F **-, -en a** *no pl* superficiality **b** (*Bemerkung*) superficial remark

O|ber-: O|ber|förs|ter(in) M(F) head forester; **O|ber|fran|ken** ['oːbəfraŋkn] NT **-s** Upper Franconia; **o|ber|gä|rig** [-gɛːrɪç] ADJ *Bier* top-fermented; **O|ber|ge|frei|te(r)** MF *decl as adj* **a** (*Heer*) lance corporal (*Brit*), private first class (*US*) **b** (*Luftwaffe*) senior aircraftsman (*Brit*), airman first class (*US*) **c** (*Marine*) seaman first class (*Brit*), seaman (*US*); **O|ber|ge|schoss** ▲ NT upper floor; (*bei zwei Stockwerken*) top floor; **im zweiten ~** on the second (*Brit*) *or* third (*US*) floor; **O|ber|gren|ze** F upper limit; **o|ber|halb** ['oːbəhalp] PREP +*gen* above; ~ **von Basel** above Basel; **wei|ter ~** further *or* higher up; **O|ber|hand** F (*fig*) upper hand; **die ~ über jdn/etw gewinnen** to get *or* gain the upper hand over sb/sth, to get the better of sb/sth; **die ~ (über jdn/etw) ha|ben/behalten** to have/keep the upper hand (over sb/sth); **O|ber|haupt** NT (= *Repräsentant*) head; (= *Anführer*) leader; **O|ber|haus** NT (*Pol*) upper house; (*in GB*) House of Lords; **O|ber|**

---

hemd NT shirt; **O|ber|herr(in)** M(F) (*old*) sovereign; **O|ber|herr|schaft** F sovereignty, supremacy (*über* +*acc* over); **unter der ~ Englands** under English rule; **O|ber|hir|te** M , **O|ber|hir|tin** F spiritual head *or* leader; **O|ber|hit|ze** F (*Cook*) top heat; **(nur) mit ~ ba|cken** to bake in the top oven; **O|ber|ho|heit** F supremacy, sovereignty; **unter UN-Oberhoheit stehen** to be under UN authority *or* control; **unter polnischer ~** under Polish sovereignty; **die ~ über jdn gewinnen** to gain *or* win supremacy over sb

O|be|rin ['oːbərɪn] F **-, -nen a** (*im Krankenhaus*) matron **b** (*Eccl*) Mother Superior

O|ber-: O|ber|in|ge|ni|eur(in) M(F) chief engineer; **O|ber|in|spek|tor(in)** M(F) senior inspector; **o|ber|ir|disch** ADJ above ground *pred* ADV above ground; **O|ber|kell|ner** M head waiter; **O|ber|kell|ne|rin** F head waitress; **O|ber|kie|fer** M upper jaw; **O|ber|kir|chen|rat¹** M (*Gremium*) church assembly; **O|ber|kir|chen|rat²** M , **O|ber|kir|chen|rä|tin** F member of the church assembly; **O|ber|klas|se** F **a** (*Sch*) **~n** top classes *or* forms **b** (*Sociol*) upper class **c ein Auto/eine Stereoanlage der ~** a top-of-the-range car/stereo; **O|ber|kleid** NT (*liter*) outer garment(s *pl*); **O|ber|klei|dung** F outer clothing; **O|ber|kom|man|die|ren|de(r)** [-kɔmandiːrəndə] MF *decl as adj* Commander-in-Chief, Supreme Commander; **O|ber|kom|man|do** NT (= *Oberbefehl*) Supreme Command; (= *Befehlsstab*) headquarters *pl*; **O|ber|kör|per** M upper part of the body; **mit bloßem ~ or freiem or nacktem ~** stripped to the waist; **den ~ freimachen** to strip to the waist; **O|ber|land** NT , *no pl* (*Geog*) uplands *pl*; **das Berner ~** the Bernese Oberland; **O|ber|lan|des|ge|richt** NT *provincial high court and court of appeal*; **O|ber|län|ge** F upstroke; (*Typ*) ascender; **o|ber|las|tig** [-lastɪç] ADJ (*Naut*) top-heavy; **O|ber|lauf** M upper reaches *pl*; **am ~ des Rheins** in the upper reaches of the Rhine; **O|ber|le|der** NT (leather) uppers *pl*; **O|ber|leh|rer(in)** M(F) (*old*) senior primary school teacher; **O|ber|lei|tung** F **a** (= *Führung*) direction; **die ~ eines Projekts haben** to be in overall charge of a project **b** (*Elec*) overhead cable; **O|ber|leut|nant** M **a** (*Heer*) lieutenant (*Brit*), first lieutenant (*US*) **b** (*Luftwaffe*) flying officer (*Brit*), first lieutenant (*US*) **c** (*Marine*) **~ zur See** lieutenant; **O|ber|licht** NT (= *hoch gelegenes Fenster*) small, high window; (= *Lüftungsklappe, über einer Tür*) fanlight, transom (window); **O|ber|lid** NT upper lid; **O|ber|li|ga** F (*Sport*) top *or* first league; **O|ber|lip|pe** F upper lip; **O|ber|maat** M (*Naut*) leading seaman; **O|ber|ma|te|ri|al** NT (*von Schuh*) upper; **O|ber|meis|ter(in)** M(F) **a** head of craft guild **b** (*bei Polizei*) ≈ sergeant; **O|ber|ös|ter|reich** NT Upper Austria; **O|ber|post|di|rek|ti|on** F (*Behörde*) regional post office (administration); (*Bezirk*) postal area *or* district; **~ Köln** Cologne postal district; **O|ber|pries|ter** M high priest; **O|ber|pries|te|rin** F high priestess; **O|ber|pri|ma** F (*dated*) top class of German grammar school, ≈ upper sixth (*Brit*), ≈ senior grade (*US*); **O|ber|pri|ma|ner(in)** M(F) (*dated*) ≈ sixth former (*Brit*), ≈ senior (*US*); **o|ber|rhei|nisch** ADJ upper Rhine; **die Oberrheinische Tiefebene** the Upper Rhine Valley; **im Oberrheinischen** along *or* around the upper Rhine; **O|ber|rich|ter(in)** M(F) (*Sw*) ≈ high court judge

O|bers ['oːbəs] NT **-**, *no pl* (*Aus*) cream

O|ber-: O|ber|schen|kel M thigh; **O|ber|schen|kel|bruch** M broken thighbone *or* femur, fracture of the thighbone *or* femur; **O|ber|schen|kel|hals** M head of the thighbone *or* femur; **O|ber|schen|kel|hals|bruch** M femoral neck fracture; **O|ber|schen|kel|kno|chen** M thighbone, femur; **O|ber|schicht** F top layer; (*Sociol*) upper strata (of society) *pl*; **o|ber|schläch|tig** [-flɛçtɪç] ADJ *Mühle* over-

---

shot; **o|ber|schlau** (*inf*) ADJ really clever ADV really cleverly; **sie redet schon wieder so ~ da|her** she's talking again as if she knows it all; **O|ber|schu|le** F (*old:* = *Gymnasium*) ≈ grammar school (*Brit*), ≈ high school (*US*); (*weiterführende Schule*) secondary school; **O|ber|schü|ler(in)** M(F) (*old:* = *Gymnasiast*) ≈ grammar school pupil (*Brit*), ≈ high school student (*US*); (*an weiterführenden Schulen*) secondary school pupil; **O|ber|schul|rat** M , **O|ber|schul|rä|tin** F school inspector, HMI (*Brit inf*); **O|ber|schur|ke** M , **O|ber|schur|kin** F (*inf*) chief villain, baddie (*inf*); **O|ber|schwes|ter** F senior nursing officer; **O|ber|sei|te** F top (side); **O|ber|se|kun|da** F (*dated*) seventh year of German secondary school; **O|ber|se|kun|da|ner(in)** M(F) (*dated*) *pupil in seventh year of German secondary school*

O|berst ['oːbəst] M **-en, -e(n) a** (*Heer*) colonel **b** (*Luftwaffe*) group captain (*Brit*), colonel (*US*)

O|ber-: O|ber|staats|an|walt M , **O|ber|staats|an|wäl|tin** F public prosecutor, procurator fiscal (*Scot*), district attorney (*US*); **O|ber|stadt** F upper town, upper part of a town; **O|ber|stadt|di|rek|tor(in)** M(F) town clerk; **O|ber|stei|ger** M head foreman (in a mine)

o|bers|te(r, s) ['oːbəstə] ADJ **a** (= *ganz oben*) *Stockwerk, Schicht* topmost, uppermost, very top; **das Oberste zuunterst kehren** to turn everything *or* things upside down **b** *Gebot, Gesetz, Prinzip* supreme; *Dienstgrad* highest, most senior, top; **die ~n Kreise der Gesellschaft** the upper circles *or* echelons of society; **Oberstes Gericht, Oberster Gerichtshof** supreme court; (*in GB*) High Court (of Justice); (*in USA*) Supreme Court

O|ber|stim|me F soprano; (= *Knabenoberstimme*) treble; (= *Diskant*) descant

O|berst|leut|nant M **a** (*Heer*) lieutenant colonel **b** (*Luftwaffe*) wing commander (*Brit*), lieutenant colonel (*US*)

O|ber-: O|ber|stüb|chen NT (*inf*) **er ist nicht ganz richtig im ~** he's not quite right up top (*inf*); **O|ber|stu|di|en|di|rek|tor** M headmaster (*esp Brit*), principal (*US*); **O|ber|stu|di|en|di|rek|to|rin** F headmistress (*esp Brit*), principal (*US*); **O|ber|stu|di|en|rat** M , **O|ber|stu|di|en|rä|tin** F senior teacher; **O|ber|stu|fe** F upper school; (*Univ*) advanced level; **O|ber|teil** M OR NT upper part, top; **O|ber|ter|tia** F (*dated*) fifth year of German secondary school; **O|ber|ter|ti|a|ner(in)** M(F) (*dated*) *pupil in fifth year of German secondary school*; **O|ber|ton** M (*Mus, fig*) overtone(s *pl*); **O|ber|trot|tel** M (*inf*) prize *or* first-class idiot; **O|ber|vol|ta** [oːbəˈvɔlta] NT **-s** Upper Volta; **O|ber|was|ser** NT *pl* **-wasser a** (*von Wehr*) backwater **b** (*fig mil*) **~ haben** to feel better; **sobald sein älterer Bruder dabei ist, hat er (wieder) ~** he feels much braver when his elder brother is around; **wieder ~ gewinnen** *or* **bekommen** to be in a better position; **O|ber|wei|te** F bust measurement; **sie hat ~ 94** ≈ she has a 38-inch bust; **die hat eine ganz schöne ~!** she's very well-endowed

Ob|frau F representative

ob|gleich [ɔpˈglaiç] CONJ although, (even) though

Ob|hut [ˈɔphuːt] F **-**, *no pl* (*geh*) (= *Aufsicht*) care; (= *Verwahrung*) keeping, care; **jdn/etw jds ~** (*dat*) **anvertrauen** to place *or* put sb/sth in sb's care; **jdn in ~ nehmen** to take care of sb, to look after sb; **jdn bei jdm in ~ geben, jdn in jds ~** (*acc*) **geben** to put *or* place sb in sb's care; **sich in jds ~** (*dat*) **befinden, unter jds ~** (*dat*) **sein** to be in sb's care

o|bi|ge(r, s) [ˈoːbɪgə] ADJ *attr* above; **vergleiche ~ Abbildung** compare the illustration above *or* the above illustration; **der Obige** (*form*) the above (*form*)

Ob|jekt [ɔp'jɛkt] NT **-(e)s, -e** (*auch Gram*) object; (*Comm: = Grundstück etc*) property; (*Phot*) subject; **das ~ der Untersuchung** the object under examination; **zum ~ der Forschung werden** to become the object of research

ob|jek|tiv [ɔpjɛk'tiːf] ADJ objective ▣ objectively; **~ Stellung nehmen** to take an objective stance; **~ über etw** (*acc*) **urteilen** to make an objective judgement about sth, to judge sth objectively; **etw ~ betrachten** to view sth objectively; **~ gesehen** *or* **betrachtet ist das falsch** seen *or* viewed objectively this is wrong

Ob|jek|tiv [ɔpjɛk'tiːf] NT **-s, -e** [-və] (*object*) lens, objective

ob|jek|ti|vie|ren [ɔpjɛkti'viːrən] ptp **objektiviert** ▣ to objectify; **~des Denken** objective thinking ▣ *Problem, Aussage* to treat objectively, to objectivize

Ob|jek|ti|vi|tät [ɔpjɛktivi'tɛːt] F **-,** *no pl* objectivity; **sich um größte ~ bemühen** to try to be as objective as possible

Ob|jekt-: Ob|jekt|satz M (*Gram*) object clause; **Ob|jekt|schutz** M protection of property; **Ob|jekt|spra|che** F (*Ling*) object language; **Ob|jekt|trä|ger** M slide

Ob|la|te [o'blaːtə] F **-, -n** wafer; (*Eccl*) host

ob|lie|gen [ɔp'liːgn̩, 'ɔp'liːgn̩] ptp **oblegen** *or* (*rare*) **obgelegen** [ɔp'leːgn̩, 'ɔpgəleːgn̩] *irreg aux* *haben or sein (+dat)* ▣ *impers insep or (rare) sep* (*form*) **es obliegt ihm, es liegt ihm ob** it is incumbent upon him (*form*); **ihm oblag die Betreuung der Flüchtlinge** he was responsible for looking after the refugees; **diese Entscheidung obliegt dem Präsidenten** this decision lies with the President ▣ *sep or insep* (*old: = sich widmen*) to apply oneself to (*form*)

Ob|lie|gen|heit [ɔp'liːgn̩haɪt] F **-, -en** (*form*) obligation, incumbency (*form*)

ob|li|gat [obli'gaːt] ADJ obligatory; **der ~e Dudelsackpfeifer** the obligatory (bag)piper; **mit ~em Cembalo** (*Mus*) with (a) cembalo obbligato

Ob|li|ga|ti|on [obliga'tsɪoːn] F **-, -en** (*auch Fin*) obligation; **die Firma übernimmt keine ~** the firm is under no obligation

ob|li|ga|to|risch [obliga'toːrɪʃ] ADJ obligatory; *Fächer, Vorlesung* compulsory; *Qualifikationen* necessary, requisite

Ob|li|go ['oːbligo, 'ɔbligo] NT **-s, -s** ▣ (*Fin*) guarantee; **ohne ~** without recourse ▣ (= *Verpflichtung*) obligation; **bei der Sicherung der Renten ist die Regierung im ~** the government has an obligation to safeguard pensions

Ob|mann ['ɔpman] M *pl* **-männer** *or* **-leute**, **Ob|män|nin** ['ɔpmɛnɪn] F **-, -nen** representative

O|boe [o'boːə] F **-, -n** oboe

O|bo|ist [obo'ɪst] M **-en, -en**, **O|bo|is|tin** [-'ɪstɪn] F **-, -nen** oboist, oboe player

O|bo|lus ['oːbolʊs] M **-, -se** contribution

Ob|rig|keit ['oːbrɪçkaɪt] F **-, -en** ▣ (*als Begriff, Konzept*) authority ▣ (= *Behörden*) **die ~** the authorities *pl*; **die geistliche/weltliche ~** the spiritual/secular authorities

ob|rig|keit|lich ['oːbrɪçkaɪtlɪç] ADJ authoritarian ▣ in an authoritarian manner

Ob|rig|keits|staat M authoritarian state

Ob|rist [o'brɪst] M **-en, -en** colonel

ob|schon [ɔp'ʃoːn] CONJ (*liter*) although, albeit (*nur in verbloser Konstruktion*)

Ob|ser|vanz [ɔpzɛr'vants] F **-, -en** observance; **ein Orden (von) der strengen ~** a strict *or* closed order

Ob|ser|va|to|ri|um [ɔpzɛrva'toːrɪʊm] NT **-s, Observatorien** [-riən] observatory

ob|ser|vie|ren [ɔpzɛr'viːrən] ptp **observiert** VT (*form*) to observe; **er ist schon einige Monate observiert worden** he has been under surveillance for several months

Ob|ses|si|on [ɔpzɛ'sɪoːn] F **-, -en** obsession

ob|ses|siv [ɔpzɛ'siːf] ADJ obsessive ▣ obsessively

ob|sie|gen [ɔp'ziːgn̩, 'ɔpziːgn̩] ptp **obsiegt** *or* (*rare*) **obgesiegt** [ɔp'ziːkt, 'ɔpgəziːkt] VI *insep or (rare) sep* (*obs, Jur*) to prevail (*+dat* over)

obs|kur [ɔps'kuːɐ] ADJ (= *fragwürdig, zweifelhaft*) *Quellen* obscure; (= *verdächtig*) *Gestalten, Kneipe, Geschäfte* suspect, dubious; **diese ~en Gestalten der Unterwelt** these twilight figures of the underworld ▣ obscurely; **~ aussehen/erscheinen** to look/seem obscure

Obs|ku|ran|tis|mus [ɔpskuran'tɪsmʊs] M **-,** *no pl* obscurantism

ob|so|let [ɔpzo'leːt] ADJ obsolete

Obst [oːpst] NT **-(e)s,** *no pl* fruit

Obst-: Obst|bau M **,** *no pl* fruit-growing; **Obst|baum** M fruit tree; **Obst|gar|ten** M orchard

obs|ti|nat [ɔpsti'naːt] ADJ (*geh*) obstinate

Obst-: Obst|jahr NT **ein gutes ~** a good year for fruit; **Obst|ku|chen** M fruit flan; (*gedeckt*) fruit tart

Obst|ler ['oːpstlɐ] M **-s, -** (*dial*) fruit schnapps

Obst-: Obst|mes|ser NT fruit knife; **Obst|sa|lat** M fruit salad

Ob|struk|ti|on [ɔpstrʊk'tsɪoːn] F **-, -en** ▣ (*Med*) obstruction, blockage ▣ (*Pol*) obstruction, filibuster; **die Gesetzesvorlage scheiterte an der ~ der Opposition** the bill failed because of the Opposition's obstructive *or* filibustering tactics *or* obstructionism; **~ betreiben** to obstruct, to block, to filibuster

Obst-: Obst|saft M fruit juice; **Obst|tag** M **legen Sie jede Woche einen ~ ein** eat only fruit one day a week; **meine Frau hat heute ihren ~** my wife's on her fruit diet today; **Obst|tor|te** F fruit flan; (*gedeckt*) fruit tart; **Obst|was|ser** NT *pl* **-wässer** fruit schnapps; **Obst|wein** M fruit wine

obs|zön [ɔps'tsøːn] ADJ obscene ▣ obscenely; **~ klingen** to sound obscene; **~ gestikulieren** to make obscene gestures

Obs|zö|ni|tät [ɔpstsøni'tɛːt] F **-, -en** obscenity

O|bus ['oːbʊs] M **-ses, -se** (*inf*) trolley (*Brit inf*), trolley bus

ob|wal|ten ['ɔpvaltn̩, ɔp'valtn̩] ptp **obwaltet** *or* (*rare*) **obgewaltet** ['ɔpˌvaltət, 'ɔpgəvaltət] VI *insep* *or* (*rare*) *sep* (*form: = herrschen*) to prevail

ob|wohl [ɔp'voːl] CONJ although, (even) though

ob|zwar [ɔp'tsvaːɐ] CONJ (*rare*) although, (even) though

Oc|ca|si|on [ɔka'zɪoːn] F **-, -en** (*Aus, Sw*) → **Okkasion**

Ochs [ɔks] M **-en, -en**, **Och|se** ['ɔksə] M **-n, -n** ▣ ox; (*junger Ochse*) bullock; **~ am Spieß** roast ox; **er stand da wie der ~ vorm** *or* **am Berg** *or* **vorm (neuen) Scheunentor** (*inf*) he stood there like a cow at a five-barred gate (*inf*) ▣ (*inf: = Dummkopf*) twit (*Brit inf*), ass (*inf*), dope (*inf*)

och|sen ['ɔksn̩] (*Sch inf*) VT to swot up (*Brit inf*), to mug up (*Brit inf*), to study up on (*US inf*) VI to swot (up) (*Brit inf*), to mug (up) (*Brit inf*), to cram (*US inf*)

Och|sen- ['ɔksn̩-]: **Och|sen|frosch** M bullfrog; **Och|sen|ge|spann** NT yoke of oxen; **Och|sen|schwanz|sup|pe** F oxtail soup; **Och|sen|tour** F (*inf*) ▣ (= *Schinderei*) slog (*inf*), sweat (*inf*) ▣ **er brauchte sich nicht über die ~ heraufzudienen** he did not have to work his way up the hard way; **Och|sen|zie|mer** M bull's pizzle, bullwhip

Öch|sle ['œkslə] NT **-s, -** *measure of alcohol content of drink according to its specific gravity*

O|cker ['ɔkɐ] M OR NT **-s, -** ochre (*Brit*), ocher (*US*)

o|cker|braun, o|cker|gelb ADJ ochre (*Brit*), ocher (*US*)

OCR-Schrift [oːtseːˈʔɛr-] F OCR font

öd [øːt] ADJ = **öde**

od. *abbr von* **oder**

O|de ['oːdə] F **-, -n** ode

ö|de ['øːdə] ADJ ▣ (= *verlassen*) *Stadt, Strand* deserted, empty, abandoned; (= *unbewohnt*) desolate, empty; (= *unbebaut*) waste, barren; **öd und leer** dreary and desolate ▣ (*fig: = fade*) dull, dreary, tedious; *Dasein* dreary; (*inf: = langweilig*) grim (*inf*)

Ö|de ['øːdə] F **-, -n** (*liter*) ▣ (= *einsame Gegend*) desert, wasteland ▣ *no pl* (= *Langeweile*) dreariness

O|dem ['oːdəm] M **-s,** *no pl* (*poet, Bibl*) breath

Ö|dem [ø'deːm] NT **-s, -e** oedema, edema

o|der ['oːdɐ] CONJ ▣ or; **~ aber** or else; **~ auch** or even, or maybe, or perhaps; **eins ~ das andere** one or the other, it's either or; **entweder ... ~** either ... or; **~ so** (*am Satzende*) or something; **~ so ähnlich** or something like that ▣ (*in Fragen*) **so wars doch, ~ (etwa) nicht?** that was what happened, wasn't it?, wasn't that how it happened?, it happened like that, didn't it?; **du kommst doch, ~?** you're coming, aren't you?; **der Mörder hat sein Opfer nie vorher gesehen, ~ doch?** the murderer had never seen his victim before, or had he?; **damit war der Fall erledigt, ~ doch nicht?** with that the case was closed, or perhaps not?; **~ soll ich lieber mitkommen?** maybe I should come along?; **lassen wir es so, ~?** let's leave it at that, right *or* OK?

O|der ['oːdɐ] F **-** Oder

O|der-Nei|ße-Gren|ze F **, O|der-Nei|ße-Li|nie** ['oːdɐˈnaɪsə-] F Oder-Neisse Line

ö|di|pal [ødi'paːl] ADJ oedipal

Ö|di|pus|kom|plex ['øːdipʊs-] M Oedipus complex

O|di|um ['oːdiʊm] NT **-s,** *no pl* (*liter*) odium

Öd|land ['øːtlant] NT wasteland

Öd|nis ['øːtnɪs] F **-, -se** (*geh*) = **Öde**

O|dys|see [ody'seː] F **-, -n** [-'seːən] (*Liter*) Odyssey; (*fig*) odyssey

OECD-Land [oːˌeːtseːˈdeː-] NT OECD member country

Oeu|vre ['øːvɐ, 'øːvrə] NT **-, -s** (*Liter*) work, works *pl*

OEZ *abbr von* **Osteuropäische Zeit**

OF *abbr von* **Originalfassung**

Öf|chen ['øːfçən] NT **-s, -** *dim von* **Ofen**

O|fen ['oːfn̩] M **-s, ⁀** ['øːfn̩] ▣ (= *Heizofen*) heater; (= *Elektroofen, Gasofen*) fire, heater; (= *Ölofen, Petroleumofen*) stove, heater; (= *Kohleofen*) stove; (= *Heizungsofen*) boiler; (= *Kachelofen*) tiled stove; **hinter dem ~ hocken** to be a stay-at-home; **jdn hinter dem ~ hervorlocken** to tempt sb; **jetzt ist der ~ aus** (*inf*) that's it (*inf*), that does it (*inf*) ▣ (= *Herd*) oven, stove; (= *Kohleofen*) stove, range; (= *Backofen*) oven ▣ (*Tech*) furnace, oven; (= *Brennofen*) kiln; (= *Trockenofen*) drying oven *or* kiln; (= *Hochofen*) blast furnace; (= *Schmelzofen*) smelting furnace; (= *Müllverbrennungsofen*) incinerator ▣ (*inf: = Motorrad*) **ein heißer ~** a fast bike (*inf*)

Ofen-: O|fen|bank F *pl* **-bänke** fireside (bench), hearth; **auf der ~** by the hearth *or* fire *or* fireside; **O|fen|blech** NT tray for catching falling coals; **O|fen|ecke** F inglenook; **o|fen|fer|tig** ADJ *Gericht* oven-ready ▣ oven-ready; **o|fen|frisch** ADJ *Brot* oven-fresh; **O|fen|hei|zung** F stove heating; **Zimmer mit ~** room with stove (heater); **O|fen|klap|pe** F ▣ (= *Ofentür*) stove door ▣ (= *Lüftungsklappe*) damper; **O|fen|loch** NT stove door; **O|fen|rohr** NT stovepipe; (*old inf: = Zylinder*) stovepipe (hat); **O|fen|röh|re** F (slow) oven; **O|fen|schirm** M firescreen; **O|fen|set|zer(in)** M(F) stove fitter; **O|fen|tür** F stove door

Off [ɔf] NT -, *no pl* (*TV, Theat*) offstage; **aus dem ~** offstage; **eine Stimme aus dem ~** a voice off; **aus dem ~ kommen** to come onstage, to come from offstage

of|fen [ˈɔfn] ADJ **a** open; *Bein* ulcerated; *Flamme, Licht* naked; *Feuer* open; *Haare* loose; **ein ~er Brief** an open letter; **er geht mit ~em Hemd** he is wearing an open-neck shirt; **der Laden hat bis 10 Uhr ~** the shop (*esp Brit*) or store is or stays open until 10 o'clock; **das Turnier ist für alle ~** the tournament is open to everybody; **die Teilnahme ist für alle ~** anyone can take part; **~er Wein** wine by the carafe/glass; **auf ~er Strecke** (*Straße*) on the open road; (*Rail*) between stations; **wir hielten auf ~er Strecke** we stopped in the middle of nowhere; **auf ~er Straße** in the middle of the street; (*Landstraße*) on the open road; **auf ~er See** on the open sea; **Beifall auf ~er Szene** spontaneous applause, an outburst of applause; **bei ~er Szene** or **Bühne verwandelt sich das Bild** the scene changed without a curtain; **~e Flanke** (*Mil*) open or exposed flank; **~e Stadt** (*Mil*) open or undefended town; **mit ~em Munde dastehen** (*fig*) to stand gaping; **mit ~em Munde atmen** to breathe with one's mouth open; **Tag der ~en Tür** open day; **ein ~es Haus haben** or **führen** to keep open house; **überall ~e Türen finden** (*fig*) to find a warm welcome everywhere; **Haus der ~en Tür** open house; **Politik der ~en Tür** open-door policy; **mit ~en Augen** or **Sinnen durchs Leben gehen** to go through life with one's eyes open; **eine ~e Hand haben** (*fig*) to be open-handed; **allem Neuen gegenüber ~ sein** to be open or receptive to (all) new ideas; **~e Handelsgesellschaft** general partnership → **Arm, Buch, Karte, Tür**

b (= *frei*) *Stelle* vacant; **~e Stellen** vacancies; **„offene Stellen"** "vacancies", "situations vacant" (*Brit*)

c (= *unerledigt, unentschieden*) *Frage, Ausgang, Partie* open; *Rechnung* outstanding

d (= *aufrichtig, freimütig*) *Mensch, Bekenntnis, Aussprache* open; **er hat einen ~en Blick** he's got an open or honest face; **er hat keinen ~en Blick** he's got a shifty look in his eyes; **ein ~es Wort mit jdm reden** to have a frank talk with sb

ADV **a** (= *freimütig*) candidly; *kritisieren, zugeben, als Lügner bezeichnen, sich zu etw bekennen* openly; **ein ~ schwul lebender Mensch** a person living openly as a homosexual; **die Karten ~ auf den Tisch legen** to lay one's cards on the table; **etw ~ aussprechen** to say sth out loud; **etw ~ einräumen** to be perfectly willing to admit sth; **sich ~ für/gegen etw aussprechen** to openly speak out for/against sth; **~ gestanden** or **gesagt** to tell you the truth, quite honestly, to be frank; **etw ~ eingestehen** or **zugeben** to confess or admit (to) sth openly or frankly; **seine Meinung ~ sagen** to speak one's mind, to say what one thinks; **sag mir ganz ~ deine Meinung** tell me your honest opinion; **~ mit jdm reden** to speak openly to sb, to be frank with sb

b (= *deutlich*) clearly; **die Probleme treten ~ zutage** the problems can be clearly identified; **damit war der Krieg ~ ausgebrochen** with that the war had clearly begun; **wir sollten den Konflikt ~ austragen** we should bring the matter out in the open

c (= *lose*) **die Haare ~ tragen** to wear one's hair loose or down; **Wein ~ verkaufen** to sell wine on draught (*Brit*) or draft (*US*); (*glasweise*) to sell wine by the glass; **Schrauben ~ kaufen** to buy screws loose

d (= *unverstellt*) **endlich lag das Ziel ~ vor ihnen (da)** at last their goal lay before them; **das Land erstreckte sich ~ vor ihnen** the countryside stretched out before them

of|fen|bar [ˈɔfn-] ADJ obvious; **sein Zögern machte ~, dass ...** it showed or was obvious from the way he hesitated that ...; **~ werden** to become obvious or clear, to emerge ADV (= *vermutlich*) apparently; **er hat ~ den Zug verpasst** he must

have missed the train; **da haben Sie sich ~ geirrt** you seem to have made a mistake

of|fen|ba|ren [ɔfn'baːrən] *insep ptp* **offenbart** or (*old*) **geoffenbart** [ɔfn'baːrɛt, gəˈɔfn'baːrɛt] VT to reveal VR **a** (= *erweisen*) to show or reveal itself/oneself; **sich als etw ~** to show oneself to be sth **b** (= *kundtun*) **sich jdm ~** to reveal oneself to sb; (= *Liebe erklären*) to reveal one's feelings to sb

Of|fen|ba|rung [ɔfn'baːrʊŋ] F -, -en revelation

Of|fen|ba|rungs|eid M (*Jur*) oath of disclosure or manifestation; **den ~ leisten** (*lit*) to swear an oath of disclosure or manifestation; (*fig*) to admit defeat; **mit diesem Programm hat die Partei ihren ~ geleistet** with this programme (*Brit*) or program (*US*) the party has revealed its political bankruptcy; **vor dem ~ stehen** (*fig*) to be on the verge of defeat

of|fen-: of|fen blei|ben ▲ VI *irreg aux sein* to remain open; **alle offen gebliebenen Probleme** all unsolved or remaining problems; **of|fen hal|ten** ▲ VT *irreg* to keep open; **die Ohren ~** to keep one's ear open or to the ground; **jdm eine Stelle** or **eine Stelle für jdn ~** to keep a job open for sb; **(sich** *dat*) **eine Option ~** to keep an option open

Of|fen|heit F -, *no pl* (*gegenüber* about) openness, frankness, candour (*Brit*), candor (*US*); **schonungslose ~** brutal frankness; **in aller** or **schöner ~** quite openly

of|fen-: of|fen|her|zig ADJ **a** open, frank, candid **b** (*hum inf*) *Kleid* revealing; **sie ist ja heute wieder sehr ~** she's being very revealing again today (*hum inf*) ADV (= *ehrlich*) openly, frankly; **Of|fen|her|zig|keit** [-hɛrtsɪçkaɪt] F -, *no pl* openness, frankness, candour (*Brit*), candor (*US*); **of|fen|kun|dig** ADJ obvious, clear; *Beweise* clear; *Lüge, Interesse* obvious, manifest; **es ist ~, dass ...** it is obvious or clear or evident that ... ADV blatantly, clearly; **of|fen las|sen** ▲ VT *irreg* to leave open; **of|fen le|gen** ▲ VT to disclose; **Of|fen|le|gung** F -, -en disclosure; **of|fen|markt|po|li|tik** F (*Fin*) free market policy; **of|fen|sicht|lich** [ˈɔfnzɪçtlɪç, ɔfnˈzɪçtlɪç] ADJ obvious; *Irrtum, Lüge auch* blatant; *Unterschied auch* clear; **es war ~, dass er uns mied** it was plain or evident or obvious he was avoiding us ADV obviously, clearly, evidently

of|fen|siv ADJ offensive ADV offensively; *verkaufen* aggressively; **sich ungewohnt ~ zeigen** to be unusually aggressive; **es wurde ~ geworben** the advertising campaign was aggressive

Of|fen|si|ve F -, -n offensive; **in die ~ gehen** to take the offensive

Of|fen|siv-: Of|fen|siv|krieg M offensive war; **Of|fen|siv|ra|ke|te** F offensive missile; **Of|fen|siv|waf|fe** F offensive weapon

of|fen ste|hen ▲ VI *irreg* (*S Ger auch: aux sein*) **a** (*Tür, Fenster*) to be open; (*Knopf*) to be undone; **der Mund stand ihr offen** her mouth was hanging open

b (*Comm: Rechnung, Betrag*) to be or remain unpaid or unsettled, to be outstanding

c **jdm ~** (*fig*: = *zugänglich sein*) to be open to sb; **uns stehen zwei Möglichkeiten offen** there are two possibilities or options open to us; **dir stehen noch alle Möglichkeiten offen** you still have plenty of options; **die (ganze) Welt steht ihm offen** he has the (whole) world at his feet, the world's his oyster; **es steht ihr offen, sich uns anzuschließen** she's free to join us; **die Teilnahme an der Veranstaltung steht auch Nichtmitgliedern offen** the function is also open to non-members

d (= *unbesetzt sein*: *Stelle*) to be available

öf|fent|lich ADJ **a** (= *allgemein zugänglich, sichtbar*) (*attr*) public; (*pred*) open to the public, public; **eine Persönlichkeit des ~en Lebens** a person in public life or in the public eye; **im ~en Leben stehen** to be in public life; **ein ~es Haus** (*euph*) a house of ill repute (*euph*)

b *attr* (= *die Allgemeinheit betreffend*) *Wohl, Inte-*

resse public; **die ~e Meinung/Moral** public opinion/morality; **die ~e Ordnung** law and order; **~es Recht** (*Jur*) public law; **Anstalt/Körperschaft des ~en Rechts** public institution/corporation or body

c (= *staatlich*) public; **~e Schule** state school, public school (*US*); **der ~e Dienst** the civil service; **die ~e Hand** (= *der Staat*) (central) government; (= *die Gemeinde*) local government; **Ausgaben der ~en Hand** public spending; **etw in die ~e Hand überführen** to take sth into public ownership, to take sth under public control

ADV publicly; **sich ~ äußern** to voice one's opinion in public; **etw ~ bekannt machen** to make sth public, to publicize sth; **~ versteigern** to sell by public auction, to auction publicly; **jdn ~ anschuldigen/hinrichten** to accuse/execute sb publicly

Öf|fent|lich|keit F -, *no pl* **a** (= *Zugänglichkeit*) **der Verteidiger bestand auf der ~ der Verhandlung** the defence (*Brit*) or defense (*US*) counsel insisted that the trial take place in public; **~ der Rechtsprechung** administration of justice in open court; **~ der Prüfungen war eine Hauptforderung der Studenten** one of the students' main demands was that exams should be open to the public; **die ~ einer Versammlung herstellen** to make a meeting public

b (= *Allgemeinheit*) (general) public; **die ~ scheuen** to shun publicity; **in** or **vor aller ~** in public; **die/eine breite ~** the/a broad public; **unter Ausschluss der ~** in secret or private; (*Jur*) in camera; **als er das erste Mal vor die ~ trat** when he made his first public appearance; **mit etw an** or **vor die ~ treten** or **gehen**, **etw vor die ~ bringen** to bring sth to public attention or into the public eye; **etw in** or **an die ~ tragen** to go public with sth; **etw der ~ übergeben** (*form*) (= *eröffnen*) to declare sth officially open; (= *veröffentlichen*) to publish sth; **etw der ~ zugänglich machen** to open sth to the public; **im Licht der ~ stehen** to be in the public eye; **ans** or **ins Licht der ~ geraten** to end up in the public eye; **das Licht der ~ scheuen** to keep out of the public eye

Öf|fent|lich|keits-: Öf|fent|lich|keits|ar|beit F public relations work; **öf|fent|lich|keits|scheu** ADJ publicity-shy; **öf|fent|lich|keits|wirk|sam** ADJ **~ sein** to be effective (as) publicity, to be good publicity ADV **wir müssen besonders ~ werben** we need particularly effective publicity

öf|fent|lich-recht|lich [ˈœfntlɪçˈrɛçtlɪç] ADJ *attr* (under) public law; **~er Rundfunk/~es Fernsehen** ≈ public-service broadcasting

of|fe|rie|ren [ɔfəˈriːrən] *ptp* **offeriert** VT (*Comm, form*) to offer

Of|fer|te [ɔˈfɛrtə] F -, -n (*Comm*) offer

Of|fi|zi|al|de|likt [ɔfiˈtsiaːl-] NT (*Jur*) offence for which proceedings are brought directly by the public prosecutor's department

of|fi|zi|ell [ɔfiˈtsiɛl] ADJ *Meinung, Erklärung, Besuch* official; *Einladung, Besuch auch* formal; **wie von ~er Seite verlautet** according to official sources; **auf dem Empfang ging es schrecklich ~ zu** the reception was extremely formal ADV officially; **etw ~ bekannt geben** to announce sth officially

Of|fi|zier[1] [ɔfiˈtsiːɐ] M -s, -e (*Chess*) piece (*except pawn*)

Of|fi|zier[2] [ɔfiˈtsiːɐ] M -s, -e, **Of|fi|zie|rin** [-ˈtsiːrɪn] F -, -nen officer; **~ werden** to become an officer, to get or be given or gain a commission; (*als Beruf*) to become or be an army officer; **ers|ter/zweiter ~** first/second officer

Of|fi|ziers-: Of|fi|ziers|an|wär|ter(in) M(F) officer cadet; **Of|fi|ziers|ka|si|no** NT officers' mess; **Of|fi|ziers|korps** NT officer corps, the officers *pl*; **Of|fi|ziers|lauf|bahn** F officer's career, career as an officer; **Of|fi|ziers|mes|se** F officers' mess; **Of|fi|ziers|pa|tent** NT (*old*) commission

of|fi|zi|ös [ɔfi'tsiøːs] ADJ semiofficial

Off-Ki|no ['ɔf-] NT art-house or repertory (US) cinema

off|line ['ɔflaɪn] ADV (Comput) off line

Off|line|be|trieb ▲ ['ɔflaɪn-] M (Comput) off--line mode

öff|nen ['œfnən] VT to open; **jdm den Blick für etw ~** to open sb's eyes to sth, to make sb a-ware or conscious of sth; **eine Leiche ~** to open (up) a corpse; **das Museum wird um 10 geöff-net** the museum is open or opens at 10; **die Messe öffnet heute ihre Tore** or **Pforten** the (trade) fair opens its doors or gates today; **„hier ~"** "open here"; **eine Datei ~** (Comput) to open a file
▪ VI to open; **es hat geklingelt, könnten Sie mal ~?** that was the doorbell, would you answer it or would you get it?; **der Nachtportier öffnete mir** the night porter opened the door for me
▪ VR (Tür, Blume, Augen) to open; (= weiter wer-den) to open out; **sich jdm ~** to confide in sb, to open up to sb; **die Erde öffnete sich** the ground opened (up); **nach Norden hin öffnete sich die Schlucht** the gully widens or opens out or is open to the north; **die Landschaft öffnet sich** the landscape opens out; **vom Bürofenster aus öffnete sich der Blick auf die Berge** the office window offered a view of the mountains

Öff|ner ['œfnɐ] M -s, - opener

Öff|nung ['œfnʊŋ] F -, -en ⓐ no pl (= das Öff-nen) opening; (von Partei, Bewegung) opening up; **~ der Leiche** postmortem, autopsy; **eine Politik der ~ gegenüber dem Westen** a policy of opening up to the West ⓑ (= offene Stelle) o-pening

Öff|nungs-: Öff|nungs|kurs M (Pol) process of opening up; **Öff|nungs|po|li|tik** F policy of openness; **Öff|nungs|zei|ten** PL hours pl of business

Off|set|druck ['ɔfsɛt-] M pl -drucke offset (printing)

oft [ɔft] ADV comp ⸗er ['œftɐ], (rare) superl **am ⸗esten** ['œftəstn] (= häufig) often, frequently; (= in kurzen Abständen) frequently; **der Bus fährt nicht ~, die Bahn verkehrt öfter** the bus doesn't go very often, the train goes more often; **schon so ~, ~ genug** often enough; **wie ~ fährt der Bus?** how often or frequently does the bus go?; **wie ~ warst du schon in Deutschland?** how of-ten or how many times have you been to Ger-many?; **wie ~ wir das schon gehört haben!** how often we've heard that!, how many times have we heard that before!; **des Öfteren** quite often or frequently; **je öfter ...** the more often ...

öf|ter(s) ['œftɐ(s)] ADV on occasion, (every) once in a while; (= wiederholt) from time to time, (every) now and then; **öfter mal was Neu-es** (inf) variety is the spice of life (prov)

oft|mals ['ɔftmaːls] ADV (geh) often, oft (poet), ofttimes (poet)

o.g. abbr von **oben genannt**

oh [oː] INTERJ = **o**

O|heim ['oːhaɪm] M -s, -e (old) uncle

OHG [oːhaː'geː] F -, -s abbr von **offene Handels-gesellschaft**

Ohm¹ [oːm] NT -(s), - ohm; **ohmsches Gesetz** Ohm's Law

Ohm² M -s, -e (old) uncle

oh|ne ['oːnə] PREP +acc ⓐ without; **~ (die) Vor-orte hat die Stadt 100.000 Einwohner** exclud-ing or not including or not counting the sub-urbs, the city has 100,000 inhabitants; **~ mich!** count me out!; **er ist nicht ~** (inf) he's not bad (inf), he's got what it takes (inf); **die Sache ist (gar) nicht (so) ~** (inf) (= interessant) it's not bad; (= schwierig) it's not that easy (inf); **ihn wären wir immer noch dort** without him or but for him or if it weren't for him we'd still be there; **~ etw sein** to be without or minus (inf) sth; **~ Auto** without a or one's car; **~ Mehrwertsteuer**

excluding VAT; **er ist ~ jede Begabung (für Mu-sik)** he lacks or is without any (musical) talent; **~ einen** or **jeden Pfennig Geld** penniless, with-out a penny or dime (US), without two ha'pen-nies to rub together; **ich rauche immer ~** (inf) I always smoke untipped cigarettes
ⓑ **ich hätte das ~ weiteres getan** I'd have done it without a second thought, I'd have done it without thinking twice about it; **so et-was kann man ~ weiteres sagen** it's quite all right to say that; **so etwas kann man in feiner Gesellschaft nicht ~ weiteres sagen** you can't say that sort of thing in polite society; **ich wür-de ~ weiteres sagen, dass ...** I would not hesi-tate to say that ...; **er hat den Brief ~ weiteres unterschrieben** he signed the letter straight a-way or just like that; **das Darlehen ist ~ weite-res bewilligt worden** the loan was granted straight away or without any bother or prob-lem; **ihm können Sie ~ weiteres vertrauen** you can trust him implicitly; **das lässt sich ~ weite-res arrangieren** that can easily be arranged; **das ist nicht (so) ~ weiteres möglich** it can't be done just like that; **hast du das Geld gekriegt? – ja, ~ weiteres** did you get the money? – yes, no problem (inf); **dem Kerl kann man nicht ~ weiteres glauben** you can't just believe any-thing or whatever that guy says; **das kann man nicht ~ weiteres voraussetzen** you can't just as-sume that automatically; **diesem Vorschlag kann ich nicht ~ weiteres zustimmen** I can't just accept the suggestion without question; **du kannst doch nicht so ~ weiteres aus der Schule weglaufen** you can't just run away from school like that
CONJ **~ zu zögern** without hesitating; **~ dass ich ihn darum gebeten hätte, kam er mich be-suchen** he came to see me without my (Brit) or me inviting him; **wer redet, ~ gefragt zu sein ...** anybody who talks without being asked ...

oh|ne-: oh|ne|dem ['oːnə'deːm] (old), **oh|ne-dies** ['oːnə'diːs] ADV = **ohnehin; oh|ne|ei|nan|der** ['oːnəlaɪ'nandɐ] ADV without one an-other, without each other; **oh|ne|glei|chen** ['oːnə'glaɪçn̩] ADJ inv unparalleled; **ein Erfolg ~** an unparalleled success; **diese Frechheit ist ~** I've never known such a nerve!; **seine Frech-heit ist ~** I've never known anybody have such a nerve; **er singt ~** as a singer he is without compare or he's in a class by himself; **oh|ne-hin** ['oːnə'hɪn] ADV anyway; **wir sind ~ zu viel Leute** there are too many of us already or as it is; **es ist ~ schon spät** it's already late, it's late enough already, it's late enough as it is; **das hat ~ keinen Zweck** there is no point in (do-ing) that anyway

Ohn|macht ['oːnmaxt] F -, -en ⓐ (Med) faint, swoon (old); **in ~ fallen** to faint, to swoon (old); **aus der ~ erwachen** to come round or to, to recover consciousness ⓑ (geh = Machtlosig-keit) powerlessness, helplessness, impotence

ohn|mäch|tig ['oːnmɛçtɪç] ADJ ⓐ (= bewusstlos) unconscious; **~ werden** to faint, to pass out; **Hilfe, sie ist ~!** help, she's fainted!; **~ sank sie in seine Arme** she fainted into his arms, she collapsed unconscious into his arms ⓑ (geh = machtlos) powerless, impotent, helpless; **~e Wut, ~er Zorn** impotent or helpless rage ADV (= hilflos) helplessly, powerlessly, impotently; **ei-ner Sache** (dat) **~ gegenüberstehen** to be help-less or powerless in the face of sth; **~ zusehen** to look on helplessly

Ohn|machts|an|fall M (lit, fig) fainting fit; **als ich das hörte, habe ich fast einen ~ bekommen** (inf) when I heard that I nearly fainted or near-ly passed out

o|ho [oː'hoː] INTERJ oho, hello → **klein**

Ohr [oːɐ] NT -(e)s, -en ear; **seine ~en sind nicht mehr so gut** his hearing isn't too good any more; **auf einem ~ taub sein** to be deaf in one ear; **auf dem ~ bin ich taub** (fig) nothing doing (inf), I won't hear of it; **auf taube/offene ~en stoßen** to fall on deaf/sympathetic ears; **bei jdm ein aufmerksames/geneigtes/offenes ~ fin-**

den to find sb a ready/willing/sympathetic lis-tener; **ein offenes ~ für jdn/etw haben** to be ready to listen to sb/sth; **jdm ein geneigtes ~ leihen** or **schenken** (geh) to lend sb an ear or a sympathetic ear; **lange ~en machen** (inf) to prick up one's ears; **ein musikalisches ~ haben** to have a musical ear or an ear for music; **ein scharfes** or **feines ~ haben** to have a good ear; **die ~en hängen lassen** (inf) to look down in the mouth (inf) or down in the dumps (inf); **die ~en steif halten** (inf) to keep one's chin up; **die ~en anlegen** to put its ears back; **mach** or **sperr die ~en auf!** (inf) wash or clean out your ears (inf); **mir klingen die ~en** my ears are burning; **seine Kritik klingt ihnen noch immer in den ~en** his criticism is still ringing in their ears; **jdm die ~en voll jammern** (inf) to keep (going) on or moaning at sb; **die Wände haben ~en** walls have ears; **ganz ~ sein** (hum) to be all ears; **sich aufs ~ legen** or **hauen** (inf) to turn in (inf), to hit the hay or the sack (inf), to kip down (Brit inf); **sitzt er auf seinen ~en?** (inf) is he deaf or something?; **jdn bei den ~en neh-men, jdm die ~en lang ziehen** (inf) to tweak sb's ear(s); **für deutsche/englische ~en klingt das komisch** that sounds odd to German/Eng-lish ears; **diese Nachricht war nicht für fremde ~en bestimmt** this piece of news was not meant for other ears; **jdm eins** or **ein paar hin-ter die ~en geben** (inf) to give sb a clip round (Brit) or a smack on the ear; **ein paar** or **eins hinter die ~en kriegen** (inf) to get a clip round (Brit) or a smack on the ear; **jdm etw um die ~en hauen** (inf) or **schlagen** (inf) to hit sb over the head with sth; **schreib es dir hinter die ~en** (inf) will you (finally) get that into your (thick) head (inf), has that sunk in? (inf); **noch nass** or **feucht** or **nicht trocken hinter den ~en sein** to be still wet behind the ears; **jdm etw ins ~ sagen** to whisper sth in sb's ear; **die Melodie geht (leicht) ins ~** the tune is very catchy; **du hast wohl Dreck** or **Watte in den ~en!** (inf) are you deaf or something?, is there something wrong with your ears?; **ich habe seine Worte noch deutlich im ~** I can still hear his words clearly, his words are still ringing in my ears; **jdm (mit etw) in den ~en liegen** to badger sb (about sth), to keep on at sb (about sth) (inf); **mit halbem ~(e) hinhören** or **zuhören** to half lis-ten, to listen with half an ear; **jdn übers ~ hau-en** to take sb for a ride (inf), to pull a fast one on sb (inf); **bis über die** or **beide ~en verliebt sein** to be head over heels in love; **bis über die** or **beide ~en verschuldet sein** to be up to one's ears or eyes (Brit) in debt; **viel um die ~en ha-ben** (inf) to have a lot on (one's plate) (inf), to be rushed off one's feet (inf); **es ist mir zu ~en gekommen** it has come to my ears (form); **zum einen ~ hinein und zum anderen wieder hinaus gehen** (inf) to go in one ear and out the other (inf); **dein Wort in Gottes ~** God willing

Öhr [øːɐ] NT -(e)s, -e eye

Oh|ren-: Oh|ren|arzt M, **Oh|ren|ärz|tin** F ear specialist; **Oh|ren|beich|te** F (auricular) confession; **oh|ren|be|täu|bend** ADJ (fig) deafening; **Lärm auch earsplitting** ADV **~ laut** deafeningly loud; **Oh|ren|ent|zün|dung** F ear infection; **Oh|ren|klap|pe** F earflap; **Oh|ren-krie|cher** M (= Ohrwurm) earwig; **Oh|ren-sau|sen** NT -s, no pl (Med) buzzing in one's ears; **Oh|ren|schmalz** NT earwax; **Oh|ren-schmaus** M **das Konzert war ein richtiger ~** the concert was a real delight to hear or a treat for the ears; **moderne Musik ist oft kein ~** modern music is often far from easy on the ear; **Oh|ren|schmer|zen** PL earache; **Oh|ren|schüt|zer** PL earmuffs pl; **Oh|ren|ses|sel** M wing chair; **Oh|ren|stöp|sel** M ear-plug; **Oh|ren|zeu|ge** M, **Oh|ren|zeu|gin** F earwitness

Ohr|fei|ge ['oːɐfaɪɡə] F -, -n slap (on or round (Brit) the face); (als Strafe) box on the ears (dated), clip round the ear (Brit), smack on the ear; **jdm eine ~ geben** or **verabreichen** or

verpassen (*inf*) to slap sb's face; **eine ~ bekommen** to get a slap round (*Brit*) or in (*US*) the face; **wenn du nicht gleich ruhig bist, bekommst du eine ~** if you don't shut up I'll box your ears (*dated*) or I'll give you a clip round the ear (*Brit*) or a smack on the ear

ohr|fei|gen ['oːɐfaign] **VT** *insep* **jdn ~** to slap or hit sb; (*als Strafe*) to box sb's ears (*dated*), to give sb a clip round the ear (*Brit*) or a smack on the ear; **ich könnte mich selbst ~, dass ich das gemacht habe** I could kick myself for doing it

Ohr|fei|gen|ge|sicht **NT** (*inf*) fish face (*inf*); **er hat so ein richtiges ~** he's got the sort of face you'd like to put your fist into

Ohr-: Ohr|ge|hän|ge **NT** (*form*) drop earrings *pl*; (*hum*) dangly earrings *pl*; **Ohr|hän|ger** M earring; **Ohr|läpp|chen** **NT** (ear)lobe; **Ohr|mu|schel** F (outer) ear, auricle (*form*)

Oh|ro|pax® ['oːropaks, oːro'paks] **NT** -, - earplugs *pl*

Ohr-: Ohr|ring M earring; **Ohr|ste|cker** M stud earring; **Ohr|wurm** M (*Zool*) earwig; **der Schlager ist ein richtiger ~** (*inf*) that's a really catchy record (*inf*)

Oi|mel ['ɔymǝl] M -s, - **a** (*inf*: = *großes Ding*) whopper (*inf*) **b** *pl* (*sl*: = *großer Busen*) knockers *pl* (*Brit inf*), hooters *pl* (*US inf*)

o.J. *abbr von* **ohne Jahr** n.d. (*no date*)

o je [o'jeː], **o je|mi|ne** [o'jeːmine], **o je|rum** [o-'jeːrʊm] **INTERJ** oh dear

OK¹ [oː'ka:] **NT** -, -s *abbr von* **Organisationskomitee**

OK² [oː'ka:] *abbr von* **organisierte Kriminalität**

o.k., O.K. [o'keː] *abbr von* **okay** OK

O|ka|pi [o'ka:pi] **NT** -s, -s okapi

o|kay [o'keː] **INTERJ** okay, OK

O|kay [o'keː] **NT** -s, -s okay, OK

Ok|ka|si|on [ɔka'zioːn] F -, -en (*Comm*) **a** (= *Ware aus zweiter Hand*) second-hand article **b** (= *Gelegenheitskauf*) (second-hand) bargain

ok|kult [ɔ'kʊlt] **ADJ** occult; **das Okkulte** the occult

Ok|kul|tis|mus [ɔkʊl'tɪsmʊs] M -, *no pl* occultism

Ok|ku|pant [ɔku'pant] M -en, -en, **Ok|ku|pan|tin** [-'pantɪn] F -, -nen occupier; **die ~en** the occupying forces or powers

Ok|ku|pa|ti|on [ɔkupa'tsioːn] F -, -en occupation

ok|ku|pie|ren [ɔku'piːrǝn] *ptp* **okkupiert** **VT** to occupy

Öko ['øːko] M -s, -s (*inf*: = *Umweltschützer*) Green

Öko- *in cpds* eco-, ecological; (= *die Umwelt betreffend auch*) environmental; **Öko-Au|dit** [-'au-dɪt] M OR NT -s, -s green or environmental audit; **Öko|bau|er** M -n, -n, **Öko|bäu|e|rin** F -, -nen (*inf*) ecologically-minded farmer; **Öko|bi|lanz** F ecological balance; **Öko|kri|mi|nel|le(r)** MF *decl as adj* environmental criminal; **Öko|kri|se** F ecological crisis; **Öko|la|den** M wholefood shop

Öko|lo|ge [øko'loːgǝ] M -n, -n, **Öko|lo|gin** [-'loːgɪn] F -, -nen ecologist

Öko|lo|gie [økolo'giː] F -, *no pl* ecology

Öko|lo|gie|be|we|gung F ecology movement

öko|lo|gisch [øko'loːgɪʃ] **ADJ** ecological, environmental **ADV** ecologically; *anbauen, aufziehen* organically; **~ wirtschaftende Betriebe** companies saving on natural resources

Öko|nom [øko'noːm] M -en, -en, **Öko|no|min** [-'noːmɪn] F -, -nen **a** economist **b** (*obs*) bailiff

Öko|no|mie [økono'miː] F -, -n **a** *no pl* (= *Wirtschaftlichkeit*) economy; **durch kluge ~ hat er das Unternehmen wieder auf die Beine gestellt** by clever economies he put the concern back on its feet again **b** (= *Wirtschaft*) economy **c**

no pl (= *Wirtschaftswissenschaft*) economics *sing*; **politische ~ studieren** to study political economy **d** (*Aus*: = *Landwirtschaftsbetrieb*) farm

öko|no|misch [øko'noːmɪʃ] **ADJ** **a** economic **b** (= *sparsam*) economic(al) **ADV** economically; **~ mit etw umgehen** to be sparing with sth; **etw ~ einsetzen** to use sth sparingly; **~ wirtschaften** to be economical

Öko-: Öko|pa|pier NT recycled paper; **Öko|par|tei** F ecology party; **Öko|pax** ['øːko-paks] M -, -e (*inf*) campaigner for peace and the environment; **Öko|pa|zi|fis|mus** M environmental pacifism; **Öko|po|li|ti|ker(in)** M(F) ecologist politician; **Öko|sie|gel** NT eco-label; **Öko|sphä|re** F ecosphere; **Öko|sys|tem** NT ecosystem

Öko|tro|pho|lo|gie [økotrofolo'giː] F -, *no pl* home economics *sing*

Ok|ta|e|der [ɔkta'eːdɐ] NT -s, - octahedron

Ok|tan|zahl [ɔk'ta:n-] F octane number *or* rating; **Benzin mit einer hohen ~** high octane petrol

Ok|tav [ɔk'ta:f] NT -s, -e [-vǝ] octavo

Ok|tav|band [-bant] M *pl* -bände octavo volume

Ok|ta|ve [ɔk'ta:vǝ] F -, -n octave

Ok|tett [ɔk'tɛt] NT -s, -e octet

Ok|to|ber [ɔk'to:bɐ] M -(s), - October → *auch* **März**

Ok|to|ber|fest NT Munich beer festival

> ### OKTOBERFEST
>
> The beer festival known as the **Oktoberfest** takes place annually in Munich from the middle of September until the first weekend in October. Beer tents representing Munich's breweries are set up on the **Wies'n**, a large festival site in the city. In the tents local people and tourists sit at long wooden tables and drink a particularly strong festival beer served only in one-litre mugs. Pretzels and various kinds of sausage are available, and people sing along with the brass bands that are often in attendance.

Ok|to|ber|re|vo|lu|ti|on F October Revolution

ok|tro|yie|ren [ɔktroa'jiːrǝn] *ptp* **oktroyiert** **VT** (*geh*) to force, to impose (*jdm etw* sth on sb)

O|ku|lar [oku'la:ɐ] NT -s, -e eyepiece, ocular

o|ku|lie|ren [oku'liːrǝn] *ptp* **okuliert** **VT** *Obstbäume, Rosen* to graft, to bud

Öku|me|ne [øku'meːnǝ] F -, *no pl* ecumenical movement

öku|me|nisch [øku'meːnɪʃ] **ADJ** ecumenical; **~es Konzil** Ecumenical Council **ADV** **~ denken** to be ecumenically minded; **~ getraut werden** *to be married by a priest and a minister together*

Ok|zi|dent ['ɔktsidɛnt, ɔktsi'dɛnt] M -s, *no pl* (*liter*) occident

Öl [øːl] NT -(e)s, -e oil; **auf Öl stoßen** to strike oil; **Öl fördern** to extract oil; **nach Öl bohren** to drill for oil; **ätherische Öle** (*Chem*) essential oils; **in Öl malen** to paint in oils; **T(h)unfisch in Öl** tuna (fish) in oil; **Öl auf die Wogen gießen** (*prov*) to pour oil on troubled waters; **Öl ins Feuer gießen** (*prov*) to add fuel to the fire (*prov*); **solche Schmeicheleien gehen ihm runter wie Öl** (*inf*) he laps up compliments like that

Öl-: Öl|ab|schei|der [-ʃaidɐ] M -s, - oil separator; **Öl|baum** M olive tree; **Öl|berg** M **a** Mount of Olives **b** (*Art*) sculpture or painting showing Christ with 12 sleeping Apostles on the Mount of Olives; **Öl|bild** NT oil painting, oil; **Öl|boh|rung** F oil drilling, drilling for oil

Ol|die ['oːldi] M -s, -s (*inf*: = *Schlager*) (golden) oldie (*inf*)

Öl-: Öl|druck M **a** *pl* -drucke (*Bild*) oleograph **b** *no pl* (*Tech*) oil pressure; **Öl|druck|brem|se** F hydraulic brake

Old|ti|mer ['ɔːldtaimɐ] M -s, - **a** (= *Auto*) veteran car; (*Rail*) historic train; (*Aviat*) veteran plane, old bus *or* crate (*pej inf*) **b** (*Sport*) veteran, old timer **c** (= *Pferd*) old *or* retired racehorse

Ole|an|der [ole'andɐ] M -s, - oleander

Öl|em|bar|go NT oil embargo

ölen ['øːlǝn] **VT** to oil; **wie geölt** (*inf*) like clockwork (*inf*)

Öl-: Öl|ex|port|land NT oil-exporting country; **Öl|far|be** F oil-based paint; (*Art*) oil (paint *or* colour (*Brit*) or color (*US*)); **mit ~n malen** to paint in oil colours (*Brit*) or colors (*US*), to paint in oils; **Öl|feld** NT oil field; **Öl|film** M film of oil; **Öl|för|der|land** NT oil-producing country; **Öl|ge|mäl|de** NT oil painting; **Öl|ge|sell|schaft** F oil company; **Öl|göt|ze** M (*inf*) **wie ein ~** like a stuffed or tailor's dummy (*inf*); **Öl|hei|zung** F oil-fired central heating

ölig ['øːlɪç] **ADJ** oily; (*fig auch*) greasy **ADV** **~ verschmierte Gesichter** faces smeared with oil or (*fettig*) grease; **~ glänzende Gesichter** shiny faces; **~ triefender Fisch** fish dripping with oil

Oli|gar|chie [oligar'çiː] F -, -n [-'çiːǝn] oligarchy

Oli|go|pol [oligo'po:l] NT -s, -e oligopoly

Öl|in|dust|rie F oil industry

oliv [o'liːf] **ADJ** *pred* olive(-green); **ein Kleid in Oliv** an olive-green dress

Oli|ve [o'liːvǝ] F -, -n olive

Oli|ven-: Oli|ven|baum M olive tree; **oli|ven|far|ben** [-farbn], **oli|ven|far|big** ADJ *attr* olive-green; **Oli|ven|hain** M olive grove; **Oli|ven|öl** NT olive oil

o|liv|grün ADJ olive-green

Öl-: Öl|ka|nal M oil duct; **Öl|kan|ne** F, **Öl|känn|chen** NT oil can; **Öl|ka|tas|tro|phe** F (= *Tankerunglück*) oil spill disaster; **Öl|kon|zern** M oil company; **Öl|kri|se** F oil crisis; **Öl|ku|chen** M oil cake; **Öl|küh|lung** F oil cooling; **mit ~** oil-cooled

oll [ɔl] **ADJ** (*N Ger inf*) old; **je ~er, je** or **desto doller** (*prov inf*) there's no fox like an old fox (*prov inf*) → **Kamelle**

Öl|la|che [-laxǝ, -'la:xǝ] F patch of oil

Ol|le(r) ['ɔlǝ] MF *decl as adj* (*N Ger*) old man/woman; (= *Chef, Chefin*) boss; **mein ~r** (*inf*) (= *Vater*) the old man (*inf*); (= *Ehemann*) my old man (*inf*); **meine ~** (*inf*) (= *Mutter, Ehefrau, Freundin*) the old lady (*inf*)

Öl-: Öl|lie|fe|rant(in) M(F) oil producer; **Öl|ma|le|rei** F oil painting; **Öl|mess|stab** ▲ M (*Aut*) dipstick; **Öl|müh|le** F oil mill; **Öl|mul|ti** M (*inf*) oil conglomerate; **Öl|ofen** M oil stove or heater; **Öl|pa|pier** NT oil paper; **Öl|pest** F oil pollution; **Öl|platt|form** F oil rig; **Öl|quel|le** F oil well; **öl|reich** ADJ *Pflanze, Gegend* oil-rich; **Öl|reich|tum** M (*von Land*) rich oil reserves *pl*; **Öl|sar|di|ne** F sardine; **6 Leute im Auto, da sitzt ihr ja wie die ~n** (*inf*) with 6 people in the car, you must be crammed in like sardines (*inf*); **Öl|schal|ter** M (*Elec*) oil switch; **Öl|scheich** M (*pej*) oil sheik; **Öl|schicht** F layer of oil; **Öl|schie|fer** M oil shale; **Öl|sper|re** F oil barrier (*for containing oil spills*); **Öl|stand** M oil level; **Öl|stands|an|zei|ger** M oil pressure gauge; **Öl|tep|pich** M oil slick

Ölung ['øːlʊŋ] F -, -en oiling; **die Letzte ~** (*Eccl*) extreme unction, the last rites

Öl-: Öl|ver|brauch M oil consumption; **Öl|ver|knap|pung** F -, -en oil shortage; **Öl|vor|kom|men** NT oil deposit; **Öl|wan|ne** F (*Aut*) sump (*Brit*), oil pan (*US*); **Öl|wech|sel** M oil change; **ich muss mit dem Auto zum ~** I must take my car in for an oil change; **den ~ machen** to change the oil, to do an oil change

Olymp [o'lʏmp] M **-s** **a** (*Berg*) Mount Olympus; **die Götter des** ~ the gods of *or* on Mount Olympus; **in den ~ der Baukunst/der Politik aufsteigen** to climb to the top of the architectural/political world **b** (*Theat*) **der ~** the gods

Olympia [o'lʏmpia] NT **-(s)**, *no pl* (*liter*) the Olympic Games *pl*, the Olympics *pl*

Olympiade [olʏm'pia:də] F **-**, **-n** a (= *Olympische Spiele*) Olympic Games *pl*, Olympics *pl* **b** (*liter: Zeitraum*) Olympiad

Olympia-: Olympiamannschaft F Olympic team; **Olympiamedaille** F Olympic medal; **Olympiasieger(in)** M(F) Olympic champion, Olympic gold medallist (*Brit*) *or* medalist (*US*); **Olympiastadion** NT Olympic stadium; **Olympiateilnehmer(in)** M(F) participant in the Olympic Games

Olympier [o'lʏmpiɐ] M **-s**, **-**, **Olympierin** [-iərɪn] F **-**, **-nen** (*liter*) Olympian (*liter*)

Olympionike [olʏmpio'ni:kə] M **-n**, **-n**, **Olympionikin** [-'ni:kɪn] F **-**, **-nen** (*liter*) Olympic athlete

olympisch [o'lʏmpɪʃ] ADJ **a** (= *den Olymp betreffend*) Olympian (*auch fig*); **die ~en Götter, die Olympischen** (*liter*) the gods of *or* on Mount Olympus, the Olympian deities (*liter*) **b** (= *die Olympiade betreffend*); **die Olympischen Spiele** the Olympic Games

Öl-: Ölzeug NT oilskins *pl*; **Ölzweig** M (*lit, fig*) olive branch

Oma [o:ma] F **-**, **-s** (*inf*) granny (*inf*), grandma (*inf*); **die alte ~ da drüben** the old dear (*inf*) *or* old granny (*inf*) over there

Oman [o:ma:n] NT **-s** Oman

Omaner [o:ma:nɐ] M **-s**, **-**, **Omanerin** [-ərɪn] F **-**, **-nen** Omani

omanisch [o:ma:nɪʃ] ADJ Omani

Ombudsfrau [ɔmbʊts-] F ombudswoman

Ombudsmann [ɔmbʊts-] M *pl* **-männer** ombudsman

Omelett [ɔm(ə)'lɛt] NT **-(e)s**, **-e** *or* **-s**, **Omelette** [ɔm(ə)'lɛt] F **-**, **-n** omelette

Omen [o:mən] NT **-s**, **-** *or* **Omina** [o:mina] o-men

ominös [omi'nø:s] (*geh*) ADJ ominous, sinister ADV ominously

Omnibus [ɔmnibʊs] M bus; (*im Überlandverkehr*) bus, coach (*Brit*)

Omnibus-: Omnibuslinie F bus route; **Omnibusverkehr** M (*Stadtverkehr*) bus service; (*Überlandverkehr*) bus or coach (*Brit*) service

omnipotent [ɔmnipo'tɛnt, 'ɔmni-] ADJ (*liter*) omnipotent

Omnipotenz [ɔmnipo'tɛnts, 'ɔmni-] F **-**, *no pl* (*liter*) omnipotence

omnipräsent [ɔmniprɛ'zɛnt] ADJ (*geh*) omnipresent

Omnipräsenz [ɔmniprɛ'zɛnts] F **-**, *no pl* (*geh*) omnipresence

Omnivore [ɔmni'vo:rə] M **-n**, **-n** *usu pl* (*Zool*) omnivore

OmU *abbr von* **Original(fassung) mit Untertiteln**

Onanie [ona'ni:] F **-**, *no pl* masturbation, o-nanism

onanieren [ona'ni:rən] *ptp* **onaniert** VI to masturbate

Onanist [ona'nɪst] M **-en**, **-en** masturbator

On-dit [õ'di:] NT **-**, **-s** (*geh*) **einem ~ zufolge** as rumour (*Brit*) *or* rumor (*US*) has it, as being noised abroad (*liter*)

ondulieren [ɔndu'li:rən] *ptp* **onduliert** VT to crimp

Onkel [ɔŋkl] M **-s**, **-** **a** uncle; **~ Sam** (= *USA*) Uncle Sam **b** (*Kindersprache: = erwachsener Mann*) uncle; **sag dem ~ guten Tag!** say hello to the nice man!; **sieh mal den komischen ~ da!** look at the funny (old) man *or* guy (*inf*) over

there!; **der ~ Doktor** the nice doctor **c** (*inf*) **der große** *or* **dicke ~** your/his *etc* big toe; **über den ~ gehen** to walk pigeon-toed

Onkel-: Onkelehe F *cohabitation of widow with a man so that she keeps pension rights etc*; **onkelhaft** ADJ avuncular (*form*) ADV avuncularly (*form*); (*pej*) patronizingly

Onkogen [ɔŋko'ge:n] NT **-s**, **-e** (*Med*) oncogene

Onkologe [ɔŋko'lo:gə] M **-n**, **-n**, **Onkologin** [-'lo:gɪn] F **-**, **-nen** oncologist

Onkologie [ɔŋkolo'gi:] F **-**, *no pl* (*Med*) oncology

online ▲ ['ɔnlaɪn] ADJ *pred* (*Comput*) on line; **~ arbeiten** to work on line

Online- ▲ ['ɔnlaɪn] *in cpds* (*Comput*) on-line; **Online-Anbieter** ▲ M on-line (service) provider; **Onlinebetrieb** ▲ M on-line mode; **Onlinedatenbank** ▲ F *pl* **-banken** on-line database; **Onlinedienst** ▲ M on-line service; **Onlineservice** ▲ [-zø:ɐvɪs, -zœrvɪs] M on-line service

ONO *abbr von* **Ostnordost** ENE

Onomasiologie [onomaziolo'gi:] F **-**, *no pl* onomastics *sing*

onomatopoetisch [onomatopo'e:tɪʃ] (*form*) ADJ onomatopoeic ADV onomatopoeically

Önorm ['ø:nɔrm] F **-**, *no pl abbr von* **Österreichische Norm** Austrian standard

ontisch ['ɔntɪʃ] ADJ ontic

Ontogenese [ɔntoge'ne:zə] F **-**, *no pl* ontogenesis, ontogeny

ontogenetisch [ɔntoge'ne:tɪʃ] ADJ ontogenetic, ontogenic

Ontologie [ɔntolo'gi:] F **-**, *no pl* ontology

ontologisch [ɔnto'lo:gɪʃ] ADJ ontological; **der ~e Gottesbeweis** the ontological proof *or* argument

Onyx ['o:nʏks] M **-(es)**, **-e** onyx

OP [o:'pe:] M **-s**, **-s** *abbr von* **Operationssaal**

o. P. *abbr von* **ordentlicher Professor**

Opa ['o:pa] M **-s**, **-s** (*inf*) grandpa (*inf*); (*fig*) old grandpa *or* grandad (*inf*); **na ~, nun mach mal schneller!** come on grandpa, hurry up! (*inf*)

opak [o'pa:k] ADJ opaque

Opal [o'pa:l] M **-s**, **-e** opal

Op-Art ▲ ['ɔp|a:rt] F **-**, *no pl* op art

Opazität [opatsi'tɛ:t] F **-**, *no pl* opacity

OPEC ['o:pɛk] F **- die ~** OPEC; **~-Länder** OPEC countries *pl*

Open Air ['o:pn ɛɐ] NT **-s**, **-s** (= *Festival*) open-air festival

Oper ['o:pɐ] F **-**, **-n** opera; (*Ensemble*) Opera; (= *Opernhaus*) opera, opera house; **in die ~ gehen** to go to the opera; **an die** *or* **zur ~ gehen** to take up opera-singing, to become an opera singer; **die Wiener/Zürcher ~** the Vienna/Zurich Opera; **quatsch keine ~!** (*inf*) stop going on! (*inf*)

Operand [opə'rant] M **-en**, **-en** (*Comput*) operand

Operateur [opəra'tø:ɐ] M **-s**, **-e**, **Operateurin** [-'tø:rɪn] F **-**, **-nen** **a** (*Med*) surgeon **b** (*old: im Kino*) projectionist

Operation [opəra'tsio:n] F **-**, **-en** operation

Operations-: Operationsnarbe F operation scar; **Operationssaal** M operating theatre (*Brit*) *or* room (*US*); **Operationsschwester** M theatre sister (*Brit*), operating room nurse (*US*); **Operationstisch** M operating table

operativ [opəra'ti:f] ADJ **a** (*Med*) operative, surgical; **das ist nur durch einen ~en Eingriff zu beseitigen** that can only be removed by (means of) surgery **b** (*Mil*) *Pläne, Planung, Stab* operational, strategic

c (*Econ*) *Ergebnis, Verluste* operational ADV **a** (*Med*) surgically; **eine Geschwulst ~ entfernen** to remove a growth surgically *or* by surgery **b** (*Mil*) strategically; **~ denken** to think strategically; **wir sollten ~ vorgehen** we should attempt to develop a strategy **c** (*Econ*) **das Unternehmen steckt ~ in den roten Zahlen** the company is operating in the red; **die Firma wirtschaftet seit geraumer Zeit ~ mit Verlust** the firm has been operating at a loss for quite some time; **unser Betrieb ist auch in den USA ~ tätig** our company also has operations in the USA; **die Behörde sollte in dieser Sache ~ tätig werden** the authorities should take action on this matter

Operator ['ɔpəreɪtə, opə'ra:to:ɐ] M **-s**, **-s**, *or* (*bei dt. Aussprache*) **Operatoren** [-'to:rən], **Operatorin** [-'to:rɪn] F **-**, **-nen** (computer) operator

Operette [opə'rɛtə] F **-**, **-n** operetta

Operettenkaiser M (*hum*) stage emperor

operieren [opə'ri:rən] *ptp* **operiert** VT *Patienten, Krebs, Magen* to operate on; **jdn am Magen ~** to operate on sb's stomach, to perform an operation on sb's stomach; **der Blinddarm muss sofort operiert werden** that appendix must be operated on at once, that appendix needs immediate surgery VI **a** (*Med*) to operate; **die Ärzte haben drei Stunden an ihm operiert** the doctors operated on him for three hours; **sich ~ lassen** to have an operation; **ambulant ~** to operate on an out-patient basis **b** (*Mil*) to operate **c** (*fig* = *agieren, arbeiten*) to operate; **Arbeiter, die mit großen Maschinen ~** workers who operate large machines; **wir müssen in den Verhandlungen sehr vorsichtig ~** we must go *or* tread very carefully in the negotiations; **ein weltweit ~des Unternehmen** a worldwide business

Opern-: Opernarie F (operatic) aria; **Opernball** M opera ball; **Opernführer** M (*Buch*) opera guide; **Opernglas** NT opera glasses *pl*; **Opernhaus** NT opera house; **Opernsänger(in)** M(F) opera singer; **Operntext** M libretto

Opfer ['ɔpfɐ] NT **-s**, **-** **a** (= *Opfergabe*) sacrifice (*auch fig*); **zum** *or* **als ~** as a sacrifice; **die Gottheit verlangte zehn Jungfrauen zum** *or* **als ~** the god demanded the sacrifice of ten virgins; **sie brachten ein ~ aus Wein und Wasser dar** they made an offering of water and wine; **jdm etw zum ~ bringen, jdm etw als ~ darbringen** to offer sth as a sacrifice to sb, to make a sacrificial offering of sth to sb; **für ihre Kinder scheut sie keine ~** she sacrifices everything for her children, for her children she considers no sacrifice too great; **ein ~ bringen** to make a sacrifice **b** (= *Geschädigte*) victim; **jdm/einer Sache zum ~ fallen** to be (the) victim of sb/sth; **sie fiel seinem Charme zum ~** she fell victim to his charm; **ein ~ einer Sache (gen) werden** to be a victim of sth, to fall victim to sth; **täglich werden 28 Kinder ~ des Straßenverkehrs** every day 28 children are the victims of road accidents; **das Erdbeben forderte viele ~** the earthquake took a heavy toll *or* claimed many victims

Opfer-: opferbereit ADJ ready *or* willing to make sacrifices; **Opferbereitschaft** F readiness *or* willingness to make sacrifices; **opferfreudig** ADJ willing to make sacrifices; **Opfergabe** F (*liter*) (sacrificial) offering; (*Eccl*) offering; **Opfergang** M *pl* **-gänge** **einen ~ antreten** (*fig liter*) to make a huge sacrifice; **Opferlamm** NT sacrificial lamb; **der Bräutigam schritt wie ein ~ zum Altar** the groom walked to the altar like a lamb to the slaughter; **Opfermut** M self-sacrifice

opfern ['ɔpfɐn] VT **a** (= *als Opfer darbringen*) to sacrifice, to immolate (*form*); *Feldfrüchte etc* to offer (up); **sein Leben ~** to give up *or* sacrifice one's life; **die soziale Idee wurde auf dem Altar des freien Marktes geopfert** the idea of social responsibility was sacrificed on the altar of the free market

b (fig: = aufgeben) to give up, to sacrifice

VI to make a sacrifice, to sacrifice; **einem Gotte ~** (liter) to pay homage to a god (liter), to worship a god

VR a sich für etw ~ (= hingeben) to devote or dedicate one's life to sth; **sich** or **sein Leben für jdn/etw ~** to sacrifice oneself or one's life for sb/sth

b (inf: = sich bereit erklären) to be a martyr (inf); **wer opfert sich und isst die Reste auf?** who's going to be a martyr and eat up the leftovers? (inf), who's going to volunteer to eat up the leftovers?

Op|fer-: Op|fer|pfen|nig M small contribution; **Op|fer|rol|le** F role of (a/the) victim; **Op|fer|stät|te** F sacrificial altar; **Op|fer|stock** M offertory box; **Op|fer|tier** NT sacrificial animal; **Op|fer|tod** M self-sacrifice, sacrificial death; **er rettete durch seinen ~ den anderen das Leben** by sacrificing his own life, he saved the lives of the others; **Christus starb den ~ (für unsere Sünden)** Christ gave up his life (for our sins)

Op|fe|rung ['ɔpfərʊŋ] F -, -en (= das Opfern) sacrifice; (Eccl) offertory

Op|fer-: Op|fer|wil|le M spirit of sacrifice; **op|fer|wil|lig** ADJ self-sacrificing, willing to make sacrifices

O|pi|at [o'pia:t] NT -(e)s, -e opiate

O|pi|um ['o:piʊm] NT -s, no pl opium

O|pi|um-: O|pi|um|han|del M opium trade or traffic(king); **O|pi|um|höh|le** F opium den; **O|pi|um|rau|cher(in)** M(F) opium smoker

ÖPNV abbr von **öffentlicher Personennahverkehr**

O|pos|sum [o'pɔsʊm] NT -s, -s (Zool) opossum, possum (inf)

Op|po|nent [ɔpo'nɛnt] M -en, -en, **Op|po|nen|tin** [-'nɛntɪn] F -, -nen opponent

op|po|nie|ren [ɔpo'ni:rən] ptp **opponiert** VI to oppose (gegen jdn/etw sb/sth), to offer opposition (gegen to); **ihr müsst auch immer ~** do you always have to oppose everything or be against everything?

op|por|tun [ɔpɔr'tu:n] ADJ (geh) opportune

Op|por|tu|nis|mus [ɔpɔrtu'nɪsmʊs] M -, no pl opportunism

Op|por|tu|nist [ɔpɔrtu'nɪst] M -en, -en, **Op|por|tu|nis|tin** [-'nɪstɪn] F -, -nen opportunist

op|por|tu|nis|tisch [ɔpɔrtu'nɪstɪʃ] ADJ opportunistic, opportunist; **~e Infektion** (Med) secondary infection **ADV** opportunistically; **~ handeln** to act in an opportunist fashion; **da hat er sehr ~ gehandelt** that was very opportunist(ic) of him

Op|por|tu|ni|tät [ɔpɔrtuni'tɛ:t] F -, -en (geh) appropriateness

Op|por|tu|ni|täts|prin|zip NT , no pl (Jur) discretionary prosecution principle (principle allowing the public prosecutor to judge whether legal proceedings are appropriate in certain cases)

Op|po|si|ti|on [ɔpozi'tsio:n] F -, -en opposition (auch Pol, Astron); **etw aus (lauter) ~ tun** to do sth out of or from (sheer) contrariness; **diese Gruppe macht ständig ~ (gegen den Klassenlehrer)** (inf) this group is always making trouble (for the teacher); **in ~ zu etw stehen** to stand in opposition to sth; **in die ~ gehen** (Pol) to go into opposition

op|po|si|ti|o|nell [ɔpozitsio'nɛl] ADJ Gruppen, Kräfte opposition

Op|po|si|ti|ons- in cpds opposition; **Op|po|si|ti|ons|bank** F pl -bänke (Pol) opposition bench; **auf der ~ sitzen** to be in the opposition, to sit on the opposition benches; **Op|po|si|ti|ons|füh|rer(in)** M(F) (Pol) opposition leader;

Op|po|si|ti|ons|par|tei F (Pol) opposition, opposition party

OP-Schwes|ter [o:'pe:-] F abbr von **Operationsschwester**

Op|ta|tiv ['ɔptati:f] M -s, -e [-və] optative

op|tie|ren [ɔp'ti:rən] ptp **optiert** VI (form: auch Pol) **~ für** to opt for

Op|tik ['ɔptɪk] F -, -en **a** no pl (Phys) optics

b (= Linsensystem) lens system; **du hast wohl einen Knick in der ~!** (inf) can't you see straight? (inf), are you blind?

c (= Sicht, Sehweise) point of view, perspective; **das ist eine Frage der ~** (fig) it depends on your point of view; **in** or **aus seiner ~** in his eyes

d (= Mode, Aussehen) look; (= Schein) appearances pl; **das ist nur hier wegen der ~** it's just here because it looks good, it's just here for visual or optical effect; **die Partei muss sehen, dass sie die ~ ihrer Politik ein bisschen verbessert** the party must try to present their policies in a better light; **etw in die rechte ~ bringen** to put sth into the right perspective

Op|ti|ker ['ɔptɪkɐ] M -s, -, **Op|ti|ke|rin** [-ərɪn] F -, -nen optician

op|ti|mal [ɔpti'ma:l] ADJ optimal, optimum attr **ADV** perfectly; **etw ~ nutzen** to put sth to the best possible use

op|ti|mie|ren [ɔpti'mi:rən] ptp **optimiert** VT to optimize

Op|ti|mis|mus [ɔpti'mɪsmʊs] M -, no pl optimism

Op|ti|mist [ɔpti'mɪst] M -en, -en, **Op|ti|mis|tin** [-'mɪstɪn] F -, -nen optimist

op|ti|mis|tisch [ɔpti'mɪstɪʃ] ADJ optimistic **ADV** optimistically; **etw ~ sehen** or **einschätzen** to be optimistic about sth

Op|ti|mum ['ɔptimʊm] NT -s, **Optima** [-ma] optimum

Op|ti|on [ɔp'tsio:n] F -, -en **a** (= Wahl) option (für in favour of) **b** (= Anrecht) option (auf +acc on)

Op|ti|ons-: Op|ti|ons|an|lei|he F optional bond; **Op|ti|ons|aus|übung** F exercise (of option); **Op|ti|ons|emp|fän|ger(in)** M(F) grantee (of an option); **Op|ti|ons|fi|xie|rer** [-fɪksi:rɐ] M -s, -, **Op|ti|ons|fi|xie|re|rin** [-ərɪn] F -, -nen option issuer; **Op|ti|ons|frist** F option period; **Op|ti|ons|ge|schäft** NT dealing in options; (einzelne Transaktion) option transaction; **Op|ti|ons|preis** M option price; **Op|ti|ons|recht** NT option right; **Op|ti|ons|schein** M warrant

op|tisch ['ɔptɪʃ] ADJ visual; Gesetze, Instrumente optical; **~er Eindruck** visual or optical impact; **~e Täuschung** optical illusion **ADV a** (= vom Eindruck her) optically, visually; **die Bepflanzung lockert die Betonbauten ~ auf** the landscaping softens the appearance of the concrete structures; **dieser Bezirk unterscheidet sich schon rein ~ von ...** the very appearance of this area distinguishes it from ... **b** (= mit optischen Mitteln) optically; **die Daten werden ~ eingelesen** the data is read in optically

o|pu|lent [opu'lɛnt] (geh) ADJ Kostüme, Geldsumme, Feier lavish; Mahl, Inszenierung auch sumptuous **ADV** lavishly, sumptuously

O|pu|lenz F -, no pl (geh) lavishness

O|pus ['o:pʊs, 'ɔpʊs] NT -, **Opera** ['o:pəra] (pl rare) work; (Mus, hum) opus; (= Gesamtwerk) (complete) works pl, opus

O|ra|kel [o'ra:kl] NT -s, - oracle; **das ~ befragen** to consult the oracle; **er spricht in ~n** (fig) he talks in riddles → **Delphi**

o|ra|kel|haft (liter) ADJ oracular, delphic (liter) **ADV** ambiguously, mysteriously; **sich ~ ausdrücken** to talk in riddles

o|ra|keln [o'ra:kln] ptp **orakelt** VI **a** (= rätseln) **wir haben lange orakelt, was der Satz bedeuten sollte** we spent a long time trying to figure out what the sentence meant or trying to decipher

the sentence **b** (über die Zukunft) to prophesy, to prognosticate (hum)

o|ral [o'ra:l] ADJ oral **ADV** orally; **~ mit jdm verkehren** to have oral sex with sb

O|ral|ero|tik F , no pl oral eroticism

O|ral|sex M oral sex

o|ran|ge [o'rɑ̃:ʒə] ADJ inv orange; **ein ~** or **~ner** (inf) **Rock** an orange skirt

O|ran|ge¹ [o'rɑ̃:ʒə] F -, -n (Frucht) orange

O|ran|ge² NT -s - or (inf) -s orange

O|ran|gea|de [orɑ̃'ʒa:də] F -, -n orangeade (esp Brit), orange juice

O|ran|geat [orɑ̃'ʒa:t] NT -s, -e candied (orange) peel

o|ran|ge(n)|far|ben [o'rɑ̃:ʒə(n)farbn], **o|ran|ge(n)|far|big** ADJ orange(-coloured) (Brit), orange(-colored) (US)

O|ran|gen- [o'rɑ̃:ʒən-]: **O|ran|gen|haut** F , no pl (Med) orange-peel skin; **O|ran|gen|mar|me|la|de** F orange marmalade; **O|ran|gen|saft** M orange juice

O|ran|ge|rie [orɑ̃ʒə'ri:] F -, -n [-'ri:ən] orangery

O|rang-U|tan ['o:raŋ-'u:tan] M -s, -s orang-utan, orang-outang

O|ra|ni|en [o'ra:niən] NT -s Orange; **Wilhelm von ~** William of Orange; **der ~-Orden** the Orange Order

O|ran|je|frei|staat [o'ranjə-] M Orange Free State

O|ra|to|ri|um [ora'to:riʊm] NT -s, **Oratorien** [-riən] **a** (Mus) oratorio **b** (= Betraum) oratory

ORB [o:ɛr'be:] M - abbr von **Ostdeutscher Rundfunk Brandenburg**

Or|bit ['ɔrbɪt] M -s, -s orbit

Or|bi|ter ['ɔrbitɐ] M -s, -s orbiter

Or|ches|ter [ɔr'kɛstɐ, (old) ɔr'ʧɛstɐ] NT -s, - **a** orchestra **b** (= Orchesterraum) orchestra (pit)

Or|ches|ter-: Or|ches|ter|be|glei|tung F orchestral accompaniment; **Or|ches|ter|fas|sung** F orchestral version; **Or|ches|ter|gra|ben** M orchestra pit

or|chest|ral [ɔrkɛs'tra:l, (old) ɔrʧɛs'tra:l] ADJ orchestral

or|chest|rie|ren [ɔrkɛs'tri:rən, (old) ɔrʧɛs'tri:rən] ptp **orchestriert** VT to orchestrate

Or|chest|rie|rung F -, -en orchestration

Or|chi|dee [ɔrçi'de:(ə)] F -, -n [-'de:ən] orchid

Or|den ['ɔrdn] M -s, - **a** (Gemeinschaft) (holy) order **b** (= Ehrenzeichen) decoration; (Mil) medal, decoration; **~ tragen** to wear one's decorations; **jdm einen ~ (für etw) verleihen** to decorate sb (for sth); **einen ~ bekommen** to be decorated, to receive a decoration

or|den|ge|schmückt [-gəʃmʏkt] ADJ decorated, covered in decorations or (Mil auch) medals

Or|dens-: Or|dens|band [-bant] NT pl -bänder ribbon; (Mil) medal ribbon; **Or|dens|bru|der** M **a** (Eccl) monk; **meine Ordensbrüder** my brother monks **b** (von Ritterorden etc) brother member (of an order); **Or|dens|burg** F medieval castle built by a religious order; **Or|dens|frau** F (old) nun; **Or|dens|geist|li|che(r)** M decl as adj priest (in a religious order); **Or|dens|ge|mein|schaft** F (= Orden) (religious) order; (= Mitglieder) (total) membership of an order; **Or|dens|kleid** NT (liter) habit; **Or|dens|meis|ter** M master of an order; **Or|dens|re|gel** F rule (of the order); **Or|dens|schwes|ter** F nun; (= Krankenschwester) (nursing) sister; **Or|dens|tracht** F habit

or|dent|lich ['ɔrdntlıç] ADJ **a** Mensch, Zimmer tidy, neat, orderly

b (= ordnungsgemäß) **~es Gericht** court of law, law court; **~es Mitglied** full member; **~er Professor** (full) professor

c (= anständig) respectable

d (inf: = tüchtig) **ein ~es Frühstück** a proper or good breakfast; **eine ~e Tracht Prügel** a real beating, a proper hiding (inf)

e (*inf*: = *richtig*) real, proper
f (= *annehmbar, ganz gut*) *Preis, Leistung* reasonable
ADV a (= *geordnet*) zusammenlegen, stapeln, untereinander schreiben neatly; **hier geht es ~ zu** we do things by the book here; **in ihrem Haushalt geht es sehr ~ zu** she runs a very orderly household; **bei ihr sieht es immer ~ aus** her house always looks neat and tidy
b (= *ordnungsgemäß*) anmelden, abmelden, regeln correctly; *studieren, lernen* seriously; **~ arbeiten** to be a thorough and precise worker
c (= *anständig*) sich kleiden appropriately; *hinlegen, aufhängen* properly, right; **sich ~ benehmen** to behave properly
d (*inf*: = *tüchtig*) **~ essen** to eat heartily, to eat (really) well; **nicht ~ essen** not to eat properly; **~ trinken** to drink a lot; **ihr habt sicher Hunger, greift ~ zu** you're sure to be hungry, tuck in (*Brit inf*) or dig in (*inf*); **alle haben ~ zugelangt** everyone got stuck in (*inf*); **jdn ~ verprügeln** to give sb a real beating; **~ was wegschaffen** (*S Ger*) to get a lot done; **wir haben ~ gearbeitet** we really got down to it; **~ fluchen** to swear like a trooper (*Brit*) or sailor (*US*); **sich ~ vertun** to be way off (*inf*); **es hat ~ geregnet** it really rained; **~ Geld verdienen** to make a pile of money (*inf*)
e (= *annehmbar*) **ganz** or **recht ~** quite well

Or|der [ˈɔrdɐ] F -, -s or -n **a** (*Comm*: = *Auftrag*) order; **an ~ lautend** made out to order **b** (*dated*: = *Anweisung*) order; **jdm ~ erteilen** to order or direct or instruct sb; **jdm die ~ geben, etw zu tun** to give sb the order to do sth; **~ erhalten** or **bekommen, etw zu tun** to receive orders to do sth; **sich an eine ~ halten** to keep to one's orders; **ich habe meine ~ und daran halte ich mich** orders are orders, I have my orders and I'm sticking to them

or|dern [ˈɔrdɐn] VT (*Comm*) to order

Or|di|na|lia [ɔrdiˈnaːlia] PL ordinals *pl*

Or|di|nal|zahl [ɔrdiˈnaːl-] F ordinal number

or|di|när [ɔrdiˈnɛːɐ] ADJ **a** (= *gemein, unfein*) vulgar, common **b** (= *alltäglich*) ordinary; **was, Sie wollen so viel für eine ganz ~e Kiste?** what, you're wanting that much for a perfectly ordinary box or for that old box? **c** (*old Comm*: = *regulär*) *Preis* regular, normal **ADV** vulgarly; **~ aussehen** to look like a tart (*Brit inf*) or tramp (*US inf*); **wenn du dich so ~ schminkst, dann ...** if you wear such tarty (*Brit*) or trampy (*US*) make-up, then ...

Or|di|na|ri|at [ɔrdinaˈriaːt] NT -(e)s, -e **a** (*Univ*) chair **b** (*erz*)bischöfliches ~ archbishop's palace; (*Amt*) bishopric

Or|di|na|ri|us [ɔrdiˈnaːriʊs] M -, Ordinarien [-riən] **a** (*Univ*) professor (*für* of) **b** (*Eccl*) bishop, ordinary **c** (*old Sch*) form or class teacher

Or|di|na|te [ɔrdiˈnaːtə] F -, -n ordinate

Or|di|na|ten|ach|se F axis of ordinates

Or|di|na|ti|on [ɔrdinaˈtsioːn] F -, -en **a** (*Eccl*) ordination, ordaining **b** (*Med*: = *Verordnung*) prescription; (*old*: = *Sprechstunde*) surgery **c** (*Aus*) (doctor's) surgery (*Brit*) or office (*US*)

or|di|nie|ren [ɔrdiˈniːrən] *ptp* **ordiniert** VT **a** (*Eccl*) to ordain; **sich ~ lassen** to be ordained **b** (*Med*) to prescribe VI (*Med*: old, *Aus*) to hold or have surgery (hours) (*Brit*) or office (hours) (*US*)

ord|nen [ˈɔrdnən] VT **a** *Gedanken, Ideen, Material* to order, to organize; *Sammlung* to sort out; *Sektor, Markt* to organize; *Akten, Finanzen, Hinterlassenschaft, Privatleben* to put in order, to straighten out; **neu ~** *Struktur, Verhältnisse* to reorganize; *Kleidung, Haar* to straighten up; **das Steuerrecht wird neu geordnet** tax law is being reformed → *auch* **geordnet**
b (= *sortieren*) to order, to arrange; (*Comput*) to sort
VR to get into order; **allmählich ordnete sich das Bild** (*fig*) the picture gradually became clear, things gradually fell into place; **die Men-**

---

ge ordnete sich zu einem Festzug the crowd formed itself into a procession

Ord|ner¹ [ˈɔrdnɐ] M -s, - (= *Aktenordner*) file

Ord|ner² [ˈɔrdnɐ] M -s, -, **Ord|ne|rin** [-ərɪn] F -, -nen steward; (*bei Demonstration auch*) marshal

Ord|nung [ˈɔrdnʊŋ] ✪ 36.1 F -, -en **a** (= *das Ordnen*) ordering; **bei der ~ der Papiere** when putting the papers in order
b (= *geordneter Zustand*) order; **~ halten** to keep things tidy; **du musst mal ein bisschen ~ in deinen Sachen halten** you must keep your affairs a bit more in order, you must order your affairs a bit more; **in dem Aufsatz sehe ich keine ~** I can see no order or coherence in the essay; **~ schaffen, für ~ sorgen** to sort things out, to put things in order, to tidy things up; **seid ruhig, sonst schaff ich gleich mal ~** (*inf*) be quiet or I'll come and sort you out (*inf*); **Sie müssen mehr für ~ in Ihrer Klasse sorgen** you'll have to keep more discipline in your class, you'll have to keep your class in better order; **auf ~ halten** or **sehen** to be tidy; **etw in ~ halten** to keep sth in order; *Garten, Haus etc auch* to keep sth in; **etw in ~ bringen** (= *reparieren*) to fix sth; (= *herrichten*) to put sth in order; (= *bereinigen*) to clear sth up, to sort sth out; **ich finde es (ganz) in ~, dass ...** I think or find it quite right that ...; **ich finde es nicht in ~, dass ...** I don't think it's right that ...; **(das ist) in ~!** (*inf*) (that's) OK (*inf*) or all right!; **geht in ~** (*inf*) sure (*inf*), that's all right or fine or OK (*inf*); **Ihre Bestellung geht in ~** we'll see to your order, we'll put your order through; **der ist in ~** (*inf*) he's OK (*inf*) or all right (*inf*); **da ist etwas nicht in ~** there's something wrong there; **mit ihm/der Maschine ist etwas nicht in ~** there's something wrong or there's something the matter with him/the machine; **die Maschine ist (wieder) in ~** the machine's fixed or in order or all right (again); **das kommt schon wieder in ~** (*inf*) that will soon sort itself out; **es ist alles in bester** or **schönster ~** everything's fine, things couldn't be better; **jetzt ist die/seine Welt wieder in ~** all is right with the/his world again; **jdn zur ~ rufen** to call sb to order; **jdn zur ~ anhalten** to tell sb to be tidy; **jdn zur ~ erziehen** to teach sb tidy habits; **~ muss sein!** we must have order!; **~ ist das halbe Leben** (*Prov*) a tidy mind or tidiness is half the battle; **hier** or **bei uns herrscht ~** we like to have a little order around here; **hier herrscht ja eine schöne ~** (*iro*) this is a nice mess → **Ruhe**
c (= *Gesetzmäßigkeit*) order; **alles muss (bei ihm) seine ~ haben** (*räumlich*) he has to have everything in its right or proper place; (*zeitlich*) he does everything according to a fixed schedule; **das Kind braucht seine ~** the child needs a routine
d (= *Vorschrift*) rules *pl*; **sich an eine ~ halten** to stick or keep to the rules; **ich frage nur der ~ halber** it's only a routine or formal question, I'm only asking as a matter of form; **der ~ gemäß** according to the rules or the rule book
e (= *Rang, auch Biol*) order; **Straße erster ~** first-class road; **das war ein Skandal erster ~** (*inf*) that was a scandal of the first water (*Brit inf*) or first order; **ein Stern fünfter ~** a star of the fifth magnitude; **die ~ der Nagetiere** the order of rodents

Ord|nungs-: **Ord|nungs|amt** NT ≈ town clerk's office; **Ord|nungs|fa|na|ti|ker(in)** M(F) fanatic for order; **nicht alle Deutschen sind ~** not all Germans have a mania or passion for order; **Ord|nungs|geld** NT = Ordnungsstrafe; **ord|nungs|ge|mäß** ADJ according to or in accordance with the regulations, proper; **ich werde mich selbst um die ~e Abwickelung Ihrer Bestellung kümmern** I will see to it myself that your order is properly or correctly dealt with **ADV** correctly, properly; **der Prozess ist ~ abgelaufen** the trial took its proper course; **ord|nungs|hal|ber** ADV as a matter of form, for the sake of form; **Ord|nungs|hü|**

---

ter(in) M(F) (*hum*) custodian of the law (*hum*); **Ord|nungs|lie|be** F love of order; **ord|nungs|lie|bend** ADJ tidy, tidy-minded; **Ord|nungs|macht** F law enforcement agency; (*im Ausland*) peacekeeper, peacekeeping power; **Ord|nungs|ruf** M call to order; **in der Debatte musste der Präsident mehrere ~ erteilen** during the debate the chairman had to call the meeting to order several times; **einen ~ erhalten** to be called to order; **Ord|nungs|sinn** M , *no pl* idea or conception of tidiness or order; **Ord|nungs|stra|fe** F fine; **jdn mit einer ~ belegen** to fine sb; **ord|nungs|wid|rig** ADJ irregular; *Parken, Verhalten (im Straßenverkehr)* illegal **ADV** parken illegally; **~ handeln** to go against or to infringe rules or regulations; (*ungesetzlich*) to act illegally; **Ord|nungs|wid|rig|keit** F infringement; **Ord|nungs|zahl** F **a** (*Math*) ordinal number **b** (*Phys*) atomic number

Or|don|nanz [ɔrdɔˈnants] F -, -en orderly

Or|don|nanz|of|fi|zier M aide-de-camp, ADC

O|re|ga|no [oˈreːɡano] M -, *no pl* (*Bot*) oregano

Or|gan [ɔrˈɡaːn] NT -s, -e **a** (*Med, Biol*) organ; **kein ~ für etw haben** (*inf*) not to have any feel for sth **b** (*inf*: = *Stimme*) voice **c** (*fig*: = *Zeitschrift*) organ, mouthpiece **d** (= *Behörde, Einrichtung*) organ, instrument; (= *Beauftragter*) agent; (*von Polizei*) branch, division; **die ausführenden ~e** the executors; **wir sind nur ausführendes ~** we are only responsible for implementing orders; **beratendes ~** advisory body; **die staatlichen ~e** state organs

Or|gan-: **Or|gan|bank** F *pl* -banken (*Med*) organ bank; **Or|gan|emp|fän|ger(in)** M(F) (*Med*) organ recipient; **Or|gan|ent|nah|me** F (*Med*) organ removal; **Or|gan|han|del** M trade in transplant organs; **Or|gan|händ|ler(in)** M(F) organ dealer

Or|ga|ni|gramm [ɔrɡaniˈɡram] NT -s, -e organization chart

Or|ga|ni|sa|ti|on [ɔrɡanizaˈtsioːn] F -, -en organization

Or|ga|ni|sa|ti|ons-: **Or|ga|ni|sa|ti|ons|plan** M organization chart; **Or|ga|ni|sa|ti|ons|pro|gram|mie|rer(in)** M(F) (*Comput*) application programmer (*Brit*) or programer (*US*); **Or|ga|ni|sa|ti|ons|talent** NT talent or flair for organization; **er ist ein ~** he has a talent or flair for organization

Or|ga|ni|sa|tor [ɔrɡaniˈzaːtoːɐ] M -s, Organisatoren [-ˈtoːrən], **Or|ga|ni|sa|to|rin** [-ˈtoːrɪn] F -, -nen organizer

or|ga|ni|sa|to|risch [ɔrɡanizaˈtoːrɪʃ] ADJ *Schwierigkeiten, Maßnahmen* organizational; **eine ~e Höchstleistung** a masterpiece of organization; **er ist ein ~es Talent** he has a talent or flair for organization **ADV** organizationally; **er betätigt sich lieber ~, die Durchführung überlässt er anderen** he prefers organizing, leaving others to carry things out; **~ hatte einiges nicht geklappt** the organization left something to be desired; **so viele Leute zu koordinieren, dürfte ~ nicht so einfach sein** coordinating everything for so many people can't be very easy to organize; **dazu brauchen wir einen ~ versierten Menschen** we need someone with good organizational skills

or|ga|nisch [ɔrˈɡaːnɪʃ] ADJ *Chemie, Verbindung, Salze* organic; *Erkrankung, Leiden* physical; **ein ~es Ganzes** an organic whole **ADV a** (*Med*) organically, physically; *gesund* physically **b** (=

sinnvoll) **sich ~ einfügen** to merge, to blend (in +acc with, into)

or|ga|ni|sie|ren [ɔrgani'ziːrən] ptp **organisiert VT|I** (= veranstalten, aufbauen) to organize; **er kann ausgezeichnet ~** he's excellent at organizing; **etw neu ~** to reorganize sth **VR** to organize

or|ga|ni|siert [ɔrgani'ziːɐt] ADJ organized; **die ~e Kriminalität** organized crime

Or|ga|nis|mus [ɔrga'nɪsmʊs] M -, **Organismen** [-mən] organism

Or|ga|nist [ɔrga'nɪst] M -en, -en, **Or|ga|nis|tin** [-'nɪstɪn] F -, -nen (Mus) organist

Or|ga|ni|zer ['ɔrganaizɐ] M -s, - (Comput) organizer

Organ-: Or|gan|kla|ge F action brought against the Bundestag or Bundesrat by a Land or political party; **Or|gan|spen|de** F organ donation; **Or|gan|spen|der(in)** M(F) donor (of an organ); **Or|gan|spen|der|aus|weis** M donor card; **Or|gan|ver|mitt|lung** F transplant coordination; **Or|gan|ver|pflan|zung** F transplant(ation) (of organs)

Or|gan|za [ɔr'gantsa] M -s, no pl organza

Or|gas|mus [ɔr'gasmʊs] M -, **Orgasmen** [-mən] orgasm

or|gas|tisch [ɔr'gastɪʃ] ADJ orgasmic **ADV ~ gestört sein** to have problems experiencing an orgasm

Or|gel ['ɔrgl] F -, -n (Mus) organ

Or|gel|mu|sik F organ music

or|geln ['ɔrgln] VI **a** (inf: = Orgel spielen) to play the organ **b** (Hunt: Hirsch) to bell **c** (= tiefes Geräusch machen) (Motor) to growl; (Wind) to howl **d** (sl: = koitieren) to screw (sl)

Or|gel|pfei|fe F organ pipe; **die Kinder standen da wie die ~n** (hum) the children were standing in order of height, the children were standing like a row of Russian dolls

or|gi|as|tisch [ɔr'giastɪʃ] (geh) ADJ orgiastic **ADV ~ feiern** to celebrate wildly

Or|gie ['ɔrgiə] F -, -n orgy; **~n feiern** (lit) to have orgies; (fig) to go wild; (Phantasie etc) to run riot

Ori|ent ['oːriɛnt, o'riɛnt] M -s, no pl **a** (liter: = der Osten) Orient; **das Denken des ~s** Eastern thought; **vom ~ zum Okzident** from east to west **b** (= arabische Welt) ≈ Middle East; **der Vordere ~** the Near East; **der Alte ~** the ancient Orient

Ori|en|ta|le [oriɛn'taːlə] M -n, -n, **Ori|en|ta|lin** [-'taːlɪn] F -, -nen person from the Middle East

ori|en|ta|lisch [oriɛn'taːlɪʃ] ADJ Middle Eastern

Ori|en|ta|list [oriɛnta'lɪst] M -en, -en, **Ori|en|ta|lis|tin** [-'lɪstɪn] F -, -nen ≈ specialist in Middle Eastern and oriental studies (= Student) ≈ student of Middle Eastern and oriental studies

Ori|en|ta|lis|tik [oriɛnta'lɪstɪk] F -, no pl ≈ Middle Eastern and oriental studies pl; **~ studieren** ≈ to do Middle Eastern and oriental studies

ori|en|tie|ren [oriɛn'tiːrən] ptp **orientiert VT a** (= unterrichten) **jdn ~** to put sb in the picture (über +acc about); **unsere Broschüre orientiert Sie über unsere Sonderangebote** our brochure gives you information on or about our special offers; **darüber ist er gut/falsch/nicht orientiert** he is well/wrongly/not informed on or about that

b (= ausrichten: lit, fig) to orient, to orientate (nach, auf +acc to, towards); **ein positivistisch orientierter Denker** a positivistically orientated thinker; **am Text orientierte Illustrationen** text-related illustrations; **links orientiert sein** to tend to the left; **links orientierte Gruppen** left-wing groups

c (= hinweisen) to orient, to orientate (nach, auf +acc to, towards)

VI (= informieren) **unsere Broschüre orientiert über unsere Sonderangebote** our brochure

gives information on or about our special offers

VR a (= sich unterrichten) to inform oneself (über +acc about, on)

b (= sich zurechtfinden) to orientate oneself (an +dat, nach by), to find or get one's bearings; **in einer fremden Stadt kann ich mich gar nicht ~ I** just can't find my way around in a strange city; **von da an kann ich mich alleine ~** I can find my own way from there

c (= sich einstellen) to adapt or orientate (oneself) (an +dat, auf +acc to)

d (= sich ausrichten) to be orientated (nach, an +dat towards); **sich nach Norden/links ~** to bear north/left

Ori|en|tie|rung F -, -en **a** (= Unterrichtung) information; **zu Ihrer ~** for your information **b** (= das Zurechtfinden) orientation; **hier fällt einem die ~ schwer** it's difficult to find or get one's bearings here; **die ~ verlieren** to lose one's bearings **c** (= das Ausrichten) orientation (an +dat according to, auf +acc towards) **d** (= Ausrichtung) orientation (an +dat towards, auf +acc to); **sexuelle/politische ~** sexual/political orientation

Ori|en|tie|rungs-: Ori|en|tie|rungs|punkt M point of reference; **Ori|en|tie|rungs|sinn** M , no pl sense of direction

---

ORIENTIERUNGSSTUFE

The **Orientierungsstufe** (also called **Förderstufe**, **Beobachtungsstufe**, **Erprobungsstufe** and **Eingangsstufe**) is a way of structuring the fifth and sixth years at school. It allows the decision about the most suitable type of secondary school for a child to be postponed for a while. However, since the **Gymnasien** in particular consider it important that they have their own lower school, the **Orientierungsstufe** is usually spent in a **Gymnasium** or a **Realschule** before the decision regarding schools is taken → GYMNASIUM, REALSCHULE

Ori|ent|tep|pich M Oriental carpet; (= Brücke) Oriental rug

Orig. abbr von **Original**

Ori|ga|mi [ori'gaːmi] NT -(s), no pl origami

Ori|ga|no [o'riːgano] M -, no pl (Bot) oregano

Ori|gi|nal [origi'naːl] ADJ original **ADV ~ Meißener Porzellan** real or genuine Meissen porcelain; **Jeans ~ aus (den) USA** original American jeans; **~ verpackt sein** to be in the original packaging; **diese Tapete ist noch ~ erhalten** this is still the original wallpaper; **einige Häuser in der Altstadt sind noch ~ erhalten** some of the houses in the old town are original

Ori|gi|nal [origi'naːl] NT -s, -e **a** original **b** (Mensch) character

Original-: Ori|gi|nal|aus|ga|be F first edition; **Ori|gi|nal|ein|zug** M (bei Kopierer) automatic sheet feed; **Ori|gi|nal|fas|sung** F original (version); **in ~** in the original; **in der englischen ~** in the original English; **ori|gi|nal|ge|treu ADV** true to the original **ADV etw ~ nachmalen** to paint a very faithful copy of sth; **die Kopie sieht sehr ~ aus** the copy looks very much like the original; **Farben werden ~ wiedergegeben** colours (Brit) or colors (US) are faithfully reproduced; **etw ~ übersetzen** to give a true translation of sth

Ori|gi|na|li|tät [originali'tɛːt] F -, no pl **a** (= Echtheit) authenticity, genuineness **b** (= Urtümlichkeit) originality

Original-: Ori|gi|nal|ton M pl **-töne** original soundtrack; **(im) ~ Thatcher** (fig) in Thatcher's own words; **Ori|gi|nal|über|tra|gung** F live broadcast; **Ori|gi|nal|ver|packung** F original packaging; **in ~** (= ungeöffnet) unopened; (= in ursprünglicher Verpackung) in the original packaging

ori|gi|när [origi'nɛːɐ] ADJ Idee, Rechte, Aufgabe original **ADV eine ~ bayerische Trachtengruppe**

an original Bavarian folk dance group; **~ katholische Bräuche** originally Catholic customs

ori|gi|nell [origi'nɛl] ADJ (= selbstständig) Idee, Argumentation, Interpretation original; (= neu) novel; (= geistreich) witty; **sie ist ein ~er Kopf** she's got an original mind; **das finde ich ~ (von ihm)** that's pretty original/witty (of him) **ADV** originally; (= witzig) wittily; **sie denkt/argumentiert ~** her way of thinking/her arguments are very original; **das hat er sich (dat) sehr ~ ausgedacht** that's a very original idea of his

Or|kan [ɔr'kaːn] M -(e)s, -e **a** hurricane; **der Sturm schwoll zum ~ an** the storm increased to hurricane force **b** (fig) storm; **ein ~ der Entrüstung brach los** a storm of indignation broke out

Orkan-: or|kan|ar|tig ADJ Wind gale-force; Beifall thunderous; Geschwindigkeit tremendous; **Or|kan|stär|ke** F hurricane force; **Or|kan|tief** NT hurricane-force depression or cyclone or low

Or|kus ['ɔrkʊs] M -, no pl (Myth) Orcus, Hades; **etw im ~ verschwinden lassen** (hum) to consign sth to oblivion

Or|na|ment [ɔrna'mɛnt] NT -(e)s, -e decoration, ornament; **der Fries ist reines ~** the frieze is purely ornamental or decorative; **eine Vase mit figürlichen ~en** a vase decorated with figures; **etw mit ~en versehen** to put ornaments on/in sth

or|na|men|tal [ɔrnamɛn'taːl] ADJ ornamental **ADV** ornamentally

or|na|men|tie|ren [ɔrnamɛn'tiːrən] ptp **ornamentiert** VT to embellish, to ornament

Or|na|men|tik [ɔrna'mɛntɪk] F -, no pl (Art) **a** (= Verzierung) ornamentation **b** (Stil eine Epoche) decorative art

Or|nat [ɔr'naːt] M -(e)s, -e regalia pl; (Eccl) vestments pl; (Jur) official robes pl; **in vollem ~** (inf) dressed up to the nines (Brit inf) or hilt (US inf)

Or|ni|tho|lo|ge [ɔrnito'loːgə] M -n, -n, **Or|ni|tho|lo|gin** [-'loːgɪn] F -, -nen ornithologist

Or|pheus ['ɔrfɔys] M -' Orpheus

or|phisch ['ɔrfɪʃ] ADJ Orphic

Ort¹ [ɔrt] M -(e)s, -e **a** (= Platz, Stelle) place; **~ des Treffens** meeting place, venue; **hier bin ich wohl nicht am rechten ~** I've obviously not come to the right place; **das Bügeleisen ist nicht an seinem ~** the iron is not in its usual place; **ein ~ der Stille/des Friedens** a place of quiet/of peace; **ein ~ der Einkehr** a place for thinking quietly; **~ der Handlung** (Theat) scene of the action; **an den ~ der Tat** or **des Verbrechens zurückkehren** to return to the scene of the crime; **hier ist nicht der ~, darüber zu sprechen** this is not the (time or) place to talk about that; **am angegebenen ~** in the place quoted, loc cit abbr; **ohne ~ und Jahr** without indication of place and date of publication; **an ~ und Stelle** on the spot, there and then; **an ~ und Stelle ankommen** to arrive (at one's destination); **das ist höheren ~(e)s entschieden worden** (hum, form) the decision came from higher places or from above; **höheren ~(e)s ist das bemerkt worden** (hum, form) it's been noticed in high places; **an ~ treten** (Sw fig) to make no progress or headway

b (= Ortschaft) place; (= Dorf) village; (= Stadt) town; **in einem kleinen ~ in Cornwall** in a little spot in Cornwall; **jeder größere ~ hat ein Postamt** a place of any size has a post office; **~e über 100.000 Einwohner** places with more than or with over 100,000 inhabitants; **er ist im ganzen ~ bekannt** everyone knows him, the whole village/town etc knows him; **wir sind mit dem halben ~ verwandt** we're related to half the people in the place; **am ~** in the place; **das beste Hotel am ~** the best hotel in town; **wir haben keinen Arzt am ~** we have no resident doctor; **am ~ wohnen** to live in the same village/town; **mitten im ~** in the centre (Brit) or center (US) (of the place/town); **der nächste ~** the next village/town *etc*; **von ~ zu ~** from place to place

Ort² M **-(e)s, ̈er** ['ɔrtə] **a** position (*auch Astron*); (*Math*) locus **b** (*Min*) coal face, (working) face; **vor ~** at the (coal) face; (*fig*) on the spot; **Wartungsarbeiten vor ~ durchführen** to carry out on-the-spot *or* on-site servicing

Ört|chen ['œrtçən] NT **-s, -** (= *kleiner Ort*) small place; **das (stille** *or* **gewisse) ~** (*inf*) the smallest room (*inf*)

or|ten ['ɔrtn] VT *U-Boot, Flugzeug* to locate, to fix the position of, to get a fix on; *Fischschwarm, Gegenstand* to locate; (*fig: = ausfindig machen*) to locate

or|tho|dox [ɔrto'dɔks] **ADJ** (*lit, fig*) orthodox **ADV a** (*Rel*) **~ leben** to lead an orthodox life; **~ heiraten** to be married in the Eastern Orthodox Church; (*jüdisch*) to be married in an orthodox Jewish ceremony **b** (= *starr*) **denken** conventionally; **~ an etw** (*dat*) **festhalten** to stick rigidly to sth

Or|tho|do|xie [ɔrtodɔ'ksiː] F **-, no pl** orthodoxy

Or|tho|gra|fie ▲ [ɔrtogra'fiː] F **-, -n** [-'fiːən] orthography

or|tho|gra|fisch ▲ [ɔrto'graːfɪʃ] **ADJ** orthographic(al) **ADV** orthographically; **ein ~ schwieriges Wort** a hard *or* difficult word to spell; **er schreibt nicht immer ~ richtig** his spelling is not always correct

Or|tho|pä|de [ɔrto'pɛːdə] M **-n, -n, Or|tho|pä|din** [-'pɛːdɪn] F **-, -nen** orthopaedist (*Brit*), orthopedist (*US*), orthopaedic (*Brit*) *or* orthopedic (*US*) specialist

Or|tho|pä|die [ɔrtopɛ'diː] F **-, no pl a** (= *Wissenschaft*) orthopaedics *pl* (*Brit*), orthopedics *pl* (*US*) **b** (*inf: = Abteilung*) orthopaedic (*Brit*) *or* orthopedic (*US*) department; **auf der ~ liegen** to be in an orthopaedic (*Brit*) *or* orthopedic (*US*) ward, to be in an orthopaedic (*Brit*) *or* orthopedic (*US*) ward

or|tho|pä|disch [ɔrto'pɛːdɪʃ] **ADJ** orthopaedic (*Brit*), orthopedic (*US*)

ört|lich ['œrtlɪç] **ADJ** local **ADV** locally; **das ist ~ verschieden** it varies from place to place; **der Konflikt war ~ begrenzt** the conflict was limited to one area; **jdn/etw ~ betäuben** to give sb/ sth a local anaesthetic (*Brit*) *or* anesthetic (*US*); **er war nur ~ betäubt** he was only under local anaesthetic (*Brit*) *or* anesthetic (*US*), he had only had a local anaesthetic (*Brit*) *or* anesthetic (*US*); **~ desorientiert sein** to be disoriented

Ört|lich|keit F **-, -en** locality; **sich mit der ~/den ~en vertraut machen** to get to know the place; **er ist mit den ~en gut vertraut** he knows his way about; **die ~en** (*euph*) the cloakroom (*euph*)

Orts-: Orts|an|ga|be F place of publication; (*bei Anschriften*) (name of the) town; (= *Standortangabe*) (name of) location; (*Theat: = Szenenbeschreibung*) location; **ohne ~** no place of publication indicated; **orts|an|säs|sig** ADJ local; **eine schon lange ~e Firma** a long established local firm; **sind Sie schon lange ~?** have you been living here *or* locally for a long time?; **die Ortsansässigen** the local residents; **Orts|aus|gang** M way out of the village/town; **am ~** as you leave the village/town; **Orts|be|reich** M local area; **im ~ München** in the Munich area; **Orts|be|stim|mung** F Fehler bei der ~ navigational error; **die ~ mit dem Kompass** getting one's bearings with a compass; **die ~ einer Partei** vornehmen to locate a party's political position; **Orts|bild** NT town's/village's apperance; (*architektonisch*) townscape; (*von Großstadt*) cityscape

Ort|schaft ['ɔrtʃaft] F **-, -en** village; (*größer*) town; **geschlossene ~** built-up *or* restricted area

Orts-: Orts|ein|gang M way into the village/ town; **orts|fest** ADJ fixed; **orts|fremd** ADJ non-local; **ich bin hier ~** I'm a stranger here;

ein Ortsfremder a stranger; **orts|ge|bun|den** ADJ local; (= *stationär*) stationary; *Person* tied to the locality *pred*; *Industrie* resources-bound; **Orts|ge|spräch** NT (*Telec*) local call; **Orts|grup|pe** F local branch *or* group; **Orts|kennt|nis** F local knowledge; **(gute) ~se haben** to know one's way around (well); **Orts|kern** M centre (*Brit*) *or* center (*US*)(of the village/town); **Orts|klas|se** F classification of area according to cost of living for estimating salary weighting allowances; **Orts|kran|ken|kas|se** F **Allgemeine ~** compulsory medical insurance scheme; **orts|kun|dig** ADJ **nehmen Sie sich einen ~en Führer** get a guide who knows his way around; **ich bin nicht sehr ~** I don't know my way around very well; **ein Ortskundiger** somebody who knows his way around *or* who knows the area; **Orts|mit|te** F centre (*Brit*), center (*US*); **Orts|na|me** M place name; **Orts|netz** NT (*Telec*) local (telephone) exchange area; (*Elec*) local grid; **Orts|netz|kenn|zahl** F (*Telec*) dialling (*Brit*) *or* dialing (*US*) code; **Orts|re|gis|ter** NT index of places; **Orts|schild** NT place name sign; **Orts|sinn** M sense of direction; **Orts|ta|rif** M (*bei Briefen*) local postal charge; (*Telec*) charge for local phone call; **orts|üb|lich** ADJ local; **~e Mieten** standard local rents; **das ist hier ~** it is usual *or* customary here, it is (a) local custom here; **Orts|um|ge|hung** F (*Straße*) bypass; **Orts|ver|band** M local committee; **Orts|ver|kehr** M local traffic; **selbst im ~ hat der Brief noch drei Tage gebraucht** even a local letter took three days; **Gebühren im ~** (*Telec*) charges for local (phone) calls; (*von Briefen*) local postage rates; **Orts|zeit** F local time; **Orts|zu|la|ge** F , **Orts|zu|schlag** M (local) weighting allowance

Or|tung ['ɔrtʊŋ] F **-, -en** locating; **bei (der) ~ eines feindlichen U-Boots ...** when locating an *or* fixing the position of *or* getting a fix on an enemy submarine ...

O-Saft ['oː-] M (*inf*) orange juice, O-J (*US inf*)

Os|car ['ɔskar] M **-(s), -s** Oscar

Os|car|preis|trä|ger(in) M(F) Oscar winner

Os|car|ver|lei|hung F Oscar award ceremony; **die ~** the Oscars *pl* (*inf*)

Ö|se ['øːzə] F **-, -n** loop; (*an Kleidung*) eye → **Haken**

Ö|sen|zan|ge F eyelet punch

Os|lo ['ɔslo] NT **-s** Oslo

Os|lo|er ['ɔsloːɐ] M **-s, -, Os|lo|e|rin** [-ərɪn] F **-, -nen** person from Oslo

Os|ma|ne [ɔs'maːnə] M **-n, -n, Os|ma|nin** [-'maːnɪn] F **-, -nen** Ottoman

os|ma|nisch [ɔs'maːnɪʃ] ADJ Ottoman; **das Osmanische Reich** the Ottoman Empire

Os|mi|um ['ɔsmiʊm] NT **-s, no pl** (*abbr* **Os**) osmium

Os|mo|se [ɔs'moːzə] F **-, no pl** osmosis

OSO *abbr von* **Ostsüdost**

Os|si ['ɔsi] M **-s, -s** (*inf*) Easterner, East German

OSSI

Ossi is the jocular (or, depending on the intonation used, derogatory) term for a citizen of the former East Germany. The 40-year separation of the two Germanies and the differences between the two political systems has meant that West and East Germans have grown apart from each other. As a result there are still many prejudices on both sides about what exactly is typical of an **Ossi** or a **Wessi** → Wᴇꜱꜱɪ

Ost [ɔst] M **-(e)s, no pl** (*liter*) **a** East; **aus ~ und West** from East and West; **von ~ nach West** from East to West; **in ~ und West** in East and West, in the East and the West; **der Wind kommt aus ~** the wind is coming from the East; **wo ~ und West zusammentreffen** where

East and West meet, where East meets West; **10 Mark ~** (*DDR Hist*) 10 East German marks **b** (*liter: = Ostwind*) east or easterly wind

Ost-, ost- *in cpds* (*bei Ländern, Erdteilen*) (*als politische Einheit*) East; (*geografisch auch*) Eastern, the East of ...; (*bei Städten, Inseln*) East; **Ost|af|ri|ka** NT East Africa

Os|tal|gie [ɔstal'giː] F **-, no pl** (*inf*) ostalgia, nostalgia for the good old days of the GDR

Ost-: Ost|asi|en NT Eastern Asia; **Ost|ber|lin** NT (*Hist*) East Berlin; **Ost|ber|li|ner** ADJ *attr* East Berlin; **Ost|ber|li|ner(in)** M(F) East Berliner; **Ost|block** M , *no pl* (*Hist*) Eastern bloc; **Ost|block|land** NT , **Ost|block|staat** M (*Hist*) country belonging to the Eastern bloc, Eastern bloc country, Iron Curtain country; **ost|deutsch** ADJ East German; **Ost|deutsch|land** NT (*Geog*) East(ern) Germany

Os|ten ['ɔstn] M **-s, no pl a** east; (*von Land*) East; **der Ferne ~** the Far East; **der Nahe ~** the Middle East, the Near East; **der Mittlere ~** *area stretching from Iran and Iraq to India*, the Middle East; **im Nahen und Mittleren ~** in the Middle East; **aus dem ~, von ~** her from the east; **Flüchtlinge aus dem ~** (*Hist: aus ehemaligen deutschen Ostgebieten*) *German refugees displaced from former German territories in the East after World War II* **gegen** *or* **gen** (*liter*) **or nach ~** east(wards), to the east; **nach ~ (hin)** to the east; **im ~ der Stadt/des Landes** in the east of the town/country; **weiter im ~** further east; **im ~ Frankreichs** in the east of France, in eastern France

b (*Pol*) **der ~** (= *Ostdeutschland*) East Germany; (*dated: = Ostblock*) the East

os|ten|ta|tiv [ɔstɛnta'tiːf] **ADJ** pointed **ADV** pointedly

Os|te|o|po|ro|se [ɔsteopo'roːzə] F **-, no pl** (*Med*) osteoporosis

Os|ter-: Os|ter|ei NT Easter egg; **Os|ter|fei|er|tag** M Easter holiday; **am 2. ~** on Easter Monday; **an den ~en** at the Easter weekend; **über die ~e fahren wir weg** we're going away over the Easter weekend; **Os|ter|fest** NT Easter; **das jüdische ~** the Jewish Feast of the Passover; **Os|ter|feu|er** NT *bonfire lit on Easter Saturday*; **Os|ter|glo|cke** F daffodil; **Os|ter|ha|se** M Easter bunny; **Os|ter|in|sel** F Easter Island; **Os|ter|ker|ze** F paschal candle; **Os|ter|lamm** NT paschal lamb

ös|ter|lich ['øːstɐlɪç] ADJ Easter

Os|ter- ['oːstɐ-]: **Os|ter|marsch** M Easter peace march; **Os|ter|mon|tag** ['oːstɐ'moːntaːk] M Easter Monday; **Os|ter|mor|gen** M Easter morning

Os|tern ['oːstɐn] NT **-, -** Easter; **frohe** *or* **fröhliche ~!** Happy Easter!; **ein verregnetes ~, verregnete ~** a rainy Easter; **an ~** on Easter Day; **zu ~** an ~ at Easter; (**zu** *or* **über**) **~ fahren wir weg** we're going away at *or* over Easter; **wenn ~ und Pfingsten auf einen Tag fällt** (*hum*) if pigs could fly (*hum*); **das ist ein Gefühl wie Weihnachten und ~ (zusammen)** it's like having Christmas and Easter rolled into one, it's like having all your Christmases come at once

Os|ter|nacht F Easter eve; (*kirchliche Feier*) Easter eve service

Ös|ter|reich ['øːstɐraɪç] NT **-s** Austria; **~-Ungarn** (*Hist*) Austria-Hungary

Ös|ter|rei|cher ['øːstɐraɪçɐ] M **-s, -, Ös|ter|rei|che|rin** [-ərɪn] F **-, -nen** Austrian; **er ist ~** he's (an) Austrian

ös|ter|rei|chisch ['øːstɐraɪçɪʃ] ADJ Austrian; **~-ungarisch** (*Hist*) Austro-Hungarian; **das Österreichische** (*Ling*) Austrian

Os|ter-: Os|ter|sonn|tag ['oːstɐ'zɔntaːk] M Easter Sunday; **Os|ter|spiel** NT Easter (passion) play

Ost|er|wei|te|rung ['ɔst-] F (*von Nato, EU*) eastward expansion

Os|ter|wo|che ['oːstɐ-] F Easter week

Ost- [ɔst-]: **Ost|eu|ro|pa** NT East(ern) Europe; **ost|eu|ro|pä|isch** ADJ East(ern) European; **Ost|frie|se** [-'fri:zə] M , **Ost|frie|sin** [-'fri:zɪn] F East Frisian; **ost|frie|sisch** ADJ East Frisian; **Ost|frie|si|sche In|seln** PL East Frisian Islands pl; **Ost|fries|land** [-'fri:slant] NT -s East Frisia; **Ost|geld** NT (DDR) East German money; **ost|ger|ma|nisch** ADJ (Ling) East Germanic; **Ost|go|ten** PL (Hist) Ostrogoths pl

os|ti|nat [ɔsti'na:t] ADJ (Mus) ostinato; **~er Bass** ground bass, bass ostinato

Os|ti|na|to [ɔsti'na:to] NT OR M -s, -s or **Osti|nati** [-ti] ostinato

Ost-: **ost|in|disch** ['ɔst'ɪndɪʃ] ADJ East Indian; **Ostindische Kompanie** East India Company; **Ost|ju|de** M , **Ost|jü|din** F East European Jew; **Ost|kir|che** F Orthodox or Eastern Church; **Ost|ko|lo|ni|sa|ti|on** F (Hist) German medieval colonization of Eastern Europe; **Ost|küs|te** F East coast

Öst|ler ['œstlɐ] M -s, -, **Öst|le|rin** [-ərɪn] F -, -nen (inf) East German

öst|lich ['œstlɪç] ADJ Richtung, Winde easterly; Gebiete eastern; **30° ~er Länge** 30° (longitude) east ADV **~ von Hamburg/des Rheins** (to the) east of Hamburg/of the Rhine PREP +gen (to the) east of

Ost- [ɔst-]: **Ost|mark** F a no pl (Hist) Austria b pl -mark (DDR Hist inf) East German Mark; **Ost|nord|ost** M , **Ost|nord|os|ten** M east-north-east; **Ost|po|li|tik** F (Hist) Ostpolitik, West German foreign policy regarding the Eastern bloc especially East Germany and East Berlin; **Ost|preu|ße** M , **Ost|preu|ßin** F East Prussian; **Ost|preu|ßen** NT East Prussia; **ost|preu|ßisch** ADJ East Prussian

Öst|ro|gen [œstro'ge:n] NT -s, -e oestrogen (Brit), estrogen (US)

Ost- [ɔst-]: **Ost|rom** NT (Hist) Eastern (Roman) Empire, Byzantine Empire; **ost|rö|misch** ADJ Byzantine

Ost|see ['ɔstze:] F die ~ the Baltic (Sea)

Ost|see- in cpds Baltic; **Ost|see|ha|fen** M Baltic port; **Ost|see|in|sel** F island in the Baltic; **Ost|see|küs|te** F Baltic coast; **Ost|see|rat** M Baltic Council

Ost- [ɔst-]: **Ost|staa|ten** PL (in USA) the Eastern states pl, the East coast states pl; **Ost|süd|ost** M , **Ost|süd|os|ten** M east-south-

-east; **Ost|ver|trä|ge** PL (Pol) political, social and economic agreements made between West Germany and some Eastern bloc countries in the early 1970s; **ost|wärts** [-vɛrts] ADV eastwards

Ost-West-: **Ost-West-Ach|se** [-'vɛst-] F East--West link; **Ost-West-Be|zie|hung|en** F pl East-West relations pl; **Ost-West-Ver|hand|lun|gen** PL East-West negotiations pl

Ost|wind M east or easterly wind

OSZE [o:ɛstsɛt'le:] F abbr von **Organisation für Sicherheit und Zusammenarbeit in Europa** OSCE

os|zil|lie|ren [ɔstsɪ'li:rən] ptp oszilliert VI to oscillate

Os|zil|lo|graf ▲ [ɔstsɪlo'gra:f] M -en, -en oscillograph

O-Ton ['o:-] M pl **-Töne** abbr von **Originalton**

Ot|ter¹ ['ɔtɐ] M -s, - otter

Ot|ter² F -, -n viper, adder

Ot|tern|ge|zücht NT (Bibl) brood of vipers

Ot|to|ma|ne [ɔto'ma:nə] F -, -n ottoman

Ot|to|mo|tor ['ɔto-] M internal combustion engine, otto engine

ÖTV [ø:te:'fau] F abbr von **Gewerkschaft Öffentliche Dienste, Transport und Verkehr** ≈ TGWU (Brit), ≈ TWU (US)

Öt|zi ['œtsi] M -s Otzi, the Iceman, frozen mummified corpse found in the Alps in 1991 (fig inf) dinosaur

out [aut] ADJ pred Mode etc out

ou|ten ['autn] (inf) VT (als Homosexuellen) to out (inf); (als Trinker, Spitzel etc) to reveal, to expose VR (als Homosexueller) to come out (inf); **du solltest dich endlich ~** you really should come out (inf); **er outete sich als Schwuler** he came out (inf)

Out|fit ['autfɪt] NT -(s), -s outfit

Ou|ting ['autɪŋ] NT -s (inf: als Homosexueller) outing (inf); **er hat Angst vor dem ~** (geoutet zu werden) he's afraid of being outed (inf); (sich zu outen) he's afraid of coming out (inf)

Out|sour|cing ['autsɔ:rsɪŋ] NT -s, no pl outsourcing

Ou|ver|tü|re [uvɛr'ty:rə] F -, -n overture

o|val [o'va:l] ADJ oval ADV **ein ~ geformter Spiegel** an oval mirror; **ein ~ gerahmtes Bild** a picture with an oval frame

O|val [o'va:l] NT -s, -e oval

O|va|ti|on [ova'tsio:n] F -, -en ovation (für jdn/ etw for sb/sth); **jdm eine ~** or **~en darbringen** to give sb an ovation or a standing ovation; **stehende ~en** standing ovations

O|ver|all- ['o:vərɔ:l] M -s, -s overalls pl

O|ver|head- ['o:vɛhɛd-]: **O|ver|head|fo|lie** F transparency; **O|ver|head|pro|jek|tor** M overhead projector

O|ver|kill ['o:vɛkɪl] M -(s) overkill

O|vo|lac|to-Ve|ge|ta|bi|le(r) [ovo'laktovegeta'bi:lə] MF decl as adj ovo-lacto-vegetarian

ÖVP [ø:fau'pe:] F - abbr von **Österreichische Volkspartei**

O|vu|la|ti|on [ovula'tsio:n] F -, -en ovulation

O|vu|la|ti|ons|hem|mer [-hɛmɐ] M -s, - ovulation inhibitor

O|xer ['ɔksɐ] M -s, - (Sport) oxer

O|xid [ɔ'ksi:t] NT -(e)s, -e, **O|xyd** [ɔ'ksy:t] NT -(e)s, -e [-də] oxide

O|xi|da|ti|on [ɔksida'tsio:n] F -, -en, **O|xy|da|ti|on** [ɔksyda'tsio:n] F -, -en oxidation

o|xi|die|ren [ɔksi'di:rən] ptp oxidiert, **o|xy|die|ren** [ɔksy'di:rən] ptp oxydiert VTI (vi: aux sein or haben) to oxidize

OZ abbr von **Oktanzahl**

O|ze|an ['o:tsea:n, otse'a:n] M -s, -e ocean; **ein ~ von Tränen** an ocean of tears

O|ze|an|damp|fer M ocean steamer

O|ze|a|ni|en [otse'a:niən] NT -s Oceania

o|ze|a|nisch [otse'a:nɪʃ] ADJ Flora, Klima oceanic; Sprachen, Kunst Oceanic

O|ze|a|no|gra|fie ▲ [otseanogra'fi:] F -, no pl oceanography

O|ze|an|rie|se M (inf) ocean liner

O|ze|lot ['o:tsɛlɔt, 'ɔtsɛlɔt] M -s, -e ocelot

O|zon [o'tso:n] NT OR (INF) M -s, no pl ozone

O|zon-, o|zon- in cpds ozone; **O|zon|a|larm** M ozone warning; **O|zon|ge|halt** M ozone content; **O|zon|hül|le** F ozone layer; **O|zon|loch** NT hole in the ozone layer; **O|zon|schicht** F ozone layer; **O|zon|schild** M , no pl ozone shield; **O|zon|the|ra|pie** F ozone therapy; **O|zon|war|nung** F ozone warning; **O|zon|wert** M ozone level

---

P

P, p [peː] NT **-, -** P, p

paar [paːɐ] ADJ *inv* **ein ~** a few; (= *zwei oder drei auch*) a couple of; **ein ~ Mal(e)** a few times; (= *zwei- oder dreimal auch*) a couple of times, once or twice; **schreiben Sie mir ein ~ Zeilen** drop me a line; **die ~ Cent, die es kostet ...** the few cents that it costs ...; **der Bus fährt alle ~ Minuten** there's a bus every few minutes; **wenn er alle ~ Minuten mit einer Frage kommt ...** if he comes along with a question every other minute ...; **du kriegst ein ~!** (*inf*) I'll land you one! (*Brit inf*), I'll kick your butt (*US inf*)

Paar [paːɐ] NT **-s, -e** pair; (= *Mann und Frau auch*) couple; **ein ~ Schuhe** a pair of shoes; **zwei ~ Socken** two pairs of socks; **ein ~ Ochsen** a yoke of oxen; **ein ~ Würstchen** two sausages; **ein ~ bilden** to make or form a pair; **ein ~ mit jdm bilden** to pair off with sb; **ein ~ werden** (*liter:* = *heiraten*) to become man and wife (*form*), to be made one (*liter*); **ein ungleiches ~** an odd pair; (*Menschen auch*) an odd or unlikely couple; **das sind zwei ~ Stiefel** or **Schuhe** (*fig*) they are two completely different things

paa|ren ['paːrən] VT *Tiere* to mate, to pair; (*Sport*) to match; (*Chem*) to pair; (*fig*) to combine; **in seinen Bemerkungen sind Witz und Geist gepaart** his remarks show a combination of wit and intellect VR (*Tiere*) to mate, to copulate; (*Chem*) to be paired; (*fig*) to be coupled or combined

Paar|hu|fer [-huːfɐ] M (*Zool*) cloven-hoofed animal, even-toed ungulate (*spec*)

paa|rig ['paːrɪç] ADJ in pairs; **~e Blätter** paired leaves

Paar-: Paar|lauf M , **Paar|lau|fen** NT pair-skating, *pairs pl*; **paar+lau|fen** VI *sep irreg aux sein infin, ptp only to* pair-skate

paar|mal △ ['paːɐmaːl] ADV → **paar**

Paar|reim M (*Poet*) rhyming couplet

Paa|rung ['paːrʊŋ] F **-, -en a** (*Sport, fig liter*) combination; (*Sport:* = *Gegnerschaft*) draw, match **b** (= *Kopulation*) mating, copulation; (= *Kreuzung*) crossing, mating

Paa|rungs|zeit F mating season

Paar-: paar|wei|se ADV in pairs, in twos; **Paar|ze|her** [-tseːɐ] M **-s, -** cloven-hoofed animal, even-toed ungulate (*spec*)

Pacht [paxt] F **-, -en** lease; (*Entgelt*) rent; **etw in ~ geben** to lease sth (out), to let out sth on lease; **etw in ~ nehmen** to take sth on lease, to lease sth; **etw in** or **zur ~ haben** to have sth on lease or (on) leasehold

Pacht|brief M lease

pach|ten ['paxtn] VT to take a lease on, to lease; **du hast das Sofa doch nicht für dich gepachtet** (*inf*) don't hog the sofa (*inf*), you haven't got a monopoly on the sofa (*inf*); **er tat so, als hätte er die Weisheit für sich (allein) gepachtet** (*inf*) he behaved as though he was the only clever person around

Päch|ter ['pɛçtɐ] M **-s, -**, **Päch|te|rin** [-ərɪn] F **-, -nen** tenant, leaseholder, lessee (*form*); **er ist ~ eines Bauernhofs** or **auf einem Bauernhof** he's a tenant farmer

Pacht-: Pacht|er|trag M net rent; **Pacht|geld** NT rent; **Pacht|grund|stück** NT leasehold property; **Pacht|gut** NT , **Pacht|hof** M smallholding

Pach|tung ['paxtʊŋ] F **-, -en** leasing

Pacht-: Pacht|ver|trag M lease; **pacht|wei|se** ADV leasehold, on lease; **Pacht|zins** M rent

Pack¹ [pak] M **-(e)s, -e** or **ꞟe** ['pɛkə] (*von Zeitungen, Büchern, Wäsche*) stack, pile; (*zusammenge-schnürt*) bundle, pack; **zwei ~(e) Spielkarten** two packs of (playing) cards

Pack² NT **-s,** *no pl* (*pej*) rabble *pl* (*pej*), riffraff *pl* (*pej*); **~ schlägt sich, ~ verträgt sich** (*Prov*) riff-raff like that are at each other's throats one minute and friends again the next (*pej*)

Pack³ NT **-s, -s** (= *Paket*) pack, package

Päck|chen ['pɛkçən] NT **-s, -** package, (small) parcel; (*Post*) small packet; (= *Packung*) packet, pack; **ein ~ Zigaretten** a packet or pack (*esp US*) of cigarettes; **ein ~ Spielkarten** a pack of (playing) cards; **ein ~ aufgeben** to post (*Brit*) or mail (*esp US*) a small parcel; **jeder hat sein ~ zu tragen** (*fig inf*) we all have our cross to bear

Pack|eis NT pack ice

pa|ckeln ['pakln] VI (*Aus inf:* = *paktieren*) to make a deal (*inf*)

pa|cken ['pakn] VT **a** *Koffer* to pack; *Paket* to make up; (= *verstauen*) to stow or pack (away); **Sachen in ein Paket ~** to make things up into a parcel; **etw ins Paket ~** to put or pack sth into the parcel; **etw in Holzwolle ~** to pack sth (up) in wood shavings; **etw in Watte ~** to pack or wrap sth (up) in cotton wool; **jdn ins Bett ~** (*inf*) to tuck sb up (in bed) → **Watte**
b (= *fassen*) to grab (hold of), to seize, to grasp; (*Gefühle*) to grip, to seize; **jdn am** or **beim Kragen ~** (*inf*) to grab or seize sb by the collar; **von der Leidenschaft gepackt** in the grip of passion; **jdn bei der Ehre ~** to appeal to sb's sense of honour (*Brit*) or honor (*US*); **den hat es aber ganz schön gepackt** (*inf*) he's got it bad (*inf*)
c (*fig:* = *mitreißen*) to grip, to thrill, to enthral; **das Theaterstück hat mich gepackt** I was really gripped by the play
d (*inf:* = *schaffen*) to manage; **hast du die Prüfung gepackt?** did you (manage to) get through the exam?; **du packst das schon** you'll manage it OK
e (*inf:* = *gehen*) **~ wirs!** let's go
VI **a** (= *den Koffer packen*) to pack
b (*fig:* = *mitreißen*) to thrill
VR **a** (*inf:* = *abhauen*) to clear off (*Brit inf*) or out (*inf*); **packt euch (fort)!** clear off! (*inf*), beat it! (*inf*); **pack dich nach Hause!** clear off home! (*Brit inf*), clear out and go home! (*inf*)
b (*inf:* = *sich hinlegen*) to crash out (*inf*); **sich aufs Sofa ~** to crash out on the couch (*inf*)

Pa|cken ['pakn] M **-s, -** heap, pile, stack; (*zusammengeschnürt*) package, bundle; **ein ~ Arbeit** (*inf*) a pile of work

Packer¹ ['pakɐ] M **-s, -** (*Hunt*) boarhound

Packer² ['pakɐ] M **-s, -**, **Pa|cke|rin** [-ərɪn] F **-, -nen** packer

Pa|cke|rei [pakə'rai] F **-, -en a** packing department **b** *no pl* (*inf*) packing

Pack-: Pack|esel M packass, packmule; (*fig*) packhorse; **Pack|lei|nen** NT , **Pack|lein-wand** F burlap, gunny, bagging; **Pack|ma|te|ri|al** NT packing material; **Pack|pa|pier** NT wrapping or brown paper; **Pack|pferd** NT packhorse; **Pack|raum** M packing room; **Pack|sat|tel** M pack-saddle; **Pack|ta|sche** F saddlebag; **Pack|tier** NT pack animal, beast of burden

Pa|ckung ['pakʊŋ] F **-, -en a** (= *Schachtel*) packet, pack; (*von Pralinen*) box; **eine ~ Zigaret-ten** a packet or pack (*esp US*) of cigarettes **b** (*Med*) compress, pack; (*Kosmetik*) face pack or mask; **sich** (*dat*) **eine ~ machen** to have a face pack or mask; **jdm eine ~ machen** to put a face pack or mask on sb **c** (*Tech*) gasket; (*Straßenbau*) pitching *no pl*, ballast *no pl* **d** (*inf:* = *Niederlage*) thrashing, hammering (*inf*)

Pa|ckungs|bei|la|ge F (*bei Medikamenten*) enclosed instructions *pl* for use

Pack-: Pack|wa|gen M luggage van (*Brit*), baggage car (*US*); **Pack|zet|tel** M packing slip, docket

Pä|da|go|ge [pɛda'goːɡə] M **-n, -n**, **Pä|da|go|gin** [-'goːɡɪn] F **-, -nen** educationalist, pedagogue (*form*)

Pä|da|go|gik [pɛda'goːɡɪk] F **-,** *no pl* education, educational theory, pedagogy (*rare*)

pä|da|go|gisch [pɛda'goːɡɪʃ] ADJ educational, pedagogical (*form*); **~e Hochschule** college of education, teacher-training college (*for primary teachers*); **eine ~e Ausbildung** a training in education, a pedagogical training; **seine ~en Fähigkeiten** his ability to teach, his teaching ability; **das ist nicht sehr ~** that's not a very educationally sound thing to do ADV educationally, pedagogically; **~ falsch** wrong from an educational point of view; **das Spielzeug ist ~ wertvoll** it is an educational toy

pä|da|go|gi|sie|ren [pɛdagogi'ziːrən] *ptp* **pä-dagogisiert** VT (= *pädagogisch ausrichten*) to bring into line with educational or pedagogical theory VI (*inf:* = *über Pädagogik reden*) to talk education

Pad|del ['padl] NT **-s, -** paddle

Pad|del-: Pad|del|boot NT canoe; **Pad|del-boot|fah|rer(in)** M(F) canoeist

pad|deln ['padln] VI *aux sein or haben* to paddle; (*als Sport*) to canoe; (= *schwimmen*) to dog-paddle

Pad|dler ['padlɐ] M **-s, -**, **Padd|le|rin** [-ərɪn] F **-, -nen** canoeist

Pä|de|rast [pɛde'rast] M **-en, -en** pederast

Pä|de|ras|tie [pɛderas'tiː] F **-,** *no pl* pederasty

Pä|di|at|rie [pɛdia'triː] F **-,** *no pl* paediatrics *sing* (*Brit*), pediatrics *sing* (*US*)

pä|di|at|risch [pɛ'diaːtrɪʃ] ADJ paediatric (*Brit*), pediatric (*US*)

Pä|do|phi|le(r) [pɛdo'fiːlə] MF *decl as adj* paedophile (*Brit*), pedophile (*US*)

Pä|do|phi|lie [pɛdofi'liː] F **-,** *no pl* paedophilia (*Brit*), pedophilia (*US*)

paff [paf] INTERJ bang

paff|fen ['pafn] (*inf*) **VT** **a** (= *heftig rauchen*) to puff away **b** (= *nicht inhalieren*) to puff; **du paffst ja bloß!** you're just puffing at it! **VT** to puff (away) at

Pa|ge ['paːʒə] M **-n, -n** (*Hist*) page; (= *Hotelpage*) page (boy), bellboy, bellhop (*US*)

Pa|gen|fri|sur F, **Pa|gen|kopf** M page-boy (hairstyle *or* haircut)

Pa|ger ['peːdʒɐ] M **-s, -** (*Telec*) pager

Pa|ging-Dienst ['peːdʒɪŋ-] M paging service

pa|gi|nie|ren [pagi'niːrən] *ptp* **paginiert** VT to paginate

Pa|gi|nie|rung [pagi'niːrʊŋ] F pagination, page numbering

Pa|go|de [pa'goːdə] F **-, -n** pagoda

pah [paː] INTERJ bah, pooh, poof

Pail|let|te [pai'jɛtə] F **-, -n** sequin

pail|let|ten|be|setzt [pai'jɛtnbəzɛtst] ADJ *attr Kleidungsstück* sequin(n)ed

Pak [pak] F **-, -s** *abbr von* **Panzerabwehrkanone** anti-tank gun

Pa|ket [pa'keːt] NT **-s, -e** (= *Bündel*) pile, stack; (*zusammengeschnürt*) bundle, package; (= *Packung*) packet; (*Post*) parcel; (*fig: von Angeboten, Gesetzesvorschlägen*) package; (= *Aktienpaket*) dossier; (*Comput*) package; **ein ~ von Maßnahmen** a package of measures

Pa|ket-: Pa|ket|ad|res|se F stick-on address label; **Pa|ket|an|nah|me** F parcels office; **Pa|ket|aus|ga|be** F parcels office; **Pa|ket|bom|be** F parcel bomb; **Pa|ket|boot** NT packet (boat), mailboat; **Pa|ket|dienst** M parcel service, parcel post; **Pa|ket|kar|te** F dispatch form; **Pa|ket|post** F parcel post; **Pa|ket|schal|ter** M parcels counter; **Pa|ket|schnur** F parcel string, twine

Pa|kis|tan ['paːkɪstaːn] NT **-s** Pakistan

Pa|kis|ta|ner [pakɪs'taːnɐ] M **-s, -**, **Pa|kis|ta|ne|rin** [-ərɪn] F **-, -nen**, **Pa|kis|ta|ni** [pakɪs'taːni] M **-(s), -(s)** *or* f **-, -s** Pakistani

pa|kis|ta|nisch [pakɪs'taːnɪʃ] ADJ Pakistani

Pakt [pakt] M **-(e)s, -e** pact, agreement; **einen ~ (ab)schließen (mit)** to make a pact *or* agreement *or* deal (*inf*) (with); **einem ~ beitreten** to enter into an agreement

pak|tie|ren [pak'tiːrən] *ptp* **paktiert** VI **a** (*old:* = *Bündnis schließen*) to make a pact *or* an agreement **b** (*pej*) to make a deal (*inf*)

Pa|la|din [pala'diːn, 'paːladiːn, 'paːladiːn] M **-s, -e** (*Hist*) paladin; (*pej*) (= *Gefolgsmann*) henchman, hireling; (= *Land*) satellite

Pa|lais [pa'lɛː] NT **-, -** palace

Pa|läo-, pa|läo- [palɛo] **PREF** palaeo- (*Brit*), paleo- (*US*); **Pa|läo|li|thi|kum** [palɛo'liːtɪkʊm] NT **-s** Palaeolithic (*Brit*), Paleolithic (*US*)

Pa|lä|on|to|lo|gie [palɛɔntolo'giː] F **-, no pl** palaeontology (*Brit*), paleontology (*US*)

Pa|last [pa'last] M **-(e)s, Paläste** [pa'lɛstə] (*lit, fig*) palace

pa|last|ar|tig ADJ palatial

Pa|läs|ti|na [palɛs'tiːna] NT **-s** Palestine

Pa|läs|ti|nen|ser [palɛsti'nɛnzɐ] M **-s, -**, **Pa|läs|ti|nen|se|rin** [-ərɪn] F **-, -nen** Palestinian

Pa|läs|ti|nen|ser|füh|rer M Palestinian leader

Pa|läs|ti|nen|ser|tuch NT *pl* **-tücher** keffiyeh (*esp Brit*), kaffiyeh

pa|läs|ti|nen|sisch [palɛsti'nɛnzɪʃ], **pa|läs|ti|nisch** [pale'stiːnɪʃ] ADJ Palestinian

Pa|last-: Pa|last|re|vo|lu|ti|on F (*lit, fig*) palace revolution; **Pa|last|wa|che** F palace guard

pa|la|tal [pala'taːl] ADJ palatal

Pa|la|tal|laut [pala'taːl-] M palatal (sound)

Pa|lat|schin|ke [pala'tʃɪŋkə] F **-, -n** (*Aus*) stuffed pancake

Pa|la|ver [pa'laːvɐ] NT **-s, -** (*lit, fig inf*) palaver (*inf*)

pa|la|vern [pa'laːvɐn] *ptp* **palavert** VI (*lit, fig inf*) to palaver (*inf*)

Pa|le|tot ['paləto] M **-s, -s** (*obs*) greatcoat, overcoat

Pa|let|te [pa'lɛtə] F **-, -n** **a** (*Malerei*) palette; (*fig*) range **b** (= *Stapelplatte*) pallet

pa|let|ti [pa'lɛti] ADV (*inf*) OK (*inf*); **alles ~!** everything's OK! (*inf*)

Pa|li|sa|de [pali'zaːdə] F **-, -n** palisade

Pa|li|sa|den|wand F, **Pa|li|sa|den|zaun** M palisade, stockade

Pa|li|san|der M **-s, -**, **Pa|li|san|der|holz** NT jacaranda

Pal|la|di|um [pa'laːdiʊm] NT **-s**, *no pl* (*abbr* **Pd**) palladium

Pal|li|a|tiv [palia'tiːf] NT **-s, -e** [-və], **Pal|li|a|ti|vum** [palia'tiːvʊm] NT **-s, Palliativa** [-va] (*Med*) palliative

Pal|me ['palmə] F **-, -n** palm; **jdn auf die ~ bringen** (*inf*) to make sb see red (*inf*), to make sb's blood boil (*inf*); **unter ~n** under (the) palm trees; **einen von der ~ locken** (*sl:* = *onanieren*) to visit palm and her five sisters (*Brit sl*), to have a date with Mrs Handy (*US sl*)

Palm|fett NT (= *Palmbutter*) palm butter; (= *Palmöl*) palm oil

Pal|min® [pal'miːn] NT **-s**, *no pl* cooking fat (*made from coconut oil*)

Palm-: Palm|kätz|chen NT pussy willow, catkin (*Brit*); **Palm|li|lie** F yucca; **Palm|öl** NT palm oil; **Palm|sonn|tag** M Palm Sunday

Palm|top ['paːmtɔp] M **-s, -s** palmtop

Palm-: Palm|we|del M palm leaf; **Palm|wein** M palm wine; **Palm|zweig** M palm leaf

Pam|pa ['pampa] F **-, -s** pampas *pl*

Pam|pas|gras ['pampas-] NT pampas grass

Pam|pe ['pampə] F **-**, *no pl* paste; (*pej*) slop (*inf*), mush (*inf*)

Pam|pel|mu|se [pampl'muːzə] F **-, -n** grapefruit

Pam|pers® ['pɛmpɐs] PL (disposable) nappies *pl* (*Brit*) *or* diapers *pl* (*US*)

Pamph|let [pam'fleːt] NT **-(e)s, -e** lampoon

pam|pig ['pampɪç] (*inf*) ADJ **a** (= *breiig*) gooey (*inf*); *Kartoffeln* soggy **b** (= *frech*) stroppy (*Brit inf*), bad-tempered **ADV** (= *frech*) **jdm ~ antworten** to talk back to sb; **jdm ~ kommen** to be stroppy (*Brit inf*) *or* bad-tempered with sb

Pan [paːn] M **-s** (*Myth*) Pan

pan- [paːn] PREF pan-; **panafrikanisch** pan-African; **panamerikanisch** pan-American; **panarabisch** pan-Arab; **Panslawismus** pan-Slavism

Pa|na|de [pa'naːdə] F **-, -en** (*Cook*) coating (*of eggs, flour and breadcrumbs*)

Pa|na|ma ['panama, 'paːnama] NT **-s, -s** **a** Panama **b** (*auch* **Panamahut**) Panama (hat)

Pa|na|ma|ka|nal M, *no pl* Panama Canal

pa|na|schie|ren [pana'ʃiːrən] *ptp* **panaschiert** VI (*Pol*) to split one's ticket **VT** **panaschierte Blätter** variegated leaves

pan|chro|ma|tisch [pankro'maːtɪʃ] ADJ panchromatic

Pan|da ['panda] M **-s, -s** panda

Pan|dä|mo|ni|um [pandɛ'moːniʊm] NT **-s, Pandämonien** [-niən] (*Myth, fig*) pandemonium

Pan|dek|ten [pan'dɛktn] PL (*Jur*) Pandects *pl*, Digest

Pan|de|mie [pande'miː] F **-, -n** [-'miːən] (*Med*) pandemic

Pa|neel [pa'neːl] NT **-s, -e** (*form*) (*einzeln*) panel; (= *Täfelung*) panelling (*Brit*), paneling (*US*), wainscoting

pa|nee|lie|ren [pane'liːrən] *ptp* **paneeliert** VT (*form*) to panel

Pan|flö|te ['paːn-] F panpipes *pl*, Pan's pipes *pl*

päng [pɛŋ] INTERJ bang

Pa|nier [pa'niːɐ] NT **-s, -e** (*obs*) banner, standard; **Freiheit sei euer ~!** (*liter*) let freedom be your slogan *or* motto! (*liter*); **unter dem ~ der Freiheit kämpfen** (*liter*) to fight under the banner of freedom; **sich** (*dat*) **etw aufs ~ schreiben** (*fig*) to take *or* adopt sth as one's motto

pa|nie|ren [pa'niːrən] *ptp* **paniert** VT to bread, to coat with breadcrumbs

Pa|nier|mehl NT breadcrumbs *pl*

Pa|nik ['paːnɪk] F **-, -en** panic; **(eine) ~ brach aus** *or* **breitete sich aus** panic broke out *or* spread, there was panic; **in ~ ausbrechen** *or* **geraten** to panic, to get into a panic; **jdn in ~ versetzen** to throw sb into a state of panic; **von ~ ergriffen** panic-stricken; **nur keine ~!** don't panic!; **kein Grund zur ~!** no reason to panic!; **die ~, die ihn zu überwältigen drohte** the feeling of panic that threatened to overwhelm him

Pa|nik-: Pa|nik|kauf M (*Comm*) panic buying; **Pa|nik|ma|che** F (*inf*) panicmongering (*Brit*), inciting panic; **Pa|nik|stim|mung** F state of panic; **Pa|nik|ver|kauf** M (*Comm*) panic selling

pa|nisch ['paːnɪʃ] **ADJ** *no pred* panic-stricken; **~e Angst** panic-stricken fear, terror; **sie hat ~e Angst vor Schlangen** she's terrified of snakes, snakes scare her out of her wits; **er hatte eine ~e Angst zu ertrinken** he was terrified of drowning; **~er Schrecken** panic **ADV** in panic, frantically; **~ reagieren** to panic; **sich ~ fürchten (vor)** to be terrified *or* petrified (by); **sie rannten ~ durcheinander** they ran about frantically *or* in panic

Pan|kre|as ['pankreas] NT **-, Pankreaten** [pankre'aːtn] (*Anat*) pancreas

Pan|ne ['panə] F **-, -n** **a** (= *technische Störung*) hitch (*inf*), breakdown, trouble *no indef art*; (= *Reifenpanne*) puncture, flat (tyre (*Brit*) *or* tire (*US*)), blow-out (*inf*); **ich hatte eine ~ mit dem Fahrrad, mein Fahrrad hatte eine ~** I had some trouble with my bike; (*Reifenpanne*) I had a puncture (*Brit*) *or* flat; **ich hatte eine ~ mit dem Auto, mein Auto hatte eine ~** my car broke down; **mit der neuen Maschine passieren dauernd ~n** things keep going wrong with the new machine, the new machine keeps breaking down

b (*fig inf*) slip, boob (*esp Brit inf*), goof (*US inf*) (*bei etw* with sth); **mit jdm/etw eine ~ erleben** to have (a bit of) trouble with sb/sth; **uns ist eine ~ passiert** we've made a slip, we've slipped up, we've boobed (*esp Brit inf*) *or* goofed (*US inf*); **da ist eine ~ passiert mit dem Brief** something has gone wrong with the letter

Pan|nen-: Pan|nen|dienst M, **Pan|nen|hil|fe** F breakdown service; **Pan|nen|kof|fer** M emergency toolkit; **Pan|nen|kurs** M car maintenance course

Pa|nop|ti|kum [pa'nɔptikʊm] NT **-s, Panoptiken** [-kn] (*von Kuriositäten*) collection of curios; (*von Wachsfiguren*) waxworks *pl*

Pa|no|ra|ma [pano'raːma] NT **-s, Panoramen** [-mən] panorama

Pa|no|ra|ma-: Pa|no|ra|ma|auf|nah|me F panorama, panoramic view; **Pa|no|ra|ma|bus** M coach with panoramic windows, panorama coach; **Pa|no|ra|ma|ge|mäl|de** NT panoramic painting; **Pa|no|ra|ma|spie|gel** M (*Aut*) panoramic mirror

pan|schen ['panʃn] **VT** to adulterate; (= *verdünnen*) to water down, to dilute **VI** (*inf*) to splash (about)

Pan|scher ['panʃɐ] M **-s, -**, **Pan|sche|rin** [-ərɪn] F **-, -nen** (*inf*) **a** (*pej*) adulterator **b** **du bist vielleicht ein ~!** you're a messy thing!

Pan|sche|rei [panʃə'rai] F **-, -en** **a** (= *Vermischen*) adulteration; (*mit Wasser*) watering down, dilution **b** (= *Herumspritzen*) splashing (about); **was für eine ~ du gemacht hast!** what a mess you've made!

Pan|sen ['panzn] M **-s, -** (*Zool*) rumen; (*N Ger inf*) belly (*inf*)

Pan|ta|lons [pɑ̃ta'lõːs] PL (*Hist*) pantaloons *pl*

Pan|ter ▲ ['pantɐ] M **-s, -** = **Panther**

Pan|the|is|mus [pante'ɪsmʊs] M -, *no pl* pantheism

Pan|the|ist [pante'ɪst] M -en, -en, **Pan|the|is|tin** [-'ɪstɪn] F -, -nen pantheist

pan|the|is|tisch [pante'ɪstɪʃ] ADJ pantheistic

Pan|ther ['pantɐ] M -s, - panther

Pan|ti|ne [pan'tiːnə] F -, -n (*N Ger*) clog → **kippen**

Pan|tof|fel [pan'tɔfl] M -s, -n slipper; **unterm ~ stehen** (*inf*) to be henpecked (*inf*); **unter den ~ kommen** *or* **geraten** (*inf*) to become henpecked (*inf*); **den ~ schwingen** to wear the trousers (*esp Brit inf*) *or* pants (*esp US inf*)

Pan|tof|fel|blu|me F slipper flower, calceolaria

Pan|töf|fel|chen [pan'tœflçən] NT -s, - slipper

Pan|tof|fel-: Pan|tof|fel|held M (*inf*) henpecked husband (*inf*); **Pan|tof|fel|ki|no** NT (*inf*) telly (*Brit inf*), (goggle)box (*Brit inf*), tube (*US inf*); **Pan|tof|fel|tier|chen** NT (*Biol*) slipper animalcule, paramecium (*spec*)

Pan|to|let|te [panto'lɛtə] F -, -n slip-on (shoe)

Pan|to|mi|me¹ [panto'miːmə] F -, -n mime

Pan|to|mi|me² [panto'miːmə] M -n, -n, **Pan|to|mi|min** [-'miːmɪn] F -, -nen mime

pan|to|mi|misch [panto'miːmɪʃ] ADJ *Darstellung* in mime ADV in mime; **sich ~ verständlich machen** to communicate with gestures *or* in mime

pant|schen ['pantʃn] VTI = **panschen**

Pan|zer ['pantsɐ] M -s, - **a** (*Mil*) tank; **die deutschen ~** the German tanks *pl* or armour *sing* (*Brit*) *or* armor *sing* (*US*) **b** (*Hist:* = *Rüstung*) armour *no indef art* (*Brit*), armor *no indef art* (*US*), suit of armo(u)r **c** (= *Panzerung*) armour (*Brit*) *or* armor (*US*) plating, armour (*Brit*) *or* armor (*US*) plate **d** (*von Schildkröte, Insekt*) shell; (= *dicke Haut*) armour (*Brit*), armor (*US*) **e** (*fig*) shield; **sich mit einem ~ (gegen etw) umgeben** to harden oneself (against sth); **sich mit einem ~ aus etw umgeben** to put up *or* erect a defensive barrier of sth; **ein ~ der Gleichgültigkeit** a wall of indifference

Pan|zer-: Pan|zer|ab|wehr F anti-tank defence (*Brit*) *or* defense (*US*); (*Truppe*) anti-tank unit; **Pan|zer|ab|wehr|hub|schrau|ber** M anti-tank helicopter; **Pan|zer|ab|wehr|ka|no|ne** F anti-tank gun; **Pan|zer|be|sat|zung** F tank crew; **pan|zer|bre|chend** ADJ armour-piercing (*Brit*), armor-piercing (*US*); **Pan|zer|di|vi|si|on** F armoured (*Brit*) *or* armored (*US*) division; **Pan|zer|fal|le** F tank trap; **Pan|zer|faust** F bazooka; **Pan|zer|glas** NT bulletproof glass; **Pan|zer|gra|ben** M anti-tank ditch; **Pan|zer|gra|na|te** F armour-piercing (*Brit*) *or* armor-piercing (*US*) shell; **Pan|zer|gre|na|dier** M armoured (*Brit*) *or* armored (*US*) infantryman; **Pan|zer|hemd** NT coat of mail; **Pan|zer|kampf|wa|gen** M armoured (*Brit*) *or* armored (*US*) vehicle; **Pan|zer|ket|te** F tank-track; **Pan|zer|kreu|zer** M (*Naut*) (armoured (*Brit*) *or* armored (*US*)) cruiser

pan|zern ['pantsɐn] VT to armour-plate (*Brit*), to armor-plate (*US*); **gepanzerte Fahrzeuge** armoured (*Brit*) *or* armored (*US*) vehicles; **gepanzerte Tiere** shell-bearing animals VR (*lit*) to put on one's armour (*Brit*) *or* armor (*US*); (*fig*) to arm oneself

Pan|zer-: Pan|zer|plat|te F armour (*Brit*) *or* armor (*US*) plating *no pl*, armour (*Brit*) *or* armor (*US*) plate; **Pan|zer|schrank** M safe; **Pan|zer|späh|wa|gen** M armoured (*Brit*) *or* armored (*US*) scout car; **Pan|zer|sper|re** F anti-tank obstacle, tank trap; **Pan|zer|trup|pe** F tanks *pl*, tank division; **Pan|zer|turm** M tank turret

Pan|ze|rung ['pantseʀʊŋ] F -, -en armour (*Brit*) *or* armor (*US*) plating; (*fig*) shield

Pan|zer-: Pan|zer|wa|gen M armoured (*Brit*) *or* armored (*US*) car; **Pan|zer|wes|te** F bulletproof vest

Pa|pa¹ ['papa] M -s, -s (*inf*) daddy (*inf*), pa (*US inf*), pop(s) (*US inf*)

Pa|pa² [pa'paː] M -s, -s papa

Pa|pa|gal|lo [papa'galo] M -s, **Papagalli** [-li] (*pej*) (Latin) wolf *or* romeo

Pa|pa|gei [papa'gai, 'papagai] M -s, -en parrot; **er plappert alles wie ein ~ nach** he repeats everything parrot fashion

Pa|pa|gei|en|krank|heit F (*Med*) parrot fever, psittacosis

Pa|pa|gei|en|tau|cher M puffin

Pa|pa|raz|zo [papa'ratso] M -s, **Paparazzi** [-tsi] (*inf*) paparazzo

Pa|pa|ya [pa'paːja] F -, -s papaya

Pa|per ['peːpɐ] NT -s, - paper

Pa|per|back ['peːpɐbɛk] NT -s, -s paperback

Pa|pe|te|rie ['papetəri-] F -, -n [-riːən] (*Sw*) stationer's

Pa|pi ['papi] M -s, -s (*inf*) daddy (*inf*), pappy (*US inf*)

Pa|pier [pa'piːɐ] NT -s, -e **a** *no pl* (*Material*) paper; **ein Blatt ~** a sheet *or* piece of paper; **~ verarbeitend** (*Industrie*) paper-processing; **das existiert nur auf dem ~** it only exists on paper; **das steht nur auf dem ~** that's only on paper, that's only in theory; **etw zu ~ bringen** to set *or* put sth down on paper *or* in writing, to commit sth to paper; **~ ist geduldig** (*Prov*) you can say what you like on paper, you can write what you like; **das Abkommen ist das ~ nicht wert, auf dem es gedruckt ist** the agreement isn't worth the paper it's written on **b** (= *politisches Dokument, Schriftstück*) paper **c Papiere** PL (identity) papers *pl*; (= *Urkunden*) documents *pl*; **er hatte keine ~e bei sich** he had no *or* he was carrying no means of identification on him; **seine ~e bekommen** (= *entlassen werden*) to get one's cards **d** (*Fin:* = *Wertpapier*) security

Pa|pier-: Pa|pier|deutsch NT officialese, gobbledygook (*inf*); **Pa|pier|ein|zug** M paper feed

pa|pie|ren [pa'piːʀən] ADJ **a** (*lit form*) paper **b** (*fig*) *Stil, Sprache* prosy, bookish ADV (*fig*) **die Sprache wirkt ~** the language seems stilted

Pa|pier-: Pa|pier|fa|brik F paper mill; **Pa|pier|fet|zen** M scrap *or* (little) bit of paper; **Pa|pier|for|mat** NT paper size; **Pa|pier|geld** NT paper money; **Pa|pier|korb** M (waste)paper basket *or* bin; **Pa|pier|kram** M bumf (*Brit inf*), stuff (to read) (*inf*); **Pa|pier|krieg** M (*inf*) **vor lauter ~ kommen wir nicht zur Forschung** there's so much paperwork we can't get on with our research; **erst nach einem langen ~** after going through a lot of red tape; **einen ~ (mit jdm) führen** to go through a lot of red tape (with sb); **pa|pier|los** ADJ *Datenverkehr, Kommunikation* paperless; **das ~e Büro** the paperless *or* paper-free office ADV **Daten ~ versenden** to send data electronically; **Pa|pier|ma|ché** [papie-ma'ʃeː] NT -s, -s = papier-mâché; **Pa|pier|man|schet|te** F paper frill; (*am Ärmel*) false cuff; **Pa|pier|ma|schee** ▲ [papie-ma'ʃeː] NT -s, -s → **Papiermaché**; **Pa|pier|müh|le** F paper mill

pa|piern [pa'piːɐn] ADJ, ADV = **papieren**

Pa|pier-: Pa|pier|sche|re F paper scissors *pl*; **Pa|pier|schlan|ge** F streamer; **Pa|pier|schnit|zel** M OR NT scrap of paper; (*pl:* = *Konfetti*) confetti; **Pa|pier|ser|vi|et|te** F paper serviette (*esp Brit*) *or* napkin; **Pa|pier|ta|schen|tuch** NT paper hankie *or* handkerchief, tissue; **Pa|pier|ti|ger** M (*fig*) paper tiger; **Pa|pier|tü|te** F paper bag; **pa|pier|ver|ar|bei|tend** △ ADJ *attr* → **Papier a**; **Pa|pier|ver|schwen|dung** F waste of paper; **Pa|pier|vor|schub** M paper feed; **Pa|pier|wäh|rung** F paper currency; **Pa|pier|wa|ren** PL stationery *no pl*; **Pa|pier|wa|ren|ge|schäft** NT , **Pa|pier|wa|ren|hand|lung** F stationer's (shop); **Pa|pier|zu|füh|rung** F (*Comput*) sheetfeed

Pa|pist [pa'pɪst] M -en, -en, **Pa|pis|tin** [-'pɪstɪn] F -, -nen (*pej*) papist (*pej*)

pa|pis|tisch [pa'pɪstɪʃ] ADJ (*Hist*) papal; (*pej*) popish

papp [pap] ADJ (*inf*) **ich kann nicht mehr ~ sagen** I'm full to bursting (*Brit inf*), I'm about to go pop (*inf*)

Papp [pap] M -s, *no pl* (*S Ger*) = **Pappe b**

Papp-: Papp|band [-bant] M *pl* -bände (*Einband*) pasteboard; (*Buch*) hardback; **Papp|be|cher** M paper cup; **Papp|de|ckel** M (thin) cardboard; **einen ~ unterlegen** to put a piece of cardboard underneath

Pap|pe ['papə] F -, -n **a** (= *Pappdeckel*) cardboard; (= *Dachpappe*) roofing felt; **dieser linke Haken war nicht von ~** (*inf*) that left hook really had some weight *or* force behind it, that was a mean left hook; **X ist ein guter Sprinter, aber Y ist auch nicht von ~** (*inf*) X is good but Y is no mean sprinter either (*Brit*), X is a fast sprinter but Y is no slacker (*esp US inf*) **b** (*S Ger inf*) (= *Leim*) glue; (= *Brei*) paste; (*pej*) slop (*pej inf*), mush (*pej inf*); **ich kann diese ~ von Porridge nicht essen** I can't eat this porridge slop (*pej inf*)

Papp|ein|band M pasteboard

Pap|pel ['papl] F -, -n poplar

Pap|pel|al|lee F avenue of poplars

päp|peln ['pɛpln] VT (*inf*) to nourish

pap|pen ['papn] (*inf*) VT to stick, to glue (*an* +*acc*, *auf* +*acc* on) VI (*inf*) (= *klebrig sein*) to be sticky; (*Schnee*) to pack; **der Leim pappt gut** the glue sticks *or* holds well; **das Hemd pappt an mir** my shirt is sticking to me

Pap|pen-: Pap|pen|de|ckel M (*S Ger*) = **Pappdeckel**; **Pap|pen|hei|mer** [-haimɐ] PL **ich kenne meine ~** (*inf*) I know you lot/that lot (inside out) (*inf*); **Pap|pen|stiel** M , *no pl* (*fig inf*) **das ist doch ein/kein ~** (= *billig*) that's chicken feed/not exactly chicken feed (*inf*); (= *leicht*) that's child's play/not exactly child's play (*inf*); (*Geldbetrag*) that's peanuts/not exactly peanuts (*inf*); **das ist keinen ~ wert** that's not worth a thing *or* a penny *or* a straw; **das hab ich für einen ~ gekauft** I bought it for a song (*inf*) *or* for next to nothing

pap|per|la|papp [papɐla'pap] INTERJ (*inf*) rubbish (*Brit inf*), (stuff and) nonsense

pap|pig ['papɪç] (*inf*) ADJ sticky; *Brot* doughy ADV **der Kartoffelbrei klebte ~ am Löffel/an meinem Gaumen** mashed potato was stuck to the spoon/to the roof of my mouth

Papp-: Papp|ka|me|rad M (*Mil sl*) silhouette target; **Papp|kar|ton** M (= *Schachtel*) cardboard box; (*Material*) cardboard; **Papp|ma|ché** ['papmaʃeː] NT -s, -s, **Papp|ma|schee** ▲ NT -s, -s papier-mâché; **Papp|na|se** F false nose; **Papp|schach|tel** F cardboard box; **Papp|schnee** M wet *or* sticky snow; **Papp|tel|ler** M paper plate

Pap|ri|ka ['paprika, 'paːprika] M -s, -(s) (*no pl:* = *Gewürz*) paprika; (= *Paprikaschote*) pepper; (*Sw:* = *Peperoni*) chilli (*Brit*), chili

Pap|ri|ka|scho|te F pepper; (= *rote Paprikaschote*) pepper, pimento (*US*); **gefüllte ~n** stuffed peppers

Paps [paps] M -, *no pl* (*inf*) dad (*inf*), daddy (*inf*), pops (*US inf*)

Papst [paːpst] M -(e)s, **-e** ['pɛːpstə] pope; (*fig*) high priest

Papst-: Papst|au|di|enz F audience with the Pope; **Papst|be|such** M papal visit

Päps|tin ['pɛːpstɪn] F -, -nen popess; (*fig*) high priestess

päpst|lich ['pɛːpstlɪç] ADJ papal; (*fig pej*) pontifical; **~er als der Papst sein** to be more Catholic than the Pope, to be more royal than the king

Papst-: Papst|tum ['paːpstuːm] NT -(e)s, *no pl* papacy; **Papst|wahl** F papal elections *pl*; **Papst|wür|de** F papal office

Pa|pua ['pa:pua, pa'puːa] M -(s), -(s) or f -, -s Papuan

Pa|pua-Neu|gui|nea ['paːpuaɔygi'neːa] NT -s Papua New Guinea

pa|pu|a|nisch [papu'aːnɪʃ] ADJ Papuan

Pa|py|rus [pa'pyːrʊs] M -, **Papyri** [-ri] papyrus

Pa|py|rus|rol|le F papyrus (scroll)

Pa|ra|bel [pa'raːbl] F -, -n a (Liter) parable b (Math) parabola, parabolic curve

pa|ra|bo|lisch [para'boːlɪʃ] ADJ a (Liter) parabolic; **eine ~e Erzählung** a parable b (Math) parabolic

Pa|ra|bol|an|ten|ne F satellite dish, parabolic receiving dish

Pa|ra|bol|spie|gel M parabolic reflector or mirror

Pa|ra|de [pa'raːdə] F -, -n a parade (auch Mil); **die ~ abnehmen** to take the salute b (Sport) (Fechten, Boxen) parry; (Ballspiele) save; (Reiten) check; **jdm in die ~ fahren** (fig) to cut sb off short

Pa|ra|de-: Pa|ra|de|an|zug M (Mil) dress uniform; (inf: = gute Kleidung) best bib and tucker (dated inf), Sunday best (inf); **Pa|ra|de|bei|spiel** NT prime example; **Pa|ra|de|bett** NT fourposter (bed)

Pa|ra|de|fall M prime example

Pa|ra|dei|ser [para'daizɐ] M -s, - (Aus) tomato

Pa|ra|de-: Pa|ra|de|kis|sen NT scatter cushion; **Pa|ra|de|marsch** M a (= Paradeschritt) parade step; (= Stechschritt) goose step; **im ~ marschieren** to march in parade step/to goose-step b (= Aufmarsch) march in parade step c (Marschmusik) (military) march; **Pa|ra|de|pferd** NT show horse; (fig) showpiece; **Pa|ra|de|platz** M parade ground; (fig) most famous role; **Pa|ra|de|rol|le** F (von Schauspieler) most famous role; **der Hamlet war seine ~** he was best known for his role as Hamlet; **Pa|ra|de|schritt** M = **Parademarsch** a; **Pa|ra|de|stück** NT (fig) showpiece; (Gegenstand auch) pièce de résistance; **Pa|ra|de|uni|form** F dress uniform

pa|ra|die|ren [para'diːrən] ptp **paradiert** VI to parade; **mit etw ~** (fig) to show off or flaunt sth

Pa|ra|dies [para'diːs] NT -es, -e [-zə] a (lit, fig) paradise; **die Vertreibung aus dem ~** the expulsion from Paradise; **das verlorene ~** the lost paradise; **hier ist es so schön wie im ~** it's like paradise here, this is paradise; **da haben sie wie im ~ gelebt** they were living in paradise; **ein ~ für Kinder** a children's paradise, a paradise for children; **das ~ auf Erden** heaven on earth b (Archit) galilee

pa|ra|die|sisch [para'diːzɪʃ] ADJ (fig) heavenly, paradisiac(al) (liter); **dort herrschen ~e Zustände für Autofahrer** it's heaven for car drivers there ADV leer blissfully; schön incredibly; **hier ist es ~ ruhig** it's incredibly peaceful here; **sich ~ wohl fühlen** to be blissfully happy, to be in paradise

Pa|ra|dies|vo|gel M bird of paradise; (fig inf) exotic creature

Pa|ra|dig|ma [para'dɪgma] NT -s, **Paradigmen** [-mən] paradigm

pa|ra|dig|ma|tisch [paradɪg'maːtɪʃ] ADJ paradigmatic

pa|ra|dox [para'dɔks] ADJ paradoxical ADV paradoxically

Pa|ra|dox [para'dɔks] NT -es, -e paradox

pa|ra|do|xer|wei|se [para'dɔksɐ'vaizə] ADV paradoxically

Pa|ra|do|xie [paradɔ'ksiː] F -, -n [-'ksiːən] paradox

Pa|ra|do|xon [pa'raːdɔksɔn] NT -s, **Paradoxa** [-ksa] (geh) paradox

Pa|raf|fin [para'fiːn] NT -s, -e (Chem) (= Paraffinöl) (liquid) paraffin; (= Paraffinwachs) paraffin wax

Pa|ra|gli|der¹ M -s, - (= Schirm) paraglider

Pa|ra|gli|der² M -s, -, **Pa|ra|gli|de|rin** F -, nen paraglider

Pa|ra|gli|ding ['paːraglaidɪŋ] NT -s, no pl paragliding

Pa|ra|graf ▲ [para'graːf] M -en, -en (Jur) section; (= Abschnitt) paragraph

---

PARAGRAF 218

Paragraf 218 of the criminal code concerns abortion. Since abortion is a highly controversial issue, **Paragraf 218** has become a by-word for the entire abortion debate. In Germany abortion is legal up to the third month of pregnancy, provided the pregnant woman has undergone thorough counselling.

Pa|ra|gra|fen- ▲: **Pa|ra|gra|fen|rei|ter(in)** ▲ M(F) (inf) pedant, stickler for the rules; **pa|ra|gra|fen|wei|se** ▲ ADV in paragraphs; **Pa|ra|gra|fen|werk** ▲ NT rules and regulations pl; **Pa|ra|gra|fen|zei|chen** ▲ NT (Typ) paragraph (marker or sign)

Pa|ral|la|xe [para'laksə] F -, -n (Math) parallax

pa|ral|lel [para'leːl] ADJ parallel (auch Comput) ADV parallel; **~ laufen** to run parallel; **der Weg (ver)läuft ~ zum Fluss** the path runs or is parallel to the river; **die Entwicklung dort verläuft ~ zu der in Deutschland** the development there is parallel to or parallels that of Germany; **~ schalten** (Elec) to connect in parallel

Pa|ral|lel|com|pu|ter [para'leːl-] M parallel computer

Pa|ral|lel|dru|cker M (Comput) parallel printer

Pa|ral|le|le [para'leːlə] F -, -n (lit) parallel (line); (fig) parallel; **eine ~/~n zu etw ziehen** (lit) to draw a line/lines parallel to sth; (fig) to draw a parallel/parallels to sth; **dafür gibt es keine ~** there are no parallels; **~n sehen zwischen ...** to see parallels between ...

Pa|ral|lel- [para'leːl-]: **Pa|ral|lel|er|schei|nung** F parallel; **Pa|ral|lel|fall** M parallel (case)

Pa|ral|le|lis|mus [paraleˈlɪsmʊs] M -, **Parallelismen** [-mən] parallelism

Pa|ral|le|li|tät [paraleli'teːt] F -, -en parallelism

Pa|ral|lel- [para'leːl-]: **Pa|ral|lel|klas|se** F parallel class; **Pa|ral|lel|kreis** M parallel (of latitude)

Pa|ral|le|lo|gramm [paralelo'gram] NT -s, -e parallelogram

Pa|ral|lel- [para'leːl-]: **Pa|ral|lel|rech|ner** M (Comput) parallel computer; **Pa|ral|lel|schal|tung** F parallel connection; **Pa|ral|lel|schwung** M (Ski) parallel turn

Pa|ra|lym|pics [para'lʏmpɪks] PL Paralympics pl

Pa|ra|ly|se [para'lyːzə] F -, -n (Med, fig) paralysis

pa|ra|ly|sie|ren [paraly'ziːrən] ptp **paralysiert** VT (Med, fig) to paralyze

Pa|ra|ly|ti|ker [para'lyːtikɐ] M -s, -, **Pa|ra|ly|ti|ke|rin** [-ərɪn] F -, -nen (Med) paralytic

pa|ra|ly|tisch [para'lyːtɪʃ] ADJ paralytic

Pa|ra|me|di|zin ['paːra-] F alternative medicine

Pa|ra|me|ter [pa'raːmetɐ] M -s, - parameter

pa|ra|mi|li|tä|risch ['paːra-] ADJ paramilitary

Pa|ra|noia [para'nɔya] F -, no pl paranoia

pa|ra|no|id [parano'iːt] ADJ paranoid

Pa|ra|no|i|ker [para'noːikɐ] M -s, -, **Pa|ra|no|i|ke|rin** [-ərɪn] F -, -nen paranoiac

pa|ra|no|isch [para'noːɪʃ] ADJ paranoiac

Pa|ra|nuss ▲ ['paːra-] F (Bot) Brazil nut

Pa|ra|phe [pa'raːfə] F -, -n (form) (= Namenszug) signature; (= Namenszeichen) initials pl; (= Stempel) signature stamp

pa|ra|phie|ren [para'fiːrən] ptp **paraphiert** VT (Pol) to initial

Pa|ra|phra|se [para-] F paraphrase; (Mus) variation

pa|ra|phra|sie|ren [parafra'ziːrən] ptp **paraphrasiert** VT to paraphrase; (Mus) to write variations on

Pa|ra|psy|cho|lo|gie ['paːra-] F parapsychology

Pa|ra|sit [para'ziːt] M -en, -en (Biol, fig) parasite

pa|ra|si|tär [parazi'tɛːɐ], **pa|ra|si|tisch** [para'ziːtɪʃ] ADJ (Biol, fig) parasitic(al) ADV **~ leben** to live parasitically

Pa|ra|sol [para'zɔːl] M OR NT -s, -s or -e (old) parasol, sunshade

pa|rat [pa'raːt] ADJ Antwort, Beispiel etc ready, prepared; Werkzeug etc handy, ready; **halte dich ~** be ready; **er hatte immer eine Ausrede ~** he always had an excuse ready or on tap (inf), he was always ready with an excuse; **seine stets ~e Ausrede** his ever-ready excuse

pa|ra|tak|tisch [para'taktɪʃ] ADJ (Ling) coordinated; (ohne Konjunktion) paratactic(al)

Pa|ra|ta|xe [para'taksə] F (Ling) coordination; (ohne Konjunktion) parataxis

Pär|chen ['pɛːɐçən] NT -s, - (courting) couple; **ihr seid mir so eine ~!** (iro) you're a fine pair!

pär|chen|wei|se ADV in pairs

Par|cours [par'kuːɐ] M -, - [-'kuːɐ(s), -'kuːɐs] (Reiten) showjumping course; (Sportart) showjumping; (= Rennstrecke, Hindernisstrecke) course; **einen ~ reiten** to jump a course; **sie reitet nicht gern ~** she doesn't like showjumping

par|dauz [par'dauts] INTERJ (old) whoops

par|don [par'dõː] INTERJ (= Verzeihung) sorry; (= nicht verstanden) sorry, beg (your) pardon, pardon me (US); **o ~!** sorry!, I'm so sorry!; (empört) excuse me!

Par|don [par'dõː] M OR NT -s, no pl a pardon; **jdn um ~ bitten** to ask sb's pardon; **jdm kei|n(en) ~ geben** (old) to show sb no mercy, to give sb no quarter b (inf) **kein ~ kennen** to be ruthless; **wenn er sich** (dat) **was in den Kopf gesetzt hat, gibts kein ~** once he's set on something he's merciless or ruthless; **das Zeug räumst du auf, da gibts kein ~** you'll clear that stuff up and that's that! (inf)

Pa|ren|the|se [parɛn'teːzə] F parenthesis; **in ~** in parenthesis or parentheses; **etw in ~ setzen** to put sth in parentheses

pa|ren|the|tisch [parɛn'teːtɪʃ] ADJ parenthetic(al)

par ex|cel|lence [par ɛksɛ'lãːs] ADV par excellence

Par|fait [par'fɛː] NT -s, -s (Art Sorbet) parfait

Par|force- [par'fɔrs-]: **Par|force|jagd** F hunt, course; (Jagdart) coursing; **wir machen eine ~** we're going hunting, we're going on a hunt; **Par|force|ritt** M forced ride

Par|fum [par'fœː] NT -s, -s, **Par|füm** [par'fyːm] NT -s, -e or -s perfume, scent

Par|fü|me|rie [parfyməˈriː] F -, -n [-'riːən] perfumery

Par|füm|fläsch|chen NT scent or perfume bottle

par|fü|mie|ren [parfy'miːrən] ptp **parfümiert** VT to scent, to perfume VR to put perfume or scent on; **du parfümierst dich zu stark** you put too much scent or perfume on

Par|füm|wol|ke F cloud of perfume

Par|füm|zer|stäu|ber M scent spray, perfume or scent atomizer

pa|ri ['paːri] ADV (Fin) par; **al ~, zu ~** at par (value), at nominal value; **über ~** above par, at a premium; **unter ~** below par, at a discount; **die Chancen stehen ~ (~)** the odds are even or fifty-fifty

Pa|ria ['paːria] M -s, -s (lit, fig) pariah

pa|rie|ren [pa'riːrən] ptp **pariert** VT a (Fechten, fig) to parry; (Ftbl) to deflect b (Reiten) to rein in VI to obey, to do what one is told; **aufs Wort ~** to jump to it

Pa|ri|kurs ['paːri-] M (Fin) par of exchange

Pa|ris [pa'riːs] NT -' Paris

Pa|ri|ser¹ [pa'riːzɐ] ADJ *attr* Parisian, Paris

Pa|ri|ser² M -s, - **a** Parisian **b** (*inf*: = *Kondom*) French letter (*inf*)

Pa|ri|se|rin [pa'riːzərɪn] F -, -nen Parisienne

Pa|ri|tät [pari'tɛːt] F -, -en (= *Gleichstellung*) parity, equality; (*in Gremium*) parity; (*von Währung*) parity, par of exchange; (*Comput*) parity

pa|ri|tä|tisch [pari'tɛːtɪʃ] ADJ equal; **~e Mitbestimmung** equal representation ADV equally; **eine Kommission ~ besetzen** to provide equal representation on a committee

Park [park] M -s, -s **a** park; (*von Schloss*) grounds *pl* **b** (*rare*: = *Fuhrpark*) fleet (of vehicles)

Par|ka ['parka] M -(s), -s or *f* -, -s parka

Park-and-ride-Sys|tem ['paːkənd'raid-] NT park and ride system

Park-: Park|an|la|ge F park; **park|ar|tig** ADJ park-like **a** like a park; **Park|aus|weis** M parking permit; **Park|bahn** F (*Space*) parking orbit; **Park|bank** F *pl* -bänke park bench; **Park|bucht** F parking bay; **Park|dau|er** F parking period; **Park|deck** NT parking level

par|ken ['parkn] VTI (*auch Comput*) to park; **ein ~des Auto** a parked car; **„Parken verboten!"** "No Parking"; **falsch ~** to park illegally; **sein Auto parkte ...** his car was parked ...

Par|kett [par'kɛt] NT -s, -e **a** (= *Fußboden*) parquet (flooring); **ein Zimmer mit ~ auslegen** to lay parquet (flooring) in a room; **sich auf jedem ~ bewegen können** (*fig*) to be able to move in any society; **auf dem internationalen ~** in international circles; **sich auf glattem ~ bewegen** (*fig*) to be skating on thin ice **b** (= *Tanzfläche*) (dance) floor; **eine tolle Nummer aufs ~ legen** (*inf*) to put on a great show → **Sohle c** (*Theat*) stalls *pl*, parquet (*US*); **das ~ klatschte Beifall** there was applause from the stalls; **im ~ sitzen** to sit in the stalls **d** (*St Ex*) trading floor; **auf dem ~** on the trading floor

Par|kett(fuß)|bo|den M parquet floor

par|ket|tie|ren [parkɛ'tiːrən] *ptp* **parkettiert** VT to lay with parquet, to lay or put down parquet in, to parquet

Par|kett|platz M , **Par|kett|sitz** M (*Theat*) seat in the stalls or parquet (*US*)

Park-: Park|ge|bühr F parking fee; **Park|haus** NT multi-storey (*Brit*) or multi-story (*US*) car park

par|kie|ren [par'kiːrən] *ptp* **parkiert** VTI (*Sw*) = **parken**

Par|king|me|ter ['parkɪŋ-] M (*Sw*) parking meter

Par|kin|son|kran|ke(r) ['paːɛkɪnzən-] MF *decl as adj* person suffering from Parkinson's disease

par|kin|son|sche Krank|heit ▲ ['paːɛkɪnzənʃə-] F Parkinson's disease

Park-: Park|kral|le F wheel clamp (*Brit*), Denver boot (*US*); **Park|land|schaft** F parkland; **Park|leit|sys|tem** NT parking guidance system; **Park|licht** [park'lɪçt] NT parking light; **Park|lü|cke** F parking space; **Park|mög|lich|keit** F parking facility; **Park|platz** M car park, parking lot (*esp US*); (*für Einzelwagen*) (parking) space (*Brit*) or spot (*US*), place to park; **bewachter/unbewachter ~** car park with/without an attendant; **Park|platz|not** F shortage of parking spaces; **Park|raum** M parking space; **Park|raum|not** F shortage of parking space; **Park|schei|be** F parking disc; **Park|schein** M car-parking ticket; **Park|schein|au|to|mat** M (*Mot*) ticket machine (*for parking*); **Park|stu|di|um** NT (*Univ*) interim course of study (*while waiting for a place*); **Park|sün|der(in)** M(F) parking offender (*Brit*), illegal parker; **Park|uhr** F parking meter; **Park|ver|bot** NT parking ban; **hier ist ~** there's no parking here, you're not allowed to park here; **im ~ stehen** to be parked illegally; **Park|ver|bots|schild**

NT no-parking sign; **Park|wäch|ter(in)** M(F) (*auf Parkplatz*) car-park attendant; (= *Politesse*) traffic warden; (*von Anlagen*) park keeper or attendant; **Park|zeit** F parking time

Par|la|ment [parla'mɛnt] NT -(e)s, -e parliament; **das ~ auflösen** to dissolve parliament; **jdn ins ~ wählen** to elect sb to parliament; **im ~ vertreten sein** to be represented in parliament

Par|la|men|tär [parlamɛn'tɛːɐ] M -s, -e, **Par|la|men|tä|rin** [-'tɛːrɪn] F -, -nen peace envoy, negotiator

Par|la|men|tär|flag|ge F flag of truce

Par|la|men|ta|ri|er [parlamɛn'taːriɐ] M -s, -, **Par|la|men|ta|rie|rin** [-iərɪn] F -, -nen parliamentarian

par|la|men|ta|risch [parlamɛn'taːrɪʃ] ADJ parliamentary; **~er Staatssekretär im Verteidigungsministerium** non-Cabinet minister with special responsibility for defence **~er Geschäftsführer** ≈ party whip; **der Parlamentarische Rat** the Parliamentary Council; **~e Demokratie** parliamentary democracy ADV **~ regieren** to govern by a parliament; **~ vertreten sein** to be represented in parliament

Par|la|men|ta|ris|mus [parlamɛnta'rɪsmʊs] M -, *no pl* parliamentarianism

Par|la|ments-: Par|la|ments|aus|schuss ▲ M parliamentary committee; **Par|la|ments|be|schluss** ▲ M vote or decision of parliament; **Par|la|ments|fe|ri|en** PL recess; **in die ~ gehen** to go into recess; **Par|la|ments|ge|bäu|de** NT parliamentary building(s *pl*); (*in London*) Houses of Parliament *pl*; (*in Washington*) Capitol; **Par|la|ments|mehr|heit** F parliamentary majority, majority in parliament; **Par|la|ments|mit|glied** NT member of parliament; (*in GB*) Member of Parliament, MP; (*in USA*) Congressman; **Par|la|ments|prä|si|dent(in)** M(F) (parliamentary) president; (*in GB*) Speaker; **Par|la|ments|sit|zung** F sitting (of parliament); **Par|la|ments|wahl** F *usu pl* parliamentary election(s *pl*)

Par|lan|do [par'lando] NT -s, -s or **Parlandi** [-di] (*Mus*) parlando

par|lie|ren [par'liːrən] *ptp* **parliert** VI to talk away; **Italienisch ~** to chat away in Italian; **er ist so schüchtern, ich hätte nie geglaubt, dass er so ~ könnte** he's so shy I'd never have believed that he could talk so fluently

Par|ma|schin|ken ['parma-] M Parma ham

Par|me|san(|kä|se) [parme'zaːn-] M -s, *no pl* Parmesan (cheese)

Par|nass [par'nas] M -es (*liter*) (Mount) Parnassus

Pa|ro|die [paro'diː] F -, -n [-'diːən] parody, take-off (*Brit*) (*auf +acc* on, *zu* of); **er ist nur noch eine ~ seiner selbst** he is now only a parody of his former self; **eine ~ von jdm geben** to do a parody or takeoff (*Brit*) of sb, to take sb off (*Brit*)

pa|ro|die|ren [paro'diːrən] *ptp* **parodiert** VT **a** (= *Parodie schreiben auf*) to parody **b** (= *karikieren*) to take off (*Brit*), to parody

Pa|ro|dist [paro'dɪst] M -en, -en, **Pa|ro|dis|tin** [-'dɪstɪn] F -, -nen parodist; (*von Persönlichkeiten*) impersonator

pa|ro|dis|tisch [paro'dɪstɪʃ] ADJ parodistic (*liter*); **~e Sendung** parody, takeoff (*Brit*); **er hat ~e Fähigkeiten** he's good at taking people off, he's a good impersonator; **~e Literatur** literary parodies

Pa|ro|don|to|se [parodən'toːzə] F -, -n periodontosis (*spec*), receding gums *pl*

Pa|ro|le [pa'roːlə] F -, -n **a** (*Mil*) password **b** (*fig* = *Wahlspruch*) motto, watchword; (*Pol*) slogan

Pa|ro|li [pa'roːli] NT **jdm ~ bieten** (*geh*) to defy sb

Par|sing ['paːɛsɪŋ] NT -s (*Comput*) parsing

Part [part] M -s, -e **a** (= *Anteil*) share **b** (*Theat*, *Mus*) part

Par|tei [par'tai] F -, -en **a** (*Pol*) party; **bei** or **in der ~** in the party; **die ~ wechseln** to change parties; **als Bundespräsident steht er über den ~en** as Federal President he takes no part in party politics **b** (*Jur*) party; **die streitenden ~en** the disputing parties; **die vertragsschließenden ~en** the contracting parties; **meine ~** my client **c** (*fig*) **~ sein** to be biased (*Brit*) or biassed; **jds ~ (acc) ergreifen, für jdn ~ ergreifen** or **nehmen** to take sb's side or part, to side with sb; **gegen jdn ~ ergreifen** or **nehmen** to side or to take sides against sb; **es mit keiner ~ halten, es mit keiner von beiden ~en halten** to be on neither side, to be neutral; **es mit beiden ~en halten** to run with the hare and hunt with the hounds (*prov*); **ein Richter sollte über den ~en stehen** a judge should be impartial **d** (*in Mietshaus*) tenant, party (*form*)

Partei-: Par|tei|ab|zei|chen NT party badge; **Par|tei|an|hän|ger(in)** M(F) party supporter; **Par|tei|ap|pa|rat** M party machinery or apparatus; **Par|tei|aus|schluss|ver|fah|ren** ▲ NT expulsion proceedings *pl*; **Par|tei|ba|sis** F rank and file, grassroots (members) *pl*; **Par|tei|bon|ze** M (*pej*) party bigwig or boss; **Par|tei|buch** NT party membership book; **das richtige/falsche ~ haben** to belong to the right/wrong party; **das ~ ab-** or **zurückgeben** to leave the party; **Par|tei|chef(in)** M(F) party leader or boss; **Par|tei|chi|ne|sisch** NT (*pej*) party jargon

Parteien-: Par|tei|en|fi|nan|zie|rung F party financing; **Par|tei|en|ge|setz** NT (*Jur*) political parties act; **Par|tei|en|land|schaft** F party (political) scene, political constellation

Partei-: Par|tei|frau F (*Pol*) female politician; **Par|tei|freund(in)** M(F) fellow party member; **Par|tei|füh|rer(in)** M(F) party leader; **Par|tei|füh|rung** F leadership of a party; (*Vorstand*) party leaders *pl* or executive; **Par|tei|gän|ger** [-gɛŋɐ] M -s, -, **Par|tei|gän|ge|rin** [-ərɪn] F -, -nen party supporter or follower; **Par|tei|ge|nos|se** M , **Par|tei|ge|nos|sin** F party member; **par|tei|in|tern** ADJ internal party *attr*; **~e Kritik** criticism from within the party ADV within the party

par|tei|isch [par'taiʃ] ADJ biased (*Brit*), biassed, partial ADV **~ urteilen** to be biased (in one's judgement)

Par|tei|kon|gress ▲ M convention, party congress

par|tei|lich [par'tailɪç] ADJ **a** (*rare*: = *parteiisch*) bias(s)ed **b** (= *eine Partei betreffend*) party *attr* ADV **~ organisiert** to belong to a (political) party; **Maßnahmen, die nicht ~ gebunden sind** measures which are independent of party politics; **ein ~ ungebundener Kandidat** an independent candidate

Par|tei|lich|keit F -, *no pl* bias, partiality

Par|tei|li|nie F party line; **auf die ~ einschwenken** to toe the party line

par|tei|los ADJ *Abgeordneter, Kandidat* independent, non-party; **der Journalist war ~** the journalist wasn't attached to or aligned with any party

Par|tei|lo|se(r) [par'tailoːzə] MF *decl as adj* independent

Par|tei|lo|sig|keit F -, *no pl* independence; **seine ~** the fact that he is not a member of any political party; **~ ist oft ein Vorteil** it's often an advantage not to belong to any party

Partei-: Par|tei|mit|glied NT party member; **Par|tei|nah|me** [-naːmə] F -, -n partisanship; **Par|tei|or|gan** NT party organ; **Par|tei|po|li|tik** F party politics *pl*; **par|tei|po|li|tisch** ADJ party political ADV as far as party politics go; **dieser Schritt ist ~ geboten** party politics demand this step; **etw ~ ausschlachten** to make party political capital out of sth; **Par|tei|prä|si|di|um** NT party executive committee; **Par|tei|pro|gramm** NT (party) manifesto, (party) programme (*Brit*) or program (*US*); **Par|tei|-**

sol|dat(in) M(F) (inf) party activist; **Par|tei|spen|de** F party donation; **Par|tei|spen|den|af|fä|re** F party donations scandal; **Par|tei|spit|ze** F party leadership, party leaders pl; **Par|tei|tag** M party conference or convention

Par|tei|un|gen [par'taiʊŋən] PL (old) factions pl

Par|tei-: Par|tei|ver|samm|lung F party meeting; **Par|tei|volk** NT grass roots pl of the party; **Par|tei|vor|sit|zen|de(r)** MF decl as adj party leader; **Par|tei|vor|stand** M party executive; **Par|tei|we|sen** NT , no pl party system; **Par|tei|zu|ge|hö|rig|keit** F party membership; **was hat er für eine ~?** what party does he belong to?

par|terre [par'tɛr] ADV on the ground (esp Brit) or first (US) floor

Par|ter|re [par'tɛr(ə)] NT -s, -s **a** (von Gebäude) ground floor (esp Brit), first floor (US); **im ~ wohnen** to live on the ground floor (esp Brit) or first floor (US) **b** (old Theat) rear stalls pl, pit (Brit), parterre (US)

Par|ter|re|woh|nung F ground-floor flat (Brit), first-floor apartment (US)

Par|tie [par'ti:] F -, -n [-'ti:ən] **a** (= Teil, Ausschnitt) part; (eines Buchs) part, section **b** (Theat) part, role; (Mus) part **c** (Sport) game; (Fechten) round; **eine ~ Schach spielen** to play or have a game of chess; **die ~ verloren geben** (lit, fig) to give the game up as lost; **eine gute/schlechte ~ liefern** to give a good/bad performance **d** (old: = Landpartie) outing, trip; **eine ~ machen** to go on an outing, to go for or on a trip **e** (Comm) lot, batch **f** (inf) catch (inf); **eine gute ~ (für jdn) sein** to be a good catch (for sb) (inf); **eine gute ~ machen** to marry (into) money **g** **mit von der ~ sein** to join in, to be in on it; **da bin ich mit von der ~** count me in, I'm with you **h** (Aus: = Arbeitergruppe) gang

par|ti|ell [par'tsiɛl] ADJ partial ADV partially, partly; **diese Lösung ist ~ richtig** this solution is partly or partially right; **~ differenzieren** (Math) to form a partial derivative

par|ti|en|wei|se [par'ti:ənvaizə] ADV (Comm) in lots

Par|ti|kel [par'ti:kl, par'tɪkl] F -, -n (Gram, Phys) particle

Par|ti|kel|schleu|der F (Phys) particle accelerator

Par|ti|ku|la|ris|mus [partikula'rɪsmʊs] M -, no pl particularism

Par|ti|ku|la|rist [partikula'rɪst] M -en, -en, **Par|ti|ku|la|ris|tin** [-'rɪstɪn] F -, -nen particularist

par|ti|ku|la|ris|tisch [partikula'rɪstɪʃ] ADJ particularistic

Par|ti|san [parti'za:n] M -s or -en, -en, **Par|ti|sa|nin** [-'za:nɪn] F -, -nen partisan

Par|ti|sa|nen-: Par|ti|sa|nen|kampf M guerrilla warfare; (Kampfhandlung) guerrilla battle; **Par|ti|sa|nen|krieg** M partisan war; (Art des Krieges) guerrilla warfare

Par|ti|ta [par'ti:ta] F -, Partiten [-tn] (Mus) partita

par|ti|tiv [parti'ti:f] ADJ (Gram) partitive

Par|ti|tur [parti'tu:ɐ] F -, -en [-'tu:rən] (Mus) score

Par|ti|zip [parti'tsi:p] NT -s, -ien [-piən] (Gram) participle; **~ I** or **Präsens** present participle; **~ II** or **Perfekt** past participle

Par|ti|zi|pa|ti|on [partitsipa'tsio:n] F -, -en participation (an +dat)

Par|ti|zi|pa|ti|ons|ge|schäft NT (Comm) transaction conducted by several parties

Par|ti|zi|pi|al- [partitsi'pia:l-]: **Par|ti|zi|pi|alkon|struk|ti|on** F participial construction; **Par|ti|zi|pi|al|satz** M participial clause

---

par|ti|zi|pie|ren [partitsi'pi:rən] ptp **partizipiert** VI to participate (an +dat in)

Part|ner ['partnɐ] M -s, -, **Part|ne|rin** [-ərɪn] F -, -nen partner; (Film) co-star; **als jds ~ spielen** (in Film) to play opposite sb; (Sport) to be partnered by sb, to be sb's partner → **Gesprächspartner**

Part|ner|look [-lʊk] M matching clothes pl

Part|ner|schaft ['partnɐʃaft] F -, -en partnership; (= Städtepartnerschaft) twinning

part|ner|schaft|lich ['partnɐʃaftlɪç] ADJ **~es Verhältnis** (relationship based on) partnership; **in unserer Ehe haben wir ein ~es Verhältnis** our marriage is a partnership; **~e Zusammenarbeit** working together as partners; **in gutem ~em Einvernehmen** in a spirit of partnership ADV **~ zusammenarbeiten** to work in partnership; **~ zusammenleben** to live together as equal partners; **das haben wir ~ gelöst** we solved it together or jointly

Part|ner-: Part|ner|staat M partner (country); **Part|ner|stadt** F twin town (Brit), sister city (US); **Part|ner|su|che** F finding a/the right partner, finding a mate (inf); **auf ~ sein** to be looking for a partner or a mate (inf); **Part|ner|tausch** M **a** (Tanz, Tennis) change of partners **b** (sexuell) partner-swopping; **Part|ner|vermitt|lung** F dating agency; (= Institut) marriage bureau; **Part|ner|wahl** F choice of partner; **jetzt ist ~** (beim Tanz) take or choose your partners, please!; **Part|ner|wech|sel** M = **Partnertausch**

par|tout [par'tu:] ADV (dated) **er will ~ nach Hause gehen** he insists on going home; **sie will ~ nicht nach Hause gehen** she just doesn't want to go home

Par|ty ['pa:ɐti] F -, -s party; **eine ~ geben** or **veranstalten** to give or have a party; **bei** or **auf einer ~** at a party; **auf eine** or **zu einer ~ gehen** to go to a party

Par|ty-: Par|ty|dro|ge F recreational drug; **Par|ty|lö|we** M , **Par|ty|lö|win** F (iro) socialite; **Par|ty|raum** M party room; **Par|ty|service** [-zœ:ɐvɪs, -zœɐvɪs] M party catering service

Par|ve|nü [parve'ny:, -və'ny:] M -s, -s (dated) parvenu, upstart

Par|ze ['partsə] F -, -n (Myth) Parca; **die ~n** the Fates

Par|zel|le [par'tsɛlə] F -, -n plot, lot, parcel of land

par|zel|lie|ren [partse'li:rən] ptp **parzelliert** VT to parcel out

Pasch [paʃ] M -(e)s, -e or ⸚e ['pɛʃə] (beim Würfelspiel) doublets pl → **Viererpasch**

Pa|scha ['paʃa] M -s, -s pasha; **wie ein ~** like Lord Muck (Brit) or His Highness (inf)

Pa|pel ['paspl] F -, -n piping no pl

pas|pe|lie|ren [paspə'li:rən] ptp **paspeliert**, **pas|peln** ['paspln] VT to pipe

Pass ▲ [pas] M -es, ⸚e ['pɛsə] **a** passport **b** (im Gebirge etc) pass **c** (Ballspiele) pass **d** (Reitsport) amble; **im ~ gehen** to amble

pas|sa|bel [pa'sa:bl] ADJ passable, reasonable; Aussehen auch presentable ADV reasonably well; schmecken passable; aussehen presentable; **mir gehts ganz ~** I'm OK (inf), I'm all right

Pas|sa|ge [pa'sa:ʒə] F -, -n (alle Bedeutungen) passage; (= Ladenstraße) arcade

Pas|sa|gier [pasa'ʒi:ɐ] M -s, -e, **Pas|sa|gie|rin** [-'ʒi:rɪn] F -, -nen passenger; **ein blinder ~** a stowaway

Pas|sa|gier-: Pas|sa|gier|damp|fer M passenger steamer; **Pas|sa|gier|flug|zeug** NT passenger aircraft, airliner; **Pas|sa|gier|lis|te** F passenger list

Pas|sah ['pasa] -s, no pl, **Pas|sah|fest** NT (Feast of the) Passover

Pas|sah|mahl NT Passover meal; (jüdisch) Seder

Pass|amt ▲ NT passport office

Pas|sant [pa'sant] M -en, -en, **Pas|san|tin** [-'santɪn] F -, -nen passer-by

Pas|sat [pa'sa:t] M -s, -e, **Pas|sat|wind** M trade wind

Pass|bild ▲ NT passport photo(graph)

Pas|se ['pasə] F -, -n yoke

pas|sé [pa'se:], **pas|see** ▲ ADJ pred passé; **diese Mode ist längst ~** this fashion went out long ago; **die Sache ist längst ~** that's all ancient history (inf), that's all in the past

pas|sen¹ [pasn] **VI a** (= die richtige Größe, Form haben) to fit; **die Schuhe ~ (mir) gut** the shoes fit (me) well, the shoes are a good fit (for me); **dieser Schlüssel passt nicht (ins Schloss)** this key doesn't or won't fit (the lock); **der Deckel passt nicht** the lid doesn't or won't fit (on) **b** (= harmonieren) **zu etw ~** to go with sth; (im Ton) to match sth; **zu jdm ~** (Mensch) to be suited to sb, to suit sb; **zueinander ~** to go together; (Menschen auch) to be suited (to each other), to suit each other, to be well matched; **sie passt gut zu ihm** she's well suited to him, she's just right for him; **das passt zu ihm, so etwas zu sagen** that's just like him to say that; **es passt nicht zu dir, Bier zu trinken** it doesn't look right for you to drink beer, you don't look right drinking beer; **es passt nicht zu ihr, dass sie so freundlich ist** it's not like her to be so friendly; **diese Einstellung passt gut zu ihm** that attitude is typical of him, that attitude is just like him; **diese Einstellung passt nicht mehr in die heutige Zeit** this attitude is not acceptable nowadays; **so ein formeller Ausdruck passt nicht in diesen Satz** such a formal expression is out of place or is all wrong in this sentence; **Streiks ~ nicht in die konjunkturelle Landschaft** strike action is inappropriate in the current economic situation; **das Rot passt da nicht** the red is all wrong there; **das Bild passt besser in das andere Zimmer** the picture would look or go better in the other room; **er passt nicht in diese Welt/in dieses Team** he doesn't fit or he is out of place in this world/in this team; **ins Bild ~** to fit the picture **c** (= genehm sein) to suit, to be suitable or convenient; **er passt mir (einfach) nicht** I (just) don't like him; **Sonntag passt uns nicht/gut** Sunday is no good for us/suits me fine; **das passt mir gar nicht** (= kommt ungelegen) that isn't at all convenient, that doesn't suit me at all; (= gefällt mir nicht) I don't like that at all, I don't think much of that; **das passt mir gar nicht, dass du schon gehst** I don't want you to go now; **wenns dem Chef passt ...** if it suits the boss ..., if the boss gets the idea into his head ...; **du kannst doch nicht einfach kommen, wann es dir passt** you can't just come when it suits you or when you like; **das könnte dir so ~!** (inf) you'd like or love that, wouldn't you?; **ihre Raucherei passt mir schon lange nicht** this smoking of hers has been annoying me for a long time

VR (inf) to be proper; **ein solches Benehmen passt sich nicht hier** you can't behave like that here

VT to fix

pas|sen² VI (Cards, fig) to pass; **(ich) passe!** (I) pass!; **~ müssen** to have to pass; **bei dieser Frage muss ich ~** I'll have to pass on this question

pas|sen³ VTI (Ftbl) to pass

pas|send ADJ **a** (in Größe, Form) gut/schlecht **~** well-/ill-fitting; **er trägt kaum mal einen ~en Anzug** he hardly ever wears a suit that fits; **ein ~er Schlüssel (zu diesem Schloss)** a key that fits or to fit (this lock) **b** (in Farbe, Stil) matching; **etwas dazu Passendes** something that goes with it or to go with it, something to match; **ich muss jetzt dazu ~e Schuhe kaufen** now I must buy some matching shoes or some shoes that go with it; **eine im Ton genau dazu ~e Tasche** a bag which matches it exactly **c** (= genehm) Zeit, Termin convenient, suitable;

er kam zu jeder ~en und unpassenden Zeit he came at any time, no matter how inconvenient **d** (= *angemessen*) *Bemerkung, Benehmen, Kleidung* suitable, appropriate, fitting; *Wort* right, proper; **sie trägt zu jeder Gelegenheit einen ~en Hut** she always wears a hat to suit *or* match the occasion; **er findet immer das ~e Wort** he always knows the right thing to say; **bei jeder ~en und unpassenden Gelegenheit** at every opportunity, whether appropriate or not **e** *Geld* exact **ADV** **a** **etw ~ machen** (*Kleidung*) to alter sth; *Brett etc* to fit sth; **etw ~ kürzen** to shorten sth to fit **b** (= *abgezählt*) **den Fahrpreis ~ bereithalten** to have the exact fare ready; **haben Sie es ~?** have you got it exactly?, have you got the right money?

Pas|se|par|tout [paspar'tu:] M OR NT **-s, -s** (*alle Bedeutungen*) passe-partout

Pass-: Pass|form ▲ F fit; **eine gute ~ haben** to be a good fit; **Pass|fo|to** ▲ NT passport photo(graph); **Pass|gang** ▲ [-gaŋ] M **-(e)s**, *no pl* amble; **im ~ gehen** to amble; **Pass|gän|ger** ▲ [-gɛŋɐ] M **-s, -** ambler; **Pass|hö|he** ▲ F top of the pass

pas|sier|bar ADJ *Brücke, Grenze* passable; *Fluss, Kanal, Pass* negotiable

pas|sie|ren [pa'si:rən] *ptp* **passiert** **VI** *aux sein* **a** (= *sich ereignen*) to happen (*mit* to); **ihm ist etwas Schreckliches passiert** something terrible has happened to him; **ihm ist beim Bergsteigen etwas passiert** he had an accident while mountaineering; **ist ihm etwas passiert?** has anything happened to him?; **beim Sturz ist ihm erstaunlicherweise nichts passiert** miraculously he wasn't hurt *or* injured in the fall; **was ist denn passiert?** what's the matter?; **es wird dir schon nichts ~** nobody's going to hurt you, nothing is going to happen to you; **es ist ein Unfall passiert** there has been an accident; **das kann auch nur mir ~!** that could only happen to me!, just my luck!; **dass mir das ja nicht mehr** *or* **nicht noch mal passiert!** see that it doesn't happen again!; **jetzt ist es passiert!** now it's happened! I warned you; **jetzt ist es passiert! jetzt kriegen wir Ärger** that's done it *or* torn it (*Brit inf*) *or* that does it, now we'll be in trouble; **so was ist mir noch nie passiert!** that's never happened to me before!; (*empört*) I've never known anything like it!

b (= *durchgehen*) to pass; (*Gesetz*) to be passed, to go through; **jdn ungehindert ~ lassen** to let sb pass

VT **a** (= *vorbeigehen an*) to pass; **der Zug passierte die Brücke** the train crossed *or* went over *or* passed over the bridge; **der Zug passierte zwei Stationen** the train went through *or* passed (through) two stations; **die Grenze ~** to cross (over) *or* pass (over *or* through) the border; **die Zensur ~** to get through the censor, to be passed by the censor; **das Parlament ~** (*Gesetz*) to be passed by parliament, to get through parliament

b (*Cook*) to strain

Pas|sier-: Pas|sier|schein M pass, permit; **Pas|sier|schlag** M (*Tennis*) passing shot; **Pas|sier|sieb** NT strainer; **Pas|sier|stel|le** F crossing point

Pas|si|on [pa'sio:n] F **-, -en** passion; (*religiös*) Passion; **er ist Jäger aus ~** he has a passion for hunting

pas|si|o|niert [pasio'ni:ɐt] ADJ enthusiastic, passionate

Pas|si|ons-: Pas|si|ons|blu|me F passion flower; **Pas|si|ons|frucht** F passion fruit; **Pas|si|ons|spiel** NT Passion play; **Pas|si|ons|wo|che** F Holy Week, Passion Week; **Pas|si|ons|zeit** F (= *Karwoche*) Holy *or* Passion Week; (= *Fastenzeit*) Lent

pas|siv [pasi:f, pa'si:f] ADJ passive; **~e Bestechung** corruption *no pl*, corrupt practices *pl*; **~es Mitglied** non-active member; **~es Rauchen**

passive smoking; **~e Sicherheit** (*Aut*) passive safety; **~er Widerstand** passive resistance; **~er Wortschatz** passive vocabulary; **~e Handelsbilanz** (*Comm*) adverse trade balance → **Wahlrecht** **ADV** passively; **sich ~ verhalten** to be passive

Pas|siv ['pasi:f] NT **-s, -e** [-və] (*Gram*) passive (voice); **das Verb steht im ~** the verb is in the passive (voice)

Pas|si|va [pa'si:va] PL, **Pas|si|ven** [-vn] PL (*Comm*) liabilities *pl*

Pas|siv-: Pas|siv|bil|dung F (*Gram*) formation of the passive; **Pas|siv|fä|hig|keit** F (*Gram*) ability to form the passive; **Pas|siv|ge|schäft** NT (*Fin*) deposit business

Pas|si|vi|tät [pasivi'tɛ:t] F **-**, *no pl* passiveness, passivity; (*Chem*) passivity

Pas|siv-: Pas|siv|pos|ten M (*Comm*) debit entry; **Pas|siv|rau|chen** NT passive smoking; **Pas|siv|sal|do** M (*Comm*) debit account; **Pas|siv|sei|te** F (*Comm*) debit side

Pas|si|vum [pa'si:vʊm] NT **-s, Passiva** [-va] (*Gram*) = **Passiv**

Pass-: Pass|kon|trol|le ▲ F passport control; **~!** (your) passports please!; **durch die ~ gehen** to go through passport control; **Pass|pho|to** NT passport photo(graph); **Pass|stel|le** ▲ F passport office; **Pass|stra|ße** ▲ F (mountain) pass

Pas|sung ['pasʊŋ] F **-, -en** (*Tech*) fit

Pas|sus ['pasʊs] M **-, -** ['pasu:s] passage

Pass|ver|län|ge|rung ▲ F passport renewal

Pass|wort ▲ NT *pl* **-wörter** (*Comput*) password

Pass|wort|schutz ▲ M password protection

Pass|zwang ▲ M, *no pl* requirement to carry a passport; **es besteht kein ~** you don't have to carry a passport

Pas|te ['pastə] F **-, -n**, **Pas|ta** ['pasta] F **-, Pasten** ['pastn] paste

Pas|tell [pas'tɛl] NT **-s, -e** pastel; (= *Pastellfarbe auch*) pastel shade *or* colour (*Brit*) *or* color (*US*); **in ~ arbeiten** to work in pastels; **ein schönes ~** a beautiful pastel (drawing)

Pas|tell-: Pas|tell|far|be F pastel (crayon); (*Farbton*) pastel (shade *or* colour (*Brit*) *or* color (*US*)); **pas|tell|far|ben** [-farbn] **ADJ** pastel (-coloured) (*Brit*), pastel(-colored) (*US*); **ADV** in pastel colours (*Brit*) *or* colors (*US*), in pastels; **etw ~ streichen** to paint sth in pastel colo(u)rs *or* in pastels; **Pas|tell|ma|ler(in)** M(F) pastellist (*Brit*), pastelist (*US*); **Pas|tell|ma|le|rei** F drawing in pastels, pastel drawing; **Pas|tell|stift** M pastel (crayon); **Pas|tell|ton** M *pl* **-töne** pastel shade *or* tone

Pas|tet|chen [pas'te:tçən] NT **-s, -** vol-au-vent

Pas|te|te [pas'te:tə] F **-, -n** **a** (= *Schüsselpastete*) pie; (= *Pastetchen*) vol-au-vent; (*ungefüllt*) vol-au-vent case **b** (= *Leberpastete etc*) pâté

Pas|teu|ri|sa|ti|on [pastøriza'tsio:n] F **-, -en** pasteurization

pas|teu|ri|sie|ren [pastøri'zi:rən] *ptp* **pasteurisiert** VT to pasteurize

Pas|teu|ri|sie|rung F **-, -en** pasteurization

Pas|til|le [pas'tɪlə] F **-, -n** pastille

Pas|ti|nak ['pastinak] M **-s, -e**, **Pas|ti|na|ke** [pasti'na:kə] F **-, -n** (*Bot*) parsnip

Pas|tor ['pasto:ɐ, pas'to:ɐ] M **-s, Pastoren** [-'to:rən], **Pas|to|rin** [-'to:rɪn] F **-, -nen** → **Pfarrer**

pas|to|ral [pasto'ra:l] ADJ pastoral

Pas|to|ra|le [pasto'ra:lə] NT **-s, -s** *or f* **-, -n** (*Mus*) pastorale; (*Art, Liter*) pastoral; **Beethovens ~** Beethoven's Pastoral Symphony

Patch|work ['pɛtʃwø:ɐk, -wœrk] NT **-s**, *no pl* (*Tex, fig*) patchwork

Pa|te ['pa:tə] M **-n, -n** **a** (= *Taufzeuge*) godfather, godparent; (= *Mafiaboss*) godfather; (= *Firmzeuge*) sponsor; **bei einem Kind ~ stehen** to be a child's godparent/sponsor; **bei etw ~ gestanden haben** (*fig*) to be the force behind sth **b** (*obs*: = *Täufling*) godchild

Pa|te|ne [pa'te:nə] F **-, -n** (*Eccl*) paten

Pa|ten-: Pa|ten|kind NT godchild; godson; goddaughter; **Pa|ten|on|kel** M godfather; **Pa|ten|schaft** ['pa:tnʃaft] F **-, -en** godparenthood; sponsorship; **er übernimmt die ~ für das Kind** he's going to be the child's godfather; **die ~ für** *or* **über jdn/etw übernehmen** (*fig*) to take on the responsibility for sb/sth; **er nahm seine ~ nicht ernst** he didn't take his responsibilities as godfather *or* godparent very seriously; **Pa|ten|sohn** M godson; **Pa|ten|stadt** F twin(ned) town (*Brit*), sister city (*US*)

pa|tent [pa'tɛnt] ADJ ingenious, clever; *Lösung auch* neat; *Werkzeug auch* nifty (*inf*); **ein ~er Kerl** a great guy/girl (*inf*); **sie ist eine ~e Frau** she's a tremendous woman

Pa|tent [pa'tɛnt] NT **-(e)s, -e** **a** (= *Erfindung, Urkunde*) patent (*für etw* for sth, *auf etw* on sth); **etw als** *or* **zum ~ anmelden**, **ein ~ auf** *or* **für etw anmelden** to apply for a patent on *or* for sth; **ein ~ auf eine Erfindung haben** to have a patent on an invention; **für etw** *or* **auf etw das ~ erteilen** to grant a patent on sth; **„(zum) ~ angemeldet"** "patent pending" **b** (= *Ernennungsurkunde*) commission **c** (*Sw*) permit, licence (*Brit*), license (*US*) **d** (*inf*: = *Mechanismus*) apparatus; **der Haken, so ein blödes ~** this hook, the stupid thing

Pa|tent-: Pa|tent|amt NT Patent Office; **Pa|tent|an|mel|dung** F application for a patent

Pa|ten|tan|te F godmother

Pa|tent-: Pa|tent|an|walt M, **Pa|tent|an|wäl|tin** F patent agent *or* attorney; **Pa|tent|dau|er** F life of a patent; **pa|tent|fä|hig** ADJ patentable; **Pa|tent|fä|hig|keit** F patentability; **Pa|tent|ge|ber(in)** M(F) patentor; **Pa|tent|ge|bühr** F (*bei Anmeldung*) (patent) filing fee; (*jährlich*) patent annuity; **Pa|tent|ge|setz** NT Patents Act

pa|ten|tier|bar ADJ patentable

pa|ten|tie|ren [patɛn'ti:rən] *ptp* **patentiert** VT to patent; **sich** (*dat*) **etw ~ lassen** to take out a patent on sth, to have sth patented

Pa|tent-: Pa|tent|in|ha|ber(in) M(F) patentee, patent-holder; **Pa|tent|lö|sung** F (*fig*) easy answer, patent remedy; **bei der Kindererziehung gibt es keine ~** there's no instant recipe for success in bringing up children

Pa|ten|toch|ter F goddaughter

Pa|tent-: Pa|tent|recht NT patent law; **pa|tent|recht|lich** ADJ, ADV under patent law; **~ geschützt** patented, protected (by patent); **Pa|tent|re|gis|ter** NT Patent Rolls *pl*; **Pa|tent|re|zept** NT (*fig*) = **Patentlösung**; **Pa|tent|schrift** F patent specification; **Pa|tent|schutz** M patent right, protection by (letters) patent; **Pa|tent|ur|kun|de** F letters patent *pl*; **Pa|tent|ver|let|zung** F patent infringement

Pa|ter ['pa:tɐ] M **-s, -** *or* **Patres** ['patre:s] (*Eccl*) Father

Pa|ter|nos|ter¹ [patɐ'nɔstɐ] NT **-s, -** (= *Gebet*) Lord's Prayer, paternoster

Pa|ter|nos|ter² M **-s, -** (= *Aufzug*) paternoster

pa|the|tisch [pa'te:tɪʃ] **ADJ** emotional; *Beschreibung auch* dramatic; *Rede, Stil auch* emotive; *Gehabe auch* histrionic **ADV** dramatically; **das war zu ~ gespielt** it was overacted

pa|tho|gen [pato'ge:n] ADJ (*Med*) pathogenic

Pa|tho|lo|ge [pato'lo:gə] M **-n, -n**, **Pa|tho|lo|gin** [-'lo:gɪn] F **-, -nen** pathologist

Pa|tho|lo|gie [patolo'gi:] F **-, -n** [-'gi:ən] pathology

pa|tho|lo|gisch [patolo'gɪʃ] (*Med, fig*) **ADJ** pathological **ADV** pathologically

Pa|thos ['pa:tɔs] NT **-**, *no pl* emotiveness, emotionalism; **ein Gedicht mit/ohne ~ vortragen** to recite a poem with great drama/without drama; **die Rede enthielt zu viel falsches ~** the speech contained too much false emotionalism; **mit viel ~ in der Stimme** in a voice charged with emotion; **mit viel ~ versuchte sie, ihn zu überzeugen** she made a highly emotional attempt to persuade him

Pa|ti|ence [pa'siã:s] F **-, -n** patience *no pl*; **~n legen** to play patience; **eine ~ legen** to play (a game of) patience

Pa|ti|ent [pa'tsiɛnt] M **-en, -en**, **Pa|ti|en|tin** [-'tsiɛntɪn] F **-, -nen** patient; **ich bin ~ von** *or* **bei Dr X** I'm Dr X's patient, I'm being treated by Dr X; **~en mit Lungenentzündung** pneumonia patients

Pa|tin ['pa:tɪn] F **-, -nen** godmother, godparent; (= *Firmpatin*) sponsor

Pa|ti|na ['pa:tina] F **-, *no pl** (lit, fig)* patina; **~ an|setzen** *(lit)* to patinate, to become coated with a patina; *(fig)* to take on a hallowed air of tradition

pa|ti|nie|ren [pati'ni:rən] *ptp* **patiniert** VT to patinate, to coat with a patina

Pa|tio ['pa:tio] M **-s, -s** *(Archit)* patio

Pa|tis|se|rie [patɪsa'ri:] F **-, Patisserien** [-'ri:ən] *(Sw)* a (= *Konditorei*) patisserie b (= *Gebäck*) pastries *pl*

Pat|res *pl von* **Pater**

Pat|ri|arch [patri'arç] M **-en, -en** *(lit, fig)* patriarch

pat|ri|ar|cha|lisch [patriar'ça:lɪʃ] *(lit, fig)* ADJ patriarchal ADV patriarchally; **er regiert ~** his rule is patriarchal; **eine noch stark ~ organisierte Gesellschaft** a still very patriarchal society

Pat|ri|ar|chat [patriar'ça:t] NT **-(e)s, -e** patriarchy

Pat|ri|ot [patri'o:t] M **-en, -en**, **Pat|ri|o|tin** [-'o:tɪn] F **-, -nen** patriot

pat|ri|o|tisch [patri'o:tɪʃ] ADJ patriotic ADV reden, sich verhalten, denken patriotically; **~ gesinnt** *or* **eingestellt** patriotically-minded, patriotic; **~ klingen** to sound patriotic

Pat|ri|o|tis|mus [patrio'tɪsmʊs] M **-, *no pl** patriotism

Pat|ri|ze [pa'tri:tsə] F **-, -n** punch

Pat|ri|zi|at [patri'tsia:t] NT **-(e)s, -e** patriciate

Pat|ri|zi|er [pa'tri:tsiɐ] M **-s, -**, **Pat|ri|zie|rin** [-iərɪn] F **-, -nen** patrician

Pat|ri|zi|er|ge|schlecht NT patrician family

pat|ri|zisch [pa'tri:tsɪʃ] ADJ patrician

Pat|ron [pa'tro:n] M **-s, -e** *(Eccl)* patron saint b (old: = *Schirmherr*) patron c *(inf)* **frecher ~** cheeky beggar *(Brit inf)*, real (impudent) so--and-so *(inf)* d *(Sw, S Ger: = Inhaber)* owner

Pat|ro|na|ge [patro'na:ʒə] F **-, -n** patronage

Pat|ro|nat [patro'na:t] NT **-(e)s, -e** patronage *(über +acc* of); **unter jds ~** *(dat)* **stehen** to be under sb's patronage

Pat|ro|ne [pa'tro:nə] F **-, -n** *(Film, Mil, von Füller, von Drucker)* cartridge; *(Tex)* point paper design

Pat|ro|nen-: Pat|ro|nen|gurt M ammunition belt; **Pat|ro|nen|gür|tel** M cartridge belt, bandolier; **Pat|ro|nen|hül|se** F cartridge case; **Pat|ro|nen|rah|men** M (cartridge) clip; **Pat|ro|nen|ta|sche** F ammunition pouch

Pat|ro|nin F **-, -nen** a *(Eccl)* patron saint b (old: = *Schirmherrin*) patron, patroness

Pat|ro|nym [patro'ny:m] NT **-s, -e**, **Pat|ro|ny|mi|kon** [patro'ny:mikɔn] NT **-s, Patronymika** [-ka] patronymic

Pat|rouil|le [pa'trʊljə] F **-, -n** patrol; **(auf) ~ ge|hen** to patrol

Pat|rouil|len- [pa'trʊljən-]: **Pat|rouil|len|boot** NT patrol boat; **Pat|rouil|len|gang** M *pl* **-gänge** patrol

pat|rouil|lie|ren [patrʊl'ji:rən] *ptp* **patrouilliert** VI to patrol

patsch [patʃ] INTERJ splash, splat; *(bei Ohrfeige)* smack; **wenn du so frech bist, machts gleich ~!** if you go on being so naughty you'll get a good smack

Patsch [patʃ] M **-es, -e** *(inf)* smack, slap

Pat|sche ['patʃə] F **-, -n** *(inf)* a (= *Hand*) paw *(inf)*, mitt *(inf)* b (= *Matsch*) mud; (= *Schneematsch*) slush; *(fig)* jam *(inf)*, fix *(inf)*, (tight) spot *(inf)*; **in der ~ sitzen** *or* **stecken** to be in a jam *(inf)*; **jdm aus der ~ helfen**, **jdn aus der ~ ziehen** to get sb out of a jam *(inf)*; **jdn in der ~ (sitzen) lassen** to leave sb in the lurch; **jdn in die ~ reiten** to get sb into a jam *(inf)* c (= *Feuerpatsche*) beater; (= *Fliegenpatsche*) swat

pat|schen ['patʃn] VI a *(mit Flüssigkeit)* to splash; **das Baby patschte mit der Hand in die Suppe** the baby went splat *or* splash with his hand in the soup; **er ist durch die Pfützen gepatscht** he splashed *or* went splashing through the puddles b *(inf: mit Hand, Fuß)* **das Baby patschte auf den Tisch/an die Möbel** the baby smacked the table/the furniture; **die Kinder ~ mit den Händen** the children clap their hands (together); **der Hund patschte über den Flur** the dog padded across the hall; **er patschte der Sekretärin auf den Hintern** he gave his secretary a pat on the bottom, he patted his secretary on the bottom

Patsch|hand F *(inf)*, **Patsch|händ|chen** NT *(inf)* paw *(inf)*, mitt *(inf)*; *(von Kindern)* (little) hand

patsch|nass ▲ ['patʃ'nas] ADJ *(inf)* soaking *or* dripping wet; **draußen ist es ~!** it's soaking wet outside

Pat|schu|li|öl [pa'tʃu:liø:l] NT **-s, -e** pa(t)chouli oil, patchouly oil

patt [pat] ADJ *pred* ADV *(Chess, fig)* in stalemate; **das Spiel endete ~** the game ended in (a) stalemate; **jetzt sind wir beide ~** now we've both reached a stalemate

Patt [pat] NT **-s, -s** *(lit, fig)* stalemate; **ein ~ errei|chen** to reach (a) stalemate, to come to (a) stalemate

Patt|si|tu|a|ti|on F *(lit, fig)* stalemate; **aus ei|ner ~ herauskommen** to get out of a stalemate, to break the deadlock

pat|zen ['patsn] VI *(inf)* to slip up, to boob *(esp Brit inf)*, to goof *(US inf)*; **der Pianist hat gepatzt** the pianist fluffed a passage *or* boobed *etc*; **der Schauspieler hat gepatzt** the actor fluffed his lines *or* boobed *etc*

Pat|zen ['patsn] M **-s, -** *(Aus)* blotch, splodge; *(Tinte auch)* blot

Pat|zer ['patsɐ] M **-s, -** *(inf: = Fehler)* slip, boob *(esp Brit inf)*, goof *(US inf)*; **mir ist ein ~ unter|laufen** I made a boob *(esp Brit inf)* or slip

pat|zig ['patsɪç] *(inf)* ADJ snotty *(inf)* ADV **jdm ~ kommen** to be snotty to sb *(inf)*

Pau|kant [pau'kant] M **-en, -en** *(Univ sl)* duellist *(Brit)*, duelist *(US)*

Pauk|bo|den M *(Univ sl)* duelling *(Brit)* or dueling *(US)* floor

Pau|ke ['paukə] F **-, -n** a *(Mus)* kettledrum; **jdn mit ~n und Trompeten empfangen** to roll out the red carpet for sb, to give sb the red-carpet treatment; **mit ~n und Trompeten durchfallen** *(inf)* to fail miserably *or* dismally; **auf die ~ hau|en** *(inf)* (= *angeben*) to blow one's own trumpet, to brag; (= *feiern*) to paint the town red b *(Sch inf: = Schule)* swot-shop *(Brit dated sl)*, school

pau|ken ['paukn] VI a *(inf: = Pauke spielen)* to drum b *(von Korpsstudenten)* to fence c *(inf: = lernen)* to swot *(Brit inf)*, to cram *(US inf)*; **meine Mutter hat immer mit mir gepaukt** my mother always helped me with my swotting *(Brit inf)* or cramming *(inf)* VT to swot up *(Brit inf)*, to study up on *(US)*; **mit jdm Geschichtszahlen ~** to help sb swot up *(Brit inf)* or study up on *(US)* their dates; **Englisch ~** to swot up on *(Brit inf)* or study up on *(US)* English

Pauken-: Pau|ken|schlag M drum beat; **wie ein ~** *(fig)* like a thunderbolt; **die Sinfonie mit dem ~** the Surprise Symphony; **Pau|ken|schlä|gel** M drumstick; **Pau|ken|schlä|ger(in)** M(F) drummer; **Pau|ken|spie|ler(in)** M(F) drummer

Pau|ker ['paukɐ] M **-s, -**, **Pau|ke|rin** [-ərɪn] F **-, -nen** a *(inf: = Paukenspieler)* timpanist b *(Sch inf: = Lehrer)* teacher; **da geht unser ~** there's sir *(Brit inf)*, there's the teach *(US inf)*

Pau|ke|rei [paukə'rai] F **-, -en** a *(inf: = das Paukespielen)* drumming b *(Sch inf)* swotting *(Brit inf)*, cramming *(inf)*; **ich hab diese ~ satt** I'm fed up with school

Pau|kist [pau'kɪst] M **-en, -en**, **Pau|kis|tin** [-'kɪstɪn] F **-en, -en** timpanist

Pau|lus|brief ['paulʊs-] M Paul's Epistle

Paus|ba|cken ['paus-] PL chubby cheeks *pl*

paus|bä|ckig ['pausbɛkɪç] ADJ chubby-cheeked

pau|schal [pau'ʃa:l] ADJ a (= *vorläufig geschätzt*) estimated; (= *einheitlich*) flat-rate *attr* only b *(fig)* Behauptung, Kritik, Urteil sweeping ADV a (= *nicht spezifiziert*) at a flat *or* set rate; **ich schätze die Baukosten ~ auf etwa eine Million Euro** I'd estimate the overall building costs to be 1 million euros; **die Werkstatt berechnet ~ pro Inspektion 100 Euro** the garage has a flat rate of 100 euros per service; **die Einkommensteuer kann ~ festgesetzt werden** income tax can be set at a flat rate; **die Gebühren werden ~ bezahlt** the charges are paid in a lump sum; **Strom berechnen wir Ihnen ~** we'll charge you a flat rate for electricity; **die Kosten verstehen sich ~** the costs are fixed; **alle bekommen ~ £20 pro Woche mehr** there will be an across--the-board increase of £20 a week, they'll get £20 a week more across the board b (= *nicht differenziert*) abwerten categorically; **so ~ kann man das nicht sagen** that's much too sweeping a statement; **ein Volk ~ verurteilen** to condemn a people wholesale, to condemn a people lock, stock and barrel; **diese Probleme hat er ganz ~ behandelt** he dealt with these problems all lumped together

Pau|schal|be|trag [pau'ʃa:l-] M lump sum; (= *Preis*) inclusive price

Pau|scha|le [pau'ʃa:lə] F **-, -n** (= *Einheitspreis*) flat rate; (= *vorläufig geschätzter Betrag*) estimated amount

Pau|schal- [pau'ʃa:l-]: **Pau|schal|ge|bühr** F (= *Einheitsgebühr*) flat rate (charge); (= *vorläufig geschätzter Betrag*) estimated charge; **Pau|schal|ho|no|rar** NT flat-rate fee

pau|scha|lie|ren [pauʃa'li:rən] *ptp* **pauschaliert** VT to estimate at a flat rate *or* in a lump sum

Pau|scha|lie|rung [pauʃa'li:rʊŋ] F a *(von Beträgen)* consolidation into a lump sum b *(Fin: = Besteuerung)* lump-sum taxation, taxation based on average figures

pau|scha|li|sie|ren [pauʃali'zi:rən] VTI *(geh)* (= *verallgemeinern*) to generalize; (= *nicht differenzieren*) to lump everything together, to tar everything with the same brush *(inf)*; **das kann man nicht ~** you can't generalize or make generalizations like that

Pau|schal- [pau'ʃa:l-]: **Pau|schal|preis** M (= *Einheitspreis*) flat rate; (= *vorläufig geschätzter Betrag*) estimated price; (= *Inklusivpreis*) inclusive or all-in price; **Pau|schal|rei|se** F package holiday *(esp Brit)* or tour; **Pau|schal|steu|er** F (= *vorläufige Steuer*) estimated tax; (= *einheitliche Steuer*) tax at a flat rate; **Pau|schal|sum|me** F lump sum; **Pau|schal|ta|rif** M flat rate; **Pau|schal|ur|laub** M package holiday; **Pau|schal|ur|teil** NT sweeping statement; **er neigt sehr zu ~en** he tends to make sweeping statements; **Pau|schal|ver|si|che|rung** F comprehensive insurance *no pl*

Pausch|be|trag ['pauʃ-] M flat rate

Pau|se¹ F **-, -n** a (= *Unterbrechung*) break; (= *Rast*) rest; (= *das Innehalten*) pause; *(Theat)* interval, intermission; *(Sch)* break, recess *(US)*; *(Pol)* recess; *(Liter)* caesura; **(eine) ~ machen**, **eine ~ einlegen** (= *sich entspannen*) to take or have or make a break; (= *rasten*) to rest, to have or take a rest; (= *innehalten*) to pause, to make a pause; **du hast jetzt mal ~!** *(inf)* now, you keep quiet!; **nach einer langen ~ sagte er ...** after a long silence he said ...; **immer wieder entstanden ~n in der Unterhaltung** the conversation was full of gaps or silences; **ohne ~ arbeiten** to work nonstop or without stopping or continuously; **die große ~** (Sch) (the) break (Brit), recess (US); (in Grundschule) playtime; **zur ~ stand es 3:1** (Ftbl) it was 3-1 at half-time

b (Mus) rest; **die ~n einhalten** to make the rests; **eine halbe/ganze ~** a minim (Brit) or half-note (US)/semibreve (Brit) or whole-note (US) rest

Pau|se² F -, -n (= Durchzeichnung) tracing; (= Fotokopie) (photo)copy

pau|sen ['pauzn] VT to trace

Pau|sen-: Pau|sen|brot NT something to eat at break; **Pau|sen|clown** M **ich bin doch hier nicht der ~!** (inf) I'm not going to play the clown; **Pau|sen|fül|ler** M stopgap; **Pau|sen|hal|le** F break or recess (US) hall; **Pau|sen|hof** M playground, schoolyard; **pau|sen|los** ADJ no pred nonstop, continuous, incessant **ADV** continuously; **er arbeitet ~** he works nonstop; **Pau|sen|pfiff** M (Sport) time-out whistle; (zur Halbzeit) half-time whistle; **Pau|sen|stand** M half-time score; score at the interval; **Pau|sen|zei|chen** NT (Mus) rest; (Rad) call sign

pau|sie|ren [pau'ziːrən] ptp **pausiert** VI to (take or have a) break; **der Torwart musste wegen einer Verletzung ~** the goalkeeper had to rest up because of injury

Paus|pa|pier ['paus-] NT tracing paper; (= Kohlepapier) carbon paper

Pa|vi|an ['paːviaːn] M -s, -e baboon

Pa|vil|lon ['paviljõ:] M -s, -s pavilion

Pay-TV ['peːtiˌviː] NT -s, no pl pay TV

Pa|zi|fik [pa'tsiːfɪk, 'paːtsifɪk] M -s Pacific

pa|zi|fisch [pa'tsiːfɪʃ] ADJ Pacific; **der Pazifische Ozean** the Pacific (Ocean); **der (asiatisch-)pazifische Raum** the Pacific Rim

Pa|zi|fis|mus [patsi'fɪsmʊs] M -, no pl pacifism

Pa|zi|fist [patsi'fɪst] M -en, -en, **Pa|zi|fis|tin** [-'fɪstɪn] F -, -nen pacifist

pa|zi|fis|tisch [patsi'fɪstɪʃ] ADJ pacifist **ADV** **~ eingestellt sein** to be a pacifist; **~ klingen** to sound pacifist; **sich ~ geben** to give the impression of being a pacifist

PC [peː'tseː] M -s, -s abbr von **Personalcomputer** PC

PC-Be|nut|zer(in) M(F) PC user

PDS [peːdeː'ɛs] F - abbr von **Partei des Demokratischen Sozialismus**

PDS

The **PDS** (Partei des Demokratischen Sozialismus) emerged in 1989/90 from the **Sozialistische Einheitspartei Deutschlands** (**SED**), which was the official ruling party of the former East Germany. The **PDS** champions people's rights in the new **Länder** and aims to establish itself as a left-wing socialist party throughout Germany.

Pech [pɛç] NT -(e)s, -e **a** (Stoff) pitch; **schwarz wie ~** (as) black as pitch; **ihr Haar ist schwarz wie ~** her hair is jet black; **die beiden halten zusammen wie ~ und Schwefel** (inf) the two are as thick as thieves (Brit) or are inseparable

b no pl (inf: = Missgeschick) bad or hard or tough (inf) luck; **bei etw ~ haben** to be unlucky in or with sth, to have bad or tough (inf) or lousy (inf) luck in or with sth; **~ gehabt!** tough! (inf); **sie ist vom ~ verfolgt** bad luck follows her around; **das ist sein ~!** that's his hard or bad or tough (inf) luck!; **so ein ~!** just my/our etc luck!; **~ im Spiel, Glück in der Liebe** (prov) unlucky at cards, lucky in love (prov)

Pech-: Pech|blen|de F (Min) pitchblende; **Pech|draht** M waxed thread; **Pech|fa|ckel** F (pitch) torch, link; **Pech|koh|le** F bituminous coal; **pech|(ra|ben)|schwarz** ADJ (inf) pitch-

-black; Haar jet-black; **Pech|sträh|ne** F (inf) run or streak of bad luck, unlucky patch; **eine ~ haben** to have a run or streak of bad luck; **Pech|vo|gel** M (inf) unlucky person, walking disaster area (hum inf); (Frau auch) Calamity Jane

Pe|dal [pe'daːl] NT -s, -e pedal; **(fest) in die ~e treten** to pedal (hard)

Pe|dant [pe'dant] M -en, -en, **Pe|dan|tin** [-'dantɪn] F -, -nen pedant

Pe|dan|te|rie [pedantə'riː] F -, -n [-'riːən] pedantry

pe|dan|tisch [pe'dantɪʃ] ADJ pedantic **ADV** pedantically

Ped|dig|rohr ['pɛdɪç-] NT cane

Pe|dell [pe'dɛl] M -s, -e (old) (Sch) caretaker, janitor; (Univ) porter

Pe|di|kü|re [pedi'kyːrə] F -, -n **a** no pl (= Fußpflege) pedicure **b** (= Fußpflegerin) chiropodist

pe|di|kü|ren [pedi'kyːrən] ptp **pedikürt** VT to give a pedicure to

Pee|ling ['piːlɪŋ] NT -s, -s (Hautpflege) peeling, exfoliation

Peep|show ▲ ['piːpʃoː] F peep show

Pe|ga|sus ['peːgazʊs] M -' Pegasus

Pe|gel ['peːgl] M -s, - (in Flüssen, Kanälen, Meer) water depth gauge; (Elec) level recorder

Pe|gel|stand M water level

Peil-: Peil|an|la|ge F direction-finding equipment, direction finder; (Naut) sounding equipment; **Peil|an|ten|ne** F directional antenna

pei|len ['pailən] VT Wassertiefe to sound, to plumb; U-Boot, Sender, Standort to get a fix on, to get or take the bearings of; Richtung to plot; (= entdecken) to detect; **die Lage ~** (inf) to see how the land lies, to see which way the wind's blowing; **über den Daumen ~** (inf) to guess roughly; **über den Daumen gepeilt** (inf) roughly speaking, at a rough estimate; **es ~** (sl: = durchblicken) to get it (inf)

Pei|ler ['pailɐ] M -s, - detector

Peil-: Peil|funk M radio direction finder; **Peil|ge|rät** NT direction finder; **Peil|lot** NT plumb line; **Peil|sen|der** M tracking device; **Peil|sta|ti|on** F direction finding station

Pei|lung ['pailʊŋ] F -, -en (von Wassertiefe) sounding, plumbing; (von U-Boot, Sender, Standort) locating; (von Richtung) plotting; **eine ~ vornehmen** to take a bearing; **was für eine ~ haben wir für das U-Boot?** what's our bearing on the submarine?

Pein [pain] F -, no pl (geh) agony, suffering; **sein Leben war eine einzige ~** his life was one long torment; **jdm das Leben zur ~ machen** to make sb's life a misery

pei|ni|gen ['painɪgŋ] VT to torture; (fig) to torment; **jdn bis aufs Blut ~** to torture sb till he bleeds; (fig) to torment sb mercilessly; **von Schmerzen/Zweifeln gepeinigt** tormented by pain/doubt, racked with pain/doubt

Pei|ni|ger ['painɪgɐ] M -s, -, **Pei|ni|ge|rin** [-ərɪn] F -, -nen (liter) torturer; (fig) tormentor

Pei|ni|gung F -, -en (liter) torture; (fig) torment

pein|lich ['painlɪç] ADJ **a** (= unangenehm) (painfully) embarrassing; Lage, Fragen auch awkward; Überraschung nasty; **ich habe das ~e Gefühl, dass ...** I have a terrible feeling that ...; **es war ihm ~(, dass ...)** he was or felt embarrassed (because ...); **es ist mir sehr ~, aber ich muss es Ihnen einmal sagen** I don't know how to put it, but you really ought to know; **es ist mir sehr ~, aber die Arbeit ist immer noch nicht fertig** I'm really sorry but the work still isn't finished; **das ist mir ja so ~** I feel awful about it; **es war so schlecht, dass es schon ~ war** (inf) it was so bad that it was (really) painful (inf)

b (= gewissenhaft) painstaking, meticulous; Sparsamkeit careful; **in seinem Zimmer/auf seinem Schreibtisch herrschte ~e or ~ste Ordnung** his room/his desk was meticulously or scrupu-

lously tidy; **jdn einem ~en Verhör unterziehen** to question sb very closely

ADV a (= unangenehm) **~ berührt sein** (hum) to be profoundly shocked (iro); **~ wirken** to be embarrassing, to cause embarrassment

b (= gründlich) painstakingly, scrupulously; **der Koffer wurde ~ genau untersucht** the case was gone through very thoroughly, the case was given a very thorough going-over (inf); **er vermied es ~st, davon zu sprechen** he was at pains not to talk about it; **etw ~st geheim halten** to keep sth strictly secret or top secret

Pein|lich|keit F -, -en (= Unangenehmheit) awkwardness; **die ~ der Situation** the awkwardness of the situation, the embarrassing or awkward situation; **die ~ seines Benehmens** his embarrassing behaviour (Brit) or behavior (US); **diese ~en auf der Bühne** these embarrassing or painful scenes on stage

pein|sam ['painzaːm] ADJ (hum) painful, embarrassing

pein|voll ['painfɔl] ADJ (old) painful

Peit|sche ['paitʃə] F -, -n whip; **er gab seinem Pferd die ~** he whipped his horse on; **mit der ~ knallen** (lit, fig) to crack the whip → **Zuckerbrot**

peit|schen ['paitʃn] VTI to whip; (fig) to lash

Peit|schen-: Peit|schen|hieb M stroke, lash; **Peit|schen|knall** M crack of a whip; **Peit|schen|leuch|te** F streetlamp; **Peit|schen|schlag** M stroke or lash of a whip; **Peit|schen|schnur** F (whip)lash, thong; **Peit|schen|stiel** M whip handle, whipstock

pe|jo|ra|tiv [pejora'tiːf] ADJ pejorative **ADV** pejoratively

Pe|ki|ne|se [peki'neːzə] M -n, -n pekinese, pekinese (inf)

Pe|king ['peːkɪŋ] NT -s Peking, Beijing

Pe|king-: Pe|king|en|te F Peking duck; **Pe|king|oper** F Peking Opera

Pek|tin [pek'tiːn] NT -s, -e pectin

pe|ku|ni|är [pekuni'ɛː] (dated) **ADJ** pecuniary, financial **ADV** financially

Pe|lar|go|nie [pelar'goːniə] F -, -n (Bot) pelargonium

Pe|le|ri|ne [peləˈriːnə] F -, -n (old) pelerine (old), cape

Pe|li|kan ['peːlikaːn, peli'kaːn] M -s, -e pelican

Pel|le ['pɛlə] F -, -n (inf) skin; (abgeschält) peel; **der Chef sitzt mir auf der ~** (inf) I've got the boss on my back (inf); **er geht mir nicht von der ~** (inf) he won't stop pestering me → **rücken**

pel|len ['pɛlən] (inf) VT Kartoffeln, Wurst to skin, to peel; Ei to take the shell off → **Ei** VR (Mensch, Körperhaut) to peel; **meine Haut pellt sich** my skin's peeling, I'm peeling; **sie pellt sich aus dem nassen Kleid** she peeled off her wet dress

Pell|kar|tof|feln PL potatoes pl boiled in their jackets or skins

Pe|lo|pon|nes [pelopɔˈneːs] M -(es) or f - Peloponnese

Pelz [pɛlts] M -es, -e fur; (nicht gegerbt auch) pelt, hide, skin; (Kleidung) fur; (fig: = Haarwuchs) fur no pl; **jdm eins auf den ~ brennen** (inf) to singe sb's hide; **sich** (dat) **die Sonne auf den ~ brennen lassen** (inf) to toast oneself (inf); **wasch mir den ~, aber mach mich nicht nass** (prov) give me all of the benefits and none of the hassle (inf) → **rücken**

Pelz-: Pelz|be|satz M fur trimming; **pelz|be|setzt** ADJ trimmed with fur, fur-trimmed; **Pelz|fut|ter** NT fur lining; **pelz|ge|füt|tert** [-gəfʏtɐt] ADJ fur-lined, lined with fur; **Pelz|händ|ler(in)** M(F) furrier; (= Fellhändler) fur trader; **Pelz|hand|schuh** M fur glove

pel|zig ['pɛltsɪç] ADJ furry; Zunge furred(-over), furry

Pelz-: Pelz|imi|ta|ti|on F imitation fur; **Pelz|jä|ger(in)** M(F) skin-hunter; (= Fallensteller)

(fur) trapper; **Pelz|kra|gen** M fur collar; **Pelz|man|tel** M fur coat; **Pelz|müt|ze** F fur hat; **Pelz|stie|fel** M fur or furry (inf) boot; (pelzgefüttert) fur-lined boot; **Pelz|stoff** M fur fabric; **Pelz|tier** NT animal with a valuable fur, animal prized for its fur; **~e jagen** to hunt animals for their fur; (mit Fallen) to go trapping; **Pelz|tier|farm** F fur farm; **Pelz|tier|jäger(in)** M(F) skin-hunter; (= Fallensteller) (fur) trapper; **Pelz|tier|zucht** F fur farming; **pelz|ver|brämt** [-fɛːbrɛːmt] ADJ (liter) = pelzbesetzt; **Pelz|wa|ren** PL furs pl; **Pelz|werk** NT fur

Pe|nal|ty ['pɛnltɪ] M -(s), -s (Sport) a (Eishockey) penalty b (Aus, Sw Ftbl) penalty

Pen-Club ['pɛn-] M PEN Club

Pen|dant [pã'dãː] NT -s, -s counterpart, opposite number

Pen|del ['pɛndl] NT -s, - pendulum; **keiner kann das ~ der Zeit aufhalten** time and tide wait for no man (prov); **das ~ schlug nach der entgegengesetzten Seite aus** (fig) the pendulum swung in the other direction

Pen|del-: Pen|del|aus|schlag M swing of a/the pendulum; **Pen|del|flug|dienst** M shuttle service

pen|deln ['pɛndln] VI a (= schwingen) to swing (to and fro), to oscillate (form); (Boxer) to weave; **er ließ die Beine ~** he let his legs dangle, he dangled his legs; **der DAX pendelte um die 3000-Marke** the DAX index fluctuated around the 3000 level b aux sein (= hin und her fahren) (Zug, Fähre etc) to shuttle; (Mensch) to commute; (fig) to vacillate, to fluctuate

Pen|del-: Pen|del|schlag M swing of the pendulum; **er spielte zum ~ des Metronoms** he played in time to the metronome; **der ~ der Zeit** the march of time; **Pen|del|schwin|gung** F swing of the pendulum; (Phys auch) oscillation (of a pendulum); **Pen|del|tür** F swing door; **Pen|del|uhr** F pendulum clock; **Pen|del|ver|kehr** M shuttle service; (= Berufsverkehr) commuter traffic

Pend|ler ['pɛndlɐ] M -s, -, **Pend|le|rin** [-ərɪn] F -, -nen commuter

Pen|do|li|no [pɛndo'liːno] M -s, -s (Rail) tilting train

pe|net|rant [pene'trant] ADJ a Gestank, Geschmack penetrating, pungent; Gestank, Parfüm auch overpowering b (fig. = aufdringlich) pushing, insistent; **der Typ war mir zu ~** he was too pushing or pushy (inf) for my liking; **seine Selbstsicherheit ist schon ~** his self-confidence is overpowering; **ein ~er Kerl** a pest (inf), a nuisance ADV a (= stark) **das Parfüm riecht ~** the perfume is overpowering; **das schmeckt ~ nach Knoblauch** you can't taste anything for garlic, it has a very strong taste of garlic b (= aufdringlich) **jdn ~ nach etw ausfragen** to ask sb insistent questions about sth; **er ist mir ~ auf die Pelle gerückt** he just wouldn't take no for an answer

Pe|net|ranz [pene'trants] F -, no pl (von Geruch, Geschmack) pungency; (fig. = Aufdringlichkeit) pushiness; **er ist von einer unausstehlichen ~** he's unbearably pushy (inf)

Pe|net|ra|ti|on [penetra'tsioːn] F -, -en penetration

pe|net|rie|ren [pene'triːrən] ptp **penetriert** VT to penetrate

peng [pɛŋ] INTERJ bang

pe|ni|bel [pe'niːbl] ADJ a (= gründlich, genau) pernickety (inf), precise, exact b (dial. = peinlich) Lage, Angelegenheit painful, embarrassing ADV sauber meticulously; **ein ~ ordentliches Zimmer** an immaculately clean and tidy room; **sie räumt ihr Zimmer immer ~ auf** she always keeps her room immaculate; **mein Mann rechnet mir jeden Cent ~ vor** my husband knows exactly where every penny I spend goes; **er macht seine Buchführung äußerst ~** he is very meticulous about his bookkeeping; **sie zählte**

~ jeden Cent einzeln nach she checked every single penny

Pe|ni|cil|lin [penitsɪ'liːn] NT -s, -e penicillin

Pe|nis ['peːnɪs] M -, -se or **Penes** ['peːneːs] penis

Pe|nis|neid M (Psych) penis envy

Pe|ni|zil|lin [penitsɪ'liːn] NT -s, -e penicillin

Pen|nä|ler [pɛ'nɛːlɐ] M -s, -, **Pen|nä|le|rin** [-ərɪn] F -, -nen (dated) high-school boy/girl, grammar-school boy/girl (Brit)

Penn|bru|der ['pɛn-] M (inf) tramp, bum (inf), hobo (US)

Pen|ne¹ ['pɛnə] F -, -n (Sch inf) school

Pen|ne² ['pɛnə] PL (= Nudeln) penne sing

pen|nen ['pɛnən] VI (inf, = schlafen) to kip (Brit inf), to sleep; (= dösen) to be half-asleep; **ich habe gerade ein bisschen gepennt** I've just been having a kip (Brit inf) or a sleep; **der Meier pennt schon wieder im Unterricht** Meier's having a little nap again during the lesson; **du bist dran, penn nicht!** it's your turn, wake up!; **was das Arbeitslosenproblem betrifft, haben die Politiker wieder einmal gepennt** as far as the unemployment problem is concerned the politicians were once again caught napping

Pen|ner ['pɛnɐ] M -s, -, **Pen|ne|rin** ['pɛnərɪn] F -, -nen (inf) a tramp, bum (inf), hobo (US) b (= verschlafener Mensch) sleepyhead (inf) c (= Blödmann) plonker (inf)

Pen|sa pl, **Pen|sen** pl von Pensum

Pen|si|on [pã'zioːn, pã'sioːn, pɛn'zioːn] F -, -en a (= Fremdenheim) guesthouse, pension b no pl (= Verpflegung, Kostgeld) board; **halbe/volle ~** half/full board; **die ~ pro Tag macht 70 Euro** half/full board is 70 euros a day c (= Ruhegehalt) pension, superannuation d no pl (= Ruhestand) retirement; **in ~ gehen** to retire, to go into retirement; **in ~ sein** to be retired, to be in retirement; **jdn in ~ schicken** to retire sb

Pen|si|o|när [pãzio'nɛːɐ, pãsio'nɛːɐ, pɛnzio'nɛːɐ] M -s, -e, **Pen|si|o|nä|rin** [-'nɛːrɪn] F -, -nen a (Pension beziehend) pensioner; (im Ruhestand befindlich) retired person b (= Pensionsgast) paying guest; (= ständiger Pensionsgast) boarder

Pen|si|o|nat [pãzio'naːt, pãsio'naːt, pɛnzio'naːt] NT -(e)s, -e (dated) boarding school

pen|si|o|nie|ren [pãzio'niːrən, pãsio'niːrən, pɛnzio'niːrən] ptp **pensioniert** VT to pension off, to retire; **sich ~ lassen** to retire; **sich vorzeitig ~ lassen** to take early retirement

pen|si|o|niert [pãzio'niːɐt, pãsio'niːɐt, pɛnzio'niːɐt] ADJ retired, in retirement

Pen|si|o|nie|rung F -, -en (Zustand) retirement; (Vorgang) pensioning-off; **das Finanzamt entschloss sich zur ~ der älteren Mitarbeiter** the tax office decided to pension off the older workers

Pen|si|o|nist [pãzio'nɪst, pãsio'nɪst, pɛnzio'nɪst] M -en, -en, **Pen|si|o|nis|tin** [-'nɪstɪn] F -, -nen (S Ger, Aus) (Pension beziehend) pensioner; (im Ruhestand befindlich) retired person

Pen|si|ons-: Pen|si|ons|al|ter NT retiring or retirement age; **Pen|si|ons|an|spruch** M right to a pension; **pen|si|ons|be|rech|tigt** ADJ entitled to a pension; **Pen|si|ons|fonds** M pension fund; **Pen|si|ons|gast** M paying guest; **Pen|si|ons|kas|se** F pension fund; **Pen|si|ons|preis** M price for full board; **~ 70 Euro** full board 70 euros; **pen|si|ons|reif** ADJ (inf) ready for retirement; **Pen|si|ons|rück|stel|lun|gen** PL pension reserve(s pl)

Pen|sum ['pɛnzʊm] NT -s, **Pensa** or **Pensen** [-za, -sn] workload; (Sch) curriculum; (= Trainingspensum) quota, programme (Brit), program (US); **tägliches ~** daily quota; **er hat sein ~ nicht geschafft** or **bewältigt** he didn't achieve his target; **ein hohes** or **großes ~ an Arbeit** a heavy workload

Pen|ta|gon [pɛnta'goːn] NT -s, -e Pentagon

Pen|ta|gramm [pɛnta'gram] NT pl **-gramme** pentagram

Pen|ta|me|ter [pɛn'taːmetɐ] M (Poet) pentameter

Pen|ta|teuch [pɛnta'tɔʏç] M -s Pentateuch

Pent|house ['pɛnthaus] NT -, -s, **Pent|house--Woh|nung** F penthouse (flat (Brit) or apartment)

Pen|ti|um® ['pɛntsiʊm] M -(s), -s (Comput) Pentium® PC; (Chip) Pentium® chip

Pen|ti|um-Pro|zes|sor® M Pentium® processor

Pen|top ['pɛntɔp] M -s, -s (Comput) pentop

Pep [pɛp] M -(s), no pl (inf) pep (inf), life; **etw mit ~ machen** to put a bit of pep (inf) or life or zip (inf) into doing sth; **das Kleid hat ~** that dress has style or flair; **auch torlose Spiele haben manchmal ~** even goalless (esp Brit) or scoreless games can be full of action

Pe|pe|ro|ni [pepe'roːni] PL chillies pl (Brit), chilies pl; (Sw: = Paprika) pepper

Pe|pi|ta [pe'piːta] M OR NT -s, -s shepherd('s) check or plaid

pep|pig ['pɛpɪç] (inf) ADJ Musik, Show lively, upbeat; Kleidung jolly ADV **die Band spielte ~** the band played lively music; **sie war ~ zurechtgemacht** she was really dolled up (inf)

Pep|sin [pɛ'psiːn] NT -s, -e pepsin

Pep|tid [pɛp'tiːt] NT -(e)s, -e [-də] peptide

per [pɛr] PREP a (= mittels, durch) by; **~ Adresse** (Comm) care of, c/o; **mit jdm ~ du sein** (inf) to be on Christian-name terms or first-name terms with sb; **~ procura** (Comm) per procura, pp abbr, for; **~ Saldo** (Fin) net; **~ pedes** (hum) on shanks's pony (Brit hum) or mare (US hum), on foot; **~ se** per se; **~ definitionem** by definition b (Comm: = gegen) against; **~ cassa** (old) **~ Kasse** (old) against cash c (Comm, Econ: = bis, am) by d (Comm: = pro) per; **~ annum** per annum

Per NT -s, no pl, **PER** [pɛr] NT -s, no pl abbr von **Perchloräthylen** perchloroethylene

Per|cus|sion [pøːɐˈkaʃn] F -, -s (Mus: = Instrumente) percussion

per|du [pɛrˈdyː] ADJ pred (inf) lost

pe|ren|nie|rend [pereˈniːrənt] ADJ perennial

per|fekt [pɛrˈfɛkt] ADJ a (= vollkommen) perfect b pred (= abgemacht) settled; **etw ~ machen** to settle or conclude sth; **die Sache ~ machen** to clinch the deal, to settle the matter; **der Vertrag ist ~** the contract is signed, sealed and delivered (inf), the contract is all settled; **damit war die Niederlage ~** total defeat was then inevitable ADV (= sehr gut) perfectly; **~ kochen** to be a perfect cook; **~ Englisch sprechen** to speak perfect English, to speak English perfectly

Per|fekt ['pɛrfɛkt] NT -s, -e perfect (tense)

Per|fek|ti|on [pɛrfɛkˈtsioːn] F -, no pl perfection; **das war Artistik in höchster ~** that was the epitome of artistry, that was perfect artistry; **etw (bis) zur ~ entwickeln** (Produkt) to hone sth; Betrugsmanöver, Ausreden etc to get sth down to a fine art

per|fek|ti|o|nie|ren [pɛrfɛktsioˈniːrən] ptp **perfektioniert** VT to perfect

Per|fek|ti|o|nis|mus [pɛrfɛktsioˈnɪsmʊs] M -, no pl perfectionism

Per|fek|ti|o|nist [pɛrfɛktsioˈnɪst] M -en, -en, **Per|fek|ti|o|nis|tin** [-ˈnɪstɪn] F -, -nen perfectionist

per|fek|ti|o|nis|tisch [pɛrfɛktsioˈnɪstɪʃ] ADJ perfectionist ADV **du musst nicht alles so ~ machen** you don't have to be such a perfectionist; **~ eingestellt sein** to be a perfectionist

per|fek|tiv [pɛrfɛkˈtiːf] ADJ perfective

Per|fek|tum ['pɛrfɛktʊm] NT -s, **Perfekta** [-ta] perfect (tense)

per|fid [pɛrˈfiːt], **per|fi|de** [pɛrˈfiːdə] (liter) ADJ perfidious (liter) ADV perfidiously (liter)

Per|fi|die [pɛrfiˈdiː] F -, -n [-ˈdiːən] (liter) perfidy

Per|fo|ra|ti|on [pɛrforaˈtsioːn] F -, -en perforation

per|fo|rie|ren [pɛrfo'riːrən] *ptp* **perforiert** VT to perforate

Per|for|mance [pœr'fɔːməns] F -, -s [-mənsɪz] (*Theat*) performance

Per|for|mance-In|dex M (*Econ, Fin*) performance indicator

Per|for|manz [pɛrfɔr'mants] F -, *no pl* (*Ling*) performance

Per|ga|ment [pɛrga'mɛnt] NT -(e)s, -e **a** (= *präparierte Tierhaut*) parchment; (= *Kalbspergament auch*) vellum; **dieses Buch ist in ~ gebunden** this book is vellum-bound *or* bound in vellum **b** (= *Handschrift*) parchment **c** (= *Pergamentpapier*) greaseproof paper

Per|ga|ment|band [-bant] M *pl* -**bände** vellum(-bound) book

per|ga|men|ten [pɛrga'mɛntn] ADJ (*liter*) parchment; (*aus Kalbshaut*) vellum

Per|ga|ment-: **Per|ga|ment|pa|pier** NT greaseproof paper; **Per|ga|ment|rol|le** F (parchment) scroll; **Per|ga|ment|rü|cken** M vellum spine

Per|go|la ['pɛrgola] F -, **Per|go|len** [-lən] arbour (*Brit*), arbor (*US*), bower

Pe|ri|o|de [pe'rioːdə] F -, -n period (*auch Physiol*); (*von Wetter auch*) spell; (*Math*) repetend; (*Elec*) cycle; **0,33** ~ 0.33 recurring; **ihre ~ ist ausgeblieben** she didn't get *or* have her period; **~n pro Sekunde** cycles per second

Pe|ri|o|den|sys|tem NT periodic system; (*Tafel*) periodic table

Pe|ri|o|di|kum [pe'rioːdikʊm] NT -s, **Periodika** [-ka] *usu pl* periodical

pe|ri|o|disch [pe'rioːdɪʃ] ADJ periodic(al); (= *regelmäßig*) regular; (*Phys*) periodic; **~er Dezimalbruch** recurring fraction ADV periodically

pe|ri|o|di|sie|ren [periodi'ziːrən] *ptp* **periodisiert** VT to divide up into periods

Pe|ri|o|di|zi|tät [periodizi'tɛːt] F -, *no pl* periodicity; (*Math: von Bruch*) recurrence

Pe|ri|pe|tie [peripe'tiː] F -, -n [-'tiːən] peripeteia

pe|ri|pher [peri'feːɐ] (*geh, Med*) ADJ peripheral ADV peripherally

Pe|ri|phe|rie [perife'riː] F -, -n [-'riːən] periphery; (*von Kreis*) circumference; (*von Stadt*) outskirts *pl*; (*von Computer*) periphery; **an der ~ Bonns** in *or* on the outskirts of Bonn

Pe|ri|phe|rie|ge|rät NT peripheral

Pe|ri|skop [peri'skoːp] NT -s, -e periscope

pe|ri|sko|pisch [peri'skoːpɪʃ] ADJ periscopic

Pe|ris|tal|tik [peri'staltɪk] F -, *no pl* peristalsis

Per|le ['pɛrlə] F -, -n **a** (= *Muschelperle*) pearl; **~n vor die Säue werfen** (*prov*) to cast pearls before swine (*prov*) → **Krone b** (*aus Glas, Holz etc*) bead; (= *Luftbläschen*) bubble; (*von Wasser, Schweiß*) bead, drop, droplet **c** (*fig*) pearl, gem; (*dated inf*: = *Hausmädchen*) maid

per|len ['pɛrlən] VI (= *sprudeln*) to sparkle, to bubble, to effervesce; (*Champagner*) to fizz; (= *fallen, rollen*) to trickle, to roll; **~des Lachen** (*liter*) rippling *or* bubbling laughter; **der Tau perlt auf den Blättern** drops *or* beads of dew glisten on the leaves; **der Schweiß perlte ihm von/auf der Stirn** beads of sweat were running down/stood out on his forehead; **Wasser perlt auf einer Fettschicht** water forms into droplets on a greasy surface

Per|len-: **Per|len|aus|ter** F pearl oyster; **per|len|be|setzt** ADJ set with pearls; **per|len|be|stickt** [-bəʃtɪkt] ADJ embroidered *or* decorated with pearls; **Per|len|fi|scher(in)** M(F) pearl fisher, pearler; **Per|len|fi|sche|rei** F pearl fishing; **Per|len|ket|te** F string of pearls, pearl necklace, pearls *pl*; **Per|len|schnur** F string of beads, beads *pl*; **Per|len|sti|cke|rei** F beadwork; **Per|len|tau|cher(in)** M(F) pearl diver

Perl-: **Perl|fang** M , *no pl* (*Sew*) knit one, purl one; **Perl|garn** NT mercerized yarn; **perl|grau** ADJ pearl-grey (*Brit*), pearl-gray (*US*);

Perl|huhn NT guinea fowl; **Perl|mu|schel** F pearl oyster; **Perl|mutt** ['pɛrlmʊt, pɛrl'mʊt] NT -s, *no pl*, **Perl|mut|ter** ['pɛrlmʊtɐ, pɛrl'mʊtɐ] F - *no pl or nt* -s, *no pl* mother-of-pearl; **Perl|mut|ter|knopf**, **Perl|mutt|knopf** M (mother-of-)pearl button; **perl|mut|tern** ['pɛrlmʊtɐn, pɛrl'mʊtɐn] ADJ mother-of-pearl; (*fig*) pearly

Per|lon® ['pɛrlɔn] NT -s, *no pl* ≈ nylon

Per|lon|strümp|fe PL nylons *pl*, nylon stockings *pl*

Perl-: **Perl|schrift** F (*Typ*) pearl; **Perl|wein** M sparkling wine; **perl|weiß** ADJ pearly white; **Perl|zwie|bel** F cocktail *or* pearl onion

Per|ma|frost ['pɛrmafrɔst] M permafrost

Per|ma|frost|bo|den M permafrost

per|ma|nent [pɛrma'nɛnt] ADJ permanent ADV constantly, continually

Per|ma|nenz [pɛrma'nɛnts] F -, *no pl* permanence; **in ~** continually, constantly

Per|man|ga|nat [pɛrmaŋga'naːt] NT -s, -e (*Chem*) permanganate

per|me|a|bel [pɛrme'aːbl] ADJ (*Bot, Phys, Tech*) permeable

per|mis|siv [pɛrmɪ'siːf] ADJ permissive

Per|mis|si|vi|tät [pɛrmɪsivi'tɛːt] F -, *no pl* permissiveness

per|ni|zi|ös [pɛrni'tsjøːs] ADJ (*Med*) malignant

Per|pen|di|kel [pɛrpɛn'diːkl] M OR NT -s, - (*von Uhr*) pendulum

per|pe|tu|ie|ren [pɛrpetu'iːrən] *ptp* **perpetuiert** VT to perpetuate

Per|pe|tu|um mo|bi|le [pɛr'peːtuʊm 'moːbilə] NT -, - -(s) perpetual motion machine

per|plex [pɛr'plɛks] ADJ dumbfounded, thunderstruck

Per|ron ['pɛrõː] M -s, -s (*old, Sw, Aus*) platform

Per|sen|ning [pɛr'zenɪŋ] F -, -e(n) tarpaulin, tarp (*US inf*)

Per|ser¹ ['pɛrzɐ] M -s, - (*inf*) (= *Teppich*) Persian carpet; (= *Brücke*) Persian rug

Per|ser² ['pɛrzɐ] M -s, -, **Per|se|rin** [-ərɪn] F -, -nen Persian

Per|ser|tep|pich M Persian carpet; (= *Brücke*) Persian rug

Per|shing ['pøːʃɪŋ, 'pœrʃɪŋ] F -, -s (*inf*), **Per|shing-Ra|ke|te** F Pershing missile

Per|si|a|ner [pɛr'ziaːnɐ] M -s, - **a** (*Pelz*) Persian lamb **b** (*auch* **Persianermantel**) Persian lamb (coat)

Per|si|en ['pɛrziən] NT -s Persia

Per|sif|la|ge [pɛrzi'flaːʒə] F -, -n pastiche, satire (+*gen, auf* +*acc* on, of)

per|sif|lie|ren [pɛrzi'fliːrən] *ptp* **persifliert** VT to satirize, to write a pastiche of

Per|sil|schein [pɛr'ziːl-] M (*Hist*) denazification certificate; (*hum inf*) clean bill of health (*inf*); **jdm einen ~ ausstellen** (*hum inf*) to absolve sb of all responsibility

per|sisch ['pɛrzɪʃ] ADJ Persian; **Persischer Golf** Persian Gulf

Per|sisch(e) NT Persian → *auch* **Deutsch(e)**

Per|son [pɛr'zoːn] F -, -en **a** (= *Einzelperson*) person, individual; (= *Charakter*) character; **~en** people, persons (*form*); **jede ~ bezahlt ...** each person *or* everybody pays ...; **eine aus 6 ~en bestehende Familie** a family of 6; **ein Vier-Personen-Haushalt** a four-person household; **pro ~** per person; **die eigene ~** oneself; **was seine (eigene) ~ betrifft** for himself; **ich für meine ~ ...** I myself ..., as for myself I ..., I for my part ...; **in (eigener) ~ erscheinen** to appear in person *or* personally; **er ist Vorsitzender und Schatzmeister in einer ~** he's the chairman and treasurer rolled into one; **jdn zur ~ vernehmen** (*Jur*) to question sb concerning his identity; **Angaben zur ~** to give one's personal details; **von ~ bekannt** (*Jur*) of known identity; **natürliche/juristische ~** (*Jur*) natural/juristic *or* artificial person; **die drei göttlichen ~en** the Ho-

ly Trinity, God in three persons; **eine hoch gestellte ~** a high-ranking personage *or* person **b** (= *Mensch*) person; (*pej:* = *Frau*) female; **sie ist die Geduld in ~** she's patience personified; **Tiere treten in Fabeln als ~en auf** animals figure in fables as human beings *or* as people; **die ~ des Königs ist unantastbar** (the person of) the king is inviolable; **es geht um die ~ des Kanzlers, nicht um das Amt** it concerns the chancellor as a person, not the office; **lassen wir seine ~ aus dem Spiel** let's leave personalities out of it; **wir müssen die ~ von der Sache trennen** we must keep the personal and the factual aspects separate **c** (*Liter, Theat*) character; **die ~en der Handlung** the characters (in the action); (*Theat auch*) the dramatis personae; **eine stumme ~** a nonspeaking part **d** (*Gram*) person; **das Verb steht in der ersten ~ Plural** the verb is in the first person plural

Per|so|nal [pɛrzo'naːl] NT -s, *no pl* personnel, staff; (= *Dienerschaft auch*) servants *pl*; (*Liter.* = *Romanfiguren*) characters *pl*; **fliegendes ~** aircrew; **ungenügend/ausreichend mit ~ versehen sein** to be understaffed/adequately staffed; **beim ~ sparen** to save money on personnel costs

Per|so|nal-: **Per|so|nal|ab|bau** M , *no pl* reductions *pl* in staff *or* in personnel, personnel *or* staff cuts *pl*; **Per|so|nal|ab|tei|lung** F personnel (department); **Per|so|nal|ak|te** F personal file; **Per|so|nal|an|ga|ben** PL particulars *pl*; **Per|so|nal|auf|wand** M personnel expenditure, staff costs *pl*; **hohen ~ erfordern** to be very labour-intensive (*Brit*) *or* labor-intensive (*US*); **Per|so|nal|aus|weis** M identity card; **Per|so|nal|be|ra|ter(in)** M(F) personnel adviser *or* consultant; **Per|so|nal|be|stand** M number of staff *or* employees *or* personnel; **Per|so|nal|bü|ro** NT personnel (department); **Per|so|nal|chef(in)** M(F) personnel manager, head of the personnel department; **Per|so|nal|com|pu|ter** M personal computer; **Per|so|nal|de|cke** F personnel cover; **eine dünne ~** a very tight personnel situation; **Per|so|nal|di|rek|tor(in)** M(F) personnel director; **Per|so|nal|ein|spa|rung** F reduction *or* cut in personnel; **Per|so|nal|ge|sell|schaft** F unlimited company

Per|so|na|lie [pɛrzo'naːliə] F -, -n **a** (= *Angabe zur Person*) personal detail; **~n** *pl* particulars *pl* **b** (= *Personalangelegenheit*) personnel matter

per|so|na|li|sie|ren [pɛrzonali'ziːrən] *ptp* **personalisiert** VTI to personalize; **er personalisiert immer alles** he always personalizes everything, he always reduces everything to a personal level

Per|so|na|li|sie|rung F -, -en personalization

Per|so|na|li|tät [pɛrzonali'tɛːt] F -, -en (*geh*) personality

Per|so|nal-: **Per|so|nal|kar|tei** F personnel index; **Per|so|nal|kos|ten** PL personnel costs *pl*; **Per|so|nal|lei|ter(in)** M(F) personnel manager, head of the personnel department; **Per|so|nal|man|gel** M staff shortage(s *pl*), shortage of staff; **an ~ leiden** to be understaffed; **Per|so|nal|pla|nung** F staff planning; **Per|so|nal|po|li|tik** F staff *or* personnel policy; **Per|so|nal|pro|no|men** NT personal pronoun; **Per|so|nal|ra|batt** M staff discount; **Per|so|nal|rat¹** M (*Ausschuss*) staff council for civil servants; **Per|so|nal|rat²** M , **Per|so|nal|rä|tin** F representative on a staff council for civil servants; **Per|so|nal|uni|on** F personnel union; **er ist Kanzler und Parteivorsitzender in ~** he is at the same time Prime Minister and party chairman; **Per|so|nal|ver|tre|tungs|ge|setz** NT employees' representation law; **Per|so|nal|we|sen** NT , *no pl* personnel (matters *pl*)

Per|so|na non gra|ta [pɛr'zoːna nɔn 'graːta] F - - -, *no pl* persona non grata

Per|sön|chen [pɛrˈzøːnçən] NT **-s, -** (inf) little lady (inf)

per|so|nell [perzoˈnɛl] ADJ staff attr, personnel attr; Konsequenzen for staff, for personnel; unsere Schwierigkeiten sind rein ~ our difficulties are simply to do with staffing or personnel ADV die Abteilung wird ~ aufgestockt more staff will be taken on in the department; ~ unzureichend/zu großzügig ausgestattet sein to be understaffed/overstaffed; die Verzögerungen der Produktion sind ~ bedingt the delays in production are caused by staff or personnel problems

Per|so|nen-: Per|so|nen|auf|zug M (passenger) lift (Brit), elevator (US); **Per|so|nen|au|to** NT car, automobile (US); **Per|so|nen|be|för|de|rung** F carriage or conveyance of passengers; die Bahn hat ein Defizit bei der ~ the railways' passenger(-carrying) services show a deficit; **Per|so|nen|be|schrei|bung** F (personal) description; **per|so|nen|be|zo|gen** ADJ Daten, Informationen personal; **Per|so|nen|fern|ver|kehr** M (esp Rail) long-distance passenger services pl; **Per|so|nen|ge|dächt|nis** NT memory for faces; **Per|so|nen|ge|sell|schaft** F partnership; **Per|so|nen|kraft|wa|gen** M (form) (private) car, motorcar (form), automobile (US); **Per|so|nen|kreis** M group of people; **Per|so|nen|kult** M personality cult; mit Che Guevara wird viel ~ getrieben a great personality cult has been built up around Che Guevara; **Per|so|nen|nah|ver|kehr** M local passenger services pl; öffentlicher ~ local public transport; **Per|so|nen|re|gis|ter** NT index of names; **Per|so|nen|ruf|an|la|ge** F pager, bleeper (Brit), beeper (esp US); **Per|so|nen|scha|den** M injury to persons; ein Unfall mit/ohne ~ an accident in which people were injured/in which nobody was injured; es gab keine ~ no-one was injured; **Per|so|nen|schutz** M personal security; **Per|so|nen|stand** M marital status; **Per|so|nen|stands|re|gis|ter** NT register of births, marriages and deaths; **Per|so|nen|ver|kehr** M passenger services pl; **Per|so|nen|ver|si|che|rung** F personal injury insurance; **Per|so|nen|ver|zeich|nis** NT register of persons); (Liter) list of characters; **Per|so|nen|waa|ge** F scales pl, pair of scales; **Per|so|nen|wa|gen** M (Aut) car, automobile (US); **Per|so|nen|zahl** F number of persons (form) or people; **Per|so|nen|zug** M (Gegensatz: Schnellzug) slow or stopping train; (Gegensatz: Güterzug) passenger train

Per|so|ni|fi|ka|ti|on [pɛrzonifikaˈtsioːn] F -, -en personification

per|so|ni|fi|zie|ren [pɛrzonifiˈtsiːrən] ptp **per|so|ni|fi|ziert** VT to personify; er läuft herum wie das personifizierte schlechte Gewissen he's going around with guilt written all over his face

Per|so|ni|fi|zie|rung F -, -en personification

per|sön|lich [pɛrˈzøːnlɪç] ❂ 33.1, 33.2, 53.5 ADJ personal; Atmosphäre, Umgangsformen friendly; ~e Auslagen out-of-pocket or personal expenses; ~e Meinung personal opinion, one's own opinion; ~es Fürwort personal pronoun; ~ werden to get personal; nun werden Sie doch nicht gleich ~! there's no need to get personal ADV personally; (auf Briefen) private (and confidential); der Chef ~ the boss himself or in person or personally; etw ~ meinen/nehmen or auffassen to mean/take sth personally; er interessiert sich ~ für seine Leute he takes a personal interest in his people; Sie müssen ~ erscheinen you are required to appear in person or personally; ~ haften (Comm) to be personally liable

Per|sön|lich|keit F -, -en **a** no pl (= Charakter) personality; (von Hotel, Einrichtung) character; er besitzt wenig ~ he hasn't got much personality **b** (= bedeutender Mensch) personality; er ist eine ~ he's quite a personality; ~en des öffentlichen Lebens public figures

Per|sön|lich|keits-: Per|sön|lich|keits|ent|fal|tung F personality development, development of the personality; **Per|sön|lich|keits|merk|mal** NT personality trait; **Per|sön|lich|keits|pro|fil** NT psychological profile; **Per|sön|lich|keits|test** M personality test; **Per|sön|lich|keits|ver|än|de|rung** F personality change; **Per|sön|lich|keits|wahl** F electoral system in which a vote is cast for a candidate rather than a party diese Wahl war eine reine ~ (inf) this election boiled down to a question of the candidates' personalities

Per|spek|tiv [pɛrspɛkˈtiːf] NT -(e)s, -e [-və] small telescope, perspective (obs)

Per|spek|ti|ve [pɛrspɛkˈtiːvə] F -, -n (Art, Opt) perspective; (= Blickpunkt) angle; (= Gesichtspunkt) point of view, angle; (fig: = Zukunftsausblick) prospects pl; aus dieser ~ wirkt das Haus viel größer the house looks much bigger from this angle; das eröffnet ganz neue ~n für uns that opens new horizons for us; für etw keine ~ sehen to see no future for sth

per|spek|ti|visch [pɛrspɛkˈtiːvɪʃ] ADJ **a** perspective attr; die Zeichnung ist nicht ~ the drawing is not in perspective; ~e Verkürzung foreshortening **b** (= auf die Zukunft gerichtet) prospective ADV in perspective; ~ verkürzt foreshortened; dieses Bild ist ~ korrekt/verzerrt the perspective in this picture is correct/distorted

per|spek|tiv|los ADJ without prospects

Per|spek|tiv|lo|sig|keit F -, no pl lack of prospects

Pe|ru [peˈruː] NT -s Peru

Pe|ru|a|ner [peˈruaːnɐ] M -s, -, **Pe|ru|a|ne|rin** [-ərɪn] F -, -nen Peruvian

pe|ru|a|nisch [peˈruaːnɪʃ] ADJ Peruvian

Pe|rü|cke [peˈrʏkə] F -, -n wig

per|vers [pɛrˈvɛrs] ADJ perverted, warped (inf); ein ~er Mensch a pervert ADV perversely; ~ veranlagt sein to be a pervert

Per|ver|si|on [pɛrvɛrˈzioːn] F -, -en perversion

Per|ver|si|tät [pɛrvɛrziˈtɛːt] F -, -en perversion

per|ver|tie|ren [pɛrvɛrˈtiːrən] ptp **pervertiert** VT to pervert, to warp VI aux sein to become or get perverted

Per|ver|tiert|heit F -, -en pervertedness, perversion

pe|sen [ˈpeːzn̩] VI aux sein (inf) to belt (inf), to charge (inf)

Pes|sar [pɛˈsaːɐ] NT -s, -e pessary; (zur Empfängnisverhütung) cap, diaphragm

Pes|si|mis|mus [pɛsiˈmɪsmʊs] M -, no pl pessimism; immer dieser ~! you're/he's etc always so pessimistic!, this eternal pessimism!; in ~ machen (inf) to be pessimistic

Pes|si|mist [pɛsiˈmɪst] M -en, -en, **Pes|si|mis|tin** [-ˈmɪstɪn] F -, -nen pessimist

pes|si|mis|tisch [pɛsiˈmɪstɪʃ] ADJ pessimistic ADV pessimistically; etw ~ beurteilen to take a pessimistic view of sth, to view sth pessimistically; ~ eingestellt sein to be pessimistic

Pest [pɛst] F -, no pl (Hist, Med) plague, pestilence, pest; (fig) plague; die Schwarze ~ the black plague; sich wie die ~ ausbreiten to spread like the plague or like wildfire; jdn/etw wie die ~ hassen (inf) to loathe (and detest) sb/sth, to hate sb's guts (inf); jdn wie die ~ meiden (inf) to avoid sb like the plague; wie die ~ stinken (inf) to stink to high heaven (inf); jdm die ~ an den Hals wünschen (inf) to wish sb would drop dead (inf)

Pest-: pest|ar|tig ADJ (Med) pestilential; (fig) Gestank fetid, miasmic (liter) ADV ~ stinken to stink to high heaven (inf); sich ~ verbreiten to spread like the plague; **Pest|beu|le** F plague spot; **Pest|ge|ruch** M , **Pest|ge|stank** M (foul) stench, stink; **Pest|hauch** M (poet) miasma (liter), fetor (liter)

Pes|ti|lenz [pɛstiˈlɛnts] F -, -en (old) pestilence

Pes|ti|zid [pɛstiˈtsiːt] NT -(e)s, -e [-də] pesticide

Pest-: pest|krank ADJ sick of the plague (old), plague-stricken; **Pest|kran|ke(r)** MF decl as adj person with the plague

PET [pɛt] NT abbr von **Polyethylenterephthalat** PET, polyethylene terephthalate

Pe|ter|si|lie [petɐˈziːliə] F -, -n parsley; du siehst aus, als hätte es dir die ~ verhagelt (inf) you look as though you've lost a pound and found a sixpence (Brit inf), you look as though you lost a buck and found a penny (US inf)

Pe|ters|kir|che [ˈpeːtɐs-] F , no pl St Peter's

Pe|ter|wa|gen [ˈpeːtɐ-] M (inf) police or patrol car, panda car (Brit)

PET-Fla|sche [ˈpɛt-] F PET bottle

Pe|ti|tes|se [petiˈtɛsə] F -, -n (geh) small or trifling matter; (Summe) small or trifling sum

Pe|ti|ti|on [petiˈtsioːn] F -, -en petition

Pe|ti|ti|ons-: Pe|ti|ti|ons|aus|schuss ▲ M committee on petitions; **Pe|ti|ti|ons|recht** NT right to petition

Pe|tri Heil [ˈpeːtri-] INTERJ (Anglergruß) tight lines!

Pe|tri|scha|le [ˈpeːtri-] F Petri dish

Pet|ro-: Pet|ro|che|mie [petroçeˈmiː, ˈpeːtro-] F petrochemistry; **pet|ro|che|misch** ADJ petrochemical; **Pet|ro|dol|lar** M petrodollar

Pet|ro|le|um [peˈtroːleʊm] NT -s, no pl paraffin (oil) (Brit), kerosene (esp US)

Pet|ro|le|um-: Pet|ro|le|um|ko|cher M paraffin (Brit) or kerosene (esp US) stove, primus (stove)® (Brit); **Pet|ro|le|um|lam|pe** F , **Pet|ro|le|um|licht** NT paraffin (Brit) or oil or kerosene (esp US) lamp

Pet|rus [ˈpeːtrʊs] M -' (Bibl) Peter

Pet|schaft [ˈpɛtʃaft] NT -s, -e (old) seal

Pet|ti|coat [ˈpɛtikoːt] M -s, -s stiff(ened) petticoat

Pet|ting [ˈpɛtɪŋ] NT -s, -s petting

pet|to [ˈpɛto] ADV etw in ~ haben (inf) to have sth up one's sleeve (inf)

Pe|tu|nie [peˈtuːniə] F -, -n petunia

Petz [pɛts] M -es, -e (liter) Meister ~ (Master) Bruin

Pet|ze [ˈpɛtsə] F -, -n (Sch inf) sneak (dated Brit Sch inf), telltale (tit) (Brit Sch inf), snitch (Sch inf)

pet|zen [ˈpɛtsn̩] (inf) VT der petzt alles he always tells; er hat gepetzt, dass ... he (went and) told that ...; er hat's dem Lehrer gepetzt he told sir (Brit Sch inf), he told the teacher VI to tell (tales) (bei to)

Pet|zer [ˈpɛtsɐ] M -s, -, **Pet|ze|rin** [-ərɪn] F -, -nen (inf) sneak (dated Brit Sch inf), telltale (tit) (Brit Sch inf), snitch (Sch inf)

peu à peu [pø a ˈpø] ADV (inf) gradually, little by little

Pf (Hist) abbr von **Pfennig**

Pfad [pfaːt] M -(e)s, -e [-də] path, track; (Comput) path; auf dem ~ der Tugend wandeln (liter) to follow the path of virtue; neue ~e in der Medizin new directions in medicine

Pfad|fin|der M , **Pfa|der** [ˈpfaːdɐ] M -s, - (Sw) (Boy) Scout; er ist bei den Pfadern he's in the (Boy) Scouts

Pfad|fin|der|be|we|gung F (Boy) Scout movement, (Boy) Scouts pl

Pfad|fin|de|rin F , **Pfa|de|rin** [-ərɪn] F -, -nen (Sw) Girl Guide (Brit), Girl Scout (US)

Pfaf|fe [ˈpfafə] M -n, -n (pej) cleric (pej), parson

pfäf|fisch [ˈpfɛfɪʃ] ADJ (pej) sanctimonious (pej)

Pfahl [pfaːl] M -s, ⁼e [ˈpfɛːlə] post; (= Zaunpfahl auch) stake; (= Stütze auch) support; (= Palisade) palisade, pale; (= Brückenpfahl) pile, pier; (= Marterpfahl) stake; jdm ein ~ im Fleisch sein (liter) to be a thorn in sb's flesh

Pfahl-: Pfahl|bau M pl **-bauten** **a** no pl (Bauweise) building on stilts; **im ~** on stilts **b** (Haus) pile dwelling, house built on stilts; **Pfahl|brü|cke** F pile bridge; **Pfahl|dorf** NT pile village

pfäh|len ['pfɛːlən] VT **a** (Hort) to stake **b** (hinrichten) to impale

Pfahl-: Pfahl|werk NT (= Stützwand) pilework; (= Palisade) palisade, paling; **Pfahl|wur|zel** F taproot

Pfalz [pfalts] F **-, -en** **a** no pl (= Rheinpfalz) Rhineland or Lower Palatinate, Rheinpfalz **b** no pl (= Oberpfalz) Upper Palatinate **c** (Hist) (= Burg) palace; (= Gebiet eines Pfalzgrafen) palatinate

Pfäl|zer¹ ['pfɛltsɐ] M **-s, -** (Wein) wine from the Rhineland Palatinate

Pfäl|zer² ['pfɛltsɐ] M **-s, -, Pfäl|ze|rin** [-ərɪn] F **-, -nen** (aus Rheinpfalz) person from the Rhineland; (aus der Oberpfalz) person from the Upper Palatinate; **er ist (ein) ~** he comes from the (Rhineland/Upper) Palatinate

Pfäl|zer³ ['pfɛltsɐ] ADJ attr Palatine, of the (Rhineland) Palatinate

Pfalz-: Pfalz|graf M (Hist) count palatine; **pfalz|gräf|lich** ADJ of a/the count palatine

pfäl|zisch ['pfɛltsɪʃ] ADJ Palatine, of the (Rhineland) Palatinate

Pfand [pfant] NT **-(e)s, ̈-er** ['pfɛndɐ] security, pledge; (beim Pfänderspiel) forfeit; (= Verpackungspfand, Nutzungspfand) deposit; (fig) pledge; **etw als ~ geben, etw zum ~ setzen** (liter) to pledge sth, to give sth as (a) security; (fig) to pledge sth; (beim Pfänderspiel) to pay sth as a forfeit; **ich gebe mein Wort als ~** I pledge my word; **etw gegen ~ leihen** to lend sth against a security or pledge; Fahrrad, Schlittschuh etc to hire (Brit) or rent (US) sth out in return for a deposit; **auf dem Glas ist ~** there's something (back) on the glass (inf), there's a deposit on the glass (inf); **auf der Flasche sind 50 Pf ~** there's 50Pf (back) on the bottle (inf); **ein ~ einlösen** to redeem a pledge; **etw als ~ behalten** to hold sth as (a) security, to hold sth in pledge

pfänd|bar ADJ (Jur) distrainable (form), attachable (form); **der Fernseher ist nicht ~** the bailiffs can't take the television

Pfand|brief M (von Bank, Regierung) bond, debenture

pfän|den ['pfɛndn] VT (Jur) to impound, to seize, to distrain upon (form); Konto, Lohn, Gehalt to seize; **man hat ihm die Möbel gepfändet** the bailiffs or they took away his furniture; **jdn ~ to** impound or seize some of sb's possessions; **jdn ~ lassen** to get the bailiffs onto sb

Pfän|der|spiel NT (game of) forfeits

Pfand-: Pfand|fla|sche F returnable bottle; **Pfand|haus** NT pawnshop, pawnbroker's; **Pfand|lei|he** F **a** (das Leihen) pawnbroking **b** (= Pfandhaus) pawnshop, pawnbroker's; **Pfand|lei|her** [-laiɐ] M **-s, -, Pfand|lei|he|rin** [-ərɪn] F **-, -nen** pawnbroker; **Pfand|pflicht** F (a) compulsory deposit (on bottles, tins, cans, etc); **Pfand|recht** NT right of distraint (an +dat upon) (form), lien (an +dat on) (form); **wenn du deine Miete nicht bezahlst, hat der Vermieter ein ~ an deinen Möbeln** if you don't pay your rent the landlord is entitled to seize or impound your furniture; **Pfand|schein** M pawn ticket

Pfän|dung ['pfɛndʊŋ] F **-, -en** seizure, distraint (form), attachment (form); **der Gerichtsvollzieher kam zur ~** the bailiff came to seize or impound their possessions

Pfän|dungs|be|fehl M , **Pfän|dungs|ver|fü|gung** F distress warrant

Pfan|ne ['pfanə] F **-, -n** (Cook) pan; (Anat) socket; (= Dachpfanne) pantile; (= Zündpfanne) pan; (= Gießpfanne) ladle; **ein paar Eier in die ~ schlagen** or **hauen** to bung a couple of eggs in the pan (Brit inf), to fry up a couple of eggs (inf); **jdn in die ~ hauen** (inf) to do the dirty on sb (inf); **etw auf der ~ haben** (inf: = in petto) to

have sth up one's sleeve (inf); **etwas auf der ~ haben** (inf: geistig) to have it up there (inf)

Pfan|nen|ge|richt NT (Cook) fry-up

Pfan|nen|ku|chen M , **Pfann|ku|chen** M (= Eierpfannkuchen) pancake; (= Berliner) (jam) doughnut (Brit) or donut (US); **aufgehen wie ein ~** (inf) to turn into or to get to be a real dumpling (Brit inf) or roly-poly (inf)

Pfarr|amt NT priest's office

Pfarr|be|zirk M , **Pfar|re** ['pfarə] F **-, -n** (old) parish

Pfar|rei [pfaˈrai] F **-, -en** (= Gemeinde) parish; (= Amtsräume) priest's office

Pfar|rer ['pfarɐ] M **-s, -, Pfar|re|rin** [-ərɪn] F **-, -nen** (katholisch, evangelisch) parish priest; (anglikanisch auch) vicar; (von Freikirchen) minister; (= Gefängnispfarrer, Militärpfarrer etc) chaplain, padre; **guten Morgen, Herr ~!** good morning, (katholisch) Father or (evangelisch, anglikanisch) Vicar or (von Freikirchen) Mr ... or (Gefängnis etc) Padre; **als nächster wird Herr ~ Schmidt sprechen** the Reverend Michael Schmidt is going to speak next

Pfarr-: Pfarr|ge|mein|de F parish; **Pfarr|ge|mein|de|rat** M (= Gremium) parish council; **Pfarr|haus** NT (anglikanisch) vicarage; (methodistisch, Scot) manse; (katholisch) presbytery; **Pfarr|hel|fer(in)** M(F) curate; **Pfarr|kind** NT parishioner; **Pfarr|kir|che** F parish church; **Pfarr|stel|le** F parish, (church) living, benefice

Pfau [pfau] M **-(e)s** or **-en, -en** peacock; **er stolziert daher wie ein ~** he struts around like a peacock; **aufgedonnert wie ein ~** (inf) dressed or done up to the nines (Brit inf) or hilt (US inf)

Pfauen-: Pfau|en|au|ge NT (= Tagpfauenauge) peacock butterfly; (= Nachtpfauenauge) peacock moth; **Pfau|en|fe|der** F peacock feather; **Pfau|en|hen|ne** F peahen

Pfef|fer ['pfɛfɐ] M **-s, -** pepper; **~ und Salz** (lit) salt and pepper; (Stoffmuster) pepper-and-salt; **das brennt wie ~** that's red-hot; (Schmerz) that really stings; **er kann hingehen** or **bleiben, wo der ~ wächst!** (inf) he can go to hell (inf), he can take a running jump (Brit inf) or flying leap (US inf); **sie hat ~ im Hintern** (inf) or **Arsch** (sl) she's a lot of get-up-and-go (inf)

pfef|fe|rig ['pfɛfərɪç] ADJ peppery

Pfef|fer-: Pfef|fer|korn NT pl **-körner** peppercorn; **Pfef|fer|ku|chen** M gingerbread; **Pfef|fer|ku|chen|häus|chen** [-hɔysçən] NT gingerbread house

Pfef|fer|minz ['pfɛfɐmɪnts, -'mɪnts] NT **-es, -(e)**, **Pfef|fer|minz|bon|bon** NT OR M peppermint

Pfef|fer|min|ze ['pfɛfɐmɪntsə, -'mɪntsə] F **-, no pl** peppermint

Pfef|fer|minz-: Pfef|fer|minz|ge|schmack M peppermint flavour (Brit) or flavor (US); **Pfef|fer|minz|li|kör** M crème de menthe; **Pfef|fer|minz|plätz|chen** NT peppermint; **Pfef|fer|minz|tee** M peppermint tea

Pfef|fer|müh|le F pepper mill

pfef|fern ['pfɛfɐn] VT **a** (Cook) to season with pepper, to pepper; (fig) to pepper → auch **gepfeffert** **b** (inf: = heftig werfen) to fling, to hurl; (= hinauswerfen) to chuck out (inf), to sling out (inf); **jdm eine ~** to give sb a clout (Brit inf) or a slap, to clout sb one (Brit inf)

Pfef|fer-: Pfef|fer|nuss ▲ F gingerbread biscuit; **Pfef|fer|steak** NT pepper steak; **Pfef|fer|strauch** M pepper (plant); **Pfef|fer|streu|er** M pepper pot or shaker; **Pfef|fer-und-Salz-Mus|ter** ['pfɛfɐʊntˈzalts-] NT pepper-and-salt (pattern)

pfeff|rig ['pfɛfrɪç] ADJ = **pfefferig**

Pfeif|chen ['pfaifçən] NT **-s, -** dim von **Pfeife** pipe; **ein ~ rauchen** to smoke or have a pipe

Pfei|fe ['pfaifə] F **-, -n** **a** whistle; (= Querpfeife) fife (esp Mil), piccolo; (= Bootsmannspfeife, Orgelpfeife) pipe; **nach jds ~ tanzen** to dance to

sb's tune **b** (zum Rauchen) pipe; **eine ~ rauchen** to smoke or have a pipe; **~ rauchen** (= Pfeifenraucher sein) to smoke a pipe, to be a pipe-smoker **c** (inf: = Versager) wash-out (inf)

pfei|fen ['pfaifn] pret **pfiff** [pfɪf], ptp **gepfiffen** [gəˈpfɪfn] **VI** to whistle (+dat for); (auf einer Trillerpfeife) to blow one's whistle; (Mus: = auf einer Pfeife spielen) to pipe; (Wind) to whistle; (Radio) to whine; **mit Pfeifen und Trommeln zogen sie durch die Stadt** they made their way through the town amid piping and drumming or with pipes piping and drums beating; **aus** or **auf dem letzten Loch ~** (inf) (= erschöpft sein) to be on one's last legs (inf); (finanziell) to be on one's beam-ends (Brit inf), to be broke (inf); **ich pfeife darauf!** (inf) I couldn't care less, I don't give a damn (inf); **ich pfeife auf seine Meinung** (inf) I couldn't care less about what he thinks; **~der Atem** wheezing; **sein Atem ging ~d** he was wheezing

VT to whistle; (Mus) to pipe; (Sport inf) Spiel to ref (inf); Abseits, Foul to give; **das ~ ja schon die Spatzen von den Dächern** that's common knowledge, it's all over town

Pfei|fen-: Pfei|fen|de|ckel M pipe lid; **Pfei|fen|kopf** M bowl (of a pipe); **Pfei|fen|rei|ni|ger** M pipe cleaner; **Pfei|fen|stän|der** M pipe stand or rack; **Pfei|fen|stiel** M pipe stem; **Pfei|fen|stop|fer** M tamper; **Pfei|fen|ta|bak** M pipe tobacco; **Pfei|fen|werk** NT pipes pl, pipework

Pfei|fer ['pfaifɐ] M **-s, -, Pfei|fe|rin** [-ərɪn] F **-, -nen** piper, fifer (esp Mil)

Pfei|fe|rei [pfaifəˈrai] F **-, -en** (inf) whistling

Pfeif|fer|sches Drü|sen|fie|ber ['pfaifɐʃəs-] NT (Med) Pfeiffer's glandular fever, infectious mononucleosis (US)

Pfeif-: Pfeif|kes|sel M whistling kettle; **Pfeif|kon|zert** NT barrage or hail of catcalls or whistles; **Pfeif|ton** M pl **-töne** whistle, whistling sound or tone

Pfeil [pfail] M **-s, -e** arrow; (bei Armbrust auch) bolt; (= Wurfpfeil) dart; **~ und Bogen** bow and arrow; **die ~e seines Spotts** (liter) the barbs of his mockery; **vergiftete ~e abschießen** (fig) to fire poisoned darts at sb; **alle seine ~e verschossen haben** (fig) to have run out of arguments, to have shot one's bolt; **Amors ~** Cupid's arrow or dart; **er schoss (schnell) wie ein ~ davon** he was off like a shot (inf); **der grüne ~** (Mot) the filter (arrow)

Pfei|ler ['pfailɐ] M **-s, -** (lit, fig) pillar; (= Brückenpfeiler auch) pier; (von Hängebrücke) pylon; (= Stützpfeiler) buttress

Pfeil-: pfeil|för|mig ADJ arrow-shaped, V-shaped; ADV **~ angeordnet** arranged in the shape of an arrow, arranged in a V; **pfeil|ge|ra|de** ADJ as straight as a die; **eine ~ Linie** a dead straight line; ADV **sie kam ~ auf uns zu** she made a beeline for us, she headed straight for us; **der Vogel flog ~ von einem Baum zum nächsten** the bird flew straight as an arrow from one tree to the next; **Pfeil|gift** NT arrow poison; **Pfeil|kö|cher** M quiver; **Pfeil|rich|tung** F **in ~** in the direction of the arrow; **in ~ gehen** to follow the arrows; **pfeil|schnell** ADJ as quick as lightning; ADV like an arrow, like a shot (inf); **er startete ~** he was off like a shot (inf); **Pfeil|schuss** ▲ M arrow shot; **durch einen ~ getötet** killed by an arrow; **Pfeil|schüt|ze** M bowman, archer; **Pfeil|schüt|zin** F archer; **Pfeil|spit|ze** F arrowhead, tip of an arrow; **Pfeil|tas|te** F (Comput) arrow key; **Pfeil|wurf|spiel** NT darts pl; **Pfeil|wurz** [-vʊrts] F **-, -en** arrowroot no pl

Pfen|nig ['pfɛnɪç] M **-s, -e** [-gə] or **-** (nach Zahlenangabe) **-** (Hist) pfennig (one hundredth of a mark); **30 ~** 30 pfennigs; **er hat keinen ~ (Geld)** he hasn't got a penny to his name, he hasn't got two pennies to rub together, he hasn't got a dime (US); **ohne einen ~ dasitzen** (inf) to be left without a penny (Brit) or cent (US); **es ist keinen ~ wert** (fig) it's not worth a thing *or* a red cent (*US*); **dem/dafür gebe ich keinen ~** (*lit*) I won't give him/it a penny; **für seine Chancen gebe ich keinen ~** I don't give much for his chances (*inf*), I wouldn't put much money on his chances (*inf*); **nicht für fünf ~** (*inf*) not the slightest (bit of); **er hat nicht für fünf ~ Anstand/Verstand** (*inf*) he hasn't an ounce of respectability/intelligence; **das interessiert mich nicht für fünf ~** (*inf*) that doesn't interest me in the slightest; **auf den ~ sehen** (*fig*) to watch or count every penny; **mit dem or jedem ~ rechnen müssen** (*fig*) to have to watch *or* count every penny; **jeden ~ (dreimal) umdrehen** (*fig inf*) to think twice about every penny one spends; **wer den ~ nicht ehrt, ist des Talers nicht wert** (*Prov*) ≈ take care of the pennies, and the pounds will take care of themselves (*Brit Prov*), ≈ a penny saved is a penny earned (*US*) → **Groschen, Heller**

Pfen|nig-: **Pfen|nig|ab|satz** M stiletto heel; **Pfen|nig|be|trag** M (*Hist, fig*) **es war nur ein ~** it was only a matter of pence or pennies; **Pfen|nig|fuchs|er** [-fʊksɐ] M **-s, -, Pfen|nig|fuch|se|rin** [-ərɪn] F **-, -nen** (*fig inf*) skinflint (*inf*), miser (*inf*); **pfen|nig|groß** ADJ **ein ~es Geschwür** a boil the size of a penny (coin) *or* a cent (*US*); **Pfen|nig|stück** NT (*Hist*) pfennig (piece); **pfen|nig|wei|se** ADV (*Hist*) penny by penny, one penny at a time

Pferch [pfɛrç] M **-es, -e** fold, pen

pfer|chen ['pfɛrçn] VT to cram, to pack

Pferd [pfeːɐt] NT **-(e)s, -e** [-də] (*Tier, Turngerät*) horse; (= *Reitpferd auch*) mount; (*Chess*) knight, horse (*US inf*); **zu ~(e)** on horseback; **aufs falsche/richtige ~ setzen** (*lit, fig*) to back the wrong/right horse; **mitten im Strom die ~e wechseln** (*fig*) to change horses in midstream; **die ~e gehen ihm leicht durch** (*fig*) he flies off the handle easily (*inf*); **immer langsam** *or* **sachte mit den jungen ~en** (*inf*) hold your horses (*inf*); **wie ein ~ arbeiten** *or* **schuften** (*inf*) to work like a Trojan; **das hält ja kein ~ aus** (*inf*) it's more than flesh and blood can stand; **keine zehn ~e brächten mich dahin** (*inf*) wild horses couldn't drag me there; **mit ihm kann man ~e stehlen** (*inf*) he's a great sport (*inf*); **er ist unser bestes ~ im Stall** he's our best man; **ich glaub, mich tritt ein ~** (*inf*) blow me down (*dated inf*), struth (*Brit inf*)

Pfer|de-: **Pfer|de|ap|fel** M piece of horse dung; **Pferdeäpfel** horse droppings *pl or* dung *no pl*; **Pfer|de|bahn** F horse-drawn tram (*esp Brit*), horsecar (*US*); **pfer|de|be|spannt** [-bəʃpant] ADJ horse-drawn; **Pfer|de|brem|se** F horsefly; **Pfer|de|cke** F horse blanket; **Pfer|de|dieb(in)** M(F) horse thief; **Pfer|de|drosch|ke** F hackney cab; **Pfer|de|fleisch** NT horse meat, horseflesh; **Pfer|de|flie|ge** F horsefly; **Pfer|de|fuhr|werk** NT horse and cart; **Pfer|de|fuß** M (*von Teufel*) cloven hoof; (*fig*) snag; **die Sache hat aber einen ~** there's just one snag; **Pfer|de|ge|biss** ▲ NT horsey mouth *or* teeth; **Pfer|de|ge|sicht** NT horsey face, face like a horse; **Pfer|de|haar** NT horsehair; **Pfer|de|händ|ler(in)** M(F) horse dealer; **Pfer|de|huf** M horse's hoof; **Pfer|de|knecht** M groom; **Pfer|de|kop|pel** F paddock; **Pfer|de|län|ge** F length; **Pfer|de|renn|bahn** F race course or track; **Pfer|de|ren|nen** NT (*Sportart*) (horse) racing; (*einzelnes Rennen*) (horse) race; **Pfer|de|schlach|ter(in)** M(F) knacker (*Brit inf*), butcher; **Pfer|de|schlach|te|rei** F knacker's (*Brit inf*), slaughterhouse; **Pfer|de|schlit|ten** M horse-drawn sleigh; **Pfer|de|schwanz** M horse's tail; (*Frisur*) ponytail; **Pfer|de|sport** M equestrian sport; **Pfer|de|stall** M stable; **Pfer|de|stär|ke** F horse power *no pl*, hp *abbr*; **Pfer|de|wa|gen** M (*für Personen*) horse and carriage, trap (*Brit*), horse buggy (*US*); (*für Lasten*) horse and cart; **Pfer|de|zucht** F horse breeding; (= *Gestüt*) stud farm; **Pfer|de|züch|ter(in)** M(F) horse breeder

pfet|zen ['pfɛtsn] VT (*S Ger*: = *kneifen*) to pinch

---

pfiff *pret von* **pfeifen**

Pfiff [pfɪf] M **-s, -e** **a** whistle; (*Theat auch*) catcall; **auf ~ reagieren** (*fig*) to obey on command **b** (= *Reiz*) flair, style; **der Soße fehlt noch der letzte ~** the sauce still needs that extra something; **einem Kleid den richtigen ~ geben** to give a dress real style; **eine Inneneinrichtung mit ~** a stylish interior **c** (*inf*: = *Trick*) knack; **jetzt hast du den ~ heraus** you've got the knack *or* hang (*inf*) of it now; **das ist ein Ding mit 'nem ~** there's a special knack to it

Pfif|fer|ling ['pfɪfɐlɪŋ] M **-, -e** chanterelle; **er kümmert sich keinen ~ um seine Kinder** (*inf*) he doesn't give a fig (*inf*) *or* couldn't care less about his children; **keinen ~ wert** (*inf*) not worth a thing

pfif|fig ['pfɪfɪç] ADJ smart, sharp, cute; **Idee** smart, clever ADV cleverly

Pfif|fig|keit F **-, no pl** sharpness, cuteness; (*von Idee*) cleverness

Pfif|fi|kus ['pfɪfikʊs] M **- or -ses, -se** (*dated*) crafty thing (*inf*)

Pfings|ten ['pfɪŋstn] NT **-, -** Whitsun (*Brit*), Pentecost; **zu** *or* **an ~** at Whitsun (*Brit*) *or* Pentecost

Pfingst-: **Pfingst|fe|ri|en** PL Whit(sun) holiday(s *pl*) (*Brit*), Pentecost holiday (*pl*) (*US*); **Pfingst|fest** NT Whitsun (*Brit*), Pentecost

pfingst|lich ['pfɪŋstlɪç] ADJ *no pred* Whit(sun) *attr* (*Brit*), Pentecost *attr* ADV **der Altar war ~ geschmückt** the altar was decorated for Whitsun (*Brit*) *or* Pentecost

Pfingst-: **Pfingst|mon|tag** M Whit Monday (*Brit*), Pentecost Monday (*US*); **Pfingst|och|se** **herausgeputzt wie ein ~** (*inf*) dressed or done up to the nines (*Brit inf*) *or* hilt (*US inf*); **Pfingst|ro|se** F peony; **Pfingst|sonn|tag** M Whit Sunday (*Brit*), Pentecost; **Pfingst|wo|che** F Whit week (*Brit*), the week of the Pentecost holiday (*US*); **Pfingst|zeit** F Whitsun (-tide) (*Brit*), the time before Pentecost

Pfir|sich ['pfɪrzɪç] M **-s, -e** peach

Pfir|sich-: **Pfir|sich|baum** M peach tree; **Pfir|sich|blü|te** F peach blossom; **pfir|sich|far|ben** [-farbn] ADJ peach(-coloured) (*Brit*), peach(-colored) (*US*); **Pfir|sich|haut** F , *no pl* (*lit*) peach skin; (*fig*) peaches-and-cream complexion

Pflanz [pflants] M **-, no pl** (*Aus inf*) fraud, swindle

Pflan|ze ['pflantsə] F **-, -n** **a** (= *Gewächs*) plant; **~n fressend** herbivorous **b** (*inf: Mensch*) **er/sie ist eine komische** *or* **seltsame ~** he/she is a strange fish (*inf*); **eine Berliner ~** (*dated*) a typical Berlin lass (*Brit*) *or* girl

pflan|zen ['pflantsn] VT to plant; **einem Kind etw ins Herz ~** (*liter*) to implant sth in the heart of a child (*liter*) VR (*inf*) to plant (*inf*) *or* plonk (*Brit inf*) oneself

Pflan|zen-: **Pflan|zen|but|ter** F vegetable butter; **Pflan|zen|farb|stoff** M vegetable dye; **Pflan|zen|fa|ser** F plant fibre (*Brit*) *or* fiber (*US*); **Pflan|zen|fett** NT vegetable fat; **pflan|zen|fres|send** △ ADJ *attr* → **Pflanze a**; **Pflan|zen|fres|ser** M herbivore; **Pflan|zen|kost** F vegetable foodstuffs *pl*; **Pflan|zen|kun|de** F , *no pl* botany; **Pflan|zen|mar|ga|ri|ne** F vegetable margarine; **Pflan|zen|öl** NT vegetable oil; **Pflan|zen|reich** NT vegetable kingdom; **Pflan|zen|schäd|ling** M pest; garden pest; **Pflan|zen|schutz** M protection of plants; (*gegen Ungeziefer*) pest control; **Pflan|zen|schutz|mit|tel** NT pesticide; **Pflan|zen|welt** F plant world; **die ~ des Mittelmeers** the plant life *or* the flora of the Mediterranean

Pflan|zer ['pflantsɐ] M **-s, -, Pflan|ze|rin** [-ərɪn] F **-, -nen** planter

Pflanz|kar|tof|fel F seed potato

pflanz|lich ['pflantslɪç] ADJ *Fette, Nahrung* vegetable *attr*; *Zellen, Organismen* plant *attr* ADV

---

sich rein ~ ernähren to eat no animal products; (*Tier*) to be a herbivore

Pflänz|ling ['pflɛntslɪŋ] M **-s, -e** seedling

Pflanz-: **Pflanz|scha|le** F planting dish; **Pflanz|trog** M plant trough

Pflan|zung ['pflantsʊŋ] F **-, -en** (= *das Pflanzen*) planting; (= *Plantage*) plantation

Pflas|ter ['pflastɐ] NT **-s, -** **a** (= *Heftpflaster*) (sticking) plaster (*Brit*), adhesive tape (*US*); (*fig*: = *Entschädigung*) sop (*auf +acc* to); **das ~ erneuern** to put on a fresh *or* new (piece of) (sticking) plaster (*Brit*) *or* adhesive tape (*US*) **b** (= *Straßenpflaster*) (road) surface; (= *Kopfsteinpflaster*) cobbles *pl*; **~ treten** (*inf*) to trudge the streets, to trudge *or* traipse around; **ein gefährliches** *or* **heißes ~** (*inf*) a dangerous place; **ein teures ~** (*inf*) a pricey place (*inf*); **das Berliner ~** (*inf*) the streets of Berlin

Pflas|te|rer ['pflastərɐ] M **-s, -, Pflas|te|rin** [-ərɪn] F **-, -nen** road worker

Pflas|ter-: **Pflas|ter|ma|ler(in)** M(F) pavement artist; **pflas|ter|mü|de** ADJ (*inf*) dead on one's feet (*inf*)

pflas|tern ['pflastɐn] VT **a** *Straße, Hof* to surface; (*mit Kopfsteinpflaster*) to cobble; (*mit Steinplatten*) to pave; **eine Straße neu ~** to resurface a road; **ihre Filmkarriere war mit unzähligen Misserfolgen gepflastert** her film career was made up of a series of failures → **Weg a** **b** (*inf*: = *ohrfeigen*) **jdm eine ~** to sock sb (one) (*inf*); **du kriegst gleich eine gepflastert** I'll sock you one in a minute (*inf*)

Pflas|ter|stein M (= *Kopfstein*) cobble(stone); (= *Steinplatte*) paving stone, flag(stone); (*inf*: = *Pfefferkuchen*) ≈ gingerbread

Pflas|te|rung F **-, -en** surfacing; (*mit Kopfsteinpflaster*) cobbling; (*mit Steinplatten*) paving; (= *Pflaster*) surface; (= *Kopfsteinpflaster*) cobbles *pl*; (= *Steinplatten*) paving *no pl*

Pflau|me ['pflaumə] F **-, -n a** plum; **getrocknete ~** prune **b** (*inf: Mensch*) dope (*inf*), twit (*inf*) **c** (*sl*: = *Vagina*) cunt (*vulg*)

Pflau|men-: **Pflau|men|baum** M plum (tree); **Pflau|men|kern** M plum stone; **Pflau|men|kom|pott** NT stewed plums *pl*; **Pflau|men|ku|chen** M plum tart; **Pflau|men|mus** NT plum jam; **pflau|men|weich** ADJ (*inf*) soft; (*pej*) *Haltung* spineless

Pfle|ge ['pfleːgə] F **-, no pl** care; (*von Kranken auch*) nursing; (*von Garten auch*) attention; (*von Beziehungen, Künsten*) fostering, cultivation; (*von Maschinen, Gebäuden*) maintenance, upkeep; **jdn/etw in ~ nehmen** to look after sb/sth; **jdn/etw in ~ geben** to have sb/sth looked after; **sie gaben den Hund bei ihrem Sohn in ~** they gave their dog to their son to look after; **ein Kind in ~ nehmen** (*dauernd*) to foster a child; **ein Kind in ~ geben** to have a child fostered; (*stundenweise*) to have a child looked after; (*Behörde*) to foster a child out (*zu jdm* with sb); **die ~ von jdm/etw übernehmen** to look after sb/sth; **der Garten/Kranke braucht viel ~** the garden/sick man needs a lot of care and attention; **das Kind/der Hund hat bei uns gute ~** the child/dog is well looked after *or* cared for by us; **jdm gute ~ angedeihen lassen** to take good care of sb, to look after sb well; **häusliche ~** care in the home

Pfle|ge-: **pfle|ge|be|dürf|tig** ADJ in need of care (and attention); **wenn alte Leute ~ werden** when old people start to need looking after; **Pfle|ge|be|dürf|tig|keit** F need for care; **Pfle|ge|be|ruf** M caring profession; **Pfle|ge|dienst** M home nursing service; **Pfle|ge|el|tern** PL foster parents *pl*; **Pfle|ge|fall** M case for nursing *or* care; **sie ist ein ~** she needs constant care; **Pfle|ge|geld** NT (*für Pflegekinder*) boarding-out allowance; (*für Kranke*) attendance allowance; **Pfle|ge|heim** NT nursing home; **Pfle|ge|kind** NT foster child; **Pfle|ge|kos|ten** PL nursing fees *pl*; **Pfle|ge|kos|ten|ver|si|che|rung** F private nursing insurance;

pfle|ge|leicht ADJ easy-care; (*fig auch*) easy to handle; **Pfle|ge|mit|tel** NT (= *Kosmetikum*) cosmetic care product; (*Aut*) cleaning product; **Pfle|ge|mut|ter** F *pl* **-mütter** foster mother

pfle|gen ['pfle:gn] VT to look after, to care for; *Kranke auch* to nurse; *Garten, Blumen, Rasen* to tend, to look after; *Haar, Bart* to groom, to look after; *Beziehungen, Kunst, Freundschaft* to foster, to cultivate; *Maschinen, Gebäude, Denkmäler* to maintain, to keep up; **etw regelmäßig ~** to attend to sth regularly, to pay regular attention to sth; **eine Creme, die die Haut pflegt** a cream which is good for the skin → *auch* **gepflegt, Umgang** [superscript]1

VI (= *gewöhnlich tun*) to be in the habit (*zu* of), to be accustomed (*zu* to); **sie pflegte zu sagen** she used to say, she was in the habit of saying; **zum Mittagessen pflegt er Bier zu trinken** he's in the habit of drinking beer with his lunch, he usually drinks beer with his lunch; **wie es so zu gehen pflegt** as usually happens; **wie man zu sagen pflegt** as they say

VR **a** (= *sein Äußeres pflegen*) to care about one's appearance

b (= *sich schonen*) to take it *or* things easy (*inf*)

Pfle|ge-: Pfle|ge|not|stand M shortage of nursing staff; **Pfle|ge|per|so|nal** NT nursing staff; **Pfle|ge|pro|dukt** NT care product; **~e für die Haut/das Auto** skin/car care products

Pfle|ger ['pfle:gɐ] M **-s, -** (*im Krankenhaus*) orderly; (*voll qualifiziert*) (male) nurse; (= *Vormund*) guardian; (= *Nachlasspfleger*) trustee

Pfle|ge|rin ['pfle:gərɪn] F **-, -nen** nurse → *auch* **Pfleger**

pfle|ge|risch ['pfle:gərɪʃ] ADJ nursing ADV **~ ausgebildet sein** to be a trained nurse; **~ tätig sein** to do nursing

Pfle|ge-: Pfle|ge|satz M hospital and nursing charges *pl*; **Pfle|ge|se|rie** F (= *Kosmetika*) line of cosmetic products; **Pfle|ge|sohn** M foster son; **Pfle|ge|sta|ti|on** F nursing ward; **Pfle|ge|toch|ter** F foster daughter; **Pfle|ge|va|ter** M foster father; **Pfle|ge|ver|si|che|rung** F nursing care insurance

---

PFLEGEVERSICHERUNG

Pflegeversicherung was introduced in Germany in 1995 and is compulsory for members of state and private health insurance schemes. It covers the costs associated with long-term nursing care, for example in the case of old age or severe disability. The **Pflegeversicherung** also pays a certain amount to those who have to care for relatives at home and covers their social security contributions. **Pflegeversicherung** costs are borne jointly by employee and employer.

---

pfleg|lich ['pfle:klɪç] ADJ careful ADV *behandeln, umgehen* carefully, with care

Pfleg|ling ['pfle:klɪŋ] M **-s, -e** foster child; (= *Mündel*) ward

Pflegs|chaft ['pfle:kʃaft] F **-, -en** (= *Vormundschaft*) guardianship, tutelage (*form*); (= *Vermögenspflegschaft*) trusteeship

Pflicht [pflɪçt] F **-, -en** **a** (= *Verpflichtung*) duty (*zu* to); **ich habe die traurige ~ ...** it is my sad duty ...; **als Abteilungsleiter hat er die ~, ...** it's his duty *or* responsibility as head of (the) department ...; **Rechte und ~en** rights and responsibilities; **seine ~ erfüllen** *or* **tun** to do one's duty; **der ~ gehorchen** (*geh*) to obey the call of duty; **jdn in die ~ nehmen** to remind sb of his duty; **eheliche ~en** conjugal *or* marital duties; **die bürgerlichen ~en** one's civic duties *or* responsibilities; **die ~ ruft** duty calls; **ich habe es mir zur ~ gemacht** I've taken it upon myself, I've made it my duty; **ich tue nur meine ~** I'm only doing my duty; **etw nur aus ~ tun** to do sth merely because one has to; **das ist ~** you have to do that, it's compulsory; **Schulbesuch ist ~** you have to go to school, going to school is compulsory; **es ist seine (verdammte**

inf) **~ und Schuldigkeit(, das zu tun)** he damn well *or* jolly well (*Brit*) ought to (do it) (*inf*)

b (*Sport*) compulsory section *or* exercises *pl*; **bei der ~** in the compulsory section *or* exercises

Pflicht-: Pflicht|be|such M duty visit; **pflicht|be|wusst** ▲ ADJ conscientious, conscious of one's duties; **er ist sehr ~** he takes his duties very seriously, he has a great sense of duty; **Pflicht|be|wusst|sein** ▲ NT sense of duty; **Pflicht|ei|fer** M zeal; **pflicht|eif|rig** ADJ zealous ADV zealously

Pflich|ten|heft NT (= *Anforderungsprofil*) (*für Geräte*) specification; (*für Arbeitsstelle*) job description

Pflich|ten|kreis M duties *pl*

Pflicht-: Pflicht|er|fül|lung F fulfilment (*Brit*) *or* fulfillment (*US*) of one's duty; **Pflicht|exem|plar** NT deposit copy; **Pflicht|fach** NT compulsory subject; **Deutsch ist ~** German is compulsory, German is a compulsory subject; **Pflicht|ge|fühl** NT sense of duty; **pflicht|ge|mäß** ADJ dutiful; **~es Ermessen** proper discretion ADV dutifully; **ich teile Ihnen ~ mit** it is my duty to inform you; **etw ~ tun müssen** to be required to do sth; **pflicht|ge|treu** ADJ dutiful ADV dutifully; **Pflicht|jahr** NT (*NS*) *a year's compulsory community service for girls during Nazi period*; **Pflicht|kür** F compulsory exercise; **Pflicht|lauf** M (*Eiskunstlauf*) compulsory figures *pl*; **Pflicht|lek|tü|re** F compulsory reading; (*Sch auch*) set book(s *pl*); **pflicht|schul|dig** ADJ dutiful ADV dutifully; **Pflicht|teil** M OR NT statutory portion (*of a deceased person's estate that must be left eg to a child*); **pflicht|treu** ADJ dutiful; **Pflicht|treue** F devotion to duty; **Pflicht|übung** F compulsory exercise; **pflicht|ver|ges|sen** ADJ neglectful of one's duty; **Pflicht|ver|ges|sen|heit** F neglect of one's duty; **Pflicht|ver|let|zung** F breach of duty; **Pflicht|ver|säum|nis** F neglect *or* dereliction of duty *no pl*; **er machte sich häufiger ~se schuldig** he was frequently guilty of neglecting his duties; **pflicht|ver|si|chert** [-fɛɐzɪçɐt] ADJ compulsorily insured; **Pflicht|ver|si|cher|te(r)** MF *decl as adj* compulsorily insured person; **Pflicht|ver|si|che|rung** F compulsory insurance; **Pflicht|ver|tei|di|ger(in)** M(F) *counsel for the defence appointed by the court and paid from the legal aid fund*; **Pflicht|vor|le|sung** F compulsory lecture; **pflicht|wid|rig** ADJ **~es Verhalten** failure to carry out one's duty ADV **er hat sich ~ verhalten** he failed to carry out his duty

Pflock [pflɔk] M **-(e)s, ⁼e** ['pflœkə] peg; (*für Tiere*) stake; **einen ~** *or* **ein paar Pflöcke zurückstecken** (*dated fig*) to back-pedal a bit; **Pflöcke** *or* **einen ~ einschlagen** (*fig*) to set standards

pflü|cken ['pflʏkn] VT to pick, to pluck; (= *sammeln*) to pick

Pflü|cker ['pflʏkɐ] M **-s, -, Pflü|cke|rin** [-ərɪn] F **-, -nen** picker

Pflück|sa|lat M picking salad, *lettuce that is picked a few leaves at a time*

Pflug [pflu:k] M **-(e)s, ⁼e** ['pfly:gə] plough (*Brit*), plow (*US*); (= *Schneepflug*) snowplough (*Brit*), snowplow (*US*); **unter dem ~ sein** to be under the plough (*Brit*) or plow (*US*)

Pflug|bo|gen M (*Ski*) snowplough (*Brit*) *or* snowplow (*US*) turn

pflü|gen ['pfly:gn] VTI (*lit, fig*) to plough (*Brit*), to plow (*US*); (*lit auch*) to till (*liter*); **das Boot pflügt durch die Brandung** the boat ploughs (*Brit*) or plows (*US*) (through) the waves

Pflü|ger ['pfly:gɐ] M **-s, -** ploughman (*Brit*), plowman (*US*)

Pflü|ge|rin ['pfly:gərɪn] F **-, -nen** ploughwoman (*Brit*), plowwoman (*US*)

Pflug-: Pflug|schar F ploughshare (*Brit*), plowshare (*US*); **Pflug|sterz** M plough handle (*Brit*), plow handle (*US*)

Pfort|ader F portal vein

Pfor|te ['pfɔrtə] F **-, -n** (= *Tor*) gate; (*Geog*) gap; **das Theater hat seine ~ für immer geschlossen** the theatre (*Brit*) or theater (*US*) has closed its doors for good; **die Messe öffnet am Sonntag ihre ~n** the (trade) fair opens its doors or gates on Sunday; **Nepal, die ~ zum Himalaya** Nepal, the gateway to the Himalayas; **die ~n des Himmels** the gates *or* portals (*liter*) of Heaven; **die Hohe ~** (*Hist*) the Sublime Porte

Pfört|ner¹ ['pfœrtnɐ] M **-s, -** (*Anat*) pylorus

Pfört|ner² ['pfœrtnɐ] M **-s, -, Pfört|ne|rin** [-ərɪn] F **-, -nen** porter; (*von Fabrik*) gateman/-woman; (*von Wohnhaus, Behörde*) doorman/-woman; (*von Schloss*) gatekeeper

Pfört|ner|lo|ge F porter's office; (*in Fabrik*) gatehouse; (*in Wohnhaus, Büro*) doorman's office

Pfos|ten ['pfɔstn] M **-s, -** post; (= *senkrechter Balken*) (= *Fensterpfosten*) (window) jamb; (= *Türpfosten*) (door) jamb, doorpost; (= *Stütze*) support, prop; (*Ftbl*) (goal)post, upright

Pfos|ten|schuss ▲ M (*Ftbl*) **das war nur ein ~** it hit the (goal)post or upright

Pföt|chen ['pfø:tçən] NT **-s, -** *dim von* **Pfote** little paw; **~ geben** (*fig inf*) to shake hands; **(gib) ~!** (*zu Hund*) give me a paw!

Pfo|te ['pfo:tə] F **-, -n** **a** paw **b** (*inf: = Hand*) mitt (*inf*), paw (*inf*); **sich** (*dat*) **die ~n verbrennen** (*inf*) to burn one's fingers; **seine ~n überall drin haben** (*fig inf*) to have a finger in every pie (*inf*) **c** (*inf: = schlechte Handschrift*) scribble, scrawl

Pfriem [pfri:m] M **-(e)s, -e** awl

Pfropf [pfrɔpf] M **-(e)s, -e** *or* **⁼e** ['pfrœpfə] (= *Stöpsel*) stopper; (= *Kork, Sektpfropf*) cork; (= *Wattepfropf etc*) plug; (*von Fass, Korbflasche*) bung; (*Med: = Blutpfropf*) (blood) clot; (*verstopfend*) blockage; **er hat einen ~ im Ohr** his ears are bunged up (*Brit inf*) or blocked up

pfrop|fen ['pfrɔpfn] VT **a** *Pflanzen* to graft **b** (= *verschließen*) *Flasche* to bung, to stop up **c** (*inf: = hineinzwängen*) to cram; **er pfropfte den Korken in die Flasche** he shoved the cork in the bottle; **gepfropft voll** jam-packed (*inf*), crammed full

Pfrop|fen ['pfrɔpfn] M **-s, -** = **Pfropf**

Pfröpf|ling ['pfrœpflɪŋ] M **-s, -e** graft, scion

Pfropf-: Pfropf|mes|ser NT grafting knife; **Pfropf|reis** NT *, no pl* graft, scion

Pfrün|de ['pfrʏndə] F **-, -n** (= *Kirchenamt*) (church) living, benefice; (*Einkünfte auch*) prebend; (*fig*) sinecure

Pfuhl [pfu:l] M **-s, -e** (*liter*) mudhole; (*fig*) (quag)mire, slough (*liter*)

Pfühl [pfy:l] M OR NT **-(e)s, -e** (*poet, dial*) (= *Kissen*) pillow; (= *weiches Bett*) downy *or* feather bed

pfui [pfui] INTERJ (*Ekel*) ugh, yuck; (*Missbilligung*) tut tut; (*zu Hunden*) oy, hey; (*Buhruf*) boo; **fass das nicht an, das ist ~** (*inf*) don't touch it, it's dirty or nasty; **~ Teufel** *or* **Deibel** *or* **Spinne** (all *inf*) ugh, yuck; **~ schäme dich** shame on you!; **da kann ich nur ~** *or* **Pfui sagen** it's simply disgraceful

Pfui|ruf M boo

Pfund [pfʊnt] NT **-(e)s, -e** [-də] *or* (*nach Zahlenangabe*) **- a** (= *Gewicht*) (*in Deutschland*) 500 grams, half a kilo(gram); (*in Großbritannien*) pound; **drei ~ Äpfel** three pounds of apples; **er bewegte seine ~e mit Mühe** he moved his great bulk with effort; **überflüssige ~e abspecken** to shed surplus pounds **b** (= *Währungseinheit*) pound; (= *türkisches Pfund*) lira; (*Hist: = irisches Pfund*) punt; **in ~** in pounds; **zwanzig ~ Sterling** twenty pounds sterling; **das ~ sinkt** the pound is falling; **mit seinem ~e** *or* **seinen ~en wuchern** (*liter*) to make the most of one's talents

Pfund- *in cpds* pound; **Pfund|be|trag** M amount in pounds, sterling sum

-pfün|der [pfʏndɐ] M **-s, -** *in cpds* -pounder; **ein Fünfpfünder** (*Fisch*) a five-pounder

---

pfun|dig ['pfʊndɪç] (*dated inf*) **ADJ** great *no adv*, fantastic, swell *no adv* (*US dated inf*) **ADV** fantastically; **sich ~ amüsieren** to have a great time; **das hast du ~ gemacht** you've made a great job of that

-pfün|dig [pfʏndɪç] **ADJ** *suf* weighing … pounds; **ein vierpfündiger Fisch** a fish weighing four pounds

Pfunds- *in cpds* (*inf*) great (*inf*), swell (*US dated inf*), super (*inf*); **Pfunds|kerl** M (*inf*) great guy (*inf*)

pfund|wei|se **ADV** by the pound

Pfusch [pfʊʃ] M -(e)s, *no pl* (*inf*) = **Pfuscherei**

Pfusch|ar|beit F, *no pl* (*inf*) slapdash work; **sie haben richtige ~ geleistet** they did a really sloppy job (*inf*)

pfu|schen ['pfʊʃn] VI **a** (= *schlecht arbeiten*) to bungle; (= *einen Fehler machen*) to slip up, to come unstuck (*inf*); **jdm ins Handwerk ~** to stick one's nose into sb's affairs (*inf*), to meddle in sb's affairs **b** (*Sch*) to cheat **c** (*Aus*: = *schwarzarbeiten*) to (do) work on the side (*esp Brit inf*), to moonlight (*inf*)

Pfu|scher ['pfʊʃɐ] M -s, - (*inf*), **Pfu|sche|rin** [-ərɪn] F -, -nen (*inf*) bungler, botcher (*inf*)

Pfu|sche|rei [pfʊʃə'raɪ] F -, -en (= *das Pfuschen*) bungling *no pl*; (= *gepfuschte Arbeit*) botch-up (*inf*), botched-up job (*inf*)

Pfüt|ze ['pfʏtsə] F -, -n puddle

PH [peː'haː] F -, -s *abbr von* **pädagogische Hochschule**

Pha|lanx ['faːlaŋks] F -, **Phalangen** [fa'laŋən] (*Hist*) phalanx; (*fig*) battery

Phal|len *pl*, **Phal|li** *pl von* **Phallus**

phal|lisch ['falɪʃ] **ADJ** phallic

Phal|lus ['falʊs] M -, -se *or* **Phalli** *or* **Phallen** ['fali, 'falən] phallus

Phal|lus-: **Phal|lus|kult** M , *no pl* phallus worship; **Phal|lus|sym|bol** NT phallic symbol

Phä|no|men [fɛno'meːn] NT -s, -e phenomenon; **dieser Mensch ist ein ~** this person is phenomenal, this person is an absolute phenomenon

phä|no|me|nal [fɛnome'naːl] **ADJ** phenomenal **ADV** phenomenally (well); **~ aussehen** to look phenomenal

Phä|no|me|no|lo|gie [fɛnomenolo'giː] F -, *no pl* phenomenology

Phä|no|typ [feno'tyːp] M -s, -en, **Phä|no|ty|pus** [feno'tyːpʊs] M phenotype

Phan|ta|sie [fanta'ziː] F -, -n [-'ziːən] = **Fantasie**

Phan|ta|sie- *in cpds* = **Fantasie-**

phan|ta|sie|ren VTI = **fantasieren**

Phan|tast [fan'tast] M -en, -en, **Phan|tas|tin** [-'tastɪn] F -, -nen = **Fantast**

Phan|tas|te|rei [fantastə'raɪ] F -, -en = **Fantasterei**

phan|tas|tisch [fan'tastɪʃ] **ADJ, ADV** = **fantastisch**

Phan|tom [fan'toːm] NT -s, -e **a** (= *Trugbild*) phantom; **einem ~ nachjagen** (*fig*) to tilt at windmills **b** (= *Modell*) (*für Unterricht*) anatomical model, manikin; (*beim Fechten*) dummy

Phan|tom-: **Phan|tom|bild** NT Identikit® (picture), Photofit® (picture); **Phan|tom|schmerz** M phantom limb pain

Pha|rao ['faːrao] M -s, **Pharaonen** [fara'oːnən] Pharaoh

Pha|rao|nen- *in cpds* of the Pharaohs; **Pharaonengräber** tombs of the Pharaohs

Pha|ri|sä|er [fari'zɛːɐ] M -s, - (*Hist*) pharisee; (*fig auch*) hypocrite

pha|ri|sä|er|haft **ADJ** pharisaic(al); (*fig auch*) holier-than-thou, self-righteous

Pha|ri|sä|er|tum [fari'zɛːɐtuːm] NT -s, *no pl* (*fig*) self-righteousness

pha|ri|sä|isch [fari'zɛːɪʃ] **ADJ** = **pharisäerhaft**

pharm. *abbr von* **pharmazeutisch**

Phar|ma- ['farma-]: **Phar|ma|her|stel|ler(in)** M(F) drug manufacturer; **Phar|ma|in|dust|rie** F pharmaceuticals industry

Phar|ma|ko|lo|ge [farmako'loːgə] M -n, -n, **Phar|ma|ko|lo|gin** [-'loːgɪn] F -, -nen pharmacologist

Phar|ma|ko|lo|gie [farmakolo'giː] F -, *no pl* pharmacology

phar|ma|ko|lo|gisch [farmako'loːgɪʃ] **ADJ** pharmacological **ADV** pharmacologically

Phar|ma- ['farma-]: **Phar|ma|markt** M pharmaceuticals market; **Phar|ma|pro|dukt** NT pharmaceutical product; **Phar|ma|pro|du|zent(in)** M(F) pharmaceuticals producer; **Phar|ma|re|fe|rent(in)** M(F) medical representative; **Phar|ma|rück|stän|de** PL pharmaceutical effluents *pl*; **Phar|ma|un|ter|neh|men** NT pharmaceuticals company

Phar|ma|zeut [farma'tsɔyt] M -en, -en, **Phar|ma|zeu|tin** [-'tsɔytɪn] F -, -nen pharmacist, druggist (*US*)

Phar|ma|zeu|tik [farma'tsɔytɪk] F -, *no pl* pharmacy, pharmaceutics *sing*

phar|ma|zeu|tisch [farma'tsɔytɪʃ] **ADJ** pharmaceutical; **~-technische Assistentin**, **~-technischer Assistent** pharmaceutical assistant **ADV** pharmaceutically

Phar|ma|zie [farma'tsiː] F -, *no pl* pharmacy, pharmaceutics *sing*

Pha|se ['faːzə] F -, -n phase

Pha|sen-: **pha|sen|gleich** **ADJ** in phase; **Pha|sen|gleich|heit** F phase coincidence; **Pha|sen|span|nung** F voltage to neutral, phase voltage; **Pha|sen|ver|schie|bung** F phase difference *or* displacement

pha|sen|wei|se **ADJ a** *attr* (*in Abschnitten*) step-by-step, stage-by-sage **b** (= *zeitweilig*) temporary **ADV a** (= *in Phasen*) in phases *or* stages, step by step, stage by stage **b** (= *zeitweise*) temporarily; (= *manchmal*) at times; (= *vereinzelt*) from time to time, now and then

-pha|sig [faːzɪç] **ADJ** *suf* -phase; **dreiphasig** three-phase

Phe|nol [fe'noːl] NT -s, *no pl* phenol

Phe|nol|gas NT phenol gas

Phe|ro|mon [fero'moːn] NT -s, -e pheromone

Phi|lan|throp [filan'troːp] M -en, -en, **Phi|lan|thro|pin** [-'troːpɪn] F -, -nen philanthropist

Phi|lan|thro|pie [filantro'piː] F -, *no pl* philanthropy

phi|lan|thro|pisch [filan'troːpɪʃ] **ADJ** philanthropic(al)

Phi|la|te|lie [filate'liː] F -, *no pl* philately

Phi|la|te|list [filate'lɪst] M -en, -en, **Phi|la|te|lis|tin** [-'lɪstɪn] F -, -nen philatelist

phi|la|te|lis|tisch [filate'lɪstɪʃ] **ADJ** philatelic

Phil|har|mo|nie [fɪlharmo'niː, fiːlharmo'niː] F -, -n [-'niːən] (= *Orchester*) philharmonia, philharmonic (orchestra); (= *Konzertsaal*) philharmonic hall

Phil|har|mo|ni|ker [fɪlhar'moːnikɐ, fiːlhar'moːnikɐ] M -s, -, **Phil|har|mo|ni|ke|rin** [-ərɪn] F -, -nen (= *Musiker*) member of a philharmonic orchestra; **die (Münchner) ~** the (Munich) philharmonic (orchestra)

phil|har|mo|nisch [fɪlhar'moːnɪʃ, fiːlhar'moːnɪʃ] **ADJ** philharmonic

Phi|lip|pi|ka [fi'lɪpika] F -, **Philippiken** [-kn] (*Hist*) Philippic; (*fig*) philippic

Phi|lip|pi|nen [filɪ'piːnən] PL Philippines *pl*, Philippine Islands *pl*

Phi|lip|pi|ner [filɪ'piːnɐ] M -s, -, **Phi|lip|pi|ne|rin** [-ərɪn] F -, -nen Filipino

phi|lip|pi|nisch [filɪ'piːnɪʃ] **ADJ** Filipino

Phi|lis|ter [fi'lɪstɐ] M -s, -, **Phi|lis|te|rin** [-ərɪn] F -, -nen (*lit*) Philistine; (*fig*) philistine

phi|lis|ter|haft [fi'lɪstɛhaft] (*fig*) **ADJ** philistine **ADV** **sich verhalten** like a philistine

Phi|lo|lo|ge [filo'loːgə] M -n, -n, **Phi|lo|lo|gin** [-'loːgɪn] F -, -nen philologist

Phi|lo|lo|gie [filolo'giː] F -, *no pl* philology

phi|lo|lo|gisch [filo'loːgɪʃ] **ADJ** philological **ADV** philologically; **~ gesehen** from a philological point of view

Phi|lo|soph [filo'zoːf] M -en, -en, **Phi|lo|so|phin** [-'zoːfɪn] F -, -nen philosopher

Phi|lo|so|phie [filozo'fiː] F -, -n [-'fiːən] philosophy

phi|lo|so|phie|ren [filozo'fiːrən] *ptp* **philosophiert** VI to philosophize (*über +acc* about)

phi|lo|so|phisch [filo'zoːfɪʃ] **ADJ** philosophical **ADV** philosophically; **~ gesehen** from a philosophical point of view

Phi|mo|se [fi'moːzə] F -, -n phimosis

Phi|o|le ['fioːlə] F -, -n phial, vial

Phleg|ma ['flɛgma] NT -s, *no pl* apathy, torpor

Phleg|ma|ti|ker [flɛ'gmaːtikɐ] M -s, -, **Phleg|ma|ti|ke|rin** [-ərɪn] F -, -nen apathetic person

phleg|ma|tisch [flɛ'gmaːtɪʃ] **ADJ** apathetic **ADV** apathetically; **~ veranlagt sein** to be apathetic (by nature)

Phlox [flɔks] M -es, -e *or* F -, -e phlox

Pho|bie [fo'biː] F -, -n [-'biːən] phobia (*vor +dat* about)

Phon [foːn] NT -s, -s phon

Pho|nem [fo'neːm] NT -s, -e phoneme

Pho|ne|tik [fo'neːtɪk] F -, *no pl* phonetics *sing*

Pho|ne|ti|ker [fo'neːtikɐ] M -s, -, **Pho|ne|ti|ke|rin** [-ərɪn] F -, -nen phonetician

pho|ne|tisch [fo'neːtɪʃ] **ADJ** phonetic; **~e Schrift** phonetic transcription *or* script **ADV** **etw ~ (um)schreiben** to write *or* transcribe sth phonetically *or* in phonetics

Phö|nix ['føːnɪks] M -(es), -e phoenix; **wie ein ~ aus der Asche steigen** to rise like a phoenix from the ashes

Phö|ni|zi|er [fø'niːtsiɐ] M -s, -, **Phö|ni|zi|e|rin** [-iərɪn] F -, -nen Phoenician

phö|ni|zisch [fø'niːtsɪʃ] **ADJ** Phoenician

Pho|no- ['fono-]: **Pho|no|bran|che** F hi-fi industry; **Pho|no|graf** ▲ [fono'graːf] M -en, -en phonograph

Pho|no|lo|gie [fonolo'giː] F -, *no pl* phonology

pho|no|lo|gisch [fono'loːgɪʃ] **ADJ** phonological

Pho|no|ty|pist [fonoty'pɪst] M -en, -en, **Pho|no|ty|pis|tin** [-'pɪstɪn] F -, -nen audiotypist

Phon- ['foːn-]: **phon|stark** **ADJ** *Lautsprecher* powerful; *Lärm* loud; **Phon|stär|ke** F decibel; **Phon|zahl** F decibel level

Phos|gen [fɔs'geːn] NT -s, *no pl* phosgene

Phos|phat [fɔs'faːt] NT -(e)s, -e phosphate

phos|phat-: **phos|phat|frei** **ADJ** phosphate-free; **phos|phat|hal|tig** **ADJ** containing phosphates

Phos|phor ['fɔsfɔɐ] M -s, *no pl* (*abbr* **P**) phosphorus

Phos|pho|res|zenz [fɔsfores'tsɛnts] F -, *no pl* phosphorescence

phos|pho|res|zie|ren [fɔsfores'tsiːrən] *ptp* **phosphoresziert** VI to phosphoresce

phos|pho|res|zie|rend [fɔsfores'tsiːrənt] *prp von* **phosphoreszieren** **ADJ** phosphorescent

phos|phor|hal|tig **ADJ** phosphorous

phos|pho|rig ['fɔsforɪç] **ADJ** **~e Säure** phosphorous acid

Phos|phor-: **Phos|phor|säu|re** F phosphoric acid; **Phos|phor|ver|gif|tung** F phosphorus poisoning

phot. *abbr von* **photographisch**

Pho|to¹ ['foːto] NT -s, -s = **Foto¹**

Pho|to² M -s, -s (*inf*) = **Foto²**

Pho|to- *in cpds von auch* **Foto-**; **Pho|to|che|mie** F photochemistry; **pho|to|elekt|risch** **ADJ** photoelectric

Pho|to|graph [foto'gra:f] M **-en, -en, Pho|to|graphin** F **-, -nen = Fotograf**

Pho|to|gra|phie [fotogra'fi:] F **-, -n** [-'fi:ən] **= Fotografie**

pho|to|gra|phie|ren [fotogra'fi:rən] ptp **photographiert** VTI = fotografieren

Pho|ton ['fo:tɔn, fo'to:n] NT **-s, -en** [-'to:nən] photon

Pho|to-: Pho|to|syn|the|se [fotozyn'te:zə, 'fo:tozynte:zə] F photosynthesis; **pho|to|trop** [foto'tro:p] ADJ phototropic; **Pho|to|vol|ta|ik** [fotovɔl'ta:ɪk] F **-,** no pl (Phys) photovoltaics sing; **pho|to|vol|ta|isch** [-vɔl'ta:ɪʃ] ADJ photovoltaic; **Pho|to|zel|le** F photoelectric cell

Phra|se ['fra:zə] F **-, -n** phrase; (pej) empty or hollow phrase; **abgedroschene ~** cliché, hackneyed phrase (Brit); **das sind alles nur ~n** that's just (so many) words, that's just talk; **leere** or **hohle ~n** empty or hollow words or phrases; **~n dreschen** (inf) to churn out one cliché after another

Phra|sen-: Phra|sen|dre|scher(in) M(F) (pej) windbag (inf); **Phra|sen|dre|sche|rei** [-drɛʃə'rai] F **-, -en** (pej) phrasemongering; (= Geschwafel) hot air; **phra|sen|haft** ADJ empty, hollow; ⏵ **er drückt sich ~ aus** he speaks in clichés; **phra|sen|reich** ADJ cliché-ridden

Phra|se|o|lo|gie [frazeolo'gi:] F **-, -n** [-'gi:ən] phraseology; (Buch) dictionary of idioms

phra|se|o|lo|gisch [frazeo'lo:gɪʃ] ADJ phraseological; **~es Wörterbuch** dictionary of idioms

phra|sie|ren [fra'zi:rən] ptp **phrasiert** VT to phrase

Phra|sie|rung F **-, -en** phrasing

pH-Wert [pe:'ha:-] M pH value

Phy|lo|ge|ne|se [fyloge'ne:zə] F **-, -n** (Biol) phylogenesis

Phy|sik [fy'zi:k] F **-,** no pl physics sing

phy|si|ka|lisch [fyzi'ka:lɪʃ] ADJ physical; **~e Experimente durchführen** to carry out physics experiments or experiments in physics; **~e Therapie** physiotherapy, physical therapy ADV physically; **das ist ~ nicht erklärbar** that can't be explained by physics; **jdn ~ behandeln** (Med) to give sb physiotherapy or physical therapy; **etw ~ therapieren** (Med) to have physiotherapy or physical therapy

Phy|si|ker ['fy:zikɐ] M **-s, -, Phy|si|ke|rin** [-ərɪn] F **-, -nen** physicist; (Student auch) physics student

Phy|sik|saal M physics lab or laboratory

Phy|si|kum ['fy:zikʊm] NT **-s,** no pl (Univ) preliminary examination in medicine

Phy|si|og|no|mie [fyziɔgno'mi:] F **-, -n** [-'mi:ən] (liter) physiognomy

phy|si|og|no|misch [fyzio'gno:mɪʃ] ADJ physiognomical ADV physiognomically

Phy|si|o|lo|ge [fyzio'lo:gə] M **-n, -n, Phy|si|o|lo|gin** [-'lo:gɪn] F **-, -nen** physiologist

Phy|si|o|lo|gie [fyziolo'gi:] F **-,** no pl physiology

phy|si|o|lo|gisch [fyzio'lo:gɪʃ] ADJ physiological ADV physiologically

Phy|si|o|the|ra|peut(in) [fyziotera'pɔyt] M(F) physiotherapist

Phy|si|o|the|ra|pie [fyziotera'pi:] F physiotherapy, physical therapy

Phy|sis ['fy:zɪs] F **-,** no pl (geh) physical constitution

phy|sisch ['fy:zɪʃ] ADJ physical ADV physically

Phy|to|plank|ton NT (Biol) phytoplankton

Phy|to|the|ra|pie [fytotera'pi:] F (Med) phytotherapy

Pi [pi:] NT **-(s), -s** pi; **etw Pi mal Daumen machen** (inf) to do sth off the top of one's head

Pia|ni|no [pia'ni:no] NT **-s, -s** pianino, cottage or piccolo piano

Pia|nist [pia'nɪst] M **-en, -en, Pia|nis|tin** [-'nɪstɪn] F **-, -nen** pianist

Pia|no¹ [pia'no] NT **-s, -s** (geh: = Klavier) piano

Pia|no² NT **-s, -s** or **Piani** piano section

pia|no ADV (Mus) piano

Pia|no|for|te [piano'fɔrte] NT **-s, -s** pianoforte

pi|cheln ['pɪçln] VI (inf) to booze (inf), to knock it back (Brit inf), to put it away (inf)

Pi|chel|stei|ner ['pɪçlʃtainɐ] M **-s,** no pl, **Pi|chel|stei|ner Topf** M **-(e)s,** no pl (Cook) meat and vegetable stew

Pi|cke ['pɪkə] F **-, -n** pick(axe) (Brit), pick(ax) (US)

Pi|ckel ['pɪkl] M **-s, -** ⓐ spot, pimple ⓑ (= Spitzhacke) pick(axe) (Brit), pick(ax) (US); (= Eispickel) ice axe (Brit), ice ax (US)

Pi|ckel-: Pi|ckel|ge|sicht NT (inf) ⓐ (Gesicht) spotty face ⓑ (pej: Person) spotty person, zit face (US pej), pizza face (pej); (Junge) pimply youth; **~er** pl (also) the acne brigade; **Pi|ckel|hau|be** F spiked (leather) helmet; **pi|cke|lig** ['pɪkəlɪç] ADJ spotty, pimply; **pi|cken** ['pɪkn] VTI to peck (nach at); **Pi|ckerl** ['pɪkɛl] NT **-s, -n** (Aus) ⓐ (= Aufkleber) sticker ⓑ (= Autobahnvignette) motorway (Brit) or tollway (US) permit (in the form of a windscreen sticker), motorway tax disc; **pick|lig** ['pɪklɪç] ADJ spotty, pimply; **Pick|nick** ['pɪknɪk] NT **-s, -s** or **-e** picnic; **zum ~ fahren** to go for a picnic; **~ machen** to have a picnic; **pick|ni|cken** ['pɪknɪkn] VI to (have a) picnic; **Pick|nick|korb** M picnic basket; (größer) picnic hamper; **pi|co|bel|lo** [piko'bɛlo] (inf) ADJ perfect, spot (Brit) or right (US) on (inf) ADV **~ gekleidet** immaculately dressed; **~ sauber** absolutely spotless; **er hat die Wohnung ~ aufgeräumt** he did a beautiful job of tidying the flat (Brit) or apartment (esp US); **das Zimmer war ~ aufgeräumt** (also) there wasn't a thing out of place (in the room); **Pi|co|gramm** [piko'gram] NT pl **-gramme** or (nach Zahlenangabe) **-** picogramme (Brit), picogram (US); **Pief|ke** ['pi:fkə] M **-s, -s** ⓐ (Aus inf: = Deutscher) Kraut (inf), Jerry (inf) ⓑ **ein kleiner ~** a (little) pipsqueak ⓒ (= Wichtigtuer) pompous idiot; **pie|ken** ['pi:kn] VTI (inf) to prick; **es hat nur ein bisschen gepiekt** it was just a bit of a prick, I/he etc just felt a bit of a prick; **piek|fein** ['pi:k'fain] (inf) ADJ posh (inf), swish (Brit inf) ADV **~ eingerichtet sein** to have classy furnishings or posh furniture (inf); **~ angezogen sein** to look snazzy (inf); **~ speisen** to have a really posh meal (inf); **piek|sau|ber** ['pi:k'zaubɐ] (inf) ADJ spotless, clean as a whistle or a new penny; **piek|sen** ['pi:ksn] VTI **= pieken; piep** [pi:p] INTERJ tweet(-tweet), chirp(-chirp), cheep(-cheep); (von Armbanduhr, Telefon) beep(-beep); **Piep** [pi:p] M **-s, -e** (= Piepgeräusch) peep, beep; (inf) **er sagt keinen ~** or **gibt keinen ~ von sich** he doesn't say a (single) word; **keinen ~ mehr machen** to have had it (inf); **du hast ja einen ~!** you're off your head (Brit) or rocker! (inf); **er traute sich nicht mal, ~ zu sagen** or **machen** (inf) he wouldn't have dared to say boo to a goose (inf); **pie|pe** ['pi:pə], **piep|egal** ['pi:p'ega:l] ADJ pred (inf) all one (inf); **das ist mir ~!** I couldn't care less (inf), it's all one to me (inf); **pie|pen** ['pi:pn] VI (Vogel) to cheep, to chirrup; (Kinderstimme) to pipe, to squeak; (Maus) to squeak; (Funkgerät etc) to bleep, to beep; **bei dir piepts wohl!** (inf) are you off your head (Brit) or rocker? (inf); **es war zum Piepen!** (inf) it was a scream! (inf); **mit ~der Stimme** in a piping voice; **Pie|pen** ['pi:pn] PL (dated sl) lolly (dated inf), dough (inf); **Piep|matz** ['pi:pmats] M **-s, Piepmätze** [-'mɛtsə] (baby-talk: = Vogel) dickybird (Brit baby-talk), birdy (baby-talk); **piep|sen** ['pi:psn] VI **= piepen; Piep|ser** ['pi:psɐ] M **-s, -** (inf) ⓐ **= Piep** ⓑ (Telec) bleeper; **piep|sig** ['pi:psɪç] (inf) ADJ Stimme squeaky ADV **~ reden** to talk in a squeaky voice; **~ klingen** to sound squeaky; **Pieps|stim|me** F (inf) squeaky voice; **Piep|ton** M bleep; **sprechen Sie bitte nach dem ~** please speak after the tone; **Piep|vo|gel** M (baby-talk) dickybird (Brit baby-talk), birdy (baby-talk); **Pier** [pi:ɐ] M **-s, -s** or **-e,** or f **-, -s**

jetty, pier; **pier|cen** ['pi:ɐsn] VT to pierce; **sich** (dat) **die Zunge ~ lassen** to get one's tongue pierced; **Pier|cing** ['pi:ɐsɪŋ] NT **-s, s** ⓐ no pl body piercing ⓑ (Körperschmuck) piece of body jewellery (Brit) or jewelry (US); **~s aus Gold** gold body jewellery (Brit) or jewelry (US); **pie|sa|cken** ['pi:zakn] VT (inf: = quälen) to torment; (= belästigen) to pester; **er piesackt mich schon den ganzen Tag, dass ich ihn mitnehmen soll** he's been pestering me all day to take him with me; **pie|seln** ['pi:zln] VI (inf) ⓐ (= nieseln) to drizzle ⓑ (= pinkeln) to pee, to have a pee; **~ gehen** to go for a pee; **Pie|se|pam|pel** ['pi:zəpampl] M **-s, -** (inf) square (inf); **Pie|ta** [pie'ta] F **-, -s, Pie|tà** F **-, -s** pietà; **Pie|tät** [pie'te:t] F **-,** no pl (= Ehrfurcht vor den Toten) reverence no pl; (= Achtung) respect (gegenüber jdm/etw, vor (dat) for sb/sth); (= Frömmelei) piety; **das verstößt gegen jede ~** this offends against a proper sense of reverence; **pie|tät|los** ADJ irreverent; (= ohne Achtung) lacking in respect, impious ADV irreverently; **~ über Tote sprechen** to speak disrespectfully of the dead; **Pie|tät|lo|sig|keit** F **-, -en** irreverence; (Tat) impiety; **das ist eine ~ sondergleichen!** that shows a complete lack of reverence!; **pie|tät|voll** ADJ pious, reverent ADV respectfully; **Pie|tis|mus** [pie'tɪsmʊs] M **-,** no pl Pietism; (pej) pietism, piety, piousness; **Pie|tist** [pie'tɪst] M **-en, -en, Pie|tis|tin** [-'tɪstɪn] F **-, -nen** Pietist; (pej auch) holy Joe (inf); **pie|tis|tisch** [pie'tɪstɪʃ] ADJ pietistic; (pej auch) pious; **piff paff** ['pɪf'paf] INTERJ bang bang, pow pow (inf); **Pig|ment** [pɪ'gmɛnt] M **-(e)s, -e** pigment; **Pig|men|ta|ti|on** [pɪgmɛnta'tsio:n] F **-, -en** pigmentation; **Pig|ment|fleck** M pigmentation mark; **pig|men|tie|ren** [pɪgmɛn'ti:rən] ptp **pigmentiert** (form) VI to become pigmented, to pigment VT to pigment; **Pik¹** [pi:k] M (inf) **einen ~ auf jdn haben** to have something or a grudge against sb; **Pik²** NT **-s, -** (Cards) (no pl: Farbe) spades pl; (= Pikkarte) spade; **~ass** ace of spades; **dastehen wie ~sieben** (inf) to look completely bewildered or at a loss; **pi|kant** [pi'kant] ADJ piquant, spicy; Witz, Geschichte auch racy ADV piquantly; **~ gewürzt** well-seasoned; **~ schmecken** to taste piquant; **Pi|kan|te|rie** [pikantə'ri:] F **-, -n** [-'ri:ən] ⓐ piquancy; (von Witz, Geschichte auch) raciness ⓑ (Bemerkung) piquant or racy remark; **pi|ka|resk** [pika'rɛsk] ADJ Roman picaresque; **Pi|ke** ['pi:kə] F **-, -n** pike; **von der ~ auf dienen** (inf) to rise from the ranks, to work one's way up; **etw von der ~ auf lernen** (fig) to learn sth starting from the bottom; **Pi|kee** [pi'ke:] M or NT **-s, -s** piqué; **pi|kfein** ['pi:k'fain] ADJ, ADV **= piekfein**; **pi|kie|ren** [pi'ki:rən] ptp **pikiert** VT ⓐ Sämlinge to prick out, to transplant; Bäume to transplant ⓑ (Sew) pad or prick stitch; **pi|kiert** [pi'ki:ɐt] (inf) ADJ put out, peeved (inf), piqued; **sie machte ein ~es Gesicht** she looked put out or peeved (inf) ADV **~ reagieren** to be put out or peeved (inf); **~ das Gesicht verziehen** to look peeved (inf); **Pik|ko|lo** ['pɪkolo] M **-s, -s** ⓐ Kellnerlehrling) apprentice or trainee waiter ⓑ (fig: = kleine Ausgabe) mini-version, baby; (auch **Pikkoloflasche**) quarter bottle of champagne ⓒ (Mus: auch **Pikkoloflöte**) piccolo; **pi|ko|bel|lo** [piko'bɛlo] (inf) ADJ immaculate, impeccable ADV immaculately, impeccably; **ein Zimmer ~ aufräumen** to make a room look immaculate; **Pik|to|gramm** [pɪkto'gram] NT pl **-gramme** pictogram; **Pi|lau** [pi'lau] M **-s,** no pl, **Pi|law** [pi'laf] M **-s,** no pl (Cook) pilau, pilaf(f); **Pil|ger** ['pɪlgɐ] M **-s, -, Pil|ge|rin** [-ərɪn] F **-, -nen** pilgrim; **Pil|ger|fahrt** F pilgrimage; **auf ~ gehen** to go on a pilgrimage; **pil|gern** ['pɪlgɐn] VI aux sein to make a pilgrimage; (inf: = gehen) to make or wend one's way; **Pil|ger|schaft** ['pɪlgɐʃaft] F **-, -en** pilgrimage

Pil|ger-: Pil|ger|stab M pilgrim's staff; **Pil|ger|zug** M procession of pilgrims

Pil|le ['pɪlə] F **-, -n** pill, tablet; (= Antibabypille) pill; **die ~ danach** the morning-after pill; **die ~**

für den Mann the male pill; **eine ~ (ein)nehmen** or **schlucken** to take a pill; **sie nimmt die ~** she's on the pill, she takes the pill; **das war eine bittere ~ für ihn** (fig) that was a bitter pill for him (to swallow); **jdm eine bittere ~ versüßen** or **verzuckern** (fig) to sugar or sweeten the pill for sb

Pil|len-: Pil|len|dre|her M (Zool) scarab; **Pil|len|dre|her(in)** M(F) (inf: = Apotheker) chemist, druggist (US); **Pil|len|knick** M slump in the birth rate caused by the pill; **Pil|len|schach|tel** F pillbox

Pi|lot [pi'lo:t] M **-en, -en, Pi|lo|tin** [-'lo:tɪn] F **-, -nen** pilot

Pi|lot-: Pi|lot|an|la|ge F pilot plant; **Pi|lot|bal|lon** M pilot balloon; **Pi|lot|film** M pilot film

Pi|lo|tin F **-, -nen** pilot

Pi|lot-: Pi|lot|pro|jekt NT pilot scheme; **Pi|lot|sen|dung** F (TV) pilot broadcast; **Pi|lot|stu|die** F pilot study; **Pi|lot|ver|such** M pilot experiment

Pils [pɪls] NT **-, -, Pil|se|ner** ['pɪlzənɐ] NT **-s, -, Pils|ner** [-znɐ] NT **-s, -** Pils, Pilsner

Pilz [pɪlts] M **-es, -e** a fungus; (giftig) toadstool; (essbar) mushroom; (= Mikropilz) mould (Brit), mold (US); (= Atompilz) mushroom cloud; **~e sammeln, in die ~e gehen** (inf) to go mushrooming or mushroom-picking; **wie ~e aus der Erde** or **aus dem Boden schießen** or **sprießen** to spring up like mushrooms, to mushroom b (= Hautpilz) fungal skin infection

pilz|för|mig ADJ mushroom-shaped ADV **der Rauch stieg ~ auf** the smoke rose to form a mushroom-shaped cloud

Pilz-: Pilz|kopf M (inf) Beatle; (Frisur) Beatle haircut; **Pilz|krank|heit** F fungal disease; **Pilz|kun|de** F, no pl mycology; **pilz|tö|tend** ADJ fungicidal; **Pilz|ver|gif|tung** F fungus poisoning

Pi|ment [pi'mɛnt] M OR NT **-(e)s, -e** (= Nelkenpfeffer) allspice, piment

Pim|mel ['pɪml] M **-s, -** (inf: = Penis) willie (inf)

pim|pe|lig ['pɪmpəlɪç] ADJ (inf) (= wehleidig) soppy (inf); (= verweichlicht auch) namby-pamby (Brit inf), sissyish

Pim|per|lin|ge ['pɪmpəlɪŋə] PL (dated inf) **die paar ~** the odd penny

pim|pern ['pɪmpɐn] (inf) VT to have it off with (Brit inf), to have it with (US sl) VI to have it off (Brit inf), to do it (inf)

Pimpf [pɪmpf] M **-(e)s, -e** a (inf) squirt (pej) b (Hist) member of Hitlerian organization for 10-14-year-olds

pimp|lig ['pɪmplɪç] ADJ = pimpelig

PIN [pɪn] F abbr von persönliche Identifikationsnummer PIN; **~-Code** PIN code; **~-Nummer** PIN number

Pin [pɪn] M **-s, -s** a (Comput: von Stecker) pin b (= Ansteckknadel) badge

Pi|na|ko|thek [pinako'te:k] F **-, -en** art gallery

pin|ge|lig ['pɪŋəlɪç] ADJ (inf) finicky (inf), fussy, nit-picking (inf)

Ping|pong ['pɪŋpɔŋ] NT **-s, -s** (inf) ping-pong

Pin|gu|in ['pɪŋguiːn] M **-s, -e** penguin

Pi|nie ['piːniə] F **-, -n** (= Baum) pine (tree); (= Holz) pine (wood)

Pi|ni|en|kern M pine nut

pink [pɪŋk] ADJ shocking pink

Pin|kel ['pɪŋkl] M **-s, -** (inf) **ein feiner** or **vornehmer ~** a swell, Lord Muck (Brit inf), His Highness (inf)

pin|keln ['pɪŋkln] VI (inf) to pee (inf), to piddle (inf); **ich muss mal ~** I need a pee (inf)

Pin|kel|pau|se F (inf) toilet break; **der Bus hielt zu einer ~** the bus made a toilet stop or a convenience stop

Pin|ke(pin|ke) ['pɪŋkə('pɪŋkə)] F **-, no pl** (dated inf) dough (inf), lolly (dated inf); **heute gibts ~** payday today!

pink|far|ben [-farbn] ADJ shocking pink

Pin|ne ['pɪnə] F **-, -n** a (inf: = Stift) pin b (für Kompassnadel) pivot c (= Ruderpinne) tiller

Pinn|wand [pɪn-] F (notice) board

Pin|scher¹ ['pɪnʃɐ] M **-s, -** pinscher

Pin|scher² ['pɪnʃɐ] M **-s, -, Pin|sche|rin** [-ərɪn] F **-, -nen** (inf) self-important little pipsqueak (inf)

Pin|sel ['pɪnzl] M **-s, -** a brush; (Hunt) tuft of hair b (inf) **ein eingebildeter ~** a self-opinionated twit (Brit inf), a jumped-up (Brit) or hopped-up (US) so-and-so (inf) c (sl: = Penis) willie (inf)

Pin|se|lei [pɪnzə'lai] F **-, -en** (pej) daubing (pej); (= Gemälde auch) daub (pej)

Pin|sel|füh|rung F brushwork

pin|seln ['pɪnzln] VTI (inf: = streichen) to paint (auch Med); (pej: = malen) to daub; (inf: = schreiben) to pen

Pin|sel|strich M stroke (of a brush), brushstroke

Pin|te ['pɪntə] F **-, -n** a (inf: = Lokal) boozer (Brit inf), bar b (Measure) pint

Pin-up-Girl [pɪn'ʔap-] NT pin-up (girl)

Pin|zet|te [pɪn'tsɛtə] F **-, -n** (pair of) tweezers pl

Pi|o|nier [pio'niːɐ] M **-s, -e, Pi|o|nie|rin** [-'niːərɪn] F **-, -nen** a (Mil) sapper, engineer b (fig) pioneer c (DDR) member of a political organization in the former GDR similar to the Boy Scouts

Pi|o|nier-: Pi|o|nier|ar|beit F, no pl pioneering work; **Pi|o|nier|geist** M, no pl pioneering spirit

Pi|pa|po [pipa'po:] NT **-s, no pl** (inf) **das ganze ~** the whole (kit and) caboodle (inf); **eine Party mit allem ~** a party with all the works

Pipe|line ['paiplain] F **-, -s** pipeline

Pi|pet|te [pi'pɛtə] F **-, -n** pipette

Pi|pi [pi'piː] NT OR M **-s, -s** (baby-talk) wee(-wee) (baby-talk); **~ machen** to do or have a wee (-wee)

Pi|pi-: Pi|pi|fax ['pɪpifaks] NT OR M **-, no pl** (inf) nonsense; **Pi|pi|mäd|chen** ['pɪpi-] NT (pej) bimbo (inf)

Pi|ran|ha [pi'ranja] M **-(s), -s** piranha

Pi|rat [pi'raːt] M **-en, -en, Pi|ra|tin** [-'raːtɪn] F **-, -nen** (lit, fig) pirate; (= Luftpirat) hijacker

Pi|ra|ten-: Pi|ra|ten|akt M act of piracy; **Pi|ra|ten|flag|ge** F Jolly Roger, skull and crossbones; **unter der ~ segeln** to sail under the skull and crossbones; **Pi|ra|ten|schiff** NT pirate ship; **Pi|ra|ten|sen|der** M pirate radio station

Pi|ra|te|rie [piratə'riː] F **-, -n** [-'riːən] (lit, fig) piracy

Pi|ra|tin F → Pirat

Pi|rog|ge [pi'rɔgə] F **-, -n** (Cook) pirogi, piroshki pl

Pi|rol [pi'roːl] M **-s, -e** oriole

Pi|rou|et|te [pi'ruɛtə] F **-, -n** pirouette

Pirsch [pɪrʃ] F **-, no pl** stalk; **auf (die) ~ gehen** to go stalking; **auf der ~ nach etw sein** (fig) to be on the lookout for sth

pir|schen ['pɪrʃn] VI to stalk, to go stalking

Pirsch|gang M pl **-gänge** stalk; **auf ~ gehen** to go stalking

pis|pern ['pɪspɐn] VI (dial) to whisper

Piss|ba|cke F (sl) nerd (inf)

Pis|se ['pɪsə] F **-, no pl** (vulg) piss (sl)

pis|sen ['pɪsn] VI (vulg) to (have a (Brit) or take a) piss; (sl: = regnen) to piss down (Brit vulg), to pour down (inf)

Piss|nel|ke F (sl) nerd (inf)

Piss|soir [pɪ'soaːɐ] NT **-s, -s** or **-e** (dated) urinal

Piss|pott ▲ ['pɪspɔt] M (sl) potty (inf)

Pis|ta|zie [pɪs'taːtsiə] F **-, -n** pistachio

Pis|ta|zi|en|kern M (shelled) pistachio

Pis|te ['pɪstə] F **-, -n** (Ski) piste, (ski) run; (= Rennbahn) track, circuit; (Aviat) runway, tarmac; (behelfsmäßig) landing strip, airstrip; (im Zirkus) barrier

Pis|ten-: Pis|ten|rau|pe F piste caterpillar or basher (inf); **Pis|ten|sau** F (Ski sl), **Pis|ten|schreck** M (Ski inf) hooligan on the piste

Pis|to|le ['pɪsto:lə] F **-, -n** a (lit) pistol; **jdn mit vorgehaltener ~ (zu etw) zwingen** to force sb (to do sth) at gunpoint; **jdn auf ~n fordern** (old) to challenge sb to a duel (with pistols); **jdm die ~ auf die Brust setzen** (fig) to hold a pistol to sb's head; **wie aus der ~ geschossen** (fig) like a shot (inf) b (Hist: Goldmünze) pistole

Pis|to|len-: Pis|to|len|griff M pistol butt; **Pis|to|len|ku|gel** F (pistol) bullet; **Pis|to|len|schuss** ▲ M pistol shot; **Pis|to|len|ta|sche** F holster

Pit-Bull-Ter|ri|er ['pɪtbʊl-] M pit bull terrier

pit|sche|nass ▲ ['pɪtʃə'nas], **pitsch|nass** ▲ ['pɪtʃ'nas] (inf) ADJ soaking (wet); Kleidung, Mensch auch dripping (wet)

pitsch, patsch ['pɪtʃ 'patʃ] INTERJ pitter-patter

pit|to|resk [pɪto'rɛsk] ADJ picturesque ADV picturesquely; **~ aussehen** to look picturesque

Pi|xel ['pɪksl] NT **-s, -s** (Comput) pixel

Piz|za ['pɪtsa] F **-, -s** or **Pizzen** ['pɪtsn] pizza

Piz|za-: Piz|za|bä|cker(in) M(F) pizza chef; **Piz|za|ge|würz** NT pizza spice; **Piz|za|ta|sche** F calzone

Piz|ze|ria [pɪtsə'riːa] F **-, -s** or **Pizzerien** [-'riːən] pizzeria

Pkw ['pe:ka:ve:, pe:ka:'ve:] M **-s, -s** abbr von Personenkraftwagen car

pl., Pl. abbr von Plural pl

Pla|ce|bo [pla'tse:bo] NT **-s, -s** placebo

Pla|ce|bo-Ef|fekt M (lit, fig) placebo effect

pla|cie|ren △ [pla'tsiːrən] ptp **placiert** VT → platzieren

Pla|cie|rung △ F **-, -en** → Platzierung

pla|cken ['plakn] VR (inf) to slave away (inf)

Pla|cken ['plakn] M **-s, -** (dial) patch

Pla|cke|rei [plakə'rai] F **-, -en** (inf) grind (inf)

pla|d|dern ['pladɐn] (N Ger) VT aux sein (Regen) to pelt (down) VI impers to pelt down

plä|die|ren [plɛ'diːrən] ptp **plädiert** VI (Jur, fig) to plead (für, auf +acc for)

Plä|do|yer [plɛdoa'je:] NT **-s, -s** (Jur) address to the jury, summation (US), summing up; (fig) plea

Pla|fond [pla'fõ:] M **-s, -s** (lit, fig) ceiling

Pla|ge ['pla:gə] F **-, -n** a plague b (fig: = Mühe) nuisance; (= Plackerei) (hard) grind (inf); **sie hat ihre ~ mit ihm** he's a trial for her; **man hat schon seine ~ mit dir** you do make life difficult, you are a nuisance; **zu einer ~ werden** to become a nuisance

Pla|ge|geist M nuisance, pest

pla|gen ['pla:gn] VT to plague, to torment; (mit Bitten und Fragen auch) to pester, to harass; **dich plagt doch was, heraus mit der Sprache** something's worrying or bothering you, out with it; **ein geplagter Mann** a harassed man; **vom schlechten Gewissen geplagt werden** to be plagued or tormented by a guilty conscience VR a (= leiden) to be troubled or bothered (mit by); **schon die ganze Woche plage ich mich mit meinem Heuschnupfen** I've been bothered or troubled all week by my hay fever, my hay fever's been bothering or troubling me all week b (= sich abrackern) to slave or slog (esp Brit) away (inf); (= sich Mühe geben) to go to or take a lot of trouble or great pains (mit over, with)

Pla|gi|at [pla'gia:t] NT **-(e)s, -e** a (= geistiger Diebstahl) plagiarism; **da hat er ein ~ begangen** that's a plagiarism, he plagiarized that b

(*Buch, Film etc*) book/film *etc* resulting from plagiarism; (= *nachgebildeter Markenartikel*) counterfeit product; **dieses Buch ist ein ~** this book is plagiarism

Pla|gi|a|tor [plaˈgiaːtoːɐ] M **-s, Plagiatoren** [-ˈtoːrən], **Pla|gi|a|to|rin** [-ˈtoːrɪn] F **-, -nen** plagiarist

pla|gi|ie|ren [plagiˈiːrən] *ptp* **plagiiert** VTI to plagiarize

Plaid [pleːt] NT OR M **-s, -s** tartan travelling rug (*Brit*) or traveling rug (*US*)

Pla|ka|far|be® [ˈplaka-] F poster paint

Pla|kat [plaˈkaːt] NT **-(e)s, -e** (*an Litfaßsäulen etc*) poster, bill; (*aus Pappe*) placard

Pla|kat-: Pla|kat|ak|ti|on F poster campaign; **Pla|kat|an|kle|ber** [-ankleːbɐ] M **-s, -, Pla|kat|an|kle|be|rin** [-ərɪn] F **-, -nen** billposter, billsticker; **Pla|kat|far|be** F poster paint

pla|ka|tie|ren [plakaˈtiːrən] *ptp* **plakatiert** VT to placard; (*fig*) to broadcast

pla|ka|tiv [plakaˈtiːf] ADJ *Wirkung, Farben* striking, bold; *Sprüche* pithy; *Gehabe* showy ADV **formuliert** catchy; **etw ~ formulieren** to express sth in a catchy phrase; **~ wirkende Lieder** catchy songs

Pla|kat-: Pla|kat|ma|ler(in) M(F) poster painter *or* artist; **Pla|kat|säu|le** F advertisement pillar; **Pla|kat|schrift** F block lettering; **Pla|kat|trä|ger(in)** M(F) sandwich man, man/woman carrying a sandwich board; **Pla|kat|wer|bung** F poster advertising

Pla|ket|te [plaˈkɛtə] F **-, -n** (= *Abzeichen*) badge; (*Münze*) commemorative coin; (*an Wänden*) plaque

plan [plaːn] ADJ flat, level; *Ebene, Fläche* plane *attr*

Plan¹ [plaːn] M **-(e)s, ⸚e** [ˈplɛːnə] **a** plan; **die Pläne zur Renovierung der Häuser** the plans for the renovation of the houses; **den ~ fassen, etw zu tun** to form the intention of doing sth, to plan to do sth; **wir haben den ~, ...** we're planning to ...; **Pläne machen** *or* **schmieden** to make plans, to plan; **nach ~ verlaufen** to run *or* go according to plan; **das passt mir nicht in den ~** (*inf*) it doesn't suit me, it's inconvenient **b** (= *Stadtplan*) (street) map, town plan; (= *Grundriss, Bauplan*) plan, blueprint; (= *Zeittafel*) schedule, timetable; (= *Wirtschaftsplan*) economic plan

Plan² M **-(e)s, ⸚e** [ˈplɛːnə] (*obs* = *ebene Fläche*) plain; **auf den ~ erscheinen, auf den ~ treten** (*fig*) to arrive *or* come on the scene; **jdn auf den ~ rufen** (*fig*) to bring sb into the arena

Pla|ne [ˈplaːnə] F **-, -n** tarpaulin, tarp (*US inf*); (*von LKW*) hood; (= *Schutzdach*) canopy, awning

Plä|ne|ma|cher(in) M(F) planner; **er ist ein großer ~** he's a great one for making plans

pla|nen [ˈplaːnən] ⚙ 35.2, 52.5 VTI to plan; *Attentat, Verbrechen auch* to plot

Pla|ner [ˈplaːnɐ] M **-s, -, Pla|ne|rin** [-ərɪn] F **-, -nen** planner

Plan|er|fül|lung F realization of a/the plan; **uns trennen nur noch 5% von der ~** we're only 5% short of our planned target

pla|ne|risch [ˈplaːnərɪʃ] ADJ planning; **~e Ausarbeitung** working out of the plans ADV **etw ~ durchdenken** to plan sth from start to finish; **~ ausgearbeitet** planned down to the last detail; **~ vorgehen** to proceed methodically; **ein Projekt ~ betreuen** to be in charge of the planning of a project; **~ hat das Team versagt** the team's planning was a failure

Pla|net [plaˈneːt] M **-en, -en** planet

pla|ne|ta|risch [planeˈtaːrɪʃ] ADJ planetary; **~er Nebel** (*Astron*) planetary nebula

Pla|ne|ta|ri|um [planeˈtaːriʊm] NT **-s, Planetarien** [-riən] planetarium

Pla|ne|ten-: Pla|ne|ten|bahn F planetary orbit; **Pla|ne|ten|sys|tem** NT planetary system

Pla|ne|to|id [planetoˈiːt] M **-en, -en** [-dn] planetoid, asteroid

Plan-: Plan|fest|stel|lungs|ver|fah|ren NT (*Build*) planning permission hearings *pl*; **plan|ge|mäß** ADJ ADV = **planmäßig**

pla|nie|ren [plaˈniːrən] VT *Boden* to level (off); *Werkstück* to planish

Pla|nier|rau|pe F bulldozer

Plan|ke [ˈplaŋkə] F **-, -n** plank, board; (= *Leitplanke*) crash barrier; **~n** (= *Umzäunung*) fencing, boarding (+*gen* round)

Plän|ke|lei [plɛŋkəˈlai] F **-, -en** (*old Mil*) skirmish; (*fig auch*) squabble

plän|keln [ˈplɛŋkln] VI (*old Mil*) to skirmish, to engage in skirmishes; (*fig*) to squabble, to have a squabble

Plank|ton [ˈplaŋktɔn] NT **-s**, *no pl* plankton

plan|los ADJ unmethodical, unsystematic; (= *ziellos*) random ADV *umherirren, durchstreifen* aimlessly; *vorgehen* without any clear direction; *durchsuchen* haphazardly; **etw ~ durchblättern** to flick aimlessly through sth

Plan|lo|sig|keit F **-**, *no pl* lack of planning

plan|mä|ßig ADJ (= *wie geplant*) as planned, according to plan; (= *pünktlich*) on schedule, as scheduled; (= *methodisch*) methodical; **~e Ankunft/Abfahrt** scheduled time of arrival/departure ADV **a** (= *systematisch*) methodically, systematically **b** (= *fahrplanmäßig*) on schedule, on time; **wir sind ~ um 7 angekommen** we arrived on schedule *or* as scheduled *or* on time at 7; **~ kommt der Zug um 7 Uhr an** the train is scheduled to arrive *or* is due in at 7 o'clock

Plan|mä|ßig|keit F (= *Methodik*) method; (= *Pünktlichkeit*) punctuality; (= *Regelmäßigkeit*) regularity

Plan|quad|rat NT grid square

Plansch|be|cken NT paddling pool (*Brit*), wading pool (*US*)

plan|schen [ˈplanʃn] VI to splash around

Plan|sche|rei [planʃəˈrai] F **-, -en** splashing around

Plan-: Plan|soll NT output target; **Plan|spiel** NT experimental game; (*Mil*) map exercise; (*Econ*) planning *or* experimental game; **Plan|stel|le** F post

Plan|ta|ge [planˈtaːʒə] F **-, -n** plantation

Plantsch|be|cken NT paddling pool (*Brit*), wading pool (*US*)

plant|schen VI to splash around

Plant|sche|rei F **-, -en** splashing around

Pla|nung [ˈplaːnʊŋ] F **-, -en** planning; **diese Straße ist noch in ~** this road is still being planned; **schon in der ~** in *or* at the planning stage

Pla|nungs-: Pla|nungs|ab|tei|lung F planning department; **Pla|nungs|aus|schuss** ▲ M planning committee; **Pla|nungs|kom|mis|si|on** F planning commission; **Pla|nungs|zeit|raum** M planning period

Plan-: Plan|wa|gen M covered wagon; **Plan|wirt|schaft** F planned economy

Plap|pe|rei [plapəˈrai] F **-, -en** (*inf*) chatter(ing), prattling (*esp Brit*)

Plap|per|maul NT (*inf*) (= *Mund*) big mouth (*inf*); (= *Kind*) chatterbox (*inf*); (= *Schwätzer*) tittle-tattler (*esp Brit inf*), windbag (*inf*)

plap|pern [ˈplapɐn] VI to prattle, to chatter; (= *Geheimnis verraten*) to talk, to blab (*inf*) VT **was plapperst du denn da für Blödsinn?** don't talk rubbish (*Brit*) *or* nonsense

Plap|per|ta|sche F (*inf*) tittle-tattler (*esp Brit inf*), windbag (*inf*)

Plaque [plak] F **-, -s** (*Med*) plaque

plär|ren [ˈplɛrən] VTI (*inf* = *weinen*) to howl, to bawl; (*Radio*) to blare (out); (= *schreien*) to yell, to shriek; (= *unschön singen*) to screech

Plä|sier [plɛˈziːɐ] NT **-s, -e** (*dated*) pleasure, delight; **nun lass ihm doch sein ~** let him have his bit of fun

Plä|sier|chen [plɛˈziːɐçən] NT **-s, -** **jedem Tierchen sein ~** (*hum*) each to his own

Plas|ma [ˈplasma] NT **-s, Plasmen** [-mən] plasma

Plast [plast] M **-(e)s, -e, Plas|te** [ˈplastə] F **-, -n** (*dial*) plastic

Plas|tik¹ [ˈplastɪk] NT **-s**, *no pl* (= *Kunststoff*) plastic

Plas|tik² F **-, -en** **a** (= *Bildhauerkunst*) sculpture, plastic art (*form*) **b** (= *Skulptur*) sculpture **c** (*Med*) plastic surgery **d** (*fig* = *Anschaulichkeit*) vividness

Plas|tik-: Plas|tik|beu|tel M plastic bag, carrier bag; **Plas|tik|bom|be** F plastic bomb; **Plas|tik|fla|sche** F plastic bottle; **Plas|tik|fo|lie** F plastic film; **Plas|tik|geld** NT (*inf*) plastic money; **mit ~ bezahlen** to pay with plastic (*inf*); **Plas|tik|ma|te|ri|al** NT plastic; **Plas|tik|spreng|stoff** M plastic explosive; **Plas|tik|tü|te** F plastic bag

Plas|ti|lin [plastiˈliːn] NT **-s, -e** Plasticine®

Plas|ti|na|ti|on [plastinaˈtsioːn] F **-**, *no pl* plastination

plas|tisch [ˈplastɪʃ] ADJ **a** (= *knetbar*) malleable, workable **b** (= *dreidimensional*) three-dimensional, 3-D; (*fig* = *anschaulich*) vivid; **~es Vorstellungsvermögen** ability to imagine things in three dimensions; **~e Sprache** vivid *or* graphic language **c** (*Art*) plastic; **die ~e Kunst** plastic art; **~e Arbeiten** sculptures, plastic works **d** (*Med*) *Chirurgie* plastic ADV **a** (*räumlich*) three-dimensionally; **~ wirken** *or* **erscheinen** to appear three-dimensional; **etw ~ ausformen** to mould (*Brit*) *or* mold (*US*) sth into shape; **~ hervortreten** to stand out **b** (*fig* = *anschaulich*) **etw ~ schildern** to give a graphic description of sth; **sich** (*dat*) **etw ~ vorstellen** to picture sth clearly; **das kann ich mir ~ vorstellen** I can just imagine *or* picture it

Plas|ti|zi|tät [plastitsiˈtɛːt] F **-**, *no pl* **a** (= *Formbarkeit*) malleability, workability **b** (*fig* = *Anschaulichkeit*) vividness, graphicness

Pla|ta|ne [plaˈtaːnə] F **-, -n** plane tree

Pla|teau [plaˈtoː] NT **-s, -s** **a** plateau **b** (*von Schuh*) platform

Pla|teau|schuh [plaˈtoː-] M platform shoe

Pla|teau|soh|le [plaˈtoː-] F platform sole

Pla|tin [ˈplaːtiːn, plaˈtiːn] NT **-s**, *no pl* (*abbr* Pt) platinum

pla|tin|blond ADJ platinum blond(e) ADV **~ gefärbtes Haar** dyed platinum blond(e) hair

Pla|ti|ne [plaˈtiːnə] F **-, -n** (*Comput*) circuit board

Pla|ti|tü|de △ [platiˈtyːdə] F **-, -n** → **Plattitüde**

Pla|to(n) [ˈplaːto, ˈplaːtɔn] M **-s** Plato

Pla|to|ni|ker [plaˈtoːnikɐ] M **-s, -, Pla|to|ni|ke|rin** [-ərɪn] F **-, -nen** Platonist

pla|to|nisch [plaˈtoːnɪʃ] ADJ Platonic, Platonist; (= *nicht sexuell*) platonic; (*geh* = *unverbindlich*) noncommittal; **~e Liebe** platonic love ADV platonically

platsch [platʃ] INTERJ splash, splosh

plat|schen [ˈplatʃn] VI (*inf*) to splash; (= *regnen*) to pelt, to pour

plät|schern [ˈplɛtʃɐn] VI (*Bach*) to babble, to splash; (*Brunnen*) to splash; (*Regen*) to patter; (= *planschen*) to splash (about (*Brit*) *or* around); **aus dem Radio plätscherte ein altes Lied** an old song was playing softly on the radio; **eine ~de Unterhaltung** light conversation

platsch|nass ▲ ADJ (*inf*) soaking (wet); *Kleidung, Mensch auch* dripping (wet), drenched

platt [plat] ADJ **a** (= *flach*) flat; **einen Platten** (*inf*) *or* **einen ~en Reifen haben** to have a flat (*inf*), to have a flat tyre (*Brit*) *or* tire (*US*); **das ~e Land** the flat country; (*nicht Stadt*) the country **b** (*fig* = *geistlos*) *Bemerkung, Witz* flat, dull; *Mensch* dull, uninspired **c** (*inf* = *verblüfft*) ~

sein to be flabbergasted (*inf*); **da bist du ~, nicht?** that surprised you, didn't it? **d** (*inf*) (= *erschöpft*) done in (*inf*), dead beat (*Brit inf*); (= *bankrott*) Betrieb bust (*inf*) **e** (*sl:* = *high*) wasted (*sl*) ▨ ADV pressen, walzen flat; **etw ~ drücken** to press sth flat, to flatten sth

Platt [plat] NT **-(s)**, *no pl* (*inf*) Low German, Plattdeutsch

Plätt|brett NT (*dial*) ironing board; (*inf*) skinny Lizzy (*Brit inf*), skinny Minnie (*US inf*)

Plätt|chen ['plɛtçən] NT **-s**, **-** little tile

platt|deutsch ADJ Low German

Platt|deutsch(e) NT Low German, Plattdeutsch → *auch* **Deutsch(e)**

Plat|te ['platə] F **-**, **-n** **a** (= *Holzplatte*) piece of wood, wood *no pl*, board; (*zur Wandverkleidung*) panel; (= *Tischtennisplatte*) ping-pong table; (= *Glasplatte/Metallplatte/Plastikplatte*) piece or sheet of glass/metal/plastic; (= *Betonplatte, Steinplatte*) slab; (*zum Pflastern*) paving stone, flag(stone); (= *Kachel, Fliese*) tile; (= *Grabplatte*) gravestone, slab; (= *Herdplatte*) hotplate; (= *Tischplatte*) (table) top; (*ausziehbare*) leaf; (= *Felsenplatte*) shelf, ledge; (*Geog:* = *ebenes Land*) flat or low land; (*Geol:* = *tektonische Platte*) (tectonic) plate; (= *Druckstock*) plate; (= *Münzrohling*) coin disc; (*Phot*) plate; (*von Gebiss*) (dental) plate; (= *Gedenktafel*) plaque; (*Comput*) disk; **ein Ereignis auf die ~ bannen** to capture an event on film **b** (= *Servierteller*) serving dish, plate; (= *Tortenplatte*) cake plate; (*mit Fuß*) cake stand; **eine ~ Aufschnitt** a plate of selected cold meats **c** (= *Schallplatte*) record, disc; **etw auf ~ sprechen/aufnehmen** to make a record of sth, to record sth; **eine ~ mit Marschmusik** a record of march music; **die ~ kenne ich schon** (*fig inf*) I've heard all that before, I know that line; **er legte die alte ~ auf** (*fig inf*) he started on his old theme; **leg doch mal eine neue ~ auf!** (*fig inf*) change the record, can't you!; **die ~ hat einen Sprung** the record's stuck **d** (= *Glatze*) bald head; (= *kahle Stelle*) bald spot or patch **e** (*Aus:* = *Verbrecherbande*) gang (of criminals) **f** (*sl*) **auf ~ sein** (= *obdachlos*) to be on the streets; **~ machen** (= *als Obdachloser schlafen*) to sleep rough (*Brit*) or on the streets

Plät|te ['plɛtə] F **-**, **-n** (*N Ger inf*) iron

Plätt|ei|sen NT (*dial*) iron; (*Hist*) smoothing iron

plät|ten ['plɛtn] VT (*dial*) to iron, to press → *auch* **geplättet**

Plat|ten-: Plat|ten|bau M *pl* **-bauten** (*inf:* = *Haus*) *building made from prefabricated slabs*; **Plat|ten|kon|den|sa|tor** M plate condenser; **Plat|ten|la|bel** NT (*Comput*) record label; **Plat|ten|lauf|werk** NT (*Comput*) disk drive; **Plat|ten|le|ger** [-le:gɐ] M **-s**, **-**, **Plat|ten|le|ge|rin** [-ərɪn] F **-**, **-nen** paver; **Plat|ten|samm|lung** F record collection; **Plat|ten|see** M der = Lake Balaton; **Plat|ten|spie|ler** M record player; **Plat|ten|tel|ler** M turntable; **Plat|ten|wechs|ler** [-vɛkslɐ] M **-s**, **-** autochanger, record changer; **Plat|ten|weg** M paved path

Plät|ter ['plɛtɐ] M **-s**, **-**, **Plät|te|rin** [-ərɪn] F **-**, **-nen** (*dial*) ironer, presser

Plät|te|rei [plɛtə'raɪ] F **-**, **-en** (*dial*) **a** (*Betrieb*) *business which does ironing* **b** (*inf:* = *das Plätten*) ironing

Platt-: Platt|fisch M flatfish; **Platt|form** F platform; (*fig:* = *Grundlage*) basis; **Platt|fuß** M flat foot; (*inf:* = *Reifenpanne*) flat (*inf*); **platt|fü|ßig** ADJ, ADV flat-footed

Platt|heit F **-**, **-en** **a** *no pl* (= *Flachheit*) flatness; (= *Geistlosigkeit*) dullness, flatness **b** *usu pl* (= *Redensart etc*) commonplace, platitude, cliché

plat|tie|ren [pla'ti:rən] *ptp* **plattiert** VT Metall to plate

Platt|ti|tü|de ▲ [plati'ty:də] F **-n**, **-n** platitude

Plätt|li ['plɛtli] NT **-**, **-** (*Sw:* = *Fliese, Kachel*) tile

---

Platt-: platt+ma|chen VT *sep* (*sl*) (= *dem Erdboden gleichmachen*) to level; (= *Pleite gehen lassen*) *Firma* to bankrupt; (= *heruntermachen*) to knock (*inf*); (= *töten*) to do in (*inf*), to take out (*inf*); (= *fertig machen*) to lay into (*inf*); **platt|na|sig** ADJ flat-nosed; **Platt|stich** M satin stitch; **Platt|sti|cke|rei** F satin stitch embroidery

Plätt|wä|sche F (*dial*) ironing

Platz [plats] M **-es**, **⸚e** ['plɛtsə] **a** (= *freier Raum*) room, space; **~ für jdn/etw schaffen** to make room for sb/sth; **~ für etw finden** to find room or space for sth; **in dem Zelt finden** or **haben zwei Personen ~** there is room for two people in the tent; **es wird ~ finden** there'll be room or space for it; **~ greifen** to spread, to gain ground; **~ einnehmen** or **brauchen** to take up or occupy room or space; **~ für etw (frei) lassen** to leave room or space for sth; **~ raubend** space-consuming; **~ sparend** space-saving *attr*; *bauen, einbauen, unterbringen* (in order) to save space; **das ist ~ sparender** that saves more space; **etw ~ sparend stapeln** to stack sth (away) with a minimum use of space; **so kann ~ sparend geparkt werden** it's a way of saving parking space; **das Buch hat keinen ~ mehr im Regal** there's no more room or space on the bookshelf for that book; **mehr als 10 Leute haben hier nicht ~** there's not room or space for more than 10 people here; **jdm den (ganzen) ~ wegnehmen** to take up all the room; **jdm ~ machen** to make room for sb; (= *vorbeigehen lassen*) to make way for sb (*auch fig*); **für etw ~ machen** or **schaffen** to make room for sth; **~ machen** to get out of the way (*inf*); **mach mal ein bisschen ~** make a bit of room; **~ für jdn/etw bieten** to hold sb/sth, to have room for sb/sth; **~ da!** (*inf*) (get) out of the way there! (*inf*), gangway! (*inf*) **b** (= *Sitzplatz*) seat; **~ nehmen** to take a seat; **bitte ~ nehmen zum Mittagessen** please take your seats for lunch; **behalten Sie doch bitte ~!** (*form*) please remain seated (*form*); **ist hier noch ein ~ frei?** is there a free seat here?; **dieser ~ ist belegt** or **besetzt** this seat's taken, this is somebody's seat; **sich von seinem ~ erheben** (*geh*) to rise (*form*); **der Saal hat 2.000 Plätze** the hall seats 2,000, the hall has seating for 2,000 or has 2,000 seats; **mit jdm den ~ tauschen** or **wechseln** to change places with sb; **erster/zweiter ~** front/rear stalls; **~!** (*zum Hund*) (lie) down! **c** (= *Stelle, Standort, Rang*) place; **das Buch steht nicht an seinem ~** the book isn't in (its) place; **etw (wieder) an seinen ~ stellen** to put sth (back) in (its) place; **fehl** or **nicht am ~(e) sein** to be out of place; **am ~(e) sein** to be appropriate; **auf die Plätze, fertig, los!** (*beim Sport*) on your marks, get set, go!, ready, steady, go! (*Brit*), ready, set, go! (*esp US*); **er wich nicht vom ~(e)** he wouldn't yield (an inch); **seinen ~ behaupten** to stand one's ground, to hold one's own; **Extremismus hat keinen ~ in der Politik** there is no place for extremism in politics; **alles hat seinen festen ~** everything has its proper place; **die Literatur hat einen festen ~ in ihrem Leben** literature is very much a part of her life; **ihr ~ ist an der Seite ihres Mannes** her (proper) place is at her husband's side; **den ersten ~ einnehmen** (*fig*) to take first place, to come first; **auf ~ zwei** in second place; **jdn auf ~ drei/den zweiten ~ verweisen** to beat sb into third/second place; **jdn auf die Plätze verweisen** (*fig*) to beat sb; **auf ~ wetten** to make a place bet; **ein ~ an der Sonne** (*lit, fig*) a place in the sun → **fehl** **d** (= *Arbeitsplatz, Studienplatz, Heimplatz etc*) place; (= *unbesetzter Arbeitsplatz*) vacancy; **im Kindergarten sind noch ein paar Plätze frei** there are still a few vacancies or places left in the kindergarten **e** (= *umbaute Fläche*) square; **auf dem ~** in or on the square; **ein freier ~ vor der Kirche** an open space in front of the church **f** (= *Sportplatz*) playing field; (*Ftbl, Hockey*)

---

pitch, field; (= *Handballplatz, Tennisplatz*) court; (= *Golfplatz*) (golf) course, (golf) links *pl*; **einen Spieler vom ~ stellen** or **verweisen** to send a player off (*Brit*), to eject a player (*US*); **auf gegnerischem ~ away**; **auf eigenem ~** at home; **jdn vom ~ fegen** (*inf:* = *vernichtend schlagen*) to wipe the floor with sb (*inf*) **g** (= *Ort*) town, place; (= *Handelsplatz*) centre (*Brit*), center (*US*); **das erste Hotel** or **Haus am ~(e)** the best hotel in town or in the place **h** (= *Lagerplatz*) (store or storage) yard **i** (= *Bauplatz*) site

Platz-: Platz|angst F (*inf:* = *Beklemmung*) claustrophobia; (*auf offenen Plätzen*) agoraphobia; **~ bekommen** to get claustrophobic or claustrophobia/agoraphobic or agoraphobia; **Platz|an|wei|ser** [-anvaizɐ] M **-s**, **-** usher; **Platz|an|wei|se|rin** [-anvaizərɪn] F **-**, **-nen** usherette

Plätz|chen ['plɛtsçən] NT **-s**, **-** **a** *dim von* **Platz** spot, little place **b** (*Gebäck*) biscuit (*Brit*), cookie (*US*)

plat|zen ['platsn] VI *aux sein* **a** (= *aufreißen*) to burst; (*Naht, Hose, Augenbraue, Haut*) to split; (= *explodieren: Granate, Stinkbombe*) to explode; (= *einen Riss bekommen*) to crack; **mir ist unterwegs ein Reifen geplatzt** I had a blowout on the way (*inf*), a tyre burst (*Brit*) or a tire blew (*US*) on the way; **ihm ist eine Ader geplatzt** he burst a blood vessel; **wenn du so weiterisst, platzt du!** if you go on eating like that you'll burst; **wir sind vor Lachen fast geplatzt** we split our sides laughing, we laughed till our sides ached or split; **ins Zimmer ~** (*inf*) to burst into the room; **jdm ins Haus ~** (*inf*) to descend on sb; **(vor Wut/Neid/Ungeduld) ~** (*inf*) to be bursting (with rage/envy/impatience); **bei ihm ist endlich der Knoten geplatzt** (*inf*) it all eventually clicked (for him) (*inf*) → **Bombe, Kragen, Naht** **b** (*inf:* = *scheitern*) (*Plan, Geschäft, Termin, Vertrag*) to fall through; (*Freundschaft, Koalition*) to break up; (*Theorie*) to fall down, to collapse; (*Wechsel*) to bounce (*inf*); **die Verlobung ist geplatzt** the engagement is (all) off; **etw ~ lassen** (*Plan, Geschäft, Termin, Vertrag*) to make sth fall through; *Freundschaft, Verlobung* to break sth off; *Koalition* to break sth up; *Vorstellung* to call sth off; *Theorie* to explode sth; *Wechsel* to make sth bounce (*inf*)

Platz-: Platz|er|spar|nis F space saving; **aus Gründen der ~** for reasons of space, to save space; **Platz|hal|ter** M place marker; (*Comput*) free variable parameter, free definable parameter; **Platz|hal|ter(in)** M(F) custodian; **Platz|her|ren** PL (*Sport inf*) home team; **Platz|hirsch** M (*lit, fig*) dominant male

plat|zie|ren ▲ [pla'tsi:rən] *ptp* **platziert** ▨ **a** (= *Platz anweisen*) *Soldaten, Wächter* to put, to place, to position; (*Tennis*) to seed; **der Kellner platzierte uns in die** or **der Nähe der Band** the waiter directed or showed us to a place or put us near the band; **„Sie werden platziert"** "please wait to be seated" **b** (= *zielen*) *Ball* to place, to position; *Schlag, Faust* to land; **gut platzierte Aufschläge** well-placed or well-positioned services; **ein (gut) platzierter Schlag** a well-placed or well-aimed blow; **platziert schießen** to position one's shots well; **er hat platziert in die rechte Torecke geschossen** he tucked the ball away neatly in the right corner of the goal **c** (= *anlegen*) *Geld* to put, to place; *Aktien* to place ▨ **a** (*inf:* = *sich setzen, stellen etc*) to plant oneself (*inf*) **b** (*Sport*) to be placed, to get a place; (*Tennis*) to be seeded; **der Läufer konnte sich gut/nicht ~** the runner was well-placed/wasn't even placed

Plat|zie|rung ▲ F (*bei Rennen*) order; (*Tennis*) seeding; (= *Platz*) place; (*von Aktien, Geld*) placing; **welche ~ hatte er?** where did he come in?, what position did he come in?

Platz-: Platz|kar|te F (*Rail*) seat reservation (ticket); **ich bestelle mir eine ~** I'll reserve (myself) a seat, I'll get a seat reservation; **Platz|kon|zert** NT open-air concert; **Platz|man|gel** M , *no pl* shortage *or* lack of space *or* room; **wir leiden sehr unter ~** we're terribly short of space *or* room, we've a space problem; **Platz|mie|te** F (*Theat*) season ticket; (*Sport*) ground rent; **Platz|pat|ro|ne** F blank (cartridge); **platz|rau|bend** △ ADJ → Platz a; **Platz|re|gen** M cloudburst; **das ist nur ein ~** it's only a (passing) shower; **Platz|re|ser|vie|rung** F seat reservation; **platz|spa|rend** △ ADJ → Platz a; **Platz|sper|re** F (*Sport*) (home) ground ban, ban on playing on one's home ground; **Platz|ver|hält|nis|se** PL (*Sport*) state *sing* of the pitch *or* field; **Platz|ver|weis** M sending-off (*Brit*), ejection (*US*); **es gab drei ~** three players were sent off (*Brit*) *or* ejected (*US*); **Platz|vor|teil** M home advantage; **Platz|wahl** F toss-up; **die ~ haben/verlieren** to win/lose the toss; **die ~ vornehmen** to toss up; **Platz|wart** [-vart] M **-s, -e**, **Platz|war|tin** [-vartɪn] F **-, -nen** (*Sport*) groundsman; **Platz|wech|sel** M change of place; (*Sport*) change of position; **Platz|wet|te** F place bet; **Platz|wun|de** F cut, laceration

Plau|de|rei [plaudə'rai] F **-, -en** chat, conversation; (*Press*) feature; (*TV, Rad*) chat show (*Brit*), talk show

Plau|de|rer ['plaudərɐ] M **-s, -**, **Plau|de|rin** [-ərɪn] F **-, -nen** conversationalist

plau|der|haft ADJ Ton conversational, chatty

plau|dern ['plaudɐn] VI to chat, to talk (*über +acc, von* about); (= *verraten*) to talk; **mit ihm lässt sich gut ~** he's easy to talk to → Schule, Nähkästchen

Plau|der-: Plau|der|stünd|chen NT , **Plau|der|stun|de** F chat; **ein angenehmes ~ zubringen** to have a pleasant chat, to have a cosy (*Brit*) *or* cozy (*US*) little chat; **Plau|der|ta|sche** F (*inf*) chatterbox (*inf*); **Plau|der|ton** M , *no pl* conversational *or* chatty tone

Plausch [plauʃ] M **-(e)s, -e** (*inf*) chat; **einen ~ halten** to have a chat; **das war ein ~** (*Sw*: = *Freude, Amüsement*) that was a good laugh

plau|schen ['plauʃn] VI (*inf*) to chat, to have a chat *or* a natter (*Brit inf*)

plau|si|bel [plau'ziːbl] ADJ Erklärung, Grund plausible (ADV plausibly; **jdm etw ~ machen** to make sth clear to sb, to explain sth to sb

Plau|si|bi|li|tät [plauzibili'tɛːt] F **-, no pl** plausibility

Plau|si|bi|li|täts|kon|trol|le F (*von Daten, Statistik*) plausibility check

plauz [plauts] INTERJ (*inf*) crash, bang

Plauz [plauts] M **-es, -e** (*inf*) (*Geräusch*) bang, crash; (= *Fall*) fall

Plau|ze ['plautsə] F **-, -n** (*dial inf*) chest; **es auf der ~ haben** (*inf*) to have a chesty (*Brit*) *or* deep (*US inf*) cough, to be chesty (*Brit inf*); **auf der ~ liegen** (*inf*) to be laid up (*inf*)

Play-: Play-back ▲ ['pleːbɛk] NT **-s, -s**, **Play-back** NT **-s, -s** (= *Band*) (*bei Musikaufnahme*) backing track; (*TV*) recording; (= *Playbackverfahren*) (*bei Musikaufnahme*) double-tracking no *pl*; (*TV*) miming no *pl*; **ein Playback von einem Lied machen** to double-track a song; (*TV*) to prerecord a song, to make a recording of a song; **etw im Playback machen** to double-track sth; (*TV*) to mime to (a recording of) sth; **Play-back singen** to mime, to lip-sync(h); **Play|boy** ['pleː-] M (*inf*) playboy; **Play|girl** ['pleː-] NT playgirl; **Play-off** [pleːˈlɔf] NT **-(s), -s** (*Sport*) play-off; **Play-off-Run|de** [pleː-ˈlɔf-] F (*Sport*) play-off round, play-offs *pl*

Pla|zen|ta [pla'tsɛnta] F **-, -s** *or* **Plazenten** [-'tsɛntn] Plazenta

Pla|zet ['plaːtset] NT **-s, -s** (*geh*) approval; **sein ~ zu etw geben** to approve sth, to give sth one's approval

Pla|zeur [pla'tsøːɐ] M **-s, -e**, **Pla|zeu|rin** [-'tsøːrɪn] F **-, -nen** (*Fin*) securities investor

pla|zie|ren △ [pla'tsiːrən] VT → platzieren

Pla|zie|rung △ F **-, -en** → Platzierung

Ple|be|jer [ple'beːjɐ] M , **Ple|be|je|rin** [-ərɪn] F **-, -nen** (*lit, fig*) plebeian, pleb (*inf*)

ple|be|jisch [ple'beːjɪʃ] ADJ (*lit*) plebeian no adv; (*fig auch*) plebby (*inf*), common ADV **sich ~ benehmen** to behave like a pleb (*inf*)

Ple|bis|zit [plebɪs'tsiːt] NT **-(e)s, -e** plebiscite

Plebs[1] [pleːps] F **-, no pl** (*Hist*) plebs *pl*

Plebs[2] M **-es, no pl** (*pej*) plebs *pl* (*inf*)

plei|te ['plaitə] ADJ pred ADV (*inf*) Mensch broke (*inf*); Firma auch bust (*inf*)

Plei|te ['plaitə] F **-, -n** (*inf*) bankruptcy, collapse; (*fig*) flop (*inf*), washout (*inf*); **~ machen** to go bankrupt *or* bust (*inf*); **damit/mit ihm haben wir eine ~ erlebt** it/he was a disaster; **~ gehen** to go bust

Plei|te|gei|er M (*inf*) **a** (= *drohende Pleite*) vulture; **über der Firma schwebt** *or* **kreist der ~** the vultures are hovering over the firm, the threat of bankruptcy is hanging over the firm **b** (= *Bankrotteur*) bankrupt

Plei|ti|er [plai'tieː] M **-s, -s** (*inf*: = *Bankrotteur*) bankrupt

Plek|tron ['plɛktrɔn] NT **-s, Plektren** *or* **Plektra** [-trən, -tra], **Plek|trum** ['plɛktrʊm] NT **-s, Plektren** *or* **Plektra** plectrum

Plem|pe ['plɛmpə] F **-, -n** (*dial*) dishwater

plem|pern ['plɛmpɐn] VI (*inf*) **a** (= *trödeln*) to dawdle **b** (= *verschütten*) to splash

plem|plem [plɛm'plɛm] ADJ pred (*inf*) nuts (*inf*), round (*Brit*) *or* around (*US*) the bend (*inf*); **jdn ~ machen** to drive sb round (*Brit*) *or* around (*US*) the bend (*inf*), to drive sb up the wall (*inf*)

Ple|na *pl von* Plenum

Ple|nar- [ple'naːɐ-]: **Ple|nar|saal** M chamber; **Ple|nar|sit|zung** F , **Ple|nar|ver|samm|lung** F plenary session

Ple|num ['pleːnʊm] NT **-s, Plena** [-na] plenum

Ple|o|nas|mus [pleo'nasmʊs] M **-, Pleonasmen** [-mən] pleonasm

ple|o|nas|tisch [pleo'nastɪʃ] ADJ pleonastic

Pleu|el|stan|ge ['plɔyəl-] F connecting rod

Ple|xi|glas® ['plɛksiglaːs] NT , *no pl* acrylic glass

plie|ren ['pliːrən], **plin|kern** ['plɪŋkɐn] VI (*N Ger*) to screw up one's eyes (*Brit*), to squint

Plis|see [plɪˈseː] NT **-s, -s** pleats *pl*, pleating no *pl*

Plis|see-: Plis|see|fal|te F pleat; **Plis|see|rock** M pleated skirt

plis|sie|ren [plɪˈsiːrən] ptp **plissiert** VT to pleat

PLO [peːˈɛlˈloː] F - PLO

PLO-Füh|rung F PLO leadership

Plom|be ['plɔmbə] F **-, -n a** (= *Siegel*) lead seal **b** (= *Zahnplombe*) filling

plom|bie|ren [plɔmˈbiːrən] ptp **plombiert** VT **a** (= *versiegeln*) to seal, to put a seal on **b** Zahn to fill; **er hat mir zwei Zähne plombiert** he did two fillings

Plom|bie|rung F **-, -en a** (= *das Versiegeln*) sealing; (*Vorrichtung*) seal **b** (*beim Zahn*) filling

Plör|re ['plœrə] F **-, -n** (*dial*) dishwater

Plo|siv [plo'ziːf] M **-s, -e**, **Plo|siv|laut** M (*Phon*) plosive

Plot [plɔt] M OR NT **-s, -s** (*Liter*) plot

Plot|ter ['plɔtɐ] M **-s, -** (*Comput*) plotter

plötz|lich ['plœtslɪç] ADJ sudden ADV suddenly, all of a sudden; **aber etwas ~!** (*inf*), **aber ein bisschen ~** (*inf*) (and) make it snappy! (*inf*), and look sharp (about it)! (*inf*); **das kommt alles so ~** (*inf*) it all happens so suddenly

Plötz|lich|keit F **-, no pl** suddenness

Plu|der|ho|se ['pluːdɐ-] F harem pants *pl*, Turkish trousers *pl* (*esp Brit*)

Plug-and-Play ['plagənd'pleː] NT **-s, no pl** (*Comput*) plug-and-play

Plu|meau [ply'moː] NT **-s, -s** eiderdown, quilt

plump [plʊmp] ADJ Figur, Hände, Form ungainly no adv; Bewegung, Gang auch awkward; Ausdruck clumsy; Bemerkung, Benehmen crass; Mittel, Schmeichelei, Lüge, Betrug, Trick obvious, crude; Film, Roman crude; **~e Annäherungsversuche** obvious and crude advances ADV sich bewegen, tanzen awkwardly; sagen, sich ausdrücken clumsily; **~ lügen** to tell a blatant lie; **jdn ~ hereinlegen** to play a blatantly obvious trick on sb; **der Film ist sehr ~ gemacht** the film is very crudely made; **sich ~ verhalten** to behave crassly

Plump|heit F **-, -en** (*von Figur, Form*) ungainliness; (*von Bewegung auch*) awkwardness; (*von Ausdruck*) clumsiness; (*von Bemerkung, Benehmen*) crassness; (*von Lüge, Trick*) obviousness

plumps [plʊmps] INTERJ bang; (*lauter*) crash; **~, da lag er** crash, he'd fallen over

Plumps [plʊmps] M **-es, -e** (*inf*) (= *Fall*) fall, tumble; (*Geräusch*) bump, thud; **einen ~ machen** (*baby-talk*) to fall; **mit einem ~ ins Wasser fallen** to fall into the water with a splash

plump|sen ['plʊmpsn] VI aux sein (*inf*) (= *fallen*) to tumble, to fall; **ich habe es ~ hören** I heard a bang *or* a thud; **ich ließ mich einfach aufs Bett ~** I just flopped (down) onto the bed; **er plumpste ins Wasser** he went splash into the water, he fell into the water with a splash

Plumps|klo(|sett) NT (*inf*) earth closet

plumpver|trau|lich ▲ ADJ overly chummy (*inf*) ADV in an overly chummy way (*inf*)

Plun|der ['plʊndɐ] M **-s, no pl** junk, rubbish (*Brit*)

Plün|de|rer ['plʏndərɐ] M **-s, -**, **Plün|de|rin** [-ərɪn] F **-nen** looter, plunderer

Plun|der|ge|bäck NT flaky pastry

plün|dern ['plʏndɐn] VTI to loot, to plunder, to pillage; (= *ausrauben*) to strip; Obstbaum to strip; **jemand hat unsere** *or* **auf unserer Obstplantage geplündert** somebody's raided our orchard

Plün|de|rung F **-, -en** looting, pillage, plunder

Plün|de|rer ['plʏndrɐ] M **-s, -**, **Plünd|re|rin** [-rarɪn] F **-, -nen** looter, plunderer

Plu|ral ['pluːraːl] M **-s, -e** plural; **im ~ stehen** to be (in the) plural; **den ~ zu etw bilden** to form the plural of sth

Plu|ra|le|tan|tum [plura:lə'tantʊm] NT **-s, -s** *or* **Pluraliatantum** [plura:lia'tantʊm] plural noun

Plu|ral|en|dung F plural ending

plu|ra|lisch [plu'raːlɪʃ] (*Gram*) ADJ plural ADV **ein Wort ~ gebrauchen** to use a word in the plural

Plu|ra|lis|mus [plura'lɪsmʊs] M **-, no pl** pluralism

plu|ra|lis|tisch [plura'lɪstɪʃ] ADJ pluralistic (*form*) ADV pluralistically (*form*); **sich ~ organisieren** to create a pluralistic system

Plu|ra|li|tät [plurali'tɛːt] F **-, -en** plurality; (= *Mehrheit*) majority, plurality (*US*)

plus [plʊs] PREP +gen plus ADV plus; **bei ~ 5 Grad** *or* **5 Grad ~** at 5 degrees (above freezing or zero); **~/minus 10** (= *mit Abweichung bis plus oder minus zehn*) plus or minus 10; **das Ergebnis war ~ minus null** nothing was gained, nothing was lost; **mit ~ minus null abschließen** to break even CONJ Karl **~ Ehefrau** (*inf*) Karl plus wife

Plus [plʊs] NT **-, - a** (= *Pluszeichen*) plus (sign); **ein ~ machen** to put a plus (sign) **b** (*Phys inf*: = *Pluspol*) positive (pole) **c** (*esp Comm*) (= *Zuwachs*) increase; (= *Gewinn*) profit; (= *Überschuss*) surplus **d** (*fig*: = *Vorteil*) advantage; **das ist ein ~ für dich** that's a point in your favour (*Brit*) *or* favor (*US*); **das können Sie als ~ für sich buchen** that's one up to *or* for you (*inf*), you've scored a point there (*inf*)

Plüsch [plyʃ, ply:ʃ] M **-(e)s, -e** plush; (pej) ostentation; **Stofftiere aus ~** soft toys made of fur fabric

Plüsch- in cpds plush; (von Plüschtier) furry; **Plüsch|bär** M furry teddy bear

plü|schig ['plyʃɪç, 'ply:ʃɪç] ADJ plush; (pej) ostentatious ADV plushly

Plüsch|tier NT ≈ soft toy

Plüsch|vor|hang M plush curtain

Plus-: Plus|pol M (Elec) positive pole; **Plus|punkt** M (Sport) point; (Sch) extra mark; (fig) advantage; **einen ~ machen** to win a point; **deine Erfahrung ist ein ~ für dich** your experience counts in your favour (Brit) or favor (US), your experience is a point in your favour (Brit) or favor (US); **~e sammeln** (inf) to score Brownie points; **Plus|quam|per|fekt** ['plʊskvampɛrfɛkt] NT pluperfect, past perfect

plus|tern ['plu:stɐn] VT Federn to fluff up VR to fluff oneself up

Plus|zei|chen NT plus sign

Plu|to|krat [pluto'kra:t] M **-en, -en, Plu|to|kra|tin** [-'kra:tɪn] F **-, -nen** plutocrat

Plu|to|kra|tie [plutokra'ti:] F **-, -n** [-'ti:ən] plutocracy

Plu|to|ni|um [plu'to:niʊm] NT **-s,** no pl (abbr **Pn**) plutonium

Plu|to|ni|um-: Plu|to|ni|um|ge|win|nung F plutonium extraction; **Plu|to|ni|um|wirt|schaft** F **-,** no pl plutonium industry

PLZ [pe:|ɛl'tsɛt] F **-** abbr von **Postleitzahl**

Pneu [pnɔø] M **-s, -s** (esp Sw) tyre (Brit), tire (US)

pneu|ma|tisch [pnɔy'ma:tɪʃ] ADJ pneumatic; **~e Kammer** pressure chamber ADV pneumatically

Po [po:] M **-s, -s** (inf) bottom, behind (inf)

Po|ba|cke F (inf) buttock, cheek (inf), bun (US inf)

Pö|bel ['pø:bl] M **-s,** no pl rabble, mob, riffraff (pej)

Pö|be|lei [pø:bə'lai] F **-, -en** vulgarity, bad language no pl

Pö|bel-: pö|bel|haft ADJ uncouth, vulgar ADV uncouthly, vulgarly; **Pö|bel|herr|schaft** F mob rule

pö|beln ['pø:bln] VI to swear, to use bad language

po|chen ['pɔxn] VI to knock; (leise auch) to tap; (heftig) to thump, to bang; (Herz) to pound, to thump; (Blut) to throb, to pound; **auf etw (acc) ~** (fig) to insist on sth; **auf sein (gutes) Recht ~** to insist on one's rights, to stand up for one's rights

po|chie|ren [pɔ'ʃi:rən] ptp **pochiert** VT Ei, Fisch to poach

Po|cke ['pɔkə] F **-, -n** a pock b **Pocken** PL smallpox

Pocken-: Po|cken|nar|be F pockmark; **po|cken|nar|big** ADJ pockmarked; **Po|cken-(schutz)|imp|fung** F smallpox vaccination

Pocket-: Po|cket|for|mat NT pocket size; **im ~** pocket-sized; **Po|cket|ka|me|ra** F pocket camera

Po|dest [po'dɛst] NT OR M **-(e)s, -e** (= Sockel) pedestal (auch fig); (= Podium) platform; (= Treppenabsatz) landing

Po|dex ['po:dɛks] M **-es, -e** (hum inf) posterior (hum inf), behind (inf)

Po|di|um ['po:diʊm] NT **-s, Podien** [-diən] (lit, fig) platform; (des Dirigenten) podium; (bei Diskussion) panel

Po|di|ums|dis|kus|si|on F , **Po|di|ums|ge|spräch** NT panel discussion, brains trust

Po|em [po'e:m] NT **-s, -e** (usu pej) poem, doggerel (pej) no indef art

Po|e|sie [poe'zi:] F **-, -n** [-'zi:ən] (lit, fig) poetry

Po|e|sie|al|bum NT autograph book

Po|et [po'e:t] M **-en, -en, Po|e|tin** [-'e:tɪn] F **-, -nen** (old: = Dichter) poet, bard (liter); (pej) poetaster, versifier

Po|e|tas|ter [poe'tastɐ] M **-s, -, Po|e|tas|te|rin** [-ərɪn] F **-, -nen** (old pej) poetaster

Po|e|tik [po'e:tɪk] F **-, -en** poetics sing

po|e|tisch [po'e:tɪʃ] ADJ poetic ADV poetically

po|fen ['po:fn] VI (dated sl) to kip (Brit inf), to sleep

Pog|rom [po'gro:m] NT OR M **-s, -e** pogrom

Pog|rom|stim|mung F bloodthirsty mood

Poin|te ['poɛ̃tə] F **-, -n** (eines Witzes) punch line; (einer Geschichte) point; **die ~ einer Geschichte begreifen** to get the (main) point of a story

poin|tie|ren [poɛ̃'ti:rən] ptp **pointiert** [poɛ̃'ti:ɐt] VT to emphasize, to stress

poin|tiert [poɛ̃'ti:ɐt] ADJ trenchant (form), pithy ADV trenchantly (form), pithily; **~ ant|worten** to give a pithy or trenchant (form) answer

Poin|til|lis|mus [pɛ̃inti'lɪsmʊs, poɛ̃ti'jɪsmʊs] M **-,** no pl (Art) pointillism

Po|kal [po'ka:l] M **-s, -e** (zum Trinken) goblet; (Sport) cup; **das Endspiel um den ~** the cup final

Po|kal-: Po|kal|run|de F round (of the cup); **Po|kal|sie|ger(in)** M(F) cup winners pl; **Po|kal|spiel** NT cup tie; **Po|kal|tur|nier** NT cup tournament

Pö|kel ['pø:kl] M **-s, -** brine, pickle

Pö|kel-: Pö|kel|fleisch NT salt meat; **Pö|kel|he|ring** M salt or pickled herring

pö|keln ['pø:kln] VT Fleisch, Fisch to salt, to pickle

Po|ker ['po:kɐ] NT **-s,** no pl poker

Po|ker|face ['po:kɐfe:s] NT **-, -s, Po|ker|ge|sicht** NT , **Po|ker|mie|ne** F poker face; **ein ~ machen** or **aufsetzen** to put on a poker-faced or deadpan expression

Po|ker|spiel NT poker; (einzelnes Spiel) game of poker

po|kern ['po:kɐn] VI to play poker; (fig) to gamble, to take a risk; **um etw ~** (fig) to haggle for sth; **hoch ~** (fig) to take a big risk

Pol [po:l] M **-s, -e** pole; **der ruhende ~** (fig) the calming influence

pol. abbr von **politisch** von **polizeilich**

Po|la|cke [po'lakə] M **-s, -n, Po|la|ckin** [po'lakɪn] F **-, -nen** (pej sl) Polack (pej)

po|lar [po'la:ɐ] ADJ a polar; **~e Kälte** arctic coldness b **~e Gegensätze** complete or exact opposites ADV **~ entgegengesetzt** diametrically opposed, poles apart pred

Po|lar-: Po|lar|kreis M polar circle; **nördlicher/südlicher ~** Arctic/Antarctic circle; **Po|lar|licht** NT polar lights pl, Northern/Southern lights pl; **Po|lar|meer** NT **Nördliches/Südliches ~** Arctic/Antarctic Ocean; **Po|lar|stern** M Pole Star, North Star, Polaris

Po|la|roid|ka|me|ra® [polaro'i:t-, pola'rɔyt-] F Polaroid® camera

Po|lar|zo|ne F Frigid Zone (esp Brit), polar region

Pol|der ['pɔldɐ] M **-s, -** polder

Pol|der|deich M polder dyke

Po|le ['po:lə] M **-n, -n** Pole; **er ist ~** he's Polish, he's a Pole

Po|le|mik [po'le:mɪk] F **-, -en** polemics sing (gegen against); (= Streitschrift) polemic; **die ~ dieses Artikels** the polemic nature of this article;

seine ~ ist kaum mehr erträglich his polemics are becoming unbearable

Po|le|mi|ker [po'le:mikɐ] M **-s, -, Po|le|mi|ke|rin** [-ərɪn] F **-, -nen** controversialist, polemicist

po|le|misch [po'le:mɪʃ] ADJ polemic(al) ADV polemically; **~ argumentieren** to be polemical

po|le|mi|sie|ren [polemi'zi:rən] ptp **polemisiert** VI to polemicize; **~ gegen** to inveigh against

po|len ['po:lən] VT to polarize

Po|len ['po:lən] NT **-s** Poland; **noch ist ~ nicht verloren** (prov) the day is not yet lost, all is not yet lost

Po|len|ta [po'lɛnta] F **-, -s** or **Polenten** (Cook) polenta

Po|len|te [po'lɛntə] F **-,** no pl (dated inf) cops pl (inf), fuzz pl (esp Brit dated inf)

Po|li|ce [po'li:sə] F **-, -n** (insurance) policy

Po|lier [po'li:ɐ] M **-s, -e** site foreman

po|lie|ren [po'li:rən] ptp **poliert** VT to polish; Schuhe auch to shine; (fig) to polish or brush up; **jdm die Fresse** or **Visage ~** (vulg) to smash sb's face in (inf)

Po|lie|rin [po'li:ərɪn] F **-, -nen** site forewoman

Po|lier-: Po|lier|mit|tel NT polish; **Po|lier|schei|be** F polishing wheel or disc; **Po|lier|tuch** NT pl **-tücher** polishing cloth; **Po|lier|wachs** NT wax polish

Po|li|kli|nik ['po:li-] F (= Krankenhaus) clinic (for outpatients only); (Abteilung) outpatients' department, outpatients sing

Po|lin ['po:lɪn] F **-, -nen** Pole, Polish woman

Po|lio [po'lio] F **-,** no pl polio, poliomyelitis

Po|lit- [po'lɪt-] in cpds (inf) political; **Po|lit|ba|ro|me|ter** NT (fig) political barometer; **Po|lit|büh|ne** F political stage; **Po|lit|bü|ro** NT Politburo

Po|li|tes|se [poli'tɛsə] F **-, -n** (woman) traffic warden

Po|li|tik [poli'ti:k] F **-, -en** a no pl politics sing; (= politischer Standpunkt) politics pl; **welche ~ vertritt er?** what are his politics?; **in die ~ ge|hen** to go into politics; **über ~ sprechen** to talk (about) politics b (= bestimmte Politik) policy; **eine ~ der starken Hand treiben** to take a tough line; **eine ~ verfolgen** or **betreiben** to pursue a policy; **ihre gesamte ~** all their policies

Po|li|ti|ka pl von **Politikum**

Po|li|ti|ker [po'li:tikɐ] M **-s, -, Po|li|ti|ke|rin** [-ərɪn] F **-, -nen** politician; **führender ~** leading politician

po|li|tik|fä|hig ADJ Partei capable of governing responsibly; **der Naturschutz muss ~ werden** conservation must become part of the political debate

Po|li|tik|fä|hig|keit F (von Partei) ability to govern responsibly

Po|li|ti|kum [po'li:tikʊm] NT **-s, Politika** [-ka] political issue

Po|li|tik-: po|li|tik|un|fä|hig ADJ Partei incapable of governing responsibly; **Po|li|tik|un|fä|hig|keit** F (von Partei) inability to govern responsibly; **po|li|tik|ver|dros|sen** ADJ tired of politics, disenchanted with politics; **Po|li|tik|ver|dros|sen|heit** F disenchantment with politics; **die wachsende ~ der Bevölkerung** the people's growing disenchantment with politics; **Po|li|tik|wis|sen|schaft** F political science, politics sing

po|li|tisch [po'li:tɪʃ] ADJ political; (= klug) politic, judicious; **er ist ein Politischer** he's a political prisoner ADV politically; **sich ~ betätigen** to be involved in politics; **~ interessiert sein** to be interested in politics; **jdn ~ schulen** to educate sb politically

po|li|ti|sie|ren [politi'zi:rən] ptp **politisiert** VI to talk politics, to politicize VT to politicize; **jdn** to make politically aware

Po|li|ti|sie|rung F **-,** no pl politicization

Po|lit|öko|no|mie [po'liːt-] F political economy

Po|li|to|lo|ge [polito'loːgə] M -n, -n, **Po|li|to|lo|gin** [-'loːgɪn] F -, -nen political scientist

Po|li|to|lo|gie [politolo'giː] F -, no pl political science, politics sing

Po|lit|pro|mi|nenz F (inf) political top brass (inf), top politicians pl

Po|li|tur [poli'tuːɐ] F -, -en (= Poliermittel) polish; (= Glanz) shine, polish; (= das Polieren) polishing

Po|li|zei [poli'tsai] F -, -en police pl; (Gebäude) police station; **auf die** or **zur ~ gehen** to go to the police; **er ist bei der ~** he's in the police (force); **die ~, dein Freund und Helfer** (usu iro) your friendly neighbourhood (Brit) or neighborhood (US) police force (iro) → **dumm**

Po|li|zei- in cpds police; **Po|li|zei|ak|ti|on** F police operation; **Po|li|zei|ap|pa|rat** M police force; **Po|li|zei|auf|ge|bot** NT police presence; **Po|li|zei|auf|sicht** F police supervision; **unter ~ stehen** to have to report regularly to the police; **Po|li|zei|be|am|te(r)** M decl as adj, **Po|li|zei|be|am|tin** F police official; (= Polizist) police officer; **sich bei der ~ anmelden** to register with the police; **Po|li|zei|be|hör|de** F police authority; **Po|li|zei|be|richt** M police report; **Po|li|zei|chef(in)** M(F) chief constable (Brit), chief of police (US); **Po|li|zei|dienst|stel|le** F (form) police station; **Po|li|zei|di|rek|ti|on** F police headquarters pl; **Po|li|zei|ein|satz** M police action or intervention; **Po|li|zei|funk** M police radio; **Po|li|zei|ge|wahr|sam** M police custody; **jdn in ~ nehmen** to take sb into police custody; **Po|li|zei|ge|walt** F **die ~ haben** to have police powers pl; **die Menge wurde mit ~ auseinander getrieben** the police dispersed the crowd by force; **Po|li|zei|griff** M wrist-hold, police hold; **jdn in den ~ nehmen** to put sb in an arm lock; **er wurde im ~ abgeführt** he was frogmarched away (Brit), they put a wrist-hold on him and took him away; **Po|li|zei|haft** F detention; **Po|li|zei|hund** M police dog; **Po|li|zei|in|spek|tor(in)** M(F) police inspector; **Po|li|zei|ket|te** F police cordon; **Po|li|zei|knüp|pel** M truncheon, billy club (esp US); **Po|li|zei|kom|mis|sar(in)** M(F) (police) inspector

po|li|zei|lich [poli'tsailɪç] ADJ police attr; **~es Führungszeugnis** certificate issued by the police, stating that the holder has no criminal record ADV **ermittelt werden by** the police; **~ überwacht werden** to be under police surveillance; **sie wird ~ gesucht** the police are looking for her; **sich ~ melden** to register with the police; **~ verboten** against the law; **„Parken ~ verboten"** "police notice - no parking"; **diese Regelung ist ~ angeordnet** this is a police regulation, this regulation is by order of the police

Po|li|zei-: **Po|li|zei|prä|si|dent(in)** M(F) chief constable (Brit), chief of police (US); **Po|li|zei|prä|si|di|um** NT police headquarters pl; **Po|li|zei|re|vier** NT **a** (= Polizeiwache) police station; **ins** or **aufs** or **zum ~ gehen** to go (down) to the (police) station **b** (Bezirk) (police) district, precinct (US), patch (inf); **Po|li|zei|schutz** M police protection; **Po|li|zei|si|re|ne** F (police) siren, heehaw (Brit inf); **Po|li|zei|spit|zel** M (police) informer, nark (inf); **Po|li|zei|staat** M police state; **Po|li|zei|strei|fe** F police patrol; **Po|li|zei|stun|de** F closing time; **Po|li|zei|ver|ord|nung** F police regulation; **Po|li|zei|wa|che** F police station; **Po|li|zei|we|sen** NT , no pl police force; **po|li|zei|wid|rig** ADJ illegal ADV **sich ~ verhalten** to break the law

Po|li|zist [poli'tsɪst] -en, -en M policeman

Po|li|zis|tin [poli'tsɪstɪn] F -, -nen policewoman

Po|liz|ze [po'lɪtsə] F -, -n (Aus: Insur) (insurance) policy

Pol|ka ['pɔlka] F -, -s polka

Pol|kap|pe F polar icecap

Pol|len ['pɔlən] M -s, - pollen

Pol|len-: **Pol|len|be|richt** M pollen forecast; **Pol|len|fal|le** F pollen trap; **Pol|len|flug** M pollen count; **Pol|len|sack** M pollen sac; **Pol|len|war|nung** F pollen warning

Pol|ler ['pɔlɐ] M -s, - capstan, bollard

Pol|lu|ti|on [polu'tsioːn] F -, -en (Med) (seminal) emission

pol|nisch ['pɔlnɪʃ] ADJ Polish; **~e Wirtschaft** (inf) shambles sing

Pol|nisch(e) ['pɔlnɪʃ] NT Polish → auch **Deutsch(e)**

Po|lo ['poːlo] NT -s, -s polo

Po|lo|hemd NT sports shirt; (für Frau) casual blouse

Po|lo|nai|se [polo'nɛːzə] F -, -n, **Po|lo|nä|se** [polo'nɛːzə] F -, -n polonaise

Po|lo|ni|um [po'loːnium] NT -s, no pl (abbr **Po**) polonium

Pols|ter ['pɔlstɐ] NT OR (AUS) M -s, - **a** cushion; (= Polsterung) upholstery no pl; (bei Kleidung) pad, padding no pl; **das ~ vom Sessel muss erneuert werden** the chair needs re-upholstering; **sich in die ~ (zurück)fallen lassen** to let oneself fall (back) into the cushions; **seine Jacke als ~ für den Kopf benutzen** to use one's jacket as a pillow **b** (fig) (= Fettpolster) flab no pl (inf), layer of fat; (= Bauch) spare tyre (Brit) or tire (US); (= Reserve) reserve, cushion; (= Geldreserve) reserves pl; **er hat ein ganz schönes ~ am Hintern** he's pretty well-upholstered or well-padded behind (Brit), he has a pretty well-upholstered or well-padded butt (US inf) **c** (esp Aus: = Kissen) cushion

Pöls|ter|chen ['pœlstɐçən] NT -s, - (inf) **a** (= Rücklage) nest egg **b** (= Fettpolster) (layer of) fat; (an Hüften) spare tyre (Brit) or tire (US); **sie hat einige ~** she's well-upholstered or well-padded

Pols|te|rer ['pɔlstərɐ] M -s, -, **Pols|te|rin** [-ərɪn] F -, -nen upholsterer

Pols|ter|gar|ni|tur F three-piece suite

Pols|ter|mö|bel PL upholstered furniture sing

pols|tern ['pɔlstɐn] VT to upholster; Kleidung, Tür to pad; **etw neu ~** to re-upholster sth; **sie ist gut gepolstert** she's well-upholstered or well-padded; **sie ist finanziell gut** or **komfortabel gepolstert** she's not short of the odd penny

Pols|ter-: **Pols|ter|ses|sel** M armchair, easy chair; **Pols|ter|sitz** M upholstered or padded seat; **Pols|ter|stoff** M upholstery or upholstering fabric; **Pols|ter|stuhl** M upholstered or padded chair; **Pols|ter|tür** F padded door

Pols|te|rung ['pɔlstərʊŋ] F -, -en (= Polster) upholstery; (= das Polstern) upholstering

Pol|ter|abend M party on the eve of a wedding, at which old crockery is smashed to bring good luck

---

POLTERABEND

Polterabend is the evening before a wedding, when crockery is smashed outside the door of the bride's parents or of the bride and groom. According to tradition, the broken pieces are supposed to bring luck to the happy couple. Often the **Polterabend** is extended into an informal party for friends and acquaintances and is sometimes held a week before the wedding to allow guests time to recover.

Pol|te|rer ['pɔltərɐ] M -s, - noisy person; (beim Sprechen) ranter, blusterer

Pol|ter|geist M poltergeist

Pol|te|rin F → **Polterer**

pol|tern ['pɔltɐn] VI **a** (= Krach machen) to crash about; (= polternd umfallen) to go crash;

die Kinder ~ oben the children are crashing about or banging about upstairs, the children are making a din or racket (inf) upstairs; **was hat da eben so gepoltert?** what was that crash or bang?; **es fiel ~d zu Boden** it crashed to the floor, it fell with a crash to the floor; **es polterte fürchterlich, als er ...** there was a terrific crash or bang when he ...; **es poltert (an der Tür/vor dem Haus)** there's a real racket (inf) or din going on (at the door/ in front of the house); **an die Tür ~** to thump or bang on the door **b** aux sein (= sich laut bewegen) to crash, to bang; **über das Pflaster ~** to clatter over the cobbles **c** (inf: = schimpfen) to rant (and rave), to carry on (inf) **d** (inf: = Polterabend feiern) to celebrate on the eve of a wedding

Poly-: **Po|ly|amid** [polyla'miːt] NT -(e)s, -e [-də] polyamide; **po|ly|chlo|riert** [polyklo'riːɐt] ADJ polychlorinated; **Po|ly|es|ter** ['poly'lɛstɐ] M -s, - polyester; **po|ly|gam** [poly'gaːm] ADJ polygamous ADV **~ leben** to be polygamous; **Po|ly|ga|mie** [polyga'miː] F -, no pl polygamy; **po|ly|glott** [poly'glɔt] ADJ polyglot no adv; **po|ly|morph** ADJ polymorphous

Po|ly|ne|si|en [poly'neːziən] NT -s Polynesia

Po|ly|ne|si|er [poly'neːziɐ] M -s, -, **Po|ly|ne|si|e|rin** [-iərɪn] F -, -nen Polynesian

po|ly|ne|sisch [poly'neːzɪʃ] ADJ Polynesian

Po|lyp [po'lyːp] M -en, -en **a** (Zool) polyp; (old: = Krake) octopus **b** (Med) **~en** adenoids **c** (dated inf: = Polizist) cop (inf)

po|ly|phon ADJ (Mus, fig) polyphonic, polyphonous

Po|ly|pho|nie F -, no pl (Mus) polyphony

po|ly|sem [poly'zeːm] ADJ (Ling) polysemous

Po|ly|se|mie [polyze'miː] F -, no pl (Ling) polysemy

Po|ly|tech|ni|kum [poly'tɛçnikʊm] NT polytechnic, poly (inf)

po|ly|tech|nisch [poly'tɛçnɪʃ] ADJ polytechnic

Po|ly|the|is|mus [polyte'ɪsmʊs] M -, no pl polytheism

Po|ma|de [po'maːdə] F -, -n hair cream; (Hist, für krause Haare) pomade

po|ma|dig [po'maːdɪç] ADJ (inf) **a** Haare greased-back (inf), Brylcreemed® **b** (= schleimig) smarmy (inf) **c** (= langsam) sluggish ADV **~ glänzendes Haar** oiled hair; **~ zurückgekämmte Haare** slicked-back hair

Po|me|ran|ze [pomə'rantsə] F -, -n Seville or bitter orange

Pom|mer ['pɔmɐ] M -n, -n, **Pom|me|rin** [-ərɪn] F -, -nen Pomeranian

pom|me|risch ['pɔmərɪʃ] ADJ , **pom|mersch** ['pɔmɐʃ] ADJ Pomeranian

Pom|mern ['pɔmɐn] NT -s Pomerania

Pom|mes ['pɔməs] PL (inf) chips pl (Brit), (French) fries pl

Pom|mes|bu|de F (inf) fast food stand, ≈ chip shop (Brit)

Pom|mes frites [pɔm 'frits] PL chips pl (Brit), French fries pl, French fried potatoes pl (form)

Pomp [pɔmp] M -(e)s, no pl pomp

pom|pös [pɔm'pøːs] ADJ grandiose ADV grandiosely

Pon|cho ['pɔntʃo] M -s, -s poncho

Pond [pɔnt] NT -s, - (Phys) weight of 1 gram mass under standard gravity

Pon|ti|fex ['pɔntifɛks] M -, **Pontifizes** [pɔn'tiːfi-tseːs] Pontifex

Pon|ti|fi|kal|amt [pɔntifi'kaːl-] NT Pontifical Mass

Pon|ti|fi|kat [pɔntifi'kaːt] NT OR M -(e)s, -e pontificate

Pon|ti|us ['pɔntsiʊs] M **von ~ zu Pilatus laufen** to rush from pillar to post (Brit) or one place to another; **jdn von ~ zu Pilatus schicken** to pass sb from pillar to post (*Brit*) *or* one place to another

Pon|ton [põˈtõ:, pɔnˈtõ:, ˈpɔntõ] M **-s, -s** pontoon

Pon|ton|brü|cke F pontoon bridge

Po|ny¹ [ˈpɔni] NT **-s, -s** pony

Po|ny² M **-s, -s** (*Frisur*) fringe (*Brit*), bangs *pl* (*US*)

Po|ny|fri|sur F hairstyle with a fringe (*Brit*) *or* with bangs (*US*); **sie hat eine ~** she has bangs (*US*) *or* a fringe (*Brit*)

Pool [pu:l] M **-s, -s** (*alle Bedeutungen*) pool; **Mitarbeiter-Pool** pool of workers

Pool|(bil|lard) [ˈpu:l-] NT **-s, no pl** pool, pocket billiards *no pl*

Pop [pɔp] M **-s, no pl** (*Mus*) pop; (*Art*) pop art; (*Mode*) pop fashion

Po|panz [ˈpo:pants] M **-es, -e** **a** (= *Schreckgespenst*) bogey; **etw/jdn als ~ hinstellen, etw/jdn zum ~ machen** to make a bogey of sth/sb **b** (= *willenloser Mensch*) puppet

Pop|corn [ˈpɔpkɔ:n] NT **-s, no pl** popcorn

Po|pe [ˈpo:pə] M **-n, -n** priest; (*pej*) cleric

Po|pel [ˈpo:pl] M **-s, -** (*inf*) (= *Nasenpopel*) bogey (*Brit inf*), booger (*US inf*), (piece of) snot (*inf*)

po|pe|lig [ˈpo:pəlɪç] (*inf*) **ADJ** **a** (= *knauserig*) stingy (*inf*); **~e zwei Euro** a lousy two euros (*inf*) **b** (= *dürftig*) crummy (*inf*) **c** (= *spießig*) small-minded, narrow-minded **ADV** **a** (= *knauserig*) stingily **b** (= *dürftig*) **~ leben** to live on the cheap (*inf*); **ihr Haus war recht ~ eingerichtet** her house had really crummy furniture (*inf*)

Po|pe|lin [popəˈli:n] M **-s, -e**, **Po|pe|li|ne** [popəˈli:nə] F **-, -** poplin

po|peln [ˈpo:pln] VI (*inf*) **(in der Nase) ~** to pick one's nose

Pop|grup|pe F pop group

pop|lig [ˈpo:plɪç] ADJ, ADV (*inf*) = **popelig**

Pop-: Pop|kon|zert NT pop concert; **Pop|mu|sik** F pop music

Po|po [po'po:] M **-s, -s** (*inf*) bottom, behind (*inf*), botty (*baby-talk*)

Po|po|schei|tel M (*inf*) middle *or* centre parting (*Brit*), center part (*US*)

pop|pen [ˈpɔpn] VI (*sl:* = *koitieren*) to pump (*sl*)

Pop|per [ˈpɔpɐ] M **-s, -**, **Pop|pe|rin** [-ərɪn] F **-, -nen** preppie

pop|pig [ˈpɔpɪç] (*inf*) **ADJ** (*Art, Mus*) pop *no adv*; *Kleidung* loud and trendy; *Farben* bright and cheerful **ADV** **sich ~ kleiden** to wear loud, trendy clothes; **das Buch war total ~ aufgemacht** the book was brightly presented

Pop-: Pop|sän|ger(in) M(F) pop singer; **Pop|star** M pop star; **Pop|sze|ne** F pop scene

po|pu|lär [popu'lɛ:ɐ] **ADJ** popular (*bei* with) **ADV** *schreiben, darstellen, sich ausdrücken* in an accessible way

po|pu|la|ri|sie|ren [populari'zi:rən] *ptp* **popularisiert** VT to popularize

Po|pu|la|ri|tät [populari'tɛ:t] F **-, no pl** popularity

po|pu|lär|wis|sen|schaft|lich **ADJ** *Buch* popular science; *Literatur* popular scientific; **seine Bücher sind mehr ~** his books are rather more popular science **ADV** **etw ~ darstellen** to present sth in a popular scientific way

Po|pu|la|ti|on [popula'tsio:n] F **-, -en** (*Biol, Sociol*) population

Po|pu|lis|mus [popu'lɪsmʊs] M **-, no pl** (*Pol*) populism

Po|pu|list [popu'lɪst] M **-en, -en**, **Po|pu|lis|tin** [-'lɪstɪn] F **-, -nen** populist

po|pu|lis|tisch [popu'lɪstɪʃ] **ADJ** populist **ADV** in a populist way; **~ argumentieren** to use populist arguments

Po|re [ˈpo:rə] F **-, -n** pore

po|rig [ˈpo:rɪç] ADJ *Gestein, Struktur* porous

-po|rig ADJ *suf* with … pores; **feinporige Haut** skin with fine pores

Por|no [ˈpɔrno] M **-s, -s** (*inf*) porn (*inf*)

Por|no- in cpds (*inf*) porn (*inf*); **Por|no|film** M porn *or* blue movie, skin flick (*US inf*); **Por|no|heft** NT porn magazine

Por|no|gra|fie ▲ [pɔrnogra'fi:] F **-, -n** [-'fi:ən] pornography

por|no|gra|fisch ▲ [pɔrno'gra:fɪʃ] **ADJ** pornographic

po|rös [po'rø:s] ADJ (= *durchlässig*) porous; (= *brüchig*) *Gummi, Leder* perished; **~ werden** to perish

Po|ro|si|tät [porozi'tɛ:t] F **-, no pl** porosity

Por|ree [ˈpɔre] M **-s, -s** leek

Port¹ [pɔrt] M **-(e)s, -e** **a** (*poet*) haven (*poet*) **b** (= *Portwein*) port

Port² M **-s, -s** (*Comput*) port

por|ta|bel [pɔrˈta:bl] ADJ (*also Comput*) portable

Por|ta|bi|li|tät [pɔrtabili'tɛ:t] F **-, no pl** (*also Comput*) portability

Por|ta|ble [ˈpɔrtəbl] NT **-s, -s** portable TV *or* television (set)

Por|tal [pɔrˈta:l] NT **-s, -e** portal

Por|te|feuille [pɔrt(ə)ˈfø:j] NT **-s, -s** (*Pol, obs*) portfolio; (*obs:* = *Brieftasche*) wallet

Por|te|mon|naie [pɔrtmɔˈne:, pɔrtmɔ'ne:] NT **-s, -s** purse

Port|fo|lio [pɔrtˈfo:lio] NT **-s, -s** **a** (*Fin, St Ex*) portfolio **b** (= *Bildbandmappe*) portfolio

Por|ti|er [pɔrˈtie:] M **-s, -s** = **Pförtner²**

por|tie|ren [pɔrˈti:rən] *ptp* **portiert** VT (*Sw Pol*) to put up

Por|ti|er|lo|ge [pɔrˈtie:lo:ʒə] F = **Pförtnerloge**

Por|ti|ers|frau [pɔrˈtie:z-] F = **Pförtnerin**

Por|ti|on [pɔrˈtsio:n] F **-, -en** **a** (*beim Essen*) portion, helping; **eine halbe ~** a half portion; (*fig inf*) a half pint (*inf*); **eine zweite ~** a second helping; **eine ~ Kaffee** a pot of coffee; **eine ~ Butter** a portion of butter **b** (*fig inf:* = *Anteil*) amount; **er besitzt eine gehörige ~ Mut** he's got a fair amount of courage; **sie brachte eine gute ~ Geduld auf** she showed a fair amount of patience (*inf*)

por|ti|o|nen|wei|se [pɔrˈtsio:nənvaizə], **por|ti|ons|wei|se** [pɔrˈtsio:nsvaizə] ADV in helpings *or* portions

por|ti|o|nie|ren [pɔrtsio'ni:rən] *ptp* **portioniert** VT to divide into portions

Por|ti|o|nie|rer [pɔrˈtsio:n] M **-s, -** (*für Eis*) scoop

Port|mo|nee ▲ [pɔrtmɔˈne:, pɔrtmɔ'ne:] NT **-s, -s** = **Portemonnaie**

Por|to [ˈpɔrto] NT **-s, -s** *or* **Porti** [-ti] postage *no pl* (*für* on, for); (*für Kisten etc*) carriage; **~ zahlt Empfänger** postage paid; **das ~ für den Brief macht** *or* **beträgt zwei Euro** the postage on *or* for the letter is two euros

Por|to-: Por|to|aus|la|gen PL postal *or* postage expenses *pl*; **por|to|frei** ADJ, ADV post-free (*Brit*), postage paid; **Por|to|kas|se** F = petty cash (*for postal expenses*); **por|to|pflich|tig** [-pflɪçtɪç] ADJ liable *or* subject to postage

Por|trät [pɔrˈtrɛ:, pɔrˈtrɛ:t] NT **-s, -s** (*lit, fig*) portrait

Por|trät|auf|nah|me F portrait photo(graph)

Por|trät|fo|to|gra|fie ▲ F portrait photography

por|trä|tie|ren [pɔrtrɛ'ti:rən] *ptp* **porträtiert** VT (*fig*) to portray; **jdn ~** to paint a portrait of sb, to paint sb's portrait; (*mit Fotoapparat*) to do a portrait of sb

Por|trä|tist [pɔrtrɛ'tɪst] M **-en, -en**, **Por|trä|tis|tin** [-'tɪstɪn] F **-, -nen** portrait painter, portraitist; (= *Fotograf*) portrait photographer

Por|rät-: Por|rät|ma|ler(in) M(F) portrait painter, portraitist; **Por|rät|ma|le|rei** F portraiture; **Por|rät|stu|die** F sketch for a portrait

Por|tu|gal [ˈpɔrtugal] NT **-s** Portugal

Por|tu|gie|se [pɔrtu'gi:zə] M **-n, -n**, **Por|tu|gie|sin** [-ˈgi:zɪn] F **-, -nen** Portuguese

por|tu|gie|sisch [pɔrtu'gi:zɪʃ] ADJ Portuguese

Por|tu|gie|sisch(e) [pɔrtu'gi:zɪʃ] NT Portuguese → *auch* **Deutsch(e)**

Port|wein [ˈpɔrt-] M port

Por|zel|lan [pɔrtse'la:n] NT **-s, -e** (*Material*) china, porcelain; (= *Geschirr*) china; **(unnötig) ~ zerbrechen** *or* **zerschlagen** (*fig*) to cause a lot of (*unnecessary*) bother *or* trouble

Por|zel|lan- in cpds china, porcelain; **Por|zel|lan|er|de** F china clay, kaolin; **Por|zel|lan|ge|schirr** NT china, crockery; **Por|zel|lan|la|den** M china shop → **Elefant**; **Por|zel|lan|ma|nu|fak|tur** F porcelain *or* china factory; (*Herstellung*) porcelain *or* china production

Po|sau|ne [po'zaunə] F **-, -n** trombone; (*fig*) trumpet; **die ~n des Jüngsten Gerichts** the last trump

po|sau|nen [po'zaunən] *ptp* **posaunt** (*inf*) **VI** (*Posaune spielen*) to play the trombone **VTI** (*fig:* = *laut sprechen*) to bellow, to bawl, to yell; **etw in alle Welt** *or* **in die Gegend ~** to shout sth from the rooftops *or* hilltops, to tell *or* proclaim sth to the whole world

Po|sau|nen-: Po|sau|nen|blä|ser(in) M(F) trombonist, trombone player; **Po|sau|nen|chor** M trombone band (*usually connected with a church*); **Po|sau|nen|en|gel** M (*lit*) cherub with a trumpet; (*fig*) (little) chubby-cheeks (*inf*)

Po|sau|nist [pozau'nɪst] M **-en, -en**, **Po|sau|nis|tin** [-'nɪstɪn] F **-, -nen** trombonist, trombone player

Po|se [ˈpo:zə] F **-, -n** pose

po|sie|ren [po'zi:rən] *ptp* **posiert** VI to pose; **er posiert in der Rolle des Wohltäters** he's playing the benefactor

Po|si|ti|on [pozi'tsio:n] F **-, -en** position; (*Comm:* = *Posten einer Liste*) item; **in gesicherter ~ sein** to have a secure position

po|si|ti|o|nie|ren [pozitsio'ni:rən] *ptp* **positioniert** VT (*Comput*) to position

Po|si|ti|o|nie|rung F **-, -en** positioning

Po|si|ti|ons-: Po|si|ti|ons|lam|pe F, **Po|si|ti|ons|licht** NT navigation light; **Po|si|ti|ons|pa|pier** NT (*Pol*) policy document

po|si|tiv [ˈpo:ziti:f, pozi'ti:f] **ADJ** positive; **eine ~e Antwort** an answer in the affirmative, an affirmative (answer); **ich weiß nichts Positives** I don't know anything definite **ADV** positively; **etw ~ wissen** to know sth for certain *or* for a fact; **~ denken** to think positively; **etw ~ (auf-)laden** (*Phys*) to put a positive charge on sth; **~ zu etw stehen** to be in favour (*Brit*) *or* favor (*US*) of sth; **sich ~ zu einer Sache äußern** to respond *or* react positively to sth

Po|si|tiv¹ [ˈpo:ziti:f, pozi'ti:f] M **-s, -e** [-və] (*Gram*) positive

Po|si|tiv² NT **-s, -e** [-və] **a** (*Phot*) positive **b** (= *Orgel*) harmonium

Po|si|ti|vis|mus [poziti'vɪsmʊs] M **-, no pl** positivism

po|si|ti|vis|tisch [poziti'vɪstɪʃ] ADJ positivist

Po|si|tiv|lis|te F **a** (*Med, Pharm*) approved drug list **b** (*allgemein*) list of recommended products/shops/procedures *etc*

Po|si|tur [pozi'tu:ɐ] F **-, -en** posture; (*stehend auch*) stance; **sich in ~ setzen/stellen** to take up a posture; **sie setzte sich vor den Fernsehkameras in ~** she posed for the TV cameras; **sich in ~ werfen** to strike a pose

Pos|se [ˈpɔsə] F **-, -n** farce

Pos|sen [ˈpɔsn] M **-s, -** (*dated*) prank, tomfoolery *no pl*; **~ reißen** to lark *or* fool *or* clown around; **jdm einen ~ spielen** to play a prank on sb; **mit jdm ~ treiben** (old) to play pranks on sb; **er tat es mir zum ~** he did it just to annoy me

Pos|sen-: pos|sen|haft ADJ farcical ADV farcically; **Pos|sen|rei|ßer** [-raisə] M **-s, -, Pos|-sen|rei|ße|rin** [-ərɪn] F **-, -nen** clown, buffoon; **Pos|sen|spiel** NT (liter) pranks pl

pos|ses|siv ['pɔsesiːf, pɔseˈsiːf] ADJ possessive

Pos|ses|siv ['pɔsesiːf, pɔseˈsiːf] NT **-s, -e, Pos|-ses|siv|pro|no|men** ['pɔsesiːf-, pɔseˈsiːf-] NT , **Pos|ses|si|vum** [pɔseˈsiːvʊm] NT **-s, Possessiva** possessive pronoun

pos|sier|lich [pɔˈsiːrlɪç] ADJ comical, funny ADV comically

Post [pɔst] F **-, -en** **a** post (Brit), mail; (= Post-amt, Postwesen) post office; **war die ~ schon da?** has the post (Brit) or mail come yet?; **ist ~ für mich da?** is there any post (Brit) or mail for me?, are there any letters for me?; **etw mit der ~ schicken** to send sth by post (Brit) or mail; **etw auf** or **in die ~ geben** to post (Brit) or mail sth; **auf die** or **zur ~ gehen** to go to the post office; **mit gleicher ~** by the same post (Brit), in the same mail (US); **mit getrennter ~** under separate cover; **mit der ersten ~ kommen** to come (with or in the) first post (Brit), to come in the first mail (US); **etw durch die ~ beziehen** to order sth by post (Brit) or by mail **b** (= Postkutsche) stagecoach; (= Postbus) post bus (Brit), mail bus; **die ~ geht ab** (fig inf) things really happen

Post|ab|ho|ler [-ʔaphoːlɐ] M **-s, -, Post|ab|-ho|le|rin** [-ərɪn] F **-, -nen** someone who collects his mail from a PO box

pos|ta|lisch [pɔsˈtaːlɪʃ] ADJ postal ADV by post (Brit) or mail

Pos|ta|ment [pɔstaˈmɛnt] NT **-(e)s, -e** pedestal, base

Post-: Post|amt NT post office; **Post|an|-schrift** F postal address; **Post|an|wei|sung** F remittance paid in at a Post Office and delivered by post; ≈ postal (Brit) or money order; **Post|aus|gang** M , no pl outgoing mail (Internet) out mail; **Post|au|to** NT post office van; (Lieferwagen) mail van (Brit) or truck (US); (Bus) post bus (Brit), mail bus; **Post|bank** F Post Office Savings Bank; **Post|be|amt|e(r)** M decl as adj, **Post|be|am|tin** F post office official; **Post|be|dien|ste|te(r)** MF decl as adj (form) post office worker; **Post|be|zirk** M postal district or area or zone (US); **Post|boot** NT mail boat, packet (boat); **Post|bo|te** M postman, mailman (US); **Post|bo|tin** F postwoman, mailwoman (US); **Post|bus** M mail bus

Pöst|chen ['pœstçən] NT **-s, -** dim von **Posten** little position or job

Post-: Post|dienst M postal service, the mail (US); **Post|ein|gang** M , no pl incoming mail

pos|ten ['pɔstn] (Sw: = einkaufen) VT to buy VI to shop

Pos|ten ['pɔstn] M **-s, -** **a** (= Anstellung) post (esp Brit), position, job **b** (Mil: = Wachmann) guard; (am Eingang) sentry, guard; (= Stelle) post; **~ stehen** to stand guard; (am Eingang auch) to stand sentry; **~ be|-ziehen** to take up one's post; **~ aufstellen** to post guards, to mount a guard **c** (fig) **auf dem ~ sein** (= aufpassen) to be a-wake; (= gesund sein) to be fit; **nicht ganz auf dem ~ sein** to be (a bit) under the weather, to be off colour (Brit) or off color (US) → **verlo|-ren, ausharren** **d** (= Streikposten) picket; **~ aufstellen** to set up pickets or a picket line **e** (Comm: = Warenmenge) quantity, lot **f** (Comm: im Etat) item, entry

Pos|ten-: Pos|ten|dienst M guard duty; **~ ha|-ben** to be on guard duty; **Pos|ten|ket|te** F cordon

Pos|ter ['pɔstɐ] NT **-s, -(s)** poster

Postf. abbr von **Postfach**

Post-: Post|fach NT post office or PO box; **Post|fach|num|mer** F (PO or post office) box number; **post|fer|tig** ADJ ready for posting (Brit) or mailing, ready for the post (Brit) or mail; **Post|flug|zeug** NT mail plane; **post|-frisch** ADJ Briefmarke mint; **Post|ge|bühr** F postal charge or rate; **Post|ge|heim|nis** NT secrecy of the post (Brit) or mail

Post|gi|ro- [-ʒiːro] (dated): **Post|gi|ro|amt** NT National Giro office (Brit), state-owned bank office (US); **Post|gi|ro|kon|to** NT National or Post Office Giro account (Brit), state-owned bank account (US)

Post-: Post|hal|te|rei [pɔsthaltəˈrai] F **-, -en** coaching house (Brit), motor inn (US); **Post|-horn** NT post horn

post|hum [pɔstˈhuːm, pɔsˈtuːm] ADJ, ADV = **postum**

pos|tie|ren [pɔsˈtiːrən] ptp **postiert** VT to post, to station, to position VR to station or position oneself

Pos|til|li|on [pɔstɪlˈjoːn, ˈpɔstɪljoːn] M **-s, -e** stagecoach driver

Pos|til|lon d'A|mour [pɔstijõ daˈmuːr] M **- -, -s -** go-between

Post|kar|te F postcard, postal card (US)

Post|kar|ten|for|mat NT , **Post|kar|ten|-grö|ße** F postcard size; **in Postkartengröße, im ~** postcard-sized

Post-: Post|kas|ten M pillar box (Brit), post-box, mailbox (US); **Post|kut|sche** F stage-coach; **post|la|gernd** ADJ, ADV poste restante (Brit), general delivery (US); **Post|leit|zahl** F post(al) code, Zip code (US)

Post|ler ['pɔstlɐ] M **-s, -, Post|le|rin** [-ərɪn] F **-, -nen**, (Sw) **Pöst|ler** ['pœstlɐ] M **-s, -, Pöst|le|-rin** [-ərɪn] F **-, -nen** (inf) post office worker

Post-: Post|meis|ter M (dated) postmaster; **Post|meis|te|rin** F (dated) postmistress; **Post|mi|nis|ter(in)** M(F) ≈ postmaster general

post|mo|dern [pɔstmoˈdɛrn] ADJ postmodern

Post|mo|der|ne [pɔstmoˈdɛrnə] F postmodern era

post|na|tal ['pɔstnaˈtaːl] ADJ attr postnatal

post|nuk|le|ar [pɔstnukleˈaːɐ] ADJ post-nuclear

Post-: Post|pa|ket NT parcel (sent by post); **Post|sa|che** F matter no pl sent postage paid; **Post|sack** M postbag (Brit), mailbag; **Post|-schal|ter** M post office counter; **Post|-scheck** M (dated) (Post Office or National) Giro cheque (Brit), state-owned bank check (US)

Post|skript [pɔstˈskrɪpt] NT **-(e)s, -e, Post|-skrip|tum** [pɔstˈskrɪptʊm] NT **-s, -e** or **Post-skripta** [-ta] postscript, PS

Post-: Post|spar|buch NT Post Office savings book; **Post|spar|kas|se** F (dated) Post Office Savings Bank; **Post|stel|le** F sub-post office; **Post|stem|pel** M postmark; **Datum des ~s** date as postmark; **Einsendungen bis zum 17. Juni (Datum des ~s)** entries to be postmarked no later than 17th June; **Post|über|wei|sung** F Girobank transfer (Brit), money transfer from a Post Office Savings Bank

Pos|tu|lat [pɔstuˈlaːt] NT **-(e)s, -e** (= Annahme) postulate; (Eccl: = Probezeit) postulancy

pos|tu|lie|ren [pɔstuˈliːrən] ptp **postuliert** VT to postulate

pos|tum [pɔsˈtuːm] ADJ posthumous ADV post-humously

Post-: Post|ver|merk M postmark; **Post|wa|-gen** M (Rail) mail car, mail coach (Brit); **Post|weg** M **auf dem ~** by mail or post (Brit), by snail mail (inf); **post|wen|dend** ADV by return (of post) (Brit), by return mail; (fig) straight away, immediately; **Post|wert|zei|-chen** NT (form) postage stamp (form); **Post|-we|sen** NT , no pl Post Office; **Post|wurf|-sen|dung** F direct-mail advertising; **Post|zug** M mail train; **Post|zu|stel|lung** F postal or

mail delivery; **Post|zu|stel|lungs|ur|kun|de** F registered post (Brit) or certified mail (US) certificate

Pot [pɔt] NT **-s**, no pl (sl: = Haschisch) pot (inf)

po|tem|kinsch [po'tɛmkɪnʃ] ADJ sham; **~e Dör-fer** façade

po|tent [po'tɛnt] ADJ **a** (sexuell) potent **b** (= leistungsfähig, stark) Gegner, Waffe, Fantasie powerful **c** (= einflussreich) high-powered; (= zah-lungskräftig) financially powerful

Po|ten|tat [poten'taːt] M **-en, -en, Po|ten|ta|-tin** [-'taːtɪn] F **-, -nen** potentate

Po|ten|ti|al [poten'tsiaːl] NT **-s, -e** = **Potenzial**

po|ten|ti|ell [poten'tsiɛl] ADJ, ADV = **potenziell**

Po|tenz [po'tɛnts] F **-, -en a** (Med) potency; (fig) ability; (wirtschaftlich etc) power; **schöpferi-sche ~** creative power **b** (Math) power; **zweite ~ square; dritte ~** cube; **eine Zahl in die sechs-te ~ erheben** to raise a number to the power of six (esp Brit) or to the sixth power; **die zwei-te/dritte ~ zu zwei ist vier/acht** the square/cube of two is four/eight, two to the power of two/three is four/eight; **die sechste ~ zu zwei** two to the power of six (esp Brit) or to the sixth power; **in höchster ~** (fig) to the highest degree

Po|ten|zi|al ▲ [poten'tsiaːl] NT **-s, -e** potential

po|ten|zi|ell ▲ [poten'tsiɛl] ADJ potential ADV potentially; **er ist ~ mein Gegner** he's a potential opponent, he's potentially my opponent

po|ten|zie|ren [poten'tsiːrən] ptp **potenziert** VT (Math) to raise to the power of; (fig: = stei-gern) to multiply, to increase; **2 hoch ~** to raise 2 to the power of 5; **3 mit 2 ~** (auch) to square 3; **4 mit 3 ~** (auch) to cube 4; **2 potenziert mit 4** 2 to the power of 4 (esp Brit), 2 to the fourth

po|tenz|stei|gernd ADJ potency-enhancing; **~es Mittel** potency pill or supplement

Pot|pour|ri ['pɔtpʊri] NT **-s, -s** (Mus) potpourri, medley (aus +dat of); (fig) potpourri, assort-ment

Pott [pɔt] M **-(e)s, ⸚e** ['pœtə] (inf) pot; (= Schiff) ship, tub (hum inf); **mit etw zu ~e kommen** to see sth through; (= anfangen) to get down to sth

Pott-: Pott|asche F potash; **Pott|fisch** M sperm whale; **pott|häss|lich ▲** (inf) ADJ ugly as sin, plug-ugly (inf) ADV **sie war ~ angezogen** the way she was dressed made her look plug-ugly (inf); **wie kann man sein Haus nur so ~ an-streichen?** who would ever paint a house like that, it's ugly as sin (inf); **Pott|wal** M sperm whale

potz Blitz ['pɔts 'blɪts], **potz|tau|send** ['pɔts-'tauznt] INTERJ (old) upon my soul (old)

Pou|lar|de [pu'lardə] F **-, -n** poulard(e)

Pou|let [pu'leː] NT **-s, -s** (Sw) chicken

pous|sie|ren [pu'siːrən] ptp **poussiert** VI (dated inf: = flirten) to flirt VT (old: = schmeicheln) **jdn ~** to curry favour (Brit) or favor (US) with sb

po|wer ['poːvɐ] ADJ (dial) poor; Essen, Geschenke meagre (Brit), meager (US)

Pow|er ['pauɐ] F **-**, no pl (inf) power

Pow|er|frau ['pauɐ-] F (inf) high-powered ca-reer woman

pow|ern ['pauɐn] VI (inf) to get things moving

Po|widl ['poːvidl] M **-**, no pl (Aus: = Pflaumenmus) plum jam

PR [peː'ɛr] abbr von **Public Relations** PR

Prä-, prä- [prɛ] PREF pre-; **Prä|am|bel** [prɛ-'ambl] F **-, -n** preamble (+gen to)

Pracht [praxt] F **-**, no pl splendour (Brit), splen-dor (US), magnificence; (fig: = Herrlichkeit) splendo(u)r; **in seiner vollen** or **ganzen ~** in all its splendo(u)r or magnificence; **große ~ entfal-ten** to put on a show or display of great splen-do(u)r; **es ist eine wahre ~** it's (really) marvel-lous (esp Brit) or marvelous (US) or fantastic; **er kann singen, dass es eine ~ ist** he can sing marvellously (esp Brit) or marvelously (US) or fantastically; **die weiße ~** (= *Schnee*) snowy splendo(u)r

Pracht-: Pracht|aus|ga|be F de luxe edition; **Pracht|bau** M *pl* **-bauten** splendid *or* magnificent building; **Pracht|ent|fal|tung** F display of splendour (*Brit*) *or* splendor (*US*), magnificent display; **zur vollen ~ kommen** to display its/their full splendour (*Brit*) *or* splendor (*US*); **Pracht|exemp|lar** NT splendid *or* prime specimen, beauty (*inf*); (*von Buch*: = *Prachtausgabe*) de luxe copy; (*fig*: *Mensch*) fine specimen; **mein ~ von Sohn** (*iro*) my brilliant son (*iro*)

präch|tig ['prɛçtɪç] ADJ (= *prunkvoll*) splendid, magnificent; (= *großartig*) splendid, marvellous (*esp Brit*), marvelous (*US*) ADV a (= *prunkvoll*) magnificently b (= *großartig*) splendidly, marvellously (*esp Brit*), marvelously (*US*); **sich ~ amüsieren** to have a splendid *or* marvellous (*esp Brit*) *or* marvelous (*US*) time

Pracht-: Pracht|kerl M (*inf*) great guy (*inf*), good bloke (*Brit inf*); (= *Prachtexemplar*) beauty (*inf*); **Pracht|stra|ße** F boulevard, magnificent avenue; **Pracht|stück** NT = **Prachtexemplar; pracht|voll** ADJ, ADV = **prächtig; Pracht|weib** NT (*inf*) fine specimen of a woman *or* of womanhood

Prä|des|ti|na|ti|on [predestinaˈtsioːn] F -, *no pl* predestination

prä|des|ti|nie|ren [predɛstiˈniːrən] *ptp* **prädestiniert** VT to predestine, to predetermine (*für* for); **sein diplomatisches Geschick prädestinierte ihn zum Politiker** with his diplomatic skill he was predestined to be a politician; **er ist für diese Aufgabe wie** *or* **geradezu prädestiniert** he seems to have been made for the job

Prä|di|kat [prediˈkaːt] NT **-(e)s, -e** (*Gram*) predicate; (= *Bewertung*) rating; (*Sch*: = *Zensur*) grade; (= *Rangbezeichnung*) title; **Wein mit ~** special quality wine

prä|di|ka|tiv ['preːdikatiːf, predikaˈtiːf] ADJ predicative ADV predicatively

Prä|di|ka|tiv ['preːdikatiːf, predikaˈtiːf] NT **-s, -e** [-və], **Prä|di|ka|tivum** [predikaˈtiːvʊm] NT **-s,** **Prädikativa** [-va] predicative noun/adjective/pronoun

Prä|di|kats-: Prä|di|kats|exa|men NT honours (*Brit*) *or* honors (*US*) degree; **Prä|di|kats|no|men** NT predicative noun/pronoun; **Prä|di|kats|wein** M top quality wine

prä|dis|po|nie|ren [predɪspoˈniːrən] *ptp* **prädisponiert** VT to predispose (*für* to)

Prä|emp|tiv|schlag [preˈlɛmpˈtiːf-] M (*Mil*) pre-emptive strike

Prä|fekt [preˈfɛkt] M **-en, -en, Prä|fek|tin** [-ˈfɛk-tɪn] F **-, -nen** prefect

Prä|fe|renz [prefeˈrɛnts] F **-, -en** (*geh*) preference

Prä|fix [preˈfɪks, ˈpreːfɪks] NT **-es, -e** prefix

Prag [praːk] NT **-s** Prague; **der ~er Frühling** (*Pol*) the Prague Spring → **Fenstersturz**

Prä|ge ['prɛːɡə] F **-, -n, Prä|ge|an|stalt** F mint

prä|gen ['prɛːɡn] VT a Münzen to mint, to strike; Leder, Papier, Metall to emboss; (= *erfinden*) Begriffe, Wörter to coin; **seine Worte prägten sich ihr ins Herz** (*liter*) his words engraved themselves on her heart (*liter*)
b (*fig*: = *formen*) Charakter to shape, to mould (*Brit*), to mold (*US*); (Erlebnis, Kummer, Erfahrungen) jdn to leave its/their mark on; **ein vom Leid geprägtes Gesicht** a face marked by suffering; **ein katholisch geprägtes Land** a predominantly Catholic country; **das moderne Drama ist durch Brecht geprägt worden** Brecht had a forming *or* formative influence on modern drama
c (= *kennzeichnen*) Stadtbild, Landschaft etc to characterize

prä|gend ADJ Erlebnis formative

PR-Agen|tur [peːˈlɛr-] F PR agency

Prä|ge-: Prä|ge|ort M *pl* **-orte** mint; **Prä|ge|stem|pel** M die, stamp; **Prä|ge|stock** M punch

Prag|ma|ti|ker [praˈɡmaːtikɐ] M **-s, -, Prag|ma|ti|ke|rin** [-ərɪn] F **-, -nen** pragmatist

prag|ma|tisch [praˈɡmaːtɪʃ] ADJ pragmatic ADV pragmatically; **~ eingestellt sein** to be pragmatic

Prag|ma|tis|mus [praɡmaˈtɪsmʊs] M **-,** *no pl* pragmatism

präg|nant [prɛˈɡnant] ADJ Worte succinct, concise; Beispiel, Unterschied striking ADV succinctly, concisely; **die Antwort ist ~ ausgefallen** the answer was concise *or* succinct

Präg|nanz [prɛˈɡnants] F **-,** *no pl* succinctness, conciseness

Prä|gung ['prɛːɡʊŋ] F **-, -en** a (= *das Prägen*) stamping; (*von Münzen*) minting, striking; (*von Leder, Papier, Metall*) embossing; (*von Begriffen, Wörtern*) coining; (*fig*: *von Charakter*) shaping, moulding (*Brit*), molding (*US*) b (*auf Münzen*) strike; (*auf Leder, Metall, Papier*) embossing c (= *Eigenart*) character; **Kommunismus sowjetischer ~ soviet-style communism**

prä|his|to|risch ADJ prehistoric

prah|len ['praːlən] VI to boast, to brag, to swank (*Brit inf*) (*mit* about)

Prah|ler ['praːlɐ] M **-s, -, Prah|le|rin** [-ərɪn] F **-, -nen** boaster, bragger, braggart

Prah|le|rei [praːləˈrai] F **-, -en** (= *Großsprecherei*) boasting *no pl*, bragging *no pl*; (= *das Zurschaustellen*) showing-off, swank (*Brit inf*); **~en** boasts; showing-off, swanking (*Brit inf*)

prah|le|risch ['praːlərɪʃ] ADJ (= *großsprecherisch*) boastful, bragging *attr*; (= *großtuerisch*) swanky (*Brit inf*), flashy (*inf*) ADV boastfully; **~ reden** to brag; **sich ~ verhalten** to swank about (*Brit inf*), to strut around (*inf*)

Prahl|hans [-hans] M **-es, -hänse** [-hɛnzə] (*inf*) show-off

Prahm [praːm] M **-(e)s, -e** *or* **-e** ['prɛːmə] barge, lighter

prä|ju|di|zie|ren [prɛjudiˈtsiːrən] *ptp* **präjudiziert** VT *insep* (*Jur*) to prejudge

Prak|tik ['praktɪk] F **-, -en** (= *Methode*) procedure, method; (*usu pl*: = *Kniff*) practice, trick; **undurchsichtige ~en** shady or dark practices

Prak|ti|ka *pl von* **Praktikum**

prak|ti|ka|bel [praktiˈkaːbl] ADJ practicable

Prak|ti|ka|bi|li|tät F **-,** *no pl* practicability

Prak|ti|kant [praktiˈkant] M **-en, -en, Prak|ti|kan|tin** [-ˈkantɪn] F **-, -nen** student doing a period of practical training, trainee

Prak|ti|ker ['praktikɐ] M **-s, -, Prak|ti|ke|rin** [-ərɪn] F **-, -nen** practical person *or* man/woman; (*auf wissenschaftlichem Gebiet auch*) practitioner; (*inf*: = *praktischer Arzt*) GP; **was hätten Sie als ~ von der Montessori-Pädagogik?** what do you, as a practising (*Brit*) *or* practicing (*US*) teacher, think of the Montessori method?; **er ist ein ~ unter den Politikern** he is a practical sort of politician

Prak|ti|kum ['praktɪkʊm] NT **-s, Praktika** [-ka] practical, (period of) practical training

---

PRAKTIKUM

A **Praktikum** is a period of practical work experience. It usually entails four to eight weeks of unpaid work in a firm and is generally a compulsory part of an employment training course. Recently, however, increasing numbers of young people and students have been using the **Praktikum** as an opportunity to sample a profession and make useful contacts.

PR-Ak|ti|on [peːˈlɛr-] F PR campaign

prak|tisch ['praktɪʃ] ADJ practical; (= *nützlich auch*) handy; **sie hat einen ~en Verstand** she's practically minded; **~er Arzt** general practition-

er; **~es Jahr** practical year; **~e Ausbildung** practical *or* in-job training; **~es Beispiel** concrete example ADV (= *in der Praxis*) in practice; (= *geschickt*) practically; (= *so gut wie*) practically, virtually

prak|ti|zie|ren [praktiˈtsiːrən] *ptp* **praktiziert** VI to practise (*Brit*), to practice (*US*); **ein ~der Katholik** a practising (*Brit*) *or* practicing (*US*) Catholic; **sie praktiziert als Ärztin/Rechtsanwältin** she is a practising (*Brit*) *or* practicing (*US*) doctor/lawyer VT a (*pej*: = *ausführen*) to put into practice, to practise (*Brit*), to practice (*US*) b (*inf*: = *geschickt an eine Stelle bringen*) to conjure

Prä|lat [preˈlaːt] M **-en, -en, Prä|la|tin** [-ˈlaːtɪn] F **-, -nen** prelate

Prä|li|mi|na|ri|en [prelimiˈnaːriən] PL preliminary talks *or* discussions *pl*

Pra|li|ne [praˈliːnə] F **-, -n,** (*Aus*) **Pra|li|né** [praliˈneː] NT **-s, -s, Pra|li|nee** [praliˈneː] NT **-s, -s** chocolate, chocolate candy (*US*)

prall [pral] ADJ Sack, Beutel, Brieftasche bulging; Segel billowing, full; Tomaten firm; Euter swollen, full; Luftballon hard; Wange full, chubby; Brüste full, well-rounded; Hintern well-rounded; Arme, Schenkel big strong *attr*; Sonne blazing; **das ~e Leben** life in all its colour (*Brit*) *or* color (*US*) *or* intensity; **sich ins ~e Leben stürzen** to live life to the full
ADV **etw ~ aufblasen** to blow sth up until it is ready to burst; **~ gefüllt** (Tasche, Kasse etc) full to bursting; Arbeitstag chock-full (*inf*); **das Segel war ~ vom Wind gefüllt** the sail billowed out in the wind; **ihre Brüste wölbten sich ~ unter dem Pullover** her breasts swelled firmly under her sweater; **die Shorts spannten sich ~ über seinem Hintern** his shorts stretched tightly over his bottom; **die Sonne brannte ~ auf den Strand** the sun blazed *or* beat down onto the beach

Prall [pral] M **-(e)s, -e** collision (*gegen* with)

prall|len ['pralən] VI *aux sein* **gegen etw ~** to collide with sth, to crash into sth; (*Ball*) to bounce against *or* off sth; **er prallte mit dem Kopf gegen die Windschutzscheibe** he hit *or* crashed his head on *or* against the windscreen; **die Sonne prallte auf** *or* **gegen die Fenster** the sun beat *or* blazed down on the windows

prall|voll ADJ full to bursting; Brieftasche bulging

Prä|lu|di|um [preˈluːdiʊm] NT **-s, Präludien** [-diən] prelude; (*sexuell*) foreplay

prä|mens|tru|ell [premɛnstruˈɛl] ADJ premenstrual; **~e Beschwerden** *pl*, **~es Syndrom** premenstrual tension, PMT, premenstrual syndrome (*esp US*), PMS (*esp US*)

Prä|mie ['prɛːmiə] F **-, -n** premium; (= *Belohnung*) bonus; (= *Preis*) prize

Prä|mi|en-: prä|mi|en|be|güns|tigt [-bəɡʏnstɪçt] ADJ carrying a premium, with benefit of premiums; **Prä|mi|en|ge|schäft** NT (*Handel*) option dealing; (*Abschluss*) option; **Prä|mi|en|los** NT winning premium bond; **prä|mi|en|spa|ren** VI *sep infin, ptp only* to save on a system benefiting from government premiums in addition to interest

prä|mie|ren [prɛˈmiːrən] *ptp* **prämiert** VT (= *auszeichnen*) to give an award; (= *belohnen*) to give a bonus; **etw mit dem ersten Preis/mit 1000 Euro ~** to award sth first prize/a prize of 1000 euros *or* a 1000-euro prize; **der prämierte Film** the award-winning film

Prä|mie|rung F **-, -en** a (= *das Prämieren*) **für diesen Film kommt eine ~ nicht in Frage** there's no question of giving this film an award b (*Veranstaltung*) presentation; **die ~ der Preisträger** the presentation to the prizewinners

prä|mi|ie|ren [prɛmiˈiːrən] *ptp* **prämiiert** VT = **prämieren**

Prä|mi|ie|rung F **-, -en** = **Prämierung**

Prä|mis|se [prɛˈmɪsə] F **-, -n** premise

German spelling reform (see supplement): ▲ new spelling △ old spelling

prä|na|tal [prena'taːl] ADJ *attr Diagnostik* prenatal; *Vorsorge, Untersuchung* antenatal, prenatal (*esp US*)

pran|gen ['praŋən] VI (*liter*) to be resplendent; **an der Tür prangte ein Schild** a notice hung resplendent on the door; **an der Tür prangte sein Name in großen Lettern** his name was emblazoned in big letters on the door

Pran|ger ['praŋɐ] M **-s, -** stocks *pl*, pillory; **jdn/ etw an den ~ stellen** (*fig*) to pillory sb/sth; **am ~ stehen** (*lit*) to be in the stocks *or* pillory; (*fig*) to be being pilloried

Pran|ke ['praŋkə] F **-, -n** (= *Tierpranke*) paw; (*inf*: = *Hand*) paw (*inf*), mitt (*inf*)

Pran|ken|hieb M swipe *or* blow from a paw; **ein ~ des Löwen streckte die Antilope nieder** one blow *or* swipe from the lion's paw brought the antelope down

PR-An|zei|ge [peːʔɛr-] F promotional advert

Prä|pa|rat [prepa'raːt] NT **-(e)s, -e** preparation; (*für Mikroskop*) slide preparation

Prä|pa|ra|tor [prepa'raːtoːɐ] M **-s, Präparatoren** [-'toːrən], **Prä|pa|ra|to|rin** [-'toːrɪn] F **-, -nen** lab technician; (= *Tierpräparator*) taxidermist

prä|pa|rie|ren [prepa'riːrən] *ptp* **präpariert** VT **a** (= *konservieren*) to preserve; *Tier* to prepare **b** (*Med*: = *zerlegen*) to dissect **c** (*geh*: = *vorbereiten*) to prepare VR (*dated*) to prepare (oneself), to do one's preparation (*für, auf +acc* for)

Prä|po|si|ti|on [prepozi'tsi̯oːn] F **-, -en** preposition

prä|po|si|ti|o|nal [prepozitsi̯o'naːl] ADJ prepositional

Prä|rie [preˈriː] F **-, -n** [-'riːən] prairie

Prä|rie|wolf M prairie wolf, coyote

Prä|sens ['preːzɛns] NT **-, Präsenzien** [preˈzɛntsi̯ən] present (tense)

prä|sent [pre'zɛnt] ADJ (= *anwesend*) present; (= *geistig rege*) alert; **etw ~ haben** to have sth at hand; **sein Name ist mir nicht ~** his name escapes me

Prä|sent [pre'zɛnt] NT **-s, -e** present, gift

prä|sen|ta|bel [prezɛn'taːbl] ADJ presentable ADV presentably; **~ aussehen** to look presentable; **etw ~ herrichten** to make sth look presentable

Prä|sen|ta|ti|on [prezɛnta'tsi̯oːn] F **-, -en** presentation

prä|sen|tie|ren [prezɛn'tiːrən] *ptp* **präsentiert** VT to present; **jdm etw ~** to present sb with sth; **jdm die Rechnung (für etw) ~** (*fig*) to make sb pay the price (for sth); **präsentiert das Gewehr!** present arms! VR (= *sich zeigen*) to present oneself; (= *sich vorstellen auch*) to introduce oneself VI (*Mil*) to present arms

Prä|sen|tier|tel|ler M (*old*) salver; **auf dem ~ sitzen** (*fig*) to be on show; **jdm etw auf dem ~ servieren** (*fig*) to hand sb sth on a plate

Prä|sent|korb M gift basket; (*mit Lebensmitteln*) (food) hamper

Prä|senz [pre'zɛnts] F **-, no pl** (*geh*) presence; **die ständig abnehmende ~ im Abgeordnetenhaus** the constantly decreasing numbers in parliament

Prä|senz|bib|li|o|thek F reference library

Prä|sen|zi|en *pl von* **Präsens**

Prä|senz|lis|te F (attendance) register

Pra|se|o|dym [prazeo'dyːm] NT **-s, no pl** (*abbr* **Pr**) praseodymium

Prä|ser ['preːzɐ] M **-s, -** (*inf*) *abbr von* **Präservativ**

Prä|ser|va|tiv [prezɛrva'tiːf] NT **-s, -e** [-və] contraceptive, condom, sheath

Prä|si|dent [prezi'dɛnt] M **-en, -en**, **Prä|si|den|tin** [-'dɛntɪn] F **-, -nen** president; **Herr ~** Mister President; **Frau ~in** Madam President

Prä|si|den|ten|wahl F presidential election

Prä|si|dent|schaft [prezi'dɛntʃaft] F **-, -en** presidency

Prä|si|dent|schafts|kan|di|dat(in) M(F) presidential candidate

Prä|si|di|al|de|mo|kra|tie F presidential democracy

prä|si|die|ren [prezi'diːrən] *ptp* **präsidiert** VI to preside; **einem Ausschuss ~** to preside over a committee, to be president of a committee

Prä|si|di|um [pre'ziːdi̯ʊm] NT **-s, Präsidien** [-di̯ən] (= *Vorsitz*) presidency; (= *Führungsgruppe*) committee; (= *Gebäude*) headquarters (building); (= *Polizeipräsidium*) (police) headquarters *pl*; **ins ~ gewählt werden** to be elected to the committee; **das ~ übernehmen** to take the chair

pras|seln ['prasln] VI **a** *aux sein* to clatter; (*Regen, Hagel*) to drum; (*fig*: *Vorwürfe, Fragen*) to rain *or* hail down **b** (*Feuer*) to crackle; **~der Beifall** thunderous applause

pras|sen ['prasn] VI (= *schlemmen*) to feast; (= *in Luxus leben*) to live the high life

Pras|ser ['prasɐ] M **-s, -**, **Pras|se|rin** [-ərɪn] F **-, -nen** glutton; (= *Verschwender*) spendthrift

Pras|se|rei [prasə'rai] F **-, -en** (= *Schlemmerei*) feasting; (= *Luxusleben*) high life

Prä|ten|dent [preten'dɛnt] M **-en, -en**, **Prä|ten|den|tin** [-'dɛntɪn] F **-, -nen** pretender

prä|ten|ti|ös [preten'tsi̯øːs] ADJ (*geh*) pretentious

Prä|te|ri|tum [preˈteːritʊm] NT **-s, Präterita** [-ta] preterite

Prat|ze ['pratsə] F **-, -n** (*S Ger inf*) paw; (*fig*: = *Hand*) paw (*inf*), mitt (*inf*)

Prä|ven|ti|on [prevɛn'tsi̯oːn] F **-, -en** prevention (*gegen* of)

prä|ven|tiv [prevɛn'tiːf] ADJ prevent(at)ive ADV prevent(at)ively; *wirken, operieren* as a prevent(at)ive measure; **etw ~ bekämpfen** to use prevent(at)ive measures against sth; **die Polizei hat ~ eingegriffen** the police took prevent(at)ive measures

Prä|ven|tiv-: **Prä|ven|tiv|be|hand|lung** F (*Med*) prevent(at)ive treatment; **Prä|ven|tiv|krieg** M prevent(at)ive *or* pre-emptive war; **Prä|ven|tiv|maß|nah|me** F prevent(at)ive measure; **Prä|ven|tiv|me|di|zin** F prevent(at)ive medicine; **Prä|ven|tiv|schlag** M (*Mil*) pre-emptive strike

Pra|xis ['praksɪs] F **-, Praxen** ['praksn] **a** *no pl* practice; (= *Erfahrung*) experience; (= *Brauch*) practice, custom; **in der ~** in practice; **die ~ sieht anders aus** the facts are different; **etw in die ~ umsetzen** to put sth into practice; **ein Mann der ~** a man with practical experience; **ein Beispiel aus der ~** an example from real life; **das lernt man erst durch die** *or* **in der ~** you only learn that by doing it, that's only learned through practical experience; **seine langjährige künstlerische ~** his long years of artistic experience **b** (*eines Arztes, Rechtsanwalts*) practice; (= *Behandlungsräume*) surgery (*Brit*), doctor's office (*US*); (= *Anwaltsbüro*) office **c** (= *Sprechstunde*) consultation (hour), surgery (*Brit*)

Pra|xis-: **Pra|xis|be|zug** M foundation in reality; **ohne ~** with no foundation in reality; **pra|xis|fern, pra|xis|fremd** ADJ *Ausbildung* lacking in practical relevance; **jdn ~ ausbilden** to provide sb with training lacking in practical relevance; **Pra|xis|fer|ne** F (*von Studium*) lack of practical relevance; (*von Nachwuchs*) lack of practical experience; **pra|xis|nah** ADJ *Ausbildung* practically relevant ADV **jdn ~ ausbilden** to provide sb with practically relevant training; **Pra|xis|nä|he** F practical relevance; **pra|xis|ori|en|tiert** [-lorienti̯ːɐt] ADJ *Ausbildung, Lösung, Software* practically orientated ADV **jdn ~ ausbilden** to provide sb with a practically orientated training; **dort wird ~er gearbeitet** their work is practically orientated

Prä|ze|denz|fall M precedent; **einen ~ schaffen** to set *or* create *or* establish a precedent

prä|zis [pre'tsiːs], **prä|zi|se** [pre'tsiːzə] ADJ precise ADV precisely; *formulieren, schneiden* exactly; **sie arbeitet sehr ~** her work is very precise

prä|zi|sie|ren [pretsi'ziːrən] *ptp* **präzisiert** VT to state more precisely; (= *zusammenfassen*) to summarize

Prä|zi|si|on [pretsi'zi̯oːn] F **-, no pl** precision

Prä|zi|si|ons- *in cpds* precision; **Prä|zi|si|ons|ar|beit** F precision work; **~ leisten** to work with precision; **Prä|zi|si|ons|ins|tru|ment** NT precision instrument

pre|di|gen ['preːdɪgn] VT **a** (*Rel*) to preach; **solche Leute ~ immer Moral** people like that are always preaching (about) *or* sermonizing about morality → **Wein b** (*fig*) **jdm etw ~** to lecture sb on sth; **sie predigt ihm andauernd, dass er sich die Zähne putzen soll** she keeps lecturing him on the importance of cleaning his teeth VI to give a sermon, to preach; (*fig*: = *mahnen*) to preach, to sermonize; **tauben Ohren ~** to preach to deaf ears

Pre|di|ger ['preːdɪgɐ] M **-s, -**, **Pre|di|ge|rin** [-ərɪn] F **-, -nen** preacher

Pre|digt ['preːdɪçt] F **-, -en** (*lit, fig*) sermon; **jdm eine lange ~ über etw** (*acc*) **halten** (*fig*) to give sb a long sermon on *or* about sth

Pre|digt|text M text for a sermon

Preis [prais] M **-es, -e** **a** price (*für* of); (= *Fahrgeld*) fare (*für* for); (= *Gebühr, Honorar*) fee (*für* of); **der ~ für die Jacke beträgt 90 Euro** the price of the jacket is 90 euros; **(weit) unter(m) ~** cut-price; **etw unter ~ verkaufen/verschleudern** to sell/flog (*Brit inf*) sth off cheap; **zum halben ~** half-price; **um jeden ~** (*fig*) at all costs; **Qualität hat ihren ~** you have to pay for quality; **ich gehe um keinen ~ hier weg** (*fig*) I'm not leaving here at any price; **auch um den ~ seines eigenen Glücks** even at the expense of his own happiness

b (*bei Wettbewerben*) prize; (= *Auszeichnung*) award; **in diesem Rennen ist kein ~ ausgesetzt** there's no prize in *or* for this race; **den ersten ~ gewinnen** to win (the) first prize; **jdm einen ~ zusprechen** *or* **zuerkennen** *or* **verleihen** to award *or* give sb a prize/to give sb an award; **der Große ~ von Deutschland** the German Grand Prix

c (= *Belohnung*) reward; **einen ~ auf jds Kopf aussetzen** to put a price on sb's head

d *no pl* (*liter*: = *Lob*) praise (*auf +acc* of); **ein Gedicht zum ~ von ...** a poem in praise of ...; **~ sei Gott** praise be to God

Preis-: **Preis|ab|bau** M **, no pl** price reduction; **Preis|ab|spra|che** F price-fixing *no pl*; **Preis|än|de|rung** F price change; **Preis|an|ga|be** F price quotation; **alle Kleider sind mit ~** all dresses are priced, the prices of all dresses are given; **Preis|an|stieg** M rise in prices; **Preis|auf|ga|be** F prize competition; **Preis|auf|schlag** M supplementary charge, supplement; **Preis|auf|trieb** M price increase; **Preis|aus|schrei|ben** NT competition; **Preis|be|we|gung** F movement of prices; **preis|be|wusst** ▲ ADJ price-conscious ADV **~ ein|kaufen** to shop around; **Preis|bil|dung** F price fixing; **Preis|bin|dung** F price fixing; **~ der zweiten Hand** retail price maintenance; **Preis|bre|cher** M (*Produkt*) (all-time) bargain, snip (*Brit inf*), steal (*inf*); (*Firma*) undercutter; **diese Firma wirkt als ~ auf dem Markt** this firm undercuts the market; **Preis|dis|zip|lin** F price restraint; **Preis|ein|bruch** M price collapse

Prei|sel|bee|re ['praizl-] F cranberry

Preis-: **Preis|emp|feh|lung** F recommended price; **unverbindliche ~** recommended retail price, rrp, RRP

preis|emp|find|lich ADJ price-sensitive

prei|sen ['praizn] *pret* **pries** [priːs], *ptp* **gepriesen** [gə'priːzn] VT (*geh*) to extol, to praise, to laud (*liter*); **Gott sei gepriesen** praise be to God;

sich glücklich ~ to consider or count or think oneself lucky

Preis-: Preis|ent|wick|lung F price trend; **Preis|er|hö|hung** F price increase; **Preis|er|mä|ßi|gung** F price reduction; **Preis|ex|plo|si|on** F price explosion; **Preis|fra|ge** F **a** question of price **b** (beim Preisausschreiben) prize question (in a competition); (inf: = schwierige Frage) sixty-four thousand dollar question (inf), big question

Preis|ga|be F (geh) (= Aufgabe) surrender, relinquishment, abandoning; (von Gebiet) abandoning; (von Geheimnis) betrayal, divulgence; **sie wurden zur ~ ihrer Position gezwungen** they were forced to surrender or abandon or relinquish their position

preis+ge|ben VT sep irreg (geh) **a** (= ausliefern) to expose, to leave to the mercy of; **jdm/einer Sache preisgegeben sein** to be exposed to sb/ sth, to be at the mercy of sb/sth **b** (= aufgeben) to abandon, to relinquish; Gebiete to surrender, to abandon **c** (= verraten) to betray; Geheimnis to divulge, to betray

Preis-: Preis|ge|fäl|le NT price gap; **Preis|ge|fü|ge** NT price structure; **preis|ge|krönt** [-ɡəkrøːnt] ADJ award-winning; **~ werden** to be given an award; **Preis|ge|richt** NT jury, team of judges; **Preis|ge|stal|tung** F pricing (bei of); **eine ganz andere ~** a totally different price structure; **Preis|gren|ze** F price limit; **preis|güns|tig** ADJ inexpensive ADV kaufen inexpensively; **etw ~ bekommen** to get sth at a low or good price; **am ~sten kauft man im Supermarkt ein** you get the most for your money at the supermarket; **Preis|in|dex** M price index; **Preis|kampf** M price war; **Preis|klas|se** F price range; **die gehobene/mittlere/untere ~** the upper/medium/lower price range; **Preis|kon|trol|le** F price control; **Preis|krieg** M price war; **Preis|la|ge** F price range; **in jeder ~** at all prices, at prices to suit every pocket; **in der mittleren ~** in the medium-priced range; **Preis|la|wi|ne** F (inf) snowballing prices pl; **Preis-Leis|tungs-Ver|hält|nis** NT cost-effectiveness

preis|lich ['praislɪç] ADJ price attr, in price; **~e Wettbewerbsfähigkeit** price competitiveness ADV **~ niedriger/vorteilhaft** lower/favourably (Brit) or favorably (US) priced; **~ günstig/höher** reasonably/higher priced; **~ vergleichbar** similarly priced; **sie sind ~ unterschiedlich** they differ in price; **dieses Angebot ist ~ sehr günstig** this offer is a bargain; **die Waren sind nur ~ verschieden** the goods only differ in price

Preis-: Preis|lis|te F price list; **Preis|nach|lass** ▲ M price reduction; **10% ~ bei Barzahlung** 10% off cash sales; **Preis|ni|veau** NT price level; **Preis|po|li|tik** F pricing policy; **Preis|rät|sel** NT prize competition; **Preis|rich|ter(in)** M(F) judge (in a competition), jury member; **Preis|schie|ßen** NT -s, no pl shooting competition or contest, shoot; **Preis|schild** NT price tag; **Preis|schla|ger** M (all-time) bargain; **Preis|schwan|kung** F price fluctuation; **Preis|sen|kung** F price cut; **Preis|span|ne** F price margin; **preis|sta|bil** ADJ stable in price; **Preis|sta|bi|li|tät** F price stability; **Preis|stei|ge|rung** F price increase; **Preis|stei|ge|rungs|ra|te** F rate of price increases; **Preis|stopp** M price freeze; **Preis|sturz** M sudden fall or drop in prices; **Preis|sys|tem** NT price or pricing system, system of prices; **Preis|trä|ger(in)** M(F) prizewinner; (= Kulturpreisträger) award-winner; **Preis|trei|ber(in)** M(F) person who forces prices up; **Preis|trei|be|rei** [-traibə'rai] F -, -en forcing up of prices; (= Wucher) profiteering; **das ist nur ein Vorwand für die ~ der Industrie** that's only an excuse for industry to force up prices; **Preis|über|wa|chung** F price control; **Preis|un|ter|schied** M difference in price(s), price differential; **Preis|ver|fall** M drop-off in prices; **Preis|ver|gleich** M price comparison; **einen ~ machen** to shop around; **Preis|ver|**

lei|hung F presentation (of prizes); (von Auszeichnung) presentation (of awards); **preis|wert** ADJ good value pred; **ein (sehr) ~es Angebot** a (real) bargain; **ein ~es Kleid** a dress which is good value (for money) ADV inexpensively; **hier kann man ~ einkaufen** you get good value (for money) here; **am ~esten kauft man im Supermarkt ein** you get the most for your money at the supermarket

pre|kär [pre'kɛːɐ] ADJ (= peinlich) awkward, embarrassing; (= schwierig) precarious

Prell-: Prell|ball M game similar to volleyball in which the ball is bounced over the net; **Prell|bock** M (Rail) buffers pl, buffer stop; **der ~ sein** (fig) to be the scapegoat or fall guy (esp US inf)

prel|len ['prɛlən] VT **a** Körperteil to bruise; (= anschlagen) to hit **b** (fig inf: = betrügen) to swindle, to cheat; **jdm um etw ~** to swindle or cheat sb out of sth → **Zeche c** (Sport) to bounce VR to bruise oneself; **ich habe mich am** or **mir den Arm geprellt** I've bruised my arm

Prel|le|rei [prɛlə'rai] F -, -en swindle, fraud

Prell|schuss ▲ M ricochet, ricocheting bullet

Prel|lung ['prɛlʊŋ] F -, -en bruise, contusion

Pre|mier [prə'mie:, pre-] M -s, -s premier

Pre|mie|re [prə'mie:rə, pre-, -'miɛːrə] F -, -n premiere

Pre|mie|ren-: Pre|mie|ren|be|su|cher PL , **Pre|mie|ren|pu|bli|kum** NT premiere audience no pl; **Pre|mie|ren|ki|no** NT first-run cinema

Pre|mier|mi|nis|ter(in) [prə'mie:-, pre-] M(F) prime minister

Pres|by|te|ri|a|ner [presbyte'ria:nɐ] M -s, -, **Pres|by|te|ri|a|ne|rin** [-ərɪn] F -, -nen Presbyterian

pres|by|te|ri|a|nisch [presbyte'ria:nɪʃ] ADJ Presbyterian

pre|schen ['prɛʃn] VI aux sein (inf) to tear, to dash

pres|sant [prɛ'sant] ADJ (inf) urgent; **es ~ haben** to be in a hurry

Pres|se ['prɛsə] F -, -n **a** (= mechanische Presse, Druckmaschine) press; **in die ~ gehen** to go to press; **frisch** or **eben aus der ~** hot from the press **b** (= Zeitungen) press; **eine gute/schlechte ~ haben** to have or get a good/bad press; **von der ~ sein** to be (a member of the) press

Pres|se-: Pres|se|agen|tur F press or news agency; **Pres|se|amt** NT press office; **Pres|se|at|ta|ché** M press attaché; **Pres|se|aus|weis** M press card; **Pres|se|be|richt** M press report; **Pres|se|bü|ro** NT press or news agency; **Pres|se|dienst** M news service; **Pres|se|emp|fang** M press reception; **Pres|se|er|klä|rung** F statement to the press; (schriftlich) press release; **Pres|se|fo|to|graf(in)** M(F) press photographer; **Pres|se|frei|heit** F freedom of the press; **Pres|se|ge|setz** NT press law; **Pres|se|jar|gon** M journalese; **Pres|se|kam|pa|gne** F press campaign; **Pres|se|kar|te** F press or review ticket; **Pres|se|kom|men|tar** M press commentary; **Pres|se|kon|fe|renz** F press conference; **Pres|se|map|pe** F press kit; **Pres|se|mel|dung** F press report; **Pres|se|mit|tei|lung** F press release or announcement

pres|sen ['prɛsn] VT **a** (= quetschen) to press; Obst, Saft to squeeze; hohe Töne to squeeze out; (fig: = zwingen) to force (in +acc, zu into); (fig dated: = unterdrücken) to oppress; **frisch gepresster Orangensaft** freshly squeezed orange juice; **eine CD ~** to press a CD; **etw auf CD-ROM ~** to put sth onto CD-ROM; **mit gepresster Stimme** in a strained voice **b** (Naut) Segel ~ to make too much sail

Pres|se-: Pres|se|no|tiz F paragraph in the press; **Pres|se|or|gan** NT press organ; **Pres|se|recht** NT press laws pl; **Pres|se|refe|rent(in)** M(F) press officer; **Pres|se|rum|mel** M (inf) press furore (Brit) or furor (US), media

frenzy; **Pres|se|spre|cher(in)** M(F) press officer; **Pres|se|stel|le** F press office; **Pres|se|stim|me** F press commentary; (kulturell) press review; **Pres|se|tri|bü|ne** F press box; (Parl) press gallery; **Pres|se|ver|tre|ter(in)** M(F) representative of the press; **Pres|se|we|sen** NT press; **Pres|se|zar(in)** M(F) (inf) press baron

Press|glas ▲ NT pressed glass

pres|sie|ren [prɛ'siːrən] ptp **pressiert** (S Ger, Aus, Sw) VI to be in a hurry VI impers **es pressiert** it's urgent; **(bei) ihm pressiert es immer** he's always in a hurry

Pres|si|on [prɛ'sio:n] F -, -en pressure

Press|kopf ▲ M , no pl → Presssack

Press|koh|le ▲ F briquette

Press|luft ▲ F compressed air

Press|luft-: Press|luft|boh|rer ▲ M pneumatic drill; **Press|luft|ham|mer** ▲ M pneumatic or air hammer

Press|sack ▲ M , no pl (Cook) brawn (Brit), headcheese (US)

Press|we|hen ▲ PL (bei Geburt) bearing-down pains pl, expulsive pains pl (spec)

Pres|ti|ge [prɛs'ti:ʒə] NT -s, no pl prestige; **~ verlieren** to lose (one's) prestige

Pres|ti|ge-: Pres|ti|ge|den|ken NT status mentality; **Pres|ti|ge|fra|ge** F question or matter of prestige; **Pres|ti|ge|ge|winn** M gain in prestige; **Pres|ti|ge|sa|che** F question or matter of prestige; **Pres|ti|ge|ver|lust** M loss of prestige

Prêt-à-por|ter- [prɛtapɔrte:] in cpds ready-to-wear; **Prêt-à-por|ter-Kol|lek|ti|on** F ready-to-wear collection

pre|ti|ös ▲ [pre'tsiø:s] ADJ (geh) = preziös

Pre|ti|o|sen [pre'tsio:zn] PL (geh) valuables pl

Preu|ße ['prɔysə] M -n, -n, **Preu|ßin** [-sɪn] F -, -nen Prussian; (fig) strict disciplinarian; **so schnell schießen die ~n nicht** (inf) things don't happen that fast

Preu|ßen ['prɔysn] NT -s Prussia

preu|ßisch ['prɔysɪʃ] ADJ Prussian

preu|ßisch|blau ADJ Prussian blue

pre|zi|ös [pre'tsiø:s] ADJ (geh) precious

PR-Fach|frau [peː'ɛr-] F , **PR-Fach|mann** M PR specialist

Pri|cke ['prɪkə] F -, -n (Naut) shallows marker

pri|ckeln ['prɪkln] VI (= kribbeln) to tingle; (= kitzeln) to tickle; (= Bläschen bilden) to sparkle, to bubble; **die Limonade prickelt in der Nase** the lemonade's tickling my nose; **ein angenehmes Prickeln auf der Haut** a pleasant tingling of the skin; **ich spürte ein Prickeln in meinem Bein** I had pins and needles in my leg; **die Atmosphäre prickelte vor Spannung** the atmosphere was electric

pri|ckelnd ADJ (= kribbelnd) tingling; (= kitzelnd) tickling; (= Bläschen bildend) sparkling, bubbling; (fig) (= würzig) piquant; (= erregend) Gefühl tingling; **der ~ Reiz der Neuheit** the thrill of novelty; **etwas Prickelndes für den Gaumen** something to titillate the taste buds (hum)

Priel [priːl] M -(e)s, -e narrow channel (in North Sea mud flats), tideway

Priem [priːm] M -(e)s, -e quid of tobacco

prie|men ['priːmən] VI to chew tobacco

pries pret von **preisen**

Pries|ter ['priːstɐ] M -s, - priest

Pries|ter|amt NT priesthood

Pries|te|rin ['priːstərɪn] F -, -nen (woman) priest; (Hist) priestess

pries|ter|lich ['priːstəlɪç] ADJ priestly no adv; Kleidung auch clerical ADV **er war ~ gekleidet** he was dressed like a priest

Pries|ter-: Pries|ter|rock M cassock; **Pries|ter|schaft** ['priːstəʃaft] F -, -en priesthood; **Pries|ter|se|mi|nar** NT seminary; **Pries|ter|**

tum ['priːstɛtuːm] NT **-s**, *no pl* priesthood; **Pries|ter|wei|he** F ordination (to the priesthood); **die ~ empfangen** to be ordained (to the priesthood *or* as a priest); **jdm die ~ spenden** to confer holy orders on sb

pri|ma ['priːma] ADJ *inv* **a** (*inf*) fantastic (*inf*), great *no adv* (*inf*) first-class, top-quality ADV (*inf:* = *sehr gut*) fantastically; **das hast du ~ gemacht** you did that fantastically (well) *or* beautifully *or* just great

Pri|ma ['priːma] F **-, Primen** [-mən] (*dated Sch*) *eighth and ninth year of German secondary school* (*Aus*) *first year of secondary school*

Pri|ma-: Pri|ma|bal|le|ri|na [primabalə'riːna] F prima ballerina; **Pri|ma|don|na** [prima'dɔna] F **-, Primadonnen** [-'dɔnən] prima donna

Pri|ma|ner [pri'maːnɐ] M **-s**, **-**, **Pri|ma|ne|rin** [-ərɪn] F **-, -nen** (*dated Sch*) ≈ sixth-former (*Brit*), ≈ twelfth grader (*US*); (*Aus*) first-former

pri|mär [pri'mɛːɐ] ADJ primary ADV primarily

Pri|mär-: Pri|mär|ener|gie F primary energy; **Pri|mär|kreis|lauf** M primary circuit

Pri|mar|leh|rer(in) [pri'maːɐ-] M(F) (*Sw*) primary school teacher

Pri|mär|li|te|ra|tur F primary literature *or* sources *pl*

Pri|mar|schu|le [pri'maːɐ-] F (*Sw*) primary *or* junior school

Pri|mas ['priːmas] M **-, -se** *or* **Primaten** [pri'maːtn] (*Eccl*) primate; (*in Zigeunerkapelle*) first violin

Pri|mat[1] [pri'maːt] M OR NT **-(e)s, -e** priority, primacy (*vor* +*dat* over); (*des Papstes*) primacy; (= *Erstgeburtsrecht*) primogeniture

Pri|mat[2] M **-en, -en** (*Zool*) primate

Pri|ma|ten *pl von* **Primas** *or* **Primat**[2]

Pri|mel ['priːml] F **-, -n** (= *Waldprimel*) (wild) primrose; (= *Schlüsselblume*) cowslip; (= *farbige Gartenprimel*) primula; (*mit verzweigtem Stiel*) polyanthus; **wie eine ~ eingehen** (*fig*) to fade *or* wither away

Pri|men *pl von* **Prima**

Pri|mi *pl von* **Primus**

pri|mi|tiv [primi'tiːf] ADJ primitive; *Maschine auch* crude ADV primitively

Pri|mi|ti|ve(r) [primi'tiːvə] MF *decl as adj* primitive

Pri|mi|ti|vi|tät [primitivi'tɛːt] F **-, -en** primitiveness; (*von Maschine auch*) crudeness

Pri|mi|tiv|ling [primi'tiːflɪŋ] M **-s, -e** (*pej inf*) peasant (*pej inf*), primitive (*pej inf*)

Pri|mus ['priːmʊs] M **-, -se** *or* **Primi** [-mi] top of the class, top *or* star pupil

Prim|zahl ['priːm-] F prime (number)

Prin|te ['prɪntə] F **-, -n** (*Gebäck*) oblong spiced biscuit

Print|me|di|um ['prɪntmeːdiʊm] NT *usu pl* printed medium; **die Werbung in Fernsehen und Printmedien** advertising on television and in printed media

Prinz [prɪnts] M **-en, -en** prince; **wie ein ~ leben** (*inf*) to live like a lord (*Brit*) *or* a king; **unser kleiner ~** (*inf:* = *Sohn*) our son and heir (*inf*); **Johann Georg ~ von Hohenzollern** Johann Georg, Prince of Hohenzollern

Prin|zen-: Prin|zen|gar|de F (*im Karneval*) King's Guard; **Prin|zen|paar** NT **a** (*Adelige*) princely couple **b** (*im Karneval*) Carnival King and Queen *or* Prince and Princess

Prin|zes|sin [prɪn'tsɛsɪn] F **-, -nen** princess; **Ag|nes ~ von Polen** Agnes, Princess of Poland; **die ~ auf der Erbse** (*Liter*) the Princess and the Pea; **eine ~ auf der Erbse** (*fig*) a hothouse plant

Prinz|ge|mahl M prince consort

Prin|zip [prɪn'tsiːp] NT **-s, -ien** [-piən] *or* (*rare*) **-e** principle; **aus ~** on principle; **das hat er aus ~ getan** he did it on principle, he did it as a matter of principle; **im ~** in principle; **das funktio|niert nach einem einfachen ~** it works on a

simple principle; **nach einem ~ handeln** to act according to a principle; **etw zum ~ erheben** *or* **machen** to make sth into a principle; **er ist ein Mann von** *or* **mit ~ien** he is a man of principle; **das ~ Hoffnung** the principle of hope

Prin|zi|pal [prɪntsi'paːl] M **-s, -e**, **Prin|zi|pa|lin** [-'paːlɪn] F **-, -nen a** (= *Theaterleiter*) theatre (*Brit*) *or* theater (*US*) director **b** (*old*) (= *Geschäftsinhaber*) proprietor; (= *Lehrherr*) master

prin|zi|pi|ell [prɪntsi'piɛl] ADJ (= *im Prinzip*) in principle; (= *aus Prinzip*) on principle ADV **a** (= *im Prinzip*) möglich theoretically; *dafür/dagegen sein* basically; **~ bin ich einverstanden** I agree in principle **b** (= *aus Prinzip*) ablehnen, gegen *etw sein, sich weigern* on principle; **das tue ich ~ nicht** I won't do that on principle

Prin|zi|pien- [prɪn'tsiːpiən-]: **prin|zi|pi|en|fest** ADJ *Mensch* firm-principled, of firm principles; *Politik* principled; **Prin|zi|pi|en|fra|ge** F matter *or* question of principle; **Prin|zi|pi|en|los** ADJ unprincipled ADV **sich ~ verhalten** to be unprincipled; **Prin|zi|pi|en|lo|sig|keit** F **-**, *no pl* lack of principle(s); **Prin|zi|pi|en|rei|ter(in)** M(F) (*pej*) stickler for one's principles; **Prin|zi|pi|en|rei|te|rei** F (*pej*) going-on about principles (*pej*); **Prin|zi|pi|en|streit** M dispute about principles

Prinz|re|gent M prince regent

Pri|on ['priːɔn] NT **-s, -e** [pri'oːnə] (*Biol*) prion

Pri|or ['priːoːɐ] M **-s, Prioren** [pri'oːrən] prior

Pri|o|rin [pri'oːrɪn] F **-, -nen** prioress

Pri|o|ri|tät [priori'tɛːt] F **-, -en a** priority; **~ vor etw** (*dat*) **haben** to have *or* take priority *or* precedence over sth; **erste** *or* **höchste ~ haben** to have top priority; **~en setzen** to establish one's priorities; **die richtigen/falschen ~en setzen** to get one's priorities right/wrong; **jdm/etw (höchste) ~ einräumen** to give sb/sth (top) priority **b Prioritäten** PL (*Comm*) preference shares *pl*, preferred stock (*US*)

Pri|o|ri|tä|ten|lis|te F list of priorities

Pri|se ['priːzə] F **-, -n a** (= *kleine Menge*) pinch; **eine ~ Salz** a pinch of salt; **eine ~ Humor** a touch of humour (*Brit*) *or* humor (*US*) **b** (*Naut*) prize

Pris|ma ['prɪsma] NT **-s, Prismen** [-mən] prism

pris|ma|tisch [prɪs'maːtɪʃ] ADJ prismatic

Pris|men *pl von* **Prisma**

Pris|men|glas NT prismatic telescope

Prit|sche ['prɪtʃə] F **-, -n a** (= *Narrenpritsche*) fool's wand **b** (*von LKW*) platform **c** (= *Liegestatt*) plank bed

prit|schen ['prɪtʃn] VT (*Volleyball*) to pass (the ball) with both hands

Prit|schen|wa|gen M platform truck

pri|vat [pri'vaːt] ADJ private; *Telefonnummer auch* home *attr*; **etw an Privat verkaufen/von Privat kaufen** (*Comm*) to sell sth to/to buy sth from private individuals; **aus ~er Hand** from private individuals

ADV **a** (= *als Privatperson*) privately; **~ wohnt sie in einer Villa** she lives in a villa; **~ ist der Chef sehr freundlich** the boss is very friendly out(side) of work; **jdn ~ sprechen** to speak to sb privately *or* in private **b** (*von Privatpersonen*) finanzieren, unterstützen privately **c** (= *individuell*) **jdn ~ unterbringen** to put sb up privately; **ich sagte es ihm ganz ~** I told him in private **d** (= *nicht gesetzlich*) **~ versichert sein** to be privately insured; **~ behandelt werden** to have private treatment; **~ liegen** to be in a private ward

Pri|vat- *in cpds* private; **Pri|vat|ad|res|se** F private *or* home address; **Pri|vat|an|ge|le|gen|heit** F private matter; **das ist eine reine ~** that's a purely *or* strictly private matter; **das ist meine ~** that's my own business, that's a private matter; **Pri|vat|aus|ga|ben** PL personal

expenses *pl*; **Pri|vat|be|sitz** M private property; **viele Gemälde sind** *or* **befinden sich in ~** many paintings are *or* are in private ownership; **in ~ befindliche Grundstü|cke** privately owned land; **Pri|vat|de|tek|tiv(in)** M(F) private detective *or* investigator *or* eye (*inf*); **Pri|vat|do|zent(in)** M(F) outside lecturer; **Pri|vat|ei|gen|tum** NT private property; **Pri|vat|fern|se|hen** NT commercial television; **Pri|vat|funk** M commercial broadcasting; **Pri|vat|ge|brauch** M private use, personal use; **die sind für den ~** they're for your own (personal) use; **Pri|vat|ge|lehr|te(r)** MF *decl as adj* scholar (*working for himself/herself*); **Pri|vat|ge|spräch** NT private conversation *or* talk; (*am Telefon*) private call; **Pri|vat|grund|stück** NT private property

Pri|va|tier [priva'tieː] M **-s, -s** (*dated*) man of independent *or* private means

Pri|vat-: Pri|vat|ini|ti|a|ti|ve F private initiative; **Pri|vat|in|te|res|se** NT private interest

pri|va|ti|sie|ren [privati'ziːrən] *ptp* **privatisiert** VT to privatize VI to live on a private income *or* on independent means

Pri|va|ti|sie|rung F **-, -en** privatization

Pri|vat-: Pri|vat|kla|ge F private action *or* suit; **Pri|vat|klä|ger(in)** M(F) private litigant; **Pri|vat|kli|nik** F private clinic *or* hospital, nursing home; **Pri|vat|le|ben** NT private life; **Pri|vat|leh|rer(in)** M(F) private tutor; **Pri|vat|mann** M *pl* **-leute** private person *or* individual; **Pri|vat|mit|tel** F (= *Privatnummer*) private means *pl*; **Pri|vat|num|mer** F (= *Telefonnummer*) private number, home number; **Pri|vat|pa|ti|ent(in)** M(F) private patient; **Pri|vat|per|son** F private individual *or* person; **Pri|vat|quar|tier** NT private quarters *pl*; **Pri|vat|recht** NT private *or* civil law; **pri|vat|recht|lich** ADJ *Klage, Verfahren* private *or* civil law *attr*; *Gesellschaft* private ADV **~ ist die Frage ganz eindeutig** the matter is quite clear in private *or* civil law; **Pri|vat|sa|che** F private matter; **das ist meine ~** that's my own business, that's a private matter; **das ist eine reine ~** that's a purely *or* strictly private matter; **Religion ist ~** religion is a private matter; **Pri|vat|schu|le** F private school; (= *Eliteschule auch*) ≈ public school (*Brit*); **Pri|vat|sek|re|tär(in)** M(F) private secretary; **Pri|vat|sek|tor** M private sector; **Pri|vat|un|ter|neh|men** NT private enterprise; **Pri|vat|un|ter|richt** M private tuition; **Pri|vat|ver|gnü|gen** NT (*inf*) private pleasure; **Pri|vat|ver|mö|gen** NT private fortune; **Pri|vat|ver|si|che|rung** F private insurance; **Pri|vat|weg** M private way; **Pri|vat|wirt|schaft** F private industry; **Pri|vat|woh|nung** F private flat (*Brit*) *or* apartment; (*Haus*) private house

Pri|vi|leg [privi'leːk] NT **-(e)s, -gien** *or* **-e** [-giən, -gə] privilege

pri|vi|le|gie|ren [privile'giːrən] *ptp* **privilegiert** VT to favour (*Brit*), to favor (*US*), to privilege; **die privilegierten Schichten** the privileged classes; **eine privilegierte Stellung innehaben** to hold a privileged position; **steuerlich privilegiert sein** to enjoy tax privileges

pro [proː] PREP per; **~ Tag/Stunde** a *or* per day/hour; **~ Jahr** per annum (*form*), a *or* per year; **~ Quadratmeter** a *or* per square metre (*Brit*) *or* meter (*US*); **~ Person** per person; **~ Kopf** per person, per capita (*form*); **~ Nase** (*inf*) a *or* per head; **~ Stück** each, apiece; **~ Kopf und Tag** per person per day

Pro [proː] NT **(das) ~ und (das) Kontra** the pros and cons *pl*

Pro|band [pro'bant] M **-en, -en** [-dn], **Pro|ban|din** [-'bandɪn] F **-, -nen** guinea pig

pro|bat [pro'baːt] ADJ *no adv* (*dated*) tried and tested

Pro|be ['proːbə] F **-, -n a** (= *Prüfung*) test; **eine ~ auf etw** (*acc*) **machen** to test sth, to do a test on sth; **die ~ (auf eine Rechnung) machen** to check a calculation; **wenn du die ~ gemacht hättest** if you'd checked it, if you'd given it a check; **ein Beamter auf ~** a probationary civil servant; **er ist auf ~ angestellt** he's employed for a probationary period; **jdn/etw auf ~ nehmen** to take sb/sth on trial; **~ fahren** to go for a test drive or run; **ein Auto ~ fahren** to test-drive a car; **jdn/etw auf die ~ stellen** to put sb/sth to the test, to try sb/sth; **meine Geduld wurde auf eine harte ~ gestellt** my patience was sorely tried; **jdn/etw einer ~ unterziehen** to subject sb/sth to a test; **zur ~** for a trial, to try out → **Exempel**

b (*Theat, Mus*) rehearsal; **~n abhalten** to rehearse, to hold rehearsals

c (= *Teststück, Beispiel*) sample; **er gab eine ~ seines Könnens** he showed what he could do

Pro|be-: **Pro|be|ab|zug** M proof; **Pro|be|alarm** M practice alarm; **heute ist ~ the** alarms will be tested today; **Pro|be|an|ge|bot** NT trial offer; **Pro|be|ar|beit** F test or specimen piece, trial work no pl; **Pro|be|be|las|tung** F stress test; **Pro|be|boh|rung** F test drill, probe; **Pro|be|druck** M pl **-drucke** trial print; **Pro|be|exem|plar** NT specimen (copy); **pro|be|fah|ren** △ **VT VI** → **Probe** a; **Pro|be|fahrt** F test drive or run; (*mit Boot*) trial sail; (*mit Fahrrad*) test ride; **eine ~ machen** to go for a test drive etc; **Pro|be|flug** M test flight; **pro|be|hal|ber** ADV for a test; **Pro|be|jahr** NT probationary year; **Pro|be|lauf** M test or trial run; (*Sport*) practice run; **Pro|be|leh|rer(in)** M(F) probationary teacher

pro|ben ['pro:bn] VTI to rehearse

Pro|ben-: **Pro|ben|ar|beit** F rehearsals pl; **Pro|ben|ent|nah|me** F sampling

Pro|be-: **Pro|be|num|mer** F trial copy; **Pro|be|pa|ckung** F sample pack; **Pro|be|sei|te** F specimen or sample page; **Pro|be|sen|dung** F (*von Ware*) sample pack; **Pro|be|stück** NT sample, specimen; **pro|be|wei|se** ADV on a trial basis; **ich habe mir ~ einen anderen Kaffee gekauft** I've bought another kind of coffee to try (out); **Pro|be|zeit** F probationary or trial period

pro|bie|ren [pro'bi:rən] ptp **probiert** **VT** **a** (= *versuchen*) to try, to have a go (*Brit*) or try at; (= *prüfen*) to try (out), to test; **~ Sie es noch mal!** try (it) again!, have another go (*Brit*) or try!; **lass (es) mich mal ~!** let me try!, let me have a go (*Brit*) or a try!

b (= *kosten*) Speisen, Getränke to try, to taste, to sample

c (= *proben*) to rehearse

VI **a** (= *versuchen*) to try, to have a go (*Brit*) or a try; **Kinder lernen durch Probieren** children learn by trial and error; **Probieren geht über Studieren** (*Prov*) the proof of the pudding is in the eating (*Prov*)

b (= *kosten*) to have a taste, to try; **probier mal** try some, have a taste

c (= *proben*) to rehearse

Pro|bie|rer [pro'bi:rɐ] M **-s,** -, **Pro|bie|re|rin** [-ərɪn] F **-,** **-nen** taster

Pro|bier|glas [pro'bi:ɐ-] NT **a** (*zum Kosten*) taster, tasting glass **b** (= *Reagenzglas*) test tube

Prob|lem [pro'ble:m] **☉** 38.3, 44.1, 53.1, 53.2, 53.3 NT **-s,** -e problem; **vor einem ~ stehen** to be faced or confronted with a problem; **das wird zum ~** it's becoming (something of) a problem; **~e wälzen** to turn problems over in one's mind

Prob|le|ma|tik [proble'ma:tɪk] F **-,** -en **a** (= *Schwierigkeit, Problem*) difficulty (+gen with); **die ~ der modernen Soziologie** the problems of modern sociology **b** (= *Fragwürdigkeit*) questionability, problematic nature

prob|le|ma|tisch [proble'ma:tɪʃ] ADJ problematic; (= *fragwürdig*) questionable

Prob|lem-: **Prob|lem|be|wusst|sein** ▲ NT appreciation of the difficulties or problem; **Prob|lem|fall** M problem (case), problematic case; **Prob|lem|kind** NT problem child; **Prob|lem|kreis** M problem area; **prob|lem|los** ADV trouble-free, problem-free ADV with-

out any problems; **~ ablaufen** to go smoothly, to go without any problems; **Prob|lem|ori|en|tiert** ADJ (*auch Comput*) problem-oriented; **Prob|lem|stel|lung** F problem; **Prob|lem|stück** NT problem play; **Prob|lem|zo|ne** F problem area

Pro|ce|de|re [pro:'tse:dərə] NT **-,** - (*geh*) proceedings pl

Pro|duct-Place|ment ▲ ['prɔdakt'ple:smənt] NT **-s,** -s, **Pro|duct|place|ment** ▲ NT **-s,** -s product placement

Pro|dukt [pro'dʊkt] NT **-(e)s,** -e (*lit, fig*) product; **landwirtschaftliche ~e** agricultural produce no pl or products; **das ~ aus 2 mal 2** the product of 2 times 2; **ein ~ seiner Phantasie** a figment of his imagination

Pro|duk|ten-: **Pro|duk|ten|han|del** M produce business or trade; **Pro|duk|ten|markt** M produce market

Pro|dukt|haf|tung F product liability

Pro|duk|ti|on [prodʊk'tsio:n] F **-,** -en production

Pro|duk|ti|ons- in cpds production; **Pro|duk|ti|ons|ab|lauf** M production process or sequence; **Pro|duk|ti|ons|an|la|gen** PL production plant; **Pro|duk|ti|ons|aus|fall** M loss of production; **Pro|duk|ti|ons|be|schrän|kung** F limitation of production; **Pro|duk|ti|ons|ge|nos|sen|schaft** F (*esp DDR*) collective, cooperative; **landwirtschaftliche ~** collective farm; **~ des Handwerks** craftsmen's cooperative; **Pro|duk|ti|ons|kos|ten** PL production costs pl; **Pro|duk|ti|ons|kraft** F production capacity; **Pro|duk|ti|ons|leis|tung** F (potential) output, production capacity; **Pro|duk|ti|ons|lei|ter(in)** M(F) production manager; **pro|duk|ti|ons|mä|ßig** ADJ production attr ADV in terms of production; **Pro|duk|ti|ons|men|ge** F output; **Pro|duk|ti|ons|mit|tel** PL means of production pl; **pro|duk|ti|ons|reif** ADJ ready to go into production; **Pro|duk|ti|ons|rei|fe** F vom Entwurf bis zur **~** from conception to production; **dieser Artikel hat die ~ noch nicht erreicht** this article is not yet ready to go into production; **Pro|duk|ti|ons|rück|gang** M drop in production; **Pro|duk|ti|ons|stand** M production level; **Pro|duk|ti|ons|stät|te** F production centre (*Brit*) or center (*US*); **Pro|duk|ti|ons|zweig** M line of production

pro|duk|tiv [prodʊk'ti:f] ADJ Autor, Arbeit etc productive

Pro|duk|ti|vi|tät [prodʊktivi'tɛ:t] F **-,** -en productivity

Pro|duk|ti|vi|täts|stei|ge|rung F increase or rise in productivity, increased productivity

Pro|duk|tiv|kräf|te PL (*Sociol*) productive forces pl, forces of production pl

Pro|duk|tiv|ver|mö|gen NT (*Econ*) productive assets pl

Pro|dukt-: **Pro|dukt|ma|na|ger(in)** M(F) product manager; **Pro|dukt|pa|let|te** F product spectrum; **Pro|dukt|pi|ra|te|rie** F product piracy

Pro|du|zent [produ'tsɛnt] M **-en,** -en, **Pro|du|zen|tin** [-'tsɛntɪn] F **-,** -nen producer

pro|du|zie|ren [produ'tsi:rən] ptp **produziert** **VT** **a** auch vi to produce; **~des Gewerbe** production industry **b** (*inf:* = *hervorbringen*) Lärm to make; Entschuldigung to come up with (*inf*); Romane to churn out (*inf*); **wer hat denn das produziert?** who's responsible for that? **VR** (*pej*) to show off

Prof [prɔf] M **-s,** -s (*Univ inf*) prof (*inf*)

Prof. abbr von **Professor**

Pro Fa|mi|lia ['pro fa'mi:lia] F **- -,** no pl family planning organization

pro|fan [pro'fa:n] ADJ (= *weltlich*) secular, profane; (= *gewöhnlich*) mundane

Pro|fan|bau M pl **-bauten** secular building

pro|fa|nie|ren [profa'ni:rən] ptp **profaniert** VT (*form*) to profane

Pro|fes|si|on [profe'sio:n] F **-,** -en (old, form) profession; **eine ~ ausüben** to ply a trade (*old*), to follow a profession (*form*)

Pro|fes|si|o|nal [pro'fɛʃənəl] M **-s,** -s professional

Pro|fes|si|o|na|li|tät [profesionali'tɛ:t] F **-,** no pl professionalism

pro|fes|si|o|nell [profesio'nɛl] ADJ professional; **eine Professionelle** (*inf*) a pro (*inf*), a tart (*inf*) ADV professionally

Pro|fes|sor [pro'fɛsoːɐ] M **-s,** Professoren [-'soːrən] **a** (= *Hochschulprofessor*) professor; **or|dentlicher ~ für Philosophie** (full) professor of philosophy; **außerordentlicher ~** professor not holding a chair, ≈ associate professor (*US*); **Herr/Frau ~!** Professor!; **Herr ~ Vogel** Professor Vogel **b** (*Aus, S Ger:* = *Gymnasiallehrer*) teacher; **Herr ~!** Sir!; **Frau ~!** Miss!

pro|fes|so|ral [profeso'ra:l] (*geh*) ADJ professorial ADV like a professor, professorially (*pej*)

Pro|fes|so|ren|schaft [profe'so:rənʃaft] F **-,** -en professors pl

Pro|fes|so|rin [profe'so:rɪn] F **-,** -nen **a** (= *Hochschulprofessorin*) professor **b** (*Aus, S Ger:* = *Gymnasiallehrerin*) teacher

Pro|fes|sur [profe'su:ɐ] F **-,** -en chair (*für* in, of)

Pro|fi ['pro:fi] M **-s,** -s (*inf*) pro (*inf*)

Pro|fi|kil|ler(in) M(F) professional or contract killer

Pro|fil [pro'fi:l] NT **-s,** -e **a** (*von Gesicht*) profile; (*Archit*) elevation; (*fig:* = *Ansehen*) image; **im ~** in profile; **~ haben** or **besitzen** (*fig*) to have a (distinctive or personal) image; **die Partei hat in den letzten Jahren mehr ~ bekommen** over the last few years the party has sharpened its image; **dadurch hat er an ~ gewonnen/verloren** that improved/damaged his image; **psychisches ~** state of mind **b** (*von Reifen, Schuhsohle*) tread **c** (= *Querschnitt*) cross section; (= *Längsschnitt*) vertical section; (*Geog*) (vertical) section; (*Aviat*) wing section; (*fig:* = *Skizze*) profile; **im ~** in section

Pro|fi|la|ger NT (*Sport inf*) **ins ~ (über)wechseln** to turn or go professional; **aus dem ~ zurückkehren** to give up being a professional, to give up professional sport

pro|fi|lie|ren [profi'li:rən] ptp **profiliert** **VT** (= *mit Profil versehen*) Schuhsohlen, Reifen to put a tread on; Blech to profile; (*fig:* = *scharf umreißen*) to give a distinctive image to **VR** (= *sich ein Image geben*) to create a distinctive image for oneself; (= *Besonderes leisten*) to distinguish oneself; **er will sich akademisch/politisch** etc **~** he wants to make a name for himself academically/in politics etc, he wants to make his mark academically/in politics etc; **sie hat sich als Expertin für Lexikografie profiliert** she made a name for herself as an expert in lexicography

pro|fi|liert [profi'li:rt] ADJ Schuhe, Reifen with a tread, treaded; (*fig:* = *scharf umrissen*) clear-cut no adv; (*fig:* = *hervorstechend*) distinctive; Persönlichkeit prominent; **ein ~er Politiker/Wissenschaftler** a politician/scientist who has made his mark

Pro|fi|lie|rung F **-,** no pl (= *das Sich-Profilieren*) making one's mark no art

pro|fil|los ADJ Politiker, Firma lacking any distinct image; Sohle, Reifen treadless

Pro|fil-: **Pro|fil|neu|ro|se** F (*hum*) neurosis about one's image, image neurosis; **Pro|fil|soh|le** F sole with a tread, treaded sole; **Pro|fil|stahl** M sectional steel

Pro|fi-: **Pro|fi|sport** M professional sport or sports pl (*US*); **Pro|fi|sport|ler(in)** M(F) professional sportsperson or sportsman/-woman; (*in Leichtathletik*) professional athlete

Pro|fit [pro'fi:t, pro'fɪt] M **-(e)s,** -e profit; **~ aus etw schlagen** or **ziehen** (*lit*) to make a profit from or out of sth; (*fig*) to reap the benefits from sth, to profit from sth; **~ machen** to make a profit; **~ bringend** (*adjektivisch*) profitable; (*adverbial*) profitably; **den/keinen ~ von etw haben** to profit/not to profit from sth; **ohne/mit ~ arbeiten** to work unprofitably/profitably

Pro|fi|ta|bel [profi'ta:bl] ADJ profitable

Pro|fi|ta|bi|li|tät F -, *no pl* profitability

Pro|fit-: pro|fit|brin|gend △ ADJ → **Profit**; **Pro|fit|cen|ter** ['profitsentɐ] NT (*Comm*) profit centre (*Brit*) or center (*US*); **Pro|fit|den|ken** NT profit orientation; **Pro|fit|gier** F greed for profit, profit lust; **pro|fit|gie|rig** ADJ greedy for profit, profit-greedy

pro|fi|tie|ren [profi'ti:rən] *ptp* **profitiert** VTI (*von* from, by) to profit; (*fig auch*) to gain; **viel/ etwas ~** (*lit*) to make a large profit/to make something of a profit; (*fig*) to profit greatly/ somewhat; **davon hat er wenig profitiert** (*lit*) he didn't make much of a profit from it; (*fig*) he didn't profit much *or* didn't gain a great deal from it; **dabei kann ich nur ~** I only stand to gain from it, I can't lose; **und was profitierst du dabei** *or* **davon?** what do you stand to gain from *or* by it?

Pro|fit-: Pro|fit|jä|ger(in) M(F) , **Pro|fit|ma|cher(in)** M(F) (*inf*) profiteer; **Pro|fit|ma|che|rei** [-maxə'rai] F -, **-en** (*inf*) profiteering; **Pro|fit|ma|xi|mie|rung** F maximization of profit(s); **Pro|fit|stre|ben** NT profit seeking

pro for|ma [pro 'fɔrma] ADV as a matter of form, for appearance's sake

Pro-for|ma-Rech|nung [pro'fɔrma-] F pro forma invoice

pro|fund [pro'fʊnt] (*geh*) ADJ profound, deep; **er ist ein ~er Kenner** +*gen* he has a profound *or* deep knowledge of …; ADV profoundly; **~ recherchiert** thoroughly researched

Prog|no|se [pro'gno:zə] F -, **-n** prediction, prognosis; (= *Wetterprognose*) forecast; **eine ~ stellen/wagen** to give *or* make/venture a prediction *or* prognosis; **genetische ~** genetic prognosis

prog|nos|tisch [pro'gnɔstɪʃ] ADJ prognostic

prog|nos|ti|zie|ren [prognɔsti'tsi:rən] *ptp* **prognostiziert** VT to predict, to prognosticate (*form*)

Pro|gramm [pro'gram] NT -s, **-e** a programme (*Brit*), program (*US*); (= *Tagesordnung*) agenda; (*TV*: = *Sender*) channel; (= *Sendefolge*) program(me)s *pl*; (= *gedrucktes Radio-Programm*) programme guide (*Brit*), TV guide; (= *Programmheft*) program(me); (= *Verlagsprogramm*) list; (*beim Pferderennen*) card; (= *Kollektion, Sortiment*) range; **nach ~** as planned; **auf dem ~ stehen** to be on the program(me)/agenda; **ein ~ für das nächste Quartal machen** to work out a programme for the next quarter; **für heute habe ich schon ein ~** I've already got something planned for today; **ein volles ~ haben** to have a full schedule; **unser ~ für den heutigen Abend** (*TV, Rad*) our program(me)s for this evening; **durch das ~ führt XY** the program(me) is presented by XY

b (*Comput*) program

Pro|gramm|an|bie|ter M (*TV*) programme (*Brit*) or program (*US*) maker

Pro|gram|ma|tik F -, *no pl* aims and objectives *pl*

pro|gram|ma|tisch [progra'ma:tɪʃ] ADJ programmatic; ADV **der Titel ist ~ zu verstehen** the title is the central theme of the programme (*Brit*) or program (*US*); **der Sprecher der Partei hat ~ verkündet, dass dieser Punkt revidiert würde** the party spokesman announced that this point was to be revised in their new programme (*Brit*) or program (*US*)

Pro|gramm-: Pro|gramm|di|rek|tor(in) M(F) (*TV, Rad*) director of programmes (*Brit*) or programs (*US*); **Pro|gramm|fol|ge** F order of programmes (*Brit*) or programs (*US*); (*Theat*) order of acts; **Pro|gramm|fül|ler** M (*inf*) (pro-

gramme (*Brit*) or program (*US*)) filler; **pro|gramm|ge|mäß** ADJ, ADV according to plan or programme (*Brit*) or program (*US*); **Pro|gramm|ge|stal|tung** F programme (*Brit*) or program (*US*) planning; **pro|gramm|ge|steuert** ADJ computer-controlled; **Pro|gramm|heft** NT programme (*Brit*), program (*US*); **Pro|gramm|hin|weis** M (*Rad, TV*) announcement; **wir bringen noch einige ~e für morgen** and now a look at some of tomorrow's programmes (*Brit*) or programs (*US*)

pro|gram|mier|bar ADJ programmable

pro|gram|mie|ren [progra'mi:rən] *ptp* **programmiert** VT a *auch vi* to programme (*Brit*), to program (*US*); (*Comput*) to program; (*fig*: = *konditionieren*) to programme (*Brit*), to program (*US*), to condition; **auf etw** (*acc*) **programmiert sein** (*fig*) to be geared *or* conditioned to sth; **programmiertes Lernen** program(m)ed learning **b** (= *entwerfen*) to draw up a programme (*Brit*) or program (*US*) for; (= *planen*) to schedule, to plan

Pro|gram|mie|rer [progra'mi:rɐ] M -s, -, **Pro|gram|mie|re|rin** [-ərɪn] F -, **-nen** programmer (*Brit*), programer (*US*)

Pro|gram|mier|feh|ler M programming (*Brit*) or programing (*US*) error

Pro|gram|mier|spra|che F programming (*Brit*) or programing (*US*) language

Pro|gram|mie|rung [progra'mi:rʊŋ] F -, **-en** programming (*Brit*), programing (*US*); (*fig auch*) conditioning

Pro|gramm-: Pro|gramm|ki|no NT arts or repertory (*US*) cinema; **Pro|gramm|mu|sik** ▲ F programme (*Brit*) or program (*US*) music; **Pro|gramm|platz** M (*TV, Rad*) programme (*Brit*) or program (*US*) slot; **Pro|gramm|punkt** M item on the agenda; (*TV*) programme (*Brit*), program (*US*); (*bei Show*) act; **Pro|gramm|spei|cher** M (*von CD-Spieler etc*) programmable memory; **Pro|gramm|über|sicht** F rundown of the programmes (*Brit*) or programs (*US*)

Programmusik △ F → **Programmmusik**

Pro|gramm-: Pro|gramm|vor|schau F preview (*für of*); (*Film*) trailer; **Pro|gramm|zeit|schrift** F (*TV*) programme (*Brit*) or TV guide; **Pro|gramm|zet|tel** M programme (*Brit*), program (*US*)

Pro|gress ▲ [pro'grɛs] M **-es, -e** progress

Pro|gres|si|on [progrɛ'sio:n] F -, **-en** progression

pro|gres|siv [progrɛ'si:f] ADJ progressive ADV **a** (= *fortschrittlich*) progressively; **~ eingestellt sein** to be progressive **b** (*in Bezug auf Steuern*) **der Steuertarif ist ~ gestaltet** the tax rates are progressive

Pro|gym|na|si|um ['pro:-] NT secondary school (*for pupils up to 16*)

Pro|hi|bi|ti|on [prohibi'tsio:n] F -, **-en** Prohibition

Pro|jekt [pro'jɛkt] NT **-(e)s, -e** project

Pro|jekt|grup|pe F project team

pro|jek|tie|ren [projɛk'ti:rən] *ptp* **projektiert** VT (= *entwerfen*) to plan, to project, to lay plans for; (= *planen*) to project

Pro|jek|til [projɛk'ti:l] NT **-s, -e** (*form*) projectile

Pro|jek|ti|on [projɛk'tsio:n] F -, **-en** projection

Pro|jek|ti|ons-: Pro|jek|ti|ons|ap|pa|rat M projector; **Pro|jek|ti|ons|ebe|ne** F plane of projection; **Pro|jek|ti|ons|flä|che** F projection surface; **Pro|jek|ti|ons|lam|pe** F projection lamp; **Pro|jek|ti|ons|schirm** M projection screen

Pro|jekt|lei|ter(in) M(F) project leader

Pro|jek|tor [pro'jɛkto:ɐ] M **-s, Projektoren** [-'to:rən] projector

Pro|jekt|un|ter|richt M (*Sch*) project-based teaching

pro|ji|zie|ren [proji'tsi:rən] *ptp* **projiziert** VT to project

Pro|kla|ma|ti|on [proklama'tsio:n] F -, **-en** proclamation

pro|kla|mie|ren [prokla'mi:rən] *ptp* **proklamiert** VT to proclaim

Pro-Kopf- [pro:'kɔpf] *in cpds* per capita; **Pro-Kopf-Ein|kom|men** NT per capita income; **Pro-Kopf-Ver|brauch** M per capita consumption

Pro|krus|tes|bett [pro'krʊstəs-] NT Procrustean bed

Pro|ku|ra [pro'ku:ra] F -, **Prokuren** [-rən] (*form*) procuration (*form*), general commercial power of attorney; **jdm ~ erteilen** to grant sb general commercial power of attorney

Pro|ku|rist [proku'rɪst] M **-en, -en**, **Pro|ku|ris|tin** [-'rɪstɪn] F -, **-nen** holder of a general power of attorney, ≈ company secretary (*Brit*)

Pro|let [pro'le:t] M **-en, -en**, **Pro|le|tin** [-'le:tɪn] F -, **-nen** (*pej*) prole (*esp Brit pej inf*), pleb (*pej inf*)

Pro|le|ta|ri|at [proleta'ria:t] NT **-(e)s**, *no pl* proletariat

Pro|le|ta|ri|er [prole'ta:riɐ] M **-s, -**, **Pro|le|ta|ri|e|rin** [-iərɪn] F -, **-nen** proletarian; **~ aller Länder, vereinigt euch!** workers of the world, unite!

pro|le|ta|risch [prole'ta:rɪʃ] ADJ proletarian

pro|le|ta|ri|sie|ren [proletari'zi:rən] *ptp* **proletarisiert** VT to proletarianize

pro|le|ten|haft (*pej*) ADJ plebeian (*pej*), plebby (*Brit pej inf*); ADV like a pleb (*inf*)

Pro|le|tin F → **Prolet**

Proll [prɔl] M **-s, -s** → **Prolo**

prol|lig ['prɔlɪç] ADJ (*pej inf*) → **proletenhaft**

Pro|lo ['pro:lo] M **-s, -s** (*pej inf*: = *Prolet*) prole (*esp Brit inf*), pleb (*pej inf*)

Pro|log [pro'lo:k] M **-(e)s, -e** [-gə] prologue (*Brit*), prolog (*US*)

Pro|lon|ga|ti|on [prolɔŋga'tsio:n] F -, **-en** (*St Ex*) carryover

Pro|lon|ga|ti|ons- (*St Ex*): **Pro|lon|ga|ti|ons|ge|schäft** NT carryover; **Pro|lon|ga|ti|ons|satz** M carryover rate

pro|lon|gie|ren [prolɔŋ'gi:rən] *ptp* **prolongiert** VT to prolong, to extend

Pro|me|na|de [promə'na:də] F -, **-n** (*old*: = *Spaziergang*) promenade, constitutional (*old, hum*); (= *Spazierweg*) promenade

Pro|me|na|den-: Pro|me|na|den|deck NT promenade deck; **Pro|me|na|den|kon|zert** NT promenade concert; **Pro|me|na|den|mi|schung** F (*hum*) mongrel, crossbreed

pro|me|nie|ren [promə'ni:rən] *ptp* **promeniert** VI *aux sein* (*geh*) to promenade

pro|me|the|isch [prome'te:ɪʃ] ADJ (*liter*) Promethean (*liter*)

Pro|me|theus [pro'me:tɔys] M **-'** Prometheus

Pro|me|thi|um [pro'me:tiʊm] NT **-s**, *no pl* (*abbr* **Pm**) promethium

Pro|mi ['pro:mi] M **-s, -s** or f **-, -s** (*inf*) VIP; (= *Politiker*) star politician

Pro|mil|le [pro'mɪlə] NT **-(s), -** thousandth; (*inf*: = *Alkoholspiegel*) alcohol level; **er hat zu viel ~ (im Blut)** he has too much alcohol in his blood, his alcohol level is too high; **0,5 ~** (Alkohol im Blut) a blood-alcohol level of 50 millilitres (*Brit*), a blood-alcohol content of 0.5 (*US*)

Pro|mil|le-: Pro|mil|le|gren|ze F legal (alcohol) limit; **Pro|mil|le|mes|ser** M **-s, -** Breathalyzer®

pro|mi|nent [promi'nɛnt] ADJ prominent

Pro|mi|nen|ten- *in cpds* VIP; (*inf*: = *vornehm*) posh; **Pro|mi|nen|ten|her|ber|ge** F (*inf*) posh hotel (*inf*); **Pro|mi|nen|ten|suite** F VIP suite

Pro|mi|nen|te(r) [promi'nɛntə] MF *decl as adj* prominent figure, VIP

Pro|mi|nenz [promi'nɛnts] F - VIPs *pl*, prominent figures *pl*

pro|misk [pro'mɪsk] ADJ promiscuous

Pro|mis|ku|i|tät [promɪskui'tɛːt] F -, *no pl* promiscuity

Pro|mo|ter [pro'moːtɐ] M -s, -, **Pro|mo|te|rin** [-ərɪn] F -, -nen promoter

Pro|mo|ti|on[1] [promo'tsioːn] F -, -en **a** (*Univ*) doctorate, PhD; (*Aus:* = *Feier*) doctoral degree ceremony; **während seiner ~** while he was doing his doctorate *or* PhD; **nach seiner ~** after he got his PhD; **jds ~ befürworten** to recommend sb for a doctorate; **das Studium mit einer ~ abschließen** to gain a doctorate *or* PhD **b** (*Sw Sch:* = *Versetzung*) moving up

Pro|mo|ti|on[2] [prə'moːʃən] F -, -s (*Comm*) promotion

Pro|mo|ti|ons|ord|nung F (*Univ*) doctoral degree regulations *pl*

Pro|mo|tor [pro'moːtoːɐ] M -s, **Promotoren** [-'toːrən], **Pro|mo|to|rin** F -, -nen promoter

pro|mo|vie|ren [promo'viːrən] *ptp* **promoviert** VI to do a doctorate *or* a doctor's degree *or* a PhD (**über** +*acc* in); (= *Doktorwürde erhalten*) to receive a doctorate *etc* VT to confer a doctorate *or* the degree of doctor on

prompt [prɔmpt] ADJ prompt ADV promptly; (= *natürlich*) naturally, of course

Prompt|heit F -, *no pl* promptness

Pro|no|men [pro'noːmən] NT -s, - *or* **Pronomina** [-mina] pronoun

pro|no|mi|nal [pronomi'naːl] ADJ pronominal

Pro|no|mi|nal-: **Pro|no|mi|nal|ad|jek|tiv** NT pronominal adjective; **Pro|no|mi|nal|ad|verb** NT pronominal adverb

pro|non|ciert [pronõ'siːɐt] (*geh*) ADJ (= *deutlich*) distinct, clear; (= *nachdrücklich*) definite ADV (= *deutlich*) clearly; (= *nachdrücklich*) definitely

Pro|pä|deu|tik [propɛ'dɔytɪk] F -, -en preparatory course

pro|pä|deu|tisch [propɛ'dɔytɪʃ] ADJ preparatory

Pro|pa|gan|da [propa'ganda] F -, *no pl* propaganda; (*dated:* = *Werbung*) publicity; **~ für/gegen etw machen** *or* **betreiben** to make propaganda for/against sth; **~ mit etw machen** to make propaganda out of sth; **das ist (doch) alles nur ~** that's just (so much) propaganda

Pro|pa|gan|da-: **Pro|pa|gan|da|ap|pa|rat** M propaganda machine; **Pro|pa|gan|da|feld|zug** M propaganda campaign; (= *Werbefeldzug*) publicity campaign; **Pro|pa|gan|da|rum|mel** M (*inf*) deluge *or* torrent *or* flood of propaganda; **pro|pa|gan|da|wirk|sam** ADJ which is effective *or* good propaganda ADV **etw ~ nutzen** to use sth as propaganda; **er hat ihre Außenpolitik ~ angegriffen** the way he attacked her foreign policy was strictly for propaganda; **etw ~ ausnutzen** to make effective propaganda out of sth

Pro|pa|gan|dist [propagan'dɪst] M -en, -en, **Pro|pa|gan|dis|tin** [-'dɪstɪn] F -, -nen **a** propagandist **b** (*Comm*) demonstrator

pro|pa|gan|dis|tisch [propagan'dɪstɪʃ] ADJ propagandist(ic) ADV as propaganda; **etw ~ ausnutzen** to use sth as propaganda

pro|pa|gie|ren [propa'giːrən] *ptp* **propagiert** VT to propagate

Pro|pan [pro'paːn] NT -s, *no pl* propane

Pro|pan|gas NT , *no pl* propane gas

Pro|pel|ler [pro'pɛlɐ] M -s, - (= *Luftschraube*) propeller, prop (*inf*); (= *Schiffsschraube*) propeller, screw

Pro|pel|ler-: **Pro|pel|ler|an|trieb** M propeller drive; **ein Flugzeug mit ~** a propeller-driven plane; **Pro|pel|ler|flug|zeug** NT , **Pro|pel|ler|ma|schi|ne** F propeller-driven plane; **Pro|pel|ler|tur|bi|ne** F turboprop

pro|per ['prɔpɐ] ADJ (*inf*) trim, neat, (clean and) tidy

Pro|phet [pro'feːt] M -en, -en prophet; **der ~ gilt nichts in seinem Vaterland** *or* **im eigenen Lande** (*Prov*) a prophet is without honour (*Brit*) *or* honor (*US*) in his own country (*Prov*); **beim Barte des ~en!** (*usu hum*) honest to God! (*inf*) → **Berg**

Pro|phe|tie [profe'tiː] F -, -n [-'tiːən] prophecy

Pro|phe|tin [pro'feːtɪn] F -, -nen prophetess

pro|phe|tisch [pro'feːtɪʃ] ADJ *Worte, Gabe* prophetic ADV prophetically

pro|phe|zei|en [profe'tsaiən] *ptp* **prophezeit** VT to prophesy; (= *vorhersagen auch*) to predict, to foretell; **jdm eine glänzende Zukunft ~** to predict a brilliant future for sb; **Kassandra hat den Trojanern ihren Untergang prophezeit** Cassandra prophesied that the Trojans would meet their downfall; **das kann ich dir ~!** I can promise you that!

Pro|phe|zei|ung F -, -en prophecy

Pro|phy|lak|ti|kum [profy'laktikʊm] NT -s, **Prophylaktika** [-ka] (*Med*) prophylactic; (= *Präservativ*) contraceptive

pro|phy|lak|tisch [profy'laktɪʃ] ADJ prophylactic (*form*), preventative ADV as a preventative measure, as a precaution

Pro|phy|la|xe [profy'laksə] F -, -n prophylaxis

Pro|por|ti|on [propɔr'tsioːn] F -, -en proportion

pro|por|ti|o|nal [propɔrtsio'naːl] ADJ proportional, proportionate; **umgekehrt ~** (*Math*) in inverse proportion ADV proportionally; **die Steuern steigen ~ mit dem Einkommen** *or* **zum Einkommen** taxes increase in proportion to *or* proportionally to income

Pro|por|ti|o|nal-: **Pro|por|ti|o|nal|druck** M , *no pl* proportional printing; **Pro|por|ti|o|nal|schrift** F proportionally spaced font; **Pro|por|ti|o|nal|zo|ne** F (*Fin*) flat rate tax bracket

pro|por|ti|o|niert [propɔrtsio'niːɐt] ADJ proportioned

Pro|porz [pro'pɔrts] M -es, -e proportional representation *no art*

Prop|pen ['prɔpn] M -s, - (*N Ger*) **a** (= *Pfropfen*) stopper; (= *Kork, Sektproppen*) cork; (*von Fass, Korbflasche*) bung **b** (*inf: Mensch*) dumpling (*inf*)

prop|pe(n)|voll ADJ (*inf*) jam-packed (*inf*)

Propst [proːpst] M -(e)s, ⸚e ['prøːpstə], **Pröps|tin** [prøːpstɪn] F -, -nen provost

Pro|rek|tor [proːrɛktoːɐ, pro'rɛktoːɐ] M , **Pro|rek|to|rin** [-'toːrɪn] F (*old Sch*) deputy rector; (*Univ*) deputy vice chancellor

Pro|sa [pro'zaː] F -, *no pl* prose; (*fig*) prosaicness

Pro|sa|dich|tung F prose writing

Pro|sa|i|ker [pro'zaːikɐ] M -s, -, **Pro|sa|i|ke|rin** [-ərɪn] F -, -nen **a** (*old:* = *Prosaist*) prose writer **b** (*fig:* = *nüchterner Mensch*) prosaic person

pro|sa|isch [pro'zaːɪʃ] ADJ **a** (= *nüchtern*) prosaic **b** (*Liter*) prose *attr*, prosaic (*form*) ADV **a** (= *nüchtern*) prosaically **b** (*Liter*) **ein Thema ~ bearbeiten** to treat a subject in prose

Pro|sa|ist [proza'ɪst] M -en, -en, **Pro|sa|is|tin** [-'ɪstɪn] F -, -nen, **Pro|sa|schrift|stel|ler(in)** M(F) prosewriter

Pro|se|lyt [proze'lyːt] M -en, -en, **Pro|se|ly|tin** [-'lyːtɪn] F -, -nen (*liter*) proselyte; **~en machen** to proselytize

Pro|se|mi|nar ['proː-] NT *introductory seminar course for students in their first and second year*

pro|sit ['proːzɪt] INTERJ your health; **~ Neujahr!** Happy New Year!, (here's to) the New Year!

Pro|sit ['proːzɪt] NT -s, -s toast; **ein ~ der Köchin!** here's to the cook!; **ein ~ auf die Treue** there's to *or* let's drink to loyalty; **auf jdn ein ~ ausbringen** to toast sb, to drink to sb, to drink

sb's health; **sie rief mir ein ~ zu** she called out "cheers" to me

Pro|so|die [prozo'diː] F -, -n [-'diːən] prosody

pro|so|disch [pro'zoːdɪʃ] ADJ prosodic

Pros|pekt [pro'spɛkt] M -(e)s, -e **a** (= *Reklameschrift*) brochure, pamphlet (+*gen* about); (= *Werbezettel*) leaflet; (= *Verzeichnis*) catalogue (*Brit*), catalog (*US*) **b** (= *Ansicht*) view, prospect (*old*) **c** (*Theat*) backdrop, backcloth (*Brit*)

pros|pek|tie|ren [prospɛk'tiːrən] *ptp* **prospektiert** VT to prospect (in)

pros|pek|tiv [prospɛk'tiːf] ADJ prospective

Pros|pekt|ma|te|ri|al NT brochures *pl*, pamphlets *pl*, literature

pros|pe|rie|ren [prospe'riːrən] *ptp* **prosperiert** VI (*geh*) to prosper

Pros|pe|ri|tät [prosperi'tɛːt] F -, *no pl* (*geh*) prosperity

prost [proːst] INTERJ cheers, cheerio (*Brit*); (*hum: beim Niesen*) bless you; **na denn ~!** (= *Prosit*) cheers then!, bottoms up! (*hum inf*); (*iro inf*) that's just great (*inf*) *or* swell (*esp US dated inf*); **~ Neujahr!** (*inf*) Happy New Year!, (here's to) the New Year! → **Mahlzeit**

Pros|ta|ta ['prɔstata] F -, *no pl* prostate gland; (*inf:* = *Prostataleiden*) prostate

Pros|ta|ta|krebs M prostate cancer

pros|ten ['proːstn] VI to say cheers

prös|ter|chen ['prøːstɐçən] INTERJ (*hum*) cheers, bottoms up (*hum inf*)

pros|ti|tu|ie|ren [prostitu'iːrən] *ptp* **prostituiert** VR (*lit, fig*) to prostitute oneself VT (*old*) to prostitute

Pros|ti|tu|ier|te(r) [prostitu'iːɐtə] MF *decl as adj* prostitute

Pros|ti|tu|ti|on [prostitu'tsioːn] F -, -en prostitution

Pro|sze|ni|um [pro'stseːniʊm] NT -s, **Proszenien** [-niən] proscenium

Pro|tac|ti|ni|um [protak'tiːniʊm] NT -s, *no pl* (*abbr* **Pa**) protactinium

Pro|ta|go|nist [protago'nɪst] M -en, -en, **Pro|ta|go|nis|tin** [-'nɪstɪn] F -, -nen (*lit, fig*) protagonist

Pro|te|gé [prote'ʒeː] M -s, -s protégé

pro|te|gie|ren [prote'ʒiːrən] *ptp* **protegiert** VT *Künstler, Persönlichkeit, Projekt* to sponsor; *Land, Regime* to support; **er wird vom Chef protegiert** he's the boss's protégé

Pro|te|in [prote'iːn] NT -s, -e protein

Pro|tek|ti|on [protɛk'tsioːn] F -, -en (= *Schutz*) protection; (= *Begünstigung*) patronage; **unter jds ~** (*dat*) **stehen** (*Schutz*) to be under sb's protection; (*Begünstigung*) to be under sb's patronage

Pro|tek|ti|o|nis|mus [protɛktsio'nɪsmʊs] M -, *no pl* **a** (*Econ*) protectionism **b** (= *Günstlingswirtschaft*) nepotism

pro|tek|ti|o|nis|tisch [protɛktsio'nɪstɪʃ] ADJ protectionist

Pro|tek|tor [pro'tɛktoːɐ] M -s, **Protektoren** [-'toːrən], **Pro|tek|to|rin** [-'toːrɪn] F -, -nen (*old:* = *Beschützer*) protector; (= *Schirmherr*) patron

Pro|tek|to|rat [protɛkto'raːt] NT -(e)s, -e (= *Schirmherrschaft*) patronage; (= *Schutzgebiet*) protectorate

Pro|test [pro'tɛst] M -(e)s, -e **a** protest; (*scharfen*) **~ gegen jdn/etw erheben** to make a (strong) protest against sb/sth; (**gegen etw**) **~ einlegen** to register a protest (about sth); **etw aus ~ tun** to do sth in protest *or* as a protest; **unter ~** protesting; (*gezwungen*) under protest; **ich machs, aber nur unter ~** I'm only doing it under protest **b** (*Fin*) protest; **~ mangels Annahme/Zahlung** protest for non-acceptance/non-payment; **einen Wechsel zu ~ gehen lassen** to protest a bill

Pro|test|ak|ti|on F protest

Pro|tes|tant [protɛsˈtant] M **-en, -en, Pro|tes|tan|tin** [-ˈtantɪn] F **-, -nen** Protestant

pro|tes|tan|tisch [protɛsˈtantɪʃ] ADJ Protestant ADV ~ **denken** to have Protestant beliefs; **Kinder ~ erziehen** to raise one's children as Protestants; ~ **heiraten** to be married in the Protestant church; ~ **beerdigt werden** to be buried as a Protestant; ~ **beeinflusst** influenced by Protestantism

Pro|tes|tan|tis|mus [protɛstanˈtɪsmʊs] M **-,** *no pl* Protestantism

Pro|test-: Pro|test|be|we|gung F protest movement; **Pro|test|de|monst|ra|ti|on** F (protest) demonstration, demo (*inf*); **Pro|test|ge|schrei** NT howls (*pl*) of protest; **Pro|test|hal|tung** F attitude of protest, rebellious attitude *or* stance

pro|tes|tie|ren [protɛsˈtiːrən] *ptp* **protestiert** VI to protest (*gegen* against, about) VT (*Fin*) to protest

Pro|test|kund|ge|bung F (protest) rally

Pro|test|ler [proˈtɛstlɐ] M **-s, -, Pro|test|le|rin** [-ərɪn] F **-, -nen** (*inf*) protester

Pro|test-: Pro|test|marsch M protest march; **Pro|test|no|te** F (*Pol*) letter of protest; **Pro|test|sän|ger(in)** M(F) protest singer; **Pro|test|schrei|ben** NT letter of protest; **Pro|test|song** M protest song; **Pro|test|stim|me** F protest vote; **Pro|test|streik** M protest strike; **Pro|test|sturm** M storm of protest; **Pro|test|ver|samm|lung** F protest meeting; **Pro|test|wäh|ler(in)** M(F) protest voter; **Pro|test|wel|le** F wave of protest

Pro|the|se [proˈteːzə] F **-, -n** **a** artificial limb *or* (*Gelenk*) joint, prosthesis (*Med, form*); (= *Gebiss*) set of dentures **b** (*Ling*) prosthesis

Pro|the|sen|trä|ger(in) M(F) **a** (*von Arm, Bein*) person with an artificial limb; (*von Auge, Nase etc*) person with an artificial eye/nose *etc*; **er ist ~** he has an artificial eye/nose etc; artificial nose etc **b** (= *Gebissträger*) denture-wearer

Pro|the|tik [proˈteːtɪk] F **-,** *no pl* (*Med*) prosthetics *sing*

pro|the|tisch [proˈteːtɪʃ] ADJ prosthetic

Pro|to|koll [protoˈkɔl] NT **-s, -e** **a** (= *Niederschrift*) record; (= *Bericht*) report; (*von Sitzung*) minutes *pl*; (*bei Polizei*) statement; (*bei Gericht*) transcript; (= *Vertragsanhang*) protocol; **das ~ aufnehmen** (*bei Sitzung*) to take (down) the minutes; (*bei Polizei*) to take (down) a statement; (*bei Gericht*) to keep a record of the proceedings; (**das**) **~ führen** (*bei Sitzung*) to take *or* keep the minutes; (*bei Gericht*) to keep a record of *or* make a transcript of the proceedings; (*beim Unterricht*) to write a report; **etw zu ~ geben** to have sth put on record; (*bei Polizei*) to say sth in one's statement; **etw zu ~ nehmen** to take sth down, to record sth; **wenn man auf Dienstreise ist, muss man über alle Ausgaben ~ führen** on a business trip one must keep a record *or* (check)list of all expenses **b** *no pl* (*diplomatisch*) protocol **c** (= *Strafzettel*) ticket **d** (*Comput*) protocol

Pro|to|koll|ant [protoˈklant] M **-en, -en, Pro|to|koll|an|tin** [-ˈlantɪn] F **-, -nen** secretary; (*Jur*) clerk (of the court)

pro|to|kol|la|risch [protoˈklaːrɪʃ] ADJ **a** (= *protokolliert*) on record; (*in Sitzung*) minuted **b** (= *zeremoniell*) ~**e Vorschriften** rules of protocol; **diese Vorschriften sind rein** ~ these are merely rules of protocol ADV **a** (= *per Protokoll*) **folgende Maßnahmen wurden ~ festgelegt** the following measures were agreed on **b** (= *zeremoniell*) according to protocol; ~ **ist das so geregelt, dass ...** protocol requires that ...

Pro|to|koll-: Pro|to|koll|chef(in) M(F) head of protocol; **Pro|to|koll|füh|rer(in)** M(F) secretary (*Jur*) clerk (of the court)

pro|to|kol|lie|ren [protokɔˈliːrən] *ptp* **protokolliert** VI (*bei Sitzung*) to take the minutes (down); (*bei Polizei*) to take a/the statement (down); (*in der Schule*) to write notes VT to take down; *Sitzung* to minute; *Unfall, Verbrechen* to take (down) statements about; *Vorgang, Vernehmung, Gerichtsverhandlung* to keep a record of; *Bemerkung* to put *or* enter in the minutes; *Stunde* to write up; (*Comput*) to keep a log of; **protokollierte Zeugenaussagen** recorded witness statements

Pro|ton [ˈproːtɔn] NT **-s, Protonen** [proˈtoːnən] proton

Pro|to|plas|ma [protoˈplasma] NT protoplasm

Pro|to|typ [ˈproːtotyːp] M (= *Erstanfertigung*) prototype; (= *Inbegriff auch*) archetype

pro|to|ty|pisch [ˈproːtotyːpɪʃ] ADJ prototypical, archetypal

Pro|to|zo|on [protoˈtsoːɔn] NT **-s, Protozoen** [-ˈtsoːən] *usu pl* (*Zool*) protozoon

Pro|tu|be|ranz [protubeˈrants] F **-, -en** (*Astron*) prominence; (*am Sonnenrand*) solar flare

Protz [prɔts] M **-es** *or* **-en, -e(n)** (*inf*) swank (*inf*)

prot|zen [ˈprɔtsn] VI (*inf*) to show off; **mit etw ~** to show off with

Prot|ze|rei [prɔtsəˈraɪ] F **-, -en** (*inf*) showing off, swanking (*inf*)

prot|zig [ˈprɔtsɪç] (*inf*) ADJ swanky (*inf*), showy (*inf*) ADV extravagantly; *wohnen* ostentatiously; ~ **auftreten** to show off

Pro|ve|ni|enz [proveˈniɛnts] F **-, -en** (*geh*) provenance

Pro|ven|za|le [provɛnˈtsaːlə, provɛnˈsaːlə, provãˈsaːlə] M **-n, -n, Pro|ven|za|lin** [-ˈtsaːlɪn, -ˈsaːlɪn] F **-, -nen** Provençal

pro|ven|za|lisch [provɛnˈtsaːlɪʃ, provɛnˈsaːlɪʃ] ADJ Provençal

Pro|vi|ant [proˈviant] M **-s,** (*rare*) **-e** provisions *pl*, supplies *pl* (*esp Mil*); (= *Reiseproviant*) food for the journey; **sich mit ~ versehen** to lay in provisions; (*für Reise*) to buy food for the journey

Pro|vi|ant|la|ger NT supply camp

Pro|vi|der [proˈvaidɐ] M **-s, -** provider

Pro|vinz [proˈvɪnts] F **-, -en** province; (*im Gegensatz zur Stadt*) provinces *pl* (*auch pej*), country; **das ist finsterste** *or* **hinterste ~** (*pej*) it's so provincial, it's a cultural backwater

Pro|vinz- *in cpds* provincial; **Pro|vinz|be|woh|ner(in)** M(F) provincial; **Pro|vinz|blatt** NT (*pej inf*) local rag (*pej inf*), provincial newspaper; **Pro|vinz|haupt|stadt** F provincial capital; **Pro|vinz|nest** NT (*pej inf*) provincial backwater (*pej*), hick town (*US pej*)

Pro|vin|zi|a|li|tät F **-,** *no pl* (*usu pej*) provinciality

pro|vin|zi|ell [provɪnˈtsiɛl] ADJ provincial (*auch pej*)

Pro|vinz|ler [proˈvɪntslɐ] M **-s, -, Pro|vinz|le|rin** [-ərɪn] F **-, -nen** (*pej*) provincial

pro|vinz|le|risch [proˈvɪntslərɪʃ] ADJ (*pej*) provincial

Pro|vi|si|on [proviˈzioːn] F **-, -en** commission; (*bei Bank*) bank charges *pl*; **auf ~** on commission

Pro|vi|si|ons|ba|sis F **,** *no pl* commission basis; **auf ~ arbeiten** to work on a commission basis

Pro|vi|sor [proˈviːzɔr] M **-s, Provisoren** [-ˈzoːrən], **Pro|vi|so|rin** [-ˈzoːrɪn] F **-, -nen** (*old*) manager of a chemist's shop

pro|vi|so|risch [proviˈzoːrɪʃ] ADJ provisional, temporary; ~**e Regierung** caretaker *or* provisional government; **das ist alles noch sehr ~ in unserem Haus** things are still very makeshift in our house; **Straßen mit ~em Belag** roads with a temporary surface ADV temporarily; **wir wollen es ~ so lassen** let's leave it like that for the time being; **ich habe den Stuhl ~ repariert** I've fixed the chair up for the time being

Pro|vi|so|ri|um [proviˈzoːriʊm] NT **-s, Provisorien** [-riən] stopgap, temporary *or* provisional arrangement

pro|vo|kant [provoˈkant] ADJ provocative, provoking ADV provocatively, provokingly

Pro|vo|ka|teur [provokaˈtøːr] M **-s, -e, Pro|vo|ka|teu|rin** [-ˈtøːrɪn] F **-, -nen** troublemaker; (*Pol auch*) agitator, agent provocateur

Pro|vo|ka|ti|on [provokaˈtsioːn] F **-, -en** provocation

pro|vo|ka|tiv [provokaˈtiːf], **pro|vo|ka|to|risch** [provokaˈtoːrɪʃ] ADJ provocative, provoking ADV provocatively, provokingly

pro|vo|zie|ren [provoˈtsiːrən] *ptp* **provoziert** VTI to provoke

Pro|ze|dur [protseˈduːr] F **-, -en** **a** (= *Vorgang*) procedure; **die Ratifizierung des Vertrages ist eine langwierige ~** ratifying the treaty is a lengthy procedure **b** (*pej*) carry-on (*inf*), palaver (*inf*); **die ganze ~, bis man endlich zur Universität zugelassen wird** all the rigmarole before you are finally admitted to university; **die ~ beim Zahnarzt** the ordeal at the dentist's **c** (*Comput*) procedure

Pro|zent [proˈtsɛnt] NT **-(e)s, -e** *or* (*nach Zahlenangaben*) **-** per cent *no pl* (*Brit*), percent *no pl* (*US*); ~**e** percentage; **fünf ~** five per cent (*Brit*) *or* percent (*US*); **wie viel ~?** what percentage?; **zu zehn ~** at ten per cent (*Brit*) *or* percent (*US*); **zu hohen ~en** at a high percentage; **etw in ~en ausdrücken** to express sth as a percentage *or* in per cent (*Brit*) *or* percent (*US*); **dieser Whisky hat 35 ~ (Alkoholgehalt)** this whisky contains 35 per cent (*Brit*) *or* percent (*US*) alcohol; ~**e bekommen** (= *Rabatt*) to get a discount

Pro|zent|ba|sis F percentage basis; (*von Vertreter auch*) commission basis; **auf ~ arbeiten** to work on a commission basis

-pro|zen|tig [protsɛntɪç] ADJ *suf* per cent; **hochprozentig** high percentage; **eine zehnprozentige Lohnerhöhung** a ten per cent (*Brit*) *or* percent (*US*) pay rise

Pro|zent-: Pro|zent|punkt M point; **Pro|zent|rech|nung** F percentage calculation; **Pro|zent|satz** M percentage; (= *Zins*) rate of interest, interest rate

pro|zen|tu|al [protsɛnˈtuaːl] ADJ percentage *attr*, ~**er Anteil** percentage ADV **etw ~ ausdrücken/rechnen** to express/calculate sth as a percentage *or* in percentages; **sich an einem Geschäft ~ beteiligen** to have a percentage (share) in a business; **~ gut abschneiden** to get a good percentage

pro|zen|tu|ell [protsɛnˈtuɛl] ADJ, ADV (*esp Aus*) = **prozentual**

Pro|zent|zei|chen NT per cent *or* percent (*esp US*) sign

Pro|zess ▲ [proˈtsɛs] M **-es, -e** **a** (= *Strafprozess*) trial (*wegen* for; *um* in the matter of); (= *Rechtsfall*) (court) case; **der ~ gegen XY** the trial of XY, the case against XY; **einen ~ gewinnen/verlieren** to win/lose a case; **gegen jdn einen ~ anstrengen** to take *or* institute legal proceedings against sb, to bring an action against sb; **er führt zur Zeit gegen fünf Firmen einen ~** at the moment he's taking five companies to court *or* he is involved in legal action against five companies; **es ist sehr teuer, einen ~ zu führen** going to court is very expensive, taking legal action is very expensive; **es zum ~ kommen lassen** to go to court; **es kann zum ~ kommen** it might come to a court case; **mit jdm im ~ liegen** to be involved in a court case *or* in a lawsuit *or* in litigation (*form*) with sb; **jdm den ~ machen** (*inf*) to take sb to court; **mit jdm/etw kurzen ~ machen** (*fig inf*) to make short work of sb/sth (*inf*) **b** (= *Vorgang*) process

Pro|zess-: Pro|zess|ak|ten ▲ PL case files *pl*; **pro|zess|fä|hig** ▲ ADJ entitled to take legal action; **Pro|zess|fä|hig|keit** ▲ F entitlement to take legal action; **pro|zess|füh|rend** ▲ ADJ **~e Partei** litigant; **die ~e Strafkammer** the criminal court conducting the case; **Pro|zess|füh|rung** ▲ F conducting of a case; **Pro|zess|geg|ner(in)** ▲ M(F) opposing party; **Pro|zess|han|sel** [-hanzl] M **-s, -** (*inf*) someone who is always going to law

pro|zes|sie|ren [protse'si:rən] *ptp* **prozessiert** VI to go to court; **er prozessiert mit fünf Firmen** he's got cases going on against five firms; **gegen jdn ~** to bring an action against sb; **sie haben jahrelang gegen mich prozessiert** they've been bringing an action against me for years, they've had a case going on against me for years; **durch alle Instanzen ~** to go through all the courts

Pro|zes|si|on [protse'sio:n] F **-, -en** procession

Pro|zess-: Pro|zess|kos|ten ▲ PL legal costs *pl*; **er musste die ~ tragen** he had to pay costs; **Pro|zess|la|wi|ne** ▲ F spate of trials

Pro|zes|sor [pro'tsɛso:ɐ] M **-s, Prozessoren** [-'so:rən] (*Comput*) processor

Pro|zess-: Pro|zess|ord|nung ▲ F code or rules *pl* of procedure, legal procedure; **Pro|zess|recht** ▲ NT procedural law; **Pro|zess|spra|che** ▲ F (*Comput*) processing language; **pro|zess|süch|tig** ▲ ADJ litigious; **pro|zess|un|fä|hig** ▲ ADJ not entitled to take legal action; **Pro|zess|un|fä|hig|keit** ▲ F lack of entitlement to take legal action; **Pro|zess|ver|schlep|pung** ▲ F protraction of a case; **Pro|zess|voll|macht** ▲ F , *no pl* power of attorney (*for a lawsuit*); (*Formular*) letter of attorney; **Pro|zess|wär|me** ▲ F heat of reaction

prü|de ['pry:də] ADJ prudish

Prü|de|rie [pry:də'ri:] F **-,** *no pl* prudishness, prudery

prü|fen ['pry:fn] VT **a** *auch vi* (*Sch, Univ*) jdn to examine; **Kenntnisse** to examine, to test; **jdn in etw** (*dat*) **~** to examine sb in sth; **wer hat bei dir geprüft?** who examined you?; **morgen wird in Englisch geprüft** the English exams are tomorrow; **schriftlich geprüft werden** to have a written examination; **ein staatlich geprüfter Dolmetscher** a state-certified interpreter

b (= *überprüfen*) to check (*auf +acc* for); (= *untersuchen*) to examine, to check; (*durch Ausprobieren*) to test; (= *auf die Probe stellen*) to test; *Geschäftsbücher* to audit, to check, to examine; *Lebensmittel, Wein* to inspect, to test; **es wird geprüft, ob alle anwesend sind** they check or there's a check to see if everyone is present; **den Wein auf sein Aroma ~** to sniff or test the bouquet of the wine; **Metall auf den Anteil an Fremdstoffen ~** to check the level of impurities in metal; **jdn auf seine Ehrlichkeit ~** to test or try sb's honesty; **wir werden die Beschwerde/Sache ~** we'll look into or investigate the complaint/matter; **sie wollte ihn nur ~** she only wanted to test him; **drum prüfe, wer sich ewig bindet** (*prov*) marry in haste, repent at leisure (*Prov*)

c (= *erwägen*) to examine, to consider; **etw nochmals ~** to reconsider or review sth

d (= *mustern*) to scrutinize; **ein ~der Blick** a searching look

e (= *heimsuchen*) to try, to afflict; **ein schwer geprüfter Vater** a sorely tried father, a much afflicted father

VI (*Sch, Univ*) to give exams; **er prüft sehr streng** he's a strict examiner

VR (*geh*) to search one's heart; **du musst dich selber ~, ob ...** you must decide for yourself or you must inquire of yourself (*liter*) whether ...

Prü|fer ['pry:fɐ] M **-s, -, Prü|fe|rin** [-ərɪn] F **-, -nen** examiner; (= *Wirtschaftsprüfer*) inspector

Prüf-: Prüf|ge|rät NT testing apparatus or equipment; **Prüf|lam|pe** F control light tester

Prüf|ling ['pry:flɪŋ] M **-s, -e** examinee, (examination) candidate

Prüf-: Prüf|röhr|chen NT test tube; **Prüf|stand** M test bed; (*Space*) test stand; **auf dem ~ stehen** to be being tested; **Prüf|stand|lauf**

M test run; **Prüf|stein** M (*fig*) touchstone (*für* of, for), measure (*für* of); **Prüf|stück** NT specimen; **kostenloses ~** (= *Buch*) inspection or specimen copy

Prü|fung ['pry:fʊŋ] F **-, -en** **a** (*Sch, Univ*) exam, examination; **eine ~ machen** or **ablegen** to take or do or sit (*Brit*) an exam

b (= *Überprüfung*) check, checking *no indef art*; (= *Untersuchung*) examination, checking *no indef art*; (*durch Ausprobieren*) test, testing *no indef art*; (*von Geschäftsbüchern*) audit, examination, checking *no indef art*; (*von Lebensmitteln, Wein*) inspection, testing *no indef art*; **eine gründliche ~ einer Maschine vornehmen** to check or examine or test a machine thoroughly, to give a machine a thorough check or examination or test; **jdn/etw einer ~ unterziehen** to subject sb/sth to an examination; **nach der ~ wird das Auto ...** after being checked or tested the car is ...; **bei nochmaliger ~ der Rechnung** on rechecking the account; **er führt ~en bei Firmen durch** (*von Geschäftsbüchern*) he audits firms' books; **nach/bei ~ Ihrer Beschwerde/dieser Sache ...** after/on looking into or investigating your complaint/the matter

c (= *Erwägung*) examination, consideration; **die ~ seiner Entscheidung** the reconsideration of one's decision

d (= *Heimsuchung*) test, trial

e (*Sport*) test

Prüfungs-: Prü|fungs|an|for|de|rung F examination requirement; **Prü|fungs|angst** F exam nerves *pl*; **Prü|fungs|ar|beit** F dissertation; **Prü|fungs|auf|ga|be** F exam(ination) question; **Prü|fungs|aus|schuss** ▲ M board of examiners, examining board; (*bei Geräten*) board of inspectors; **Prü|fungs|er|geb|nis** NT (*Sch, Univ*) exam(ination) results *pl*; (*Tech*) test result; **Prü|fungs|fra|ge** F examination question; **Prü|fungs|ge|bühr** F examination fee; **Prü|fungs|kan|di|dat(in)** M(F) examinee, (examination) candidate; **Prü|fungs|kom|mis|si|on** F = Prüfungsausschuss; **Prü|fungs|ord|nung** F exam(ination) regulations *pl*; **Prü|fungs|ter|min** M (*Sch, Univ*) date of examination or test; (*Jur*) meeting of creditors; **Prü|fungs|un|ter|la|gen** PL exam(ination) papers *pl*; **Prü|fungs|zeug|nis** NT exam(ination) certificate

Prüf|ver|fah|ren NT test procedure

Prü|gel ['pry:gl] M **-s, -** **a** *pl auch* **-n** (= *Stock*) club, cudgel (*Brit*) **b** *pl* (*inf:* = *Schläge*) beating, thrashing; **~ bekommen** or **beziehen** (*lit, fig*) to get a beating or thrashing; **~ einstecken** to take a beating; **jetzt gibt** or **setzt es ~** you're/he's *etc* in for a (good) thrashing → **Tracht c** (*sl:* = *Penis*) tool (*sl*)

Prü|ge|lei [pry:gə'lai] F **-, -en** (*inf*) fight, punch-up (*Brit inf*)

Prü|gel|kna|be M (*fig*) whipping boy

prü|geln ['pry:gln] VT to beat; **unser Lehrer prügelt grundsätzlich nicht** our teacher doesn't use corporal punishment on principle; **jdn zu Tode ~** to beat sb to death VR **sich mit jdm ~** to fight sb; **Eheleute, die sich ~** married people who come to blows; **sich um etw** (*acc*) **~** to fight over sth

Prügel-: Prü|gel|stra|fe F corporal punishment; **Prü|gel|sze|ne** F fight; (*Theat*) fight scene

Prunk [prʊŋk] M **-s,** *no pl* (= *Pracht*) splendour (*Brit*), splendor (*US*), magnificence, resplendence; (*von Saal, Rokoko auch*) sumptuousness; (*von Stadt, Gebäude auch*) grandeur; (*von höfischer Zeremonie, Fest auch*) pomp and pageantry; **Protz und ~** pomp and splendo(u)r; **Ludwig XIV liebte ~** Louis XIV had a passion for grandeur; **der ~ im Saal** the splendo(u)r or magnificence or resplendence of the hall; **die Schlösser sind voller ~** the castles are sumptuously appointed; **großen ~ entfalten** to put on a show of great splendo(u)r

Prunk- *in cpds* magnificent, resplendent; **Prunk|bau** M *pl* **-bauten** magnificent building; **Prunk|bett** NT magnificent bed; (= *Himmelbett*) four-poster bed

prun|ken ['prʊŋkn] VI to be resplendent; **an der Decke prunkt ein Gipsbaldachin** on the ceiling is a resplendent plaster baldachin; **mit etw ~** to flaunt sth, to make a great show of sth

Prunk-: Prunk|ge|mach NT state apartment; **prunk|los** ADV unostentatious, modest ADV modestly, unostentatiously; **Prunk|saal** M sumptuous or palatial room; **Prunk|stück** NT showpiece; **Prunk|sucht** F great love of splendour (*Brit*) or splendor (*US*), passion for the grand scale; **prunk|süch|tig** ADJ **~ sein** to have a craving for splendour (*Brit*) or splendor (*US*); **prunk|voll** ADJ splendid, magnificent ADV splendidly, magnificently

prus|ten ['pru:stn] VI (*inf*) to snort; **vor Lachen ~** to snort with laughter; **sie prustete laut vor Lachen** she gave a loud snort (of laughter)

PS [pe:'ɛs] NT **-, -** *abbr von* **Pferdestärke** hp

P.S., PS [pe:'ɛs] NT **-, -** *abbr von* **Postskript(um)** PS

Psalm [psalm] M **-s, -en** psalm

Psal|mist [psal'mɪst] M **-en, -en, Psal|mis|tin** [-'mɪstɪn] F **-, -nen** psalmist

Psal|ter ['psaltɐ] M **-s, -** **a** (*Eccl*) psalter **b** (*Mus*) psaltery

pseu|do- ['psɔydo] *in cpds* pseudo

Pseu|do|krupp [-krʊp] M **-,** *no pl* (*Med*) pseudocroup

Pseu|do|nym [psɔydo'ny:m] NT **-s, -e** pseudonym; (*eines Schriftstellers auch*) nom de plume, pen name

psst [pst] INTERJ psst; (*ruhig*) sh, hush

Psy|cha|go|ge [psyça'go:gə] M **-n, -n, Psy|cha|go|gin** [-'go:gɪn] F **-, -nen** educational psychotherapist

Psy|che ['psy:çə] F **-, -n** psyche; (*Myth*) Psyche

psy|che|de|lisch [psyçə'de:lɪʃ] ADJ psychedelic

Psy|chi|a|ter [psy'çia:tɐ] M **-s, -, Psy|chi|a|te|rin** [-ərɪn] F **-, -nen** psychiatrist

Psy|chi|at|rie [psyçia'tri:] F **-, -n** [-'tri:ən] psychiatry

psy|chi|at|risch [psy'çia:trɪʃ] ADJ psychiatric ADV psychiatrically; *behandeln, untersuchen* by a psychiatrist; **~ betrachtet** from a psychiatric point of view, (considered) psychiatrically; **~ behandelt werden** to be under psychiatric treatment

psy|chisch ['psy:çɪʃ] ADJ *Belastung, Auswirkungen, Defekt* emotional, psychological; *Phänomen, Erscheinung* psychic; *Vorgänge* psychological; **~e Erkrankung** mental illness; **~ unter großem Druck stehen, unter großem ~en Druck stehen** to be under a great deal of emotional or psychological pressure

ADV *abnorm, auffällig* psychologically; *krank, gestört, labil* mentally; **~ gesund/unauffällig** psychologically normal; **sich ~ auswirken** to have psychological effects; **~ belastet sein** to be under psychological pressure; **~ erschöpft** emotionally exhausted; **sich ~ schlecht fühlen** to feel bad; **eine ~ bedingte Krankheit** a psychosomatic illness; **~ gestört** emotionally or psychologically disturbed; **jdn ~ beanspruchen** to make emotional or psychological demands on sb; **er ist ~ völlig am Ende** his nerves can't take any more

Psy|cho-, psy|cho- ['psy:ço] *in cpds* psycho-; **Psy|cho|ana|ly|se** [psyço-] F psychoanalysis; **Psy|cho|ana|ly|ti|ker(in)** [psyço-] M(F) psychoanalyst; **psy|cho|ana|ly|tisch** [psyço-] ADJ psychoanalytic(al) ADV *behandeln* to psychoanalyze sb; **Psy|cho|di|ag|nos|tik** [psyço-] F psychodiagnostics *sing*; **Psy|cho|dra|ma** ['psy:ço-] NT psychodrama; **psy|cho|gen** [psyço'ge:n] ADJ psychogenic; **Psy|cho|gramm** [psyço-] NT *pl* **-gramme** profile (*auch fig*), psychograph; **Psy|cho|ki|ne|se** [psyçoki'ne:zə] F -, no pl psychokinesis; **Psy|cho|lo|ge** [psyçо-'lo:gə] M -n, -n, **Psy|cho|lo|gin** [-'lo:gɪn] F -, -nen psychologist; **Psy|cho|lo|gie** [psyçolo'gi:] F -, no pl psychology; **psy|cho|lo|gisch** [psy-ço'lo:gɪʃ] ADJ psychological; ~e Kriegsführung psychological warfare ADV psychologically; ~ erfahrene Kräfte personnel with experience in psychology; **psy|cho|lo|gi|sie|ren** [psycologi-'zi:rən] ptp **psychologisiert** VT to psychologize; **Psy|cho|neu|ro|se** [psyço-] F psychoneurosis; **Psy|cho|path** [psyço'pa:t] M -en, -en, **Psy|cho|pa|thin** [-'pa:tɪn] F -, -nen psychopath; **Psy|cho|pa|thie** [psyçopa'ti:] F -, -n [-'ti:ən] psychopathy; **psy|cho|pa|thisch** [psyço'pa:tɪʃ] ADJ psychopathic ADV like a psychopath; ~ reagieren to react psychopathically; **Psy|cho|phar|ma|kon** [psyço'farmakɔn] NT -s, -pharmaka [-ka] usu pl psychiatric drug

Psy|cho|se [psy'ço:zə] F -, -n psychosis

Psy|cho-: Psy|cho|so|ma|tik [psyçozo'ma:tɪk] F -, no pl psychosomatics sing; **psy|cho|so|ma|tisch** [psyçozo'ma:tɪʃ] ADJ psychosomatic ADV psychosomatically; **psy|cho|so|zi|al** ADJ (Psych, Sociol) psychosocial; **Psy|cho|ter|ror** ['psy-ço-] M psychological terror; **Psy|cho|test** ['psy-ço-] M psychological test; **Psy|cho|the|ra|peut(in)** [psyço-] M(F) psychotherapist; **psy|cho|the|ra|peu|tisch** [psyço-] ADJ psychotherapeutic ADV psychotherapeutically; **Psy|cho|the|ra|pie** [psyço-] F psychotherapy; **Psy|cho|thril|ler** [psyço-] M psychological thriller

Psy|cho|ti|ker [psy'ço:tikɐ] M -s, -, **Psy|cho|ti|ke|rin** [-ərɪn] F -, -nen psychotic

psy|cho|tisch [psy'ço:tɪʃ] ADJ psychotic

PTA¹ [pe:te:'ʔa:] M -s, -s abbr von pharmazeutisch-technischer Assistent

PTA² [pe:te:'ʔa:] F -, -s abbr von pharmazeutisch--technische Assistentin

pto|le|mä|isch [ptole'me:ɪʃ] ADJ Ptolemaic

Pto|le|mä|us [ptole'me:ʊs] M -' Ptolemy

pu|ber|tär [pubɐr'tɛ:ɐ] ADJ of puberty, adolescent; **ein Junge im ~ Alter** a boy in puberty ADV **~ bedingte Störungen** disorders caused by puberty, adolescent disorders

Pu|ber|tät [pubɐr'tɛ:t] F -, no pl puberty; **er steckt mitten in der ~** he's going through his adolescence

Pu|ber|täts-: Pu|ber|täts|al|ter NT age of puberty; **im ~** at the age of puberty; **Pu|ber|täts|er|schei|nung** F symptom of puberty or adolescence; **Pu|ber|täts|stö|run|gen** pl adolescent disturbances pl, growing-up problems pl (inf); **Pu|ber|täts|zeit** F puberty (period)

pu|ber|tie|ren [pubɐr'ti:rən] ptp **pubertiert** VI to reach puberty; **~d** pubescent

Pu|blic-Do|main-Pro|gramm [pablɪkdɔ'me:n-] NT (Comput) public domain program

Pu|bli|ci|ty [pa'blɪsɪti] F -, no pl publicity

pu|bli|ci|ty-: pu|bli|ci|ty|scheu ADJ **er ist ~** he shuns publicity; **pu|bli|ci|ty|träch|tig** ADJ which generates (a lot of) publicity

Pub|lic Re|la|tions [pablɪk rɪ'le:ʃəns] PL public relations pl

pu|blik [pu'bli:k] ADJ pred public; **~ werden** to become public knowledge; **etw ~ machen** to make sth public; **die Sache ist längst ~** that's long been common knowledge

Pu|bli|ka|ti|on [publika'tsi̯o:n] F -, -en publication

Pu|bli|kum ['pu:blikʊm] NT -s, no pl public; (= Zuschauer, Zuhörer) audience; (= Leser) readers pl; (Sport) crowd; **er muss ja immer ein ~ haben** (fig) he always has to have an audience; **das ~ in dem Restaurant ist sehr gemischt** you get a very mixed group of people using this restaurant, this restaurant's customers are very mixed; **in diesem Restaurant verkehrt ein sehr schlechtes ~** this restaurant attracts a very bad type of customer or a very bad clientele; **sein ~**

finden to find a public; **vor eigenem ~** (Sport) in front of a home crowd

Pu|bli|kums-: Pu|bli|kums|er|folg M success with the public, popular success; **Pu|bli|kums|ge|schmack** M public or popular taste; **Pu|bli|kums|in|te|res|se** NT interest of the public; **Pu|bli|kums|lieb|ling** M darling of the public; **Pu|bli|kums|mag|net** M crowd puller; **Pu|bli|kums|ren|ner** M (inf) hit with the public (inf); **Pu|bli|kums|ver|kehr** M ~ **im Rathaus ist von 8 bis 12 Uhr** the town hall is open to the public from 8 till 12 o'clock; **„heute kein ~"** "closed today for public business"; **für den ~ geschlossen/geöffnet sein** to be closed/open to the public; **wir haben heute viel ~** we've a lot of people coming in today; **pu|bli|kums|wirk|sam** ADJ **~ sein** to have public appeal; **sehr ~e Tricks** tricks with great public appeal, tricks which appeal to the public ADV **ein Stück ~ inszenieren** to produce a play in a popular way or with a view to public appeal

pu|bli|zie|ren [publi'tsi:rən] ptp **publiziert** VTI a (= veröffentlichen) to publish; **er hat in verschiedenen Fachzeitschriften publiziert** he's had things or work published or he has been published in various journals b (= publik machen) to publicize

Pu|bli|zist [publi'tsɪst] M -en, -en, **Pu|bli|zis|tin** [-'tsɪstɪn] F -, -nen publicist; (= Journalist) journalist

Pu|bli|zis|tik [publi'tsɪstɪk] F -, no pl journalism

pu|bli|zis|tisch [publi'tsɪstɪʃ] ADJ journalistic ADV **ausschlachten** in the media; **sich ~ betätigen** to write for newspapers

Pu|bli|zi|tät [publitsi'tɛ:t] F -, no pl publicity

Pu|bli|zi|täts|pflicht F (St Ex) duty of public disclosure

pu|bli|zi|täts|pflich|tig [-pflɪçtɪç] ADJ declarable

Puck [pʊk] M -s, -s puck

pu|ckern ['pʊkɐn] VI (inf) to throb; **es puckert im Zahn** my tooth's throbbing

Pud|ding ['pʊdɪŋ] M -s, -s or -e a thick custard-based dessert often tasting of vanilla, chocolate etc, ≈ blancmange; **kaltgerührter ~** instant whip; **Beine/Arme wie ~ haben** to have legs/arms like jelly

Pud|ding|pul|ver NT custard powder

Pu|del ['pu:dl] M -s, - a (= Hund) poodle; **das ist des ~s Kern** (fig) that's what it's really all about → **begossen** b (inf: = Fehlwurf beim Kegeln) miss

Pu|del-: Pu|del|müt|ze F bobble cap or hat, pompom hat (inf); **pu|del|nackt** ADJ (inf) stark-naked, starkers pred (Brit inf); **pu|del-naß** ▲ ADJ dripping or soaking wet, drenched; **pu|del|wohl** ADJ (inf) **sich ~ fühlen** to feel completely contented; **nach der Sauna fühle ich mich ~** after the sauna I feel like a million dollars (inf) or I feel on top of the world (inf)

Pu|der ['pu:dɐ] M OR (INF) NT -s, - powder

Pu|der|do|se F powder tin; (für Gesichtspuder) (powder) compact

pu|de|rig ['pu:dərɪç] ADJ powdery

pu|dern ['pu:dɐn] VT to powder; **sich** (dat) **das Gesicht ~** to powder one's face; **ich muss mir noch die Nase ~** (euph) I just have to powder my nose VR (= Puder auftragen) to powder oneself; (= Puder benutzen) to use powder; **ich muss mich noch ~** I still have to powder my nose or face; **sich stark ~** to use a lot of powder

Pu|der-: Pu|der|quas|te F powder puff; **Pu|der|zu|cker** M icing sugar

pu|e|ril [pue'ri:l] ADJ (geh) puerile; (= knabenhaft) boyish

Pu|er|to|ri|ca|ner [pʊɐrtori'ka:nɐ] M -s, -, **Pu|er|to|ri|ca|ne|rin** [-ərɪn] F -, -nen Puerto Rican

pu|er|to|ri|ca|nisch [pʊɐrtori'ka:nɪʃ] ADJ Puerto Rican

Pu|er|to Ri|co [pu'ɛrto 'ri:ko] NT - -s Puerto Rico

puff [pʊf] INTERJ bang

Puff¹ [pʊf] M -(e)s, ⸚e [pʏfə] a (= Stoß) thump, blow; (in die Seite) prod, dig; (vertraulich) nudge; **einen ~** or **einige Püffe aushalten können** (fig) to be thick-skinned b (Geräusch) phut (inf)

Puff² M -(e)s, -e a (= Wäschepuff) linen basket b (= Bausch) puff c (= Sitzpuff) pouffe (Brit), pouf (US)

Puff³ M OR NT -s, -s (inf) brothel, whorehouse (inf), cathouse (esp US inf)

Puff|är|mel M puff(ed) sleeve

puf|fen ['pʊfn] VT a (= schlagen) to thump, to hit; (in die Seite) to prod, to dig; (= vertraulich stoßen) to nudge b Rauch to puff c Ärmel to puff d Mais to pop VI (inf) (Dampflokomotive, Rauch, Abgase) to puff; (= puff machen) to go phut (inf)

Puf|fer ['pʊfɐ] M -s, - a (Rail, Comput) buffer b (Cook: = Kartoffelpuffer) potato fritter

Puf|fer|funk|ti|on F (Comput) buffer function

puf|fern ['pʊfɐn] VT to buffer

Puf|fer-: Puf|fer|spei|cher M (Comput) buffer memory; **Puf|fer|staat** M buffer state; **Puf|fer|zo|ne** F buffer zone

Puff-: Puff|ge|gend F (inf) red-light district; **Puff|mais** M popcorn; **Puff|mut|ter** F pl -mütter (inf) madam(e), bawd; **Puff|reis** M puffed rice; **Puff|stra|ße** F (inf) brothel street

puh [pu:] INTERJ (Abscheu) ugh; (Erleichterung) phew

pu|len ['pu:lən] VI (inf) to pick; **in der Nase ~** to pick one's nose; **an einem Loch/einem Etikett/einer Narbe ~** to pick at a hole/a label/a scar VT (N Ger) Krabben to shell; Erbsen, Bohnen auch to pod; **etw aus etw ~** to pick sth out of sth

Pulk [pʊlk] M -s, -s or (rare) -e a (Mil) group b (= Menge) (von Menschen) throng; (von Dingen) pile; **im ~** in a throng

Pull-down-Me|nü [pʊl'daun-] NT (Comput) pull-down menu

Pul|le ['pʊlə] F -, -n (inf) bottle; **eine ~ Schnaps** a bottle of schnapps; **ein Schluck aus der ~** (fig) a fair whack (Brit inf) or share; **volle ~ fahren/arbeiten** (inf) to drive/work flat out (esp Brit) or at full speed; **das Radio volle ~ aufdrehen** (inf) to turn the radio on at full blast

pul|len¹ ['pʊlən] VI (Naut) to row

pul|len² VI , **pul|lern** ['pʊlɐn] VI (inf) to pee (inf)

Pul|li ['pʊli] M -s, -s (inf), **Pull|o|ver** [pʊ'lo:vɐ] M -s, - jumper (Brit), pullover, sweater, jersey

Pul|lun|der [pʊ'lʊndɐ, pʊl'ʊndɐ] M -s, - tank top, slipover

Puls [pʊls] M -es, -e [-zə] pulse; **sein ~ geht** or **schlägt regelmäßig** his pulse is regular; **jdm den ~ fühlen** (lit) to feel or take sb's pulse; (fig) to take sb's pulse; **am ~ der Zeit sein** to have one's finger on the pulse of the time(s)

Puls|ader F artery; **sich** (dat) **die ~(n) aufschneiden** to slash one's wrists

Pul|sar [pʊl'za:ɐ] M -s, -e (Astron) pulsar

pul|sen ['pʊlzn] VI (liter) to pulse, to pulsate, to throb

pul|sie|ren [pʊl'zi:rən] ptp **pulsiert** VI (lit, fig) to pulsate; **~der Gleichstrom** intermittent direct current

Puls-: Puls|schlag M pulse beat; (fig) pulse; (= das Pulsieren) throbbing, pulsing, pulsation; **an der Börse fühlt man den ~ der Wirtschaft** at the stock exchange you have your finger on the pulse of the economy; **in Schwabing spürte sie den ~ der Großstadt** in Schwabing she felt the throbbing or puls(at)ing of the city; **den ~ der Zeit spüren** to feel life pulsing around one;

Puls|wär|mer [-vɛrmɐ] M **-s, -** wristlet; **Puls|zahl** F pulse count

Pult [pʊlt] NT **-(e)s, -e** desk

Pul|ver ['pʊlfɐ, -vɐ] NT **-s, -** powder; (= *Schießpulver*) gunpowder, powder; **er hat das ~ nicht erfunden** (*fig*) he'll never set the Thames on fire (*prov*); **sein ~ verschossen haben** (*fig*) to have shot one's bolt → **Schuss**

Pul|ver-: Pul|ver|dampf M gunsmoke, gunpowder smoke; **Pul|ver|fab|rik** F gunpowder factory; **Pul|ver|fass** ▲ NT barrel of gunpowder, powder barrel or keg; (*fig*) powder keg, volcano; **(wie) auf einem ~ sitzen** (*fig*) to be sitting (on top of) a volcano; **Russland gleicht einem ~** Russia is like a powder keg; **die Lunte ans ~ legen** (*fig*) to ignite an explosive situation; **pul|ver|fein** ADJ finely ground ADV mahlen finely

pul|ve|rig ['pʊlfɐrɪç, -vɐrɪç] ADJ powdery *no adv* ADV **den Kaffee ~ mahlen** to grind the coffee to a powder

Pul|ve|ri|sa|tor [pʊlveri'za:toːɐ] M **-s, Pulverisatoren** [-'to:rən] pulverizer

pul|ve|ri|sie|ren [pʊlveri'zi:rən] *ptp* **pulverisiert** VT to pulverize, to powder

Pul|ver-: Pul|ver|kaf|fee M (*inf*) instant coffee; **Pul|ver|kam|mer** F (*Hist*), **Pul|ver|ma|ga|zin** NT magazine; **Pul|ver|müh|le** F gunpowder factory

pul|vern ['pʊlfɐn, -vɐn] VT to pulverize, to powder; **zu Silvester werden Millionenbeträge in die Luft gepulvert** on New Year's Eve vast sums of money go up in smoke VI (*inf*) to shoot

Pul|ver-: Pul|ver|schnee M powder snow; **Pul|ver|turm** M (*Hist*) magazine

pulv|rig ['pʊlfrɪç, -vrɪç] ADJ, ADV = **pulverig**

Pu|ma ['pu:ma] M **-s, -s** puma (*Brit*), cougar (*US*)

Pum|mel ['pʊml] M **-s, -** (*inf*), **Pum|mel|chen** ['pʊmlçən] NT **-s, -** (*inf*) dumpling (*Brit inf*), pudding (*Brit inf*), roly-poly (*inf*)

pum|me|lig ['pʊməlɪç], **pumm|lig** ['pʊmlɪç] ADJ (*inf*) chubby, plump

Pump [pʊmp] M **-(e)s,** *no pl* (*inf*) credit, tick (*Brit inf*); **etw auf ~ kaufen** to buy sth on tick (*Brit inf*) or on credit; **auf ~ leben** to live on tick (*Brit inf*) or on credit

Pum|pe ['pʊmpə] F **-, -n** a pump b (*inf*: = *Herz*) ticker (*inf*)

pum|pen ['pʊmpn] VT a (*mit Pumpe*) to pump b (*inf*: = *entleihen*) to borrow; (= *verleihen*) to lend, to loan; (**sich** *dat*) **Geld bei jdm ~** to borrow money from or off (*inf*) sb VI to pump

Pum|pen|schwen|gel M pump handle

pum|pern ['pʊmpɐn] VI (*inf: S Ger, Aus*) to thump, to hammer; **sein Herz pumperte vor Aufregung** his heart was thumping (away) or hammering away with excitement

Pum|per|ni|ckel ['pʊmpɐnɪkl] M **-s, -** pumpernickel

Pump|ho|se F baggy breeches *pl*, knickerbockers *pl*; (= *Unterhose*) bloomers *pl*

Pumps [pœmps] M **-, -** pump

Pump-: Pump|spei|cher|kraft|werk NT , **Pump|spei|cher|werk** NT pumped storage works *sing or pl*; **Pump|spray** NT pump (action) spray; **Pump|sta|ti|on** F pumping station

Punch [pantʃ] M **-s, -s** (*Boxen*) punch; **einen harten ~ haben** to pack a hard punch, to be a hard puncher

punc|to ['pʊŋkto] PREP +*gen* = **punkto**

Pu|ni|er ['pu:niɐ] M **-s, -**, **Pu|ni|e|rin** [-iərɪn] F **-, -nen** Phoenician

pu|nisch ['pu:nɪʃ] ADJ Punic; **die Punischen Kriege** the Punic Wars

Punk [paŋk] M **-s,** *no pl* punk

Pun|ker ['paŋkɐ] M **-s, -**, **Pun|ke|rin** ['paŋkərɪn] F **-, -nen** punk

Punkt [pʊŋkt] M **-(e)s, -e** a (= *Tupfen*) spot, dot; **grüne ~e in den Augen** green flecks in one's eyes; **das Schiff war nur noch ein kleiner ~ in der Ferne** the ship was only a small speck or dot or spot in the distance

b (= *Satzzeichen*) full stop (*Brit*), period (*esp US*); (*Typ*) point; (*auf dem i, Mus:* = *Auslassungszeichen, von Punktlinie, Comput, E-Mail-Adresse*) dot; **einen ~ setzen** or **machen** to put a full stop (*Brit*) or a period (*esp US*); **der Satz endet mit drei ~en** the sentence ends with a row of dots or with suspension points (*Brit*) or with the ellipsis mark; **der ~ auf dem i sein** (*fig*) to be the final touch; **nun mach aber mal einen ~!** (*inf*) come off it! (*inf*); **einen ~ hinter eine Angelegenheit setzen** to make an end to a matter; **ohne ~ und Komma reden** (*inf*) to talk nineteen to the dozen (*Brit inf*), to rattle on and on (*inf*), to talk up a storm (*US inf*); **und sagte, ~, ~, ~** and said dot, dot, dot

c (= *Stelle, Zeitpunkt, auch Math*) point; **zwischen den ~en A und B** between (the) points A and B; **~ 12 Uhr** at 12 o'clock on the dot; **wir sind auf** or **an dem ~ angelangt, wo ...** we have reached the stage or point where ...; **ein dunkler ~** (*fig*) a dark chapter; **bis zu einem gewissen ~** up to a certain point → **tot**

d (= *Bewertungseinheit*) point, mark; (*bei Prüfung*) mark; (*bei Verkehrsvergehen*) point; **nach ~en siegen/führen** to win/lead on points

e (*bei Diskussion, von Vertrag etc*) point; **in diesem ~** on this point; **etw ~ für ~ widerlegen** to disprove sth point by point; **etw in allen ~en widerlegen** to refute sth in every respect; **der strittige ~** the disputed point, the area of dispute; **sein Aufsatz ist in vielen ~en anfechtbar** many points in his essay are disputable; **etw auf den ~ bringen** to get to the heart of sth; **damit brachte er das Problem auf den ~** he put his finger on it or on the problem

Punkt|ball M punchball (*Brit*), punchbag (*US*), punching ball or bag (*US*)

Pünkt|chen ['pʏŋktçən] NT **-s, -** little dot or spot; **drei ~** three dots; **da fehlt aber auch nicht das ~ auf dem i!** (*fig*) it's got every i dotted and every t crossed

punk|ten ['pʊŋktn] VI (*Sport*) to score (points); (*fig: = Erfolg haben*) to score a hit → *auch* **gepunktet**

Punkt-: Punkt|feu|er NT (*Mil*) precision fire; **punkt|gleich** ADJ (*Sport*) level (*mit* with) ADV **die Mannschaften haben ~ gespielt/abgeschnitten** the score was even, it was a draw (*esp Brit*); **die beiden Mannschaften liegen ~** the two teams are lying level (on points) or are level pegging (*Brit*), the two teams are even; **der Boxkampf ging ~ aus** the fight ended in a draw or was a draw; **Punkt|gleich|heit** F (*Sport*) level score; **bei ~** if the scores are level; **wegen ~** because the score was level

punk|tie|ren [pʊŋk'ti:rən] *ptp* **punktiert** VT a (*Med*) to aspirate b (= *mit Punkten versehen*) to dot; (*Mus*) *Note* to dot; **einen Umriss ~** to dot in an outline; **punktierte Linie** dotted line; **punktierte Rhythmen** dotted rhythms

Punk|ti|on [pʊŋk'tsio:n] F **-, -en** (*Med*) aspiration

Punkt|lan|dung F precision landing

pünkt|lich ['pʏŋktlɪç] ADJ a punctual b (= *genau*) exact, precise, meticulous ADV on time; **er kam ~ um 3 Uhr** he came punctually at 3 o'clock or at 3 o'clock sharp; **der Zug kommt immer sehr ~** the train is always dead on time or very punctual; **~ da sein** to be there on time; **es wird ~ erledigt** it will be promptly dealt with; (= *rechtzeitig*) it will be dealt with on time

Pünkt|lich|keit F **-,** *no pl* punctuality; **~ ist die Höflichkeit der Könige** (*Prov*) punctuality is the politeness of princes

Punkt-: Punkt|li|nie F dotted line; **Punkt|mat|rix** F (*Comput*) dot matrix; **Punkt|nie|der|la|ge** F defeat on points, points defeat

punk|to ['pʊŋkto] PREP +*gen* in ~ with regard to, as regards; **~ X** where X or as far as X is concerned; **~ meiner Anfrage** concerning or reference (*Comm*) or re (*Comm*) my inquiry

Punkt-: Punkt|rich|ter(in) M(F) judge; **Punkt|schrift** F Braille; **punkt+schwei|ßen** VTI *sep infin, ptp only* (*Tech*) to spot-weld; **Punkt|sieg** M win on points, points win; **Punkt|sie|ger(in)** M(F) winner on points; **Punkt|spiel** NT league game, game decided on points

punk|tu|ell [pʊŋk'tuɛl] ADJ *Maßnahmen, Streik* selective; *Zusammenarbeit* on certain points; **ei|nige ~e Ergänzungen anbringen** to expand a few points; **~e Verkehrskontrollen** spot checks on traffic ADV *kritisieren* in a few points; **wir haben uns nur ~ mit diesem Thema befasst** we only dealt with certain or selected points of this topic; **die Kontrollen erfolgten nur ~** they only did spot checks

Punk|tum ['pʊŋktʊm] INTERJ and that's flat, and that's that; **Schluss, aus, ~!** and that's the end of that!

Punkt-: Punkt|ver|lust M loss of points; **Punkt|wer|tung** F points system; **in der ~ liegt er vorne** he's leading on points; **Punkt|zahl** F score

Punsch [pʊnʃ] M **-es, -e** (hot) punch

Punsch|glas NT punch cup

Pun|ze ['pʊntsə] F **-, -n** a (*Tech*) punch b (= *Güte-, Herstellerzeichen*) hallmark

pun|zen ['pʊntsn] VT a (*Tech*) to punch b *Gold* to hallmark

Pup [pu:p] M **-(e)s, -e** (*inf*) (= *Furz, Geräusch*) rude noise; (= *Geruch*) nasty smell

pu|pen ['pu:pn] VI (*inf*) to let off (*Brit inf*), to pass gas (*US inf*)

Pu|pil|le [pu'pɪlə] F **-, -n** pupil

Pu|pil|len-: Pu|pil|len|er|wei|te|rung F dilation of the pupil; **Pu|pil|len|ver|en|gung** F contraction of the pupil, miosis (*spec*)

Püpp|chen ['pʏpçən] NT **-s, -** a (= *kleine Puppe*) little doll or puppet b (= *hübsches Mädchen*) little sweetie; (= *Teenagerin*) dolly bird (*dated inf*); **ein süßes kleines ~** a sweet little thing

Pup|pe ['pʊpə] F **-, -n** a (= *Kinderspielzeug*) doll, dolly (*inf*); (= *Marionette*) puppet, marionette; (= *Schaufensterpuppe, Mil:* = *Übungspuppe*) dummy; (*inf:* = *Mädchen*) doll (*inf*), bird (*esp Brit inf*); (*als Anrede*) baby (*inf*), doll (*esp US inf*); **die ~n tanzen lassen** (*inf*) to paint the town red (*inf*), to live it up (*inf*); **bis in die ~n schlafen** (*inf*) to sleep to all hours b (*Zool*) pupa

Puppen- *in cpds* doll's; **Pup|pen|dok|tor** M , **Pup|pen|dok|to|rin** F dolls' doctor; **Pup|pen|gesicht** NT baby-doll face; **pup|pen|haft** ADJ doll-like; **Pup|pen|haus** NT doll's house (*Brit*), dollhouse (*US*); **Pup|pen|kü|che** F doll's kitchen (*Brit*), dollkitchen (*US*); **Pup|pen|spiel** NT puppet show; **Pup|pen|spie|ler(in)** M(F) puppeteer; **Pup|pen|stu|be** F doll's house (*Brit*), dollhouse (*US*); **Pup|pen|the|ater** NT puppet theatre (*Brit*) or theater (*US*); **Pup|pen|wa|gen** M doll's pram (*Brit*), toy baby carriage (*US*)

pup|pern ['pʊpɐn] VI (*inf*) (= *zittern*) to tremble, to shake, to quake; (= *klopfen*) to thump, to thud

pup|pig ['pʊpɪç] ADJ (*inf*) a (= *niedlich*) cute b (= *einfach*) easy

Pups [pu:ps] M **-es, -e** (*inf*) = **Pup**

pup|sen ['pu:psn] VI (*inf*) to let off (*Brit inf*), to pass gas (*US inf*)

Pup|ser M **-s, -** (*inf*) = **Pup**

pur [pu:ɐ] ADJ (= *rein*) pure; (= *unverdünnt*) neat, straight; (= *bloß, völlig*) sheer, pure; **~er Unsinn** absolute nonsense; **~er Wahnsinn** sheer or pure or absolute madness; **~er Zufall** sheer or mere coincidence; **Whisky ~** straight or neat whisky ADV *anwenden* pure, undiluted; *trinken* straight

Pü|ree [pyˈreː] NT **-s, -s** puree; (= *Kartoffelpüree*) mashed *or* creamed potatoes *pl*

Pur|ga|to|ri|um [pʊrgaˈtoːriʊm] NT **-s**, *no pl* purgatory

pü|rie|ren [pyˈriːrən] *ptp* **püriert** VT to puree

Pü|rier|stab M masher

pu|ri|fi|zie|ren [purifiˈtsiːrən] *ptp* **purifiziert** VT (*liter*) to purify

Pu|ris|mus [puˈrɪsmʊs] M **-**, *no pl* purism

Pu|rist [puˈrɪst] M **-en, -en**, **Pu|ris|tin** [-ˈrɪstɪn] F **-, -nen** purist

pu|ris|tisch [puˈrɪstɪʃ] ADJ puristic

Pu|ri|ta|ner [puriˈtaːnɐ] M **-s, -**, **Pu|ri|ta|ne|rin** [-ərɪn] F **-, -nen** Puritan

pu|ri|ta|nisch [puriˈtaːnɪʃ] ADJ (*Hist*) Puritan; (*pej*) puritanical ADV (*pej*) puritanically; **bei uns geht es ~ zu** ours is a puritanical household; **sie verhält sich sehr ~** she is really puritanical

Pu|ri|ta|nis|mus [puritaˈnɪsmʊs] M **-**, *no pl* Puritanism

Pur|pur [ˈpʊrpʊr] M **-s**, *no pl* crimson; (= *purpurner Umhang*) purple; **den ~ tragen** (*fig*) to wear the purple

Pur|pur-: **pur|pur|far|ben** [-farbn], **pur|pur|far|big** ADJ crimson; **der Morgenhimmel strahlte ~** the morning sky shone a deep crimson; **Pur|pur|man|tel** M purple robe

pur|purn [ˈpʊrpʊrn] ADJ (*liter*) crimson

pur|pur|rot ADJ crimson (red)

Pur|zel|baum [ˈpʊrtslbaum] M somersault; **ei|nen ~ machen** *or* **schlagen** *or* **schießen** to turn *or* do a somersault

pur|zeln [ˈpʊrtsln] VI *aux sein* to tumble; **über etw** (*acc*) **~** to trip *or* fall over sth

pu|schen, pu|shen [ˈpʊʃn] VT (*inf*) to push

Pu|schen [ˈpʊʃn] M **-s, -** (N Ger) slipper

Pus|sel|ar|beit [ˈpʊsl-] F (*inf*) fiddly *or* finicky work *no art*

pus|se|lig [ˈpʊsəlɪç] ADJ (*inf*) *Mensch* pernickety (*inf*), finicky (*inf*), fussy; *Arbeit, Aufgabe* fiddly (*Brit inf*), awkward

pus|seln [ˈpʊsln] VI (*inf*) **a** (= *geschäftig sein*) to fuss; **sie pusselt den ganzen Tag im Haus** she fusses about the house all day **b** (= *herumbasteln*) to fiddle around (*an etw* (*dat*) with sth)

Puß|ta △ [ˈpʊsta] F **-**, **Pußten** [-tn] → **Puszta**

Pus|te [ˈpʊstə] F **-**, *no pl* (*inf*) puff (*inf*), breath; **aus der** *or* **außer ~ kommen** *or* **geraten** to get out of breath; **außer ~ sein** to be puffed out (*inf*), to be out of puff (*inf*); **(ja) ~!** (*inf*) no chance! (*inf*) → **ausgehen**

Pus|te|blu|me F (*inf*) dandelion clock

Pus|te|ku|chen INTERJ (*inf*) fiddlesticks (*dated inf*); **(ja) ~!** (*inf*) no chance! (*inf*)

Pus|tel [ˈpʊstl] F **-, -n** (= *Pickel*) spot, pimple; (*Med*) pustule

pus|ten [ˈpuːstn] (*inf*) VI (= *blasen*) to puff, to blow; (= *keuchen*) to puff (and pant) VT **a** (= *blasen*) to puff, to blow; **die Fabrik pustet seit Jahren Dreck in die Luft** the factory has been puffing (out) *or* blowing (out) filth into the air for years **b** (*inf*) **dem werd' ich was ~!** I'll tell him where he can get off! (*inf*)

Pus|te|rohr NT (*inf*) peashooter

Pusz|ta ▲ [ˈpʊsta] F **-**, **Puszten** [-tn] puszta, Hungarian plain

pu|ta|tiv [putaˈtiːf] ADJ (*geh*) putative

Pu|te [ˈpuːtə] F **-, -n** turkey (hen); **dumme ~** (*inf*) silly goose (*inf*); **eingebildete ~** (*inf*) conceited *or* stuck-up little madam (*Brit inf*) *or* missy (*US inf*)

Pu|ten-: **Pu|ten|fleisch** NT (*Cook*) turkey (meat) *no pl*; **Pu|ten|schnit|zel** NT (*Cook*) turkey breast in breadcrumbs

Pu|ter [ˈpuːtɐ] M **-s, -** turkey (cock)

pu|ter|rot ADJ scarlet, bright red; **~ werden** to go as red as a beetroot (*inf*), to go scarlet, to go bright red

put put [ˈpʊt ˈpʊt] INTERJ chick, chick, chick

Putsch [pʊtʃ] M **-(e)s, -e** coup (d'état), revolt, putsch

put|schen [ˈpʊtʃn] VI to rebel, to revolt; **in Südamerika wird permanent geputscht** they're always having coups *or* revolts in South America; **sich an die Macht ~** to take power by a military coup

Put|schist [pʊˈtʃɪst] M **-en, -en**, **Put|schis|tin** [-ˈtʃɪstɪn] F **-, -nen** rebel

Putsch|ver|such M attempted coup (d'état)

Pütt [pʏt] M **-s, -s** (*dial*) pit, mine

Put|te [ˈpʊtə] F **-, -n** (*Art*) cherub

put|ten [ˈpʊtn] VT to putt

putt putt [ˈpʊt ˈpʊt] INTERJ chick, chick, chick

Putz [pʊts] M **-es**, *no pl* **a** (*dated*) (= *Kleidung*) finery; (= *Besatz*) frills and furbelows *pl*; **in vollem ~ erscheinen** to arrive all dressed up in one's Sunday best **b** (*Build*) plaster; (= *Rauputz*) roughcast; **eine Mauer mit ~ verkleiden** *or* **bewerfen** to plaster *or* roughcast a wall; **unter ~** under the plaster **c** **auf den ~ hauen** (*inf*) (= *angeben*) to show off; (= *ausgelassen feiern*) to have a rave-up (*inf*); (= *meckern*) to kick up a fuss (*inf*)

Putz|dienst M cleaning duty; (= *Dienstleistung*) cleaning service; **~ haben** to be on cleaning duty

put|zen [ˈpʊtsn] VT **a** (= *säubern*) to clean; (= *polieren*) to polish; (= *wischen*) to wipe; *Pferd* to brush down, to groom; *Docht* to trim; **die Schuhe ~** to clean *or* polish one's shoes; **Fenster ~** to clean the windows; **sich** (*dat*) **die Nase ~** to wipe one's nose; (= *sich schnäuzen*) to blow one's nose; **sich** (*dat*) **die Zähne ~** to clean (*Brit*) *or* brush one's teeth; **einem Baby den Hintern/die Nase ~** to wipe a baby's bottom/nose; **~ gehen** to work as a cleaner **b** (*dated*: = *schmücken*) to decorate **c** *Mauer* to roughcast, to plaster **d** (*Aus*: = *chemisch reinigen*) to dry-clean VR **a** (= *sich säubern*) to wash *or* clean oneself **b** (*dated*: = *sich schmücken*) to dress *or* do oneself up

Put|ze|rei [pʊtsəˈrai] F **-, -en** **a** *no pl* (*inf*) cleaning; **hör doch endlich mal auf mit der ~!** will you stop all this damn cleaning! (*inf*) **b** (*Aus*: = *Reinigung*) dry cleaner's

Putz-: **Putz|fim|mel** M , *no pl* (*inf*) cleaning mania *or* bug; **einen ~ haben** to be a cleaning maniac; **Putz|frau** F cleaner, cleaning lady, char(woman) (*Brit*)

put|zig [ˈpʊtsɪç] (*inf*) ADJ (= *komisch*) funny, comical, amusing; (= *niedlich*) cute; (= *merkwürdig*) funny, strange, odd ADV (= *niedlich*) cutely; **das klingt ganz ~** that sounds so cute

Putz-: **Putz|ko|lon|ne** F team of cleaners; **Putz|lap|pen** M cloth; (= *Staubtuch*) duster; **Putz|le|der** NT chamois *or* chammy (leather), wash-leather; **Putz|ma|che|rin** F (*dated*) milliner; **Putz|mann** M *pl* **-männer** cleaning man; **Putz|mit|tel** NT (*zum Scheuern*) cleanser, cleansing agent; (*zum Polieren*) polish; (*pl*) cleaning things *pl*; **putz|mun|ter** [ˈpʊtsˈmʊntɐ] ADJ (*inf*) full of beans (*Brit inf*), lively; **Putz|sche|re** F wick trimmer; **Putz|stel|le** F cleaning job; **Putz|tag** M cleaning day; **Putz|teu|fel** M (*inf*) **sie ist ein richtiger ~** she's excessively house-proud (*Brit*), she's a neat-freak (*US sl*); **vom ~ besessen sein**, **den ~ haben** to have a mania for keeping things clean, to have the cleaning bug (*inf*); **Putz|tuch** NT *pl* **-tücher** (= *Staubtuch*) duster; (= *Wischlappen*) cloth; **Putz|wol|le** F wire *or* steel wool; **Putz|wut** F obsession with cleaning; **Putz|zeug** NT cleaning things *pl*

puz|zeln [pasəln] VI to do a jigsaw (puzzle)

Puz|zle [ˈpazl, ˈpasl] NT **-s, -s** jigsaw (puzzle)

Puz|zle- [ˈpazl-, ˈpasl-]: **Puz|zle|spiel** NT jigsaw (puzzle); **Puz|zle|teil** NT (*lit, fig*) piece of a/the puzzle; **die ~e wollen nicht passen** the pieces of the puzzle won't fit together

PVC [peːfauˈtseː] NT **-(s)** PVC

PX-La|den [peːˈʔɪks-] M (*US Mil*) PX store

Pyg|mäe [pʏˈɡmɛːə] M **-n, -n**, **Pyg|mä|in** [pʏˈɡmɛːɪn] F **-, -nen** Pygmy

pyg|mä|en|haft [pʏˈɡmɛːən-] ADJ pygmy-like, pygmy *attr*

Py|ja|ma [pʏˈdʒaːma, pʏˈʒaːma, piˈdʒaːma, piˈʒaːma] M **-s, -s** pair of pyjamas (*Brit*) *or* pajamas (*US*) *sing*, pyjamas *pl* (*Brit*), pajamas *pl* (*US*); **er öffnete die Tür im ~** he opened the door in his pyjamas (*Brit*) *or* pajamas (*US*)

Py|ja|ma|ho|se F pyjama trousers *or* bottoms *pl* (*Brit*), pajama bottoms *pl* (*US*)

Pyk|ni|ker [ˈpʏknikɐ] M **-s, -**, **Pyk|ni|ke|rin** [-ərɪn] F **-, -nen** stocky person

pyk|nisch [ˈpʏknɪʃ] ADJ stockily built, pyknic (*spec*)

Py|lon [pʏˈloːn] M **-en, -en**, **Py|lo|ne** [pʏˈloːnə] F **-, -n** (*Archit, von Brücke, Eingangstor*) pylon; (= *Absperrmarkierung*) traffic cone

Py|ra|mi|de [pyraˈmiːdə] F **-, -n** pyramid

py|ra|mi|den|för|mig [pyraˈmiːdən-] ADJ pyramid-shaped *no adv*, pyramidal (*form*) ADV in the shape of a pyramid; **die Artisten hatten sich ~ aufgebaut** the acrobats had formed a pyramid

Py|re|nä|en [pyreˈnɛːən] PL **die ~** the Pyrenees *pl*

Py|re|nä|en|halb|in|sel F Iberian Peninsula

Py|ro-: **Py|ro|ly|se** [pyroˈlyːzə] F **-, -n** pyrolysis; **Py|ro|ma|ne** [pyroˈmaːnə] M **-n, -n**, **Py|ro|ma|nin** [-ˈmaːnɪn] F **-, -nen** pyromaniac; **Py|ro|ma|nie** [pyromaˈniː] F , *no pl* pyromania; **Py|ro|tech|nik** [pyroˈtɛçnɪk] F pyrotechnics *sing*; **Py|ro|tech|ni|ker(in)** [pyroˈtɛçnikɐ, -ərɪn] M(F) pyrotechnist; **py|ro|tech|nisch** [pyroˈtɛçnɪʃ] ADJ pyrotechnic

Pyr|rhus|sieg [ˈpʏrʊs-] M Pyrrhic victory

py|tha|go|re|isch [pytaɡoˈreːɪʃ] ADJ Pythagorean; **~er Lehrsatz** Pythagoras's theorem, law of Pythagoras

Py|thon [ˈpyːtɔn] M **-s, -s** python

Py|thon|schlan|ge [ˈpyːtɔn-] F python

Q

Q, q [kuː] NT **-, -** Q, q

qkm *abbr von* **Quadratkilometer**

qm *abbr von* **Quadratmeter**

qua [kva:] ADV *(geh)* qua

quab|be|lig ['kvabəlɪç] ADJ *Frosch, Qualle* slimy; *Pudding* wobbly

quab|beln ['kvabln] VI to wobble

Qua|cke|lei [kvakə'lai] F **-, -en** *(inf)* nattering *(Brit inf)*, chattering, blethering *(inf)*

Quack|sal|ber ['kvakzalbɐ] M **-s, -**, **Quack|sal|be|rin** [-ərɪn] F **-, -nen** *(pej)* quack (doctor)

Quack|sal|be|rei [kvakzalbə'rai] F **-, -en** quackery, quack medicine

quack|sal|bern ['kvakzalbɐn] VI *insep* to quack *(rare)*; **sowas nenne ich ~** I'd call that quack medicine or quackery

Quad|del ['kvadl] F **-, -n** hives pl, rash; *(durch Insekten)* bite; *(von Sonne)* heat spot

Qua|der ['kva:dɐ] M **-s, -** *or* f **-, -n** *(Math)* cuboid, rectangular solid; *(Archit: auch* **Quaderstein***)* ashlar, square stone block

Qua|der|stein M ashlar, square stone block

Quad|rant [kva'drant] **-en, -en** M quadrant

Quad|rat¹ ['kva'dra:t] NT **-(e)s, -e** *a no pl (Fläche)* square; **drei Meter im ~** three metres *(Brit)* or meters *(US)* square **b** *no pl (Potenz)* square; **eine Zahl ins ~ erheben** to square a number; **vier zum ~** four squared; **die Geschwindigkeit steigt im ~ zur Entfernung** the speed increases in proportion to the square of the distance; **Pech im ~** *(fig)* incredibly bad luck **c** *(= quadratische Fläche)* square; **magisches ~** magic square

Quad|rat² NT **-(e)s, -e(n)** *(Typ)* quad, quadrat

Quad|rat- *in cpds* square; **Quad|rat|fuß** M square foot

quad|ra|tisch [kva'dra:tɪʃ] ADJ *Form* square; *(Math) Gleichung* quadratic

Quad|rat-: **Quad|rat|ki|lo|me|ter** M square kilometre *(Brit)* or kilometer *(US)*; **Quad|rat|lat|schen** PL *(inf)* *(= Schuhe)* clodhoppers pl *(inf)*, beetle-crushers pl *(Brit inf)*; *(= Füße)* plates of meat pl *(Brit inf)*; **Quad|rat|me|ter** M OR NT square metre *(Brit)* or meter *(US)*; **Quad|rat|me|ter|preis** M price per square metre *(Brit)* or meter *(US)*; **Quad|rat|schä|del** M *(inf: = Kopf)* big head, great bonce *(Brit inf)*

Quad|ra|tur [kvadra'tu:ɐ] F **-, -en** quadrature; **die ~ des Kreises** *or* **Zirkels** the squaring of the circle; **das käme der ~ des Kreises** *or* **Zirkels gleich** that's like trying to square the circle

Quad|rat-: **Quad|rat|wur|zel** F square root; **Quad|rat|zahl** F square number

quad|rie|ren [kva'dri:rən] ptp **quadriert** VT **a** *Zahl, Kreis* to square **b** *Wand* to divide into squares

Quad|ri|ga [kva'dri:ga] F **-, Quadrigen** [-gn] four-horsed chariot

Quad|ril|le [kva'drɪljə, ka-] F **-, -n** quadrille

Quad|ro|pho|nie [kvadrofo'ni:] F **-, no pl** quadrophonic sound, quadrophony; **in ~ in** quadrophonic, in quad *(inf)*

quad|ro|pho|nisch [kvadro'fo:nɪʃ] ADJ quadrophonic

Quai [keː, keː] M OR NT **-s, -s** quay; *(= Uferdamm auch)* waterfront

quak [kva:k] INTERJ *(von Frosch)* croak; *(von Ente)* quack

qua|ken ['kva:kn] VI *(Frosch)* to croak; *(Ente)* to quack; *(inf: Mensch)* to squawk *(inf)*, to screech *(inf)*

quä|ken ['kvɛːkn] VTI *(inf)* to screech, to squawk

Quä|ker ['kvɛːkɐ] M **-s, -**, **Quä|ke|rin** [-ərɪn] F **-, -nen** Quaker

Qual [kva:l] F **-, -en** *(= Schmerz) (körperlich)* pain, agony; *(seelisch)* agony, anguish; **tapfer ertrug er alle ~en** he bore all his suffering or pain bravely; **jds ~(en) lindern** or **mildern** *(liter)* to lessen sb's suffering; **~en erleiden** or **leiden** to suffer agonies; **unter großen ~en sterben** to die in agony or great pain; **sein Leben war eine einzige ~** his life was a living death; **die letzten Monate waren für mich eine (einzige) ~** the last few months have been sheer agony for me; **es ist eine ~, das mit ansehen zu müssen** it is agonizing to watch; **er machte ihr den Aufenthalt/das Leben/die Tage zur ~** he made her stay/her life/her days a misery; **(jdm) zur ~ werden** to be agony (for sb); **es bereitete ihm ~en, sie so leiden zu sehen** it tormented him to see her suffering so; **die ~en des Gewissens** *(geh)*/**des Zweifels** agonies of conscience/of doubt or indecision; **die ~en, die sie seinetwegen** *or* **um ihn ausgestanden hat** the suffering she has gone through because of him → **Wahl**

quä|len ['kvɛːlən] VT to torment; *Tiere auch* to tease; *(inf) Motor* to punish; *(mit Bitten etc)* to pester, to plague; **jdn zu Tode ~** to torture sb to death → *auch* **gequält**

VR **a** *(seelisch)* to torture or torment oneself; *(= leiden)* to suffer, to be in agony

b *(= sich abmühen)* to struggle; **sie quälte sich in das enge Kleid** she struggled into or squeezed herself into her tight dress; **er musste sich ~, damit er das schaffte** it took him a lot of effort to do it, it was a struggle for him to do it; **sich durch ein Buch/die Unterlagen ~** to struggle or plough *(Brit)* or plow *(US)* through a book/the documents; **ich quäle mich jeden Morgen aus dem Bett** it's a struggle for me to get out of bed every morning; **er quälte sich aus dem Sessel** he heaved himself out of the chair; **das Auto quälte sich über den Berg** the car laboured *(Brit)* or labored *(US)* or struggled over the hill

quä|lend ADJ agonizing; *Erinnerungen auch* tormenting; *Krankheit auch* excruciating; **~e Ungewissheit/Zweifel** agonizing uncertainty/doubts, agonies of uncertainty/doubt; **~er Schmerz** agonizing or excruciating pain ADV agonizingly; **~ langsam** agonizingly slow

Quä|le|rei [kvɛːlə'rai] F **-, -en** **a** *(= Grausamkeit)* atrocity, torture *no pl*; *(= seelische, nervliche Belastung)* agony, torment; **diese Tierversuche sind in meinen Augen ~** in my view these experiments on animals are cruel; **das ist doch eine ~ für das Tier** that is cruel to the animal; **die**

letzten Monate waren eine einzige ~ the last few months were sheer agony **b** *(= mühsame Arbeit)* struggle; **das war vielleicht eine ~!** that was really a struggle or hard going

quä|le|risch ['kvɛːlərɪʃ] ADJ *attr* tormenting, agonizing

Quäl|geist M *(inf)* pest *(inf)*

Qua|li¹ ['kva:li] M *(Sch inf)* special secondary school leaving certificate

Qua|li² ['kva:li] F *abbr von* **Qualifikation** *(Sport inf)* qualification; *(= Runde)* qualifying round

Qua|li|fi|kant [kvalifi'kant] M **-en, -en**, **Qua|li|fi|kan|tin** [-ɪn] F **-, -nen** *(Sport)* qualifier

Qua|li|fi|ka|ti|on [kvalifika'tsio:n] F **-, -en** qualification; *(= Ausscheidungswettkampf)* qualifying round, qualifier; **für diese Arbeit fehlt ihm die nötige ~** he lacks the necessary qualifications for this work; **er hat die ~ zu diesem Amt** he has the qualifications or he is qualified for this office; **die ~ für** or **zu etw schaffen** to qualify for sth; **zur ~ fehlten ihr nur wenige Sekunden** she only failed to qualify by a few seconds

Qua|li|fi|ka|ti|ons-: **Qua|li|fi|ka|ti|ons|run|de** F qualifying round; **Qua|li|fi|ka|ti|ons|spiel** NT qualifying match or game

qua|li|fi|zie|ren [kvalifi'tsi:rən] ptp **qualifiziert** VT **a** *(= befähigen)* to qualify *(für, zu* for) **b** *(geh: = differenzieren)* to qualify **c** *(geh: = einstufen)* to characterize, to label VR **a** *(allgemein, Sport)* to qualify; **er hat sich zum Facharbeiter qualifiziert** he qualified as a specialist; **sich wissenschaftlich ~** to gain academic qualifications **b** *(= sich erweisen)* to show or reveal oneself *(als* to be)

qua|li|fi|ziert [kvalifi'tsi:ɐt] ADJ **a** *Arbeiter, Nachwuchs* qualified; *Arbeit* expert, professional **b** *(Pol) Mehrheit* requisite

Qua|li|tät [kvali'tɛːt] F **-, -en** quality; **dieses Leder ist in der ~ besser** this leather is better quality; **von der ~ her** as far as quality is concerned, (as) for quality; **die Ware ist von ausgezeichneter ~** the product is top quality, this is a top-quality product; **er kauft nur ~** he only buys quality (goods)

qua|li|ta|tiv [kvalita'ti:f] ADJ qualitative ADV qualitatively; **~ hochwertige Produkte** high-quality products; **~ ausgezeichnet/minderwertig sein** to be of (an) excellent/(a) substandard quality; **etw ist ~ verbesserungsfähig** the quality of sth could be improved

Qua|li|täts- *in cpds* quality; **Qua|li|täts|ar|beit** F quality work; **unsere Firma hat sich durch (ihre) ~ einen Namen gemacht** our firm made its name by the quality of its work, our firm has got itself a reputation for quality; **Qua|li|täts|er|zeug|nis** NT quality product; **Qua|li|täts|kon|trol|le** F quality check or control; **Qua|li|täts|ma|nage|ment** NT quality management; **Qua|li|täts|merk|mal** NT mark of quality; **Qua|li|täts|si|che|rung** F *, no pl* quality assurance *no pl*; **Qua|li|täts|un|ter|schied** M difference in quality; **Qua|li|täts|wa|re** F quality goods pl; **Qua|li|täts|wein** M *wine of certified origin and quality*

Qual|le ['kvalə] F -, -n jellyfish

Qualm [kvalm] M -(e)s, no pl (thick or dense) smoke; (= Tabaksqualm) fug

qual|men ['kvalmən] VI a (Feuer) to give off smoke; (Ofen, Schornstein) to (give off) smoke; **es qualmt aus dem Schornstein/hinten aus dem Auto** clouds of smoke are coming or billowing from the chimney/from the back of the car; **ihm ~ die Socken** (inf) he's rushing around all over the place b (inf: Mensch) to smoke; **sie qualmt einem die ganze Bude voll** she fills the whole place with smoke → **Schlot** VT (inf) Zigarette, Pfeife to puff away at (inf)

Qual|me|rei [kvalmə'rai] F -, -en (inf) smoking; (von Ofen, Auto) smoke

qual|mig ['kvalmɪç] ADJ Zimmer smoke-filled, smoky; Flamme smoky

qual|voll ADJ painful; Schmerzen agonizing, excruciating; Vorstellung, Gedanke agonizing; Anblick harrowing ADV ~ **sterben** to die an agonizing death

Quant [kvant] NT -s, -en quantum

Quänt|chen ▲ ['kvɛntçən] NT -s, - (old) tiny bit, spot; **ein ~ Salz** a speck or dash of salt; **ein ~ Mut** a scrap of courage; **kein ~** not a jot, not an iota; **das letzte ~ Glück/Hoffnung** the last little bit of luck/hope

quan|teln ['kvantln] VT to quantize

Quan|ten ['kvantn] pl von **Quant** von **Quantum**

Quan|ten-: Quan|ten|me|cha|nik F quantum mechanics sing; **Quan|ten|phy|sik** F quantum physics sing; **Quan|ten|sprung** M quantum leap; **Quan|ten|the|o|rie** F quantum theory

quan|ti|fi|zie|ren [kvantifi'tsi:rən] ptp **quantifiziert** VT to quantify

Quan|ti|tät [kvanti'tɛ:t] F -, -en quantity

quan|ti|ta|tiv [kvantita'ti:f] ADJ quantitative ADV quantitatively

Quan|tum ['kvantʊm] NT -s, **Quanten** [-tn] (= Menge, Anzahl) quantum, quantity; (= Anteil) quota, quantum (an +dat of)

Quap|pe ['kvapə] F -, -n a (= Kaulquappe) tadpole b (= Aalquappe) burbot

Qua|ran|tä|ne [karan'tɛ:nə] F -, -n quarantine; **in ~ liegen** or **sein** to be in quarantine; **unter ~ stellen** (Personen) to put in quarantine; Gebiet, Stadt auch to put under quarantine, to quarantine off; **unter ~ stehen** (Person) to be in quarantine; (Gebiet, Stadt auch) to be under quarantine, to be quarantined off; **über das Gebiet wurde sofort ~ verhängt** the area was immediately placed under quarantine or was immediately quarantined off

Qua|ran|tä|ne|sta|ti|on F quarantine or isolation ward

Quark¹ [kvark] M -s, no pl a (= Käse) quark b (inf) (= Unsinn) rubbish (Brit), nonsense; (= unbedeutende Sache) (little) trifle; **so ein ~!** stuff and nonsense!; **~ reden** to talk rubbish (Brit) or nonsense; **das geht ihn einen ~ an!** it's none of his business!; **getretener ~ wird breit, nicht stark** (Prov) it's quality not quantity that counts

Quark² [kvaːk] NT -s, -s (Phys) quark

Quark-: Quark|ku|chen M ≈ cheesecake; **Quark|spei|se** F uncooked pudding made with quark, sugar, milk, fruit etc; **Quark|ta|sche** F, **Quark|teil|chen** NT curd cheese turnover

Quart¹ [kvart] F -, -en a (Mus: auch **Quarte**) fourth; **ein Sprung über eine ~ nach oben/unten** a jump up/down a fourth; **verminderte/reine ~** diminished/perfect fourth b (Fechten) quarte

Quart² NT -s, -e a (old: Maß) ≈ quart b no pl (Typ: = Format) quarto (format)

Quar|ta ['kvarta] F -, **Quarten** [-tn] (dated Sch) third year of German secondary school

Quar|tal [kvar'ta:l] NT -s, -e quarter; **Kündigung zum ~** quarterly notice date; **es muss jedes ~**

bezahlt werden it has to be paid quarterly or every quarter

Quar|tal(s)-: Quar|tal(s)|ab|schluss ▲ M end of the quarter; **Quar|tal(s)|säu|fer(in)** M(F) (inf) periodic heavy drinker; **sein Vater ist ein ~** every so often his father goes on a binge (inf); **quar|tal(s)|wei|se** ADJ quarterly ADV quarterly

Quar|ta|ner [kvar'ta:nɐ] M -s, -, **Quar|ta|ne|rin** [-ərɪn] F -, -nen (dated Sch) pupil in third year of German secondary school

Quar|tär [kvar'tɛ:ɐ] NT -s, no pl quaternary

Quart|band [-bant] M pl **-bände** quarto volume

Quar|te ['kvartə] F -, -n = **Quart¹** a

Quar|ten pl von **Quart¹** von **Quarta** von **Quarte**

Quar|tett [kvar'tɛt] NT -(e)s, -e a (Mus) quartet b (Cards) (= Spiel) ≈ happy families; (= Karten) set of four cards

Quart|for|mat ['kvart-] NT quarto (format)

Quar|tier [kvar'ti:ɐ] NT -s, -e a (= Unterkunft) accommodation (Brit), accommodations pl (US); **wir sollten uns ein ~ suchen** we should look for accommodation(s) or a place to stay; **die Jugendlichen sind in verschiedenen ~en untergebracht/auf mehrere ~e verteilt worden** the youngsters have been accommodated or have been given accommodation(s) or have been put up in various places; **wir hatten unser ~ in einem alten Bauernhof** we stayed in an old farmhouse b (Mil) quarters pl, billet; **bei jdm in ~ liegen** to be quartered or billeted with or on sb; **~ machen** to arrange quarters or billets; **~ nehmen** to put up, to stop; **(sein) ~ beziehen** to take up (one's) quarters c (= Stadtviertel) district, quarter

Quar|tier-: Quar|tier|ma|cher(in) M(F) (Mil) billeting officer; **Quar|tier|meis|ter** M (old Mil) quartermaster; **Quar|tier|su|che** F **auf ~ sein** to be looking for accommodation or a place to stay

Quarz [kvarts] M -es, -e quartz

Quarz-: Quarz|glas NT quartz glass; **quarz|hal|tig** ADJ quartziferous (form), which contains quartz; **Quarz|lam|pe** F quartz lamp; **Quarz|sand** M quartz sand; **Quarz|uhr** F quartz clock; (= Armbanduhr) quartz watch

Qua|sar [kva'za:ɐ] M -s, -e quasar

qua|si ['kva:zi] ADV virtually PREF quasi; **~-wissenschaftlich** quasi-scientific

Quas|sel-: Quas|sel|bu|de F (pej inf: = Parlament etc) talking shop (inf); **Quas|sel|strip|pe** F (inf) chatterbox (inf); (beleidigend) windbag (inf), blabbermouth (inf)

Quas|se|lei [kvasə'lai] F -, -en (inf) gabbling (Brit inf), gabbing (inf), blathering (inf)

quas|seln ['kvasln] VTI to gabble (Brit inf), to blather (inf); **was quasselst du denn da für ein dummes Zeug?** what are you blathering about now? (inf)

Quast [kvast] M -(e)s, -e (dial) wide paint brush

Quas|te ['kvastə] F -, -n (= Troddel) tassel; (von Pinsel) brush, bristles pl; (= Schwanzquaste) tuft; (= Puderquaste) powder puff

Quas|ten|flos|ser [-flɔsɐ] M -s, - (Zool) coelacanth

Quäs|tur [kvɛs'tu:ɐ] F -, -en (Univ) bursary

Qua|tem|ber [kva'tɛmbɐ] M -s, - (Eccl) Ember day

quatsch [kvatʃ] INTERJ squelch

Quatsch [kvatʃ] M -es, no pl (inf) a (= Unsinn) rubbish (Brit), nonsense; **das ist der größte ~, den ich je gehört habe** that is the biggest load of rubbish (Brit) or nonsense I have ever heard; **ach ~!** rubbish! (Brit), nonsense!; **ohne ~!** (= ehrlich) no kidding! (inf); **alles ~!, so ein ~!** what (a load of) rubbish (Brit) or nonsense; **~ mit Soße!** stuff and nonsense! b (= Dummheiten) nonsense; **hört doch endlich**

mit dem ~ auf! stop being so stupid or silly!; **was soll denn der ~!** what's all this nonsense in aid of then!; **lass den ~** cut it out! (inf); **~ machen** to mess about (Brit) or around (inf); **etw aus ~ machen** to do sth for a laugh or for fun; **mach damit keinen ~** don't mess about (Brit) or around with it (inf), don't do anything stupid with it; **mach keinen ~, sonst knallts** don't try anything funny or I'll shoot; **mach keinen ~, du kannst doch jetzt nicht schwanger werden** don't be silly, you can't get pregnant now!

quat|schen¹ ['kvatʃn] (inf) VTI (= dummes Zeug reden) to gab (away) (inf), to blather (inf), to gabble (Brit inf); **sie quatscht mal wieder einen Blödsinn** she's talking a load of rubbish (Brit) or nonsense again VI a (= plaudern) to blather (inf), to chatter, to natter (Brit inf); **er hat stundenlang gequatscht** he blathered or gabbled (Brit) on for hours (inf); **ich hab mit ihm am Telefon gequatscht** I had a good natter (Brit inf) or chat with him on the phone b (= etw ausplaudern) to squeal (inf), to talk

quat|schen² ['kva:tʃn] VI (Schlamm) to squelch

Quat|sche|rei [kvatʃə'rai] F -, -en (inf) blathering (inf), yacking (inf); (in der Schule) chattering

Quatsch-: Quatsch|kopf M (pej inf) (= Schwätzer) windbag (inf); (= Dummkopf) fool, twit (inf); **quatsch|nass** ▲ ADJ (inf) soaking or dripping wet

Que|cke ['kvɛkə] F -, -n couch grass

Queck|sil|ber ['kvɛkzɪlbɐ] NT a (abbr **Hg**) mercury, quicksilver (dated); (inf: = Thermometer) mercury (inf); **~ im Leib haben** (fig) to have ants in one's pants (inf) b (dated: Mensch) fidget

Queck|sil|ber- in cpds mercury; **Queck|sil|ber|dampf|lam|pe** F mercury-vapour (Brit) or mercury-vapor (US) lamp; **queck|sil|ber|hal|tig** ADJ mercurial

queck|sil|be|rig, queck|silb|rig ADJ (fig) fidgety, restless

Queck|sil|ber-: Queck|sil|ber|säu|le F mercury (column); **die ~ ist auf 30 Grad geklettert** the mercury has risen to 30 degrees; **Queck|sil|ber|ver|gif|tung** F mercury poisoning

Quell [kvɛl] M -(e)s, -e (poet) spring, source

Quell-: Quell|be|wöl|kung F (Met) cumulus clouds pl; **Quell|code** M (Comput) source code

Quel|le ['kvɛlə] F -, -n a spring; (von Fluss) spring, source; (= Erdölquelle, Gasquelle) well; **heiße ~n** hot springs; **eine ~ erschließen** to develop or exploit a source b (fig) (= Ursprung, Informant) source; (für Waren) source (of supply), supplier; **die ~ allen Übels** the root of all evil; **eine ~ der Freude** a source of pleasure; **~n der Weisheit** fountain of knowledge; **aus zuverlässiger/sicherer ~** from a reliable/trustworthy source; **an der ~ sitzen** (fig) to be well-placed; (in Organisation) to be able to get inside information; **kannst du mir einige Bücher besorgen, du sitzt doch an der ~?** can you get me some books, after all you can get them at source

quel|len ['kvɛlən] VI pret **quoll** [kvɔl], ptp **gequollen** [gə'kvɔlən] aux sein a (= herausfließen) to pour, to stream (aus out of); **der Bauch quillt ihm über die Hose** his stomach hangs out or bulges out over his trousers (esp Brit) or pants (esp US); **die Augen quollen ihm aus dem Kopf** his eyes were popping out of his head b (Holz, Reis, Erbsen) to swell; **lassen Sie die Bohnen über Nacht ~** leave the beans to soak overnight VT pret **quellte** ['kvɛltə], ptp **gequellt** [gə'kvɛlt] (rare) Erbsen to soak

Quel|len-: Quel|len|an|ga|be F reference; **achten Sie bei der ~ darauf, dass ...** make sure when doing or giving the references that ...; **das Material wurde ohne ~ verwendet** the material was used without reference to its source; **Quel|len|for|schung** F source research;

Quel|len|kri|tik F verification of sources; **Quel|len|nach|weis** M (= Quellenangabe) reference; (Auflistung der Quellen) bibliography, list of sources; **Quel|len|samm|lung** F (collection of) source material; (= Quellenwerk) source book; **Quel|len|steu|er** F (Econ) tax at source; **Quel|len|stu|di|um** NT study of sources; **ich bin immer noch mit dem ~ beschäftigt** I am still studying the sources

Quell-: **Quell|fluss** ▲ M source (river); **quell|frisch** ADJ Wasser spring-fresh attr, fresh from the spring pred; **Quell|ge|biet** NT headwaters pl; **Quell|pro|gramm** NT (Comput) source program; **Quell|spra|che** F source language; **Quell|was|ser** NT spring water

Quen|ge|lei [kvɛŋəˈlaɪ] F -, -en (inf) whining

quen|ge|lig [ˈkvɛŋəlɪç], **queng|lig** [ˈkvɛŋlɪç] ADJ whining; **die Kinder wurden ~** the children started to whine; **er ist sonst nicht so ~** he doesn't usually whine so much

quen|geln [ˈkvɛŋln] VI (inf) to whine

Quen|gler [ˈkvɛŋlɐ] M -s, -, **Queng|le|rin** [-ərɪn] F -, -nen (inf) whiner

Quent|chen △ [ˈkvɛntçən] NT -s, - → **Quänt|chen**

quer [kveːɐ] ADV (= schräg) crossways, crosswise, diagonally; (= rechtwinklig) at right angles; **~ gestreift** horizontally striped, cross-striped; **sollen wir den Teppich lieber ~ legen?** why don't we lay the carpet crosswise or crossways or diagonally?; **er legte sich ~ aufs Bett** he lay down across the bed; **die Spur verläuft ~ zum Hang** the path runs across the slope; **die Straße/Linie verläuft ~** the road/the line runs at right angles; **der Wagen stand ~ zur Fahrbahn** the car was at right angles to the road; **der Lastzug lag ~ über der Straße** the truck was lying (diagonally/at right angles) across the road; **wenn Sie sich ~ stellen, habe ich mit meinem Wagen auch noch Platz** if you park diagonally/at right angles I'll have room to park my car too; **~ durch etw gehen/laufen** etc to cross sth, to go through sth; **~ über etw** (acc) **gehen/laufen** to cross sth, to go across sth; **der Hund ist ~ über den Rasen gelaufen** the dog ran straight or right across the lawn; **die Kamera ~ nehmen** to hold the camera lengthways or crossways; **den Stoff ~ nehmen** to use the cross-grain of the material → **kreuz**

Quer-: **quer|ab** [kveːɐˈlap] ADV (Naut) abeam; **Quer|ach|se** F transverse axis; **Quer|bal|ken** M (von Türrahmen) transom, lintel; (Sport) crossbar; (Her) bar; (Mus) line joining quavers etc; **quer|beet** [kveːɐˈbeːt, ˈkveːɐbeːt] ADV (inf) (= wahllos) at random; (= durcheinander) all over the place (inf); (= querfeldein) across country; **Quer|den|ker(in)** M(F) open-minded thinker; **quer|durch** [kveːɐˈdʊrç] ADV straight through

Que|re [ˈkveːrə] F -, no pl **der ~ nach** widthways, breadthways; **jdm in die ~ kommen** (= begegnen) to cross sb's path; (auch fig: = in den Weg geraten) to get in sb's way; **es muss ihm etwas in die ~ gekommen sein, sonst hätte er sich nicht verspätet** something must have come up otherwise he would not be late

Quer|ein|stei|ger(in) M(F) lateral entry employee; **sie ist (eine) ~in** she comes from a totally different profession; **bei uns gibt es viele ~** many of our employees or colleagues come from a different professional or educational background

Que|re|le [kveˈreːlə] F -, -n usu pl (geh) dispute, quarrel

que|ren [ˈkveːrən] VTI to cross

quer|feld|ein [kveːɐfɛltˈlaɪn] ADV across country

Quer|feld|ein-: **Quer|feld|ein|lauf** M cross-country (run); (Wettbewerb) cross-country (race); **Quer|feld|ein|ren|nen** NT cross-country; (Autorennen) autocross; (Motorradren-

nen) motocross; (Fahrradrennen) cyclecross; (Pferderennen) point-to-point

Quer-: **Quer|flö|te** F (transverse) flute; **Quer|for|mat** NT landscape format; **im ~** in landscape format; **quer ge|hen** ▲ VI irreg aux sein (inf) to go wrong; **heute geht mir alles quer** I can't do a thing right today; **quer|ge|streift** △ ADJ attr → **quer**; **Quer|holz** NT crossbeam; (von Türrahmen) transom, lintel; **Quer|kopf** M (inf) awkward so-and-so (inf) or customer (inf); **quer|köp|fig** ADJ awkward, perverse; **Quer|la|ge** F (Med) transverse presentation, crossbirth; **Quer|lat|te** F crossbar; **quer le|gen** ▲ VR (fig inf) to be awkward; **Quer|li|nie** F diagonal line; **Quer|pass** ▲ M cross; **Quer|pfei|fe** F fife; **Quer|ru|der** NT aileron; **quer schie|ßen** ▲ VI irreg (inf) to be awkward, to spoil things; **Quer|schiff** NT transept; **Quer|schlä|ger** M ricochet (shot)

Quer|schnitt M (lit, fig) cross section

Quer|schnitt(s)-: **quer|schnitt(s)|ge|lähmt** ADJ paraplegic; **seit dem Autounfall ist er ~** since the car accident he has been paralyzed from the waist down; **Quer|schnitt(s)|ge|lähm|te(r)** [-gəlɛːmtə] MF decl as adj paraplegic; **Quer|schnitt(s)|läh|mung** F paraplegia; **Quer|schnitt(s)|zeich|nung** F sectional drawing

Quer-: **quer schrei|ben** ▲ VT irreg (Fin) Wechsel to accept, to underwrite; **Quer|schuss** ▲ M (fig) objection; **quer stel|len** ▲ VR (fig inf) to be awkward; **Quer|stra|ße** F (= Nebenstraße) side street; (= Abzweigung) turning; **das ist eine ~ zur Hauptstraße** it runs at right angles to the main street; **in dieser ~ muss das Geschäft sein** the shop must be down this turning; **bei** or **an der zweiten ~ fahren Sie links ab** take the second road or turning on your left; **die ~n zur Königstraße sehen alle gleich aus** the streets (going) off Königstraße all look the same; **Quer|strei|fen** M horizontal stripe; **Quer|strich** M (horizontal) stroke or line; (Typ inf: = Gedankenstrich) dash; (= Bruchstrich) line; **einen ~ durch etw machen** to put a line through sth; (= streichen auch) to cross sth out; **er macht beim T nie die ~e** he always forgets to cross his T's; **Quer|sum|me** F (Math) sum of digits (of a number); **die ~ bilden** to add the digits in a number; **Quer|trei|ber(in)** M(F) (inf) troublemaker, awkward customer (inf); **Quer|trei|be|rei** [kveːɐtraɪbəˈraɪ] F -, -en (inf) awkwardness, troublemaking

Que|ru|lant [kveruˈlant] M -en, -en, **Que|ru|lan|tin** [-ˈlantɪn] F -, -nen grouser (Brit inf), grumbler

que|ru|lie|ren [kveruˈliːrən] ptp **queruliert** VI to grouse (Brit inf), to grumble

Quer-: **Quer|ver|bin|dung** F connection, link; (von Eisenbahn) connecting line; (von Straße) link road; **hier lässt sich doch eine ~ zur deutschen Geschichte herstellen** you can surely make a connection here with German history, you can surely link this up with German history; **Quer|ver|weis** M cross-reference

quet|schen [ˈkvɛtʃn] VT (= drücken) to squash, to crush; (aus einer Tube) to squeeze; Kartoffeln to mash; (Med:) usu pass to crush; Stimme to strain; **etw in etw** (acc) **~** to squeeze or squash sth into sth; **jdn halbtot ~** to crush sb (nearly) to death; **jdm/sich den Finger ~** to squash sb's/one's finger; **ich hab mir den Finger in der Tür gequetscht** you caught my finger in the door VR (= sich klemmen) to be caught or squashed or crushed; (= sich zwängen) to squeeze (oneself); **du kannst dich noch ins Auto ~** you can still squeeze into the car

Quetsch-: **Quetsch|fal|te** F (Fashion) box pleat; **Quetsch|kom|mo|de** F (hum inf) squeeze-box (inf)

Quet|schung [ˈkvɛtʃʊŋ] F -, -en, **Quetsch|wun|de** F (Med) bruise, contusion (form); **~en erleiden** to suffer bruising; **der Fahrer kam**

mit ~en davon the driver escaped with bruises or bruising; **~ innerer Organe** internal bruising

Queue [køː] NT OR M -s, -s (Billard) cue

Quiche [kɪʃ] F -, -s quiche

quick [kvɪk] ADJ (esp N Ger) lively

Qui|ckie [ˈkvɪki] M -s, -s (inf: = Sex) quickie (inf)

quick|le|ben|dig ADJ (inf) Kind lively, active; ältere Person auch spry

quiek [kviːk] INTERJ squeak

quie|ken [ˈkviːkən], **quiek|sen** [ˈkviːksn] VI to squeal, to squeak

quiet|schen [ˈkviːtʃn] VI (Tür, Schloss, Schuhe) to squeak; (Reifen, Straßenbahn, Mensch) to squeal; Bremsen to screech; **das Kind quietschte vergnügt** or **vor Vergnügen** the child squealed with delight; **das** or **es war zum Quietschen!** (inf) it was a (real) scream! (inf)

quietsch- [ˈkviːtʃ-]: **quietsch|fi|del** → **quietschvergnügt**; **quietsch|le|ben|dig** ADJ (inf) Kind full of beans pred (inf); (= sehr wach) wide awake pred; **quietsch|ver|gnügt** ADJ (inf) happy as a sandboy

quillt [kvɪlt] 3. pers sing pres von **quellen**

Quilt [kvɪlt] M -s, -s quilt

Quint [kvɪnt] F -, -en a (Mus) fifth b (Fechten) quinte

Quin|ta [ˈkvɪnta] F -, **Quinten** [-tn] (dated Sch) second year of German secondary school

Quin|ta|ner [kvɪnˈtaːnɐ] M -s, -, **Quin|ta|ne|rin** [-ərɪn] F -, -nen (dated Sch) pupil in second year of German secondary school

Quin|te [ˈkvɪntə] F -, -n (Mus) fifth

Quin|ten pl von **Quinta** von **Quinte**

Quin|tes|senz [ˈkvɪntɛsɛnts] F quintessence

Quin|tett [kvɪnˈtɛt] NT -(e)s, -e quintet

Quin|tol|le [kvɪnˈtɔlə] F -, -n quintuplet

Quirl [kvɪrl] M -s, -e a (Cook) whisk, beater b (Bot) whorl, verticil c (dated inf: Mensch) live wire (inf)

quir|len [ˈkvɪrlən] VT to whisk, to beat

quir|lig [ˈkvɪrlɪç] ADJ Mensch, Stadt lively, exuberant

Quis|ling [ˈkvɪslɪŋ] M -s, -e (Pol pej) quisling

quitt [kvɪt] ADJ **~ sein (mit jdm)** to be quits or even (with sb); **jdn/etw ~ sein** (dial) to be rid of sb/sth

Quit|te [ˈkvɪtə] F -, -n quince

quit|te(n)|gelb ADJ (sickly) yellow

Quit|ten|ge|lee NT quince jelly

quit|tie|ren [kvɪˈtiːrən] ptp **quittiert** VT a (= bestätigen) Betrag, Rechnung, Empfang to give a receipt for; **lassen Sie sich** (dat) **die Rechnung ~** get a receipt for the bill b (= beantworten) to meet, to answer, to counter (mit with) c (= verlassen) Dienst to quit, to resign VI a (= bestätigen) to sign b (old: = zurücktreten) to quit, to resign

Quit|tung [ˈkvɪtʊŋ] F -, -en a receipt; **gegen ~** on production of a receipt; **eine ~ über 500 Euro** a receipt for 500 euros; **eine ~ ausstellen (über** or **für etw)** to make out or give a receipt (for sth); **jdm eine ~ für etw ausstellen** to give sb a receipt for sth; **können Sie mir bitte eine ~ geben?** could I have a receipt please? b (fig) **das ist die ~ für Ihre Unverschämtheit** that is what you get for being so insolent, that's what comes of being so insolent; **das ist die ~ dafür, dass ...** that's the price you have to pay for ...; **jetzt haben Sie die ~!** now you have paid the penalty!; **die ~ für etw bekommen** or **erhalten** to pay the penalty for sth; **du wirst schon noch die ~ für deine Faulheit/Frechheit bekommen** you'll pay the penalty for your laziness/impudence or for being so lazy/impudent

Quit|tungs|block M pl -blöcke, **Quit|tungs|buch** NT pl -bücher receipt book

Qui|vive [kiˈviːf] NT , no pl **auf dem ~** on the qui vive, on the alert

Quiz [kvɪs] NT **-, -** quiz

Quiz- [kvɪs-]: **Quiz|fra|ge** F quiz question; **Quiz|mas|ter** ['kvɪsmaːstɐ] M **-s, -,** **Quiz|-mas|te|rin** [-ərɪn] F **-, -nen** quizmaster; **Quiz|-sen|dung** F quiz show; (*mit Spielen*) gameshow

quoll *pret von* **quellen**

Quo|rum ['kvoːrʊm] NT **-s,** *no pl* quorum

Quo|te ['kvoːtə] F **-, -n** **a** (*Statistik*) (= *Anteilsziffer*) proportion; (= *Rate*) rate; (*TV etc*) ratings *pl* **b** (*Econ:* = *Quantum*) quota

QUOTE
In German-speaking countries the word **Quote** generally refers to two things. Firstly, it denotes the ratings for a particular television programme. If the **Quote** is not high e- nough, then the programme in question is likely to be doomed, whether it is on a state or a commercial channel. Secondly, **Quoten** refer to the quota system for the allocation of jobs. This is a commitment on the part of the government, employers and political parties to reserve a certain proportion of available jobs for women, the disabled and members of ethnic minorities. Quota systems, especially those relating to women, are controversial and have given rise to derogatory terms such as **Quotenfrauen**.

Quo|te|lung ['kvoːtəlʊŋ] F **-, -en** apportionment

Quo|ten|frau F (*pej inf*) *woman who has been given a post just to fulfil the quota system requirements*

Quo|ten|re|ge|lung F quota system

Quo|ti|ent [kvoˈtsiɛnt] M **-en, -en** quotient

quo|tie|ren [kvoˈtiːrən] *ptp* **quotiert** VT (*Comm*) Preis, Kurs to quote; (= *Verhältnis regeln*) to set quotas/a quota on; **die Ministerposten sind quotiert** the allocation of ministerial posts (*esp Brit*) or positions is subject to quotas

Quo|tie|rung F **-, -en** (*Comm*) quotation; (= *Regelung des Verhältnisses*) setting of quotas/a quota

QWER|TY-Tas|ta|tur ['kvɛrti-] F QWERTY keyboard

QWERTZ-Tas|ta|tur ['kvɛrts-] F QWERTZ keyboard

R

R, r [ɛr] NT **-, -** R, r; **das R rollen** to roll one's r's; **R wie Richard** R for Richard

Ra|batt [ra'bat] M **-(e)s, -e** discount (*auf* on); **mit 10% ~** at *or* with (a) 10% discount

Ra|bat|te [ra'batə] F **-, -n** (= *Beet*) border

Ra|batt|mar|ke F (*Comm*) (trading) stamp

Ra|batz [ra'bats] M **-es, no pl** (*inf*) = **Radau**

Ra|bau|ke [ra'baukə] M **-n, -n** (*inf*) hooligan, lout (*inf*), rowdy (*Brit inf*), punk (*US inf*)

Ra|bau|ken|tum [ra'baukntu:m] NT **-s, no pl** hooliganism, rowdyism (*Brit*)

Rab|bi [ˈrabi] M **-(s), -s** *or* **Rabbinen** [ra'bi:nən] rabbi

Rab|bi|ner [ra'bi:nɐ] M **-s, -, Rab|bi|ne|rin** [-ərɪn] F **-, -nen** rabbi

rab|bi|nisch [ra'bi:nɪʃ] ADJ rabbinical

Ra|be [ˈra:bə] M **-n, -n** raven; **wie ein ~ stehlen** (*inf*) to thieve like a magpie; **ein weißer ~** (*fig*) a rare bird, a rara avis

Ra|ben-: Ra|ben|aas NT (*dated inf*) bad lot (*Brit inf*), bad character (*esp US inf*); **Ra|ben|el|tern** PL (*inf*) bad parents *pl*; **Ra|ben|mut|ter** F *pl* **-mütter** (*inf*) bad mother; **ra|ben|schwarz** ADJ *Nacht* pitch-black, black as pitch; *Augen, Seele auch* coal-black, black as coal; *Haare* jet-black, raven(-black); (*fig*) *Tag, Humor* black; **Ra|ben|va|ter** M (*inf*) bad father

ra|bi|at [ra'bia:t] **ADJ** *Kerl* violent, rough; *Autofahrer* breakneck, wild; *Geschäftsleute* ruthless; *Umgangston* aggressive; *Methoden, Konkurrenz* ruthless, cut-throat; **~ werden** (*wütend*) to go wild; (*aggressiv*) to get violent *or* physical (*inf*) **ADV** (= *rücksichtslos*) roughly; *vorgehen* ruthlessly; (= *aggressiv*) violently

Ra|bu|list [rabu'lɪst] M **-en, -en, Ra|bu|lis|tin** [-'lɪstɪn] F **-, -nen** sophist, quibbler

Ra|bu|lis|te|rei [rabulɪstə'rai] F **-, -en, Ra|bu|lis|tik** [rabu'lɪstɪk] F **-, no pl** sophistry, quibbling

ra|bu|lis|tisch [rabu'lɪstɪʃ] ADJ sophistic, quibbling

Ra|che [ˈraxə] F **-, no pl** revenge, vengeance; **die ~ des kleinen Mannes** (*inf*) sweet revenge; **Tag der ~** (*liter*) day of reckoning; **das ist die ~ für deine Untat** this is the retribution for your misdeed; **auf ~ sinnen** to contemplate *or* plot revenge; **~ schwören** to swear vengeance; **(an jdm) ~ nehmen** *or* **üben** to take revenge *or* to have one's revenge (on *or* upon sb); **etw aus ~ tun** to do sth in revenge; **~ ist Blutwurst** (*inf*) you'll/he'll *etc* be sorry (*inf*); **~ ist süß** (*prov*) revenge is sweet (*prov*); **Montezumas ~** (*hum inf*: = *Durchfall*) Montezuma's revenge (*hum*)

Ra|che-: Ra|che|akt M act of revenge *or* vengeance; **Ra|che|durst** M thirst *or* longing for revenge *or* vengeance; **ra|che|durs|tig** ADJ thirsting *or* longing for revenge *or* vengeance; **Ra|che|en|gel** M avenging angel; **Ra|che|feld|zug** M retaliation campaign; **Ra|che|ge|fühl** NT feeling of bitter resentment; **-e gegen etw/jdn haben** to feel bitter resentment at sth/against *or* toward(s) sb; **Ra|che|göt|tin** F wie **eine ~** like a Fury

Ra|chen [ˈraxn] M **-s, -** throat, pharynx (*spec*); (*von großen Tieren*) jaws *pl*; (*fig*) jaws *pl*, abyss, maw; **jdm etw in den ~ werfen** *or* **schmeißen** (*inf*) to shove sth down sb's throat (*inf*); **jdm den ~ stopfen** (*inf*) to give sb what he/she wants

rä|chen [ˈrɛçn] **VT** *jdn, Untat* to avenge (*etw an jdm* sth on sb); **er schwor, dieses Unrecht zu ~** he swore to seek vengeance for this injustice, he swore to avenge this injustice; **dieses Unrecht werde ich noch an ihm ~** I intend to avenge myself on him for this injustice **VR** (*Mensch*) to get one's revenge, to take revenge *or* vengeance (*an jdm für etw on sb for sth*); (*Schuld, Sünde, Untat*) to have dire consequences; **deine Faulheit/Unehrlichkeit wird sich ~** you'll pay for being so lazy/dishonest

Ra|chen-: Ra|chen|blüt|ler [-bly:tlɐ] M **-s, -** (*Bot*) figwort; **Ra|chen|höh|le** F pharynx, pharyngeal cavity; **Ra|chen|ka|tarr(h)** M pharyngitis; **Ra|chen|man|del** F pharyngeal tonsil; **Ra|chen|put|zer** [-pʊtsɐ] M **-s, -** (*hum inf*) gut rot (*inf*)

Ra|che|plan M plan of revenge; **Rachepläne schmieden** to plot revenge

Rä|cher [ˈrɛçɐ] M **-s, -, Rä|che|rin** [-ərɪn] F **-, -nen** avenger

Ra|che|schwur M oath of revenge *or* vengeance

Rach-: Rach|gier F vindictiveness; **rach|gie|rig ADJ** vindictive **ADV** vindictively

Ra|chi|tis [ra'xi:tɪs] F **-, Rachitiden** [raxi'ti:dn] rickets, rachitis (*spec*)

ra|chi|tisch [ra'xi:tɪʃ] ADJ *Kind* with rickets, rickety, rachitic (*spec*); *Symptom* of rickets

Rach-: Rach|sucht F vindictiveness; **rach|süch|tig** ADJ vindictive

Ra|cker [ˈrakɐ] M **-s, -** (*inf*: *Kind*) rascal, scamp, monkey (*all inf*)

Ra|cke|rei [rakə'rai] F **-, -en** (*inf*) grind (*inf*)

ra|ckern [ˈrakɐn] VIR (*inf*) to slave (away) (*inf*)

Ra|cket [ˈrɛkət, ra'kɛt] NT **-s, -s** (*Aus*) racket, racquet (*Brit*)

Rac|lette [ˈraklɛt] NT OR F **-s, -s** raclette

Rad[1] [ra:t] NT **-(e)s, ⸚er** [ˈrɛːdɐ] **a** wheel; (= *Rolle*) caster; (= *Zahnrad*) gearwheel; (*Sport*) cartwheel; **~ schlagen** to do *or* turn cartwheels; **ein ~ schlagen** to do *or* turn a cartwheel; **der Pfau schlägt ein ~** the peacock is fanning out its tail *or* spreading its tail *or* opening its fan; **jdn aufs ~ flechten** (*Hist*) to break sb on the wheel; **alle Räder greifen ineinander** (*fig*) **ein ~ greift ins andere** (*fig*) it all knits together, all the parts knit together; **nur ein ~** *or* **Rädchen im Getriebe sein** (*fig*) to be only a cog in the works; **das ~ der Geschichte** the wheels of history; **das ~ der Geschichte** *or* **Zeit lässt sich nicht zurückdrehen** you can't turn *or* put the clock back; **unter die Räder kommen** *or* **geraten** (*inf*) to get *or* fall into bad ways; **ein großes ~ drehen** (*fig*) to be a big businessman/businesswoman; **das ~ neu** *or* **noch einmal erfinden** to reinvent the wheel; **das fünfte ~ am Wagen sein** (*inf*) to be in the way; **ein ~ abhaben** (*inf*) to have a screw loose (*inf*)

b (= *Fahrrad*) bicycle, bike (*inf*), cycle; **~ fahren** to cycle; (*pej inf*: = *kriechen*) to crawl (*Brit inf*), to suck up (*inf*); **ich fahre ~** I ride a bicycle; **kannst du ~ fahren?** can you ride a bike?; **mit dem ~ fahren/kommen** to go/come by bicycle

Rad[2] NT **-(s), -** (*Maßeinheit*) rad

Rad|ach|se F axle(tree)

Ra|dar [ra'da:ɐ, 'ra:da:ɐ] M OR NT **-s, -e** radar

Ra|dar- *in cpds* radar; **Ra|dar|ab|wehr|netz** NT (*Mil*) radar defence (*Brit*) *or* defense (*US*) network; **Ra|dar|an|la|ge** F radar (equipment) *no indef art*; **Ra|dar|fal|le** F speed trap; **Ra|dar|ge|rät** NT radar unit; **ra|dar|ge|steu|ert** [-gəʃtɔyɐt] ADJ radar-controlled; **Ra|dar|kon|trol|le** F radar speed check; **Ra|dar|schirm** M radar screen, radarscope; **Ra|dar|sta|ti|on** F radar station; **Ra|dar|über|wach|ung** F radar monitoring

Ra|dau [ra'dau] M **-s, no pl** (*inf*) row, din, racket (*inf*); **~ machen** *or* **schlagen** to kick up a row; (= *Unruhe stiften*) to cause *or* make trouble; (= *Lärm machen*) to make a racket

Ra|dau|bru|der M (*inf*) hooligan, yobbo (*Brit inf*)

Rad|auf|hän|gung F (*Aut*) (wheel) suspension

Ra|dau|ma|cher(in) M(F) (*inf*) hooligan, yobbo (*Brit inf*)

Rad|ball M **, no pl** bicycle polo

Räd|chen [ˈrɛːtçən] NT **-s, -** *dim von* Rad small wheel; (*für Schnittmuster*) tracing wheel; (*Cook*) pastry wheel → **Rad a**

Rad|damp|fer M paddle steamer

Ra|de [ˈra:də] F **-, -n** corncockle

ra|de|bre|chen [ˈra:dəbrɛçn] *insep* **VI** to speak broken English/German *etc* **VT** **Englisch/ Deutsch ~** to speak broken English/German; **er radebrechte auf Italienisch, er wolle ...** he said in broken Italian that he wanted ...

ra|deln[1] [ˈra:dln] **VI** *aux sein* (*inf*) to cycle

ra|deln[2], rä|deln [ˈrɛːdln] VT *Schnittmuster* to trace; (*Cook*) to cut out with a/the pastry wheel

Rä|dels|füh|rer(in) [ˈrɛːdls-] M(F) ringleader

-rä|de|rig [rɛdərɪç] ADJ *suf* -wheeled; **zwei-/vierräderig** two-/four-wheeled

rä|dern [ˈrɛːdɐn] VT (*Hist*) to break on the wheel → *auch* **gerädert**

Rä|der|werk NT (*Mech*) mechanism, works *pl*; (*fig*) machinery, cogs *pl*

rad+fah|ren △ [ˈra:tfa:rən] VI *sep irreg aux sein* → **Rad b**

Rad|fah|ren NT **-s, no pl** → **verboten** no cycling

Rad|fah|rer(in) M(F) **a** cyclist **b** (*pej inf*) crawler (*Brit inf*), brown-noser (*esp US sl*)

Rad|fahr-: Rad|fahr|sport M cycling; **Rad|fahr|weg** M cycleway; (*in der Stadt*) cycle lane

Rad|ga|bel F fork

Rad|helm M cycle helmet

Ra|di [ˈra:di] M **-s, -** (*S Ger, Aus*) white radish; **ei|nen ~ kriegen** (*inf*) to get a rocket (*Brit inf*), to catch it (*inf*)

ra|di|al [ra'dia:l] **ADJ** radial **ADV** radially

Ra|di|al|ge|schwin|dig|keit F (*Phys, Astron*) radial velocity

Ra|di|al|rei|fen M radial (tyre (*Brit*) or tire (*US*))

Ra|di|a|tor [ra'dia:to:ɐ] M **-s, Radiatoren** [-'to:rən] radiator

Ra|dic|chio [ra'dɪkjo] M **-s, Radicchis** [-'diki] radicchio

ra|die|ren [ra'di:rən] *ptp* **radiert** VT a (*mit Radiergummi*) to rub out (*esp Brit*), to erase; (*mit Messer*) to erase b (*Art*) to etch VI a (*mit Radiergummi*) to erase, to rub out (*esp Brit*); **auf dieser Seite hat er dreimal radiert** he's rubbed three things out (*esp Brit*) or he's erased three things on this page b (*Art*) to etch

Ra|die|rer[1] [ra'di:rɐ] M **-s, -** (*inf*) rubber (*Brit*), eraser (*esp US, form*)

Ra|die|rer[2] [ra'di:rɐ] M **-s, -, Ra|die|re|rin** [-ərɪn] F **-, -nen** (*Art*) etcher

Ra|dier-: Ra|dier|gum|mi M rubber (*Brit*), eraser (*esp US, form*); **Ra|dier|kunst** F (*Art*) etching; **Ra|dier|mes|ser** NT (steel) eraser, erasing knife; **Ra|dier|na|del** F (*Art*) etching needle

Ra|die|rung [ra'di:rʊŋ] F **-, -en** (*Art*) etching

Ra|dies|chen [ra'di:sçən] NT **-s, -** radish; **sich** (*dat*) **die ~ von unten ansehen** or **besehen** (*hum*) to be pushing up the daisies (*hum*)

ra|di|kal [radi'ka:l] ADJ radical; *Vereinfachung, Methode auch* drastic; *Vertilgung, Entfernen* total; *Verneinung* categorical; *Ablehnung* flat, categorical

ADV a (*Pol*) **sich verhalten** radically; **~ denken, ~ eingestellt** or **gesinnt sein** to be politically radical

b (*= völlig*) *ausrotten, beseitigen, mit jdm brechen* radically; *ablehnen* flatly; *verneinen* categorically

c (*= tief greifend*) *ändern, verfahren* radically; **mit diesem Missbrauch muss ~ Schluss gemacht werden** a definitive stop must be put to this abuse; **etw ~ verneinen** to deny sth categorically; **etw ~ ablehnen** to refuse sth flatly; **~ vorgehen** to be drastic; **~ gegen etw vorgehen** to take radical steps against sth

Ra|di|kal [radi'ka:l] NT **-s, -e** (*Math*) root; (*Chem*) radical

Ra|di|ka|len|er|lass ▲ M *ban on the employment of teachers and civil servants who are considered to be radical*

Ra|di|ka|le(r) [radi'ka:lə] MF *decl as adj* radical

ra|di|ka|li|sie|ren [radikali'zi:rən] *ptp* **radikalisiert** VT to radicalize

Ra|di|ka|li|sie|rung F **-, -en** radicalization

Ra|di|ka|lis|mus [radika'lɪsmʊs] M **-, no pl** (*Pol*) radicalism

Ra|di|ka|li|tät [radikali'tɛ:t] F **-, no pl** (*Wesenszug*) radical nature; (*Maßnahmen*) drastic nature; (*in Meinung*) radical approach or views *pl*

Ra|di|kal|kur F (*inf*) drastic remedy, kill-or-cure remedy

Ra|dio ['ra:dio] NT OR (SW, S GER AUCH) M **-s, -s** radio, wireless (*esp Brit old*); (*= Station*) radio; **~ hören** to listen to the radio; **im ~, am ~** (*Sw*) on the radio; **etw aus dem ~ erfahren** to hear sth on the radio; **aus dem ~ ertönte ein Beatles-Hit** a Beatles hit was playing on the radio

Ra|dio- *in cpds* radio; **ra|di|o|ak|tiv** [radio-ak'ti:f] ADJ radioactive; **~er Niederschlag** (radioactive) fallout ADV radioactively; **~ verseucht** contaminated with radioactivity; **Ra|di|o|ak|ti|vi|tät** [radioaktivi'tɛ:t] F radioactivity; **Ra|di|o|ama|teur(in)** M(F) radio ham (*inf*) or amateur; **Ra|di|o|ap|pa|rat** M radio (set); **Ra|di|o|as|tro|no|mie** F radio astronomy; **Ra|di|o|bi|o|lo|gie** F radiobiology; **Ra|di|o|che|mie** F radiochemistry; **Ra|di|o|durch|sa|ge** F radio announcement; **Ra|di|o|emp|fän|ger** M radio (set); (*von Funkamateur*) radio receiver; **Ra|di|o|ge|häu|se** NT radio cabinet; (*von Kofferradio*) radio casing; **Ra|di|o|ge|rät** NT radio (set); **Ra|di|o|gra|fie** ▲ [radiogra'fi:] F **-, -n** [-'fi:ən] radiography; **Ra|di|o|gramm** [radio-

'gram] NT *pl* **-gramme** (*Med*) X-ray (photograph), radiograph (*esp US*); **Ra|di|o|iso|top** NT radioisotope; **Ra|di|o|kar|bon|me|tho|de** [radiokar'bo:n-] F radiocarbon (dating) technique or method; **Ra|di|o|kom|pass** ▲ M (*Aviat, Naut*) radio compass, automatic direction finder

Ra|di|o|lo|ge [radio'lo:gə] M **-n, -n, Ra|di|o|lo|gin** [-'lo:gɪn] F **-, -nen** (*Med*) radiologist

Ra|di|o|lo|gie [radiolo'gi:] F **-, no pl** (*Med*) radiology

ra|di|o|lo|gisch [radio'lo:gɪʃ] ADJ radiological ADV radiologically; **~ behandelt werden** to undergo radiotherapy; **~ untersucht werden** to undergo a radiological examination

Ra|di|o|ly|se [radio'ly:zə] F **-, -n** radiolysis

Ra|di|o-: Ra|di|o|me|cha|ni|ker(in) M(F) radio technician or engineer; **Ra|di|o|met|rie** [radiome'tri:] F **-, no pl** radiometry; **Ra|di|o|nuk|lid** M (*Phys*) radionuclide; **Ra|di|o|quel|le** F (*Astron*) radio source; **Ra|di|o|re|kor|der** M radio recorder; **Ra|di|o|röh|re** F radio valve (*esp Brit*) or tube (*esp US*); **Ra|di|o|sen|der** M (*= Rundfunkanstalt*) radio station; (*= Sendeeinrichtung*) radio transmitter; **Ra|di|o|sen|dung** F radio programme (*Brit*) or program (*US*); **Ra|di|o|sko|pie** [radiosko'pi:] F **-, -n** [-'pi:ən] radioscopy; **Ra|di|o|son|de** F (radio-equipped) weather balloon, radiosonde; **Ra|di|o|sta|ti|on** F radio or broadcasting station; **Ra|di|o|strah|lung** F radio signal; **Ra|di|o|tech|nik** F radio technology; **Ra|di|o|tech|ni|ker(in)** M(F) radio technician or engineer; **Ra|di|o|te|le|gra|fie** F radiotelegraphy; **Ra|di|o|te|le|skop** NT radio telescope; **Ra|di|o|the|ra|peut(in)** M(F) radiotherapist; **Ra|di|o|the|ra|pie** F radiotherapy; **Ra|di|o|über|tra|gung** F (radio) broadcast or transmission; **Ra|di|o|we|cker** M radio alarm (clock); **Ra|di|o|wel|len** PL radio waves *pl*

Ra|di|um ['ra:diʊm] NT **-, no pl** (*abbr* Ra) radium

Ra|di|um-: Ra|di|um|be|hand|lung F, **Ra|di|um|be|strah|lung** F (*Med*) radium therapy or treatment; **ra|di|um|hal|tig** ADJ containing radium; **~ sein** to contain radium; **Ra|di|um|strah|len** PL (*Phys, Med*) radium rays *pl*; **Ra|di|um|the|ra|pie** F radium therapy or treatment

Ra|di|us ['ra:diʊs] M **-, Radien** [-diən] radius

Rad-: Rad|kap|pe F hubcap; **Rad|kas|ten** M wheel casing; (*Naut*) paddle box; **Rad|kral|le** F wheel clamp, (*Denver*) boot (*US*); **Rad|kranz** M rim (of a/the wheel); **Rad|la|ger** NT wheel bearing

Rad|ler ['ra:dlɐ] M **-s, -, Rad|le|rin** [-ərɪn] F **-, -nen** (*inf*) cyclist

Rad|ler|ho|se F cycling shorts *pl*

Rad|ler|maß F (*S Ger inf*) shandy (*esp Brit*), radler (*US*)

Rad-: Rad|ma|cher(in) M(F) wheelwright; **Rad|man|tel** M (*= Bereifung*) bicycle tyre (*Brit*) or tire (*US*); **Rad|na|be** F (wheel) hub

Ra|don ['ra:dɔn, ra'do:n] NT **-s, no pl** (*abbr* Rn) radon

Rad-: Rad|renn|bahn F cycle (racing) track; **Rad|ren|nen** NT (*Sportart*) cycle racing; (*einzelnes Rennen*) cycle race; **Rad|renn|fah|rer(in)** M(F) racing cyclist; **Rad|renn|sport** M cycle racing

-räd|rig [rɛ:drɪç] ADJ *suf* = -räderig

Rad-: Rad|schau|fel F blade (of a wheel); **rad+schla|gen** △ ['ra:tʃla:gn] VI *sep irreg* → **Rad** a; **Rad|sport** M cycling; **Rad|sport|ler(in)** M(F) cyclist; **Rad|stand** M (*Aut, Rail*) wheelbase; **Rad|sturz** M (*Aut*) camber; **Rad|tour** F bike ride; (*länger*) cycling or cycle tour; **Rad|wech|sel** M wheel change; (*einen*) **~ machen** (*= Bauteil wechseln*) to change a wheel, to do a wheel change; (*= Fahrrad wechseln*) to change bicycles; **Rad|weg** M cycleway

RAF [ɛra:'ʔɛf] F **-, no pl** *abbr von* **Rote-Armee-Fraktion**

Raf|fel [rafl] F **-, -n** (*dial*) a (*= Reibeisen*) grater b (*Tex*) hackle, flax comb

raf|feln [rafln] VTI a (*= raspeln*) to grate b (*Tex*) to comb, to hackle

raf|fen [rafn] VT a (*= anhäufen*) to pile, to heap; (*hastig*) to grab, to snatch; **er will immer nur (Geld) ~** he's always after money; **sein ganzes Leben hat er nur (Geld) gerafft** he spent his whole life making money; **etw an sich** (*acc*) **~** to grab or snatch sth b *Stoff, Gardine* to gather; *langes Kleid, Rock* to gather up c (*zeitlich*) to shorten, to cut down d (*sl: = verstehen*) to get (*inf*), to work out

Raff-: Raff|gier ['rafgi:ɐ] F greed, avarice; **raff|gie|rig** ['rafgi:rɪç] ADJ greedy, grasping

Raf|fi|na|de [rafi'na:də] F **-, -n** (*Zucker*) refined sugar

Raf|fi|na|ti|on [rafina'tsio:n] F **-, -en** (*von Öl, Zucker, Metall*) refining

Raf|fi|ne|ment [rafinə'mã:] NT **-s, -s** (*geh*) cunning *no pl*, craftiness *no pl*, wiliness *no pl*; **mit allen ~s** with all one's cunning

Raf|fi|ne|rie [rafinə'ri:] F **-, -n** [-'ri:ən] refinery

Raf|fi|nes|se [rafi'nɛsə] F **-, -n** a (*= Feinheit*) refinement, finesse *no pl*; **ein Auto mit allen ~n** a car with all the refinements b (*= Schlauheit, Durchtriebenheit*) cunning *no pl*, craftiness *no pl*, wiliness *no pl*; **mit aller ~** with all one's cunning

raf|fi|nie|ren [rafi'ni:rən] *ptp* **raffiniert** VT *Zucker, Öl, Metall* to refine

raf|fi|niert [rafi'ni:ɐt] ADJ a *Zucker, Öl* refined b *Methoden, Techniken, Mechanismen, Apparat* sophisticated; (*inf*) *Kleid, Frisur, Kleidung* stylish c (*= schlau*) clever, cunning; (*= durchtrieben*) crafty; **sie ist eine ~e Frau** she knows all the tricks in the book; **ein ~es Luder** or **Weib** (*pej*) a sly cow (*Brit pej inf*) or bitch (*US sl*) ADV a (*= durchtrieben*) cleverly; **~ vorgehen** to be cunning; **da musst du dich ~er anstellen** you have to be a little more clever; **~ einfach** cunningly simple b (*= ausgesucht*) *gewürzt* exquisitely; **sie kleidet sich sehr ~** she certainly knows how to dress

Raf|fi|niert|heit F **-, no pl** a (*von Kleidung, Frisur*) stylishness b (*= Schlauheit*) cleverness; (*= Durchtriebenheit*) cunning, craftiness

Raff|ke ['rafkə] M **-s, -s** (*inf*) money-grubber (*inf*)

RAF- [ɛra:'ʔɛf-]: **RAF-Ka|der** M unit of the Red Army Faction; **RAF-Mit|glied** NT member of the Red Army Faction

Ra|ge ['ra:ʒə] F **-, no pl** a (*= Wut*) rage, fury; **jdn in ~ bringen** to infuriate sb; **in ~ kommen** or **geraten** to get or become furious, to fly into a rage or fury; **sich in ~ reden** to talk oneself into a rage b (*inf: = Aufregung, Eile*) hurry, rush

ra|gen ['ra:gn] VI to rise, to tower, to loom; (*= herausragen*) to jut

Ra|gi|o|nen|buch [ra'dʒo:nən-] NT (*Sw*) business register

Rag|lan- ['ragla:n] *in cpds* raglan; **Rag|lan|är|mel** M raglan sleeve; **Rag|lan|schnitt** M raglan style

Ra|gout [ra'gu:] NT **-s, -s** ragout

Rag|time ['rɛgtaim] M **-(s), no pl** ragtime

Rah [ra:] F **-, -en, Ra|he** ['ra:ə] F **-, -en** (*Naut*) yard

Rahm [ra:m] M **-(e)s, no pl** (*dial*) cream → **abschöpfen**

Rähm|chen ['rɛ:mçən] NT **-s, -** *dim von* **Rahmen** (*= Diarähmchen*) mount

rah|men ['ra:mən] VT to frame; *Dias* to mount

Rah|men ['ra:mən] M **-s, -** a frame; (*vom Schuh*) welt b (*fig*) (*= Bereich, Liter: = Rahmenhandlung*) framework; (*= Atmosphäre*) setting; (*= Größe*) scale; **den ~ zu** or **für etw bilden** to provide a backdrop for sth; **im ~ within the framework** (+*gen* of); **seine Verdienste wurden im ~ einer kleinen Feier gewürdigt** his services were honoured (*Brit*) or honored (*US*) in a small ceremony; **im ~ des Möglichen** within the bounds of possibility; **im ~ bleiben, sich im ~ halten** to keep within the limits; **aus dem ~ fallen** to be strikingly different; **musst du denn immer aus dem ~ fallen!** do you always have to show yourself up?; **ein Geschenk/Getränk, das aus dem ~ des Üblichen fällt** a present/drink with a difference; **dieses Buch fällt aus dem ~ unserer normalen Produktion** this book is outside our usual line (of business); **in den ~ von etw passen, sich in den ~ von etw einfügen** to fit (in) or blend in with sth, to go with sth; **den ~ von etw sprengen, über den ~ von etw hinausgehen** to go beyond the scope of sth; **das würde den ~ sprengen** it would be beyond my/our *etc* scope; **einer Feier einen würdigen** or **den richtigen ~ geben** to provide the appropriate setting for a celebration; **in größerem/kleinerem ~** on a large/small scale; **die Feier fand nur in engem** or **in engstem ~ statt** the celebration was just a small-scale affair

Rah|men-: Rah|men|ab|kom|men NT (*Pol*) outline agreement; **Rah|men|an|ten|ne** F frame aerial (*esp Brit*) or antenna; **Rah|men|be|din|gung** F basic condition; **Rah|men|er|zäh|lung** F (*Liter*) framework story; **Rah|men|ge|setz** NT *general outline of a law providing guidelines for specific elaboration*; **Rah|men|hand|lung** F (*Liter*) background story, story which forms the framework; **Rah|men|plan** M framework, outline plan; **Rah|men|pro|gramm** NT **a** (*von Veranstaltung etc*) supporting programme (*Brit*) or program (*US*) **b** = *Rahmenplan*) framework, outline plan; **Rah|men|richt|li|ni|en** PL guidelines *pl*; **Rah|men|ta|rif|ver|trag** M ≈ general agreement on conditions of employment; **Rah|men|ver|an|stal|tung** F umbrella event; **Rah|men|ver|trag** M (*Ind*) general agreement

rah|mig ['ra:mɪç] ADJ (*dial*) creamy

Rahm-: Rahm|kä|se M cream cheese; **Rahm|spi|nat** M creamed spinach (*with sour cream*)

Rah|se|gel ['ra:-] NT (*Naut*) square sail

Rain [raɪn] M -(e)s, -e (*liter*) margin, marge (*poet*)

rä|keln ['rɛ:kln] VR = rekeln

Ra|kel|tief|druck ['ra:kl-] M , *no pl* photogravure, rotogravure

Ra|ke|te [ra'ke:tə] F -, -n rocket (*auch Space*); (*Mil auch*) missile; **ferngelenkte** or **ferngesteuerte ~** guided missile; **wie eine ~ einschlagen** (*inf: Idee etc*) to be a big hit (*inf*)

Ra|ke|ten-, ra|ke|ten- *in cpds* rocket; (*Mil auch*) missile; **Ra|ke|ten|ab|schuss** ▲ M (rocket) launching (*Brit*) or launch; **Ra|ke|ten|ab|schuss|ba|sis** ▲ F (*Mil*) missile or rocket base; (*Space*) launching (*Brit*) or launch site

Ra|ke|ten|ab|wehr F antimissile defence (*Brit*) or defense (*US*)

Ra|ke|ten|ab|wehr-: Ra|ke|ten|ab|wehr|ra|ke|te F antimissile missile; **Ra|ke|ten|ab|wehr|schirm** M nuclear defence (*Brit*) or defense (*US*) umbrella; **Ra|ke|ten|ab|wehr|stel|lung** F antimissile position; **Ra|ke|ten|ab|wehr|sys|tem** NT missile defence (*Brit*) or defense (*US*) system; **Ra|ke|ten|ab|wehr|waf|fe** F antimissile weapon

Ra|ke|ten-: Ra|ke|ten|an|trieb M rocket propulsion; **mit ~** rocket-propelled; **Ra|ke|ten|ap|pa|rat** M rocket(-line) apparatus; **Ra|ke|ten|ba|sis** F = Raketenabschussbasis; **ra|ke|ten|be|stückt** [-bəʃtʏkt] ADJ missile-carrying, missile-equipped; **Ra|ke|ten|flug|zeug** NT rocket-propelled aircraft; **Ra|ke|ten|ge|schoss** ▲ NT missile; **Ra|ke|ten|satz** M set of rockets; (*Mil auch*) set of missiles; **Ra|ke|ten|si|lo** M rocket silo; **Ra|ke|ten|spreng|kopf** M (*Mil*) missile warhead; **Ra|ke|ten-**

start M (rocket) launching (*Brit*) or launch; (= *Start mittels Raketen*) rocket-assisted takeoff; **Ra|ke|ten|stu|fe** F stage (of a rocket or (*Mil auch*) missile); **Ra|ke|ten|stütz|punkt** M missile base; **Ra|ke|ten|ver|suchs|ge|län|de** NT rocket range; (*Space*) launching (*Brit*) or launch site; **Ra|ke|ten|wer|fer** M rocket launcher; **Ra|ke|ten|zeit|al|ter** NT space age

Ra|kett [ra'kɛt] NT -s, -s or -e (*old Sport*) racket, racquet (*Brit*)

Ral|lye ['rali, 'rɛli] F -, -s rally; **eine ~ fahren** to drive in a rally; **~ fahren** to go rallying

Ral|lye|fah|rer(in) M(F) rally driver

RAM [ram] NT -s, -s (*Comput*) RAM

Ra|ma|dan [rama'da:n] M , -e Ramadan

Ram|ba|zam|ba ['ramba'tsamba] NT -s, *no pl* (*inf*) **~ machen** to kick up a fuss

Ram|bo ['rambo] M -s, -s Rambo, tough guy (*inf*)

Ramm-: Ramm|bock M ram(mer); (*für Pfähle*) pile-driver; **ramm|dö|sig** ['ramdø:zɪç] ADJ (*inf*) giddy, dizzy

Ram|me ['ramə] F -, -n ram(mer); (*für Pfähle*) pile-driver

Ram|me|lei [ramə'laɪ] F -, -en **a** (*inf*: = *Gedränge*) crush, scrum (*Brit inf*) **b** (*sl*) banging away (*inf*)

ram|meln ['ramln] VT → gerammelt VIR (*dial*: = *herumtoben*) to charge about (*Brit*) or around VI (*Hunt*) to mate; (*sl*) to have it off or away (*Brit inf*), to do it (*inf*)

ram|men ['ramən] VT to ram

Rammler ['ramlɐ] M -s, - **a** (= *Kaninchen*) buck **b** (*sl*: = *Mann*) stud (*inf*)

Ram|pe ['rampə] F -, -n **a** ramp **b** (*Theat*) a-pron, forestage

Ram|pen|licht NT (*Theat*) footlights *pl*; (*fig*) limelight; **sie möchte im ~ stehen** (*Theat*) she'd like to go on the stage; (*fig*) she wants to be in the limelight; **im ~ der Öffentlichkeit stehen** (*fig*) to be in the limelight; **ins ~ treten** or **rü|cken** (*Theat*) to come down to the footlights; (*fig*) to step into the limelight

ram|po|nie|ren [rampo'ni:rən] ptp **ramponiert** VT (*inf*) to ruin; *Möbel* to bash about (*inf*); **er sah ziemlich ramponiert aus** he looked the worse for wear (*inf*)

Ramsch [ramʃ] M -(e)s, *no pl* **a** (*inf*) junk, rubbish (*Brit*), trash **b** (*Skat*) **(einen) ~ spielen** to play (a) ramsch

ram|schen ['ramʃn] VI **a** (*inf*) to buy cheap junk **b** (*beim Skat*) to play (a) ramsch VT (*Comm*) to buy up

Ramsch-: Ramsch|händ|ler(in) M(F) (*pej*) junk dealer; **Ramsch|la|den** M (*pej*) junk shop; **Ramsch|ver|kauf** M oddments sale; **Ramsch|wa|re** F (*pej*) trashy goods *pl*, rubbish (*Brit*)

RAM-Spei|cher ['ram-] M (*Comput*) RAM memory

ran [ran] INTERJ (*inf*) come on, go it (*inf*); **~ an den Feind!** let's go get 'em! (*inf*); **~ an die Arbeit!** down to work, shoulders to the wheel → *auch* heran

Ranch [rɛntʃ, ra:ntʃ] F -, -(e)s ranch

Ran|cher ['rɛntʃɐ, 'ra:ntʃɐ] M -s, -(s), **Ran|che|rin** [-ərɪn] F -, -nen rancher

Rand¹ [rant] M -es, ⸚er ['rɛndɐ] **a** edge; (*von Weg, Straße, Schwimmbecken etc*) side, edge; (*von Brunnen, Gefäß, Tasse*) top, rim, brim; (*von Abgrund*) brink; **voll bis zum ~** full to the brim, brimful; **am ~e** (*erwähnen, zur Sprache kommen*) by the way, in passing; *interessieren* marginally; *beteiligt sein* marginally, on the fringe; *miterleben* from the sidelines; **etw am ~e bemerken** or **vermerken** to mention sth in passing or in parentheses; **am ~e des Waldes** at the edge of the forest; **am ~e der Stadt** on the outskirts of the town; **am ~e der Veranstaltung** on the fringe(s) of the event; **am ~e der Verzweiflung/des Wahn-**

sinns on the verge of despair/madness; **am ~e des Grabes** or **Todes stehen** to be at death's door; **am ~e des Untergangs** or **Ruins** on the brink or verge of ruin; **am ~e eines Krieges** on the brink of war; **die Schweizer haben den Krieg nur am ~e miterlebt** the Swiss were only marginally involved in the war, the Swiss only experienced the war from the sidelines; **er hat die Russische Revolution noch am ~e miterlebt** he was around at the beginning/end of the Russian Revolution; **eine kleine Szene am ~e des Krieges** a small incident on the fringe of the war; **am ~e der Gesellschaft/der politischen Landschaft** on the fringes of society/the political scene; **an den ~ der Gesellschaft gedrängt werden** to be marginalized by society; **am äußersten rechten ~ des politischen Spektrums** on the extreme right of the political spectrum **b** (= *Umrandung*) border; (= *Tellerrand*) edge, side; (= *Brillenrand*) rim; (*von Hut*) brim; (= *Seitenrand, Buchrand, Heftrand*) margin; **wenn er so über die Ränder seiner Brille schielt** when he peers over the top of his glasses like that; **mit schwarzem ~** black-edged, with a black border; **etw an den ~ schreiben** to write sth in the margin **c** (= *Schmutzrand*) ring; (*um Augen*) circle, ring; **rote Ränder um die Augen haben** to have red rims around one's eyes **d** (*fig*) **das versteht sich am ~e** that goes without saying; **sie waren außer ~ und Band** there was no holding them, they were going wild; (*sl*) **halt den ~!** (*sl*) shut your face! (*sl*); **zu ~e** = zurande

Rand² M -s, -(s) (= *Währung*) rand

Ran|da|le [ran'da:lə] F -, *no pl* rioting; **~ machen** to riot

ran|da|lie|ren [randa'li:rən] ptp **randaliert** VI to rampage (about); **~de Jugendliche** (young) hooligans; **~de Studenten** rioting students; **die Jugendlichen zogen ~d durch die Straßen** the youths rampaged or went on the rampage or ran wild through the streets; **die Gefangenen fingen an zu ~** the prisoners started to go on the rampage

Ran|da|lie|rer [randa'li:rɐ] M -s, -, **Ran|da|lie|re|rin** [-ərɪn] F -, -nen hooligan, troublemaker

Rand-: Rand|aus|gleich M (*Comput*) justification; **Rand|aus|lö|ser** M margin release; **Rand|be|mer|kung** F (*schriftlich: auf Seite*) note in the margin, marginal note; (*mündlich, fig*) (passing) comment; **etw in einer ~ erwähnen** (*fig*) to mention sth in passing; **Rand|be|zirk** M outlying district

Ran|de ['randə] F -, -n (*Sw*) beetroot

Rand|ein|stel|lung F margin setting

rän|deln ['rɛndln] VT *Münze* to mill

rän|dern ['rɛndɐn] VT to edge, to border

Rand-: Rand|er|schei|nung F marginal or peripheral matter; (= *Nebenwirkung*) side effect; **Rand|fi|gur** F minor figure; **Rand|ge|biet** NT (*Geog*) edge, fringe; (*Pol*) border territory; (*fig*) subsidiary; **rand|ge|näht** [-gənɛ:t] ADJ *Schuhe* welted; **Rand|glos|se** F marginal note; **Rand|grup|pe** F fringe group

-ran|dig [randɪç] ADJ *suf* -edged; **goldrandig** (*Rahmen*) gold-edged; *Tasse* gold-rimmed

Rand-: rand|los ADJ *Brille* rimless; *Hut* brimless ADV (*Comput*) *drucken, bedrucken* without margins; **Rand|no|tiz** F marginal note; **Rand|staat** M border state; **die ~en des Mittelmeers** the countries around or bordering on the Mediterranean; **die ~en der Nordsee** the North Sea countries; **rand|stän|dig** ADJ *Personen, Position* marginal(ized); *Bevölkerungsgruppen* minority; **Rand|stän|di|ge(r)** [-ʃtɛndɪgə] MF *decl as adj* person marginalized by society; **die ~n der deutschen Gesellschaft** the marginalized in German society; **Rand|stän|dig|keit** F -, *no pl* marginality; **Rand|stein** M kerb; **den ~ mit|nehmen** (*inf*) to hit the kerb; **Rand|stel|ler** [-ʃtɛlɐ] M -s, - margin stop; **rand|voll** ADJ *Glas* full to the brim; *Behälter* full to the top; *Flug-*

zeug, Aktenordner packed; *(fig)* **Terminkalender, Programm** packed; *(inf: = betrunken)* smashed *(inf)*; **Rand|zo|ne** F peripheral zone *or* area; *(fig)* fringe; **in der ~** on the periphery; **diese Staaten sind vorerst noch ~n der Weltpolitik** these states are still on the periphery *or* perimeter of world politics

Ranft [ranft] M **-(e)s, ~e** ['rɛnftə] *(dial)* crust *(Brit)*, heel *(US, Scot)*

rang *pret von* **ringen**

Rang [raŋ] M **-(e)s, ~e** ['rɛŋə] **a** *(Mil)* rank; *(in Firma)* position; *(= gesellschaftliche Stellung)* position, rank; *(in Wettbewerb)* place, position; **im ~(e) eines Hauptmanns stehen** to have the rank of captain; **im ~ höher/tiefer stehen** to have a higher/lower rank/position, to rank higher/lower; **einen hohen ~ bekleiden** to hold a high office; *(Mil)* to have a high rank; **ein Mann von ~ und Würden** a man of considerable *or* high standing, a man of status; **ein Mann ohne ~ und Namen** a man without any standing *or* reputation; **alles, was ~ und Namen hat** everybody who is anybody; **jdm den ~ streitig machen** *(fig)* to challenge sb's position; **jdm den ~ ablaufen** *(fig)* to outstrip sb **b** *(= Qualität)* quality, class; **ein Künstler/Wissenschaftler von ~** an artist/scientist of standing, a top artist/scientist; **von hohem ~** high-class; **eine Touristenattraktion ersten ~es** a first-class *or* first-rate tourist attraction; **ein Skandal ersten ~es** a scandal of the highest order; **mindern ~es** low-class, second-rate **c** *(Theat)* circle; **erster/zweiter ~** dress/upper circle, first/second circle; **wir sitzen (erster/zweiter) ~ Mitte** *(inf)* we're sitting in the middle of the (dress/upper) circle; **vor leeren/überfüllten Rängen spielen** to play to an empty/a packed house **d Ränge** PL *(Sport: = Tribünenränge)* stands *pl* **e** *(= Gewinnklasse)* prize category

Rang-: Rang|ab|zei|chen NT *(Mil)* badge of rank, insignia; **Rang|äl|tes|te(r)** MF *decl as adj* *(Mil)* senior officer

Ran|ge ['raŋə] F **-, -n** urchin

ran+ge|hen ['rangeːən] VI *sep irreg aux sein* **a** *(inf)* to get stuck in *(inf)*; **geh ran!** go on! → *auch* **herangehen** **b** *(sl: = Frau anbaggern)* **der Typ geht schwer ran** that guy's really giving it the chat *(inf)*

Ran|ge|lei [raŋə'lai] F **-, -en** *(inf)* = **Gerangel**

ran|geln ['raŋln] *(inf)* **VI** to scrap; *(um Sonderangebote auch)* to tussle *(um* for); *(um Posten)* to wrangle *(um* for) **VR** to sprawl about

Rang-: Rang|fol|ge F order of rank *(esp Mil)* *or* standing; *(in Sport, Wettbewerb)* order of placing; *(von Problemen, Prioritäten)* order of importance; **nach der ~, der ~ nach** in order of rank *(esp Mil)* *or* standing; *(in Sport, Wettbewerb)* in order of placing; *(von Problemen, Prioritäten)* in order of importance; **rang|hoch** ADJ senior; *(Mil auch)* high-ranking; **Rang|höchs|te(r)** MF *decl as adj* senior person; *(Mil)* highest-ranking officer

Ran|gier|bahn|hof [rã'ʒiːɐ-] M marshalling *(Brit)* *or* marshaling *(US)* yard

ran|gie|ren [rã'ʒiːrən] *ptp* **rangiert** **VT** **a** *(Rail)* to shunt *(Brit)*, to switch *(US)* **b** *(inf: = abschieben)* to shove *(inf)*, to shunt *(inf)* **VI** *(inf: = Rang einnehmen)* to rank; **er rangiert gleich hinter** *or* **unter dem Abteilungsleiter** he comes directly beneath the head of department; **seine Familie rangiert in seinem Leben nur am Rande** his family take second place (in his life); **Mathilde rangiert bei mir unter „ferner liefen"** *(inf)* as far as I'm concerned Mathilde is an "also-ran" *(esp Brit)* *or* "has-been" *(inf)*; **der Intelligenz nach rangiert er ganz vorne** he's quite high up the list as far as intelligence goes; **an erster/letzter Stelle ~** to come first/last, to take first/last place

Ran|gie|rer [rã'ʒiːrɐ] M **-s, -, Ran|gie|re|rin** [-ərɪn] F **-, -nen** *(Rail)* shunter *(Brit)* *or* switcher *(US)* driver

Ran|gier- [rã'ʒiːɐ-]: **Ran|gier|gleis** NT siding, sidetrack *(US)*; **Ran|gier|lok** F , **Ran|gier|lo|ko|mo|ti|ve** F , **Ran|gier|ma|schi|ne** F shunter *(Brit)*, switcher *(US)*

Rang-: Rang|lis|te F **a** *(Mil)* active list **b** *(Sport, fig)* (results) table; **er steht auf der ~ der weltbesten Boxer** he ranks among the world's top boxers; **Rang|lo|ge** F *(Theat)* box (in the circle); **rang|mä|ßig** ADJ according to rank **ADV** höher in rank; **jdm ~ übergeordnet/untergeordnet sein** to be sb's superior/subordinate; **~ entspricht der Admiral dem General** the rank of admiral corresponds to the rank of general; **~ stehe ich unter ihm** I'm lower than him in rank; **Rang|ord|nung** F hierarchy; *(Mil)* (order of) ranks; **Rang|stu|fe** F rank; **auf der gleichen ~ stehen** to be of *or* to have the same rank; **Rang|un|ter|schied** M social distinction; *(Mil)* difference of rank; **wir machen hier keine ~e** we're not status-conscious here

ran+hal|ten ['ranhaltn] VR *sep irreg* *(inf)* **a** *(= sich beeilen, sich umtun)* to get a move on *(inf)* **b** *(= schnell zugreifen)* to dig in *(inf)*, to get stuck in *(inf)*

rank [raŋk] ADJ *(liter)* **~ und schlank** slender and supple; *Mädchen auch* slim and sylphlike

Rank [raŋk] M **-(e)s, Ränke** ['rɛŋkə] *(Sw: = Kurve)* curve; **den ~ finden** *(fig: = zurechtkommen)* to cope, to manage; **den ~ zueinander finden** to get on (with each other) → *auch* **Ränke**

Ran|ke ['raŋkə] F **-, -n** tendril; *(von Brom-, Himbeeren)* branch; *(von Erdbeeren)* stalk; *(von Weinrebe)* shoot

Rän|ke ['rɛŋkə] PL *(liter)* intrigue, cabal *(liter)*; **~ schmieden** to hatch a plot, to intrigue, to cabal *(liter)*

ran|ken ['raŋkn] **VR** **sich um etw ~** to entwine itself around sth; *(fig: Geschichten etc)* to have grown up around sth **VI** *aux haben* *or* **sein an etw** *(dat)* **~** to entwine itself around sth

Ran|ken-: Ran|ken|ge|wächs NT climbing plant, climber; *(= Efeu etc)* creeper; **Ran|ken|werk** NT *(Art)* arabesques *pl*; *(fig)* embellishment

Rän|ke-: Rän|ke|schmied(in) M(F) *(liter)* intriguer; **Rän|ke|spiel** NT *(liter)* intrigue, cabal *(liter)*; **rän|ke|süch|tig, rän|ke|voll** ADJ *(liter)* scheming, caballing *(liter)*

ran|kig ['raŋkɪç] ADJ *(Bot)* climbing

Ran|king ['rɛŋkɪŋ] NT **-s, -s** *(inf: = Rangordnung)* ranking

ran+klot|zen ['ranklɔtsn] VI *sep* *(inf)* to get stuck in *(inf)*

ran+kom|men ['rankɔmən] VI *sep irreg aux sein* *(inf)* **an etw** *(acc)* **~** to get at sth; **an die Helga ist nicht ranzukommen** you won't get anywhere with Helga *(inf)*; **an unseren Chef ist schwer ranzukommen** our boss isn't very easy to get at *(inf)*; **niemanden an sich ~ lassen** to be standoffish *(inf)*, to keep oneself to oneself *(inf)*; **nichts an sich ~ lassen** not to be fazed by anything → *auch* **herankommen, drankommen**

ran+krie|gen ['rankriːgn] VT *sep* *(inf)* **a** *(= verpflichten)* **jdn ~** *(zur Arbeit)* to make sb knuckle under *(inf)*; *(stärker)* to put sb through the mill *(inf)*; *(zur Mitarbeit)* to make sb pull his *or* her weight *(inf)*; *(zur Verantwortung)* to get sb to take responsibility **b** *(= reinlegen)* **jdn ~** to con sb *(inf)*, to take sb for a ride *(fig)*

Ran|kü|ne [raŋ'kyːnə] F **-, *no pl*** *(geh, old)* grudge, rancour *(Brit)*, rancor *(US)*

ran+las|sen ['ranlasn] VT *sep irreg* *(inf)* **jdn ~** *(an Aufgabe etc)* to let sb have a go *(esp Brit)* *or* a try *(inf)*; **sie lässt jeden ran** *(inf)* she's anybody's *(inf)*, she's an easy lay *(sl)*; **sie lässt keinen mehr (an sich** *acc)* **ran** *(inf)* she won't let anybody near her

ran+ma|chen ['ranmaxn] VR *sep* *(inf)* = **heranmachen**

rann *pret von* **rinnen**

ran+neh|men ['ranneːmən] VT *sep irreg* *(inf)* **a** *(= fordern)* **jdn ~** to put sb through his *or* her paces; **der neue Lehrer nimmt uns ganz schön ran** the new teacher really gives us a hard time **b** *(= zurechtweisen)* **jdn ~** to let sb have it **c** *(= aufrufen)* **Schüler** to pick on

rann|te *pret von* **rennen**

Ran|schmei|ße ['ranʃmaisə] F **-, *no pl*** *(inf)* **er hat den Job durch ~ bekommen** he got the job by being a complete crawler *(Brit inf)* *or* brown-noser *(esp US sl)*

ran+schmei|ßen ['ranʃmaisn] VR *sep irreg* *(inf)* **sich an jdn ~** to throw oneself at sb *(inf)*

Ra|nun|kel [ra'nʊŋkl] F **-, -n** *(Bot)* ranunculus

Rän|zel ['rɛntsl] NT OR M **-s, -** *(old, dial)* knapsack, pack; **sein** *or* **das ~ schnüren** *(liter)* to pack up one's belongings

Ran|zen ['rantsn] M **-s, -** **a** *(= Schulranzen)* satchel **b** *(inf: = Bauch)* belly *(Brit inf)*, gut *(inf)*; **sich** *(dat)* **den ~ voll schlagen** to stuff oneself *(inf)* *or* one's face *(inf)* **c** *(inf: = Buckel)* hunchback, hump(back); **jdm (ordentlich) den ~ voll hauen** to give sb a (good) thrashing

ran|zig ['rantsɪç] ADJ rancid **ADV** **~ schmecken/riechen** to taste/smell rancid

Rap [rɛp] M **-(s), -s** *(Mus)* rap

ra|pid [ra'piːt], **ra|pi|de** [ra'piːdə] ADJ rapid **ADV** rapidly

Ra|pier [ra'piːɐ] NT **-s, -e** rapier

Rap|pe ['rapə] M **-n, -n** black horse → **Schuster**

Rap|pel ['rapl] M **-s, -** *(inf)* **a** *(= Fimmel)* craze; *(= Klaps)* crazy mood; **seinen ~ kriegen** *or* **bekommen** to go completely crazy; **du hast wohl einen ~!** you must be crazy! **b** *(= Wutanfall)* **einen ~ haben** to be in a foul *or* filthy mood *or* temper; **einen ~ kriegen** *or* **bekommen** to throw a fit; **dabei kann man ja einen ~ kriegen** it's enough to drive you mad *or* up the wall *(inf)*

rap|pel|dürr ['rapl'dʏr] ADJ *(inf)* thin as a rake

rap|pe|lig ['rapəlɪç] ADJ *(inf)* **a** *(= verrückt)* crazy, cracked *(inf)*; **bei dem Lärm kann man ja ~ werden** the noise is enough to drive you crazy *(inf)* *or* round the twist *(Brit inf)* **b** *(= nervös, unruhig)* jumpy *(inf)*

rap|peln ['rapln] VI *(inf)* *(= lärmen)* to rattle; *(Aus: = verrückt sein)* to be crazy; **es rappelt an der Tür** somebody's shaking *or* rattling the door; **bei dir rappelt's wohl!** *(inf)* are you crazy?; **bei dem rappelt's manchmal** *(inf)* he just flips (out) sometimes *(inf)*

rap|pel|voll ['rapl'fɔl] ADJ *(inf)* jampacked *(inf)*, chock-a-block *(inf)*

rap|pen ['rɛpn] VI *(Mus)* to rap

Rap|pen ['rapn] M **-s, -** *(Sw)* centime

Rap|per ['rɛpɐ] M **-s, -, Rap|pe|rin** [-ərɪn] F **-, -nen** *(Mus)* rapper; *(= Fan)* rap fan

rapp|lig ['raplɪç] ADJ = **rappelig**

Rap|port [ra'pɔrt] M **-(e)s, -e** **a** report; **sich zum ~ melden** to report; **jdn zum ~ bestellen** to ask sb to present a report **b** *(Psych)* rapport **c** *(Mil old)* report; **sich zum ~ melden** to report; **er ist beim Kommandeur zum ~** he's making a report to the commander

Raps [raps] M **-es, -e** *(Bot)* rape

Raps|öl NT rape(seed) oil

Rap|tus ['raptus] M **-, -se** *(Med)* fit, raptus *(spec)*

Ra|pun|zel [ra'pʊntsl] F **-, -n** **a** *(Bot)* corn salad, lamb's lettuce **b** *(Märchen)* Rapunzel

Ra|pun|zel|sa|lat M corn salad

rar [raːɐ] ADJ rare; **sich ~ machen** *(inf)* to keep *or* stay away; *(= sich zurückziehen)* to make oneself scarce

Ra|ri|tät [rari'tɛːt] F **-, -en** rarity

Ra|ri|tä|ten-: Ra|ri|tä|ten|händ|ler(in) M(F) dealer in rare objects; **Ra|ri|tä|ten|ka|bi|nett** NT collection of rare objects

ra|sant [ra'zant] ADJ **a** *Tempo, Spurt* terrific, lightning *attr* (*inf*); *Auto, Fahrer* fast; *Aufstieg, Karriere* meteoric; *Entwicklung, Wachstum, Fortschritt, Abnahme, Zerfall* rapid; **das ist vielleicht ein ~es Auto** this car really can shift (*inf*); **sie haben das Presto in ~em Tempo gespielt** they really raced *or* rattled (*inf*) through the presto **b** (= *imponierend*) *Frau* vivacious; *Leistung* terrific **c** *Schuss-, Flugbahn* level, flat ADV **a** (= *sehr schnell*) fast; **sie fuhr ~ die Straße hinunter** she tore *or* raced down the street **b** (= *stürmisch*) dramatically

Ra|sanz [ra'zants] F -, *no pl* **a** (= *Geschwindigkeit*) speed; **er jagte mit unheimlicher ~ davon** he tore off at a terrific lick (*Brit inf*) *or* speed; **er nahm die Kurve mit gekonnter ~** he took the bend with daredevil skill **b** (= *Schwung*) panache

rasch [raʃ] ADJ **a** (= *schnell*) quick, rapid, swift; *Tempo* great **b** (= *übereilt*) rash, (over-)hasty ADV **a** (= *schnell*) quickly, rapidly, swiftly; **nicht so ~!** not so fast *or* quick; **~ machen** to hurry (up), to get a move on (*inf*); **es muss ~ gehen** it's got to be fast; **ich habe so ~ wie möglich gemacht** I was as quick *or* fast as I could be; **ein bisschen ~, bitte!** make it quick, be quick **b** (= *vorschnell*) **mit etw ~ bei der Hand sein** to be rash *or* (over-)hasty about sth, to be too quick off the mark with sth (*inf*)

ra|scheln ['raʃln] VI to rustle; **es raschelt (im Stroh/Laub)** there's something rustling (in the straw/leaves); **mit etw ~** to rustle sth

Rasch|heit F -, *no pl* **a** (= *Schnelligkeit*) rapidity, swiftness **b** (= *Übereiltheit*) rashness, (over-)hastiness

ra|sen ['raːzn] VI **a** (= *wüten, toben*) to rave; (*Sturm*) to rage; **er raste vor Schmerz** he was going wild with pain; **er raste vor Wut** he was mad with rage; **er raste vor Eifersucht** he was half-crazed with jealousy; **die Zuschauer rasten vor Begeisterung** the spectators were wild with excitement **b** *aux sein* (= *sich schnell bewegen*) to race, to tear; (*Puls, Herz*) to race; **der Rennwagen raste in die Menge/gegen einen Baum** the racing car crashed *or* smashed into the crowd/a tree; **das Auto raste in den Fluss** the car crashed into the river; **ras doch nicht so!** (*inf*) don't go so fast!; **die Zeit rast** time flies **c** *aux sein* (*inf*: = *herumhetzen*) to race *or* run around

Ra|sen ['raːzn] M -s, - lawn, grass *no indef art, no pl*; (*von Sportplatz*) turf, grass; (= *Sportplatz*) field, pitch; (*Tennis*) court; **einen ~ anlegen** to lay (down) a lawn; **„bitte den ~ nicht betreten"** "please keep off the grass"; **jetzt deckt ihn der kühle** *or* **grüne ~ zu** (*liter*) now he lies beneath the green sward (*liter*); **unter dem grünen ~ ruhen** (*liter*) to be at rest in God's green acre (*liter*)

Rasen-: Rasen|bank F *pl* -bänke grassy bank; **ra|sen|be|deckt, ra|sen|be|wach|sen** ADJ grassy, grass-covered, covered with grass

ra|send ADJ **a** (= *enorm*) terrific; *Eile* terrific, tearing; *Durst* raging, terrific; *Beifall* wild, rapturous; *Eifersucht* burning; *Schmerz* excruciating, terrific; **~e Kopfschmerzen** a splitting headache **b** (= *wütend*) furious, livid, raging; **jdn ~ machen** to make sb furious *or* livid *or* wild (*inf*); **er macht mich noch ~** he'll drive me crazy (*inf*); **ich könnte ~ werden** I could scream; **es ist zum Rasendwerden** it's absolutely infuriating *or* maddening ADV (*inf*) terrifically, enormously; *schnell* incredibly; *wehtun, sich beeilen, applaudieren* like mad (*inf*) *or* crazy (*inf*); *lieben, verliebt, eifersüchtig sein* madly (*inf*); **~ viel Geld** heaps *or* pots of money (*inf*); **~ gern!** I'd simply love to!

Ra|sen|de(r) ['raːzndə] MF *decl as adj* madman/-woman, maniac

Rasen-: Ra|sen|flä|che F lawn; **Ra|sen|mä|her** M , **Ra|sen|mäh|ma|schi|ne** F lawn mower; **Ra|sen|platz** M (*Ftbl etc*) field, pitch; (*Tennis*) grass court; **Ra|sen|spiel** M (*Sport*) game played on grass, outdoor game; **Ra|sen|sport** M sport played on grass, outdoor sport; **Ra|sen|spren|ger** [-ʃprɛŋɐ] M -s, - (lawn) sprinkler; **Ra|sen|stück** NT patch of grass; **Ra|sen|wal|ze** F (lawn) roller

Ra|ser ['raːzɐ] M -s, -, **Ra|se|rin** [-ərɪn] F -, -nen (*inf*) speed maniac (*esp Brit inf*) *or* merchant (*Brit inf*), speed demon (*US inf*)

Ra|se|rei [raːzə'raɪ] F -, -en **a** (= *Wut*) fury, rage, frenzy **b** (*inf*: = *schnelles Fahren, Gehen*) mad rush

Ra|sier- [ra'ziːɐ] *in cpds* shaving; **Ra|sier|ap|pa|rat** M razor; (*elektrisch auch*) shaver; **Ra|sier|creme** F shaving cream

ra|sie|ren [ra'ziːrən] *ptp* **rasiert** VT **a** *Haare, Kopf, Bart* to shave; **sich ~ lassen** to get a shave; **sie rasiert sich** (*dat*) **die Beine** she shaves her legs **b** (*inf*: = *streifen*) to scrape VR to (have a) shave; **sich nass ~** to have a wet shave; **sich trocken ~** to use an electric shaver

Ra|sie|rer [ra'ziːrɐ] M -s, - (*inf*) (electric) razor *or* shaver

Rasier-: Ra|sier|klin|ge F razor blade; **Ra|sier|mes|ser** NT (open) razor, cut-throat razor; **Ra|sier|pin|sel** M shaving brush; **Ra|sier|schau|m** M shaving foam; **Ra|sier|sei|fe** F shaving soap; **Ra|sier|was|ser** NT *pl* -wasser *or* -wässer aftershave (lotion); (*vor der Rasur*) pre-shave (lotion); **Ra|sier|zeug** NT *pl* -zeuge shaving things *pl* or tackle (*inf*) or equipment

Rä|son [rɛ'zõː] F -, *no pl* **er will keine ~ annehmen** he refuses to listen *or* won't listen to reason; **jdn zur ~ bringen** to make sb listen to reason, to make sb see reason *or* sense; **jdn zur ~ rufen** to call on sb to see reason *or* sense; **zur ~ kommen** to see reason *or* sense

rä|so|nie|ren [rɛzo'niːrən] *ptp* **räsoniert** VI (*old*) to grumble

Ras|pel ['raspl] F -, -n **a** (= *Holzfeile*) rasp **b** (*Cook*) grater

ras|peln ['raspln] VT to grate; *Holz* to rasp → **Süßholz**

rass ▲ [ras], **räss** ▲ [rɛs] (*S Ger, Sw*) ADJ *Most, Speise* tart; *Witz* earthy; *Pferd* fiery; *Kellnerin* buxom; (*Sw*) *Mensch* wild ADV **~** *or* **räss schmecken** to taste tart

Ras|se ['rasə] F -, -n (= *Menschenrasse*) race; (= *Tierrasse*) breed; (*fig*) spirit, hot-bloodedness; **das Mädchen hat ~** she's a hot-blooded girl; **das Pferd/der Hund hat ~** that horse/dog has race

Rasse-: Ras|se|hund M pedigree *or* thoroughbred dog; **Ras|se|kat|ze** F pedigree cat

Ras|sel ['rasl] F -, -n rattle

Ras|sel|ban|de F (*dated inf*) mischievous bunch (*inf*)

ras|seln ['rasln] VI **a** (= *Geräusch erzeugen*) to rattle; **mit** *or* **an etw** (*dat*) **~** to rattle sth **b** *aux sein* (*inf*) **durch eine Prüfung ~** to flunk an exam (*inf*)

Ras|sen- *in cpds* racial; **Ras|sen|be|wusst|sein** ▲ NT racial consciousness; **Ras|sen|dis|kri|mi|nie|rung** F racial discrimination; **Ras|sen|dokt|rin** F racial doctrine; **Ras|sen|for|schung** F ethnogeny (*form*), racial research; **Ras|sen|fra|ge** F race *or* racial problem; **Ras|sen|ge|set|ze** PL (*NS*) racial *or* race laws *pl*; **Ras|sen|gleich|heit** F racial equality; **Ras|sen|hass** ▲ M race *or* racial hatred; **Ras|sen|hy|gie|ne** F (*NS*) eugenics *sing*; **ras|sen|hy|gie|nisch** ADJ (*NS*) eugenical; **Ras|sen|kampf** M racial struggle; **Ras|sen|kon|flikt** M racial conflict; **Ras|sen|kra|wall** M race *or* racial riot; **Ras|sen|kreu|zung** F (*von Tieren*) crossbreeding; (*Tier*) crossbreed, crossbred; **Ras|sen|kun|de** F ethnogeny (*form*), study of race; **Ras|sen|merk|mal** NT racial characteris-

tic; **Ras|sen|mi|schung** F mixture of races; (*bei Tieren*) crossbreeding; (*Tier*) crossbreed, crossbred; **Ras|sen|po|li|tik** F racial policy; **Ras|sen|prob|lem** NT race *or* racial problem; **Ras|sen|schan|de** F *Nazi term for sexual relations with a non-Aryan*; **Ras|sen|schran|ke** F racial barrier, barrier of race; (*Farbige betreffend*) colour (*Brit*) *or* color (*US*) bar; **Ras|sen|theo|rie** F racial theory, theory of race; **Ras|sen|tren|nung** F racial segregation; **Ras|sen|un|ru|hen** PL racial disturbances *pl*; **Ras|sen|vor|ur|teil** NT racial prejudice; **~e haben** to be racially biased

Ras|se-: Ras|se|pferd NT thoroughbred (horse); **ras|se|rein** ADJ = **reinrassig**; **Ras|se|rein|heit** F racial purity; **Ras|se|vieh** NT thoroughbred *or* purebred animal(s); **Ras|se|weib** NT (*pej inf*) hot-blooded woman

ras|sig ['rasɪç] ADJ *Pferd, Auto* sleek; *Frau* vivacious and hot-blooded; *Erscheinung, Gesichtszüge* sharp, striking; *Wein* spirited, lively; *Zigeuner, Südländer* fiery, hot-blooded

ras|sisch ['rasɪʃ] ADJ racial ADV racially; **~ anders sein** not to belong to the same race; **jdn ~ verfolgen** to persecute sb because of his/her race

Ras|sis|mus [ra'sɪsmʊs] M -, *no pl* racialism, racism

Ras|sist [ra'sɪst] M -en, -en, **Ras|sis|tin** [-'sɪstɪn] F -, -nen racist

ras|sis|tisch [ra'sɪstɪʃ] ADJ racist, racialist ADV **sich ~ äußern** to make racist remarks; **sich ~ verhalten** to act like a racist; **~ eingestellt sein** to be a racist; **~ angehauchte Texte** racist sounding texts

Rast [rast] F -, -en rest, repose (*liter*); (*auf Autofahrt*) stop (for a rest); **~ machen** to stop (for a rest); (*Mil*) to make a halt; **die schöne Aussicht lädt zur ~** (*liter*) the beautiful view invites repose (*liter*); **er gönnt sich keine ~** he won't rest, he allows himself no respite; **ohne ~ und Ruh** (*liter*) without pause for rest, without respite

Ras|ta ['rasta] M -s, -s, **Ras|ta|fa|ri** [rasta'faːri] M -s, -s Rasta, Rastafarian

Ras|ta|lo|cken ['rasta-] PL dreadlocks *pl*, dreads *pl* (*inf*)

Ras|te ['rastə] F -, -n notch

ras|ten ['rastn] VI to rest; (*Mil*) to make a halt; **er hat nicht gerastet und geruht, bis ...** (*liter*) he did not rest until ...; **wer rastet, der rostet** (*Prov*) a rolling stone gathers no moss (*Prov*)

Ras|ter ['rastɐ] NT -s, - (*Archit: auf Landkarte*) grid; (*Typ*) halftone *or* raster screen; (*Phot:* = *Gitter*) screen; (*TV*) raster; (*fig*) framework; **es passt nicht in das ~, es fällt durch das ~** (*fig*) it doesn't fit into the scheme of things; **ein grobes ~** (*fig*) a rough criterion

Raster-: Ras|ter|ät|zung F halftone (engraving); **Ras|ter|bild** NT (*Typ*) halftone picture; (*TV*) frame; **Ras|ter|druck** M *pl* -drucke (*Typ*) halftone printing; **Ras|ter|fahn|dung** F computer search

ras|tern ['rastɐn] VT (*Typ*) to print in halftone; (*TV*) to scan

Ras|ter|punkt M (*Typ*) (halftone) dot; (*TV*) picture element

Ras|te|rung F -, -en (*TV*) scanning

Rast-: Rast|haus NT (travellers' (*Brit*) *or* travelers' (*US*)) inn; (*an Autobahn: auch* **Rasthof**) service area (including motel), rest area; **rast|los** ADJ (= *unruhig*) restless; (= *unermüdlich*) tireless, untiring; *Arbeiten, Bemühen* tireless, ceaseless ADV tirelessly; **~ tätig sein** to work tirelessly *or* ceaselessly; **Rast|lo|sig|keit** F -, -en restlessness; **Rast|platz** M resting place, place to rest; (*an Autostraßen*) picnic area; **Rast|stät|te** F (*Mot*) service area, services *pl*

Ra|sur [ra'zuːɐ] F -, -en **a** (= *Bartrasur*) shave; (= *das Rasieren*) shaving **b** (= *radierte Stelle*) erasure

Rat¹ ✪ 28.1, 29, 38.3 [raːt] M **-(e)s** a pl **Ratschläge** ['raːtʃɛːɡə] (= *Empfehlung*) advice *no pl*, counsel *no pl* (*liter*); **ein ~** a piece of advice; **jdm einen ~ geben** to give sb a piece of advice; **jdm den ~ geben, etw zu tun** to advise sb to do sth; **jdn um ~ fragen** or **bitten, sich** (*dat*) **bei jdm ~ holen** to ask sb's advice or sb for advice; **bei jdm ~ suchen** to seek sb's advice; **~ suchend** seeking advice; **sich ~ suchend an jdn wenden** to turn to sb for advice; **~ Suchende** or those seeking advice; **gegen jds ~ handeln** to go against or act against or ignore sb's advice; **einem ~ folgen, einen ~ befolgen** to take a piece of advice; **auf jds ~** (*acc*) or following sb's advice; **jdm mit ~ und Tat beistehen** or **zur Seite stehen** to support sb or back sb up in (both) word and deed; **da ist guter ~ teuer** it's hard to know what to do; **zu ~e = zurate**

b *no pl* (*liter*: = *Beratung*) **mit jdm ~ halten** or **pflegen** to take counsel with sb (*liter*)

c *no pl* (= *Abhilfe*) **~ (für etw) wissen** to know what to do (about sth); **~ schaffen** (*liter*) to show what is to be done; **sie wusste sich** (*dat*) **keinen ~ mehr** she was at her wits' end; **sich** (*dat*) **keinen ~ mit etw wissen** not to know what to do about sth; **kommt Zeit, kommt ~** (*Prov*) things work themselves out, given time

d pl **Räte** ['rɛːtə] (= *Körperschaft*) council; (= *Ratsmitglied*) councillor (*Brit*), councilor (*US*), council member; **der ~ der Gemeinde/Stadt** ≈ the district council; **der Große ~** (*Sw*) the cantonal parliament; **der Hohe ~** (*Bibl*) the Sanhedrin; **den ~ einberufen** to call a council meeting; **im ~ sitzen** to be on the council

Rat² M **-(e)s, ⸚e**, **Rätin** ['rɛːtɪn] F **-, -nen** senior official; (= *Titel*) Councillor (*Brit*), Councilor (*US*) → **wissenschaftlich, geheim**

rät [rɛːt] 3. pers sing pres von **raten**

Ra|te ['raːtə] F **-, -n** a (= *Geldbetrag*) instalment (*Brit*), installment (*US*); **auf ~n kaufen** to buy in instal(l)ments, to buy on hire purchase (*Brit*) or on the installment plan (*US*); **auf ~n** (*fig*) bit by bit; **Tod auf ~n** slow death; **in ~n zahlen** to pay in instal(l)ments b (= *Verhältnis*) rate

ra|ten ['raːtn̩] ✪ 29.1, 29.2 pret **riet** [riːt], ptp **geraten** [ɡəˈraːtn̩] VTI a (= *Ratschläge geben*) to advise; **jdm ~** to advise sb; **jdm gut/richtig/schlecht ~** to give sb good/correct/bad advice; (**jdm**) **zu etw ~** to recommend sth (to sb); **jdm ~, etw nicht zu tun** to advise sb not to do sth, to advise sb against doing sth; **zu dieser langen Reise kann ich dir nicht ~** I must advise you against making this long journey; **das würde ich dir nicht ~** I wouldn't advise or recommend it; **das möchte ich dir nicht ~** or **nicht geraten haben** I wouldn't advise or recommend it, I wouldn't if I were you; **das möchte ich dir auch geraten haben!** you better had (*inf*); **was or wozu ~ Sie mir?** what do you advise or recommend?; **lass dir ~!** take some advice, be advised; **ich weiß mir nicht zu ~** (*dated*) I'm at a loss; **wem nicht zu ~ ist, dem ist auch nicht zu helfen** (*prov*) a bit of advice never hurt anybody

b (= *erraten, herausfinden*) to guess; *Kreuzworträtsel etc* to solve, to do; **hin und her ~** to make all sorts of guesses; **rate mal!** (have a) guess; **dreimal darfst du ~** I'll give you three guesses (*auch iro*); **das rätst du nie!** you'll never guess!; **(gut) geraten!** good guess!; **falsch geraten!** wrong!; **das kann ich nur ~** I can only make a guess, I can only guess at it; **das hab ich nur so geraten** I was only guessing, it was only a guess

Raten-: Ra|ten|kauf M (= *Kaufart*) hire purchase (*Brit*), HP (*Brit inf*), the installment plan (*US*); **sie tätigte Ratenkäufe** she bought things on hire purchase (*Brit*) or on HP (*Brit inf*) or on the installment plan (*US*); **durch viele Ratenkäufe verschuldet sein** to have hire purchase (*Brit*) or installment plan (*US*) debts; **Ra|ten|spar|ver|trag** M (*Fin*) premium-aided

saving; **ra|ten|wei|se** ADV in instalments (*Brit*) or installments (*US*); **Ra|ten|zah|lung** F (= *Zahlung einer Rate*) payment of an instalment (*Brit*) or installment (*US*); (= *Zahlung in Raten*) payment by instal(l)ments

Ra|ter ['raːtɐ] M **-s, -**, **Ra|te|rin** [-ərɪn] F **-, -nen** guesser; (*von Rätsel*) solver

Rä|te|re|gie|rung F soviet government

Ra|te|rei [raːtəˈraɪ] F **-, -en** a (= *das Schätzen*) guessing; **lass mal die ~** must we have these guessing games? b (= *Rätselraten*) puzzle-solving

Rä|te|re|pub|lik F soviet republic (*esp in Bavaria 1919*)

Ra|te|spiel NT guessing game; (*TV*) quiz; (*Beruferaten etc*) panel game, quiz

Rat-: Rat|ge|ber M (*Buch, TV-Sendung etc*) guide; **ein ~ für den Garten** a book of gardening tips; **Rat|ge|ber(in)** M(F) adviser, counsellor (*Brit form*), counselor (*US form*); **Rat|haus** NT town hall; (*einer Großstadt*) city hall; **Rat|haus|platz** M town or city (*esp US*) hall square; **Rat|haus|saal** M council chamber; **Konzert im ~** concert in the town hall

Ra|ti|fi|ka|ti|on [ratifikaˈtsioːn] F **-, -en** ratification

Ra|ti|fi|ka|ti|ons-: Ra|ti|fi|ka|ti|ons|klau|sel F ratification clause; **Ra|ti|fi|ka|ti|ons|urkun|de** F ratification document

ra|ti|fi|zie|ren [ratifiˈtsiːrən] ptp **ratifiziert** VT to ratify

Ra|ti|fi|zie|rung F **-, -en** ratification

Rä|tin F → **Rat²**

Ra|tio ['raːtsio] F **-,** *no pl* (*geh*) reason; **es ist ein Gebot der ~, zu ...** reason demands that ..., it's only rational to ...

Ra|ti|on [raˈtsioːn] F **-, -en** ration; **jeder bekommt eine bestimmte ~** everyone gets fixed rations

ra|ti|o|nal [ratsioˈnaːl] ADJ rational ADV rationally

ra|ti|o|na|li|sie|ren [ratsionaliˈziːrən] ptp **rationalisiert** VTI to rationalize

Ra|ti|o|na|li|sie|rung F **-, -en** rationalization

Ra|ti|o|na|li|sie|rungs-: Ra|ti|o|na|li|sierungs|fach|frau F, **Ra|ti|o|na|li|sie|rungsfach|mann** M efficiency expert, time and motion (study) expert; **Ra|ti|o|na|li|sie|rungsmaß|nah|me** F rationalization or efficiency measure; **Ra|ti|o|na|li|sie|rungs|schutz** M job protection measures *pl*

Ra|ti|o|na|lis|mus [ratsionaˈlɪsmʊs] M **-,** *no pl* rationalism

Ra|ti|o|na|list [ratsionaˈlɪst] M **-en, -en**, **Ra|tio|na|lis|tin** [-lɪstɪn] F **-, -nen** rationalist

ra|ti|o|na|lis|tisch [ratsionaˈlɪstɪʃ] ADJ rationalist(ic)

Ra|ti|o|na|li|tät [ratsionaliˈtɛːt] F **-,** *no pl* rationality; (= *Leistungsfähigkeit*) efficiency

ra|ti|o|nell [ratsioˈnɛl] ADJ *Methode, Energienutzung etc* efficient ADV efficiently

ra|ti|o|nen|wei|se [raˈtsioːnənvaɪzə] ADV in rations

ra|ti|o|nie|ren [ratsioˈniːrən] ptp **rationiert** VT to ration

Ra|ti|o|nie|rung F **-, -en** rationing

Ra|ti|o|nie|rungs|sys|tem NT rationing system

ra|ti|ons|wei|se [raˈtsioːnsvaɪzə] ADV = **rationenweise**

rat|los ADJ helpless; **ich bin völlig ~(, was ich tun soll)** I'm at a complete loss (as to what to do), I just don't know what to do; **~e Eltern** parents who are at a loss to know what to do with their children; **sie machte ein ~es Gesicht** she looked helpless or at a loss ADV helplessly; **einer Sache** (*dat*) **~ gegenüberstehen** to be at a loss when faced with sth

Rat|lo|sig|keit F **-,** *no pl* helplessness; **in meiner ~ ...** not knowing what to do ..., being at a loss ...

Rä|to|ro|ma|ne [retoroˈmaːnə] M **-n, -n**, **Rä|toro|ma|nin** [-ˈmaːnɪn] F **-, -nen** Rhaetian

rä|to|ro|ma|nisch [retoroˈmaːnɪʃ] ADJ Rhaetian; *Sprache* Rhaeto-Romanic

Rä|to|ro|ma|nisch(e) [retoroˈmaːnɪʃ] NT Rhaeto-Romanic → *auch* **Deutsch(e)**

rat|sam [ˈraːtzaːm] ADJ advisable; **ich halte es für ~, das zu tun** I think it (would be) advisable to do that

Rats|be|schluss ▲ M decision of the local council

ratsch [ratʃ] INTERJ rip

Rat|sche [ˈraːtʃə] F **-, -n** (*S Ger, Aus*), **Rät|sche** [ˈrɛːtʃə] F **-, -n** (*Sw*) rattle

rat|schen [ˈraːtʃn̩] VI , **rät|schen** [ˈrɛːtʃn̩] VI (*Sw*) a (*mit der Ratsche*) to rattle b (*inf*: = *schwatzen*) to blather (*inf*)

Rat|schlag ✪ 29.2 M piece or bit of advice; **Ratschläge** advice; **drei Ratschläge** three pieces of advice; **ein guter ~** a good piece of advice, good advice; **deine klugen Ratschläge kannst du dir sparen** keep your advice for yourself; **jdm einen ~ geben** or **erteilen** to give sb a piece of advice or some advice; **jds ~** (*dat*) **folgen, jds ~ befolgen** to take sb's advice

rat|schla|gen [ˈraːtʃlaːɡn̩] VI *insep* to deliberate, to consult (together)

Rat|schluss ▲ M (*liter*) decision; **Gottes ~** the will of God; **Gottes unerforschlichem ~ hat es gefallen ...** it has pleased the Lord in his mysterious wisdom ...

Rats|die|ner M (*old*) (town hall) porter

Rät|sel [ˈrɛːtsl̩] NT **-s, -** a riddle; (= *Kreuzworträtsel*) crossword (puzzle); (= *Silbenrätsel, Bilderrätsel etc*) puzzle; **in ~n sprechen** to talk in riddles; **jdm ein ~ aufgeben** to give or ask sb a riddle b (*fig*: = *Geheimnis*) riddle, mystery, enigma (*um of*); **die Polizei konnte das ~ lösen** the police have solved the riddle or mystery; **vor einem ~ stehen** to be faced with a riddle or mystery, to be baffled; **das plötzliche Verschwinden des Zeugen gab der Polizei ~ auf** the sudden disappearance of the witness baffled the police; **es ist mir ein ~, wie ...** it's a mystery to me how ..., it baffles or beats (*inf*) me how ...; **er ist mir ein ~** he's a mystery or an enigma to me; (**jdm**) **ein ~ bleiben** to remain a mystery (to sb); **das ist des ~s Lösung!** that's the answer

Rätsel-: Rät|sel|ecke F puzzle corner; **Rät|sel|fra|ge** F (= *Quizfrage*) question; **rät|sel|haft** ADJ mysterious; *Gesichtsausdruck, Lächeln auch* enigmatic; **auf ~e Weise** mysteriously; **es ist mir ~** it's a mystery to me, it baffles me; **Rät|sel|haf|tig|keit** [ˈrɛːtsl̩haftɪçkaɪt] F **-,** *no pl* mysteriousness; **Rät|sel|heft** NT puzzle book; **Rät|sel|lö|ser** [-løːzɐ] M **-s, -**, **Rät|sel|lö|serin** [-ərɪn] F **-, -nen** puzzle-solver

rät|seln [ˈrɛːtsl̩n] VI to puzzle (over sth), to rack one's brains

Rät|sel-: Rät|sel|ra|ten NT **-s,** *no pl* guessing game; (= *Rätseln*) guessing; **rät|sel|voll** ADJ (*geh*) mysterious; **Rät|sel|zei|tung** F puzzle book

Rats-: Rats|herr(in) M(F) (*dated*) councillor (*esp Brit*), councilman (*US*); **Rats|kel|ler** M rathskeller (*US*), *restaurant under the town hall*; **Rats|sit|zung** F council meeting; **Rats|stu|be** F *bar/restaurant near the town hall*

rat|su|chend △ ADJ → **Rat¹**

Rat|su|chen|de(r) MF *decl as adj* **~** people or those seeking advice

Rats|ver|samm|lung F a (= *Sitzung*) council meeting b (= *Rat*) council

Rat|tan [ˈratan] NT **-s,** *no pl* rattan

Rat|te [ˈratə] F **-, -n** a (= *Tier*) rat; **die ~n verlassen das sinkende Schiff** (*prov*) the rats are deserting the sinking ship → **schlafen** b (*inf*: =

Mensch) rat *(inf)*; **eine widerliche ~** a dirty rat *(inf)*

Rat|ten-: Rat|ten|be|kämp|fung F rat control; **Rat|ten|fän|ger(in)** M(F) rat-catcher; *(Hund)* ratter; *(fig)* rabble-rouser; **der ~ von Hameln** the Pied Piper of Hamelin; **Rat|ten|gift** NT rat poison; **Rat|ten|schwanz** M **a** *(lit)* rat's tail **b** *usu pl (inf: = Zopf)* bunch **c** *(fig inf: = Serie, Folge)* string

rat|tern ['ratən] VI *(als Bewegungsverb: aux sein)* to rattle, to clatter; *(Maschinengewehr)* to chatter

Rat|ze|fum|mel ['ratsəfʊml] M -s, - *(inf: Schülersprache)* rubber *(Brit)*, eraser

rat|ze|kahl ['ratsə'ka:l] ADV *(inf)* completely, totally; **alles ~ aufessen** *(Vorräte)* to eat the cupboard bare *(inf)*; *Portion* to polish off the lot *(inf)*; **die Raupen fraßen die Laubbäume ~** the caterpillars ate all the leaves off the trees

rat|zen¹ VI *(dial inf)* to kip *(Brit inf)*, to sleep; **ich hab vielleicht geratzt** I had a really good kip *(Brit inf)* or sleep

rat|zen² VT to scratch

ratz|fatz ['rats'fats] ADV *(inf: sehr schnell)* in no time, in a flash *(beide nachgestellt)*

rau ▲ [rau] ADJ **a** rough; **eine ~e Schale haben** *(fig)* to be a rough diamond; **~e Schale, weicher Kern** *(fig)* tough exterior, soft centre *(Brit)* or center *(US)* **b** *Hals, Kehle* sore; *Stimme* husky; *(= heiser)* hoarse **c** *(= nicht mild, streng) Wetter* inclement; *Wind, Luft* raw; *See* rough; *Klima, Winter* harsh, raw; *(= unwirtlich) Gebiet* bleak; *Stadt* tough; **im ~en Norden** in the rugged north; **(die) ~e Wirklichkeit** harsh reality, the hard facts *pl* **d** *(= barsch, grob) Benehmen, Wesen* rough; *(= hart) Mann* tough, rugged; *Ton* harsh; *Worte, Behandlung* rough, harsh; **~, aber herzlich** bluff; **Begrüßung, Ton** rough but jovial; **er ist ~, aber herzlich** he's a rough diamond; **in unserer Familie geht es ~, aber herzlich zu** we're a pretty hale and hearty lot in our family; **hier herrschen ja ~e Methoden** their/his *etc* methods are brutal **e** *(inf)* **in ~en Mengen** by the ton *(inf)*, galore *(inf)*; **Zucker in ~en Mengen** sugar by the ton *(inf)*, sugar galore *(inf)*

Raub [raup] M -(e)s [-bəs] *no pl* **a** *(= das Rauben)* robbery; *(= Diebstahl)* theft; **auf ~ ausgehen** *(Tiere)* to go out hunting or on the prowl; *(Räuber)* to go out pillaging; **schwerer ~** aggravated robbery **b** *(= Entführung)* abduction; **der ~ der Sabinerinnen** the rape of the Sabine women **c** *(= Beute)* booty, loot, spoils *pl*; **ein ~ der Flammen werden** *(liter)* to fall victim to the flames

Raub-: Raub|bau M , *no pl* overexploitation *(of natural resources)*; *(am Wald)* overfelling; *(an Äckern)* overcropping; *(an Weideland)* overgrazing; *(an Fischbeständen)* overfishing; **~ an etw** *(dat)* **treiben** to overexploit *etc* sth; **am Fischbestand eines Flusses ~ treiben** to overfish a river; **mit seiner Gesundheit ~ treiben** to ruin one's health; **Raub|druck** M pl **-drucke** pirate(d) copy; *(= das Drucken)* pirating

Rau-: Rau|bein ▲ NT *(inf)* rough diamond; **rau|bei|nig** ▲ ADJ *(inf)* rough-and-ready

rau|ben ['raubn] VT **a** *(= wegnehmen)* to steal; **jdm etw ~** to rob sb of sth **b** *(= entführen)* to abduct, to carry off **c** *(fig)* **jdm etw ~** to rob sb of sth; **das hat uns viel Zeit geraubt** it cost us a lot of time; **jdm einen Kuss ~** to steal a kiss from sb; **jdm den Schlaf/den Verstand ~** to rob sb of his/her sleep/reason; **jdm den Atem ~** to take sb's breath away; **jdm die Unschuld ~** *(obs, iro)* to take sb's virginity; **du raubst mir noch den letzten Nerv!** you'll drive me mad or crazy *(inf)* **VI** to rob, to plunder, to pillage

Räu|ber ['rɔybɐ] M -s, -, **Räu|be|rin** [-ərɪn] F -, -nen robber, brigand *(old)*; *(bei Bankübberfall etc)* robber, raider; *(= Wegelagerer)* highwayman; *(inf: = Kind)* rascal *(inf)*; **Ali Baba und die vierzig ~** Ali Baba and the forty thieves; **unter die ~**

fallen or *geraten* to fall among thieves; **der Fuchs ist ein ~** the fox is a beast of prey, the fox is a predator; **~ und Gendarm** cops and robbers

Räu|ber|ban|de F robber band, band of robbers; *(pej)* bunch of thieves

Räu|be|rei [rɔybə'rai] F -, -n *(inf)* robbery

Räu|ber-: Räu|ber|ge|schich|te F **a** story about robbers **b** *(fig)* cock-and-bull story *(inf)*; **Räu|ber|ge|sin|del** NT *(pej)* thieving riffraff; **Räu|ber|haupt|mann** M robber-chief; **Räu|ber|höh|le** F **a** *(lit)* robbers' cave **b** *(fig inf)* *(= Spelunke)* low dive *(inf)*; *(= Durcheinander)* pigsty

Räu|be|rin F → **Räuber**

räu|be|risch ['rɔybərɪʃ] ADJ rapacious, predatory; **~r Diebstahl** *(Jur)* theft in which force or the threat of violence is used to remain in possession of the stolen goods **~e Erpressung** *(Jur)* armed robbery; **in ~er Absicht** with intent to rob

räu|bern ['rɔybɐn] VI *(inf)* to thieve; **in der Speisekammer ~** to raid the larder

Räu|ber-: Räu|ber|pis|to|le F cock-and-bull story *(inf)*; **Räu|ber|zi|vil** NT *(hum inf)* scruffy old clothes *pl (inf)*

Raub-: Raub|fisch M predatory fish, predator; **Raub|gier** F *(liter)* rapacity; **raub|gie|rig** ADJ *(liter)* rapacious; **Raub|kat|ze** F *(predatory)* big cat; **Raub|ko|pie** F pirate(d) copy; **Raub|krieg** M war of conquest; **der ~ gegen unser Land** the rape of our country; **Raub|mord** M robbery with murder; **Raub|mör|der(in)** M(F) robber and murderer; **Raub|pres|sung** F pirate(d) copy; **Raub|rit|ter** M robber baron

Raub|tier NT predator, beast of prey

Raub|tier-: Raub|tier|haus NT lion house; **Raub|tier|kä|fig** M lion's/tiger's *etc* cage

Raub-: Raub|über|fall M robbery; *(auf Bank etc auch)* raid *(auf on)*; **einen ~ auf jdn begehen** or **verüben** to hold sb up; **„Raubüberfall auf Taxifahrer"** "taxi driver attacked and robbed"; **Raub|vo|gel** M bird of prey, predator; **Raub|wild** NT *(Hunt)* predatory game; **Raub|zeug** NT *(Hunt)* vermin *pl*; **Raub|zug** M series *sing* of robberies; *(pej: = Angriffskrieg)* rape *(nach, gegen* of); *(= Plünderung)* raid *(auf +acc* on); *(von Tieren)* hunting excursion; **auf ~ gehen** *(Einbrecher)* to commit a series of robberies; *(Tier)* to go hunting or on the prowl

Rauch [raux] M -(e)s, *no pl* smoke; *(giftig auch)* fumes *pl*; **in ~ und Flammen aufgehen** to go up in smoke or flames; **in ~ aufgehen** *(lit, fig)* **sich in ~ auflösen** *(fig)* to go up in smoke; **Würste in den ~ hängen** to hang sausages up to smoke; **kein ~ ohne Feuer** *(Prov)* there's no smoke without fire *(prov)*

Rauch-: Rauch|ab|zug M smoke outlet; **rauch|arm** ADJ smokeless; **rauch|bar** ADJ smok(e)able; **hast du was Rauchbares?** have you got anything to smoke?; **Rauch|bil|dung** F production or formation of smoke; **mit großer ~ verbrennen** to burn giving off a lot of smoke; **Rauch|bom|be** F smoke bomb

rau|chen ['rauxn] **VI** *(= Rauch abgeben)* to smoke, to give off smoke; **sie sah, dass es aus unserer Küche rauchte** she saw smoke coming from our kitchen; **mir raucht der Kopf** my head's spinning **VTI** *(Mensch)* to smoke; **möchten Sie ~?** do you want to smoke?; *(Zigarette anbietend)* would you like a cigarette?; **darf ich ~?** do you mind if I smoke?, may I smoke?; **nach dem Essen rauche ich gern** I like a or to smoke after a meal; **eine ~** to have a smoke; **haben Sie mal zu ~?** have you got a smoke?; **„Rauchen verboten"** "no smoking"; **sich** *(dat)* **das Rauchen angewöhnen/abgewöhnen** to take up/give up smoking; **viel** or **stark ~** to be a heavy smoker, to smoke a lot; **~ Sie?** do you smoke?

Rauch|ent|wick|lung F production or formation of smoke; **mit starker/geringer ~** giving off high/low smoke levels

Rau|cher¹ ['rauxɐ] M -s, - *(Rail: = Raucherabteil)* smoker, smoking compartment

Rau|cher² ['rauxɐ] M -s, -, **Rau|che|rin** [-ərɪn] F -, -nen smoker; **sind Sie ~?** do you smoke?, are you a smoker?

Rau|cher|aal ['rɔyçɐ-] M smoked eel

Raucher-: Rau|cher|ab|teil NT smoking compartment, smoker; **Rau|cher|bein** NT hardening of the arteries (in the leg) *(caused by smoking)*; **Rau|cher|ecke** F smokers' corner

Räu|cher-: Räu|cher|fass ▲ ['rɔyçɐ-] NT *(Eccl)* censer; **Räu|cher|fisch** ['rɔyçɐ-] M smoked fish; **Räu|cher|ge|fäß** ['rɔyçɐ-] NT incense burner; **Räu|cher|he|ring** ['rɔyçɐ-] M kipper, smoked herring

Rau|cher|hus|ten M smoker's cough

Rau|che|rin F smoker → *auch* **Raucher²**

Räu|cher-: Räu|cher|kam|mer ['rɔyçɐ-] F smoking chamber, smokehouse; **Räu|cher|ker|ze** ['rɔyçɐ-] F incense cone; **Räu|cher|lachs** ['rɔyçɐ-] M smoked salmon

Rau|cher|lun|ge F smoker's lung

Räu|cher|männ|chen ['rɔyçɐ-] NT smoking man *(usu wooden figure containing an incense cone)*

räu|chern ['rɔyçɐn] **VT** to smoke **VI** *(inf: mit Weihrauch)* to burn incense

Räu|cher-: Räu|cher|schin|ken M smoked ham; **Räu|cher|speck** M ≈ smoked bacon; **Räu|cher|stäb|chen** NT joss stick; **Räu|cher|wa|ren** PL smoked foods *pl*

Rau|cher-: Rau|cher|zim|mer NT smoking room; **Rau|cher|zo|ne** F smoking area

Rauch-: Rauch|fah|ne F smoke trail, trail of smoke; **Rauch|fang** M **a** *(= Rauchabzug)* chimney hood **b** *(Aus)* chimney; **Rauch|fang|keh|rer** [-ke:rɐ] M -s, -, **Rauch|fang|keh|re|rin** [-ərɪn] F -, -nen *(Aus)* (chimney) sweep; **rauch|far|ben** [-farbn], **rauch|far|big** ADJ smoke-coloured *(Brit)*, smoke-colored *(US)*; **Rauch|fass** ▲ NT *(Eccl)* censer; **Rauch|fleisch** NT smoked meat; **rauch|frei** ADJ Zone smokeless; *Aufenthaltsraum* no-smoking; **Rauch|ga|se** PL fumes *pl*; **Rauch|gas|ent|schwe|fe|lung** F flue gas desulphurization *(Brit)* or desulfurization *(US)*; **Rauch|gas|ent|schwe|fe|lungs|an|la|ge** F flue gas desulphurization *(Brit)* or desulfurization *(US)* plant; **rauch|ge|schwän|gert** [-gəʃvɛŋɐt] ADJ *Zimmer* smoke-filled; *Luft* heavy with smoke; **rauch|ge|schwärzt** [-gəʃvɛrtst] ADJ blackened by smoke, smoke-blackened; **Rauch|glas** NT smoked glass; **Rauch|glo|cke** F pall of smoke

rau|chig ['rauxɪç] ADJ *Geruch, Geschmack, Stimme* smoky

Rauch-: rauch|los ADJ smokeless; **Rauch|mel|der** M smoke alarm or detector; **Rauch|pilz** M mushroom cloud; **Rauch|quarz** M smoky quartz, cairngorm; **Rauch|sa|lon** M smoking or smoke room; **Rauch|säu|le** F column or pillar of smoke; **Rauch|schlei|er** M veil of smoke; **Rauch|schwa|den** PL drifts *pl* of smoke; **Rauch|schwal|be** F swallow; **Rauch|ser|vice** [-zɛrviːs] NT smoker's set; **Rauch|sig|nal** NT smoke signal; **Rauch|ta|bak** M *(form)* tobacco; **Rauch|tisch** M smoker's table; **Rauch|tisch|chen** NT smoker's table; **Rauch|to|pas** M smoky quartz, cairngorm; **Rauch|uten|si|li|en** PL smoker's requisites *pl*; **Rauch|ver|bot** NT smoking ban, ban on smoking; **hier herrscht ~** smoking is not allowed here, there's no smoking here; **Rauch|ver|gif|tung** F fume poisoning; **eine ~ erlei|den** to be overcome by fumes; **Rauch|ver|zeh|rer** [-fɛɐtseːrɐ] M -s, - smoke dispeller, *small, often ornamental device for neutralizing tobacco smoke*; **Rauch|vor|hang** M , **Rauch|wand** F smokescreen; **Rauch|wa|ren¹** PL tobacco (products *pl*); **Rauch|wa|ren²** PL

(= *Pelze*) furs *pl*; **Rauch|wa|ren|händ|ler(in)** M(F) furrier; **Rauch|wol|ke** F cloud of smoke; **Rauch|zei|chen** NT smoke signal; **Rauch|zim|mer** NT smoking *or* smoke room

Räu|de ['rɔydə] F -, -n (*Vet*) mange

räu|dig ['rɔydɪç] ADJ mangy; **du ~er Hund!** (*old inf*) you dirty dog!

rau|en ▲ ['rauən] VT to roughen (up); (*Tex*) *Stoff* to nap

rauf [rauf] ADV (*inf*) ~! (get) up! → *auch* **herauf, hinauf**

Rau|fa|ser|ta|pe|te ▲ F woodchip paper

Rauf|bold ['raufbɔlt] M -(e)s, -e [-də] (*dated*) ruffian, roughneck

Rau|fe ['raufə] F -, -n hayrack

rau|fen ['raufn] VT *Unkraut* to pull up; *Flachs* to pull; **sich** (*dat*) **die Haare ~** to tear (at) one's hair VIR to scrap, to fight; **sich um etw ~** to fight over sth

Rau|fe|rei [raufə'rai] F -, -en scrap, roughhouse (*inf*); **nur eine harmlose ~** just a harmless little scrap

Rauf-: **Rauf|han|del** M (*old, form*) affray (*form*); **Rauf|lust** F pugnacity; **rauf|lus|tig** ADJ ready for a fight *or* scrap, pugnacious

Rau|fut|ter ▲ NT roughage

rauh △ [rau] ADJ → **rau**

Rauh- △: **Rauh|bein** △ NT → **Raubein**; **rauh|bei|nig** △ ADJ → **raubeinig**

Rau|haar|da|ckel ▲ M wire-haired dachshund

rau|haa|rig ▲ ADJ coarse-haired; *Hund auch* wire-haired; *Fell, Wolle* coarse

Rau|heit ['rauhait] F -, *no pl* a roughness b (*von Hals, Kehle*) soreness; (*von Stimme*) huskiness; (= *Heiserkeit*) hoarseness c (= *Strenge*) (*von Wind, Luft*) rawness; (*von See*) roughness; (*von Klima, Winter*) harshness; (*von Gegend*) bleakness; **die ~ des schottischen Wetters** the inclement Scottish weather d (= *Barschheit, Grobheit*) roughness; (= *Härte*) toughness

rau|hen △ ['rauən] VT → **rauen**

Rauh- △: **Rauh|fa|ser|ta|pe|te** △ F → **Raufasertapete**; **Rauh|fut|ter** △ NT → **Raufutter**; **Rauh|haar|da|ckel** △ M → **Rauhaardackel**; **rauh|haa|rig** △ ADJ → **rauhaarig**; **Rauh|putz** △ M → **Rauputz**; **Rauh|reif** △ M , *no pl* → **Raureif**

Rau|ke ['raukə] F (*Bot*) rocket

Raum [raum] M -(e)s, **Räume** ['rɔymə] a *no pl* (= *Platz*) room, space; (= *Weite*) expanse; **~ schaffen** to make some space *or* room; **~ sparend** space-saving *attr*; *bauen, einbauen, unterbringen* to save space; **das ist ~ sparender** that saves more space; **etw ~ sparend stapeln** to stack sth (away) with a minimum use of space; **auf engstem ~ leben** to live in a very confined space; **einer Sache** (*dat*) **~ geben** (*geh*) to yield to sth; **eine Frage in den ~ stellen** to pose a question; **eine Frage im ~ stehen lassen** to leave a question unresolved *or* hanging; **den ~ decken** (*Sport*) to cover the area b (= *Spielraum*) room, scope c (= *Zimmer*) room d (= *Gebiet, Bereich*) area; (*größer*) region; (*fig*) sphere; **der ~ Frankfurt** the Frankfurt area; **der mitteleuropäische ~** the Central European region; **im ländlichen ~** in rural areas; **im geistigen ~** in the intellectual sphere; **~ gewinnen** (*Mil, fig*) to gain ground e *no pl* (*Phys, Space*) space *no art*; **der offene** *or* **leere ~** the void → **luftleer**

Raum-: **Raum|an|zug** M spacesuit; **Raum|auf|tei|lung** F floor plan; **Raum|aus|stat|ter** [-ausʃtatɐ] M -s, -, **Raum|aus|stat|te|rin** [-ərɪn] F -, -nen interior decorator; **Raum|bild** NT stereoscopic *or* 3-D picture; **Raum|bild|ver|fah|ren** NT stereoscopy

Räum|boot NT minesweeper

Raum|ein|heit F unit of volume

räu|men ['rɔymən] VT a (= *verlassen*) *Gebäude, Gebiet, Posten* to vacate; (*Mil: Truppen*) to move out of, to withdraw from; *Wohnung* to vacate, to move out of; *Hotelzimmer* to vacate, to check out of; *Sitzplatz* to vacate, to give up; **wir müssen das Haus bis Mittwoch ~** we have to be out of the house by Wednesday → **Feld** b (= *leeren*) *Gebäude, Straße, Warenlager* to clear (*von of*); **„wir ~"** "clearance sale" c (= *woanders hinbringen*) to shift, to move; (= *entfernen*) *Schnee, Schutt* to clear (away), to shift; *Minen* to clear; (*auf See*) to sweep, to clear; **räum deine Sachen in den Schrank** put your things away in the cupboard; **er hat seine Sachen aus dem Schrank geräumt** he cleared his things out of the cupboard → **Weg** VI (= *aufräumen*) to clear up; (= *umräumen*) to rearrange things; **in etw** (*dat*) **~** to rummage around in sth

Raum-: **Raum|ent|wei|ser** [-ɛntveːzɐ] M -s, -, **Raum|ent|wei|se|rin** [-ərɪn] F -, -nen (*form*) pest exterminator; **Raum|er|spar|nis** F space-saving; **aus Gründen der ~** to save space, for reasons of space; **Raum|fäh|re** F space shuttle; **Raum|fah|rer(in)** M(F) spaceman/-woman, astronaut; (*russisch*) cosmonaut

Raum|fahrt F space travel *no art or* flight *no art*; **die Ausgaben für die ~ erhöhen** to increase the space budget; **das Zeitalter der ~** the space age; **die bemannte ~** manned space travel *or* flight

Raumfahrt- *in cpds* space; **Raum|fahrt|be|hör|de** F space authority; **Raum|fahrt|in|ge|ni|eur(in)** M(F) astronautical engineer; **Raum|fahrt|me|di|zin** F space medicine; **Raum|fahrt|pro|gramm** NT space programme; **Raum|fahrt|sta|ti|on** F space station; **Raum|fahrt|tech|nik** F space technology; **Raum|fahrt|zeit|al|ter** NT space age; **Raum|fahrt|zent|rum** NT space centre (*Brit*) *or* center (*US*)

Raum|fahr|zeug NT spacecraft

Räum|fahr|zeug NT bulldozer; (*für Schnee*) snow-clearer

Raum-: **Raum|flug** M space flight; (*Forschungsflug auch*) space mission; **Raum|for|schung** F space research; **Raum|ge|stal|tung** F interior design; **Raum|ge|winn** M extra space gained; **der ~ war nicht sehr groß** we didn't gain much space; **Raum|git|ter** NT (*Min*) (crystal *or* space) lattice; **Raum|glei|ter** M orbiter; **raum|grei|fend** ADJ far-reaching, extensive; *Schritt* long, lengthy; **eine ~e Skulptur** a sculpture of great presence; **Raum|in|halt** M volume, (cubic) capacity; **Raum|kap|sel** F space capsule; **Raum|klang** M stereophonic sound; **Raum|kli|ma** NT indoor climate, *room temperature and air quality*; **Raum|la|bor** NT space lab; **Raum|leh|re** F geometry

räum|lich ['rɔymlɪç] ADJ a (= *den Raum betreffend*) spatial; **~e Verhältnisse** physical conditions; **~e Nähe** physical closeness, spatial proximity; **~e Entfernung** physical distance b (= *dreidimensional*) three-dimensional; **~es Anschauungsvermögen** capacity to think in three dimensions ADV a (= *platzmäßig*) **~ beschränkt sein** to have very little room; **sich ~ beschränken** to make do with very little room; **wir haben ~ keine Probleme** we have no problem with room; **wir wohnen ~ sehr beengt** we live in very cramped conditions; **rein ~ ist das unmöglich** (just) from the point of view of space it's impossible b (= *dreidimensional*) **~ sehen** to see in three dimensions, to see three-dimensionally; **Menschen, die auf einem Auge blind sind, können nicht ~ sehen** people who are blind in one eye have no depth perception; **ich kann mir das nicht ~ vorstellen** I can't really picture it

Räum|lich|keit F -, -en a *no pl* three-dimensionality b (= *Zimmer*) room; **~en** *pl* premises *pl*; **dazu fehlen uns die ~en** we don't have the premises for it/them

Raum-: **Raum|man|gel** M lack of space *or* room; **Raum|maß** NT unit of volume; **Raum|me|ter** M OR NT cubic metre (*Brit*) *or* meter (*US*) (*of stacked wood*); **Raum|mis|si|on** F space mission; **Raum|not** F shortage of space; **Raum|ord|nung** F environmental planning; **Raum|ord|nungs|plan** M development plan; **Raum|pfle|ger(in)** M(F) cleaner

Räum|pflug M snowplough (*Brit*), snowplow (*US*)

Raum-: **Raum|pla|nung** F (*das Planen*) development planning; (*Plan*) development plan; **Raum|schiff** NT spaceship; **Raum|schiff|fahrt** F = **Raumfahrt**; **Raum|son|de** F space probe; **raum|spa|rend** △ ADJ → **Raum a**; **Raum|sta|ti|on** F space station; **Raum|tei|ler** M room divider; (*dünne Trennwand*) partition; **Raum|tem|pe|ra|tur** F room temperature; **Raum|trans|por|ter** M space shuttle

Räum|trupp M clearance gang *or* workers *pl*

Räu|mung ['rɔymʊŋ] F -, -en clearing; (*von Wohnung, Gebäude, Stelle, Posten*) vacation; (*wegen Gefahr etc*) evacuation; (*unter Zwang*) eviction; (*Mil: von besetztem Gebiet*) withdrawal (*gen* from); (*von Lager, Vorräten, Geschäft*) clearance; **„wegen ~ alle Preise radikal herabgesetzt!"** "all prices reduced to clear"

Räu|mungs-: **Räu|mungs|ar|bei|ten** PL clearance operations *pl*; **Räu|mungs|be|fehl** M eviction order; **Räu|mungs|frist** F (period of) notice; **Räu|mungs|kla|ge** F action for eviction; **Räu|mungs|ver|kauf** M clearance sale

Raum|ver|schwen|dung F waste of space

rau|nen ['raunən] VTI (*liter*) to whisper; **es ging ein Raunen durch die Menge** a murmur went through the crowd

raun|zen ['rauntsn] VI (*inf: S Ger, Aus*) to grouse (*Brit inf*), to grouch (*inf*)

Raun|zer ['rauntse] M -s, - (*inf: S Ger, Aus*) grouse(r) (*Brit inf*), grouch(er) (*inf*)

Rau|pe ['raupə] F -, -n a caterpillar b (= *Planierraupe*) caterpillar®; (= *Kette*) caterpillar® track *or* tread

Rau|pen-: **Rau|pen|fahr|zeug** NT caterpillar® (vehicle); **Rau|pen|ket|te** F caterpillar® track; **Rau|pen|schlep|per** M caterpillar® (tractor)

Rau|putz ▲ M roughcast

Rau|reif ▲ M hoarfrost, white frost; (= *gefrorener Nebel*) rime

raus [raus] ADV (*inf*) ~! (get) out! → *auch* **heraus, hinaus**

Rausch [rauʃ] M -(e)s, **Räusche** ['rɔyʃə] a (= *Trunkenheit*) intoxication, inebriation; (= *Drogenrausch*) drugged(-up) state, high (*inf*); **sich** (*dat*) **einen ~ antrinken** to get drunk; **einen ~ haben** to be drunk; **etw im ~ tun/sagen** to do/say sth while under the influence (of alcohol *or* drink); **seinen ~ ausschlafen** to sleep it off b (*liter*) (= *Ekstase*) ecstasy, transport (*liter*), rapture; (= *Blutrausch, Mordrausch etc*) frenzy; **im ~ der Leidenschaft** inflamed with passion; **im ~ der Gefühle** in an ecstasy of emotion; **der ~ der Geschwindigkeit** the thrill of speed

rausch|arm ADJ (*Rad*) low-noise

Rau|sche|bart M (*inf*) big bushy beard; (*Mann*) man with a big bushy beard, beardy (*hum inf*)

rau|schen ['rauʃn] VI a (*Wasser, Meer, Wasserfall*) to roar; (*sanft*) to murmur; (*Brandung*) to boom, to roar; (*Baum, Wald*) to rustle; (*Wind*) to murmur; (*Seide*) to rustle, to swish; (*Korn*) to swish; (*Regen*) to pour down; (*Radio, Lautsprecher etc*) to hiss; (*Muschel*) to sing; (*Applaus*) to resound; **weißes Rauschen** (*Rad*) white noise b *aux sein* (= *sich schnell bewegen*) (*Bach*) to rush; (*Bumerang, Geschoss*) to whoosh (*inf*); (*Auto etc*) to whoosh (*inf*), to whizz (*inf*) c *aux sein* (*inf: Mensch*) to sweep; **sie rauschte in das/**

aus dem Zimmer she swept into/out of the room

rau|schend ADJ *Fest* grand; *Beifall, Erfolg* resounding; **im ~en Walde** in the gently murmuring forest; **mit ~en Flügeln** with a swish or swoosh of its wings; **eine ~e Ballnacht** a glittering ball

Rau|scher ['rauʃɐ] M **-s, -** (*dial*) sweet cider (*half fermented*)

rausch|frei ADJ (*Rad, Tech*) noiseless

Rausch|gift NT drug, narcotic; (= *Drogen*) drugs *pl*, narcotics *pl*; **~ nehmen** to take drugs; (*regelmäßig auch*) to be on drugs; **mit ~ handeln** to deal in drugs

Rausch|gift-: Rausch|gift|de|zer|nat NT narcotics or drug squad; **Rausch|gift|han|del** M drug trafficking; **Rausch|gift|händ|ler(in)** M(F) drug trafficker; **Rausch|gift|sucht** F drug addiction; **rausch|gift|süch|tig** ADJ drug-addicted; **er ist ~** he's addicted to drugs, he's a drug addict; **Rausch|gift|süch|ti|ge(r)** MF *decl as adj* drug addict

Rausch-: Rausch|gold NT gold foil; **Rausch|gold|en|gel** M ≈ Christmas tree fairy; **rausch|haft** ADJ (*fig*) ecstatic; **Rausch|mit|tel** NT (*form*) intoxicant (*form*); **Rausch|zu|stand** M (*form*) state of intoxication, intoxicated state

raus+ekeln ['raus|eːkln] VT *sep* (*inf*) to freeze out (*inf*)

raus+feu|ern ['rausfɔyɐn] VT *sep* (*inf*) to chuck out (*inf*), to sling out (*Brit inf*)

raus+flie|gen ['rausfliːgn] VI *sep irreg aux sein* (*inf*) to be chucked or slung out (*inf*); (= *entlassen werden auch*) to be given the boot (*inf*) or the push (*Brit inf*)

raus+hau|en ['raushauən] VT *sep* (*fig inf*) = **rauspauken**

raus+krie|gen ['rauskriːgn] VT *sep* (*inf*) = **herausbekommen**

raus+pau|ken ['rauspaukn] VT *sep* (*inf*) **jdn ~** to get sb out of trouble, to get sb off the hook (*inf*); **mein Anwalt hat mich rausgepaukt** my lawyer got me off

räus|pern ['rɔyspɐn] VR to clear one's throat

raus+rei|ßen ['rausraisn] VT *sep irreg* (*inf*) **jdn ~** to save sb, to save sb's bacon (*Brit inf*), to get sb out of trouble (*inf*); **der Torwart/das hat noch alles rausgerissen** the goalkeeper/that saved the day → *auch* **herausreißen**

raus+schmei|ßen ['rausʃmaisn] VT *sep irreg* (*inf*) to chuck or sling or kick out (*aus* of) (*all inf*); (= *entlassen auch*) to give the boot (*inf*); (= *wegwerfen*) to chuck out or away (*inf*); *Geld* to chuck away (*inf*), to chuck down the drain (*Brit inf*); **das ist rausgeschmissenes Geld** that's money down the drain (*inf*)

Raus|schmei|ßer[1] ['rausʃmaisɐ] M (*inf*: = *letzter Tanz*) last number or dance

Raus|schmei|ßer[2] ['rausʃmaisɐ] M **-s, -**, **Raus|schmei|ße|rin** [-ərɪn] F **-, -nen** (*inf*) bouncer

Raus|schmiss A ['rausʃmɪs] M **-es, -e** (*inf*) booting out (*inf*); **man drohte uns mit dem ~** they threatened us with the boot (*inf*) or push (*Brit inf*)

Rau|te ['rautə] F **-, -n a** (*Bot*) rue **b** (*Math*) rhombus; (*Her*) lozenge

rau|ten|för|mig ADJ rhomboid, diamond--shaped, lozenge-shaped

Rau|ten|mus|ter NT diamond pattern

Rave [reːv] M OR NT **-(s), -s a** (= *Party*) rave **b** *no pl* (*Musikrichtung*) rave (music)

Rave-Par|ty ['reːv-] F rave (party)

Ra|ver ['reːvɐ] M **-s, -**, **Ra|ve|rin** [-ərɪn] F **-, -nen** raver

Ra|vi|o|li [ravi'oːli] PL ravioli *sing*

Ra|yon [rɛ'jõː] M **-s, -s** (*Aus*) department; (*old*) region

Raz|zia ['ratsia] F **-, Raz|zien** [-tsiən] raid, swoop (*inf*) (*gegen* on); **eine ~ durchführen** to carry

out a raid; **die Polizei machte in ein paar Loka|len ~** the police swooped on (*inf*) or carried out a raid on or raided three or four bars

Re [reː] NT **-s, -s** (*Cards*) redouble; **Re ansagen** to redouble

Rea|der ['riːdɐ] M **-s, -** (= *Lehrbuch*) reader

Re|a|gens [re'aːgɛns, re'a:gɛns] NT **-, Reagenzi|en** [rea'gɛntsiən], **Re|a|genz** [rea'gɛnts] NT **-es, -ien** [-tsiən] (*Chem*) reagent

Re|a|genz|glas NT , **Re|a|genz|röhr|chen** NT (*Chem*) test tube

re|a|gie|ren [rea'giːrən] *ptp* **reagiert** VI to react (*auf +acc* to; *mit* with); (*Chem*) to react (*mit* with); **miteinander ~** (*Chem*) to react (together); **auf etw** (*acc*) **verärgert** or **mit Verärgerung ~** to react angrily or with anger to sth

Re|ak|ti|on [reak'tsioːn] F **-, -en a** reaction (*auf +acc* to); (*Chem*) reaction (*mit* with) **b** (*Pol pej*) reaction; **ein Vertreter der ~** a representative of reactionary thinking

re|ak|ti|o|när [reaktsio'nɛːɐ] (*Pol pej*) ADJ reactionary ADV **~ denken** to be a reactionary

Re|ak|ti|o|när [reaktsio'nɛːɐ] M **-(e)s, -e**, **Re|ak|ti|o|nä|rin** [-'nɛːrɪn] F **-, -nen** (*pej*) reactionary

Re|ak|ti|ons-: Re|ak|ti|ons|fä|hig|keit F ability to react; (*Chem, Physiol*) reactivity; **Alkohol vermindert die ~** alcohol slows down the or one's reactions; **re|ak|ti|ons|freu|dig** ADJ highly reactive; **Re|ak|ti|ons|ge|schwin|dig|keit** F speed of reaction; **re|ak|ti|ons|schnell** ADJ with fast reactions; **~ sein** to have fast reactions ADV **er bremste ~** he reacted quickly and braked; **Re|ak|ti|ons|schnel|lig|keit** F speed of reaction; **re|ak|ti|ons|trä|ge** ADJ of low reactivity; **Re|ak|ti|ons|ver|lauf** M (*Chem*) course of the reaction; **Re|ak|ti|ons|wär|me** F (*Chem*) heat of reaction; **Re|ak|ti|ons|zeit** F reaction time

re|ak|tiv [reak'tiːf] (*geh*) ADJ reactive ADV **er ver|hält sich nur ~** he doesn't act, he only reacts

re|ak|ti|vie|ren [reakti'viːrən] *ptp* **reaktiviert** VT (*Sci*) to reactivate; (*Agr, Biol, fig*) to revive; *Kenntnisse, Können* to brush up, to polish up; *Kontakte* to renew, to revive; *Markt* to revive; *Gliedmaßen* to rehabilitate; (*Mil*) to call up again; *Sportler, Beamte* to bring back

Re|ak|ti|vie|rung F **-, -en** (*Sci*) reactivation; (*Agr, Biol, fig*) revival; (*von Kenntnissen, Können*) brushing or polishing up; (*von Gliedmaßen*) rehabilitation; (*Mil*) new call-up

Re|ak|tor [re'aktoːɐ] M **-s, Reaktoren** [-'toːrən] reactor

Re|ak|tor-: Re|ak|tor|block M *pl* **-blöcke** reactor block; **Re|ak|tor|ge|bäu|de** NT reactor housing or dome, concrete sheet; **Re|ak|tor|kern** M reactor core; **Re|ak|tor|si|cher|heit** F reactor safety; **Re|ak|tor|un|glück** NT nuclear disaster

re|al [re'aːl] ADJ real; (= *wirklichkeitsbezogen*) realistic ADV *sinken, steigen* actually; **der ~ existie|rende Sozialismus** socialism as it exists in reality

Re|al-: Re|al|bü|ro NT (*Aus*) estate agency (*Brit*), real estate agency (*US*); **Re|al|ein|kom|men** NT real income; **Re|al|en|zy|klo|pä|die** F specialist encyclopaedia; **Re|al|gym|na|si|um** NT ≈ grammar school (*Brit*), ≈ high school (*esp US*) (*stressing modern languages, maths and science*)

Re|a|li|en [re'aːliən] PL realities *pl*, real facts *pl*; (*old Sch*) science and modern languages *pl*

Re|al-: Re|al|in|dex M (*dated*) subject index; **Re|al|in|ju|rie** [re'aːlʔɪnjuˑriə] F **-, -n** (*Jur*) ≈ assault

Re|a|li|sa|ti|on [realiza'tsioːn] F **-, -en** (= *Verwirk|lichung, auch Fin*) realization; (*TV, Rad, Theat*) production

re|a|li|sier|bar ADJ **a** *Idee, Projekt* practicable, feasible, realizable **b** (*Fin*) realizable

Re|a|li|sier|bar|keit [reali'ziːɐbaɐkait] F **-, no pl** feasibility, practicability

re|a|li|sie|ren [reali'ziːrən] *ptp* **realisiert** VT **a** *Pläne, Ideen, Programm, Projekt* to carry out; (*TV, Rad, Theat*) to produce **b** (*Fin*) to realize; *Verkauf* to make, to conclude **c** (= *erkennen*) to realize

Re|a|li|sie|rung F **-, -en** = **Realisation**

Re|a|lis|mus [rea'lɪsmʊs] M **-, no pl** realism

Re|a|list [rea'lɪst] M **-en, -en**, **Re|a|lis|tin** [-'lɪs|tɪn] F **-, -nen** realist

re|a|lis|tisch [rea'lɪstɪʃ] ADJ realistic ADV realistically

Re|a|li|tät [reali'tɛːt] F **-, -en a** reality; **der ~** (*dat*) **entsprechen** to correspond to reality or the facts; **die ~ anerkennen** to face facts; **die ~en** *pl* (= *Gegebenheiten*) the realities *pl*, the facts *pl*; **virtuelle ~** virtual reality **b Realitä|ten** PL (*Aus*: = *Immobilien*) real estate

Re|a|li|tä|ten|händ|ler(in) M(F) , **Re|a|li|tä|ten|ver|mitt|ler(in)** M(F) (*Aus*) estate agent (*Brit*), realtor (*US*), real estate agent (*US*)

Re|a|li|täts-: re|a|li|täts|feind|lich ADJ (*pej*) **~** to refuse to accept the realities of the situation; **re|a|li|täts|fern** ADJ unrealistic; **Re|a|li|täts|fer|ne** F lack of contact with reality; **re|a|li|täts|fremd** ADJ out of touch with reality; **re|a|li|täts|nah** ADJ realistic; **Re|a|li|täts|nä|he** F contact with reality; **Re|a|li|täts|sinn** M sense of realism; **er hat einen ausgeprägten ~** he has a firm hold on reality; **Re|a|li|täts|ver|lust** M (*Psych*) derealization

re|a|li|ter [re'aːlitɐ] ADV (*geh*) in reality, in (point of) fact

Re|a|li|ty-Fern|se|hen [ri'ɛliti-] NT , **Re|a|li|ty-TV** [ri'ɛlititiˑviˑ] NT real-life TV, reality TV (*esp US*)

Re|al-: Re|al|kanz|lei F (*Aus*) estate agency (*Brit*), real estate agency (*US*); **Re|al|ka|pi|tal** NT physical assets *pl*, non-monetary capital; **Re|al|ka|ta|log** M subject catalogue (*Brit*) or catalog (*US*); **Re|al|kon|kur|renz** F (*Jur*) **in ~ mit** in conjunction with; **Re|al|kre|dit** [-kre'diːt] M (*Fin*) collateral loan; **Re|al|le|xi|kon** NT specialist dictionary; **Re|al|lohn** M real wages *pl*

Re|a|lo [re'aːlo] M **-s, -s** (*Pol sl*) political realist (*of the Green Party*)

Re|al-: Re|al|po|li|tik F political realism, Realpolitik; **Re|al|po|li|ti|ker(in)** M(F) political realist; **re|al|po|li|tisch** ADJ politically realistic, pragmatic; **Re|al|sa|ti|re** F real-life satire; **Re|al|schu|le** F ≈ secondary school, ≈ secondary modern school (*Brit*); **Re|al|schü|ler(in)** M(F) ≈ secondary modern pupil (*Brit*), ≈ student in secondary school (*US*); **Re|al|tei|lung** F (*Jur*) division of (land/property *etc*); **Re|al|wert** M (*Fin*) real value; **Re|al|zins** M (*Fin*) real interest rate

---

REALSCHULE

A **Realschule** is a type of German secondary school. It normally covers a period of six school years (only four years in many **Länder** that have a separate **Orientierungsstufe**) and is designed to provide a general education that goes beyond that of a **Hauptschule**. Pupils work towards the **mittlere Reife**, after which they can for example try for a **Fachabi|tur** at a **Fachoberschule** or serve an apprenticeship. If pupils from a **Realschule** achieve good examination results, they may move up to the eleventh year of a **Gymnasium** and try for the **Abitur**.

In Austria the functions of **Realschulen** are performed by **mathematische Realgymnasien** and extended **Hauptschulen** → Abitur, Gymnasium, Hauptschule, mittlere Reife, Orientierungsstufe

---

Re|a|ni|ma|ti|on [reanima'tsioːn] F (*Med*) resuscitation

re|ani|mie|ren [reˌani'miːrən] *ptp* **reanimiert** VT (*Med*) to resuscitate

Re|be ['reːbə] F **-, -n** (= *Ranke*) shoot; (= *Weinstock*) vine

Re|bell [re'bɛl] M **-en, -en**, **Re|bel|lin** [-'bɛlɪn] F **-, -nen** rebel

re|bel|lie|ren [rebe'liːrən] *ptp* **rebelliert** VI to rebel, to revolt

Re|bel|li|on [rebɛ'lioːn] F **-, -en** rebellion, revolt

re|bel|lisch [re'bɛlɪʃ] ADJ rebellious

Re|ben|saft M (*liter*) wine, juice of the vine (*liter*), grape (*liter*)

Reb-: **Reb|huhn** ['reːp-, 'rɛp-] NT (common) partridge; **Reb|laus** ['reːp-] F phylloxera (*spec*), vine pest; **Reb|ling** ['reːplɪŋ] M **-s, -e** young vine; **Reb|schnur** ['reːp-] F (*Aus*) rope; **Reb|sor|te** ['reːp-] F type of vine; **Reb|stock** ['reːp-] M vine

Re|bus ['reːbʊs] M OR NT **-, -se** rebus, picture puzzle

Re|chaud [re'ʃoː] M OR NT **-s, -s** hotplate; (*für Tee/Kaffee*) tea/coffee warmer; (*für Fondue*) spirit burner (*Brit*), ethanol burner (*US*)

re|chen ['rɛçn] VT (*S Ger*) to rake

Re|chen ['rɛçn] M **-s, -** (*S Ger*) (= *Harke*) rake; (= *Gitter an Bächen, Flüssen*) grill

Re|chen-: **Re|chen|an|la|ge** F computer; **Re|chen|art** F type of calculation; **die vier ~en** the four arithmetical operations; **Re|chen|auf|ga|be** F sum (*esp Brit*), (arithmetical) problem; **Re|chen|au|to|mat** M (automatic) adding machine, Comptometer® (*Brit*); **Re|chen|brett** NT abacus; **Re|chen|buch** NT arithmetic book; **Re|chen|exem|pel** NT sum (*esp Brit*), arithmetical problem; **das ist doch ein ganz einfaches ~** it's a matter of simple arithmetic; **Re|chen|feh|ler** M miscalculation, (arithmetical) error or mistake; **Re|chen|funk|ti|on** F (*Comput*) computational function; **Re|chen|ge|schwin|dig|keit** F (*Comput*) processing speed; **Re|chen|heft** NT arithmetic book; **Re|chen|künst|ler(in)** M(F) mathematical genius or wizard (*inf*); **Re|chen|leh|rer(in)** M(F) arithmetic teacher; **Re|chen|ma|schi|ne** F adding machine; **Re|chen|ope|ra|ti|on** F calculation

Re|chen|schaft ['rɛçnʃaft] F **-, no pl** account; **jdm über etw** (*acc*) **~ geben** *or* **ablegen** to account to sb for sth, to give *or* render account to sb for sth (*liter*); **sich** (*dat*) **über etw** (*acc*) **~ ablegen** to account to oneself for sth; **jdm ~ schuldig sein** *or* **schulden** to be accountable to sb, to have to account to sb; **dafür bist du mir ~ schuldig** you owe me an explanation for that; **jdn (für etw) zur ~ ziehen** to call sb to account (for *or* over sth); **(von jdm) ~ verlangen** *or* **fordern** to demand an explanation *or* account (from sb)

Re|chen|schafts-: **Re|chen|schafts|be|richt** M report; **Re|chen|schafts|le|gung** [-leːgʊŋ] F **-, no pl** report; **jdm gegenüber zur ~ verpflichtet sein** to be accountable to sb; **Re|chen|schafts|pflicht** F accountability

Re|chen-: **Re|chen|schie|ber** M slide rule; **Re|chen|schwä|che** F (*Psych*) difficulty in dealing with numbers, dyscalculia (*spec*); **Re|chen|stab** M slide rule; **Re|chen|stun|de** F arithmetic lesson; **Re|chen|ta|bel|le** F ready reckoner; **Re|chen|ta|fel** F arithmetic slate; (*an der Wand*) (squared) blackboard; **Re|chen|werk** NT (*Comput*) arithmetic unit; **Re|chen|zeit** F (*Comput*) computer time; **Re|chen|zent|rum** NT computer centre (*Brit*) *or* center (*US*)

Re|cher|che [re'ʃɛrʃə, rə-] F **-, -n** investigation, inquiry; (*in Datenbank, Katalog*) search; **~n anstellen** to make investigations *or* inquiries (*über etw* (*acc*) about *or* into sth)

Re|cher|chen|jour|na|lis|mus [re'ʃɛrʃən-, rə-] M investigative journalism

re|cher|chie|ren [reʃɛr'ʃiːrən, rə-] *ptp* **recherchiert** VTI to investigate

rech|nen ['rɛçnən] **VT** **a** (= *addieren etc*) to work out, to calculate; **Aufgabe** to work out; **wir ~ gerade Additionen** we're doing addition at the moment; **rund gerechnet** in round figures; **was für einen Unsinn hast du da gerechnet!** how did you get that absurd result?, how did you work that out?

b (= *einstufen*) to count; **jdn/etw zu etw ~**, **jdn/etw unter etw** (*acc*) **~** to count sb among sth, to class sb/sth as sth; **er wird zu den größten Physikern** *or* **unter die größten Physiker gerechnet** he is rated as one *or* is reckoned to be one of the greatest physicists, he is counted among the greatest physicists

c (= *veranschlagen*) to estimate, to reckon; **wir hatten nur drei Tage gerechnet** we were only reckoning on three days; **für vier Personen rechnet man ca. zwei Pfund Fleisch** for four people you should reckon on about two pounds of meat; **das ist zu hoch/niedrig gerechnet** that's too high/low (an estimate)

d (= *einberechnen*) to include, to count, to take into account; **alles in allem gerechnet** all in all, taking everything into account; **den Ärger/die Unkosten mit dazu gerechnet** what with all the trouble/expense too *or* on top of that

VI **a** (= *addieren etc*) to do *or* make a calculation/calculations; (*esp Sch*) to do sums (*esp Brit*) *or* adding; **falsch ~** to go wrong *or* to make a mistake (in one's calculations); **richtig ~** to calculate correctly; **(da hast du) falsch gerechnet!** you got that wrong; **gut/schlecht ~ können** to be good/bad at arithmetic *or* with figures; (*esp Sch*) to be good/bad at sums (*esp Brit*) *or* adding; **~ lernen** to learn arithmetic; **mit Variablen/Zahlen ~** to do (the) calculations using variables/numbers

b (= *eingestuft werden*) to count; **er rechnet noch als Kind** he still counts as a child

c (= *sich verlassen*) **auf jdn/etw ~** to count on sb/sth

d **mit jdm/etw ~** (= *erwarten, einkalkulieren*) to reckon on *or* with sb/sth; (= *berücksichtigen*) to reckon with sb/sth; **es wird damit gerechnet, dass ...** it is reckoned *or* expected that ...; **du musst damit ~, dass es regnet** you must reckon on *or* with it raining; **mit ihm/dieser Partei wird man ~ müssen** he/this party will have to be reckoned with; **damit hatte ich nicht gerechnet** I wasn't expecting that, I hadn't reckoned on *or* with that; **mit so etwas muss man ~** you have to reckon on *or* with that sort of thing happening; **er rechnet mit einem Sieg** he reckons he'll win; **mit allem/dem Schlimmsten ~** to be prepared for anything/the worst; **wir hatten nicht mehr mit ihm** *or* **seinem Kommen gerechnet** we hadn't reckoned on him coming any more; **damit ~ müssen, dass ...** to have to be prepared for the fact that ..., to have to expect that ...; **ich rechne morgen fest mit dir** I'll be expecting you tomorrow

e (*inf*: = *haushalten*) to count the pennies, to be thrifty; **seine Frau kann gut ~** his wife knows how to count the pennies, his wife is thrifty → **Pfennig**

VR to pay off, to turn out to be profitable; **etw rechnet sich/rechnet sich nicht** sth is economical/not economical

Rech|nen ['rɛçnən] NT **-s, no pl** arithmetic; (*esp Sch*) sums *pl* (*Brit*), arithmetic

Rech|ner¹ ['rɛçnɐ] M **-s, -** (= *Elektronenrechner*) computer; (= *Taschenrechner*) calculator

Rech|ner² ['rɛçnɐ] M **-s, -**, **Rech|ne|rin** [-ərɪn] F **-, -nen** arithmetician; **ein guter ~ sein** to be good at arithmetic *or* figures

Rech|ne|rei [rɛçnə'raɪ] F **-, -en** (*inf*) calculation; **das ist eine furchtbare ~** it's incredibly difficult to work out; **die ganze ~ überlasse ich ihm** I leave all the calculations *or* figure-work to him

rech|ner-: **rech|ner|ge|steu|ert** [-gəʃtɔyɐt] ADJ computer-controlled; **rech|ner|ge|stützt** [-gəʃtʏtst] ADJ computer-aided

Rech|ne|rin F → **Rechner²**

rech|ne|risch ADJ arithmetical; (*Pol*) **Mehrheit** numerical; **ein ~es Beispiel** an example with some figures ADV **a** (= *kalkulatorisch*) **~ falsch sein** to be wrongly calculated; **~ richtig** correctly calculated; **rein ~** just on the basis of the figures; **ich bin rein ~ überzeugt, aber ...** I'm convinced as far as the figures go but ... **b** (= *durch Rechnen*) by *or* through calculation

Rech|ner|netz NT (*Comput*) computer network

Rech|ner|ver|bund M computer network; **um den ~ zu erleichtern** to make networking easier; **sie arbeiten im ~** they use networking *or* a computer network

Rech|nung ['rɛçnʊŋ] ☼ 47.5 F **-, -en** **a** (= *Berechnung*) calculation; (*als Aufgabe*) sum; **die ~ geht nicht auf** (*lit*) the sum doesn't work out; (*fig*) it won't work (out); **eine ~ aufmachen** to work it out → **Strich**

b (= *schriftliche Kostenforderung*) bill (*Brit*), check (*US*); (*esp von Firma*) invoice; (*für Kundenkonto*) statement of account; **das geht auf meine ~** I'm paying, this one's on me; **auf ~ kaufen/bestellen** to buy/order on account; **laut ~ vom 5. Juli** as per our invoice of July 5th; **auf** *or* **für eigene ~** on one's own account; **(jdm) etw in ~ stellen** to charge (sb) for sth; **einer Sache** (*dat*) **~ tragen, etw in ~ ziehen** to take sth into account, to bear sth in mind; **auf seine ~ kommen** to get one's money's worth; **mit jdm noch eine ~ offen haben** (*fig*) to have a score to settle with sb; **aber er hatte die ~ ohne den Wirt gemacht** (*inf*) but there was one thing he hadn't reckoned with → **begleichen**

Rech|nungs-: **Rech|nungs|ab|schluss** ▲ M making-up of (the) accounts; **den ~ machen** to do the books, to make up the accounts; **Rech|nungs|amt** NT audit office; **Rech|nungs|art** F = **Rechenart**; **Rech|nungs|be|trag** M → **Rechnung b** (total) amount of a bill (*Brit*) *or* check (*US*)/invoice/account; **Rech|nungs|buch** NT account(s) book *or* ledger; **Rech|nungs|ein|heit** F unit of account; **Rech|nungs|füh|rer(in)** M(F) chief accountant; **Rech|nungs|füh|rung** F accounting; **Rech|nungs|hof** M ≈ Auditor General's office (*Brit*), ≈ audit division (*US*); **Rech|nungs|jahr** NT financial *or* fiscal year; **Rech|nungs|le|gung** [-leːgʊŋ] F **-, -en** tendering of account; **Rech|nungs|prü|fer(in)** M(F) auditor; **Rech|nungs|prü|fung** F audit; **Rech|nungs|sum|me** F amount payable; **Rech|nungs|we|sen** NT (*Führung*) accountancy, bookkeeping; (*Prüfung*) auditing

recht [rɛçt] ☼ 36.2 ADJ **a** (= *richtig*) right; **es soll mir ~ sein, mir soll's ~ sein** (*inf*) it's all right *or* OK (*inf*) by me; **ganz ~!** quite right; **ist schon ~!** (*inf*) that's all right, that's OK (*inf*); **alles, was ~ ist** (*empört*) there's a limit, fair's fair; (*anerkennend*) you can't deny it; **ich will zum Bahnhof, bin ich hier ~?** (*esp S Ger*) I want to get to the station, am I going the right way?; **bin ich hier ~ bei Schmidts?** (*esp S Ger*) is this the Schmidts' place (all right (*inf*))?; **hier geht es nicht mit ~en Dingen zu** there's something odd *or* not right here; **ich habe keine ~e Lust** I don't particularly feel like it; **ein ~er Narr** (*old*) a real *or* right (*Brit*) fool; **nichts Rechtes** no good; **aus dem Jungen kann nichts Rechtes werden** that boy will come to no good; **aus ihm ist nichts Rechtes geworden** (*beruflich etc*) he never really made it; **er hat nichts Rechtes gelernt** he didn't learn any real trade; **nach dem Rechten sehen** to see that everything's OK (*inf*); **Tag, ich wollte nur mal nach dem Rechten sehen** hello, I just thought I'd come and see how you're doing *or* how things are; **es ist nicht mehr als ~ und billig** it's only right and proper; **was dem einen ~ ist, ist dem andern billig** (*Prov*) what's sauce for the goose is sauce for the goose (*Brit Prov*), what's good for the goose is good for the gander (*US Prov*)

b **~ haben/bekommen/behalten/geben** →

Recht d

ADV **a** (= *richtig*) properly; (= *wirklich*) really; **verstehen Sie mich ~** don't get me wrong (*inf*), don't misunderstand me; **ich verstehe ihn nicht so ~, wie kann er nur ...?** I just don't understand him, how can he ...?; **wenn ich Sie ~ verstehe** if I understand you rightly *or* aright (*form*); **sehe/höre ich ~?** am I seeing/hearing things?; **ich werde daraus nicht ~ klug** I don't really *or* rightly know what to make of it; **das geschieht ihm ~** it serves him right; **nun** *or* **jetzt mache ich es erst ~/erst ~ nicht** now I'm definitely/definitely not going to do it; **du kommst gerade ~, um ...** you're just in time to ...; **das ist** *or* **kommt mir gerade ~** (*inf*) that suits me fine; **du kommst mir gerade ~** (*iro*) you're all I needed; **gehe ich ~ in der Annahme, dass ...?** am I right *or* correct in assuming that ...?; **es hat mir nicht mehr ~ gefallen** I didn't really like it any more; **hat es dir gefallen? – nicht so ~** did you like it? – not really; **ich weiß nicht ~ I** don't really *or* rightly know; **man kann ihm nichts ~ machen** you can't do anything right for him; **man kann es nicht allen ~ machen** you can't please all of the people all of the time; **ich mache es Ihnen (auch) ~** (*inf*) I'll make it worth your while; **sie versuchte, es ihm immer ~ zu machen** she always tried to do everything right for him; **~ daran tun, zu ...** to be *or* do right to ...

b (= *ziemlich, ganz*) quite, fairly, pretty (*inf*); **~ viel** quite a lot

c (= *sehr*) very, right (*Brit dial*); **~ herzlichen Dank!** thank you very much indeed

Recht [rɛçt] ✪ 38.1, 40.3, 53.6 NT **-(e)s, -e** **a** (= *Rechtsordnung, sittliche Norm*) law; (= *Gerechtigkeit*) justice; **~ sprechen** to administer *or* dispense justice; **nach geltendem ~** in law; **nach englischem ~** in *or* under *or* according to English law; **~ muss ~ bleiben** (= *Naturrecht*) fair's fair; (= *Gesetz*) the law's the law; **für das ~ kämpfen** to fight for justice; **das Schwurgericht hat für ~ erkannt ...** the court has reached the following verdict *or* has decided ...; **von ~s wegen** legally, as of right; (*inf:* = *eigentlich*) by rights (*inf*)

b Rechte PL (*form*: = *Rechtswissenschaft*) jurisprudence; **Doktor der** *or* **beider ~e** Doctor of Laws **c** (= *Anspruch, Berechtigung*) right (*auf* +*acc* to, *zu* to); **sein ~ fordern** to demand one's rights; **seine ~e geltend machen** to insist on one's rights; **ich nehme mir das ~, das zu tun I** shall make so bold as to do that; **sein ~ bekommen** *or* **erhalten** *or* **kriegen** (*inf*) to get one's rights, to get what is one's by right; **zu seinem ~ kommen** (*lit*) to gain one's rights; (*fig*) to come into one's own; **auch das Vergnügen muss zu seinem ~ kommen** there has to be a place for pleasure too; **der Körper verlangt sein ~ auf Schlaf** the body demands its rightful sleep; **gleiches ~ für alle!** equal rights for all!; **gleiche ~e, gleiche Pflichten** equal rights, equal duties; **das ~ des Stärkeren** the law of the jungle; **mit** *or* **zu ~** rightly, with justification; **und (das) mit ~** and rightly so; **Sie stellen diese Frage ganz zu ~** you are quite right to ask this question; **im ~ sein** to be in the right; **das ist mein gutes ~** it's my right; **es ist unser gutes ~, zu erfahren ...** we have every right to know ...; **woher nimmt er das ~, das zu sagen?** what gives him the right to say that?; **mit welchem ~?** by what right? → **vorbehalten**

d **~ haben** to be right; **er hat ~ bekommen** he was right; **~ behalten** to be right; **er will immer ~ behalten** he always has to be right; **ich hatte ~, und ich habe ~ behalten** I was right and I'm still right; **jdm ~ geben** to agree with sb, to admit that sb is right

Rechte [rɛçtə] F *decl as adj* **a** (*Hand*) right hand; (*Seite*) right(-hand) side; (*Boxen*) right; **zur ~n (des Königs) saß ...** to the right (of the king) *or* on the (king's) right sat ... **b** (*Pol*) **die ~** the Right

Recht-: Recht|eck NT rectangle; **recht|eckig** ADJ rectangular

Rech|te|hand|re|gel F (*Phys*) right-hand rule

rech|ten [ˈrɛçtn] VI (*geh*) to argue, to dispute

rech|tens ▲ [ˈrɛçtns] ADJ (*form*) **es ist ~/nicht ~, dass er das gemacht hat** he was/was not within his rights to do that; **die Sache war nicht ~** the matter was not right *or* (*Jur*) legal; **etw für ~ erklären** to declare sth legal

rech|te(r, s) [ˈrɛçtə] ADJ *attr* **a** right; *Rand, Spur etc auch* right-hand; **auf der ~n Seite** on the right-hand side, on the right; **jds ~ Hand sein** to be sb's right-hand man **b** **ein ~r Winkel** a right angle **c** (= *konservativ*) right-wing, rightist; **der ~ Flügel** the right wing **d** (*beim Stricken*) plain; **eine ~ Masche stricken** to knit one

rech|ter|seits [ˈrɛçtzaits] ADV on the right-hand side

rech|fer|ti|gen [ˈrɛçtfɛrtɪɡn] *insep* **VT** to justify; (= *berechtigt erscheinen lassen auch*) to warrant; **das ist durch nichts zu ~** that can in no way be justified, that is completely unjustifiable **VR** to justify oneself

Recht|fer|ti|gung F justification; **zu meiner ~** in my defence (*Brit*) *or* defense (*US*), in justification of what I did/said *etc*; **etw zur ~ vorbringen** to say sth in one's defence (*Brit*) *or* defense (*US*), to say sth to justify oneself

Recht|fer|ti|gungs-: Recht|fer|ti|gungs|grund M (*Jur*) justification; **Recht|fer|ti|gungs|schrift** F apologia; **Recht|fer|ti|gungs|ver|such** M attempt at self-justification

Recht-: recht|gläu|big [ˈrɛçtɡlɔybɪç] ADJ orthodox; **der Rechtgläubige** the orthodox person; **Recht|gläu|big|keit** F orthodoxy; **Recht|ha|ber** [ˈrɛçthaːbɐ] M **-s, -, Recht|ha|be|rin** [-ərɪn] F **-, -nen** (*pej*) know-all (*Brit inf*), know-it-all (*US inf*), self-opinionated person; **Recht|ha|be|rei** [rɛçthaːbəˈrai] F **-, *no pl*** (*pej*) know-all (*Brit inf*) *or* know-it-all (*US inf*) attitude, self-opinionatedness; **recht|ha|be|risch** [ˈrɛçthaːbərɪʃ] ADJ know-all (*Brit inf*), know-it-all *attr* (*US inf*), self-opinionated; **er ist so ~** he's such a know-all (*Brit inf*) *or* know-it-all (*US inf*), he's so self-opinionated **ADV** **~ bestand er darauf** he insisted on it in his self-opinionated way

recht|lich [ˈrɛçtlɪç] ADJ **a** (= *gesetzlich*) legal **b** (*old:* = *redlich*) honest, upright, upstanding (*old*) **ADV** **a** (= *gesetzlich*) legally; **~ verpflichtet** bound by law, legally obliged; **~ zulässig** permissible in law; **~ nicht zulässig** not permissible in law; **~ unmöglich** impossible for legal reasons; **jdn ~ belangen** to take sb to court, to take legal action against sb **b** (*old:* = *redlich*) honestly; **~ denken/handeln** to think/act in an honest way

Recht-: recht|los ADJ **a** without rights **b** *Zustand* lawless; **Recht|lo|se(r)** [ˈrɛçtloːzə] MF *decl as adj* person with no rights; (= *Vogelfreier*) outlaw; **Recht|lo|sig|keit** F **-, *no pl*** **a** (*von Mensch*) lack of rights; **in völliger ~ leben** to have no rights whatever **b** (*in Land*) lawlessness; **recht|mä|ßig** ADJ **a** (= *legitim*) lawful, legitimate; *Erben, Thronfolger, Besitzer auch* rightful; (= *dem Gesetz entsprechend*) legal, in accordance with the law; **etw für ~ erklären** to legitimize sth; to declare sth legal **ADV** legally; **jdm etw ~ zuerkennen** to recognize sb's legal right *or* entitlement to sth; **jdm ~ zustehen** to belong to sb legally; **~ gewählt** legally elected, elected in accordance with the law; **Recht|mä|ßig|keit** [ˈrɛçtmɛːsɪçkait] F **-, *no pl*** (= *Legitimität*) legitimacy; (= *Legalität*) legality

rechts [rɛçts] ADV **a** on the right; **nach ~** (to the) right; **von ~** from the right; **~ von etw** (on *or* to the right) of sth; **~ von jdm** to *or* on sb's right; (*Pol*) to the right of sb; **weiter ~** further to the right; **sich ~ einordnen** to move into *or* take the right-hand lane; **~ vor links** right before left (*rule of the priority system for driving*); **sich ~ halten** to keep (to the) right; **Augen ~!** (*Mil*) eyes right!; **~ schwenkt, marsch!** (*Mil*) right wheel! (*Brit*), right about-face! (*US*); **~ um!** (*Mil*) right about turn!; **~ stehen** *or* **sein** (*Pol*) to be right-wing *or* on the right *or* a right-winger; **~ stehend** right-hand, on the right; (*Pol*) right-wing, on the right; **ich weiß nicht mehr, wo ~ und links ist** (*inf*) I don't know whether I'm coming or going (*inf*)

b **~ stricken** to knit (plain); **ein ganz ~ gestrickter Pullover** a pullover knitted in garter stitch; **zwei ~, zwei links** (*beim Stricken*) knit two, purl two, two plain, two purl

PREP +*gen* **~ des Rheins** to *or* on the right of the Rhine

Rechts- *in cpds* (*Jur*) legal; **Rechts|ab|bie|ger¹** M **-s, -** (= *Spur*) right-hand turn-off lane; **Rechts|ab|bie|ger²** M **-s, -, Rechts|ab|bie|ge|rin** [-ərɪn] F **-, -nen** motorist/cyclist/car *etc* turning right; **die Spur für ~** the right-hand turn-off lane; **Rechts|ab|bie|ger|spur** F right-hand turn-off lane; **Rechts|ab|tei|lung** F legal department; **Rechts|ab|weich|ler(in)** M(F) (*Pol inf*) right-wing dissenter; **Rechts|an|ge|le|gen|heit** F legal matter; **Rechts|an|schau|ung** F legal view; **Rechts|an|spruch** M legal right *or* entitlement; **einen ~ auf etw (*acc*) haben** to be legally entitled to sth, to have a legal right to sth; **aus etw einen ~ ableiten** to derive a legal right from sth

Rechts|an|walt M , **Rechts|an|wäl|tin** F lawyer, attorney (*US*); (*als Berater auch*) solicitor (*Brit*), attorney (*US*); (*vor Gericht auch*) barrister (*Brit*), advocate (*Scot*), attorney (*US*); **sein ~ behauptete vor Gericht, ...** his counsel maintained in court ...; **sich (*dat*) einen ~ nehmen** to get a lawyer *etc*

Rechts|an|walts-: Rechts|an|walts|ge|hil|fe M , **Rechts|an|walts|ge|hil|fin** F legal secretary; **Rechts|an|walts|kam|mer** F Law Society (*Brit*), Bar Association (*US*); **Rechts|an|walts|kanz|lei** F lawyer's *or* solicitor's (*Brit*) *or* attorney's (*US*) office; (*Firma auch*) law firm

Rechts-: Rechts|auf|fas|sung F **a** conception of legality **b** (= *Auslegung*) interpretation of the law; **Rechts|aus|kunft** F legal advice; **Rechts|aus|le|ger** M (*Boxen*) southpaw; **Rechts|aus|le|ger(in)** M(F) (*Pol hum*) extreme right-winger (of a party); **Rechts|aus|schuss** ▲ M (*Pol*) committee on legal affairs, judiciary committee; **Rechts|au|ßen** [-ˈlausn] M **-, -** (*Ftbl*) outside-right; (*Pol inf*) extreme right-winger; **Rechts|bei|stand** M legal advice; (*Mensch*) legal adviser; **Rechts|be|leh|rung** F legal information; (*der Geschworenen*) directions *pl*, instruction (of the jury) (*US*); **Rechts|be|ra|ter(in)** M(F) legal adviser; **Rechts|be|ra|tung** F **a** legal advice **b** (*auch* **Rechtsberatungsstelle**) legal advice office, ≈ citizens' advice bureau (*Brit*), ≈ ACLU (*US*); **Rechts|beu|gung** F perversion of the course of justice; **Rechts|bre|cher(in)** M(F) lawbreaker, criminal; **Rechts|bruch** M breach *or* infringement of the law; **rechts|bün|dig** (*Typ*) ADJ ranged *or* flush right (*Brit*), right-aligned ADV flush right (*Brit*), aligned right

recht|schaf|fen [ˈrɛçtʃafn] ADJ **a** (= *ehrlich, redlich*) honest, upright **b** (*inf:* = *stark, groß*) **~en Durst/Hunger haben** to be really thirsty/hungry, to be parched (*inf*)/starving (*inf*) **ADV** **a** (= *redlich*) honestly, uprightly **b** (*inf:* = *sehr*) really; **sich ~ bemühen** to try really hard

Recht|schaf|fen|heit F **-, *no pl*** honesty, uprightness

recht|schrei|ben [ˈrɛçtʃraibn] VI *infin only* to spell

Recht|schrei|ben [ˈrɛçtʃraibn] NT spelling

Recht|schreib-: Recht|schreib|feh|ler M spelling mistake; **Recht|schreib|hil|fe** F (*Comput*) spelling aid; **Recht|schreib|kon|trol|le** F , **Recht|schreib|prü|fung** F (*Comput*) spell check; (= *Programm*) spellchecker; **Recht|schreib|re|form** F spelling reform

Recht|schrei|bung F spelling

Rechts-: Rechts|drall M (im Gewehrlauf) clockwise rifling; (von Geschoss, Billardball) swerve to the right; (von Auto, Pferd) pull to the right; (Pol inf) leaning to the right; **einen ~ haben** to swerve/pull/lean to the right; **rechts|drehend** ADJ (Chem) dextrorotatory (spec); **Rechts|dre|hung** F turn to the right

Rechts|ein|wand M objection, demurrer (spec)

rechts|sei|tig [-zaitç] ADJ = rechtsseitig

Rechts|emp|fin|den NT sense of justice

Recht|ser ['rɛçtsɐ] M -s, -, **Recht|se|rin** [-ərɪn] F -, -nen (dial) = Rechtshänder

Rechts-: rechts|ext|rem ADJ right-wing extremist attr; **Rechts|ext|re|mis|mus** M right-wing extremism; **Rechts|ext|re|mist(in)** M(F) right-wing extremist; **rechts|ext|re|mis|tisch** ADJ right-wing extremist attr; **rechts|fä|hig** ADJ (Jur) legally responsible, having legal capacity (form); **Rechts|fä|hig|keit** F (Jur) legal responsibility or capacity (form); **Rechts|fall** M court case; (in der Rechtsgeschichte auch) legal case; **Rechts|form** F legal form; **Rechts|fra|ge** F legal question or issue; **rechts|frei** ADJ ~er Raum unlegislated area; **Rechts|frie|den** M (Jur) peace under the law; **Rechts|gang¹** M , no pl (Jur) legal procedure; **im ersten ~** at the first court case; **Rechts|gang²** M pl -gänge (Tech) right-handed thread; **rechts|gän|gig** ADJ (Tech) right-handed; **Rechts|ge|fühl** NT sense of justice; **Rechts|ge|lehr|sam|keit** F (old) jurisprudence; **Rechts|ge|lehr|te(r)** MF decl as adj jurist, legal scholar; **rechts|ge|rich|tet** [-gərɪçtət] ADJ (Pol) right-wing; **Rechts|ge|schäft** NT legal transaction; **einseitiges/mehrseitiges ~** unilateral/multilateral legal transaction; **~e tätigen** to carry out legal transactions; **Rechts|ge|schich|te** F legal history; (= Geschichte der Rechtswissenschaft auch) history of law; **Rechts|ge|win|de** NT right-handed thread; **Rechts|grund** M legal justification; **Rechts|grund|la|ge** F legal basis; **Rechts|grund|satz** M legal maxim; **rechts|gül|tig** ADJ legally valid, legal; Vertrag auch legally binding; **Rechts|gül|tig|keit** F legal validity, legality; **~ erlangen** to become legally valid; **Rechts|gut** NT something enjoying legal protection, legally protected right; **Rechts|gut|ach|ten** NT legal report; **Rechts|ha|ken** M (Boxen) right hook; **Rechts|han|del** M (liter) lawsuit; **Rechts|hän|der** [-hɛndɐ] M -s, -, **Rechts|hän|de|rin** [-ərɪn] F -, -nen right-handed person, right-hander (esp Sport); **~ sein** to be right-handed; **rechts|hän|dig** ADJ ADV right-handed; **Rechts|hän|dig|keit** F -, no pl right-handedness; **Rechts|hand|lung** F legal act; **rechts|hän|gig** ADJ (Jur) sub judice pred; **Rechts|hän|gig|keit** F -, no pl state of being sub judice; **rechts|her** ['rɛçtshɛːɐ] ADV from the right; **rechts|he|ran** ['rɛçtsheran] ADV over to the right; **rechts|he|rum** ['rɛçtsherʊm] ADV (round) to the right; sich drehen etc auch clockwise; **Rechts|hil|fe** F (mutual) assistance in law enforcement; **Rechts|hil|fe|ab|kom|men** NT law enforcement treaty; **rechts|hin** ['rɛçtshɪn] ADV (old) (to the) right; **Rechts|klar|heit** F clear legal principles pl; **~ über etw (acc) schaffen** to clearly define the legal position with regard to sth; **Rechts|kraft** F , no pl (von Gesetz, Urteil) legal force, force of law; (= Gültigkeit: von Vertrag etc) legal validity; **~ erlangen** (Gesetz) to become law, to come into force; (Urteil) to come into force; **rechts|kräf|tig** ADV having the force of law; Urteil final; Vertrag legally valid; **~ sein/werden** (Verordnung) to have the force of law/to become law; (Urteil) to be/become final; (Gesetz) to be in/come into force ADV **~ verurteilt sein** to be issued with a final sentence; **rechts|kun|dig** ADJ familiar with or versed in the law; **Rechts|kur|ve** F (von Straße) right-hand bend; (von Bahn auch) right-hand curve; **Rechts|la|ge** F legal position; **rechts|las|tig**

[-lastıç] ADJ listing to the right; Auto auch down at the right; (fig) leaning to the right; **~ sein** to list to/be down at/lean to the right; **rechts|läu|fig** ADJ Gewinde right-handed; Schrift left-to-right; **Rechts|leh|re** F jurisprudence; **Rechts|leh|rer(in)** M(F) (form) professor of jurisprudence (form); **Rechts|miss|brauch** ▲ M abuse of the law; **Rechts|mit|tel** NT means sing of legal redress; **~ einlegen** to lodge an appeal; **auf ~ verzichten** to relinquish one's right to appeal; **Rechts|mit|tel|be|leh|rung** F statement of rights of redress or appeal; **Rechts|nach|fol|ge** F legal succession; **Rechts|nach|fol|ger(in)** M(F) legal successor; **Rechts|norm** F legal norm; **Rechts|ord|nung** F eine ~ a system of laws; **die ~** the law; **die staatliche ~** state laws pl; **Rechts|par|tei** F right-wing party; **Rechts|pfle|ge** F administration of justice; **Rechts|pfle|ger(in)** M(F) official with certain judicial powers; **Rechts|phi|lo|so|phie** F philosophy of law

Recht|spre|chung ['rɛçtʃprɛçʊŋ] F -, -en **a** (= Rechtspflege) administration of justice; (= Gerichtsbarkeit) jurisdiction **b** (= richterliche Tätigkeit) administering or dispensation of justice **c** (= bisherige Urteile) precedents pl

Rechts-: rechts|ra|di|kal ADJ radical right-wing; **die Rechtsradikalen** the right-wing radicals ADV **~ eingestellt sein** to be a right-wing radical; **~ klingen** to sound radically right-wing; **Rechts|ra|di|ka|lis|mus** M right-wing radicalism; **Rechts|re|fe|ren|dar(in)** M(F) articled clerk (Brit), legal intern (US); **~ sein** to be under articles (Brit), to be a legal intern (US); **rechts|rhei|nisch** ADJ to or on the right of the Rhine; **Rechts|ruck** M , **Rechts|rutsch** M (Pol) swing to the right; **rechts|rum** ['rɛçtsrʊm] ADV (inf) = rechtsherum; **Rechts|sa|che** F legal matter; (= Fall) case; **Rechts|schutz** M legal protection; **Rechts|schutz|ver|si|che|rung** F legal costs insurance; **Rechts|schwenk** M (Pol) swing to the right; **rechts|sei|tig** [-zaitıç] ADJ, ADV on the right(-hand) side; **~ gelähmt** paralyzed on the right side; **~ blind** blind in the right eye; **er war ~ amputiert worden** his right arm/leg had been amputated; **Rechts|si|cher|heit** F , no pl legal certainty; **~ schaffen** to create legal certainty; **Rechts|spra|che** F legal terminology or language; **Rechts|spruch** M verdict; **Rechts|staat** M state under the rule of law; **Rechts|staat|lich** ADJ of a state under the rule of law; **~e Ordnung** law and order; **seine ~e Gesinnung** his predisposition for law and order; **Rechts|staat|lich|keit** F -, no pl rule of law; (einer Maßnahme) legality; **rechts|ste|hend** △ ADJ attr → rechts ADV a; **Rechts|stel|lung** F legal position; **Rechts|steu|e|rung** F right-hand drive; **Rechts|streit** M lawsuit; **Rechts|sys|tem** NT judicial system; **Rechts|ti|tel** M legal title

recht|su|chend ADJ attr seeking justice

rechts|um ['rɛçts'ʊm] ADV (Mil) to the right; **~ (kehrt)!** right about turn!

Rechts-: Rechts|un|si|cher|heit F legal uncertainty; **rechts|ver|bind|lich** ADJ legally binding; Auskunft legally valid ADV **~ festgelegt** laid down so as to be legally binding; **Rechts|ver|bind|lich|keit** F (von Auskunft) legal validity; **Rechts|ver|dre|her** M -s, -, **Rechts|ver|dre|he|rin** [-ərɪn] F -, -nen (pej) shyster (inf), Philadelphia lawyer (US); (hum inf) legal eagle (inf); **Rechts|ver|glei|chung** F comparative law; **Rechts|ver|hält|nis** NT facts pl of the case; **Rechts|ver|kehr¹** M driving on the right no def art; **in Deutschland ist ~ in** Germany they drive on the right; **im ~ muss man ...** when driving on the right one must ...; **Rechts|ver|kehr²** M (Jur) legal dealings pl; **Rechts|ver|let|zung** F infringement or breach of the law; **Rechts|ver|ord|nung** F ≈ statutory order; **Rechts|ver|tre|ter(in)** M(F) legal representative; **Rechts|vor|schrift** F ≈ legal provision; **Rechts|weg** M legal action;

den ~ beschreiten or **einschlagen** to have recourse to or to take legal action, to go to law; **auf dem ~** by recourse to legal action, by taking legal action; **unter Ausschluss des ~es** without possibility of recourse to legal action; **der ~ ist ausgeschlossen** ≈ the judges' decision is final; **rechts|wid|rig** ADJ illegal ADV illegally; **Rechts|wid|rig|keit** F **a** no pl illegality **b** (Handlung) illegal act, breach of the law; **Rechts|wis|sen|schaft** F jurisprudence

Recht-: recht|win|ke|lig, recht|wink|lig ADJ right-angled; **recht|zei|tig** ADJ (= früh genug) timely; (= pünktlich) punctual; **um ~e Anmeldung wird gebeten** you are requested to apply in good time ADV (= früh genug) in (good) time; (= pünktlich) on time; **gerade noch ~ ankommen** to arrive or be just in time; **Recht|zei|tig|keit** F ['rɛçtsaitçkait] F -, no pl timeliness; (= Pünktlichkeit) punctuality

Re|ci|tal [rı'saitl] NT -s, -s (Mus) recital

Reck [rɛk] NT -(e)s, -e (Sport) horizontal bar

Re|cke ['rɛkə] M -n, -n (old) warrior

re|cken ['rɛkn] VT **a** (= aus-, emporstrecken) to stretch; **den Kopf** or **Hals ~** to crane one's neck; **die Glieder ~** to stretch (oneself), to have a stretch; **die Arme in die Höhe ~** to raise one's arms in the air **b** (dial: = glatt ziehen) etw ~ to pull the creases out of sth VR to stretch (oneself); **sich ~ und strecken** to have a good stretch

Reck-: Reck|stan|ge F horizontal bar; **Reck|tur|nen** NT bar exercises pl

Re|cor|der △ [re'kɔrdɐ] M -s, - → Rekorder

re|cy|cel|bar [rı'saikəlbaːɐ] ADJ recyclable

re|cy|celn [rı'saikln] ptp recycelt [rı'saiklt] VT to recycle

Re|cyc|ling [rı'saiklıŋ] NT -s, no pl recycling

Re|cyc|ling- [rı'saiklıŋ-]: **Re|cyc|ling|hof** M transfer facility for recyclable waste; **Re|cyc|ling|pa|pier** NT recycled paper; **Re|cyc|ling|werk** NT recycling plant

Red. **a** abbr von Redakteur ed **b** abbr von Redaktion

Re|dak|teur [redak'tøːɐ] M -s, -e, **Re|dak|teu|rin** [-'tø:rɪn] F -, -nen editor

Re|dak|ti|on [redak'tsio:n] F -, -en **a** (= das Redigieren) editing; **die ~ dieses Buches hatte ...** this book was edited by ...; **~: XY** editor: XY **b** (= Personal) editorial staff **c** (= Büro) editorial office(s); **der Reporter rief seine ~ an** the reporter phoned his office or paper

re|dak|ti|o|nell [redaktsio'nɛl] ADJ editorial; **die ~e Leitung im Ressort Wirtschaft hat Herr Müller** Mr Müller is the editor responsible for business and finance; **Leserbriefe stellen keine ~en Meinungsäußerungen dar** readers' letters do not necessarily reflect the views of the editor ADV **überarbeiten** editorially; **ein Projekt ~ betreuen** to be the editor of a project; **etw ~ bearbeiten** to edit sth

Re|dak|ti|ons-: Re|dak|ti|ons|ge|heim|nis NT press secret; **Re|dak|ti|ons|kon|fe|renz** F editorial conference; **Re|dak|ti|ons|schluss** ▲ M time of going to press; (= Einsendeschluss) copy deadline; **bei ~** at the time of going to press; **diese Nachricht ist vor/nach ~ eingegangen** this news item arrived before/after the paper went to press or bed (inf)

Re|dak|tor [re'dakto:ɐ] M -s, **Redaktoren** [-'to:rən], **Re|dak|to|rin** [-'to:rɪn] F -, -nen (Sw) editor

Re|dak|tri|ce [redak'tri:sə] F -, -n (Aus) editor

Re|de ['re:də] F -, -n **a** speech; (= Ansprache) address; **die Kunst der ~** (form) the art of rhetoric; **eine ~ halten** or **schwingen** (inf) to make or give a speech; **die ~ des Bundeskanzlers** the speech given by the Chancellor; **die Kanzlerin...** the Chancellor's speech; **in freier ~** without (consulting) notes; **der langen ~ kurzer Sinn** (prov) the long and the short of it **b** (= Äußerungen, Worte) words pl, language no *pl*; **seine frechen ~n** his cheek (*Brit*) or impudence; **große ~n führen** or **schwingen** (*inf*) to talk big (*inf*); **das ist meine ~!** that's what I've always said; **jds stehende ~ sein** to be sb's stock saying; **das ist nicht der ~ wert** it's not worth mentioning; **(es ist) nicht der ~ wert!** don't mention it, it was nothing

c (= *das Reden, Gespräch*) conversation, talk; **jdm in die ~ fallen** to interrupt sb; **die ~ fiel** or **kam auf** (+*acc*) the conversation or talk turned to; **die in ~ stehende Person** (*form*) the person in question or under discussion; **es war von einer Gehaltserhöhung die ~** there was talk or mention of a salary increase; **von Ihnen war eben die ~** we were just talking about you; **aber davon war doch nie die ~** but no-one was ever talking about that; **wovon ist die ~?** what are you/we *etc* talking about?; **von einer Gehaltserhöhung kann keine** or **kann nicht die ~ sein** there can be no question of a salary increase; **von Großzügigkeit kann keine** or **kann nicht die ~ sein, das war nur ...** there's no question of it being generosity, it was just ...; **davon kann keine** or **kann nicht die ~ sein** it's out of the question

d (*Ling, Liter*) speech; **direkte** or **wörtliche/indirekte ~** direct/indirect speech or discourse (*US*); **gebundene ~** verse; **ungebundene ~** prose

e (= *Gerücht, Nachrede*) rumour (*Brit*), rumor (*US*); **kümmere dich doch nicht um die ~n der Leute!** don't worry (about) what people say; **es geht die ~, dass** there's a rumo(u)r that, rumo(u)r has it that; **von ihr geht die ~, dass sie ...** people say or it is said (about her) that she ...

f (= *Rechenschaft*) **(jdm) ~ (und Antwort) stehen** to justify oneself (to sb); **(jdm) Rede für etw ~ und Antwort stehen** to account (to sb) for sth; **jdn zur ~ stellen** to take sb to task

Re|de-: Re|de|du|ell NT verbal exchange or duel; **Re|de|fi|gur** F (*Liter*) figure of speech; **Re|de|fluss** ▲ M flow of words; **er stockte plötzlich in seinem ~** he suddenly stopped in mid-flow; **ich will Ihren ~ nicht unterbrechen, aber ...** I don't wish to interrupt your flow but ...; **Re|de|frei|heit** F freedom of speech; **Re|de|ga|be** F eloquence; **re|de|ge|wandt** ADJ eloquent; **Re|de|kunst** F **die ~** rhetoric

re|den ['reːdn̩] **VI a** (= *sprechen*) to talk, to speak; **Reden während des Unterrichts** talking in class; **mit sich selbst/jdm ~** to talk or speak to oneself/sb; **wie red(e)st du denn mit deiner Mutter!** that's no way to talk or speak to your mother; **so lasse ich nicht mit mir ~!** I won't be spoken to like that!; **sie hat geredet und geredet** she talked and talked; **mit jdm über jdn/etw ~** to talk or speak to or with sb about sb/sth; **~ wir nicht mehr davon** or **darüber** let's not talk or speak about it any more, let's drop it (*inf*); **~ Sie doch nicht!** (*inf*) come off it! (*inf*); **(viel) von sich ~ machen** to become a (very much) a talking point; **das Buch/er macht viel von sich ~** everyone is talking about the book/him; **viel Redens von einer Sache machen** to make a great to-do about sth (*inf*); **du hast gut** or **leicht ~!** it's all very well for you (to talk); **ich habe mit Ihnen zu ~!** I would like to speak or talk to you, I would like a word with you; **ich rede gegen eine Wand** or **Mauer** it's like talking to a brick wall (*inf*); **darüber lässt** or **ließe sich ~** that's a possibility; (*über Preis, Bedingungen*) I think we could discuss that; **darüber lässt** or **ließe sich eher ~** that's more like it, now you're talking; **er lässt mit sich ~** he could be persuaded; (*in Bezug auf Preis*) he's open to offers; (= *gesprächsbereit*) he's open to discussion; **sie lässt nicht mit sich ~** she is adamant; (*bei eigenen Forderungen auch*) she won't take no for an answer; **Reden ist Silber, Schweigen ist Gold** (*Prov*) (speech is silver but) silence is golden (*Prov*); **das ist ja mein Reden (seit 33)** (*inf*) I've been saying that for (donkey's (*Brit inf*)) years → **Wasserfall**

b (= *klatschen*) to talk (*über* +*acc* about); **schlecht von jdm ~** to talk or speak ill of sb; **in so einem Dorf wird natürlich viel geredet** in a village like that naturally people talk a lot

c (= *eine Rede halten*) to speak; **er redet nicht gerne öffentlich** he doesn't like public speaking; **er kann gut ~** he is a good speaker; **frei ~** to speak extempore, to speak without notes

d (*euph.* = *gestehen, aussagen*) to talk; **jdn zum Reden bringen** to get sb to talk, to make sb talk; **er will nicht ~** he won't talk

VT a (= *sagen*) to say; *Worte* to say; **einige Worte ~** to say a few words; **kein Wort ~** not to say or speak a word; **sich** (*dat*) **etw von der Seele** or **vom Herzen ~** to get sth off one's chest

b (= *klatschen*) to say; **es kann dir doch nicht egal sein, was über dich geredet wird** it must matter to you what people say about you; **Schlechtes von jdm** or **über jdn ~** to say bad things about sb; **damit die Leute wieder was zu ~ haben** so that people have something to talk about again

VR sich heiser ~ to talk oneself hoarse; **sich in Zorn** or **Wut ~** to talk oneself into a fury

Re|dens|art F (= *Phrase*) hackneyed expression (*Brit*), cliché; (= *Redewendung*) expression, idiom; (= *Sprichwort*) saying; (= *leere Versprechung*) empty promise; **das ist nur so eine ~** it's just a way of speaking; **bloße ~en** empty talk

Re|den|schrei|ber(in) M(F) speechwriter

Re|de|rei [reːdəˈraɪ] F -, -en **a** (= *Geschwätz*) chattering *no pl*, talking *no pl*; **du mit deiner ~, du bist doch zu feige dazu** you're all talk, you're too scared to do it **b** (= *Klatsch*) gossip *no pl*, talk *no pl*; **zu ~en Anlass geben** to make people talk, to give rise to gossip

Re|de-: Re|de|schwall M torrent or flood of words; **Re|de|strom** M flow of words; **Re|de|ver|bot** NT ban on speaking; **jdm ~ erteilen** to ban sb from speaking; **(allgemeines) ~!** (= *keine Gespräche erlaubt*) no talking!; **Re|de|wei|se** F style or manner (of speaking); **Re|de|wen|dung** F idiom, idiomatic expression

re|di|gie|ren [rediˈɡiːrən] *ptp* **redigiert** VT to edit

Re|dis|kont|ge|schäft [redɪsˈkɔnt-] NT rediscount

Re|dis|kon|tie|rung [redɪskɔnˈtiːrʊŋ] F -, -en rediscounting

red|lich ['reːtlɪç] ADJ honest ADV **a** (= *ehrlich*) honestly; **~ denken** to be honest; **~ handeln** to be honest, to act honestly; **er meint es ~** he is being honest; **sich** (*dat*) **etw ~ verdient haben** to have really or genuinely earned sth; *Geld, Gut* to have acquired sth by honest means; **~ (mit jdm) teilen** to share (things) equally (with sb); **sich ~ durchs Leben schlagen** to make an honest living; **~** (= *ziemlich*) **sich bemühen, sich anstrengen, sich einsetzen** really

Red|lich|keit F -, *no pl* honesty

Red|ner ['reːdnɐ] M -s, -, **Red|ne|rin** [-ərɪn] F -, -nen speaker; (= *Rhetoriker*) orator; **ich bin kein (großer) ~** I'm not much of a speaker

Red|ner-: Red|ner|büh|ne F platform, rostrum; **Red|ner|ga|be** F gift of oratory

red|ne|risch ['reːdnərɪʃ] ADJ rhetorical, oratorical; **~e Begabung** talent for public speaking; ADV rhetorically; **~ begabt sein** to be a gifted speaker

Red|ner|pult NT lectern

red|se|lig ['reːtzeːlɪç] ADJ talkative

Red|se|lig|keit F -, *no pl* talkativeness

Re|duk|ti|on [redʊkˈtsi̯oːn] F -, -en **a** (= *Einschränkung*) reduction (+*gen* in) **b** (= *Zurückführung*) reduction (*auf* +*acc* to) **c** (*Chem*) reduction

Re|duk|ti|ons-: Re|duk|ti|ons|mit|tel NT (*Chem*) reducing agent; **Re|duk|ti|ons|ofen** M (*Metal*) reducing furnace

re|dun|dant [redʊnˈdant] ADJ redundant (*auch Comput*); ADV **schreiben** redundantly; **er drückt**

sich ~ aus a lot of what he says is redundant; **das ist ~ formuliert** it's redundant

Re|dun|danz [redʊnˈdants] F -, -en redundancy, redundance *no pl*

Re|dup|li|ka|ti|on [reduplikaˈtsi̯oːn] F reduplication

re|dup|li|zie|ren [redupliˈtsiːrən] *ptp* **redupliziert** VT to reduplicate

re|du|zier|bar, re|du|zi|bel [reduˈtsiːbl̩] ADJ reducible (*auf* +*acc* to)

re|du|zie|ren [reduˈtsiːrən] *ptp* **reduziert** VT **a** (= *einschränken*) to reduce **b** (= *zurückführen*) to reduce (*auf* +*acc* to) **c** (*Chem*) to reduce VR to decrease, to diminish

Re|du|zie|rung F -, -en = Reduktion

Ree|de ['reːdə] F -, -n (*Naut*) roads *pl*, roadstead; **auf der ~ liegen** to be (lying) in the roads

Ree|der ['reːdɐ] M -s, -, **Ree|de|rin** [-ərɪn] F -, -en shipowner

Ree|de|rei [reːdəˈraɪ] F -, -en shipping company

Ree|de|rei|flag|ge F house flag

re|ell [reˈɛl] ADJ **a** (= *ehrlich*) honest, straight, on the level (*inf*); (*Comm*) *Geschäft, Firma* solid, sound; *Preis* realistic, fair; *Bedienung* good; **das ist etwas Reelles!** it's pretty much on the level! (*inf*) **b** (= *wirklich, echt*) *Chance* real **c** (*Math*) *Zahlen* real ADV (= *tatsächlich*) when it comes down to it; (= *nicht betrügerisch*) on the level (*inf*)

Reep [reːp] NT -(e)s, -e (*N Ger*) rope

Reet [reːt] NT -s, *no pl* (*N Ger*) reed

Reet-: Reet|dach NT thatched roof; **reet|ge|deckt** ADJ thatched

REFA-Fach|frau F , **REFA-Frau** ['reːfa-] F (*inf*) time and motion expert or woman

REFA-Fach|mann M , **REFA-Mann** ['reːfa-] M (*inf*) time and motion expert or man

Re|fek|to|ri|um [refɛkˈtoːri̯ʊm] -s, **Refektorien** [-ri̯ən] NT (*Eccl*) refectory

Re|fe|rat [refeˈraːt] NT -(e)s, -e **a** (*Univ*) seminar paper; (*Sch*) project; (= *Vortrag*) paper; **ein ~ vortragen** or **halten** to give or read or present a seminar paper/to present a project/to give or read or present a paper **b** (*Admin*: = *Ressort*) department

Re|fe|ren|dar [referɛnˈdaːɐ] M -s, -e trainee (in civil service); (= *Studienreferendar*) student teacher; (= *Gerichtsreferendar*) articled clerk (*Brit*), legal intern (*US*)

Re|fe|ren|da|ri|at [referɛndaˈri̯aːt] NT -(e)s, -e probationary training period

Re|fe|ren|da|rin [-ˈdaːrɪn] F -, -nen → **Referendar**

Re|fe|ren|dar|zeit F traineeship; (= *Studienreferendarzeit*) teacher training; (= *Gerichtsreferendarzeit*) time under articles (*Brit*), legal internship (*US*)

Re|fe|ren|dum [refeˈrɛndʊm] NT -s, **Referenden** or **Referenda** [-dn̩, -da] referendum

Re|fe|rent [refeˈrɛnt] M -en, -en, **Re|fe|ren|tin** [-ˈrɛntɪn] F -, -nen (= *Sachbearbeiter*) consultant, expert; (= *Redner, Berichterstatter*) speaker; (*Univ*: = *Gutachter*) examiner

Re|fe|renz [refeˈrɛnts] F -, -en reference (*auch Comput*); **jdn als ~ angeben** to give sb as a referee

re|fe|rie|ren [refe'riːrən] *ptp* **referiert** VI to (give a) report, to give a review (*über +acc* on)

Reff [rɛf] NT **-(e)s, -e** (*Naut*) reef

ref|fen ['rɛfn] VT (*Naut*) to reef

Re|fi|nan|zie|rung [refinan'tsiːrʊŋ] F financing of financing, rediscounting

Re|flek|tant [reflɛk'tant] M **-en, -en, Re|flek|tan|tin** [-'tantɪn] F **-, -nen** (*old*) (= *Kauflustiger*) prospective purchaser; (= *Stellungsbewerber*) applicant

re|flek|tie|ren [reflɛk'tiːrən] *ptp* **reflektiert** VT **a** (*lit, fig*: *widerspiegeln*) to reflect **b** (*überdenken*) to reflect on, to ponder (on) VI **a** (*Phys*) to reflect **b** (= *nachdenken*) to reflect, to ponder (*über +acc* on)**j/on) c** (= *streben nach*) **auf etw** (*acc*) ~ to be interested in sth

Re|flek|tor [re'flɛktoːɐ] M **-s, Reflektoren** [-'toːrən] reflector

re|flek|to|risch [reflɛk'toːrɪʃ] ADJ **a** (*motorisch*) reflex **b** (*geistig*) reflective ADV by reflex action

Re|flex [re'flɛks] M **-es, -e a** (*Phys*) reflection **b** (*Physiol*) reflex **c** (*Soziol*) reflection

Re|flex|be|we|gung F reflex action

Re|fle|xi|on [reflɛ'ksioːn] F **-, -en a** (*lit, Phys*) reflection **b** (= *Überlegung*) reflection (*über* on); **über etw** (*acc*) **~en anstellen** to reflect on sth

Re|fle|xi|ons|win|kel M (*Phys*) angle of reflection

re|fle|xiv [reflɛ'ksiːf] (*Gram*) ADJ reflexive ADV reflexively

Re|fle|xiv [reflɛ'ksiːf] NT **-s, -e** [-və], **Re|fle|xi|vum** [reflɛ'ksiːvʊm] NT **-s, Reflexiva** [-va] NT reflexive (pronoun/verb)

Re|fle|xiv|pro|no|men NT reflexive pronoun

Re|flex|zo|nen|mas|sa|ge F reflexology

Re|form [re'fɔrm] F **-, -en** reform

Re|for|ma|ti|on [refɔrma'tsioːn] F **-, -en** Reformation

Re|for|ma|ti|ons|tag M Reformation Day

REFORMATIONSTAG

Reformationstag, celebrated on October 31st, is a public holiday in some (predominantly Protestant) regions of Germany. It commemorates Martin Luther's nailing of his 95 theses to the church door at Wittenberg in 1517, an action which marked the beginning of the Reformation.

Re|for|ma|tor [refɔr'maːtoːɐ] M **-s, Reformatoren** [-'toːrən], **Re|for|ma|to|rin** [-'toːrɪn] F **-, -nen** Reformer

re|for|ma|to|risch [refɔrma'toːrɪʃ] ADJ (= *reformierend*) reforming; (= *aus der Zeit der Reformation*) Reformation *attr*

Re|form-: Re|form|be|darf M need for reform; **Re|form|be|dürf|tig** ADJ in need of reform; **Re|form|be|stre|bun|gen** PL striving for *or* after reform; **Re|form|be|we|gung** F reform movement; **Re|form|ei|fer** M reforming zeal

Re|for|mer [re'fɔrmɐ] M **-s, -**, **Re|for|me|rin** [-ərɪn] F **-, -nen** reformer

re|for|me|risch [re'fɔrmərɪʃ] ADJ reforming

Re|form-: re|form|freu|dig ADJ eager for reform; **Re|form|ge|setz** NT reform bill *or* law; **Re|form|haus** NT health-food shop

---

REFORMHAUS

Reformhaus sells everything for a healthy diet and lifestyle, including **Reformkost** (natural foodstuffs without chemical additives), health products such as essential oils and natural bath salts, and medicinal herbs. The first **Reformhäuser** were established as early as 1890 out of a desire to encourage healthy

---

living. Nowadays, however, they have to contend with competition from the **Bioläden**
→ **BIOLÄDEN**

re|for|mie|ren [refɔr'miːrən] *ptp* **reformiert** VT to reform

re|for|miert [refɔr'miːɐt] ADJ (*Eccl*) Reformed

Re|for|mier|te(r) [refɔr'miːɐtə] MF *decl as adj* member of the Reformed Church

Re|for|mis|mus [refɔr'mɪsmʊs] M **-, no pl** (*Pol*) reformism

Re|for|mist [refɔr'mɪst] M **-en, -en, Re|for|mis|tin** [-'mɪstɪn] F **-, -nen** (*Pol*) reformist

re|for|mis|tisch [refɔr'mɪstɪʃ] ADJ (*Pol*) reformist

Re|form-: Re|form|kurs M policy of reform; **einen ~ steuern** to follow a policy of reform; **auf ~ gehen** to embark on a policy of reform; **Re|form|plan** M plan for reform; **Re|form|stau** M (*Pol*) reform bottleneck

Ref|rain [rə'frɛ̃ː, re-] M **-s, -s** (*Mus*) chorus, refrain

re|frak|tär [refrak'tɛːɐ] ADJ (*Med, liter*) refractory

Re|frak|ti|on [refrak'tsioːn] F **-, -en** (*Phys*) refraction

Re|frak|tor [re'fraktoːɐ] M **-s, Refraktoren** [-'toːrən] (*Phys, Opt*) refractor

Re|fu|gi|um [re'fuːgiʊm] NT **-s, Refugien** [-giən] (*geh*) refuge

Re|gal¹ [re'gaːl] NT **-s, -e a** (= *Bord*) shelves *pl*; (*Typ*) stand **b** (*Mus*) (= *tragbare Orgel*) regal; (*Orgelteil*) vox humana

Re|gal² NT **-s, -ien** [-liən] (*Jur*) regale (*spec*)

Re|gal-: Re|gal|sys|tem NT shelving system; **Re|gal|wand** F wall unit; (*nur Regale*) wall-to-wall shelving

Re|gat|ta [re'gata] F **-, Regatten** [-tn] regatta

Re|gat|ta|stre|cke F regatta course

Reg. Bez. *abbr von* **Regierungsbezirk**

re|ge ['reːgə] ADJ **a** (= *betriebsam*) active, busy; *Verkehr* busy; *Handel* flourishing; *Briefwechsel* lively; **ein ~s Treiben** a busy to-and-fro, a hustle and bustle; **auf dem Marktplatz herrschte ein ~s Treiben** the market place was bustling with activity *or* life; **Tendenz ~** (*St Ex*) brisk activity; **~ werden** to become active **b** (= *lebhaft*) lively; *Unterhaltung* animated, lively; *Fantasie* vivid; *Interesse auch* avid; **ein ~r Geist** a lively soul; (= *Verstand*) an active mind; **körperlich und geistig ~ sein** to be mentally and physically active; **noch sehr ~ sein** to be very active still; **in ihm wurde der Gedanke ~** (*liter*) the thought stirred within him; **~ Beteiligung** lively participation; (*zahlreich*) good attendance *or* turnout **c** (= *zahlreich*) numerous; (= *häufig*) frequent; **~r Besuch** high attendance ADV (= *lebhaft*) **das Museum wurde nach der Eröffnung ~ besucht** when it opened the museum was very well visited; **sich ~ an etw** (*dat*) **beteiligen** to actively take part in sth; **an etw** (*dat*) **~ Anteil nehmen** to take an active interest in sth

Re|gel ['reːgl] F **-, -n a** (= *Vorschrift, Norm*) rule; (= *Verordnung*) regulation; **die ~n der ärztlichen Kunst** the rules of the medical profession; **nach allen ~n der Kunst** (*fig*) thoroughly; **sie überredete ihn nach allen ~n der Kunst, ...** she used every trick in the book to persuade him ... **b** (= *Gewohnheit*) habit, rule; **sich** (*dat*) **etw zur ~ machen** to make a habit *or* rule of sth; **in der *or* aller ~** as a rule; **zur ~ werden** to become a habit **c** (= *Monatsblutung*) period; **die ~ haben/bekommen** to have/get one's period; **sie hat mit zehn ihre ~ bekommen** her periods started when she was ten

Re|gel-: Re|gel|ar|beits|zeit F core working hours *pl*; **re|gel|bar** ADJ (= *steuerbar*) adjustable; (= *klärbar*) easily arranged; **Re|gel|blu|tung** F (*euph*) (monthly) period, monthly cy-

---

cle; **Re|gel|det|ri** [reːgl'deːtriː] F **-, no pl** (*Math*) rule of three; **Re|gel|fall** M rule; **im ~** as a rule; **re|gel|mä|ßig** ADJ regular; *Lebensweise auch* well-ordered, orderly ADV **a** (*in gleichmäßiger Folge*) regularly; **das Herz schlägt ~** the heartbeat is normal; **sein Herz schlägt wieder ~er** his heartbeat is more regular now; **etw ~ jeden Tag tun** to do sth every day; **~ spazieren gehen** to take regular walks **b** (= *andauernd*) always; **er kommt ~ zu spät** he's always late; **Re|gel|mä|ßig|keit** ['reːglmɛːsɪçkait] F **-, no pl** regularity; **er kommt mit starrer ~ zu spät** he is persistently late; **in *or* mit schöner ~** with clockwork regularity, as regular as clockwork

re|geln ['reːgln] VT **a** (= *regulieren*) *Prozess, Vorgang, Temperatur* to regulate, to control; *Verkehr* to control → *auch* **geregelt** **b** (= *erledigen*) to see to; (*endgültig*) to settle; *Problem etc* to sort out; (= *in Ordnung bringen*) *Unstimmigkeiten* to settle, to resolve; *Finanzen* to put in order; *Nachlass* to settle; *Finanzierung* to deal with; **das lässt sich ~** that can be arranged; **das werde ich schon ~** I'll see to it **c** (= *festsetzen, einrichten*) to settle; **wir haben die Sache so geregelt ...** we have arranged things like this ...; **dieses Gesetz regelt ...** this law deals with ...; **gesetzlich geregelt sein** to be laid down by law VR to sort itself out, to resolve itself

Re|gel-: re|gel|recht ADJ real, proper; *Betrug, Erpressung, Beleidigung etc* downright; **er wollte einen ~en Prozess** he wanted a full-blown trial; **das Spiel artete in eine ~e Schlägerei aus** the match degenerated into a regular brawl ADV really; *unverschämt, beleidigend* downright; (= *buchstäblich*) literally; **Re|gel|schu|le** F ordinary school; **Re|gel|stu|di|en|zeit** F *period of time within which a student should complete his studies*; **Re|gel|tech|nik** F control engineering; **Re|gel|tech|ni|ker(in)** M(F) control engineer

Re|ge|lung ['reːgəlʊŋ] F **-, -en a** (= *Regulierung*) regulation, control(ling) **b** (= *Erledigung*) settling, settlement; (*von Unstimmigkeiten*) resolution; (*von Nachlass*) settling, settlement; **ich habe die ~ meiner finanziellen Angelegenheiten meinem Bruder übertragen** I have entrusted my brother with the management of my financial affairs; **ich werde für die ~ dieser Angelegenheit sorgen** I shall see to this matter **c** (= *Abmachung*) arrangement; (= *Bestimmung*) ruling; **gesetzliche ~en** legal *or* statutory regulations; **wir haben eine ~ gefunden** we have come to an arrangement

Re|ge|lungs|tech|nik F control engineering

Re|gel-: Re|gel|werk NT rules *pl* (and regulations *pl*), set of rules; **re|gel|wid|rig** ADJ against the rules; (= *gegen Verordnungen verstoßend*) against the regulations; **~es Verhalten im Verkehr** breaking the traffic regulations; **~e Transaktion** irregular transaction; **ein ~er Einwurf** a foul throw-in; **ein ~er Elfmeter** an improperly taken penalty ADV **~ spielen** to infringe the rules; (= *foulen*) to commit a foul; **Re|gel|wid|rig|keit** F irregularity; (= *Regelverstoß auch*) breach of the rules; (= *Verstoß gegen Verordnungen auch*) breach of regulations

re|gen ['reːgn] VT (= *bewegen*) to move; **keinen Finger (mehr) ~** (*fig*) not to lift a finger (any more) VR (*Mensch, Glied, Baum etc*) to move, to stir; (*Gefühl, Gewissen, Zweifel, Widerstand, Wind etc*) to stir; **unter den Zuhörern regte sich Widerspruch** there were mutterings of disapproval from the audience; **im Bundestag regt sich Widerstand gegen das Gesetz** opposition to the bill is beginning to make itself felt in the Bundestag; **kein Lüftchen regt sich** (*poet*) not a breeze stirs the air; **reg dich!** look lively!; **er kann sich nicht/kaum ~** he is not/hardly able to move; **sich ~ bringt Segen** (*Prov*) hard work brings its own reward

---

Re|gen ['re:gn] M **-s, -** rain; (fig: von Schimpfwörtern, Blumen etc) shower; **in den ~ kommen** to be caught in the rain; **es gibt bald ~** it's going to rain soon; **so ein ~!** what or some rain!; **in** or **bei strömendem ~** in the pouring rain; **bei ~ entfällt das Konzert** if it rains the concert will be cancelled (esp Brit) or canceled (US); **ein warmer ~** (fig) a windfall; **jdn im ~ stehen lassen** (fig) to leave sb out in the cold; **vom ~ in die Traufe kommen** (prov) to jump out of the frying pan into the fire (prov)

Re|gen-: re|gen|arm ADJ Jahreszeit, Gegend dry; **Re|gen|bö** F rainy squall

Re|gen|bo|gen M rainbow

Re|gen|bo|gen-: Re|gen|bo|gen|far|ben PL colours pl (Brit) or colors pl (US) of the rainbow; **in allen ~ schillern** to shine like shot silk, to iridesce (liter); **re|gen|bo|gen|far|ben** [-farbn], **re|gen|bo|gen|far|big** ADJ rainbow--coloured (Brit), rainbow-colored (US); **Re|gen|bo|gen|fo|rel|le** F rainbow trout; **Re|gen|bo|gen|haut** F (Anat) iris; **Re|gen|bo|gen|haut|ent|zün|dung** F iritis (spec), inflammation of the iris; **Re|gen|bo|gen|pres|se** F trashy (inf) or pulp magazines pl; **Re|gen|bo|gen|tri|kot** NT (Sport) rainbow jersey

Re|gen-: Re|gen|dach NT canopy; (hum: = Regenschirm) brolly (Brit inf), bumbershoot (US inf); **re|gen|dicht** ADJ rainproof

Re|ge|ne|ra|ti|on [regenera'tsio:n] F regeneration; (fig auch) revitalization

re|ge|ne|ra|ti|ons|fä|hig ADJ capable of regeneration; (fig auch) capable of regenerating itself or of revitalization

re|ge|ne|ra|tiv [regenera'ti:f] ADJ regenerative

Re|ge|ne|ra|tor [regene'ra:tɐ] M (Tech) regenerator

re|ge|ne|rie|ren [regene'ri:rən] ptp **regeneriert VR** (Biol) to regenerate; (fig) to revitalize or regenerate oneself/itself; (nach Anstrengung, Schock etc) to recover **VT** (Biol) to regenerate; (fig auch) to revitalize

Re|ge|ne|rie|rung F **-, -en** regeneration; (fig auch) revitalization

Re|gen-: Re|gen|fall M usu pl (fall of) rain; **ein ~ rain**, a shower; **tropische Regenfälle** tropical rains; **heftige Regenfälle** heavy rain; **Re|gen|fass ▲** NT water butt, rain barrel; **Re|gen|flut** F usu pl torrential rain usu sing, torrent of rain; **re|gen|frei** ADJ Tag without rain; **Re|gen|guss ▲** M downpour; **Re|gen|haut®** F plastic mac (Brit inf) or raincoat; **Re|gen|hut** M waterproof hat, rain hat; **Re|gen|klei|dung** F rainwear; **Re|gen|man|tel** M raincoat, mackintosh (esp Brit), mac (Brit inf); **Re|gen|pfei|fer** M plover; **re|gen|reich** ADJ Jahreszeit, Region rainy, wet; **Re|gen|rin|ne** F gutter; **Re|gen|schat|ten** M (Geog) rain shadow; **Re|gen|schau|er** M shower (of rain); **Re|gen|schirm** M umbrella → **gespannt**; **re|gen|schwer** ADJ **-e Wolken** black or rain clouds, clouds heavy with rain

Re|gent [re'gɛnt] M **-en, -en, Re|gen|tin** [-'gɛntɪn] F **-, -nen** sovereign, reigning monarch; (= Stellvertreter) regent

Re|gen-: Re|gen|tag M rainy day; **Re|gen|ton|ne** F water butt, rain barrel; **Re|gen|trop|fen** M raindrop

Re|gent|schaft [re'gɛntʃaft] F **-, -en** reign; (= Stellvertretung) regency; **die ~ antreten** or **übernehmen** to ascend the throne; (als Stellvertreter) to become regent; **die ~ übernehmen** to take over as regent

Re|gen-: Re|gen|wald M (Geog) rain forest; **Re|gen|was|ser** NT , no pl rainwater; **Re|gen|wet|ter** NT rainy weather, rain; **er macht ein Gesicht wie drei** or **sieben Tage ~** (inf) he's got a face as long as a month of Sundays (inf); **Re|gen|wol|ke** F rain cloud; **Re|gen|wurm** M earthworm; **Re|gen|zeit** F rainy season, rains pl

Reg|gae ['rɛge:] M **-(s)**, no pl reggae

Re|gie [re'ʒi:] F **-**, no pl **a** (= künstlerische Leitung) direction; (Theat, Rad, TV) direction, production; **die ~ bei etw haben** or **führen** to direct/ produce sth; (fig) to be in charge of sth; **die ~ bei diesem Film/dieser Sendung führte** or **hatte Heinz Krüger** this film was directed/this programme (Brit) or program (US) was produced by Heinz Krüger; **unter der ~ von** directed/produced by; **„Regie: A.G. Meier"** "Director/Producer A.G. Meier"

b (= Leitung, Verwaltung) management; **unter jds ~** under sb's control; **etw in eigener ~ führen** to control sth directly or personally; **etw in eigene ~ nehmen** to take or assume direct or personal control of sth; **etw in eigener ~ tun** to do sth oneself

Re|gie-: Re|gie|an|wei|sung F (stage) direction; **Re|gie|as|sis|tent(in)** M(F) assistant director; (Theat, Rad, TV auch) assistant producer; **Re|gie|be|trieb** M (Admin) state-owned factory; **Re|gie|feh|ler** M (fig) slip-up; **Re|gie|film** M **sein erster ~** the first film he directed; **Re|gie|pult** NT (Rad) control desk (Brit) or console

re|gie|ren [re'gi:rən] ptp **regiert VI** (= herrschen) to rule; (Monarch auch, fig) to reign; **der Regierende Bürgermeister von Berlin** the Mayor of Berlin **VT** (= beherrschen, lenken) Staat to rule (over), to govern; (Monarch auch) to reign over; Markt to control; (Gram) to govern; **SPD-regierte Länder** states governed by the SPD → **Geld**

Re|gie|rung [re'gi:roŋ] F **-, -en a** (= Kabinett) government; **die ~ Blair** the Blair government **b** (= Herrschaft) government; (= Zeitabschnitt) period of government; (nicht demokratisch) rule; (von Monarch) reign; (= Führung) leadership; **an die ~ kommen** to come to power; (durch Wahl auch) to come into or take office; **jdn an die ~ bringen** to put sb into power; (durch Wahl auch) to put sb into office; **die ~ antreten** to take power; (nach Wahl auch) to take office; **die ~ ausüben** to exercise power

Re|gie|rungs-: Re|gie|rungs|ab|kom|men NT agreement between governments, international agreement; **re|gie|rungs|amt|lich** ADJ governmental; **Re|gie|rungs|an|hän|ger(in)** M(F) government supporter; **Re|gie|rungs|an|tritt** M coming to power; (nach Wahl auch) taking of office; **bei ~** when the government took power/office; **Re|gie|rungs|aus|schuss ▲** M government committee; **Re|gie|rungs|bank** F pl -bänke government bench; **Re|gie|rungs|be|am|te(r)** M decl as adj, **Re|gie|rungs|be|am|tin** F government official; **Re|gie|rungs|be|zirk** M primary administrative division of a Land, ≈ region (Brit), ≈ county (US); **Re|gie|rungs|bil|dung** F formation of a government; **Re|gie|rungs|chef(in)** M(F) head of a/the government; **der belgische ~** the head of the Belgian government; **Re|gie|rungs|di|rek|tor(in)** M(F) senior government official; **Re|gie|rungs|er|klä|rung** F inaugural speech; (in GB) King's/Queen's Speech; **re|gie|rungs|fä|hig** ADJ Partei able to govern; Mehrheit workable; **Re|gie|rungs|fä|hig|keit** F ability to govern; **re|gie|rungs|feind|lich** ADJ anti-government no adv **ADV sich ~ verhalten/ äußern** to act/speak against the government; **Re|gie|rungs|form** F form or type of government; **re|gie|rungs|freund|lich** ADJ pro-government no adv **ADV sich ~ verhalten/äußern** to act/speak in support of the government; **Re|gie|rungs|ge|schäf|te** PL government business sing; **Re|gie|rungs|haupt|stadt** F administrative capital; **Re|gie|rungs|koa|li|ti|on** F ruling coalition; **Re|gie|rungs|krei|se** PL government circles pl; **Re|gie|rungs|kri|se** F government(al) crisis; **re|gie|rungs|kri|tisch ADJ** critical of the government **ADV sich ~ äußern** to make statements critical of the government, to speak critically of the government; **re|gie|rungs|nah** ADJ Kreise close to the government; Zeitung pro-government; **Re|gie-**

rungs|par|tei F ruling or governing party, party in power; **Re|gie|rungs|prä|si|dent(in)** M(F) chief administrator of a Regierungsbezirk, ≈ chairman/-woman of the regional council (Brit), ≈ county manager (US); **Re|gie|rungs|prä|si|di|um** NT highest authority in a Regierungsbezirk, ≈ regional council (Brit) or board (US); **Re|gie|rungs|rat[1]** M (Sw: Organ) legislature; **Re|gie|rungs|rat[2]** M , **Re|gie|rungs|rä|tin** F senior civil servant; **Re|gie|rungs|sitz** M seat of government; **Re|gie|rungs|spre|cher(in)** M(F) government spokesperson or spokesman/-woman; **Re|gie|rungs|sys|tem** NT system of government, governmental system; **re|gie|rungs|treu** ADJ loyal to the government; **Re|gie|rungs|um|bil|dung** F cabinet reshuffle; **Re|gie|rungs|vor|la|ge** F government bill; **Re|gie|rungs|wech|sel** M change of government; **Re|gie|rungs|zeit** F rule; (von Monarch auch) reign; (von gewählter Regierung, Präsident) period or term of office

Re|gime [re'ʒi:m] NT **-s, -s** (pej) regime

Re|gime-: Re|gime|an|hän|ger(in) M(F) supporter of the regime; **Re|gime|geg|ner(in)** M(F) opponent of the regime; **Re|gime|kri|ti|ker(in)** M(F) critic of the regime, dissident

Re|gi|ment [regi'mɛnt] NT **-(e)s, -e** or (Einheit) **-er a** (old: = Herrschaft) rule; **das ~ führen** (inf) to be the boss (inf), to give the orders; **ein strenges** or **straffes ~ führen** (inf) to be strict; (Vorgesetzter etc auch) to run a tight ship (inf); **der Winter führt ein strenges ~** the winter is harsh and stern **b** (Mil) regiment

Re|gi|ments- in cpds regimental; **Re|gi|ments|kom|man|deur(in)** M(F) regimental commander

Re|gi|on [re'gio:n] F **-, -en** region → **schweben**

re|gi|o|nal [regio'na:l] **ADJ** regional **ADV** regionally; **~ verschieden** or **unterschiedlich sein** to vary from one region to another

Re|gi|o|nal|bahn F (Rail) local railway (Brit) or railroad (US)

Re|gi|o|na|lis|mus [regiona'lɪsmʊs] M **-, Regionalismen** [-mən] regionalism

Re|gi|o|nal-: Re|gi|o|nal|li|ga F regional league (lower leagues of professional clubs); **Re|gi|o|nal|pro|gramm** NT (TV, Rad) regional station or (TV auch) channel; (Sendung) regional programme (Brit) or program (US); **Re|gi|o|nal|schnell|bahn** F (Rail) high-speed regional railway (Brit) or railroad (US); **Re|gi|o|nal|ver|kehr** M regional transport or transportation (esp US)

Re|gis|seur [reʒɪ'søːɐ] M **-s, -e, Re|gis|seu|rin** [-'søːrɪn] F **-, -nen** director; (Theat, Rad, TV) producer

Re|gis|ter [re'gɪstɐ] NT **-s, - a** (= amtliche Liste) register; **ein ~ (über etw acc) führen** to keep a register (of sth); **etw ins ~ (eines Amtes etc) eintragen** to register sth (with an office etc) **b** (= Stichwortverzeichnis) index **c** (Mus) register; (von Orgel) stop, register; **alle ~ ziehen** or **spielen lassen** (fig) to pull out all the stops; **andere ~ ziehen** (fig inf) to get tough **d** (fig inf) **ein langes/altes ~** a tall/an old type (inf)

Re|gis|ter-: Re|gis|ter|ton|ne F (Naut) register ton; **Re|gis|ter|zug** M (Mus: bei Orgel) stop

Re|gis|tra|tor [regɪs'tra:tɐ] M **-s, Registratoren** [-'to:rən], **Re|gis|tra|to|rin** [-'to:rɪn] F **-, -nen** (old) registrar

Re|gis|tra|tur [regɪstra'tu:ɐ] F **-, -en a** (= das Registrieren) registration **b** (Büro) records office **c** (= Aktenschrank) filing cabinet **d** (Mus: bei Orgel) stops pl

Re|gis|trier|bal|lon M (Met) sounding balloon

re|gis|trie|ren [regɪs'tri:rən] ptp **registriert** VT **a** (= erfassen) to register; (= zusammenzählen) to calculate; **amtlich registriert** officially registered; **sie ist registriert** (als Prostituierte) she is a registered prostitute **b** (= *feststellen*) to note; **sie hat überhaupt nicht registriert, dass ich nicht da war** the fact that I wasn't there didn't register with her at all **c** (*Mus: bei Orgel*) to push the stops; **ein Orgelstück ~** to set the stops for an organ piece

Re|gist|rier-: Re|gist|rier|kas|se F cash register; **Re|gist|rier|stel|le** F registration office

Re|gist|rie|rung F -, -en registration

Reg|le|ment [rɛglə'mã:] NT -s, -s (*old*) rules *pl*, conventions *pl*

reg|le|men|ta|risch [rɛglɛmɛn'taːrɪʃ] **ADJ** regulation **ADV** according to (the) regulations; **etw ~ festlegen** to make a regulation about sth

reg|le|men|tie|ren [rɛglɛmɛn'tiːrən] *ptp* **reglementiert** VT to regulate; *jdn* to regiment; **staatlich reglementiert** state-regulated

Reg|le|men|tie|rung F -, -en regulation

reglement- [rɛglə'mã:-]: **reg|le|ment|mä|ßig** (*old*) **ADJ** according to regulation(s) **ADV** ~ **gekleidet sein** to be in regulation dress; ~ **grüßen** to give a regulation greeting; **sich ~ verhalten** to behave according to regulation; **reg|le|ment|wid|rig** (*old*) ADJ, ADV contrary to regulations

Reg|ler ['reːglɐ] M -s, - regulator; (*an Fernseher, Stereoanlage etc*) control; (*von Elektromotor, Fernsteuerung*) control(ler); (*von Benzinmotor*) governor

Reg|let|te [re'glɛtə] F -, -n (*Typ*) lead

reg|los ['reːkloːs] ADJ, ADV motionless

reg|nen ['reːgnən] VTI *impers* to rain; **es regnet in Strömen** it's pouring (with rain); **es regnet Glückwünsche/Proteste** congratulations/protests are pouring in; **es regnete Vorwürfe** reproaches hailed down → **Bindfaden**

reg|ne|risch ['reːgnərɪʃ] ADJ *Wetter, Tag* rainy

Re|gress ▲ [re'grɛs] M -es, -e **a** (*Philos*) regress **b** (*Jur*) recourse, redress; ~ **anmelden** to seek recourse *or* redress; **einen ~ auf jdn *or* an jdm nehmen**, *jdn* **in ~ nehmen** to have recourse against sb

Re|gress|an|spruch ▲ M (*Jur*) claim for compensation

Re|gress|for|de|rung ▲ F (*Jur*) recourse demand *or* claim

Re|gres|si|on [regrɛ'sioːn] F -, -en regression, retrogression

re|gres|siv [regrɛ'siːf] ADJ (*Biol*) regressive, retrogressive; (*fig*) retrograde, retrogressive **ADV** ~ **verlaufen** (= *abnehmen*) to drop off

Re|gress-: Re|gress|pflicht ▲ F liability for compensation; **re|gress|pflich|tig** ▲ [-pflɪçtɪç] ADJ liable for compensation

reg|sam ['reːkzaːm] ADJ active; **geistig ~** mentally active

Reg|sam|keit F activity; **geistige ~** mental activity

re|gu|lär [regu'lɛːɐ] **ADJ** (= *üblich*) normal; (= *vorschriftsmäßig*) proper, regular; *Arbeitszeit* normal, basic, regular; **~e Truppen** regular troops, regulars; **~e Bankgeschäfte** normal banking transactions; **die ~e Spielzeit** (*Sport*) normal time **ADV** (= *zum normalen Preis*) normally; **etw ~ kaufen/verkaufen** (= *zum normalen Preis*) to buy/sell sth at the normal price; (= *auf normale Weise*) to buy/sell sth in the normal way

Re|gu|la|ti|on [regula'tsioːn] F -, -en (*Biol*) regulation

Re|gu|la|ti|ons-: Re|gu|la|ti|ons|stö|rung F (*Biol*) malfunction of a regulatory system; **Re|gu|la|ti|ons|sys|tem** NT (*Biol*) regulatory system

re|gu|la|tiv [regula'tiːf] **ADJ** regulatory, regulative **ADV** **in etw** (*acc*) ~ **eingreifen** to regulate sth

Re|gu|la|tiv [regula'tiːf] NT -s, -e [-və] regulating agent; **als ~ wirken, ein ~ bilden** to have a regulating effect

Re|gu|la|tor [regu'laːtoːɐ] M -s, **Regulatoren** [-'toːrən] wall clock

re|gu|lier|bar ADJ regul(at)able, adjustable

re|gu|lie|ren [regu'liːrən] *ptp* **reguliert** VT (= *einstellen*) to regulate; (= *nachstellen*) to adjust VR to regulate itself; **sich (von) selbst ~** to regulate itself

Re|gu|lier|he|bel M (*Tech*) regulating lever

Re|gu|lie|rung F -, -en regulation; (= *Nachstellung*) adjustment

Re|gu|lie|rungs|be|hör|de F regulatory body *or* authority

Re|gung ['reːgʊŋ] F -, -en (= *Bewegung*) movement; (*des Gefühls, des Gewissens, von Mitleid*) stirring; **ohne jede ~** without a flicker of emotion; **einer ~ des Herzens folgen** (*liter*) to follow the dictates of one's heart (*liter*); **zu keiner ~ fähig sein** (*fig*) to be paralyzed; **eine menschliche ~ verspüren** (*hum*) to have to answer a call of nature (*hum*)

re|gungs|los ADJ, ADV motionless

Re|gungs|lo|sig|keit F -, *no pl* motionlessness

Reh [reː] NT -s, -e deer; (*im Gegensatz zu Hirsch etc*) roe deer; **scheu wie ein ~** (as) timid as a fawn

Re|ha- ['reːha] *in cpds abbr von* **Rehabilitations-**

Re|ha|bi|li|tand [rehabili'tant] M -en, -en [-dn], **Re|ha|bi|li|tan|din** [-'tandɪn] F -, -nen (*form*) person undergoing rehabilitation

Re|ha|bi|li|ta|ti|on [rehabilita'tsioːn] F rehabilitation; (*Jur, Ehre*) vindication

Re|ha|bi|li|ta|ti|ons-: Re|ha|bi|li|ta|ti|ons|kli|nik F rehabilitation clinic; **Re|ha|bi|li|ta|ti|ons|zent|rum** NT rehabilitation centre (*Brit*) *or* center (*US*)

re|ha|bi|li|tie|ren [rehabili'tiːrən] *ptp* **rehabilitiert** VT to rehabilitate; **das Gericht rehabilitierte ihn** the court overturned his conviction VR to rehabilitate oneself

Re|ha|bi|li|tie|rung F -, -en rehabilitation

Reh-: Reh|bock M roebuck; **Reh|bra|ten** M roast venison; **reh|braun** ADJ russet; *Augen* hazel; **Reh|geiß** F doe (*of the roe deer*); **Reh|kalb** NT , **Reh|kitz** NT fawn *or* kid (*of the roe deer*); **Reh|keu|le** F (*Cook*) haunch of venison; **Reh|le|der** NT deerskin; **reh|le|dern** ADJ deerskin

Reh|ling ['reːlɪŋ] M -s, -e (*Bot dial*) chanterelle

Reh-: Reh|nüss|chen ▲ NT (*Cook*) medallion of venison, venison medallion; **Reh|pos|ten** M (*Hunt*: = *grober Schrot*) buckshot; **Reh|rü|cken** M (*Cook*) saddle of venison; **Reh|wild** NT (*Hunt*) roe deer

Rei|bach ['raibax] M -s, *no pl* (*inf*) killing (*inf*); **einen ~ *or* den großen ~ machen** (*inf*) to make a killing (*inf*)

Rei|be ['raibə] F -, -n (*Cook*) grater

Rei|bei|sen NT rasp; (*Cook*) grater; (*fig*: = *zänkisches Weib*) shrew; **rau wie ein ~** (*inf*) like sandpaper; *Stimme* rasping

Rei|be-: Rei|be|ku|chen M (*Cook dial*) ≈ potato fritter; **Rei|be|laut** M (*Ling*) fricative

rei|ben ['raibn] *pret* **rieb** [riːp], *ptp* **gerieben** [gə'riːbn] VT **a** (= *frottieren*) to rub; **etw blank ~** to rub sth till it shines; **sich** (*dat*) **die Augen (vor Müdigkeit) ~** to rub one's eyes (because one is tired); **sie rieb dem Kranken die Salbe in die Haut** she rubbed the ointment into the patient's skin; **jdm den Rücken ~** to rub sb's back; **sich** (*dat*) **die Hände ~** (*lit, fig*) to rub one's hands → **Nase a, Schlaf**
b (= *zerkleinern*) to grate
VI **a** (= *frottieren*) to rub; **an etw** (*dat*) **~** to rub sth
b (= *zerkleinern*) to grate
VR to rub oneself (*an +dat* on, against); (= *sich verletzen*) to scrape oneself (*an +dat* on); **ich würde mich ständig an ihm ~** there would always be friction between him and me; **sich an etw** (*dat*) **wund ~** to rub oneself raw on sth; **ich**

habe mich beim Radfahren wund gerieben I got chafed cycling → *auch* **gerieben**

Rei|be|rei [raibə'rai] F -, -en *usu pl* (*inf*) friction *no pl*; (**kleinere**) **~en** (short) periods of friction; **ihre ständigen ~en** the constant friction between them; **zwischen den beiden Gruppen kam es zu ~en** friction developed between the two groups

Reib|flä|che F (*für Streichholz*) striking surface; (*von Reibe*) scraping surface

Rei|bung ['raibʊŋ] F -, -en **a** (= *das Reiben*) rubbing; (*Phys*) friction **b** (*fig*) friction *no pl*; **es kommt zu ~en** friction occurs

Rei|bungs-: Rei|bungs|elekt|ri|zi|tät F frictional electricity; **Rei|bungs|flä|che** F (*fig*) source of friction; (**viele**) **~n bieten** to be a potential cause of friction; **rei|bungs|los** **ADJ** frictionless; (*fig inf*) trouble-free **ADV** (= *problemlos*) smoothly; **~ verlaufen** to go off smoothly *or* without a hitch; **Rei|bungs|ver|lust** M friction(al) loss; **Rei|bungs|wär|me** F (*Phys*) frictional heat; **Rei|bungs|wi|der|stand** M (*Phys*) frictional resistance

reich [raiç] **ADJ** **a** (= *vermögend, wohlhabend*) rich, wealthy; *Erbschaft* substantial; *Partie, Heirat* good
b (= *kostbar*) costly *no adv*, rich; *Schmuck* costly *no adv*, expensive
c (= *ergiebig, üppig*) rich, copious; *Ernte auch* bountiful, abundant; *Mahl* sumptuous, lavish; **~ an etw** (*dat*) **sein** to be rich in sth; **~ an Fischen/Wild/Steinen** abounding with *or* full of fish/game/stones; **er ist ~ an Erfahrungen** he has had a wealth of experiences; **er ist ~ an guten Einfällen** he is full of good ideas
d (= *groß, vielfältig*) large, copious; *Auswahl* wide, large; *Erfahrungen, Kenntnisse* wide; *Blattwerk, Vegetation* rich, luxuriant; **eine ~e Fülle** a rich abundance; **in ~em Maße vorhanden sein** to abound, to be found in large quantities
ADV **a** (= *wohlhabend*) **~ heiraten** (*inf*) to marry (into) money; **~ begütert** wealthy, affluent
b (= *großzügig*) *jdn* **~ belohnen** to reward sb well, to give sb a rich reward; **damit bin ich ~ belohnt** (*fig*) I am richly *or* amply rewarded; *jdn* **~ beschenken** to shower sb with presents; **eine mit Kindern ~ beschenkte Familie** a family blessed with many children
c (= *reichhaltig*) richly; **ein ~ ausgestattetes Haus** a richly *or* lavishly furnished house; **eine ~ ausgestattete Bibliothek** a well-stocked library; **~ mit Vorräten ausgestattet** well *or* amply stocked up with supplies; **~ illustriert** richly *or* copiously illustrated; **~ geschmückt** (*Gebäude, Gegenstand*) richly decorated *or* adorned; **~ verziert** richly ornamented

Reich [raiç] NT -(e)s, -e **a** (= *Herrschaft(sgebiet), Imperium*) empire; (= *Königreich*) realm, kingdom; **das ~ der aufgehenden Sonne** (*liter*) the land of the rising sun; **das Deutsche ~** the German Reich; (*bis 1918 auch*) the German Empire; **das Dritte ~** the Third Reich; **das ~ der Mitte** the Middle Kingdom; **das himmlische ~** (*liter*) the Kingdom of Heaven, the Heavenly Kingdom; **das ~ Gottes** the Kingdom of God
b (= *Bereich, Gebiet*) realm; **das ~ der Tiere/Pflanzen** the animal/vegetable kingdom; **das ~ der Natur** the world *or* nature of nature; **das ist mein ~** (*fig*) that is my domain; **da bin ich in meinem ~** that's where I'm in my element; **etw ins ~ der Fabel verweisen** to consign sth to the realms of fantasy

reich|be|gü|tert △ ADJ → **reich** ADV a

rei|chen ['raiçn] ✪ 41 VI **a** (= *sich erstrecken*) to stretch, to extend (*bis zu* to), to reach (*bis zu etw* sth); (*Stimme*) to carry (*bis zu* to), to reach (*bis zu jdm/etw* sb/sth); (*Kleidungsstück*) to reach (*bis zu etw* sth); **sein Swimmingpool reicht bis an mein Grundstück** his swimming pool comes right up to my land; **der Garten reicht bis ans Ufer** the garden stretches *or* extends *or* goes right down to the riverbank; **das Wasser reicht mir bis zum Hals** (*lit*) the water comes up to my neck; **jdm bis zur Schulter ~** to come up to sb's shoulder; **er reicht mit dem Kopf bis zur Decke** his head reaches *or* touches the ceiling; **so weit der Himmel reichte** in the whole sky; **das Spektrum reicht von der Volksmusik bis zum Jazz** the spectrum ranges from folk music to jazz; **so weit ~ meine Beziehungen nicht** my connections are not that extensive; **so weit ~ meine Fähigkeiten nicht** my skills are not that wideranging; **... aber sein Arm reichte nicht so weit** ... but his arm wouldn't reach that far; **so weit das Auge reicht** as far as the eye can see

b (= *langen*) to be enough, to suffice (*form*); **der Saal reicht nicht für so viele Leute** the room isn't big enough *or* won't suffice (*form*) for so many people; **der Zucker reicht nicht** there won't be enough sugar; **reicht mein Geld noch bis zum Monatsende?** will my money last until the end of the month?; **reicht das Licht zum Lesen?** is there enough light to read by?; **dazu reicht meine Geduld nicht** I haven't got enough patience for that; **dazu ~ meine Fähigkeiten nicht** I'm not skilled enough for that; **das muss für vier Leute ~** that will have to be enough *or* to suffice (*form*) *or* to do (*inf*) for four people; **das sollte eigentlich ~** that should be enough, that should do (*inf*); **mir reichts** (*inf*) (= *habe die Nase voll*) I've had enough (*inf*); (= *habe genug gehabt*) that's enough for me; **als das dann noch passierte, reichte es ihm** when that happened it was just too much for him; **jetzt reichts (mir aber)!** that's the last straw!; (= *Schluss!*) that's enough!; **das reicht ja, um den Geduldigsten aus der Fassung zu bringen!** it's enough to try the patience of a saint!; **es reichte ja schon, dass er faul war** it was bad enough that he was lazy, his being lazy was bad enough

c (*inf*) **mit dem Essen/der Zeit** *etc* **~** to have enough food/time *etc*

VT (= *entgegenhalten*) to hand; (= *geben auch*) to give; (= *herüberreichen, hinüberreichen auch*) to pass (over); (= *anbieten*) to serve; (*Eccl*) *Abendmahl* to give, to administer; **jdm etw ~** to hand/give/pass sb sth, to hand/give/pass sth to sb; **sie reichte mir die Wange zum Kuss** she proffered her cheek for a kiss; **jdm die Hand ~** to hold out one's hand to sb; (*fig*) to extend the hand of friendship to sb; **sich die Hände ~** to join hands; (*zur Begrüßung*) to shake hands; **es wurden Erfrischungen gereicht** refreshments were served

Rei|che(r) [ˈraiçə] MF *decl as adj* rich *or* wealthy man/woman *etc*; **~n** the rich *or* wealthy

Reich-: **reich|ge|schmückt** △ [-gəʃmʏkt] ADJ *attr* → **reich** ADV c; **reich|hal|tig** ADJ extensive; *Auswahl, Angebot auch* wide, large; *Essen* rich; *Informationen* comprehensive; *Programm* varied; **Reich|hal|tig|keit** [ˈraiçhaltiçkait] F -, *no pl* extensiveness; (*von Angebot auch*) wideness; (*von Essen*) richness; (*von Programm etc*) variety; **die ~ der Auswahl** the range of choice

reich|lich [ˈraiçlɪç] **ADJ** **a** (= *sehr viel, groß*) ample, large, substantial; *Vorrat* plentiful, ample, substantial; *Portion, Trinkgeld* generous; *Alkoholgenuss* substantial; *Geschenke* numerous

b (= *mehr als genügend*) *Zeit, Geld, Platz* ample, plenty of; *Belohnung* ample

c (*inf*: = *mehr als*) good; **eine ~e Stunde** a good hour

ADV **a** (= *sehr viel*) belohnen, sich eindecken amply; *verdienen* richly; **jdn ~ beschenken** to give sb lots of *or* numerous presents; **~ Trinkgeld geben** to tip generously

b (= *mehr als genügend*) **~ Zeit/Geld haben** to have plenty of *or* ample time/money; **~ vorhanden sein** to abound, to exist in plenty; **mehr als ~ belohnt** more than amply rewarded; **mehr als ~ bezahlt** paid more than enough; **der Mantel ist ~ ausgefallen** the coat is on the big side; **das war ~ gewogen/abgemessen** that was very generously weighed out/measured out; **das ist ~ gerechnet** that's a generous estimate

c (*inf*: = *mehr als*) **~ 1.000 Euro** a good 1,000 euros

d (*inf*: = *ziemlich*) pretty

Reichs-: **Reichs|abt** M (*Hist*) abbot of an abbey under imperial protection; **Reichs|acht** F (*Hist*) outlawry in the Emperor's name; **Reichs|ad|ler** M (*Her, Hist*) imperial eagle; **Reichs|ap|fel** M (*Her, Hist*) imperial orb; **Reichs|bahn** F state railway (*Brit*) *or* railroad (*US*); (*DDR*) East German State Railways (*Brit*) *or* Railroad System (*US*); **Reichs|ge|biet** NT territory of the (German) Reich; **im ~** within the boundaries of the (German) Reich; **Reichs|ge|richt** NT (*Hist*) German supreme court (*until 1945*); **Reichs|gren|ze** F border of the empire, prewar German border; **Reichs|grün|dung** F foundation of the Reich *or* Prussian Empire; **Reichs|haupt|stadt** F (*1933-45*) capital of the Reich; (*vor 1933*) imperial capital; **Reichs|in|sig|ni|en** PL (*Hist*) imperial regalia *pl*; **Reichs|kanz|ler** M (*bis 1918*) Imperial Chancellor; (*1918-34*) German Chancellor; **Reichs|klein|o|di|en** PL (*Hist*) imperial regalia *pl*; **Reichs|kon|kor|dat** NT Reich Concordat; **Reichs|kris|tall|nacht** F (*Hist*) → **Kristallnacht**; **Reichs|mark** F *pl* **-mark** (*Hist*) reichsmark, (old) German mark; **Reichs|prä|si|dent** M German president (*until 1934*); **Reichs|re|gie|rung** F German government (*until 1945*); **Reichs|stadt** F (*Hist*) free city (of the Holy Roman Empire); **freie ~** free city; **Reichs|stän|de** PL (*Hist*) estates of the Empire *pl*; **Reichs|tag** M Parliament; (*in Deutschland 1871-1945*) Reichstag; (*in Deutschland vor 1871, in Japan*) Imperial Diet; **Reichs|tags|brand** M burning of the Reichstag; **reichs|un|mit|tel|bar** ADJ (*Hist*) self-governing under the Kaiser; **Reichs|vogt** M (*Hist*) protector; **Reichs|wehr** F German army (*1921-35*)

Reich|tum [ˈraiçtuːm] M -s, **Reichtümer** [-tyːmɐ] **a** wealth *no pl*, richness *no pl*; (= *Besitz*) riches *pl*; **zu ~ kommen** to become rich, to make one's fortune; **Reichtum erwerben** to gain riches; **die Reichtümer der Erde/des Meeres** the riches of the earth/sea; **der innere** *or* **seelische ~** richness of spirit; **damit kann man keine Reichtümer gewinnen** you won't get rich that way **b** (*fig*: = *Fülle, Reichhaltigkeit*) wealth, abundance (*an +dat* of); **der ~ an Fischen** the abundance of fish

reich|ver|ziert △ [-fɛɐtsiːɐt] ADJ *attr* → **reich** ADV c

Reich|wei|te F (*von Geschoss, Sender, Tankfüllung, Batterie*) range; (= *greifbare Nähe*) reach; (*fig*: = *Einflussbereich*) scope; **in ~** within range/reach (+*gen* of); **jd ist in ~** sb is nearby *or* around; **in ~ rücken** (*fig*) to come within reach; **außer ~** out of range/reach (+*gen* of); (*fig*) out of reach; **innerhalb der ~** (+*gen*) within range/the scope of; **außerhalb der ~** (+*gen*) outside the range of/beyond the scope of

reif [raif] ADJ **a** (= *voll entwickelt*) *Früchte, Getreide* ripe; *Mensch, Ei* mature; **der Pickel/das Geschwür ist ~** (*inf*) the spot/abscess has formed a head

b (= *erfahren, älter*) mature; **in ~(er)em Alter, in den ~eren Jahren** in one's mature(r) years; **die ~ere Jugend** those of mellower years; **im ~eren Alter von ...** at the ripe old age of ...

c (= *vorbereitet*) ready, ripe; (= *durchdacht*) *Urteil, Arbeit, Gedanken* mature; **~ zur Veröffentlichung** ready *or* ripe for publication; **die Zeit ist ~/noch nicht ~** the time is ripe/not yet ripe; **eine ~e Leistung** (*inf*) a brilliant achievement

d **für etw ~ sein** (*inf*) to be ready for sth; **~ sein** (*inf*) to be for the high jump (*inf*); (*sl*: *für Geschlechtsverkehr*) to be gagging (*Brit*) *or* dying for it (*sl*)

Reif¹ [raif] M **-(e)s**, *no pl* (= *Raureif*) hoarfrost, white frost; (= *gefrorener Nebel*) rime

Reif² M **-(e)s, -e** (*old, liter*) (= *Stirnreif, Diadem*) circlet; (= *Armreif*) bangle; (= *Fingerring*) ring; (*im Rock*) hoop

Rei|fe [ˈraifə] F -, *no pl* **a** (= *das Reifen*) ripening **b** (= *das Reifsein*) ripeness; (= *Geschlechtsreife, von Ei*) maturity; **zur ~ kommen** to ripen; (*geh: Mädchen*) to come to *or* reach maturity; **zur ~ bringen** to ripen **c** (*fig: von Menschen, Gedanken etc*) maturity; **ihm fehlt die (sittliche) ~** he lacks maturity, he's too immature **d** (*Sch*) **Zeugnis der ~** (*form*) = **Reifezeugnis** → **mittlere(r,s)**

Rei|fe|grad M degree of ripeness

rei|fen¹ [ˈraifn] VI *impers* **es reift** there has been/will be a frost

rei|fen² **VT** *Obst* to ripen; *jdn* to mature; **das hat ihn zum Manne gereift** (*liter*) that made a man out of him → *auch* **gereift** **VI** *aux sein* **a** (*Obst*) to ripen; (*Mensch, Ei*) to mature; **er reifte zum Manne** (*liter*) he became a man → *auch* **gereift** **b** (*fig: Plan, Entscheidung*) to mature; **zur Wirklichkeit ~** to come to fruition, to become reality; **zur Gewissheit ~** to turn into certainty; **die Erkenntnis ist gereift, dass ...** the realization has grown that ...; **langsam reifte in ihm der Entschluss, ...** he slowly reached the decision ...

Rei|fen [ˈraifn] M **-s, -** tyre (*Brit*), tire (*US*); (= *Spielreifen, von Fass, von Rock*) hoop; (= *Armreifen*) bangle; **(den) ~ treiben** *or* **spielen** to bowl *or* roll a hoop

Reifen-: **Rei|fen|de|fekt** M = **Reifenpanne**; **Rei|fen|druck** M *pl* **-drücke** tyre (*Brit*) *or* tire (*US*) pressure; **Rei|fen|pan|ne** F puncture (*Brit*), flat (*inf*); (*geplatzt auch*) blowout (*inf*); **Rei|fen|pro|fil** NT tyre (*Brit*) *or* tire (*US*) tread; **Rei|fen|scha|den** M **a** (= *schadhafter Reifen*) faulty tyre (*Brit*) *or* tire (*US*) **b** = **Reifenpanne**; **Rei|fen|wech|sel** M tyre (*Brit*) *or* tire (*US*) change

Reife-: **Rei|fe|prü|fung** F (*Sch*) → **Abitur**; **Rei|fe|zeit** F ripening time; (*von Ei*) period of incubation; (= *Pubertät*) puberty *no def art*; **Rei|fe|zeug|nis** NT (*Sch*) *Abitur* certificate, ≈ A Level certificate (*Brit*), ≈ high school diploma (*US*)

reif|lich [ˈraiflɪç] **ADJ** thorough, careful; **nach ~er Überlegung** after careful consideration, upon mature reflection (*liter*) **ADV** *nachdenken* thoroughly; **sich** (*dat*) **etw ~ überlegen** to consider sth carefully

Reif|rock M (*Hist*) farthingale, hoop skirt

Rei|fung [ˈraifʊŋ] F -, *no pl* (*von Obst*) ripening; (*von Ei*) maturing, maturation; (*von Käse, Bier*) maturing; (*von Mensch*) maturing

Rei|fungs|pro|zess ▲ M (*von Obst*) ripening process; (*von Ei*) maturation process; (*von Käse, Bier*) maturing process; (*von Mensch*) maturing process

Rei|gen [ˈraign] M **-s, -** round dance, roundelay (*old*); (*fig geh*) round; **den ~ eröffnen** *or* **anführen** (*fig geh*) to lead off; **er eröffnete den ~ der Ansprachen** (*fig geh*) he led off with his speech; **den ~ beschließen** (*fig geh*) to bring up the rear; **ein bunter ~ von Melodien** a varied selection of melodies

Rei|he [ˈraiə] F **-, -n** **a** (= *geregelte Anordnung*) row, line; (= *Sitzreihe, beim Stricken*) row; **in ~(n) antreten** to line up; (*Mil*) to fall in; **in ~n zu (je) drei antreten/marschieren** to line up/march in rows of three *or* in threes; **sich in einer ~ aufstellen** to line up, to form a row *or* line; **sich in die ~ stellen** to join the row *or* line; **sich in einer ~ stellen** to line up; (*Mil*) to fall in; **in einer ~ stehen** to stand in a row *or* line; **in Reih und Glied antreten** to line up in formation; **sie standen in Reih und Glied vor dem Lehrer** they stood lined up in front of their teacher; **aus der ~ tanzen** (*fig inf*) to be different; (= *gegen Konventionen verstoßen*) to step out of line; **die ~ herumgehen** (*Gegenstand*) to be passed around, to go the rounds; **die ~n schließen** (*Mil*) to close ranks; **die ~n lichten sich** (*fig*) the ranks are thinning; **in den eigenen ~n** within our/their *etc* own ranks; **die ~ eröffnen** (*fig*) to start off; **in einer ~ mit jdm stehen** (*fig*) to be on a par with sb; **sich in eine ~ mit jdm stellen** (*fig*) to put oneself on a par *or* on an equal footing with sb; **in die erste ~ (vor)rücken** (*fig*) to move into the top rank; **in der vordersten ~ stehen** (*fig*) to be in the topmost rank

b (= *Reihenfolge*) **er ist an der ~** it's his turn, he's next; (*beim Spiel etc auch*) it's his go; **die ~ ist an jdm** it's sb's turn; **er kommt an die ~** he's next, it's his turn next, it's him next (*inf*); **warte, bis du an die ~ kommst** wait till it's your turn/go; **er kommt immer außer der ~** he always comes just when he pleases; **der ~ nach, nach der ~** in order, in turn; **sie sollen der ~ nach hereinkommen** they are to come in one by one *or* one at a time; **erzähl mal der ~ nach, wie alles war** tell us how it was in the order it all happened; **außer der ~** out of order; (*bei Spielen auch*) out of turn; (= *zusätzlich, nicht wie gewöhnlich*) out of the usual way of things; **wenn ich das Auto mal außer der ~ brauche** if I should happen to need the car at a time when I don't normally have it; **es kommt ganz selten vor, dass ich mal außer der ~ da bin** it's very rare for me to be there out of my routine

c (= *Serie, Math, Mus*) series *sing*; (*Biol*: = *Ordnung*) order

d (= *unbestimmte Anzahl*) number; **in die ~ der Mitgliedsstaaten eintreten** to join the ranks of the member states; **in der ~ der Stars** amongst the ranks of the stars; **eine ganze ~ (von)** a whole lot (of); **eine ganze ~ von Beispielen** a whole string of examples

e (*inf*: = *Ordnung*) **aus der ~ kommen** (= *in Unordnung geraten*) to get out of order; (= *verwirrt werden*) to lose one's equilibrium; (*gesundheitlich*) to fall ill; **jdn aus der ~ bringen** to muddle *or* confuse sb; **wieder in die ~ kommen** to get one's equilibrium back; (*gesundheitlich*) to get back on form; **nicht in der ~ sein** to be unwell (*esp Brit*), not to be one hundred per cent (*Brit inf*) *or* percent (*US inf*); **in die ~ bringen** to put in order, to put straight; **nicht alle auf der ~ haben** (*sl*) to have a screw loose (*inf*); **etw auf die ~ kriegen** (*inf*) to handle sth

rei|hen ['raɪən] **VT a** **Perlen auf eine Schnur ~** to string beads (on a thread); **sie reihte die Pilzstücke auf einen Faden** she strung the pieces of mushroom up (on a thread) **b** (*Sew*) to tack **VR etw reiht sich an etw** (*acc*) sth follows (after) sth; **eine Enttäuschung reihte sich an die andere** letdown followed letdown

Rei|hen ['raɪən] M **-s, -** (*S Ger*) instep

Reihen-: Rei|hen|dorf NT *village built along a road*, ribbon development (*spec*); **Rei|hen|fabri|ka|ti|on** F, **Rei|hen|fer|ti|gung** F serial production

Rei|hen|fol|ge F order; (= *notwendige Aufeinanderfolge*) sequence; **der ~ nach** in sequence; **in zwangloser ~** in no particular *or* special order; **in umgekehrter ~** in reverse order; **alphabetische/zeitliche ~** alphabetical/chronological order

Reihen-: Rei|hen|haus NT terraced house (*Brit*), town house (*esp US*); **Rei|hen|(haus)|sied|lung** F estate of terraced houses (*Brit*) *or* town houses (*esp US*); **Rei|hen|schal|tung** F (*Elec*) series connection; **in ~** in series; **Rei|hen|un|ter|su|chung** F mass screening; **rei|hen|wei|se** ADV **a** (= *in Reihen*) in rows **b** (*fig*: = *in großer Anzahl*) by the dozen; **sie sind ~ ohnmächtig geworden** they fainted by the dozen, dozens of them fainted; **Rei|hen|zahl** F (*Math*) member of a series

Rei|her ['raɪɐ] M **-s, -** heron

Reiher-: Rei|her|fe|der F heron's feather; (*als Hutschmuck*) aigrette; **Rei|her|horst** M heron's nest

rei|hern ['raɪɐn] VI (*sl*) to puke *or* spew (up) (*inf*)

Rei|her|schna|bel M (*Bot*) common storksbill

Reih|garn ['raɪ-] NT tacking thread

-rei|hig [raɪç] ADJ *suf* -rowed; **zweireihige Jacke** double-breasted jacket

---

reih|um [raɪ'ʊm] ADV round; **es geht ~** everybody takes their turn; **etw ~ gehen lassen** to pass sth round

Reim [raɪm] M **-(e)s, -e** rhyme; **ein ~ auf „Hut"** a rhyme for "hat"; **~e bilden** *or* **machen** *or* **drechseln** (*hum*) *or* **schmieden** (*hum*) to make *or* write rhymes, to versify (*hum*); **etw in ~e bringen** to make sth rhyme; **sich** (*dat*) **einen ~ auf etw** (*acc*) **machen** (*inf*) to make sense of sth; **ich mache mir so meinen ~ darauf** (*inf*) I can put two and two together (*inf*); **ich kann mir keinen ~ darauf machen** (*inf*) I can't make head (n)or tail of it, I can see no rhyme (n)or reason in it

Reim|art F type of rhyme

rei|men ['raɪmən] **VT** to rhyme (*auf +acc, mit* with); **ich kann das Wort nicht ~** I can't find a rhyme for this word, I can't find anything to rhyme with this word **VI** to make up rhymes, to rhyme (*liter*), to versify (*hum*) **VR** to rhyme (*auf +acc, mit* with); **das reimt sich nicht** (*fig*) it doesn't hang together *or* make sense

Rei|mer ['raɪmɐ] M **-s, -**, **Rei|me|rin** [-ərɪn] F **-, -nen** (*pej*) rhymester, versifier

Rei|me|rei [raɪmə'raɪ] F **-, -en a** (= *das Reimen*) versifying **b** (= *Gedicht*) doggerel *no pl*; **eine ~** a piece of doggerel

Reim-: Reim|le|xi|kon NT rhyming dictionary; **reim|los** ADJ unrhymed, non-rhyming; **Reim|paar** NT rhyming couplet

Re|im|port [reɪm'pɔrt, 'reɪmpɔrt] M (*Fin, Comm*) reimportation

Reim-: Reim|sche|ma NT rhyming pattern, rhyme scheme; **Reim|schmied(in)** M(F) (*hum*) rhymester, versifier; **Reim|wort** NT *pl* **-wörter** rhyme; **ein ~ zu etw finden** to find a rhyme for sth *or* a word to rhyme with sth

rein¹ [raɪn] ADV (*inf*) = **herein, hinein**

rein² [ADJ] **a** pure; (= *absolut, völlig*) pure, sheer; *Wahrheit* plain, straight, unvarnished; *Gewinn* clear; **das ist die ~ste Freude/der ~ste Hohn** *etc* it's pure *or* sheer joy/mockery *etc*; **er ist der ~ste Künstler/Akrobat** he's a real artist/acrobat; **das Kind ist der ~ste Vater** (*dial*) the child is just like his father; **er ist die ~ste Bestie** he's an absolute *or* downright brute; **mit ihren Kindern hat sie nicht immer die ~ste Freude** she sometimes finds her children a mixed blessing; **die ~e Arbeit kostet ...** the work alone costs ...; **er ist ein Demokrat ~sten Wassers** *or* **von ~stem Wasser** he is the archetypal *or* a pure democrat; **eine ~e Jungenklasse** an all boys' class; **eine ~e Industriestadt** a purely industrial town

b (= *sauber*) clean; *Haut, Teint* clear, pure; **etw ~ machen** to clean sth; **~ Schiff!** (*Naut*) ≈ swab the decks!; **~en Tisch machen** (*fig*) to get things straight, to sort things out; **ich habe ~e Hände** (*fig*) my hands are clean; **die Hände ~ behalten** (*fig*) to keep one's nose clean (*inf*) → **Weste**

c (= *klar, übersichtlich*) **etw ins Reine schreiben** to write out a fair copy of sth, to write sth out neatly; **etw ins Reine bringen** to clear sth up; **die Sache ist ins Reine gekommen** things are cleared up, things have cleared themselves up; **mit sich selbst ins Reine kommen** to get things straight with oneself, to straighten *or* sort things out with oneself; **mit etw ins Reine kommen** to get straight about sth; **mit jdm/sich selbst im Reinen sein** to have got things straightened *or* sorted out with sb/oneself; **mit etw im Reinen sein** to have got sth straightened *or* sorted out; **mit seinem Gewissen im Reinen sein** to have a clear conscience; **er ist mit sich selbst nicht im Reinen** he is at odds with himself

d (= *unschuldig*) pure; *Gewissen* clear; **er ist ~ von Schuld** (*old*) he is free of guilt; **dem Reinen ist alles ~** (*prov*) to the pure all things are pure **ADV a** (= *ausschließlich*) purely; **~ hypothetisch gesprochen** speaking purely hypothetically **b** (= *pur*) **~ leinen** pure linen; **~ seiden** pure silk; **~ wollen** pure wool **c** (= *sauber*) **~ klingen** to make a pure sound;

~ singen to have a pure voice

d (*inf*: = *ganz, völlig*) absolutely; **~ alles/unmöglich** absolutely everything/impossible; **~ gar nichts** absolutely nothing

Rein F **-, -en** (*S Ger, Aus*: Cook) ≈ casserole

rein+bei|ßen VT *sep irreg* (*inf*) to bite into (*in +acc*); **zum Reinbeißen aussehen** to look scrumptious

Rei|nec|lau|de [rɛːnə'kloːdə] F **-, -n** greengage

Rein|ein|nah|me F net profit(s *pl*) *or* proceeds *pl*

Rei|ne|ke Fuchs ['raɪnəkə] M **- -** (*Liter*) Reynard the Fox

Rei|ne|ma|che|frau F cleaner, cleaning lady

Rei|ne|ma|chen NT **-s**, *no pl* (*inf*) cleaning

Rein-: rei|n|er|big ADJ (*Biol*) homozygous (*spec*); **Rein|er|lös** M, **Rein|er|trag** [M] net profit(s *pl*) *or* proceeds *pl*

Rei|net|te [rɛ'nɛtə] F **-, -n** rennet

rei|ne|weg ['raɪnəvɛk] ADV (*inf*) completely, absolutely; **das ist ~ Freiheit/erlogen** it's downright cheek (*Brit*) *or* impudence/a downright lie; **das ist ~ zum Verrücktwerden** it's enough to drive you absolutely mad

Rein|fall M (*inf*) disaster (*inf*); (= *Pleite auch*) flop (*inf*); **mit der Waschmaschine/dem Kollegen haben wir einen ~ erlebt** we had real problems with the washing machine/this colleague; **unsere Reise war vielleicht ein ~!** our journey was a real disaster

rein+fal|len ['raɪnfalən] VI *sep irreg aux sein* (*inf*) = **hereinfallen, hineinfallen**

Re|in|fek|ti|on [reɪɪnfɛk'tsioːn] F reinfection

Rein|ge|schmeck|te(r) ['raɪngəʃmɛktə] MF *decl as adj* (*S Ger*) outsider

Rein-: Rein|ge|wicht NT net(t) weight; **Rein|ge|winn** M net(t) profit; **Rein|hal|tung** F keeping clean; (*von Wasser, Luft auch, von Sprache*) keeping pure; **die ~ des Spielplatzes** keeping the playground clean

rein+hän|gen VR *sep* (*sl*: = *sich anstrengen*) to get stuck in (*inf*)

Rein|heit F **-**, *no pl* purity, pureness; (= *Sauberkeit*) cleanness; (*von Haut*) clearness; (= *Unschuld*) purity, pureness; **Rohstoffe in hoher ~** high-purity raw materials

Rein|heits-: Rein|heits|ge|bot NT purity law (*regulating the production of beer and various other food and drink items*); **Rein|heits|grad** M (*Chem*) (degree of) purity

rei|ni|gen ['raɪnɪgn] **VT a** (= *sauber machen, putzen*) to clean; **etw chemisch ~** to dry-clean sth; **sich** (*dat*) **die Hände ~** to clean one's hands

b (= *säubern*) to purify; *Metall* to refine; *Blut* to purify, to cleanse; **ein ~des Gewitter** (*fig inf*) a row which clears the air

c (= *zensieren*) *Text* to clean up, to bowdlerize; *Sprache* to purify; **eine Sprache/einen Text von etw ~** to purify *or* purge a language/text of sth **VR** to clean itself; (*Mensch*) to cleanse oneself; **normalerweise kann ein Fluss sich von selbst ~** normally a river can cleanse itself *or* keep itself clean; **sich von einer Schuld ~** (*liter*) to cleanse oneself of a sin (*liter*); **sich von einem Verdacht ~** (*liter*) to clear oneself of suspicion

Rei|ni|ger ['raɪnɪgɐ] M **-s, -** cleaner

Rei|ni|gung ['raɪnɪgʊŋ] F **-, -en a** (= *das Saubermachen*) cleaning **b** (= *chemische Reinigung*) (*Vorgang*) dry cleaning; (*Anstalt*) (dry) cleaner's **c** (= *das Säubern*) purification; (*von Metall*) refining; (*von Blut*) purification, cleansing **d** (*von Text*) cleaning up, bowdlerization; (*von Sprache*) purification **e** (*Rel*) purification

Rei|ni|gungs-: Rei|ni|gungs|cre|me F cleansing cream; **Rei|ni|gungs|milch** F cleansing milk; **Rei|ni|gungs|mit|tel** NT cleansing agent

Re|in|kar|na|ti|on [reɪnkarna'tsioːn] F reincarnation

---

rein+krie|gen ['rainkri:gn] VT *sep* (*inf*) = **hereinbekommen**

Rein|kul|tur F (*Biol*) pure culture; **~en der Bierhefe** pure beer-yeast cultures; **Kitsch/Faschismus** *etc* **in ~** (*inf*) pure unadulterated kitsch/fascism *etc*

rein+le|gen ['rainle:gn] VT *sep* (*inf*) = **hereinlegen, hineinlegen**

rein|lei|nen △ ['rain'lainən] ADJ → **rein²** ADV b

rein|lich ['rainlıç] **ADJ** **a** (= *sauberkeitsliebend*) cleanly **b** (= *ordentlich*) neat, tidy **c** (= *gründlich, klar*) clear **ADV** **a** (= *sauber*) cleanly **b** (= *genau*) *trennen, unterscheiden* clearly

Rein|lich|keit F -, *no pl* **a** (= *Sauberkeitsliebe*) cleanliness **b** (= *Ordentlichkeit*) neatness, tidiness

Rein-: Rein|luft|ge|biet NT pollution-free zone; **Rein|ma|che|frau** ['rainmaxə-] F cleaner, cleaning lady; **rein|ras|sig** ADJ of pure race, pure-blooded; *Tier* purebred, thoroughbred; (*fig*) *Sportwagen etc* thoroughbred; **Rein|ras|sig|keit** F -, *no pl* racial purity; (*von Tier*) pure breeding; **Rein|raum** clean room; **rein+rei|ten** ['rainraitn] VT *sep irreg* **jdn (ganz schön) ~** (*inf*) to get sb into a (right) mess (*inf*); **Rein|schiff** NT (*Naut*) **~ machen** ≈ to swab the decks; **rein+schnup|pern** VI *sep* (*inf*) = **hineinschnuppern**; **Rein|schrift** F writing out a fair copy *no art*; (*Geschriebenes*) fair copy; **etw in ~ schreiben** to write out a fair copy of sth; **Notizen in ~ schreiben** to write up notes; **rein|schrift|lich** ADJ **~es Exemplar** fair copy; **rein|sei|den** △ ADJ → **rein²** ADV **b**; **rein+sem|meln** VT *sep* (*inf*) **jdm eine ~** (= *schlagen*) to give sb a thump, to land sb one (*inf*); (= *hereinlegen*) to do the dirty on sb (*inf*)

Reinst|raum ['rainst-] M clean room

Rein-: rein+stres|sen VR *sep* (*sl*) to get stressed out (*inf*); (= *hart arbeiten*) to work like hell (*inf*); **rein+tun** ['raintu:n] VT (*inf*) **sich** (*dat*) **etw ~** to imagine sth; **das muss man sich mal ~** just imagine that → *auch* **hineintun**; **Rein|ver|dienst** M net earnings *pl*; **Rein|ver|mö|gen** NT net assets *pl*

Re|in|ves|ti|ti|on [reinvesti'tsio:n] F -, -en reinvestment

Rein-: rein wa|schen ▲ ['rainvaʃn] *irreg* **VT** (*von of*) to clear; (*von Sünden*) to cleanse; *schmutziges Geld* to launder **VR** (*fig*) to clear oneself; (*von Sünden*) to cleanse oneself; **rein|weg** ['rainvɛk] ADV = **reineweg**; **rein|wol|len** △ VI *sep* (*inf*) → **rein²** ADV **b**; **rein+wür|gen** ['rainvvrgn] VT (*inf*) *Essen etc* to force down; **jdm einen** *or* **eins ~** to do the dirty on sb (*inf*); **rein+zie|hen** ['raintsi:ən] VT (*inf*) **sich** (*dat*) **etw ~** (*Drogen*) to take sth; *Musik* to listen to sth; *Film, Video* to watch sth; *Getränk* to knock sth back (*inf*); *Essen* to guzzle sth down; (= *vorstellen*) to imagine sth; (= *akzeptieren*) to take sth in → *auch* **hineinziehen**; **Rein|zucht** F (*von Tieren*) inbreeding; (*von Bakterien*) cultivation of pure cultures

Reis¹ [rais] NT **-es, -er** [-zə] (*old, liter*) (= *Zweig*) twig, sprig; (= *Pfropfreis*) scion

Reis² M **-es, -e** [-zə] rice; **Huhn auf ~** chicken with rice

Reis-: Reis|auf|lauf M rice pudding; **Reis|bau** M , *no pl* rice-growing *no art*, cultivation of rice; **Reis|be|sen** M besom; **Reis|brannt|wein** M rice spirit; **Reis|brei** M = creamed rice; **Reis|bün|del** NT bundle of twigs, faggot (*Brit*)

Rei|se ['raizə] F -, **-n** journey, trip; (= *Schiffsreise*) voyage; (*Space*) voyage, journey; (= *Geschäftsreise*) trip; **seine ~n durch Europa** his travels through Europe; **seine ~ nach Spanien** his trip to Spain; **eine ~ mit der Eisenbahn/dem Auto** a train/car journey, a journey by rail/car; **eine ~ zu Schiff** a sea voyage; (= *Kreuzfahrt*) a cruise; **er plant eine ~ durch Afrika** he's planning to travel through Africa; **eine ~ machen** to go on a journey; **wir konnten die geplante ~ nicht**

machen we couldn't go away as planned; **er hat in seinem Leben viele interessante ~n gemacht** he has travelled (*Brit*) *or* traveled (*US*) to a lot of interesting places in his lifetime; **wann machst du die nächste ~?** when are you off (on your travels) again?, when's the next trip?; **ich muss mal wieder eine ~ machen** I must go away again; **die ~ nach Afrika habe ich allein gemacht** I travelled (*Brit*) *or* traveled (*US*) to Africa by myself; **auf ~n sein** to be a-way (travelling (*Brit*) *or* traveling (*US*)); **er ist viel auf ~n** he does a lot of travelling (*Brit*) *or* traveling (*US*); **jeden Sommer gehen wir auf ~n** we go away every summer; **er geht viel auf ~n** he travels a lot; **jdn auf die ~ schicken** to see sb off on his/her journey; **etw auf die ~ schicken** (*Brief etc*) to send sth off; **wohin geht die ~?** where are you off to?; **die letzte ~ antreten** (*euph liter*) to enter upon one's last journey (*liter*); **glückliche** *or* **gute ~!** bon voyage!, have a good journey!; **wenn einer eine ~ tut, so kann er was erzählen** (*prov*) strange things happen when you're abroad; **die ~ nach Jerusalem** (= *Spiel*) musical chairs *sing*; **Gullivers ~n** (*Liter*) Gulliver's Travels

Rei|se-: Rei|se|an|den|ken NT souvenir; **Rei|se|an|tritt** M start of a/the journey; **vor/bei ~** before/at the start of a/the journey; **Rei|se|apo|the|ke** F first-aid kit; **Rei|se|be|darf** M travel requisites *pl*; **Rei|se|be|glei|ter(in)** M(F) travelling (*Brit*) *or* traveling (*US*) companion; (= *Reiseleiter*) courier; (*für Kinder*) chaperon; **Rei|se|be|kannt|schaft** F acquaintance made while travelling (*Brit*) *or* traveling (*US*); **Rei|se|be|richt** M report *or* account of one's journey; (*Buch*) travel story; (*Film*) travel film, travelogue (*Brit*), travelog (*US*); (*in Tagebuch*) holiday diary (*Brit*), travel journal (*US*); **Rei|se|be|schrän|kun|gen** PL travel restrictions *pl*; **Rei|se|be|schrei|bung** F description of one's travels; (*Liter*) traveller's (*Brit*) *or* traveler's (*US*) tale; (*Film*) travelogue (*Brit*), travelog (*US*); **Rei|se|bü|ro** NT travel agency; **Rei|se|bü|ro|kauf|frau** F, **Rei|se|bü|ro|kauf|mann** M travel agent; **Rei|se|car** M (*Sw*) coach (*Brit*), bus; **Rei|se|ein|drü|cke** PL travel impressions *pl*; **Rei|se|er|leich|te|run|gen** PL easing of travel restrictions; **Rei|se|fach|kraft** F travel agent; **rei|se|fer|tig** ADJ ready (to go *or* leave); **~e Gäste warten bitte in der Hotelhalle** would guests who are ready to leave please wait in the hotel foyer; **Rei|se|fie|ber** NT (*fig*) travel nerves *pl*; **Rei|se|flug|hö|he** F cruising altitude; **Rei|se|füh|rer** M (*Buch*) guidebook; **Rei|se|füh|rer(in)** M(F) tour guide, courier; **Rei|se|ge|fähr|te** M , **Rei|se|ge|fähr|tin** F travelling (*Brit*) *or* traveling (*US*) companion; **Rei|se|geld** NT fare; **Rei|se|ge|neh|mi|gung** F travel permit; **Rei|se|ge|päck** NT luggage, baggage (*esp US, Aviat*); **Rei|se|ge|päck|ver|si|che|rung** F baggage insurance; **Rei|se|ge|schwin|dig|keit** F cruising speed; **Rei|se|ge|sell|schaft** F (*tourist*) party; (*im Bus auch*) coach party; (*inf*: = *Veranstalter*) tour operator; **eine japanische ~** a party of Japanese tourists; **Rei|se|grup|pe** F (*tourist*) group *or* party; (*im Bus auch*) coach party; **Rei|se|kof|fer** M suitcase

Rei|se|kos|ten PL travelling (*Brit*) *or* traveling (*US*) expenses *pl*

Rei|se|kos|ten-: Rei|se|kos|ten|ab|rech|nung F claim for travelling (*Brit*) *or* traveling (*US*) expenses; **Rei|se|kos|ten|ver|gü|tung** F payment *or* reimbursement of travelling (*Brit*) *or* traveling (*US*) expenses; **die Firma übernimmt volle ~** the firm will pay all (your) travelling (*Brit*) *or* traveling (*US*) expenses; **250 Euro** = 250 euros (in respect of) travelling (*Brit*) *or* traveling (*US*) expenses

Rei|se-: Rei|se|kran|ken|ver|si|che|rung F travel health(care) insurance; **Rei|se|krank|heit** F travel sickness; **Rei|se|land** NT holiday (*esp Brit*) *or* travel destination; **Rei|se|lei|ter(in)** M(F) tour guide, courier; **Rei-**

tung F (*das Leiten*) organization of a/the tourist party; (= *Reiseleiter*) courier(s); **möchten Sie die ~ für eine Englandtour übernehmen?** would you like to take a party for a tour of England?; **wegen schlechter ~** because of the poor way in which the party was run; **Rei|se|lek|tü|re** F reading matter (for a journey); **etw als ~ mitnehmen** to take sth to read on the journey; **Rei|se|lust** F travel urge, wanderlust; **mich packt die ~** I've got itchy feet (*inf*), I've got the travel bug (*inf*); **rei|se|lus|tig** ADJ fond of *or* keen on travel *or* travelling (*Brit*) *or* traveling (*US*), travel-mad (*Brit inf*), travel-crazy (*esp US inf*); **Rei|se|mit|bring|sel** NT souvenir

rei|sen ['raizn] VI *aux sein* to travel; **in den Urlaub ~** to go away on holiday (*esp Brit*) *or* vacation (*US*); **in etw** (*dat*) **~** (*Comm*) to travel in sth; **viel gereist sein** to have travelled (*Brit*) *or* traveled (*US*) a lot, to be well-travelled (*Brit*) *or* well-traveled (*US*)

Rei|sen|de(r) ['raizndə] MF *decl as adj* traveller (*Brit*), traveler (*US*); (= *Fahrgast*) passenger; (*Comm*) (commercial) traveller (*Brit*) *or* traveler (*US*), travelling (*Brit*) *or* traveling (*US*) salesman/-woman

Rei|se-: Rei|se|ne|ces|saire NT (*für Nagelpflege*) travelling (*Brit*) *or* traveling (*US*) manicure set; (= *Nähzeug*) travelling (*Brit*) *or* traveling (*US*) sewing kit; **Rei|se|on|kel** M (*hum inf*) globetrotter (*hum*); **Rei|se|pass** ▲ M passport; **Rei|se|plan** M *usu pl* travel plans *pl*; **meine Mutter schmiedet dauernd irgendwelche Reisepläne** my mother is always planning some journey *or* trip *or* other; **Rei|se|pros|pekt** M travel brochure; **Rei|se|pro|vi|ant** M food for the journey, provisions *pl* (*usu hum*)

Rei|se|rei [raizə'rai] F -, -en (endless) travelling (*Brit*) *or* traveling (*US*) around

Rei|se-: Rei|se|rou|te F route, itinerary; **Rei|se|rück|tritts|ver|si|che|rung** F travel *or* holiday (*esp Brit*) *or* vacation (*US*) cancellation insurance; **Rei|se|ruf** M personal message; **Rei|se|scheck** M traveller's cheque (*Brit*), traveler's check (*US*); **Rei|se|schil|de|rung** F = Reisebericht; **Rei|se|schreib|ma|schi|ne** F portable typewriter; **Rei|se|spe|sen** PL travelling (*Brit*) *or* traveling (*US*) expenses *pl*; **Rei|se|sti|pen|di|um** NT travelling (*Brit*) *or* traveling (*US*) scholarship; **Rei|se|tab|let|te** F travel sickness pill; **Rei|se|ta|ge|buch** NT travel *or* holiday diary (*Brit*), travel journal (*US*); **Rei|se|tan|te** F (*hum inf*) globetrotter (*hum*); **Rei|se|ta|sche** F holdall, travelling (*Brit*) *or* traveling (*US*) bag; **Rei|se|un|ter|la|gen** PL travel documents *pl*; **Rei|se|ver|an|stal|ter(in)** M(F) tour operator; **Rei|se|ver|kehr** M holiday (*esp Brit*) *or* vacation (*US*) traffic; **Rei|se|ver|si|che|rung** F travel insurance; **Rei|se|vor|be|rei|tun|gen** PL travel preparations *pl*, preparations *pl* for a/the journey; **Rei|se|we|cker** M travelling (*Brit*) *or* traveling (*US*) alarm clock; **Rei|se|wel|le** F (surge of) holiday traffic; **die ~ setzt ein** the holiday season is under way; **die ~ nach Süden** the wave of holiday-makers (*Brit*) *or* vacationers (*US*) heading south, the surge of holiday-makers (*Brit*) *or* vacationers (*US*) to the south; **Rei|se|wet|ter** NT travelling (*Brit*) *or* traveling (*US*) weather; **Rei|se|wet|ter|be|richt** M holiday (*Brit*) *or* travel weather forecast; **Rei|se|zeit** F (= *günstige Zeit*) time for travelling (*Brit*) *or* traveling (*US*); (= *Saison*) holiday (*esp Brit*) *or* vacation (*US*) period *or* season; (= *Fahrzeit, Fahrtdauer*) travelling (*Brit*) *or* travel time; **die beste ~ für Ägypten** the best time to go to Egypt; **Rei|se|ziel** NT destination

Reis-: Reis|feld NT paddy field; **Reis|holz** NT (*old*) brushwood, twigs *pl*

Rei|sig ['raizıç] NT **-s**, *no pl* brushwood, twigs *pl*

Rei|sig-: Rei|sig|be|sen M besom; **Rei|sig|bün|del** NT bundle of twigs, faggot (*Brit*)

Reis-: Reis|korn NT pl **-körner** grain of rice; **Reis|mehl** NT ground rice; **Reis|pa|pier** NT (Art, Cook) rice paper

Reiß|aus [raisˈaus] M ~ **nehmen** (inf) to clear off (Brit inf) or out (inf), to make oneself scarce (inf)

Reiß-: Reiß|blei [ˈrais-] NT graphite; **Reiß|brett** [ˈrais-] NT drawing board; **Reiß|brett|stift** [ˈrais-] M drawing pin (Brit), thumb tack (US)

Reis-: Reis|schleim M rice water; **Reis|schnaps** M rice spirit

rei|ßen [ˈraisn̩] pret **riss** [rɪs], ptp **gerissen** [ɡəˈrɪsn̩]
▮VT▮ **a** (= zerreißen) to tear, to rip; **ein Loch ins Kleid ~** to tear or rip a hole in one's dress
b (= abreißen, entreißen, herunterreißen, wegreißen) to tear, to pull, to rip (etw von etw sth off sth); (= mitreißen, zerren) to pull, to drag; **jdn zu Boden ~** to pull or drag sb to the ground; **jdn/etw in die Tiefe ~** to pull or drag sb/sth down into the depths; **der Fluss hat die Brücke mit sich gerissen** the river swept the bridge away; **jdm etw aus den Händen/der Hand ~** to snatch sth from or out of sb's hands/hand; **jdn aus der Gefahr ~** to snatch sb from danger; **aus diesem Leben gerissen** snatched from this life; **jdn aus seinen Gedanken ~** to interrupt sb's thoughts; (= aufmuntern) to make sb snap out of it; **jdn aus dem Schlaf/seinen Träumen ~** to wake sb from his sleep/dreams; **in etw (dat) Lücken ~** to make gaps in sth; **jdn ins Verderben ~** to ruin sb; **jdn in den Tod ~** to claim sb's life; (Flutwelle, Lawine) to sweep sb to his/her death; **hin und her gerissen werden/sein** (fig) to be torn → **Zusammenhang**
c etw an sich (acc) ~ to seize sth; Macht auch to usurp sth; Unterhaltung to monopolize sth → **Nagel**
d (Sport) (Gewichtheben) to snatch; (Hochsprung, Pferderennen) to knock off or down
e (= töten) to take, to kill
f (inf: = machen) Witze to crack (inf); Possen to play
g (Aus sl) **jdm eine ~** to clout sb (one) (Brit inf), to slap sb; **einen Stern ~** to fall; **damit kannst du nichts ~** that's not going to impress anybody
h (= Wunde beibringen) **sich** (dat) **eine Wunde an etw** (dat) ~ to cut oneself on sth; **sich** (dat) **etw blutig ~** to tear sth open
i → **gerissen**
▮VI▮ **a** aux sein (= zerreißen) to tear, to rip; (Muskel, Bänder) to tear; (Seil) to tear, to break, to snap; (Risse bekommen) to crack; **mir ist die Kette/der Faden gerissen** my chain/thread has broken or snapped; **da riss mir die Geduld** or **der Geduldsfaden** then my patience gave out or snapped; **es reißt mir in allen Gliedern** (inf) I'm aching all over; **wenn alle Stricke** or **Stränge ~** (fig inf) if the worst comes to the worst, if all else fails
b (= zerren) (an +dat at) to pull, to tug; (wütend) to tear
c (Sport) (Gewichtheben) to snatch; (Hochsprung) to knock the bar off or down; (Springreiten) to knock the bar/top brick(s) etc off or down
▮VR▮ **a** (= sich verletzen) to cut oneself (an +dat on)
b (= sich losreißen) to tear oneself
c (inf) **sich um jdn/etw ~** to scramble to get sb/sth

Rei|ßen [ˈraisn̩] NT **-s**, no pl **a** (Gewichtheben) snatch **b** (inf: = Gliederreißen) ache

rei|ßend ADJ Fluss torrential, raging; Tier rapacious; Schmerzen searing; Verkauf, Absatz massive; **-en Absatz finden** to sell like hot cakes (inf)

Rei|ßer [ˈraisɐ] M **-s**, - (inf) (Theat, Film, Buch) thriller; (Ware) hot item (inf) or line (inf), big seller

rei|ße|risch [ˈraisərɪʃ] ADJ Bericht, Titel sensational ADV sensationally

Reiß- [ˈrais-]: **Reiß|fe|der** F (Art) (drawing) pen; **reiß|fest** ADJ tear-proof; **Reiß|fes|tig|keit** F (tensile) strength; **Reiß|koh|le** F (Art) charcoal; **Reiß|lei|ne** F ripcord; **Reiß|na|gel** M drawing pin (Brit), thumbtack (US); **Reiß|schie|ne** F T-square; **Reiß|stift** M drawing pin (Brit), thumbtack (US); **Reiß|ver|schluss** ▲ M zip (fastener) (Brit), zipper (US); **den ~ an etw** (dat) **zumachen** or **zuziehen** to zip sth up; **den ~ an etw** (dat) **aufmachen** or **aufziehen** to unzip sth; **Reiß|ver|schluss|prin|zip** ▲ NT principle of alternation; **Reiß|wolf** M shredder, shredding machine; **Reiß|wol|le** F shoddy; **Reiß|zahn** M fang, carnassial (tooth) (spec); **Reiß|zeug** NT pl **-zeuge** drawing instruments pl; **Reiß|zir|kel** M drawing compass(es pl); **Reiß|zwe|cke** F drawing pin (Brit), thumbtack (US)

Reis-: Reis|tag M day of eating only rice (as part of a diet); **Reis|ter|ras|se** F rice terrace, terraced paddy field; **Reis|wein** M rice wine

Reit-: Reit|an|zug M riding habit; **Reit|bahn** F arena

rei|ten [ˈraitn̩] pret **ritt** [rɪt], ptp **geritten** [ɡəˈrɪtn̩]
▮VI▮ aux sein **a** (auf Tier) to ride; **auf etw** (dat) ~ to ride (on) sth; **auf einer Welle ~** (lit, fig) to ride (on) a wave; **im Schritt/Trab/Galopp ~** to ride at a walk/trot/gallop; **geritten kommen** to ride up, to come riding up; **das Schiff reitet vor Anker** (Naut) the ship is riding at anchor; **auf diesem Messer kann man (nach Köln) ~!** (inf) you couldn't cut butter with this knife!
b (sl: = koitieren) to ride (sl)
▮VT▮ to ride; **Schritt/Trab/Galopp ~** to ride at a walk/trot/gallop; **ein schnelles Tempo ~** to ride at a fast pace; **sich** (dat) **Schwielen ~** to get saddle-sore; **jdn zu Boden** or **über den Haufen** (inf) ~ to trample sb down; **jdn in die Patsche** or **den Schlamassel ~** (inf) to get sb into a jam (inf) or mess; **Prinzipien ~** (inf) to insist on one's principles; **was hat dich denn da geritten, dass du so ausfällig geworden bist?** what was eating you to make you so obnoxious? (inf)

rei|tend ADJ mounted; **~e Artillerie** horse artillery

Rei|ter [ˈraitɐ] M **-s**, - **a** rider, horseman; (Mil) cavalryman; **ein Trupp preußischer ~** a troop of Prussian horse (Brit) or horses (US) → auch **Reiterin b** (an Waage) rider; (= Karteireiter) index tab **c** (Mil: = Absperrblock) barrier; **spanische ~** pl barbed-wire barricade

Reiter-: Rei|ter|an|griff M cavalry charge; **Rei|ter|auf|zug** M cavalcade

Rei|te|rei [raitəˈrai] F **-**, **-en a** (Mil) cavalry **b** (inf: = das Reiten) riding

Rei|te|rin [ˈraitərɪn] F **-**, **-nen** rider, horsewoman

Rei|ter|re|gi|ment NT cavalry regiment

Rei|ters|mann M pl **-männer** (liter) horseman

Rei|ter|stand|bild NT equestrian statue

Reit-: Reit|ger|te F riding crop; **Reit|ho|se** F riding breeches pl; (Hunt, Sport) jodhpurs pl; **Reit|ja|cke** F riding jacket; **Reit|kleid** NT riding habit; **Reit|knecht** M (old) groom; **Reit|kunst** F horsemanship, riding skill; **Reit|peit|sche** F riding whip; **Reit|pferd** NT saddle horse, mount; **Reit|sat|tel** M (riding) saddle; **Reit|schu|le** F riding school; **Reit|sitz** M riding position; (rittlings) straddling position; **im ~ sitzen** to sit astride (auf etw dat sth); **Reit|sport** M (horse-)riding, equestrian sport (form); **Reit|stall** M riding stable; **Reit|stie|fel** M riding boot; **Reit|stun|de** F riding lesson; **Reit|tier** NT mount, animal used for riding; **Reit|tur|nier** NT horse show; (Geländereiten) point-to-point; **Reit- und Fahr|tur|nier** NT horse show; **Reit|un|ter|richt** M riding lessons pl; **Reit|weg** M bridle path; **Reit|zeug** NT pl **-zeuge** riding equipment or things pl

Reiz [raits] M **-es**, **-e a** (Physiol) stimulus; **einen ~ auf etw** (acc) **ausüben** to act as a stimulus on sth **b** (= Verlockung) attraction, appeal; (des Unbekannten, Fremdartigen, der Großstadt) lure, appeal; (= Zauber) charm; **der ~ des Neuen/des Verbotenen** the lure or appeal of novelty/forbidden fruits; **(auf jdn) einen ~ ausüben** to have or hold great attraction(s) (for sb); **das erhöht den ~** it adds to the thrill or pleasure; **einen/keinen ~ für jdn haben** to appeal/not to appeal to sb; **diese Idee hat auch ihren ~** this idea also has its attractions; **seinen** or **den ~ verlieren** to lose all one's/its charm; **an ~ verlieren** to be losing one's/its charm or attraction or appeal, to begin to pall; **seine ~e spielen lassen** to display one's charms; **weibliche ~e** feminine charms; **seine ~e zeigen** (euph iro) to reveal one's charms

Reiz-: Reiz|aus|lö|ser M stimulant; (von krankhaftem Zustand) irritant; **reiz|bar** ADJ (= empfindlich) sensitive, touchy (inf); (Med) irritable, sensitive; (= erregbar) irritable; **leicht ~ sein** to be very sensitive/irritable; (= ständig erregbar auch) to be quick-tempered or hot-tempered; **~e Schwäche** (Med) irritability; (fig) sensitive spot or point; **Reiz|bar|keit** [ˈraitsbaːɐkait] F **-**, no pl (= Empfindlichkeit) sensitiveness, sensitivity, touchiness (inf); (Med) irritability, sensitivity; (= Erregbarkeit) irritability; **Reiz|be|hand|lung** F (Med) stimulation therapy; **reiz|emp|fäng|lich** ADJ responsive; (Physiol) receptive to stimuli; **Reiz|emp|fäng|lich|keit** F responsiveness to stimuli; (Physiol) receptiveness to stimuli

rei|zen [ˈraitsn̩] ▮VT▮ **a** (Physiol) to irritate; (= stimulieren) to stimulate
b (= verlocken) to appeal to; **jds Gaumen ~** to make sb's mouth water; **den Gaumen ~** to waken or rouse sb's desire; **es würde mich ja sehr ~, ...** I'd love to ...; **es reizt mich, nach Skye zu fahren** I've got an itch to go to Skye; **es hat mich ja immer sehr gereizt, ...** I've always had an itch to ...; **Ihr Angebot reizt mich sehr** I find your offer very tempting; **sie versteht es, Männer zu ~** she knows how to appeal to men; **was reizt Sie daran?** what do you like about it?
c (= ärgern) to annoy; Tier to tease, to annoy; (= herausfordern) to provoke; **ein gereiztes Nashorn ...** a rhinoceros when provoked ...; **jds Zorn ~** to arouse sb's anger; **jdn bis aufs Blut ~** to push sb to breaking point; **die Kinder reizten sie bis zur Weißglut** the children really made her see red → auch **gereizt**
d (Skat) to bid
▮VI▮ **a** (Med) to irritate; (= stimulieren) to stimulate; **auf der Haut** etc ~ to irritate the skin etc; **der Rauch reizt zum Husten** the smoke makes you cough; **zum Widerspruch ~** to invite contradiction
b (Cards) to bid; **hoch ~** (lit, fig) to make a high bid

rei|zend ADJ charming, lovely; **es ist ~ (von dir)** it's charming or lovely (of you); **das ist ja ~** (iro) (that's) charming ADV **einrichten, schmücken** attractively; **~ aussehen** to look charming; **sie haben sich ~ um uns gekümmert** they took such good care of us; **er hat mich ~ umsorgt** he was so considerate to me

Reiz-: Reiz|fi|gur F controversial figure; **er ist eine politische ~** he is a politically controversial figure; **Reiz|gas** NT irritant gas; **Reiz|hus|ten** M chesty (Brit) or deep (US) cough; (nervös) nervous cough

Reiz|ker [ˈraitskɐ] M **-s**, - (Bot) saffron milk cap

Reiz-: Reiz|kli|ma NT bracing climate; (fig) charged atmosphere; **reiz|los** ADJ dull, uninspiring; **das ist ja ~** that's no fun; **Reiz|lo|sig|keit** F **-**, no pl dullness, uninspiring nature; **Reiz|mit|tel** NT (Med) stimulant; **Reiz|schwel|le** F (Physiol) stimulus or absolute threshold; (Comm) sales resistance; **Reiz|stoff** M irritant; **Reiz|the|ma** NT controversial issue; **Reiz|the|ra|pie** F (Med) stimulation therapy; **Reiz|über|flu|tung** F overstimulation

Rei|zung ['raitsʊŋ] F -, -en **a** (Med) stimulation; (krankhaft) irritation **b** (= Herausforderung) provocation

Reiz-: reiz|voll ADJ charming, delightful; Aufgabe, Beruf attractive; die Aussicht ist nicht gerade ~ the prospect is not particularly enticing or appealing; es wäre ~, mal dahin zu fahren it would be lovely to go there some time; es wäre ~, das ganz anders zu machen it would be interesting to do it quite differently; **Reiz|wäsche** F (inf) sexy underwear; **Reiz|wort** NT pl -wörter emotive word

Re|ka|pi|tu|la|ti|on [rekapitula'tsioːn] F recapitulation

re|ka|pi|tu|lie|ren [rekapitu'liːrən] ptp **rekapituliert** VT to recapitulate

Re|ke|lei [reːkə'lai] F -, -en (inf) lolling about (Brit) or around (inf)

re|keln ['reːkln] VR (inf) (= sich herumlümmeln) to loll about (Brit) or around (inf); (= sich strecken) to stretch; **sich noch ein paar Minuten im Bett ~** to stretch out in bed for a few more minutes; **er rekelte sich im behaglichen Sessel vor dem Feuer** he snuggled down in the comfy chair in front of the fire; **die Katze rekelte sich genüsslich in der Sonne** the cat stretched out contentedly in the sun

Re|kla|ma|ti|on [reklama'tsioːn] F -, -en query; (= Beschwerde) complaint; „spätere ~en können nicht anerkannt werden" "please check your change/money immediately since mistakes cannot be rectified later"

Re|kla|me [re'klaːmə] F -, -n **a** (= Werbewesen, Werbung) advertising; ~ für jdn/etw machen to advertise sb/sth; (fig) to do a bit of advertising for sb/sth; mit jdm ~ machen (pej) to show sb off; ~ mit etw machen (pej) to show off about sth; das ist keine gute ~ für die Firma it's not a very good advertisement for the company **b** (= Einzelwerbung) advertisement, advert (Brit inf), ad (inf); (esp TV, Rad) commercial

Re|kla|me-: Re|kla|me|ar|ti|kel M free gift, sales gimmick (often pej); (= Probe) (free) sample; **Re|kla|me|bro|schü|re** F (advertising) brochure, handout; **-n** advertising literature; **Re|kla|me|feld|zug** M advertising campaign; **Re|kla|me|film** M advertising film, commercial; **Re|kla|me|pla|kat** NT (advertising) poster, advertisement; **Re|kla|me|rum|mel** M (pej) advertising frenzy (inf); **Re|kla|me|schild** NT pl -schilder advertising sign; **Re|kla|me|sen|dung** F (TV, Rad) commercial break, commercials pl; (= Postwurfsendung) mailshot (Brit), mailing; eine verkappte ~ a disguised commercial; **Re|kla|me|spot** M (advertising) spot, commercial; **Re|kla|me|ta|fel** F hoarding; **Re|kla|me|trick** M sales trick; **Re|kla|me|trom|mel** F die ~ für jdn/etw rühren (inf) to beat the (big) drum for sb/sth; **Re|kla|me|zet|tel** M (advertising) leaflet, hand-out

re|kla|mie|ren [rekla'miːrən] ptp **reklamiert** VI (= Einspruch erheben) to complain, to make a complaint; bei jdm wegen etw ~ to complain to sb about sth; die Rechnung kann nicht stimmen, da würde ich ~ the bill can't be right, I would query it VT **a** (= bemängeln) to complain about (etw bei jdm sth to sb); (= infrage stellen) Rechnung, Rechnungsposten to query (etw bei jdm sth with sb); **b** (= in Anspruch nehmen) to claim; jdn/etw für sich ~ to lay claim to sb/sth, to claim sb/sth as one's own

re|kom|man|die|ren [rekɔman'diːrən] ptp **rekommandiert** VT (Aus) Brief, Sendung to register; einen Brief rekommandiert aufgeben to register a letter, to send a letter by registered post (Brit) or certified mail (US) VR (obs, Aus) sich jdm ~ to pay one's compliments to sb

Re|kom|pens [rekɔm'pɛns] -, -en [-zn] (Aus), **Re|kom|penz** [rekɔm'pɛnts] F -, -en (Admin) compensation

re|kon|stru|ie|ren [rekɔnstru'iːrən] ptp **rekonstruiert** VT to reconstruct

Re|kon|struk|ti|on [rekɔnstrʊk'tsioːn] F reconstruction

Re|kon|va|les|zent [rekɔnvalɛs'tsɛnt] M -en, -en, **Re|kon|va|les|zen|tin** [-'tsɛntɪn] F -, -nen convalescent

Re|kon|va|les|zenz [rekɔnvalɛs'tsɛnts] F -, -en convalescence

Re|kord [re'kɔrt] M -s, -e [-də] record; einen ~ aufstellen to set a record; das Zeitalter der ~e the age of superlatives; (des Fortschritts) the age of achievement

Rekord- in cpds record; **Re|kord|bre|cher(in)** M(F) record breaker

Re|kor|der [re'kɔrdɐ] M -s, - (cassette) recorder

Re|kord-: Re|kord|er|geb|nis NT record result(s) pl; **Re|kord|hal|ter(in)** M(F), **Re|kord|ha|ber(in)** M(F) record holder; **Re|kord|lauf** M record(-breaking) run

Re|kord|ler [re'kɔrtlɐ] M -s, -, **Re|kord|le|rin** [-ərɪn] F -, -nen (inf) record holder

Re|kord-: Re|kord|mar|ke F (Sport, fig) record; die bisherige ~ im Weitsprung war … till now the long-jump record stood at or was …; auf der ~ (von) at the record or (fig) record level (of); **Re|kord|tief** NT (St Ex) record or all-time low; **Re|kord|ver|lust** M (Fin, Comm) record(-breaking) losses pl; **Re|kord|ver|such** M attempt on the/a record; **Re|kord|zeit** F record time

Rek|rut [re'kruːt] M -en, -en, **Rek|ru|tin** [-'kruːtɪn] F -, -nen (Mil) recruit

Rek|ru|ten-: Rek|ru|ten|aus|bil|dung F (Mil) basic training; **Rek|ru|ten|aus|he|bung** F (old Mil) levy (old); **Rek|ru|ten|schu|le** F (Sw Mil) recruit school

rek|ru|tie|ren [rekru'tiːrən] ptp **rekrutiert** VT (Mil, fig) to recruit VR (fig) sich ~ aus to be recruited or drawn from

Rek|ru|tie|rung F -, -en recruitment, recruiting

Rek|ru|tie|rungs|stel|le F (Mil) recruiting centre (Brit) or center (US)

Rek|ru|tin F -, -nen (Mil) recruit

Rek|ta pl von **Rektum**

rek|tal [rek'taːl] ADJ (Med) rectal ADV ~ einführen to insert through the rectum; die Temperatur ~ messen to take the temperature rectally

Rek|ti|fi|ka|ti|on [rektifika'tsioːn] F -, -en **a** (old) correction; (= Berichtigung) correction, rectification **b** (Chem, Math) rectification

rek|ti|fi|zie|ren [rektifi'tsiːrən] ptp **rektifiziert** VT **a** (old) to correct; (= berichtigen) to correct, to rectify **b** (Chem, Math) to rectify

Rek|ti|on [rek'tsioːn] F -, -en (Gram) government; die ~ eines Verbs the case governed by a verb

Rek|tor ['rektoːɐ] M -s, Rektoren [-'toːrən], **Rek|to|rin** [-'toːrɪn, 'rektorɪn] F -, -nen (Sch) head teacher, principal (esp US); (Univ) vice chancellor (Brit), rector (US); (von Fachhochschule) principal; (von kirchlicher Einrichtung) rector

Rek|to|rat [rekto'raːt] NT -(e)s, -e (Sch) (= Amt, Amtszeit) headship, principalship (esp US); (= Zimmer) headmaster's/headmistress's study, principal's room (esp US); (Univ) vice chancellorship (Brit), rectorship (US); (von Fachhochschule) principalship; principal's office

Rek|to|rats|re|de F (Univ) (vice chancellor's (Brit) or rector's (US)) inaugural address

Rek|tum ['rektʊm] NT -s, Rekta [-ta] (form) rectum

re|kur|rie|ren [rekʊ'riːrən] ptp **rekurriert** VI **a** (old Jur) to appeal **b** (liter: = auf etw zurückkommen) to return (auf +acc to)

Re|kurs [re'kʊrs] M -es, -e [-zə] (old Jur) appeal

Rel. abbr von **Religion**

Re|lais [rə'lɛː] NT -, - [rə'lɛː(s), rə'lɛːs] (Elec) relay

Re|lais|schal|tung [rə'lɛː-] F (Elec) relay circuit or connection

Re|lais|sta|ti|on [rə'lɛː-] F (Elec) relay station

Re|la|ti|on [rela'tsioːn] F -, -en relation; in einer/keiner ~ zu etw stehen to bear some/no relation to sth; etw in ~ (zu or mit etw) setzen to compare sth (to or with sth)

re|la|ti|o|nal [relatsio'naːl] (Comput) ADJ relational ADV relationally

re|la|tiv [rela'tiːf] ADJ relative; ~e Mehrheit (Parl) simple majority; alles ist ~ everything is relative ADV relatively

Re|la|tiv [rela'tiːf] NT -s, -e [-və] relative pronoun

re|la|tiv|ad|verb NT relative adverb

re|la|ti|vie|ren [relati'viːrən] ptp **relativiert** (geh) VT Begriff, Behauptung etc to qualify VI to see things or to think in relative terms VR to become relative

Re|la|ti|vis|mus [relati'vɪsmʊs] M -, no pl relativism

re|la|ti|vis|tisch [relati'vɪstɪʃ] ADJ relativistic

Re|la|ti|vi|tät [relativi'tɛːt] F -, no pl relativity

Re|la|ti|väts|the|o|rie F theory of relativity, relativity theory no art

Re|la|tiv-: Re|la|tiv|pro|no|men NT relative pronoun; **Re|la|tiv|satz** M relative clause

Re|la|ti|vum [rela'tiːvʊm] NT -s, Relativa [-va] (form) relative pronoun

Re|launch ['riːloːntʃ] M OR NT -(e)s, -(e)s relaunch

re|la|xen [ri'lɛksn] VI (inf) to take it easy (inf), to relax

re|laxt [ri'lɛkst] (inf) ADJ relaxed, laid-back (inf) ADV ~ auf etw (acc) reagieren to be laid-back about sth (inf); an etw (acc) ~ herangehen to be laid-back (inf) or relaxed about tackling sth; sie ist alles andere als ~ in die Prüfung gegangen she was anything but relaxed when she went to sit (Brit) or take her exam

Re|le|ga|ti|on [relega'tsioːn] F -, -en (form) expulsion

re|le|gie|ren [rele'giːrən] ptp **relegiert** VT (form) to expel

re|le|vant [rele'vant] ADJ relevant

Re|le|vanz [rele'vants] F -, no pl relevance

Re|li ['reːli] F -, no pl (Sch inf: = Religion) RE

Re|li|ef [reli'ɛf] NT -s, -s or -e relief

Re|li|ef-: Re|li|ef|druck M pl -drucke relief printing; **Re|li|ef|kar|te** F relief map

Re|li|gi|on [reli'gioːn] F -, -en (lit, fig) religion; (Schulfach) religious instruction or education, RI, RE; seine ~ ausüben to practise (Brit) or practice (US) one's religion; ~ sehr gut, Kopfrechnen schwach (inf) virtuous but stupid

Re|li|gi|ons-: Re|li|gi|ons|be|kennt|nis NT denomination; **Re|li|gi|ons|buch** NT religion or religious textbook; **Re|li|gi|ons|er|satz** M substitute for religion; **Re|li|gi|ons|frei|heit** F religious freedom, freedom of worship; **Re|li|gi|ons|frie|de(n)** M religious peace; **Re|li|gi|ons|füh|rer(in)** M(F) religious leader; **Re|li|gi|ons|ge|mein|schaft** F religious community; **Re|li|gi|ons|ge|schich|te** F history of religion; **Re|li|gi|ons|krieg** M religious war, war of religion; **Re|li|gi|ons|leh|re** F religious education or instruction; **Re|li|gi|ons|leh|rer(in)** M(F) teacher of religious education, RI or RE teacher; **re|li|gi|ons|los** ADJ not religious; (= bekenntnislos) nondenominational; **Re|li|gi|ons|stif|ter(in)** M(F) founder of a religion; **Re|li|gi|ons|streit** M religious controversy; **Re|li|gi|ons|stun|de** F religious education or instruction lesson, RI or RE lesson; **Re|li|gi|ons|un|ter|richt** M religious education or instruction; (Sch) religious education or instruction lesson, RE or RI lesson; **Re|li|gi|ons|wis|sen|schaft** F religious studies pl; vergleichende ~ comparative religion; **Re|li|gi|ons|zu|ge|hö|rig|keit** F religious affiliation, religion

re|li|gi|ös [reli'giø:s] **ADJ** religious **ADV** ~ **motiviert** religiously motivated or inspired; **sie werden ~ verfolgt** they are being persecuted because of their religion; ~ **erzogen werden** to have or receive a religious upbringing

Re|li|gi|o|si|tät [religiozi'tɛ:t] F -, no pl religiousness; **ein Mensch von tiefer ~** a deeply religious person

Re|likt [re'lɪkt] NT -(e)s, -e relic

Re|ling ['re:lɪŋ] F -, -s or -e (Naut) (deck) rail

Re|li|qui|ar [relikvi'a:ɐ] NT -s, -e reliquary

Re|li|quie [re'li:kviə] F -, -n relic

Re|li|qui|en|schrein M reliquary

Re|lo|cate-Funk|ti|on [ri:lo'ke:t-] F relocate function

Rem NT , **rem** [rɛm] NT -, - (= Einheit) rem

Re|make ['ri:me:k] NT -s, -s remake

Re|ma|nenz [rema'nɛnts] F -, no pl (Phys) remanence, residual magnetism

Rem|bours [rã'bu:ɐ] M -, - (Fin) reimbursement, payment

Rem|bours|ge|schäft [rã'bu:ɐ-] NT (Fin) documentary credit trading; (Einzelgeschäft) documentary credit transaction

Re|mig|rant [remi'grant] M -en, -en, **Re|mig|ran|tin** [-'grantɪn] F -, -nen returned emigrant; (= Heimkehrender) returning emigrant

re|mi|li|ta|ri|sie|ren [remilitari'zi:rən] ptp **remilitarisiert** VTI to remilitarize

Re|mi|nis|zenz [reminɪs'tsɛnts] F -, -en (geh) = Erinnerung) memory (an +acc of); (= Ähnlichkeit) similarity, resemblance (an +acc to); **ich habe aus seinem Vortrag ~en an Spengler herausgehört** I found his lecture in some ways reminiscent of Spengler

re|mis [rə'mi:] ADJ inv drawn; ~ **spielen** to draw; **die Partie ist ~** the game has ended in a draw or has been drawn; **die Vereine trennten sich ~** the clubs held each other to a draw

Re|mis [rə'mi:] NT - [rə'mi:(s)] - or -en [rə'mi:s, rə'mi:zn] a (Chess, Sport) draw; **gegen jdn ein ~ erzielen** to hold sb to a draw b (fig) stalemate, deadlock; **mit einem ~** in stalemate or deadlock

Re|mi|se [rə'mi:zə] F -, -n (old) shed, outbuilding

Re|mis|si|on [remi'sio:n] F -, -en (Med old: = Erlass) remission; (Comm) remittance

Re|mit|ten|de [remɪ'tɛndə] F -, -n (Comm) return

Re|mit|tent [remɪ'tɛnt] M -en, -en, **Re|mit|ten|tin** [-'tɛntɪn] F -, -nen (Fin) payee

re|mit|tie|ren [remɪ'ti:rən] ptp **remittiert** VT (Comm) Waren to return; Geld to remit VI (Med: = nachlassen) to remit (form)

Re|mi|dem|mi ['remi'dɛmi] NT -s, no pl (inf) (= Krach) row, rumpus (inf); (= Trubel) to-do (inf); ~ **machen** to make a row etc

Re|mou|la|de [remu'la:də] F -, -n, **Re|mou|la|den|so|ße** F (Cook) remoulade

Rem|pe|lei [rɛmpə'lai] F -, -en (inf) barging (inf), jostling, pushing and shoving; (im Sport) pushing

rem|peln ['rɛmpln] (inf) VT to barge (jdn into sb); (= anstoßen) to jostle, to elbow; (im Sport) to barge (jdn into sb) (inf); (= foulen) to push VI to barge (inf), to jostle; (Sport) to barge (inf); (= foulen) to push

REM-Pha|se ['rɛm-] F REM sleep

Rem|pler ['rɛmplɐ] M (inf: = Stoß) push, shove

Rem(p)|ter ['rɛm(p)tɐ] M -s, - (in Klöstern) refectory; (in Burgen) banquet(ing) hall

Re|mu|ne|ra|ti|on [remunera'tsio:n] F -, -en (Aus) (= Gratifikation) bonus; (= Vergütung) remuneration

Ren [rɛn, re:n] NT -s, -e or -s ['re:nə, rɛns] reindeer

Re|nais|sance [rəne'sã:s] F -, -en a (Hist) renaissance b (fig) revival, rebirth; (von Kunstfor-

men) renaissance, revival; **eine ~ erleben** to enjoy or experience a revival

Re|nais|sance- [rəne'sã:s] in cpds renaissance; **Re|nais|sance|mensch** M renaissance man no art

Re|na|tu|rie|rung [renatu'ri:roŋ] F -, -en die ~ **von Flüssen** the restoration of rivers to their natural state

Ren|dez|vous [rãde'vu:, 'rã:devu] NT -, - [-'vu:(s), -'vu:s] rendezvous (liter, hum), date (inf); (Space) rendezvous

Ren|dez|vous|ma|nö|ver [rãde'vu:-] NT (Space) rendezvous manoeuvre (Brit) or maneuver (US)

Ren|di|te [rɛn'di:tə] F -, -n (Fin) yield, return on capital

Re|ne|gat [rene'ga:t] M -en, -en, **Re|ne|ga|tin** [-'ga:tɪn] F -, -nen (Eccl, Pol) renegade

Re|nek|lo|de [re:nə'klo:də] F -, -n greengage

Re|net|te [re'nɛtə] F -, -n rennet

re|ni|tent [reni'tɛnt] ADJ refractory, defiant **ADV** defiantly

Re|ni|tenz [reni'tɛnts] F -, -en refractoriness, defiance

Ren|ke ['rɛŋkə] F -, -n whitefish

Renn- in cpds race; **Renn|bahn** F (race)track; **Renn|boot** NT powerboat

ren|nen ['rɛnən] pret **rannte** ['rantə], ptp **gerannt** [gə'rant] VI aux sein a (= schnell laufen) to run; (Sport) (Mensch, Tier) to run, to race; (Auto etc) to race; **um die Wette ~** to have a race; **(aufs Klo) ~** (inf) to run to the loo (Brit inf) or bathroom (US); **(mit offenen Augen) ins Verderben** or **Unglück ~** to rush into disaster (with one's eyes wide open)

b (inf: = hingehen) to run (off); **sie rennt wegen jeder Kleinigkeit zum Chef** she goes running (off) to the boss at the slightest little thing; **er rennt zu jedem Fußballspiel** he goes to every football match; **sie rennt jeden Tag in die Kirche** she goes running off to church every day

c (= stoßen) **an** or **gegen jdn/etw ~** to run or bump or bang into sb/sth; **er rannte mit dem Kopf gegen ...** he bumped or banged his head against ...; **mit dem Kopf durch** or **gegen die Wand ~** (fig) to bang one's head against a brick wall

VT a aux haben or sein (Sport) to run; **einen neuen Rekord über 100 Meter ~** to set a new record for the 100 metres (Brit) or meters (US)

b **jdn zu Boden** or **über den Haufen ~** to knock sb down or over; **sich** (dat) **(an etw) ein Loch in den Kopf ~** to crack one's head (against sth)

c (= stoßen) Messer etc to run

Ren|nen ['rɛnən] NT -s, - running; (Sport) (Vorgang) racing; (Veranstaltung) race; (fig) race (um for); **totes ~** dead heat; **gehst du zum ~?** (bei Pferderennen, Hunderennen etc) are you going to the races?, are you going racing?; (bei Autorennen etc) are you going to the racing?; **gut im ~ liegen** (lit, fig) to be well-placed; **das ~ ist gelaufen** (lit) the race is over; (fig) it's all over; **das ~ machen** (lit, fig) to win (the race); **aus dem ~ ausscheiden** (lit, fig) to drop out; **jdn aus dem ~ werfen** (lit) to put sb out of the race; (fig) to put sb out of the running; **das ~ aufgeben** (lit) to drop out (of the race); (fig auch) to throw in the towel

Ren|ner ['rɛnɐ] M -s, - (inf: = Verkaufsschlager) winner, world-beater (Brit); (Pferd auch) flier

Ren|ne|rei [rɛnə'rai] F -, -en (inf) (lit, fig: = das Herumrennen) running around; (= Hetze) mad chase (inf); **die ~, bis ich endlich meinen Pass gekriegt habe** all that running around until I finally got my passport; **nach meinem Umzug hatte ich tagelange ~en** after moving I was running around for days; **diese ~ zum Klo** this running to the loo (Brit inf) or bathroom (US)

Renn-: Renn|fah|rer(in) M(F) (= Radrennfahrer) racing cyclist; (= Motorradrennfahrer) racing motorcyclist; (= Autorennfahrer) racing driver;

Renn|jacht F racing yacht; **Renn|lei|ter(in)** M(F) race organizer; **Renn|lei|tung** F organization of a race meeting; (= die Rennleiter) race organizers pl; **Renn|lenk|stan|ge** F drop handlebars pl; **Renn|ma|schi|ne** F racer; **Renn|pferd** NT racehorse; **aus einem Ackergaul kann man kein ~ machen** (prov) you can't make a silk purse out of a sow's ear (Prov); **Renn|pis|te** F (race)track; **Renn|platz** M racecourse; **Renn|rad** NT racing bicycle or bike (inf); **Renn|ro|deln** NT -s, no pl bob (-sleigh) racing; **Renn|schlit|ten** M bob (-sleigh), bobsled; **Renn|schu|he** PL (Sport) spikes pl; **Renn|sport** M racing; **Renn|stall** M (Tiere, Zucht) stable; (Rennsport, Radrennen) team; **Renn|stre|cke** F (= Rennbahn) (race-) track; (= zu laufende Strecke) course, distance; **eine ~ von 100km** a 100 km course, a distance of 100km; **Renn|tag** M race day; **das Rennen erstreckt sich über drei ~e** the race is a three-day event; **Renn|ver|an|stal|tung** F races pl, race meeting; **Renn|wa|gen** M racing car; **Renn|wet|te** F bet (on a race); **Ergebnisse der ~n** betting results

Re|nom|mee [rɛnɔ'me:] NT -s, -s reputation, name

re|nom|mie|ren [rɛnɔ'mi:rən] ptp **renommiert** VI to show off, to swank (Brit inf); (= aufschneiden auch) to brag

Re|nom|mier-: Re|nom|mier|fi|gur F famous name; **Re|nom|mier|klub** M posh club (inf); **Re|nom|mier|schu|le** F (inf) posh or classy school (inf); **Re|nom|mier|stück** NT pride and joy, showpiece

re|nom|miert [rɛnɔ'mi:rt] ADJ (wegen for) renowned, famed, famous

re|no|vie|ren [reno'vi:rən] ptp **renoviert** VT to renovate; (= tapezieren etc) to redecorate, to do up (inf)

Re|no|vie|rung F -, -en renovation

ren|ta|bel [rɛn'ta:bl] ADJ profitable; **es ist nicht ~, das reparieren zu lassen** it is not worth (-while) having it repaired; **das ist eine rentable Sache** or **Angelegenheit** it will pay (off) **ADV** profitably; ~ **wirtschaften** (= gut einteilen) to spend one's money sensibly; (= mit Gewinn arbeiten) to make or show a profit; ~ **kalkulieren** (= gut einteilen) to budget sensibly; (= Gewinn einplanen) to think in terms of profit(s), to go for profit(s)

Ren|ta|bi|li|tät [rɛntabili'tɛ:t] F -, -en profitability

Ren|ta|bi|li|täts-: Ren|ta|bi|li|täts|ge|sichts|punk|te PL profitability point of view; **Ren|ta|bi|li|täts|gren|ze** F limit of profitability; **Ren|ta|bi|li|täts|prü|fung** F investigation into profitability; **Ren|ta|bi|li|täts|rech|nung** F profitability calculation; **Ren|ta|bi|li|täts|schwel|le** F breakeven point

Rent|amt NT (old Admin) bursary

Ren|te ['rɛntə] F -, -n (= Altersrente, Invalidenrente) pension; (aus Versicherung = Lebensrente) annuity; (aus Vermögen) income; (St Ex = Rentenpapier) fixed-interest security; **in** or **auf** (inf) ~ **gehen** to start drawing one's pension; **in** or **auf** (inf) ~ **sein** to be on a pension; **jdn in ~ schicken** (inf) to pension sb off (inf)

Ren|ten-: Ren|ten|al|ter NT retirement age; **Ren|ten|an|he|bung** F pension increase; **Ren|ten|an|pas|sung** F tying of pensions to the national average wage; **Ren|ten|an|pas|sungs|ge|setz** NT law tying pensions to the national average wage; **Ren|ten|an|spruch** M pension entitlement; **Ren|ten|ba|sis** F annuity basis; **Ren|ten|bei|trag** M pension contribution; **ständig steigende Rentenbeiträge** pl ever-increasing pension contributions pl, steady increase in pension contributions; **Ren|ten|be|mes|sungs|grund|la|ge** F basis of calculation of a pension/the pensions; **Ren|ten|be|rech|nung** F calculation of a pension/the pensions; **ren|ten|be|rech|tigt** ADJ entitled to a pension; Alter pensionable;

Ren|ten|be|scheid M notice of the amount of one's pension; **Ren|ten|be|steu|e|rung** F taxation of pensions; **Ren|ten|be|zü|ger(in)** M(F) (Sw) pensioner; **Ren|ten|ein|tritts|al|ter** NT retirement age; **Ren|ten|emp|fän|ger(in)** M(F) pensioner; **Ren|ten|er|hö|hung** F pension increase; **Ren|ten|fi|nan|zie|rung** F financing of pensions; **Ren|ten|fonds** M fixed-income fund; **Ren|ten|for|mel** F pension formula; **Ren|ten|kas|se** F pension fund (paying out pensions); (= Rentenversicherung) pension scheme (Brit), retirement plan (US); **Milliardenloch in der ~** pension fund announces or expects etc multibillion deficit; **Ren|ten|mark** F (Hist) rentenmark; **Ren|ten|markt** M market in fixed-interest securities; **Ren|ten|op|ti|ons|han|del** M bond option dealing; **Ren|ten|pa|pier** NT fixed-interest security; **ren|ten|pflich|tig** [-pflɪçtɪç] ADJ responsible for paying a pension; **Ren|ten|po|li|tik** F pension policy; **Ren|ten|re|form** F reform of pensions; **Ren|ten|si|che|rung** F safeguarding of pensions; **Ren|ten|sys|tem** NT pensionsystem; **Ren|ten|ver|si|che|rung** F pension scheme (Brit), retirement plan (US); **Ren|ten|ver|si|che|rungs|bei|trag** M pension scheme (Brit) or retirement plan (US) contribution

---

RENTENVERSICHERUNG

Many Germans are provided for in their old age by the state **Rentenversicherung**, to which all employees are required to contribute. The **Rentenversicherung** is funded by the contributions of both employees and employers and by a subsidy from the Federal Government. The amount of the pension depends on the period and level of contribution, with allowances made for time spent in education or bringing up children. In addition, many firms pay a **Betriebsrente** (occupational pension) to employees.

Ren|ten-: **Ren|ten|wer|te** PL fixed-interest securities pl; **Ren|ten|zahl|tag** M pension day
Ren|tier[1] ['rɛntiːɐ, 'rɛntiːɐ] NT (Zool) reindeer
Ren|tier[2] [rɛn'tieː] M -s, -s (old) man of private means, gentleman of leisure; (mit staatlicher Rente) pensioner
ren|tie|ren [rɛn'tiːrən] ptp **rentiert** VI to be worthwhile; (Wertpapier) to yield a return VR to be worthwhile; (Geschäft, Unternehmen etc auch, Maschine) to pay; **es hat sich doch rentiert, dass ich noch ein bisschen dageblieben bin** it was worth(while) staying on a bit; **das rentiert sich nicht** it's not worth it; **ein Auto rentiert sich für mich nicht** it's not worth my having a car
ren|tier|lich [rɛn'tiːrlɪç] ADJ profitable
Rent|ner ['rɛntnɐ] M -s, -, **Rent|ne|rin** [-ərɪn] F -, -nen pensioner; (= Altersrentner auch) senior citizen, old age pensioner (Brit)
re|ok|ku|pie|ren [rɛɔku'piːrən] ptp **reokkupiert** VT (Mil) to reoccupy
Re|or|ga|ni|sa|ti|on [rɛɔrganiza'tsioːn] F , **Re|or|ga|ni|sie|rung** F -, -en reorganization
re|or|ga|ni|sie|ren [rɛɔrgani'ziːrən] ptp **reorganisiert** VT to reorganize
Rep [rɛp] M -s, -s(e) usu pl (inf) abbr von **Republikaner** Republican, member of the right-wing German Republikaner party
re|pa|ra|bel [repa'raːbl] ADJ repairable
Re|pa|ra|ti|on [repara'tsioːn] F -, -en usu pl reparations pl; **~en leisten** or **zahlen** to pay or make reparations
Re|pa|ra|ti|ons-: **Re|pa|ra|ti|ons|aus|schuss** ▲ M reparations committee; **Re|pa|ra|ti|ons|zah|lun|gen** PL reparations pl
Re|pa|ra|tur [repara'tuːɐ] F -, -en repair; **~en am Auto** car repairs; **~en am Haus vornehmen** or **ausführen** to do some repairs on or to the house; **in ~** being repaired; **er übernimmt ~en von Schuhen** he does shoe repairs, he mends

shoes; **etw in ~ geben** to have sth repaired or mended; Auto, Fahrrad to have sth repaired
Re|pa|ra|tur-: **re|pa|ra|tur|an|fäl|lig** ADJ prone to break down; **Re|pa|ra|tur|ar|bei|ten** PL repairs pl, repair work no pl; **re|pa|ra|tur|be|dürf|tig** ADJ in need of repair; **Re|pa|ra|tur|kos|ten** PL repair costs pl; **Re|pa|ra|tur|set** NT repair kit; **Re|pa|ra|tur|werk|statt** F workshop; (= Autowerkstatt) garage, auto repair shop (US)
re|pa|rie|ren [repa'riːrən] ptp **repariert** VT to repair, to mend; Auto, Fahrrad to repair; **etw not|dürftig ~** to repair sth in a makeshift way
Re|par|tie|rung [repar'tiːrʊŋ] F -, -en (Fin) scaling down, allotment
re|pat|ri|ie|ren [repatri'iːrən] ptp **repatriiert** VT **a** (= wieder einbürgern) to renaturalize **b** (= heimschicken) to repatriate
Re|pat|ri|ie|rung F -, -en (= Einbürgerung) renaturalization; (= Zurückschicken) repatriation
Re|per|toire [reper'toaːɐ] NT -s, -s repertory, repertoire (auch fig)
Re|per|toire- [reper'toaːɐ-]: **Re|per|toire|stück** NT repertory or stock play; **Re|per|toire|the|a|ter** NT repertory theatre (Brit) or theater (US), rep (inf)
Re|pe|tent [repe'tɛnt] M -en, -en, **Re|pe|ten|tin** F -, -nen (Aus form) pupil who has to repeat a year
re|pe|tie|ren [repe'tiːrən] ptp **repetiert** VT **a** (old) Stoff, Vokabeln to revise **b** (= wiederholen) to repeat; (Aus form) Klasse to repeat, to take again; Jahr to repeat, to stay down for VI **a** (old) to do revision, to revise **b** (Aus form) to stay down, to repeat a class
Re|pe|tier|ge|wehr NT (old) repeating rifle
Re|pe|ti|ti|on [repeti'tsioːn] F -, -en **a** (old: von Stoff etc) revision **b** (= Wiederholung) repetition
Re|pe|ti|tor [repe'tiːtoːɐ] M -s, **Repetitoren** [-'toːrən], **Re|pe|ti|to|rin** [-'toːrɪn] F -, -nen (Univ) coach, tutor, crammer (esp Brit inf)
Re|pe|ti|to|ri|um [repeti'toːriʊm] NT -s, **Repetitorien** [-riən] (Buch) revision book; (Unterricht) revision or cramming (Brit inf) or tutorial (US) course
Rep|lik [re'pliːk] F -, -en **a** (Jur) replication; (fig geh) riposte, reply **b** (Art) replica
rep|li|zie|ren [repli'tsiːrən] ptp **repliziert** VT **a** auch vi (Jur) to reply; (fig geh) to riposte, to reply **b** (Art) to make a replica of
Re|port [re'pɔrt] M -(e)s, -e **a** report **b** (Fin) contango
Re|por|ta|ge [repɔr'taːʒə] F -, -n report
Re|por|ter [re'pɔrtɐ] M -s, -, **Re|por|te|rin** [-ərɪn] F -, -nen reporter; **Sport-/Wirtschaftsreporter** sports/economics correspondent
Re|port|ge|schäft NT (Fin) contango
Re|po|si|ti|on [repozi'tsioːn] F (Med) resetting
re|prä|sen|ta|bel [reprezɛn'taːbl] ADJ impressive, prestigious; Frau (highly) presentable
Re|prä|sen|tant [reprezɛn'tant] M -en, -en, **Re|prä|sen|tan|tin** [-'tantɪn] F -, -nen representative
Re|prä|sen|tan|ten|haus NT (US Pol) House of Representatives
Re|prä|sen|tanz [reprezɛn'tants] F -, -en **a** (Pol) representation **b** (= Geschäftsvertretung) branch
Re|prä|sen|ta|ti|on [reprezɛnta'tsioːn] F **a** (= Vertretung, Vorhandensein) representation; (von Firma) office **b** (= Darstellung) **der ~ dienen** to create a good image, to have good prestige value, to make the right impression; **die Diplomatenfrau fand die Pflichten der ~ sehr anstrengend** the diplomat's wife found her life of official functions very tiring; **die einzige Funktion des Monarchen ist heute die ~** the sole function of the monarch today is that of an official figurehead

re|prä|sen|ta|tiv [reprezɛnta'tiːf] ADJ **a** (= stellvertretend, typisch) representative (für of); **~e Umfrage** representative survey **b** Haus, Auto, Ausstattung prestigious; Erscheinung presentable; **die ~en Pflichten eines Botschafters** the social duties of an ambassador; **der ~e Aufwand des Königshauses/der Firma** the expenditure for maintaining the royal household's/company's image; **ein großes Konferenzzimmer für ~e Zwecke** a large conference room to provide a suitable setting for functions ADV **bauen** prestigiously; **sie sind sehr ~ eingerichtet** their decor is very impressive
Re|prä|sen|ta|tiv|um|fra|ge F representative survey
re|prä|sen|tie|ren [reprezɛn'tiːrən] ptp **repräsentiert** VT to represent VI to perform official duties
Re|pres|sa|lie [repre'saːliə] F -, -n reprisal; **~n anwenden** or **ergreifen** to take reprisals
Re|pres|si|on [reprɛ'sioːn] F -, -en repression
re|pres|si|ons|frei ADJ free of repression
re|pres|siv [reprɛ'siːf] ADJ repressive
Re|pri|se [re'priːzə] F -, -n **a** (Mus) recapitulation; (TV, Rad) repeat; (Film, Theat) rerun; (nach längerer Zeit) revival **b** (Mil) recapture
Re|pri|va|ti|sie|rung [reprivati'ziːrʊŋ] F denationalization
Re|pro ['reːpro] F -, -s (Typ sl) abbr von **Reproduktion**
Re|pro|duk|ti|on [reprodʊk'tsioːn] F reproduction; (Typ auch) repro (inf)
Re|pro|duk|ti|ons-: **Re|pro|duk|ti|ons|fak|tor** M (Econ) production factor; **Re|pro|duk|ti|ons|me|di|zin** F reproductive medicine; **Re|pro|duk|ti|ons|pro|zess** ▲ M reproductive process; **Re|pro|duk|ti|ons|tech|nik** F reproduction technology
re|pro|duk|tiv [reprodʊk'tiːf] ADJ reproductive ADV **er arbeitet rein ~** he merely reproduces what others have done
re|pro|du|zier|bar ADJ reproducible
re|pro|du|zier|bar|keit [reprodu'tsiːrbaːɐkait] F -, no pl reproducibility
re|pro|du|zie|ren [reprodu'tsiːrən] ptp **reproduziert** VT to reproduce
Re|pro-: **re|pro|fä|hig** ADJ camera-ready ADV **etw ~ ausgeben/vorlegen** to produce camera-ready copy; **Re|pro|film** M repro film; **Re|pro|fo|to|gra|fie** F repro photography; **Re|pro|gra|fie** ▲ [reprogra'fiː] F -, -en [-'fiːən] (Typ) reprography
Rep|til [rɛp'tiːl] NT -s, -ien [-liən] reptile
Rep|ti|li|en|fonds M slush fund
Re|pub|lik [repu'bliːk] F -, -en republic
Re|pub|li|ka|ner [republi'kaːnɐ] M -s, -, **Re|pub|li|ka|ne|rin** [-ərɪn] F -, -nen republican; (Pol) Republican

---

REPUBLIKANER

Founded in 1983, the **Republikaner** are a political party on the right of the electoral spectrum. The party stands for nationalist values and advocates populist economic policies, repressive law-and-order policies and social policies which exclude foreigners. Its increasingly aggressive nationalism and xenophobia have led to its being officially classified as a right-wing extremist party hostile to the constitution.

---

re|pub|li|ka|nisch [republi'kaːnɪʃ] ADJ republican
Re|pub|lik-: **Re|pub|lik|flucht** F (DDR) illegal crossing of the border; **re|pub|lik|flüch|tig** ADJ (DDR) illegally emigrated; **~ werden** to cross the border illegally; **Re|pub|lik|flücht|ling** M (DDR) illegal emigrant
Re|pun|ze [re'pʊntsə] F -, -n hallmark, platemark

Re|pu|ta|ti|on [reputa'tsi̯oːn] F -, *no pl* (*old*) (good) reputation

re|pu|tier|lich [repu'tiːɐlɪç] (*old*) ADJ reputable, of good *or* high renown (*old, liter*) ADV ~ **le-ben** to lead a respectable life

Re|qui|em ['reːkvi̯ɛm] NT **-s, -s** *or* (*Aus*) **Requien** [-vi̯ən] requiem

re|qui|rie|ren [rekvi'riːrən] *ptp* **requiriert** VT (*Mil*) to requisition, to commandeer

Re|qui|sit [rekvi'ziːt] NT **-s, -en** equipment *no pl*, requisite (*form*); **ein unerlässliches ~** an indispensable piece of equipment; **~en** (*Theat*) props, properties (*form*)

Re|qui|si|teur [rekvizi'tøːɐ] M **-s, -e, Re|qui-si|teu|rin** [-'tøːrɪn] F **-, -nen** (*Theat*) props *or* property manager

Re|qui|si|ti|on [rekvizi'tsi̯oːn] F **-, -en** requisition(ing), commandeering

Re|qui|si|ti|ons|schein M (*Mil*) requisition order

resch [rɛʃ] ADJ (*Aus*) (= *knusprig*) Brötchen *etc* crisp, crunchy, crispy; (*fig*: = *lebhaft*) Frau dynamic

Re|se|da [re'zeːda] F **-, Rese|den** [-dn], **Re|se|de** [re'zeːdə] F **-, -n** (*Gattung*) reseda; (= *Gartenrese-da*) mignonette

re|ser|vat [rezɛr'vaːt] ADJ (*Aus*) classified

Re|ser|vat [rezɛr'vaːt] NT **-(e)s, -e** a (= *Natur-schutzgebiet*) reserve; (*fig*) preserve b (*für India-ner, Ureinwohner etc*) reservation c (*old*: = *Son-derrecht*) right, discretionary power; **sich** (*dat*) **das ~ vorbehalten, etw zu machen** to reserve the right to do sth

Re|ser|va|ti|on [rezɛrva'tsi̯oːn] F **-, -en** a (*old*: = *Sonderrecht*) = **Reservat** a b (*für Indianer, Urein-wohner etc*) reservation

Re|ser|vat|recht [rezɛr'vaːt-] NT discretionary power

Re|ser|ve [re'zɛrvə] F **-, -n** a (= *Vorrat*) reserve(s *pl*) (*an* +*dat* of); (= *angespartes Geld*) savings *pl*; (= *Kapitalrücklagen*) reserve(s *pl*); (*Mil, Sport*) reserves *pl*; **offene ~n** (*Fin*) disclosed reserves; **(noch) etw/jdn in ~ haben** to have sth/sb (still) in reserve; **in ~ liegen** (*Mil*) to stay back in reserve b (= *Zurückhaltung*) reserve; (= *Bedenken*) reservation; **jdn aus der ~ locken** to break down sb's reserve, to bring sb out of his shell (*inf*); **aus der ~ heraustreten** to lose one's reserve, to come out of one's shell (*inf*)

Re|ser|ve-: Re|ser|ve|bank F *pl* **-bänke** (*Sport*) substitutes *or* reserves bench; **er saß nur auf der ~** he only sat on the bench; **Re|ser|ve-fonds** M reserve fund; **Re|ser|ve|ka|nis|ter** M spare can; **Re|ser|ve|mann** M *pl* **-männer** *or* **-leute** (*Sport*) reserve; **Re|ser|ve|of|fi|zier(in)** M(F) reserve officer; **Re|ser|ve|rad** NT spare (wheel); **Re|ser|ve|rei|fen** M spare (tyre (*Brit*) *or* tire (*US*)); **Re|ser|ve|spie|ler(in)** M(F) (*Sport*) reserve; **Re|ser|ve|tank** M reserve tank; **Re|ser|ve|trup|pen** PL reserves *pl*; **Re|ser|ve|übung** F (army) reserve training *no pl*

re|ser|vie|ren [rezɛr'viːrən] *ptp* **reserviert** VT to reserve

re|ser|viert [rezɛr'viːɐt] ADJ Platz, Mensch reserved

Re|ser|viert|heit F **-, no pl** reserve, reservedness

Re|ser|vie|rung ✪ 48.3 F **-, -en** reservation

Re|ser|vist [rezɛr'vɪst] M **-en, -en, Re|ser|vis-tin** [-'vɪstɪn] F **-, -nen** reservist

Re|ser|voir [rezɛr'voaːɐ] NT **-s, -e** reservoir; (*fig auch*) pool

Re|set-Tas|te [riː'sɛt-] F (*Comput*) reset key

re|si|dent [rezi'dɛnt] ADJ (*Comput*) resident

Re|si|dent [rezi'dɛnt] M **-en, -en, Re|si|den|tin** [-'dɛntɪn] M **-, -nen** envoy, resident (*rare*)

Re|si|denz [rezi'dɛnts] F **-, -en** a (= *Wohnung*) residence, residency b (= *Hauptstadt*) royal seat *or* capital

Re|si|denz|stadt F royal seat *or* capital

re|si|die|ren [rezi'diːrən] *ptp* **residiert** VI to reside

re|si|du|al [rezi'dua̯ːl] ADJ (*geh*) residual

Re|si|du|um [re'ziːdu̯ʊm] NT **-s, Residuen** [-du̯ən] (*geh*) residue, residuum (*form*)

Re|sig|na|ti|on [rezɪgna'tsi̯oːn] F **-, no pl** (*geh*) resignation; (**über etw** *acc*) **in ~ verfallen, sich der ~ überlassen** to become resigned (to sth); **in der Partei macht sich ~ breit** a feeling of resignation is spreading through the party

re|sig|na|tiv [rezɪgna'tiːf] ADJ resigned

re|sig|nie|ren [rezɪg'niːrən] *ptp* **resigniert** VI to give up; **resigniert** resigned; **... sagte er ~d** *or* **resigniert** ... he said with resignation *or* in a resigned way

re|sis|tent [rezɪs'tɛnt] ADJ (*auch Med*) resistant (*gegen* to)

Re|sis|tenz [rezɪs'tɛnts] F **-, -en** (*auch Med*) resistance (*gegen* to)

re|sis|tie|ren [rezɪs'tiːrən] *ptp* **resistiert** VI (*Med*) to resist

re|so|lut [rezo'luːt] ADJ resolute, determined ADV resolutely, determinedly

Re|so|lut|heit [rezo'luːthait] F **-, -en** resolute-ness; (= *Entschlossenheit*) determination

Re|so|lu|ti|on [rezolu'tsi̯oːn] F **-, -en** (*Pol*) (= *Beschluss*) resolution; (= *Bittschrift*) petition

Re|so|nanz [rezo'nants] F **-, -en** a (*Mus, Phys*) resonance b (*fig*) response (*auf* +*acc* to); **keine/wenig/große ~ finden** to meet with *or* get no/little/a good response; **(bei jdm) auf positi-ve ~ stoßen** to meet with *or* get a positive response (from sb)

Re|so|nanz-: Re|so|nanz|bo|den M sound-ing board; **Re|so|nanz|kas|ten** M soundbox

Re|so|pal® [rezo'paːl] NT **-s, no pl** Formica®

re|sor|bie|ren [rezɔr'biːrən] *ptp* **resorbiert** VT to absorb

Re|sorp|ti|on [rezɔrp'tsi̯oːn] F **-, -en** absorption

re|so|zia|li|sie|ren [rezotsi̯ali'ziːrən] *ptp* **reso-zialisiert** VT to rehabilitate

Re|so|zia|li|sie|rung F rehabilitation

resp. *abbr von* **respektive**

Re|spekt [re'spɛkt, res'pɛkt] ✪ 40.4 M **-s, no pl** (= *Achtung*) respect; (= *Angst*) fear; **jdm ~ einflö-ßen** (*Achtung*) to command *or* inspire respect from sb; (*Angst*) to put the fear of God into sb; **~ einflößend** authoritative; **ein wenig ~ einflö-ßender Mensch** a person who commands *or* inspires little respect; **vor jdm den ~ verlieren** to lose one's respect for sb; **bei allem ~ (vor jdm/etw)** with all due respect (to sb/for sth); **vor jdm/etw ~ haben** (*Achtung*) to respect sb/sth, to have respect for sb/sth; (*Angst*) to be afraid of sb/sth; **~ heischend** demanding respect; **jdn/etw mit ~ behandeln** to treat sb/sth with respect; **jdm mit ~ begegnen** to behave respect-fully toward(s) sb, to treat sb with respect; **sich** (*dat*) **~ verschaffen** to make oneself respected; **allen ~!** well done!

res|pek|ta|bel [rɛspɛk'taːbl̩, res-] ADJ respecta-ble

res|pekt-: res|pekt|ein|flö|ßend △ ADJ → **Respekt; res|pekt|hei|schend** △ ADJ → **Res-pekt**

res|pek|tie|ren [rɛspɛk'tiːrən, res-] *ptp* **respek-tiert** VT to respect; Wechsel to honour (*Brit*), to honor (*US*)

res|pek|ti|ve [rɛspɛk'tiːvə, res-] ADV (*geh, Comm*) a (= *jeweils*) and ... respectively; **Fritz und Franz verdienen 100 ~ 150 Euro pro Tag** Fritz and Franz earn 100 and 150 euros per day respectively b (= *anders ausgedrückt*) or rather; (= *genauer gesagt*) (or) more precisely c (= *oder*) or

Re|spekt-: res|pekt|los ADJ disrespectful ADV disrespectfully; **Res|pekt|lo|sig|keit** F **-, -en** a (*no pl: Verhalten*) disrespect(fulness), lack of respect b (*Bemerkung*) disrespectful remark *or* comment

Res|pekts|per|son F person to be respected; (= *Beamter etc*) person in authority

Re|spekt-: Re|spekt|ta|ge PL (*Comm*) days *pl* of grace; **res|pekt|voll** ADJ respectful ADV respectfully; **res|pekt|wid|rig** ADJ disrespect-ful, irreverent

Re|spi|ra|ti|on [respira'tsi̯oːn, res-] F **-, no pl** (*form*) respiration

Re|spi|ra|ti|ons|ap|pa|rat M , **Re|spi|ra|tor** [respi'raːtoːɐ, res-] M **-s, Respiratoren** [-'toːrən] respirator

re|spi|rie|ren [respi'riːrən, res-] *ptp* **respiriert** VI (*form*) to respire

Res|sen|ti|ment [resãti'mãː, rə-] NT **-s, -s** resentment *no pl*, feeling of resentment (*gegen* against)

Res|sort [re'soːɐ] NT **-s, -s** department; **in das ~ von jdm fallen** to be sb's/sth's department; **das ~ Finanzen** *etc* the finance *etc* department

Res|sort-: Res|sort|lei|ter(in) M(F) depart-ment head, head of department; **Res|sort|mi-nis|ter(in)** M(F) department minister; **der ~ für die Polizei** the minister responsible for the police

Res|sour|ce [re'sʊrsə] F **-, -n** (*auch Comput*) re-source; **erneuerbare ~n** renewable resources

Rest [rest] M **-(e)s, -e** a rest; **die ~ einer Kir-che/Stadt/Kultur** the remains *or* remnants of a church/city/civilization; **der ~ der Welt** the rest of the world; **90% sind schon fertig, den ~ ma-che ich** 90% is done, I'll do the rest *or* remain-der; **am Anfang hatte ich 25 Schüler, die 3 hier sind noch der ~ (davon)** at the beginning I had 25 pupils, these 3 are what's left *or* all that is left; **der letzte ~** the last bit; **der letzte ~ vom Schützenfest** (*hum*) the last little bit; **bis auf ei-nen ~** except for a little bit *or* a small amount; **dieser kleine ~** this little bit that's left (over); **der kümmerliche** *or* **klägliche** *or* **schäbige ~** (*von meinem Geld*) all that's left, the miserable re-mains; (*vom Essen*) the sad remnants; **der ~ ist Schweigen** the rest is silence; **der ~ ist für Sie** (*beim Bezahlen*) keep the change; **jdm/einer Sa-che den ~ geben** (*inf*) to finish sb/sth off; **sich** (*dat*) **den ~ holen** (*inf*) to make oneself really ill (*Brit*) *or* sick b **Reste** PL (= *Essensreste*) leftovers *pl* c (= *Stoffrest*) remnant d (*Math*) remainder; **2 ~ 3** 2 and 3 over, 2 remainder 3

Rest- *in cpds* remaining; **Rest|ab|schnitt** M remaining part; **Rest|al|ko|hol** M , *no pl* re-sidual alcohol

Res|tant¹ [res'tant] M **-en, -en** (*Comm*: = *Laden-hüter*) slow *or* slow-moving line

Res|tant² [res'tant] M **-en, -en, Res|tan|tin** [-'tantɪn] F **-, -nen** (*Comm*: = *Schuldner*) defaulter

Rest|auf|la|ge F remainder(ed) stock, remain-ders *pl*

Res|tau|rant [resto'rãː] NT **-s, -s** restaurant

Res|tau|ra|teur [restora'tøːɐ] M **-s, -e, Res|-tau|ra|teu|rin** [-'tøːrɪn] F **-, -nen** (*old*) restaura-teur

Res|tau|ra|ti|on¹ [restora'tsi̯oːn, res-] F **-, -en** restoration; **die ~** (*Hist*) the Restoration

Res|tau|ra|ti|on² [restora'tsi̯oːn] F **-, -en** (*old, Aus*) inn, tavern (*old*); (*im Bahnhof*) refreshment rooms *pl*

Res|tau|ra|ti|ons-: Res|tau|ra|ti|ons|be-trieb M catering business; **Res|tau|ra|ti|ons-zeit** F period of ultraconservatism; **die ~** (*Hist*) the Restoration

Res|tau|ra|tor [restau'raːtoːɐ, res-] M **-s, Restau-ratoren** [-'toːrən], **Res|tau|ra|to|rin** [-'toːrɪn] F **-, -nen** restorer

res|tau|rie|ren [restau'riːrən, res-] *ptp* **restauriert** VT to restore VR (*old*) to partake of some refreshment (*old form*)

Res|tau|rie|rung F **-, -en** restoration

Rest-: Rest|be|stand M remaining stock; (*fig*) remnant; **wir haben noch einen kleinen ~ an Bi-**

kinis we still have a few bikinis left; **Rest|be|trag** M balance

Res|te-: Res|te|es|sen NT leftovers pl; **Res|te|ver|kauf** M remnants sale

Rest|for|de|rung F residual claim

re|sti|tu|ie|ren [restitu'i:rən, rɛs-] ptp **restituiert** VT (form) to make restitution of (form)

Re|sti|tu|ti|on [restitu'tsio:n, rɛs-] F -, -en (form) restitution (form)

Re|sti|tu|ti|ons-: Re|sti|tu|ti|ons|edikt NT Edict of Restitution; **Re|sti|tu|ti|ons|kla|ge** F action for a retrial

Rest|lauf|zeit F (Fin) remaining term

rest|lich ['rɛstlɪç] ADJ remaining, rest of the ...; **die ~e Welt** the rest of the world; **die ~en** the rest

Rest|lie|fe|rung F (Comm) rest of the/a delivery

rest|los ADJ complete, total ADV completely, totally; **ich war ~ begeistert** I was completely bowled over (inf)

Rest-: Rest|men|ge F residue; **Rest|pos|ten** M a (Comm) remaining stock; **ein ~** remaining stock; **ein großer ~ Bücher/Zucker** a lot of books/sugar left in stock; **„Restposten"** "reduced to clear" b (Fin: in Bilanz) residual item

Rest|rik|ti|on [rɛstrɪk'tsio:n, rɛs-] F -, -en (form) restriction

Rest|rik|ti|ons|maß|nah|me F restriction, restrictive measure

rest|rik|tiv [rɛstrɪk'ti:f, rɛs-] (geh) ADJ restrictive ADV restrictively; **die Werbebeschränkungen wurden ~ gehandhabt** advertising restrictions were rigorously applied

Rest-: Rest|ri|si|ko NT residual risk; **Rest|sum|me** F balance, amount remaining; **Rest|ur|laub** M unused holiday (esp Brit) or vacation (US), remaining holiday (esp Brit) or vacation (US, form) (entitlement); **ich habe noch (10 Tage) ~** I've still got (ten days') holiday owing or vacation owed (US) to me; **Rest|wär|me** F residual heat; **Rest|wert** M residual; **Rest|zah|lung** F final payment, payment of the balance

Re|sul|tan|te [rezʊl'tantə] F -, -n (Math) resultant

Re|sul|tat [rezʊl'ta:t] NT -(e)s, -e result; (von Prüfung auch) results pl; **zu einem ~ kommen** to come to or arrive at a conclusion; **gute ~e erzielen** to achieve good results

re|sul|tat|los ADJ fruitless, without result ADV **das Spiel verlief ~** the game was undecided or ended in a draw

re|sul|tie|ren [rezʊl'ti:rən] ptp **resultiert** VI (geh) to result (in +dat in); (Sw: sich ergeben) to result; **aus etw ~** to be the result of sth, to result from sth; **aus dem Gesagten resultiert, dass ...** from what was said one must conclude that ...; **die daraus ~den ...** the resulting ...; **daraus resultiert ...** the result of (this) is ...

Re|sul|tie|ren|de [rezʊl'ti:rəndə] F decl as adj (Math) resultant

Re|sü|mee [rezy'me:] NT -s, -s, (Aus, Sw) **Re|su|mé** [rezy'me:] NT -s, -s (geh) summary, résumé; (am Ende einer Rede auch) recapitulation

re|sü|mie|ren [rezy'mi:rən] ptp **resümiert** VTI (geh) to summarize, to sum up; (am Ende einer Rede auch) to recapitulate

Re|tar|da|ti|on [retarda'tsio:n] F -, -en retardation

re|tar|die|ren [retar'di:rən] ptp **retardiert** VT to retard; **ein ~des Moment** a delaying factor or element; **retardiert** (= geistig zurückgeblieben) retarded

re|ti|rie|ren [reti'ri:rən] ptp **retiriert** VI aux sein (old Mil, hum) to beat a retreat

Re|tor|te [re'tɔrtə] F -, -n (Chem) retort; **aus der ~** (fig inf) synthetic; **Baby aus der ~** test-tube baby

Re|tor|ten|ba|by NT test-tube baby

Re|tor|ten|stadt F (pej inf) ≈ new town (Brit), purpose-built town

re|tour [re'tu:ɐ] ADV (Aus, dial) back

Re|tour|bil|lett [re'tu:ɐbɪl'jet] NT (Sw) return (ticket) (esp Brit), round-trip ticket (US)

Re|tou|re [re'tu:rə] F -, -n usu pl return

Re|tour- [re'tu:ɐ-: **Re|tour|gang** M pl -gänge (Aus) reverse (gear); **Re|tour|kar|te** F (Aus) return (ticket) (esp Brit), round-trip ticket (US); **Re|tour|kut|sche** F (inf) (Worte) retort; (Handlung) retribution

re|tour|nie|ren [retʊr'ni:rən] ptp **retourniert** VT (old, Aus) to return

Re|tour|spiel [re'tu:ɐ-] NT (Aus) return (match)

ret|ro|spek|tiv [retrospɛk'ti:f] (liter) ADJ retrospective ADV in retrospect

Ret|ro|spek|ti|ve [retrospɛk'ti:və] F -, -n (liter) retrospective

Ret|ro|vi|rus [retro'vi:rʊs] NT OR M retrovirus

ret|ten ['rɛtn] VT to save; (aus Gefahr auch, = befreien) to rescue; (Comput) Datei to recover; **jdn/etw vor jdm/etw ~** to save sb/sth from sb/sth; **jdm das Leben ~** to save sb's life; **ein ~der Gedanke** a bright idea that saved the situation or his/our etc bacon (inf); **der Patient/die alte Kirche ist noch/nicht mehr zu ~** the patient/the old church can still be saved or is not yet past saving/is past saving; **wir sollten ~, was noch zu ~ ist** we should salvage what we can; **er hat wieder geheiratet? er ist nicht mehr zu ~** he got married again? he's beyond redemption or past saving or past helping; **bist du noch zu ~?** (inf) are you out of your mind?, have you gone completely round the bend? (Brit inf)

VR to escape; **sich auf/unter etw** (acc)/**aus etw ~** to escape onto/under/from sth; **sich vor jdm/etw ~** to escape (from) sb/sth; **sich durch die Flucht ~** to escape; **sich vor etw nicht mehr ~ können** or **zu ~ wissen** (fig) to be swamped with sth; **rette sich, wer kann!** (it's) every man for himself!

Ret|ter ['rɛtɐ] M -s, -, **Ret|te|rin** F -, -nen (aus Notlage) rescuer, deliverer (liter); **der ~** (Rel) the Saviour (Brit) or Savior (US); **ach mein ~!** oh my hero!; **der ~ des Unternehmens/von 1000 Arbeitsplätzen** the saviour (Brit) or savior (US) of the business/of 1000 jobs → **Not**

Ret|tich ['rɛtɪç] M -s, -e radish

Ret|tung ['rɛtʊŋ] F -, -en (aus Notlage) rescue, deliverance (liter); (= Erhaltung) saving; (von Waren) recovery; (Rel) salvation, deliverance; **die ~ und Erhaltung historischer Denkmäler** the saving and preservation of historical monuments; **Gesellschaft zur ~ Schiffbrüchiger** Lifeboat Service; **die ~ kam in letzter Minute** the situation was saved at the last minute; (für Schiffbrüchige etc) help came in the nick of time; **auf ~ hoffen** to hope to be saved, to hope for deliverance (liter); **an seine (eigene) ~ denken** to worry about one's own safety; **für den Patienten/unsere Wirtschaft gibt es keine ~ mehr** the patient/our economy is beyond saving, our economy is beyond salvation; **das war meine ~** that saved me, that was my salvation; **es war meine ~, dass ...** I was saved by the fact that ...; **das war meine letzte ~** that was my last hope; (= hat mich gerettet) that was my salvation, that saved me

Ret|tungs-: Ret|tungs|ak|ti|on F rescue operation; **Ret|tungs|an|ker** M sheet anchor; (fig) anchor; **Ret|tungs|arzt** M , **Ret|tungs|ärz|tin** F emergency doctor; **Ret|tungs|bo|je** F life belt; (= Hosenboje) breeches buoy; **Ret|tungs|boot** NT lifeboat; **Ret|tungs|dienst** M rescue service; **Ret|tungs|fahr|zeug** NT rescue vehicle; **Ret|tungs|floß** NT life raft; **Ret|tungs|flug|wacht** F air rescue service; **Ret|tungs|flug|zeug** NT rescue aircraft; **Ret|tungs|ge|rät** NT rescue equipment no pl or apparatus no pl; **Ret|tungs|gür|tel** M life belt; **Ret|tungs|hub|schrau|ber** M rescue helicopter; **Ret|tungs|in|sel** F inflatable life raft; **Ret|tungs|kom|man|do** NT rescue squad; **Ret|tungs|lei|ne** F lifeline; **Ret|tungs|lei|ter** F rescue ladder; **ret|tungs|los** ADJ beyond saving; Lage hopeless, irredeemable; Verlust irrecoverable ADV verloren hopelessly, irretrievably; **er ist ihr ~ verfallen** he is completely under her spell; **Ret|tungs|mann|schaft** F rescue team or party; **Ret|tungs|me|dail|le** F lifesaving medal; **Ret|tungs|ring** M life buoy, life belt; (hum: = Bauch) spare tyre (Brit hum), spare tire (US hum); **Ret|tungs|sa|ni|tä|ter(in)** M(F) paramedic; **Ret|tungs|schuss** ▲ M finaler ~ fatal shot (fired by the police); **Ret|tungs|schwim|men** NT lifesaving; **Ret|tungs|schwim|mer(in)** M(F) lifesaver; (an Strand, Pool) lifeguard; **Ret|tungs|sta|ti|on** F , **Ret|tungs|stel|le** F rescue centre (Brit) or center (US); (für erste Hilfe) first-aid post; (mit Rettungsbooten) lifeboat or coastguard station; **Ret|tungs|trupp** M rescue squad; **Ret|tungs|ver|such** M rescue attempt or bid; (von Arzt etc) attempt to save sb; **Ret|tungs|wa|che** F rescue station; (kleiner) rescue post; **Ret|tungs|wa|gen** M ambulance; **Ret|tungs|we|sen** NT rescue services pl

Re|tu|sche [re'tʊʃə] F -, -n (Phot) retouching

Re|tu|scheur [retu'ʃø:ɐ] M -s, -e, **Re|tu|scheu|rin** [-'ʃø:rɪn] F -, -nen retoucher

re|tu|schie|ren [retu'ʃi:rən] ptp **retuschiert** VT (Phot) to retouch, to touch up (inf, auch fig)

Reue ['rɔyə] F -, no pl remorse (über +acc at, about), repentance (auch Rel) (über +acc of), rue (old, liter) (über +acc at, of); (= Bedauern) regret (über +acc at, about)

reue|los ADJ unrepentant

reu|en ['rɔyən] VT (liter) etw reut jdn sb regrets or rues (liter, old) sth; **es reut mich, dass ich das getan habe** I regret or rue (liter, old) having done that

reue|voll ADJ, ADV = reumütig

reu|ig ['rɔyɪç] ADJ, ADV (liter) = reumütig

reu|mü|tig ['rɔymy:tɪç] ADJ (= voller Reue) remorseful, repentant; Sünder contrite, penitent; (= betreten, zerknirscht) rueful ADV gestehen, bekennen full of remorse; **du wirst bald ~ zu mir zurückkommen** you'll soon come back to me feeling sorry

Reu|se ['rɔyzə] F -, -n fish trap

re|üs|sie|ren [rely'si:rən] ptp **reüssiert** VI (old) to succeed, to be successful (bei, mit with)

Re|van|che [re'vã:ʃ(ə)] F -, -n a (Sport) revenge (für for); (= Revanchepartie) return match (Brit), rematch (US); **du musst ihm ~ geben!** you'll have to let him have or get his revenge, you'll have to give him a return match (Brit) or a rematch (US); (für etw) ~ **nehmen** to have or get one's revenge (for sth) b no pl (= Rache) revenge, vengeance

Re|van|che- [re'vã:ʃə-]: **Re|van|che|krieg** M war of revenge; **re|van|che|lüs|tern** ADJ revanchist; **Re|van|che|par|tie** F (Sport) return match (Brit), rematch (US); **Re|van|che|po|li|tik** F (pej) revanchist policy; **Re|van|che|spiel** NT (Sport) return match (Brit), rematch (US)

re|van|chie|ren [revã'ʃi:rən] ptp **revanchiert** VR a (= sich rächen) to get or have one's revenge, to get one's own back (Brit) (bei jdm für etw on sb for sth); (Sport) to get or have one's revenge b (= sich erkenntlich zeigen) to reciprocate; **ich werde mich bei Gelegenheit mal ~** I'll return the compliment some time; (für Hilfe) I'll do the same for you one day, I'll return the favour (Brit) or favor (US) one day; **das Problem bei Geschenken ist, dass man meint, sich ~ zu müssen** the problem with getting presents is that one always feels one has to give something in return; **sich bei jdm für eine Einladung/seine Gastfreundschaft ~** to return sb's invitation/hospitality

Re|van|chis|mus [revã'ʃɪsmʊs] M -, *no pl* revanchism

Re|van|chist [revã'ʃɪst] M **-en, -en**, **Re|van|chis|tin** [-'ʃɪstɪn] F **-, -nen** revanchist

re|van|chis|tisch [revã'ʃɪstɪʃ] ADJ revanchist

Re|ve|renz [reve'rɛnts] F **-, -en** (*old*) (= *Hochachtung*) reverence; (= *Geste der Hochachtung*) gesture of respect; (= *Verbeugung*) obeisance, reverence (*old*); **jdm seine ~ erweisen** to show one's reverence or respect for sb; **seine ~en machen** to make one's obeisances (*old*), to bow

Re|vers¹ [re'vɛːɐ, re'vɛːɐ, rə'-] NT OR (AUS) M **-,** [-ɐ(s), -əs] (*an Kleidung*) lapel, revere, revers (*esp US*)

Re|vers² [re'vɛrs] M **-es, -e** [-zə] **a** (= *Rückseite*) reverse **b** (= *Erklärung*) declaration

re|ver|si|bel [revɛr'ziːbl] ADJ reversible

Re|ver|si|on [revɛr'zioːn] F **-, -en** (*Biol, Psych*) reversion

re|vi|die|ren [revi'diːrən] *ptp* **revidiert** VT to revise; (*Comm*) to audit, to check; **die Wachstumsprognosen wurden nach oben/unten revidiert** the growth forecasts were revised upwards/downwards

Re|vier [re'viːɐ] NT **-s, -e** **a** (= *Polizeidienststelle*) (police) station, station house (*US*); (= *Dienstbereich*) beat, district, precinct (*US*), patch (*inf*); (*von Prostituierter*) beat, patch (*inf*) **b** (*Zool*: = *Gebiet*) territory; **die Küche ist mein ~** the kitchen is my territory or preserve **c** (*Hunt*: = *Jagdrevier*) hunting ground, shoot **d** (*old*: = *Gebiet, Gegend*) district, area **e** (*Mil*: = *Krankenrevier*) sickbay; **auf dem or im ~ liegen** to be in the sickbay **f** (*Min*: = *Kohlenrevier*) (coal) mines *pl*, coalfields *pl*; **im ~ an der Ruhr** in the mines of the Ruhr; **das ~** (= *Ruhrgebiet*) the Ruhr; (= *Saarland*) the Saar

Re|vier-: Re|vier|förs|ter(in) M(F) forester, forest ranger (*US*); **Re|vier|förs|te|rei** F forester's lodge; **re|vier|krank** ADJ (*Mil*) hospitalized, in the sickbay; **Re|vier|wa|che** F duty room; **Re|vier|wacht|meis|ter(in)** M(F) station sergeant

Re|vi|re|ment [revirə'mãː, revɪr'mãː] NT **-s, -s** (*Pol*) reshuffle

Re|vi|si|on [revi'zioːn] F **-, -en** **a** (*von Meinung, Politik etc*) revision; **sich in ~ befinden** to be undergoing revision **b** (*Comm*: = *Prüfung*) audit **c** (*Typ*: = *letzte Überprüfung*) final (proof)read; **~ lesen** to do the final (proof)read **d** (*Jur*: = *Urteilsanfechtung*) appeal (*an +acc* to); **in die ~ gehen, ~ einlegen** to lodge an appeal, to appeal

Re|vi|si|o|nis|mus [revizio'nɪsmʊs] M **-,** *no pl* (*Pol*) revisionism

Re|vi|si|o|nist [revizio'nɪst] M **-en, -en**, **Re|vi|si|o|nis|tin** [-'nɪstɪn] F **-, -nen** (*Pol*) revisionist

re|vi|si|o|nis|tisch [revizio'nɪstɪʃ] ADJ (*Pol*) revisionist

Re|vi|si|ons-: Re|vi|si|ons|an|trag M (*Jur*) notice of appeal; **Re|vi|si|ons|bo|gen** M page proof; **Re|vi|si|ons|frist** F time for appeal; **Re|vi|si|ons|ge|richt** NT court of appeal, appeal court; **Re|vi|si|ons|ver|fah|ren** NT (*Jur*) appeal proceedings *pl*; **Re|vi|si|ons|ver|hand|lung** F appeal hearing

Re|vi|sor [re'viːzoːɐ] M **-s, Revisoren** [-'zoːrən], **Re|vi|so|rin** [-'zoːrɪn] F **-, -nen** (*Comm*) auditor; (*Typ*) proofreader

Re|vol|te [re'vɔltə] F **-, -n** revolt

re|vol|tie|ren [revɔl'tiːrən] *ptp* **revoltiert** VI to revolt, to rebel (*gegen* against); (*fig: Magen*) to rebel

Re|vo|lu|ti|on [revolu'tsioːn] F **-, -en** (*lit, fig*) revolution; **eine ~ der Moral** a moral revolution, a revolution in morals; **die sanfte/friedliche ~** the velvet/peaceful revolution

re|vo|lu|ti|o|när [revolutsio'nɛːɐ] ADJ (*lit, fig*) revolutionary **ADV** **etw als ~ betrachten** to view sth as revolutionary; **etw als ~ bezeichnen** to call sth revolutionary

Re|vo|lu|ti|o|när [revolutsio'nɛːɐ] M **-s, -e**, **Re|vo|lu|ti|o|nä|rin** [-'nɛːrɪn] F **-, -nen** revolutionary

re|vo|lu|ti|o|nie|ren [revolutsio'niːrən] *ptp* **revolutioniert** VT to revolutionize

Re|vo|lu|ti|ons- *in cpds* revolutionary; **Re|vo|lu|ti|ons|füh|rer(in)** M(F) revolutionary leader; **Re|vo|lu|ti|ons|re|gie|rung** F revolutionary government

Re|vo|luz|zer [revo'lʊtsɐ] M **-s, -**, **Re|vo|luz|ze|rin** [-ərɪn] F **-, -nen** (*pej*) would-be revolutionary

Re|vol|ver [re'vɔlvɐ] M **-s, -** revolver, gun

Re|vol|ver-: Re|vol|ver|blatt NT (*pej*) scandal sheet; **Re|vol|ver|griff** M butt (of a/the revolver); **Re|vol|ver|held(in)** M(F) (*pej*) gunslinger; **Re|vol|ver|lauf** M barrel (of a/the revolver); **Re|vol|ver|mün|dung** F mouth (of a/the revolver); **plötzlich starrte er in eine ~** he suddenly found himself staring down the barrel of a revolver; **Re|vol|ver|pres|se** F (*pej*) gutter press

Re|vue [rə'vyː] F **-, -n** [-'vyːən] **a** (*Theat*) revue **b** (*rare*: = *Zeitschrift*) review **c** (*old, Mil*) review; **etw ~ passieren lassen** (*fig*) to let sth parade before one, to pass sth in review

Re|vue|tän|zer(in) [rə'vyː-] M(F) chorus boy/girl

Reyk|ja|vik ['raikjaviːk] NT **-s** Reykjavik

Re|zen|sent [retsɛn'zɛnt] M **-en, -en**, **Re|zen|sen|tin** [-'zɛntɪn] F **-, -nen** reviewer

re|zen|sie|ren [retsɛn'ziːrən] *ptp* **rezensiert** VT to review

Re|zen|si|on [retsɛn'zioːn] F **-, -en** review, write-up (*inf*)

Re|zen|si|ons|exem|plar NT review copy

re|zent [re'tsɛnt] ADJ **a** (*Biol*) living; (*Ethnologie*) *Kulturen* surviving **b** (*dial*: = *säuerlich, pikant*) tart, sour **c** (*geh*: = *neuerlich*) recent

Re|zept [re'tsɛpt] NT **-(e)s, -e** **a** (*Med*) prescription; (*fig*: = *Heilmittel*) cure, remedy (*für, gegen* for); **auf ~** on prescription **b** (*Cook, fig*: = *Anleitung*) recipe (*zu* for)

Re|zept-: Re|zept|block M *pl* **-blöcke** or **-blocks** prescription pad; **re|zept|frei** ADJ available without prescription **ADV** over the counter, without a prescription; **Re|zept|ge|bühr** F prescription charge

Re|zep|ti|on [retsɛp'tsioːn] F **-, -en** **a** (*liter. von Gedankengut, Kultur*) adoption; (*von Buch, Musikstück*) reception **b** (*von Hotel*: = *Empfang*) reception

re|zep|tiv [retsɛp'tiːf] ADJ receptive; **der Kritiker als ~er Mensch** the critic as one who assimilates or receives ideas

Re|zep|tor [re'tsɛptoːɐ] M **-s, Rezeptoren** (*Biol, Physiol*) receptor

Re|zept-: Re|zept|pflicht F prescription requirement; **der ~ unterliegen** or **unterstehen** to be available only on prescription; **dafür besteht jetzt keine ~ mehr** you don't need a prescription for it any more; **re|zept|pflich|tig** [-pflɪçtɪç] ADJ available only on prescription, ethical (*spec*); **etw ~ machen** to put sth on prescription

Re|zep|tur [retsɛp'tuːɐ] F **-, -en** (*form*) dispensing

Re|zess ▲ [re'tsɛs] M **-es, -e** (*Jur*) written settlement or agreement

Re|zes|si|on [retsɛ'sioːn] F **-, -en** (*Econ*) recession

re|zes|siv [retsɛ'siːf] ADJ **a** (*Biol*) recessive **b** (*Econ*) recessionary **ADV** (*Biol*) **Erbanlagen, die ~ vorhanden sind** genetic traits which are recessive, recessive genetic traits

Re|zi|pi|ent [retsipi'ɛnt] M **-en, -en**, **Re|zi|pi|en|tin** [retsipi'ɛntɪn] F **-, -nen** **a** (*form: Person*) recipient **b** (*Chem, Phys*) recipient

re|zi|pie|ren [retsi'piːrən] *ptp* **rezipiert** VT *Ideen etc* to adopt, to accept; *Text, Buch* to apprehend

re|zip|rok [retsi'proːk] ADJ (*Math, Gram*) reciprocal **ADV** **sich ~ zueinander verhalten** to be in a reciprocal relationship

Re|zi|ta|ti|on [retsita'tsioːn] F **-, -en** recitation

Re|zi|ta|ti|ons|abend M poetry evening

Re|zi|ta|tiv [retsita'tiːf] NT **-s, -e** [-və] (*Mus*) recitative

Re|zi|ta|tor [retsita'toːɐ] M **-s, Rezitatoren** [-'toːrən], **Re|zi|ta|to|rin** [-'toːrɪn] F **-, -nen** reciter

re|zi|tie|ren [retsi'tiːrən] *ptp* **rezitiert** VTI to recite

R-Ge|spräch ['ɛr-] NT transfer or reverse charge call (*Brit*), collect call (*US*); **ein ~ führen** to make a transfer charge call *etc*, to transfer or reverse the charges, to call collect (*US*)

rh [ɛr'haː] *abbr von* **Rhesusfaktor negativ**

Rh [ɛr'haː] *abbr von* **Rhesusfaktor positiv**

Rha|bar|ber¹ [ra'barbɐ] M **-s**, *no pl* rhubarb

Rha|bar|ber² NT **-s**, *no pl* (*inf*: = *Gemurmel*) rhubarb

Rhap|so|die [rapso'diː, rapzo'diː] F **-, -n** [-'diːən] (*Mus, Liter*) rhapsody

rhap|so|disch [rap'soːdɪʃ, rap'zoːdɪʃ] ADJ (*Mus, Liter*) rhapsodic(al)

Rhein [rain] M **-s** Rhine

Rhein-: rhein|ab(wärts) [rain'lap(vɛrts)] ADV down the Rhine; **Rhein|ar|mee** F British Army of the Rhine; **rhein|auf(wärts)** [rain'lauf (-vɛrts)] ADV up the Rhine; **Rhein|bund** M, *no pl* (*Hist*) Confederation of the Rhine; **Rhein|fall** M Rhine Falls *pl*, Falls *pl* of the Rhine

rhei|nisch ['rainɪʃ] ADJ *attr* Rhenish, Rhineland

Rhein-: Rhein|län|der¹ ['rainlɛndɐ] M **-s, -** (= *Tanz*) ≈ schottische; **Rhein|län|der²** ['rainlɛndɐ] M **-s, -**, **Rhein|län|de|rin** [-ərɪn] F **-, -nen** Rhinelander; **rhein|län|disch** ['rainlɛndɪʃ] ADJ Rhenish, Rhineland; **Rhein|land-Pfalz** ['rainlant'pfalts] NT Rhineland-Palatinate; **Rhein|wein** M Rhine wine, Rhenish (wine); (*weißer auch*) hock

Rhe|ni|um ['reːniʊm] NT **-s**, *no pl* (*abbr* **Re**) rhenium

Rhe|sus-: Rhe|sus|af|fe M rhesus monkey; **Rhe|sus|fak|tor** M (*Med*) rhesus or Rh factor; **Rhesus(faktor) positiv/negativ** rhesus positive/negative

Rhe|to|rik [re'toːrɪk] F **-, -en** rhetoric

Rhe|to|ri|ker [re'toːrikɐ] M **-s, -**, **Rhe|to|ri|ke|rin** [-ərɪn] F **-, -nen** rhetorician (*form*), master of rhetoric; (= *Redner*) orator

rhe|to|risch [re'toːrɪʃ] ADJ rhetorical; **~e Frage** rhetorical question **ADV** **a** (*als Redner*) rhetorically; **~ begabt sein** to have a gift for rhetoric **b** **rein ~** rhetorically; **verstehen Sie diese Frage bitte rein ~** of course, you understand this question is purely rhetorical

Rheu|ma ['rɔyma] NT **-s**, *no pl* rheumatism

Rheu|ma|mit|tel NT (*inf*) cure for rheumatism or the rheumatics (*inf*)

Rheu|ma|ti|ker [rɔy'maːtikɐ] M **-s, -**, **Rheu|ma|ti|ke|rin** [-ərɪn] F **-, -nen** rheumatic, rheumatism sufferer

rheu|ma|tisch [rɔy'maːtɪʃ] ADJ rheumatic **ADV** **~ bedingte Schmerzen** rheumatic pains

Rheu|ma|tis|mus [rɔyma'tɪsmʊs] M **-, Rheumatismen** [-mən] rheumatism

Rheu|ma|to|lo|ge [rɔymato'loːgə] M **-n, -n**, **Rheu|ma|to|lo|gin** [-'loːgɪn] F **-, -nen** rheumatologist

Rhi|no|ze|ros [ri'noːtsɛros] NT **-(ses), -se** rhinoceros, rhino (*inf*); (*inf*: = *Dummkopf*) fool, twit (*inf*), sap (*inf*)

Rhi|zom [ri'tsoːm] NT **-s, -e** (*Bot*) rhizome

Rho|de|si|en [ro'deːziən] NT **-s** (*Hist*) Rhodesia

Rho|de|si|er [ro'deːziɐ] M **-s, -**, **Rho|de|si|e|rin** [-iərɪn] F **-, -nen** (*Hist*) Rhodesian

rho|de|sisch [ro'deːzɪʃ] ADJ (*Hist*) Rhodesian

Rho|di|um ['ro:diʊm] NT **-s**, *no pl* (*abbr* **Rh**) rhodium

Rho|do|dend|ron [rodo'dɛndrɔn] M OR NT **-s,** **Rhododendren** [-drən] rhododendron

Rho|dos ['ro:dɔs, 'rɔdɔs] NT **-'** Rhodes

Rhom|ben *pl von* **Rhombus**

rhom|bisch ['rɔmbɪʃ] ADJ rhomboid(al)

Rhom|bo|id [rɔmbo'i:t] NT **-(e)s, -e** [-də] rhomboid

Rhom|bus ['rɔmbʊs] M **-,** **Rhomben** [-bn] rhombus, rhomb

Rhön|rad ['rø:nra:t] NT (*Turnen*) aero wheels *pl*

Rhyth|mik ['rʏtmɪk] F **-, -en** rhythmics *sing*; (*inf*: = *Rhythmus*) rhythm

Rhyth|mi|ker ['rʏtmɪkɐ] M **-s, -,** **Rhyth|mi|ke|rin** [-ərɪn] F **-, -nen** rhythmist

rhyth|misch ['rʏtmɪʃ] ADJ rhythmic(al); ~**e Pro|sa** rhythmic prose; ~**e (Sport)gymnastik** rhythmic gymnastics *sing*, music and movement ADV rhythmically; **sie bewegten sich ~ zum Schlagen der Trommeln** they moved to the rhythm of the drums

rhyth|mi|sie|ren [rʏtmi'zi:rən] *ptp* **rhythmisiert** VT to make rhythmic, to put rhythm into; **rhythmisiert** rhythmic

Rhyth|mus ['rʏtmʊs] M **-, Rhythmen** [-mən] (*Mus, Poet, fig*) rhythm

Rhyth|mus|ins|tru|ment NT rhythm instrument

RIAS ['ri:as] M *abbr von* **Rundfunk im amerikanischen Sektor** broadcasting station in the American sector (of Berlin)

Ri|bi|sel ['ri:bi:zl] F **-, -n**, **Ri|bisl** ['ri:bi:zl] F **-, -n** (*Aus*: = *Johannisbeere*) (*rot*) redcurrant; (*schwarz*) blackcurrant

Ri|bo|nuk|le|in|säu|re [ribonukle'i:n-] F (*abbr* **RNS**) ribonucleic acid

Ri|bo|se [ri'bo:zə] F **-, -n**, **Ri|bo|som** [ribo-'zo:m] NT **-s, -e** ribosome

Richt-: Richt|an|ten|ne F directional aerial (*esp Brit*) or antenna; **Richt|baum** M *tree used in the topping-out ceremony*; **Richt|beil** NT executioner's axe (*Brit*) or ax (*US*); **Richt|blei** NT plumb line, plummet

rich|ten ['rɪçtn] VT **a** (= *lenken*) to direct (*auf +acc* towards), to point (*auf +acc* at, towards); *Augen, Blicke, Aufmerksamkeit, Kamera* to direct, to turn (*auf +acc* towards), to focus (*auf +acc* on); *Pläne, Wünsche, Tun* to direct (*auf +acc* towards); **den Kurs nach Norden/Osten** *etc* ~ to set or steer a northerly/easterly *etc* course; **die Augen gen Himmel ~** (*liter*) to raise or lift one's eyes heavenwards (*liter*) or to heaven (*liter*); **richt euch!** (*Mil*) right dress!; (*Sch*) get in a straight line!; **einen Verdacht gegen jdn ~** to suspect sb → **zugrunde**

b (= *ausrichten*) **etw nach jdm/etw ~** to suit or fit sth to sb/sth; *Lebensstil, Verhalten* to orientate sth to sb/sth

c (= *adressieren*) *Briefe, Anfragen* to address, to send (*an +acc* to); *Bitten, Forderungen, Gesuch* to address, to make (*an +acc* to); *Kritik, Vorwurf* to level, to direct, to aim (*gegen* at, against); **das Wort an jdn ~** to address sb

d (*esp S Ger* = *zurechtmachen*) to prepare, to get ready; *Essen auch* to get, to fix; (= *in Ordnung bringen*) to do, to fix; (= *reparieren*) to fix; *Haare* to do; *Tisch* to lay (*Brit*), to set; *Betten* to make, to do; **jdm ein Bad ~** (*form, S Ger*) to draw (*form*) or run a bath for sb

e (= *einstellen*) to set; (*S Ger*: = *gerade biegen*) to straighten (out), to bend straight; **einen Knochenbruch ~** to set a fracture

f (*Aus*: = *erreichen*) **sichs** (*dat*) ~ to do nicely for oneself (*inf*)

g (*old*: = *hinrichten*) to execute, to put to death; **sich selbst ~** (*liter*) to find death by one's own hand (*liter*); **sich von selbst ~** (*fig*) to condemn oneself

VR **a** (= *sich hinwenden*) to focus, to be focussed (*auf +acc* on), to be directed (*auf +acc*

towards); (*Gedanken, Augen, Blick*) to turn, to be directed (*auf +acc* towards); (*Hoffnungen*) to be focussed (*auf +acc* on); (*Protest, Kritik*) to be directed or aimed (*gegen* at)

b (= *sich wenden*) to consult (*an jdn* sb); (*Maßnahme, Vorwurf etc*) to be directed or aimed (*gegen* at)

c (= *sich anpassen*) to follow (*nach jdm/etw* sb/sth); **sich nach den Vorschriften ~** to go by the rules; **sich nach jds Wünschen ~** to comply with or go along with sb's wishes; **mir ist es egal, ob wir früher oder später gehen, ich richte mich nach dir** I don't mind if we go earlier or later, I'll fit in with you or I'll do what you do; **wir ~ uns ganz nach unseren Kunden** we are guided entirely by our customers' wishes; **warum sollte die Frau sich immer nach dem Mann ~?** why should the woman always do what the man wants?; **sich nach den Sternen/der Wettervorhersage/dem, was er behauptet, ~** to go by the stars/the weather forecast/what he maintains; **und richte dich (gefälligst) danach!** (*inf*) (kindly) do as you're told

d (= *abhängen von*) to depend (*nach* on)

e (*esp S Ger*: = *sich zurechtmachen*) to get ready; **für die Party brauchst du dich nicht extra zu ~** you don't have to get specially done up for the party (*inf*)

VI (*liter*: = *urteilen*) to judge (*über jdn* sb), to pass judgement (*über +acc* on); **milde/streng ~** to be mild/harsh in one's judgement; **richtet nicht, auf dass ihr nicht gerichtet werdet!** (*Bibl*) judge not, that ye be not judged (*Bibl*)

Rich|ter ['rɪçtɐ] M **-s, -, Rich|te|rin** [-ərɪn] F **-, -nen** judge; **jdn/einen Fall vor den ~ bringen** or **zerren** to bring sb/a case before a judge; **die verfassungsrechtlich verankerte Garantie des gesetzlichen ~s** the constitutional right to a fair trial; **der vorsitzende ~** the presiding judge; **die ~** the Bench, the judiciary, the judges *pl*; **die Karlsruher ~** the judges of the Federal Constitutional Court; **das Buch der ~** (*Bibl*) (the Book of) Judges; **sich zum ~ aufwerfen** or **machen** (*fig*) to set (oneself) up in judgement; **der höchste ~** (*liter*: = *Gott*) the Supreme Judge; **vor dem höchsten ~ stehen** (*liter*: = *vor Gott*) to stand before the Judgement Seat or the Throne of Judgement

Rich|ter-: Rich|ter|amt NT judicial office; (*Sw*: = *Behörde*) court; **das ~ ausüben** to sit on the Bench; **Rich|ter|ge|setz** NT *law defining the functions and powers of judges*; **rich|ter|lich** ['rɪçtɐlɪç] ADJ *attr* judicial; **Rich|ter|ro|be** F judge's robe (*pl*); **Rich|ter|schaft** ['rɪçtɐʃaft] F **-, -en** judiciary, Bench

Rich|ter-Ska|la ['rɪçtɐ-] F (*Geol*) Richter scale

Rich|ter-: Rich|ter|spruch M **a** (*Jur*) ≈ judgement **b** (*Sport*) judges' decision; (*Pferderennen*) stewards' decision; **Rich|ter|stuhl** M Bench; (= *Richteramt*) judicial office; **auf dem ~ sitzen** to be on the Bench; **der ~ (Gottes)** the Judgement Seat, the Throne of Judgement

Richt-: Richt|fest NT topping-out ceremony; **Richt|feu|er** NT (*Naut*) leading lights *pl*; (*Aviat*) approach lights *pl*

Richt|funk M directional radio

Richt|funk-: Richt|funk|ba|ke F (*Naut*) directional radio beacon; **Richt|funk|ver|bin|dung** F microwave link

Richt|ge|schwin|dig|keit F recommended speed

rich|tig ['rɪçtɪç] ○ 38.1, 40.2, 41, 53.6 ADJ **a** right *no comp*; (= *zutreffend*) correct, right; **eine ~e Erkenntnis/Voraussetzung** *etc* a correct realization/presupposition *etc*; **der ~e Mann am ~en Ort** the right man for the job; **ich halte es für ~/das Richtigste, ...** I think it would be right/best ...; **nicht ganz ~ (im Kopf) sein** (*inf*) to be not quite right (in the head) (*inf*); **bin ich hier ~ bei Müller?** (*inf*) is this right for the Müllers?; **der Junge ist ~** (*inf*) that boy's all right (*inf*) or OK (*inf*)

b (= *wirklich, echt*) real, proper; **der ~e Vater**

the real father; **die ~e Mutter** the real mother; **ein ~er Idiot** a real or proper or right (*inf*) idiot ADV **a** (= *korrekt*) correctly, right; *passen, funktionieren, liegen etc* properly, correctly, right; **ich habe ihn ~ eingeschätzt** I was right about him; **~ gehend** (*Uhr, Waage*) accurate; **die Uhr geht ~** the clock is right or correct; **habe ich ~ gehört?** (*iro*) do my ears deceive me?, am I hearing things?; (*Gerücht betreffend*) is it right what I've heard?; **wenn man es ~ nimmt** (*inf*) really, actually, properly speaking; **du kommst gerade ~!** you're just in time; (*iro*) you're just what I need **b** (*inf*: = *ganz und gar*) really, real (*esp US inf*); *sich schämen, verlegen* thoroughly, really, real (*esp US inf*) **c** (= *wahrhaftig*) right, correct; **du bist doch Konrads Schwester – ~!** you're Konrad's sister – (that's) right; **das ist doch Paul! – ach ja, ~** that's Paul – oh yes, so it is; **wir dachten, es würde gleich regnen, und ~, kaum ...** we thought it would soon start raining and, sure enough, scarcely ...

Rich|ti|ge(r) ['rɪçtɪgə] MF *decl as adj* right person, right man/woman *etc*; (*zum Heiraten auch*) Mr/Miss Right; **du bist mir der ~!** (*iro*) you're a fine one (*inf*); **an den ~n/die ~ geraten** or **kommen** to come to the right person; **sechs ~ im Lotto** six right in the lottery

Rich|ti|ge(s) ['rɪçtɪgə] NT *decl as adj* right thing; **das ist das ~** that's right; **das ist genau das ~** that's just right or the thing or the job (*inf*); **das ist auch nicht das ~** that's not right either; **ich habe nichts ~s gegessen** I haven't had a proper meal; **ich habe nichts ~s gelernt** I didn't really learn anything; **ich habe noch nicht das ~ gefunden** I haven't found anything right or suitable; **ich habe endlich was ~s gefunden** at last I've found something suitable

rich|tig|ge|hend ADJ *attr* (*inf*: = *regelrecht*) real, regular (*inf*), proper → *auch* **richtig** ADV **a** ADV (*inf*) → **intelligent** really intelligent; **das ist ja ~ Betrug** that's downright deceit

Rich|tig|keit F **-,** *no pl* correctness, accuracy; (*von Verhalten, Vorgehen, Meinung*) correctness; (*von Entscheidung*) rightness, correctness; **an der ~ von etw zweifeln, bei etw an der ~ zweifeln** (*inf*) to doubt whether sth is correct or right; **die ~ einer Abschrift bescheinigen** to certify a copy as being accurate; **damit hat es or das hat schon seine ~** that's (quite) right; **es wird schon seine ~ haben** it's bound to be right or OK (*inf*)

rich|tig-: richtig lie|gen ▲ VI *irreg* (*inf*) to fit in; (= *recht haben*) to be right; **bei jdm ~** to get on well with sb → **liegen** f; **richtig stel|len** ▲ VT to correct; **ich muss Ihre Behauptung ~** I must put you right there; **Rich|tig|stel|lung** F correction

Richt-: Richt|ka|no|nier(in) M(F) (*Mil*) gunlayer; **Richt|kranz** M **,** **Richt|kro|ne** F (*Build*) *wreath used in the topping-out ceremony*; **Richt|li|nie F**, **Richt|li|ni|en|kom|pe|tenz** F (*Pol*) authority in matters of general policy; **Richt|maß** NT standard measure; (= *Gewicht*) standard weight; (*fig*) standard; **Richt|mik|ro|fon** ▲ NT directional microphone or mike (*inf*); **Richt|platz** M place of execution; **Richt|preis** M (*unverbindlicher*) ~ recommended price; **Richt|scheit** NT (*Build*) (spirit) level; **Richt|schnur** F **a** (*Build*) guide line; (*senkrecht*) plumb line **b** (*fig*: = *Grundsatz*) guiding principle; **Richt|spruch** M (*old*) judgement; **Richt|stät|te** F (*old*) place of execution; **Richt|strah|len|an|ten|ne** F, **Richt|strah|ler** M beam or directional antenna

Rich|tung ['rɪçtʊŋ] F **-, -en** **a** direction; **in ~ Hamburg** towards (*Brit*) or toward (*US*) Hamburg, in the direction of Hamburg; (*auf Autobahn*) towards (*Brit*) or toward (*US*) Hamburg; **in ~ Süden** towards (*Brit*) or toward (*US*) the south, in a southerly direction; (*auf Autobahn*) on the southbound carriageway (*Brit*) or lane;

in **nördliche ~** northwards, towards (*Brit*) or toward (*US*) the north, in a northerly direction; **die Autobahn/der Zug ~ Hamburg** the Hamburg autobahn/train; **nach allen ~en, in alle ~en** in all directions; **in umgekehrter ~** in the opposite or other direction; **die ~ ändern** or **wechseln** to change direction(s); **die ~ anzeigen** to indicate the direction, to point the way; (*mit Fahrzeug*) to indicate which way one is going to turn; **eine ~ nehmen** or **einschlagen** to head or drive/walk *etc* in a direction; **eine neue ~ bekommen** to change course, to take a new turn or direction; **einem Gespräch eine bestimmte ~ geben** to turn a conversation in a particular direction; **in die gleiche ~ gehen** or **zielen** (*fig*) to point in the same direction; **er will sich nach keiner ~ hin festlegen** he won't commit himself in any way at all; **ein Schritt in die richtige/falsche ~** a step in the right/wrong direction; **ein Schritt in ~ Frieden und Stabilität** a step toward(s) peace and stability; **in jeder ~** each way, in each direction; (*fig: = in jeder Hinsicht*) in every respect; **irgend etwas in der** or **dieser ~** something along those lines

b (= *Tendenz*) trend; (*in der Kunst, einer Partei*) line, trend; (= *die Vertreter einer Richtung*) movement; (= *Denkrichtung, Lehrmeinung*) school of thought; **die herrschende ~** the prevailing trend; **Picasso begann eine völlig neue ~ in der Malerei** Picasso started a completely new direction in painting; **die beiden ~en in der katholischen Kirche** the two lines of thought in the Catholic church; **sie gehören den verschiedensten politischen ~en an** they have the most varied political sympathies; **die ganze ~ passt uns nicht!** that's not the sort of thing we want

rich|tung|ge|bend ADJ pointing the way; (*in der Mode*) trendsetting; **für jdn/etw ~ sein** to set the pattern for sb/sth

Rich|tungs-: **Rich|tungs|än|de|rung** F change of or in direction; **Rich|tungs|kampf** M (*Pol*) factional dispute; **rich|tungs|los** ADJ lacking a sense of direction; **Rich|tungs|lo|sig|keit** F -, *no pl* lack of a sense of direction; **Rich|tungs|pfeil** M (*Mot*) lane indication arrow; **Rich|tungs|streit** M (*Pol*) factional dispute; **Rich|tungs|wech|sel** M (*lit, fig*) change of direction

rich|tung(s)|wei|send ADJ pointing the way; **~ sein** to point the way (ahead)

Richt-: **Richt|waa|ge** F spirit level; **Richt|wert** M guideline; **Richt|zahl** F approximate figure

Ri|cke ['rɪkə] F -, -n doe

rieb *pret von* **reiben**

rie|chen ['riːçn] *pret* **roch** [rɔx], *ptp* **gerochen** [gə'rɔxn] **VT** to smell; **ich rieche Gas** I (can) smell gas; **ich rieche das Gewürz gern** I like the smell of this spice; **Lunte** or **den Braten ~** (*inf*) to smell a rat (*inf*); **ich kann das nicht ~** (*inf*) I can't stand the smell of it; (*fig: = nicht leiden*) I can't stand it; **jdn nicht ~ können** (*inf*) not to be able to stand sb, to hate sb's guts (*inf*); **das konnte ich doch nicht ~!** (*inf*) how was I (supposed) to know?, I'm not psychic (*inf*) → **Mei|le**

VI **a** (= *Geruchssinn haben*) to have a sense of smell, to be able to smell; **nicht mehr ~ können** to have lost one's sense of smell; **Hunde können gut ~** dogs have a good sense of smell
b (= *bestimmten Geruch haben*) to smell; **gut/schlecht ~** to smell good/bad; **nach etw ~** to smell of sth; **aus dem Mund ~** to have bad breath; **das riecht nach Betrug/Verrat** (*fig inf*) that smacks of deceit/treachery
c (= *schnüffeln*) to smell, to sniff; (*Tier*) to sniff; **an jdm/etw ~** to smell sb/sth, to sniff (at) sb/sth; (*Tier*) to sniff (at) sb/sth; **riech mal** have a sniff or smell

VI *impers* to smell; **es riecht angebrannt** there's a smell of burning, there's a burning smell; **es riecht nach Gas** there's a smell of gas

Rie|cher ['riːçɐ] M -s, - (*inf*) **einen ~ (für etw) haben** to have a nose (for sth); **einen guten** or

den richtigen ~ (für etw) haben to have a good nose (for sth) (*inf*); **da habe ich doch den richtigen ~ gehabt!** I knew it all along!

Riech-: **Riech|fläsch|chen** NT (bottle of) smelling salts *pl*; **Riech|kol|ben** M (*inf*) hooter (*Brit inf*), conk (*Brit inf*), honker (*US inf*); **Riech|nerv** M olfactory nerve; **Riech|or|gan** NT organ of smell, olfactory organ; **Riech|salz** NT smelling salts *pl*; **Riech|stoff** M aromatic substance

Ried [riːt] NT -s, -e [-də] **a** (= *Schilf*) reeds *pl* **b** (*S Ger: = Moor*) marsh

Ried|gras NT sedge

rief *pret von* **rufen**

Rie|fe ['riːfə] F -, -n groove, channel; (*in Säulen*) flute

Rie|ge ['riːgə] F -, -n (*Sport*) team, squad; (*fig: = Gruppe*) team

Rie|gel ['riːgl] M -s, - **a** (= *Verschluss*) bolt; **den ~ an etw** (*dat*) **vorlegen** to bolt sth; **vergiss nicht, den ~ vorzulegen!** don't forget to bolt the door *etc*; **den ~ an etw** (*dat*) **zurückschieben** to unbolt sth; **einer Sache** (*dat*) **einen ~ vorschieben** or (*Sw*) **schieben** (*fig*) to put a stop to sth, to clamp down on sth; **ein ~ gegen aggressive Politik** a restraint on or against aggressive policies → **Schloss b** **b** (= *Schokoladenriegel*) bar; (= *Seifenstück*) cake, bar **c** (*Sew*) (= *Lasche*) tab; (*von Jackett*) strap; (*für Haken*) eye; (*am Knopfloch*) bar tack

Rie|gel-: **Rie|gel|bau** M *pl* -bauten (*Sw*) half-timbering; (*Gebäude*) half-timbered building; **Rie|gel|stel|lung** F (*Mil*) switch line or position; **Rie|gel|werk** NT (*dial*) half-timbering

Rie|gen-: **Rie|gen|füh|rer(in)** M(F) team or squad leader or captain; **rie|gen|wei|se** ADV in teams or squads

Riem|chen|schuh ['riːmçən-] M strap shoe

Rie|men¹ ['riːmən] M -s, - (= *Treibriemen, Gürtel*) belt; (*an Schuhen, Kleidung, Koffer, Gepäck*) strap; (= *Schnürsenkel*) leather shoelace; (= *Peitschenriemen*) thong; (*vulg: = Penis*) prick (*sl*), cock (*sl*); **jdn mit einem ~ verdreschen** to strap sb, to give sb the strap or belt; **den ~ enger schnallen** (*fig*) to tighten one's belt; **sich am ~ reißen** (*fig inf*) to get a grip on oneself

Rie|men² M -s, - (*Sport*) oar; **die ~ einlegen** to ship oars; **sich in die ~ legen** (*lit, fig*) to put one's back into it

Rie|men-: **Rie|men|an|trieb** M belt drive; **Rie|men|werk** NT strapping

Ries [riːs] NT -es, -e [-zə] (*Measure*) German ream, ≈ 2 reams

Rie|se¹ ['riːzə] **das macht nach Adam ~ EUR 3,50** (*hum inf*) the way I learned it at school that makes EUR 3.50

Rie|se² M -n, -n (*lit, fig*) giant; (*sl Hist: = Tausendmarkschein*) 1000 mark note, big one (*inf*); **ein böser ~** an ogre; **ein ~ von Mensch** or **von einem Menschen** a giant of a man/woman; **roter ~** (*Astron*) red giant

Rie|sel|fel|der PL sewage farm

rie|seln ['riːzln] VI *aux sein* (*Wasser, Sand*) to trickle; (*Regen*) to drizzle; (*Schnee*) to float or flutter down; (*Staub*) to fall down; (*Musik*) to filter; **der Kalk rieselt von der Wand** lime is crumbling off the wall; **Schuppen ~ ihm vom Kopf** dandruff is flaking off his head; **ein angenehmes Lustgefühl rieselte durch seinen Körper** a pleasurable sensation ran or thrilled through his body; **ein Schauder rieselte mir über den Rücken/durch alle Glieder** a shiver went down my spine/through me

Rie|sen- PREF gigantic, enormous, colossal; (*Zool, Bot etc auch*) giant; **Rie|sen|amei|se** F carpenter ant; **Rie|sen|ar|beit** F (= *Pensum*) gigantic etc job; (= *Anstrengung*) gigantic etc effort; **Rie|sen|ba|by** NT (*Kind*) huge baby; (*fig pej inf: = Mann*) lumbering hulk (*inf*); (= *Hund*) huge hound; **Rie|sen|chan|ce** F tremendous chance; **Rie|sen|dumm|heit** F (*inf*) monu-

mental stupidity or mistake, mega boo-boo (*US inf*); **Rie|sen|er|folg** M gigantic etc success; (*Theat, Film*) smash hit; **Rie|sen|fräu|lein** NT giantess; **Rie|sen|ge|bir|ge** NT (*Geog*) Sudeten Mountains *pl*; **Rie|sen|ge|stalt** F **a** (*Größe*) gigantic etc frame **b** (= *Riese*) giant; **Rie|sen|ge|winn** M huge profits *pl*; (*beim Spiel*) huge winnings *pl*; **einen ~ erzielen** to win a fortune; **rie|sen|groß, rie|sen|haft** ADJ = riesig; **Rie|sen|hai** M basking shark; **Rie|sen|hun|ger** M (*inf*) enormous appetite; **ich habe einen ~** (*inf*) I could eat a horse (*inf*); **Rie|sen|kraft** F colossal or enormous strength *no pl*; **mit Riesenkräften** (= *mit enormer Anstrengung*) with a colossal or an enormous effort; **Rie|sen|por|ti|on** F (*inf*) giant portion; **eine ~ Fleisch** a huge piece of meat; **Rie|sen|rad** NT big or Ferris wheel; **Rie|sen|sa|la|man|der** M giant salamander; **Rie|sen|schild|krö|te** F giant tortoise; **Rie|sen|schlan|ge** F boa; **Rie|sen|schreck** M **einen ~ kriegen** (*inf*) to get a terrible fright; **ich habe einen ~ gekriegt** I got such a fright; **Rie|sen|schritt** M giant step or stride; **wir nähern uns mit ~en dem amerikanischen System** we are moving swiftly toward(s) the American system; **Weihnachten nähert sich mit ~en** Christmas is fast approaching; **einer Sache** (*dat*) **einen ~ näher kommen** to take a giant step or stride towards sth; **Rie|sen|sla|lom** M giant slalom; **Rie|sen|tra|ra** NT (*inf*) great fuss or to-do (*inf*); **Rie|sen|werk** NT colossal work; (= *Gesamtwerk*) colossal works *pl*; **Rie|sen|wuchs** M giantism; (*Med auch*) gigantism; **Rie|sen|wut** F **eine ~ (im Bauch) haben** (*inf*) to be wild with rage

rie|sig ['riːzɪç] **ADJ** **a** (= *sehr groß, gigantisch*) enormous, huge; *Spaß* tremendous **b** (*inf: = toll*) terrific, fantastic **ADV** (*inf: = sehr, überaus*) tremendously, incredibly

Rie|sin ['riːzɪn] F -, -nen giantess

Ries|ling ['riːslɪŋ] M -s, -e Riesling

riet *pret von* **raten**

Riff¹ [rɪf] NT -(e)s, -e (= *Felsklippe*) reef

Riff² M -(e)s, -s (*Mus*) riff

Rif|fel ['rɪfl] F -, -n (*Tex*) (flax) hackle, flax comb

rif|feln ['rɪfln] VT **a** *Flachs* to comb **b** (*Tech*) to groove, to channel; *Säule* to flute

Rigg [rɪg] NT -s, -s (*Naut*) rigging

Rig|gung ['rɪgʊŋ] F -, -en (*Naut*) rigging

ri|gi|de [ri'giːdə] ADJ (*geh*) rigid

Ri|gi|di|tät [rigidi'tɛːt] F -, *no pl* (*Med, Psych*) rigidity

Ri|gips|plat|te® ['riːgɪpsplatə] F type of plasterboard, gypsum wallboard, dry wall (*US*), Sheetrock® (*US*)

Ri|go|le [ri'goːlə] F -, -n (*Agr*) (drainage) trench

Ri|go|ris|mus [rigo'rɪsmʊs] M -, *no pl* (*geh*) rigour (*Brit*), rigor (*US*)

ri|go|ris|tisch [rigo'rɪstɪʃ] ADJ (*geh*) rigorous

ri|go|ros [rigo'roːs] **ADJ** rigorous; **ich bleibe dabei, da bin ich ganz ~** I'm sticking to that, I'm adamant **ADV** *ablehnen* rigorously; *kürzen auch* drastically; **~ durchgreifen** to take decisive action

Ri|go|ro|si|tät [rigorozi'tɛːt] F -, *no pl* rigour (*Brit*), rigor (*US*)

Ri|go|ro|sum [rigo'roːzʊm] NT -s, Rigorosa or (*Aus*) Rigorosen [-za, -zn] (*Univ*) (doctoral or PhD) viva (*Brit*) or oral

Rik|scha ['rɪkʃa] F -, -s rickshaw

Ril|le ['rɪlə] F -, -n groove; (*in Säule*) flute

Ril|len-: **ril|len|för|mig** ADJ groove-like; **Ril|len|pro|fil** NT tread

ril|lig ['rɪlɪç] ADJ (*rare*) fluted

Ri|mes|se [ri'mɛsə] F -, -n (*Fin*) remittance

rin- ['rɪn] PREF (*dial*) = **herein-, hinein-**

Rind [rɪnt] NT -(e)s, -er [-də] **a** (= *Tier*) cow; (= *Bulle*) bull; **~er** cattle *pl*; **10 ~er** 10 head of cattle; **die Inkubationszeit beim ~** the incubation period in cattle **b** (*inf: = Rindfleisch*) beef; **vom**

~ beef *attr*; **Hackfleisch vom ~** minced (*esp Brit*) or ground (*US*) beef, mince

Rin|de ['rɪndə] F **-, -n** (= *Baumrinde*) bark; (= *Brotrinde*) crust; (= *Käserinde*) rind; (*Anat*) cortex

rin|den|los ADJ *Baum* barkless; *Käse* rindless

Rin|der-: Rin|der|bouil|lon F beef stock or bouillon (*form*); **Rin|der|bra|ten** M (*roh*) joint of beef; (*gebraten*) roast beef *no indef art*; **Rin|der|brem|se** F horsefly; **Rin|der|brü|he** F beef broth; **Rin|der|brust** F brisket (of beef); **Rin|der|fi|let** NT fillet of beef; **Rin|der|her|de** F herd of cattle; **Rin|der|hirt(in)** M(F) cowherd; (*in Nordamerika*) cowboy/-girl; (*in Südamerika*) gaucho; (*in Australien*) drover; **Rin|der|len|de** F beef tenderloin

rin|dern ['rɪndɐn] VI (*Kuh*) to be on (*Brit*) or in heat

Rin|der-: Rin|der|pest F (*Vet*) rinderpest; **Rin|der|seuche** F epidemic cattle disease; (= *BSE*) mad cow disease; **Rin|der|talg** M beef tallow; **Rin|der|wahn(sinn)** M mad cow disease; **Rin|der|zucht** F cattle farming or raising; **Rin|der|zun|ge** F ox tongue

Rind-: Rind|fleisch NT beef; **Rind|fleisch|brü|he** F beef broth

Rinds- *in cpds* (*Aus, S Ger*) = **Rinder-: Rinds|le|der** NT cowhide; **rinds|le|dern** ADJ *attr* cowhide; **Rinds|stück** NT (*Cook*) joint of beef

Rind|vieh NT **a** *no pl* cattle; **10 Stück ~** 10 head of cattle **b** *pl* **Rindviecher** (*inf:* = *Idiot*) ass (*inf*)

Ring [rɪŋ] M **-(e)s, -e a** ring; (= *Kettenring*) link; (= *Wurfring*) quoit; (= *Einweckring*) seal, rubber; (= *Rettungsring*) life buoy, life belt; **die ~e tauschen** or **wechseln** to exchange rings **b** (= *Kreis*) (= *Jahresring, Rauchring*) ring; (*auf dem Wasser, von Menschen*) circle, ring; (= *Ringstraße*) ring road; **(dunkle) ~e unter den Augen haben** to have (dark) rings under one's eyes **c** (*Sport*) (= *Boxring*) ring; (*von Schießscheibe*) ring, circle; **~e** (*Turnen*) rings; **acht ~e schießen** to score an eight; **~ frei!** seconds out or away!; (*fig*) clear the decks!; **in den ~ steigen** (*lit*) to climb into the ring; (*fig*) to enter the lists or the fray **d** (*Astron, Met, Chem*) ring **e** (= *Vereinigung*) circle, group; (*von Großhändlern, Erzeugern*) group; (= *Bande*) ring; (*Theat:* = *Abonnentenring*) theatre-goers' (*Brit*) or theatergoers' (*US*) group **f** (*liter:* = *Kreislauf*) circle, cycle; **der ~ schließt sich** the circle is completed or closed, the wheel comes or turns full circle **g** (= *Sagenzyklus*) cycle; **der ~ (des Nibelungen)** the Ring (of the Nibelung)

Ring-: ring|ar|tig ADJ ring-like; **Ring|bahn** F circle line; **Ring|buch** NT ring binder; **Ring|buch|ein|la|ge** F loose-leaf pad

Rin|gel ['rɪŋl] M **-s, -** ring; (= *Locke*) ringlet

Rin|gel|blu|me F marigold

Rin|gel|chen ['rɪŋlçən] NT **-s, -** (*inf*) little ring

Rin|gel|gans F Brent goose

rin|ge|lig ['rɪŋəlɪç] ADJ ringleted

Rin|gel|lo|cke F ringlet; **~n tragen** to wear one's hair in ringlets, to have ringlets

rin|geln ['rɪŋln] VT (*Pflanze*) to (en)twine; *Schwanz etc auch* to curl → *auch* **geringelt** VR to go curly, to curl; (*Rauch*) to curl up(wards); **die Schlange ringelte sich durch das Unterholz** the snake wriggled through the undergrowth; **der Schwanz des Schweins ringelt sich** the pig has a curly tail; **die Schlange ringelte sich um den Baum** the snake coiled or curled itself around the tree

Rin|gel|-: Rin|gel|nat|ter F grass snake; **Rin|gel|pie(t)z** ['rɪŋlpiːts] M **-es, -e** (*hum inf*) hop (*inf*); **~ mit Anfassen** hop (*inf*); **Rin|gel|rei|gen** M , **Rin|gel|rei|hen** [-raiən] M **-s, -** ring-a-ring-o' roses; **einen ~ tanzen** to play ring-a-ring-o' roses; **Rin|gel|schwanz** M , **Rin|gel|schwänz|chen** NT (*inf*) curly tail;

Rin|gel|so|cke F hooped or striped sock; **Rin|gel|spiel** NT (*Aus*) merry-go-round, roundabout (*Brit*); **Rin|gel|tau|be** F wood pigeon, ringdove; **Rin|gel|wurm** M ringed worm, annelid (*spec*)

rin|gen ['rɪŋən] *pret* **rang** [raŋ], *ptp* **gerungen** [gə'rʊŋən] VT **die Hände ~** to wring one's hands; **er rang ihr das Messer aus der Hand** he wrenched or wrested the knife from her hand; **ein Schluchzen rang sich aus ihrer Brust** (*liter*) a sob was wrung from her breast (*liter*) VI **a** (*lit, fig:* = *kämpfen*) to wrestle (*mit* with); **mit sich/dem Tode ~** to wrestle with oneself/death; **mit den Tränen ~** to struggle or fight to keep back one's tears **b** (= *streben*) **nach** or **um etw ~** to struggle for sth; **er rang um Fassung** he struggled to maintain his composure; **ums Überleben ~** (*liter*) to struggle to survive

Rin|gen ['rɪŋən] NT **-s**, *no pl* (*Sport*) wrestling; (*fig*) struggle

Rin|ger ['rɪŋɐ] M **-s, -**, **Rin|ge|rin** [-ərɪn] F **-, -nen** wrestler

Rin|ger|griff M wrestling hold

rin|ge|risch ['rɪŋərɪʃ] ADJ *Fähigkeiten* as a wrestler; **mit ~em Geschick** with the skill of a wrestler

Ring-: Ring|fahn|dung F dragnet; **Ring|fin|ger** M ring finger; **ring|för|mig** ADJ ring-like; **~e Verbindungen** (*Chem*) cyclic or ring compounds ADV in a ring or circle; **die Truppen schlossen die Festung ~** the troops surrounded the fortress; **die Straße führt ~ um die Stadt herum** the road encircles the town; **der Wallgraben umschließt die Stadt ~** the rampart rings or encircles the town; **Ring|hef|ter** M ring binder; **Ring|kampf** M fight; (*Sport*) wrestling match; **Ring|kämp|fer(in)** M(F) wrestler

Ring|lein ['rɪŋlain] NT **-s, -** ring

Ring|lei|tung F (*Elec etc*) ring main

ring|lig ['rɪŋlɪç] ADJ ringleted

Ring|glot|te ['rɪŋˈglɔtə] F **-, -n** (*Aus:* = *Reneklode*) greengage

Ring-: Ring|mau|er F circular wall; **die ~ rund um die Burg** the wall encircling or surrounding the castle; **Ring|mus|kel** M sphincter; **Ring|ord|ner** M ring binder; **Ring|pan|zer** M articulated or jointed armour (*Brit*) or armor (*US*); **Ring|rich|ter(in)** M(F) (*Sport*) referee

rings [rɪŋs] ADV (all) around; **die Stadt ist ~ von Bergen umgeben** the town is completely surrounded or encircled by mountains, there are mountains all around the town; **ich bin ~ um die Kirche gegangen** I went all the way (a)round (the outside of) the church; **wir mussten uns alle ~ im Kreis aufstellen** we all had to get into or make a circle

Ring-: Ring|schei|be F (*Sport*) target (*marked with concentric rings*); **Ring|sen|dung** F (*Rad, TV*) link up (transmission)

rings|he|rum ['rɪŋshɛ'rʊm] ADV all (the way) around

Ring|stra|ße F ring road

rings-: rings|um ['rɪŋs'ʊm] ADV (all) around; **~ konnte ich nichts sehen** I could see nothing around me; **rings|um|her** ['rɪŋsʊm'heːɐ] ADV around

Ring-: Ring|tausch M exchange (*between three or more people*); (*bei Heirat*) exchanging of rings; **Ring|ten|nis** NT (*Sport*) quoits *sing*, deck tennis; **Ring|vor|le|sung** F *series of lectures by different speakers*; **Ring|wall** M = **Ringmauer**

Rin|ne ['rɪnə] F **-, -n** (= *Rille*) groove; (= *Furche, Abflussrinne, Fahrrinne*) channel; (= *Dachrinne, inf:* = *Rinnstein*) gutter; (*Geog*) gap

rin|nen ['rɪnən] *pret* **rann** [ran], *ptp* **geronnen** [gə'rɔnən] VI *aux* **sein** (= *fließen*) to run; **das Blut rann ihm in Strömen aus der Wunde** blood streamed from his wound; **die Zeit rinnt (dahin)** (*liter*) time is slipping away (*liter*); **das Geld**

rinnt ihm durch die Finger (*fig*) money slips through his fingers

Rinn-: Rinn|sal ['rɪnzaːl] NT **-(e)s, -e** rivulet; **Rinn|stein** M (= *Gosse*) gutter; (*old:* = *Ausguss*) drain; **jdn aus dem ~ holen** or **auflesen** (*fig*) to pick sb out of the gutter; **im ~ enden** to come to a sorry end

Ripp|chen ['rɪpçən] NT **-s, -** (*Cook*) slightly cured pork rib

Rip|pe ['rɪpə] F **-, -n a** (*Anat, Cook*) rib; **bei ihm kann man die ~n zählen** (*inf*) you could play a tune on his ribs (*inf*); **er hat nichts auf den ~n** (*inf*) he's just skin and bones; **... damit du was auf die ~n kriegst** (*inf*) ... to put a bit of flesh on you; **ich kann es mir nicht aus den ~n schneiden** (*inf*) I can't just produce it from nowhere → **leiern b** (*von Blatt, Gewölbe etc, in Stoffmuster*) rib **c** (*von Heizkörper, Kühlaggregat*) fin **d** (*von Apfelsine*) segment; (*von Schokolade*) row (of squares)

rip|pen ['rɪpn] VT to rib → *auch* **gerippt**

Rip|pen-: Rip|pen|bo|gen M (*Anat*) costal arch; **Rip|pen|bruch** M broken or fractured rib; **Rip|pen|fell** NT pleura; **Rip|pen|fell|ent|zün|dung** F pleurisy; **Rip|pen|ge|wöl|be** M (*Archit*) ribbed vaulting; **Rip|pen|qual|le** F comb jelly, ctenophorane (*spec*); **Rip|pen|speer** M OR NT (*Cook*) spare rib; **Kass(e)ler** ≈ *slightly cured pork spare rib*; **Rip|pen|stoß** M nudge, dig (*Brit*) or poke in the ribs; (*schmerzhaft*) thump (*inf*) or dig (*Brit inf*) or poke in the ribs; **ein freundschaftlicher ~** (*fig*) a quiet or friendly word; **Rip|pen|strick|pul|li** M ribbed sweater; **Rip|pen|stück** NT (*Cook*) *joint of meat including ribs*

Rip|pli ['rɪpli] PL (*Sw*) ribs *pl*

Ripp|speer ['rɪp-] M = **Rippenspeer**

rips [rɪps] INTERJ **~, raps!** rip!

Rips [rɪps] M **-es, -e** (*Tex*) rep

Ri|si|ko ['riːziko] NT **-s, -s** or **Risiken** or (*Aus*) **Ris|ken** ['riːzikn, 'rɪskn] risk; **auf eigenes ~** at one's own risk; **bitte, Sie können das machen, aber auf eigenes ~** do it by all means, but on your own head be it; **ohne ~** without risk; **etw ohne ~ tun** to do sth without taking a risk; **es ist nicht ohne ~, das zu tun** there is a risk involved in doing that, doing that is not without risk; **die Sache ist ohne ~** there's no risk involved; **als gutes ~ gelten** to be a good (credit) risk

Ri|si|ko-: Ri|si|ko|be|reit|schaft F readiness to take risks; **sie hat eine hohe ~** she is prepared to take big risks; **Ri|si|ko|fak|tor** M risk factor; **Ri|si|ko|freu|de** F readiness to take risks; **sie ist sehr ~** she likes to take risks; **Ri|si|ko|ge|burt** F (*Med*) high-risk birth; **Ri|si|ko|grup|pe** F (high-)risk group; **Ri|si|ko|ka|pi|tal** NT (*Fin*) risk or venture capital; **Ri|si|ko|le|bens|ver|si|che|rung** F (renewable) term life insurance; **Ri|si|ko|pa|ti|ent(in)** M(F) high-risk patient; **ri|si|ko|scheu** ADJ unwilling to take risks; **Ri|si|ko|schwan|ger|schaft** F (*Med*) high-risk pregnancy; **Ri|si|ko|stu|die** F risk analysis; **Ri|si|ko|trä|ger(in)** M(F) (*von Krankheit*) high-risk carrier; (*Insur, Fin*) risk bearer; **~ von Lungenkrebs sein** to be in a high-risk category for lung cancer; **Ri|si|ko|ver|si|che|rung** F term insurance; **Ri|si|ko|vor|sor|ge** F (*auch Econ*) risk provision, provision for risks; **Ri|si|ko|zu|la|ge** F danger money, ≈ hazard pay (*US*); **Ri|si|ko|zu|schlag** M (*bei Versicherung*) excess, loading

ris|kant [rɪs'kant] ADJ risky, chancy (*inf*); **das ist mir zu ~** that's too risky or chancy (*inf*) for me

ris|kie|ren [rɪs'kiːrən] *ptp* **riskiert** VT **a** (= *aufs Spiel setzen*) to risk; **etwas/nichts ~** to take risks or chances/no risks or chances; **seine Stellung/sein Geld ~** to risk losing one's job/money, to put one's job/money at risk; **sein Geld bei etw**

~ to risk one's money on sth **b** (= *wagen*) to venture; **traust du dich, hier runterzuspringen? – ja, ich riskiere!** do you think you dare jump down? – yes, I'll risk or chance it!; **in Gegenwart seiner Frau riskiert er kein Wort** when his wife is present he dare not say a word → **Lippe**

Ri|sot|to [ri'zɔto] M OR NT **-(s), -s** risotto

Ris|pe ['rɪspə] F **-, -n** (*Bot*) panicle

ris|pen|för|mig, ris|pig ['rɪspɪç] ADJ (*Bot*) panicled, paniculate

riss ▲ *pret von* **reißen**

Riss ▲ [rɪs] M **-es, -e** **a** (*in Stoff, Papier etc*) tear, rip; (*in Erde, Gestein*) crevice, fissure; (= *Sprung*: *in Wand, Behälter etc*) crack; (= *Hautriss*) chap; (*fig*: = *Kluft*) rift, split; **die Freundschaft hat einen (tiefen) ~ bekommen** a (deep) rift has developed in their friendship; **durch das Volk geht ein tiefer ~** there is a deep split in the people, the people are deeply divided **b** (*Archit*: = *Zeichnung*) sketch, sketch plan **c** (*Hunt*: = *Raubwildbeute*) kill

ris|sig ['rɪsɪç] ADJ *Boden, Wand, Leder* cracked; *Haut, Hände, Lippen* chapped

Riss|wun|de ▲ F laceration, lacerated wound

Rist [rɪst] M **-(e)s, -e** **a** (*am Fuß*) instep; (*an der Hand*) back (of the hand) **b** (*beim Pferd*) withers *pl*

ri|te ['riːtə] ADV (*Univ*) lowest pass grade in doctoral examinations

Ri|ten *pl von* **Ritus**

ritsch [rɪtʃ] INTERJ **~, ratsch!** rip!

ritt *pret von* **reiten**

Ritt [rɪt] M **-(e)s, -e** ride; **einen ~ machen** to go for a ride; **in scharfem ~ jagte er über die Felder** he rode furiously across the fields; **ein ~ über den Bodensee** (*fig geh*) a leap in the dark

Ritt|ber|ger ['rɪtbɛrgə] M **-s, -** (*Eiskunstlauf*) Rittberger

Rit|ter ['rɪtə] M **-s, -** **a** (*im Mittelalter, im alten Rom*) knight; (= *Kavalier*) cavalier; (*fig, hum*: = *Kämpfer*) champion; **fahrender ~** knight errant; **jdn zum ~ schlagen** to knight sb, to dub sb knight; **der ~ von der traurigen Gestalt** the Knight of the Sorrowful Countenance; **ein ~ ohne Furcht und Tadel** (*lit*) a doughty knight; (*fig*) a knight in shining armour (*Brit*) or armor (*US*) **b** (*Adelstitel*) ≈ Sir; **X ~ von Y** ≈ Sir X of Y **c** (= *Ordensträger*) knight **d** (= *Schmetterling*) swallowtail **e** (*Cook*) **arme ~** *pl* ≈ bread-and--butter pudding

Ritter-: Rit|ter|burg F knight's castle; **Rit|ter|gut** NT ≈ manor; **Rit|ter|guts|be|sit|zer(in)** M(F) ≈ lord/lady of the manor; **rit|ter|haft** ADJ = **ritterlich**; **Rit|ter|kreuz** NT (*Mil*) Knight's Cross; **~ mit Eichenlaub** Knight's Cross with bar; **Rit|ter|kreuz|trä|ger** M holder of the Knight's Cross; **rit|ter|lich** ['rɪtɐlɪç] (*lit*) knightly; (*fig*) chivalrous; **Rit|ter|lich|keit** F **-, -en** chivalry, chivalrousness; **Rit|ter|or|den** M order of knights; **der Deutsche ~** the Teutonic Order; **Rit|ter|ro|man** M (*Liter*) romance of chivalry; **Rit|ter|rüs|tung** F knight's armour (*Brit*) or armor (*US*); **Rit|ter|schaft** ['rɪtɐʃaft] F **-, -en** **a** (= *die Ritter*) knights *pl*, knighthood **b** (= *Ritterehre*) knighthood; **Rit|ter|schlag** M (*Hist*) dubbing; (*fig*) ennoblement; **den ~ empfangen** to be knighted, to be dubbed knight; **(jdm) den ~ erteilen** to confer a knighthood (on sb)

Rit|ters|mann M *pl* **-leute** (*poet*) knight

Ritter-: Rit|ter|sporn M *pl* **-sporne** (*Bot*) larkspur, delphinium; **Rit|ter|stand** M knighthood; **in den ~ erhoben werden** to be raised to the knighthood, to be knighted; **Rit|ter|tum** ['rɪtɐtuːm] NT **-s**, *no pl* knighthood; **Rit|ter--und-Räu|ber-Ro|man** M (*Liter*) late eighteenth century sentimental novel about knights and robbers, romance of chivalry; **Rit|ter|we|sen** NT , *no pl* knighthood; **Rit|ter|zeit** F Age of Chivalry

ritt|lings ['rɪtlɪŋs] ADV astride (*auf etw* (*dat*) sth)

Ritt|meis|ter M (*old Mil*) cavalry captain, captain (of horse)

Ri|tu|al [ri'tuaːl] NT **-s, -e** *or* **-ien** [-liən] (*lit, fig*) ritual

Ri|tu|a|le [ri'tuaːlə] NT **-**, *no pl* (*Eccl*) ritual (*book*); **~ Romanum** missal

Ri|tu|al|hand|lung F ritual act

Ri|tu|a|li|en PL (*Eccl*) ritual objects *pl*

Ri|tu|al|mord M ritual murder

ri|tu|ell [ri'tuɛl] ADJ (*Rel, fig*) ritual

Ri|tus ['riːtʊs] M **-**, **Riten** [-tn] rite; (*fig*) ritual

Ritz [rɪts] M **-es, -e** **a** (= *Kratzer*) scratch **b** (= *Spalte*) chink, crack

Rit|ze ['rɪtsə] F **-, -n** (= *Riss, Poritze*) crack; (= *Fuge*) join, gap; **auf der ~ schlafen** (*hum inf*) to sleep in the middle

Rit|zel ['rɪtsl] NT **-s, -** (*Tech*) pinion

rit|zen ['rɪtsn] VT to scratch; (= *einritzen*) *Initialen, Namen etc auch* to carve → *auch* **geritzt** VR to scratch oneself

Rit|zer ['rɪtsə] M **-s, -** (*inf*) scratch

Ri|va|le [ri'vaːlə] M **-n, -n**, **Ri|va|lin** [ri'vaːlɪn] F **-, -nen** rival

ri|va|li|sie|ren [rivali'ziːrən] *ptp* **rivalisiert** VI **mit jdm (um etw) ~** to compete with sb (for sth); **34 ~de Parteien** 34 rival parties

Ri|va|li|tät [rivali'tɛːt] F **-, -en** rivalry

Ri|va|ner [ri'vaːnɐ] M **-, -** (= *Wein*) riesling-silvaner

Ri|vi|e|ra [ri'vieːra] F **-** Riviera

Ri|zi|nus ['riːtsinʊs] M **-, -** *or* **-se** **a** (*Bot*) castor--oil plant **b** (*auch* **Rizinusöl**) castor oil

RNS [ɛrʔɛn'ʔɛs] F **-**, *- abbr von* **Ribonukleinsäure** RNA

Roa|die ['roːdɪ] M **-s, -s** roadie

Road|show ['roːʃoː] F **-, -s**, **Road-Show** F **-, -s** road show

Roads|ter ['roːdstɐ] M **-s, -** roadster

Roast|beef ['roːstbiːf] NT **-s, -s** (*roh*) beef; (*gebraten*) roast beef

Rob|be ['rɔbə] F **-, -n** seal

rob|ben ['rɔbn] VI *aux sein* (*Mil*) to crawl

Robben-: Rob|ben|fang M sealing, seal hunting; **Rob|ben|fän|ger(in)** M(F) sealer, seal hunter; **Rob|ben|jagd** F sealing, seal hunting; **Rob|ben|ster|ben** NT (high number of) seal deaths *pl*; **das ~ an der Nordsee** the high number of seal deaths in the North Sea

Ro|be ['roːbə] F **-, -n** **a** (= *Abendkleid*) evening gown; **in großer ~** in evening dress **b** (= *Amtstracht*) (official) robe *or* robes *pl*

Ro|bi|nie [ro'biːniə] F **-, -n** robinia

Ro|bin|so|na|de [robɪnzo'naːdə] F **-, -n** Robinsonade; (*Sport*) flying save (*towards attacker*)

Ro|bot|bild ['rɔbɔt-] NT (*Sw*) Identikit® (picture)

Ro|bo|ter ['rɔbɔtɐ] M **-s, -** **a** robot **b** (*Sport*) ball-feeder

Ro|bo|ter|tech|nik F, **Ro|bo|tik** [ro'boːtɪk] F **-**, *no pl* robotics *sing or pl*

ro|bust [ro'bʊst] ADJ *Mensch, Gesundheit, Konjunktur* robust; *Material* tough

Ro|bust|heit F **-**, *no pl* (*von Mensch, Gesundheit, Konjunktur*) robustness; (*von Material*) toughness

roch *pret von* **riechen**

Ro|cha|de [rɔ'xaːdə, rɔ'ʃaːdə] F **-, -n** (*Chess*) castling; (*Ftbl*) switch-over, change of position; (*fig*) switch; **die kleine** *or* **kurze/große** *or* **lange ~** castling king's side/queen's side

rö|cheln ['rœçln] VI to groan; (*Sterbender*) to give the death rattle; **~d atmen** to breathe with a rasping sound

Rö|cheln NT **-s**, *no pl* groan; (= *Todesröcheln*) death rattle; **das ~ der Verletzten** the groans *or* groaning of the wounded

Ro|chen ['rɔxn] M **-s, -** ray

ro|chie|ren [rɔ'xiːrən, rɔ'ʃiːrən] *ptp* **rochiert** VI to castle; (*Ftbl*) to change or switch positions

Rock¹ [rɔk] M **-(e)s, ¨e** ['rœkə] **a** (= *Damenrock*) skirt; (= *Schottenrock*) kilt; (*Sw*: = *Kleid*) dress **b** (*geh*: = *Herrenrock*) jacket; **der grüne ~ (des Försters)** (*old*) the green coat of a forester; **der schwarze ~ (des Geistlichen)** (*old*) the black gown *or* cassock of a priest; **den bunten ~ anziehen** (*old*) to take the King's/Queen's shilling (*Brit old*), to enlist in the army; **den bunten ~ ausziehen** (*old*) to come out of the army

Rock² M **-s**, *no pl* (*Mus*) rock

Rock-: Rock|auf|schlag M lapel; **Rock|band** [-bɛnt] F *pl* **-bands** rock band; **Rock|bar|de** M rock poet; **Rock|bar|din** F rock poetess

Röck|chen ['rœkçən] NT **-s, -** *dim von* **Rock¹**

ro|cken ['rɔkn] VI (*Mus*) to rock

Ro|cken ['rɔkn] M **-s, -** (*Tex*) distaff

Ro|cker ['rɔkɐ] M **-s, -** rocker

Rocker-: Ro|cker|ban|de F gang of rockers; **Ro|cker|braut** F (*inf*) rocker's moll (*inf*)

Ro|cke|rin [-ərɪn] F **-, -nen** → **Rocker**

Rock-: Rock|fal|te F (*von Damenrock*) inverted pleat; (*von Jackett*) vent; **Rock|fes|ti|val** NT rock festival; **Rock|fut|ter** NT skirt lining; **Rock|grup|pe** F rock band

ro|ckig ['rɔkɪç] ADJ *Musik* which sounds like (hard) rock ADV **~ klingender Blues** blues which sounds like (hard) rock; **die Band spielt mir zu ~** I don't like this band because their music sounds too much like (hard) rock

Rock-: Rock|mu|sik F rock music; **Rock|röh|re** F (*Press sl*) rock singer; **Rock|saum** M hem of a/the skirt; **Rock|schoß** M coat-tail; **an jds Rockschößen hängen** (*inf*) **sich an jds Rockschöße klammern** (*inf*) to cling to sb's coat-tails (*inf*); **Rock|star** M rock star; **Rock|zip|fel** M **unter ihrem Mantel guckt ein ~ hervor** part of her skirt is hanging down below her coat; **der Mutter am ~ hängen, an Mutters ~ hängen** (*inf*) to be tied to (one's) mother's apron strings (*inf*); **an jds ~** (*dat*) **hängen** (*inf*) to cling to sb's coat-tails (*inf*)

Ro|de|ha|cke F mattock

Ro|del ['roːdl] M **-s, -** (*S Ger, Aus*) F **-, -n** sledge (*Brit*), sled (*esp US*), toboggan, sleigh

Ro|del|bahn F toboggan run

ro|deln ['roːdln] VI *aux sein or haben* to toboggan (*auch Sport*), to sledge

Rodel-: Ro|del|schlit|ten M toboggan, sledge (*Brit*), sled (*esp US*); **Ro|del|sport** M tobogganing

ro|den ['roːdn] VT *Wald, Land* to clear; *Kartoffeln* to lift

Ro|deo [ro'deːo, 'rodeo] M OR NT **-s, -s** rodeo

Rod|ler ['roːdlɐ] M **-s, -**, **Rod|le|rin** [-ərɪn] F **-, -nen** tobogganer; (*Sport auch*) tobogganist

Ro|dung ['roːdʊŋ] F **-, -en** (= *das Roden, Siedlung*) clearing

Ro|gen ['roːgn] M **-s, -** roe

Ro|ge|ner ['roːgənɐ] M **-s, -** spawner

Ro|gen|stein ['roːgn-] M (*Geol*) oolite, oolitic limestone

ro|ger ['rɔdʒɐ] ADV **a** (*Rad*: = *verstanden*) roger **b** (*inf*: = *einverstanden*) roger, OK; **alles ~!** all agreed!

Rog|gen ['rɔgn] M **-s**, *no pl* rye

Rog|ner ['roːgnɐ] M **-s, -** spawner

roh [roː] ADJ **a** (= *ungebraten, ungekocht*) raw; *Milch* unpasteurized → **Ei** **b** (= *unbearbeitet*) *Bretter, Stein etc* rough; *Diamant* uncut, rough; *Eisen, Metall* crude; *Felle* untreated; **etw aus dem Rohen arbeiten** (*Art*) to work sth from the rough; **die Statue/das Bild/das Manuskript ist im Rohen fertig** the rough shape of the statue/the rough sketch of the picture/the rough draft of the manuscript is finished **c** (= *unkultiviert, brutal*) rough; **~e Gewalt** brute force; **wo ~e Kräfte sinnlos walten ...** (*prov*) brute force does it

ADV **a** (= *ungekocht*) raw **b** (= *grob*) *behauen, zusammen nageln* roughly **c** (= *brutal*) brutally

Roh-: Roh|bau M *pl* **-bauten a** (*Bauabschnitt*) shell or carcass (of a/the building); **das Haus ist im ~ fertig (gestellt)** the house is structurally complete **b** (*Ind: von Fahrzeug*) shell; **Roh|baum|wol|le** F raw cotton; **Roh|ben|zin** NT naphtha; **Roh|bi|lanz** F trial balance sheet; **Roh|bo|gen** M unbound sheet; **Roh|dia|mant** M rough or uncut or unpolished diamond; **Roh|ein|nah|me** F gross proceeds *pl*; **Roh|ei|sen** NT pig iron

Ro|heit △ ['ro:hait] F -, -en → **Rohheit**

Roh-: Roh|ent|wurf M rough draft; **Roh|er|trag** M gross proceeds *pl*

ro|her|wei|se ['ro:ɐˈvaizə] ADV roughly

Roh-: Roh|fa|ser F raw fibre (*Brit*) or fiber (*US*); **Roh|fas|sung** F rough draft; **Roh|ge|wicht** NT gross weight; **Roh|gum|mi** M OR NT raw rubber; **Roh|heit** ▲ ['ro:hait] F -, -en **a** *no pl* (*Eigenschaft*) roughness; (= *Brutalität*) brutality **b** (*Tat*) brutality **c** (= *ungekochter Zustand*) rawness; **Roh|kost** F raw fruit and vegetables *pl*; **Roh|köst|ler** M -s, -, **Roh|köst|le|rin** [-ərɪn] F -, -nen person *who prefers fruit and vegetables uncooked*; **Roh|le|der** NT rawhide, untanned leather; **Roh|ling** ['ro:lɪŋ] M -s, -e **a** (= *Grobian*) brute, ruffian **b** (*Tech*) blank; **CD-Rohling** blank CD; **Roh|ma|te|ri|al** NT raw material; **Roh|milch|kä|se** M unpasteurized cheese; **Roh|öl** NT crude oil; **Roh|pro|dukt** NT raw material; **Roh|pro|duk|ten|händ|ler(in)** M(F) scrap dealer or merchant

Rohr [ro:ɐ] NT -(e)s, -e **a** (= *einzelnes Schilfrohr*) reed; (= *Röhricht, Schilf*) reeds *pl*; (= *Zuckerrohr*) cane; (*für Stühle etc*) cane, wicker *no pl*; **aus ~ geflochtene Stühle** wicker(work) or basketwork or cane (*esp Brit*) chairs; **wie ein schwankendes ~ im Wind** (*liter*) like a reed in the wind (*liter*); **spanisches ~** (*old*) cane **b** (*Tech, Mech*) pipe; (= *Geschützrohr*) (gun) barrel; (= *Blasrohr*) blowpipe; **aus allen ~en feuern** (*lit*) to fire with all its guns; (*fig*) to use all one's fire power; **volles ~** (*inf*) flat out (*Brit*), at full speed **c** (*S Ger, Aus: = Backröhre*) oven

Rohr-: Rohr|am|mer F (*Orn*) reed bunting; **Rohr|blatt** NT (*Mus*) reed; **Rohr|bruch** M burst pipe

Röhr|chen ['rø:ɐçən] NT -s, - tube; (*Chem*) test tube; (*inf: zur Alkoholkontrolle*) Breathalyzer®; **ins ~ blasen** (*inf*) to be breathalyzed

Rohr|dom|mel ['ro:ɐdɔml] F -, -n (*Orn*) bittern

Röh|re ['rø:ɐə] F -, -n **a** (*Ofenröhre*) warming oven; (= *Backröhre*) oven; (= *Drainageröhre*) drainage pipe; **in die ~ gucken** (*inf*) to be left out **b** (= *Neonröhre*) (neon) tube or strip; (= *Elektronenröhre*) valve (*Brit*), tube (*US*); (= *Fernsehröhre*) tube; (*fig*: = *Fernseher*) telly (*Brit inf*), box (*esp Brit inf*), tube (*US inf*); **in die ~ gucken or glotzen** (*inf*) to watch telly (*Brit inf*), to watch the tube (*US inf*), to sit in front of the box (*esp Brit inf*) **c** (= *Höhlung, Hohlkörper*) tube; (*in Knochen*) cavity; (*von Tunnel, U-Bahn*) tube **d** (*Hunt: = Gang im Tierbau*) gallery

röh|ren ['rø:rən] VI (*Hunt*) to bell; (*Motorrad, Mensch*) to roar; **der ~de Hirsch** (*als Sinnbild*) ≈ the Monarch of the Glen

Röh|ren|blüt|ler [-bly:tlɐ] PL (*Bot*) tubiflorae *pl* (*spec*); **röh|ren|för|mig** ADJ tubular; *Hosenbein* drainpipe *attr*; **Röh|ren|ho|se** F (*inf*) drainpipe trousers *pl* (*esp Brit*), drainpipes *pl*; **Röh|ren|kno|chen** M long bone; **Röh|ren|pilz** M boletus

Rohr-: Rohr|flö|te F (*Mus*) reed pipe; (*von Orgel*) rohrflöte, rohr flute; (= *Panrohrflöte*) panpipes *pl*; **Rohr|ge|flecht** NT wickerwork, basketwork

Röh|richt ['rø:rɪçt] NT -s, -e (*old*) reeds *pl*, reed bed

Rohr-: Rohr|kol|ben M (*Bot*) reed mace, cat's tail; **Rohr|krepie|rer** [-krepi:rɐ] M -s, - (*Mil sl*) barrel burst; **zum ~ werden** (*fig*) **ein ~ sein** (*fig*) to backfire; **Rohr|le|ger** [-le:gɐ] M -s, -, **Rohr|le|ge|rin** [-ərɪn] F -, -nen pipe fitter; **Rohr|lei|tung** F pipe, conduit; **Rohr|lei|tungs|sys|tem** NT network or system of pipes

Röhr|ling ['rø:ɐlɪŋ] M -s, -e (*Bot*) boletus

Rohr-: Rohr|mat|te F rush or reed mat; **Rohr|mö|bel** PL cane (*esp Brit*) or wicker furniture *sing*; **Rohr|muf|fe** F (*Tech*) socket; **Rohr|netz** NT network of pipes; **Rohr|pal|me** F calamus; **Rohr|post** F pneumatic dispatch system; **Rohr|sän|ger** M (*Orn*) warbler; **Rohr|spatz** M **schimpfen wie ein ~** (*inf*) to make a fuss; (= *Schimpfwörter gebrauchen*) to curse and swear; **Rohr|stock** M cane; **Rohr|stuhl** M basketwork or wickerwork chair; **Rohr|zan|ge** F pipe wrench; **Rohr|zu|cker** M cane sugar

Roh-: Roh|sei|de F wild silk; **roh|sei|den** ADJ wild silk

Roh|stoff M raw material; (*St Ex*) commodity

Roh|stoff-: roh|stoff|arm ADJ *Land* poor or lacking in raw materials; **Roh|stoff|bör|se** F commodities market; **Roh|stoff|fonds** M commodity fund; **Roh|stoff|man|gel** M shortage of raw materials; **Roh|stoff|markt** M commodities market; **Roh|stoff|preis** M commodity price; **Roh|stoff|quel|le** F source of raw materials; **roh|stoff|reich** ADJ *Land* rich in raw materials; **Roh|stoff|re|ser|ven** PL reserves *pl* of raw materials

Roh-: Roh|ta|bak M tobacco; (*ungetrocknet*) uncured tobacco; (*ungeschnitten*) leaf tobacco; **Roh|über|set|zung** F rough translation; **Roh|zu|cker** M crude or unrefined sugar; **Roh|zu|stand** M natural state or condition; **im ~** (*Denkmal etc*) in its initial stages; (*Übersetzung*) in its first draft

ro|jen ['ro:jən] VTI (*Naut*) to row

Ro|ko|ko ['rɔkoko, ro'koko, roko'ko:] NT -(s), *no pl* Rococo period; (= *Stil*) Rococo, rococo

Rol|la|den △ M → **Rollladen**

Roll-: Roll|bahn F (*Aviat*) taxiway; (= *Start-, Landebahn*) runway; **Roll|bra|ten** M (*Cook*) roast; **Roll|brett** NT (*Sport*) skateboard

Röll|chen ['rœlçən] NT -s, - little roll; (*von Garn*) reel

Rol|le ['rɔlə] F -, -n **a** (= *Zusammengerolltes*) roll; (= *Garnrolle, Zwirnrolle*) reel, bobbin (*spec*); (= *Papierrolle*) (= *Urkunde*) scroll; **eine ~ Bindfaden or Garn or Zwirn** a reel of thread; **eine ~ Toilettenpapier** a toilet roll, a roll of toilet paper; **eine ~ Drops** a tube of fruit drops; **eine ~ Film** a roll of film; (*im Kino*) a reel of film

b (= *kleines Rad, Walze*) roller; (*an Möbeln, Kisten*) caster, castor; (*an Flaschenzug*) pulley; (= *Gardinenrolle*) runner; **von der ~ sein** (*fig inf*) to have lost it (*inf*)

c (*Sport, Aviat*) roll; **eine ~ machen** to do a roll; **eine ~ vorwärts/rückwärts** a forward/backward roll

d (*Theat, Film, fig*) role, part; (*Sociol*) role; **es war ein Spiel mit vertauschten ~n** (*fig*) it was a situation where the roles were reversed; **ein Stück mit verteilten ~n lesen** to read a play with the parts cast; (*in Schule*) to read a play with the parts given out; **der literarische Kreis liest jeden Dienstag ein Stück mit verteilten ~n** the literary circle has a play-reading every Tuesday; **eine Ehe mit streng verteilten ~n** a marriage with strict allocation of roles; **jds ~ sein** or **in etw** (*dat*) sb's role or part in sth; **in der ~ von jdm/etw auftreten** to appear in the role of sb/sth; **er gefällt sich** (*dat*) **in der ~ des ...** (*fig*) he likes to think of or see himself in the role of the ...; **sich in die ~ eines anderen versetzen** (*fig*) to put oneself in sb else's place; **bei** or **in etw** (*dat*) **eine ~ spielen** to play a part in sth; (*Mensch auch*) to play a role in sth; **als Lehrer hat er eine klägliche ~ gespielt** as a teacher he was not up to much or he left much to be

---

desired; **etw spielt eine große ~ (bei jdm)** sth is very important (to sb); **es spielt keine ~, (ob) ...** it doesn't matter (whether) ..., it doesn't make any difference (whether) ..., whether ... doesn't come into it; **das spielt hier keine ~** that is irrelevant; **bei ihm spielt Geld keine ~** with him money is no object; **aus der ~ fallen** (*fig*) to do/say the wrong thing; **du bist aber gestern wirklich aus der ~ gefallen!** you really behaved badly yesterday!; **seine ~ ausgespielt haben** (*fig*) to have played one's part

e (*dial: = Wäschemangel*) roller iron

rol|len ['rɔlən] VI **a** *aux sein* to roll; (*Flugzeug*) to taxi; **der Stein kommt ins Rollen** (*fig*) the ball has started rolling; **die Ermittlungen sind ins Rollen gekommen** the investigation has gathered momentum; **etw/den Stein ins Rollen bringen** (*fig*) to set or start sth/the ball rolling; **es werden einige Köpfe ~** heads will roll; **die Privatisierungswelle rollt** privatizations are in full flow **b** **mit den Augen ~** to roll one's eyes **VT** to roll; *Teig* to roll out; *Teppich, Papier* to roll up; (*dial: = mangeln*) *Wäsche, Betttücher* to roll **VR** to curl up; (*Schlange auch*) to curl itself up

Rol|len-: Rol|len|be|set|zung F (*Theat, Film*) casting; **Rol|len|bild** NT (*Sociol*) role model; **Rol|len|er|war|tung** F (*Sociol*) role expectation; **Rol|len|fach** NT (*Theat*) character or type part; **der jugendliche Liebhaber ist sein ~** he's a character actor specializing in the young lover; **rol|len|för|mig** ADJ cylindrical; **Rol|len|ge|dicht** NT (*Liter*) dramatic monologue (*Brit*) or monolog (*US*); **rol|len|ge|la|gert** ADJ mounted on roller bearings; **Rol|len|kon|flikt** M role conflict; **Rol|len|la|ger** NT roller bearings *pl*; **Rol|len-Off|set-Ver|fah|ren** NT rotary offset process; **Rol|len|prüf|stand** M (*Tech*) rolling road dynamometer; **rol|len|spe|zi|fisch** ADJ role-specific; **Rol|len|spiel** NT role play; **Rol|len|tausch** M exchange of roles, role reversal; **Rol|len|ver|hal|ten** NT (*Sociol*) behavioural (*Brit*) or behavioral (*US*) role; **Rol|len|ver|ständ|nis** NT understanding of one's role; **Rol|len|ver|tei|lung** F (*Sociol*) role allocation; **Rol|len|zug** M block and tackle; **Rol|len|zwang** M role constraint(s *pl*)

Rol|ler ['rɔlɐ] M -s, - **a** (= *Motorroller, für Kinder*) scooter **b** (*Naut: = Welle*) roller **c** (*Aus: = Rollo*) (roller) blind **d** (*Orn*) Harzer ~ canary, roller **e** (= *Walze*) roller

Rol|ler|blades® ['rɔləbleːdz] PL Rollerblades® *pl*

Rol|ler|fah|ren NT -s, *no pl* riding a scooter

rol|lern ['rɔlɐn] VI *aux sein* to ride one's scooter

Rol|ler|skates ['roːləskeːts] PL rollerskates *pl*

Roll-: Roll|feld NT runway; **Roll|film** M roll film; **Roll|fuhr|dienst** M road-rail haulage; **Roll|geld** NT carriage, freight charge; **Roll|gers|te** F (*Agr*) pot barley, hulled barley; **Roll|gut** NT (*Rail*) freight; **Roll|ho|ckey** NT roller-skate hockey

Rol|li ['rɔli] M -s, -s (*Fashion inf*) rollneck

rol|lig ['rɔlɪç] ADJ (*inf*) *Katze* on (*Brit*) or in heat; (*sl*) *Mensch* horny

Roll-: Roll|kom|man|do NT raiding party; **Roll|kra|gen** M rollneck, polo neck; **Roll|kra|gen|pul|lo|ver** M polo-neck sweater; **Roll|kunst|lauf** M roller skating; **Roll|kur** F (*Med*) treatment for stomach disorders where the patient takes medicine, lies for 5 minutes on his back, 5 minutes on his side, then on his front etc; **Roll|la|den** ▲ M (*an Fenster, Tür etc*) (roller) shutters *pl*; (*von Schreibtisch*) roll top; (*von Schrank*) roll front; **Roll|mops** M rollmops

Rol|lo ['rɔlo, rɔ'lo:] NT -s, -s (roller) blind

Roll-: Roll|schin|ken M smoked ham; **Roll|schnell|lauf** ▲ M speed (roller-)skating; **Roll|schrank** M roll-fronted cupboard

Roll|schuh M roller skate; **~ laufen** to roller-skate

Roll|schuh-: Roll|schuh|bahn F roller-skating rink; **Roll|schuh|lau|fen** NT -s, *no pl* roller--skating; **Roll|schuh|läu|fer(in)** M(F) roller skater; **Roll|schuh|sport** M roller-skating

Roll-: Roll|sitz M (*im Rennboot*) sliding seat; **Roll|splitt** M loose chippings *pl*; **Roll|sport** M roller-skating; **Roll|steg** M travolator, moving pavement (*Brit*), mobile walkway (*US*); (*Naut*) gangplank, gangway

Roll|stuhl M wheelchair

Roll|stuhl-: Roll|stuhl|fah|rer(in) M(F) wheelchair user; **roll|stuhl|ge|recht** ADJ, ADV suitable *or* accessible for wheelchairs

Roll-: Roll|ta|bak M tobacco plug; **Roll|trep|-pe** F escalator; **Roll|werk** NT (*Archit*) cartouche, scrollwork

Rom [roːm] NT -s Rome; ~ **ist auch nicht an einem Tag erbaut worden** (*Prov*) Rome wasn't built in a day (*Prov*); **viele** *or* **alle Wege führen nach ~** (*Prov*) all roads lead to Rome (*Prov*); **das sind Zustände wie im alten ~** (*inf*) (*unmoralisch*) it's disgraceful; (*primitiv*) it's medieval (*inf*)

ROM [rɔm] NT -s, -s (*Comput*) ROM

Ro|ma ['roːma] PL (= *Zigeuner*) Romanies *pl*

Ro|mag|na-Sa|lat [roˈmanja-] M romaine lettuce

Ro|man [roˈmaːn] M -s, -e novel; (*höfisch, ritterlich etc auch*) romance; **ich könnte einen ~ schreiben!** (*inf*) I could write a book about it!; (*jdm*) **einen ganzen ~ erzählen** (*inf*) to give sb a long rigmarole (*inf*); **erzähl keine ~e!** (*inf*) don't tell stories! (*inf*)

ro|man|ar|tig ADJ novelistic

Ro|man|au|tor(in) M(F), **Ro|man|ci|er** [romãˈsie] M -s, -s novelist

Ro|man|die [romanˈdiː] F - (*esp Sw*) **die ~** French-speaking Switzerland

Ro|ma|ne [roˈmaːnə] M -n, -n, **Ro|ma|nin** [-ˈmaːnɪn] F -, -nen person speaking a Romance language

Ro|ma|nen|tum [roˈmaːnəntuːm] NT -s, *no pl* Latin nature

Ro|man-: Ro|man|fi|gur F character (in a novel); **ro|man|haft** ADJ like a novel; **Ro|man|heft** NT cheap pulp novel, penny dreadful (*dated Brit*); **Ro|man|held** M hero of a/the novel; **Ro|man|hel|din** F heroine of a/the novel

Ro|ma|nik [roˈmaːnɪk] F -, *no pl* (*Archit, Art*) Romanesque period; (*Stil*) Romanesque (style)

Ro|ma|nin F ▷ **Romane**

ro|ma|nisch [roˈmaːnɪʃ] ADJ *Volk, Sprache* Romance; (*Art, Archit*) Romanesque

Ro|ma|nist [romaˈnɪst] M -en, -en, **Ro|ma|nis|tin** [-ˈnɪstɪn] F -, -nen (*Univ*) student of *or* (*Wissenschaftler*) expert on Romance languages and literature

Ro|ma|nis|tik [romaˈnɪstɪk] F -, *no pl* (*Univ*) Romance languages and literature

ro|ma|nis|tisch [romaˈnɪstɪʃ] ADJ Romance; **~es Institut** (*Univ*) Institute for Romance Languages and Literature

Ro|man-: Ro|man|le|ser(in) M(F) novel reader; **Ro|man|li|te|ra|tur** F fiction, novels *pl*; **Ro|man|schrei|ber(in)** M(F) (*inf*) novelist; (*pej*) scribbler; **Ro|man|schrift|stel|ler(in)** M(F) novelist

Ro|man|tik [roˈmantɪk] F -, *no pl* **a** (*Liter, Art, Mus*) Romanticism; (*Epoche*) Age of Romanticism, Romantic period **b** (*fig*) (*Gefühl, Einstellung*) romanticism; **keinen Sinn für ~ haben** to have no sense of romance

Ro|man|ti|ker [roˈmantɪkɐ] M -s, -, **Ro|man|ti|ke|rin** [-ərɪn] F -, -nen (*Liter, Art, Mus*) Romantic; (*fig*) romantic

ro|man|tisch [roˈmantɪʃ] ADJ romantic; (*Liter etc*) Romantic ADV romantically; **~ liegen** to be in a romantic spot; **die Halle war ~ ausgestattet** the hall was decorated to give it a romantic feel

ro|man|ti|sie|ren [romantiˈziːrən] *ptp* **romantisiert** VT to romanticize

ro|mantsch [roˈmantʃ] ADJ = **rätoromanisch**

Ro|man|ze [roˈmantsə] F -, -n (*Liter, Mus, fig*) romance

ro|maun(t)sch [roˈmaun(t)ʃ] ADJ = **rätoromanisch**

Rö|mer¹ ['røːmɐ] M -s, - *wineglass with clear glass bowl and green or brown coiled stem*

Rö|mer² M -s *der* ~ *town hall of Frankfurt am Main*

Rö|mer³ ['røːmɐ] M -s, -, **Rö|me|rin** [-ərɪn] F -, -nen Roman; **die alten ~** the (ancient) Romans

Rö|mer-: Rö|mer|brief M Letter *or* Epistle of Paul to the Romans, Romans *sing, no art*; **Rö|mer|reich** NT Roman Empire; **Rö|mer|stra|ße** F Roman road; **Rö|mer|topf®** M (*Cook*) clay casserole dish; **Rö|mer|tum** ['røːmɐtuːm] NT -s, *no pl* Roman culture *etc*; **die Haupttugenden des ~s** the main virtues of Rome; **das ~ hat zahlreiche griechische Elemente absorbiert** Rome absorbed many elements from Greece

Rom|fah|rer(in) M(F) pilgrim to Rome

rö|misch ['røːmɪʃ] ADJ Roman; **~ 12** 12 in Roman numerals

rö|misch-ka|tho|lisch ['røːmɪʃkaˈtoːlɪʃ] ADJ Roman Catholic

Rom|mé [rɔˈmeː, 'rɔmeː] NT -s, -s, **Rom|mee** ▲ NT -s, -s rummy

Ron|deau NT -s, -s **a** [rõˈdoː] (*Liter, Mus*) rondeau, rondel **b** [rɔnˈdoː] (*Aus:* = *Rondell*) circular flowerbed

Ron|dell [rɔnˈdɛl] NT -s, -e **a** (*Archit*) round tower **b** circular flowerbed

Ron|do ['rɔndo] NT -s, -s (*Mus*) rondo

rönt|gen ['rœntgn] VT to X-ray; *Körperteil auch* to take an X-ray of

Rönt|gen NT -s, *no pl* X-raying; **er ist gerade beim ~** he's just being X-rayed

Rönt|gen-: Rönt|gen|ap|pa|rat M X-ray equipment *no indef art, no pl*; **Rönt|gen|auf|nah|me** F X-ray (plate); **Rönt|gen|au|gen** PL (*hum*) X-ray eyes *pl* (*hum*); **Rönt|gen|be|hand|lung** F, **Rönt|gen|be|strah|lung** F radiotherapy, X-ray treatment *or* therapy; **Rönt|gen|bild** NT , X-ray; **Rönt|gen|di|ag|nos|tik** F X-ray diagnosis; **Rönt|gen|film** M X-ray film

rönt|ge|ni|sie|ren [rœntgeniˈziːrən] *ptp* **röntgenisiert** VT (*Aus*) to X-ray; *Körperteil auch* to take an X-ray of

Rönt|gen|la|ser M X-ray laser

Rönt|ge|no|gramm [rœntgenoˈgram] NT *pl* -gramme X-ray (plate), radiograph (*esp US*)

Rönt|ge|no|gra|fie ▲ [rœntgenograˈfiː] F -, -n [-ˈfiːən] radiography

Rönt|ge|no|lo|ge [rœntgenoˈloːgə] M -n, -n, **Rönt|ge|no|lo|gin** [-ˈloːgɪn] F -, -nen radiologist, roentgenologist (*form*)

Rönt|ge|no|lo|gie [rœntgenoloˈgiː] F -, *no pl* radiology, roentgenology (*form*)

Rönt|ge|no|sko|pie [rœntgenoskoˈpiː] F -, -n [-ˈpiːən] radioscopy

Rönt|gen-: Rönt|gen|pass ▲ M X-ray registration card; **Rönt|gen|rei|hen|un|ter|su|chung** F X-ray screening; **Rönt|gen|röh|re** F X-ray tube; **Rönt|gen|strah|len** PL X-rays *pl*; **jdn mit ~ behandeln** to treat sb with X-rays, to give sb X-ray treatment; **Rönt|gen|the|ra|pie** F radiotherapy, X-ray treatment *or* therapy; **Rönt|gen|un|ter|su|chung** F X-ray examination

Ror|schach|test M (*Psych*) Rorschach test

ro|sa ['roːza] ADJ *inv* pink; **ein ~** *or* **~es** (*inf*) **Kleid** a pink dress; **die Welt durch eine ~(rote) Brille sehen** to see the world through rose-coloured (*Brit*) or rose-colored (*US*) or rose-tinted glasses; **in ~(rotem) Licht** in a rosy light; **er malt die Zukunft ~rot** he paints a rosy picture of the future

Ro|sa ['roːza] NT -s, -s pink

ro|sa|far|ben [-farbn], **ro|sa|far|big**, **ro|sa|rot** ADJ = **rosa**

rösch [røʃ] ADJ (*S Ger:* = *knusprig*) *Brot* crusty; *Fleisch* crisp; *Mädchen* bonnie (*esp N Engl, Scot*), pretty

Rös|chen ['røːsçən] NT -s, - (little) rose; (*von Broccoli, Blumenkohl*) floret; (*von Rosenkohl*) sprout

Ro|se ['roːzə] F -, -n **a** (*Blume*) rose; (*Archit*) rose window; **er ist nicht auf ~n gebettet** (*fig*) life isn't a bed of roses for him; **keine ~ ohne Dornen** (*prov*) no rose without a thorn (*prov*) **b** (*Med*) erysipelas (*spec*), rose **c** (*Hunt: am Hirschgeweih*) burr

ro|sé [roˈzeː] ADJ *inv* pink; **Schuhe in ~** pink shoes

Ro|sé [roˈzeː] M -s, -s rosé (wine)

Ro|sen-: ro|sen|ar|tig ADJ rose-like, rosaceous (*spec*); **Ro|sen|blatt** NT rose petal; **Ro|sen|duft** M scent *or* perfume of roses; **ro|sen|far|ben** [-farbn], **ro|sen|far|big** ADJ rose-coloured (*Brit*), rose-colored (*US*), pink, rosy; **Ro|sen|gar|ten** M rose garden; **Ro|sen|ge|wächs|e** M rosaceae *pl* (*spec*); **Ro|sen|holz** NT rosewood; **Ro|sen|kä|fer** M rose chafer, rose beetle; **Ro|sen|knos|pe** F rosebud; **Ro|sen|kohl** M Brussels(s) sprouts *pl*; **Ro|sen|kranz** M (*Eccl*) rosary; **den ~ beten** to say a rosary; **Ro|sen|kreu(t)|zer** [-krɔytsɐ] PL (*Rel*) Rosicrucians *pl*; **Ro|sen|krie|ge** PL (*Hist*) the Wars of the Roses *pl*; **Ro|sen|mon|tag** M *Monday preceding Ash Wednesday*; **Ro|sen|mon|tags|zug** M *Carnival parade which takes place on the Monday preceding Ash Wednesday*

ROSENMONTAG

Rosenmontag is the last Monday of **Karneval**. Traditional processions take place on this day: bands and carnival club members go through the streets wearing costumes and throwing toffees (**Kamellen**), sweets and flowers into the crowd, who are also dressed up for the occasion. There are also big carnival floats which pass comment on the year's events and carry huge papier-mâché figures which poke fun at local and national politicians → **KARNEVAL**

Ro|sen-: Ro|sen|öl NT attar of roses; **Ro|sen|quarz** M rose quartz; **ro|sen|rot** ADJ *Wangen, Lippen* rosy (red); **Schneeweißchen und Rosenrot** (*Liter*) Snow White and Rose Red; **Ro|sen|stock** M rose (tree); **Ro|sen|strauch** M rosebush; **Ro|sen|was|ser** NT rosewater; **Ro|sen|zucht** F rose-growing; **Ro|sen|züch|ter(in)** M(F) rose-grower

Ro|set|te [roˈzɛtə] F -, -n rosette

Ro|sé|wein M rosé wine

ro|sig ['roːzɪç] ADJ (*lit, fig*) rosy; *Braten* pink; **etw in ~em Licht sehen** (*inf*) to see sth in a rosy light; **etw in ~en Farben schildern** (*inf*) to paint a glowing *or* rosy picture of sth, to show sth in a rosy light

Ro|si|ne [roˈziːnə] F -, -n raisin; (*große*) **~n im Kopf haben** (*inf*) to have big ideas; **sich** (*dat*) **die (besten** *or* **größten) ~n (aus dem Kuchen) herauspicken** (*inf*) to take the pick of the bunch

Ro|si|nen-: Ro|si|nen|bom|ber M (*hum*) *plane which flew food etc into Berlin during the 1948 airlift*; **Ro|si|nen|bröt|chen** NT ≈ currant bun

Rös|lein ['røːslain] NT -s, - (little) rose

Ros|ma|rin ['roːsmariːn, roːsmaˈriːn] M -s, *no pl* rosemary

Ross ▲ [rɔs] NT -es, -e *or* (*S Ger, Aus, Sw*) **Rösser** ['rœsɐ] (*liter*) steed; (*S Ger, Aus, Sw*) horse; (*inf:* = *Dummkopf*) dolt (*inf*); **~ und Reiter nennen** (*fig geh*) to name names; **der Ritter hoch zu ~** (*liter*) the knight astride his steed (*liter*); **auf dem ho-**

hen ~ sitzen (fig) to be on one's high horse; hoch zu ~ on horseback

Ross-: Ross|ap|fel ▲ M (hum inf) horse droppings pl; **Ross|brei|ten** ▲ PL (Naut) horse latitudes pl

Rös|sel ['rœsl] NT -s, - (Chess) knight; (S Ger: = Pferd) horse

Ros|se|len|ker ['rɔsə-] M (poet) reinsman (liter)

Rös|sel|sprung M **a** (Chess) knight's move **b** (= Rätsel) type of puzzle in which certain individual letters or syllables make up a phrase or saying

Ross-: Ross|haar ▲ NT horsehair; **Ross|haar|mat|rat|ze** ▲ F horsehair mattress; **Ross|kä|fer** ▲ M dung beetle; **Ross|ta|nie** ▲ F horse chestnut; **Ross|kas|ta|ni|en|ex|trakt** ▲ M extract of horse chestnut used as a medicament for varicose veins; **Ross|kur** ▲ F (hum) drastic cure, kill-or-cure remedy; **eine ~ (durch)machen** to follow a drastic cure

Rössl ['rœsl] NT -s, - (Chess) knight; (S Ger: = Pferd) horse

Röss|li|spiel ▲ ['rœsli-] NT (Sw) merry-go--round, roundabout (Brit)

Ross-: Ross|schläch|ter(in) ▲ M(F) horse butcher; **Ross|schläch|te|rei** ▲ F horse butchery; **Ross|täu|scher(in)** ▲ M(F) (old, fig) horse trader; **Ross|täu|sche|rei** ▲ [-tɔyʃə-'rai] F -, -en (fig) horse trading no pl

Rost[1] [rɔst] M -(e)s, no pl (auch Bot) rust; **~ an|setzen** to start to rust

Rost[2] M -(e)s, -e (= Ofenrost) grill; (= Gitterrost) grating, grille; (dial: = Bettrost) base, frame; **auf dem ~ braten** (Cook) to barbecue, to grill over charcoal

Rost-: Rost|an|satz M signs pl of rust; **rost|be|stän|dig** ADJ rust-resistant; **Rost|bil|dung** F rust formation; **Rost|bra|ten** M (Cook) ≈ roast; **Rost|brat|wurst** F barbecue sausage; **rost|braun** ADJ russet; Haar auburn

Röst|brot [(S Ger) 'rø:st-] [(N Ger) 'rœst-] NT toast

Rös|te [(S Ger) 'rø:stə] [(N Ger) 'rœstə] F -, -n (Metal) roasting

ros|ten ['rɔstn] VI aux sein or haben to rust, to get rusty (auch fig); **alte Liebe rostet nicht** (Prov) true love never dies (prov) → **rasten**

rös|ten [(S Ger) 'rø:stn] [(N Ger) 'rœstn] VT **a** Kaffee, Erdnüsse, Kastanien to roast; Brot to toast; **sich in der Sonne ~ lassen** to lie in the sun and bake **b** Erz to roast, to calcine

Rös|te|rei [(S Ger) 'rø:stə'rai] [(N Ger) 'rœstə'rai] F -, -en roast(ing) house; **frisch aus der ~** fresh from the roast, freshly roasted

Rost-: rost|far|ben, rost|far|big ADJ = rostbraun; **Rost|fleck** M spot or patch of rust, rust spot or patch; **Rost|fraß** M rust corrosion; **rost|frei** ADJ Stahl stainless

röst|frisch [(S Ger) 'rø:st-] [(N Ger) 'rœst-] ADJ Kaffee freshly roasted

Rös|ti [(S Ger) 'rø:sti] [(N Ger) 'rœsti] PL fried grated potatoes

ros|tig ['rɔstɪç] ADJ (lit, fig) rusty

Rös|ti|gra|ben M (esp Sw, hum) lack of understanding between the German-speaking and French-speaking Swiss

Röst|kar|tof|feln [(S Ger) 'rø:st-] [(N Ger) 'rœst-] PL fried or sauté potatoes pl

Rost-: Rost|krank|hei|ten PL (Bot) rust diseases pl; **Rost|lau|be** F (hum) rust-heap (hum); **rost|rot** ADJ rust-coloured (Brit), rust-colored (US), russet; **Rost|schutz** M antirust protection; **Rost|schutz|far|be** F antirust paint; **Rost|schutz|mit|tel** NT rustproofer; **Rost|um|wand|ler** [-ʊmvandlɐ] M -s, - (Aut) rust converter

Röst|zwie|beln [(S Ger) 'rø:st-] [(N Ger) 'rœst-] PL fried onions pl

rot [ro:t] ADJ comp **röter** ['rø:tɐ], superl **röteste(r, s)** ['rø:təstə] red (auch Pol); **Rote Bete** or **Rüben** beetroot (Brit), beets pl (US); **~e Karte** (Ftbl) red card; **das Rote Kreuz** the Red Cross; **der Rote Halbmond** the Red Crescent; **der Rote Löwe** the Red Lion; **der Rote Platz** Red Square; **das Rote Meer** the Red Sea; **die Rote Armee** the Red Army; **die Roten** (pej) the reds; **~e Zahlen schreiben, in den ~en Zahlen stecken** to be in the red; **Gewalt zieht sich wie ein ~er Faden durch die Geschichte** violence runs like a thread through history; **~ werden** to blush, to go red (inf); **bis über beide Ohren ~ werden** to blush furiously, to turn crimson; **~ wie ein Krebs** red as a lobster; **~e Ohren bekommen** (hum) **einen ~en Kopf bekommen** or **kriegen** (inf) to blush, to go red (inf); **~ sein** (Pol inf) to be a socialist → **Grütze, rotsehen, Tuch, Hahn**

ADV comp **röter**, superl **am rötesten** **a** (= mit roter Farbe) anmalen red; schreiben, unterstreichen, anstreichen in red; **die Lippen ~ schminken** to use a red lipstick; **sich** (dat) **etw ~ (im Kalender) anstreichen** (inf) to make sth a red-letter day; **den Tag werde ich mir ~ im Kalender anstreichen** that will be a red-letter day

b (= in roter Farbe) glühen, leuchten a bright red; **~ anlaufen** to turn red; **seine Ohren glühten** ~ his ears glowed red; **~ gerändert** red-rimmed; ~ **glühend** (Metall) red-hot; **der ~ glühende Abendhimmel** the red glow of the evening sky; **~ verheulte Augen** eyes red from crying

c (Pol inf) **~ angehaucht sein** to have left-wing leanings

Rot [ro:t] NT -s, -s or - red; (= Wangenrot) rouge; **bei** or **auf** at red; **bei ~ anhalten!** stop (when the lights are) at red, stop when the lights are (at) red; **die Ampel stand auf ~** the lights were (at) red; **bei ~ über die Ampel fahren/gehen** to jump (Brit) or go through the lights/cross at a red light

Röt [rø:t] NT -(e)s, no pl (Geol) upper layer of bunter sandstone

Ro|ta|ri|er [ro'ta:riɐ] M -s, -, **Ro|ta|ri|e|rin** [-iərɪn] F -, -nen Rotarian

Rot|ar|mist ['ro:tˌarmɪst] M -en, -en, **Rot|ar|mis|tin** [-mɪstɪn] F -, -nen soldier in or of the Red Army; **die ~en zogen auf ihrem Vormarsch durch die Stadt** the Red Army advanced through the town

Ro|ta|ry Club ['ro:tari, 'ro:tɐri, ro'ta:ri] M Rotary Club

Ro|ta|ti|on [rota'tsio:n] F -, -en (Phys, Pol) rotation; (Math auch) curl

Ro|ta|ti|ons-: Ro|ta|ti|ons|ach|se F (Math, Phys) axis of rotation; **Ro|ta|ti|ons|druck** M pl -drucke (Typ) rotary (press) printing; **Ro|ta|ti|ons|flä|che** F (Math, Phys) surface of revolution; **Ro|ta|ti|ons|ma|schi|ne** F, **Ro|ta|ti|ons|pres|se** F (Typ) rotary press; **Ro|ta|ti|ons|prin|zip** NT (Pol) rota system

Rot-: Rot|au|ge NT (Zool) roach; **rot|ba|ckig** [-bakɪç], **rot|bä|ckig** [-bɛkɪç] ADJ rosy--cheeked; **Rot|barsch** M rosefish; **Rot|bart** M red-beard; **Kaiser ~** Emperor Frederick Barbarossa; **rot|bär|tig** ADJ red-bearded; **rot|blond** ADJ (Männer)haar sandy; Mann sandy--haired; Frau, Tönung strawberry blonde; **rot|braun** ADJ reddish brown; **Rot|bu|che** F (common) beech; **Rot|dorn** M pl -dorne hawthorn

Rö|te ['rø:tə] F -, no pl redness, red; (= Erröten) blush; **die ~ des Abendhimmels** the red glow of the evening sky; **die ~ stieg ihr ins Gesicht** her face reddened

Ro|te-Ar|mee-Frak|ti|on [ro:təˌarˈme:-] F Red Army Faction

Ro|te Khmer [kme:ɐ] PL Khmer Rouge pl

Rö|tel ['rø:tl] M -s, - red chalk

Rö|teln ['rø:tln] PL German measles sing

rö|ten ['rø:tn] VT to redden, to make red; Himmel to turn red; **die frische Luft rötete ihre Wangen** the fresh air gave her rosy cheeks or

made her cheeks (go) red; **ein gerötetes Gesicht** a flushed face; **gerötete Augen** red eyes

VR to turn or become red

Rot-: Rot|fil|ter NT OR M (Phot) red filter; **Rot|front** F (Pol) red front; **Rot|fuchs** M red fox; (Pferd) sorrel or bay (horse); (fig inf) carrot--top (inf); **Rot|gar|dist(in)** M(F) Red Guard; **rot|ge|rän|dert** △ [-gərɛndɐt] ADJ → **rot** ADV **b**; **rot|ge|sich|tig** [-gəzɪçtɪç] ADJ florid, red--faced; **rot|glü|hend** △ ADJ → **rot** ADV **b**; **Rot|glut** F (Metal) red heat; **rot|grün** ▲ ADJ red--green; **die ~e Koalition** the Red-Green coalition; **Rot|grün|blind|heit** F red-green colour (Brit) or color (US) blindness; **Rot|guss** ▲ M (Metal) red brass; **rot|haa|rig** ADJ red-haired; **Rot|haa|ri|ge(r)** ['ro:tˌhaːrɪgə] MF decl as adj redhead; **Rot|haut** F (dated hum) redskin; **Rot|hirsch** M red deer

ro|tie|ren [ro'ti:rən] ptp **rotiert** VI (auch Pol) to rotate; (inf: = hektisch handeln) to flap (inf); **an|fangen zu ~** (inf) to get into a flap (inf); **am Rotieren sein** (inf) to be in a flap (inf)

Rot-: Rot|ka|bis M (Sw) red cabbage; **Rot|käpp|chen** [-kɛpçən] NT -s, no pl (Liter) Little Red Riding Hood; **Rot|kehl|chen** [-ke:lçən] NT -s, - robin; **Rot|kohl** M red cabbage; **Rot|kopf** M (inf) redhead; **Rot|kraut** NT (S Ger, Aus) red cabbage

Rot|kreuz- [ro:t'krɔyts-]: **Rot|kreuz|lot|te|rie** F Red Cross lottery; **Rot|kreuz|samm|lung** F Red Cross appeal or collection; **Rot|kreuz|schwes|ter** F Red Cross nurse

Rot|lauf M, no pl (Vet) swine erysipelas (spec)

röt|lich ['rø:tlɪç] ADJ reddish → **schimmern**

Rot|licht NT red light

Rot|licht-: Rot|licht|mi|lieu NT demimonde; **Rot|licht|re|vier** NT, **Rot|licht|vier|tel** NT red-light district

Ro|tor ['ro:tor] M -s, Rotoren [-'to:rən] rotor

Ro|tor|flü|gel M (Aviat) rotor blade

Rot-: Rot|schwanz M, **Rot|schwänz|chen** NT redstart; **rot|se|hen** ['ro:tze:ən] VI sep irreg (inf) to see red (inf); **Rot|se|hen** NT -s, no pl (Med) erythropsia (spec); **Rot|specht** M spotted woodpecker; **Rot|stift** M red pencil; **den ~ ansetzen** (fig) to cut back drastically; **dem ~ zum Opfer fallen** (fig) to be scrapped or rejected, to be cancelled (Brit) or canceled (US); **Rot|tan|ne** F Norway spruce

Rot|te ['rɔtə] F -, -n gang; (bei Jugendorganisation) troop; (Mil) rank; (Mil Aviat, Mil Naut) pair (of planes/ships operating together); (von Hunden etc) pack; (Hunt: von Sauen) herd, sounder (spec)

rot|ten|wei|se ['rɔtnvaizə] ADV in groups; **die Hunde fielen ~ über das Reh her** packs of dogs attacked the deer

Rott|wei|ler ['rɔtvailɐ] M -s, - Rottweiler

Ro|tun|de [ro'tʊndə] F -, -n (Archit) rotunda

Rö|tung ['rø:tʊŋ] F -, -en reddening

Rot-: rot|ver|heult △ ADJ → **rot** ADV **b**; **rot|wan|gig** [-vaŋɪç] ADJ Mensch, Apfel rosy--cheeked; **Rot|wein** M red wine; **rot|welsch** ['ro:tvɛlʃ] ADJ argot, thieves' cant; **Rot|welsch(e)** ['ro:tvɛlʃ] NT argot, thieves' cant → auch Deutsch(e); **Rot|wild** NT red deer; **Rot|wurst** F ≈ black pudding

Rotz [rɔts] M -es, no pl **a** (inf) snot (inf); **~ und Wasser heulen** (inf) to blubber; **Baron** or **Graf ~** (inf) Lord Muck (Brit inf), His Highness (inf) **b** (Vet) glanders sing, farcy; **den ~ haben** to have glanders **c** (Bot) soft rot

Rotz|ben|gel M, (S Ger, Aus) **Rotz|bub** M (inf) snotty-nosed brat (inf)

rotz|be|sof|fen ADJ (sl) wrecked (Brit sl), wasted (sl)

rot|zen ['rɔtsn] VI (sl: = spucken) to spit

Rotz-: Rotz|fah|ne F (sl) snot-rag (inf); **rotz|frech** (inf) ADJ cocky (inf) ADV **~ antworten** to give a cocky answer (inf); **~ auftreten** to act cocky (inf); **Rotz|gö|re** F (inf) **a** (= kleines

Mädchen) snotty little madam (*inf*) **b** (= *kleines Kind*) snotty-nosed brat (*inf*)

rot|zig ['rɔtsɪç] ADJ **a** (*inf: lit, fig*) snotty (*inf*) **b** (*Vet*) glanderous

Rotz-: Rotz|jun|ge M (*inf*) snotty-nosed kid (*inf*); **Rotz|ko|cher** M (*pej*) pipe; **Rotz|löf|fel** M (*inf*) cheeky (*Brit*) or impudent brat (*inf*); **Rotz|na|se** F **a** (*inf*) snotty nose (*inf*) **b** (*inf: = Kind*) snotty-nosed brat (*inf*); **rotz|nä|sig** [-nɛːzɪç] ADJ (*inf*) **a** snotty-nosed (*inf*) **b** (= *frech*) snotty (*inf*); **Rotz|ni|gel** ['rɔtsniːgl] M **-s, -** (*Aus inf*) snotty-nosed brat (*inf*)

Rot|zun|ge F (*Zool*) witch flounder

Rouge [ruːʒ] NT **-s, -s** rouge, blusher

Rou|la|de [ruˈlaːdə] F **-, -n** (*Cook*) beef olive

Rou|leau [ruˈloː] NT **-s, -s** (roller) blind

Rou|lett [ruˈlɛt] NT **-(e)s, -e** or **-s**, **Rou|let|te** [ruˈlɛtə] NT **-s, -s** roulette

rou|lie|ren [ruˈliːrən] ptp **rouliert** VT (*Sew*) to roll

Rou|te ['ruːtə] F **-, -n** route (*auch Comput*); **wir sind die ~ über Bremen gefahren** we took the Bremen route

Rou|ti|ne [ruˈtiːnə] F **-, -n** **a** (= *Erfahrung*) experience; (*Gewohnheit, Trott*) routine; **das ist (bei mir) zur ~ geworden** that has become routine (for me) **b** (*Comput*) routine

Rou|ti|ne-: Rou|ti|ne|an|ge|le|gen|heit F routine matter; **Rou|ti|ne|ar|beit** F routine (work); **rou|ti|ne|mä|ßig** ADJ routine ADV **ich gehe ~ zum Zahnarzt** I make routine visits to the dentist's; **das wird ~ überprüft** it's checked as a matter of routine; **ich werde das ~ abwickeln** I'll deal with it in the usual way; **Rou|ti|ne|sa|che** F routine matter; **Rou|ti|ne|un|ter|su|chung** F routine examination

Rou|ti|ni|er [rutiˈnieː] M **-s, -s** old hand

rou|ti|niert [rutiˈniːrt] ADJ experienced ADV expertly; **die Kunstfertigkeit der Verse wirkt ~** such skilful verse is made to seem effortless

Row|dy ['raudi] M **-s, -s** hooligan; (*zerstörerisch*) vandal; (*lärmend*) rowdy (type); (= *Verkehrsrowdy*) road hog (*inf*)

Row|dy|tum ['raudituːm] NT **-s**, *no pl* hooliganism; (*zerstörerisch*) vandalism; **das ~ im Verkehr bekämpfen** to combat or fight road rage

Ro|ya|lis|mus [roajaˈlɪsmʊs] M **-**, *no pl* royalism

Ro|ya|list [roajaˈlɪst] M **-en, -en**, **Ro|ya|lis|tin** [-ˈlɪstɪn] F **-, -nen** royalist

ro|ya|lis|tisch [roajaˈlɪstɪʃ] ADJ royalist

Rub|bel- [ˈrʊbl-]: **Rub|bel|karte** F , **Rub|bel|los** NT scratch card; **Rub|bel|lot|te|rie** F scratch card lottery; **Rub|bel|mas|sa|ge** F body scrub

rub|beln [ˈrʊbln] VTI to rub; *Los* to scratch

Rüb|chen ['ryːpçən] NT **-s, -** *dim von* **Rübe** small turnip; **Teltower ~** (*Cook*) glazed turnip with bacon

Rü|be ['ryːbə] F **-, -n** **a** turnip; **Gelbe ~** (*S Ger, Sw*: = *Mohrrübe*) carrot; **Rote ~** beetroot (*Brit*), beet (*US*); **Weiße ~** white turnip; **jdn über die ~n jagen** (*inf*) to send sb packing (*inf*) → **Kraut b** (*inf: = Kopf*) nut (*inf*); **nichts in der ~ haben** to have nothing up top (*inf*); **jdm die ~ abhacken** (*fig*) to have sb's guts for garters (*inf*); **~ ab!** off with his/her head!

Ru|bel ['ruːbl] M **-s, -** rouble; **der ~ rollt** (*inf*) the money's rolling in (*inf*)

Rü|ben-: rü|ben|ar|tig ADJ turnip-like; **Rü|ben|saft** M , **Rü|ben|kraut** NT sugar beet syrup; **Rü|ben|zu|cker** M beet sugar

rü|ber- ['ryːbɐ-] *in cpds* (*inf*) → *auch* **herüber-, hinüber-: rü|ber+brin|gen** VT *sep irreg* (*inf*) *Botschaft, Feeling* to get across, to communicate; **rü|ber+kom|men** VI *sep* **a** → **herüberkommen b** (*inf*) to come across; **sie kam gut rüber** she came across or over well; **mit etw ~** to come out with sth; **rü|ber+wach|sen** *sep irreg* VI → **lassen** (*inf, Geld etc*) to come up with; **rü|ber+zie|hen** *sep irreg* VTI → **herüberziehen** VTI

(*inf: = schlagen*) **jdm eine ~** to give sb one (*inf*), to stick one on sb (*inf*)

Rü|be|zahl ['ryːbətsaːl] M **-s** *spirit of the Sudeten Mountains*

Ru|bi|di|um [ruˈbiːdiʊm] NT **-s**, *no pl* (*abbr* **Rb**) rubidium

Ru|bi|kon ['ruːbikɔn] M **-s** Rubicon; **den ~ überschreiten** (*fig geh*) to cross the Rubicon

Ru|bin [ruˈbiːn] M **-s, -e** ruby

ru|bin|rot ADJ ruby-red, ruby

Rüb-: Rüb|kohl ['ryːpkoːl] M kohlrabi; **Rüb|öl** ['ryːpøːl] NT rapeseed oil, rape oil

Rub|rik [ruˈbriːk] F **-, -en** **a** (= *Kategorie*) category; **das gehört in die ~ „Militaria"** this belongs under the category or heading "military"; **das läuft unter der ~ Spesen** that comes under expenses **b** (= *Zeitungsrubrik*) section; **wir berichteten unter** or **in der ~ Frauen und Politik** we ran a report in the Women and Politics section

rub|ri|zie|ren [rubriˈtsiːrən] ptp **rubriziert** VT to categorize, to put under a heading/headings

Rub|ri|zie|rung F **-, -en** categorization

Rüb|sa|me(n) ['ryːpzaːmə(n)] M **-(n)s**, *no pl* (*Bot*) rape

Ruch [ruːx, rʊx] M **-(e)s, ⸚e** ['ryːçə, 'rʏçə] (*geh*) **jdn/etw in den ~ der Bestechlichkeit bringen** to pin allegations of corruption on sb/sth; **ein ~ von Korruption** the smell or whiff of corruption; **in den ~ der Korruption geraten** to become tainted by corruption; **ihm haftet der ~ der Unfehlbarkeit an** he can't shake off his air of infallibility

Ruch-: ruch|bar ADJ **~ werden** (*geh*) to become known; **ruch|los** ADJ (*old, liter*) dastardly (*liter*); **Ruch|lo|sig|keit** F **-, -en** (*old, liter*) dastardliness (*liter*)

ruck [rʊk] INTERJ → **hau ruck, ruck, zuck**

Ruck [rʊk] M **-(e)s, -e** jerk, tug; (*von Fahrzeug*) jolt, jerk; (*Pol*) swing, shift; **auf einen** or **ein einem ~** in one go, with one heave; **er stand mit einem ~ auf** he sprang to his feet, he stood up suddenly; **sich** (*dat*) **einen ~ geben** (*inf*) to make an effort, to give oneself a kick up the backside (*Brit inf*) or in the ass (*US sl*); **etw in einem ~ erledigen** to do sth at one fell swoop; **durch die Gesellschaft muss ein ~ gehen** society needs to be pulled out of its complacency

Rück-: Rück|an|sicht F back or rear view; **Rück|ant|wort** F reply, answer; **um ~ wird gebeten** please reply; **Telegramm mit ~** reply-paid telegram

ruck|ar|tig ADJ jerky; **das Auto machte einige ~e Bewegungen** the car jerked a few times ADV jerkily; **er stand ~ auf** he shot to his feet; **sie drehte sich ~ um** she turned round jerkily

Rück-: Rück|äu|ße|rung F reply, answer; **Rück|be|ru|fung** F recall; **Rück|be|sin|nung** F **eine ~ auf die Werte der Vergangenheit** a return to past values; **rück|be|züg|lich** ADJ (*Gram*) reflexive; **Rück|bil|dung** F (*Ling*) back formation; (*Biol*) degeneration; **Rück|bil|dungs|gym|nas|tik** F (*nach der Geburt*) postnatal exercise(s *pl*); **Rück|blen|de** F flashback; **Rück|blick** M look back (*auf +acc* at); **im ~ auf etw** (*acc*) looking back on sth; **im ~ lässt sich sagen ...** looking back or in retrospect one can say ...; **einen ~ auf etw** (*acc*) **werfen** to look back on or at sth; **rück|bli|ckend** ADJ retrospective; **ein auf das vergangene Jahr ~er Bericht** a report that looks back at or over the last year ADV in retrospect, looking back; **~ lässt sich sagen, dass ...** looking back or in retrospect one can say that ...; **rück|da|tie|ren** ['rʏkdatiːrən] ptp **rückdatiert** VT *sep infin, ptp only* to backdate; **Rück|de|ckungs|ver|si|che|rung** F (*Econ*) firm's private pension plan for employees; **rück|dre|hend** ADJ (*Met*) *Wind* backing

ru|cken ['rʊkn] VI (*inf*) to jerk; (*Fahrzeug*) to jerk, to jolt; (*Taube*) to coo; **in den Schultern ~** to jerk one's shoulders back

rü|cken ['rʏkn] VI *aux sein* to move; (= *Platz machen*) to move up or (*zur Seite auch*) over; (= *weiterrücken: Zeiger*) to move on (*auf +acc* to); **näher ~** to move or come closer; (*Zeit*) to come or get closer; **ins Feld ~** (*old*) to take the field; **ins Manöver ~** (*old*) to go off on manoeuvres (*Brit*) or maneuvers (*US*); **an die Front ~** (*old*) to go up to the front; **mit etw ~** to move sth; **sie rückten ungeduldig mit den Stühlen** they shuffled their chairs about impatiently; **an etw** (*dat*) **~** (*an Uhrzeiger*) to move sth; *an Krawatte* to pull sth (straight); (= *schieben*) to push at sth; (= *ziehen*) to pull at sth; **an jds Seite** (*acc*) **~** to move up close beside sb; **an jds Stelle** (*acc*) **~** to take sb's place; **nicht von der Stelle ~** not to budge an inch (*inf*); **in weite Ferne ~** (*lit, fig*) to recede into the distance; **in den Vordergrund ~** (*lit*) to move into the foreground; (*fig*) to come to the fore; **in den Mittelpunkt ~** (*lit*) to move into the centre (*Brit*) or center (*US*); (*fig*) to become the focus of attention; **in den Hintergrund ~** (*lit*) to move into the background; (*fig*) to be pushed into the background; **in greifbare Nähe ~** (*fig*) to come within reach; **jdm auf den Leib** or **Pelz** (*inf*) or **Balg** (*inf*) or **die Pelle** (*inf*) **~** (= *zu nahe kommen*) to crowd sb; (= *sich jdm vornöpfen*) to get on at sb; (*hum: = besuchen*) to move in on sb; **einer Sache** (*dat*) **zu Leibe ~** to have a go at sth (*Brit*), to tackle sth → **Bude c, Bewusstsein a**; **VT** to move → **Licht b**

Rü|cken ['rʏkn] M **-s, -** (= *Stuhlrücken, Handrücken, auch Anat, Sew*) back; (= *Nasenrücken*) ridge; (= *Fußrücken*) instep; (= *Messerrücken*) blunt edge, back; (= *Hügelrücken, Bergrücken*) crest; (= *Buchrücken*) spine; **auf dem/den ~** on one's back; **ich bin ja auf den ~ gefallen!** (*fig*) you could have knocked me down with a feather (*inf*); **den Feind im ~ haben** to have the enemy to one's rear; **die Sonne im ~ haben** to have the sun behind one or on one's back; **den Wind im ~ haben** to have a tail or following (*Brit*) wind; **er hat doch die Firma des Vaters im ~** but he's got his father's firm behind him; **ich habe nicht gern jemanden im ~** I don't like having somebody sitting/standing right behind my back; **jdm die Hände auf den ~ binden** to tie sb's hands behind his back; **mit dem ~ zur Tür/Wand** with one's back to the door/wall; **mit dem ~ zur Wand stehen** (*fig*) (*aus Feigheit*) to cover oneself; (*aus Unterlegenheit*) to have one's back to the wall; **der verlängerte ~** (*hum inf*) one's posterior (*hum inf*); **~ an ~** back to back; **ein schöner ~ kann auch entzücken** (*hum inf*) you've/she's *etc* got a lovely back; **hinter jds ~** (*dat*) (*fig*) behind sb's back; **jdm/einer Sache den ~ kehren** (*lit, fig*) or **zuwenden** (*lit*) or **wenden** (*fig*) or **zudrehen** (*lit*) to turn one's back on sb/sth (*lit, fig*); **den ~ wenden** to turn one's back; **jdm in den ~ fallen** (*fig*) to stab sb in the back; (*Mil*) to attack sb from the rear; **den ~ frei haben** (*fig*) to be free of ties; **sich** (*dat*) **den ~ freihalten** (*inf*) or **decken** to cover oneself; **jdm den ~ decken** (*fig inf*) to back sb up (*inf*); **auf seinen ~ geht viel** (*inf*) he can take it; **die Sparpolitik wird auf dem ~ der Sozialhilfeempfänger ausgetragen** the cost-cutting policy is being carried out at the expense of people on benefit; **jdm den ~ stärken** or **steifen** (*fig inf*) to give sb encouragement → **breit ADJ**

Rücken-: Rücken|de|ckung F (*fig*) backing; **jdm ~ geben** to back sb; **Rücken|flos|se** F dorsal fin; **Rücken|flug** M (*Aviat*) inverted flight; **rücken|frei** ADJ *Kleid* backless, low-backed; **Rücken|gym|nas|tik** F back exercise(s *pl*); **rücken+krau|len** VI *sep infin only* to do or swim backstroke or back crawl; **Rücken|krau|len** NT **-s**, *no pl* (*Sport*) backstroke, back crawl; **Rücken|la|ge** F supine position; **er musste 3 Monate in ~ verbringen** he had to spend 3 months lying (flat) on his back or lying in a supine position (*form*); **er schläft in ~** he sleeps on his back; **in der ~ schwimmen** to swim on one's back; **Rücken|-**

leh|ne F back, back rest; **Rü|cken|mark** NT spinal cord; **Rü|cken|mark(s)|ent|zün|dung** F myelitis; **Rü|cken|mus|kel** M back muscle; **Rü|cken|mus|ku|la|tur** F back muscles *pl*, muscles *pl* of the/one's back; **Rü|cken|schmer|zen** PL backache; **ich habe ~** I've got backache, my back aches; **Rü|cken|schu|le** F , *no pl* programme (*Brit*) or program (*US*) of back exercises; **rü|cken+schwim|men** ['rʏkn̩ʃvɪmən] VI *sep infin only* to swim on one's back, to do the *or* swim backstroke; **Rü|cken|schwim|men** NT backstroke, swimming on one's back; **Rü|cken|stär|kung** F (*fig*) moral support; **Rü|cken|stück** NT (*Cook*) (*vom Rind, Schwein*) chine; (*vom Reh, Hammel*) saddle; **ein schönes ~** a nice piece of back; **Rü|cken|tra|ge** F carrying frame

Rück|ent|wick|lung F (*allgemein*) fall-off (+*gen* in); (*Biol*) degeneration

Rück-: **Rü|cken|wind** M tail *or* following wind; **Rü|cken|wir|bel** M dorsal vertebra

Rück-: **Rück|er|in|ne|rung** F memory (*an* +*acc* of); **rück+er|stat|ten** ['rʏklɛɐ̯ʃtatn̩] *ptp* **rückerstattet** VT *sep infin, ptp only* to refund; *Ausgaben* to reimburse; **Rück|er|stat|tung** F refund; (*von Ausgaben*) reimbursement; **Rück|fahr|kar|te** F , **Rück|fahr|schein** M return ticket, round-trip ticket (*US*); **Rück|fahr|schein|wer|fer** M (*Aut*) reversing light; **Rück|fahrt** F return journey; **Rück|fall** M (*Med, fig*) relapse; (*Jur*) subsequent offence (*Brit*) or offense (*US*), repetition of an/the offence (*Brit*) or offense (*US*); **ein ~ in alte Gewohnheiten** a relapse into one's old habits; **Diebstahl im ~** a repeated case of theft; **rück|fäl|lig** ADJ (*Med, fig*) relapsed; (*Jur*) recidivistic (*form*); **ein ~er Dieb** a thief who repeats his offence (*Brit*) or offense (*US*); **~ werden** (*Med*) to have a relapse; (*fig*) to relapse; (*Jur*) to lapse back into crime; **Rück|fäl|li|ge(r)** ['rʏkfɛlɪɡə] MF *decl as adj* (*Med, fig*) person who has relapsed; (*Jur*) subsequent offender, recidivist (*form*); **Rück|fall|tä|ter(in)** M(F) recidivist (*form*), recidivistic offender (*form*); **Rück|fens|ter** NT (*im Auto*) rear window; **Rück|flug** M return flight; **Rück|fluss** ▲ M reflux, flowing back; (*von Investitionen, Kapital*) return; **Rück|for|de|rung** F **~ des Geldes/des Buches** demand for the return of the money/the book; **Rück|fracht** F return load; **Rück|fra|ge** F question; **nach ~ bei der Zentrale ...** after querying *or* checking this with the exchange ...; **bei jdm wegen etw ~ halten** to query sth with sb; **auf ~ wurde uns erklärt ...** when we queried this, we were told ...; **rück+fra|gen** ['rʏkfraːɡn̩] VI *sep infin, ptp only* to inquire, to check; **ich habe an der Rezeption rückgefragt** I inquired *or* checked at reception; **ich muss beim Chef ~** I'll have to check with the boss *or* query it with the boss; **Rück|front** F back, rear façade; **Rück|führ|ge|bühr** F (*bei Leihwagen*) drop-off charge; **Rück|füh|rung** F **a** (= *Deduktion*) tracing back; **die ~ der Probleme auf** (+*acc*) tracing the problems back to **b** (*von Menschen*) repatriation, return **c** (*Fin: von Kredit, Schulden*) repayment; (= *Senkung*) reduction **d** (= *Zurückgabe*) restitution; **Rück|ga|be** F return; **Rück|ga|be|recht** NT (*Comm*) right of return; **mit ~ bestellen** to order on a sale or return basis; **Rück|gang** M *pl* -**gänge** fall, drop (+*gen* in); **einen ~** *or* **Rückgänge zu verzeichnen haben** to report a drop *or* fall; **rück|gän|gig** ADJ **a** (= *zurückgehend*) declining, falling, dropping **b** **~ machen** (= *widerrufen*) to undo; *Bestellung, Geschäft, Vertrag, Termin* to cancel; *Entscheidung* to go back on; *Verlobung, Hochzeit* to call off; *chemischen Prozess* to reverse; **Rück|gän|gig|ma|chung** ['rʏkɡɛnɪçmaxʊŋ] F -, -**en** (*form*) cancellation; (*Chem*) reversal; **Rück|ge|bäu|de** NT rear building; **rück|ge|bil|det** ADJ (*Biol*) degenerate; **Rück|ge|win|nung** F recovery; (*von Land, Gebiet*) reclaiming, reclamation; (*aus verbrauchten Stoffen*) recycling; **Rück|glie|de|rung** F (*Pol*) reintegration

Rück|grat ['rʏkɡraːt] NT -(e)s, -e spine, backbone; **er ist ein Mensch ohne ~** (*fig*) he's a spineless creature, he's got no backbone; **das ~ der Wirtschaft** the backbone *or* mainstay of the economy; **jdm das ~ stärken** (*fig inf*) to give sb encouragement *or* a boost; **jdm das ~ brechen** (*fig*) to break *or* ruin sb

Rück|grat|ver|krüm|mung F curvature of the spine

Rück-: **Rück|griff** M **a** **durch einen** *or* **unter ~ auf jdn/etw** by reverting to sb/sth; **wenn ein ~ auf vorhandene Reserven nicht möglich ist** if it is not possible to fall back on available resources; **erlauben Sie mir einen ~ auf bereits Gesagtes** allow me to revert to something that has already been said **b** (*Jur*) = **Regress** b; **Rück|halt** M **a** (= *Unterstützung*) support, backing; **um jdm einen ~ haben** to find a support in sb; **keinen/starken ~ haben** to have no/strong support **b** (= *Einschränkung*) **ohne ~** without reservation; **Rück|hal|te|be|cken** NT storage pond; **rück|halt|los** ADJ complete; *Unterstützung auch* unqualified, wholehearted; *Vertrauen auch* implicit ADV completely; *unterstützen auch* wholeheartedly; *ermitteln* thoroughly; **sich ~ zu etw bekennen** to proclaim one's total allegiance to sth; **Rück|hand** F (*Sport*) backhand; **~ spielen** to play backhand; **er kann erstklassig ~ spielen** he has a first-rate backhand; **den Ball (mit der) ~ schlagen** to hit the ball (on one's backhand); **Rück|hand|schlag** M (*Sport*) backhand (stroke)

ru|cki|zu|cki ['rʊkiˈtsʊki] ADV (*inf*) = **ruck, zuck**

Rück|kampf M (*Sport*) return match

Rück|kauf M repurchase

Rück|kaufs-: **Rück|kaufs|recht** NT right of repurchase; **Rück|kaufs|wert** M repurchase value

Rück|kehr ['rʏkkeːɐ̯] F -, *no pl* return; **bei seiner ~** on his return; **jdn zur ~ (nach X/zu jdm) bewegen** to persuade sb to return (to X/to sb)

Rück|kehr-: **Rück|kehr|för|de|rungs|ge|setz** NT , **Rück|kehr|hil|fe|ge|setz** NT *law encouraging the return of immigrants to their native country*; **rück|kehr|wil|lig** ADJ willing to return

Rück-: **rück+kop|peln** ['rʏkkɔpln̩] VTI *sep infin, ptp only* (*alle Bedeutungen*) to feed back; **Rück|kop|pe|lung** F , **Rück|kopp|lung** F feedback; **Rück|kreu|zung** F backcross; (*Vorgang*) backcrossing; **Rück|kunft** ['rʏkkʊnft] F -, *no pl* (*liter*) return; **Rück|la|ge** F (*Fin:* = *Reserve*) reserve, reserves *pl*; (= *Ersparnisse auch*) savings *pl*; **Rück|lauf** M , *no pl* (*Tech*) reverse running; (*von Maschinenteil*) return travel; (= *Gegenströmung*) countercurrent; (*TV*) flyback; (*Naut*) slip; (*beim Tonband*) fast rewind; (*von Schusswaffe*) recoil; (*von Fragebögen, Waren*) returns *pl*; **ein guter ~** a good number of returns; **rück|läu|fig** ADJ declining, falling, dropping; *Tendenz* downward; **eine ~e Entwicklung** a decline, a falling off; **Rück|licht** NT tail-light, rear light; (*bei Fahrrad auch*) back light; **rück|lings** ['rʏklɪŋs] ADV (= *rückwärts*) backwards; (= *von hinten*) from behind; (= *auf dem Rücken*) on one's back; **Rück|marsch** M (*Mil*) march back; (= *Rückzug*) retreat

Rück|mel|de-: **Rück|mel|de|frist** F (*Univ*) re-registration period; **Rück|mel|de|ge|büh|ren** PL (*Univ*) re-registration fee

Rück-: **Rück|mel|dung** F **a** (*Univ*) re-registration **b** (*Comput*) echo; **Rück|nah|me** [-naːmə] F -, -**n** taking back; (*von Verordnung, Gesetz*) revocation, revoking; (*von Geldkürzungen*) reversal; (= *Senkung*) reduction; **die ~ des Gerätes ist unmöglich** it is impossible for us to take this set back; **ich bestehe auf der ~ des Gerätes** I must insist that you take this set back; **Rück|nah|me|preis** M repurchase price; **Rück|pass** ▲ M (*Sport*) return pass; **Rück|por|to** NT return postage; **Rück|prall** M rebound; (*von Kugel, Stein etc*) ricochet; **Rück|prä|mie** F (*Fin*) put

premium; **Rück|prä|mi|en|ge|schäft** NT (*Fin*) put

Rück|rei|se F return journey

Rück|rei|se-: **Rück|rei|se|ver|kehr** M homebound traffic; **Rück|rei|se|vi|sum** NT return visa; **Rück|rei|se|wel|le** F surge of homebound traffic, rush of returning holidaymakers

Rück-: **Rück|ruf** M **a** (*am Telefon*) **Herr X hat angerufen und bittet um ~** Mr X called and asked you to call (him) back; **automatischer ~** automatic callback **b** (*Jur*) rescission of permission to manufacture under licence (*Brit*) *or* license (*US*) **c** (*von Botschafter, Auto, Waren*) recall; **Rück|ruf|ak|ti|on** F call-back campaign; **Rück|run|de** F (*Sport*) second half of the season; (= *Rückspiel*) return match *or* leg

Ruck|sack ['rʊkzak] M rucksack

Ruck|sack|tou|rist(in) M(F) backpacker

Rück-: **Rück|schalt|tas|te** F backspace key; **Rück|schau** F reflection (*auf* +*acc* on); (*in Medien*) review (*auf* +*acc* of); **~ halten** to reminisce, to reflect; **auf etw** (*acc*) **~ halten** to look back on sth; **in ~ auf das vergangene Jahr ...** looking back on the past year ...; **Rück|schein** M ≈ recorded delivery slip; **Rück|schlag** M **a** (*von Ball*) rebound; (*von Gewehr*) recoil; (*fig*) setback; (*bei Patient*) relapse **b** (*Biol*) atavism **c** (*Sw:* = *Defizit*) deficit; **Rück|schlä|ger(in)** M(F) (*Sport*) receiver; **Rück|schlag|ven|til** NT check valve; **Rück|schluss** ▲ M conclusion; **den ~ gestatten, dass ...** to admit of the conclusion that ...; **den ~ ziehen, dass ...** to draw the conclusion that ..., to conclude that ...; **Rückschlüsse auf etw** (*acc*) **zulassen** to allow conclusions to be drawn about sth; **Rückschlüsse ziehen** to draw one's own conclusions (*aus* from); **Rück|schritt** M (*fig*) retrograde step, step backwards, retrogression (*form*); **ein gesellschaftlicher ~** a retrograde *or* retrogressive (*form*) social step, a social step backwards; **rück|schritt|lich** ['rʏkʃrɪtlɪç] ADJ reactionary; *Entwicklung* retrograde

Rück|sei|te F back; (*von Blatt Papier, Geldschein auch*) reverse; (*von Planet auch*) far side; (*von Gebäude auch*) rear; (*von Buchseite, Münze*) reverse, verso; (*von Zeitung*) back page; **siehe ~** see over(leaf)

rück|sei|tig ['rʏkzaitɪç] ADJ on the back *or* reverse; **die ~en Bemerkungen** the remarks overleaf ADV (= *auf der Rückseite*) on the back; **das Papier soll auch ~ beschrieben werden** you should write on both sides of the paper; **der Garten liegt ~** the garden is at the back

ruck|sen ['rʊksn̩] VI (*Taube*) to coo

Rück|sen|dung F return

Rück|sicht ['rʏkzɪçt] F -, -**en** **a** (= *Schonung, Nachsicht*) consideration; **aus** *or* **mit ~ auf jdn/etw** out of consideration for sb/sth; **ohne ~ auf jdn/etw** with no consideration for sb/sth; **ohne ~ auf Verluste** (*inf*) regardless; **auf jdn/etw ~ nehmen** to consider sb/sth, to show consideration for sb/sth; **er kennt keine ~** he's ruthless; **da kenne ich keine ~!** I can be ruthless **b** **Rücksichten** PL (= *Gründe, Interessen*) considerations *pl*

rück|sicht|lich ['rʏkzɪçtlɪç] PREP +*gen* (*old*) in view of

Rück|sicht|nah|me [-naːmə] F -, *no pl* consideration

Rück|sichts-: **rück|sichts|los** ADJ **a** inconsiderate, thoughtless; (*im Verkehr*) reckless **b** (= *unbarmherzig*) ruthless ADV **a** (= *ohne Nachsicht*) inconsiderately, thoughtlessly; **er verfolgt ~ seine Interessen** he follows his own interests without consideration for others **b** (= *schonungslos*) ruthlessly; **Rück|sichts|lo|sig|keit** F -, -**en a** (= *rücksichtslose Tat*) inconsiderate act; **das ist doch eine ~!** how inconsiderate *or* thoughtless **b** *no pl* (= *das Rücksichtslossein*) lack of consideration, thoughtlessness; (= *Unbarmherzigkeit*) ruthlessness; **rück|sichts|voll** ADJ considerate, thoughtful (*gegenüber, gegen* towards) **ADV** considerately, thoughtfully; **behandeln Sie ihn etwas ~er** show him a little more consideration

Rück-: Rück|sitz M (*von Fahrrad, Motorrad*) pillion; (*von Auto*) back seat; **Rück|spie|gel** M (*Aut*) rear(-view) *or* driving mirror; (*außen*) outside mirror; **Rück|spiel** NT (*Sport*) return match; **Rück|spra|che** F consultation; **nach ~ mit Herrn Müller ...** after consulting Mr Müller ...; **~ mit jdm halten** *or* **nehmen** to confer with *or* consult (with) sb

Rück|spul|au|to|ma|tik F (*von Kamera, Video etc*) automatic rewind

rück+spu|len [ˈrʏkʃpuːlən] VT *sep infin, ptp only Tonband, Film* to rewind

Rück|spul|knopf M (*von Kamera*) rewind knob

Rück|spul|tas|te F (*von Tonbandgerät etc*) rewind key

Rück|stand [ˈrʏkʃtant] M **a** (= *Überrest*) remains *pl*; (*bei Verbrennung:* = *Bodensatz*) residue **b** (= *Verzug*) delay; (*bei Aufträgen*) backlog; (*bei Entwicklung*) slow progress; **im ~ sein** to be behind; (*bei Zahlungen auch*) to be in arrears *pl*; **in ~ geraten** to fall behind; (*bei Zahlungen auch*) to get in arrears *pl*; **seinen ~ aufholen** to make up for one's delay; (*bei Aufträgen*) to catch up on a backlog; (*bei Zahlungen*) to catch up on one's payments; (*in Leistungen*) to catch up **c** (= *Außenstände*) arrears *pl*; **wie hoch ist mein ~?** how much are my arrears?; **Rückstände eintreiben/bezahlen** to collect/pay arrears **d** (*Sport*) amount by which one is behind; **mit 0:2 (Toren) im ~ sein** to be 2-0 down; **ihr ~ auf den Tabellenführer beträgt 4 Punkte** they are 4 points behind the leader; **seinen ~ aufholen** to catch up, to close the gap

rück|stän|dig [ˈrʏkʃtɛndɪç] ADJ **a** (= *überfällig*) *Betrag* overdue; *Mensch* in arrears; **~er Betrag** amount overdue **b** (= *zurückgeblieben*) *Land, Mensch* backward; *Methoden, Ansichten* backward, antiquated **ADV** **~ denken** to have antiquated ideas

Rück|stän|dig|keit F -, *no pl* backwardness

rück|stand(s)|frei ADJ residue-free; *Verbrennung auch* clean **ADV** **ein Diamant verbrennt ~** a diamond burns without leaving any residue; **dieses Öl verbrennt nahezu ~** this oil burns cleanly

Rück-: Rück|stau M (*von Wasser*) backwater; (*von Autos*) tailback; (*von Unerledigtem*) backlog; **Rück|stell|tas|te** F (*an Tastatur*) backspace key; **Rück|stell|lung** F (*Fin*) reserve; **Rück|stoß** M repulsion; (*bei Gewehr*) recoil; (*von Rakete*) thrust; **Rück|stoß|an|trieb** M (*Aviat*) reaction propulsion; **rück|stoß|frei** ADJ *Geschütze* recoilless; **Rück|strah|ler** M reflector; **Rück|strom** M (*Elec*) reverse current; (*von Menschen, Fahrzeugen*) return; **der ~ der Urlauber aus Italien** the stream of holiday-makers (*Brit*) *or* vactioners (*US*) returning from Italy; **Rück|ta|bu|la|tor** M (*an Schreibmaschine*) tab left (key); **Rück|tas|te** F (*an Tastatur*) backspace key; **Rück|trans|port** M return transport; (*bei Schreibmaschine*) return

Rück|tritt M **a** (= *Amtsniederlegung*) resignation; (*von König*) abdication; **seinen ~ einreichen** *or* **erklären** to hand in *or* tender (*form*) one's resignation **b** (*Jur*) (*von Vertrag*) withdrawal (*von* from), rescission (*form*) (*von* of); **~ vom Versuch** abandonment of intent **c** (*inf: = Bremse*) backpedal *or* coaster brake

Rück|tritt|brem|se F backpedal *or* coaster brake

Rück|tritts-: Rück|tritts|dro|hung F threat to resign; (*von König*) threat to abdicate; **Rück|tritts|er|klä|rung** F announcement of one's resignation, resignation announcement; (*schriftlich*) letter of resignation; **Rück|tritts|for|de|rung** F demand for his *or* her resignation; **Rück|tritts|frist** F period for withdrawal; **Rück|tritts|ge|such** NT resignation; **das ~**

---

einreichen to tender one's resignation (*form*); **Rück|tritts|klau|sel** F withdrawal clause; **Rück|tritts|recht** NT right of withdrawal; **Rück|tritts|vor|be|halt** M option of withdrawal

Rück-: rück+über|set|zen [ˈrʏkyːbɛzɛtsn̩] ptp **rückübersetzt** VT *sep infin, ptp only* to translate back into the original language; **Rück|über|set|zung** F retranslation into the original language; **Rück|um|schlag** M reply-paid *or* business reply (*US*) envelope; **adressierter und frankierter ~** stamped addressed envelope; **rück+ver|gü|ten** [ˈrʏkfɛɐgyːtn̩] ptp **rückvergütet** VT *sep infin, ptp only* to refund (*jdm etw* sb sth); **Rück|ver|gü|tung** F refund; **Rück|ver|si|che|rer** M reinsurer; (*fig*) hedger; **rück+ver|si|chern** [ˈrʏkfɛɐzɪçɐn] ptp **rückversichert** sep **VTI** to reinsure **VR** to check (up *or* back); **Rück|ver|si|che|rung** F reinsurance; **Rückversicherungsvertrag** M (*Hist*) Reinsurance Treaty; **Rück|ver|weis** M reference back; **rück+ver|wei|sen** [ˈrʏkfɛɐvaɪzn̩] ptp **rückverwiesen** VTI *sep irreg infin, ptp only* to refer back; **Rück|wand** F (*von Zimmer, Gebäude etc*) back wall; (*von Möbelstück etc*) back; **Rück|wan|de|rer** M , **Rück|wan|de|rin** F returning emigrant, remigrant; **Rück|wan|de|rung** F re-migration; **rück|wär|tig** [ˈrʏkvɛrtɪç] ADJ back; *Tür, Eingang, Ausgang auch* rear; (*Mil*) rear; **~e Verbindungen** (*Mil*) lines of communication

rück|wärts [ˈrʏkvɛrts] ADV **a** (= *zurück, rücklings*) backwards; **Rolle ~** backward roll; **Salto ~** back somersault; **~ einparken** to back *or* reverse into a parking space; **~ gewandt** backward-looking, retrogressive **b** (*Aus:* = *hinten*) behind, at the back; **von ~** from behind

Rück|wärts-: Rück|wärts|dre|hung F reverse turn; **Rück|wärts|fah|ren** NT -s, *no pl* reversing; **Rück|wärts|gang** M *pl* **-gänge** (*Aut*) reverse gear; **den ~ einlegen** to change (*Brit*) *or* shift (*US*) into reverse, to put the car *etc* into reverse; **im ~ fahren** to reverse; **sich im ~ bewegen** (*fig*) to go backwards, to regress (*form*); **rück|wärts|ge|wandt** △ ADJ (*fig*) → **rückwärts a**

Rück|weg M way back; **auf dem ~ vorbeikommen** to call in on one's way back; **den ~ antreten, sich auf den ~ begeben** to set off back; **sich auf den ~ machen** to head back; **jdm den ~ abschneiden** to cut off sb's line of retreat

ruck|wei|se [ˈrʊkvaɪzə] ADV jerkily; **sich ~ bewegen** to jerk, to move jerkily

Rück-: Rück|wen|dung F return (*zu, auf +acc* to); **rück|wir|kend** [ˈrʏkvɪrknt] ADJ (*Jur*) retrospective; *Lohn-, Gehaltserhöhung* backdated **ADV** **es wird ~ vom 1. Mai bezahlt** it will be backdated to 1st May; **das Gesetz tritt ~ vom** *or* **zum 1. Januar in Kraft** the law is made retrospective to 1st January; **etw ist ~ fällig** sth is backdated; **die Erhöhung der Renten gilt ~ zum 1. Januar** the rise in pensions is backdated to 1st January; **Rück|wir|kung** F repercussion; **~en auf etw** (*acc*) **haben** to have repercussions on sth; **eine Zahlung/Gesetzesänderung mit vom ...** a payment backdated to/an amendment made retrospective to (*...*); **rück|zahl|bar** ADJ repayable; **Rück|zah|lung** F repayment; **Rück|zie|her** [ˈrʏktsiːɐ] M -s, - (*inf*) backing down; **einen ~ machen** to back down; **rück|zie|lend** ADJ (*Gram rare*) reflexive

Ruck|zuck [ˈrʊktsʊk] NT -s, *no pl* (*inf*) **etw mit ~ machen** to do sth at the double (*inf*)

ruck, zuck [ˈrʊktsʊk] **INTERJ** (*beim Ziehen*) heave; (*beim Schieben*) push **ADV** in a flash; (*Imperativ*) jump to it; **das geht ~** it won't take a second; **wenn er nicht gehorcht, fliegt er raus, das geht ~** if he doesn't obey he'll be out, just like that

Rück|zug M (*Mil*) retreat; (*fig*) withdrawal; **geordneter/ungeordneter ~** (*lit, fig*) orderly/disorderly retreat; **auf dem ~** in the retreat; **den ~ antreten** (*lit, fig*) to retreat, to beat a retreat;

---

den ~ ins Private antreten to withdraw into oneself → **blasen VI**

Rück|zugs-: Rück|zugs|ge|biet NT retreat; **Rück|zugs|ge|fecht** NT (*Mil, fig*) rearguard action

Ru|co|la [ˈruːkola] F (*esp Sw Bot*) (garden *or* salad) rocket, rucola

rü|de [ˈryːdə], (*Aus*) **rüd** [ryːt] ADJ impolite; *Antwort* curt, brusque; *Methoden* crude; *Angriff, Foul* rough; **das war sehr ~ von dir** that was very rude of you **ADV** rudely

Rü|de [ˈryːdə] M **-n, -n** (= *Männchen*) dog, male; (= *Hetzhund*) hound

Ru|del [ˈruːdl̩] NT **-s, -** (*von Hunden, Wölfen*) pack; (*von Wildschweinen, Hirschen*) herd; (*fig dated*) swarm, horde; **in ~n auftreten** to go (a)round in packs/herds/swarms *or* hordes

ru|del|wei|se ADV → **Rudel** in packs/herds/ swarms *or* hordes

Ru|der [ˈruːdɐ] NT **-s, -** (*von Ruderboot, Galeere etc*) oar; (*Naut, Aviat:* = *Steuerruder*) rudder; (*fig:* = *Führung*) helm; **das ~ fest in der Hand haben** (*fig*) to be in control of the situation; **am ~ sein** (*lit, fig*) to be at the helm; **ans ~ kommen** *or* **das ~ übernehmen** (*lit, fig*) to take over (at) the helm; **sich in die ~ legen** (*lit, fig*) to put one's back into it; **sich für etw in die ~ legen** (*fig*) to put one's back into sth; **das ~ herumwerfen** *or* **herumreißen** (*fig*) to change course *or* tack; **aus dem ~ laufen** (*fig*) to get out of hand

Ru|der-: Ru|der|bank F *pl* **-bänke** rowing seat; (*in Galeere*) rowing bench; **Ru|der|blatt** NT (oar) blade; **Ru|der|boot** NT rowing boat (*Brit*), rowboat (*US*); **Ru|der|dol|le** F rowlock

Ru|de|rer [ˈruːdərɐ] M **-s, -** oarsman, rower

Ru|der|gän|ger [-gɛŋɐ] M **-s, -**, **Ru|der|gän|ge|rin** [-ərɪn] F **-, -nen** (*Naut*) helmsman/woman

Ru|der|haus NT (*Naut*) wheelhouse, pilot house

Ru|de|rin [ˈruːdərɪn] F oarswoman, rower

ru|dern [ˈruːdɐn] **VI** **a** *aux* **haben** *or* **sein** to row (*Schwimmvögel*) to paddle; (*fig*) to struggle; **mit den Armen ~** (*fig*) to flail *or* wave one's arms about **VT** to row

Ru|der-: Ru|der|pin|ne F tiller; **Ru|der|re|gat|ta** F rowing regatta; **Ru|der|schlag** M stroke; **Ru|der|sport** M rowing *no def art*; **Ru|der|stan|ge** F tiller

Ru|di|ment [rudiˈmɛnt] NT **-(e)s, -e** rudiment

ru|di|men|tär [rudimɛnˈtɛːɐ] ADJ rudimentary; (*Biol*) *Organ auch* vestigial **ADV** rudimentarily; **~ ausgebildet** rudimentary; **~ vorhanden sein** to be vestigial

Rud|rer [ˈruːdrɐ] M **-s, -**, **Rud|re|rin** [-ərɪn] F **-, -nen** = **Ruderer, Ruderin**

Ruf [ruːf] M **-(e)s, -e** **a** (= *Ausruf, Vogelruf, fig:* = *Aufruf*) call (*nach* for); (*lauter*) shout; (= *gellender Schrei*) cry; **ein ~ ertönte** a cry rang out; **in den ~ „...." ausbrechen** to burst into cries *or* shouts of „..."; **der ~ des Muezzins** the call of the muezzin; **der ~ der Wildnis** the call of the wild; **dem ~ des Herzens/Gewissens folgen** (*fig*) to obey the voice of one's heart/conscience; **der ~ nach Freiheit/Gerechtigkeit** the call for freedom/justice; **der ~ zu den Waffen** the call to arms; **der ~ zur Ordnung** (*fig*) the call to order **b** (= *Ansehen, Leumund*) reputation; **einen guten ~ haben** *or* **genießen, sich eines guten ~es erfreuen** (*geh*) to have *or* enjoy a good reputation; **einen schlechten ~ haben** to have a bad reputation; **dem ~ nach** by reputation; **eine Firma von ~** a firm with a good reputation, a firm of high repute, a firm with a good name; **sich** (*dat*) **einen ~ als etw erwerben** to build up a reputation for oneself as sth, to make a name for oneself as sth; **seinem ~ (als etw) gerecht werden** to live up to one's reputation (as sth); **ein Mann von schlechtem ~** a man with a bad reputation, a man with a bad name; **von üblem**

---

or **zweifelhaftem ~** with a bad reputation; **von übelm** *or* **zweifelhaftem ~ sein** to have a bad reputation; **jdn/etw in schlechten ~ bringen** to give sb/sth a bad name; **jdn bei jdm in schlechten ~ bringen** to bring sb into disrepute with sb; **sie/das ist besser als ihr/sein** = she/it is better than she/it is made out to be, she/it is not as black as she/it is painted; **ist der ~ erst ruiniert, lebt man völlig ungeniert** (*prov*) you live freely if you haven't a reputation to lose

c (*Univ: = Berufung*) offer of a chair *or* professorship; **er hat einen ~ nach Mainz erhalten** he has been offered a chair *or* professorship at Mainz

d (*= Fernruf*) telephone number; „**Ruf: 2785**" "Tel 2785"

Ru|fe ['ruːfə] F **-, -n**, **Rü|fe** ['ryːfə] F **-, -n** (*Sw*) **a** (*= Steinlawine*) rock fall; (*= Erdrutsch*) landslide **b** (*auch S Ger: auf Wunde*) scab

ru|fen ['ruːfn] *pret* **rief** [riːf], *ptp* **gerufen** [gə'ruːfn]
VI **a** (*= rufen*); (*Mensch: = laut rufen*) to call; (*Gong, Glocke, Horn etc*) to sound (*zu* for); **um Hilfe ~** to call *or* cry for help; **die Pflicht ruft** duty calls; **die Arbeit ruft** my/your *etc* work is waiting; **nach jdm/etw ~** to call for sb/sth
VI *impers* **es ruft eine Stimme** a voice is calling; **es hat gerufen** somebody called
VT (*= laut sagen*) **a** to call; (*= ausrufen*) to cry; (*Mensch: = laut rufen*) to shout; **jdm etw in Erinnerung** *or* **ins Gedächtnis ~** to bring back (memories of) sth to sb; **sich** (*dat*) **etw in Erinnerung** *or* **ins Gedächtnis ~** to recall sth; **jdn zur Ordnung ~** to call sb to order; **jdn zur Sache ~** to bring sb back to the point; **jdn zu den Waffen ~** to call sb to arms; **bravo/da capo ~** to shout hooray (*Brit*) *or* bravo/encore; **sich heiser ~** to shout oneself hoarse
b (*= kommen lassen*) to send for; **Arzt, Polizei** to send for, to call; **Taxi** to call; **jdn zu sich ~** to send for sb; **Gott hat sie zu sich gerufen** God has called her to Him; **Sie haben mich ~ lassen?** you called, sir/madam?; **~ Sie ihn bitte!** please send him to me; **jdn zu Hilfe ~** to call on sb to help; **du kommst wie gerufen** you're just the man/woman I wanted; **das kommt mir wie gerufen** that's just what I needed; (*= kommt mir gelegen*) that suits me fine (*inf*)

Ru|fen NT **-s**, *no pl* calling *no indef art*; (*von Mensch: laut*) shouting *no indef art*; **haben Sie das ~ nicht gehört?** didn't you hear him/her *etc* calling/shouting?

Ru|fer ['ruːfə] M **-s, - der ~ im Streit** (*liter*) the leader in battle; **der (einsame) ~ in der Wüste** the (lone) voice (crying) in the wilderness

Ru|fe|rei [ruːfə'rai] F **-, -en** (*inf*) = **Rufen**

Rüf|fel ['rʏfl] M **-s, -** (*inf*) telling-off (*inf*), ticking-off (*Brit inf*)

rüf|feln ['rʏfln] VT (*inf*) to tell *or* tick (*Brit*) off (*inf*)

Ruf-: **Ruf|mord** M character assassination; **Ruf|mord|kam|pag|ne** F smear campaign; **Ruf|na|me** M forename (by which one is generally known); **Ruf|num|mer** F telephone number; **Ruf|num|mern|spei|cher** M (*von Telefon*) memory; **Ruf|säu|le** F (*für Taxi*) telephone; (*Mot: = Notrufsäule*) emergency telephone; **ruf|schä|di|gend** ADJ **~ sein** to be damaging to one's reputation; **Ruf|schä|di|gung** F defamation; **Ruf|um|lei|tung** F (*Telec*) call diversion; **Ruf|wei|te** F **in ~** within earshot, within calling distance; **außer ~** out of earshot; **Ruf|zei|chen** NT **a** (*Telec*) call sign; (*von Telefon*) ringing tone **b** (*Aus*) exclamation mark

Rug|by ['rakbi] NT **-**, *no pl* rugby, rugger (*Brit inf*)

Rug|by|spiel ['rakbi-] NT (*Veranstaltung*) rugby match; **das ~** (*Sportart*) rugby

Rü|ge ['ryːɡə] F **-, -n** (*= Verweis*) reprimand, rebuke (*für jdn* for sb); (*= Kritik*) criticism *no indef art*; (*= scharfe Kritik*) censure *no indef art*; **jdm eine ~ erteilen** to reprimand *or* rebuke/criticize/censure sb (*für, wegen* for)

rü|gen ['ryːɡn] VT (*form*) **jdn** to reprimand (*wegen, für* for); **etw** to reprehend; **ich muss dein Verhalten ~** I must reprimand you for your behaviour (*Brit*) *or* behavior (*US*)

rü|gens|wert ADJ reprehensible

Ru|he ['ruːə] F **-**, *no pl* **a** (*= Schweigen, Stille*) quiet, silence; **~!** quiet!, silence!; **~, bitte!** quiet, please; **gebt ~!** be quiet!; **ihr sollt ~ geben!** once and for all: (will you) be quiet!; **jdn zur ~ ermahnen** to tell sb to be quiet; **sich** (*dat*) **~ verschaffen** to get quiet *or* silence; **es herrscht ~** all is silent, silence reigns (*liter*); (*fig: = Disziplin, Frieden*) **~ halten** (*lit, fig*) to keep quiet *or* silent; **die ~ der Natur** the stillness of nature; **himmlische ~** heavenly peace; **~ und Frieden** peace and quiet; **in ~ und Abgeschiedenheit** in peaceful seclusion; **die ~ vor dem Sturm** (*fig*) the calm before the storm

b (*= Ungestörtheit, Frieden*) peace, quiet; (*= Ruhestätte*) resting place; **~ ausstrahlen** to radiate a sense of calm; **in ~ und Frieden leben** to live a quiet life; **~ und Ordnung** law and order; **nach tagelangen Krawallen ist wieder ~ eingekehrt** after days of rioting, order *or* calm has returned; **~ ist die erste Bürgerpflicht** (*prov*) the main thing is to keep calm; **die ~ wieder herstellen** to restore order; **ich brauche meine ~** I need a bit of peace; **lass mich in ~!** leave me in peace, stop bothering me; **ich will meine ~ haben!** leave *or* let me alone *or* be; **dann hat die liebe Seele Ruh** (*prov*) then perhaps we'll get a bit of peace; **vor jdm ~ haben wollen** to want a rest from sb; (*endgültig*) to want to get *or* be rid of sb; **jdm keine ~ lassen** *or* **gönnen** (*Mensch*) not to give sb any peace; **keine ~ geben** to keep on and on; **das lässt ihm keine ~** he can't stop thinking about it; **zur ~ kommen** to get some peace; (*solide werden*) to settle down; **jdn zur ~ kommen lassen** to give sb a chance to rest; **keine ~ finden (können)** to know no peace, not to be able to find any peace of mind; **jdn zur letzten** *or* **ewigen ~ betten** (*liter*) to lay sb to rest (*liter*); **die letzte ~ finden** (*liter*) to be laid to rest (*liter*)

c (*= Erholung*) rest, repose (*liter*); (*= Ruhestand*) retirement; (*= Stillstand*) rest; **der Patient braucht viel ~** the patient needs a great deal of rest; **das Pendel befindet sich in ~** the pendulum is stationary; **jdm keine ~ gönnen** not to give sb a minute's rest; **sich zur ~ begeben** (*form*) **zur ~ gehen** to retire (to bed) (*form*); **angenehme ~!** sleep well!; **sich zur ~ setzen** to retire

d (*= Gelassenheit*) calm(ness); (*= Disziplin*) quiet, order; **die ~ weghaben** (*inf*) to be unflappable (*inf*); **~ bewahren** to keep calm; **die ~ selbst sein** to be calmness itself; **jdn aus der ~ bringen** to throw sb (*inf*); **sich nicht aus der ~ bringen lassen, nicht aus der ~ zu bringen sein** not to (let oneself) get worked up; **in aller ~** calmly; **er trank noch in aller ~ seinen Kaffee** he drank his coffee as if he had all the time in the world; **überlege es dir in (aller) ~** take your time and think about it; **sich** (*dat*) **etw in ~ ansehen** to look at sth in one's own time; **immer mit der ~** (*inf*) don't panic

Ru|he-: **Ru|he|bank** F *pl* **-bänke** bench, seat; **Ru|he|be|dürf|nis** NT need for rest; **ru|he|be|dürf|tig** ADJ in need of rest; **Ru|he|bett** NT bed; **Ru|he|ge|halt** NT (*form*) superannuation (*Brit*), retirement pension; **Ru|he|geld** NT (*form*), (*Aus*) **Ru|he|ge|nuss** ▲ M pension; **Ru|he|kis|sen** NT bolster → **Gewissen**; **Ru|he|la|ge** F (*von Mensch*) reclining position; (*Med: bei Bruch*) immobile position; (*Tech*) (*von Maschine*) resting position; (*von Zeiger*) neutral position; (*= Unbeweglichkeit*) immobility; **sich in ~ befinden** (*Mensch, Maschine*) to be at rest; (*Wein*) to be kept still; (*= unbeweglich sein*) to be immobile; **ru|he|lie|bend** ADJ fond of peace and quiet; **ru|he|los** ADJ restless; **eine ~e Zeit** a time of unrest; **Ru|he|lo|sig|keit** F **-**, *no pl* restlessness; **Ru|he|mas|se** F (*Phys*) rest mass

ru|hen ['ruːən] **VI** **a** (*= ausruhen*) to rest; **nach dem Essen soll man ruhn oder tausend Schritte tun** (*Prov*) after a meal one should either rest or take some exercise; **ich möchte etwas ~** I want to take a short rest, I want to rest a little; **nicht (eher)** *or* **nicht ~ und rasten, bis ...** (*fig*) not to rest until ...; **ich wünsche wohl zu ~!** (*form*) I wish you a good night (*form*); **(ich) wünsche, wohl geruht zu haben!** (*form*) I trust that you slept well (*form*)

b (*geh. = liegen*) to rest (*an* or *auf +dat* on); (*Gebäude*) to be supported (*auf +dat* by), to rest (*auf +dat* on); (*Fluch*) to lie (*auf +dat* on); **unsere Hoffnung ruht auf ...** (*dat*) our hopes rest on ...; **möge Gottes Segen auf dir ~** may God's blessing be with you; **auf ihm ruht ein Verdacht** suspicion hangs over him (*liter*)

c (*= stillstehen*) to stop; (*Maschinen*) to stand idle; (*Arbeit*) to stop, to cease; (*Verkehr*) to be at a standstill; (*Waffen*) to be laid down; (*= unterbrochen sein: Verfahren, Verhandlung, Vertrag*) to be suspended; **lass die Arbeit jetzt ~** (*geh*) leave your work now

d (*= tot und begraben sein*) to lie, to be buried; „**hier ruht (in Gott) ...**" "here lies ..."; „**ruhe in Frieden!**" "Rest in Peace"; „**ruhe sanft!**" "rest eternal"
VR *impers* **hier ruht es sich gut** this is good to rest on

ru|hend ADJ resting; *Kapital* dormant; *Maschinen* idle; *Verkehr* stationary; **~e Venus** Venus reclining → **Pol**

ru|hen las|sen ▲ VT *ptp* **ruhen lassen** *or (rare)* **ruhen gelassen** *irreg* *Vergangenheit, Angelegenheit* to let rest; *Verhandlungen, Prozess* to adjourn; *Teig* to allow to rest; *Amt* to leave temporarily vacant

Ru|he-: **Ru|he|pau|se** F break; (*wenig Betrieb, Arbeit*) slack *or* quiet period; **eine ~ einlegen** to take *or* have a break; **Ru|he|platz** M resting place; **Ru|he|pos|ten** M sinecure; **Ru|he|punkt** M place of rest; **Ru|he|raum** M rest room; **Ru|he|sitz** M (*Haus*) retirement home; **er hat seinen ~ in Ehlscheid aufgeschlagen** has retired to Ehlscheid; **Ru|he|stand** M retirement; **im ~ sein** *or* **leben** to be retired; **er ist Bankdirektor im ~** he is a retired bank director; **in den ~ treten** *or* **gehen** to retire, to go into retirement; **jdn in den ~ versetzen** to retire sb; **er wurde in den ~ verabschiedet** a retirement ceremony was held for him; **Ru|he|ständ|ler** [-ʃtɛndlɐ] M **-s, -**, **Ru|he|ständ|le|rin** [-ərɪn] F **-, -nen** retired person; **Ru|he|stands|be|am|te(r)** M *decl as adj*, **Ru|he|stands|be|am|tin** F retired civil servant; **Ru|he|statt** F *pl* **-stät|ten** [-ʃtɛtn], **Ru|he|stät|te** F resting place; **letzte Ruhestätte** last *or* final resting place; **Ru|he|stel|lung** F (*von Körper*) resting position; (*von beweglichem Gegenstand*) resting point; (*von Maschinen*) off position; **der Arm muss in ~ bleiben** the arm must not be moved; **ru|he|stö|rend** ADJ **~er Lärm** (*Jur*) disturbance of the peace; **Ru|he|stö|rer(in)** M(F) (*Jur*) disturber of the peace; **Ru|he|stö|rung** F (*Jur*) disturbance of the peace; **Ru|he|tag** M rest day, day off; (*von Geschäft etc*) closing day; **einen ~ einlegen** to have a day's rest, to take a day off; „**Mittwoch ~**" "closed (on) Wednesdays"; **Ru|he|zeit** F rest period; (*= Nebensaison*) off season; **Ru|he|zu|stand** M state of rest; (*Tech*) idle state; **im ~** (when) at rest; (*Tech*) when idle

ru|hig ['ruːɪç] ADJ **a** (*= still*) quiet; *Wetter, Meer* calm; **seid ~!** be quiet!; **ihr sollt ~ sein!** (will you) be quiet!

b (*= geruhsam*) quiet; *Urlaub, Feiertage, Leben* quiet, peaceful; *Farbe* restful; (*= ohne Störung*) *Überfahrt, Verlauf* smooth; (*Tech*) smooth; **gegen 6 Uhr wird es ~er** it quietens (*Brit*) *or* quiets (*US*) down around 6 o'clock; **alles geht seinen ~en Gang** everything is going smoothly → **Kugel a**

c (*= gelassen*) calm; *Gewissen* easy; **nur ~ (Blut)** keep calm, take it easy (*inf*); **bei ~er Überlegung** on (mature) consideration; **du wirst auch**

noch **~er!** you'll calm down one day; **du kannst/Sie können ganz ~ sein** I can assure you → **Blut**

d (= *sicher*) *Hand, Blick* steady **e** (= *teilnahmslos*) calm **ADV a** (= *still*) *sitzen, stehenbleiben, dastehen* still; **sitz doch ~!** sit still!

b (= *untätig*) **mitansehen** to stand by and watch sth; **~ dabeistehen** just to stand by; **ich kann doch nicht ~ mit ansehen, wie er so etwas tut** I can't just stand there and watch him do a thing like that; **sich ~ verhalten** to keep calm

c (*inf*) **du kannst ~ hier bleiben** feel free to stay here, you're welcome to stay here if you want; **ihr könnt ~ gehen, ich passe schon auf** you just go and I'll look after things; **man kann ~ behaupten/sagen/annehmen, dass ...** (= *mit Recht*) one may well assert/say/assume that ..., one need have no hesitation in *or* about asserting/saying/assuming that ...; **die können ~ etwas mehr zahlen** (= *leicht*) they could easily pay a little more; **wir können ~ darüber sprechen** we can talk about it if you want; **du könntest ~ mal etwas für mich tun!** it's about time you did something for me!

d (= *ohne Turbulenzen*) *laufen* very quietly; **das Flugzeug liegt ~ in der Luft** the plane is flying smoothly; **ihr Leben verläuft sehr ~** she leads a very quiet life

e (= *gelassen*) **wenn du etwas ~er überlegen würdest** if you took more time to think things over; **lass uns ~ nachdenken** let's think things over calmly

f (= *beruhigt*) *schlafen* peacefully; **du kannst ~ ins Kino gehen** go ahead, go to the cinema; **jetzt kann ich ~ in Urlaub fahren** now I can go on holiday (*esp Brit*) *or* vacation (*US*) with an easy mind

ru|hig stel|len ▲ VT **a** (*Med*) (*bei Knochenbruch etc*) to immobilize; (*mit Drogen*) to sedate **b** (*fig*: = *beruhigen*) to pacify, to calm

Ruhm [ruːm] M **-(e)s**, *no pl* glory; (= *Berühmtheit*) fame; (= *Lob*) praise; **des ~es voll sein** to be full of praise (**über** +*acc* for); **jds ~ begründen** to establish *or* make sb's name, to make sb famous; **zu ~ gelangen** to find fame, to become famous; **mit etw keinen ~ ernten** (*inf*) not to win any medals with *or* for sth; **sich in seinem ~ sonnen** to rest on one's laurels → **bekleckern VR**

ruhm|be|deckt ADJ covered with glory

rüh|men ['ryːmən] **VT** (= *preisen, empfehlen*) to praise, to sing the praises of; *Tugenden, Schönheit auch* to extol; **jdn ~d erwähnen** to give sb an honourable (*Brit*) *or* honorable (*US*) mention; **etw ~d hervorheben** to single sth out for *or* give sth special praise **VR sich einer Sache** (*gen*) **~** (= *prahlen*) to boast about sth; (= *stolz sein*) to pride oneself on sth; **sich einer Sache** (*gen*) **~ können** to be able to boast of sth; **die Stadt rühmt sich eines eigenen Schwimmbads** (*iro*) the town boasts its own swimming pool; **ohne mich zu ~** without wishing to boast

rüh|mens|wert ADJ praiseworthy, laudable

Ruh|mes-: **Ruh|mes|blatt** NT (*fig*) glorious chapter; **Ruh|mes|hal|le** F hall of fame; **Ruh|mes|tag** M glorious day; **Ruh|mes|tat** F glorious deed

rühm|lich ['ryːmlɪç] ADJ praiseworthy, laudable; *Ausnahme* notable; **kein ~es Ende finden** *or* **nehmen** to meet a bad end; **sich ~ hervortun** to distinguish oneself

Ruhm-: **ruhm|los** ADJ inglorious; **ruhm|reich** ADJ (*liter*) glorious; **Ruhm|sucht** F thirst for glory; **ruhm|süch|tig** ADJ thirsting for glory; **ruhm|voll** ADJ glorious

Ruhr¹ [ruːr] F - (*Geog*) Ruhr

Ruhr² F -, *no pl* (*Krankheit*) dysentery

Rühr|ei ['ryːrʔai] NT scrambled egg; (*als Gericht*) scrambled eggs *pl*

rüh|ren ['ryːrən] **VT a** (= *umrühren*) to stir; **sie rührte in ihrem Kaffee** she stirred her coffee

b an etw (*acc or dat*) **~** (= *anfassen*) to touch sth; (*fig*: = *erwähnen*) to touch on sth; **daran wollen wir nicht ~** let's not go into it; (*in Bezug auf Vergangenes*) let sleeping dogs lie; **rührt nicht daran!** (*liter*) let us not dwell on that; **die Sache rührte an ihren Herzen** the matter touched their hearts

c von etw ~ to stem from sth; **das rührt daher, dass ...** that is because ...; **daher rührt sein Misstrauen!** so that is the reason for his distrust!

VT a (= *umrühren*) *Teig, Farbe etc* to stir; (= *schlagen*) *Eier* to beat

b (= *bewegen*) to move; **er rührte kein Glied** he didn't stir at all; **er rührte keinen Finger** *or* **keine Hand, um mir zu helfen** (*inf*) he didn't lift a finger to help me (*inf*)

c (= *Gemüt bewegen*) to move; *Herz* to stir; **das kann mich nicht ~!** that leaves me cold; (= *stört mich nicht*) that doesn't bother me; **jdn zu Tränen ~** to move sb to tears; **sie war äußerst gerührt** she was extremely moved *or* touched

d (*Mus*) *Trommel* to strike, to beat

e ihn hat der Schlag gerührt (*inf*) he was thunderstruck; **ich glaubte, mich rührt der Schlag** (*inf*) you could have knocked me down with a feather (*inf*) → **Donner**

VR a (= *sich bewegen*) (*Blatt, Mensch*) to stir; (*Körperteil*) to move; (= *sich von der Stelle bewegen*) to move; (= *sich beeilen*) to buck up (*inf*); (= *sich beeilen*) to bestir oneself, to get a move on (*inf*); **rührt euch!** (*Mil*) at ease!; **~ lassen** (*Mil*) to give the order to stand at ease; **kein Lüftchen rührte sich** the air was still, there was not the slightest breeze; **er rührt sich nicht mehr** (*inf*) he won't get up again; **hier kann man sich nicht ~** you can't move in here; **sich vor Muskelkater/ Kisten kaum ~ können** to be hardly able to move because of stiffness/for boxes; **nichts hat sich gerührt** nothing happened → **Stelle a**

b (*Gewissen, Mitleid, Reue*) to stir, to be awakened; (*inf*: = *sich melden*) to say something; **sie hat sich schon zwei Jahre nicht gerührt** (*inf*) she hasn't been in touch for two years

Rüh|ren NT **-s**, *no pl* stirring; **ein menschliches ~ (verspüren)** (= *feel*) a stirring of human pity; (*hum*) (= *have to answer*) a *or* the call of nature (*hum*)

rüh|rend ADJ touching; **das ist ~ von Ihnen** that is sweet of you **ADV sie kümmert sich ~ um das Kind** it's touching how she looks after the child

Ruhr|ge|biet NT , *no pl* Ruhr (area)

rüh|rig ['ryːrɪç] ADJ active

ruhr|krank ADJ suffering from dysentery

Rühr-: **Rühr|ku|chen** M stirred cake; **Rühr|löf|fel** M mixing spoon; **Rühr|ma|schi|ne** F mixer; (*in Bäckerei*) mixing machine; **Rühr-mich|nicht|an** ['ryːrʔɪmɪçnɪçtʔan] NT -, - (*Bot*) touch-me-not

Ruhr|pott M , *no pl* (*inf*) Ruhr (Basin *or* Valley)

Rühr-: **Rühr|schüs|sel** F mixing bowl; **rühr-se|lig** ADJ (*pej*) touching, tear-jerking (*pej inf*); *Person* weepy; *Stimmung* sentimental; **Rühr|se|lig|keit** F , *no pl* sentimentality; **Rühr|stück** NT (*Theat*) melodrama; **Rühr-teig** M sponge mixture

Rüh|rung ['ryːrʊŋ] F -, *no pl* emotion; **vor ~ nicht sprechen können** to be choked with emotion

Ru|in [ruˈiːn] M **-s**, *no pl* ruin; **vor dem ~ stehen** to be on the brink *or* verge of ruin; **jdn in den ~ treiben** to ruin sb; **seinem/dem ~ entgegengehen** to be on the way to ruin; **das ist mein ~!** that will be my ruin *or* the ruin of me; **du bist noch mein ~!** (*hum inf*) you'll be the ruin of me

Ru|i|ne [ruˈiːnə] F -, **-n** (*lit, fig*) ruin

Ru|i|nen-: **Ru|i|nen|feld** NT sea of debris; **ru|i|nen|haft** ADJ ruined; **Ru|i|nen|stadt** F ruined city

ru|i|nie|ren [ruiˈniːrən] *ptp* **ruiniert** VT to ruin; **sich ~** to ruin oneself

ru|i|nös [ruiˈnøːs] ADJ *Wettbewerb, Gebäude* ruinous

Rülps [rʏlps] M **-es**, **-e** (*dial inf*) belch

rülp|sen ['rʏlpsn] VI to belch; **das Rülpsen** belching

Rülp|ser ['rʏlpsɐ] M **-s**, - (*inf*) belch

rum [rʊm] ADV (*inf*) = **herum**

Rum [rʊm, (*S Ger, Aus auch*) ruːm] M **-s**, **-s** rum

Ru|mä|ne [ruˈmɛːnə] M **-n**, **-n**, **Ru|mä|nin** [-ˈmɛː-nɪn] F -, **-nen** Romanian

Ru|mä|ni|en [ruˈmɛːniən] NT **-s** Romania

ru|mä|nisch [ruˈmɛːnɪʃ] ADJ Romanian

Ru|mä|nisch(e) [ruˈmɛːnɪʃ] NT Romanian → *auch* **Deutsch(e)**

Rum|ba ['rʊmba] F -, **-s** *or* (*inf*) m **-s**, **-s** rumba; **~ tanzen** to (dance the) rumba

Rum|ba|ku|gel F , **Rum|ba|ras|sel** F maraca

rum+flach|sen ['rʊmflaksn] VI *sep* (*inf*) to have a laugh, to joke around

rum+gam|meln VI *sep* (*inf*) to loaf *or* bum (*US*) around *or* about (*inf*)

rum+gif|ten VI *sep* (*sl*) to bitch (*inf*)

rum+gra|ben VI *sep irreg* (*sl*: = *Annäherungsversuche machen*) to try it on (*inf*)

rum+gur|ken VI *sep* (*sl*: = *herumfahren*) to drive around

rum+hän|gen VI *sep irreg aux haben or sein* (*inf*) (**in** +*dat* in) to hang around; **sie hängt zurzeit nur so rum** she's just killing time at the moment; **er hängt ständig mit diesen Typen rum** he's always hanging around with that lot

rum+kom|men ['rʊmkɔmən] VI *sep irreg* (*inf*) **a** = **herumkommen b dabei kommt nichts rum** nothing will come out of it

rum+krie|gen ['rʊmkriːgn] VT *sep* (*inf*) **jdn ~** to talk sb round (*Brit*), to bring sb around (*US*)

Rum|ku|gel F rum truffle

rum+ma|chen ['rʊmmaxn] VI *sep* (*inf*) to mess about (*Brit*) *or* around (*mit jdm* with sb, *an etw dat* with sth)

Rum|mel ['rʊml] M **-s**, *no pl* **a** (*inf*) (= *Betrieb*) (hustle and) bustle; (= *Getöse*) racket (*inf*); (= *Aufheben*) fuss (*inf*); **der ganze ~** the whole business *or* carry-on (*inf*); **den ~ kennen** to know all about it; **großen ~ um jdn/etw machen** *or* **veranstalten** to make a great fuss *or* to-do about sb/sth (*inf*) **b** (= *Rummelplatz*) fair; **auf den ~ gehen** to go to the fair

Rum|mel|platz M (*inf*) fairground

rum+mot|zen VI *sep* (*inf*) to moan

Rum|my ['rœmi] NT **-s**, **-s** (*Aus*) rummy

rum+nüs|sen ['rʊmnʏsn] VI *sep* (*sl*: = *Sex haben*) to shag (*sl*)

ru|mo|ren [ruˈmoːrən] *ptp* **rumort** **VI** to make a noise; (*Mensch*) to rumble about; (*Magen, Vulkan*) to rumble; (*Gewissen*) to play up; (*Gedanke*) to float about; **etw rumort in den Köpfen** sth is going through people's minds **VI** *impers* **es rumort in meinem Magen** *or* **Bauch** my stomach's rumbling; **es rumort in der Mannschaft** (*fig*) there is growing unrest in the team

rum+or|geln VI *sep* (*sl*: = *Sex haben*) to screw (*sl*)

rum|pe|lig ['rʊmpəlɪç] ADJ (*inf*) *Weg, Pflaster* bumpy

Rum|pel|kam|mer F (*inf*) junk room (*inf*)

rum|peln ['rʊmpln] VI **a** (= *Geräusch machen*) to rumble; **er fiel ~d die Treppe hinunter** he fell down the stairs with a clatter **b** *aux sein* (= *sich polternd bewegen*) to rumble; (*Mensch*) to clatter

Rum|pel|stilz|chen ['rʊmplʃtɪltsçən] NT **-s** Rumpelstiltskin

Rumpf [rʊmpf] M **-(e)s**, **⸚e** [ˈrʏmpfə] trunk; (*Sport*) body; (*von geschlachtetem Tier*) carcass; (*von Statue*) torso; (*von Schiff*) hull; (*von Flugzeug*) fuselage; **~ beugt!** (*Sport*) bend!; **~ streckt!** (*Sport*) stretch

Rumpf|beu|ge F forward bend

rümp|fen ['rʏmpfn] VT **die Nase ~** to turn up one's nose (*über +acc* at)

Rumpf|par|la|ment NT (*Hist*) Rump (Parliament)

rump|lig ['rʊmplɪç] ADJ *Weg, Pflaster* bumpy

Rump|steak ['rʊmpsteːk] NT rump steak

rums [rʊms] INTERJ bang

rum|sen ['rʊmzn] VI (*inf*) to bang

rum+stän|kern VI *sep* (*inf*) to stir (*inf*)

Rum-: Rum|topf M rumpot (*soft fruit in rum*); **Rum|ver|schnitt** M blended rum

rum+zi|cken ['rʊmtsɪkn] VI *sep* (*sl*) to turn awkward

Run [ran] M **-s, -s** run (*auf +acc* on)

rund [rʊnt] ADJ round; *Figur, Arme* plump; *Ton, Klang* full; *Wein* mellow; **du wirst mit jedem Jahr ~er** you're getting bigger *or* plumper every year; **~e 50 Jahre/2000 Euro** a good 50 years/2,000 euros; **ein ~es Dutzend Leute** a dozen *or* more people; **das Kind machte ~e Augen** the child's eyes grew round; **~er Tisch** round table; **Konferenz am ~en Tisch** round-table talks *pl*; **die Sache wird ~** it all works out; **das ist eine ~e Sache** that's pretty good

   ADV **a** (= *herum*) (a)round; **~ um** right (a)round; **~ um die Uhr** right (a)round the clock

   b (= *ungefähr*) (round) about, roughly; **~ gerechnet 200** call it 200

   c (*fig*: = *glattweg*) *abschlagen, ablehnen* flatly

   d (*Aut*) **der Motor läuft ~** the engine runs smoothly

Rund-: Rund|bank F *pl* **-bänke** circular bench; **Rund|bau** M *pl* **-bauten** rotunda; **Rund|blick** M panorama; **Rund|bo|gen** M (*Archit*) round arch; **Rund|brief** M circular; **Rund|bürs|te** F curved brush

Run|de ['rʊndə] F **-, -n a** (= *Gesellschaft*) company; (*von Teilnehmern*) circle; **sich zu einer gemütlichen ~ treffen** to meet informally

   b (= *Rundgang*) walk, turn; (*von Wachmann*) rounds *pl*; (*von Briefträger etc*) round; **die/seine ~ machen** to do the/one's rounds; (*Gastgeber*) to circulate; (= *herumgegeben werden*) to be passed round; **das Gerücht machte die ~** the rumour did the rounds (*Brit*), the rumour (*Brit*) *or* rumor (*US*) went around; **eine ~ durch die Lokale machen** to go on a pub crawl (*Brit*), to go bar-hopping (*US*); **eine ~ machen** to go for a walk; (*mit Fahrzeug*) to go for a ride; **eine ~ um etw machen** to go for a walk (a)round sth, to take a turn (a)round sth; (*mit Fahrzeug*) to ride (a)round sth; **zwei ~ um etw machen** to do two circuits of sth; **eine ~ um den Block machen** to walk around the block

   c (= *Gesprächsrunde, Verhandlungsrunde*) round; (*Cards*) game; (*Golf*) round; (*Sport*) (*bei Rennen*) lap; (*von Turnier, Wettkampf*) round; **seine ~n drehen** *or* **ziehen** to do one's laps; **über die ~n kommen** (*Sport, fig*) to pull through; **etw über die ~ bringen** (*fig*) to manage sth, to get through sth; **eine ~ schlafen** (*inf*) to have a kip (*Brit inf*) *or* nap

   d (*von Getränken*) round; (**für jdn**) **eine ~ spendieren** *or* **ausgeben** *or* **schmeißen** (*inf*) to buy *or* stand (*Brit*) (sb) a round

   e (*liter*: = *Umkreis*) surroundings *pl*; **in die/der ~** round about

run|den ['rʊndn] VT Lippen to round; Zahl (= *abrunden*) to round down; (= *aufrunden*) to round up; **nach oben/unten ~** (*Math*) to round up/down VR (*lit*: = *rund werden*) (*Bauch*) to become round; (*Gesicht auch*) to become full; (*Lippen*) to grow round; (*fig*: = *konkrete Formen annehmen*) to take shape; **sich zu etw ~** (*fig*) to develop into sth

Rund-: Rund|er|lass ▲ M circular (directive); **rund+er|neu|ern** ['rʊntʔɛɐnɔyɐn] *ptp* **runderneuert** VT *sep infin, ptp only* (*lit, fig*) to remould (*Brit*), to remold (*US*); **runderneuerte Reifen** remoulds (*Brit*), remolds (*US*); **Rund|er|neue|rung** F remoulding (*Brit*), remolding (*US*);

Rund|fahrt F tour; **eine ~ machen, an einer ~ teilnehmen** to go on a tour; **Rund|flug** M (= *Besichtigungsflug*) sightseeing flight; (= *Reiseroute*) round trip; **Rund|fra|ge** F survey (*an +acc, unter +dat* of)

Rund|funk M broadcasting; (= *Hörfunk*) radio, wireless (*esp Brit dated*); (= *Organisation*) broadcasting company *or* corporation; **der ~ überträgt etw** sth is broadcast; **im/über ~ sein** on the radio; **~ hören** to listen to the radio; **beim ~ arbeiten** *or* (**tätig**) **sein** to work *or* be in broadcasting

Rund|funk- *in cpds* radio; **Rund|funk|an|sager(in)** M(F) (radio) announcer; **Rund|funk|an|stalt** F (*form*) broadcasting corporation; **Rund|funk|durch|sa|ge** F special announcement (on the radio); **Rund|funk|emp|fang** M radio reception; **Rund|funk|emp|fän|ger** M radio receiver; **Rund|funk|ge|bühr** F radio licence (*Brit*) *or* license (*US*) fee; **Rund|funk|ge|rät** NT radio set (*Brit*), radio; **Rund|funk|ge|sell|schaft** F broadcasting company; **Rund|funk|hö|rer(in)** M(F) (radio) listener; **Rund|funk|or|ches|ter** NT radio orchestra; **Rund|funk|pro|gramm** NT (= *Kanal, inf*: = *Sendung*) radio programme (*Brit*) *or* program (*US*); (= *Sendefolge*) radio programmes (*Brit*) *or* programs (*US*); (= *gedrucktes Rundfunkprogramm*) radio programme (*Brit*) *or* program (*US*) guide; **Rund|funk|sa|tel|lit** M TV satellite; **Rund|funk|sen|der** M **a** (= *Sendeanlage*) radio transmitter **b** (= *Sendeanstalt*) radio station; **Rund|funk|sen|dung** F radio programme (*Brit*) *or* program (*US*); **Rund|funk|spre|cher(in)** M(F) radio announcer; **Rund|funk|sta|ti|on** F radio station; **Rund|funk|tech|nik** F radiotechnology; **Rund|funk|tech|ni|ker(in)** M(F) radio engineer; **Rund|funk|teil|neh|mer(in)** M(F) (*form*) owner of a radio set (*Brit*) *or* radio; **Rund|funk|über|tra|gung** F radio broadcast; **Rund|funk|zeit|schrift** F radio programme (*Brit*) *or* program (*US*) guide

Rund|gang M *pl* **-gänge a** (= *Spaziergang*) walk; (*zur Besichtigung*) tour (*durch* of); (*von Wachmann*) rounds *pl*; (*von Briefträger etc*) round; **einen ~ machen** to go for a walk; to go on a tour; **seinen ~ machen** to do one's rounds/round **b** (*Archit*) circular gallery

rund+ge|hen ['rʊntgeːən] VI *sep irreg* (*inf*) **a** **jetzt gehts rund** this is where the fun starts (*inf*); **wenn er das erfährt, gehts rund** all hell will break loose when he finds out (*inf*); **es geht rund, wenn sie zu Besuch kommen** there's never a dull moment when they come to visit; **es geht rund im Büro** there's a lot (going) on at the office **b** (= *herumgehen*) to do the rounds (*Brit*), to go around; **die Neuigkeit ist schon rundgegangen** the news has already got (a)round

Rund-: Rund|ge|sang M (*Mus*) chorus song (*in which a different person sings each verse*); (= *Kanon*) round; **Rund|hals|pul|lo|ver** M crew-neck sweater; **Rund|heit** F **-, -** *no pl* roundness; **rund|he|raus** ['rʊnthɛ'raʊs] ADV straight out; *sagen, fragen auch* bluntly; *ablehnen auch* flatly; **~ gesagt** frankly; **rund|he|rum** ['rʊnthɛ'rʊm] ADV all round (*Brit*), all around (*US*); (*fig inf*: = *völlig*) totally; **Rund|kopf|schrau|be** F round-headed *or* button-head (*US*) screw; **Rund|kurs** M circuit; **rund|lich** ['rʊntlɪç] ADJ *Mensch, Gesicht* plump, chubby; *Form* rounded; **Rund|lich|keit** F **-, -** *no pl* (*von Mensch*) plumpness; **Rund|ling** ['rʊntlɪŋ] M **-s, -e** *circular village grouped around a green*; nuclear village; **Rund|rei|se** F tour (*durch* of); **Rund|rü|cken** M (*Med*) round shoulders *pl*; **Rund|ruf** M per ~ with a series of phone calls; **Rund|schä|del** M shorthead; **Rund|schau** F (*Rad, TV*) magazine programme (*Brit*), news magazine (show) (*US*); **Rund|schnitt** M round haircut; **Rund|schrei|ben** NT circular; **Rund|sicht** F panorama; **Rund|strick|na|del** F circular needle; **Rund|stück** NT (*N Ger: Brötchen*) roll

rund|um ['rʊnt'ʊm] ADV all around; (*fig*) completely, totally

Rund|um-: Rund|um|er|neu|e|rung F general overhaul; **Rund|um|schlag** M (*lit, fig*) sweeping blow; **Rund|um|sicht** F panoramic view

Run|dung ['rʊndʊŋ] F **-, -en** curve

Rund-: Rund|wan|der|weg M circular route; **rund|weg** ['rʊnt'vɛk] ADV = **rundheraus**; **Rund|zan|ge** F round-nosed pliers *pl*

Ru|ne ['ruːnə] F **-, -n** rune

Ru|nen- *in cpds* runic; **Ru|nen|rei|he** F runic alphabet; **Ru|nen|schrift** F runic writing; **Ru|nen|stein** M rune stone; **Ru|nen|zei|chen** NT runic character

Run|ge ['rʊŋə] F **-, -n** stake

Run|kel ['rʊŋkl] F **-, -n** (*Aus*), **Run|kel|rü|be** F mangelwurzel

Ru|no|lo|ge [runo'loːgə] M **-n, -n**, **Ru|no|lo|gin** [-'loːgɪn] F **-, -nen** runologist

run|ter ['rʊntɐ] ADV (*inf*) = **herunter, hinunter** **~!** down!

run|ter- PREF (*inf*) down; **run|ter+hau|en** ['rʊntɐhaʊən] VT *sep* (*inf*) **a** (= *ohrfeigen*) **jdm eine** *or* **ein paar ~** to give sb a clip round (*Brit*) *or* a smack on the ear **b** (= *schreiben*) **einen Text ~** to bang out a text (*inf*); **run|ter+ho|len** ['rʊntɐhoːlən] VT *sep* to get down; **jdm/sich einen ~** (*inf*) to jerk sb/(oneself) off (*sl*) → *auch* **herunterholen**; **run|ter+kom|men** ['rʊntɐkɔmən] VI *sep irreg aux sein* (*inf: von Drogen/Heroin etc*) **von etw ~** to come off sth → *auch* **herunterkommen**; **run|ter+las|sen** ['rʊntɐlasn] VT *sep irreg* = **herunterlassen die Hosen ~** (*sl*) to come clean (*inf*)

run|ter sein ▲ VI *sep irreg aux sein* (*inf*: = *erschöpft sein*) to be run down; **von etw ~** (*inf*: *von Drogen/Heroin etc*) to be off sth; **gesundheitlich ~** to be under the weather (*inf*), to feel off (*inf*); **mit den Nerven ~** to be at the end of one's tether (*Brit inf*) *or* rope (*US inf*)

Run|zel ['rʊntsl] F **-, -n** wrinkle; (*auf Stirn auch*) line; **~n bekommen** (*Mensch*) to get wrinkles; (*Haut*) to get *or* become wrinkled

run|ze|lig ['rʊntsəlɪç] ADJ wrinkled; *Stirn auch* lined

run|zeln ['rʊntsln] VT *Stirn* to wrinkle, to crease; *Brauen* to knit VR to become wrinkled

runz|lig ['rʊntslɪç] ADJ = **runzelig**

Rü|pel ['ryːpl] M **-s, -** lout, yob(bo) (*Brit inf*)

Rü|pe|lei [ryːpə'laɪ] F **-, -en** (= *rüpelhafte Art*) loutishness; (= *rüpelhafte Handlung/Bemerkung*) loutish act/remark *etc*

rü|pel|haft ADJ loutish ADV **sich ~ benehmen** to behave like a lout

rup|fen ['rʊpfn] VT *Geflügel, Federn* to pluck; *Gras, Unkraut* to pull up; **jdn ~** (*fig inf*) to fleece sb (*inf*), to take sb to the cleaners (*inf*); **sie sieht aus wie ein gerupftes Huhn** (= *schlecht frisiert*) she looks as if she's been dragged through a hedge backwards; (= *schlechter Haarschnitt*) she looks like a half-shorn sheep

Ru|pfen ['rʊpfn] M **-s, -** (*Tex*) gunny; (*für Wandbehänge*) hessian

Ru|pie ['ruːpiə] F **-, -n** rupee

rup|pig ['rʊpɪç] ADJ (= *grob*) rough; *Antwort* gruff; *Aktion* reckless; **sein ~es Äußeres** his rough-looking exterior; **~es Benehmen** uncouth behaviour (*Brit*) *or* behavior (*US*) ADV *behandeln, sagen* gruffly; *Auto fahren* recklessly; **~ spielen** to play rough; **~ antworten** to give a gruff answer; **sich ~ benehmen** to behave in an uncouth way

Rup|pig|keit F **-, -en a** *no pl* (= *Benehmen*) gruff manner; (*von Antwort*) gruffness; (*von Fahrer*) thuggishness; **die ~ seines Fahrstils** his thuggish driving **b** (= *Handlung*) **~en** *pl* rough behaviour (*Brit*) *or* behavior (*US*); **zwischen den beiden kam es zu ~en** things got rough between the two of them

Ru|precht ['ruːprɛçt] M **-s** Rupert → **Knecht c**

Rü|sche ['ry:ʃə] F -, -n ruche, frill
Rush|hour ▲ ['raʃlauɐ] F -, -s, **Rush-hour** △ F -, -s rush hour
Ruß [ru:s] M -es, no pl soot; (von Kerze) smoke; (von Petroleumlampe) lampblack; (von Dieselmotor) exhaust particulate (spec)
ruß|be|deckt ADJ covered in or with soot
Rus|se ['rʊsə] M -n, -n, **Rus|sin** ['rʊsɪn] F -, -nen Russian
Rüs|sel ['rʏsl] M -s, - (auch inf: = Nase) snout; (von Elefant) trunk; (von Insekt) proboscis
rüs|sel|för|mig ADJ → **Rüssel** snoutlike; trunklike; proboscidean (spec)
ru|ßen ['ru:sn] VI (Öllampe, Kerze) to smoke; (Ofen) to produce soot; **es rußt** there's a lot of soot; **eine stark ~de Lampe** a very smoky lamp VT (Sw, S Ger) **den Ofen ~** to clean the soot out of the stove; **den Kamin ~** to sweep the chimney
Rus|sen-: rus|sen|freund|lich ADJ pro-Russian; **Rus|sen|kit|tel** M smock; **Rus|sen|stie|fel** M Cossack boot
Ruß-: ruß|far|ben [-farbn], **ruß|far|big** ADJ soot-black; **Ruß|fil|ter** M (esp Aut) particulate filter (spec); **Ruß|fleck** M sooty mark; **Ruß|flo|cke** F soot particle; **ruß|ge|schwärzt** [-gəʃvɛrtst] ADJ soot-blackened
ru|ßig ['ru:sɪç] ADJ sooty
Rus|sin F -, -nen Russian
rus|sisch ['rʊsɪʃ] ADJ Russian; **~es Roulett** Russian roulette; **~e Eier** (Cook) egg(s) mayonnaise; **~er Salat** (Cook) Russian salad
Rus|sisch|brot ▲ NT (Cook) alphabet biscuits pl (Brit) or cookies pl (US)
Rus|sisch(e) ['rʊsɪʃ] NT Russian → auch **Deutsch(e)**
Russ|land ▲ ['rʊslant] NT -s Russia
Russ|land|deut|sche(r) ▲ MF decl as adj ethnic German living in Russia and the Republics
rüs|ten ['rʏstn] VI (Mil) to arm; (fig) to arm oneself; **zum Krieg/Kampf ~** to arm for war/battle; **gut/schlecht gerüstet sein** to be well/badly armed; (fig) to be well/badly prepared; **um die Wette ~** to be involved in an arms race VR to prepare (zu for); (lit, fig: = sich wappnen) to arm oneself (gegen for); **sich zur Abreise ~** to get ready to leave; **sich zum Fest ~** to prepare for the festival VT a (old: = vorbereiten) to prepare; Nachtlager auch to make ready b (Build) Haus to scaffold
Rüs|ter ['rʏstɐ] F -, -n elm
rüs|tern ['rʏstɐn] ADJ attr elm

Rüs|ter(n)|holz NT elm (wood)
rüs|tig ['rʏstɪç] ADJ sprightly; **geistig/körperlich ~** mentally/physically active
Rüs|tig|keit F -, no pl sprightliness
rus|ti|kal [rʊsti'ka:l] ADJ Möbel rustic; Speisen country-style, farmhouse attr ADV wohnen rustically; **sich ~ einrichten** to furnish one's home in a rustic or farmhouse style
Rüst|kam|mer F (Mil, fig) armoury (Brit), armory (US)
Rüs|tung ['rʏstʊŋ] F -, -en a (= das Rüsten) armament; (= Waffen) arms pl, weapons pl b (= Ritterrüstung) armour (Brit), armor (US)
Rüs|tungs- in cpds arms; **Rüs|tungs|aus|ga|ben** PL defence (Brit) or defense (US) spending sing; **Rüs|tungs|be|gren|zung** F arms limitation; **Rüs|tungs|be|gren|zungs|ver|hand|lun|gen** PL arms limitation talks pl; **Rüs|tungs|be|schrän|kung** F arms limitation; **Rüs|tungs|be|trieb** M , **Rüs|tungs|fab|rik** F armaments or ordnance factory; **Rüs|tungs|geg|ner(in)** M(F) supporter of disarmament; **Rüs|tungs|in|dust|rie** F armaments industry; **Rüs|tungs|kon|trol|le** F arms control; **Rüs|tungs|kon|troll|ver|hand|lun|gen** PL arms control talks pl; **Rüs|tungs|pro|duk|ti|on** F arms production; **Rüs|tungs|wett|lauf** M arms race
Rüst|zeug NT , no pl a (old: = Handwerkszeug) tools pl b (fig) skills pl
Ru|te ['ru:tə] F -, -n a (= Gerte) switch; (= esp Stock zum Züchtigen) cane, rod; (= Birkenrute) birch (rod); (von Gertenbündel) birch; **jdn mit einer ~ schlagen** to cane/birch sb, to beat sb with a cane/birch; **mit eiserner ~ regieren** (fig) to rule with a rod of iron b (= Wünschelrute) (divining or dowsing) rod; (= Angelrute) (fishing) rod; **mit der ~ gehen** to go divining c (Hunt: = Schwanz) tail d (= Tierpenis) penis; (dated sl: von Mann) cock (sl), prick (sl) e (Aus: = Schneebesen) whisk f (old: Measure) rod
Ru|ten-: Ru|ten|bün|del NT (Hist) fasces pl; **Ru|ten|gän|ger** M -s, -, **Ru|ten|gän|ge|rin** [-ərɪn] F -, -nen diviner, dowser; **Ru|ten|ge|hen** NT dowsing; **Ru|ten|hieb** M stroke (of the birch)
Ru|the|ni|um [ru'te:niʊm] NT -s, no pl (abbr **Ru**) ruthenium
Rüt|li|schwur ['ry:tli-] M , no pl (Hist) oath taken on the Rütli Mountain by the founders of Switzerland
rutsch [rʊtʃ] INTERJ whee, whoomph
Rutsch [rʊtʃ] M -es, -e slip, slide, fall; (= Erdrutsch) landslide; (von Steinen) rock fall; (fig)

(Pol) shift, swing; (Fin) slide, fall; (inf: = Ausflug) trip, outing; **guten ~!** (inf) have a good New Year!; **in einem ~** in one go
Rutsch|bahn F , **Rut|sche** ['rʊtʃə] F -, -n (Mech) chute; (= Kinderrutschbahn) slide
rut|schen ['rʊtʃn] VI aux sein a (= gleiten) to slide; (= ausrutschen, entgleiten) to slip; (Aut) to skid; (fig) (Preise, Kurse) to slip; (Regime, Hierarchie) to crumble; **auf dem Stuhl hin und her ~** to fidget (around) or shift around on one's chair; **ins Rutschen kommen** or **geraten** (lit, fig) to start to slip; (Unternehmen) to start to go downhill
b (inf: = rücken) to move or shove (inf) up; **zur Seite ~** to move or shove (inf) up or over; **ein Stück(chen) ~** to move or shove (inf) up a bit
c (= herunterrutschen) to slip down; (Essen, Tablette) to go down
d (auf Rutschbahn) to slide; **darf ich mal ~?** can I have a go on the slide?
e (= rutschend kriechen) to crawl; **auf den Knien ~** (lit) to go along on one's knees; **auf den Knien gerutscht kommen** (fig inf) to go down on bended knee
Rut|scher ['rʊtʃɐ] M -s, - (Aus) (= Abstecher) small detour; (= kleine Strecke) stone's throw
Rutsch-: rutsch|fest ADJ nonslip; **Rutsch|ge|fahr** F danger of skidding; „**Rutschgefahr**" "slippery road"
rut|schig ['rʊtʃɪç] ADJ slippery, slippy (inf)
Rutsch-: Rutsch|par|tie F (hum inf) (= das Ausrutschen) slip; (von Auto) skid; (auf Rutschbahn) slide; **eine ~ machen** (= ausrutschen) to slip; (mit Auto) to skid; (auf Rutschbahn) to slide; **das war eine schöne ~** (auf vereister Straße) we were sliding all over the place; **rutsch|si|cher** ADJ nonslip
Rüt|te|lei [rʏtə'lai] F -, no pl shaking; (von Fahrzeug, Zug) jolting; (von Fenstern, Türen) rattling; **die Fahrt war eine einzige ~** we were jolted about the whole way
rüt|teln ['rʏtln] VT to shake (about); Getreide etc to riddle, to sieve; **jdn am Arm/an der Schulter ~** to shake sb's arm/shoulder, to shake sb by the arm/shoulder → auch **gerüttelt** VI to shake; (Fahrzeug) to jolt; (Fenster, Tür: im Wind) to rattle; **an etw** (dat) **~** (an Tür, Fenster etc) to rattle (at) sth; (fig) an Grundsätzen, Ergebnis etc to call sth into question; **daran ist nicht zu ~,** **daran gibt es nichts zu ~** (inf) there's no doubt about that
Rüt|tel|sieb NT sieve, riddle

S

S, s [ɛs] NT **-, -** S, s

s. *abbr von* **siehe** see

S *abbr von* **Süden** S

S. *abbr von* **Seite** p

SA [ɛs'|aː] F **-,** *no pl* (*NS*) *abbr von* **Sturmabteilung**

s. a. *abbr von* **siehe auch**

Saal [zaːl] M **-(e)s, Säle** ['zɛːlə] hall; (*für Sitzungen etc*) room; (= *Lesesaal*) reading room; (= *Tanzsaal, Ballsaal*) ballroom; (*für Hochzeiten, Empfänge*) function suite; (= *Theatersaal*) auditorium

Saal-: Saal|mie|te F hall hire *or* rental (*US*) charge; **Saal|ord|ner** M usher; **Saal|ord|ne|rin** F usherette; **Saal|schlacht** F (*inf*) brawl, punch-up (*inf*); **Saal|toch|ter** F (*Sw*) waitress

Saar [zaːɐ] F **-** Saar

Saar-: Saar|ge|biet NT , **Saar|land** NT **-s** Saarland; **Saar|län|der** ['zaːɐlɛndɐ] M **-s, -,** **Saar|län|de|rin** [-ərɪn] F **-, -nen** Saarlander; **saar|län|disch** ['zaːɐlɛndɪʃ] ADJ (of the) Saarland

Saat [zaːt] F **-, -en** **a** (= *das Säen*) sowing **b** (= *Samen, Saatgut*) seed(s) (*auch fig*); **die ~ ist aufgegangen** (*lit*) the seed has begun to grow; (*fig*) the seeds have borne fruit; **die ~ für etw legen** (*fig*) to sow the seed(s) of sth; **wie die ~, so die Ernte** (*prov*) **ohne ~ keine Ernte** (*prov*) as you sow, so shall you reap (*Prov*) **c** (= *junges Getreide*) young crop(s *pl*), seedlings *pl*

Saat|beet NT bed of seedlings, seedling bed

Saa|ten|stand M state of the crop(s)

Saat-: Saat|feld NT cornfield (*Brit*), grain field; **Saat|gut** NT , *no pl* seed(s); **Saat|kar|tof|fel** F seed potato; **Saat|korn** NT *pl* **-kör-ner** seed corn; **Saat|krä|he** F rook; **Saat|zeit** F seedtime, sowing time

Sa|ba ['zaːba] NT **-s** (*Hist*) Sheba; **die Königin von ~** the Queen of Sheba

Sạb|bat ['zabat] M **-s, -e** Sabbath

Sạb|bat-: Sạb|bat|jahr NT sabbatical year; **Sạb|bat|schän|der** [-ʃɛndɐ] M **-s, -,** **Sạb|bat|schän|de|rin** [-ərɪn] F **-, -nen** desecrator of the Sabbath

Sạb|bel ['zabl] M **-s,** *no pl* (*dial*) slobber, saliva, slaver

sạb|beln ['zabln] VTI (*dial*) = **sabbern**

Sạb|ber ['zabɐ] M **-s,** *no pl* (*dial*) slobber, saliva, slaver

Sạb|be|rei [zabə'rai] F **-, -en** (*inf*) (*dial*) slobber-ing; (*fig*: = *Geschwätz*) drivel (*inf*)

Sạb|ber|lätz|chen NT (*dial*) bib

sạb|bern ['zabɐn] (*inf*) VI to slobber, to slaver; **vor sich hin ~** (*fig*) to mutter away to oneself VT (*inf*), to blether; **dummes Zeug ~** to talk drivel (*inf*)

Sä|bel ['zɛːbl] M **-s, -** sabre (*Brit*), saber (*US*); (= *Krummsäbel*) scimitar; **jdn auf ~ fordern** to challenge sb to a (sabre (*Brit*) *or* saber (*US*)) duel; **mit dem ~ rasseln** (*fig*) to rattle the sabre (*Brit*) *or* saber (*US*)

Sä|bel-: Sä|bel|bei|ne PL (*inf*) bow *or* bandy (*Brit*) legs *pl*; **sä|bel|bei|nig** ADJ (*inf*) bow-legged, bandy-legged (*Brit*); **Sä|bel|fech|ten** NT **-s,** *no pl* sabre (*Brit*) *or* saber (*US*) fencing;

Sä|bel|ge|ras|sel [-gərasl] NT **-s,** *no pl* sabre-rattling (*Brit*), saber-rattling (*US*); **Sä|bel|hieb** M stroke of one's sabre (*Brit*) *or* saber (*US*)

sä|beln ['zɛːbln] (*inf*) VT to saw away at VI to saw away (*an +dat* at)

Sä|bel-: Sä|bel|ras|seln NT **-s,** *no pl* sabre-rat-tling (*Brit*), saber-rattling (*US*); **sä|bel|ras|selnd** ADJ sabre-rattling (*Brit*), saber-rattling (*US*); **Sä|bel|rass|ler** ▲ [-raslɐ] M **-s, -,** **Sä|bel|rass|le|rin** ▲ [-ərɪn] F **-, -nen** sabre-rattler (*Brit*), saber-rattler (*US*)

Sa|bi|ner M **-s, -,** **Sabinerin** F **-, -nen** Sabine; **der Raub der ~innen** the rape of the Sabines *or* the Sabine women

Sa|bo|ta|ge [zabo'taːʒə] F **-, -n** sabotage (*an +dat* of); **~ treiben** to perform acts of sabotage

Sa|bo|ta|ge|akt M act of sabotage

Sa|bo|teur [zabo'tøːɐ] M **-s, -e,** **Sa|bo|teu|rin** [-'tøːrɪn] F **-, -nen** saboteur

sa|bo|tie|ren [zabo'tiːrən] *ptp* **sabotiert** VT to sabotage

Sa(c)|cha|rin [zaxa'riːn] NT **-s,** *no pl* saccharin

Sach-: Sach|an|la|ge|ver|mö|gen NT (*Econ*) tangible fixed assets *pl*; **Sach|aus|ga|ben** PL material costs *pl*; **Sach|be|ar|bei|ter(in)** M(F) specialist; (= *Beamter*) official in charge (*für* of); **der ~ für Anträge ist nicht da** the person who deals with applications isn't here; **Sach|be|reich** M (specialist) area; **Sach|be|schä|di|gung** F damage to property; **sach|be|zo|gen** ADJ *Wissen, Fragen, Angaben, Politik* relevant, pertinent ADV with reference to the relevant issue/issues; **Sach|be|zü|ge** PL pay-ment *or* contributions *pl* in kind; **Sach|buch** NT nonfiction book; **sach|dien|lich** ADJ *Hinweise* useful; **es ist nicht ~, wenn ...** it won't help the matter if ...

Sạche ['zaxə] ✪ 33.2 F **-, -n** **a** thing; (= *Gegenstand*) object, thing; (*Jur*: = *Eigentum*) article of property; **der Mensch wird zur ~** man is re-duced to *or* becomes an object; **~n gibts(, die gibts gar nicht)!** (*inf*) would you credit it! (*inf*) **b** **Sachen** PL (*inf*: = *Zeug*) things *pl*; (*Jur*) property; **seine ~n packen** to pack ones bags **c** (= *Angelegenheit*) matter; (= *Rechtsstreit, Fall*) case; (= *Aufgabe*) job; **eine ~ der Polizei/der Be-hörden** a matter for the police/authorities; **es ist ~ der Polizei/der Behörden, das zu tun** it's up to the police/authorities *or* it's for the po-lice/authorities to do that; **das mit dem Prä-sidenten war eine unangenehme ~** that was an unpleasant business with the president; **das ist eine ganz tolle/unangenehme ~** it's really fantastic/unpleasant; **die ~ macht sich** (*inf*) things are coming along; **ich habe mir die ~ an-ders vorgestellt** I had imagined things differ-ently; **das ist eine andere ~** that's a different matter, that's a different kettle of fish (*inf*), that's a different cup of tea (*US inf*); **das ist meine/seine ~** that's my/his affair *or* business; **in eigener ~** on one's own account; **in ~ A ge-gen B** (*Jur*) in the case (of) A versus B; **das ist nicht jedermanns ~** it's not every-one's cup of tea (*inf*); **er versteht seine ~** he knows what he's doing *or* what he's about (*inf*); **er macht seine ~ gut** he's doing very well;

(*beruflich*) he's doing a good job; **diese Frage können wir nicht hier mitbesprechen, das ist eine ~ für sich** we can't discuss this question now, it's a separate issue all to itself; **und was hat deine Frau gesagt?/was meinen Sie zu die-sen Streiks? – das ist eine ~ für sich** and what did your wife say?/what do you think about these strikes? – that's another story; **das ist so eine ~** (*inf*) it's a bit tricky, it's a bit of a prob-lem; **das ist 'ne ~** (*inf*: = *prima*) great (*inf*); **der ~ zuliebe** for the love of it; **die ~ mit der Bank ist also geplatzt** so the bank job fell through; **er ist für illegale ~n nicht zu haben** you won't get him to do anything illegal; **solche ~n liegen mir nicht** I don't like things like that

d (= *Vorfall*) business, affair; **~n** PL (= *Vor-kommnisse*) things *pl*; **die ~ mit dem verschwun-denen Schlüssel** the business *or* affair with the disappearing key; **machst du bei der ~ mit?** are you with us?; **bei der ~ mache ich nicht mit** I'll have nothing to do with it; **was hat die Polizei zu der ~ gesagt?** what did the police say about it *or* about all this business?; **das ist (eine) be-schlossene ~** it's (all) settled; **die ~ hat ge-klappt/ist schief gegangen** everything *or* it worked/went wrong; **mach keine ~n!** (*inf*) don't be daft (*Brit inf*) *or* silly!; **was machst du bloß für ~n!** (*inf*) the things you do!; **was sind denn das für ~n?** what's all this?

e (= *Frage, Problem*) matter, question; (= *Thema*) subject; (= *Ideal, Anliegen*) cause; **eine ~ der Er-ziehung/des Geschmacks** a matter *or* question of education/taste; **mehr kann ich zu der ~ nicht sagen** that's all I can say on the subject; **um die ~ herumreden** to talk (all) round the subject; **zur ~!** let's get on with it; (*Parl, Jur etc*) come to the point!; **zur ~ kommen** to come to the point; **zur ~ gehen** (*inf*) to come to the crunch (*inf*); (*Sport*) to get stuck in (*inf*); **das tut nichts zur ~** that doesn't matter; **sich** (*dat*) **seiner ~ sicher** *or* **gewiss sein** to be sure of one's ground; **bei der ~ sein** to be with it (*inf*), to be on the ball (*inf*); **sie war nicht bei der ~** her mind was elsewhere; **bei der ~ bleiben** to keep one's mind on the job; (*bei Diskussion*) to keep to the point

f (= *Sachlage*) things *pl, no art*; **so steht die ~ also** so that's the way things are; **die ~ ist die, dass ...** the thing is that ...; **jdm sagen, was ~ ist** (*inf*) to tell sb what's what; **neben der ~ lie-gen** to be beside the point

g (= *Tempo*) **mit 60/100 ~n** (*inf*) at 60/100

-sa|che F *suf in cpds* a matter of ...; **das ist An-sichtssache/Geschmackssache** that's a matter of opinion/taste

Sach|ein|la|ge F (*Econ*) contribution in kind

Sa|chen|recht NT (*Jur*) law of property

Sa|cher|tor|te ['zaxɐ-] F *rich chocolate cake,* sachertorte

Sach-: Sach|fahn|dung F search for lost or stolen property; **Sach|fra|ge** F question regarding the matter itself; **Sach- und Personal-fragen** questions relating to work and to per-sonnel matters; **sach|fremd** ADJ irrelevant; **Sach|ge|biet** NT subject area; **sach|ge|mäß,** **sach|ge|recht** ADJ proper; **bei ~er Anwen-dung** if used properly ADV properly; **etw ~ ma-**

chen to do sth properly; **Sach|ka|ta|log** M subject index; **Sach|ken|ner(in)** M(F) expert (*in +dat* on); **~ auf einem** *or* **für ein Gebiet sein** to be an expert in a field; **Sach|kennt|nis** F (*in Bezug auf Wissensgebiet*) knowledge of the/his subject; (*in Bezug auf Sachlage*) knowledge of the facts; **Sach|kun|de** M *no pl* **a** = **Sachkenntnis b** (*Schulfach*) general knowledge; **sach|kun|dig** ADJ (well-)informed; *Beratung, Information* expert; *Erklärung* competent; **sich ~ machen** to inform oneself ADV **~ antworten** to give an informed answer; **jdn ~ beraten** to give sb expert advice; **etw ~ erklären** to give a competent explanation of sth; **Sach|kun|di|ge(r)** [-kʊndɪɡə] MF *decl as adj* = **Sachkenner(in)**; **Sach|la|ge** F situation, state of affairs; **Sach|leis|tung** F payment in kind; (*bei Krankenkasse etc*) benefit in kind

sach|lich ['zaxlɪç] ADJ **a** (= *faktisch*) *Irrtum, Angaben* factual; *Unterschied* material, factual; *Grund, Einwand* practical; (*sachbezogen*) *Frage, Wissen* relevant **b** (= *objektiv*) *Kritik, Bemerkung* objective; (= *nüchtern*) unemotional, matter-of-fact; **bleiben Sie mal ~** don't get carried away; (= *nicht persönlich werden*) don't get personal, stay objective **c** (= *schmucklos*) functional, businesslike ADV **a** (= *faktisch*) *unzutreffend* factually; **die Auskunft war ~ falsch/richtig** the information was wrong/correct; **rein ~ hast du Recht** from a purely factual point of view you are right **b** (= *objektiv*) objectively

säch|lich ['zɛçlɪç] ADJ (*Gram*) neuter

Sach|lich|keit F, *- no pl* **a** (= *Objektivität: von Kritik, Bemerkung*) objectivity; (= *Nüchternheit*) matter-of-factness; **mit ~ kommt man weiter** you get on better if you stay objective **b** (= *Schmucklosigkeit*) functionality; **die Neue ~** (*Art, Archit*) the new functionalism

Sach-: Sach|män|gel PL material defects *pl*; **Sach|män|gel|haf|tung** F liability for material defects; **Sach|mit|tel** PL (*form*) materials *pl*; (= *Zubehör*) equipment *no pl*; **Sach|re|gis|ter** NT subject index; **Sach|scha|den** M damage (to property); **bei dem Unfall hatte ich nur ~** only the car was damaged in the accident; **es entstand ~ in Höhe von …** there was damage amounting to …

Sach|se ['zaksə] M **-n, -n**, **Säch|sin** ['zɛksɪn] F **-, -nen** Saxon

säch|seln ['zɛksln] VI (*inf*) (*mit Akzent*) to speak with a Saxon accent; (*in Mundart*) to speak in the Saxon dialect

Sach|sen ['zaksn] NT **-s** Saxony

Sach|sen-An|halt ['zaksn|ʔanhalt] NT **-s** Saxony-Anhalt

säch|sisch ['zɛksɪʃ] ADJ Saxon; **die Sächsische Schweiz** *area southeast of Dresden known for its health resorts and unusual rock formations*

Säch|sisch(e) ['zɛksɪʃ] NT Saxon (dialect) → *auch* **Deutsch(e)**

Sach|spen|de F gift; **wir bitten um Geld- und ~n** we are asking for donations of money and goods

sacht [zaxt], **sach|te** ['zaxtə] ADJ (= *leise*) soft; (= *sanft*) gentle; (= *vorsichtig*) cautious, careful; (= *allmählich*) gentle, gradual; **mit ~en Schritten** softly ADV softly, gently; *ansteigen, abfallen* gently; (= *vorsichtig*) *anfragen* carefully; **~e, ~e!** (*inf*) take it easy!

Sach-: Sach|ver|halt [-fɛɐhalt] M **-(e)s, -e** facts *pl* (of the case); **Sach|ver|stand** M expertise; **Sach|ver|stän|di|gen|aus|schuss** ▲ M committee of experts; **Sach|ver|stän|di|gen|gut|ach|ten** NT specialist report; **Sach|ver|stän|di|ge(r)** [-fɛɐʃtɛndɪɡə] MF *decl as adj* expert, specialist; (*Jur*) expert witness; **Sach|ver|zeich|nis** NT subject index; **Sach|wal|ter** ['zaxvaltɐ] M **-s, -**, **Sach|wal|te|rin** [-ərɪn] F **-, -nen** (*geh*) (= *Verwalter*) agent; (= *Treuhänder*)

trustee; (*fig: = Fürsprecher*) champion; **Sach|wert** M real *or* intrinsic value; **~e** *pl* material assets *pl*; **Sach|wör|ter|buch** NT specialist dictionary; **~ der Kunst/Botanik** dictionary of art/botany, art/botanical dictionary; **Sach|zu|sam|men|hang** M factual connection; **Sach|zwang** M practical constraint; **Sachzwängen unterliegen, unter Sachzwängen** (*dat*) **stehen** to be constrained by circumstances

Sack [zak] M **-(e)s, ⸚e** ['zɛkə] **a** sack; (*aus Papier, Plastik*) bag; **drei ~ Kartoffeln/Kohlen** three sacks of potatoes/sacks *or* bags of coal; **in ~ und Asche** in sackcloth and ashes; **in ~ und Tüten sein** (*inf*) to be in the bag (*inf*), to be all wrapped up (*inf*); **etw im ~ haben** (*inf*) to have sth in the bag (*inf*); **mit ~ und Pack** (*inf*) with bag and baggage; **den ~ schlägt man, und den Esel meint man** (*Prov*) to kick the dog and mean the master (*prov*); **jdn in den ~ stecken** (*fig inf*) to put sb in the shade (*Brit*), to outdo sb **b** (*Anat, Zool*) sac **c** (*S Ger, Aus: = Hosentasche*) (trouser (*Brit*) *or* pants (*US*)) pocket; **Geld im ~ haben** to have money in one's pocket **d** (*vulg: = Hoden*) balls *pl* (*sl*); **jdm auf den ~ gehen** (*sl*) to get on sb's tits (*sl*) **e** (*inf: = Kerl, Bursche*) sod (*Brit inf*), bastard (*sl*), cunt (*vulg*); **fauler ~** lazy bugger (*Brit inf*) *or* bastard (*sl*); **alter ~** old bastard (*sl*)

Sack|bahn|hof M terminus

Sä|ckel ['zɛkl] M **-s, -** (*S Ger* = *Beutel*) bag; (= *Hosentasche*) pocket; (= *Geldsäckel*) money bag; (*old, hum* = *Staatssäckel*) national coffers *pl*; **tief in den ~ greifen müssen** to have to dig deep (into one's pockets); **sich** (*dat*) **den ~ füllen** to line one's (own) pockets

sa|cken¹ ['zakn], **sä|ckeln** ['zɛkln] (*dial*) VT to put into sacks, to sack

sa|cken² VI *aux sein* (*lit, fig*) to sink; (*Flugzeug*) to lose height; (= *durchhängen*) to sag; **in die Knie ~** to sag at the knees; **die Aktienkurse sackten in den Keller** share prices went through the floor *or* hit rock bottom

sa|cker|lot [zakɐ'loːt], **sa|cker|ment** [zakɐ'mɛnt] INTERJ (*old*) stap me (*Brit old*), upon my soul (*old*)

sä|cke|wei|se ['zɛkəvaizə] ADJ, ADV → **Sack a** by the sack/bag

Sack-: sack|för|mig ADJ like a sack, sack-like ADV like a sack; **Sack|gas|se** F dead end, blind alley; cul-de-sac (*esp Brit*); (*fig*) dead end; **in eine ~ geraten** (*fig*) to finish up a blind alley; (*Verhandlungen*) to reach an impasse; **in einer ~ stecken** (*fig*) to be (stuck) up a blind alley; (*mit Bemühungen etc*) to have come to a dead end; **die Verhandlungen in die ~ führen** (*fig*) to lead the negotiations into an impasse; **die Verhandlungen aus der ~ führen** (*fig*) to end the impasse in the negotiations; **Sack|hüp|fen** NT **-s**, *no pl* sack race; **Sack|kar|re** F barrow, handcart; **Sack|kleid** NT sack dress; **Sack|lei|nen** NT, **Sack|lein|wand** F sacking, burlap (*US*); **Sack|mes|ser** NT (*Sw, S Ger*: = *Taschenmesser*) pocketknife, penknife; **Sack|pfei|fe** F bagpipes *pl*; **Sack|tuch** NT *pl* **-tücher a** (= *Sackleinen*) sacking, burlap (*US*) **b** (*S Ger, Aus, Sw*: = *Taschentuch*) handkerchief; **Sack|wich|ser** M (*sl*) wanker (*vulg*)

Sa|dis|mus [za'dɪsmʊs] M **-**, **Sadismen** [-mən] **a** *no pl* sadism **b** (*Handlung*) sadistic act

Sa|dist [za'dɪst] M **-en, -en**, **Sa|dis|tin** [-dɪstɪn] F **-, -nen** sadist

sa|dis|tisch [za'dɪstɪʃ] ADJ sadistic ADV sadistically

Sa|do|ma|so [zado'maːzo] M **-**, *no pl* (*sl*) SM

Sa|do|ma|so|chis|mus [zadomazoˈxɪsmʊs] M sadomasochism

sä|en ['zɛːən] VTI to sow; (*fig*) to sow (the seeds of); **dünn** *or* **spärlich** *or* **nicht dick gesät** (*fig*) thin on the ground, few and far between → **Wind a**

Sa|fa|ri [za'faːri] F **-, -s** safari; **eine ~ machen** to go on safari

Sa|fa|ri-: Sa|fa|ri|an|zug M safari suit; **Sa|fa|ri|look** [-lʊk] M safari look; **Sa|fa|ri|park** M safari park

Safe [zeːf] M OR NT **-s, -s** safe

Sa|fer|sex ▲ ['zeːfɐzɛks] M **- -(es)**, *no pl*, **Sa|fer Sex** M **- -(es)**, *no pl* safe sex

Saf|fi|an ['zafian, 'zafiaːn] M **-s**, *no pl*, **Saf|fi|an|le|der** NT morocco (leather)

Saf|ran ['zafraːn, 'zafran] M **-s, -e** (= *Krokus, Gewürz*) saffron

saf|ran|gelb ADJ saffron (yellow)

Saft [zaft] M **-(e)s, ⸚e** ['zɛftə] **a** (= *Obstsaft*) (fruit) juice; (= *Pflanzensaft*) sap; (= *Bratensaft, Fleischsaft*) juice; (= *Flüssigkeit*) liquid; (= *Hustensaft etc*) syrup; (= *Magensaft*) juices *pl*; (*old*: = *Körpersaft*) humour (*Brit old*), humor (*US old*); (*inf*: = *Strom, Benzin*) juice (*inf*); (*sl*: = *Sperma*) spunk (*vulg*); **roter ~** lifeblood; **Blut ist ein ganz besonderer ~** blood is a very special stuff; **der ~ der Reben** the juice of the grape; **voll im ~ stehen** to be full of sap; **die Säfte der Natur** (*liter*) the vital forces of nature; **von ~ und Kraft** (*fig*) dynamic, vital, vibrant; **ohne ~ und Kraft** (*fig*) wishy-washy (*inf*), effete → **schmoren VI a**

Saft|bra|ten M (*Cook*) roast

Säft|chen ['zɛftçən] NT **-s, -** *dim von* **Saft** (= *Fruchtsäftchen*) juice; (*pej*: = *Arznei*) mixture, medicine

Saft|fot|ze F (*pej vulg*) cunt (*vulg*)

saf|tig ['zaftɪç] ADJ **a** (= *voll Saft*) *Obst, Fleisch* juicy; *Wiese, Grün* lush **b** (= *kräftig*) *Witz* juicy (*inf*); *Rechnung, Strafe, Ohrfeige* hefty (*inf*); *Brief, Antwort, Ausdrucksweise* potent; **da habe ich ihm einen ~en Brief geschrieben** so I wrote him a pretty potent letter *or* one hell of a letter (*inf*)

Saf|tig|keit F **-**, *no pl* (*von Obst, Fleisch, Witz*) juiciness; (*von Wiese etc*) lushness

Saft-: Saft|kur F fruit-juice diet; **Saft|la|den** M (*pej inf*) dump (*pej inf*); **saft|los** ADJ **a** not juicy, juiceless **b** (*fig*: = *kraftlos*) feeble; **saft- und kraftlos** (*Mensch*) washed-out; *Bild, Gedicht etc* lifeless ADV (*fig*) feebly; **Saft|pres|se** F fruit press; **Saft|sack** M (*inf*) stupid bastard (*sl*) *or* bugger (*Brit inf*); **Saft|tag** M juice day; **einen ~ haben/einlegen** to have a day on juices only

Sa|ga ['zaːga] F **-, -s** saga

sag|bar ADJ sayable

Sa|ge ['zaːɡə] F **-, -n** legend; (*altnordische*) saga; **es geht die ~, dass …** legend has it that …; (= *Gerücht*) rumour (*Brit*) *or* rumor (*US*) has it that …

Sä|ge ['zɛːɡə] F **-, -n a** (*Werkzeug*) saw **b** (*Aus*: = *Sägewerk*) sawmill

Säge-: Sä|ge|blatt NT saw blade; **Sä|ge|bock** M sawhorse; **Sä|ge|fisch** M sawfish; **Sä|ge|ma|schi|ne** F mechanical saw; **Sä|ge|mehl** NT sawdust; **Sä|ge|mes|ser** NT serrated knife; **Sä|ge|müh|le** F sawmill

---

sa|gen ['zaːɡn]

TRANSITIVES VERB

a = *äußern* to say; **wie kannst du so etwas sagen?** how can you say such things?; **wie ich schon sagte** as I said before; **wie gesagt** as I say; **das kann ich Ihnen nicht sagen** I couldn't say; **das kann ich noch nicht sagen** I can't say yet; **das sage ich nicht!** I'm not saying!; **so was sagt man doch nicht!** you can't say things like that!; (*bei Schimpfen, Fluchen*) (mind your) language!; **haben Sie dazu etwas zu sagen?** do you have anything to say (about that)?; **was soll man dazu sagen?** what can you say?; **was sagen Sie dazu?** what do you think about it?; **sich** (*dat*) **etw sagen** to say sth to oneself; **das möchte** *or* **will ich nicht sagen** I wouldn't say

that; **um nicht zu sagen ...** not to say ...; **das würde ich (wieder) nicht sagen** I wouldn't say that; **ich sags ja immer ...** I always say ...; **ich möchte fast sagen, ...** I'd almost say ..., one could almost say ...; **wenn ich so sagen darf** if I may say so; **sag, was du willst, ...** (*inf*) say what you like ...; **damit ist alles gesagt** that says it all; **sag bloß!** you don't say!; **was Sie nicht sagen!** you don't say!; **ich sage gar nichts mehr!** I'm not saying another word!; (*verblüfft*) good heavens!; **das kann man wohl sagen!** you can say that again!; **ich muss schon sagen** I must say; **wie man so sagt** as they say, as the saying goes; **das ist nicht gesagt** that's by no means certain; **leichter gesagt als getan** easier said than done; **gesagt, getan** no sooner said than done; **ich bin, sagen wir, in einer Stunde da** I'll be there in an hour, say; **da soll noch einer sagen, wir Deutschen hätten keinen Humor!** never let it be said that we Germans have no sense of humour (*Brit*) or humor (*US*)!

> Das englische Verb **to tell** kann von einem Personalpronomen gefolgt werden, **to say** jedoch nicht.

jdm etw sagen to say sth to sb, to tell sb sth; **was hast du ihm gesagt?** what did you say to him?, what did you tell him?; **könnten Sie mir sagen, was das kosten soll?** could you tell me how much it will cost?; **ich sags ihm** I'll tell him; **ich kann dir sagen ...** (*inf*) I can tell you ...; **sag mir, was du liest, und ich sage dir, wer du bist** (*prov*) tell me what you read and I'll tell you what kind of person you are; **ich sage, wie es ist** I'm telling you the way it is; **das ist schnell gesagt** I can tell you in two words; **wem sagen Sie das!** you don't need to tell ME that!, tell me about it! (*inf*); **sag an, ...** (*old, liter*) pray tell, ... (*old*)

b = bedeuten, meinen to mean; **was will er damit sagen?** what does he mean (by that)?; **das hat nichts zu sagen** that doesn't mean anything; **sagt dir der Name etwas?** does the name mean anything to you?; **ich will damit nicht sagen, dass ...** I don't mean to imply or to say that ...; **damit ist nichts gesagt** that doesn't mean anything; **damit ist nicht gesagt, dass ...** that doesn't mean (to say) that ...; **willst du vielleicht sagen, dass ...** are you trying to say that ...?; **sein Gesicht sagte alles** it was written all over his face

c = befehlen to tell; **jdm sagen, er solle etw tun** to tell sb to do sth; **du hast hier (gar) nichts zu sagen** it's not your job to tell us what to do, you're not the boss; **hat er im Betrieb etwas zu sagen?** does he have a say in the firm?; **das Sagen haben** to be the boss; **hier habe ich das Sagen** I'm the boss here

♦ **sagen lassen:** ich habe mir sagen lassen, ... (= *ausrichten lassen*) I've been told ...; **was ich mir von ihm nicht alles sagen lassen muss!** the things I have to take from him!; **lass dir von mir sagen** or **gesagt sein, ...** let me tell you ...; **lass dir das gesagt sein** let me tell you; **er lässt sich** (*dat*) **nichts sagen** he won't be told, you can't tell him anything; **das lass ich mir von dem nicht sagen** I won't take that from him; **sie ließen es sich** (*dat*) **nicht zweimal sagen** they didn't need to be told twice

d andere Redewendungen **das hättest du dir selbst sagen können** or **müssen!** you might have known that!; **im Vertrauen gesagt** in confidence; **unter uns gesagt** between you and me; **genauer/deutlicher gesagt** to put it more precisely/clearly; **sag nicht so etwas** or **so was!** (*inf*) don't talk like that!; **sag das nicht!** (*inf*) don't you be so sure!; **was ich noch sagen wollte, ...** another point I would like to make is that ...; **was ich noch sagen wollte, vergiss nicht ...** (*inf*) by the way, don't forget ...; **dann will ich nichts gesagt haben** in that case forget I said anything; **es ist nicht zu sagen!** it doesn't bear thinking about!; (*entrüstet*) there aren't any words to describe it!; **das muss man**

sagen you have to admit that; **sage und schreibe 100 Euro** 100 euros, would you believe it

♦ **sag mal/sagen Sie mal du, Veronika, sag mal, wollen wir ...** hey Veronika, listen, shall we ...; **sag mal, Peter, kannst du mir fünf Euro leihen?** hey Peter, can you lend me five euros?; **sag mal, willst du nicht endlich Schluss machen?** come on, isn't it time to stop?; **nun sagen Sie/sag mal selber, ist das nicht unpraktisch?** you must admit that's impractical → **offen, Dank, Meinung**

sä|gen ['zɛːgn] **VT** to saw **VI** (*inf*: = schnarchen) to snore, to saw wood (*US inf*)

Sa|gen-: Sa|gen|dich|tung F sagas *pl*; **sa|gen|haft ADJ a** (= *nach Art einer Sage*) legendary **b** (= *enorm*) Summe fabulous **c** (*inf*: = *hervorragend*) fantastic (*inf*), terrific (*inf*) **ADV** (*inf*: = *unglaublich*) unbelievably, incredibly; **Sa|gen|kreis** M group of sagas; **sa|gen|um|wo|ben** [-ʊmvoːbn] ADJ legendary; **Sa|gen|welt** F mythology, legend

Sä|ge|rei [zɛːgəˈraɪ] F -, -en **a** (= *Sägewerk*) sawmill **b** *no pl* (*inf*: = das Sägen) sawing

Sä|ge-: Sä|ge|spä|ne PL wood shavings *pl*; **Sä|ge|werk** NT sawmill; **Sä|ge|zahn** M sawtooth

Sa|go ['zaːgo] M OR NT -s, *no pl* sago

Sa|go|pal|me F sago palm

sah *pret von* **sehen**

Sa|ha|ra [zaˈhaːra, ˈzaːhara] F - Sahara (Desert)

Sa|hel [zaˈheːl, ˈzaːhɛl] M -(s) Sahel

Sa|hel-Zo|ne F , **Sa|hel|zo|ne** F Sahel region

Sah|ne ['zaːnə] F -, *no pl* cream; **(aller)erste ~ sein** (*inf*) to be top-notch (*inf*)

Sah|ne-: Sah|ne|bai|ser NT cream meringue; **Sah|ne|bon|bon** M OR NT toffee; **Sah|ne|eis** NT ice cream; **Sah|ne|häub|chen** NT (*lit*) cream topping; (*fig*) icing on the cake; **Sah|ne|kä|se** M cream cheese; **Sah|ne|meer|ret|tich** M creamy or creamed horseradish; **Sah|ne|quark** [-kvark] M creamy quark; **Sah|ne|so|ße** F cream sauce; **Sah|ne|tor|te** F cream gateau

sah|nig ['zaːnɪç] ADJ creamy **ADV etw ~ schlagen** to whip or beat sth until creamy

Saib|ling ['zaɪplɪŋ] M -s, -e char(r)

Sai|son [zɛˈzõː, zɛˈzɔŋ, (Aus) zɛˈzoːn] F -, -s or (Aus) -en [-ˈzɔːnən] season; **außerhalb der ~, in der stillen** or **toten ~** in the off season; **~ haben** (Obst, Gemüse) to be in season; (*inf*: Konsumgüter*) to be in demand

Sai|son- [zɛˈzõː, zɛˈzɔŋ, (Aus) zɛˈzoːn] *in cpds* seasonal

sai|so|nal [zezoˈnaːl] ADJ seasonal

Sai|son- [sɛˈzõː, zɛˈzɔŋ]: **Sai|son|ar|beit** F seasonal work; **Sai|son|ar|bei|ter(in)** M(F) seasonal worker; **sai|son|be|dingt** ADJ seasonal; **Sai|son|be|ginn** M start of the season; **sai|son|be|rei|nigt** [-bəraɪnɪçt] ADJ Zahlen etc seasonally adjusted; **Sai|son|be|schäf|ti|gung** F seasonal job; **Sai|son|be|trieb** M (= Hochsaison) high season; (= Saisongeschäft) seasonal business; **Sai|son|er|öff|nung** F opening of the season; **Sai|son|ge|schäft** NT seasonal business; **Sai|son|ge|wer|be** NT seasonal trade; **Sai|son|in|dus|trie** F seasonal industry; **Sai|son|kenn|zei|chen** NT (Aut) vehicle number plate valid only for certain months of the year; **Sai|son|schluss** ▲ M end of the season; **Sai|son|schwan|kung** F seasonal fluctuation; **in ~ gehen** to take a seasonal job; **Sai|son|wan|de|rung** F (Econ) seasonal movement of labour (Brit) or labor (US); **Sai|son|zu|schlag** M in-season supplement

Sai|te ['zaɪtə] F -, -n **a** (Mus, Sport) string **b** (fig liter) **eine ~ in jdm berühren** or **anschlagen, eine ~ in jdm zum Klingen bringen** to strike a chord in sb; **andere ~n aufziehen** (inf) to get tough

Sai|ten-: Sai|ten|in|stru|ment NT string(ed) instrument; **Sai|ten|klang** M (liter) sound of strings; **Sai|ten|spiel** NT , *no pl* playing of a stringed instrument; **Sai|ten|wurst** F type of frankfurter

-sai|tig [zaɪtɪç] ADJ *suf* -string(ed); **eine zwölfsaitige Gitarre** a twelve-string(ed) guitar

Sait|ling ['zaɪtlɪŋ] M -s, -e sausage skin (for frankfurters)

Sak|ko ['zako] M OR NT -s, -s sports jacket (esp Brit), sport coat (US); (aus Samt etc) jacket

sak|ra ['zakra] INTERJ (S Ger, Aus) good God, my God

sak|ral [zaˈkraːl] ADJ sacred

Sak|ral-: Sak|ral|bau M *pl* -bauten sacred building; **~ten** *pl* (also) ecclesiastical or sacred architecture *sing*; **Sak|ral|kunst** F religious art, sacral art

Sak|ra|ment [zakraˈmɛnt] NT -(e)s, -e sacrament; **das ~ der Taufe** the sacrament of baptism; **die ~e spenden** to administer the sacraments; **~ (noch mal)!** (inf) Jesus Christ! (sl); **Himmel, Herrgott, ~!** (inf) Christ Almighty! (sl)

sak|ra|men|tal [zakramɛnˈtaːl] ADJ sacramental

Sak|ra|men|t(s)|häus|chen [-hɔysçən] NT tabernacle

Sak|ri|leg [zakriˈleːk] NT -s, -e [-gə], **Sak|ri|le|gi|um** [zakriˈleːgiʊm] NT -s, Sakrilegien [-giən] (geh) sacrilege

sak|risch ['zakrɪʃ] ADV (dial inf) damned (inf); schreien like hell (inf)

Sak|ris|tei [zakrɪsˈtaɪ] F -, -en sacristy

sak|ro|sankt [zakroˈzaŋkt] ADJ sacrosanct

sä|ku|lar [zɛkuˈlaːɐ] ADJ **a** (= weltlich) secular **b** (= zeitüberdauernd) timeless

Sä|ku|la|ri|sa|ti|on [zɛkulariza'tsioːn] F -, -en secularization

sä|ku|la|ri|sie|ren [zɛkulariˈziːrən] *ptp* säkularisiert VT to secularize

Sä|ku|lum ['zɛːkulʊm] NT -s, Säkula [-la] (geh) century

Sa|la|man|der [zalaˈmandɐ] M -s, - salamander

Sa|la|mi [zaˈlaːmi] F -, -s salami

Sa|la|mi|tak|tik F (inf) policy of small steps

Sa|lär [zaˈlɛːɐ] NT -s, -e (old, Sw) salary

Sa|lat [zaˈlaːt] M -(e)s, -e **a** (= Pflanze, Kopfsalat) lettuce **b** (= Gericht) salad; **da haben wir den ~!** (inf) now we're in a fine mess or in a pickle (inf)

Sa|lat-: Sa|lat|be|steck NT salad servers *pl*; **Sa|lat|dres|sing** [-drɛsɪŋ] NT -s, -s salad dressing; **Sa|lat|gur|ke** F cucumber; **Sa|lat|kar|tof|fel** F potato (used for potato salad); **Sa|lat|kopf** M (head of) lettuce; **Sa|lat|öl** NT salad oil; **Sa|lat|pflan|ze** F **a** (= Setzling) lettuce (plant) **b** (= Sorte) salad; **Sa|lat|plat|te** F salad; **Sa|lat|schleu|der** F salad drainer (Brit) or strainer (US); **Sa|lat|schüs|sel** F salad bowl; **Sa|lat|so|ße** F salad dressing

Sal|ba|de|rei [zalbadəˈraɪ] F -, -en (pej geh) sanctimonious prating

sal|ba|dern [zalˈbaːdɐn] *ptp* salbadert VI to prate

Sal|be ['zalbə] F -, -n ointment

Sal|bei ['zalbaɪ, zalˈbaɪ] M -s or f , *no pl* sage

Sal|bei|bon|bon NT sage cough sweet or drop (US)

sal|ben ['zalbn] VT (liter) to anoint; **jdn zum König ~** to anoint sb king

Salb|öl NT consecrated oil

Sal|bung ['zalbʊŋ] F -, -en (liter) anointing, unction

sal|bungs|voll (pej) ADJ Worte, Ton unctuous (pej) ADV sprechen, predigen unctuously (pej)

Sal|chow ['zalço] M -s, -s (Eiskunstlauf) salchow

sal|die|ren [zalˈdiːrən] *ptp* saldiert VT (Comm) to balance; (Aus) to confirm payment

Sal|do ['zaldo] M **-s, -s** or **Saldi** or **Salden** [-di, -dn] (Fin) balance; **per saldo** (lit, fig) on balance; **per saldo bezahlen** or **remittieren** to pay off the balance in full; **in saldo bleiben/sein** to stay/be in debt

Sal|do|über|trag M , **Sal|do|vor|trag** M (Fin) balance brought forward or carried forward

Sä|le pl von **Saal**

Sa|li|ne [za'li:nə] F **-, -n** saltworks sing or pl

sa|lisch ['za:lɪʃ] ADJ (Hist) Salian, Salic

Sa|li|zyl|säu|re [zali'tsy:l-] F salicylic acid

Salm [zalm] M **-(e)s, -e** a (= Lachs) salmon b (inf: = Gerede) rigmarole (inf)

Sal|mi|ak [zal'miak, 'zalmiak] M OR NT **-s**, no pl sal ammoniac, ammonium chloride

Sal|mi|ak-: Sal|mi|ak|geist M , no pl (liquid) ammonia; **Sal|mi|ak|pas|til|le** F bitter-tasting lozenge, liquorice imp® (Brit)

Sal|mo|nel|len [zalmo'nɛlən] PL salmonellae pl

Sal|mo|nel|len|ver|gif|tung F salmonella (poisoning)

Sal|mo|nel|lo|se [zalmonɛ'lo:zə] F **-, -n** salmonellosis

Sa|lo|mo(n) ['za:lomo, 'za:lomən] M **-s** or (geh) **Salomonis** ['za:'lo:monis] Solomon

sa|lo|mo|nisch [zalo'mo:nɪʃ] ADJ of Solomon; **Urteil** worthy of a Solomon; **ein wahrhaft ~es Urteil!** a real judgement of Solomon!

Sa|lon [sa'lō:, za'lɔŋ, (Aus) za'lo:n] M **-s, -s** a (= Gesellschaftszimmer) drawing room; (Naut) saloon b (= Friseursalon, Modesalon, Kosmetiksalon etc) salon c (Hist: = literarischer etc Zirkel) salon d (= Messe, Ausstellung) show; (= Messestand) stand, exhibition stand e (= Kunstsalon) exhibition room

Sa|lon- [sa'lō:-, za'lɔŋ-]: **Sa|lon|anar|chist(in)** M(F) (pej) drawing-room revolutionary; **sa|lon|fä|hig** ADJ (iro) socially acceptable; **Leute, Aussehen** presentable; **ein nicht ~er Witz** an objectionable joke; (= unanständig auch) a rude or naughty joke; **nicht ~e Ausdrucksweise** uncouth language, not the sort of language to be used in polite society; **Sa|lon|fä|hig|keit** F social acceptability; **Sa|lon|lö|we** M , **Sa|lon|lö|win** F socialite, society man/woman; **Sa|lon|mu|sik** F palm court music; **Sa|lon|wa|gen** M (Rail) Pullman (carriage), special coach

sa|lopp [za'lɔp] ADJ a (= nachlässig) sloppy, slovenly; Manieren slovenly; Ausdruck, Sprache slangy b (= ungezwungen) casual ADV sich kleiden, sich ausdrücken casually; **~ gesagt, ...** to put it crudely ...

Sal|pe|ter [zal'pe:tɐ] M **-s**, no pl saltpetre (Brit), saltpeter (US), nitre (Brit), niter (US)

sal|pe|te|rig [zal'pe:tərɪç] ADJ (Chem) Säure nitrous

Sal|pe|ter|säu|re F nitric acid

sal|pet|rig [zal'pe:trɪç] ADJ (Chem) Säure nitrous

Sal|sa [zalza] M **-**, no pl (Mus) salsa

Sal|sa-Mu|sik F , **Sal|sa|mu|sik** F salsa (music)

Sal|to ['zalto] M **-s, -s** or **Salti** [-ti] somersault; (Turmspringen auch) turn; **~ vorwärts/rückwärts** forward/backward somersault; **ein anderthalb-facher ~** a one-and-a-half somersault; **dreifacher ~** triple somersault; **~ mortale** (im Zirkus) death-defying leap; **einen ~ mortale machen** (im Zirkus) to perform a death-defying leap; (Aviat) to loop the loop; **ein logischer/gedanklicher ~ mortale** a logical/an intellectual leap

Sa|lut [za'lu:t] M **-(e)s, -e** (Mil) salute; **~ schie-Ben** or **feuern** to fire a salute; **21 Schuss ~** 21--gun salute

sa|lu|tie|ren [zalu'ti:rən] ptp **salutiert** VTI (Mil) to salute

Sa|lut|schuss ▲ M **man gab** or **feuerte fünf Sa-lutschüsse ab** a five-gun salute was fired

Sal|ve ['zalvə] F **-, -n** salvo, volley; (= Ehrensalve) salute; (fig) (= Lachsalve) burst of laughter; (von Applaus) volley, burst; (von Vorwürfen) volley; **ei-ne ~ auf jdn abschießen** (lit, fig) to fire a salvo or volley at sb

sal|vie|ren [zal'vi:rən] ptp **salviert** VT (geh) to exculpate

Salz [zalts] NT **-es, -e** salt; **jodiertes ~** iodized salt; **das ~ der Erde** (liter) the salt of the earth; **das ist das ~ in der Suppe** (fig) that's what gives it that extra something; **wie eine Suppe ohne ~** (fig) like ham or bacon without eggs (hum); **er gönnt einem nicht das ~ in der Sup-pe** he even begrudges you the air you breathe; **in ~ legen** to salt down or away → **Wunde**

Salz-: salz|arm ADJ (Cook) low-salt, with a low salt content ADV **~ essen** to eat low-salt food; **~ leben** to live on a low-salt diet; **~ ko-chen** to use very little salt in one's cooking; **Salz|berg|werk** NT salt mine; **Salz|bre|zel** F pretzel

sal|zen ['zaltsn] ptp **gesalzen** [gə'zaltsn] VT to salt → auch **gesalzen**

Salz-: Salz|fass ▲ NT , **Salz|fäss|chen** ▲ NT saltcellar; **Salz|fleisch** NT (Cook) salt meat; **salz|frei** ADJ salt-free; Diät auch no-salt attr ADV **~ essen** not to eat salt; **~ kochen** to cook without salt; **Salz|ge|bäck** NT savoury (Brit) or savory (US) biscuits pl; **Salz|gur|ke** F pick-led gherkin, pickle (US); **salz|hal|tig** ADJ Boden, Luft, Wasser salty, saline; **Salz|he|ring** M salted herring

sal|zig ['zaltsɪç] ADJ Speise, Wasser salty

Sal|zig|keit F **-**, no pl saltiness

Salz-: Salz|kar|tof|feln PL boiled potatoes pl; **Salz|korn** NT pl **-körner** grain of salt; **Salz|la-ke** F brine; **salz|los** ADJ salt-free ADV **~ es-sen** not to eat salt; **~ kochen** to cook without salt; **Salz|lö|sung** F saline solution; **Salz|man|del** F salted almond; **Salz|säu|le** F **zur ~ erstarren** (Bibl) to turn into a pillar of salt; (fig) to stand as though rooted to the spot; **Salz|säu|re** F hydrochloric acid; **Salz|see** M salt lake; **Salz|sie|der** [-zi:dɐ] M **-s, -**; **Salz|sie|de|rin** [-ərɪn] F **-, -nen** (Hist) salt-maker; **Salz|sie|de|rei** [-zi:də'rai] F **-, -en** (Hist) salt-works sing or pl; **Salz|sol|le** F brine; **Salz|stan|ge** F pretzel stick; **Salz|stock** M salt mine; **Salz|streu|er** [-ʃtrɔyɐ] M **-s, -** salt shak-er, saltcellar; **Salz|teig** M salt dough; **Salz|was|ser** NT , no pl salt water; **Salz|wüs|te** F salt desert, salt flat

Sä|mann ['zɛ:man] M pl **-männer** (old liter) sower

SA-Mann [ɛs'a:-] M pl **SA-Leute** storm trooper, SA-man

Sa|ma|ri|ter¹ [zama'ri:tɐ] M **-s, -** (Bibl) Samari-tan; **der Barmherzige ~** the good Samaritan

Sa|ma|ri|ter² [zama'ri:tɐ] M **-s, -**, **Sa|ma|ri|te-rin** [-ərɪn] F **-, -nen** (fig) a (= barmherziger Mensch) Samaritan b (= Sanitäter) first-aid vol-unteer

Sa|ma|ri|ter|dienst M a act of mercy; **jdm einen ~ erweisen** to be a good Samaritan to sb b (= Sanitätsdienst) first-aid service

Sa|ma|ri|um [za'ma:riʊm] NT **-s**, no pl (abbr **Sm**) samarium

Sam|ba ['zamba] M **-s, -s** or f **-, -s** samba

Sam|be|si [zam'be:zi] M **-(s)** Zambezi

Sam|bia ['zambia] NT **-s** Zambia

Sam|bier ['zambiɐ] M **-s, -**, **Sam|bie|rin** [-iərɪn] F **-, -nen** Zambian

sam|bisch ['zambɪʃ] ADJ Zambian

Sa|me ['za:mə] M **-ns, -n** (liter) = **Samen**

Sa|men ['za:mən] M **-s, -** a (Bot, fig) seed; **~ tra-gend** seed-bearing b (= Menschensamen, Tiersa-men) sperm c (liter, Bibl: = Nachkommen) seed (liter, Bibl)

Samen-: Sa|men|an|la|ge F (Bot) ovule; **Sa|men|bank** F pl **-banken** sperm bank; **Sa|men|bla|se** F seminal vesicle; **Sa|men|er-guss** ▲ M ejaculation, emission of semen, seminal discharge or emission; **Sa|men|fa|den** M spermatozoon; **Sa|men|flüs|sig|keit** F se-men, seminal fluid; **Sa|men|händ|ler(in)** M(F) seed merchant; **Sa|men|hand|lung** F seed shop; **Sa|men|kap|sel** F seed capsule; **Sa|men|korn** NT pl **-körner** seed; **Sa|men|lei|ter** M vas deferens; **Sa|men|spen|der** M sperm donor; **Sa|men|strang** M spermatic cord; **sa|men|tra|gend** △ ADJ → **Samen** a; **Sa|men|zel|le** F sperm cell; **Sa|men|zwie-bel** F seed onion

Sä|me|rei|en [zɛ:mə'raiən] PL seeds pl

sä|mig ['zɛ:mɪç] ADJ Soße thick

Sä|misch|le|der ['zɛ:mɪʃ-] NT chamois (leather)

Säm|ling ['zɛ:mlɪŋ] M **-s, -e** seedling

Sam|mel-: Sam|mel|al|bum NT (collector's) album; **Sam|mel|an|schluss** ▲ M (Telec) pri-vate (branch) exchange; (von Privathäusern) par-ty line; **Sam|mel|band** [-bant] M pl **-bände** anthology; **Sam|mel|be|cken** NT collecting tank; (Geol) catchment area; (fig) melting pot (von for); **Sam|mel|be|griff** M (Gram) collec-tive name or term; **Sam|mel|be|stel|lung** F joint or collective order; **Sam|mel|be|zeich-nung** F collective name or term; **Sam|mel-büch|se** F collecting tin or box; **Sam|mel-de|pot** NT (Fin) collective securities deposit; **Sam|mel|fahr|schein** M , **Sam|mel|kar|te** F (für mehrere Fahrten) multi-journey ticket; (für mehrere Personen) group ticket; **Sam|mel|kon-to** NT combined account; **Sam|mel|map|pe** F folder

sam|meln ['zamln] VT to collect; Holz, Ähren, Fakten, Material, Erfahrungen auch to gather; Blu-men, Pilze etc to pick, to gather; Truppen, Anhän-ger to gather, to assemble; **neue Kräfte ~** to build up one's energy again; **seine Gedanken ~** to collect one's thoughts; **Punkte ~** (Sport, fig) to score points VR a (= zusammenkommen) to gather, to collect; (Menschenmenge) to gather; (= sich anhäufen: Wasser, Geld etc) to collect, to ac-cumulate; (Lichtstrahlen) to converge, to meet b (= sich konzentrieren) to collect or compose oneself or one's thoughts → auch **gesammelt** VI to collect (für for)

Sam|mel-: Sam|mel|na|me M collective name or term; **Sam|mel|num|mer** F (Telec) private exchange number, switchboard number; **Sam|mel|pass** ▲ M group passport; **Sam|mel-platz** M a (= Treffpunkt) assembly point b (= Lagerplatz) collecting point; (= Deponie) dump; **Sam|mel|punkt** M a (= Treffpunkt) assembly point b (Opt) focus c (= Lagerplatz) collecting point; **Sam|mel|sen|dung** F joint consign-ment; **Güter als ~ schicken** to send goods part-load; **Sam|mel|ste|cker** M (Elec) plugboard; **Sam|mel|stel|le** F = **Sammelplatz**

Sam|mel|su|ri|um [zaml'zu:riʊm] NT **-s, Sam-melsurien** [-riən] conglomeration

Sam|mel-: Sam|mel|tas|se F ornamental cup, saucer and plate; **Sam|mel|ta|xi** NT share-a--ride taxi; **Sam|mel|trans|port** M (von Gütern) general shipment; (von Personen) group trans-port; **Sam|mel|vi|sum** NT collective visa; **Sam|mel|wut** F collecting mania

Sam|met ['zamət] M **-s, -** (obs, Sw) velvet

Samm|ler ['zamlɐ] M **-s, -**, **Samm|le|rin** [-ərɪn] F **-, -nen** collector; (von Beeren) picker; (von Holz) gatherer → **Jäger** a

Samm|ler|fleiß M collector's enthusiasm; **die-se Kollektion ist mit großem ~ zusammenge-tra-gen** it has taken a lot of hard work to put this collection together

Samm|lung ['zamlʊŋ] F **-, -en** a collection b (fig: = Konzentration) composure; **ihm fehlt die innere ~** he lacks composure; **zur ~ (meiner Gedanken)** to collect myself or my thoughts

Samm|lungs|be|we|gung F coalition movement

Sa|mos|\(wein) ['za:mɔs-] M -, - Samian wine, wine from Samos

Sa|mo|war ['zamova:ɐ, zamo'va:ɐ] M -s, -e samovar

Samp|ler ['zamplɐ] M -s, - (= Gerät, CD) sampler

Sams|tag ['zamsta:k] M Saturday → auch **Dienstag**

sams|tä|gig ['zamstə:gɪç] ADJ Saturday

sams|tags ['zamsta:ks] ADV on Saturdays

samt [zamt] **PREP** +dat along or together with; **sie kam ~ Katze** (hum) she came complete with cat **ADV** **~ und sonders** the whole lot (of them/us/you), the whole bunch (inf); **die Teilnehmer wurden ~ und sonders verhaftet** all the participants were arrested, the whole lot of them

Samt [zamt] M -(e)s, -e velvet; **in ~ und Seide** (liter) in silks and satins; **zart wie ~ und Seide** (liter) as soft as silk

Samt- in cpds velvet; **samt|ar|tig** ADJ velvety, like velvet; **Samt|band** [-bant] NT pl **-bänder** velvet ribbon; **Samt|blu|me** F (Bot) marigold

sam|ten ['zamtn] ADJ (liter) velvet

Samt|hand|schuh M velvet glove; **jdn mit ~en anfassen** (inf) to handle sb with kid gloves (inf)

sam|tig ['zamtɪç] ADJ velvety

sämt|lich ['zɛmtlɪç] **ADJ** (= alle) all; (= vollständig) complete; **~e Unterlagen waren verschwunden** all the or every one of the documents had disappeared, the documents had all disappeared; **Schillers ~e Werke** the complete works of Schiller; **~e Anwesenden** all those present; **sie mussten ~en Besitz zurücklassen** they had to leave all their possessions behind **ADV** all; **die Unterlagen waren ~ verschwunden** all the or every one of the documents had disappeared, the documents had all disappeared

Samt-: Samt|pföt|chen NT (inf) velvet paw; **~ machen** (Katze) to draw in its claws; (fig) to go all soft; **wie auf ~ gehen** to tread softly; **Samt|schlei|fe** F velvet bow; **samt|weich** ADJ (as) soft as velvet, velvet-soft, velvety

Sa|na|to|ri|um [zana'to:riʊm] NT -s, **Sanatorien** [-riən] sanatorium (Brit), sanitarium (US)

Sand [zant] M -(e)s, -e [-də] sand; (= Scheuersand) scouring powder; **mit ~ bestreuen** to sand; **das/die gibts wie ~ am Meer** (inf) there are heaps of them (inf); **auf ~ laufen** or **geraten** to run aground; **auf ~ bauen** (fig) to build upon sandy ground; **jdm ~ in die Augen streuen** (fig) to throw dust (Brit) or dirt (US) in sb's eyes; **~ ins Getriebe streuen** (Brit) to throw a spanner in the works (Brit), to throw a (monkey) wrench into the works (US); **im ~e verlaufen** (inf) to peter out, to come to naught or nothing; **den Kopf in den ~ stecken** to stick or bury or hide one's head in the sand; **etw in den ~ setzen** (inf, Projekt, Prüfung) to blow sth (inf); Geld to squander sth

San|da|le [zan'da:lə] F -, -n sandal

San|da|let|te [zanda'lɛtə] F -, -n high-heeled sandal

Sand-: Sand|bank F pl **-bänke** sandbank, sandbar; **Sand|bo|den** M sandy soil; **Sand|burg** F sandcastle; **Sand|dorn** M pl **-dorne** (Bot) sea buckthorn

San|del|holz ['zandl-] NT sandalwood

san|deln ['zandln] VI (S Ger, Aus, Sw) to play in the sand

San|del|öl ['zandl-] NT sandalwood oil

Sand-: sand|far|ben [-farbn], **sand|far|big** ADJ sand-coloured (Brit), sand-colored (US); **Sand|förm|chen** NT sand mould (Brit), sand mold (US); **Sand|gru|be** F sandpit (esp Brit), sandbox (US); (Golf) bunker, sand trap (esp US); **Sand|hau|fen** M pile or heap of sand; (= Sandkasten) sandpit (esp Brit), sandbox (US);

Sand|ho|se F sand column or spout, dust devil

san|dig ['zandɪç] ADJ sandy

San|di|nist [zandi'nɪst] M -en, -en, **San|di|nis|tin** [-'nɪstɪn] F -, -nen Sandinista

Sand-: Sand|kas|ten M sandpit (esp Brit), sandbox (US); (Mil) sand table; **Sand|kas|ten|spie|le** PL (Mil) sand-table exercises pl; (fig) tactical manoeuvrings (Brit) or maneuverings (US) pl; **Sand|korn** NT pl **-körner** grain of sand; **Sand|ku|chen** M (Cook) sand cake (a Madeira-type cake); (von Kindern) mud pie; **Sand|mann** M , no pl, **Sand|männ|chen** NT , no pl (in Geschichten) sandman; **Sand|meer** NT (geh) sea of sand; **Sand|pa|pier** NT sandpaper; **Sand|platz** M (Tennis) clay court; **Sand|sack** M sandbag; (Boxen) punchbag (Brit), punching bag (US)

Sand|stein M sandstone; **ein Haus aus rotem ~** a red sandstone house, a brownstone (house) (US)

Sand|stein- in cpds sandstone; **Sand|stein|fel|sen** M sandstone cliff

Sand-: Sand|strahl M jet of sand; **etw mit ~ abblasen** or **reinigen** to sandblast sth; **sand|strah|len** ptp **gesandstrahlt** or (or spec) **sandgestrahlt** VTI to sandblast; **Sand|strahl|ge|blä|se** NT sandblasting equipment no indef art, no pl; **Sand|strand** M sandy beach; **Sand|sturm** M sandstorm

sand|te pret von **senden** [1]

Sand-: Sand|uhr F hourglass; (= Eieruhr) egg timer; **Sand|weg** M dirt road, track

Sand|wich ['zɛntvɪtʃ] NT OR M -(s), -(e)s sandwich

Sand|wich- ['zɛntvɪtʃ-]: **Sand|wich|bau|wei|se** F sandwich construction; **Sand|wich|mann** M pl **-männer** (hum) sandwich man; **Sand|wich|we|cken** M (Aus) long thin white loaf, French loaf

Sand|wüs|te F sandy waste; (Geog) (sandy) desert

sanft [zanft] **ADJ** gentle; Berührung, Stimme, Farbe, Licht, Wind, Regen auch, Haut soft; Schlaf, Tod peaceful; **mit ~er Gewalt** gently but firmly; **mit ~er Hand** with a gentle hand; **von ~er Hand** by a woman's fair hand; **sie schaute das Kind mit ~en Augen an** she looked tenderly at the child; **~ wie ein Lamm** (as) gentle as a lamb; **~er Tourismus** green tourism → **ruhen** **ADV** softly; abfallen, ansteigen, sich winden auch gently; lächeln softly; tadeln, ermahnen mildly; hinweisen gently; **sie lächelte ~** she smiled softly; **sich ~ anfühlen** to feel soft; **~ mit jdm umgehen** to be gentle with or to sb; **~ schlafen** to be sleeping peacefully; **er ist ~ entschlafen** he passed away peacefully, he fell gently asleep (auch iro)

Sänf|te ['zɛnftə] F -, -n litter; (esp im 17., 18. Jh. Europas) sedan chair; (in Indien) palanquin; (auf Elefant) howdah

Sänf|ten|trä|ger(in) M(F) → **Sänfte** litter bearer; sedan bearer; palanquin bearer

Sanft|heit F -, no pl gentleness; (von Stimme, Farbe, Licht auch) softness

sänf|ti|gen ['zɛnftɪgn] VT (obs) = **besänftigen**

Sanft|mut F -, no pl (liter) gentleness

sanft|mü|tig ['zanftmy:tɪç] ADJ (liter) gentle; (Bibl) meek

sang pret von **singen**

Sang [zaŋ] M -(e)s, ⸚e ['zɛŋə] (old liter) (= Gesang) song; (= das Singen) singing; **mit ~ und Klang** (lit) with drums drumming and pipes piping; (fig iro) durchfallen disastrously, catastrophically; entlassen werden with a lot of hullaballoo; **ohne ~ und Klang** (inf) without any ado, quietly; **ohne ~ und Klang verschwinden** to just simply disappear

Sän|ger [zɛŋɐ] M -s, - **a** singer; (= esp Jazzsänger, Popsänger) vocalist **b** (old liter. = Dichter)

bard (old), poet; **da(rüber) schweigt des ~ Höflichkeit** modesty forbids me to say **c** (= Singvogel) songbird, songster

Sän|ger-: Sän|ger|bund M pl **-bünde** choral union; **Sän|ger|fest** NT choral festival

Sän|ge|rin ['zɛŋərɪn] F singer; (= esp Jazzsängerin, Popsängerin) vocalist

Sang|es-: Sang|es|bru|der M (inf) chorister; **Sang|es|freu|de** F , **Sang|es|lust** F (dated) love of song or singing; **sang|es|freu|dig**, **sang|es|lus|tig** ADJ (dated) fond of singing, song-loving; **Sang|es|schwes|ter** F (inf) chorister

Sang|ria [zaŋ'gri:a, 'zaŋgria] F -, -s sangria

San|gu|i|ni|ker [zaŋ'gui:nikɐ] M -s, -, **San|gu|i|ni|ke|rin** [-ərɪn] F -, -nen (Psych) sanguine person

san|gu|i|nisch [zaŋ'gui:nɪʃ] ADJ (Psych) sanguine

sang- und klang|los ADV (inf) without any ado, quietly; **sie ist ~ verschwunden** she just simply disappeared

Sa|ni ['zani] M -s, -s (Mil inf) medical orderly

sa|nie|ren [za'ni:rən] ptp **saniert** **VT** **a** (= gesunde Lebensverhältnisse schaffen) Gebäude to renovate; Stadtteil, Gelände to redevelop; Fluss to clean up **b** (Econ) Unternehmen, Wirtschaft to put (back) on its feet, to rehabilitate; Haushalt to turn round **VR** **a** (inf: Mensch) to line one's own pocket (inf); **bei dem Geschäft hat er sich saniert** he made a killing on the deal (inf) **b** (Unternehmen, Wirtschaft, Industrie) to put itself (back) in good shape

Sa|nie|rung F -, -en **a** (von Gebäude) renovation; (von Stadtteil) redevelopment; (von Fluss) cleaning-up **b** (Econ) rehabilitation; (von Rentensystem etc) modernization; **Maßnahmen zur ~ des Dollars** measures to put the dollar back on an even keel or on its feet again **c** (inf: = Bereicherung) self-enrichment; **er ist nur auf die eigene ~ bedacht** he is only interested in lining his own pocket (inf)

Sa|nie|rungs-: Sa|nie|rungs|ge|biet NT redevelopment area; **Sa|nie|rungs|ge|winn** M profit from property speculation in a redevelopment area; **Sa|nie|rungs|maß|nah|me** F (für Gebiete etc) redevelopment measure; (Econ) rehabilitation measure; **Sa|nie|rungs|plan** M redevelopment plan or scheme; (Econ) rehabilitation plan

sa|ni|tär [zani'tɛ:r] **ADJ** no pred sanitary; **~e Anlagen** sanitation (facilities), sanitary facilities **ADV** **ein Haus ~ ausstatten** to install sanitation in a house

Sa|ni|tär|an|la|gen PL sanitary or sanitation facilities pl

Sa|ni|tät [zani'tɛ:t] F -, -en (Aus, Sw) **a** medical service; (= Krankenpflege) nursing **b** (inf: = Krankenwagen) ambulance

Sa|ni|tä|ter [zani'tɛ:tɐ] M -s, -, **Sa|ni|tä|te|rin** [-ərɪn] F -, -nen first-aid attendant; (Mil) (medical) orderly; (in Krankenwagen) ambulanceman/-woman

Sa|ni|täts-: Sa|ni|täts|au|to NT ambulance; **Sa|ni|täts|dienst** M (Mil) medical duty; (= Heeresabteilung) medical corps; **Sa|ni|täts|flug|zeug** NT ambulance plane, air ambulance; **Sa|ni|täts|ge|frei|te(r)** MF decl as adj (medical) orderly; **Sa|ni|täts|kas|ten** M first-aid box (esp Brit) or kit; **Sa|ni|täts|kom|pa|nie** F medical company; **Sa|ni|täts|of|fi|zier(in)** M(F) (Mil) Medical Officer, MO; **Sa|ni|täts|trup|pe** F medical corps; **Sa|ni|täts|wa|gen** M ambulance; **Sa|ni|täts|we|sen** NT (Mil) medical service; **Sa|ni|täts|zelt** NT first-aid tent

sank pret von **sinken**

San|ka ['zaŋka] M -s, -s (Mil inf) ambulance

Sankt [zaŋkt] ADJ inv saint; **~ Nikolaus** Santa (Claus), Father Christmas; (Rel) St or Saint Nicholas

Sankt-Flo|ri|ans-Prin|zip [zaŋkt'floːriaːns-] NT (*inf*) not-in-my-back-yard attitude

Sankt Gal|len [zaŋkt 'galən] NT - -s (= *Kanton, Stadt*) St Gall

Sank|ti|on [zaŋk'tsioːn] F -, -en sanction

sank|ti|o|nie|ren [zaŋktsio'niːrən] *ptp* **sanktio|niert** VT to sanction

Sank|ti|o|nie|rung F -, -en sanctioning

Sankt-Lo|renz-Strom [zaŋkt'loːrɛnts-] M St Lawrence river

Sankt-Nim|mer|leins-Tag [zaŋkt'nɪmɐlains-] M never-never day; **ja ja, am ~** yes yes, and pigs might fly (*hum*); **etw auf den ~ verschieben** to put sth off indefinitely

sann *pret von* **sinnen**

Sann|ya|si [zan'jaːzi] MF -, -n sannyasi(n)

San|se|vie|ria [zanze'vieːria] F -, **Sansevierien**, **San|se|vie|rie** [zanze'vieːriə] F -, -n (*Bot*) sansevieria

San|si|bar ['zanzibaːɐ, zanzi'baːɐ] NT -s Zanzibar

Sans|krit ['zanskrɪt] NT -s, *no pl* Sanskrit

San|ya|si [zan'jaːzi] MF -, -n sannyasi(n)

Sap|phir ['zafɪr, 'zaˌfiːɐ, zaˈfiːɐ] M -s, -e sapphire

sap|per|lot [zapɐ'loːt], **sap|per|ment** [zapɐ'mɛnt] INTERJ (*old*) stap me (*old*), upon my soul (*old*)

sap|phisch ['zapfɪʃ, 'zafɪʃ] ADJ Sapphic

Sa|ra|ban|de [zara'bandə] F -, -n (*Mus*) saraband

Sa|ra|ze|ne [zara'tseːnə] M -n, -n, **Sa|ra|ze|nin** [-'tseːnɪn] F -, -nen Saracen

sa|ra|ze|nisch [zara'tseːnɪʃ] ADJ Saracen

Sar|de ['zardə] M -n, -n, **Sar|din** ['zardɪn] F -, -nen Sardinian

Sar|del|le [zar'dɛlə] F -, -n anchovy

Sar|del|len-: Sar|del|len|but|ter F anchovy butter; **Sar|del|len|pas|te** F anchovy paste

Sar|din F -, -nen Sardinian

Sar|di|ne [zar'diːnə] F -, -n sardine

Sar|di|nen|büch|se F sardine tin; **wie in einer ~** (*fig inf*) like sardines (*inf*)

Sar|di|ni|en [zar'diːniən] NT -s Sardinia

Sar|di|ni|er [zar'diːniɐ] M -s, -, **Sar|di|ni|e|rin** [-iərɪn] F -, -nen Sardinian

sar|di|nisch [zar'diːnɪʃ], **sar|disch** ['zardɪʃ] ADJ Sardinian

sar|do|nisch [zar'doːnɪʃ] (*liter*) ADJ sardonic ADV sardonically

Sarg [zark] M -(e)s, ⸚e ['zɛːrgə] coffin, casket (*US*); **ein Nagel zu jds ~ sein** (*hum inf*) to be a nail in sb's coffin; **du kannst dir schon deinen ~ machen lassen** (*hum inf*) you'd better start arranging your funeral

Sarg-: Sarg|de|ckel M coffin lid, casket lid (*US*); **Sarg|na|gel** M coffin nail; (*fig inf auch:* = *Zigarette*) cancer stick (*hum inf*); **ein letzter/der letzte ~ für etw sein** to be the final nail in the coffin of sth; **Sarg|tisch|ler(in)** M(F) coffin-maker, casket-maker (*US*); **Sarg|trä|ger(in)** M(F) pallbearer

Sa|ri ['zaːri] M -(s), -s sari

Sa|rin [za'riːn] NT -s, *no pl* (*Chem*) sarin

Sar|kas|mus [zar'kasmʊs] M -, **Sarkasmen** [-mən] *no pl* sarcasm ⓑ (= *Bemerkung*) sarcastic comment or remark

sar|kas|tisch [zar'kastɪʃ] ADJ sarcastic ADV sarcastically

Sar|kom [zar'koːm] NT -s, -e (*Med*) sarcoma

Sar|ko|phag [zarko'faːk] M -(e)s, -e [-gə] sarcophagus

Sa|rong ['zaːrɔŋ] M -(s), -s sarong

saß *pret von* **sitzen**

Sa|tan ['zaːtan] M -s, -e (*Bibl, fig*) Satan; **dieses Weib ist ein ~** this woman is a (she-)devil

sa|ta|nisch [za'taːnɪʃ] ADJ satanic ADV satanically

Sa|ta|nis|mus [zata'nɪsmʊs] M -, *no pl* Satanism

Sa|tans-: Sa|tans|bra|ten M (*hum inf*) young devil; **Sa|tans|kult** M satan cult; **Sa|tans|pilz** M Satan's mushroom, boletus satanas (*spec*)

Sa|tel|lit [zatɛ'liːt] M -en, -en (*alle Bedeutungen*) satellite

Sa|tel|li|ten- *in cpds* satellite; **Sa|tel|li|ten|ab|wehr|waf|fe** F antisatellite weapon; **Sa|tel|li|ten|an|ten|ne** F (*TV*) satellite dish; **Sa|tel|li|ten|bahn** F satellite orbit; **Sa|tel|li|ten|bild** NT (*TV*) satellite picture; **Sa|tel|li|ten|fern|se|hen** NT satellite television; **Sa|tel|li|ten|fo|to** NT (*TV*) satellite picture; **Sa|tel|li|ten|schüs|sel** F (*TV inf*) satellite dish; **Sa|tel|li|ten|sen|der** M satellite (TV) station; **Sa|tel|li|ten|staat** M satellite state; **Sa|tel|li|ten|stadt** F satellite town; **Sa|tel|li|ten|sta|ti|on** F space station; **Sa|tel|li|ten|über|tra|gung** F (*Rad, TV*) satellite transmission

Sa|tin [za'tɛ̃ː] M -s, -s satin; (= *Baumwollsatin*) sateen

sa|ti|nie|ren [zati'niːrən] *ptp* **satiniert** VT *Papier* to glaze; (*Typ*) to satin-coat

Sa|tin|pa|pier [za'tɛ̃ː-] NT glazed paper

Sa|ti|re [za'tiːrə] F -, -n satire (*auf +acc* on)

Sa|ti|ri|ker [za'tiːrikɐ] M -s, -, **Sa|ti|ri|ke|rin** [-ərɪn] F -, -nen satirist

sa|ti|risch [za'tiːrɪʃ] ADJ satirical ADV satirically

Sa|tis|fak|ti|on [zatɪsfak'tsioːn] F -, -en (*old*) satisfaction; **ich verlange** *or* **fordere ~!** I demand satisfaction

sa|tis|fak|ti|ons|fä|hig ADJ (*old*) capable of giving satisfaction

Sat|rap [za'traːp] M -en, -en (*Hist*) satrap

satt [zat] ⊘ 41 ADJ ⓐ (= *gesättigt*) *Mensch* replete (*hum, form*), full (up) (*inf*); *Magen, Gefühl* full; **~ sein** to have had enough (to eat), to be full (up) (*inf*); **~ werden** to have enough to eat; **von so was kann man doch nicht ~ werden** it's not enough to satisfy you *or* to fill you up; **das macht ~** it's filling; **sich (an etw** *dat*) **~ essen** to eat one's fill (of sth); (= *überdrüssig werden auch*) to have had one's fill (of sth); **wie soll sie ihre Kinder ~ kriegen?** (*inf*) how is she supposed to feed her children?; **er ist kaum ~ zu kriegen** (*inf: lit, fig*) he's insatiable; **er konnte sich an ihr nicht ~ sehen** he could not see enough of her; **sie konnte sich an der Musik nicht ~ hören** she could not get enough of the music; **~ sank er in den Sessel zurück** having eaten his fill he sank back into his chair; **wie ein ~er Säugling** (*inf*) with a look of contentment, like a contented cow (*inf*)

ⓑ **jdn/etw ~ haben** *or* **sein** to be fed up with sb/sth (*inf*); **jdn/etw ~ bekommen** *or* **kriegen** (*inf*) to get fed up with sb/sth (*inf*)

ⓒ (= *blasiert, übersättigt*) well-fed; (= *selbstgefällig*) smug

ⓓ (= *kräftig, voll*) *Farben, Klang* rich, full; (*inf*) *Applaus* resounding; (*inf*) *Mehrheit* comfortable; **~e 10 Prozent/1000 Euro** (*inf*) a cool 10 per cent (*Brit*) *or* percent (*US*)/1000 euros (*inf*)

ⓔ (*inf:* = *im Überfluss*) **...** ≈ ... galore, ... in abundance

ADV (*inf*) *verdienen, da sein* more than enough; **es gab Champagner ~** there was more than enough champagne; **sie haben nicht ~ zu essen** they don't have enough to eat

Sat|tel ['zatl] M -s, ⸚ ['zɛtl] ⓐ saddle; **ohne/mit ~ reiten** to ride bareback *or* without a saddle/with a saddle; **sich in den ~ schwingen** to swing (oneself) into the saddle; (*auf Fahrrad*) to jump onto one's bicycle; **in den ~ steigen** (= *reiten, radfahren*) to ride; **sich im ~ halten** (*lit, fig*) to stay in the saddle; **jdn aus dem ~ heben** (= *herunterhelfen*) to help sb (to) dismount; (*lit, fig:* = *zu Fall bringen*) to unseat sb; **jdn in den ~ heben** (*lit*) to lift sb into the saddle; (*fig*) to help sb to power; **er ist in allen Sätteln gerecht** *or* **sicher** (*fig*) he can turn his hand to anything; **fest im ~ sitzen** (*fig*) to be firmly in the saddle

ⓑ (= *Bergsattel*) saddle; (= *Geigensattel*) nut; (= *Nasensattel*) bridge

Sat|tel-: Sat|tel|dach NT saddle roof; **Sat|tel|de|cke** F saddlecloth; **sat|tel|fest** ADJ **~ sein** (*Reiter*) to have a good seat; **in etw** (*dat*) **~ sein** (*fig*) to have a firm grasp of sth; **Sat|tel|gurt** M girth; **Sat|tel|knopf** M pommel

sat|teln ['zatln] VT *Pferd* to saddle (up); **für etw gesattelt sein** (*fig*) to be ready for sth

Sat|tel-: Sat|tel|na|se F saddlenose; **Sat|tel|pferd** NT saddle horse; **Sat|tel|platz** M paddock; **Sat|tel|schlep|per** M articulated lorry (*Brit*), artic (*Brit inf*), semitrailer (*US*), semi (*US inf*); **Sat|tel|ta|sche** F saddlebag; (= *Gepäcktasche am Fahrrad, aus Stroh*) pannier; **Sat|tel|zeug** NT *pl* -zeuge saddlery; **Sat|tel|zug** M = Sattelschlepper

Satt|heit F -, *no pl* ⓐ (*Gefühl*) full feeling, feeling of being full ⓑ (*von Farben, Klang*) richness, fullness

sät|ti|gen ['zɛtign] VT ⓐ *Hunger, Neugier* to satisfy, to satiate; *jdn* to make replete; (= *ernähren*) to feed, to provide with food; **ich bin gesättigt** I am *or* feel replete ⓑ (*Comm, Chem*) to saturate → *auch* **gesättigt** VI to be filling VR **sich an etw** (*dat*) *or* **mit etw ~** to eat one's fill of sth

sät|ti|gend ADJ *Essen* filling

Sät|ti|gung F -, -en ⓐ (*geh:* = *Sattsein*) repletion; **die** = **der Hungrigen** the feeding of the hungry; **das Essen dient nicht nur der ~** eating does not only serve to satisfy hunger ⓑ (*Chem, Comm, von Farbe*) saturation

Sät|ti|gungs-: Sät|ti|gungs|bei|la|ge F filling vegetables, trimmings *pl* (*inf*); **Sät|ti|gungs|grad** M degree of saturation; **Sät|ti|gungs|punkt** M saturation point

Satt|ler ['zatlɐ] M -s, -, **Satt|le|rin** [-ərɪn] F -, -nen (= *Polsterer*) upholsterer

Satt|le|rei [zatlə'rai] F -, -en (= *Polsterei*) upholstery; (= *Werkstatt*) saddler's; upholsterer's

Satt|ler|meis|ter(in) M(F) master saddler; (= *Polsterer*) master upholsterer

satt|sam ['zatzaːm] ADV amply; *bekannt* sufficiently

sa|tu|rie|ren [zatu'riːrən] *ptp* **saturiert** VT (*liter*) to satisfy, to content VR (*geh*) to do well for oneself

sa|tu|riert [zatu'riːɐt] (*geh*) ADJ *Markt* saturated; *Klasse* prosperous ADV **~ leben** to prosper, to live prosperously

Sa|turn [za'tʊrn] M -s (*Myth, Astron*) Saturn; **die Ringe des ~s** the rings of Saturn

Sa|tur|na|li|en [zatʊr'naːliən] PL (*Hist*) Saturnalia *pl*

Sa|tyr ['zaːtyr] M -s *or* -n, -n *or* -e satyr

Satz [zats] M -es, ⸚e ['zɛtsə] ⓐ sentence; (= *Teilsatz*) clause; (*Jur:* = *Gesetzabschnitt*) clause; **ich kann nur ein paar Sätze Italienisch** I only know a few phrases of Italian; **mitten im ~** in mid-sentence; **abhängiger/selbstständiger ~** subordinate/principal clause; **eingeschobener ~** appositional phrase

ⓑ (= *Lehrsatz, auch Philos*) proposition; (*Math*) theorem; **der ~ des Pythagoras** Pythagoras' theorem

ⓒ (*Typ*) (= *das Setzen*) setting; (= *das Gesetzte*) type *no pl*; **etw in ~ geben** to send sth for setting; **in ~ gehen** to go for setting; **das Buch ist im ~** the book is being set

ⓓ (*Mus*) (= *Abschnitt*) movement; (= *Kompositionsweise*) composition

ⓔ (= *Bodensatz*) dregs *pl*; (= *Kaffeesatz*) grounds *pl*; (= *Teesatz*) leaves *pl*, dregs *pl*

ⓕ (= *Zusammengehöriges*) set; (*Comput:* = *Datensatz*) record; (*Hunt:* = *Wurf*) litter

ⓖ (*Sport*) set; (*Tischtennis, Badminton*) game

ⓗ (= *Tarifsatz*) charge; (= *Spesensatz*) allowance; (= *Zinssatz*) rate

ⓘ (= *Sprung*) leap, jump; **einen ~ machen** *or* **tun**

to leap, to jump; **mit einem ~** in one leap or bound

Satz-: Satz|aus|sa|ge F (Gram) predicate; **Satz|ball** M (Sport) set point; (Tischtennis) game point; **Satz|bau** M, no pl sentence construction; **Satz|be|fehl** M (Typ) typographical command; **Satz|er|gän|zung** F (Gram) object; **Satz|feh|ler** M (Typ) printer's error; **Satz|fet|zen** M sentence fragment; **Satz|ge|fü|ge** NT (Gram) complex sentence; **Satz|ge|gen|stand** M (Gram) subject; **Satz|glied** NT part of a/the sentence; **Satz|her|stel|lung** F (Typ) typesetting

-sät|zig [zɛtsɪç] ADJ suf (Mus) in ... movements; **eine dreisätzige Sonate** a sonata in three movements

Satz-: Satz|leh|re F (Gram) syntax; **Satz|me|lo|die** F (Phon) intonation; **Satz|mus|ter** NT (Ling) sentence pattern; **Satz|rei|he** F compound sentence; **Satz|spie|gel** M (Typ) type area, area of type; **Satz|teil** M part or constituent of a/the sentence

Sat|zung ['zatsʊŋ] F -, -en constitution, statutes pl; (von Verein) rules pl

sat|zungs|ge|mäß ADJ, ADV → **Satzung** according to the statutes/rules

Satz-: Satz|ver|bin|dung F clause construction; **Satz|ver|lust** M (Tennis) loss of a set; **satz|wei|se** ADJ a (Ling) sentence by sentence b (Tech) in sets ADV a (Ling) sentence by sentence; **sprechen Sie mir ~ nach** repeat after me; **eine Sprache lernt man besser ~** you are better to learn a language in phrases b (= in Sets) in sets; **Satz|zei|chen** NT punctuation mark; **Satz|zu|sam|men|hang** M context of the sentence

Sau [zau] F -, **Säue** ['zɔʏə] or (Hunt) -en a sow; (inf: = Schwein) pig; (Hunt) wild boar; **die ~ rauslassen** (fig inf) to let it all hang out (inf); **wie eine gestochene ~ bluten** (sl) to bleed like a (stuck) pig (inf); **wie eine gesengte ~** (inf) **wie die ~** (inf) like a maniac (inf) b (pej inf) (= Schmutzfink) dirty swine (inf); **du ~!** you dirty swine! (inf); **du alte ~!** (vulg) you dirty bastard (sl), you son of a bitch (sl); (Frau auch) you dirty bitch (sl); **miese ~ bastard** (sl); **dumme ~** stupid cow (inf) c (fig inf) **da war keine ~ zu sehen** there wasn't a bloody (Brit inf) or goddamn (inf) soul to be seen; **das interessiert keine ~** nobody gives a damn about that (inf); **jdn zur ~ machen** to bawl sb out (inf); **unter aller ~** bloody (Brit inf) or goddamn (inf) awful or lousy; **wie die ~** (= wie verrückt) like mad or crazy

Sau-: Sau|ban|de F (inf) gang of hoodlums (inf) or gang-bangers (US sl); **Sau|bär** M (sl: = gemeiner Typ) bastard (sl)

sau|ber ['zaubɐ] ADJ a (= rein, reinlich) clean; ~ **sein** (Hund etc) to be house-trained; (Kind) to be (potty-)trained b (= ordentlich) neat, tidy; (Aus, Sw, S Ger: = hübsch) Mädel pretty; (= exakt) accurate c (= anständig) honest, upstanding; ~ **bleiben** to keep one's hands clean; **bleib ~!** (inf) keep your nose clean (inf) d (inf: = großartig) fantastic, great; ~! **~!** that's the stuff! (inf); **du bist mir ja ein ~er Freund!** (iro) a fine friend YOU are! (iro); **eine ~e Gesellschaft!** (iro) a bunch of crooks; **das ist ja ~!** (iro) that's great (iro) ADV a (= rein) **etw ~ putzen** to clean sth; ~ **singen/spielen** to sing/play on key b (= sorgfältig) very thoroughly, well c (= genau) analysieren, darstellen carefully; **etw ~ lösen** to find a neat solution for sth d (Aus, S Ger: verstärkend) really and truly

Sau|ber|frau F (fig inf) decent and upstanding sort; (in Politik etc) squeaky-clean woman (inf)

sau|ber hal|ten ▲ VT irreg to keep clean

Sau|ber|keit F -, no pl a (= Hygiene, Ordentlichkeit) cleanliness; (= Reinheit) (von Wasser, Luft etc) cleanness; (von Tönen) accuracy b (= Anständig-

keit) honesty, upstandingness; (im Sport) fair play

Sau|ber|keits|fim|mel M (pej) mania for cleanliness, thing about cleanliness (inf)

säu|ber|lich ['zɔʏbɐlɪç] ADJ neat and tidy ADV neatly; auseinander halten, trennen clearly; **fein ~** neatly and tidily

sau|ber ma|chen ▲ VT to clean

Sau|ber|mann M pl **-männer** (fig inf) decent and upstanding sort; (in Politik etc) Mr Clean (inf), squeaky-clean man (inf); **die Saubermänner** the squeaky-clean brigade (inf)

säu|bern ['zɔʏbɐn] VT a (= reinigen) to clean; **er säuberte seinen Anzug von den Blutflecken** he cleaned the bloodstains off his jacket; **das Wasser (von Verschmutzung) ~** to cleanse the water b (fig euph) Partei, Buch to purge (von of); Saal to clear (von of); (Mil) Gegend to clear (von of); **eine Region ethnisch ~** to ethnically cleanse a region

Säu|be|rung F -, -en a (= Reinigung) cleaning; (von Wasser) cleansing b (fig: von Partei, Buch) purging; (von Gegend) clearing; (Pol: Aktion) purge; **ethnische ~** ethnic cleansing

Säu|be|rungs|ak|ti|on F cleaning-up operation; (Pol) purge

Sau-: sau|blöd, sau|blö|de (inf) ADJ bloody (Brit inf) or damn (inf) stupid ADV **sich ~ anstellen** to behave like a bloody (Brit sl) or damn idiot (inf); ~ **fragen** to ask a damn stupid question (inf); **Sau|boh|ne** F broad bean, horse bean

Sau|ce ['zo:sə] F -, -n sauce; (= Bratensauce) gravy

Sau|ci|ere [zo'sie:rə, zo:si'e:rə] F -, -n sauce boat

Sau|di ['zaudi, za'u:di] M -(s), -(s) or f -, -s Saudi

Sau|di-: Sau|di|ara|ber(in) ['zaudi'arabɐ, 'zaudila'ra:bə] M(F) Saudi; **Sau|di-Ara|bi|en** ['zaudi'ara:biən] NT Saudi Arabia; **sau|di-ara|bisch** ADJ Saudi attr, Saudi Arabian

sau|disch ADJ Saudi attr, Saudi Arabian

sau|dumm (inf) ADJ damn stupid (inf) ADV **sich ~ benehmen** to behave like a stupid idiot (inf); ~ **fragen** to ask a damn stupid question (inf)

sau|en ['zauən] VI a (= Ferkel bekommen) to litter b (inf: = Dreck machen) to make a mess c aux sein (S Ger, inf: = rennen) to run

sau|er ['zauɐ] ADJ a (= nicht süß) sour, sharp; Wein acid(ic); **saure Drops** acid drops → **aufstoßen**, **Apfel** b (= verdorben) off pred (Brit), bad; Milch sour, off pred (Brit); Geruch sour, sickly; ~ **werden** (Milch, Sahne) to go off (Brit) or sour, to turn (sour) c (= mit Säure zubereitet) Gurke, Hering pickled; Sahne soured d (= sumpfig) Wiese, Boden acidic e (Chem) acid(ic); **saurer Regen** acid rain f (inf: = schlecht gelaunt) (auf +acc with) mad (inf), cross; **eine ~e Miene machen** to look sour or annoyed g (= unerfreulich) **jdm das Leben ~ machen** to make sb's life a misery, to make life miserable for sb ADV a (= verdorben) **es roch so ~** there was a sickly smell b (Cook) ~ **einlegen** to pickle c (Chem) ~ **reagieren** to react acidically d (= mühselig) **das habe ich mir ~ erworben** I got that the hard way; ~ **erworbenes Geld** hard-earned money; **mein ~ erspartes Geld** money I had painstakingly saved e (inf: = übel gelaunt) ~ **reagieren** to get annoyed; ~ **antworten** to give a cross answer

Sau|er-: Sau|er| amp|fer M sorrel; **Sau|er|bra|ten** M braised beef (marinated in vinegar, sauerbraten (US)); **Sau|er|brun|nen** M a (= Heilquelle) acidic spring b (= Wasser) acidic mineral water

Sau|e|rei [zauə'rai] F -, -en (inf) a (= Unflätigkeit) **-en erzählen** to tell filthy stories; **eine ein-**

zige ~ a load of filth b (= Gemeinheit) **das ist eine ~!, so eine ~!** it's a bloody (Brit inf) or downright disgrace or scandal c (= Dreck, Unordnung) mess; **(eine) ~ machen** to make a mess

Sau|er-: Sau|er|kir|sche F sour cherry; **Sau|er|klee** M wood sorrel, oxalis; **Sau|er|kohl** M (dial), **Sau|er|kraut** NT sauerkraut, pickled cabbage

säu|er|lich ['zɔʏɐlɪç] ADJ (lit, fig) sour; Wein auch sharp; Obst auch sharp, tart ADV a (Cook) ~ **schmecken** to taste a little sour b (= übellaunig) ~ **reagieren** to get peeved (inf); ~ **antworten** to answer in a peeved tone

Säu|er|lich|keit F -, no pl (lit, fig) sourness

Säu|er|ling ['zɔʏɐlɪŋ] M -s, -e a = **Sauerbrunnen** b (Bot) = **Sauerampfer**

Sau|er|milch F sour milk

säu|ern ['zɔʏɐn] VT Brot, Teig to leaven; Kohl, Gurken to pickle; Fisch to put vinegar/lemon juice on VI to go or turn sour, to sour

Sau|er|rahm M thick sour(ed) cream

Sau|er|stoff M, no pl (abbr **O**) oxygen

Sau|er|stoff- in cpds oxygen; **Sau|er|stoff|ap|parat** M breathing apparatus; **sau|er|stoff|arm** ADJ low in oxygen; (zu wenig) oxygen-deficient; **Sau|er|stoff|ent|zug** M (Med) oxygen deficiency; (Chem) deoxygenation; **Sau|er|stoff|fla|sche** F oxygen cylinder or (kleiner) bottle; **Sau|er|stoff|ge|halt** M oxygen content; **Sau|er|stoff|ge|rät** NT breathing apparatus; (Med) (für künstliche Beatmung) respirator; (für erste Hilfe) resuscitator; **sau|er|stoff|hal|tig** ADJ containing oxygen; **Sau|er|stoff|man|gel** M lack of oxygen; (akut) oxygen deficiency; **Sau|er|stoff|mas|ke** F oxygen mask; **Sau|er|stoff|pat|ro|ne** F oxygen cartridge; **Sau|er|stoff|zelt** NT oxygen tent; **Sau|er|stoff|zu|fuhr** F oxygen supply; **mittels ~** by supplying oxygen

Sau|er-: sau|er|süß ADJ, ADV = **süßsauer**; **Sau|er|teig** M sour dough; **Sau|er|topf** M (old hum) sourpuss (inf); **sau|er|töp|fisch** [-tœpfɪʃ] ADJ (old hum) sour; Mensch auch sour-faced

Säu|e|rung F -, -en leavening

Sauf-: Sauf|aus ['zauflaus] M -, -, **Sauf|bold** ['zaufbɔlt] M -(e)s, -e [-də] (old pej) sot (old), drunkard; **Sauf|bru|der** M (pej inf) (= Kumpan) drinking companion or buddy (esp US inf); (= Säufer) soak (inf), boozer (inf)

sau|fen ['zaufn] pret **soff** [zɔf], ptp **gesoffen** [gə'zɔfn] VTI a (Tiere) to drink b (inf: Mensch) to booze (inf), to drink; **das Saufen** boozing; **sich zu Tode ~** to drink oneself to death; **wie ein Loch** or **Bürstenbinder** (dated) ~ to drink like a fish

Säu|fer ['zɔʏfɐ] M -s, -, **Säu|fe|rin** [-ərɪn] F -, -nen (inf) boozer (inf), drunkard

Sau|fe|rei [zaufə'rai] F -, -en (inf) a (= Trinkgelage) booze-up (inf) b no pl (= Trunksucht) boozing (inf)

Säu|fer-: Säu|fer|le|ber F (inf) gin-drinker's liver (inf); **Säu|fer|na|se** F boozer's nose; **Säu|fer|wahn|(sinn)** M the DTs pl (inf)

Sauf-: Sauf|ge|la|ge NT (pej inf) drinking bout or binge, booze-up (inf); **Sauf|kum|pan(in)** M(F), **Sauf|kum|pel** M (pej inf) drinking pal (inf)

säuft [zɔʏft] 3. pers sing pres von **saufen**

Sauf|tour F (inf) drinking binge (inf), pub crawl (esp Brit inf), bar hop (US inf); **eine ~ machen** to go on a pub crawl (esp Brit inf) or bar hop (US inf)

Säug|am|me F (old) wet nurse

Saug|bag|ger M suction dredger

sau|gen ['zaugn] pret **sog** or **saugte** [zo:k, 'zaukta], ptp **gesogen** or **gesaugt** [gə'zo:gn, gə'zaukt] VTI to suck; (Pflanze, Schwamm) to draw up, to absorb; (inf: mit Staubsauger) to vacuum; **an etw** (dat) ~ to suck sth; an Pfeife to draw on sth → **Finger**

säu|gen ['zɔygn] VT to suckle

Sau|ger ['zauge] M **-s, -** **a** (*auf Flasche*) teat (*Brit*), nipple (*US*); (= *Schnuller*) dummy (*Brit*), pacifier (*US*) **b** (*von Krake*) sucker **c** (*inf*: = *Staubsauger*) vacuum (cleaner)

Säu|ger ['zɔyge] M **-s, -**, **Säu|ge|tier** NT mammal

Saug-: saug|fä|hig ADJ absorbent; **Saug|fä|hig|keit** F absorbency; **Saug|fla|sche** F (*form*) feeding bottle; **Saug|glo|cke** F **a** (*Med*) vacuum extractor, ventouse (*spec*) **b** (*zur Abflussreinigung*) plunger; **Saug|glo|cken|ge|burt** F (*Med*) suction or ventouse (*spec*) delivery; **Saug|kraft** F suction (force)

Säug|ling ['zɔyklɪŋ] M **-s, -e** baby, infant (*form*)

Säug|lings- *in cpds* baby, infant (*form*); **Säug|lings|al|ter** NT babyhood; **das Kind ist noch im ~** the child is still a baby; **Säug|lings|für|sor|ge** F infant welfare; **Säug|lings|heim** NT home for babies; **Säug|lings|nah|rung** F baby food(s *pl*); **Säug|lings|pfle|ge** F babycare; **Säug|lings|schwes|ter** F infant nurse; **Säug|lings|sta|ti|on** F neonatal care unit; **Säug|lings|sterb|lich|keit** F infant mortality

Saug-: Saug|mas|sa|ge F suction or vacuum massage; **Saug|napf** M sucker; **Saug|or|gan** NT suctorial organ (*form*); **Saug|pum|pe** F suction pump; (*für Brust*) breast pump; **Saug|re|flex** M sucking reflex; **Saug|rohr** NT , **Saug|röhr|chen** NT pipette; **Saug|rüs|sel** M **a** (*Zool*) proboscis **b** (*an Tanksäule*) flexible tube fitted around pump nozzle for drawing off fumes; **Saug|wurm** M trematode (*spec*)

Sau-: Sau|hatz F (*Hunt*) wild boar hunt; **Sau|hau|fen** M (*inf*) bunch of layabouts (*Brit inf*) or slobs; **Sau|hirt(in)** M(F) (*old*) swineherd (*old*); **Sau|hund** M (*dated sl*) bastard (*sl*); **Sau|jagd** F wild boar hunt; **sau|kalt** ADJ (*inf*) bloody (*Brit inf*) or damn (*inf*) cold; **Sau|käl|te** F (*inf*) bloody (*Brit inf*) or damn (*inf*) freezing weather; **Sau|kerl** M (*inf*) bastard (*sl*); **Sau|klaue** F (*inf*) scrawl (*inf*)

Säu|le ['zɔylə] F **-, -n** column; (= *Rauchsäule, Wassersäule auch, inf:* = *Pfeiler, fig:* = *Stütze*) pillar; **ei|ne/die tragende ~ sein** (*fig*) to be a/the mainstay; **die ~n des Herkules** the Pillars of Hercules

Säu|len-: Säu|len|ab|schluss ▲ M capital; **Säu|len|bau** M *pl* **-bauten** building with columns; **Säu|len|di|a|gramm** NT bar chart; **säu|len|för|mig** ADJ like a column/columns, columnar (*form*); **Säu|len|fuß** M base; **Säu|len|gang** M *pl* **-gänge** colonnade; (*um einen Hof*) peristyle; **Säu|len|hal|le** F columned hall; **Säu|len|hei|li|ge(r)** MF *decl as adj* stylite; **Säu|len|ord|nung** F order (of columns); **die dorische ~** the Doric Order; **Säu|len|por|tal** NT colonnaded doorway; **Säu|len|rei|he** F row of columns; **Säu|len|schaft** M shaft of a column; **Säu|len|tem|pel** M colonnaded temple

Sau|lus ['zaulʊs] M **-'** (*Bibl*) Saul; **vom ~ zum Paulus werden** (*fig*) to have seen the light

Saum [zaum] M **-(e)s, Säume** ['zɔymə] **a** (*Stoffumschlag*) hem; (= *Naht*) seam; (*fig:* = *Waldsaum etc*) edge; **ein schmaler ~ am Horizont** a thin band of cloud (*Brit*) or clouds (*US*) on the horizon

sau|mä|ßig ['zaumɛːsɪç] (*inf*) ADJ lousy (*inf*); (*zur Verstärkung*) hell of a (*inf*) ADV lousily (*inf*); (*zur Verstärkung*) damn (*inf*); **das hat er ~ gemacht** he made a real mess of it

säu|men¹ ['zɔymən] VT (*Sew*) to hem; (*fig geh*) to line

säu|men² VI (*liter*) to tarry (*liter*)

säu|mig ['zɔymɪç] ADJ (*geh*) *Schuldner* defaulting; *Zahlung* late, overdue; *Schüler* dilatory; **~ sein/bleiben/werden** to be/remain/get behind

Säum|nis ['zɔymnɪs] F **-, -se** (*obs*) delay

Säum|nis|ge|bühr F , **Säum|nis|zu|schlag** M late payment charge, extra charge (for late payment)

Saum-: Saum|pfad M mule track; **saum|se|lig** ['zaumze:lɪç] ADJ (*old liter*) dilatory; **Saum|se|lig|keit** F (*old liter*) dilatoriness; **Saum|stich** M hemstitch; **Saum|tier** NT pack animal

Sau|na ['zauna] F **-, -s** *or* **Saunen** [-nən] sauna

sau|nie|ren [zau'ni:rən] *ptp* **sauniert** VI to have a sauna

Sau|pack NT (*pej inf*) scum (*pej inf*)

Sau|preu|ße M , **Sau|preu|ßin** F (*S Ger inf*) Prussian swine

Säu|re ['zɔyrə] F **-, -n** **a** (= *Magensäure, auch Chem*) acid **b** (= *saurer Geschmack*) sourness; (*von Wein, Bonbons*) acidity, sharpness; (*von Obst*) sharpness; **dieser Wein hat zu viel ~** this wine is too sharp

Säu|re-: säu|re|arm ADJ low in acid; **Säu|re|bad** NT acid bath; **säu|re|be|stän|dig**, **säu|re|fest** ADJ acid-resistant; **säu|re|frei** ADJ acid-free; **Säu|re|ge|halt** M acid content

Säu|re-: säu|re|hal|tig ADJ acidic; **säu|re|lös|lich** ADJ acid-soluble

Sau|re(s) ['zaurə] NT *decl as adj* **gib ihm ~s!** (*inf*) let him have it! (*inf*)

Säu|re-: Säu|re|schutz|man|tel M (*von Haut*) hydrolipidic film (*spec*); **Säu|re|ver|gif|tung** F acid poisoning; **Säu|re|zün|der** M acid fuse

Sau|ri|er ['zauriɐ] M **-s, -** dinosaur, saurian (*spec*)

Saus [zaus] M **in ~ und Braus leben** to live like a lord (*Brit*) or king

Sau|se ['zauzə] F **-, -n** (*inf*) **a** (= *Party*) bash (*inf*) **b** (= *Kneipentour*) pub crawl (*esp Brit inf*), bar hop (*US inf*); **eine ~ machen** to go on a pub crawl (*esp Brit inf*) or bar hop (*US inf*)

sau|sen ['zauzn] VI **a** (*Ohren, Kopf*) to buzz; (*Wind*) to whistle; (*Sturm*) to roar; **ihr sauste das Blut in den Ohren** (*geh*) the blood pounded in her ears; **mir ~ die Ohren, es saust mir in den Ohren** my ears are buzzing **b** *aux sein* (*Geschoss, Peitsche*) to whistle **c** *aux sein* (*inf: Mensch*) to tear (*inf*), to charge (*inf*); (*Fahrzeug*) to roar; (*Schlitten, Gegenstand*) to hurtle; **saus mal schnell zum Bäcker** nip round (*Brit*) or run round to the baker's; **in den Graben ~** to fly into the ditch

sau|sen las|sen ▲ *ptp* **sausen lassen** *or* (*rare*) **sausen gelassen** VT *irreg* (*inf*) **a** **jdn ~** to drop sb; **etw ~** to let sth go; *Termin* to skip sth; **die Party heute Abend lass ich sausen** I'll not bother going to the party tonight **b** **einen ~** (*inf*) to let off (*inf*)

Sau|ser ['zauzɐ] M **-s, -** (*S Ger*) fermented apple/grape juice

Sau|se|wind M **a** (*dated inf*) (*lebhaft*) live wire (*inf*); (*unstet*) restless person; **wie ein ~** (= *sehr schnell*) like a whirlwind **b** (*baby-talk:* = *Wind*) wind

Sau-: Sau|stall M (*inf*) (*unordentlich*) pigsty (*inf*); (*chaotisch*) mess; **sau|teu|er** ADJ (*inf*) incredibly expensive

sau|tie|ren [zo'ti:rən] *ptp* **sautiert** VT (*Cook*) to sauté

Sau-: Sau|wet|ter NT (*inf*) bloody (*Brit inf*) or damn (*inf*) awful weather; **sau|wohl** ADJ *pred* (*inf*) bloody (*Brit inf*) or really good; **mir ist ~, ich fühle mich ~** I feel bloody (*Brit inf*) or really good; **Sau|wut** F (*inf*) absolute rage (*inf*); **eine ~ (im Bauch) haben** to be flaming mad (*inf*); **eine ~ auf jdn/etw haben** to be flaming mad at sb/sth

Sa|van|ne [za'vanə] F **-, -n** savanna(h)

sa|ven ['se:vn] VTI (*Comput inf*) to save

Sa|voy|en [za'vɔyən] NT **-s** Savoy

Sa|xo|fon ▲ [zakso'fo:n, 'zaksofo:n] NT **-(e)s, -e**, **Sa|xo|phon** NT **-(e)s, -e** saxophone, sax (*inf*)

Sa|xo|pho|nist [zakso'fɔnɪst] M **-en, -en**, **Sa|xo|pho|nis|tin** [-'nɪstɪn] F **-, -nen** saxophone player, saxophonist

SB- [ɛs'be:] *in cpds* self-service

S-Bahn ['ɛs-] F *abbr von* **Schnellbahn** *von* **Stadtbahn**

S-Bahn|hof ['ɛs-] M suburban line station

S-Bahn-Li|nie ['ɛs-] F suburban rail line

S-Bahn-Netz ['ɛs-] NT suburban rail network

SBB [ɛsbe:'be:] F *- abbr von* **Schweizerische Bundesbahn**

s. Br. *abbr von* **südlicher Breite**

SB- [ɛs'be:-]: **SB-Tank|stel|le** F self-service petrol (*Brit*) or gas (*US*) station; **SB-Wa|ren|haus** NT superstore, hypermarket (*Brit*)

Scam|pi ['skampi] PL scampi *pl*

scan|nen ['skɛnən] VT to scan

Scan|ner ['skɛnɐ] M **-s, -** (*Med, Comput*) scanner

Scan|ner-Kas|se ['skɛnɐ-] F , **Scan|ner|kas|se** F electronic scanning cash register

sch [ʃ] INTERJ shh; (*zum Fortscheuchen*) shoo

Scha|bau [ʃa'bau] M **-s, -s** (*dial*) spirits *pl*

Scha|be [ʃa'bə] F **-, -n** cockroach

Scha|be|fleisch NT (*Cook dial*) minced steak (*Brit*), ground beef (*US*) (*often eaten raw*)

Scha|be|mes|ser NT scraping knife, scraper

scha|ben ['ʃa:bn] VT to scrape; *Fleisch* to chop finely; *Leder, Fell* to shave

Scha|ber ['ʃa:bɐ] M **-s, -** scraper

Scha|ber|nack ['ʃa:bɐnak] M **-(e)s, -e** **a** prank, practical joke; **jdm einen ~ spielen, mit jdm einen ~ treiben** to play a prank on sb; **al|lerlei ~ treiben** to get up to all sorts of pranks; **ich bin zu jedem ~ bereit** I'm always ready for a laugh **b** (*Kind*) monkey (*inf*)

schä|big ['ʃɛːbɪç] ADJ **a** (= *unansehnlich*) *Wohnung, Teppich, Aussehen* shabby **b** (= *niederträchtig*) mean, shabby **b** (= *geizig*) mean, stingy; *Bezahlung* poor, shabby ADV **a** (= *unansehnlich*) shabbily; **~ aussehen** to look shabby **b** (= *gemein*) **jdn ~ behandeln** to treat sb shabbily **b** (= *dürftig*) *bezahlen* poorly

Schä|big|keit F **-, -en** **a** (= *Unansehnlichkeit*) shabbiness **b** (= *Niederträchtigkeit*) meanness, shabbiness; (*Verhalten*) mean or shabby behaviour (*Brit*) or behavior (*US*) *no pl*

Scha|blo|ne [ʃa'blo:nə] F **-, -n** stencil; (= *Muster*) template; (*Comput*) template **b** (*fig pej*) (*bei Arbeit, Arbeitsweise*) routine, pattern; (*beim Reden*) cliché; **in ~n denken** to think in a stereotyped way; **in ~n reden** to speak in clichés; **nicht in die ~ passen** not to fit the stereotype; **etw in ~n pressen** to stereotype sth; **etw geht nach ~** sth follows the same routine; **der Präsident lächelte, aber das war reine ~** the President smiled but it was just a matter of convention; **das ist alles nur ~** that's all just for show

schab|lo|nen|haft ADJ (*pej*) *Denken, Vorstellungen, Argumente* stereotyped; *Ausdrucksweise* clichéd ADV in stereotypes/clichés

Schab|mes|ser NT scraping knife, scraper

Schab|ra|cke [ʃa'brakə] F **-, -n** **a** (= *Satteldecke*) saddlecloth **b** (= *altes Pferd*) nag **c** (= *Querbehang*) pelmet

Schab|sel ['ʃa:psl] PL shavings *pl*

Schach [ʃax] NT **-s, no pl** chess; (= *Stellung im Spiel*) check; **kannst du ~ (spielen)?** can you play chess?; **~ (dem König)!** check; **~ (und) matt** checkmate; **im ~ stehen** or **sein** to be in check; **jdm ~ bieten** (*lit*) to put sb in check, to check sb; (*fig*) to thwart sb; **jdn in ~ halten** (*fig*) to keep sb in check; (*mit Pistole etc*) to cover sb, to keep sb covered

Schach-: Schach|auf|ga|be F chess problem; **Schach|brett** NT chessboard; **schach|brett|ar|tig** ADJ chequered (*Brit*), checkered (*US*) ADV **Platten ~ anlegen** to lay tiles in a chequered (*Brit*) or checkered (*US*) pattern or like a chessboard; **die Straßen sind ~ angeordnet** the roads are laid out like a grid; **~ gemustert** chequered (*Brit*), checkered (*US*); **Schach|brett|mus|ter** NT chequered (*Brit*) or checkered (*US*) pattern; **Schach|com|pu|ter** M chess computer

Scha|cher ['ʃaxɐ] M -s, *no pl* (*pej*) (= *das Feilschen*) haggling (*um over* or *about*); (= *Wucher*) sharp practice; (*fig Pol*) haggling (*um over* or *about*), horse trading (*um over* or *about*); **~ treiben** to indulge in haggling *etc*

Schä|cher ['ʃɛçɐ] M -s, - (*Bibl*) thief

Scha|che|rei [ʃaxəˈrai] F -, -en (*pej*) = Schacher

Scha|che|rer ['ʃaxərɐ] M -s, -, **Scha|che|rin** [-ərɪn] F -, -nen (*pej*) haggler; (= *Wucherer*) sharper; (*Pol*) horse trader

scha|chern ['ʃaxɐn] VI (*pej*) **um etw ~** to haggle over sth

Schach-: Schach|er|öff|nung F chess opening; **Schach|feld** NT square (on a chessboard); **Schach|fi|gur** F chesspiece, chessman; (*fig*) pawn; **Schach|groß|meis|ter(in)** M(F) chess grandmaster; **schach|matt** ADJ (*lit*) (check)mated; (*fig*: = *erschöpft*) exhausted, shattered (*Brit inf*); **~!** (check)mate; **jdn ~ setzen** (*lit*) to (check)mate sb; (*fig*) to snooker sb (*inf*); **Schach|par|tie** F game of chess; **Schach|prob|lem** NT chess problem; **Schach|spiel** NT (= *Spiel*) game of chess; (= *Spielart*) chess *no art*; (= *Brett und Figuren*) chess set; **Schach|spie|ler(in)** M(F) chess player

Schacht [ʃaxt] M -(e)s, ⸚e ['ʃɛçtə] shaft; (= *Brunnenschacht*) well; (= *Straßenschacht*) manhole; (= *Kanalisationsschacht*) drain; (*Comput: von Laufwerk*) bay, slot; (= *Druckerschacht*) tray

Schach|tel ['ʃaxtl] F -, -n a box; (= *Zigarettenschachtel*) packet; **eine ~ Streichhölzer/Pralinen** a box of matches/chocolates b (*inf*: = *Frau*) **alte ~** old bag (*inf*) c (*Fin: auch* **Schachtelbeteiligung**) participation in an affiliated company (*minimum of 25%*)

Schach|tel-: Schach|tel|halm M (*Bot*) horsetail; **Schach|tel|satz** M complicated or multiclause sentence

schäch|ten ['ʃɛçtn] VT to slaughter according to religious rites; **das rituelle Schächten von Tieren** the ritual slaughter of animals

Schach-: Schach|tur|nier NT chess tournament; **Schach|uhr** F chess clock; **Schach|zug** M (*fig*) move

scha|de ['ʃaːdə] ✪ 45.3 ADJ **pred** **(das ist aber) ~!** what a pity or shame; **es ist (zu) ~, dass ...** it's a (real) pity or shame that ...; **es ist ~ um jdn/etw** it's a pity or shame about sb/sth; **um ihn ist es nicht ~** he's no great loss; **für etw ~ sein** to be too good for sth; **sich** (*dat*) **für etw zu ~ sein** to consider oneself too good for sth; **sich** (*dat*) **für nichts zu ~ sein** to consider nothing to be beneath one

Scha|de ['ʃaːdə] M (*old*) **es soll dein ~ nicht sein** it will not be to your disadvantage

Schä|del ['ʃɛːdl] M -s, - skull; **ein kahler ~** a bald head; **jdm den ~ einschlagen** to beat sb's skull or head in; **jdm den ~ spalten/zertrümmern** to split or cleave/crush sb's skull; **sich** (*dat*) **den ~ einrennen** (*inf*) to crack one's skull; **mir brummt der ~** (*inf*) my head is going round and round; (*vor Kopfschmerzen*) my head is throbbing; **einen dicken ~ haben** (*fig inf*) to be stubborn

Schä|del-: Schä|del|ba|sis|bruch M fracture at the base of the skull; **Schä|del|bruch** M fractured skull; **Schä|del|de|cke** F top of the skull; **Schä|del-Hirn-Trau|ma** NT (*Med*) head trauma; **Schä|del|la|ge** F vertex presentation; **Schä|del|naht** F suture

scha|den ['ʃaːdn] VI +*dat* to damage, to harm; **einem Menschen** to harm, to hurt; **jds Ruf** to damage; **das Rauchen schadet Ihrer Gesundheit/Ihnen** that/smoking is bad for your health/you; **das schadet nichts** it does no harm; (= *macht*

nichts) that doesn't matter; **das kann nicht(s) ~** that won't do any harm, it wouldn't hurt; **es kann nicht(s) ~, wenn ...** it would do no harm if ...; **das schadet dir gar nichts** it serves you right; **was schadet es, wenn ...?** what harm can it do if ...?; **mehr ~ als nützen** to do more harm than good VR **sich** (*dat*) **selbst ~** to harm or hurt oneself, to do oneself harm

Scha|den ['ʃaːdn] M -s, ⸚ ['ʃɛːdn] a (= *Beschädigung, Zerstörung*) damage *no pl, no indef art* (*durch* caused by, *an* +*dat* to); (= *Personenschaden*) injury; (= *Verlust*) loss; (= *Unheil, Leid*) harm; **einen ~ verursachen, ~/Schäden anrichten** to cause damage; **den ~ begrenzen** to limit the damage; **ich habe einen ~ am Auto** my car has been damaged; **zu jds ~ gereichen** (*geh*) to be to sb's detriment; **es soll sein ~ nicht sein** it will not be to his disadvantage; **es ist nicht zu deinem ~** it won't do you any harm; **den ~ von etw haben** to suffer for sth; **zu ~ kommen** to suffer; (*physisch*) to be hurt or injured; **nicht zu ~ kommen** not to come to any harm; **an etw** (*dat*) **~ nehmen** to damage or harm sth; **jdm ~ zufügen** to harm sb; **einer Sache** (*dat*) **~ zufügen** to harm or damage sth; **geringe/einige Schäden aufweisen** to have suffered little/some damage; **aus** or **durch ~ wird man klug** (*Prov*) you learn by or from your mistakes; **wer den ~ hat, braucht für den Spott nicht zu sorgen** (*Prov*) don't mock the afflicted

b (= *Defekt*) fault; (= *körperlicher Mangel*) defect; **Schäden an der Lunge** lung damage; **Schäden aufweisen** to be defective; (*Organ*) to be damaged; **ein ~ an der Leber** a damaged liver; **du hast wohl 'nen ~!** (*inf*) you're not quite right in the head! (*inf*)

Scha|den-: Scha|den|er|satz M = Schadensersatz; **Scha|den|fall** M = Schadensfall; **Scha|den|fest|stel|lung** F assessment of damage; **Scha|den|frei|heits|ra|batt** M no-claims bonus; **Scha|den|freu|de** F malicious joy, gloating; **... sagte er mit einer gewissen ~ ...** he gloated; **scha|den|froh** ADJ gloating ADV with malicious delight; *sagen* gloatingly

Schadens-: Schadens|be|gren|zung F damage limitation; **Schadens|bi|lanz** F total damage or loss

Scha|dens|er|satz M damages *pl*, compensation; **jdn auf ~ verklagen** to sue sb for damages or compensation; **~ leisten** to pay damages or compensation

Scha|dens|er|satz-: Scha|dens|er|satz|an|spruch M claim for damages or compensation; **Scha|dens|er|satz|kla|ge** F action for damages or compensation; **scha|dens|er|satz|pflich|tig** [-pflɪçtɪç] ADJ liable for damages or compensation

Scha|dens-: Scha|dens|fall M (*Insur*) case of damage; **im ~** in the event of damage; **Scha|dens|re|gu|lie|rung** F settlement of damages; **Scha|dens|sum|me** F amount of damages

schad|haft ADJ *no adv* faulty, defective; (= *beschädigt*) damaged; (= *abgenutzt*) *Kleidung* worn; *Zähne* decayed; *Gebäude* dilapidated

schä|di|gen ['ʃɛːdɪɡn] VT to damage; *Gesundheit, Umwelt auch* to harm; *jdn* to hurt, to harm; *Firma, Ansehen* to damage, to hurt; **man muss die Firma ~, wo man nur kann** (*iro*) you've got to get what you can out of the firm

Schä|di|gung F -, -en (+*gen* done to) damage; (*von Menschen*) hurt, harm

schäd|lich ['ʃɛːtlɪç] ADJ harmful; *Wirkung, Einflüsse* detrimental, damaging; **~ für etw sein** to be damaging to sth; **~es Tier** pest

Schäd|lich|keit F -, *no pl* harmfulness

Schäd|ling ['ʃɛːtlɪŋ] M -s, -e pest

Schäd|lings-: Schäd|lings|be|fall M (pest) infestation; **Schäd|lings|be|kämp|fung** F pest control *no art*; **Schäd|lings|be|kämp|fungs|mit|tel** NT pesticide

schad|los ADJ a **sich an jdm/etw ~ halten** to take advantage of sb/sth; **wir halten uns dafür**

am Bier ~ (*hum*) ... but we'll make up for it on the beer b (= *keine Schäden verursachend*) Müllbeseitigung etc without damage to the environment; **etw ~ überstehen** to survive sth unharmed

Scha|dor [ʃaˈdoːɐ] M -s, -s (= *Schleier*) chador

Schad|stoff M harmful substance

Schad|stoff-: schad|stoff|arm ADJ **~ sein** to contain a low level of harmful substances; **ein ~es Auto** a clean-air car; **Schad|stoff|aus|stoß** M noxious emission; (*von Auto*) exhaust emission; **Schad|stoff|be|las|tung** F (*von Umwelt*) pollution; **Schad|stoff|ge|halt** M level of harmful substances (+*gen* in); (*der Luft*) pollution content (+*gen* of); **Schad|stoff|kon|zen|tra|ti|on** F concentration of harmful substances

Schaf [ʃaːf] NT -(e)s, -e sheep; (*inf*: = *Dummkopf*) twit (*Brit inf*), dope (*inf*); **das schwarze ~ sein** to be the black sheep (*in* +*dat, gen* of); **~e zählen** (*fig*) to count sheep → **Bock¹ a**

Schaf|bock M ram

Schäf|chen ['ʃɛːfçən] NT -s, - lamb, little sheep; (*inf*: = *Dummerchen*) silly-billy (*inf*); **~ pl** (= *Gemeinde, Anvertraute*) flock *sing*; **sein ~ ins Trockene bringen** (*prov*) to look after or take care of number one (*inf*); **sein ~ im Trockenen haben** to have looked after or taken care of number one (*inf*)

Schäf|chen|wol|ken PL cotton wool clouds *pl*, fleecy clouds *pl*

Schä|fer ['ʃɛːfɐ] M -s, - shepherd

Schä|fer|dich|tung F (*Liter*) pastoral poetry

Schä|fe|rei [ʃɛːfəˈrai] F -, -en a (= *Schafhaltung*) sheep rearing, sheep farming b (*Betrieb*) sheep farm

Schä|fer|hund M Alsatian (dog) (*Brit*), German shepherd (dog) (*US*)

Schä|fe|rin ['ʃɛːfərɪn] F -, -nen shepherdess

Schä|fer-: Schä|fer|ro|man M (*Liter*) pastoral novel; **Schä|fer|stünd|chen** NT (*euph hum*) bit of hanky-panky (*hum inf*)

Schaf|fell NT sheepskin

schaf|fen¹ ['ʃafn] *pret* **schuf** [ʃuːf], *ptp* **geschaffen** [ɡəˈʃafn] VT a (= *hervorbringen*) to create; **die ~de Natur** the creative power of nature; **der ~de Mensch** the creative human being; **dafür ist er wie geschaffen** he's just made for it; **wie ihn Gott geschaffen hatte** as God made him

b *pret auch* **schaffte** ['ʃaftə] (= *herstellen*) to make; *Bedingungen, Möglichkeiten, System, Methode, Arbeitsplätze* to create; (= *verursachen*) *Ärger, Unruhe, Verdruss* to cause, to create; **Raum** or **Platz ~** to make room; **Probleme ~** to create problems; **Ruhe ~** to establish order; **Klarheit ~** to provide clarification; **Linderung ~** to bring relief (*für* to) → **Blut**

schaf|fen² VT a (= *bewältigen, zustande bringen*) *Aufgabe, Hürde, Portion etc* to manage; *Prüfung* to pass; **~ wir das zeitlich?** are we going to make it?; **schaffst dus noch?** (*inf*) can you manage?; **wir habens geschafft** we've managed it; (= *Arbeit erledigt*) we've done it; (= *gut angekommen*) we've made it; **so, das hätten wir** or **das wäre geschafft!** there, that's done; **das ist nicht zu ~** that can't be done; **das hast du wieder mal geschafft** you've done it again; **wir haben nicht viel geschafft** we haven't managed to do much or haven't got much done; **er schafft es noch, dass ich ihn rauswerfe/er rausgeworfen wird** he'll end up with me throwing him out/(by) being thrown out

b (*inf*: = *überwältigen*) *jdn* to see off (*inf*); **das hat mich geschafft** it took it out of me; (*nervlich*) it got on top of me; **geschafft sein** to be shattered (*Brit inf*) or exhausted

c (= *bringen*) **etw in etw** (*acc*) **~** to put sth in sth; **wie sollen wir das in den Keller/auf den Berg ~?** how will we manage to get that into the cellar/up the mountain?; **etw aus etw ~** to get sth out of sth; **einen Koffer zum Bahnhof ~** to take a (suit)case to the station; **alte Zeitun-**

gen auf den Boden ~ to put old newspapers in the attic; **etw aus der Welt ~** to settle sth (for good); **sich** (dat) **jdn/etw vom Hals(e)** or **Leib(e) ~** to get sb/sth off one's back → **beiseite**

VI **a** (= tun) to do; **ich habe damit nichts zu ~** that has nothing to do with me; **ich habe nichts mit ihm zu ~** I don't have anything to do with him; **was haben Sie dort zu ~?** what do you think you're doing (there)?; **sich** (dat) **an etw** (dat) **zu ~ machen** to fiddle about with sth; **sich mit etw zu ~ machen** to busy oneself with sth

b (= zusetzen) **jdm** (**sehr** or **schwer**) **zu ~ machen** to cause sb (a lot of) trouble; (= bekümmern) to worry sb (a lot); **das macht ihr heute noch zu ~** she still worries about it today

c (S Ger: = arbeiten) to work

Scha̲f|fen NT -s, no pl **die Freude am ~** the joy of creation; **sein musikalisches/künstlerisches ~** his musical/artistic works pl or creations pl; **der Künstler bei seinem ~** the artist at work; **auf dem Höhepunkt seines ~s** at the peak of his creative powers or prowess

Scha̲f|fens-: Scha̲f|fens|drang M energy; (von Künstler) creative urge; **Scha̲f|fens|freu-de** F (creative) zest or enthusiasm; **scha̲f-fens|freu|dig** ADJ (creatively) enthusiastic; Künstler creative; **Scha̲f|fens|kraft** F creativity

Scha̲f|fer ['ʃafɐ] M -s, -, **Scha̲f|fe|rin** [-ərɪn] F -, -nen (inf) hard worker

Schaff|hau̲|sen [ʃaf'hauzn] NT -s (Kanton, Stadt) Schaffhausen

Scha̲f|fleisch NT mutton

Scha̲ff|ner ['ʃafnɐ] M -s, -, **Scha̲ff|ne|rin** [-ərɪn] F -, -nen **a** (im Bus) conductor/conductress; (Rail) ticket collector; (im Zug) guard (Brit), conductor (US); (im Schlafwagen) attendant; (= Fahrkartenkontrolleur) ticket inspector **b** (old: = Verwalter) steward, estate manager

Scha̲f|fung ['ʃafʊŋ] F -, -en creation

Scha̲f- → auch **Schafs-: Scha̲f|gar|be** F yarrow; **Scha̲f|her|de** F flock of sheep; **Scha̲f|hirt** M shepherd; **Scha̲f|hir|tin** F shepherdess; **Scha̲f|hür|de** F sheep pen, (sheep)fold

Scha̲f|kopf M , no pl = **Schafskopf b**

Schä̲f|lein ['ʃɛːflaɪn] NT -s, - (lit, fig) lamb; (pl fig) flock sing or pl

Scha|fo̲tt [ʃa'fɔt] NT -(e)s, -e scaffold

Scha̲f-: Scha̲f|pelz M sheepskin; **Scha̲f-sche|rer** [-ʃeːrɐ] M -s, -, **Scha̲f|sche|re|rin** [-ərɪn] F -, -nen sheepshearer; **Scha̲f|schur** F sheepshearing

Scha̲fs-: Scha̲fs|kä|se M sheep's milk cheese; **Scha̲fs|kopf** M **a** sheep's head; (pej: = Dummkopf) blockhead, dolt, numskull **b** no pl (Cards) German card game, a simplified version of skat; **Scha̲fs|milch** F sheep's milk; **Scha̲fs|pelz** M sheepskin → **Wolf**

Scha̲f|stall M sheepfold

Schaft [ʃaft] M -(e)s, ⸚e ['ʃɛftə] **a** shaft (auch Archit); (von Gewehr) stock; (von Stiefel) leg; (von Schraube, Schlüssel) shank; (Bot) stalk **b** (Sw, S Ger) (= Regal) shelves pl; (= Schrank) cupboard

Scha̲ft|stie|fel PL high boots pl; (Mil) jackboots pl

Scha̲f-: Scha̲f|wei|de F sheep pasture; **Scha̲f-wol|le** F sheep's wool; **Scha̲f|zucht** F sheep breeding no art

Schah [ʃaː] M -s, -s Shah

Scha|kal [ʃa'kaːl] M -s, -e jackal

Schä̲|ker ['ʃɛːkɐ] M -s, - (inf) flirt; (= Witzbold) joker

Schä̲|ke|rei [ʃɛːkəˈraɪ] F -, -en (inf) flirting; (= Witzelei) fooling around

Schä̲|ke|rin ['ʃɛːkərɪn] F -, -nen (inf) flirt, coquette; (= Witzbold) joker

schä̲|kern ['ʃɛːkɐn] VI to flirt; (= necken) to play about

schal [ʃaːl] ADJ Getränk flat; Wasser, Geschmack stale; (fig: = geistlos) Witz weak; Leben empty; Gerede vapid, empty

Schal [ʃaːl] M -s, -s or -e scarf; (= Umschlagtuch) shawl

Schä̲l|chen ['ʃɛːlçən] NT -s, - dim von **Schale** [1] (small) bowl

Scha̲|le [1] ['ʃaːlə] F -, -n bowl; (flach, zum Servieren etc) dish; (von Waage) pan; (= Sektschale) champagne glass; (esp S Ger, Aus: = Tasse) cup

Scha̲|le [2] F -, -n (von Obst, Gemüse) skin; (abgeschält) peel no pl; (= Rinde) (von Käse) rind; (von Nuss, Ei, Muschel, Krebs) shell; (von Getreide) husk, hull; (Hunt) hoof; (fig: = äußeres Auftreten) appearance; **sich in ~ werfen** or **schmeißen** (inf) to get dressed up; (Frau auch) to get dolled up (inf); **in seiner rauen ~ steckt ein guter Kern** beneath that rough exterior (there) beats a heart of gold (prov)

schä̲|len ['ʃɛːlən] VT to peel; Tomate, Mandel to skin; Erbsen, Eier, Nüsse to shell; Getreide to husk **VR** to peel; **sich aus den Kleidern ~** to peel off (one's clothes); **ich schäle mich auf der Nase** my nose is peeling

Scha̲|len-: Scha̲|len|obst NT nuts pl; **Scha̲|len|ses|sel** M shell chair; **Scha̲|len|sitz** M bucket seat; **Scha̲|len|tier** NT shellfish; **~e** shellfish pl; **Scha̲|len|wild** NT hoofed game

Scha̲l|heit F -, no pl (von Getränk) flatness; (von Wasser, Geschmack) staleness

Scha̲l|holz NT shuttering wood

Scha̲lk [ʃalk] M -(e)s, -e or ⸚e ['ʃɛlkə] joker; **ihm sitzt der ~ im Nacken** he's in a devilish mood; **ihr schaut der ~ aus den Augen** she (always) has a roguish or mischievous look on her face

scha̲lk|haft ADJ roguish, mischievous ADV roguishly, mischievously

Scha̲lk|haf|tig|keit ['ʃalkhaftɪçkaɪt] F -, no pl roguishness, mischievousness

Scha̲l|kra|gen M shawl collar; (mit losen Enden) scarf collar

Schall [ʃal] M -(e)s, -e or ⸚e ['ʃɛlə] sound; **Ruhm vergeht wie ~ und Rauch** (geh) fame is but a transient shadow; **Name ist ~ und Rauch** (Prov) what's in a name?; **das ist alles ~ und Rauch** it's all hollow words

Schall-: Schall|be|cher M (Mus) bell; **Schall|bo|den** M sound(ing) board; **schall|däm|men** VT to soundproof; **schall|däm-mend** ADJ sound-deadening; **Schall|däm-mung** F sound absorption; (= Abdichtung gegen Schall) soundproofing; **schall|däm|pfend** ADJ Wirkung sound-muffling, sound-deadening; Material soundproofing; **Schall|däm|pfer** M sound absorber; (von Auto) silencer (Brit), muffler (US); (von Gewehr etc) silencer; (Mus) mute; **Schall|däm|pfung** F sound absorption; (= Abdichtung gegen Schall) soundproofing; (von Auto etc) silencing; **schall|dicht** ADJ soundproof ADV **~ abgeschlossen sein** to be fully soundproofed

Schall|lei|ter △ M → **Schallleiter**

scha̲l|len ['ʃalən] pret schallte or (old) scholl ['ʃaltə, ʃɔl], ptp geschallt or (old) geschollen [gəˈʃalt, gəˈʃɔlən] VI to sound; (Stimme, Glocke, Beifall) to ring (out); (= widerhallen) to resound, to echo; **das Schlagen der Turmuhr schallte zu uns herüber** we could hear the church clock ring out

scha̲l|lend ADJ Beifall, Ohrfeige resounding; Gelächter ringing ADV **~ lachen** to roar with laughter; **jdn ~ ohrfeigen** to give sb a resounding slap

Schall-: Schall|ge|schwin|dig|keit F speed of sound; **Schall|gren|ze** F sound barrier; **Schall|lei|ter** △ M conductor of sound; **Schall|mau|er** F sound barrier; **Schall|mes-sung** F sound ranging

Schall|plat|te F record

Schall|plat|ten-: Schall|plat|ten|al|bum NT record case; **Schall|plat|ten|ar|chiv** NT

(gramophone) record archive; **Schall|plat-ten|auf|nah|me** F (gramophone) recording

Schall-: schall|schlu|ckend ADJ sound-absorbent; Material soundproofing; **Schall-schutz|fens|ter** NT soundproof window; **schall|si|cher** ADJ soundproof; **schall|tot** ADJ Raum completely soundproof, anechoic (spec); **Schall|trich|ter** M horn; (von Trompeten etc) bell; **Schall|wand** F baffle (of loudspeaker etc); **Schall|wel|le** F sound wave; **Schall|wort** NT pl -wörter onomatopoeic word

Schal|mei [ʃalˈmaɪ] F -, -en shawm

Scha̲l|obst NT nuts pl

Scha|lot|te [ʃaˈlɔtə] F -, -n shallot

schalt pret von **schelten**

Schalt-: Scha̲lt|an|la|ge F switchgear; **Scha̲lt|bild** NT circuit diagram, wiring diagram; **Scha̲lt|brett** NT switchboard, control panel

scha̲l|ten ['ʃaltn] VT **a** Gerät to switch, to turn; (= in Gang bringen) to switch or turn on; Leitung to connect; **etw auf „2" ~** to turn or switch sth to "2"; **etw auf die höchste Stufe ~** to turn sth on full, to turn sth full on or up; **in Reihe/paral-lel ~** (Elec) to connect in series/in parallel; **das Gerät lässt sich schwer ~, das Gerät schaltet sich schwer** this device has a difficult switch (to operate); **das Auto schaltet sich leicht** it's easy to change (esp Brit) or shift (US) gear in this car

b Werbung, Anzeige to place; Hotline to set up **VI** **a** (Gerät, Ampel) to switch (auf +acc to); (Aut) to change (esp Brit) or shift (US) gear; **in den 2. Gang ~** to change (esp Brit) or shift (US) into 2nd gear; **auf stur ~** (inf) to dig one's heels in

b (= verfahren, handeln) **~ und walten** to bustle around; **frei ~ (und walten) können** to have a free hand (to do as one pleases); **jdn frei ~ und walten lassen** to give sb a free hand, to let sb manage things as he sees fit

c (inf) (= begreifen) to latch on (inf), to get it (inf), to get the message (inf); (= reagieren) to react

Scha̲l|ter ['ʃaltɐ] M -s, - **a** (Elec etc) switch **b** (in Post, Bank, Amt) counter; (im Bahnhof) ticket window

Scha̲l|ter-: Scha̲l|ter|be|am|te(r) M decl as adj, **Scha̲l|ter|be|am|tin** F counter clerk; (im Bahnhof) ticket clerk; **Scha̲l|ter|dienst** M counter duty; **Scha̲l|ter|hal|le** F (in Post) hall; (in Bank) (banking) hall; (im Bahnhof) booking or ticket hall; **Scha̲l|ter|leis|te** F (Comput) toolbar; **Scha̲l|ter|raum** M = **Schalterhalle**; **Scha̲l|ter|schluss** ▲ M (einer Bank, Behörde) closing time; **~ ist um vier** offices close at four; **nach ~** after hours; **Scha̲l|ter|stun|den** PL hours pl of business, business hours pl

scha̲lt|faul ADJ (inf) reluctant to change (esp Brit) or shift (US) gear; **~es Fahren** driving without changing (esp Brit) or shifting (US) gear

Schalt-: Scha̲lt|flä|che F (Comput) button; **Scha̲lt|ge|trie|be** NT manual transmission, stick shift (US); **Scha̲lt|he|bel** M switch lever; (Aut) gear lever (Brit), gear shift (US); **an dem ~ der Macht sitzen** to hold the reins of power; **Scha̲lt|jahr** NT leap year; **alle ~e** (inf) once in a blue moon; **Scha̲lt|kas|ten** M switch box; **Scha̲lt|knüp|pel** M (Aut) gear lever (Brit), gear shift (US); (Aviat) joystick; **Scha̲lt|kreis** M (Tech) (switching) circuit; **Scha̲lt|pau|se** F (TV, Rad) pause (before going over to another region or station); **Scha̲lt|plan** M circuit diagram, wiring diagram; **Scha̲lt|pult** NT control desk; **Scha̲lt-satz** M (Ling) parenthetic clause; **Scha̲lt-schritt** M (von Schreibmaschine) horizontal spacing; **Scha̲lt|skiz|ze** F circuit diagram, wiring diagram; **Scha̲lt|stel|le** F (fig) coordinating point; **Scha̲lt|ta|fel** F switchboard, control panel; **Scha̲lt|tag** M leap day

Schal|tung ['ʃaltʊŋ] F **-, -en** switching; (*Elec*) wiring; (*Aut*) gear change (*Brit*), gearshift (*US*)

Schalt|zent|ra|le F (*lit*) control centre (*Brit*) or center (*US*); (*fig*) nerve centre (*Brit*) or center (*US*)

Scha|lung ['ʃaːlʊŋ] F **-, -en** formwork, shuttering

Schal|up|pe [ʃaˈlʊpə] F **-, -n** sloop

Schal|wild ['ʃaːl-] NT hoofed game

Scham [ʃaːm] F **-,** *no pl* **a** shame; **er wurde rot vor ~** he went red with shame; **die ~ stieg ihm ins Gesicht** (*old*) a blush of shame mounted to his cheeks; **ich hätte vor ~ (in den Boden) versinken können** I wanted the floor to swallow me up or to open up under me; **er versteckte sich vor ~** he hid himself in shame; **aus falscher ~** from a false sense of shame; **nur keine falsche ~!** (*inf*) no need to feel or be embarrassed!, no need for embarrassment!; **sie hat kein bisschen ~ (im Leibe)** she doesn't have an ounce of shame (in her); **ohne ~** unashamedly; **alle ~ verlieren** to lose all sense of shame **b** (*geh*: = *Genitalien*) private parts *pl*; (*von Frau*) pudenda *pl*

Scha|ma|ne [ʃaˈmaːnə] M **-n, -n, Scha|ma|nin** [-ˈmaːnɪn] F **-, -nen** shaman

Scham-: Scham|bein NT pubic bone; **Scham|berg** M (*geh*) mount of Venus, mons veneris (*form*); **Scham|bo|gen** M pubic arch

schä|men ['ʃɛːmən] VR to be ashamed; **du solltest dich ~!, du sollst dich was ~** (*inf*) you ought to be ashamed of yourself!; **sich einer Sache** (*gen*) or **für** or **wegen etw ~** to be a-shamed of sth; **sich jds/einer Sache** or **wegen jdm/etw** (*inf*) ~ to be ashamed of sb/sth; **sich für jdn** (*inf*) ~ to be ashamed for sb; **sich vor jdm ~** to be or feel ashamed in front of sb; **ich schäme mich so vor ihm** he makes me feel so ashamed; **schäme dich!** shame on you!

Scham-: Scham|frist F decent interval; **Scham|fu|ge** F pubic symphysis (*spec*); **Scham|ge|fühl** NT sense of shame; **ganz ohne ~ sein** to have no (sense of) shame; **Scham|ge|gend** F pubic region; **Scham|gren|ze** F bounds *pl* of what is acceptable; **keine ~ haben** to have no sense of shame; **die ~ überschreiten** to go beyond the bounds of what is acceptable; **da liegt meine ~** that's going too far for me; **Scham|haar** NT pubic hair; **scham|haft** ADJ modest; (= *verschämt*) bashful, coy; **die heutige Jugend ist nicht sehr ~** today's young people have very little modesty ADV modestly; (= *verschämt*) bashfully, coyly; **Scham|haf|tig|keit** ['ʃaːmhaftɪçkait] F **-,** *no pl* modesty; **Scham|hü|gel** M mount of Venus, mons veneris (*form*); **Scham|lip|pen** PL labia *pl*, lips *pl* of the vulva; **scham|los** ADJ shameless; (= *unanständig auch*) indecent; (= *unverschämt auch*) brazen; *Frechheit, Lüge* brazen, barefaced; **~e Reden führen** to make indecent remarks ADV shamelessly; **sich ~ zeigen** to flaunt oneself brazenly or shamelessly; **sich ~ kleiden** to dress indecently; **Scham|lo|sig|keit** F **-, -en** shamelessness; (= *Unanständigkeit auch*) indecency; (= *Unverschämtheit auch*) brazenness

Scha|mott [ʃaˈmɔt] M **-s,** *no pl* **a** (*inf*) junk (*inf*), trash (*inf*), rubbish **b** (*Aus, S Ger*: = *Ton*) fireclay

Scha|mot|te [ʃaˈmɔtə] F **-,** *no pl* fireclay

Scha|mot|te-: Scha|mot|te|stein M firestone; **Scha|mot|te|zie|gel** M firebrick

scha|mot|tie|ren [ʃamɔˈtiːrən] *ptp* **schamottiert** VT to line with firebricks

Scham|pus ['ʃampʊs] M **-s,** *no pl* (*dated inf*) champers *sing* (*dated Brit inf*), bubbly (*inf*)

Scham-: scham|rot ADJ red (with shame); **~ werden** or **anlaufen** to turn red or to blush or flush with shame; **Scham|rö|te** F flush or blush of shame; **die ~ stieg ihr ins Gesicht** her face flushed with shame; **Scham|tei|le** PL private parts *pl*, genitals *pl*

schand|bar ADJ shameful, disgraceful ADV **a** (= *schändlich*) shamefully, disgracefully **b** (*dial*: = *sehr*) awfully; *wehtun* terribly

Schan|de ['ʃandə] F **-,** *no pl* disgrace; (= *Unehre auch*) shame, ignominy; **er ist eine ~ für seine Familie** he is a disgrace to his family; **das ist eine (wahre) ~!** this is a(n absolute) disgrace!; **~!** (*euph inf*) sugar! (*euph inf*), hell! (*inf*); **es ist doch keine ~, Gefühle zu zeigen** or **wenn man Gefühle zeigt** there is no shame or disgrace in showing one's feelings; **~ über jdn bringen** to bring disgrace or shame upon sb, to disgrace sb; **~ über dich!** (*dated*) shame on you!; **jdm/einer Sache ~ machen** to be a disgrace to sb/sth; **mach mir keine ~** don't show me up (*inf*), don't be a disgrace to me; **zu meiner (großen) ~ muss ich gestehen, ...** to my great or eternal shame I have to admit that ...; **zu ~n = zuschanden →** **Schimpf**

schän|den ['ʃɛndn] VT *Leichnam* to violate, to defile; *Heiligtum, Grab, Friedhof, Denkmal auch* to desecrate; *Sabbat, Sonntag etc* to violate, to desecrate; *Frauen, Kinder* to violate; *Ansehen, Namen* to dishonour (*Brit*), to dishonor (*US*), to discredit, to sully

Schand-: Schand|fleck M blot (*in* +*dat* on); (*Gebäude etc auch*) eyesore; **er war der ~ der Familie** he was the disgrace of his family; **Schand|geld** NT ridiculous or extortionate price

schänd|lich ['ʃɛndlɪç] ADJ disgraceful, shameful ADV shamefully; *behandeln* disgracefully; **jdn ~ betrügen** to deceive sb shamefully; **er hat sie ~ verlassen** it was a disgrace the way he left her

Schänd|lich|keit F **-, -en** shamefulness

Schand-: Schand|mal NT *pl* **-male** brand, stigma; **Schand|maul** NT (*pej*) malicious or evil tongue; **er ist ein ~** he has a malicious or an evil tongue; **Schand|pfahl** M pillory; **Schand|tat** F scandalous or disgraceful deed; (*hum*) prank, escapade; **zu jeder ~ bereit sein** (*inf*) to be always ready for mischief or a lark (*inf*)

Schän|dung ['ʃɛndʊŋ] F **-, -en** (*von Leichnam*) violation, defilement; (*von Heiligtum, Grab, Denkmal auch*) desecration; (*von Sabbat, Frauen, Kindern*) violation; (*von Namen, Ansehen*) dishonouring (*Brit*), dishonoring (*US*), discrediting, sullying

schang|hai|en [ʃaŋˈhaiən, ˈʃaŋhaiən] *ptp* **schanghait** VT (*Naut*) to shanghai

Scha|ni ['ʃaːni] M **-s, -** (*Aus inf*) **a** (= *Freund*) mate (*inf*), buddy (*US inf*) **b** (= *Diener*) servant

Scha|ni|gar|ten ['ʃaːni-] M (*Aus*) pavement café (*Brit*), sidewalk café (*US*)

Schänk [ʃaŋk] F **-, -en** (*Aus*) bar

Schänk-: Schänk|be|trieb M bar service; **nach 24 Uhr kein ~ mehr** the bar closes at 12 midnight; **Schänk|bier** NT draught (*Brit*) or draft (*US*) beer

Schän|ke ▲ ['ʃɛŋkə] F **-, -n** tavern, inn

Schän|ker ['ʃɛŋkɐ] M **-s, -** chancre

Schänk-: Schänk|er|laub|nis F licence (*of publican*) (*Brit*), excise license (*US*); **Schänk|fräu|lein** NT (*Aus*) barmaid; **Schänk|kon|zes|si|on** F licence (*of publican*) (*Brit*), excise license (*US*); **Schänk|stu|be** F (*public*) bar (*esp Brit*), saloon (*US dated*); **Schänk|tisch** M bar; **Schänk|wirt(in)** M(F) (*old*) taverner (*old*), publican (*Brit*), saloon keeper (*US dated*), barkeeper (*US*); **Schänk|wirt|schaft** F (*old, Aus*) tavern (*old*), public house (*Brit*), saloon (*US dated*)

Schanz-: Schanz|ar|beit F *usu pl* trench digging *no pl*, trench work *no pl*; **Schanz|bau** M , *no pl* construction of fieldwork or entrenchments

Schan|ze ['ʃantsə] F **-, -n** (*Mil*) fieldwork, entrenchment; (*Naut*) quarterdeck; (*Sport*) (ski) jump; (*für Skateboarder*) ramp; **kleine/große ~** (*Sport*) 90-/120-metre (*Brit*) or meter (*US*) (ski)

jump; **sein Leben in die ~ schlagen** (*geh*) to risk one's life, to put one's life at risk or in jeopardy

schan|zen ['ʃantsn] VI (*Mil*) to dig (trenches)

Schan|zen-: Schan|zen|bau M , *no pl* construction of fieldwork or entrenchments; **Schan|zen|re|kord** M (*Sport*) ski-jump record; **Schan|zen|tisch** M (*Sport: Skispringen*) take-off area

Schanz|werk NT entrenchment

Schar¹ [ʃaːr] F **-, -en** crowd, throng (*liter*); (*von Vögeln*) flock; (*von Insekten, Heuschrecken etc*) swarm; (= *Reiterschar, Soldatenschar etc*) band, company; (*von Jägern*) party; (*von Pfadfindern*) company, troop; (*von Engeln*) host, band, throng (*liter*); **~en von Hausfrauen stürzten sich auf die Sonderangebote** hordes or crowds of housewives descended on the special offers; **die Fans verließen das Stadion in (hellen) ~en** the fans left the stadium in droves; **der Partei laufen die Mitglieder in ~en davon** members are leaving the party in droves; **die Menschen kamen in (hellen) ~en nach Lourdes** people flocked to Lourdes

Schar² F **-, -en** (= *Pflugschar*) (plough)share (*Brit*), (plow)share (*US*)

Scha|ra|de [ʃaˈraːdə] F **-, -n** charade; **~ spielen** to play charades

Schar|bocks|kraut ['ʃaːrbɔks-] NT (lesser) celandine

Schä|re ['ʃɛːrə] F **-, -n** skerry

scha|ren ['ʃaːrən] VT **Menschen/Anhänger um sich ~** to gather people/to rally supporters around one VR **sich um jdn/etw ~** to gather around sb/sth; (*Anhänger auch*) to rally around sb/sth

scha|ren|wei|se ADV (*in Bezug auf Menschen*) in droves; **die Heuschrecken/Vögel fielen ~ über die Saat her** swarms of locusts/whole flocks of birds descended on the seedcrop; **~ drängten sich die Leute vor die Schaufenster** people crowded or thronged in front of the shop window

scharf [ʃarf] ADJ *comp* **=er** ['ʃɛrfə], *superl* **=ste(r, s)** ['ʃɛrfstə] **a** *Messer, Kante, Kurve* sharp; (= *durchdringend*) *Wind* keen, biting, cutting; *Kälte* biting; *Luft* raw, keen; *Frost* sharp, keen; *Ton* piercing, shrill; **das ~e S** (*Aus inf*) the "scharfes s" (*German symbol ß*), ess-tset; **ein Messer ~ machen** to sharpen a knife

b (= *stark gewürzt*) hot; *Geruch, Geschmack* pungent, acrid; *Käse* strong, sharp; *Alkohol* (= *stark*) strong; (= *brennend*) *Waschmittel, Lösung* caustic; **~e Sachen** (*inf*) hard stuff (*inf*)

c (= *hart, streng*) *Mittel, Maßnahmen* tough, severe, drastic; (*inf*) *Prüfung, Untersuchung* strict, tough; *Lehrer, Polizist* tough; *Bewachung* close, tight; *Hund* fierce

d (= *schonungslos, stark*) *Worte, Kritik* sharp, biting, harsh; *Widerstand, Konkurrenz* fierce, tough; *Gegner, Protest* strong, fierce; *Auseinandersetzung* bitter, fierce; **eine ~e Zunge haben** to have a sharp tongue, to be sharp-tongued; **jdn/etw in ~er Form kritisieren** to criticize sb/sth in strong terms; **etw in schärfster Form** or **aufs Schärfste** or **aufs schärfste verurteilen** to condemn sth in the strongest possible terms

e (= *deutlich, klar, genau*) sharp; *Unterschied* sharp, marked; *Brille, Linse* sharply focusing; *Augen* sharp, keen; *Töne* clear, precise; *Verstand, Intelligenz, Gehör* sharp, keen, acute; *Beobachter* keen; **ein ~es Auge für etw haben** (*fig*) to have a keen or sharp eye for sth; **mit ~em Blick** (*fig*) with penetrating insight

f (= *heftig, schnell*) *Ritt, Trab* hard; **ein ~es Tempo fahren** (*inf*) to drive hell for leather (*Brit*) or like a bat out of hell (*inf*), to drive at quite a lick (*Brit inf*); **einen ~en Stil fahren** (*inf*) to drive hard

g (= *echt*) *Munition etc, Schuss* live; **etw ~ machen** to arm sth; **~e Schüsse abgeben** to shoot or fire live bullets

h (*inf*: = *geil*) randy (*Brit inf*), horny (*inf*); **jdn ~ machen** to turn sb on (*inf*); **~ werden** to get turned on (*inf*), to get randy (*Brit inf*) or horny (*inf*); **auf jdn/etw ~ sein** to be keen on (*inf*) or hot for (*inf*) sb/sth, to fancy sb/sth (*inf*); **der Kleine/Alte ist ~ wie Nachbars Lumpi** or **tausend Russen** or **sieben Sensen** (*dated*) he's a randy (*Brit*) or horny little/old bugger (*inf*) → *auch* **scharfmachen**

ADV *comp* **-er**, *superl* **am -sten a** (= *intensiv*) ~ **nach etw riechen** to smell strongly of sth; ~ **würzen** to season highly, to make hot (*inf*); **Fleisch ~ anbraten** to sear meat; **sie kocht sehr ~** her cooking is very spicy; **sie hat das Curry ~ zubereitet** she made the curry hot

b (= *schneidend*) **etw ~ schleifen** to sharpen or hone sth to a fine edge; **schärfer geschliffen** more finely sharpened; **das „s" wird oft ~ ausgesprochen** "s" is often voiceless, "s" is often pronounced as an "s" and not a "z"

c (= *heftig*) **attackieren, kritisieren** sharply; **ablehnen** adamantly; **protestieren** emphatically; **etw ~ verurteilen** to criticize sth sharply

d (= *konzentriert*) **zuhören** closely; ~ **beobachten** to be very observant; **etw ~ unter die Lupe nehmen** to examine sth carefully; **etw ~ betrachten** to look at sth intensely; ~ **aufpassen** to pay close attention; ~ **zuhören** to listen closely; **jdn ~ ansehen** to give sb a scrutinizing look; (*missbilligend*) to look sharply at sb; ~ **nachdenken** to have a good or long think, to think long and hard

e (= *präzise*) **analysieren** carefully, in detail; **etw ~ umreißen** (*fig*) to outline sth precisely or clearly

f (= *genau*) **etw ~ einstellen** (*Bild, Diaprojektor etc*) to bring sth into focus; **Sender** to tune sth in (properly); **eingestellt**, in (sharp) focus, (properly) tuned in; ~ **sehen/hören** to have sharp eyes/ears

g (= *schnell*) **fahren, marschieren** fast; ~ **galoppieren** to ride at a full gallop; ~ **reiten** to ride hard

h (= *abrupt*) **bremsen** sharply, hard; ~ **links abbiegen** to take a hard left; ~ **kehrtmachen** to turn on one's heel

i (= *hart*) ~ **vorgehen/durchgreifen** to take decisive action; **etw ~ bekämpfen** to take strong measures against sth

j (= *streng*) **bewachen** closely; **jdn ~ kontrollieren** to examine sb thoroughly

k (= *knapp*) ~ **kalkulieren** to reduce one's profit margin; **schärfer kalkulieren** to reduce one's profit margin even more; ~ **rechnen** to figure it out carefully

l (= *fein*) **hören, sehen** clearly, well

m (*Mil*) **das Gewehr war ~ geladen** the rifle was loaded with live ammunition; ~ **schießen** (*lit*) (= *mit scharfer Munition*) to shoot with live ammunition; (= *auf den Mann*) to aim to hit; (*fig*) to let fly; **in der Diskussion wurde ziemlich ~ geschossen** (*inf*) the discussion became rather heated, sparks flew in the discussion

Scharf|blick M (*fig*) perspicacity, keen insight, penetration

Schär|fe ['ʃɛrfə] F **-, -n a** (*von Messer, Kante, Kurve*) sharpness; (*von Wind, Frost*) keenness; (*von Ton*) shrillness

b (*von Essen*) spiciness; (*von Geruch, Geschmack*) pungency; (*von Lösung*) causticity

c (= *Härte, Strenge*) toughness, severity; **mit ~ vorgehen** to take tough or severe measures

d (*von Worten, Kritik*) sharpness, harshness; (*von Widerstand, Konkurrenz*) toughness; (*von Protest*) strength; (*von Auseinandersetzung*) bitterness; **ich möchte in aller ~ sagen, dass ...** I'm going to be quite harsh (about this) and say that ...; **etw/jdn in** or **mit aller ~ kritisieren** to be sharply critical of sth/sb; **der Konflikt hat an ~ zugenommen** the conflict has become more bitter

e (= *Deutlichkeit*) sharpness; (*von Brille, Linse*) strength; (*von Augen*) sharpness, keenness; (*von Gehör, Verstand*) keenness; (*an Kamera, Fernsehen*) focus; (*an Radio*) tuning; **dem Bild fehlt die ~**

the picture lacks sharpness (of focus) or definition

Scharf|ein|stel|lung F focusing

schär|fen ['ʃɛrfn] VT (*lit, fig*) to sharpen

Schär|fen|ein|stel|lung F focusing control

Scharf-: scharf|kan|tig ADJ with sharp edges, sharp-edged; **scharf+ma|chen** VT *sep* (*inf*, = *aufstacheln*) to stir up, to get up in arms; (= *aufreizen*) to turn on (*inf*); **Scharf|ma|cher(in)** M(F) (*inf*) rabble-rouser, agitator; **Scharf|ma|che|rei** [-maxə'raɪ] F **-, -en** (*inf*) rabble-rousing, agitation; **Scharf|rich|ter** M executioner; **Scharf|schüt|ze** M marksman; **Scharf|schüt|zin** F markswoman; **scharf|sich|tig** [-zɪçtɪç] ADJ keen-sighted, sharp-sighted; (*fig*) perspicacious, clear-sighted; **Scharf|sinn** M astuteness, acumen, keen perception; **scharf|sin|nig** ADJ *Bemerkung* astute, penetrating; *Detektiv etc* astute, sharp-witted ADV astutely; **wie er ~ bemerkte** as he so astutely remarked

Schär|fung ['ʃɛrfʊŋ] F **-**, *no pl* (*lit, fig*) sharpening

Scha|ria [ʃa'riːa] F **-**, *no pl* (= *islamische Rechtsordnung*) sharia

Schar|lach ['ʃarlax] M **-s**, *no pl* **a** (*Farbe*) scarlet **b** (= *Scharlachfieber*) scarlet fever

Schar|lach-: schar|lach|far|ben [-farbn] ADJ scarlet; **Schar|lach|fie|ber** NT scarlet fever; **schar|lach|rot** ADJ scarlet (red)

Schar|la|tan ['ʃarlatan] M **-s, -e** charlatan; (= *Arzt auch*) quack

Schar|la|ta|ne|rie [ʃarlatanə'riː] F **-, -n** [-'riːən] charlatanism

Schar|müt|zel [ʃa:r'mʏtsl] NT **-s, -** skirmish, brush with the enemy

Schar|nier [ʃar'niːɐ] NT **-s, -e**, **Schar|nier|ge|lenk** NT hinge

Schär|pe ['ʃɛrpə] F **-, -n** sash

schar|ren ['ʃarən] VTI to scrape; (*Pferd, Hund*) to paw; (*Huhn*) to scratch; (= *verscharren*) to bury (hurriedly); **mit dem Huf ~** to paw the ground; **mit den Füßen ~** to shuffle one's feet

Schar|te ['ʃartə] F **-, -n** nick; (*in Bergkamm*) wind gap; (= *Schießscharte*) embrasure; (*in Kampfwagen*) gun-port; **eine ~ auswetzen** (*fig*) to make amends, to patch things up

Schar|te|ke [ʃar'teːkə] F **-, -n** (*pej*) (old) hag; (= *Buch*) tattered old volume

schar|tig ['ʃartɪç] ADJ jagged, notched

schar|wen|zeln [ʃar'vɛntsln] *ptp* **scharwenzelt** VI *aux sein* or *haben* (*inf*) to dance attendance (*um* upon)

Schasch|lik ['ʃaʃlɪk] NT **-s, -s** (shish) kebab

schas|sen ['ʃasn] VT (*inf*) to chuck out (*inf*), to boot out (*inf*)

Schat|ten ['ʃatn] M **-s, -** (*lit, fig*) shadow; (= *schattige Stelle*) shade; (= *Geist*) shade; **im ~ sitzen** to sit in the shade; **40 Grad im ~** 40 degrees in the shade; ~ **geben** or **spenden** to give or provide shade; ~ **spendend** (*Baum, Dach*) shady; **einen ~ auf etw** (*acc*) **werfen** (*lit*) to cast a shadow on sth; (*fig*) to cast a shadow or cloud (up)on sth; **aus dem ~ (ans Licht) treten** (*lit, fig*) to come out of the shadows; **große Ereignisse werfen ihre ~ voraus** great events are often foreshadowed; **in jds ~** (*dat*) **stehen** (*fig*) to stand or be in sb's shadow; **im ~ bleiben** (*fig*) to remain in the background or shadows; **jdn/etw in den ~ stellen** (*fig*) to put sb/sth in the shade, to overshadow or eclipse sb/sth; **jdm wie ein ~ folgen** (*fig*) to follow sb like a shadow; **man kann nicht über seinen eigenen ~ springen** (*fig*) the leopard cannot change his spots (*prov*); **sich vor seinem eigenen ~ fürchten** (*fig*) to be afraid of one's own shadow; **nur noch ein ~ (seiner selbst) sein** to be (only) a shadow of one's former self; **die ~ des Todes/der Nacht** (*liter*) the shades of death/night (*liter*); **Reich der ~** (*liter*) realm of shades (*liter*); **es fiel nicht der leiseste ~ des Verdachts auf ihn** not a shadow of suspicion fell on him;

nicht der ~ eines Beweises not the slightest proof; ~ **unter den Augen** shadows under the eyes; **du hast ja einen ~** (*sl*) you must be nuts (*inf*) → **Licht a**

Schat|ten-: Schat|ten|bild NT silhouette; (*in Schattenspiel*) shadow picture, shadow(graph); **Schat|ten|bo|xen** NT shadow-boxing; **Schat|ten|da|sein** NT shadowy existence; **Schat|ten|druck** M *pl* **-drucke** (*Comput*) shadow printing; **schat|ten|haft** ADJ shadowy, shadow-like; (*fig*: = *vage*) shadowy, fuzzy, vague ADV **sehen, erkennen** vaguely; **sichtbar** barely; **im Dunkeln zeichneten sich die Umrisse nur ~ ab** the silhouettes were shadowy in the dark; **Schat|ten|ka|bi|nett** NT (*Pol*) shadow cabinet; **schat|ten|los** ADJ shadowless; **Schat|ten|mo|rel|le** [-mɔrɛlə] F **-, -n** morello cherry; **Schat|ten|par|ker** [-parkɐ] M (*sl: Schimpfwort*) tosser (*sl*); **schat|ten|reich** ADJ shady; **Schat|ten|reich** NT (*liter*) realm of shadows (*liter*) or shades (*liter*); **Schat|ten|riss** ▲ M silhouette; **Schat|ten|sei|te** F ▲ shady side; (*von Planeten*) dark side; (*fig*: = *Nachteil*) drawback, disadvantage; **die ~(n) des Lebens** the dark side of life, life's dark side; (*in Milieu, Slums etc*) the seamy side of life; **schat|ten|spen|dend** △ ADJ *attr* → **Schatten**; **Schat|ten|spiel** NT shadow play or show; (*Art*) contrast, shadow play; **Schat|ten|the|a|ter** NT shadow theatre (*Brit*) or theater (*US*); **Schat|ten|wirt|schaft** F black economy

schat|tie|ren [ʃa'tiːrən] *ptp* **schattiert** VT to shade

Schat|tie|rung F **-, -en** (*lit, fig*) shade; (= *das Schattieren*) shading; **aller politischen ~en** of every political shade; **in allen ~en** (*fig*) of every shade

schat|tig ['ʃatɪç] ADJ shady

Scha|tul|le [ʃa'tʊlə] F **-, -n** casket; (= *Geldschatulle*) coffer; (*pej inf*) bag (*inf*)

Schatz [ʃats] M **-es, -̈e** ['ʃɛtsə] (*lit, fig*) treasure; **Schätze** *pl* (= *Bodenschätze*) natural resources *pl*; (= *Reichtum*) riches *pl*, wealth *sing*; **nach Schätzen graben** to dig for (buried) treasure; **du bist ein ~!** (*inf*) you're a (real) treasure or gem!; **für alle Schätze der Welt** (*fig*) for all the money in the world, for all the tea in China **b** (= *Liebling*) sweetheart; (*als Anrede*) sweetheart, darling

Schatz-: Schatz|amt NT Treasury; **Schatz|an|wei|sung** F treasury bond

schätz|bar ADJ assessable; **gut/schlecht/schwer ~** easy/hard/difficult to assess or estimate

Schätz|chen ['ʃɛtsçən] NT **-s, -** darling

schät|zen ['ʃɛtsn] ✪ 40.4 **VT a** (= *veranschlagen*) to estimate, to assess (*auf +acc* at); *Wertgegenstand, Gemälde etc* to value, to appraise; (= *annehmen*) to reckon, to think; **die Besucherzahl wurde auf 500.000 geschätzt** the number of visitors was estimated at or to be 500,000; **wie alt ~ Sie mich denn?** how old do you reckon I am then?, how old would you say I am, then?; **was schätzt du, wie lange/wie viele/wie alt ...?** how long/how many/how old do you reckon or would you say ...?; **was/wie viel schätzt du denn?** what/how much do you reckon it is?, what/how much would you say it was?; **ich hätte sie älter geschätzt** I'd have said or thought she was older, I'd have thought her older (*esp Brit*) → **hoch 2 d**

b (= *würdigen*) to regard highly, to value; **jdn ~** to think highly of sb, to hold sb in high regard or esteem; **mein geschätzter Kollege** (*form*) my esteemed colleague (*form*); **etw besonders ~** to hold sth in very high esteem; **etw zu ~ wissen** to appreciate sth; **das schätzt er (überhaupt) nicht** he doesn't care for or appreciate that (at all); **sich glücklich ~** to consider or deem (*form*) oneself lucky

VI (= *veranschlagen, raten*) to guess; **schätz mal** have a guess

schät|zen ler|nen ▲ VT to come to appreciate or value

schät|zens|wert ADJ estimable

Schät|zer M **-s**, **-**, **Schät|ze|rin** [-ərɪn] F **-**, **-nen** valuer; (*Insur*) assessor

Schatz-: **Schatz|fund** M find (*of treasure*), treasure-trove (*Jur*); **Schatz|grä|ber** [-grɛ:bɐ] M **-s**, **-**, **Schatz|grä|be|rin** [-ərɪn] F **-**, **-nen** treasure hunter; **Schatz|kam|mer** F treasure chamber *or* vault; **Schatz|kanz|ler(in)** M(F) (*Pol*) minister of finance, Chancellor of the Exchequer (*Brit*), Secretary of the Treasury (*US*); **Schatz|käst|chen** NT , **Schatz|käst|lein** [-kestlaɪn] NT **-s**, **-** casket, (small) treasure chest; (*fig: als Buchtitel etc*) treasury; **Schatz|meis|ter(in)** M(F) treasurer; **Schatz|ob|li|ga|ti|on** F (*Fin*) treasury bond

Schätz|preis M valuation price

Schatz-: **Schatz|schein** M (*Fin*) treasury note; **Schatz|su|che** F treasure hunt(ing); **auf ~ gehen** to go on a treasure hunt, to go treasure hunting

Schät|zung [ˈʃɛtsʊŋ] F **-**, **-en** estimate; (= *das Schätzen*) estimation; (*von Wertgegenstand*) valuation, appraisal; **nach meiner ~ ...** I reckon that ...; (= *ungefähr*) approximately, roughly

schät|zungs|wei|se ADV (= *so vermutet man*) it is estimated *or* thought; (= *ungefähr*) approximately, roughly; (= *so schätze ich*) I think, I reckon; **die Inflationsrate wird sich ~ verdoppeln** it is thought *or* estimated (that) the rate of inflation will double; **es werden ~ 3.000 Zuschauer kommen** an estimated 3,000 spectators will come; **das wird ~ länger dauern** I think *or* reckon (that) that'll take longer; **wann wirst du ~ kommen?** when do you think *or* reckon you'll come?

Schatz|wech|sel M (*Fin*) Treasury bill

Schätz|wert M estimated value

Schau [ʃau] F **-**, **-en** **a** (= *Vorführung*) show; (= *Ausstellung*) show, display, exhibition; **etw zur ~ stellen** (= *ausstellen*) to put sth on show, to display *or* exhibit *or* show sth; (*fig*) to make a show of sth; (= *protzen mit*) to show off sth; **zur ~ gestellter Wohlstand** display of wealth; **sich zur ~ stellen** to make a spectacle *or* exhibition of oneself; **etw zur ~ tragen** to display sth

b (*inf*) **eine ~ abziehen** to put on a display *or* show; (= *Theater machen*) to make a big show (*inf*); **das war eine ~!** that was really great *or* fantastic (*inf*); **das ist nur ~** it's only show; **er macht nur (eine) ~** he's (only) putting it on; **jdm die ~ stehlen** *or* **klauen** to steal the show from sb

Schau-: **Schau|bild** NT diagram; (= *Kurve*) graph; **Schau|bu|de** F (show) booth; **Schau|büh|ne** F (*old*) theatre (*Brit*), theater (*US*); (*fig*) stage, scene

Schau|der [ˈʃaudɐ] M **-s**, **-** shudder; (*vor Angst, Kälte auch*) shiver; **~ erregend** terrifying, fearsome, horrifying; (*Vorstellung, Vision, Geschichte auch*) hair-raising; **jdm einen ~ über den Rücken jagen** to send a shudder/shiver down sb's spine; **ein ~ lief mir über den Rücken** a shudder/shiver ran down my spine

schau|der-: **schau|der|er|regend** △ ADJ → **Schauder**; **schau|der|haft** ADJ (*lit*) horrible, ghastly, terrible; (*fig inf*) terrible, dreadful, awful ADV **verstümmeln** gruesomely; (*fig inf*) horribly, awfully; **er spricht ~ schlecht Italienisch** his Italian is terrible

schau|dern [ˈʃaudɐn] VI (*vor Grauen, Abscheu*) to shudder; (*vor Kälte, Angst auch*) to shiver; (*vor Ehrfurcht*) to tremble, to quiver; **mich schauderte bei dem Anblick/Gedanken** I shuddered/shivered/trembled *or* quivered at the sight/thought (of it); **ihr schaudert vor ihm** he makes her shudder/shiver; **mit Schaudern** with a shudder

schau|en [ˈʃauən] VI (*esp dial*) to look; **verärgert/traurig** etc **~** to look angry/sad etc; **auf etw** (*acc*) **~** to look at sth; **um sich ~** to look around (one); **die Sonne schaut durch die Wolken** the sun is peeping *or* shining through the clouds *or* from behind the clouds; **jdm (fest) in die Augen ~** to look sb (straight) in the eye; **jdm verliebt in die Augen ~** to gaze adoringly into sb's eyes; **ihm schaut der Ärger/Zorn/Schrecken aus den Augen** annoyance/anger/fright is written all over his face; **nach jdm/etw ~** (= *suchen*) to look for sb/sth; (= *sich kümmern um*) to look after sb/sth; **da schaust du aber!** there, see!, there you are!; **schau, schau!** (*inf*) well, well!, what do you know! (*inf*), how about that! (*inf*); **schau, dass du ...** see *or* mind (that) you ...
◆ VT (*geh*) to see, to behold (*old, liter*); (= *erkennen*) to see; **Gott ~** to see God

Schau|er [ˈʃauɐ] M **-s**, **-** **a** (= *Regenschauer*) shower **b** = **Schauder**

Schau|er|ge|schich|te F horror story; (*Liter*) gothic tale *or* story; (*inf: = Lügengeschichte*) horror story

Schau|er|leu|te pl von **Schauermann**

schau|er|lich [ˈʃauɐlɪç] ADJ **a** horrific, horrible; *Schrei* bloodcurdling, spine-chilling; (= *gruselig*) eerie, creepy (*inf*) **b** (*inf: = fürchterlich*) terrible, dreadful, awful ADV *entstellt, verstümmelt* horribly; (*fig inf auch*) dreadfully; **sie spricht ~ schlecht Englisch** her English is terrible

Schau|er-: **Schau|er|mann** M pl **-leute** docker, longshoreman (*US*); **Schau|er|mär|chen** NT (*inf*) horror story

schau|ern [ˈʃauɐn] VI impers **es schauert** it's just a shower VI = **schaudern**

Schau|er|ro|man M (*lit, fig inf*) horror story; (*Liter auch*) Gothic novel

Schau|fel [ˈʃaufl] F **-**, **-n** shovel; (*kleiner. für Mehl, Zucker*) scoop; (= *Kehrichtschaufel*) dustpan; (*von Bagger*) scoop; (*von Schaufelrad*) paddle; (*von Wasserrad, Turbine*) vane; (= *Geweihschaufel*) palm; (*Hunt: von Auerhahn*) fan; **zwei ~n (voll) Sand/Kies** two shovel(ful)s of sand/gravel

Schäu|fe|le [ˈʃɔyfələ] NT **-s**, **-** (*S Ger Cook*) cured shoulder of pork; (*gebraten*) roast shoulder of pork

schau|fel|för|mig ADJ shaped like a shovel, shovel-shaped

schau|feln [ˈʃaufln] VTI to shovel; *Grab, Grube* to dig → **Grab**

Schau|fel-: **Schau|fel|rad** NT (*von Dampfer*) paddle wheel; (*von Turbine*) vane wheel, impeller; (*von Bagger*) bucket wheel; **Schau|fel|rad|damp|fer** M paddle steamer; **schau|fel|wei|se** ADV in shovelfuls

Schau|fens|ter NT display window; (*von Geschäft auch*) shop window; (*fig*) shop window

Schau|fens|ter-: **Schau|fens|ter|aus|la|ge** F window display; **Schau|fens|ter|bum|mel** M window-shopping expedition; **einen ~ machen** to go window-shopping; **Schau|fens|ter|de|ko|ra|teur(in)** M(F) window-dresser; **Schau|fens|ter|de|ko|ra|ti|on** F (= *Dekoration*) window decorations pl; (= *das Dekorieren*) window dressing; **Schau|fens|ter|front** F shop front, storefront (*US*); **Schau|fens|ter|ge|stal|tung** F window-dressing; **Schau|fens|ter|krank|heit** F intermittent claudication; **Schau|fens|ter|pup|pe** F display dummy, mannequin

Schau-: **Schau|flie|gen** NT **-s**, no pl stunt flying; (*Veranstaltung*) air display; **Schau|flug** M stunt flight; **Schau|ge|schäft** NT show business; **Schau|kampf** M exhibition bout *or* fight; **Schau|kas|ten** M showcase

Schau|kel [ˈʃaukl] F **-**, **-n** swing

schau|ke|lig [ˈʃaukəlɪç] ADJ *Brücke* swaying attr; *Überfahrt* rough; *Auto, Fahrt* bouncy; **ein ~es Boot** a boat which rocks

schau|keln [ˈʃaukln] VI **a** (*mit Schaukel*) to swing; (*im Schaukelstuhl*) to rock; **die Kinder wollen ~** the children want to play on the swings; **auf** *or* **mit dem Stuhl ~** to swing *or* rock back and forth in one's chair, to tip one's chair back and forth

b (= *sich hin und her bewegen*) to swing *or* sway (to and fro *or* back and forth); (= *sich auf und ab bewegen*) to rock up and down; (*Fahrzeug*) to bounce (up and down); (*Schiff*) to rock, to pitch and toss; (*Aktienkurse*) to go up and down, to fluctuate

c *aux sein* (= *sich schaukelnd bewegen: Schiff*) to pitch and toss; (= *gemütlich fahren*) to jog along ◆ VT to rock; **jdn durch die Gegend ~** (*inf*) to take sb for a spin round the place (*inf*); **wir werden das Kind** *or* **die Sache** *or* **das schon ~** (*inf*) we'll manage it

◆ VI impers **bei der Überfahrt hat es geschaukelt** the boat pitched and tossed on the way over; **im Auto hat es geschaukelt** it was a bouncy ride

Schau|kel-: **Schau|kel|pferd** NT rocking horse; **Schau|kel|po|li|tik** F seesaw(ing) policy; **Schau|kel|stuhl** M rocking chair

schauk|lig [ˈʃauklɪç] ADJ = **schaukelig**

Schau-: **Schau|lau|fen** NT **-s**, no pl exhibition skating; (*Veranstaltung*) skating display; **schau|lus|tig** ADJ curious; **Schau|lus|ti|ge** [-lʊstɪgə] PL decl as adj (curious) onlookers pl, rubbernecks pl (*US inf*)

Schaum [ʃaum] M **-s**, **Schäume** [ˈʃɔymə] foam, froth; (= *Seifenschaum, Shampooschaum*) lather; (*von Waschmittel*) suds pl; (*zum Feuerlöschen*) foam; (*Cook, auf Speisen, Getränken*) froth; (*auf Marmelade, Flüssen, Sümpfen*) scum; (*von Bier*) head, froth; **~ vor dem Mund haben** (*lit, fig*) to froth *or* foam at the mouth; **etw zu ~ schlagen** (*Cook*) to beat *or* whip sth until frothy; **~ schlagen** (*fig inf*) to be all hot air

Schaum-: **Schaum|bad** NT bubble *or* foam bath; **Schaum|bla|se** F bubble

schäu|men [ˈʃɔymən] VI to foam, to froth; (*Seife, Shampoo, Waschmittel*) to lather (up); (*Limonade, Wein*) to bubble; (*inf: = wütend sein*) to foam at the mouth; **das Waschmittel schäumt stark/schwach** it's a high-lather/low-lather detergent; **vor Wut ~** to be foaming at the mouth ◆ VT **Kunststoff ~** to produce foam synthetics

Schaum-: **Schaum|fes|ti|ger** M mousse; **Schaum|feu|er|lö|scher** M foam fire-extinguisher; **Schaum|gum|mi** NT OR M foam rubber

schau|mig [ˈʃaumɪç] ADJ foamy, frothy; *Seife, Shampoo* lathery; *Waschmittel* lathery, sudsy; *Speise, Getränk, Bier* frothy; *Marmelade, Fluss, Sumpf* scummy; **ein Ei ~ schlagen** to beat an egg until frothy

Schaum-: **Schaum|kel|le** F skimmer; **Schaum|kro|ne** F whitecap, white crest *or* horse; **Schaum|löf|fel** M skimmer; **Schaum|lö|scher** M , **Schaum|lösch|ge|rät** NT foam extinguisher

Schäum|mit|tel NT foaming agent

Schaum-: **Schaum|rei|ni|ger** M foam cleaner; **Schaum|schlä|ger(in)** M(F) (*fig inf*) hot-air merchant (*Brit inf*), person full of hot air (*inf*); **Schaum|schlä|ge|rei** F (*fig inf*) hot air (*inf*); **Schaum|stoff** M foam material; **Schaum|tö|nung** F colour (*Brit*) *or* color (*US*) mousse; **Schaum|wein** M sparkling wine

Schau-: **Schau|platz** M scene; **vom ~ berichten** to give an on-the-spot report; **am ~ sein** to be on *or* at the scene *or* on the spot; **auf dem ~ erscheinen** to appear on the scene; **vom ~ (der Politik) abtreten** to leave the (political) scene *or* arena; **Schau|pro|zess** ▲ M show trial

schau|rig [ˈʃaurɪç] ADJ gruesome; *Schrei* spine-chilling, bloodcurdling; (*inf: = sehr schlecht*) dreadful, abysmal (*inf*); awful ADV (*inf*) terribly, dreadfully; **er spricht ~ schlecht Japanisch** his Japanese is terrible

schau|rig-schön ADJ gruesomely beautiful; (= *unheimlich*) eerily beautiful

Schau|spiel NT **a** (*Theat*) (= *Stück*) drama, play; (= *Theater*) **Leipziger ~** Leipzig Playhouse

ⓑ (*fig*) spectacle; **wir wollen doch den Leuten kein ~ bieten** or **geben** let's not make a spectacle of ourselves

Schau|spieler M actor, player; (*fig*) (play-)actor

Schau|spie|le|rei F acting; (*fig*: = *Verstellung*) play-acting

Schau|spie|le|rin F (*lit*) actress; (*fig*) (play-)actress

schau|spie|le|risch ADJ acting *attr*; Talent for acting; **eine überzeugende ~e Leistung** a convincing piece of acting ADV as regards acting, as far as (the) acting is/was concerned

schau|spie|lern ['ʃauʃpiːlɐn] VI *insep* to act; (*fig*) to (play-)act

Schauspiel-: Schau|spiel|haus NT playhouse, theatre (*Brit*), theater (*US*); **Schau|spiel|kunst** F dramatic art, drama; (*in Bezug auf Schauspieler*) acting; **Schau|spiel|schu|le** F drama school; **Schau|spiel|schü|ler(in)** M(F) drama student; **Schau|spiel|un|ter|richt** M acting or drama lessons *pl* or classes *pl*

Schau-: Schau|stel|ler ['ʃauʃtɛlɐ] M -s, -, **Schau|stel|le|rin** [-ərɪn] F -, -nen showman; **Schau|stück** NT showpiece; **Schau|ta|fel** F (*zur Information*) (notice) board; (= *Schaubild*) diagram; **Schau|tanz** M exhibition dance; **Schau|tur|nen** NT gymnastic display

Scheck [ʃɛk] M -s, -s or (*rare*) -e cheque (*Brit*), check (*US*); **mit (einem)** or **per ~ bezahlen** to pay by cheque (*Brit*) or check (*US*); **ein ~ auf** or **über EUR 200** a cheque (*Brit*) or check (*US*) for 200 euros

Scheck-: Scheck|be|trug M cheque (*Brit*) or check (*US*) fraud; **Scheck|be|trü|ger(in)** M(F) cheque (*Brit*) or check (*US*) fraud; **Scheck|buch** NT chequebook (*Brit*), checkbook (*US*)

Sche|cke ['ʃɛka] M -n, -n or f -, -n (= *Pferd*) dappled horse/pony; (= *Rind*) spotted ox/bull/cow

Scheck-: Scheck|fäl|schung F cheque (*Brit*) or check (*US*) forgery; **Scheck|heft** NT chequebook (*Brit*), checkbook (*US*)

sche|ckig ['ʃɛkɪç] ADJ spotted; Pferd dappled; (*inf*) (= *kunterbunt*) gaudy; (= *verfärbt*) blotchy, patchy; **sich ~ lachen** (*inf*) to laugh oneself silly (*inf*)

Scheck-: Scheck|kar|te F cheque card (*Brit*), check card (*US*), banker's card; **Scheck|ver|kehr** M cheque (*Brit*) or check (*US*) transactions *pl*

scheel [ʃeːl] ADJ ⓐ (*old*: = *schielend*) cross-eyed ⓑ (= *missgünstig*) envious, jealous; (= *abschätzig*) disparaging; **ein ~er Blick** a dirty look ADV **jdn ~ ansehen** to give sb a dirty look; (= *abschätzig*) to look askance at sb

Schef|fel ['ʃɛfl] M -s, - (= *Gefäß, Hohlmaß*) ≈ bushel, (= *Flächenmaß*) area between 12 and 42 acres; **sein Licht unter den ~ stellen** (*inf*) to hide one's light under a bushel

schef|feln ['ʃɛfln] VT Geld to rake in (*inf*); Gold, Orden to pile up, to accumulate VI **er scheffelt seit Jahren** he's been raking it in for years (*inf*)

schef|fel|wei|se ADV in large quantities, by the sackful; **~ Geld verdienen** to be raking it in (*inf*)

scheib|chen|wei|se ['ʃaipçənvaizə] ADV (*fig*) bit by bit, little by little, a bit or little at a time

Schei|be ['ʃaiba] F -, -n ⓐ disc (*esp Brit*), disk; (= *Schießscheibe*) target; (*Eishockey*) puck; (= *Wählscheibe*) dial; (*Tech*) (= *Unterlegscheibe, Dichtungsscheibe*) washer; (= *Kupplungsscheibe, Bremsscheibe*) disc (*esp Brit*), disk; (= *Töpferscheibe*) wheel; (*inf*: = *Schallplatte*) disc (*esp Brit inf*), disk ⓑ (= *abgeschnittene Scheibe*) slice; (= *Längsscheibe: von Orange etc*) segment; **etw in ~n schneiden** to slice sth (up), to cut sth into slices; **von ihm könntest du dir eine ~ abschneiden** (*fig inf*) you could take a leaf out of his book (*inf*)

ⓒ (= *Glasscheibe*) (window)pane; (= *Fenster, auch von Auto*) window; (*inf*: = *Windschutzscheibe*) windscreen (*Brit*), windshield (*US*); (= *Spiegelscheibe*) glass ⓓ (*euph inf*) **~!** sugar! (*euph inf*)

Scheiben-: Schei|ben|brem|se F disc (*esp Brit*) or disk brake; **Schei|ben|ho|nig** M comb honey; **~!** (*euph inf*) sugar! (*euph inf*); **Schei|ben|kleis|ter** INTERJ (*euph inf*) sugar! (*euph inf*); **Schei|ben|kupp|lung** F disc (*esp Brit*) or disk or plate clutch; **Schei|ben|schie|ßen** NT -s, *no pl* target shooting; **Schei|ben|wasch|an|la|ge** F windscreen (*Brit*) or windshield (*US*) washers *pl*; **schei|ben|wei|se** ['ʃaibnvaizə] ADV in slices; **Schei|ben|wi|scher** M windscreen (*Brit*) or windshield (*US*) wiper; **Schei|ben|wi|scher|blatt** NT windscreen (*Brit*) or windshield (*US*) wiper blade

Scheich [ʃaiç] M -s, -e sheik(h); (*inf*) bloke (*Brit inf*), guy (*inf*)

Scheich|tum ['ʃaiçtuːm] NT -s, -e, Scheichtümer [-tyːmə] sheik(h)dom

Schei|de ['ʃaidə] F -, -n ⓐ sheath; (*von Schwert*) sheath, scabbard; (= *Vagina*) vagina; **das Schwert aus der ~ ziehen** to unsheathe or draw one's sword; **das Schwert in die ~ stecken** to put up or sheathe one's sword ⓑ (*obs, fig*: = *Grenze*) border

Scheide-: Schei|de|an|stalt F separating works *sing* or *pl*; **Schei|de|li|nie** F (*lit*) border(line); (*fig*) dividing line; **Schei|de|mit|tel** NT (*Chem*) separating agent

schei|den ['ʃaidn] *pret* **schied** [ʃiːt], *ptp* **geschieden** [gə'ʃiːdn] VT ⓐ (= *auflösen*) Ehe to dissolve; Eheleute to divorce; **sich ~ lassen** to get divorced, to get a divorce; **er will sich von ihr ~ lassen** he wants to divorce her or to get a divorce (from her); **er lässt sich nicht von ihr ~** he won't give her a divorce → *auch* **geschieden** ⓑ (*geh*: = *trennen*) to separate; (*Chem*) to separate (out) → **Geist c** VI *aux sein* (*liter*) (= *sich trennen*) to part; (= *weggehen*) to depart; **aus dem Dienst/Amt ~** to retire from service/office; **aus dem Leben ~** to depart this life; **Scheiden tut weh** (*Prov*) parting is such sweet sorrow (*Prov*) VR (*Wege*) to divide, to part, to separate; (*Meinungen*) to diverge, to part company

Scheiden-: Schei|den|ab|strich M vaginal smear (*esp Brit*), Pap smear; **Schei|den|krampf** M vaginal cramp, vaginismus (*form*); **Schei|den|vor|fall** M prolapse of the vagina

Scheide-: Schei|de|wand F partition; (*von Nase, Herz*) septum (*spec*); (*fig*) barrier; **Schei|de|was|ser** NT *pl* **-wässer** (*Chem*) nitric acid, aqua fortis; **Schei|de|weg** M (*fig*) crossroads *sing*; **am ~ stehen** to be at a crossroads

Schei|dung ['ʃaidʊŋ] F -, -en ⓐ (= *das Scheiden*) separation ⓑ (= *Ehescheidung*) divorce; **die ~ dieser Ehe** the dissolution of this marriage; **in ~ leben** or **liegen** to be in the middle of divorce proceedings, to be getting a divorce; **die ~ einreichen** to file a petition for divorce

Scheidungs-: Schei|dungs|grund M grounds *pl* for divorce; (*hum*: *Mensch*) reason for his/her *etc* divorce; **Schei|dungs|kla|ge** F petition for divorce; **Schei|dungs|pro|zess** ▲ M divorce proceedings *pl*; **Schei|dungs|recht** NT divorce law(s *pl*); **Schei|dungs|rich|ter(in)** M(F) divorce judge; **Schei|dungs|ur|kun|de** F divorce certificate; **Schei|dungs|ur|teil** NT decree of divorce; **Schei|dungs|wai|se** F (*inf*) child of divorced parents

Schein¹ [ʃain] M -s, *no pl* ⓐ (= *Licht*) light; (*matt*) glow; (*von Gold, Schwert etc*) gleam, glint; **einen (hellen) ~ auf etw** (*acc*) **werfen** to shine (brightly) on sth, to cast a (bright) light on sth ⓑ (= *Anschein*) appearances *pl*; (= *Vortäuschung*) pretence, sham; **~ und Sein/Wirklichkeit** appearance and reality; **das ist mehr ~ als Sein** it's all (on the) surface; **der ~ trügt** or **täuscht**

appearances are deceptive; **dem ~ nach** on the face of it, to all appearances; **den ~ wahren** to keep up appearances; **etw nur zum ~ tun** only to pretend to do sth, to make only a pretence or a show of doing sth

Schein² M -s, -e (= *Geldschein*) note, bill (*US*); (= *Bescheinigung*) certificate; (*Univ*) credit; (= *Fahrschein*) ticket; **~e machen** (*Univ*) to get credits

Schein-: Schein|an|griff M feint (attack); **Schein|asy|lant(in)** M(F) bogus asylum-seeker; **schein|bar** ADJ apparent, seeming *attr*; (= *vorgegeben*) feigned, ostensible ADV apparently, seemingly; **er hörte ~ interessiert zu** he listened with apparent or seeming/feigned interest; **Schein|blü|te** F illusory flowering; (*Econ*) illusory boom; **Schein|da|sein** NT phantom existence; **Schein|ehe** F fictitious or sham marriage

schei|nen ['ʃainən] ☉ 33.2, 38.2, 39.2, 41, 53.4, 53.5 *pret* **schien** [ʃiːn], *ptp* **geschienen** [gə'ʃiːnən] VI ⓐ (= *leuchten*) to shine ⓑ *auch vi impers* (= *den Anschein geben*) to seem, to appear; **es scheint, dass .../als (ob) ...** it seems or appears that .../as if ...; **mir scheint, (dass) ...** it seems or appears to me that ...; **wie es scheint** as it seems, as it would appear, apparently; **es scheint nur so** it only seems or appears to be like that; **er kommt scheints nicht mehr** (*dial inf*) it would seem that he won't come now, seemingly he's not coming now; **du hast scheints vergessen, dass ...** (*dial inf*) you seem to have forgotten that ...

Schein-: Schein|fir|ma F dummy or fictitious firm; **Schein|frie|de** M phoney peace, peace in name only, semblance *no pl* of peace; **Schein|ge|fecht** NT mock or sham fight; **Schein|ge|schäft** NT bogus transaction; **Schein|grund** M spurious reason; (= *Vorwand*) pretext; **schein|hei|lig** ADJ hypocritical; (= *Arglosigkeit vortäuschend*) innocent ADV fragen, sagen, grinsen innocently; **~ tun** to be hypocritical; (= *Arglosigkeit vortäuschen*) to act innocent, to play or act the innocent; **Schein|hei|li|ge(r)** MF *decl as adj* hypocrite; (*Arglosigkeit vortäuschend*) sham; **Schein|hei|lig|keit** F hypocrisy; (= *vorgetäuschte Arglosigkeit*) feigned innocence; **Schein|hei|rat** F sham or bogus marriage; **Schein|hin|rich|tung** F mock execution; **Schein|schwan|ger|schaft** F false pregnancy; **Schein|selbst|stän|di|ge(r)** ▲ MF *decl as adj* person who has adopted freelance status so that his employer avoids paying social security contributions; **Schein|selbst|stän|dig|keit** ▲ F freelance status (*to avoid employer paying social security contributions*); **Schein|tod** M apparent death, suspended animation; **schein|tot** ADJ in a state of apparent death or of suspended animation; (*fig*) Mensch, Partei on one's/its last legs; **Schein|to|te(r)** MF *decl as adj* apparent corpse, apparently dead person; **Schein|welt** F illusory world

Schein|wer|fer M (*zum Beleuchten*) floodlight; (*im Theater*) spotlight; (= *Suchscheinwerfer*) searchlight; (*Aut*) (head)light, headlamp

Schein|wer|fer|licht NT floodlight(ing); (*im Theater*) spotlight; (*von Suchscheinwerfer*) searchlight (beam); (*Aut*) light or beam of the headlights or headlamps; (*fig*) limelight; **im ~ (der Öffentlichkeit) stehen** (*fig*) to be in the glare of publicity; **ein Problem ins ~ rücken** to spotlight or highlight a problem

Schein|wi|der|stand M sham resistance; (*Elec*) impedance, apparent resistance

Scheiß [ʃais] M -, *no pl* (*sl*) shit (*sl*), crap (*sl*); **ein ~ a load of shit** (*sl*) or crap (*sl*); **einen ~** (= *nichts*) fuck-all (*vulg*); **~ machen** (= *herumalbern*) to bugger about (*Brit sl*), to mess around (*inf*); (= *Fehler machen*) to make a balls-up (*Brit sl*), to screw up (*sl*); **mach keinen ~!** don't do anything so bloody (*Brit inf*) or damn (*inf*) silly; **red doch keinen ~!** don't talk crap! (*esp Brit* *inf*), cut (out) the crap! (*inf*); **was soll der ~?** what the hell's the matter with you/him *etc*? (*inf*)

Scheiß- in cpds (*inf*) **a** (= *verdammt*) damn(ed) (*inf*), bloody (*Brit inf*), fucking (*vulg*); **diese Scheißpolitiker!** those damn(ed) *etc* politicians! **b** (= *miserabel*) awful, crap(py) (*sl*), shitty (*sl*); **so ein Scheißwetter!** what awful *etc* weather!

Scheiß|dreck M (*vulg*: = *Kot*) shit (*sl*), crap (*sl*); (*sl* = *blödes Gerede, schlechtes Buch, schlechte Ware etc*) load of shit (*sl*); (= *unangenehme Sache, Arbeit*) effing thing (*sl*), bloody thing (*Brit inf*); (= *Angelegenheiten*) effing business (*sl*), bloody business (*Brit inf*); **~!** shit! (*sl*); **wegen jedem ~** about every effing (*sl*) or bloody (*Brit sl*) little thing; **das geht dich einen ~** it's none of your effing (*sl*) or bloody (*Brit inf*) business, it's got bugger all (*Brit inf*) or shit (*US vulg*) to do with you; **einen ~ werd ich tun!** like (bloody (*Brit inf*)) hell I will!; **sich einen ~ um jdn/etw kümmern** not to give a shit (*sl*) or a damn (*inf*) about sb/sth

Schei|ße F -, no pl (*vulg*: = *Kot*) shit (*sl*), crap (*sl*); (*inf*: = *unangenehme Lage*) mess (*sl*); (*inf*: = *Unsinn*) crap (*sl*); **(echt) ~ sein** (*inf*) to be bloody awful (*Brit inf*) or goddamn (*inf*) awful; (= *ärgerlich*) to be a bloody (*inf*) or goddamn (*inf*) nuisance; **das ist doch alles ~** (*inf*) it's all a bloody mess (*Brit inf*), it's all shit (*sl*); (= *Unsinn*) it's all a load of shit (*sl*); **in der ~ sitzen** (*inf*) to be in the shit (*sl*), to be up shit creek (*sl*); **~ bauen** (*inf*) to make a balls-up (*Brit sl*), to screw up (*sl*) → *auch* **Scheiß**

scheiß|egal [ˈʃaisʔeˈgaːl] ADJ (*inf*) **das ist mir doch ~!** I don't give a shit (*sl*) or a damn (*inf*)

schei|ßen [ˈʃaisn̩] pret **schiss** [ʃɪs], ptp **geschissen** [gəˈʃɪsn̩] VI (*vulg*) to shit (*sl*), to crap (*sl*); **auf jdn/etw** (*acc*) **~** (*fig sl*) not to give a shit about sb/sth (*sl*) VR (*vulg*) **sich** (*dat*) **vor Angst in die Hosen ~** to have or get the shits (*sl*), to shit oneself (*sl*)

Schei|ßer [ˈʃaisɐ] M -s, -, **Schei|ße|rin** [-ərɪn] F -, -nen (*sl*: = *Arschloch*) arsehole (*Brit sl*), asshole (*US sl*); (*inf*: *Kosename*) chubby cheeks *sing* (*hum inf*)

Schei|ße|rei [ʃaisəˈrai] F -, -en (*inf*) **die ~** the runs (*inf*), the shits (*sl*)

Schei|ße|ri|tis [ʃaisəˈriːtɪs] F -, no pl (*hum inf*) = **Scheißerei**

Scheiß-: scheiß|freund|lich [ˈʃaisˈfrɔyntlɪç] ADJ (*inf*) as nice as pie (*iro inf*); **Scheiß|haus** NT (*inf*) shithouse (*sl*); **Scheiß|kerl** M (*inf*) bastard (*sl*), sod (*Brit inf*), son of a bitch (*sl*), mother(fucker) (*US vulg*); **Scheiß|wut** F (*sl*) **eine ~ (auf jdn/etw) haben** to be mad as hell (with sb/sth) (*inf*)

Scheit [ʃait] M -(e)s, -e or (*Aus, Sw*) -er log, piece of wood

Schei|tel [ˈʃaitl̩] M -s, - **a** (= *Haarscheitel*) parting (*Brit*), part (*US*); (*liter*: = *Haupthaar*) locks pl; **vom ~ bis zur Sohle** (*fig*) through and through **b** (= *höchster Punkt*) vertex

schei|teln [ˈʃaitl̩n] VT to part

Scheitel-: Schei|tel|punkt M vertex; **Schei|tel|wert** M peak (value); **Schei|tel-win|kel** M vertical angle

schei|ten [ˈʃaitn̩] VT (*Sw*) Holz to chop

Schei|ter|hau|fen [ˈʃaitɐ-] M (funeral) pyre; (*Hist*: *zur Hinrichtung*) stake; **die Hexe wurde auf dem ~ verbrannt** the witch was burned at the stake

schei|tern [ˈʃaitɐn] VI aux sein **a** (an +dat because of) (*Mensch, Unternehmen, Versuch*) to fail; (*Plan, Vorhaben auch*) to fall through; (*Verhandlungen, Ehe*) to break down; (*Regierung*) to founder (an +dat on); (*Mannschaft*) to be defeated (an +dat by); **die Partei scheiterte an der Fünf-Prozent-Hürde** the party fell at the five-percent hurdle → **Existenz b** (*dated*: *Schiff*) to be wrecked

Schei|tern [ˈʃaitɐn] NT -s, no pl **a** (*von Menschen, Unternehmen*) failure; (*von Plan, Vorhaben auch*) falling through; (*von Verhandlungen, Ehe*) breakdown; (*von Regierung*) foundering; (*von Mannschaft*) defeat; **das war zum ~ verurteilt** that was doomed to failure; **etw zum ~ bringen** to make sth fail/fall through/break down **b** (*von Schiff*) wrecking

Scheit|holz NT firewood

Schelf [ʃɛlf] M OR NT -s, -e (*Geog*) (continental) shelf

Schelf|meer NT shelf sea

Schel|lack [ˈʃɛlak] M -(e)s, -e shellac

Schel|le [ˈʃɛlə] F -, -n **a** bell; (*dial*: = *Klingel*) (door)bell **b** (*Tech*) clamp **c** (= *Handschelle*) handcuff **d** (*dial*) = **Ohrfeige e** **Schellen** PL (*Cards*) ≈ diamonds *sing or pl* (*shaped like bells on traditional German cards*)

schel|len [ˈʃɛlən] VI to ring (*nach jdm for sb*); **es hat geschellt** the bell has gone; **bei jdm** or **an jds Tür** (*dat*) **~** to ring at sb's door

Schel|len-: Schel|len|baum M (*Mus*) Turkish crescent, pavillon chinois; **Schel|len|bu|be** M ≈ jack or knave (*Brit*) of diamonds; **Schel|len|ge|läut** NT , **Schel|len|ge|läu|te** NT jingling (*of bells*); **mit ~(e) fuhr der Pferdeschlit-ten vorbei** the sleigh passed by with its bells jingling; **Schel|len|kap|pe** F cap and bells, fool's cap; **Schel|len|kö|nig** M ≈ king of diamonds; **Schel|len|ober** M ≈ queen of diamonds (*a man on traditional German cards*); **Schel|len|un|ter** [-ʊntɐ] M -s, - ≈ jack or knave (*Brit*) of diamonds

Schell|fisch [ˈʃɛl-] M haddock

Schelm [ʃɛlm] M -(e)s, -e (*dated*: = *Spaßvogel*) joker, wag (*dated*); (*obs*: = *Gauner*) knave (*Brit obs*), scoundrel; (*Liter*) picaro; **den ~ im Nacken haben** to be up to mischief; **ein ~, der Böses dabei denkt** (*prov*) honi soit qui mal y pense (*prov*), evil to him who evil thinks (*prov*)

Schel|men-: Schel|men|ge|sicht NT mischievous face; **Schel|men|ro|man** M picaresque novel; **Schel|men|streich** M (*dated*) roguish prank, dirty trick; **Schel|men|stück** NT (*dated*) knavery (*esp Brit old*), trickery; (*obs*: = *Missetat*) villainous deed (*old*)

schel|misch [ˈʃɛlmɪʃ] ADJ Blick, Lächeln mischievous ADV mischievously

Schel|te [ˈʃɛltə] F -, -n scolding; (= *Kritik*) attack; **er hat ~ bekommen** he got a scolding

schel|ten [ˈʃɛltn̩] pret **schalt** [ʃalt], ptp **gescholten** [gəˈʃɔltn̩] VT to scold, to chide; **jdn einen Dummkopf ~** to call sb an idiot; **(als) faul gescholten werden** to be called lazy VI (= *schimpfen*) to curse; **über** or **auf jdn/etw ~** to curse sb/sth, to rail at sb/sth (*old*); **mit jdm ~** to scold sb

Schelt|wort NT pl -worte or -wörter word of abuse; **-e** words of abuse, invective *sing*

Sche|ma [ˈʃeːma] NT -s, **Schemen** or -ta [-mən, -ta] scheme; (= *Darstellung*) diagram; (= *Ordnung, Vorlage*) plan; (= *Muster*) pattern; (*Philos, Psych*) schema; **nach ~ F** in the same (old) way; **etw nach einem ~ machen** to do sth according to a pattern

sche|ma|tisch [ʃeˈmaːtɪʃ] ADJ schematic; (= *mechanisch*) mechanical ADV **etw ~ darstellen** to show sth schematically; **etw ~ umreißen** to give a general outline of sth; **~ vorgehen** to work methodically; **er arbeitet zu ~** he works too mechanically

sche|ma|ti|sie|ren [ʃemati'ziːrən] ptp **schematisiert** VTI to schematize

Sche|ma|tis|mus [ʃemaˈtɪsmʊs] M -, **Schematis-men** [-mən] schematism

Sche|mel [ˈʃeːml̩] M -s, - stool

Sche|men [ˈʃeːmən] M -s, - silhouette; (= *Gespenst*) spectre

sche|men|haft [ˈʃeːmən-] ADJ shadowy; *Erinnerungen* hazy ADV **etw ~ sehen/erkennen** to see/make out the outlines of sth; **etw ~ zeichnen** to sketch

sth; **die Bäume hoben sich ~ gegen den Himmel ab** the trees were silhouetted against the sky

Schen|ke [ˈʃɛŋkə] F -, -n tavern, inn

Schen|kel [ˈʃɛŋkl̩] M -s, - **a** (*Anat*) (= *Oberschenkel*) thigh; (= *Unterschenkel*) lower leg; **sich** (*dat*) **auf die ~ schlagen** to slap one's thighs; **dem Pferd die ~ geben** to press a horse on **b** (*von Zirkel*) leg; (*von Zange, Schere*) shank; (*Math: von Winkel*) side

Schen|kel-: Schen|kel|bruch M fracture of the thigh(bone) or femur; **Schen|kel|hals** M neck of the femur; **Schen|kel|hals|bruch** M fracture of the neck of the femur

schen|ken [ˈʃɛŋkn̩] VT **a** (= *Geschenk geben*) **jdm etw ~** to give sb sth or give sth to sb (as a present or gift); **sich** (*dat*) **(gegenseitig) etw ~** to give each other sth (as a present or gift); **etw geschenkt bekommen** to get sth as a present or gift; **etw zum Geburtstag/zu Weihnachten geschenkt bekommen** to get sth for one's birthday/for Christmas; **zu Weihnachten hat er nichts geschenkt bekommen** he didn't get anything or any presents for Christmas; **so was kaufe ich nicht, das lasse ich mir immer ~** I don't buy anything like that, I always like to get these things as presents; **ich möchte nichts geschenkt haben!** (*lit*) I don't want any presents!; (*fig*: = *bevorzugt werden*) I don't want any special treatment!; **ich nehme nichts geschenkt!** I'm not accepting any presents!; **das ist geschenkt!** (*inf*) (= *ist ein Geschenk*) it's a present; (= *nicht der Rede wert*) that's no great shakes (*inf*); (*sl*: = *nichts wert*) forget it! (*inf*); **das ist (fast or glatt) geschenkt!** (*inf*: = *billig*) that's dirt cheap (*inf*) or a giveaway (*inf*); **das möchte ich nicht mal geschenkt haben!** I wouldn't want it if it was given to me; **einem geschenkten Gaul sieht man nicht ins Maul** (*Prov*) don't look a gift horse in the mouth (*Prov*)

b (= *erlassen*) **jdm etw ~** to let sb off sth; **ihm ist nie etwas geschenkt worden** (*fig*) he never had it easy

c **sich** (*dat*) **etw ~** to skip sth (*inf*); **deine Komplimente kannst du dir ~!** you can keep your compliments (*inf*); **sich** (*dat*) **die Mühe ~** to save oneself the trouble; **er hat sich** (*dat*) **nichts geschenkt** he spared no pains; **die beiden haben sich nichts geschenkt** neither was giving anything away

d (*in Verbindung mit n siehe auch dort*) **jdm das Leben ~** (= *begnadigen*) to spare sb's life; **einem Kind das Leben ~** (*geh*) to give birth to a child; **jdm die Freiheit ~** to set sb free; **jdm seine Lie-be/seine Aufmerksamkeit** *etc* **~** to give sb one's love/one's attention *etc*; **jdm/einer Sache Glau-ben/keinen Glauben ~** to give credence/no credence to sb/sth; **jdm Vertrauen ~** to put one's trust in sb

VI to give presents

VR **sich jdm ~** (*liter: Frau*) to give oneself to sb

Schen|kung [ˈʃɛŋkʊŋ] F -, -en (*Jur*) gift

Schen|kungs-: Schen|kungs|steu|er F gift tax; **Schen|kungs|ur|kun|de** F deed of gift

schep|pern [ˈʃɛpɐn] VI (*dial*) to clatter; **es hat gescheppert** there was a clatter; (*loser Gegen-stand*) there was a rattle; (*Autounfall*) there was a bang; (*Ohrfeige*) he/she got a clip round (*Brit*) or a slap on (*US*) the ear

Scher [ʃeːɐ] M -(e)s, -e (*S Ger, Aus, Sw*) mole

Scher|be [ˈʃɛrbə] F -, -n fragment, (broken) piece; (= *Glasscherbe/Porzellanscherbe/Keramik-scherbe*) broken piece of glass/china/pottery; (*Archeol*) shard, potsherd; **etw in ~n schlagen** to shatter sth; **in ~n gehen** to break, to shatter; (*fig*) to fall or go to pieces; **~n machen** to break something; (*fig*) to put one's foot in it; **die ~n zusammenkehren** to sweep up the (broken) pieces; (*fig*) to pick up the pieces; **es hat ~n ge-geben** (*fig*) there was lots of trouble; (*bei Streit*) sparks flew; **die ~n unseres Glücks** the shattered remains of our happiness; **~n bringen Glück** (*Prov*) broken crockery brings you luck

Scherben ['ʃɛrbn] M **-s, -** (*S Ger, Aus*) = **Scherbe**

Scherben-: Scherben|gericht NT ostracism; **über jdn ein ~ abhalten** (*geh*) to take sb to task; **Scherben|hau|fen** M pile of smashed crockery; **wir stehen vor einem ~** (*fig*) it's all gone to pot (*inf*), it's all come to nothing; **er stand vor dem ~ seiner Ehe** he was faced with the ruins of his marriage; **einen ~ hinterlassen** (*fig*) to leave behind a complete mess

Sche|re ['ʃeːrə] F **-, -n** a (*Werkzeug*) (*klein*) scissors *pl*; (*groß*) shears *pl*; (= *Drahtschere*) wire-cutters *pl*; (*fig*: = *Kluft*) divide; **eine ~** a pair of scissors/shears/wire-cutters b (*Zool*) pincer; (*von Hummer, Krebs etc*) claw, pincer c (*Turnen, Ringen*) scissors *sing*

sche|ren[1] ['ʃeːrən] *pret* **schor** [ʃoːɐ], *ptp* **geschoren** [gə'ʃoːrən] VT to clip; *Schaf* to shear; (*Tech*) to shear; *Haare* to crop; *Bart* (= *rasieren*) to shave; (= *stutzen*) to trim; **er schor/sie hat seine/ihre Haare waren kurz geschoren** his hair was cropped short → **kahl scheren, Kamm** a

sche|ren[2] VTR (= *kümmern*) **sich nicht um jdn/ etw ~** not to care or bother about sb/sth; **was schert mich das?** what do I care (about that)?, what's that to me?; **er scherte sich nicht im Geringsten darum** he couldn't have cared less about it (*inf*) **über dich (weg)!** scram! (*inf*), beat it! (*inf*); **scher dich heim!** go home!; **scher dich ins Bett!** get to bed!; **es ist Zeit, dass du dich nach Hause scherst** it's time you were off (to (*US*)) home → **Teufel** b, **Kuckuck** c

Sche|ren-: Sche|ren|fern|rohr NT binocular periscope; **Sche|ren|git|ter** NT concertina barrier; **Sche|ren|schlag** M scissors kick; **Sche|ren|schlei|fer(in)** M(F) scissor(s) grinder, knife grinder; **Sche|ren|schnitt** M silhouette

Sche|re|rei [ʃeːrə'rai] F **-, -en** *usu pl* (*inf*) trouble *no pl*

Scher|ge ['ʃɛrgə] M **-n, -n** a (*geh*: = *Büttel*) thug b (*obs*: = *Häscher*) henchman

Scher|gen|dienst M dirty work

Scher-: Scher|kopf M shaving head; **Scher|maus** F (*Aus, S Ger*) vole; (*Sw*) mole; **Scher|mes|ser** NT shearing knife; **Scher|wind** M (*Met*) wind shear; **Scher|wol|le** F fleece

Scherz[1] [ʃɛrts] M **-es, -e** joke, jest; (= *Unfug*) tomfoolery *no pl*; **aus** or **zum ~** as a joke; **im ~** in jest; **einen ~ machen** to make a joke; (= *Streich*) to play a joke; **mach keine ~e!** (*inf*) you're joking!, you must be kidding! (*inf*); **mit so etwas macht man keine ~e** you don't joke or make jokes about things like that; **zu ~en aufgelegt sein** to be in a joking mood; **seine ~e über jdn/etw machen** to make or crack jokes about sb/sth; **seine ~e (mit jdm) treiben** to play jokes; **sich** (*dat*) **(mit jdm) einen (schlechten) ~ erlauben** to play a (dirty) trick (on sb); **... und solche ~e** (*inf*) ... and what have you (*inf*); **(ganz) ohne ~!** (*inf*) no kidding! (*inf*); **~ beiseite!** joking aside or apart!

Scherz[2] M **-es, -e**, **Scher|zel** ['ʃɛrtsl] NT **-s, -** (*Aus*) hunk of bread; (= *Endstück*) heel

Scherz|ar|ti|kel M *usu pl* joke (article)

Scherz|bold [-bɔlt] M **-(e)s, -e** (*inf*) joker (*inf*)

scher|zen ['ʃɛrtsn] VI (*old, geh*) to joke, to jest; (= *albern*) to banter; (= *nicht ernst nehmen*) to trifle (*mit* with); **mir scheint, du scherzt** you can't be serious; **ich scherze nicht** (*old, geh*) I'm not joking; **Sie belieben wohl zu ~!** (*old, geh*) surely you are in jest (*old, liter*), surely you're joking; **mit jdm/etw ist nicht zu ~** one can't trifle with sb/sth

Scherz-: Scherz|fra|ge F riddle; **Scherz|ge|dicht** NT humorous poem; **scherz|haft** ADJ jocular, jovial; *Angelegenheit* joking; (= *spaßig*) *Einfall* playful; ADV jokingly; **etw ~ sagen** to say

sth jokingly or as a joke or in jest; **etw ~ meinen** to mean sth as a joke; **etw ~ aufnehmen** to take sth as a joke; **Scherz|keks** M (*inf*) joker

Scher|zo ['skɛrtso] NT **-s, -s** or **Scherzi** [-tsi] scherzo

Scherz|wort NT *pl* **-worte** witticism, jocular or joking remark

sche|sen ['ʃeːzn] VI *aux sein* (*dial*) to rush

scheu [ʃɔy] ADJ (= *schüchtern*) shy; (= *ängstlich*) *Reh, Tier auch* timid; (= *zaghaft*) *Versuche, Worte* cautious; **jdn ~ machen** to make sb shy; (= *ängstigen*) to frighten or scare sb; **mach doch die Pferde** or **Gäule nicht ~** (*fig inf*) keep your hair on (*Brit*) or head (*US*) or shirt on (*inf*); **~ werden** (*Pferd*) to be frightened ADV shyly, timidly

Scheu [ʃɔy] F **-, no pl** fear (*vor* +*dat* of); (= *Schüchternheit*) shyness; (*von Reh, Tier*) shyness, timidity; (= *Hemmung*) inhibition; (= *Ehrfurcht*) awe; **seine ~ verlieren** to lose one's inhibitions; **ohne jede ~** without any inhibition; **sprechen** quite freely

scheu|chen ['ʃɔyçn] VT to shoo (away); (= *verscheuchen*) to frighten or scare away or off; (= *antreiben*) *Tiere* to drive; *Menschen* to shoo (along)

scheu|en ['ʃɔyən] VT *Kosten, Arbeit, Vergleich, Konflikt, Risiko* to shy away from; *Menschen, Licht* to shun; **weder Mühe noch Kosten ~** to spare neither trouble nor expense; **keine Mühe(n) ~** to go to endless trouble; **wir brauchen den Vergleich mit ihnen nicht zu ~** we don't have to be afraid of the comparison with them VR **sich vor etw** (*dat*) **~** (= *Angst haben*) to be afraid of sth; (= *zurückschrecken*) to shy away from sth; **sich (davor) ~, etw zu tun** (= *Angst haben*) to be afraid of doing sth; (= *zurückschrecken*) to shrink back from doing sth; **und ich scheue mich nicht, das zu sagen** and I'm not afraid of saying it VI (*Pferd etc*) to shy (*vor* +*dat* at)

Scheu|er ['ʃɔyɐ] F **-, -n** barn

Scheu|er-: Scheu|er|be|sen M scrubbing (*Brit*) or scrub (*US*) broom; **Scheu|er|bürs|te** F scrubbing (*Brit*) or scrub (*US*) brush; **Scheu|er|frau** F char (*Brit*), cleaning woman; **Scheu|er|lap|pen** M floorcloth; **Scheu|er|leis|te** F skirting board (*Brit*), baseboard (*US*); **Scheu|er|mit|tel** NT scouring agent

scheu|ern ['ʃɔyɐn] VTI a (= *putzen*) to scour; (*mit Bürste*) to scrub b (= *reiben*) to chafe; **der Rucksack scheuert mich am Rücken** the rucksack is chafing my back; **der Kragen scheuert am Hals** the collar chafes at the neck VT (*inf*) **jdm eine ~** to smack sb one (*inf*) VR **sich (an etw** *dat*) **~** to rub (against sth); **sich** (*acc*) **(wund) ~** to chafe oneself

Scheu|er-: Scheu|er|sand M scouring powder; **Scheu|er|tuch** NT *pl* **-tücher** floor cloth

Scheu|klap|pe F blinker (*Brit*), blinder (*US*); **~n haben** or **tragen** (*lit, fig*) to be blinkered (*Brit*), to wear blinkers (*Brit*) or blinders (*US*); **mit ~n herumlaufen** or **durchs Leben laufen** to be wearing blinkers (*Brit*) or blinders (*US*)

Scheu|ne ['ʃɔynə] F **-, -n** barn

Scheu|nen-: Scheu|nen|dre|scher M **wie ein ~ fressen** (*inf*) to eat like a horse (*inf*); **Scheu|nen|tor** NT barn door → **Ochse**

Scheu|re|be ['ʃɔyreːbə] F **-, -n** a *no pl* (*Rebsorte*) Scheurebe grape b (*Wein*) Scheurebe wine

Scheu|sal ['ʃɔyzaːl] NT **-s, -e** or (*inf*) **Scheusäler** [-zɛːlɐ] monster

scheuß|lich ['ʃɔyslɪç] ADJ dreadful; (= *abstoßend hässlich*) hideous ADV a (= *widerlich*) *kochen* terribly; *speisen* badly; **~ riechen/schmecken** to smell/taste terrible b (= *gemein*) *sich benehmen* dreadfully, terribly c (*inf*: = *furchtbar*) dreadfully; **es hat ~ wehgetan** it hurt dreadfully, it was horribly or terribly painful

Scheuß|lich|keit F **-, -en** a *no pl* (= *das Scheußlichsein*) dreadfulness; (= *Hässlichkeit*) hideousness b (= *Greueltat etc*) monstrosity

Schi [ʃiː] M **-s, -er** [ʃiːɐ] or **-** = **Ski**

Schicht [ʃɪçt] F **-, -en** a (= *Lage*) layer; (= *dünne Schicht*) film; (*Geol, Sci*) layer, stratum; (= *Farbschicht*) coat; (*der Gesellschaft*) level, stratum; **breite ~en der Bevölkerung** large sections of the population; **aus allen ~en (der Bevölkerung)** from all walks of life b (= *Arbeitsabschnitt, -gruppe etc*) shift; **er hat jetzt ~** (*inf*) er ist auf **~** (*inf*) he's on shift; **zur ~ gehen** to go on shift; **er muss ~ arbeiten** he has to work shifts

Schicht-: Schicht|ar|beit F shiftwork; **Schicht|ar|bei|ter(in)** M(F) shiftworker; **Schicht|be|trieb** M shift operation; **im ~ ar|beiten** to work in shifts; **Schicht|dienst** M shiftwork; **~ haben** to be working shifts

schich|ten ['ʃɪçtn] VT to layer; *Holz, Steine, Bücher etc* to stack VR (*Geol*) to form layers; (*Gestein*) to stratify

schich|ten|spe|zi|fisch ADJ (*Sociol*) specific to a particular social stratum

Schicht-: Schicht|kä|se M *low-fat quark with an interposed layer of high-fat quark*; **Schicht|lohn** M shift(work) rates *pl*; **Schicht|stoff** M laminate; **Schicht|stoff|plat|te** F laminated sheet

Schich|tung ['ʃɪçtʊŋ] F **-, -en** layering; (*von Holz, Heu, Büchern etc*) stacking; (*Sociol, Geol, Met*) stratification

Schicht-: Schicht|un|ter|richt M teaching in shifts; **Schicht|wech|sel** M change of shifts; **um 6 Uhr ist ~ bei uns** we change or switch (*US*) shifts at six o'clock; **schicht|wei|se** ADV in layers; (*Farbe, Lack*) in coats

schick [ʃɪk] ADJ elegant, smart; *Haus, Wohnung auch, Möbel* stylish; *Frauenmode, Kleidung* chic; *Auto* smart; (*inf*: = *prima*) great (*inf*) ADV stylishly, smartly

Schick [ʃɪk] M **-s, no pl** style; (*von Frauenmode, Frau auch*) chic

schi|cken ['ʃɪkn] ☼ 48.1, 48.3 VTI to send; **(jdm) etw ~** to send (sb) to send (sb) sth; **jdn einkaufen ~** to send sb to do the shopping; **jdn Bier holen ~** to send sb to fetch some beer or for some beer, to send sb on a beer run (*US*); **(jdn) nach jdm/etw ~** to send (sb) for sb/ sth; **jdn in den Ruhestand ~** to pension sb off VR *impers* (= *sich ziemen*) to be fitting or proper; **das schickt sich nicht für ein Mädchen** it does not befit or become a girl VR (*old*: = *sich abfinden*) **sich in etw** (*acc*) **~** to resign or reconcile oneself to sth; **schließlich schickte er sich drein** eventually he became reconciled to this

Schi|cke|ria [ʃɪkə'riːa] F **-, no pl** (*iro*) in-crowd (*inf*)

Schi|cki|mi|cki [ʃɪki'mɪki] M **-(s), -s** (*inf*) trendy

schick|lich ['ʃɪklɪç] ADJ *Kleidung* proper, fitting; *Verhalten* seemly, becoming; **es ist nicht ~ zu pfeifen** it is unseemly or unbecoming to whistle ADV properly, as one should

Schick|lich|keit F seemliness; **sobald die ~ es zulässt** as soon as it is seemly to do so

Schick|sal ['ʃɪkzaːl] NT **-s, -e** fate, destiny; (= *Pech*) fate; **das ~ wollte es, (dass) ...** as fate would have it, ...; **~ spielen** to influence fate; **die ~e der Flüchtlinge** the fate of the refugees; **manche schweren ~e** many a difficult fate; **das sind (schwere) ~e** those are tragic cases; **er hat ein schweres ~ gehabt** or **durchgemacht** fate has been unkind to him; **(das ist) ~** (*inf*) that's life; **jdn seinem ~ überlassen** to leave or abandon sb to his fate; **sein ~ herausfordern** to tempt fate or providence; **dem ~ haben wir es zu verdanken, dass ...** we have to thank our good fortune that ...; **das ~ hat es gut mit uns gemeint** fortune has smiled on us

schick|sal|haft ADJ fateful

Schick|sals-: schick|sals|er|ge|ben ADJ resigned to one's fate *pred*; **Schick|sals|fra|ge** F fateful question; **Schick|sals|ge|fähr|te** M , **Schick|sals|ge|fähr|tin** F companion in misfortune; **Schick|sals|ge|mein|schaft** F **wir waren eine ~** we shared a common destiny; **Schick|sals|glau|be** M fatalism; **Schick|sals|göt|tin** F goddess of destiny; **die ~nen** the Fates; (= *Nornen*) the Norns; **Schick|sals|schlag** M great misfortune, stroke of fate; **Schick|sals|tra|gö|die** F tragedy of fate *or* destiny; **Schick|sals|wen|de** F change in fortune

Schick|se ['ʃɪksə] F -, -n (*pej inf*) floozy (*pej inf*)

Schi|ckung ['ʃɪkʊŋ] F -, -en (*liter*) act of providence (*esp Brit*) or God

Schie|be-: Schie|be|büh|ne F traverser; (*Theat*) sliding stage; **Schie|be|dach** NT sunroof; **Schie|be|fens|ter** NT sliding window

schie|ben ['ʃiːbn] *pret* **schob** [ʃoːp], *ptp* **gescho-ben** [ɡəˈʃoːbn] **VT** a (= *bewegen*) to push, to shove; *Fahrrad, Rollstuhl etc* to push, to wheel; *Auto* to push; (*in den Ofen*) to put; **etw von sich (dat) ~** (*fig*) to put sth aside; *Schuld, Verantwortung* to reject sth; **etw vor sich (dat) her ~** (*fig*) to put off sth; **etw von einem Tag auf den an-dern ~** to put sth off from one day to the next; **etw auf jdn/etw ~** to blame sb/sth for sth, to put the blame onto sb/sth; **die Schuld auf jdn ~** to put the blame on sb; **die Verantwortung auf jdn ~** to put the responsibility at sb's door; **Bedenken beiseite ~** to push doubts aside **b** (= *stecken*) to put; *Hände* to slip, to put; **jdm/ sich etw in den Mund ~** to put sth into sb's/one's mouth **c** (*inf*: = *handeln mit*) to traffic in; *Drogen* to push (*inf*) **d** (*inf*) **Dienst/Wache ~** to do duty/guard duty → **Kohldampf e** (*Rail*) to shunt **VI** a (= *drücken, schubsen*) to push, to shove **b** (*inf*) **mit etw ~** to traffic in sth; **mit Drogen ~** to push drugs (*inf*) **c** (*inf*: = *begünstigen*) to wangle (*inf*); **da wurde viel geschoben** there was a lot of wangling going on (*inf*) **VR** a (*mit Anstrengung*) to push, to shove; **sich an die Spitze ~** to push one's way to the front **b** (= *sich bewegen*) to move

Schie|ber¹ ['ʃiːbɐ] M -s, - a slide; (*am Ofen etc*) damper; (= *Bettpfanne*) bedpan; (= *Essbesteck für Kinder*) pusher **b** (*inf*: = *Tanz*) shuffle

Schie|ber² ['ʃiːbɐ] M -s, -, **Schie|be|rin** [-ərɪn] F -, -nen (= *Schwarzhändler*) black marketeer; (= *Waffenschieber*) gunrunner; (= *Drogenschieber*) pusher (*inf*)

Schie|be|rei [ʃiːbəˈraɪ] F -, -en (*inf*) a (= *Drängelei*) pushing, shoving **b** (= *Begünstigung*) string-pulling *no pl* **c** (= *Schwarzhandel*) black marketeering; (*mit Waffen*) gunrunning

Schie|ber|ge|schäft NT shady deal; (= *Schwarzhandel*) black marketeering

Schie|ber|müt|ze F flat cap

Schie|be-: Schie|be|sitz M sliding seat; **Schie|be|tür** F sliding door; **Schie|be|wand** F sliding partition (wall)

Schieb|leh|re F calliper (*Brit*) or caliper (*US*) rule

Schie|bung ['ʃiːbʊŋ] F -, -en (= *Begünstigung*) string-pulling *no pl*; (*Sport*) rigging; (= *Schieber-geschäfte*) shady deals *pl*; **der ~ bezichtigt wer-den** to be accused of rigging; **das war doch ~** that was rigged, that was a fix; **die Zuschauer riefen „Schiebung!"** the spectators shouted "fix!"

schiech [ʃiːç] ADJ (*Aus*) a (= *hässlich*) ugly **b** (= *bang*) **jdm wird ~** sb gets scared

schied *pret von* **scheiden**

schied|lich ['ʃiːtlɪç] ADV **~ und friedlich** amicably

Schieds-: Schieds|frau F arbitrator, arbiter; **Schieds|ge|richt** NT , **Schieds|ge|richts-**

hof M court of arbitration; **schieds|ge-richt|lich** ADJ arbitral ADV by arbitration; **Schieds|ge|richts|bar|keit** F arbitral jurisdiction; **Schieds|mann** M *pl* **-leute** arbitrator, arbiter; **Schieds|rich|ter(in)** M(F) arbitrator, arbiter; (*Fußball, Eishockey, Boxen*) referee; (*Hockey, Tennis, Federball, Kricket, Mil*) umpire; (= *Preisrichter*) judge; **Schieds|rich|ter|ent-schei|dung** F (*Sport*) referee's/umpire's decision; **schieds|rich|ter|lich** ADJ arbitrational, arbitral; (*bei Hockey, Federball, Kricket, Tennis*) umpiring; (*Fußball, Eishockey, Boxen*) refereeing ADV **das muss ~ entschieden werden** the arbitrator/referee *etc* decides; **schieds|rich|tern** ['ʃiːtsrɪçtɐn] VI *insep* (*inf*) → **Schiedsrichter(in)** to arbitrate/referee/umpire/judge; **Schieds|rich-ter|stuhl** M (*Tennis etc*) umpire's chair; **Schieds|spruch** M (arbitral) award; **Schieds|stel|le** F arbitration service; **Schieds|ver|fah|ren** NT arbitration proceedings *pl*

schief [ʃiːf] ADJ crooked, not straight *pred*; (= *nach einer Seite geneigt*) lopsided, tilted; *Winkel* oblique; *Blick, Lächeln* wry; *Absätze* worn (-down); (*fig*: = *unzutreffend*) inappropriate; *Deu-tung* wide of the mark, inappropriate; *Bild* distorted; **~e Ebene** (*Phys*) inclined plane; **auf die ~e Bahn geraten** *or* **kommen** (*fig*) to leave the straight and narrow; **einen ~en Mund** *or* **ein ~es Gesicht ziehen** (*fig inf*) to pull a (wry) face; **der Schiefe Turm von Pisa** the Leaning Tower of Pisa → **Licht** ADV a (= *schräg*) *halten, wachsen* crooked; *hin-stellen* at an angle; **er hatte den Hut ~ auf** he wore his hat at an angle; **~ laufen** to walk lop-sidedly; **das Bild hängt ~** the picture is crooked or isn't straight **b** (= *scheel*) **jdn ~ ansehen** (*fig*) to look askance at sb; **sie lächelte ~** she gave him a crooked smile **c** (= *unrichtig*) *übersetzen* badly; **etw ~ schil-dern/wiedergeben** to give a distorted version of sth; **du siehst die Sache ganz ~!** (*fig*) you're looking at it all wrong!; **~ gewickelt** on the wrong track; **da bist du ~ gewickelt** you've got a surprise coming to you there (*inf*)

Schie|fe ['ʃiːfə] F -, *no pl* crookedness; (= *Nei-gung*) lopsidedness, tilt; (*von Ebene*) inclination; (*von Winkel*) obliqueness

Schie|fer ['ʃiːfɐ] M -s, - (*Gesteinsart*) slate; (*esp Aus*: = *Holzsplitter*) splinter

Schie|fer-: Schie|fer|bruch M slate quarry; **Schie|fer|dach** NT slate roof; **schie|fer|grau** ADJ slate-grey; **Schie|fer|kas|ten** M pencil box; **Schie|fer|plat|te** F slate; **Schie|fer|stift** M slate pencil; **Schie|fer|ta|fel** F slate

schief-: schief ge|hen ▲ VI *irreg aux sein* to go wrong; **es wird schon ~!** (*hum*) it'll be OK (*inf*); **schief|ge|wi|ckelt** △ [-ɡəvɪklt] ADJ *pred* → **schief** ADV c; **schief+la|chen** VR *sep* (*inf*) to kill oneself (laughing) (*inf*); **Schief|la|ge** F (*fig*) difficulties *pl*; **schief lau|fen** ▲ *irreg* **VI** **schief treten** ▲ VI *aux sein* (*inf*) to go wrong; **schief lie|gen** ▲ VI *irreg* (*inf*) to be wrong; **mit einer Meinung ~** to be on the wrong track; **schief tre|ten** ▲ VT *irreg Absätze* to wear down; **die Schuhe ~** to wear down the heels of one's shoes; **schief|win|ke|lig, schief|wink-lig** ADJ oblique-angled

schiel|äu|gig ADJ cross-eyed, squint-eyed, boss-eyed (*Brit*)

schie|len ['ʃiːlən] VI to squint, to be cross-eyed or boss-eyed (*Brit*); **auf** *or* **mit einem Auge ~** to have a squint in one eye; **auf etw** (*acc*) **~** (*inf*) to steal a glance at sth; **nach jdm/etw ~** (*inf*) to look at sb/sth out of the corner of one's eyes; (*begehrlich*) to eye sb/sth up (*Brit*), to look sb/sth up and down; (*heimlich*) to sneak a look at sb/sth

schien *pret von* **scheinen**

Schien|bein ['ʃiːnbaɪn] NT shin; (= *Schienbein-knochen*) shinbone; **jdm gegen** *or* **vor das ~ tre-ten** to kick sb on *or* in (*esp US*) the shin(s)

Schien|bein|scho|ner M , **Schien|bein|schutz** M , **Schien|bein|schüt|zer** [-ʃʏtsɐ] M -s, - shin pad, shin guard

Schie|ne ['ʃiːnə] F -, -n a rail; (*Med*) splint; (*von Lineal*) edge, guide; (*von Winkelmesser*) blade; **auf oberster ~ backen** (*im Backofen*) to bake at the top of the oven **b Schienen** PL (*Rail*) track *sing*, rails *pl*; **aus den ~n springen** to leave *or* jump the rails; **Verkehr auf die ~(n) verlagern** to transfer traffic onto the rails **c** (*fig*) **auf der politischen ~** along political lines; **ein Problem auf der pragmatischen/politischen ~ lösen** to solve a problem pragmatically/by political means; **auf der emotionalen ~** on an emotional level

schie|nen ['ʃiːnən] VT *Arm, Bein* to put in a splint/splints, to splint; *Bruch* to splint

Schie|nen-: Schie|nen|bahn F a (*Transport-system*) track transport **b** (*Fahrzeug*) track vehicle; **Schie|nen|brem|se** F slipper brake; **Schie|nen|bus** M rail bus; **Schie|nen|er-satz|ver|kehr** M (*Rail*) alternative transport(ation) (*when trains or trams are not run-ning*); **Schie|nen|fahr|zeug** NT track vehicle; **schie|nen|gleich** ADJ *or* **Straßenüber-gang** level crossing (*Brit*), grade crossing (*US*); **Schie|nen|netz** NT (*Rail*) rail network; **Schie|nen|räu|mer** [-rɔʏmɐ] M -s, - track clearer; **Schie|nen|strang** M (section of) track; **Schie|nen|weg** M railway (*Brit*) or rail-road (*US*) line; **etw auf dem ~ versenden** to send sth by rail

schier¹ ['ʃiːɐ] ADJ pure; (*fig*) sheer

schier² ADV (= *beinahe*) nearly, almost

Schier|ling ['ʃiːɐlɪŋ] M -s, -e hemlock

Schier|lings|be|cher M (cup of) hemlock

Schieß-: Schieß|be|fehl M order to fire *or* shoot; **Schieß|bu|de** F shooting gallery; **Schieß|bu|den|fi|gur** F target figure *or* doll; (*fig inf*) clown; **du siehst ja aus wie eine ~** you look like something out of a pantomime; **Schieß|ei|sen** NT (*hum inf*) shooting iron (*inf*)

schie|ßen ['ʃiːsn] *pret* **schoss** [ʃɔs], *ptp* **gescho-ssen** [ɡəˈʃɔsn] **VT** to shoot; *Kugel, Rakete* to fire (*auf jdn/etw at sb/sth*); (*Ftbl etc*) to kick; *Tor* to score; (*mit Stock, Schläger*) to hit; **jdn in den Kopf ~** to shoot sb in the head; **etw an der Schießbude ~** to win sth at the shooting galle-ry; **ein paar Bilder ~** (*Phot inf*) to shoot a few pictures, to take a few shots; **eine Filmszene ~** (*inf*) to shoot a film scene; **sie hat ihn zum Krüppel geschossen** she shot and crippled him **VI** a (*mit etw ~*) to shoot; **auf jdn/etw ~** to shoot at sb/sth; **nach etw ~** to shoot at sth; **aufs Tor/ins Netz ~** to shoot *or* kick at goal/in-to the net; **es wurde scharf geschossen** there was shooting with live ammunition; **das ist zum Schießen** (*inf*) that's a scream (*inf*) **b** *aux sein* (= *in die Höhe schießen*) to shoot up; (*Bot*: = *Samenstand entwickeln*) to run (*Brit*) or go to seed; **die Pflanzen/Kinder sind in die Höhe geschossen** the plants/children have shot up; **die Preise schossen in die Höhe** prices rocketed; (**wie Pilze**) **aus dem Boden ~** (*lit, fig*) to spring or sprout up → **Kraut b c** *aux sein* (*inf*: = *sich schnell bewegen*) to shoot; **er ist** *or* **kam um die Ecke geschossen** he shot round the corner; **jdm durch den Kopf ~** (*fig*) to flash through sb's mind **d** *aux sein* (*Flüssigkeit*) to shoot; (= *spritzen*) to spurt; **das Blut schoss ihm ins Gesicht** blood rushed *or* shot to his face; **die Tränen schossen ihr in die Augen** tears flooded her eyes **e** *aux sein* (*S Ger, Aus*: = *verbleichen*) to fade **VR** to have a shoot-out

Schie|ße|rei [ʃiːsəˈraɪ] F -, -en gun battle, shoot-out; (= *das Schießen*) shooting; **bei einer ~ getötet werden** to be killed in a shoot-out

Schieß-: Schieß|ge|wehr NT (*hum*) gun; **Schieß|hund** M **wie ein ~ aufpassen** (*inf*) to keep a close watch, to watch like a hawk; **Schieß|kunst** F marksmanship *no pl*;

Schieß|platz M (shooting or firing) range; **Schieß|prü|gel** M (sl) iron (inf); **Schieß|pul|ver** NT gunpowder; **Schieß|schar|te** F embrasure; **Schieß|schei|be** F target; **Schieß|sport** M shooting; **Schieß|stand** M shooting range; (= Schießbude) shooting gallery; **Schieß|übung** F shooting or target practice no pl

Schiet [ʃiːt] M -s, no pl (N Ger inf) = **Scheiße**

Schiff [ʃɪf] NT -(e)s, -e **a** ship; **das ~ der Wüste** (geh) the ship of the desert; **das ~ des Staates** (geh) the ship of state → **klar b** (Archit) (= Mittelschiff) nave; (= Seitenschiff) aisle; (= Querschiff) transept **c** (in Kohleherd) boiler **d** (Typ: = Setzschiff) galley

Schiffahrt △ F → **Schifffahrt**

Schiff-: schiff|bar ADJ Gewässer navigable; **Schiff|bar|keit** [ˈʃɪfbaːɐkait] F -, no pl navigability; **Schiff|bar|ma|chung** [ˈʃɪfbaːɐmaxʊŋ] F -, -en (von Fluss) canalization; **Schiff|bau** M , no pl shipbuilding; **Schiff|bau|er(in)** M(F) pl -bauer(innen) shipwright; **Schiff|bruch** M shipwreck; **~ erleiden** (lit) to be shipwrecked; (fig) to fail; (Firma) to founder; **schiff|brü|chig** ADJ shipwrecked; **~ werden** to be shipwrecked; **Schiff|brü|chi|ge(r)** [-bʁʏçɪɡə] MF decl as adj person who has/had been shipwrecked

Schiff|chen [ˈʃɪfçən] NT -s, - **a** (zum Spielen) little boat **b** (Mil, Fashion) forage cap **c** (Tex, Sew) shuttle **d** (Bot) keel, carina (spec) **e** (für Weihrauch) boat

schiff|fen [ˈʃɪfn̩] **VI a** aux sein (old) (= Schiff fahren) to ship (old), to go by ship; (= Schiff steuern) to steer **b** (sl: = urinieren) to piss (sl) **VI** impers (sl: = regnen) to piss down (Brit inf), to pour down

Schiff|fer [ˈʃɪfɐ] M -s, -, **Schiff|fe|rin** [-ərɪn] F -, -nen boatman, sailor; (von Lastkahn) bargee; (= Kapitän) skipper

Schiff|fer-: Schiff|fer|kla|vier NT accordion; **Schiff|fer|kno|ten** M sailor's knot; **Schiff|fer|müt|ze** F yachting cap

Schiff|fahrt ▲ F shipping; (= Schifffahrtskunde) navigation; **die ~ wurde eingestellt** all shipping movements were halted

Schiff|fahrts-: Schiff|fahrts|ge|sell|schaft ▲ F shipping company; **Schiff|fahrts|kun|de** ▲ F navigation; **Schiff|fahrts|li|nie** ▲ F **a** (= Schiffsweg) shipping route **b** (= Unternehmen) shipping line; **Schiff|fahrts|recht** ▲ NT maritime law; **Schiff|fahrts|stra|ße** ▲ F , **Schiff|fahrts|weg** ▲ M (= Kanal) waterway; (= Schifffahrtslinie) shipping route or lane

Schiffs- in cpds ship's; **Schiffs|an|le|ge|stel|le** F ship's berth, ship's mooring point; **Schiffs|arzt** M , **Schiffs|ärz|tin** F ship's doctor; **Schiffs|bauch** M bilge; **Schiffs|be|sat|zung** F ship's company

Schiff|schau|kel F swingboat

Schiffs-: Schiffs|eig|ner(in) M(F) (form) shipowner; **Schiffs|füh|rer(in)** M(F) (form) boatman; (= Kapitän) master, skipper; **Schiffs|hy|po|thek** F ship mortgage; **Schiffs|jun|ge** M ship's boy; **Schiffs|ka|pi|tän(in)** M(F) ship's captain; **Schiffs|kar|te** F chart; **Schiffs|koch** M , **Schiffs|kö|chin** F ship's cook; **Schiffs|kör|per** M (form) hull; **Schiffs|la|dung** F shipload; **Schiffs|mak|ler(in)** M(F) ship-broker; **Schiffs|mann|schaft** F ship's crew; **Schiffs|mo|dell** NT model ship; **Schiffs|pa|pie|re** PL ship's papers pl; **Schiffs|raum** M hold; **Schiffs|re|gis|ter** NT register of shipping; **Schiffs|rumpf** M hull; **Schiffs|schna|bel** M bow; **Schiffs|schrau|be** F ship's propeller; **Schiffs|ta|ge|buch** NT ship's log; **Schiffs|tau** NT (ship's) rope; **Schiffs|tau|fe** F christening or naming of a/the ship; **Schiffs|trans|port** M maritime transport; **Schiffs|un|fall** M , **Schiffs|un|glück** NT shipping accident; (Zusammenstoß) ship collision; **Schiffs|ver|bin|dung** F connecting boat service; **Schiffs-**

ver|kehr M shipping; **Schiffs|werft** F shipyard; **Schiffs|zwie|back** M ship's biscuit

Schi|is|mus [ʃiˈɪsmʊs] M -, no pl Shiism

Schi|it [ʃiˈiːt] M -en, -en, **Schi|i|tin** [-ˈiːtɪn] F -, -nen Shiite

schi|i|tisch [ʃiˈiːtɪʃ] ADJ Shiite

Schi|ka|ne [ʃiˈkaːnə] F -, -n **a** harassment; (von Mitschülern) bullying no pl; **diese neuerlichen ~n an der Grenze** this recent harassment at the border; **das hat er aus reiner ~ gemacht** he did it out of sheer bloody-mindedness (Brit) or pig-headedness; **die Schüler brauchen sich nicht alle ~n gefallen zu lassen** the pupils don't have to put up with being messed around (inf) **b mit allen ~n** (inf) with all the trimmings **c** (Sport) chicane

schi|ka|nie|ren [ʃikaˈniːrən] ptp **schikaniert** VT to harass, to bully; Ehepartner, Freundin etc to mess around; Mitschüler to bully; **ich lasse mich nicht weiter von diesem Weibsstück ~** I won't let this female mess me around any more (inf); **er hat mich einmal so schikaniert, dass ...** he once gave me such a rough time that ...

schi|ka|nös [ʃikaˈnøːs] ADJ Mensch bloody-minded (Brit), pig-headed; Maßnahme etc harassing; Mitschüler, Ehemann, Vorgesetzter bullying; **~e Behandlung** harassment; bullying **ADV jdn ~ behandeln** to give sb a rough time, to harass/bully sb

Schi|ko|ree ▲ [ˈʃɪkoreː] F - or m -s, no pl chicory

Schild¹ [ʃɪlt] M -(e)s, -e **a** shield; (= Wappenschild) escutcheon; (von Schildkröte) shell, carapace (spec); **etwas im ~e führen** (fig) to be up to something; **nichts Gutes im ~e führen** (fig) to be up to no good; **jdn auf den ~ heben** (fig) to make sb one's leader

Schild² NT -(e)s, -er [-dɐ] (= Aushang, Warenschild, Verkehrsschild) sign; (= Wegweiser) signpost; (= Namensschild, Türschild) nameplate; (= Kennzeichen) number plate (Brit), license plate (US); (= Preisschild) ticket; (= Etikett: an Käfig, Gepäck etc) label; (= Plakette) badge; (= Plakat) placard; (von Plakatträger) plaque; (an Monument, Haus, Grab) plaque; (von Mütze) peak; **im Fenster stand ein ~** there was a sign or notice in the window

Schild|bür|ger(in) M(F) (Liter) ≈ Gothamite; (hum) fool

Schild|bür|ger|streich M foolish act; **das war ein ~** that was a stupid thing to do

Schild|chen [ˈʃɪltçən] NT -s, - → **Schild²** small sign; small plate etc

Schild|drü|se F thyroid gland; **an der ~ leiden** to have a thyroid complaint

Schild|drü|sen-: Schild|drü|sen|hor|mon NT thyroid hormone; **Schild|drü|sen|über|funk|ti|on** F overactive thyroid, hyperthyroidism (spec); **Schild|drü|sen|un|ter|funk|ti|on** F underactive thyroid, hypothyrosis (spec)

Schil|de|rer [ˈʃɪldərɐ] M -s, -, **Schil|de|rin** [-ərɪn] F -, -nen portrayer

Schil|der|haus NT , **Schil|der|häus|chen** [-hɔysçən] NT sentry box

Schil|der|ma|ler(in) M(F) sign writer

schil|dern [ˈʃɪldɐn] VT Ereignisse, Situation, Erlebnisse, Vorgänge to describe; (= skizzieren) to outline; Menschen, Landschaften to portray; **es ist kaum zu ~** it's almost impossible to describe; **es ist kaum zu ~, wie frech er war** he was indescribably cheeky (Brit) or fresh (US); **~ Sie den Verlauf des Unfalls** give an account of how the accident happened → **Farbe a**

Schil|de|rung [ˈʃɪldərʊŋ] F -, -en (= Beschreibung) description; (= Bericht: auch von Zeuge) account; (= literarische Schilderung) portrayal

Schil|der|wald M (hum) forest or jungle of traffic signs

Schild-: Schild|knap|pe M (Hist) squire, shield-bearer; **Schild|krö|te** F (= Landschildkröte) tortoise; (= Wasserschildkröte) turtle; **Schild|krö|ten|sup|pe** F turtle soup; **Schild|laus** F scale insect; **Schild|müt|ze** F

peaked cap; **Schild|patt** [ˈʃɪltpat] NT -s, no pl tortoiseshell; **Schild|wa|che** F (old) sentry; **~ stehen** to stand sentry

Schilf [ʃɪlf] NT -(e)s, -e reed; (= mit Schilf bewachsene Fläche) reeds pl

Schilf-: Schilf|dach NT thatched roof; **Schilf|gras** NT , **Schilf|rohr** NT reed

Schil|ler [ˈʃɪlɐ] M -s, no pl **a** (= Schimmer, Glanz) shimmer **b** (Wein) rosé (wine)

Schil|ler-: Schil|ler|kra|gen M Byron collar; **Schil|ler|lo|cke** F **a** (Gebäck) cream horn **b** (Räucherfisch) strip of smoked rock salmon

schil|lern [ˈʃɪlɐn] VI to shimmer

schil|lernd ADJ Farben, Stoffe shimmering; (in Regenbogenfarben) iridescent; (fig) Charakter enigmatic; **~e Seide** shot silk

Schil|ler|wein M rosé (wine)

Schil|ling [ˈʃɪlɪŋ] M -s, - or (bei Geldstücken) -e shilling; (Hist: Aus) schilling

schil|pen [ˈʃɪlpn̩] VI to twitter, to chirp

schilt [ʃɪlt] 3. pers sing pres von **schelten**

Schi|mä|re [ʃiˈmɛːrə] F -, no pl chimera

schi|mä|risch [ʃiˈmɛːrɪʃ] ADJ chimerical

Schim|mel¹ [ˈʃɪml̩] M -s, - (= Pferd) white horse, grey (Brit), gray (US); **ein weißer ~** (hum) a pleonasm

Schim|mel² M -s, no pl (auf Nahrungsmitteln) mould (Brit), mold (US); (auf Leder, Papier etc) mildew

Schim|mel|bil|dung F formation of mould (Brit) or mould (US) or mildew

schim|me|lig [ˈʃɪmlɪç] ADJ Nahrungsmittel mouldy (Brit), moldy (US); Leder, Papier etc mildewy; **~ riechen** to smell mo(u)ldy; **~ werden** (Nahrungsmittel) to go mo(u)ldy; (Leder, Papier etc) to become covered with mildew

schim|meln [ˈʃɪml̩n] VI aux sein or haben (Nahrungsmittel) to go mouldy (Brit) or moldy (US); (Leder, Papier etc) to go mildewy; **die Wand schimmelt** the wall has mould (Brit) or mold (US) on it

Schim|mel-: Schim|mel|pilz M mould (Brit), mold (US); **Schim|mel|rei|ter** M (Myth) ghost rider

Schim|mer [ˈʃɪmɐ] M -s, no pl glimmer, gleam; (von Licht auf Wasser, von Perlen, Seide) shimmer; (von Metall) gleam; (im Haar) sheen; **beim ~ der Lampe/Kerzen** by or in the soft glow of the lamp/glimmer of the candles; **blassen** or **nicht den geringsten ~ von etw haben** (inf) not to have the slightest or the faintest (inf) idea about sth

schim|mern [ˈʃɪmɐn] VI to glimmer, to gleam; (Licht auf Wasser auch, Perlen, Seide) to shimmer; (Metall) to gleam; **der Stoff/ihr Haar schimmert rötlich** the material/her hair has a tinge of red; **ihre Augen schimmerten feucht** her eyes glistened moistly

schim|mlig [ˈʃɪmlɪç] ADJ = **schimmelig**

Schim|pan|se [ʃɪmˈpanzə] M -n, -n, **Schim|pan|sin** [-panzɪn] F -, -nen chimpanzee, chimp (inf)

Schimpf [ʃɪmpf] M -(e)s, no pl (liter) insult, affront; **mit ~ und Schande** in disgrace

schimp|fen [ˈʃɪmpfn̩] VI to get angry; (= sich beklagen) to moan, to grumble, to bitch (inf); (= fluchen) to swear, to curse; (Vögel, Affen etc) to bitch (inf); **mit jdm ~** to scold sb, to tell sb off; **heute hat der Lehrer geschimpft, weil ich ...** the teacher told me off today because I ... (inf); **auf** or **über jdn/etw ~** to bitch about sb/sth (inf), to curse (about or at) sb/sth; **vor sich hin ~** to grumble → **Rohrspatz** VT (= ausschimpfen) to tell off, to scold; **jdn einen Idioten ~** to call sb an idiot VR **sich etw ~** (inf) to call oneself sth

Schimp|fe|rei [ʃɪmpfəˈrai] F -, -en cursing and swearing; (= Geschimpfe) scolding; (= Beschimpfung) row, set-to (Brit inf), slanging match (Brit inf); (= das Murren) moaning, grumbling, bitching (*inf*); (*von Vögeln, Affen etc*) bitching (*inf*)

Schimpf|ka|no|na|de F barrage of abuse

schimpf|lich ['ʃɪmpflɪç] (*geh*) **ADJ** (= *beleidigend*) insulting; (= *schmachvoll*) humiliating **ADV** jdn ~ **verjagen** to drive sb away in disgrace

Schimpf-: Schimpf|na|me M insulting nickname; **Slick Willie war sein ~** they dubbed him Slick Willie; **Schimpf|wort** NT *pl* **-wörter** swearword; **mit Schimpfwörtern um sich werfen** to curse and swear

Schi|na|kel [ʃiˈnaːkl] NT **-s, -(n)** (*Aus inf*) (= *Ruderboot*) rowing boat; (= *klappriges Fahrzeug*) rattletrap (*inf*)

Schind|an|ger ['ʃɪntaŋɐ] M (*old*) knacker's yard (*Brit*), slaughterhouse

Schin|del ['ʃɪndl] F **-, -n** shingle

Schin|del|dach NT shingle roof

schin|den ['ʃɪndn] *pret* **schindete** or (*rare*) **schund** ['ʃɪndətə, ʃʊnt], *ptp* **geschunden** [ɡəˈʃʊndn] **VT a** (= *quälen*) Gefangene, Tiere to maltreat; (= *ausbeuten*) to overwork, to drive hard; Maschine, Motor, Auto to flog; **jdn zu Tode ~** to work sb to death → *auch* **geschunden b** (*inf*: = *herausschlagen*) Zeilen to pad (out); Arbeitsstunden to pile up; **Zeit ~** to play for time; (**bei jdm**) **Eindruck ~** to make a good impression (on sb), to impress (sb); **Mitleid ~** to get some sympathy **c** (*old*: = *abdecken*) Tier to flay, to skin **VR** (= *hart arbeiten*) to struggle; (= *sich quälen*) to strain; **sich mit etw ~** to slave away at sth

Schin|der ['ʃɪndɐ] M **-s, -, Schin|de|rin** [-ərɪn] F **-, -nen a** (*old*: = *Abdecker*) knacker (*Brit*), butcher **b** (*fig*: = *Quäler*) slave-driver

Schin|de|rei [ʃɪndəˈraɪ] F **-, -en a** (*old*: = *Abdeckerei*) knacker's yard (*Brit*), slaughterhouse **b** (= *Plackerei*) struggle; (= *Arbeit*) slavery *no indef art* **c** (= *Quälerei*) maltreatment *no pl*

Schind|lu|der ['ʃɪntluːdɐ] NT (*inf*) **mit jdm ~ treiben** to make sb suffer; **mit etw ~ treiben** to misuse sth; **mit seiner Gesundheit/seinen Kräften ~ treiben** to abuse one's health/strength

Schind|mäh|re ['ʃɪntmɛːrə] F (*old*) nag

Schin|ken ['ʃɪŋkn] M **-s, - a** ham; (*gekocht und geräuchert*) gammon, ham **b** (*pej inf*) hackneyed and clichéd play/book/film; (= *großes Buch*) tome; (= *großes Bild*) great daub (*pej inf*)

Schin|ken-: Schin|ken|brot NT ham sandwich; (*offen*) open ham sandwich; **Schin|ken|bröt|chen** NT ham roll; **Schin|ken|nu|deln** PL *noodles \$ with (pieces of) ham*; **Schin|ken|röll|chen** NT roll of ham; **Schin|ken|speck** M bacon; **Schin|ken|wurst** F ham sausage

Schinn [ʃɪn] M **-s**, *no pl*, **Schin|nen** ['ʃɪnən] PL (*N Ger*) dandruff *no pl*

Schin|to|is|mus [ʃɪntoˈɪsmʊs] M **-**, *no pl* (*Rel*) Shintoism

Schip|pe ['ʃɪpə] F **-, -n a** (*esp N Ger*: = *Schaufel*) shovel, spade; **jdn auf die ~ nehmen** (*fig inf*) to pull sb's leg (*inf*); **dem Tod von der ~ springen** (*inf*) to be snatched from the jaws of death **b** ~ *pl* (*Cards*) spades *pl*

schip|pen ['ʃɪpn] VT to shovel; **Schnee ~** to shovel the snow away

schip|pern ['ʃɪpɐn] VI *aux sein* (*inf*) to sail

Schi|ri ['ʃiːri] M **-s, -s** (*Ftbl inf*) ref (*inf*)

Schirm [ʃɪrm] M **-(e)s, -e a** (= *Regenschirm*) umbrella; (= *Sonnenschirm*) sunshade, parasol; (*von Pilz*) cap **b** (= *Mützenschirm*) peak; **eine Mütze mit ~** a peaked cap **c** (= *Röntgenschirm, Wandschirm, Ofenschirm*) screen; (= *Lampenschirm*) shade **d** (*liter*: = *Schutz*) umbrella; **unter seinem Schutz** ~ under his protection; **jdm** or **jds ~ und Schild sein** to be sb's protector; **der nukleare** or **atomare ~ der USA** the nuclear umbrella of the USA **e** (= *Bildschirm*) screen

Schirm-: Schirm|aka|zie F umbrella thorn; **Schirm|bild** NT X-ray (picture); **Schirm|**-

bild|auf|nah|me F (*form*) X-ray; **Schirm|bild|stel|le** F X-ray unit

schir|men ['ʃɪrmən] VT (*geh*) to shield, to protect (*vor +dat* from, *gegen* against)

Schirm-: Schirm|fut|te|ral NT umbrella cover or case; **Schirm|herr(in)** M(F) patron; (*Frau auch*) patroness; **Schirm|herr|schaft** F patronage; **unter der ~ von** under the patronage of; (*von Organisation*) under the auspices of; **die ~ übernehmen** to become patron; **Schirm|hül|le** F umbrella cover; **Schirm|müt|ze** F peaked cap; **Schirm|pilz** M parasol mushroom; **Schirm|stän|der** M umbrella stand

Schi|rok|ko [ʃiˈrɔko] M **-s, -s** sirocco

Schis|ma ['ʃɪsma, 'sçɪ-] NT **-s, Schismen** or (*geh*) **-ta** [-mən, -ta] (*Eccl, Pol*) schism

Schis|ma|ti|ker [ʃɪsˈmaːtikɐ, sçɪ-] M(F) **-s, -, Schis|ma|ti|ke|rin** [-ərɪn] F **-, -nen** (*liter*) schismatic

schis|ma|tisch [ʃɪsˈmaːtɪʃ, sçɪ-] ADJ (*geh*) schismatic

schiss ▲ *pret von* **scheißen**

Schiss ▲ [ʃɪs] M **-es**, *no pl* (*sl*) **(fürchterlichen) ~ haben** to be scared to death (*vor +dat* of) (*inf*); **~ kriegen** to get scared

schi|zo|phren [ʃitsoˈfreːn, sçi-] **ADJ a** (*Med*) schizophrenic **b** (*pej*: = *widersinnig*) contradictory, topsy-turvy **ADV** (*pej*) schizophrenically

Schi|zo|phre|nie [ʃitsofreˈniː, sçi-] F **-**, *no pl* **a** (*Med*) schizophrenia **b** (*pej*: = *Widersinn*) contradictoriness; **das ist die reinste ~** that's a flat contradiction

Schlab|be|rei [ʃlabəˈraɪ] F **-, -en** (*inf*) slurping, slobbering

Schlab|ber|ho|se F baggy pants *pl* or trousers *pl* (*esp Brit*)

schlab|be|rig ['ʃlabərɪç] ADJ (*inf*) Brei, Suppe watery; Pullover, Hose baggy; (= *glitschig*) slithery

Schlab|ber-: Schlab|ber|look M [-lʊk] (*inf*) baggy look; **Schlab|ber|maul** NT (*inf*: *von Hund*) slobbery mouth

schlab|bern ['ʃlabɐn] (*inf*) **VI a** (*geräuschvoll*) to slurp; **er schlabberte beim Essen** he slurped his food **b** (= *kleckern*) to make a mess **c** (= *zu weit sein*: Rock, Hose) to flap **d** (*dial inf*: = *sich unterhalten*) **mit jdm ~** to blether with sb **VT** (= *schlürfend essen/trinken*) to slurp

schlab|brig ADJ (*inf*) = **schlabberig**

Schlacht [ʃlaxt] F **-, -en** battle; **die ~ bei** or **um X** the battle of X; **in die ~ gehen** or **ziehen** to go into battle; **jdm eine ~ liefern** to fight sb, to battle with sb; **die Kelten lieferten den Römern eine ~, die …** the Celts gave the Romans a battle that … → **schlagen** VT f

Schlacht|bank F **jdn (wie ein Lamm) zur ~ führen** to lead sb (like a lamb) to the slaughter

schlach|ten ['ʃlaxtn] **VT** Schwein, Kuh to slaughter, to butcher; Huhn, Kaninchen, Opfertier etc to slaughter, to kill; (*hum*) Sparschwein to break into; **heilige Kühe ~** (*fig*) to kill or slaughter sacred cows **VI** to do one's slaughtering; **unser Fleischer schlachtet selbst** our butcher does his own slaughtering; **heute wird geschlachtet** we're/they're etc slaughtering today

Schlach|ten-: Schlach|ten|bumm|ler(in) M(F) (*Sport inf*) visiting or away supporter or fan; **Schlach|ten|ma|ler(in)** M(F) painter of battle scenes

Schlach|ter ['ʃlaxtɐ] M **-s, -, Schlach|te|rin** [-ərɪn] F **-, -nen** (*esp N Ger*) butcher

Schläch|ter ['ʃlɛçtɐ] M **-s, -, Schläch|te|rin** [-ərɪn] F **-, -nen** (*dial, fig*) butcher

Schlach|te|rei [ʃlaxtəˈraɪ] F **-, -en** (*esp N Ger*) butcher's (shop)

Schläch|te|rei [ʃlɛçtəˈraɪ] F **-, -en a** (*dial*) butcher's (shop) **b** (*fig*: = *Blutbad*) slaughter, butchery *no pl*, massacre

Schlacht-: Schlacht|feld NT battlefield; **auf dem ~ bleiben** (*lit*) to fall in battle; (*fig*) (*nach Schlägerei etc*) to be left lying; (*esp Pol*) to be fin-

ished; **das ~ räumen** (= *aufräumen*) to clear the (battle)field; (= *verlassen*) to leave the (battle-)field; (*fig*) to drop out of contention; **das Zimmer sieht aus wie ein ~** the room looks like a battlefield, the room looks as if a bomb has hit it (*inf*); **Schlacht|fest** NT country feast to eat up meat from freshly slaughtered pigs; **Schlacht|ge|sang** M battle song; **Schlacht|ge|tüm|mel** NT thick of the battle, fray; **Schlacht|ge|wicht** NT dressed weight; **Schlacht|ge|wühl** NT thick of the battle, fray; **Schlacht|haus** NT , **Schlacht|hof** M slaughterhouse, abattoir (*esp Brit*); **Schlacht|kreu|zer** M battle cruiser; **Schlacht|li|nie** F battle line; **Schlacht|mes|ser** NT butcher's knife; **Schlacht|op|fer** NT sacrifice; (*Mensch*) human sacrifice; **Schlacht|ord|nung** F battle formation; **Schlacht|plan** M battle plan; (*für Feldzug*) campaign plan; (*fig*) plan of action, battle plan; **Schlacht|plat|te** F (*Cook*) ham and German sausage made with meat from freshly slaughtered pigs and served with sauerkraut; **schlacht|reif** ADJ (*lit, fig*) ready for the slaughter; **Schlacht|ross** ▲ NT (*liter*) warhorse, charger; (*fig inf*) heavyweight; **Schlacht|ruf** M battle cry; **Schlacht|schiff** NT battleship; **Schlacht|schüs|sel** F (*Cook*) selection of boiled pork, pork sausages etc from freshly slaughtered pigs, served with sauerkraut; **Schlacht|tag** M slaughtering day

Schlach|tung ['ʃlaxtʊŋ] F **-, -en** (*von Schwein, Kuh*) slaughter(ing), butchering; (*von Huhn, Kaninchen, Opfertier*) killing

Schlacht|vieh NT , *no pl* animals *pl* for slaughter; (= *Rinder auch*) beef cattle *pl*

Schla|cke ['ʃlakə] F **-, -n** (= *Verbrennungsrückstand*) clinker *no pl*; (= *Aschenteile auch*) cinders *pl*; (*Metal*) slag *no pl*; (*Geol*) scoria *pl* (*spec*), slag *no pl*; (*Physiol*) waste products *pl*

Schla|cken-: Schla|cken|bahn F (*Sport*) cinder track; **schla|cken|frei**, **schla|cken|los** **ADJ** (= *ohne Verbrennungsrückstand*) non-clinker *attr*, clinker-free; (= *ohne Stoffwechselrückstand*) free of waste products **ADV** **Anthrazit brennt ~** anthracite burns without clinkering

schla|ckern ['ʃlakɐn] VI (*inf*) to tremble, to shake; (*vor Angst auch*) to quake; (*Kleidung*) to hang loosely, to be baggy; **mit den Knien ~** to tremble at the knees; **mit den Ohren ~** (*fig*) to be (left) speechless

Schlaf [ʃlaːf] M **-(e)s**, *no pl* sleep; (= *Schläfrigkeit auch*) sleepiness; **einen leichten/festen/tiefen ~ haben** to be a light/sound/deep sleeper; **keinen ~ finden** to be unable to sleep; **um seinen ~ kommen** or **gebracht werden** to lose sleep; (= *überhaupt nicht schlafen*) not to get any sleep; **jdm den ~ rauben** to rob or deprive sb of his/her sleep; **jdn um seinen ~ bringen** to keep sb awake; **im ~** (= *während des Schlafens*) while he sleeps/they slept etc; **halb im ~e** half asleep; **im ~ reden** to talk in one's sleep; **ein Kind in den ~ singen** to sing a child to sleep; **sich** (*dat*) **den ~ aus den Augen reiben** to rub the sleep out of one's eyes; **in einen unruhigen/tiefen ~ fallen** to fall into a troubled/deep sleep; **in tiefstem ~ liegen** to be sound or fast asleep; **aus dem ~ erwachen** (*geh*) to awake, to waken (from sleep); **den ewigen** or **letzten ~ schlafen** (*euph*) to sleep one's last sleep; **den Seinen gibts der Herr im ~** (*Prov*) the devil looks after his own; **es fällt mir nicht im ~(e) ein, das zu tun** I wouldn't dream of doing that; **das macht** or **tut** or **kann er (wie) im ~** (*fig inf*) he can do that in his sleep → **ge-recht a**

Schlaf-: Schlaf|an|zug M pyjamas *pl* (*Brit*), pajamas *pl* (*US*); **schlaf|be|dürf|tig** ADJ (*besonders*) ~ **sein** to need a lot of sleep; **Kinder sind ~er als Erwachsene** children need more sleep than adults

Schläf|chen ['ʃlɛːfçən] NT **-s, -** nap, snooze; **ein ~ machen** to have a nap or snooze

Schlaf|couch F studio couch, sofa bed

Schlä|fe [ˈʃlɛːfə] F -, -n temple; **graue ~n** greying (*Brit*) or graying (*US*) temples

schla|fen [ˈʃlaːfn̩] *pret* **schlief** [ʃliːf], *ptp* **geschla-fen** [ɡəˈʃlaːfn̩] **VI** to sleep; (= *nicht wach sein auch*) to be asleep; (*euph*: = *tot sein*) to be asleep (*euph*); (*geh*: *Stadt, Land*) to be quiet, to slumber (*liter*); (*inf*: = *nicht aufpassen*) (*bei bestimmter Gelegenheit*) to be asleep; (*immer*) not to pay attention; **er schläft immer noch** he's still asleep, he's still sleeping; **tief** or **fest ~** (*zu diesem Zeitpunkt*) to be fast or sound asleep; (*immer*) to be a deep or sound sleeper; **~ gehen** to go to bed; **sich ~ legen** to lie down to sleep; **jdn ~ legen** to put sb to bed; **schläfst du schon?** are you asleep?; **jetzt wird (aber) geschlafen!** go to sleep this minute!; **lange ~** to sleep for a long time; (= *spät aufstehen*) to sleep late, to have a long lie (in) (*Brit*); **schlaf gut** or (*geh*) **wohl** sleep well; **hast du gut geschlafen?** did you sleep well?, did you have a good sleep? (*Brit*); **mittags** or **über Mittag ~** to have an afternoon nap; **~ wie ein Murmeltier** or **Bär** or **Sack** or **Stein** or **eine Ratte** (*all inf*) to sleep like a log; **bei jdm ~** (*inf*) to stay overnight with sb; **wir können ruhig ~** (*fig*) we can sleep easy; **er kann nachts nicht mehr ~** (*fig*) he can't sleep nights; **ich konnte die ganze Nacht nicht ~** I couldn't sleep at all last night; **das lässt ihn nicht ~** (*fig*) it preys on his mind, it gives him no peace; **da-rüber muss ich erst mal ~** (*fig*: = *überdenken*) I'll have to sleep on it; **mit jdm ~** (*euph*) to sleep with sb; **miteinander ~** (*euph*) to sleep with each other; **sie schläft mit jedem** she sleeps around; **schlaf nicht!** wake up!

VR *impers* **auf dieser Matratze schläft es sich schlecht** this mattress is terrible to sleep on

Schlä|fen|bein NT temporal bone

schla|fend ADJ sleeping; **im ~en Zustand** asleep → **Hund** ADV asleep; **sich ~ stellen** to pretend to be asleep

Schla|fen|ge|hen NT -s, *no pl* going to bed; **vor dem ~** before going to bed

Schlä|fen|lo|cke F sidelock

Schla|fens|zeit F bedtime

Schlaf|ent|zug M sleep deprivation

Schlä|fer [ˈʃlɛːfɐ] M -s, -, **Schlä|fe|rin** [-ərɪn] F -, -nen (*inf*) (*fig*) dozy person (*inf*)

schlaff [ʃlaf] ADJ limp; (= *locker*) *Seil, Segel* loose, slack; *Moral* lax, loose; *Disziplin* lax; *Haut* flabby, loose; *Muskeln* flabby; (= *erschöpft*) worn-out, shattered (*Brit inf*), exhausted; (= *energielos*) listless, floppy ADV limply; (*bei Seil, Segel*) loosely

Schlaff|heit F -, *no pl* limpness; (*von Seil*) looseness, slackness; (*von Haut, Muskeln*) flabbiness; (= *Erschöpftheit*) exhaustion; (= *Energielosigkeit*) listlessness

Schlaf|fi [ˈʃlafi] M -s, -s (*inf*) wimp (*inf*)

Schlaf-: Schlaf|ge|le|gen|heit F place to sleep; **wir haben ~ für mehrere Leute** we can sleep several people (*Brit*), we have room for several people to sleep over; **Schlaf|ge|mach** NT (*liter*) bedchamber (*liter*)

Schla|fitt|chen [ʃlaˈfɪtçən] NT **jdn am** or **beim ~ nehmen** or **kriegen** (*inf*) to take sb by the scruff of the neck; (= *zurechtweisen*) to give sb a dressing down (*esp Brit inf*), to reprimand sb

Schlaf-: Schlaf|kam|mer F (*dial*) bedroom; **Schlaf|krank|heit** F sleeping sickness; **Schlaf|lied** NT lullaby; **schlaf|los** ADJ (*lit, fig*) sleepless; **~ liegen** to lie awake; **jdm ~e Nächte bereiten** to give sb many a sleepless night ADV sleeplessly; **Schlaf|lo|sig|keit** F -, *no pl* sleeplessness, insomnia; **sie verbrachte die folgenden Nächte in ~** she spent the following nights unable to sleep; **Schlaf|mit|tel** NT sleeping drug; (*fig iro*) soporific; **diese Zeitung ist das reinste ~** this newspaper just sends you to sleep; **Schlaf|mit|tel|ver|gif-tung** F (poisoning from an) overdose of sleeping pills, ≈ barbiturate poisoning; **Schlaf|müt-ze** F **a** nightcap **b** (*inf*: *Person*) dozy devil

(*inf*); (= *jd, der viel schläft*) sleepyhead (*inf*); **die-se ~n im Parlament** that dozy lot in Parliament (*inf*); **schlaf|müt|zig** [-mʏtsɪç] ADJ (*inf*) dozy (*inf*), dopey (*inf*); **Schlaf|müt|zig|keit** F (*inf*) doziness (*inf*), dopiness (*inf*); **Schlaf|pil|le** F (*inf*) sleeping pill; **Schlaf|raum** M dormitory, dorm (*inf*)

schläf|rig [ˈʃlɛːfrɪç] ADJ sleepy, drowsy; (*fig*: = *träge*) sleepy

Schläf|rig|keit F -, *no pl* sleepiness, drowsiness; (*fig*: = *Trägheit*) sleepiness

Schlaf-: Schlaf|rock M dressing gown; **Äpfel im ~** baked apples in puff pastry; **Würstchen im ~** ≈ sausage roll; **Schlaf|saal** M dormitory; **Schlaf|sack** M sleeping bag; **Schlaf|sack|tou|rist(in)** M(F) backpacker; **Schlaf|ses|sel** M reclining seat; **Schlaf|so|fa** NT sofa bed, bed-settee (*Brit*), hideaway bed (*US*); **Schlaf-stadt** F dormitory town; **Schlaf|stel|le** F place to sleep; **Schlaf|stö|rung** F sleeplessness, insomnia; **Schlaf|stu|be** F (*dial*) bedroom; **Schlaf|sucht** F hypersomnia

schläft [ʃlɛːft] 3. *pers sing pres von* **schlafen**

Schlaf-: Schlaf|tab|let|te F sleeping pill; **Schlaf|trunk** M (*old*) sleeping draught (*Brit*) or draft (*US*, *old*); (*hum inf*: *Alkohol*) nightcap; **schlaf|trun|ken** (*geh*) ADJ drowsy, half asleep ADV drowsily, half-asleep

Schlaf|wa|gen M sleeping car, sleeper

Schlaf|wa|gen-: Schlaf|wa|gen|kar|te F sleeper ticket; **Schlaf|wa|gen|platz** M berth; **Schlaf|wa|gen|schaff|ner(in)** M(F) sleeping-car attendant

Schlaf-: schlaf|wan|deln VI *insep aux sein* or *haben* to sleepwalk, to walk in one's sleep, to somnambulate (*form*); **Schlaf|wand|ler** [-vandlɐ] M -s, -, **Schlaf|wand|le|rin** [-ərɪn] F -, -nen sleepwalker, somnambulist (*form*); **schlaf|wand|le|risch** [-vandlərɪʃ] ADJ sleepwalking *attr*, somnambulatory (*form*); **~er Sicherheit** (*wählen, Fragen beantworten*) intuitively, instinctively; **das Kind lief mit ~er Sicherheit durch den dichten Verkehr** the child ran through the heavy traffic with instinctive assurance; **Schlaf|zim|mer** NT bedroom; **Schlaf|zim|mer|blick** M (*hum inf*) come-to-bed eyes *pl* (*inf*); **Schlaf|zim|mer|ein|rich-tung** F bedroom furniture *sing*; (*Garnitur*) bedroom suite; **Schlaf|zim|mer|ge|schich|te** F (*inf*) sexual adventure, bedroom antic (*inf*)

Schlag [ʃlaːk] M -(e)s, ¨-e [ˈʃlɛːɡə] **a** (*lit, fig*) blow (*gegen* against); (= *Faustschlag auch*) punch; (*mit der Handfläche*) smack, slap; (*leich-ter*) pat; (= *Handkantenschlag, auch Judo etc*) chop (*inf*); (= *Ohrfeige*) cuff, clout (*inf*), slap; (*mit Rohrstock etc*) stroke; (= *Peitschenschlag*) stroke, lash; (= *einmaliges Klopfen*) knock; (*dumpf*) thump, thud; (= *leichtes Pochen*) tap; (= *Glockenschlag*) chime; (= *Standuhrschlag*) stroke; (*von Metronom*) tick, beat; (= *Gehirnschlag, Schlaganfall, Kolbenschlag, Ruderschlag, auch Schwimmen, Tennis*) stroke; (= *Herzschlag, Pulsschlag, Trommelschlag, Wellenschlag*) beat; (= *Blitzschlag*) bolt, stroke; (= *Donnerschlag*) clap; (= *Stromschlag*) shock; (= *Militärschlag*) strike; **man hörte die Schläge des Hammers/der Trommeln** you could hear the clanging of the hammer/beating of the drums; **Schläge kriegen** to get a hiding or thrashing or beating; **zum entscheidenden ~ ausholen** (*fig*) to strike the decisive blow; **~ auf ~** (*fig*) in quick succession, one after the other; **~ acht Uhr** (*inf*) at eight on the dot (*inf*), on the stroke of eight; **jdm/einer Sache einen schweren ~ versetzen** (*fig*) to deal a severe blow to sb/sth; **ein ~ ins Gesicht** (*lit, fig*) a slap in the face; **ein ~ ins Kontor** (*dated inf*) a nasty shock or surprise; **ein ~ ins Wasser** (*inf*) a washout (*inf*), a letdown (*inf*); **ein ~ aus heiterem Himmel** a bolt from the blue; **mit einem** or **auf einen ~** (*inf*) all at once; (= *auf einmal, zugleich auch*) in one go; **mit einem ~ berühmt werden** to become famous overnight; **die haben keinen ~ getan** (*inf*) they haven't done a stroke (of work); **einen ~**

weghaben (*sl*: = *blöd sein*) to have a screw loose (*inf*); **ihn hat der ~ getroffen** (*Med*) he had a stroke; **ich dachte, mich rührt** or **trifft der ~** (*inf*) I was flabbergasted (*inf*) or thunderstruck; **ich glaube, mich trifft der ~** I don't believe it; **wie vom ~ gerührt** or **getroffen sein** to be flabbergasted (*inf*) or thunderstruck (*inf*)

b (= *Wesensart*) type (of person etc); **vom ~ der Südländer sein** to be a Southern type; **vom gleichen ~ sein** to be cast in the same mould (*Brit*) or mold (*US*); (*pej*) to be tarred with the same brush; **vom alten ~** of the old school

c (= *Vogelschlag*) song

d (*dated*: = *Wagenschlag*) door

e (= *Taubenschlag*) cote, pigeon cage

f (*Aus*: = *Schlagsahne*) cream

g (*inf*: = *Portion*) helping

h (= *Hosenschlag*) flare; **eine Hose mit ~** flared trousers *pl* (*esp Brit*) or pants *pl* (*esp US*), flares *pl* (*inf*)

Schlag-: Schlag|ab|tausch M (*Boxen*) exchange of blows; (*fig*) (verbal) exchange; **offe-ner ~** public exchange (of views); **Schlag|ader** F artery; **Schlag|an|fall** M stroke; **schlag|ar-tig** ADJ sudden, abrupt ADV suddenly; **Schlag|ball** M (*Spiel*) rounders *sing*; (*Ball*) rounders ball; **schlag|bar** ADJ beatable; **diese Mannschaft ist durchaus ~** this team is by no means invincible or unbeatable; **Schlag|baum** M barrier; **Schlag|boh|rer** M , **Schlag-bohr|ma|schi|ne** F hammer drill; **Schlag-bol|zen** M firing pin

Schlä|ge *pl von* **Schlag**

Schlä|gel [ˈʃlɛːɡl̩] M -s, - **a** (*Min*) (miner's) hammer; **~ und Eisen** crossed hammers (miner's symbol) **b** stick; (= *Trommelschlägel*) (drum)stick

schla|gen [ˈʃlaːɡn̩] *pret* **schlug** [ʃluːk], *ptp* **ge-schlagen** [ɡəˈʃlaːɡn̩] **VTI** **a** (= *zuschlagen, prü-geln*) to hit; (= *hauen*) to beat; (= *einmal zuschla-gen, treffen*) to hit, to strike; (*mit der flachen Hand*) to slap, to smack; (*leichter*) to pat; (*mit der Faust*) to punch; (*mit Schläger*) to hit; (= *treten*) to kick; (*mit Hammer, Pickel etc*) *Loch* to knock; **die Bombe schlug ein Loch in die Straße** the bomb blew a hole in the road; **jdn bewusstlos ~** to knock sb out or unconscious; (*mit vielen Schlägen*) to beat sb unconscious; **etw in Stücke** or **kurz und klein ~** to smash sth up or to pieces; **nach jdm/etw ~** to hit out or lash out at sb/sth; **um sich ~** to lash out; **mit dem Hammer auf den Nagel ~** to hit the nail with the ham-mer; **mit der Faust an die Tür/auf den Tisch ~** to beat or thump on the door/table with one's fist; **gegen die Tür ~** to hammer on the door; **jdm** or (*rare*) **jdn auf die Schulter ~** to slap sb on the back; (*leichter*) to pat sb on the back; **jdm** or (*rare*) **jdn auf den Kopf ~** to hit sb on the head; **jdm ein Buch** or **mit einem Buch auf den Kopf ~** to hit sb on the head with a book; **jdm etw aus der Hand ~** to knock sth out of sb's hand; **jdm** or (*rare*) **jdn ins Gesicht ~** to hit/slap/punch sb in the face; **ihm schlug das Ge-wissen** his conscience pricked (*Brit*) or both-ered him; **einer Sache** (*dat*) **ins Gesicht ~** (*fig*) to be a slap in the face for sth; **na ja, ehe ich mich ~ lasse!** (*hum inf*) yes, I don't mind if I do, I suppose you could twist my arm (*hum inf*) → **grün, Fass, Wahrheit** etc

b (= *läuten*) to chime; *Stunde* to strike; **die Uhr hat 12 geschlagen** the clock has struck 12; **ei-ne geschlagene Stunde** a full hour; **wissen, was es** or **die Uhr** or **die Glocke** or **die Stunde ge-schlagen hat** (*fig inf*) to know what's what (*inf*) → **dreizehn**

c (= *heftig flattern*) **mit den Flügeln ~**, **die Flügel ~** (*liter*) to beat or flap its wings

VT **a** (= *besiegen, übertreffen*) *Gegner, Konkurrenz, Rekord* to beat; **jdn in etw** (*dat*) **~** to beat sb at sth; **unsere Mannschaft schlug den Gegner (mit) 2:1** our team beat their opponents (by) 2-1; **sich geschlagen geben** to admit that one is beaten, to admit defeat

b *Teig, Eier* to beat; (*mit Schneebesen*) to whisk;

Sahne to whip; **ein Ei in die Pfanne ~** to crack an egg into the pan; **ein Ei in die Suppe ~** to beat an egg into the soup

c (*Chess*) to take, to capture

d (*liter: = treffen*) **das Schicksal schlug sie hart** fate dealt her a hard blow; **ein vom Schicksal geschlagener Mann** a man dogged by fate

e (*Bibl: = bestrafen*) to strike (down), to smite (*Bibl*); **mit Blindheit geschlagen sein** (*lit, fig*) to be blind; **mit Dummheit geschlagen sein** to be dumb

f (*= fällen*) to fell

g (*= fechten*) *Mensuren* to fight

h (*liter: = krallen, beißen*) **seine Fänge/Zähne in etw** (*acc*) **~** to sink one's talons/teeth into sth

i (*Hunt: = töten*) to kill

j (*= spielen*) *Trommel* to beat; (*liter*) *Harfe, Laute* to pluck, to play; **das Schlagen der Trommeln** the beat(ing) of the drums

k (*dated: = prägen*) *Münzen etc* to mint, to coin

l (*= hinzufügen*) to add (*auf +acc, zu* to); *Gebiet* to annexe

m (*in Verbindung mit n siehe auch dort*) *Kreis, Bogen* to describe; *Purzelbaum, Rad* to do; *Alarm, Funken* to raise; *Krach* to make; **Profit aus etw ~** to make a profit from sth; (*fig*) to profit from sth; **eine Schlacht ~** to fight a battle

n den Kragen nach oben ~ to turn up one's collar; **die Hände vors Gesicht ~** to cover one's face with one's hands

o (*= wickeln*) to wrap

VI a (*Herz, Puls*) to beat; (*heftig*) to pound, to throb; **sein Puls schlug unregelmäßig** his pulse was irregular; **ihr Herz schlägt für den FC Bayern** she's passionate about FC Bayern; **jds Herz höher ~ lassen** (*fig*) to make sb's heart beat faster, to set sb's pulse racing

b *aux sein* (*= auftreffen*) **mit dem Kopf auf/gegen etw** (*acc*) **~** to hit one's head on/against sth

c *aux sein* (*= gelangen*) **ein leises Wimmern schlug an sein Ohr** he could hear a faint whimpering

d (*Regen*) to beat; (*Wellen*) to pound, to beat → **Welle a**

e *aux sein or haben* (*Flammen*) to shoot out (*aus* of); (*Rauch*) to pour out (*aus* of)

f (*Blitz*) to strike (*in etw acc* sth)

g (*= singen: Nachtigall, Fink*) to sing

h *aux sein* (*inf: = ähneln*) **er schlägt sehr nach seinem Vater** he takes after his father a lot → **Art a**

i (*= betreffen*) **in jds Fach/Gebiet** (*acc*) **~** to be in sb's field/line

j *aux sein* (*esp Med: = in Mitleidenschaft ziehen*) **auf die Augen/Nieren etc ~** to affect the eyes/kidneys *etc*; **jdm auf die Augen ~** to affect sb's eyes *etc* → **Magen**

VR a (*= sich prügeln*) to fight; (*= sich duellieren*) to duel (*auf +dat* with); **als Schuljunge habe ich mich oft geschlagen** I often had fights when I was a schoolboy; **sich mit jdm ~** to fight (with) sb, to have a fight with sb; (*= duellieren*) to duel with sb; **sich um etw ~** (*lit, fig*) to fight over sth; **er schlägt sich nicht um die Arbeit** he's not too keen on work (*Brit*), he's not crazy about work (*inf*)

b (*= sich selbst schlagen*) to hit or beat oneself

c (*= sich bewähren*) to do, to fare; **sich tapfer or gut ~** to make a good showing

d (*= sich begeben*) **sich nach rechts/links/Norden ~** to strike out to the right/left/for the North; **sich auf jds Seite** (*acc*) **~** to side with sb; (*= die Fronten wechseln*) to go over to sb; **sich zu einer Partei ~** to throw in one's lot with a party → **Leben a, Busch**

e (*Mech*) **sich auf etw** (*acc*) **~** to affect sth

schla|gend **ADJ** (*= treffend*) *Bemerkung, Vergleich* apt, appropriate; (*= überzeugend*) *Beweis* striking, convincing → **Verbindung, Wetter²** **ADV** **etw ~ beweisen/widerlegen** to prove/refute sth convincingly

Schla|ger ['ʃlaːgɐ] **M -s, -** **a** (*Mus*) pop song; (*erfolgreich*) hit song, hit **b** (*inf*) (*= Erfolg*) hit; (=

Waren) bargain; (*= Verkaufsschlager, Buch*) bestseller; **der ~ in der Bundesliga** the big match in the (German) national league

Schlä|ger¹ ['ʃlɛːgɐ] **M -s, -** **a** (*= Tennisschläger, Federballschläger*) racquet (*Brit*), racket (*US*); (*= Hockeyschläger, Eishockeyschläger*) stick; (*= Golfschläger*) club; (*= Kricketschläger, Baseballschläger*) bat; (*= Tischtennisschläger*) bat, paddle; (*= Poloschläger*) mallet **b** (*= Waffe*) straight-bladed sabre used by students in duelling bouts

Schlä|ger² ['ʃlɛːgɐ] **M -s, -, Schlä|ge|rin** [-ərɪn] **F -, -nen** **a** (*= Spieler*) (*Kricket*) batsman; (*Baseball*) batter **b** (*= Raufbold*) thug, ruffian

Schlä|ger|ban|de **F** gang of thugs

Schlä|ge|rei [ʃlɛːgə'raɪ] **F -, -en** fight, brawl

Schlä|ger|mu|sik **F** pop music

Schlä|ger|müt|ze **F** cap

Schlager-: Schla|ger|pa|ra|de **F** hit parade; **Schla|ger|sän|ger(in)** **M(F)** pop singer; **Schla|ger|sen|dung** **F** pop music programme (*Brit*) or program (*US*); **Schla|ger|text** **M** (pop music) lyrics *pl*; **Schla|ger|tex|ter(in)** **M(F)** writer of pop music lyrics, pop lyricist

Schlä|ger|trupp **M** , **Schlä|ger|trup|pe** **F** (*inf*) gang of thugs

Schlä|ger|typ **M** (*inf*) thug

Schlag-: schlag|fer|tig **ADJ** *Antwort* quick and clever; **er ist ein ~er Mensch** he is always ready with a quick (-witted) reply **ADV** **~ reagieren** to give a quick-witted reply; **~ antworten** to be quick with an answer; **... bemerkte sie ~** ... she said smartly; **Schlag|fer|tig|keit** **F** , *no pl* (*von Mensch*) quick-wittedness; (*von Antwort*) cleverness; **Schlag|ho|se** **F** flared trousers *pl* (*esp Brit*) or pants *pl* (*esp US*), flares *pl* (*inf*); **Schlag|in|stru|ment** **NT** percussion instrument; **Schlag|kraft** **F** (*lit, fig*) power; (*Boxen*) punch(ing power); (*Mil*) strike power; **schlag|kräf|tig** **ADJ** *Boxer, Armee, Argumente* powerful; *Beweise* clear-cut; **Schlag|licht** **NT** (*Art, Phot*) highlight; **ein ~ auf etw** (*acc*) **werfen** (*lit, fig*) to highlight sth; **schlag|licht|ar|tig** **ADV** **etw ~ beleuchten** to give a sudden insight into sth; **~ deutlich werden** to become clear at a stroke; **Schlag|loch** **NT** pothole; **Schlag|mann** **M** *pl* **-männer** (*Rudern*) stroke; (*Kricket*) batsman; (*Baseball*) batter; **Schlag|obers** ['ʃlaːklo:bɐs] **NT -, -** (*Aus*), **Schlag|rahm** **M** (*S Ger*) (whipping) cream; (*geschlagen*) whipped cream; **Schlag|ring** **M** **a** knuckle-duster **b** (*Mus*) plectrum; **Schlag|sah|ne** **F** (whipping) cream; (*geschlagen*) whipped cream; **Schlag|schat|ten** **M** (*Art, Phot*) shadow (*of person or object*); **Schlag|sei|te** **F** (*Naut*) list; **~ haben** (*Naut*) to be listing, to have a list; (*fig*) to be one-sided; (*hum inf: = betrunken sein*) to be half seas over (*Brit inf*), to be three sheets to the wind (*inf*); **Schlag|stock** **M** (*form*) truncheon, baton, nightstick (*US*); **Schlagstöcke einsetzen** to charge with batons; **Schlag|stock|ein|satz** **M** (*form*) baton charge

schlägt [ʃlɛːkt] *3. pers sing pres von* **schlagen**

Schlag-: Schlag|werk **NT** striking mechanism (*of a clock*); **Schlag|wet|ter** **NT** (*Min*) firedamp; **Schlag|wort** **NT** *a* *pl* **-wörter** (*= Stichwort*) headword **b** *pl* **-worte** (*= Parole*) catchword, slogan; **Schlag|wort|ka|ta|log** **M** subject catalogue (*Brit*) or catalog (*US*); **Schlag|zei|le** **F** headline; **~ machen** (*inf*) to hit the headlines; **in die ~n geraten** to make the headlines; **für ~n sorgen** to make headlines; **etw/jdn aus den ~n bringen** to get sth/sb out of the media spotlight; **aus den ~n verschwinden** not to be big news anymore; **schlag|zei|len** ['ʃlaːktsaɪlən] **VT** to headline; **Schlag|zeug** **NT** *pl* **-zeuge** drums *pl*; (*in Orchester*) percussion *no pl*; **Schlag|zeu|ger** [-tsɔygɐ] **M -s, -, Schlag|zeu|ge|rin** [-ərɪn] **F -, -nen** drummer; (*inf: in Orchester*) percussionist; **Schlag|zeug|spie|ler(in)** **M(F)** percussionist

schlak|sig ['ʃlaːksɪç] (*esp N Ger inf*) **ADJ** gangling, gawky **ADV** in a gangling way, gawkily

Schla|mas|sel [ʃla'masl] **M OR NT -s, -** (*inf*) (*= Durcheinander*) mix-up; (*= missliche Lage*) mess (*inf*); **der** or **das ganze ~** (*Zeug*) the whole lot (*inf*), the whole (kit and) caboodle (*inf*); **da haben wir den** or **das ~** now we're in a right mess (*inf*); **im ~ stecken** to be in a mess (*inf*); **jdn aus dem ~ ziehen** to get sb out of the mess he/she is in (*inf*); **jdn in den ~ bringen** or **reiten** to get sb into a mess (*inf*)

Schlamm [ʃlam] **M -(e)s, -e** or **¨e** ['ʃlɛmə] mud; (*= Schlick auch*) sludge

Schlamm|bad **NT** mud bath

schläm|men ['ʃlɛmən] **VT** **a** (*= reinigen*) *Hafenbecken* to dredge; *Kreide* to wash **b** (*= weißen*) *Wand* to whitewash

schlam|mig ['ʃlamɪç] **ADJ** muddy; (*= schlickig auch*) sludgy

Schlämm|krei|de **F** whiting

Schlamm|la|wi|ne **F** mudflow, mudslide

Schlamm|schlacht **F** (*inf*) mud bath

Schlam|pe ['ʃlampə] **F -, -n** (*pej inf*) slut (*inf*)

schlam|pen ['ʃlampn] **VI** (*inf*) to be sloppy (in one's work); **bei einer Arbeit ~** to do a piece of work sloppily; **die Behörden haben wieder einmal geschlampt** (once again) the authorities have done a sloppy job

Schlam|per ['ʃlampɐ] **M -s, -, Schlam|pe|rin** [-ərɪn] **F -, -nen** (*S Ger inf*) sloppy person; (*unordentlich*) untidy person

Schlam|pe|rei [ʃlampə'raɪ] **F -, -en** (*inf*) sloppiness; (*= schlechte Arbeit*) sloppy work; (*= Unordentlichkeit*) untidiness; **das ist eine ~!** that's a disgrace!

schlam|pig ['ʃlampɪç], (*Aus, S Ger*) **schlam|pert** ['ʃlampɐt] **ADJ** sloppy, careless; *Arbeit auch* slipshod; (*= unordentlich*) untidy; (*= liederlich*) slovenly (*= nachlässig*) carelessly, sloppily; (*= ungepflegt*) slovenly; **die Arbeit ist ~ erledigt worden** the work has been sloppily or carelessly done, the work has been done in a slipshod manner

Schlam|pig|keit **F -,** *no pl* (*inf*) sloppiness, carelessness; (*= Unordentlichkeit*) untidiness; (*= Liederlichkeit*) slovenliness

schlang *pret von* **schlingen¹** *von* **schlingen²**

Schlan|ge ['ʃlaŋə] **F -, -n** **a** snake, serpent (*liter*); (*fig: = Frau*) Jezebel; **die ~** (*Astron*) Serpens, the Serpent; **eine falsche ~** a snake in the grass; **sich winden wie eine ~** (*fig*) to go through all sorts of contortions **b** (*= Menschenschlange, Autoschlange*) queue (*Brit*), line (*US*); **~ stehen** to queue (up) (*Brit*), to stand in line (*US*) **c** (*Tech*) coil

schlän|ge|lig ['ʃlɛŋəlɪç] **ADJ** *Weg* winding

Schlän|gel|li|nie **F** wavy line

schlän|geln ['ʃlɛŋln] **VR** (*Weg, Menschenmenge*) to wind (its way), to snake; (*Fluss auch*) to meander; (*Schlange*) to wriggle; **sich um etw ~** to wind around sth; **sich durch etw ~** (*fig*) to worm one's way or wriggle through sth; **eine geschlängelte Linie** a wavy line

Schlangen-: schlan|gen|ar|tig **ADJ, ADV** snake-like; **Schlan|gen|be|schwö|rer** [-bəʃvø:rɐ] **M -s, -, Schlan|gen|be|schwö|re|rin** [-ərɪn] **F -, -nen** snake charmer; **Schlan|gen|biss ▲** **M** snakebite; **Schlan|gen|brut** **F** (*old liter*) brood of vipers; **Schlan|gen|fraß** **M** (*pej inf*) muck *no indef art*; **Schlan|gen|ge|zücht** **NT** brood of vipers; **Schlan|gen|gift** **NT** snake venom or poison; **Schlan|gen|gur|ke** **F** snake cucumber or gourd; **Schlan|gen|haft** **ADJ** snake-like; **Schlan|gen|haut** **F** snake's skin; (*= Leder*) snakeskin; **Schlan|gen|le|der** **NT** snakeskin; **Schlan|gen|li|nie** **F** wavy line; (*beim Fahren*) to swerve about; **Schlan|gen|mensch** **M** contortionist

Schlan|ge|ste|hen **NT -s,** *no pl* queueing (*Brit*), standing in line (*US*)

schlank [ʃlaŋk] **ADJ** **a** slim; *Hals, Bäume auch* slender; **~ werden** to slim; **ihr Kleid macht sie ~** her dress makes her look slim; **Jog(h)urt macht**

~ yoghurt is slimming, yoghurt is good for the figure; **sich ~ machen** (fig) to breathe in → **Linie b** (fig: = effektiv) lean; **~er Staat** (Pol) lean or slimmed-down state

Schlank|heit F -, no pl slimness

Schlank|heits|kur F diet; (Med) course of slimming treatment; **eine ~ machen/anfangen** to be/go on a diet; **eine ~ für den Staat** (fig) slimming down the state

Schlank|ma|cher M slimming agent

schlank|weg ['ʃlaŋkvɛk] ADV (inf) ablehnen, sagen point-blank, flatly

schlank|wüch|sig ['ʃlaŋkvyːksɪç] ADJ Person tall and slim, willowy; Baum tall and slender

schlapp [ʃlap] ADJ (inf) (= erschöpft, kraftlos) worn-out, shattered (Brit inf); (= energielos) listless, floppy (inf); (nach Krankheit etc) run-down; (= feige) Haltung, Mensch lily-livered (inf), yellow (inf); (= gering, unbedeutend) measly (inf); **sich ~ lachen** (inf) to laugh oneself silly; **~e 300 Euro** a mere or measly 300 euros

Schläpp|chen ['ʃlɛpçən] NT -s, - usu pl (für Gymnastik, Ballett) slipper

Schlap|pe ['ʃlapə] F -, -n (inf) setback; (esp Sport) defeat; **eine ~ einstecken (müssen)** or **erleiden** to suffer a setback/defeat; **jdm eine ~ beibringen** or **erteilen** to defeat sb

schlap|pen ['ʃlapn̩] VI aux sein or haben (inf) (= lose sitzen) to be baggy; (Schuhe) to flap; (= latschen) to slouch VT (Tier) to lap (up)

Schlap|pen ['ʃlapn̩] M -s, - (inf) slipper

Schlapp|heit F -, no pl (= Erschöpfung) exhaustion; (= Energielosigkeit) listlessness; (= Feigheit) cowardice

Schlapp-: Schlapp|hut M floppy hat; **schlapp+machen** VI sep (inf) to wilt; (= zusammenbrechen, ohnmächtig werden) to collapse; **die meisten Manager machen mit 40 schlapp** most managers are finished by the time they're 40; **Leute, die bei jeder Gelegenheit ~, können wir nicht gebrauchen** we can't use people who can't take it or who can't stand the pace (inf); **Schlapp|ohr** NT **a** (hum: = Kaninchen) bunny (rabbit) (inf) **b** **Schlappohren** PL floppy ears pl; **Schlapp|schwanz** M (pej inf) wimp (inf)

Schla|raf|fen|land NT Cockaigne, land of milk and honey

schlau [ʃlau] ADJ clever, smart; Mensch, Idee auch shrewd; (= gerissen) cunning, crafty, wily; Sprüche clever; **er ist ein ~er Kopf** he has a good head on his shoulders; **ein ~er Bursche** a crafty or cunning devil (inf); **ein ~es Buch** (inf) a clever book; **sich über etw** (acc) **~ machen** (inf) to inform oneself about sth; **ich werde nicht ~ aus ihm/dieser Sache** I can't make him/it out → **Fuchs** ADV cleverly; **sie tut immer so ~** she always thinks she's so clever or smart; **etw ~ anfangen** or **anstellen** to manage sth cleverly

Schlau|be ['ʃlaubə] F -, -n (dial) skin

Schlau|ber|ger ['ʃlaubɛrɡə] M -s, -, **Schlau|ber|ge|rin** [-ərɪn] F -, -nen (inf) clever Dick (Brit inf), smart aleck (US)

Schlau|ber|ge|rei [ʃlaubɛrɡə'rai] F -, no pl (iro inf) know-all attitude

Schlauch [ʃlaux] M -(e)s, **Schläuche** ['ʃlɔyçə] hose; (Med) tube; (= Gartenschlauch) hose (pipe); (= Fahrradschlauch, Autoschlauch) (inner) tube; (= Weinschlauch etc) skin; **das Zimmer ist ein richtiger ~** the room is really narrow; **auf dem ~ stehen** (inf) (= nicht begreifen) not to have a clue (inf) (= nicht weiterkommen) to be stuck (inf)

Schlauch-: schlauch|ar|tig ADJ tube-like, tubular; Zimmer narrow; **Schlauch|boot** NT rubber dinghy

schlau|chen ['ʃlauxn̩] VT (inf) jdn (Reise, Arbeit etc) to wear out; (Chef, Feldwebel etc) to drive hard VI (inf: = Kraft kosten) to wear you/one etc out, to take it out of you/one etc (inf); **das schlaucht echt!** it really takes it out of you (inf)

schlauch|los ADJ Reifen tubeless

Schläue ['ʃlɔyə] F -, no pl cunning, craftiness, slyness

schlau|er|wei|se ['ʃlauɐ'vaizə] ADV cleverly, shrewdly; (= gerissen) craftily, cunningly, slyly; **wenn du das wusstest, hättest du mich ~ benachrichtigen können** if you knew about it, you should have had the sense to tell me

Schlau|fe ['ʃlaufə] F -, -n (an Kleidungsstück, Schuh etc) loop; (= Aufhänger) hanger; (= Strecke) loop

Schlau|fuchs M → **Schlauberger**

Schlau|heit ['ʃlauhait] F -, -en, **Schlau|ig|keit** ['ʃlauɪçkait] F -, -en (rare) **a** no pl cleverness, smartness; (von Mensch, Idee auch) shrewdness; (= Gerissenheit) cunning, craftiness **b** (= Bemerkung) clever remark

Schlau|kopf M , (S Ger) **Schlau|le** ['ʃlaulə] (inf) NT -s, -, **Schlau|mei|er** [-maiɐ] M -s, - clever Dick (Brit inf), smart aleck (inf)

Schla|wi|ner [ʃla'viːnɐ] M -s, - (hum inf) villain, rogue

schlecht [ʃlɛçt] ADJ **a** bad; Zustand, Aussprache, Geschmack, Zensur, Leistung poor, bad; Qualität poor, bad, inferior; Luft stale, bad; Zeiten bad, hard; **das Schlechte in der Welt/im Menschen** the evil in the world/in man; **das ist ein ~er Scherz** that is a dirty trick; **er ist in Latein ~er als ich** he is worse at Latin than I am; **sich zum Schlechten wenden** to take a turn for the worse; **nur Schlechtes von jdm** or **über jdn sagen** not to have a good word to say for sb → **Dienst c, Eltern, Licht b**

b pred (= ungenießbar) off pred (Brit), bad; **die Milch/das Fleisch ist ~** the milk/meat has gone off or is off (Brit), the milk/meat has gone bad or is bad; **~ werden** to go off (Brit) or bad

c (gesundheitlich etc) Zustand poor; Nieren, Herz bad; Durchblutung bad, poor; **jdm ist (es) ~** sb feels sick or ill; **in ~er Verfassung sein** to be in a bad way; **~ aussehen** (Mensch) to look bad or sick or ill; (Lage) to look bad; **mit jdm/etw sieht es ~ aus** sb/sth looks in a bad way; **damit sieht es ~ aus** things look bad → **schlecht gehen**

ADV **a** badly; **~ beraten sein** to be ill-advised; **~ bezahlt** (Person, Job) low-paid, badly paid; **sich ~ vertragen** (Menschen) to get along badly; (Dinge, Farben etc) not to go well together; **die beiden können sich ~ leiden** the two of them don't get along (with each other); **an jdm ~ handeln** to do sb wrong, to wrong sb; **~ über jdn sprechen/von jdm denken** to speak/think ill of sb; **~ gelaunt** bad-tempered; **~ gelaunt sein** to be in a bad mood

b (= mit Schwierigkeiten) hören, sehen badly; lernen, begreifen with difficulty; **er kann ~ nein** or **Nein sagen** he finds it hard to say no, he can't say no; **da kann man ~ nein** or **Nein sagen** you can hardly say no to that, it's hard to say no to that; **heute geht es ~** today is not very convenient; **das lässt sich ~ machen, das geht ~** that's not really possible or on (inf); **er ist ~ zu verstehen** he is hard to understand; **sie kann sich ~ anpassen** she finds it difficult or hard to adjust; **das kann ich ~ sagen** it's hard to say, I can't really say; **sie kann es sich ~ leisten, zu …** she can ill afford to …; **ich kann sie ~ sehen** I can't see her very well

c (in festen Redewendungen) **auf jdn/etw ~ zu sprechen sein** not to have a good word to say for sb/sth; **~ gerechnet** at the very least; **~ und recht** (hum) **mehr ~ als recht** (hum) after a fashion

d (inf) **er hat nicht ~ gestaunt** he wasn't half surprised (Brit inf), he was very surprised

schlecht-: schlecht|be|ra|ten △ [-bera:tn̩] ADJ attr → **schlecht ADV a**; **schlecht|be|zahlt** △ ADJ attr → **schlecht ADV a**

schlech|ter|dings ['ʃlɛçtɐdɪŋs] ADV (= völlig) absolutely; (= nahezu) virtually

schlecht-: schlecht ge|hen ▲ VI impers irreg aux sein **es geht jdm schlecht** sb is in a bad way; (finanziell) sb is doing badly; **wenn er das**

erfährt, gehts dir schlecht if he hears about that you'll be for it (inf); **schlecht|ge|launt** △ ADJ attr → **schlecht ADV a**; **schlecht|hin** ['ʃlɛçt'hɪn] ADV (= vollkommen) quite, absolutely; (= als solches, in seiner Gesamtheit) as such, per se; **er gilt als** or **er ist der romantische Komponist ~** he is the epitome of the Romantic composer; **Studenten/die deutsche Sprache ~** students/the German language as such or per se

Schlech|tig|keit ['ʃlɛçtɪçkait] F -, -en **a** no pl badness; (esp qualitativ) inferiority **b** (= schlechte Tat) misdeed

Schlecht-: schlecht ma|chen ▲ VT (= herabsetzen) to denigrate, to run down; **schlecht|weg** ['ʃlɛçtvɛk] ADV = **schlechthin**; **Schlecht|wet|ter** NT bad weather; **Schlecht|wet|ter|geld** NT bad-weather money or pay; **Schlecht|wet|ter|pe|ri|o|de** F spell of bad weather

schle|cken ['ʃlɛkn̩] (Aus, S Ger) VTI = **lecken ²** VI (= Süßigkeiten essen) to eat sweets (esp Brit) or candies (US); **Lust auf was zum Schlecken haben** to feel like eating something sweet

Schle|cke|rei [ʃlɛkə'rai] F -, -en (Aus, S Ger) **a** no pl (= das Lecken) licking **b** no pl (= das Naschen) eating sweet things; **die ~ der Kinder** the children eating sweet things **c** (= Leckerbissen) delicacy; (= Süßigkeit) sweet (esp Brit), sweetie (Brit inf), candy (US)

Schle|cker|maul NT (hum inf) **sie ist ein richtiges ~** she really has a sweet tooth

Schle|gel ['ʃle:ɡl] M -s, - (S Ger, Aus: Cook) leg; (von Geflügel) drumstick, leg → auch **Schlägel**

Schleh|dorn ['ʃle:dɔrn] M pl -dorne blackthorn, sloe

Schle|he ['ʃle:ə] F -, -n sloe

Schlei [ʃlai] M -(e)s, -e (Zool) tench

schlei|chen ['ʃlaiçn̩] pret **schlich** [ʃlɪç], ptp **geschlichen** [ɡə'ʃlɪçn̩] VI aux sein to creep; (heimlich auch) to sneak, to steal; (Fahrzeug) to crawl; (fig: Zeit) to crawl (by); **um das Haus ~** to prowl around the house VR **a** (= leise gehen) to creep, to sneak, to steal; (fig: Misstrauen) to enter; **sich in jds Vertrauen** (acc) **~** to worm one's way into sb's confidence; **sich in jds Herz** (acc) **~** (Zweifel etc) to enter sb's heart **b** (S Ger, Aus: = weggehen) to go away; **schleich dich** get lost (inf)

schlei|chend ADJ attr creeping; Krankheit, Gift insidious; Fieber lingering

Schlei|cher ['ʃlaiçɐ] M -s, -, **Schlei|che|rin** [-ərɪn] F -, -nen hypocrite

Schlei|che|rei [ʃlaiçə'rai] F -, -en hypocrisy, insincerity

Schleich-: Schleich|han|del M illicit trading (mit in); **der ~ mit Waffen** gunrunning; **der ~ mit Alkohol** bootlegging; **Schleich|händ|ler(in)** M(F) illicit trader; **Schleich|pfad** M , **Schleich|weg** M secret or hidden path; (= wenig befahrene Straßenverbindung) short cut (avoiding traffic); **auf Schleichwegen** (fig) on the quiet, surreptitiously; **Schleich|wer|bung** F a plug; **~ vermeiden** to avoid making plugs

Schleie ['ʃlaiə] F -, -n (Zool) tench

Schlei|er ['ʃlaiɐ] M -s, - (lit, fig) veil; (von Wolken, Nebel auch) haze; **das Foto hat einen ~** the photo is foggy or fogged; **die Berggipfel waren in ~ von Nebel gehüllt** the mountain tops were veiled in mist; **einen ~ vor den Augen haben, wie durch einen ~ sehen** to have a mist in front of one's eyes; **den ~ (des Geheimnisses) lüften** to lift the veil of secrecy; **einen ~ über etw** (acc) **ziehen** or **breiten** (fig) to draw a veil over sth; **der ~ des Vergessens** the veil of oblivion; **den ~ nehmen** (liter) to take the veil

Schlei|er-: Schlei|er|eu|le F barn owl; **Schlei|er|fahn|dung** F (police search involving) spot checks pl; **schlei|er|haft** ADJ (inf) baffling, mysterious; **es ist mir völlig ~** it's a complete mystery to me; **Schlei|er|kraut** NT (Bot) gypsophila; **Schlei|er|schwanz** M goldfish; **Schlei|er|tanz** M veil dance; **Schlei|er-wol|ke** F usu pl (Met) cirrostratus (spec)

Schleif|bank F pl **-bänke** grinding machine

Schlei|fe ['ʃlaifə] F **-, -n a** (auch Aviat, Comput, beim Schlittschuhlaufen); (= Flussschleife) bow, horseshoe bend; (= Straßenschleife) twisty bend **b** (von Band) bow; (= Schuhschleife) bow(knot); (= Fliege) bow tie; (= Kranzschleife) ribbon

schlei|fen¹ ['ʃlaifn] **VT a** (lit, fig) to drag; (= ziehen) to haul, to drag; (Mus) Töne, Noten to slur; **jdn vor Gericht ~** (fig) to drag or haul sb into court; **jdn ins Konzert ~** (hum inf) to drag sb along to a concert **b** (= niederreißen) to raze (to the ground) **VI a** aux sein or haben to trail, to drag **b** (= reiben) to rub; **die Kupplung ~ lassen** (Aut) to slip the clutch; **die Zügel ~ lassen** (lit, fig) to slacken the reins; **wir haben die Sache ~ lassen** (fig) we let things slide

schlei|fen² pret **schliff** [ʃlif], ptp **geschliffen** [gə'ʃlifn] VT **a** Rasiermesser, Messer, Schere to sharpen, to whet; Beil, Sense to grind, to whet; Werkstück, Linse to grind; Parkett to sand; Edelstein, Glas, Spiegel to cut → auch **geschliffen b** (inf: = drillen) **jdn ~** to drill sb hard

Schlei|fer¹ ['ʃlaife] M (= Mus) slurred note

Schlei|fer² ['ʃlaife] M **-s, -**, **Schlei|fe|rin** [-ərɪn] F **-, -nen a** grinder; (= Edelsteinschleifer) cutter **b** (Mil sl) slave-driver

Schlei|fe|rei [ʃlaifə'rai] F **-, -en a** (Werkstatt) grinding shop; (für Edelstein, Glas) cutting shop **b** (Mil sl: = Drill) square-bashing (Brit inf), drill on barrack square

Schleif-: Schleif|lack M (coloured (Brit) or colored (US)) lacquer or varnish; **Schleif|lack|mö|bel** PL lacquered furniture sing; **Schleif|ma|schi|ne** F grinding machine; **Schleif|mit|tel** NT abrasive (agent); **Schleif|pa|pier** NT abrasive paper; **Schleif|rad** NT , **Schleif|schei|be** F grinding wheel; **Schleif|spur** F blutig etc trail; **Schleif|stein** M grinding stone, grindstone; **er sitzt da wie ein Affe auf dem ~** (dated inf) he looks a proper idiot or a proper Charlie (Brit inf) sitting there

Schlei|fung ['ʃlaifʊŋ] F **-, -en** razing

Schleim [ʃlaim] M **-(e)s, -e a** slime; (Med) mucus; (in Atemorganen) phlegm, mucus; (Bot) mucilage **b** (Cook) gruel

Schleim-: Schleim|ab|son|de|rung F mucous secretion; **Schleim|beu|tel** M (Physiol) bursa (spec); **Schleim|drü|se** F mucous gland; (von Schnecken etc) slime gland

schlei|men ['ʃlaimən] VI to leave a coating or film; (fig inf: = schmeicheln) to fawn, to crawl (inf)

Schlei|mer ['ʃlaime] M **-s, -**, **Schlei|me|rin** [-ərɪn] F **-, -nen** (inf) crawler (inf)

Schlei|mhaut F mucous membrane

schlei|mig ['ʃlaimɪç] ADJ slimy; (Med) mucous; (Bot) mucilaginous **b** (pej: = unterwürfig) slimy (inf)

Schlei|mig|keit F **-, no pl** (pej) sliminess (inf)

Schleim-: schleim|lö|send ADJ expectorant; **Schleim|pilz** M slime mould (Brit) or mold (US), slime fungus; **Schleim|schei|ßer(in)** M(F) (inf) bootlicker (inf), arse licker (Brit sl), ass licker (US sl); **Schleim|sup|pe** F gruel

Schle|mihl [ʃle'mi:l, 'ʃle:mi:l] M **-s, -s** (geh: = Pechvogel) unlucky devil (inf), schlemiel (inf); (inf: = Schlitzohr) crafty customer (inf)

schlem|men ['ʃlɛmən] VI (= üppig essen) to feast, to have a feast; (= üppig leben) to live it up **VT** to feast on

Schlem|mer ['ʃlɛme] M **-s, -**, **Schlem|me|rin** [-ərɪn] F **-, -nen** gourmet, bon vivant

Schlem|me|rei [ʃlɛmə'rai] F **-, -en** feasting; (= Mahl) feast

schlem|mer|haft, **schlem|me|risch** ['ʃlɛmərɪʃ] ADJ gourmandizing, gluttonous (pej)

Schlem|mer|mahl NT feast, banquet

---

schlen|dern ['ʃlɛndɐn] VI aux sein to stroll, to amble

Schlend|ri|an ['ʃlɛndria:n] M **-(e)s, no pl** (inf) casualness, inefficiency; (= Trott) rut

Schlen|ker ['ʃlɛŋke] M **-s, -** swerve; (= Abstecher) detour; **einen ~ machen** to swerve; (= einen Abstecher machen) to make a detour

schlen|kern ['ʃlɛŋken] **VT/I** to swing, to dangle; **mit den Beinen/Armen ~, die Beine/Arme ~** to swing or dangle one's legs/arms **VI** (Auto) to swerve, to sway

schlen|zen ['ʃlɛntsn] VI (Sport) to scoop

Schlepp [ʃlɛp] M (Naut, fig) **jdn/etw in ~ neh|men** to take sb/sth in tow; **in** or **im ~ haben** to have in tow

Schlepp|damp|fer M tug(boat)

Schlep|pe ['ʃlɛpə] F **-, -n a** (von Kleid) train **b** (Hunt) drag

schlep|pen ['ʃlɛpn] **VT a** (= tragen) Lasten, Gepäck to lug, to schlepp (US sl); (= zerren) to drag, to haul, to schlepp (US sl); Auto, Schiff to tow (to) drag; Flüchtlinge to smuggle; **jdn vor den Richter ~** to haul sb (up) before the judge; **etw mit sich ~** (fig, Verantwortung etc) to carry sth on one's shoulders, to be burdened with sth **VT** (inf: = nachschleifen) to drag, to trail **VR** to drag or haul oneself; (Verhandlungen etc) to drag on

schlep|pend **ADJ** Gang dragging, shuffling; Bedienung, Abfertigung sluggish, slow; Absatz, Nachfrage, Geschäft slack, sluggish; Stimme drawling; Gesang dragging, slow; **wehmütig ~e Klänge** melancholy languorous sounds; **nach ein paar Stunden wurde die Unterhaltung immer ~er** after a few hours the conversation began to drag **ADV** nur **~ vorankommen** to progress very slowly; **die Unterhaltung kam nur ~ in Gang** conversation was very slow to start or started sluggishly

Schlep|pen|trä|ger(in) M(F) trainbearer

Schlep|per¹ ['ʃlɛpe] M **-s, - a** (Aut) tractor **b** (Naut) tug

Schlep|per² ['ʃlɛpe] M **-s, -**, **Schlep|pe|rin** [-ərɪn] F **-, -nen a** (sl: für Lokal) tout **b** (= Fluchthelfer) somebody who smuggles people across borders

Schlep|per|ban|de F people or refugee smuggling ring

Schlep|pe|rei [ʃlɛpə'rai] F **-, no pl** (inf) lugging around or about

Schlep|per|or|ga|ni|sa|ti|on F , **Schlep|per|ring** M ring or syndicate of touts; (= Fluchthelfer) people or refugee smuggling ring

Schlepp-: Schlepp|kahn M lighter, (canal) barge; **Schlepp|lift** M ski tow; **Schlepp|lohn** M (Naut) towage; **Schlepp|netz** NT trawl (net); **Schlepp|netz|fahn|dung** F dragnet; **Schlepp|schiff** NT tug(boat); **Schlepp|tau** NT (Naut) tow rope; (Aviat) dragrope, trail rope; **ein Schiff/jdn ins ~ nehmen** to take a ship/sb in tow

Schle|si|en ['ʃle:ziən] NT **-s** Silesia

Schle|si|er ['ʃle:ziɐ] M **-s, -**, **Schle|si|e|rin** [-iərɪn] F **-, -nen** Silesian

schle|sisch ['ʃle:zɪʃ] ADJ Silesian

Schles|wig-Hol|stein ['ʃle:svɪç'hɔlʃtain] NT **-s** Schleswig-Holstein

Schleu|der ['ʃlɔydɐ] F **-, -n a** (Waffe) sling; (= Wurfmaschine) catapult, onager; (= Zwille) catapult (Brit), slingshot (US) **b** (= Zentrifuge) centrifuge; (für Honig) extractor; (= Wäscheschleuder) spin-dryer

Schleu|der-: Schleu|der|ball M (Sport) **a** heavy leather ball with a strap attached, swung round the head and then thrown **b** no pl a game using such a ball; **Schleu|der|gang** M (bei Waschmaschine) spin (cycle); **Schleu|der|ge|fahr** F (Mot) risk of skidding; **„Achtung ~"** "slippery road ahead"; **Schleu|der|ho|nig** M extracted honey; **Schleu|der|ma|schi|ne** F (= Wurfmaschine) catapult, ona-

---

ger; (für Milch etc) centrifuge; (für Honig) extractor

schleu|dern ['ʃlɔydɐn] **VT/I a** (= werfen) to hurl, to sling, to fling; **durch die Luft geschleudert werden** to be flung through the air; **jdm etw ins Gesicht** or **an den Kopf ~** (lit) to hurl or fling sth in sb's face; (fig) to throw sth in sb's face; **jdn zu Boden ~** to hurl or fling sb to the ground **b** (Tech) to centrifuge, to spin; Honig to extract; Wäsche to spin-dry; **kalt geschleuderter Honig** cold-pressed honey **VI** aux sein or haben to skid; **ins Schleudern kommen** or **geraten** to go into a skid; (fig inf) to run into trouble

Schleu|der-: Schleu|der|preis M giveaway price, throwaway price; **Schleu|der|sitz** M (Aviat) ejection or ejector seat; (fig) hot seat; **Schleu|der|spur** F skid mark; **Schleu|der|start** M (Aviat) catapult start; **Schleu|der|trau|ma** NT (Med) whiplash (injury); **Schleu|der|wa|re** F cut-price goods pl, cheap goods pl; **Schleu|der|wä|sche** F **ist das ~?** are those clothes for spinning?

schleu|nig ['ʃlɔynɪç] ADJ attr usu superl prompt, speedy; Schritte quick, rapid; **nur ~stes Eingreifen kann jetzt helfen** only immediate measures can help now

schleu|nigst ['ʃlɔynɪçst] ADV at once, straight away, immediately; **verschwinde, aber ~!** beat it, on the double!; **ein Bier, aber ~!** a beer, and make it snappy! (inf)

Schleu|se ['ʃlɔyzə] F **-, -n** (für Schiffe) lock; (zur Regulierung des Wasserlaufs) sluice, floodgate; (für Abwasser) sluice; (= Sicherheitsschleuse) double door system; **die ~n öffnen** (fig) to open the floodgates; **der Himmel öffnete seine ~n** (liter) the heavens opened (fig), the rain sluiced down

schleu|sen ['ʃlɔyzn] VT Schiffe to pass through a lock, to lock; Wasser to channel; (langsam) Menschen to filter; Antrag to channel; (fig: heimlich) Flüchtlinge to smuggle; **er wurde in den Saal geschleust** he was smuggled into the hall

Schleu|sen-: Schleu|sen|geld NT lock dues pl, lockage; **Schleu|sen|kam|mer** F (lock) basin; **Schleu|sen|meis|ter(in)** M(F) lock keeper; **Schleu|sen|tor** NT (für Schiffe) lock gate; (zur Regulierung des Wasserlaufs) sluicegate, floodgate; **Schleu|sen|wär|ter(in)** M(F) lock keeper

Schleu|ser ['ʃlɔyze] M **-s, -**, **Schleu|se|rin** [-ərɪn] F **-, -nen** = Schlepper² b

Schleu|sung ['ʃlɔyzʊŋ] F **-, -en** lockage, locking; (von Menschen) smuggling; **bei der ~ größerer Schiffe** when putting bigger ships through the locks

schlich pret von schleichen

Schlich [ʃlɪç] M **-(e)s, -e** usu pl ruse, trick, wile usu pl; **alle ~e kennen** to know all the tricks; **jdm auf** or **hinter die ~e kommen** to catch on to sb, to get on to sb, to get wise to sb (inf)

schlicht [ʃlɪçt] **ADJ** simple; **die ~e Wahrheit/Tatsache** the plain or simple truth/fact; **~ und einfach** plain and simple; **der ~e Menschenverstand** basic common sense; **das geht über den ~en Menschenverstand** this is beyond the normal human mind or beyond human comprehension; **diese Gedichte sind ~ und ergreifend** (iro) these poems are not exactly brilliant; **unser Abschied war ~ und ergreifend** our parting was short and sweet **ADV a** (= einfach) simply **b** (= glattweg) gelogen, erfunden simply; falsch simply, just; vergessen completely **c** **das ist ~ und einfach nicht wahr** that's just simply not true; **er sagte ~ und ergreifend nein** or **Nein** he said quite simply no

schlich|ten ['ʃlɪçtn] **VT/I a** Streit (= vermitteln) to mediate, to arbitrate (esp Ind); (= beilegen) to settle **b** (= glätten) Werkzeug, Leder, Gewebe to dress; Holz to smooth (off) **VI** to mediate, to arbitrate (esp Ind); **zwischen zwei Ländern ~** to mediate between two countries; **er wollte ~d in den Streit eingreifen** he wanted to intervene in the quarrel (to settle it)

Schlich|ter [ˈʃlɪçtɐ] M **-s, -**, **Schlich|te|rin** [-ərɪn] F **-, -nen** mediator; (*Ind*) arbitrator

Schlich|ter|spruch M (= *Schiedsspruch*) (arbitral) award

Schlicht|fei|le F smooth-cut file

Schlicht|heit F **-**, *no pl* simplicity

Schlicht|ho|bel M smoothing plane

Schlich|tung [ˈʃlɪçtʊŋ] F **-, -en** (= *Vermittlung*) mediation, arbitration (*esp Ind*); (= *Beilegung*) settlement

Schlich|tungs-: **Schlich|tungs|aus|schuss** ▲ M arbitration *or* conciliation commission; **Schlich|tungs|stel|le** F arbitration *or* conciliation board; **Schlich|tungs|ver|fah|ren** NT , **Schlich|tungs|ver|hand|lun|gen** PL arbitration (proceedings *pl*); **Schlich|tungs|ver|such** M attempt at mediation *or* arbitration

schlicht|weg [ˈʃlɪçtˈvɛk] ADV → **schlechthin**

Schlick [ʃlɪk] M **-(e)s, -e** silt, ooze; (= *Ölschlick*) slick

schli|ckig [ˈʃlɪkɪç] ADJ muddy, slimy

schli|dern [ˈʃliːdɐn] VI *aux* haben *or* sein (*N Ger*) = **schlittern**

schlief *pret von* **schlafen**

Schlie|re [ˈʃliːrə] F **-, -n** streak, schlieren *pl* (*Tech*)

schließ|bar ADJ (*rare*) closable; (= *zuschließbar*) lockable

Schlie|ße [ˈʃliːsə] F **-, -n** fastening, fastener

schlie|ßen [ˈʃliːsn] *pret* **schloss** [ʃlɔs], *ptp* **geschlossen** [ɡəˈʃlɔsn] VT **a** (= *zumachen*) to close, to shut; (= *verriegeln*) to bolt; (= *Betrieb einstellen*) to close *or* shut down; *Stromkreis* to close; **seine Pforten ~** to close its doors; **eine Lücke ~** (*lit*) to close a gap; (*fig auch*) to fill a gap; **die Reihen ~** (*Mil*) to close ranks
b (= *beenden*) *Versammlung* to close, to conclude, to wind up; *Brief* to conclude, to close
c (= *eingehen*) *Vertrag* to conclude; *Frieden* to make; *Bündnis* to enter into; *Freundschaft* to form; **wo wurde Ihre Ehe geschlossen?** where did your marriage take place?; **wer hat Ihre Ehe geschlossen?** who married you?
d (*geh*: = *umfassen*) **etw in sich** (*dat*) **~** to contain sth, to include sth; (*indirekt*) to imply sth; **jdn in die Arme ~** to embrace sb; **lass dich in die Arme ~** let me embrace you; **jdn/etw in sein Herz ~** to take sb/sth to one's heart
e (= *befestigen*) **etw an etw** (*acc*) **~** to fasten sth to sth; **daran schloss er eine Bemerkung** he added a remark (to this)
VR (= *zugehen*) to close, to shut; *Wunde* to close; (*fig geh*: *Wunde*) to heal; **daran schließt sich eine Diskussion** this is followed by a discussion; **sich um etw ~** to close around sth
VI **a** (= *zugehen*) to close, to shut; (= *Betrieb einstellen*) to close *or* shut down; (*Schlüssel*) to fit; **die Tür schließt nicht** the door doesn't *or* won't close *or* shut; **„geschlossen"** "closed"
b (= *enden*) to close, to conclude; (*St Ex*) to close; **leider muss ich jetzt ~** (*in Brief*) I'm afraid I must conclude *or* close now; **die Börse schloss fester/schwächer** the market closed stronger/weaker
c (= *schlussfolgern*) to infer; **aus etw auf etw** (*acc*) **~** to infer sth from sth; **auf etw** (*acc*) **~ lassen** to indicate sth, to suggest sth; **von sich auf andere ~** to judge others by one's own standards → *auch* **geschlossen**

Schlie|ßer [ˈʃliːsɐ] M **-s, -**, **Schlie|ße|rin** [-ərɪn] F **-, -nen** (*inf*) jailer, warder (*Brit*)

Schließ-: **Schließ|fach** NT (= *Postschließfach*) post office box, PO box; (= *Bankschließfach*) safe-deposit box, safety-deposit box; **Schließ|korb** M hamper

schließ|lich [ˈʃliːslɪç] ❂ 53.2, 53.5 ADV (= *endlich*) in the end, finally, eventually; (= *immerhin*) after all; **er kam ~ doch** he came after all;

~ und endlich at long last; **~ und endlich bist du doch kein Kind mehr** after all you're not a child any more

Schließ|mus|kel M (*Anat*) sphincter

Schlie|ßung [ˈʃliːsʊŋ] F **-, -en a** (= *das Schließen*) closing, shutting; (= *Betriebseinstellung*) closure **b** (= *Beendigung*) (*einer Versammlung*) closing, breaking-up; (*von Debatte etc*) conclusion, closing; (= *Geschäftsschluss*) closing (time); (*Parl*) closure **c** (= *Vereinbarung*) (*von Frieden, Vertrag, Ehe*) conclusion; (*von Bündnis*) conclusion, forming

schliff *pret von* **schleifen**[2]

Schliff [ʃlɪf] M **-(e)s, -e** (*von Glas, von Edelstein*) (*Prozess*) cutting; (*Ergebnis*) cut; (*von Linse*) grinding; (*fig* = *Umgangsformen*) refinement, polish; **jdm ~ beibringen** *or* **geben** to give sb some polish *or* refinement; **jdm den letzten ~ geben** (*fig*) to perfect sb; **einer Sache den letzten ~ geben** (*fig*) to put the finishing touch(es) to sth

schlimm [ʃlɪm] ADJ **a** *Mensch* bad, wicked; (= *unartig*) naughty, bad; **es gibt Schlimmere als ihn** there are worse than him; **ein ~er Bösewicht** (*old*) an out-and-out villain; **Sie sind ja ein ganz Schlimmer!** (*hum*) you ARE naughty *or* wicked
b (*inf*: = *krank, entzündet*) bad
c (= *übel*) bad; *Krankheit* nasty, bad; *Wunde* nasty, bad, ugly; *Nachricht* awful, terrible, bad; **~, ~!** terrible, terrible!; **das war ~** that was awful *or* terrible; **~ genug, dass ...** it is/was bad enough that ...; **das finde ich nicht ~** I don't find that so bad; **eine ~e Geschichte** (*inf*) a nasty state of affairs; **eine ~e Zeit** bad times *pl*; **das ist halb so** *or* **nicht so ~!** that's not so bad!, it doesn't matter!; **zu Anfang war es ~ für ihn** in the beginning he had a hard time of it; **ist es ~ oder etwas Schlimmes?** is it bad?; **wenn es nichts Schlimmeres ist!** if that's all it is!; **es gibt Schlimmeres** it *or* things could be worse; **~er kann es nicht mehr werden** things can hardly get any worse; **im ~sten Fall** if (the) worst comes to (the) worst; **das Schlimmste** the worst; **was aber das Schlimmste ist, ...** but the worst of it is that ...; **das Schlimmste liegt hinter uns** the worst (of it) is behind us
ADV **a** (= *gravierend*) **sich täuschen, sich irren** really
b (= *äußerst schlecht*) **sich benehmen, zurichten** horribly; *zerstören* totally; **sie haben ~ gehaust** they wreaked *or* created havoc; **mit der neuen Frisur siehst du ~ aus** you look awful with that new hairdo; **es steht ~ (um ihn)** things aren't looking too good (for him)
c (*Med*) **sich verletzen, entzündet** badly; **~ eitern** to abscess badly
d (= *übel*) **er ist ~ dran** (*inf*) he's in a bad way; **wenn es ganz ~ kommt** if things get really bad; **es hätte ~er kommen können** it *or* things could have been worse; **umso** *or* **desto ~er** all the worse

schlimms|ten|falls [ˈʃlɪmstnˌfals] ADV at (the) worst; **~ wird er nur sein Geld verlieren** at worst, he will only lose his money; **~ kann ich dir £ 100 leihen** if (the) worst comes to (the) worst I can lend you £100

Schlin|ge [ˈʃlɪŋə] F **-, -n** loop; (*an Galgen*) noose; (*Med*: = *Armbinde*) sling; (= *Falle*) snare; **~n legen** to set snares; **den Kopf** *or* **sich aus der ~ ziehen** (*fig*) to get out of a tight spot (*inf*); **(bei jdm) die ~ zuziehen** (*fig*) to tighten the noose (on sb); **die ~ um seinen Hals zieht sich langsam zu** (*fig*) the noose is slowly tightening on him

Schlin|gel [ˈʃlɪŋl] M **-s, -** rascal

schlin|gen[1] [ˈʃlɪŋən] *pret* **schlang** [ʃlaŋ], *ptp* **geschlungen** [ɡəˈʃlʊŋən] (*geh*) VT (= *binden*) Knoten to tie; (= *umbinden*) *Schal etc* to wrap (*um +acc* around); **die Arme um jdn ~** to wrap one's arms around sb, to hug sb VR **sich um etw ~** to coil (itself) around sth; (*Pflanze auch*) to twine (itself) around sth

schlin|gen[2] *pret* **schlang** [ʃlaŋ], *ptp* **geschlungen** [ɡəˈʃlʊŋən] VI to gobble, to gulp, to bolt one's food

Schlin|ger|be|we|gung F rolling (motion)

Schlin|ger|kurs M (*fig*) wavering course; (*Pol*) wavering policy; **auf ~** wavering *or* vacillating from one possibility to another; (*Pol*) wavering in his/her *etc* policy; **einen ~ steuern/verfolgen** to steer/follow a wavering course; (*Pol*) to pursue a wavering policy

schlin|gern [ˈʃlɪŋɐn] VI (*Schiff*) to roll; (*Auto etc*) to lurch from side to side; **ins Schlingern geraten** (*Auto etc*) to go into a skid; (*fig*) to run into trouble

Schling|ge|wächs NT , **Schling|pflan|ze** F creeper

Schlips [ʃlɪps] M **-es, -e** tie, necktie (*US*); **mit** *or* **in ~ und Kragen** (*inf*) wearing a collar and tie → **treten** VI **c**

Schlit|ten [ˈʃlɪtn] M **-s, - a** sledge, sled; (= *Pferdeschlitten*) sleigh; (= *Rodelschlitten*) toboggan; (= *Rennschlitten*) bobsleigh; **~ fahren** to go tobogganing; **mit jdm ~ fahren** (*inf*) to have sb on the carpet (*inf*), to bawl sb out (*inf*) **b** (*Tech*) (= *Schreibmaschinenschlitten*) carriage; (*zum Stapellauf*) cradle **c** (*inf*: = *Auto*) big car

Schlit|ten-: **Schlit|ten|bahn** F toboggan run; **Schlit|ten|fah|ren** NT **-s**, *no pl* sledging; (= *Rodeln*) tobogganing; (*mit Pferdeschlitten etc*) sleighing; **Schlit|ten|fahrt** F sledge ride; (*mit Rodel*) toboggan ride; (*mit Pferdeschlitten etc*) sleigh ride; **Schlit|ten|hund** M sledge *or* sled dog; (= *Eskimohund*) husky; **Schlit|ten|par|tie** F sleigh ride

Schlit|ter|bahn F slide

schlit|tern [ˈʃlɪtɐn] VI **a** *aux* sein *or* haben (*absichtlich*) to slide **b** *aux* sein (= *ausrutschen*) to slide, to slip; (*Wagen*) to skid; (*fig*) to slide, to stumble; **in den Konkurs/Krieg ~** to slide into bankruptcy/war

Schlitt|schuh M (ice) skate; **~ laufen** *or* **fahren** (*inf*) to (ice-)skate

Schlitt|schuh-: **Schlitt|schuh|bahn** F ice rink; **Schlitt|schuh|lau|fen** NT **-s**, *no pl* (ice-)skating; **Schlitt|schuh|läu|fer(in)** M(F) (ice-)skater; **Schlitt|schuh|schritt** M skating step

Schlitz [ʃlɪts] M **-es, -e** slit; (= *Einwurfschlitz*) slot; (= *Hosenschlitz*) fly, flies *pl* (*Brit*); (= *Kleiderschlitz*) slit; (= *Jackettschlitz*) vent; **die Augen zu einem ~ zusammenkneifen** to narrow one's eyes to slits

Schlitz-: **Schlitz|au|ge** NT slit *or* slant eye; (*pej*: = *Chinese*) Chink (*pej*); **schlitz|äu|gig** ADJ slit-eyed, slant-eyed ADV **er grinste ~** he grinned a slant-eyed *or* slit-eyed grin

schlit|zen [ˈʃlɪtsn] VT to slit

Schlitz-: **Schlitz|ohr** NT (*fig*) sly fox; **schlitz|oh|rig** ADJ [-lo:rɪç] (*fig inf*) sly, crafty; **Schlitz|oh|rig|keit** F **-**, *no pl* (*fig inf*) slyness, craftiness; **Schlitz|schrau|be** F slotted screw; **Schlitz|ver|schluss** ▲ M (*Phot*) focal plane shutter

schloh|weiß [ˈʃloːˈvais] ADJ *Haare* snow-white

schloss ▲ *pret von* **schließen**

Schloss ▲ [ʃlɔs] NT **-es, ⸚er** [ˈʃlœsə] **a** (= *Gebäude*) castle; (= *Palast*) palace; (= *großes Herrschaftshaus*) mansion, stately home; (*in Frankreich*) château; **~ Nymphenburg** Nymphenburg Palace; **Schlösser und Burgen** castles and stately homes; **Schlösser im Mond** (*fig*) castles in the air, castles in Spain (= *Türschloss, Gewehrschloss etc*) lock; (= *Vorhängeschloss*) padlock; (*an Handtasche etc*) clasp; **ins ~ fallen** to click shut *or* to; **die Tür ins ~ werfen** to slam the door shut; **hinter ~ und Riegel sitzen/bringen** to be/put behind bars

Schloss-: **schloss|ar|tig** ▲ ADJ palatial; **Schloss|berg** ▲ M castle *etc* hill; **Schloss|be|sit|zer(in)** ▲ M(F) owner of a castle *etc*

Schlöss|chen ▲ [ˈʃlœsçən] NT **-s, -** *dim von* **Schloss** small castle *etc*

Schlos|ser ['ʃlɔsɐ] M **-s, -**, **Schlos|se|rin** [-ərɪn] F **-, -nen** fitter, metalworker; (für Schlösser) locksmith

Schlos|se|rei [ʃlɔsə'raɪ] F **-, -en** a (= Schlossereihandwerk) metalworking b (= Schlossereiwerkstatt) metalworking shop

Schlos|ser|hand|werk NT metalworking

Schlos|ser-: **Schlos|ser|meis|ter(in)** M(F) master fitter; **Schlos|ser|werk|statt** F metalworking shop

Schloss-: **Schloss|gar|ten** ▲ M castle etc gardens pl; **Schloss|herr(in)** ▲ M(F) owner of a castle etc; (= Adliger) lord/lady of the castle; **Schloss|hof** ▲ M courtyard; **Schloss|ho|tel** ▲ NT castle hotel; (kleiner) country house hotel (Brit); **Schloss|hund** ▲ M (obs: = Kettenhund) watchdog; **heulen wie ein ~** (inf) to howl one's head off (inf); **Schloss|ka|pel|le** ▲ F castle etc chapel; **Schloss|park** ▲ M castle etc grounds pl, estate; **Schloss|platz** ▲ M castle etc square; **Schloss|vogt** ▲ M (Hist) castellan; **Schloss|wa|che** ▲ F castle etc guard

Schlot [ʃloːt] M **-(e)s, -e** or (rare) **-e** ['ʃløːtə] a (= Schornstein) chimney (stack), smokestack; (Naut, Rail) funnel, chimney (stack); (von Vulkan) chimney; **rauchen** or **qualmen wie ein ~** (inf) to smoke like a chimney (inf) b (inf: = Flegel) slob (inf), peasant (inf)

schlot|te|rig ['ʃlɔtərɪç] ADJ (inf) a (= zitternd) shivering attr; (vor Angst, Erschöpfung) trembling attr b Kleider baggy

schlot|tern ['ʃlɔtɐn] VI a (vor with) (= zittern) to shiver; (vor Angst, Erschöpfung) to tremble; **an allen Gliedern ~** to shake all over; **ihm schlotterten die Knie** he was shaking at the knees, his knees were knocking or shaking b (Kleider) to hang loose, to be baggy

schlott|rig ['ʃlɔtrɪç] ADJ = **schlotterig**

schlot|zen ['ʃlɔtsn] VTI (S Ger inf: = lutschen) to suck; (= trinken) to slurp; (mit Genuss) to savour (Brit), to savor (US); **ein Viertele ~** to sip a quarter litre (Brit) or liter (US) of wine

Schlucht [ʃlʊxt] F **-, -en** gorge, ravine

schluch|zen ['ʃlʊxtsn] VTI (lit, fig) to sob

Schluch|zer ['ʃlʊxtsɐ] M **-s, -** sob

Schluck [ʃlʊk] M **-(e)s, -e** or (rare) **-e** ['ʃlʏkə] drink; (= ein bisschen) drop; (= das Schlucken) swallow; (großer) gulp; (kleiner) sip; **der erste ~ war mir ungewohnt** the first mouthful tasted strange; **er stürzte das Bier in einem ~ herunter** he downed the beer in one gulp or in one go; **etw ~ für ~ austrinken** to drink every drop; **einen (kräftigen) ~ nehmen** to take a (long) drink or swig (inf); **einen ~ aus der Flasche/dem Glas nehmen** to take a drink or swig (inf) from or out of the bottle/the glass; **ein ~ aus der Pulle** (fig inf) a fair whack (inf)

Schluck|auf ['ʃlʊkʔaʊf] M **-s,** no pl hiccups pl; **einen/den ~ haben** to have (the) hiccups

Schluck|be|schwer|den PL difficulties pl in swallowing

Schlück|chen ['ʃlʏkçən] NT **-s, -** dim von **Schluck** drop; (von Alkohol auch) nip

schlück|chen|wei|se ADV in short sips; **~ trinken** to sip

schlu|cken ['ʃlʊkn] VT a (= hinunterschlucken) to swallow; (hastig) to gulp down; **Alkohol ~** (sl) to booze (inf); **Pillen ~** (sl) to pop pills (inf) → **Kröte** a b (Comm, inf: = absorbieren) to swallow up; **Benzin, Öl** to guzzle c (inf: = hinnehmen) **Beleidigung** to swallow, to take d (inf: = glauben) to swallow VI (inf: = schlucken) (hastig) to gulp; **da musste ich erst mal (trocken or dreimal) ~** (inf) I had to take a deep breath, I had to count to ten; **daran hatte er schwer zu ~** (fig) he found that difficult to swallow

Schlu|cken ['ʃlʊkn] M **-s,** no pl = **Schluckauf**

Schlu|cker ['ʃlʊkɐ] M **-s, -** (inf) **armer ~** poor devil

Schluck-: **Schluck|imp|fung** F oral vaccination; **Schluck|specht** M (dated inf) boozer (inf); **schluck|wei|se** ADV in sips

Schlu|der|ar|beit F (inf) botched-up or sloppy job (inf)

Schlu|de|rei [ʃluːdə'raɪ] F **-, -en** (inf) sloppiness; **das ist eine ~!** how sloppy can you get!

schlu|de|rig ['ʃluːdərɪç] (inf) ADJ **Arbeit** sloppy, slipshod no adv ADV **schreiben, Hausaufgaben machen** sloppily; **arbeiten auch** in a slipshod way

Schlu|de|rig|keit F **-, -en** (inf) sloppiness

schlu|dern ['ʃluːdɐn] (inf) VT to skimp; **das ist geschludert!** this is a sloppy piece of work! VI to do sloppy work, to work sloppily

schlud|rig ['ʃluːdrɪç] ADJ ADV (inf) = **schluderig**

Schlud|rig|keit F **-, -en** (inf) sloppiness

schlug pret von **schlagen**

Schlum|mer ['ʃlʊmɐ] M **-s,** no pl (liter) (light) slumber (liter)

Schlum|mer|lied NT (geh) cradlesong (esp Brit), lullaby

schlum|mern ['ʃlʊmɐn] VI (geh) to slumber (liter); (fig auch) to lie dormant

Schlum|mer-: **Schlum|mer|rol|le** F bolster; **Schlum|mer|tas|te** F (an Radiowecker) snooze button; **Schlum|mer|trunk** M nightcap

Schlumpf [ʃlʊmpf] M **-(e)s, -e** ['ʃlʏmpfə] (inf: = komischer Kauz) odd bod (Brit inf), oddball (inf); **„die Schlümpfe"** "the Smurfs"

Schlund [ʃlʊnt] M **-(e)s, -e** ['ʃlʏndə] (Anat) pharynx, gullet; (fig liter) maw (liter)

schlun|zen ['ʃlʊntsn] VI (dial) to do sloppy work, to work sloppily

Schlupf [ʃlʊpf] M **-(e)s,** no pl (Elec, Naut) slip; (Tech) slip, slippage

schlüp|fen ['ʃlʏpfn] VI aux sein to slip; (Küken) to hatch (out)

Schlüp|fer ['ʃlʏpfɐ] M **-s, -** panties pl, knickers pl (Brit)

Schlupf|lid NT hooded (eye)lid

Schlupf|loch NT hole, gap; (= Versteck) hideout, lair; (fig) loophole; **ein ~ stopfen** (fig) to close a loophole

schlüp|frig ['ʃlʏpfrɪç] ADJ a slippery b (fig) **Bemerkung** suggestive

Schlüp|frig|keit F **-, -en** a no pl slipperiness; (fig: von Bemerkung) suggestiveness b (Bemerkung) suggestive remark

Schlupf-: **Schlupf|wes|pe** F ichneumon fly or wasp; **Schlupf|win|kel** M hiding place; (fig) quiet corner

schlur|fen ['ʃlʊrfn] VI aux sein to shuffle

schlür|fen ['ʃlʏrfn] VT to slurp; (mit Genuss) to savour (Brit), to savor (US); **er schlürfte die letzten Tropfen** he slurped up the last drops VI to slurp

Schluss ▲ [ʃlʊs] M **-es, -e** ['ʃlʏsə] a no pl (= Ende) end; (eines Romans, Gedichts, Theaterstücks) end, ending, conclusion; (= hinterer Teil) back, end, rear; **~ damit!** that'll do!, stop!; **für heute!** that's it or all for today, that'll do for today; **~ damit!** stop it!, that'll do!; **... und damit ~!** ... and that's that!, ... and that's the end of it!; **nun ist aber ~!** that's enough now!; **dann ist ~** that'll be it; **~ folgt** to be concluded; **am/zum ~ des Jahres** at the end of the year; **fünf Minuten vor ~ des Spiels** five minutes before the end of the game; **zum ~ sangen wir ...** at the end we sang ...; **zum ~ hat sies dann doch erlaubt** finally or in the end she allowed it after all; **bis zum ~ bleiben** to stay to the end; **zum ~ kommen** to conclude; **zum ~ möchte ich noch darauf hinweisen, dass ...** to conclude or in conclusion I would like to point out that ...; **~ machen** (inf: = aufhören) to finish, to call it a day (inf); (= zumachen) to close, to shut; (= Selbstmord begehen) to put an end to oneself, to end it all; (= Freundschaft beenden) to break or call it off; **ich muss ~ machen** (in Brief) I'll have to finish off now; (am Telefon) I'll have

to go now; **mit etw ~ machen** to stop or end sth, to finish with sth (inf); **mit der Arbeit ~ machen** to stop or leave off work b no pl (= das Schließen) closing c (= Folgerung) conclusion; **zu dem ~ kommen, dass ...** to come to the conclusion or to conclude that ...; **aus etw den ~ ziehen, dass ...** to draw the conclusion or to conclude from sth that ...; **aus etw die richtigen/falschen Schlüsse ziehen** to draw the right/wrong conclusions from sth; **ich ziehe meine Schlüsse daraus!** I can draw my own conclusions! → **Weisheit** a d (Tech) **die Tür hat einen guten/schlechten ~** the door is a good/bad fit e (Mus) cadence f (St Ex) minimum amount allowed for dealing

Schluss-: **Schluss|ab|rech|nung** ▲ F final statement or account; **Schluss|ak|kord** ▲ M final chord; **Schluss|akt** ▲ M (lit, fig) final act; **Schluss|ak|te** ▲ F (Pol) final agreement; **Schluss|an|spra|che** ▲ F closing address or speech; **Schluss|be|mer|kung** ▲ F final observation, concluding remark; **Schluss|be|stim|mung** ▲ F final clause; **Schluss|bi|lanz** ▲ F (lit) final balance (sheet); (fig) final position; **Schluss|di|vi|den|de** ▲ F (St Ex) final dividend

Schlüs|sel ['ʃlʏsl] M **-s, -** (lit, fig) key (zu to); (= Chiffrenschlüssel auch) cipher; (Sch: = Lösungsschlüssel) key; (Tech) spanner (Brit), wrench; (= Verteilungsschlüssel) ratio (of distribution); (Mus) clef

Schlüs|sel-: **Schlüs|sel|an|hän|ger** M keyring pendant; **Schlüs|sel|bart** M bit, ward; **Schlüs|sel|be|griff** M (= Wort) keyword; (= Konzept) key concept; **Schlüs|sel|bein** NT collarbone, clavicle (form); **Schlüs|sel|blu|me** F cowslip; **Schlüs|sel|brett** NT keyboard; **Schlüs|sel|bund** M OR NT pl **-bunde** keyring, bunch of keys; **Schlüs|sel|dienst** M key cutting service; **Schlüs|sel|er|leb|nis** NT (Psych) crucial experience; **schlüs|sel|fer|tig** ADJ **Neubau** ready for moving into, ready for occupancy; **Schlüs|sel|fi|gur** F key figure; **Schlüs|sel|ge|walt** F (Jur) a wife's power to represent her husband in matters concerning the household; (Eccl) power of the keys; **Schlüs|sel|in|dust|rie** F key industry; **Schlüs|sel|kind** NT (inf) latchkey kid (inf); **Schlüs|sel|loch** NT keyhole; **Schlüs|sel|loch|chi|rur|gie** F keyhole surgery; **Schlüs|sel|po|si|ti|on** F key position; **Schlüs|sel|qua|li|fi|ka|ti|on** F key qualification; **Schlüs|sel|reiz** M (Psych) key stimulus; **Schlüs|sel|ring** M keyring; **Schlüs|sel|ro|man** M roman à clef; **Schlüs|sel|stel|lung** F key position; **Schlüs|sel|ta|sche** F key wallet; **Schlüs|sel|wort** NT pl **-wörter** keyword; (für Schloss) combination, code

Schluss-: **schluss|end|lich** ▲ ADV (geh) to conclude, in conclusion or closing; **Schluss|er|geb|nis** ▲ NT final result; **schluss|fol|gern** ▲ ✪ 53.4 VI insep to conclude, to infer; **Schluss|fol|ge|rung** ▲ ✪ 38.1, 53.4 F conclusion, inference; **Schluss|for|mel** ▲ F (in Brief) complimentary close; (bei Vertrag) final clause

schlüs|sig ['ʃlʏsɪç] ADJ **Beweis** conclusive; **Konzept** logical; **sich** (dat) **(über etw** acc**) ~ sein** to have made up one's mind (about sth) ADV **be|gründen** conclusively

Schlüs|sig|keit F **-,** no pl conclusiveness

Schluss-: **Schluss|ka|pi|tel** ▲ NT concluding or final chapter; **Schluss|kom|mu|ni|qué** ▲ NT, **Schluss|kom|mu|ni|keé** ▲ NT final communiqué; **Schluss|kund|ge|bung** ▲ F (Pol: bei Wahlen) final (election) rally; **Schluss|kurs** ▲ M (St Ex) closing prices pl; **Schluss|läu|fer(in)** ▲ M(F) last runner; (in Staffel) anchor(man/-woman); **Schluss|licht** ▲ NT rear light (Brit), tail-light; (inf: bei Rennen etc) tailender (Brit), back marker; **~ der Tabelle/in der Klasse sein** to be bottom of the table/class; **das ~ bilden** (fig) (beim Laufen etc) to bring up the rear; (*in einer Tabelle*) to be bottom of the league; **Schluss|mann** ▲ M *pl* **-männer** (*Sport sl*) goalie (*inf*), keeper (*Brit inf*); **Schluss|no|tie|rung** ▲ F (*St Ex*) closing quotation; **Schluss|pfiff** ▲ M final whistle; **Schluss|pha|se** ▲ F final stages *pl*; **Schluss|punkt** ▲ M **einen ~ unter etw** (*acc*) **setzen** to round off sth; (*bei etwas Unangenehmem*) to write sth off; **Schluss|rech|nung** ▲ F **a** (*Comm*) final account or settlement **b** (*Math: = Dreisatz*) computation using the rule of three; **Schluss|re|dak|ti|on** ▲ F final edit(ing); **Schluss|run|de** ▲ F (*Boxen, Golf etc, fig*) final round; (*in Rennsport, Leichtathletik*) final lap; (*bei Ausscheidungskämpfen*) final heat; (*= Endausscheidung*) final(s); **Schluss|run|den|teil|neh|mer(in)** ▲ M(F) finalist; **Schluss|satz** ▲ M closing or concluding sentence; (*Logik*) conclusion; (*Mus*) last or final movement; **Schluss|schein** ▲ M (*Comm*) contract note; **Schluss|sprung** ▲ M standing jump; (*beim Turnen*) finishing jump; **Schluss|stand** ▲ M final result; (*von Spiel auch*) final score; (*von Aktienindex etc*) closing price; **Schluss|stein** ▲ M (*Archit, fig*) keystone; **Schluss|strich** ▲ M (*fig*) final stroke; **einen ~ unter etw** (*acc*) **ziehen** to consider sth finished; **Schluss|tag** ▲ M (*St Ex*) settlement day; **Schluss|ver|kauf** ▲ M (end-of-season) sale (*Brit*), season close-out sale (*US*); **Schluss|wort** ▲ NT *pl* **-worte** closing words or remarks *pl*; (*= Schlussrede*) closing or concluding speech; (*= Nachwort*) postscript

Schmach [ʃmaːx] F -, *no pl* (*geh*) disgrace, ignominy, shame *no indef art*; (*= Demütigung auch*) humiliation; **etw als ~ empfinden** to see sth as a disgrace; to feel humiliated by sth

schmach|ten [ʃmaxtn] VI (*geh*) **a** (*= leiden*) to languish; **vor Durst ~** to be parched; **vor Hunger ~** to starve; **vor Liebeskummer ~** to pine with love **b** (*= sich sehnen*) **nach jdm/etw ~** to pine or yearn for sb/sth

schmach|tend ADJ *Stimme, Blick* yearning, soulful; *Liebhaber* languishing

Schmacht|fet|zen M (*dated hum*) tear-jerker (*inf*)

schmäch|tig [ʃmɛçtɪç] ADJ slight, weedy (*pej inf*)

Schmäch|tig|keit F -, *no pl* slightness, weediness (*pej inf*)

Schmacht-: Schmacht|lap|pen M (*dated hum*) Romeo (*inf*); **Schmacht|lo|cke** F (*dated hum*) kiss curl (*Brit*), spit curl (*US*)

schmach|voll (*geh*) ADJ *Niederlage* ignominious; (*= demütigend auch*) *Frieden* humiliating ADV *verlieren* ignominiously

Schma|ckes [ʃmakəs] PL (*dial inf*) **a** (*= Schläge*) **~ kriegen** to get a smacking **b** (*= Schwung*) **er knallte das Buch mit ~ auf den Tisch** he slammed or banged (*inf*) the book down on the table; **das muss man mit ~ machen!** (*= richtig zuschlagen*) give it a good clout (*esp Brit inf*) or bang (*inf*)

schmack|haft ADJ (*= wohlschmeckend*) tasty; (*= appetitanregend*) appetizing; **jdm etw ~ machen** (*fig*) to make sth palatable to sb

Schmack|haf|tig|keit F -, *no pl* tastiness

Schmäh [ʃmɛː] M -s, -(s) (*Aus inf*) **a** (*= Trick*) con (*inf*), dodge (*inf*); **jdn am ~ halten** to make a fool out of sb **b** (*= Scherzhaftigkeit*) jokiness; **einen ~ führen** (*= Witze machen*) to clown around

Schmäh|brief M defamatory or abusive letter

schmä|hen [ʃmɛːən] VT (*geh*) to abuse, to revile (*liter*), to vituperate against (*liter*)

schmäh|lich [ʃmɛːlɪç] (*geh*) ADJ ignominious, shameful; (*= demütigend*) humiliating ADV *shamefully*; *versagen* miserably; **~ im Stich gelassen werden** to be left in the lurch in a humiliating way

Schmäh-: Schmäh|re|de F (*geh*) invective, diatribe; **~n (gegen jdn) führen** to launch dia-

tribes (against sb); **Schmäh|schrift** F defamatory piece of writing; (*= Satire*) lampoon

Schmä|hung [ʃmɛːʊŋ] F -, -en (*geh*) abuse, vituperation (*liter*); (**gegen jdn**) **~en ausstoßen** to hurl abuse (at sb)

Schmäh|wort NT *pl* **-worte** (*liter*) abusive word, term of abuse; **~e** abuse *sing*, invective *sing*

schmal [ʃmaːl] ADJ *comp* **-er** or **¨er** [ʃmɛːlɐ], *superl* **-ste(r, s)** or **¨ste(r, s)** [ʃmɛːlstə], *adv superl* **am -sten** or **¨sten** **a** *narrow*; *Hüfte, Taille* slim, slender, narrow; *Mensch* slim, slender; *Band, Buch* slim; *Gelenke, Lippen* thin; **er ist sehr ~ geworden** he has got (*Brit*) or gotten (*US*) very thin **b** (*fig: = karg*) meagre (*Brit*), meager (*US*), slender; **~e Kost** slender fare; **einen ~en Geldbeutel haben** (*fig*) to have to watch the pennies

schmal|brüs|tig [-brʏstɪç] ADJ narrow-chested; (*fig*) limited

schmä|lern [ʃmɛːlɐn] VT to diminish, to reduce, to lessen; (*= heruntermachen*) to detract from, to belittle, to belittle

Schmä|le|rung F -, -en diminishing, reduction, lessening; (*= Schlechtmachen*) detraction, belittlement; **eine ~ seines Ruhms** a detraction from or a diminishing of his fame

Schmal-: Schmal|film M cine film (*Brit*), movie film (*US*); **Schmal|film|ka|me|ra** F cine camera (*Brit*), movie camera (*US*); **Schmal|hans** M (*inf*) **bei ihnen/uns ist ~ Küchenmeister** their/our cupboard is nearly always bare; **schmal|lip|pig** [-lɪpɪç] ADJ thin-lipped; (*fig: = schweigsam*) tight-lipped; **schmal|schul|te|rig, schmal|schult|rig** ADJ narrow-shouldered; **Schmal|sei|te** F narrow side

Schmal|spur F (*Rail*) narrow gauge

Schmal|spur- *in cpds* (*Rail*) narrow-gauge; (*pej*) small-time; **Schmal|spur|aka|de|mi|ker(in)** M(F) (*pej*) small-time academic; **Schmal|spur|bahn** F narrow-gauge railway

schmal|spu|rig [-ʃpuːrɪç] ADJ (*Rail*) *Strecke* narrow-gauge; (*fig*) *Fachmann* overspecialized ADV *ausgebildet* narrowly; **der Lehrplan ist sehr ~ angelegt** the curriculum is very narrow

Schmalz¹ [ʃmalts] NT -es, -e **a** (*= Schweineschmalz*) lard; (*= Bratenschmalz*) dripping (*Brit*), drippings *pl* (*US*) **b** (*= Ohrenschmalz*) earwax

Schmalz² M -es, *no pl* (*pej inf*) schmaltz (*inf*)

schmal|zen [ʃmaltsn] VTI to drool; *Lied* to croon

Schmalz-: Schmalz|fleisch NT rillettes *pl*, potted meat; **Schmalz|ge|bäck** NT ', **Schmalz|ge|ba|cke|ne(s)** [-gəbakənə] NT *decl as adj* deep-fried pastry

schmal|zig [ʃmaltsɪç] (*pej inf*) ADJ schmaltzy (*inf*), slushy (*inf*) ADV **er singt mir zu ~** his songs are too schmaltzy for me (*inf*); **seine Liebesbriefe sind ziemlich ~ geschrieben** his love letters are pretty schmaltzy (*inf*)

Schmalz|ler [ʃmaltslɐ] M -s, - (*S Ger*) snuff

Schmalz|topf M pot of lard; **tief in den ~ greifen** (*fig inf*) to lay on the sentiment with a trowel

Schmand [ʃmant] M **-(e)s** [-dəs] *no pl* sour(ed) cream

Schman|kerl [ʃmaŋkɐl] NT **-s, -n** (*S Ger, Aus*) **a** (*= Speise*) delicacy, titbit (*Brit*), tidbit (*US*) **b** (*fig*) gem

Schmant [ʃmant] M **-(e)s**, *no pl* (*dial*) **a** (*= Sahne*) cream **b** (*= Matsch*) muck

schma|rot|zen [ʃmaˈrɔtsn] *ptp* **schmarotzt** VI to sponge, to scrounge (*Brit*), to freeload (*esp US*) (**bei** on, off); (*Biol*) to be parasitic (**bei** on)

Schma|rot|zer¹ [ʃmaˈrɔtsɐ] M **-s, -** (*Biol*) parasite

Schma|rot|zer² [ʃmaˈrɔtsɐ] M **-s, -**, **Schma|rot|ze|rin** F **-, -nen** (*fig*) sponger, scrounger (*Brit*), freeloader (*esp US*)

schma|rot|zer|haft, **schma|rot|ze|risch** [ʃmaˈrɔtsərɪʃ] ADJ (*Biol, fig*) parasitic

Schma|rot|zer|tum [ʃmaˈrɔtsetuːm] NT **-s**, *no pl* (*Biol, fig*) parasitism

Schmar|re [ʃmarə] F **-, -n** (*dial*) cut, gash; (*= Narbe*) scar

Schmar|ren [ʃmarən] M **-s, -**, **Schmarrn** [ʃmarn] M **-s, -** **a** (*S Ger, Aus: Cook*) pancake cut up into small pieces **b** (*inf: = Quatsch*) rubbish (*Brit*), tripe (*inf*); **das geht dich einen ~ an!** that's none of your business!

Schmatz [ʃmats] M **-es, -e** (*inf: = Kuss*) smacker (*inf*)

schmat|zen [ʃmatsn] VI (*beim Essen*) to eat noisily, to smack (*US*); (*beim Trinken*) to slurp; (*in Morast etc*) to squelch; **er aß ~d seine Suppe** he slurped his soup; **schmatz nicht so!** don't make so much noise when you eat!, don't smack when you eat! (*US*); **mit den Lippen ~** to smack one's lips; **Oma küsste das Kind ~d** grandma gave the child a real smacker of a kiss (*inf*)

schmau|chen [ʃmauxn] VT to puff away at VI to puff away

Schmauch|spur F *usu pl* traces *pl* of powder

Schmaus [ʃmaus] M **-es, Schmäuse** [ʃmɔyzə] (*dated*) meal

schmau|sen [ʃmauzn] VI (*geh*) to feast VT to feast on

schme|cken [ʃmɛkn] VI **a** (*= Geschmack haben*) to taste (**nach** of); (*= gut schmecken*) to be good, to taste good or lovely; (*= probieren*) to taste, to have a taste; **ihm schmeckt es** (*= gut finden*) he likes it; (*= Appetit haben*) he likes his food; **ihm schmeckt es nicht** (*= keinen Appetit haben*) he's lost his appetite, he's off his food (*esp Brit*); **das schmeckt ihm nicht** (*lit, fig*) he doesn't like it; **diese Arbeit schmeckt ihm nicht** this work doesn't agree with him, he has no taste for this work; **wie schmeckt die Ehe?** how does marriage agree with you?; **nach etw ~** (*fig*) to smack of sth; **das schmeckt nach nichts** it's tasteless; **das schmeckt nach mehr!** (*inf*) it tastes moreish (*Brit hum inf*), it tastes like I want some more; **schmeckt es (Ihnen)?** do you like it?, is it good?, are you enjoying your food or meal? (*esp form*); **das hat geschmeckt!** that was good; **und das schmeckt!** and it tastes so good, and it's so good; **das schmeckt nicht (gut)** it doesn't taste good or nice; **es schmeckt mir ausgezeichnet** it is or it tastes really excellent; **Hauptsache, es schmeckt** (*inf*) the main thing is it tastes nice; **es sich** (*dat*) **~ lassen** to tuck in; **sich** (*dat*) **etw ~ lassen** to tuck into sth **b** (*S Ger, Aus, Sw: = riechen*) to smell VT **a** (*= den Geschmack wahrnehmen von*) to taste; (*= probieren*) to taste, to have a taste of; **etw zu ~ bekommen** (*fig inf*) to have a taste of sth **b** (*S Ger, Aus, Sw: = riechen*) to smell; (*fig: = ahnen*) to sense

Schmei|che|lei [ʃmaɪçaˈlaɪ] F **-, -en** flattery; (*= Kompliment auch*) flattering remark, compliment; **so eine ~!** such flattery!

schmei|chel|haft ADJ flattering; *Bemerkung auch* complimentary; **wenig ~** not very flattering/complimentary

schmei|cheln [ʃmaɪçln] VI **a jdm ~** to flatter sb; (*um etw zu erreichen*) to flatter sb, to butter sb up (*Brit inf*); **es schmeichelt mir, dass ... ** it flatters me that ..., I find it flattering that ...; **~ sagte sie ~d ...** she wheedled **b** (*= verschönen*) to flatter; **das Bild ist aber geschmeichelt!** the picture is very flattering VR **sich** (*dat*) **~ ...** (*geh*) to flatter oneself (that) ...

Schmei|chel|wort NT *pl* **-worte** (*geh*) flattery, honeyed word, sweet nothing *usu pl*

Schmeich|ler [ʃmaɪçlɐ] M **-s, -**, **Schmeich|le|rin** [-ərɪn] F **-, -nen** flatterer; (*= Kriecher*) sycophant, fawner

schmeich|le|risch [ʃmaɪçlərɪʃ] ADJ flattering; (*= lobhudelnd auch*) unctuous, fawning, sycophantic

---

Deutsche Rechtschreibreform (siehe Anhang): ▲ neue Schreibung △ alte Schreibung | + trennbare Verben

schmei|ßen ['ʃmaisn] pret **schmiss** [ʃmɪs], ptp **geschmissen** [gə'ʃmɪsn] (inf) **VT a** (= werfen) to sling (inf), to chuck (inf), to fling; **die Tür (ins Schloss) ~** to slam the door; **Pillen ~** (sl) to be a pill-popper (inf) **b** (inf: = spendieren) **eine Runde** or **Lage ~** to stand a round; **eine Party ~** to throw a party **c** (= managen) **den Laden ~** to run the (whole) show; **die Sache ~** to handle it **d** (= aufgeben) Ausbildung, Schule, Job etc to chuck in (inf) **VI** (= werfen) to throw, to chuck (inf); **mit Steinen ~** to throw or chuck (inf) stones; **mit etw um sich ~** to throw sth about, to chuck sth around (inf); **mit dem Geld (nur so) um sich ~** to throw or chuck (inf) money around; **mit Fremdwörtern um sich ~** to bandy foreign words about **VR sich auf etw** (acc) **~** to throw oneself into sth; **die Kunden schmissen sich auf die Sonderangebote** the customers made a rush for the special offers; **sich jdm an den Hals ~** (fig) to throw oneself at sb; **er schmiss sich mutig zwischen die beiden** he courageously flung or threw or hurled himself between the two

Schmeiß|flie|ge F bluebottle

Schmelz [ʃmɛlts] M -(e)s, -e (= Glasur) glaze; (= Zahnschmelz) enamel; (geh, einer Farbe) lustre (Brit), luster (US), glow; (= Wohlklang) melodiousness, mellifluousness

Schmelz-: schmelz|bar ADJ fusible, meltable; **Eisen ist leicht ~** iron is easily melted or melts easily; **Schmelz|bar|keit** ['ʃmɛltsbaːɐkait] F -, no pl fusibility

Schmel|ze ['ʃmɛltsə] F -, -n **a** (Metal, Geol) melt **b** (= Schmelzen) melting; (Metal: von Erz) smelting **c** (= Schmelzhütte) smelting plant or works sing or pl

schmel|zen ['ʃmɛltsn] pret **schmolz** [ʃmɔlts], ptp **geschmolzen** [gə'ʃmɔltsn] **VI** aux sein (lit, fig: = erweichen) to melt; (Reaktormasse) to melt down; (fig: = schwinden) to melt (away); **es ist ihr gelungen, sein hartes Herz zum Schmelzen zu bringen** she succeeded in melting his heart of stone **VT** Metall, Fett, Schnee to melt; Erz to smelt

schmel|zend ADJ (geh) Gesang, Ton, Stimme mellifluous

Schmel|ze|rei [ʃmɛltsə'rai] F -, -en smelting plant or works sing or pl

Schmelz-: Schmelz|far|be F (Tech) vitrifiable pigment or colour (Brit) or color (US); **Schmelz|glas** NT enamel; **Schmelz|hüt|te** F smelting plant or works sing or pl; **Schmelz|kä|se** M cheese spread; **Schmelz|ofen** M melting furnace; (für Erze) smelting furnace; **Schmelz|punkt** M melting point; **Schmelz|tie|gel** M (lit, fig) melting pot; **Schmelz|wär|me** F (Metal) heat of fusion; **Schmelz|was|ser** NT pl **-wasser** melted snow and ice; (Geog, Phys) meltwater

Schmer [ʃmeːɐ] M OR NT -s, no pl (old, dial) pork fat

Schmer-: Schmer|bauch M (inf) paunch, potbelly; **schmer|bäu|chig** [-bɔʏçɪç] ADJ (inf) paunchy, potbellied

Schmer|le ['ʃmɛrlə] F -, -n loach

Schmerz [ʃmɛrts] M -es, -en pain pl rare; (= Kummer auch) grief no pl; **ihre ~en** her pain; **chronische ~en** chronic pain; **dumpfer ~** dull pain; **stechender ~** stabbing pain; **sie schrie vor ~en** she cried out in pain; **~en haben** to be in pain; **~en in der Nierengegend haben** to have a pain in the kidneys; **~en in den Ohren haben** to have (an (US)) earache; **~en im Hals haben** to have a sore throat; **wo haben Sie ~en?** where does it hurt?, where's the pain?; **wenn der Patient wieder ~en bekommt ...** if the patient starts feeling pain again ...; **von ~en geplagt werden** to be racked with pain; **jdm ~en bereiten** to cause sb pain; (seelisch auch) to pain sb; **mit ~en** (fig) regretfully; **jdn/etw mit ~en erwarten** to wait impatiently for sb/sth; **unter ~en** while

in pain; (fig) regretfully; **jdn mit ~(en) erfüllen** (fig) to grieve or hurt sb

Schmerz-: schmerz|be|täu|bend ADJ pain-killing; **Schmerz|emp|fin|den** NT sensation or experience of pain; **schmerz|emp|find|lich** ADJ Mensch sensitive to pain; Wunde, Körperteil sensitive, tender; **Schmerz|emp|find|lich|keit** F sensitivity to pain; (von Wunde) sensitivity, tenderness

schmer|zen ['ʃmɛrtsn] (geh) **VT** to hurt, to pain; (körperlich) to hurt **VI** to hurt; (Kopf, Bauch auch, Wunde) to be sore, to ache; **mir schmerzt der Kopf** my head aches; **es schmerzt** (lit, fig) it hurts; **eine ~de Stelle** a painful spot or area

-schmer|zen PL suf in cpds -ache; **Bauch-/Kopfschmerzen haben** to have stomach ache/a headache; **Herzschmerzen haben** to have pains in the chest; **ich habe Halsschmerzen** I have a sore throat

Schmer|zens-: Schmer|zens|geld NT (Jur) damages pl; **Schmer|zens|laut** M (geh) cry of pain; **Schmer|zens|schrei** M scream of pain

Schmerz-: schmerz|er|füllt [-ɛɐfʏlt] ADJ (geh) racked with pain; (seelisch) grief-stricken; **schmerz|frei** ADJ free of pain; Operation painless; **Schmerz|frei|heit** F freedom from pain; **Schmerz|gren|ze** F (lit, fig) pain barrier; **schmerz|haft** ADJ (lit, fig) painful; **Schmerz|kran|ke(r)** MF decl as adj person suffering from chronic pains; **schmerz|lich** ['ʃmɛrtslɪç] (geh) ADJ painful; Lächeln sad; **es ist mir sehr ~, Ihnen mitteilen zu müssen, dass ...** it is my painful duty to inform you that ... **ADV** entbehren painfully; **etw/jdn ~ vermissen** to miss sth/sb dreadfully; **schmerz|lin|dernd** ADJ pain-relieving, analgesic (Med); **Schmerz|lin|de|rung** F relief or alleviation of pain; **schmerz|los** ADJ (lit, fig) painless; **~er es** painful → **kurz**; **Schmerz|lo|sig|keit** F -, no pl (lit, fig) painlessness; **Schmerz|mit|tel** NT pain-killing drug, painkiller, ≈ aspirin (esp US inf); **Schmerz|schwel|le** F pain threshold; **schmerz|stil|lend** ADJ pain-killing, pain-relieving, analgesic (Med); **~es Mittel** pain-killing drug, painkiller, analgesic (Med); **Schmerz|tab|let|te** F painkiller, ≈ aspirin (esp US inf); **schmerz|un|emp|find|lich** ADJ insensitive to pain; **schmerz|ver|zerrt** [-fɛɐtsɛrt] ADJ Gesicht twisted or distorted with pain; **mit ~em Gesicht** his/her face twisted with pain; **schmerz|voll** ADJ (fig) painful

Schmet|ter|ball M smash

Schmet|ter|ling ['ʃmɛtɐlɪŋ] M -s, -e (Zool, inf: Schwimmart) butterfly; **kannst du ~ schwimmen?** can you do the butterfly?

Schmet|ter|lings-: Schmet|ter|lings|blüt|ler [-blyːtlɐ] M -s, - **die ~** the papilionaceae (spec); **ein ~** a member of the papilionaceae family (spec); **Schmet|ter|lings|netz** NT butterfly net; **Schmet|ter|lings|stil** M butterfly stroke

schmet|tern ['ʃmɛtɐn] **VT a** (= schleudern) to smash; Tür to slam; (Sport) Ball to smash; **etw in Stücke ~** to smash sth to pieces **b** Lied, Arie to bellow out; (Vogel) to sing, to warble **VI a** (Sport) to smash, to hit a smash (esp Brit) **b** (Trompete etc) to blare (out) (Sänger) to bellow; (Vogel) to sing, to warble

Schmied [ʃmiːt] M -(e)s, -e [-də], **Schmie|din** ['ʃmiːdɪn] F -, -nen (black)smith → **Glück a**

schmied|bar ADJ malleable

Schmie|de ['ʃmiːdə] F -, -n smithy, forge

Schmiede-: Schmie|de|ar|beit F (= das Schmieden) forging; (Gegenstand) piece of wrought-iron work; **Schmie|de|ei|sen** NT wrought iron; **schmie|de|ei|sern** ADJ wrought-iron; **Schmie|de|ham|mer** M blacksmith's hammer; **Schmie|de|kunst** F skill in wrought-iron work

schmie|den ['ʃmiːdn] **VT** (lit, fig) to forge (zu into); (= ersinnen) Plan, Komplott to hatch, to concoct; (hum) Verse to concoct; **geschmiedet sein** (Gartentür etc) to be made of wrought iron; **jdn in Ketten ~** (liter) to bind sb in chains

Schmie|din ['ʃmiːdɪn] F -, -nen (black)smith

schmie|gen ['ʃmiːgn] **VR sich an jdn ~** to cuddle or snuggle up to sb; **sich an/in etw** (acc) **~** to nestle or snuggle into sth; **die Weinberge/Häuser ~ sich an die sanften Hänge** the vineyards/houses nestle into the gentle slopes; **sich um etw ~** to hang gracefully on sth; (Haare) to fall gracefully (a)round sth **VT etw an/in etw** (acc) **~** to nestle sth into sth; **etw um etw ~** to wrap sth around sth; **die an den Felsen geschmiegte Kapelle** the chapel nestled or nestling in the cliffs

schmieg|sam ['ʃmiːkzaːm] ADJ supple; Stoff soft; (fig: = anpassungsfähig) adaptable, flexible

Schmie|re ['ʃmiːrə] F -, -n **a** (inf) grease; (= Salbe) ointment; (= feuchter Schmutz) mud, grease; (pej: = Schminke) paint; (= Aufstrich) spread **b** (pej: = Wanderbühne) (troop of) barnstormers pl; (= schlechtes Theater) fleapit **c** (inf) **~ stehen** to be the look-out

schmie|ren ['ʃmiːrən] **VT a** (= streichen) to smear; Butter, Aufstrich to spread; Brot (mit Butter) to butter; Salbe, Make-up to rub in (in +acc -to); (= einfetten, ölen) to grease; (Tech) Achsen, Gelenke etc to grease, to lubricate; **sie schmierte sich ein Brot** she made herself a sandwich; **es geht** or **läuft wie geschmiert** it's going like clockwork; **jdm eine ~** (inf) to smack sb one (inf) **b** (pej: = schreiben) to scrawl; (= malen) to daub **c** (inf: = bestechen) **jdn ~** to grease sb's palm (inf) **d** (Cards) Ass, Zehn to discard (on a trick which one's partner is winning) **VI a** (pej) (= schreiben) to scrawl; (= malen) to daub **b** (Stift, Radiergummi, Scheibenwischer) to smear **c** (inf: = bestechen) to give a bribe/bribes **d** (Cards) to discard a high-value card on a trick which one's partner is winning

Schmie|ren-: Schmie|ren|ko|mö|di|ant(in) M(F) (pej) (actor/actress); **Schmie|ren|ko|mö|die** F (pej) slapstick farce, pantomime; (fig) pantomime, farce; **Schmie|ren|schau|spie|ler(in)** M(F) barnstormer; (pej) ham (actor/actress); **Schmie|ren|the|a|ter** NT (pej) (troop of) barnstormers pl; (= schlechtes Theater) fleapit; (fig) farce

Schmie|rer ['ʃmiːrɐ] M -s, -, **Schmie|re|rin** [-ərɪn] F -, -nen (inf) scrawler, scribbler; (von Parolen) slogan dauber; (in Toiletten, an Gebäuden) graffiti writer; (= Maler) dauber; (= Autor, Journalist) hack, scribbler

Schmie|re|rei [ʃmiːrə'rai] F -, -en (pej inf) (= Geschriebenes) scrawl, scribble; (= Parolen etc) graffiti pl; (= Malerei) daubing; (= Schriftstellerei) scribbling; (= das Schmieren von Parolen etc) scrawling, scribbling; (von Stift, Scheibenwischer etc) smearing

Schmie|re|ste|hen NT (inf) keeping lookout

Schmier-: Schmier|fett NT (lubricating) grease; **Schmier|fink** M (pej) **a** (= Autor, Journalist) hack, scribbler; (= Skandaljournalist) muckraker (inf) **b** (= Schüler) messy writer, scrawler; **Schmier|geld** NT bribe, bribe money

Schmier|geld-: Schmier|geld|af|fä|re F bribery case or affair; **Schmier|geld|zah|lung** F bribe payment

Schmier|heft NT jotter (Brit), rough book (Brit), sketchbook

schmie|rig ['ʃmiːrɪç] ADJ greasy; Restaurant auch grimy; (fig) (= unanständig) dirty, filthy; (= schleimig) greasy, smarmy (Brit inf)

Schmier-: Schmier|in|fek|ti|on F (Med) infection (passed on through touch); **Schmier|kä|se** M (dated) cheese spread; **Schmier|mit|tel** NT lubricant; **Schmieröl**

NT lubricating oil; **Schmier|pa|pier** NT rough *or* jotting paper (*Brit*), scratch paper (*US*); **Schmier|sei|fe** F soft soap

Schmie|rung [ˈʃmiːrʊŋ] F -, -en lubrication

Schmier|zet|tel M piece of rough *or* jotting paper (*Brit*), piece of scratch paper (*US*)

schmilzt [ʃmɪltst] *3. pers sing pres von* **schmelzen**

Schmin|ke [ˈʃmɪŋkə] F -, -n make-up

schmin|ken [ˈʃmɪŋkn] VT to make up; **sich** (*dat*) **die Lippen/Augen ~** to put on lipstick/eye make-up VR to make oneself up, to put on make-up; **sich selten ~** to wear make-up rarely; **sich stark ~** to wear a lot of make-up

Schmink|-: Schmink|kof|fer M vanity case; **Schmink|täsch|chen** [-tɛʃçən] NT make-up bag; **Schmink|tisch** M dressing table

Schmir|gel [ˈʃmɪrɡl] M -s, *no pl* emery

schmir|geln [ˈʃmɪrɡln] VT to sand, to rub down (*esp Brit*) **~ an** to sand

Schmir|gel|-: Schmir|gel|pa|pier NT sandpaper; **Schmir|gel|schei|be** F sanding disc

schmiss ▲ *pret von* **schmeißen**

Schmiss ▲ [ʃmɪs] M -es, -e **a** (= *Fechtwunde*) gash, wound; (= *Narbe*) duelling scar **b** (*dated*: = *Schwung*) dash, élan; **~ haben** (*Musik etc*) to go with a swing; (*Mensch*) to have go (*inf*)

schmis|sig [ˈʃmɪsɪç] ADJ (*dated*) dashing (*dated*); *Musik auch* spirited

Schmock [ʃmɔk] M -(e)s, -e *or* -s (*pej*) hack

Schmok [ʃmoːk] M -s, *no pl* (*N Ger*) smoke

schmö|ken [ˈʃmøːkən] VTI (*N Ger*) to smoke

Schmö|ker [ˈʃmøːkɐ] M -s, - book (*usu of light literature*); (*dick*) tome

schmö|kern [ˈʃmøːkɐn] (*inf*) VI to bury oneself in a book/magazine *etc*; (= *in Büchern blättern*) to browse VT to bury oneself in sth

Schmoll|ecke F = **Schmollwinkel**

schmol|len [ˈʃmɔlən] VI to pout; (= *gekränkt sein*) to sulk; **mit jdm ~** to be annoyed with sb

Schmoll|-: Schmoll|mund M pout; **einen ~ machen** to pout; **Schmoll|win|kel** M (*inf*) **im ~ sitzen** to have the sulks (*Brit inf*), to sulk; **sich in den ~ zurückziehen** to go off into a corner to sulk; **aus dem ~ herauskommen** to stop sulking

schmolz *pret von* **schmelzen**

Schmon|zes [ˈʃmɔntsəs] M -, - (*dated*) balderdash (*Brit dated*), tripe (*inf*)

Schmon|zet|te [ʃmɔnˈtsɛtə] F -, -n (*inf*) kitschy film/book *etc*

Schmor|-: Schmor|brand M smouldering (*Brit*) *or* smoldering (*US*) fire; **Schmor|bra|ten** M pot roast

schmo|ren [ˈʃmoːrən] VT to braise; *Braten auch* to pot-roast; **geschmorte Kalbshaxe** braised knuckle of veal VI **a** (*Cook*) to braise; (*inf*: = *schwitzen*) to roast, to swelter; **jdn (im eigenen Saft *or* Fett) ~ lassen** to leave sb to stew (in his/her own juice); **in der Hölle ~** to roast in hell **b** (= *unbearbeitet liegen*) to moulder (*Brit*), to molder (*US*)

Schmor|-: Schmor|fleisch NT (*Cook*) braising steak; (*Braten*) pot roast; **Schmor|topf** M casserole

Schmu [ʃmuː] M -s, *no pl* (*inf*) cheating; (*esp mit Geld auch*) fiddling (*inf*); **das ist ~!** that's cheating *or* fiddling! (*inf*); **~ machen** to cheat, to fiddle (*inf*); **bei der Abrechnung ~ machen** to fiddle the expenses; **bei der Prüfung ~ machen** to cheat in the exam

schmuck [ʃmʊk] ADJ (*dated*) *Haus etc* neat, tidy; *Schiff* neat, trim; *Bursche, Mädel* smart, spruce; *Paar* smart

Schmuck [ʃmʊk] M -(e)s, (*rare*) -e **a** (= *Schmuckstücke*) jewellery (*Brit*) *no pl*, jewelry (*US*) *no pl* **b** (= *Verzierung*) decoration; (*fig*) embellishment; **der ~ am Christbaum** the decorations on the Christmas tree; **im ~ der Blumen/Fahnen** (*liter*) decked with flowers/flags;

Natürlichkeit ist der schönste ~ eines Mädchens naturalness is the greatest adornment a girl can have

schmü|cken [ˈʃmʏkn] VT to decorate, to adorn; *Baum* to decorate; *Rede* to embellish; **die mit Blumenkränzen geschmückten Tänzerinnen** the dancers adorned with garlands of flowers; **mit Juwelen geschmückt** bejewelled (*US*), bejeweled (*US*); **~des Beiwerk/Beiwort** embellishment VR (*zum Fest etc*) (*Mensch*) to adorn oneself; (*Stadt*) to be decorated; **sich mit etw ~** (*lit, fig*) to adorn oneself with sth; **sich mit Blumenkränzen ~** to garland oneself with flowers → **fremd a**

Schmuck|-: Schmuck|ge|gen|stand M ornament; (= *Ring etc*) piece of jewellery (*Brit*) *or* jewelry (*US*); **Schmuck|kas|set|te** F, **Schmuck|käst|chen** NT , **Schmuck|kas|ten** M jewellery (*Brit*) *or* jewelry (*US*) box; **ihr Haus war ein Schmuckkästchen** her house was a picture; **schmuck|los** ADJ plain; *Fassade* unadorned; *Einrichtung, Stil* simple, plain; *Prosa* simple, unadorned; **Schmuck|lo|sig|keit** F -, *no pl* plainness; (*von Einrichtung, Stil, Prosa*) simplicity; **Schmuck|sa|chen** PL jewellery (*Brit*) *sing*, jewelry (*US*) *sing*; **Schmuck|stein** M (= *Edelstein*) precious stone, gem; (= *Halbedelstein*) semiprecious stone; **Schmuck|stück** NT (= *Ring etc*) piece of jewellery; (= *Schmuckgegenstand*) ornament; (*fig*: = *Prachtstück*) gem; (*fig inf*: = *Frau*) better half (*hum inf*); **Schmuck|wa|ren** PL jewellery (*Brit*) *sing*, jewelry (*US*) *sing*

Schmud|del [ˈʃmʊdl] M -s, *no pl* (*N Ger inf*) = *Schmutz*) mess; (*auf Straße*) dirt, mud

Schmud|de|lei [ʃmʊdəˈlai] F -, -en (*inf*) mess *no pl*

schmud|de|lig [ˈʃmʊdəlɪç] ADJ messy; (= *schmutzig auch*) dirty; (= *schmierig, unsauber*) filthy; (= *schlampig*) *Bedienung* sloppy; *Frau, Schüler* sloppy, slovenly

Schmud|del|-: Schmud|del|kind NT (*fig*) (street) urchin; **Schmud|del|look** M (*iro*) urchin look (*iro*); **Schmud|del|wet|ter** NT lousy *or* mucky weather

schmud|dlig [ˈʃmʊdlɪç] ADJ = **schmuddelig**

Schmug|gel [ˈʃmʊɡl] M -s, *no pl* smuggling; (= *einzelne Schmuggeloperation*) smuggling operation; **~ treiben** to smuggle; **der ~ von Heroin** heroin smuggling

Schmug|ge|lei [ʃmʊɡəˈlai] F -, -en smuggling *no pl*; **seine kleinen ~en** his small-scale smuggling

schmug|geln [ˈʃmʊɡln] VTI (*lit, fig*) to smuggle; **mit etw ~** to smuggle sth

Schmug|geln NT -s, *no pl* smuggling

Schmug|gel|wa|re F smuggled goods *pl*, contraband *no pl*

Schmugg|ler [ˈʃmʊɡlɐ] M -s, -, **Schmugg|le|rin** [-ərɪn] F -, -nen smuggler; **~ von Rauschgift** drug smuggler; **~ von Waffen** arms smuggler, gunrunner

Schmugg|ler|-: Schmugg|ler|ban|de F smuggling ring, ring of smugglers; **Schmugg|ler|pfad** M smugglers' path; **Schmugg|ler|ring** M → **Schmugglerbande**

schmun|zeln [ˈʃmʊntsln] VI to smile

Schmun|zeln NT -s, *no pl* smile

Schmus [ʃmuːs] M -es, *no pl* (*inf*) (= *Unsinn*) nonsense; (= *Schmeicheleien*) soft soap (*Brit inf*), cajolery; **~ erzählen** to talk nonsense

Schmu|se|-: Schmu|se|decke F (*inf*) comfort blanket; **Schmu|se|kat|ze** F (*fig inf*: = *Person*) cuddly type; (= *Kind*) cuddly little thing; **Schmu|se|kurs** M (*inf*) friendly overtures *pl*; **mit jdm auf ~ gehen** to cosy up to sb; **der ~ zwischen SPD und Unternehmern** the friendly noises between the SPD and the employers; **sich mit jdm auf ~ begeben** to try to ingratiate oneself with sb; **Schmu|se|me|lo|die** F (*inf*) smoochy ballad (*inf*); **Schmu|se|tier** NT (= *Stofftier*) cuddly toy *or* animal

---

schmu|sen [ˈʃmuːzn] VI (*inf*) (= *zärtlich sein*) to cuddle; (*mit Freund, Freundin*) to cuddle, to canoodle (*Brit inf*); **mit jdm ~** to cuddle sb/canoodle (*Brit inf*) with sb

Schmu|se|pup|pe F (*inf*) cuddly toy

Schmu|ser [ˈʃmuːzɐ] M -s, -, **Schmu|se|rin** [-ərɪn] F -, -nen (*inf*: = *zärtlicher Mensch*) affectionate person; **er ist ein kleiner ~** he likes a cuddle

schmu|se|weich ADJ (*inf*) velvet-soft

schmu|sig [ˈʃmuːzɪç] ADJ (*inf*) smoochy (*inf*)

Schmutz [ʃmʊts] M -es, *no pl* **a** dirt; (= *Schlamm auch*) mud; **die Handwerker haben viel ~ gemacht** the workmen have made a lot of mess; **sie leben in ~** they live in real squalor; **der Stoff nimmt leicht ~ an** the material dirties easily **b** (*fig*) filth, dirt, smut; **~ und Schund** obscene *or* offensive material; **jdn/etw in den ~ ziehen *or* zerren** to drag sb/sth through the mud → **bewerfen a**

schmutz|ab|wei|send [adj] dirt-repellent; *Kleidung, Teppich etc* stain-resistant

Schmutz|blatt NT (*Typ*) half-title (page)

schmut|zen [ˈʃmʊtsn] VI to get dirty

Schmutz|-: Schmutz|fän|ger M dust trap; **Schmutz|fink** M (*inf*) (= *unsauberer Mensch*) dirty slob (*inf*); (= *Kind*) mucky pup (*Brit inf*), messy thing (*esp US inf*); (*fig*) (= *Mann*) dirty old man; (= *Journalist*) muckraker (*inf*); **Schmutz|fleck** M dirty mark; **Schmutz|fracht** F dirty cargo

schmut|zig [ˈʃmʊtsɪç] ADJ (= *unsauber, unanständig*) dirty; *Geschäft* dirty, sordid; *Witze, Geschichten* smutty, dirty; **sich ~ machen** to get oneself dirty; **Geld ist doch nicht ~** money is money no matter where it comes from; **~e Wäsche (vor anderen Leuten) waschen** to wash (*Brit*) *or* air (*US*) one's dirty linen in public; **~e Reden führen** to use bad *or* foul language

Schmut|zig|keit F -, -en **a** *no pl* (= *Unsauberkeit*) dirtiness **b** (= *Witz*) dirty joke; (= *Bemerkung*) dirty remark

Schmutz|-: Schmutz|kam|pag|ne F smear campaign; **Schmutz|li|te|ra|tur** F dirty *or* smutty literature; **Schmutz|schicht** F layer of dirt; **Schmutz|ti|tel** M (*Typ*) half-title; **Schmutz|wä|sche** F dirty washing; **Schmutz|was|ser** NT *pl* -**wässer** dirty water

Schna|bel [ˈʃnaːbl] M -s, = [ˈʃnɛːbl] **a** (= *Vogelschnabel*) beak, bill **b** (*von Kanne*) spout; (*von Krug*) lip; (*von Schiff*) prow **c** (*Mus*: = *Mundstück*) mouthpiece **d** (*inf*: = *Mund*) mouth; **halt den ~!** shut your mouth (*inf*) *or* trap! (*inf*); **mach doch den ~ auf** say something; **reden, wie einem der ~ gewachsen ist** to say exactly what comes into one's head; (*unaffektiert*) to talk naturally

Schnä|be|lei [ʃnɛːbəˈlai] F -, -en (*lit, fig*) billing and cooing

Schna|bel|hieb M peck

schnä|beln [ˈʃnɛːbln] VI (*lit, fig*) to bill and coo

Schna|bel|-: Schna|bel|schuh M pointed shoe (with turned-up toe); **Schna|bel|tas|se** F feeding cup; **Schna|bel|tier** NT duckbilled platypus

schna|bu|lie|ren [ʃnabuˈliːrən] *ptp* **schnabuliert** VI (*inf*: = *essen*) to nibble

Schnack [ʃnak] M -(e)s, -s (*N Ger, inf*) (= *Unterhaltung*) chat; (= *Ausspruch*) silly *or* amusing phrase; **das ist ein dummer ~** that's a silly phrase

schna|ckeln [ˈʃnakln] VI (*S Ger*) (*Mensch*) to shake; **mit den Fingern ~** to snap *or* click one's fingers; **jdm ~ die Knie** sb's knees are trembling *or* shaking; **es hat (bei jdm) geschnackelt** it's clicked

schna|cken [ˈʃnakn] VI (*N Ger*) to chat

Schna|ckerl [ˈʃnakəl] M OR NT -s, *no pl* (*Aus*) hiccup; **den ~ haben** to have (the) hiccups

Schna|ke [ˈʃnaːkə] F **-, -n** **a** (*inf*: = *Stechmücke*) gnat, midge (*Brit*), mosquito **b** (= *Weberknecht*) daddy-longlegs

Schna|ken|stich M mosquito bite

Schnal|le [ˈʃnalə] F **-, -n** **a** (= *Schuhschnalle, Gürtelschnalle*) buckle **b** (an *Handtasche, Buch*) clasp **c** (*Aus, S Ger*: = *Türklinke*) handle **d** (*sl*: = *Frau, Mädchen*) bird (*esp Brit inf*), chick (*esp US inf*) **e** (*vulg*: = *Vagina*) fanny (*sl*)

schnal|len [ˈʃnalən] VT **a** (= *befestigen*) to strap; *Gürtel* to buckle, to fasten → **Gürtel b** (*inf*: = *begreifen*) **etw ~** to catch on to sth; **hast du das noch immer nicht geschnallt?** have you still not caught on?

Schnal|len|schuh M buckled shoe

schnal|zen [ˈʃnaltsn] VI **mit der Peitsche ~** to crack one's whip, to give a crack of one's whip; **mit der Zunge ~** to click one's tongue

Schnal|zer [ˈʃnaltsɐ] M **-s, -** (*inf*) (*mit Zunge*) click; (*von Peitsche*) crack

Schnalz|laut M (*Ling*) click

schnapp [ʃnap] INTERJ snap → **schnipp**

Schnäpp|chen [ˈʃnɛpçən] NT **-s, -** bargain; **ein ~ machen** to get a bargain

Schnäpp|chen|jä|ger(in) M(F) (*inf*) bargain hunter

schnap|pen [ˈʃnapn] **VI a nach jdm/etw ~** to snap at *or* take a snap at sb/sth; (= *greifen*) to snatch at *or* grab at sb/sth → **Luft b** **b** *aux sein* (= *sich bewegen*) to spring up; **die Tür schnappt ins Schloss** the door snaps *or* clicks shut VT (*inf*) **a** (= *ergreifen*) to snatch, to grab; **jdn am Arm ~** to grab sb's arm *or* sb by the arm; **sich** (*dat*) **jdn/etw ~** to grab sb/sth (*inf*) → **Luft b** **b** (= *fangen*) to catch, to nab (*inf*)

Schnap|per [ˈʃnapɐ] M **-s, -** (*inf: von Hund etc*) snap

Schnäp|per [ˈʃnɛpɐ] M **-s, -** (*Med*) lancet

Schnapp-: Schnapp|fe|der F spring catch; **Schnapp|hahn** M (*Hist*) highwayman; **Schnapp|mes|ser** NT clasp knife; **Schnapp|schloss ▲** NT (an *Tür*) spring lock; (an *Schmuck*) spring clasp; **Schnapp|schuss ▲** M (= *Foto*) snap(shot); **Schnapp|ver|schluss ▲** M snap lock

Schnaps [ʃnaps] M **-es, ⁼e** [ˈʃnɛpsə] (= *klarer Schnaps*) schnapps; (*inf*) (= *Branntwein*) spirits *pl*; (= *Alkohol*) drink, booze (*inf*), liquor (*esp US inf*)

Schnaps-: Schnaps|bren|ner(in) M(F) distiller; **Schnaps|bren|ne|rei** F **a** (*Gebäude*) distillery **b** *no pl* (= *das Brennen*) distilling of spirits *or* liquor; **Schnaps|bru|der** M (*inf*) boozer (*inf*)

Schnäps|chen [ˈʃnɛpsçən] NT **-s, -** (*inf*) little drink, wee dram (*esp Scot*)

Schnaps|dros|sel F (*inf, hum*) boozer (*inf*), lush (*esp US inf*)

schnap|sen [ˈʃnapsn], (*Aus*) **schnap|seln** [ˈʃnapsln] VI (*inf*) to booze (*inf*)

Schnaps-: Schnaps|fah|ne F (*inf*) boozy breath (*inf*); **Schnaps|fla|sche** F bottle of booze (*inf*) *or* spirits *or* liquor; **Schnaps|glas** NT small glass for spirits; **Schnaps|idee** F (*inf*) crazy *or* crackpot idea; **Schnaps|la|den** M off-licence (*Brit*), liquor store (*US*); **Schnaps|lei|che** F (*inf*) drunk; **Schnaps|na|se** F (*inf*) boozer's nose (*inf*); **Schnaps|zahl** F (*inf*) *multidigit number with all digits identical*

schnar|chen [ˈʃnarçn] VI to snore

Schnar|cher [ˈʃnarçɐ] M **-s, -**, **Schnar|che|rin** [-ərɪn] F **-, -nen** snorer

Schnar|re [ˈʃnarə] F **-, -n** rattle

schnar|ren [ˈʃnarən] VI (*Wecker, Radio, Saite etc*) to buzz; (*Maschine, Spinnrad etc*) to clatter; (*Uhrwerk*) to creak; (*Vogel, Frosch*) to croak; **mit ~der Stimme** in a rasping *or* grating voice

Schnat|ter|gans F, **Schnat|ter|lie|se** [-liːzə] F **-, -n**, **Schnat|ter|maul** NT (*all inf*) chatterbox (*inf*)

schnat|tern [ˈʃnatɐn] VI (*Gans*) to gabble; (*Ente*) to quack; (*Affen*) to chatter, to gibber; (*inf*: = *schwatzen*) to natter (*inf*); **sie schnattert vor Kälte** her teeth are chattering with (the) cold

schnau|ben [ˈʃnaubn] *pret* **schnaubte** *or* (*old*) **schnob** [ˈʃnauptə, ʃnoːp], *ptp* **geschnaubt** *or* (*old*) **geschnoben** [gəˈʃnaupt, gəˈʃnoːbn] **VI a** (*Tier*) to snort **b** (= *fauchen*) to snort; **vor Wut/Entrüstung ~** to snort with rage/indignation VT **a** (= *schnäuzen*) **sich** (*dat*) **die Nase ~** to blow one's nose **b** (= *fauchen*) to snort; **Unverschämtheit, schnaubte er** disgraceful, he snorted **c** (*liter: Pferd etc*) to breathe VR **sich ~** to blow one's nose

schnau|fen [ˈʃnaufn] VI **a** (= *schwer atmen*) to wheeze; (= *keuchen*) to puff, to pant; (*fig*) (*Lokomotive*) to puff; (*inf: Auto*) to struggle **b** (*esp S Ger*: = *atmen*) to breathe **c** *aux sein* (= *sich keuchend bewegen*) (*Auto*) to struggle; (*Lokomotive*) to puff; **ich bin in den fünften Stock geschnauft** (*inf*) I went puffing and panting up to the fifth floor

Schnau|fer [ˈʃnaufɐ] M **-s, -** (*inf*) breath; **ein ~ frische Luft** a breath of fresh air; **seinen letzten ~ tun** to breathe one's last, to kick the bucket (*inf*), to snuff it (*Brit inf*)

Schnau|ferl [ˈʃnaufɐl] NT **-s, -** *or* (*Aus*) **-n** (*hum*: = *Oldtimer*) veteran car

Schnauf|pau|se F (*Aus, S Ger*) short breather (*inf*)

Schnauz|bart M walrus moustache (*Brit*) *or* mustache (*US*)

Schnäuz|chen [ˈʃnɔytsçən] NT **-s, -** dim von **Schnauze** nose

Schnau|ze [ˈʃnautsə] F **-, -n** **a** (*von Tier*) snout, muzzle; **eine feuchte ~ haben** to have a wet nose; **mit einer Maus in der ~** with a mouse in its mouth **b** (= *Ausguss*) (an *Kaffeekanne etc*) spout; (an *Krug etc*) lip **c** (*inf*) (*von Fahrzeugen*) front; (*von Flugzeug, Schiff*) nose **d** (*inf*) (= *Mund*) gob (*Brit inf*), trap (*inf*); (= *respektlose Art zu reden*) bluntness; (**halt die**) **~!** shut your gob (*Brit inf*) *or* trap! (*inf*); **auf die ~ fallen** (*lit*) to fall flat on one's face; (*fig auch*) to come a cropper (*Brit inf*); **jdm die ~ polieren** to smash sb's face in (*inf*); **die ~ (von jdm/etw) (gestrichen) voll haben** to be fed up to the back teeth (with sb/sth) (*inf*); **eine große ~ haben** to have a big mouth, to be a bigmouth (*inf*); **die ~ halten** to hold one's tongue; **etw frei nach ~ machen** to do sth any old (*Brit*) *or* ole (*US*) how (*inf*); **Berliner ~** endearing Berlin bluntness

schnau|zen [ˈʃnautsn] VI (*inf*) to shout; (= *jdn anfahren*) to snap, to bark

schnäu|zen ▲ [ˈʃnɔytsn] VR to blow one's nose VT **einem Kind/sich die Nase ~** to blow a child's/one's nose

Schnau|zer [ˈʃnautsɐ] M **-s, -** **a** (= *Hundeart*) schnauzer **b** (*inf*: = *Schnauzbart*) walrus moustache (*Brit*) *or* mustache (*US*)

Schneck [ʃnɛk] M **-s, -en** (*Aus, S Ger*) = **Schnecke a, b**

Schne|cke [ˈʃnɛkə] F **-, -n** **a** (*Zool, fig*) snail; (= *Nacktschnecke*) slug; (*Cook*) escargot, snail; **wie eine ~ kriechen** to crawl at a snail's pace; **jdn zur ~ machen** (*inf*) to give sb a real bawling-out (*inf*), to bawl sb out (*inf*) **b** (*Anat*) cochlea (*spec*) **c** (*Archit: an Säule*) volute (= *Treppe*) spiral staircase **d** (*Tech*) (= *Schraube*) worm, endless screw; (= *Förderschnecke*) worm *or* screw conveyor **e** *usu pl* (*Frisur*) earphone **f** (*Cook: Gebäck*) ≈ Chelsea bun **g** (*Mus: an Geige etc*) scroll

Schne|cken-: schne|cken|för|mig ADJ spiral; (*Archit*) Ornament scroll-shaped; **Schne|cken|ge|häu|se** NT, **Schne|cken|haus** NT snail shell; **sich in sein Schneckenhaus zurückziehen** (*fig inf*) to retreat into one's shell; **Schne|cken|korn** NT, *no pl* slug pellets *pl*; **Schne|cken|post** F (*inf*) snail mail (*inf*); **du bist wohl mit der ~ gefahren?** you must have crawled your way here; **Schne|cken|tem|po** NT (*inf*) **im ~** at a snail's pace; **dein ~ kenn ich schon** I know how slowly you do things

Schnee [ʃneː] M **-s,** *no pl* **a** (*auch TV*) snow; **vom ~ eingeschlossen sein** to be snowbound; **im Jahre ~** (*Aus*) ages ago; **das ist ~ von gestern** (*inf*) that's old hat **b** (= *Eischnee*) whisked egg white; **Eiweiß zu ~ schlagen** to whisk the egg white(s) till stiff **c** (*inf*: = *Heroin, Kokain*) snow (*sl*)

Schnee-: Schnee|an|zug M snowsuit; **schnee|arm** ADJ *Gebiet, Winter* with little snow

Schnee|ball M snowball; (*Bot*) snowball, guelder rose

Schnee|ball-: Schnee|ball|ef|fekt M snowball effect; **Schnee|ball|prin|zip** NT snowball effect; **Schnee|ball|schlacht** F snowball fight; **eine ~ machen** to have a snowball fight; **Schnee|ball|sys|tem** NT accumulative process; (*Comm*) pyramid selling; **ein Gewinnspiel/ Geldgeschäft nach dem** *or* **im ~** a prize game/ financial transaction involving a pyramid scheme; **das vermehrt sich nach dem ~** it snowballs

Schnee-: schnee|be|deckt ADJ snow-covered; *Berg auch* snowcapped; **Schnee|be|sen** M (*Cook*) whisk; **schnee|blind** ADJ snow-blind; **Schnee|blind|heit** F snow blindness; **Schnee|brett** NT windslab (*Brit*), snow/ice slab (*US*); **Schnee|brett|ge|fahr** F danger of windslab (*Brit*) *or* snow/ice slab (*US*) avalanches; **Schnee|bril|le** F snow goggles *pl*; **Schnee|de|cke** F blanket *or* (*Met*) covering of snow; **Schnee-Eu|le** F snowy owl; **Schnee|fall** M snowfall, fall of snow; **dichter ~ behindert die Sicht** heavy falling snow is impairing visibility; **Schnee|flo|cke** F snowflake; **Schnee|frä|se** F snow blower; **schnee|frei** ADJ *Gebiet, Bergpass* free of snow; **in der ~en Zeit** when there is no snow; **Schnee|gans** F snow goose; **Schnee|ge|stö|ber** NT (*leicht*) snow flurry; (*stark*) snowstorm; **Schnee|glät|te** F hard-packed snow *no pl*; **Schnee|glöck|chen** NT snowdrop; **Schnee|gren|ze** F snow line; **Schnee|ha|se** M blue hare; **Schnee|hemd** NT (*Mil*) white coat for camouflage in snow; **Schnee|hüt|te** F hut made of snow; **Schnee|ka|no|ne** F snow cannon; **Schnee|ket|te** F (*Aut*) snow chain; **Schnee|ket|ten|pflicht** F (*Aut*) obligation to fit snow chains, chain law (*US*); **Schnee|kö|nig** M **sich freuen wie ein ~** to be as pleased as Punch; **Schnee|kris|tall** M snow crystal; **Schnee|land|schaft** F snowy landscape; **Schnee|mann** M *pl* **-männer** snowman; **Schnee|matsch** M slush; **Schnee|mensch** M abominable snowman, yeti; **Schnee|mo|bil** [-moBiːl] NT **-s, -e** snowmobile; **Schnee|pflug** M (*Tech, Ski*) snowplough (*Brit*), snowplow (*US*); **Schnee|rau|pe** F snow cat; **Schnee|re|gen** M sleet; **Schnee|schau|fel** F, **Schnee|schie|ber** M, **Schnee|schip|pe** F snow shovel, snowpusher (*US*); **Schnee|schlä|ger** M whisk; **Schnee|schmel|ze** F thaw; **Schnee|schuh** M snowshoe; (*dated Ski*) ski; **schnee|si|cher** ADJ **~e Gebiete** areas that are assured of snow; **Schnee|sturm** M snowstorm; (*stärker*) blizzard; **Schnee|trei|ben** NT driving snow; **Schnee|ver|hält|nis|se** PL snow conditions *pl*; **Schnee|ver|we|hung** F snowdrift; **Schnee|wäch|te ▲** F [-vɛçtə] F **-, -n** snow cornice; **Schnee|was|ser** NT, *no pl* water from melting snow, snowmelt (*US*); **Schnee|we|he** F snowdrift; **schnee|weiß** ADJ snow-white, as white as snow; *Haare* snowy-white; *Hände* lily-white; *Gewissen* clear; **Schnee|weiß|chen**

[-'vaisçən] **NT** **-s**, *no pl*, **Schnee|witt|chen** [-'vɪtçən] **NT** **-s**, *no pl* Snow White

Schneid [ʃnait] **M** -(e)s [-dəs] (*S Ger, Aus*) f -, *no pl* (*inf*) guts *pl* (*inf*), nerve, courage; **~/keinen ~ haben** to have/not to have guts (*inf*); **den ~ verlieren** to lose one's nerve; **jdm den ~ abkaufen** (*fig*) to knock the stuffing out of sb (*inf*), to take the fight out of sb

Schneid|brenn|ner **M** (*Tech*) oxyacetylene cutter, cutting torch

Schnei|de ['ʃnaidə] **F** -, -n (sharp *or* cutting) edge; (*von Messer, Schwert*) blade → **Messer**

Schnei|de|brett **NT** chopping *or* cutting board

schnei|den [ʃnaidn] *pret* **schnitt** [ʃnɪt], *ptp* **geschnitten** [gə'ʃnɪtn] **VI** to cut; (*Med*) to operate; (*bei Geburt*) to do an episiotomy; **jdm ins Gesicht/in die Hand** etc → to cut sb on the face/on the hand etc; **der Wind schneidet** the wind is biting; **die Kälte schneidet** it is bitingly cold; **jdm ins Herz** or **in die Seele ~** to cut sb to the quick

VT **a** *Papier etc, Haare, Hecke* to cut; *Getreide* to mow, to cut; (= *klein schneiden*) *Schnittlauch, Gemüse etc* to chop; (*Sport*) *Ball* to slice, to cut; (= *schnitzen*) *Namen, Figuren* to carve; (*Math*) to intersect with, to cut; (*Weg*) to cross; **eine Kurve ~** to cut a corner; **jdn ~** (*beim Überholen*) to cut in on sb; (= *ignorieren*) to cut sb dead (*Brit*) or off; **sein schön/scharf geschnittenes Gesicht** his clean-cut/sharp features *or* face; **Gesichter** *or* **Grimassen ~** to make *or* pull faces; **die Luft ist zum Schneiden (dick)** (*fig inf*) the air is very bad; **die Atmosphäre ist zum Schneiden** (*fig inf*) you could cut the atmosphere with a knife; **weit/eng geschnitten sein** (*Sew*) to be cut wide/narrow

b *Film, Tonband* to edit

c (*inf*: = *operieren*) to operate on; *Furunkel* to lance; **jdn ~** to cut sb open (*inf*); (*bei Geburt*) to give sb an episiotomy; **geschnitten werden** (*bei Geburt*) to have an episiotomy

d (*fig*: = *meiden*) to cut

VR **a** (*Mensch*) to cut oneself; **sich in den Finger ~** to cut one's finger etc → **Fleisch a**

b (*inf*: = *sich täuschen*) **da hat er sich aber geschnitten!** he's made a big mistake, he's very mistaken

c (*Linien, Straßen etc*) to intersect

schnei|dend **ADJ** biting; *Hohn, Bemerkung auch* cutting; *Wind, Kälte auch* piercing, bitter; *Schmerz* sharp, searing; *Stimme, Ton* piercing

Schnei|der¹ ['ʃnaidə] **M** -s, - **a** (*Cards*) **einen ~ machen** to score half (the full) points; **im ~ sein** to have less than half points; **aus dem ~ sein** to have slightly more than half points; (*fig*) to be out of the woods **b** (*Gerät*) cutter; (*inf*: für Brot etc*) slicer **c** (= *Schnake*) gnat; (= *Weberknecht*) daddy-longlegs

Schnei|der² ['ʃnaidə] **M** -s, -, **Schnei|de|rin** ['ʃnaidərɪn] **F** -, -nen tailor; (= *Damenschneider auch*) dressmaker → **frieren VI a**

Schnei|de|raum **M** (= *Filmschneideraum*) cutting room, editing suite

Schnei|de|rei [ʃnaidə'rai] **F** -, -en **a** *no pl* (*Handwerk*) tailoring; (*für Damen*) dressmaking **b** (*Werkstatt*) tailor's/dressmaker's

Schnei|der-: **Schnei|der|ge|sel|le** **M** , **Schnei|der|ge|sel|lin** **F** → **Schnei|der²** journeyman tailor/dressmaker; **Schnei|der|werk** **NT** tailoring *no art*; (*für Damenkleidung*) dressmaking *no art*; **Schnei|der|kos|tüm** **NT** tailored suit; **Schnei|der|krei|de** **F** tailor's chalk; **Schnei|der|leh|re** **F** tailoring apprenticeship; (*für Damenmode*) dressmaking apprenticeship; **Schnei|der|lehr|ling** **M** → **Schneider²** tailor's/dressmaker's apprentice; **Schnei|der|meis|ter(in)** **M(F)** → **Schneider²** master tailor/dressmaker

schnei|dern ['ʃnaidən] **VI** (*beruflich*) to be a tailor; (*Damenschneider*) to be a dressmaker; (*als Hobby*) to do dressmaking **VT** to make, to sew; *Anzug, Kostüm* to tailor; to make; (*fig*) *Plan, Programm* to draw up; **jdm (wie) auf den Leib geschneidert sein** (*fig*) to be tailor-made for sb

Schnei|der-: **Schnei|der|pup|pe** **F** → **Schnei|der²** tailor's/dressmaker's dummy; **Schnei|der|sitz** **M** **im ~ sitzen** to sit cross-legged; **Schnei|der|werk|statt** **F** → **Schneider²** tailor's/dressmaker's workshop

Schnei|de-: **Schnei|de|tisch** **M** (*Film*) editing *or* cutting table; **Schnei|de|werk|zeug** **NT** cutting tool; **Schnei|de|zahn** **M** incisor

schnei|dig ['ʃnaidɪç] **ADJ** *Mensch* dashing; *Musik, Rede* rousing; *Tempo* fast

schnei|en ['ʃnaiən] **VI** *impers* to snow **VT** *impers* **es schneit dicke Flocken** big flakes (of snow) are falling; **es schneite Konfetti** confetti rained down **VI** *aux sein* (*fig*) to rain down; **jdm ins Haus ~** (*inf*) (*Besuch*) to drop in on sb; (*Rechnung, Brief*) to arrive through sb's letter box (*Brit*) or mailbox (*US*), to arrive in the post (*Brit*) or mail for sb

Schnei|se ['ʃnaizə] **F** -, -n break; (= *Waldschneise*) aisle, lane; (= *Feuerschneise*) firebreak; (= *Flugschneise*) path; **eine ~ schlagen** (*lit*) to cut a lane; **der Toleranz** (*dat*) **eine ~ schlagen** to pave the way for tolerance

schnell [ʃnɛl] **ADJ** quick; *Bedienung, Fahrt, Tempo, Läufer auch* fast; *Schritte, Puls, Verbesserung auch* fast, rapid; *Auto, Zug, Verkehr, Fahrer, Strecke* fast; *Abreise, Bote, Hilfe* speedy; *Antwort* quick, speedy, prompt; *Genesung, Besserung* quick, rapid, speedy; **etw in ~em Tempo singen** to sing sth quickly *or* fast; **er kam in ~em Lauf dahergerannt** he came running up quickly; **er ist sehr ~ mit seinem Urteil/seiner Kritik** he's very quick to judge/to criticize; **~es Geld (machen)** (*inf*) (to make) a fast buck → **Schnelle, Truppe a**

ADV **a** (= *mit hoher Geschwindigkeit*) quickly, fast; **~er als der Schall fliegen** to fly faster than the speed of sound; **wie ~ ist er die 100 Meter gelaufen?** how fast did he run the 100 metres (*Brit*) or meters (*US*)?; **geh ~er!** hurry up!; **nicht so ~!** not so fast!; **sein Puls ging ~** his pulse was very fast

b (= *zügig*) *arbeiten, handeln, durchführen, erwärmen* fast, quickly; **das geht ~** (*grundsätzlich*) it doesn't take long; **das mache ich gleich, das geht ~** I'll do that now, it won't take long; **das ging ~** that was quick; **mach ~/~er!** hurry up!; **es ist mit dem Patienten ~ gegangen** it was all over quickly; **mit dicker Wolle geht es ~, einen Pullover zu stricken** knitting a pullover with thick wool is very quick; **an der Grenze ist es ~ gegangen** things went very quickly at the border; **das ging alles viel zu ~** it all happened much too quickly or fast; **das werden wir ~ erledigt haben** we'll soon have that finished; **das werden wir ~ sehen** (= *bald*) we'll soon see about that

c (= *leicht*) **das sagt sich so ~** that's easy to say; **sie wird ~ böse, sie ist ~ verärgert** she loses her temper quickly, she is quick to get angry; **das werde ich so ~ nicht vergessen/wieder tun** I won't forget that/do that again in a hurry; **diese dünnen Gläser gehen ~ kaputt** these thin glasses break easily

d (= *kurz*) **ich gehe noch ~ beim Bäcker vorbei** I'll just stop by at the baker's; **kannst du das vorher noch ~ machen?** (*inf*) can you do that quickly first?; **ich muss mir nur noch ~ die Haare kämmen** I must just give my hair a quick comb

Schnellläufer △ **M** → **Schnellläufer, Schnellläufer(in)**

Schnell-: **Schnell|bahn** **F** (= *S-Bahn*) suburban railway (*Brit*), city railroad (*US*); **Schnell|bau|wei|se** **F** high-speed building methods *pl*; **Schnell|boot** **NT** speedboat; (*Mil*) motor torpedo boat (*Brit*), PT boat (*US*); **Schnell|den|ker(in)** **M(F)** (*inf*: = *intelligenter Mensch*) bright or clever person, brainbox (*Brit inf*); **Schnell|dienst** **M** express service; **Schnell|dru|cker** **M** high-speed printer

Schnel|le ['ʃnɛlə] **F** -, -n **a** *no pl* (= *Schnelligkeit*) quickness, speed **b** (= *Stromschnelle*) rapids *pl* **c** **etw auf die ~ machen** to do sth quickly or in a rush; **das lässt sich nicht auf die ~ machen** we can't rush that, that will take time; **Sex/ein Bier auf die ~** (*inf*) a quickie (*inf*)

schnelllebig △ **ADJ** → **schnelllebig**

Schnelllebigkeit △ **F** → **Schnelllebigkeit**

schnel|len ['ʃnɛlən] **VI** *aux sein* (*lit, fig*) to shoot; **in die Höhe ~** to shoot up; **ein Gummiband ~ lassen** to flick a rubber band

Schnell|feu|er **NT** (*Mil*) rapid fire

Schnell|feu|er-: **Schnell|feu|er|ge|schütz** **NT** automatic rifle; **Schnell|feu|er|ge|wehr** **NT** automatic pistol; **Schnell|feu|er|waf|fe** **F** rapid-fire weapon

Schnell-: **schnell|fü|ßig** **ADJ** (*geh*) fleet-footed (*liter*), fleet of foot (*liter*); **Schnell|gast|stät|te** **F** fast-food restaurant, cafeteria, fast-food store (*US*); **Schnell|ge|richt** **NT** **a** (*Jur*) summary court **b** (*Cook*) convenience food; **Schnell|hef|ter** **M** spring folder

Schnell|lig|keit ['ʃnɛlɪçkait] **F** -, -en (*von Auto, Verkehr, Abreise*) speed; (*von Bewegung, Tempo auch*) quickness; (*von Schritten, Besserung, Verbesserung, Entwicklung auch, von Puls*) rapidity; (*von Bote, Hilfe*) speediness; (*von Antwort*) speediness, promptness

Schnell-: **Schnell|im|biss** ▲ **M** **a** (*Essen*) (quick) snack **b** (*Raum*) snack bar; **Schnell|koch|plat|te** **F** high-speed ring; **Schnell|koch|topf** **M** (= *Dampfkochtopf*) pressure cooker; (= *Wasserkochtopf*) ≈ electric kettle; **Schnell|kraft** **F** (*von Feder, Sprungbrett*) springiness, resilience; (*von Sportler, Fischen*) ability to jump; **Schnell|kurs** **M** crash course; **Schnell|läu|fer** ▲ **M** (*Astron*) high-velocity star; (*Tech*) high-speed machine; **Schnell|läu|fer(in)** ▲ **M(F)** (*Sport*) sprinter; **schnell|le|big** ▲ [-le:bɪç] **ADJ** *Zeit, Geschäft, Markt* fast-moving; **Schnell|le|big|keit** ▲ [-le:bɪç-] **F** -, *no pl* fast-moving nature; **Schnell|pa|ket** **NT** express parcel; **Schnell|pres|se** **F** high-speed printing machine or press; **Schnell|rei|ni|gung** **F** express cleaning service; **Schnell|res|tau|rant** **NT** fast-food restaurant; **Schnell|rück|lauf** **M** fast rewind; **Schnell|schrift** **F** (*Comput*) draft quality; **Schnell|schuss** ▲ **M** (*inf*: = *vorschnelle Handlung*) hasty reaction; (*Buch, Fernsehsendung etc*) rush job; **ei|nen ~ machen** to react too hastily

schnells|tens ['ʃnɛlstns] **ADV** as quickly as possible

schnellst|mög|lich ['ʃnɛlst-] **ADJ** *attr* fastest or quickest possible *attr* **ADV** as quickly as possible

Schnell-: **Schnell|stra|ße** **F** expressway; **Schnell|such|lauf** **M** rapid search; **Schnell|ver|fah|ren** **NT** (*Jur*) summary trial; (*Mil*) summary court martial; **im ~ abgeurteilt werden** to be sentenced by a summary trial/court martial; **Schnell|ver|kehr** **M** fast-moving traffic; (*im Transportwesen*) express service; **etw im ~ schicken** to send sth express delivery; **Schnell|vor|lauf** **M** fast forward; **Schnell|zug** **M** fast train; **Schnell|zug|zu|schlag** **M** supplementary or extra charge for travel on a fast train; (*inf*: = *Zuschlagkarte*) supplementary ticket

Schnep|fe ['ʃnɛpfə] **F** -, -n snipe; (*pej inf*) silly cow (*inf*)

schnet|zeln ['ʃnɛtsln] **VT** (*S Ger, Sw*) *Frucht, Gemüse* to slice; *Fleisch* to mince

schneu|zen △ ['ʃnɔytsn] **VTR** → **schnäuzen**

Schnick|schnack ['ʃnɪkʃnak] **M** -s, *no pl* (*inf*) (= *Unsinn*) twaddle (*inf*) *no indef art*, poppycock (*inf*) *no indef art*; (= *Kinkerlitzchen*) paraphernalia (*inf*) *no indef art*; (= *dated*) balderdash! (*Brit dated inf*), fiddlesticks! (*dated inf*)

Schnick|se ['ʃnɪksə] **F** -, -n (*sl*: = *Frau, Mädchen*) bird (*esp Brit inf*), chick (*esp US inf*)

Schnie|del ['ʃniːdl] M **-s, -, Schnie|del|wutz** ['ʃniːdlwʊts] M **-es, -e** (hum inf: = Penis) willy (Brit hum inf), weenie (US hum inf)

schnie|fen ['ʃniːfn] VI (dial) (bei Schnupfen) to sniff(le); (beim Weinen) to sniffle, to snivel

schnie|geln ['ʃniːgln] (inf) **VT** Kleidung, Kinder, Auto to spruce up **VR** to get spruced up, to spruce oneself up → auch **geschniegelt**

schnie|ke ['ʃniːkə] ADJ (N Ger, inf: = schick) swish (inf)

schnipp [ʃnɪp] INTERJ snip; ~, **schnapp** snip, snip (Brit), snip, snap (US)

Schnipp|chen ['ʃnɪpçən] NT **-s, -** (inf) jdm ein ~ **schlagen** to play a trick on sb, to trick sb; **dem Tod ein ~ schlagen** to cheat death

Schnip|pel ['ʃnɪpl] M OR NT **-s, -** (inf) scrap; (= Papierschnipsel) scrap or bit of paper

schnip|peln ['ʃnɪpln] **VI** to snip (an +dat at); (mit Messer) to hack (an +dat at); **an ihr haben die Ärzte schon was geschnippelt!** she has already been hacked about a bit by the doctors (inf) **VT** to snip; (mit Messer) to hack; Gemüse to chop up

schnip|pen ['ʃnɪpn] **VI** mit den Fingern ~ to snap one's fingers **VT** etw (von etw) ~ to flick sth (off or from sth)

schnip|pisch ['ʃnɪpɪʃ] ADJ saucy, pert ADV saucily, pertly

Schnip|sel ['ʃnɪpsl] M OR NT **-s, -** (inf) scrap; (= Papierschnipsel) scrap or bit of paper

schnip|seln ['ʃnɪpsln] VTI (inf) = **schnippeln**

schnip|sen ['ʃnɪpsn] VTI (inf) = **schnippen**

schnitt pret von **schneiden**

Schnitt [ʃnɪt] M **-(e)s, -e a** cut; (= Kerbe) notch, nick; (Med) incision, cut; (von Heu, Getreide) crop; **Blumen für den ~** flowers pl (suitable) for cutting
b (= Haarschnitt) (hair)cut; **einen kurzen ~ bitte** cut it short please
c (Sew) cut; (= Schnittmuster) pattern
d (= Form) (von Edelstein) cut; (von Gesicht, Augen) shape; (von Profil) line
e (Film) editing no pl; **der Film ist jetzt beim ~** the film is now being edited or cut; **schnelle ~e** quick cutting; **~: L. Schwarz** editor - L. Schwarz
f (Math) (= Schnittpunkt) (point of) intersection; (= Schnittfläche) section; (inf: = Durchschnitt) average; **im ~** on average; **unter/über dem ~** below/above average
g (Längsschnitt, Querschnitt) section; **im ~ gezeichnet** drawn in section
h (= Gewinn) profit
i (Typ) (= das Beschneiden) cut; (= Buchrand) (trimmed) edge; **dann kommt das gebundene Buch zum ~** then the bound book is cut or trimmed
j (Hort: von Bäumen etc) cutting no indef art

Schnitt-: Schnitt|blu|men PL cut flowers pl; (im Garten) flowers pl (suitable) for cutting; **Schnitt|boh|nen** PL French or green beans pl

Schnit|te ['ʃnɪtə] F **-, -n a** slice; (belegt) open sandwich; (zusammengeklappt) sandwich; **womit soll ich dir die ~ belegen?** what shall I put on your (slice of) bread? **b** (sl: = Frau, Mädchen) bird (esp Brit inf), chick (esp US inf)

Schnitt|ebe|ne F (Math) sectional plane

Schnit|ter ['ʃnɪtɐ] M **-s, -, Schnit|te|rin** [-ərɪn] F **-, -nen** reaper

Schnitt-: schnitt|fest ADJ Tomaten, Käse etc firm; **Schnitt|flä|che** F section

schnit|tig ['ʃnɪtɪç] ADJ smart; Mann, Auto, Formen auch stylish; Mund, Lippen finely shaped; Tempo auch snappy (inf); **er ist ganz schön ~ gefahren** he nipped or zipped along (inf)

Schnitt-: Schnitt|kä|se M slicing cheese; (= aufgeschnittener Käse) cheese slices pl; **Schnitt|lauch** M , no pl chives pl; **Schnitt|lauch|lo|cken** PL (hum inf) straight hair no pl; **Schnitt|li|nie** F (Math) line of intersection;

(Sew) cutting line; **Schnitt|men|ge** F (Math) intersection; **Schnitt|mus|ter** NT (Sew) (paper) pattern; **Schnitt|mus|ter|bo|gen** M (Sew) pattern chart; **Schnitt|punkt** M (von Straßen) intersection; (Math auch) point of intersection; (fig) interface; **Schnitt|stel|le** F cut; (Comput, fig) interface; **Schnitt|ver|let|zung** F = Schnittwunde; **Schnitt|win|kel** M angle of intersection; **Schnitt|wun|de** F cut; (tief) gash

Schnitz [ʃnɪts] M **-es, -e** (S Ger, Aus) piece; (von Orange auch) segment; (von Apfel auch) slice

Schnitz|ar|beit F (wood)carving

Schnit|zel[1] ['ʃnɪtsl] NT OR M **-s, - a** (= Papierschnitzel) bit or scrap of paper; (= Holzschnitzel) shaving; (= Fetzen, Karottenschnitzel, Kartoffelschnitzel) shred, sliver **b Schnitzel** PL (= Abfälle) scraps pl

Schnit|zel[2] NT **-s, -** (Cook) veal/pork cutlet, schnitzel

Schnit|zel|jagd F paper chase

schnit|zeln ['ʃnɪtsln] VT Gemüse to shred; Holz to chop (up) (into sticks)

schnit|zen ['ʃnɪtsn] VTI to carve; **wir haben in der Schule Schnitzen gelernt** we learned woodcarving at school → **Holz a**

Schnit|zer[1] ['ʃnɪtsɐ] M **-s, -** (inf) (in Benehmen) blunder, boob (esp Brit inf), goof (US inf); (= Fauxpas) gaffe, clanger (Brit inf); (= Fehler) howler (Brit inf), blooper (US inf); **ein grober ~** an awful blunder; (= Fauxpas) a real gaffe or clanger (Brit inf)

Schnit|zer[2] ['ʃnɪtsɐ] M **-s, -, Schnit|ze|rin** ['ʃnɪtsərɪn] F **-, -nen** woodcarver

Schnit|ze|rei ['ʃnɪtsə'rai] F **-, -en** (wood)carving

Schnitz-: Schnitz|kunst F (art of) woodcarving; **Schnitz|mes|ser** NT woodcarving knife; **Schnitz|werk** NT (wood)carving

schnob (old) pret von **schnauben**

schnöd [ʃnøːt] ADJ, ADV = **schnöde**

schno|de|rig ['ʃnøːdərɪç], **schnodd|rig** ['ʃnɔdrɪç] ADJ (inf) Mensch, Bemerkung brash

Schno|de|rig|keit F **-, -en, Schnodd|rig|keit** F **-, -en** (inf) brashness

schnö|de ['ʃnøːdə] ADJ (= niederträchtig) despicable, contemptible, base; Geiz, Verrat base; Gewinn vile; Behandlung, Ton, Antwort contemptuous, disdainful; **~r Mammon, ~s Geld** filthy lucre ADV **behandeln** despicably; **jdn ~ verlassen** to leave sb in a most despicable fashion; **jdn ~ verraten** to betray sb in a despicable way; **er wurde ~ entlassen** it was despicable the way they fired him

Schnö|dig|keit ['ʃnøːdɪçkait] F **-, -en a** (= Gemeinheit) baseness; (= Geringschätzung) contempt no pl, disdain no pl **b** (= gemeine Handlung/Bemerkung) despicable or contemptible thing to do/say)

Schnor|chel ['ʃnɔrçl] M **-s, -** (von U-Boot, Taucher) snorkel; (= Schnorchelmaske) snorkel mask

schnor|cheln ['ʃnɔrçln] VI to snorkel, to go snorkelling (Brit) or snorkeling (US)

Schnör|kel ['ʃnœrkl] M **-s,-** flourish; (an Möbeln, Säulen) scroll; (fig: = Unterschrift) squiggle (hum), signature

schnör|ke|lig ['ʃnœrkəlɪç] ADJ ornate; Schrift auch full of flourishes; Rede auch flowery

schnör|kel|los ADJ without frills; Eleganz simple; Einfachheit unadorned; Sprache plain, simple

schnor|ren ['ʃnɔrən] VTI (inf) to cadge (Brit inf), to scrounge (inf) (bei from)

Schnor|rer ['ʃnɔrɐ] M **-s, -, Schnor|re|rin** [-ərɪn] F **-, -nen** (inf) cadger (Brit inf), scrounger (inf)

Schnö|sel ['ʃnøːzl] M **-s, -** (inf) snotty(-nosed) little upstart (inf)

schnö|se|lig ['ʃnøːzəlɪç] (inf) ADJ Benehmen, Jugendlicher snotty (inf), snotty-nosed (inf) ADV **sich benehmen** snottily

---

Schnö|se|lig|keit F **-, no pl** (inf) snottiness (inf)

Schnu|ckel|chen ['ʃnʊklçən] NT **-s, -** (inf) sweetheart, pet, baby (esp US)

schnu|cke|lig ['ʃnʊkəlɪç] (inf) ADJ (= gemütlich) snug, cosy; Wärme cosy; (= niedlich) cute ADV ~ **warm** warm and cosy

Schnüf|fe|lei ['ʃnʏfə'lai] F **-, -en** (inf) **a** (von Hund) snuffling no pl, sniffing no pl; (von Mensch) sniffing no pl **b** (fig: = das Spionieren) snooping no pl (inf)

schnüf|feln ['ʃnʏfln] **VI a** (= schnuppern, riechen) to sniff; (Hund) to sniff, to snuffle; **an etw** (dat) ~ to sniff (at) sth **b** (bei Erkältung etc) to sniffle, to snuffle **c** (fig inf: = spionieren) to snoop around (inf), to nose around (inf) **d** (von Drogen, Klebstoff) to sniff **VT** Drogen, Klebstoff to sniff

Schnüff|ler ['ʃnʏflɐ] M **-s, -, Schnüff|le|rin** [-ərɪn] F **-, -nen** (inf) (fig) snooper (inf), nosey parker (Brit inf), curious George (US); (= Detektiv) sleuth (inf), private eye (inf); (von Drogen, Klebstoff) glue-sniffer

Schnul|ler ['ʃnʊlɐ] M **-s, -** (inf) dummy (Brit), pacifier (US); (auf Flasche) teat (Brit), nipple (US)

Schnul|ze ['ʃnʊltsə] F **-, -n** (inf) schmaltzy film/book/song (inf); **das sind alles ~n** it's all schmaltz (inf)

Schnul|zen|sän|ger(in) M(F) (pej inf) crooner (pej)

schnul|zig ['ʃnʊltsɪç] (inf) ADJ slushy, soppy, schmaltzy (all inf) ADV **schreiben** soppily (inf); **er singt so ~** his songs are so schmaltzy (inf)

schnup|fen ['ʃnʊpfn] VTI Kokain to snort, to sniff; Tabak ~ to take snuff; **willst du auch ~?** would you like some snuff too?

Schnup|fen ['ʃnʊpfn] M **-s, -** cold, head cold; **(einen) ~ bekommen, sich** (dat) **einen ~ holen** (inf) to catch a cold; **(einen) ~ haben** to have a cold

Schnup|fer ['ʃnʊpfɐ] M **-s, -, Schnup|fe|rin** [-ərɪn] F **-, -nen** snuff-taker

Schnupf-: Schnupf|ta|bak M snuff; **Schnupf|ta|bak(s)|do|se** F snuffbox; **Schnupf|tuch** NT pl **-tücher** (S Ger) handkerchief, hanky (inf)

schnup|pe ['ʃnʊpə] ADJ pred (inf) jdm ~ **sein** to be all the same to sb; **das Wohl seiner Angestellten ist ihm völlig ~** he couldn't care less about the welfare of his employees (inf)

Schnup|per- in cpds (inf) trial, taster; **Schnup|per|kurs** M (inf) taster course

schnup|pern ['ʃnʊpɐn] **VI** to sniff; (Hund auch) to snuffle; **an etw** (dat) ~ to sniff (at) sth; **wir kamen nur zum Schnuppern** (fig inf) we only came to get a taste of it **VT** to sniff; (fig) Atmosphäre etc to sample

Schnup|per|preis M (inf) (special) introductory price

Schnur [ʃnuːɐ] F **-, ⁻e** ['ʃnyːrə] (= Bindfaden) string; (= Kordel, an Vorhang) cord; (= Litze) braid no indef art, no pl, piping no indef art, no pl; (= Zeltschnur) guy (rope); (= Angelschnur) (fishing) line; (= Kabel) flex, lead

Schnür-: Schnür|band [-bant] NT pl **-bänder** lace; **Schnür|bo|den** M (Theat) flies pl

Schnür|chen ['ʃnyːɐçən] NT **-s, -** dim von **Schnur** bit of string; **es läuft** or **geht** or **klappt alles wie am ~** everything's going like clockwork; **etw wie am ~ hersagen** to say or recite sth off pat (Brit) or on cue

schnü|ren ['ʃnyːrən] **VT** Paket, Strohbündel to tie up; Schuhe auch, Mieder to lace (up); Körper to lace in; (fig) Maßnahmenpaket etc to put together; **Schuhe zum Schnüren** lace-up shoes, lace-ups **VI a** (inf: = eng sein) to be too tight **b** aux sein (Hunt) to run in a straight line **VR** (Frauen) to lace oneself up or in

Schnur-: schnur|ge|ra|de ADJ (dead) straight ADV (perfectly) straight, straight as an arrow; ~

---

auf jdn/etw zugehen to make a beeline for sb/sth *(inf)*, to go straight up to sb/sth; **Schnur|ke|ra|mik** F *(Archeol)* string ceramics *sing*

Schnür|leib|chen NT lace-up corset

schnur|los ADJ *Telefon, Apparat* cordless ADV **~ telefonieren** to use a cordless phone

Schnürl- [ˈʃnyːɐl-] *(Aus)*: **Schnürl|re|gen** M pouring *or* streaming rain; **Schnürl|samt** M corduroy

Schnür|mie|der NT lace-up corset

Schnurr|bart M moustache *(Brit)*, mustache *(US)*

schnurr|bär|tig ADJ with a moustache *(Brit)* or mustache *(US)*, mustachioed *(esp Brit)*, mustached *(US)*

Schnur|re [ˈʃnʊrə] F **-, -n** **a** (= *Erzählung*) funny story **b** (= *Posse*) farce

schnur|ren [ˈʃnʊrən] VI *(Katze)* to purr; *(Spinnrad etc)* to hum, to whir(r)

Schnurr|haa|re PL whiskers *pl*

Schnür|rie|men M shoelace; *(für Stiefel)* bootlace

schnur|rig [ˈʃnʊrɪç] ADJ amusing, droll; *alter Mann* quaint, funny ADV drolly

Schnür-: **Schnür|schuh** M lace-up *or* laced shoe; **Schnür|sen|kel** M shoelace; *(für Stiefel)* bootlace; **Schnür|stie|fel** M lace-up *or* laced boot

schnur|stracks [ˈʃnuːɐˈʃtraks] ADV straight, directly; **du gehst jetzt ~ nach Hause!** you are to go straight home (now), you are to go home directly; **~ auf jdn/etw zugehen** to make a beeline for sb/sth, to go straight up to sb/sth

schnurz [ʃnʊrts], **schnurz|(piep)|egal** ADJ *(inf)* **das ist ihm ~** he couldn't care less (about it) *(inf)*, he couldn't give a damn (about it) *(inf)*; **das ist ~!** it doesn't matter a damn! *(inf)*

Schnu|te [ˈʃnuːtə] F **-, -n** *(inf)* (= *Mund*) mouth, (= *Schmollmund*) pout, *(pej: = Mundwerk)* big mouth *(inf)*; **eine ~ ziehen** *or* **machen** to pout, to pull a face

Scho|ah [ʃoˈaː, ˈʃoːa] F **-, no pl** (= *Holocaust*) Shoah

schob pret von **schieben**

Scho|ber [ˈʃoːbɐ] M **-s, -** *(S Ger, Aus)* **a** (= *Scheune*) barn **b** (= *Heuhaufen*) haystack, hayrick

Schock¹ [ʃɔk] NT **-(e)s, -e** *(obs)* three score *(old)*

Schock² M **-(e)s, -s** *or (rare)* **-e** (= *Schreck, elektrisch*) shock; **unter ~ stehen** to be in (a state of) shock

scho|ckant [ʃɔˈkant] *(dated)* ADJ shocking ADV shockingly

Schock-: **Schock|be|hand|lung** F shock therapy; *(elektrisch auch)* electroconvulsive therapy; **Schock|ein|wir|kung** F state of shock; **unter ~ stehen** to be in (a state of) shock

scho|cken [ˈʃɔkn] VT *(inf)* to shock; **jdn elektrisch ~** *(Med)* to give sb an electric shock, to administer an electric shock to sb *(form)*

Scho|cker [ˈʃɔkɐ] M **-s, -** *(inf: = Film/Roman)* shock film/novel, film/novel aimed to shock

Schock|far|be F electric colour *(Brit)* or color *(US)*

scho|ckie|ren [ʃɔˈkiːrən] ptp **schockiert** VTI to shock; *(stärker)* to scandalize; **sich leicht ~ lassen** to be easily shocked; **schockiert sein** to be shocked *(über +acc* at)

Schock-: **Schock|the|ra|pie** F shock therapy; *(elektrisch auch)* electroconvulsive therapy; **schock|wei|se** ADV *(obs)* by the three score *(old)*

scho|fel [ˈʃoːfl], **scho|fe|lig** [ˈʃoːfəlɪç] *(inf)* ADJ *Behandlung, Ausrede* mean, rotten *no adv (inf)*; *Spende, Geschenk, Mahlzeit* miserable ADV miserably

Schöf|fe [ˈʃœfə] M **-n, -n**, **Schöf|fin** [ˈʃœfɪn] F **-, -nen** ≈ juror

Schöf|fen-: **Schöf|fen|amt** NT ≈ jury service; **Schöf|fen|bank** F *pl* **-bänke** ≈ jury bench; **Schöf|fen|ge|richt** NT court *(with jury)*; **einen Fall vor einem ~ verhandeln** ≈ to try a case by jury

Schöf|fin F **-, -nen** ≈ juror

schof|lig [ˈʃoːflɪç] ADJ, ADV *(inf)* = **schofel**

Scho|ko|la|de [ʃokoˈlaːdə] F **-, -n** chocolate

Scho|ko|la|den- *in cpds* chocolate; **scho|ko|la|den|braun** ADJ chocolate-coloured *(Brit)*, chocolate-colored *(US)*; **Scho|ko|la|den|ei** NT chocolate egg; **Scho|ko|la|den|guss** ▲ M chocolate icing; **Scho|ko|la|den|ras|pel** F chocolate flake; **Scho|ko|la|den|rie|gel** M chocolate bar; **Scho|ko|la|den|sei|te** F *(fig)* attractive side; **sich von seiner ~ zeigen** to show oneself at one's best

Scho|ko|rie|gel [ˈʃoko-] M chocolate bar

Scho|las|tik [ʃoˈlastɪk] F **-, no pl** scholasticism

Scho|las|ti|ker [ʃoˈlastikɐ] M **-s, -**, **Scho|las|ti|ke|rin** [-ərɪn] F **-, -nen** scholastic

scho|las|tisch [ʃoˈlastɪʃ] ADJ scholastic

scholl *(old)* pret von **schallen**

Schol|le¹ [ˈʃɔlə] F **-, -n** *(Fisch)* plaice

Schol|le² F **-, -n** (= *Eisscholle*) (ice) floe; (= *Erdscholle*) clod (of earth); **mit der ~ verbunden sein** *(fig)* to be a son of the soil

Schol|len|fi|let NT (= *Fisch*) plaice fillet, fillet of plaice

Schol|li [ˈʃɔli] M **mein lieber ~!** *(inf)* *(drohend)* now look here!; *(erstaunt)* my goodness me!, my oh my!

Schöll|kraut NT *(Bot)* celandine

schon [ʃoːn]

ADVERB

a = bereits already; **Sie kommen erst nächste Woche? aber ich warte doch schon drei Wochen!** you'll come next week? but I've already been waiting three weeks!; **schon vor 100 Jahren kämpften Frauen um das Wahlrecht** 100 years ago women were already fighting for the vote

Im Englischen wird **schon** oft nicht übersetzt.

er ist schon hier! he's (already) here!; **danke, ich habe schon** *(inf)* no thank you, I have (already) got some; **ich habe den Film schon gesehen** I've (already) seen that film; **es ist schon 11 Uhr** it's (already) 11 o'clock; **wie schon erwähnt** as has (already) been mentioned; **ich warte nun schon seit drei Wochen!** I've been waiting three whole weeks!; **ich bin schon drei Jahre alt** I'm THREE (years old); **der Milchmann kommt schon um 6 Uhr!** the milkman comes at 6 o'clock!; **ich finde das Buch toll, ich habe es schon zweimal gelesen!** I love that book, I've read it twice!; **das habe ich dir doch schon hundertmal gesagt** I've told you that a hundred times; **schon vor drei Wochen** three weeks ago; **schon am frühen Morgen** early in the morning; **ich werde schon bedient** I'm being served; **er wollte schon die Hoffnung aufgeben, als ...** he was about to give up hope when ...; **das haben wir schon gestern** *or* **gestern schon gemacht** we did that yesterday; **schon damals** even then; **schon damals, als ...** even when ...; **schon früher wusste man ...** even in years gone by they knew ...; **schon im 13. Jahrhundert** as early as the 13th century; **schon am nächsten Tag** the very next day; **das habe ich schon oft gehört** I've often heard that; **das ist schon längst erledigt** that was done a long time ago; **ich bin schon lange fertig** I've been ready for ages; **wie schon so oft** as ever; **schon immer** always; **ich hatte schon immer dunkle Haare** I've always had dark hair

♦ **schon einmal, schon mal** before; (= *je: in Fragen*) ever; **ich habe das schon mal gehört** I've heard that before; **warst du schon (ein)mal**

dort? have you ever been there?; **ich habe Sie schon (ein)mal gesehen** I've seen you before somewhere; **ich habe dir schon (ein)mal gesagt, dass ...** I've already told you once that ...

♦ **schon wieder** schon wieder zurück back already; **da sie schon wieder** (= *zum x-ten Male*) there she is again, she's back again; (= *schon zurück*) she's back already; **was, schon wieder?** what - AGAIN?; **was denn nun schon wieder?** what is it NOW?

b = bereits: in Fragen *(= überhaupt schon)* ever; *(= je)* ever; **ist er schon hier?** is he here yet?; **warst du schon dort?** have you been there (yet)?; *(= je)* have you (ever) been there?; **musst du schon gehen?** must you go so soon?

In Fragesätzen wird **schon** oft nicht übersetzt.

kommt er schon heute? is he coming today?; **wie lange wartest du schon?** how long have you been waiting?; **wartest du schon lange?** have you been waiting long?

c = allein, bloß just; **der braucht kein Geld, der hat** *(ohnehin)* **schon genug** he doesn't need any money, he's got (quite) enough as it is; **allein schon der Gedanke, dass ...** just the thought that ...; **schon die Tatsache, dass ...** just the fact that ...; **wenn ich das schon sehe/höre/lese!** if I even see/hear/read that!; **schon deswegen** if only because of that; **schon weil** if only because

d = bestimmt all right; **du wirst schon sehen** you'll see (all right); **das wirst du schon noch lernen** you'll learn that one day; **sie wird es schon machen** (don't worry), she'll do it; (= *schaffen*) she'll manage (it) all right

e = tatsächlich, allerdings really; **das ist schon eine Frechheit!** that's real impudence!; **das ist schon etwas, (wenn ...)** it's really something (if ...); **da gehört schon Mut/Geschick etc dazu** that takes real courage/skill *etc*; **da müssten wir schon großes Glück haben** we'd be very lucky; **du müsstest schon etwas mehr arbeiten** you really ought to work a bit harder; **das ist schon möglich** that's quite possible; **das musst du schon machen!** you really ought to do that!

f ungeduldig **hör schon auf damit!** will you stop that!; **so antworte schon!** come on, answer!; **geh schon** go on; **nun sag schon!** come on, tell me/us *etc*!; **mach schon!** get a move on! *(inf)*; **wenn doch schon ...!** if only ...!; **ich komme ja schon!** I'm just coming!

g einschränkend **schon** *or* **ja schon, aber ...** *(inf)* yes (well), but ...; **da haben Sie schon Recht, aber ...** yes, you're right (there), but ...

h in rhetorischen Fragen **was macht das schon, wenn ...** what does it matter if ...; (= *was hilft das schon*) what(ever) use is it if ...; **wer fragt schon danach, ob ...** who wants to know if ...; **aber wer fragt schon danach** *(resignierend)* but no-one wants to know; **10 Euro, was ist das schon?** was sind heute schon 10 Euro? what's 10 euros these days?; **die paar Tropfen, was ist das schon, das ist doch kein Regen** a few drops, what are you talking about, that's not rain; **3 Seiten schreiben, was ist das schon?** write 3 pages? that's nothing!

i Füllwort *(inf)* **schon gut!** all right!, okay! *(inf)*; **ich verstehe schon** I understand; **ich weiß schon** I know; **danke, es geht schon** thank you, I'll/we'll *etc* manage; **so kannst du das schon gar nicht machen!** you CERTAINLY can't do that!; **für Krimis gebe ich kein Geld aus und für Pornoheftchen schon gar nicht** I won't spend money on thrillers and certainly not on pornography

j bedingt → **wenn, wennschon**

schön [ʃøːn] ADJ **a** (= *hübsch anzusehen*) beautiful, lovely; *Mann* handsome; **das Schöne** beauty; **~es Fräulein** *(old, hum)* my pretty one *(old)* or maid *(Brit old)*; **na, ~es Kind** *(inf)* well then, beautiful *(inf)* → **Auge a**

b (= *nett, angenehm*) good; *Erlebnis, Stimme, Musik, Wetter* good, lovely; *Gelegenheit* great, splendid; **die ~en Künste** the fine arts; **die ~e Litera-**

tur belles-lettres *sing*; **das ist ein ~er Tod** that's a good way to die; **eines ~en Tages** one fine day; **(wieder) in ~ster Ordnung** *(nach Krach etc)* back to normal (again); **in ~ster Eintracht** or **Harmonie** in perfect harmony; **das Schöne beim Skilaufen ist ...** the nice thing about skiing is ...; **das Schönste daran ist ...** the beauty of it is ..., the nicest or best thing about it is ...; **~ Ferien!**, **~en Urlaub!** have a good or nice holiday *(esp Brit)* or vacation *(US)*; **~es Wochenende** have a good or nice weekend; **~en guten Tag** a very good morning/afternoon/evening to you; **war es ~ im Urlaub?** did you have a nice or good holiday *(esp Brit)* or vacation *(US)?*; **war es ~ bei Tante Veronika?** did you have a nice or good time at Aunt Veronika's?; **~, dass du gekommen bist** nice of you to come; **~er, heißer Kaffee** nice hot coffee; **ein ~er frischer Wind** a nice fresh wind

c *(iro)* Unordnung fine, nice, lovely; *Überraschung, Wetter* lovely; *Unsinn, Frechheit* absolute; **da hast du etwas Schönes angerichtet** you've made a fine or nice or lovely mess; **du bist mir ein ~er Freund/Vater/Held** *etc* a fine friend/father/hero *etc* you are, you're some friend/father/hero *etc*; **du machst** or **das sind mir ja ~e Sachen** or **Geschichten** here's or this is a pretty state of things, here's a pretty kettle of fish *(inf)*; **von dir hört man ~e Sachen** or **Geschichten** I've been hearing some nice or fine things about you; **das wäre ja noch ~er** *(inf)* that's (just) too much!; **es wird immer ~er** *(inf)* things are going from bad to worse → **Bescherung**

d *(inf: = gut)* nice; **das war nicht ~ von dir** *(inf)* that wasn't very nice of you; **zu ~, um wahr zu sein** *(inf)* too good to be true; **~, ~, (also) ~, sehr ~, na ~** fine, okay, all right; **~ und gut, aber ...** (that's) all well and good but ..., that's all very well but ...

e *(= beträchtlich, groß)* Erfolg great; *Strecke, Stück Arbeit, Alter* good; **ein ~es Stück weiterkommen** to make good progress; **eine ganz ~e Leistung** quite an achievement; **eine ganz ~e Arbeit** quite a lot of work; **eine ganz ~e Menge** quite a lot; **das hat eine ~e Stange Geld gekostet** *(inf)* that cost a pretty penny

ADV a *(bei Verben)* *(= gut)* well; *sich waschen, verarbeiten lassen* easily; *scheinen* brightly; *schreiben* beautifully; *(= richtig, genau)* ansehen, durchlesen *etc* carefully; **sich ~ anziehen** to get dressed up; **es ~ haben** to be well off; *(im Urlaub etc)* to have a good time (of it); **etw am ~sten machen** to do sth best → **danke, bitte**

b *(= angenehm)* **weich/warm/stark** *etc* nice and soft/warm/strong *etc*

c *(bei Wünschen)* **schlaf ~** sleep well; **amüsiere dich ~** have a nice or good time; **erhole dich ~** have a good rest → **grüßen**

d *(inf: = brav, lieb)* nicely; **iss mal ~ deinen Teller leer** eat it all up nicely (now), be a good girl/boy and eat it all up; **sag ~ "Guten Tag"** say "hello" nicely; **sei ~ still/ordentlich** *etc (als Aufforderung)* be nice and quiet/tidy *etc*; **sei ~ brav** be a good boy/girl; **fahr ~ langsam** drive nice and slowly → **bleiben lassen**

e *(inf: = sehr, ziemlich)* really; **sich (dat) ~ wehtun** to hurt oneself a lot; **sich ~ täuschen** to make a big mistake; **sich ~ ärgern** to be very angry; **jdn ~ erschrecken** to give sb quite a or a real fright; **ganz ~ teuer/kalt** pretty expensive/cold; **(ganz) ~ weit weg** a long or good way off, quite a distance away; **ganz ~ lange** quite a while; **(ganz) ~ viel Geld kosten** to cost a pretty penny

Schon|be|zug M *(für Matratzen)* mattress cover; *(für Möbel)* loose cover; *(für Autositz)* seat cover

Schön|druck M *pl* **-drucke** *(Typ)* first printing

Schö|ne ['ʃøːnə] F *decl as adj (liter, hum: = Mädchen)* beauty, belle *(esp Brit liter, hum)*; **nun, ihr beiden ~n** *(inf)* now, my beauties *(inf)*

scho|nen ['ʃoːnən] **VT** *Gesundheit, Herz, Körperteil, Buch, Kleider* to look after, to take care of; *Ressourcen, eigene Kraft* to save, to conserve; *Um-* welt to protect, to conserve; *eigene Nerven* to go easy on; *jds Nerven, Gefühle, Kraft* to spare; *Gegner, Kind* to be easy on; *(= nicht stark beanspruchen)* Teppich, Schuhsohlen, Füße to save; *Bremsen, Auto, Batterie* to go easy on; *(iro)* Gehirn to spare; *(= schützen)* to protect; **ein Waschmittel, das die Hände/Wäsche schont** a detergent that is kind to your hands/washing; **ein Licht, das die Augen schont** lighting that is easy on the eyes; **sie trägt eine Schürze, um ihre Kleider zu ~** she wears an apron to save her clothes; **er muss den Arm noch ~** he still has to be careful with his arm, he still has to be easy on his arm; **um seine Nerven/die Nerven seiner Mutter zu ~** for the sake of his/his mother's nerves; **ein Beruf, der die Nerven nicht gerade schont** a job that isn't exactly easy on the nerves; **du brauchst mich nicht zu ~, sag ruhig die Wahrheit** you don't need to spare me or my feelings - just tell me the truth

VR to look after oneself, to take care of oneself; *(Patient auch)* to take things easy; **er schont sich für das nächste Rennen** he's saving himself for the next race

schö|nen ['ʃøːnən] **VT a** Wein to clarify **b** Statistik, Zahlen to dress up

scho|nend **ADJ** gentle; *(= rücksichtsvoll)* considerate; *Waschmittel, Politur* mild; *Nutzung (von Ressourcen etc)* sparing, careful **ADV** **jdm etw ~ beibringen** to break sth to sb gently; **jdn ~ behandeln** to be or go easy on sb; *Kranken* to treat sb gently; **etw ~ behandeln** to treat sth with care, to look after sth

Scho|ner¹ ['ʃoːnɐ] M **-s, -** *(Naut)* schooner

Scho|ner² M **-s, -** cover; *(für Rückenlehnen)* antimacassar, chairback; *(= Ärmelschoner)* sleeve-protector

Schön-: schön+fär|ben *sep* **VT** *(fig)* to gloss over **VI** to gloss things over; **Schön|fär|ber(in)** M(F) *(fig)* **ein ~ sein** to tend to gloss things over; **Schön|fär|be|rei** F *(fig)* glossing things over

Schon-: Schon|frist F period of grace; **eine ~ von 12 Tagen** 12 days' grace; **Schon|gang** M *pl* **-gänge** *(bei Waschmaschine)* gentle action wash

Schön|geist M aesthete

schön|geis|tig **ADJ** aesthetic; **~e Literatur** belletristic literature

Schön|heit F **-, -en** beauty

Schön|heits-: Schön|heits|chi|rur|gie F cosmetic surgery; **Schön|heits|farm** F beauty farm; **Schön|heits|fehler** M blemish; *(von Gegenstand)* flaw; **Schön|heits|fleck** M beauty spot; **Schön|heits|ide|al** NT ideal of beauty; **Schön|heits|kö|ni|gin** F beauty queen; **Schön|heits|kon|kur|renz** F beauty contest; **Schön|heits|kor|rek|tur** F correction of an imperfection/imperfections; *(fig)* cosmetic alteration; **Schön|heits|ope|ra|ti|on** F cosmetic operation *(Brit)* or surgery; **Schön|heits|pfläs|ter|chen** [-pflɛstɐçən] NT **-s, -** (artificial) beauty spot; **Schön|heits|pfle|ge** F beauty care; **Schön|heits|sa|lon** M beauty parlour *(Brit)* or parlor *(US)*, beauty salon; **Schön|heits|sinn** M sense of beauty; **Schön|heits|wett|be|werb** M beauty contest

Schon-: Schon|kaf|fee M mild coffee; **Schon|kost** F light diet; *(= Spezialdiät)* special diet

Schön|ling ['ʃøːnlɪŋ] M **-s, -e** *(pej)* pansy *(inf)*, pretty boy *(inf)*

Schön-: schön+ma|chen *sep* **VT** Kind to dress up; *Wohnung, Straßen* to decorate **VR** to get dressed up, to dress (oneself) up; *(= sich schminken)* to make (oneself) up **VI** *(Hund)* to sit up (and beg); **schön+rech|nen** NT *sep* **etw ~** to make the figures for sth seem better than they are; **schön+re|den** *sep* **VI** to use flattery; **das Schönreden** smooth talking, flattery **VT** **etw ~** to make sth seem better than it is; **Schön|red|ner(in)** M(F) flatterer, smooth-talker

Schön|schreib|dru|cker M letter-quality printer

Schön|schrei|ben NT **, no pl** *(Sch)* writing

Schön|schreib|heft NT writing book; *(mit vorgedruckten Buchstaben)* copybook

Schön|schrift F **, no pl** **in ~** in one's best (copybook) (hand)writing

schöns|tens ['ʃøːnstns] **ADV** most beautifully; *bitten, fragen* respectfully

Schön-: Schön|tu|e|rei [ʃøːntuːəˈrai] F flattery, blandishments *pl*, soft soap *(Brit inf)*; **schön+tun** **VI** *sep irreg* **jdm ~** *(= schmeicheln)* to flatter sb, to soft-soap sb *(Brit inf)*, to sweet-talk sb *(inf)*; *(= sich lieb Kind machen)* to pay court to sb *(dated)*, to play up to sb, to suck up to sb *(inf)*

Scho|nung ['ʃoːnʊŋ] F **-, -en a** *(= Waldbestand)* (protected) forest plantation area **b** *no pl (= das Schonen)* *(von Gefühlen, Kraft)* sparing; *(von Teppich, Schuhsohlen, Kleider)* saving; *(von Umwelt)* protection, conservation; *(von Ressourcen)* saving, conservation; *(= das Schützen)* protection; **der Patient/Arm braucht noch ein paar Wochen ~** the patient/arm still needs looking after for a few weeks; **zur ~ meiner Gefühle/der Gefühle anderer** to spare my feelings/the feelings of others; **auf ~ seiner Gesundheit Wert legen** to value one's health; **zur ~ des Magens sollten Sie nur Tee trinken** in order not to irritate your stomach you should only drink tea; **zur ~ Ihrer Augen/Waschmaschine** to look after your eyes/washing machine; **zur ~ des Getriebes** to give your gears a longer life **c** *no pl (= Nachsicht, Milde)* mercy

Scho|nungs-: scho|nungs|be|dürf|tig **ADJ** in need of care; *(in Bezug auf Gefühle, Nerven)* in need of careful handling; **scho|nungs|los** **ADJ** ruthless, merciless; *Wahrheit* blunt; *Ehrlichkeit, Offenheit* brutal; *Kritik* savage **ADV** ruthlessly; **jdm ~ die Wahrheit sagen** to tell sb the truth with no holds barred; **Scho|nungs|lo|sig|keit** F **-, no pl** ruthlessness; *(von Kritik)* savageness; **mit einer solchen ~** so ruthlessly, so mercilessly; **so savagely;** **scho|nungs|voll** **ADJ** gentle; **~er Umgang mit der Umwelt** treating the environment with care **ADV** gently; **er geht jetzt ~er mit ihr um** he treats her more kindly now

Schon|wald M protected woodland

Schön|wet|ter NT *(lit)* fine weather; **~ machen** *(fig inf)* to smooth things over; **bei jdm um ~ bitten** *(fig inf)* to be as nice as pie to sb *(inf)*

Schön|wet|ter-: Schön|wet|ter|front F warm front; **Schön|wet|ter|pe|ri|o|de** F period of fine weather; **Schön|wet|ter|wol|ke** F *(inf)* cloud that means good weather

Schon|zeit F close season; *(fig)* honeymoon period

Schopf [ʃɔpf] M **-(e)s, ¨e** ['ʃœpfə] (shock of) hair; *(von Vogel)* tuft, crest; **jdn beim ~ packen** to grab sb by the hair; **eine Gelegenheit beim ~ ergreifen** or **packen** or **fassen** to seize or grasp an opportunity with both hands

schöp|fen ['ʃœpfn] **VT a** *auch vi (aus from)* Wasser to scoop; *Suppe* to ladle; *Papier* to dip; **Wasser aus einem Boot ~** to bale out a boat **b** Mut, Kraft to summon up; *Vertrauen, Hoffnung* to find; **Atem ~** to draw breath, to take a breath; **Verdacht ~** to become suspicious; *Vertrauen/Hoffnung/Mut etc* **aus etw ~** to draw confidence/hope/courage *etc* from sth → **voll ADJ a** **c** *auch vi (= schaffen)* Kunstwerk to create; *neuen Ausdruck, Wörter* to coin, to create

Schöp|fer¹ ['ʃœpfɐ] M **-s, -** **a** *(inf: = Schöpflöffel)* ladle **b** *(= Papierschöpfer)* paper maker

Schöp|fer² ['ʃœpfɐ] M **-s, -, Schöp|fe|rin** [-ərɪn] F **-, -nen** creator; *(= Gott)* Creator; **sei|nem ~ danken** to thank one's Maker or Creator

Schöp|fer-: Schöp|fer|geist M creative spirit; *(Rel)* Holy Spirit; **Schöp|fer|hand** F *(Rel)* Hand of the Creator

schöp|fe|risch ['ʃœpfərɪʃ] **ADJ** creative; **~er Augenblick** moment of inspiration, creative moment; **~e Pause** (hum) pause for inspiration **ADV** creatively; **~ tätig sein** to do creative work; **~ begabt sein** to be creative; **sie ist ~ veranlagt** she is creative; (= *künstlerisch*) she is artistic

Schöp|fer|kraft F creative power, creativity

Schöpf|kel|le F , **Schöpf|löf|fel** M ladle

Schöp|fung ['ʃœpfʊŋ] F -, **-en** creation; (= *Wort, Ausdruck*) coinage, invention; **die ~** (Rel) the Creation; (= *die Welt*) Creation → **Herr a, Krone b**

Schöp|fungs-: Schöp|fungs|be|richt M , **Schöp|fungs|ge|schich|te** F story of the Creation; **Schöp|fungs|tag** M (Rel) day of the Creation

schöp|peln ['ʃœpln] VTI (dial) **(einen) ~** to have a drink

Schop|pen ['ʃɔpn] M -s, - **a** (old: *Flüssigkeitsmaß*) half-litre (Brit) or half-liter (US) (measure); (S Ger: = *Glas Wein*) glass of wine; (S Ger: = *Glas Bier*) ≈ half-pint of beer, ≈ glass of beer **b** (dial: = *Beisammensein*) **zum ~ gehen** to go for a drink; **sich beim ~ treffen** to meet for or over a drink **c** (S Ger, Sw: = *Babyfläschchen*) bottle

Schop|pen|wein M (dial) wine by the glass

schop|pen|wei|se ADV (dial) by the glass(-ful)

Schöps [ʃœps] M -es, -e (Aus) = **Hammel**

Schöp|ser|ne(s) ['ʃœpsənə] NT decl as adj (Aus) mutton

schor pret von **scheren** [1]

Schorf [ʃɔrf] M -(e)s, -e **a** crust, scaly skin; (= *Wundschorf*) scab **b** (= *Pflanzenkrankheit*) scab

schor|fig ['ʃɔrfɪç] ADJ **a** *Wunde* that has formed a scab; *Haut* scaly **b** *Pflanzen* scabby

Schor|le ['ʃɔrlə] F -, **-n** or NT -s, -s spritzer

Schorn|stein ['ʃɔrnʃtain] M chimney; (von Fabrik auch) stack; (von Schiff, Lokomotive) funnel, (smoke)stack; **etw in den ~ schreiben** (inf) to write sth off (as a dead loss (inf)); **damit der ~ raucht** (inf) to keep body and soul together

Schorn|stein-: Schorn|stein|brand M chimney fire; **Schorn|stein|fe|ger** [-fe:gə] M -s, -, **Schorn|stein|fe|ge|rin** [-ərɪn] F -, **-nen**, **Schorn|stein|keh|rer** [-ke:rə] M -s, -, **Schorn|stein|keh|re|rin** [-ərɪn] F -, **-nen** chimney sweep

Scho|se ['ʃo:zə] F -, **-n** (dated inf) = **Chose**

schoss ▲ pret von **schießen**

Schoss ▲ [ʃɔs] M -es, -e (Bot) shoot

Schoß¹ [ʃo:s] -es, **=e** ['ʃø:sə] M **a** lap; **die Hände in den ~ legen** (lit) to put one's hands in one's lap, (fig) to sit back (and take it easy); **das ist ihm nicht in den ~ gefallen** (fig) it wasn't handed (to) him on a plate, it didn't just fall into his lap → **Abraham b** (liter) (= *Mutterleib*) womb; (= *Scheide*) vagina; **im ~ der Familie/Kirche** in the bosom of one's family/of the church; **im ~ der Erde** in the bowels of the earth; **in den ~ der Familie/Kirche zurückkehren** (fig) to return to the bosom of one's family/the church **c** (an Kleidungsstück) tail

Schoß² [ʃo:s] F -, **-en** or **=e** ['ʃø:sə] (Aus) skirt

Schöß|chen ['ʃø:sçən] NT -s, - dim von **Schoß¹** **c**

Schöß|chen|ja|cke F peplum jacket

Schoß-: Schoß|hund M lapdog; **Schoß|kind** NT spoiled child (esp Brit); **Mamas ~** mummy's (Brit) or mamma's (US) little boy/girl; **ein ~ des Glücks** (geh) a child of Fortune

Schöss|ling ▲ ['ʃœslɪŋ] M -s, -e (Bot) shoot

Schot [ʃo:t] F -, **-en** (Naut) sheet

Scho|te ['ʃo:tə] F -, **-n a** (Bot) pod; **~n** (inf: = *Erbsen*) peas (in the pod) **b** (inf) yarn, tall story **c** (Naut) sheet

Schott [ʃɔt] NT -(e)s, -e(n) (Naut) bulkhead; **die ~en dichtmachen** (inf) to close up shop

---

Schot|te ['ʃɔtə] M -n, -n Scot, Scotsman; **er ist ~** he's a Scot, he's Scottish; **die ~n** the Scots, the Scottish

Schot|ten-: Schot|ten|ka|ro NT , **Schot|ten|mus|ter** NT tartan; **Rock mit** or **im ~** tartan skirt; **Schot|ten|preis** M (hum) rock-bottom price; **Schot|ten|rock** M tartan skirt; (= *Kilt*) kilt

Schot|ter ['ʃɔtə] M -s, - gravel; (im Straßenbau) (road) metal; (Rail) ballast; (inf: = *Geld*) dough (inf)

Schot|ter|de|cke F gravel surface

schot|tern ['ʃɔtɐn] VT to gravel (over); (im Straßenbau) to metal; (Rail) to ballast

Schot|ter-: Schot|ter|stra|ße F gravel road; **Schot|ter|weg** M gravel path

Schot|tin ['ʃɔtɪn] F -, **-nen** Scot, Scotswoman; **sie ist ~** she's a Scot, she's Scottish; **die ~nen** Scottish women, Scotswomen

schot|tisch ['ʃɔtɪʃ] ADJ Scottish; *Sprache* Scots

Schott|land ['ʃɔtlant] NT -s Scotland

schraf|fie|ren [ʃra'fi:rən] ptp **schraffiert** VT to hatch

Schraf|fie|rung F -, **-en**, **Schraf|fur** [ʃra'fu:ɐ] F -, **-en** hatching

schräg [ʃrɛ:k] ADJ **a** (= *schief, geneigt*) sloping; *Schrift* sloping, slanting; *Augen* slanted, slanting; *Kante* bevelled (Brit), beveled (US) **b** (= *nicht gerade, nicht parallel*) oblique; *Linie* oblique, diagonal **c** (inf: = *verdächtig*) suspicious, fishy (inf) **d** (inf: = *seltsam*) *Musik, Vorstellung, Leute* weird; **ein ~er Vogel** a queer fish (Brit inf), a strange bird (US)

ADV a (= *geneigt*) at an angle; **halten** on the slant, slanting; (= *krumm*) slanting, skewwhiff (Brit inf); **den Hut ~ aufsetzen** to put one's hat on at an angle; **~ stehende Augen** slanting or slanted eyes

b (= *nicht gerade, nicht parallel*) obliquely; **überqueren, gestreift** diagonally; (Sew) on the bias; **schneiden** on the cross or bias; **~ gegenüber/hinter** diagonally opposite/behind; **~ rechts/links** diagonally to the right/left; **~ rechts/links abbiegen** (Auto, Fähre) to bear or fork right/left; **die Straße biegt ~ ab** the road forks off; **~ gedruckt** in italics; **~ laufend** diagonal, oblique; **den Kopf ~ halten** to hold one's head at an angle or cocked to one side; **~ parken** to park at an angle; **die Sonne schien ~ ins Fenster** the sun slanted in through the window; **jdn ~ ansehen** or **angucken** (lit) to look at sb out of the corner of one's eye; (fig) to look askance at sb; **~ zum Hang queren/fahren** to traverse; **~ zum Fadenlauf** on the bias

Schräg|band [-bant] NT pl **-bänder** bias binding

Schräg|dach NT pl **-dächer** pitched roof

Schrä|ge ['ʃrɛ:gə] F -, **-n a** (= *schräge Fläche*) slope, sloping surface; (= *schräge Kante*) bevel, bevelled (Brit) or beveled (US) edge **b** (= *Schrägheit*) slant, angle; (von Dach) pitch, slope; (im Zimmer) sloping ceiling; **eine ~ haben** to be on the slant, to slope, to slant; (Zimmer) to have a sloping ceiling

schrä|gen ['ʃrɛ:gn] VT to chamfer; *Kanten* to bevel

Schräg|heck NT (am Auto) coupé back; (= *Auto*) coupé

Schräg|heit F -, no pl slant, angle; (von Wand auch) slope; (von Dach) pitch, slope, slant; (von Schrift, Augen) slant

Schräg-: Schräg|kan|te F bevelled (Brit) or beveled (US) edge; **Schräg|la|ge** F angle, slant; (von Flugzeug) bank(ing); (im Mutterleib) oblique position; **etw in ~ bringen/aufbewahren** to put/keep sth at an angle or on the slant; **das Baby ist in ~** the baby is in an oblique position; **schräg|lau|fend** △ ADJ → **schräg laufend** ADV bei **schräg**; **Schräg|li|nie** F diagonal line, oblique (line); **Schräg|schrift** F (Handschrift) slanting

---

hand(writing) or writing; (Typ) italics pl; **Schräg|strei|fen** M **a** (Muster) diagonal stripe **b** (Sew) bias binding; **Schräg|strich** M (Typ) (forward) slash, oblique; **umgekehrter ~** backslash; **doppelter umgekehrter ~** double backslash

schrak (old) pret von **schrecken**

Schram|me ['ʃramə] F -, **-n** scratch

Schram|mel|mu|sik ['ʃraml-] F popular Viennese music for violins, guitar and accordion

Schram|meln ['ʃramln] PL (Aus) quartet playing Schrammelmusik

schram|men ['ʃramən] VT to scratch; **sich** (dat) **den Arm/sich ~** to scratch one's arm/oneself VI **über den Boden ~** to scrape across the floor; **haarscharf am Bankrott ~** to come within an inch of bankruptcy

Schrank [ʃraŋk] M -(e)s, **=e** ['ʃrɛŋkə] cupboard (Brit), closet (US); (im Wohnzimmer, = *Vitrinenschrank, Mülizinschrank auch*) cabinet; (= *Küchenschrank*) cupboard; (= *Kleiderschrank*) wardrobe (Brit), closet (US); (für Bücher) bookcase; (= *Plattenschrank*) record cabinet; (= *Umkleideschrank, Mil*: = *Spind*) locker; (inf: Mann) giant → **Tasse**

Schrank|bett NT foldaway bed

Schränk|chen ['ʃrɛŋkçən] NT -s, - dim von **Schrank** small cupboard (Brit) or closet (US); (= *Arzneischränkchen, im Badezimmer*) cabinet; (neben dem Bett) bedside cupboard or cabinet (Brit), night stand (US)

Schran|ke ['ʃraŋkə] F -, **-n a** barrier; (= *Barrikade*) barricade; (fig) (= *Grenze*) limit; (= *Hindernis*) barrier; **die ~ ist zu/auf** (Rail) the barrier is down/up; **vor den ~n des Gerichts** before the court; **keine ~n kennen** to know no bounds; (Mensch) not to know when to stop; **er kennt keine ~n mehr** there's no restraining him; **sich in ~n halten** to keep or to remain within reasonable limits; **meine Begeisterung hält sich in ~n** I'm not exactly overwhelmed by it; **etw in ~n halten** to keep sth within reasonable limits or bounds; **einer Sache** (dat) **(enge) ~n setzen** to put a limit on sth; **seiner Geduld sind keine ~n gesetzt** his patience knows no bounds **b** **Schranken** PL (Hist) lists pl; **jdn in die ~n fordern** (fig) to challenge sb; **jdn in seine** or **die ~n (ver)weisen** (fig) to put sb in his place

Schran|ken ['ʃraŋkn] M -s, - (Aus) (level-crossing (Brit) or grade-crossing (US)) barrier

Schran|ken-: schran|ken|los ADJ (fig) *Weiten* boundless, unbounded, unlimited; *Egoismus, Glück* unbounded, boundless; *Vertrauen* total; *Verhalten, Forderungen, Ansprüche* unrestrained, unbridled; **Schran|ken|lo|sig|keit** F -, no pl (fig) boundlessness; (von Forderungen etc) lack of restraint (+gen in); **Schran|ken|wär|ter(in)** M(F) attendant (at level crossing)

Schrank-: Schrank|fach NT shelf; **im obersten ~** on the top shelf; **schrank|fer|tig** ADJ *Wäsche* washed and ironed; **Schrank|kof|fer** M wardrobe (Brit) or clothes trunk; **Schrank|spie|gel** M wardrobe (Brit) or vanity (US) mirror; **Schrank|tür** F cupboard (Brit) or closet (US) door; (von Kleiderschrank) wardrobe door; **Schrank|wand** F wall unit

Schränk|zan|ge ['ʃrɛŋk-] F saw set pliers pl

Schran|ze ['ʃrantsə] F -, **-n** (pej inf) toady (inf), lackey (pej)

Schrap|nell [ʃrap'nɛl] NT -s, -e or -s shrapnel no pl

Schrap|per ['ʃrapɐ] M -s, - scraper

Schrat [ʃra:t] M -(e)s, -e, **Schratt** [ʃrat] M -(e)s, -e forest demon

Schraub|de|ckel M screw(-on) lid

Schrau|be ['ʃraubə] F -, **-n a** screw; (ohne Spitze) bolt; **bei ihr ist eine ~ locker** (inf) she's got a screw loose (inf) **b** (Naut, Aviat) propeller, prop (inf) **c** (Sport) twist **d alte ~** (pej inf) old bag (inf)

schrau|ben ['ʃraubn] VTI to screw; **etw höher/ niedriger ~** to screw sth in/out; **etw fester ~** to screw sth tighter; **etw in die Höhe ~** (*fig, Preise, Rekorde, Gewinn*) to push sth up; *Ansprüche, Erwartungen* to raise; **etw niedriger ~** (*fig*) to lower sth; **das Flugzeug schraubte sich in die Höhe** the plane spiralled (*esp Brit*) or spiraled (*US*) upwards → *auch* **geschraubt**

Schrau|ben-: Schrau|ben|bol|zen M bolt; **Schrau|ben|damp|fer** M propeller-driven steamer; **Schrau|ben|dre|her** M screwdriver; **Schrau|ben|ge|win|de** NT screw thread; **Schrau|ben|kopf** M screw head; **Schrau|ben|mut|ter** F pl -muttern nut; **Schrau|ben|schlüs|sel** M spanner (*Brit*), wrench (*US*); **Schrau|ben|win|dung** F screw thread; (= *Umdrehung*) turn; **Schrau|ben|zie|her** [-tsi:ɐ] M -s, - screwdriver

Schraub-: Schraub|fas|sung F screw fitting (*on light bulb*); **Schraub|glas** NT screw-top jar; **Schraub|stock** M vice; **etw wie ein ~ umklammern** (*fig*) to clasp sth in a vicelike grip; **Schraub|ver|schluss** ▲ M screw top or cap; **Schraub|zwin|ge** F screw clamp

Schre|ber|gar|ten ['ʃreːbɐ-] M allotment (*Brit*), garden plot

Schreck [ʃrɛk] M -s, (*rare*) -e fright, scare; (= *Schreckfigur*) terror; **vor ~** in fright; *zittern* with fright; **zu meinem großen ~(en)** to my great horror or dismay; **einen ~(en) bekommen** to get a fright or scare; **jdm einen ~(en) einjagen** to give sb a fright or scare; **der ~ fuhr mir in die Glieder** or **Knochen** my knees turned to jelly (*inf*); **mir sitzt** or **steckt der ~ noch in den** or **allen Gliedern** or **Knochen** my knees are still like jelly (*inf*); **auf den ~ (hin)** to get over the fright; **sich vom ersten ~ erholen** to recover from the initial shock; **mit dem ~(en) davonkommen** to get off or escape with no more than a fright; **ach du ~!** (*inf*) (oh) crumbs! (*inf*), blast! (*inf*); **(o) ~, lass nach!** (*hum inf*) for goodness sake! (*inf*), for heaven's sake! (*inf*)

Schreck|bild NT terrible or awful vision, nightmare

schre|cken ['ʃrɛkn] *pret* **schreckte** [ʃrɛktə], *ptp* **geschreckt** [gə'ʃrɛkt] VT a (= *ängstigen*) to frighten, to scare; (*stärker*) to terrify; **jdn aus dem Schlaf/aus seinen Träumen ~** to startle sb out of his sleep/dreams b (*Cook*) to dip quickly in cold water ◆ *pret auch* (*old*) **schrak** [ʃraːk], *ptp auch* (*old*) **geschrocken** [gə'ʃrɔkn] VI a *aux sein* **aus dem Schlaf ~** to be startled out of one's sleep; **aus den Gedanken ~** to be startled b (*Hunt*) to start up

Schre|cken ['ʃrɛkn] M -s, - a (= *plötzliches Erschrecken*) → **Schreck** b (= *Furcht, Entsetzen*) terror, horror; **~ erregend** terrifying, horrifying; **einer Sache** (*dat*) **den ~ nehmen** to make a thing less frightening or terrifying; **er war der ~ der ganzen Lehrerschaft** he was the terror of all the teachers; **das Gleichgewicht des ~s** the balance of terror; **jdn in Angst und ~ versetzen** to frighten and terrify sb; **ein Land in Angst und ~ versetzen** to spread fear and terror throughout a country → **Ende**

schre|cken|er|re|gend △ [-ˈɛːrəːgnt] ADJ → **Schrecken b**

Schre|ckens-: schre|ckens|blass ▲, **schre|ckens|bleich** ADJ as white as a sheet or ghost; **Schre|ckens|bot|schaft** F terrible or alarming piece of news; **Schre|ckens|herr|schaft** F (reign of) terror; **Schre|ckens|kam|mer** F chamber of horrors; **Schre|ckens|mel|dung** F , **Schre|ckens|nach|richt** F shock news *sing*; **Schre|ckens|nacht** F night of horror; **Schre|ckens|tat** F atrocity; **Schre|ckens|vi|si|on** F terrifying or terrible vision, nightmare

Schreck-: Schreck|ge|spenst NT nightmare; **das ~ des Krieges/der Inflation** the bogey of war/inflation; **schreck|haft** ADJ easily startled; *Mensch auch* jumpy (*inf*); **Schreck|-**

haf|tig|keit ['ʃrɛkhaftɪçkait] F -, *no pl* nervousness; (*von Mensch auch*) jumpiness (*inf*)

schreck|lich ['ʃrɛklɪç] ADJ terrible, dreadful; (*inf:* = *sehr, groß auch*) awful; *Freude* great; **er war ~ in seinem Zorn** (*geh*) his wrath was terrible (to behold) (*liter*) ADV a (= *entsetzlich*) horribly; **~ schimpfen** to swear dreadfully or terribly b (*inf:* = *sehr*) terribly; **sich ~ freuen** to be terribly or awfully pleased; **~ gerne!** I'd absolutely love to; **~ viel** an awful lot (of); **~ wenig** very little; **~ nett** (*usu iro*) terribly nice

Schreck|nis ['ʃrɛknɪs] NT -ses, -se (*old*) horror(s *pl*), terror(s *pl*)

Schreck-: Schreck|schrau|be F (*pej inf*) (*old*) battle-axe (*Brit inf*) or battle-ax (*US inf*); (*in Bezug auf Äußeres*) dolled-up old bag (*inf*); **Schreck|schuss** ▲ M (*lit*) warning shot; **einen ~ abgeben** (*lit, fig*) to give or fire a warning shot; **Schreck|schuss|pis|to|le** ▲ F blank gun; **Schreck|se|kun|de** F moment of shock

Schred|der ['ʃrɛdɐ] M -s, - shredder

Schrei [ʃrai] M -(e)s, -e cry, shout; (*brüllender*) yell; (*gellender*) scream; (*kreischender*) shriek; (*von Vogel, von Wild*) cry, call; (*von Esel*) bray; (*von Eule etc*) screech; (*von Hahn*) crow; **einen ~ ausstoßen** to give a cry or shout/yell/scream/ shriek; **einen ~ unterdrücken** to suppress a cry; **ein spitzer ~** a sharp cry; **der ~ nach Freiheit/ Rache** the call for freedom/revenge; **ein ~ der Entrüstung** an (indignant) outcry; **der letzte ~** (*inf*) the latest thing, all the rage (*inf*); **nach dem letzten ~ gekleidet** (*inf*) dressed in the latest style or in the height of fashion

Schreib-: Schreib|ar|beit F (*einzeln*) written assignment; (*kollektiv,* = *Verwaltungsarbeit*) paperwork *no pl*; **Schreib|art** F style; **Schreib|be|darf** M writing materials *pl*, stationery *no pl*; **alles, was Sie für Ihren ~ brauchen** everything you need in the way of stationery or writing materials; **Schreib|block** M pl -blöcke or -blocks (writing) pad; **Schreib|blo|ckade** F writer's block *no art*; **Schreib|bü|ro** NT typing pool

Schrei|be ['ʃraibə] F -, -en (*inf*) writing

schrei|ben ['ʃraibn] ✪ 48.1, 48.2 *pret* **schrieb** [ʃriːp], *ptp* **geschrieben** [gə'ʃriːbn] VT a (= *ausstellen*) *Scheck* to write (out), to make out; *Rechnung* to make out, to write out; (*mit Schreibmaschine*) to type (out); *Klassenarbeit, Übersetzung, Examen* to do; (= *niederschreiben*) to write (down); **sie schreibt einen guten Stil** she has or writes a good style; **jdm** or **an jdn einen Brief ~** to write a letter to sb, to write sb a letter; **jdm ein paar Zeilen ~** to write or drop sb a few lines, to write a few lines to sb; **schwarze/rote Zahlen ~** (*Comm*) to be in the black/red; **etw auf Diskette ~** or *disk* to write to or save sth to disk; **sich** (*dat*) **etw von der Seele** or **dem Herzen ~** to get sth off one's chest; **wo steht das geschrieben?** where does it say that?; **es steht geschrieben** (*Rel*) it is written; **es steht Ihnen im Gesicht** or **auf der Stirn geschrieben** it's written all over your face → **Handschrift a, Stern¹ a**
b (*orthografisch*) to spell; **ein Wort falsch ~** to misspell a word, to spell a word wrong(ly); **wie schreibt man das?** how do you spell that?, how is that spelled? → **großschreiben, kleinschreiben**
c (*Datum*) **wir ~ heute den 10. Mai** today is the 10th May; **den Wievielten ~ wir heute?** what is the date today?; **man schrieb das Jahr 1939** the year was 1939, it was (in) 1939
d (= *verbuchen*) **jdm etw auf sein (Bank)konto ~** to credit sth to sb's (bank) account; **jdm etw auf die Rechnung ~** to put sth on sb's bill
VI to write; (= *Schriftsteller sein*) to write, to be a writer; (= *tippen*) to type; (= *berichten*) to say; **jdm ~** to write to sb, to write sb (*US*); **ich schrieb ihm, dass ...** I wrote and told him that ...; **er schreibt orthografisch richtig** his spelling is correct; **an einem Roman** *etc* **~** to be working on or writing a novel *etc*; **über etw** (*acc*) **~** (= *ab-*

handeln) to write about sth; (*Univ auch*) to work on sth; **ich kann nicht mit der Maschine ~** I can't type; **wie viel Anschläge schreibt sie pro Minute?** what is her (typing) speed?; **mit Bleistift ~** to write in pencil, to write with a pencil; **mit Tinte ~** to write in ink; **hast du was zum Schreiben?** have you something or anything to write with?
VR *impers* to write; **mit diesem Bleistift schreibt es sich gut/schlecht** this pencil writes well/ doesn't write properly; **auf diesem Papier schreibt es sich gut/schlecht** this paper is easy or good/difficult to write on
VR a (= *korrespondieren*) to write (to one another or to each other), to correspond; **ich schreibe mich schon lange mit ihm** (*inf*) I've been writing to him for a long time
b (= *geschrieben werden*) to be spelt (*esp Brit*) or spelled (*US*); **wie schreibt er sich?** how does he spell his name?, how is his name spelled?; **wie schreibt sich das?** how is that spelled?, how do you spell that?
c (*dated:* = *heißen*) to call oneself; **seit wann schreibst du dich wieder mit deinem Mädchennamen?** how long have you been calling yourself by your maiden name again?

Schrei|ben ['ʃraibn] NT -s, - a *no pl* writing b (= *Mitteilung*) communication (*form*); (= *Brief*) letter

Schrei|ber¹ ['ʃraibɐ] M -s, - a (*inf:* = *Schreibgerät*) writing implement; **einen/keinen ~ haben** to have something/nothing to write with b (*Tech*) (= *Fahrtenschreiber*) tachograph; (*an Messgerät*) recording instrument, recorder; (= *Fernschreiber*) teleprinter, telex

Schrei|ber² ['ʃraibɐ] M -s, -, **Schrei|be|rin** [-ərɪn] F -, -nen (= *Verfasser*) writer, author; (= *Briefschreiber*) (letter-)writer; (*Hist*) scribe; (= *Angestellter, Gerichtsschreiber*) clerk/clerkess; (*Sw:* = *Schriftführer*) secretary; (*pej:* = *Schriftsteller*) scribbler

Schrei|be|rei [ʃraibə'rai] F -, -en (*inf*) (= *das Schreiben, Geschriebenes*) writing *no indef art*; (= *Schriftverkehr*) paperwork *no indef art, no pl*; (*pej: von Schriftsteller*) scribbling

Schrei|ber|ling ['ʃraibɐlɪŋ] M -s, -e (*pej*) (= *Schriftsteller*) scribbler; (= *kleiner Angestellter*) pen-pusher

Schreib-: schreib|faul ADJ lazy (about letter writing); **ich bin ~** I'm no great letter writer, I'm a poor correspondent; **Schreib|faul|heit** F laziness (about letter writing); **Schreib|fe|der** F (pen) nib; (= *Federhalter*) ink pen; (= *Gänseschreibfeder*) quill (pen); **Schreib|feh|ler** M (spelling) mistake; (*aus Flüchtigkeit*) slip of the pen; (= *Tippfehler*) (typing) mistake or error; **Schreib|ge|rät** NT writing implement; (*Tech*) recording instrument, recorder; **schreib|ge|schützt** ADJ (*Comput*) write-protected; **Schreib|heft** NT exercise book; (= *Schönschreibheft*) copybook; **Schreib|kraft** F typist; **Schreib|krampf** M writer's cramp; **einen ~ (in der Hand) bekommen** to get writer's cramp; **Schreib-/Le|se|kopf** M (*Comput*) read-write head; **Schreib|ma|schi|ne** F typewriter; **auf** or **mit der ~ schreiben** to type; **mit der ~ geschrieben** typewritten, typed; **Schreib|maschi|nen|pa|pier** NT typing paper; **Schreib|ma|te|ri|al** NT writing materials *pl*, stationery *no pl*; **Schreib|pa|pier** NT (typing) paper; (= *Briefpapier*) writing paper, letter paper, notepaper; **Schreib|pult** NT (writing) desk; **Schreib|schrift** F cursive (hand)writing, script; (*Typ*) script; **Schreib|schutz** M (*Comput*) write protection; **schreib|schüt|zen** VT (*Comput*) to write-protect; **Schreib|stel|le** F (*Comput*) (cursor) position; **Schreib|stel|len|mar|ke** F (*Comput:* = *Cursor*) cursor; **Schreib|stift** M (*auch Comput*) pen; **Schreib|stu|be** F (*Hist*) writing room; (= *Büro*) (typists') office, typing room; (*inf*) orderly room; **Schreib|ta|fel** F (*Hist*) tablet; (*für Schüler*) slate; (= *Wandtafel*) blackboard; **Schreib|tisch** M desk; **Schreib|tisch|stuhl** M office or desk chair;

Schreib|tisch|tä|ter(in) M(F) mastermind or brains sing behind the scenes (of a/the crime); **Schreib|übung** F writing exercise

Schrei|bung [ˈʃraɪbʊŋ] F -, -en spelling; **falsche ~ eines Namens** misspelling of a name

Schreib-: schreib|un|kun|dig ADJ unable to write; **Schreib|un|ter|la|ge** F pad; (auf Schreibtisch) desk pad; **ein Buch als ~ benutzen** to use a book to rest (one's paper) on; **Schreib|wa|ren** PL stationery sing, writing materials pl; **Schreib|wa|ren|händ|ler(in)** M(F) stationer; **Schreib|wa|ren|hand|lung** F stationer's (shop), stationery shop; **Schreib|wei|se** F (= Stil) style; (= Rechtschreibung) spelling; **Schreib|werk** NT typing mechanism; **Schreib|zeug** NT pl -zeuge writing things pl; **Schreib|zim|mer** NT (= Büro) (typists') office, typing room; (von Schriftsteller) study

schrei|en [ˈʃraɪən] pret **schrie** [ʃriː], ptp **ge-schrie(e)n** [ɡəˈʃriː(ə)n] VI to shout, to cry out; (gellend) to scream; (vor Angst, vor Schmerzen) to cry out/to scream; (kreischend) to shriek; (= brüllen) to yell; (inf: = laut reden) to shout; (inf: = schlecht und laut singen) to screech; (= heulen, weinen: Kind) to howl; (= jammern) to moan; (Esel) to bray; (Vogel, Wild) to call; (Eule, Käuzchen etc) to screech; (Hahn) to crow; **vor Lachen ~** to roar or hoot with laughter; (schrill) to scream with laughter; **es war zum Schreien** (inf) it was a scream (inf) or a hoot (inf); **nach jdm ~** to shout for sb; **nach etw ~** (fig) to cry out for sth → **Hilfe a**

▪ VT Befehle etc to shout (out); **jdm etw ins Ge-sicht ~** to shout sth in sb's face; **sich** (dat) **die Kehle heiser** or **aus dem Hals ~** (inf) to shout oneself hoarse, to shout one's head off (inf)

▪ VR **sich heiser ~** to shout oneself hoarse; (Ba-by) to cry itself hoarse

schrei|end ADJ Farben loud, garish, gaudy; Un-recht glaring, flagrant

Schrei|er [ˈʃraɪə] M -s, -, **Schrei|e|rin** [-ərɪn] F -, -nen (inf: = Baby) bawler (inf); (= Unruhestifter) rowdy, noisy troublemaker; (fig: = Nörgler) moaner, grouser (inf)

Schrei|e|rei [ʃraɪəˈraɪ] F -, -en (inf) bawling (inf) no pl, yelling no pl

Schrei-: Schrei|hals M (inf) (= Baby) bawler (inf); (= Unruhestifter) rowdy, noisy troublemak-er; **Schrei|krampf** M screaming fit

Schrein [ʃraɪn] M -(e)s, -e (geh) shrine; (= Reli-quienschrein auch) reliquary; (old: = Sarg) coffin, casket (US)

Schrei|ner [ˈʃraɪnə] M -s, -, **Schrei|ne|rin** [-ərɪn] F -, -nen (esp S Ger) carpenter

schrei|nern VI (esp S Ger) VI to do car-pentry; **mein Mann kann gut ~** my husband is good at carpentry or woodwork, my husband is a good carpenter ▪ VT to make

schrei|ten [ˈʃraɪtn] pret **schritt** [ʃrɪt], ptp **geschrit-ten** [ɡəˈʃrɪtn] VI aux sein (geh) (= schnell gehen) to stride; (= feierlich gehen) to walk; (vorwärts) to proceed; (= stolzieren) to strut, to stalk; **im Zim-mer auf und ab ~** to stride or pace up and down the room; **zu etw ~** (fig) to get down to sth, to proceed with sth; **es wird Zeit, dass wir zur Tat ~** it's time we got down to work or action; **zum Äußersten ~** to take extreme mea-sures; **zur Abstimmung/Wahl ~** to proceed or go to a vote

schrie pret von **schreien**

schrieb pret von **schreiben**

Schrieb [ʃriːp] M -s, -e [-bə] (inf) missive (hum)

Schrift [ʃrɪft] F -, -en a writing; (= Handschrift) (hand)writing; (= Schriftsystem) script; (Typ) type, typeface, font; **gotische ~ schreiben** to write in Gothic script; **er hat eine schlechte ~** he has bad handwriting, he writes or has a poor hand **b** (= Schriftstück) document; (= Be-richt) report; (= Eingabe) petition **c** (= Broschüre) leaflet; (= Buch) work; (= kürzere Abhandlung) pa-per; **seine früheren ~en** his early writings or works; **Schopenhauers sämtliche ~en** the com-

plete works of Schopenhauer; **die (Heilige) ~** the (Holy) Scriptures pl

Schrift-: Schrift|art F (= Handschrift) script; (Typ) type, typeface; **Schrift|aus|le|gung** F (Bibl) interpretation (of the Bible); **Schrift|bild** NT script; **Schrift|deutsch** NT (nicht Um-gangssprache) written German; (nicht Dialekt) standard German; **Schrift|deu|tung** F grap-hology

Schrift|ten|nach|weis M , **Schrift|ten|ver-zeich|nis** NT bibliography

Schrift-: Schrift|form F (Jur) **dieser Vertrag erfordert die ~** this contract may be drawn up in writing; **Schrift|füh|rer(in)** M(F) secretary; (= Protokollführer auch) clerk; **Schrift|ge|lehr-te(r)** M decl as adj (Bibl) scribe; **Schrift|gie-ßer(in)** M(F) typefounder; **Schrift|grad** M type size; **Schrift|guss** ▲ M typefounding; **Schrift|hö|he** F x-height (spec), height of the type; **Schrift|kunst** F calligraphy; **Schrift-lei|ter(in)** M(F) editor; **Schrift|lei|tung** F (= Redaktionsstab) editorial staff pl; (= Redaktionslei-tung) editorship; **Schrift|le|sung** F (Eccl) les-son

schrift|lich [ˈʃrɪftlɪç] ADJ written; **in ~er Form** in writing; **auf ~em Wege** in writing; **die ~e Prü-fung, das Schriftliche** (inf) the written exam; **ich habe nichts Schriftliches darüber** I haven't got anything in writing ADV in writing; **ich bin ~ eingeladen worden** I have had a written invita-tion; **ich muss mich bei ihm ~ für das Geschenk bedanken** I must write and thank him for the present; **etw ~ festhalten/niederlegen/machen** (inf) to put sth down in writing; **das kann ich Ihnen ~ geben** (fig inf) I can tell you that for free (inf)

Schrift-: Schrift|li|nie F (Typ) type line; **Schrift|pro|be** F (von Handschrift) sample of one's handwriting; (Typ) sample (proof); **Schrift|rol|le** F scroll; **Schrift|sach|ver-stän|di|ge(r)** M decl as adj handwriting ex-pert; **Schrift|satz** M a (Jur) legal document **b** (Typ) form(e); **Schrift|set|zer(in)** M(F) typesetter, compositor, comp (Typ sl); **Schrift-spra|che** F (= nicht Umgangssprache) written language; (= nicht Dialekt) standard language; **die französische ~** written/(good) standard French; **schrift|sprach|lich** ADJ Ausdruck, Kon-struktion used in the written language ADV **würde man ... sagen** in the written language one would say ...; **~ reden** to speak as it would be written

Schrift|stel|ler [-ʃtɛlə] M -s, - author, writer **Schrift|stel|le|rei** [-ʃtɛləˈraɪ] F -, no pl writing **Schrift|stel|le|rin** [-ʃtɛlərɪn] F -, -nen author (-ess), writer

schrift|stel|le|risch [-ʃtɛlərɪʃ] ADJ Arbeit, Werk, Talent literary ADV **~ tätig sein** to write; **er ist ~ begabt** he has literary talent, he has talent as a writer

schrift|stel|lern [-ʃtɛlən] VI insep (inf) to try one's hand at writing or as an author; **der ~de General Patschke** General Patschke, who also writes in his free time

Schrift|stel|ler|na|me M pen name, nom de plume

Schrift-: Schrift|stück NT paper; (Jur) docu-ment; **Schrift|tum** [ˈʃrɪftuːm] NT -s, no pl lite-rature; **Schrift|ver|kehr** M , **Schrift|wech-sel** M correspondence; **im ~ stehen** to be in correspondence; **Schrift|zei|chen** NT charac-ter; **Schrift|zug** M usu pl stroke; (= Duktus) hand

schrill [ʃrɪl] ADJ Ton, Stimme shrill; (fig) () Misston, Missklang jarring; Fest, Musik, Persönlichkeit brash; Farbe, Accessoires, Outfit garish; **er reagierte mit ~en Tönen** his reaction was quite strident ADV shrilly; gekleidet loudly; **sie lachte ~ auf** she gave a shriek or screech of laughter

schril|len [ˈʃrɪlən] VI to shrill; (Stimme auch) to sound shrill; (Telefon, Wecker) to ring shrilly

Schrip|pe [ˈʃrɪpə] F -, -n (dial) (bread) roll

schritt pret von **schreiten**

Schritt [ʃrɪt] M -(e)s, -e **a** (lit, fig) step (zu to-wards); (weit ausholend) stride; (hörbar) footstep; **mit schnellen/langsamen ~en** quickly/slowly, with quick/slow steps; **mit schleppenden ~en** dragging one's feet, with dragging feet; **sie nä-herte sich ihm mit trippelnden ~en** she tripped towards him; **einen ~ zurücktreten** to step back; **einen ~ zur Seite gehen** to step aside or to one side; **~ vor ~ setzen** to put one foot in front of the other; **ein paar ~e spazieren gehen** to go for or take a short walk or stroll; **einen ~ machen** or **tun** to take a step; **kleine** or **kurze/ große** or **lange ~e machen** to take small steps/ long strides; **ich habe seit Wochen keinen/kaum einen ~ aus dem Haus getan** I haven't/have hardly set foot outside the house for weeks; **die ersten ~e machen** or **tun** to take one's first steps; (fig) to take the first step; **den ersten ~ tun** (fig) to make the first move; (= etw begin-nen) to take the first step; **den zweiten ~ vor dem ersten tun** (fig) to put the cart before the horse; **den ~ tun** (fig) to take the plunge; **~e gegen jdn/etw unternehmen** to take steps a-gainst sb/sth; **ich würde sogar noch einen ~ weiter gehen und behaupten ...** I would go e-ven further and maintain ...; **im gleichen ~ und Tritt** (lit, fig) in step; **auf ~ und Tritt** (lit, fig) wherever or everywhere one goes; **~ für** or **um ~** step by step; (fig auch) little by little, gradually; **Politik der kleinen ~e** step-by-step or gradualis-tic policy; **ein ~ in Richtung Frieden** a step to-wards peace

b (= Gang) walk, gait; (= Tempo) pace; **~ halten** (lit, fig) to keep pace, to keep up; **mit der Zeit ~ halten** to keep abreast of the times; **einen schnellen/unwahrscheinlichen ~ am Leib** (inf) or **an sich** (dat) **haben** to walk quickly/incredibly quickly; **gemessenen/leichten/langsamen ~es** (geh) with measured/light/slow step(s) or tread; **seinen ~** or **seine ~e beschleunigen/verlangsa-men** (geh) to increase/slow one's pace, to speed up/slow down; **den ~ anhalten** to stop

c (= Schrittgeschwindigkeit) walking pace; **(im) ~ fahren** to go at a crawl, to drive at walking speed; „**Schritt fahren**" "dead slow" (Brit), "slow"; **im ~ reiten/gehen** to go at a walk

d (Maßangabe) = yard; **mit zehn ~** or **~en Ab-stand** at a distance of ten paces; **sich** (dat) **jdn drei ~(e) vom Leib halten** (inf) to keep sb at arm's length

e (= Hosenschritt) crotch; (= Schrittweite) crotch measurement

Schrittempo △ NT → **Schritttempo**

Schritt-: Schritt|fol|ge F (beim Tanzen) se-quence of steps, step sequence; **Schritt|ge-schwin|dig|keit** F walking pace; **mit ~ fahren** to drive at a walking pace or a crawl; **Schritt-kom|bi|na|ti|on** F (Sport) combination of steps; **Schritt|län|ge** F length of one's stride; **Schritt|ma|cher** M (Med) pacemaker; **Schritt|ma|cher(in)** M(F) (Sport) pacemaker (esp Brit), pacer; (fig auch) pacesetter; **die Uni-versitäten waren ~ der Revolution** the universi-ties were in the vanguard of or led the way in the revolution; **Schritt|ma|cher|diens|te** PL (fig) **jdm ~ leisten** to smooth the path or way for sb; **Schritt|ma|cher|ma|schi|ne** F (Sport) pacemaker (esp Brit), pacer; **Schritt|tem|po** ▲ NT walking speed; **im ~ fahren** to crawl a-long; „**Schritttempo**" "dead slow" (Brit), "slow"; **Schritt|wei|se** ADV gradually, little by little ADJ gradual; **Schritt|wei|te** F (Sew) (von Hose) (waist-to-)crotch measurement; (von Kleid, Rock) hemline; **Schritt|zäh|ler** M pedometer

schroff [ʃrɔf] ADJ (= rau, barsch) curt, brusque; (= krass, abrupt) Übergang, Bruch abrupt; (= steil, jäh) Fels, Klippe precipitous, steep; **das ~e Ne-beneinander von Arm und Reich** the stark jux-taposition of rich and poor; **~e Gegensätze** stark or sharp contrasts ADV **a** (= barsch) curtly, gruffly; zurückweisen, ablehnen curtly, brusquely **b** (= steil) steeply

Schroff|heit F -, -en **a** no pl (= Rauheit, Barschheit) curtness, brusqueness **b** (= schroffes Wort) curt remark

schröp|fen ['ʃrœpfn] VT (= Blut absaugen) to bleed, to cup (old); **jdn ~** (fig) to fleece sb (inf), to rip sb off (inf)

Schröpf|kopf M (Med) cupping glass

Schrot [ʃroːt] M OR NT -(e)s, -e **a** grain (coarsely ground); (= Weizenschrot) ≈ wholemeal (Brit), ≈ whole-wheat (US); **ein Schotte von echtem ~ und Korn** a true Scot; **er ist ein Bauer von echtem ~ und Korn** he is a farmer through and through; **vom alten ~ und Korn** (fig) of the old school **b** (Hunt) shot; **einem Hasen eine Ladung ~ aufbrennen** (inf) to pepper a hare with shot

Schrot-: Schrot|brot NT bread made from coarsely-ground grain (aus Weizenschrot) ≈ wholemeal (Brit) or whole-wheat (US) bread; **Schrot|büch|se** F (Hunt) shotgun; **Schrot|ef|fekt** M (Elec) shot effect

schro|ten ['ʃroːtn] VT Getreide to grind coarsely; Alteisen to break up

Schrot-: Schrot|flin|te F shotgun; **Schrot|korn** NT pl **-körner** **a** grain **b** (Hunt) pellet; **Schrot|ku|gel** F pellet; **Schrot|la|dung** F round of shot; **Schrot|mehl** NT coarsely-ground flour; (= Weizenmehl) ≈ wholemeal (Brit) or whole-wheat (US) flour; **Schrot|mei|ßel** M blacksmith's chisel; **Schrot|sä|ge** F crosscut saw; **Schrot|schuss** ▲ M round of shot or pellets

Schrott [ʃrɔt] M -(e)s, no pl scrap metal; (aus Eisen auch) old iron; (fig) rubbish (Brit), garbage, trash → fahren 2 a

Schrott-: Schrott|au|to NT car that is ready for the scrap heap; **Schrott|hal|de** F scrap heap; **Schrott|han|del** M scrap trade; **Schrott|händ|ler(in)** M(F) scrap dealer or merchant; **Schrott|hau|fen** M (lit) scrap heap; (fig: = Auto) pile or heap of scrap; **Schrott|mö|bel** PL (fig) trashy furniture; **Schrott|platz** M scrap yard; **schrott|reif** ADJ ready for the scrap heap, only fit for scrap → fahren 2 a; **Schrott|wert** M scrap value

schrub|ben ['ʃrʊbn] **VTI** to scrub; **das Deck ~** to swab or scrub the deck/decks **VR** to scrub oneself

Schrub|ber ['ʃrʊbɐ] M -s, - (long-handled) scrubbing (Brit) or scrub (US) brush

Schrul|le ['ʃrʊlə] F -, -n **a** quirk; **was hast du dir denn da für eine ~ in den Kopf gesetzt?** (inf) what strange idea have you got into your head now? **b** (pej: = alte Frau) old crone

schrul|len|haft **ADJ** odd, cranky (Brit) **ADV** sich benehmen oddly

Schrul|len|haf|tig|keit ['ʃrʊlənhaftɪçkait] F -, no pl oddness, crankiness (Brit)

schrul|lig ['ʃrʊlɪç] **ADJ** odd, cranky (Brit) **ADV** sich benehmen oddly

Schrul|lig|keit F -, -en oddness, crankiness (Brit)

Schrum|pel ['ʃrʊmpl] F -, -n (dial) wrinkle

schrum|pe|lig ['ʃrʊmpəlɪç] ADJ (inf) Haut, Apfel wrinkled

schrum|peln ['ʃrʊmpln] VI aux sein (inf) to go wrinkled

schrump|fen ['ʃrʊmpfn] VI aux sein **a** (lit) to shrink; (Leber, Niere) to atrophy; (Muskeln) to waste, to atrophy; (Metall, Gestein etc) to contract; (= runzlig werden) to get wrinkled **b** (fig) to shrink; (Exporte, Mitgliederschaft, Interesse) to dwindle; (Währung) to depreciate; (Industriezweig) to decline

Schrumpf-: Schrumpf|kopf M shrunken head; **Schrumpf|le|ber** F cirrhosis of the liver; **Schrumpf|nie|re** F cirrhosis of the kidney

Schrump|fung ['ʃrʊmpfʊŋ] F -, -en shrinking; (= Raumverlust) shrinkage; (von Fundamenten, Metall) contraction; (Med) atrophy(ing); (von Kapital, Arbeitskräften, Exporten) dwindling, diminu-

tion; (von Währung) depreciation; (von Industriezweig etc) decline

schrum|plig ['ʃrʊmplɪç] ADJ (inf) Haut, Apfel wrinkled

Schrund [ʃrʊnt] M -(e)s, ⸚e ['ʃrʏndə] (= Bergschrund) crevasse

Schrun|de ['ʃrʊndə] F -, -n (in der Haut) crack; (durch Kälte) chap; (= Felsschrunde, Gletscherspalte) crevasse

schrun|dig ['ʃrʊndɪç] ADJ Haut, Hände cracked; (durch Kälte) chapped; Papier rough; Weg creviced

schrup|pen ['ʃrʊpn] VT **a** (Tech) (mit Feile) to rough-file; (mit Hobel) to rough-plane; (mit Maschine) to rough-machine **b** (= schrubben) to scrub

Schrupp-: Schrupp|fei|le F rough file; **Schrupp|ho|bel** M jack plane

Schub [ʃuːp] M -(e)s, ⸚e ['ʃyːbə] **a** (= Stoß) push, shove **b** (Phys) (= Vortriebskraft) thrust; (= Scherung) shear; (fig: = Impuls, Anstoß) impetus; **einer Sache neuen ~ geben** (fig) to give sth new impetus or momentum **c** (Med) phase **d** (= Anzahl) batch **e** (= Kegelschub) throw; **alle neune auf einen ~** a strike; **auf zwei Schübe** in two throws **f** (inf: = Schubfach) drawer

schub|bern ['ʃubɐn] VTI (N Ger) to scratch

Schu|ber ['ʃuːbɐ] M -s, - slipcase

Schub-: Schub|fach NT drawer; **Schub|haft** F (Jur) = Abschiebehaft; **Schub|kar|re** F , **Schub|kar|ren** M wheelbarrow; **Schub|kas|ten** M drawer; **Schub|kraft** F (Phys) thrust; (= Scherung) shearing stress

Schub|la|de ['ʃuːplaːdə] F -, -n drawer; (fig) pigeonhole, compartment; **in der ~ liegen** (fig) to be in reserve

Schub|la|den-: Schub|la|den|den|ken NT pigeonholing, stereotyped thinking; **Schub|la|den|ge|setz** NT (Pol pej) law kept in reserve to deal with a special situation

Schub|lad|kas|ten M (Aus) chest of drawers

Schub|leh|re F vernier calliper

Schubs [ʃups] M -es, -e (inf) shove (inf), push; (Aufmerksamkeit erregend) nudge; **jdm einen ~ geben** to give sb a shove (inf) or push/nudge; (fig) to give sb a prod

Schub|schiff NT tug (boat) (which pushes)

schub|sen ['ʃupsn] VTI (inf) to shove (inf), to push; (Aufmerksamkeit erregend) to nudge

Schub|um|kehr F (Aviat) thrust reverser

schub|wei|se ADV in batches; (Med) in phases

schüch|tern ['ʃʏçtɐn] **ADJ** shy; (= scheu auch) bashful; **einen ~en Versuch unternehmen** (iro) to make a half-hearted attempt **ADV** shyly; (= scheu auch) bashfully

Schüch|tern|heit F -, no pl shyness; (= Scheu auch) bashfulness

schu|ckeln ['ʃʊkln] VI (dial) = wackeln a

schuf pret von **schaffen** [1]

Schu|fa ['ʃuːfa] F -, no pl abbr von **Schutzgemeinschaft für allgemeine Kreditsicherung** ≈ credit investigation company (Brit), ≈ credit bureau (US)

Schuft [ʃʊft] M -(e)s, -e heel (inf), cad, blackguard (old)

schuf|ten ['ʃʊftn] VI (inf) to graft (away) (inf), to slave away; **wie ein Pferd ~** (inf) to work like a Trojan (Brit) or a horse

Schuf|te|rei [ʃʊftə'rai] F -, -en (inf) graft (inf), hard work

schuf|tig ['ʃʊftɪç] **ADJ** mean, shabby **ADV** behandeln meanly, shabbily; **sich jdm gegenüber ~ verhalten** to behave meanly toward(s) sb

Schuf|tig|keit F -, -en meanness, shabbiness; **das war eine ~ von ihm** that was a mean thing he did, that was mean of him

Schuh [ʃuː] M -(e)s, -e **a** shoe; **jdm etw in die ~e schieben** (inf) to lay the blame for sth at sb's door, to put the blame for sth on sb; **wis-**

sen, **wo jdn der ~ drückt** to know what is bothering or troubling sb; **wo drückt der ~?** what's the trouble?, what's bothering you?; **umgekehrt wird ein ~ d(a)raus** (fig) exactly the opposite is the case **b** (= Bremsschuh etc) shoe

Schuh- in cpds shoe; **Schuh|ab|satz** M heel (of a/one's shoe); **Schuh|an|zie|her** [-lantsiːɐ] M -s, - shoehorn; **Schuh|band** [-bant] NT pl -bänder shoelace; **Schuh|bürs|te** F shoe brush

Schüh|chen ['ʃyːçən] NT -s, - dim von **Schuh**

Schuh-: Schuh|cre|me F shoe polish or cream; **Schuh|grö|ße** F shoe size; **Schuh|haus** NT shoe shop; **Schuh|kar|ton** M shoebox; **Schuh|löf|fel** M shoehorn; **Schuh|ma|cher(in)** M(F) shoemaker; (= Flickschuster) cobbler; **Schuh|num|mer** F (inf) shoe size; **jds ~ sein** (fig) to be sb's cup of tea (inf); **ein paar oder mindestens zwei ~n zu groß für jdn** (fig) out of sb's league; **Schuh|platt|ler** [-platlɐ] M -s, - Bavarian folk dance; **Schuh|put|zer** [-pʊtsɐ] M -s, -, **Schuh|put|ze|rin** [-ərɪn] F -, -nen bootblack, shoeshine boy/girl (US); **jdn wie einen ~ behandeln** to treat sb like dirt; **ich bin doch nicht dein ~!** I'm not your slave!; **Schuh|putz|mit|tel** NT shoe polish; **Schuh|rie|men** M strap (of a/one's shoe); (= Schnürsenkel) shoelace; **Schuh|soh|le** F sole of a/one's shoe); **~n sparen** to save shoe leather; **Schuh|span|ner** M shoetree; **Schuh|wa|ren** PL footwear (pl); **Schuh|werk** NT , no pl footwear; **Schuh|wich|se** F (inf) shoe polish; **Schuh|zeug** NT , no pl footwear

Schu|ko-® ['ʃuːko-]: **Schu|ko|steck|do|se** F safety socket; **Schu|ko|ste|cker** M safety plug

Schul-: Schul|ab|gän|ger [-lapgɛŋɐ] M -s, -, **Schul|ab|gän|ge|rin** [-ərɪn] F -, -nen school-leaver (Brit), graduate (US); **Schul|ab|schluss** ▲ M school-leaving qualification, ≈ high school diploma (US); **Schul|al|ter** NT school age; **im ~** of school age; **ins ~ kommen** to reach school age; **Schul|amt** NT education authority; **Schul|an|fang** M beginning of (the (esp US)) term; (= Schuleintritt) first day at school; **morgen ist ~** school starts tomorrow; **Schul|an|fän|ger(in)** M(F) child just starting school; **Schul|ar|beit** F **a** usu pl homework no pl, prep no pl (Brit inf) **b** (Aus, S Ger) test; **Schul|art** F type of school; **Schul|arzt** M , **Schul|ärz|tin** F school doctor; **Schul|auf|ga|ben** PL homework usu pl; **Schul|auf|satz** M class essay; **Schul|auf|sicht** F supervision of schools; **die ~ obliegt dem Kultusministerium** the ministry of education is responsible for schools; **Schul|auf|sichts|be|hör|de** F education authority; **Schul|aus|flug** M school outing (esp Brit) or trip, field trip (US); **Schul|aus|ga|be** F school edition; **Schul|bank** F pl -bänke school desk; **die ~ drücken** (inf) to go to school; **Schul|be|ginn** M (= Schuljahrsbeginn) beginning of the school year; (nach Ferien) beginning of (the (esp US)) term; (der) ~ **ist um neun** school starts at nine; **Schul|be|hör|de** F education authority; **Schul|bei|spiel** NT (fig) classic example (für of); **Schul|be|such** M school attendance; **Schul|bil|dung** F (school) education; **Schul|bub** M (S Ger, Aus) schoolboy; **Schul|buch** NT schoolbook, textbook; **Schul|buch|ver|lag** M educational publishing company; **Schul|bus** M school bus

schuld [ʃʊlt] ADJ pred ~ **sein** to be to blame (an +dat for); **er war ~ an dem Streit** the argument was his fault, he was to blame for the argument; **das Wetter/ich war ~ daran, dass wir zu spät kamen** the weather/I was to blame for us being late, it was the fault of the weather/my fault that we were late; **bin ich denn ~, wenn ...?** is it my fault if ...?; **du bist selbst ~** that's your own fault, that's nobody's fault but your own

Schuld [ʃʊlt] ✪ 45.2 F -, -en [-dn] **a** *no pl* (= *Ursache, Verantwortlichkeit*) **die ~ an etw** (*dat*) **haben** or **tragen** (*geh*) to be to blame for sth; **~ haben** to be to blame (**an** +*dat* for); **er hatte ~ an dem Streit** the argument was his fault, he was to blame for the argument; **du hast selbst ~** that's your own fault, that's nobody's fault but your own; **die ~ auf sich** (*acc*) **nehmen** to take the blame; **jdm die ~ geben** or **zuschreiben** to blame sb; **die ~ auf jdn abwälzen** or **schieben** to put the blame on sb; **die ~ bei anderen suchen** to try to blame somebody else; **die ~ liegt bei mir** I am to blame (for that); **das ist meine/deine ~** that is my/your fault, I am/you are to blame (for that); **das ist meine eigene ~** it's my own fault, I've nobody but or only myself to blame; **durch meine/deine ~** because of me/you; **jdm/einer Sache ~ geben** to blame sb/sth; **er gab ihr ~, dass es nicht klappte** he blamed her for it not working, he blamed her for the fact that it didn't work

b *no pl* (= *Schuldhaftigkeit, Schuldgefühl*) guilt; (= *Unrecht*) wrong; (*Rel*: = *Sünde*) sin; (*im Vaterunser*) trespasses *pl*; **die Strafe sollte in einem angemessenen Verhältnis zur ~ stehen** the punishment should be appropriate to the degree of culpability; **sich frei von ~ fühlen** to consider oneself completely blameless; **ich bin mir keiner ~ bewusst** I'm not aware of having done anything wrong; **ich bin mir meiner ~ bewusst** I know that I have done wrong; **ihm konnte seine ~ nicht nachgewiesen werden** his guilt could not be proved; **ihm konnte keine ~ nachgewiesen werden** it couldn't be proved that he had done anything wrong; **~ auf sich** (*acc*) **laden** to burden oneself with guilt; **für seine ~ büßen** to pay for one's sin/sins; **~ und Sühne** crime and punishment; *see* **zuschulden**

c (= *Zahlungsverpflichtung*) debt; **ich stehe tief in seiner ~** (*lit*) I'm deeply in debt to him; (*fig*) I'm deeply indebted to him; **~en machen** to run up debts; **~en haben** to be in debt; **EUR 10.000 ~en haben** to have debts totalling (*Brit*) or totaling (*US*) or of 10,000 euros, to be in debt to the tune of 10,000 euros; **in ~en geraten** to get into debt; **mehr ~en als Haare auf dem Kopf haben** (*inf*) **bis über beide Ohren in ~en stecken** (*inf*) to be up to one's ears in debt (*inf*); **das Haus ist frei von ~en** the house is unmortgaged

Schuld-: Schuld|an|er|kennt|nis NT admission of one's guilt; (= *Schuldschein*) promissory note, IOU; **Schuld|be|kennt|nis** NT confession; **schuld|be|laden** [-bəladn] ADJ burdened with guilt; **Schuld|be|weis** M proof or evidence of one's guilt; **schuld|be|wusst** ▲ ADJ *Mensch* feeling guilty; *Gesicht, Miene* guilty ADV **jdn ~ ansehen** to give sb a guilty look; **~ erröten** to turn red with guilt (*Brit*), to blush from guilt; **Schuld|be|wusst|sein** ▲ NT feelings *pl* of guilt; **Schuld|buch** NT (*Econ*) Debt Register; **Schuld|buch|for|de|rung** F (*Econ*) Debt Register Claims; **Schuld|ein|ge|ständ|nis** NT admission of guilt

schuld|den [ʃʊldn] VT to owe; **das schulde ich ihm** I owe him that, I owe it to him; **jdm Dank ~** to owe sb a debt of gratitude

Schuld|den-: Schuld|den|berg M mountain of debts; **Schuld|den|dienst** M (*Econ*) debt servicing; **Schuld|den|er|lass** ▲ M (*Econ*) debt relief, waiving of debts; **schuld|den|frei** ADJ free of debt(s); *Besitz* unmortgaged; **Schuld|den|kri|se** F debt crisis; **Schuld|den|last** F debts *pl*; **Schuld|den|ma|cher(in)** M(F) (*inf*) habitual debtor; **er ist ein notorischer ~** he is notorious for running up debts; **Schuld|den|ma|nage|ment** NT debt management; **Schuld|den|mas|se** F (*Jur*) aggregate liabilities *pl*; **Schuld|den|til|gung** F discharge of one's debt(s)

Schuld-: schuld|fä|hig ADJ (*Jur*) criminally responsible; **voll/vermindert ~** fully/not fully responsible; **Schuld|fä|hig|keit** F (*Jur*) criminal responsibility; **verminderte ~** diminished responsibility; **Schuld|for|de|rung** F claim; **Schuld|fra|ge** F question of guilt; **schuld|frei** ADJ blameless; **Schuld|ge|fäng|nis** NT (*Hist*) debtors' prison; **Schuld|ge|fühl** NT sense *no pl* or feeling of guilt; **Schuld|ge|ständ|nis** NT → **Schuldbekenntnis**; **schuld|haft** (*Jur*) ADJ culpable ADV culpably; **jdm etw ~ nachweisen** to prove sb's culpability for sth; **Schuld|haft** F (*Hist*) imprisonment for debt

Schul-: Schul|die|ner M (*old*) school janitor or caretaker; **Schul|dienst** M (school)teaching *no art*; **in den ~ treten** or **gehen** to go into teaching; **im ~ (tätig) sein** to be a teacher, to be in the teaching profession

schul|dig [ʃʊldɪç] ADJ **a** (= *schuldhaft, straffällig, schuldbeladen*) guilty; (= *verantwortlich*) to blame pred (**an** +*dat* for); (*Rel*) sinful; **einer Sache** (*gen*) **~ sein** to be guilty of sth; **jdn einer Tat** (*gen*) **(für) ~ erklären** or **befinden** (*Jur*) to find sb guilty of or to convict sb of an offence (*Brit*) or offense (*US*); **jdn einer Sache** (*gen*) **~ machen** to be guilty of sth; **jdn ~ sprechen** to find or pronounce sb guilty, to convict sb; **sich ~ bekennen** to admit one's guilt; (*Jur*) to plead guilty; **jdn ~ werden** (*geh*) to wrong sb

b (*geh*: = *gebührend*) due; **jdm die ~e Achtung/den ~en Respekt zollen** to give sb the attention/respect due to him

c (= *verpflichtet*) **jdm etw** (*acc*) **~ sein** (*lit, fig*) to owe sb sth; **ich muss Ihnen 2 Euro ~ bleiben** I'll have to owe you 2 euros; **was bin ich Ihnen ~?** how much or what do I owe you?; **jdm Dank ~ sein** to owe sb a debt of gratitude; **sie blieb mir die Antwort ~** she didn't answer me, she didn't have an answer; **sie blieb mir die Antwort nicht ~** she hit back at me; **er blieb ihr nichts ~** (*fig*) he gave (her) as good as he got

ADV **~ geschieden sein** to be the guilty party in a/the divorce

Schul|di|ge(r) [ʃʊldɪgə] MF *decl as adj* guilty person; (*zivilrechtlich*) guilty party

Schul|di|ger [ʃʊldɪgɐ] M -s, - (*Bibl*) trespasser; **wie auch wir vergeben unseren ~n** as we forgive those who trespass against us

Schul|dig|keit F -, *no pl* duty; **seine ~ tun** to do one's duty → **Mohr**

Schul|di|spre|chung [-ʃpreçʊŋ] F -, -en conviction

Schul|di|rek|tor(in) M(F) headteacher (*esp Brit*), headmaster/headmistress, principal

Schul-: Schul|kom|plex M guilt complex; **schuld|los** ADJ (*an Verbrechen*) innocent (**an** +*dat* of); (*an Fehler, Unglück etc*) blameless, free from blame; **er war vollständig ~ an dem Unglück** he was in no way to blame for the accident; **jdn ~ in etw geraten** innocently; **~ in einen Unfall verwickelt sein** to be involved in an accident without being at fault; **~ geschieden sein** to be the innocent party in a/the divorce; **Schuld|lo|sig|keit** F -, *no pl* innocence

Schuld|ner [ʃʊldnɐ] M -s, -, **Schuld|ne|rin** [-ərɪn] F -, -nen debtor

Schuld|ner-: Schuld|ner|be|ra|tung F advisory service for debtors, debt advisory service, credit counseling (*US*); **Schuld|ner|staat** M debtor nation; **Schuld|ner|ver|zeich|nis** NT (*Jur*) (court) register of outstanding debts

Schuld-: Schuld|prin|zip NT (*Jur*) principle of the guilty party; **Schuld|recht** NT (*Jur*) law of contract; **Schuld|schein** M IOU, promissory note; **Schuld|schein|dar|le|hen** F loan against borrower's note; **Schuld|spruch** M verdict of guilty; **Schuld|turm** M (*Hist*) debtors' prison; **Schuld|über|nah|me** F assumption of debt; **schuld|un|fä|hig** ADJ (*Jur*) not criminally responsible; **Schuld|un|fä|hig|keit** F (*Jur*) lack of criminal responsibility; **Schuld|ver|hält|nis** NT (*Jur*) relationship of debenture; **Schuld|ver|schrei|bung** F (*Fin*) debenture bond; **Schuld|zins** M debt interest; **Schuld|zu|wei|sung** F accusation, assignment of guilt

Schu|le [ʃuːlə] F -, -n **a** (= *Lehranstalt, Lehrmeinung, künstlerische Richtung*) school; **in die** or **zur ~ kommen** to start school; **in die** or **zur ~ gehen** to go to school; **er hat nie eine ~ besucht** he has never been to school; **auf** or **in der ~** at school; **die ~ wechseln** to change schools; **von der ~ abgehen** to leave school; **die ~ ist aus** school is over, the schools are out; **sie ist an der ~** (= *sie ist Lehrerin*) she is a (school)teacher; **~ des Violinspiels** (= *Lehrwerk*) violin tutor; **er ist bei Brecht in die ~ gegangen** (*fig*) he was greatly influenced by Brecht; (= *wurde von Brecht unterrichtet*) he was a student of Brecht's; **darin hat er bei seinen Eltern eine gute ~ gehabt** his parents have given him a good schooling in that; **durch eine harte ~ gegangen sein** (*fig*) to have learned in a hard school; **~ machen** to become the accepted thing; **aus der ~ plaudern** to tell tales (out of school (*Brit inf*)); **ein Kavalier der alten ~** a gentleman of the old school

b (*Reiten*) school of riding → **hoch 1 g**

schu|len [ʃuːlən] VT to train; *Auge, Gedächtnis, Pferd auch* to school; (*Pol*) to give political instruction to

Schul-: Schul|eng|lisch NT schoolboy/schoolgirl English; **zwei Jahre ~** two years' English at school; **mein ~** the English I learned at school; **schul|ent|las|sen** ADJ kaum ~, begann er ... hardly had he left school when he began ...; **die ~e Jugend** the young people who have recently left school; **Schul|ent|las|se|ne** [-lɛntlasnə] PL *decl as adj* school-leavers *pl* (*Brit*), ≈ graduates *pl* (*US*); **Schul|ent|las|sung** F **der Tag der ~** the day one leaves (*Brit*) or graduates from (*US*) school; **nach seiner/der ~** after leaving (*Brit*) or graduating from (*US*) school; **Schul|ent|las|sungs|fei|er** F school-leavers' day (*Brit*), ≈ graduation day (*US*)

Schü|ler [ʃyːlɐ] M -s, -, **Schü|le|rin** [-ərɪn] F -, -nen schoolboy/-girl; (*einer bestimmten Schule, eines Künstlers*) pupil; (*einer Oberschule*) pupil, student; (= *Jünger*) follower, disciple; **als ~ habe ich ...** when I was at school I ...; **alle ~ und ~innen dieser Stadt** all the schoolchildren of this town; **ein ehemaliger ~ (der Schule)** an old boy or pupil (of the school)

Schüler-: Schü|ler|aus|tausch M school or student exchange; **Schü|ler|aus|weis** M (school) student card; **Schü|ler|er|mä|ßi|gung** F reduction or concession for pupils or students, student discount (*US*); **schü|ler|haft** ADJ schoolboyish/-girlish; (*pej*) childish, puerile ADV childishly; **sein Behemen wirkte ~** his behaviour (*Brit*) or behavior (*US*) seemed childish; **Schü|ler|heim** NT (school) boarding house

Schü|le|rin F → **Schüler**

Schüler-: Schü|ler|kar|te F school season ticket; **Schü|ler|lot|se** M , **Schü|ler|lot|sin** F *pupil acting as warden at a crossing*, lollipop man/lady (*Brit inf*); **Schü|ler|mit|ver|wal|tung** F school or student council; **Schü|ler|par|la|ment** NT interschool student council; **Schü|ler|schaft** [ʃyːlɐʃaft] F -, -en pupils *pl*; **Schü|ler|spra|che** F school slang; **Schü|ler|ver|tre|tung** F pupil or student representation; **Schü|ler|zahl** F number of pupils or students; **zurückgehende ~en** falling pupil numbers or school enrollment (*US*); **Schü|ler|zei|tung** F school magazine or newspaper

Schul-: Schul|er|zie|hung F schooling; **Schul|fach** NT school subject; **Schul|fei|er** F school function; **Schul|fe|ri|en** PL school holidays *pl* (*Brit*) or vacation (*US*); **Schul|fern|se|hen** NT schools' or educational television; **Schul|fest** NT school function; **Schul|film** M educational film; **schul|frei** ADJ **ein ~er Nachmittag** an afternoon when one doesn't have to go to school; **an ~en Samstagen** on Saturdays when there's no school; **nächsten Samstag ist ~** there's no school next Saturday; **die Kinder haben morgen ~** the children don't have to go to school tomorrow; **Schul|freund(in)** M(F) schoolfriend; **Schul|funk** M schools' radio; **Schul|ge|bäu|de** NT school building; **Schul|ge|brauch** M zum or für den ~ for use in schools; **Schul|ge|gen|stand** M (Aus) school subject; **Schul|ge|län|de** NT school grounds pl; **Schul|geld** NT school fees pl; **Schul|ge|lehr|sam|keit** F (pej) book-learning; **Schul|ge|setz** NT education act; **Schul|gram|ma|tik** F (school) grammar book or grammar (inf); **Schul|haus** NT schoolhouse; **Schul|heft** NT exercise book; **Schul|hof** M school playground, schoolyard

schu|lisch ['ʃuːlɪʃ] ADJ Leistungen, Probleme, Verbesserung at school; (= rein akademisch) scholastic; Bildung, Einrichtung school attr; **seine ~en Leistungen/Probleme** his progress/problems at school; **~e Angelegenheiten** school matters; **aus ~er Sicht** from the school angle ADV scholastically; **er hat ~ große Fortschritte gemacht** he has improved greatly at school

Schul-: Schul|jahr NT school year; (= Klasse) year; **ihre ~e** her school days; **Schul|ju|gend** F schoolchildren pl; **Schul|jun|ge** M schoolboy; **Schul|ka|me|rad(in)** M(F) schoolmate (Brit), schoolfriend; **Schul|kennt|nis|se** PL knowledge sing acquired at school; **Schul|kind** NT schoolchild; **Schul|kin|der|gar|ten** M establishment for children whose primary school entry has been delayed for a year; **Schul|klas|se** F (school) class; **Schul|land|heim** NT country house used by school classes for short visits; **Schul|leh|rer(in)** M(F) schoolteacher; **Schul|lei|ter** M headmaster, principal; **Schul|lei|te|rin** F headmistress, principal; **Schul|lek|tü|re** F book/books read in school; **~ sein** to be read in schools; **Schul|mäd|chen** NT schoolgirl; **Schul|map|pe** F schoolbag; **schul|mä|ßig** ADJ **a** Unterricht, Kurs, Lehrbuch didactic **b** (fig: = wie im Lehrbuch) textbook attr; **ein ~es Tor** a textbook goal ADV **machen** strictly by the book; **gekleidet** for school; **reglementiert** just like in school; **weniger ~ ausgedrückt** to say it less technically or formally; **Schul|me|di|zin** F orthodox medicine; **Schul|me|di|zi|ner(in)** M(F) orthodox medical practitioner; **Schul|mei|nung** F received opinion; **Schul|meis|ter** M (old, hum, pej) schoolmaster; **schul|meis|ter|lich** (pej) ADJ schoolmasterish ADV like a schoolmaster; **sich ~ aufspielen** to play the schoolmaster; **Schul|meis|tern** ['ʃuːlmaɪstɐn] insep VT to lecture (at or to) VI to lecture; **Schul|mö|bel** PL school furniture sing; **Schul|ord|nung** F school rules pl; **Schul|pflicht** F compulsory school attendance no art; **allgemeine ~** compulsory school attendance for all children; **es besteht ~** school attendance is compulsory; **schul|pflich|tig** [-pflɪçtɪç] ADJ Kind required to attend school; **im ~en Alter** of school age; **Schul|po|li|tik** F education policy; **Schul|psy|cho|lo|ge** M , **Schul|psy|cho|lo|gin** F educational psychologist; **Schul|ran|zen** M (school) satchel; **Schul|rat** M , **Schul|rä|tin** F schools inspector (Brit), ≈ school board superintendent (US); **Schul|re|form** F educational reform; **Schul|rei|fe** F school readiness (spec); **die ~ haben** to be ready to go to school; **Schul|rei|fe|test** M school readiness test; **Schul|sa|chen** PL school things pl, things pl for school; **seine ~ packen** to get one's things ready for school; **Schul|schiff** NT training ship; **Schul|schluss** ▲ M , no pl end of school; (vor den Ferien) end of term; **~ ist um 13.10** school finishes at 13.10; **kurz nach ~** just after school finishes; **Schul|schwän|zen** NT -s, no pl truancy; **Schul|schwän|zer** [-ʃvɛntsɐ] M -s, -, **Schul|schwän|ze|rin** [-ərɪn] F -, -nen truant; **Schul|se|na|tor(in)** M(F) schools minister (in Berlin, Hamburg and Bremen); **Schul|spei|sung** F free school meals pl; **Schul|sport** M school sport; **Schul|spre|cher** M head boy (Brit), school representative; **Schul|spre|che|rin** F

head girl (Brit), school representative; **Schul|spren|gel** M (Aus) (school) catchment (Brit) or service (US) area; **Schul|stress** ▲ M stress at school; **im ~ sein** to be under stress at school; **Schul|stun|de** F (school) period or lesson; **Schul|sys|tem** NT school system; **Schul|tag** M school day; **der erste ~** the/one's first day at school; **Schul|ta|sche** F schoolbag

Schul|ter ['ʃʊltɐ] F -, -n shoulder; **mit gebeugten/hängenden ~n dastehen** to stand there with sloping/drooping shoulders; (fig: = niedergeschlagen sein) to be careworn/downcast; **breite ~n haben** (lit) to be broad-shouldered, to have broad shoulders; (fig) to have a broad back; **er ließ die ~n hängen** he was slouching; (niedergeschlagen) he hung his head; **sich** (dat) **eine Jacke über die ~n hängen** to put a jacket round one's shoulders; **sich** (dat) **den Fotoapparat über die ~ hängen** to sling one's camera over one's shoulder; **jdm die Hand auf die ~ legen** to put one's hand on sb's shoulder; **jdm auf die ~ klopfen** or **schlagen** to give sb a slap on the back, to clap sb on the back; (lobend) to pat sb on the back; **sich** (dat) **selbst auf die ~ klopfen** (fig) to blow one's own trumpet; **jdm** or **jdn um die ~ fassen** to put one's arm round sb's shoulders; **~ an ~** (= dicht gedrängt) shoulder to shoulder; (= gemeinsam, solidarisch) side by side; **die** or **mit den ~n zucken** to shrug one's shoulders; **jdn auf die ~ legen** or **werfen** to get sb in a shoulder-press; **dem Künstler beim Arbeiten über die ~ sehen** to look over the artist's shoulder while he works; **die Verantwortung ruht auf seinen ~n** the responsibility rests on his shoulders or lies at his door; **die Arbeit sollte auf mehr/mehrere ~n verteilt werden** the work should be shared out between more/several people; **etw auf die leichte ~ nehmen** to take sth lightly → **kalt**

Schul|ter-: Schul|ter|blatt NT shoulder blade; **schul|ter|frei** ADJ Kleid off-the-shoulder; (ohne Träger) strapless; (mit Nackenträger) halterneck; **sie war/kam ~** her shoulders were bare, she was wearing a dress which left her shoulders bare; **Schul|ter|ge|lenk** NT shoulder joint; **Schul|ter|hö|he** F shoulder height; **in ~** at shoulder level or height

-schul|te|rig [-ʃʊltərɪç] ADJ suf -shouldered; **breitschulterig** broad-shouldered; **schmalschulterig** with narrow shoulders

Schul|ter-: Schul|ter|klap|pe F (Mil) epaulette; **Schul|ter|klop|fen** NT -s, no pl slap on the shoulder; (fig: = Lob) pat on the shoulder; **schul|ter|lang** ADJ shoulder-length

schul|tern ['ʃʊltɐn] VT (lit, fig) to shoulder; **das Gewehr ~** to shoulder arms

Schul|ter-: Schul|ter|pols|ter NT shoulder pad; **Schul|ter|rie|men** M shoulder strap; **Schul|ter|schluss** ▲ M , no pl shoulder-to--shoulder stance, solidarity; (= Solidarisierung) closing of ranks; **Schul|ter|sieg** M (Sport) fall; **Schul|ter|stand** M (Sport) shoulder stand; **Schul|ter|stück** NT **a** (Mil) epaulette **b** (Cook) piece of shoulder; **Schul|ter|wurf** M (Sport) shoulder-throw; **Schul|ter|zu|cken** NT -s, no pl shrug (of the shoulders); **die Antwort war ein ~** he/she answered with a shrug, he/she shrugged in reply

Schul|t|heiß ['ʃʊlthais] M -en, -en (Hist) mayor

Schul|trä|ger(in) M(F) (form) **der ~ (dieser Schule) ist der Staat** the school is supported or maintained by the State

-schul|t|rig [-ʃʊltrɪç] ADJ suf -schulterig

ents. It is intended to help children overcome any fears they may have about starting school.

Schul|typ M type of school

Schu|lung ['ʃuːlʊŋ] F -, -en (= Ausbildung, Übung) training; (von Auge, Gedächtnis, Pferd auch) schooling; (Pol) political instruction

Schu|lungs-: Schu|lungs|dis|ket|te F tutorial diskette; **Schu|lungs|kurs** M training course; **Schu|lungs|la|ger** NT training camp

Schul-: Schul|uni|form F school uniform; **Schul|un|ter|richt** M school lessons pl; **Schul|ver|sa|ger(in)** M(F) failure at school; **Schul|wan|de|rung** F school outing; **Schul|weg** M way to/from school; (Entfernung) distance to school; (Route) route to school; **ich habe einen ~ von 20 Minuten** it takes me 20 minutes to get to school; **Schul|weis|heit** F (pej) book-learning; **Schul|we|sen** NT school system; **Schul|wis|sen** NT knowledge acquired at school; **Schul|wör|ter|buch** NT school dictionary

Schul|ze ['ʃʊltsə] M -n, -n (Hist) mayor

Schul-: Schul|zeit F (= Schuljahre) school days pl; **nach 13-jähriger ~** after 13 years at school; **seit der ~** since we/they were at school, since our/their school days; **Schul|zei|tung** F school magazine or newspaper; **Schul|zent|rum** NT school complex; **Schul|zeug|nis** NT school report; **Schul|zwang** M = Schulpflicht; **Schul|zwe|cke** PL für ~n for school; (= als geeignetes Lehrmittel) for use in schools

schu|meln ['ʃʊmln] VI (inf) to cheat; **in Latein/beim Kartenspiel ~** to cheat in Latin/at cards

schum|me|rig ['ʃʊmərɪç] ADJ Beleuchtung dim; Raum dimly-lit; **bei ~em Licht** in the half-light; **es war schon ~** it was already getting dark

schum|mern ['ʃʊmɐn] VI impers (N Ger) **es schummert** dusk is falling VT (Geog) to shade (in)

Schum|mer|stun|de F (N Ger) twilight hour

Schum|me|rung ['ʃʊmərʊŋ] F -, -en (Geog) shading

schumm|rig ['ʃʊmrɪç] ADJ = schummerig

Schund (rare) pret von schinden

Schund [ʃʊnt] M -(e)s [-dəs] no pl (pej) trash, rubbish (Brit), garbage; **was für ~/einen ~ hast du denn da?** what's that trash/trashy book you're reading? → Schmutz **b**

Schund-: Schund|li|te|ra|tur F trash, trashy or pulp literature; **Schund|ro|man** M trashy or pulp novel

Schun|kel|lied NT German drinking song

schun|keln ['ʃʊŋkln] VI to link arms and sway from side to side

Schup|fen ['ʃʊpfn] M -s, - (esp S Ger) shed

Schup|fer ['ʃʊpfɐ] M -s, - (Aus) = Schubs

Schupf|nu|deln ['ʃʊpf-] PL (Cook) finger--shaped potato dumplings

Schu|po¹ ['ʃuːpo] F -, no pl abbr von Schutzpolizei

Schu|po² M -s, -s (dated inf) abbr von Schutzpolizist cop (inf), copper (esp Brit inf)

Schup|pe ['ʃʊpə] F -, -n **a** (Bot, Zool) scale; (von Ritterrüstung, Tierpanzer) plate; **es fiel mir wie ~n von den Augen** the scales fell from my eyes **b** **Schuppen** PL (= Kopfschuppen) dandruff sing

schup|pen ['ʃʊpn] VT Fische to scale VR to flake

Schup|pen ['ʃʊpn] M -s, - **a** (= Flugzeugschuppen) hangar **b** (inf) (= Haus, Wohnung etc) joint (inf), hole (pej inf), hovel (pej); (= übles Lokal) dive (inf) **c** (sl: = Disko etc) club

Schup|pen-: schup|pen|ar|tig ADJ scale-like ADV **die Ziegel sind ~ angeordnet** the tiles are arranged so that they overlap; **Schup|pen|bil|dung** F , no pl dandruff; **Schup|pen|flech|te** F (Med) psoriasis (spec); **schup|-**

pen|för|mig ADJ ADV = **schuppenartig**; **Schup|pen|pan|zer** M scale armour (Brit) or armor (US); **Schup|pen|tier** NT scaly anteater

schup|pig ['ʃʊpɪç] ADJ scaly; (= abblätternd auch) flaking ADV **die Haut löst sich ~ ab** his etc skin is flaking (off); **~ abblättern** to scale off

Schups [ʃʊps] M -es, -e = **Schubs**

schup|sen ['ʃʊpsn] VTI (inf) = **schubsen**

Schur [ʃuːɐ̯] F -, -en (= das Scheren) shearing; (= geschorene Wolle) clip

Schür|ei|sen NT poker

schü|ren ['ʃyːrən] VT a Feuer, Glut to rake, to poke b (fig) to stir up; Zorn, Eifersucht, Leidenschaft, Hass to fan the flames of

schür|fen ['ʃyrfn] VI (Min) to prospect (nach for); **tief ~** (fig) to dig deep VT Bodenschätze to mine VR to graze oneself; **sich** (dat) **die Haut ~, sich ~** to graze oneself or one's skin; **sich am Knie ~** to graze one's knee

Schürf-: Schürf|gru|be F , **Schürf|loch** NT (Min) test pit; **Schürf|recht** NT mining rights pl; **Schürf|wun|de** F graze, abrasion

Schür|ha|ken M poker

schu|ri|geln ['ʃuːriːgln] VT (inf) (= hart anfahren) to lay into (inf); (= schikanieren) to bully

Schur|ke ['ʃʊrkə] M -n, -n, **Schur|kin** ['ʃʊrkɪn] F -, -nen (dated) villain, scoundrel, rogue

Schur|ken|staat M (Pol) rogue state or nation

Schur|ken|streich M , **Schur|ken|tat** F , **Schur|ke|rei** [ʃʊrkə'raɪ] F -, -en (old) (piece of) villainy

schur|kisch ['ʃʊrkɪʃ] (dated) ADJ base, despicable ADV despicably

schur|ren ['ʃʊrən] VI (dial) (Schlitten) to grate; **mit den Füßen ~** to shuffle one's feet; (beim Gehen) to drag one's feet

Schur|wol|le ['ʃuːɐ̯-] F virgin wool; „**reine ~**" "pure new wool"

Schurz [ʃʊrts] M -es, -e loincloth; (von Schmied, Arbeiter etc, dial) apron

Schür|ze ['ʃʏrtsə] F -, -n apron; (= Frauenschürze, Kinderschürze mit Latz auch) pinafore, pinny (Brit inf); (= Kittelschürze) overall; **sich** (dat) **eine ~ umbinden** to put an apron on; **er ist hinter jeder ~ her** (dated inf), **er läuft jeder ~ nach** (dated inf) he runs after anything in a skirt (inf)

schür|zen ['ʃʏrtsn] VT a (dated) Rock to gather (up) b (geh: = schlingen) Knoten to tie; **einen Knoten ~** to tie a knot in c (geh: = aufwerfen) **die Lippen/den Mund ~** (zum Pfeifen) to purse one's lips; (verführerisch) to pout; **ihr geschürzter Mund** her pursed lips; her pout

Schür|zen-: Schür|zen|band [-bant] NT pl -bänder = **Schürzenzipfel**; **Schür|zen|jä|ger** M (inf) philanderer, one for the girls (inf); **Schür|zen|zip|fel** M apron string; **er hängt der Mutter noch am ~** he's still tied to his mother's apron strings

Schuss ▲ [ʃʊs] M -es, ⸚e ['ʃʏsə] a shot; (= Schuss Munition) round; **sechs ~** or **Schüsse** six shots/rounds; **einen ~ auf jdn/etw abgeben** to fire a shot at sb/sth; **zum ~ kommen** to have a chance to shoot; **ein ~ ins Schwarze** (lit, fig) a bull's-eye; **weit** (ab) **vom ~ sein** (fig) to be miles from where the action is (inf); **er ist keinen ~ Pulver wert** (fig) he is not worth tuppence (Brit inf) or two cents (US inf); **das war ein (schöner) ~ vor den Bug** (fig) that was a warning not to be ignored; **der ~ ging nach hinten los** it backfired; **ein ~ in den Ofen** (inf) a complete waste of time

b (Min: = Sprengung) blast, charge

c (Ftbl) kick; (esp zum Tor) shot; **zum ~ kommen** to get the ball; (zum Tor) to get a chance to shoot

d (Ski) schuss; **im ~ fahren** to schuss

e (= Spritzer) (von Wein, Essig etc) dash; (von Whisky) shot; (von Humor, Leichtsinn etc) touch, dash

f (Tex: = Querfäden) weft, woof

g (inf: mit Rauschgift) shot; (sich dat) **einen ~ setzen** to shoot up (inf); **sich** (dat) **den goldenen ~ setzen** to OD (inf)

h (inf) **in ~ sein/kommen** to be in/get into (good) shape; (Mensch, Sportler auch) to be on form/get into good form; (Schüler, Klasse) to be/get up to the mark (esp Brit) or up to snuff; (Party) to be going well/get going; **etw in ~ bringen/halten** to knock sth into shape/keep sth in good shape; Schulklasse to bring/keep sth up to the mark (esp Brit) or up to snuff; Party to get/keep sth going

i (sl) **einen ~ (an der Waffel) haben** to be off one's nut (inf)

Schuss-: Schuss|be|reich ▲ M (firing) range; **im ~** within range; **schuss|be|reit** ▲ ADJ ready to fire; Gewehr auch cocked

Schüs|sel ['ʃʊsl] M -s, - (inf) or f -, -n (inf) dolt (inf); (zerstreut) scatterbrain (inf); (ungeschickt) clumsy clot (inf)

Schüs|sel ['ʃʏsl] F -, -n bowl; (= Servierschüssel auch, = Satellitenschüssel) dish; (= Waschschüssel) basin; **vor leeren ~n sitzen** (nach dem Essen) to sit staring at the dirty dishes; (in Notzeit) to go hungry

schus|se|lig ['ʃʊsəlɪç] ADJ (= zerstreut) scatterbrained (inf), muddleheaded (Brit inf); (= ungeschickt) clumsy, all thumbs pred

Schus|se|lig|keit F -, -en (= Zerstreutheit) muddleheadedness (Brit inf), emptyheadedness; (= Ungeschick) clumsiness

schus|seln ['ʃʊsln] VI (inf) (= zerstreut sein) to be scatterbrained (inf) or muddle-headed (Brit inf); (= ungeschickt vorgehen) to be clumsy; (= sich ungeschickt bewegen) to bumble (inf)

Schus|ser ['ʃʊsɐ] M -s, - (dial) marble

Schuss-: Schuss|fa|den ▲ M (Tex) weft thread; **Schuss|fahrt** ▲ F (Ski) schuss; (= das Schussfahren) schussing; **Schuss|feld** ▲ NT field of fire; (= Übungsplatz) firing range; **schuss|fest** ▲ ADJ Glas, Weste bulletproof; **Schuss|ge|schwin|dig|keit** ▲ F velocity (of bullet etc); **Schuss|ka|nal** ▲ M (Med) path of a/the bullet through the body

schuss|lig ▲ ['ʃʊslɪç] ADJ (inf) = **schusselig**

Schuss|lig|keit ▲ F -, -en (inf) = **Schusseligkeit**

Schuss-: Schuss|li|nie ▲ F line of fire; (fig auch) firing line; **Schuss|rich|tung** ▲ F direction of fire; **schuss|si|cher** ▲ ADJ Glas, Weste bulletproof; **Schuss|ver|let|zung** ▲ F bullet wound; **Schuss|waf|fe** ▲ F firearm; **Schuss|waf|fen|ge|brauch** ▲ M (form) use of firearms; **Schuss|wech|sel** ▲ M exchange of shots or fire; **Schuss|wei|te** ▲ F range (of fire); **in/außer ~** within/out of range; **Schuss|win|kel** ▲ M angle of fire; **Schuss|wun|de** ▲ F bullet wound; **Schuss|zahl** ▲ F (Tex) number of weft threads

Schus|ter ['ʃuːstɐ] M -s, -, **Schus|te|rin** [-ərɪn] F -, -nen shoemaker; (= Flickschuster) cobbler; **auf ~s Rappen** (inf) by shanks's pony (Brit) or mare (US); **~, bleib bei deinem Leisten!** (Prov) cobbler, stick to your last (Prov)

Schus|ter-: Schus|ter|ah|le F shoemaker's awl; **Schus|ter|draht** M waxed thread

Schus|te|rei [ʃuːstə'raɪ] F -, -en a (Werkstatt) shoemaker's; (von Flickschuster) cobbler's b (pej inf: = Pfuscherei) botching (inf)

Schus|ter|hand|werk NT shoemaking, cobbling

Schus|te|rin F → **Schuster**

Schus|ter|jun|ge M a (old) (= Schusterlehrling) shoemaker's apprentice; (= Flickschuster) cobbler's apprentice b (Typ) widow

schus|tern ['ʃuːstɐn] VI (= Schusterarbeit machen) to cobble or repair or mend shoes VT (pej inf: = zusammenpfuschen) to cobble together (inf)

Schus|ter-: Schus|ter|pech NT shoemaker's or cobbler's wax; **Schus|ter|pfriem** M , **Schus|ter|pfrie|men** M shoemaker's awl; **Schus|ter|werk|statt** F shoemaker's workshop; (Flickschuster) cobbler's workshop

Schu|te ['ʃuːtə] F -, -n a (Naut) lighter b (= Damenhut) poke (bonnet)

Schutt [ʃʊt] M -(e)s, no pl (= Trümmer, Bauschutt) rubble; (Geol) debris, detritus (spec); „**Schutt abladen verboten**" "no tipping" (Brit), "no dumping" (US); **eine Stadt in ~ und Asche legen** to reduce a town to rubble; **in ~ und Asche liegen** to be in ruins

Schutt|ab|la|de|platz M tip (Brit), dump

Schütt-: Schütt|be|ton M cast concrete; **Schütt|bo|den** M strawloft; (für Getreide) granary

Schüt|te ['ʃʏtə] F -, -n a (= Bund) stock b (Behälter) wall-mounted drawer-like canister for sugar, flour etc

Schüt|tel-: Schüt|tel|be|cher M (cocktail) shaker; **Schüt|tel|frost** M (Med) shivering fit, fit of the shivers (inf); **Schüt|tel|läh|mung** F (Med) Parkinson's disease

schüt|teln ['ʃʏtln] VT to shake; (= rütteln) to shake about, to jolt (about); **den** or **mit dem Kopf ~** to shake one's head; **von Angst geschüttelt werden** to be gripped with fear; **von Fieber geschüttelt werden** to be racked with fever → **Hand a, Staub** VR to shake oneself; (vor Kälte) to shiver (vor with); (vor Ekel) to shudder (vor with, in); **sich vor Lachen ~** to shake with laughter

Schüt|tel-: Schüt|tel|reim M goat rhyme, rhyme in which the consonants of the rhyming syllables are transposed in the next line; **Schüt|tel|rut|sche** F (Tech) vibrating chute; **Schüt|tel|sieb** NT riddle

schüt|ten ['ʃʏtn] VT to pour; (= verschütten) to spill VI impers (inf) **es schüttet** it's pouring (with rain), it's pouring (down), it's bucketing (down) (Brit inf), it's coming down in buckets (US inf)

schüt|ter ['ʃʏtɐ] ADJ Haar, Schneedecke, Pflanzen thin; Gruppe small and pitiful

Schütt|gut NT , no pl bulk goods pl

Schutt-: Schutt|hal|de F (= Schutthaufen) rubble tip (Brit) or heap; (Geol) scree slope; **Schutt|hau|fen** M pile or heap of rubble; **etw in einen ~ verwandeln** to reduce sth to a pile of rubble; **Schutt|ke|gel** M (Geol) cone of scree or debris; **Schutt|mul|de** F skip (Brit), Dumpster® (US); **Schutt|platz** M tip (Brit)

Schütt-: Schütt|stein M (S Ger, Sw) sink; **Schütt|stroh** NT bedding straw

Schutz [ʃʊts] M -es, no pl protection (vor +dat, gegen against, from); (= Zuflucht auch) shelter, refuge (vor +dat, gegen from); (der Natur, Umwelt etc) protection, conservation; (esp Mil: = Deckung) cover; **jdn um ~ bitten** to ask sb for protection; **~ suchend** seeking protection; (nach Obdach) seeking refuge or shelter; **bei jdm ~ suchen** to look to sb for protection, to seek shelter or refuge with sb; **unter einem Baum ~ suchen** to shelter under a tree, to seek refuge under a tree; **im ~(e) der Nacht** or **Dunkelheit/des Artilleriefeuers** under cover of night or darkness/artillery fire; **zum ~ von Leib und Leben** for the protection of life and limb; **jdn/etw als ~ mitnehmen** to take sb/sth with one for protection; **zum ~ der Augen** to protect the eyes; **jdn in ~ nehmen** (fig) to take sb's part, to stand up for sb; **etw unter ~ stellen** (= unter Denkmalschutz, Naturschutz) to give sth protected status; **zu ~ und Trutz zusammenstehen** (old, liter) to stand together

Schutz-: Schutz|an|strich M protective coat; **Schutz|an|zug** M protective clothing no indef art, no pl; **Schutz|är|mel** M sleeve-protector; **Schutz|auf|sicht** F (Jur) supervision by a social worker; **schutz|be|dürf|tig** ADJ in need of protection; **Schutz|be|dürf-**

tig|keit F need for protection; **Schutz|be|foh|le|ne(r)** [-bəfo:lənə] MF decl as adj protégé; (= esp Kind) charge; **Schutz|be|haup|tung** F lie to cover oneself; **Schutz|blech** NT mudguard; **Schutz|brief** M **a** (letter of) safe-conduct **b** = **Auslandsschutzbrief**; **Schutz|bril|le** F protective goggles pl; **Schutz|bünd|nis** NT defensive alliance; **Schutz|dach** NT porch; (an Haltestelle) shelter; **Schutz|deck** NT shelter deck

Schüt|ze [ˈʃʏtsə] M **-n, -n** **a** marksman; (= Schießsportler) rifleman; (Hunt) hunter; (= Bogenschütze) archer; (Hist) bowman, archer; (Ftbl: = Torschütze) scorer; **er ist der beste ~** he is the best shot **b** (Mil: = Dienstgrad) private; (= Maschinengewehrschütze) gunner **c** (Astrol, Astron) Sagittarius no art; **sie ist ~** she's Sagittarius or a Sagittarian **d** (= Weberschiffchen) shuttle

schüt|zen [ˈʃʏtsn] **VT** to protect (vor +dat, gegen from, against); Umwelt auch to conserve; (= Zuflucht bieten auch) to shelter (vor +dat, gegen from); (= absichern: Versicherung etc auch) to safeguard; (esp Mil: = Deckung geben) to cover; **urheberrechtlich geschützt** protected by copyright; **gesetzlich geschützt** registered; **patentrechtlich geschützt** patented; **vor Hitze/Sonnenlicht ~!** keep away from heat/sunlight; **vor Nässe ~!** keep dry; **Gott schütze dich!** (old) (may) the Lord protect or keep you → auch **geschützt**
VI to give or offer protection (vor +dat, gegen from, against); (= Zuflucht bieten auch) to give or offer shelter (vor +dat, gegen from); (esp Mil: = Deckung geben) to give cover
VR to protect oneself (vor +dat, gegen from, against); (= sich absichern auch) to safeguard oneself (vor +dat, gegen against); **er weiß sich zu ~** he knows how to look after himself

Schüt|zen [ˈʃʏtsn] M **-s, -** (Tex) shuttle

Schüt|zen-: **Schüt|zen|an|ger** M = **Schützenwiese**; **Schüt|zen|bru|der** M member of a rifle club

schüt|zend **ADJ** protective; **ein ~es Dach** (gegen Wetter) a shelter; **ein ~es Dach über sich** (dat) **haben** to be under cover; **der ~e Hafen** (lit) the protection of the harbour (Brit) or harbor (US); (fig) a/the safe haven; **seine ~e Hand über jdn halten** or **breiten** to take sb under one's wing **ADV** protectively

Schüt|zen|fest NT fair featuring shooting matches

SCHÜTZENFEST

The **Schützenfest** is celebrated in rural areas, particularly in Austria and Southern Germany. Archery competitions are held and the winners become the **Schützenkönig** and **Schützenkönigin**. Their prize is usually a chain which is placed around their neck and which they keep until the following year. Usually there is also a parade and a small fair.

Schutz|en|gel M guardian angel
Schüt|zen-: **Schüt|zen|ge|sell|schaft** F , **Schüt|zen|gil|de** F rifle or shooting club; **Schüt|zen|gra|ben** M trench; **Schüt|zen|haus** NT clubhouse (of a rifle club); **Schüt|zen|hil|fe** F (fig) support; **jdm ~ geben** to back sb up, to support sb; **Schüt|zen|ket|te** F (Mil) firing line; **Schüt|zen|kö|nig(in)** M(F) champion rifleman/-woman at a Schützenfest; **Schüt|zen|li|nie** F (Mil) firing line; **Schüt|zen|loch** NT (Mil) foxhole; **Schüt|zen|pan|zer|(wa|gen)** M armoured (Brit) or armored (US) personnel carrier; **Schüt|zen|platz** M = **Schützenwiese**; **Schüt|zen|schwes|ter** F member of a rifle club; **Schüt|zen|ver|ein** M rifle or shooting club; **Schüt|zen|wie|se** F fairground at which a rifle club holds its competitions; **Schüt|zen|zug** M procession (Brit) or parade of riflemen

Schutz-: **Schutz|far|be** F , **Schutz|fär|bung** F (Biol) protective or adaptive colouring (Brit) or coloring (US); **Schutz|film** M protective

layer or coating; **Schutz|folie** F protective film; **Schutz|frist** F term of copyright; **Schutz|ge|biet** NT (Pol) protectorate; **Schutz|ge|bühr** F (token) fee; **Schutz|geist** M (Myth) protecting or tutelary (liter) spirit; **Schutz|ge|län|der** NT guardrail; **Schutz|geld** NT protection money; **Schutz|geld|er|pres|sung** F extortion of protection money; **Schutz|ge|wahr|sam** M (Jur) protective custody; **Schutz|git|ter** NT (um Denkmal etc) protective barrier; (vor Maschine, Fenster, Tür) protective grill(e); (um Leute zu schützen) safety barrier/grill(e); (vor Kamin) (fire)guard; (Elec) screen grid; **Schutz|gott** M (Myth) tutelary god (liter); **Schutz|göt|tin** F (Myth) tutelary goddess (liter); **Schutz|ha|fen** M port of refuge; (= Winterhafen) winter harbour (Brit) or harbor (US); **Schutz|haft** F (Jur) protective custody; (Pol) preventive detention; **Schutz|hand|schuh** M protective glove; **Schutz|hau|be** F protective hood; (für Schreibmaschine) cover; **Schutz|haut** F protective covering; **Schutz|hei|li|ge(r)** MF decl as adj patron saint; **Schutz|helm** M safety helmet; (von Bauarbeiter auch) hard hat (inf); **Schutz|herr** M patron; **Schutz|her|rin** F patron, patroness; **Schutz|herr|schaft** F (Pol) protection, protectorate; (= Patronat) patronage; **Schutz|hül|le** F protective cover; (= Buchumschlag) dust cover or jacket; **Schutz|hüt|te** F shelter, refuge; **schutz|imp|fen** pret **schutzimpfte**, ptp **schutzgeimpft** VT to vaccinate, to inoculate; **Schutz|imp|fung** F vaccination, inoculation

Schüt|zin [ˈʃʏtsɪn] F **-, -nen** markswoman; (= Schießsportlerin) riflewoman; (Hunt) huntress; (= Bogenschützin) archer; (Ftbl: = Torschützin) scorer

Schutz-: **Schutz|kap|pe** F (protective) cap; **Schutz|kar|ton** M cardboard box; (für Buch) slipcase; **Schutz|klau|sel** F protective or let-out clause; **Schutz|klei|dung** F protective clothing; **Schutz|kon|takt** M (Elec) safety contact; **Schutz|kon|takt|(steck|)do|se** F (Elec) safety socket; **Schutz|kon|takt|ste|cker** M (Elec) safety plug; **Schutz|leis|te** F protective strip; (bei Maschine) guardrail

Schütz|ling [ˈʃʏtslɪŋ] M **-s, -e** protégé; (esp Kind) charge

schutz|los **ADJ** (= wehrlos) defenceless (Brit), defenseless (US); (gegen Kälte etc) without protection, unprotected **ADV** **jdm/einer Sache ~ ausgeliefert** or **preisgegeben sein** to be at the mercy of sb/sth, to be defenceless (Brit) or defenseless (US)/without protection against sb/sth

Schutz|lo|sig|keit F **-, no pl** defencelessness (Brit), defenselessness (US)

Schutz-: **Schutz|macht** F (Pol) protecting power, protector; **Schutz|mann** M pl **-leute** policeman, constable (Brit); **Schutz|man|tel** M (Tech) protective casing; (gegen Strahlen) radiation shield; (der Haut) protective layer; **Schutz|mar|ke** F trademark; **Schutz|mas|ke** F (protective) mask; **Schutz|maß|nah|me** F precaution, precautionary measure; (vorbeugend) preventive measure; **Schutz|mau|er** F protecting wall; (von Festung) defensive wall; **Schutz|me|cha|nis|mus** M (esp Psych) protective mechanism; **Schutz|mit|tel** NT means of protection sing; (Substanz) protective substance, prophylactic (Med) (gegen for); **Schutz|netz** NT (im Zirkus) safety net; (an Damenfahrrad) skirt guard; (gegen Stechmücken etc) mosquito net; **Schutz|pat|ron** M , **Schutz|pat|ro|nin** F patron saint; **Schutz|po|li|zei** F (form) police force, constabulary (Brit form); **Schutz|po|li|zist(in)** M(F) (form) police officer, (police) constable (Brit), policeman/-woman; **Schutz|pro|gramm** NT **a** conservation programme (Brit) or program (US) **b** (Comput) (= Virenschutzprogramm) antivirus program; (= Datenschutzprogramm) privacy and security program; **Schutz|raum** M shelter; **Schutz|schicht** F protective layer; (= Überzug) protective coating; **Schutz|schild** M pl **-schil-**

de shield; (an Geschützen) gun shield; **Schutz|schirm** M (Tech) protective screen; **Schutz|staf|fel** F (Hist) SS; **schutz|su|chend** △ ADJ → Schutz; **Schutz|trup|pe** F protection force; (Hist) colonial army or force; **Schutz|um|schlag** M dust cover or jacket; **Schutz-und-Trutz-Bünd|nis** NT (old) defensive and offensive alliance; **Schutz|ver|band** M **a** protective association; **der ~ der ...** (in Namen) the Association for the Protection of ... **b** (Med) protective bandage or dressing; **Schutz|vor|rich|tung** F safety device; **Schutz|wald** M barrier woodland; **Schutz|wall** M protective wall (gegen to keep out), barrier; **Schutz|weg** M (Aus) pedestrian crossing (Brit), crosswalk (US); **Schutz|wes|te** F protective jacket; (= schusssichere Weste) bulletproof vest; **schutz|wür|dig** ADJ Interessen worth protecting; Gebäude, Sitten, Status worth preserving; **Schutz|wür|dig|keit** F **die ~ eines Gebäudes in Frage stellen** to question whether a building is worth preserving; **die ~ des Lebens sollte im Grundgesetz festgeschrieben werden** it should be laid down in the constitution that life must be protected; **Schutz|zoll** M protective duty or tariff; **Schutz|zo|ne** F (= Sicherheitszone, um Gefahrenherd) safety zone; (= militärische Schutzzone) safe haven; (= Naturschutzzone) conservation area; (im Seerecht) exclusion zone

Schwa [ʃva:] NT **-s, no pl** (Ling) schwa
schwab|be|lig [ˈʃvabəlɪç] ADJ (inf) Körperteil flabby; Gelee wobbly
schwab|beln [ˈʃvabln] VI (inf) to wobble (about)
Schwab|bel|schei|be F (Tech) buffing wheel
Schwa|be [ˈʃvaːbə] M **-n, -n**, **Schwä|bin** [ˈʃvɛ:bɪn] F **-, -nen** Swabian
schwä|beln [ˈʃvɛːbln] VI (inf) to speak Swabian or the Swabian dialect; (mit Akzent) to speak with a Swabian accent
Schwa|ben [ˈʃvaːbn] NT **-s** Swabia
Schwa|ben|streich M piece of folly
Schwä|bin F **-, -nen** Swabian (woman/girl)
schwä|bisch [ˈʃvɛːbɪʃ] ADJ Swabian; **die Schwäbische Alb** the Swabian mountains pl; **das Schwäbische Meer** (hum) Lake Constance

schwach [ʃvax] **ADJ** comp **=er** [ˈʃvɛçɐ], superl **=ste(r, s)** [ˈʃvɛçstə] weak (auch Gram); Mensch, Greis, Begründung, Versuch, Aufführung, Alibi, Widerstand auch feeble; Konstitution auch frail; Gesundheit, Beteiligung, Gedächtnis poor; Ton, Anzeichen, Hoffnung, Bewegung faint, slight; Gehör poor, dull; Stimme weak, faint; Licht poor, dim; Wind light; (Comm) Nachfrage, Geschäft slack, poor; **~e Augen** weak or poor (eye)sight; **das ist ein ~es Bild** (inf) or **eine ~e Leistung** (inf) that's a poor show (inf); **ein ~es Lob** faint praise; **jds ~e Seite/Stelle** sb's weak point/spot; **ein ~er Trost** cold or small comfort; **in einem ~en Augenblick, in einer ~en Stunde** in a moment of weakness, in a weak moment; **jdn ~ machen** (inf) to soften sb up, to talk sb round (esp Brit); **mach mich nicht ~!** (inf) don't say that! (inf); **in etw** (dat) **~ sein** to be weak in sth; **auf ~en Beinen** or **Füßen stehen** (fig) to be on shaky ground; (Theorie) to be shaky; **alles, was in meinen ~en Kräften steht** everything within my power; **jdn an seiner ~en** or **schwächsten Stelle treffen** to strike at or hit sb's weak spot; **mir wird ~** (lit) I feel faint; (fig inf) it makes me sick (inf); **nur nicht ~ werden!** don't weaken!; **schwächer werden** to grow weaker, to weaken; (Augen) to fail, to grow worse; (Stimme) to grow fainter; (Licht) to (grow) dim; (Ton) to fade; (Nachfrage) to fall off, to slacken; **die Schwachen** the weak; **der Schwächere** the weaker (person); (gegenüber Gegner) the underdog
ADV comp **=er**, superl **am =sten** **a** (= leicht) schlagen weakly; vibrieren, radioaktiv slightly; spüren, riechen, hören barely
b (= spärlich) besucht, bestückt poorly; **~ besiedelt** or **bevölkert** sparsely populated; **das Stadi-**

on war nur ~ besetzt there were only a few people in the stadium **c** (= *geringfügig*) klatschen weakly; *sich interessieren* slightly; *sich beteiligen* very little; **sich immer schwächer beteiligen** to participate less and less; ~ **aktiv** (*Atommüll etc*) low-level; ~ **radioaktiv** with low-level radioactivity; ~ **betont** weakly stressed; ~ **bewegt** (*Meer*) gently rolling; **schon bei ~ bewegtem Meer werde ich seekrank** as soon as there's the slightest swell I get seasick **d** (= *mild*) salzen, süßen slightly; würzen lightly; pfeffern mildly

schwach-: schwach|ak|tiv △ ADJ → **schwach ADV c**; **schwach|be|sie|delt** △ [-bəzi:dlt] ADJ *attr* → **schwach ADV b**; **schwach|be|tont** △ ADJ *attr* → **schwach ADV c**; **schwach|be|völ|kert** △ [-bəfœlkɛt] ADJ *attr* → **schwach ADV b**; **schwach|be|wegt** △ ADJ *attr* → **schwach ADV c**; **schwach|brüs|tig** [-brʏstɪç] ADJ (*hum*) feeble

Schwä|che [ʃvɛçə] ✪ 34.2 F **-, -n** **a** *no pl* weakness; (*von Stimme*) feebleness, faintness; (*von Licht*) dimness; (*von Wind*) lightness; **sie brach vor ~ zusammen** she was so weak she collapsed; **die zunehmende ~ seines Gehörs** his increasing deafness **b** (= *Schwächeanfall*) feeling of weakness **c** (= *Nachteil, Fehler*) weakness **d** (= *Vorliebe*) weakness (*für for*) **e** (= *Charaktermangel*) weakness, failing; **menschliche ~n** human failings *or* frailties; **jeder Mensch hat seine ~n** we all have our little weaknesses *or* failings

Schwä|che-: Schwä|che|an|fall M sudden feeling of weakness; **Schwä|che|ge|fühl** NT feeling of weakness

schwä|cheln [ʃvɛçln] VI (*inf*) to weaken slightly; **geistig ~** to begin to go a bit gaga; **der Dollar schwächelt** the dollar is showing signs of weakness

schwä|chen [ʃvɛçn] VT (*lit, fig*) to weaken **VR** to weaken oneself **VI** **etw schwächt** sth has a weakening effect

Schwä|che-: Schwä|che|punkt M low point; **einen ~ erreichen** to reach a low point *or* a low ebb; **Schwä|che|zu|stand** M condition of weakness *or* debility (*spec*), weak condition

Schwach|heit F **-, -en** **a** *no pl* (*fig*) weakness, frailty; **~, dein Name ist Weib** (*prov*) frailty, thy name is woman! (*prov*) **b** *no pl* (*rare*) = **Schwäche a c** (*inf*) **bilde dir nur keine ~en ein!** don't fool *or* kid yourself! (*inf*)

Schwach-: Schwach|kopf M (*inf*) dimwit (*inf*), idiot, thickie (*Brit inf*); **schwach|köp|fig** (*inf*) **ADJ** daft (*Brit inf*), idiotic **ADV** idiotically

schwäch|lich [ʃvɛçlɪç] ADJ weakly; (= *zart auch*) puny

Schwäch|lich|keit F **-**, *no pl* weakness

Schwäch|ling [ʃvɛçlɪŋ] M **-s, -e** (*lit, fig*) weakling

Schwach|ma|ti|kus [ʃvax'ma:tikʊs] M **-, -se**, **Schwach|ma|ti|ker** [ʃvax'ma:tike] M **-s, -** (*hum inf*) weakling

Schwach-: Schwach|punkt M weak point; **schwach|ra|dio|ak|tiv** ADJ △ → **schwach ADV c**; **schwach|sich|tig** [-zɪçtɪç] ADJ (*Med*) poor- *or* weak-sighted; **Schwach|sich|tig|keit** F **-**, *no pl* (*Med*) poor vision, amblyopia (*spec*); **Schwach|sinn** M (*Med*) mental deficiency, feeble-mindedness (*dated*); (*fig inf*) (= *unsinnige Tat*) idiocy *no indef art*; (= *Quatsch*) rubbish (*Brit inf*), garbage; **leichter/mittelschwerer/schwerer ~** mild/severe to moderate/profound mental deficiency, moronism/imbecility/idiocy (*Med*); **schwach|sin|nig** ADJ (*Med*) mentally deficient, feeble-minded (*dated*); (*fig inf*) daft (*Brit inf*), idiotic **ADV** (*fig inf*) idiotically; **Schwach|sin|ni|ge(r)** MF [ʃvaxzɪnɪgə] *decl as adj* mental defective; (*fig inf*) moron (*inf*), imbecile (*inf*); **Schwach|stel|le** F weak point

Schwach|strom M (*Elec*) low-voltage *or* weak current

Schwach|strom-: Schwach|strom|lei|tung F low-voltage (current) line; **Schwach|strom|tech|nik** F (*dated*) communications engineering *or* technology

Schwä|chung [ʃvɛçʊŋ] F **-, -en** weakening

schwach|win|dig ADV **morgen ~** (*Met*) light winds tomorrow

Schwa|de [ʃva:də] F **-, -n** swath(e), windrow (*spec*)

Schwa|den [ʃva:dn] M **-s, -** **a** *usu pl* (= *Dunst*) cloud **b** (= *Abgemähtes*) swath(e), windrow (*spec*)

Schwad|ron [ʃva'dro:n] F **-, -en** (*Mil Hist*) squadron

schwad|ro|neur [ʃvadro'nøːɐ] M **-s, -e** blusterer

schwad|ro|nie|ren [ʃvadro'ni:rən] *ptp* **schwadroniert** VI to bluster

Schwa|fe|lei [ʃvafə'laɪ] F **-, -en** (*pej inf*) drivel *no pl* (*inf*), twaddle *no pl* (*inf*); (= *das Schwafeln*) drivelling (*Brit*) *or* driveling (*US*) *or* blathering on (*inf*)

schwa|feln [ʃva:fln] (*pej inf*) VI to drivel (on), to blather (on), to talk drivel (*all inf*); (*in einer Prüfung*) to waffle (*inf*) **VT** **dummes Zeug ~** to talk drivel (*inf*); **was schwafelst du da?** what are you drivelling (*Brit*) *or* driveling (*US*) *or* blathering on about? (*inf*)

Schwaf|ler [ʃva:flɐ] M **-s, -**, **Schwaf|le|rin** [-ərɪn] F **-, -nen** (*pej inf*) windbag, gasbag, blather-er (*all inf*)

Schwa|ger [ʃva:gɐ] M **-s, ̈** [ʃvɛːgə] **a** brother-in-law **b** (*obs*: = *Postillion*) coachman

Schwä|ge|rin [ʃvɛːgərɪn] F **-, -nen** sister-in-law

Schwä|ger|schaft [ʃvɛːgəʃaft] F **-, -en** (*Jur*) relationship by marriage, affinity (*spec*)

Schwai|ge [ʃvaɪgə] F **-, -n** (*S Ger, Aus*) Alpine dairy hut

Schwai|ger [ʃvaɪgɐ] M **-s, -** (*S Ger, Aus*) (Alpine) dairyman

Schwai|ge|rin F **-, -nen** (*S Ger, Aus*) (Alpine) dairymaid

Schwälb|chen [ʃvɛlpçən] NT **-s, -** *dim von* **Schwalbe**

Schwal|be [ʃvalbə] F **-, -n** swallow; **eine ~ ma-chen** (*Ftbl sl*) to take a dive; **eine ~ macht noch keinen Sommer** (*Prov*) one swallow doesn't make a summer (*Prov*)

Schwal|ben-: Schwal|ben|nest NT **a** swallow's nest **b** (*Mil*) (bandsman's) epaulette **c** (*Naut*) sponson **d** (*Cook*) bird's nest soup; **Schwal|ben|nest|sup|pe** F bird's nest soup; **Schwal|ben|schwanz** M **a** (*Zool*) swallowtail (butterfly) **b** (*inf*) (= *Frack*) swallow-tailed coat, swallowtails *pl*, cutaway; (= *Frackschoß*) (swallow)tails *pl* **c** (*Tech*) dovetail; **mit einem ~ verbinden** to dovetail; **Schwal|ben|wurz** [-vʊrts] F **-, -e** (*Bot*) swallowwort

Schwall [ʃval] M **-(e)s, -e** flood, torrent; (*von Worten auch*) effusion

schwal|len [ʃvalən] (*sl*) VI to chatter on **VT** to chatter about

schwamm *pret von* **schwimmen**

Schwamm [ʃvam] M **-(e)s, ̈e** [ʃvɛmə] **a** sponge; **etw mit dem ~ abwischen** to sponge sth (down), to wipe sth with a sponge; **~ drüber!** (*inf*) (let's) forget it! **b** (*dial*: = *Pilz*) fungus; (*essbar*) mushroom; (*giftig*) toadstool **c** (= *Hausschwamm*) dry rot; **den ~ haben** to have dry rot **d** (= *Feuerschwamm*) touchwood, tinder, punk *all no pl* **e** (*Zool*) sponge

Schwämm|chen [ʃvɛmçən] NT **-s, -** **a** *dim von* **Schwamm b** (*Med*) thrush

Schwamm|merl [ʃvamɐl] NT **-s, -(n)** (*inf*: *S Ger, Aus*) = **Schwamm b**

schwam|mig [ʃvamɪç] **ADJ** **a** (*lit*) spongy **b** (*fig*) Gesicht, Hände puffy, bloated; (= *vage*) Be-

griff, Gesetz, Regelung woolly **ADV** (= *vage*) vaguely

Schwamm|tuch NT *pl* **-tücher** sponge cloth

Schwan [ʃva:n] M **-(e)s, ̈e** [ʃvɛːnə] swan; **mein lieber ~** (*inf*) (*überrascht*) my goodness!; (*drohend*) my boy/girl

schwand *pret von* **schwinden**

schwa|nen [ʃva:nən] VI *impers* **ihm schwante etwas** he had forebodings, he sensed something might happen; **mir schwant nichts Gutes** I don't like it, I've a feeling something bad is going to happen

Schwa|nen-: Schwa|nen|ge|sang M (*fig*) swan song; **Schwa|nen|hals** M swan's neck; (*fig*) swanlike neck; (*Tech*) gooseneck, swan neck; **Schwa|nen|jung|frau** F (*Myth*) swan maiden; **Schwa|nen|see** M Swan Lake; **Schwa|nen|teich** M swan pond; **schwa|nen|weiß** ADJ (*geh*) lily-white

schwang *pret von* **schwingen**

Schwang [ʃvaŋ] M **im ~(e) sein** to be in vogue, to be "in" (*inf*); (= *in der Entwicklung*) to be a-foot; **in ~ kommen** to come into vogue

schwan|ger [ʃvaŋɐ] ADJ pregnant; **~ sein** *or* **gehen** to be pregnant; **mit etw ~ gehen** (*fig*) to be big with sth; **mit großen Ideen ~ gehen** (*fig*) to be full of great ideas

Schwan|ge|re [ʃvaŋərə] F *decl as adj* pregnant woman

schwän|gern [ʃvɛŋɐn] VT to make pregnant, to impregnate (*form*); **mit etw geschwängert sein** (*fig*) to be impregnated with sth; **die Luft war mit Rauch/Weihrauch geschwängert** the air was thick with smoke/heavy *or* impregnated with incense

Schwan|ger|schaft [ʃvaŋɐʃaft] F **-, -en** pregnancy

Schwan|ger|schafts-: Schwan|ger|schafts|ab|bruch M termination of pregnancy, abortion; **Schwan|ger|schafts|gym|nas|tik** F antenatal (*esp Brit*) *or* prenatal exercises *pl*; **Schwan|ger|schafts|kon|flikt|be|ra|tung** F counselling (*Brit*) *or* counseling (*US*) on pregnancy options; **Schwan|ger|schafts|mo|nat** M month of pregnancy; **im dritten ~ sein** to be three months pregnant; **Schwan|ger|schafts|nach|weis** M pregnancy test; **Schwan|ger|schafts|nar|be** F , **Schwan|ger|schafts|strei|fen** M stretchmark; **Schwan|ger|schafts|test** M pregnancy test; **Schwan|ger|schafts|un|ter|bre|chung** F termination of pregnancy; **Schwan|ger|schafts|ver|hü|tung** F contraception; **Schwan|ger|schafts|wo|che** F week of pregnancy

Schwän|ge|rung [ʃvɛŋərʊŋ] F **-, -en** die ~ einer Frau making a woman pregnant

schwank [ʃvaŋk] ADJ (*poet*) ~en Schrittes with faltering steps, shakily, falteringly

Schwank [ʃvaŋk] M **-(e)s, ̈e** [ʃvɛŋkə] (*Liter*) merry *or* comical tale (*esp Brit*), comical story; (*Theat*) farce; **ein ~ aus der Jugendzeit** (*hum*) a tale of one's youthful exploits

schwan|ken [ʃvaŋkn] VI **a** (= *wanken, sich wiegen*) to sway; (*Schiff*) (*auf und ab*) to pitch; (*seitwärts*) to roll; (= *beben*) to shake, to rock; **der Boden schwankte unter meinen Füßen** (*lit, fig*) the ground rocked beneath my feet **b** *aux sein* (= *gehen*) to stagger, to totter **c** (*Preise, Temperatur, Stimmung etc*) to fluctuate, to vary; (*Gebrauch, Schätzungen, Angaben*) to vary; (*Phys, Math*) to fluctuate (*Kompassnadel etc*) to swing, to oscillate **d** (= *hin und her gerissen werden*) to vacillate; (= *wechseln*) to alternate; **sie schwankte zwischen Stolz und Mitleid** she alternated between pride and pity **e** (= *zögern*) to hesitate; (= *sich nicht schlüssig sein*) to waver, to vacillate; **~, ob** to hesitate as to whether, to be undecided (as to) whether **f** **ins Schwanken kommen** *or* **geraten** (*Baum, Gebäude etc*) to start to sway; (*Erde*) to start to shake *or* rock; (*Preise, Kurs, Temperatur etc*) to start to fluctuate or vary; (Autorität, Überzeugung etc) to begin to waver; (Institution) to begin to totter

schwan|kend ADJ **a** (= wankend, sich wiegend) swaying; Schiff (auf und ab) pitching; (seitwärts) rolling; (= bebend) shaking, rocking; **auf ~en Füßen stehen** (fig) to be shaky; **auf ~em Boden stehen** (fig) to be on shaky ground **b** Mensch staggering; Gang rolling; Schritt unsteady **c** Preise, Temperatur, Stimmung etc fluctuating esp attr; Gebrauch varying; Kompassnadel etc oscillating **d** (= unschlüssig) uncertain, wavering attr; (= zögernd) hesitant; (= unbeständig) vacillating, unsteady; **jdn ~ machen** to make sb waver; **~ werden** to waver; **sie ist sehr ~ in ihren Entschlüssen** she vacillates a lot

Schwan|kung F **-, -en** **a** (hin und her) swaying no pl; (auf und ab) shaking no pl, rocking no pl; **um die ~en des Turms zu messen** to measure the extent to which the tower sways **b** (von Preisen, Temperatur, Stimmung etc) fluctuation, variation (+gen in); (von Kompassnadel etc) oscillation; **seelische ~en** fluctuations in one's mental state, mental ups and downs (inf)

Schwan|kungs|be|reich M range

Schwanz [ʃvants] M **-es, ⸚e** [ˈʃvɛntsə] **a** (lit, fig) tail; (inf: von Zug) (tail) end; **den ~ zwischen die Beine klemmen und abhauen** (lit, fig sl) to put one's tail between one's legs and run; **den ~ hängen lassen** (lit) to let its tail droop; (fig inf) to be down in the dumps (inf); **das Pferd or den Gaul beim or am ~ aufzäumen** to do things back to front; **kein ~** (inf) not a (blessed) soul (inf) → **treten** VI **c** **b** (sl: = Penis) prick (sl), cock (sl)

Schwänz|chen [ˈʃvɛntsçən] NT **-s, -** dim von **Schwanz**

Schwän|ze|lei [ʃvɛntsəˈlai] F **-, no pl** (fig pej: von Mensch) crawling (inf)

schwän|zeln [ˈʃvɛntsln] VI **a** (Hund: = mit dem Schwanz wedeln) to wag its tail **b** (fig pej: Mensch) to crawl (inf) **c** aux sein (= geziert gehen) to sashay (inf)

schwän|zen [ˈʃvɛntsn] (inf) **VT** Stunde, Vorlesung to skip (inf), to cut (inf); Schule to play truant (esp Brit) or hooky (esp US inf) from, to skive off (Brit inf) **VI** to play truant (esp Brit), to play hooky (esp US inf), to skive (Brit inf)

Schwanz-: **Schwanz|en|de** NT end or tip of the tail; (fig) tail end; (von Flugzeug) tail; **Schwanz|fe|der** F tail feather; **Schwanz|flos|se** F tail or caudal fin; (Aviat) tail fin; **schwanz|ge|steu|ert** ADJ (vulg pej) dick-driven (vulg pej); **schwanz|las|tig** [-lastıç] ADJ (Aviat) tail-heavy; **schwanz|los** ADJ tailless (auch Aviat); **Schwanz|lurch** M (Zool) caudate (spec), urodele (spec); **Schwanz|lut|scher** M (sl) prick (sl); **Schwanz|mei|se** M (Orn) long-tailed tit; **Schwanz|spit|ze** F tip of the/its tail; **Schwanz|sta|chel** M (Zool) sting (in the tail); **Schwanz|wir|bel** M (Anat) caudal vertebra

schwapp [ʃvap] INTERJ slosh, splash; (= schwups) slap, smack

Schwapp [ʃvap] M **-(e)s, -e** slosh, splash

schwap|pen [ˈʃvapn] VI **a** (Flüssigkeit) to slosh around **b** aux sein (= überschwappen) to splash, to slosh; (fig) to spill; **die Modewelle schwappt nach Europa** the fashion spills over into Europe

schwaps [ʃvaps] INTERJ = **schwapp**

Schwaps [ʃvaps] M **-(e)s, -e** slosh, splash

Schwä|re [ˈʃvɛːrə] F (liter) abscess, boil

schwä|ren [ˈʃvɛːrən] VI (liter) to fester; **eine ~de Wunde** (lit, fig) a festering sore

Schwarm [ʃvarm] M **-(e)s, ⸚e** [ˈʃvɛrmə] **a** swarm; (= Flugzeugformation) flight **b** (inf: = Angebeteter) idol; (= Schauspieler, Popsänger) idol, heart-throb (inf); (= Vorliebe) passion, big thing (inf); **der neue Englischlehrer ist ihr ~** she's got a crush on the new English teacher (inf)

schwär|men [ˈʃvɛrmən] VI **a** aux sein to swarm **b** (= begeistert reden) to enthuse (von about), to go into raptures (von about); **für jdn/etw ~** (= außerordentlich angetan sein) to be mad or wild or crazy about sb/sth (inf); (= verliebt sein, verehren auch) to worship sb/sth, to be smitten with sb/sth (liter, hum); **ins Schwärmen kommen** or **geraten** to go or fall into raptures; **ich schwärme nicht gerade für ihn** (iro) I'm not exactly crazy about him (inf)

Schwär|mer¹ [ˈʃvɛrmɐ] M **-s, -** **a** (Zool) hawk moth (esp Brit), sphinx moth (US) **b** (= Feuerwerkskörper) jumping jack

Schwär|mer² [ˈʃvɛrmɐ] M **-s, -**, **Schwär|me|rin** [-ərın] F **-, -nen** (= Begeisterter) enthusiast, zealot; (= Fantast) dreamer, visionary; (= sentimentaler Schwärmer) sentimentalist

Schwär|me|rei [ʃvɛrməˈrai] F **-, -en** (= Begeisterung) enthusiasm; (in Worten ausgedrückt) effusion no pl; (= Leidenschaft) passion; (= Verzückung) rapture; **sich in ~en über jdn/etw ergehen** to go into raptures over sb/sth; **sich in ~en verlieren** to get or become carried away

schwär|me|risch [ˈʃvɛrmərıʃ] ADJ (= begeistert) enthusiastic; Worte, Übertreibung effusive; (= verliebt) infatuated, gooey (inf); (= verzückt) enraptured; Illusion, Glaube, Gemüt fanciful; **die Romantiker hatten alle etwas Schwärmerisches** the Romantics were all filled with a great emotional passion ADV enthusiastically; (verliebt) infatuated; **seine Stimme klang ~** he sounded captivated

Schwarm-: **Schwarm|geist** M (= Fantast) visionary; (= Eiferer) zealot; **schwarm|wei|se** ADV in swarms

Schwärm|zeit F swarming time

Schwar|te [ˈʃvartə] F **-, -n** **a** (= Speckschwarte) rind; (Hunt: = Haut) skin, hide; (= Abfallholz) slab; **arbeiten, dass or bis die ~ kracht** (inf) or **knackt** (inf) to work oneself into the ground (inf) **b** (inf) (Buch) old book, tome (hum); (Gemälde) daub(ing) (pej)

Schwar|ten|ma|gen M (Cook) brawn

schwar|tig [ˈʃvartıç] ADJ (rare) rindy

schwarz [ʃvarts] ADJ comp **⸚er** [ˈʃvɛrtsə], superl **⸚este(r, s)** [ˈʃvɛrtsəstə] **a** (lit, fig) black; (= schmutzig) dirty, black; (= stark sonnengebräunt) deeply tanned, brown; **~e Blattern** or **Pocken** smallpox; **~e Diamanten** black diamonds; **der Schwarze Erdteil** the Dark Continent; **der Schwarze Freitag** Black Friday; **~es Gold** (fig) black gold; **~er Humor** black humour (Brit) or humor (US); **~er Kaffee/Tee** black coffee/tea; **die ~e Kunst** (= Buchdruckerkunst) (the art of) printing; (= Magie) the Black Art; **~e Liste** blacklist; **jdn auf die ~e Liste setzen** to blacklist sb, to put sb on the blacklist; **~es Loch** black hole; **~e Magie** black magic; **der ~e Mann** (= Schornsteinfeger) the (chimney) sweep; (= Kinderschreck) the bogeyman; (dated: = die schwarze Rasse) the Black Man, the Negro; **das Schwarze Meer** the Black Sea; **eine ~e Messe** a black mass; **Schwarzer Peter** (Cards) children's card game, ≈ old maid; **jdm den ~en Peter zuschieben** or **zuspielen** (fig) (= die Verantwortung abschieben) to pass the buck to sb (inf), to leave sb holding the baby (Brit) or bag (US); (= etw Unangenehmes abschieben) to give sb the worst of the deal; **das ~e Schaf (in der Familie)** the black sheep (of the family); **eine ~e Seele** a black or evil soul; **~er Star** (Med) amaurosis (spec); **ein ~er Tag** a black day; **der ~e Tod** the Black Death; **die Schwarze Witwe** the Black Widow (spider); **etw ~ auf weiß haben** to have sth in black and white; **etw in den schwärzesten Farben** or **~ in ~ schildern/darstellen** to describe/present sth in the blackest terms; **~ von Menschen** crowded or black with people; **~ wie die Nacht/wie Ebenholz** jet-black; **in den ~en Zahlen sein, ~e Zahlen schreiben** (Comm) to be in the black; **sich ~ ärgern** to get extremely annoyed, to get hopping mad (esp Brit inf); **er wurde ~ vor Ärger** his face went black; **mir wur-**

de ~ vor den Augen everything went black, I blacked out; **~ werden** (Cards) to lose every trick, to be whitewashed (inf); **da kannst du warten, bis du ~ wirst** (inf) you can wait till the cows come home (inf); **da kannst du schreien, bis du ~ wirst** (inf) you can shout until you're blue in the face (inf)
b (= ungesetzlich) illicit; **der ~e Markt** the black market; **~e Geschäfte machen** to do shady deals; **~es Konto** secret account
c (pej inf) (= katholisch) Catholic, Papist (pej); (Pol: = konservativ) Conservative
ADV comp **⸚er**, superl **am ⸚esten** **a** (= mit schwarzer Farbe) anstreichen, färben, lackieren black; einrichten, sich kleiden in black; **~ gestreift** with black stripes
b (= illegal) erwerben, über die Grenze gehen illegally; **sich** (dat) **etw ~ besorgen** to get sth illicitly; (= auf dem Schwarzmarkt) to get sth on the black market; **etw ~ verdienen** to earn sth on the side (inf)
c (= konservativ) **~ wählen** to vote Conservative; **dort wählen alle ~** they all vote Conservative there

Schwarz [ʃvarts] NT **-, no pl** inv black; **in ~ gehen** to wear black

Schwarz-: **Schwarz|af|ri|ka** NT Black Africa; **Schwarz|ar|beit** F illicit work, work on the side (inf); (nach Feierabend) moonlighting (inf); **schwarz+ar|bei|ten** VI sep to do illicit work, to work on the side (inf); (nach Feierabend) to moonlight (inf); **Schwarz|ar|bei|ter(in)** M(F) person doing illicit work or doing work on the side (inf); (nach Feierabend) moonlighter (inf); **schwarz|äu|gig** ADJ dark-eyed; Schönheit auch sloe-eyed (liter); **Schwarz|bee|re** F (S Ger, Aus: = Heidelbeere) bilberry (Brit), blueberry (esp US); **schwarz|blau** ADJ bluish black, inky blue; Tinte blue-black; **Schwarz|blech** NT black plate; **schwarz|braun** ADJ dark brown; **Schwarz|bren|ner(in)** M(F) illicit distiller, moonshine distiller (inf), moonshiner (inf); **Schwarz|bren|ne|rei** F illicit still, moonshine still (inf); **Schwarz|brot** NT (braun) brown rye bread; (schwarz, wie Pumpernickel) black bread, pumpernickel; **Schwarz|bun|te** [ˈʃvartsbʊntə] F decl as adj Friesian; **Schwarz|dorn** M pl **-dorne** (Bot) blackthorn; **Schwarz|dros|sel** F blackbird

Schwarze [ˈʃvartsə] F decl as adj black woman/girl; (= Schwarzhaarige) black-haired woman/girl

Schwär|ze [ˈʃvɛrtsə] F **-, -n** **a** (no pl: = Dunkelheit) blackness **b** (Farbe) black dye; (= Druckerschwärze) printer's ink

schwär|zen [ˈʃvɛrtsn] VTR to blacken

Schwar|ze(r) [ˈʃvartsə] M decl as adj black; (= Schwarzhaariger) dark(-haired) man/boy; (pej sl: = Katholik) Catholic, Papist (pej); (Aus: = schwarzer Mokka) black (mocha) coffee; **die ~n** (pej inf) the Conservatives

Schwarz|er|de F (Geol) black earth

Schwar|ze(s) [ˈʃvartsə] NT decl as adj black; (auf Zielscheibe) bull's-eye; **das kleine ~** (inf) one's/a little black dress; **ins ~ treffen** (lit, fig) to score a bull's-eye; **jdm nicht das ~ unter den Nägeln gönnen** (dated) to begrudge sb the very air he/she breathes

Schwarz-: **schwarz+fah|ren** VI sep aux sein (ohne zu zahlen) to travel without paying, to dodge paying the fare (inf); (ohne Führerschein) to drive without a licence (Brit) or license (US); **Schwarz|fah|rer(in)** M(F) fare dodger (inf); (ohne Führerschein) driver without a licence (Brit) or license (US); **Schwarz|fahrt** F ride without paying; (ohne Führerschein) drive without a licence (Brit) or license (US); **sie wurde bei einer ~ geschnappt** she was caught travelling (Brit) or traveling (US) without a ticket or taking a free ride (inf)/driving without a licence (Brit) or license (US); **Schwarz|fäu|le** F (Bot) black rot; **Schwarz|film** M (Typ) film; **Schwarz|fil|ter** M (Phot) black filter;

Schwarz|geld NT illegal earnings *pl*; **schwarz|ge|streift** △ ADJ *attr* → **schwarz** ADV a; **schwarz|grau** ADJ grey-black (*Brit*), gray-black (*US*), greyish-black (*Brit*), grayish-black (*US*); **schwarz|haa|rig** ADJ black-haired; **eine Schwarzhaarige** a black-haired woman/girl; **Schwarz|han|del** M *no pl* black market; (= *Tätigkeit*) black marketeering; **im ~** on the black market; **Schwarz|händ|ler(in)** M(F) black marketeer; **Schwarz|hem|den** PL (*Hist*) Blackshirts *pl*; **schwarz|hö|ren** △ *sep* (*Rad*) to use a radio without having a licence (*Brit*) or license (*US*); **Schwarz|hö|rer(in)** M(F) (*Rad*) radio-owner without a licence (*Brit*) or license (*US*); **Schwarz|kit|tel** M (*inf*) wild boar; (*pej*: = *Geistlicher*) priest

Schwarz|kon|to NT secret account

schwärz|lich ['ʃvɛrtslɪç] ADJ blackish; *Haut* dusky

Schwarz-: schwarz ma|len ▲ ▼ to be pessimistic ▼ to be pessimistic about; **Schwarz|ma|ler(in)** M(F) pessimist; **Schwarz|ma|le|rei** F pessimism; **Schwarz|markt** M black market; **Schwarz|markt|händ|ler(in)** M(F) black marketeer; **Schwarz|markt|preis** M black-market price; **Schwarz|meer|flot|te** F Black Sea fleet; **Schwarz|pap|pel** F black poplar; **Schwarz|pul|ver** NT black (gun)powder; **Schwarz|rock** M (*pej*) priest; **Schwarz|rot|gold** ▲ NT, **Schwarz-Rot-Gold** NT **die Far-ben/Fahne Schwarz-Rot-Gold** the black-red-and-gold colours (*Brit*) or colors (*US*)/flag (of Germany); **schwarz|rot|gol|den**, **schwarz-rot-gol|den** ▲ ADJ *Fahne* black-red-and-gold; **schwarz+schlach|ten** *sep* ▼ to slaughter pigs *etc* illegally or illicitly ▼ to slaughter illegally or illicitly; **schwarz se|hen** ▲ *irreg* ▼ to be pessimistic about ▼ to be pessimistic; **für jdn/ etw ~** to be pessimistic about sb/sth; **schwarz+sehen** ▼ *sep irreg* (*TV*) to watch TV without a licence (*Brit*) or license (*US*); **Schwarz|se|her(in)** M(F) a pessimist b (*TV*) somebody watching TV without a licence, (*TV*) licence-dodger (*Brit inf*); **Schwarz|se|he|rei** [-zeːəˈraɪ] F *no pl* pessimism; **schwarz|se|he|risch** ADJ pessimistic, gloomy; **Schwarz|sen|der** M pirate (radio) station; **Schwarz|specht** M black woodpecker; **Schwarz|storch** M black stork; **Schwarz|tee** M black tea

Schwär|zung ['ʃvɛrtsʊŋ] F -, -en blackening

Schwarz-: Schwarz|wald M Black Forest; **Schwarz|wäl|der** [-vɛldɐ] ADJ *attr* Black Forest; **~ Kirschtorte** Black Forest gateau (*Brit*) or cake (*US*); **~ Kirschwasser** kirsch; **Schwarz|wäl|der** M -s, -, **Schwarz|wäl|de|rin** [-ərɪn] F -, -nen person from the Black Forest

schwarz|weiß, **schwarz-weiß** ▲ ADJ black-and-white *attr*, black and white; **~ gepunktet/gestreift** with black and white polka dots/stripes

Schwarz|weiß-: Schwarz|weiß|auf|nah|me F black-and-white (shot); **Schwarz|weiß|emp|fän|ger** M black-and-white or monochrome set; **Schwarz|weiß|fern|se|hen** NT black-and-white or monochrome television; **Schwarz|weiß|fern|se|her** M black-and-white or monochrome television (set); **Schwarz|weiß|film** M black-and-white film; **Schwarz|weiß|fo|to** NT black-and-white (photo); **Schwarz|weiß|ge|rät** NT black-and-white or monochrome set; **schwarz|weiß ma|len** ▲, **schwarz-weiß ma|len** ▲ VTI *sep* (*fig*) to depict in black and white (terms); **das kann man doch nicht so ~** it's not as black and white as that; **Schwarz|weiß|ma|le|rei** F (*fig*) black-and-white portrayal; **die ~ älterer Geschichtsbücher** the way older history books make everything seem black and white or reduce everything to black and white (terms); **schwarz|weiß-rot**, **schwarz-weiß-rot** ▲ ADJ black-white-and-red (*relating to the German imperial*

flag); **Schwarz|weiß|rot** NT, **Schwarz--weiß-rot** ▲ NT **die Farben/Fahne ~** the black-white-and-red colours (*Brit*) or colors (*US*)/flag; **Schwarz|weiß|zeich|nung** F black-and-white (drawing)

Schwarz-: Schwarz|wild NT wild boars *pl*; **Schwarz|wur|zel** F viper's grass; (*Cook*) salsify

Schwatz [ʃvats] M -es, -e (*inf*) chat, chinwag (*Brit inf*); **auf einen ~ kommen** to come (round *Brit*) or by) for a chat

Schwatz|ba|se F, (*S Ger*) **Schwätz|ba|se** F (*inf*) gossip

Schwätz|chen ['ʃvɛtsçən] NT -s, - *dim von* **Schwatz**

schwat|zen ['ʃvatsn] ▼ to talk; (*pej*) (*unaufhörlich*) to chatter; (*über belanglose, oberflächliche Dinge, kindisch*) to prattle; (= *Unsinn reden*) to blather (*inf*); (= *klatschen*) to gossip; **über Politik ~** to prattle on about politics (*pej*) ▼ to talk; **dummes Zeug ~** to talk a lot of rubbish (*esp Brit inf*) or drivel (*inf*)

schwät|zen ['ʃvɛtsn] VTI (*S Ger, Aus*) = **schwatzen**

Schwät|zer ['ʃvɛtsɐ] M -s, -, **Schwät|ze|rin** [-ərɪn] F -, -nen (*pej*) chatterer, chatterbox (*inf*); (= *Schwafler*) windbag, gasbag, blether (*all inf*); (= *Klatschmaul*) gossip

Schwät|ze|rei [ʃvɛtsəˈraɪ] F -, -en (*pej*) (= *Gerede, im Unterricht*) talk, chatter; (*über Belanglosigkeiten, kindisch*) prattle; (= *Unsinn*) drivel (*inf*); (= *Klatsch*) gossip

schwät|ze|risch ['ʃvɛtsərɪʃ] ADJ windy (*inf*), gassy (*inf*)

schwatz|haft ADJ (= *geschwätzig*) talkative, garrulous; (= *klatschsüchtig*) gossipy

Schwatz|haf|tig|keit ['ʃvatshaftɪçkaɪt] F -, *no pl* (= *Geschwätzigkeit*) garrulousness, talkativeness; (= *Klatschsucht*) gossipy nature

Schwe|be ['ʃveːbə] F -, *no pl* **sich in der ~ halten** (*Ballon*) to hover, to float in the air; (*Waage*) to balance; (*fig*) to hang in the balance; **in der ~ sein/bleiben** (*fig*) to be/remain in the balance, to be/remain undecided; (*Jur, Comm*) to be/remain pending

Schwe|be-: Schwe|be|bahn F suspension railway; (= *Seilbahn*) cable railway; **Schwe|be|bal|ken** M, **Schwe|be|baum** M (*Sport*) beam

schwe|ben ['ʃveːbn] ▼ a (= *frei im Raum stehen, hängen*) (*Nebel, Rauch*) to hang; (*in der Luft*) to hang, to float; (*Wolke*) to float; (*in Flüssigkeit*) to float; (*an Seil etc*) to hang, to dangle; (= *sich unbeweglich in der Luft halten: Geier etc*) to hover; (= *nachklingen, zurückbleiben: Klänge, Parfüm*) to linger (on); **und der Geist Gottes schwebte über den Wassern** (*Bibl*) and the Spirit of the Lord moved over the waters (*Bibl*); **und über allem schwebt ...** and over everything there hangs ...; **ihr war, als ob sie schwebte** she felt she was walking or floating on air; **etw schwebt jdm vor Augen** (*fig*) sb envisages sth, sb has sth in mind; (*Bild*) sb sees sth in his mind's eye; **in großer Gefahr ~** to be in great danger; **der Verletzte schwebt in Lebensgefahr** the injured man is in a critical condition; **in höheren Regionen** or **Sphären ~**, **über** or **in den Wolken ~** (*fig*) to have one's head in the clouds b *aux sein* (= *durch die Luft gleiten*) to float, to sail; (= *hochschweben*) to soar; (= *niederschweben*) to float down; (*an Seil etc*) to swing; (*mit Fahrstuhl*) to soar, to zoom; (= *sich leichtfüßig bewegen*) to glide, to float c (= *schwanken*) to hover, to waver; (*Angelegenheit*) to hang or be in the balance, to be undecided; (*Jur*) to be pending

schwe|bend ADJ (*Tech, Chem*) suspended; (*fig*) *Fragen etc* unresolved, undecided; (*Musik, Rhythmus*) floating; (*Jur*) *Verfahren* pending; (*Comm*) *Geschäft* pending; *Schulden* floating; (*Poet*) *Betonung* hovering

Schwe|be-: Schwe|be|zug M hovertrain; **Schwe|be|zu|stand** M (*fig*) state of suspense; (*zwischen zwei Stadien*) in-between state

Schweb-: Schweb|flie|ge F hover fly, ≈ sweat bee (*US*); **Schweb|staub** M floating dust; **Schweb|stoff** M suspended matter; (*in Luft*) airborne particles *pl*

Schwe|de ['ʃveːdə] M -n, -n, **Schwe|din** ['ʃveːdɪn] F -, -nen Swede; **alter ~** (*inf*) (my) old fruit (*Brit inf*) or chap (*inf*) or buddy (*esp US inf*)

Schwe|den ['ʃveːdn] NT -s Sweden

Schwe|den-: Schwe|den|plat|te F (*Cook*) smorgasbord; **Schwe|den|punsch** M arrack punch, Swedish punch; **Schwe|den|stahl** M Swedish steel

Schwe|din F -, -nen Swede, Swedish woman/girl

schwe|disch ['ʃveːdɪʃ] ADJ Swedish; **hinter ~en Gardinen** (*inf*) behind bars; **hinter ~e Gardinen kommen** (*inf*) to be put behind bars

Schwe|disch(e) ['ʃveːdɪʃ] NT Swedish → *auch* **Deutsch(e)**

Schwe|fel ['ʃveːfl] M -s, *no pl* (*abbr* **S**) sulphur (*Brit*), sulfur (*US*), brimstone (*old, Bibl*)

Schwe|fel- *in cpds* sulphur (*Brit*), sulfur (*US*); **schwe|fel|ar|tig** ADJ sulphur(e)ous (*Brit*), sulfurous (*US*); **Schwe|fel|blu|me** F, **Schwe|fel|blü|te** F flowers of sulphur (*Brit*) or sulfur (*US*); **Schwe|fel|di|o|xid** NT sulphur (*Brit*) or sulfur (*US*) dioxide; **schwe|fel|gelb** ADJ sulphurous (*Brit*) or sulfurous (*US*) yellow; **schwe|fel|hal|tig** ADJ containing sulphur (*Brit*) or sulfur (*US*), sulphur(e)ous (*Brit*), sulfurous (*US*); **Schwe|fel|hölz|chen** NT (*old*) match, lucifer (*old*)

schwe|fe|lig ['ʃveːfəlɪç] ADJ, ADV = **schweflig**

Schwe|fel-: Schwe|fel|kies M iron pyrites *sing* or *pl*; **Schwe|fel|koh|len|stoff** M carbon disulphide (*Brit*) or disulfide (*US*)

schwe|feln ['ʃveːfln] VT to sulphurize (*Brit*), to sulfurize (*US*)

schwe|fel|sau|er ADJ (*Chem*) sulphuric (*Brit*), sulfuric (*US*); (*in bestimmten Verbindungen auch*) sulphate (*Brit*) or sulfate (*US*) of

Schwe|fel|säu|re F sulphuric (*Brit*) or sulfuric (*US*) acid

Schwe|fe|lung F -, -en sulphurization (*Brit*), surfurization (*US*)

Schwe|fel-: Schwe|fel|ver|bin|dung F sulphur (*Brit*) or sulfur (*US*) compound; **Schwe|fel|was|ser|stoff** M hydrogen sulphide (*Brit*) or sulfide (*US*), sulphuretted (*Brit*) or sulfureted (*US*) hydrogen

schwef|lig ['ʃveːflɪç] ADJ sulphurous (*Brit*), sulfurous (*US*) ADV **es roch ~** there was a smell of sulphur (*Brit*) or sulfur (*US*)

Schweif [ʃvaɪf] M -(e)s, -e (*auch Astron*) tail

schwei|fen ['ʃvaɪfn] ▼ *aux sein* (*lit geh, fig*) to roam, to wander, to rove; **warum in die Ferne ~?** why roam so far afield?; **seine Gedanken in die Vergangenheit ~ lassen** to let one's thoughts roam or wander over the past; **seinen Blick ~ lassen** to let one's eyes wonder (*über etw acc* over sth) ▼ *Bretter, Blechgefäß* to curve → *auch* **geschweift**

Schweif-: Schweif|haar NT tail hair(s *pl*); **Schweif|sä|ge** F fret saw; **Schweif|stern** M comet

Schwei|fung ['ʃvaɪfʊŋ] F -, -en curving; (= *geschweifte Form*) curve

schweif|we|deln ['ʃvaɪfveːdln] VI *insep* (*Hund*) to wag its tail; (*fig old*: = *liebedienern*) to fawn

Schwei|ge-: Schwei|ge|an|ruf M *telephone call during which the caller remains silent*, silent call; **Schwei|ge|geld** NT hush money; **Schwei|ge|marsch** M silent march (of protest); **Schwei|ge|mi|nu|te** F one minute('s) silence

schwei|gen ['ʃvaɪgn] *pret* **schwieg** [ʃviːk], *ptp* **ge|schwiegen** [gəˈʃviːgn] VI to be silent; (= *still sein* *auch*) to keep quiet; (= *sich nicht äußern auch*) to remain silent, to say nothing; (= *aufhören: Musik, Geräusch, Wind*) to cease, to stop; **~ Sie!** be silent *or* quiet!; **kannst du ~?** can you keep a secret?; **seit gestern ~ die Waffen** yesterday the guns fell silent; **plötzlich schwieg er** suddenly he fell *or* went silent; **er kann ~ wie ein Grab** he knows how to keep quiet; **auf etw** (*acc*)**/zu etw ~** to make no reply to sth; **ganz zu ~ von ..., von ... ganz zu ~** to say nothing of ...

Schwei|gen NT **-s**, *no pl* silence; **jdn zum ~ bringen** to silence sb (*auch euph*); (**es herrscht**) **~ im Walde** (there is) dead silence → **reden** VI a

schwei|gend ADJ silent; **die ~e Mehrheit** the silent majority ADV in silence, silently; **~ verharren** to remain silent; **~ über etw** (*acc*) **hinweggehen** to pass over sth in silence

Schwei|ge|pflicht F pledge of secrecy; (*von Anwalt*) requirement of confidentiality; **die ärztliche ~** medical confidentiality *or* secrecy; **die priesterliche ~** a priest's duty to remain silent; **unter ~ stehen** to be bound to observe confidentiality; **jdn von der ~ entbinden** to release sb from his/her duty of confidentiality

Schwei|ger [ˈʃvaigɐ] M **-s**, **-**, **Schwei|ge|rin** [-ərɪn] M **-, -nen** man/woman of few words; **der große ~** the strong silent type; (*als Beiname*) **the silent**

schweig|sam [ˈʃvaikzaːm] ADJ silent, quiet; (*als Charaktereigenschaft*) silent, taciturn; (= *verschwiegen*) discreet

Schweig|sam|keit F **-**, *no pl* silence, quietness; (*als Charaktereigenschaft*) silent manner, taciturnity

Schwein [ʃvain] NT **-s**, **-e** a pig, hog (*US*); (*Fleisch*) pork; **sich wie die ~e benehmen** (*inf*) to behave like pigs (*inf*); **bluten wie ein ~** (*inf*) to bleed like a stuck pig; **mit jdm (zusammen) ~e gehütet haben** (*inf*) to be on familiar terms (with sb); **ich glaub, mein ~ pfeift!** (*dated sl*) blow me down! (*dated inf*), well kiss my ass! (*US sl*) b (*inf: Mensch*) pig (*inf*), swine; (= *Schweinehund*) swine (*inf*), bastard (*sl*); **ein armes/faules ~** a poor/lazy sod (*Brit sl*) *or* bastard (*sl*); **kein ~** nobody, not one single person c *no pl* (= *Glück*) ~ **haben** to be lucky; **~ gehabt!** that's a stroke of luck

Schwein|chen [ˈʃvainçən] NT **-s**, **-** *dim von* **Schwein** little pig, piglet; (*baby-talk*) piggy(-wiggy) (*baby-talk*); (*fig inf*) = *kleiner Schmutzfink*) mucky pup (*inf*), messy thing (*esp US inf*)

Schwei|ne-: **Schwei|ne|ar|beit** F (*inf*) (*schmutzig*) dirty work; (*schwierig*) ghastly job; **Schwei|ne|ba|cke** F (*sl*: = *Mann*) fat bastard (*sl*); **Schwei|ne|ban|de** F (*fig inf*) pack; **Schwei|ne|bauch** M (*Cook*) belly of pork; **Schwei|ne|bra|ten** M joint of pork; (*gekocht*) roast pork; **Schwei|ne|bucht** F (*Geog*) **die ~** the Bay of Pigs; **Schwei|ne|fett** NT pig fat; **Schwei|ne|fi|let** NT fillet of pork; **Schwei|ne|fleisch** NT pork; **Schwei|ne|fraß** M (*fig inf*) muck (*inf*); **Schwei|ne|fut|ter** NT pig feed; (*flüssig*) pig swill; **Schwei|ne|geld** NT (*inf*) **ein ~** a packet (*Brit inf*), a fistful (*US inf*); **Schwei|ne|hal|tung** F pig-keeping; **Schwei|ne|hirt(in)** M(F) , **Schwei|ne|hir|te** M (*esp liter*) swineherd (*esp old, liter*); **Schwei|ne|hund** M (*inf*) bastard (*sl*), swine (*inf*); **den inneren ~ überwinden** (*inf*) to conquer one's weaker self; **Schwei|ne|kerl** M (*inf*) swine (*inf*), bastard (*sl*); **Schwei|ne|ko|ben** [-koːbn] M **-s**, **-**, **Schwei|ne|ko|fen** [-koːfn] M **-s**, **-** pigsty, pigpen (*esp US*); **Schwei|ne|ko|te|lett** NT pork chop; **Schwei|ne|len|de** F pork tenderloin; **~ in Blätterteig** tenderloin en croute; **Schwei|ne|mast** F pig-fattening; (*Futter*) pig food; **Schwei|ne|mäs|te|rei** F piggery; **Schwei|ne|mett** NT (*N Ger Cook*) minced (*esp Brit*) *or* ground (*US*) pork; **Schwei|ne|pack** NT (*pej inf*) vermin; **Schwei|ne|pest** F (*Vet*) swine fever; **Schwei|ne|pries|ter** M (*pej inf*) bastard (*sl*)

Schwei|ne|rei [ʃvainəˈrai] F **-**, **-en** (*inf*) a *no pl* mess; **es ist eine ~, wenn ...** it's disgusting if ...; **so eine ~!** how disgusting!; **Fische zu schuppen ist eine ~** scaling fish is a messy business b (= *Skandal*) scandal; (= *Gemeinheit*) dirty *or* mean trick (*inf*); **ich finde es eine ~, wie er sie behandelt** I think it's disgusting the way he treats her; (**so eine**) **~!** what a dirty trick! (*inf*) c (= *Zote*) smutty *or* dirty joke; (= *unzüchtige Handlung*) indecent act; **~en machen** to do dirty *or* filthy things; **das Buch besteht nur aus ~en** the book is just a lot of dirt *or* filth d (*iro: = Leckerbissen*) delicacy

Schwei|ne-: **Schwei|ne|ripp|chen** NT (*Cook*) cured pork chop; **Schwei|ne|rot|lauf** M (*Vet*) swine erysipelas (*spec*)

schwei|nern [ˈʃvainɐn] ADJ pork; **Schweinernes** pork

Schwei|ne-: **Schwei|ne|rüs|sel** M pig's snout; **Schwei|ne|schmalz** NT dripping (*Brit*), drippings *pl* (*US*); (*als Kochfett*) lard; **Schwei|ne|schnit|zel** NT pork cutlet, escalope of pork; **Schwei|ne|stall** M (*lit, fig*) pigsty, pigpen (*esp US*); (= *korruptes System*) corrupt shambles *sing*; **Schwei|ne|zucht** F pig-breeding; (*Hof*) pig farm; **Schwei|ne|züch|ter(in)** M(F) pig-breeder

Schwein|igel [ˈʃvainˌiːgl] M (*inf*) dirty pig (*inf*) *or* so-and-so (*inf*)

Schwein|ige|lei [ʃvainiːgəˈlai] F **-**, **-en** (*inf*) (*Witz*) dirty *or* smutty joke; (*Bemerkung*) dirty *or* smutty remark; (= *das Schweinigeln*) dirty *or* smutty jokes *pl*/remarks *pl*

schwein|igeln [ˈʃvainiːgln] VI *insep* (*inf*) (= *Witze erzählen*) to tell dirty jokes; (= *Bemerkungen machen*) to make dirty *or* smutty remarks; (= *Schmutz machen*) to make a mess

schwei|nisch [ˈʃvainɪʃ] (*inf*) ADJ *Benehmen* piggish (*inf*), swinish (*inf*); *Witz* dirty ADV like a pig; **benimm dich nicht so ~!** stop behaving like a pig!

Schwein|kram M (*inf*) dirt, filth

Schweins-: **Schweins|au|gen** PL , **Schweins|äug|lein** [-ɔyklain] PL (*inf*) piggy eyes *pl* (*inf*); **Schweins|bla|se** F pig's bladder; **Schweins|bors|te** F pig's bristle; **Schweins|fü|ße** PL (*Cook dial*) (pig's) trotters *pl*; **Schweins|ga|lopp** M **im ~ davonlaufen** (*hum inf*) to go galumphing (*esp Brit*) *or* galloping off (*inf*); **Schweins|ha|xe** F (*S Ger Cook*) knuckle of pork; **Schweins|kopf** M (*Cook*) pig's head; **Schweins|le|der** NT pigskin; **schweins|le|dern** ADJ pigskin; **Schweins|ohr** NT a pig's ear; (*Gebäck*) (kidney-shaped) pastry b (*Bot*) (= *Kalla*) calla (lily); (*Pilz*) cantharellus clavatus (*spec*); **Schweins|stel|ze** F (*Aus*) (pig's) trotters *pl*

Schweiß [ʃvais] M **-es**, *no pl* sweat; (*von Mensch auch*) perspiration; (*Hunt*) blood; **in ~ geraten** *or* **kommen** to break into a sweat, to start sweating/perspiring; **der ~ brach ihm aus allen Poren** he was absolutely dripping with sweat; **der ~ brach ihm aus** he broke out in a sweat; **nass von ~** soaked with perspiration *or* sweat; **kalter ~** cold sweat; **das hat viel ~ gekostet** it was a sweat (*inf*); **im ~e seines Angesichts** (*Bibl, liter*) in the sweat of his brow (*Bibl*); (*liter*) **die Früchte seines ~es** (*liter*) the fruits of his toil *or* labour(s) (*Brit*) *or* labor (*US*)

Schweiß-: **Schweiß|ab|son|de|rung** F perspiration; **Schweiß|ap|pa|rat** M welding equipment *no indef art, no pl*; **Schweiß|aus|bruch** M sweating *no indef art, no pl*; **Schweiß|band** [-bant] NT *pl* **-bänder** sweatband; **schweiß|bar** ADJ (*Tech*) weldable; **schweiß|be|deckt** ADJ covered in sweat; **schweiß|bläs|chen** [-blɛːsçən] PL (*Med*) prickly heat *sing*, miliaria *sing* (*spec*); **Schweiß|bren|ner** M (*Tech*) welding torch; **Schweiß|bril|le** F (*Tech*) welding goggles *pl*; **Schweiß|draht** M (*Tech*) welding rod *or* wire; **Schweiß|drü|se** F (*Anat*) sweat *or* perspiratory (*form*) gland

schwei|ßen [ˈʃvaisn] VT (*Tech*) to weld VI a (*Tech*) to weld b (*Hunt*) to bleed

Schwei|ßer [ˈʃvaisɐ] M **-s**, **-**, **Schwei|ße|rin** [-ərɪn] F **-, -nen** (*Tech*) welder

Schweiß-: **Schweiß|fähr|te** F (*Hunt*) trail of blood, blood track; **Schweiß|flam|me** F welding flame; **Schweiß|fleck** M sweat stain, perspiration mark; **Schweiß|fuß** M sweaty foot; **schweiß|ge|ba|det** [-gəbaːdət] ADJ bathed in sweat; *Mensch auch* bathed in perspiration; **Schweiß|ge|ruch** M smell of sweat *or* perspiration; **Schweiß|hand** F sweaty palm; **Schweiß|hund** M (*Hunt*) bloodhound

schwei|ßig [ˈʃvaisɪç] ADJ sweaty; (*Hunt*) *Tier* bleeding; *Fährte* bloody

Schweiß-: **Schweiß|naht** F (*Tech*) weld, welded joint; **schweiß|nass** ▲ ADJ sweaty; **Schweiß|per|le** F bead of perspiration *or* sweat; **Schweiß|ro|bo|ter** M welding robot; **Schweiß|stahl** M welding steel; **Schweiß|stel|le** F weld; **Schweiß|tech|nik** F welding (engineering); **schweiß|trei|bend** ADJ *Tätigkeit* that makes one sweat, sudorific (*spec*); **~es Mittel** sudorific (*spec*); **schweiß|trie|fend** ADJ dripping with perspiration *or* sweat; **Schweiß|trop|fen** M drop of sweat *or* perspiration; **Schweiß|tuch** NT *pl* **-tücher** a (*obs:* = *Taschentuch*) handkerchief b **das ~ der Veronika** the sudarium, Veronica's veil; **schweiß|über|strömt** [-lyːbəʃtrøːmt] ADJ streaming *or* running with sweat

Schwei|ßung [ˈʃvaisʊŋ] F **-**, **-en** welding; (*Naht, Stelle*) weld

Schweiz [ʃvaits] F **die ~** Switzerland

Schwei|zer[1] [ˈʃvaitsɐ] M **-s**, **-** a (= *Melker*) dairyman b (*Eccl:* = *Pförtner*) beadle, usher c (= *päpstlicher Leibgardist*) Swiss Guard ADJ *attr* Swiss; **~ Käse** Swiss cheese

Schwei|zer[2] [ˈʃvaitsɐ] M **-s**, **-**, **Schwei|ze|rin** [-ərɪn] F **-, -nen** Swiss

Schwei|zer-: **Schwei|zer|de|gen** M (*Typ*) compositor-printer; **schwei|zer|deutsch** ADJ Swiss-German; **Schwei|zer|deutsch(e)** NT Swiss German → *auch* **Deutsch(e)**; **Schwei|zer|fran|ken** M Swiss franc; **Schwei|zer|gar|de** F Swiss Guard

Schwei|ze|rin F **-, -nen** Swiss (woman/girl)

schwei|ze|risch [ˈʃvaitsərɪʃ] ADJ Swiss

Schwei|zer|mes|ser NT Swiss army knife

Schwell|brand M smouldering (*Brit*) *or* smoldering (*US*) fire

schwel|len [ˈʃveːlən] VI (*lit, fig*) to smoulder (*Brit*), to smolder (*US*) VT *Rasen* to burn off (slowly); *Koks* to carbonize at a low temperature

schwel|gen [ˈʃvɛlgn] VI to indulge oneself (*in* +*dat* in); **von Schwelgen und Prassen hat er nichts gehalten** he had no time for self-indulgence and feasting; **wir schwelgten in Kaviar und Sekt** we feasted on caviar and champagne; **in Erinnerungen ~** to revel in reminiscences; **in Farben/Worten ~** to revel in colour (*Brit*) *or* color (*US*)/in the sound of words; **im Überfluss ~** to live in the lap of luxury; **in Gefühlen** *etc* **~** to revel in one's emotions

Schwel|ge|rei [ʃvɛlgəˈrai] F **-**, **-en** high living *no pl*, indulgence *no pl*; (= *Schlemmerei*) feasting *no pl*

schwel|ge|risch [ˈʃvɛlgərɪʃ] ADJ (= *üppig*) *Mahl, Farbe* sumptuous; *Akkorde auch* voluptuous; (= *genießerisch*) self-indulgent

Schwel-: **Schwel|koh|le** F high-bituminous brown coal; **Schwel|koks** M low-temperature coke

Schwel|le [ˈʃvɛlə] F **-**, **-n** a (= *Türschwelle, fig, Psych*) threshold; (= *Stein etc*) sill; (*auf Straße*) ramp, bump; **einen/keinen Fuß über die ~ setzen** to set foot/not to set foot in sb's house; **du darfst mir nie wieder über die ~ kommen, er darf meine ~ nie wieder betreten** he shall *or* may not darken my door again (*liter*), he may not cross my threshold again (*liter*); **an der ~ (zu) einer neuen Zeit** on the threshold of a new era; **an der ~ des Grabes** or **Todes** at death's door **b** (*Rail*) sleeper (*Brit*), cross-tie (*US*) **c** (*Geog*) rise

schwel|len [ˈʃvɛlən] **VI** *pret* **schwoll** [ʃvɔl], *ptp* **geschwollen** [gəˈʃvɔlən] *aux sein* to swell; (*lit: Körperteile auch*) to swell up; **der Wind schwoll zum Sturm** the wind grew into a storm; **ihm schwoll der Kamm** (*inf*) (*vor Eitelkeit, Übermut*) he got swollen-headed (*esp Brit*) or swell-headed (*esp US*), he got above himself (*Brit*); (*vor Wut*) he saw red → *auch* **geschwollen VT** (*geh*) *Segel* to swell or belly (out); (*fig*) *Brust* to swell

Schwel|len|angst F (*Psych*) fear of entering a place; (*fig*) fear of embarking on something new

schwel|lend ADJ (*geh*) swelling; *Lippen* full

Schwel|len-: Schwel|len|land NT fast-developing nation; **Schwel|len|macht** F rising power; **Schwel|len|preis** M (*Econ*) threshold price; **Schwel|len|wert** M (*Phys, Psych*) threshold value

Schwel|ler [ˈʃvɛlɐ] M -s, - (*Mus*) swell

Schwell|kör|per M (*Anat*) erectile tissue

Schwel|lung [ˈʃvɛlʊŋ] F -, -en swelling; (*von Penis*) tumescence (*spec*)

Schwe|lung [ˈʃveːlʊŋ] F -, -en (*Tech*) low-temperature carbonization

Schwemm|bo|den M alluvial land

Schwem|me [ˈʃvɛmə] F -, -n **a** (*für Tiere*) watering place **b** (= *Überfluss*) glut (*an +dat* of) **c** (= *Kneipe*) bar, public bar (*Brit*) **d** (*Aus: im Warenhaus*) bargain basement

-schwem|me F *suf in cpds* glut of; **Akademikerschwemme** glut of university graduates

schwem|men [ˈʃvɛmən] VT (= *treiben*) *Sand etc* to wash; *Vieh* to water; (= *wässern*) *Felle* to soak; (*Aus: = spülen*) *Wäsche* to rinse; **etw an(s) Land ~** to wash sth ashore

Schwemm-: Schwemm|land NT alluvial land; **Schwemm|sand** M alluvial sand

Schwen|gel [ˈʃvɛŋl] M -s, - (= *Glockenschwengel*) clapper; (= *Pumpenschwengel*) handle; (*inf: = Penis*) dong (*US sl*), tool (*sl*)

Schwenk [ʃvɛŋk] M -(e)s, -s (= *Drehung*) wheel; (*Film*) pan, panning shot; (*fig*) about-turn; **einen ~ machen** (*Kolonne*) to swing or wheel around

Schwenk-: Schwenk|arm M swivel arm; **schwenk|bar** ADJ swivelling (*Brit*), swiveling (*US*); *Lampe auch* swivel *attr*; *Geschütz* traversable; **Schwenk|be|reich** M jib range

schwen|ken [ˈʃvɛŋkən] **VT a** (= *schwingen*) to wave; (= *herumfuchteln mit*) to brandish **b** *Lampe etc* to swivel, to swing; *Kran* to swing, to slew; *Geschütz* to traverse, to swivel; *Kamera* to pan (*Cook*) *Kartoffeln, Nudeln* to toss **2** *Tanzpartnerin* to swing round, to spin (round) **VI** *aux sein* to swing; (*Kolonne von Soldaten, Autos etc*) to wheel; (*Geschütz*) to traverse, to swivel; (*Kamera*) to pan, (*fig*) to swing over, to switch; **links schwenkt!** (*Mil*) left wheel!

Schwen|ker [ˈʃvɛŋkɐ] M -s, - balloon glass

Schwenk-: Schwenk|flü|gel M (*Tech*) swing-wing; **Schwenk|kar|tof|feln** PL sauté potatoes *pl*; **Schwenk|kran** M swing crane; **Schwenk|so|ckel** M (*Comput*) swivel base

Schwen|kung [ˈʃvɛŋkʊŋ] F -, -en swing; (*Mil*) wheel; (*von Kran*) slewing, swing; (*von Geschütz*) traverse; (*von Kamera*) pan(ning); **eine ~ vollziehen** (*Mil*) to wheel; (*fig*) to swing around

schwer [ʃveːɐ] ✪ 33.3, 53.3, 53.6 **ADJ a** (*lit, fig*) heavy; (= *massiv*) *Gold* solid; **ein 10 kg ~er Sack** a sack weighing 10 kgs, a sack 10 kgs in weight; **die Beine wurden mir ~** my legs grew heavy; **er ist fünf Millionen ~** (*inf*) he is worth five million → **Herz b, Kapee, Magen, Stand a b** (= *stark*) *Fahrzeug, Maschine* powerful; *Artillerie, Kavallerie, Wein, Parfüm* heavy; *Zigarre* strong; (= *nährstoffreich*) *Boden* rich; **~es Wasser** (*Phys*) heavy water → **Geschütz**

c (= *heftig*) *Sturm, See, Angriff, Artilleriefeuer* heavy; *Winter* hard, severe

d (= *ernst*) *Sorge, Bedenken, Unrecht, Unfall, Verlust, Krankheit, Beleidigung* serious, grave; *Fehler, Enttäuschung* serious, grave, big; *Zeit, Leben, Schicksal* hard; *Leiden, Belastungsprobe, Strafe, Buße* severe; *Musik* heavy; **~e Verluste** heavy losses; **Schweres erlebt** or **durchgemacht haben** to have been through (some) hard times, to have had a hard time (of it); **das war ein ~er Schlag für ihn** it was a hard blow for him → **Stunde, Junge** ¹

e (= *hart, anstrengend*) *Amt, Aufgabe, Dienst, Arbeit, Tag* hard; *Geburt, Tod* difficult; **es ~ haben** to have a hard time (of it) → **Anfang, Geburt**

f (= *schwierig*) *Frage, Entscheidung, Übung* hard, difficult, tough

g (*inf: = enorm*) **~es Geld machen** to make a packet (*inf*)

ADV a (= *mit schwerer Last*) *beladen, bepackt, bewaffnet* heavily; **~ auf jdm/etw liegen/lasten** to lie/weigh heavily on sb/sth; **~ an etw** (*dat*) **zu tragen haben** (*sich abschleppen*) to be loaded down with sth; (*fig*) *an Schuld etc* to be heavily burdened with sth; **an den 50 Sack hast du viel zu ~ zu tragen** these 50 sacks are too much for you to carry; **das Bewusstsein, ihr Unrecht getan zu haben, lastet ~ auf ihm** knowing that he did her an injustice is hard for him to bear

b (= *hart*) *arbeiten, schuften* hard; *bestrafen, tadeln, missbilligen* severely; **~ geprüft sein** to be sorely tried; **~ verdientes Geld** hard-earned money; **es ~ haben** to have a hard time of it; **es mit jdm ~ haben** to have a hard time with sb

c (= *ernstlich*) *verletzen, verwunden* seriously; *krank* seriously, critically; *behindert* severely; *beleidigen, kränken, treffen, gekränkt* deeply; **~ beschädigt** severely disabled; **~ kriegsbeschädigt** seriously disabled (*in war*); **~ erkältet sein** to have a bad cold; **~ stürzen** to have a bad fall; **~ verunglücken** to have a serious accident

d (= *nicht einfach*) **~ zu sehen/sagen** hard or difficult to see/say; **es lässt sich ~ abschätzen/voraussagen** it's hard to estimate/to predict

e (= *mit Mühe*) **sich ~ entschließen können** to find it hard or difficult to decide; **er lernt ~** he's a slow learner; **~ hören** to be hard of hearing; **~ löslich** (*attr*) not easily dissoluble; **etw ist ~ löslich** sth is not easy to dissolve; **jd ist ~ erziehbar** sb has behavioural (*Brit*) or behavioral (*US*) problems; **ein ~ erziehbares Kind** a maladjusted child; **~ verdaulich** (*Speisen*) indigestible; (*fig auch*) difficult; **etw ist ~ verdaulich** sth is hard to digest; **~ verständlich** difficult or hard to understand, incomprehensible; **~ verträglich sein** (*Speise*) to be indigestible; (*Medikament*) to have side effects; (*Klima*) to be unhealthy; **ein ~ verträgliches Medikament** medicine which has side effects

f (*inf: = sehr*) really; **da musste ich ~ aufpassen** I really had to watch out; **~ betrunken** completely drunk, rolling drunk (*Brit inf*); **~ verdienen** to earn a packet (*Brit inf*) or a fistful (*US inf*); **sich ~ blamieren** to make a proper fool (*Brit*) or an ass (*esp US*) of oneself; **ich werde mich ~ hüten** there's no way (I will) (*inf*); **~ im Irrtum sein** to be badly or seriously mistaken; **er ist ~ in Ordnung** he's OK (*inf*), he's a good bloke (*Brit inf*) or guy (*inf*)

Schwer-: Schwer|ar|beit F heavy labour (*Brit*) or labor (*US*); **Schwer|ar|bei|ter(in)** M(F) labourer (*Brit*), laborer (*US*); **Schwer|ath|let(in)** M(F) weightlifter; boxer; wrestler; **Schwer|ath|le|tik** F *weightlifting sports, boxing, wrestling etc*; **schwer|be|hin|dert △** ADJ → **schwer** ADV c; **Schwer|be|hin|der|te(r)** MF *decl as adj* severely disabled person; **Schwer|be|hin|der|ten|aus|weis** M disabled pass or ID; **schwer|be|la|den △** [-bəla:dn] ADJ *attr* → **schwer** ADV a; **Schwer|ben|zin** NT heavy benzene (*Brit*), naphtha (*US*); **schwer|be|packt △** [-bəpakt] ADJ *attr* → **schwer** ADV a; **schwer|be|schä|digt △** [-bəʃeːdɪçt] ADJ *attr* → **schwer** ADV c; **Schwer|be|schä|dig|te(r)** MF

decl as adj severely disabled person; **schwer|be|waff|net △** ADJ *attr* → **schwer** ADV a; **schwer|blü|tig** ADJ serious, ponderous; **ein ~er Mensch** a ponderous (sort of) person

Schwe|re [ˈʃveːrə] F -, *no pl* **a** heaviness **b** (= *Ernsthaftigkeit, von Krankheit*) seriousness, gravity; **die ganze ~ des Gesetzes** the full severity of the law **c** (= *Schwierigkeit*) difficulty; **das hängt von der ~ der Aufgabe ab** it depends on how difficult the task is **d** (*Phys: = Schwerkraft*) gravitation

Schwe|re-: Schwe|re|feld NT field of gravity, gravitational field; **schwe|re|los** ADJ weightless; **Schwe|re|lo|sig|keit** F -, *no pl* weightlessness

Schwe|re|nö|ter [ˈʃveːrənøːtɐ] M -s, -, **Schwe|re|nö|te|rin** [-ərɪn] F -, -nen (*dated*) philanderer

schwer|er|zieh|bar △ ADJ *attr Kind* → **schwer** ADV e

Schwer|er|zieh|ba|re(r) MF *decl as adj* difficult or problem child

schwer fal|len ▲ VI *irreg aux sein* to be difficult or hard (*jdm* for sb); **das dürfte dir doch nicht ~ fallen** you shouldn't find that too difficult or hard

schwer|fäl|lig ADJ (= *unbeholfen*) *Gang, Bewegungen* heavy (in one's movements); (= *langsam*) *Verstand* slow, ponderous; *Stil, Übersetzung* ponderous; *Verwaltung, Staatsapparat* cumbersome; **~ sein** (*Mensch*) to move heavily **ADV** *sprechen* ponderously; *sich bewegen* with difficulty; **du bewegst dich so ~** you seem to have so much trouble moving

Schwer|fäl|lig|keit F (= *Unbeholfenheit: von Gang, Bewegungen*) heaviness; (= *Langsamkeit: von Verstand*) slowness, ponderousness; **die ~ seines Stils** his ponderous style

Schwer-: schwer|ge|prüft △ [-gəpry:ft] ADJ *attr* → **schwer** ADV b; **Schwer|ge|wicht** NT **a** (*Sport, fig*) heavyweight **b** (= *Nachdruck*) stress, emphasis; **das ~ verlagern** to shift the emphasis or emphasis on sth; **das ~ auf etw** (*acc*) **legen** to put the stress or emphasis on sth; **schwer|ge|wich|tig** ADJ (*lit, fig*) heavyweight; **Schwer|ge|wicht|ler** [-gəvɪçtlɐ] M -s, -, **Schwer|ge|wicht|le|rin** [-ərɪn] F -, -nen (*Sport*) heavyweight; **schwer|hö|rig** ADJ hard of hearing; **du bist wohl ~!** (*inf*) are you deaf? (*inf*); **Schwer|hö|ri|ge(r)** MF *decl as adj* person with hearing difficulties or impaired hearing, hearing-impaired person; **Schwer|hö|rig|keit** F hardness of hearing; **Schwer|in|dust|rie** F heavy industry; **Schwer|in|dust|ri|el|le(r)** MF *decl as adj* industrialist (*in heavy industry*); **Schwer|kraft** F -, *no pl* gravity; **schwer|krank △** ADJ *attr* → **schwer** ADV c; **Schwer|kran|ke(r)** MF *decl as adj* seriously or critically ill patient; **schwer|kriegs|be|schä|digt △** ADJ *attr* → **schwer** ADV c; **Schwer|kriegs|be|schä|dig|te(r)** MF *decl as adj* seriously disabled ex-serviceman/ex-servicewoman, seriously disabled war veteran (*US*); **Schwer|last|ver|kehr** M heavy vehicle traffic

schwer|lich [ˈʃveːlɪç] ADV hardly, scarcely

Schwer-: schwer|lös|lich △ ADJ → **schwer** ADV e; **schwer ma|chen △** VT a **jdm das Herz ~** to make sb's heart sad or heavy; **jdm das Leben ~** to make life difficult or hard for sb **b** **es jdm/sich ~** to make it or things difficult or hard for sb/oneself; **Schwer|me|tall** NT heavy metal

Schwer|mut [ˈʃveːmuːt] F -, *no pl* melancholy

schwer|mü|tig [ˈʃveːmyːtɪç] ADJ *Mensch, Geschichte, Musik* melancholy

schwer neh|men ▲ VT *sep irreg* **etw ~** to take sth hard

Schwer|öl NT heavy oil

Schwer|punkt M (*Phys*) centre (*Brit*) or center (*US*) of gravity; (*fig*) (= *Zentrum*) centre (*Brit*), center (*US*), main focus; (= *Hauptgewicht*) main emphasis or stress; **politische/thematische ~e** main political/thematic emphases; **er hat Fran-**

zösisch mit ~ **Linguistik studiert** he studied French with the main emphasis or main stress on linguistics; **den ~ einer Sache** (gen) **bilden** to occupy the central position in sth; **den ~ auf etw** (acc) **legen** to put the main emphasis or stress on sth; **~e setzen** to set priorities

Schwer|punkt-: Schwer|punkt|bil|dung F concentration; **Schwer|punkt|in|dust|rie** F main industry; **schwer|punkt|mä|ßig** ADJ **ei-ne ~e Betrachtung** a look at the main points ADV **sich mit etw ~ befassen** to concentrate on sth; **~ konzentrieren wir uns auf …** principally we concentrate on …; **Schwer|punkt|pro-gramm** NT programme (Brit) or program (US) or plan of main points of emphasis; **Schwer-punkt|streik** M pinpoint strike; **Schwer-punkt|the|ma** NT main (discussion) topic; (in Prüfung) special subject; **Schwer|punkt|ver-la|ge|rung** F shift of emphasis

Schwer-: schwer|reich ADJ (inf) stinking rich (inf); **Schwer|spat** M heavy spar, barite, ba-rytes sing

Schwerst- [ʃveːɐst-]: **Schwerst|ar|bei|ter(in)** M(F) heavy labourer (Brit), hard laborer (US); **schwerst|be|hin|dert** ADJ totally disabled; **Schwerst|be|hin|der|te(r)** MF decl as adj to-tally disabled person

Schwert [ʃveːɐt] NT **-(e)s, -er** [a] sword; **das ~ ziehen** or **zücken** to draw one's sword; **sich mit dem ~ gürten** (liter) to gird (on) one's sword [b] (von Segelboot) centreboard (Brit), centerboard (US)

Schwert|adel M (Hist, fig) military nobility

Schwer|ter-: Schwer|ter|ge|klirr NT (liter) ring(ing) or clash(ing) of swords; **Schwer|ter-tanz** M sword dance

Schwert-: Schwert|fisch M swordfish; **schwert|för|mig** ADJ sword-shaped; Blatt auch gladiate (spec); **Schwert|griff** M (sword) hilt; **Schwert|hieb** M sword stroke, stroke or blow of the sword; **Schwert|klin|ge** F sword blade; **Schwert|knauf** M (sword) pommel; **Schwert|lei|te** [-laitə] F -, -n (Hist) accolade; **Schwert|li|lie** F (Bot) iris

Schwer|trans|port M (Ladung) heavy load; (= Transporter) → **Schwertransporter**

Schwer|trans|por|ter M heavy truck or lorry (Brit), heavy goods or heavy weight (US) vehicle (form), HGV (Brit)

Schwert-: Schwert|schlu|cker(in) M(F) sword-swallower; **Schwert|streich** M sword stroke, stroke or blow of the sword

Schwert|tanz M sword dance

Schwert|trä|ger M (Zool) swordtail

schwer tun ▲ VR irreg (inf) **sich** (dat) **mit** or **bei etw ~** to make heavy weather of sth (Brit inf), to make a big deal of sth (inf)

Schwert|wal M killer whale

Schwer-: Schwer|ver|bre|cher(in) M(F) crim-inal, felon (esp Jur); **schwer|ver|dau|lich** △ ADJ attr → **schwer** ADV e; **schwer|ver|dient** △ ADJ attr → **schwer** ADV b; **Schwer|ver|kehr** M heavy goods traffic; **Schwer|ver|kehrs|ab|ga-be** F heavy goods vehicle supplement; **schwer|ver|letzt** △ [-fɛɐlɛtst] ADJ attr → **schwer** ADV c; **Schwer|ver|letz|te(r)** MF decl as adj serious casualty; **schwer|ver|ständ-lich** △ ADJ attr → **schwer** ADV e; **schwer|ver|träg-lich** △ ADJ attr → **schwer** ADV e; **schwer|ver|wun|det** △ ADJ attr → **schwer** ADV c; **Schwer|ver|wun|de|te(r)** MF decl as adj major casual-ty; **Schwer|was|ser|re|ak|tor** M heavy water reactor; **schwer|wie|gend** ADJ (fig) Fehler, Mängel, Folgen serious

Schwes|ter [ʃvɛstɐ] F -, -n sister; (= Kranken-schwester) nurse; (= Stationsschwester) sister; (= Ordensschwester) nun, sister; (= Gemeindeschwes-ter) district nurse; (inf: = Schwesterfirma) sister or associate(d) company

Schwes|ter|chen [ʃvɛstɐçən] NT -s, - little sis-ter, baby sister

Schwes|ter-: Schwes|ter|fir|ma F sister or as-sociate(d) company; **Schwes|ter|herz** NT (inf) (dear) sister, sis (inf)

Schwes|ter|lein [ʃvɛstɐlain] NT -s, - little sis-ter, baby sister

schwes|ter|lich [ʃvɛstəlɪç] ADJ sisterly ADV like sisters; **ich bin ihr ~ verbunden** she's like a sister to me

Schwes|ter|lie|be F sisterly love

Schwes|tern-: Schwes|tern|heim NT nurses' home; **Schwes|tern|hel|fer(in)** M(F) nursing auxiliary (Brit) or assistant (US); **Schwes|tern|lie|be** F sisterly love; **Schwes|tern|or-den** M sisterhood; **Schwes|tern|paar** NT two sisters pl; **Schwes|tern|schaft** F [ʃvɛstɐn-ʃaft] F -, -en nursing staff; (von Orden) sister-hood; **Schwes|tern|schu|le** F nurses' training college; **Schwes|tern|schü|le|rin** F student nurse; **Schwes|tern|tracht** F nurse's uniform; **Schwes|tern|wohn|heim** NT nurses' home

Schwes|ter-: Schwes|ter|par|tei F sister par-ty; **Schwes|ter|schiff** NT sister ship

Schwib|bo|gen [ʃvɪpboːgn] M (Archit) flying buttress

schwieg pret von **schweigen**

Schwie|ger- [ʃviːgə-]: **Schwie|ger|el|tern** PL parents-in-law pl; **Schwie|ger|leu|te** PL (inf) in-laws pl; **Schwie|ger|ma|ma** [-mama:] F (inf), **Schwie|ger|mut|ter** F pl -mütter mother-in-law; **Schwie|ger|pa|pa** [-papa:] M (inf) father-in-law; **Schwie|ger|sohn** M son-in-law; **Schwie|ger|toch|ter** F daughter-in--law; **Schwie|ger|va|ter** M father-in-law

Schwie|le [ʃviːlə] F -, -n callus; (= Vernarbung) welt

schwie|lig [ʃviːlɪç] ADJ Hände callused

schwie|me|lig [ʃviːməlɪç], **schwiem|lig** [ʃviːm-lɪç] ADJ (dial inf) dizzy

schwie|rig [ʃviːrɪç] ADJ difficult; (= schwer zu ler-nen etc auch) hard; **er ist ein ~er Fall** he is a problem ADV **zu übersetzen** difficult to translate; **das Gespräch verlief ~** the discussion didn't go well; **die Klärung seiner Identität ge-staltete sich ~** it was difficult to identify him

Schwie|rig|keit F -, -en difficulty; **in ~en gera-ten** or **kommen** to get into difficulties or trou-ble; **auf ~en stoßen** to meet with difficulties; **jdm ~en machen** to make trouble for sb; **es macht mir keine ~en** it's no trouble at all; it's not at all difficult for me; **warum musst du bloß immer ~en machen!** why must you always be diffi-cult!; **jdn in ~en** (acc) **bringen** to create difficul-ties for sb; **mach keine ~en!** (inf) don't be diffi-cult, don't make any trouble; **ohne ~en** with-out any difficulty; **ohne große ~(en)** without any great difficulty; **~en haben, etw zu tun** to have difficulties doing sth

Schwie|rig|keits|grad M degree of difficulty

schwillt [ʃvɪlt] 3. pers sing pres von **schwellen**

Schwimm-: Schwimm|bad NT swimming pool; (= Hallenbad) swimming baths pl; **Schwimm|bag|ger** M dredger; **Schwimm|bahn** F lane; **Schwimm|bas|sin** NT , **Schwimm|be|cken** NT (swimming) pool; **Schwimm|be|we|gun|gen** PL swimming ac-tion sing; (= Schwimmzüge) swimming strokes pl; **Schwimm|bla|se** F (Zool) air bladder; **Schwimm|bril|le** F swimming goggles pl; **Schwimm|dock** NT floating dock

schwim|men [ʃvɪmən] pret **schwamm** [ʃvam], ptp **geschwommen** [gəˈʃvɔmən] aux sein VI [a] auch aux haben to swim; **~ gehen** to go swimming, to go for a swim; **er ist über den Fluss ge-schwommen** he swam (across) the river [b] (= auf dem Wasser treiben) to float; **seine Schiffe ~ auf allen Meeren** his ships are afloat on every ocean [c] (inf: = überschwemmt sein, triefen) (Boden) to be swimming (inf), to be awash; **in Fett** (dat) **~** to be swimming in fat; **in seinem Blut ~** to be soaked in blood; **in Tränen ~** to be bathed in tears; **in** or **im Geld ~** to be rolling in it or in

money (inf) [d] (fig: = unsicher sein) to be at sea, to flounder [e] **es schwimmt mir vor den Augen** I feel giddy or dizzy, everything's going round VT auch aux haben (Sport) to swim

Schwim|men NT -s, no pl swimming; **zum ~ ge-hen** to go swimming; **ins ~ geraten** or **kommen** (fig) to begin to flounder

schwim|mend ADJ floating; **~es Fett** deep fat; **im ~en Fett aufbraten** to deep-fry

Schwim|mer¹ [ʃvɪmɐ] M -s, - (Tech, Angeln) float

Schwim|mer² [ʃvɪmɐ] M -s, -, **Schwim|me|rin** [-ərɪn] F -, -nen swimmer

Schwim|mer|be|cken NT swimmer's pool

Schwimm-: schwimm|fä|hig ADJ Material buoyant; Fahrzeug, Flugzeug amphibious; Boot, Floß floatable; **~ sein** to be able to float; (Materi-al) to float, to be buoyant; **Schwimm|fest** NT swimming gala; **Schwimm|flos|se** F fin; (von Taucher auch, von Wal, Robbe) flipper; **Schwimm|flü|gel** M water wing; **Schwimm-fuß** M webfoot, webbed foot; **Schwimm|gür-tel** M swimming or cork belt; **Schwimm|hal-le** F swimming bath (s pl), (indoor) swimming pool; **Schwimm|haut** F (Orn) web; **Schwimm|hil|fe** F swimming aid; **Schwimm-kä|fer** M diving beetle; **Schwimm|kis|sen** NT water wing; **Schwimm|kran** M floating crane; **Schwimm|kurs** M swimming course or lessons pl; **Schwimm|la|ge** F swimming posi-tion; **Schwimm|leh|rer(in)** M(F) swimming instructor; **Schwimm|rei|fen** M [a] (zum Schwimmen) rubber ring [b] (fig hum: = Hüftspeck) spare tyre (Brit) or tire (US) (hum), love han-dles pl (hum); **Schwimm|sport** M swimming no art; **Schwimm|sta|di|on** NT swimming stadium, international swimming pool; **Schwimm|stil** M stroke; (= Technik) (swim-ming) style; **Schwimm|stoß** M stroke; **Schwimm|übun|gen** PL swimming exercises pl; **Schwimm|un|ter|richt** M swimming les-sons pl; **Schwimm|ver|ein** M swimming club; **Schwimm|ver|such** M (fig) **die ersten ~e** the/one's first tentative steps; **Schwimm|vo-gel** M water bird, waterfowl; **Schwimm|wes-te** F life jacket

Schwin|del [ʃvɪndl] M -s, no pl [a] (= Gleichge-wichtsstörung) dizziness; (esp nach Drehen) giddi-ness; **~ erregend** (Höhe) dizzy, vertiginous (form); Tempo dizzying; (inf) Preise astronomical; **in ~ erregender Höhe** at a dizzy height [b] (= Lüge) lie; (= Betrug) swindle, fraud; (= Ver-trauensmissbrauch) con (inf); **die Berichte über das perfekte Haarwuchsmittel sind reiner ~** the reports about this perfect hair-restorer are a complete swindle or fraud or con (inf); **das ist alles ~, was er da sagt** what he says is all a pack of lies or a big con (inf); **glaub doch nicht an diesen ~!** don't be taken in!; **den ~ kenne ich!** (inf), **auf den ~ falle ich nicht herein!** (inf) that's an old trick; **mit Subventionen wird viel ~ getrieben** a lot of swindling or cheating goes on with subsidies [c] (inf: = Kram) **der ganze ~** the whole (kit and) caboodle (inf) or shoot (inf); **ich will von dem ganzen ~ nichts mehr wissen!** I don't want to hear another thing about the whole damn business (inf)

Schwin|del|an|fall M dizzy turn, attack of dizziness

Schwin|de|lei [ʃvɪndəˈlai] F -, -en (inf) (= leichte Lüge) fib (inf); (= leichter Betrug) swindle; **seine ständige ~** his constant fibbing (inf)

Schwin|del-: schwin|del|er|re|gend △ ADJ → **Schwindel** a; **Schwin|del|fir|ma** F bogus firm or company; **schwin|del|frei** ADJ Wendy **ist kein ~** Wendy can't stand heights, Wendy suffers from vertigo; **sie ist völlig ~** she has a good head for heights, she doesn't suffer from vertigo at all; **Schwin|del|ge|fühl** NT feeling of dizziness; (esp nach Drehen) feeling of giddi-ness

schwin|de|lig ['ʃvɪndəlɪç] ADJ dizzy; (esp nach Drehen) giddy; **mir ist** or **ich bin ~** I feel dizzy/giddy; **mir wird leicht ~** I get dizzy/giddy easily

schwin|deln ['ʃvɪndln] VI **a** **mir** or **mich** (rare) **schwindelt** I feel dizzy or (esp vom Drehen) giddy; **mir schwindelte der Kopf, mein Kopf schwindelte** my head was reeling; **der Gedanke macht mich ~** (fig) my head reels or I was fibbing at the thought; **in ~der Höhe** at a dizzy height; **ein ~der Abgrund** a yawning abyss or chasm **b** (inf: = lügen) to fib (inf), to tell fibs (inf) VT (inf) **das hat sie geschwindelt** she was fibbing (inf) or telling fibs (inf); **das ist alles geschwindelt** it's all lies VR **sich durch die Kontrollen/in den Saal ~** to con or wangle one's way through the checkpoint/into the hall (inf); **sich durchs Leben/durch die Schule ~** to con one's way through life/school

Schwin|del-: Schwin|del|preis M astronomical or exorbitant price; **Schwin|del|unter|neh|men** NT bogus firm or company

schwin|den ['ʃvɪndn] pret **schwand** [ʃvant], ptp **geschwunden** [gə'ʃvʊndn] VI aux sein **a** (= abnehmen) to dwindle; (Schönheit) to fade, to wane; (= allmählich verschwinden) (Hoffnung) to fade away, to dwindle; (Erinnerung, Angst, Chance, Zeit) to fade away; (Kräfte) to fade, to fail; **im Schwinden begriffen sein** to be dwindling; (Schönheit) to be on the wane; **ihm schwand der Mut, sein Mut schwand** his courage failed him; **ihm schwanden die Sinne** (liter) he grew faint; **aus den Augen ~** to fade from view; **aus der Erinnerung/dem Bewusstsein ~** to fade from (one's) memory/one's consciousness **b** (= verblassen: Farben) to fade; (= leiser werden: Ton) to fade (away); (= sich auflösen: Dunkelheit) to fade away, to retreat (liter) **c** (Tech: Holz, Metall, Ton) to shrink, to contract

Schwind|ler ['ʃvɪndlɐ] M **-s, -**, **Schwind|le|rin** [-ərɪn] F **-, -nen** swindler; (= Hochstapler) con man, con merchant (Brit inf); (= Lügner) liar, fibber (inf), fraud

schwind|le|risch ['ʃvɪndlərɪʃ] ADJ fraudulent

schwind|lig ['ʃvɪndlɪç] ADJ = schwindelig

Schwind|sucht ['ʃvɪnt-] F (dated) consumption; **die (galoppierende) ~ haben** (dated) to have galloping consumption; (fig hum) to suffer from a sort of wasting disease

schwind|süch|tig ADJ (dated) consumptive; (fig hum) shrinking, ailing

schwind|süch|ti|ge(r) MF decl as adj (dated) consumptive

Schwing|be|sen M (Sw Cook) whisk

Schwing|bo|den M sprung floor

Schwin|ge ['ʃvɪŋə] F **-, -n** (liter: = Flügel) wing, pinion (poet); **auf den ~n der Poesie/Begeisterung** on wings of poetry/passion

schwin|gen ['ʃvɪŋən] pret **schwang** [ʃvaŋ], ptp **geschwungen** [gə'ʃvʊŋən] VT **a** Schläger (swing); (drohend) Schwert, Stock etc to brandish; Hut, Zauberstab, Fahne to wave; **die Gläser** or **den Becher ~** (hum) to quaff a glass (old, hum); **Rahm ~** (Sw) to whip cream → auch **geschwungen**, **Rede a**, **Tanzbein**, **Zepter** VR **sich auf etw** (acc) **~** to leap or jump onto sth, to swing oneself onto sth; **sich über etw** (acc) **~** to vault across or over sth, to swing oneself over sth; **sich in etw** (acc) **~** to vault into sth, to swing oneself into sth; **sich in die Luft** or **Höhe ~** (geh) to soar (up) into the air; **der Aktienindex schwang sich auf Rekordhöhe** the share index leapt or jumped to a record high; **die Brücke schwingt sich elegant über das Tal** the bridge sweeps elegantly over the valley VI **a** (= sich hin- und herbewegen) to swing **b** (vibrieren) (Brücke, Saite) to vibrate; (Wellen) to oscillate **c** (geh) (= nachklingen) to linger; **in ihren Worten schwang leichte Kritik** her words had a

tone of mild criticism **d** (Ski) to swing

Schwin|gen NT **-s**, no pl (Sw Sport) (kind of) wrestling

Schwin|ger[1] ['ʃvɪŋɐ] M **-s, -** (Boxen) swing

Schwin|ger[2] ['ʃvɪŋɐ] M **-s, -**, **Schwin|ge|rin** [-ərɪn] F **-, -nen** (Sw) wrestler

Schwing-: Schwing|flü|gel M casement window; **Schwing|he|bel** M (Aut) rocker arm; **Schwing|schlei|fer** M (orbital) sander; **Schwing|tür** F swing door

Schwin|gung ['ʃvɪŋʊŋ] F **-, -en** (Phys) vibration; (von Wellen) oscillation; (fig) vibration; **in ~ kommen** to begin to swing or (Saite) to vibrate or (Wellen) to oscillate; **etw in ~(en) versetzen** to set sth swinging; to start sth vibrating; to start sth oscillating

Schwin|gungs-: Schwin|gungs|dämp|fer M (Tech) vibration damper; **Schwin|gungs|dau|er** F (Phys) time of vibration, period (of oscillation); **Schwin|gungs|kreis** M (Rad) resonant circuit; **Schwin|gungs|wei|te** F (Phys) amplitude; **Schwin|gungs|zahl** F (Phys) frequency of oscillation

schwipp [ʃvɪp] INTERJ **~, schwapp** splish-splash

Schwipp- ['ʃvɪp-]: **Schwipp|schwa|ger** M (inf) sister-in-law's husband; sister-in-law's brother/brother-in-law's brother; **Schwipp|schwä|ge|rin** F (inf) brother-in-law's wife; brother-in-law's/sister-in-law's sister

Schwips [ʃvɪps] M **-es, -e** (inf) **einen (kleinen) ~ haben** to be tiddly (Brit inf) or (slightly) tipsy

schwir|ren ['ʃvɪrən] VI aux sein to whizz (Brit), to whiz; (Bienen, Fliegen etc) to buzz; **unzählige Gerüchte ~ durch die Presse** the press is buzzing with countless rumours (Brit) or rumors (US); **die Gedanken/Zahlen schwirrten mir durch den Kopf** thoughts/figures were whirling around in my head or buzzing through my head; **mir schwirrt der Kopf** my head is buzzing

Schwitz|bad NT Turkish bath; (= Dampfbad) steam bath

Schwit|ze ['ʃvɪtsə] F **-, -n** (Cook) roux

schwit|zen ['ʃvɪtsn] VI (lit, fig) to sweat; (Mensch auch) to perspire; (Fenster) to steam up; **Gott sei Dank, dass du kommst, wir haben vielleicht geschwitzt!** (inf) thank God you've come, we were really in a sweat (inf) VT **a** Harz to sweat → **Rippe a**, **Blut b** (Cook) Mehl to brown in fat VR **sich halb tot ~** (inf) to get drenched in sweat; **wir schleppen diese Kisten und ~ uns halb tot** (inf) we've been sweating away with these crates (inf); **sich nass ~** to get drenched in sweat

Schwit|zen NT **-s**, no pl sweating; (von Mensch auch) perspiration; **ins ~ kommen** or **geraten** (lit) to break out in a sweat; (fig) to get into a sweat; **jdn ins ~ bringen** (lit, fig) to make sb sweat

schwit|zig ['ʃvɪtsɪç] ADJ = verschwitzt

Schwitz-: Schwitz|kas|ten M (Ringen) headlock; **jdn in den ~ nehmen** to get sb in a headlock, to put a headlock on sb; **Schwitz|kur** F sweating cure; **Schwitz|pa|ckung** F hot pack; **Schwitz|was|ser** NT , no pl condensation

Schwof [ʃvoːf] M **-(e)s, -e** (inf) hop (inf), shindig (dated inf), dance

schwo|fen ['ʃvoːfn] VI (inf) to dance; **~ gehen** to go to a hop (inf) or shindig (dated inf) or dance

schwoll pret von **schwellen**

schwö|ren ['ʃvøːrən] pret **schwor** [ʃvoːɐ], ptp **geschworen** [gə'ʃvoːrən] VT to swear; Eid auch to take; **ich schwöre es(, so wahr mir Gott helfe)** I swear it (so help me God); **er schwor bei Gott/seiner Ehre, nichts davon gewusst zu haben** he swore by God/by or on his honour (Brit) or honor (US) that he knew nothing about it; **ich kann darauf ~, dass ...** I could swear to it that ...; **ich hätte ~ mögen** or **hätte geschworen, dass ...** I could have sworn that ...; **jdm/sich**

etw ~ to swear sth to sb/oneself; **ich spreche nie mehr mit ihm, das habe ich mir geschworen** I have sworn never to speak to him again; **er macht das nie wieder, das hat er ihr geschworen** he has sworn to her that he'll never do it again; **aber das hast du mir geschworen!** but you swore ...!; **sie schworen sich** (dat) **ewige Liebe** they swore (each other) eternal love VI to swear; **auf jdn/etw ~** (fig) to swear by sb/sth; **auf die Bibel/die Verfassung** etc **~** to swear on the Bible/the Constitution etc

Schwuch|tel ['ʃvʊxtl] F **-, -n** (pej inf) queen (sl); (sl: Schimpfwort) dick (sl)

schwul [ʃvuːl] ADJ (inf) gay, queer (pej inf)

schwül [ʃvyːl] ADJ (lit, fig) Wetter, Tag etc sultry, close, muggy; Träume, Fantasien sensuous; Beleuchtung murky

Schwü|le ['ʃvyːlə] F **-**, no pl (lit, fig) sultriness; (von Wetter, Tag auch) closeness, mugginess; **in dieser ~** in this sultry weather

Schwu|len- (inf): **Schwu|len|bar** F gay bar; **Schwu|len|ehe** F gay marriage; **Schwu|len|lo|kal** NT gay bar; **Schwu|len|strich** M (inf) gay or queer (pej inf) beat (inf); **Schwu|len|sze|ne** F gay scene

Schwu|le(r) ['ʃvuːlə] MF decl as adj gay

Schwu|li|tät ['ʃvuːliːtɛːt] F **-, -en** (inf) trouble no indef art, difficulty; **in ~en geraten** or **kommen** to get in a fix (inf); **jdn in ~en bringen** to get sb into trouble or hot water (inf)

Schwulst [ʃvʊlst] M **-(e)s, no pl** (pej) (in der Sprache) bombast, fustian, pompousness; (in der Kunst) bombast, ornateness, floridness

schwuls|tig ['ʃvʊlstɪç] ADJ, ADV **a** = geschwollen **b** (esp Aus) = schwülstig

schwüls|tig ['ʃvʏlstɪç] (pej) ADJ Stil, Redeweise bombastic, fustian, pompous ADV bombastically, pompously

schwum|me|rig ['ʃvʊmə101rɪç], **schwumm|rig** ['ʃvʊmrɪç] ADJ (inf) (= nervös) uneasy, apprehensive; (dial) (= schwindelig) dizzy, giddy; (= unwohl) funny (inf); **mir wird ~** I feel uneasy/dizzy/funny (inf)

Schwund [ʃvʊnt] M **-(e)s** [-dəs] no pl **a** (= Abnahme, Rückgang) decrease (+gen in), decline (+gen in), dwindling (+gen of) **b** (von Material) shrinkage; (Tech: = Abfall) waste; **~ machen** (inf) to produce scrap **c** (Rad) fading **d** (Med) atrophy **e** (Ling: von Vokal etc) loss

Schwund-: Schwund|aus|gleich M (Rad) automatic frequency control, anti-fade device; **Schwund|stu|fe** F (Ling) zero grade

Schwung [ʃvʊŋ] M **-(e)s, ¨e** ['ʃvʏŋə] **a** swing; (= ausholende Handbewegung) flourish; (= Sprung) leap; **jdm/einer Sache einen ~ geben** to give sb/sth a push; **etw in ~ setzen** to set sth in motion **b** no pl (lit: = Antrieb) momentum; (fig: = Elan) verve, zest; **~ holen** (lit, fig) to get up or build up momentum; **in ~ kommen** (lit: Schlitten etc) to gather or gain momentum; (fig auch) to get going; **an ~ gewinnen/verlieren** (lit, fig) to gain/lose momentum; **jdn/etw in ~ bringen** (lit, fig) to get sb/sth going; **die Sache** or **den Laden in ~ bringen** (inf) to get things going; **~ in die Sache** or **den Laden bringen** (inf) to put a bit of life into things, to liven things up; **jdm/einer Sache ~ geben** or **verleihen** (lit) to give sb/sth momentum; (fig auch) to get sb/sth going; **in ~ sein** (lit: Schlitten etc) to be going full pelt (esp Brit inf) or at full speed; (fig) to be in full swing; **etw mit ~ tun** (fig) to do sth with zest; **voller/ohne ~** (fig) full of/lacking life or verve or zest **c** (= Linienführung) sweep **d** no pl (inf: = Menge) (Sachen) stack, pile (inf); (Leute) bunch

Schwung-: Schwung|fe|der F (Orn) wing feather; **schwung|haft** ADJ Handel flourishing, roaring ADV **sich ~ entwickeln** to grow hand over fist; **Schwung|kraft** F centrifugal force; **schwung|los** ADJ lacking in verve or zest, lacking life; Absatz, Konjunktur sluggish, slack

---

ADV sluggishly, slackly; **im Endspiel wirkte Brasilien ~** Brazil seemed sluggish in the final; **Schwung|rad** NT flywheel

schwung|voll ADJ **a** *Linie, Bewegung, Handschrift* sweeping **b** (= *mitreißend*) *Rede, Aufführung* lively **ADV a** (= *mit Schwung*) *auf etw zugehen, aufstehen, hereinkommen, sich an die Arbeit machen* energetically; *werfen, schaukeln* powerfully; *etw ~ unterschreiben* to sign sth with a flourish **b** *spielen* with verve or zest; **die Aufführung war ~ inszeniert** it was a very lively performance; **etw ~er spielen** to play sth with more verve or zest

schwupp [ʃvʊp] INTERJ in a flash, as quick as a flash; **~! da ist er hingefallen** bang! down he fell; **und ~ hatte der Zauberer ...** and (hey (*Brit*)) presto, the conjurer had ...

Schwupp [ʃvʊp] M **-s, -e** (*inf:* = *Stoß*) push; **in einem ~** in one fell swoop

schwupp|di|wupp [ʃvʊpdiˈvʊp], **schwups** [ʃvʊps] INTERJ = **schwupp**

Schwups [ʃvʊps] M **-es, ⸚e** [ˈʃvʏpsə] (*inf*) = **Schwupp**

Schwur [ʃvuːɐ] M **-(e)s, ⸚e** [ˈʃvyːrə] (= *Eid*) oath; (= *Gelübde*) vow

Schwur-: Schwur|fin|ger PL thumb, first finger and second finger, raised in swearing an oath; **Schwur|ge|richt** NT court with a jury **vor das ~ kommen** to be tried by jury; **Schwur|ge|richts|ver|fah|ren** NT trial by jury *no def art*

Schwyz [ʃviːts] NT **-** (= *Kanton*) Schwyz

Schwy|zer|dütsch [ˈʃviːtsədy:tʃ] NT , **Schwy|zer|tütsch** [-ty:tʃ] NT **-(s)**, *no pl* (*Sw*) Swiss German

Sci|ence|fic|tion ▲ [ˈsaiəns'fikʃn] F **-, -s** science fiction, sci-fi (*inf*)

Sci|en|to|lo|ge [saiəntoˈloːgə] M **-n, -n, Sci|en|to|lo|gin** [-ˈloːgɪn] F **-, -nen** Scientologist

sci|en|to|lo|gisch [saiəntoˈloːgɪʃ] ADJ Scientologist

Sci|en|to|lo|gy [saiənˈtɔlədʒi] F **-, *no pl*** Scientology

Sci|en|to|lo|gy-Kir|che F Church of Scientology

Sci|roc|co [ʃiˈrɔko] M **-s, -s** sirocco

Scotch|ter|rier [ˈskɔtʃtɛriɐ] M Scotch terrier, Scottie

Scrib|ble [ˈskrɪbl] NT **-s, -s** (*spec:* = *Entwurf*) first draft (*of a publicity visual*)

scrol|len [ˈskrɔlən] VTI (*Comput*) to scroll

Scro|tum [ˈskroːtʊm] NT **-s, Scrota** [-ta] (*Med*) scrotum

Scyl|la [ˈstsʏla] F **-, *no pl*** (*Myth*) = **Szylla**

SD¹ [ɛsˈdeː] M **-, *no pl*** (*NS*) abbr von **Sicherheitsdienst** Security Service

SD² [ɛsˈdeː] F **-, -s** abbr von **Super Density Disc** SD

SDR [ɛsdeːˈɛr] M **-** abbr von **Süddeutscher Rundfunk**

SDS [ɛsdeːˈɛs] M **-** abbr von **Sozialistischer Deutscher Studentenbund**

Seal [siːl] M OR NT **-s, -s** sealskin

Seal|skin [ˈsiːlskɪn] M OR NT **-s, -s a** sealskin **b** imitation sealskin

Sé|an|ce [zeˈã:s(ə)] F **-, -n** séance

Se|bor|rhöe [zebɔˈrøː] F **-, -n** [-ˈrøːən] dandruff, seborrh(o)ea (*spec*)

sec abbr von **Sekunde**

sechs [zɛks] NUM six → *auch* **vier**

Sechs- [zɛks] in cpds six → *auch* **vier-; Sechs|ach|tel|takt** M (*Mus*) six-eight time; **Sechs|eck** NT hexagon; **sechs|eckig** ADJ hexagonal

Sech|ser [ˈzɛksɐ] M **-s, - a** (*obs*) six-kreutzer/six-groschen *etc* piece; (*Hist dial inf*) five-pfennig piece; **nicht für einen ~ Verstand haben** not to have a scrap or a ha'p'orth (*Brit*) of sense **b** six → *auch* **Vierer**

---

sech|ser|lei [ˈzɛksɐˈlai] ADJ *inv* six kinds of → *auch* **viererlei**

Sech|ser|pack [-pak] M **-s, -s** six-pack

Sechs- [ˈzɛks-]: **sechs|fach** **ADJ** sixfold **ADV** sixfold, six times → *auch* **vierfach; Sechs|fü|ßer** [-fyːsɐ] M **-s, -** (*Zool*) hexapod; **sechs|hun|dert** NUM six hundred; **Sechs|kampf** M *gymnastic competition with six events*; **sechs|mal** ADV six times; **Sechs|ta|ge|krieg** M (*Hist*) Six Day War; **Sechs|ta|ge|ren|nen** NT six-day (bicycle) race; **sechs|tä|gig** ADJ six-day; **sechs|tau|send** NUM six thousand; **ein Sechstausender** *a mountain six thousand metres in height*

Sechs|tel [ˈzɛkstl] NT **-s, -** sixth → *auch* **Viertel ¹**

sechs|tens [ˈzɛkstns] ADV sixth(ly), in the sixth place

sechs|te(r, s) [ˈzɛkstə] ADJ sixth; **einen ~n Sinn für etw haben, den ~n Sinn haben** to have a sixth sense (for sth) → *auch* **vierte(r, s)**

Sechs|und|sech|zig [ˈzɛksʊntˈzɛçtsɪç] NT **-, *no pl*** (*Cards*) sixty-six

Sechs|zy|lin|der [ˈzɛks-] M (*Auto*) six-cylinder car; (*Motor*) six-cylinder engine

sech|zehn [ˈzɛçtseːn] NUM sixteen → *auch* **vierzehn**

Sech|zehn|tel [ˈzɛçtseːntl] NT **-s, -** (*Mus*) semiquaver (*Brit*), sixteenth note (*US*)

Sech|zehn|tel|no|te F (*Mus*) semiquaver (*Brit*), sixteenth note (*US*)

sech|zig [ˈzɛçtsɪç] NUM sixty → *auch* **vierzig**

Sech|zi|ger [ˈzɛçtsɪgɐ] M **-s, -, Sech|zi|ge|rin** [-ərɪn] F **-, -nen** sixty-year-old, sexagenarian

Se|cond|hand- [sɛkəndˈhɛnd] *in cpds* second-hand; **Se|cond|hand|la|den** M second-hand shop

SED [ɛsleˈdeː] F **-** (*DDR*) abbr von **Sozialistische Einheitspartei Deutschlands**

Se|da|tiv [zedaˈtiːf] NT **-s, -e** [-və], **Se|da|ti|vum** [zedaˈtiːvʊm] NT **-s, Sedativa** [-va] (*Pharm*) sedative

Se|dez|for|mat [zeˈdeːts-] NT (*Typ*) sextodecimo

se|die|ren [zeˈdiːrən] ptp **sediert** VTI (*Med*) to sedate

Se|di|ment [zediˈmɛnt] NT **-(e)s, -e** (*Geol*) sediment

se|di|men|tär [zedimɛnˈtɛːɐ] ADJ (*Geol*) sedimentary

Se|di|ment|ge|stein NT (*Geol*) sedimentary rock

See¹ [zeː] F **-, -n** [ˈzeːən] sea; **raue** or **schwere ~** rough or heavy seas; **an der ~** by the sea, at the seaside; **an die ~ fahren** to go to the sea(side); **auf hoher ~** on the high seas; **auf ~** at sea; **in ~ gehen** or **stechen** to put to sea; **zur ~ fahren** to be a merchant seaman; **zur ~ gehen** to go to sea

See² [zeː] M **-s, -n** lake; (*in Schottland*) loch; (= *Teich*) pond

See-: See|aal M **a** (*Zool*) conger (eel) **b** (*Comm*) dogfish; **See|ad|ler** M sea eagle; **See|al|pen** PL (*Geog*) Maritime Alps *pl*; **See|amt** NT (*Admin*) maritime court; **See|ane|mo|ne** F sea anemone; **See|bad** NT **a** (= *Kurort*) seaside resort **b** (= *Bad im Meer*) bathe or swim in the sea; **See|bär** M **a** (*hum inf*) seadog (*inf*) **b** (*Zool*) fur seal; **See|bar|be** F (*Zool*) red mullet; **See|be|ben** NT seaquake; **see|be|schä|digt** [-bəfɛːdɪçt] ADJ (*form*) *Schiff* damaged at sea; **See|blick** M view of the sea/lake; **ein Zimmer mit ~** (*am Meer*) a room with sea view; (*am See*) a room overlooking the lake; **See|bo|den** M bottom or bed of a/the lake; (*von Meer*) bottom or bed of a/the sea; **der ~ des Loch Ness** the bottom or bed of Loch Ness; **See-Ele|fant** M , **See|ele|fant** ▲ M sea elephant; **see|er|fah|ren** ADJ *Volk* experienced at navigation or seafaring; **see|fah|rend** ADJ *attr Volk* seafaring; **See|fah-**

---

rer(in) M(F) seafarer; **Sindbad der ~** Sinbad the Sailor

See|fahrt F **a** (= *Fahrt*) (sea) voyage; (= *Vergnügungsseefahrt*) cruise **b** (= *Schifffahrt*) seafaring *no art*; **ungeeignet für die ~ in ...** unsuited for navigation or sailing in ...; **die ~ lernen** to learn to sail; **die Regeln der ~** the rules of the sea → *auch* **christlich**

See|fahrts-: See|fahrts|amt NT shipping board; **See|fahrts|buch** NT (*seaman's*) registration book; **See|fahrts|schu|le** F merchant navy (*Brit*) or merchant marine (*US*) training college

See-: see|fest ADJ **a** *Mensch* not subject to seasickness; **~ sein** to be a good sailor **b** = **seetüchtig c** *Ladung* fit for sea transport; **See|fisch** M saltwater fish; **See|fi|sche|rei** F sea fishing; **See|fracht** F sea freight; **See|fracht|brief** M (*Comm*) bill of lading; **See|frau** F sailor, mariner (*esp liter*); **See|funk (-|dienst)** M shipping radio service; **See|gang** [-gaŋ] M , *no pl* swell; **starker** or **hoher ~** heavy or rough seas or swell; **See|ge|fahr** F (*Comm*) sea risk; **See|ge|fecht** NT sea or naval battle; **See|gel|tung** F (*Hist*) naval prestige; **See|ge|mäl|de** NT seascape; **see|ge|stützt** [-gəʃtʏtst] ADJ (*Mil*) sea-based; *Flugkörper auch* sea-launched; **See|gras** NT (*Bot*) eelgrass, sea grass or hay; **See|gras|mat|rat|ze** F sea grass mattress; **see|grün** ADJ sea-green; **See|gur|ke** F (*Zool*) sea cucumber; **See|ha|fen** M seaport; **See|han|del** M maritime trade; **See|ha|se** M lumpsucker; **See|herr|schaft** F naval or maritime supremacy; **See|hö|he** F sea level; **See|hund** M seal; **See|hunds|fell** NT sealskin; **See|igel** M sea urchin; **See|jung|fer** F (*Zool*) dragonfly; **See|jung|frau** F (*Myth*) mermaid; **See|ka|dett(in)** M(F) (*Mil*) naval cadet; **See|ka|nal** M (maritime) canal; **See|kar|te** F sea or nautical chart; **See|kat|ze** F catfish; **see|klar** ADJ ready to sail; **See|kli|ma** NT maritime climate; **see|krank** ADJ seasick; **Paul wird leicht ~** Paul is a bad sailor; **See|krank|heit** F seasickness; **See|krieg** M naval war; **See|kriegs|recht** NT laws *pl* of naval warfare; **See|kuh** F (*Zool*) sea cow, manatee; **See|lachs** M (*Zool*) pollack; (*Cook*) rock salmon; **See|lachs|fi|let** NT (*Cook*) rock salmon fillet

See|lamt NT (*Sw Eccl*) requiem

See|land [ˈzeːlant] NT **-s** (*Geog*) **a** (*dänisch*) Zealand, Seeland **b** (*niederländisch*) Zeeland

See|lchen [ˈzeːlçən] NT **-s, -** (*inf*) dear soul

See|le [ˈzeːlə] F **-, -n a** (*Rel, fig*) soul; (= *Herzstück, Mittelpunkt*) life and soul; **seine ~ aushauchen** (*euph liter*) to breathe one's last (*liter*); **in tiefster** or **innerster ~** (*geh*) in one's heart of hearts; **mit ganzer ~** with all one's soul; **von ganzer ~** with all one's heart (and soul); **aus tiefster** or **innerster ~** with all one's heart and with all one's soul; *danken* from the bottom of one's heart; **jdm aus der ~ sprechen** to express exactly what sb feels; **das liegt mir auf der ~** it weighs heavily on my mind; **sich (*dat*) etw von der ~ reden** to get sth off one's chest; **sich (*dat*) die ~ aus dem Leib reden/schreien** (*inf*) to talk/shout until one is blue in the face (*inf*); **das tut mir in der ~ weh** I am deeply distressed; **zwei ~n und ein Gedanke** (*prov*) two minds with but a single thought; **zwei ~n wohnen in meiner Brust** (*liter*) I am torn; **dann/nun hat die liebe** or **arme ~ Ruh** that'll put him/us *etc* out of his/our misery; **meiner Seel!** (*old*) upon my soul! (*old*) **b** (= *Mensch*) soul; **eine ~ von Mensch** or **von einem Menschen** an absolute dear **c** (*von Feuerwaffen*) bore **d** (*von Tau*) core

See|len-: See|len|ach|se F axis (of the bore); **See|len|adel** M (*liter*) nobility of mind; **See|len|amt** NT (*Eccl*) requiem; **See|len|arzt** M , **See|len|ärz|tin** F (*hum*), **See|len|dok|tor** M , **See|len|dok|to|rin** F (*hum inf*) head-

---

shrinker (*hum inf*), shrink (*inf*), trick cyclist (*Brit hum sl*); **See|len|dra|ma** NT psychological drama; **See|len|for|scher(in)** M(F) psychologist; **See|len|freund(in)** M(F)   (*geh*) soul mate; **See|len|frie|de(n)** M (*geh*) peace of mind; **See|len|grö|ße** F (*geh*) greatness of mind, magnanimity; **see|len|gut** ADJ kindhearted; **See|len|gü|te** F (*geh*) kind-heartedness; **See|len|heil** NT spiritual salvation, salvation of one's soul; (*fig*) spiritual welfare; **See|len|hirt(in)** M(F) , **See|len|hir|te** M (*geh, iro*) pastor; **See|len|klemp|ner(in)** M(F) (*pej inf: = Psychiater*) head shrinker (*hum inf*), shrink (*inf*), trick cyclist (*Brit hum sl*); **See|len|kun|de** F (*dated*) psychology; **See|len|la|ge** F (*von Individuum*) inner state; (*politisch, von Nation, Partei etc auch*) inner feeling; **See|len|land|schaft** F (*inf*) mindset; (*künstlerisch, literarisch*) landscape of the soul; **See|len|le|ben** NT inner life; **er versteht ihr ~ überhaupt nicht** he does not understand her emotions *or* feelings at all; **See|len|leh|re** F (*dated*) psychology; **see|len|los** ADJ soulless; **See|len|mas|sa|ge** F (*hum inf*) gentle persuasion; **See|len|mes|se** F (*Eccl*) requiem mass; **See|len|not** F , **See|len|pein** F , **See|len|qual** F (*geh*) (mental) anguish; **See|len|re|gung** F sign of emotion, emotional reaction *or* response; **See|len|ru|he** F calmness, coolness; **in aller ~** calmly; (*= kaltblütig*) as cool as you please (*Brit*), as cool as ice; **see|len|ru|hig** ADJ calm; (*= kaltblütig*) as cool as you please, as cool as a cucumber (*inf*) ADV calmly; (*= kaltblütig*) callously; **See|len|trös|ter** M (*hum: = Schnaps*) pick-me-up (*inf*); **See|len|trös|ter(in)** M(F) (*Mensch*) comforter; **See|len|ver|käu|fer** M (*Hist*) seller of souls; (*fig pej*) (*= Heuerbaas*) press-gang officer; (*Schiff*) death trap; **see|len|ver|wandt** ADJ congenial (*liter*); **sie waren ~** they were kindred spirits; **See|len|ver|wandt|schaft** F affinity, congeniality of spirit (*liter*); **see|len|voll** ADJ Blick, Tonfall soulful ADV soulfully, passionately; **See|len|wan|de|rung** F (*Rel*) transmigration of souls, metempsychosis; **See|len|wär|mer** [-vɛrmɐ] M **-s, -** (*hum: = Schnaps*) pick-me-up (*inf*); **See|len|zu|stand** M psychological *or* mental state

See-: **See|leu|te** pl von Seemann; **See|li|lie** F sea lily

see|lisch [ˈzeːlɪʃ] ADJ (*Rel*) spiritual; (*= geistig*) Gesundheit, Gleichgewicht mental; Schaden psychological; Erschütterung, Belastung emotional; Grausamkeit mental; **~e Kraft zu etw haben** to have the strength of mind for sth; **~e Abgründe** the blackest depths of the human soul ADV psychologically; **~ bedingt sein** to have psychological causes; **~ krank** mentally ill; **jdn ~ misshandeln** to ill-treat sb psychologically

See-: **See|lot|se** M , **See|lot|sin** F pilot; **See|lö|we** M sea lion

Seel|sor|ge [ˈzeːlzɔrgə] F , no pl spiritual welfare; **in der ~ arbeiten** to do spiritual welfare work with a church

Seel|sor|ger [-zɔrgɐ] M **-s, -**, **Seel|sor|ge|rin** [-ərɪn] F -, -nen pastor

seel|sor|ge|risch [-zɔrgərɪʃ], **seel|sor|ger|lich** [-zɔrgɐlɪç], **seel|sorg|lich** ADJ Tätigkeit, Betreuung pastoral ADV **~ tätig sein** to do pastoral work; **jdn ~ betreuen** to be a religious counsellor (*Brit*) *or* counselor (*US*) to sb

See-: **See|luft** F sea air; **See|macht** F naval *or* sea *or* maritime power

See|mann M pl **-leute** sailor, seaman, mariner (*esp liter*)

see|män|nisch [-mɛnɪʃ] ADJ Ausbildung, Sprache etc nautical; Tradition auch seafaring; **das ist typisch ~** that is typical of sailors ADV nautically; **~ heißen sie ...** in nautical *or* sailors' language they are called ...

Seemanns-: **See|manns|amt** NT shipping board; **See|manns|aus|druck** M pl **-ausdrü|cke** nautical *or* sailors' term; **See|manns|brauch** M seafaring custom; **See|manns|**

---

gang [-gaŋ] M , no pl sailor's walk *or* swagger; **See|manns|garn** NT , no pl (*inf*) sailor's yarn; **~ spinnen** to spin a yarn; **See|manns|grab** NT watery grave, Davy Jones' *or* Jones's locker; **ein ~ finden** to go to a watery grave; **See|manns|heim** NT sailors' home; **See|manns|lied** NT sea shanty; **See|manns|los** NT a sailor's lot; **See|manns|mis|si|on** F mission to seamen, seamen's mission; **See|manns|spra|che** F nautical *or* sailors' slang; **See|manns|tod** M sailor's death; **den ~ sterben** to die a sailor's death

See-: **see|mä|ßig** ADJ Verpackung seaworthy; **See|mei|le** F nautical *or* sea mile; **See|mi|ne** F (sea) mine; **See|mö|we** F seagull; **See|nel|ke** F sea anemone

Seen|ge|biet [ˈzeːən-] NT , **Seen|land|schaft** F lakeland area

See|not F , no pl distress; **in ~ geraten** to get into distress

See|not-: **See|not|kreu|zer** M (motor) lifeboat; **See|not(ret|tungs)|dienst** M sea rescue service; **See|not|zei|chen** NT nautical distress signal

Seen|plat|te [ˈzeːən-] F lowland plain full of lakes

See-: **See|nym|phe** F mermaid; **See|ot|ter** M sea otter; **See|pferd** M , **See|pferd|chen** [-pfeːɐtçən] NT **-s,** - sea horse; **See|räu|ber(in)** M(F) pirate; (*in Mittelamerika im 17., 18. Jh. auch*) buccaneer; **See|räu|be|rei** F piracy; **See|räu|ber|schiff** NT pirate (ship); buccaneer; **See|recht** NT maritime law; **See|rei|se** F (sea) voyage; (*= Kreuzfahrt*) cruise; **See|ro|se** F water lily; **See|sack** M seabag, sailor's kitbag (*Brit*); **See|salz** NT sea salt; **See|sand** M sea sand; **See|scha|den** M damage at sea, average (*spec*); **See|schiff** NT seagoing *or* ocean-going ship *or* vessel; **See|schiff|fahrt** F maritime *or* ocean shipping; **See|schild|krö|te** F sea turtle; **See|schlacht** F naval *or* sea battle; **See|schlan|ge** F sea snake; (*Myth*) sea serpent; **See|schwal|be** F tern; **See|sieg** M naval victory; **See|sper|re** F naval blockade; **See|stadt** F seaside town; **See|stern** M (*Zool*) starfish; **See|stra|ße** F sea route, shipping lane; **See|stra|ßen|ord|nung** F rules pl of the road (at sea), international regulations pl for preventing collisions at sea (*form*); **See|streit|kräf|te** PL naval forces pl, navy; **See|stück** NT (*Art*) seascape; **See|tang** M seaweed; **See|tau|cher** M (*Orn*) grebe; **See|teu|fel** M (*Zool*) angler, allmouth; (*am Meeresboden lebend*) monkfish; **See|trans|port** M shipment *or* transport by sea, sea transport; **see|tüch|tig** ADJ seaworthy; **See|tüch|tig|keit** F seaworthiness; **See|ufer** NT lakeside; (*von großem See auch*) (lake) shore; **See|un|ge|heu|er** NT sea monster; **see|un|tüch|tig** ADJ unseaworthy; **See|ver|kehr** M maritime traffic; **See|ver|si|che|rung** F marine insurance; **See|vo|gel** M sea bird; **See|volk** NT (*Nation*) seafaring nation *or* people; (*inf: = Seeleute*) seafaring people pl; **See|wal|ze** F (*Zool*) sea cucumber; **see|wärts** [ˈzeːvɛrts] ADV (*= in Richtung Meer*) seaward(s), toward(s) the sea; (*= in Richtung (Binnen)see*) toward(s) the lake; **See|was|ser** NT , no pl (*= Meerwasser*) sea water; (*= Wasser eines Sees*) lake water; **See|weg** M sea route; **auf dem ~ reisen** to go *or* travel by sea; **See|we|sen** NT maritime affairs pl, no art; **See|wet|ter|dienst** M meteorological service, Met Office (*Brit inf*); **See|wind** M sea breeze, onshore wind; **See|wolf** M (*Zool*) wolffish; **See|zei|chen** NT navigational aid; **See|zun|ge** F sole

Se|gel [ˈzeːgl] NT **-s,** - sail; **die ~ setzen** to set the sails; **mit vollen ~n** under full sail *or* canvas; (*fig*) with gusto; **unter ~ gehen** (*Naut*) to set sail; **die ~ streichen** (*Naut*) to strike sail; (*fig*) to give in → **Wind a**

Segel-: **Se|gel|boot** NT sailing boat (*Brit*), sailboat (*US*); **Se|gel|fahrt** F sail; **se|gel|flie|-**

---

gen VI infin only to glide; **~ gehen** to go gliding; **Se|gel|flie|gen** NT **-s**, no pl gliding; **Se|gel|flie|ger(in)** M(F) glider pilot; **Se|gel|flie|ge|rei** F gliding; **Se|gel|flug** M (*no pl: = Segelfliegerei*) gliding; (*= Flug*) glider flight; **Se|gel|flug|platz** M gliding field; **Se|gel|flug|zeug** NT glider; (*leichter gebaut auch*) sailplane; **Se|gel|jacht** F (sailing) yacht, sailboat (*US*); **Se|gel|kar|te** F chart; **se|gel|klar** ADJ pred ready to sail; **Se|gel|klas|se** F (*Sport*) (yacht) class; **Se|gel|klub** M sailing club; **Se|gel|ma|cher(in)** M(F) sailmaker

se|geln [ˈzeːgln] VTI aux haben or sein (lit, fig) to sail; **eine Strecke ~** to sail a course; **eine Regatta ~** to sail in a regatta; **als junger Mensch hat** *or* **ist er viel gesegelt** in his younger days he did a lot of sailing *or* he sailed a lot; **~ gehen** VI aux sein (*inf*) to go for a sail; **durch eine Prüfung ~** to flop in an exam (*Brit inf*), to fail an exam

Se|geln NT **-s**, no pl sailing

Segel-: **Se|gel|oh|ren** PL (*hum*) flappy ears pl (*inf*); **Se|gel|par|tie** F sail, sailing trip; **Se|gel|re|gat|ta** F sailing *or* yachting regatta; **Se|gel|schiff** NT sailing ship *or* vessel; **Se|gel|schu|le** F sailing school; **Se|gel|schul|schiff** NT training sailing ship; **Se|gel|sport** M sailing no art; **Se|gel|törn** M cruise (on a yacht etc); **Se|gel|tuch** NT pl **-tuche** canvas

Se|gen [ˈzeːgn] M **-s, -** **a** (lit, fig) blessing; (*Eccl: = Gnadengebet*) blessing, benediction; **es ist ein ~, dass ...** it is a blessing that ...; **über jdn/etw den ~ sprechen** to give sb/sth one's blessing; (*Eccl auch*) to pronounce one's blessing upon sb/sth; **jdm den ~ erteilen** *or* **spenden** to give one's blessing *or* benediction; **~ spendend** beneficent; **jdm/einer Sache seinen ~ erteilen** *or* **geben** (*fig*) to give sb/sth one's blessing; **meinen ~ hat er, er hat meinen ~** he has my blessing

b (*= Heil, Erfolg*) blessing, boon, godsend; **das bringt keinen ~** no good will come of it; **~ bringend** beneficent; **ein wahrer ~** a real blessing *or* boon; **zum ~ der Menschheit werden** to be for *or* to redound to (*liter*) the benefit of mankind; **zum ~ des Unternehmens handeln** to act for the good of the company; **jdm zum ~ gereichen** to be a blessing *or* boon *or* godsend to sb

c (*liter: = Ertrag, Lohn*) fruits pl

d (*inf*) **der ganze ~** the whole lot *or* shoot (*inf*)

Segen-: **se|gen|brin|gend** △ ADJ → Segen b; **Se|gen|er|tei|lung** F (*Eccl*) benediction, blessing; **se|gen|spen|dend** △ ADJ → Segen b

Segens-: **se|gens|reich** ADJ beneficial; Tätigkeit beneficent; **Se|gens|wunsch** M (*liter*) blessing; **herzliche Segenswünsche** congratulations and best wishes

Seg|ler¹ [ˈzeːglɐ] M **-s, -** **a** (*= Schiff*) sailing vessel **b** (*Orn*) swift

Seg|ler² [ˈzeːglɐ] M **-s, -**, **Seg|le|rin** [-ərɪn] F -, -nen (*= Segelsportler*) yachtsman/-woman, sailor

Seg|ler|müt|ze F sailor's cap

Seg|ment [zɛˈgmɛnt] NT **-(e)s, -e** segment

seg|men|tal [zɛgmɛnˈtaːl] ADJ segmental

seg|men|tär [zɛgmɛnˈtɛːɐ] ADJ segmentary

seg|men|tie|ren [zɛgmɛnˈtiːrən] ptp **segmentiert** VT to segment

Seg|men|tie|rung F -, -en segmentation

seg|nen [ˈzeːgnən] VT (*Rel*) to bless; **~d die Hände erheben** to raise one's hands in blessing → auch **gesegnet**

Seg|nung F -, -en (*Rel*) blessing, benediction

Se|gre|ga|ti|on [zegregaˈtsi̯oːn] F -, -en (*Sociol*) segregation

seh|be|hin|dert ADJ partially sighted

Seh|be|hin|de|rung F impaired vision *or* sight

se|hen ['ze:ən]

pret **sah** [za:], *ptp* **gesehen** [gə'ze:ən]

1 TRANSITIVES VERB	3 INTRANSITIVES VERB
2 REFLEXIVES VERB	

1 – TRANSITIVES VERB

a | = mit den Augen wahrnehmen | to see; (= *ansehen*) to look at, to see; **siehst du irgendwo mein Buch?** can you see my book anywhere?; **Sie sehen jetzt eine Direktübertragung ...** we now bring you a live broadcast ...; **Sie sahen eine Direktübertragung ...** that was a live broadcast ...; **ich sehe was, was du nicht siehst** (= *Spiel*) I spy (with my little eye (*Brit*)); **gut zu sehen sein** to be clearly visible; **schlecht zu sehen sein** to be difficult to see; **sieht man das?** does it show?; **das kann man sehen** you can see that; **von ihm war nichts mehr zu sehen** he was no longer to be seen; **da gibt es nichts zu sehen** there is nothing to see; **darf ich das mal sehen?** can I have a look at that?; **jdn kommen/weggehen sehen** to see sb coming/leaving; **jdn/etw zu sehen bekommen** to get to see sb/sth; **sich/jdn als etw sehen** to see oneself/sb as sth; **etw in jdm sehen** to see sb as sth; **Sie sah in ihm ihren Nachfolger** she saw him as her successor; **das Kind sah in ihm den Beschützer** the child saw him as a protector; **ich kann den Mantel/Mann nicht mehr sehen** (= *nicht mehr ertragen*) I can't stand the sight of that coat/the man any more; **das muss man gesehen haben** it has to be seen to be believed; (= *lässt sich nicht beschreiben*) you have to see it for yourself; **den möchte ich sehen, der ...** I'd like to meet the man who ...; **hat man so was schon gesehen!** (*inf*) did you ever see anything like it!

♦ **sich sehen lassen** to put in an appearance; **er hat sich schon lange nicht mehr zu Hause sehen lassen** he hasn't put in an appearance at home for a long time; **er lässt sich kaum noch bei uns sehen** he hardly ever comes to see us now, we hardly ever see him these days; **lassen Sie sich doch mal wieder sehen!** do come again!; **er kann sich in dieser Gegend nicht mehr sehen lassen** he can't show his face in the area any more; **kann mich in diesem Anzug sehen lassen?** do I look all right in this suit?; **mit diesem eleganten Kostüm kann sie sich überall sehen lassen** she'd look fine anywhere in this smart suit; **mit diesem Mann kannst du dich doch nirgends sehen lassen!** you don't want to be seen with this man!; **mit diesem Ergebnis kann sich die Mannschaft sehen lassen** the team can be proud of this result

b | = treffen | to see; **sich** *or* **einander sehen** to see each other; **ich freue mich, Sie zu sehen!** nice to see you!; **also, wir sehen uns morgen** right, I'll see you tomorrow; **sie sehen sich in letzter Zeit oft** they've been seeing a lot of each other lately

c | = feststellen | to see; **das wird man noch sehen** we'll see; **ob er tatsächlich kommt, das wird man noch sehen** we'll see if he actually comes; **das wollen wir (doch) erst mal sehen!** we'll see about that!; **das wollen wir (doch) erst mal sehen, ob ...** we'll see if ...; **das müssen wir erst mal sehen** that remains to be seen; **da sieht man es mal wieder!** that's typical!; **das sehe ich noch nicht** (*inf*) I still don't see that happening

d | = beurteilen | to see; **wie siehst du das?** how do you see it?; **das sehe ich anders, so sehe ich das nicht** that's not how I see it; **du hast wohl keine Lust, oder wie sehe ich das?** (*inf*) you don't feel like it, do you?; **das darf man nicht so sehen** that's not the way to look at it; **du siehst das/ihn nicht richtig** you've got it/him wrong; **seit dieser Unterhaltung sehe ich sie anders** since this conversation I see her differently; **rein menschlich/wirtschaftlich gesehen** from a purely personal/economic point of view; **so gesehen** looked at in this way

2 – REFLEXIVES VERB

♦ **sich sehen sich betrogen/getäuscht sehen** to see oneself cheated/deceived; **sich enttäuscht sehen** to feel disappointed; **sich genötigt** *or* **veranlasst sehen, zu ...** to find it necessary to ...; **sich gezwungen sehen, zu ...** to find oneself obliged to ...; **sich in der Lage sehen, zu ...** (*form*) to find oneself in a position to ... (*form*)

3 – INTRANSITIVES VERB

a | mit den Augen | to see; **er sieht gut/schlecht** he can/cannot see very well; **er sieht nur mit einem** *or* **auf einem Auge** he only has sight in one eye; **seit diesem Unfall sehe ich doppelt** I've been seeing double *or* I've had double vision since the accident; **nichts mehr sehen** (*sl*: = *betrunken sein*) to be wrecked (*Brit*) *or* wasted (*sl*); **durchs Schlüsselloch sehen** to look through the keyhole; **jdm tief in die Augen sehen** to look deep into sb's eyes; **jdm über die Schulter sehen** to look over sb's shoulder; **siehe oben/unten** see above/below; **sieh(e) da!** (*liter*) behold! (*liter*); **siehst du (wohl)!, siehste!** (*inf*) you see!; **sieh doch!** look (here)!; **sehen Sie mal!** look!; **siehe!, sehet!** (*old, liter, Bibl*) lo! (*Bibl*), behold! (*Bibl*); **willst du mal sehen?** do you want to have a look?; **lass mal sehen** let me see, let me have a look; **sehenden Auges** (*geh*) with one's eyes open; **das Boot sah kaum aus dem Wasser** the boat hardly showed above the water

b | = feststellen | **na siehst du** (there you are,) you see?; **wie ich sehe ...** I see that ...; **wie ich sehe, hast du schon angefangen** I see you have already started; **Sie sind beschäftigt, wie ich sehe** I can see you're busy; **ich sehe schon, du willst nicht** I can see you don't want to; **wir werden schon sehen** we'll see; **da kann man mal sehen, da kannste mal sehen** (*inf*) that just goes to show (*inf*); **wir wollen sehen** we'll have to see; **mal sehen, ob ...** (*inf*) let's see if ...; **mal sehen!** (*inf*) we'll see; **jeder muss sehen, wo er bleibt** (it's) every man for himself; **sieh, dass du ...** make sure you..., see (that) you ...

♦ **auf etw** (*acc*) **sehen** (= *hinsehen*) to look at sth; (= *achten*) to consider sth important; **auf die Uhr sehen** to look at one's watch; **jdm auf den Mund sehen** to watch sb's lips; **das Fenster sieht auf den Garten** the window looks onto the garden; **darauf sehen, dass ...** to make sure (that) ...; **er sieht auf Pünktlichkeit** he's a stickler for punctuality; **er sieht auf gute Umgangsformen** he thinks good manners are important; **er sieht nur auf seinen eigenen Vorteil** he only cares about what's good for him

♦ **sehen nach nach jdm sehen** (= *betreuen*) to look after sb; (= *besuchen*) to go to see sb; **nach etw sehen** to look after sth; **ich muss nur mal eben nach den Kartoffeln sehen** I've just got to have a look at the potatoes; **nach der Post sehen** to see if there are any letters

Se|hen NT -s, *no pl* seeing; (= *Sehkraft*) sight, vision; **als Fotograf muss man richtiges, bewusstes – lernen** as a photographer one has to learn to see correctly and consciously; **ich kenne ihn nur vom –** I only know him by sight

se|hens|wert, se|hens|wür|dig ADJ worth seeing; **ein –es Schloss** a castle (which is) worth seeing

Se|hens|wür|dig|keit [-vyrdɪçkaɪt] F -, -en sight; **dieses Gebäude ist wirklich eine –!** that building is really (a sight) worth seeing!; **die –en (einer Stadt) besichtigen** to go sightseeing (in a city), to see the sights (of a city)

Se|her¹ ['ze:ɐ] M -s, - (*Hunt*) eye

Se|her² ['ze:ɐ] M -s, -, **Se|he|rin** [-ərɪn] F -, -nen (*liter*) seer

Se|her-: Se|her|blick M (*geh*) prophetic eye; **den – haben** to have a prophetic eye; **Se|her|ga|be** F (*geh*) gift of prophecy, prophetic gift

se|he|risch ['ze:ərɪʃ] ADJ *attr Fähigkeit* prophetic

Seh-: Seh|feh|ler M visual *or* sight defect; **Seh|feld** NT field of vision, visual field; **Seh|hil|fe** F seeing aid; **Seh|kraft** F , *no pl* (eye)sight; **Seh|kreis** M = **Gesichtskreis**; **Seh|loch** NT (*Opt*) pupil

Seh|ne ['ze:nə] F -, -n **a** (*Anat*) tendon, sinew **b** (= *Bogensehne*) string **c** (*Math*) chord

seh|nen ['ze:nən] VR **sich nach jdm/etw ~** to long *or* yearn (*liter*) for sb/sth; (*schmachtend*) to pine for sb/sth; **mit ~dem Verlangen** (*geh*) with longing *or* yearning

Seh|nen NT -s, *no pl* = **Sehnsucht**

Seh|nen-: Seh|nen|re|flex M tendon reflex; **Seh|nen|schei|den|ent|zün|dung** F tendinitis, tendonitis; **Seh|nen|zer|rung** F pulled tendon

Seh|nerv M optic nerve

seh|nig ['ze:nɪç] ADJ *Gestalt, Mensch* sinewy, wiry; *Fleisch* stringy

sehn|lich ['ze:nlɪç] ADJ *Wunsch* ardent; *Erwartung* eager; **sein ~ster Wunsch** his fondest *or* most ardent (*liter*) wish ADV *hoffen, wünschen* ardently; **sich** (*dat*) **etw ~(st) wünschen** to long for sth with all one's heart; **wir alle hatten sie ~(st) erwartet** we had all been (most) eagerly awaiting her

Sehn|sucht ['ze:nzʊxt] F longing, yearning (*nach* for); (*schmachtend*) pining; **~ haben** to have a longing *or* yearning

sehn|süch|tig ADJ longing, yearning; *Verlangen, Wunsch etc* ardent; *Erwartung, Ungeduld* eager; *Brief* full of longing *or* yearning; **der dritte Satz hat etwas seltsam Sehnsüchtiges** the third movement has a strangely yearning quality ADV *hoffen, wünschen* ardently; **~ auf jdn warten** to yearn for sb; **~ auf etw** (*acc*) **warten** to long for sth

sehn|suchts|voll ADJ longing, yearning; *Blick, Augen, Brief, Schilderung, Musik* wistful ADV *betrachten, denken* longingly; *singen* yearningly; **~ auf etw** (*acc*) **warten** to long for sth

Seh|or|gan NT visual organ

sehr [ze:ɐ] ADV *comp* (**noch**) **mehr** [me:ɐ], *superl* **am meisten** ['maɪstn] **a** (*mit adj, adv*) very; **~ verbunden!** (*dated form*) much obliged; **er ist ~ dafür** he is very much in favour (*Brit*) *or* favor (*US*) of it, he is all for it; **er ist ~ dagegen** he is very much against it; **hat er ~ viel getrunken?** did he drink very much?; **er hat ~ viel getrunken** he drank a lot; **~ zu meiner Überraschung** very much to my surprise; **es geht ihm ~ viel besser** he is very much better; **wir haben ~ viel Zeit/Geld** we have plenty of time/money, we have a lot of time/money, we have lots of time/money; **wir haben nicht ~ viel Zeit/Geld** we don't have very much time/money

b (*mit vb*) very much, a lot; **so ~** so much; **jdn so ~ schlagen/zusammenschlagen, dass ...** to hit sb so hard that/to beat sb up so much *or* so badly that ...; **sich über etw** (*acc*) **so ~ ärgern/freuen, dass ...** to be so (very) annoyed/pleased about sth that ...; **~ verwurzelt sein** to be very deeply rooted; **wie ~** how much; **wie ~ er sich auch ...** however much he ...; **sich ~ vorsehen** to be very careful, to be very much on the lookout; **sich** (*dat*) **etw ~ überlegen** to consider sth very carefully; **sich ~ anstrengen** to try very hard; **es lohnt sich ~** it's very *or* well worthwhile; **~ weinen** to cry a lot *or* a great deal; **hat sie ~ geweint?** did she cry very much *or* a lot?; **es regnet ~** it's raining hard *or* heavily; **regnet es ~?** is it raining very much?, is it raining a lot?; **freust du dich? – ja, ~!** are you pleased? – yes, very; **freust du dich darauf? – ja, ~** are you looking forward to it? – yes, very much; **tut es weh? – ja, ~/nein, nicht ~** does it hurt? – yes, a lot/no, not very much *or* not a lot; **~ sogar!** yes, very much so (in fact); **zu ~** too much; **man sollte sich nicht zu ~ ärgern** one shouldn't get too annoyed

seh|ren ['ze:rən] VT (*old, dial*) = **verletzen**

Seh-: **Seh|rohr** NT periscope; **Seh|schär|fe** F keenness of sight, visual acuity; **Seh|schlitz** M slit; (von Panzer etc) observation slit; **Seh|schwä|che** F poor eyesight; **Seh|stö|rung** F visual defect; **wenn ~en auftreten** when the vision becomes disturbed; **Seh|test** M eye test; **Seh|ver|mö|gen** NT powers pl of vision; **Seh|wei|te** F = Sichtweite

sei [zai] imper sing, 1. and 3. pers sing subjunc von **sein**

sei|bern ['zaibən] VI (dial) = sabbern

Seich [zaiç] M -(e)s, no pl, **Sei|che** F ['zaiçə] F -, no pl **a** (dial sl) piss (sl) **b** (inf: = Geschwätz) claptrap (inf)

sei|chen ['zaiçn] VI **a** (dial sl) to piss (sl) **b** (inf) = schwafeln

seicht [zaiçt] ADJ (lit, fig) shallow; Unterhaltung, TV-Programm trivial; **die ~e Stelle** the shallows pl

Seicht|heit F -, -en (lit, fig) shallowness

seid [zait] 2. pers pl pres, imper pl von **sein**

Sei|de ['zaidə] F -, -n silk

Sei|del ['zaidl] NT -s, - **a** (Gefäß) stein, (beer) mug **b** (S Ger: altes Maß) half-litre (Brit), half-liter (US), ≈ pint

Sei|del|bast M (Bot) daphne

sei|den ['zaidn] ADJ attr (= aus Seide) silk, silken (liter)

Sei|den- in cpds silk; **sei|den|ar|tig** ADJ silky, silk-like; **Sei|den|at|las** M pl -se silk satin; **Sei|den|band** [-bant] NT pl -bänder silk ribbon; **Sei|den|fa|den** M silk thread; **Sei|den|ge|we|be** NT silk fabric; **Sei|den|glanz** M silky or silken sheen; **Sei|den|ma|le|rei** F silk painting; **sei|den|matt** ADJ Foto semi-matt; **Sei|den|pa|pier** NT tissue paper; (Phot) satin-finished paper; **Sei|den|rau|pe** F silkworm; **Sei|den|rau|pen|zucht** F silkworm breeding; **Sei|den|schwanz** M (Orn) waxwing; **Sei|den|spin|ner** M (Zool) silk(worm) moth; **Sei|den|spin|ne|r(in)** M(F) silk spinner; **Sei|den|spin|ne|rei** **b** (Betrieb) silk mill; **Sei|den|stoff** M silk cloth or fabric; **Sei|den|stra|ße** F (Hist) silk road; **Sei|den|strumpf** M silk stocking; **Sei|den|tuch** NT silk scarf; **sei|den|weich** ADJ soft as silk, silky soft

sei|dig ['zaidiç] ADJ (= wie Seide) silky, silken

Sei|en|de(s) ['zaiəndə] NT decl as adj (Philos) being no art

Sei|fe ['zaifə] F -, -n **a** soap **b** (Geol) alluvial deposit

sei|fen ['zaifn] VT **a** (= einseifen, abseifen) to soap **b** (Min) to wash

Sei|fen-: **Sei|fen|bla|se** F soap bubble; (fig) bubble; **~n machen** to blow (soap) bubbles; **Sei|fen|flo|cken** PL soap flakes pl; **Sei|fen|kis|ten|ren|nen** NT soapbox derby; **Sei|fen|lau|ge** F (soap)suds pl; **Sei|fen|napf** M shaving mug; **Sei|fen|oper** F (inf) soap (opera); **Sei|fen|pul|ver** NT soap powder; **Sei|fen|scha|le** F soap dish; **Sei|fen|schaum** M lather; **Sei|fen|spen|der** M soap dispenser; **Sei|fen|was|ser** NT , no pl soapy water

sei|fig ['zaifiç] ADJ soapy; (fig) soppy

Sei|ger|schacht ['zaigɐ-] M (Min) perpendicular shaft

Sei|he ['zaiə] F -, -n = Seiher

sei|hen ['zaiən] VT (= sieben) to sieve; (S Ger, Aus: = Flüssigkeit abgießen von) to strain

Sei|her ['zaiɐ] M -s, - (esp S Ger, Aus) strainer, colander

Seih|tuch NT pl -tücher (muslin) cloth

Seil [zail] NT -(e)s, -e rope; (= Kabel) cable; (= Hochseil) tightrope, high wire; **auf dem ~ tanzen** (fig) to be walking a tightrope

Seil-: **Seil|bahn** F cable railway; (= Bergseilbahn auch) funicular; **Seil|brü|cke** F rope bridge

Sei|ler ['zailɐ] M -s, -, **Sei|le|rin** [-ərɪn] F -, -nen ropemaker

Sei|ler|bahn F ropewalk

Sei|le|rei [zailə'rai] F -, -en **a** (= Seilerhandwerk) ropemaking **b** (= Seilerwerkstatt) ropewalk, ropery (rare)

Sei|ler|wa|ren PL rope goods pl

Seil-: **Seil|fäh|re** F cable ferry; **seil+hüp|fen** VI sep aux sein, usu infin or ptp to skip; **Seil|schaft** ['zailʃaft] F -, -en (Bergsteigen) rope, roped party; (fig: in Politik, Industrie etc) clique, coterie; **Seil|schwe|be|bahn** F cable railway; (= Bergseilbahn auch) funicular; **seil+sprin|gen** VI sep aux sein, usu infin or ptp to skip; **Seil|tanz** M tightrope or high-wire act; **seil+tan|zen** VI sep, usu infin or ptp to walk the tightrope or high wire; **Seil|tän|zer(in)** M(F) tightrope walker, high-wire performer; **Seil|win|de** F winch; **Seil|zie|hen** NT tug-of-war; **Seil|zug** M (Tech) cable control

Seim [zaim] M -(e)s, -e viscous or glutinous substance

sei|mig ['zaimiç] ADJ viscous, glutinous

sein¹ [zain] pres **ist** [ɪst], pret **war** [vaːɐ], ptp **gewesen** [gə'veːzn] aux sein **VI** **a** (= in einem Zustand sein, sich befinden) to be; **wir waren** we were; **wir sind gewesen** we have been, we've been; **sei (mir)/seien Sie (mir) nicht böse, aber ...** don't be angry (with me) but ...; **sei/seid so nett und ...** be so kind as to ...; **du bist wohl verrückt!** (inf) you must be crazy (inf); **ist das heiß/kalt!** that's really hot/cold!, is that hot/cold! (inf); **das wäre gut** that would or that'd (inf) be a good thing; **es wäre schön gewesen** it would or it'd (inf) have been nice; **die Arbeit will sofort erledigt ~** (geh) this work must be done immediately; **er ist Lehrer/Inder/ein Verwandter/der Chef** he is a teacher/(an) Indian/a relative/the boss; **was sind Sie (beruflich)?** what do you do?; **er ist immer noch nichts** he still hasn't become anything; **wir sind wieder wer** we're somebody again; **Liverpool ist Fußballmeister/eine große Stadt** Liverpool are football champions/is a large town; **in der Küche sind noch viele** there's (inf) or there are still plenty in the kitchen; **drei und vier ist** or **sind sieben** three and four is or are seven; **x sei 4** let x be or equal 4; **wenn ich Sie wäre** if I were or was you/him or he (form); **er war es nicht** it wasn't him; **niemand will es gewesen ~** nobody admits that it was him/her or them (inf); **ich will mal nicht so ~ und ...** I don't want to be awkward and ...; **das kann schon ~** that may well be; **und das wäre?** and what would or might that be?; **das wärs!** that's all, that's it; **wie war das noch?** what was that again?; **wie war das noch mit dem Witz?** how did that joke go now?; **bist dus/ist ers?** is that you/him?; **wer ist da?** who's there?; **ist da jemand?** is (there) anybody there?; **er ist aus Genf/aus guter Familie** he is or comes from Geneva/a good family; **morgen bin ich im Büro/in Rom** I'll or I will or I shall be in the office/in Rome tomorrow; **waren Sie (schon) mal in Rom?** have you ever been to Rome?; **wir waren baden/essen** we went swimming/out for a meal; **wo warst du so lange?** where have you been all this time?, what kept you?; **er war vier Jahre hin, bevor er ... he** had been here for four years before he ...; **es sind über zwanzig Jahre her, dass ...** it is more than twenty years since ...; **was nicht ist, kann ja noch werden** anything can happen, things can change → auch **gewesen**

b (mit infin +zu) **du bist nicht zu sehen** you cannot be seen; **das war ja vorauszusehen** that was to be expected; **das war nicht vorauszusehen** we couldn't have known that; **der Brief ist persönlich abzugeben** the letter is to be delivered by hand; **wie ist das zu verstehen?** how is that to be understood?; **er ist nicht zu ersetzen** he cannot be replaced; **ein eigener Garten ist nicht zu unterschätzen** a garden of one's own is not to be underestimated; **mit ihr ist ja nicht zu sprechen** you can't talk to her

c **was ist?** what's the matter?, what is it?, what's up (inf); **ist was?** what is it?; (= passt dir was nicht) is something the matter?; **was ist mit dir/ihm?** what or how about you/him?; (= was hast du/hat er?) what's wrong or the matter or up (inf) with you/him?; **das kann nicht ~** that can't be (true); **wie wäre es mit ...?** how about ...?, what about ...?; **sei es, dass ..., sei es, dass ...** whether ... or ...; **es sei denn ...** unless ...; **nun, wie ist es?** well, how or what about it?; **wie wäre es, wenn wir ihn besuchen würden?** what about or how about going to see him?, why don't we go to see him?; **das brauchte nicht zu ~** (= hätte nicht passieren müssen) it need not or it need never have happened or have been (Brit dial, liter), it didn't have to happen

d (= da sein, existieren) to be; **wenn du nicht gewesen wärst ...** if it hadn't been for you ...; **er ist nicht mehr** (euph) he is no more (euph liter); **alles, was (bis jetzt/damals) war** all that has/had been (liter)

e (in unpersönlicher Konstruktion) **mir ist schlecht** or **übel** I feel ill; **mir ist kalt** I'm cold; **was ist Ihnen?** what's the matter with you?; **mir ist, als wäre ich zehn Jahre jünger** I feel ten years younger; **mir ist, als hätte ich ihn früher schon einmal gesehen** I have a feeling I've seen him before

V AUX to have; **er ist/war jahrelang krank gewesen** he has/had been or he's/he'd been ill for years; **sie ist gestern nicht zu Hause gewesen** she was not or wasn't at home yesterday; **er ist verschwunden** he has disappeared; **er ist gestern verschwunden** he disappeared yesterday; **er ist eben nach Hause gekommen** he has just come home; **er ist gestern nach Hause gekommen** he came home yesterday; **er ist geschlagen worden** he has been beaten

sein² **POSS PRON** **a** (adjektivisch) (bei Männern) his; (bei Dingen, Abstrakta) its; (bei Mädchen) her; (bei Tieren) its, his/her; (bei Ländern, Städten) its, her; (bei Schiffen) her, its; (auf „man" bezüglich) one's, his (US), your; **wenn man ~ Leben betrachtet** when one looks at one's or his (US) life, when you look at your life; **jeder hat ~e Probleme** everybody has his or their (inf) problems; **~e komische Frau** that peculiar wife of his, his peculiar wife; **mein und ~ Freund** my friend and his; **~e zwanzig Zigaretten** his/her/one's twenty cigarettes; **er wiegt gut ~e zwei Zentner** (inf) he weighs a good two hundred pounds; **er ist gut ~e zwei Meter** (inf) he's a good two metres (Brit) or meters (US)

b (old: substantivisch) his

PERS PRON gen von **er** von **es**¹ (old, poet) **ich werde ewig ~ gedenken** I shall remember him forever

Sein [zain] NT -s, no pl being no art; (Philos) (= Existenz, Dasein auch) existence no art; (= Wesen, Sosein) essence, suchness; **~ und Schein** appearance and reality; **~ oder Nichtsein** to be or not to be

sei|ner ['zainɐ] PERS PRON gen von **er** von **es**¹ (geh) **gedenke ~** remember him; **er war ~ nicht mächtig** he was not in command of himself

sei|ne(r, s) ['zainə] POSS PRON (substantivisch) his; **der/die/das ~** or **Seine** (geh) his; **das ~** or **Seine tun** (geh) to do one's or his (US) bit; **er hat das ~** or **Seine getan** (geh) he did his bit; **jedem das ~** or **Seine** each to his own (Brit); **jedem das ~** or **Seine** each to his own; **sie ist die ~** or **Seine geworden** (geh) she has become his (liter); **die ~n** or **Seinen** (geh) his family, his people; (auf „man" bezüglich) one's or his (US) family or people; **das ~** or **Seine** (geh: = Besitz) what is his; (auf „man" bezüglich) what is one's own or his (US) → **Schlaf**

sei|ner-: **sei|ner|seits** ['zainɐzaits] ADV (= von ihm) on his part; (= er selbst) for his part; **sei|ner|zeit** ['zainɐtsait] ADV at that time; (rare: künftig) one day; **sei|ner|zei|tig** ['zainɐtsaitɪç] ADJ attr (Aus) then attr

sei|nes ['zaɪnəs] POSS PRON → **seine(r, s)**

sei|nes|glei|chen ['zaɪnəs'glaɪçn̩] PRON *inv* (*gleichgestellt*) his equals *pl*; (*auf „man" bezüglich*) one's *or* his (*US*) equals; (*gleichartig*) his kind *pl*; of one's own kind; (*pej*) the likes of him *pl*; **jdn wie ~ behandeln** to treat sb as an equal *or* on equal terms; **das hat nicht** *or* **das sucht ~** it is unparalleled; (*Kunstwerk auch*) it has no equal

sei|net-: sei|net|hal|ben ['zaɪnət'halbn̩] (*dated*), **sei|net|we|gen** ['zaɪnət've:gn̩] ADV **a** (= *wegen ihm*) because of him, on account of him, on his account; (= *ihm zuliebe*) for his sake; (= *um ihn*) about him; (= *für ihn*) on his behalf **b** (= *von ihm aus*) as far as he is concerned; **sei|net|wil|len** ['zaɪnət'vɪlən] ADV **um ~** for his sake, for him

sei|ni|ge ['zaɪnɪɡə] POSS PRON **der/die/das ~** *or* **Seinige** (*form, old*) → **seine(r, s)**

sein las|sen ▲ *ptp* **sein lassen** VT *irreg* **etw ~** (= *aufhören*) to stop sth/doing sth; (= *nicht tun*) to drop sth, to leave sth; **jdn/etw ~** to leave sb/sth alone, to let sb/sth be; **lass das sein!** stop that!; **du hättest es ~ sollen** you should have left well (enough (*US*)) alone; **sie kann es einfach nicht ~** she just can't stop herself

seins [zaɪns] POSS PRON his

Seins|leh|re F (*Philos*) ontology

seis|misch ['zaɪsmɪʃ] ADJ seismic

Seis|mo|graf ▲ [zaɪsmo'gra:f] M **-en, -en** seismograph

Seis|mo|gramm [zaɪsmo'gram] NT *pl* **-gramme** seismogram

Seis|mo|lo|ge [zaɪsmo'lo:ɡə] M **-n, -n, Seis|mo|lo|gin** [-'lo:ɡɪn] F **-, -nen** seismologist

Seis|mo|lo|gie [zaɪsmolo'gi:] F **-, no pl** seismology

seit [zaɪt] PREP **+dat** (*in Bezug auf Zeitpunkt*) since; (*in Bezug auf Zeitdauer*) for, in (*esp US*); **~ wann?** since when?; **~ Jahren** for years; **ich habe ihn ~ Jahren nicht gesehen** I haven't seen him for *or* in (*esp US*) years; **ich bin ~ zwei Jahren hier** I have been here for two years; **schon ~ zwei Jahren nicht mehr** not for two years, not since two years ago; **wir warten schon ~ zwei Stunden** we have been *or* we've been waiting (for) two hours; **~ etwa einer Woche** since about a week ago, for about a week ⬛CONJ⬛ since

seit|dem [zaɪt'de:m] ADV since then; **~ ist die Strecke nicht mehr in Betrieb** the line has been closed down since then ⬛CONJ⬛ since

Sei|te ['zaɪtə] F **-, -n a** (= *auch Abstammungslinie, Charakterzug*) side; **die hintere/vordere ~** the back/front; **zu** *or* **auf beiden ~n des Fensters/des Hauses/der Straße** on both sides of the window/house/street; **mit der ~ nach vorn** sideways; **~ an ~** side by side; **an jds ~** (*dat*) **gehen** to walk at *or* by sb's side, to walk beside sb; **halt dich an meiner ~!** stay by my side; **er ging** *or* **wich uns nicht von der ~** he never left our side; **ich kann mich nicht an Ihrer ~ zeigen** I can't be seen with you; **jdn von der ~ ansehen** to give sb a sidelong glance; **auf die** *or* **zur ~ gehen** *or* **treten** to step aside; **an der ~ (einer Reihe) sitzen** to sit at the end of (a row); **zur ~ sprechen/sehen** to speak/look to one side; **zur ~** (*Theat*) aside; **die ~n wechseln** (*Sport*) to change ends *or* over; (*fig*) to change sides; **jdn auf seine ~ bringen** *or* **ziehen** (*fig*) to get sb on one's side; **auf einer ~ gelähmt sein** to be paralyzed down one side; **die Hände in die ~n gestemmt** with arms akimbo, with one's hands on one's hips; **jedes Ding** *or* **alles hat zwei ~n** there are two sides to everything; **jdm zur ~ stehen** (*fig*) to stand by sb's side; **jdn jdm an die ~ stellen** (= *gleichstellen*) to put sb on a level with sb; (*zur Unterstützung*) to put sb alongside sb; **auf jds** (*dat*) **~ stehen** *or* **sein** (*fig*) to be on sb's side; **das Recht ist auf ihrer ~** she has right on her side; **etw auf die ~ legen** (*lit, fig*) to put sth on one side, to put sth aside; (= *umkippen*) to put sth on its side; **etw zur ~** *or* **auf die ~ schaffen** (*inf*) to help oneself to sth; **jdn zur ~** *or*

auf die ~ schaffen (*inf*) to get rid of sb; **jdn zur ~ nehmen** to take sb aside *or* on one side; **auf der einen ~..., auf der anderen (~) ...** on the one hand ..., on the other (hand) ...; **jds starke ~** sb's forte, sb's strong point; **jds schwache ~** sb's weakness, sb's weak spot; **sich von seiner besten ~ zeigen** to show oneself at one's best; **neue ~n an jdm/etw entdecken** to discover new sides to sb/sth; **von dieser ~ kenne ich ihn gar nicht** I didn't know that side of him; **einer Sache** (*dat*) **die beste ~ abgewinnen** to make the best of sth **b** (= *Richtung*) **von allen ~n** (*lit, fig*) from all sides; **nach allen ~n auseinander gehen** to scatter in all directions; **sich nach allen ~n umsehen** to look around on all sides; **sich nach allen ~n vergewissern** to check up on all sides; **das habe ich von einer anderen ~ erfahren** (*fig*) I heard it from another source *or* from elsewhere; **er erfuhr es von dritter ~** (*fig*) he heard it from a third party; **bisher wurden von keiner ~ Einwände erhoben** so far no objections have been voiced from any quarter; **die Behauptung wurde von keiner ~ bestritten** nobody challenged the claim; **die Behauptung wurde von allen/beiden ~n bestritten** the claim was challenged by all/both parties; **von meiner ~ aus** (*fig*) on my part; **von kirchlicher ~ (aus)** on the part of the church; **auf ~n +gen = aufseiten von ~n +gen = vonseiten**

c (= *Buchseite, Zeitungsseite*) page; **die erste/letzte ~** the first/last page; (*von Zeitung*) the front/back page

Sei|ten- *in cpds* side; (*esp Tech, Sci etc*) lateral; **Sei|ten|air|bag** M (*Aut*) side-impact airbag; **Sei|ten|al|tar** M side altar; **Sei|ten|an|ga|be** F page reference; **Sei|ten|an|sicht** F side view; (*Tech*) side elevation; (*Comput*) page view; **Sei|ten|arm** M branch, feeder; (*von Fluss*) branch; **Sei|ten|auf|prall|schutz** M (*Aut*) side impact protection system, SIPS; **Sei|ten|aus|gang** M side exit; **Sei|ten|be|schrei|bungs|spra|che** F (*Comput*) page description language; **Sei|ten|blick** M sidelong glance; **mit einem ~ auf** (+*acc*) (*fig*) with one eye on; **Sei|ten|ein|gang** M side entrance; **Sei|ten|ein|stei|ger(in)** M(F) (*fig*) person who comes in through the back door; **Sei|ten|flä|che** F (*Tech*) lateral face *or* surface; **Sei|ten|flos|se** F (*Aviat*) fin; **Sei|ten|flü|gel** M side wing; (*von Altar*) wing; **Sei|ten|gang** M *pl* **-gänge** (*Naut*) side strake; (*Rail*) (side) corridor; **Sei|ten|gas|se** F side street, backstreet; **Sei|ten|ge|bäu|de** NT side building; (*auf Hof*) outhouse; (= *Anbau*) annex(e); **Sei|ten|ge|wehr** NT bayonet; **Sei|ten|hal|bie|ren|de** [-halbi:rəndə] F *decl as adj* (*Math*) median; **Sei|ten|hieb** M (*Fechten*) side cut; (*fig*) sideswipe; **Sei|ten|kan|te** F lateral edge; **Sei|ten|la|ge** F side position; **in ~ schlafen** to sleep on one's side; **stabile ~** recovery position; **sei|ten|lang** ⬛ADJ⬛ several pages long, going on for pages ⬛ADV⬛ **darstellen** over pages and pages; **etw ~ beschreiben** to devote pages to describing sth; **sich ~ über etw** (*acc*) **auslassen** to go on for pages about sth; **sie hat mir ~ geschrieben** she wrote me a long letter; **Sei|ten|län|ge** F length of a/the side; **ein gleichseitiges Dreieck mit der ~ 4,5 cm** an equilateral triangle whose sides are 4.5 cm long; **Sei|ten|lay|out** NT (*Typ*) page layout; **Sei|ten|leh|ne** F arm(rest); **Sei|ten|leit|werk** NT (*Aviat*) rudder (assembly); **Sei|ten|li|nie** F **a** (*Rail*) branch line **b** (*von Fürstengeschlecht*) collateral line **c** (*Tennis*) sideline; (*Ftbl etc*) touchline (*Brit*), sideline; **Sei|ten|mo|rä|ne** F (*Geol*) lateral moraine; **Sei|ten|pfad** M bypath; **Sei|ten|rand** M margin; **Sei|ten|riss** ▲ M (*Tech*) side elevation; **Sei|ten|ru|der** NT (*Aviat*) rudder

sei|tens ['zaɪtns] PREP **+gen** (*form*) on the part of

Sei|ten-: Sei|ten|schei|tel M side parting (*Brit*), side part (*US*); **Sei|ten|schiff** NT (*Archit*) (side) aisle; **Sei|ten|schnei|der** M side

cutters *pl*, cutting pliers *pl*; **Sei|ten|schwel|ler** M (*Aut*) side skirt; **Sei|ten|sprung** M (*fig*) bit on the side (*inf*) *no pl*, (little) infidelity; **die Versuchung, Seitensprünge zu machen** the temptation to have a bit on the side (*inf*); **Sei|ten|ste|chen** NT , *no pl* stitch; **~ haben/be|kommen** to have/get a stitch; **Sei|ten|sti|che** PL = **Seitenstechen**; **Sei|ten|stra|ße** F side street, side road; **Sei|ten|strei|fen** M verge; (*der Autobahn*) hard shoulder (*Brit*), shoulder (*US*); **„Seitenstreifen nicht befahrbar"** "soft verges" (*Brit*), "soft shoulder" (*US*); **Sei|ten|tal** NT valley; **Sei|ten|ta|sche** F side pocket; **Sei|ten|teil** M OR NT side; **Sei|ten|um|bruch** M (*Typ*) page make-up; **sei|ten|ver|kehrt** ADJ, ADV the wrong way round; **Sei|ten|vor|schub** M (*beim Drucker*) form feed; **Sei|ten|wa|gen** M sidecar; **Sei|ten|wand** F side wall; (*von Schiff*) side; **Seitenwände** *pl* (*Theat*) wings *pl*; **Sei|ten|wech|sel** M (*Sport*) changeover; **Sei|ten|weg** M side road, byway, back road; **~e gehen** (*fig*) to indulge in clandestine activities; **sei|ten|wei|se** ADV (*viele Seiten*) pages (and pages) of; **~ vorgehen** (= *Seite für Seite vorgehen*) to proceed a page at a time; **Sei|ten|wind** M crosswind; **Sei|ten|zahl** F **a** page number **b** (= *Gesamtzahl*) number of pages

seit|her [zaɪt'he:ɐ] ADV since then

seit|he|rig [zaɪt'he:rɪç] ADJ = **bisherig**

seit|lich ['zaɪtlɪç] ⬛ADJ⬛ lateral (*esp Sci, Tech*), side *attr*; **die ~e Begrenzung der Straße wird durch einen weißen Streifen markiert** the side of the road is marked by a white line; **bei starkem ~en Wind** in a strong crosswind ⬛ADV⬛ at the side; (= *von der Seite*) from the side; **~ von** at the side of; **~ stehen** to stand sideways on; **etw/sich ~ stellen** to put sth/stand sideways on; **die Kisten sind ~ grün bemalt** the sides of the boxes are painted green; **er ist mir ~ ins Auto gefahren** he crashed into the side of my car ⬛PREP⬛ **+gen** to *or* at the side of

seit|lings ['zaɪtlɪŋs] ADV (*obs*) (= *zur Seite*) sideways; (= *auf der Seite*) on one's side

seit|wärts ['zaɪtvɛrts] ADV sideways; **sich ~ halten** to keep to the side

Sek., sek. *abbr von* **Sekunde** sec

Se|kans ['ze:kans] M **-, -** *or* **Sekanten** [ze'kantn̩], **Se|kan|te** [ze'kantə] F **-, -n** (*Math*) secant

Se|kond [ze'kɔnt] F **-, -en** [-dn] (*Fechten*) seconde

Sekret¹ [ze'kre:t] NT **-(e)s, -e** (*Physiol*) secretion

Sekret² F **-, no pl** (*Eccl*) secret (of the mass)

Sek|re|tär¹ [zekre'tɛ:ɐ] M **-s, -e a** (= *Schreibschrank*) bureau (*Brit*), secretaire (*Brit*), secretary desk (*US*) **b** (*Orn*) secretary bird

Sek|re|tär² [zekre'tɛ:ɐ] M **-s,-e, Sek|re|tä|rin** [-'tɛ:rɪn] F **-, -nen** secretary

Sek|re|ta|ri|at [zekreta'ria:t] NT **-(e)s, -e** office

Sek|re|ti|on [zekre'tsio:n] F **-, -en** (*Physiol*) secretion

Sekt [zɛkt] M **-(e)s, -e** sparkling wine, champagne

Sek|te ['zɛktə] F **-, -n** sect

Sekt|emp|fang M champagne reception

Sek|ten-: Sek|ten|be|auf|trag|te(r) MF *decl as adj* religious sects adviser; **Sek|ten|füh|rer(in)** M(F) sect leader; **Sek|ten|we|sen** NT sectarianism

Sekt-: Sekt|früh|stück NT champagne breakfast; **Sekt|glas** NT champagne glass

Sek|tie|rer [zɛk'ti:rɐ] M **-s, -, Sek|tie|re|rin** [-ərɪn] F **-, -nen** sectarian

sek|tie|re|risch [zɛk'ti:rərɪʃ] ⬛ADJ⬛ sectarian ⬛ADV⬛ in a sectarian way; **~ denken** to think in a sectarian way

Sek|tie|rer|tum [zɛk'ti:rətu:m] NT **-s**, *no pl* sectarianism

Sek|ti|on [zɛkˈtsioːn] F **-, -en** **a** section; (= Abteilung) department **b** (= Obduktion) postmortem (examination), autopsy

Sek|ti|ons-: Sek|ti|ons|be|fund M postmortem or autopsy findings pl; **Sek|ti|ons|chef|in** M(F) (von Abteilung) head of department; **Sek|ti|ons|saal** M dissection room; **sek|ti|ons|wei|se** ADV in sections

Sekt-: Sekt|kelch M champagne flute; **Sekt|kor|ken** M champagne cork; **Sekt|küh|ler** M champagne bucket or cooler

Sek|tor [ˈzɛktoːɐ] M **-s, Sektoren** [-ˈtoːrən] sector (auch Comput); (= Sachgebiet) field

Sek|to|ren|gren|ze F sector boundary

Sekt|schale F champagne glass

Se|kund [zeˈkʊnt] F **-, -en** [-dn] (Mus) second

Se|kun|da [zeˈkʊnda] F **-, Sekunden** [-dn] (dated Sch) sixth and seventh year of German secondary school

Se|kund|ak|kord M (Mus) third inversion (of the seventh chord)

Se|kun|da|ner [zekʊnˈdaːnɐ] M **-s, -, Se|kun|da|ne|rin** [-ərɪn] F **-, -nen** (dated Sch) pupil in sixth and seventh year of German secondary school

Se|kun|dant [zekʊnˈdant] M **-en, -en, Se|kun|dan|tin** [-ˈdantɪn] F **-, -nen** second

se|kun|där [zekʊnˈdɛːɐ] ADJ secondary ADV secondarily; **nur ~ von Bedeutung sein** to be of secondary importance; **nur ~ eine Rolle spielen** to play only a secondary role

Se|kun|där- in cpds secondary; **Se|kun|där|ener|gie** F secondary energy; **Se|kun|där|kreis|lauf** M (in Atomkraftwerk) secondary circuit

Se|kun|där|leh|rer(in) [zekʊnˈdɛːɐ-] M(F) (Sw) secondary or high (esp US) school teacher

Se|kun|där|li|te|ra|tur F secondary literature

Se|kun|där|markt M (Econ) aftermarket; (Fin) secondary market

Se|kun|där- [zekʊnˈdɛːɐ-]: **Se|kun|där|schu|le** F (Sw) secondary school; **Se|kun|där|stu|fe** F secondary or high (esp US) school level

Se|kun|de [zeˈkʊnda] F **-, -n** (auch Mus, Math) second; **eine ~, bitte!** just a or one second, please; **auf die ~ genau** to the second

Se|kun|den pl von **Sekunda** von **Sekunde**

Se|kun|den-: Se|kun|den|bruch|teil M split second, fraction of a second; **Se|kun|den|ge|schwin|dig|keit** F **in ~** in a matter of seconds; **Se|kun|den|kle|ber** M superglue, instant glue; **Se|kun|den|lang** ADJ of a few seconds ADV for a few seconds; **Se|kun|den|schlaf** M (am Steuer) momentary nodding off, microsleep (spec); **se|kun|den|schnell** ADJ Reaktion, Entscheidung split-second attr, lightning attr; Antwort quick-fire attr ADV **sich ~ entscheiden müssen** to have to make a snap decision; **alles ging ~** it all happened in a matter of seconds; **Se|kun|den|schnel|le** F **in ~** in a matter of seconds; **Se|kun|den|tod** M (Med) sudden death, sudden adult death syndrome; **Se|kun|den|zei|ger** M second hand

se|kun|die|ren [zekʊnˈdiːrən] ptp **sekundiert** VI +dat to second; (= unterstützen auch) to back up; **jdm (bei einem Duell) ~** to act as or be sb's second (in a duel)

se|kund|lich [zeˈkʊntlɪç], **se|künd|lich** [zeˈkʏntlɪç] ADJ (rare) Abstand one-second ADV every second

Se|ku|rit® [zekuˈriːt] NT **-s, no pl** Triplex®

sel. abbr von **selig**

Se|la [ˈzeːla] NT **-s, -s** (Bibl) selah

sel|ber [ˈzɛlbɐ] DEM PRON = **selbst** DEM PRON

sel|be(r, s) [ˈzɛlbə] PRON → **derselbe, dieselbe, dasselbe**

Sel|ber|ma|chen NT **-s**, no pl do-it-yourself, DIY (inf); (von Kleidern etc) making one's own; **Möbel zum ~** do-it-yourself furniture; **Spielzeug zum ~** build-it-yourself toy

sel|big [ˈzɛlbɪç] PRON (obs, Bibl) the same

selbst [zɛlpst] DEM PRON **a ich ~** I myself; **er ~** he himself; **Sie ~** (sing) you yourself; (pl) you yourselves; **sie ~** she herself; **das Haus ~** the house itself; **die Katze ~** the cat itself; **wir ~** we ourselves; **sie ~** they themselves; **die Häuser ~** the houses themselves; **er ist gar nicht mehr er ~** he's not himself any more; **du Esel! ~ ~ einer** (inf) you idiot! – same to you (inf); **sie ist die Güte/Tugend ~** she's kindness/virtue itself; **~ ist der Mann/die Frau!** self-reliance is the name of the game (inf); **er wäscht seine Wäsche ~** he does his washing himself, he does his own washing; **was man von sich ~ hält** what one thinks of oneself; **zu sich ~ kommen** to collect one's thoughts; **eine Sache um ihrer ~ willen tun** to do sth for its own sake; **sie tut mir ~ Leid** I feel very sorry for her myself
b (= ohne Hilfe) alone, by oneself/himself/yourself etc, on one's/his/your etc own
c von ~ by myself/yourself/himself/itself/ourselves etc; **das funktioniert von ~** it works by itself, it works automatically; **das regelt sich alles von ~** it'll sort itself out (by itself); **er kam ganz von ~** he came of his own accord, he came off his own bat (Brit inf); **das hat er ganz von ~ entschieden** he decided that all by himself
ADV **a** (= eigen) **~ ernannt** self-appointed; (in Bezug auf Titel) self-styled; **~ gebacken** home-baked, home-made; **~ gebastelt** home-made; **~ gebaut** self-built; Haus self-built; **~ gebraut** (Bier) home-brewed; **~ gemacht** home-made; **~ gesponnen** homespun; **~ gestrickt** (Pullover etc) hand-knitted; (inf) Methode etc homespun, amateurish; **ist das ~ gestrickt?** did you knit it yourself?; **~ gezogen** (Rosen etc) home-cultivated; Kerzen home-made; **~ verdientes Geld** money one has earned oneself; **sein ~ verdientes Motorrad** the motorbike he bought with the money he earned; **~ verfasst** of one's own composition; **alle seine Reden sind ~ verfasst** he writes all his speeches himself
b (= sogar) even; **~ der Minister/Gott** even the Minister/God (himself); **~ wenn** even if

Selbst [zɛlpst] NT **-**, no pl self

Selbst-: Selbst|ab|ho|ler [-laphoːlɐ] M **-s, -, Selbst|ab|ho|le|rin** [-ərɪn] F **-, -nen ~ sein** to collect one's own mail; **Selbst|ach|tung** F self-respect, self-esteem; **Selbst|ana|ly|se** F self-analysis

selb|stän|dig [ˈzɛlpʃtɛndɪç] ADJ, ADV = **selbstständig**

Selb|stän|di|ge(r) [ˈzɛlpʃtɛndɪgə] MF decl as adj = **Selbstständige(r)**

Selb|stän|dig|keit F **-**, no pl = **Selbstständigkeit**

Selbst-: Selbst|an|kla|ge F self-accusation; **Selbst|an|zei|ge** F **a** (steuerlich) voluntary declaration **b ~ erstatten** to come forward oneself; **Selbst|auf|ga|be** F surrender of one's identity, self-abnegation; **Selbst|auf|op|fe|rung** F self-sacrifice; **Selbst|aus|kunft** F (one's own) personal details pl; **Selbst|aus|lö|ser** M (Phot) delayed-action shutter release, delay timer; **Selbst|be|die|nung** F self-service; (fig: finanziell) helping oneself to funds; **Selbst|be|die|nungs|la|den** M self-service shop (esp Brit) or store; **Selbst|be|fle|ckung** F (old, Rel) self-abuse; **Selbst|be|frei|ung** F self-liberation; (Jur) prison escape without outside assistance; **Selbst|be|frie|di|gung** F masturbation; (fig auch) self-gratification; **Selbst|be|fruch|tung** F (Biol) self-fertilization; **Selbst|be|halt** [-bəhalt] M **-(e)s, -e a** (Insur: Selbstbeteiligung) (percentage) excess **b** (= Medikamentenzuzahlung) patient's contribution; **Selbst|be|haup|tung** F self-assertion; **Selbst|be|herr|schung** F self-control; **die ~ wahren/verlieren** to keep/lose one's self-control or temper; **Selbst|be|kennt|nis** NT confession; **Selbst|be|kös|ti|gung** F (dated) self-catering; **Selbst|be|obach|tung** F self-

-observation; **Selbst|be|schei|dung** [-bəʃaidʊŋ] F **-**, no pl (geh) self-denial; **Selbst|be|sin|nung** F self-contemplation; **zur ~ kommen** to reflect; **hier ist es unmöglich, zur ~ zu kommen** that there is no opportunity (afforded) here for self-contemplation; **Selbst|be|spie|ge|lung** [-bəʃpiːgəlʊŋ] F **-, -en** (pej) self-admiration; **Selbst|be|stä|ti|gung** F self-affirmation; **das empfand er als ~** it boosted his ego; **man braucht ab und zu eine ~** now and then you need something to boost your ego; **Lob dient der ~ der Kinder** praise boosts the children's confidence; **Selbst|be|stäu|bung** F (Bot) self-pollination; **selbst|be|stimmt** ADJ self-determined; **~ leben** to be independent, to live an independent life; **sein Wunsch nach ~em Sterben** his desire to determine his own death; **Selbst|be|stim|mung** F self-determination; **Selbst|be|stim|mungs|recht** NT right of self-determination; **Selbst|be|tei|li|gung** F (Insur) (percentage) excess; **Selbst|be|trug** M self-deception; **Selbst|be|weih|räu|che|rung** [-bəvairoʏçərʊŋ] F **-, -en** (pej) self-congratulation, self-promotion, self-admiration; **Selbst|be|wun|de|rung** F self-admiration; **selbst|be|wusst** ▲ ADJ **a** (= selbstsicher) self-assured, self-confident; **b** (= eingebildet) self-important **b** (Philos) self-aware, self-conscious ADV self-confidently; **Selbst|be|wusst|sein** ▲ NT **a** self-assurance, self-confidence; (= Einbildung) self-importance **b** (Philos) self-awareness, self-consciousness; **selbst|be|zo|gen** ADJ self-centred (Brit), self-centered (US), egocentric (geh); **sein ~** the way he sees himself; **Selbst|bild** NT (Psych) self-image; **sein ~** the way he sees himself; **Selbst|bild|nis** NT self-portrait; **Selbst|bräu|ner** [-broʏnɐ] M **-s, -** self-tanning lotion; **Selbst|bu|cher** [-buːxɐ] M **-s, -, Selbst|bu|che|rin** [-ərɪn] F **-, -nen** (Post) person/firm etc with own franking machine; **Selbst|dar|stel|lung** F **a** (= Selbstpräsentation) self-presentation; (= Selbstbeweihräucherung) self-promotion **b** (= Selbstbildnis) self-portrait; **Selbst|dis|zip|lin** F self-discipline; **Selbst|ein|schät|zung** F self-assessment; **eine gesunde ~** a healthy self-awareness; **Selbst|ent|fal|tung** F self-development; (Philos) unfolding; **Selbst|ent|lei|bung** [-lɛntlaibʊŋ] F **-, -en** (liter) suicide; **Selbst|ent|zün|dung** F spontaneous combustion; **Selbst|er|fah|rung** F self-awareness; **Selbst|er|fah|rungs|grup|pe** F encounter group; **Selbst|er|hal|tung** F self-preservation, survival; **Selbst|er|hal|tungs|trieb** M survival instinct, instinct of self-preservation; **Selbst|er|kennt|nis** F self-knowledge; **~ ist der erste Schritt zur Besserung** (prov) self-knowledge is the first step toward(s) self-improvement; **selbst|er|nannt** △ [-lɛɐnant] ADJ → **selbst** ADV a; **Selbst|er|nied|ri|gung** F self-abasement; **Selbst|er|zie|hung** F self-discipline; **~ zur Pünktlichkeit** teaching oneself to be punctual; **Selbst|fah|rer** (= Krankenfahrstuhl) self-propelling wheelchair; **Selbst|fah|rer(in)** M(F) (Aut) person who rents a car and drives it himself Autovermietung für ~ self-drive car hire (Brit), car rental; **wir vermieten nur an ~** we only have self-drive (Brit); **Selbst|fahr|la|fet|te** F (Mil) self-propelled gun; **selbst|fi|nan|zie|rend** ADJ self-financing; **Selbst|fi|nan|zie|rung** F self-financing; **in** or **durch ~** with one's own resources or means; **Selbst|fin|dung** [-fɪndʊŋ] F **-**, no pl finding one's self; **Selbst|gän|ger** [-gɛŋɐ] M **-s, -** (inf, fig) **a** (= etwas, das von alleine funktioniert) Existenzgründungen in der Internetbranche sind keine ~ mehr Internet start-ups no longer generate automatic success without any hitches; **ich halte Bayern München nicht für einen ~** I don't think Bayern München is hooked on success forever; **keine Unternehmensgemeinschaft ist ein ~** no merger runs that smoothly; **sind diese bevorzugten Industriestandorte nicht ~?** are these preferred industrial locations not self-perpetuating?; **ein ~ wird die neue Saison bestimmt nicht** we can't expect the new season to become a sweeping success (without a great deal of effort on our part); **Beach Volleyball ist kein ~ mehr** beach volleyball is no longer a popular game that easily attracts crowds; **für Sven als Legastheniker ist die Schule kein ~** Sven being dyslexic, going to school is no mean feat for him **b** (= *etwas Selbstverständliches*) **sein fünfter WM-Titel sei keinesfalls ein ~ gewesen** his fifth world title was by no means to be taken for granted; **glückliche Ehen sind heute nicht unbedingt ~** happy marriages aren't necessarily a matter of course nowadays; **es ist ein ~, dass die bestehenden Gesetze auch anzuwenden sind** it is self-evident that existing laws have to be applied; **erfolgreiche Öffentlichkeitsarbeit ist kein ~** successful PR work is by no means a self-fulfilling prophecy; **wir dachten, die Liebe wäre ein ~** we thought love would stay forever **c** (= *etwas, das sich notgedrungen ergeben muss*) **das war doch ein ~** (*bei schwacher gegnerischer Mannschaft etc*) they were a walk-over **d** (= *etwas, das logischerweise zu erwarten ist*) **das zu erwartende Urteil wäre ein ~** the judgement would be the sort one would have expected; **Nein, das ist kein ~** (*bei Rückgängigmachung einer Schiedsrichterentscheidung etc*) No, I don't think this can be taken for granted **e** (= *etwas, das sich leicht erfolgreich vermarkten lässt*) **ein ~ in Sachen Unterhaltung** an instant success in terms of entertainment; **unser neues Versicherungspaket ist konkurrenzlos - ein ~** our new insurance package is unrivalled: sure seller; **wie die Soap „Big Brother" zum ~ wurde** how the soap opera "Big Brother" became a regular feature on TV; **ein US-College-Radio-Selbstgänger** a piece of music very often played by US college radio stations **f** (= *etwas, das nicht viel Können erfordert*) **das Gelände war für die Radsportler dennoch kein ~** nevertheless, the terrain wasn't that easy to tackle for the cyclists; **bei Hobby-Zauberkünstlern kommen oft ~ zum Einsatz** amateur magicians often use tricks that don't really afford much skill and are nevertheless impressive **g** (= *ein Muss*) **diese Punk-Jazz-Nummer ist ein ~ für Musikfreaks** this punkjazz piece is a must for music-lovers; **selbst|ge|ba|cken** △ ADJ → **selbst** ADV a; **selbst|ge|bas|telt** △ ADJ → **selbst** ADV a; **selbst|ge|baut** △ ADJ → **selbst** ADV a; **selbst|ge|braut** △ [-gəbraut] ADJ → **selbst** ADV a; **Selbst|ge|dreh|te** [-gədreːtə] F *decl as adj* roll-up (*inf*); **~ rauchen** to roll one's own; **selbst|ge|fäl|lig** ADJ self-satisfied, smug, complacent ADV smugly, complacently; **Selbst|ge|fäl|lig|keit** F self-satisfaction, smugness, complacency; **selbst|ge|fühl** NT self-esteem; **ein übertriebenes ~ besitzen** to have an exaggerated opinion of oneself, to have an oversized ego (*inf*); **selbst|ge|macht** △ ADJ → **selbst** ADV a; **selbst|ge|nüg|sam** ADJ **a** (= *bescheiden*) modest (in one's demands) **b** (= *sich selbst genug*) self-sufficient; **Selbst|ge|nüg|sam|keit** F modesty (in one's demands); **selbst|ge|recht** ADJ self-righteous ADV self-righteously; **Selbst|ge|rech|tig|keit** F self-righteousness; **selbst|ge|spon|nen** △ ADJ → **selbst** ADV a; **Selbst|ge|spräch** NT **~e führen** or **halten** to talk to oneself; **selbst|ge|strickt** △ [-gəʃtrɪkt] ADJ → **selbst** ADV a; **selbst|ge|zo|gen** △ ADJ → **selbst** ADV a; **Selbst|hass** ▲ M self-hate, self-hatred; **Selbst|hei|lungs|kraft** F self-healing power; **selbst|herr|lich** (*pej*) ADJ **a** (= *eigenwillig*) high-handed **b** (= *selbstgefällig, selbstgerecht*) arrogant ADV **a** (= *eigenwillig*) high-handedly **b** (= *selbstgefällig*) arrogantly; **Selbst|herr|lich|keit** F (*pej*) **a** (= *Eigenwilligkeit*) high-handedness **b** (= *Selbstgerechtigkeit*) arrogance; **Selbst|herr|schaft** F (*rare*) autocracy; **Selbst|herr|scher(in)** M(F) (*rare*) autocrat; **Selbst|hil|fe** F self-help; **zur ~ greifen** to take matters into one's own hands; **Selbst|hil|fe|grup|pe** F self-help group; **Selbst|in|sze|nie|rung** F self-promotion, self-glorification;

ihr Auftreten ist eine gigantische ~ the way she carries on is all one great act of self--promotion; **Selbst|in|ter|pre|ta|ti|on** F image of oneself, self-image; **Selbst|iro|nie** F self-mockery, self-irony

selbst|tisch [ˈzɛlbstɪʃ] ADJ (*geh*) selfish

Selbst-: **Selbst|iso|lie|rung** F self-isolation; **Selbst|jus|tiz** F arbitrary law; **~ üben** to take the law into one's own hands; **Selbst|kle|be|eti|kett** NT self-adhesive label; **selbst|kle|bend** ADJ self-adhesive; **Selbst|kon|trol|le** F check on oneself; (*von Computer*) automatic check; **zur ~** to keep a check on oneself; **der Computer hat ~** the computer is self-checking, the computer has an automatic check

Selbst|kos|ten PL (*Econ*) prime costs *pl*

Selbst|kos|ten-: **Selbst|kos|ten|be|tei|li|gung** F (*Insur*) excess; **Selbst|kos|ten|preis** M cost price; **zum ~** at cost

Selbst-: **Selbst|kri|tik** F self-criticism; **selbst|kri|tisch** ADJ self-critical ADV self-critically; **Selbst|la|der** [-laːdɐ] M **-s, ~** self-loader, semiautomatic weapon *or* firearm; **Selbst|läu|fer** M (*inf*) **a** (= *eigenständiger Erfolg*) surefire success (*inf*) **b** → **Selbstgänger**; **Selbst|laut** M vowel; **selbst|lau|tend** ADJ vocalic; **Selbst|ler|ner(in)** M(F) autodidact (*form*); **er ist ~** he is self-taught; **dies Buch ist geeignet für ~** this book is suitable for people teaching themselves; **Selbst|lob** NT self-importance, vaingloriousness; **selbst|los** ADJ *Mensch, Liebe, Motiv* selfless ADV selflessly; **Selbst|lo|sig|keit** F -, *no pl* selflessness; **Selbst|me|di|ka|ti|on** [-medikatsioːn] F -, *no pl* self-medication; **Selbst|mit|leid** NT self-pity

Selbst|mord M (*lit, fig*) suicide

Selbst|mord|an|schlag M suicide attack

Selbst|mör|der(in) M(F) suicide; **ich bin doch kein ~!** (*inf*) I have no desire to commit suicide

selbst|mör|de|risch ADJ (*lit, fig*) suicidal; **in ~er Absicht** intending to commit suicide

Selbst|mord-: **Selbst|mord|ge|dan|ken** PL suicidal thoughts *pl*; **sich mit ~ tragen** to contemplate suicide; **selbst|mord|ge|fähr|det** ADJ suicidal; **Selbst|mord|kom|man|do** NT suicide squad; **Selbst|mord|ver|such** M suicide attempt, attempted suicide

Selbst-: **Selbst|pflü|cker(in)** M(F) *usu pl* customer who picks his/her own; **Selbst|port|rät** NT self-portrait; **selbst|quä|le|risch** ADJ self-tormenting; **selbst|re|dend** ADV of course, naturally; **Selbst|re|gie|rung** F self--government; **Selbst|rei|ni|gungs|kraft** F self--purifying power; **Selbst|schuld|ner(in)** M(F) (*Jur*) directly suable guarantor; **selbst|schuld|ne|risch** ADJ (*Jur*) *Bürgschaft* directly enforceable; *Bürge* directly suable; **Selbst|schuss** ▲ M set gun, spring gun; **Selbst|schutz** M self-protection; **selbst|si|cher** ADJ self-assured, self-confident ADV self-confidently; **Selbst|si|cher|heit** F self-assurance, self-confidence; **selbst|stän|dig** ▲ [ˈzɛlpstʃtɛndɪç] ADJ independent; (*beruflich*) self-employed; (*rare*: = *getrennt*) separate; **~ sein** (*beruflich*) to be self-employed, to have set up on one's own; **sich ~ machen** (*beruflich*) to set up on one's own, to start one's own business; (*hum*) to go off on its own; (= *verschwinden*) to grow legs (*hum*) ADV independently, on one's own; **~ denken** to think for oneself; **das entscheidet er ~** he decides that on his own *or* by himself *or* independently; **Selbst|stän|di|ge(r)** ▲ [ˈzɛlpstʃtɛndɪgə] MF *decl as adj* self-employed person; **die ~n** the self-employed; **Selbst|stän|dig|keit** ▲ F -, *no pl* independence; (*beruflich*) self-employment; **in großer ~ handeln** (*beruflich*) to act on one's own (initiative); **~ im Denken lernen** to learn to think for oneself; **Selbst|stu|di|um** NT private study; **etw im ~ lernen** to learn sth by studying on one's own; **Selbst|sucht** F , *no pl* egoism; **selbst|süch|tig** ADJ egoistic; **selbst|tä|tig**

ADJ **a** (= *automatisch*) automatic, self-acting **b** (= *eigenständig*) independent ADV (= *automatisch*) automatically; **damit sich nicht ~ ein Schuss lösen kann** so that a gun can't fire by itself; **Selbst|täu|schung** F self-deception; **Selbst|test** M (*von Maschine*) self-test; **Selbst|tor** NT own goal; **Selbst|tö|tung** F suicide; **Selbst|über|schät|zung** F overestimation of one's abilities; **das ist eine ~, wenn er meint ...** he's overestimating himself *or* his abilities if he thinks ...; **Selbst|über|win|dung** F willpower; **das war echte ~** that shows real willpower; **selbst bei der größten ~ könnte ich das nicht tun** I simply couldn't bring *or* force myself to do it; **Selbst|ver|ach|tung** F self-contempt; **selbst|ver|ant|wort|lich** ADJ autonomous, independent ADV **etw ~ entscheiden/leiten** to be personally responsible for a decision on sth/in charge of sth; **Selbst|ver|ant|wor|tung** F in ~ (= *entscheiden*) on one's own responsibility; **Selbst|ver|brau|cher** M Verkauf nur an ~ goods not for resale; **Selbst|ver|bren|nung** F sich durch ~ töten to burn oneself to death; **„zwei ~en in einem Monat"** "two people burn themselves to death in one month"; **selbst|ver|dient** △ ADJ → **selbst** ADV a; **selbst|ver|fasst** △ [-fɛfast] ADJ → **selbst** ADV a; **selbst|ver|ges|sen** ADJ absent--minded; *Blick* faraway ADV **~ dasitzen** to sit there lost to the world; **Selbst|ver|ges|sen|heit** F absent-mindedness; **in seinem Blick lag völlige ~** he looked totally lost to the world; **Selbst|ver|göt|te|rung** F self-glorification; **Selbst|ver|lag** M **im ~ erschienen** published oneself, published at one's own expense; **Selbst|ver|leug|nung** F self-denial; **selbst|ver|liebt** ADJ narcissistic ADV narcissistically; **Selbst|ver|liebt|heit** F self-love, narcissism; **Selbst|ver|nich|tung** F self-destruction; **Selbst|ver|pfle|ger** [-fɛɐpfleːgɐ] M **-s, ~**, **Selbst|ver|pfle|ge|rin** [-ərɪn] F -, **-nen** self-caterer; **Ferien für ~** self-catering holiday(s); **Selbst|ver|pfle|gung** F self-catering; **Selbst|ver|schul|den** NT one's own fault; **wenn ~ vorliegt ...** if the claimant is himself at fault ...; **selbst|ver|schul|det** [-fɛɐʃʊldət] ADJ *Unfälle, Notlagen* for which one is responsible *or* to blame; **der Unfall war ~** the accident was his/her own fault; **wenn der Unfall/Verlust ~ ist** if the claimant is himself/herself responsible *or* to blame for the accident/loss; **Selbst|ver|si|che|rung** F personal insurance; **Selbst|ver|sor|ger(in)** M(F) **a** **~ sein** to be self-sufficient *or* self-reliant **b** (*im Urlaub etc*) sb who is self-catering (*Brit*) *or* self-sufficient; **Appartements für ~** self-catering apartments (*Brit*), condominiums (*US*); **Selbst|ver|sor|gung** F self-sufficiency, self-reliance; (*in Urlaub etc*) self-catering (*Brit*), self-sufficiency; **selbst|ver|ständ|lich** ADJ *Freundlichkeit* natural; *Wahrheit* self-evident; **das ist doch ~!** this goes without saying, that's obvious; **vielen Dank für Ihre Hilfe - aber das ist doch ~** thanks for your help - it's no more than anybody would have done; **kann ich mitkommen? - aber das ist doch ~** can I come too? - but of course; **es war für uns ~, dass Sie ...** we took it for granted that you ...; **das ist keineswegs ~** it's by no means a matter of course, it cannot be taken for granted; **etw für ~ halten, etw als ~ annehmen** to take sth for granted ADV of course; **wie ~** as if it were the most natural thing in the world; **Selbst|ver|ständ|lich|keit** [-fɛɐʃtɛntlɪçkait] F -, **-en** naturalness; (= *Unbefangenheit*) casualness *no indef art*; (*von Wahrheit*) self-evidence; (*von Wahrheit etc*) self-evident truth *etc*; **nichts zu danken, das war doch eine ~** think nothing of it, it was no more than anyone would have done; **das war doch eine ~, dass wir ...** it was only natural that we ...; **etw für eine ~ halten** to take sth as a matter of course; **Meinungsfreiheit ist für uns eine ~** we take freedom of speech for granted; **das sind heute ~en** those are things we take for granted today; **mit der**

größten ~ as if it were the most natural thing in the world; **Selbst|ver|ständ|nis** NT jds ~ the way sb sees himself/herself; **nach seinem eigenen ~** as he sees himself; **Selbst|ver|stüm|me|lung** F self-inflicted wound; (= *das Verstümmeln*) self-mutilation; **Selbst|ver|such** M experiment on oneself; **Selbst|ver|tei|di|gung** F self-defence (*Brit*), self-defense (*US*); **Selbst|ver|trau|en** NT self-confidence; **Selbst|ver|wal|tung** F self-administration; (*Verwaltungskörper*) self-governing body; **Selbst|ver|wirk|li|chung** F self-realization; **Selbst|vor|wurf** M self-reproach; **Selbst|wähl|fern|dienst** M (*Telec*) automatic dialling (*Brit*) or dialing (*US*) service, subscriber trunk dialling (*Brit*), STD (*Brit*); **Selbst|wähl|fern|ver|kehr** M (*Telec*) automatic dialling (*Brit*) or dialing (*US*), STD system (*Brit*); **Selbst|wert|ge|fühl** NT feeling of one's own worth or value, self-esteem; **Selbst|zer|flei|schung** [-tseeflaiʃʊŋ] F -, -en self-destruction; **selbst|zer|stö|re|risch** ADJ self-destructive ADV self-destructively; **Selbst|zer|stö|rung** F self-destruction; **selbst|zu|frie|den** ADJ self-satisfied ADV complacently, smugly; **Selbst|zu|frie|den|heit** F self-satisfaction; **selbst|zün|dend** ADJ self-igniting; **Selbst|zün|der** M (*Aut inf, Motor, Fahrzeug*) diesel; **Selbst|zweck** M end in itself; **als ~** as an end in itself; **Selbst|zwei|fel** M usu pl self-doubt no pl

sel|chen ['zɛlçn] VTI (*S Ger, Aus*) Fleisch to smoke

Sel|cher ['zɛlçɐ] M -s, -, **Sel|che|rin** [-ərɪn] F -, -nen (*S Ger, Aus*) (pork) butcher

Selch|fleisch NT (*S Ger, Aus*) smoked meat

se|lek|tie|ren [zelɛk'tiːrən] ptp **selektiert** VT to select

Se|lek|ti|on [zelɛk'tsioːn] F -, -en selection

Se|lek|ti|ons|leh|re F , **Se|lek|ti|ons|the|o|rie** F theory of natural selection

se|lek|tiv [zelɛk'tiːf] ADJ selective ADV selectively

Se|lek|ti|vi|tät [zelɛktivi'tɛːt] F -, no pl (*Rad, Biol, Psych*) selectivity; (*fig*) selectiveness

Se|len [ze'leːn] NT -s, no pl (*abbr* **Se**) selenium

Se|len|zel|le F (*Phot*) selenium cell

Self|made|man ['sɛlfmeːdmən] M -s, **Self|mademen** self-made man

se|lig [ze'lɪç] ADJ a (*Rel*) blessed; (*old:* = *verstorben*) late; **(sind) die Armen im Geiste, denn …** (*Bibl*) blessed are the poor in spirit, for … (*Bibl*); **bis an mein ~es Ende** (*old, hum*) until the day I die; **mein Vater ~** (*old*), **mein ~er Vater** (*old*) my late father → **Angedenken, geben, Gefilde, glauben** b (= *überglücklich*) overjoyed; *Lächeln* blissful, beatific (*liter*); *Stunden* blissful; (*inf*: = *beswipst*) tipsy (*inf*), merry (*Brit inf*) ADV ~ **entschlafen** (*liter*) departed this life; **Gott hab ihn ~** (*old*) God rest his soul b (= *glücklich*) blissfully; ~ **schlafen** to sleep blissfully

Se|li|ge(r) ['zeːlɪɡə] MF decl as adj a (*Eccl*) blessed (*inf*); **die ~n** the Blessed b (*old*) **mein/Ihr ~r** my/your late husband

Se|lig|keit F -, -en a no pl (*Rel*) salvation; **ewige ~** eternal salvation b (= *Glück*) (supreme) happiness, bliss

Se|lig-: se|lig prei|sen ▲ irreg VT a (*Bibl*) to bless b (*liter*: = *verherrlichen*) to glorify VR to thank one's lucky stars; **Se|lig|prei|sung** [-praizʊŋ] F -, -en (*Bibl*) Beatitude; (*liter*) glorification; **se|lig spre|chen** ▲ VT irreg (*Eccl*) to beatify; **Se|lig|spre|chung** ['zeːlɪçʃprɛçʊŋ] F -, -en (*Eccl*) beatification

Sel|le|rie ['zɛlərɪ] M -s, -(s) or f -, - celeriac; (= *Stangensellerie*) celery

sel|ten ['zɛltn] ADJ rare; (= *kaum vorkommend auch*) scarce; **du bist ja in letzter Zeit ein ~er Gast** you're a stranger here these days → **Erde, Vogel** ADV a (= *nicht oft*) rarely, seldom; (= *be-sonders*) exceptionally; **nur/höchst ~** very/

extremely rarely or seldom; **~ so gelacht!** (*inf*) what a laugh! (*inf*)

Sel|ten|heit F -, -en a no pl (= *seltenes Vorkommen*) rareness, rarity b (= *seltene Sache*) rarity; **das ist keine ~ bei ihr** it's nothing unusual with her

Sel|ten|heits|wert M rarity value

Sel|ters ['zɛltɐs] NT -, - (*inf*), **Sel|ter(s)|was|ser** NT pl -wässer soda (water)

selt|sam ['zɛltzaːm] ADJ strange; (= *komisch auch*) odd, peculiar ADV strangely; ~ **berührt** strangely moved; ~ **klingen/aussehen/schmecken/riechen** to sound/look/taste/smell strange; **es schimmerte ~ grünlich** it had a strange green shimmer to it

selt|sa|mer|wei|se ['zɛltzaːmɐ'vaizə] ADV strangely enough

Selt|sam|keit F -, -en a no pl (= *Sonderbarkeit*) strangeness b (= *seltsame Sache*) oddity

Se|man|tik [ze'mantɪk] F -, no pl semantics sing

se|man|tisch [ze'mantɪʃ] ADJ semantic ADV semantically

Se|ma|phor [zema'foːɐ] NT OR M -s, -e (*Naut, Rail*) semaphore

Se|ma|si|o|lo|gie [zemazio'ɡiː] F -, no pl (*Ling*) semasiology

Se|mes|ter [ze'mɛstɐ] NT -s, - (*Univ*) semester (*esp US*), term (*of a half-year's duration*); **im 7./8. ~ sein** to be in one's 4th year; **die älteren ~** the older or senior students; **ein älteres ~** a senior student; (*hum*) an old boy/girl; **sie ist auch schon ein älteres ~** she's no spring chicken (*inf*)

Se|mes|ter- (*Univ*): **Se|mes|ter|be|ginn** M zu ~ at the beginning of term or semester (*esp US*); **Se|mes|ter|en|de** NT zu ~ at the end of term or semester (*esp US*); **Se|mes|ter|fe|ri|en** PL vacation sing; **se|mes|ter|lang** ADJ, ADV for years; **Se|mes|ter|schluss** ▲ M end of term, end of the semester (*esp US*); **Se|mes|ter|ti|cket** NT student ticket (*valid during term*)

-se|mes|trig [zemɛstrɪç] ADJ suf **ein acht-/zehn-semestriges Studium** a four-/five-year course

Se|mi-, se|mi- ['zemi] in cpds semi-; **Se|mi|fi|na|le** ['zemi-] NT (*Sport*) semifinal(s); **Se|mi|ko|lon** [zemi'koːlɔn] NT -s, -s or Semikola [-la] semicolon

Se|mi|nar [zemi'naːɐ] NT -s, -e or (*Aus*) -rien [-iən] a (*Univ*) department; (= *Seminarübung*) seminar b (= *Priesterseminar*) seminary c (= *Lehrerseminar, Studienseminar*) teacher training college, college of education

Se|mi|nar- (*Univ*): **Se|mi|nar|ap|pa|rat** M seminar course books pl; **Se|mi|nar|ar|beit** F seminar paper

Se|mi|na|rist [zemina'rɪst] M -en, -en, **Se|mi|na|ris|tin** [-'rɪstɪn] F -, -nen (*Eccl*) seminarist

se|mi|na|ris|tisch [zemina'rɪstɪʃ] ADJ a (*Univ*) *Struktur* departmental; **~e Ausbildung** (= *in Gruppen*) training through seminars b (*Eccl*) seminary

Se|mi|nar- (*Univ*): **Se|mi|nar|schein** M *certificate of attendance for one semester or half year*; **Se|mi|nar|übung** F seminar

Se|mi|o|lo|gie [zemiolo'ɡiː] F -, no pl semiology

Se|mi|o|tik [zemi'oːtɪk] F -, no pl semiotics sing

se|mi|per|me|a|bel ADJ semipermeable

Se|mit [ze'miːt] M -en, -en, **Se|mi|tin** [-'miːtɪn] F -, -nen Semite

se|mi|tisch [ze'miːtɪʃ] ADJ Semitic

Se|mi|tist [zemi'tɪst] M -en, -en, **Se|mi|tis|tin** [-'tɪstɪn] F -, -nen Semitist

Se|mi|tis|tik [zemi'tɪstɪk] F -, no pl Semitics sing

Se|mi|vo|kal ['zemi-] M semivowel

Sem|mel ['zɛml] F -, -n (*dial*) roll; **geriebene ~** breadcrumbs pl

Sem|mel-: sem|mel|blond ADJ (*dated*) flaxen-haired; **Sem|mel|brö|sel(n)** [-brøːzl(n)] PL breadcrumbs pl; **Sem|mel|kloß** M , (*S Ger, Aus*) **Sem|mel|knö|del** M bread dumpling; **Sem|mel|mehl** NT breadcrumbs pl

sen. abbr von **senior** sen.

Se|nat [ze'naːt] M -(e)s, -e a (*Pol, Univ*) senate b (*Jur*) Supreme Court

Se|na|tor [ze'naːtoːɐ] M -s, **Senatoren** [-'toːrən], **Se|na|to|rin** [-'toːrɪn] F -, -nen senator

Se|nats- in cpds of the senate; **Se|nats|aus|schuss** ▲ M senate committee; **se|nats|ei|gen** ADJ belonging to the senate; **Se|nats|prä|si|dent(in)** M(F) chairman/-woman of the senate; **Se|nats|wah|len** PL elections pl to the senate

Send-: Send|bo|te M (*Hist*) emissary, ambassador (*old*); **Send|brief** M (*liter*) circular letter

Sen|de-: Sen|de|an|la|ge F transmitting installation; **Sen|de|an|stalt** F broadcasting organization or station; **Sen|de|an|ten|ne** F transmitting aerial (*esp Brit*) or antenna (*US*); **Sen|de|be|reich** M transmission range; **Sen|de|ein|rich|tung** F transmitting facility; **Sen|de|fol|ge** F a (= *Sendung in Fortsetzungen*) series sing; (= *einzelne Folge*) episode b (= *Programmfolge*) programmes pl (*Brit*), programs pl (*US*); **Sen|de|ge|biet** NT transmission area; **Sen|de|lei|ter(in)** M(F) producer; **Sen|de|mast** M radio or transmitter mast, broadcasting tower (*US*)

sen|den¹ ['zɛndn] ◯ 50.2 pret **sandte** or **sende|te** ['zantə, 'zɛndətə], ptp **gesandt** or **gesendet** [ɡə'zant, ɡə'zɛndət] VT to send (*an* +acc to); **jdm etw ~** to send sb sth, to send sth to sb VI **nach jdm ~** to send for sb

sen|den² VTI (*Rad, TV*) to broadcast; *Signal etc* to transmit

Sen|de|pau|se F interval; (*fig inf*) deathly silence; **danach tritt eine ~ bis 6 Uhr ein** afterwards we shall be going off the air until 6 o'clock; **auf meine Frage hin herrschte ~** my question was met by deathly silence

Sen|der ['zɛndɐ] M -s, - transmitter; (= *Senderkanal*) (*Rad*) station; (*TV*) channel (*esp Brit*), station (*esp US*); **der ~ Prag** Radio Prague; **über den ~ gehen** to go on the air

Sen|de-: Sen|de|raum M studio; **Sen|de|rei|he** F (*radio/television*) series

Sen|der-: Sen|der|ein|stel|lung F tuning; **Sen|der-Emp|fän|ger** M transceiver; **Sen|der|such|lauf** M search tuning

Sen|de-: Sen|de|saal M studio; **Sen|de|schluss** ▲ M (*Rad, TV*) close-down, end of broadcasts; **und nun bis ~** and now until we close down; **Sen|de|turm** M radio tower; **Sen|de|zei|chen** NT call sign; **Sen|de|zeit** F broadcasting time; **und damit geht unsere heutige ~ zu Ende** and that concludes our programmes (*Brit*) or programs (*US*) for today; **in der besten ~** in prime time

Send|schrei|ben NT (*liter*) circular letter

Sen|dung ['zɛndʊŋ] F -, -en a no pl (= *das Senden*) sending b (= *Postsendung*) letter; (= *Päckchen*) packet; (= *Paket*) parcel; (*Comm*) consignment c (*TV*) programme (*Brit*), program (*US*); (*Rad*) broadcast, programme (*Brit*), program (*US*); (= *das Senden*) broadcasting; (*von Signal etc*) transmission; **auf ~ gehen/sein** to go/be on the air d (*liter:* = *Aufgabe*) mission

Sen|dungs|be|wusst|sein ▲ NT sense of mission

Se|ne|gal¹ ['zeːneɡal] M -(s) **der ~** the Senegal (River)

Se|ne|gal² NT -s Senegal

Se|ne|ga|ler [zeneˈɡaːlɐ] M -s, -, **Se|ne|ga|le|rin** [-ərɪn] F -, -nen, **Se|ne|ga|le|se** [zenegaˈleːzə] M -n, -n, **Se|ne|ga|le|sin** [-ˈleːzɪn] F -, -nen Senegalese

se|ne|ga|le|sisch [zenegaˈleːzɪʃ], **se|ne|ga-lisch** [zeneˈgaːlɪʃ] ADJ Senegalese

Se|ne|schall [ˈzeːnəʃal] M **-s, -e** (Hist) seneschal

Se|nes|zenz [zenɛsˈtsɛnts] F **-,** no pl (Med) senescence

Senf [zɛnf] M **-(e)s, -e** mustard; **seinen ~ dazu-geben** (inf) to get one's three ha'p'orth (Brit) or two cents (US) in (inf), to have one's say

Senf-: senf|far|ben [-farbn], **senf|far|big** ADJ mustard(-coloured) (Brit), mustard(-colored) (US); **Senf|gas** NT (Chem) mustard gas; **Senf|gur|ke** F gherkin pickled with mustard seeds; **Senf|korn** NT pl **-körner** mustard seed; **Senf|mehl** NT flour of mustard; **Senf|pa-ckung** F (Med) mustard poultice; **Senf-pflas|ter** NT (Med) mustard plaster; **Senf-so|ße** F , **Senf|tun|ke** F (dial) mustard sauce; **Senf|um|schlag** M (Med) mustard poultice

Sen|ge [ˈzɛŋə] PL (dated inf) **~ kriegen** to get a good hiding

sen|gen [ˈzɛŋən] VT to singe VI to scorch; **~d und brennend** (old liter) with fire and sword

se|nil [zeˈniːl] ADJ (pej) senile

Se|ni|li|tät [zeniliˈtɛːt] F **-,** no pl senility

se|ni|or [ˈzeːnioːɐ] ADJ **Franz Schulz ~** Franz Schulz senior

Se|ni|or [ˈzeːnioːɐ] M **-s, Senioren** [zeˈnioːrən], **Se|ni|o|rin** [zeˈnioːrɪn] F **-, -nen** a (auch **Seni-orchef(in)**) boss; **kann ich mal den ~ spre-chen?** can I speak to Mr X senior? b (Sport) senior player; **die ~en** the seniors, the senior team c **Senioren** PL senior citizens pl; (hum) old folk pl

Se|ni|o|ren-: Se|ni|o|ren|ho|tel NT hotel for the elderly; **Se|ni|o|ren|kar|te** F pensioner's ticket, senior citizen's ticket; **Se|ni|o|ren-mann|schaft** F senior team; **Se|ni|o|ren-pass** ▲ M senior citizen's travel pass; **Se|ni-o|ren|tel|ler** M dish for senior citizens; **Se|ni-o|ren(wohn)|haus** NT , **Se|ni|o|ren-(wohn)|heim** NT old people's home

Se|ni|o|rin F → **Senior**

Se|ni|or|part|ner(in) M(F) senior partner

Senk|blei NT plumb line; (= Gewicht) plummet

Sen|ke [ˈzɛŋkə] F **-, -n** valley

Sen|kel [ˈzɛŋkl] M **-s, -** a (= Schnürsenkel) lace; **jdm auf den ~ gehen** (fig: inf) to get on sb's wick (Brit inf) or nerves b (= Senklot) plumb line; (= Gewicht) plummet; **jdn in den ~ stellen** (fig inf) to put sb in his/her place

sen|ken [ˈzɛŋkn] VT to lower; Lanze, Fahne to dip; Kopf to bow; Preis, Steuern, Kosten to de-crease, to lower; (Tech) Schraube, Loch, Schacht to sink; (Hort) Schösslinge, Wurzeln etc to plant; **den Blick ~** to lower one's gaze VR to sink; (Grab, Haus, Boden, Straße auch) to subside; (Was-serspiegel auch) to go down, to fall; (Decke) to sag; (Flugzeug) to descend; (Stimme) to drop; (li-ter: Nacht, Nebel) to fall, to descend (über, auf +acc on); **dann senkte sich ihr Blick** then she looked down, then she lowered her eyes or her gaze (liter)

Senk-: Senk|fuß M (Med) fallen arches pl; **Senk|fuß|ein|la|ge** F arch support; **Senk-gru|be** F cesspit; **Senk|kas|ten** M caisson; **Senk|kopf|schrau|be** F countersunk screw; **Senk|lot** NT plumb line; (= Gewicht) plummet

senk|recht [ˈzɛŋkrɛçt] ADJ vertical; (Math) per-pendicular; (in Kreuzworträtsel) down; **immer schön ~ bleiben!** (inf) keep your end up (inf) ADV vertically, perpendicularly; aufsteigen, in die Höhe steigen straight up; **sie stehen ~ aufeinan-der** they are perpendicular to each other

Senk|rech|te [ˈzɛŋkrɛçtə] F decl as adj vertical; (Math) perpendicular

Senk|recht|star|ter M (Aviat) vertical takeoff aircraft

Senk|recht|star|ter(in) M(F) (fig inf) whiz(z) kid (inf)

Sen|kung [ˈzɛŋkʊn] F **-, -en** a sinking; (von Bo-den, Straße) subsidence; (von Wasserspiegel) fall (+gen in), drop (+gen in); (als Maßnahme) low-ering; (von Decke) sag(ging); (von Stimme) lower-ing; (von Preisen, Steuern) lowering (von of), de-crease (von in); (von Arbeitslosigkeit) fall, drop (von in) b (= Vertiefung) hollow, valley c (Po-et) thesis d (Med) = **Blutsenkung**

Sen|kungs|ge|schwin|dig|keit F (Med) rate of sedimentation

Senk|waa|ge F hydrometer

Senn [zɛn] M **-(e)s, -e, Sen|ne**[1] M **-n, -(S Ger, Aus)** Alpine dairyman

Sen|ne[2] [ˈzɛnə] F **-, -n** (S Ger, Aus) Alpine pas-ture

Sen|ner [ˈzɛnɐ] M **-s, -** (S Ger, Aus) Alpine dairy-man

Sen|ne|rei [zɛnəˈrai] F **-, -en** (S Ger, Aus, Gebäu-de) Alpine dairy; (Wirtschaftsform) Alpine dairy farming

Sen|ne|rin [ˈzɛnərɪn] F **-, -nen** (S Ger, Aus) Al-pine dairymaid

Sen|nes|blät|ter [ˈzɛnəs-] PL senna leaves pl

Senn|hüt|te F Alpine dairy hut

Sen|sa|ti|on [zɛnzatsiˈoːn] F **-, -en** sensation

sen|sa|ti|o|nell [zɛnzatsioˈnɛl] ADJ sensational ADV sensationally; **er wurde ~ Dritter** he came a sensational third; **~ schnell** incredibly fast

Sen|sa|ti|ons-: Sen|sa|ti|ons|be|dürf|nis NT need for sensation; **Sen|sa|ti|ons|blatt** NT sensational paper; **Sen|sa|ti|ons|gier** F (pej) sensation-seeking; **aus ~** for the sheer sensa-tion; **Sen|sa|ti|ons|lust** F desire for sensa-tion; **sen|sa|ti|ons|lüs|tern** ADJ sensation--seeking; **sen|sa|ti|ons|lus|tig** ADJ sensation--loving; **Sen|sa|ti|ons|ma|che** F (inf) sensa-tionalism; **Sen|sa|ti|ons|mel|dung** F , **Sen-sa|ti|ons|nach|richt** F sensational news sing; **eine Sensationsnachricht** a sensation, a scoop, a sensational piece of news; **Sen|sa|ti|ons-pres|se** F sensational papers pl, yellow press; **Sen|sa|ti|ons|pro|zess** ▲ M sensational trial

Sen|se [ˈzɛnzə] F **-, -n** a scythe b (inf) **jetzt/ dann ist ~!** that's the end!; **es ist nichts mehr da, ~!** there's none left, all gone!

Sen|sen|mann M pl **-männer der ~** the Grim Reaper

sen|si|bel [zɛnˈziːbl] ADJ sensitive; (= heikel auch) problematic, delicate ADV schildern sensi-tively; **~ auf etw** (acc) **reagieren** to be sensitive to sth; **~ mit jdm umgehen** to treat sb sensi-tively

Sen|si|bel|chen [zɛnˈziːblçən] NT **-s, -** (inf, usu pej) sensitive soul

Sen|si|bi|li|sa|tor [zɛnzibiliˈzaːtoːɐ] M **-s, Sen-sibilisatoren** [-ˈtoːrən] (Phot) sensitizer

sen|si|bi|li|sie|ren [zɛnzibiliˈziːrən] ptp **sensibi-lisiert** VT to sensitize

Sen|si|bi|li|sie|rung F **-, -en** sensitization

Sen|si|bi|li|tät [zɛnzibiliˈtɛːt] F **-,** no pl sensitivi-ty; (= Feingefühl auch) sensibility

sen|si|tiv [zɛnziˈtiːf] ADJ (geh, Comput) sensitive

Sen|si|ti|vi|tät [zɛnzitiviˈtɛːt] F **-,** no pl (geh, Comput) sensitivity

Sen|sor [ˈzɛnzoːɐ] M **-s, Sensoren** [-ˈzoːrən] sen-sor

sen|so|ri|ell [zɛnzoˈriɛl] ADJ, ADV = **sensorisch**

Sen|so|ri|en [zɛnˈzoːriən] PL sensoria pl

sen|so|risch [zɛnˈzoːrɪʃ] ADJ sensory ADV akti-vieren, steuern by a sensor; **~ gestört sein** to have a sensory disability

Sen|sor|tas|te F touch-sensitive button

Sen|su|a|lis|mus [zɛnzuaˈlɪsmʊs] M **-,** no pl (Phi-los) sensualism, sensationalism

Sen|su|a|li|tät [zɛnzualiˈtɛːt] F **-,** no pl sensuali-ty

sen|su|ell [zɛnˈzuɛl] ADJ sensory

Sen|tenz [zɛnˈtɛnts] F **-, -en** aphorism

sen|ten|zi|ös [zɛntɛnˈtsiøːs] ADJ sententious

Sen|ti|ment [zãtiˈmãː] NT **-s, -s** (liter) feeling

sen|ti|men|tal [zɛntimɛnˈtaːl], **sen|ti|men|ta-lisch** [zɛntimɛnˈtaːlɪʃ] (old) ADJ sentimental ADV sentimentally; **~ klingen** to sound senti-mental; **sich jdm gegenüber ~ verhalten** to be sentimental about sb; **der Brief war ~ ange-haucht** the letter had a sentimental tone to it

Sen|ti|men|ta|li|tät [zɛntimɛntaliˈtɛːt] F **-, -en** sentimentality

se|pa|rat [zepaˈraːt] ADJ separate; (= in sich abge-schlossen) Wohnung, Zimmer self-contained ADV separately

Se|pa|rat-: Se|pa|rat(ab)|druck M pl **-drucke** offprint; **Se|pa|rat|frie|de(n)** M separate peace

Se|pa|ra|tis|mus [zeparaˈtɪsmʊs] M **-,** no pl (Pol) separatism

Se|pa|ra|tist [zeparaˈtɪst] M **-en, -en, Se|pa|ra-tis|tin** [-ˈtɪstɪn] F **-, -nen** (Pol) separatist

se|pa|ra|tis|tisch [zeparaˈtɪstɪʃ] ADJ (Pol) sepa-ratist

Sé|pa|rée [zepaˈreː] NT **-s, -s, Se|pa|ree** ▲ NT **-s, -s** private room; (= Nische) private booth

se|pa|rie|ren [zepaˈriːrən] ptp **separiert** VT (rare) to separate; (= isolieren) to isolate

se|pa|riert [zepaˈriːɐt] ADJ (esp Aus) Zimmer self-contained

se|pia [ˈzeːpia] ADJ inv sepia

Se|pia [ˈzeːpia] F **-, Sepien** [-piən] a (Zool) cut-tlefish b no pl (Farbstoff) sepia (ink)

Se|pia-: Se|pi|a|scha|le F cuttlefish shell; **Se-pi|a|zeich|nung** F sepia (drawing)

Se|pi|en [ˈzeːpiən] pl von **Sepia**

Sepp [zɛp] M **-s (S Ger) abbr von Josef**

Sepp|pel-: Sepp|pel|ho|se [ˈzɛpl-] F (inf) leder-hosen pl, leather shorts pl; **Sepp|pel|hut** [ˈzɛpl-] M (inf) traditional Bavarian hat

Sep|sis [ˈzɛpsɪs] F **-, Sepsen** [ˈzɛpsn] (Med) sepsis

Sep|tem|ber [zɛpˈtɛmbɐ] M **-(s), -** September → auch **März**

Sep|tett [zɛpˈtɛt] NT **-(e)s, -e** (Mus) septet(te)

Sep|ti|me [zɛpˈtiːmə] F **-, -en** (Aus) **Sep|tim** [zɛpˈtiːm] F **-, -en** (Mus) seventh

sep|tisch [ˈzɛptɪʃ] ADJ (Med) septic

Sep|tu|a|gin|ta [zɛptuaˈgɪnta] F **-** (Eccl) Septua-gint

se|quen|ti|ell [zekvɛnˈtsiɛl] ADJ, ADV = **sequen-ziell**

Se|quenz [zeˈkvɛnts] F **-, -en** sequence; (Cards auch) flush, run

Se|quen|zer [ˈziːkvɛntsɐ] M **-s, -** (Tech) se-quencer

se|quen|zi|ell ▲ [zekvɛnˈtsiɛl] ADJ, ADJ sequen-tial ADV sequentially

se|quest|rie|ren [zekvɛsˈtriːrən] ptp **sequest-riert** VT (Jur) to sequester, to sequestrate

Se|ra pl von **Serum**

Se|rail [zeˈraːj, zeˈrai(l)] NT **-s, -s** seraglio

Se|raph [ˈzeːraf] M **-s, -e** or **-im** [-fiːm] seraph

Ser|be [ˈzɛrbə] M **-n, -n, Ser|bin** [ˈzɛrbɪn] F **-, -nen** Serbian

Ser|bi|en [ˈzɛrbiən] NT **-s** Serbia

Ser|bin F **-, -nen** Serbian (woman/girl)

ser|bisch [ˈzɛrbɪʃ] ADJ Serbian

Ser|bo|kro|a|tisch(e) [zɛrbokroˈaːtɪʃ] NT Ser-bo-Croat → auch **Deutsch(e)**

Se|ren PL von **Serum**

Se|re|na|de [zereˈnaːdə] F **-, -n** serenade

Ser|geant [zɛrˈʒant] M **-en, -en** (dated Mil) ser-geant

Se|rie [ˈzeːriə] F **-, -n** series sing; (von Waren auch) line; (Billard) break; **13 Siege in ~** 13 wins in a row; **in ~ gehen** to go into production, to go onto the production line; **in ~ hergestellt werden** to be mass-produced; **das Gesetz der ~** the law of averages; **in ~ schalten** (Elec) to con-nect in series

---

se|ri|ell [zeˈriɛl] **ADJ** *Herstellung* series *attr*; (*Comput*) serial; **~e Musik** serial music **ADV** serially; **~ hergestellt werden** to be mass-produced

Se|rien- [ˈzeːriən-]: **Se|rien|au|to** NT mass-produced car; **Se|rien|brief** M (*Comput*) mail-merge letter; **Se|rien|fab|ri|ka|ti|on** F, **Se|ri|en|fer|ti|gung** F, **Se|ri|en|her|stel|lung** F series production; **se|rien|fax** NT mail-merge fax; **se|ri|en|mä|ßig** **ADJ** *Autos* production *attr*; *Ausstattung* standard; *Herstellung* series *attr* **ADV** *herstellen* in series; **das wird ~ eingebaut** it's a standard fitting; **Se|ri|en|mör|der** M(F) serial killer; **Se|ri|en|num|mer** F serial number; **Se|ri|en|pro|duk|ti|on** F series production; **in ~ gehen** to go into production, to go onto the production line; **se|ri|en|reif** ADJ (*esp Aut*) ready to go into production; **Se|ri|en|reife** F readiness for production; **etw zur ~ entwickeln** to develop sth so that it is ready for production; **Se|ri|en|schal|tung** F (*Elec*) series connection; **Se|ri|en|tä|ter(in)** M(F) serial offender; **se|ri|en|weise** [-vaizə] **ADV** *produzieren* in series; (*inf*: = *in Mengen*) wholesale

Se|ri|fe [zeˈriːfə] F -, -n (*Typ*) serif

se|ri|fen|los ADJ (*Typ*) sanserif

Se|ri|gra|fie ▲ [zerigraˈfiː] F -, -n [-ˈfiːən] **a** (*Verfahren*) silk-screen printing, serigraphy (*spec*) **b** (*Bild*) silk-screen print, serigraph (*spec*)

se|ri|ös [zeˈriøːs] **ADJ** serious; (= *anständig*) respectable, (= *anständig*) respectable; *Firma* reputable **ADV ~ auftreten** to appear respectable; **~ wirken** to give the impression of being respectable; **~ klingen** to sound serious

Se|ri|o|si|tät [zerioziˈtɛːt] F -, no pl seriousness; (= *Anständigkeit*) respectability, (*von Firma*) integrity; **von zweifelhafter ~** of doubtful reputation

Ser|mon [zɛrˈmoːn] M -s, -e (*pej*) sermon, lecture

Se|ro|di|ag|nos|tik [zero-] F serodiagnosis

Se|ro|lo|gie [zeroloˈgiː] F -, no pl serology

se|ro|lo|gisch [zeroˈloːgɪʃ] ADJ serological

se|ro|ne|ga|tiv [zero-] ADJ HIV negative, seronegative (*spec*)

se|ro|po|si|tiv ADJ HIV positive, seropositive (*spec*)

Ser|pen|tin [zɛrpɛnˈtiːn] M -s, -e (*Miner*) serpentine

Ser|pen|ti|ne [zɛrpɛnˈtiːnə] F -, -n winding road, zigzag; (= *Kurve*) double bend; **die Straße führt in** *or* **den Berg hinauf** the road winds *or* zigzags its way up the mountain

Ser|pen|ti|nen|stra|ße F winding *or* serpentine road

Se|rum [ˈzeːrʊm] NT -s, Seren *or* Sera [ˈzeːrən, ˈzeːra] serum

Se|rum|be|hand|lung F, **Se|rum|the|ra|pie** F serotherapy, serum therapy

Ser|ver [ˈzœrvə] M -s, - (*Comput*) server

Ser|vice¹ [zɛrˈviːs] NT -(s), - [-ˈviːs(əs), -ˈviːs(ə)] (= *Essgeschirr*) dinner service; (= *Kaffee-/Teeservice*) coffee/tea service; (= *Gläserservice*) set

Ser|vice² [ˈsøːɛvɪs, ˈzœrvɪs] M OR NT -, -s (*Comm*) service; (*Sport*) service, serve

Ser|vice- [ˈzœrvɪs-, ˈsøːɛvɪs-]: **Ser|vice|leis|tung** [ˈzœrvɪs-, ˈsøːɛvɪs-] F service; **Ser|vice|pro|vi|der** [ˈzœrvɪsprɔˈvaidɐ, ˈsøːɛvɪs-] M -s, - (*für Mobilfunk, Internet*) service provider; **Ser|vice|te|le|fon** [ˈzœrvɪs-, ˈsøːɛvɪs-] NT customer service hotline

Ser|vier|brett [zɛrˈviːɐ-] NT tray

ser|vie|ren [zɛrˈviːrən] ptp **serviert** **VT** to serve (*jdm etw* sb sth, sth to sb); (*inf*: = *anbieten*) to serve up (*inf*) (*jdm* for sb); (*Tennis*) to serve; **jdm etw auf dem Silbertablett ~** (*fig*) to hand sth to sb on a plate (*Brit*) *or* on a silver platter; **jdm den Ball ~** (*Ftbl etc*) to pass the ball to sb; (*Tennis*) to hit the ball right to sb; **er bekam den Ball toll serviert** the ball was beautifully set up for him **VI a** to serve; **nach 24 Uhr wird nicht**

mehr serviert there is no waiter service after midnight; **es ist serviert!** lunch/dinner *etc* is served **b** (*Tennis*) to serve

Ser|vie|re|rin [zɛrˈviːrərɪn] F -, -nen waitress

Ser|vier- [zɛrˈviːɐ-]: **Ser|vier|tisch** M serving table; **Ser|vier|toch|ter** F (*Sw*) waitress; **Ser|vier|vor|schlag** M (*auf Verpackungen*) serving suggestion; **Ser|vier|wa|gen** M trolley

Ser|vi|et|te [zɛrˈvieta] F -, -n serviette (*Brit*), napkin

Ser|vi|et|ten-: **Ser|vi|et|ten|knö|del** M (*Cook*) dumpling cooked in a napkin; **Ser|vi|et|ten|ring** M serviette (*Brit*) *or* napkin ring

ser|vil [zɛrˈviːl] (*geh*) **ADJ** servile **ADV** servilely

Ser|vi|li|tät [zɛrviliˈtɛːt] F -, no pl (*geh*) servility

Ser|vo- [ˈzɛrvo-] (*Tech*): **Ser|vo|brem|se** F power brake, servo(-assisted) brake; **Ser|vo|len|kung** F power steering, servo(-assisted) steering; **Ser|vo|mo|tor** M servomotor

ser|vus [ˈzɛrvʊs] INTERJ (*Aus, S Ger*) (*beim Treffen*) hello; (*beim Abschied*) goodbye, so long (*inf*), cheerio (*Brit inf*), see ya (*esp US inf*)

Se|sam [ˈzeːzam] M -s, -s sesame; **~, öffne dich!** open Sesame!

Se|sam|stra|ße® F, no pl (*TV: Kindersendung*) Sesame Street®

Ses|sel [ˈzɛsl] M -s, - easy chair; (= *Polstersessel*) armchair; (*Aus*: = *Stuhl*) chair; **am ~ kleben** (*fig*) to cling to one's position; **seinen ~ räumen** (*fig*) to clear one's desk

Ses|sel-: **Ses|sel|leh|ne** F (*chair*) arm; **Ses|sel|lift** M chairlift

sess|haft ▲ **ADJ** settled; (= *ansässig*) resident; **~ werden, sich ~ machen** to settle down

Sess|haf|tig|keit ▲ [ˈzɛshaftɪçkait] F -, no pl settled existence; (*von Lebensweise mit festem Wohnsitz*) settledness; **die sprichwörtliche ~ der Holsteiner** the Holsteiners' proverbial lack of wanderlust

Ses|si|on [zɛˈsioːn] F -, -en (*Parl*) session; (*Jur*) term

Set¹ [zɛt, sɛt] M OR NT -s, -s **a** (*Tennis*: = *Satz*) set **b** (= *Deckchen*) place mat, table mat

Set² M -(s), -s (*TV, Film*) set

Set|ter [ˈzɛtɐ] M -s, - setter

Setz|ei [ˈzɛtsai] NT fried egg

set|zen [ˈzɛtsn] **VT a** (= *hintun, hinbringen*) to put, to place, to set; (= *sitzen lassen*) to sit, to place, to put; **etw auf die Rechnung/Speisekarte** *etc* **~** to put sth on the bill/menu *etc*; **etw an den Mund/die Lippen ~** to put sth to one's mouth/lips; **jdn an Land ~** to put *or* set sb ashore; **jdn über den Fluss ~** to take sb across the river; **Fische in einen Teich ~** to stock a pond with fish; **ein Stück auf den Spielplan ~** to put on a play; **etw auf die Tagesordnung ~** to put sth on the agenda; **etw in die Zeitung ~** to put sth in the paper; **jdn über jemanden anders/andere ~** to put *or* set sb above somebody else/others; **sich** (*dat*) **etw in den Kopf** *or* **Schädel ~** (*inf*) to take sth into one's head; **dann setzt es was** *or* **Hiebe** *or* **Prügel** (*all inf*) there'll be trouble; **seine Hoffnung/sein Vertrauen in jdn/etw ~** to put *or* place one's hopes/trust in sb/sth; **seine Ehre in etw** (*acc*) **~** to make sth a point of honour (*Brit*) *or* honor (*US*); **seinen Ehrgeiz in etw** (*acc*) **~** to make sth one's goal; **sein Leben an etw** (*acc*) **~** (*geh*) to devote one's life to sth → **Druck¹ a**
b (*Hort*: = *pflanzen*) to set, to plant; (= *aufziehen*) *Ständer, Laternen* to put up; (*Naut*) *Segel* to set; (*Typ*) to set; (*geh*: = *formulieren*) *Worte* to choose; **ein Gedicht/einen Text in Musik ~** to set a poem/words to music
c *Preis, Summe* to put (*auf +acc* on); (*bei Gesellschaftsspielen*: = *spielen, ziehen*) *Stein, Figur* to move; **Geld auf ein Pferd ~** to put *or* place *or* stake money on a horse; **auf seinen Kopf sind 100.000 Dollar gesetzt** there's 100,000 dollars on his head
d (= *errichten, aufstellen*) to build; *Denkmal auch*

to erect, to put *or* set up; (*fig*) *Norm etc* to set; **jdm ein Grabmal/Denkmal ~** to put *or* set up *or* build a monument to sb; **sich** (*dat*) **ein Denkmal ~** (*fig*) to ensure that one will not be forgotten
e (= *schreiben*) *Komma, Punkt* to put; **seinen Namen unter etw** (*acc*) **~** to put one's signature to sth
f (= *bestimmen*) *Ziel, Grenze, Termin, Preis, Prioritäten etc* to set; **jdm/sich ein Ziel/eine Frist ~** to set sb/oneself a goal/deadline; **den Fall ~** to make the assumption
g **jdm eine Spritze ~** to give sb an injection; **sich** (*dat*) **einen Schuss ~** (*inf*) to shoot up (*inf*)
h (= *einstufen*) *Sportler* to place; (*Tennis*) to seed; **sie wurde auf Platz zwei gesetzt** she was placed/seeded second; **der an Nummer eins/zwei gesetzte Spieler** (*Tennis*) the top-seeded/second-seeded player
i (*Hunt*: = *gebären*) to bear, to produce
j = **gesetzt**
VR a (= *Platz nehmen*) to sit down; (*Vogel*) to perch, to alight; **sich auf einen Stuhl/seinen Platz ~** to sit down on a chair/at one's place; **sich ins Auto ~** to get into the car; **sich in die Sonne/ins Licht ~** to sit in the sun/light; **sich jdm auf den Schoß ~** to sit on sb's lap; **sich zu jdm ~** to sit with sb; **wollen Sie sich nicht zu uns ~?** won't you join us?; **darf ich mich zu Ihnen ~?** may I join you?; **bitte ~ Sie sich** please sit down, please take a seat, please be seated (*form*); **setz dich doch** sit yourself down (*inf*)
b (*Kaffee, Tee, Lösung*) to settle
c (= *sich festsetzen*: *Staub, Geruch, Läuse*) to get (*in +acc* into)
VI a (*bei Glücksspiel, Wetten*) to bet; **auf ein Pferd ~** to bet on *or* to place a bet on *or* to back a horse; **auf jdn/etw ~** (*lit, fig*) to put one's money on sb/sth, to back sb/sth; **hoch/niedrig ~** to play for high/low stakes
b (*Typ*) to set
c (= *springen*) (*Pferd, Läufer*) to jump; (*Mil*) to cross; **über einen Graben/Zaun/ein Hindernis ~** to jump (over) *or* clear a ditch/fence/hurdle; **über einen Fluss ~** to cross a river

Set|zer [ˈzɛtsɐ] M -s, -, **Set|ze|rin** [-ərɪn] F -, -nen (*Typ*) typesetter

Set|ze|rei [zɛtsəˈrai] F -, -en (= *Firma*) typesetter's

Setz-: **Setz|feh|ler** M (*Typ*) printer's error, literal; **Setz|ha|se** M (*Hunt*) doe hare; **Setz|kas|ten** M case; **Setz|lat|te** F (*Surv*) aligning pole; **Setz|ling** [ˈzɛtslɪŋ] M -s, -e **a** (*Hort*) seedling **b** (= *Fisch*) fry; **Setz|ma|schi|ne** F typesetting machine, typesetter; **Setz|schiff** NT (*Typ*) galley; **Setz|waa|ge** F spirit level

Seu|che [ˈzɔyçə] F -, -n epidemic; (*fig pej*) scourge

Seu|chen-: **seu|chen|ar|tig** **ADJ** epidemic **ADV** **sich ~ ausbreiten** to spread like an epidemic; **Seu|chen|be|kämp|fung** F epidemic control; **Seu|chen|ge|biet** NT epidemic *or* infested area *or* zone; **Seu|chen|ge|fahr** F danger of epidemic; **Seu|chen|herd** M centre (*Brit*) *or* center (*US*) of an/the epidemic

seuf|zen [ˈzɔyftsn] VTI to sigh

Seuf|zer [ˈzɔyftsɐ] M -s, - sigh

Seuf|zer|brü|cke F Bridge of Sighs

Sex [zɛks] M -(es), no pl sex; **sie hat viel ~** she's very sexy

Sex-: **sex|ak|tiv** ADJ sexually active; **Sex-Appeal** [-ləˈpiːl] M -s, no pl sex appeal; **sex|be|ses|sen** ADJ sex-obsessed; **Sex|bom|be** F (*inf*) sex bomb (*inf*); **Sex|film** M sex film, skin flick (*inf*); **Sex|fo|to** NT sexy photo

Se|xis|mus [zɛˈksɪsmʊs] M -, **Se|xis|men** [-mən] sexism

Se|xist [zɛˈksɪst] M -en, -en, **Se|xis|tin** [-ˈksɪstɪn] F -, -nen sexist

se|xis|tisch [zɛˈksɪstɪʃ] **ADJ** sexist **ADV** **~ eingestellt sein** to be sexist; **sich ~ verhalten** to act in a sexist way; **sich ~ geben** to give the impression of being sexist; **~ klingen** to sound sexist

Sex-: Sex|kon|trol|le F sex check; **Sex|ma-ga|zin** NT sex magazine; **Sex|muf|fel** M (*hum inf*) sexless person; **Sex|objekt** NT sex object

Se|xo|lo|ge [zɛkso'loːgə] M **-n, -n**, **Se|xo|lo-gin** [-'loːgɪn] F **-, -nen** sexologist

Se|xo|lo|gie [zɛksolo'giː] F **-, no pl** sexology

Sex-: Sex|protz M (*hum inf*) sexual athlete; **Sex|shop** ['zɛksʃɔp] M **-s, -s** sex shop

Sex|ta ['zɛksta] F **-, Sexten** [-tn] (*dated Sch*) first year in a secondary school (*Aus Sch*) top year in a secondary school

Sex|ta|ner [zɛks'taːnɐ] M **-s, -**, **Sex|ta|ne|rin** [-ərɪn] F **-, -nen** (*dated Sch*) pupil in the first year of a secondary school (*Aus Sch*) pupil in the top year of a secondary school

Sex|ta|ner|bla|se F (*hum inf*) weak or Chinese (*hum sl*) bladder

Sex|tant [zɛks'tant] M **-en, -en** (*Naut*) sextant

Sex|te ['zɛkstə] F **-, -n** (*Mus*) sixth

Sex|ten pl von **Sexta**

Sex|tett [zɛks'tɛt] NT **-(e)s, -e** (*Mus*) sextet(te)

Sex|til|li|on [zɛkstɪ'lioːn] F **-, -en** sextillion (*Brit*), undecillion (*US*)

Sex-: Sex|tou|ris|mus M sex tourism; **Sex-tou|rist(in)** M(F) sex tourist

se|xu|al [zɛ'ksuaːl] ADJ (*rare*) sexual

Se|xu|al-: Se|xu|al|at|las M illustrated sex handbook; **Se|xu|al|emp|fin|den** NT sexual feeling; **Se|xu|al|er|zie|hung** F sex education; **Se|xu|al|ethik** F sexual ethics pl; **Se|xu|al-for|scher(in)** M(F) sexologist; **Se|xu|al|for-schung** F sexology; **Se|xu|al|hor|mon** NT sex hormone; **Se|xu|al|hy|gie|ne** F sex(ual) hygiene

se|xu|a|li|sie|ren [zɛksuali'ziːrən] ptp **sexuali-siert** VT to eroticize

Se|xu|a|li|sie|rung F **-, -en** eroticization

Se|xu|a|li|tät [zɛksuali'tɛːt] F **-, no pl** sexuality

Se|xu|al-: Se|xu|al|kun|de F (*Sch*) sex education; **Se|xu|al|le|ben** NT sex life; **Se|xu|al-lock|stoff** M pheromone; **Se|xu|al|mo|ral** F sexual morals pl; **Se|xu|al|mord** M sex murder; **Se|xu|al|mör|der(in)** M(F) sex murderer; **Se|xu|al|neu|ro|se** F sex neurosis; **Se|xu|al-objekt** NT sex object; **Se|xu|al|pä|da|go-gik** F sex education; **Se|xu|al|part|ner(in)** M(F) sexual partner; **Se|xu|al|prak|tik** F sexual practice usu pl; **Se|xu|al|straf|tä|ter** M , **Se|xu|al|tä|ter** M sex offender; **Se|xu|al-trieb** M sex(ual) drive; **Se|xu|al|ver|bre-chen** NT sex(ual) offence (*Brit*) or offense (*US*); **Se|xu|al|ver|hal|ten** NT sexual behaviour (*Brit*) or behavior (*US*); **Se|xu|al|ver|kehr** M sexual intercourse; **Se|xu|al|wis|sen|schaft** F sexology

se|xu|ell [zɛ'ksuɛl] ADJ sexual ADV sexually

Se|xus ['zɛksʊs] M **-, -** ['zɛksuːs] (*geh*) sexuality

se|xy ['zɛksi] ADJ inv (*inf*) sexy (*inf*)

Sey|chel|len [zeˈʃɛlən] PL (*Geog*) Seychelles pl

Se|zes|si|on [zetse'sioːn] F **-, -en** secession

Se|zes|si|o|nist [zetsesio'nɪst] M **-en, -en**, **Se-zes|si|o|nis|tin** [-'nɪstɪn] F **-, -nen** secessionist

se|zes|si|o|nis|tisch [zetsesio'nɪstɪʃ] ADJ secessionist

Se|zes|si|ons|krieg M American Civil War

se|zie|ren [ze'tsiːrən] ptp **seziert** VTI (*lit, fig*) to dissect

Se|zier|saal M dissecting room

SFB [ɛsɛf'beː] M **-** abbr von **Sender Freies Berlin**

SFOR, Sfor ['ɛsfɔːɐ] F abbr von **Stabilization Force** SFOR

S-för|mig ['ɛs-] ADJ S-shaped

sfr abbr von **Schweizer Franken** sfr

Sgraf|fi|to [sgra'fiːto] NT **-s, -s** or **Sgraffiti** [-ti] (*Art*) sgraffito

---

Shag [ʃɛk] M **-s, -s** (= *Tabak*) shag

Shake|hands ['ʃeːkhɛndz] NT **-, -** (*inf*) handshake; **~ machen** to shake hands, to press the flesh (*hum inf*)

Shake|speare|büh|ne ['ʃeːkspiːɐ-] F Elizabethan stage

shake|spea|resch ['ʃeːkspiːrɛʃ], **shake|spea-risch** ['ʃeːkspiːrɪʃ] ADJ Shakespearean

Sham|poo [ʃampuː, 'ʃampoː] NT **-s, -s**, **Sham-poon** [ʃam'poːn, ʃɛm'puːn] NT **-s, -s** shampoo

sham|poo|nie|ren [ʃampoˈniːrən, ʃampuˈniːrən] ptp **shampooniert** VT to shampoo

Shan|ty ['ʃɛnti, 'ʃanti] NT **-s, -s** shanty

Share|ware ['ʃɛːɐvɛːɐ] F **-, no pl** (*Comput*) shareware

Share|ware-Pro|gramm ['ʃɛːɐvɛːɐ-] NT shareware program

She|riff ['ʃɛrɪf] M **-s, -s** sheriff

Sher|pa ['ʃɛrpa] M **-s, -s** Sherpa

Sher|ry ['ʃɛri] M **-s, -s** sherry

Shet|land- ['ʃɛtlant-]: **Shet|land|in|seln** PL Shetland Islands pl, Shetlands pl; **Shet|land-po|ny** NT Shetland pony; **Shet|land|wol|le** F Shetland wool

Shift-Tas|te ['ʃɪft-] F , **Shift|tas|te** F (*Comput*) shift key

Shin|to|is|mus [ʃinto'ɪsmʊs] M **-, no pl** (*Rel*) Shintoism, Shinto

shin|to|is|tisch [ʃinto'ɪstɪʃ] ADJ Shinto, Shintoistic

Shit [ʃɪt] NT **-s, no pl** (*sl*: = *Haschisch*) dope (*inf*)

sho|cking ['ʃɔkɪŋ] ADJ pred shocking

Shoo|ting|star ['ʃuːtɪŋstaːɐ] M shooting star, whiz(z) kid (*inf*)

shop|pen ['ʃɔpn] VI to shop; **~ gehen** to go shopping

Shop|ping ['ʃɔpɪŋ] NT **-s, no pl** shopping (*for luxury items*); **~ gehen** or **machen** (*inf*) to go shopping (*for luxury items*)

Shop|ping|cen|ter ['ʃɔpɪŋsɛntɐ] NT **-s, -** shopping centre (*Brit*) or center (*US*)

Shorts [ʃɔːɐts, ʃɔrts] PL (pair of) shorts pl

Shor|ty ['ʃɔːɐti, 'ʃɔrti] NT **-s, -s** shorty pyjamas pl (*Brit*) or pajamas pl (*US*)

Show [ʃoː] F **-, -s** show; **eine ~ abziehen** (*inf*) to put on a show (*inf*)

Show-: Show-down ▲ ['ʃoːdaun] M OR NT **-(s), -s**, **Showdown** M OR NT **-(s), -s** showdown; **Show|ein|la|ge** ['ʃoː-] F entertainment section (*of a programme*); **Show|ge|schäft** ['ʃoː-] NT show business; **Show|man** ['ʃoːmən] M **-s, -men** showman; **Show|mas|ter** ['ʃoːmaːstɐ] M **-s, -**, **Show|mas|te|rin** [-ərɪn] F **-, -nen** compère, emcee (*US*)

Shred|der ['ʃrɛdɐ] M **-s, -**, **Shred|der|an|la|ge** F shredder, shredding machine

Shunt [ʃant] M **-s, -s** (*Med*) shunt

Shut|tle ['ʃatl] M **-s, -s** (*Aut, Aviat, Space*) shuttle

Shut|tle-Flug ['ʃatl-] M (*Space*) shuttle flight

Si|am ['ziːam] NT **-s** (*Hist*) Siam

Si|a|me|se [zia'meːzə] M **-n, -n**, **Si|a|me|sin** [-'meːzɪn] F **-, -nen** (*Hist*) Siamese

si|a|me|sisch [zia'meːzɪʃ] ADJ **a** (*Hist*) Siamese **b** **~e Katze** Siamese cat; **~e Zwillinge** Siamese twins

Si|am|kat|ze F Siamese (cat)

Si|bi|ri|en [zi'biːriən] NT **-s** Siberia

si|bi|risch [zi'biːrɪʃ] ADJ Siberian; **~e Kälte** Siberian or arctic conditions pl

Si|byl|la [zi'bʏla] F **-, Sibyllen**, **Si|byl|le** [zi'bʏlə] F **-, Sibyllen** sibyl

si|byl|li|nisch [zibʏ'liːnɪʃ] (*geh*) ADJ sibylline, sibyllic ADV prophetically; **sich ausdrücken** mysteriously; (= *drohend*) ominously

sich [zɪç] REFL PRON **a** (*acc*) (+infin, bei „man") oneself; (*3. pers sing*) himself; herself; itself; (*Höflichkeitsform sing*) yourself; (*Höflichkeitsform pl*) yourselves; (*3. pers pl*) themselves

---

b (*dat*) (+infin, bei „man") to oneself; (*3. pers sing*) to himself; to herself; to itself; (*Höflichkeitsform sing*) to yourself; (*Höflichkeitsform pl*) to yourselves; (*3. pers pl*) to themselves; **~ die Haa-re waschen/färben** to wash/dye etc one's hair; **er hat ~ das Bein gebrochen** he has broken his leg; **sie hat ~ einen Pulli gekauft/ge-strickt** she bought/knitted herself a pullover, she bought/knitted a pullover for herself; **wann hat sie ~ das gekauft?** when did she buy that?

c (*acc, dat* (*mit prep*) (+infin, bei „man") one; (*3. pers sing*) him, her, it; (*Höflichkeitsform*) you; (*3. pers pl*) them; **wenn man keinen Pass bei ~** (*dat*) **hat** if one hasn't a passport with one or him (*US*), if you haven't got a passport with you; **nur an ~** (*acc*) **denken** to think only of oneself; **wenn er jemanden zu ~** (*dat*) **einlädt** if he invites somebody round to his place

d (= *einander*) each other, one another; **sie schreiben ~ schon viele Jahre** they have been writing to each other or to one another for many years

e (*impers*) **hier sitzt/singt es ~ gut** it's good to sit/sing here; **diese Wolle strickt ~ gut** this wool knits well; **dieses Auto fährt ~ gut** this car drives well

Si|chel ['zɪçl] F **-, -n** sickle; (= *Mondsichel*) crescent

Si|chel|zel|len|anä|mie F (*Med*) sickle cell anaemia (*Brit*) or anemia (*US*)

si|cher ['zɪçɐ] ✪ 42.1, 43.1, 53.6 ADJ **a** (= *ge-wiss*) certain, sure; **der ~e Tod/Sieg** certain death/victory; (*sich dat*) **einer Sache** (*gen*) **~ sein** to be sure or certain of sth; **sich** (*dat*) **jds/seiner selbst ~ sein** to be sure of sb/oneself; (*sich dat*) **seiner Sache** (*gen*) **~ sein** to be sure of what one is doing/saying; **so viel ist ~** this much is certain; **ist das ~?** is that certain?; **man weiß nichts Sicheres** we don't know anything certain; **das ist uns ~** that is for sure; **mit der guten Zeit ist uns der zweite Platz ~** with such a good time we're sure or certain of second place → **Leben a**

b (= *geschützt, gefahrlos*) safe; (= *geborgen*) secure; *Investition* secure, safe; **vor jdm/etw ~ sein** to be safe from sb/sth; **~ ist** you can't be too sure

c (= *zuverlässig*) reliable; *Methode* reliable, surefire attr (*inf*); *Verhütungsmethode* safe, reliable; *Fahrer, Schwimmer* safe; (= *fest*) *Gefühl, Zusage* certain, definite; *Hand, Einkommen, Job* steady; *Stellung* secure; **ein ~er Schütze** a sure shot; **~ auf den Beinen sein** to be steady on one's legs; **mit ~em Instinkt** with a sure instinct

d (= *selbstbewusst*) (self-)confident, (self-)assured

ADV **a** fahren, aufbewahren etc safely; **~ wirkend** reliable; **~ leben** to live or lead a secure life; **~ schießen** to be a reliable shot; **sehr ~ Ski fah-ren** to ski extremely well

b (= *selbstbewusst*) **~ wirken/auftreten** to give an impression of (self-)confidence or (self-)assurance

c (= *natürlich*) of course; **~!** of course, sure (*esp US*)

d (= *bestimmt*) **das wolltest du ~ nicht sagen** surely you didn't mean that; **du hast dich ~ verrechnet** you must have counted wrong; **das weiß ich ganz ~** I know that for certain or for sure; **das ist ganz ~ das Beste** it's quite certainly the best; **aber er kommt ~ noch** I'm sure or certain he'll come; **das hat er ~ vergessen** I'm sure he's forgotten it; (= *garantiert*) he's sure to have forgotten it; **er kommt ~ auch mit** he's bound or sure or certain to want to come too

si|cher+ge|hen VI sep irreg aux sein to be sure; (= *sich vergewissern auch*) to make sure

Si|cher|heit ✪ 42.1, 43.1 F **-, -en** **a** no pl (= *Gewissheit*) certainty; **sich** (*dat*) **darüber ver-schaffen, dass …** to assure oneself that …; **ver-schaffen Sie sich persönlich ~ darüber** you have to make certain for yourself; **woher nimmst du die ~, …?** how can you be so sure …?; **mit an ~ grenzender Wahrscheinlichkeit** almost certainly, probably if not certainly; **das ist mit ~ richtig** that is definitely right; **das lässt sich nicht mit ~ sagen/beweisen** that cannot be said/proved with any degree of certainty

b _no pl_ (= _Schutz, das Sichersein_) safety; (_als Aufgabe von Sicherheitsbeamten etc_) security; **~ und Ordnung** law and order; **die öffentliche ~** public safety _or_ security; **innere ~** internal security; **die ~ der Bevölkerung** the safety _or_ security of the people; **soziale ~** social security; **jdn/etw in ~ bringen** to get sb/sth to safety; **sich in ~ bringen** to get (oneself) to safety; **es gelang mir in letzter Minute, mich im Keller in ~ zu bringen** at the last minute I managed to get to the safety of the cellar; **~ im Straßen-/Flugverkehr** road/air safety; **in ~ sein, sich in ~ befinden** to be safe; **sich in ~ wiegen** _or_ **wähnen** to think oneself safe; **jdn in ~ wiegen** to lull sb into a (false) sense of security; **jdn in ~ wähnen** to think sb safe; **der ~ (geh) halber** in the interests of safety; (= _um sicherzugehen_) to be on the safe side; **schnallen Sie sich zu Ihrer ~ an** fasten your seat belt for your own safety

c _no pl_ (= _Zuverlässigkeit_) (_von Mittel, Methode, Geschmack, Instinkt_) reliability, sureness; (= _Festigkeit_) (_von Hand, beim Balancieren etc_) steadiness; (_von Fahrer, Schwimmer_) competence; (_von Hand, Job, Einkommen_) steadiness; (_von Stellung_) security; **mit tödlicher ~** with deadly accuracy

d (= _Treffsicherheit im Umgang mit Sprache_) sureness

e _no pl_ (= _Selbstsicherheit_) (self-)confidence, (self-)assurance; **~ im Auftreten** self-confident _or_ self-assured manner

f (_Comm, Fin_) security; (= _Pfand_) surety; **~ leisten** (_Comm, Fin_) to offer security; (_Jur_) to stand _or_ go bail; **etw als ~ hinterlegen** (_Comm, Fin_) to deposit _or_ lodge sth as security; (_Jur_) to put up sth as bail

Si|cher|heits-: **Si|cher|heits|ab|stand** M safe distance; **Si|cher|heits|au|to** NT safe car; **Si|cher|heits|be|am|te(r)** M _decl as adj,_ **Si|cher|heits|be|am|tin** F security officer; (_Pol auch_) security agent; **Si|cher|heits|be|häl|ter** M (_von Atomreaktor_) containment dome; **Si|cher|heits|be|hör|de** F security service; (b) **Si|cher|heits|be|ra|ter(in)** M(F) safety adviser; **Si|cher|heits|be|stim|mun|gen** PL safety regulations _pl_; (_betrieblich, Pol etc_) security controls _pl or_ regulations _pl_; **Si|cher|heits|bin|dung** F (_Ski_) safety binding; **Si|cher|heits|bü|gel** M (_an Sessellift_) safety bar; **Si|cher|heits|fak|tor** M security factor; **Si|cher|heits|ga|ran|tie** F safety guarantee; **Si|cher|heits|glas** NT safety glass; **Si|cher|heits|gurt** M (_in Flugzeug_) seat belt; (_in Auto auch_) safety belt; **Si|cher|heits|hal|ber** ADV to be on the safe side; **Si|cher|heits|hül|le** F (_von Atomreaktor_) shell; **Si|cher|heits|ket|te** F safety chain; **Si|cher|heits|kon|trol|le** F security check; (b) (_Comput_) backup copy; **Si|cher|heits|ko|pie** F (_Comput_) backup copy; **Si|cher|heits|kräf|te** PL security forces _pl_; **Si|cher|heits|lam|pe** F (_Min_) safety lamp; **Si|cher|heits|leis|tung** F (_Comm_) surety; (_Jur_) bail; **Si|cher|heits|maß|nah|me** F safety precaution _or_ measure; (_betrieblich, Pol etc_) security measure; **Si|cher|heits|na|del** F safety pin; **Si|cher|heits|rat** M security council; **Si|cher|heits|ri|si|ko** NT security risk; **Si|cher|heits|schleu|se** F security door system; **Si|cher|heits|schloss** ▲ NT safety _or_ Yale® lock; **Si|cher|heits|schlüs|sel** M special key (_for safety locks_), Yale® key; **Si|cher|heits|trup|pen** PL security troops _pl_; **si|cher|heits|über|prü|fen** VT _ptp_ **sicherheitsüberprüft** _Bedienstete, Mitarbeiter_ to vet; **Si|cher|heits|über|prü|fung** F (a) (_Tech_) safety check (b) (_von Bediensteten, Mitarbeitern_) vetting; **Si|cher|heits|ven|til** NT safety valve; **Si|cher|heits|ver|schluss** ▲ M safety catch; **Si|cher|heits|vor|keh|rung** F safety precaution; (_betrieblich, Pol etc_) security precaution; **die ~en waren sehr gut** security was _or_ the security precautions were very good

---

si|cher|lich ['zɪçɐlɪç] ADV = **sicher** ADV c, d

si|chern ['zɪçɐn] VT (a) (_gegen, vor +dat_ against) to safeguard; (= _absichern_) to protect; (= _sicher machen_) _Tür, Wagen, Fahrrad, Unfallstelle_ to secure; _Bergsteiger etc_ to belay, to secure; (_Mil_) to protect, to cover; (_Comput_) _Daten_ to save; **eine Feuerwaffe ~** to put the safety catch of a firearm on; **den Frieden ~** to maintain the peace (b) **jdm/sich etw ~** to get _or_ secure sth for sb/oneself; **diese beiden Flaschen habe ich extra für mich gesichert** I've made sure of _or_ I've set aside these two bottles for myself

VR to protect oneself; (_Bergsteigen_) to belay _or_ secure oneself; **sich vor etw** (_dat_) _or_ **gegen etw ~** to protect oneself against sth, to guard against sth

VI (_Hunt_) to scent

si|cher+stel|len VT _sep_ (a) (= _in Gewahrsam nehmen_) _Waffen, Drogen_ to take possession of; _Beweismittel_ to secure; **das Tatfahrzeug wurde sichergestellt** the vehicle used in the crime was found (and taken in) (b) (= _garantieren_) to guarantee

Si|cher|stel|lung F (a) (_von Waffen, Drogen_) taking possession; (= _Auffinden, von Fahrzeug_) finding (b) (= _Garantie_) guarantee

Si|che|rung ['zɪçərʊŋ] F -, -en (a) _no pl_ (= _das Sichern_) (_gegen, vor +dat_ against) safeguarding; (= _Absicherung_) protection; (_von Tür, Wagen, Fahrrad_) securing (b) (= _Schutz_) safeguard (c) (_Elec_) fuse; (_von Waffe_) safety catch; **da ist (bei) ihm die ~ durchgebrannt** (_fig inf_) he blew a fuse (_inf_)

Si|che|rungs-: **Si|che|rungs|ko|pie** F (_Comput_) backup copy; **Si|che|rungs|über|eig|nung** F (_Jur_) transfer of ownership as security on a debt; **Si|che|rungs|ver|kauf** M (_Fin_) hedge selling; **Si|che|rungs|ver|wah|rung** F (_Jur_) preventive detention

Sicht [zɪçt] F -, _no pl_ (a) (= _Sehweite_) visibility; **die ~ betrug teilweise nur 20 Meter** at times visibility was down to 20 metres (_Brit_) _or_ meters (_US_); **eine ~ von 30 Metern** 30 metres' (_Brit_) _or_ meters' (_US_) visibility; **in ~ sein/kommen** to be in/come into sight; **aus meiner/seiner etc ~** (_fig_) as I see/he sees it, from my/his point of view; **aus heutiger ~** from today's standpoint _or_ perspective; **auf lange/kurze ~** (_fig_) in the long/short term; _planen_ for the long/short term; **auf lange ~ ausgebucht** fully booked for a long time ahead → **Land a** (b) (= _Ausblick_) view (c) (_Comm_) **auf** _or_ **bei ~** at sight; **acht Tage nach ~** one week after sight

sicht|bar ADJ (_lit, fig_) visible; **etw ~ machen** to make sth visible; (_fig_) to make sth clear; **~ werden** (_fig_) to become apparent; **allmählich wurden Fortschritte ~** it could gradually be seen that progress was being made ADV _altern_ visibly; _Fortschritte machen_ obviously; _sich verändern_ noticeably; _sich verbessern, sich verschlechtern_ clearly; **sie hat ~ abgenommen/zugenommen** it's obvious that she's lost/gained weight

Sicht|bar|keit ['zɪçtbaːɐkaɪt] F -, _no pl_ visibility

Sicht|bar|wer|den ['zɪçtbaːɐveːɐdn] NT -s, _no pl_ (_lit, fig_) appearance; **um das ~ früherer Fehler zu verhindern** to prevent earlier mistakes from becoming apparent

Sicht-: **Sicht|be|ton** M exposed concrete; **Sicht|ein|la|ge** F (_Fin_) sight (_esp Brit_) _or_ demand deposit

sich|ten ['zɪçtn] VT (a) (= _erblicken_) to sight (b) (= _durchsehen_) to look through, to examine, to inspect; (= _ordnen_) to sift through

Sicht-: **Sicht|feld** NT field of view _or_ vision; **Sicht|fens|ter** NT window; **Sicht|flug** M contact flight; **Sicht|ge|rät** NT monitor; (_Comput_) VDU, visual display unit; **Sicht|gren|ze** F visibility limit; **Sicht|kar|tei** F visible card index; **Sicht|kon|takt** M eye contact

sicht|lich ['zɪçtlɪç] ADJ obvious ADV obviously; _beeindruckt_ visibly

Sicht|schutz M privacy fence _or_ screen

Sich|tung ['zɪçtʊŋ] F -, -en sighting; (= _Prüfung_) examination, inspection

Sicht-: **Sicht|ver|hält|nis|se** PL visibility _sing_; **Sicht|ver|merk** M endorsement; (_im Pass_) visa stamp; **Sicht|wech|sel** M (_Fin_) bill payable on demand; **Sicht|wei|se** F view (of things); **Sicht|wei|te** F visibility _no art_; **außer ~** out of sight

Si|cker|gru|be F soakaway

si|ckern ['zɪkɐn] VI _aux sein_ to seep; (_dickere Flüssigkeit auch_) to ooze; (_in Tropfen_) to drip; (_fig_) to leak out; **in die Presse ~** to be leaked to the press

Si|cker|was|ser NT , _no pl_ water seeping through the ground

Side|board ['saɪdbɔːɐd] NT -s, -s sideboard

si|de|risch [zi'deːrɪʃ] ADJ (_Astron_) sidereal

sie [ziː] PERS PRON 3. pers (a) _sing gen_ **ihrer** ['iːrɐ], _dat_ **ihr** [iːɐ], _acc_ **sie** (_von Frau, weiblichem Tier_) (_nom_) she; (_acc_) her; (_von Dingen_) it; (_von Behörde, Organ_) (_nom_) they _pl_; (_acc_) them _pl_; **wenn ich ~ wäre ...** if I were her or she (_form_) ...; **~ ist es** it's her, it is she (_form_); **wer hat das gemacht? – ~** who did that? – she did _or_ her!; **wer ist der Täter? – ~** who is the culprit? – she is _or_ her!; **~ war es nicht, ich wars** it wasn't her, it was me; **~ und du** you and she; **~ und ich** she and I; **unser Hund ist eine ~** our dog is a she

(b) _pl gen_ **ihrer** ['iːrɐ], _dat_ **ihnen** ['iːnən], _acc_ **sie** (_nom_) they; (_acc_) them; **~ sind es** it's them; **~ sind es, die ...** it's them or it is they (_form_) who ...; **wer hats zuerst bemerkt? – ~** who noticed it first? – they did _or_ them (_inf_)

(c) (_obs: als Anrede_) **Sie** (_sing_) you, thee (_obs_); (_pl_) you

Sie [ziː] PERS PRON 2. pers sing or pl with 3. pers pl _vb gen_ **Ihrer** ['iːrɐ], _dat_ **Ihnen** ['iːnən], _acc_ **Sie** you; (_im Imperativ: nicht übersetzt_) **beeilen ~ sich!** hurry up!; **he, ~!** (_inf_) hey, you!; **~ wissen ~ was ...** (_inf_) do you know what ... NT -s, _no pl_ polite _or_ "Sie" form of address; **jdn per** _or_ **mit ~ anreden** to use the polite form of address to sb, to call sb "Sie"

Sieb [ziːp] NT -(e)s, -e [-bə] sieve; (_für Erde auch_) riddle; (_für Korn, Gold auch_) screen; (= _Teesieb_) strainer; (= _Gemüsesieb_) colander; **ein Gedächtnis wie ein ~ haben** to have a memory like a sieve

Sieb-: **Sieb|bein** NT (_Anat_) ethmoid (bone); **Sieb|druck** M _pl_ -drucke (silk-)screen print; (= _Siebdruckverfahren_) (silk-)screen printing

sie|ben¹ ['ziːbn] VT to pass through a sieve; _Korn, Gold_ to screen; (_Cook_) to sift, to sieve; **gesiebte Luft atmen** (_inf: = im Gefängnis sein_) to do time (_inf_), to be inside (_inf_) VI (_fig inf_) **solche Unternehmen ~ sehr** organizations like that pick and choose very carefully _or_ are very selective; **es wird stark gesiebt** they pick and choose, they are very selective; **bei der Prüfung wird stark gesiebt** the exam will weed a lot of people out

sie|ben² NUM seven; **die Sieben Weisen** the Seven Sages; **die ~ freien Künste** the humanities, the (seven) liberal arts; **die ~ Todsünden** _or_ **Hauptsünden** the seven deadly sins; **die ~ fetten und die ~ mageren Jahre** (_Bibl_) the seven fat and the seven lean years → _auch_ **vier**

Sie|ben ['ziːbn] F -, - _or_ -en seven → **Vier**

sie|ben-, Sie|ben- _in cpds_ → _auch_ **Vier-:** **sie|ben|ar|mig** ADJ _Leuchter_ seven-armed; **Sie|ben|bür|gen** [ziːbn'bʏrgn] NT -s (_Geog_) Transylvania; **Sie|ben|eck** NT heptagon; **Sie|ben|ge|stirn** NT (_Astron_) Pleiades _pl_; **Sie|ben|hü|gel|stadt** F city of the seven hills; **sie|ben|hun|dert** ['ziːbn'hʊndɐt] NUM seven hundred; **sie|ben|jäh|rig** ADJ seven-year-old; (= _sieben Jahre dauernd_) seven-year _attr_; **der Sie|ben|jäh|rige Krieg** the Seven-Years' War; **sie|ben|mal** ['ziːbnmaːl] ADV seven times; **Sie|ben|mei|len|stie|fel** PL (_Liter_) seven-league boots _pl_; **Sie|ben|me|ter** M (_Sport_) penalty;

Sie|ben|mo|nats|kind NT seven-month baby; **Sie|ben|sa|chen** PL (inf) belongings pl, things pl; **seine ~ packen** to pack one's bits and pieces; **Sie|ben|schläf|er** M **a** (Zool) edible or fat dormouse; **Gemeiner ~** common dormouse **b** 27th June (day which is said to determine the weather for the next seven weeks); **sie|ben|tau|send** ['zi:bn'tauznt] NUM seven thousand

Sie|ben|tel ['zi:bntl] NT -s, -, **Sieb|tel** ['zi:ptl] NT -s, - seventh

sie|ben|tens ['zi:bntəns], **sieb|tens** ['zi:ptns] ADV seventh(ly), in seventh place

sie|ben|te(r, s) ['zi:bntə] ADJ = **siebte(r, s)**

sieb|te(r, s) ['zi:ptə] ADJ seventh → auch **vierte(r, s)**

sieb|zehn ['zi:ptse:n] NUM seventeen; **Siebzehn und Vier** (Cards) pontoon → auch **vierzehn**

sieb|zig ['zi:ptsɪç] NUM seventy → auch **vierzig**

Sieb|zi|ger ['zi:ptsɪgɐ] M -s, -, **Sieb|zi|ge|rin** [-ərɪn] F -, -nen, **Sieb|zig|jäh|ri|ge(r)** [-jɛ:rɪgə] MF decl as adj seventy-year-old, septuagenarian

siech [zi:ç] ADJ (liter) infirm; (fig) Wirtschaft, Unternehmen ailing

sie|chen ['zi:çn] VI (rare) = **dahinsiechen**

Siech|tum ['zi:çtu:m] NT -s, no pl (liter) infirmity; (fig: von Wirtschaft, Unternehmen) ailing state

Sie|del|land NT settlement area

sie|deln ['zi:dln] VI to settle

sie|den ['zi:dn] pret **siedete** or **sott** ['zi:dətə, zɔt], ptp **gesiedet** or **gesotten** [gə'zi:dət, gə'zɔtn] **VI** (Wasser, Zucker etc) to boil; (Aus, S Ger: = köcheln) to simmer; **Scandium siedet bei 2830°C** scandium boils at 2830°C; **da siedet einem das Blut** it makes your blood boil; **~d heiß** boiling or scalding hot; **~de Hitze** boiling or scalding heat; (von Klima auch) sweltering hot; **~de Hitze** boiling or scalding heat; (von Klima auch) sweltering heat **VT** Seife, Leim to produce by boiling; (Aus, S Ger: = köcheln lassen) to simmer → auch **gesotten**

Sie|de-: **Sie|de|punkt** M (Phys, fig) boiling point; **Sie|de|was|ser|re|ak|tor** M boiling-water reactor

Sied|ler ['zi:dlɐ] M -s, -, **Sied|le|rin** [-ərɪn] F -, -nen settler; (= Bauer) smallholder

Sied|lung ['zi:dlʊŋ] F -, -en **a** (= Ansiedlung) settlement **b** (= Siedlerstelle) smallholding **c** (= Wohnsiedlung) housing scheme (Brit) or estate or development (US)

Sied|lungs-: **Sied|lungs|dich|te** F population density; **Sied|lungs|haus** NT house in a housing scheme

Sieg [zi:k] M -(e)s, -e [-gə] victory (über +acc over); (in Wettkampf auch) win (über +acc over); **um den ~ kämpfen** to fight for victory; **den ~ davontragen** or **erringen** to be victorious; (in Wettkampf auch) to be the winner; **einer Sache** (dat) **zum ~ verhelfen** to help sth to triumph; **von ~ zu ~ schreiten** (geh) to heap victory upon victory

Sie|gel ['zi:gl] NT -s, - seal; **unter dem ~ der Verschwiegenheit** under the seal of secrecy → **Buch a, Brief a**

Sie|gel|lack M sealing wax

sie|geln ['zi:gln] VT Urkunde to affix a/one's seal to; (= versiegeln) Brief to seal

Sie|gel-: **Sie|gel|ring** M signet ring; **Sie|gel|wachs** NT sealing wax

sie|gen ['zi:gn] VI (Mil) to be victorious; (fig auch) to triumph; (in Wettkampf auch) to win; **über jdn/etw ~** (Mil) to vanquish sb/sth; (fig) to triumph over sb/sth; (in Wettkampf) to beat sb/sth, to win against sb/sth; **ich kam, sah und siegte** I came, I saw, I conquered

Sie|ger ['zi:gɐ] M -s, -, **Sie|ge|rin** [-ərɪn] F -, -nen victor; (in Wettkampf) winner; **zweiter ~** runner-up; **~ werden** to be the winner, to win; **als ~ hervorgehen** to emerge victorious

Sie|ger-: **Sie|ger|eh|rung** F (Sport) presentation ceremony; **Sie|ger|kranz** M victor's laur-

els pl; **im ~** crowned with the victor's laurels; **Sie|ger|macht** F usu pl (Pol) victorious power; **Sie|ger|po|dest** NT (Sport) winners' podium or rostrum; **Sie|ger|po|se** F victory pose; **Sie|ger|stra|ße** F road to victory; **Sie|ger|trepp|chen** NT winners' rostrum (Brit) or podium; **Sie|ger|ur|kun|de** F (Sport) winner's certificate

Sie|ges-: **sie|ges|be|wusst** ▲ ADJ confident of victory; **Sie|ges|bot|schaft** F news sing of victory; **Sie|ges|denk|mal** NT victory monument; **Sie|ges|fei|er** F victory celebrations pl; (Sport) victory celebration; **Sie|ges|ge|schrei** NT (pej) shouts pl of victory; **sie|ges|ge|wiss** ▲ ADJ certain or sure of victory; **sie|ges|ge|wohnt** ADJ = **sieggewohnt**; **Sie|ges|göt|tin** F goddess of victory; **Sie|ges|kranz** M victor's laurels pl; **Sie|ges|pal|me** F palm (of victory); **Sie|ges|preis** M winner's prize; (Boxen) winner's purse; **Sie|ges|säu|le** F victory column; **Sie|ges|se|rie** F series sing of victories; (bei Wettkämpfen auch) series sing of wins; **sie|ges|si|cher** ADJ certain or sure of victory ADV confidently; **Sie|ges|tau|mel** M triumphant euphoria; **im ~** euphoric with their etc victory or triumph; **Sie|ges|tor** NT **a** (= Bauwerk) triumphal arch **b** (Sport) winning goal; **sie|ges|trun|ken** ADJ drunk with victory; **Sie|ges|zug** M triumphal march

sieg-: **sieg|ge|wohnt** ADJ used to victory; (bei Wettkämpfen auch) used to winning; **sieg|haft** ADJ = **siegesbewusst**; **sieg|reich** ADJ victorious, triumphant; (in Wettkampf) winning attr, successful ADV triumphantly, victoriously

sieh [zi:], **sie|he** ['zi:ə] imper sing von **sehen**

siehs|te ['zi:stə] (inf) 2. pers sing pres von **sehen** (inf) (you) see

sieht ['zi:t] 3. pers sing pres von **sehen**

Siel [zi:l] NT OR M -(e)s, -e (= Schleuse) sluice; (= Abwasserkanal) sewer

Sie|le ['zi:lə] F -, -n trace; **in den ~n sterben** (fig) to die in harness

sie|len ['zi:lən] VR (dial) to wallow

sie|na ['zie:na] ADJ inv sienna

Si|er|ra [si'ɛra] F -, -s or **Sierren** [si'ɛrən] (Geog) sierra

Si|es|ta [zi'ɛsta] F -, -s or **Siesten** [zi'ɛstn] siesta, afternoon nap or snooze (inf); **~ halten** to have a siesta or an afternoon nap or snooze (inf)

Sie|vert ['zi:vɐt] NT -, - (Phys) (abbr **Sv**) sievert

sie|zen ['zi:tsn] VT **jdn/sich ~** to use the formal term of address to sb/each other, to address sb/each other as "Sie" → auch **duzen**

Siff [zɪf] M -s, no pl, **Sif|fe** ['zɪfə] F -, no pl (pej sl) (= Dreck) filth; (= Zustand) mess

sif|fen ['zɪfn] VI (pej sl, = Dreck machen) to make a filthy mess

sif|fig ['zɪfɪç] ADJ (pej sl) filthy

Sight|see|ing ['saitsi:ɪŋ] NT -, no pl sightseeing; **~ machen** to do some sightseeing

Sig|nal [zɪ'gna:l] NT -s, -e (auch Rail) signal; **(ein) ~ geben** to give a signal; **mit der Hupe ein ~ geben** to hoot (as a signal); **~e setzen** (fig) to blaze a trail; **falsche ~e setzen** (fig) to point in the wrong direction

Sig|nal|an|la|ge F signals pl, set of signals

Sig|na|le|ment [zɪgnalə'mãː, -'mɛnt] NT -s, -s (Sw) (personal) description

Sig|nal-: **Sig|nal|far|be** F striking colour (Brit) or color (US); **Sig|nal|flag|ge** F signal flag; **Sig|nal|gast** M signalman; **Sig|nal|horn** NT (Hunt) hunting horn; (Mil) bugle

sig|na|li|sie|ren [zɪgnali'zi:rən] ptp **signalisiert** VT (lit, fig) to signal

Sig|nal-: **Sig|nal|kel|le** F signalling (Brit) or signaling (US) disc; **Sig|nal|lam|pe** F, **Sig|nal|la|ter|ne** F signalling (Brit) or signaling (US) lamp; (installiert) signal lamp; **Sig|nal-**

mast M signal mast; **Sig|nal|pfei|fe** F whistle; **Sig|nal|pis|to|le** F Very® pistol; **Sig|nal|tech|nik** F signalling (Brit), signaling (US); **Sig|nal|wir|kung** F signal; **davon ging eine ~ aus** this acted as a signal

Sig|na|tar [zɪgna'ta:ɐ] M -s, -e, **Sig|na|ta|rin** [-'ta:rɪn] F -, -nen (form) signatory (+gen to)

Sig|na|tar|mäch|te PL signatory powers pl

Sig|na|tur [zɪgna'tu:ɐ] F -, -en **a** (= Unterschrift, Buchsignatur) signature **b** (auf Landkarten) symbol **c** (= Bibliothekssignatur) shelf mark

Sig|net [zɪ'gnɛt, zɪ'gnet, zɪn'je:] NT -s, -s (Typ) publisher's mark

sig|nie|ren [zɪ'gni:rən] ptp **signiert** VT to sign; (mit Anfangsbuchstaben auch) to initial

Sig|nie|rung F -, -en signing; (mit Anfangsbuchstaben) initialling

sig|ni|fi|kant [zɪgnifi'kant] (geh) ADJ significant ADV significantly

Sig|ni|fi|kanz [zɪgnifi'kants] F -, no pl (geh) significance

Sikh [zi:k] M -(s), -s Sikh

Si|la|ge [zi'la:ʒə] F -, no pl (Agr) silage

Sil|be ['zɪlbə] F -, -n syllable; **~ für ~** (fig) word for word; **er hat es mit keiner ~ erwähnt/verraten** he didn't say/breathe a word about it

Sil|ben-: **Sil|ben|rät|sel** NT word game in which the answers are obtained by combining syllables from a given list; **Sil|ben|schrift** F syllabary; **Sil|ben|trenn|pro|gramm** NT (Typ, Comput) hyphenation program; **Sil|ben|trenn|ung** F syllabification; (Typ, Comput) hyphenation; **sil|ben|wei|se** ADV in syllables; **Sil|ben|zahl** F number of syllables

Sil|ber ['zɪlbɐ] NT -s, no pl (abbr **Ag**) silver; (= Tafelbesteck auch) silverware; (Her) argent; **aus ~ made of silver → reden VI a**

Sil|ber- in cpds silver; **Sil|ber|ar|beit** F silverwork no pl; **Sil|ber|be|steck** NT silver(ware), silver cutlery; **Sil|ber|blick** M (inf) squint; **Sil|ber|dis|tel** F carline thistle; **sil|ber|far|ben** [-farbn], **sil|ber|far|big** ADJ silver(-coloured) (Brit), silver(-colored) (US); (Her) argent; **Sil|ber|fisch|chen** [-fɪʃçən] NT -s, - silverfish; **Sil|ber|fo|lie** F silver foil; **Sil|ber|fuchs** M silver fox; **Sil|ber|ge|halt** M silver content; **Sil|ber|geld** NT silver; **Sil|ber|ge|schirr** NT silver(ware); **Sil|ber|glanz** M (Miner, Chem) silver glance, argentite, silver sulphide (Brit) or sulfide (US); (poet) silvery gleam; **sil|ber|grau** ADJ silver(y)-grey (Brit), silver(y)-gray (US); **Sil|ber|haar** NT (poet) silver(y) hair; (von Mann auch) hoary head (poet); **sil|ber|hal|tig** ADJ silver-bearing, argentiferous (spec); **sil|ber|hell** ADJ Stimme, Lachen silvery ADV **~ lachen** to give a silvery laugh; **Sil|ber|hoch|zeit** F silver wedding (anniversary); **Sil|ber|hüt|te** F silverworks sing or pl

sil|be|rig ['zɪlbərɪç] ADJ, ADV = **silbrig**

Sil|ber-: **Sil|ber|klang** M (poet) silvery sound; **Sil|ber|ling** ['zɪlbɐlɪŋ] M -s, -e (Bibl) piece of silver; **Sil|ber|lö|we** M puma (esp Brit), mountain lion; **Sil|ber|me|dail|le** F silver medal; **Sil|ber|mö|we** F herring gull

sil|bern ['zɪlbɐn] ADJ silver; (liter) Licht, Stimme, Haare silvery (liter), silvern (poet); **~e Hochzeit** silver wedding (anniversary) ADV **~ schimmern** to have a silvery gleam

Sil|ber-: **Sil|ber|pa|pier** NT tin foil, silver paper (esp Brit); **Sil|ber|pap|pel** F white poplar; **Sil|ber|schmied(in)** M(F) silversmith; **Sil|ber|schmuck** M silver jewellery (Brit) or jewelry (US); **Sil|ber|sti|cke|rei** F (Kunst) silver embroidery; (Produkt) silver-embroidered garment/cushion etc; **Sil|ber|streif** [-ʃtraif] M -en, -en, **Sil|ber|strei|fen** M (fig) **es zeichnete sich ein ~(en) am Horizont ab** you/they etc could see light at the end of the tunnel; **das war wie ein ~(en) am Horizont** that was a ray of sunshine; **Sil|ber|stück** NT silver coin; **Sil|-**

ber|tan|ne F noble fir; **Sil|ber|wäh|rung** F currency based on the silver standard; **Sil|ber|wa|ren** PL silver *sing*; **sil|ber|weiß** ADJ silvery white; **Sil|ber|zeug** NT , *no pl* silver *sing*

-sil|big [zɪlbɪç] ADJ *suf* **fünfsilbig/zehnsilbig sein** to have five/ten syllables; **ein sechssilbiges Wort** a word with six syllables

silb|rig ['zɪlbrɪç] ADJ silvery ADV **~ schimmern/glänzen** to shimmer/gleam like silver; **~ weißes Haar** silvery white hair

Sil|hou|et|te [zi'lʊɛtə] F -, -n silhouette; **sich als ~ gegen etw abheben** *or* **abzeichnen** to be silhouetted against sth

Si|li|cat [zili'kaːt] NT -(e)s, -e (*spec*), **Si|li|kat** [zili'kaːt] NT -(e)s, -e silicate

Si|li|kon [zili'koːn] NT -s, -e silicone

Si|li|ko|se [zili'koːzə] F -, -n (*Med*) silicosis

Si|li|zi|um [zi'liːtsiʊm] NT -s, *no pl* (*abbr* **Si**) silicon

Si|li|zi|um|schei|be F silicon chip

Si|lo ['ziːlo] M -s, -s silo

Si|lur [zi'luːɐ] NT -s, *no pl* (*Geog*) Silurian

Sil|va|ner [zɪl'vaːnɐ] M -s, - (= *Traubensorte*) Sylvaner (grape); (= *Wein*) Sylvaner (wine)

Sil|ves|ter [zɪl'vɛstɐ] M OR NT -s, - New Year's Eve, Hogmanay (*esp Scot*)

SILVESTER

December 31st is known as **Silvester** after the saint commemorated on that day. The old year is seen out with friends, often with a special **Silvester** meal. At midnight **Sekt** is drunk and fireworks let off to welcome the New Year. There is also the custom of **Bleigießen**, in which small amounts of lead are melted down and dropped into cold water. The resulting shapes are used as the basis for prophecies about the coming year. In some parts of Switzerland the old year is seen out with noisy processions in which the participants wear traditional masks.

Sil|ves|ter-: Sil|ves|ter|abend M New Year's Eve, Hogmanay (*esp Scot*); **Sil|ves|ter|fei|er** F New Year's Eve party, New Year party, Hogmanay party (*esp Scot*); **Sil|ves|ter|nacht** F night of New Year's Eve *or* Hogmanay (*esp Scot*)

Sim|bab|we [zɪm'bapvə] NT -s Zimbabwe

Sim|mer|ring® ['zɪmerɪŋ] M (*Tech*) shaft seal

Si|mo|nie [zimo'niː] F -, -n [-'niːən] simony

sim|pel ['zɪmpl] ADJ simple; *Mensch auch* simple-minded; (= *vereinfacht*) simplistic ADV simply

Sim|pel ['zɪmpl] M -s, - (*inf*) simpleton

Sim|plex ['zɪmplɛks] NT -, -e *or* **Simplizia** [zɪm'pliːtsia] (*Gram*) simplex

Sim|pli|fi|ka|ti|on [zɪmplifika'tsioːn] F -, -en (*geh*) simplification

sim|pli|fi|zie|ren [zɪmplifi'tsiːrən] *ptp* **simplifiziert** VT (*geh*) to simplify

Sim|pli|zi|tät [zɪmplitsi'tɛːt] F -, *no pl* (*geh*) simplicity

Sims [zɪms] M OR NT -es, -e [-zə] (= *Fenstersims*) (window)sill; (*außen auch*) (window) ledge; (= *Gesims*) ledge; (= *Kaminsims*) mantelpiece

sim|sen ['zɪmzn] VTI (*Telec: inf*) to text (*inf*), to send a text message/text messages

Si|mu|lant [zimu'lant] M -en, -en, **Si|mu|lan|tin** [-'lantɪn] F -, -nen malingerer

Si|mu|la|ti|on [zimula'tsioːn] F -, -en simulation

Si|mu|la|tor [zimu'laːtoːɐ] M -s, **Simulatoren** [-'toːrən] (*Sci*) simulator

si|mu|lie|ren [zimu'liːrən] *ptp* **simuliert** VI (= *sich krank stellen*) to feign illness; **er simuliert nur** he's shamming; (*um sich zu drücken auch*) he's malingering VT **a** (*Sci, Tech, Comput*) to simu-

late **b** (= *vorgeben*) *Krankheit* to feign, to sham; *Empörung, Frohsinn* to feign

si|mul|tan [zimʊl'taːn] ADJ simultaneous ADV simultaneously

Si|mul|tan-: Si|mul|tan|dol|met|schen NT -s, *no pl* simultaneous translation; **Si|mul|tan|dol|met|scher(in)** M(F) simultaneous translator

Si|mul|ta|ne|i|tät [zimʊltanei'tɛːt] F -, -en, **Si|mul|ta|ni|tät** [zimʊltani'tɛːt] F -, -en (*geh*) simultaneity

sin. *abbr von* Sinus

Si|nai ['ziːnai] M -(s), **Si|nai|halb|in|sel** F Sinai (Peninsula)

sind [zɪnt] *1. and 3. pers pl, with* Sie *sing and pl pres von* sein

Si|ne|ku|re [zine'kuːrə] F -, -n (*liter*) sinecure

si|ne tem|po|re ['ziːnə'tɛmpore] ADV (*abbr* **s. t.**) (*Univ*) punctually

Sin|fo|nie [zɪnfo'niː] F -, -n [-'niːən] symphony

Sin|fo|nie-: Sin|fo|nie|kon|zert NT symphony concert; **Sin|fo|nie|or|ches|ter** NT symphony orchestra

Sin|fo|ni|ker [zɪn'foːnikɐ] M -s, -, **Sin|fo|ni|ke|rin** [-ərɪn] F -, -nen member of a symphony orchestra; **die Bamberger ~** the Bamberg Symphony Orchestra

sin|fo|nisch [zɪn'foːnɪʃ] ADJ symphonic; **~e Dichtung** symphonic poem

Sing|aka|de|mie F choral society

Sin|ga|pur ['zɪŋgapuːɐ] NT -s Singapore

Sing-: sing|bar ADJ singable; **schwer ~ sein** to be hard to sing; **Sing|dros|sel** F song thrush

sin|gen ['zɪŋən] *pret* **sang** [zaŋ], *ptp* **gesungen** [gə'zʊŋən] VI **a** (*lit, fig*) to sing; (*esp Eccl*: *eintönig, feierlich*) to chant; (*Dynamo*) to hum; (*Telegrafendrähte*) to hum, to sing; **zur Gitarre/Mandoline ~** to sing to the guitar/mandoline; **ein ~der Tonfall** a lilt, a lilting accent; **singe, wem Gesang gegeben** (*dated prov*) if God gave you a good voice you should use it → **Alte(r)**
b (*inf*: = *gestehen*) to squeal (*inf*), to sing (*inf*), to talk
VT (*lit, fig*) to sing; (*esp Eccl*) *Psalmen, Kanon* to chant; **jdn in den Schlaf** *or* **Schlummer** (*liter*) **~** to sing sb to sleep; **das kann ich schon ~** (*inf*) I know it backwards (*Brit*), I know it backwards and forwards (*US*)
VR **sich heiser/in den Schlaf ~** to sing oneself hoarse/to sleep; **sich müde ~** to sing until one is tired; **das Lied singt sich leicht** it's an easy song to sing

Sin|gen NT -s, *no pl* singing (*also Sch*); (*eintönig, feierlich*) chanting; (*von Dynamo, Telegrafendrähten*) humming

Sin|ge|rei [zɪŋə'rai] F -, -en (*inf*) singing

Sin|gha|le|se [zɪŋga'leːzə] M -n, -n, **Sin|gha|le|sin** [-'leːzɪn] F -, -nen Sin(g)halese

sin|gha|le|sisch [zɪŋga'leːzɪʃ] ADJ Sin(g)halese

Sin|gle¹ ['sɪŋgl] F -, -(s) (= *Schallplatte*) single

Sin|gle² NT -, -(s) (*Tennis etc*) singles *sing*

Sin|gle³ M -s, -s (= *Alleinlebender*) single; **Urlaub für ~s** singles' holiday (*Brit*), vacation for singles (*US*)

Sin|gle|bar F singles' bar

Sin|gle|da|sein NT singledom, singlehood

Sin|gle|haus|halt M single(-person) household, one-person houshold

Sin|gle|woh|nung F apartment *or* flat (*Brit*) for single occupation

Sing-: Sing|sang ['zɪŋzaŋ] M -s, -s **a** (= *Liedchen*) ditty **b** (= *Gesang*) monotonous singing **c** (= *singende Sprechweise*) singsong; **Sing|spiel** NT lyrical drama; **Sing|stim|me** F vocal part

Sin|gu|lar ['zɪŋgulaːɐ] M -s, -e (*Gram*) singular; **im ~ stehen** to be (in) the singular; **den ~ zu etw bilden** to form the singular of sth

sin|gu|lär [zɪŋgu'lɛːɐ] ADJ (*geh*) unique

sin|gu|la|risch [zɪŋgu'laːrɪʃ] ADJ (*Gram*) singular

Sin|gu|la|ri|tät [zɪŋgulari'tɛːt] F -, *no pl* (*geh*) uniqueness

Sing-: Sing|vo|gel M songbird; **Sing|wei|se** F way of singing

si|nis|ter [zi'nɪstɐ] ADJ (*geh*) sinister

sin|ken ['zɪŋkn] *pret* **sank** [zaŋk], *ptp* **gesunken** [gə'zʊŋkn] VI *aux* **sein a** (*Mensch, Gegenstand*) to sink; (*Schiff*) to sink, to go down; (*Ballon*) to descend; (*Nebel*) to come down, to descend (*liter*); **auf den Grund ~** to sink to the bottom; **auf einen Stuhl/zu Boden ~** to sink into a chair/to the ground; **ins Bett ~** to fall into bed; **in Schlaf ~** to sink into a sleep; **an jds Brust** (*acc*) *or* **jdm an die Brust ~** (*liter*) to fall upon sb's breast; **in Ohnmacht ~** (*geh*) to swoon (*old*), to fall into a faint (*esp Brit*), to faint; **ich hätte in die Erde ~ mögen** I wished that the earth would (open and) swallow me up; **sein Stern ist im** *or* **am Sinken** (*geh*) his star is waning; **die Arme/den Kopf ~ lassen** to let one's arms/head drop
b (*Boden, Gebäude*) to subside, to sink; (*Fundament*) to settle; **das Haus war ein Meter tiefer gesunken** the house had sunk one metre (*Brit*) *or* meter (*US*); **in Staub** *or* **Trümmer ~** (*geh*) to fall into ruin(s); **in Schutt und Asche ~** (*geh*) to be reduced to a pile of rubble
c (= *niedriger werden*: *Wasserspiegel, Temperatur, Preise etc*) to fall, to drop
d (= *schwinden*) (*Ansehen, Vertrauen*) to diminish; (*Einfluss*) to wane, to decline, to diminish; (*Hoffnung, Stimmung*) to sink; **den Mut/die Hoffnung ~ lassen** to lose courage/hope
e (*moralisch*) to sink; **tief gesunken sein** to have sunk low; **in jds Meinung/Achtung** (*dat*) **~** to go down in sb's estimation

Sinn [zɪn] M -(e)s, -e **a** (= *Wahrnehmungsfähigkeit*) sense; **die ~e** (= *sinnliche Begierde*) one's desires; **seiner ~e** (*gen*) **nicht mehr mächtig sein**, **nicht mehr Herr seiner ~e** (*gen*) **sein** to have lost all control over oneself → **fünf, sechste(r, s)**
b Sinne PL (= *Bewusstsein*) senses *pl*, consciousness; **er war von ~en, er war nicht bei ~en** he was out of his senses *or* mind; **wie von ~en** like one demented; **bist du noch bei ~en?** have you taken leave of your senses? **c** (= *Gedanken, Denkweise*) mind; **sich** (*dat*) **jdn/etw aus dem ~ schlagen** to put (all idea of) sb/sth out of one's mind, to forget all about sb/sth; **es kommt** *or* **geht** *or* **will mir nicht aus dem ~** (*geh*) I can't get it out of my mind; **es kam** *or* **fuhr mir plötzlich in den ~** it suddenly came to me; **das will mir einfach nicht in den ~** I just can't understand it; **jdm durch den ~ gehen** to occur to sb; **etw im ~ haben** to have sth in mind; **mit etw nichts im ~ haben** to want nothing to do with sth; **anderen ~es werden** (*geh*) to change one's mind; **(mit jdm) eines ~es sein** (*geh*) to be of the same mind (as sb)
d (= *Wunsch*) inclination; **ihr ~ ist auf ...** (*acc*) **gerichtet** (*geh*) her inclination is for ...; **danach steht ihm der ~** (*geh*) that is his wish; **mir steht der ~ nach Tanzen** (*geh*) I feel like dancing
e (= *Verständnis, Empfänglichkeit*) feeling; **dafür fehlt ihm der ~** he has no feeling for that sort of thing; **~ für Proportionen/Gerechtigkeit** *etc* **haben** to have a sense of proportion/justice *etc*; **~ für Kunst/Literatur/das Höhere haben** to appreciate art/literature/higher things
f (= *Geist*) spirit; **im ~e des Gesetzes** according to the spirit of the law; **in jds ~e** (*dat*) **handeln** to act as sb would have wished; **im ~e des Verstorbenen** in accordance with the wishes of the deceased; **das ist nicht in meinem/seinem ~e** that is not what I myself/he himself would have wished; **das wäre nicht im ~e unserer Kunden** it would not be in the interests of our customers; **das ist nicht im ~e des Erfinders** (*inf*) that's not what was originally intended
g (= *Zweck*) point; **das ist nicht der ~ der Sa-**

che that is not the point, that is not the object of the exercise; **~ und Zweck einer Sache** (*gen*) the (aim and) object of sth; **~ und Unsinn dieser Maßnahmen/des Geschichtsunterrichts** reasoning or lack of it behind these measures/behind history teaching; **der ~ des Lebens** the meaning of life; **ohne ~ und Verstand sein** to make no sense at all; **das hat keinen ~** there is no point or sense in that; **was hat denn das für einen ~?** what's the point of or in that?, what's the sense in that? **h** (= *Bedeutung*) meaning; (*von Wort, Ausdruck*) sense, meaning; **im übertragenen/weiteren ~** in the figurative/broader sense; **~ machen** to make sense; **das macht keinen/wenig ~** that makes no/little sense; **der Satz (er)gibt** or **macht keinen ~** the sentence doesn't make sense; **~ stiftend** (*geh*) meaningful

Sinn-: **sinn|be|tö|rend** ADJ (*liter*) sensuously intoxicating; **Sinn|bild** NT symbol; **sinn|bild|lich** ADJ symbolic(al) ADV symbolically

sin|nen ['zɪnən] *pret* **sann** [zan], *ptp* **gesonnen** [gə'zɔnən] (*geh*) **VI a** (= *nachdenken*) to meditate, to ponder, to muse; (= *grübeln*) to brood; **über etw** (*acc*) **~** to reflect on sth; (= *grübeln*) to brood over sth **b** (= *planen*) **auf etw** (*acc*) **~** to devise sth, to think sth up, to think of sth; **auf Abhilfe ~** to think up or devise a remedy; **auf Verrat/Rache ~** to plot treason/revenge; **all sein Sinnen und Trachten** all his mind and energies → *auch* **gesonnen** VT (*old liter*) Verrat, Rache to plot

Sinnen-: **Sin|nen|freu|de** F enjoyment of the pleasures of life; **sin|nen|freu|dig, sin|nen|froh** ADJ **ein ~er Mensch** a person who enjoys the pleasures of life; **Sin|nen|ge|nuss ▲** M sensual pleasure; **Sin|nen|lust** F (*liter*) sensuality; **Sin|nen|mensch** M sensuous person; **Sin|nen|rausch** M (*liter*) sensual passion

sinn-: **sinn|ent|leert** [-lɛ:ɐt] ADJ bereft of content; **sinn|ent|stel|lend** ADJ **~ sein** to distort the meaning ADV **~ übersetzt** translated so that the meaning is/was distorted; **etw ~ zitieren** to quote sth in a way that distorts the meaning

Sin|nen|welt F (*liter*) material world

Sin|nes-: **Sin|nes|än|de|rung** F change of mind or heart; **Sin|nes|art** F (*geh*) = **Gesinnung**; **Sin|nes|ein|druck** M sensory impression, impression on the senses; **Sin|nes|nerv** M sensory nerve; **Sin|nes|or|gan** NT sense organ; **Sin|nes|reiz** M sensory stimulus; **Sin|nes|stö|rung** F sensory disorder; **Sin|nes|täu|schung** F hallucination; **Sin|nes|wahr|neh|mung** F sensory perception *no pl*; **Sin|nes|wan|del** M change of mind or heart

Sinn-: **sinn|fäl|lig** ADJ Beispiel, Symbol manifest, obvious; **Sinn|fra|ge** F question of the meaning or purpose of life; **Sinn|ge|bung** [-ge:bʊŋ] F -, -en (*geh*) giving meaning (+*gen* to); (= *Sinn*) meaning; **Sinn|ge|dicht** NT epigram; **sinn|ge|mäß** ADJ **a** (= *inhaltlich*) **eine ~e Zusammenfassung** a summary which gives the gist (of it) **b** (*esp Jur*: = *analog*) corresponding, analogous ADV **a** (= *dem Sinn nach*) etw ~ wiedergeben to give the gist of sth **b** (*Jur*) etw ~ anwenden to apply sth by analogy; **sinn|ge|treu** ADJ Übersetzung faithful (to the sense or meaning) ADV **etw ~ übersetzen** to do a faithful translation of sth

sin|nie|ren [zɪ'ni:rən] *ptp* **sinniert** VI to brood (*über* +*acc* over), to ruminate (*über* +*acc* about)

sin|nig ['zɪnɪç] ADJ apt; Vorrichtung practical; (*iro*: = *wenig sinnvoll*) clever

sin|ni|ger|wei|se ADV (*iro*) naturally (*iro*)

Sinn|kri|se F identity crisis

sinn|lich ['zɪnlɪç] ADJ **a** (*Philos*) Empfindung, Eindrücke sensory, sensorial; **die ~e Welt** the material world; **~e Anschauung** perception (by the senses) **b** (= *vital, sinnenfroh*) sensuous; (= *erotisch*) sensual; **~e Liebe** sensual love ADV **a** (= *sexuell*) sexually **b** (= *mit den Sinnen*) **wahr-**

nehmbar perceptible by the senses; **Menschen können diesen Ton nicht ~ wahrnehmen** this tone is not perceptible to humans

Sinn|lich|keit F -, *no pl* **a** (*Philos*) sensory or sensorial nature **b** (= *Vitalität, Sinnenfreude*) sensuousness; (= *Erotik*) sensuality

sinn|los ADJ **a** (= *unsinnig*) Redensarten, Geschwätz meaningless; Verhalten, Töten senseless **b** (= *zwecklos*) pointless, futile, senseless; Hoffnung forlorn; **es ist/wäre ~, zu ...** it is/would be pointless or futile to ...; **das ist völlig ~** there's no sense in that, that's completely pointless **c** Wut blind; Hast desperate ADV **a** (= *ohne Sinn*) zerstören, morden senselessly; **ich habe mich ~ bemüht, ihm das beizubringen** I tried in vain to teach him that **b** (= *äußerst*) **~ betrunken** blind drunk; **sich ~ betrinken** to get blind drunk

Sinn|lo|sig|keit F -, -en **a** (= *Unsinnigkeit*) (*von Redensart, Geschwätz*) meaninglessness; (*von Verhalten, Töten*) senselessness **b** (= *Zwecklosigkeit*) pointlessness, futility, senselessness; (*von Hoffnung*) forlornness

Sinn-: **sinn|reich** ADJ Deutung meaningful; (= *zweckdienlich*) Einrichtung, Erfindung useful; **Sinn|spruch** M epigram; **sinn|stif|tend** △ ADJ → **Sinn h**; **sinn|ver|wandt** ADJ synonymous; **~e Wörter** synonyms; **Sinn|ver|wandt|schaft** F synonymity; **sinn|voll** ADJ **a** Satz meaningful **b** (*fig*) (= *vernünftig*) sensible; (= *nützlich*) useful ADV **sein Geld ~/-er anlegen** to invest one's money sensibly/more sensibly; **seine Zeit ~/-er nutzen** to do something sensible/more constructive with one's time; **seine Fähigkeiten ~ einsetzen** to use one's capabilities intelligently; **sein Geld ~ verwenden** to use one's money for something useful; **sinn|wid|rig** ADJ nonsensical, absurd; **Sinn|wid|rig|keit** F absurdity

Si|no|lo|ge [zino'lo:gə] M -n, -n, **Si|no|lo|gin** [-'lo:gɪn] F -, -nen Sinologist

Si|no|lo|gie [zinolo'gi:] F -, *no pl* Sinology

sin|te|mal ['zɪntə'ma:l] CONJ (*obs, hum*) because, since

Sin|ter ['zɪntɐ] M -s, - (*Miner*) sinter

sin|tern ['zɪntɐn] VTI to sinter

Sint|flut ['zɪntflu:t] F (*Bibl*) Flood; **nach mir/uns die ~** (*inf*) it doesn't matter what happens when I've/we've gone

sint|flut|ar|tig ADJ **~e Regenfälle** torrential rain

Sin|to ['zɪnto] M -, Sinti ['zɪnti] *usu pl* Sinto (gypsy); **Sinti und Roma** Sinti and Romanies

Si|nus ['zi:nʊs] M -, -se or - [-nu:s] **a** (*Math*) sine **b** (*Anat*) sinus

Si|nus-: Si|nus|kur|ve F sine curve; **Si|nus|satz** M sine theorem

Si|oux ['zi:uks] M -, - Sioux

Si|phon ['zi:fõ, zi'fõ:, zi'fo:n] M -s, -s siphon; (*Aus inf*) soda (water)

Sip|pe ['zɪpə] F -, -n (= *extended*) family, kinship group (*inf*: = *Verwandtschaft*) family, clan (*inf*); (*Zool*) species *sing*

Sip|pen-: Sip|pen|äl|tes|te(r) MF *decl as adj* head of the family; **Sip|pen|for|schung** F genealogy, genealogical research; **Sip|pen|haft** F (*inf*), **Sip|pen|haf|tung** F (*Jur*) liability of all the members of a family for the crimes of one member; **Sip|pen|ver|band** M kinship group

Sipp|schaft ['zɪpʃaft] F -, -en (*pej inf*) (= *Familie*) tribe (*inf*); (= *Bande, Gesindel auch*) bunch (*inf*)

Sire [si:r] INTERJ (*old liter*) Sire (*old*)

Si|re|ne [zi're:nə] F -, -n (*Myth, Tech, fig*) siren; (*Zool*) sirenian

Si|re|nen-: Si|re|nen|ge|heul NT wail of a/the siren/sirens; **Si|re|nen|ge|sang** M siren song

Si|ri|us ['zi:riʊs] M - (*Astron*) Sirius

sir|ren ['zɪrən] VI → **surren**

Si|rup ['zi:rʊp] M -s, -e syrup; (*schwarz, aus Zuckerrohr auch*) treacle

Si|sal|(hanf) ['zi:zal-] M -s sisal (hemp)

Si|sal|tep|pich M sisal mat

sis|tie|ren [zɪs'ti:rən] *ptp* **sistiert** VT (*Jur*) Verdächtigen to detain; Verfahren to adjourn

Si|sy|phus|ar|beit ['zi:zyfʊs-] F Sisyphean task (*liter*), never-ending task

Sit-in [sɪt'ɪn] NT -(s), -s sit-in; **ein ~ machen** to have or stage or hold a sit-in

Sit|te ['zɪtə] F -, -n **a** (= *Brauch*) custom; (= *Mode*) practice; **~ sein** to be the custom/the practice; **~n und Gebräuche** customs and traditions; **was sind denn das für ~n?** what's all this?; **hier reißen ja ~n ein!** (*inf*) the things people have started doing! **b** *usu pl* (= *gutes Benehmen*) manners *pl*; (= *Sittlichkeit*) morals *pl*; **gegen die (guten) ~n verstoßen** to offend common decency; **gute ~n** good manners *pl*; **was sind denn das für ~n?** what sort of a way is that to behave! **c** (*sl*: = *Sittenpolizei*) vice squad

Sitten-: Sit|ten|apos|tel M (*pej*) moralizer; **Sit|ten|bild** NT (*Art*) genre picture; **Sit|ten|de|zer|nat** NT vice squad; **Sit|ten|ge|mäl|de** NT genre picture; **Sit|ten|ge|schich|te** F Roms history of Roman life and customs; **Sit|ten|ge|setz** NT moral law; **Sit|ten|ko|dex** M moral code; **Sit|ten|leh|re** F ethics *sing*; **sit|ten|los** ADJ immoral; **Sit|ten|lo|sig|keit** F -, *no pl* immorality; **Sit|ten|po|li|zei** F vice squad; **Sit|ten|pre|di|ger(in)** M(F) moralist, sermonizer; **Sit|ten|rich|ter(in)** M(F) judge of public morals; **sit|ten|streng** ADJ highly moral; **Sit|ten|stren|ge** F strict morality; **Sit|ten|strolch** M (*Press inf*) sex fiend; **Sit|ten|ver|fall** M decline or drop in moral standards; **Sit|ten|wäch|ter(in)** M(F) (*iro*) guardian of public morals; **sit|ten|wid|rig** ADJ (*form*) immoral; **Sit|ten|wid|rig|keit** F (*form*) immorality

Sit|tich ['zɪtɪç] M -s, -e parakeet

sitt|lich ['zɪtlɪç] ADJ moral; **ihm fehlt der ~e Halt** he lacks moral fibre (*Brit*) or fiber (*US*); **ihm fehlt die ~e Reife** he's morally immature; **er verlor jeden ~en Halt** he became morally unstable; **das Sittliche** morality

Sitt|lich|keit F -, *no pl* morality

Sitt|lich|keits-: Sitt|lich|keits|de|likt NT sexual offence (*Brit*) or offense (*US*); **Sitt|lich|keits|ver|bre|chen** NT sex crime; **Sitt|lich|keits|ver|bre|cher(in)** M(F) sex offender

sitt|sam ['zɪtza:m] ADJ demure ADV demurely

Sitt|sam|keit F -, *no pl* demureness

Si|tu|a|ti|on [zitua'tsio:n] F -, -en situation; (= *persönliche Lage auch*) position

Si|tu|a|ti|ons-: Si|tu|a|ti|ons|be|richt M report on the situation; **Si|tu|a|ti|ons|ko|mik** F comicalness or comedy of the situation/situations; (= *Art der Komik*) situation comedy, sitcom (*inf*)

si|tu|iert [zitu'i:ɐt] ADJ **a** gut ~ (*attr*) well-off; **gut/schlecht ~ sein** to be well/poorly situated financially **b** (*S Ger, esp Aus*: = *sich befindend*) situated

Sitz [zɪts] M -es, -e **a** (= *Sitzplatz, Parl*) seat; **~ und Stimme haben** to have a seat and a vote **b** (*von Regierung, Herrscher, Universität, fig*) seat; (= *Wohnsitz*) residence, domicile (*form*); (*von Firma, Verwaltung*) headquarters *pl*; **die Welthandelsorganisation hat ihren ~ in Genf** the World Trade Organization has its headquarters in Geneva **c** *no pl* (*Tech, von Kleidungsstück*) sit; (*von der Größe her*) fit; **einen guten ~ haben** to sit/fit well; **einen schlechten ~ haben** to sit/fit badly **d** *no pl* (*von Reiter*) seat

Sitz-: Sitz|bad NT sitz or hip (*esp Brit*) bath; **Sitz|ba|de|wan|ne** F sitz or hip (*esp Brit*) bath; **Sitz|bank** F *pl* -bänke bench; **Sitz|blo|cka|de** F sit-in; **Sitz|de|monstrant(in)**

M(F) sit-down demonstrator; **Sitz|e|cke** F corner seating unit

sit|zen ['zɪtsn] *pret* **saß** [za:s], *ptp* **gesessen** [gə'zesn] **VI** *aux* haben *or* (Aus, S Ger, Sw) sein **a** (*Mensch, Tier*) to sit; (*Vogel*) to perch; ~ **Sie bequem?** are you comfortable?; **hier sitzt man sehr bequem** it's very comfortable sitting here; **auf der Toilette** ~ to be on (*inf*) *or* in the toilet; **etw im Sitzen tun** to do sth sitting down; **beim Frühstück/Mittagessen** ~ to be having breakfast/lunch; **beim Wein/Schach** ~ to sit over a glass of wine/a game of chess; **an einer Aufgabe/über den Büchern/über einer Arbeit** ~ to sit over a task/one's books/a piece of work → *auch* **sitzen bleiben**

b (= *Modell sitzen*) to sit (*jdm* for sb)

c (= *seinen Sitz haben*) (*Regierung, Gericht etc*) to sit; (*Firma*) to have its headquarters

d (= *Mitglied sein*) (*im Parlament*) to have a seat (*in +dat* in); (*im Vorstand, Aufsichtsrat etc*) to be *or* sit (*in +dat* on)

e (*inf:* = *im Gefängnis sitzen*) to be inside (*inf*); **gesessen haben** to have done time (*inf*), to have been inside (*inf*); **er musste zwei Jahre** ~ he had to do two years (*inf*)

f (= *sein*) to be; **er sitzt in Bulgarien/im Kultusministerium** (*inf*) he's in Bulgaria/the ministry of culture; **er sitzt in der Äußeren Mongolei (und kann nicht weg)** (*inf*) he's stuck in outer Mongolia (*inf*); **er sitzt im Gefängnis** (*inf*) he's in prison; **die Verfolger saßen uns auf den Fersen** our pursuers were hard on our heels; **auf der Bank** ~ (*Sport*) to be *or* sit on the bench

g (= *angebracht sein: Deckel, Schraube etc*) to sit; **der Deckel sitzt fest** the lid is on tightly; **die Schraube sitzt fest** the screw is in tightly; **locker** ~ to be loose

h (= *stecken*) to be (stuck); **fest** ~ to be stuck tight(ly); **der Splitter saß fest in meinem Fuß** the splinter was stuck in my foot

i (= *im Gedächtnis sitzen*) to have sunk in

j (= *seinen Herd haben*) (*Infektion, Schmerz*) to be; (*fig: Übel, Hass, Schmerz*) to lie, to be

k (*Kleid, Frisur*) to sit; **deine Krawatte sitzt nicht richtig** your tie isn't straight; **sein Hut saß schief** his hat was (on) crooked

l (*inf:* = *treffen*) to hit home; **das saß!, das hat gesessen!** that hit home

m **einen** ~ **haben** (*inf*) to have had one too many (*inf*)

sit|zen blei|ben ▲ **VI** *irreg aux* sein (*inf*) **a** (= *nicht aufstehen*) to remain seated; **bleiben Sie bitte sitzen!, bitte bleiben Sie sitzen!** please don't get up **b** (*Sch*) to stay down (a year), to have to repeat a year **c** **auf einer Ware** ~ to be left with a product **d** (*Mädchen*) (*beim Tanz*) to be left sitting; (= *nicht heiraten*) to be left on the shelf (*inf*)

Sit|zen|blei|ber [-blaibɐ] M **-s,** -, **Sit|zen|blei|be|rin** [-ərɪn] F **-, -nen** (*inf*) pupil who has to repeat a year

sit|zend **ADJ** *attr Lebensweise etc* sedentary **ADV** sitting down, seated; **er hat mich** ~ **begrüßt** he greeted me without getting up; **ich verbringe die meiste Zeit** ~ I sit most of the time

sit|zen las|sen ▲ *ptp* **sitzen lassen** *or* (*rare*) **sitzen gelassen VT** *irreg* (*inf*) **a** (*Sch:* = *nicht versetzen*) to keep down (a year) **b** (= *hinnehmen*) **eine Beleidigung etc auf sich** (*dat*) ~ to stand for or take an insult *etc* **c** **jdn** ~ (= *im Stich lassen*) to leave sb in the lurch; (= *warten lassen*) to leave sb waiting; **Freund(in)** (*durch Nichterscheinen*) to stand sb up; (*für immer*) to walk out on sb **d** (= *nicht heiraten*) to jilt, to walk out on

-sit|zer [zɪtsɐ] M *suf* **-s,** - *in cpds* -seater; **ein Zweisitzer** a two-seater

Sit|ze|rei [zɪtsə'rai] F **-,** *no pl* (*inf*) sitting about

Sitz-: **Sitz|fleisch** NT (*inf*) ability to sit still; ~ **haben** to be able to sit still; (*hum: Besucher*) to stay a long time; **Sitz|gar|ni|tur** F living-room suite; (*dreiteilig auch*) three-piece suite; **Sitz|ge|le|gen|heit** F seats *pl*, seating (accommodation); **eine** ~ **suchen** to look for somewhere

to sit, to look for a seat; **Sitz|kis|sen** NT (*floor*) cushion; **Sitz|ord|nung** F seating plan; **Sitz|pin|kler** [-pɪŋklɐ] M **-s,** - (*sl: Schimpfwort*) tosser (*sl*); **Sitz|platz** M seat; **Sitz|rei|he** F row of seats; **Sitz|rie|se** M (*hum*) short person with a long body who looks tall when sitting down; **Sitz|streik** M sit-down strike

Sit|zung ['zɪtsʊŋ] F **-, -en a** (= *Konferenz*) meeting; (*Jur:* = *Gerichtsverhandlung*) session; (= *Parlamentssitzung*) sitting **b** (= *Einzelsitzung*) (*bei Künstler*) sitting; (*bei Zahnarzt*) visit; (*inf:* = *Toilettenbesuch*) session; **spiritistische** ~ séance

Sit|zungs-: **Sit|zungs|be|richt** M minutes *pl*; **Sit|zungs|geld** NT (*Parl*) attendance allowance; **Sit|zungs|ma|ra|thon** M (*inf*) marathon session *or* meeting; **Sit|zungs|pe|ri|o|de** F (*Parl*) session; (*Jur*) term; **Sit|zungs|saal** M conference hall; (*Jur*) courtroom; **Sit|zungs|zim|mer** NT conference room

six|ti|nisch [zɪks'ti:nɪʃ] **ADJ** Sistine

Si|zi|li|a|ner [zitsi'lia:nɐ] M **-s,** -, **Si|zi|li|a|ne|rin** [-ərɪn] F **-, -nen** Sicilian

si|zi|li|a|nisch [zitsi'lia:nɪʃ] **ADJ** Sicilian

Si|zi|li|en [zi'tsi:liən] NT **-s** Sicily

Skai® [skai] NT **-(s)**, *no pl* imitation leather

Ska|la ['ska:la] F **-, Skalen** ['ska:lən] *or* **-s** (= *Gradeinteilung, auch Mus*) scale; (= *Reihe gleichartiger Dinge*) range; (*fig*) gamut, range

Ska|lar [ska'la:ɐ] M **-s,** -e (*Math*) scalar

Ska|lar|pro|dukt NT (*Math*) scalar product

Skal|de ['skaldə] M **-n,** -n skald

Skal|den|dich|tung F skaldic poetry

Skalp [skalp] M **-s,** -e scalp

Skal|pell [skal'pɛl] NT **-s,** -e scalpel

skal|pie|ren [skal'pi:rən] *ptp* **skalpiert VT** to scalp

Skan|dal [skan'da:l] M **-s,** -e scandal; (*inf:* = *Krach*) to-do (*inf*), fuss; **einen** ~ **machen** to create *or* cause a scandal; to make a to-do (*inf*) *or* fuss; **das ist ein** ~! it's scandalous *or* a scandal

Skan|dal-: **Skan|dal|blatt** NT (*pej*) scandal sheet; **Skan|dal|ge|schich|te** F (bit *or* piece of) scandal; **Skan|dal|nu|del** F (*hum*) **sie ist eine richtige** ~ she's always involved in some scandal *or* other

skan|da|lös [skanda'lø:s] **ADJ** scandalous **ADV** scandalously

Skan|dal-: **Skan|dal|pres|se** F (*pej*) gutter press (*Brit*), tabloids *pl*; **Skan|dal|pro|zess** ▲ M sensational trial *or* case; **skan|dal|süch|tig ADJ** (*pej*) *Publikum, Leser* fond of scandal; *Klatschtante, Presse etc auch* scandalmongering *attr*; **skan|dal|träch|tig ADJ** potentially scandalous; **skan|dal|um|wit|tert ADJ** (*Press*) surrounded by scandal

skan|die|ren [skan'di:rən] *ptp* **skandiert VTI** to scan

Skan|di|na|vi|en [skandi'na:viən] NT **-s** Scandinavia

Skan|di|na|vi|er [skandi'na:viɐ] M **-s,** -, **Skan|di|na|vi|e|rin** [-iərɪn] F **-, -nen** Scandinavian

skan|di|na|visch [skandi'na:vɪʃ] **ADJ** Scandinavian

Skan|di|um ['skandiʊm] NT **-s,** *no pl* (*abbr* **Sc**) scandium

Ska|ra|bä|us [skara'bɛːʊs] M **-, Skarabäen** [-'bɛːən] scarab

Skat [ska:t] M **-(e)s,** -e (*Cards*) skat; ~ **spielen** *or* **dreschen** (*inf*) *or* **kloppen** (*sl*) to play skat

ing decided every year. Since 1927 **Skat** has had its own special panel in Altenburg for settling disputes.

Skat|brü|der PL (*inf*) fellow skat players *pl*

Skate|board ['ske:tbɔːɐd] NT **-s,** -s skateboard

Skate|board-: **Skate|board|bahn** ['ske:tbɔːɐd-] F skateboard rink; **Skate|board|fah|rer(in)** ['ske:tbɔːɐd-] M(F) skateboarder

ska|ten ['ske:tn] **VI** (*inf*) to play skat

Skat|spie|ler(in) M(F) skat player

Ske|le|ton ['skɛlətn, 'skɛlətɔn] M **-s,** -s (*Sport*) skeleton

Ske|lett [ske'lɛt] NT **-(e)s,** -e (*lit, fig*) skeleton; **er war bis aufs** ~ **abgemagert**, er war nur noch ein ~ he was like a skeleton

Skep|sis ['skɛpsɪs] F **-,** *no pl* scepticism (*Brit*), skepticism (*US*); **mit** *or* **voller** ~ sceptically (*Brit*), skeptically (*US*)

Skep|ti|ker ['skɛptikɐ] M **-s,** -, **Skep|ti|ke|rin** [-ərɪn] F **-, -nen** sceptic (*Brit*), skeptic (*US*)

skep|tisch ['skɛptɪʃ] **ADJ** sceptical (*Brit*), skeptical (*US*) **ADV** sceptically (*Brit*), skeptically (*US*); **das Ergebnis muss** ~ **stimmen** the results must make you sceptical (*Brit*) *or* skeptical (*US*)

Skep|ti|zis|mus [skɛpti'tsɪsmʊs] M **-,** *no pl* (*esp Philos*) scepticism (*Brit*), skepticism (*US*)

skep|ti|zis|tisch [skɛpti'tsɪstɪʃ] **ADJ** (*esp Philos*) sceptic(al) (*Brit*), skeptic(al) (*US*)

Sketch [skɛtʃ] M **-(es),** -e(s) (*Art, Theat*) sketch

Ski [ʃiː] M **-s,** - *or* **-er** [ʃiːɐ] ski; ~ **laufen** *or* **fahren** to ski

Ski-: *in cpds* ski; **Ski|an|zug** M ski suit; **Ski|aus|rüs|tung** F skiing gear; **eine komplette** ~ a complete set of skiing gear; **Ski|bin|dung** F ski binding; (*pl auch*) ski fittings *pl*; **Ski|bob** M skibob; **Ski|bril|le** F ski goggles *pl*

Skier *pl von* **Ski**

Ski-: **Ski|fah|rer(in)** M(F) skier; **Ski|flie|gen** NT **-s,** *no pl*, **Ski|flug** M ski flying; **Ski|ge|biet** NT ski(ing) area; **Ski|ge|län|de** NT ski (-ing) area; **Ski|gym|nas|tik** F skiing exercises *pl*; **Ski|ha|se** M , **Ski|ha|serl** [-hazɛl] NT **-s, -n** (*hum inf*) girl skier; **Ski|ho|se** F (pair of) ski pants *pl*; **Ski|hüt|te** F ski hut *or* lodge (*US*); **Ski|kurs** M skiing course; **Ski|lang|lauf** M → Langlauf; **Ski|lauf** M skiing; **Ski|lau|fen** NT skiing; **zum** ~ **fahren** to go skiing; **Ski|läu|fer(in)** M(F) skier; **Ski|leh|rer** M ski instructor; **Ski|lift** M ski lift

Skin [skɪn] M **-s,** -s (*inf*) skin (*inf*)

Skin|head ['skɪnhɛd] M **-s,** -s skinhead

Ski-: **Ski|pass** ▲ M ski pass; **Ski|pis|te** F ski run; **Ski|schan|ze** F ski jump; **Ski|schuh** M ski boot; **Ski|schu|le** F ski school; **Ski|sport** M skiing; **Ski|sprin|gen** NT ski jumping; **Ski|sprin|ger(in)** M(F) ski jumper; **Ski|stie|fel** M ski boot; **Ski|stock** M ski stick; **Ski|trä|ger** M (*Aut*) ski rack, ski roof carrier (*US*); **Ski|ur|laub** M skiing holiday (*esp Brit*) *or* vacation (*US*); **Ski|zir|kus** M ski circus

Skiz|ze ['skɪtsə] F **-, -n** sketch; (*fig:* = *Grundriss*) outline, plan

Skiz|zen-: **Skiz|zen|block** M *pl* **-blöcke** *or* **-blocks** sketchpad; **Skiz|zen|buch** NT sketchbook; **skiz|zen|haft ADJ** *Zeichnung etc* roughly sketched; *Beschreibung etc* (given) in broad outline **ADV** **etw** ~ **zeichnen** to sketch sth roughly; **etw** ~ **beschreiben** to describe sth in broad outline

skiz|zie|ren [skɪ'tsi:rən] *ptp* **skizziert VT** to sketch; (*fig*) *Plan etc* to outline

Skiz|zie|rung F **-, -en** sketching; (*fig: von Plan etc*) outlining

Skla|ve ['skla:və, 'skla:fə] M **-n,** -n, **Skla|vin** ['skla:vɪn, 'skla:fɪn] F **-, -nen** slave; ~ **einer Sache** (*gen*) **sein** (*fig*) to be a slave to sth; **jdn zum**

~n machen to make a slave of sb; *(fig)* to enslave sb, to make sb one's slave

Skla|ven-: Skla|ven|ar|beit F slavery; (= *Arbeit von Sklaven*) work of slaves; **Skla|ven|dienst** M slavery; **Skla|ven|ga|lee|re** F slave galley; **Skla|ven|hal|ter(in)** M(F) slaveholder, slave owner; **Skla|ven|hal|ter|ge|sell|schaft** F slave-owning society; **Skla|ven|han|del** M slave trade; **~ betreiben** to deal in slaves; **Skla|ven|händ|ler(in)** M(F) slave-trader, slaver *(esp Brit)*; **Skla|ven|markt** M slave market; **Skla|ven|trei|ber(in)** M(F) *(lit, fig)* slave-driver

Skla|ve|rei [skla:və'rai, skla:fə'rai] F -, *no pl (lit, fig)* slavery *no art*; **jdn in die ~ führen** to take sb into slavery

Skla|vin F *(lit, fig)* slave → *auch* **Sklave**

skla|visch ['skla:vɪʃ, 'skla:fɪʃ] ADJ slavish ADV slavishly

Skle|ro|se [skle'ro:zə] F -, **-n** *(Med)* sclerosis

Sko|li|o|se [skoli'o:zə] F -, **-n** *(Med)* scoliosis

skon|tie|ren [skɔn'ti:rən] *ptp* **skontiert** VT **jdm etw ~** to give sb a cash discount on sth

Skon|to ['skɔnto] NT OR M **-s, -s** *or* **Skonti** [-ti] cash discount; **bei Barzahlung 3% ~** 3% discount for cash; **jdm ~ geben** *or* **gewähren** *(form)* to give *or* allow sb a cash discount *or* a discount for cash

Skor|but [skɔr'buːt] M **-(e)s**, *no pl* scurvy

Skor|pi|on [skɔr'pioːn] M **-s, -e** *(Zool)* scorpion; *(Astrol)* Scorpio

Skri|bent [skri'bɛnt] M **-en, -en, Skri|ben|tin** [-'bɛntɪn] F **-, -nen** *dated pej* hack, scribbler

Skript [skrɪpt] NT **-(e)s, -e** *or* **a** *pl usu* **-s** *(Film)* (film) script **b** *(Univ)* (set of) lecture notes *pl*; **ein ~ anfertigen** to take lecture notes

Skript|girl ['skrɪpt-] NT script girl

Skrip|tum ['skrɪptʊm] NT **-s, Skripten** *or* **Skripta** [-tn, -ta] *(esp Aus Univ)* (set of) lecture notes *pl*; **ein ~ anfertigen** to take lecture notes

Skro|tum ['skro:tʊm] NT **-s, Skrota** [-ta] *(Med)* scrotum

Skru|pel ['skru:pl] M **-s,** *usu pl* scruple; **keine ~ haben** *or* **kennen** to have no scruples; **er hatte keine ~, das zu tun** he didn't scruple to do it; **ohne (jeden) ~** without (the slightest) scruple

Skru|pel-: skru|pel|los ADJ unscrupulous ADV unscrupulously; **Skru|pel|lo|sig|keit** F -, *no pl* unscrupulousness

skru|pu|lös [skrupu'løːs] *(geh)* ADJ scrupulous ADV scrupulously

Skull|boot ['skʊlbo:t] NT sculling boat

skul|len ['skʊlən] VI *(Sport)* to scull

Skulp|tur [skʊlp'tu:ɐ] F -, **-en** sculpture

Skunk [skʊŋk] M **-s, -s** *or* **-e** skunk

skur|ril [skʊ'ri:l] ADJ *(geh)* droll, comical

Skur|ri|li|tät [skʊrili'tɛːt] F -, **-en** *(geh)* drollery

S-Kur|ve ['ɛs-] F S-bend

Skye|ter|ri|er ['skaiterie] M Skye terrier

Sky|sur|fing ['skai-] NT -, *no pl* sky surfing

Sla|lom ['sla:lɔm] M **-s, -s** slalom; **(im) ~ fahren** *(fig inf)* to drive a crazy zigzag course *(inf)*

Slang [slɛŋ] M **-s,** *no pl* slang

Slap|stick ['slɛpstɪk] M **-s, -s** slapstick

S-Laut ['ɛs-] M *(stimmlos)* `s`-sound; *(stimmhaft)* `z`-sound

Sla|we ['sla:və] M **-n, -n, Sla|win** ['sla:vɪn] F **-, -nen** Slav

sla|wisch ['sla:vɪʃ] ADJ Slavonic, Slavic

Sla|wist [sla'vɪst] M **-en, -en, Sla|wis|tin** [-'vɪstɪn] F **-, -nen** Slavonicist, Slavist

Sla|wis|tik [sla'vɪstɪk] F -, *no pl* Slavonic studies *sing*

Sli|bo|witz ['sli:bovɪts] M **-(e)s, -e** slivovitz

Slip [slɪp] M **-s, -s** (pair of) briefs *pl*; (= *Damenslip auch*) (pair of) panties *pl*

Slip|ein|la|ge F panty liner

Slip|per ['slɪpɐ] M **-s, -** slip-on shoe

Slo|gan ['slo:gn] M **-s, -s** slogan

Slot [slɔt] M **-s, -s** *(Comput, Aviat)* slot

Slo|wa|ke [slo'va:kə] M **-n, -n, Slo|wa|kin** [-'va:kɪn] F **-, -nen** Slovak

Slo|wa|kei [slova'kai] F - **die ~** Slovakia

slo|wa|kisch [slo'va:kɪʃ] ADJ Slovakian, Slovak

Slo|wa|kisch(e) NT Slovak → *auch* **Deutsch(e)**

Slo|we|ne [slo've:nə] M **-n, -n, Slo|we|nin** [-'ve:nɪn] F **-, -nen** Slovene

Slo|we|ni|en [slo've:niən] NT **-s** Slovenia

slo|we|nisch [slo've:nɪʃ] ADJ Slovenian, Slovene

Slo|we|nisch(e) NT Slovene, Slovenian → *auch* **Deutsch(e)**

Slow|fox ['slo:fɔks] M **-(es), -e** slow foxtrot

Slum [slam] M **-s, -s** slum

sm *abbr von* **Seemeile**

SM [ɛs'ɛm] M **-(s)** *abbr von* **Sadomasochismus**

S. M. *abbr von* **seine(r) Majestät** HM

Small|talk ▲ ['smɔːltɔːk] M **-(s)**, *no pl*, **Small Talk** M - **-(s)**, *no pl* small talk

Sma|ragd [sma'rakt] M **-(e)s, -e** [-də] emerald

sma|ragd|grün ADJ emerald-green

smart [sma:ɐt, smart] *(inf)* ADJ smart ADV *gekleidet* smartly; **~ klingen** to sound smart

Smart-Card F -, -s, **Smart|card** ['sma:ɐtka:ɐd] F -, -s *(inf)* smart card

Smi|ley¹ ['smaili] NT **-s, -s** *(Comput)* smiley

Smi|ley² ['smaili] M **-s, -s** *(pej:* = *ständig lächelnder Mensch)* grinner, smiler

Smog [smɔk] M **-(s), -s** smog

Smog-: Smog|alarm M smog alert; **Smog|alarm|stu|fe** F **~ 1** smog warning level 1; **Smog|ver|ord|nung** F smog regulations *pl*

Smok|ar|beit F *(Sew)* smocking

smo|ken ['smo:kn] VTI *(Sew)* to smock

Smo|king ['smo:kɪŋ] M **-s, -s** dinner jacket, dj *(inf)*, tuxedo *(esp US)*, tux *(esp US inf)*

SMS [ɛs'ɛm'ɛs] F **-, -** *abbr von* **Short Message Service** text message; **jdm eine ~ schicken** to text sb

SMS|en ['zɪmzn] VTI → **simsen**

Smut|je ['smʊtjə] M **-s, -s** *(Naut)* ship's cook

SMV [ɛs'ɛm'fau] -, *no pl abbr von* **Schülermitverwaltung** *or* **-mitverantwortung** school council

Smyr|na|tep|pich ['smyrna-] M Smyrna (carpet)

Snack [snɛk] M **-s, -s** snack (meal)

snif|fen ['snɪfn] VI *(sl) (von Drogen)* to sniff; *(von Kokain auch)* to snort

Snob [snɔp] M **-s, -s** snob

Sno|bis|mus [sno'bɪsmʊs] M -, **Snobismen** [-mən] **a** *no pl* snobbery, snobbishness **b** (= *Bemerkung*) snobbish remark *or* comment

sno|bis|tisch [sno'bɪstɪʃ] ADJ snobbish

Snow-: Snow|board ['sno:bɔːɐd] NT **-s, -s** snowboard; **Snow|boar|den** ['sno:bɔːɐdn] NT **-s,** *no pl*, **Snow|boar|ding** ['sno:bɔːɐdɪŋ] NT **-s,** *no pl* snowboarding; **Snow|boar|der** ['sno:bɔːɐdɐ] M **-s, -**, **Snow|boar|de|rin** [-ərɪn] F **-, -nen** snowboarder; **Snow|mo|bil** ['sno:mobi:l] NT **-s, -e** snowmobile; **Snow|raf|ting** ['sno:ra:ftɪŋ] NT **-s,** *no pl* snow rafting

SO [zo:] ADV **a** *(mit adj, adv)* so; *(mit vb:* = *so sehr)* so much; **so groß** etc so big etc; **eine so große Frau** such a big woman; **es ist gar nicht so einfach** it's really not so easy; **so groß** etc **wie ...** as big etc as ...; **so groß** etc**, dass ...** so big etc that ...; **sie hat ihn so geschlagen, dass ...** she hit him so hard that ...; **er ist so gelaufen** he ran so fast; **ich habe so gearbeitet** I worked so hard; **so gut es geht** as best *or* well as I/he etc can; **er ist nicht so dumm, das zu glauben** he's not so stupid as to believe that, he's not stupid enough to believe that; **sie hat sich so gefreut** she was so *or* really pleased;

das hat ihn so geärgert, dass ... that annoyed him so much that ...; **ich wusste nicht, dass es ihn so ärgern würde** I didn't know that it would annoy him so *or* that much; **ich freue mich so sehr, dass du kommst** I'm so pleased you're coming

b (= *auf diese Weise, von dieser Art)* like this/that, this/that way, thus *(form)*; **mach es nicht so, sondern so** don't do it like this but like that; **du sollst es so machen, ...** do it like this ..., do it this way ...; **mach es so, wie er es vorgeschlagen hat** do it the way *or* as *or* like *(inf)* he suggested; **ist es dort tatsächlich so?** is it really like that there?; **ist das tatsächlich so?** is that really so?; **so ist sie nun einmal** that's the way she is, that's what she's like; **sei doch nicht so** don't be like that; **so ist es nicht gewesen** it wasn't like that, that's not how it was; **es ist vielleicht besser so** perhaps it's better like that *or* that way; **so IST das!** that's the way things are, that's how it is; **(ach) so** I see!; **ist das so?** is that so?; **so oder** *or* **und so** either way; **und so weiter (und so fort)** and so on (and so forth); **gut so!** fine!, good!; **das ist gut so** that's fine; **das ist auch gut so!** (and) a good thing too!; **mir ist (es) so, als ob ...** it seems to me as if ...; **so geht es, wenn ...** that's what happens if ...; **... und so ist es also geschehen** ... and so that is what happened; **das kam so ...** this is what happened ..., it happened like this ...; **es verhält sich so ...** the facts are thus *(form)* *or* as follows ...; **das habe ich nur so gesagt** I didn't really mean it; **so genannt** as it/he etc is called; (= *angeblich)* so-called

c (= *etwa)* about, *or* so; **ich komme so um 8 Uhr** I'll come at about 8, I'll come at 8 *or* so *or* or thereabouts; **sie heißt doch Malitzki oder so** she's called Malitzki *or* something

d *(inf:* = *umsonst)* for nothing

e *(als Füllwort: nicht übersetzt)* **so dann und wann** now and then; **so bist du also gar nicht dort gewesen?** *(geh)* so you weren't there after all?; **so beeil dich doch!** do hurry up!; **so mancher** a number of people *pl*, quite a few people *pl*

f (= *solch)* **so ein Gebäude/Fehler** a building/mistake like that, such a building/mistake; **so ein guter Lehrer/schlechtes Bild** etc such a good teacher/bad picture etc; **so ein Idiot!** what an idiot!; **hast du so etwas schon einmal gesehen?** have you ever seen anything like it?; **so (et-) was ist noch nie vorgekommen** nothing like that has ever happened; **sie ist doch Lehrerin oder so was** she's a teacher *or* something like that; **na so was!** well I never!, no!; **so etwas Schönes** something as beautiful as that, such a beautiful thing; **so einer wie ich/er** somebody like *or* a person such as myself *or* me/him; **er ist so einer wie ich** he's like me → **umso, viel, weit, wenig**

CONJ **a** **so dass, sodass** so that

b **so wie es jetzt ist** as *or* the way things are at the moment

c **so klein er auch sein mag** however small he may be; **so wahr ich lebe** as true as I'm standing here

d **kaum hatte er ..., so ...** scarcely had he ... when ...

e *(old:* = *falls)* if, provided that; **so (der Herr-)gott will, sehen wir uns wieder** God willing, we shall see one another again

INTERJ so; (= *wirklich)* oh, really; *(abschließend)* well, right; **er ist schon da – so?** he's here already – is he? *or* oh! *or* really?; **ich kann nicht mitkommen – so?** I can't come with you – can't you? *or* oh!; **so, das wärs für heute** well *or* right *or* so, that's it for today; **so, jetzt habe ich die Nase voll** I've had enough; **so, so!** well well → **ach**

SO *abbr von* **Südosten** SE

s. o. *abbr von* **siehe oben**

so|bald [zo'balt] CONJ as soon as

Söck|chen ['zœkçən] NT **-s, -** *dim von* **Socke**

So|cke ['zɔkə] F -, -n sock; **sich auf die ~n machen** (inf) to get going (inf); **von den ~n sein** (inf) to be flabbergasted (inf), to be knocked for six (Brit inf)

So|ckel ['zɔkl] M -s, - base; (von Denkmal, Statue) plinth, pedestal, socle (spec); (Elec) socket; (für Birne) holder

So|ckel-: So|ckel|be|trag M basic sum; **So|ckel|ren|te** F basic pension

So|cken ['zɔkn] M -s, - (S Ger, Aus) sock

So|cken|hal|ter M (sock) suspender (Brit), garter

So|da ['zoːda] F -, no pl or nt -s, no pl soda

so|dann [zoˈdan] ADV (old) thereupon (old, form), then

so|dass ▲ [zoˈdas] CONJ → **so CONJ a**

So|da|was|ser NT pl -wässer soda water

Sod|bren|nen ['zoːtbrɛnən] NT -s, no pl heartburn

So|de ['zoːdə] F -, -n (= Rasenstück, Torfscholle) turf, sod

So|dom ['zoːdɔm] NT -s Sodom; **~ und Gomorrha** (lit, fig) Sodom and Gomorrah

so|do|mie [zodoˈmiː] F -, no pl buggery, bestiality

so|do|mi|tisch [zodoˈmiːtɪʃ] ADJ bestial

so|eben [zoˈleːbn] ADV just (this moment); **~ hören wir** or **haben wir gehört ...** we have just (this moment) heard ...; **~ erschienen** just out or published

So|fa ['zoːfa] NT -s, -s sofa, settee (esp Brit)

So|fa-: So|fa|bett NT bed-settee (Brit), sofa bed, hideaway bed (US); **So|fa|ecke** F corner of the/a sofa; **So|fa|kis|sen** NT sofa cushion

so|fern [zoˈfɛrn] CONJ provided (that); **~ ... nicht** if ... not

soff pret von **saufen**

So|fia ['zɔfia, zoˈfiːa] NT -s (Geog) Sofia

So|fi|o|ter [zoˈfiːɔtɐ] M -s, -, **So|fi|o|te|rin** [-ərɪn] F -, -nen Sofian

so|fort [zoˈfɔrt] ADV immediately, straight or right away, at once; **~ nach ...** immediately after ...; **komm hierher, aber ~** or **und zwar ~!** come here this instant or at once!; **(ich) komme ~!** (I'm) just coming!; (Kellner etc) I'll be right with you

So|fort-: So|fort|bild|ka|me|ra F Polaroid® camera, instant camera; **So|fort|hil|fe** F emergency relief or aid

so|for|tig [zoˈfɔrtɪç] ADJ immediate, instant

So|fort|maß|nah|me F immediate measure

Soft|drink ['zɔftdrɪŋk] M -s, -s, **Soft Drink** M - -s, - -s soft drink

Soft|eis ['zɔftlais] NT soft ice cream

Sof|tie ['zɔfti] M -s, -s (inf) caring type

Soft|ware ['sɔftwɛːɐ] F -, -s (Comput) software

Soft|ware-: Soft|ware|ent|wick|ler(in) ['sɔftwɛːɐ-] M(F) software developer; **Soft|ware|pa|ket** ['sɔftwɛːɐ-] NT software package; **Soft|ware|un|ter|neh|men** ['sɔftwɛːɐ-] NT software company or firm

sog pret von **saugen**

Sog [zoːk] M -(e)s, -e [-gə] (= saugende Kraft) suction; (bei Schiff) wake; (bei Flugzeug, Fahrzeug) slipstream; (von Strudel) vortex; (von Brandungswelle) undertow; (fig) maelstrom

sog. abbr von **so genannt**

so|gar [zoˈgaːɐ] ADV even; **er kam ~** he even came; **jedes Getränk, ja ~ schon ein kleines Bier, kostet sehr viel** every drink, even a small glass of beer or a small glass of beer, even, costs a lot; **schön, ~ sehr schön** beautiful, in fact very beautiful; **ich kann sie gut leiden, ich finde sie ~ sehr nett** I like her, in fact I think she's very nice; **ich habe sie nicht nur gesehen, sondern ~ geküsst** I didn't just see her, I actually kissed her (as well)

so|ge|nannt △ ['zoːgənant] ADJ attr → **so ADV b**

so|gleich [zoˈglaɪç] ADV = **sofort**

Sog|wir|kung F suction; (fig) knock-on effect

Soh|le ['zoːlə] F -, -n **a** (= Fußsohle etc) sole; (= Einlage) insole; **auf leisen ~n** (poet) softly, noiselessly; **mit nackten ~n** barefoot; **es brennt ihm unter den ~n** he has itchy feet (inf), his feet are itching (inf); **eine kesse ~ aufs Parkett legen** (inf hum) to put up a good show on the dance floor → **heften VR b, Scheitel a b** (= Boden) bottom; (= Talsohle) floor, bottom **c** (Min) (= Grubenboden) floor; (= Stollen) level

sohlen ['zoːlən] VT to sole

Soh|len|le|der NT , **Sohl|le|der** NT sole leather

Sohn [zoːn] M -(e)s, ⸚e ['zøːnə] (lit, fig) son; **Gottes ~** (Bibl) **der ~ Gottes** (Bibl) the Son of God; **des Menschen ~** (Bibl) the Son of Man; **na, mein ~** well, son or sonny → **verloren ADJ b**

Söhn|chen ['zøːnçən] NT -s, - dim von **Sohn**

Soh|ne|mann ['zoːnəman] M pl -männer (dial inf) son, sonny

Söhn|lein ['zøːnlain] NT -s, - dim von **Sohn**

soig|niert [soanˈjiːɛt] ADJ (geh) elegant; **Frau auch** soignée; **Mann auch** soigné

Soi|ree [soaˈreː] F -, -n [-ˈreːən] soirée

So|ja ['zoːja] F -, **Sojen** ['zoːjən] soya (esp Brit), soy

So|ja-: So|ja|boh|ne F soya bean (esp Brit), soybean; **So|ja|boh|nen|kei|me** PL → **Sojasprossen**; **So|ja|so|ße** F soya (esp Brit) or soy sauce; **So|ja|spros|sen** PL soya bean (esp Brit) or soybean sprouts pl

So|ko ['zoːko] F -, -s abbr von **Sonderkommission**

Sok|ra|tes ['zoːkrates] M -' Socrates

sok|ra|tisch [zoˈkraːtɪʃ] ADJ Socratic

so|lang [zoˈlaŋ], **so|lan|ge** [zoˈlaŋə] CONJ as or so long as

So|lar- [zola-ɐ-] in cpds solar; **So|lar|an|trieb** M solar drive; **so|lar|be|trie|ben** ADJ solar-powered, driven by solar power pred; **So|lar|ener|gie** F solar energy

So|la|ri|um [zoˈlaːriʊm] NT -s, **Solarien** [-riən] solarium

So|lar|mo|bil NT solar-powered vehicle

So|lar|ple|xus [zola-ɐˈplɛksʊs] M -, - (Anat) solar plexus

So|lar-: So|lar|strom M , no pl solar electricity; **So|lar|zel|le** F solar cell

Sol|bad ['zoːlbaːt] NT (= Bad) saltwater or brine bath; (= Badeort) saltwater spa

solch [zɔlç] ADJ inv, **sol|che(r, s)** ['zɔlçə] ADJ such; **ein ~er Mensch, ~ ein Mensch** such a person, a person like that; **~e Menschen** people like that, such people; **~es Wetter/Glück** such weather/luck; **wir haben ~en Durst/~e Angst** we're so thirsty/afraid; **~ langer Weg** such a long way; **der Mensch als ~er** man as such; **~es** that kind of thing; **~e (Leute)** such people; **Experten und ~e, die es werden wollen** experts and people who would like to be experts; **Rechtsanwälte gibt es ~e und ~e** there are lawyers and lawyers; **ich hätte gern ~e und ~e (Bonbons)** I'd like some of those (sweets) and some of those

sol|cher-: sol|cher|art ['zɔlçəla-ɐt] ADJ attr inv (geh) such; **sol|cher|ge|stalt** ['zɔlçəgəˈʃtalt] ADV (geh) = **dergestalt**; **sol|cher|lei** ['zɔlçɐˈlai] ADJ attr inv (geh) such; **sol|cher|ma|ßen** ['zɔlçɐˈmaːsn] ADV to such an extent, so; **~ ermutigt, wagten wir ...** thus emboldened, we ventured ...

Sold [zɔlt] M -(e)s [-dəs] no pl (Mil) pay; **in jds ~** (dat) **stehen** (old) to be in sb's employ; (pej) to be in sb's pay

Sol|dat [zɔlˈdaːt] M -en, -en, **Sol|da|tin** [-ˈdaːtɪn] F -, -nen soldier; **bei den ~en sein** (dated) to be in the army, to be a soldier; **zu den ~en kommen** (dated), **~ werden** to join the army, to join up (inf), to become a soldier; **~ spielen** to play soldiers → **Grabmal**

Sol|da|ten-: Sol|da|ten|fried|hof M military cemetery; **Sol|da|ten|ge|setz** military regulations pl, no art; **Sol|da|ten|lied** NT army or soldier's song; **Sol|da|ten|rat** M soldiers' council; (= Sowjet) soldiers' soviet; **Sol|da|ten|rock** M (old) military or soldier's uniform; **Sol|da|ten|spra|che** F military or soldier's slang; **Sol|da|ten|stie|fel** M army or soldier's (esp Brit) boot; **Sol|da|ten|tum** [zɔlˈdaːtntuːm] NT -s, no pl soldiership no art, soldiery no art; (Tradition) military tradition

Sol|da|tes|ka [zɔldaˈtɛska] F -, **Soldatesken** [-tɛskn] (pej) band of soldiers

Sol|da|tin F -, -nen soldier → auch **Soldat**

sol|da|tisch [zɔlˈdaːtɪʃ] ADJ (= militärisch) military; (= soldatengemäß) soldierly ADV **sich verhalten** like a soldier; **~ stramm stehen** to stand up straight like a soldier; **~ grüßen** to salute

Sold|buch NT (Hist) military passbook

Söld|ner ['zœldnɐ] M -s, -, **Söld|ne|rin** [-ərɪn] F -, -nen mercenary

Söld|ner|heer NT army of mercenaries, mercenary army

Söld|ner|trup|pe F mercenary force

So|le ['zoːlə] F -, -n brine, salt water

Sol|ei ['zoːllai] NT pickled egg

So|li¹ pl von **Solo**

So|li² ['zoːli] M -s, no pl (inf) = **Solidaritätszuschlag**

so|lid [zoˈliːt] ADJ, ADV = **solide**

So|li|dar- [zoliˈdaːɐ-]: **So|li|dar|bei|trag** M (von Interessengemeinschaft) supportive contribution (to public funds, social services etc); **So|li|dar|ge|mein|schaft** F (mutually) supportive society; (= Beitragszahler) contributors pl; **der ~ zur Last fallen** to be a burden on the social security system

so|li|da|risch [zoliˈdaːrɪʃ] ADJ showing solidarity; **sich mit jdm ~ erklären** to declare one's solidarity with sb; **eine ~e Haltung** to show (one's) solidarity; **in ~er Übereinstimmung** in complete solidarity; **sich mit jdm ~ fühlen** to feel solidarity with sb ADV in/showing solidarity; **~ mit jdm handeln** to act in solidarity with sb

so|li|da|ri|sie|ren [zolidari'ziːrən] ptp **solidarisiert** VR **sich ~ mit** to show (one's) solidarity with

So|li|da|ri|tät [zolidari'tɛːt] F -, no pl solidarity; **~ üben** to show solidarity

So|li|da|ri|täts-: So|li|da|ri|täts|ad|res|se F message of solidarity; **So|li|da|ri|täts|be|kun|dung** F usu pl declaration of solidarity; **So|li|da|ri|täts|fonds** M solidarity fund; **So|li|da|ri|täts|ge|fühl** NT feeling of solidarity; **So|li|da|ri|täts|prin|zip** NT principle of solidarity; **So|li|da|ri|täts|streik** M sympathy strike; **So|li|da|ri|täts|zu|schlag** M (Fin) solidarity surcharge on income tax (for the reconstruction of eastern Germany)

So|li|dar|pakt [zoliˈdaːɐ-] M solidarity pact or agreement

so|li|de [zoˈliːdə] ADJ **Haus, Möbel etc** solid, sturdy; **Arbeit, Wissen, Mechaniker, Politik, Basis, Finanzen** sound; **Ausbildung** sound, solid; **Mensch, Le-**

ben, Lokal respectable; *Firma, Mehrheit* solid; *Preise* reasonable **ADV** **a** (= *untadelig*) ~ **leben** to lead a well-ordered life **b** (= *stabil*) ~ **gebaut** solidly built; ~ **konstruiert** well-constructed **c** (= *gründlich*) arbeiten thoroughly; ~ **ausgebildet** well-trained **d** (= *überzeugend*) begründen solidly; ~ **argumentieren** to have well-founded arguments

So|li|di|tät [zolidi'tɛːt] F -, no pl (*von Haus, Möbeln etc*) solidness, sturdiness; (*von Arbeit, Wissen, Finanzen*) soundness; (*von Firma*) solidness

So|lip|sis|mus [zolɪp'sɪsmʊs] M -, no pl (*Philos*) solipsism

So|list [zo'lɪst] M -en, -en, **So|lis|tin** [-'lɪstɪn] F -, -nen (*Mus*) soloist

so|lis|tisch [zo'lɪstɪʃ] ADJ, ADV solo

So|li|tär [zoli'tɛːɐ] M -s, -e solitaire; (= *Diamant*) diamond solitaire, solitaire diamond

Soll [zɔl] NT -(s), -(s) **a** (= *Schuld*) debit; (= *Schuldseite*) debit side; ~ **und Haben** debit and credit **b** (*Comm:* = *Planaufgabe*) target

Soll|bruch|stel|le F (*Tech*) predetermined breaking point

---

sol|len ['zɔlən]
✪ 28.1, 29, 30, 37.2, 41, 43.1, 43.2, 47.1, 53.2, 53.6

1 HILFSVERB	3 TRANSITIVES VERB
2 INTRANSITIVES VERB	

1 – HILFSVERB
pret **sollte** ['zɔltə], *ptp* **sollen**

a Befehl, Verpflichtung, Plan **was soll ich/er tun?** what shall *or* should I/should he do?; (= *was sind meine/seine Aufgaben auch*) what do I/does he have to do?; **kannst du mir helfen? – klar, was soll ich tun?** can you help me? – of course, what shall I do?; **soll ich Ihnen helfen?** can I help you?; **soll ich dir mal sagen, wie ...?** shall *or* will I tell you how ...?; **soll ich (gehen/singen)? – ja, du sollst (gehen/singen)** shall I (go/sing)? – yes, do; **du weißt, dass du das nicht tun sollst** you know that you're not supposed to do that; **er weiß nicht, was er tun soll** he doesn't know what to do; (= *kennt seine Aufgaben nicht auch*) he doesn't know what he's meant to do; **sie sagte ihm, er solle draußen warten** she told him (that he was) to wait outside; **er wurde wütend, weil er draußen warten sollte** he was livid that he had to wait outside; **sie sagte mir, was ich tun sollte/was ich alles tun soll** she told me what to do *or* what I should do/everything I should do; **was ich (nicht) alles tun/wissen soll!** the things I'm meant *or* supposed to do/know!; **so soll es nicht wieder vorkommen** it won't happen again; **er soll reinkommen** tell him to come in; **der soll nur kommen!** just let him come!; **und da soll man nicht böse werden/nicht lachen!** and then they expect you/me *etc* not to get cross/not to laugh; **niemand soll sagen, dass ...** let no-one say that ...; **ich soll Ihnen sagen, dass ...** I've been asked to tell you that ...; **ich soll dir schöne Grüße von Renate bestellen** Renate asked me to give you her best wishes; **du sollst nicht töten** (*Bibl*) thou shalt not kill; **so soll es sein** that's how it should be; **das Haus soll nächste Woche gestrichen werden** the house is to be painted next week; **das Gebäude soll ein Museum werden** the building is (meant) to become a museum

b konjunktivisch **was sollte ich/er deiner Meinung nach tun?** what do you think I/he should do *or* ought to do?; **so etwas sollte man nicht tun** one shouldn't do that, one oughtn't to do that (*esp Brit*); **das hättest du nicht tun sollen** you shouldn't have *or* oughtn't to have (*esp Brit*) done that; **das hättest du sehen sollen!** you should have seen it!; **er hätte (gehen/singen) sollen** he should have (gone/sung); **du solltest lieber etwas früher kommen/zu Hause bleiben** it would be better if you came early/stayed at home

---

c konditional **sollte das passieren, ...** if that should happen ..., should that happen ...; **sollte ich Unrecht haben, tut es mir Leid** I'm sorry if I am wrong

d Vermutung, Erwartung to be supposed *or* meant to; **er soll heute kommen** he should *or* come today, he is supposed *or* meant to come today; **sie soll krank/verheiratet sein** apparently she's ill/married; **er soll angeblich sehr reich sein** he's supposed to be very rich; **Xanthippe soll zänkisch gewesen sein** Xanthippe is supposed to have been quarrelsome; **das soll gar nicht so einfach sein** they say it's not that easy; **was soll das heißen?** what's that supposed to mean?; **wer soll das sein?** who is that supposed *or* meant to be?

e = können, mögen **gut, Sie sollen Recht haben!** all right, have it your own way (*inf*), all right, whatever you say; **mir soll es gleich sein** it's all the same to me; **so etwas soll es geben** these things happen; **man sollte glauben, dass ...** you would think that ...; **sollte das möglich sein?** is that possible?

f in Prophezeihung (*geh*) **er sollte sie nie wiedersehen** he was never to see her again; **es hat nicht sollen sein** it wasn't to be; **Jahre sollten vergehen, bevor ...** years were to pass before ...; **es sollte nicht lange dauern, bis ...** it was not to be long until ...

2 – INTRANSITIVES VERB
pret **sollte** ['zɔltə], *ptp* **gesollt** [ɡə'zɔlt]

(= *bewirken, bedeuten, in Fragen*) **was soll das?** what's all this?; (= *warum denn das*) what's that for?; **was solls!** (*inf*) what the hell! (*inf*); **was soll der Quatsch** *or* **Mist?** (*inf*) what's this stupid nonsense? (*inf*); **was soll ich dort?** what would I do there?

3 – TRANSITIVES VERB
pret **sollte** ['zɔltə], *ptp* **gesollt** [ɡə'zɔlt]

das sollst/solltest du nicht you shouldn't do that; **das hast du nicht gesollt** you shouldn't have done that; **was man nicht alles soll** *or* **sollte!** (*inf*) the things you're expected to do!

Söl|ler ['zœlɐ] M -s, - balcony

Soll-: Soll|sei|te F (*Fin*) debit side; **Soll|stär|ke** F required *or* authorized strength; **Soll|zin|sen** PL (*Fin*) interest owing *sing*

so|lo ['zoːlo] ADV (*Mus*) solo; (*fig inf*) on one's own, alone

So|lo ['zoːlo] NT -s, **Soli** ['zoːli] (*alle Bedeutungen*) solo

So|lo- in *cpds* solo; **So|lo|auf|tritt** M (*auf Bühne etc*) solo performance *or* appearance; **So|lo|ge|sang** M solo; **So|lo|ge|schäft** NT (*St Ex*) outright transaction; **So|lo|in|stru|ment** NT solo instrument; **So|lo|kar|rie|re** F career as a soloist; **So|lo|künst|ler(in)** M(F) solo artist; **So|lo|stim|me** F (= *Stimme*) solo voice; (= *Part*) solo part; **So|lo|tän|zer(in)** M(F) solo dancer; (*im Ballett*) principal dancer

So|lo|thurn ['zoːloturn] NT -s (= *Kanton, Stadt*) Solothurn

sol|vent [zɔl'vɛnt] ADJ (*Fin*) solvent

Sol|venz [zɔl'vɛnts] F -, -en (*Fin*) solvency

So|ma|li [zo'maːli] M -(s), -(s) *or* f -, -s Somali

So|ma|lia [zo'maːlia] NT -s Somalia

So|ma|li|er [zo'maːliɐ] M -s, -, **So|ma|li|e|rin** [-iərɪn] F -, -nen Somali

So|ma|li|halb|in|sel F , **So|ma|li|land** NT -(e)s Somaliland

so|ma|lisch [zo'maːlɪʃ] ADJ Somali

so|ma|tisch [zo'maːtɪʃ] (*Med*) **ADJ** somatic **ADV** *krank* somatically; ~ **bedingt sein** to have a somatic cause

Somb|re|ro [zɔm'breːro] M -s, -s sombrero

so|mit [zo'mɪt, 'zoːmɪt] ADV consequently, therefore

Som|me|li|er [zɔmə'lieː] M -s, -s, **Som|me|li|e|re** [zɔmə'lieːrə] F -, -n wine waiter (*Brit*), wine server (*US*)

Som|mer ['zɔmɐ] M -s, - summer; **im** ~, **des ~s** (*geh*) in (the) summer; **im nächsten** ~ next summer; **im** ~ **(des Jahres) 1951** in the summer of 1951; ~ **wie** *or* **und Winter** all year round

Som|mer- in *cpds* summer; **Som|mer|abend** M summer('s) evening; **Som|mer|an|fang** M beginning of summer; **Som|mer|fahr|plan** M summer timetable; **Som|mer|fell** NT (*Zool*) summer coat; **Som|mer|fe|ri|en** PL summer holidays *pl* (*Brit*) *or* vacation (*US*); (*Jur, Parl*) summer recess; **in die** ~ **fahren** to go away for the *or* one's summer holidays (*Brit*) *or* vacation (*US*); **in die** ~ **gehen** to begin one's summer holidays (*Brit*) *or* vacation (*US*) (*Sch auch*) to break up for the summer (holidays) (*Brit*); (*Univ*) to go down for the summer; (*Jur, Parl*) to go into the summer recess; **Som|mer|fest** NT summer party; **Som|mer|flug|plan** M summer flight schedule; **Som|mer|fri|sche** F (*dated*) **a** no pl (= *Sommerurlaub*) summer holiday (*esp Brit*) *or* vacation (*US*) *or* break; **in die** ~ **gehen** to go away for a summer holiday *etc* **b** (*Ort*) summer resort; **Som|mer|frisch|ler** [-frɪʃlɐ] M -s, -, **Som|mer|frisch|le|rin** [-ərɪn] F -, -nen (*dated*) summer holiday-maker (*Brit*) *or* vacationist (*US*); **Som|mer|gast** M summer guest; **Som|mer|gers|te** F spring barley; **Som|mer|ge|trei|de** NT spring cereal; **Som|mer|halb|jahr** NT summer semester, ≈ summer term (*Brit*); **Som|mer|haus** NT holiday home (*esp Brit*); **Som|mer|kleid** NT **a** (*Kleidungsstück*) summer dress **b** (= *Sommerfell*) summer coat; (*von Vögeln*) summer plumage; **Som|mer|klei|dung** F summer clothing; (*esp Comm*) summerwear

som|mer|lich ['zɔmɐlɪç] **ADJ** (= *sommerartig, heiter*) summery; (= *Sommer-*) summer *attr* **ADV** **es ist** ~ **warm** it's as warm as it is in summer; ~ **heiße Temperaturen** hot summery temperatures; ~ **gekleidet sein** to be in summer clothes

Som|mer-: Som|mer|loch NT (*inf*) silly (*Brit*) *or* off (*US*) season; **Som|mer|mo|nat** M summer month; **Som|mer|nacht** F summer('s) night; **Som|mer|olym|pi|a|de** F Summer Olympics *pl*; **Som|mer|pau|se** F summer break; (*Jur, Parl*) summer recess; **Som|mer|rei|fen** M normal tyre (*Brit*) *or* tire (*US*)

som|mers ['zɔmɐs] ADV (*geh*) in summer; ~ **wie winters** all year round

Som|mer-: Som|mer|sai|son F summer season; **Som|mer|schluss|ver|kauf** ▲ M summer sale; **Som|mer|se|mes|ter** NT (*Univ*) summer semester, ≈ summer term (*Brit*); **Som|mer|sitz** M summer residence; **Som|mer|son|nen|wen|de** F summer solstice; **Som|mer|spie|le** PL Summer Games *pl*; **die Olympischen** ~ the Summer Olympics, the Summer Olympic Games; **Som|mer|spros|se** F freckle; **som|mer|spros|sig** [-ʃprɔsɪç] ADJ freckled

som|mers|über ['zɔmɐsʔyːbɐ] ADV during summer

Som|mer-: Som|mer|tag M summer's day; **Som|mer|the|a|ter** NT open-air theatre (*Brit*) *or* theater (*US*); **Som|mer|wei|zen** M spring wheat; **Som|mer|wet|ter** NT summer weather; **Som|mer|woh|nung** F holiday flat (*Brit*), vacation apartment (*US*); **Som|mer|zeit** F summer time *no art*; (*geh:* = *Sommer*) summertime, summertide (*liter*); **zur** ~ (*geh*) in summertime

som|nam|bul [zɔmnam'buːl] ADJ (*spec*) somnambulary

Som|nam|bu|le(r) [zɔmnam'buːlə] MF *decl as adj* (*spec*) somnambulist

Som|nam|bu|lis|mus [zɔmnambu'lɪsmʊs] M -, no pl (*spec*) somnambulism

so|nach [zo'naːx, 'zoːnaːx] ADV (*old*) = **somit**

So|nar [zo'naːɐ] NT -s, -e sonar

So|nar|ge|rät NT sonar (device)

So|na|te [zo'naːtə] F **-, -n** sonata

So|na|ti|ne [zona'tiːnə] F **-, -n** sonatina

Son|de ['zɔndə] F **-, -n** (Space, Med: zur Untersuchung) probe; (Med: zur Ernährung) tube; (Met) sonde

son|der ['zɔndɐ] PREP +acc (obs) without

Son|der- ['zɔndɐ-] in cpds special; **Son|der|ab|druck** M (Typ) offprint; **Son|der|ab|fall** M hazardous or special waste; **Son|der|ab|ga|be** F special tax, special impost (spec); **Son|der|ab|schrei|bung** F (von Steuern) special depreciation allowance; **Son|der|an|fer|ti|gung** F special model; **eine ~ sein** to have been made specially; **Son|der|an|ge|bot** NT special offer; **im ~ sein** to be on special offer; **Son|der|aus|bil|dung** F specialist or special training; **Son|der|aus|füh|rung** F special model or version; (Auto auch) custom-built model; **Son|der|aus|ga|be** F **a** special edition **b** **Son|der|aus|ga|ben** PL (Fin) additional or extra expenses pl; **Son|der|aus|stel|lung** F special exhibition

son|der|bar ADJ strange, peculiar, odd ADV strangely; **~ klingen** to sound strange; **sich ~ benehmen** to act strangely or (esp US) strange

son|der|ba|rer|wei|se ['zɔndɐbaːrɐˈvaɪzə] ADV strangely enough, strange to say

Son|der-: **Son|der|be|auf|trag|te(r)** MF decl as adj (Pol) special emissary; **Son|der|be|richt|er|stat|ter(in)** M(F) (Press) special correspondent; **Son|der|bot|schaf|ter(in)** M(F) ambassador/ambassadress extraordinary; **Son|der|druck** M pl **-drucke** offprint; **Son|der|ein|satz** M special action; **Son|der|er|laub|nis** F special permission; (= Schriftstück) special permit; **Son|der|er|mitt|ler(in)** M(F) special investigator; **Son|der|fahrt** F special excursion or trip; **„Sonderfahrt"** (auf Schild) "special"; **Son|der|fall** M special case; (= Ausnahme) exception; **Son|der|ge|neh|mi|gung** F special permission; (Schein) special permit; **Son|der|ge|richt** M special court; **Son|der|glei|chen** ['zɔndɐˈglaɪçn̩] ADJ inv **eine Geschmacklosigkeit ~** the height of bad taste; **mit einer Arroganz ~** with unparalleled arrogance; **Son|der|klas|se** F special class; (von Obst etc) top grade; **Son|der|kom|man|do** NT special unit; **Son|der|kom|mis|si|on** F special commission; **Son|der|kon|to** NT special account

son|der|lich ['zɔndɐlɪç] ADJ attr particular, especial, special; **ohne ~e Begeisterung** without any particular enthusiasm, without much enthusiasm ADV particularly, especially

Son|der|ling ['zɔndɐlɪŋ] M **-s, -e** eccentric

Son|der-: **Son|der|mar|ke** F special issue (stamp); **Son|der|ma|schi|ne** F special plane or aircraft; **Son|der|mel|dung** F (Rad, TV) special announcement; **Son|der|müll** M hazardous waste; **Son|der|müll|de|po|nie** F hazardous waste depot

son|dern¹ ['zɔndɐn] CONJ but; **~?** where/who/what etc then?; **wir fahren nicht nach Spanien, ~ nach Frankreich** we're not going to Spain, we're going to France; **nicht nur …, ~ auch** not only … but also

son|dern² VT (old, geh) to separate (von from) → auch **gesondert**

Son|der- ['zɔndɐ-]: **Son|der|num|mer** F (Press) special edition or issue; **Son|der|pä|da|go|gik** F remedial or special education; **Son|der|par|tei|tag** M special party conference or convention; **Son|der|preis** M special reduced price; **Son|der|recht** NT (special) privilege; **Son|der|re|ge|lung** F special provision

son|ders ['zɔndɐs] ADV → **samt**

Son|der- ['zɔndɐ-]: **Son|der|schicht** F special shift; (zusätzlich) extra shift; **Son|der|schu|le** F special school; **Son|der|schul|leh|rer(in)** M(F) teacher at a special school

---

SONDERSCHULE

A **Sonderschule** is a school for disabled and special-needs children. By offering support and assistance and by focusing on the children's disabilities, the aim is to develop their abilities and help to compensate for their disability. Opportunities also exist for children to move to a conventional school at a later stage. There are different kinds of **Sonderschulen** catering for the physically and mentally disabled, and for blind, deaf and developmentally retarded children.

Son|der- ['zɔndɐ-]: **Son|der|sen|dung** F special broadcast; **Son|der|sit|zung** F special session; (von Vorstand) special meeting; **Son|der|stel|lung** F special position; **Son|der|stem|pel** M (bei der Post) special postmark; **Son|der|ur|laub** M (Mil) special leave; (für Todesfall etc) compassionate leave; **Son|der|voll|macht** F emergency powers pl; **Son|der|wün|sche** PL special requests pl; **Son|der|zah|lung** F special payment; **Son|der|zei|chen** NT (Comput) special character; **Son|der|zie|hungs|rech|te** PL (Fin) special drawing rights pl; **Son|der|zug** M special train; **Son|der|zu|la|ge** F special bonus

son|die|ren [zɔn'diːrən] ptp **sondiert** VT to sound out; **das Terrain or Gelände ~** to spy out the land; **die Lage ~** to find out how the land lies VI to sound things out; **~, ob …** to try to sound out whether …

Son|die|rung F **-, -en** sounding out no pl; **die ~ des Terrains** spying out the land; **ohne gründliche ~** without sounding things out thoroughly

Son|die|rungs|ge|spräch NT exploratory discussion or talk

So|nett [zɔ'nɛt] NT **-(e)s, -e** sonnet

Song [zɔŋ] M **-s, -s** song

Sonn|abend ['zɔnaːbnt] M Saturday → auch **Dienstag**

sonn|abends ['zɔnaːbnts] ADV on Saturdays, on a Saturday → auch **dienstags**

Son|ne ['zɔnə] F **-, -n** **a** sun; (= Sonnenlicht) sun(light); **die liebe ~** (poet, inf) **Frau ~** (poet) the sun; **unter der ~** (fig geh) under the sun; **an or in die ~ gehen** to go out in the sun(shine); **er kommt viel/wenig an die ~** he gets/doesn't get a lot of sun, he goes/doesn't go out in the sun a lot; **geh mir aus der ~!** (inf) stop blocking my view!, get out of the way!; (= aus dem Licht) get out of the or my light!; **das Zimmer hat wenig ~** the room doesn't get much sun(light); **die ~ bringt es an den Tag** (prov) truth will out (prov); **keine ~ sehen** (inf) not to have a hope in hell (inf); **das Reich or Land der aufgehenden ~** the Land of the Rising Sun

b (= Heizsonne) electric fire

son|nen ['zɔnən] VT **Betten** to put out in the sun VR to sun oneself; **sich in etw** (dat) **~** (fig) to bask in sth

Son|nen-: **Son|nen|an|be|ter(in)** M(F) (lit, fig) sun worshipper; **Son|nen|auf|gang** M sunrise, sunup (inf); **den ~ abwarten** to wait for the sun to rise; **Son|nen|bad** NT sunbathing no pl; **ein fünfständiges ~** five hours in the sun, five hours' sunbathing; **ein ~ nehmen** to sunbathe, to bask in the sun; **son|nen|ba|den** VI sep infin, ptp only to sunbathe; **Son|nen|bahn** F sun's path; **Son|nen|ball** M (liter) fiery orb (liter); **Son|nen|bank** F pl **-bän|ke** sun bed; **Son|nen|blen|de** F (Aut) sun visor; (Phot) lens hood

Son|nen|blu|me F sunflower

Son|nen|blu|men-: **Son|nen|blu|men|kern** M sunflower seed; **Son|nen|blu|men|öl** NT sunflower oil

Son|nen-: **Son|nen|brand** M sunburn no art; **Son|nen|bräu|nung** F suntan; **Son|nen|bril|le** F (pair of) sunglasses pl, shades pl (esp US inf); **Son|nen|creme** F suntan cream or lo-

tion; **Son|nen|dach** NT awning, sun blind; (Aut dated) sun or sunshine (Brit) roof; **Son|nen|deck** NT (Naut) sun deck; **son|nen|durch|flu|tet** [-dʊrçfluːtət] ADJ (geh) sunny, with the sun streaming in; **Son|nen|ein|strah|lung** F solar radiation; **Son|nen|ener|gie** F solar energy; **Son|nen|fer|ne** F (Astron) aphelion; **Son|nen|fins|ter|nis** F solar eclipse, eclipse of the sun; **Son|nen|fleck** M (Astron) sunspot; **son|nen|ge|bräunt** ADJ suntanned; **Son|nen|ge|flecht** NT (Physiol) solar plexus; **Son|nen|gel** NT suntan gel; **Son|nen|ge|ne|ra|tor** M (an Satellit) solar generator; **Son|nen|glanz** M (poet), **Son|nen|glut** F (geh) blazing heat of the sun; **Son|nen|gott** M sun-god; **Son|nen|gür|tel** M (der Erde) Torrid Zone; **son|nen|halb** ['zɔnənhalp] ADV (Sw) = **sonnseitig**; **son|nen|hell** ADJ sunny, sunlit; **Son|nen|hit|ze** F heat of the sun; **son|nen|hung|rig** ADJ hungry for the sun; **Son|nen|hung|ri|ge** [-hʊŋriɡə] PL decl as adj sun-seekers pl; **Son|nen|hut** M sunhat; **Son|nen|jahr** NT (Astron) solar year; **son|nen|klar** ADJ (inf) clear as daylight, crystal-clear; **Son|nen|kol|lek|tor** M solar panel; **Son|nen|kö|nig** M (Hist) Sun King, Roi Soleil; **Son|nen|kraft|werk** NT solar power station; **Son|nen|kult** M sun cult; **Son|nen|licht** NT sunlight; **Son|nen|milch** F suntan lotion; **Son|nen|nä|he** F (Astron) perihelion; **Son|nen|öl** NT suntan oil; **Son|nen|pad|del** NT (inf: = Sonnengenerator) solar paddle (inf); **Son|nen|rad** NT (Hist) (representation of the) sun; **Son|nen|schein** M sunshine; **bei ~** in the sunshine; **bei strahlendem ~** in brilliant sunshine; **Son|nen|schirm** M sunshade; (für Frauen auch) parasol; **Son|nen|schutz** M protection against the sun; **Son|nen|schutz|fak|tor** M protection factor; **Son|nen|schutz|mit|tel** NT sunscreen; **Son|nen|se|gel** NT **a** (= Schutzdach) awning **b** (bei Raumfahrzeug) solar sail; **Son|nen|sei|te** F side facing the sun, sunny side (auch fig); **Son|nen|stand** M position of the sun; **Son|nen|stich** M heatstroke no art, sunstroke no art; **du hast wohl einen ~!** (inf) you must have been out in the sun too long!; **Son|nen|strahl** M sunbeam, ray of sunshine; (esp Astron, Phys) sun ray; **Son|nen|stu|dio** NT tanning salon (esp US) or studio, solarium; **Son|nen|sys|tem** NT solar system; **Son|nen|tag** M sunny day; (Met auch) day of sunshine; (Astron) solar day; **Son|nen|ter|ras|se** F sun terrace or deck (US); **Son|nen|uhr** F sundial; **Son|nen|un|ter|gang** M sunset, sundown; **den ~ abwarten** to wait for the sun to set; **son|nen|ver|brannt** ADJ Vegetation scorched; Mensch sunburnt; **Son|nen|wen|de** F solstice; **Son|nen|wend|fei|er** F = **Sonnwendfeier**; **Son|nen|wind** M (Phys) solar wind

son|nig ['zɔnɪç] ADJ (lit, fig) sunny

Sonn-: **Sonn|sei|te** F (Aus) side facing the sun, sunny side (auch fig); **sonn|sei|tig** ['zɔnzaɪtɪç] ADV (Aus) **~ gelegen** facing the sun

Sonn|tag ['zɔntaːk] M Sunday → auch **Dienstag**

sonn|tä|gig ['zɔntɛːgɪç] ADJ attr Sunday; **die gestrigen ~en Verhandlungen …** the negotiations yesterday, Sunday …

sonn|täg|lich ['zɔntɛːklɪç] ADJ Sunday attr ADV **~ gekleidet** dressed in one's Sunday best; **~ ruhig** as quiet as a Sunday

sonn|tags ['zɔntaːks] ADV on Sundays, on a Sunday → auch **dienstags**

Sonn|tags- in cpds Sunday; **Sonn|tags|ar|beit** F Sunday working; **Sonn|tags|aus|flug** M Sunday trip; **Sonn|tags|bei|la|ge** F Sunday supplement; **Sonn|tags|bra|ten** M Sunday roast; **Sonn|tags|dienst** M (von Polizist etc) Sunday duty; **~ haben** (Apotheke) to be open on Sundays; **Sonn|tags|fah|rer(in)** M(F) (pej) Sunday driver; **Sonn|tags|fahr|ver|bot** NT Sunday driving ban; **Sonn|tags|fra|ge** F (inf) question about voting intentions; **Sonn|tags-**

kind NT (*lit*) Sunday's child; **ein ~ sein** (*fig*) to have been born under a lucky star; **Sonn|tags|klei|dung** F Sunday clothes *pl*; **Sonn|tags|ma|ler(in)** M(F) Sunday painter; **Sonn|tags|re|de** (*iro*) **~n halten** to get up on one's soapbox from time to time; **Sonn|tags|red|ner(in)** M(F) (*iro*) soapbox speaker; **Sonn|tags|ru|he** F **die ~ stören/einhalten** to contravene the observance of/to observe Sunday as a day of rest; **Sonn|tags|schu|le** F Sunday school; **Sonn|tags|staat** M (*hum*) Sunday best; **in vollem ~** in one's Sunday best; **Sonn|tags|zei|tung** F Sunday paper

Sonn- und Fei|er|ta|ge PL Sundays and public holidays *pl*

sonn- und fei|er|tags [ˈzɔnʊntˈfaiɐtaːks] ADV on Sundays and public holidays

Sonn|wend-: Sonn|wend|fei|er F (*im Sommer*) midsummer celebrations *pl*; (*im Winter*) midwinter celebrations *pl*; **Sonn|wend|feu|er** NT *bonfire at midsummer/midwinter celebrations*

Son|ny|boy [ˈzɔnibɔy] M **-s, -s** (*inf*) blue-eyed boy (*inf*)

So|no|gra|fie ▲ [zonograˈfiː] F **-, -n** [-ˈfiːən] (*Med*) sonography

so|nor [zoˈnoːɐ] ADJ sonorous

So|no|ri|tät F **-, no pl** sonority (*form*), sonorousness

sonst [zɔnst] ADV **a** (= *außerdem*) (*mit pron, adv*) else; (*mit n*) other; **~ keine Besucher/Zeitungen** *etc* no other visitors/papers *etc*; **~ noch Fragen?** any other questions?; **wer/wie** *etc* (**denn**) **~?** who/how *etc* else?; **bringst du all deine Freunde mit?** – **was denn ~** are you bringing all your friends? – of course; **~ niemand** *or* **keiner/(noch) jemand** *or* **wer** (*inf*) nobody/somebody else; **das kannst du ~ jemandem** *or* **wem** (*inf*) **erzählen** tell that to the marines (*Brit inf*) *or* to the judge (*US*); **der Text ist von Handke oder ~ jemandem** *or* **wem** (*inf*) the text is by Handke or somebody; **da kann ~ wer kommen, wir machen keine Ausnahme** (*inf*) it doesn't matter who it is, we're not making any exceptions; **das kannst du ~ wem schenken** (*inf*) you can give that to some other sucker (*inf*) *or* to somebody else; **es könnte ~ wer kommen** (*inf*) anybody might come; **ich will weder dich noch ~ jemanden** *or* **wen** (*inf*) **sehen** I don't want to see you or anyone else; **er und ~ keiner** nobody else but he, he and nobody else, he and he alone; **wenn du ~ irgendjemanden kennst** if you know somebody else *or* anybody else *or* any other person; **~ wann** (*inf*) some other time; **wenn du ~ irgendwann mal kommen kannst** if you can come some or any other time; **er denkt, er ist ~ wer** (*inf*) he thinks he's somebody special, he thinks he's the bee's knees (*Brit inf*) *or* the cat's whiskers (*Brit inf*) *or* the cat's meow (*US inf*); **~ nichts/noch etwas** nothing/something else; **da kann ja ~ was passieren** (*inf*) anything could happen; **von mir aus kannst du ~ was machen** (*inf*) as far as I'm concerned you can do whatever you like; **ich habe ~ was versucht** (*inf*) I've tried everything; **ich werde weder das tun noch ~ was** (*inf*) I won't do that or anything else; **~ noch etwas?** is that all?, anything else?; (*in Geschäft auch*) will there be anything else?, will that be all?; **ja ~ noch was?** (*iro inf*) that'd be right! (*inf*); **~ wie** (*inf*) (in) some other way; (= *sehr*) like mad (*inf*) *or* crazy (*inf*); **~ wo** somewhere else; **~ wo, nur nicht hier** anywhere (else) but here; **~ wohin** somewhere else; **wo soll ich hingehen? – von mir aus ~ wohin** where should I go? – (as far as I'm concerned,) anywhere you like; **das kannst du dir ~ wohin stecken!** (*inf*) you can stuff that! (*inf*), you know where you can put that! (*inf*); **~ bist du gesund?** (*iro inf*) **gehts dir gut?** (*iro inf*) are you feeling okay? (*inf*); **~ willst du nichts?** (*iro inf*) anything else you'd like?; **und wer weiß was ~ noch alles** and goodness knows what else; **wo warst du ~ überall?** where else were

you? **b** (= *andernfalls, im übrigen*) otherwise; **wie gehts ~?** how are things otherwise *or* apart from that? **c** (= *in anderer Hinsicht*) in other ways; **wenn ich Ihnen ~ noch behilflich sein kann** if I can help you in any *or* some other way **d** (= *gewöhnlich*) usually; **genau wie es ~ ist** just as it usually is; **genau wie ~** the same as usual; **anders als ~** different from usual; **mehr/weniger als ~** more/less than usual; **der ~ so mürrische Herr Grün war heute direkt freundlich** Mr Grün, who is usually so grumpy, was really friendly today **e** (= *früher*) **alles war wie ~** everything was as it always used to be; **war das auch ~ der Fall?** was that always the case?; **wenn er ~ zu Besuch hier war** when he has visited us before **CONJ** otherwise, or (else)

sons|tig [ˈzɔnstɪç] ADJ *attr* other; *Fragen, Auskünfte etc* further; **aber ihr ~es Verhalten ist/ihre ~en Leistungen sind verhältnismäßig gut** but her behaviour (*Brit*) *or* behavior (*US*)/performance otherwise is quite good; **„Sonstiges"** "other"

sonst-: sonst|je|mand △ INDEF PRON (*inf*) → **sonst** ADV a; **sonst|wann** △ ADV → **sonst** ADV a; **sonst|was** △ INDEF PRON → **sonst** ADV a; **sonst|wer** △ INDEF PRON → **sonst** ADV a; **sonst|wie** △ ADV → **sonst** ADV a; **sonst|wo** △ ADV → **sonst** ADV a; **sonst|wo|hin** △ ADV → **sonst** ADV a

so|oft [zoˈɔft] CONJ whenever

Soor [zoːɐ] M **-(e)s, -e** (*Med*) thrush *no art*

So|phis|mus [zoˈfɪsmʊs] M **-, Sophismen** [-mən] sophism

So|phist [zoˈfɪst] M **-en, -en, So|phis|tin** [-ˈfɪstɪn] F **-, -nen** sophist

So|phis|te|rei [zofɪstəˈrai] F **-, -en** sophistry

So|phis|tik [zoˈfɪstɪk] F **-, no pl** sophistry

So|phok|les [ˈzoːfokles] M **-'** Sophocles

Sop|ran [zoˈpraːn] M **-s, -e** soprano; (= *Knabensopran, Instrumentensopran auch*) treble; (*Chorstimmen*) sopranos *pl*/trebles *pl*

Sop|ra|nist [zopraˈnɪst] M **-en, -en** treble

Sop|ra|nis|tin [zopraˈnɪstɪn] F **-, -nen** soprano

Sor|be [ˈzɔrbə] M **-n, -n, Sor|bin** [ˈzɔrbɪn] F **-, -nen** Sorb

Sor|bet [zɔrˈbeː] M OR NT **-s, -s, Sor|bett** [zɔrˈbet] M OR NT **-(e)s, -e** (*Cook*) sorbet

Sor|bin|säu|re [zɔrˈbiːn-] F sorbic acid

sor|bisch [ˈzɔrbɪʃ] ADJ Sorbian

Sor|bisch(e) [ˈzɔrbɪʃ] NT *decl as adj* (*Ling*) Sorbian → **Deutsch(e)**

So|re [ˈzoːrə] F **-, no pl** (*sl*) loot, swag (*hum*)

Sor|ge [ˈzɔrgə] F **-, -n** **a** worry; (= *Ärger*) trouble; (= *Kummer*) care, worry; **frei von ~n** free of care *or* worries; **keine ~!** (*inf*) don't (you) worry!; **~ haben, ob/dass ...** to be worried whether/that ...; **wir betrachten diese Entwicklung mit ~** we view this development with concern; **~n haben** to have problems; **nichts als ~n haben** to have nothing but problems (*inf*); **ich habe solche ~** I'm so worried; **du hast ~n!** (*iro*) **deine ~ möchte ich haben!** (*iro*) I wish that's all you've got problems!; **~n haben die Leute!** the worries people have!; **mit ihm/damit haben wir nichts als ~n** we've had nothing but trouble with him/that; **ich habe andere ~n, als ...** I have other things to worry about than ...; **jdm ~n machen** *or* **bereiten** (= *Kummer bereiten*) to cause sb a lot of worry; (= *beunruhigen*) to worry sb; **es macht mir ~n, dass ...** it worries me that ...; **in ~ (dat) sein** to be worried; **sich (dat) ~n machen** to worry; **wir haben uns solche ~n gemacht** we were so worried; **machen Sie sich deshalb keine ~n** don't worry about that; **seien Sie ohne ~!** (*geh*) do not fear (*liter*) or worry; **lassen Sie das meine ~ sein** let me worry about that; **das ist nicht meine ~** that's not my problem; **für etw ~ tragen** (*geh*) to attend or see to

sth, to take care of sth; **dafür ~ tragen, dass ...** (*geh*) to see to it that ... **b** (= *Fürsorge, auch Jur*) care

Sor|ge-: sor|ge|be|rech|tigt ADJ **~ sein** to have custody; **Sor|ge|be|rech|tig|te(r)** [-bərɛçtɪçtə] MF *decl as adj* person having custody

sor|gen [ˈzɔrgn] VR to worry; **sich ~ um** to be worried about, to worry about **VI ~ für** (= *sich kümmern um*) to take care of, to look after; (= *betreuen auch*) to care for; (= *vorsorgen für*) to provide for; (= *herbeischaffen*) *Proviant, Musik* to provide; (= *bewirken*) to ensure; *Aufregung* to cause; **dafür ~, dass ...** to see to it that ..., to make sure that ...; **für Schlagzeilen ~** to make headlines; **für Wirbel ~** to cause a commotion; **für Ruhe/einen reibungslosen Ablauf ~** to make sure that things are quiet/go smoothly; **für Aufsehen ~** to cause a sensation; **das reichlich fließende Bier sorgte für Stimmung** the plentiful supply of beer made sure that things went with a swing; **dafür ist gesorgt** that's taken care of

Sor|gen-: Sor|gen|fal|te F worry line; **sor|gen|frei** ADJ free of care; (= *heiter, sich keine Sorgen machend*) carefree; **~ leben** to live a carefree life; **Sor|gen|kind** NT (*inf*) problem child; (*fig auch*) biggest headache (*inf*); **Aktion ~** (*dated*) charity for people with disabilities; **Sor|gen|last** F (*geh*) burden of one's cares; **sor|gen|los** ADJ, ADV = **sorgenfrei**; **Sor|gen|püpp|chen** NT worry doll; **sor|gen|schwer** ADJ *Stimme, Blick* troubled; *Leben* full of cares; **Sor|gen|te|le|fon** NT helpline; **sor|gen|voll** ADJ *Blick, Miene* worried; *Leben* full of worries ADV *sagen* worried, with worry; **~ seufzen** to give a worried sigh; **..., seufzte er ~ ...**, he said with a worried sigh; **etw ~ betrachten** to view sth with concern; **einer Sache ~ entgegensehen** to await sth with concern

Sor|ge|recht NT (*Jur*) custody

Sorg|falt [ˈzɔrkfalt] F **-, no pl** care; **ohne ~ arbeiten** to work carelessly; **viel ~ auf etw** (*acc*) **verwenden** to take a lot of care over sth

sorg|fäl|tig [ˈzɔrkfɛltɪç] ADJ careful ADV carefully

Sorg|falts|pflicht F (*Jur*) duty of care to a child; **Verletzung der ~** negligence of one's duties as a parent *or* (*als Vormund*) as a guardian

sorg|los ADJ (= *unbekümmert*) carefree; (= *leichtfertig, nachlässig*) careless ADV carelessly; **in a carefree way**; **jdm ~ vertrauen** to trust sb implicitly; **sie geht ganz ~ mit den Kindern um** she gets along with the children so easily

Sorg|lo|sig|keit F **-, no pl** (= *Unbekümmertheit*) carefreeness; (= *Leichtfertigkeit*) carelessness

sorg|sam [ˈzɔrkzaːm] ADJ careful ADV carefully; **ein ~ gehütetes Geheimnis** a well-guarded secret

Sor|te [ˈzɔrtə] F **-, -n** **a** sort, type, kind; (*von Waren*) variety, type; (= *Qualität, Klasse*) grade; (= *Marke*) brand; **beste** *or* **erste ~** top quality *or* grade; **diese Psychiater sind eine ganz komische ~** these psychiatrists are quite a peculiar bunch (*inf*) **b** (*Fin*) *usu pl* foreign currency

Sor|ten-: Sor|ten|ge|schäft NT, **Sor|ten|han|del** M (*Fin*) foreign currency trading; **Sor|ten|kurs** M (*Fin*) exchange rate (*for notes and coins*)

sor|ten|rein ADJ *Materialien* unmixed ADV **Materialien ~ trennen** to separate out materials

Sor|ter [ˈzɔrtɐ] M **-s, -** sorting machine, sorter

sor|tie|ren [zɔrˈtiːrən] *ptp* **sortiert** VT to sort (*auch Comput*); *Waren (nach Qualität, Größe auch*) to grade; **etw in einen Schrank/ein Regal** *etc* **~** to sort sth and put it in a cupboard/bookcase *etc*

Sor|tie|rer [zɔrˈtiːrɐ] M **-s, -, Sor|tie|re|rin** [-ərɪn] F **-, -nen** sorter

Sor|tier-: Sor|tier|feld NT (*Comput*) sort field; **Sor|tier|lauf** M (*Comput*) sort run; **Sor|tier-**

ma|schi|ne F sorting machine, sorter; **Sor|tier|schlüs|sel** M (*Comput*) sort key

Sor|tie|rung [zɔrˈtiːrʊŋ] F **-, -en** sorting; (*Comput: von Daten*) sort

Sor|tier|wert M (*Comput*) sort value

Sor|ti|ment [zɔrtiˈmɛnt] NT **-(e)s, -e a** assortment; (*von Waren*) range, assortment; (= *Sammlung*) collection; **etw ins ~ nehmen** to add sth to one's range; **etw aus dem ~ nehmen** to drop sth from one's range **b** (= *Buchhandel*) retail book trade

Sor|ti|men|ter [zɔrtiˈmɛntɐ] M **-s, -**, **Sor|ti|men|te|rin** [-ərɪn] F **-, -nen** retail bookseller, book retailer

Sor|ti|ments-: Sor|ti|ments|buch|han|del M retail book trade; **Sor|ti|ments|buch|händ|ler(in)** M(F) retail bookseller, book retailer; **Sor|ti|ments|buch|hand|lung** F retail bookshop (*esp Brit*) or bookstore (*esp US*)

SOS [ɛsloːˈlɛs] NT **-, -** SOS; **~ funken** to put out an SOS

so|sehr [zoˈzeːɐ] CONJ however much, no matter how much

So|sein [ˈzoːzaɪn] NT (*Philos*) essence

SOS-Kin|der|dorf NT *children's home organized into family units*

so|so [zoˈzoː] **ADV** (*inf*: = *einigermaßen*) so-so (*inf*), middling (*inf*) **INTERJ** **~!** I see!; (*indigniert, iro auch*) really!; (*interessiert-gelassen auch*) oh yes?; (*erstaunt*) well well!; (*drohend*) well!

SOS-Ruf M (*lit*) SOS (call), Mayday; (*fig*) SOS

So|ße [ˈzoːsə] F **-, -n** sauce; (= *Bratensoße*) gravy; (*pej inf*) gunge (*Brit inf*), goo (*US inf*); (*sl:* = *Sperma*) spunk (*sl*), come (*sl*)

So|ßen|löf|fel M gravy spoon

sott *pret von* **sieden**

Soub|ret|te [zuˈbrɛtə] F **-, -n** soubrette

Souff|lé [zuˈfleː] NT **-s, -s**, **Souff|lee** ▲ NT **-s, -s** (*Cook*) soufflé

Souff|leur [zuˈfløːɐ] M **-s, -e** (*Theat*) prompter

Souff|leur|kas|ten [zuˈfløː-] M (*Theat*) prompt box

Souff|leu|se [zuˈfløːzə] F **-, -n** (*Theat*) prompter

souff|lie|ren [zuˈfliːrən] *ptp* **souffliert** VTI (*Theat*) to prompt; **jdm (den Text) ~** to prompt sb

Soul [soːl] M **-s**, *no pl* (*Mus*) soul

Sound [saʊnd] M **-s, -s** (*inf*) sound

Sound|kar|te F (*Comput*) sound card

so|und|so [ˈzoːlʊntzo] ADV **~ lange** for such and such a time; **~ groß/breit** of such and such a size/width; **~ oft** n (number of) times; **~ viele** so and so many; **Paragraf ~** article such-and-such or so-and-so; **er sagte, mach das ~** he said, do it in such and such a way

So|und|so [ˈzoːlʊntzo] M **-s, -s** or f **-, -s der ~** whatshisname; **die ~** whatshername; **Herr/Frau ~** Mr/Mrs So-and-so; **eine Margot ~ hat gesagt ...** a Margot Something-or-other said ...

so|und|so|viel|te(r, s) [ˈzoːlʊntzoˈfiːltə] ADJ umpteenth; **am/bis zum Soundsovielten** (*Datum*) on such and such a date; **er ist der Soundsovielte, der ...** he's the umpteenth person who ... (*inf*)

Sound|track [ˈsaʊndtrɛk] M **-s, -s** (*inf*) soundtrack (music)

Sou|per [zuˈpeː] NT **-s, -s** (*geh*) dinner

sou|pie|ren [zuˈpiːrən] *ptp* **soupiert** VI (*geh*) to dine

Sou|ta|ne [zuˈtaːnə] F **-, -n** (*Eccl*) cassock

Sou|ter|rain [zutɛˈrɛ̃, ˈzuːtɛrɛ̃] NT **-s, -s** basement

Sou|ve|nir [zuvəˈniːɐ] NT **-s, -s** souvenir

Sou|ve|nir-: Sou|ve|nir|jä|ger(in) M(F) (*inf*) souvenir hunter; **Sou|ve|nir|la|den** M souvenir shop

sou|ve|rän [zuvəˈrɛːn] ADJ sovereign *no adv*; (*fig*) supremely good; (= *überlegen*) (most) superior *no adv*; *Sieg* commanding; **das Land wurde ~** the country became a sovereign state

ADV **a ~ regieren** to rule as (the) sovereign, to have sovereign power, to be sovereign **b** (= *überlegen*) handhaben supremely well; **etw ~ meistern** to resolve sth masterfully; **~ siegen** to win a commanding victory; **sein Gebiet ~ beherrschen** to have a commanding knowledge of one's field; **die Lage ~ beherrschen** to be in full command of the situation; **eine Sprache ~ beherrschen** to have a superb command of a language; **er ist ganz ~ darüber hinweggegangen** he blithely ignored it

Sou|ve|rän [zuvəˈrɛːn] M **-s, -e** sovereign; (= *Parlament, Organisation*) sovereign power

Sou|ve|rä|ni|tät [zuvərɛniˈtɛːt] F **-**, *no pl* sovereignty; (*fig*) (= *Überlegenheit*) superiority; (= *Leichtigkeit*) supreme ease

so|viel [zoˈfiːl] △ **ADV** → **viel a CONJ** as or so far as; **~ ich weiß, nicht!** not as or so far as I know; **~ ich auch ...** however much I ...

so|viel|mal [zoˈfiːlmaːl] **ADV** so many times **CONJ** **~ ... auch ...** no matter how many times ..., however many times ...

so|weit [zoˈvaɪt] △ **ADV** → **weit 1 d 2 d CONJ** as or so far as; (= *insofern*) in so far as; **~ ich sehe** as or so far as I can tell or see

so|we|nig [zoˈveːnɪç] △ **ADV** → **wenig ADJ a CONJ** however little, little ...; **~ ich auch ...** however little I ...

so|wie [zoˈviː] CONJ **a** (= *sobald*) as soon as, the moment (*inf*) **b** (= *und auch*) as well as

so|wie|so [zoviˈzoː] ADV anyway, anyhow, in any case; **wir sind ~ nicht gegangen** we didn't go anyway or anyhow or in any case; **das ~!** obviously!, of course!, that goes without saying

Sow|jet [zɔˈvjɛt, ˈzɔvjɛt] M (*Hist*) **-s, -s** Soviet

Sow|jet|ar|mee F (*Hist*) Soviet Army

Sow|jet|bür|ger(in) M(F) (*Hist*) Soviet citizen

sow|je|tisch [zɔˈvjɛtɪʃ, zɔˈvjeːtɪʃ] ADJ (*Hist*) Soviet

Sow|jet- (*Hist*): **Sow|jet|macht** F Soviet power *no art*; **Sow|jet|mensch** M Soviet citizen; **Sow|jet|re|pub|lik** F Soviet Republic; **Union der Sozialistischen ~en** Union of Soviet Socialist Republics; **Sow|jet|rus|se** M , **Sow|jet|rus|sin** F Soviet Russian; **Sow|jet|staat** M Soviet State; **Sow|jet|stern** M Soviet star, star of the Soviets; **Sow|jet|uni|on** F Soviet Union; **Sow|jet|zo|ne** F (*Hist*) Soviet zone

so|wohl [zoˈvoːl] CONJ **~ ... als** or **wie (auch)** both ... and, ... as well as

So|zi [ˈzoːtsi] M **-s, -s** (*pej inf*) Socialist

So|zia [ˈzoːtsia] F **-, -s a** (= *Partner*) partner **b** (*usu hum:* = *Beifahrerin*) pillion rider or passenger

so|zi|al [zoˈtsiaːl] ADJ social; (= *sozial bewusst*) socially conscious; (= *das Gemeinwohl denkend*) public-spirited; **die ~en Berufe** the caring professions; **~e Dienste** social services; **~er Wohnungsbau** ≈ council (*Brit*) or public (*US*) housing; **~es Jahr** year spent by young person as voluntary assistant in hospitals, with social services etc **~e Indikation** (*bei Abtreibung*) social factor; **~er Friede** social harmony; **~e Marktwirtschaft** social market economy; **~e Sicherheit** social security (*as a concept*); **ich habe heute meinen ~en Tag!** (*inf*) I'm feeling charitable today

ADV **~ eingestellt sein** to be public-spirited; **~ handeln** to act for the good of all; **~ denken** to be socially minded

So|zi|al-: So|zi|al|ab|bau M , *no pl* cuts *pl* in social services; **So|zi|al|ab|ga|ben** PL social security (*Brit*) or social welfare (*US*) contributions *pl*; **So|zi|al|amt** NT social security (*Brit*) or social welfare (*US*) office; **So|zi|al|ar|beit** F social work; **So|zi|al|ar|bei|ter(in)** M(F) social worker; **So|zi|al|aus|ga|ben** PL public spending *sing*; **So|zi|al|aus|schuss** ▲ M social committee; **So|zi|al|bei|trä|ge** PL social

security (*Brit*) or social welfare (*US*) contributions *pl*; (*Parl*) welfare report; **So|zi|al|be|ruf** M caring profession; **So|zi|al|bin|dung** F social obligation scheme (*restricting rents etc to a socially acceptable level*), rent control regulations *pl*; **unter die ~ fallen** to come under the social obligation scheme or under rent control regulations; **So|zi|al|dar|wi|nis|mus** M social Darwinism; **So|zi|al|de|mo|krat(in)** M(F) social democrat; **So|zi|al|de|mo|kra|tie** F social democracy; **so|zi|al|de|mo|kra|tisch** ADJ social democratic **ADV** **die ~ regierten Bundesländer** the states controlled by the Social Democrats; **~ wählen** to vote for the Social Democrats; **der ~ orientierte Flügel** the Social Democratic wing; **So|zi|al|de|mo|kra|tis|mus** [-demokraˈtɪsmʊs] M **-**, *no pl* (*pej*) social democracy; **So|zi|al|ein|rich|tun|gen** PL social facilities *pl*; **So|zi|al|ethik** F social ethics *sing*; **so|zi|al|ethisch** ADJ social-ethical; **So|zi|al|ex|per|te** M , **So|zi|al|ex|per|tin** F social affairs expert; **So|zi|al|fall** M hardship case; **So|zi|al|fa|schis|mus** M socialist fascism; **So|zi|al|fonds** M social capital; **So|zi|al|for|schung** F social research; **So|zi|al|für|sor|ge** F (*dated*) income support (*Brit*), welfare (aid) (*US*); **So|zi|al|ge|fü|ge** NT social fabric; **So|zi|al|ge|richt** NT (social) welfare tribunal; **So|zi|al|ge|schich|te** F social history; **So|zi|al|ge|setz|ge|bung** F social welfare legislation; **So|zi|al|hil|fe** F income support (*Brit*), welfare (aid) (*US*); **So|zi|al|hil|fe|emp|fän|ger(in)** M(F) person receiving income support (*Brit*) or welfare (aid) (*US*); **So|zi|al|hy|gie|ne** F public health or hygiene; **So|zi|al|im|pe|ri|a|lis|mus** M social imperialism

So|zi|a|li|sa|ti|on [zotsializaˈtsioːn] F **-**, *no pl* (*Psych, Sociol*) socialization

so|zi|a|li|sie|ren [zotsialiˈziːrən] *ptp* **sozialisiert** VT (*Psych, Sociol, Ind*) to socialize; (*Pol:* = *verstaatlichen*) to nationalize

So|zi|a|li|sie|rung F **-, -en** socialization; (= *Verstaatlichung*) nationalization

So|zi|a|lis|mus [zotsiaˈlɪsmʊs] M **-, Sozialismen** [-mən] socialism

So|zi|a|list [zotsiaˈlɪst] M **-en, -en**, **So|zi|a|lis|tin** [-ˈlɪstɪn] F **-, -nen** socialist

so|zi|a|lis|tisch [zotsiaˈlɪstɪʃ] **ADJ** socialist **ADV** socialistically

So|zi|al-: So|zi|al|kun|de F (*Schulfach*) social studies *pl*; **So|zi|al|leis|tun|gen** PL employers' contribution (*sometimes including pension scheme payments*); **So|zi|al|neid** M social envy; **so|zi|al|öko|no|misch** ADJ socio-economic; **So|zi|al|ord|nung** F social order; **So|zi|al|pä|da|go|ge** M , **So|zi|al|pä|da|go|gin** F social education worker; **So|zi|al|pä|da|go|gik** F social education; **So|zi|al|part|ner** PL unions and management *pl*; **wenn einer der ~ ...** if either unions or management ...; **So|zi|al|plan** M redundancy payments scheme; **So|zi|al|po|li|tik** F social policy; **so|zi|al|po|li|tisch** ADJ socio-political; **So|zi|al|pres|ti|ge** NT social standing; **So|zi|al|pro|dukt** NT national product; **So|zi|al|psy|cho|lo|gie** F social psychology; **So|zi|al|recht** NT social legislation; **So|zi|al|re|form** F social reform; **So|zi|al|ren|te** F social security pension; **So|zi|al|staat** M welfare state; **So|zi|al|sta|ti|on** F health and advice centre (*Brit*) or center (*US*); **So|zi|al|struk|tur** F social structure; **So|zi|al|sys|tem** NT social system; **So|zi|al|ta|rif** M subsidized rate; **So|zi|al|ver|si|che|rung** F national insurance (*Brit*), social security (*US*); **So|zi|al|ver|si|che|rungs|aus|weis** M ≈ national insurance card (*Brit*), ≈ social security card (*US*); **so|zi|al|ver|si|che|rungs|frei** ADJ exempt from social insurance or national insurance (*Brit*) or social security (*US*) *pred*; **so|zi|al|ver|si|che|rungs|pflich|tig** ADJ liable for social insurance or national insurance (*Brit*) or social security (*US*) *pred*;

So|zi|al|ver|si|che|rungs|trä|ger M ≈ Department of Social Security

So|zi|al-: **so|zi|al|ver|träg|lich** ADJ socially acceptable; **So|zi|al|wahl** F *election to the representative bodies of the state pension and health insurance schemes*; **So|zi|al|we|sen** NT social services *pl*; **So|zi|al|wis|sen|schaf|ten** PL social sciences *pl*; **so|zi|al|wis|sen|schaft|ler(in)** M(F) social scientist; **so|zi|al|wis|sen|schaft|lich** ADJ *attr* social science; **So|zi|al|woh|nung** F ≈ council flat (*Brit*), state-subsidized apartment; **So|zi|al|zu|la|ge** F (welfare) allowance

So|zie|tät [zotsie'tɛ:t] F **-, -en** **a** (*von Anwälten, Ärzten etc*) joint practice **b** (*Sociol: Gruppe*) social group, (branch of) society

so|zio- PREF socio-

So|zio-: **So|zio|gramm** [zotsio'gram] NT *pl* **-gramme** sociogram; **So|zio|gra|fie** ▲ [zotsiogra'fi:] F **-**, *no pl* sociography; **so|zio|kul|tu|rell** [sotsiokʊltu'rɛl] ADJ socio-cultural ADV socio-culturally; **So|zio|lekt** [zotsio'lɛkt] M **-(e)s, -e** sociolect; **So|zio|lin|guis|tik** [zotsiolɪŋ'ɡʊɪstɪk] F sociolinguistics *sing*; **so|zio|lin|guis|tisch** [zotsiolɪŋ'ɡʊɪstɪʃ] ADJ sociolinguistic

So|zio|lo|ge [zotsio'lo:ɡə] M **-n, -n**, **So|zio|lo|gin** [-'lo:ɡɪn] F **-, -nen** sociologist

So|zio|lo|gie [zotsiolo'ɡi:] F **-**, *no pl* sociology

so|zio|lo|gisch [zotsio'lo:ɡɪʃ] ADJ sociological ADV sociologically; **~ gesehen/betrachtet** from a sociological point of view

So|zio-: **So|zio|me|trie** [zotsiome'tri:] F **-**, *no pl* sociometry; **so|zi|o|öko|no|misch** [zotsiolø-ko'no:mɪʃ] ADJ socioeconomic ADV socioeconomically; **sein Sozialismus ist eher religiös als ~ fundiert** religious conviction rather than socioeconomic principle underpins his socialism

So|zi|us ['zo:tsiʊs] M **-, -se** **a** (= *Partner*) partner **b** (= *Beifahrer*) pillion rider *or* passenger **c** (*inf*: = *Soziussitz*) pillion (seat)

So|zi|us|sitz M pillion (seat)

so|zu|sa|gen [zo:tsu'za:gn, 'zo:tsuza:gn] ADV so to speak, as it were

Spach|tel ['ʃpaxtl] M **-s, -** *or* f **-, -n** **a** (*Werkzeug*) spatula **b** (*spec*: = *Spachtelmasse*) filler

Spach|tel|mas|se F filler

spach|teln ['ʃpaxtln] VT Mauerfugen, Ritzen to fill (in), to smooth over, to stop VI to do some filling; (*inf*: = *essen*) to tuck in (*inf*), to dig in (*US inf*)

Spa|gat¹ [ʃpa'ɡa:t] M OR NT **-(e)s, -e** (*lit*) splits *pl*; (*fig*) balancing act; **~ machen** to do the splits

Spa|gat² M **-(e)s, -e** (*S Ger, Aus*: = *Bindfaden*) string

Spa|get|ti¹ ▲ [ʃpa'ɡɛti, sp-] PL , **Spa|ghet|ti¹** PL spaghetti *sing*

Spa|get|ti² ▲ M , **Spa|ghet|ti²** M **-(s), -s**, **Spa|g(h)et|ti|fres|ser** M **-s, -**, **Spa|g(h)et|ti|fres|se|rin** F **-, -nen** (*pej inf*: = *Italiener*) wop (*pej sl*), Eyetie (*Brit pej sl*), dago (*pej sl*)

Spa|g(h)et|ti|trä|ger M (*Fashion*) shoestring (*Brit*) *or* spaghetti strap

Spa|g(h)et|ti|wes|tern M (*inf*) spaghetti western

spä|hen ['ʃpɛ:ən] VI to peer; (*durch Löcher etc auch*) to peep; (*vorsichtig auch*) to peek; (= *Mil*) to reconnoitre (*Brit*), to reconnoiter (*US*), to scout; **nach jdm/etw ~** to look out for sb/sth

Spä|her ['ʃpɛ:ɐ] M **-s, -**, **Spä|he|rin** [-ərɪn] F **-, -nen** (*old Mil*) scout; (= *Posten*) lookout

Späh|trupp M (*Mil*) reconnaissance *or* scouting party *or* patrol

spa|kig ['ʃpa:kɪç] ADJ (*N Ger*) Bettwäsche, Matratze mildewed

Spa|lier [ʃpa'li:ɐ] NT **-s, -e** **a** trellis; **am ~ zie|hen** to trellis, to train on a trellis **b** (*von Menschen*) row, line; (*zur Ehrenbezeigung*) guard of honour (*Brit*), honor guard (*US*); **~ stehen/ein ~ bilden** to form a guard of honour (*Brit*) *or* honor guard (*US*)

Spa|lier|obst NT wall fruit

Spalt [ʃpalt] M **-(e)s, -e** **a** (= *Öffnung*) gap, opening; (= *Riss*) crack; (= *Felsspalt*) crevice, fissure; **die Tür stand einen ~ offen** the door was slightly ajar; **die Tür/Augen einen ~ öffnen** to open the door/one's eyes slightly **b** (*fig*: = *Kluft*) split

spalt|bar ADJ (*Phys*) Material fissile

Spalt|bar|keit ['ʃpaltba:ɐkait] F **-**, *no pl* (*Phys*) fissionability

spalt|breit ADJ **ein ~er Schlitz** a narrow crack

Spalt|breit ['ʃpaltbrait] M **etw einen ~ öffnen** *etc* to open *etc* sth slightly

Spal|te ['ʃpaltə] F **-, -n** **a** (*esp Geol*) fissure; (= *esp Felsspalte*) cleft, crevice; (= *Gletscherspalte*) crevasse; (*in Wand*) crack; (*sl*: = *Vagina*) hole (*sl*) **b** (*Typ, Press*) column

spal|ten ['ʃpaltn] *ptp auch* **gespalten** VT (*lit, fig*) to split; (*Chem*) Öl to crack (*spec*); Holz to chop **Schädel** VR to split; (*Meinungen*) to be split → *auch* **gespalten**

Spalt-: **Spalt|ma|te|ri|al** NT fissile material; **Spalt|pilz** M (*old*) *usu pl* bacterium; **Spalt|pro|dukt** NT fission product

Spal|tung ['ʃpaltʊŋ] F **-, -en** (*lit, fig*) splitting; (*von Atomkernen auch*) fission; (*von Öl*) cracking (*spec*); (*in Partei etc*) split; (*eines Landes*) split, division; **die ~ der Persönlichkeit/des Bewusstseins** the split in his *etc* personality/mind

Spam|ming ['spɛmɪŋ] NT **-(s)**, *no pl* (*Comput, Internet*) spamming

Span [ʃpa:n] M **-(e)s, ⸚e** ['ʃpɛ:nə] (= *Hobelspan*) shaving; (= *Bohrspan auch*) boring; (*zum Feueranzünden*) piece of kindling; (= *Metallspan*) filing; **arbeiten, dass die Späne fliegen** to work furiously

spä|nen ['ʃpɛ:nən] VT Holzboden to scour with steel wool

Span|fer|kel NT sucking pig

Span|ge ['ʃpaŋə] F **-, -n** clasp; (= *Haarspange*) hair slide (*Brit*), barrette (*US*); (= *Schuhspange*) strap, bar; (= *Schnalle*) buckle; (= *Armspange*) bangle, bracelet

Span|gen|schuh M bar shoe

Spa|ni|el ['ʃpa:niəl] M **-s, -s** spaniel

Spa|ni|en ['ʃpa:niən] NT **-s** Spain

Spa|ni|er ['ʃpa:niɐ] M **-s, -**, **Spa|ni|e|rin** [-iərɪn] F **-, -nen** Spaniard; **die ~** the Spanish, the Spaniards; **stolz wie ein ~ sein** (*prov*) to be (very) proud

spa|nisch ['ʃpa:nɪʃ] ADJ Spanish; **Spanische Fliege** Spanish fly; **~e Wand** (folding) screen; **das kommt mir ~ vor** (*inf*) that seems odd to me

Spa|nisch(e) ['ʃpa:nɪʃ] NT Spanish → *auch* **Deutsch(e)**

Span|korb M chip basket

spann *pret von* **spinnen**

Spann [ʃpan] M **-(e)s, -e** instep

Spann-: **Spann|be|ton** M prestressed concrete; **Spann|bett|tuch** ▲ NT fitted sheet

Span|ne ['ʃpanə] F **-, -n** (*altes Längenmaß*) span; (*geh*: = *Zeitspanne*) while; (= *Verdienstspanne*) margin; **eine ~ Zeit** (*geh*) a space *or* span of time

span|nen ['ʃpanən] VT **a** Saite, Seil, Geigenbogen to tighten, to tauten; Bogen to draw; Feder to tension; Muskeln to tense, to flex; Strickteile, Wolle to stretch; Gewehr, Abzugshahn, Kameraverschluss to cock; **einen Tennisschläger ~** to put a tennis racket in a/the press **b** (= *straff befestigen*) Werkstück to clamp; Wäscheleine to put up; Netz, Plane, Bildleinwand to stretch; **einen Bogen in die Schreibmaschine ~** to insert *or* put a sheet in the typewriter **c** Zugtier to hitch up (an *+acc*, vor *+acc* to); **sich vor jds Karren ~ lassen** (*fig*) to let oneself be used by sb **d** (*fig*) **seine Erwartungen zu hoch ~** to set one's expectations too high; **die Ausstellung spannt einen weiten thematischen Bogen** the exhibition spans *or* covers a wide range of themes → **Folter** **e** → **gespannt** **f** (*S Ger, Aus inf*: = *merken*) to catch on to (*inf*), to get wise to (*inf*) VR **a** (*Haut*) to go *or* become taut; (*Muskeln*) to tense **b** **sich über etw** (*acc*) **~** (*Regenbogen, Brücke*) to span sth; (*Haut*) to stretch over sth VI **a** (*Kleidung*) to be (too) tight; (*Haut*) to be taut **b** (= *Gewehr spannen*) to cock; (= *Kamera spannen*) to cock the shutter

span|nend ADJ exciting; (*stärker*) thrilling; (*inf*: = *interessant*) fascinating; **machs nicht so ~!** (*inf*) don't keep me/us in suspense ADV full of suspense; **der Bericht liest sich ~** the report is thrilling to read; **er kann ~ erzählen** his stories are thrilling

Span|ner ['ʃpanɐ] M **-s, -** **a** (*für Tennisschläger*) press; (= *Hosenspanner*) hanger; (= *Schuhspanner*) shoetree; (= *Stiefelspanner*) boot tree **b** (*Zool*) geometer moth; (= *Raupe*) looper **c** (*inf*: = *Voyeur*) peeping Tom

-spän|ner [ʃpɛnɐ] *suf* **-s, -** *in cpds* **Vierspänner** *etc* four-in-hand *etc*

Span|ne|rin ['ʃpanərɪn] F **-, -nen** (*inf*: = *Voyeurin*) female peeping Tom

-spän|nig [ʃpɛnɪç] ADJ *suf* **vierspännig fahren** to drive a four-in-hand

Spann-: **Spann|kraft** F (*von Feder, Bremse*) tension; (*von Muskel*) tone, tonus (*spec*); (*fig*) vigour (*Brit*), vigor (*US*); **spann|kräf|tig** ADJ (*fig*) vigorous

Span|nung ['ʃpanʊŋ] F **-, -en** **a** *no pl* (*von Seil, Feder, Muskel etc*) tension, tautness; (*Mech*: = *innerer Druck*) stress; **wegen der zu großen ~ riss das Seil** the rope broke because the strain (on it) was too great **b** (*Elec*) voltage, tension; **unter ~ stehen** to be live **c** *no pl* (*fig*) excitement; (= *Spannungsgeladenheit*) suspense, tension; **mit großer/atemloser ~** with great/breathless excitement; **in erwartungsvoller ~** full of excited anticipation, full of excitement; **etw mit ~ erwarten** to await sth full of suspense; **seine mit ~ erwarteten Memoiren sind endlich erschienen** his eagerly awaited

---

memoirs have appeared at last **d** _no pl_ (= _innerliche, nervliche Anspannung_) tension **e** _usu pl_ (= _Feindseligkeit_) tension _no pl_

Span|nungs-: Span|nungs|ab|fall M voltage drop; **Span|nungs|feld** NT (_lit_) electric field; (_fig_) area of conflict; **span|nungs|frei** ADJ (_lit_) _Metall, Glas_ unstressed; (_fig_) relaxed; **Span|nungs|ge|biet** NT (_Pol_) flash point, area of tension; **Span|nungs|kopf|schmerz** M _usu pl_ tension headache; **Span|nungs|mes|ser** M **-s, -** (_Elec_) voltmeter; **Span|nungs|mo|ment** NT (_fig_) suspense-creating factor; **Span|nungs|prü|fer** M voltage detector; **Span|nungs|reg|ler** M voltage regulator; **Span|nungs|stoß** M surge; **Span|nungs|ver|hält|nis** NT tense or strained relationship; (_Pol auch_) tense or strained relations _pl_

Spann|wei|te F (_Math_) range; (_Archit_) span; (_Aviat_) (wing)span; (_von Vogelflügeln_) wing-spread, (wing)span

Span-: Span|plat|te F chipboard; **Span|schach|tel** F _small box made from very thin strips of wood_

Spant¹ [ʃpant] NT **-(e)s, -en** (_Naut_) rib

Spant² M **-(e)s, -en** (_Aviat_) frame

Spar-: Spar|brief M (_Fin_) savings certificate; **Spar|buch** NT savings book; (_bei Bank auch_) bankbook; **Spar|büch|se** F , **Spar|do|se** F piggy bank; **Spar|eck|zins** M basic savings rate; **Spar|ein|la|ge** F savings deposit

spa|ren [ʃpaːrən] **VT** to save; _Energie auch_ to conserve; **dadurch habe ich (mir) viel Geld/Zeit/Arbeit gespart** I saved (myself) a lot of money/time/work that way; **keine Kosten/Mühe ~** to spare no expense/effort; **spar dir deine guten Ratschläge!** (_inf_) you can keep your advice!; **diese Mühe/diese Kosten/das hätten Sie sich** (_dat_) **~ können** you could have saved or spared yourself the trouble/this expense/the bother; **diese Bemerkung hätten Sie sich** (_dat_) **~ können!** you should have kept that remark to yourself! **VI** to save; (= _sparsam sein, Haus halten_) to economize, to make savings; **an etw** (_dat_) **~** to be sparing with sth; (= _mit etw Haus halten_) to economize or save on sth; **bei etw ~** to save on sth; **er hatte nicht mit Lob gespart** he was unstinting or lavish in his praise; **für** or **auf etw** (_acc_) **~** to save up for sth; **am falschen Ort ~** to make false economies, to make savings in the wrong place; **spare in der Zeit, so hast du in der Not** (_Prov_) waste not, want not (_Prov_)

Spa|rer [ʃpaːrɐ] M **-s, -**, **Spa|re|rin** [-ərɪn] F **-, -nen** (_bei Bank etc_) saver

Spa|rer|frei|be|trag M (_Steuern_) savers' tax-free amount, allowance on savings

Spar|flam|me F low flame; (= _Zündflamme_) pilot light; **auf ~** (_fig inf_) just ticking over (_Brit inf_) or coming along (_US_); **auf ~ kochen** (_fig_) to soft-pedal (_inf_), to go easy

Spar|gel [ʃpargl] M **-s, -** or (_Sw_) **f -, -n** asparagus

Spar|gel|der PL savings _pl_

Spar|gel|spit|ze F asparagus tip

Spar-: Spar|gro|schen M nest egg; **Spar|gut|ha|ben** NT savings account; **Spar|kas|se** F savings bank; **Spar|kas|sen|buch** NT savings book, bankbook; **Spar|kon|to** NT savings or deposit account; **Spar|kurs** M economy drive (_Brit_), budget (_US_); **einen strikten ~ einhalten** to be on a strict economy drive (_Brit_) or budget (_US_)

spär|lich [ʃpɛːrlɪç] **ADJ** sparse; _Ausbeute, Reste, Einkünfte, Kenntnisse_ sketchy, scanty; _Beleuchtung_ poor; _Kleidung_ scanty, skimpy; _Mahl_ meagre (_Brit_), meager (_US_); _Nachfrage_ low **ADV** _bevölkert_ sparsely, thinly; _beleuchtet, besucht_ poorly; _eingerichtet_ sparsely; **~ bekleidet** scantily clad or dressed; **die Geldmittel fließen nur ~** the money is only coming slowly or in dribs and drabs

Spär|lich|keit F **-, no pl** sparseness; (_von Nachfrage_) low level; **die ~ meiner Kenntnisse auf dem Gebiet** my sketchy or scanty knowledge in this area

Spar-: Spar|maß|nah|me F economy (_Brit_) or budgeting (_US_) measure; **Spar|pa|ckung** F economy size (pack); **Spar|pa|ket** NT savings package; (_Pol_) package of austerity measures; **Spar|pfen|nig** M (_fig_) nest egg; **Spar|po|li|tik** F cost-cutting policy; **Spar|prä|mie** F savings premium; **Spar|preis** M economy price; **Spar|quo|te** F , **Spar|ra|te** **F** rate of saving

Spar|ren [ʃpaːrən] M **-s, -** rafter; **du hast ja einen ~ (zu viel im Kopf)** (_inf_) you must have a screw loose (_inf_)

Spar|ring [ʃpaːrɪŋ, 'sp-] NT **-s, no pl** (_Boxen_) sparring

Spar|rings-: Spar|rings|kampf M sparring bout; **Spar|rings|partner(in)** M(F) sparring partner

spar|sam [ʃpaːrzaːm] **ADJ** _Mensch_ thrifty; (= _haushälterisch, wirtschaftlich_) _Hausfrau, Motor, Verbrauch_ economical; **~ im Verbrauch** economical; **von einer Möglichkeit nur ~en Gebrauch machen** to make little use of an opportunity **ADV** _leben, essen_ economically; _verwenden_ sparingly; **~ wirtschaften** to keep expenses as low as possible; **~er wirtschaften** to spend less money; **mit etw ~ umgehen** or **sein** to be economical or sparing with sth; **von etw nur ~ Gebrauch machen** to make little use of sth

Spar|sam|keit F **-, no pl** thrift; (= _sparsames Haushalten_) economizing; **~ im Verbrauch** economy

Spar|schwein NT piggy bank

Spar|strumpf M money sock

Spar|ta|ki|a|de [ʃparta'kia:də, sp-] F **-, -n** Spartakiad

Spar|ta|kus|bund [ʃpartakʊs-, 'sp-] M , _no pl_ Spartacus league

Spar|ta|ner [ʃpar'ta:nɐ, sp-] M **-s, -**, **Spar|ta|ne|rin** [-ərɪn] F **-, -nen** Spartan

spar|ta|nisch [ʃpar'ta:nɪʃ, sp-] **ADJ** (_lit_) Spartan; (_fig auch_) spartan **ADV** spartanly; **~ leben** to lead a Spartan or spartan life

Spar|ta|rif M discount price; (_bei Strom, Gas etc_) economy rate; (_Telec_) reduced rate; **zum ~ einkaufen** to shop at discount prices

Spar|te [ʃpartə] F **-, -n a** (_Comm_) (= _Branche_) line of business; (= _Teilgebiet_) branch, area **b** (= _Rubrik_) section

Spar|ten|ka|nal M (_TV_) specialist channel

Spar-: Spar|ver|trag M savings agreement; **Spar|vo|lu|men** NT targeted savings figure; **Spar|zins** M interest _no pl_ (on a savings account); **Spar|zu|la|ge** F savings bonus

spas|misch [ʃpasmɪʃ, 'sp-], **spas|mo|disch** [ʃpas'mo:dɪʃ, sp-] ADJ (_Med_) spasmodic, spasmic

Spaß [ʃpaːs] M **-es, ⸚e** [ʃpɛːsə] (_no pl_: = _Vergnügen_) fun; (= _Scherz_) joke; (= _Streich_) prank, lark (_Brit inf_); **lass die dummen Späße!** stop fooling around!; **~ beiseite** joking apart; **viel ~!** have fun! (_auch iro_), have a good time!, enjoy yourself/yourselves!; **wir haben viel ~ gehabt** we had a lot of fun, we had a really good time, we enjoyed ourselves a lot; **an etw** (_dat_) **~ haben** to enjoy sth; **er hat viel ~ an seinem Garten** his garden gives him a lot of pleasure; **es macht mir ~/keinen ~ (, das zu tun)** it's fun/no fun (doing it), I enjoy or like/don't enjoy or like (doing) it; **wenns dir ~ macht** if you want to, if it turns you on (_inf_); **Hauptsache, es macht ~** the main thing is to have fun or to enjoy yourself; **~/keinen ~ machen** to be fun/no fun; **ich hab doch nur ~ gemacht!** I was only joking or kidding (_inf_)!, it was only (in (_Brit_)) or for) fun; **(nur so,) zum** or **aus ~** (just) for fun, (just) for the fun or hell of it (_inf_); **etw aus** or **im** or **zum ~ sagen** to say sth as a joke or in (_Brit_) or for fun; **das sage ich nicht bloß zum ~** I'm not say-

ing that for the fun of it, I kid you not (_hum inf_); **aus ~ an der Freude** (just) for the fun of it; **da hört der ~ auf, das ist kein ~ mehr** that's going beyond a joke; **aus (dem) ~ wurde Ernst** the fun turned deadly earnest; **~ muss sein** there's no harm in a joke; (_als Aufheiterung_) all work and no play (makes Jack a dull boy) (_prov_); **es war ein ~, ihm bei der Arbeit zuzusehen** it was a joy to see him at work; **sich** (_dat_) **einen ~ daraus machen, etw zu tun** to get enjoyment or a kick (_inf_) out of doing sth; **seinen ~ mit jdm treiben** to make fun of sb; (= _sich mit jdm vergnügen_) to have one's fun with sb; **lass** or **gönn ihm doch seinen** or **den ~!** let him enjoy himself, let him have his fun; **er versteht keinen ~** he has no sense of humour (_Brit_) or humor (_US_); (= _er lässt nicht mit sich spaßen_) he doesn't stand for any nonsense; **da verstehe ich keinen ~!** I won't stand for any nonsense; **das war ein teurer ~** (_inf_) that was an expensive business (_inf_)

Spaß|bad NT leisure pool

Späß|chen [ʃpɛːsçən] NT **-s, -** _dim von_ **Spaß** little joke

spa|ßen [ʃpaːsn] VI (_dated_) to joke, to jest; **mit Blutvergiftung ist nicht zu ~** blood poisoning is no joke or no joking matter; **mit radioaktivem Material ist nicht zu ~** radioactive material is no joke; **mit der aufgebrachten Menge ist nicht zu ~** an angry mob is not to be trifled with; **mit ihm ist nicht zu ~, er lässt nicht mit sich ~** he doesn't stand for any nonsense

spa|ßes|hal|ber ADV for the fun of it, for fun

spaß|haft, spa|ßig [ʃpaːsɪç] ADJ funny, droll

Späß|lein [ʃpɛːslain] NT **-s, -** little joke

Spaß-: Spaß|ma|cher(in) M(F) (= _Spaßvogel_) joker; (_im Zirkus_) clown; **Spaß|ver|der|ber** [-fɛɐdɛrbə] M **-s, -**, **Spaß|ver|der|be|rin** [-ərɪn] F **-, -nen** spoilsport, wet blanket (_inf_), killjoy; **Spaß|vo|gel** M joker

Spas|ti [ʃpasti] M **-s, -s** (_sl_) spastic (_sl_)

Spas|ti|ker [ʃpastikɐ, 'sp-] M **-s, -**, **Spas|ti|ke|rin** [-ərɪn] F **-, -nen** spastic

spas|tisch [ʃpastɪʃ, 'sp-] **ADJ** spastic **ADV** _sich bewegen_ spastically; **~ gelähmt** suffering from spastic paralysis

Spat [ʃpaːt] M **-(e)s, -e a** (_Miner_) spar **b** _no pl_ (_Vet_) spavin

spät [ʃpɛːt] **ADJ** late; _Reue, Ruhm, Glück_ belated; **am ~en Nachmittag** in the late afternoon; **im ~en 18. Jahrhundert** in the late 18th century; **die Werke des ~en Shakespeare, die ~en Werke Shakespeares** the works of the late(r) Shakespeare, Shakespeare's late(r) works; **ein ~es Mädchen** (_inf_) an old maid **ADV** late; **~ in der Nacht/am Tage** late at night/in the day; **es ist schon ~** it is late; **es wird schon ~** it is getting late; **heute Abend wird es ~** it'll be a late night tonight; (_nach Hause kommen_) I/he _etc_ will be late this evening; **gestern ist es (bei der Arbeit) ~ geworden** I worked late yesterday; **wir hatten gestern eine Party und da ist es ziemlich ~ geworden** we had a party yesterday and it went on fairly late; **wie ~ ist es?** what's the time?; **zu ~** too late; **er kommt morgens regelmäßig fünf Minuten zu ~** he's always five minutes late in the mornings; **der Zug ist zu ~ angekommen** the train arrived late; **wir sind ~ dran** we're late; **er hat erst ~ mit dem Schreiben angefangen** he only started writing late in life; **besser ~ als nie** (_prov_) better late than never (_prov_) → _auch_ **später**

Spät- _in cpds_ late; **Spät|auf|ste|her(in)** [-lauf-ʃteːɐ, -ɪn] M(F) late riser; **Spät|aus|sied|ler(in)** M(F) _emigrant of German origin from Eastern European state_; **Spät|bur|gun|der** M (= _Rebsorte_) pinot noir; **~ Rotwein/Weißherbst** (= _Wein_) red/rosé wine made from pinot noir grapes

Spa|tel [ʃpaːtl] M **-s, -** spatula

Spa|ten [ʃpaːtn] M **-s, -** spade

Spa|ten|stich M cut of the spade; **den ersten ~ tun** to turn the first sod

Spät|ent|wick|ler(in) M(F) late developer

spä|ter ['ʃpɛːtɐ] *comp von* **spät** ADJ later; (= *zukünftig*) future; **in der ~en Zukunft** further on in the future; **die Späteren** (*liter*) posterity *sing* ADV later (on); **das werden wir ~ erledigen** we'll settle that later (on); **ein paar Minuten ~** a few minutes later; **~ als** later than; **das war viel ~ als Augustus** that was much later (on) than Augustus; **was will er denn ~ (einmal) werden?** what does he want to do later (on)?; **an ~ denken** to think of the future; **bis ~!, also dann, auf ~!** see you later!

spä|ter|hin ['ʃpɛːtɐhɪn] ADV (*liter*) later (on)

spä|tes|tens ['ʃpɛːtəstns] ADV at the latest; **~ morgen/in einer Stunde** tomorrow/in one hour at the latest; **~ um 8 Uhr** not later than 8 o'clock, by 8 o'clock at the latest; **bis ~ in einer Woche** in one week at the latest

Spät-: **Spät|fol|ge** F *usu pl* late effect; **Spät|ge|bä|ren|de** [-gəbɛːrəndə] F *decl as adj* woman having her (first) child around forty, elderly prim (*Brit*); **Spät|ge|burt** F late birth; **Spät|go|tik** F late Gothic; **Spät|heim|keh|rer(in)** M(F) late returnee (*from a prisoner-of-war camp*); **Spät|herbst** M late autumn, late fall (*US*); **Spät|jahr** NT (*liter*) autumn, fall (*US*); **Spät|ka|pi|ta|lis|mus** M late capitalism; **Spät|le|se** F late vintage; **Spät|nach|mit|tag** M late afternoon; **Spät|nach|rich|ten** PL late(-night) news *sing*; **Spät|scha|den** M *usu pl* long-term damage; **Spät|schicht** F late shift; **Spät|som|mer** M late summer; **Spät|vor|stel|lung** F late show

Spatz [ʃpats] M **-en, -en** ⓐ sparrow; **wie ein ~ essen** to peck at one's food; **besser ein ~ in der Hand als eine Taube auf dem Dach** (*Prov*) a bird in the hand is worth two in the bush (*Prov*) → **pfeifen** ⓑ (*inf*: = *Kind*) tot, mite (*Brit*), halfpint (*US inf*); (= *Anrede*) darling, honey

Spätz|chen ['ʃpɛtsçən] NT **-s, -** *dim von* **Spatz** little sparrow; (*inf*, = *Kind*) tot, mite (*Brit*), halfpint (*US inf*); (= *Anrede*) honeybun (*inf*), sweetie pie (*inf*)

Spat|zen|hirn NT (*pej*) birdbrain (*inf*)

Spätz|le ['ʃpɛtslə] PL (*S Ger Cook*) spaetzle (*sort of pasta*)

Spät-: **Spät|zün|der(in)** M(F) (*hum inf*) **~ sein** (= *schwer von Begriff sein*) to be slow on the uptake; (= *spät im Leben mit etw anfangen*) to be a late starter; **Spät|zün|dung** F retarded ignition; **~ haben** (*inf*) to be slow on the uptake

spa|zie|ren [ʃpa'tsiːrən] *ptp* **spaziert** VI *aux sein* to stroll; (= *stolzieren*) to strut; **wir waren ~** we went for a walk or stroll

spa|zie|ren fah|ren ▲ *irreg* VI *aux sein* (*im Auto*) to go for a drive or ride or run; (*mit Fahrrad, Motorrad*) to go for a ride; **ich will nur ein bisschen ~** I just want to go for a little drive or ride or run; VT **jdn ~** to take sb for a drive or ride or run; **das Baby (im Kinderwagen) ~** to take the baby for a walk (in the pram (*Brit*) or baby carriage (*US*))

spa|zie|ren füh|ren ▲ VT **jdn ~** to take sb for a walk; **sie hat ihr neues Kleid/ihren Fotoapparat spazieren geführt** (*inf*) she paraded her new dress/her camera

spa|zie|ren ge|hen ▲ VI *irreg aux sein* to go for a walk or stroll; **ich gehe jetzt ein bisschen spazieren** I'm going to go for a little walk or stroll now

Spazier-: **Spa|zier|fahrt** F (*im Auto*) ride, drive, run; (*mit Fahrrad, Motorrad*) ride; **eine ~ machen** to go for a ride *etc*; **Spa|zier|gang** M *pl* **-gänge** walk, stroll; (*fig*) child's play *no art*, doddle (*Brit inf*); (*Match*) walkover; **einen ~ machen** to go for a walk or stroll; **~ im All** space walk, walk in space; **Spa|zier|gän|ger** [-gɛŋɐ] M **-s, -**, **Spa|zier|gän|ge|rin** [-ərɪn] F **-, -nen** stroller; **Spa|zier-**

zier|stock M walking stick; **Spa|zier|weg** M path, walk

SPD [espeː'deː] F - *abbr von* **Sozialdemokratische Partei Deutschlands**

SPD

Re-founded in 1945, the SPD (Sozialdemokratische Partei Deutschlands) is one of the large popular parties in Germany. It is traditionally a workers' party and supports social justice within a social market economy.

Specht [ʃpɛçt] M **-(e)s, -e** woodpecker

Speck [ʃpɛk] M **-(e)s, -e** (= *Schweinespeck*) bacon fat; (= *Schinkenspeck, durchwachsener Speck*) bacon; (= *Walspeck*) blubber; (*inf: bei Mensch*) fat, flab (*inf*), **mit ~ fängt man Mäuse** (*Prov*) you have to use a sprat to catch a mackerel (*prov*); **~ ansetzen** (*inf*) to get fat, to put on weight, to put it on (*inf*); **~ auf den Knochen haben** (*inf*) **~ drauf haben** (*inf*) to be fat; (*an Hüften*) to be broad in the beam (*inf*); **ran an den ~** (*inf*) let's get stuck in (*inf*)

Speck-: **Speck|bauch** M (*inf*) potbelly (*inf*), paunch; **speck|bäu|chig** [-bɔyçɪç] ADJ (*inf*) potbellied (*inf*); **Speck|gür|tel** M (*fig*) affluent areas outside city boundaries

spe|ckig ['ʃpɛkɪç] ADJ *Kleidung, Haar* greasy

Speck-: **Speck|na|cken** M fat neck; **speck|na|ckig** ADJ fat-necked; **Speck|schei|be** F (*bacon*) rasher; **Speck|schwar|te** F bacon rind; **wie eine ~ glänzen** (*inf*) to shine greasily; **Speck|sei|te** F side of bacon; **Speck|stein** M (*Miner*) soapstone, steatite

Spe|di|teur [ʃpedi'tøːɐ] M **-s, -e**, **Spe|di|teu|rin** [-'tøːrɪn] F **-, -nen** carrier, haulier, haulage contractor; (= *Zwischenspediteur*) forwarding agent; (*von Schiffsfracht*) shipper, shipping agent; (= *Umzugsfirma*) furniture remover

Spe|di|ti|on [ʃpedi'tsioːn] F **-, -en** ⓐ (= *das Spedieren*) carriage, transporting; (*auf dem Wasserweg*) shipping ⓑ (= *Firma*) haulage contractor; (= *Zwischenspedition*) forwarding agency; (= *Schiffskontor*) shipping agency; (= *Umzugsfirma*) removal firm; (= *Versandabteilung*) forwarding department

Speditions-: **Spe|di|ti|ons|bran|che** F haulage business; **Spe|di|ti|ons|fir|ma** F , **Spe|di|ti|ons|ge|schäft** NT haulage contractor; (= *Zwischenspediteur*) forwarding agency; (= *Schiffskontor*) shipping agency; (= *Umzugsfirma*) removal firm; **Spe|di|ti|ons|kauf|frau** F , **Spe|di|ti|ons|kauf|mann** M forwarding agent; **Spe|di|ti|ons|kos|ten** PL haulage (costs *pl*)

Speed¹ [spiːd] NT **-s, -s** (*inf: = Droge*) speed (*inf*)

Speed² [spiːd] M **-s, -s** (*Sport: = Spurt*) burst of speed

Speer [ʃpeːɐ] M **-(e)s, -e** spear; (*Sport*) javelin

Speer-: **Speer|spit|ze** F (*lit, fig*) spearhead; **Speer|wer|fen** NT **-s,** *no pl* (*Sport*) **das ~** the javelin, throwing the javelin; **im ~** in the javelin; **Speer|wer|fer(in)** M(F) (*Sport*) javelin thrower

Spei|che ['ʃpaɪçə] F **-, -n** ⓐ spoke; **dem Schicksal in die ~n greifen** or **fallen** (*fig*) to try to stop the wheel of fate ⓑ (*Anat*) radius

Spei|chel ['ʃpaɪçl] M **-s,** *no pl* saliva, spittle

Speichel-: **Spei|chel|drü|se** F salivary gland; **Spei|chel|fluss** ▲ M salivation; **Spei|chel|le|cker** [-lɛke] M **-s, -**, **Spei|chel|le|cke|rin** [-ərɪn] F **-, -nen** (*pej*) lickspittle, toady, bootlicker (*inf*); **Spei|chel|le|cke|rei** F (*pej inf*) toadying, bootlicking (*inf*)

Spei|cher ['ʃpaɪçɐ] M **-s, -** (= *Lagerhaus*) storehouse; (*im Haus*) loft, attic; (= *Wasserspeicher*) tank, reservoir; (*Comput*) memory, store; **auf dem ~** in the loft or attic

Speicher-: **Spei|cher|bat|te|rie** F storage battery, accumulator (*Brit*); **Spei|cher|be|cken** NT reservoir; **Spei|cher|chip** M (*Com-*

put) memory chip; **Spei|cher|dich|te** F (*Comput*) storage density; **Spei|cher|ein|heit** F (*Comput*) (= *Gerät*) storage device; (= *Einheit*) storage unit; **Spei|cher|er|wei|te|rung** F (*Comput*) memory expansion; **Spei|cher|funk|ti|on** F (*Comput*) memory function; **Spei|cher|ka|pa|zi|tät** F storage capacity; (*Comput*) memory capacity; **Spei|cher|kraft|werk** NT storage power station; **Spei|cher|mo|dul** [-moduːl] NT (*Comput*) memory module

spei|chern ['ʃpaɪçɐn] VT *Vorräte, Energie, Daten* to store; (= *abspeichern*) to save; (*fig*) *Gefühle* to store up VR to accumulate

Spei|cher-: **Spei|cher|ofen** M storage heater; **Spei|cher|plat|te** F (*Comput*) storage disk; **Spei|cher|platz** M (*Comput*) storage space; **spei|cher|re|si|dent** ADJ (*Comput*) memory-resident; **Spei|cher|schreib|ma|schi|ne** F memory typewriter; **Spei|cher|schutz** M (*Tech*) memory protection

Spei|che|rung ['ʃpaɪçərʊŋ] F **-, -en** storing, storage

Spei|cher|ver|wal|tung F (*Comput*) memory management

spei|en ['ʃpaɪən] *pret* **spie** [ʃpiː], *ptp* **gespie(e)n** [gə'ʃpiː(ə)n] VT to spit, to expectorate (*spec*); *Lava, Feuer* to spew (forth); *Wasser* to spout; *Flammen, Dämpfe* to belch (forth or out); (= *erbrechen*) to vomit; **der Drache spie Feuer** the dragon breathed fire → **Gift** VI (= *sich übergeben*) to vomit

Speis [ʃpaɪs] M **-es** [-zəs] *no pl* (*S Ger. = Mörtel*) mortar

Spei|se ['ʃpaɪzə] F **-, -n** ⓐ (*geh: = Nahrung*) food, fare (*liter*); (= *Gericht*) dish; (= *Süßspeise*) sweet (*Brit*), dessert; **~n und Getränke** meals and beverages; **vielen Dank für Speis und Trank** (*hum*) many thanks for the meal; **kalte und warme ~n** hot and cold meals; **erlesene ~n** choice dishes ⓑ *no pl* (= *Mörtel*) mortar ⓒ (*Metal*) speiss; (= *Glockenspeise*) bell metal

Speise-: **Spei|se|brei** M chyme; **Spei|se|eis** NT ice cream; **Spei|se|fett** NT cooking or edible fat; **Spei|se|kam|mer** F larder (*esp Brit*), pantry; **Spei|se|kar|te** F menu; **Spei|se|lei|tung** F (*Elec*) feeder, supply main; **Spei|se|lo|kal** NT restaurant

spei|sen ['ʃpaɪzn] *ptp also* (*hum*) **gespiesen** [gə'ʃpiːzn] VI (*geh*) to eat, to dine (*form*); **zu Abend ~** to have dinner, to dine (in the evening) (*form*); **zu Mittag ~** to have lunch; **wünsche wohl zu ~** I hope you enjoy your meal VT ⓐ (= *essen*) to eat, to dine on (*form*); **was wünschen Sie zu ~?** what do you wish to eat, sir/madam? ⓑ (*liter, Tech*) to feed; (*old*) *Gast* to dine VR **sich aus etw ~** (= *seinen Ursprung haben*) to have its source in sth; (= *finanziert werden*) to be financed by sth

Speisen-: **Spei|sen|auf|zug** M dumb waiter, service lift; **Spei|sen|fol|ge** F order of the menu or the courses

Spei|se-: **Spei|se|öl** NT salad oil; (*zum Braten*) cooking or edible oil; **Spei|se|plan** M today's/this week's *etc* menu; **Spei|se|quark** [-kvark] M quark; **Spei|se|res|te** PL leftovers *pl*; (*zwischen den Zähnen*) food particles *pl*; **Spei|se|röh|re** F (*Anat*) gullet; **Spei|se|saal** M dining hall; (*in Hotel etc*) dining room; (*auf Schiffen*) dining saloon; **Spei|se|salz** NT table salt; **Spei|se|schrank** M larder (*esp Brit*), pantry; **Spei|se|stär|ke** F cornflour (*Brit*), cornstarch (*US*); **Spei|se|wa|gen** M (*Rail*) dining car, restaurant car, diner (*esp US*); **Spei|se|wär|mer** [-vɛrmɐ] M **-s, -** hotplate; **Spei|se|zet|tel** M menu; **Spei|se|zim|mer** NT dining room

Spei|sung ['ʃpaɪzʊŋ] F **-, -en** (*geh*) feeding; (*Tech auch*) supply; **die ~ der fünftausend** the feeding of the five thousand

spei|übel ['ʃpaɪy:bl] ADJ **mir ist ~** I think I'm going to be sick or to throw up (*inf*); **da kann**

einem ~ **werden, wenn man das sieht** the sight of that is enough to make you feel sick

Spek|ta|bi|li|tät [ʃpɛktabili'tɛːt, sp-] F **-, -en** (dated Univ) (Mr) Dean

Spek|ta|kel¹ [ʃpɛk'taːkl] M **-s, -** (inf) row, rumpus (inf); (= Aufregung) fuss, palaver (inf)

Spek|ta|kel² [ʃpɛk'taːkl, sp-] NT **-s, -** (old) spectacle, show

spek|ta|ku|lär [ʃpɛktaku'lɛːɐ, sp-] **ADJ** spectacular **ADV** spectacularly

Spekt|ra pl von **Spektrum**

Spekt|ral- [ʃpɛk'traːl-, sp-]: **Spekt|ral|ana|ly|se** F spectrum analysis; **Spekt|ral|far|be** F colour (Brit) or color (US) of the spectrum

Spekt|ren pl von **Spektrum**

Spekt|ro|skop [ʃpɛktro'skoːp, sp-] NT **-s, -e** spectroscope

Spekt|rum ['ʃpɛktrʊm, 'sp-] NT **-s, Spektren** or **Spektra** [-trən, -tra] spectrum

Spe|ku|lant [ʃpeku'lant] M **-en, -en, Spe|ku|lan|tin** [-'lantɪn] F **-, -nen** speculator

Spe|ku|la|ti|on [ʃpekula'tsioːn] F **-, -en** a (Fin) speculation (mit in); b **mit Grundstücken** property speculation b (= Vermutung) speculation (über about); **das ist reine ~** that's pure or mere speculation; **~en anstellen** to speculate

Spe|ku|la|ti|ons-: **Spe|ku|la|ti|ons|ge|schäft** NT speculative transaction or operation; **es war ein ~, aber es hat sich gelohnt** it was a gamble but it was worth it; **Spe|ku|la|ti|ons|ge|winn** M speculative gains pl or profit; **Spe|ku|la|ti|ons|objekt** NT object of speculation; **Spe|ku|la|ti|ons|steu|er** F windfall tax, tax on speculative profits

Spe|ku|la|ti|us [ʃpeku'laːtsiʊs] M **-, -** spiced biscuit (Brit) or cookie (US)

spe|ku|la|tiv [ʃpekula'tiːf, sp-] **ADJ** speculative

spe|ku|lie|ren [ʃpeku'liːrən] ptp **spekuliert** VI a (Fin) to speculate (mit in) → **Baisse, Hausse** b (= Vermutungen anstellen) to speculate; **auf etw** (acc) **~** (inf) to have hopes of sth

Spell|che|cker ['spɛltʃɛkɐ] M **-s, -** (Comput) spellchecker

Spe|lun|ke [ʃpe'lʊŋkə] F **-, -n** (pej inf) dive (inf)

Spelz [ʃpɛlts] M **-es, -e** (Agr) spelt

Spel|ze ['ʃpɛltsə] F **-, -n** (Bot) husk; (von Gras) glume

spen|da|bel [ʃpɛn'daːbl] **ADJ** (inf) generous, open-handed

Spen|de ['ʃpɛndə] F **-, -n** donation; (= Beitrag) contribution; **eine ~ geben** or **machen** to give a donation/contribution, to donate/contribute something; **bitte eine kleine ~!** please give or donate or contribute something (for charity)

spen|den ['ʃpɛndn] VT Lebensmittel, Blut, Geld, Hilfsgüter to donate, to give; (= beitragen) Geld to contribute; Abendmahl, Segen to administer; Schatten to afford, to offer; Trost to give → **Beifall, Lob** VI to donate; (= Geld beitragen) to contribute; **bitte ~ Sie für das Rote Kreuz!** please donate/contribute something to or for the Red Cross

Spen|den-: **Spen|den|af|fä|re** F donations scandal; **Spen|den|ak|ti|on** F fund-raising or charity drive, fun-raiser; **Spen|den|auf|kom|men** NT revenue from donations; **Spen|den|auf|ruf** M charity appeal; **Spen|den|be|schaf|fung** F procuring of donations; **Spen|den|be|schei|ni|gung** F charitable donation certificate; **Spen|den|kon|to** NT donations account; **Spen|den|samm|ler(in)** M(F) fundraiser; **Spen|den|wasch|an|la|ge** F (Pol) donation-laundering scheme

Spen|der¹ ['ʃpɛndɐ] M **-s, -** (= Seifenspender etc) dispenser

Spen|der² ['ʃpɛndɐ] M **-s, -, Spen|de|rin** [-ərɪn] F **-, -nen** donator; (Med) donor; **wer war der edle ~?** (inf) to whom am I indebted?

Spen|der- in cpds (Med) donor; **Spen|der|aus|weis** M donor card; **Spen|der|blut** NT donor blood; **Spen|der|herz** NT donor heart

spen|die|ren [ʃpɛn'diːrən] ptp **spendiert** VT to buy, to get (jdm etw sb sth, sth for sb); **spendierst du mir einen?** (inf) are you going to buy or stand (esp Brit) me a drink?; **lass mal, das spendiere ich** forget it, it's on me

Spen|dier|ho|sen PL (inf) **seine ~ anhaben** to be in a generous mood, to be feeling generous

Speng|ler ['ʃpɛŋlɐ] M **-s, -, Speng|le|rin** [-ərɪn] F **-, -nen** (dial: = Klempner) plumber

Spen|zer ['ʃpɛntsɐ] M **-s, -** long-sleeved vest; (= kurze Jacke) short jacket

Sper|ber ['ʃpɛrbɐ] M **-s, -** sparrowhawk

Spe|renz|chen [ʃpe'rɛntsçən] PL , **Spe|ren|zi|en** [ʃpe'rɛntsiən] PL (inf) **~ machen** to make trouble, to be difficult

Sper|ling ['ʃpɛrlɪŋ] M **-s, -e** sparrow

Sper|ma ['ʃpɛrma, 'sp-] NT **-s, Spermen** or **-ta** [-mən, -ta] sperm

Sper|mio|gramm [ʃpɛrmio'gram, sp-] NT pl **-gramme** spermiogram

sper|mi|zid [ʃpɛrmi'tsiːt, sp-] **ADJ** spermicidal

Sper|mi|zid [ʃpɛrmi'tsiːt, sp-] NT **-(e)s, -e** [-də] spermicide

Sperrad △ NT → **Sperrrad**

sperr|an|gel|weit ['ʃpɛr'aŋl'vait] **ADV** (inf) **~ offen** wide open

Sperr-: **Sperr|bal|lon** M (Mil) barrage balloon; **Sperr|be|zirk** M no-go area, prohibited area; **Sperr|dif|fe|ren|zi|al** ▲ NT (Aut) locking differential

Sper|re ['ʃpɛrə] F **-, -n** a (= Hindernis, Schlagbaum, Bahnsteigsperre etc) barrier; (= Polizeisperre) roadblock; (Mil) obstacle; (Tech) locking device b (= Verbot, auch Sport) ban; (= Blockierung) blockade; (Comm) embargo; (= Nachrichtensperre) (news) blackout c (Psych) mental block; **ei|ne psychologische/emotionale ~** a mental/emotional block

sper|ren ['ʃpɛrən] VT a (= schließen) Grenze, Hafen, Straße, Brücke, Tunnel etc to close; Platz, Gegend to close (off); (Tech) to lock; **Tunnel gesperrt!** tunnel closed; **etw für jdn/etw ~** to close sth to sb/sth
b (Comm) Konto, Gelder to block, to freeze; Scheck, Kreditkarte to stop; (Comput) Daten, Zugriff to lock
c (Sport: = ausschließen) to ban
d (Sport: = behindern) Gegner to obstruct, to block
e (= verbieten) Einfuhr, Ausfuhr to ban; **jdm das Gehalt ~** to stop sb's salary; **jdm den Ausgang ~** (Mil) to confine sb to barracks
f (= abstellen) Gas, Strom, Telefon to cut off, to disconnect; **jdm den Strom/das Telefon ~** to cut off or disconnect sb's electricity/telephone
g (= einschließen) **jdn in etw** (acc) **~** to shut or lock sb in sth
h (Typ) to space out
VR **sich (gegen etw) ~** to ba(u)lk or jib (at sth); **jetzt lass dir doch auch einmal etwas schenken und sperr dich nicht so** can't you just accept a present for once and not be so ungracious
VI a (= nicht schließen: Tür, Fenster) to stick, to jam; (= blockiert sein: Räder) to lock
b (Sport) to obstruct; **Sperren ist nicht zulässig** obstruction is not allowed

Sperr-: **Sperr|feu|er** NT (Mil, fig) barrage; **sein Vorschlag geriet ins ~ der Kritik** his suggestion came in for a barrage of criticism; **Sperr|frist** F waiting period (auch Jur); (Sport) (period of) suspension; **Sperr|ge|biet** NT no-go area, prohibited area or zone; **Sperr|ge|trie|be** NT locking mechanism; **Sperr|gut** NT , no pl bulky freight or goods pl; **Sperr|holz** NT plywood

sper|rig ['ʃpɛrɪç] **ADJ** bulky; (= unhandlich) unwieldy; (fig) Slogan, Sprache unwieldy, clum-

sy; Text, Musik unwieldy; Thema, Charakter awkward; **sich ~ zeigen** to be awkward

Sperr-: **Sperr|ket|te** F chain; (an Haustür) safety chain; **Sperr|klau|sel** F exclusion clause; **Sperr|klin|ke** F pawl; **Sperr|kon|to** NT blocked account; **Sperr|kreis** M (Rad) wave trap; **Sperr|mau|er** F wall; **Sperr|mi|no|ri|tät** F (Fin) blocking minority; **Sperr|müll** M bulky refuse; **Sperr|müll|ab|fuhr** F removal of bulky refuse; **Sperrrad** ▲ NT ratchet wheel; **Sperr|schrift** M (Typ) spaced type; **Sperr|sitz** M (im Kino) back seats pl; (im Zirkus) front seats pl; (old: im Theater) stalls pl, orchestra; **Sperr|stück** M (Fin) blocked security; **Sperr|stun|de** F closing time

Sper|rung ['ʃpɛrʊŋ] F **-, -en** a (= Schließung) closing; (von Platz, Gegend) closing off; (Tech) locking; (von Konto) blocking; (von Scheck) stopping; (Sport: = Ausschluss) banning, barring; (= Verbot) banning; (von Urlaub, Gehalt) stopping, stoppage; (von Strom, Gas, Telefon) cutting off, disconnection, disconnecting; (Typ) spacing b = **Sperre** b

Sperr-: **Sperr|ver|merk** M (in Dokumenten) restricted notice; **Sperr|ver|trag** M (Pol) blocking treaty; **Sperr|zoll** M prohibitive tariff; **Sperr|zo|ne** F no-go area, prohibited area or zone

Spe|sen ['ʃpeːzn] PL (auch Fin) expenses pl; **auf ~ reisen/essen** to travel/eat on expenses; **außer ~ nichts gewesen** nothing doing, no joy (esp Brit inf)

Spe|sen-: **Spe|sen|ab|rech|nung** F calculation of expenses; **spe|sen|frei** **ADJ** free of charge; **Spe|sen|kon|to** NT expense account; **Spe|sen|rech|nung** F statement of expenses; **Spe|sen|rit|ter** M (inf) expense-account type (inf)

Spe|ze|rei [ʃpeːtsə'rai] F **-, -en** usu pl (old) spice; (= Delikatesse) exotic delicacy

Spe|zi¹ ['ʃpeːtsi] M **-s, -s** (S Ger inf) pal (inf), mate (Brit inf), buddy (esp US inf)

Spe|zi² NT **-s, -s** (Getränk) cola and orangeade

Spe|zi|al- [ʃpe'tsiaːl-]: **Spe|zi|al|arzt** M , **Spe|zi|al|ärz|tin** F specialist; **Spe|zi|al|aus|bil|dung** F specialized training; **Spe|zi|al|aus|füh|rung** F special model or version; **ein Modell in ~** a special version; **Spe|zi|al|dis|zip|lin** F special discipline; **Spe|zi|al|ef|fekt** M special effect; **Spe|zi|al|ein|heit** F special unit, special task force; **Spe|zi|al|fach** NT special subject; **Spe|zi|al|fahr|zeug** NT special-purpose vehicle; **Spe|zi|al|fall** M special case; **Spe|zi|al|ge|biet** NT special field or topic; **Spe|zi|al|ge|schäft** NT specialist shop; **ein ~ für Sportkleidung** a sportswear specialist's

spe|zi|a|li|sie|ren [ʃpetsiali'ziːrən] ptp **spezialisiert** VR **sich (auf etw** acc**) ~** to specialize (in sth) VT (old: = spezifizieren) to specify, to itemize

Spe|zi|a|li|sie|rung F **-, -en** specialization

Spe|zi|a|list [ʃpetsia'lɪst] M **-en, -en, Spe|zi|a|lis|tin** [-'lɪstɪn] F **-, -nen** specialist (für in)

Spe|zi|a|lis|ten|tum [ʃpetsia'lɪstntuːm] NT **-s**, no pl specialization

Spe|zi|a|li|tät [ʃpetsiali'tɛːt] F **-, -en** a speciality (Brit), specialty (US) b **Spezialitäten** PL (Cook) specialities pl; **~ des Hauses** (auf Speisekarte) speciality (Brit) or specialty (US) of the house

Spe|zi|a|li|tä|ten|res|tau|rant NT speciality (Brit) or specialty (US) restaurant

Spe|zi|al-: **Spe|zi|al|sla|lom** M special slalom; **Spe|zi|al|voll|macht** F special authorization

spe|zi|ell [ʃpe'tsiɛl] **ADJ** special; **auf Ihr (ganz) Spezielles!** (to) your good health!; **er ist mein ganz ~er Freund** he's a very special friend of mine (auch iro) **ADV** (e)specially

Spe|zi|es ['ʃpeːtsies, 'sp-] F **-, -** (Biol) species sing; **die ~ Mensch** the human species

---

Spe|zi|fi|ka|ti|on [ʃpetsifikaˈtsioːn, sp-] F -, -en specification; (= *Aufgliederung*) classification

Spe|zi|fi|kum [ʃpeˈtsiːfikʊm] NT -s, Spezifika [-ka] (*geh*: = *Besonderheit*) specific feature; (*Med*) specific

spe|zi|fisch [ʃpeˈtsiːfɪʃ, sp-] ADJ specific ADV specifically; (= *typisch*) typically

spe|zi|fi|zie|ren [ʃpetsifiˈtsiːrən, sp-] ptp **spezifiziert** VT to specify; (= *einzeln aufführen auch*) to itemize

Spe|zi|fi|zie|rung [ʃpetsifiˈtsiːrʊŋ, sp-] F -, -en specification, specifying; (= *Einzelaufführung auch*) itemization, itemizing

Sphä|re [ˈsfɛːrə] F -, -n (*lit, fig*) sphere → **schweben a**

Sphä|ren-: **Sphä|ren|har|mo|nie** F harmony of the spheres; **Sphä|ren|mu|sik** F music of the spheres

sphä|risch [ˈsfɛːrɪʃ] ADJ spherical; *Klänge, Musik* celestial

Sphinx [sfɪŋks] F -, -e sphinx

Spick-: **Spick|aal** M smoked eel; **Spick|bra|ten** M larded (*esp Brit*) or basted roast

spi|cken [ˈʃpɪkn] VT (*Cook*) Braten to lard (*esp Brit*), to baste; (*inf*: = *bestechen*) to bribe, to square (*Brit inf*); **eine (gut) gespickte Brieftasche** a well-lined wallet; **mit Zitaten gespickt** larded (*esp Brit*) or peppered with quotations; **mit Fehlern gespickt** peppered with mistakes VI (*Sch inf*) to copy, to crib (*Brit inf*) (*bei off, from*)

Spick|er [ˈʃpɪkɐ] M -s, - (*inf*), **Spick|zet|tel** M crib (*Brit*), cheat sheet (*US*)

spie pret von **speien**

Spie|gel [ˈʃpiːgl] M -s, - **a** mirror, glass (*old*); (*Med*) speculum; (*fig*) mirror; **in den ~ schauen** or **sehen** to look in the mirror; **glatt wie ein ~** like glass; **im ~ der Öffentlichkeit** or **der öffentlichen Meinung** as seen by the public, as reflected in public opinion; **jdm den ~ vorhalten** (*fig*) to hold up a mirror to sb **b** (= *Wasserspiegel, Alkoholspiegel, Zuckerspiegel*) level; (= *Wasseroberfläche*) surface **c** (= *Aufschlag*) lapel; (*Mil*: = *Kragenspiegel*) tab **d** (*Archit*: *von Decke, Tür*) panel **e** (*Hunt*) (*bei Rotwild*) escutcheon; (*bei Vögeln*) speculum **f** (*Liter*: = *Sammlung von Regeln, Gesetzen etc*) code **g** (*Typ*) type area

Spie|gel-: **Spie|gel|bild** NT (*lit, fig*) reflection; (= *seitenverkehrtes Bild*) mirror image; **die Schrift im ~** the mirror image of the writing; **spie|gel|bild|lich** ADJ (*lit, fig*) mirror image; **~ dazu ...** as a direct contrast, ... ADV **~ schreiben** to do mirror writing; **~ gleich sein** (*zwei Dinge*) to be the mirror image of each other; **spie|gel|blank** ADJ glossy, shining ADV **etw ~ putzen/polieren/reiben/wienern** to polish sth until it shines

Spie|gel|ei [ˈʃpiːgllai] NT fried egg

Spie|gel-: **Spie|gel|fech|te|rei** [-fɛçtəˈrai] F -, -en (*fig*) (= *Scheingefecht*) shadow-boxing; (= *Heuchelei, Vortäuschung*) sham, bluff; **Spie|gel|fern|rohr** NT reflector (telescope); **Spie|gel|fo|lie** F mirror foil; **spie|gel|frei** ADJ *Brille, Bildschirm etc* nonreflecting; **Spie|gel|glas** NT mirror glass; **spie|gel|glatt** ADJ *Fahrbahn, Meer etc* like glass pred, glassy; **spie|gel|gleich** ADJ symmetrical; **Spie|gel|gleich|heit** F symmetry; **Spie|gel|heck** NT (*Naut*) square stern; **Spie|gel|karp|fen** M mirror carp

spie|geln [ˈʃpiːgln] VI (= *reflektieren*) to reflect (the light); (= *glitzern*) to gleam, to shine VT to reflect, to mirror VR to be mirrored or reflected; (= *sich betrachten*) to look at one's reflection

Spie|gel-: **Spie|gel|re|flex|ka|me|ra** F reflex camera; **Spie|gel|schrift** F mirror writing; **etw in ~ schreiben** to write sth backwards

Spie|ge|lung [ˈʃpiːgəlʊŋ] F -, -en reflection; (= *Luftspiegelung*) mirage

spie|gel|ver|kehrt ADJ back-to-front, backward (*US*); **~e Abbildung** mirror image ADV **abbilden** in mirror image

Spie|ker [ˈʃpiːkɐ] M -s, - **a** (*N Ger.* = *Nagel*) nail; (*Naut*) spike **b** (*N Ger.* = *Speicher*) storehouse

Spiel [ʃpiːl] NT -(e)s, -e **a** (= *Unterhaltungsspiel, Glücksspiel, Sport, Tennis*) game; (= *Wettkampfspiel, Fußballspiel*) game, match; (*Theat*: = *Stück*) play; (*fig*: = *eine Leichtigkeit*) child's play *no art*; **ein ~ spielen** (*lit, fig*) to play a game; **im ~ sein** (*lit*) to be in the game; (*fig*) to be involved or at work; **die Kräfte, die hier mit im ~ waren** the forces which were at play here; **das Leben ist kein ~** life is not a game; **das ~ verloren geben** to give the game up for lost; (*fig*) to throw in the towel; **machen Sie ihr ~!** place your bets!, faites vos jeux; **das ~ machen** (*Sport*) to make the play; **jdn ins ~ schicken** (*Sport*) to send sb on; **jdn aus dem ~ nehmen** (*Sport*) to take sb off **b** (= *das Spielen, Spielweise*) play(ing); (*Mus, Theat*) playing; (*Sport*) play; (*bei Glücksspielen*) gambling; **das ~ ist für die Entwicklung des Kindes wichtig** play(ing) is important for children's development; **stör die Kinder nicht beim ~** don't disturb the children while they're playing or at play; **stummes ~** miming **c** (= *Bewegung, Zusammenspiel*) play; **~ der Hände** hand movements; **das (freie) ~ der Kräfte** the (free) (inter)play of forces; **~ der Lichter** play of lights; **das ~ der Wellen** the play of the waves **d** **ein ~ des Schicksals** or **Zufalls** a whim of fate **e** (= *Spielzubehör*) game; (*Cards*) deck, pack; (= *Satz*) set; **führen Sie auch ~e?** do you have games?; **das Monopolyspiel ist nicht mehr vollständig** the Monopoly® set has something missing **f** (*von Stricknadeln*) set **g** (*Tech*) (free) play; (= *Spielraum*) clearance **h** (*Hunt*) tail **i** (*fig*) **das ist ein ~ mit dem Feuer** that's playing with fire; **leichtes ~ (mit** or **bei jdm) haben** to have an easy job of it (with sb); **bei den einfachen Bauern hatten die Betrüger leichtes ~** the simple peasants were easy prey for the swindlers; **das ~ ist aus** the game's up; **die Hand** or **Finger im ~ haben** to have a hand in it; **jdn/etw aus dem ~ lassen** to leave or keep sb/sth out of it; **aus dem ~ bleiben** to stay or keep out of it; **jdn/etw ins ~ bringen** to bring sb/sth into it; **etw aufs ~ setzen** to put sth at stake or on the line (*inf*), to risk sth; **auf dem ~(e) stehen** to be at stake; **sein ~ mit jdm treiben** to play games with sb

Spiel-: **Spiel|al|ter** NT playing stage; **Spiel|an|zug** M playsuit, rompers pl; **Spiel|art** F variety; **Spiel|au|to|mat** M gambling or gaming machine; (*zum Geldgewinnen*) fruit machine, one-armed bandit (*hum inf*); **Spiel|bahn** F (*Golf*) fairway; **Spiel|ball** M (*Volleyball*) match ball, game ball (*US*); (*Tennis*) game point; (*Billard*) cue ball; (*fig*) plaything; **ein ~ der Wellen sein** (*geh*) to be at the mercy of the waves, to be tossed about by the waves; **Spiel|bank** F pl -banken casino; **spiel|bar** ADJ playable; *Theaterstück* actable; **Spiel|be|ginn** M start of play; **gleich nach ~** just after the start of play; **Spiel|bein** NT free leg; **spiel|be|reit** ADJ ready to play; **Spiel|brett** NT board; (*Basketball*) backboard

Spiel|chen [ˈʃpiːlçən] NT -s, - (*inf*) little game

Spiel|com|pu|ter M (*für Computerspiele*) games computer; (= *Lerncomputer*) educational computer

Spiel|do|se F musical box (*Brit*), music box

Spie|le|com|pu|ter M = Spielcomputer

spie|len [ˈʃpiːlən] VT to play; **Klavier/Flöte ~** to play the piano/the flute; **was wird heute im Theater/Kino gespielt?** what's on at the theatre (*Brit*) or theater (*US*)/cinema today?, what's playing at the theatre (*Brit*) or theater (*US*)/ what's showing at the cinema today?; **sie ~ einen Film von ...** they're showing a film by ...; **das Stück war sehr gut gespielt** the play was very well acted or performed or done; **wir haben die Mutter Courage in Stuttgart gespielt** we played Mother Courage in Stuttgart; **den Unschuldigen ~** to play the innocent; **den Beleidigten ~** to act all offended; **sie spielt die große Dame** she's playing or acting the grand lady or the grand old dame (*US*); **am Sonntag musste ich mal wieder Klempner ~** on Sunday I had to do my plumber's act again; **was wird hier gespielt?** (*inf*) what's going on here? → **Herr c, Schicksal**

VI to play; (*Theat*) (*Schauspieler*) to act, to play; (*Stück*) to be on, to be playing; (*Film*) to be on, to be showing; (*beim Glücksspiel*) to gamble; **die Mannschaft hat gut/schlecht etc gespielt** the team had a good/bad etc game, the team played well/badly etc; **bei ihm spielt das Radio den ganzen Tag** he has the radio on all day; **seine Beziehungen ~ lassen** to bring one's connections to bear or into play; **seine Muskeln ~ lassen** to ripple one's muscles; **wie das Leben so spielt** life's funny like that; **in der Hauptrolle spielt X** X is playing the lead; **das Stück spielt im 18. Jahrhundert/in Italien** the play is set in the 18th century/in Italy; **nervös spielte er mit dem Bleistift** he played or toyed nervously with the pencil; **mit dem Gedanken ~, etw zu tun** to toy or play with the idea of doing sth; **mit jdm/jds Liebe/Gefühlen ~** to play (around) with sb/sb's affections/feelings; **ein Lächeln spielte um ihre Lippen** a smile played about her lips; **ihr Haar spielt ins Rötliche** her hair has a reddish tinge

VR **sich müde ~** to tire oneself out playing; **sich warm ~** to warm up; **sich in den Vordergrund ~** to push oneself into the foreground; **auf nassem Boden spielt es sich schlecht** (*Sport*) wet ground isn't very good to play on → *auch* **gespielt**

spie|lend ADJ playing ADV easily; **das ist ~ leicht** that's very easy

Spiel|en|de [ˈʃpiːlˌlɛndə] NT end of play; **kurz vor ~** just before the end of play

Spie|ler [ˈʃpiːlɐ] M -s, -, **Spie|le|rin** [-ərɪn] F -, -nen player; (*Theat auch*) actor/actress; (= *Glücksspieler*) gambler

Spie|le|rei [ʃpiːləˈrai] F -, -en **a** no pl (= *das Spielen*) playing; (*beim Glücksspiel*) gambling; (= *das Herumspielen*) playing or fooling or fiddling (*inf*) about (*Brit*) or around; (= *Kinderspiel*) child's play no pl, doddle (*Brit inf*); **das ist nur ~** I am/he is etc just playing or fooling about (*Brit*) or around; **hör mit der ~ am Fernseher auf!** stop playing or fooling or fiddling (*inf*) about (*Brit*) or around with the TV! **b** (= *Gegenstand*) frivolity; (= *Gerät*) gadget

spie|le|risch [ˈʃpiːlərɪʃ] ADJ **a** (= *verspielt*) Geste, Katze etc playful **b** **mit ~er Leichtigkeit** with the greatest of ease, with consummate ease **c** (*Sport*) playing; (*Theat*) acting; **~es Können** playing/acting ability; **die ~e Leistung** the playing/acting ADV **a** (= *verspielt*) playfully **b** (= *mit Leichtigkeit*) with the greatest of ease, with consummate ease **c** (*Sport*) in playing terms; (*Theat*) in acting terms **d** (= *im Spiel*) **etw ~ lernen** to learn sth through play(ing)

Spie|ler-: **Spie|ler|na|tur** F gambler; **Spie|ler|wech|sel** M substitution

Spiel-: **Spiel|feld** NT field, pitch (*Brit*); (*Tennis, Squash, Basketball*) court; **Spiel|feld|hälf|te** F half (of the field or pitch (*Brit*)); (*Tennis, Squash, Basketball*) half (of the court); **Spiel|feld|rand** M touchline; **Spiel|fi|gur** F piece; **Spiel|film** M feature film; **Spiel|flä|che** F playing area; (*bei Gesellschaftsspielen*) playing surface; **Spiel|fol|ge** F (*Sport*) order of play; (*Theat*) programme (*Brit*), program (*US*); **spiel|frei** ADJ (*Theat, Sport*) **~er Tag** rest day;

die ~e Zeit the close season; **der Sonntag ist ~** there is no performance on Sundays; (*Sport*) there is no game on Sundays; **spiel|freu|dig** ADJ keen, enthusiastic; **Spiel|füh|rer(in)** M(F) (team) captain; **Spiel|ge|fähr|te** M , **Spiel|ge|fähr|tin** F playmate, playfellow (*Brit*); **Spiel|geld** NT a (= *Einsatz*) stake b (= *unechtes Geld*) play money, toy money (*Brit*); **Spiel|ge|nos|se** M , **Spiel|ge|nos|sin** F playmate, playfellow (*Brit*); **Spiel|ge|sche-hen** NT (*Sport*) play, action; **das gesamte ~** all of the play or action; **Spiel|ge|stal|ter** [-gəʃtaltɐ] M -s, -, **Spiel|ge|stal|te|rin** [-ərɪn] F -, -nen (*Sport*) key player; **Spiel|hal|le** F amusement arcade (*Brit*), arcade; **Spiel|höl|le** F gambling den; **Spiel|ka|me|rad(in)** M(F) playmate, playfellow (*Brit*); **Spiel|kar|te** F playing card; **Spiel|ka|si|no** NT (gambling) casino; **Spiel|klas|se** F division; **Spiel|kon-so|le** F game(s) console; **Spiel|lei|den-schaft** F passion for gambling, gambling mania; **Spiel|lei|ter(in)** M(F) a (= *Regisseur*) director; (*Theat, Rad, TV auch*) producer (*Brit*) b (*Sport*) organizer c (= *Conférencier*) master of ceremonies, emcee (*esp US inf*); **Spiel|ma-cher(in)** M(F) key player; **Spiel|mann** M pl -leute Minstrel; (= *Mitglied eines Spiel-mannszuges*) bandsman; **Spiel|manns|zug** M (brass) band; **Spiel|mar|ke** F chip, counter; **Spiel|ma|te|ri|al** NT (*von Brettspielen etc*) game components pl; (*fig: = Spielzeug*) plaything; **Spiel|mi|nu|te** F minute of play)

Spie|lo|thek [ʃpiːloˈteːk] F -, -en amusement arcade (*Brit*), arcade

Spiel-: Spiel|plan M (*Theat, Film*) programme (*Brit*), program (*US*); **ein Stück vom ~ absetzen** to drop a play (from the programme (*Brit*) or program (*US*)); **Spiel|platz** M (*für Kinder*) playground; (*Sport*) playing field; **Spiel|raum** M room to move; (*fig*) scope; (*zeitlich*) time; (*bei Planung etc*) leeway; (*Tech*) clearance, (free) play; **jedes Kind braucht einen gewissen ~, um sich frei entwickeln zu können** all children need a certain amount of scope to be able to develop freely; **Spiel|rausch** M gambling fever; **Spiel|re|gel** F (*lit, fig*) rule of the game; **sich an die ~ halten** (*lit, fig*) **die ~ beachten** (*lit, fig*) to stick to the rules of the game, to play the game; **gegen die ~ verstoßen** (*lit, fig*) to break the rules, not to play the game; **Spiel-run|de** F round; **Spiel|saal** M gambling hall; **Spiel|sa|chen** PL toys pl, playthings pl; **Spiel|sai|son** F (*Theat, Sport*) season; **Spiel-schuld** F gambling debt; **Spiel|stand** M score; **bei einem ~ von ...** with the score (standing) at ...; **Spiel|stät|te** F play area; **Spiel|stra|ße** F a (= *verkehrsberuhigte Zone*) play street b (*auf Kinderfest*) play area; **Spiel-sucht** F compulsive gambling; **Spiel|süch|ti-ge(r)** MF decl as adj compulsive gambler; **Spiel|tag** M (*Ftbl etc*) day; **Spiel|teu|fel** M gambling urge or bug (*inf*); **vom ~ besessen sein** (*inf*) to have the gambling bug (*inf*); **Spiel|tisch** M games table; (*beim Glücksspiel*) gaming or gambling table; **Spiel|trieb** M play instinct; **Spiel|uhr** F musical box (*Brit*), music box; **Spiel|ver|bot** NT (*Sport*) ban; **~ haben** to be banned; **Spiel|ver|der|ber** [-feːɐdɛrbə] M -s, -, **Spiel|ver|der|be|rin** [-ərɪn] F -, -nen spoilsport; **Spiel|ver|län|ge|rung** F extra time (*Brit*), overtime (*US*); (*wegen Verletzung auch*) injury time (*Brit*); **es gab eine ~ (von 30 Minu-ten)** (30 minutes') extra time *etc* was played; **Spiel|ver|lauf** M action, play; **Spiel|wa|ren** PL toys pl; **Spiel|wa|ren|ge|schäft** NT , **Spiel|wa|ren|hand|lung** F toy shop (*esp Brit*) or store (*esp US*); **Spiel|wei|se** F way of playing; **offensive/defensive/unfaire ~** attack-ing/defensive/unfair play; **Spiel|werk** NT mu-sical mechanism; **Spiel|wie|se** F playing field; **Spiel|zeit** F a (= *Saison*) season b (= *Spiel-dauer*) playing time; **die normale ~** (*Sport*) nor-mal time; **nach dreimonatiger ~ wurde das**

Stück abgesetzt the play was taken off after a three-month run

Spiel|zeug NT pl -zeuge toys pl, playthings pl; (*einzelnes*) toy; **er hat viel ~** he has a lot of toys

Spiel|zeug- in cpds toy; **Spiel|zeug|ei|sen-bahn** F (toy) train set

Spiel|zim|mer NT playroom

Spie|re [ˈʃpiːrə] F -, -n (*Naut*) spar, boom

Spier|ling [ˈʃpiːrlɪŋ] M -s, -e (= *Eberesche*) ser-vice tree

Spieß [ʃpiːs] M -es, -e a (= *Stich- und Wurfwaf-fe*) spear; (= *Bratspieß*) spit; (*kleiner*) skewer; **am ~ gebraten** roasted on the spit, spit-roast(ed); **Lamm am ~** spit-roast(ed) lamb; **wie am ~(e) schreien** (*inf*) schreien als ob man am ~ steckt (*inf*) to squeal like a stuck pig; **den ~ umkehren** or **umdrehen** (*fig*) to turn the tables → **brüllen** b (*Mil sl*) sarge (*inf*) c (*Hunt*) spike d (*Typ*) spacing mark, work-up (*US*)

Spieß-: Spieß|bock M (*Hunt*) brocket, spike buck; **Spieß|bra|ten** M joint roasted on a spit

Spieß|bür|ger(in) M(F) (*pej*) (petit) bour-geois; **ihre Eltern sind richtige ~** her parents are typically middle-class

spieß|bür|ger|lich (*pej*) ADJ middle-class, (petit) bourgeois ADV **denken, sich benehmen, le-ben** in a middle-class or bourgeois way

Spieß|bür|ger|tum NT -s (*pej*) (petit-)bourgeois conformism, middle-class values pl

spie|ßen [ˈʃpiːsn] VT **etw auf etw** (acc) ~ (*auf Pfahl etc*) to impale sth on sth; (*auf Gabel etc*) to skewer sth on sth; (*auf größeren Bratspieß*) to spit sth on sth; (*auf Nadel*) to pin sth on sth

Spie|ßer¹ [ˈʃpiːsɐ] M -s, - (*Hunt*: = *Spießbock*) brocket, spike buck

Spie|ßer² [ˈʃpiːsɐ] M -s, -, **Spie|ße|rin** [-ərɪn] F -, -nen (*pej*) = **Spießbürger(in)**

Spieß|ge|sel|le M (*old*) companion; (*hum: = Komplize*) crony (*inf*)

spie|ßig [ˈʃpiːsɪç] ADJ, ADV (*pej*) = **spießbürger-lich**

Spieß|ru|te F switch; **~n laufen** (*fig*) to run the gauntlet

Spieß|ru|ten|lauf M (*fig*) running the gaunt-let; **für ihn wird jeder Gang durch die Stadt zum ~** every time he walks through town it's like running the gauntlet

Spikes [ʃpaiks, sp-] PL (= *Sportschuhe, Stifte*) spikes pl; (= *Autoreifen*) studded tyres pl (*Brit*) or tires pl (*US*); (= *Stifte an Reifen*) studs pl

Spill [ʃpɪl] NT -(e)s, -e (*Naut*) capstan

spil|le|rig [ˈʃpɪlərɪç] ADJ (*N Ger*) spindly

spi|nal [ʃpiˈnaːl, sp-] ADJ (*Med*) spinal; **~e Kin-derlähmung** poliomyelitis; **~er Muskelschwund** spinal muscular atrophy

Spi|nat [ʃpiˈnaːt] M -(e)s, no pl spinach

Spi|nat|wach|tel F (*pej inf*) old cow (*inf*) or baggage (*inf*)

Spind [ʃpɪnt] M OR NT -(e)s, -e [-də] (*Mil, Sport*) locker; (*old: = Vorratskammer*) cupboard

Spin|del [ˈʃpɪndl] F -, -n spindle; (= *Treppenspin-del*) newel

spin|del|dürr ADJ (*pej*) spindly, thin as a rake (*Brit*) or rail (*US*); **~e Beine** spindleshanks (*inf*), spindly legs

spin|del|för|mig ADJ spindle-shaped

Spi|nett [ʃpiˈnɛt] NT -s, -e (*Mus*) spinet

Spin|na|ker [ˈʃpɪnakɐ] M -s, - (*Naut*) spinnaker

Spin|ne [ˈʃpɪnə] F -, -n spider; (= *Wäschespinne*) rotary clothesline

Spin|ne|feind ▲ M (*inf*) **sich** or **einander** (*dat*) **~ sein** to be deadly enemies

spin|nen [ˈʃpɪnən] pret **spann** [ʃpan], ptp **gespon-nen** [gəˈʃpɔnən] VT to spin; (*old liter.* = *ersinnen*) **Verrat, Ränke** to plot; **Lügen** to concoct, to in-vent; **Geschichte** to spin; **ein Netz von Lügen ~, ein Lügengewebe ~** to weave a web of lies; **das ist alles gesponnen** (*inf*) it's all fairy tales; **Fä-**

den ~ (*fig*) to create a network of contacts → **Garn** a, **Seemannsgarn**

VI a (*lit*) to spin
b (*inf*) (= *leicht verrückt sein*) to be crazy or nutty or screwy (*all inf*); (= *Unsinn reden*) to talk rub-bish (*Brit inf*) or garbage (*inf*); (= *Lügengeschich-ten erzählen*) to make it up, to tell tall stories; **stimmt das oder spinnst du?** is that true, or are you having me on (*inf*) or putting me on (*US inf*)?; **sag mal, spinn ich, oder ...?** am I imagin-ing things or ...?; **ich denk ich spinn** I don't be-lieve it; **ich spinn doch nicht** no way (*inf*); **spinn doch nicht!** come off it! (*inf*); **du spinnst wohl!, spinnst du?** you must be crazy!, are you crazy!; **ich dein Auto waschen?, du spinnst wohl!** me clean your car?, you've got to be jok-ing or kidding! (*inf*)

Spin|nen-: Spin|nen|fa|den M spider's thread; **Spin|nen|ge|we|be** NT cobweb, spi-der's web; **Spin|nen|netz** NT cobweb, spider's web

Spin|ner¹ [ˈʃpɪnɐ] M (*Zool*) silkworm moth

Spin|ner² [ˈʃpɪnɐ] M -s, -, **Spin|ne|rin** [-ərɪn] F -, -nen a (*Tex*) spinner b (*inf*) nutcase (*inf*), screwball (*esp US inf*); **du ~, das stimmt doch nicht!** are you crazy? that's not true at all!

Spin|ne|rei [ʃpɪnəˈrai] F -, -en a (= *das Spinnen*) spinning b (= *Spinnwerkstatt*) spinning mill c (*inf*) crazy behaviour (*Brit*) or behavior (*US*) no pl, crazy thing; (= *Unsinn*) rubbish (*Brit inf*), garbage (*inf*); **das ist doch eine ~, so was zu machen** it's crazy to do that; **deine ~en glaubt dir doch kein Mensch!** nobody's going to be-lieve all that rubbish (*Brit inf*) or garbage (*inf*)

spin|nert [ˈʃpɪnɐt] (*S Ger, Aus: inf*) ADJ crazy (*inf*) ADV crazily; **~ daherreden** to talk daft (*Brit inf*) or crazy (*US inf*)

Spinn-: Spinn|fa|ser F spinning fibre (*Brit*) or fiber (*US*); **Spinn|ge|we|be** NT cobweb, spi-der's web; **Spinn|ma|schi|ne** F spinning ma-chine; **Spinn|rad** NT spinning wheel; **Spinn-ro|cken** [-rɔkn] M -s, - distaff; **Spinn|stu|be** F spinning room; **Spinn|we|be** [-veːbə] F -, -n, (*Aus, S Ger*) **Spinn|web** [-veːp] NT OR M -(e)s, -e [-bə] cobweb, spider's web

spi|nös [ʃpiˈnøːs, sp-] ADJ crackpot attr (*inf*)

spin|ti|sie|ren [ʃpɪntiˈziːrən] ptp **spintisiert** VI (*inf*) to ruminate, to muse

Spi|on¹ [ʃpiˈoːn] M -s, -e (*inf*) (= *Guckloch*) spy-hole, peephole; (= *Fensterspiegel*) window mir-ror

Spi|on² [ʃpiˈoːn] M -s, -e, **Spi|o|nin** [ˈʃpioːnɪn] F -, -nen spy

Spi|o|na|ge [ʃpioˈnaːʒə] F -, no pl spying, espio-nage; **~ treiben** to spy, to carry on espionage; **unter dem Verdacht der ~ für ...** on suspicion of spying for ...

Spi|o|na|ge-: Spi|o|na|ge|ab|wehr F counter-intelligence or counterespionage (service); **Spi|o|na|ge|dienst** M (*inf*) secret service; **Spi|o|na|ge|netz** NT spy network; **Spi|o|na-ge|ring** M spy ring; **Spi|o|na|ge|sa|tel|lit** M spy satellite

spi|o|nie|ren [ʃpioˈniːrən] ptp **spioniert** VI to spy; (*fig inf: = nachforschen*) to snoop or poke a-bout (*inf*)

Spi|o|nin F -, -nen spy

Spi|ral|block F pl -blöcke or -blocks spiral notebook

Spi|ra|le [ʃpiˈraːlə] F -, -n spiral; (*geometrisch, Sci auch*) helix; (*Med*) coil

Spi|ral-: Spi|ral|fe|der F coil spring; **spi|ral-för|mig** ADJ spiral ADV in a spiral; **das Flug-zeug schraubte sich ~ in den Himmel hinauf** the plane spiralled (*Brit*) or spiraled (*US*) up into the sky

spi|ra|lig [ʃpiˈraːlɪç] ADJ (*rare*) spiral, helical

Spi|ral|ne|bel M (*Astron*) spiral nebula

Spi|rans [ˈʃpiːrans, 'sp-] F -, **Spiranten** [-'rantn], **Spi|rant** [ʃpiˈrant, sp-] M -en, -en (*Ling*) frica-tive, spirant

Spi|ri|tis|mus [ʃpiri'tɪsmʊs, sp-] M -, *no pl* spiritualism, spiritism

Spi|ri|tist [ʃpiri'tɪst, sp-] M -en, -en, **Spi|ri|tis|tin** [-'tɪstɪn] F -, -nen spiritualist

spi|ri|tis|tisch [ʃpiri'tɪstɪʃ, sp-] ADJ ~e Sitzung seance

Spi|ri|tu|al ['spɪrɪtjʊəl] M OR NT -s, -s (negro) spiritual

Spi|ri|tu|a|lis|mus [ʃpiritua'lɪsmʊs, sp-] M -, *no pl* spiritualism

spi|ri|tu|a|lis|tisch [ʃpiritua'lɪstɪʃ, sp-] ADJ spiritualist

Spi|ri|tu|ell [ʃpiri'tuɛl, sp-] [ADJ] spiritual [ADV] spiritually

Spi|ri|tu|o|sen [ʃpiri'tuo:zn, sp-] PL spirits *pl*

Spi|ri|tus M -, *no pl* **a** ['ʃpi:rɪtʊs] (= Alkohol) spirit; **mit ~ kochen** to cook with *or* on a spirit stove; **etw in ~ legen** to put sth in alcohol **b** ['spi:rɪtʊs] (Ling) spiritus

Spi|ri|tus-: Spi|ri|tus|ko|cher M spirit stove; **Spi|ri|tus|lam|pe** F spirit lamp

Spi|tal [ʃpi'ta:l] NT -s, Spitäler [-'tɛ:lɐ] (old, Aus, Sw: = Krankenhaus) hospital, spital (obs); (rare: = Altersheim) old people's home

spitz [ʃpɪts] [ADJ] **a** (= mit einer Spitze) pointed; (= nicht stumpf) Bleistift, Nadel etc sharp; (Math) Winkel acute; **die Feder dieses Füllhalters ist nicht ~ genug** the nib on this fountain pen is too broad; **~e Schuhe** pointed shoes, winklepickers (Brit hum inf), elf-shoes (US hum inf); **~e Klammern** angle brackets; **mit dem ~en Bleistift rechnen** (fig) to work everything out (down) to the last penny; **etw mit ~en Fingern anfassen** (inf) to pick sth up gingerly; **über einen ~en Stein stolpern** (hum) to pronounce "sp" and "st" as in English

b (= gehässig) Bemerkung pointed, barbed; Zunge sharp → Feder b

c (= kränklich) Aussehen, Gesicht pinched, haggard, peaky

d (sl: = lüstern) randy (Brit inf), horny (inf); **~ wie Nachbars Lumpi** *or* **wie ein Turnschuh** *or* **wie Rettich** as randy (Brit) *or* horny as (Frau) a bitch in heat *or* (Mann) an old goat (all inf); **jdn ~ machen** to turn sb on (inf)

[ADV] **a** feilen, zuhauen to a point

b (= V-förmig) zulaufen, vorstehen, abgehen to a point, sharply; **der Ausschnitt des Kleides lief unten ~ zu** the dress had a V-shaped neckline

c (= spitzzüngig) bemerken, kontern, antworten sharply

d (= knapp) ~ kalkulieren *or* rechnen to calculate very carefully

Spitz [ʃpɪts] M -es, -e (Hunderasse) spitz, pomeranian

Spitz-: Spitz|bart M goatee; **spitz|bär|tig** ADJ with a goatee, goateed; **Spitz|bauch** M potbelly (inf); **spitz+be|kom|men** ptp spitzbekommen VT sep irreg (inf) etw ~ to cotton (Brit) *or* catch on to sth (inf), to get wise to sth (inf); **~, dass ...** to cotton (Brit) *or* catch on *or* get wise to the fact that ... (inf); **Spitz|bo|gen** M pointed arch, ogive (spec); **Spitz|bub** M , **Spitz|bu|be** M , **Spitz|bü|bin** [-'by:bɪn] F -, -nen (old) villain, rogue; (dial inf: = Schlingel) scamp (inf), scallywag (inf); **Spitz|bu|ben|ge|sicht** NT (old) villainous *or* roguish face; **Spitz|bu|ben|streich** M (dated) nasty *or* knavish (Brit old) trick; **spitz|bü|bisch** [ADJ] roguish, mischievous [ADV] roguishly, mischievously; **Spitz|dach** NT (Archit) pointed roof

Spit|ze ['ʃpɪtsə] F -, -n **a** (= Schwertspitze, Nadelspitze, Pfeilspitze, Bleistiftspitze, Kinnspitze) point; (= Schuhspitze) toe; (= Fingerspitze, Nasenspitze, Bartspitze, Spargelspitze) tip; (= Zigarrenspitze, Haarspitze) end; (= Bergspitze, Felsspitze) peak, top; (= Baumspitze, Turmspitze, Giebelspitze) top; (= Pyramidenspitze) top, apex (form); (= Dreiecksspitze) top, vertex (form); **auf der ~ stehen** to be upside down; **etw auf die ~ treiben** to carry sth too far *or* to extremes; **einer Sache** (dat) **die ~ abbrechen** *or* **nehmen** (fig) to take the sting

out of sth

b (fig) (= Höchstwert) peak; (inf: = Höchstgeschwindigkeit) top speed; **dieser Sportwagen fährt 200 ~** (inf) ≈ this sports car has a top speed of 125

c (= Führung) head; (= vorderes Ende) front; (esp Mil: von Kolonne etc) head; (= Tabellenspitze) top; **die ~n der Gesellschaft** the leading lights of society; **an der ~ stehen** to be at the head; (auf Tabelle) to be (at) the top (of the table); **an der ~ liegen** (Sport, fig) to be in front, to be in the lead; **Ruritanien liegt im Lebensstandard an der ~** Ruritania has the highest standard of living; **die ~ halten** (Sport, fig) to keep the lead; **sich an die ~ setzen** to put oneself at the head; (in Wettbewerb etc, Sport) to go into *or* take the lead; (auf Tabelle) to go to the top (of the table); (im Pferderennen) to take up the running; **er wurde an die ~ des Unternehmens gestellt** he was put at the top *or* head of the company

d (= Zigaretten-/Zigarrenhalter) (cigarette/cigar) holder

e (fig: = Stichelei) dig (esp Brit), cut (US); **das ist eine ~ gegen Sie** that's a dig (esp Brit) *or* cut (US) at you, that's directed at you; **die ~ zurückgeben** to give tit for tat

f (Comm: = Überschuss) surplus

g (Gewebe) lace; **Höschen mit ~n** panties with lace borders

h (inf: = prima) great (inf); **das war einsame** *or* **absolute ~!** that was really great! (inf)

Spit|zel ['ʃpɪtsl] M -s, - (= Informant) informer; (= Spion) spy; (= Schnüffler) snooper; (= Polizeispitzel) police informer, nark (inf)

Spit|zel|diens|te PL informing *no pl*; **für jdn ~ leisten** to act as an informer for sb

spit|zeln ['ʃpɪtsln] VI to spy; (= Spitzeldienste leisten) to act as an informer

spit|zen ['ʃpɪtsn] [VT] (= spitz machen) Bleistift to sharpen; Lippen, Mund to purse; (zum Küssen) to pucker (up); Ohren (lit, fig) to prick up; **spitzt doch die Ohren, dann versteht ihr auch, was ich sage!** open your ears and then you'll understand what I'm saying! (inf) [VIR] (sich) auf etw (acc) ~ to look forward to sth (inf) [VI] (dial inf) (= aufpassen) to keep a lookout, to keep one's eyes peeled (inf); (= heimlich spähen) to peek

Spit|zen- in cpds top; (= aus Spitze) lace; **Spit|zen|an|ge|bot** NT top-of-the-range *or* top-of-the-line (US) offer; **Spit|zen|be|darf** M peak demand; **Spit|zen|be|las|tung** F peak (load); **die Zeit der ~** the peak period; **Spit|zen|be|satz** M lace trimming; **Spit|zen|blu|se** F lace blouse; **Spit|zen|deck|chen** NT , **Spit|zen|de|cke** F lace doily; **Spit|zen|ein|kom|men** NT top income; **Spit|zen|er|zeug|nis** NT top(-quality) product; **Spit|zen|feld** NT (Sport) leaders *pl*, leading group; **im ~ amongst the leaders**, in the leading group; **Spit|zen|funk|ti|o|när(in)** M(F) top official; **Spit|zen|gar|ni|tur** F set of lace underwear; **Spit|zen|ge|halt** NT top salary; **Spit|zen|ge|schwin|dig|keit** F top speed; **Spit|zen|ge|spräch** NT top-level talks *pl*; (Pol: = Gipfel) summit (meeting); **Spit|zen|gre|mi|en** PL leading *or* top committees *pl*; **Spit|zen|grup|pe** F top group; (Sport: = Spitzenfeld) leading group; **Spit|zen|hös|chen** [-hø:sçən] NT lace panties *pl*; **Spit|zen|jahr|gang** M (von Wein) top-quality *or* outstanding(ly good) vintage; **Spit|zen|kan|di|dat(in)** M(F) top candidate; **Spit|zen|klas|se** F top class; **Sekt/ein Auto** etc **der ~** top-class champagne/a top-class car etc; **~!** (inf) great! (inf); **Spit|zen|kön|ner(in)** M(F) ace, first-rate *or* top-class talent; **Spit|zen|kra|gen** M lace collar; **Spit|zen|leis|tung** F top performance; (von Maschine, Auto) peak performance; (bei der Herstellung von Produkten, Energie) peak output; (fig: = ausgezeichnete Leistung) top-class *or* first-rate performance; (Sport: = Rekord) record (performance); **Spit|zen|lohn** M top wage(s *pl*); **spit|zen|mä|ßig** (inf) [ADJ] fantastic (inf), great (inf) [ADV] fantastically (inf); **Spit|zen|mo|dell** NT top

model; **Spit|zen|or|ga|ni|sa|ti|on** F leading organization *or* group; **Spit|zen|po|si|ti|on** F leading *or* top position; **Spit|zen|prei|se** PL (Comm) top prices *pl*; **Spit|zen|qua|li|tät** F top quality; **Spit|zen|rei|ter(in)** M (Ware) top seller; (Film, Stück etc) hit; (= Schlager) top of the pops, number one; **Spit|zen|rei|ter(in)** M(F) (Sport) leader; (fig: Kandidat) frontrunner; **Spit|zen|sport|ler(in)** M(F) top(-class) sportsman/-woman; **Spit|zen|stel|lung** F leading position; **Spit|zen|steu|er|satz** M top rate of income tax; **Spit|zen|sti|cke|rei** F lace embroidery; **Spit|zen|tanz** M dance on points, toe dance (US); **Spit|zen|tech|no|lo|gie** F state-of-the-art technology; **Spit|zen|tref|fen** NT summit meeting; **Spit|zen|tuch** NT *pl* -tücher lace cloth, piece of lace; (= Taschentuch) lace handkerchief; **Spit|zen|ver|band** M leading organization *or* group; **Spit|zen|ver|die|ner(in)** M(F) top earner; **Spit|zen|ver|kehrs|zeit** F peak period; **Spit|zen|ver|tre|ter(in)** M(F) usu *pl* (der Wirtschaft etc) leading representative; **Spit|zen|wein** M top-quality wine; **Spit|zen|wert** M peak; **Spit|zen|zeit** F (Sport) record time

Spit|zer ['ʃpɪtsɐ] M -s, - (inf) (pencil) sharpener

Spitz-: Spitz|fei|le F taper file; **spitz|fin|dig** [ADJ] over(ly)-subtle, over(ly)-precise; (= haarspalterisch auch) hairsplitting, nit-picking (inf); Unterschied auch over(ly)-nice [ADV] in an over(ly)-subtle way; **er argumentiert immer sehr ~** he always splits hairs; **Spitz|fin|dig|keit** ['ʃpɪtsfɪndɪçkaɪt] F -, -en over-subtlety, over-precision *no pl*; (= Haarspalterei auch) hairsplitting *no pl*, nit-picking *no pl* (inf); **zu behaupten, dass das Wort hier seine Bedeutung ändert, ist eine ~** it's splitting hairs *or* it's nit-picking (inf) to claim that the word changes its meaning here; **spitz|gie|b(e)|lig** ADJ with pointed gables; **spitz+ha|ben** vt sep irreg (inf) etw ~ to have cottoned (Brit) *or* caught on to sth (inf), to have got wise to sth (inf); **~, dass ...** to have cottoned (Brit) *or* caught on *or* to have got wise to the fact that ... (inf); **Spitz|ha|cke** F pickaxe (Brit), pickax (US)

spit|zig ['ʃpɪtsɪç] ADJ, ADV (old, dial) = spitz

Spitz-: Spitz|keh|re F (Rail) switchback turn; (Ski) kick turn; **Spitz|kopf** M pointed head; **spitz+krie|gen** sep (inf) = spitzbekommen; **Spitz|küh|ler** M (Aut) pointed *or* V-shaped radiator; (hum inf) potbelly (inf); **Spitz|mar|ke** F (Typ) sidehead; **Spitz|maus** F shrew; **du bist eine richtige ~ geworden** (inf) you've got (Brit) *or* gotten (US) so thin; **Spitz|na|me** M nickname; **mit dem ~n** nicknamed; **Spitz|we|ge|rich** M ribwort; **spitz|win|ke|lig, spitz|wink|lig** [ADJ] (Math) Dreieck acute-angled; Gasse sharp-cornered, angular [ADV] abzweigen, auslaufen at a sharp angle; **spitz|zün|gig** [-tsyŋɪç] [ADJ] sharp-tongued; Bemerkung sharp [ADV] antworten sharply

Spleen [ʃpli:n] M -s, -s (inf) (= Angewohnheit) strange *or* crazy habit, eccentricity, quirk (of behaviour (Brit) *or* behavior (US)); (= Idee) crazy idea *or* notion; (= Fimmel) obsession; **die Psychologen haben doch alle irgendeinen ~!** these psychologists are all quacks!; **du hast ja einen ~!** you're round the bend (Brit inf), you're off your head (Brit inf) *or* rocker (inf)

splee|nig ['ʃpli:nɪç] ADJ (inf) crazy, nutty (inf)

splei|ßen ['ʃplaɪsn] pret **spliss** [ʃplɪs], ptp **gesplissen** [gə'ʃplɪsn] VT **a** (dial, old) Holz to split **b** (Naut) Taue, Leinen to splice

splen|did [ʃplɛn'di:t, sp-] ADJ (geh) generous; Behandlung etc auch handsome

Splint [ʃplɪnt] M -(e)s, -e cotter (pin), split pin

Splin|ten|trei|ber M pin punch

spliss ▲ pret von **spleißen**

Spliss ▲ [ʃplɪs] M -es, -e **a** (dial: = Splitter) splinter **b** *no pl* (= gespaltene Haarspitzen) split ends *pl*

---

splis|sig ['ʃplɪsɪç] ADJ ~**e (Haar)spitzen** split ends

Splitt [ʃplɪt] M **-(e)s, -e** stone chippings pl; (= Streumittel) grit

Split|ter ['ʃplɪtɐ] M **-s, -** (= Holzsplitter, Metallsplitter, Knochensplitter) splinter; (= Glassplitter auch, Granatsplitter) fragment; **der ~ in deines Bruders Auge** (Bibl) the mote that is in thy brother's eye (Bibl)

Split|ter-: Split|ter|bom|be F (Mil) fragmentation bomb; **split|ter|fa|ser|nackt** ADJ (inf) stark-naked, starkers pred (Brit hum inf); **Split|ter|frak|tur** F (Med) splintered or comminuted (spec) fracture; **split|ter|frei** ADJ Glas shatterproof; **Split|ter|gra|ben** M (Mil) slit trench; **Split|ter|grup|pe** F (Pol) splinter group

split|te|rig ['ʃplɪtərɪç] ADJ splintering

split|tern ['ʃplɪtɐn] VI aux sein or haben (Holz, Glas, Knochen) to splinter

split|ter|nackt ADJ = splitterfasernackt

Split|ter|par|tei F (Pol) splinter party

Split|ting ['ʃplɪtɪŋ, 'sp-] NT **-s, -s** **a** (von Aktien) splitting **b** (Pol: bei Wahlen) distribution of first and second votes among the parties **c** (Fin) → Splittingsystem

Split|ting|sys|tem ['ʃplɪtɪŋ-, 'sp-] NT (Fin) tax system in which husband and wife each pay income tax on half the total of their combined incomes

splitt|rig ['ʃplɪtrɪç] ADJ splintering

SPÖ [ɛsˈpeːˈøː] F - abbr von Sozialdemokratische Partei Österreichs

Spoi|ler ['ʃpɔylɐ, 'sp-] M **-s, -** spoiler

Spö|ken|kie|ker ['ʃpøːknkiːkɐ] M **-s, -**, **Spö|ken|kie|ke|rin** [-ərɪn] F **-, -nen** (N Ger) psychic, clairvoyant, person who has second sight

spon|sern ['ʃpɔnsɐn, 'sp-] VT to sponsor

Spon|si|on [ʃpɔnˈzioːn] F (Aus: Univ) academic degree ceremony in which the title of Magister is awarded

Spon|sor ['ʃpɔnzɐ, 'sp-] M **-s, Sponsoren** [-ˈzoːrən], **Spon|so|rin** [-ˈzoːrɪn] F **-, -nen** sponsor

Spon|so|ring ['ʃpɔnzorɪŋ, 'sp-] NT **-s**, no pl sponsorship

spon|tan [ʃpɔnˈtaːn, sp-] ADJ spontaneous ADV spontaneously

Spon|ta|ne|i|tät [ʃpɔntaneiˈtɛːt, sp-] F **-**, no pl spontaneity

Spon|tan|hei|lung F (Med) spontaneous recovery

Spon|tan|kauf M impulse buy or purchase; **Spontankäufe** pl (regelmäßig) impulse buying no pl

Spon|ti ['ʃpɔnti] M **-s, -s** (Pol sl) member of alternative movement rejecting traditional procedures

spo|ra|disch [ʃpoˈraːdɪʃ, sp-] ADJ sporadic ADV sporadically

Spo|re ['ʃpoːrə] F **-, -n** (Biol) spore

Spo|ren pl von **Sporn** von **Spore**

spo|ren|klir|rend ADV (old) with a clatter of spurs

Spo|ren|tier|chen PL (Biol) sporozoa pl

Sporn [ʃpɔrn] M **-(e)s, Sporen** ['ʃpoːrən] usu pl (auch Zool, Bot) spur; (Naut auch) ram; (am Geschütz) trail spade; (Aviat: = Gleitkufe) tailskid; (Rad) tail wheel; **einem Pferd die Sporen geben** to spur a horse, to give a horse a touch of the spurs; **sich** (dat) **die (ersten) Sporen verdienen** (fig) to win one's spurs

spor|nen ['ʃpɔrnən] VT (geh) to spur; (fig) to spur on → gestiefelt b

sporn|streichs ['ʃpɔrnʃtraiçs] ADV (old) posthaste, straight away

Sport [ʃpɔrt] M **-(e)s**, (rare) **-e** sport; (= Zeitvertreib) hobby, pastime; **treiben Sie ~?** do you do any sport?; **er treibt viel ~** he goes in for or he

does a lot of sport; **etw aus** or **zum ~ betreiben** to do sth as a hobby or for fun; **sich** (dat) **einen ~ aus etw machen** (inf) to get a kick out of sth (inf)

Sport-: Sport|ab|zei|chen NT sports certificate; **Sport|ang|ler(in)** M(F) angler; **Sport|an|la|ge** F sports complex; **Sport|an|zug** M sports clothes pl; (= Trainingsanzug) tracksuit; **Sport|art** F (kind of) sport; **Sport|ar|ti|kel** M **a** (pl) sports equipment with sing vb; **ein ~** a piece of sports equipment **b** (inf: = Sportbericht) sports report; **Sport|arzt** M , **Sport|ärz|tin** F sports physician; **sport|be|geis|tert** ADJ keen on sport, sports-mad (Brit inf), crazy about sports (US inf); **ein Sportbegeisterter** a sports enthusiast or fan; **Sport|bei|la|ge** F sports section or page(s pl); **Sport|be|richt** M sports report; **Sport|be|richt|er|stat|tung** F sports reporting

spor|teln ['ʃpɔrtln] VI (inf) to do a bit of sport(s), to dabble in sport(s)

Sport-: Sport|er|eig|nis NT sporting event; **Sport|fech|ten** NT **-s**, no pl fencing; **Sport|feld** NT sports ground; **Sport|fest** NT sports festival; **Sport|flie|ger(in)** M(F) amateur pilot; **Sport|flug|zeug** NT sporting aircraft; **Sport|freund(in)** M(F) sport(s) fan; **Sport|geist** M sportsmanship; **Sport|ge|rät** NT piece of sports equipment; **~s** sports equipment; **Sport|ge|schäft** NT sports shop, sporting goods store (US); **Sport|hal|le** F sports hall; **Sport|hemd** NT casual or sports shirt; **Sport|hoch|schu|le** F college of physical education

spor|tiv [ʃpɔrˈtiːf, ʃp-] ADJ Mensch, Kleidung, Auto sporty

Sport-: Sport|ja|ckett NT sports jacket or coat; **Sport|kar|re** F (N Ger) pushchair (Brit), (baby) stroller (US); **Sport|klei|dung** F sportswear; **Sport|klub** M sports club; **Sport|leh|rer(in)** M(F) sports instructor; (Sch) PE or physical education teacher

Sport|ler ['ʃpɔrtlɐ] M **-s, -** sportsman, athlete

Sport|ler|herz NT athlete's heart

Sport|le|rin ['ʃpɔrtlərɪn] F **-, -nen** sportswoman, (woman) athlete

sport|lich ['ʃpɔrtlɪç] ADJ **a** (= den Sport betreffend) Veranstaltung, Wettkampf, Leistung, Erfolg sporting **b** Mensch sporty; (= durchtrainiert) athletic **c** (= fair) sporting, sportsmanlike no adv **d** Kleidung casual; (= sportlich-schick) natty (inf), snazzy (inf), smart but casual; (= wie Sportkleidung aussehend) sporty; **eine ~e Note** a sporty touch **e** Auto sporty ADV **a** **sich ~ betätigen, ~ aktiv sein** to do sport; **~ gesehen, ...** from a sporting point of view ... **b** (= fair) sportingly; **er hat sich ihr gegenüber nicht besonders ~ verhalten** he wasn't particularly sporting in his behaviour (Brit) or behavior (US) toward(s) her **c** (= leger) casually; **~ gekleidet** casually dressed; **~ wearing** smart but casual clothes, smartly but casually dressed **d** (= rasant) fahren fast

Sport|lich|keit F **-**, no pl **a** (von Menschen) sportiness **b** (= Fairness) sportsmanship **c** (von Auto) sportiness

Sport-: Sport|man|tel M casual coat; **sport|mä|ßig** ADJ, ADV = sportsmäßig; **Sport|me|di|zin** F sports medicine; **Sport|mel|dung** F , **Sport|nach|richt** F , **Sport|nach|rich|ten** PL sports news with sing vb or reports pl; **eine wichtige ~** or **Sportnachricht** an important piece of sports news; **Sport|platz** M sports field; (in der Schule) playing field(s pl); **Sport|rad** NT sports cycle or bike (inf); **Sport|re|dak|teur(in)** M(F) sports editor; **Sport|re|por|ta|ge** F sports reporting; (= Bericht) sports report; **die ~ über die Weltmeisterschaft** the coverage of the world championships; **Sport-**

schlit|ten M racing toboggan; **Sport|schuh** M casual shoe

Sports-: Sports|frau F sportswoman; **Sports|freund(in)** M(F) (fig inf) buddy (inf); **wenn der ~ da ...** if this guy ... (inf); **Sports|ka|no|ne** F (inf) sporting ace (inf); **Sports|mann** M pl **-männer** or **-leute** (dated) sportsman; (inf, als Anrede) sport (esp Austral inf), mate (Brit inf), buddy (inf); **sports|mä|ßig** ADJ sporty ADV **sich ~ betätigen** to do sport; **wie siehts denn dort ~ aus?** what sort of sporting facilities are there?

Sport-: Sport|un|fall M sporting accident; **Sport|ver|an|stal|tung** F sporting event; **Sport|ver|ein** M sports club; **Sport|ver|let|zung** F sports injury; **Sport|wa|gen** M sports car; (für Kind) pushchair (Brit), (baby) stroller (US); **Sport|zei|tung** F sports paper; **Sport|zeug** NT , no pl (inf) sport(s) things pl (Brit) or stuff

Spot [spɔt, ʃpɔt] M **-s, -s** commercial, advertisement, ad (inf)

Spot- ['spɔt-]: **Spot|ge|schäft** NT (Fin) spot transaction; **Spot|light** ['spɔtlait] NT **-s, -s** spotlight; **Spot|markt** M (Fin) spot market

Spott [ʃpɔt] M **-(e)s**, no pl mockery; (höhnisch auch) ridicule, derision; **jdn dem ~ preisgeben** to hold sb up to ridicule; **dem ~ preisgegeben sein** to be held up to ridicule, to be made fun of; **seinen ~ mit jdm treiben** to make fun of sb; **Gegenstand des allgemeinen ~es** object of general ridicule, laughing stock; **zum ~ der Nachbarn werden** to become the laughing stock of the neighbourhood (Brit) or neighborhood (US) → Schaden a

Spott-: Spott|bild NT (fig) travesty, mockery; **das ~ eines Präsidenten** a travesty etc of a president; **spott|bil|lig** (inf) ADJ dirt-cheap (inf) ADV **das habe ich ~ gekauft** I bought it for a song (inf) or for practically nothing, I bought it dirt-cheap (inf); **Spott|dros|sel** F mockingbird; (dated fig: = Spötter) tease, mocker

Spöt|te|lei [ʃpœtəˈlai] F **-, -en** (= das Spotten) mocking; (= ironische Bemerkung) mocking remark

spöt|teln ['ʃpœtln] VI to mock (über jdn/etw sb/sth), to poke gentle fun (über jdn/etw at sb/sth)

spot|ten ['ʃpɔtn] VI **a** (= sich lustig machen) to mock, to poke fun; (= höhnen) to mock, to ridicule, to be derisive; **über jdn/etw ~** to mock sb/sth, to poke fun at sb/sth, to ridicule sb/sth; (höhnisch auch) to deride sb/sth, to ridicule sb/sth; **du hast leicht ~!**, **spotte (du) nur!** it's easy for you to mock or laugh!, it's all very well for you to mock; **..., spottete er** ..., he mocked **b** +gen (old, liter: = Hohn sprechen) to mock; (geh: = missachten) der Gefahr to be contemptuous of, to scorn; **das spottet jeder Beschreibung** that simply defies or beggars description

Spöt|ter ['ʃpœtɐ] M **-s, -**, **Spöt|te|rin** [-ərɪn] F **-, -nen** (= satirischer Mensch) wit, satirist; (= jd, der über etw spottet) mocker

Spott-: Spott|fi|gur F joke figure, ludicrous character; **eine ~ sein** to be a figure of fun, to be an object of ridicule; **Spott|ge|burt** F (liter) freak, monstrosity; **Spott|ge|dicht** NT satirical poem, lampoon; **Spott|ge|läch|ter** NT mocking laughter

spöt|tisch ['ʃpœtɪʃ] ADJ Blick, Lächeln, Bemerkung mocking; (höhnisch auch) derisive ADV mockingly

Spott-: Spott|lied NT satirical song; **Spott|lust** F love of mockery, inclination to mock; **spott|lus|tig** ADJ given to mockery, inclined to mock; **Spott|na|me** M derisive nickname; **Spott|preis** M ridiculously or ludicrously low price; **für einen ~** for a song (inf); **Spott|re|de** F satirical or lampooning speech; **~n führen** to make satirical or lampooning speeches; **Spott|sucht** F , no pl compulsive mocking;

spott|süch|tig ADJ ~ **sein** to delight in (constant) mockery; **Spott|vers** M satirical verse

sprach pret von **sprechen**

Sprach-: Sprach|at|las M linguistic atlas; **Sprach|aus|ga|be|sys|tem** NT (Comput) audio response system; **Sprach|au|to|no|mie** F (Pol) linguistic autonomy; **Sprach|bar|ri|e|re** F language barrier; **Sprach|bau** M , no pl linguistic structure; **sprach|be|gabt** ADJ good at languages, linguistically talented or gifted; **Sprach|be|ga|bung** F talent for languages, linguistic talent; **Sprach|com|pu|ter** M computer with speech synthesizer; (= Taschenübersetzer) pocket electronic dictionary; **Sprach|denk|mal** NT linguistic monument

Spra|che ['ʃpraːxə] F -, -n language; (= das Sprechen) speech; (= Sprechweise) speech, way of speaking; (= Fähigkeit, zu sprechen) power or faculty of speech; **eine/die ~ sprechen** to (be able to) speak a language/the language or lingo (inf); **die ~ analysieren** to analyze language; **die ~ der Musik** the language of music; **in französischer** etc **~** in French etc; **die gleiche ~ sprechen** (lit, fig) to speak the same language; **das spricht eine klare** or **deutliche ~** (fig) that speaks for itself, it's obvious what that means; **er spricht jetzt eine ganz andere ~** (fig) he's changed his tune now; **mit der ~ herausrücken** to come out with it; **heraus mit der ~!** (inf) come on, out with it!; **die ~ auf etw** (acc) **bringen** to bring the conversation (a)round to sth; **zur ~ kommen** to be mentioned or brought up, to come up; **etw zur ~ bringen** to bring sth up, to mention sth; **die ~ verlieren** to lose the power of speech; **hast du die ~ verloren?** have you lost your tongue?, has the cat got your tongue? (inf); **die ~ wiederfinden** to be able to speak again; **es raubt** or **verschlägt einem die ~** it takes your breath away; **mir blieb die ~ weg** I was speechless

Sprach-: Sprach|ei|gen|tüm|lich|keit F linguistic peculiarity or idiosyncrasy; **Sprach|ein|heit** F **a** (Ling) linguistic unit **b** (= Einheitlichkeit) linguistic unity

Spra|chen-: Spra|chen|ge|wirr NT babel of tongues (usu hum), mixture or welter of languages; **Spra|chen|schu|le** F language school; **Spra|chen|zent|rum** NT (Univ) language centre (Brit) or center (US)

Sprach-: Sprach|er|ken|nung F (Comput) speech recognition; **Sprach|er|werb** M language acquisition; **Sprach|er|zie|hung** F (form) language education; **Sprach|fa|mi|lie** F family of languages, language family; **Sprach|feh|ler** M speech defect or impediment; **Sprach|for|scher(in)** M(F) linguist(ic researcher); (= Philologe) philologist; **Sprach|for|schung** F linguistic research; (= Philologie) philology; **Sprach|füh|rer** M phrase book; **Sprach|ge|biet** NT language area; **ein französisches** etc **~** a French-speaking etc area; **Sprach|ge|brauch** M (linguistic) usage; **mo|derner deutscher ~** modern German usage; **Sprach|ge|fühl** NT feeling for language; **Sprach|ge|lehr|te(r)** MF decl as adj linguist; **Sprach|ge|mein|schaft** F speech community; **Sprach|ge|nie** NT linguistic genius; **Sprach|ge|schich|te** F , no pl linguistic history; **die ~ des Mongolischen** the history of the Mongolian language; **Sprach|ge|set|ze** PL linguistic laws pl; **sprach|ge|steu|ert** [-gəʃtɔyɐt] ADJ (Comput) voice-activated; **Sprach|ge|walt** F power of expression, eloquence; **sprach|ge|wal|tig** ADJ eloquent; **ein ~er Redner** a powerful speaker; **sprach|ge|wandt** ADJ articulate, fluent; **Sprach|gren|ze** F linguistic or language boundary; **Sprach|gut** NT , no pl linguistic heritage; **ein Wörterbuch kann nicht das gesamte ~ widerspiegeln** a dictionary cannot reflect the whole wealth of a language

-spra|chig [ʃpraːxɪç] ADJ suf **a** (= in einer Sprache) -language; (= sprechend) -speaking; **eng-**

lischsprachig (Film, Buch) English-language; Mensch English-speaking **b** Wörterbuch, Mensch -lingual; **einsprachig** monolingual; **zweisprachig** bilingual; **mehrsprachig** multilingual

Sprach-: Sprach|in|sel F linguistic enclave or island; **Sprach|kennt|nis|se** PL knowledge sing of languages/the language/a language; **mit englischen ~n** with a knowledge of English; **haben Sie irgendwelche ~?** do you know any languages?; **~ erwünscht** (knowledge of) languages desirable; **Sprach|kom|pe|tenz** F linguistic competence; **Sprach|kri|tik** F linguistic criticism; **sprach|kun|dig** ADJ (in mehreren Sprachen) proficient in or good at (foreign) languages; (in einer bestimmten Sprache) linguistically proficient; **es ist schwer, sich in diesem Land zurechtzufinden, wenn man nicht ~ ist** it's very difficult to get along in this country if you don't know the language or if you are not familiar with the language; **Sprach|kurs** M , **Sprach|kur|sus** M language course; **Sprach|la|bor** NT language laboratory or lab (inf); **Sprach|läh|mung** F paralysis of the organs of speech or the speech organs; **Sprach|land|schaft** F linguistic geography; **Sprach|leh|re** F (= Grammatik, Grammatikbuch) grammar; **Sprach|leh|rer(in)** M(F) language teacher; **Sprach|lehr|gang** M language course

sprach|lich ['ʃpraːxlɪç] ADJ Eigenheit, Kommunikation, Minderheit linguistic; Unterricht, Schwierigkeiten language attr; Fehler grammatical ADV linguistically; **~ hatten die Einwanderer keine Schwierigkeiten** the immigrants had no language difficulties; **~ falsch/richtig** ungrammatical/grammatical, grammatically incorrect/correct; **eine intelligente Analyse, auch ~ gut** an intelligent analysis, well written too

sprach|los ADJ (= ohne Sprache) speechless; (= erstaunt) speechless, dumbfounded; **ich bin ~!** I'm speechless; **da ist man (einfach) ~** (inf) that's quite or really something (inf)

Sprach|lo|sig|keit F -, no pl speechlessness

Sprach-: Sprach|me|lo|die F intonation, speech melody; **Sprach|miss|brauch** ▲ M misuse of language; **Sprach|mitt|ler(in)** M(F) translator and interpreter; **Sprach|mo|dul** [-moduːl] NT (Comput) (in Textverarbeitung) language module; (zur Umwandlung in Gesprochenes) speech synthesizer; **Sprach|pfle|ge** F concern for the purity of language; **aktive ~ betreiben** to be actively concerned with the purity of a language; **Sprach|phi|lo|so|phie** F philosophy of language; **Sprach|psy|cho|lo|gie** F psychology of language; **Sprach|raum** M = Sprachgebiet; **Sprach|re|gel** F grammatical rule, rule of grammar; (für Aussprache) pronunciation rule; (Ling) linguistic rule, rule of language; **die einfachsten ~n des Lateinischen** the most elementary rules of Latin; **Sprach|re|ge|lung** F **a** (= Bestimmung) linguistic ruling **b** (= Version) offizielle ~ official version; **Sprach|reg|ler(in)** M(F) linguistic arbiter; **Sprach|rein|heit** F linguistic purity; **Sprach|rei|se** F language(-learning) holiday (esp Brit) or trip; **Sprach|rohr** NT (= Megafon) megaphone; (fig) mouthpiece; **sich zum ~ einer Sache/Gruppe machen** to become the spokesperson for or mouthpiece (usu pej) of sth/a group; **Sprach|schatz** M (geh) vocabulary; **dem englischen ~ fehlt ein Wort für ...** the English language has no word for ...; **Sprach|schön|heit** F linguistic beauty, beauty of language; **die ~ Rimbauds** the beauty of Rimbaud's language; **Sprach|schöp|fer(in)** M(F) linguistic innovator; **Sprach|schöp|fe|risch** ADJ innovatory, (linguistically) creative; **Sprach|schöp|fung** F linguistic innovation; **Sprach|schu|le** F language school; **Sprach|sil|be** F syllable; **Sprach|so|zi|o|lo|gie** F sociology of language; **Sprach|stamm** M (language) stock; **Sprach|stil** M style, way one uses language; **Sprach|stö|rung** F speech disorder; **Sprach|struk|tur** F linguistic structure; **Sprach|stu|di|um** NT study of languages/a language, lin-

guistic or language studies pl; **Sprach|ta|lent** NT talent or gift for languages; **Sprach|the|o|rie** F theory of language; **Sprach|übung** F linguistic or language exercise; **Sprach|un|ter|richt** M language teaching or instruction; **der französische ~** French teaching, the teaching of French; **~/französischen ~ erteilen** to give language lessons/French lessons; **Sprach|ur|laub** M language-learning holiday (esp Brit) or trip; **Sprach|ver|ar|bei|tung** F (Comput) speech or voice processing; **Sprach|ver|ein** M language society; **Sprach|ver|fall** M decay of language; **Sprach|ver|glei|chung** [-fɛɐglaiçʊŋ] F -, -en comparative analysis (of languages); **Sprach|ver|mö|gen** NT faculty of language; **Sprach|ver|wandt|schaft** F linguistic relationship or kinship; **Sprach|ver|wir|rung** F confused mixture of languages, confusion of tongues (Bibl) → **babylonisch**; **Sprach|wis|sen|schaft** F linguistics sing; (= Philologie) philology; **vergleichende ~en** comparative linguistics/philology; **Sprach|wis|sen|schaft|ler(in)** M(F) linguist; (= Philologe) philologist; **sprach|wis|sen|schaft|lich** ADJ linguistic ADV linguistically; **~ interessierte Menschen** people interested in linguistics; **Sprach|zent|rum** NT (Univ) language centre (Brit) or center (US); **Sprach|zweig** M (language) branch

sprang pret von **springen**

Spray [ʃpreː, spreː] M OR NT -s, -s spray

Spray|do|se ['ʃpreː-, 'spreː-] F aerosol (can), spray

spra|yen ['ʃpreːən, 'sp-] VTI to spray

Spra|yer ['ʃpreːɐ, 'sp-] M -s, -, **Spra|ye|rin** [-ərɪn] F -, -nen sprayer

Sprech-: Sprech|akt M (Ling) speech act; **Sprech|an|la|ge** F intercom; **Sprech|bla|se** F balloon; **Sprech|büh|ne** F theatre (Brit), theater (US), stage; **Sprech|chor** M chorus; (fig) chorus of voices; **im ~ rufen** to shout in unison, to chorus; **Sprech|ein|heit** F (Telec) unit

spre|chen ['ʃpreçn] ✪ 27, 28.1, 46.2, 53.2, 53.3, 53.6 pret **sprach** [ʃpraːx], ptp **gesprochen** [gəˈʃprɔxn] VI to speak (über +acc, von about, of); (= reden, sich unterhalten) to talk (über +acc, von about); **viel ~** to talk a lot; **frei ~** to extemporize, to speak off the cuff (inf); **er spricht wenig** he doesn't say or talk very much; **sprich!** (liter) speak! (liter); **~ Sie!** (form) speak away!; **sprich doch endlich!** (geh) say something; **also sprach ...** (liter, Bibl) thus spoke ..., thus spake ... (liter, Bibl); **im Traum** or **Schlaf ~** to talk in one's sleep; **gut/schön ~** to speak well/beautifully; **im Rundfunk/Fernsehen ~** to speak on the radio/on television; **es spricht ...** the speaker is ...; **es ~ ...** the speakers are ...; **die Vernunft ~ lassen** to listen to reason, to let the voice of reason be heard; **sein Herz ~ lassen** to follow the dictates of one's heart; **schlecht** or **nicht gut auf jdn/etw zu ~ sein** not to have a good thing to say about sb/sth; **mit jdm ~** to speak or talk with or to sb; **mit sich selbst ~** to talk to oneself; **ich muss mit dir ~** I must talk or speak to you; **ich habe mit dir zu ~** I want to have a word or a few words with you; **wie sprichst du mit mir?** who do you think you're talking to?; **so spricht man nicht mit seinem Großvater** that's no way to talk or speak to your grandfather; **sie spricht nicht mit jedem** she doesn't speak or talk to just anybody; **wir ~ nicht mehr miteinander** we are no longer on speaking terms, we're not speaking any more; **mit wem spreche ich?** to whom am I speaking, please?; **~ wir nicht mehr darüber!** let's not talk about that any more, let's drop the subject; **darüber spricht man nicht** one doesn't talk about or speak of such things; **ich weiß nicht, wovon Sie ~** I don't know what you're talking about; **~ wir von etwas anderem** let's talk about something else, let's change the subject; **wir haben gerade von dir gesprochen** we were just talking about you; **es wird kaum**

noch von ihm gesprochen he's hardly mentioned now; **auf jdn/etw zu ~ kommen** to get to talking about sb/sth; **für jdn/etw ~** to speak for sb/sth, to speak on behalf of sb/sth; **gegen jdn/etw ~** to speak against sb/sth; **es spricht für jdn/etw(, dass ...)** it says something for sb/sth (that ...), it speaks well for sb/sth (that ...); **das spricht für ihn** that's a point in his favour (Brit) or favor (US), that says something for him; **es spricht nicht für die Firma, dass so was passieren konnte** it doesn't say much for the firm that something like that could happen; **das spricht für sich (selbst)** that speaks for itself; **es spricht vieles dafür/dagegen** there's a lot to be said for/against it; **es spricht vieles dafür, dass ...** there is every reason to believe that ...; **was spricht dafür/dagegen?** what is there to be said for/against it?; **aus seinen Worten sprach Verachtung/Hoffnung** his words expressed contempt/hope; **er sprach vor den Studenten/dem Ärztekongress** he spoke to the students/the medical conference; **ganz allgemein gesprochen** generally speaking

VT **a** (= sagen) to say, to speak; eine Sprache, Mundart to speak; (= aufsagen) Gebet to say; Gedicht to recite; **es wurde viel gesprochen** a lot of talking was done; **alles, was er sprach ...** everything he said ...; **~ Sie Japanisch?** do you speak Japanese?; **hier spricht man Spanisch** Spanish spoken, we speak Spanish → **Sprache**

b Urteil to pronounce → **Recht a, schuldig ADJ a**

c (= mit jdm reden) to speak to; **kann ich bitte Herrn Kurz ~?** may I speak to Mr Kurz, please?; **er ist nicht zu ~** he can't see anybody; **ich bin für niemanden zu ~** I can't see anybody, I'm not available; **ich hätte gern Herrn Bremer gesprochen** could I speak to Mr Bremer?; **kann ich Sie einen Augenblick** or **kurz ~?** can I see you for a moment?, can I have a quick word?; **für Sie bin ich jederzeit zu ~** I'm always at your disposal; **wir ~ uns noch!** you haven't heard the last of this!

spre|chend ADJ Augen, Gebärde eloquent

Spre|cher ['ʃprɛçɐ] M -s, -, **Spre|che|rin** [-ərɪn] F -, -nen speaker; (= Nachrichtensprecher) newscaster, newsreader; (für Dokumentarfilme, Stücke etc) narrator; (= Ansager) announcer; (= Wortführer) spokesperson; **sich zum ~ von jdm/etw machen** to become the spokesperson for sb/sth

Sprech-: **Sprech|er|zie|hung** F speech training, elocution; **sprech|faul** ADJ taciturn; **sei doch nicht so ~!** haven't you got a tongue in your head!; **morgens ist sie besonders ~** she's not exactly talkative in the mornings; **Sprech|feh|ler** M slip of the tongue; **Sprech|fens|ter** NT grille; **Sprech|funk** M radiotelephone system; **Sprech|funk|ge|rät** NT radiotelephone; (tragbar auch) walkie-talkie; **Sprech|funk|ver|kehr** M local radio traffic; **den ~ unterbrechen** to interrupt radiotelephone communications; **Sprech|ge|bühr** F (Telec) call (Brit) or calling (US) charge; **Sprech|ge|sang** M (Mus) speech song, sprechgesang; **Sprech|kun|de** F study of speech; **Sprech|me|lo|die** F intonation, speech melody; **Sprech|mu|schel** F (Telec) mouthpiece; **Sprech|or|gan** NT organ of speech, speech organ; **Sprech|plat|te** F spoken-word record; **Sprech|pro|be** F voice trial; **Sprech|pup|pe** F talking or speaking doll; **Sprech|rol|le** F speaking part; **Sprech|schu|lung** F voice training; **Sprech|sil|be** F (Ling) (phonetic) syllable; **Sprech|stim|me** F speaking voice; (Mus) sprechstimme, speech voice; **Sprech|stun|de** F consultation (hour); (von Arzt) surgery (Brit), consultation (US); **~n** consultation hours; (von Arzt) surgery (Brit) or consulting hours (US); **~ halten** to hold surgery (Brit); **Sprech|stun|den|hil|fe** F (doctor's) receptionist; **Sprech|tas|te** F "talk" button or switch; **Sprech|the|a|ter** NT theatre (Brit) or

theater (US) of the spoken word, straight theatre (Brit) or theater (US); **Sprech|übung** F speech exercise; **Sprech|un|ter|richt** M elocution lessons pl; **Sprech|wei|se** F way of speaking; **Sprech|werk|zeu|ge** PL organs pl of speech, speech organs pl; **Sprech|zeit** F **a** (= Sprechstunde) consulting time; (von Arzt) surgery time (Brit) **b** (= Besuchszeit: in Gefängnis, Kloster) visiting time **c** (Telec) call time; **Sprech|zim|mer** NT consulting room

Sprei|ßel¹ ['ʃpraɪsl] NT -s, - (Aus: zum Feuermachen) kindling no pl

Sprei|ßel² M -s, - (esp S Ger: = Splitter) splinter

Sprei|te ['ʃpraɪtə] F -, -n (leaf) blade

Spreiz|dü|bel M cavity plug

Sprei|ze ['ʃpraɪtsə] F -, -n **a** (Build) strut **b** (Sport) straddle

sprei|zen ['ʃpraɪtsn] **VT** Flügel, Gefieder to spread; Finger, Zehen auch to splay (out); Beine auch to open; (Sport) to straddle → auch **gespreizt VR** (= sich sträuben) to kick up (inf); (= sich aufplustern) to give oneself airs, to put on airs; **sich wie ein Pfau ~** to puff oneself up, to put on airs; **sich gegen etw ~** to kick against sth

Spreiz-: **Spreiz|fuß** M splayfoot; **Spreiz|schritt** M (Sport) straddle; **im ~ stehen** to stand with one's legs apart

Spreng-: **Spreng|ar|bei|ten** PL blasting operations pl; **„Sprengarbeiten"** "blasting"; **Spreng|bom|be** F high-explosive bomb

Spren|gel ['ʃprɛŋl] M -s, - (= Kirchspiel) parish; (= Diözese) diocese

spren|gen ['ʃprɛŋən] **VT a** (mit Sprengstoff) to blow up; Fels to blast; **etw in die Luft ~** to blow sth up **b** Türschloss, Tor to force (open); Tresor to break open; Bande, Fesseln to burst, to break; Eisdecke, Versammlung to break up; (Spiel)bank to break; **die Grenzen von etw ~** (fig) to go beyond the boundaries of sth → **Rahmen b c** (= bespritzen) to sprinkle; Beete, Rasen to water; Wäsche to sprinkle (with water); (= verspritzen) Wasser to sprinkle, to spray **VI a** (= Sprengarbeiten vornehmen) to blast **b** aux sein (liter: = kraftvoll reiten) to thunder

Spreng-: **Spreng|kam|mer** F demolition chamber; **Spreng|kap|sel** F detonator; **Spreng|kom|man|do** NT demolition squad; (zur Bombenentschärfung) bomb disposal squad; **Spreng|kopf** M warhead; **Spreng|kör|per** M explosive device; **Spreng|kraft** F explosive force; **Spreng|la|dung** F explosive charge; **Spreng|meis|ter(in)** M(F) (in Steinbruch) blaster; (bei Abbrucharbeiten) demolition expert; (zur Bombenentschärfung) bomb disposal expert; **Spreng|satz** M explosive device

Spreng|stoff M explosive; (fig) dynamite

Spreng|stoff|an|schlag M , **Spreng|stoff|at|ten|tat** NT bomb attack; (erfolgreich auch) bombing; **auf ihn wurde ein ~ verübt** he was the subject of a bomb attack; **auf das Haus wurde ein ~ verübt** there was a bomb attack on the house

Spren|gung ['ʃprɛŋʊŋ] F -, -en **a** blowing-up; (von Felsen) blasting **b** (von Tür, Schloss) forcing (open); (von Tresor) breaking open; (von Fesseln) bursting, breaking; (von Eisdecke, Versammlung) breaking-up **c** (= Bespritzen) sprinkling; (von Beeten, Rasen) watering

Spreng-: **Spreng|wa|gen** M water(ing) cart, street sprinkler; **Spreng|we|del** M (Eccl) aspergillum; **Spreng|wir|kung** F explosive effect

Spren|kel ['ʃprɛŋkl] M -s, - **a** (= Tupfen) spot, speckle **b** (= Vogelschlinge) snare

spren|keln ['ʃprɛŋkln] **VT** Farbe to sprinkle spots of → auch **gesprenkelt**

Spreu [ʃprɔy] F -, no pl chaff; **wie (die) ~ im Wind** (Bibl) like chaff in the wind (Bibl); **die ~ vom Weizen trennen** or **sondern** (fig) to separate the wheat from the chaff

spricht [ʃprɪçt] 3. pers sing pres von **sprechen**

Sprich|wort NT pl -wörter proverb

sprich|wört|lich ADJ (lit, fig) proverbial

sprie|ßen ['ʃpriːsn] pret **spross** or **sprießte** [ʃprɔs, 'ʃpriːstə], ptp **gesprossen** [gə'ʃprɔsn] **VI** aux sein (aus der Erde) to come up, to spring up; (Knospen, Blätter) to shoot; (fig geh: Liebe, Zuneigung) to burgeon (liter) → **Pilz a**

Spriet [ʃpriːt] NT -(e)s, -e (Naut) sprit

Spring|brun|nen M fountain

sprin|gen ['ʃprɪŋən] pret **sprang** [ʃpraŋ], ptp **gesprungen** [gə'ʃprʊŋən] **VI** aux sein **a** (lit, fig, Sport, bei Brettspielen) to jump; (esp mit Schwung) to leap, to spring; (beim Stabhochsprung) to vault; (Raubtier) to pounce; (= sich springend fortbewegen) to bound; (= hüpfen, seilhüpfen) to skip; (= auf einem Bein hüpfen) to hop; (Ball etc) to bounce; (Wassersport) to dive; (S Ger inf: = eilen) to nip (Brit inf), to pop (inf); **tanzen und ~** to dance and leap about; **jdm an den Hals** or **die Kehle** or **die Gurgel** (inf) **~** to leap or fly at sb's throat; (fig) to fly at sb, to go for sb; **ich hätte ihm an die Kehle ~ können** I could have strangled him; **aus dem Gleis** or **aus den Schienen ~** to jump the rails; **ins Aus ~** (Sport) to go out (of play) → **Auge a, Bresche, Klinge, Schatten**

b etw ~ lassen (inf) to fork out for sth (inf); Runde to stand sth; Geld to fork out sth; **für jdn etw ~ lassen** (inf) to treat sb to sth; **das hat der Chef ~ lassen!** (inf) that was on the boss! (inf)

c (geh: = hervorsprudeln) to spring; (Wasserstrahl, Quelle) to spring, to spurt; (Blutstrahl) to spurt; (Funken) to leap

d (Glas, Porzellan, Saite) to break; (= Risse bekommen) to crack; (= sich lösen: Knopf) to come off (von etw sth)

e (geh: = aufplatzen) to burst (forth) **VT** aux haben **einen (neuen) Rekord ~** (Sport) to make a record jump

Sprin|gen NT -s, - (Sport) jumping; (= Stabhochspringen) vaulting; (Wassersport) diving

sprin|gend ADJ der ~e Punkt the crucial point

Sprin|ger¹ ['ʃprɪŋɐ] M -s, - (Chess) knight

Sprin|ger² ['ʃprɪŋɐ] M -s, -, **Sprin|ge|rin** [-ərɪn] F -, -nen **a** jumper; (= Stabhochspringer) vaulter; (Wassersport) diver **b** (Ind) stand-in

Sprin|ger|stie|fel PL Doc Martens® (boots) pl

Spring-: **Spring|flut** F spring tide; **Spring|form** F (Cook) springform

Spring|ins|feld ['ʃprɪŋɪnsfɛlt] M -(e)s, -e [-də] madcap

Spring-: **Spring|kraut** NT , no pl (Bot) touch-me-not; **spring|le|ben|dig** ADJ lively, full of beans (esp Brit inf), antsy (US) ADV in a lively manner, full of beans (esp Brit inf); **Spring|pferd** NT jumper; **Spring|rei|ten** NT -s, no pl show jumping; **Spring|rol|lo** NT roller blind; **Spring|seil** NT skipping-rope (Brit), jump rope (US); **über ein ~ springen** (= seilspringen) to skip; **Spring|tur|nier** NT show jumping competition

Sprink|ler ['ʃprɪŋklɐ] M -s, - sprinkler

Sprink|ler|an|la|ge F sprinkler system

Sprint [ʃprɪnt] M -s, -s sprint

sprin|ten ['ʃprɪntn] VTI aux sein to sprint

Sprin|ter ['ʃprɪntɐ] M -s, -, **Sprin|te|rin** [-ərɪn] F -, -nen sprinter

Sprint|stre|cke F sprint distance

Sprit [ʃprɪt] M -(e)s, -e (inf: = Benzin) gas (inf), juice (inf); (= Rohspiritus) neat spirit (Brit), pure alcohol

Spritz-: **Spritz|be|steck** NT (für Drogen) needles pl; **Spritz|beu|tel** M icing or piping bag; **Spritz|dü|se** F nozzle; (Tech) jet

Sprit|ze ['ʃprɪtsə] F -, -n syringe; (= Feuerspritze, Gartenspritze) hose; (= Injektion) injection, jab

(*Brit inf*); **eine ~ bekommen** to have an injection *or* a jab (*Brit inf*)

sprit|zen ['ʃprɪtsn] **VT a** *Flüssigkeit* to spray; (*in einem Strahl*) *Wasser* to squirt, to spray; (*Cook*) *Zuckerguss etc* to pipe; (= *verspritzen*) *Wasser, Schmutz etc* to splash; (*Fahrzeug*) to spray, to spatter; **die Feuerwehr spritzte Wasser in das brennende Gebäude** the firemen directed their hoses into the burning building; **das vorbeifahrende Auto spritzte mir Wasser ins Gesicht** the passing car sprayed *or* spattered water in my face **b** (= *lackieren*) *Auto, Gegenstand* to spray **c** *Wein* to dilute with soda water; **er trinkt Rotwein gespritzt** he drinks red wine and soda → **Gespritzte(r)**

d (= *injizieren*) *Serum etc* to inject; *Heroin etc* to inject, to shoot (up) (*inf*); (= *eine Injektion geben*) to give injections/an injection; **wir müssen (dem Kranken) Morphium ~** we have to give (the patient) a morphine injection; **sich** (*dat*) **Heroin ~** to inject (oneself with) heroin, to shoot up (*inf*)

VI a *aux haben or sein* (*Wasser, Schlamm*) to spray, to splash; (*heißes Fett*) to spit; (*Blut*) to spray; (*in einem Strahl*) to spurt; (*aus einer Tube, Wasserpistole etc*) to squirt; **es spritzte gewaltig, als er ins Wasser plumpste** there was an enormous splash when he fell into the water; **die Feuerwehr spritzte in das brennende Gebäude** the firemen directed their hoses into the burning building **b** (= *lackieren*) to spray **c** (= *sich injizieren*) to inject oneself; **er spritzt seit einem Jahr** (*inf*) he has been shooting (up) *or* mainlining for a year (*sl*); (*Diabetiker*) he has been injecting himself for a year **d** *aux sein* (*inf*: = *eilen*) to dash, to nip (*Brit inf*)

Sprit|zen-: Sprit|zen|haus NT fire station; **Sprit|zen|wa|gen** M (*old*) fire engine

Sprit|zer ['ʃprɪtsɐ] M -s, - (= *Farbspritzer, Wasserspritzer*) splash; (*von Parfüm, Mineralwasser auch*) dash

Spritz-: Spritz|fahrt F (*inf*) spin (*inf*); **eine ~ machen** to go for a spin (*inf*); **Spritz|ge|bäck** NT (*Cook*) ≈ Viennese whirl/whirls *pl*; **Spritz|guss** ▲ M injection moulding (*Brit*) *or* molding (*US*); (*Metal*) die-casting

sprit|zig ['ʃprɪtsɪç] **ADJ** *Wein* tangy; *Auto* lively, nippy (*Brit inf*), zippy (*inf*); *Aufführung, Dialog etc* sparkling, lively; (= *witzig*) witty; **das Kabarett war ~ und witzig** the cabaret was full of wit and sparkle **ADV** *aufführen, darstellen* with sparkle; *schreiben* racily; (= *witzig*) wittily

Sprit|zig|keit F liveliness; **aufgrund seiner ~ eignet sich dieser Wein besonders für ...** its tangy flavour (*Brit*) *or* flavor (*US*) means this wine goes especially well with ...

Spritz-: Spritz|ku|chen M (*Cook*) cruller; **Spritz|lack** M spray paint; **Spritz|la|ckie|rung** F spraying; **Spritz|pis|to|le** F spray gun; **Spritz|schutz** M guard; **Spritz|tour** F = Spritzfahrt; **Spritz|tül|le** F nozzle

spröd [ʃprøːt], **sprö|de** ['ʃprøːdə] **ADJ** *Glas, Stein, Haar* brittle; *Haut* rough; *Stimme* thin; (*fig*) *Material* obdurate, recalcitrant; (= *abweisend*) *Mensch* aloof, standoffish (*inf*); *Charakter* aloof; *Sprache, Worte* offhand; *Atmosphäre, Stimmung* chilly; *Charme* austere; *Text, Musik etc* unwieldy

spross ▲ *pret von* **sprießen**

Spross ▲ [ʃprɔs] M -es, -e shoot; (*fig*: = *Nachkomme*) scion (*liter*)

Spros|se ['ʃprɔsə] F -, -n (*lit, fig*) rung; (= *Fenstersprosse*) (*senkrecht*) mullion; (*waagerecht*) transom; (= *Geweihsprosse*) branch, point, tine

spros|sen VI *aux sein* (*liter*) = **sprießen**

Spros|sen-: Spros|sen|fens|ter NT lattice window; **Spros|sen|wand** F (*Sport*) wall bars *pl*

Spröss|ling ▲ ['ʃprœslɪŋ] M -s, -e shoot; (*fig hum*) offspring *pl*

Sprot|te ['ʃprɔtə] F -, -n sprat

Spruch [ʃprʊx] M -(e)s, ⸚e ['ʃprʏçə] **a** saying; (= *Sinnspruch*) saying, aphorism; (= *Maxime*) adage, maxim; (= *Wahlspruch*) motto; (= *Bibelspruch*) quotation, quote; (*Poet*: = *Gedicht*) medieval lyric poem; **die Sprüche Salomos** (*Bibl*) (the Book of) Proverbs; **Sprüche** (*inf*: = *Gerede*) patter *no pl* (*inf*); **flotte Sprüche** wisecracks; **Sprüche klopfen** (*inf*) to talk fancy (*Brit inf*); (= *angeben*) to talk big (*inf*); (*Verkäufer*) to give one's patter (*Brit inf*) *or* spiel (*inf*); **mach keine Sprüche!** come off it! (*inf*); **das sind doch nur Sprüche!** that's just talk **b** (= *Richterspruch*) judgement; (= *Freispruch/Schuldspruch*) verdict; (= *Strafurteil*) sentence; (= *Schiedsspruch*) ruling

Spruch|band [-bant] NT *pl* **-bänder** banner

Spruch|dich|tung F (*Poet*) medieval lyric poetry

Sprü|che|klop|fer(in) M(F) (*inf*) patter merchant (*Brit inf*), smooth talker (*esp US inf*); (= *Angeber*) big talker (*inf*)

Sprüch|lein ['ʃprʏçlain] NT -s, - *dim von* **Spruch**; **sein ~ hersagen** to say one's (little) piece

spruch|reif ADJ (*inf*) **die Sache ist noch nicht ~** it's not definite yet so we'd better not talk about it; **die Sache wird erst ~, wenn ...** we can only start talking about it definitely when ...; **es gibt noch keine ~e Lösung** there is still no solution to speak of

Spru|del ['ʃpruːdl] M -s, - (= *saurer Sprudel*) mineral water; (= *süßer Sprudel*) fizzy drink

Spru|del|bad NT whirlpool (bath), jacuzzi

spru|deln ['ʃpruːdln] **VI a** (= *schäumen*) (*Wasser, Quelle*) to bubble; (*Sekt, Limonade*) to effervesce, to fizz; (*fig*: *vor Freude, guten Ideen etc*) to bubble **b** *aux sein* (= *hervorsprudeln*) (*Wasser etc*) to bubble; (*fig*) (*Worte*) to pour out; (*Steuern, Einnahmen*) to pour in **VT** (*Aus*: = *quirlen*) to whisk

spru|delnd ADJ (*lit*) *Getränke* fizzy, effervescent; *Quelle* bubbling; (*fig*) *Temperament, Witz* bubbly, effervescent; *Geldquelle, Gewinne* inexhaustible

Spru|del|tab|let|te F effervescent tablet

Sprud|ler ['ʃpruːdlɐ] M -s, - (*Aus*) whisk

Sprüh-: Sprüh|ak|ti|on F slogan-spraying operation; **Sprüh|do|se** F spray (can); (*unter Druck stehend auch*) aerosol (can)

sprü|hen ['ʃpryːən] **VI a** *aux haben or sein* to spray; (*Funken*) to fly **b** (*fig*) (*vor Witz, Ideen etc*) to bubble over (*vor +dat* with); (*Augen*) (*vor Freude etc*) to sparkle (*vor +dat* with); (*vor Zorn etc*) to flash (*vor +dat* with) **VT** to spray; (*fig*: *Augen*) to flash; **er sprühte Lack auf die beschädigte Stelle** he sprayed the damaged spot with paint

sprü|hend ADJ *Laune, Temperament etc* bubbly, effervescent; *Energie* bubbly; *Witz* sparkling, bubbly

Sprüh-: Sprüh|flug|zeug NT crop-spraying plane; **Sprüh|ne|bel** M mist; **Sprüh|re|gen** M drizzle, fine rain

Sprung [ʃprʊŋ] M -(e)s, ⸚e ['ʃprʏŋə] **a** jump; (*schwungvoll, fig*: = *Gedankensprung*) leap, jump; (= *Hüpfer*) skip; (*auf einem Bein*) hop; (= *Satz*) bound; (*von Raubtier*) pounce; (= *Stabhochsprung*) vault; (*Wassersport*) dive; **einen ~ machen** to jump; **einen kleinen ~ machen** to do a small jump; **zum ~ ansetzen** (*lit*) to get ready to jump *etc*; (*fig*) to get ready to pounce; **sie wagte den ~ (ins kalte Wasser) nicht** (*fig*) she didn't dare (to) take the plunge; **ein großer ~ nach vorn** (*fig*) a great leap forward; **damit kann man keine großen Sprünge machen** (*inf*) you can't exactly live it up on that (*inf*); **auf dem ~ sein** *or* **stehen, etw zu tun** to be about to do sth; **immer auf dem ~ sein** (*inf*) to be always on the go (*inf*); (= *aufmerksam*) to be always on the ball (*inf*); **jdm auf die Sprünge helfen** (*wohlwollend*) to give sb a (helping) hand; (*drohend*) to show sb what's what **b** (*inf*: = *kurze Strecke*) stone's throw (*inf*); **bis**

zum Postamt ist es nur ein ~ the post office is only a stone's throw from here (*inf*); **auf einen ~ bei jdm vorbeikommen/-gehen** to drop in to see sb (*inf*) **c** (= *Riss*) crack; (= *Kratzer*) scratch; **einen ~ haben** to be cracked/scratched; **einen ~ bekommen** to crack; **einen ~ in der Schüssel haben** (*fig inf*: = *verrückt sein*) to be off one's rocker (*inf*) **d** (*Geol*) fault **e** (*Hunt*: = *Rudel*) herd **f** (*Agr*: = *Begattung*) mounting; **dieser Hengst eignet sich nicht zum ~** this stallion isn't suitable for stud purposes; **es kam nicht zum ~** they didn't mate

Sprung-: Sprung|bein NT **a** (*Anat*) anklebone **b** (*Sport*) takeoff leg; **sprung|be|reit** ADJ ready to jump; *Katze* ready to pounce; (*fig hum*) ready to go; **Sprung|brett** NT (*lit, fig*) springboard; **Sprung|de|ckel** M spring lid; **Sprung|fe|der** F spring; **Sprung|fe|der|mat|rat|ze** F spring mattress; **Sprung|ge|lenk** NT ankle joint; (*von Pferd*) hock; **Sprung|gru|be** F (*Sport*) (landing) pit; **sprung|haft** ADJ **a** *Mensch, Charakter* volatile; *Denken* disjointed **b** (= *rapide*) *Aufstieg, Entwicklung, Zunahme etc* rapid; *Preisanstieg* sharp, rapid **ADV** *ansteigen, entwickeln* by leaps and bounds; **Sprung|haf|tig|keit** ['ʃprʊŋhaftɪçkait] F -, *no pl* **a** (*von Mensch*) volatility **b** (*von Entwicklung etc*) rapidity, rapidness; **Sprung|kraft** F (*Sport*) takeoff power, leg power; **Sprung|lauf** M (*Ski*) ski-jumping; **Sprung|netz** NT (jumping) net, life net (*US*), safety net; **Sprung|schan|ze** F (*Ski*) ski jump; **Sprung|stab** M (vaulting) pole; **Sprung|tuch** NT *pl* **-tücher** jumping sheet *or* blanket, life net (*US*), safety net; **Sprung|turm** M diving platform; **sprung|wei|se** ADV in bounds *or* jumps; (*fig*) by leaps and bounds

Spu|cke ['ʃpʊkə] F -, *no pl* (*inf*) spittle, spit; **da bleibt einem die ~ weg!** (*inf*) it's flabbergasting (*inf*); **als ich das hörte, blieb mir die ~ weg** when I heard that I was flabbergasted (*inf*), when I heard that you could have knocked me down with a feather (*inf*); **mit Geduld und ~** (*hum inf*) with blood, sweat and tears (*hum*)

spu|cken ['ʃpʊkn] **VT** to spit; (*inf*: = *erbrechen*) to throw *or* bring up (*inf*); *Lava, Flammen* to spew (out) **VI** to spit; (*inf*: *sich übergeben*) to throw up (*inf*), to be sick (*inf*: *Motor, Maschine etc*) to give the occasional hiccup (*inf*); **in die Hände ~** (*lit*) to spit on one's hands; (*fig*) to roll up one's sleeves

Spuck|napf M spittoon

Spuck|tü|te F (*inf*: *esp Aviat*) sick bag

Spuk [ʃpuːk] M -(e)s, -e **a** (= *Geistererscheinung*) **der ~ fing um Mitternacht an** the ghosts started to walk at midnight; **ich glaube nicht an diesen ~** I don't believe the place is haunted **b** (*fig*) (= *Lärm*) din, racket (*inf*); (= *Aufheben*) fuss, to-do (*inf*), palaver (*inf*)

spu|ken VI to haunt; **an einem Ort/in einem Schloss ~** to haunt *or* walk a place/castle; **es spukt auf dem Friedhof/im alten Haus** *etc* the cemetery/old house *etc* is haunted; **hier spukt es** this place is haunted; **durch den Film spukten wunderliche Gestalten/eigenartige Ideen** the film was haunted by weird and wonderful apparitions/strange ideas; **das spukt noch immer in den Köpfen** *or* **durch die Köpfe** that still has a hold on people's minds

Spuk-: Spuk|ge|schich|te F ghost story; **spuk|haft** ADJ eerie; **Spuk|schloss** ▲ NT haunted castle

Spül-: Spül|au|to|mat M (automatic) dishwasher; **Spül|bad** NT rinse; **Spül|be|cken** NT sink; **Spül|bürs|te** F washing-up (*Brit*) *or* dishwashing (*US*) brush

Spu|le ['ʃpuːlə] F -, -n **a** spool, reel; (= *Nähmaschinenspule, Ind*) bobbin; (*Elec*) coil **b** (= *Federkiel*) quill

Spü|le ['ʃpyːlə] F -, -n sink

spu|len [ˈʃpuːlən] VT to spool (*auch Comput*), to reel; (= *aufspulen auch*) to wind onto a spool or reel *or* (*auf Nähmaschinenspule, Ind*) bobbin

spü|len [ˈʃpyːlən] **VT a** (= *ausspülen, abspülen*) *Mund* to rinse; *Wunde* to wash; *Darm* to irrigate; *Vagina* to douche; (= *abwaschen*) *Geschirr* to wash up **b** (*Wellen etc*) to wash; (*fig*) *Menschen* to bring; **etw an Land ~** to wash sth ashore; **Geld in die Kassen ~** to bring money pouring into the coffers **VI** (*Waschmaschine*) to rinse; (= *Geschirr spülen*) to wash up; (*auf der Toilette*) to flush; **du spülst und ich trockne ab** you wash and I'll dry; **vergiss nicht zu ~** don't forget to flush the toilet

Spü|ler [ˈʃpyːlɐ] M **-s, -**, **Spü|le|rin** [-ərɪn] F **-, -nen** dishwasher, washer-up (*inf*)

Spü|licht [ˈʃpyːlɪçt] NT **-s, -e** (*old*) dishwater

Spül-: Spül|kas|ten M cistern; **Spül|klo|sett** NT flush toilet, water closet (*dated*); **Spül|lap|pen** M dishcloth; **spül|ma|schi|ne** F (*automatic*) dishwasher; **spül|ma|schi|nen|fest** ADJ dishwasher-proof; **Spül|mit|tel** NT washing-up liquid; **Spül|pro|gramm** NT wash programme (*Brit*) *or* program (*US*); (*von Waschmaschine*) rinse cycle

Spul|rad NT bobbin winder

Spül-: Spül|schüs|sel F washing-up bowl; **Spül|tisch** M sink (unit); **Spül|tuch** NT *pl* **-tücher** dishcloth

Spü|lung [ˈʃpyːlʊŋ] F **-, -en** rinsing; (= *Mundspülung*) rinse; (= *Wasser-, Toilettenspülung*) flush; (= *Spülkasten*) cistern, tank (*esp US*); (= *Haarspülung*) conditioner; (*Med*) (= *Darm-, Nasenspülung etc*) irrigation; (= *Vaginalspülung*) douche; (*Aut*) scavenging

Spül|was|ser NT *pl* **-wässer** (*beim Abwaschen*) dishwater, washing-up water; (*beim Wäschewaschen*) rinsing water

Spul|wurm M roundworm, ascarid (*Med*)

Spund¹ [ʃpʊnt] M **-(e)s, ⁼e** [ˈʃpʏndə] bung (*Brit*), stopper, spigot; (*Holztechnik*) tongue

Spund² [ʃpʊnt] M **-(e)s, -e** [-də] **junger ~** (*dated inf*) young pup (*dated inf*)

spun|den [ˈʃpʊndn̩] VT *Fass* to bung (*Brit*), to stop up

Spund-: Spund|loch NT bunghole (*Brit*), cork hole; **Spund|wand** F (*Build*) bulkhead

Spur [ʃpuːɐ] F **-, -en a** (= *Abdruck im Boden etc*) track; (*Hunt*) track, spoor *no pl*; (= *hinterlassenes Zeichen*) trace; (= *Bremsspur*) skidmarks *pl*; (= *Blutspur, Schleimspur etc, Fährte zur Verfolgung*) trail; **von den Tätern fehlt jede ~** there is no clue as to the whereabouts of the persons responsible; **der Täter hat keine ~en hinterlassen** the culprit left no traces or marks; **jds ~ aufnehmen** to take up sb's trail; **auf der richtigen/falschen ~ sein** (*lit, fig*) to be on the right/wrong track; **jdn auf jds ~ bringen** to put sb onto sb's trail or onto sb; **jdn auf die richtige ~ bringen** (*fig*) to put sb on(to) the right track; **jdm/einer Sache auf der ~ sein/auf die ~ kommen** to be/get onto sb/sth; **die Polizei ist ihm jetzt auf der ~** the police are onto him now; **auf** *or* **in jds ~en wandeln** (*fig*) to follow in sb's footsteps; **(seine) ~en hinterlassen** (*fig*) to leave its mark; **~en hinterlassen** (*fig*) to leave one's/its mark; **ohne ~(en) an jdm vorübergehen** to have no effect on sb; **nicht ohne ~(en) an jdm vorübergehen** to leave its mark on sb

b (*fig: = kleine Menge, Überrest*) trace; (*von Pfeffer, Paprika etc*) touch, soupçon; (*von Vernunft, Anstand, Talent etc*) scrap, ounce; **von Anstand/Takt keine ~** (*inf*) no decency/tact at all; **von Liebe keine ~** (*inf*) love doesn't/didn't come into it; **keine ~!** (*inf*) not at all; **keine ~ davon ist wahr** (*inf*) there's not a scrap *or* an ounce of truth in it; **wir hatten nicht die ~ einer Chance** we didn't have a ghost of a chance (*inf*); **eine ~ zu laut/grell** a shade *or* a touch too loud/garish

c (= *Fahrbahn*) lane; **auf der linken ~ fahren** to

drive in the left-hand lane; **in der ~ bleiben** to keep in lane; **die ~ wechseln** to change lanes **d** (*Aut*: = *gerade Fahrtrichtung*) tracking; **~ halten** (*beim Bremsen etc*) to hold its course; (*nach Unfall*) to track properly; **aus der ~ geraten** *or* **kommen** (*durch Seitenwind*) to go off course; (*beim Bremsen etc*) to skid

e (= *Spurweite*) (*Rail*) gauge; (*Aut*) track **f** (*Comput*) track

spür|bar ADJ noticeable, perceptible ADV noticeably, perceptibly

Spur|brei|te F (*Rail*) gauge

Spur|bus M guided bus (*which travels on road and rails*)

spu|ren [ˈʃpuːrən] VT (*Ski*) *Loipe* to make, to lay VI (*Ski*) to make or lay a track; (*Aut*) to track; (*inf*) to obey; (= *sich fügen*) to toe the line; (= *funktionieren: Maschine, Projekt*) to run smoothly, to go well; **jetzt wird gespurt!** (*inf*) I want a little obedience; **bei dem Lehrer wird gespurt** (*inf*) he makes you obey, that teacher

spü|ren [ˈʃpyːrən] VT to feel; (= *intuitiv erfassen*) *jds Hass, Zuneigung, Unwillen etc auch* to sense; **sie spürte, dass der Erdboden leicht bebte** she felt the earth trembling underfoot; **sie ließ mich ihr Missfallen ~** she made no attempt to hide her displeasure, she let me know that she was displeased; **etw in allen Gliedern ~** (*lit, fig*) to feel sth in every bone of one's body; **davon ist nichts zu ~** there is no sign of it, it's not noticeable; **etw zu ~ bekommen** (*lit*) to feel sth; (*fig*) to feel the (full) force of sth; *jds Spott, Anerkennung etc* to meet with sth; (= *bereuen*) to suffer for sth, to regret sth; **es zu ~ bekommen, dass ...** to feel the effects of the fact that ...; **ihr werdet es noch zu ~ bekommen, dass ihr so faul seid** some day you'll regret being so lazy; **sie bekamen es deutlich zu ~, dass sie Weiße waren** they were made very conscious *or* aware of the fact that they were whites

VTI (*Hunt*) (**nach**) **etw ~** to track sth, to follow the scent of sth

Spu|ren-: Spu|ren|ele|ment NT trace element; **Spu|ren|gas** NT trace gas; **Spu|ren|si|che|rung** F securing of evidence; **die Leute von der ~** the forensic people

Spür|hund M tracker dog; (*inf: Mensch*) sleuth

spur|los ADJ, ADV without trace; **~ verschwinden** to disappear or vanish without trace, to vanish into thin air; **~ an jdm vorübergehen** to have no effect on sb; (*Ereignis, Erfahrung etc auch*) to wash over sb; **das ist nicht ~ an ihm vorübergegangen** it left its mark on him

Spür|na|se F (*Hunt*) nose; **eine ~ für etw haben** (*fig inf*) to have a (good) nose for sth

Spür|pan|zer M (*Mil*) NBC (*nuclear, biological, and chemical*) reconnaissance system

Spur|ril|le F (*Mot*) rut

Spür|sinn M , *no pl* (*Hunt, fig*) nose; (*fig*: = *Gefühl*) feel

Spurt [ʃpʊrt] M **-s, -s** *or* **-e** spurt; (= *Endspurt, fig*) final spurt; **zum ~ ansetzen** (*lit, fig*) to make a final spurt

spur|ten [ˈʃpʊrtn̩] VI *aux sein* (*Sport*) to spurt; (= *zum Endspurt ansetzen*) to make a final spurt; (*inf: = rennen*) to sprint, to dash

Spur|wech|sel M (*Mot*) lane change; **ein ~ war unmöglich** it was impossible to change lanes

Spur|wei|te F (*Rail*) gauge; (*Aut*) track

spu|ten [ˈʃpuːtn̩] VR (*old, dial*) to hurry, to make haste (*old, liter*)

Sput|nik [ˈʃpʊtnɪk, ˈsp-] M **-s, -s** sputnik

Squash [skvɔʃ] NT **-, no pl** squash

Squash- [ˈskvɔʃ-]: **Squash|hal|le** F squash courts *pl*; **Squash|schlä|ger** M squash racket

SR M **-s**, *no pl abbr von* **Saarländischer Rundfunk**

SRG is the Schweizerische Radio- und Fernsehgesellschaft, founded in 1931. It is a private company but is non-profit-making. Altogether it transmits ten radio and three television channels in the four national languages of German, French, Italian and Rhaeto-Romanic. SRG is funded by licence fees and television advertising and aims to provide balanced and diverse political and cultural broadcasting.

Sri Lan|ka [ˈsriː ˈlaŋka] NT **- -s** Sri Lanka

Sri|lan|ker [sriːˈlaŋkɐ] M **-s, -**, **Sri|lan|ke|rin** [-ərɪn] F **-, -nen** Sri Lankan

sri|lan|kisch [sriːˈlaŋkɪʃ] ADJ Sri Lankan

SS¹ [ɛsˈʔɛs] NT **-, -** (*Univ*) *abbr von* **Sommersemester**

SS² [ɛsˈʔɛs] F **-, *no pl** (*NS*) *abbr von* **Schutzstaffel** SS

SSO *abbr von* **Südsüdost** SSE

SSV [ɛsɛsˈfaʊ] M **-s, -s** *abbr von* **Sommerschlussverkauf**

SSW *abbr von* **Südsüdwest** SSW

st INTERJ (*Aufmerksamkeit erregend*) psst; (*Ruhe gebietend*) shh

s. t. [ɛsˈteː] ADV *abbr von* **sine tempore**

St. *abbr von* **Stück** *abbr von* **Sankt** St

Staat [ʃtaːt] M **-(e)s, -en a** state; (= *Land*) country; **die ~en** (*inf*) the States (*inf*); **im deutschen ~ in** Germany; **die beiden deutschen ~en** (*Hist*) the two Germanies *or* German states; **ein ~ im ~e** a state within a state; **von ~s wegen** on a governmental level; **im Interesse des ~es** in the national interest, in the interests of the state; **zum Wohl des ~es** for the good of the nation; **beim ~ arbeiten** *or* **sein** (*inf*) to be employed by the government *or* state; **so wenig ~ wie möglich** minimal government; **der schlanke ~** the slimmed-down *or* lean state; **~ ist** the state's the state; **der ~ bin ich** (*prov*) l'État, c'est moi

b (= *Ameisenstaat, Bienenstaat*) colony

c (*fig: = Pracht*) pomp; (= *Kleidung, Schmuck*) finery; **in vollem ~** in all one's finery; (*Soldaten*) in full dress; (*Würdenträger*) in full regalia; (*großen*) **~ machen (mit etw)** to make a show (of sth); **damit ist kein ~ zu machen, damit kann man nicht gerade ~ machen** that's nothing to write home about (*inf*); **ohne großen ~ damit zu machen** without making a big thing about it (*inf*)

Staa|ten-: Staa|ten|bund M *pl* **-bünde** confederation (of states); **Staa|ten|ge|mein|schaft** F community of states; **staa|ten|los** ADJ stateless; **Staa|ten|lo|se(r)** [ˈʃtaːtn̩loːzə] MF *decl as adj* stateless person; **Staa|ten|lo|sig|keit** F **-, *no pl** statelessness

staatl. gepr. *abbr von* **staatlich geprüft**

staat|lich [ˈʃtaːtlɪç] ADJ state *attr*; *Gelder, Unterstützung etc auch* government *attr*; (= *staatseigen*) *Betrieb, Güter auch* state-owned; (= *staatlich geführt*) state-run ADV by the state; **~ subventioniert** subsidized by the state, state-subsidized; **~ anerkannt** state-approved; **~ geprüft** state-certified

staat|li|cher|seits [ˈʃtaːtlɪçɐzaits] ADV on the part of the state

Staats-: Staats|ab|ga|ben PL (government) taxes *pl*; **Staats|af|fä|re** F **a** (*lit*) affair of state **b** (*fig*) major operation; **Staats|akt** M (*lit*) state occasion; (*fig inf*) song and dance (*inf*); **er wurde in or mit einem feierlichen ~ verabschiedet** his farewell was a state occasion; **Staats|ak|ti|on** F major operation; **Staats|amt** NT public office; **Staats|an|ge|hö|ri|ge(r)** MF *decl as adj* national; (*einer Monarchie auch*) subject; **Staats|an|ge|hö|rig|keit** [-ˌlaŋɡəhøːrɪçkait] F **-, -en** nationality; **Staats|an|ge|hö|rig|keits|nach|weis** M proof of nationality; **Staats|an|ge|le|gen|heit** F state affair; **Staats|an|lei|he** F government bond;

Staats|an|walt M , **Staats|an|wäl|tin** F district attorney (US), public prosecutor (esp Brit); **der ~ forderte ...** the prosecution called for ...; **Staats|an|walt|schaft** F district attorney's office (US), public prosecutor's office (esp Brit); (= Anwälte) district attorneys pl (US), public prosecutors pl (esp Brit); **Staats|ap|pa|rat** M apparatus of state; **Staats|ar|chiv** NT state archives pl; **Staats|aus|ga|ben** PL public spending sing or expenditure sing; **Staats|bahn** F state-owned or national railway(s pl) (Brit), state-owned or national railroad(s pl) (US); **Staats|bank** F pl -banken national or state bank; **Staats|bank|rott** M national bankruptcy; **Staats|be|am|te(r)** M decl as adj, **Staats|be|am|tin** F public servant; **Staats|be|gräb|nis** NT state funeral; **Staats|be|sitz** M state property; **(in) ~ sein** to be state-owned; **Staats|be|such** M state visit; **Staats|be|trieb** M state-owned or nationalized enterprise; **Staats|bi|bli|o|thek** F national library; **Staats|bür|ger(in)** M(F) citizen; **Staats|bür|ger|kun|de** F (Sch) civics sing; **staats|bür|ger|lich** ADJ attr Pflicht civic; Rechte civil; **Staats|bür|ger|schaft** F nationality; **doppelte ~** dual nationality; **Staats|chef(in)** M(F) head of state; **Staats|die|ner(in)** M(F) public servant; **Staats|dienst** M civil service; **staats|ei|gen** ADJ state-owned; **Staats|ei|gen|tum** NT state property no art, property of the state; **Staats|ein|nah|men** PL public revenue sing; **Staats|emp|fang** M state reception; **staats|er|hal|tend** ADJ conducive to the wellbeing of the state; **Staats|exa|men** NT state exam(ination), ≈ first degree, university degree required for the teaching profession

> ## STAATSEXAMEN
>
> The **Staatsexamen**, or **Staatsprüfung** to give it its official name, is an examination set by state-run examination boards. It has to be taken by everyone trying to get into certain professions, such as those of lawyer, teacher, doctor, pharmacist or nurse. A course of study, if required, leads to the first **Staatsexamen**. This is followed by a two- to three-year period of practical training and the second **Staatsexamen** or, in the case of doctors and pharmacists, the **Approbation**.

Staats-: Staats|fei|er|tag M national holiday; **Staats|feind(in)** M(F) enemy of the state; **staats|feind|lich** ADJ Person, Gruppe hostile to the state; Tätigkeit, Hetze against the state ADV **sich ~ betätigen** to engage in activities hostile to the state; **Staats|fi|nan|zen** PL public finances pl; **Staats|flag|ge** F national flag; **Staats|form** F type of state; **Staats|ge|biet** NT national territory no art; **staats|ge|fähr|dend** ADJ threatening the security of the state; **Staats|ge|fähr|dung** F threat to the security of the state; **Staats|ge|heim|nis** NT (lit, fig hum) state secret; **Staats|gel|der** PL public funds pl; **Staats|ge|richts|hof** M constitutional court; **Staats|ge|walt** F authority of the state; **Staats|gren|ze** F state frontier or border; **Staats|haus|halt** M national budget; **Staats|ho|heit** F sovereignty; **Staats|idee** F conception of a state; **Staats|in|te|res|se** NT interests pl of (the) state; **Staats|kanz|lei** F state chancellery; **Staats|ka|pi|ta|lis|mus** M state capitalism; **Staats|ka|ros|se** F state carriage; **Staats|kas|se** F treasury, public purse; **Staats|kir|che** F state church; **Staats|klug|heit** F (liter) statesmanship; **Staats|kne|te** F (inf) public money; **Staats|kom|mis|sar(in)** M(F) state commissioner; **Staats|kos|ten** PL public expenses pl; **auf ~** at the public expense; **Staats|kunst** F (liter) statesmanship, statecraft; **Staats|leh|re** F political science; **Staats|lot|te|rie** F national or state lottery; **Staats|macht** F state power; **Staats|mann**

M pl -männer statesman; **staats|män|nisch** [-mɛnɪʃ] ADJ statesmanlike ADV in a statesmanlike manner; **Staats|mi|nis|ter(in)** M(F) state minister; **Staats|mo|no|pol** NT state monopoly; **Staats|ober|haupt** NT head of state; **Staats|ord|nung** F system of government; **Staat- und Gesellschaftsordnung** social system and system of government; **Staats|or|gan** NT organ of the state; **Staats|par|tei** F official party; **staats|po|li|tisch** ADJ political; **Staats|po|li|zei** F ≈ FBI (US), ≈ Special Branch (Brit); **die Geheime ~** (Hist) the Gestapo; **Staats|prä|si|dent(in)** M(F) president; **Staats|prü|fung** F (form) = Staatsexamen; **Staats|rai|son** [-rɛzõ:] F -, no pl, **Staats|rä|son** F reasons of state; **Staats|rat¹** M council of state; (Sw) cantonal government; **Staats|rat²** M , **Staats|rä|tin** F councillor (Brit) or councilor (US) of state; (Sw) member of the cantonal government; **Staats|rats|vor|sit|zen|de(r)** MF decl as adj (DDR) head of state; **Staats|recht** NT , no pl ⓐ national law ⓑ (= Verfassungsrecht) constitutional law; **Staats|recht|lich** ADJ ⓐ Entscheidung, Überlegung of national law ⓑ (= verfassungsrechtlich) constitutional ADV according to national law; (= verfassungsrechtlich) constitutionally; **~ unterscheiden sich ...** in national law there are differences between ...; **Staats|re|gie|rung** F state government; **Staats|re|li|gi|on** F state religion; **Staats|ren|te** F state or government pension; **Staats|ru|der** NT (geh) helm of (the) state; **Staats|sä|ckel** M (old, hum) national coffers pl; **Staats|schatz** M national treasury; **Staats|schiff** NT (liter) ship of state; **Staats|schuld** F (Fin) national debt; **Staats|sek|re|tär(in)** M(F) (= Beamter) ≈ permanent secretary (Brit), ≈ undersecretary (US); **Staats|si|cher|heit** F national or state security; **Staats|si|cher|heits|dienst** M (DDR) national or state security service; **Staats|so|zia|lis|mus** M state socialism; **Staats|streich** M coup (d'état); **Staats|the|a|ter** NT state theatre (Brit) or theater (US); **staats|tra|gend** ADJ Politiker representing the interests of the state; Partei established; Rede statesmanlike ADV **~ ausgedrückt** expressed in a statesmanlike manner; **Staats|trau|er|tag** M national day of mourning; **Staats|un|ter|neh|men** NT state-owned enterprise; **Staats|ver|bre|chen** NT political crime; (fig) major crime; **Staats|ver|dros|sen|heit** F dissatisfaction or disenchantment with the state; **Staats|ver|fas|sung** F (national) constitution; **Staats|ver|leum|dung** F slander or (schriftlich) libel of the state; **Staats|ver|mö|gen** NT national or public assets pl; **Staats|ver|schul|dung** F national debt; **Staats|ver|trag** M international treaty; **Staats|ver|wal|tung** F administration of the state; **Staats|wald** M state-owned forest; **Staats|we|sen** NT , no pl state; **Staats|wis|sen|schaft** F , **Staats|wis|sen|schaf|ten** PL (dated) political science; **Staats|wohl** NT public welfare; **Staats|zu|schuss** ▲ M state or government grant

Stab [ʃtaːp] M -(e)s, ⸚e ['ʃtɛːbə] ⓐ rod; (= Gitterstab) bar; (= Spazierstock, Wanderstab) stick; (= Bischofsstab) crosier; (= Hirtenstab) crook; (= Marschallstab, Dirigentenstab, für Staffellauf, von Majorette etc) baton; (als Amtszeichen) mace; (für Stabhochsprung, = Zeltstab) pole; (= Messstab) (measuring) rod or stick; (Aut) dipstick; (= Zauberstab) wand; **den ~ über jdn brechen** (fig) to condemn sb; **den ~ führen** (Mus geh) to conduct ⓑ (= Mitarbeiterstab, Mil) staff; (von Experten) panel; (Mil: = Hauptquartier) headquarters sing or pl

Stäb|chen [ʃtɛːpçən] NT -s, - dim von Stab (= Essstäbchen) chopstick; (= Kragenstäbchen) (collar) stiffener; (= Korsettstäbchen) bone; (Anat: der Netzhaut) rod; (beim Häkeln) treble; (inf: = Zigarette) cig (esp US), ciggy (inf)

Stab-: stab|för|mig ADJ rod-shaped; **Stab|füh|rung** F (Mus) conducting; **unter der ~ von** conducted by, under the baton of; **Stab|heu|**

schre|cke F stick insect; **Stab|hoch|sprin|ger(in)** M(F) pole-vaulter; **Stab|hoch|sprung** M pole vault

stabil [ʃtaˈbiːl, st-] ADJ Möbel, Schuhe, Kind sturdy, robust; Währung, Beziehung, Charakter stable; Gesundheit sound; (euph: = korpulent) well-built, solid ADV gebaut solidly, sturdily

Sta|bi|li|sa|ti|on [ʃtabilizaˈtsjoːn, st-] F -, -en stabilization

Sta|bi|li|sa|tor [ʃtabiliˈzaːtoːɐ, st-] M -s, Stabilisatoren [-ˈtoːrən] stabilizer

sta|bi|li|sie|ren [ʃtabiliˈziːrən, st-] ptp stabilisiert VT to stabilize VR to stabilize, to become stable

Sta|bi|li|tät [ʃtabiliˈtɛːt, st-] F -, no pl (von Währung, Land, Situation) stability

Sta|bi|li|täts|pakt [ʃtabiliˈtɛːts-, st-] M (Pol, Econ) stability pact

Stab-: Stab|kir|che F stave church; **Stab|lam|pe** F (electric) torch, flashlight; **Stab|mag|net** M bar magnet; **Stab|reim** M alliteration

Stabs-: Stabs|arzt M , **Stabs|ärz|tin** F (Mil) captain in the medical corps; **Stabs|chef(in)** M(F) (Mil inf) Chief of Staff; **Stabs|feld|we|bel(in)** M(F) (Mil) warrant officer class II (Brit), master sergeant (US); **Stabs|of|fi|zier(in)** M(F) (Mil) staff officer; (Rang) field officer; **Stabs|stel|le** F specialist team; (Mil) staff

Stab|wech|sel M (Sport) baton change, changeover

Stac|ca|to [staˈkaːto, ʃt-] NT -s, -s or Staccati [-ti] staccato

stach pret von stechen

Sta|chel ['ʃtaxl] M -s, -n (von Rosen, Ginster etc) thorn, prickle; (von Kakteen, Stachelhäutern, Igel) spine; (von Stachelschwein) quill, spine; (auf Stacheldraht) barb; (zum Viehantrieb) goad; (= Giftstachel: von Bienen etc) sting; (fig liter) (von Ehrgeiz, Neugier etc) spur; (von Vorwurf, Hass) sting; **sei|nen ~ verlieren** (fig) to lose its sting; **Tod, wo ist dein ~?** (Bibl) Death where now thy sting?; **der ~ des Fleisches** (liter) the urges pl of the body; **ein ~ im Fleisch** (liter) a thorn in the flesh or side → löcken

Sta|chel-: Sta|chel|bee|re F gooseberry; **Sta|chel|beer|strauch** M gooseberry bush

Sta|chel|draht M barbed wire

Sta|chel|draht-: Sta|chel|draht|ver|hau M barbed-wire entanglement; **Sta|chel|draht|zaun** M barbed-wire fence

Sta|chel-: Sta|chel|flos|ser [-flɔsɐ] M -s, - (Zool) spiny-finned fish; **sta|chel|för|mig** ADJ spiky; (Biol) spiniform no adv; **Sta|chel|hals|band** NT spiked (dog) collar; **Sta|chel|häu|ter** [-hɔytɐ] M -s, - (Zool) echinoderm (spec)

sta|che|lig ['ʃtaxəlɪç] ADJ Rosen, Ginster etc thorny; Kaktus, Igel etc spiny; (= sich stachelig anfühlend) prickly; Kinn, Bart bristly; Draht spiky, barbed

sta|cheln ['ʃtaxln] VT = anstacheln

Sta|chel-: Sta|chel|ro|chen M stingray; **Sta|chel|schne|cke** F murex; **Sta|chel|schwein** NT porcupine

stach|lig ['ʃtaxlɪç] ADJ = stachelig

Sta|del ['ʃtaːdl] M -s, - (S Ger, Aus, Sw) barn

Sta|di|on ['ʃtaːdiɔn] NT -s, Stadien [-diən] stadium

Sta|di|um ['ʃtaːdiʊm] NT -s, Stadien [-diən] stage; **im vorgerückten/letzten ~** (Med) at an advanced/terminal stage; **er hat Krebs im vorgerückten/letzten ~** he has advanced/terminal cancer

Stadt [ʃtat] F -, ⸚e ['ʃtɛːtə, 'ʃtɛta] ⓐ town; (= Großstadt) city; **die ~ Paris** the city of Paris; **Me|xiko-Stadt** Mexico City; **~ und Land** town and country; **in ~ und Land** throughout the land, the length and breadth of the land; **die ganze ~ spricht davon** it's all over town, the whole town is talking about it, it's the talk of the town; **in die ~ gehen** to go into town **b** (= *Stadtverwaltung*) (town) council; (*von Großstadt*) (city) council; **bei der ~ angestellt sein** to be working for the council; **die ~ Ulm** Ulm City Council; **die ~ Güstrow** Güstrow Town Council

städt. *abbr von* **städtisch**

Stadt-: Stadt|adel M town nobility; **stadt|aus|wärts** ADV out of town; **für den Verkehr ~ gesperrt** closed to traffic going out of town; **Stadt|au|to|bahn** F urban motorway (*Brit*) or freeway (*US*); **Stadt|bad** NT municipal baths *pl* (*Brit*) or swimming pool; **Stadt|bahn** F suburban railway (*Brit*), city railroad (*US*); **Stadt|be|hör|de** F municipal authority; **stadt|be|kannt** ADJ well-known, known all over town; **Stadt|be|sich|ti|gung** F town/city (sightseeing) tour, tour of a/the town/city; **Stadt|be|woh|ner(in)** M(F) town dweller (*esp Brit*) or resident; (*von Großstadt*) city dweller (*esp Brit*) or resident; **~ pl** townspeople *pl*; (*von Großstadt*) city people *pl*; **Stadt|be|zirk** M municipal district; **Stadt|bild** NT urban features *pl*, townscape; cityscape; **das ständig wechselnde ~ Bonns** the constantly changing face of Bonn; **Stadt|bü|che|rei** F → *Stadt a* municipal or town/city (lending) library, public library; **Stadt|bum|mel** M stroll in the or through town

Städt|chen ['ʃtɛːtçən, 'ʃtɛtçən] NT **-s, -** *dim von* **Stadt** small town

Stadt-: Stadt|chro|nik F → *Stadt a* town/city chronicles *pl*; **Stadt|di|rek|tor(in)** M(F) → *Stadt a* town clerk (*Brit*), town/city manager (*US*)

Städ|te-: Städ|te|bau M , *no pl* urban development; **städ|te|bau|lich** ADJ *Entwicklung* of urban building; *Maßnahme* for urban development; *Veränderungen* in urban development; ADV as regards urban development

stadt|ein|wärts ADV into town; **für den Verkehr ~ gesperrt** closed to traffic going into town

Städ|te-: Städ|te|part|ner|schaft F town twinning (*Brit*), sister city agreement (*US*); **Städ|te|pla|nung** F town or urban planning

Städ|ter ['ʃtɛːtɐ, 'ʃtɛtɐ] M **-s, -**, **Städ|te|rin** [-ərɪn] F **-, -nen** urban dweller (*Brit*) or resident; (= *Großstädter*) city dweller (*Brit*) or resident

Städ|te|tag M convention or congress of municipal authorities

Stadt-: Stadt|fahrt F → *Stadt a* journey within a/the town/city; **Stadt|flucht** F exodus from the cities; **Stadt|füh|rung** F guided tour of a/the town/city; **Stadt|gas** NT , *no pl* town gas; **Stadt|ge|biet** NT municipal area; (*von Großstadt auch*) city zone; **Stadt|ge|mein|de** F municipality; **Stadt|ge|spräch** NT **a** (*das*) **sein** to be the talk of the town **b** (*Telec*) local call; **Stadt|gren|ze** F → *Stadt a* town/city boundary; **Stadt|gue|ril|la** F urban guerrilla; **Stadt|haus** NT townhouse

städ|tisch ['ʃtɛːtɪʃ, 'ʃtɛtɪʃ] ADJ municipal, town *attr*; (= *einer Großstadt auch*) city *attr*; (= *nach Art einer Stadt*) urban; **die ~e Bevölkerung** the town/city or town population; **die ~e Lebensweise** the urban way of life, town/city life

Stadt-: Stadt|käm|me|rer M , **Stadt|käm|me|rin** F → *Stadt a* town/city treasurer; **Stadt|kas|se** F → *Stadt a* town/city treasury; **Stadt|kern** M → *Stadt a* town/city centre (*Brit*) or center (*US*); **Stadt|kind** NT → *Stadt a* town/city kid (*inf*); **Stadt|kom|man|dant(in)** M(F) → *Stadt a* military governor (of a town/city); **Stadt|kreis** M → *Stadt a* town/city borough; **Stadt|land|schaft** F → *Stadt a* town/city landscape, townscape/cityscape; **Stadt|luft** F → *Stadt a* town/city air; **~ macht frei** (*Hist*) *principle whereby a serf became a freeman if he stayed in a town/city for a year and a day*; **Stadt|ma|ga|zin** NT listings magazine, entertainment and events guide; **Stadt-**

mau|er F city wall; **Stadt|mensch** M → *Stadt a* town/city person; **Stadt|mis|si|on** F city mission; **Stadt|mit|te** F → *Stadt a* town/city centre (*Brit*) or center (*US*); **Stadt|ober|haupt** NT → *Stadt a* head of a/the town/city; **Stadt|park** M → *Stadt a* town/city or municipal park; **Stadt|par|la|ment** NT city council; **Stadt|plan** M → *Stadt a* (street) map of a/the town/city); (*Archit*) town/city plan; **Stadt|pla|nung** F town planning; **Stadt|rand** M → *Stadt a* outskirts *pl* (of a/the town/city); **am ~** on the outskirts of a/the town/city); **Stadt|rand|sied|lung** F suburban housing scheme; **Stadt|rat¹** M → *Stadt a* (town/city) council; **Stadt|rat²** M , **Stadt|rä|tin** F → *Stadt a* (town/city) councillor (*Brit*) or councilor (*US*); **Stadt|recht** NT (*Hist*) town charter; **Stadt|rund|fahrt** F → *Stadt a* (sightseeing) tour of a/the town/city; **eine ~ machen** to go on a (sightseeing) tour of a/the town/city; **Stadt|rund|gang** M → *Stadt a* walking tour of a/the town/city, town/city walking tour; **Stadt|schrei|ber(in)** M(F) (*obs, Sw*) town clerk; **Stadt|staat** M city state; **Stadt|strei|cher** [-ʃtraɪçɐ] M **-s, -**, **Stadt|strei|che|rin** [-ərɪn] F **-, -nen** (*von a/the town/city*) tramp; **Stadt|strei|che|rei** [-ʃtraɪçə'raɪ] F **-**, *no pl* urban vagrancy; **Stadt|teil** M → *Stadt a* district, part of town/city; **Stadt|the|a|ter** NT municipal theatre (*Brit*) or theater (*US*); **Stadt|tor** NT → *Stadt a* town/city gate; **Stadt|vä|ter** PL (*old, hum*) city fathers *pl* or elders *pl*; **Stadt|ver|kehr** M → *Stadt a* (= *Straßenverkehr*) town/city traffic **b** (= *örtlicher Nahverkehr*) local town/city transport; **Stadt|ver|ord|ne|te(r)** [-fɛɐlɔrdnətə] MF *decl as adj* → *Stadt a* town/city councillor (*Brit*) or councilor (*US*); **Stadt|ver|wal|tung** F → *Stadt a* (town/city) council; **Stadt|vier|tel** NT → *Stadt a* district, part of town/city; **Stadt|wap|pen** NT municipal coat of arms; **Stadt|wer|ke** PL → *Stadt a* town's/city's department of works; **Stadt|woh|nung** F → *Stadt a* town/city apartment or flat (*Brit*); **Stadt|zen|trum** NT → *Stadt a* town/city centre (*Brit*) or center (*US*)

Sta|fet|te [ʃta'fɛtə] F **-, -n** (*Hist*) courier, messenger

Staf|fa|ge [ʃta'faːʒə] F **-, -n** (*Art* = *Beiwerk*) staffage; (*fig*) window-dressing

Staf|fel ['ʃtafl] F **-, -n a** (= *Formation*) (*Mil, Naut, Aviat*) echelon; (*Aviat* = *Einheit*) squadron; **~ flie|gen** to fly in echelon formation **b** (*Sport*) relay (race); (= *Mannschaft*) relay team; (*fig*) relay; **~ lau|fen/schwim|men** to run/swim in a relay (race) **c** (= *Stufe, Sprosse*) rung; (*S Ger* = *Steintreppe*) stone steps *pl*

Staf|fe|lei [ʃtafə'laɪ] F **-, -en** easel

Staf|fel-: Staf|fel|lauf M relay (race); **Staf|fel|mie|te** F graduated rent

staf|feln ['ʃtafln] VT **a** *Gehälter, Tarife, Fahrpreise* to grade, to graduate; *Anfangszeiten, Startplätze* to stagger; **nach Dienstalter gestaffelte Gehälter** salaries graded according to years of service; **die Gehaltserhöhung wird zeitlich gestaffelt** the salary increase is being phased (over a period of time); **diese Zahlungen werden sozial gestaffelt** these payments are graded according to need; **die Startplätze gestaffelt anordnen** to stagger the starting places **b** (= *in Formation bringen*) to draw up in an echelon; **gestaffelte Formation** (*Aviat*) echelon formation

Staf|fel-: Staf|fel|schwim|men NT relay swimming; **Staf|fel|ta|rif** M graduated or differential tariff

Staf|fe|lung ['ʃtafəlʊŋ] F **-, -en**, **Stafflung** ['ʃtaflʊŋ] F **-, -en a** (*von Gehältern, Tarifen, Preisen*) grading, graduating; (*von Zeiten, Startplätzen*) staggering **b** (*in Formation*) drawing up in an echelon

Staf|fel|zins M (*Fin*) graduated interest *sing*

Stag [ʃtaːk] NT **-(e)s, -e(n)** [-gə, -gn] (*Naut*) stay

Stag|fla|ti|on [ʃtakflaˈtsioːn, st-] F **-, -en** (*Econ*) stagflation

Stag|na|ti|on [ʃtagnaˈtsioːn, st-] F **-, -en** stagnation, stagnancy; **es kam zu einer ~** there was a period of stagnation or stagnancy

stag|nie|ren [ʃtaˈgniːrən, st-] *ptp* **stagniert** VI to stagnate

Stag|nie|rung F **-, -en** = **Stagnation**

stahl *pret von* **stehlen**

Stahl [ʃtaːl] M **-(e)s, -e** or **Stähle** ['ʃtɛːlə] steel; (*old liter.* = *Schwert auch*) blade; **Nerven aus** or **wie ~** nerves of steel

Stahl- *in cpds* steel; **Stahl|bau** M *pl* **-bauten** steel-girder construction; **Stahl|be|ton** M reinforced concrete; **stahl|blau** ADJ steel-blue; **Stahl|blech** NT sheet steel; (*Stück*) steel sheet; **Stahl|bram|me** [-bramə] F **-, -n** steel girder

stäh|len ['ʃtɛːlən] VT *Körper, Muskeln, Nerven, Charakter* to harden, to toughen; **seinen Mut ~** to steel oneself VR to toughen or harden oneself; (= *sich wappnen*) to steel oneself

stäh|lern ['ʃtɛːlɐn] ADJ *Waffen, Ketten* steel; (*fig*) *Muskeln, Wille* of iron, iron *attr*; *Nerven* of steel; *Blick* steely

Stahl-: Stahl|fe|der F steel nib; **Stahl|ge|rüst** NT tubular steel scaffolding; (= *Gerippe*) steel-girder frame; **stahl|grau** ADJ steel-grey (*Brit*), steel-gray (*US*); **stahl|hart** ADJ *Mensch, Muskeln* (as) hard as steel; *Blick* steely; **Stahl|helm** M (*Mil*) steel helmet; **Stahl|helm-Frak|ti|on** F (*Pol*) hawks *pl*, hardliners *pl*; **Stahl|in|dus|trie** F , *no pl* steel industry; **Stahl|kam|mer** F strongroom; **Stahl|ko|cher(in)** M(F) steelworker; **Stahl|man|tel|ge|schoss** ▲ NT steel jacket bullet; **Stahl|rohr** NT tubular steel; (*Stück*) steel tube; **Stahl|rohr|mö|bel** PL tubular steel furniture *sing*; **Stahl|ross** ▲ NT (*hum*) bike (*inf*), velocipede (*form, hum*); **Stahl|stich** M (*Art*) steel engraving; **Stahl|trä|ger** M steel girder; **Stahl|wa|ren** PL steel goods *pl*, steelware *sing*; **Stahl|werk** NT steelworks *sing* or *pl*; **Stahl|wol|le** F steel wool

stak (*geh*) *pret von* **stecken** VI

Stake ['ʃtaːkə] F **-, -n** (*N Ger*) (barge)pole; (*für Stechkahn*) (punt) pole

sta|ken ['ʃtaːkn] VTI → (*N Ger*) (*vi: aux sein*) to pole; *Stechkahn auch* to punt; (*fig*) to stalk

Sta|ken ['ʃtaːkn] M **-s, -** (*N Ger*) = **Stake**

Sta|ket [ʃtaˈkeːt] NT **-(e)s, -e**, **Sta|ke|ten|zaun** M paling, picket fence

Stak|ka|to [ʃtaˈkaːto, st-] NT **-s, -s** or **Stakkati** [-ti] staccato

stak|sen ['ʃtaːksn] VI *aux sein* (*inf*) to stalk; (*unsicher*) to teeter; (*steif*) to hobble; **mit ~den Schritten gehen** to stalk/teeter/hobble

stak|sig ['ʃtaːksɪç] ADJ *Beine* spindly; (= *unbeholfen*) gawky ADV **~ gehen** (*steif*) to hobble; (= *unsicher*) to teeter; **jdm ~ entgegenkommen** to teeter toward(s) sb

Sta|lag|mit [ʃtalaˈgmiːt, ʃt-, -mɪt] M **-en** or **-s, -en** stalagmite

Sta|lak|tit [ʃtalakˈtiːt, ʃt-, -tɪt] M **-en** or **-s, -en** stalactite

Sta|li|nis|mus [ʃtaliˈnɪsmʊs, ʃt-] M , *no pl* Stalinism

Sta|li|nist [ʃtaliˈnɪst, ʃt-] M **-en, -en**, **Sta|li|nis|tin** [-ˈnɪstɪn] F **-, -nen** Stalinist

sta|li|nis|tisch [ʃtaliˈnɪstɪʃ, ʃt-] ADJ Stalinist; ADV *geführt* along Stalinist lines; in a Stalinist way; **~ klingend** Stalinist sounding; **~ gesinnt** Stalinist; **~ beeinflusst** influenced by (the teachings of) Stalin

Sta|lin|or|gel ['ʃtaːlin-, ʃt-] F multiple rocket launcher

Stall [ʃtal] M **-(e)s, ⸚e** ['ʃtɛlə] **a** (= *Pferdestall, Gestüt, Aut* = *Rennstall, fig*) stable; (= *Kuhstall*) cowshed, (cow) barn (*US*), byre (*Brit*); (= *Hühnerstall*) henhouse, coop; (= *Kaninchenstall*) hutch; (= *Schafstall*) (sheep)cote; (= *Schweinestall*) (pig)sty, (pig)pen (*US*); **den ~ ausmisten** to clean out the stable *etc*; (*fig*) to clean out the Augean stables; **ein (ganzer) ~ voll Kinder** (*inf*) a (whole) pack of children **b** (*inf*: = *Hosenschlitz*) flies *pl* (*Brit*), fly

Stallaterne △ F → **Stalllaterne**

Stall-: Stall|bur|sche M = **Stallknecht**; **Stall|dung** M , **Stall|dün|ger** M farmyard manure; **Stall|ge|ruch** M farmyard smell; (*fig*: = *Merkmale*) characteristics *pl*; **Stall|ha|se** M rabbit; **Stall|knecht** M farm hand; (*für Pferde*) stableman, stable lad *or* hand; (*für Kühe*) cowhand; **Stall|la|ter|ne** ▲ F stable lamp; **Stall|magd** F farm girl; (*für Pferde*) stable maid; (= *Kuhmagd*) milkmaid; **Stall|meis|ter(in)** M(F) stable boy, equerry; **Stall|mist** M farmyard manure

Stal|lung ['ʃtaluŋ] F **-**, **-en**, **Stal|lun|gen** PL stables *pl*

Stall|wa|che F (*fig*) watchdog

Stamm [ʃtam] M **-(e)s**, **⸚e** ['ʃtɛmə] **a** (= *Baumstamm*) trunk → **Apfel**
b (*Ling*) stem
c (= *Volksstamm*) tribe; (= *Abstammung*) line; (*Biol*) phylum; (= *Bakterienstamm*) strain; **der ~ der Massai** the Masai tribe; **der ~ der Bourbonen** the house of Bourbon; **aus königlichem ~** of royal blood *or* stock *or* lineage; **aus dem ~e Davids** of the line of David, of David's line; **vom ~e Nimm sein** (*hum*) to be one of the takers of this world
d (= *Kern, fester Bestand*) regulars *pl*; (= *Kunden*) regular customers *pl*; (*von Mannschaft*) regular team members *pl*; (= *Arbeiter*) regular *or* permanent workforce; (= *Angestellte*) permanent staff *pl*; **ein fester ~ von Kunden** regular customers, regulars; **zum ~ gehören** to be one of the regulars *etc*
e *usu pl* (*St Ex*) ordinary *or* common share

Stamm-: Stamm|ak|tie F (*St Ex*) ordinary *or* common share; **Stamm|baum** M family *or* genealogical tree; (*Biol*) phylogenetic tree; (*von Zuchttieren*) pedigree; (*Ling*) tree; **einen guten ~ haben** (*lit, hum*) to have a good pedigree; **Stamm|be|leg|schaft** F permanent *or* regular workforce; (= *Angestellte*) regular staff *pl*; **Stamm|buch** NT **a** *book recording family events with some legal documents* **b** (*fig*) **jdm etw ins ~ schreiben** to make sb take note of sth; **Stamm|burg** F ancestral castle; **Stamm|da|ten** PL (*Comput*) master data; **Stamm|ein|la|ge** F (*Fin*) capital investment in ordinary shares *or* in common stock (*US*)

stam|meln ['ʃtamln] VTI to stammer

Stamm|el|tern PL progenitors *pl*

stam|men ['ʃtamən] VI to come (*von, aus* from); (*zeitlich*) to date (*von, aus* from); (*Gram*) to be derived (*von, aus* from), to come (*von, aus* from); **woher ~ Sie?** where do you come from (originally)?; **die Bibliothek/Uhr stammt von seinem Großvater** the library/watch originally belonged to his grandfather

Stam|mes- *in cpds* tribal; **Stam|mes|be|wusst|sein** ▲ NT tribal spirit; **Stam|mes|füh|rer** M , **Stam|mes|fürst** M (tribal) chieftain; **Stam|mes|ge|nos|se** M , **Stam|mes|ge|nos|sin** F member of a/the tribe, tribesman/-woman; **Stam|mes|ge|schich|te** F (*Biol*) phylogeny; **stam|mes|ge|schicht|lich** ADJ (*Biol*) phylogenetic; **Stam|mes|kun|de** F (*Hist*) ethnology; **Stam|mes|zu|ge|hö|rig|keit** F tribal membership

Stamm-: Stamm|form F base form; **Stamm|gast** M regular; **Stamm|ge|richt** NT standard meal; **Stamm|gut** NT *pl* **-güter** family estate; **Stamm|hal|ter** M son and heir; **Stamm|haus** NT (*Comm*) parent branch; (= *Muttergesellschaft*) parent company; (= *Fabrik*) parent factory; **Stamm|hirn** NT (*Anat*) brainstem; **Stamm|holz** NT trunk wood

stäm|mig ['ʃtɛmɪç] ADJ (= *gedrungen*) stocky, thickset *no adv*; (= *kräftig*) sturdy

Stamm-: Stamm|ka|pi|tal NT (*Fin*) ordinary share *or* common stock (*US*) capital; **Stamm|knei|pe** F (*inf*) local (*Brit inf*), local bar;

Stamm|kun|de M , **Stamm|kun|din** F regular (customer); **Stamm|kund|schaft** F regulars *pl*, regular customers *pl*; **Stamm|land** NT place of origin

Stamm|ler ['ʃtamlɐ] M **-s**, **-**, **Stamm|le|rin** [-ərɪn] F **-**, **-nen** stammerer

Stamm-: Stamm|lo|kal NT favourite (*Brit*) *or* favorite (*US*) café/restaurant *etc*; (= *Kneipe*) local (*Brit inf*), local bar; **Stamm|mut|ter** ▲ F *pl* **-mütter** progenitrix (*form*); **Stamm|per|so|nal** NT permanent staff *pl*; **Stamm|platz** M usual *or* regular seat; **Stamm|pu|bli|kum** NT (*im Theater*) regular audience; (*im Lokal*) regulars *pl*, regular customers *pl*; (*Mil*) muster roll; **Stamm|sil|be** F radical, root syllable; **Stamm|sitz** M (*von Firma*) headquarters *sing or pl*; (*von Geschlecht*) ancestral seat; (*im Theater etc*) regular seat; **Stamm|ta|fel** F genealogical table; **Stamm|tisch** M (= *Tisch in Gasthaus*) table reserved for the regulars; (= *Stammtischrunde*) group of regulars; **er hat mittwochs seinen ~** Wednesday is his night for meeting his friends at the pub; **Stamm|tisch|po|li|ti|ker(in)** M(F) (*pej*) armchair politician; **Stamm|tisch|run|de** F group of regulars

Stammutter △ F *pl* **-mütter** → **Stammmutter**

Stamm-: Stamm|va|ter M progenitor (*form*); **stamm|ver|wandt** ADJ related; *Wörter* cognate, derived from the same root; **Stamm|vo|kal** M radical *or* root vowel; **Stamm|wäh|ler(in)** M(F) (*Pol*) staunch supporter, loyal voter; **Stamm|wür|ze** F original wort; **Stamm|zel|le** F stem cell; **adulte/embryonale ~** adult/embryonic stem cell; **Stamm|zel|len|for|schung** F stem cell research

Sta|mo|kap ['ʃta:mokap] M **-s**, *no pl* (*Pol*) *abbr von* **staatsmonopolistischer Kapitalismus**

Stam|per ['ʃtampɐ] M **-s**, **-**, **Stam|perl** ['ʃtampɐl] NT **-s**, **-n** (*S Ger, Aus*) *stemless schnapps glass*

stamp|fen ['ʃtampfn] **VI** **a** (= *laut auftreten*) to stamp; (= *auf und nieder gehen: Maschine*) to pound; **mit dem Fuß ~** to stamp one's foot; **mit den Hufen ~** to paw (*Brit*) *or* stamp (*US*) the ground (with its hooves) **b** *aux sein* (= *gehen*) (*mit schweren Schritten*) to tramp; (*wütend*) to stomp; (= *stapfen*) to trudge **c** *aux haben or sein* (*Schiff*) to pitch, to toss **VT** **a** (= *festtrampeln*) *Lehm, Sand* to stamp; *Trauben* to press; (*mit den Füßen*) to tread → **Boden a** **b** (*mit Stampfer*) to mash; (*im Mörser*) to pound

Stamp|fer ['ʃtampfɐ] M **-s**, **-** (= *Stampfgerät*) pounder; (= *Saugkolben*) plunger; (*pej inf*: = *Bein*) tree trunk (*inf*)

Stampf|kar|tof|feln PL (*dial*) mashed potato(es *pl*)

stand *pret von* **stehen**

Stand [ʃtant] M **-(e)s**, **⸚e** ['ʃtɛndə] **a** *no pl* (= *Stehen*) standing position; (= *Standfläche*) place to stand; (*für Gegenstand*) stand; **aus dem ~** from a standing position; **ein Sprung/Start aus dem ~** a standing jump/start; **bei jdm** *or* **gegen jdn/bei etw einen schweren ~ haben** (*fig*) to have a hard time with sb/in sth; **aus dem ~ (heraus)** (*fig inf*) off the cuff
b (= *Marktstand etc*) stand; (= *Taxistand*) stand, rank
c *no pl* (= *Lage*) state; (= *Niveau, Fin*: = *Kurs*) level; (= *Zählerstand, Thermometerstand, Barometer-*

stand etc) reading, level; (= *Kassenstand, Kontostand*) balance; (*von Gestirnen*) position; (*Sport*: = *Spielstand*) score; **beim jetzigen ~ der Dinge** the way things stand *or* are at the moment; **nach letztem ~ der Dinge** from the way things stood *or* were when we *etc* last heard; **der neueste ~ der Forschung** the latest developments in research; **etw auf den neuesten ~ bringen** to bring sth up to date; **auf dem neuesten ~ der Technik sein** (*Gerät*) to be state-of-the-art technology; **im ~ der Sklaverei/Knechtschaft** in a state of slavery/bondage; **~ November 1997** as at November 1997; **außer ~e** = **außerstande im ~e** = **imstande in** ~ = **instand zu** ~ = **zustande**
d (= *soziale Stellung*) station, status; (= *Klasse*) rank, class; (= *Beruf, Gewerbe*) profession; (= *Reichsstand*) estate; **Name und ~** (*old*) name and profession; **die niederen/vornehmen** *or* **höheren Stände** (*old*) the lower/upper classes; **ein Mann von (hohem) ~** (*old*) a man of (high) rank; **in den ~ der Ehe treten** (*geh*) to enter into the state of matrimony

Stan|dard ['ʃtandart, 'st-] M **-s**, **-s** standard

Stan|dard- *in cpds* standard; **Stan|dard|aus|stat|tung** F standard equipment; **Stan|dard|brief** M standard *or* regular (*US*) letter (size)

stan|dar|di|sie|ren [ʃtandardi'zi:rən, st-] *ptp* **standardisiert** VT to standardize

Stan|dar|di|sie|rung F **-**, **-en** standardization

Stan|dard-: Stan|dard|si|tu|a|ti|on F (*esp Ftbl*) set piece; **Stan|dard|tanz** M standard dance; **Stan|dard|werk** NT standard work

Stan|dar|te [ʃtan'dartə] F **-**, **-n** **a** (*Mil, Pol*) standard **b** (*Hunt*) brush

Stand-: Stand|bein NT (*Sport*) pivot leg; (*Art*) standing leg; (*fig*) pillar; **Stand|bild** NT statue; (*TV*) freeze frame

Stand-by- ['stɛndbai] *in cpds* stand-by; **Stand-by-Be|trieb** M (*Comput*) stand-by; **Stand-by-Mo|dus** M (*Comput*) stand-by mode; **Stand-by-Ti|cket** NT (*Aviat*) stand-by ticket

Länd|chen ['ʃtɛntçən] NT **-s**, **-** serenade; **jdm ein ~ bringen** to serenade sb

Stän|de-: Stän|de|ord|nung F system of estates; **Stän|de|or|ga|ni|sa|ti|on** F professional organization; **Stän|de|par|la|ment** NT parliament of estates

Stan|der ['ʃtandɐ] M **-s**, **-** pennant

Stän|der ['ʃtɛndɐ] M **-s**, **-** (= *Hutständer, Notenständer, Kartenständer etc*) stand; (= *Pfeifenständer, Schallplattenständer etc auch*) rack; (= *Pfeiler*) upright; (*Elec*) stator; (*inf*: = *Erektion*) hard-on (*sl*), stiffy (*inf*)

Stän|de|rat¹ M (*Sw Parl*) upper chamber

Stän|de|rat² M , **Stän|de|rä|tin** F (*Sw Parl*) member of the upper chamber

Stan|des-: Stan|des|amt NT registry office (*Brit*), *official building where civil marriages take place* **auf dem ~** at the registry office (*Brit*); **stan|des|amt|lich** ADJ ~**e Trauung** registry office (*Brit*) *or* civil wedding **sich ~ trauen lassen** to get married in a registry office (*Brit*), to have a registry office (*Brit*) *or* civil wedding; **Stan|des|be|am|te(r)** M *decl as adj*, **Stan|des|be|am|tin** F registrar; **Stan|des|be|wusst|sein** ▲ NT status consciousness; **Stan|des|dün|kel** M snobbishness, snobbery; **Stan|des|eh|re** F marriage between people of the same rank; **Stan|des|eh|re** F honour (*Brit*) *or* honor (*US*) as a nobleman *etc*; (*von Ärzten, Handwerkern etc*) professional honour (*Brit*) *or* honor (*US*); **stan|des|ge|mäß** ADJ befitting one's rank *or* station (*dated*) **ADV** in a manner befitting one's rank *or* station (*dated*); **Stan|des|hei|rat** F marriage between people of the same rank; **Stan|des|herr** M (*Hist*) mediatized prince; **Stan|des|or|ga|ni|sa|ti|on** F professional association; **Stan|des|per|son** F (*old*) person of quality (*old*); **Stan|des|pri|vi|leg** NT class privilege

Stän|de|staat M (*Hist*) corporate *or* corporative state

Stan|des-: Stan|des|tracht F (official) robes *pl*; **Stan|des|un|ter|schied** M class difference; **stan|des|wid|rig** ADJ socially degrading; (*beruflich*) unprofessional; **~es Verhalten** (*im Beruf*) unprofessional conduct **ADV** **sich ~ verhalten** to behave unprofessionally

Stand-: stand|fest ADJ *Tisch, Leiter* stable, steady; (*fig*) steadfast; **Stand|fes|tig|keit** F stability (*auch Sci*); (*fig*) steadfastness; **Stand|fo|to** NT still (photograph); **Stand|gas** NT (*Aut*) idling mixture; **Stand|geld** NT stallage; **Stand|ge|richt** NT (*Mil*) drumhead court martial; **vor ein ~ gestellt werden** *or* **kommen** to be summarily court-martialled (*Brit*) *or* court-martialed (*US*); **stand|haft** ADJ steadfast, strong **ADV** **etw ~ verteidigen** *or* **vertreten** to defend sth staunchly; **er weigerte sich ~, er lehnte ~ ab** he staunchly *or* steadfastly refused; **Stand|haf|tig|keit** F ['ʃtanthaftɪçkaɪt] F -, *no pl* steadfastness; **stand+hal|ten** ['ʃtanthaltn] ✪ 32.3, 53.3, 53.6 VI *sep irreg* (*Mensch*) to stand firm; (*Gebäude, Brücke etc*) to hold; **jdm ~** to stand up to sb; **einer Sache** (*dat*) **~** to withstand sth; **der Versuchung** (*dat*) **~** to resist temptation; **einer/der Prüfung ~** to stand up to *or* bear close examination; **Stand|hei|zung** F (*Aut*) stationary heating

stän|dig ['ʃtɛndɪç] ADJ **a** (= *dauernd*) permanent; *Praxis, Regel* established; *Korrespondent (von Zeitung)* resident; *Mitglied* permanent; *Einkommen* regular; **~er Ausschuss** standing committee **b** (= *unaufhörlich*) constant, continual **ADV** **a** (= *andauernd*) constantly; **müssen Sie mich ~ unterbrechen?** must you keep (on) interrupting me?, must you continually *or* constantly interrupt me?; **sie kommt ~ zu spät** she's constantly *or* always late; **sie beklagt sich ~** she's forever *or* always complaining; **sie ist ~ krank** she's always ill; **passiert das oft? – ~** does it happen often? – always *or* all the time **b** (= *permanent*) **wohnen** permanently; **sich ~ niederlassen** to settle (down)

stän|disch ['ʃtɛndɪʃ] ADJ corporate, corporative

Stand|lei|tung F (*Telec*) direct line

Stand|licht NT sidelights *pl*; **mit ~ fahren** to drive on sidelights

Stand|mie|te F (*auf Messe*) stand rent

Stand|ort M *pl* **-orte** location; (*von Schütze, Schiff etc*) position; (*Mil*) garrison; (*Bot*) habitat; (*von Pflanzungen, Industriebetrieb*) site; (*fig*) position; **den ~ der Schule in der Gesellschaft bestimmen** to define the position *or* place of the school in society; **die Division hat ihren ~ in ...** the division is based *or* garrisoned in ...

Stand|ort-: Stand|ort|äl|tes|te(r) MF *decl as adj* (*Mil*) senior officer (*of a garrison*), post senior officer (*US*); **Stand|ort|ana|ly|se** F (*Comm*) location study; **Stand|ort|be|din|gung** F *usu pl* local conditions *pl*; **Stand|ort|be|stim|mung** F (*fig*) definition of the position; **Stand|ort|fak|tor** M *usu pl* (*Econ*) locational factor; **Stand|ort|ka|ta|log** M shelf catalogue (*Brit*) *or* catalog (*US*), shelf list; **Stand|ort|nach|teil** M (*Comm*) locational disadvantage; **Stand|ort|si|che|rung** F (*Comm*) investment incentives *pl* (*provided by government to attract business to an area*); **Stand|ort|vor|teil** M (*Comm*) locational advantage; **Stand|ort|wahl** F (*Comm*) choice of site *or* location; **Stand|ort|zei|chen** NT shelf mark

Stand-: Stand|pau|ke F (*inf*) lecture (*inf*), telling-off (*esp Brit inf*); **jdm eine ~ halten** to

give sb a lecture (*inf*) *or* telling-off (*esp Brit inf*), to tell sb off (*inf*); **Stand|platz** M stand; (*für Taxis*) rank (*Brit*), stand; **Stand|punkt** M **a** (*rare*: = *Beobachtungsplatz*) vantage point, viewpoint **b** (= *Meinung*) point of view, standpoint; **auf dem ~ stehen** *or* **den ~ vertreten** *or* **sich auf den ~ stellen, dass ...** to take the view that ...; **jdm seinen ~ klarmachen** to make one's point of view clear to sb; **von meinem ~ aus** from my point of view; **das ist vielleicht ein ~!** (*iro*) what kind of attitude is that!; **Stand|quar|tier** NT (*Mil*) base; **Stand|recht** NT , *no pl* (*Mil*) military law (*invoked in times of emergency*); **~ verhängen** to impose military law (*über +acc on*); **stand|recht|lich** ADJ **eine ~e Erschießung** an on-the-spot execution **ADV** **~ erschießen** to put straight before a firing squad; **stand|si|cher** ADJ *Gebäude, Konstruktion* stable; *Mensch* steady; **Stand|si|cher|heit** F (*von Gebäude, Konstruktion*) stability; (*von Mensch*) steadiness; **Stand|spur** F (*Aut*) hard shoulder (*Brit*), shoulder (*US*); **Stand|uhr** F grandfather clock; **Stand|vo|gel** M non-migratory bird

Stan|ge ['ʃtaŋə] F -, **-n** **a** (= *langer, runder Stab*) pole; (= *Querstab*) bar; (= *Ballettstange*) barre; (= *Kleiderstange, Teppichstange*) rail; (= *Gardinenstange, Leiste für Treppenläufer*) rod; (= *Vogelstange*) perch; (= *Hühnerstange*) perch, roost; (= *Gebissstange*) bit; (*Hunt*) (= *Schwanz*) brush; (= *Geweihteil*) branch (of antlers); (*fig*: = *dünner Mensch*) beanpole (*inf*)
b (= *länglicher Gegenstand*) stick; **eine ~ Zigaretten** a carton of 200 cigarettes
c (= *zylinderförmiges Glas*) tall glass
d (*Redewendungen*) **ein Anzug von der ~** a suit off the peg (*Brit*) *or* rack (*US*); **von der ~ kaufen** to buy off the peg (*Brit*) *or* rack (*US*); **jdn bei der ~ halten** (*inf*) to keep *or* hold sb; **bei der ~ bleiben** (*inf*) to stick at it (*inf*); **jdm die ~ halten** (*inf*) to stick up for sb (*inf*), to stand up for sb (*inf*); **eine (schöne** *or* **ganze) ~ Geld** (*inf*) a tidy sum (*inf*)

Stän|gel ▲ ['ʃtɛŋl] M -s, - stem, stalk; **vom ~ fallen** (*inf*) (= *Schwächeanfall haben*) to collapse; (= *überrascht sein*) to be staggered (*inf*); **fall nicht vom ~!** (*inf*) prepare yourself for a shock!; **er fiel fast vom ~** (*inf*) he almost fell over backwards (*inf*)

stän|gel|los ▲ ADJ stemless

Stan|gen-: Stan|gen|boh|ne F runner (*Brit*) *or* pole (*US*) bean; **Stan|gen|brot** NT French bread; (= *Laib*) French loaf; **Stan|gen|sel|le|rie** M OR F celery; **Stan|gen|spar|gel** M asparagus spears *pl*

stank *pret von* **stinken**

Stän|ker ['ʃtɛŋkɐ] M -s, - (*inf*) grouser

Stän|ke|rei [ʃtɛŋkə'raɪ] F -, **-en** (*inf*) grousing

Stän|ke|rer ['ʃtɛŋkərɐ] M -s, -, **Stän|ke|rin** [-ərɪn] F -, **-nen** (*inf*) grouser

stän|kern ['ʃtɛŋkɐn] VI (*inf*) **a** (= *Unfrieden stiften*) to stir things up (*inf*) **b** (= *Gestank verbreiten*) to make a stink (*inf*)

Stan|ni|ol [ʃta'njoːl, st-] NT -s, **-e** silver foil

Stan|ni|ol|pa|pier NT silver paper

stan|te pe|de ['ʃtantə 'peːdə] ADV (*geh, Jur*) instanter

Stan|ze ['ʃtantsə] F -, **-n** **a** (*für Prägestempel, Bleche*) die, stamp; (= *Lochstanze*) punch **b** (*Poet*) eight-line stanza

stan|zen ['ʃtantsn] VT to press; (= *prägen*) to stamp, to emboss; *Löcher* to punch

Stan|zer ['ʃtantsɐ] M -s, -, **Stan|ze|rin** [-ərɪn] F -, **-nen** press worker

Sta|pel ['ʃtaːpl] M -s, - **a** (= *geschichteter Haufen, fig:* = *Vorrat*) stack, pile **b** (*Comm*) (= *Stapelplatz*) store, depot; (= *Handelsplatz*) trading centre (*Brit*) *or* center (*US*), emporium **c** (*Naut*: = *Schiffsstapel*) stocks *pl*; **auf ~ legen** to lay down; **auf ~ liegen** to be on the stocks; **vom ~ laufen** to be launched; **vom ~ lassen** to launch; (*fig*) to

come out with (*inf*) **d** (*von Wolle, Baumwolle*) staple

Stapel-: Sta|pel|kas|ten M crate; **Sta|pel|lauf** M (*Naut*) launching

sta|peln ['ʃtaːpln] **VT** to stack; (= *lagern*) to store **VR** to pile up

Sta|pel-: Sta|pel|platz M store, depot; **Sta|pel|stuhl** M stackable chair

Sta|pe|lung ['ʃtaːpəlʊŋ] F -, **-en** stacking; (= *Lagerung*) storing

Sta|pel-: Sta|pel|ver|ar|bei|tung F (*Comput*) batch processing; **Sta|pel|wa|re** F staple commodity; **sta|pel|wei|se** ADV in piles; **bei ihm liegen ~ die Computerhefte herum** he's got piles *or* stacks of computer magazines lying around

Stap|fe ['ʃtapfə] F -, **-n**, **Stap|fen** ['ʃtapfn] M -s, - footprint

stap|fen ['ʃtapfn] VI *aux sein* to trudge, to plod

Star[1] [ʃtaːɐ] M **-(e)s, -e** (*Orn*) starling

Star[2] [ʃtaːɐ] M **-(e)s, -e** (*Med*) **grauer ~** cataract; **grüner ~** glaucoma; **schwarzer ~** amaurosis (*spec*); **jdm den ~ stechen** (*fig*) to tell sb some home truths

Star[3] [ʃtaːɐ, staːɐ] M **-s, -s** (*Film etc*) star; (*fig auch*) leading light; **er trat wie ein ~ auf** he put on a big star act

Star- [ʃtaːɐ-, 'staːɐ-]: **Star|al|lü|ren** ['ʃtaːɐ-, 'staːɐ-] PL (*inf*) airs and graces *pl*; **~ an den Tag legen** to put on *or* to give oneself airs and graces; **Star|an|walt** ['ʃtaːɐ-, 'staːɐ-] M ; **Star|an|wäl|tin** F (*inf*) star *or* top lawyer *or* attorney (*US*), rainmaker (*US sl*); **Star|auf|ge|bot** ['ʃtaːɐ-, 'staːɐ-] NT (*Film, Ereignis*) gathering of stars; **mit einem riesigen ~** with a whole galaxy of stars

starb *pret von* **sterben**

Star-: Star|be|set|zung ['ʃtaːɐ-, 'staːɐ-] F star cast; **Star|bril|le** ['ʃtaːɐ-] F (pair of) glasses *pl* fitted with cataract lenses

Sta|ren|kas|ten M **a** nesting box (for starlings) **b** (*Aut inf*: = *Überwachungsanlage*) police camera

Star- [ʃtaːɐ-, 'staːɐ-] (*Press*): **Star|ga|ge** F top fee; **Star|gast** M star guest

stark [ʃtark] ADJ comp **=er** ['ʃtɛrkɐ], superl **=ste(r, s)** ['ʃtɛrkstə] **a** (= *kräftig, konzentriert*) strong (*auch Gram*); (= *mächtig*) *Stimme, Staat, Partei* strong, powerful; **~ bleiben** to be strong; (*im Glauben*) to hold firm; **sich für etw ~ machen** (*inf*) to stand up for sth; **den ~en Mann spielen** *or* **markieren** *or* **mimen** (*all inf*) to play the big guy (*inf*); **das ist seine ~e Seite** that is his strong point *or* his forte; **das ist ~ or ein ~es Stück!** (*inf*) that's a bit much!; (= *eine Unverschämtheit auch*) that's a bit thick! (*inf*)
b (= *dick*) thick; (*euph:* = *korpulent*) *Dame, Herr* large, well-built (*euph*); *Arme, Beine* large, strong (*euph*); **Kostüme für stärkere Damen** suits for the fuller figure
c (= *beträchtlich, heftig*) *Schmerzen, Kälte* intense; *Frost* severe, heavy; *Regen, Schneefall, Verkehr, Raucher, Trinker, Druck* heavy; *Sturm* violent; *Erkältung* bad, heavy; *Wind, Strömung, Eindruck* strong; *Appetit, Esser* hearty; *Beifall* hearty, loud; *Fieber, Nachfrage* high; *Trauer* deep; *Übertreibung, Widerhall, Bedenken* considerable, great; **~e Abneigung** strong dislike
d (= *leistungsfähig*) *Motor* powerful; *Sportler* able; *Mannschaft, Brille, Arznei* strong; **er ist in Englisch nicht sehr ~** he's quite weak in English
e (= *zahlreich*) *Auflage, Gefolge* large; *Nachfrage* great, big; **wir hoffen auf ~e Beteiligung** we are hoping that a large number of people will take part; **zehn Mann ~** ten strong; **das Buch ist 300 Seiten ~** the book is 300 pages long
f (*inf:* = *hervorragend*) *Leistung, Werk* great (*inf*)
Meatloafs stärkstes Album Meatloaf's greatest album (*inf*)
ADV comp **=er** ['ʃtɛrkɐ], superl **am =sten** **a** (*mit vb*) very; *applaudieren* loudly; *pressen, drücken, ziehen* hard; *regnen* heavily; *rau-*

chen a lot, heavily; beeindrucken greatly; vertreten, dagegen sein strongly; abgenutzt, beschmutzt, beschädigt, entzündet etc badly; bluten profusely; vergrößert, verkleinert greatly; **es hat ~ gestürmt** there was a severe storm; **es hat ~ gedonnert** there was a loud clap of thunder; **es donnert nicht mehr so** – the thunder is not as loud now; **~ wirken** to have a strong effect; **~ wirkend** (Medikament, Alkohol) potent; **~ gesalzen** very salty; **~ gewürzt** highly spiced; **~ verschuldet** heavily or deeply in debt; **~ behaart sein** to be very hairy; **stärker befahrene Straßen** busier roads; **die Ausstellung wurde ~ besucht** the exhibition was well attended; **das Auto zieht ~ nach links** the car is pulling badly to the left; **er ist ~ erkältet** he has a bad or heavy cold; **er hat das Schmerzmittel zu ~ dosiert** the painkillers he prescribed were too strong; **Frauen sind stärker vertreten** there are more women; **der Artikel wird immer stärker verkauft** sales of this product continue to increase

　b (inf: = hervorragend) really well; **die singt unheimlich ~** she's a really great singer (inf), she sings really well

Star|kas|ten M = Starenkasten

Stark|bier NT strong beer

Stär|ke¹ ['ʃtɛrkə] F -, -n **a** strength (auch fig); (von Stimme, Land, Regierung) power

　b (= Dicke, Durchmesser) thickness

　c (= Heftigkeit) (von Strömung, Wind, Einfluss) strength; (von Eindruck, Leid, Kälte, Schmerzen, Druck) intensity; (von Regen, Verkehr) heaviness; (von Sturm, Abneigung) violence; (von Erkältung) severity; (von Appetit) heartiness

　d (= Leistungsfähigkeit) (von Motor) power; (von Sportmannschaft, Arznei, Brille) strength

　e (= Anzahl) (von Gefolge, Heer, Mannschaft) size, strength; (von Klasse) size; (von Beteiligung, Nachfrage) level; (von Auflage) size

　f (fig: = starke Seite) strength, strong point

Stär|ke² F -, -n (Chem) starch

Stär|ke|mehl NT (Cook) thickening agent, ≈ cornflour (Brit), ≈ cornstarch (US)

stär|ken ['ʃtɛrkn] **VT a** (= kräftigen) (lit, fig) to strengthen; Selbstbewusstsein to boost, to increase; Gesundheit to improve; **gestärkt** (Mensch) strengthened → **Rückgrat b** (= erfrischen) to fortify **c** Wäsche to starch **VI** to be fortifying; **das stärkt** it fortifies you; **~des Mittel** tonic **VR** to fortify oneself

Stär|ke|zu|cker M glucose

stark|glied|rig [-gli:drɪç], **stark|kno|chig** ADJ heavy-boned

Stark|strom M (Elec) heavy current

Stark|strom- in cpds power; **Stark|strom|ka|bel** NT power cable; **Stark|strom|lei|tung** F power line; (= Kabel) power lead; **Stark|strom|tech|nik** F branches of electrical engineering not connected with telecommunications

Star|kult ['ʃta:ɐ̯-, 'sta:ɐ̯-] M star cult

Stär|kung ['ʃtɛrkʊŋ] F -, -en **a** strengthening (auch fig); (des Selbstbewusstseins) boosting; **das dient der ~ der Gesundheit** it is beneficial to the health **b** (= Erfrischung) refreshment; **eine ~ zu sich nehmen** to take or have some refreshment

Stär|kungs|mit|tel NT (Med) tonic

stark-: stark|wan|dig ADJ Schiff thick-walled; **stark|wir|kend** △ ADJ attr → **stark ADV a**

Star|let ['ʃta:ɐ̯lɛt, 'st-] NT -s, -s (Film) starlet

Star|ope|ra|ti|on F cataract operation

starr [ʃtar] **ADJ a** stiff; (= unbeweglich) rigid; **~ vor Frost** stiff with frost; **meine Finger sind vor Kälte ganz ~** my fingers are frozen stiff or are stiff with cold

　b (= unbewegt) Augen glassy; Blick fixed

　c (= regungslos) paralyzed; **~ vor Schrecken/Entsetzen** paralyzed with fear/horror; **~ vor Staunen** dumbfounded

　d (= nicht flexibel) Regelung, Prinzip inflexible, rigid; Haltung inflexible, intransigent

ADV a (= unbeweglich) **~ miteinander verbunden** joined rigidly; **~ abstehen** to stand up stiffly

　b (= bewegungslos) lächeln stiffly; **jdn ~ ansehen** to stare at sb

　c (= rigide) **~ an etw** (dat) **festhalten** to cling to sth

Star|re ['ʃtarə] F -, no pl stiffness, rigidity

star|ren ['ʃtarən] **VI a** (= starr blicken) to stare (auf +acc at); **ins Leere ~** to stare or gaze into space; **jdm ins Gesicht ~** to stare sb in the face; **vor sich** (acc) **hin ~** to stare straight ahead; **was ~ Sie so?** what are you staring at? → **Loch b von Gewehren ~** to bristle with guns **c** (= steif sein) to be stiff (von, vor +dat with); **Moskau starrt vor Kälte** Moscow is in the grip of the cold; **vor Dreck ~** to be thick or covered with dirt; (Kleidung) to be stiff with dirt **d** (= aufragen) to jut up

Starr|flüg|ler [-fly:glɐ] M -s, - (Aviat) fixed-wing aircraft

Starr|heit F -, no pl **a** (von Gegenstand) rigidity

　b (= Sturheit) inflexibility, rigidity; (von Haltung auch) intransigence

Starr-: Starr|kopf M (= Mensch) stubborn or obstinate mule; **einen ~ haben** to be stubborn or obstinate; **starr|köp|fig** ADJ stubborn, obstinate **ADV** stubbornly, obstinately; **Starr|köp|fig|keit** [-kœpfɪçkait] F -, no pl stubbornness, obstinacy; **Starr|krampf** M (Med) tetanus, lockjaw; **Starr|sinn** M , no pl stubbornness, mulishness; **starr|sin|nig** ADJ stubborn, mulish **ADV** stubbornly, mulishly; **Starr|sin|nig|keit** [-zɪnɪçkait] F -, no pl stubbornness, mulishness; **Starr|sucht** F (Med) catalepsy

Start [ʃtart] M -s, -s **a** (lit, fig) start; **das Zeichen zum ~ geben** to give the starting signal; **einen guten/schlechten ~ haben** to get (off to) a good/bad start **b** (= Startplatz, Startlinie) start(ing line); (bei Pferderennen) start(ing post); (bei Autorennen) (starting) grid; **am ~ sein, an den ~ gehen** to be at the start/on or at the starting line/at the start(ing post)/on the (starting) grid; (Läufer) to be in one's blocks **c** (Aviat) takeoff; (= Raketenstart) launch; (= Startplatz) runway; **der Maschine den ~ freigeben** to clear the plane for takeoff

Start-: Start|ab|bruch M (Aviat) aborted takeoff; **Start|auf|la|ge** F (Press) initial (print) run; **Start|au|to|ma|tik** F (Aut) automatic choke; **Start|bahn** F (Aviat) runway; **Start- und Landebahn** runway; **start|be|rech|tigt** ADJ (Sport) eligible (to enter); **start|be|reit** ADJ (Sport, fig) ready to start or go, ready for (the) off (inf); (Aviat) ready for takeoff; (Space) ready for liftoff; **Start|block** M pl -blöcke (Sport) starting block

star|ten ['ʃtartn] **VI** aux sein to start; (Aviat) to take off; (= zum Start antreten) to take part; to run; to swim; (bei Pferde-/Autorennen) to race; (inf: = abreisen) to set off; **in die letzte Runde ~** to go into or enter the last lap **VT** Satelliten, Rakete to launch; Unternehmen, Kampagne auch, Motor, Computer, Programm, Versuch, Rennen to start; Expedition to get under way

Star|ter¹ ['ʃtartɐ] M -s, - (Aut) starter

Star|ter² ['ʃtartɐ] M -s, -, **Star|te|rin** [-ərɪn] F -, -nen (Sport) starter

Star|ter|klap|pe F (Aut) choke

Start-: Start|er|laub|nis F (Sport) permission to take part; (Aviat) clearance for takeoff; **Start|flag|ge** F starting flag; **Start|frei|ga|be** F clearance for takeoff; **Start|geld** NT (Sport) entry fee; **Start|ge|rät** NT (für Raketen) launcher; **Start|hil|fe** F (Aviat) rocket-assisted takeoff; (fig) initial aid; **im Winter braucht mein Auto ~** my car won't start on its own in winter; **jdm ~ geben** to help sb get off the ground; **Start|hil|fe|ka|bel** NT jump leads pl (Brit), jumper cables pl (US); **Start|ka|pi|tal** NT starting capital; **start|klar** ADJ (Aviat) clear(ed) for takeoff; (Sport, fig) ready to start, ready for the off; **Start|kom|man|do** NT

(Sport) starting signal; (Aviat) takeoff command; **Start|li|nie** F (Sport) starting line; **Start|loch** NT (Sport) starting hole; **in den Startlöchern** on their marks; **Start|ma|schi|ne** F (Sport) starting gate; **Start|num|mer** F number; **Start|platz** M (Sport) starting place; (für Läufer) marks pl; (Autorennen) starting grid; **Start|ram|pe** F (Space) launch(ing) pad; **Start|schleu|der** F (Aviat) catapult; **Start|schuss** ▲ M (Sport) starting signal; (fig) signal (zu for); **vor dem ~** before the gun; **den ~ geben** to fire the (starting) pistol; (fig) to open the door; (= Erlaubnis geben) to give the go-ahead; **Start|sei|te** F (Comput) start(up) page (of a website); **Start|sprung** M racing dive; **Start|ver|bot** NT (Aviat) ban on takeoff; (Sport) ban; **~ bekommen** to be banned or barred; **Start-Ziel-Sieg** M (Sport) runaway victory

Sta|si ['ʃta:zi] M -, no pl (DDR) abbr von Staatssicherheitsdienst Stasi

State|ment ['ste:tmənt] NT -s, -s statement; **ein ~ abgeben** to issue a statement

Sta|tik ['ʃta:tɪk, 'st-] F -, no pl **a** (Sci) statics sing **b** (Build) structural engineering

Sta|ti|ker ['ʃta:tikɐ, 'st-] M -s, -, **Sta|ti|ke|rin** [-ərɪn] F -, -nen (Tech) structural engineer

Sta|ti|on [ʃtatsio:n] F -, -en **a** station; (= Haltestelle) stop; (fig: = Abschnitt) (von Reise) stage; (von Leben) phase; **~ machen** to stop off **b** (= Krankenstation) ward; **er liegt/arbeitet auf ~ drei** he is in/works on ward three

sta|ti|o|när [ʃtatsio:nɛ:ɐ̯] ADJ (Astron, Comput, Sociol) stationary; (Med) Behandlung, Pflegeeinrichtungen inpatient attr; **~er Patient** inpatient **ADV** entbinden in hospital; **jdn ~ behandeln** to treat sb in hospital or as an inpatient; **er liegt ~ bei Dr. Weiß** he is being treated by Dr Weiß as an inpatient; **jdn ~ einweisen** to hospitalize sb; **jdn ~ aufnehmen** to admit sb to hospital

sta|ti|o|nie|ren [ʃtatsio:ni:rən] ptp **stationiert** VT Truppen, Beobachter to station; Atomwaffen etc to deploy

Sta|ti|o|nie|rung F -, -en (von Truppen) stationing; (von Atomwaffen etc) deployment

Sta|ti|o|nie|rungs|kos|ten PL stationing costs pl

Sta|ti|ons-: Sta|ti|ons|arzt M , **Sta|ti|ons|ärz|tin** F ward doctor; **Sta|ti|ons|schwes|ter** F ward sister (Brit), senior nurse (in a ward); **Sta|ti|ons|vor|ste|her(in)** M(F) (Rail) stationmaster; **Sta|ti|ons|wahl|tas|te** F tuning button

sta|tisch ['ʃta:tɪʃ, 'st-] ADJ (lit, fig) static; Gesetze of statics **ADV** das Gebäude ist ~ einwandfrei the building is structurally sound; **die Brücke ist ~ falsch berechnet** the design of this bridge is structurally unsound; **etw ~ berechnen** to do the structural design work for sth; **meine Haare haben sich ~ aufgeladen** my hair is full of static electricity

Sta|tist ['ʃta:tɪst] M -en, -en, **Sta|tis|tin** [-'tɪstɪn] F -, -nen (Film) extra; (Theat) supernumerary; (fig) cipher; **er war nur ein kleiner ~** (fig) he only played a minor role

Sta|tis|ten|rol|le F (lit, fig) minor role; (Film, Theat auch) walk-on part, bit part

---

Sta|tis|te|rie [ʃtatɪstəˈriː] F -, -n [-ˈriːən] (Film) extras pl; (Theat) supernumeraries pl

Sta|tis|tik [ʃtaˈtɪstɪk] F -, -en statistics sing; **eine ~** a set of statistics sing; **die ~en** the statistics pl

Sta|tis|ti|ker [ʃtaˈtɪstɪkɐ] M -s, -, **Sta|tis|ti|ke|rin** [-ərɪn] F -, -nen statistician

Sta|tis|tin F → Statist

sta|tis|tisch [ʃtaˈtɪstɪʃ] ADJ statistical; **~es Amt** statistics office **ADV** statistically; **~ gesehen** statistically → **erfassen**

Sta|tiv [ʃtaˈtiːf] NT -s, -e [-və] tripod

statt [ʃtat] **PREP** +gen or (old, inf, wenn kein Artikel) +dat instead of; **~ meiner/seiner/ihrer** etc in my/ his/her etc place, instead of me/him/her etc; **~ Urlaub(s)** in lieu of or instead of holiday (Brit), instead of vacation (US); **~ Karten** heading of an announcement expressing thanks for condolences in place of individual replies **an meiner/seiner/ihrer ~** in my/his/her stead (form) or place; **an Kindes ~ annehmen** (Jur) to adopt; **an Zahlungs ~** (Comm) in lieu of payment → **Eid, stattdessen**
▪ **CONJ** instead of; **~ zu bleiben** instead of staying; **~ zu bleiben, wollte ich lieber ...** rather than stay I wanted to ...

statt|des|sen ▲ ADV instead

Stät|te [ˈʃtɛtə] F -, -n place; **eine bleibende ~** a permanent home

Statt-: **statt|fin|den** [ˈʃtatfɪndn] VI sep irreg to take place; (Veranstaltung, Wahlen auch) to be held; (Ereignis auch) to occur; **statt|ge|ben** [ˈʃtatgeːbn] VI sep irreg +dat (form) to grant → **Einspruch; statt|haft** [ˈʃtathaft] ADJ pred permitted, allowed; **Statt|hal|ter(in)** M(F) governor; **Statt|hal|ter|schaft** [ˈʃtathaltɐʃaft] F -, no pl governorship

statt|lich [ˈʃtatlɪç] ADJ **a** (= hochgewachsen, groß) Tier magnificent; Bursche strapping, powerfully built; (= eindrucksvoll) Erscheinung, Fünfziger imposing; (= ansehnlich) Gebäude, Anwesen, Park magnificent, splendid; **ein ~er Mann** a fine figure of a man **b** (= umfangreich) Sammlung impressive; Familie large; (= beträchtlich) Summe, Anzahl, Einnahmen handsome, considerable

Statt|lich|keit F -, no pl (= Größe) magnificence; (= Eindrücklichkeit) imposing appearance; (= Ansehnlichkeit) (von Gebäude) splendour (Brit), splendor (US); (von Mann) imposing presence; **die ~ seiner Erscheinung** his imposing appearance

Sta|tue [ˈʃtaːtuə, ˈʃt-] F -, -n statue

sta|tu|en|haft **ADJ** statuesque; (= unbeweglich) like a statue, statue-like **ADV** like statues/a statue

Sta|tu|et|te [ʃtatuˈɛtə, ʃt-] F -, -n statuette

sta|tu|ie|ren [ʃtatuˈiːrən, ʃt-] ptp **statuiert** VT **a ein Exempel an jdm ~** to make an example of sb; **ein Exempel mit etw ~** to use sth as a warning; **um ein Exempel zu ~** as an example or warning to others; **wir müssen da ein Exempel ~** we will have to make an example of somebody **b** (= festlegen) to lay down

Sta|tur [ʃtaˈtuːɐ] F -, Staturen build

Sta|tus [ˈʃtaːtʊs, ˈʃt-] M -, - [-tuːs] status; **~ quo** status quo; → **quo ante** status quo

Sta|tus-: **Sta|tus|sym|bol** NT status symbol; **Sta|tus|zei|le** F (Comput) status line

Sta|tut [ʃtaˈtuːt, ʃt-] NT -(e)s, -en statute

sta|tu|ta|risch [ʃtatuˈtaːrɪʃ, ʃt-] **ADJ** statutory **ADV das ist ~ nicht möglich** that is excluded by statute

Stau [ʃtau] M -(e)s, -e or -s **a** (= Wasserstauung) build-up; (= Windstau) barrier effect; (= Verkehrsstauung) traffic jam; **ein ~ von 3 km** a 3km tailback (Brit), a 3km backup (of traffic) (US) **b** = **Stauung**

Stau|an|la|ge F dam

Staub [ʃtaup] M -(e)s, -e or **Stäube** [-bə, ˈʃtɔybə] dust; (Bot) pollen; **~ saugen** to vacuum, to hoover® (Brit); **~ wischen** to dust; **zu ~ werden** (li-

ter) to turn to dust; (wieder) to return to dust (liter); **sich vor jdm in den ~ werfen** to throw oneself at sb's feet; **vor jdm im ~ kriechen** (lit, fig) to grovel before sb, to grovel at sb's feet; **sich aus dem ~(e) machen** (inf) to clear off (inf); **den ~ (eines Ortes/Landes) von den Füßen schütteln** (liter) to shake the dust (of a place/ country) off one's feet → **aufwirbeln**

Staub- in cpds dust; **Staub|beu|tel** M **a** (Bot) anther **b** (von Staubsauger) dustbag; **Staub|blatt** NT (Bot) stamen

Stäub|chen [ˈʃtɔypçən] NT -s, - speck or particle of dust

Staub|be|cken NT reservoir

stau|ben [ˈʃtaubn] VI to be dusty; (= Staub machen, aufwirbeln) to make or create a lot of dust; **bei Trockenheit staubt es mehr** there's a lot more dust around when it's dry

stäu|ben [ˈʃtɔybn] **VT Mehl/Puder** etc **auf etw** (acc) **~** to dust sth with flour/powder etc (esp Brit), to sprinkle flour/powder etc on sth **VI** aux sein (rare) (= zerstieben) to scatter; (Wasser) to spray

Staub|be|ra|ter(in) M(F) traffic problem adviser

Staub-: **Staub|fa|den** M (Bot) filament; **Staub|fän|ger** M (inf) dust collector; **die vielen Bücher sind bloß ~** all those books just lie around collecting dust; **Staub|fet|zen** M (Aus) duster; **Staub|flo|cke** F piece of fluff; **Staub|ge|bo|re|ne(r)** [-gəbo:rənə] MF decl as adj (old, liter) mortal (being); **Staub|ge|fäß** NT (Bot) stamen

stau|big [ˈʃtaubɪç] ADJ dusty

Staub-: **Staub|kamm** M fine-tooth comb; **Staub|korn** NT pl **-körner** speck of dust, dust particle; **Staub|lap|pen** M duster; **Staub|lun|ge** F (Med) dust on the lung; (von Kohlenstaub) black lung, silicosis; **staub|sau|gen** [ˈʃtaupzaugn] ptp **staubgesaugt** [ˈʃtaupgəzaukt] VI insep to vacuum, to hoover® (Brit); **Staub|sau|ger** M vacuum cleaner, Hoover® (Brit); **Staub|sau|ger|ver|tre|ter(in)** M(F) vacuum cleaner salesman/-woman, (pej) door-to-door salesman/-woman; **Staub|schicht** F layer of dust; **staub|tro|cken** [ˈʃtaup-] ADJ **a** (lit) Lack etc ≈ touch-dry; Landschaft etc parched **b** (fig inf) dry as dust pred; **Staub|tuch** NT pl **-tücher** duster; **Staub|we|del** M feather duster; **Staub|wol|ke** F cloud of dust

stau|chen [ˈʃtauxn] VT **a** (= zusammendrücken) to compress (auch Tech), to squash (inf); (rare: = verstauchen) to sprain **b** (inf: = zusammenstauchen) to give a dressing-down (inf)

Stau|damm M dam

Stau|de [ˈʃtaudə] F -, -n (Hort) herbaceous perennial (plant); (= Busch) shrub; (= Bananenstaude, Tabakstaude, Rosenkohlstaude) plant

stau|en [ˈʃtauən] **VT** a Wasser, Fluss to dam (up); Blut to stop or stem the flow of **b** (Naut) to stow (away) **VR** (= sich anhäufen) to pile up; (= ins Stocken geraten) to get jammed; (Verkehr) to build up; (Wasser, fig) to build up; (Menschen) to form a crowd; (Blut) to accumulate; (durch Abbinden) to be cut off; **die Menschen stauten sich in den Gängen** people were jamming the corridors; **der Verkehr staute sich** or **die Autos stauten sich über eine Strecke von 2 km** there was a 2km tailback (Brit) or backup (of traffic) (US)

Stau|en|de NT (Mot) end of the tailback (Brit) or backup (US)

Stau|er [ˈʃtauɐ] M -s, -, **Stau|e|rin** [-ərɪn] F -, -nen (Naut) stevedore

Stau-: **Stau|ge|fahr** F risk of congestion; **„Staugefahr"** "delays likely"; **Stau|mau|er** F dam wall; **Stau|mel|dung** F (Mot) congestion or traffic report

stau|nen [ˈʃtaunən] VI to be astonished or amazed (über +acc at); **~d** in astonishment or amazement; **ich staune(, ich staune)!** (inf) well, I never!, well well!; **man staunt, wie ...** it's

amazing how ...; **da kann man nur noch ~** it's just amazing; **da staunst du, was?** (inf) you didn't expect that, did you!; **da hat er nicht schlecht gestaunt** (inf) he was flabbergasted (inf) → **Bauklotz**

Stau|nen NT -s, no pl astonishment, amazement (über +acc at); **jdn in ~ versetzen** to amaze or astonish sb

stau|nens|wert ADJ astonishing, amazing **ADV** astonishingly, amazingly

Stau|pe [ˈʃtaupə] F -, -n (Vet) distemper

Stau-: **Stau|raum** M storage space; **Stau|see** M reservoir, artificial lake; **Stau|stu|fe** F (in Flüssen) barrage (forming one of a series)

Stau|ung [ˈʃtauʊŋ] F -, -en **a** (= Stockung) pileup; (in Lieferungen, Post etc) hold-up; (von Menschen) jam; (von Verkehr) tailback (Brit), backup (US); **bei einer ~ der Schiffe im Hafen** when the harbour (Brit) or harbor (US) gets congested; **eine ~ des Verkehrs** a traffic jam **b** (von Wasser) build-up (of water); **ein durch ~ geschaffener See** a lake created by damming a river; **~en sind hier sehr häufig** the water often builds up here; **zur ~ eines Flusses** to dam a river **c** (= Blutstauung) congestion no pl; **bei ~(en) (des Blutes) in den Venen** when the veins become congested, when blood becomes congested in the veins

Std. abbr von **Stunde** hr

stdl. abbr von **stündlich**

Steak [steːk, ʃteːk] NT -s, -s steak

Ste|a|rin [ʃteaˈriːn, st-] NT -s, -e stearin

Stech-: **Stech|ap|fel** M (Bot) thorn apple; **Stech|be|cken** NT (Med) bedpan; **Stech|bei|tel** M chisel

ste|chen [ˈʃtɛçn] pret **stach** [ʃtaːx], ptp **gestochen** [gəˈʃtɔxn] **VI** **a** (Dorn, Stachel etc) to prick; (Wespe, Biene) to sting; (Mücken, Moskitos) to bite; (mit Messer etc) to (make a) stab (nach at); (Sonne) to beat down; (mit Stechkarte) bei Ankunft) to clock in or on; (bei Weggang) to clock out or off; **die Sonne sticht in die Augen** the sun hurts one's eyes; **der Geruch sticht in die Nase** the smell stings one's nose; **mit etw in etw** (acc) **~** to stick sth in(to) sth; **jdm durch die Ohrläppchen ~** to pierce sb's ears **b** (Cards) to trump **c** (Sport) to have a play-off; (bei Springreiten) to have a jump-off **d** (Farbe: = spielen) **die Farbe sticht ins Rötliche** the colour (Brit) or color (US) has a tinge of red or a reddish tinge
▪ **VT** **a** (Dorn, Stachel etc) to prick; (Wespe, Biene) to sting; (Mücken, Moskitos) to bite; (mit Messer etc) to stab; Löcher to pierce; **die Kontrolluhr ~** to clock on or in; (beim Hinausgehen) to clock out or off **b** (Cards) to trump **c** (= ausschneiden, herauslösen) Spargel, Torf, Rasen to cut **d** (= abstechen) Schwein, Kalb to stick, to kill; (Angeln) Aale to spear **e** (= gravieren) to engrave → auch **gestochen**
▪ **VR** to prick oneself (an +dat on, mit with); **sich** (acc or dat) **in den Finger ~** to prick one's finger
▪ **VTI** impers **es sticht** it is prickly; **es sticht mir** or **mich im Rücken** I have a sharp pain in my back

Ste|chen NT -s, - **a** (Sport) play-off; (bei Springreiten) jump-off **b** (= Schmerz) sharp pain

ste|chend ADJ piercing; Sonne scorching; (= durchdringend) Augen, Blick piercing, penetrating; (= jäh) Schmerz sharp; (= beißend) Geruch pungent **ADV jdn ~ ansehen** to give sb a piercing look; **~ heiß** burning hot

Ste|cher [ˈʃtɛçɐ] M -s, - (sl: = Freund) shagging partner (sl)

Stech-: **Stech|flie|ge** F stable fly; **Stech|gins|ter** M (Bot) gorse; **Stech|kar|te** F clocking-in card; **Stech|mü|cke** F gnat, midge (Brit), mosquito; **Stech|-**

pal|me F holly; **Stech|schritt** M (Mil) goose step; **Stech|uhr** F time clock; **Stech|zir|kel** M (pair of) dividers

Steck-: Steck|brief M "wanted" poster; (fig) personal description; **steck|brief|lich** ADV jdn ~ **verfolgen** to put up "wanted" posters for sb; ~ **gesucht werden** to be wanted, to be on the wanted list; **Steck|do|se** F (Elec) (wall) socket

ste|cken ['ʃtɛkn] **VI** pret **steckte** or (geh) **stak** ['ʃtɛktə, ʃtaːk] ptp **gesteckt** [gə'ʃtɛkt] **a** (= festsitzen) to be stuck; (= an- or eingesteckt sein) to be; (Nadel, Splitter etc) to be (sticking); (Brosche, Abzeichen etc) to be (pinned); **eine Blume im Knopfloch ~ haben** to have a flower in one's buttonhole; **einen Ring am Finger ~ haben** to have a ring on one's finger; **der Stecker steckt in der Dose** the plug is in the socket; **er steckte in einem neuen Anzug** (hum) he was all done up in a new suit (inf); **der Schlüssel steckt** the key is in the lock

b (= verborgen sein) to be (hiding); **wo steckt er?** where has he got to?; **wo hast du die ganze Zeit gesteckt?** where have you been (hiding) all this time?; **darin steckt viel Mühe** a lot of work or trouble has gone into that or has been put into that; **da steckt etwas dahinter** (inf) there's something behind it; **in ihm steckt etwas** he certainly has it in him; **zeigen, was in einem steckt** to show what one is made of, to show one's mettle

c (= strotzen vor) **voll** or **voller Fehler/Nadeln/ Witz** etc ~ to be full of mistakes/pins/wit etc

d (= verwickelt sein in) **in Schwierigkeiten** ~ to be in difficulties; **tief in Schulden** ~ to be deep(ly) in debt; **in einer Krise** ~ to be in the throes of a crisis; **in der Pubertät** ~ to be an adolescent

VT pret **steckte**, ptp **gesteckt** [gə'ʃtɛkt] **a** (= hineinstecken) to put; Haare to put up; Brosche to pin (an +acc onto); **die Hände in die Taschen** ~ to put or stick (inf) one's hands in one's pockets; **das Hemd in die Hose** ~ to tuck one's shirt in (one's trousers esp Brit) or pants (esp US); **jdn ins Bett** ~ (inf) to put sb to bed (inf); **jdn ins Gefängnis** ~ (inf) to stick sb in prison (inf), to put sb away or inside (inf); **jdn in Uniform** ~ (inf) to put sb in uniform; **etw in den Backofen/ Kasten** ~ (inf) to put or stick (inf) sth in the oven/ box

b (Sew) to pin; **den Saum eines Kleides** ~ to pin up the hem of a dress

c (inf: = investieren) Geld, Mühe to put (in +acc into); Zeit to devote (in +acc to)

d (sl: = aufgeben) to jack in (Brit inf), to chuck (inf)

e jdm etw ~ (inf) to tell sb sth; **es jdm** ~ (inf) to give sb a piece of one's mind

f (= pflanzen) to set

Ste|cken ['ʃtɛkn] M **-s, -** stick

Ste|cken-: ste|cken blei|ben ▲ VI irreg aux sein to stick fast, to get stuck; (Kugel) to be lodged; (in der Rede) to falter; (beim Gedichtaufsagen etc) to get stuck; **etw bleibt jdm im Halse stecken** (lit, fig) sth sticks in sb's throat; **ste|- cken las|sen** ▲ ptp **stecken lassen** or (rare) **stecken gelassen** VT irreg to leave; **den Schlüssel** ~ to leave the key in the lock; **lass dein Geld stecken!** leave your money where it is!, leave your money in your pocket!; **Ste|cken- pferd** NT (lit, fig) hobbyhorse; **sein** ~ **reiten** (fig) to be on one's hobbyhorse

Ste|cker ['ʃtɛkɐ] M **-s, -** (Elec) plug

Steck-: Steck|kar|te F (Comput) expansion card; **Steck|kis|sen** NT papoose; **Steck|- kon|takt** M (Elec) plug

Steck|ling ['ʃtɛklɪŋ] M **-s, -e** (Hort) cutting

Steck|na|del F pin; **etw mit ~n befestigen** to pin sth (an +dat to); **keine ~ hätte zu Boden fallen können** (fig) there wasn't room to breathe; **man hätte eine ~ fallen hören können** (fig) you could have heard a pin drop; **jdn/etw wie eine ~ suchen** (fig) to hunt high and low

for sb/sth; **eine ~ im Heuhaufen** or **Heuschober suchen** (fig) to look for a needle in a haystack

Steck|na|del|kis|sen NT pincushion

Steck-: Steck|platz M (Comput) (expansion) slot; **Steck|reis** NT (Hort) cutting; **Steck|rü- be** F swede, rutabaga (US); **Steck|schach** NT travelling (Brit) or traveling (US) chess set; **Steck|schloss** ▲ NT bicycle lock; **Steck|- schlüs|sel** M box spanner; **Steck|schuss** ▲ M bullet lodged in the body; **Steck|tuch** NT pl -tücher (esp Aus) breast-pocket handkerchief; **Steck|zi|ga|ret|te** F (cigarette formed out of a) ready-made paper tube into which one inserts tobacco; **Steck|zwie|bel** F bulb

Ste|fan ['ʃtɛfan] M **-s** Stephen

Steg [ʃteːk] M **-(e)s, -e** [-gə] **a** (= Brücke) footbridge; (= Landungssteg) landing stage; (old: = Pfad) path **b** (Mus, = Brillensteg) bridge; (Tech: an Eisenträgern) vertical plate, web **c** (= Hosensteg) stirrup **d** (Typ) furniture

Steg|ho|se F stirrup pants pl

Steg|reif ['ʃteːkraif] M **aus dem ~ spielen** (Theat) to improvise, to ad-lib; **eine Rede aus dem ~ halten** to make an impromptu or off- -the-cuff or ad-lib speech; **etw aus dem ~ tun** to do sth just like that

Steg|reif-: Steg|reif|dich|ter(in) M(F) extempore poet; **Steg|reif|ko|mö|die** F improvised comedy; **Steg|reif|re|de** F impromptu speech; **Steg|reif|spiel** NT (Theat) improvisation; **Steg|reif|vor|trag** M impromptu lecture

Steh- in cpds stand-up

Steh|auf|männ|chen ['ʃteːʔauf-] NT (Spielzeug) tumbler; (fig) somebody who always bounces back; **er ist ein richtiges** ~ he always bounces back, you can't keep a good man down (prov)

Steh-: Steh|aus|schank M stand-up bar; **Steh|ca|fé** NT stand-up café; **Steh|emp|fang** M stand-up reception

ste|hen ['ʃteːən]

pret **stand** [ʃtant], ptp **gestanden** [gə'ʃtandn] aux haben or (S Ger, Aus, Sw) sein

1 INTRANSITIVES VERB	3 REFLEXIVES VERB
2 TRANSITIVES VERB	4 UNPERSÖNLICHES VERB

1 – INTRANSITIVES VERB

a = in aufrechter Stellung sein to stand; (= warten) to wait; (Penis) to be erect; **fest/sicher stehen** to stand firm(ly)/securely; (Mensch) to have a firm/safe foothold; **unter der Dusche stehen** to be in the shower; **an der Bushalte- stelle stehen** to stand or wait at the bus stop; **vor der Tür stand ein Fremder** there was a stranger (standing) at the door; **neben jdm zu stehen kommen** (Mensch) to end up beside sb; **ich kann nicht mehr stehen** I can't stay on my feet any longer; **so wahr ich hier stehe** as sure as I'm standing here; **hier stehe ich, ich kann nicht anders!** (prov) here I stand, I can do no other; **mit jdm/etw stehen und fallen** to depend on sb/sth; **mit ihm steht und fällt die Firma** he's the kingpin of the organization; **sein Hemd steht vor Dreck** (inf) his shirt is stiff with dirt; **der Kaffee ist so stark, dass der Löffel drin steht** the coffee's so strong a spoon will stand up in it; **der Weizen steht gut** the wheat is growing well; **er hat einen stehen** (inf) he has a hard-on (sl)

b = sich befinden to be; **die Vase/Tasse steht auf dem Tisch** the vase/cup is on the table; **meine alte Schule steht noch** my old school is still standing; **auf der Fahrbahn stand Wasser** there was water on the road; **ihm steht der Schweiß auf der Stirn** his forehead is covered in sweat; **am Himmel stehen** to be in the sky; **der Mond steht am Himmel** the moon is shining; **die Son- ne steht abends tief/im Westen** in the evening the sun is low/in the west; **kurz vor dem Krieg stehen** to be on the brink of war; **im 83. Le-**

bensjahr stehen to be in one's 83rd year; **unter Schock stehen** to be in a state of shock; **unter Drogen/Alkohol stehen** to be under the influence of drugs/alcohol; **man muss wissen, wo man steht** you have to know where you stand; **vor einer Entscheidung stehen** to be faced with a decision; **die Frage steht vor der Entschei- dung** the question is about to be decided; **ich tue, was in meinen Kräften/meiner Macht steht** I'll do everything I can/in my power; **das steht zu erwarten/fürchten** (geh) that is to be expected/feared → **Leben a**

c = geschrieben, gedruckt sein to be; **was steht da/in dem Brief?** what does it/the letter say?; **es stand im „Kurier"** it was in the "Courier"; **das steht bei Nietzsche** Nietzsche says that; **das steht in der Bibel (geschrieben)** it says that in the Bible; **es steht geschrieben** (Bibl) it is written (Bibl); **das steht im Gesetz** that is what the law says; **darüber steht nichts im Ge- setz** the law says nothing about that

d = angehalten haben to have stopped; **meine Uhr steht** my watch has stopped; **der ganze Verkehr steht** traffic is at a complete standstill; **wo stehen Sie?** (inf: = geparkt) where are or have you parked?

e = bewertet werden (Währung, Kurs) to be or stand (auf +dat at); **wie steht das Pfund?** what's its exchange rate for the pound?; **das Pfund steht auf EUR 1,40** the pound stands at EUR 1.40; **am besten steht der Schweizer Fran- ken** the Swiss franc is strongest

f = in bestimmter Position sein (Rekord) to stand (auf +dat at); (Mannschaft etc) to be (auf +dat in); **der Pegel des Rheins ist stark gestiegen und steht inzwischen auf 3,84 m** the level of the Rhein has risen sharply and now stands at 3.48 m; **der Zeiger steht auf 4 Uhr** the clock says 4 (o'clock); **die Kompassnadel steht auf** or **nach Norden** the compass needle is pointing north; **wie steht das Spiel?** what is the score?; **es steht 2:1 für München** the score is or it is 2-1 to Munich

g = passen zu jdm stehen to suit sb; **Gelb/dieses Kleid steht ihr (gut)** yellow/this dress suits her; **ich finde, diese Farbe steht mir gar nicht** I don't think this colour (Brit) or color (US) suits me

h grammatikalisch (bei Satzstellung) to come; (bei Zeit, Fall, Modus) to be; (= gefolgt werden von) to take; **das Adjektiv steht im Deutschen vor dem Substantiv** in German the adjective comes before the noun; **dieses Verb steht im Perfekt** this verb is in the perfect; **nach „in" steht der Akkusativ oder der Dativ** "in" takes the accusative or the dative; **mit dem Dativ/Akkusativ stehen** to take the dative/accusative

i Belohnung, Strafe **auf Betrug steht Gefängnis** or **eine Gefängnisstrafe** fraud is punishable by imprisonment; **auf sachdienliche Hinweise steht eine Belohnung** there is a reward for useful information

j → **gestanden**

k Redewendungen **das/die Sache steht** (inf) that/the whole business is settled; **es/die Sa- che steht mir bis hier (oben)** (inf) I've had it up to here with it (inf); **für etw stehen** to stand for sth; **hinter jdm/etw stehen** to be behind sb/ sth; **das steht (ganz) bei Ihnen** (form) that is (entirely) up to you; **auf jdn/etw stehen** (inf) to be mad about sb/sth (inf)

♦ **stehen zu zu jdm stehen** to stand or stick by sb; **zu seinem Versprechen stehen** to stand by one's promise; **zu seinen Behauptungen/seiner Überzeugung stehen** to stand by what one says/by one's convictions; **zu dem, was man gesagt hat, stehen** to stick to what one has said; **zum Sozialismus stehen** to be a staunch socialist; **wie stehen Sie dazu?** what are your views on that?, what is your opinion on that?

2 – TRANSITIVES VERB

Posten stehen to stand guard; **Wache stehen** to mount watch; **Spalier stehen** to form a guard of honour (Brit), to form an honor guard (*US*); **sich müde stehen, sich** (*dat*) **die Beine in den Bauch stehen** (*inf*) to stand until one is ready to drop

3 – REFLEXIVES VERB

♦ **sich stehen**

a unpersönlich **hier steht es sich nicht gut** this isn't a very good place to stand

b in bestimmten Verhältnissen leben **sich gut/ schlecht stehen** to be well/badly off; **sich bei** or **mit jdm/etw gut/schlecht stehen** to be well/ badly off with sb/sth; **mit diesem Billigflug stehst du dich schlecht** this cheap flight isn't a good choice

c = sich verstehen **sich mit jdm gut/schlecht stehen** to get on well/badly with sb

4 – UNPERSÖNLICHES VERB

wie stehts? how are or how's things?; **so steht es also!** so that's how it is!; **wie steht es damit?** how about it?; **wie steht es mit ...?** what's the state of play with ...?; **es steht schlecht/ gut/besser um jdn** (*bei Aussichten*) things look or it looks bad/good/better for sb; (*gesundheitlich, finanziell*) sb is doing badly/well/better; **es steht schlecht/gut/besser um etw** things look or it looks bad/good/better for sth, sth is doing badly/well/better

Ste|hen NT **-s**, *no pl* **a** standing; **das viele ~ all** this standing; **etw im ~ tun** to do sth standing up **b** (= *Halt*) stop, standstill; **zum ~ bringen** to stop; *Lokomotive, LKW, Verkehr, Produktion auch* to bring to a standstill or halt or stop; *Heer, Vormarsch auch* to halt; **zum ~ kommen** to stop; (*Lokomotive, LKW, Verkehr, Produktion auch*) to come to a standstill or halt or stop

ste|hen blei|ben ▲ VI *irreg aux sein* **a** (= *anhalten*) to stop; (*Zug, LKW, Verkehr, Produktion*) to stop, to come to a standstill or halt or stop; (*Aut: Motor*) to cut out, to stop; **~! stop!**; (*Mil*) halt! **b** (= *nicht weitergehen*) (*Mensch, Tier*) to stay; (*Uhr, Entwicklung*) to stop; (*Zeit*) to stand still; (*Auto, Zug*) to stand **c** (= *vergessen/zurück gelassen werden*) to be left (behind); **mein Regenschirm muss im Büro stehen geblieben sein** I must have left my umbrella in the office **d** (= *unverändert bleiben*) to be left (in); **soll das so ~?** should that stay or be left as it is?; **im Raum ~** (*Vorwurf etc*) to be left hanging in the air

ste|hend ADJ *attr Fahrzeug* stationary; *Wasser, Gewässer* stagnant; (= *ständig*) *Heer* standing, regular; *Start (Radfahren)* standing; **~e Redensart** stock phrase; **aus dem Fuße** (*liter*) without delay; **~es Gut** (*Naut*) standing rigging

ste|hen las|sen ▲ *ptp* **stehen lassen** or (*rare*) **stehen gelassen** VT *irreg* to leave; (= *zurücklassen, vergessen auch*) to leave behind; (*Cook*) to let stand; *Essen, Getränk* to leave (untouched); *Fehler* to leave (in); **lasst das (an der Tafel) stehen** leave it (on the board); **alles stehen und liegen lassen** to drop everything; (*Flüchtlinge etc*) to leave everything behind; **jdn einfach ~** to leave sb standing (there), to walk off and leave sb; **sich** (*dat*) **einen Bart ~** to grow a beard; **jdn vor der Tür/in der Kälte ~** to leave sb standing outside/in the cold; **das Auto ~ und zu Fuß gehen** to leave the car behind and walk → **Regen**

Ste|her¹ [ˈʃteːɐ] M **-s**, **-** (*Pferderennen, fig*) stayer

Ste|her² [ˈʃteːɐ] M **-s**, **-**, **Ste|he|rin** [-ərɪn] F **-**, **-nen** (*Radfahren*) motor-paced rider

Ste|her|ren|nen NT (*Radfahren*) motor-paced race

Steh-: Steh|gei|ger(in) M(F) café violinist; **Steh|im|biss** ▲ M stand-up snack bar; **Steh|knei|pe** F stand-up bar; **Steh|kon|vent** M (*hum*) stand-up do (*inf*); **Steh|kra|gen** M stand-up collar; (*von Geistlichen auch*) dog col-

lar; (= *Vatermörder*) wing collar; **Steh|lam|pe** F standard lamp; **Steh|lei|ter** F stepladder

steh|len [ˈʃteːlən] *pret* **stahl** [ʃtaːl], *ptp* **gestohlen** [gəˈʃtoːlən] **VTI** **a** (= *stehlen*); **hier wird viel gestohlen** there's a lot of stealing around here; **jdm die Ruhe ~** to disturb sb; **jdm die Zeit ~** to waste sb's time → **Elster, Schau b** **VR** to steal; **sich in das/aus dem Haus ~** to steal into/out of the house; **sich aus der Verantwortung ~** to evade one's responsibility; **die Sonne stahl sich durch die Wolken** (*liter*) the sun stole forth from behind the clouds (*liter*) → *auch* **gestohlen**

Steh|ler [ˈʃteːlɐ] M **-s**, **-**, **Steh|le|rin** [-ərɪn] F **-**, **-nen** → **Hehler(in)**

Stehl|gut NT (*form*) stolen goods *pl*

Steh-: Steh|lo|kal NT stand-up café; **Steh|par|ty** F buffet party; **Steh|platz** M ich bekam nur noch einen ~ I had to stand; **ein ~ kostet 8 Euro** a ticket for standing room costs 8 euros, it costs 8 euros to stand; **Stehplätze** standing room *sing*; **zwei Stehplätze, bitte** two standing, please; **die Anzahl der Stehplätze ist begrenzt** only a limited number of people are allowed to stand; **Steh|pult** NT high desk; **Steh|satz** M (*Typ*) standing or line type; **Steh|ver|mö|gen** NT staying power, stamina

Stei|er|mark [ˈʃtaɪɐmaʁk] F **-** Styria

steif [ʃtaɪf] **ADJ** **a** stiff; *Grog* stiff, strong; *Penis* hard, stiff, erect; **~ vor Kälte** stiff or numb with cold; **eine ~e Brise** a stiff breeze; **ein ~er Hals** a stiff neck; **ein ~er Hut** a homburg (hat); (= *Melone*) a bowler (hat), a derby (*US*); **sich ~ (wie ein Brett) machen** to go rigid; **ein Steifer** (*inf*: = *Erektion*) a stiffy (*inf*), a hard-on (*sl*); (*sl*: = *Toter*) a stiff (*inf*) **b** (= *gestärkt*) starched **c** (= *förmlich*) *Stil; Empfang, Konventionen, Begrüßung, Abend* formal **ADV** **a** (= *hart*) **das Eiweiß ~ schlagen** to beat the egg white until stiff; **~ und fest auf etw** (*dat*) **beharren** to insist stubbornly or obstinately on sth; **sie behauptete ~ und fest, dass ...** she insisted that ...; **etw ~ und fest glauben** to be convinced of sth **b** (= *förmlich*) stiffly; **~ lächeln** to smile stiffly; **jdn ~ behandeln** to be standoffish to sb

Stei|fe [ˈʃtaɪfə] F **-**, **-n** **a** *no pl* stiffness **b** (= *Stärkemittel*) starch

stei|fen [ˈʃtaɪfn] VT to stiffen; *Wäsche* to starch → **Nacken**

Steiff|tier® [ˈʃtaɪf-] NT soft toy (animal)

Steif|heit F **-**, *no pl* stiffness; (= *Förmlichkeit auch*) formality

Steif|lei|nen NT buckram

Steig [ʃtaɪk] M **-(e)s**, **-e** [-ɡə] steep track

Steig|bü|gel M stirrup; **jdm den ~ halten** (*fig*) to help sb on

Steig|bü|gel|hal|ter(in) M(F) (*esp Pol pej*) jds ~ sein to help sb to come to power

Stei|ge [ˈʃtaɪɡə] F **-**, **-n** (*dial*) **a** (= *Steig*) steep track **b** (= *Treppe*) (narrow) staircase **c** (= *Lattenkiste*) crate

Steig|ei|sen NT climbing iron *usu pl*; (*Bergsteigen*) crampon; (*an Mauer*) rung (in the wall)

stei|gen [ˈʃtaɪɡn] *pret* **stieg** [ʃtiːk], *ptp* **gestiegen** [gəˈʃtiːɡn] *aux sein* **VI** **a** (= *klettern*) to climb; **auf einen Berg/Turm/Baum/eine Leiter ~** to climb (up) a mountain/tower/tree/ladder; **aufs Fahrrad ~** to get on(to) the/one's bicycle; **aufs Pferd ~** to get on(to) or mount the/one's horse; **ins Bett/in die Straßenbahn ~** to get into bed/on the tram; **in die Badewanne ~** to climb or get into the bath; **in die Kleider ~** (*inf*) to put on one's clothes; **vom Fahrrad/Pferd ~** to get off or dismount from the/one's bicycle/horse; **aus dem Wasser/der Badewanne/dem Bett ~** to get out of the water/the bath/bed; **aus dem Zug/ Bus/Flugzeug ~** to get off the train/bus/plane; **in den Zug/Bus ~** to get on the train/bus; **wer hoch steigt, fällt tief** (*Prov*) the bigger they come the harder they fall (*prov*) **b** (= *sich aufwärts bewegen*) to rise; (*Vogel*) to

rise, to soar; (*Flugzeug, Straße*) to climb; (= *sich erhöhen*) (*Preis, Zahl, Gehalt etc*) to increase, to go up, to rise; (*Fieber*) to go up; (= *zunehmen*) (*Chancen, Misstrauen, Ungeduld etc*) to increase; (*Spannung*) to increase, to mount; (= *sich aufbäumen: Pferd*) to rear; (= *sich auflösen: Nebel*) to lift; **Drachen ~ lassen** to fly kites; **der Gestank/ Duft stieg ihm in die Nase** the stench/smell reached his nostrils; **das Blut stieg ihm in den Kopf/das Gesicht** the blood rushed to his head/face; **in jds Achtung** (*dat*) **~** to rise in sb's estimation; **die allgemeine Stimmung stieg** the general mood improved; **meine Stimmung stieg** my spirits rose **c** (*inf*: = *stattfinden*) to be; **steigt die Demo/Prüfung oder nicht?** is the demo/exam on or not?; **bei Helga steigt Sonnabend eine Party** Helga's having a party on Saturday **VT** *Treppen, Stufen* to climb (up)

Stei|ger [ˈʃtaɪɡɐ] M **-s**, **-** (*Min*) pit foreman

Stei|ge|rer [ˈʃtaɪɡərɐ] M **-s**, **-**, **Stei|ge|rin** [-ərɪn] F **-**, **-nen** bidder

stei|gern [ˈʃtaɪɡɐn] **VT** **a** (= *erhöhen*) to increase (*auf +acc* to, *um* by); *Wirkung* to increase, to heighten; (= *verschlimmern*) *Übel, Zorn* to aggravate; (= *verbessern*) *Leistung* to improve **b** (*Gram*) *Adjektiv* to compare **c** (= *ersteigern*) to buy at an auction **VR** **a** (= *sich erhöhen*) to increase; (*Zorn, Übel*) to be aggravated, to worsen; **sein Ärger steigerte sich zu Zorn** his annoyance turned into rage; **seine Schmerzen steigerten sich ins Unerträgliche** his pain became unbearable **b** (= *sich verbessern*) to improve **c** (= *hineinsteigern*) **sich in etw** (*acc*) **~** to work oneself (up) into sth

Stei|ge|rung [ˈʃtaɪɡərʊŋ] F **-**, **-en** **a** (= *das Steigern*) increase (+*gen* in); (*von Wirkung auch*) heightening; (*von Farbe*) intensification, heightening; (= *Verschlimmerung*) aggravation; (= *Verbesserung*) improvement **b** (*Gram*) comparative

Stei|ge|rungs-: stei|ge|rungs|fä|hig ADJ improvable; **Stei|ge|rungs|form** F (*Gram*) (= *Komparativ*) comparative form; (= *Superlativ*) superlative form; **Stei|ge|rungs|stu|fe** F (*Gram*) degree of comparison

Steig-: Steig|fä|hig|keit F , *no pl* (*Aut*) hill-climbing or pulling capacity; (*Aviat*) climbing capacity; **~ beweisen** to pull well; **Steig|flug** M (*Aviat*) climb, ascent; **Steig|schwin|dig|keit** F rate of climb or ascent; **Steig|rie|men** M stirrup leather

Stei|gung [ˈʃtaɪɡʊŋ] F **-**, **-en** (= *Hang*) slope; (*von Hang, Straße, Math*) gradient (*Brit*), grade (*esp US*); (= *Gewindesteigung*) pitch; **eine ~ von 10%** a gradient (*Brit*) or grade (*esp US*) of one in ten, a gradient (*Brit*) or grade (*esp US*) of 10%

Stei|gungs-: Stei|gungs|grad M gradient (*Brit*), grade (*esp US*); **Stei|gungs|win|kel** M angle of gradient (*Brit*) or grade (*esp US*)

steil [ʃtaɪl] **ADJ** **a** *Abhang, Treppe* steep; (*fig*) *Anstieg, Rückgang* steep, rapid; **eine ~e Karriere** (*fig*) a rapid rise **b** (= *senkrecht*) upright **c** (*Sport*) **~e Vorlage, ~er Pass** through ball **d** (*dated sl*) super (*inf*), smashing (*inf*); **ein ~er Zahn** (*inf*) a smasher (*inf*) **ADV** steeply; **sich ~ aufrichten** to sit/stand up straight

Steil-: Steil|hang M steep slope; **Steil|heck** NT hatchback; **Steil|heit** F , *no pl* steepness; **Steil|küs|te** F steep coast; (= *Klippen*) cliffs *pl*; **Steil|pass** ▲ M , **Steil|vor|la|ge** F (*Sport*) through ball; **Steil|wand** F steep face; **Steil|wand|fah|rer(in)** M(F) wall-of-death rider; **Steil|wand|zelt** NT frame tent

Stein [ʃtaɪn] M **-(e)s**, **-e** (*auch Bot, Med*) stone; (= *Feuerstein*) flint; (= *Edelstein*) jewel, stone; (*in Uhr*) jewel; (= *Spielstein*) piece; **heißer ~** (*Cook*) hot stone; **der ~ der Weisen** (*lit, fig*) the philosophers' stone; **es blieb kein ~ auf dem anderen** everything was smashed to pieces; (*bei Gebäuden, Mauern*) not a stone was left standing; **das könnte einen ~ erweichen** that would move the hardest heart to pity; **mir fällt ein ~ vom Herzen!** (*fig*) that's a load off my mind!; **bei jdm einen ~ im Brett haben** (*fig inf*) to be well in with sb (*inf*); **jdm einen ~ aus dem Weg räumen** (*fig*) to remove an obstacle from sb's path; **den ersten ~ (auf jdn) werfen** (*fig*) to cast the first stone (at sb) → **Anstoß c, rollen VI a**

b (= *Baustein, Naturstein*) stone; (*groß, esp Hohlblock*) block; (*kleiner, esp Ziegelstein*) brick

c *no pl* (*Material*) stone; **ein Haus aus ~** a house made of stone, a stone house; **ein Herz aus ~** (*fig*) a heart of stone; **es friert ~ und Bein** (*fig inf*) it's freezing cold outside; **~ und Bein schwören** (*fig inf*) to swear blind (*Brit inf*), to swear to God (*inf*); **zu ~ erstarren** *or* **werden** to turn to stone; (*fig*) to be as if turned to stone

Stein-: Stein|ad|ler M golden eagle; **stein|alt** ADJ ancient, as old as the hills; **Stein|bau** M **a** *no pl* building in stone *no art* **b** *pl* **-bauten** (= *Gebäude*) stone building; **Stein|bock** M **a** (*Zool*) ibex **b** (*Astrol*) Capricorn; **Stein|boden** M stone floor; **Stein|boh|rer** M masonry drill; (= *Gesteinsbohrer*) rock drill; **Stein|bruch** M quarry; **Stein|bruch|ar|bei|ter(in)** M(F) quarry worker; **Stein|butt** M (*Zool*) turbot; **Stein|druck** M *pl* **-drucke** (*Typ*) lithography; **Stein|dru|cker(in)** M(F) lithographer; **Stein|ei|che** F holm oak, holly oak

stei|nern ['ʃtainɐn] ADJ stone, (*fig*) stony; **ein ~es Herz** a heart of stone

Stein-: Stein|er|wei|chen NT **zum ~ weinen** to cry heartbreakingly; **stein|er|wei|chend** ADJ heart-rending, heartbreaking **ADV** heart-rendingly, heartbreakingly; **Stein|fraß** M stone erosion; **Stein|frucht** F stone fruit; **Stein|fuß|bo|den** M stone floor; **Stein|gar|ten** M rockery, rock garden; **Stein|geiß** F female ibex; **stein|grau** ADJ stone-grey (*Brit*), stone-gray (*US*); **Stein|gut** NT , *no pl* stoneware; **Stein|ha|gel** M hail of stones

Stein|hä|ger® [-hɛːgɐ] M **-s, -** Steinhäger®, *type of schnapps*

stein|hart ADJ (as) hard as a rock, rock hard

stei|nig ['ʃtainɪç] ADJ stony; **ein ~er Weg** (*fig*) a path of trial and tribulation

stei|ni|gen ['ʃtainɪgn] VT to stone

Stei|ni|gung F **-, -en** stoning

Stein|koh|le F hard coal

Stein|koh|len-: Stein|koh|len|berg|bau M coal mining; **Stein|koh|len|berg|werk** NT coal mine, colliery; **Stein|koh|len|re|vier** NT coal-mining area

Stein-: Stein|krug M (= *Kanne*) stoneware jug; (= *Becher*) earthenware/stoneware mug; (*für Bier*) stein; **Stein|lei|den** NT (= *Nieren-/Blasensteine*) kidney/bladder stones *pl*; (= *Gallensteine*) gallstones *pl*; **ein ~ haben** to suffer from kidney *etc* stones; **Stein|mei|ßel** M stone chisel; **Stein|metz** [-mɛts] M **-en, -en**, **Stein|met|zin** [-mɛtsɪn] F **-, -nen** stonemason; **Stein|obst** NT stone fruit; **Stein|pilz** M boletus edulis (*spec*); **Stein|plat|te** F stone slab; (*zum Pflastern*) flagstone; **stein|reich** ADJ (*inf*) stinking rich (*Brit inf*), rolling in it (*inf*); **Stein|salz** NT rock salt; **Stein|schlag** M **a** rockfall; **„Achtung ~"** "danger falling stones" **b** *no pl* (= *Schotter*) broken stone; (*zum Straßenbau*) (road) metal; **Stein|schlag|ge|fahr** F danger of rockfall(s); **Stein|schleu|der** F catapult (*Brit*), slingshot (*US*); **Stein|schnei|der(in)** M(F) gem cutter; **Stein|schnitt** M **a** cut (gem)stone **b** *no pl* (*Verfahren*) gem cutting; **Stein|ta|fel** F stone tablet; **Stein|topf** M stoneware pot; **Stein|wild** NT (*Hunt*) ibexes *pl*; **Stein|wurf** M **a** (*fig*) stone's throw **b** (*lit*) **mit einem ~** by throwing a stone; **Stein|wüs|te** F stony desert; (*fig*) concrete jungle; **Stein|zeit** F (*lit, fig*) Stone Age; **stein|zeit|lich** ADJ Stone Age *attr*; **Stein|zeug** NT , *no pl* stoneware

Stei|rer ['ʃtaire] M **-s, -**, **Stei|re|rin** [-ərɪn] F **-, -nen** Styrian

stei|risch ['ʃtairɪʃ] ADJ Styrian

Steiß [ʃtais] M **-es, -e** (*Anat*) coccyx; (*hum inf*) tail (*inf*), behind

Steiß-: Steiß|bein NT (*Anat*) coccyx; **Steiß|ge|burt** F (*Med*) breech birth *or* delivery; **Steiß|la|ge** F (*Med*) breech presentation

Ste|le ['steːlə, 'ʃt-] F **-, -n** (*Bot, Archeol*) stele

Stell|la|ge [ʃtɛ'laːʒə] F **-, -n** (*inf*: = *Gestell*) rack, frame; (*dial inf*: = *Beine*) legs *pl*, pins *pl* (*inf*)

stel|lar [ʃtɛ'laːɐ, st-] ADJ (*Astron*) stellar

Stell|dich|ein ['ʃtɛldɪçʔain] NT **-(s), -(s)** (*dated*) rendezvous, tryst (*old*); **sich** (*dat*) **ein ~ geben** (*fig*) to come together

Stel|le ['ʃtɛlə] ✪ 28.1, 28.2, 29.1, 29.2, 46.1, 46.5, 46.6, 53.2 F **-, -n** **a** place, spot; (= *Standort*) place; (*Fleck: rostend, nass, faul etc*) patch; **an dieser ~** in this place, on this spot; **eine gute ~ zum Parken/Picknicken** a good place *or* spot to park/for a picnic; **legen Sie das an eine andere ~** put it in a different place; **diese ~ muss repariert werden** this bit needs repairing, it needs to be repaired here; **eine kahle ~ am Kopf** a bald patch on one's head; **eine entzündete ~ am Finger** an inflammation on one's finger, an inflamed finger; **Salbe auf die wunde/aufgeriebene ~ auftragen** apply ointment to the affected area; **eine empfindliche ~** (*lit*) a sensitive spot *or* place; (*fig*) a sensitive point; **eine schwache ~** a weak spot; (*fig auch*) a weak point; **auf der ~ laufen** to run on the spot; **auf der ~ treten** (*lit*) to mark time; (*fig*) not to make any progress *or* headway; **auf der ~** (*fig*: = *sofort*) on the spot; *kommen, gehen* straight *or* right away; **nicht von der ~ kommen** not to make any progress *or* headway; (*fig auch*) to be bogged down; **etw nicht von der ~ kriegen** (*inf*) to be unable to move *or* shift sth; **sich nicht von der ~ rühren** *or* **bewegen**, **nicht von der ~** to refuse to budge (*inf*) *or* move; **zur ~ sein** to be on the spot; (= *bereit, etw zu tun*) to be at hand; **X zur ~!** (*Mil*) X reporting!; **sich bei jdm zur ~ melden** (*Mil*) to report to sb → **Ort¹ a**

b (*in Buch etc*) place; (= *Abschnitt*) passage; (= *Textstelle, esp beim Zitieren*) reference; (= *Bibelstelle*) verse; (*Mus*) passage; **an dieser ~** here; **an anderer ~** elsewhere, in another place

c (= *Zeitpunkt*) point; **an dieser ~** at this point *or* juncture; **an anderer ~** on another occasion; **an früherer/späterer ~** earlier/later; (= *an anderem Tag auch*) on an earlier/a later occasion; **an passender ~** at an appropriate moment

d (*in Reihenfolge, Ordnung, Liste*) place; (*in Tabelle, Hierarchie*) place, position; **an erster ~** in the first place, first; **an erster/zweiter ~ geht es um ...** in the first instance *or* first/secondly it's a question of ...; **(bei jdm) an erster/letzter ~ kommen** to come first/last (for sb); **an erster/zweiter etc ~ stehen** to be first/second *etc*, to be in first/second *etc* place; (*in Bezug auf Wichtigkeit*) to come first/second *etc*; **an führender/einflussreicher ~ stehen** to be in *or* have a leading/an influential position

e (*Math*) figure, digit; (*hinter Komma*) place; **drei ~n hinter dem Komma** three decimal places; **eine Zahl mit drei ~n** a three-figure number

f (= *Lage, Platz, Aufgabenbereich*) place; **an ~ von** in place of, instead of; **an jds ~** (*acc*)**/an die ~ einer Sache** (*gen*) **treten** to take sb's place/the place of sth; **das erledige ich an deiner ~** I'll do that for you; **ich gehe an deiner ~** I'll go in your place; **ich möchte jetzt nicht an seiner ~ sein** I wouldn't like to be in his position *or* shoes now; **an deiner ~ würde ich ...** in your position I would ..., if I were you I would ... → *auch* **anstelle**

g (= *Posten*) job; (= *Ausbildungsstelle*) place; **eine freie** *or* **offene ~** a vacancy; **ohne ~** without a job; **wir haben zur Zeit keine ~n zu vergeben** we haven't any vacancies at present

h (= *Dienststelle*) office; (= *Behörde*) authority; **da bist du bei mir/uns an der richtigen ~!** (*inf*) you've come to the right place; **bei ihm/ihnen bist du an der richtigen ~!** (*inf*) you went to the right place; **sich an höherer ~ beschweren** to

---

complain to somebody higher up, to complain to a higher authority

stel|len ['ʃtɛlən] VT **a** (= *hinstellen*) to put; (= *an bestimmten Platz legen*) to place, to put; **jdm etw auf den Tisch ~** to put sth on the table for sb; **jdn über/unter jdn ~** (*fig*) to put *or* place sb above/below sb; **auf sich** (*acc*) **selbst** *or* **allein gestellt sein** (*fig*) to have to fend for oneself

b (= *in senkrechte Position bringen*) to stand; **die Ohren ~** to prick up its ears; **du solltest es ~, nicht legen** you should stand it up, not lay it down

c (= *Platz finden für*) **etw nicht ~ können** (= *unterbringen*) not to have room *or* space for sth; **etw gut ~ können** to have a good place for sth

d (= *anordnen*) to arrange; **das sollten Sie anders ~** you should put it in a different position

e (= *erstellen*) **(jdm) eine Diagnose ~** to provide (sb with) a diagnosis, to make a diagnosis (for sb); **jdm sein Horoskop ~** to draw up *or* cast sb's horoscope

f (= *arrangieren*) *Szene* to arrange; *Aufnahme* to pose; **gestellt** (*Bild, Foto*) posed; **die Szene war gestellt** they posed for the scene; **eine gestellte Pose** a pose

g (= *beschaffen, aufbieten*) to provide; **die CDU stellt zwei Minister** the CDU has two ministers

h (= *einstellen*) to set (*auf +acc* at); *Uhr etc* to set (*auf +acc* for); **das Radio lauter/leiser ~** to turn the radio up/down; **die Heizung höher/kleiner ~** to turn the heating up/down

i (*finanziell*) **gut/besser/schlecht gestellt sein** to be well/better/badly off

j (= *erwischen*) to catch; (*fig inf*) to corner → **Rede f**

k (*in Verbindung mit n siehe auch dort*) *Aufgabe, Thema, Bedingung, Termin* to set (*jdm* sb); *Frage* to put (*jdm, an jdn* to sb); *Antrag, Forderung* to make

l (*in Redewendungen*) **etw in jds Belieben** *or* **Ermessen** (*acc*) **~** to leave sth to sb's discretion, to leave sth up to sb; **jdn unter jds Aufsicht** (*acc*) **~** to place *or* put sb under sb's care; **jdn vor ein Problem/eine Aufgabe** *etc* **~** to confront sb with a problem/task *etc*; **jdn vor eine Entscheidung ~** to put sb in the position of having to make a decision

VR **a** (= *sich hinstellen*) to (go and) stand (*an +acc* at, by); (= *sich aufstellen, sich einordnen*) to position oneself; (= *sich aufrecht hinstellen*) to stand up; **sich auf (die) Zehenspitzen ~** to stand on tiptoe; **sich auf den Standpunkt ~, ...** to take the view ...; **sich gegen jdn/etw ~** (*fig*) to oppose sb/sth; **sich hinter jdn/etw ~** (*fig*) to support *or* back sb/sth, to stand by sb/sth; **sich jdm in den Weg ~** (*lit, fig*) to stand in sb's way; **sich jdm vor die Nase ~** to stand right in front of sb

b (*Gegenstand, Körperteil*) **sich senkrecht ~** to stand *or* come up; **sich in die Höhe ~** to stand up; (*Ohren*) to prick up

c (*fig*: = *sich verhalten*) **sich positiv/anders zu etw ~** to have a positive/different attitude toward(s) sth; **wie stellst du dich zu ...?** how do you regard ...?, what do you think of ...?; **sich gut mit jdm ~** to put oneself on good terms with sb

d (*inf: finanziell*) **sich gut/schlecht ~** to be well/badly off

e (= *sich einstellen: Gerät etc*) to set itself (*auf +acc* at); **die Heizung stellt sich von selbst kleiner** the heating turns itself down

f (= *sich ausliefern*) to give oneself up, to surrender (*jdm* to sb); **sich der öffentlichen Kritik ~** to lay oneself open to public criticism; **sich den Journalisten ~** to make oneself available to the reporters; **sich den Fragen der Journalisten ~** to be prepared to answer reporters' questions; **sich einer Herausforderung ~** to take up a challenge; **sich einem Herausforderer ~** to take on a challenger; **sich (jdm) zum Kampf ~** to be prepared to do battle (with sb), to announce one's readiness to fight (sb)

g (= *sich verstellen*) **sich krank/schlafend** *etc* **~** to pretend to be ill/asleep *etc* → **dumm, taub,**

tot

h (*fig*: = *entstehen*) to arise (*für* for); **es stellten sich uns** (*dat*) **allerlei Probleme** we were faced or confronted with all sorts of problems; **es stellt sich die Frage, ob ...** the question arises whether ...

Stellen-: Stellen|ab|bau M staff cuts *pl* or reductions *pl*, reduction(s *pl*) in staff; **Stellen|an|ge|bot** M offer of employment (*Brit*), job offer; **"Stellenangebote**" "situations vacant", "vacancies"; **Stellen|an|zei|ge** F, **Stellen|aus|schrei|bung** F job advertisement or ad (*inf*); **Stellen|be|schrei|bung** F job description; **Stellen|be|set|zung** F appointment, filling a/the position *no art*; **Stellen|ein|spa|rung** F *usu pl* job cut; **Stellen|ge|such** NT advertisement seeking employment, "employment wanted" advertisement; **„Stellengesuche**" "situations wanted" (*Brit*), "employment wanted"; **Stellen|markt** M employment (*Brit*) or job market; (*in Zeitung*) appointments section; **Stellen|nach|weis** , **Stellen|ver|mitt|lung** F employment bureau (*Brit*), employment centre (*Brit*) or center (*US*); (*privat auch*) employment agency; **Stellen|strei|chun|gen** PL job cuts *pl*; **stellen|wei|se** ADV in places, here and there; ~ **Schauer** scattered showers, showers in places; **Stellen|wert** M (*Math*) place value; (*fig*) status; **einen hohen ~ haben** to play an important role

Stell|flä|che F area; **10.000 Quadratmeter ~** an area of 10,000 square metres (*Brit*) or meters (*US*); **der Drucker benötigt nur eine kleine ~** the printer does not take up much space

-stel|lig [ʃtɛlɪç] ADJ *suf* (*bei Zahlen*) -figure, -digit; (*hinter Komma*) -place; **ein dreistelliger Dezimalbruch** a number with three decimal places

Stell- [ʃtɛl-]: **Stell|ma|cher(in)** M(F) (*N Ger*) (= *Wagenbauer*) cartwright; (*esp von Wagenrädern*) wheelwright; **Stell|ma|che|rei** [ʃtɛlmaxəˈraɪ] F, **-en** → **Stellmacher(in)** cart-making; (*Werkstatt*) cartwright's/wheelwright's (work)shop; **Stell|platz** M (*für Auto*) parking space; **Stell|pro|be** F (*Theat*) blocking rehearsal; **Stell|schrau|be** F (*Tech*) adjusting or set screw

Stel|lung [ʃtɛlʊŋ] F **-, -en** **a** (*lit, fig, Mil*) position; **in ~ bringen/gehen** to bring/get into position; **die ~ halten** (*Mil*) to hold one's position; (*hum*) to hold the fort; **~ beziehen** (*Mil*) to move into position; (*fig*) to declare one's position, to make it clear where one stands; **zu etw ~ nehmen** or **beziehen** to give one's opinion on sth, to comment on sth; **ich möchte dazu nicht ~ nehmen** I would rather not comment on that; **für jdn ~ nehmen** or **beziehen** to come out in favour (*Brit*) or favor (*US*) of sb; (= *verteidigen*) to take sb's part; **für etw ~ nehmen** or **beziehen** to defend sth; **gegen jdn/etw ~ neh|men** or **beziehen** to come out against sth/sb; **b** (= *Rang*) position; **in führender/untergeord|neter ~** in a leading/subordinate position; **in meiner ~ als ...** in my capacity as ...; **die rechtli|che ~ des Mieters** the legal status of the tenant; **gesellschaftliche ~** social status or standing; **eine marktbeherrschende ~ innehaben** to occupy a dominant position in the market **c** (= *Posten*) position, post (*esp Brit*), situation (*dated, form*); **bei jdm in ~ sein** to be in sb's employment (*Brit*) or employ (*form*); **ohne ~ sein** to be without employment, to be unemployed

Stel|lung|nah|me [-naːmə] F **-, -n** statement (*zu* on); **eine ~ zu etw abgeben** to make a statement on sth; **sich** (*dat*) **seine ~ vorbehal|ten, sich einer ~** (*gen*) **enthalten** to decline to comment; **was ist Ihre ~ dazu?** what is your position on this?

Stel|lungs-: Stel|lungs|be|fehl M (*Mil*) call-up (*Brit*), draft papers *pl* (*US*); **Stel|lungs|fehler** M (*Sport*) positional error; **Stel|lungs|krieg** M positional warfare *no indef*

art; **stel|lungs|los** ADJ without employment, unemployed; **Stel|lungs|spiel** NT (*Sport*) positional play *no indef art*; **Stel|lungs|su|che** F search for employment; **auf ~ sein** to be looking for employment or a position; **Stel|lungs|wech|sel** M change of employment (*esp Brit*), change of job

stellv. *abbr von* **stellvertretend**

Stell-: stell|ver|tre|tend ADJ (*von Amts wegen*) deputy *attr*; (= *vorübergehend*) acting *attr* ADV ~ **für jdn** for sb; (*Rechtsanwalt*) on behalf of sb; **ich bin ~ für ihn da** I'm here in his place; ~ **für jdn handeln** to deputize or act for sb; ~ **für etw stehen** to stand in place of sth; **Stell|ver|tre|ter(in)** M(F) (acting) representative; (*von Amts wegen*) deputy; (*von Arzt*) locum; **der ~ Christi (auf Erden)** the Vicar of Christ; **Stell|ver|tre|tung** F (= *Stellvertreter*) representative; (*von Amts wegen*) deputy; (*von Arzt*) locum; **die ~ für jdn übernehmen** to represent sb; (*von Amts wegen*) to stand in or deputize for sb; **in ~** (+*gen*) for, on behalf of; **Stell|wand** F partition wall; **Stell|werk** NT (*Rail*) signal box (*Brit*), signal or switch tower (*US*)

stelz|bei|nig ADJ (*fig*) (= *steif*) stiff ADV **er kam ~ auf uns zu** he came towards (*Brit*) or toward (*US*) us with long lanky strides; **der Storch stolzierte ~ durch den Sumpf** the stork paraded on long thin legs through the swamp

Stel|ze [ˈʃtɛltsə] F **-, -n** **a** stilt; (*inf:* = *Bein*) leg, pin (*inf*); **auf ~n gehen** to walk on stilts; (*fig: Lyrik etc*) to be stilted **b** (*Orn*) wagtail **c** (*Aus:* = *Schweinsstelze*) pig's trotter

stel|zen [ˈʃtɛltsn] VI *aux sein* (*inf*) to stalk → *auch* **gestelzt**

Stel|zen|lau|fen NT **-s**, *no pl* walking *no art* on stilts; ~ **lernen** to learn to walk on stilts

Stelz-: Stelz|fuß M wooden leg, peg (*inf*), peg leg (*inf*); (*Mensch*) peg leg (*inf*); **Stelz|vo|gel** M (*Orn*) wader

Stemm|bo|gen M (*Ski*) stem turn

Stemm|ei|sen NT crowbar

stem|men [ˈʃtɛmən] VT **a** (= *stützen*) to press; *Ellenbogen* to prop; **die Arme in die Seiten** or **Hüften gestemmt** with arms akimbo; **die Arme** or **die Hände in die Hüften ~** to put one's hands on one's hips; **er hatte die Arme in die Hüften gestemmt** he stood with arms akimbo **b** (= *hochstemmen*) to lift (above one's head); **einen ~** (*inf*) to have a few (*inf*); **Gewichte ~** to lift weights **c** (= *meißeln*) to chisel; (*kräftiger*) *Loch* to knock (*in* +*acc* in) VR **sich gegen etw ~** to brace oneself against sth; (*fig*) to set oneself against sth, to oppose sth VI (*Ski*) to stem

Stemm|schwung M (*Ski*) stem turn

Stem|pel [ˈʃtɛmpl] M **-s, -** **a** (= *Gummistempel*) (rubber) stamp **b** (= *Abdruck*) stamp; (= *Post|stempel*) postmark; (= *Viehstempel*) brand, mark; (*auf Silber, Gold*) hallmark; **jdm/einer Sache** (*dat*) **einen/seinen ~ aufdrücken** or **aufprägen** (*fig*) to make a/one's mark on sb/sth; **den ~ von jdm/etw tragen**, **jds ~/den ~ einer Sache** (*gen*) **tra|gen** to bear the stamp of sb/sth **c** (*Tech*) (= *Prägestempel*) die; (*stangenförmig,* = *Lochstempel*) punch **d** (*Tech:* von *Druckpumpe* etc) piston, plunger **e** (*Min*) prop **f** (*Bot*) pistil

Stem|pel-: Stem|pel|far|be F stamping ink; **Stem|pel|geld** NT (*inf*) dole (money) (*Brit inf*), welfare (*US*); **Stem|pel|kar|te** F punch card; **Stem|pel|kis|sen** NT ink pad

stem|peln [ˈʃtɛmpln] VT to stamp; *Brief* to postmark; *Briefmarke* to frank; *Gold, Silber* to hall|mark; **jdn zum Lügner/Verbrecher ~** (*fig*) to brand sb (as) a liar/criminal; **jdn zum Sünden|bock ~** (*fig*) to make a scapegoat of sb VI (*inf*) **a** ~ **gehen** (= *arbeitslos sein*) to be on the dole (*Brit inf*), to be on welfare (*US*); (= *sich arbeits|los melden*) to go on the dole (*Brit inf*) or on welfare (*US*) **b** (= *Stempeluhr betätigen*) (*beim Hereinkommen*) to clock on or in; (*beim Hinausge|hen*) to clock off or out

Stem|pel-: Stem|pel|schnei|der(in) M(F) punch cutter; **Stem|pel|stän|der** M rubber--stamp holder; **Stem|pel|uhr** F time clock

Stem|pe|lung [ˈʃtɛmpəlʊŋ] F **-, -en** stamping; (*von Brief*) postmarking; (*von Briefmarke*) frank|ing; (*von Gold, Silber*) hallmarking

Sten|gel △ [ˈʃtɛŋl] M **-s, -** → **Stängel**

sten|gel|los △ ADJ → **stängellos**

Ste|no [ˈʃteːno] F **-**, *no pl* (*inf*) shorthand

Steno-: Ste|no|block M *pl* **-blöcke** or **-blocks** shorthand pad; **Ste|no|graf** ▲ [ʃtenoˈɡraːf] M **-en, -en**, **Ste|no|gra|fin** ▲ [-ˈɡraːfɪn] F **-, -nen** (*im Büro*) shorthand secretary; (*esp in Gericht, bei Konferenz etc*) stenographer; **Ste|no|gra|fie** ▲ [ʃtenoɡraˈfiː] F **-**, *no pl* shorthand, stenography (*dated, form*); **ste|no|gra|fie|ren** ▲ [ʃtenoɡraˈfiːrən] *ptp* **stenografiert** VT to take down in shorthand VI to take shorthand; **können Sie ~?** can you take shorthand?; **ste|no|gra|fisch** ▲ [ʃtenoˈɡraːfɪʃ] ADJ shorthand *attr* ADV **etw ~ notieren** to take sth down in shorthand; **Ste|no|gramm** [ʃtenoˈɡram] NT *pl* **-gramme** text in shorthand; (= *Diktat*) shorthand dictation; **ein ~ aufnehmen** to take shorthand; **Ste|no|gramm|block** M *pl* **-blöcke** or **-blocks** short|hand pad; **Ste|no|stift** M shorthand pencil; **Ste|no|ty|pist** [ʃtenotyˈpɪst] M **-en, -en**, **Ste|no|ty|pis|tin** [-ˈpɪstɪn] F **-, -nen** shorthand typ|ist

Sten|tor|stim|me [ˈʃtɛntoːɐ̯-, -ˈstɪ-] F (*geh*) sten|torian voice

Stenz [ʃtɛnts] M **-es, -e** (*dated*) dandy

Step △ [ʃtɛp, st-] M **-s, -s** → **Stepp**

Step|eisen △ NT → **Steppeisen**

Ste|phan [ˈʃtefan] M **-s**, **Ste|phen** [ˈʃtefn] M **-s** Stephen, Steven

Stepp ▲ [ʃtɛp, st-] M **-s, -s** tap dance; ~ **tanzen** to tap-dance

Stepp|ano|rak M quilted anorak (*Brit*) or jacket

Stepp|de|cke F quilt

Step|pe [ˈʃtɛpə] F **-, -n** steppe

Stepp|ei|sen ▲ NT tap (*on tap-dancing shoes*)

step|pen[1] [ˈʃtɛpn] VTI to (machine-)stitch; *wat|tierten Stoff* to quilt

step|pen[2] [ˈʃtɛpn, 'st-] VI to tap-dance

Stepp|en-: Stepp|en|brand M steppe fire; **Stepp|en|kä|se** M (= *hochfat* (*hard*) *cheese*); **Stepp|en|wolf** M (*Zool*) prairie wolf, coyote

Stepp-: Stepp|fuß M foot; **Stepp|ja|cke** F quilted jacket

Stepp|ke [ˈʃtɛpkə] M **-(s), -s** (*N Ger inf*) nipper (*Brit inf*), whippersnapper (*US*), (little) laddie (*Brit inf*)

Stepp-: Stepp|naht F (*Sew*) backstitch seam; (*mit Maschine*) lockstitch seam; **Stepp|stich** M (*Sew*) backstitch; (*mit Maschine*) lockstitch; **Stepp|tanz** ▲ [ˈʃtɛp-, 'st-] M tap dance; **Stepp|tän|zer(in)** ▲ M(F) tap-dancer

Ster [ʃteːɐ] NT **-s, -s** or **-e** stere

Ster|be-: Ster|be|al|ter NT age of death; **was war sein ~?** what was his age at the time of his death?; **Ster|be|be|glei|tung** F terminal care; **Ster|be|bett** NT deathbed; **auf dem ~ liegen** to be on one's deathbed; **Ster|be|buch** NT register of deaths; **Ster|be|da|tum** NT date of death; **Ster|be|fall** M death; **Ster|be|geld** NT death benefit; **Ster|be|glo|cke** F funeral bell; **das Läuten der ~** the death knell; **Ster|be|hemd** NT (*burial*) shroud; **Ster|be|hil|fe** F **a** death benefit **b** (= *Euthanasie*) eu|thanasia; **jdm ~ geben** or **gewähren** to adminis|ter euthanasia to sb (*form*); **Ster|be|kas|se** F death benefit fund; **Ster|be|kli|nik** F hospice; **Ster|be|la|ger** NT (*geh*) deathbed

ster|ben [ˈʃtɛrbn] *pret* **starb** [ʃtarp], *ptp* **gestor|ben** [ɡəˈʃtɔrbn] VTI *aux sein* to die; **jung/als Christ ~** to die young/a Christian; **einen schnel|len Tod ~** to die quickly; **einen leichten Tod ~**

to have an easy death; **eines natürlichen/gewaltsamen Todes ~** to die a natural/violent death; **an einer Krankheit/Verletzung ~** to die of an illness/from an injury; **daran wirst du nicht ~!** (hum) it won't kill you!; **vor Angst/Durst/Hunger ~** to die of fright/thirst/hunger (auch fig); **er stirbt vor Angst** (fig) he's frightened to death, he's scared stiff (inf); **vor Langeweile/Neugierde ~** to die of boredom/curiosity; **tausend Tode ~** to die a thousand deaths; **so leicht stirbt man nicht!** (hum) you'll/he'll etc survive!; **gestorben sein** to be dead, to be deceased (Jur, form); (fig: Projekt) to be over and done with; **gestorben!** (Film sl) print it!, I'll buy it! (Brit), it's a wrap! (inf); **er ist für mich gestorben** (fig inf) he might as well be dead or he doesn't exist as far as I'm concerned; **und wenn sie nicht gestorben sind, so leben sie noch heute** and they lived happily ever after

Ster|ben NT -s, no pl death; **Angst vor dem ~** fear of death or dying; **wenn es ans ~ geht** when it comes to dying; **im ~ liegen** to be dying; **zum ~ langweilig** (inf) deadly boring or dull, deadly (Brit inf); **zum Leben zu wenig, zum ~ zu viel** barely enough to keep body and soul together

Ster|bens-: Ster|bens|angst F (inf) mortal fear; **ster|bens|elend** (inf) wretched, ghastly; **ich fühle mich ~** I feel wretched or ghastly, I feel like death (inf); **ster|bens|krank** ADJ mortally ill; **ster|bens|lang|wei|lig** (inf) deadly boring or dull, deadly (Brit inf); **Ster|bens|wort** NT, **Ster|bens|wört|chen** NT (inf) **er hat kein ~ gesagt** or **verraten** he didn't say a (single) word; **ich wer|de kein ~ davon sagen** I won't breathe a word

Ster|be-: Ster|be|ort M pl **-orte** place of death; **Ster|be|ra|te** F death rate; **Ster|be|sak|ra|men|te** PL last rites pl or sacraments pl; **Ster|be|stun|de** F last hour, dying hour; **Ster|be|ur|kun|de** F death certificate; **Ster|be|zif|fer** F mortality or death rate; **Ster|be|zim|mer** NT death chamber (liter, form); **Goethes ~** the room where Goethe died

sterb|lich [ˈʃtɛrplɪç] ADJ mortal; **jds ~e Hülle** or **(Über)reste** sb's mortal remains pl ADV (inf) terribly (inf), dreadfully (inf)

Sterb|li|che(r) [ˈʃtɛrplɪçə] MF decl as adj mortal

Sterb|lich|keit F -, no pl mortality; (Zahl) mortality (rate), death rate

ste|reo [ˈʃteːreo, ˈst-] ADV (in) stereo

Ste|reo [ˈʃteːreo, ˈst-] NT -s, -s in ~ in stereo

Ste|reo- in cpds stereo; (= stereoskopisch) stereoscopic; **Ste|re|o|an|la|ge** F stereo unit or system, stereo (inf); **Ste|re|o|auf|nah|me** F stereo recording; **Ste|re|o|box** F speaker; **ste|re|o|fon** ▲ [ʃtereoˈfoːn, st-] ADJ = stereophon; **Ste|re|o|fo|nie** ▲ [ʃtereoˈniː, st-] F -, no pl = Stereophonie; **ste|re|o|fo|nisch** ▲ [ʃtereoˈfoː-nɪʃ, st-] ADJ, ADV = stereophonisch; **Ste|re|o|ge|rät** NT stereo unit; **Ste|re|o|ka|me|ra** F stereoscopic camera; **Ste|re|o|met|rie** [ʃtereome'triː, st-] F -, no pl stereometry, solid geometry; **ste|re|o|phon** [ʃtereoˈfoːn, st-] ADJ stereophonic ADV stereophonically; **Ste|re|o|pho|nie** [ʃtereoˈniː, st-] F -, no pl stereophony; **ste|re|o|pho|nisch** [ʃtereoˈfoːnɪʃ, st-] ADJ stereophonic ADV stereophonically; **Ste|re|o|skop** [ʃtereoˈskoːp, st-] NT -s, -e stereoscope; **Ste|re|o|sko|pie** [ʃtereoskoˈpiː, st-] F -, no pl stereoscopy; **ste|re|o|sko|pisch** [ʃtereoˈskoːpɪʃ, st-] ADJ stereoscopic; (= dreidimensional) 3-D, three-dimensional; **Ste|re|o|turm** M hi-fi stack; **ste|re|o|typ** [ʃtereoˈtyːp, st-] ADJ (fig) stereotyped, stereotypical; Lächeln (= gezwungen) stiff; (= unpersönlich) impersonal ADV in stereotyped fashion; **~ darstellen** to represent as stereotypes; **Ste|re|o|typ** NT (Psych) stereotype; **Ste|re|o|typ|druck** M pl **-drucke** stereotype; **Ste|re|o|ty|pie** [ʃtereotypiː, st-] F -, -n [-ˈpiːən] (Psych) stereotypy (Typ auch) stereotype printing; (Werkstatt) stereotype printing shop

ste|ril [ʃteˈriːl, st-] ADJ (lit, fig) sterile

Ste|ri|li|sa|ti|on [ʃteriliza'tsio:n, st-] F -, -en sterilization

ste|ri|li|sie|ren [ʃteriliˈziːrən, st-] ptp **sterilisiert** VT to sterilize

Ste|ri|li|tät [ʃteriliˈtɛːt, st-] F -, no pl (lit, fig) sterility

Ster|ling [ˈʃtɛrlɪŋ, ˈst-] M -s, -e sterling; **30 Pfund ~** 30 pounds sterling

Stern¹ [ʃtɛrn] M -(e)s, -e **a** star; **dieser ~** (poet: = die Erde) this earth or orb (poet); **mit ~en übersät** star-spangled attr; Himmel auch starry attr, **unter fremden ~en sterben** (poet) to die in foreign climes (liter); **in den ~en lesen** (Astrol) to read the stars; **in den ~en (geschrieben) stehen** (fig) to be (written) in the stars; **das steht (noch) in den ~en** (fig) it's in the lap of the gods; **nach den ~en greifen** (fig) to reach for the stars; **er wollte die ~e vom Himmel holen** he wanted the moon (and the stars), he wanted the stars in the sky; **für sie holt er die ~e vom Himmel** he would do anything for her, he would go to the ends of the earth and back again for her; **der ~ der Weisen** (Bibl) the Star of Bethlehem; **sein ~ geht auf** or **ist im Aufgehen/sinkt** or **ist im Sinken** his star is in the ascendant/on the decline; **mein guter ~** my lucky star; **unter einem guten** or **glücklichen** or **günstigen ~ geboren sein** to be born under a lucky star; **unter einem guten** or **glücklichen** or **günstigen ~ stehen** to be blessed with good fortune; **unter einem unglücklichen ~ stehen** to be ill-starred or ill-fated; **mit ihr ging am Theaterhimmel ein neuer ~ auf** with her coming a new star was born in the theatrical world; **~e sehen** (inf) to see stars (inf)

b (= Abzeichen, auch an Uniform) star; **ein Hotel/Cognac mit drei ~en** a three-star hotel/brandy; **ein Vier-Sterne-General** a four-star general

Stern² M -s, -e (Naut) stern

Stern-: Stern|anis M star aniseed; **stern|be|deckt** ADJ starry, star-spangled; **Stern|bild** NT (Astron) constellation; (Astrol) sign (of the zodiac)

Stern|chen [ˈʃtɛrnçən] NT -s, - dim von **Stern¹** **a** little star **b** (Typ) asterisk, star (Brit) **c** (Film) starlet

Stern-: Stern|deu|ter(in) M(F) astrologer, stargazer (hum); **Stern|deu|te|rei** F -, no pl astrology, stargazing (hum); **Stern|deu|tung** F astrology, stargazing (hum)

Ster|ne-: Ster|ne|koch M, **Ster|ne|kö|chin** F (Cook) (Michelin-)starred chef; **Ster|ne|lo|kal** NT, **Ster|ne|res|tau|rant** NT (Cook) (Michelin-)starred restaurant

Ster|nen-: Ster|nen|ban|ner NT Star-Spangled Banner, Stars and Stripes sing; **ster|nen|be|deckt** ADJ starry, star-covered; **ster|nen|ge|wölb|te** NT (poet) starry vault (poet); **Ster|nen|glanz** M (poet) starshine (liter); **der Himmel erstrahlte im ~** the heavens shone with the light of the stars (liter); **Ster|nen|him|mel** M starry sky; **Veränderungen am ~** changes in the star formation; **ster|nen|klar** ADJ Himmel, Nacht starry attr, starlit; **Ster|nen|krieg** M (Pol) Star Wars pl; **ster|nen|los** ADJ starless; **Ster|nen|zelt** NT (poet) starry firmament (liter)

Stern-: Stern|fahrt F (Mot, Pol) rally (where participants commence at different points); **eine ~ nach Ulan Bator** a rally converging on Ulan Bator; **stern|för|mig** ADJ star-shaped, stellate (spec) ADV **~ angelegte Straßen, die vom Platz wegführen** streets radiating out from the square; **~ angelegte Gebäudekomplexe** buildings laid out like the spokes of a wheel; **~ vernetzt** (Comput) in a star-type network; **Stern|for|scher(in)** M(F) astronomer; **Stern|frucht** F star fruit; **Stern|ge|wöl|be** NT (Archit) stellar vault; **Stern|gu|cker** [-ɡʊkɐ] M -s, -, **Stern|gu|cke|rin** [-ərɪn] F -, -nen (hum) stargazer (hum); **stern|ha|gel|voll** [ˈʃtɛrn-haːɡl̩fɔl] ADJ (inf) roaring drunk (inf), blotto pred (Brit sl); **Stern|hau|fen** M (Astron) star

cluster; **stern|hell** ADJ starlit, starry attr; **Stern|jahr** NT sidereal year; **Stern|kar|te** F (Astron) celestial chart, star or stellar map or chart; **stern|klar** ADJ Himmel, Nacht starry attr, starlit; **Stern|kons|tel|la|ti|on** F (stellar) constellation; **Stern|kun|de** F astronomy; **Stern|marsch** M (Pol) protest march with marchers converging on assembly point from different directions; **Stern|mo|tor** M radial engine; **Stern|schnup|pe** [-ʃnʊpə] F -, -n shooting star; **Stern|sin|ger** PL carol singers pl; **Stern|stun|de** F great moment; **das war meine ~** that was a great moment in my life; **Stern|sys|tem** NT galaxy; **Stern|tag** M (Astron) sidereal day; **Stern|war|te** F observatory; **Stern|zei|chen** (Astrol) sign of the zodiac; **im ~ der Jungfrau** under the sign of Virgo; **Stern|zeit** F (Astron) sidereal time

Ste|ro|id [ʃteroˈiːt] NT -(e)s, -e [-də] steroid

Stert [ʃteːrt] M -(e)s, -e (N Ger), **Sterz** [ʃtɛrts] M -es, -e **a** (= Schwanzende) tail; (Cook) parson's nose (inf) **b** (= Pflugsterz) handle

stet [ʃteːt] ADJ attr constant; Fleiß auch steady; Arbeit, Wind auch steady, continuous; **~er Tropfen höhlt den Stein** (Prov) constant dripping wears away the stone

Ste|tho|skop [ʃteto'sko:p, st-] NT -s, -e stethoscope

ste|tig [ˈʃteːtɪç] ADJ steady; (Math) Funktion continuous; **~es Meckern** constant moaning ADV wachsen, sinken etc steadily; **~ steigende Bedeutung** ever-increasing or steadily increasing importance

Ste|tig|keit F -, no pl steadiness; (Math, von Funktion) continuity; **er arbeitet mit bewundernswerter ~** you have to admire how consistently he works

stets [ʃteːts] ADV always; **~ zu Ihren Diensten** (form) always or ever (form) at your service; **~ der Ihre** (old form) yours ever

Steu|er¹ [ˈʃtɔyɐ] NT -s, - (Naut) helm, tiller; (Aut) (steering) wheel; (Aviat) control column, controls pl; **am ~ stehen** (Naut) or **sein** (fig) to be at the helm; **am ~ sitzen** or **sein, hinter dem ~ sitzen** (inf) (Aut) to be at or behind the wheel, to drive; (Aviat) to be at the controls; **jdn ans ~ lassen** (Aut) to let sb drive, to let sb take the wheel; **das ~ übernehmen** (lit, fig) to take over; (lit auch) to take (over) (the helm/wheel/controls; (fig auch) to take the helm; **das ~ fest in der Hand haben** (fig) to be firmly in control, to have things firmly under control; **das ~ herumwerfen** or **herumreißen** (fig) to turn the tide of events

Steu|er² F -, -n **a** (= Abgabe) tax; (an Gemeinde) council tax (Brit), local tax (US); (von Firmen) rates pl (Brit), corporate property tax (US); **~n** tax; (= Arten von Steuern) taxes; **~n zahlen** to pay tax; **ich bezahle 35% ~n** I pay 35% tax; **in Schweden zahlt man hohe ~n** in Sweden tax is very high, in Sweden people are highly taxed; **die ~n herabsetzen** to reduce taxation, to cut tax or taxes; **der ~ unterliegen** (form) to be liable or subject to tax, to be taxable; **Gewinn vor/nach ~n** pre-/after-tax profit, profit before/after tax

b (inf: = Steuerbehörde) **die ~** the tax people pl (inf) or authorities pl, the Inland Revenue (Brit), the Internal Revenue Service (US)

Steu|er-: Steu|er|auf|kom|men NT tax revenue, tax yield; **Steu|er|aus|fall** M (Fin) tax or revenue loss; **Steu|er|aus|gleich** M (Fin) tax equalization

steu|er|bar ADJ **a** (= versteuerbar) taxable, liable or subject to tax **b** (= lenkbar, bedienbar) controllable; Schiff, Auto steerable; Flugzeug flyable; **leicht/schwer ~** easy/difficult to control/steer/fly

Steu|er-: Steu|er|be|am|te(r) M decl as adj, **Steu|er|be|am|tin** F tax officer or official; **steu|er|be|güns|tigt** [-bəɡʏnstɪçt] ADJ Investitionen, Hypothek, Spende tax-deductible; Waren taxed at a lower rate; **~es Sparen** form of sav-

ing entitling the saver to tax relief **Investitionen sind** ~ you get tax relief on investments; **Steu|er|be|güns|ti|gung** F tax concession (+*gen* on); **Steu|er|be|hör|de** F tax authorities *pl*, Inland Revenue (*Brit*), Internal Revenue Service (*US*); **Steu|er|be|mes|sungs|grund|la|ge** F (*Fin*) basis of tax assessment, tax base; **Steu|er|be|ra|ter(in)** M(F) tax consultant; **Steu|er|be|scheid** M tax assessment; **Steu|er|be|trug** M tax evasion *or* dodging; **Steu|er|be|voll|mäch|tig|te(r)** MF *decl as adj* tax expert *or* consultant; **Steu|er|bord** [ˈʃtɔyɐbɔrt] NT **-s**, *no pl* (*Naut*) starboard; **steu|er|bord(s)** [ˈʃtɔyɐbɔrt(s)] ADV (*Naut*) to starboard; **steu|er|ehr|lich** ADJ ~ **sein** to be honest in tax matters; **Steu|er|ehr|lich|keit** F honesty in tax matters; **Steu|er|ein|nah|men** PL revenue from taxation; **Steu|er|ein|neh|mer(in)** M(F) (*Hist*) tax collector; **Steu|er|er|hö|hung** F tax increase; **Steu|er|er|klä|rung** F tax return, tax declaration (*Brit*); **Steu|er|er|lass** ▲ M tax exemption; **Steu|er|er|leich|te|rung** F *usu pl* tax relief *no pl*; **Steu|er|er|mä|ßi|gung** F tax allowance *or* relief; **Steu|er|er|stat|tung** F tax rebate; **Steu|er|fahn|dung** F investigation of (suspected) tax evasion; (*Behörde*) commission for investigation of suspected tax evasion; **Steu|er|flucht** F tax evasion (*by leaving the country*); **Steu|er|flücht|ling** M tax exile; **Steu|er|frau** F (*Rudern*) cox(swain); **steu|er|frei** ADJ tax-free, exempt from tax [ADV] tax-free; **Abfindungen können ~ vereinnahmt werden** settlements are tax-free; **er hat den Nebenverdienst ~ kassiert** he didn't pay taxes on his additional earnings; **Steu|er|frei|be|trag** M tax-free allowance; **Steu|er|frei|heit** F tax exemption, exemption from tax; ~ **genießen** to be exempt from tax; **Steu|er|gel|der** PL tax money, taxes *pl*; **warum soll das aus ~n finanziert werden?** why should it be paid for with taxpayers' money?, why should the taxpayer have to pay for it?; **Veruntreuung von ~n** tax embezzlement; **Steu|er|ge|rät** NT tuner-amplifier; (*Comput*) control unit; **Steu|er|har|mo|ni|sie|rung** F harmonization of taxes; **Steu|er|hin|ter|zie|hung** F tax evasion; **Steu|er|ho|heit** F right to levy tax(es); **Steu|er|in|spek|tor(in)** M(F) tax inspector; **Steu|er|jahr** NT tax year; **Steu|er|kar|te** F *notice of pay received and tax deducted*; **Steu|er|ket|te** F (*an Motorrad*) timing chain; **Steu|er|ket|ten|span|ner** M timing chain tightener; **Steu|er|klas|se** F tax bracket *or* group; **Steu|er|knüp|pel** M control column; (*Aviat auch*) joystick; **Steu|er|last** F tax burden

steu|er|lich [ˈʃtɔyɐlɪç] ADJ tax *attr*; ~**e Belastung** tax burden; **aus ~en Überlegungen** for tax reasons [ADV] **es ist ~ günstiger …** for tax purposes it is better …; **das wirkt sich ~ ganz günstig aus** from the tax point of view *or* taxwise it works out very well; **das ist ~ vorteilhaft** that's a good way to save on taxes; ~ **abzugsfähig** tax-deductible; ~ **stark belastet werden** (*Mensch*) to pay high taxes; ~ **entlastet werden** (*Mensch*) to get a tax reduction *or* break; **etw wird ~ berücksichtigt** sth is tax-deductible

steu|er|los ADJ rudderless, out of control; (*fig*) leaderless

Steu|er|mann M *pl* **-männer** *or* **-leute** helmsman; (*als Rang*) (first) mate; (*Rudern*) cox (-swain); **Zweier mit/ohne ~** coxed/coxless pairs

Steu|er|manns|pa|tent NT (*Naut*) mate's ticket (*inf*) *or* certificate

Steu|er-: Steu|er|mar|ke F revenue *or* tax stamp; (*für Hunde*) dog licence disc (*Brit*), dog tag (*US*); **steu|er|min|dernd** ADJ tax-reducing; **etw (als) ~ geltend machen** to offset sth against tax; **Steu|er|mit|tel** PL tax revenue(s) *pl*; **etw aus ~n finanzieren** to finance sth out of public funds; **Steu|er|mo|ral** F honesty in tax matters

steu|ern [ˈʃtɔyɐn] [VT] [a] *Schiff* to steer, to navigate; *Flugzeug* to pilot, to fly; *Auto* to steer; (*fig*) *Wirtschaft, Politik* to run, to control, to manage; (*Comput*) to control; **staatlich gesteuert** state-controlled, under state control; **einen Kurs ~** (*lit, fig*) to steer a course; (*fig auch*) to take *or* follow a line; **eine Diskussion/die Wirtschaft in eine bestimmte Richtung ~** to steer a discussion/the economy in a certain direction
[b] (= *regulieren*) to control
[VI] [a] *aux sein* to head; (*Aut*) to drive, to head; (*Naut*) to make *or* head for, to steer; **wohin steuert die Wirtschaft?** where is the economy heading *or* headed (for)?
[b] = *am Steuer sein* (*Naut*) to be at the helm; (*Aut*) to be at the wheel; (*Aviat*) to be at the controls

Steu|er-: Steu|er|nach|zah|lung F additional tax payment; **Steu|er|num|mer** F tax(payer's) reference number; **Steu|er|oa|se** F , **Steu|er|pa|ra|dies** NT tax haven; **Steu|er|pflicht** F liability to tax; (*von Person auch*) liability to pay tax; **der ~ unterliegen** to be liable to tax, to be taxable; **Steu|er|pflich|tig** [-pflɪçtɪç] ADJ *Einkommen* taxable, liable to tax; *Person auch* liable to (pay) tax; **Steu|er|pflich|ti|ge(r)** [-pflɪçtɪɡə] MF *decl as adj* taxpayer; **Steu|er|po|li|tik** F tax *or* taxation policy; **steu|er|po|li|tisch** ADJ relating to tax policy; ~**e Maßnahmen der Regierung** government tax measures; **aus ~en Gründen** for tax *or* taxation reasons [ADV] **es wäre ~ unklug …** it would be unwise tax policy …; **sich ~ profilieren wollen** to try and make a good impression with tax policy; ~ **notwendige Maßnahmen** tax policies; **Steu|er|pro|gres|si|on** F progressive taxation; **Steu|er|prü|fer(in)** M(F) tax inspector, tax auditor (*esp US*); **Steu|er|prü|fung** F tax inspector's investigation (*Brit*), tax audit (*esp US*); **Steu|er|rad** NT (*Aviat*) control wheel; (*Aut*) (steering) wheel; **Steu|er|recht** NT tax law; **steu|er|recht|lich** ADJ relating to tax law; **ein ~er Fachmann** a tax expert [ADV] **das ist ~ unmöglich** the tax laws make that impossible; **er ist ~ versiert** he is familiar with tax law; ~ **bedenkliche Maßnahmen** (*von Person*) dubious accounting practices; (*von Staat*) dubious tax policies; ~ **zulässig** allowed by tax law; **Steu|er|re|form** F tax reform; **Steu|er|rück|zah|lung** F tax rebate; **Steu|er|ru|der** NT rudder; **Steu|er|sa|che** F tax matter; **Helfer in ~n** tax consultant; **Steu|er|satz** M rate of taxation; **Steu|er|schät|zung** F tax estimate; **steu|er|scho|nend** ADJ tax-saving; **Steu|er|schrau|be** F **die ~ anziehen** to put the screws on the taxpayer, to squeeze the taxpayer; **Steu|er|schuld** F tax(es *pl*) owing *no indef art*, tax liability; **Steu|er|sen|kung** F tax cut; **Steu|er|spar|mo|dell** NT tax relief scheme; **Steu|er|sün|der(in)** M(F) tax evader; **Steu|er|sys|tem** NT tax system; **Steu|er|tas|te** F (*Comput*) control key; **steu|er|un|ehr|lich** ADJ ~ **sein** to be dishonest in tax matters

Steu|e|rung [ˈʃtɔyərʊŋ] F **-**, **-en** [a] *no pl* (= *das Steuern*) (*von Schiff*) steering, navigation; (*von Flugzeug*) piloting, flying; (*fig*) (*von Politik, Wirtschaft*) running, control, management; (*Comput*) control; (= *Regulierung*) control, regulation; (= *Bekämpfung*) control [b] (= *Steuervorrichtung*) (*Aviat*) controls *pl*; (*Tech*) steering apparatus *or* mechanism; (*elektronisch*) control; **automatische ~** (*Aviat*) automatic pilot, autopilot; (*Tech*) automatic steering (device)

Steu|e|rungs-: Steu|e|rungs|fä|hig|keit F (*Psych*) ability to control oneself; **Steu|e|rungs|tas|te** F (*Comput*) control key; **Steu|e|rungs|zei|chen** NT (*Comput*) control character

Steu|er-: Steu|er|ver|an|la|gung F tax assessment; **Steu|er|ver|ge|hen** NT tax evasion *or* dodging *no pl*; **Steu|er|ver|güns|ti|gung** F tax break *or* concession; ~**en** *pl* (*auch*) tax relief; **Steu|er|vor|teil** M tax advantage *or* benefit;

Steu|er|werk NT (*Comput*) control unit; **Steu|er|zah|ler(in)** M(F) taxpayer

Ste|ven [ˈʃteːvn] M **-s**, **-** (*Naut*) (= *Vordersteven*) prow; (= *Achtersteven*) stern

Ste|ward [ˈstjuːɐt, ˈʃt-] M **-s**, **-s** (*Naut, Aviat*) steward

Ste|war|dess [ˈstjuːɐdɛs, stjuːˈɐˈdɛs, ˈʃt-] F **-**, **-en** stewardess

StGB [ɛsteːɡeːˈbeː] NT **-s** *abbr von* **Strafgesetzbuch**

sti|bit|zen [ʃtiˈbɪtsn] *ptp* **stibitzt** VT (*dated hum*) to swipe (*inf*), to pinch (*inf*)

stich [ʃtɪç] *imper sing von* **stechen**

Stich [ʃtɪç] M **-(e)s**, **-e** [a] (= *das Stechen*) (= *Insektenstich*) sting; (= *Mückenstich*) bite; (= *Nadelstich*) prick; (= *Messerstich*) stab
[b] (= *Stichwunde*) (*von Messer etc*) stab wound; (*von Insekten*) sting; (*von Mücken*) bite; (= *Einstichloch*) prick
[c] (= *stechender Schmerz*) piercing *or* shooting *or* stabbing pain; (= *Seitenstich*) stitch; (*fig*) pang; ~**e haben** to have a stitch; **es gab mir einen ~ (ins Herz)** I was cut to the quick (*esp Brit*) *or* to the heart (*US*)
[d] (*Sew*) stitch
[e] (= *Kupferstich, Stahlstich*) engraving
[f] (= *Schattierung*) tinge, shade (*in* +*acc* of); (= *Tendenz*) hint, suggestion (*in* +*acc* of); **ein ~ ins Rote** a tinge of red, a reddish tinge; **ein ~ ins Gewöhnliche/Vulgäre** a hint *or* suggestion of commonness/vulgarity
[g] (*Cards*) trick; **einen ~ machen** *or* **bekommen** to get a trick
[h] **jdn im ~ lassen** to let sb down; (= *verlassen*) to abandon *or* desert sb, to leave sb in the lurch; **etw im ~ lassen** to abandon sth
[i] ~ **halten** to hold water, to be valid *or* sound
[j] **einen ~ haben** (*Esswaren*) to be off (*Brit*) *or* bad, to have gone off (*Brit*) *or* bad; (*Butter auch*) to be *or* have gone rancid; (*Milch*) to be *or* have gone off (*Brit*) *or* sour; (*inf: Mensch* = *verrückt sein*) to be nuts (*inf*), to be round the bend (*Brit inf*)

Stich-: Stich|bahn F (*Rail*) branch terminal line; **Stich|blatt** NT [a] (*von Degen*) guard [b] (*Cards*) trump (card)

Sti|chel [ˈʃtɪçl] M **-s**, **-** (*Art*) gouge

Sti|che|lei [ʃtɪçəˈlai] F **-**, **-en** [a] (= *Näherei*) sewing [b] (*pej inf*: = *boshafte Bemerkung*) snide *or* sneering remark, gibe, dig; **deine ständigen ~en kannst du dir sparen** stop getting at me (*Brit*), stop making digs (*Brit*) *or* pokes (*US*) at me

sti|cheln [ˈʃtɪçln] VI [a] (= *nähen*) to sew; (= *sticken*) to embroider [b] (*pej inf*: = *boshafte Bemerkungen machen*) to make snide *or* sneering remarks; **gegen jdn ~** to make digs (*Brit*) *or* pokes (*US*) at sb

Stich-: Stich|ent|scheid M (*Pol*) result of a/the runoff (*US*), final ballot; (*Sport*) result of a/the play-off; **stich|fest** ADJ → **hiebfest**; **Stich|flam|me** F tongue of flame; **stich+hal|ten** [ˈʃtɪçhaltn] VI *sep irreg* (*Aus*) → **Stich i**; **stich|hal|tig**, (*Aus*) **stich|häl|tig** ✿ 53.3 [ADJ] *Argument, Grund* sound, valid; *Erklärung* valid; *Beweis* conclusive; **sein Alibi ist nicht ~** his alibi doesn't hold water [ADV] conclusively; **Stich|hal|tig|keit** [ˈʃtɪçhaltɪçkait] F **-**, *no pl* (*von Argument, Grund*) soundness, validity; (*von Erklärung*) validity; (*von Beweis*) conclusiveness; **Stich|kampf** M (*Sport*) play-off

Stich|ling [ˈʃtɪçlɪŋ] M **-s**, **-e** (*Zool*) stickleback

Stich|pro|be F spot check; (*Sociol*) (random) sample survey; ~**n machen** to carry out *or* make spot checks; (*Sociol*) to carry out a (random) sample survey; **bei der ~ wurde festgestellt, dass …** the spot check/sampling revealed that …

Stich|pro|ben-: Stich|pro|ben|er|he|bung F (*Sociol*) (random) sample survey; **stich|pro|ben|wei|se** ADV on a random basis; **es wer-**

---

den nur ~ Kontrollen gemacht only spot checks are made

Stich-: Stich|punkt M (= *Schlüsselbegriff*) key word or point; **~e** *pl* (*als Gedächtnisstütze für Vortrag etc.*) notes *pl*; **sich** (*dat*) **ein paar ~e machen** to jot down a few notes; **Stich|sä|ge** F fret saw; **Stich|stra|ße** F cul-de-sac

sticht [ʃtɪçt] *3. pers sing pres von* **stechen**

Stich-: Stich|tag M qualifying date; **Stich|-ver|let|zung** F stab wound, knife wound; **Stich|waf|fe** F stabbing weapon; **Stich|wahl** F (*Pol*) final ballot, runoff (*US*)

Stich|wort NT **a** *pl* **-wörter** (*in Nachschlagewerken*) headword **b** *pl* **-worte** (*Theat, fig*) cue **c** *pl* **-worte** *usu pl* notes *pl*; (*bei Nacherzählung etc*) key words *pl*

Stich|wort-: stich|wort|ar|tig ADJ abbreviated, shorthand; **eine ~e Gliederung** an outline ADV **etw ~ zusammenfassen** to summarize the main points of sth; **etw ~ wiedergeben** to recount sth in a shorthand *or* an abbreviated fashion; **jdn ~ über etw** (*acc*) **informieren** to give sb a brief outline of sth; **Stich|wort|ge|ber(in)** M(F) (*Theat*) stooge; (*fig*) person raising issues/the issue; **Stich|wort|ka|ta|log** M classified catalogue (*Brit*) *or* catalog (*US*); **Stich|wort|ver|zeich|nis** NT index

Stich|wun|de F stab wound

Stick|ar|beit F embroidery; **sie saß gerade an einer ~** she was sitting embroidering

sti|cken [ˈʃtɪkn] VTI to embroider

Sti|cker [ˈʃtɪkɐ, ˈst-] M **-s, -** (*inf: = Aufkleber*) sticker

Sti|cke|rei [ʃtɪkəˈraɪ] F **-, -en** **a** *no pl* (= *das Sticken*) embroidery, embroidering **b** (*Gegenstand*) embroidery

Sti|cke|rin [ˈʃtɪkərɪn] F **-, -nen** embroideress, embroiderer

Stick|garn NT embroidery thread *or* silk

sti|ckig [ˈʃtɪkɪç] ADJ *Luft, Zimmer* stuffy, close; *Klima* sticky, humid; (*fig*) *Atmosphäre* stifling, oppressive

Stick-: Stick|ma|schi|ne F embroidery machine; **Stick|mus|ter** NT embroidery pattern; **Stick|na|del** F embroidery needle; **Stick|oxid** [ˈʃtɪkɔksiːt] NT , **Stick|oxyd** [ˈʃtɪkʔɔksyːt] NT nitric oxide; **Stick|rah|men** M embroidery frame

Stick|stoff [ˈʃtɪkʃtɔf] M (*abbr* **N**) nitrogen

Stick|stoff-: Stick|stoff|dün|ger M nitrogen fertilizer; **stick|stoff|hal|tig** ADJ containing nitrogen, nitrogenous (*spec*)

stie|ben [ˈʃtiːbn] *pret* **stob** *or* **stiebte** [ʃtoːp, ˈʃtiːptə], *ptp* **gestoben** *or* **gestiebt** [ɡəˈʃtoːbn, ɡəˈʃtiːpt] VI **a** *aux haben or sein* (= *sprühen*) (*Funken, Staub etc*) to fly; (*Schnee*) to spray, to fly; (*Wasser*) to spray **b** *aux sein* (= *jagen, rennen*) to flee; (= *auseinander stieben*) to scatter

Stief|bru|der [ˈʃtiːf-] M stepbrother

Stie|fel [ˈʃtiːfl] M **-s, -** **a** (*boot*): **der italienische ~** the Italian boot, the boot of Italy; **das sind zwei Paar ~** (*fig*) they are two completely different things; **jdm die ~ lecken** (*fig*) to lick sb's boots **b** (*inf*) **seinen (alten) ~ arbeiten** *or* **weitermachen** to carry on as usual, to carry on in the same old way; **einen ~ zusammenreden** to talk a lot of nonsense *or* a load of rubbish (*Brit inf*) **c** (= *Trinkgefäß*) large, boot-shaped beer glass holding 2 litres **einen (ordentlichen) ~ vertragen** (*inf*) to be able to hold one's drink (*Brit*) *or* hold one's liquor

Stie|fel-: Stie|fel|ab|satz M (boot) heel; **Stie|fel|an|zie|her** [-lantsiːɐ] M **-s, -** boot hook

Stie|fe|let|te [ʃtiːfəˈlɛtə] F **-, -n** (= *Frauenstiefelette*) bootee (*= Männerstiefelette*) half-boot

Stie|fel|knecht M bootjack

stie|feln [ˈʃtiːfln] VI *aux sein* (*inf*) to hoof it (*inf*) → **gestiefelt**

Stie|fel|schaft M bootleg, leg of a/the boot

Stief|el|tern [ˈʃtiːf-] PL step-parents *pl*

Stie|fel|wich|se F (*dated*) boot polish, boot-blacking

Stief- [ˈʃtiːf-]: **Stief|ge|schwis|ter** PL stepbrother(s *pl*) and sister(s *pl*); **Stief|kind** NT stepchild; (*fig*) poor cousin; **sie fühlt sich immer als ~ des Glücks** she always feels that fortune never smiles upon her; **Stief|mut|ter** F *pl* **-mütter** stepmother; **Stief|müt|ter|chen** NT (*Bot*) pansy; **stief|müt|ter|lich** ADV (*fig*) *jdn/etw ~ behandeln* to pay little attention to sb/sth, to put sb/sth in second place; **die Natur hat ihn ~ behandelt** Nature has not been kind to him; **Stief|schwes|ter** F stepsister; **Stief|sohn** M stepson; **Stief|toch|ter** F stepdaughter; **Stief|va|ter** M stepfather

stieg *pret von* **steigen**

Stieg [ʃtiːk] M **-(e)s, -e** [-ɡə] steep track

Stie|ge [ˈʃtiːɡə] F **-, -n** **a** (= *schmale Treppe*) (narrow) flight of stairs, (narrow) staircase **b** (*old:* = *20 Stück*) score; **eine ~ Eier** a score of eggs **c** (= *Lattenkiste*) crate

Stie|gen|haus NT (*S Ger, Aus*) staircase

Stieg|litz [ˈʃtiːɡlɪts] M **-es, -e** goldfinch

stiehlt [ʃtiːlt] *3. pers sing pres von* **stehlen**

stie|kum [ˈʃtiːkʊm] ADV (*N Ger.* = *heimlich*) on the sly (*inf*) *or* fly (*inf*)

Stiel [ʃtiːl] M **-(e)s, -e** **a** (= *Griff*) handle; (= *Pfeifenstiel, Blütenstiel*) stem **b** (= *Stängel*) stalk; (= *Blütenstiel*) stalk, stem, peduncle (*spec*); (= *Blattstiel*) leafstalk, petiole (*spec*)

Stiel|au|gen PL (*fig inf*) **~ machen** *or* **kriegen** to gawk (*inf*), to gawp (*Brit inf*), to goggle (*inf*); **er machte ~** his eyes (nearly) popped out of his head

Stiel-: Stiel|glas NT stemmed glass; **Stiel|kamm** M tail comb; **stiel|los** ADJ *Gerät* handleless, without a handle; *Pflanze, Blatt* stalkless; *Glas* stemless; **Stiel|pfan|ne** F frying pan with a (long) handle; **Stiel|topf** M long-handled pan

stier [ʃtiːɐ] ADJ **a** (= *stumpfsinnig*) *Blick* vacant, blank **b** (*inf: Aus, Sw*) *Geschäft* slack, slow; *Mensch* broke (*inf*) ADV *starren* vacantly; **~ bli|cken** to have a blank stare

Stier [ʃtiːɐ] M **-(e)s, -e** **a** bull; (= *junger Stier*) bullock; **wütend wie ein ~ (sein)** (to be) beside oneself with rage *or* fury; **wie ein ~ brüllen** to bawl one's head off (*inf*), to bellow like a bull; **den ~ bei den Hörnern packen** *or* **fassen** (*prov*) to take the bull by the horns (*prov*) **b** (*Astrol*) Taurus *no art*; **ich bin (ein) ~** I'm (a) Taurus

stie|ren [ˈʃtiːrən] VI (*auf +acc* at) to stare; (*neugierig auch*) to gape; (**lüstern**) **auf jdn ~** to ogle sb (*inf*), to eye sb up (*Brit*); **sein Blick stierte ins Leere** he stared vacantly into space

Stier-: Stier|kampf M bullfight; **Stier|kampf|are|na** F bullring; **Stier|kämp|fer(in)** M(F) bullfighter; **Stier|na|cken** M neck like a bull, thick neck; **stier|na|ckig** ADJ bull-necked; **Stier|op|fer** NT sacrifice of a bull

Stie|sel [ˈʃtiːzl] M **-s, -** (*inf*) boor, lout (*inf*)

stie|se|lig [ˈʃtiːzəlɪç], **sties|lig** [ˈʃtiːzlɪç] (*inf*) ADJ boorish, loutish (*inf*) ADV **sich ~ benehmen** to behave like a boor *or* lout

Stie|se|lig|keit [ˈʃtiːzəlɪçkaɪt] F **-, no pl**, **Sties|lig|keit** [ˈʃtiːzlɪçkaɪt] F **-, no pl** (*inf*) boorishness, loutishness (*inf*)

stieß *pret von* **stoßen**

Stift¹ [ʃtɪft] M **-(e)s, -e** **a** (= *Metallstift*) pin; (= *Holzstift*) peg, pin; (= *Nagel*) tack **b** (= *Bleistift*) pencil; (= *Buntstift*) pencil, crayon; (= *Filzstift*) felt-tip, felt-tipped pen; (= *Kugelschreiber*) ballpoint (pen), Biro® (*Brit*); (*Comput*) pen **c** (*inf*) (= *Lehrling*) apprentice (boy); (= *Knirps*) nipper (*Brit inf*), whippersnapper (*US inf*)

Stift² NT **-(e)s, -e** (= *Domstift*) cathedral chapter; (= *Theologiestift*) seminary; (*old:* = *Heim, Anstalt*) home; (*in Namen*) foundation; (*old:* = *Bistum*) diocese

stif|ten [ˈʃtɪftn] VT **a** (= *gründen*) *Kirche, Universität* to found, to establish; (= *spenden, spendieren*) to donate; *Geld, Summe* to put up, to donate; *Preis, Stipendium etc* to endow **b** *Verwirrung* to cause; *Unfrieden, Unheil* to cause, to bring about; *Identität* to create; *Frieden* to bring about; *Ehe* to arrange; **Gutes/Schaden ~** to do good/damage

stif|ten ge|hen VI *irreg aux sein* (*inf*) to hop it (*Brit inf*), to move it (*US inf*)

Stif|ten|kopf [ˈʃtɪftn-] M (*dated inf*) crew cut; (*Mensch*) person with a crew cut

Stif|ter [ˈʃtɪftɐ] M **-s, -**, **Stif|te|rin** [-ərɪn] F **-, -nen** (= *Gründer*) founder; (= *Spender*) donator

Stif|ter|re|li|gi|on F religion founded by a particular person eg Buddha, Jesus

Stifts-: Stifts|da|me F (*Eccl*) canoness; **Stifts|herr** M (*Eccl*) canon; **Stifts|hüt|te** F (*Bibl*) Tabernacle; **Stifts|kir|che** F collegiate church

Stif|tung [ˈʃtɪftʊŋ] F **-, -en** **a** (= *Gründung*) foundation, establishment; (= *Schenkung*) donation; (*von Universität, Stipendium etc*) endowment **b** (= *Organisation*) foundation

Stif|tungs-: Stif|tungs|fest NT Founder's Day celebration; **Stif|tungs|ur|kun|de** F foundation charter

Stift|zahn M post crown

Stig|ma [ˈʃtɪɡma, st-] NT **-s, -ta** [-ta] (*Biol, Rel, fig*) stigma

stig|ma|ti|sie|ren [ʃtɪɡmatiˈziːrən, st-] *ptp* **stigmatisiert** [-ˈziːɐt] VT (*Rel, auch fig*) to stigmatize (*als* as), to brand (*als* as) (*fig*)

Stig|ma|ti|sier|te(r) [ʃtɪɡmatiˈziːɐtə, st-] MF *decl as adj* (*Biol, Rel*) stigmatic; (*fig*) stigmatized person

Stil [ʃtiːl, stiːl] M **-(e)s, -e** style; (= *Eigenart*) way, manner; **in großem ~, im großen ~, großen ~s** in a big way; **... alten ~s** old-style ...; **schlechter ~** bad style; **das ist schlechter ~** (*fig*) that is bad form; **~ haben** (*fig*) to have style; **er fährt einen rücksichtslosen ~** he drives recklessly *or* in a reckless manner; **er schreibt einen sehr schwerfälligen ~** his writing style is very clumsy

Stil-: Stil|ana|ly|se F (*Art, Liter*) stylistic analysis; **stil|bil|dend** ADJ (*für jdn*) **~ sein** to improve sb's style; **~ sein/wirken** (*einen Stil kreieren*) to help set a style; **Stil|blü|te** F (*hum*) stylistic howler (*Brit inf*) *or* blooper (*US inf*); **Stil|bruch** M stylistic incongruity *or* inconsistency; (*in Roman etc*) abrupt change in style; **das ist ein glatter ~** that is really incongruous; **Stil|ebe|ne** F (*Liter, Ling*) style level; **stil|echt** ADJ authentic(-style); *Möbel* period *attr* ADV in an authentic style; **~ eingerichtet** with period furniture; **Stil|ele|ment** NT stylistic element; **Stil|emp|fin|den** NT feeling for style, sense of style

Sti|lett [ʃtiˈlɛt, st-] NT **-s, -e** stiletto

Stil-: Stil|feh|ler M stylistic lapse; **Stil|fi|gur** F stylistic device; **Stil|ge|fühl** NT feeling for style, sense of style; **stil|ge|recht** ADJ appropriate to *or* in keeping with a/the style; **stil|ge|treu** ADJ true to *or* in the original style

sti|li|sie|ren [ʃtili:ˈziːrən, st-] *ptp* **stilisiert** VT to stylize

Sti|li|sie|rung F **-, -en** stylization

Sti|list [ʃtiˈlɪst, st-] M **-en, -en**, **Sti|lis|tin** [-lɪstɪn] F **-, -nen** stylist

Sti|lis|tik [ʃtiˈlɪstɪk, st-] F **-, -en** (*Liter*) stylistics *sing*; (= *Handbuch*) guide to good style

sti|lis|tisch [ʃtiˈlɪstɪʃ, st-] ADJ stylistic ADV **ich muss meine Vorlesung ~ überarbeiten** I must go over my lecture from the point of view of style; **etw ~ ändern/verbessern** to change/improve the style of sth; **~ gesehen** *or* **betrachtet ist der Artikel brillant** the style of this article is brilliant

Stil|kun|de F stylistics *sing*; (= *Handbuch*) guide to good style

still [ʃtɪl] ADJ **a** (= *ruhig*) quiet, silent; (= *lautlos*) *Seufzer* quiet; *Gebet* silent; (= *schweigend*) *Vor-*

wurf, Beobachter silent; **~ werden** to go quiet, to fall silent; **im Saal wurde es ~, der Saal wurde ~** the room fell silent; **um ihn/darum ist es ~ geworden** you don't hear anything about him/it any more; **es blieb ~** there was no sound, silence reigned; **Stille Nacht** Silent Night; **in ~em Gedenken** in silent tribute; **in ~em Schmerz/in ~er Trauer** in silent suffering/grief; **im Stillen** without saying anything, quietly; **ich dachte mir im Stillen** I thought to myself; **die Stillen im Lande** the quiet ones; **sei doch ~!** be *or* keep quiet; **~e Messe** silent mass

b (= *unbewegt*) *Luft* still; *See* calm, still; (= *ohne Kohlensäure*) *Mineralwasser* still; **der Stille Ozean** the Pacific (Ocean); **~e Wasser sind tief** (*Prov*) still waters run deep (*Prov*); **er ist ein ~es Wasser** he's a deep one, he's a dark horse

c (= *einsam, abgeschieden*) *Dorf, Tal, Straße* quiet; **ein ~es Eckchen** a quiet corner; **ein ~es Plätzchen** a quiet spot

d (= *heimlich*) secret; **im Stillen** in secret; **er ist dem ~en Suff ergeben** (*inf*) he drinks on the quiet, he's a secret drinker

e (*Comm*) *Gesellschafter, Teilhaber* sleeping (*Brit*), silent (*US*); *Reserven, Rücklagen* secret, hidden; **~e Beteiligung** sleeping partnership (*Brit*), non-active interest

ADV **a** (= *leise*) *weinen, arbeiten, nachdenken* quietly; *leiden* in silence; *auseinander gehen, weggehen* silently; **~ lächeln** to give a quiet smile

b (= *unbewegt*) *daliegen, dasitzen, liegen bleiben* still; **~ halten** to keep *or* hold still; **~ sitzen** to sit *or* keep still; **den Kopf/die Hände/Füße halten** to keep one's head/hands/feet still; **ein Glas/Tablett ~ halten** to hold a glass/tray steady; **vor uns lag ~ die Ägäis** before us lay the calm waters of the Aegean

c (= *ohne viel Trubel*) *vor sich hin leben, arbeiten* quietly; **ganz ~ und leise** (*etw erledigen*) discreetly; **er hat sich ~ und leise aus dem Staub gemacht** he just disappeared

Still-BH [ˈʃtɪlbeːhaː] M nursing bra

stil|le [ˈʃtɪlə] ADJ, ADV (*old*) = **still**

Stil|le [ˈʃtɪlə] F -, *no pl* **a** (= *Ruhe*) quiet(ness), peace(fulness), (= *Schweigen*) silence; **in der ~ der Nacht** in the still of the night; **in aller ~** quietly, calmly; **die Beerdigung fand in aller ~ statt** it was a quiet funeral; **jdn in aller ~ begraben** to give sb a quiet burial **b** (= *Unbewegtheit*) calm(ness); (*der Luft*) stillness **c** (= *Einsamkeit, Abgeschiedenheit*) quiet, seclusion **c** (= *Heimlichkeit*) secrecy; **in aller ~** in secret, secretly

Stilleben △ NT → **Stillleben**

stillegen △ VT → **stilllegen**

Stillegung △ F -, -en → **Stilllegung**

Stil|leh|re F stylistics *sing*

Still|ein|la|ge F (*für BH*) nursing pad

stil|len [ˈʃtɪlən] VT **a** (= *zum Stillstand bringen*) *Tränen* to stop; *Schmerzen* to ease, to relieve, to allay; *Blutung* to staunch, to stop **b** (= *befriedigen*) *Neugier, Begierde, Verlangen, Hunger* to satisfy, to still (*liter*); *Durst* to quench **c** *Säugling* to breast-feed, to nurse ► VI to breast-feed; **~de Mutter** nursing mother

Still|geld NT nursing mothers' allowance

still|ge|stan|den INTERJ (*Mil*) halt

Still|grup|pe F mothers' group

Still|hal|te|ab|kom|men NT (*Fin, fig*) moratorium

still+hal|ten VI *sep irreg* **a** △ → **still** ADV b **b** (*fig*) to keep quiet

Still|hal|ter(in) M(F) (*St Ex*) taker of an option

stilliegen △ VI → **stillliegen**

Still-: **Still|le|ben** ▲ NT still life; **still+le|gen** ▲ VT *sep* to close down, to shut down; *Schiff* to lay up; **stillgelegtes Bergwerk** disused *or* abandoned mine; **Still|le|gung** ▲ [-leːɡʊŋ] F -, -en closure, shutdown; (*von Schiff*) laying-up; **still+lie|gen** ▲ VI *sep irreg aux sein or haben* **a** (*= außer Betrieb sein*) to be closed down, to be shut down **b** (= *lahm liegen*) to be at a stand-

still, to have been brought to a standstill, to have come to a halt

still|los ADJ lacking in style; (= *fehl am Platze*) incongruous; **eine völlig ~e Zusammenstellung von Möbelstücken** a collection of furniture completely lacking (in) any sense of style ADV with no sense of style; **völlig ~ servierte sie Hummersuppe in Teetassen** showing absolutely no sense of style she served up lobster soup in tea cups

Still|lo|sig|keit F -, -en lack of style *no pl*; **solche ~en ist man von ihr gewohnt** we're used to her having no sense of style

still+schwei|gen VI *sep irreg* to remain silent; **zu etw ~** to remain silent in the face of sth; **schweig still!** be silent *or* quiet

Still|schwei|gen NT silence; **auf sein ~ kann man sich verlassen** one can rely on his keeping silent; **jdm ~ auferlegen, jdn zum ~ verpflichten** to swear sb to silence; **beide Seiten haben ~ vereinbart** both sides have agreed not to say anything; **über etw** (*acc*) **~ bewahren** to observe *or* maintain silence about sth; **etw mit ~ übergehen** to pass over sth in silence

still|schwei|gend ADJ silent; *Einverständnis* tacit ADV tacitly; **über etw** (*acc*) **~ hinweggehen** to pass over sth in silence; **etw ~ hinnehmen** to accept sth silently *or* without protest

still+sit|zen △ VI *sep irreg aux sein or haben* → **still** ADV b

Still|stand M standstill; (*von Betrieb, Produktion, Verhandlungen etc auch*) stoppage; (*vorübergehend*) interruption; (*in Entwicklung*) halt; **bei ~ der Maschine ...** when the machine is stopped ...; **ein ~ des Herzens** a cardiac arrest; **Hauptsache ist, dass kein ~ in der Produktion eintritt** the main thing is that production is not interrupted; **zum ~ kommen** (*Verkehr*) to come to a standstill *or* stop; (*Produktion auch, Maschine, Motor, Herz, Blutung*) to stop; (*Wirtschaft*) to come to a standstill *or* halt; (*Prozess, Entwicklung*) to come to a halt; **etw zum ~ bringen** (*Verkehr*) to bring sth to a standstill *or* stop; *Produktion auch, Maschine, Motor* to stop sth; *Blutung* to stop *or* check sth; *Prozess, Entwicklung* to bring sth to a halt; **~ ist Rückgang** (*prov*) if you don't go forwards, you go backwards

still+ste|hen VI *sep irreg aux sein or haben* **a** (*Produktion, Handel etc*) to be at a standstill; (*Fabrik, Maschine*) to be *or* stand idle; (*Verkehr*) to be stopped, to be at a standstill; (*Herz*) to have stopped; **die Zeit schien stillzustehen** time seemed to stand still *or* to stop; **alle Räder stehen still** (*fig*) everything has ground to a halt **b** (= *stehen bleiben*) to stop; (*Maschine*) to stop working; **keinen Moment ~** not to stop for a moment; **mein Herz stand still vor Schreck** I was so frightened my heart stood still

still+ver|gnügt ADJ contented ADV happily, contentedly

Still|zeit F lactation period

Stil-: **Stil|merk|mal** NT stylistic feature; **Stil|mit|tel** NT stylistic device; **Stil|mö|bel** PL period furniture *sing*; **Stil|pro|be** F specimen *or* sample of written work; **stil|rein** ADJ stylistically correct; **Stil|rich|tung** F style; **stil|si|cher** ADJ stylistically confident ADV **~ schrei|ben** to write with a good consistent style; **sich ~ ausdrücken** to be a stylistically confident speaker; **Stil|übung** F exercise in stylistic composition; **stil|voll** ADJ *Einrichtung, Ambiente* stylish ADV stylishly; **stil|wid|rig** ADJ (stylistically) incongruous *or* inappropriate; **Stil|wör|ter|buch** NT dictionary of correct usage

Stimm-: **Stimm|ab|ga|be** F voting; **sie kommen zur ~** they come to vote *or* cast their votes; **Stimm|auf|wand** M vocal effort; **Stimm|band** [-bant] NT *pl* **-bänder** *usu pl* vocal chord; **seine Stimmbänder strapazieren** to strain one's voice; (*fig*) to talk one's head off; **stimm|be|rech|tigt** ADJ entitled to vote; **Stimm|be|rech|tig|te(r)** [-bərɛçtɪçtə] MF *decl as adj* person entitled to vote; **Stimm|be|zirk** M con-

stituency; **Stimm|bil|dung** F **a** voice production **b** (= *Ausbildung*) voice training; **Stimm|bruch** M = **Stimmwechsel**; **Stimm|bür|ger(in)** M(F) voter, elector

Stim|me [ˈʃtɪmə] F -, -n **a** voice; (*Mus:* = *Part*) part; (= *Orgelstimme*) register; (*fig*) (= *Meinungsäußerung*) voice; (= *Sprachrohr*) mouthpiece, voice; (*liter:* = *Ruf*) call; **mit leiser/lauter ~** in a soft/loud voice; **gut/nicht bei ~ sein** to be in good/bad voice; **erste/zweite/dritte ~** (*in Chor*) first/second/third part; **bei einem Lied die erste/zweite ~ singen** to sing the top part *or* melody of the descant to a song; **die ~n mehren sich, die ...** there is a growing body of (public) opinion that ..., there is a growing number of people calling for ...; **die ~(n) der Glocken/Geigen** (*liter*) the sound of the bells/violins; **die ~ der Öffentlichkeit** (*geh*) public opinion; **die ~ des Volkes** (*geh*) the voice of the people; **die ~ der Wahrheit** the voice of truth; **eine ~ aus dem Dunkel/Exil** a voice out of the darkness/from exile; **der ~ der Natur folgen** (*euph hum*) (= *seine Notdurft verrichten*) to answer the call of nature; (= *dem Geschlechtstrieb nachgeben*) to give way to a natural urge; **der ~ des Gewissens folgen** to act on *or* according to one's conscience; **der ~ des Herzens folgen** to follow the leanings *or* dictates of one's heart; **der ~ der Vernunft folgen** to be guided by reason, to listen to the voice of reason

b (= *Wahlstimme, Votum*) vote; **eine ~ haben** to have the vote; (= *Mitspracherecht*) to have a say *or* voice; **keine ~ haben** not to be entitled to vote; (= *Mitspracherecht*) to have no say *or* voice; **seine ~ abgeben** to cast one's vote, to vote; **jdm/einer Partei seine ~ geben** to vote for sb/a party; **die abgegebenen ~n** the votes cast; **40% der ~n erhalten** to receive 40% of the vote(s) → **enthalten** VR b

stim|men [ˈʃtɪmən] ♦ 38.1 VI **a** (= *richtig sein*) to be right *or* correct; **stimmt es, dass ...?** is it true that ...?; **das stimmt** that's right; **das stimmt nicht** that's not right, that's wrong; **hier stimmt was nicht!** there's something wrong here; **mit ihr stimmt etwas nicht** there's something wrong *or* the matter with her; **das stimmt schon, aber ...** that's true, but ...; **stimmts, oder hab ich recht?** (*hum, inf*) am I right or am I right? (*hum*); **stimmt so!** that's all right, keep the change

b (= *zusammenpassen*) to go (together) **c** (= *wählen, sich entscheiden*) to vote; **für/gegen jdn/etw ~** to vote for/against sb/sth

VT *Instrument* to tune; **etw höher/niedriger ~** to raise/lower the pitch of sth, to tune sth up/down, to sharpen/flatten sth; **jdn froh/traurig ~** to make sb (feel) cheerful/sad; **jdn gegen etw ~** (*geh*) to prejudice *or* turn sb against sth → *auch* **gestimmt**

Stim|men-: **Stim|men|aus|zäh|lung** F count (of votes); **Stim|men|fang** M (*inf*) canvassing, vote-getting (*inf*); **auf ~ sein/gehen** to be/go canvassing; **Stim|men|ge|wirr** NT babble of voices; **Stim|men|gleich|heit** F tie, tied vote; **bei ~** in the event of a tie *or* tied vote; **Stim|men|hö|ren** NT (*Psych, Med*) hearing voices; **Stim|men|kauf** M vote-buying, buying votes; **Stim|men|mehr|heit** F majority (of votes); **Stim|men|split|ting** [-ʃplɪtɪŋ, -sp-] NT **-s**, *no pl* (*Pol*) splitting one's vote

Stimm|ent|hal|tung F abstention

Stim|men|wer|bung F canvassing

Stim|mer [ˈʃtɪmɐ] M -s, -, **Stim|me|rin** [-ərɪn] F -, -nen (*Mus*) tuner

Stimm-: **Stimm|ga|bel** F tuning fork; **stimm|ge|wal|tig** ADJ (*geh*) with a strong *or* powerful voice; **stimm|haft** (*Ling*) ADJ voiced ADV **~ ausgesprochen werden** to be voiced

stim|mig [ˈʃtɪmɪç] ADJ *Umfeld* ordered; *Argumente* coherent

Stim|mig|keit F -, *no pl* coherence

Stim|mla|ge F (*Mus*) voice, register

stimm|lich [ˈʃtɪmlɪç] **ADJ** vocal; **ihre ~en Quali-täten** the quality of her voice **ADV ~ hat er nicht viel zu bieten** he doesn't have much of a voice; **sie hat ~ nachgelassen** the quality of her voice has declined

Stimm-: Stimm|lis|te F voting list; **stimm|los** (*Ling*) **ADJ** voiceless, unvoiced **ADV ~ ausge-sprochen werden** not to be voiced; **Stimm|recht** NT right to vote; **Stimm|rit|ze** F glottis; **Stimm|schlüs|sel** M (*Mus*) tuning hammer *or* key; **Stimm|um|fang** M vocal range

Stim|mung [ˈʃtɪmʊŋ] F **-, -en a** (= *Gemütszu-stand*) mood; (= *Atmosphäre*) atmosphere; (*bei der Truppe, unter den Arbeitern*) morale; **in (guter) ~** in a good mood; **in gehobener ~** in high spirits; **in schlechter ~** in a bad mood; **wir hatten eine tolle ~** we were in a tremendous mood; **in ~ kommen** to liven up; **für ~ sorgen** to make sure there is a good atmosphere; **in ~ sein** to be in a good mood; **ich bin nicht in der ~ zum Tanzen** I'm not in the mood for dancing; **sehr von ~en abhängig sein** to be moody, to be subject to mood swings; **~!** enjoy yourselves!, have a good time!

b (= *Meinung*) opinion; **~ gegen/für jdn/etw machen** to stir up (public) opinion against/in favour (*Brit*) *or* favor (*US*) of sb/sth

c (*St Ex*) mood

d (*Mus*) (= *das Stimmen*) tuning; (= *das Ge-stimmtsein*) pitch

Stim|mungs-: Stim|mungs|ba|ro|me|ter NT (*esp Pol*) barometer of public opinion; **Stim|mungs|bild** NT atmospheric picture; **dieser Bericht gibt ein eindrucksvolles ~** this report conveys the general atmosphere extremely well; **stim|mungs|för|dernd** ADJ **~es Mittel** anti-depressant (drug); **Stim|mungs|ka|no|ne** F (*inf*) life and soul of the party; **eine richtige ~** the life and soul of the party; **Stim|mungs|ka|pel|le** F band which plays light music; **Stim|mungs|la|ge** F atmosphere; **Stim|mungs|ma|che** F , *no pl* (*pej*) cheap propaganda; **Stim|mungs|mensch** M moody person; **Stim|mungs|mu|sik** F light music; **Stim|mungs|tief** NT (*auch St Ex, Econ*) depressed mood; (*einer Person*) low; **er steckt in einem ~, he's going through a low (patch)**; **Stim|mungs|um|schwung** M change of atmosphere; (*Pol*) swing (in public opinion); (*St Ex*) change in trend; **stim|mungs|voll** ADJ *Bild* idyllic; *Atmosphäre* tremendous; *Gedicht, Musik-stück, Beschreibung* full of atmosphere, atmospheric; **Stim|mungs|wan|del** M , **Stim|mungs|wech|sel** M change of atmosphere; (*Pol*) change or shift in (public) opinion

Stimm-: Stimm|ver|zer|rer [-fɛɛtsɛrɐ] M **-s, -** voice distorter; **Stimm|vieh** NT (*pej*) gullible voters *pl*; **Stimm|volk** NT voters *pl*, electorate; **Stimm|wech|sel** M **nach dem ~** after one's voice has broken; **er ist im ~** his voice is breaking; **Stimm|werk|zeu|ge** PL vocal organs *pl*; **Stimm|zet|tel** M ballot paper

Sti|mu|lans [ˈʃtiːmulans, ˈstː-] NT **-, Stimulantia** *or* **Stimulanzien** [ʃtimuˈlantsia, ʃtimuˈlantsiən, stː-] (*Med, fig*) stimulant

Sti|mu|la|ti|on [ʃtimulaˈtsioːn, stː-] F **-, -en** (*Med, fig*) stimulation

Sti|mu|li *pl von* **Stimulus**

sti|mu|lie|ren [ʃtimuˈliːrən, stː-] *ptp* **stimuliert** VT (*Med, fig*) to stimulate

Sti|mu|lie|rung F **-, -en** (*Med, fig*) stimulation

Sti|mu|lus [ˈʃtiːmulʊs, ˈstː-] M **-, Stimuli** [-liː] (*Psych*) stimulus; (*fig auch*) stimulant

Stin|ka|do|res [ʃtɪŋkaˈdoːrɛs] F **-, -** (*inf*) smelly cigar

Stink-: Stink|bom|be F stink bomb; **Stink|drü|se** F (*Zool*) scent gland

Stin|ke|fin|ger M (*inf*) finger (*inf*) (*held up as rude gesture*); **jdm den ~ zeigen** to give sb the finger (*inf*) *or* the bird (*US inf*)

stin|ken [ˈʃtɪŋkn] *pret* **stank** [ʃtaŋk], *ptp* **gestun-ken** [ɡəˈʃtʊŋkn] VI **a** (*nach of*) to stink, to

reek, to pong (*Brit inf*); **er stinkt nach Kneipe** he smells of drink; **wie ein Bock** *or* **Wiedehopf** *or* **eine Wachtel** *or* **die Pest ~** (*inf*) to stink to high heaven (*inf*)

b (*fig inf*) **er stinkt nach Geld** he's stinking rich (*inf*); **er stinkt vor Faulheit** he's bone idle; **das stinkt zum Himmel** it's an absolute scandal, it's absolutely appalling; **an der Sache stinkt etwas** there's something fishy about it (*inf*); **das stinkt nach Verrat** that smells of treachery; **die Sache stinkt mir** (*inf*), **mir stinkts (gewaltig)!** (*inf*) I'm fed up to the back teeth (with it) (*Brit inf*) *or* to the back of my throat (with it) (*US inf*)

stin|kend ADJ stinking, foul-smelling

stink|faul ADJ (*inf*) bone idle (*Brit*), extremely lazy

stin|kig [ˈʃtɪŋkɪç] ADJ (*inf*) stinking (*inf*); (= *ver-ärgert*) pissed off (*sl*)

Stink-: stink|lang|wei|lig ADJ (*inf*) deadly boring *or* dull; **Stink|lau|ne** F (*inf*) stinking (*inf*) *or* foul mood; **stink|nor|mal** ADJ (*inf*) boringly normal *or* ordinary; **stink|reich** ADJ (*inf*) stinking rich (*Brit inf*), rolling in it (*inf*); **stink|sau|er** ADJ (*sl*) pissed off (*inf*); **Stink-stie|bel** [ˈʃtɪŋkʃtiːbl] M **-s, -** (*dial, inf*), **Stink-stie|fel** M (*inf*) stinking pig (*inf*); (*hum:* = *Kumpel*) mate (*inf*); **Stink|tier** NT skunk; **stink|vor|nehm** (*inf*) **ADJ** posh (*inf*), swanky (*inf*); *Lokal* posh (*inf*), swish (*Brit inf*) **ADV** *spei-sen, wohnen* regally; **sie tut so ~** she acts so posh (*inf*); **Stink|wut** F (*inf*) raging temper; **eine ~ (auf jdn) haben** to be livid (with sb)

Stint [ʃtɪnt] M **-(e)s, -e** (*Zool*) smelt, sparling

Sti|pen|di|at [ʃtipɛnˈdiaːt] M **-en, -en**, **Sti|pen|di|a|tin** [-ˈdiaːtɪn] F **-, -nen →** Stipendium scholarship holder, person receiving a scholar-ship/grant

Sti|pen|di|um [ʃtiˈpɛndiʊm] NT **-s, Stipendien** [-diən] (*als Auszeichnung etc erhalten*) scholar-ship; (*zur allgemeinen Unterstützung des Studiums*) grant

Stip|pe [ˈʃtɪpə] F **-, -n** (*dial*) sauce

stip|pen [ˈʃtɪpn] VTI (*dial*) to dip, to dunk

Stipp|vi|si|te [ˈʃtɪp-] F (*inf*) flying visit

Sti|pu|la|ti|on [ʃtipulaˈtsioːn, stː-] F **-, -en** (*Jur*) stipulation

sti|pu|lie|ren [ʃtipuˈliːrən, stː-] *ptp* **stipuliert** VT to stipulate; **von Arbeitgeberseite wurden neue Verhandlungen stipuliert** the employers insisted on new talks

stirbt [ʃtɪrpt] 3. *pers sing pres von* **sterben**

Stirn [ʃtɪrn] F **-, -en** forehead, brow (*esp liter*); **die ~ runzeln** to wrinkle one's brow; **sich/jdm das Haar aus der ~ streichen** to brush one's/sb's hair out of one's/his/her face; **den Hut in die ~ drücken** to pull one's hat down over one's eyes; **es steht ihm auf der ~ geschrie-ben** it is written all over his face; **die ~ haben** *or* **besitzen, zu ...** to have the effrontery *or* nerve *or* gall to ...; **jdm/einer Sache die ~ bie-ten** (*geh*) to stand up to sb/sth, to defy sb/sth **→ eisern b**

Stirn-: Stirn|ader F vein in the/one's temple; **Stirn|au|ge** NT (*Zool*) ocellus; **Stirn|band** [-bant] NT *pl* **-bänder** headband; **Stirn|bein** NT frontal bone; **Stirn|fal|te** F wrinkle (on one's forehead; **Stirn|glat|ze** F receding hair-line; **Stirn|höh|le** F frontal sinus; **Stirn|höh-len|ka|tarrh** M , **Stirn|höh|len|ver|ei|te-rung** F sinusitis; **Stirn|la|ge** F (*Med*) brow presentation; **Stirn|lo|cke** F quiff (*Brit*), cow-lick; **Stirn|rad** NT (*Tech*) spur wheel; **Stirn-re|flek|tor** M (*Med*) forehead mirror; **Stirn-rie|men** M brow band; **Stirn|run|zeln** NT **-s**, *no pl* frown; **Stirn|sei|te** F end wall, gable end; **Stirn|spie|gel** M (*Med*) forehead mirror; **Stirn|wand** F end wall

Stoa [ˈʃtoːa, ˈstː-] F **-, *no pl*** (*Philos*) Stoics *pl*, Stoic school

stob *pret von* **stieben**

stö|bern [ˈʃtøːbən] VI to rummage (*in +dat* in, *durch* through)

Sto|cher|kahn M punt

sto|chern [ˈʃtɔxɐn] VI to poke (*in +dat* at); (*im Essen*) to pick (*in +dat* at); **er stocherte mit ei-nem Schürhaken im Feuer** he poked the fire; **sich** (*dat*) **in den Zähnen ~** to pick one's teeth

Stock¹ [ʃtɔk] M **-(e)s, ≈e** [ˈʃtœkə] **a** stick; (= *Rohrstock*) cane; (= *Taktstock*) baton; (= *Zeige-stock*) pointer; (= *Billardstock*) cue; **er stand da (steif) wie ein ~** *or* **als ob er einen ~ verschluckt hätte** he stood there as stiff as a poker; **am ~ gehen** to walk with (the aid of) a stick; (*fig inf*) to be in a bad way *or* in bad shape; (*nach viel Arbeit*) to be dead beat (*Brit inf*) *or* dead (*US inf*); (*finanziell*) to be in difficulties; **~ und Hut** (*dated*) hat and stick

b (= *Wurzelstock*) roots *pl*; **über ~ und Stein** up hill and down dale (*Brit*), over stick and stone (*US*)

c (*Pflanze*) (= *Rebstock*) vine; (= *Rosenstock*) rose bush; (*Bäumchen*) rose tree; (= *Blumenstock*) pot plant

d (= *Bienenstock*) hive

e (*Geol:* = *Gesteinsmasse*) massif, rock mass

f (*Hist*) stocks *pl*; **jdn in den ~ legen** to put sb in the stocks

g *pl* **-** (= *Stockwerk*) floor, storey (*Brit*), story (*US*); **das Haus hat drei ~** *or* **ist drei ~ hoch** the house is three storeys (*Brit*) *or* three stories (*US*) high; **im ersten ~** on the first floor (*Brit*), on the second floor (*US*)

h (*Sw:* = *Kartoffelbrei*) mashed potato(es *pl*)

Stock² [stɔk] M **-s, -s** (*Econ*) stock

Stock-: stock|be|sof|fen (*inf*) ADJ dead drunk (*inf*); **ein Stockbesoffener** a drunk; **Stock|bett** NT bunk bed; **stock|blind** ADJ (*inf*) as blind as a bat, completely blind

Stöck|chen [ˈʃtœkçən] NT **-s, -** dim von **Stock a, c**

stock-: stock|dumm ADJ (*inf*) thick (as two short planks) (*Brit inf*), dumb as a doorknob (*US inf*); **stock|dun|kel** ADJ (*inf*) pitch-dark; **im Stockdunkeln** in the pitch dark

Stö|ckel¹ [ˈʃtœkl] M **-s, -** (*inf*) stiletto

Stö|ckel² F **-s, -** (*Aus*) outhouse, outbuilding

Stö|ckel|ab|satz M stiletto heel

stö|ckeln [ˈʃtœkln] VI *aux sein* (*inf*) to trip, to mince

Stö|ckel|schuh M stiletto, stiletto-heeled shoe

sto|cken [ˈʃtɔkn] VI **a** (*Herz, Puls*) to miss *or* skip a beat; (*Gedanken, Worte*) to falter; (= *nicht vorangehen*) (*Arbeit, Entwicklung*) to make no pro-gress; (*Unterhaltung, Gespräch*) to flag; (*Verhand-lungen*) to grind to a halt; (*Konjunktur, Geschäfte, Handel*) to stagnate; (*Verkehr*) to be held up *or* halted; **ihm stockte das Herz/der Puls** his heart/pulse missed *or* skipped a beat; **ihm stockte der Atem** he caught his breath; **ins Stocken geraten** *or* **kommen** (*Unterhaltung, Ge-spräch*) to begin to flag; (*Entwicklung*) to make no progress; (*Verhandlungen*) to grind to a halt; (*Konjunktur etc*) to stagnate

b (= *innehalten*) (*in der Rede*) to falter; (*im Satz*) to break off, to stop short; **ihre Stimme stockte** she *or* her voice faltered

c (= *gerinnen*) (*Blut*) to thicken; (*S Ger, Aus: Milch*) to curdle, to go sour; **das Blut stockte ihm in den Adern** (*geh*) the blood froze in his veins

d (= *stockig werden*) (*Wäsche, Papier, Bücher*) to become mildewed, to go mouldy (*Brit*) *or* moldy (*US*)

sto|ckend **ADJ** *Stimme, Deutsch* faltering, hesi-tant; *Konjunktur, Verhandlungen* faltering; *Verkehr* stop-go **ADV** *sprechen* haltingly; **der Verkehr kam nur ~ voran** traffic was stop and go

Stock|en|te F mallard

Stock-: stock|fins|ter ADJ (*inf*) pitch-dark, pitch-black; **Stock|fisch** M dried cod; (*pej: Mensch*) dull old stick (*Brit*), stick-in-the-mud

---

(pej inf); **Stock|fleck** M *mark caused by mould or mildew*; **stock|fle|ckig** ADJ mouldy *(Brit)*, moldy *(US)*, mildewed; **Stock|haus** NT *(Hist)* gaol; **Stock|hieb** M blow (from a stick); *(mit Rohrstock)* stroke of the cane

Stock|holm ['ʃtɔkhɔlm] NT **-s** Stockholm

Stock|hol|mer¹ ['ʃtɔkhɔlmɐ] ADJ Stockholm *attr*

Stock|hol|mer² ['ʃtɔkhɔlmɐ] M **-s, -**, **Stock|hol|me|rin** [-ərɪn] F **-, -nen** native of Stockholm; *(Einwohner)* inhabitant of Stockholm

sto|ckig ['ʃtɔkɪç] ADJ *Geruch, Luft* musty; *Papier, Wäsche* mildewed, mouldy *(Brit)*, moldy *(US)*

-stö|ckig ['ʃtœkɪç] *suf* -storey *attr (Brit)*, -storeyed *(Brit)*, -story *attr (US)*, -storied *(US)*; **ein zweistöckiges Haus** a two-stor(e)y house

Stock-: **stock|ka|tho|lisch** ADJ *(inf)* Catholic through and through; **stock|kon|ser|va|tiv** ADJ *(inf)* archconservative; **stock|nüch|tern** ADJ *(inf)* stone-cold sober *(inf)*; **stock|sau|er** ADJ *(inf)* pissed off *(inf)*; **Stock|schirm** M walking-length umbrella; **Stock|schlag** M blow (from a stick); *(mit Rohrstock)* stroke of the cane; **Stock|schnup|fen** M permanent cold; **stock|steif** *(inf)* ADJ as stiff as a poker **ADV** as stiff as a statue; **sie bewegt sich ~** she moves very stiffly; **stock|taub** ADJ *(inf)* as deaf as a post

Sto|ckung ['ʃtɔkʊŋ] F **-, -en** **a** (= *vorübergehender Stillstand*) interruption, holdup (+*gen, in* +*dat* in); (= *Verkehrsstockung*) congestion, traffic jam, hold-up; **der Verkehr läuft wieder ohne ~en** traffic is flowing smoothly again **b** *(von Verhandlungen)* breakdown (+*gen* of, in); *(von Geschäften, Handel)* slackening or dropping off (+*gen* in) **c** (= *Pause, Unterbrechung*) *(im Gespräch)* break, lull; *(in der Rede)* pause, hesitation **d** (= *Gerinnung*) thickening; *(von Milch)* curdling

Stock|werk NT floor, storey *(Brit)*, story *(US)*; **im 5. ~** on the 5th *(Brit)* or 6th *(US)* floor; **ein Haus mit vier ~en** a four-storeyed *(Brit)* or four-storied *(US)* building

Stock|zahn M *(Aus)* molar (tooth)

Stoff [ʃtɔf] M **-(e)s, -e** **a** material, fabric; *(als Materialart)* cloth **b** *(no pl: = Materie)* matter; **~ und Form** *(Philos)* matter and form **c** (= *Substanz, Chem*) substance; (= *Papierstoff*) pulp; **tierische ~e** animal substance; **pflanzliche ~e** vegetable matter; **radioaktive ~e** radioactive substances; **aus härterem ~ gemacht sein** *(fig)* to be made of sterner stuff **d** (= *Gegenstand, Thema*) subject (matter); (= *Unterhaltungsstoff, Diskussionsstoff*) topic, subject; (= *Material*) material; **~ für ein** or **zu einem Buch sammeln** to collect material for a book; **der Vortrag bot reichlich ~ für eine Diskussion** the lecture provided plenty of material or topics for discussion; **~ zum Lesen** reading matter; **~ zum Nachdenken** food for thought **e** *(inf: = Rauschgift)* dope *(inf)*, stuff *(inf)*

Stoff-: **Stoff|bahn** F length of material; **Stoff|bal|len** M roll or bolt of material or cloth; **stoff|be|spannt** [-bəʃpant] ADJ fabric-covered

Stof|fel ['ʃtɔfl] M **-s, -** *(pej inf)* lout *(inf)*, boor

stof|fe|lig ['ʃtɔfəlɪç] *(pej inf)* ADJ uncouth, boorish **ADV** *sich benehmen* uncouthly

Stoff-: **Stoff|fet|zen** ▲ M scrap of cloth; **Stoff|fül|le** F wealth of material; **Stoff|ge|biet** NT *(Sch)* subject area; **Stoff|hand|schuh** M fabric glove

stoff|lich ['ʃtɔflɪç] ADJ **a** *(Philos, Chem)* material; **~e Verwertung** use of materials **b** (= *den Inhalt betreffend*) as regards subject matter **ADV** **a** *(Chem)* **etw ~ (wieder) verwerten** to (re)use the materials in sth **b** *(von der Materie her)* **ein ~ hochinteressanter Bericht** a report with a very interesting subject matter

Stoff|lich|keit F **-, -** *no pl (Philos)* materiality

stoff|lig ADJ, ADV *(pej inf)* = **stoffelig**

Stoff-: **Stoff|pup|pe** F rag doll; **Stoff|rest** M remnant; **Stoff|samm|lung** F *(zu einem Buch etc)* gathering of material; **Stoff|tier** NT soft toy

Stoff|fül|le △ F → **Stofffülle**

Stoff|wahl F choice of subject

Stoff|wech|sel M metabolism

Stoff|wech|sel-: **Stoff|wech|sel|krank|heit** F metabolic disease or disorder; **Stoff|wech|sel|stö|rung** F metabolic disturbance

Stoff|zu|ga|be F extra material

stöh|nen ['ʃtøːnən] VI to groan; (= *klagen auch*) to moan; **~d** with a groan

Stöh|nen NT **-s**, *no pl (lit, fig)* groaning *no pl*; (= *Stöhnlaut*) groan

Sto|i|ker ['ʃtoːikɐ, st-] M **-s, -**, **Sto|i|ke|rin** [-ərɪn] F **-, -nen** *(Philos)* Stoic (philosopher); *(fig)* stoic

sto|isch ['ʃtoːɪʃ, st-] ADJ *(Philos)* Stoic; *(fig)* stoic(al) **ADV** *(fig)* stoically

Sto|i|zis|mus [ʃtoi'tsɪsmʊs, st-] M **-**, *no pl (Philos)* Stoicism; *(fig)* stoicism

Sto|la ['ʃtoːla, 'st-] F **-, Sto|len** [-lən] stole

Stol|le ['ʃtɔlə] F **-, -n** *(Cook)* fruit loaf *(eaten at Christmas)*, stollen

Stol|len ['ʃtɔlən] M **-s, - a** *(Min, Mil)* gallery, tunnel **b** *(Cook)* fruit loaf *(eaten at Christmas)*, stollen **c** (= *Zapfen*) *(an Hufeisen)* calk(in); (= *Schuhstollen*) stud **d** *(Poet)* stollen, one of the two equal sections forming the "Aufgesang" in "Minnesang"

STOLLEN

Stollen, or **Christstollen**, is a baked Christmas loaf made from a heavy yeast dough mixed with a lot of butter, dried fruit and almonds. There are also varieties which use marzipan or quark. The best-known **Stollen** comes from Dresden, where it has been baked since the early Middle Ages.

Stol|per|draht M tripwire; *(fig)* stumbling block

stol|pe|rig ['ʃtɔlpərɪç] ADJ *Gang* stumbling; *Weg* uneven, bumpy

stol|pern ['ʃtɔlpɐn] VI *aux sein* to stumble, to trip *(über +acc over)*; *(fig: = zu Fall kommen)* to come a cropper *(Brit inf)*, to fall flat on one's face *(inf)*, to come unstuck *(esp Brit inf)*; **ins Stolpern geraten** or **kommen** to come a cropper *(Brit inf)*, to fall flat on one's face *(inf)*; *(fig auch)* to slip up; **jdn zum Stolpern bringen** *(lit)* to trip sb up, to make sb trip; *(fig)* to be sb's downfall; **über einen Hinweis ~** *(fig)* to stumble upon a clue; **über einen Bekannten ~** *(fig)* to bump or run into an acquaintance; **über einen Strohhalm ~** *(fig)* to come to grief over a trifle

Stol|per|stein M *(fig)* stumbling block

stolp|rig ['ʃtɔlprɪç] ADJ = **stolperig**

stolz [ʃtɔlts] ADJ **a** proud *(auf +acc of)*; **~ wie ein Pfau** as proud as a peacock; **warum so ~?** why so proud?; *(bei Begegnung)* don't you know me any more?; **darauf kannst du ~ sein** that's something to be proud of; **der ~e Besitzer** the proud owner **b** (= *imposant*) *Bauwerk, Schiff* majestic, impressive; *(iro: = stattlich) Preis, Summe* princely **ADV** proudly; **~ erhebt sich die Burg über der kleinen Stadt** the castle rises proudly above the little town

Stolz [ʃtɔlts] M **-es**, *no pl* pride; **sein Garten/Sohn etc ist sein ganzer ~** his garden/son etc is his pride and joy; **voller ~ auf etw** *(acc)* **sein** to be very proud of sth; **voller ~ auf etw meinen ~ –** I do have my pride; **aus falschem/verletztem ~ handeln** to act out of false/wounded pride; **seinen ~ in etw** *(acc)* **setzen** to take a pride in sth

stol|zie|ren [ʃtɔl'tsiːrən] *ptp* **stolziert** VI *aux sein* to strut, to swagger; *(hochmütig, beleidigt)* to stalk

stop [ʃtɔp, st-] INTERJ stop; *(auf Verkehrsschild auch)* halt *(esp Brit)*

Stop-and-go-Ver|kehr [stɔpənd'goː-] M stop-and-go traffic, slow-moving traffic

Stopf-: **Stopf|büch|se** F , **Stopf|buch|se** F *(Tech)* stuffing box; **Stopf|ei** ['ʃtɔpflai] NT ≈ darning mushroom

stop|fen ['ʃtɔpfn] VT **a** (= *ausstopfen, füllen*) to stuff; *Pfeife, Loch, Wurst* to fill; *(inf) Taschen* to stuff, to cram; **jdm den Mund** *(inf)* or **das Maul** *(inf)* **~ silence sb **b** (= *hineinstopfen*) to stuff; *Korken auch* to ram; **sich** *(dat)* **Watte in die Ohren ~** to plug one's ears with cotton wool *(Brit)* or cotton *(US)*, to put cotton-wool *(Brit)* or cotton *(US)* plugs in one's ears; **gierig stopfte er alles in sich hinein, was man ihm auftischte** he greedily stuffed down everything they served up **c** (= *verstopfen*) *Trompete etc* to mute; *(mit Stöpsel)* to plug, to stop **d** (= *ausbessern, flicken*) *Loch, Strümpfe etc* to darn, to mend; *(fig) Haushaltslöcher etc* to plug → *auch* **gestopft** VI **a** *(Speisen)* (= *verstopfen*) to cause constipation, to constipate; (= *sättigen*) to be filling **b** *(inf: = gierig essen)* to bolt or wolf (down) one's food, to stuff oneself *(inf)* **c** (= *flicken*) to darn, to do darning

Stop|fen ['ʃtɔpfn] M **-s, -** *(dial)* stopper; (= *Korken*) cork

Stop|fer ['ʃtɔpfɐ] M **-s, -** (= *Pfeifenstopfer*) tamper

Stopf-: **Stopf|garn** NT darning cotton or thread; **Stopf|na|del** F darning needle; **Stopf|pilz** M *(Sew)* darning mushroom

stopp [ʃtɔp] INTERJ stop

Stopp [ʃtɔp] M **-s, -s** stop, halt; (= *Lohnstopp*) freeze

Stopp|ball ▲ M *(Tennis etc)* dropshot

Stop|pel¹ ['ʃtɔpl] F **-, -n** (= *Getreidestoppel, Bartstoppel*) stubble

Stop|pel² M **-s, -** *(Aus)* = **Stöpsel**

Stop|pel-: **Stop|pel|bart** M stubbly beard, stubble; **Stop|pel|feld** NT stubble field; **Stop|pel|haar** NT bristly hair

stop|pe|lig ['ʃtɔpəlɪç] ADJ *Bart* stubbly; *Kinn auch* bristly

stop|pen ['ʃtɔpn] VT **a** (= *anhalten, aufhalten*) to stop; *(Ftbl) Ball* to trap, to stop **b** (= *Zeit abnehmen*) to time; **er hat die Laufzeit/Zeit genau gestoppt** he timed exactly how long it took VI **a** (= *anhalten*) to stop **b** **ihr beide lauft und ich stoppe** you two run and I'll time you

Stop|per¹ ['ʃtɔpɐ] M **-s, - a** *(Naut)* stopper **b** *(an Gardinenstange)* curtain stop, end piece

Stop|per² ['ʃtɔpɐ] M **-s, - a** *(Ftbl)* centre *(Brit)* or center *(US)* half **b** (= *Zeitnehmer*) timekeeper

Stopp|licht NT stoplight, red light; *(Aut)* brake light

stopp|lig ['ʃtɔplɪç] ADJ = **stoppelig**

Stopp-: **Stopp|schild** NT *pl* **-schilder** stop or halt *(esp Brit)* sign; **Stopp|stra|ße** F road with stop signs, secondary road, stop street *(US)*; **Stopp|uhr** F stopwatch

Stöp|sel ['ʃtœpsl] M **-s, -** *(Aus)* stopper; (= *Korken*) cork

Stöp|sel ['ʃtœpsl] M **-s, -** *(von Waschbecken, Badewanne etc)* plug; *(Telec auch)* jack; (= *Pfropfen*) stopper; (= *Korken*) cork; *(inf: = Knirps)* little fellow

stöp|seln ['ʃtœpsln] VTI *(Telec)* to connect

Stop|sel|zie|her [-tsiː-] M **-s, -** *(Aus)* corkscrew

Stör¹ [ʃtøːɐ] M **-(e)s, -e** *(Zool)* sturgeon

Stör² F *(Aus)* **in** or **auf die ~ gehen** to work at the customer's home

Stör-: **Stör|ak|ti|on** F disruptive action *no pl*; **stör|an|fäl|lig** ADJ *Technik, Bauteil, Kraftwerk* susceptible to faults; *Gerät, Verkehrsmittel* liable to break down; *Zündung, Lenkung etc* unreliable;

(fig) Verhältnis shaky; **Stör|an|fäl|lig|keit** F (von Technik, Bauteil, Kraftwerk) susceptibility to faults; (von Gerät, Verkehrsmittel) liability to break down; (von Zündung, Lenkung etc) unreliability; (fig: von Verhältnis) shakiness

Storch [ʃtɔrç] M -(e)s, ⸗e [ˈʃtœrçə] stork; **wie der ~ im Salat gehen** (inf) to pick one's way carefully; **der ~ hat sie ins Bein gebissen** (dated hum) she's expecting a little stranger (hum)

Stor|chen|nest NT stork's nest

Stör|chin [ˈʃtœrçɪn] F -, -nen female stork

Storch|schna|bel M **a** (Bot) cranesbill **b** (Tech) pantograph

Store [ʃtoːɐ, ʃtoːɐ] M -s, -s usu pl net curtain; (Sw) shutters pl

stö|ren [ˈʃtøːrən] ✪ 27.7, 36.1 **VT** **a** (= beeinträchtigen) Schlaf, öffentliche Ordnung, Frieden etc to disturb; Verhältnis, Harmonie, Gesamteindruck etc to spoil; Rundfunkempfang to interfere with; (absichtlich) to jam; **jds Pläne ~** to interfere with sb's plans → auch **gestört**
b Handlungsablauf, Prozess, Vorlesung, Feier to disrupt
c (= unangenehm berühren) to disturb, to bother; **was mich an ihm/daran stört** what I don't like about him/it; **entschuldigen Sie, wenn ich Sie störe** I'm sorry to bother you, I'm sorry if I'm disturbing you; **störe mich jetzt nicht!** don't bother or disturb me now!; **lassen Sie sich nicht ~!** don't let me disturb you, don't mind me; **stört es Sie, wenn ich rauche?** do you mind if I smoke?, does it bother you if I smoke?; **würden Sie bitte aufhören zu rauchen, es stört mich** would you mind not smoking, I find it annoying; **das stört mich nicht** that doesn't bother me, I don't mind; **sie stört uns nicht** she doesn't bother us, we don't mind her; **sie lässt sich durch nichts ~** she doesn't let anything bother her
VR **sich an etw** (dat) **~** to be bothered about sth; **ich störe mich an seiner Unpünktlichkeit** I take exception to his unpunctuality
VI **a** (= lästig sein, im Weg sein) to get in the way; (= unterbrechen) to interrupt; (= Belästigung darstellen: Musik, Lärm etc) to be disturbing; **bitte nicht ~!** please do not disturb!; **ich möchte nicht ~** I don't want to be in the way or to be a nuisance, I don't want to interrupt; (in Privatsphäre etc) I don't want to intrude; **störe ich?** am I disturbing you?; **wenn ich nicht störe** if I'm not in the way, if I'm not disturbing you; **stört das sehr, wenn ich jetzt fernsehe?** would it disturb you if I watch television?; **etw als ~d empfinden** to find sth bothersome; **sich ~d bemerkbar machen** to be all too noticeable or obvious; **ein ~der Lärm** a disturbing noise; **ein ~der Umstand** a nuisance, an annoyance; **eine ~de Begleiterscheinung** a troublesome side effect; **ein ~der Besucher** an unwelcome visitor
b (= unangenehm auffallen) to spoil the effect, to stick out; **ein hübsches Gesicht, aber die große Nase stört doch etwas** a pretty face, though the big nose does spoil the effect

Stö|ren|fried [-friːt] M -(e)s, -e [-də], **Stö|rer** [ˈʃtøːrɐ] M -s, -, **Stö|re|rin** [-ərɪn] F -, -nen troublemaker

Stör-: Stör|fak|tor M source of friction, disruptive factor; **Stör|fall** M (in Kernkraftwerk etc) malfunction, accident; **stör|frei** ADJ free from interference; **Stör|ge|räusch** NT (Rad, TV) interference; **Stör|ma|nö|ver** NT disruptive action

Stor|ni pl von Storno

stor|nie|ren [ʃtɔrˈniːrən, st-] ✪ 47.4, 48.3 ptp **storniert** VTI (Comm) Auftrag, Reise, Flug to cancel; Buchungsfehler to reverse

Stor|no [ˈʃtɔrno, ˈst-] M OR NT -s, Storni [-ni] (Comm) (von Buchungsfehler) reversal; (von Auftrag) cancellation

Stor|no|ge|bühr F (Comm) cancellation fee or charge

stör|risch [ˈʃtœrɪʃ], **störrig** (rare) [ˈʃtœrɪç] ADJ stubborn, obstinate; Kind unmanageable, disobedient; Pferd restive, refractory; Haare unmanageable → Esel **ADV** **sich ~ verhalten** or **anstellen** to act stubborn

Stör|sen|der M (Rad) jamming transmitter, jammer

Stö|rung [ˈʃtøːrʊŋ] F -, -en **a** disturbance
b (von Ablauf, Verhandlungen etc) disruption; **die Demonstranten beschlossen die ~ der Parlamentssitzung** the demonstrators decided to disrupt the parliamentary session
c (= Verkehrsstörung) holdup; **es kam immer wieder zu ~en des Verkehrs** there were continual holdups (in the traffic), the traffic was continually held up
d (Tech) fault, trouble no indef art; **eine ~ trouble, a fault; **in der Leitung muss eine ~ sein** there must be a fault on the line
e (Astron) perturbation
f (Met) disturbance
g (Rad) interference; (absichtlich) jamming; **atmosphärische ~en** atmospherics pl
h (Med) disorder; **gesundheitliche/psychische ~en** physical/mental disorders; **nervöse ~en** nervous disorders, nervous trouble

Störungs-: Störungs|an|zei|ge F fault indicator; **Störungs|feu|er** NT (Mil) harassing fire; **stö|rungs|frei** ADJ trouble-free; (Rad) free from interference; **der Verkehr ist** or **läuft wieder ~** the traffic is moving freely again; **Stö|rungs|stel|le** F (Telec) faults service

Sto|ry [ˈstɔːri, ˈstɔri] F -, -s story; (inf: von Verkäufer etc) spiel (inf)

Stoß [ʃtoːs] M -es, ⸗e [ˈʃtøːsə] **a** push, shove (inf); (leicht) poke; (mit Faust) punch; (mit Fuß) kick; (mit Ellbogen) nudge, dig; (mit Kopf, Hörnern) butt; (= Dolchstoß) stab, thrust; (Kugelstoßen) put, throw; (Fechten) thrust; (= Schwimmstoß) stroke; (= Atemstoß) gasp; (= Koitusbewegung) thrust; **einen ~ vertragen können** (lit, fig) to be able to take a knock (or two); **sich** (dat) **or seinem Herzen einen ~ geben** to pluck up or take courage; **das gab ihm den letzten ~** (fig) that was the last straw or final blow (for him)
b (= Anprall) impact; (= Erdstoß) tremor; (eines Wagens) jolt, bump
c (Med) intensive course of drugs
d (= Stapel) pile, stack
e (Rail: = Schienenstoß) (rail) joint
f (Sew: = Stoßband) selvage; (Tech: = Kante) butt joint; **auf ~** edge to edge
g (Mil: = Feuerstoß) volley, burst of fire; (Mil: = Angriff) strike; (= Trompetenstoß etc) blast, blow (in +acc on)
h (Min) stope, face
i (Hunt) tail feathers pl

Stoß-: stoß|ar|tig ADJ Bewegung, Fahrt jerky; Lachen staccato; (= spasmodisch) spasmodic **ADV** fahren in starts and stops; sich fortbewegen jerkily; **~ atmen** to gasp for breath; **Stoß|band** [-bant] NT pl -bänder (Sew) selvage; **Stoß|dämp|fer** M (Aut) shock absorber

Stö|ßel [ˈʃtøːsl] M -s, -, pestle; (Aut: = Ventilstößel) tappet

stoß|emp|find|lich ADJ susceptible or sensitive to shock; Obst easily damaged; **diese Uhr ist ~** this watch is not shockproof

sto|ßen [ˈʃtoːsn] pret **stieß** [ʃtiːs], ptp **gestoßen** [ɡəˈʃtoːsn] **VT** **a** (= einen Stoß versetzen) to push, to shove (inf); (leicht) to poke; (mit Faust) to punch; (mit Fuß) to kick; (mit Ellbogen) to nudge, to dig (Brit), to poke; (mit Kopf, Hörnern) to butt; (= stechen) Dolch to plunge, to thrust; (vulg) to fuck (vulg), to shag (Brit sl), to poke (sl); **sich** (dat) **den Kopf** etc or **sich** (acc) **an etw** (dat) **~** to hit one's head etc; **jdm** or **jdn in die Seite ~** to nudge sb, to dig (Brit) or poke sb in the ribs; **jdn von sich ~** to push sb away; (fig) to cast sb aside; **jdn/etw zur Seite ~** to push sb/sth aside; (mit Fuß) to kick sb/sth aside or to one side; **er stieß den Ball mit dem Kopf ins Tor** he headed the ball into the goal (Brit),

he hit the ball into the goal with his head; **ein Loch ins Eis ~** to make or bore a hole in the ice **b** (= werfen) to push; (Sport) Kugel to put; **jdn von der Treppe/aus dem Zug ~** to push sb down the stairs/out of or off the train; **jdn aus dem Haus ~** (fig) to throw or turn sb out (of the house); **jdn ins Elend ~** (liter) to plunge sb into misery
c (= zerkleinern) Zimt, Pfeffer, Zucker to pound
d (Sw: = schieben, drücken) to push
VR to bump or bang or knock oneself; **sich an etw** (dat) **~** (lit) to bump etc oneself on or against sth; (fig) to take exception to sth, to disapprove of sth; **er stößt sich daran, wenn Männer Ohrringe tragen** he takes exception to men wearing earrings
VI **a** aux sein (= treffen, prallen) to run or bump into (auch fig); (= herabstoßen: Vogel) to swoop down (auf +acc); **an etw** (acc) **~** to bump into or hit sth; (= grenzen) to border on sth; **gegen etw ~** to run into sth; **zu jdm ~** to meet up with sb, to join sb; **auf jdn ~** to bump or run into sb; **auf etw** (acc) **~** (Straße) to lead into or onto sth; (Schiff) to hit sth, to run into or against sth; (fig: = entdecken) to come upon or across sth; **auf Erdöl ~** to strike oil; **auf Grundwasser ~** to discover underground water; **auf Widerstand ~** to meet with or encounter resistance; **auf Ablehnung/Zustimmung ~** to meet with disapproval/approval; **an seine Grenzen ~** to reach one's limits
b (mit den Hörnern) to butt (nach at)
c (Tech) to butt (an +acc against)
d (Gewichtheben) to jerk
e (old: = blasen) to blow, to sound → Horn b

Stoß-: stoß|fest ADJ shockproof; **Stoß|ge|bet** NT quick prayer; **ein ~ zum Himmel schicken** to say a quick prayer; **Stoß|ge|schäft** NT business with short periods of peak activity; (= Saisonarbeit) seasonal business; **Stoß|kar|ret|te** F (Sw: = Schubkarre) wheelbarrow; **Stoß|kraft** F force; (von Aufprall) impact; (Mil) combat strength; **Stoß|rich|tung** F (Mil, fig) thrust; **die ~ seines Angriffs ging auf ...** (fig) the main thrust of his attack was aimed at ...; **Stoß|seuf|zer** M deep sigh; **stoß|si|cher** ADJ shockproof; **Stoß|stan|ge** F (Aut) bumper

stößt [ʃtøːst] 3. pers sing pres von **stoßen**

Stoß-: Stoß|the|ra|pie F (Med) intensive course of drug treatment; **Stoß|trupp** M (Mil) raiding party; **Stoß|ver|kehr** M rush-hour (traffic); **Stoß|waf|fe** F thrust weapon; **stoß|wei|se** ADV **a** (= ruckartig) spasmodically, by fits and starts; **~ atmen** to pant; **die Autoschlange bewegte sich ~ vorwärts** the line of cars moved forward by fits and starts **b** (= stapelweise) by the pile; **Stoß|zahl** F (Phys) impact coefficient; **Stoß|zahn** M tusk; **Stoß|zeit** F (im Verkehr) rush hour; (in Geschäft etc) peak period, busy time

Stot|te|rei [ʃtɔtəˈrai] F -, -en (inf) stuttering; (fig) stuttering and stammering

Stot|te|rer [ˈʃtɔtərɐ] M -s, -, **Stot|te|rin** [-ərɪn] F -, -nen stutterer

stot|tern [ˈʃtɔtɐn] VTI to stutter; (Motor) to splutter; **leicht/stark ~** to have a slight/bad stutter, to stutter slightly/badly; **ins Stottern kommen** to start stuttering

Stot|zen [ˈʃtɔtsn] M -s, - (esp S Ger) **a** (= Baumstumpf) (tree) stump **b** (= Bottich) tub, vat

Stöv|chen [ˈʃtøːfçən] NT -s, - (teapot etc) warmer

StPO [este:pe:ˈloː] F - abbr von **Strafprozessordnung**

Str. abbr von **Straße** St

Stra|ban|zer [ʃtraˈbantsɐ] M -s, -, **Stra|ban|ze|rin** [-ərɪn] F -, -nen (Aus inf: = Strolch, Nichtsnutz) loafer (inf)

stracks [ʃtraks] ADV straight

Straf-: Straf|an|dro|hung F threat of punishment; **unter ~** on or under threat of penalty;

Straf|an|stalt F penal institution, prison; **Straf|an|trag** M action, legal proceedings *pl*; ~ **stellen** to institute legal proceedings; **einen ~ zurückziehen** to withdraw an action; **Straf|an|tritt** M commencement of (prison) sentence; **sein ~** the commencement of his (prison) sentence; **Straf|an|zei|ge** F ~ **gegen jdn erstatten** to bring a charge against sb; **Straf|ar|beit** F (*Sch*) punishment; (*schriftlich*) lines *pl*; **Straf|auf|he|bungs|grund** M (*Jur*) ground for exemption from punishment; **Straf|auf|schub** M (*Jur*) suspension of sentence; (*von Todesstrafe*) reprieve; **Straf|aus|schlie|ßungs|grund** M (*Jur*) ground for exemption from punishment; **Straf|aus|set|zung** F (*Jur*) suspension of sentence; ~ **zur Bewährung** probation; **Straf|bank** F *pl* -**bänke** (*Sport*) penalty bench, sin bin (*inf*)

straf|bar ADJ *Vergehen* punishable; ~**e Handlung** punishable offence (*Brit*) or offense (*US*); **das ist ~!** that's an offence (*Brit*) or offense (*US*); **sich ~ machen** to commit an offence (*Brit*) or offense (*US*)

Straf|bar|keit [ˈʃtraːfbaːɐkait] F -, *no pl* **er war sich** (*dat*) **der ~ seines Verhaltens nicht bewusst** he didn't realize that what he was doing was a punishable offence (*Brit*) or offense (*US*)

Straf-: Straf|ba|tail|lon NT (*Mil*) punishment battalion; **Straf|be|fehl** M (*Jur*) order of summary punishment; ~ **ergeht gegen ...** ... is being prosecuted; **Straf|be|scheid** M (*Jur*) notification of penalty for a tax offence (*Brit*) or offense (*US*); **Straf|be|stim|mung** F (*Jur*) penal laws *pl*, legal sanction

Stra|fe [ˈʃtraːfə] F -, -n punishment; (*Jur, Sport*) penalty; (= *Geldstrafe*) fine; (= *Gefängnisstrafe*) sentence; **etw bei ~ verbieten** to make sth punishable by law, to prohibit sth by law; **... bei ~ verboten** ... forbidden; **es ist bei ~ verboten, ...** it is a punishable *or* prosecutable offence (*Brit*) or offense (*US*) ...; **etw unter ~ stellen** to make sth a punishable offence (*Brit*) or offense (*US*); **unter ~ stehen** to be a punishable offence (*Brit*) or offense (*US*); **bei ~ von** on pain *or* penalty of; **seine ~ abbüßen** *or* **absitzen** *or* **ab-brummen** (*inf*) to serve one's sentence, to do one's time (*inf*); **eine ~ von drei Jahren Gefängnis** a three-year prison sentence; ~ **zahlen** to pay a fine; **100 Dollar ~ zahlen** to pay a 100 dollar fine, to be fined 100 dollars; **zur ~ as a punishment; ~ muss sein!** discipline is necessary; **seine verdiente** *or* **gerechte ~ bekommen** to get one's just deserts, to be duly punished; **die ~ folgte auf dem Fuße** punishment was swift to come; **das ist die (gerechte) ~ dafür(, dass du gelogen hast)** that's your punishment (for lying), that's what you get (for lying); **etw als ~ empfinden** (= *als lästig*) to find sth a bind (*Brit inf*) *or* chore; (= *als Bestrafung*) to see sth as a punishment; **es ist eine ~, ihr zuhören zu müssen** it's a pain in the neck having to listen to her (*inf*); **dieses Kind/Wetter ist eine ~** this child/weather is a pain (in the neck) (*inf*)

stra|fen [ˈʃtraːˑfn] VT (= *bestrafen*) to punish; **jdn (für etw/mit etw) ~** to punish sb (for sth/with sth); **mit etw gestraft sein** to be cursed with sth; **mit seinen Kindern ist er wirklich gestraft** his children are a real trial to him; **mit dieser Arbeit ist er wirklich gestraft** his work is a real bind (*Brit inf*) *or* a chore; **sie ist vom Schicksal gestraft** she is cursed by Fate, she has the curse of Fate upon her; **er ist gestraft genug** he has been punished enough → **Verachtung, Lüge** VR to punish; **orientalische Richter ~ hart** oriental judges give severe sentences; **das Stra-fen** punishment

stra|fend ADJ *attr* punitive; *Blick, Worte* reproachful; **die ~e Gerechtigkeit** (*liter*) avenging justice ADV **jdn ~ ansehen** to give sb a reproachful look

Straf-: Straf|ent|las|se|ne(r) [-ɛntlasˑənə] MF *decl as adj* ex-convict, discharged prisoner; **Straf|ent|las|sung** F discharge, release (from

prison); **Straf|er|lass** ▲ M remission (of sentence); **straf|er|schwe|rend** ADJ *Umstand* aggravating ADV **(als) ~ kam hinzu, dass ...** the offence (*Brit*) or offense (*US*) was compounded by the fact that ...; **als ~ wurde gewertet, dass der Täter keine Reue gezeigt hat** the accused's lack of remorse led to the passing of a heavier sentence; **straf|exer|zie|ren** *ptp* **strafexerziert** VI *insep* (*Mil*) to do punishment drill; **Straf|ex|pe|di|ti|on** F punitive expedition

straff [ʃtraf] ADJ *Seil* tight, taut; *Haut* smooth; *Busen* firm; *Haltung, Gestalt* erect; (= *straff sitzend*) *Hose etc* tight, close-fitting; (*fig*: = *streng*) *Disziplin, Organisation* strict, tight; *Politik* strict; *Zeitplan* tight ADV (= *stramm*) tightly; (= *streng*) *organisieren, reglementieren* strictly; ~ **sitzen** to fit tightly, to be close-fitting *or* tight; **etw ~ spannen** *or* **ziehen** to tighten sth; *Decke, Laken etc* to pull sth tight; **die Leine muss ~ gespannt sein** the line has to be tight; **das Haar ~ zurückste-cken** to tie one's hair back tightly

straff|fäl|lig ADJ ~ **werden** to commit a criminal offence (*Brit*) or offense (*US*); **wenn Sie wieder ~ werden ...** if you commit a further offence (*Brit*) or offense (*US*) ...

Straf|fäl|li|ge(r) [ˈʃtraːffɛlɪɡə] MF *decl as adj* offender

straf|fen [ˈʃtrafn] VT to tighten; (= *spannen*) *Seil, Leine auch* to tauten; (= *raffen*) *Handlung, Darstellung* to make more taut, to tighten up; **sich** (*dat*) **die Gesichtshaut ~ lassen** to have a face-lift; **sich** (*dat*) **den Busen ~ lassen** to have one's breasts lifted; **die Zügel ~** (*fig*) to tighten the reins VR to tighten, to become taut; (*Haut*) to become smooth; (*Busen*) to become firm; (= *sich aufrichten*) to stiffen

Straff|heit F -, *no pl* (*von Haut*) smoothness; (*von Busen*) firmness; (*fig*: = *Strenge*) strictness

Straf-: straf|frei ADJ ADV not subject to prosecution; ~ **bleiben** *or* **ausgehen** to go unpunished; **Straf|frei|heit** F immunity from prosecution; **Straf|ge|bühr** F surcharge; **Straf|ge|fan|ge|ne(r)** MF *decl as adj* detainee, prisoner; **Straf|geld** NT fine; **Straf|ge|richt** NT criminal court; **ein ~ abhalten** to hold a trial; **das göttliche** *or* **himmlische ~** divine judgement; **das ~ Gottes** *or* **des Himmels** (*liter*) the judgement of God; **ein ~ brach über ihn herein** (*fig*) the wrath of God descended upon him; **Straf|ge|richts|bar|keit** F criminal jurisdiction; **Straf|ge|setz** NT criminal *or* penal law; **Straf|ge|setz|buch** NT Criminal *or* Penal Code; **Straf|ge|setz|ge|bung** F penal legislation; **Straf|ge|walt** F legal authority; **Straf|jus|tiz** F criminal justice *no art*; **Straf|kam|mer** F division for criminal matters (of a court); **Straf|ko|lo|nie** F penal colony; **Straf|kom|pa|nie** F (*Mil*) punishment battalion; **Straf|la|ger** NT disciplinary *or* punishment camp

sträf|lich [ˈʃtrɛːflɪç] ADJ (*lit, fig*) criminal ADV *vernachlässigen etc* criminally; **sich ~ blamieren** to make a terrible fool of oneself, to make a proper charlie of oneself (*Brit inf*)

Sträf|ling [ˈʃtrɛːflɪŋ] M -s, -e prisoner

Sträf|lings|klei|dung F prison clothing

Straf-: straf|los ADJ, ADV = **straffrei**; **Straf|man|dat** NT ticket; **Straf|maß** NT sentence; **das höchste ~** the maximum penalty *or* sentence; **straf|mil|dernd** ADJ extenuating, mitigating; **Straf|mil|de|rung** F mitigation *or* commutation of the/a sentence; **Straf|mi|nu|te** F (*Sport*) penalty minute; **straf|mün|dig** ADJ of the age of criminal responsibility; **ein kleines Kind ist nicht ~** a small child is under the age of criminal responsibility; **Straf|mün|dig|keit** F age of criminal responsibility; **Straf|nach|lass** ▲ M remission; **Straf|por|to** NT excess postage; **Straf|pre|digt** F reprimand, dressing-down (*inf*); **jdm eine ~ halten** to give sb a lecture *or* dressing-down (*inf*); **Straf|pro|zess** ▲ M criminal proceedings *pl*, criminal action *or* case; **Straf|pro|zess|ord-**

nung ▲ F code of criminal procedure; **Straf|punkt** M (*Sport*) penalty point; **Straf|rah-men** M range of sentences; **Straf|raum** M (*Sport*) penalty area *or* (*Ftbl auch*) box; **Straf|recht** NT criminal law; **Straf|recht|ler** [-rɛçtlɐ] M -s, -, **Straf|recht|le|rin** [-ərɪn] F -, -**nen** expert in criminal law, penologist; **straf|recht|lich** ADJ criminal; **das ist aber kein ~es Problem** but that is not a problem of criminal law ADV **jdn/etw ~ verfolgen** *or* **belangen** to prosecute sb/sth; **Straf|rechts|pfle|ge** F criminal justice; **Straf|re|de** F reprimand, dressing-down (*inf*); **Straf|re|gis|ter** NT police *or* criminal records *pl*; (*hum inf*) record; **ein Eintrag im ~** an entry in the police or criminal records *pl*; **einen Eintrag im ~ haben** to have a record; **er hat ein langes ~** he has a long (criminal) record; (*hum inf*) he's got a bad record; **Straf|rich|ter(in)** M(F) criminal judge (*Brit*), judge who hears criminal cases; **Straf|sa|che** F criminal matter; **Straf|schuss** ▲ M (*Sport*) penalty (shot); **Straf|se|nat** M criminal division (*of the Court of Appeal and Federal Supreme Court*); **Straf|stoß** M (*Ftbl etc*) penalty (kick); (*Hockey etc*) penalty (shot); **Straf|tat** F criminal offence (*Brit*) or offense (*US*), criminal act; **Straf|tat|be|stand** M (*Jur*) **das erfüllt den ~ der Verleumdung** *etc* that constitutes calumny *or* libel *etc*; **Straf|tä|ter(in)** M(F) offender, criminal; **Straf|um|wand|lung** F (*Jur*) commutation of a/the penalty; **Straf|ur|teil** NT (*Jur*) conviction and sentence, penal judgement; **Straf|ver|bü|ßung** F serving of a sentence; **nach seiner ~** after serving his sentence; **Straf|ver|fah|ren** NT criminal proceedings *pl*, criminal action *or* case; **Straf|ver|fol|gung** F criminal prosecution; **Straf|ver|fü|gung** F (*Jur*) ticket; **straf|ver|schär|fend** ADJ, ADV = **straferschwerend**; **Straf|ver|schär|fung** F increase in the severity of the/a penalty *or* sentence; **das führte zu einer ~** this led to the passing of a heavier sentence; **straf|ver|set-zen** *ptp* **strafversetzt** VT *insep Beamte* to transfer for disciplinary reasons; **Straf|ver|set-zung** F (disciplinary) transfer; **Straf|ver|tei-di|ger(in)** M(F) counsel for the defence (*Brit*) *or* defense (*US*), defence (*Brit*) *or* defense (*US*) counsel *or* lawyer; **Straf|voll|stre|ckung** F execution of the/a sentence; **Straf|voll|zug** M penal system; **offener ~** non-confinement; **Straf|voll|zugs|an|stalt** F (*form*) penal institution; **straf|wür|dig** ADJ (*form*) punishable; **Straf|wurf** M (*Sport*) penalty throw; **Straf|zet|tel** M (*Jur*) ticket

Strahl [ʃtraːl] M -(e)s, -en a (*lit, fig*) ray; (= *Lichtstrahl*) ray *or* shaft *or* beam (of light); (= *Sonnenstrahl*) shaft of light; (= *Radiostrahl, Laserstrahl etc*) beam; (*poet*: = *das Leuchten*) light; **im ~ einer Taschenlampe** by the light *or* in the beam of a torch; **ein ~ der Hoffnung** (*liter*) a ray of hope b (= *Wasserstrahl, Luftstrahl*) jet

Strahl|an|trieb M (*Aviat*) jet propulsion

Strah|le|mann M *pl* -**männer** (*inf*) golden boy (*inf*)

strah|len [ˈʃtraːlən] VI a (*Sonne, Licht etc*) to shine; (*Sender*) to beam; (= *glühen*) to glow (*vor +dat* with); (*Heizofen etc*) to radiate; (*radioaktiv*) to give off radioactivity b (= *leuchten*) to gleam, to sparkle; (*fig*) (*Gesicht*) to beam; (*Augen*) to shine; **der Himmel strahlte** the sky was bright; **das ganze Haus strahlte vor Sauberkeit** the whole house was sparkling clean; **was strahlst du so?** what are you beaming about?, what are you so happy about?; **er strahlte vor Freude** he was beaming with happiness; **er strahlte (übers ganze Gesicht)** he was beaming all over his face → **strahlend**

sträh|len [ˈʃtrɛːlən] VT (*S Ger, Sw*) to comb

Strahlen-: Strah|len|be|hand|lung F (*Med*) ray treatment; **Strah|len|be|las|tung** F radiation; **Strah|len|bi|o|lo|gie** F radiobiology; **Strah|len|bre|chung** F refraction; **Strah|len|bün|del** NT pencil of rays

strah|lend ADJ radiant; *Gesicht auch* beaming; *Wetter, Tag* bright, glorious; *Farben* brilliant, bright; (= *radioaktiv*) radioactive; **~es Lachen** beaming smile, beam; **mit ~en Augen** with bright *or* shining eyes; **mit ~em Gesicht** with a beaming face; (*von Frau, Kind auch*) with a radiant face ADV **jdn ~ ansehen** (= *lächelnd*) to beam at sb; (= *glücklich*) to look at sb, beaming *or* radiant with happiness; **der Tag war ~ schön, es war ein ~ schöner Tag** it was a glorious day

Strah|len-: Strah|len|do|sis F dose of radiation; **strah|len|för|mig** ADJ radial ADV **sich ~ ausbreiten** to radiate out; **~ von etw wegführen** to radiate from sth; **strah|len|ge|schä|digt** [-gəʃɛːdɪçt] ADJ suffering from radiation damage; *Organ* damaged by radiation; **die Strahlengeschädigten** the radiation victims; **Strah|len|heil|kun|de** F radiotherapy; **strah|len|krank** ADJ radiation sick; **Strah|len|kran|ke(r)** MF *decl as adj* person suffering from radiation sickness; **Strah|len|krank|heit** F radiation sickness; **Strah|len|op|fer** NT radiation victim; **Strah|len|pilz** M ray fungus; **Strah|len|quel|le** F source of radiation; **Strah|len|schä|den** PL radiation injuries *pl*; (*von Organ auch*) radiation damage *sing*; **Strah|len|schutz** M radiation protection; **Strah|len|the|ra|pie** F radiotherapy; **Strah|len|tier|chen** NT radiolarian; **Strah|len|tod** M death through radiation; **strah|len|ver|seucht** [-fɛɐ̯-zɔyçt] ADJ contaminated (with radiation); **Strah|len|waf|fe** F laser weapon

Strah|ler [ˈʃtraːlɐ] M -s, - (= *Lampe*) spotlight

strah|lig [ˈʃtraːlɪç] ADJ (*Bot*) radial

-strah|lig ADJ *suf* **ein zweistrahliges/vierstrahliges Düsenflugzeug** a two-engined/four-engined jet plane

Strahl-: Strahl|kraft F radiation intensity; (*fig*) (*von Stimme, Begriff*) force, power; (*von Mensch*) charisma; **Strahl|ma|te|rial** NT radioactive material; **Strahl|trieb|werk** NT jet engine; **Strahl|tur|bi|ne** F turbojet

Strah|lung [ˈʃtraːlʊŋ] F -, -en radiation

Strah|lungs-: strah|lungs|arm ADJ *Bildschirm, Monitor* low-radiation; **Strah|lungs|ener|gie** F radiation *or* radiant energy; **Strah|lungs|gür|tel** M Van Allen belt; **der ~ der Erde** the Van Allen belt; **Strah|lungs|in|ten|si|tät** F dose of radiation; **Strah|lungs|wär|me** F radiant heat

Strahl|ver|fah|ren NT (jet-)blasting

Strähn|chen [ˈʃtrɛːnçən] NT -s, - streak

Sträh|ne [ˈʃtrɛːnə] F -, -n, (*Aus*) **Strähn** [ʃtrɛːn] M -(e)s, -e (= *Haarsträhne*) strand; (*Längenmaß,* = *Wollsträhne, Garnsträhne*) skein, hank; **ich habe schon eine weiße ~** I already have a white streak

sträh|nig [ˈʃtrɛːnɪç] ADJ *Haar* straggly ADV **das Haar fiel ihr ~ auf die Schultern** her hair straggled down over her shoulders

Stra|min [ʃtraˈmiːn] M -s, -e even-weave (embroidery) fabric

stramm [ʃtram] ADJ (= *straff*) *Seil, Hose* tight; *Seil auch* taut; (= *schneidig*) *Haltung, Soldat* erect, upright; (= *kräftig, drall*) *Mädchen, Junge* strapping; *Junge, Beine* sturdy; *Brust* firm; (*inf*) (= *tüchtig*) *Marsch, Arbeit* strenuous, tough, hard; *Tag, Programm* packed; (= *überzeugt*) staunch; (*dated inf*: = *betrunken*) tight (*inf*); **~e Haltung annehmen** to stand to attention; **~er Max** *open sandwich of boiled ham and fried egg* (*mit Hackfleisch*) *open sandwich of seasoned raw minced pork with egg and onion* ADV binden tightly; **~ sitzen** to be tight *or* close-fitting, to fit tightly; **~ arbeiten** (*inf*) to work hard, to get down to it (*inf*); **~ marschieren** (*inf*) to march hard; **~ an etw** (*dat*) **festhalten** to stick to sth; **~ konservativ** (*inf*) staunchly conservative, true blue (*Brit*); **das Land wird ~ kommunistisch regiert** (*inf*) the country has a staunchly communist government; **die Politi-**

ker sind weiter ~ auf Atomkurs (*inf*) the politicians are continuing to support nuclear power unreservedly

stramm-: stramm+ste|hen VI *sep irreg* (*Mil inf*) to stand to attention; **stramm zie|hen** ▲ VT *sep irreg Seil, Hose* to pull tight, to tighten; *Socken* to pull up; **jdm den Hosenboden** *or* **die Hosen ~** (*inf*) to give sb a good hiding (*inf*)

Stram|pel|an|zug M romper suit

Stram|pel|hös|chen [-høːsçən] NT rompers *pl*

stram|peln [ˈʃtrampln] VI **a** (*mit Beinen*) to flail *or* thrash about; (*Baby*) to thrash about; **das Baby strampelte mit Armen und Beinen** the baby was kicking its feet and waving its arms about **b** *aux sein* (*inf*: = *Rad fahren*) to pedal **c** (*inf*: = *sich abrackern*) to (sweat and) slave

Stram|pel|sack M (*für Säuglinge*) carry-nest (*Brit*), pup sack (*US*)

Stram|pler [ˈʃtramplɐ] M romper suit

Strand [ʃtrant] M -(e)s, ⸚e [ˈʃtrɛndə] (= *Meeresstrand*) beach, strand (*poet*); (= *Seeufer*) shore; (*poet*: = *Flussufer*) bank; **am ~** (= *am Meer*) on the beach; (= *am Seeufer*) on the shore; **auf ~ geraten** *or* **laufen** to run aground; **auf ~ setzen** to beach

Strand-: Strand|an|zug M beach suit; **Strand|bad** NT (seawater) swimming pool; (= *Badeort*) bathing resort; **Strand|dis|tel** F sea holly

stran|den [ˈʃtrandn] VI *aux sein* to run aground, to be stranded; (*fig*) to fail

Strand-: Strand|gers|te F sea barley; **Strand|gut** NT , *no pl* (*lit, fig*) flotsam and jetsam; **Strand|ha|fer** M marram (grass); **Strand|hau|bit|ze** F **blau** *or* **voll wie eine ~** (*inf*) as drunk as a lord (*Brit inf*) *or* a sailor (*US inf*), rolling drunk (*inf*); **Strand|ho|tel** NT seaside hotel; **Strand|kie|fer** F (*Bot*) maritime pine, cluster pine; **Strand|klei|dung** F beachwear; **Strand|korb** M wicker beach chair with a hood; **Strand|läu|fer** M (*Orn*) sandpiper; **Strand|pro|me|na|de** F promenade; **Strand|raub** M beachcombing; **Strand|räu|ber(in)** M(F) beachcomber; **Strand|recht** NT right of salvage

Stran|dung [ˈʃtrandʊŋ] F -, -en running a-ground

Strand-: Strand|vogt M beach warden (*Brit*); **Strand|wa|che** F lifeguard; (= *Dienst*) lifeguard duty; **Strand|wäch|ter(in)** M(F) lifeguard; **Strand|weg** M beach path

Strang [ʃtraŋ] M -(e)s, ⸚e [ˈʃtrɛŋə] (= *Nervenstrang, Muskelstrang*) cord; (= *DNA-Strang*) strand; (= *Strick*) rope; (= *Wollstrang, Garnstrang*) hank, skein; (*am Pferdegeschirr*) trace, tug; (*Rail*: = *Schienenstrang*) track; **jdn zum Tod durch den ~ verurteilen** to sentence sb to be hanged; **der Tod durch den ~** death by hanging; **an einem** *or* **am gleichen** *or* **an demselben ~ ziehen** (*fig*) to pull together; **über die Stränge schlagen** *or* **hauen** (*inf*) to run riot *or* wild (*inf*), to get carried a-way (*inf*) → **reißen VI a**

Stran|gu|la|ti|on [ʃtraŋgulaˈtsi̯oːn, st-] F -, -en strangulation

stran|gu|lie|ren [ʃtraŋguˈliːrən, st-] *ptp* **strangu-liert** VT to strangle

Stra|pa|ze [ʃtraˈpaːtsə] F -, -n strain

stra|paz|fä|hig ADJ (*Aus*) = strapazierfähig

stra|pa|zie|ren [ʃtrapaˈtsiːrən] *ptp* **strapaziert** VT to be a strain on, to take a lot out of; *Schuhe, Kleidung* to be hard on, to give a lot of hard wear to; (*fig*) *Redensart, Begriff* to flog (to death) (*inf*); *Nerven* to strain, to try; *Geduld* to try; **er sah strapaziert aus** he looked worn out *or* exhausted VR to tax oneself

stra|pa|zier|fä|hig ADJ *Schuhe, Kleidung, Material* hard-wearing, durable; (*fig inf*) *Nerven* strong

Stra|pa|zier|fä|hig|keit F durability; **das übersteigt die ~ meiner Nerven** that's more than my nerves can stand

stra|pa|zi|ös [ʃtrapaˈtsi̯øːs] ADJ (*lit, fig*) wearing, exhausting

Straps [ʃtraps] M -es, -e suspender belt (*Brit*), garter belt (*US*)

Strass ▲ [ʃtras] M - *or* -es, *no pl* paste

straß|auf [ʃtras'ʔaʊf] ADV ~, **straßab** up and down the street

Straß|burg [ˈʃtraːsbʊrk] NT -s Strasbourg, Strassburg

Sträß|chen [ˈʃtrɛːsçən] NT -s, - *dim von* **Straße**

Stra|ße [ˈʃtraːsə] F -, -n **a** road; (*in Stadt, Dorf*) street, road; (= *kleine Landstraße*) lane; **an der ~** by the roadside; **auf die ~ gehen** (*lit*) to go out on the street; (*als Demonstrant*) to take to the streets, to go out into the streets; (*als Prostituierte*) to go on *or* walk the streets; **auf der ~ liegen** (*fig inf*) to be out of work; (*als Wohnungsloser*) to be on the streets; (*als Faulenzer, Asozialer etc*) to hang around the streets, to hang around street corners; (*Kraftfahrer*) to have broken down; **auf die ~ gesetzt werden** (*inf*) to be turned out (on-to the streets); (*als Arbeiter*) to be sacked (*Brit inf*), to get the sack (*Brit inf*), to be *or* get fired (*inf*); **über die ~ gehen** to cross (the road/street); **er wohnt drei ~n weiter** he lives three blocks further on; **mit etw auf die ~ gehen** to take to the streets about sth; **er ist aus unserer ~** he's from our street; **davon spricht die ganze ~** the whole street's talking about it; **die ~n der Großstadt** the city streets; **Verkauf über die ~** takeaway (*Brit*) *or* takeout (*US*) sales; (*von Getränken*) off-licence sales *pl* (*Brit*), package store sales *pl* (*US*); **etw über die ~ verkaufen** to sell sth to take away (*Brit*) *or* to take out (*US*); **das Geld liegt auf der ~** money is there for the asking; **das Geld liegt nicht auf der ~** money doesn't grow on trees; **ein Mädchen von der ~** a lady of pleasure; **der Mann auf der ~** (*fig*) the man in the street

b (= *Meerenge*) strait(s *pl*); **die ~ von Dover/Gibraltar/Messina** *etc* the Straits of Dover/Gibraltar/Messina *etc*

c (= *Mob, Pöbel*) **die ~** the masses *pl*, the rabble; **die Herrschaft der ~** mob rule

d (*Tech*) (= *Fertigungsstraße*) (production) line; (= *Walzstraße*) train

Stra|ßen-: Stra|ßen|an|zug M lounge suit (*Brit*), business suit (*US*); **Stra|ßen|ar|bei|ten** PL roadworks *pl*; **Stra|ßen|ar|bei|ter(in)** M(F) roadworker

Stra|ßen|bahn F (= *Wagen*) tram (*esp Brit*), streetcar (*US*); (= *Netz*) tramway(s) (*esp Brit*), streetcar system (*US*); **mit der ~** by tram (*esp Brit*) *or* streetcar (*US*)

Stra|ßen|bah|ner [-baːnɐ] M -s, -, **Stra|ßen|bah|ne|rin** [-ərɪn] F -, -nen (*inf*) tramway (*esp Brit*) *or* streetcar (*US*) employee

Stra|ßen|bahn-: Stra|ßen|bahn|fah|rer(in) M(F) , **Stra|ßen|bahn|füh|rer(in)** M(F) tram (*esp Brit*) *or* streetcar (*US*) driver; **Stra|ßen|bahn|hal|te|stel|le** F tram (*esp Brit*) *or* streetcar (*US*) stop; **Stra|ßen|bahn|li|nie** F tramline (*esp Brit*), tram route (*esp Brit*), streetcar line (*US*); **mit der ~ 11 fahren** to take the number 11 tram (*esp Brit*) *or* streetcar (*US*); **Stra|ßen|bahn|schaff|ner(in)** M(F) tram (*esp Brit*) *or* streetcar (*US*) conductor/conductress; **Stra|ßen|bahn|schie|ne** F tramline (*esp Brit*), tram (*esp Brit*) *or* streetcar (*US*) rail; **Stra|ßen|bahn|wa|gen** M tram (*esp Brit*), streetcar (*US*)

Stra|ßen-: Stra|ßen|bau M , *no pl* road construction; **Stra|ßen|bau|amt** NT highways *or* (*städtisch*) roads department, ≈ Department of Transportation (*US*); **Stra|ßen|bau|ar|bei|ten** PL roadworks *pl*; **Stra|ßen|be|kannt|schaft** F passing *or* nodding acquaintance; **Stra|ßen|be|lag** M road surface; **Stra|ßen|be|leuch|tung** F street lighting; **Stra|ßen|be|nut|zungs|ge|bühr** F (road) toll; **Stra|ßen|bild** NT street scene; **Stra|ßen|bö|schung** F embankment; **Stra|ßen|brei|te** F width of a/the road; **Stra|ßen|ca|fé** NT pave-

---

ment café (*Brit*), sidewalk café (*US*); **Stra|ßen|de|cke** F road surface; **Stra|ßen|dir|ne** F (*dated, form*) common prostitute, streetwalker; **Stra|ßen|dorf** NT linear village; **Stra|ßen|ecke** F street corner; **ein paar ~n weiter** a few blocks further; **Stra|ßen|ein|mün|dung** F road junction; **Stra|ßen|fe|ger** [-fe:gɐ] M **-s, -**, **Stra|ßen|fe|ge|rin** [-ərɪn] F **-, -nen** road sweeper; **Stra|ßen|fest** NT street party; **Stra|ßen|füh|rung** F route; **Stra|ßen|ga|be|lung** F fork (in a/the road); **Stra|ßen|glät|te** F slippery road surface; **Stra|ßen|gra|ben** M ditch; **Stra|ßen|han|del** M street trading; **Stra|ßen|händ|ler(in)** M(F) street trader; (*mit Obst, Fisch etc auch*) costermonger (*Brit*); **Stra|ßen|jun|ge** M (*pej*) street urchin, street Arab (*Brit liter*); **Stra|ßen|kampf** M street fighting *no pl*; **ein ~** a street fight or battle; **Stra|ßen|kämp|fer(in)** M(F) street fighter; **Stra|ßen|kar|te** F road map; **Stra|ßen|keh|rer** [-ke:rɐ] M **-s, -**, **Stra|ßen|keh|re|rin** [-ərɪn] F **-, -nen** road sweeper; **Stra|ßen|klei|dung** F streetwear; **Stra|ßen|kon|trol|le** F (road) checkpoint; **Stra|ßen|kreu|zer** M (*inf*) limo (*inf*), limousine; **Stra|ßen|kreu|zung** F crossroads *sing or pl*, intersection (*US*); **Stra|ßen|kri|mi|na|li|tät** F street crime; **Stra|ßen|la|ge** F (*Aut*) road holding; **dieses Auto hat eine gute ~** this car holds the road well, this car has good road holding; **Stra|ßen|lärm** M street noise; **Stra|ßen|la|ter|ne** F streetlamp; **Stra|ßen|mäd|chen** NT streetwalker, prostitute; **Stra|ßen|meis|te|rei** [-maɪstə'raɪ] F **-, -en** road maintenance department (*Brit*), ≈ City Road Maintenance Office (*US*); **Stra|ßen|musi|kant(in)** M(F) street musician; **Stra|ßen|na|me** M street name; **Stra|ßen|netz** NT road network or system; **Stra|ßen|rand** M roadside; **Stra|ßen|raub** M mugging (*inf*), street robbery; (*durch Wegelagerer*) highway robbery; **Stra|ßen|räu|ber(in)** M(F) mugger (*inf*), thief; (= *Wegelagerer*) highwayman; **Stra|ßen|rei|ni|gung** F street cleaning; **Stra|ßen|ren|nen** NT road race; **Stra|ßen|samm|lung** F street collection; **Stra|ßen|sän|ger** M street singer; **Stra|ßen|schä|den** PL damage *sing* to the road surface; **„Achtung ~"** "uneven road surface"; **Stra|ßen|schild** NT *pl* **-schilder** street sign; **Stra|ßen|schlacht** F street battle; **Stra|ßen|schuh** M walking shoe; **Stra|ßen|sei|te** F side of a/the road; **Stra|ßen|sper|re** F roadblock; **Stra|ßen|sper|rung** F closing (off) of a/the road; **eine ~ vornehmen** to close (off) the road; **Stra|ßen|strich** M (*inf*) walking the streets, streetwalking; (*Gegend*) red-light district; **auf den ~ gehen** to walk the streets; **Stra|ßen|the|a|ter** NT street theatre (*Brit*) or theater (*US*); **Stra|ßen|tun|nel** M (road) tunnel; **Stra|ßen|über|füh|rung** F footbridge, pedestrian bridge; **Stra|ßen|un|ter|füh|rung** F underpass, subway; **Stra|ßen|ver|hält|nis|se** PL road conditions *pl*; **Stra|ßen|ver|kauf** M street trading; (= *Außerhausverkauf*) takeaway (*Brit*) or takeout (*US*) sales *pl*; (*von alkoholischen Getränken*) off-licence sales *pl* (*Brit*), package store sales *pl* (*US*); (= *Verkaufsstelle*) takeaway (*Brit*), takeout (*US*); (*für alkoholische Getränke*) off-licence (*Brit*), package store (*US*); **Zeitungen werden im ~ angeboten** newspapers are sold on the streets; **Stra|ßen|ver|käu|fer(in)** M(F) street seller or vendor; (*von Obst, Fisch etc*) street seller or vendor, costermonger (*Brit*); **Stra|ßen|ver|kehr** M traffic; **Stra|ßen|ver|kehrs|ord|nung** F ≈ Highway Code (*Brit*), traffic rules and regulations *pl*; **Stra|ßen|ver|zeich|nis** NT index of street names; (*in Buchform auch*) street directory; **Stra|ßen|wacht** F road patrol; **Stra|ßen|wal|ze** F roadroller, steamroller; **Stra|ßen|zoll** M road toll; **Stra|ßen|zug** M street; **Stra|ßen|zu|stand** M road conditions *pl*; **Stra|ßen|zu|stands|be|richt** M road report

Sträß|lein ['ʃtrɛ:slaɪn] NT **-s, -** *dim von* **Straße**

Strass|schmuck ▲ ['ʃtras-] M paste jewellery (*Brit*) *no pl*, paste jewelry (*US*) *no pl*

Stra|te|ge [ʃtra'te:gə, st-] M **-n, -n**, **Stra|te|gin** [-'te:gɪn] F **-, -nen** strategist; **na, alter ~** (*fig inf*) well, you old fox (*inf*)

Stra|te|gie [ʃtrate'gi:, st-] F **-, -n** [-'gi:ən] strategy

Stra|te|gie|pa|pier NT (*Pol*) strategy document

stra|te|gisch [ʃtra'te:gɪʃ, st-] ADJ strategic **ADV** strategically

Stra|ti|fi|ka|ti|on [ʃtratifika'tsio:n, st-] F **-, -en** stratification

stra|ti|fi|zie|ren [ʃtratifi'tsi:rən, st-] *ptp* **stratifiziert** VT (*Geol, Agr*) to stratify

Stra|to|sphä|re [ʃtrato'sfɛ:rə, st-] F , *no pl* stratosphere

stra|to|sphä|risch [ʃtrato'sfɛ:rɪʃ, st-] ADJ stratospheric

Stra|tus ['ʃtra:tʊs, 'st-] M **-, Strati** [-ti], **Stra|tus|wol|ke** F (*Met*) stratus (cloud)

sträu|ben ['ʃtrɔʏbn] **VR** **a** (*Haare, Fell*) to stand on end; (*Gefieder*) to become ruffled; **der Katze sträubt sich das Fell** (*aggressiv*) the cat raises its hackles; **da ~ sich einem die Haare** it's enough to make your hair stand on end **b** (*fig*) to resist (*gegen etw* sth); **die Feder/die Zunge sträubt sich, das zu schildern** (*geh*) one hesitates to put it down on paper/to say it; **es sträubt sich alles in mir, das zu tun** I am most reluctant to do it **VT** *Gefieder* to ruffle

Strauch [ʃtraux] M **-(e)s, Sträucher** ['ʃtrɔʏçɐ] bush, shrub

Strauch|dieb(in) M(F) (*old*) footpad (*old*), thief

strau|cheln ['ʃtrauxln] VI *aux sein* **a** (*geh*: = *stolpern*) to stumble, to trip **b** (*fig*) (= *auf die schiefe Bahn geraten*) to transgress; (*moralisch*) to go astray; **ins Straucheln kommen** or **geraten** (*fig*) to come to grief; **an etw** (*dat*) **~** to come to grief over sth; **die Gestrauchelten** the reprobates

Strauch-: Strauch|rit|ter M (*old*) footpad (*old*), thief; **Strauch|to|ma|te** F vine-ripened tomato, tomato ripened on the vine; **Strauch|werk** NT , *no pl* (= *Gebüsch*) bushes *pl*, shrubs *pl*; (= *Gestrüpp*) undergrowth

Strauß¹ [ʃtraus] M **-es, -e** ostrich; **wie der Vogel ~** like an ostrich

Strauß² M **-es, Sträuße** ['ʃtrɔʏsə] **a** bunch; (= *Blumenstrauß*) bunch of flowers; (*als Geschenk*) bouquet, bunch of flowers; (= *kleiner Strauß, Biedermeierstrauß*) posy; **einen ~ binden** to make up a bouquet **b** (*old*: = *Kampf, auch fig*) struggle, battle; **mit jdm einen harten ~ ausfechten** (*lit, fig*) to have a hard struggle or fight with sb

Sträuß|chen ['ʃtrɔʏsçən] NT **-s, -** *dim von* **Strauß²**

Strau|ßen|fe|der F ostrich feather or plume

Strau|ßen|wirt|schaft F (*S Ger, Aus*) = **Besenwirtschaft**

Strauß|vö|gel PL struthionidae *pl* (*spec*), struthioids *pl* (*spec*)

Strauß|wirt|schaft F = **Straußenwirtschaft**

Strea|mer ['stri:mɐ] M **-s, -** (*Comput*) streamer

Streb [ʃtre:p] M **-(e)s, -e** [-bə] (*Min*) coalface; **im ~ arbeiten** to work at the coalface

Stre|be ['ʃtre:bə] F **-, -n** brace, strut; (= *Deckenstrebe*) joist; (*von Flugzeug*) strut

Stre|be-: Stre|be|bal|ken M diagonal brace or strut; **Stre|be|bo|gen** M flying buttress

stre|ben ['ʃtre:bn] VI (*geh*) **a** (= *den Drang haben, sich bemühen*) to strive (*nach, an +acc, zu* for); (*Sch pej*) to swot (*inf*); **danach ~, etw zu tun** to strive to do sth; **die Pflanze strebt nach dem Licht** the plant seeks the light; **der Fluss strebt zum Meer** the river flows towards (*Brit*) or toward (*US*) the sea; **in die Ferne ~** to be drawn to distant parts; **sich ~d bemühen** to strive one's hardest **b** *aux sein* (= *sich bewegen*)

---

nach or **zu etw ~** to make one's way to sth; (*Armee*) to push toward(s) sth; **aus etw ~** to make one's way out of sth **c** *aux sein* **in die Höhe** or **zum Himmel ~** to rise or soar aloft

Stre|ben NT **-s**, *no pl* **a** (= *Drängen, Sinnen*) striving (*nach* for); (*nach Ruhm, Geld*) aspiration (*nach* to); (= *Bemühen*) efforts *pl* **b** (= *Tendenz*) shift, movement

Stre|be|pfei|ler M buttress

Stre|ber ['ʃtre:bɐ] M **-s, -**, **Stre|be|rin** [-ərɪn] F **-, -nen** (*pej inf*) pushy person; (*Sch*) swot (*Brit inf*), grind (*US inf*)

Stre|be|rei [ʃtre:bə'raɪ] F **-**, *no pl* (*pej inf*) pushiness; (*Sch*) swotting (*Brit inf*), cramming (*inf*)

Stre|ber-: Stre|ber|na|tur F (*pej*) pushy nature; (*Mensch*) pushy person; (*Sch*) swot (*Brit inf*), grind (*US inf*); **Stre|ber|tum** ['ʃtre:bɐtu:m] NT **-s**, *no pl* pushiness (*inf*); (*Sch*) swotting (*Brit inf*), cramming (*inf*)

streb|sam ['ʃtre:pza:m] ADJ assiduous, industrious

Streb|sam|keit F **-**, *no pl* assiduity, industriousness

Stre|bung ['ʃtre:bʊŋ] F **-, -en** (*esp Psych*) tendency

Streck|bett NT (*Med*) orthopaedic (*Brit*) or orthopedic (*US*) bed (*with traction facilities*)

Stre|cke ['ʃtrɛkə] F **-, -n** **a** (= *Entfernung zwischen zwei Punkten, Sport*) distance; (*Math*) line (*between two points*); **eine ~ zurücklegen** to cover a distance; **eine ziemliche** or **gute ~ entfernt sein** (*lit, fig*) to be a long way away; **bis zum Ende des Projekts ist es noch eine ziemliche** or **lange ~** there is still quite a good way to go until the end of the project **b** (= *Abschnitt*) (*von Straße, Fluss*) stretch; (*von Bahnlinie*) section **c** (= *Weg, Route, Flugstrecke*) route; (= *Straße*) road; (= *Bahnlinie, Sport*: = *Bahn*) track; (*fig*: = *Passage*) passage; **welche ~ bist du gekommen?** which way or route did you come?; **für die ~ London-Glasgow brauchen wir 5 Stunden** the journey from London to Glasgow will take us 5 hours; **auf der ~ sein** to be in the race; **auf** or **an der ~ Paris-Brüssel** on the way from Paris to Brussels; **die ~ Wien-München führt durch ...** the road/track *etc* between Vienna and Munich goes through ...; **in einer ~** in one go (*inf*), without stopping; **auf freier** or **offener ~** (*esp Rail*) on the open line, between stations; **auf weite ~n (hin)** (*lit, fig*) for long stretches; **auf der ~ bleiben** (*bei Rennen*) to drop out of the running; (*in Konkurrenzkampf*) to fall by the wayside **d** (*Hunt*) (= *Jagdbeute*) bag, kill; **zur ~ bringen** to bag, to kill; (*fig*) *Verbrecher* to hunt down **e** (*Min*) gallery

stre|cken ['ʃtrɛkn] **VT** **a** *Arme, Beine, Oberkörper* to stretch; *Hals* to crane; (*Sch*: *um sich zu melden*) *Finger, Hand* to raise, to put up; **die Zunge aus dem Mund ~** to stick out one's tongue; **den Kopf aus dem Fenster/durch die Tür ~** to stick one's head out of the window/through the door; **jdn zu Boden ~** to knock sb to the floor → **Waffe** **b** (*im Streckverband*) *Bein, Arm* to straighten **c** (*Metal*) *Blech, Eisen* to hammer out **d** (*inf*: = *absichtlich verlängern*) *Vorräte, Geld* to eke out, to stretch; *Arbeit* to drag out (*inf*); *Essen, Suppe* to make go further; (= *verdünnen*) to thin down, to dilute **e** → **gestreckt** **VR** **a** (= *sich recken*) to have a stretch, to stretch; (*inf*: = *wachsen*) to shoot up (*inf*); **sich ins Gras/aufs Bett ~** to stretch out on the grass/the bed **b** (= *sich hinziehen*) to drag on

Strecken-: Stre|cken|ab|schnitt M (*Rail*) section of the line or track, track section; **Stre|cken|ar|bei|ter(in)** M(F) (*Rail*) platelayer; **Stre|cken|be|ge|hung** F (*Rail*) track inspection; **Stre|cken|füh|rung** F (*Rail*) route;

Stre|cken|netz NT rail network; **Stre|cken|-pos|ten** M (*Sport*) (race) marshal; (= *Kontrollstelle*) checkpoint control; (= *Verpflegungsposten*) supply station; **Stre|cken|re|kord** M (*Sport*) track record; **Stre|cken|still|le|gung** ▲ F (*Rail*) line closure; **Stre|cken|wär|ter(in)** M(F) (*Rail*) track inspector; **stre|cken|wei|se** ADV in parts or places

Stre|cker [ˈʃtrɛkɐ] M **-s, -**, **Streck|mus|kel** M (*Anat*) extensor (muscle)

Streck|ver|band M (*Med*) bandage used in traction

Street|ball [ˈstriːtbɔːl] M **-s**, *no pl* streetball

Street|wor|ker [ˈstriːtwɔːɐkɐ, -wœrkɐ] M **-s, -**, **Street|wor|ke|rin** [-ərɪn] F **-, -nen** (= *Sozialarbeiter*) outreach worker

Streich [ʃtraiç] M **-(e)s, -e** **a** (= *Schabernack*) prank, trick; **jdm einen ~ spielen** to play a trick on sb; **immer zu ~en aufgelegt sein** to be always up to pranks or tricks **b** (*old, liter*) blow; (*mit Rute, Peitsche*) stroke, lash; **jdm einen ~ versetzen** to strike sb; **auf einen** or **mit einem ~** (*lit*) with one blow; (*fig*) in one blow

Strei|chel|ein|hei|ten PL (= *Zärtlichkeit*) tender loving care *sing*; (= *Lob, Anerkennung*) words *pl* of praise

strei|cheln [ˈʃtraiçln] VTI to stroke; (= *liebkosen*) to caress; **jdm die Wange/das Haar ~** to stroke/caress sb's cheek/hair

strei|chen [ˈʃtraiçn] *pret* **strich** [ʃtrɪç], *ptp* **gestrichen** [gəˈʃtrɪçn] **▮VT▮** **a** (*mit der Hand*) to stroke; **etw glatt ~** to smooth sth (out); **sich** (*dat*) **die Haare aus dem Gesicht/der Stirn ~** to push one's hair back from one's face/forehead
b (= *auftragen*) *Butter, Marmelade etc* to spread; *Salbe, Farbe etc* to apply, to put on; **sich** (*dat*) **ein Brot (mit Butter) ~** to butter oneself a slice of bread; **sich ~ lassen** (*Butter etc*) to spread easily
c (= *anstreichen*: *mit Farbe*) to paint; **frisch gestrichen!** wet (*Brit*) or fresh (*US*) paint; **gestrichenes Papier** coated paper
d *Geige, Cello* to bow
e (= *tilgen*) *Zeile, Satz* to delete, to cross out, to strike; *Auftrag, Plan, Zug, freier Tag etc* to cancel; *Schulden* to write off; *Zuschuss, Gelder, Arbeitsplätze etc* to cut; **etw aus dem Protokoll ~** to delete or strike sth from the minutes; **jdn/etw von** or **aus der Liste ~** to take sb/sth off the list, to delete or strike sb/sth from the list; **etw aus seinem Gedächtnis ~** (*geh*) to erase sth from one's memory
f (*Naut*) *Segel, Flagge, Ruder* to strike
g → **gestrichen**
▮VI▮ **a** (= *über etw hinfahren*) to stroke; **mit der Hand über etw** *acc* **~** to stroke sth (with one's hand); **sie strich ihm über die Hand/das Haar** she stroked his hand/hair
b *aux sein* (= *streifen*) to brush past (*an* +*dat* sth); (*Wind*) to waft; **um/durch etw ~** (= *herumstreichen*) to prowl around/through sth; **die Katze strich mir um die Beine** the cat rubbed against my legs; **durch den Wald/die Felder ~** (*old, geh*) to ramble or wander through the woods/fields
c *aux sein* (*Vögel*) to sweep (*über* +*acc* over)
d (= *schmieren*) to spread
e (= *malen*) to paint

Strei|cher [ˈʃtraiçɐ] PL (*Mus*) strings *pl*

Streich-: **streich|fä|hig** ADJ *Butter* spreadable, easy to spread; **streich|fer|tig** ADJ ready to use or apply; **Streich|holz** NT match; **Streich|holz|schach|tel** F matchbox; **Streich|in|stru|ment** NT string(ed) instrument; **die ~e** the strings; **Streich|kä|se** M cheese spread; **Streich|mu|sik** F music for strings; **Streich|or|ches|ter** NT string orchestra; **Streich|quar|tett** NT string quartet; **Streich|quin|tett** NT string quintet; **Streich|rie|men** M strop

Strei|chung [ˈʃtraiçʊŋ] F **-, -en** (= *Tilgung*) (*von Zeile, Satz*) deletion; (= *Kürzung*) cut; (*von Auf-*

trag, Plan, Zug, freiem Tag etc) cancellation; (*von Schulden*) writing off; (*von Zuschüssen, Arbeitsplätzen etc*) cutting; **die drastischen ~en bei den Subventionen** the drastic cuts in subsidies

Streich|wurst F sausage for spreading, ≈ meat paste

Streif|band [ˈʃtraifbant] NT *pl* **-bänder** wrapper; **im** or **unter** (*Sw*) **~** posted in a wrapper at reduced rate

Streif|band-: **Streif|band|de|pot** NT (*Fin*) individual safe-deposit or safety-deposit box room; **Streif|band|zei|tung** F newspaper sent at printed paper rate

Strei|fe [ˈʃtraifə] F **-, -n** **a** (= *Patrouille*) patrol; **auf ~ gehen/sein** to go/be on patrol; **seine ~ machen** to do one's rounds, to patrol; **ein Polizist auf ~** a policeman on his beat **b** (*Hunt*) = **Streifjagd**

strei|fen [ˈʃtraifn] **▮VT▮** **a** (= *flüchtig berühren*) to touch, to brush (against); (*Kugel*) to graze; (*Billardkugel*) to kiss; (*Auto*) to scrape; **jdn an der Schulter ~** to touch sb on the shoulder; **jdn mit einem Blick ~** to glance fleetingly at sb; **ein flüchtiger Blick streifte mich** he/she glanced fleetingly at me
b (*fig*: *flüchtig erwähnen*) to touch (up)on
c (= *abstreifen, überziehen*) **die Butter vom Messer ~** to scrape the butter off the knife; **die Schuhe von den Füßen ~** to slip one's shoes off; **den Ring vom Finger ~** to slip or take the ring off one's finger; **sich** (*dat*) **die Handschuhe über die Finger ~** to pull on one's gloves; **er streifte sich** (*dat*) **den Pullover über den Kopf** (= *an-/ausziehen*) he slipped the pullover over his head; **die Blätter von den Zweigen ~** to strip the leaves from the twigs; **die Ärmel in die Höhe ~** to pull up one's sleeves
▮VI▮ (*geh*) **a** *aux sein* (= *wandern*) to roam, to wander; (*Fuchs*) to prowl; **(ziellos) durch das Land/die Wälder ~** to roam the country/the forests
b *aux sein* (= *flüchtig berühren*: *Blick etc*) **sie ließ ihren Blick über die Menge ~** she scanned the crowd; **sein Blick streifte über seine Besitztümer** he gazed at his possessions
c (*fig*: = *grenzen*) to border (*an* +*acc* on)

Strei|fen [ˈʃtraifn] M **-s, -** **a** (= *Stück, Band, Landstreifen*) strip; (= *Speckstreifen*) rasher; **ein ~ Land/Speck** a strip of land/bacon **b** (= *Strich*) stripe; (= *Farbstreifen*) streak **c** (= *Lochstreifen, Klebestreifen etc*) tape **d** (= *Tresse*) braid; (*Mil*) stripe **e** (*Film*) film; (= *Abschnitt*) strip of film **f** (= *Linie*) line

Streifen-: **Strei|fen|dienst** M patrol duty; **Strei|fen|kar|te** F multi-journey ticket; **Strei|fen|mus|ter** NT stripy design or pattern; **ein Anzug mit ~** a striped suit; **Strei|fen|po|li|zei** F patrol police (*Brit*) or officers (*US*); **Strei|fen|po|li|zist(in)** M(F) policeman/-woman on patrol; **Strei|fen|wa|gen** M patrol car

strei|fig [ˈʃtraifɪç] ADJ streaky

Streif-: **Streif|jagd** F walk-up, hunt where beaters and guns walk together flushing out game; **Streif|licht** NT (*fig*) highlight; **ein ~ auf etw** (*acc*) **werfen** to highlight sth; **Streif|schuss** ▲ M graze; **Streif|zug** M raid; (= *Bummel*) expedition; (*fig*: = *kurzer Überblick*) brief survey (*durch* of)

Streik [ʃtraik] M **-(e)s, -s** or (*rare*) **-e** strike; **zum ~ aufrufen** to call a strike; **jdn zum ~ aufrufen** to call sb out on strike; **in (den) ~ treten** to come out or go on strike

Streik-: **Streik|auf|ruf** M strike call; **Streik|bre|cher** [-brɛçɐ] M **-s, -**, **Streik|bre|che|rin** [-ərɪn] **F -, -nen** strikebreaker, blackleg (*pej*); scab (*pej*)

strei|ken [ˈʃtraikn] VI to be on strike, to strike; (= *in Streik treten*) to come out on or go on strike, to strike; (*hum inf*) (= *nicht funktionieren*) to pack up (*inf*); (*Magen*) to protest; (*Gedächtnis*) to fail; **die Waschmaschine/das Auto streikt schon wieder** (*inf*) the washing machine/car

has packed up again (*inf*); **als er noch einen Schnaps eingoss, habe ich gestreikt** (*inf*) when he poured out another schnapps I refused it; **wenn ich heute abwaschen soll, streike ich** (*inf*) if I have to do the washing-up today, I'll go on strike (*inf*); **da streike ich** (*inf*) I refuse!, count me out (*inf*)

Strei|ken|de(r) [ˈʃtraikndə] MF *decl as adj* striker

Streik-: **Streik|geld** NT strike pay; **Streik|kas|se** F strike fund; **Streik|pos|ten** M picket; **~ aufstellen** to put up pickets; **~ stehen** to picket; **Streik|recht** NT right or freedom to strike; **Streik|wel|le** F wave or series of strikes

Streit [ʃtrait] M **-(e)s, -e** **a** argument (*um, über* +*acc* about, over); (*leichter*) quarrel, squabble; (*zwischen Eheleuten, Kindern*) fight, argument; (= *Fehde*) feud; (= *Auseinandersetzung*) dispute; **~ haben** to be arguing or quarrelling (*Brit*) or quarreling (*US*); **wegen etw mit jdm (einen) ~ haben** to argue with sb about sth, to have an argument with sb about sth; **die Nachbarn haben seit Jahren ~** the neighbours (*Brit*) or neighbors (*US*) have been arguing or fighting for years; **wegen einer Sache ~ bekommen** to get into an argument over sth; **~ anfangen** to start an argument; **~ suchen** to be looking for an argument or a quarrel; **in ~ liegen** (*Gefühle*) to conflict; **mit jdm in ~ liegen** to be at loggerheads with sb → **Zaun**
b (*old, liter*: = *Kampf*) battle; **zum ~(e) rüsten** to arm oneself for battle

Streit|axt F (*Hist*) battle-axe (*Brit*), battle-ax (*US*); **die ~ begraben** (*fig*) to bury the hatchet

streit|bar ADJ **a** (= *streitlustig*) pugnacious **b** (*old*: = *tapfer*) valiant

strei|ten [ˈʃtraitn] *pret* **stritt** [ʃtrɪt], *ptp* **gestritten** [gəˈʃtrɪtn] **▮VI▮** **a** (= *eine Auseinandersetzung haben*) to argue (*um, über* +*acc* about, over); (*leichter*) to quarrel, to squabble; (*Eheleute, Kinder*) to fight, to argue; (*Jur*: = *prozessieren*) to take legal action; **mit Waffen/Fäusten ~** to fight with weapons/one's fists; **Scheu und Neugier stritten in ihr** she had conflicting feelings of shyness and curiosity; **die Streitenden** the arguers, the people fighting; **es wird immer noch gestritten, ob ...** the argument about whether ... is still going on
b (= *debattieren*) **über** or **um etw** (*acc*) **~** to dispute or argue about or over sth; (*Jur*) to go to court over sth; **darüber kann man** or **lässt sich ~** that's a debatable or moot point; **die ~den Parteien** (*Jur*) the litigants
c (*old, liter*) (= *kämpfen*) to fight; (*in Wettbewerb*) to compete (*um* for)
▮VR▮ to argue; (*leichter*) to quarrel, to squabble; (*Eheleute, Kinder auch*) to fight, to argue; **habt ihr euch schon wieder gestritten?** have you been fighting again?; **wir wollen uns deswegen nicht ~!** don't let's fall out over that!; **man streitet sich, ob ...** there is argument as to whether ...

Strei|ter [ˈʃtraitɐ] M **-s, -**, **Strei|te|rin** [-ərɪn] **F -, -nen** (*geh*) fighter (*für* for); (*für Prinzip etc auch*) champion (*für* of)

Strei|te|rei [ʃtraitəˈrai] F **-, -en** (*inf*) arguing *no pl*, quarrelling *no pl* (*Brit*), quarreling *no pl* (*US*); (*zwischen Eheleuten, Kindern auch*) fighting *no pl*; **eine ~** an argument

Streit-: **Streit|fall** M dispute, conflict; (*Jur*) case; **im ~** in case of dispute or conflict; **im ~ Müller gegen Braun** in the case of Müller versus Braun; **Streit|fra|ge** F dispute; **Streit|ge|gen|stand** M matter in dispute; (= *strittiger Punkt*) matter of dispute; **Streit|ge|spräch** NT debate, discussion; (*Liter, Univ auch*) disputation; **Streit|grund** M cause of the/an argument; **Streit|hahn** M (*inf*) squabbler; **Streit|ham|mel** M , (*S Ger, Aus*) **Streit|han|sel** [-hanzl] **▮M▮** (*inf*) quarrelsome person

strei|tig [ˈʃtraitɪç] ADJ **jdm das Recht auf etw** (*acc*) **~ machen** to dispute sb's right to sth; **jdm das Geschäft/den ersten Platz ~ machen** to vie (*form*) or compete with sb for business/for first place; **das/seine Kompetenz kann man ihm nicht ~ machen** that/his competence is indisputable

Strei|tig|kei|ten PL quarrels *pl*, squabbles *pl*

Streit-: Streit|kräf|te PL forces *pl*, troops *pl*; **Streit|kul|tur** F culture of debate; **eine ~ ent-wickeln** to debate things in a civilized manner; **Streit|lust** F (*liter*) argumentative disposition; (= *Aggressivität*) aggressive disposition; **streit|lus|tig** ADJ (*geh*) argumentative; (= *aggressiv*) aggressive; **Streit|macht** F armed forces *pl*; **Streit|ob|jekt** NT matter in dispute; (= *strittiger Punkt*) matter of dispute; **Streit|punkt** M contentious issue; **Streit|ross** ▲ NT warhorse; **Streit|sa|che** F dispute; (*Jur*) case; **Streit|schrift** F polemic; **Streit|sucht** F quarrelsomeness; **streit|süch|tig** ADJ quarrelsome; **Streit|wa|gen** M (*Hist*) chariot; **Streit|wert** M (*Jur*) amount in dispute

streng [ʃtrɛŋ] ♦ 36.3, 46.5 **ADJ a** strict; *Regel, Kontrolle* strict, stringent; *Maßnahmen* stringent; *Bestrafung* severe; *Anforderungen* rigorous; *Ausdruck, Blick, Gesicht* stern; *Sitten, Disziplin* rigid, strict; *Stillschweigen, Diskretion* absolute; *Mode, Schnitt* severe; *Kritik, Urteil* harsh, severe; *Richter* severe, stern; *Lebensführung, Schönheit, Form* austere; *Examen* stiff; **~ gegen sich selbst sein** to be strict or severe on or with oneself; **~ aber gerecht** severe but just → **Regiment a**

b (= *durchdringend*) *Geruch, Geschmack* pungent; *Frost, Kälte, Winter* intense, severe

c (= *strenggläubig*) *Katholik, Moslem etc* strict

ADV a (= *unnachgiebig*) *befolgen, einhalten* strictly, rigidly; *tadeln, bestrafen* severely; *vertraulich, wissenschaftlich* strictly; **~ genommen** strictly speaking; (= *eigentlich*) actually; **~ gegen jdn/etw vorgehen** to deal severely with sb/sth; **~ durchgreifen** to take rigorous or stringent action; **~ geheim** top secret; **~ nach Vorschrift** strictly according to regulations; **~(stens) verboten!** strictly prohibited; **sie kleidet sich sehr ~** she wears very severe clothes

b (= *intensiv*) **riechen/schmecken** to have a pungent smell/taste; **der Käse schmeckt mir zu ~** this cheese tastes too strong for me

c (*Sw*) **es ~ haben** to be under a lot of pressure

Stren|ge [ˈʃtrɛŋə] F -, *no pl* **a** strictness; (*von Regel, Kontrolle, Maßnahmen*) stringency; (*von Bestrafung*) severity; (*von Ausdruck, Blick*) sternness; (*von Kritik, Urteil*) harshness, severity; (*von Richter*) severity, sternness; **mit ~ regieren** to rule strictly **b** (= *Schärfe*) (*von Geruch, Geschmack*) pungency; (*von Kälte*) intensity; (*von Frost, Winter*) severity

streng-: streng|ge|nom|men △ ADV → **streng** ADV a; **streng|gläu|big** ADJ strict; **streng neh|men** ▲ VT *sep irreg* to take seriously; **es mit etw ~** to be strict about sth; **wenn man es streng nimmt** strictly speaking

Strep|to|kok|ken [ʃtrɛptoˈkɔkn, st-] PL (*Med*) streptococci *pl*

Strep|to|my|cin [ʃtrɛptomyˈtsiːn, st-] NT -s, *no pl* (*Med*) streptomycin

Stre|se|mann [ˈʃtreːzəman] M -s, *no pl* formal, *dark suit with striped trousers*

Stress ▲ [ʃtrɛs, st-] M **-es, -e** (*alle Bedeutungen*) stress; **der tägliche ~ im Büro** the daily stress or hassle (*inf*) in the office; (**voll**) **im ~ sein/stehen** to be under a (lot of) stress; **ich bin heute im ~** I'm feeling hassled today (*inf*)

Stress|be|wäl|ti|gung ▲ F stress management

stres|sen [ˈʃtrɛsn] VT to put under stress; **gestresst sein** to be under stress

stress-: stress|frei ▲ ADJ stress-free; **stress|ge|plagt** ▲ [-ɡəplaːkt] ADJ under stress; **~e Manager** highly stressed executives, executives suffering from stress; **Stress|hor|mon** ▲ NT stress hormone

stres|sig [ˈʃtrɛsɪç] ADJ (*inf*) stressful

Stress-: Stress|krank|heit ▲ F stress disease; **Stress|si|tu|a|ti|on** ▲ F stress situation

Stret|ching [ˈstrɛtʃɪŋ] NT **-s**, *no pl* (*Gymnastik*) stretching exercises *pl*

Stretch|stoff [ˈstrɛtʃ-] M stretch fabric

Streu [ʃtrɔy] F -, *no pl* straw; (*aus Sägespänen*) sawdust

Streu-: Streu|be|sitz M (*St Ex*) widely spread shareholdings *pl*, widely held stock; **Streu|dienst** M (*im Winter*) (road-)gritting service, (road) maintenance crew (*US*); **„kein ~!"** "untreated road"

streu|en [ˈʃtrɔyən] VT Futter, Samen to scatter; *Blumen auch* to strew; *Dünger, Stroh, Sand, Kies* to spread; *Gewürze, Zucker etc* to sprinkle; *Straße, Gehweg etc* (*mit Sand*) to grit; (*mit Salz*) to salt; (*fig*) *Gerüchte etc* to spread; *Aktien* to make widely available; **die Regierung ließ ~, dass ...** the government gave reason to believe that ... **VI** **a** (= *Streumittel anwenden*) to grit; to put down salt **b** (*Salzstreuer etc*) to sprinkle **c** (*Linse, Gewehr etc*) to scatter

Streu|er [ˈʃtrɔyɐ] M **-s, -** shaker; (= *Salzstreuer*) cellar; (= *Pfefferstreuer*) pot

Streu-: Streu|fahr|zeug NT gritter; **Streu|gut** NT , *no pl* (road) grit

streu|nen [ˈʃtrɔynən] VI **a** (= *nicht sesshaft sein*) to roam about, to wander about or around; (*Hund, Katze*) to stray **b** aus sein durch etw/in etw (*dat*) ~ to roam or wander through/around sth

Streu|ner [ˈʃtrɔynɐ] M **-s, -** (= *Tier*) stray; (= *Person*) tramp, vagrant

Streu-: Streu|obst|wie|se F meadow orchard; **Streu|pflicht** F obligation on householder to keep area in front of house gritted in icy weather; **Streu|pul|ver** NT grit or (*Salz*) salt (*for icy roads*); **Streu|salz** NT salt (*for icy roads*); **Streu|sand** M sand; (*für Straße*) grit

Streu|sel [ˈʃtrɔyzl] NT **-s, -** (*Cook*) crumble (*Brit*) or crumb (*US*) (*mixture*)

Streu|sel|ku|chen M thin sponge cake with crumble topping

Streu|ung [ˈʃtrɔyʊŋ] F **-, -en** (*Statistik*) mean variation; (*Phys*) scattering

Streu-: Streu|ver|lust M (*Phys*) loss of intensity due to scattering; (*fig*) loss due to a scatter-shot approach; **Streu|wa|gen** M (road) gritter; **Streu|zu|cker** M (*grob*) granulated sugar; (*fein*) castor sugar

strich *pret von* **streichen**

Strich [ʃtrɪç] M **-(e)s, -e a** line; (= *Querstrich*) dash; (= *Schrägstrich*) oblique, slash; (= *Federstrich, Pinselstrich*) stroke; (*von Land*) stretch; **etw mit wenigen ~en skizzieren** or **zeichnen** (*lit, fig*) to sketch or outline sth with a few brief strokes; **einen ~ durch die Rechnung/einen Plan machen** to thwart sb's plans/plan; **einen ~ (unter etw** *acc*) **machen** or **ziehen** (*fig*) to forget sth; **unterm ~ sein** (*inf*) not to be up to scratch (*Brit*) or up to snuff (*US*); **unterm ~** at the final count; **er kann noch auf dem ~ gehen** (*inf*) he can still walk along a straight line; **dünn wie ein ~** (*inf*) as thin as a rake (*Brit inf*) or rail (*US inf*); **sie ist nur noch ein ~ (in der Landschaft** *hum*) (*inf*) she's as thin as a rake (*Brit*) or rail (*US*) now (*inf*); **keinen ~ tun** (*inf*) not to do a stroke (of work)

b *no pl* (= *Kompassstrich*) point

c (*von Teppich*) pile; (*von Samt*) pile, nap; (*von Gewebe*) nap; (*von Fell, Haar*) direction of growth; **gegen den ~ bürsten** (*lit*) to brush the wrong way; **es geht (mir) gegen den ~** (*inf*) it goes against the grain; **nach ~ und Faden** (*inf*) good and proper (*inf*), thoroughly; **jdn nach ~ und Faden versohlen** (*inf*) to give sb a thorough or good hiding (*inf*)

d (*Mus*: = *Bogenstrich*) stroke, bow; **einen harten/weichen ~ haben** to bow heavily/lightly

e (*inf*: = *Prostitution*) prostitution *no art*; (= *Bordellgegend*) red-light district; **auf den ~ gehen**

to be on the game (*Brit inf*), to be a prostitute **f** (*von Schwalben etc*) flight

Strich-: Strich|ät|zung F (*Typ*) line etching; **Strich|code** M = **Strichkode**

stri|cheln [ˈʃtrɪçln] **VI** to sketch it in; (= *schraffieren*) to hatch **VT** to sketch in; to hatch; **eine gestrichelte Linie** a broken line

Stri|cher [ˈʃtrɪçɐ] M **-s, -** (*pej inf*) rent boy (*Brit*), boy prostitute

Stri|che|rin [ˈʃtrɪçərɪn] F **-, -nen** (*pej inf*) tart (*inf*), hooker (*esp US inf*)

Strich-: Strich|jun|ge M (*inf*) rent boy (*Brit*), boy prostitute; **Strich|ko|de** M barcode (*Brit*), universal product code (*US*); **Strich|lis|te** F check list; **eine ~ führen** (*auch fig*) to keep a careful record or account (*über +acc* of); **Strich|mäd|chen** NT (*inf*) tart (*inf*), hooker (*esp US inf*); **Strich|männ|chen** NT matchstick man, stick man; **Strich|punkt** M semicolon; **strich|wei|se** ADV (*auch Met*) here and there; **~ Regen** rain in places; **Strich|zeich|nung** F line drawing

Strick¹ [ʃtrɪk] M **-(e)s, -e** a rope; (*dünner, als Gürtel*) cord; **jdm aus etw einen ~ drehen** to use sth against sb; **zum ~ greifen** (*inf*) to hang oneself; **dann kann ich mir einen ~ nehmen** or **kaufen** (*inf*) I may as well pack it all in (*inf*); **am gleichen** or **an einem ~ ziehen** (*fig*) to pull together → **reißen VI a b** (*inf*: = *Schelm*) rascal; **fauler ~** lazybones *sing* (*inf*), lazy so-and-so (*inf*)

Strick² NT **-(e)s**, *no pl* (*inf*) knitwear

Strick-: Strick|ar|beit F knitting *no pl*; **eine ~** a piece of knitting; **Strick|beu|tel** M knitting bag

stri|cken [ˈʃtrɪkn] VTI to knit; (*fig*) to construct; **an etw** (*dat*) **~** (*lit, fig*) to work on sth

Stri|cker [ˈʃtrɪkɐ] M **-s, -**, **Stri|cke|rin** [-ərɪn] F **-, -nen** knitter

Stri|cke|rei [ʃtrɪkəˈrai] F **-, -en** a knitting *no indef art, no pl* **b** (*Betrieb*) knitwear factory

Strick-: Strick|garn NT knitting wool; **Strick|hand|schu|he** PL knitted gloves *pl*; **Strick|ja|cke** F cardigan; **Strick|kleid** NT knitted dress; **Strick|lei|ter** F rope ladder; **Strick|ma|schi|ne** F knitting machine; **Strick|mus|ter** NT (*lit*) knitting pattern; (*fig*) pattern; **Strick|na|del** F knitting needle; **Strick|wa|ren** PL knitwear *sing*; **Strick|wes|te** F knitted waistcoat; (*mit Ärmeln*) cardigan; **Strick|wol|le** F knitting wool; **Strick|zeug** NT , *no pl* knitting

Strie|gel [ˈʃtriːɡl] M **-s, -** currycomb

strie|geln [ˈʃtriːɡln] **VT** **a** Tier to curry(comb); (*fig inf*: = *kämmen*) to comb → *auch* **gestriegelt b** (*inf*: = *hart behandeln*) **jdn ~** to put sb through the hoop (*inf*) **VR** (*inf*) to spruce oneself up

Strie|me [ˈʃtriːmə] F **-, -n**, **Strie|men** [ˈʃtriːmən] M **-s, -** weal

strie|mig [ˈʃtriːmɪç] ADJ Haut marked with weals

Strie|zel [ˈʃtriːtsl] M **-s, -** (*dial Cook*) plaited Danish pastry

strikt [ʃtrɪkt, st-] ADJ strict; Ablehnung categorical **ADV** strictly; *ablehnen* categorically; **~ gegen etw sein** to be totally opposed to sth

strin|gent [ʃtrɪnˈgɛnt, st-] (*geh*) ADJ stringent; *Politik, Entscheidungen, Konzept* rigorous; *Schlussfolgerung* compelling; *Handlung* tight **ADV** argumentieren, durchführen stringently; **etw ~ nachweisen** to provide compelling proof for sth

Strip [ʃtrɪp, st-] M **-s, -s** (*inf*) strip(tease)

Strip|pe [ˈʃtrɪpə] F **-, -n** (*inf*) **a** (= *Bindfaden*) string; **die ~n ziehen** (*fig*) to pull the strings **b** (= *Telefonleitung*) phone, blower (*Brit inf*); **an der ~ hängen** to be on the phone or blower (*Brit sl*); **sich an die ~ hängen** to get on the phone or blower (*Brit sl*); **jdn an der ~ haben** to have sb on the line or phone or blower (*Brit sl*)

---

strip|pen ['ʃtrɪpn, 'st-] VI to strip, to do a strip-tease act

Strip|pen|zie|her ['ʃtrɪpəntsiːɐ] M **-s, -**, **Strip-pen|zie|he|rin** [-ərɪn] F (inf) **er war der ~** he was the one pulling the strings

Strip|per ['ʃtrɪpɐ, 'st-] M **-s, -**, **Strip|pe|rin** [-ərɪn] F **-, -nen** (inf) stripper

Strip|tease ['ʃtrɪptiːs, 'st-] M OR NT **-, no pl** striptease

Strip|tease|tän|zer(in) ['ʃtrɪptiːs-, st-] M(F) stripper

stritt pret von **streiten**

strit|tig ['ʃtrɪtɪç] ADJ contentious, controversial; **noch ~** still in dispute

Striz|zi ['ʃtrɪtsi] M **-s, -s** (Aus inf) pimp

Stro|bo|skop [ʃtrobo'skoːp, st-] NT **-s, -e** stroboscope

Stro|bo|skop|blitz M stroboscopic light

stro|bo|sko|pisch [ʃtrobo'skoːpɪʃ, st-] ADJ stroboscopic

Stro|bo|skop|lam|pe F strobe light

Stroh [ʃtroː] NT **-(e)s, no pl** straw; (= Dachstroh) thatch; **~ im Kopf haben** (inf) to have sawdust between one's ears (inf) → **dreschen a**

Stroh-: **Stroh|bal|len** M bale of straw; **stroh|blond** ADJ Mensch flaxen-haired; Haare flaxen, straw-coloured (Brit), straw-colored (US); **Stroh|blu|me** F strawflower; **Stroh|bund** NT pl **-bunde** bundle of straw; **Stroh|dach** NT thatched roof; **stroh|dumm** ADJ thick (inf); **stroh|far|ben** [-farbn] ADJ straw-coloured (Brit), straw-colored (US); Haare auch flaxen; **Stroh|feu|er** NT **ein ~ sein** (fig) to be a passing fancy; **Stroh|frau** F (fig) front woman; **stroh|ge|deckt** ADJ thatched; **stroh|gelb** ADJ straw-coloured; Haare auch flaxen; **Stroh|halm** M straw; **sich an einen ~ klammern, nach einem ~ greifen** to clutch at straws; **Stroh|hut** M straw hat; **Stroh|hüt|te** F thatched hut

stro|hig ['ʃtroːɪç] ADJ Gemüse tough; Orangen etc dry; Haar dull and lifeless

Stroh-: **Stroh|kopf** M (inf) blockhead (inf); **Stroh|la|ger** NT pallet, straw mattress; **Stroh|mann** M pl **-männer** (= Strohpuppe) scarecrow; (fig) front man; (Cards) dummy; **Stroh|mat|te** F straw mat; **Stroh|pup|pe** F scarecrow; **Stroh|sack** M palliasse; **heiliger ~!** (dated inf) good(ness) gracious (me)!; **stroh|tro|cken** ADJ very dry; (fig: = langweilig) (as) dry as dust; **Stroh|wit|we** F grass widow; **Stroh|wit|wer** M grass widower

Strolch [ʃtrɔlç] M **-(e)s, -e** (dated pej) rogue, rascal

strol|chen ['ʃtrɔlçn] VI aux sein to roam about; **durch etw/in etw** (dat) **~** to roam through/around sth

Strom [ʃtroːm] M **-(e)s, ~e** ['ʃtrøːmə] **a** (large) river; (= Strömung) current; (von Schweiß, Blut) river; (von Besuchern, Flüchen etc) stream; **ein rei-ßender ~** a raging torrent; **Ströme und Flüsse Europas** rivers of Europe; **ein ~ von Tränen** (geh) floods of tears pl; **in dem** or **im ~ der Vergessenheit versinken** (geh) to sink or pass into oblivion; **es regnet in Strömen** it's pouring (with rain); **der Wein floss in Strömen** the wine flowed like water; **der ~ seiner Rede** (geh) the torrent or flood of his words; **der ~ der Zeit** (geh) the flow of time; **der ~ der Geschichte** (geh) the course of history; **mit dem/gegen den ~ schwimmen** (lit) to swim with/against the current; (fig) to swim or go with/against the tide **b** (Elec) **(elektrischer) ~** current; (= Elektrizität) electricity; **~ führen** to be live; **~ führend** (Elec, Leitung) live; **unter ~ stehen** (lit) to be live; (fig) to be high (inf); **mit ~ heizen** to have electric heating; **der ~ ist ausgefallen** the power or electricity is off

Strom-: **strom|ab** [ʃtroːm'lap] ADV downstream; **Strom|ab|neh|mer** M (Rail etc) pantograph; **Strom|ab|neh|mer(in)** M(F) (= Verbraucher) user or consumer of electricity;

strom|ab|wärts [ʃtroːm'lapverts] ADV downstream; **Strom|an|bie|ter** M electricity supplier or provider; **Strom|an|schluss** ▲ M **~ haben** to be connected to the electricity mains; **strom|auf(wärts)** [ʃtroːm'lauf(verts)] ADV upstream; **Strom|aus|fall** M power failure; **Strom|bett** NT riverbed

strö|men ['ʃtrøːmən] VI aux sein to stream; (Blut auch, Gas) to flow; (Menschen) to pour (in into, aus out of); **bei ~dem Regen** in (the) pouring rain

Stro|mer ['ʃtroːmɐ] M **-s, -**, **Stro|me|rin** [-ərɪn] F **-, -nen** (inf) rover; (= Landstreicher) tramp, hobo (esp US)

stro|mern ['ʃtroːmɐn] VI aux sein (inf) to roam or wander about

Strom-: **Strom|er|zeu|ger** M (electricity) generator; **strom|füh|rend** △ ADJ attr → **Strom b**; **Strom|ka|bel** NT electric or power cable; **Strom|kreis** M (electrical) circuit; **Strom|lei|tung** F electric cables pl; **Strom|li|ni|en|form** F streamlined design; (von Auto auch) streamlined body; **strom|li|ni|en|för|mig** ADJ (lit, fig) streamlined ADV (fig) **sich ~ verhalten** to be a conformist; **Parteimitglieder, die ~ denken** party members who think exactly along party lines; **sich einer Sache** (dat) **~ anpassen, sich ~ in etw** (acc) **einfügen** to adapt (oneself) to sth; **Strom|mes|ser** M **-s, -** (Elec) ammeter; **Strom|netz** NT electricity or power supply system; **Strom|quel|le** F source of power or electricity; **Strom|schie|ne** F (Rail) live or conductor rail; **Strom|schlag** M electric shock; **Strom|schnel|le** F rapids pl; **Strom|span|nung** F voltage; **Strom|spei|cher** M (storage) battery; **Strom|sper|re** F power cut; **Strom|stär|ke** F strength of the/an electric current; **Strom|stoß** M electric shock

Strö|mung ['ʃtrøːmʊŋ] F **-, -en** current; (fig auch) trend

Strö|mungs|leh|re F (von Flüssigkeiten) hydrodynamics sing; (von Luft und Gasen) aerodynamics sing

Strom-: **Strom|ver|brauch** M electricity or power consumption; **Strom|ver|sor|gung** F electricity or power supply; **Strom|wen|der** [-vendɐ] M **-s, -** commutator; **Strom|zäh|ler** M electricity meter

Stron|ti|um ['ʃtrɔntsiʊm, 'st-] NT **-s, no pl** (abbr **Sr**) strontium

Stro|phe ['ʃtroːfə] F **-, -n** verse; (in Gedicht auch) stanza

-stro|phig [ʃtroːfɪç] ADJ suf **dreistrophig/vierstrophig sein** (Gedicht) to have three/four stanzas or verses; (Lied) to have three/four verses

stro|phisch ['ʃtroːfɪʃ] ADJ stanzaic ADV in stanzas

strot|zen ['ʃtrɔtsn] VI to be full (von, vor +dat of), to abound (von, vor +dat with); (von Kraft, Gesundheit, Lebensfreude) to be bursting (von with); (vor Ungeziefer) to be teeming or crawling (vor +dat with); (von Waffen) to be bristling (von with); **von Schmutz ~** to be thick or covered with dirt

strub|be|lig ['ʃtrʊbəlɪç] ADJ (inf) Haar, Fell tousled

Strub|bel|kopf M ['ʃtrʊbl-] M (inf) tousled hair; (Mensch) tousle-head; **einen ~ haben, ein ~ sein** to have tousled hair

strubb|lig ['ʃtrʊblɪç] ADJ (inf) Haar, Fell tousled

Stru|del ['ʃtruːdl] M **-s, -** **a** (lit, fig) whirlpool; (von Ereignissen, Vergnügen) whirl **b** (Cook) strudel

stru|deln ['ʃtruːdln] VI to whirl, to swirl

Stru|del|teig M (esp S Ger, Aus: Cook) strudel pastry

Struk|tur [ʃtrʊk'tuːɐ, st-] F **-, -en** structure; (von Stoff etc) texture; (in Webart) weave

Struk|tu|ra|lis|mus [ʃtrʊktura'lɪsmʊs, st-] M **-, no pl** structuralism

struk|tu|ra|lis|tisch [ʃtrʊktura'lɪstɪʃ, st-] ADJ structuralist ADV **etw ~ interpretieren** to interpret sth according to structuralist methods

Struk|tur|ana|ly|se F structural analysis

struk|tu|rell [ʃtrʊktu'rɛl, st-] ADJ Probleme, Veränderungen structural; **~e Arbeitslosigkeit** structural unemployment ADV **~ bedingt** structurally; **~ gesehen** looking at the infrastructure; **sich ~ auswirken** to have an effect on the infrastructure; **ein ~ schwaches Gebiet** a region with a weak infrastructure

Struk|tur|for|mel F (Chem) structural formula

struk|tu|rie|ren [ʃtrʊktu'riːrən, st-] ptp **strukturiert** VT to structure

Struk|tu|rie|rung F **-, -en** structuring

Struk|tur-: **Struk|tur|kri|se** F structural crisis; **Struk|tur|po|li|tik** F structural policy; **Struk|tur|prob|lem** NT structural problem; **Struk|tur|re|form** F structural reform; **struk|tur|schwach** ADJ lacking in infrastructure; **die ~en Gebiete Bayerns** the parts of Bavaria with less well-developed infrastructure; **Struk|tur|schwä|che** F lack of infrastructure; **Struk|tur|wan|del** M structural change (+gen in)

strul|lern ['ʃtrʊlɐn] VI (sl: = pinkeln) to have a slash (Brit inf), to take a leak (inf)

Strumpf [ʃtrʊmpf] M **-(e)s, ~e** ['ʃtrʏmpfə] **a** sock; (= Damenstrumpf) stocking; **ein Paar Strümpfe** a pair of socks/stockings; **auf Strümpfen** in one's stockinged feet **b** (= Sparstrumpf) **sein Geld im ~ haben** ≈ to keep one's money under the mattress **c** (= Glühstrumpf) mantle

Strumpf-: **Strumpf|band** [-bant] NT pl **-bänder** garter; **Strumpf|fab|rik** F hosiery factory; **Strumpf|ge|schäft** NT hosiery shop (esp Brit) or store (esp US); **Strumpf|hal|ter** M suspender (Brit), garter (US); **Strumpf|hal|ter|gür|tel** M suspender belt (Brit), garter belt (US); **Strumpf|ho|se** F tights pl (esp Brit), pantihose; **eine ~** a pair of tights (esp Brit) or pantihose; **Strumpf|mas|ke** F stocking mask; **Strumpf|wa|ren** PL hosiery sing; **Strumpf|wir|ker** [-vɪrkɐ] M **-s, -**, **Strumpf|wir|ke|rin** [-ərɪn] F **-, -nen** hosiery worker

Strunk [ʃtrʊŋk] M **-(e)s, ~e** ['ʃtrʏŋkə] stalk

strup|pig ['ʃtrʊpɪç] ADJ unkempt; Tier shaggy

Struw|wel|kopf ['ʃtruːvl-] M (inf) = **Strubbelkopf**

Struw|wel|pe|ter ['ʃtruːvl-] M tousle-head; **der ~** (Liter) shock-headed Peter, Struwwelpeter

Strych|nin [ʃtrʏç'niːn, st-] NT **-s, no pl** strychnine

Stub|ben ['ʃtʊbn] M **-s, -** (N Ger) tree stump

Stüb|chen ['ʃtyːpçən] NT **-, -** dim von **Stube** little room

Stu|be ['ʃtuːbə] F **-, -n** (dated, dial) room; (dial: = Wohnzimmer) lounge; (in Kaserne) barrack room (Brit), quarters; (Sch) study; (= Schlafsaal) dormitory; **auf der ~** (Mil) in one's barrack room (Brit), in one's quarters; (Sch) in one's study/dormitory; **die gute ~** the parlour (dated Brit) or parlor (dated US); **(immer) herein in die gute ~!** (hum inf) come right in!; **in der ~ hocken** (inf) to sit around indoors

Stü|bel ['ʃtyːbl] NT **-s, -** (Aus) small room

Stu|ben-: **Stu|ben|äl|tes|te(r)** MF decl as adj → **Stube** (Mil) senior soldier in a/the barrack room (Brit) or in the quarters; (Sch) study/dormitory prefect; **Stu|ben|ap|pell** M → **Stube** (Mil) barrack-room inspection (Brit), inspection of quarters; (Sch) study/dormitory inspection; **Stu|ben|ar|rest** M confinement to one's room or (Mil) quarters; **~ haben** to be confined to one's room/quarters; **Stu|ben|dienst** M → **Stube** (Mil) fatigue duty, barrack-room duty (Brit); (Sch) study/dormitory cleaning duty; **~ haben** to be on fatigue duty etc; **Stu|ben|flie|ge** F (common) housefly; **Stu|ben|ge|lehr|te(r)** MF decl as adj (pej) armchair scholar;

Stu|ben|ho|cker [-hɔkɐ] M **-s, -, Stu|ben|-**
ho|cke|rin [-ərɪn] F **-, -nen** (*pej inf*) stay-at-
home; **er ist ein richtiger ~** he sits at home
all the time; **Stu|ben|ka|me|rad(in)** M(F)
(*esp Mil*) roommate (*Brit*), bunkmate (*US*);
Stu|ben|kü|cken NT (*Cook*) young chick
(*six to eight weeks old*); **Stu|ben|mäd|-**
chen NT (*dated*) chambermaid; **stu|ben|-**
rein ADJ *Katze, Hund* house-trained; (*hum*)
Witz clean

Stü|berl ['ʃtyːbəl] NT **-s, -** (*Aus*) small room

Stuck [ʃtʊk] M **-(e)s**, *no pl* stucco; (*zur Zimmer-*
verzierung) moulding (*Brit*), molding (*US*)

Stück [ʃtʏk] NT **-(e)s, -e** *or* (*nach Zahlenangaben*)
- ⓐ piece; (*von Vieh, Wild*) head; (*von Zucker*)
lump; (= *Ausstellungsstück*) item, piece; (= *Seifen-*
stück) bar, cake; (= *abgegrenztes Land*) plot; **ich**
nehme fünf ~ I'll take five; **12 ~ (Eier)** twelve *or*
a dozen (eggs); **20 ~ Vieh** 20 head of cattle;
sechs ~ von diesen Apfelsinen six of these oranges; **12 ~, ~er 12** (*hum*) 12 all told; **10 Cent**
das ~, pro ~ 10 Cent 10 cents each; **im** *or* **am ~**
in one piece; *Käse, Wurst auch* unsliced; **etw**
nach ~ verkaufen to sell sth by the piece; **aus**
einem ~ in one piece; **~ für ~** (= *ein Exemplar*
nach dem andern) one by one; **nach ~ bezahlt**
werden (*Stücklohn erhalten*) to do piecework;
das größte/beste ~ (*Fleisch etc*) the biggest/
best piece (of meat *etc*); **ein ~ Garten** a patch
of garden; **das ist unser bestes ~** (*hum*) that is
our pride and joy
ⓑ (= *Teil, Abschnitt*) piece, bit; (*von Buch, Rede,*
Reise etc) part; (*von Straße etc*) stretch; **ich möch-**
te nur ein kleines ~ I only want a little bit *or* a
small piece; **~ für ~** (= *einen Teil um den andern*)
bit by bit; **in ~e gehen/zerspringen** to be bro-
ken/smashed to pieces; **etw in ~e schlagen** to
smash sth to pieces; **etw in ~e reißen** to tear
sth to pieces *or* shreds; **sich für jdn in ~e reißen**
lassen to do anything for sb; **ein ~ Heimat** a
piece of home; **in allen ~en** on every matter;
übereinstimmen auch in every detail; **ich komme**
ein ~ (des Weges) mit I'll come some *or* part of
the way with you
ⓒ **ein ~ spazieren gehen** to go for a walk; **ein**
gutes ~ weiterkommen to make considerable
progress *or* headway; **ein schweres ~ Arbeit** a
tough job; **ein schönes ~ Geld** (*inf*) a tidy sum,
a pretty penny (*inf*); **das ist (doch) ein starkes**
~! (*inf*) that's a bit much (*inf*); **große ~e auf jdn**
halten to think much *or* highly of sb, to have a
high opinion of sb; **große ~e auf etw** (*acc*) **hal-**
ten to be very proud of sth; **aus freien ~en** of
one's own free will
ⓓ (*Fin*) share
ⓔ (= *Bühnenstück*) play; (= *Musikstück*) piece
ⓕ (*inf: Mensch*) beggar (*esp Brit inf*), so-and-so
(*inf*); **mein bestes ~** (*hum inf*) my pride and joy;
ein ~ Dreck (*inf*) (*Frau*) a bitch (*sl*), a cow (*inf*);
(*Mann*) a bastard (*sl*)

Stück|ak|kord M piecework

Stück|ar|beit F stucco work *no pl*; (*in Zimmer*)
moulding (*Brit*), molding (*US*)

Stück|ar|beit F piecework

Stu|cka|teur ▲ [ʃtʊkaˈtøːɐ] M **-s, -e, Stu|cka|-**
teu|rin ▲ [-ˈtøːrɪn] F **-, -nen** plasterer (*who*
works with stucco)

Stuck|a|tur ▲ [ʃtʊkaˈtuːɐ] F **-, -en** stucco
(work), ornamental plasterwork

Stück|chen ['ʃtʏkçən] NT **-s, -** *dim von* **Stück a,**
b, e

Stuck|de|cke F stucco(ed) ceiling

stü|ckeln ['ʃtʏkl̩n] VT to patch VI to patch it
together

Stü|cke|lung F **-, -en** (= *Aufteilung*) splitting up;
(*von Geld, Aktien*) denomination; **in kleiner ~**
(*Geldbetrag*) in small denominations

stu|cken ['ʃtʊkn̩] VI (*Aus inf*) to swot (*Brit inf*),
to cram (*inf*)

Stü|cke|schrei|ber(in) M(F) dramatist, play-
wright

Stück|fass ▲ NT (*Weinmaß*) measure of wine
containing 1,200 litres

Stück-: Stück|gut NT (*Rail*) parcel service;
etw als ~ schicken to send sth as a parcel
(*Brit*) *or* package; **Stück|kos|ten** PL unit cost
sing; **Stück|leis|tung** F production capacity;
Stück|lohn M piece(work) rate; **Stück|no|**
tie|rung F quotation per unit; **Stück|preis**
M unit price; **stück|wei|se** ADV bit by bit, lit-
tle by little; **~ verkaufen** to sell individually;
Stück|werk NT , *no pl* incomplete *or* unfin-
ished work; **~ sein/bleiben** to be/remain in-
complete *or* unfinished; **Stück|zahl** F number
of pieces *or* items; **Stück|zeit** F production
time per piece *or* item; **Stück|zins** M (*Fin*) ac-
crued interest

stud. *abbr von* **studiosus ~ med./phil.** *etc* student
of medicine/humanities *etc*

Stu|dent [ʃtuˈdɛnt] M **-en, -en** student; (*Aus*: =
Schüler) schoolboy; (*einer bestimmten Schule*) pupil → *auch* **Studentin**

Stu|den|ten-: Stu|den|ten|aus|weis M stu-
dent (ID) card; **Stu|den|ten|be|we|gung** F
student movement; **Stu|den|ten|blu|me** F
French marigold; **Stu|den|ten|bu|de** F (*inf*)
student digs *pl* (*Brit*) *or* housing; **Stu|den|-**
ten|fut|ter NT nuts and raisins *pl*; **Stu|den|-**
ten|ge|mein|de F student religious society;
Stu|den|ten|heim NT hall of residence
(*Brit*), student hostel, dormitory (*US*); **Stu|-**
den|ten|le|ben NT student life; **Stu|den|-**
ten|lie|be F student romance; **Stu|den|ten|-**
lied NT student song; **Stu|den|ten|lo|kal**
NT students' pub; **Stu|den|ten|pfar|rer(in)**
M(F) university/college chaplain; **Stu|den|-**
ten|ra|batt NT student discount; **Stu|den|-**
ten|re|vol|te F student revolt; **Stu|den|ten|-**
schaft [ʃtuˈdɛntn̩ʃaft] F **-, -en** students *pl*, stu-
dent body; **Stu|den|ten|spra|che** F student
slang; **Stu|den|ten|ver|bin|dung** F students'
society *or* association; (*für Männer auch*) frater-
nity (*US*); (*für Frauen auch*) sorority (*US*); **Stu|-**
den|ten|werk NT student administration;
Stu|den|ten|wohn|heim NT hall of residence
(*Brit*), student hostel, dormitory (*US*)

Stu|den|tin [ʃtuˈdɛntɪn] F **-, -nen** student; (*Aus*:
= *Schülerin*) schoolgirl; (*einer bestimmten Schule*)
pupil

stu|den|tisch [ʃtuˈdɛntɪʃ] ADJ *attr* student *attr*;
~e Hilfskraft student assistant

Stu|die ['ʃtuːdiə] F **-, -n** study (*über +acc* of); (=
Entwurf auch) sketch; (= *Abhandlung*) essay (*über*
+acc on)

Stu|dien-: Stu|di|en|ab|bre|cher(in) M(F)
dropout, *student who fails to complete his/*
her course of study; **Stu|di|en|ab|schluss** ▲
M completion of a course of study; **Volkswirt-**
schaftler mit ~ graduate economist; **die Univer-**
sität ohne ~ verlassen to leave university with-
out graduating; **Stu|di|en|an|fän|ger(in)**
M(F) first year (student), freshman (*US*), fresh-
er (*Brit*); **Stu|di|en|an|ge|bot** NT range of
(degree) courses, (degree) courses on offer;
Stu|di|en|as|ses|sor(in) M(F) *graduate*
teacher who has recently completed his/her
training; **Stu|di|en|auf|ent|halt** M study vis-
it; **Stu|di|en|aus|ga|be** F (= *Buch*) student's
edition; **Stu|di|en|be|ra|tung** F course guid-
ance service; **Stu|di|en|buch** NT *book in*
which the courses one has attended are en-
tered; **Stu|di|en|di|rek|tor(in)** M(F) (*von*
Fachschule) principal; (*in Gymnasium*) ≈ deputy *or*
vice principal; **Stu|di|en|fach** NT subject;
Stu|di|en|fahrt F study trip; (*Sch*) educational
trip; **Stu|di|en|för|de|rung** F study grant; (*an*
Universität) university grant; **Stu|di|en|-**
freund(in) M(F) university/college friend;
Stu|di|en|gang M *pl* **-gänge** course of studies;
Stu|di|en|ge|büh|ren PL tuition fees *pl*; **stu|-**
di|en|hal|ber ADV for the purpose of study *or*
studying; **Stu|di|en|in|hal|te** PL course con-
tents *pl*; **Stu|di|en|jahr** NT academic year;
Stu|di|en|jah|re PL university/college years

---

pl; **Stu|di|en|plan** M course of study; **Stu|-**
di|en|platz M university/college place; **ein ~**
in Medizin a place (at university/college) to
study medicine; **Stu|di|en|rat** M , **Stu|di|en-**
rä|tin F teacher at a secondary school; **Stu|-**
di|en|re|fe|ren|dar(in) M(F) student teacher;
Stu|di|en|re|form F university/college re-
form; **Stu|di|en|rei|se** F study trip; (*Sch*) ed-
ucational trip; **Stu|di|en|se|mi|nar** NT teach-
er training course; **sie ist im ~ in Essen** she is
doing her teacher training in Essen; **Stu|di|-**
en|zeit F ⓐ student days *pl* ⓑ (= *Dauer*) du-
ration of a/one's course of studies; **Stu|di|en|-**
zeit|be|gren|zung F limitation on the length
of courses of studies; **Stu|di|en|zweck** M **für**
~e, zu ~en for the purposes of study, for study
purposes

stu|die|ren [ʃtuˈdiːrən] *ptp* **studiert** VI to study;
(= *Student sein*) to be a student, to be at univer-
sity/college, to be at school (*US inf*); **ich stu-**
diere an der Universität Bonn I am (a student)
at Bonn University; **nicht jeder kann ~** not everyone can go to university/college; **wo haben**
Sie studiert? what university/college did you
go to?; **bei jdm ~** to study under sb; **jdn ~ las-**
sen to send sb to university/college VT to
study; (*an Uni auch*) to read; (= *genau betrachten*)
to scrutinize; **sie hat vier Semester Jura studiert**
she has studied law for two years

Stu|die|ren|de(r) [ʃtuˈdiːrəndə] MF *decl as adj*
student

stu|diert [ʃtuˈdiːɐt] ADJ (*inf*) **~ sein** to have
been to university/college

Stu|dier|te(r) [ʃtuˈdiːɐtə] MF *decl as adj* univer-
sity-educated person; **er ist ein ~r** he is univer-
sity-educated; (*pej inf*) he's an intellectual

Stu|dier|zim|mer NT study

Stu|dio ['ʃtuːdio] NT **-s, -s** studio

Stu|di|o|büh|ne F studio theatre (*Brit*) *or* the-
ater (*US*)

Stu|di|o|sus [ʃtuˈdioːzʊs] M **-s, Studiosi** [-zi]
(*old, hum*) student

Stu|di|um ['ʃtuːdiʊm] NT **-s, Studien** [-diən]
study; (= *Hochschulstudium*) studies *pl*; (= *genaue*
Betrachtung) scrutiny, study; **sein ~ beginnen** *or*
aufnehmen (*form*) to begin one's studies, to go
to university/college; **das ~ hat fünf Jahre ge-**
dauert the course (of study) lasted five years;
das ~ ist kostenlos/teuer studying (at university) is free/expensive; **während seines ~s** while
he is/was *etc* a student *or* at university/college;
er ist noch im ~ he is still a student; **das ~ der**
Mathematik, das mathematische ~ the study of
mathematics, mathematical studies *pl*; **archäo-**
logische/psychologische Studien treiben to
study archaeology/psychology; **er war gerade**
beim ~ des Börsenberichts, als ... he was just
studying the stock exchange report when ...;
seine Studien zu etw machen to study sth

Stu|di|um ge|ne|ra|le ['ʃtuːdiʊm genəˈraːlə,
'st-] NT **- -**, *no pl* general course of studies; **ein**
~ machen to do a general degree

Stu|fe ['ʃtuːfə] F **-, -n** ⓐ step; (= *Geländestufe*
auch) terrace; (*Mus*: = *Tonstufe*) degree; (*an Rock,*
Kleid etc) tier; (*zum Kürzen*) tuck; (*im Haar*) layer;
(*von Rakete*) stage; **mehrere ~n auf einmal neh-**
men to run up the stairs two or three at a time
ⓑ (*fig* = *Phase*) stage; (= *Niveau*) level; (= *Rang*)
grade; (*Gram*: = *Steigerungsstufe*) degree; **eine ~**
höher als ... a step up from ...; **die höchste ~**
the height *or* pinnacle; **die tiefste ~** the depths
pl; **mit jdm auf gleicher ~ stehen** to be on a
level with sb; **jdn/sich mit jdm/etw auf die glei-**
che *or* **eine ~ stellen** to put *or* place sb/oneself
on a level *or* on a par with sb/sth

stu|fen ['ʃtuːfn̩] VT *Schüler, Preise, Gehälter* to
grade; *Haare* to layer; *Land etc* to terrace → *auch*
gestuft

Stu|fen-: Stu|fen|bar|ren M asymmetric bar;
Stu|fen|dach NT stepped roof; **stu|fen|för|-**
mig ADJ (*lit*) stepped; *Landschaft* terraced; (*fig*)
gradual ADV (*lit*) in steps; *angelegt* in terraces;

(*fig*) in stages, gradually; **Stu|fen|füh|rer|schein** M (graded) motorcycle licence (*Brit*) or license (*US*); **Stu|fen|heck** NT **ein Auto mit ~** a saloon car; **Stu|fen|lei|ter** F (*fig*) ladder (+*gen* to); **stu|fen|los** ADJ *Schaltung, Regelung* infinitely variable; (*fig*: = *gleitend*) smooth; **Stu|fen|ord|nung** F successive order; **Stu|fen|plan** M step-by-step plan (*zu* for); **Stu|fen|ra|ke|te** F multi-stage rocket; **Stu|fen|schal|ter** M (*Elec*) sequence switch; **Stu|fen|schnitt** M (*von Haaren*) layered cut; **Stu|fen|ta|rif** M (*Econ*) graduated tariff; **Stu|fen|ta|rif|ver|trag** M graduated wage agreement; **stu|fen|wei|se** ADV step by step, gradually ◨ ADJ *attr* gradual

stu|fig [ˈʃtuːfɪç] ADJ stepped; *Land etc* terraced; *Haar* layered ◨ ADV **das Haar ~ schneiden** to layer sb's hair

-stu|fig ADJ *suf* -stage *attr*; **dreistufig** (*Rakete, Plan, Verfahren*) three-stage *attr*

Stu|fung [ˈʃtuːfʊŋ] F -, -en gradation

Stuhl [ʃtuːl] M -(e)s, ̈e [ˈʃtyːlə] ◨ chair; **ist dieser ~ noch frei?** is this chair taken?, is this somebody's chair?; **sich zwischen zwei Stühle setzen** (*fig*) zwischen zwei Stühlen sitzen (*fig*) to fall between two stools; **ich wäre fast vom ~ gefallen** (*inf*) I nearly fell off my chair (*inf*); **jdm den ~ vor die Tür setzen** (*fig*) to kick sb out (*inf*)
◨ (= *Königsstuhl*) throne; **der Apostolische** or **Heilige** or **Päpstliche ~** the Apostolic or Holy or Papal See; **der ~ Petri** the See of Rome; **vor Gottes ~ gerufen werden** to be called before one's Maker
◨ (= *Lehramt*) chair (+*gen* of, *für* of, in)
◨ (= *Stuhlgang*) bowel movement; (= *Kot*) stool; **~/keinen ~ haben** to have had/not to have had a bowel movement

Stuhl-: **Stuhl|bein** NT chair leg; **Stuhl|drang** M *, no pl* (*form*) urgent need to empty the bowels; **Stuhl|ent|lee|rung** F (*form*) evacuation of the bowels; **Stuhl|gang** M [-gaŋ] *, no pl* bowel movement; **regelmäßig ~ haben** to have regular bowels; **~/keinen ~ haben** to have had/ not to have had a bowel movement; **Stuhl|leh|ne** F back of a chair; **Stuhl|rei|he** F row of chairs; **Stuhl|ver|hal|tung** F (*form*) retention of faeces (*Brit*) or feces (*US*)

Stu|ka [ˈʃtuːka, ˈʃtɔka] M -s, -s *abbr von* **Sturzkampfflugzeug** stuka, dive bomber

Stuk|ka|teur △ [ʃtʊkaˈtøːɐ] M -s, -e, **Stuk|ka|teu|rin** △ [-ˈtøːrɪn] F -, -en → **Stuckateur**

Stuk|ka|tur △ [ʃtʊkaˈtuːɐ] F -, -en → **Stuckatur**

Stul|le [ˈʃtʊlə] F -, -n (*N Ger*) slice of bread and butter; (= *Doppelstulle*) sandwich

Stul|pe [ˈʃtʊlpə] F -, -n cuff; (*von Handschuh*) gauntlet

stül|pen [ˈʃtʏlpn] VT **den Kragen nach oben ~** to turn up one's collar; **etw auf/über etw** (*acc*) **~** to put sth on/over sth; **etw nach innen/außen ~** to turn sth to the inside/outside; **sich** (*dat*) **den Hut auf den Kopf ~** to put on one's hat

Stul|pen-: **Stul|pen|hand|schuh** M gauntlet; **Stul|pen|stie|fel** M top boot

Stülp|na|se F snub or turned-up nose

stumm [ʃtʊm] ADJ ◨ (*lit, fig*) dumb; **die ~e Kreatur** (*geh*) the dumb creatures *pl*; **~ vor Schmerz** in silent agony; **~ vor Zorn** speechless with anger; **~er Diener** (= *Servierwagen*) dumbwaiter; (= *Kleiderständer*) valet ◨ (= *schweigend*) mute; **Anklage, Blick, Gebet** silent; **~ bleiben** to stay silent → **Fisch** ◨ (*Gram*) mute, silent ◨ *Rolle* nonspeaking; *Film, Szene* silent ◨ (= *schweigend*) mutely, silently; **sie sah mich ~ an** she looked at me without saying a word or without speaking

Stum|mel [ˈʃtʊml] M -s, - ◨ (= *Zigarettenstummel, Zigarrenstummel*) end, stub, butt; (= *Kerzenstummel*) stub; (*von Gliedmaßen, Zahn*) stump ◨ (= *Stummelschwanz*) dock

Stum|mel|pfei|fe F short-stemmed pipe

Stum|me(r) [ˈʃtʊmə] MF *decl as adj* dumb or mute person; **die ~n** the dumb

Stumm|film M silent film

Stumm|film|zeit F silent film era

Stum|pen [ˈʃtʊmpn] M -s, - cheroot

Stüm|per [ˈʃtʏmpɐ] M -s, -, **Stüm|pe|rin** [-ərɪn] F -, -nen (*pej*) ◨ amateur ◨ (= *Pfuscher*) bungler

Stüm|pe|rei [ʃtʏmpəˈrai] F -, -en (*pej*) ◨ amateur work ◨ (= *Pfuscherei*) bungling; (= *stümperhafte Arbeit*) botched (*inf*) or bungled job

stüm|per|haft (*pej*) ADJ (= *nicht fachmännisch*) amateurish; (= *schlecht auch*) botched (*inf*), bungled ◨ ADV *ausführen, malen* crudely; *arbeiten* poorly; *übersetzen* clumsily, crudely; **~ vorgehen** to be clumsy

stüm|pern [ˈʃtʏmpɐn] VI (*auf Klavier, bei Schach etc*) to play in an amateurish way (*auf* +*dat* on); **bei einer Arbeit ~** to do a job in an amateur way; **er stümpert nur** he's just an amateur; (= *pfuschen*) he's just a bungler

stumpf [ʃtʊmpf] ADJ ◨ *Messer* blunt; *Nase* snub, turned-up; **Rhabarber macht die Zähne ~** rhubarb sets the teeth on edge ◨ (*fig*) *Haar, Farbe, Mensch* dull; *Blick, Sinne* dulled, dull; **einer Sache gegenüber ~ sein** to remain impassive about sth ◨ (*Math*) *Winkel* obtuse; *Kegel etc* truncated ◨ (*Poet*) *Reim* masculine ◨ ADV *ansehen* dully; **~ vor sich hin brüten** to sit brooding impassively

Stumpf [ʃtʊmpf] M -(e)s, ̈e [ˈʃtʏmpfə] stump; (= *Bleistiftstumpf*) stub; **etw mit ~ und Stiel ausrotten** to eradicate sth root and branch

Stumpf|heit F -, *no pl* bluntness; (*fig*) dullness

Stumpf-: **Stumpf|sinn** M *, no pl* mindlessness; (= *Langweiligkeit*) monotony, tedium; **das ist doch ~** that's a tedious business; **stumpf|sin|nig** ADJ mindless; (= *langweilig*) monotonous, tedious; **Stumpf|sin|nig|keit** [ʃtʊmpfzɪnɪçkait] F -, *no pl* = **Stumpfsinn**; **stumpf|win|ke|lig, stumpf|wink|lig** ADJ (*Math*) *Winkel, Dreieck* obtuse

Stünd|chen [ˈʃtʏntçən] NT -s, - *dim von* **Stunde** **ein paar ~** for an hour or so

Stun|de [ˈʃtʊndə] F -, -n ◨ hour; **eine viertel ~** a quarter of an hour; **eine halbe ~** half an hour; **eine ganze/gute ~** a whole/good hour; **eine knappe ~** barely an hour; **eine halbe ~ Pause** a half-hour break, a break of half an hour; **drei ~n lang** for three hours; **eine ~ entfernt** an hour away; **eine Reise von zwei ~n** a two-hour journey; **jede ~** every hour; **~ um ~, ~n um ~n** hour after hour; **von ~ zu ~** hourly, from hour to hour; **sein Befinden wird von ~ zu ~ schlechter** his condition is becoming worse hour by hour or worse every hour; **130 Kilometer in der ~** 130 kilometres (*Brit*) or kilometers (*US*) per or an hour → *auch* **Achtstundentag**
◨ (= *Augenblick, Zeitpunkt*) time; **zu dieser ~** at this/that time; **zu jeder ~** at any time; **zu später ~** at a late hour; **zur ~** at the present moment or time, at present; **bis zur ~** up to the present moment, as yet; **von Stund an** (*old*) from henceforth; **die ~ X** (*Mil*) the impending onslaught; **sich auf die ~ X vorbereiten** (*fig*) to prepare for the inevitable; **eine schwache ~** a moment of weakness; **eine schwere ~** a time of difficulty; **seine ~ kommen** or **nahen fühlen** (*geh*: = *Tod*) to feel one's hour (of death) approaching; **seine ~ hat geschlagen** (*fig*) his hour has come; **seine schwerste ~** his darkest hour; **die ~ der Entscheidung/Wahrheit** the moment of decision/ truth
◨ (= *Unterricht*) lesson; (= *Unterrichtsstunde*) class, period, lesson; **sonnabends haben wir vier ~n** on Saturday we have four lessons; **in der zweiten ~ haben wir Latein** in the second period we have Latin; **~n geben/nehmen** to give/have or take lessons

stun|den [ˈʃtʊndn] VT **jdm etw ~** to give sb time to pay sth; **jdm etw zwei Wochen/bis Mitt-** woch **~** to give sb two weeks/until Wednesday to pay sth

Stun|den-: **Stun|den|buch** NT (*Hist Liter*) book of hours; **Stun|den|ge|bet** NT *prayer said at any of the canonical hours eg matins, vespers*; **Stun|den|ge|schwin|dig|keit** F speed per hour; **eine ~ von 90 km** a speed of 90 km per hour; **Stun|den|glas** NT hourglass; **Stun|den|ho|tel** NT *hotel where rooms are rented by the hour*; **Stun|den|ki|lo|me|ter** PL kilometres *pl* (*Brit*) or kilometers *pl* (*US*) per or an hour; **stun|den|lang** ADJ lasting several hours; **eine ~e Verspätung** a delay of several hours; **nach ~em Warten** after hours of waiting ◨ ADV for hours; **Stun|den|lohn** M hourly wage; **~ bekommen** to be paid by the hour; **Stun|den|plan** M (*Sch*) timetable; **Stun|den|satz** M (= *Bezahlung*) hourly rate; **Stun|den|schlag** M striking of the hour; **Stun|den|takt** M hourly frequency; **im ~** at hourly intervals; **stun|den|wei|se** ADV (= *pro Stunde*) by the hour; (= *stündlich*) every hour; **Kellner ~ gesucht** part-time waiters required; **der Patient darf ~ aufstehen** the patient may get up for an hour at a time; **Wasser gibt es nur ~** water is only available for a few hours at a time; **Stun|den|zei|ger** M hour hand

-stün|dig [ʃtʏndɪç] ADJ *suf* **eine halbstündige/ zweistündige Fahrt** a half-hour/two-hour journey, a journey of half an hour/two hours

Stünd|lein [ˈʃtʏntlain] NT -s, - **ein ~** a short while; **sein letztes ~ hat geschlagen** (= *er stirbt*) his last hour has come; (*fig inf*) he's had it (*inf*)

stünd|lich [ˈʃtʏntlɪç] ADJ hourly ◨ ADV hourly, every hour

-stünd|lich ADV *suf* **zweistündlich/dreistündlich** every two/three hours

Stun|dung [ˈʃtʊndʊŋ] F -, -en deferment of payment

Stunk [ʃtʊŋk] M -s, *no pl* (*inf*) stink (*inf*), row (*inf*); **~ machen** to kick up a stink (*inf*); **dann gibt es ~** then there'll be a stink (*inf*)

Stunt [stant] M -s, -s stunt

Stunt|man [ˈstantmən] M -s, **Stuntmen** [-mən] stunt man

Stunt|wo|man [ˈstantvʊmən] F -, **Stuntwomen** [-vɪmɪn] stunt woman

stu|pend [ʃtuˈpɛnt, st-] ADJ (*geh*) astounding, tremendous

stu|pid [ʃtuˈpiːt, st-], **stu|pi|de** [ʃtuˈpiːdə, st-] ADJ (*geh*) mindless

Stu|pi|di|tät F (*geh*) mindlessness

Stups [ʃtʊps] M -es, -e nudge

stup|sen [ˈʃtʊpsn] VT to nudge

Stups|na|se F snub nose

stur [ʃtuːɐ] ADJ pig-headed, stubborn; *Nein, Arbeiten* dogged; **sich ~ stellen** (*inf*) **auf ~ stellen** or **schalten** (*inf*) to dig one's heels in; **ein ~er Bock** (*inf*) a pig-headed fellow ◨ ADV *beharren, bestehen* stubbornly; **~ weitermachen/weiterreden/ weitergehen** to carry on regardless or doggedly; **er fuhr ~ geradeaus/in der Mitte der Straße** he just carried straight on/carried on driving in the middle of the road

Stur|heit F -, *no pl* pig-headedness, stubbornness

Sturm [ʃtʊrm] M -(e)s, ̈e [ˈʃtʏrmə] ◨ (*lit, fig*) storm; **in ~ und Regen** in wind and rain; **das Barometer steht auf ~** (*lit*) the barometer is indicating stormy weather; (*fig*) there's a storm brewing; **die Ruhe** or **Stille vor dem ~** the calm before the storm; **ein ~ im Wasserglas** (*fig*) a storm in a teacup (*Brit*), a tempest in a teapot (*US*); **~ läuten** to keep one's finger on the doorbell; (= *Alarm schlagen*) to ring or sound the alarm bell; **die Stürme des Lebens** the storms of life, the ups and downs of life; **ein ~ der Begeisterung/Entrüstung** a wave of enthusiasm/ indignation; **im ~ der Leidenschaft** (*geh*) in the throes of passion; **~ und Drang** (*Liter*) Storm and Stress, Sturm und Drang; (*fig*) emotion

---

b (= *Angriff*) attack (*auf* on); (*Mil*) assault, attack; (*Sport*: = *Stürmerreihe*) forward line; **etw im ~ nehmen** (*Mil, fig*) to take sth by storm; **zum ~ blasen** (*Mil, fig*) to sound the attack; **gegen etw ~ laufen** (*fig*) to be up in arms against sth; **ein ~ auf die Banken/Aktien** a run on the banks/shares; **ein ~ auf die Karten/Plätze** a rush for tickets/seats; **der ~ auf die Festung/Bastille** the storming of the stronghold/Bastille → **erobern**

Sturm-: Sturm|ab|tei|lung F (*NS*) Storm Troopers *pl*; **Sturm|an|griff** M (*Mil*) assault (*auf* +*acc* on); **sturm|be|wegt** ADJ stormy, storm-tossed (*liter*); **Sturm|bö** F squall; **Sturm|bock** M (*Mil*) battering ram; **Sturm|boot** NT (*Mil*) assault boat; **Sturm|deck** NT hurricane deck

stür|men ['ʃtʏrmən] VI **a** (*Meer*) to rage; (*Wind auch*) to blow; (*Mil*) to attack, to assault (*gegen etw* sth) **b** (*Sport*) (= *als Stürmer spielen*) to play forward; (= *angreifen*) to attack **c** *aux sein* (= *rennen*) to storm VI *impers* to be blowing a gale VT (*Mil, fig*) to storm; *Bank etc* to make a run on

Stür|mer ['ʃtʏrmɐ] M **-s, -**, **Stür|me|rin** [-ərɪn] F **-, -nen** (*Sport*) forward; (*Ftbl auch*) striker; (*fig*: = *Draufgänger*) go-getter (*inf*); **~ und Dränger** (*Liter*) writer of the Storm and Stress *or* Sturm und Drang period; (*fig*) ≈ angry young man

sturm|er|probt ADJ (*fig geh*) battle-tried

Stür|mer|rei|he F (*Sport*) forward line

Sturm-: Sturm|fah|ne F warning flag; (*Mil Hist*) standard; **sturm|fest** ADJ (*lit*) stormproof; (*fig*) steadfast; **Sturm|flut** F storm tide; **sturm|frei** ADJ (*lit*) storm-free; (*Mil*) unassailable; **bei mir ist heute Abend ~e Bude** (*inf*) it's open house at my place tonight; **ich habe eine ~e Bude** (*inf*) where I live I can do as I please; **Sturm|ge|päck** NT combat *or* light pack; **sturm|ge|peitscht** [-gəpaɪʃt] ADJ (*geh*) storm-lashed (*liter*); **Sturm|ge|wehr** NT submachine gun; **Sturm|hau|be** F **a** (*Hist*) helmet, morion **b** (*Zool*) whelk shell; **Sturm|hut** M (*Bot*) aconite

stür|misch ['ʃtʏrmɪʃ] ADJ **a** *Meer, Überfahrt* rough, stormy; *Wetter, Tag* blustery; (*mit Regen*) stormy **b** (*fig*) tempestuous; (= *aufregend*) *Zeit, Jugend* stormy, turbulent; *Entwicklung, Wachstum* rapid; *Liebhaber* passionate, ardent; *Jubel, Beifall* tumultuous, frenzied; **nicht so ~** take it easy ADV enthusiastically; **jdn ~ bejubeln/feiern** to give sb a tumultuous reception

Sturm-: Sturm|la|ter|ne F hurricane lamp; **Sturm|lauf** M trot; **im ~** at a trot; **Sturm|lei|ter** F scaling ladder; **sturm|reif** ADJ (*Mil*): **~ sein** to be ripe for attack (*für* by); **etw ~ schie|ßen** (*Mil*) to weaken sth in preparation for an attack; (*fig*) to undermine sth and expose it to attack; **Sturm|scha|den** M storm damage *no pl*; **Sturm|schritt** M (*Mil, fig*) double-quick pace; **im ~** at the double; **Sturm|se|gel** NT storm sail; **Sturm|spit|ze** F (*Mil, Sport*) spearhead; **sturm|stark** ADJ (*Sport*) **eine ~e Mannschaft** a team with a strong forward line; **Sturm|tief** NT (*Met*) deep depression; **Sturm|trupp** M (*Mil*) assault troop; **Sturm-und-Drang-Zeit** F (*Liter*) Storm and Stress *or* Sturm und Drang period; **Sturm|vo|gel** M petrel; (= *Albatros*) albatross; **Sturm|war|nung** F gale warning; **Sturm|wind** M whirlwind

Sturz [ʃtʊrts] M **-es, ⁼e** ['ʃtʏrtsə] **a** (*von, from, off*) (*aus* out of) fall; **einen ~ tun** to have a fall **b** (*in Temperatur, Preis*) drop, fall; (*von Börsenkurs*) slump **c** (*von Regierung, Minister*) fall; (*durch Coup, von König*) overthrow **d** (*Archit*) lintel **e** (= *Radsturz*) camber **f** (*S Ger, Aus*: = *Glassturz*) cover

Sturz-: Sturz|acker M (*Agr*) newly ploughed (*Brit*) *or* plowed (*US*) field; **Sturz|bach** M (*lit*) fast-flowing stream; (*fig*) stream, torrent; **sturz|be|sof|fen** (*inf*), **sturz|be|trun|ken** (*inf*) ADJ pissed as a newt (*Brit inf*), drunk as a sailor (*US inf*)

stür|zen ['ʃtʏrtsn] VI *aux sein* **a** (= *fallen*) to fall (*von* from, off); (*geh*: = *steil abfallen*) to plunge; (= *hervorstürzen*) to stream; **ins Wasser ~** to plunge into the water; **vom Pferd ~** to fall off a/one's horse; **zu Boden ~** to crash to the ground; **zu Tode** *or* **in den Tod ~** to fall to one's death; **er ist schwer** *or* **heftig/unglücklich gestürzt** he had a heavy/bad fall; **die Tränen stürzten ihm aus den Augen** (*geh*) tears streamed from his eyes **b** (*fig*: = *abgesetzt werden*) to fall **c** (= *rennen*) to rush, to dash; **sie kam ins Zimmer gestürzt** she burst *or* came bursting into the room; **jdm in die Arme ~** to fling oneself into sb's arms VT **a** (= *werfen*) to fling, to hurl; **jdn aus dem Fenster ~** to fling *or* hurl sb out of the window; **jdn ins Unglück** *or* **Verderben ~** to bring disaster to sb; **jdn/etw in eine Krise ~** to plunge sb/sth into a crisis **b** (= *kippen*) to turn upside down; *Pudding* to turn out; **„nicht ~!"** "this side up"; **etw über etw** (*acc*) **~** to put sth over sth **c** (= *absetzen*) *Regierung, Minister* to bring down; (*durch Coup*) to overthrow; *König* to depose VR **sich zu Tode ~** to fall to one's death; (*absichtlich*) to jump to one's death; **sich auf jdn/etw ~** to pounce on sb/sth; *auf Essen* to fall on sth; *auf Zeitung etc* to grab sth; *auf den Feind* to attack sb/sth; **sich ins Wasser ~** to fling *or* hurl oneself into the water; (= *sich ertränken*) to drown oneself; **sich in die Arbeit ~** to throw oneself into one's work; **sich in Schulden ~** to plunge into debt; **sich ins Unglück/Verderben ~** to plunge headlong into disaster/ruin; **sich ins Vergnügen ~** to fling oneself into a round of pleasure; **sich in Unkosten ~** to go to great expense

Sturz-: Sturz|flug M (nose) dive; **etw im ~ angreifen** to dive and attack sth; **Sturz|ge|burt** F (*Med*) precipitate delivery; **Sturz|gut** NT (*form*) goods unloaded by tipping; **Sturz|helm** M crash helmet; **Sturz|kampf|flug|zeug** NT dive bomber; **Sturz|see** F (*Naut*) breaker

Stuss ▲ [ʃtʊs] M **-es**, *no pl* (*inf*) nonsense, rubbish (*Brit inf*), codswallop (*Brit inf*); **was für ein ~** what a load of nonsense etc (*inf*); **~ lallen** (*sl*) to talk shite (*Brit sl*) *or* crap (*inf*)

Stut|buch ['ʃtuːt-] NT studbook

Stu|te ['ʃtuːtə] F **-, -n** mare

Stu|ten-: Stu|ten|foh|len NT , **Stu|ten|fül|len** NT filly; **Stu|ten|zucht** F stud farm; (= *Züchtung*) stud farming

Stutz [ʃtʊts] M **-es, Stütze** ['ʃtʏtsə] (*Sw inf*: = *Franken*) (Swiss) franc

Stütz-: Stütz|ap|pa|rat M calliper (*Brit*), caliper (*US*), brace; (*für Kopf*) collar; **Stütz|bal|ken** M beam; (*in Decke*) joist; (*quer*) crossbeam

Stüt|ze ['ʃtʏtsə] F **-, -n** **a** support; (= *Pfeiler*) pillar; (*für Wäscheleine etc*) prop; (= *Buchstütze*) rest **b** (= *Halt*) support; (= *Fußstütze*) footrest **c** (*fig*) (= *Hilfe*) help, aid (*für* to); (= *Beistand*) support; (= *wichtiger Mensch*) mainstay; (*dated*: = *Hausgehilfin*) (domestic) help; **als ~ für seinen Kreislauf** as an aid for *or* to aid his circulation; **die ~n der Gesellschaft** the pillars of society **d** (*inf*: = *Arbeitslosengeld*) dole (*Brit inf*), welfare (*US*); **~ bekommen** to be on the dole (*Brit inf*), to be on welfare (*US*)

stut|zen¹ ['ʃtʊtsn] VI to stop short; (= *zögern*) to hesitate

stut|zen² VT to trim; *Baum auch* to prune; *Flügel, Ohren, Hecke* to clip; *Schwanz* to dock

Stut|zen ['ʃtʊtsn] M **-s, -** **a** (= *Gewehr*) carbine **b** (= *Rohrstück*) connecting piece; (= *Endstück*) nozzle **c** (= *Strumpf*) woollen (*Brit*) *or* woolen (*US*) gaiter

stüt|zen ['ʃtʏtsn] VT (= *Halt geben*) to support; *Gebäude, Mauer* to shore up; *Währung* to back, to support; (*fig*: = *untermauern*) to back up, to support; **einen Verdacht durch etw ~** to back

up *or* support a suspicion with sth; **einen Verdacht auf etw** (*acc*) **~** to base *or* found a suspicion on sth; **die Ellbogen auf den Tisch ~** to prop *or* rest one's elbows on the table; **den Kopf in die Hände ~** to hold one's head in one's hands VR **sich auf jdn/etw ~** (*lit*) to lean on sb/sth; (*fig*) to count on sb/sth; (*Beweise, Verteidigung, Theorie etc*) to be based on sb/sth; **können Sie sich auf Fakten ~?** can you produce facts to bear out what you're saying?; **er konnte sich auf eigene Erfahrungen ~** he had his own experiences to fall back on; **in seiner Dissertation stützte er sich weitgehend auf diese Theorie** he based his thesis closely on this theory

Stut|zer ['ʃtʊtsɐ] M **-s, -** **a** (*dated pej*) fop (*dated*), dandy **b** (= *Mantel*) three-quarter length coat

stut|zer|haft ADJ (*dated pej*) foppish (*dated*), dandified ADV gekleidet, sich kleiden foppishly (*dated*)

Stütz|flü|gel M baby grand (piano)

Stütz|ge|we|be NT (*Med*) stroma (*spec*)

stut|zig ['ʃtʊtsɪç] ADJ pred **~ werden** (= *argwöhnisch*) to become *or* grow suspicious; (= *verwundert*) to begin to wonder; **jdn ~ machen** to make sb suspicious; **das hat mich ~ gemacht** that made me wonder; (= *argwöhnisch*) that made me suspicious

Stütz-: Stütz|kor|sett NT support corset; **Stütz|kurs** M (*Sch*) extra classes *pl*; **Stütz|mau|er** F retaining wall; **Stütz|pfei|ler** M supporting pillar *or* column; (*von Brücke auch*) pier; **Stütz|preis** M (*Econ*) support price; **Stütz|punkt** M (*Mil, fig*) base; (= *Ausbildungsstätte*) centre; **Stütz|rad** NT (*an Fahrrad*) stabilizer; **Stütz|stan|ge** F supporting pole; **Stütz|strumpf** M support stocking

Stüt|zung ['ʃtʏtsʊŋ] F **-, -en** support

Stüt|zungs-: Stüt|zungs|käu|fe PL purchases to support share prices, currency rate etc; **Stüt|zungs|maß|nah|me** F supporting measure

Stütz|ver|band M support bandage

StVO [ɛsteːfauˈʔoː] *abbr von* **Straßenverkehrsordnung**

sty|len ['staɪlən] VT *Wagen, Wohnung* to design; *Frisur* to style; *Kleidung* to design, to style; *jdn* to do up VR to do oneself up

Styling ['staɪlɪŋ] NT **-s**, *no pl* styling

Styro|por® [ʃtyroˈpoːɐ, st-] NT **-s** polystyrene

Styx [ʃtʏks, st-] M **-** (*Myth*) Styx

SU [ɛsˈʔuː] F *abbr von* **Sowjetunion**

s. u. *abbr von* **siehe unten**

Su|a|da ['zuaːda] F **-, Suaden** [-dn], **Su|a|de** ['zuaːdə] F **-, -n** (*liter*) torrent of words

Su|a|he|li¹ [zuaˈheːli] M **-(s), -(s)** *or* f **-, -(s)** Swahili

Su|a|he|li² NT **-(s)**, *no pl* (*Ling*) Swahili → auch **Deutsch(e)**

Sub-, sub- *in cpds* sub-; **sub|al|tern** [zʊpalˈtɛrn] ADJ (*pej*) *Stellung, Beamter* subordinate; *Gesinnung* obsequious, subservient; (= *unselbstständig*) unselfreliant; **sub|ato|mar** [zʊplatoˈmaːɐ] ADJ (*Phys*) subatomic; **Sub|do|mi|nan|te** [zʊpdomiˈnantə, ˈzʊp-] F (*Mus*) subdominant

Sub|jekt [zʊpˈjɛkt, ˈzʊp-] NT **-(e)s, -e** **a** subject **b** (*pej*: = *Mensch*) customer (*inf*), character (*inf*)

sub|jek|tiv [zʊpjɛkˈtiːf, ˈzʊp-] ADJ subjective ADV subjectively

Sub|jek|ti|vis|mus [zʊpjɛktiˈvɪsmʊs] M **-**, *no pl* (*Philos*) subjectivism

Sub|jek|ti|vi|tät [zʊpjɛktiviˈtɛːt] F **-**, *no pl* subjectivity

Sub|jekt|satz M (*Gram*) noun clause as subject

Sub-: Sub|kon|ti|nent M subcontinent; **Sub|kul|tur** F subculture; **sub|ku|tan** [zʊpkuˈtaːn]

(*Med*) **ADJ** subcutaneous **ADV** *spritzen* subcutaneously

sub|lim [zu'bli:m] ADJ (*geh*) sublime, lofty; *Einfühlungsvermögen, Charakter* refined; *Interpretation* eloquent

Sub|li|mat [zubli'ma:t] NT **-(e)s, -e** (*Chem*) **a** (= *Niederschlag*) sublimate **b** (= *Quecksilberverbindung*) mercuric chloride

Sub|li|ma|ti|on [zublima'tsio:n] F **-, -en** (*Chem*) sublimation

sub|li|mie|ren [zubli'mi:rən] *ptp* **sublimiert** VT **a** (*Psych*) to sublimate **b** (*Chem*) to sublimate, to sublime

Sub|li|mie|rung F **-, -en** sublimation

sub|ma|rin [zupma'ri:n] ADJ submarine, underwater

Sub|or|di|na|ti|on [zup|ɔrdina'tsio:n] F subordination

Sub|si|di|a|ri|tät [zupzidiari'tɛ:t] F **-, -en** (*Pol*) subsidiarity

Sub|si|di|a|ri|täts|prin|zip NT (*Pol*) subsidiarity principle

Sub|sis|tenz|wirt|schaft [zupzɪs'tɛnts-] F subsistence farming

Sub|skri|bent [zupskri'bɛnt] M **-en, -en, Sub|skri|ben|tin** [-'bɛntɪn] F **-, -nen** subscriber

sub|skri|bie|ren [zupskri'bi:rən] *ptp* **subskribiert** VTI **(auf) etw** (*acc*) ~ to subscribe to sth

Sub|skrip|ti|on [zupskrɪp'tsio:n] F **-, -en** subscription (+*gen, auf* +*acc* to)

Sub|skrip|ti|ons|preis M subscription price

sub|stan|ti|ell [zupstan'tsiɛl] ADJ = **substanziell**

Sub|stan|tiv ['zupstanti:f] NT **-s, -e** *or* (*rare*) **-a** [-və, -va] noun

sub|stan|ti|vie|ren [zupstanti'vi:rən] *ptp* **substantiviert** VT to nominalize

sub|stan|ti|visch ['zupstanti:vɪʃ] ADJ nominal **ADV** *verwenden* nominally, as a noun/as nouns

Sub|stanz [zup'stants] F **-, -en** **a** substance; (= *Wesen*) essence; **die ~ des Volkes** the (essential) character of the people; **etw in seiner ~ treffen** to affect the substance of sth **b** (*Fin*) capital assets *pl*; **von der ~ zehren** *or* **leben** to live on one's capital

sub|stan|zi|ell [zupstan'tsiɛl] ADJ **a** (*Philos*) (= *stofflich*) material; (= *wesenhaft*) essential **b** (*fig geh*: = *bedeutsam, inhaltlich*) fundamental **c** (= *nahrhaft*) substantial, solid **ADV** (= *wesentlich*) substantially; **die Aussagen waren ~ verschieden** the essence of the statements was completely different; **~ an etw** (*dat*) **beteiligt sein** to own a substantial part of sth

Sub|stanz-: sub|stanz|los ADJ insubstantial; **sub|stanz|reich** ADJ solid; *Aufsatz auch* meaty (*inf*); **Sub|stanz|ver|lust** M loss of volume; (= *Gewichtsverlust*) loss of weight; (*fig*) loss of significance *or* importance

sub|sti|tu|ie|ren [zupstitu'i:rən] *ptp* **substituiert** VT (*geh*) **A durch B** ~ to substitute B for A, to replace A with B

Sub|sti|tut [zupsti'tu:t] M **-en, -en, Sub|sti|tu|tin** [-'tu:tɪn] F **-, -nen** deputy *or* assistant departmental manager

Sub|sti|tu|ti|on [zupstitu'tsio:n] F **-, -en** (*geh*) **die ~ von A durch B** the substitution of B for A, the replacement of A by B

Sub|strat [zup'stra:t] NT **-(e)s, -e** substratum

sub|su|mie|ren [zupzu'mi:rən] *ptp* **subsumiert** VT to subsume (*unter* +*dat* to)

sub|til [zup'ti:l] (*geh*) ADJ subtle **ADV** subtly; **es wird ~ unterschieden zwischen ...** there is a subtle difference between ...

Sub|ti|li|tät [zupti'li'tɛ:t] F **-, -en** (*geh*) subtlety

Sub|tra|hend [zuptra'hɛnt] M **-en, -en** [-dn] (*Math*) subtrahend

sub|tra|hie|ren [zuptra'hi:rən] *ptp* **subtrahiert** VTI to subtract

Sub|trak|ti|on [zuptrak'tsio:n] F **-, -en** subtraction

Sub|trak|ti|ons|zei|chen NT subtraction sign

Sub|tro|pen PL subtropics *pl*

sub|tro|pisch ADJ subtropical

Sub|un|ter|neh|mer(in) M(F) subcontractor

Sub|ven|ti|on [zupvɛn'tsio:n] F **-, -en** subsidy; (*von Regierung, Behörden auch*) subvention

sub|ven|ti|o|nie|ren [zupvɛntsio'ni:rən] *ptp* **subventioniert** VT to subsidize

Sub|ven|ti|o|ni|tis [zupvɛntsio'ni:tɪs] F **-, *no pl*** (*hum*) compulsive subsidization

Sub|ven|ti|ons|ab|bau M cutback on subsidies

Sub|ver|si|on [zupvɛr'zio:n] F **-, -en** (*Pol*) subversion

sub|ver|siv [zupvɛr'zi:f] ADJ subversive **ADV** **sich ~ betätigen** to engage in subversive activities

Such-: Such|ak|ti|on F search operation; **Such|an|zei|ge** F missing person/dog *etc* report; **eine ~ aufgeben** to report sb/sth missing; **Such|be|fehl** M (*Comput*) search command; **Such|be|griff** M (*Comput*) search item; **Such|bild** NT (*form*) searching image; (= *Rätsel*) picture puzzle; **Such|dau|er** F (*Comput*) search time; **Such|dienst** M missing persons tracing service

Su|che ['zu:xə] F **-, *no pl*** search (*nach* for); **auf die ~ nach jdm/etw gehen, sich auf die ~ nach jdm/etw machen** to go in search of sb/sth; **auf der ~ nach etw sein** to be looking for sth

-su|che F *suf in cpds* **auf ...suche sein** to be looking for a ...

su|chen ['zu:xn] **VT a** (*um zu finden*) to look for; (*stärker, intensiv*) to search for (*auch Comput*); **Abenteuer ~** to go out in search of adventure; **die Gefahr ~** to look for *or* seek danger; **sich** (*dat*) **einen Mann/eine Frau ~** to look for a husband/wife (for oneself); **Verkäufer(in) gesucht** sales person wanted; **gesucht!** wanted (*wegen* for); **er wurde mit *or* per Haftbefehl gesucht** there was a warrant out for his arrest; **Streit/Ärger (mit jdm) ~** to be looking for trouble/a quarrel (with sb); **Schutz vor etw** (*dat*) ~ to seek shelter from sth; **Zuflucht ~ bei jdm** to seek refuge with sb; **etw zu tun ~** (*geh*) to seek *or* strive to do sth; **was suchst du hier?** what are you doing here?; **du hast hier nichts zu ~** you have no business being here; **seinesgleichen ~** to be unparalleled → *auch* **gesucht**

b (= *wünschen, streben nach*) to seek; (= *versuchen*) to strive, to try; **er sucht die tragischen Erlebnisse zu vergessen** he is trying to forget the tragic events; **sein Recht/seinen Vorteil ~** to be out for one's rights/one's own advantage; **ein Gespräch ~** to try to have a talk

VI to search, to hunt; **nach etw ~** to look for sth; (*stärker*) to search *or* hunt for sth; **nach Worten ~** to search for words; (= *sprachlos sein*) to be at a loss for words; **Suchen und Ersetzen** (*Comput*) search and replace; **such!** (*zu Hund*) seek!, find!; **sucht, so werdet ihr finden!** (*Bibl*) seek and ye shall find (*Bibl*)

Su|cher[1] ['zu:xɐ] M **-s, -** (*Phot*) viewfinder; (*Astron*) finder

Su|cher[2] ['zu:xɐ] M **-s, -, Su|che|rin** [-ərɪn] F **-, -nen** (*geh*) seeker

Su|che|rei [zu:xə'rai] F **-, -en** (*inf*) searching

Such-: Such|funk|ti|on F (*Comput*) search function; **Such|lauf** M (*bei Hi-Fi-Geräten*) search; **Such|lauf|funk|ti|on** F search function; **Such|mann|schaft** F search party; **Such|ma|schi|ne** F (*Comput*) search engine; **Such|mas|ke** F (*Comput*) search panel; **Such|mel|dung** F SOS message; (*von Suchdienst*) missing person announcement; **Such|mo|dus** M (*Comput*) search mode; **Such|pro|gramm** NT (*Comput*) search program; **Such|schein|wer|fer** M searchlight

Sucht [zuxt] F **-, ̈e** ['zʏçtə] addiction (*nach* to); (*fig*) obsession (*nach* with); **~ erzeugend** addictive; **eine krankhafte ~ haben, etw zu tun** (*fig*) to be obsessed with doing sth; **das kann zur ~ werden** you'll get *or* become addicted to that; **das Trinken ist bei ihm zur ~ geworden** he has become addicted to drink; **an einer ~ leiden** to be an addict

-sucht F , *no pl suf in cpds* **Drogensucht** addiction to drugs; **Trinksucht** addiction to drink

Sucht-: Sucht|be|auf|trag|te(r) MF *decl as adj* anti-drugs coordinator; **Sucht|be|ra|ter(in)** M(F) addiction counsellor (*Brit*) *or* counselor (*US*); **Sucht|dro|ge** F addictive drug; **sucht|er|zeu|gend** △ ADJ → **Sucht**; **Sucht|for|scher(in)** M(F) addiction researcher; **Sucht|ge|fahr** F danger of addiction

süch|tig ['zʏçtɪç] ADJ addicted (*nach* to); **von *or* nach etw ~ werden/sein** to get *or* become/be addicted to sth; **~ machen** (*Droge*) to be addictive; **davon wird man nicht ~** that's not addictive

Süch|ti|ge(r) ['zʏçtɪɡə] MF *decl as adj* addict

Süch|tig|keit F **-, *no pl*** addiction (*nach* to)

Sucht-: Sucht|kli|nik F detox(ification) centre (*Brit*) *or* center (*US*); **Sucht|kran|ke(r)** MF *decl as adj* addict; **Sucht|krank|heit** F addictive illness; **Sucht|mit|tel** NT addictive drug; **Sucht|mit|tel|miss|brauch** ▲ M drug abuse

Sud [zu:t] M **-(e)s, -e** [-də] liquid; (*esp von Fleisch, für Suppe*) stock; **der ~ des Gemüses** the vegetable water

Süd [zy:t] M **-(e)s,** (*rare*) **-e** [-də] **a** (*Naut, Met, liter*) south; **aus *or* von/nach ~** from/to the south **b** (*liter: Wind*) south wind, southerly (wind)

Süd- *in cpds* (*in Ländernamen, politisch*) South; (*geografisch auch*) the South of ..., Southern; **Süd|af|ri|ka** NT South Africa; **Süd|ame|ri|ka** NT South America

Su|dan [zu'da:n, 'zu:dan] M **-s** **der ~** the Sudan

Su|da|ner [zu'da:nɐ] M **-s, -, Su|da|ne|rin** [-ərɪn] F **-, -nen, Su|da|ne|se** [zuda'ne:zə] M **-n, -n, Su|da|ne|sin** [-'ne:zɪn] F **-, -nen** Sudanese

su|da|ne|sisch [zuda'ne:zɪʃ], **su|da|nisch** [zu'da:nɪʃ] ADJ Sudanese

Süd-: süd|deutsch ADJ South German; *Dialekt, Spezialität, Mentalität auch* Southern German; **die Süddeutschen** the South Germans; **Süd|deutsch|land** NT South(ern) Germany, the South of Germany

Su|del ['zu:dl] M **-s, -** (*Sw*: = *Kladde*) draft, rough outline; **im ~** in draft (form)

Su|de|lei [zu:də'lai] F **-, -en** (*geschrieben*) scrawling; (*gezeichnet*) daubing; (*an Mauern etc*) graffiti

su|deln ['zu:dln] VTI (= *schreiben*) to scrawl; (= *zeichnen*) to daub

Sü|den ['zy:dn] M **-s, *no pl*** south; (*von Land*) South; **aus dem ~, vom ~ her** from the south; **gegen *or* gen** (*liter*) **~** *or* **nach ~** south(wards), to the south; **nach ~ hin** to the south; **im ~ der Stadt/des Landes** in the south of the town/country; **im tiefen ~** in the deep *or* far south; **weiter *or* tiefer im ~** further south; **im ~ Frankreichs** in southern France

Süd|eng|land NT the South of England

Su|de|ten [zu'de:tn] PL (*Geog*) **die ~** the Sudeten(land)

Su|de|ten|land NT das **~** the Sudetenland

Süd-: Süd|eu|ro|pa NT Southern Europe; **Süd|frank|reich** NT the South of France; **Süd|früch|te** PL citrus and tropical fruit(*s pl*); **Süd|halb|ku|gel** F southern hemisphere; **auf der ~** in the southern hemisphere

Sud|haus ['zu:t-] NT (*in Brauerei*) brewing room

Süd-: Süd|ita|li|en NT Southern Italy; **Süd|je|men** M South Yemen; **Süd|ko|rea** NT South Korea; **Süd|küs|te** F south(ern) coast; **die ~ Englands** the south coast of England; **Süd|la|ge** F southern aspect; **Süd|län|der**

['zy:tlɛndə] M **-s, -**, **Süd|län|de|rin** [-ərɪn] F **-, -nen** southerner; (= *Italiener, Spanier etc*) Mediterranean *or* Latin type; **süd|län|disch** [-lɛndɪʃ] ADJ southern; (= *italienisch, spanisch etc*) Mediterranean, Latin; *Temperament* Latin ADV **~ aussehen** to look Mediterranean

süd|lich ['zy:tlɪç] ADJ a southern; *Kurs, Wind, Richtung* southerly; **der ~e Polarkreis** the Antarctic Circle; **der ~e Wendekreis** the Tropic of Capricorn; **52 Grad ~er Breite** 52 degrees south; **~es Eismeer** Antarctic Ocean b (= *mediterran*) Mediterranean, Latin; *Temperament* Latin ADV (to the) south; **~ von Wien (gelegen)** (to the) south of Vienna; **es liegt ~er** *or* **weiter ~** it is further (to the) south PREP **+gen** (to the) south of

Süd-: Süd|licht NT , *no pl* southern lights *pl*, aurora australis; (*fig hum: Mensch*) Southerner; **Süd-Nord-Gefäl|le** NT North-South divide

Süd|ost [zy:t'ɔst] M a **-en,** *no pl* (*Met, Naut, liter*) southeast, sou'-east (*Naut*); **aus** *or* **von ~** from the southeast; **nach ~** to the southeast, southeast(wards) b **-(e)s, -e** (*liter: Wind*) southeast(erly) (wind), sou'-easterly (*Naut*)

Süd|ost- *in cpds* southeast; (*bei Namen*) Southeast

Süd|os|ten [zy:t'ɔstn] M southeast; (*von Land*) South East; **aus** *or* **von ~** from the southeast; **nach ~** to the southeast, southeast(wards)

Süd|ost|eu|ro|pa NT Southeast(ern) Europe

süd|öst|lich [zy:t'œstlɪç] ADJ *Gegend* southeastern; *Wind* southeasterly ADV (to the) southeast (*von of*) PREP **+gen** (to the) southeast of

Süd-: Süd|pol M South Pole; **Süd|po|lar|ge|biet** NT Antarctic (region), area of the South Pole; **Süd|po|lar|meer** NT Antarctic Ocean; **Süd|pol|ex|pe|di|ti|on** F South Pole *or* Antarctic expedition; **Süd|see** ['zy:tze:] F South Seas *pl*, South Pacific; **Süd|see|in|su|la|ner(in)** M(F) South Sea Islander; **Süd|sei|te** F south(ern) side; (*von Berg*) south(ern) face; **Süd|staat** M southern state; **die ~en** (*US*) the Southern States; **Süd|staat|ler** ['zy:tʃta:tlɐ] M **-s, -**, **Süd|staat|le|rin** [-ərɪn] F **-, -nen** (*US*) Southerner; (*US Hist*) Confederate

Süd|süd-: Süd|süd|ost M a (*Naut, Met, liter*) south-southeast, sou'-sou'-east (*Naut*) b (*liter: Wind*) sou'-sou'-easterly; **Süd|süd|os|ten** M south-southeast, sou'-sou'-east (*Naut*); **süd|süd|öst|lich** ADJ south-southeast(erly), sou'-sou'-east(erly) (*Naut*); **Süd|süd|west** M a (*Naut, Met, liter*) south-southwest, sou'-sou'-west (*Naut*) b (*liter: Wind*) sou'-sou'-westerly; **Süd|süd|wes|ten** M south-southwest, sou'-sou'-west (*Naut*); **süd|süd|west|lich** ADJ south-southwest(erly), sou'-sou'-west(erly) (*Naut*)

Süd-: Süd|ti|rol NT South(ern) Tyrol; **Süd|ti|ro|ler(in)** M(F) South Tyrolean; **Süd|vi|et|nam** M (*Hist*) South Vietnam; **Süd|wand** F (*von Berg*) south face

süd|wärts ['zy:tvɛrts] ADV south(wards); **der Wind dreht ~** the wind is moving round to the south

Süd|wein M Mediterranean wine

Süd|west M a (*Naut, Met, liter*) southwest; **aus ~** from the southwest b (*liter: = Wind*) southwest(erly) wind, southwester(ly), sou'-wester (*Naut*)

Süd|west- *in cpds* south-west; (*bei Namen*) South-West; **Süd|west|af|ri|ka** NT South-West Africa

Süd|wes|ten [zy:t'vɛstn] M southwest; (*von Land*) South West; **aus** *or* **von ~** from the southwest; **nach ~** to the southwest, southwest(-wards)

Süd|wes|ter [zy:t'vɛstɐ] M **-s, -** (*Hut*) sou'wester

süd|west|lich [zy:t'vɛstlɪç] ADJ *Gegend* southwestern; *Wind* southwest(erly) ADV (to the) southwest (*von of*) PREP **+gen** (to the) southwest of

Süd|wind M south wind

Su|es|ka|nal ['zu:ɛs-] M Suez Canal

Suff [zʊf] M **-(e)s,** *no pl* (*inf*) **dem ~ verfallen** to hit the bottle (*inf*); **dem ~ ergeben** *or* **verfallen sein** to be on the bottle (*inf*); **im ~** while under the influence (*inf*); **im ~ ist er unberechenbar** there's no knowing what he'll do when he's had a few (*inf*)

süf|feln ['zyfln] VI (*inf*) to tipple (*inf*)

süf|fig ['zyfɪç] ADJ *Wein, Bier* drinkable, that goes down well; *Melodie, Ballade* lovely

Süf|fi|sance [zyfi'zã:s] F **-,** *no pl* (*geh*) smugness, complacency

süf|fi|sant [zyfi'zant] ADJ smug ADV smugly

Suf|fix [zʊ'fɪks, 'zʊfɪks] NT **-es, -e** suffix

Suf|fra|get|te [zʊfra'gɛtə] F **-, -n** suffragette

Su|fi ['zu:fi] M **-(s), -s** Sufi

Su|fis|mus [zu'fɪsmʊs] M **-,** *no pl* Sufism

sug|ge|rie|ren [zʊge'ri:rən] *ptp* **suggeriert** VT to suggest; **jdm etw ~** to influence sb by suggesting sth; **jdm ~, dass ...** to get sb to believe that ...; **jdm Zweifel an seinen Fähigkeiten ~** to get sb to doubt his own abilities

sug|ges|ti|bel [zʊges'ti:bl] ADJ suggestible

Sug|ges|ti|bi|li|tät F suggestibility

Sug|ges|ti|on [zʊges'tio:n] F **-, -en** suggestion

sug|ges|tiv [zʊges'ti:f] ADJ suggestive ADV suggestively

Sug|ges|tiv|fra|ge F leading question

Suh|le ['zu:lə] F **-, -n** muddy pool

suh|len ['zu:lən] VR (*lit, fig*) to wallow

Süh|ne ['zy:nə] F **-, -n** (*Rel, geh*) atonement; (*von Schuld*) expiation; **als ~ für etw** to atone for sth; **das Verbrechen fand seine ~** the crime was atoned for; **~ leisten** to atone (*für for*) → **Schuld**

süh|nen ['zy:nən] VT *Unrecht, Verbrechen* to atone for; **seine Schuld ~** to expiate one's guilt *or* sins, to atone for one's sins VI to atone

Süh|ne-: Süh|ne|op|fer NT (*Rel*) expiatory sacrifice; **Süh|ne|ter|min** M (*Jur*) conciliatory hearing

Sui|te ['svi:tə, 'zui:tə] F **-, -n** suite; (= *Gefolge*) retinue

Su|i|zid [zui'tsi:t] M OR NT **-(e)s, -e** [-də] (*form*) suicide

su|i|zi|dal [zuitsi'da:l] ADJ (*form*) suicidal

Su|i|zid-: Su|i|zid|ge|fahr F risk of suicide; **su|i|zid|ge|fähr|det** ADJ suicidal; **Su|i|zid|ge|fähr|de|te(r)** [-gəfɛ:rdətə] MF *decl as adj* suicidal man/woman; **die ~n** the suicidal; **Su|i|zid|tä|ter(in)** M(F) (*form*) suicide; **Su|i|zid|ver|such** M suicide attempt

Su|jet [sy'ʒe:] NT **-s, -s** (*geh*) subject

Suk|ka|de [zʊ'ka:də] F **-, -n** candied peel

suk|zes|siv [zʊktse'si:f], **suk|zes|si|ve** [zʊktse'si:və] ADJ gradual ADV gradually

Sul|fat [zʊl'fa:t] NT **-(e)s, -e** sulphate (*Brit*), sulfate (*US*)

Sul|fid [zʊl'fi:t] NT **-(e)s, -e** [-də] sulphide (*Brit*), sulfide (*US*)

Sul|fit [zʊl'fi:t] NT **-s, -e** sulphite (*Brit*), sulfite (*US*)

Sul|fo|na|mid [zʊlfona'mi:t] NT **-(e)s, -e** [-də] sulphonamide (*Brit*), sulfonamide (*US*)

Sul|ky ['zʊlki, 'zalki] NT **-s, -s** sulky

Süll [zyl] M OR NT **-(e)s, -e**, **Süll|bord** M , **Süll|rand** M (*Naut*) coaming

Sul|tan [zʊlta:n] M **-s, -e** sultan

Sul|ta|nat [zʊlta'na:t] NT **-(e)s, -e** sultanate

Sul|ta|nin [zʊltanɪn, zʊl'ta:nɪn] F **-, -nen** sultana

Sul|ta|ni|ne [zʊlta'ni:nə] F **-, -n** (= *Rosine*) sultana

Sül|ze ['zyltsə] F **-, -n**, (*esp S Ger, Aus, Sw*) **Sulz** [zʊlts] F **-, -en** brawn

sül|zen ['zyltsn] VT a (*sl*) to go on and on about (*inf*) b (*Cook*) to pickle in aspic VI (*sl*) to go on and on (*inf*)

---

sul|zig ['zʊltsɪç] ADJ *Schnee* slushy

Sülz|ko|te|lett NT cutlet in aspic

Su|mat|ra[1] [zu'ma:tra, 'zu:matra] NT **-s** Sumatra

Su|mat|ra[2] F **-, -s** *mild cigar originally from Sumatra*

Su|me|rer [zu'me:rɐ] M **-s, -**, **Su|me|re|rin** [-ərɪn] F **-, -nen** (*Hist*) Sumerian

su|me|risch [zu'me:rɪʃ] ADJ (*Hist*) Sumerian

summ [zʊm] INTERJ buzz; **~ machen** to buzz

sum|ma cum lau|de ['zʊma kʊm 'laudə] ADV (*Univ*) summa cum laude (*US*), with distinction

Sum|mand [zʊ'mant] M **-en, -en** [-dn] (*Math*) summand

sum|ma|risch [zʊ'ma:rɪʃ] ADJ (*auch Jur*) summary; *Zusammenfassung* summarizing ADV **etw ~ zusammenfassen** to summarize sth; **~ lässt sich sagen, dass ...** to summarize, we can say that ...

sum|ma sum|ma|rum ['zʊma zʊ'ma:rʊm] ADV (*geh*) all in all, on the whole

Sümm|chen ['zʏmçən] NT **-s, -** *dim von* **Summe** **ein nettes ~** (*hum*) a tidy sum (*inf*), a pretty penny (*inf*)

Sum|me ['zʊmə] F **-, -n** sum; (= *Gesamtsumme auch*) total; (*fig*) sum total; **die ~ aus etw ziehen** to sum up *or* evaluate sth

sum|men ['zʊmən] VT *Melodie etc* to hum VI to buzz; (*Mensch, Motor, Gerät*) to hum VI *impers* **es summt** there is a buzzing/humming noise

Sum|mer ['zʊmɐ] M **-s, -** buzzer

sum|mie|ren [zʊ'mi:rən] *ptp* **summiert** VT to sum up VR to mount up; **das summiert sich** it (all) adds *or* mounts up

Summ|ton M *pl* **-töne**, **Summ|zei|chen** NT buzz, buzzing sound

Su|mo ['zu:mo] NT **-,** *no pl* sumo

Su|mo|rin|gen NT sumo wrestling

Su|mo|rin|ger M sumo wrestler

Sumpf [zʊmpf] M **-(e)s, ⸚e** ['zʏmpfə] marsh; (= *Morast*) mud; (*in tropischen Ländern*) swamp; (*fig*) morass; **im ~ der Großstadt** in the squalor and corruption of the big city

Sumpf-: Sumpf|blü| F *sb who or sth which flourishes in a decaying society*; **Sumpf|bo|den** M marshy ground; **Sumpf|dot|ter|blu|me** F marsh marigold

sump|fen ['zʊmpfn] VI (*inf*) to live it up (*inf*)

Sumpf-: Sumpf|fie|ber NT malaria; **Sumpf|huhn** NT moorhen; (*inf: = unsolider Mensch*) fast-liver (*inf*)

sump|fig ['zʊmpfɪç] ADJ marshy, swampy

Sumpf-: Sumpf|land NT marshland; (*in tropischen Ländern*) swampland; **Sumpf|ot|ter** M mink; **Sumpf|pflan|ze** F marsh plant; **Sumpf|vo|gel** M wader; **Sumpf|zyp|res|se** F deciduous cypress

Sund [zʊnt] M **-(e)s, -e** [-də] sound, straits *pl*

Sün|de ['zʏndə] F **-, -n** sin; **eine ~ begehen** to sin, to commit a sin; **jdm seine ~n vergeben** to forgive sb his sins; **es ist eine ~ und Schande** (*inf*) it's a crying shame; **ökologische ~n** ecological sins *or* crimes

Sün|den-: Sün|den|ba|bel [-ba:bl] NT **-s, -** hotbed of vice; **Sün|den|be|kennt|nis** NT confession of one's sins; (*Gebet*) confession (of sins); **Sün|den|bock** M (*inf*) scapegoat, whipping boy; **jdn zum ~ machen** to make sb one's scapegoat; **Sün|den|fall** M (*Rel*) Fall (of Man); (*fig*) sin; **sün|den|frei** ADJ free from sin, without sin; **Sün|den|pfuhl** M den of iniquity; **Sün|den|re|gis|ter** NT (*fig*) list of sins; **jds ~** the list of sb's sins; **jdm ein langes/ sein ~ vorhalten** to list all sb's sins; **Sün|den|ver|ge|bung** F forgiveness *or* remission of sins

Sün|der ['zʏndɐ] M **-s, -**, **Sün|de|rin** [-ərɪn] F **-, -nen** sinner; **armer ~** (*Eccl*) miserable sinner; (*old*) *criminal under sentence of death* (*fig*)

---

poor wretch; **na, alter ~!** (*dated inf*) well, you old rogue! (*inf*)

Sün|der|mie|ne F shamefaced expression; **jdn mit einer ~ ansehen** to look at sb shamefaced(ly)

Sünd|flut F , *no pl* = **Sintflut**

sünd|haft ADJ (*lit*) sinful; (*fig inf*) *Preise* wicked; **ein ~es Geld** (*inf*) a ridiculous amount of money ADV (*inf*) **~ teuer** wickedly expensive

Sünd|haf|tig|keit ['zynthaftɪçkait] F -, *no pl* sinfulness

sün|dig ['zyndɪç] ADJ sinful; **~ werden** to sin (*an +dat* against)

sün|di|gen ['zyndɪgn] VI to sin (*an +dat* against); (*hum*) to indulge; **gegen Gott ~** to sin against God; **gegen die Natur ~** to commit a crime against nature; **gegen seine Gesundheit ~** to jeopardize one's health

sünd|teu|er ADJ (*Aus*) wickedly expensive

Sun|nit [zʊˈniːt] M -en, -en, **Sun|ni|tin** [zʊˈniːtɪn] F -, -nen Sunnite

su|per ['zuːpɐ] (*inf*) ADJ *inv* super, smashing, great (*all inf*) ADV (*mit adj*) really, incredibly (*inf*); (*mit vb*) really *or* incredibly (*inf*) well

Su|per ['zuːpɐ] NT -s, *no pl* (= *Benzin*) ≈ four-star (petrol) (*Brit*), ≈ premium (*US*)

Super- [zuːpɐ-] *in cpds* super-; (= *sehr*) ultra-; **Su|per-8-Film** [zuːpɐˈlaxt-] M Super 8 film

su|perb [zuˈpɛrp], **sü|perb** [zyˈpɛrp] (*dated geh*) ADJ splendid, superb, superlative ADV superbly; **~ schmecken** to taste superb; **sich ~ unterhalten** to have a splendid time

Super-: **Su|per|ben|zin** NT = **Super**; **Su|per-CD** F super CD; **Su|per|chip** M (*Comput*) superchip; **su|per|fein** ADJ *Qualität* top *attr*; *Esswaren etc* top-quality; (*inf*) posh (*inf*); **Su|per|frau** F superwoman; **Su|per-G** ['zuːpɐdʒiː] M -(s), -(s) (*Ski*) super G; **Su|per-GAU** M ultimate MCA; (*fig*) total meltdown; **Su|per|in|ten|dent** [zuːpɐʔɪntɛnˈdɛnt, 'zuːpɐ-] M -en, -en, **Su|per|in|ten|den|tin** [-'dɛntɪn] F -, -nen (*Eccl*) superintendent

Su|pe|ri|or [zuˈpeːrioːɐ] M -s, **Superioren** [-'rioːrən], **Su|pe|ri|o|rin** [-'rioːrɪn] F -, -nen superior

Su|pe|ri|o|ri|tät [zuperioriˈtɛːt] F -, *no pl* (*geh*) superiority

su|per|klug ADJ (*iro inf*) brilliant; **du bist ein Superkluger** (= *Besserwisser*) you are a (real) know-all (*Brit inf*) *or* know-it-all (*US inf*); (= *Dummkopf*) you're brilliant, you are (*iro*); (= *das ist nichts Neues*) you're not telling us anything new

Su|per|la|tiv ['zuːpɐlatiːf] M -s, -e [-və] (*Gram, fig*) superlative

su|per|la|ti|visch ['zuːpɐlatiːvɪʃ] ADJ (*Gram*) superlative; (*fig*) grand; **ins Superlativische geraten** to assume massive proportions, to snowball in a big way (*inf*); **er bedient sich einer ~en Ausdrucksweise** his speech is full of superlatives

Super-: **su|per|leicht** ADJ (*inf*) *Zigaretten* extra mild; (= *kinderleicht*) dead easy (*Brit inf*), very easy; (= *wenig wiegend*) ultralight; **Su|per|macht** F superpower; **Su|per|mann** M *pl* -männer superman; **Su|per|markt** M supermarket; **Su|per|mi|nis|ter(in)** M(F) (*inf*) super minister (*inf, who takes on several different portfolios*); **su|per|mo|dern** [-modɛrn] (*inf*) ADJ ultramodern ADV ultramodernly; **sich ~ ausdrücken** to use ultramodern expressions; **Su|per|no|va** ['zuːpɐˈnoːva] F -, **Supernovä** [-'noːvɛ] supernova; **su|per|schnell** (*inf*) ADJ ultrafast ADV incredibly fast (*inf*); **Su|per|schnell|zug** M high-speed train; **Su|per|star** M (*inf*) superstar; **su|per|stark** ADJ (*inf*) brilliant

Süpp|chen ['zypçən] NT -s, - *dim von* **Suppe sein eigenes ~ kochen** (*fig*) to do one's own thing (*inf*); **sein ~ am Feuer anderer kochen** (*fig*) to exploit *or* use other people

Sup|pe ['zʊpə] F -, -n soup; (*sämig mit Einlage*) broth; (= *klare Brühe*) bouillon; (*fig inf*: = *Nebel*) peasouper (*Brit inf*), dense fog; **klare ~** consommé; **jdm ein schöne ~ einbrocken** (*fig inf*) to get sb into a pickle (*inf*) *or* nice mess; **du musst die ~ auslöffeln, die du dir eingebrockt hast** (*inf*) you've made your bed, now you must lie on it (*prov*); **jdm die ~ versalzen** (*inf*) jdm in die ~ spucken (*inf*) to put a spoke in sb's wheel (*inf*), to queer sb's pitch (*Brit inf*); **du siehst aus, als ob dir jemand in die ~ gespuckt hätte** you look as though you've lost a pound and found sixpence (*Brit*), you look as though you've lost your best friend (*US*) → **Haar** c, **Salz**

Sup|pen- *in cpds* soup; **Sup|pen|fleisch** NT meat for making soup; (= *gekochtes Rindfleisch*) boiled beef; **Sup|pen|ge|mü|se** NT vegetables *pl* for making soup; **Sup|pen|grün** NT herbs and vegetables *pl* for making soup; **Sup|pen|huhn** NT boiling fowl; **Sup|pen|kas|par** [-kaspar] M -s, -e, **Sup|pen|kas|per** M (*inf*) poor eater; (= *Suppenfreund*) soup fan (*inf*); **Sup|pen|kel|le** F soup ladle; **Sup|pen|kü|che** F soup kitchen; **Sup|pen|löf|fel** M soup spoon; **Sup|pen|nu|del** F vermicelli *pl*, noodles *pl*; **Sup|pen|schüs|sel** F tureen; **Sup|pen|tas|se** F soup bowl; **Sup|pen|tel|ler** M soup plate; **Sup|pen|wür|fel** M stock cube; **Sup|pen|wür|ze** F soup seasoning

Sup|ple|ment [zʊpleˈmɛnt] NT -(e)s, -e (*geh*) supplement

Sup|ple|ment-: **Sup|ple|ment|band** [-bant] M *pl* **-bände** supplementary volume; **Sup|ple|ment|win|kel** M supplementary angle

Sup|po|si|to|ri|um [zʊpoziˈtoːriʊm] NT -s, **Suppositorien** [-riən] NT (*Med*) suppository

Sup|ra- ['zuːpra-]: **sup|ra|lei|tend** ADJ (*Phys*) superconductive; **Sup|ra|lei|ter** M (*Phys*) superconductor; **Sup|ra|lei|tung** F (*Phys*) superconductivity; **sup|ra|na|ti|o|nal** [zupranatioˈnaːl, 'zuːpra-] ADJ supranational ADV supranationally; **Sup|ra|na|tu|ra|lis|mus** [zupranaturaˈlɪsmʊs, 'zuːpra-] M supernaturalism

Sup|re|mat [zupreˈmaːt] M OR NT -(e)s, -e, **Sup|re|ma|tie** [zupremaˈtiː] F -, -n [-'tiːən] (*geh*) supremacy

Su|re ['zuːrə] F -, -n (*im Koran*) sura(h)

Surf|brett ['zøːɐf-, 'zœrf-, s-] NT surfboard

sur|fen ['zøːɐfn, 'zœrfn, s-] VI to surf; **im Internet ~** to surf the Internet

Sur|fer ['zøːɐfɐ, 'zœrfɐ, s-] M -s, -, **Sur|fe|rin** [-ərɪn] F -, -nen surfer

Sur|fing ['zøːɐfɪŋ, 'zœr-, s-] NT -s, *no pl* (*Sport*) surfing

Su|ri|nam [zuriˈnam] NT -s Dutch Guiana

sur|re|al ['zʊreaːl, 'zʏ-] ADJ surreal

Sur|re|a|lis|mus [zʊreaˈlɪsmʊs, zʏ-] M , *no pl* surrealism

sur|re|a|lis|tisch [zʊreaˈlɪstɪʃ, zʏ-] ADJ surrealistic(ic)

sur|ren ['zʊrən] VI **a** (*Projektor, Computer*) to hum; (*Motor*) to hum, to whir(r); (*Ventilator, Kamera*) to whir(r) **b** *aux sein* (= *sich bewegen: Insekt*) to buzz

Sur|ro|gat [zʊroˈgaːt] NT -(e)s, -e surrogate

Su|se ['zuːzə] F -s, **Su|si** ['zuːzi] F -s *contr von* **Susanne**

sus|pekt [zʊsˈpɛkt] ADJ suspicious; **jdm ~ sein** to seem suspicious to sb

sus|pen|die|ren [zʊspɛnˈdiːrən] *ptp* **suspendiert** VT to suspend (*von* from)

Sus|pen|si|on [zʊspɛnˈzioːn] F -, -en (*alle Bedeutungen*) suspension

sus|pen|siv [zʊspɛnˈziːf] ADJ (*Jur*) suspensory

Sus|pen|so|ri|um [zʊspɛnˈzoːriʊm] NT -s, **Suspensorien** [-riən] (*Med*) suspensory

süß [zyːs] ADJ (*lit, fig*) sweet; **etw ~ machen** to sweeten sth; *Tee, Kaffee* (*mit Zucker*) to sugar sth; **sie ist eine Süße** (*inf*) (= *isst gerne süß*) she has a sweet tooth; (= *ist nett*) she's a sweetie-(pie)

(*inf*); **das ~e Leben** the good life; **es auf die ~e Tour versuchen, es auf die Süße versuchen** (*inf*) to turn on the charm; **(mein) Süßer, (meine) Süße** (*inf*) my sweetheart; (*als Anrede auch*) my sweet, sweetie(-pie) (*inf*) → **Geheimnis, Rache** ADV **sich bedanken, sagen** sweetly; **gern ~ essen** to have a sweet tooth, to be fond of sweet things; **den Kaffee ~ trinken** to put sugar in one's coffee; **etw sehr ~ zubereiten** to make sth very sweet; **~ duften** to smell sweet; **~ aussehen** to look sweet; **sie haben uns ganz ~ betreut** (*inf*) they were so sweet to us

Sü|ße ['zyːsə] F -, *no pl* (*lit, fig*) sweetness

sü|ßen ['zyːsn] VT to sweeten; (*mit Zucker*) *Tee, Kaffee* to sugar VI **mit Honig** *etc* **~** to use honey *etc* as a sweetener

Süß|holz NT liquorice (*Brit*), licorice (*US*); **~ raspeln** (*fig*) to turn on the blarney; **du kannst aufhören, ~ zu raspeln** you can stop sucking up to *or* soft-soaping (*Brit*) me/him *etc* (*inf*)

Süß|holz|rasp|ler [-rasplɐ] M -s, -, **Süß|holz|rasp|le|rin** [-ərɪn] F -, -nen (*hum*) soft-soaper (*Brit inf*), sweet-talker

Sü|ßig|keit ['zyːsɪçkait] F **a** -en **a** *no pl* (*lit, fig*) sweetness **b** **~en** PL sweets *pl* (*Brit*), candy (*US*)

Süß-: **Süß|kar|tof|fel** F sweet potato; **Süß|kir|sche** F sweet cherry; **Süß|klee** M hedysarum (*spec*)

süß|lich ['zyːslɪç] ADJ **a** *Geruch, Geschmack* (= *leicht süß*) sweetish, slightly sweet; (= *unangenehm süß*) sickly (sweet), cloying **b** (*fig*) *Töne, Miene, Worte* sweet; *Lächeln, Schlager* sugary; *Farben, Modegeschmack* pretty-pretty (*Brit inf*), overly pretty; (= *kitschig*) mawkish, tacky

Süß-: **Süß|most** M unfermented fruit juice; **Süß|rahm|but|ter** F creamery butter; **süß|sau|er** ADJ sweet-and-sour; *Gurken etc* pickled; (*fig*: = *gezwungen freundlich*) *Lächeln* forced; *Miene* artificially friendly; **Ente ~** sweet-and-sour duck ADV **würzen, einlegen** in a sweet-and-sour sauce; **~ schmecken** to taste sweet-and-sour; **~ lächeln** to give a bittersweet smile; **Süß|spei|se** F sweet dish, dessert; **Süß|stoff** M sweetener; **Süß|wa|ren** PL confectionery *sing*; **Süß|wa|ren|ge|schäft** NT sweetshop (*Brit*), candy store (*US*), confectioner's; **Süß|was|ser** NT *pl* **-wasser** freshwater; **Süß|was|ser|fisch** M freshwater fish; **Süß|wein** M dessert wine

Su|ta|ne [zuˈtaːnə] F -, -n (*Eccl*) cassock

Süt|ter|lin|schrift ['zʏtɐliːn-] F *old-fashioned style of German handwriting*

SV [ɛsˈfau] M - *abbr von* **Sportverein** SC; **der SV Mannheim** Mannheim SC

SVP [ɛsfauˈpeː] F - *abbr von* **Schweizerische Volkspartei**

SW *abbr von* **Südwesten** SW

Swap [svɔp] M -s, -s (*Fin*) swap

Swa|si|land ['svaːzilant] NT -s Swaziland

Swas|ti|ka ['svastika] F -, **Swastiken** [-kn] swastika

Sweat|shirt ['svɛtʃœrt, -ʃøːɛt] NT -s, -s sweatshirt

SWF [ɛsveːˈʔɛf] M - *abbr von* **Südwestfunk**

Swim|ming|pool ['svɪmɪŋpuːl] M -s, -s swimming pool

Swin|egel ['sviːnˌeːgl] M -s, - (*dial*) hedgehog

Swing [svɪŋ] M -s, *no pl* (*Mus, Fin*) swing

swin|gen ['svɪŋən] VI (*Mus*) to swing

Swin|ger-Club ['svɪŋɐ-] M (*inf*) swingers' bar (*inf*)

SWR [ɛsveːˈʔɛr] M - *abbr von* **Südwestdeutscher Rundfunk**

syl|la|bisch [zʏˈlaːbɪʃ] ADJ syllabic

Syl|lo|gis|mus [zʏloˈgɪsmʊs] M -, **Syllogismen** [-mən] (*Philos*) syllogism

Syl|phe ['zʏlfə] M -n, -n *or* f -, -n (*Myth*) sylph

Sylt [zʏlt] NT -s Sylt

Syl|va|ner [zyl'va:nɐ] M **-s, -** (= *Traubensorte*) Sylvaner (grape); (= *Wein*) Sylvaner (wine)

Syl|ves|ter [zyl'vɛstɐ] NT **-s, -** = **Silvester**

Sym|bi|o|se [zym'bio:zə] F **-, -n** symbiosis

sym|bi|o|tisch [zym'bio:tɪʃ] ADJ symbiotic ADV ~ **zusammenleben** to have a symbiotic relationship; (*Menschen*) to live together symbiotically

Sym|bol [zym'bo:l] NT **-s, -e** symbol

Sym|bol|fi|gur F symbol, symbolic figure

Sym|bol|ge|halt M symbolic content

sym|bol|haft ADJ symbolic(al)

Sym|bo|lik [zym'bo:lɪk] F **-, no pl** symbolism

sym|bo|lisch [zym'bo:lɪʃ] ADJ symbolic(al) (*für* of) ADV symbolically

sym|bo|li|sie|ren [zymboli'zi:rən] ptp **symbolisiert** VT to symbolize

Sym|bo|lis|mus [zymbo'lɪsmʊs] M **-, no pl** symbolism

Sym|bo|list [zymbo'lɪst] M **-en, -en**, **Sym|bo|lis|tin** [-'lɪstɪn] F **-, -nen** symbolist

sym|bo|lis|tisch [zymbo'lɪstɪʃ] ADJ symbolist(ic)

Sym|bol-: Sym|bol|kraft F symbolic force or power; **sym|bol|kräf|tig** ADJ strongly or richly symbolic; **Sym|bol|leis|te** F (*Comput*) toolbar; **sym|bol|träch|tig** ADJ heavily symbolic, full of symbolism

Sym|met|rie [zyme'tri:] F **-, -n** [-'tri:ən] symmetry

Sym|met|rie-: Sym|met|rie|ach|se F axis of symmetry; **Sym|met|rie|ebe|ne** F plane of symmetry

sym|met|risch [zy'me:trɪʃ] ADJ symmetric(al) ADV symmetrically

Sym|pa|thie [zympa'ti:] F **-, -n** [-'ti:ən] (= *Zuneigung*) liking; (= *Mitgefühl, Solidaritätsgefühl*) sympathy; **für jdn/etw ~ haben** to have a liking for/a certain amount of sympathy with sb/sth; **jdm große** or **viel ~ entgegenbringen** to have a lot of sympathy for sb; **diese Maßnahmen haben meine volle ~** I sympathize completely with these measures; **durch seine Unverschämtheit hat er meine ~/hat er sich** (*dat*) **alle ~(n) verscherzt** he has turned me/everyone against him with his rudeness; **~n gewinnen** to win favour (*Brit*) or favor (*US*); **seine ~n gelten nicht der extremen Rechten** he isn't sympathetic to the extreme right

Sym|pa|thie-: Sym|pa|thie|äu|ße|rung F expression of support; **Sym|pa|thie|kund|ge|bung** F demonstration of support; **Sym|pa|thie|streik** M sympathy strike; **in ~ (mit jdm) treten** to come out in sympathy (with sb); **Sym|pa|thie|trä|ger(in)** M(F) popular figure; **Sym|pa|thie|wer|te** PL popularity rating *sing*

Sym|pa|thi|kus [zym'pa:tikʊs] M **-, no pl** (*Physiol*) sympathetic nerve

Sym|pa|thi|sant [zympati'zant] M **-en, -en**, **Sym|pa|thi|san|tin** [-'zantɪn] F **-, -nen** sympathizer

sym|pa|thisch [zym'pa:tɪʃ] ADJ a pleasant, nice, simpatico (*esp US inf*); **er/es ist mir ~** I like him/it; **er/es war mir gleich ~** I liked him/it at once, I took to him/it at once, I took an immediate liking to him/it; **das ist mir gar nicht ~** I don't like it at all b (*Anat, Physiol*) sympathetic

sym|pa|thi|sie|ren [zympati'zi:rən] ptp **sympathisiert** VI to sympathize (*mit* with)

Sym|pho|nie [zymfo'ni:] F **-, -n** [-'ni:ən] = **Sinfonie**

Sym|pho|nie- *in cpds* = **Sinfonie-**

Sym|pho|ni|ker [zym'fo:nikɐ] M **-s, -**, **Sym|pho|ni|ke|rin** [-ərɪn] F **-, -nen** = **Sinfoniker**

sym|pho|nisch [zym'fo:nɪʃ] ADJ = **sinfonisch**

Sym|po|si|on [zym'po:zion] NT **-s, Symposien** [-ziən], **Sym|po|si|um** [zym'po:ziʊm] NT **-s, Symposien** [-ziən] symposium

Symp|tom [zymp'to:m] NT **-s, -e** symptom

symp|to|ma|tisch [zympto'ma:tɪʃ] ADJ symptomatic (*für* of)

Sy|na|go|ge [zyna'go:gə] F **-, -n** synagogue

Sy|nap|se [zy'napsə, zyn'lapsə] F **-, -n** (*Anat, Physiol*) synapse

Syn|äs|the|sie [zynɛsteˈziː, zynˈlɛs-] F **-, -n** (*Med, Psych, Liter*) synaesthesia (*Brit*), synesthesia (*US*)

syn|chron [zyn'kro:n] ADJ synchronous; (*Ling*) synchronic ADV synchronologically

Syn|chron|ge|trie|be NT (*Aut*) synchromesh gearbox

Syn|chro|ni|sa|ti|on [zynkroniza'tsio:n] F **-, -en** (*Film, TV*) synchronization; (= *Übersetzung*) dubbing

syn|chro|ni|sie|ren [zynkroni'zi:rən] ptp **synchronisiert** VT to synchronize; (= *übersetzen*) *Film* to dub

Syn|chron-: Syn|chron|schwim|men NT synchronized swimming; **Syn|chron|spre|cher(in)** M(F) dubbing artist; **Syn|chron|uhr** F synchronous or mains-synchronized clock; **Syn|chron|ver|schluss** ▲ M (*Phot*) flash-synchronized shutter

Syn|di|ka|lis|mus [zyndika'lɪsmʊs] M **-, no pl** syndicalism

syn|di|ka|lis|tisch [zyndika'lɪstɪʃ] ADJ syndicalist(ic)

Syn|di|kat [zyndi'ka:t] NT **-(e)s, -e** (= *Kartell*) syndicate

Syn|di|kus ['zyndikʊs] M **-, Syndiken** or **Syndizi** [-kn, -tsi] (= *Geschäftsführer*) syndic; (= *Justitiar*) (company *etc*) lawyer

Syn|drom [zyn'dro:m] NT **-s, -e** syndrome

Sy|ner|gie [zynɛr'gi:, zynɛr'gi:] F **-, no pl** synergy

Sy|ner|gie|ef|fekt M (*Chem, Phys*) synergistic effect; (*fig*) synergy effect

Syn|ko|pe F **-, -n** a ['zynkopə] syncope, syncopation b [zyn'ko:pə] (*Mus*) syncopation

syn|ko|pie|ren [zynko'pi:rən] ptp **synkopiert** VT to syncopate

syn|ko|pisch [zyn'ko:pɪʃ] ADJ syncopic, syncopated (*esp Mus*)

Syn|kre|tis|mus [zynkre'tɪsmʊs] M **-, no pl** syncretism

Sy|no|da|le(r) [zyno'da:lə] MF *decl as adj* (*Eccl*) synod member

Sy|no|de [zy'no:də] F **-, -n** (*Eccl*) synod

sy|no|nym [zyno'ny:m], **sy|no|ny|misch** [zyno'ny:mɪʃ] ADJ synonymous

Sy|no|nym [zyno'ny:m] NT **-s, -e** synonym

Sy|no|nym|wör|ter|buch NT dictionary of synonyms, thesaurus

Sy|nop|se [zy'nɔpsə, zyn'lɔpsə] F **-, -n**, **Sy|nop|sis** [zy'nɔpsɪs, 'zynlɔpsɪs] F **-, Synopsen** [-sn] synopsis; (*Bibl*) synoptic Gospels *pl*, Synoptics *pl*

Sy|nop|ti|ker [zy'nɔptikɐ, zyn'lɔptikɐ] PL (*Bibl*) Synoptics *pl*; (= *Apostel*) Synoptists *pl*

Syn|tag|ma [zyn'tagma] NT **-s, Syntagmen** or **-ta** [-mən, -ta] (*Ling*) syntactic construction

syn|tak|tisch [zyn'taktɪʃ] ADJ syntactic(al) ADV **das ist ~ korrekt/falsch** the syntax (of this) is correct/wrong; **~ schwierige Übersetzungen** translations with difficult syntax

Syn|tax ['zyntaks] F **-, -en** syntax

Syn|the|se [zyn'te:zə] F **-, -n** synthesis

Syn|the|si|zer ['zyntəsaizɐ] M **-s, -** synthesizer

Syn|the|tik [zyn'te:tɪk] F **-, no pl** a (*Math*) synthesis b (= *Kunstfaser*) synthetic fibre (*Brit*) or fiber (*US*)

syn|the|tisch [zyn'te:tɪʃ] ADJ synthetic; *Stoff, Faser auch* man-made ADV **etw ~ herstellen** to make or produce sth synthetically

syn|the|ti|sie|ren [zynteti'zi:rən] ptp **synthetisiert** VT to syntheticize

Sy|phi|lis ['zy:filɪs] F **-, no pl** syphilis

sy|phi|lis|krank ADJ syphilitic, suffering from syphilis; **~ sein** to have syphilis

Sy|phi|li|ti|ker [zyfi'li:tikɐ] M **-s, -**, **Sy|phi|li|ti|ke|rin** [-ərɪn] F **-, -nen** syphilitic

sy|phi|li|tisch [zyfi'li:tɪʃ] ADJ syphilitic

Sy|ra|kus [zyra'ku:s] NT **-'** Syracuse

Sy|rer ['zy:rɐ] M **-s, -**, **Sy|re|rin** [-ərɪn] F **-, -nen** Syrian

Sy|ri|en ['zy:riən] NT **-s** Syria

Sy|ri|er ['zy:riɐ] M **-s, -**, **Sy|ri|e|rin** [-iərɪn] F **-, -nen** Syrian

sy|risch ['zy:rɪʃ] ADJ Syrian

Sy|risch(e) ['zy:rɪʃ] NT Syriac → *auch* **Deutsch(e)**

Sys|tem [zys'te:m] NT **-s, -e** system (*auch Comput*); (= *Ordnung, Ordnungsprinzip auch*) method; **etw mit ~ machen** to do sth systematically; **etw mit einem ~ machen** to do sth according to a system; **hinter dieser Sache steckt ~** there's method behind it; **~ in etw** (*acc*) **bringen** to get or bring some system into sth; **Apparate verschiedener ~e** machinery of different designs; **ein ~ von Straßen/Kanälen** a road/canal system

Sys|tem-: Sys|tem|ab|sturz M (*Comput*) system crash; **gelegentlich treten Systemabstürze auf** occasionally the system crashes; **Sys|tem|analy|se** F systems analysis; **Sys|tem|ana|ly|ti|ker(in)** M(F) systems analyst

Sys|te|ma|tik [zyste'ma:tɪk] F **-, no pl** a (= *systematisches Ordnen*) system b (= *Lehre, Klassifikation*) systematology

Sys|te|ma|ti|ker [zyste'ma:tikɐ] M **-s, -**, **Sys|te|ma|ti|ke|rin** [-ərɪn] F **-, -nen** systematist; (*fig*) systematic person

sys|te|ma|tisch [zyste'ma:tɪʃ] ADJ systematic ADV systematically

sys|te|ma|ti|sie|ren [zystemati'zi:rən] ptp **systematisiert** VT to systematize

Sys|tem-: sys|tem|be|dingt ADJ determined by the system; **Sys|tem|be|treu|er(in)** M(F) (*Comput*) systems administrator; **Sys|tem|dis|ket|te** F systems disk; **Sys|tem|feh|ler** M (*Comput*) system error; **sys|tem|ge|recht** ADV in accordance with the system; **sys|tem|im|ma|nent** ADJ inherent in the system; **dem Kapitalismus ~ sein** to be inherent in the capitalist system

sys|te|misch [zys'te:mɪʃ] ADJ systemic

Sys|tem-: sys|tem|kon|form ADJ in conformity with the system ADV **sich ~ verhalten** to conform to the system; **sich ~ geben** to give the impression of conforming to the system; **Sys|tem|kri|ti|ker(in)** M(F) critic of the system; **sys|tem|kri|tisch** ADJ critical of the system ADV **sich ~ äußern** to make remarks critical of the system; **~ eingestellt sein** to be critical of the system; **~ schreiben** to write critically about the system; **sys|tem|los** ADJ unsystematic ADV unsystematically; **Sys|tem|ma|na|ger** M (*Comput*: = *Programm*) system manager program; **Sys|tem|soft|ware** F systems software; **Sys|tem|spe|zi|a|list(in)** M(F) (*Comput*) systems specialist; **Sys|tem|tech|ni|ker(in)** M(F) (*Comput*) systems engineer; **Sys|tem|treue** F loyalty to the system; **Sys|tem|ver|än|de|rer** [-fɛɛlɛndərə] M **-s, -**, **Sys|tem|ver|än|de|rin** [-ərɪn] F **-, -nen** (*Pol pej*) **die Partei besteht aus lauter ~n** the whole party is just a bunch of people out to change the system; **Sys|tem|ver|än|de|rung** F change in the system; **Sys|tem|wech|sel** M change of system; **Sys|tem|zwang** M obligation to conform to the system

Sys|to|le ['zystolə, -'to:lə] F **-, -n** (*Med*) systole

Sze|na|re [stse'na:rɛ] NT **-s, -e**, **Sze|na|rio** [stse'na:rio] NT **-s, -s**, **Sze|na|ri|um** [stse'na:riʊm] NT **-s, Szenarien** [-riən] scenario

Sze|ne ['stse:nə] F **-, -n** a (*Theat, fig*) scene; (*Theat*: = *Bühnenausstattung*) scene (*inf*); (*sl*: = *Drogenszene etc*) scene (*inf*); (*sl*: = *Milieu*) subculture; (*sl*: *der Leute, die in sind*) in places *pl* (*inf*); **Beifall**

auf offener ~ applause during the performance; **hinter der ~** backstage; (*fig*) behind the scenes; **in ~** (*acc*) **gehen** to be staged; **etw in ~ setzen** (*lit, fig*) to stage sth; **sich in ~ setzen** (*fig*) to play to the gallery; **die ~ beherrschen** (*fig*) to dominate the scene (+*gen* in); (= *meistern*) to control things; **sich in der ~ auskennen** (*inf*) to know the scene (*inf*); **die rechte/linke ~** (*inf*) the right-/left-wing scene

b (*fig*: = *Zank, Streit*) scene; **jdm eine ~ machen** to make a scene in front of sb; **mach bloß keine ~** don't go making a scene, I don't want a scene

-sze|ne F *suf in cpds* (*inf*) scene (*inf*); **die Drogenszene** the drugs (*Brit*) *or* drug scene

Sze|ne- *in cpds* (*inf*) in-; **ein Szenekenner** somebody who knows the in places (*inf*)

Sze|ne|knei|pe F (*inf*) hip bar (*inf*), *bar fashionable with a certain clique*

Sze|nen- *in cpds*: **Sze|nen|ap|plaus** M spontaneous applause; **Sze|nen|bild** NT (stage) set, stage setting; **Sze|nen|fol|ge** F sequence of scenes; **Sze|nen|wech|sel** M scene change

Sze|ne|rie [stsenə'riː] F -, -n [-'riːən] (*Theat, fig*) scenery

sze|nisch ['stseːnɪʃ] **ADJ** (*Theat*) scenic; *Lesung, Aufführung* staged **ADV** **etw ~ aufführen** to act sth out; **etw ~ umsetzen** to adapt sth for the stage

Szep|ter ['stsɛptɐ] NT -s, - (*dated, Aus*) sceptre (*Brit*), scepter (*US*)

Szil|la ['stsɪla] F -, Szillen [-lən] (*Bot*) scilla

Szin|ti-: **Szin|ti|graf** ▲ [stsɪntiˈɡraːf] M -en, -en scintigraph; **Szin|ti|gra|fie** ▲ [stsɪntiɡraˈfiː] F -, -n [-'fiːən] scintigraphy; **Szin|ti|gramm** [stsɪntiˈɡram] NT *pl* -gramme scintigram

Szyl|la ['stsʏla] F - (*Myth*) Scylla; **zwischen ~ und Charybdis** (*liter*) between Scylla and Charybdis

T

T, t [teː] NT **-, -** T, t

t *abbr von* **Tonne**

Tab [tɛb] M **-s, -s** tab

Ta|bak [ˈtaːbak, ˈtabak, (*Aus*) taˈbak] M **-s, -e** tobacco; (= *Schnupftabak*) snuff

Ta|bak- [ˈtaːbak] *in cpds* tobacco; **Ta|bak|beu|tel** M tobacco pouch; **Ta|bak|do|se** F tobacco tin; (*für Schnupftabak*) snuffbox; **Ta|bak|ge|nuss** ▲ M (tobacco) smoking; **Ta|bak|händ|ler(in)** M(F) (*im Großhandel*) tobacco merchant; (*im Einzelhandel*) tobacconist; **Ta|bak|la|den** M tobacconist's, tobacco shop; **Ta|bak|mi|schung** F blend (of tobaccos), (tobacco) mixture; **Ta|bak|mo|no|pol** NT tobacco monopoly, monopoly on tobacco; **Ta|bak|pfei|fe** F pipe; **Ta|bak|qualm** M (*pej*) fug; **Ta|bak|rauch** M tobacco smoke

Ta|baks-: Ta|baks|beu|tel M tobacco pouch; **Ta|baks|do|se** F tobacco tin; (*für Schnupftabak*) snuffbox; **Ta|baks|pfei|fe** F pipe

Ta|bak-: Ta|bak|steu|er F duty on tobacco; **Ta|bak|tra|fik** [taˈbak-] F (*Aus*) tobacconist's, tobacco shop; **Ta|bak|tra|fi|kant(in)** [taˈbak-] M(F) (*Aus*) tobacconist; **Ta|bak|wa|ren** PL tobacco; **Ta|bak|wa|ren|la|den** M tobacconist's

Ta|ba|tie|re [tabaˈtiːrə] F **-, -n** (*Aus*) tobacco tin; (*old*: = *Schnupftabakdose*) snuffbox

ta|bel|la|risch [tabɛˈlaːrɪʃ] ADJ tabular; **bitte fügen Sie einen ~en Lebenslauf bei** please write out your curriculum vitae (*Brit*) or résumé (*US*) in tabular form ADV in tabular form, in tables/a table

ta|bel|la|ri|sie|ren [tabɛlariˈziːrən] *ptp* **tabellarisiert** VT to tabulate

Ta|bel|le [taˈbɛlə] F **-, -n** table; (= *Diagramm*) chart; (*Sport*) (league) table

Ta|bel|len-: Ta|bel|len|en|de NT (*Sport*) bottom of the league or table; **am ~ stehen** to be at the bottom of the league or table, to be cellar-dwelling (*US inf*); **Ta|bel|len|form** F **in ~** in tabular form, in tables/a table; (*Diagramm*) as a chart, in chart form; **ta|bel|len|för|mig** ADJ tabular, in tabular form, in the form of a table; (= *als Diagramm*) as a chart, in chart form ADV in a table; as a chart; **Ta|bel|len|füh|rer(in)** M(F) (*Sport*) league leaders *pl*; **~ sein** to be at the top of the (league) table; **Ta|bel|len|füh|rung** F (*Sport*) league leadership, position at the top of the table; **die ~ abgeben/verteidigen/zurückerobern** to give up/defend/regain the lead; **Ta|bel|len|ge|stal|tung** F (*an Schreibmaschine*) tabulation; **Ta|bel|len|kal|ku|la|ti|on** F (*Comput*) spreadsheet; **Ta|bel|len|kal|ku|la|ti|ons|pro|gramm** NT (*Comput*) spreadsheet (program); **Ta|bel|len|platz** M (*Sport*) place or position in the league; **auf den letzten ~ fallen** to drop to the bottom of the table; **Ta|bel|len|spit|ze** F (*Sport*) top position in the (league) table, top of the league or table; **an der ~ stehen** to be at the top of the league or table; **Ta|bel|len|stand** M (*Sport*) league situation; **~ auf Seite 15** league tables on page 15

Ta|ber|na|kel [tabɛrˈnaːkl] NT OR M **-s, -** tabernacle

Tab|lett [taˈblɛt] NT **-(e)s, -s** *or* **-e** tray; **jdm etw auf einem silbernen ~ servieren** (*fig*: = *einfach machen*) to hand sb sth on a plate (*Brit*) or on a silver platter; **muss man dir alles auf einem silbernen ~ servieren?** do you have to have everything done for you?

Tab|let|te [taˈblɛtə] F **-, -n** tablet, pill

Tab|let|ten-: Tab|let|ten|form F **in ~** in tablet form; **Tab|let|ten|miss|brauch** ▲ M pill abuse; **Tab|let|ten|röh|re** F tube of tablets or pills; **Tab|let|ten|sucht** F addiction to pills, compulsive pill-taking; **tab|let|ten|süch|tig** ADJ addicted to pills; **Tab|let|ten|süch|ti|ge(r)** MF *decl as adj* pill addict, pill-popper (*inf*)

ta|bu [taˈbuː, ˈtaːbu] ADJ *pred* taboo

Ta|bu [taˈbuː, ˈtaːbu] NT **-s, -s** taboo

ta|bu|ie|ren [tabuˈiːrən] *ptp* **tabuiert** VT to make taboo, to taboo

ta|bu|i|sie|ren [tabuiˈziːrən] *ptp* **tabuisiert** VT to make taboo, to taboo

Ta|bu|i|sie|rung F **-, -en** taboo(ing)

Ta|bu|la ra|sa [ˈtabula ˈraːza] F **- -**, *no pl* (*Philos*) tabula rasa; **~ machen** (*inf*) to make a clean sweep

Ta|bu|la|tor [tabuˈlaːtoːr] M **-s, Tabulatoren** [-ˈtoːrən] tabulator, tab (*inf*)

Ta|bu-: ta|bu|los ADJ taboo-free; **Ta|bu|schran|ke** F taboo; **Ta|bu|wort** NT *pl* **-wörter** taboo word or expression

Ta|che|les [ˈtaxələs] *no art* (*inf*) **(mit jdm) ~ reden** to have a talk (with sb); **nun wollen wir beide mal ~ reden** let's do some straight talking, let's talk turkey (*dated US inf*)

ta|chi|nie|ren [taxiˈniːrən] *ptp* **tachiniert** VI (*Aus inf*) to laze or loaf about (*inf*)

Ta|chi|nie|rer [taxiˈniːrɐ] M **-s, -, Ta|chi|nie|re|rin** [-ərɪn] F **-, -nen** (*Aus inf*) layabout (*Brit inf*), loafer (*inf*), do-nothing (*US inf*)

Ta|cho [ˈtaxo] M **-s, -s** (*inf*) speedo (*Brit inf*), speedometer

Ta|cho|me|ter [taxoˈmeːtɐ] M OR NT **-s, -** speedometer

Ta|cho|me|ter|stand M, **Ta|cho|stand** M (*inf*) mileage, number of kilometres (*Brit*) or kilometers (*US*)/miles on the clock; **beim ~ von 10.000 km** at 10,000 km, after clocking up 10,000 km

Ta|cker [ˈtakɐ] M **-s, -** (*inf*) stapler

Ta|del [ˈtaːdl] M **-s, -** (= *Verweis*) reprimand; (= *Vorwurf*) reproach; (= *Kritik*) criticism, censure; (*geh*: = *Makel*) blemish, taint; (*Sch*: = *Eintragung ins Klassenbuch*) black mark; **ein Leben ohne je|den ~** (*geh*) an unblemished or spotless or blameless life; **ihn trifft kein ~** (*geh*) he is above or beyond reproach

ta|del|los ADJ perfect; *Deutsch etc auch* faultless; *Benehmen, Haltung auch* faultless, irreproachable; *Leben* blameless; (*inf*) splendid, first-class ADV perfectly; *sprechen auch* faultlessly; *sich benehmen auch* irreproachably; *gekleidet* immaculately

ta|deln [ˈtaːdln] VT *jdn* to rebuke, to reprimand; *jds Benehmen* to criticize, to express one's disapproval of

ta|delnd ADJ *attr* reproachful; **ein ~er Blick** a reproachful look, a look of reproach

ta|delns|wert, ta|delns|wür|dig ADJ (*geh*) reprehensible, blameworthy

Ta|dels|an|trag M (*Parl*) motion of censure, censure motion

Ta|fel [ˈtaːfl] F **-, -n** ⓐ (= *Platte*) slab; (= *Holztafel*) panel; (= *Tafel Schokolade etc*) bar; (= *Gedenktafel*) plaque; (= *Wandtafel*) (black)board; (= *Schiefertafel*) slate; (*Elec*: = *Schalttafel*) control panel, console; (= *Anzeigetafel*) board; (= *Verkehrstafel*) sign ⓑ (= *Bildseite*) plate ⓒ (*form*: = *festlicher Speisetisch*) table; (= *Festmahl*) meal; (*mittags*) luncheon (*form*); (*abends*) dinner; **jdn zur ~ bitten** to ask sb to table; **die ~ aufheben** to officially end the meal

Ta|fel-: Ta|fel|ap|fel M eating apple; **Ta|fel|auf|satz** M centrepiece (*Brit*), centerpiece (*US*); **Ta|fel|berg** M (*Geog*) table mountain; **Ta|fel|be|steck** NT (best) silver; **Ta|fel|bild** NT panel; **Ta|fel|dienst** M (*Sch*) **wer hat ~?** who's the blackboard monitor?, who's in charge of the board?; **ta|fel|fer|tig** ADJ ready to serve; **ta|fel|för|mig** ADJ slab-like; *Hochplateau* table-shaped; **Ta|fel|freu|den** PL (*geh*) delicacies *pl*, culinary delights *pl*; (= *Freude am Essen*) pleasures *pl* of the table; **Ta|fel|ge|schäft** NT (*Fin*) counter transactions *pl*; **Ta|fel|ge|schirr** NT tableware; **Ta|fel|glas** NT sheet glass, plate glass; **Ta|fel|land** NT plateau, tableland; **Ta|fel|lap|pen** M (blackboard) duster; **Ta|fel|ma|le|rei** F panel painting; **Ta|fel|mu|sik** F musical entertainment

ta|feln [ˈtaːfln] VI (*geh*) to feast; **mit jdm ~** to dine with sb

tä|feln [ˈtɛːfln] VT *Wand* to wainscot; *Decke, Raum* to panel, to line with wooden panels

Ta|fel-: Ta|fel|obst NT (dessert) fruit; **Ta|fel|öl** NT cooking oil; (= *Salatöl*) salad oil; **Ta|fel|run|de** F company (at table); (*Liter*) Round Table; **die ganze ~ applaudierte** the whole table applauded; **eine festliche ~ saß beisammen** a festive banquet was in progress; **Ta|fel|salz** NT table salt; **Ta|fel|sil|ber** NT silver; **Ta|fel|spitz** M (*Cook*) soured boiled rump

Tä|fe|lung [ˈtɛːfəluŋ] F **-, -en** (*von Wand*) wainscoting; (*von Decke*) (wooden) panelling (*Brit*) or paneling (*US*)

Ta|fel-: Ta|fel|was|ser NT *pl* **-wässer** mineral water, table water; **Ta|fel|wein** M table wine

Täf|lung [ˈtɛːfluŋ] F **-, -en** = **Täfelung**

Taft [taft] M **-(e)s, -e** taffeta

taf|ten [ˈtaftn] ADJ taffeta

Tag [taːk] M **-(e)s, -e** [-gə] ⓐ day; **am ~(e) des/der ...** (on) the day of ...; **am ~** during the day; **alle ~e** (*inf*) **jeden ~** every day; **am vorigen ~(e), am ~(e) vorher** the day before, the previous day; **auf den ~ (genau)** to the day; **auf ein paar ~e** for a few days; **auf seine alten ~e** at his age; **bis auf seine letzten ~e** to his dying day, right up to the very end; **bei ~ und Nacht** night and day, day and night; **bis in unsere ~e** up to the present day; **in den letzten ~en** in the last few days, in recent days; **bis die ~e!** (inf) so long (inf), cheerio (Brit inf), see ya (inf); **diese** (inf) or **dieser ~e** (= bald) in the next few days; **den ganzen ~ (lang)** (lit, fig) all day long, the whole day; **eines ~es** one day; **eines ~es wirst du ...** one day or one of these days you'll ...; **eines schönen** or **guten ~es** one fine day; **sich** (dat) **einen schönen/faulen ~ machen** to have a nice/lazy day; **~ für** or **um ~** day by day; **in unseren ~en, in den heutigen ~en** these days, nowadays; **unter ~s** (dial) during the daytime; **von ~ zu ~** from day to day, every day; **~ der Arbeit** Labour Day (Brit), Labor Day (US); **~ der Republik/Befreiung** (DDR) Republic/Liberation Day; **~ des Herrn** (Eccl) the Lord's Day; **welcher ~ ist heute?** what day is it today?; **ein ~ wie jeder andere** a day like any other; **guten ~!** hello (inf), good day (dated form); (vormittags auch) good morning; (nachmittags auch) good afternoon; (esp bei Vorstellung) how-do-you-do; **~!** (inf) hello, hi (inf); morning (inf); afternoon (inf); **ich wollte nur Guten** (or **guten**) **~ sagen** I just wanted to have a chat; **zweimal am ~ (-e)** or **pro ~** twice daily or a day; **von einem ~ auf den anderen** overnight; **der Lärm des ~es** the bustle of the world; **der ~ X** D-Day (fig); **er erzählt** or **redet viel, wenn der ~ lang ist** (inf) he'll tell you anything if you let him; **seinen guten/schlechten ~ haben** to have a good/bad or off day, to have one of one's good/bad or off days; **das war heute wieder ein ~!** (inf) what a day!; **das Ereignis/Thema des ~es** the event/talking point of the day; **Sie hören jetzt die Nachrichten des ~es** and now the or today's news; **in den ~ hinein leben** to take each day as it comes, to live from day to day; **~ und Nacht** night and day, day and night; **das ist ein Unterschied wie ~ und Nacht** they are as different as chalk and cheese (Brit) or night and day (US); **~ und Stunde bestimmen** to fix a precise time → **Abend a**

b (= Tageslicht) **bei ~(e)** (ankommen) while it's light; arbeiten, reisen during the day; **es wird schon ~** it's getting light already; **es ist ~** it's light; **solange (es) noch ~ ist** while it's still light; **an den ~ kommen** (fig) to come to light; **etw an den ~ bringen** to bring sth to light; **er legte großes Interesse an den ~** he showed great interest; **zu ~e** zutage

c (inf: = Menstruation) **meine/ihre ~e** my/her period; **sie hat ihre ~e (bekommen)** it's her time of the month (Brit), she has her period (US)

d (Min) **über ~e arbeiten** to work above ground, to work on or at the surface; **unter ~e arbeiten** to work underground or below ground, to work below the surface; **etw unter ~e abbauen** to mine sth; **etw über ~e abbauen** to quarry (esp Brit) or excavate sth

-tag M suf in cpds (= Konferenz) conference; **Weltfrauentag** International Women's Conference

Tag- (S Ger, Aus, Sw) in cpds = **Tage-**

tag|ak|tiv ADJ (Zool) diurnal (spec)

tag|aus [taːkˈaus] ADV → **tagein**

Tag|blatt NT = Tageblatt

Tag|chen [ˈtaxçən] INTERJ (hum) hello there, hi(ya) (inf)

Tag|dienst M = Tagesdienst

Tage-: **ta|ge|bau** M pl -baue (Min) opencast mining; **Ta|ge|blatt** NT daily (news)paper; **Göttinger ~** Göttingen Daily News; **Ta|ge|buch** NT diary, journal (liter, form); **über etw** acc **~ führen** to keep a diary (of sth); **Ta|ge|dieb(in)** M(F) (dated) idler (Brit), wastrel (liter), loafer (inf); **Ta|ge|geld** NT daily allowance

tag|ein [taːkˈain] ADV **~, tagaus** day in, day out, day after day

Ta|ge-: **ta|ge|lang** ADJ lasting for days; **nach ~er Unterbrechung** after an interruption of several days, after an interruption lasting several days; **~e Regenfälle** several days' rain ADV for

days; **Ta|ge|lohn** M (dated) daily wage(s); **im ~ arbeiten** or **stehen** to be paid by the day; **Ta|ge|löh|ner** [-løːnɐ] M -s, -, **Ta|ge|löh|ne|rin** [-ərɪn] F -, -nen (dated) day labourer (Brit) or laborer (US), temporary worker

ta|gen [ˈtaːgn̩] VI impers (geh) **es tagt** day is breaking or dawning; **es begann schon zu ~** day was breaking or dawning, (the) dawn was breaking VI (Parlament, Rat, Gericht) to sit; (Minister, Leiter) to meet; **wir haben noch bis in den frühen Morgen getagt** (fig inf) we stayed up enjoying ourselves until the early hours

Ta|ge|rei|se F day's journey

Tages-: **Ta|ges|ab|lauf** M day; **Ta|ges|an|bruch** M daybreak, dawn; **Ta|ges|ar|beit** F day's work; **Ta|ges|auf|trag** M (St Ex) day order; **Ta|ges|aus|flug** M day trip or excursion, day's outing; **Ta|ges|be|darf** M daily requirement; **Ta|ges|be|fehl** M (Mil) order of the day; **Ta|ges|creme** F day cream; **Ta|ges|de|cke** F bedspread; **Ta|ges|dienst** M day duty; **~ haben** to be on day shift; **Ta|ges|ein|nah|men** PL day's takings pl; **Ta|ges|er|eig|nis** NT event of the day; **Ta|ges|fest|preis** M fixed daily rate; **Ta|ges|form** F (Sport etc) form of the day; **Ta|ges|fra|gen** PL issues pl of the day, day-to-day matters pl; **Ta|ges|geld** NT (Fin) overnight money; **Ta|ges|ge|schäft** NT (Econ, Comm) routine business, day-to-day business; (= Einzeltransaktion) day order; **Ta|ges|ge|sche|hen** NT events pl of the day; **Ta|ges|ge|spräch** NT talk of the town; **Ta|ges|hälf|te** F half of the day; **Ta|ges|höchst|tem|pe|ra|tur** F (day's) maximum temperature; (an bestimmtem Tag) highest temperature (of the day); **Ta|ges|kar|te** F **a** (= Speisekarte) menu of the day (Brit), specialties pl of the day (US) **b** (= Fahr-, Eintrittskarte) day ticket; **Ta|ges|kas|se** F **a** (Theat) box office **b** (Econ) day's takings pl; **Ta|ges|kli|nik** F day clinic; **Ta|ges|kurs** M (St Ex) (von Effekten) current price; (von Devisen) current rate; **Ta|ges|lauf** M day; **Ta|ges|leis|tung** F daily workload; (von Maschine, Schriftsteller etc) daily output; (von Milchkuh) daily yield; (Sport) performance of the day; **Ta|ges|licht** NT , no pl daylight; **ans ~ kommen** (fig) to come to light; **das ~ scheuen** to be a creature of the night, to shun the daylight; **Ta|ges|licht|pro|jek|tor** M overhead projector; **Ta|ges|lohn** M day's wages; **Ta|ges|lo|sung** F (Mil) password of the day; **Ta|ges|marsch** M day's march; **zwei Tagesmärsche entfernt** two days' march away; **Ta|ges|me|nü** NT menu of the day (Brit), specialties pl of the day (US); **Ta|ges|mut|ter** F pl -mütter child minder (Brit), nanny; **Ta|ges|nach|rich|ten** PL (today's) news sing; **die wichtigsten ~** the (main) headlines; **Ta|ges|ord|nung** F agenda, order of the day (form); **zur ~!** keep to the agenda!; **etw auf die ~ setzen** to put sth on the agenda; **auf der ~ stehen** to be on the agenda; **zur ~ übergehen** to proceed to the agenda; (= an die Arbeit gehen) to get down to business; (= wie üblich weitermachen) to carry on as usual; **an der ~ sein** (fig) to be the order of the day; **Ta|ges|ord|nungs|punkt** M item on the agenda; **Ta|ges|pau|scha|le** F fixed daily amount; **Ta|ges|preis** M (Comm) current price; **gestern betrug der ~ ...** yesterday's price was ...; **Tages- und Abendpreise** daytime and nighttime prices; **Ta|ges|pres|se** F daily (news)papers pl or press; **Ta|ges|ra|ti|on** F daily rations pl; **Ta|ges|raum** M day room; **Ta|ges|rei|se** F **a** (= Entfernung) day's journey **b** (= Ausflug) day trip; **Ta|ges|satz** M daily rate; **Ta|ges|schau** F (TV) news sing; **Ta|ges|stät|te** F (für Kinder) daycare centre (Brit) or center (US); **Ta|ges|sup|pe** F soup of the day; **Ta|ges|tour** F day trip; **Ta|ges|um|satz** M (= Durchschnittswert) daily turnover; (des aktuellen Tages) day's turnover; **Ta|ges|ver|lauf** M course of the day; **im ~** (auch) as the day went on; **Ta|ges|zeit** F time (of day); **zu jeder Tages- und Nachtzeit** at all hours of the

day and night; **zu dieser ~ kommst du nach Hause?!** what sort of time do you call this to come home!; **Ta|ges|zei|tung** F daily (paper)

Ta|ge|tes [taˈɡeːtɛs] F -, - (Bot) tagetes (spec), marigold

Tage-: **ta|ge|wei|se** [ˈtaːgəvaizə] ADV for a few days at a time; **Ta|ge|werk** NT (geh) day's work

Tag-: **Tag|fahrt** F (Min) ascent; **tag|hell** ADJ (as) bright as day; **es war schon ~** it was already broad daylight ADV **etw ~ erleuchten** to light sth up very brightly; **der Blitz erhellte die Nacht ~** the lightning lit up the night sky

-tä|gig [tɛːgɪç] ADJ suf -day; **eine dreitägige Konferenz** a three-day conference

tägl. abbr von **täglich**

täg|lich [ˈtɛːglɪç] ADJ daily; (attr: = gewöhnlich) everyday; **~e Gelder** (Comm) call money; **~e Zinsen** (Comm) daily interest; **das reicht gerade fürs ~e Leben** it's just about enough to get by on; **sein ~(es) Brot verdienen** to earn a living; **das ist unser ~(es) Brot** (fig: Ärger etc) it is our stock in trade; **das ist so wichtig wie das ~e Brot** it's as important as life itself; **unser ~ Brot gib uns heute** (Bibl) give us this day our daily bread ADV every day; **einmal ~** once a day, once daily

-täg|lich ADJ suf **sechstäglich** every six days

Tag|mem [taˈɡmeːm] NT -s, -e (Ling) tagmeme

tags [taːks] ADV **a** **~ zuvor** the day before, the previous day; **~ darauf** or **danach** the next or following day **b** (= bei Tag) in the daytime, by day

Tag|schicht F day shift; **~ haben** to be on (the) day shift

tags|über [ˈtaːksˌyːbɐ] ADV during the day

Tag-: **tag|täg|lich** ADJ daily ADV every (single) day; **Tag|traum** M daydream; **Tag|träu|mer(in)** M(F) daydreamer; **Tag|und|nacht|glei|che** [ˈtaːkˈunt|naxtˌglaiçə] F decl as adj equinox

Ta|gung [ˈtaːgʊŋ] F -, -en conference; (von Ausschuss) sitting, session

Tagungs-: **Ta|gungs|ort** M pl -orte venue (of a/the conference); **Ta|gungs|raum** M conference room; (größer auch) conference hall; **Ta|gungs|stät|te** F = Tagungsort; **Ta|gungs|teil|neh|mer(in)** M(F) conferee, person attending a conference; **Ta|gungs|zent|rum** NT conference centre (Brit) or center (US)

Tag-: **Tag|wa|che¹** F (Aus, Sw: Mil) **a** reveille **b** **~!** rise and shine!; **Tag|wa|che²** F , **Tag|wacht** F (Aus, Sw) day guard

Ta|hi|ti [taˈhiːti] NT -s Tahiti

Ta|hi|ti|a|ner [tahiˈtiaːnɐ] M -s, -, **Ta|hi|ti|a|ne|rin** [-ərɪn] F -, -nen, **Ta|hi|ti|er** [taˈhiːtiɐ] M -s, -, **Ta|hi|ti|e|rin** [-iərɪn] F -, -nen Tahitian

ta|hi|tisch [taˈhiːtɪʃ] ADJ Tahitian

Tai Chi (Chuan) [ˈtai ˈtʃiː (ˈtʃuan)] NT -, no pl t'ai chi (ch'uan)

Tai|fun [taiˈfuːn] M -s, -e typhoon

Tai|ga [ˈtaiga] F -, no pl taiga

Tail|le [ˈtaljə] F -, -n waist; (bei Kleidungsstücken auch) waistline; **auf seine ~ achten** to watch one's waistline; **in der ~ zu eng** too tight at the waist; **ein Kleid auf ~** a fitted dress

Tail|len|wei|te [ˈtaljən-] F waist measurement

tail|lie|ren [ta(l)ˈjiːrən] ptp **tailliert** VT to fit (at the waist)

tail|liert [ta(l)ˈjiːɐt] ADJ waisted, fitted; **Hemd auch** slim-fit

Tai|wan [ˈtaivan, taiˈva(ː)n] NT -s Taiwan

Tai|wa|ne|se [taivaˈneːzə] M -n, -n, **Tai|wa|ne|sin** [-ˈneːzɪn] F -, -nen Taiwanese

tai|wa|ne|sisch [taivaˈneːzɪʃ] ADJ Taiwan(ese)

Take [teːk] NT OR M , -s (Film, TV) take

Ta|kel [ˈtaːkl̩] NT -s, - (Naut) tackle

Ta|ke|la|ge [takəˈlaːʒə] F -, -n (Naut) rigging, tackle

ta|keln ['ta:kln] VT (*Naut*) to rig

Ta|ke|lung ['ta:kəlʊŋ] F -, -en rigging

Takt [takt] M -(e)s, -e **a** (= *Einheit*) (*Mus*) bar; (*Phon, Poet*) foot; **mit jdm ein paar ~e reden** (*inf*: = *die Meinung sagen*) to give sb a good talking-to (*inf*) **b** (= *Rhythmus*) time; **den ~ schlagen** to beat time; (**den**) **~ halten** to keep time; **im ~ bleiben** to stay in time; **den ~ verlieren** to lose the beat; **den ~ wechseln** to change the beat, to change (the) time; **im ~ singen/tanzen** to sing/dance in time (to (*Brit*) or with the music); **gegen den ~** out of time (with the music); **im/gegen den ~ marschieren** to be in/out of step; **den ~ angeben** (*lit*) to give the beat or time; (*fig*) to call the tune; **im ~ der Musik** in time to (*Brit*) or with music; **das Publikum klatschte den ~ dazu** the audience clapped in time to the music; **wenn alle Kolben im ~ arbeiten** if all the pistons are in phase **c** (*Aut*) stroke **d** (*Ind*) phase **e** *no pl* (= *Taktgefühl*) tact; **mit dem ihm eigenen ~** with his great tact(fulness); **er hat keinen ~ im Leibe** (*inf*) he hasn't an ounce of tact in him **f** (= *Taktverkehr*) regular service; **im ~ fahren** to go at regular intervals; **alle Linien verkehren im Einstundentakt** there is an hourly service on all routes **g** (*Comput*) (clock) pulse or signal

Takt|be|zeich|nung F time signature

tak|ten ['taktn] VT (*Comput*) to clock; **ein mit 60 MHz getakteter Prozessor** a processor with a clock speed of 60 MHz

Takt-: Takt|fahr|plan M (*Rail*) timetable of departures at regular intervals; **takt|fest** ADJ **a** (*Mus*) able to keep time **b** (*inf*) (*gesundheitlich*) fighting fit (*Brit inf*), in fighting shape (*US*); (*sicher*) sure of his etc stuff (*inf*); **Takt|fol|ge** F (*form*) sequence; **Takt|fre|quenz** F (*Comput*) clock speed; **Takt|ge|fühl** NT **a** sense of tact **b** (*rare: Mus*) sense of rhythm or time

tak|tie|ren [tak'ti:rən] *ptp* **taktiert** VI **a** (= *Taktiken anwenden*) to manoeuvre (*Brit*), to maneuver (*US*); **so kann man nicht ~** you can't use those tactics **b** (*rare: Mus*) to beat time

Tak|tik ['taktɪk] F -, -en tactics *pl*; **eine ~ tactics** *pl*, a tactical approach; **man muss mit ~ vorgehen** you have to use tactics; **der verbrannten Erde** (*Mil*) scorched earth policy

Tak|ti|ker ['taktɪkɐ] M -s, -, **Tak|ti|ke|rin** [-ərɪn] F -, -nen tactician

tak|tisch ['taktɪʃ] ADJ tactical ADV tactically; **~ vorgehen** to use tactics; **~ klug** good tactics

Takt-: takt|los ADJ tactless ADV tactlessly; **Takt|lo|sig|keit** F -, -en tactlessness; **es war eine ~ sondergleichen** it was a particularly tactless thing to do/say; **Takt|maß** NT (*Mus*) time; **Takt|mes|ser** M -s, - (*Mus*) metronome; **Takt|stock** M baton; **den ~ schwingen** (*inf*) to wield the baton; **Takt|strich** M (*Mus*) bar (line); **Takt|ver|kehr** M (*Rail etc*) regular service; **die Züge fahren im ~** the trains go at regular intervals; **einstündiger ~** hourly service; **takt|voll** ADJ tactful ADV tactfully; **benimm dich bitte ~er** please be more tactful; **Takt|wech|sel** M (*Mus*) change of time, time change

Tal [ta:l] NT -(e)s, ⁼er ['tɛ:lə] valley, vale (*poet*); **zu ~e** into the valley

tal|ab|(wärts) [ta:l'|ap(vɛrts)] ADV **a** down into the valley **b** (= *flussabwärts*) downriver, downstream

Ta|lar [ta'la:ɐ] M -s, -e (*Univ*) gown; (*Eccl auch*) cassock; (*Jur*) robe(s *pl*)

tal|auf|(wärts) ADV **a** up the valley **b** (= *flussaufwärts*) upriver, upstream

Tal-: Tal|brücke F bridge over a valley; **Tal|en|ge** F narrow part of a/the valley, gorge

Ta|lent [ta'lɛnt] NT -(e)s, -e **a** (= *Begabung*) talent (*zu* for); **ein großes ~ haben** to be very tal-ented; **sie hat viel ~ zum Singen/zur Schauspielerin** she has a great talent or gift for singing/acting; **da saß** or **stand er nun mit seinem ~** (*inf*) he was left looking a right charlie (*Brit inf*) **b** (= *begabter Mensch*) talented person; **junge ~e** young talent; **er ist ein großes ~** he is very talented **c** (*Hist*: = *Geld*) talent

ta|len|tiert [talɛn'ti:ɐt] ADJ talented, gifted; **die Mannschaft lieferte ein ~es Spiel** the team played a game of great skill or a brilliant game

Talent-: ta|lent|los ADJ untalented; **Ta|lent|pro|be** F audition; **Ta|lent|scout** [-skaʊt] M -(s), -s talent scout; **Ta|lent|su|che** F search for talent; **wir sind auf ~** we are looking for new talent; **ta|lent|voll** ADJ talented; **das war nicht sehr ~** (*inf*) that wasn't very clever or bright

Ta|ler ['ta:lɐ] M -s, - (*Hist*) T(h)aler; (*inf*) euro, ≈ quid (*Brit inf*), ≈ buck (*US inf*)

Tal|fahrt F (*bergabwärts*) descent; (*flussabwärts*) downriver trip; (*fig*) decline

Talg [talk] M -(e)s, -e [-gə] tallow; (*Cook*) suet; (= *Hautabsonderung*) sebum

Talg|drü|se F (*Physiol*) sebaceous gland

Ta|li|ban [tali'ba:n] F -, - Taliban, Taleban

Ta|lis|man ['talɪsman] M -s, -e talisman, (lucky) charm; (= *Maskottchen*) mascot

Tal|je ['taljə] F -, -n (*Naut*) block and tackle

Talk [talk] M -(e)s, *no pl* talc(um)

tal|ken ['tɔːkn] VI (*inf*) to talk

Talk|kes|sel M basin, hollow

Talk|mas|ter ['tɔːkmasːtɐ] M -s, -, **Talk|mas|te|rin** [-ərɪn] F -, -nen talk show or chat show (*Brit*) host

Talk|pu|der M OR NT talcum powder

Talk|show ▲ ['tɔːkʃəʊ] F (*TV*) talk show, chat show (*Brit*)

Tal|kum ['talkʊm] NT -s, *no pl* **a** (= *Talk*) talc(um) **b** (= *Puder*) talc, talcum powder

Tal|land|schaft F valley; (*mit mehreren Tälern*) valleys *pl*

Tal|mi ['talmi] NT -s, *no pl* (*geh*) pinchbeck; (*fig*) rubbish (*Brit inf*), trash (*inf*); **~-Religion** sham religion

Tal|mi|gold NT pinchbeck gold

Tal|mud ['talmu:t] M -(e)s, -e [-də] Talmud

Tal|mul|de F basin, hollow

Ta|lon [ta'lɔ:] M -s, -s (*St Ex*) renewal coupon

Tal-: Tal|schaft ['ta:lʃaft] F -, -en (*Sw, Aus*) valley inhabitants *pl* or dwellers *pl* or folk; **Tal|sen|ke** F hollow (of a/the valley); **Tal|soh|le** F bottom of a/the valley, valley bottom; (*fig*) rock bottom; **in der ~** (*fig*) at rock bottom, in the doldrums; **Tal|sper|re** F dam; **Tal|sta|ti|on** F base camp; (*von Skilift etc*) station at the bottom of a ski lift; **tal|wärts** ['ta:lvɛrts] ADV down to the valley

Ta|ma|rin|de [tama'rɪndə] F -, -n tamarind

Ta|ma|ris|ke [tama'rɪskə] F -, -n tamarisk

Tam|bour ['tambuːɐ] M -s, -e drummer

Tam|bour|ma|jor ['tambuːɐ-] M drum major

Tam|bu|rin [tambu'riːn, 'tam-] NT -s, -e tambourine

Ta|mi|le [ta'miːlə] M -n, -n, **Ta|mi|lin** [-'miːlɪn] F -, -nen Tamil

ta|mi|lisch [ta'miːlɪʃ] ADJ Tamil

Ta|mi|lisch(e) NT Tamil → *auch* **Deutsch(e)**

Tamp [tamp] M -s, -e, **Tam|pen** ['tampn] M -s, - (*Naut*) rope end

Tam|pon ['tampɔn, tam'po:n] M -s, -s tampon; (*für Wunde auch*) plug

tam|po|nie|ren [tampo'niːrən] *ptp* **tamponiert** VT to plug, to tampon

Tam|tam [tam'tam, 'tam-] NT -s, -s (*Mus*) tom-tom; (= *Wirbel*) fuss, to-do (*inf*), ballyhoo (*Brit inf*); (= *Lärm*) row, din (*inf*); **der Faschings-zug zog mit großem ~ durch die Straßen** the

Fasching procession paraded loudly through the streets

Tand [tant] M -(e)s [-dəs] *no pl* (*liter*) trinkets *pl*, knick-knacks *pl*; **alles Menschenwerk ist doch nur ~** all human works are but dross (*liter*)

Tän|de|lei [tɛndə'laɪ] F -, -en (*liter*) (= *Spielerei*) (dilly-)dallying, trifling (*Brit*), lallygagging (*US*); (= *Liebelei*) dalliance (*liter*)

Tan|del|markt ['tandl-] M (*Aus*), **Tän|del|markt** ['tɛndl-] M (*dial*) flea market

tän|deln ['tɛndln] VI (*liter*) (= *liebeln*) to dally (*liter*); (= *trödeln*) to (dilly-)dally, to trifle (*Brit*), to lallygag (*US*)

Tan|dem ['tandɛm] NT -s, -s tandem

Tand|ler ['tandlə] M -s, -, **Tand|le|rin** [-ərɪn] F -, -nen (*Aus*) **a** (= *Trödler*) second-hand dealer **b** (= *langsamer Mensch*) slowcoach (*Brit inf*), slowpoke (*US inf*)

Tang [taŋ] M -(e)s, -e seaweed

Tan|ga ['taŋga] M -s, -s tanga, thong (*US*)

Tan|gan|ji|ka [taŋgan'ji:ka] NT -s Tanganyika

Tan|ga-Slip M, **Tan|ga|slip** M tanga, thong (*US*)

Tan|gens ['taŋgɛns] M -, - (*Math*) tan(gent)

Tan|gens|kur|ve F (*Math*) tan wave

Tan|gen|te [taŋ'gɛntə] F -, -n (*Math*) tangent; (= *Straße*) ring road (*Brit*), expressway, beltway (*US*)

tan|gen|ti|al [taŋgɛn'tsia:l] ADJ tangential

Tan|ger ['taŋɐ, 'tandʒɐ] NT -s Tangier(s)

tan|gie|ren [taŋ'gi:rən] *ptp* **tangiert** VT **a** (*Math*) to be tangent to **b** (= *berühren*) Problem to touch on; Stadt, Gebiet to skirt; **das tangiert das Problem nur** that is merely tangential or peripheral to the problem **c** (= *betreffen*) to affect; (*inf*: = *kümmern*) to bother

Tan|go ['taŋgo] M -s, -s tango

Tank [taŋk] M -(e)s, -s or -e (= *Behälter, Panzer*) tank

Tank-: Tank|an|zei|ge F fuel gauge; **Tank|de|ckel** M filler cap (*Brit*), gas cap (*US*)

tan|ken ['taŋkn] VI **a** (*Autofahrer*) to get petrol (*Brit*) or gas (*US*); (*Rennfahrer, Flugzeug*) to refuel; **wo kann man hier ~?** where can I get petrol (*Brit*) or gas (*US*) (a)round here?; **hier kann man billig ~** you can get cheap petrol (*Brit*) or gas (*US*) here; **ich muss noch ~** I have to get some petrol (*Brit*) or gas (*US*); **wir hielten an, um zu ~** we stopped for petrol (*Brit*) or gas (*US*); **ich tanke nur für 20 Euro** I'll just put 20 euros' worth in; **hast du getankt?** have you filled up or tanked up?, have you put petrol (*Brit*) or gas (*US*) in? ▶ VT **a** Super, Diesel to get; **ich tanke bleifrei** I use unleaded; **ich habe 30 Liter getankt** I put 30 litres (*Brit*) or liters (*US*) in (the tank) **b** (*fig inf*) frische Luft to get, to fill one's lungs with; Sonne, Selbstvertrauen, neue Kräfte to get **c** (*inf*: = *viel trinken*) **er hat einiges** or **ganz schön getankt** he's had a few, he's really tanked up (*inf*)

Tan|ker ['taŋkɐ] M -s, - (*Naut*) tanker

Tan|ker|flot|te F tanker fleet, fleet of tankers

Tan|ker|un|glück NT (oil) tanker disaster

Tank-: Tank|fahr|zeug NT (*Aut*) tanker; **Tank|füll|men|ge** F tank capacity; **Tank|fül|lung** F tankful; **mit einer ~ komme ich bis nach München** I can get to Munich on a tankful or on one tank; **Tank|in|halt** M contents *pl* of the tank; **der ~ beträgt ...** the tank holds ..., the tank capacity is ... (*form*); **Tank|la|ger** NT oil or petrol (*Brit*) or gas (*US*) depot; **Tank|las|ter** M, **Tank|last|zug** M tanker; **Tank|mög|lich|keit** F letzte ~ vor ... last petrol (*Brit*) or gas (*US*) station before ...; **Tank|säu|le** F petrol pump (*Brit*), gas(oline) pump (*US*); **Tank|schiff** NT tanker; **Tank|stel|le** F filling or petrol (*Brit*) or gas(oline) (*US*) station; **Tank|stut|zen** M filler pipe; **Tank|uhr** F fuel gauge; **Tank|ver|schluss** ▲ M petrol (*Brit*) or gas (US) cap; **Tank|wa|gen** M tanker; (Rail) tank wagon or car; **Tank|wart(in)** M(F) petrol pump (Brit) or gas station (US) attendant; **Tank|zug** M tanker

Tann [tan] M -(e)s, -e (poet) forest

Tänn|chen ['tɛnçən] NT -s, - dim von **Tanne**

Tan|ne ['tanə] F -, -n fir; (Holz) pine, deal; **sie ist schlank wie eine ~** she is as slender as a reed

Tan|nen-: Tan|nen|baum M **a** fir tree **b** (= Weihnachtsbaum) Christmas tree; **Tan|nen|na|del** F fir needle; **Tan|nen|wald** M fir forest; **Tan|nen|we|del** M fir(-twig) broom; **Tan|nen|zap|fen** M fir cone; **Tan|nen|zweig** M fir branch; (kleiner) sprig of fir

Tan|nin [ta'niːn] NT -s, no pl tannin

Tann|zap|fen M fir cone

Tan|sa|nia [tanza'niːa, tan'zaːnia] NT -s Tanzania

Tan|sa|ni|er [tan'zaːniɐ] M -s, -, **Tan|sa|ni|e|rin** [-ərɪn] F -, -nen Tanzanian

tan|sa|nisch [tan'zaːnɪʃ] ADJ Tanzanian

Tan|tal [tantal] NT -s, no pl (abbr **Ta**) tantalum

Tan|ta|lus|qua|len ['tantalʊs-] PL (geh) torments pl of Tantalus (liter); **ich litt ~** it was tantalizing, I suffered torments (liter); **jdm ~ bereiten** to tantalize sb

Tant|chen ['tantçən] NT -s, - (inf) **a** (Verwandte) auntie, aunty **b** (= alte Dame) old dear (Brit inf) or lady

Tan|te ['tantə] F -, -n **a** (Verwandte) aunt, aunty, auntie **b** (pej inf: = Frau) woman (inf), old dear (Brit inf) or lady **c** (baby-talk) (= Frau) lady; (= Kindergartenschwester etc) teacher; (= Krippenschwester) nurse; **~ Schneider/Monika** aunty or auntie Schneider/Monika

Tan|te-Em|ma-La|den [tantə'ɛma-] M (inf) corner shop

tan|ten|haft ADJ **a** (inf) old-maidish **b** (pej: = betulich) Ausdruck(sweise) twee ADV **sie benimmt sich so richtig ~** she acts like a real old maid or maiden aunt (Brit)

Tan|tie|me [tãˈtieːmə, -ˈtieːmə] F -, -n percentage (of the profits); (für höhere Angestellte) director's fee; (für Künstler) royalty

Tant|ra ['tantra] NT -(s), no pl Tantra

Tanz [tants] M -es, ⸚e ['tɛntsə] **a** dance; **dort ist heute Abend ~** there's a dance or (für Jugendliche) disco there this evening; **im Goldenen Ochsen ist neuerdings auch ~** they now have dancing too at the Golden Ox; **zum ~ aufspielen** (dated) to strike up a dance (tune) (dated); **jdn zum ~ auffordern** to ask sb to dance or for a dance → **golden** ADJ **b** (fig geh: von Licht, Schatten) play; **der ~ der Boote auf den Wellen** the boats' dancing (liter) or bobbing on the waves; **ein ~ auf dem Vulkan** (fig) living on the edge **c** (inf: = Aufheben) fuss; **einen ~ um jdn machen** to make a fuss of (esp Brit) or over sb

Tanz-: Tanz|abend M dance; **Tanz|bar** F bar with dancing; **Tanz|bär** M dancing bear; **Tanz|bein** NT (mit jdm) **das ~ schwingen** (hum) to trip the light fantastic (with sb) (hum); **Tanz|bo|den** M (= Tanzfläche) dance floor; (= Saal) dance hall; (dated: Veranstaltung) dance; **Tanz|ca|fé** NT restaurant with dancing

Tänz|chen ['tɛntsçən] NT -s, - dim von **Tanz** (dated hum) dance; **ein ~ wagen** to venture onto the floor

Tanz|die|le F (dated) (Raum) dance hall; (= Tanzfläche) dance floor

tän|zeln ['tɛntsln] VI aux haben or (bei Richtungsangabe) sein to mince (Brit), to sashay (esp US), to trip; (Boxer) to skip; (Pferd) to step delicately

tan|zen ['tantsn] **VI** aux haben or (bei Richtungsangabe) sein to dance; (Boot auch) to bob; (Kreisel) to spin; (hüpfen) to hop; **gehen, zum Tanzen gehen** to go dancing → **Pfeife a, Reihe a** **VT** Walzer, Tango etc to dance; **er hat mit mir ei-**

nen Walzer getanzt he danced or did a waltz with me

Tän|zer ['tɛntsɐ] M -s, -, **Tän|ze|rin** [-ərɪn] F -, -nen dancer; (= Tanzpartner) (dancing) partner; (= Balletttänzer) ballet dancer

Tan|ze|rei [tantsə'rai] F -, -en **a** dancing; (pej) prancing about **b** (Aus) dancing party

tän|ze|risch ['tɛntsərɪʃ] ADJ Grazie, Beschwingtheit etc dance-like; **eine große ~e Leistung** a tremendous piece of dancing; **~e Darbietungen** dance acts; **sein ~es Können** his dancing ability ADV **~ veranlagt sein** to have a talent for dancing; **~ ausgebildet** trained as a dancer; **~ gestaltete Gymnastik** gymnastics done in a dance-like way or as a dance; **die Darsteller waren ~ hervorragend** the dancing was excellent; **die Kür war ~ miserabel** the dance technique in the free section was terrible

Tanz-: Tanz|flä|che F dance floor; **Tanz|grup|pe** F dance group; (bei Revue, TV-Show auch) chorus; **Tanz|ka|pel|le** F dance band; **Tanz|kunst** F art of dancing, dance; **Tanz|kurs** M , **Tanz|kur|sus** M dancing course; **Tanz|leh|rer(in)** M(F) dancing teacher; **Tanz|lied** NT dance tune; **Tanz|lo|kal** NT café with dancing; **tanz|lus|tig** ADJ fond of or keen on dancing; **einige ~e Paare blieben noch** a few couples who wanted to dance stayed on; **Tanz|mu|sik** F dance music; **Tanz|or|ches|ter** NT dance orchestra; **Tanz|part|ner(in)** M(F) dancing partner; **Tanz|plat|te** F record of dance music; **Tanz|platz** M (open-air) dance floor; **Tanz|saal** M dance hall; (in Hotel etc) ballroom; **Tanz|schritt** M (dance) step; **Tanz|schuh** M dancing shoe; **Tanz|schu|le** F dancing or dance school, school of dancing; **Tanz|sport** M competitive dancing; **Tanz|spra|che** F (Zool) dance language; **Tanz|stun|de** F dancing lesson or class; **sie haben sich in der ~ kennengelernt** they met at dancing lessons or classes; **Tanz|tee** M thé dansant, tea dance; **Tanz|tur|nier** NT dancing or dance contest or competition; **Tanz|ver|an|stal|tung** F , **Tanz|ver|gnü|gen** NT dance

Ta|o|is|mus [ta'ɪsmʊs, tau-] M -, no pl Taoism

Ta|per|greis(in) M(F) (pej inf) old dodderer (pej inf)

ta|pe|rig ['taːpərɪç] ADJ (pej inf) doddering, doddery

ta|pern ['taːpɐn] VI (inf) to totter

Ta|pet [ta'peːt] NT (inf) **etw aufs ~ bringen** to bring sth up; **aufs ~ kommen** to be brought up, to come up

Ta|pe|te [ta'peːtə] F -, -n wallpaper; **ohne ~n** without wallpaper; **die ~n wechseln** (fig inf) to have a change of scenery or surroundings

Ta|pe|ten-: Ta|pe|ten|bahn F strip of wallpaper; **Ta|pe|ten|rol|le** F roll of wallpaper; **Ta|pe|ten|tür** F concealed door; **Ta|pe|ten|wech|sel** M (inf) change of scenery or surroundings

Ta|pe|zier [tape'tsiːɐ] M -s, -e, **Ta|pe|zie|rin** [-'tsiːərɪn] F -, -nen (esp S Ger) = **Tapezierer**

Ta|pe|zier-: Ta|pe|zier|ar|beit F wallpapering; **Ta|pe|zier|bürs|te** F wallpaper brush

ta|pe|zie|ren [tape'tsiːrən] ptp **tapeziert** VT to (wall)paper; (inf: mit Bildern) to plaster (inf); **neu ~** to repaper

Ta|pe|zie|rer [tape'tsiːrɐ] M -s, -, **Ta|pe|zie|re|rin** [-ərɪn] F -, -nen **a** paperhanger, decorator **b** (= Polsterer) upholsterer

Ta|pe|zier-: Ta|pe|zier|na|gel M tack; **Ta|pe|zier|tisch** M trestle table

tap|fer ['tapfɐ] ADJ brave, courageous; Soldat, Versuch auch bold; (= wacker) steadfast ADV bravely, courageously; **wir marschierten immer ~ weiter, ohne zu merken ...** we marched on blithely, not realizing ...; **halt dich or bleib ~!** (inf) be brave; **sich ~ schlagen** (inf) to put on a brave show

Tap|fer|keit F -, no pl bravery, courage; (von Soldat auch) boldness

Tap|fer|keits|me|dail|le F medal for bravery

Ta|pi|o|ka [ta'pio:ka] F -, no pl tapioca

Ta|pir ['taːpiːɐ] M -s, -e (Zool) tapir

Ta|pis|se|rie [tapɪsə'riː] F -, -n [-'riːən] **a** tapestry **b** (old, Sw) drapery

tapp [tap] INTERJ tap

tap|pen ['tapn] VI **a** aux sein (= tapsen) to go falteringly; (Bär) to lumber, to lollop (Brit inf); (dial: = gehen) to wander; **~de Schritte** faltering steps; **er ist in eine Pfütze getappt** (inf) he walked smack into a puddle (inf); **in eine Falle ~** (fig) to walk or fall into a trap **b** (= tasten) **nach etw ~** to grope for sth; **im Finstern** or **Dunkeln ~** (fig) to grope in the dark

täp|pisch ['tɛpɪʃ], **tapp|pig** ['tapɪç] (dial) ADJ awkward, clumsy ADV **sich ~ anstellen** to act awkwardly or clumsily

tap(p)|rig ['taprɪç] ADJ (dial) = **taperig**

Taps [taps] M -es, -e (dial) clumsy oaf (inf); **kleiner ~** little bundle

tap|sen ['tapsn] VI aux sein (inf) (Kind) to toddle; (Bär) to lumber, to lollop (Brit inf); (Kleintier) to waddle

tap|sig ['tapsɪç] (inf) ADJ awkward, clumsy ADV awkwardly, clumsily

Ta|ra ['taːra] F -, Taren [-rən] (Comm) tare

Ta|ran|tel [ta'rantl] F -, -n tarantula; **wie von der ~ gestochen** as if stung by a bee, as if bitten by a snake

Ta|ran|tel|la [taran'tɛla] F -, -s or **Tarantellen** [-'tɛlən] tarantella

ta|rie|ren [ta'riːrən] ptp **tariert** VT to tare

Ta|rif [ta'riːf] M -(e)s, -e rate; (= Wassertarif, Gastarif etc auch) tariff; (= Gebühr auch) charge; (= Fahrpreis) fare; **die ~e für Telefonanschlüsse** telephone line rental; **neue ~e für Löhne/Gehälter** new wage rates/salary scales; **die Gewerkschaft hat die ~e für Löhne und Gehälter gekündigt** the union has put in a new wage claim; **nach/über/unter ~ bezahlen** to pay according to/above/below the (union) rate(s)

Ta|rif-: Ta|rif|ab|schluss ▲ M wage settlement; **Ta|rif|aus|ei|nan|der|set|zung** F wage dispute; **Ta|rif|au|to|no|mie** F (right to) free collective bargaining; **Ta|rif|er|hö|hung** F **a** (= Gebührenerhöhung) increase in rates or charges, rate or charge increase; (= Fahrpreiserhöhung) fare(s) increase or hike (US) **b** (= Lohnerhöhung) increase in pay rates, (across-the-board) pay increase, pay rise (Brit) or raise (US); **Ta|rif|ge|halt** M salary, rates pl; **Ta|rif|ge|mein|schaft** F **a** (Econ) tariff community **b** (in Verkehrsverbund) fare(s) cooperative; **Ta|rif|grup|pe** F grade; **Ta|rif|kom|mis|si|on** F joint working party on pay; **Ta|rif|kon|flikt** M wage dispute

ta|rif|lich [ta'riːflɪç] ADJ Arbeitszeit, Regelung agreed; **der ~e Mindestlohn** the agreed minimum wage ADV **die Gehälter sind ~ festgelegt** there are fixed rates for salaries; **etw ~ festschreiben** to include sth in the labour (Brit) or labor (US) contract; **~ vereinbart sein** to be in the labour (Brit) or labor (US) contract

Ta|rif-: Ta|rif|lohn M standard wage; **ta|rif|los** ADJ **~er Zustand** period when new rates are being negotiated; **ta|rif|mä|ßig** ADJ, ADV = **tariflich**; **Ta|rif|ord|nung** F (für Löhne) wage scale; (für Gehälter) salary scale; **Ta|rif|par|tei** F party to a wage agreement; **die ~en** unions and management; **Ta|rif|part|ner(in)** M(F) party to the wage or (für Gehälter) salary agreement; **die ~** union and management; (= Sozialpartner) both sides of industry; **Ta|rif|po|li|tik** F (Zoll) tariff policy; (bei Lohnforderungen) wage policy; **Ta|rif|run|de** F pay round; **Ta|rif|ver|hand|lun|gen** PL negotiations pl on pay; (für Löhne auch) wage negotiations pl; (für Gehälter auch) salary negotiations pl; **Ta|rif|ver|**

trag M pay agreement; (*für Löhne auch*) wage agreement; **Ta|rif|zo|ne** F fare zone

Tarn-: **Tarn|an|strich** M camouflage; **Tarn|an|zug** M (*Mil*) camouflage battledress

tar|nen ['tarnən] **VT** to camouflage; (*fig*) *Absichten, Identität etc* to disguise; **Saunas sind oft getarnte Bordelle** saunas are often a cover for brothels; **als Polizist getarnt** disguised as a policeman **VR** (*Tier*) to camouflage itself; (*Mensch*) to disguise oneself

Tarn-: **Tarn|far|be** F camouflage colour (*Brit*) or color (*US*); (*Anstrich*) camouflage paint; **Tarn|kap|pe** F magic hat; **Tarn|kap|pen|bom|ber** M Stealth bomber; **Tarn|kleid** NT (*Zool*) protective camouflage; **Tarn|na|me** M cover name; **Tarn|netz** NT (*Mil*) camouflage netting

Tar|nung ['tarnʊŋ] F -, -en camouflage; (*von Agent etc*) disguise; **die Arztpraxis ist nur eine ~** the doctor's practice is just a cover; **er fuhr zur ~ erst eine Station mit der U-Bahn** as a cover he first went one stop on the subway

Ta|rock [ta'rɔk] M OR NT -s, -s tarot

Ta|rot [ta'ro:] NT OR M -s, -s tarot

Tar|tan|bahn ['tartan-] F (*Sport*) tartan track

Tar|tar¹ [tar'ta:ɐ] NT -(s), *no pl*, **Tar|tar|beef|steak** NT steak tartare

Tar|tar² [tar'ta:ɐ] M -en, -en, **Tar|ta|rin** [-'ta:rɪn] F -, -nen Tartar

Täsch|chen ['tɛʃçən] NT -s, - *dim von* Tasche

Ta|sche ['taʃə] F -, -n **a** (= *Handtasche*) bag (*Brit*), purse (*US*); (= *Reisetasche etc*) bag; (= *Backentasche*) pouch; (= *Aktentasche*) case **b** (*bei Kleidungsstücken*, = *Billardtasche*) pocket; **sich** (*dat*) **die ~n füllen** (*fig*) to line one's own pockets; **in die eigene ~ arbeiten** *or* **wirtschaften** to line one's own pockets; **etw in der ~ haben** (*inf*) to have sth in the bag (*inf*); **die Hand auf die ~ halten** (*dated inf*) **die ~ zuhalten** (*dated inf*) to keep a tight grip on the purse strings; **jdm das Geld aus der ~ locken** *or* **ziehen** *or* **lotsen** to get sb to part with his money; **etw aus der eigenen ~ bezahlen** to pay for sth out of one's own pocket; **etw in die eigene ~ stecken** (*fig*) to put sth in one's own pocket, to pocket sth; **sich** (*dat*) **etwas in die ~ lügen** (*inf*) to kid oneself (*inf*); **jdm auf der ~ liegen** (*inf*) to live off sb, to live at sb's expense; **die Hände in die ~n stecken** (*lit*) to put one's hands in one's pockets; (*fig*) to stand idly by; **jdn in die ~ stecken** (*inf*) to put sb in the shade (*inf*); **jdm in die ~ greifen** (*fig*) to get money out of sb → **tief** ADV **a**

Ta|schel|zie|her ['taʃltsi:ɐ] M -s, -, **Ta|schel|zie|he|rin** [-ərɪn] F -, -nen (*Aus, inf: = Taschendieb*) pickpocket

Ta|schen-: **Ta|schen|aus|ga|be** F pocket edition; **Ta|schen|buch** NT paperback (book); **Ta|schen|buch|aus|ga|be** F paperback (edition); **Ta|schen|dieb(in)** M(F) pickpocket; **Ta|schen|dieb|stahl** M pickpocketing; **Ta|schen|fahr|plan** M (pocket) timetable; **Ta|schen|fei|tel** M (*Aus inf*) penknife, pocketknife; **Ta|schen|for|mat** NT pocket size; **Tran|sistorradio im ~** pocket-size(d) transistor (radio); **Ta|schen|geld** NT pocket money; **Ta|schen|ka|len|der** M pocket diary; **Ta|schen|kamm** M pocket comb; **Ta|schen|krebs** M edible crab; **Ta|schen|lam|pe** F torch, flashlight; **Ta|schen|mes|ser** NT pocketknife, penknife; **wie ein ~ zusammenklappen** (*inf*) to double up; **Ta|schen|rech|ner** M pocket calculator; **Ta|schen|schirm** M collapsible umbrella; **Ta|schen|spie|gel** M pocket mirror; **Ta|schen|spie|ler(in)** M(F) conjurer (*esp Brit*), magician; **Ta|schen|spie|le|rei** F sleight of hand *no pl*; **Ta|schen|spie|ler|trick** M (*fig*) sleight of hand *no indef art, no pl*; **Ta|schen|tuch** NT *pl* **-tücher** handkerchief, hanky (*inf*); **Ta|schen|uhr** F pocket watch; **Ta|schen|vei|tel** [-faitl] M -s, - (*Aus inf*) penknife, pocket-

knife; **Ta|schen|wör|ter|buch** NT pocket dictionary

Täsch|ner ['taʃnɐ] M -s, -, **Täsch|ne|rin** [-ərɪn] F -, -nen, **Täsch|ner** ['tɛʃnɐ] M -s, -, **Täsch|ne|rin** [-ərɪn] F -, -nen bag-maker (*Brit*), purse-maker (*US*)

Tas|ma|ni|en [tas'ma:niən] NT -s Tasmania

Tas|ma|ni|er [tas'ma:niɐ] M -s, -, **Tas|ma|ni|e|rin** [- iərɪn] F -, -nen Tasmanian

tas|ma|nisch [tas'ma:nɪʃ] ADJ Tasmanian

Täss|chen ▲ ['tɛsçən] NT -s, - *dim von* Tasse (little) cup; **ein ~ Tee** a quick cup of tea

Tas|se ['tasə] F -, -n cup; (*mit Untertasse*) cup and saucer; (= *Henkeltasse*) mug; (= *Suppentasse*) bowl; **eine ~ Kaffee** a cup of coffee; **er hat nicht alle ~n im Schrank** (*inf*) he's a sandwich short of a picnic (*Brit inf*), he's one card shy of a full deck (*US inf*); **eine trübe ~** (*inf*) a wet blanket (*inf*); **hoch die ~n!** (*inf*) bottoms up (*inf*)

Tas|ta|tur [tasta'tu:ɐ] F -, -en keyboard

tast|bar ADJ palpable; **eine ~e Beule** a raised bump

Tas|te ['tastə] F -, -n key; (= *Knopf an Gerät auch*) button; **in die ~n greifen** (*inf*) to play the piano; **auf die ~n hauen** *or* **hämmern** (*inf*) to hammer away at the keyboard; „**Taste drücken**" "push button"

Tast-: **Tast|emp|fin|den** NT sense of touch; **Tast|emp|fin|dung** F tactual sensation

tas|ten ['tastn] **VI** to feel; **nach etw ~** (*lit, fig*) to feel *or* grope for sth; **vorsichtig ~d** feeling *or* groping one's way carefully; **~de Schritte** (*lit, fig*) tentative steps **VR** to feel *or* grope one's way **VT** (= *drücken*) to press, to punch; *Nummer auch* to punch out; *Telex etc* to key; (*Typ:* = *setzen*) to key(board)

Tas|ten-: **Tas|ten|feld** NT (*Comput*) keypad, keys *pl*; **Tas|ten|in|stru|ment** NT (*Mus*) keyboard instrument; **Tas|ten|te|le|fon** NT push-button telephone

Tas|ter ['tastɐ] M -s, - **a** (*Zool*) organ of touch, tactile organ **b** (*Typ:* = *Tastatur*) keyboard

Tast-: **Tast|or|gan** NT organ of touch, tactile organ; **Tast|sinn** M sense of touch; **Tast|werk|zeug** NT organ of touch, tactile organ; **Tast|zir|kel** M (outside) callipers *pl* (*Brit*) *or* calipers *pl* (*US*)

tat *pret von* tun

Tat [ta:t] F -, -en (= *das Handeln*) action; (= *Einzeltat auch*) act; (= *Heldentat, Untat*) deed; (= *Leistung*) feat; (= *Verbrechen*) crime; **ein Mann der ~** a man of action; **keine Worte, sondern ~en** not words but deeds *or* actions; **seinen Worten ~en folgen lassen** to follow up one's words with actions, to suit the action to the word (*liter*); **eine ~ der Verzweiflung/Nächstenliebe** an act of desperation/charity; **als er sah, was er mit dieser ~ angerichtet hatte** when he saw what he had done by this; **eine geschichtliche/verbrecherische ~** an historic/a criminal act *or* deed; **eine gute/böse ~** a good/wicked deed; **eine eindrucksvolle ~ vollbringen** to do something impressive; **Leben und ~en des ...** the life and exploits of ...; **etw in die ~ umsetzen** to put sth into action; **zur ~ schreiten** to proceed to action; (*hum*) to get on with it; **in der ~** indeed; (*wider Erwarten, erstaunlicherweise etc*) actually

Ta|tar¹ [ta'ta:ɐ] M -(s), *no pl*, **Ta|tar|beef|steak** NT steak tartare

Ta|tar² [ta'ta:ɐ] M -en, -en, **Ta|ta|rin** [-'ta:rɪn] F -, -nen Tartar

Tat-: **Tat|be|stand** M (*Jur*) facts *pl* (of the case); (= *Sachlage*) facts *pl* (of the matter); **den ~ des Betrugs erfüllen** (*Jur*) to constitute fraud; **Tat|ein|heit** F (*Jur*) **in ~ mit** concomitantly with

Ta|ten-: **Ta|ten|drang** M thirst for action, energy; **Ta|ten|durst** M (*old, hum*) thirst for action; **ta|ten|durs|tig** ADJ (*old, hum*) eager for action; **ta|ten|froh** (*dated*) ADJ enthusiastic

ADV enthusiastically; **ta|ten|los** ADJ idle ADV **~ herumstehen** to stand idly by, to stand by and do nothing; **~ abwarten** to sit idly and wait; **wir mussten ~ zusehen** we could only stand and watch; **Ta|ten|lo|sig|keit** F -, *no pl* inaction

Tä|ter ['tɛ:tɐ] M -s, -, **Tä|te|rin** [-ərɪn] F -, -nen culprit; (*Jur*) perpetrator (*form*); **als ~ verdächtigt werden** to be a suspect; **als ~ in Frage kommen** to be a possible suspect; **nach dem ~ wird noch gefahndet** the police are still searching for the person responsible *or* the person who committed the crime; **wer war der ~?** who did it?; **unbekannte ~** person or persons unknown; **jugendliche ~** young offenders

Tä|ter|pro|fil NT suspect profile

Tä|ter|schaft ['tɛ:tɐʃaft] F -, *no pl* ~en guilt; **die Frage (nach) der ~** (*form*) the question of who was responsible *or* of who committed the crime; **die ~ leugnen/zugeben** to deny/admit one's guilt; **(vor Gericht)** to plead not guilty/guilty

Tat-: **Tat|form** F (*Gram*) active (voice); **tat|froh** ADJ, ADV = tatenfroh; **Tat|her|gang** M sequence of events; (*bei Verbrechen auch*) particulars *pl*

tä|tig ['tɛ:tɪç] ADJ **a** *attr* active; **dadurch hat er ~e Reue bewiesen** he showed his repentance in a practical way; **~e Nächstenliebe** practical charity; **in einer Sache ~ werden** (*form*) to take action in a matter **b** (= *arbeitend*) **~ sein** to work; **als was sind Sie ~?** what do you do?; **er ist im Bankwesen ~** he's in banking

tä|ti|gen ['tɛ:tɪgn] VT (*Comm*) to conclude, to effect; *Geschäft auch* to transact; (*geh*) *Einkäufe* to carry out; (*geh*) *Anruf* to make

Tä|tig|keit ['tɛ:tɪçkait] F -, -en activity; (= *Beschäftigung*) occupation; (= *Arbeit*) work; (= *Beruf*) job; **während meiner ~ als Lehrer** while I was working as a teacher; **zur Zeit übt er eine andere ~ aus** at present he has a different occupation; **auf eine langjährige ~ (als ...) zurückblicken** to look back on many years of active life (as ...); **in ~ treten** to come into operation; (*Mensch*) to act, to step in; **in ~ sein** (*Maschine*) to be operating *or* running; **in ~ setzen** (*Maschine*) to set going *or* in motion; *Alarmanlage* to activate; **außer ~ setzen** (*Maschine*) to stop; *Alarmanlage* to put out of action

Tä|tig|keits-: **Tä|tig|keits|be|reich** M field of activity; **Tä|tig|keits|be|richt** M progress report; **Tä|tig|keits|be|schrei|bung** F job description; **Tä|tig|keits|form** F (*Gram*) active (voice); **Tä|tig|keits|merk|ma|le** PL job characteristics *pl*; **Tä|tig|keits|wort** NT *pl* -wörter (*Gram*) verb

Tä|ti|gung ['tɛ:tɪgʊŋ] F -, *rare* -en conclusion, effecting; (*von Geschäft auch*) transaction; (*von Einkäufen*) carrying out; (*von Anruf*) making

Tat-: **Tat|kraft** F , *no pl* energy, vigour (*Brit*), vigor (*US*), drive; **tat|kräf|tig** ADJ energetic; *Hilfe* active ADV actively; **etw/jdn ~ unterstützen** to actively support sth/sb

tät|lich ['tɛ:tlɪç] ADJ violent; **~e Beleidigung** (*Jur*) assault (and battery); **~ werden** to become violent; **gegen jdn ~ werden** to assault sb ADV **jdn ~ angreifen** to attack sb physically, to assault sb

Tät|lich|keit F violent act, act of violence; **~en** violence *sing*; **es kam zu ~en** there was violence

Tat-: **Tat|mensch** M man/woman of action; **Tat|mo|tiv** NT motive (for the crime); **Tat|ort** M *pl* -orte scene of the crime

tä|to|wie|ren [tɛto'vi:rən] *ptp* tätowiert VT to tattoo; **sich ~ lassen** to have oneself tattooed

Tä|to|wie|rung F -, -en **a** *no pl* (= *das Tätowieren*) tattooing **b** (= *Darstellung*) tattoo

Tat|sa|che ✪ 44.1 F fact; **~ ist aber, dass ...** but the fact of the matter *or* the truth is that ...; **~?** (*inf*) really?, no!; **das stimmt, ~!** (*inf*) it's true, really; **das ist ~** (*inf*) that's a fact; **nackte ~n** (*inf*) the hard facts; (*hum*) girlie pictures; **vollendete ~n schaffen** to create a fait accompli; **jdn vor vollendete ~n stellen** to present sb with a fait accompli; **vor der vollendeten ~ stehen** to be faced with a fait accompli; **(unter) Vorspiegelung falscher ~n** (under) false pretences (Brit) or pretenses (US)

Tat|sa|chen-: Tat|sa|chen|be|richt M documentary (report); **Tat|sa|chen|ma|te|ri|al** NT facts pl

tat|säch|lich ['ta:tzɛçlıç, ta:t'zɛçlıç] **ADJ** attr real, actual **ADV** **a** (= in Wirklichkeit, objektiv) actually, really, in fact; **~ war es aber ganz anders** it (in actual) fact or actually or really it was quite different **b** (= sage und schreibe) really, actually; **willst du das ~ tun?** are you really or actually going to do it?; **~?** really?; **~!** oh yes, so it/he etc is/was etc; **da kommt er! – ~!** here he comes! – so he does!

tat|scheln ['tɛtʃln] VT to pat

tat|schen ['tatʃn] VI (pej inf) **auf etw** (acc) **~** to paw sth

Tat|ter|greis(in) ['tatɐ-] M(F) (pej inf) old dodderer, doddering old man/woman (pej)

Tat|te|rich ['tatərıç] M -(e)s, no pl (inf) **den ~ haben/bekommen** to have/get the shakes (inf)

tat|te|rig ['tatərıç], **tatt|rig** ['tatrıç] ADJ (inf) Mensch doddering, doddery; Hände, Schriftzüge shaky, quivery

ta|tü|ta|ta [ta:ty:ta:ta:] INTERJ **~! die Feuerwehr ist da!** da-da-da-da! here comes the fire engine!; **das Tatütata des Polizeiautos** the (wailing) siren of the police car

Tat-: Tat|ver|dacht M suspicion (of having committed a crime); **unter ~ stehen** to be under suspicion; **tat|ver|däch|tig** ADJ suspected; **Tat|ver|däch|ti|ge(r)** MF decl as adj suspect; **Tat|waf|fe** F weapon (used in the crime); (= bei Mord) murder weapon

Tat|ze ['tatsə] F -, -n (lit, fig) paw

Tat-: Tat|zeit F time of the incident or crime; **Tat|zeu|ge** M , **Tat|zeu|gin** F witness (to the incident or crime)

Tau¹ [tau] M -(e)s, no pl dew; **vor ~ und Tag** (poet) at break of day (poet)

Tau² NT -(e)s, -e (= Seil) rope; (Naut auch) hawser

taub [taup] ADJ deaf; Glieder numb; Gestein dead; Metall dull; Ähre unfruitful; Nuss empty; **sich ~ stellen** to pretend not to hear; **gegen** or **für etw ~ sein** (fig) to be deaf to sth → **Ohr, Nuss**

Täub|chen ['tɔypçən] NT -s, - dim von **Taube mein ~!** my little dove

Tau|be ['taubə] F -, -n **a** (Zool) pigeon; (= Turteltaube) dove, pigeon; **hier fliegen einem die gebratenen ~n nicht ins Maul** (prov) this isn't exactly the land of milk and honey **b** (fig, als Symbol) dove; **~n und Falken** (Pol inf) hawks and doves

Tau|ben-: tau|ben|blau ADJ blue-grey (Brit), blue-gray (US); **Tau|ben|ei** ['taubnlai] NT , **Taube** a pigeon's/dove's egg; **tau|ben|ei|groß** ADJ the size of a golf ball

tau|be|netzt [-bənɛtst] ADJ (liter) dewy, dew-covered

Tau|ben-: tau|ben|grau ADJ dove grey (Brit) or gray (US); **Tau|ben|haus** NT dovecot(e); (für Brieftauben) pigeon loft; **Tau|ben|post** F **mit der ~** by pigeon post (esp Brit); **Tau|ben|schie|ßen** NT -s, no pl (Sport) pigeon shooting; **Tau|ben|schlag** M **a** (lit) = Taubenhaus **b** (fig) **hier geht es zu wie im ~** it's mobbed here (inf); **Tau|ben|sport** M pigeon racing; **Tau|ben|zucht** F pigeon fancying (Brit) or breeding

Tau|be(r) ['taubɐ] MF decl as adj deaf person or man/woman etc; **die ~n** the deaf

Tau|ber ['taubɐ] M -s, -, **Täu|ber** ['tɔybɐ] M -s, -, **Täu|be|rich** ['tɔybərıç] M -s, -e cock pigeon

Taub|heit F -, no pl **a** deafness **b** (von Körperteil) numbness

Täub|ling ['tɔyplıŋ] M -s, -e (Bot) russula (toadstool)

Taub-: Taub|nes|sel F dead-nettle; **taub|stumm** ADJ deaf and dumb, deaf-mute attr; **Taub|stum|men|spra|che** F sign language; **Taub|stum|me(r)** [-ʃtʊmə] MF decl as adj deaf-mute; **Taub|stumm|heit** F -, no pl deaf-mutism

Tauch|boot NT submersible

tau|chen ['tauxn] **VI** **a** aux haben or sein to dive (nach for); (= kurz tauchen) to duck under; (= unter Wasser sein) to stay under water; (U-Boot) to submerge, to dive **b** aux sein (fig) to disappear (in +acc into); (Boxen: = abducken) to duck; **die Sonne tauchte langsam ins Meer/hinter den Horizont** the sun sank slowly into the sea/beneath the horizon **VT** (= kurz tauchen) to dip; Menschen, Kopf to duck; (= eintauchen, auch bei Taufe) to immerse; **in Licht getaucht** (geh) bathed in light

Tau|chen NT -s, no pl diving

Tau|cher ['tauxɐ] M -s, -, **Tau|che|rin** [-ərın] F -, -nen diver

Tau|cher-: Tau|cher|an|zug M diving (Brit) or dive (US) suit; **Tau|cher|aus|rüs|tung** F diving (Brit) or dive (US) equipment or gear; **Tau|cher|bril|le** F diving (Brit) or dive (US) goggles pl; **Tau|cher|flos|se** F (diving (Brit) or dive (US)) flipper; **Tau|cher|glo|cke** F diving (Brit) or dive (US) bell; **Tau|cher|helm** M diving (Brit) or dive (US) helmet, diver's helmet

Tau|che|rin F -, -nen diver

Tauch-: Tauch|gang M dive; **Tauch|mas|ke** F pl -gänge diving (Brit) or dive (US) mask; **Tauch|sie|der** [-zi:dɐ] M -s, - immersion coil (for boiling water); **Tauch|sport** M (skin) diving; **Tauch|sta|ti|on** F **auf ~ gehen** (U-Boot) to dive; (hum: in Schützengraben etc) to duck, to get one's head down; (fig: = sich verstecken) to make oneself scarce; **auf ~ sein** (U-Boot) to be submerged; **Tauch|tie|fe** F depth; (Naut: von Fluss) navigable depth

tau|en¹ ['tauən] VTI (vi: aux haben or sein) (Eis, Schnee) to melt, to thaw; **es taut** it is thawing; **der Schnee taut von den Bergen/Dächern** the snow on the mountains/roofs is melting or thawing

tau|en² VT (N Ger, Naut) to tow

Tau|en|de ['tauɛndə] NT (Naut) end of a piece of rope

Tauf-: Tauf|akt M baptism or christening (ceremony); **Tauf|be|cken** NT font; **Tauf|buch** NT baptismal register

Tau|fe ['taufə] F -, -n baptism; (christliche auch, esp von Kindern) christening; (= Schiffstaufe) launching (ceremony); **die ~ empfangen** to be baptized or christened; **jdm die ~ spenden** to baptize or christen sb; **ein Kind aus der ~ heben** (old) to stand sponsor to a child (old); **etw aus der ~ heben** (hum, Verein, Firma) to start sth up; Zeitung, Projekt to launch sth

tau|fen ['taufn] VT to baptize; (bei Äquatortaufe) to duck; (= nennen) Kind, Schiff, Hund etc to christen; **sich ~ lassen** to be baptized; **jdn auf den Namen Rufus ~** to christen sb Rufus

Täu|fer ['tɔyfɐ] M -s, - **Johannes der ~** John the Baptist; **die ~** (Eccl) the Baptists

tau|feucht ADJ dewy, wet with dew

Tauf-: Tauf|for|mel F baptism formula; **Tauf|ge|lüb|de** NT baptismal vows pl; **Tauf|ka|pel|le** F baptistry; **Tauf|kleid** NT christening robe

Täuf|ling ['tɔyflıŋ] M -s, -e child/person to be baptized

Tauf-: Tauf|na|me M Christian name; **Tauf|pa|te** M godfather; **Tauf|pa|tin** F godmother; **Tauf|re|gis|ter** NT baptismal register

tau|frisch ADJ (geh) dewy; (fig) fresh; (= fit für sein Alter) sprightly

Tauf-: Tauf|schein M certificate of baptism; **Tauf|stein** M (baptismal) font; **Tauf|zeu|ge** M , **Tauf|zeu|gin** F godparent

tau|gen ['taugn] VI **a** (= geeignet sein) to be suitable (zu, für for); **wozu soll denn das ~?** what is that supposed to be for?; **er taugt zu gar nichts** he is useless; **er taugt nicht zum Arzt** he wouldn't make a good doctor; **in der Schule taugt er nichts** he's useless or no good at school; **er taugt nicht zu harter Arbeit** he's not much good at hard work; (wegen Faulheit) he's not keen on hard work **b** (= wert sein) **etwas ~** to be good or all right; **nichts** or **nicht viel ~** to be not much good or no good or no use; **taugt der Neue etwas?** is the new bloke any good or use?; **der Bursche taugt nicht viel/gar nichts** that bloke is a (real) bad lot (inf); **als Mensch taugt er gar nichts** he is worthless as a person

Tau|ge|nichts ['taugənıçts] M -(es), -e (dated) good-for-nothing, ne'er-do-well (old)

taug|lich ['tauklıç] ADJ Kandidat, Bewerber, Material suitable (zu for); (Mil) fit (zu for); **jdn für ~ erklären** (Mil) to declare or certify sb fit for service

Taug|lich|keit F -, no pl suitability; (Mil) fitness (for service)

Taug|lich|keits|grad M (Mil) physical fitness rating (for military service)

Tau|mel ['tauml] M -s, no pl (geh: = Schwindel) (attack of) dizziness or giddiness; (liter: = Rausch) frenzy; **im ~ der Ereignisse sein** (liter) to be caught up in the whirl of events; **im ~ des Glücks** (liter) in a transport of happiness (liter); **im ~ der Sinne** or **Leidenschaft** (liter) in the fever of his/her etc passion; **wie im ~** (geh) in a daze

tau|me|lig ['tauməlıç] ADJ dizzy, giddy

tau|meln ['taumln] VI aux sein to stagger; (zur Seite) to sway

taum|lig ['taumlıç] ADJ = taumelig

Tau-: Tau|per|le F (liter) dewdrop; **Tau|punkt** M dew point

Tausch [tauʃ] M -(e)s, -e exchange, swap; (= Tauschhandel) barter; **im ~ gegen** or **für etw** in exchange for sth; **etw in ~ geben** to exchange or swap/barter sth; (bei Neukauf) to give sth in part exchange; **jdm etw zum ~ für etw anbieten** to offer to exchange or swap sth for sth; **etw in ~ nehmen** to take sth in exchange; **einen guten/schlechten ~ machen** to get a good/bad deal

Tausch|bör|se F barter exchange, bartering centre (Brit) or center (US); (im Internet) online exchange service

tau|schen ['tauʃn] **VT** to exchange, to swap; Güter to barter; (= austauschen) Briefmarken, Münzen etc to swap; Geschenke to exchange; Geld to change (in +acc into); (inf: = umtauschen) Gekauftes to change; **einen Blick mit jdm ~** (geh) to exchange glances with sb; **die Rollen ~** to swap roles; **Küsse ~** (geh) to kiss; **wollen wir die Plätze ~?** shall we change or swap places? **VI** to swap; (in Handel) to barter; **wollen wir ~?** shall we swap (places etc)?; **wir haben getauscht** we swapped, we did a swap; **ich möchte nicht mit ihm ~** I wouldn't like to change places with him

täu|schen ['tɔyʃn] **VT** to deceive; **mit dieser Fälschung täuschte er sogar die Experten** he even deceived or fooled the experts with this forgery; **man kann ihn nicht ~** you can't fool him; **er wurde in seinen Erwartungen/Hoffnungen getäuscht** his expectations/hopes were disappointed; **wenn mich mein Gedächtnis nicht täuscht** if my memory serves me right; **wenn mich nicht alles täuscht** unless I'm completely wrong; **sie lässt sich leicht/nicht ~** she is easily/not easily fooled (durch by) **VR** to be wrong or mistaken (in +dat, über +acc about); **darin ~ Sie sich** you are mistaken there, that's where you're wrong; **dann hast du**

dich getäuscht! then you are mistaken; **so kann man sich ~!** it shows how wrong you can be

VI **a** (= *irreführen*) (*Aussehen etc*) to be deceptive; (*Sport*) to feint; **das täuscht** that is deceptive; **wenn (mich) nicht alles täuscht, ...** unless I'm very much mistaken, ...; **der Eindruck täuscht** things are not what they seem

b (*Sch form* = *betrügen*) to cheat

täu|schend **ADJ** *Nachahmung* remarkable; *Ähnlichkeit auch* striking; **eine ~e Ähnlichkeit mit jdm haben** to look remarkably like sb **ADV** **sich** (*dat*) **~ ähnlich sehen/sein** to look/be remarkably alike, to look/be almost identical; **jdm ~ ähnlich sehen** to look remarkably like sb, to be the spitting image of sb; **eine ~ echte Fälschung/Nachahmung** a remarkably convincing fake/imitation

Täu|scher ['tɔʏʃɐ] **M** -s, -, **Täu|sche|rin** [-ərɪn] **F** -, -nen phoney (*inf*)

Tau|sche|rei [tauʃə'rai] **F** -, -en (*inf*) exchanging, swapping

Tausch-: **Tausch|ge|schäft** **NT** exchange, swap; (= *Handel*) barter (deal); **mit etw ein ~ machen** to exchange/barter sth; **Tausch|ge|sell|schaft** **F** barter society; **Tausch|han|del** **M** barter; **~ treiben** to barter; **Tausch|mit|tel** **NT** medium of exchange; **Tausch|objekt** **NT** barter *no pl*, barter object; **Tausch|part|ner(in)** **M(F)** **~ für 2-Zimmer-Wohnung gesucht** exchange or swap wanted for two-room(ed) flat (*Brit*) or apartment

Täu|schung ['tɔʏʃʊŋ] **F** -, -en **a** (= *das Täuschen*) deception; **das tat er zur ~** he did that in order to deceive **b** (= *Irrtum*) mistake, error; (= *Irreführung*) deceit; (= *falsche Wahrnehmung*) illusion; (= *Selbsttäuschung*) delusion; **er gab sich einer ~ hin** he was deluding himself; **darüber darf man sich keiner ~** (*dat*) **hingeben** one must not delude oneself (about that)

Täuschungs-: **Täu|schungs|ab|sicht** **F** intention to deceive; **Täu|schungs|ma|nö|ver** **NT** (*Sport*) feint; (*inf*) ploy; **Täu|schungs|ver|such** **M** attempted deception

Tausch-: **Tausch|wert** **M** (*Sociol*) exchange value, value in exchange; **Tausch|wirt|schaft** **F** , *no pl* (*Econ*) barter economy

tau|send ['tauznt] **NUM** a or one thousand; **~ Dank/Grüße/Küsse** a thousand thanks/greetings/kisses → *auch* **hundert**

Tau|send¹ ['tauznt] **F** -, -en [-dn] (*Zahl*) thousand

Tau|send² **NT** -s, -e [-də] thousand; **vom ~** in a or per thousand; **ei der ~!** (*obs*) zounds! (*obs*) → *auch* **Hundert²**

Tau|sen|der ['tauzndɐ] **M** -s, - **a** (= *Zahl*) **ein ~** a figure in the thousands; **die ~** the thousands **b** (= *Geldschein*) thousand (euro/dollar *etc* note *or* bill)

tau|sen|der|lei ['tauzndɐ'lai] **ADJ** *inv* a thousand kinds of

Tau|send-: **Tau|send|fü|ßer** [-fy:sɐ] **M** -s, - (*form*), **Tau|send|füß|ler** [-fy:slɐ] **M** -s, - centipede; **die ~** the myriapods (*spec*) **Tau|send|jahr|fei|er** **F** millenary; **tau|send|jäh|rig** *attr* thousand-year-old; (= *tausend Jahre lang*) thousand-year(-long); **nach mehr als ~er Unterdrückung** after more than a thousand years of oppression; **das ~e Reich** (*Bibl*) the millennium; **Hitlers „tausendjähriges Reich"** Hitler's "thousand-year empire"; **Tau|send|künst|ler(in)** **M(F)** jack of all trades; **tau|send|mal** **ADV** a thousand times; **ich bitte ~ um Entschuldigung** a thousand pardons; **viel ~** (*old*) times without number → *auch* **hundertmal**; **Tau|send|sa|sa** ['tauzntsasa] **M** -s, -(s), **Tau|send|sas|sa** ['tauzntsasa] **M** -s, -(s) (*dated inf*) hell of a chap (*Brit dated inf*) or guy (*inf*); **Tau|send|schön** ['tauzntʃøːn] **NT** -s, -e, **Tau|send|schön|chen** [-ʃøːnçən] **NT** -s, - daisy

Tau|sends|tel ['tauzntstl] **NT** -s, - thousandth → *auch* **Hundertstel**

tau|sends|te(r, s) ['tauzntstə] **ADJ** thousandth → *auch* **hundertste(r, s)**

Tau|send-: **tau|send|und|ei|ne(r, s)** ['tauznt-unt'lainə] **ADJ** a thousand and one; **Märchen aus Tausendundeiner Nacht** Tales of the Thousand and One Nights, the Arabian Nights; **tau|send|(und)|eins** ['tauznt(lunt)'lains] **NUM** one thousand and one

Tau|to|lo|gie [tautolo'giː] **F** -, -n [-'giːən] tautology

tau|to|lo|gisch [tauto'loːgɪʃ] **ADJ** tautological, tautologous **ADV** *sich ausdrücken, formulieren* tautologically

Tau-: **Tau|trop|fen** **M** dewdrop; **Tau|werk** **NT** , *no pl* (*Naut*) rigging; **Tau|wet|ter** **NT** thaw; (*fig auch*) relaxation; **wir haben** *or* **es ist ~** it is thawing; **bei ~** during a thaw, when it thaws; **es herrschte ein kulturelles/politisches ~** there was a period of cultural/political relaxation; **Tau|zie|hen** **NT** -s, *no pl* (*lit, fig*) tug-of-war

Ta|ver|ne [ta'vɛrnə] **F** -, -n (*old*) tavern (*old*), inn; (*in Italien*) taverna

Ta|xa|me|ter [taksa'meːtɐ] **M** -s, - taximeter, clock (*inf*)

Ta|xa|tor [ta'ksaːtoːɐ] **M** -s, Taxatoren [-'toːrən], **Ta|xa|to|rin** [-'toːrɪn] **F** -, -nen (*Comm*) valuer

Ta|xe ['taksə] **F** -, -n **a** (= *Schätzung*) valuation, estimate **b** (= *Gebühr*) charge; (= *Kurtaxe etc*) tax; (= *Gebührenordnung*) scale of charges **c** (*dial*) = **Taxi**

Ta|xi ['taksi] **NT** -s, -s taxi, cab, taxicab (*form*); **sich** (*dat*) **ein ~ nehmen** to take a taxi, to go by taxi; **~ fahren** to drive a taxi; (*als Fahrgast*) to go by taxi

Ta|xi|chauf|feur(in) **M(F)** taxi or cab driver

ta|xie|ren [ta'ksiːrən] *ptp* **taxiert** **VT** **a** *Preis, Wert* to estimate (*auf +acc* at); *Haus, Gemälde etc* to value (*auf +acc* at); **etw zu hoch ~** to overestimate/overvalue sth; **etw zu niedrig ~** to underestimate/undervalue sth; **er hat mich richtiggehend taxiert** he looked me up and down **b** (*geh* = *einschätzen*) *Situation* to assess

Ta|xi-: **Ta|xi|fah|rer(in)** **M(F)** taxi or cab driver, cabby (*inf*); **Ta|xi|fahrt** **F** taxi ride; **Ta|xi|stand** **M** taxi rank (*Brit*) or stand

Tax|kurs ['taks-] **M** rate of taxation

Tax|ler ['takslɐ] **M** -s, -, **Tax|le|rin** [-ərɪn] **F** -, -nen (*Aus inf*) cabby (*inf*)

Tax|preis ['taks-] **M** estimated price (*according to valuation*)

Ta|xus ['taksʊs] **M** -, - yew (tree)

Tax|wert ['taks-] **M** estimated value

Tb(c) [teː(')beː(ʼtseː)] **F** -, -s *abbr von* **Tuberkulose** TB

Tb(c)-krank [teː(')beː(ʼtseː)-] **ADJ** **~ sein** to have TB; **die ~en Patienten** patients with TB, TB patients or cases

Teak|holz ['tiːk-] **NT** teak; **ein Tisch aus ~** a teak table

Team [tiːm] **NT** -s, -s team

Team-: **Team|ar|beit** **F** teamwork; **etw in ~ machen** to do sth as a team or through teamwork; **das wird in ~ gemacht** it's done through teamwork; **team|fä|hig** **ADJ** able to work in a team; **sie ist nicht ~** she's not a team player; **Team|fä|hig|keit** **F** ability to work in a team; **Team|geist** **M** team spirit; **Team|work** ['tiːmwøːɐk, -wœrk] **NT** -s, *no pl* = **Teamarbeit**

Tech|ne|ti|um [tɛçˈneːtsiʊm] **NT** -s, *no pl* (*abbr* **Tc**) technetium

Tech|nik ['tɛçnɪk] **F** -, -en **a** (*no pl*: = *Technologie*) technology; (*esp als Studienfach*) engineering; **der Mensch und die ~** man and technology; **das Zeitalter der ~** the technological age, the age of technology; **verfluchte ~!** stupid technology! **b** (= *Arbeitsweise, Verfahren*) technique; **jdn mit der ~ von etw vertraut machen** to familiarize sb

with the techniques *or* skills of sth; **die ~ des Dramas/der Musik** dramatic/musical techniques **c** (*no pl*: = *Funktionsweise und Aufbau*) (*von Auto, Motor etc*) mechanics *pl* **d** (*Sch*: = *Schulfach*) (= *Haushaltslehre*) home economics; (= *Werken*) technical studies **e** (*inf*: = *technische Abteilung*) technical department, back-room boys *pl* (*inf*) **f** (*Aus, inf*: = *Technische Hochschule*) institute of technology

tech|nik|be|geis|tert **ADJ** technology-mad (*Brit inf*), techno-crazy (*US inf*)

tech|nik|be|ses|sen **ADJ** obsessed with new technology

Tech|ni|ker ['tɛçnikɐ] **M** -s, -, **Tech|ni|ke|rin** [-ərɪn] **F** -, -nen engineer; (= *Beleuchtungstechniker, Labortechniker*) technician; (*fig*: = *Fußballspieler, Künstler*) technician; **ich bin kein ~, ich verstehe das nicht** I am not technically minded, I don't understand that; **er ist mehr Theoretiker als ~** he is more concerned with theoretical than practical matters

tech|nik|feind|lich **ADJ** hostile to new technology, technophobic

Tech|nik|feind|lich|keit **F** hostility to new technology, technophobia

Tech|nik|fol|gen|ab|schät|zung **F** , **Tech|nik|fol|gen-Ab|schät|zung** **F** technology assessment

tech|nik|freund|lich **ADJ** receptive to new technology

Tech|ni|kum ['tɛçnikʊm] **NT** -s, Technika [-ka] college of technology

tech|nisch ['tɛçnɪʃ] **ADJ** **a** (= *technologisch*) technological; *Studienfach* technical; **~e Hochschule/Universität** technological university, Institute of (Science and) Technology; **~e Chemie/Medizin** chemical/medical engineering; **das ~e Zeitalter** the technological age, the age of technology; **Technisches Hilfswerk → THW** **b** (= *die Ausführung betreffend*) *Schwierigkeiten, Gründe* technical; (= *mechanisch*) mechanical; **~er Zeichner** engineering draughtsman (*Brit*) or draftsman (*US*); **~e Leiter** technical director; **~e Einzelheiten** (*fig*) technicalities, technical details; **~e Daten** specifications **ADV** technically; **er ist ~ begabt** he is technically minded; **~ versiert sein** to have technical skills; **~ sehr anspruchsvoll** technically very demanding; **~ machbar** technically feasible or possible; **das ist ~ unmöglich** it is technically impossible; (*inf*: = *das geht nicht*) it is absolutely impossible

tech|ni|sie|ren [tɛçniˈziːrən] *ptp* **technisiert** **VT** to mechanize

Tech|ni|sie|rung **F** -, -en mechanization

Tech|no ['tɛçno] **M** -, *no pl* (*Mus*) techno

Tech|no|krat [tɛçnoˈkraːt] **M** -en, -en, **Tech|no|kra|tin** [-ˈkraːtɪn] **F** -, -nen technocrat

Tech|no|kra|tie [tɛçnokraˈtiː] **F** -, *no pl* technocracy

tech|no|kra|tisch [tɛçnoˈkraːtɪʃ] **ADJ** technocratic **ADV** technocratically

Tech|no|lo|ge [tɛçnoˈloːgə] **M** -n, -n, **Tech|no|lo|gin** [-ˈloːgɪn] **F** -, -nen technologist

Tech|no|lo|gie [tɛçnoloˈgiː] **F** -, -n [-ˈgiːən] technology

Tech|no|lo|gie-: **Tech|no|lo|gie|park** **M** technology park; **Tech|no|lo|gie|trans|fer** **M** technology transfer; **Tech|no|lo|gie|zent|rum** **NT** technology park

Tech|no|lo|gin **F** -, -nen technologist

tech|no|lo|gisch [tɛçnoˈloːgɪʃ] **ADJ** technological **ADV** technologically; **eine ~ führende Nation** a leading technological nation

Tech|no-Mu|sik **F** , **Tech|no|mu|sik** **F** techno music

Tech|no-Par|ty **F** , **Tech|no|par|ty** **F** techno party

Tech|tel|mech|tel [tɛçtl'mɛçtl] NT **-s, -** (inf) affair, carry-on (inf); **mit jdm ein ~ haben** to be carrying on with sb (inf)

Te|ckel ['tɛkl] M **-s, -** dachshund

Ted [tɛt] M **-(s), -s** (inf: Mensch) ted (inf)

TED [tɛt] M **-(s)** abbr von **Teledialog** computer used to work out results of telephone polls

Ted|dy ['tɛdi] M **-s, -s** a (auch **Teddybär**) teddy (bear) b (auch **Teddystoff**) fur fabric

Ted|dy|fut|ter NT fleecy or fur-fabric lining

Te|de|um [te'de:ʊm] NT **-s, -s** Te Deum

TEE [te:e:'e:] M **-, -(s)** (Rail) abbr von **Trans-Europ(a)-Express**

Tee [te:] M **-s, -s** tea; **einen im ~ haben** (inf) to be tipsy (inf); **einen ~ geben** (dated) to give a tea party

Tee-: Tee|beu|tel M tea bag; **Tee|blatt** NT tea leaf; **Tee-Ei** NT , **Tee|ei** ▲ NT (tea) infuser (esp Brit), tea ball (esp US); **Tee|fil|ter** M tea filter; **Tee|ge|bäck** NT , no pl sweet biscuits pl (Brit), cookies pl (esp US); **Tee|glas** NT tea glass; **Tee|hau|be** F tea cosy (Brit) or cozy (US); **Tee|haus** NT teahouse; **Tee|kan|ne** F teapot; **Tee|kes|sel** M a kettle b (= Gesellschaftsspiel) guessing game based on puns; **Tee|kü|che** F kitchenette; **Tee|licht** NT night-light; **Tee|löf|fel** M teaspoon; (Menge) teaspoonful; **tee|löf|fel|wei|se** ADV by the teaspoonful; **Tee|ma|schi|ne** F tea urn; **Tee|mi|schung** F blend of tea

Teen [ti:n] M **-s, -s** (Press sl) teenager

Tee|na|ger ['ti:ne:dʒɐ] M **-s, -** teenager

Tee|netz NT tea filter

Tee|ny ['ti:ni] M **-s, -s** (inf) teenybopper (inf)

Tee|pau|se F tea break

Teer [te:ɐ] M **-(e)s, -e** tar

Teer-: Teer|dach|pap|pe F (bituminous) roofing felt; **Teer|de|cke** F tarred (road) surface

tee|ren ['te:rən] VT to tar; **~ und federn** to tar and feather

Teer-: Teer|far|ben PL , **Teer|farb|stof|fe** PL aniline dyes pl; **Teer|ge|halt** M tar content; **teer|hal|tig** ADJ **eine wenig/stark ~e Zigarette** a low/high tar cigarette; **~ sein** to contain tar

Tee|ro|se F tea rose

Teer-: Teer|pap|pe F (bituminous) roofing felt; **Teer|stra|ße** F tarred road

Tee|rung ['te:rʊŋ] F **-, -en** tarring

Tee-: Tee|ser|vice [-zɛrviːs] NT tea set; **Tee|sieb** NT tea strainer; **Tee|sor|te** F (type or sort of) tea; **Tee|strauch** M tea bush; **Tee|strumpf** M tea filter; **Tee|stu|be** F tearoom; **Tee|stun|de** F afternoon tea (time) (Brit); **Tee|tas|se** F teacup; **Tee|wa|gen** M tea trolley; **Tee|wär|mer** [-vɛrmɐ] M **-s, -** tea cosy (Brit) or cozy (US); **Tee|was|ser** NT **das ~ aufsetzen** to put the water or kettle (Brit) on for (some) tea; **Tee|wurst** F smoked German sausage for spreading

Tef|lon® ['tɛflɔːn, tɛf'lɔːn] NT **-s** Teflon®

Te|he|ran ['te:həraːn, tehə'raːn] NT **-s** Teh(e)ran

Teich [taɪç] M **-(e)s, -e** pond; **der große ~** (dated inf) the (herring) pond (hum)

Teich-: Teich|molch M smooth newt; **Teich|ro|se** F yellow water lily

Teig [taɪk] M **-(e)s, -e** [-gə] (= Hefeteig, Knetteig, Nudelteig) dough; (= Mürbteig, Blätterteig etc) pastry; (= Pfannkuchenteig) batter

tei|gig ['taɪgɪç] ADJ **~ Teig** doughy; (= voller Teig) Hände covered in dough/pastry

Teig-: Teig|mas|se F → Teig (Cook) dough; pastry; batter; mixture; **Teig|schüs|sel** F mixing bowl; **Teig|ta|sche** F pastry case; **Teig|wa|ren** PL (= Nudeln) pasta sing

Teil¹ [taɪl] M **-(e)s, -e** a part; (von Strecke) stretch, part; (von Stadt) part, district, area; (von Gebäude) part, area, section; (von Zeitung) section; **der Bau/das Projekt ist zum ~ fertig** the building/project is partly finished; **wir hörten**

zum ~ interessante Reden some of the speeches we heard were interesting; **200 Menschen wurden zum ~ schwer verletzt** 200 people were injured, some of them badly; **zum ~ ...**, **zum ~ ...** partly ..., partly ...; **zum großen/größten ~** for the most part, mostly; **er hat die Bücher darüber zum großen/größten ~ gelesen** he has read many/most of the books about that; **die Studenten wohnen zum größten ~ bei ihren Eltern** for the most part the students live with their parents; **der größere ~ ihres Einkommens** the bulk of her income; **ein großer ~ stimmte dagegen** a large number (of people) voted against it; **der dritte/vierte/fünfte** etc **~** (= ein Drittel/Viertel/Fünftel etc) a third/quarter/fifth etc (von of); **in zwei ~e zerbrechen** to break in two or half

b (Jur. = Partei, Seite) party

c auch nt (= Anteil) share; **ein gut ~ Arbeit** (dated) quite a bit of work; **ein gut ~ der Leute** (dated) many or a lot of people; **zu gleichen ~en erben** to get an equal share of an inheritance; **zu gleichen ~en beitragen** to make an equal contribution; **er hat sein(en) ~ dazu beigetragen** he did his bit or share; **er hat sein(en) ~ bekommen** or **weg** (inf) he has (already) had his due; **sich** (dat) **sein(en) ~ denken** (inf) to draw one's own conclusions

d auch nt **ich für mein(en) ~** for my part, I ..., I, for my part ...

Teil² NT **-(e)s, -e** a part; (= Bestandteil) component, part; (= Ersatzteil) spare, (spare) part; (sl: = Ding) thing; **etw in seine ~e zerlegen** (Tier, Leiche) to cut sth up; Motor, Möbel etc to take sth apart or to bits or to pieces b → Teil¹ c d

Teil-: Teil|ab|kom|men NT partial agreement; **Teil|an|sicht** F partial view; **Teil|as|pekt** M aspect, part; **teil|bar** ADJ divisible, which can be divided (durch by); **Teil|bar|keit** ['taɪlbaːrkaɪt] F **-,** no pl divisibility; **Teil|be|reich** M part; (in Abteilung) section; **Teil|be|trag** M part (of an amount); (auf Rechnung) item; (= Rate) instalment; (= Zwischensumme) subtotal

Teil|chen ['taɪlçən] NT **-s, -** particle; (dial: = Gebäckstück) cake

Teil-: Teil|chen|be|schleu|ni|ger M (Phys) particle accelerator; **Teil|chen|phy|sik** F particle physics sing

Tei|le|fer|ti|gung F (Ind) manufacture of parts or components

tei|len ['taɪlən] VT a (= zerlegen, trennen) to divide up; (Math) to divide (durch by); **27 lässt sich durch 9 ~** 27 can be divided by 9; **27 geteilt durch 9** 27 divided by 9; **etw in drei Teile ~** to divide sth in(to) three (parts); **der Fluss teilt das Land in der Mitte** the river divides the country down the middle; **(politisch) geteilter Meinung sein** to have different (political) opinions; **darüber sind die Meinungen geteilt** opinions differ on that; **darüber kann man geteilter Meinung sein** one can disagree about that; **das Schiff teilte die Wellen** or **Wogen** (liter) the ship forged its way through the waves

b (= aufteilen) to share (out) (unter +dat amongst); **etw mit jdm ~** to share sth with sb

c (= an etw teilhaben) to share; **sie haben Freud und Leid miteinander geteilt** they shared the rough and the smooth (Brit) or the good and bad times; **geteilte Freude ist doppelte Freude** (prov) a joy shared is a joy doubled (prov); **geteilter Schmerz ist halber Schmerz** (prov) a trouble shared is a trouble halved (prov); **sie teilten unser Schicksal** or **Los** they shared the same fate as us; **sie teilten das Zimmer mit ihm** they shared the room with him

VR a (in Gruppen) to split up

b (Straße, Fluss) to fork, to divide; (Vorhang) to part

c **sich** (dat) **etw ~** to share or split sth; **teilt euch das!** share or split that between you; **sich in etw** (acc) **~** (geh) to share sth

d (fig: = auseinander gehen) **in diesem Punkt ~ sich die Meinungen** opinion is divided on this

VI to share; **er teilt nicht gern** he doesn't like sharing

Tei|ler ['taɪlɐ] M **-s, -** (Math) factor

Teil-: Teil|er|folg M partial success; **Teil|er|geb|nis** NT partial result; **einige ~se sind schon bekannt** we already know some of the results; **Teil|er|rich|tungs|ge|neh|mi|gung** F restricted planning permission; **Teil|fab|ri|kat** NT component; **Teil|fra|ge** F part (of a question); **Teil|ge|biet** NT a (= Bereich) branch b (räumlich) area; **Teil|ge|neh|mi|gung** F partial permission; **Teil|ha|be** F (liter) participation, sharing (an +dat in); (esp an Gott) communion (an +dat with); **teil+ha|ben** VI sep irreg (an +dat in) (= mitwirken) to have a part, to participate; (liter: = teilnehmen) to share; **Teil|ha|ber** ['taɪlhaːbɐ] M **-s, -, Teil|ha|be|rin** [-ərɪn] F **-, -nen** (Comm) partner; **Teil|ha|ber|schaft** ['taɪlhaːbɐʃaft] F **-, -en** (Comm) partnership; **teil|haf|tig** ADJ (old) **eines großen Glücks/einer großen Ehre** etc **~ werden** to be blessed with great good fortune/a great honour (Brit) or honor (US) etc (liter)

-tei|lig [taɪlɪç] ADJ suf (von Kleidung, Geschirr etc) -piece; **ein zweiteiliges Kostüm** a two-piece suit; **ein dreiteiliges Fernsehspiel** a three-part TV drama

Teil|kas|ko-: teil|kas|ko|ver|sichert [-fɛɐzɪçɐt] ADJ **~ sein** to be insured third party, fire and theft; **Teil|kas|ko|ver|si|che|rung** F third party, fire and theft

Teil-: Teil|men|ge F (Math) subset; **teil|möb|liert** [-møbliːɐt] ADJ partially furnished

Teil|nah|me [-naːmə] F **-, -n** a (= Anwesenheit) attendance (an +dat at); (= Beteiligung an Wettbewerb etc) participation (an +dat in); **seine ~ absagen** to withdraw; **jdn zur ~ an etw** (dat) **aufrufen** to urge sb to take part or participate in sth; **~ am Straßenverkehr** (form) road use b (= Interesse) interest (an +dat in); (= Mitgefühl) sympathy; **jdm seine herzliche** or **aufrichtige ~ aussprechen** to offer sb one's heartfelt condolences

Teil|nah|me-: teil|nah|me|be|rech|tigt ADJ eligible; **Teil|nah|me|be|rech|ti|gung** F eligibility; **von der ~ ausgeschlossen sein** to be ineligible, not to be eligible

Teil|nahms-: teil|nahms|los ADJ (= gleichgültig) indifferent, apathetic; (= stumm leidend) listless ADV indifferently, apathetically; (= stumm leidend) listlessly; **Teil|nahms|lo|sig|keit** F **-,** no pl indifference, apathy; **teil|nahms|voll** ADJ compassionate, sympathetic ADV compassionately, sympathetically

teil+neh|men VI sep irreg a **an etw** (dat) **~** (= sich beteiligen) to take part or participate in sth; (= anwesend sein) to attend sth; **an Wettkampf, Preisausschreiben** etc to take part in sth, to enter sth, to go in for sth; **er hat nicht teilgenommen** he did not take part etc; **an einem Ausflug ~** to go on an outing; **am Krieg ~** to fight in the war; **am Unterricht ~** to attend classes; **lebhaft am Unterricht ~** to take an active part in the lessons; **an einem Kurs ~** to do a course; **an den Wahlen ~** (Partei, Kandidat) to stand in the elections; (Wähler) to vote in the elections

b (= Anteil nehmen) to share (an +dat in)

teil|neh|mend ADJ compassionate, sympathetic; **~e Beobachtung** (Sociol) participatory observation

Teil|neh|mer ['taɪlne:mɐ] M **-s, -, Teil|neh|me|rin** [-ərɪn] F **-, -nen** a (= Beteiligter bei Kongress etc) participant; (= Kriegsteilnehmer) combatant; (bei Wettbewerb, Preisausschreiben etc) competitor, contestant; (= Kursteilnehmer) student; (bei Ausflug etc) member of a party; **alle ~ an dem Ausflug** all those going on the outing b (Telec) subscriber; **der ~ meldet sich nicht** there is no reply

Teil|neh|mer|lis|te F list of participants; (Sport auch) list of entrants

Teil|neh|mer|zahl F attendance

Teil|pe|rü|cke F toupee; (*für Damen*) hairpiece

teils [tails] ADV partly; ~ ... ~ ... partly ... partly ...; (*inf*: = sowohl ... als auch*) both ... and ...; **die Demonstranten waren ~ Arbeiter, ~ Studenten** some of the demonstrators were workers and the others were students; **~ heiter, ~ wolkig** cloudy with sunny periods; **~, ~** (*als Antwort*) half and half; (*inf*) sort of (*inf*); **wie geht es dir? – ~, ~** how are you? – so-so (*inf*)

Teil-: Teil|schuld|ver|schrei|bung F (*Fin*) bond (forming part of a loan issue); **Teil|staat** M region, state; **Teil|stre|cke** F stretch (of road/railway *etc*); (*bei Reise*) stage; (*bei Rennen*) leg, stage; (*bei öffentlichen Verkehrsmitteln*) (fare) stage; **Teil|strich** M secondary graduation line; **Teil|stück** NT part; (= Teilstrecke *auch*) stretch

Teil|lung ['tailʊŋ] F **-, -en** division

Teil|lungs-: Tei|lungs|ar|ti|kel M (*Gram*) partitive article; **Tei|lungs|zei|chen** NT (*Math*) division sign

Teil|ver|lust M partial loss

teil|wei|se ['tailvaizə] ADV partly; (= *manchmal*) sometimes; **nicht alle Schüler sind so faul, ~ sind sie sehr interessiert** not all the pupils are so lazy, some of them are very interested; **der Film war ~ gut** the film was good in parts; **~ be-wölkt** cloudy in parts; **morgen tritt ~ eine Wet-terbesserung ein** there will be a partial improvement in the weather tomorrow ◆ ADJ *attr* partial

Teil|zah|lung F hire-purchase (*Brit*), install-ment plan (*US*); (= *Rate*) instalment (*Brit*), in-stallment (*US*); **auf ~** on hire-purchase (*Brit*) or (an) installment plan (*US*)

Teil|zah|lungs-: Teil|zah|lungs|ge|schäft NT hire purchase business, credit selling; (= *Trans-aktion*) hire purchase or credit transaction; **Teil|zah|lungs|kauf** M hire purchase (*Brit*), installment plan (*US*); **Teil|zah|lungs|preis** M hire-purchase price (*Brit*)

Teil|zeit-: Teil|zeit|ar|beit F part-time work; (= *Stelle*) part-time job; **Teil|zeit|ar|beits-platz** M part-time job; **teil|zeit|be|schäf-tigt** ADJ employed part time; **Teil|zeit|be-schäf|tig|te(r)** MF *decl as adj* part-time em-ployee; **Teil|zeit|be|schäf|ti|gung** F part--time work; (= *Stelle*) part-time job; **Teil|zeit-kraft** F part-time worker; **Teil|zeit|re|ge-lung** F part-time working arrangements *pl*

Teint [tɛ̃:] M **-s, -s** complexion

T-Ei|sen ['te:-] NT t-iron, tee-iron

Tek|to|nik [tɛk'to:nɪk] F **-**, *no pl* (*Archit, Geol*) tectonics *pl*

tek|to|nisch [tɛk'to:nɪʃ] ADJ tectonic

Tel. *abbr von* Telefon

Te|le- ['te:lə-]: **Te|le|ar|beit** F telecommuting, teleworking; **Te|le|ar|bei|ter(in)** M(F) tele-commuter, teleworker; **Te|le|ar|beits|platz** M job for telecommuters or teleworkers; **Te|le|ban|king** [-bɛŋkɪŋ] NT **-s**, *no pl* telebanking; **Te|le|brief** M telemessage, mailgram (*US*); **Te|le|di|a|log** M telephone poll; **Te|le|fax** NT (= *Kopie, Gerät*) fax; **te|le|fa|xen** VTI *insep* to fax; **Te|le|fax|ge|rät** NT fax machine; **Te|le|fax|teil|neh|mer(in)** M(F) fax subscriber

Te|le|fon [tele'fo:n, 'te:lefo:n] NT **-s, -e** (tele-)phone; **am ~** (*verlangt werden*) (to be wanted) on the phone; **~ haben** to be on the phone; **jdn ans ~ rufen** to get sb (to come) to the phone; **ans ~ gehen** to answer the phone

Te|le|fon- *in cpds* (tele)phone → *auch* **Fern-sprech-; Te|le|fon|an|ruf** M (tele)phone call; **Te|le|fon|an|sa|ge** F telephone information service; **Te|le|fon|an|schluss** ▲ M telephone connection, telephone line; (= *Nebenanschluss*) extension (line); **Te|le|fon|ap|pa|rat** M tele-phone

Te|le|fo|nat [telefo'na:t] NT **-(e)s, -e** (tele-) phone call

Te|le|fon-: Te|le|fon|aus|kunft F directory in-quiries *pl* (*Brit*) or assistance (*US*), information (*US*); **Te|le|fon|ban|king** [-bɛŋkɪŋ] NT **-s**, *no pl* telephone banking, telebanking; **Te|le|fon|buch** NT (tele)phone book; **Te|le|fon|draht** M telephone line; **Te|le|fon|ge|bühr** F call charge; (= *Grundgebühr*) telephone rental; **Te|le|fon|ge|spräch** NT (tele)phone call; (= *Un-terhaltung*) telephone conversation; **Te|le|fon|haupt|an|schluss** ▲ M telephone line; **Te|le|fon|häus|chen** [-hɔysçən] NT (*inf*) phone box (*Brit*) or booth; **Te|le|fon|hö|rer** M (tele-phone) receiver

te|le|fo|nie|ren [telefo'ni:rən] *ptp* **telefoniert** ◆ VI to make a (tele)phone call; **wir haben stun-denlang telefoniert** we talked or were on the phone for hours; **mit jdm ~** to speak to sb on the phone; **miteinander ~** to speak (to each other) on the phone; **bei jdm ~** to use sb's phone; **es wird entschieden zu viel telefoniert** the phones are definitely used too much; **ins Ausland ~** to make an international call; **am Ort ~** to make a local call; **nach Amerika/Ham-burg ~** to call America/Hamburg; **er telefoniert den ganzen Tag** he is on the phone all day long ◆ VT (*inf, Sw*) to phone, to ring (up) (*Brit*), to call; **jdm etw ~** to call or phone and tell sb sth

te|le|fo|nisch [tele'fo:nɪʃ] ADJ telephonic; **~e Auskunft/Beratung** telephone information/ad-vice service; **eine ~e Mitteilung** a (tele)phone message; **die ~e Zeitangabe** the Speaking Clock (*Brit*), TIME (*US*) ◆ ADV *Auskunft geben* o-ver the phone; *beraten, erpressen, bedrohen* on the phone; **jdm etw ~ mitteilen** to tell sb sth o-ver the phone; **~ anfragen** to call to ask; **er hat sich ~ entschuldigt** he phoned to apologize; **jdn ~ belästigen** to make crank phone calls to sb; **ich bin ~ erreichbar** or **zu erreichen** I can be contacted by phone; **bitte melden Sie sich ~ unter ...** please phone on ...

Te|le|fo|nist [telefo'nɪst] M **-en, -en**, **Te|le|fo|nis|tin** [-'nɪstɪn] F *-, -nen* telephonist; (*in Betrieb auch*) switchboard operator

Te|le|fo|ni|tis [telefo'ni:tɪs] F **-**, *no pl* (*hum inf*) **die ~ haben** to be telephone-mad (*Brit inf*) or a telephone addict (*inf*)

Te|le|fon-: Te|le|fon|kar|te F phonecard; **Te|le|fon|ket|te** F telephone tree; **Te|le|fon|kon|fe|renz** F telephone conference, telecon-ference; **Te|le|fon|kun|de** M , **Te|le|fon|kun|din** F telephone customer; **Te|le|fon|lei|tung** F telephone line; **Te|le|fon|mar|ke|ting** NT telemarketing; **Te|le|fon|netz** NT tele-phone network; **Te|le|fon|num|mer** F (tele-) phone number; **Te|le|fon|rech|nung** F (tele-) phone bill; **Te|le|fon|sa|tel|lit** M telecommu-nications satellite; **Te|le|fon|seel|sor|ge** F ≈ Samaritans *pl* (*Brit*), ≈ advice hotline (*US*); **Te|le|fon|sex** M telephone sex; **Te|le|fon|ter|ror** M telephone harassment; (*bedrohlicher*) threatening phone calls *pl*; **Te|le|fon|über|wa|chung** F telephone tapping, wiretapping; **Te|le|fon|ver|bin|dung** F telephone line; (*zwi-schen Orten*) telephone link → *auch* **Verbindung** c; **Te|le|fon|ver|stär|ker** M telephone ampli-fier; **Te|le|fon|ver|zeich|nis** NT telephone di-rectory; **Te|le|fon|wer|bung** F telephone adver-tising; (*im Wahlkampf*) telephone canvassing; **Te|le|fon|zel|le** F (tele)phone box (*Brit*) or booth; **Te|le|fon|zent|ra|le** F (telephone) switchboard

te|le|gen [tele'ge:n] ADJ telegenic

Te|le|graf [tele'gra:f] M **-en, -en** telegraph

Te|le|gra|fen-: Te|le|gra|fen|amt NT (tele-graph) office; **Te|le|gra|fen|ap|pa|rat** M tele-graph; **Te|le|gra|fen|bü|ro** NT (*dated*) news agency; **Te|le|gra|fen|mast** M telegraph pole

Te|le|gra|fie [telegra'fi:] F **-**, *no pl* telegraphy

te|le|gra|fie|ren [telegra'fi:rən] *ptp* **telegrafiert** VTI to send a telegram, to cable, to wire

te|le|gra|fisch [tele'gra:fɪʃ] ADJ telegraphic ◆ ADV **jdm ~ Geld überweisen** to wire sb money

Te|le|gramm [tele'gram] NT *pl* **-gramme** tele-gram; (= *Auslandstelegramm auch*) cable

Te|le|gramm-: Te|le|gramm|ad|res|se F tele-graphic address; **Te|le|gramm|bo|te** M , **Te|le|gramm|bo|tin** F telegram boy/girl; **Te|le|gramm|for|mu|lar** NT telegram form; **Te|le|gramm|stil** M staccato or telegram style, tele-graphese

Te|le|graph *etc* M = Telegraf *etc*

Te|le-: Te|le|ki|ne|se [teleki'ne:zə] F **-**, *no pl* tel-ekinesis; **te|le|ki|ne|tisch** [teleki'ne:tɪʃ] ADJ telekinetic ◆ ADV *bewegen* telekinetically, through telekinesis; **Te|le|kol|leg** ['te:lə-] NT ≈ Open University (*esp Brit*), ≈ Distance Educa-tion (*US*)

Te|le|kom ['te:lekɔm] F **-**, *no pl* **die ~** German telecommunications service

Te|le-: Te|le|kom|mu|ni|ka|ti|on F tele-communications *pl* or (*als Fachgebiet*) *sing*; **Te|le|ko|pie** F fax; **Te|le|ko|pie|rer** M fax machine

Te|le|mark ['te:ləmark] M **-s, -s** (*Ski*) telemark

Te|le|ob|jek|tiv ['te:lə-] NT (*Phot*) telephoto lens

Te|le|o|lo|gie [teleolo'gi:] F **-**, *no pl* (*Philos*) tele-ology

te|le|o|lo|gisch [teleo'lo:gɪʃ] ADJ (*Philos*) teleo-logical

Te|le|or|dern ['te:lə-] NT **-s**, *no pl* teleordering

Te|le|path [tele'pa:t] M **-en, -en**, **Te|le|pa|thin** [-'pa:tɪn] F **-, -nen** telepathist

Te|le|pa|thie [telepa'ti:] F **-**, *no pl* telepathy

te|le|pa|thisch [tele'pa:tɪʃ] ADJ telepathic ◆ ADV telepathically

Te|le|phon *etc* NT = Telefon *etc*

Te|le|phon- *in cpds* = Telefon-

Te|le|promp|ter ['te:leprɔmptɐ] M **-s, -** Auto-cue® (*Brit*), Teleprompter® (*US*)

Te|le|shop|ping ['te:lə-] NT teleshopping

Te|le|skop [tele'sko:p] NT **-s, -e** telescope

Te|le|skop|au|ge NT telescope eye

te|le|sko|pisch [tele'sko:pɪʃ] ADJ telescopic

Te|le-: Te|le|spiel ['te:lə-] NT video game; **Te|le|tex** ['te:lətɛks] NT **-**, *no pl* teletex; **Te|le|vi|si|on** [televi'zio:n] F **-**, *no pl* = Fernsehen

Te|lex ['te:lɛks] NT **-, -e** telex

Te|lex|an|schluss ▲ M telex link

te|le|xen ['te:lɛksn] VTI to telex

Tel|ler ['tɛlɐ] M **-s, - a** plate; **ein ~ Suppe** a plate of soup **b** (*sl*: = Plattenteller*) turntable **c** (*Ski*) basket

Tel|ler-: Tel|ler|ei|sen NT (*Hunt*) steel trap; **Tel|ler|fleisch** NT (*Cook*) boiled beef/pork (pieces); **tel|ler|för|mig** ADJ plate-shaped; **Tel|ler|ge|richt** NT one-course meal; **Tel|ler|mi|ne** F (*Mil*) flat antitank mine; **Tel|ler|rand** M rim or edge of a/the plate; **nicht zum Blick über den ~ fähig sein** (*fig*) to be una-ble to see beyond the end of one's own nose; **Tel|ler|wär|mer** [-vɛrmɐ] M **-s, -** plate warmer; **Tel|ler|wä|scher(in)** M(F) dishwasher; **Tel|ler|wä|scher|kar|ri|e|re** F (*inf*) rags-to-riches career

Tel|lur [tɛ'lu:ɐ] NT **-s**, *no pl* (*abbr* **Te**) tellurium

Tem|pel ['tɛmpl] M **-s, -** temple (*auch fig*)

Tem|pel-: Tem|pel|bau M *pl* **-bauten** (*Gebäu-de*) temple; **Tem|pel|herr** M , **Tem|pel|rit|ter** M (*Hist*) (Knight) Templar; **Tem|pel|schän-dung** F desecration of a temple; **Tem|pel|tanz** M temple dance; **Tem|pel|tän|ze|rin** F temple dancer

Tem|pe|ra ['tɛmpera] F **-, -s** tempera (colour (*Brit*) or color (*US*))

Tem|pe|ra-: Tem|pe|ra|far|be F tempera (col-our (*Brit*) or color (*US*)); **Tem|pe|ra|ma|le|rei** F (= *Maltechnik*) painting in tempera; (= *Gemäl-de*) tempera painting(s *pl*)

Tem|pe|ra|ment [tɛmpera'mɛnt] NT **-(e)s, -e a** (= *Wesensart*) temperament; **die vier ~e** (*old*) the four humours (*Brit old*) or humors (*US old*); **ein hitziges ~ haben** to be hot-tempered **b** *no pl* (= *Lebhaftigkeit*) vitality, vivacity; **viel/kein ~ haben** to be very/not to be vivacious *or* lively; **sein ~ ist mit ihm durchgegangen** he lost his temper; **sie konnte ihr ~ nicht mehr zügeln** she could control herself *or* her temper no longer

Tem|pe|ra|ment-: tem|pe|ra|ment|los ADJ lifeless, spiritless ADV listlessly; **Tem|pe|ra|ment|lo|sig|keit** F -, *no pl* lifelessness

Tem|pe|ra|ments|aus|bruch M temperamental fit *or* outburst

tem|pe|ra|ment|voll ADJ vivacious, lively; *Aufführung auch* spirited; *Auto, Fahrer* nippy (*Brit inf*), speedy (*US inf*) ADV exuberantly; **ein Lied ~ vortragen** to give a spirited rendering of a song

Tem|pe|ra|tur [tɛmpəra'tuːɐ] F -, -en temperature; **erhöhte ~ haben** to have a *or* be running a temperature; **die ~en sind angestiegen/gesunken** the temperature has risen/fallen; **bei diesen/solchen ~en** in these/such temperatures; **bei ~en von bis zu 42 Grad Celsius** in temperatures of up to 42°C

Tem|pe|ra|tur-: Tem|pe|ra|tur|ab|fall M drop *or* fall in temperature; **Tem|pe|ra|tur|an|stieg** M rise in temperature; **Tem|pe|ra|tur|reg|ler** M thermostat; **Tem|pe|ra|tur|rück|gang** M fall in temperature; **Tem|pe|ra|tur|schwan|kung** F variation in temperature; **Tem|pe|ra|tur|ska|la** F temperature scale; **Tem|pe|ra|tur|sturz** M sudden drop *or* fall in temperature

Tem|pe|renz|ler [tɛmpə'rɛntslɐ] M -s, -, **Tem|pe|renz|le|rin** [-ərɪn] F -, -nen member of a/the temperance league

tem|pe|rie|ren [tɛmpə'riːrən] *ptp* **temperiert** VT **etw ~** (= *auf die richtige Temperatur bringen*) to make sth the right temperature; (= *anwärmen*) to warm sth up; **der Raum ist angenehm temperiert** the room is at a pleasant temperature, the room is pleasantly warm; **Rotwein leicht temperiert trinken** to drink red wine at room temperature

Temp|ler ['tɛmplɐ] M -s, - (Knight) Templar

Temp|ler|or|den M Order of the Knights Templar

Tem|po ['tɛmpo] NT -s, -s **a** (= *Geschwindigkeit*) speed; (= *Arbeitstempo, Schritttempo*) pace, speed; **~!** (*inf*) hurry up!; **bei jdm ~** (*dahinter or hinter etw acc*) **machen** (*inf*) to make sb get a move on (with sth) (*inf*); **nun mach mal ein bisschen ~!** (*inf*) get a move on! (*inf*); **~ 100** speed limit (of) 100 km/h; **mit vollem/hohem ~** at full/a high speed; **im ~ zulegen** to speed up; **~ nachlassen** to slow down; **aufs ~ drücken** (*inf*) to step on the gas (*inf*)
b (*Mus*) *pl* **Tempi** ['tɛmpi] tempo; **das ~ halten** to keep time; **das ~ angeben** to set the tempo; (*fig*) to set the pace
c **~®** (*inf*: = *Taschentuch*) paper handkerchief, tissue, Kleenex®

Tem|po-30-Zo|ne [tɛmpo'draisɪç-] F ≈ 20 mph zone

Tem|po|li|mit NT speed limit

Tem|po|mat [tɛmpo'maːt] M -en, -en (*Aut*) cruise control

Tem|po|ra *pl von* **Tempus**

tem|po|ral [tɛmpo'raːl] ADJ (*Gram*) temporal

Tem|po|ral|satz M temporal clause

tem|po|rär [tɛmpo'rɛːɐ] (*geh*) ADJ temporary ADV temporarily

Tem|po-: Tem|po|sün|der(in) M(F) person caught for speeding; **Tem|po|ta|schen|tuch®** NT paper handkerchief, tissue, Kleenex®; **Tem|po|über|schrei|tung** [-ly:bəʃraitʊŋ] F -, -en speeding

Tem|pus ['tɛmpʊs] NT -, **Tempora** ['tɛmpora] (*Gram*) tense

Ten|denz [tɛn'dɛnts] F -, -en trend (*auch St Ex*); (= *Neigung*) tendency; (= *Absicht*) intention;

(*no pl*: = *Parteilichkeit*) bias, slant; **die ~ haben, zu ...** to tend to ..., to have a tendency to ...; **die ~ zeigen, zu ...** to show a tendency to ...; **er hat nationalistische ~** he has nationalist leanings; **vier Millionen Menschen sind arbeitslos, ~ steigend** the number of people out of work is four million and rising

ten|den|zi|ell [tɛndɛn'tsiɛl] ADJ **eine ~e Veränderung** a change in direction ADV **~ ist Ruritanien ein faschistischer Staat** Ruritania is a country which shows fascist tendencies; **die Ziele der beiden Parteien unterscheiden sich ~ kaum voneinander** the aims of the two parties are broadly similar (in direction)

ten|den|zi|ös [tɛndɛn'tsiøːs] ADJ tendentious ADV tendentiously; **etw ist ~ gefärbt** sth has a tendentious cast to it

Tendenz-: Ten|denz|stück NT tendentious play; **Ten|denz|wen|de** F change of direction; (= *Wendepunkt*) turning point

Ten|der ['tɛndɐ] M -s, - (*Naut, Rail*) tender

ten|die|ren [tɛn'diːrən] *ptp* **tendiert** VI **a dazu ~, etw zu tun** (= *neigen*) to tend to do sth; (= *beabsichtigen*) to be moving toward(s) doing sth; **zum Kommunismus/Katholizismus ~** to have leanings toward(s) communism/Catholicism, to have communist/Catholic leanings *or* tendencies; **zu Erkältungen/Wutausbrüchen ~** to tend to get colds/fits of anger; **seine Begabung tendiert mehr ins Künstlerische** his talents tend more toward(s) the artistic **b** (*Fin, St Ex*) to tend; **freundlich/fester/schwächer ~** to show a favourable (*Brit*) *or* favorable (*US*)/stronger/weaker tendency

Te|ne|rif|fa [tene'rɪfa] NT -s Tenerife

Ten|ne ['tɛnə] F -, -n, (*Sw*) **Tenn** [tɛn] M -s, -e threshing floor

Ten|nis ['tɛnɪs] NT -, *no pl* tennis

Tennis- *in cpds* tennis; **Ten|nis|arm** M tennis elbow; **Ten|nis|ball** M tennis ball; **Ten|nis|hal|le** F indoor tennis centre (*Brit*) *or* center (*US*); **Ten|nis|platz** M tennis court; **Ten|nis|schlä|ger** M tennis racquet (*esp Brit*) *or* racket; **Ten|nis|schuh** M tennis shoe; **Ten|nis|spie|ler(in)** M(F) tennis player; **Ten|nis|zir|kus** M tennis circus

Ten|no¹ ['tɛno] M -s, -s Emperor of Japan

Te|nor¹ ['teːnoːɐ] M -s, *no pl* tenor

Te|nor² [te'noːɐ] M -s, **≈e** [-'nøːrə] (*Mus*) tenor

Te|no|rist [teno'rɪst] M -en, -en tenor (singer)

Te|nor|schlüs|sel [te'noːɐ-] M tenor clef

Ten|sid [tɛn'ziːt] NT -(e)s, -e [-də] (*Chem*) surfactant

Ten|ta|kel [tɛn'takl] M OR NT -s, - tentacle

Te|nu|is ['teːnuɪs] F -, **Tenues** ['teːnueːs] (*Phon*) tenuis

Tep|pich ['tɛpɪç] M -s, -e **a** carpet (*auch fig*); (*inf*: = *Brücke auch*) rug; (= *Gobelin*) tapestry; (*inf*: = *Wandbehang*) wall hanging; (= *Ölteppich*) (oil) slick; **etw unter den ~ kehren** *or* **fegen** (*lit, fig*) to sweep sth under the carpet; **bleib auf dem ~!** (*inf*) be realistic!, be reasonable!; **den roten ~ ausrollen** to bring out the red carpet **b** (*dial inf*: = *Decke*) blanket; (*kleiner*) rug

Teppich-: Tep|pich|bo|den M carpet(ing); **das Zimmer ist mit ~ ausgelegt** the room has wall-to-wall carpeting *or* a fitted carpet; **Tep|pich|flie|se** F carpet tile; **Tep|pich|keh|rer** [-keːrɐ] M -s, -, **Tep|pich|kehr|ma|schi|ne** F carpet-sweeper; **Tep|pich|klop|fer** M carpet-beater; **Tep|pich|schnee** M carpet foam; **Tep|pich|stan|ge** F *frame for hanging carpets over for beating*

Ter|bi|um ['tɛrbiʊm] NT -s, *no pl* (*abbr* **Tb**) terbium

Term [tɛrm] M -s, -e (*Math, Phys, Ling*) term

Ter|min [tɛr'miːn] M -s, -e date; (*für Fertigstellung*) deadline; (*Comm*: = *Liefertag*) delivery date; (*bei Arzt, Besprechung etc*) appointment; (*Sport*) fixture; (*Jur*: = *Verhandlung*) hearing; **der letzte ~** the deadline, the last date; (*bei Bewerbung etc*)

the closing date; **sich** (*dat*) **einen ~ geben lassen** to make an appointment; **sich** (*dat*) **einen ~ in der Autowerkstatt geben lassen** to book one's car/van *etc* into the garage; **schon einen anderen ~ haben** to have a prior engagement

Ter|min|ab|spra|che F (= *Frist*) negotiation of a/the deadline, deadline negotiation(s *pl*); (= *Zeitpunkt*) agreeing (on) a date *or* time

Ter|mi|nal ['tøːɐmɪnəl, 'tœr-] NT OR M -s, -s terminal

Ter|min-: Ter|min|bör|se F futures market, forward exchange (*Brit*); **Ter|min|druck** M time pressure, deadline pressure; **unter ~ stehen** (= *Zeitdruck haben*) to have a very tight schedule; (= *Termin einhalten müssen*) to have to meet a (strict) deadline; **Ter|min|ein|la|ge** F (*Fin*) time deposit; **Ter|min|geld** NT fixed-term deposit; **ter|min|ge|mäß**, **ter|min|ge|recht** ADJ, ADV on schedule, according to schedule; **Ter|min|ge|schäft** NT deal on the forward (*Brit*) *or* futures market; **~e** futures; **Ter|min|grund** M **aus Termingründen** because of problems with one's schedule

Ter|mi|ni *pl von* **Terminus**

Ter|min|ka|len|der M (appointments *or* engagements) diary

Ter|min|kon|trakt [-kɔntrakt] M -(e)s, -e (*St Ex*) futures contract

ter|min|lich [tɛr'miːnlɪç] ADJ **aus ~en Gründen absagen** to cancel because of problems with one's schedule; **~e Verpflichtungen** commitments; **ich habe schon zu viele ~e Verpflichtungen** I have too many prior commitments ADV **etw ~ einrichten** to fit sth in (to one's schedule); **~ in Anspruch genommen sein** to have a full schedule; **diese Woche bin ich ~ zu** *or* **voll** (*inf*) this week I'm booked up; **das ist ~ zu schaffen** the scheduling is no problem

Ter|min|markt M (*St Ex*) forward (*Brit*) *or* futures market

ter|min|mä|ßig ADJ, ADV = **terminlich**

Ter|mi|no|lo|gie [tɛrminolo'giː] F -, -n [-'giːən] terminology

ter|mi|no|lo|gisch [tɛrmino'loːgɪʃ] ADJ terminological ADV terminologically; **~ arbeiten** to work in terminology; **sich ~ abstimmen** to agree on the terminology one is using; **das ist ~ nicht sauber** the terms here are not used correctly

Ter|min-: Ter|min|pla|nung F time scheduling; **Ter|min|schwie|rig|kei|ten** PL scheduling difficulties *pl*

Ter|mi|nus ['tɛrminʊs] M -, **Termini** [-ni] term; **~ technicus** technical term

Ter|min-: Ter|min|ver|ein|ba|rung F agreement on a deadline/on deadlines, deadline agreement; (*für Zeitpunkt*) agreement on a time/date; (*für Termin*) agreed deadline, agreed time/date; **Ter|min|ver|schie|bung** F postponement

Ter|mi|te [tɛr'miːtə] F -, -n termite, white ant

Ter|mi|ten-: Ter|mi|ten|hü|gel M termites' nest, termitarium (*form*); **Ter|mi|ten|staat** M colony of termites

Ter|pe|ne [tɛr'peːnə] PL terpenes *pl*

Ter|pen|tin [tɛrpɛn'tiːn] NT OR (*AUS*) M -s, -e turpentine; (*inf*: = *Terpentinöl*) turps (*inf*)

Ter|pen|tin|öl NT oil of turpentine, turps *sing* (*inf*)

Ter|rain [tɛ'rɛ̃ː] NT -s, -s land, terrain; (*fig*) territory; **das ~ sondieren** (*Mil*) to reconnoitre (*Brit*) *or* reconnoiter (*US*) the terrain; (*fig*) to see how the land lies; **sich auf neuem ~ bewegen** to be exploring new ground; **sich auf unsicheres ~ begeben** to get onto shaky ground; **verlorenes ~ (wieder) gutmachen** *or* **zurückerobern** (*lit, fig*) to regain lost ground

Ter|ra|kot|ta [tɛra'kɔta] F -, **Terrakotten** [-tn] terracotta

Ter|ra|ri|um [tɛ'raːriʊm] NT -s, **Terrarien** [-riən] terrarium

Ter|ras|se [tɛˈrasə] F **-, -n** [a] (Geog) terrace [b] (= Veranda) terrace, patio; (= Dachterrasse) roof garden

Ter|ras|sen-: ter|ras|sen|ar|tig, ter|ras|sen|för|mig ADJ terraced ADV in terraces; **Ter|ras|sen|gar|ten** M terraced garden; **Ter|ras|sen|haus** NT house built on a terraced slope (modern) split-level house

Ter|raz|zo [tɛˈratso] M **-s, Terrazzi** [-tsi] terrazzo

ter|res|trisch [tɛˈrɛstrɪʃ] ADJ terrestrial

Ter|rier [ˈtɛriɐ] M **-s, -** terrier

Ter|ri|ne [tɛˈriːnə] F **-, -n** tureen

ter|ri|to|ri|al [tɛritoˈriaːl] ADJ territorial

Ter|ri|to|ri|al-: Ter|ri|to|ri|al|ar|mee F territorial army; **Ter|ri|to|ri|al|ge|wäs|ser** PL territorial waters pl; **Ter|ri|to|ri|al|ho|heit** F territorial sovereignty

Ter|ri|to|ri|um [tɛritoˈriʊm] NT **-s, Territorien** [-riən] territory

Ter|ror [ˈtɛrɔr] M **-s,** no pl terror; (= Terrorismus) terrorism; (= Terrorherrschaft) reign of terror; (= brutale Einschüchterung) intimidation; (= Belästigung) menace; **die Stadt steht unter dem ~ der Mafia** the town is being terrorized by the Mafia; **blutiger ~** terrorism and bloodshed; **organisierter ~** organized terrorism/intimidation; **~ machen** (inf) to raise hell (inf)

Ter|ror-: Ter|ror|akt M act of terrorism, terrorist act; **Ter|ror|an|griff** M terrorist raid; **Ter|ror|an|schlag** M terrorist attack; **Ter|ror|herr|schaft** F reign of terror

ter|ro|ri|sie|ren [tɛroriˈziːrən] ptp **terrorisiert** VT to terrorize; Untergebene etc auch to intimidate

Ter|ro|ris|mus [tɛroˈrɪsmʊs] M **-,** no pl terrorism

Ter|ro|ris|mus-: Ter|ro|ris|mus|be|kämp|fung F counterterrorism; **Ter|ro|ris|mus|ex|per|te** M , **Ter|ro|ris|mus|ex|per|tin** F expert on terrorism

Ter|ro|rist [tɛroˈrɪst] M **-en, -en, Ter|ro|ris|tin** [-ˈrɪstɪn] F **-, -nen** terrorist

ter|ro|ris|tisch [tɛroˈrɪstɪʃ] ADJ terrorist attr

Ter|ror-: Ter|ror|jus|tiz F brutal, intimidatory justice; **Ter|ror|or|ga|ni|sa|ti|on** F terrorist organization

Ter|tia [ˈtɛrtsia] F **-, Tertien** [-tsiən] [a] (dated Sch) (= Unter-/Obertertia) fourth/fifth year of German secondary school [b] no pl (Typ) 16 point type

Ter|ti|a|ner [tɛrtsiˈaːnɐ] M **-s, -, Ter|ti|a|ne|rin** [-ərɪn] F **-, -nen** → Tertia a (dated Sch) pupil in fourth/fifth year of German secondary school

ter|ti|är [tɛrˈtsiɛː] ADJ tertiary

Ter|ti|är [tɛrˈtsiɛː] NT **-s,** no pl (Geol) tertiary period

Ter|ti|är|be|reich M tertiary education

Ter|ti|en pl von Tertia

Terz [tɛrts] F **-, -en** (Mus) third; (Fechten) tierce; **große/kleine ~** (Mus) major/minor third

Ter|zett [tɛrˈtsɛt] NT **-(e)s, -e** (Mus) trio

Ter|zi|ne [tɛrˈtsiːnə] F **-, -n** (Poet) tercet

Te|sa|film® [ˈteːza-] M Sellotape® (Brit), Scotch tape® (esp US)

Tes|sin [tɛˈsiːn] NT **-s** das ~ Ticino

Test [tɛst] M **-(e)s, -s** or **-e** test

Tes|ta|ment [tɛstaˈmɛnt] NT **-(e)s, -e** [a] (Jur) will; (fig) legacy; **das ~ eröffnen** to read the will; **sein ~ machen** to make one's will; **du kannst dein ~ machen!** (inf) you'd better make your will! (inf); **ohne Hinterlassung eines ~s** intestate [b] (Bibl) Testament; **Altes/Neues ~** Old/New Testament

tes|ta|men|ta|risch [tɛstamɛnˈtaːrɪʃ] ADJ testamentary; **eine ~e Verfügung** an instruction in the will ADV in one's will; **etw ~ festlegen** or **verfügen** to write sth in one's will; **~ festgelegt** (written) in the will; **jdm etw ~ vermachen** to will sth to sb

Tes|ta|ments-: Tes|ta|ments|er|öff|nung F reading of the will; **Tes|ta|ments|voll|stre|cker(in)** M(F) executor; (Frau auch) executrix

Tes|tat [tɛsˈtaːt] NT **-(e)s, -e** (Univ) certificate (awarded for successful completion of a course)

Tes|ta|tor [tɛsˈtaːtoːɐ] M **-s, Testatoren** [-ˈtoːrən], **Tes|ta|to|rin** [-ˈtoːrɪn] F **-, -nen** (= Erblasser) testator

Test-: Test|be|trieb M trial (operation); (Comput) test mode; **Test|bild** NT (TV) test card; **Test|bo|gen** M test paper

tes|ten [ˈtɛstn] VT to test (auf +acc for); **jdn auf seine Intelligenz ~** to test sb's intelligence

Tes|ter [ˈtɛstɐ] M **-s, -, Tes|te|rin** [-ərɪn] F **-, -nen** tester

Test-: Test|er|geb|nis NT result(s pl) of a/the test; **Test|fah|rer(in)** M(F) test driver; **Test|fall** M test case; **Test|fra|ge** F test question

tes|tie|ren [tɛsˈtiːrən] ptp **testiert** VT [a] (= bescheinigen) to certify; **sich** (dat) **etw ~ lassen** to get oneself a certificate of sth; **jdm etw ~** to certify sth for sb [b] (Jur: = letztwillig verfügen) to will

Tes|ti|kel [tɛsˈtiːkl] M **-s, -** testicle

Tes|tos|te|ron [tɛstosteˈroːn] NT **-s** testosterone

Test-: Test|per|son F subject (of a test); **Test|pi|lot(in)** M(F) test pilot; **Test|pro|gramm** NT (Comput) test program; **Test|rei|he** F , **Test|se|rie** F series of tests; **Test|stopp** M test ban; **Test|stopp|ab|kom|men** NT test ban treaty or agreement; **Test|ver|fah|ren** NT method of testing; **Test|wahl** F (inf) test election; **Kommunalwahlen kann man häufig als ~en ansehen** local elections can often be regarded as a test of electoral feeling

Te|ta|nus [ˈteːtanʊs, ˈtɛtanʊs] M **-,** no pl tetanus

Te|te [ˈteːtə, ˈtɛtə] F **-, -n** (Mil) head of a column

Tête-à-tête [tɛːtaˈtɛːt] NT **-, -s, Tete-à-tete** ▲ NT **-, -s** [a] (hum: = Schäferstündchen) **ein ~** a bit of hanky-panky (hum inf) [b] tête-à-tête (esp Brit), private conversation between two people

Tet|ra-: Tet|ra|eder [tetraˈeːdɐ] NT **-s, -** (Math) tetrahedron; **Tet|ra|gon** [tetraˈgoːn] NT **-s, -e** (Math) tetragon; **Tet|ra|lo|gie** [tetraloˈgiː] F **-, -n** [-ˈgiːən] tetralogy

teu|er [ˈtɔyɐ] ADJ expensive, dear usu pred; (fig) dear; **etw für teures Geld kaufen** to pay good money for sth; **teurer werden** to go up (in price); **Brot wieder teurer!** bread up again; **in Tokio ist das Leben ~** life is expensive in Tokyo, Tokyo is expensive; **~ aber gut** expensive but well worth the money; **das ist mir (lieb und) ~** (liter) that's very dear or precious to me; **mein Teurer** or **Teuerster, meine Teure** or **Teuerste** (old, hum) my dearest; (von Mann zu Mann) my dearest friend → Vergnügen a, Spaß, Pflaster b
ADV anbieten, speisen expensively; **etw ~ kaufen/verkaufen** to buy/sell sth for or at a high price; **etw zu ~ kaufen** to pay too much for sth; **in Tokio lebt man ~** life is expensive in Tokyo; **das wird ihn ~ zu stehen kommen** (fig) that will cost him dear; **einen Sieg ~ erkaufen** to pay dearly for victory; **erkauft** dearly bought; **etw ~ bezahlen** (fig) to pay a high price for sth; **sich** (dat) **etw ~ bezahlen lassen** to charge a high price for sth

Teu|e|rung [ˈtɔyərʊŋ] F **-, -en** rise in prices, rising prices pl

Teu|e|rungs-: Teu|e|rungs|aus|gleich M adjustment for inflation; **Teu|e|rungs|ra|te** F rate of price increases; **Teu|e|rungs|wel|le** F wave or round of price increases; **Teu|e|rungs|zu|la|ge** F cost of living bonus or supplement; **Teu|e|rungs|zu|schlag** M surcharge

Teu|fel [ˈtɔyfl] M **-s, -** [a] (lit, fig) devil; **den ~ durch Beelzebub austreiben** to replace one evil with another; **den ~ im Leib haben** to be possessed by the devil; **der ~ der Eifersucht** etc a jealous etc devil; **ein ~ von einem Mann/einer Frau** (old) a devil of a man/woman
[b] (inf) **~ (noch mal** or **aber auch)!** damn it (all)! (inf), confound it! (inf); **~ auch** (bewundernd) well I'll be damned (inf) or blowed (Brit inf), I'll be a sun-of-a-gun (US inf); **scher dich** or **geh zum ~, hol dich der ~!** go to blazes (inf) or hell!; **der ~ soll ihn/es holen!, hol ihn/es der ~** damn (or) or blast (inf) him/it!, to hell with him/it (inf); **jdn zum ~ wünschen** to wish sb in hell; **jdn zum ~ jagen** or **schicken** to send sb packing (inf); **zum ~!** damn! (inf), blast! (inf); **wer zum ~?** who the devil (inf) or the hell?; **zum ~ mit dem Ding!** damn or blast the thing! (inf), to hell with the thing! (inf); **zum ~ sein** (= kaputt sein) to have had it (inf); (= verloren sein) to have gone west (Brit inf), to have gone to the devil (inf); **den ~ an die Wand malen** (= schwarz malen) to think or imagine the worst; (= Unheil heraufbeschwören) to tempt fate or providence; **wenn man vom ~ spricht(, dann ist er nicht weit)** (prov) talk (Brit) or speak of the devil (and he's sure to appear) (inf); **das müsste schon mit dem ~ zugehen** that really would be a stroke of bad luck; **ihn muss der ~ geritten haben** he must have had a devil in him; **welcher ~ reitet ihn denn?** what's got into him?; **dann kommst** or **gerätst du in ~s Küche** then you'll be in a hell of a mess (inf); **wie der ~** like hell (inf), like the devil (inf); **er ist hinter dem Geld her wie der ~** hinter der armen Seele he's money mad (Brit inf), he loves money like the devil loves souls (US); **jdn/etw fürchten wie der ~ das Weihwasser** to be absolutely terrified of sb/sth; **jdn/etw meiden wie der ~ das Weihwasser** to avoid sb/sth like the plague (inf); **auf ~ komm raus** like crazy (inf); **ich mache das auf ~ komm raus** I'll do that come hell or high water; **da ist der ~ los** all hell's been let loose (inf); **bist du des ~s?** (old) have you taken leave of your senses?; **sich den ~ um etw kümmern** or **scheren** not to give a damn (inf) or a fig (Brit inf) about sth; **den ~ werde ich (tun)!** I'll be damned if I will! (inf), like hell I will! (inf); **der ~ steckt im Detail** the devil is or lies in the detail

Teu|fe|lei [tɔyfaˈlai] F **-, -en** (inf) devilish trick; (= Streich) piece of devilry

Teu|fels-: Teu|fels|aus|trei|bung F casting out no pl of devils, exorcism; **Teu|fels|be|schwö|rung** F exorcism; (Anrufen) invocation of the devil; **Teu|fels|bra|ten** M (old inf) devil; **Teu|fels|brut** F (old) devil's or Satan's brood; **Teu|fels|kerl** M (inf) daredevil; **Teu|fels|kir|sche** F (Bot) deadly nightshade, belladonna; **Teu|fels|kreis** M vicious circle; **Teu|fels|kult** M devil worship; **Teu|fels|mes|se** F black mass; **Teu|fels|weib** NT (dated) devil of a woman

teuf|lisch [ˈtɔyflɪʃ] ADJ fiendish, devilish, diabolical ADV fiendishly, devilishly, diabolically

Teu|to|ne [tɔyˈtoːnə] M **-n, -n, Teu|to|nin** [-ˈtoːnɪn] F **-, -nen** Teuton

teu|to|nisch [tɔyˈtoːnɪʃ] ADJ Teutonic

Text [tɛkst] M **-(e)s, -e** text; (einer Urkunde auch, eines Gesetzes) wording; (von Lied) words pl; (von Schlager) lyrics pl; (von Film, Hörspiel, Rede etc) script; (Mus: = Operntext) libretto; (unter Bild) caption; (auf Plakat) words pl; **weiter im ~** (inf) (let's) get on with it; **ein Telegramm mit folgendem ~ ...** a telegram which said or read ...

Text-: Text|auf|ga|be F problem; **Text|bau|stein** M (Comput) template; **Text|buch** NT script; (für Lieder) songbook; **Text|dich|ter(in)** M(F) (von Liedern) songwriter; (bei Oper) librettist; **Text|ein|ga|be** F (Comput) text input

tex|ten [ˈtɛkstn] VT to write songs/copy VI → Texter to write songs/copy

Tex|ter [ˈtɛkstɐ] M **-s, -, Tex|te|rin** [-ərɪn] F **-, -nen** (für Schlager) songwriter; (für Werbesprüche) copywriter

Text|er|fas|ser [-ɛɐfasɐ] M **-s, -, Text|er|fas|se|rin** [-ərɪn] F **-, -nen** keyboarder

Tex|til- [tɛks'tiːl] in cpds textile; **Tex|til|ar|bei|ter(in)** M(F) textile worker; **Tex|til|bran|che** F textile trade; **Tex|til|fab|rik** F textile factory; (für Textilien aus Naturfasern auch) textile mill

Tex|ti|li|en [tɛks'tiːliən] PL linen, clothing, fabrics etc (Ind) textiles pl

Tex|til-: **Tex|til|in|dust|rie** F textile industry; **Tex|til|wa|ren** PL textiles pl

Text-: **Text|kri|tik** F textual criticism; **Text|lin|gu|is|tik** F (Ling) text linguistics sing; **Text|mo|dus** M (Comput) text mode; **Text|se|man|tik** F (Ling) textual semantics sing; **Text|spei|cher** M (Comput) memory; **Text|stel|le** F passage; **Text|sys|tem** NT (Comput) word processor, word processing system

Tex|tur [tɛks'tuːɐ] F -, -en texture

Text|ver|ar|bei|tung F word processing

Text|ver|ar|bei|tungs-: **Text|ver|ar|bei|tungs|an|la|ge** F word processor, word processing system; **Text|ver|ar|bei|tungs|pro|gramm** NT word processor, word processing program; **Text|ver|ar|bei|tungs|sys|tem** NT word processor, word processing system

Te|zett ['teːtset, te'tset] NT (inf) jdn/etw bis ins or zum ~ kennen to know sb/sth inside out (inf)

TH [teː'haː] F -, -s abbr von **Technische Hochschule**

Thai¹ [tai] M -(s), -(s) Thai

Thai² [tai] F -, - Thai

Thai³ [tai] NT -, no pl (Ling) Thai

Thai|land ['tailant] NT -s Thailand

Thai|län|der ['tailɛndɐ] M -s, -, **Thai|län|de|rin** [-ərɪn] F -, -nen Thai

thai|län|disch ['tailɛndɪʃ] ADJ Thai

Thal|las|so|the|ra|pie [talaso-] F (Med) thalassotherapy

Thal|li|um ['taliʊm] NT -s, no pl (abbr **Tl**) thallium

The|a|ter [te'aːtɐ] NT -s, - **a** theatre (Brit), theater (US); (= Schauspielbühne) theatre (Brit) or theater (US) company; (= Zuschauer) audience; **beim** or **am ~ arbeiten** to work in the theatre (Brit) or theater (US); **er ist** or **arbeitet beim Ulmer ~** he's with the Ulm theatre (Brit) or theater (US) company; **heute Abend wird im ~ „Othello" gezeigt** or **gegeben** "Othello" is on or is playing at the theatre (Brit) or theater (US) tonight; **das ~ fängt um 8 Uhr an** the performance begins at 8 o'clock; **zum ~ gehen** to go on the stage; **ins ~ gehen** to go to the theatre (Brit) or theater (US); **das französische ~** French theatre (Brit) or theater (US); **~ spielen** (lit) to act; (= Stück aufführen) to put on a play; (fig) to put on an act, to play-act; **jdm ein ~ vormachen** or **vorspielen** (fig) to put on an act for sb's benefit; **das ist doch alles nur ~** (fig) it's all just play-acting

b (fig) to-do (inf), fuss; **das war vielleicht ein ~, bis ich ...** what a palaver or performance or carry-on I had to ... (inf); **das ist (vielleicht) immer ein ~, wenn er kommt** there's always a big fuss when he comes; **(ein) ~ machen** (= Umstände) to make a (big) fuss (mit jdm of sb); (= Szene auch) to make a song and dance (inf) or a scene

The|a|ter- in cpds theatre (Brit), theater (US); **The|a|ter|abon|ne|ment** NT theatre subscription; **The|a|ter|auf|füh|rung** F stage production; (= Vorstellung, Darbietung) performance; **The|a|ter|be|such** M visit to the theatre; **The|a|ter|be|su|cher(in)** M(F) theatregoer (Brit), theatergoer (US); **The|a|ter|dich|ter(in)** M(F) dramatist, playwright; **The|a|ter|ge|bäu|de** NT theatre; **The|a|ter|kar|te** F theatre ticket; **The|a|ter|kas|se** F theatre box office; **The|a|ter|kri|ti|ker(in)** M(F) theatre or drama critic; **The|a|ter|pro|be** F rehearsal; **The|a|ter|stück** NT (stage) play; **The|a|ter|vor|stel|lung** F (stage) performance; **The|a|ter|wis|sen|schaft** F theory of

drama; (= Studienfach) theatre (Brit) or theater (US) studies pl

the|at|ra|lisch [tea'traːlɪʃ] **ADJ** theatrical, histrionic **ADV** theatrically

The|is|mus [te'ɪsmʊs] M -, no pl theism

The|ke ['teːkə] F -, -n (= Schanktisch) bar; (= Ladentisch) counter

T-Hel|fer-Zel|le ['teː-] F T helper cell

The|ma ['teːma] NT -s, **Themen** or -ta [-mən, -ta] (= Gegenstand) subject, topic; (= Leitgedanke, auch Mus) theme; **interessant vom ~ her** interesting as far as the subject matter is concerned; **beim ~ bleiben** to stick to the subject or point; **vom ~ abschweifen** to stray from or wander off the subject or point; **das ~ wechseln** to change the subject; **ein/kein ~ sein** to be/not to be an issue; **Geld ist für sie kein ~** money is no object for her; **aus etw ein ~ machen** to make an issue of sth; **zum ~ werden** to become an issue; **wir wollen das ~ begraben** (inf) let's not talk about it any more, let's forget the whole subject; **das ~ ist (für mich) erledigt** (inf) as far as I'm concerned the matter's closed

The|ma|ta pl von **Thema**

The|ma|tik [te'maːtɪk] F -, -en topic

the|ma|tisch [te'maːtɪʃ] **ADJ** thematic; (= vom Thema her) as regards subject matter; **~es Verzeichnis** subject index **ADV** ~ **interessant sein** to be an interesting subject; **der Aufsatz ist ~ unbedeutend** the subject of this essay is trivial; **~ geordnet** arranged according to subject

the|ma|ti|sie|ren [tematiˈziːrən] ptp **thematisiert** VT (geh) to pick out as a central theme

The|ma|wech|sel M change of subject; **~: ...** moving on or switching to another subject now ...

The|men pl von **Thema**

The|men-: **The|men|be|reich** M , **The|men|kreis** M topic; **in den ~ „Tiere" gehören** to come under the heading of "animals"; **The|men|park** M theme park; **The|men|stel|lung** F subject; **The|men|wahl** F choice of subject or topic; **The|men|wech|sel** M → Themawechsel

Them|se ['tɛmzə] F - **die ~** the Thames

The|o|lo|ge [teo'loːgə] M -n, -n, **The|o|lo|gin** [-'loːgɪn] F -, -nen theologian

The|o|lo|gie [teolo'giː] F -, no pl theology; **Doktor der ~** Doctor of Divinity (Brit), Doctor of Theology (US)

the|o|lo|gisch [teo'loːgɪʃ] **ADJ** theological **ADV** theologically; **sich ~ gut auskennen** to know quite a bit about theology; **~ interessiert sein** to be interested in theology; **eine ~ interessante Frage** a question which is interesting from a theological point of view; **sich ~ weiterbilden** to learn more about theology

The|o|rem [teo're:m] NT -s, -e theorem

The|o|re|ti|ker [teo're:tikɐ] M -s, -, **The|o|re|ti|ke|rin** [-ərɪn] F -, -nen theorist, theoretician

the|o|re|tisch [teo're:tɪʃ] **ADJ** theoretical **ADV** theoretically; **~ gesehen** in theory, theoretically

the|o|re|ti|sie|ren [teoreti'ziːrən] ptp **theoretisiert** VI to theorize

The|o|rie [teo'riː] F -, -n [-'riːən] theory → **grau**

The|o|so|phie [teozo'fiː] F -, -n [-'fiːən] theosophy

The|ra|peut [tera'pɔyt] M -en, -en, **The|ra|peu|tin** [-'pɔytɪn] F -, -nen therapist

The|ra|peu|tik [tera'pɔytɪk] F -, no pl therapeutics sing

the|ra|peu|tisch [tera'pɔytɪʃ] **ADJ** therapeutic(al) **ADV** therapeutically; **~ umstrittene Methoden** controversial therapeutic methods

The|ra|pie [tera'piː] F -, -n [-'piːən] therapy (auch fig), treatment; (= Behandlungsmethode) (method of) treatment (gegen for)

The|ra|pie|er|folg M success of or with a therapy, therapeutic success

The|ra|pie|platz M place in therapy

the|ra|pie|ren [tera'piːrən] ptp **therapiert** VT to give therapy to, to treat

The|ra|pie|zen|trum NT treatment centre (Brit) or center (US)

Ther|mal-: **Ther|mal|bad** NT thermal bath; (Gebäude) thermal baths pl; (= Badeort) spa, watering place (old); **jdm Thermalbäder verschreiben** to prescribe hydrotherapy for sb; **Ther|mal|quel|le** F thermal spring

Ther|me ['tɛrmə] F -, -n (= Quelle) thermal or hot spring; **die ~n** the thermals; (Hist) the (thermal) baths

Ther|mik ['tɛrmɪk] F -, no pl (Met) thermal activity, thermals pl

ther|misch ['tɛrmɪʃ] ADJ attr (Phys) thermal

Ther|mo- ['tɛrmo] in cpds thermo-; **Ther|mo|che|mie** F thermochemistry; **Ther|mo|dru|cker** M thermal printer; **Ther|mo|dy|na|mik** F thermodynamics sing; **ther|mo|dy|na|misch** ADJ thermodynamic; **ther|mo|elekt|risch** ADJ thermoelectric(al); **Ther|mo|ho|se** F thermal trousers pl (esp Brit) or pants pl (esp US); **Ther|mo|kan|ne** F Thermos® jug or container

Ther|mo|me|ter NT -s, - thermometer

Ther|mo|me|ter|stand M temperature; **bei ~ 60°** when the temperature reaches 60°, when the thermometer reads 60°

ther|mo|nuk|le|ar ADJ thermonuclear

Ther|mo|pa|pier NT thermal paper

Ther|mos|fla|sche® F Thermos® (flask or bottle (US)), vacuum flask or bottle (US)

Ther|mos|tat [tɛrmo'staːt] M -(e)s, -e thermostat

the|sau|rie|ren [tezau'riːrən] VT (Econ, St Ex) to accumulate; **~der Fonds** accumulated fund

The|sau|rie|rung F -, -en (Econ, St Ex) accumulation

The|sau|rus [te'zaurʊs] M -, **Thesauri** or **Thesauren** [-ri, -rən] thesaurus

The|se ['teːzə] ○ 53.2 F -, -n hypothesis, thesis; (inf: = Theorie) theory; **Luthers 95 ~n** Luther's 95 propositions

The|sen|pa|pier NT (Sch, Univ) academic or research paper; (= Zusammenfassung) synopsis (of a lecture)

Thing [tɪŋ] NT -(e)s, -e (Hist) thing

Thing|platz M (Hist) thingstead

Tho|ra ['toːra] F -, no pl (Rel) Torah

Tho|ra-: **Tho|ra|rol|le** F (Rel) Torah scroll; **Tho|ra|schrein** M (Rel) ark of the Law

Tho|ri|um ['toːriʊm] NT -s, no pl (abbr **Th**) thorium

Thril|ler ['θrɪlɐ] M -s, - thriller

Throm|bo|se [trɔm'boːzə] F -, -n thrombosis

Throm|bo|se|strumpf M compression stocking

throm|bo|tisch [trɔm'boːtɪʃ] ADJ thrombotic

Thron [troːn] M -(e)s, -e throne; (hum inf: = Nachttopf) pot; **von seinem ~ herabsteigen** (fig) to come down off one's high horse

Thron-: **Thron|an|wär|ter(in)** M(F) claimant to the throne; (= Thronfolger) heir apparent; **Thron|be|stei|gung** F accession (to the throne)

thro|nen ['troːnən] VI (lit: = auf dem Thron sitzen) to sit enthroned; (fig: = in exponierter Stellung sitzen) to sit in state; (liter: = überragen) to stand in solitary splendour (Brit) or splendor (US)

Thron-: **Thron|er|be** M , **Thron|er|bin** F heir to the throne; **Thron|fol|ge** F line of succession; **die ~ antreten** to succeed to the throne; **Thron|fol|ger** [-fɔlgɐ] M -s, -, **Thron|fol|ge|rin** [-ərɪn] F -, -nen heir to the throne, heir apparent; **Thron|him|mel** M canopy; **Thron|räu|ber(in)** M(F) usurper; **Thron|re|de** F King's/Queen's speech at the opening of parliament; **Thron|saal** M throne room

Thu|ja ['tu:ja] F **-, Thujen** [-jən] arbor vitae, thu-
ja

Thu|li|um ['tu:liʊm] NT **-s,** *no pl* (*abbr* **Tm**) thu-
lium

Thun|fisch ['tu:n-] M tuna (fish)

Thur|gau ['tu:ɐgau] M **-s der ~** the Thurgau

Thü|rin|gen ['ty:rɪŋən] NT **-s** Thuringia

Thü|rin|ger¹ ['ty:rɪŋɐ] ADJ Thuringian; **der ~
Wald** the Thuringian Forest

Thü|rin|ger² ['ty:rɪŋɐ] M **-s, -, Thü|rin|ge|rin**
[-ərɪn] F **-, -nen** Thuringian

thü|rin|gisch ['ty:rɪŋɪʃ] ADJ Thuringian

Thus|nel|da [tʊs'nɛlda] F **-, -s** (*inf*) bird (*esp
Brit inf*), chick (*inf*)

THW [te:ha:'ve:] *abbr von* **Technisches Hilfswerk**

THW

THW – short for **Technisches Hilfswerk** – was
founded in 1950, under the organizational
control of the Ministry of the Interior. It provides technical assistance in response to cases
of civil defence, major accidents and natural
disasters both in Germany and abroad. It also
supports humanitarian relief work outside the
country. It has about 80,000 voluntary helpers.

Thy|mi|an ['ty:mian] M **-s, -e** thyme

Thy|mus|drü|se ['ty:mʊs-] F thymus (gland)

Ti|a|ra ['tia:ra] F **-, Tiaren** [-ən] tiara, triple
crown

Ti|bet ['ti:bɛt, ti'be:t] NT **-s** Tibet

Ti|be|ta|ner [tibe'ta:nɐ] M **-s, -, Ti|be|ta|ne|rin**
[-ərɪn] F **-, -nen** Tibetan

ti|be|ta|nisch [tibe'ta:nɪʃ], **ti|be|tisch** [ti'be:tɪʃ]
ADJ Tibetan

tick [tɪk] INTERJ tick; **~ tack!** ticktock!

Tick [tɪk] M **-(e)s, -e** **a** (*Med*) tic; **nervöser ~**
nervous tic **b** (*inf: = Schrulle*) quirk (*inf*); **Uhren
sind sein ~** he has a thing about clocks (*inf*);
einen ~ haben (*inf*) to be crazy; **er hat einen ~
mit seiner Ordnung** he has this thing about tidiness (*inf*); **einen ~ besser/schneller** *etc* **sein**
(*inf*) to be a shade better/faster *etc*

-tick M *suf in cpds* (*inf*) **ein Autotick** a thing a-
bout cars (*inf*)

ti|cken ['tɪkn] VI to tick (away); **anders ~** (*fig
inf*) to have a different mentality; **du tickst ja
nicht richtig** (*inf*) you're off your rocker! (*inf*)
VT (*Press sl: = zusammenschlagen*) to bash (*inf*)

Ti|cker ['tɪkɐ] M **-s, -** (*inf*) telex (machine), ticker
(*US*)

ti|ckern ['tɪkɐn] (*inf*) VI **aus dem Fernschreiber ~**
to come out of the telex VI to telex

Ti|cket ['tɪkət] NT **-s, -s** (plane) ticket

Ti|de ['ti:də] F **-, -n** (*N Ger*) tide

Ti|den|hub M (*N Ger*) tidal range

Tie-Break M **-s, -s, Tie|break** ['taibre:k] M **-s,
-s** (*Tennis*) tie-break (*esp Brit*), tie-breaker

tief [ti:f] ADJ **a** (*= weit reichend*) Tal, Wasser, Wurzeln, Schnee, Wunde, Seufzer deep; Verbeugung,
Ausschnitt low; **~er Teller** soup plate; **ein ~er
Eingriff in jds Rechte** (*acc*) a gross infringement
of sb's rights; **die ~eren Ursachen** the underlying causes; **aus ~stem Herzen** from the bottom
of one's heart; **aus ~ster Seele** from the depths
of one's soul

b (*= sehr stark, groß*) Ohnmacht, Schlaf, Erröten,
Gefühl deep; Schmerz intense; Not dire; Verlassenheit, Einsamkeit, Elend utter; **bis in den ~sten
Winter, bis ~ in den Winter** (till) well into winter; **bis in die ~ste Nacht, bis ~ in die Nacht hinein** (till) late into the night

c *auch adv* (*= mitten in etwas liegend*) **er wohnt ~
in den Bergen** he lives deep in the mountains;
~ im Wald, im ~en Wald deep in the forest, in
the depths of the forest; **~ im Winter, im ~en
Winter** in the depths of winter; **~ in der Nacht,
in der ~en Nacht** at dead of night; **~ in Afrika,
im ~sten Afrika** in darkest Africa; **~ im Innern,**

im ~sten Innern in one's heart of hearts

d (*= tiefgründig*) deep, profound; **der ~ere Sinn**
the deeper meaning

e (*= niedrig*) Lage, Stand, Temperatur low

f (*= dunkel*) Farbton, Stimme deep; (*Mus*) low;
Ton low

ADV **a** (*= weit nach unten, innen, hinten*) a long
way; bohren, graben, eindringen, tauchen deep;
sich bücken low; untersuchen in depth; **~ in etw**
(*acc*) **einsinken** to sink deep into sth, to sink
down a long way into sth; **3 m ~ fallen** to fall 3
metres (*Brit*) or meters (*US*); **~ gehend** (*lit, fig*)
deep; Schmerz extreme, acute; Kränkung ex-
treme; **~ sinken** (*fig*) to sink low; **~ fallen** (*fig*)
to go downhill; **~ liegend** (*Augen*) deep-set;
(*nach Krankheit*) sunken; (*fig*) Gefühl, Problem
deep-seated, deep-rooted; **bis ~ in etw** (*acc*) **hinein** (*örtlich*) a long way down/deep into sth;
(*ganz*) **~ unter uns** a long way below us, far below us; **seine Augen liegen ~ in den Höhlen** his
eyes are like hollows in his face; **~ verschneit**
deep with snow; **~ in Gedanken (versunken)**
deep in thought; **~ in Schulden stecken** to be
deep in debt; **jdm ~ in die Augen sehen** to look
deep into sb's eyes; **~ in die Tasche** *or* **den Beutel greifen müssen** (*inf*) to have to reach *or* dig
deep in one's pocket; **das geht bei ihm nicht
sehr ~** (*inf*) it doesn't go very deep with him →
Schuld c, blicken

b (*= sehr stark*) verletzen, atmen, erröten, schockieren, erschüttern, betrübt, bewegt, erschüttert, empfunden deeply; schlafen soundly, deeply; fühlen,
empfinden acutely, deeply; bedauern deeply, profoundly; erschüttern terribly; **~ greifend** (*Reform,
Veränderung*) far-reaching; sich verändern significantly; reformieren thoroughly; **die Gesellschaft
hat sich ~ greifend gewandelt** society has done
a basic turnaround; **~ erschüttert** deeply disturbed

c (*= tiefgründig*) nachdenken deeply; **etw ~er begründen** to find a deeper reason for sth; **~ blickend** (*fig*) perceptive, astute; **~ schürfend** profound

d (*= niedrig*) low; **ein Stockwerk ~er** one floor
down or lower, on the floor below; **Hanau liegt
~er als Schlüchtern** Hanau is lower-lying than
Schlüchtern; **das Haus liegt ~er als die Straße**
the house lies below (the level of) the road; **~
liegend** (*Gegend, Häuser*) low-lying; **im Winter
steht die Sonne ~er** the sun is lower (in the
sky) in winter

e (*= mit tiefer Stimme*) sprechen in a deep voice;
so ~ kann ich nicht singen I can't sing that
low; **~er singen** to sing lower; **etw zu ~ singen**
to sing sth flat; **~er spielen** to play in a lower
key, to play lower; **~er stimmen** to tune down

Tief [ti:f] NT **-(e)s, -e** **a** (*Met*) depression; (*im
Kern, fig*) low; **ein moralisches ~** (*fig*) a low **b**
(*Naut: = Rinne*) deep (*spec*), channel

Tief-: Tief|bau M , *no pl* civil engineering (*ex-
cluding the construction of buildings*) →
Hoch- und Tiefbau; **tief|be|trübt** △ ADJ *attr* →
tief ADV b; **tief|be|wegt** △ ADJ *attr* → tief
ADV b; **tief|blau** ADJ *attr* deep blue; **tief|bli-
ckend** △ ADJ *attr* → tief ADV c

Tief|druck M **a** *no pl* (*Met*) low pressure **b** *pl*
-drucke (*Typ*) gravure

Tief|druck-: Tief|druck|ge|biet NT (*Met*) ar-
ea of low pressure, depression; **Tief|druck|-
keil** M (*Met*) trough of low pressure; **Tief|-
druck|rin|ne** F (*Met*) depression

Tie|fe ['ti:fə] F **-, -n** **a** (*= Ausdehnung nach unten*)
depth; (*von Verbeugung, Ausschnitt*) lowness; **unten in der ~** far below; **in die ~ blicken** to look
down into the depths or a long way; **in der ~
versinken** to sink into the depths; **das U-Boot
ging auf ~** the submarine dived; **in 450 Metern
~** at a depth of 450 metres (*Brit*) or meters
(*US*); **aus der ~ meines Herzens** from the
depths of my heart

b (*= Intensität*) deepness; (*von Schmerz*) intensity; (*von Not*) direness; (*von Elend*) depths *pl*

c (*von Wald*) depths *pl*

d (*= Tiefgründigkeit*) deepness, profundity

e (*= niedriger Stand*) lowness

f (*von Farbton, Stimme*) deepness; (*von Ton*) lowness

g (*Art, Phot*) depth

Tief-: Tief|ebe|ne F lowland plain; **die Ober-
rheinische ~** the Upper Rhine Valley; **tief|-
emp|fun|den** △ ADJ *attr* → tief ADV b

Tie|fen-: Tie|fen|be|strah|lung F deep ray
therapy; **Tie|fen|ge|stein** NT plutonic rock,
pluton; **Tie|fen|psy|cho|lo|ge** M , **Tie|fen|-
psy|cho|lo|gin** F depth psychologist; **Tie|-
fen|psy|cho|lo|gie** F depth psychology; **Tie|-
fen|rausch** M (*Med*) rapture(s) of the
deep; **Tie|fen|schär|fe** F (*Phot*) depth of field;
Tie|fen|wir|kung F deep action; (*Art, Phot*) ef-
fect of depth

Tief-: tief|er|schüt|tert △ [-ɛɐʃʏtɐt] ADJ *attr* →
tief ADV b; **Tief|flie|ger** M low-flying aircraft,
hedgehopper (*inf*); **geistiger ~** (*pej inf*) num-
skull (*inf*), dummy (*inf*); **Tief|flug** M low-level
or low-altitude flight; **er überquerte den Kanal
im ~** he crossed low over the Channel; **Tief|-
flug|übung** F low-flying exercise; **Tief|gang**
[-gaŋ] M , *no pl* (*Naut*) draught (*Brit*), draft
(*US*); (*fig inf*) depth; **Tief|ga|ra|ge** F under-
ground car park (*Brit*), underground parking
garage (*esp US*); **tief|ge|frie|ren** VT *irreg* to
(deep-)freeze; **tief|ge|fro|ren** ADJ (deep-)fro-
zen ADV **Spinat ~ kaufen** to buy frozen spinach; **~ halten Erdbeeren ein Jahr** frozen straw-
berries can be stored for a year; **tief|ge|hend**
△ ADJ → tief ADV b; **tief|ge|kühlt** ADJ (*= ge-
froren*) frozen; (*= sehr kalt*) chilled ADV **Spinat
~ kaufen** to buy frozen spinach; **~ halten Erdbeeren ein Jahr** frozen strawberries can be stored
for a year; **~ servieren** to serve frozen; **tief|-
greifend** △ ADJ → tief ADV b; **tief|grün|dig**
[-gryndɪç] ADJ profound, deep; (*= durchdacht*)
well-grounded

Tief|kühl-: Tief|kühl|fach NT freezer com-
partment; **Tief|kühl|kost** F frozen food;
Tief|kühl|tru|he F (chest) freezer

Tief-: Tief|la|der [-la:dɐ] M **-s, -, Tief|la|de|-
wa|gen** M low-loader; **Tief|land** NT low-
lands *pl*; **tief|lie|gend** △ ADJ *attr* → tief ADV
a, d; **Tief|punkt** M low; **Tief|schlaf** M deep
sleep; **sich im ~ befinden** to be in a deep sleep,
to be fast asleep; **Tief|schlag** M (*Boxen, fig*)
hit below the belt; **jdm einen ~ verpassen** (*lit,
fig*) to hit sb below the belt; **das war ein ~** (*lit,
fig*) that was below the belt; **Tief|schnee** M
deep powder, deep (powder) snow; **tief|-
schür|fend** △ ADJ → tief ADV c

Tief|see F deep sea

Tief|see- *in cpds* deep-sea; **Tief|see|gra|ben** M
ocean *or* deep-sea trench; **Tief|see|tau|-
cher(in)** M(F) deep-sea diver

Tief-: Tief|sinn M profundity; **tief|sin|nig** ADJ
profound; **Tief|sin|nig|keit** F ['ti:fzɪnɪçkait] F **-,**
no pl profundity; **Tief|stand** M low; **Tief|sta|-
pe|lei** [-ʃta:pə'lai] F **-, -en** understatement; (*auf
eigene Leistung bezogen*) modesty; **tief|sta|peln**
VI *sep* to understate the case; to be modest;
Tief|start M crouch start

Tiefst- ['ti:fst-]: **Tiefst|preis** M lowest price;
„**Tiefstpreise**“ "rock bottom prices"; **Tiefst|-
tem|pe|ra|tur** F lowest temperature; **Tiefst|-
wert** M lowest value

tief|trau|rig ADJ very sad

Tie|gel ['ti:gl] M **-s, -** (*zum Kochen*) (sauce)pan;
(*in der Chemie*) crucible; (*= Tiegeldruckpresse*)
platen (press)

Tier [ti:ɐ] NT **-(e)s, -e** animal; (*= großes Tier auch*)
beast; (*= Haustier auch*) pet; (*inf: = Ungeziefer*)
bug (*inf*); (*inf: = Mensch*) (grausam) brute; (*grob*)
animal; (*gefräßig*) pig (*inf*); **großes** *or* **hohes ~**
(*inf*) big shot (*inf*); **das ~ im Menschen** the beast
in man; **da wird der Mensch zum ~** it brings
out man's bestiality; **sich wie die ~e benehmen**
to behave like animals

Tier- *in cpds* animal; (*Med*) veterinary; (*für Haustie-
re*) pet; **Tier|arzt** M , **Tier|ärz|tin** F vet, veter-

---

inary surgeon (form), veterinarian (US); **Tier|asyl** NT (animal) pound

Tier|chen ['tiːɐçən] NT **-s, -** dim von **Tier** little animal; **ein niedliches ~** a sweet little creature → **Pläsierchen**

Tier-: Tier|fabrik F (pej) animal factory; **Tier|freund(in)** M(F) animal lover; (von Haustier auch) pet lover; **Tier|fut|ter** NT animal food or fodder; (für Haustiere) pet food; **Tier|gar|ten** M zoo; **Tier|hal|ter(in)** M(F) (von Haustieren) pet owner; (von Nutztieren) livestock owner; **Tier|hand|lung** F pet shop; **Tier|heil|kun|de** F veterinary medicine; **Tier|heim** NT animal home

tie|risch ['tiːrɪʃ] ADJ animal attr; (fig) Rohheit, Grausamkeit bestial; (= unzivilisiert) Benehmen, Sitten animal attr; (fig inf: = unerträglich) deadly (inf), terrible; **~er Ernst** (inf) deadly seriousness **ADV** (inf: = ungeheuer) horribly (inf); wehtun, nerven like hell (inf); ernst deadly; gut incredibly; **ich habe mich ~ geärgert** I got really furious; **~ schaffen** to work like a dog/like dogs; **~ schwitzen** to sweat like a pig/like pigs (inf); **~ wenig verdienen** to earn practically nothing

Tier-: Tier|kämp|fe PL animal fights pl; **Tier|kör|per|be|sei|ti|gungs|an|stalt** F carcass disposal plant; **Tier|kreis** M zodiac; **Tier|kreis|zei|chen** NT sign of the zodiac; **im ~ des Skorpions geboren sein** to be born under Scorpio; **Tier|kun|de** F zoology; **tier|lieb** ADJ animal-loving attr, fond of animals pred; **~ sein** to like animals; (stärker) to love animals; **Tier|lie|be** F love of animals; **tier|lie|bend** ADJ fond of animals, animal-loving attr, (= Haustiere liebend) pet-loving attr; **Tier|me|di|zin** F veterinary medicine; **Tier|mehl** NT meat and bone meal; **Tier|park** M zoo; **Tier|pfle|ger(in)** M(F) zoo keeper; **Tier|quäler** [-kvɛːlɐ] M **-s, -**, **Tier|quäle|rin** [-ərɪn] F **-, -nen** person who is cruel to animals; **Tier|quäle|rei** F cruelty to animals; (fig inf) cruelty to dumb animals; **Tier|reich** NT animal kingdom; **Tier|schutz** M protection of animals; **Tier|schüt|zer** [-ʃʏtsɐ] M **-s, -**, **Tier|schüt|ze|rin** [-ərɪn] F **-, -nen** animal conservationist; **Tier|schutz|ver|ein** M society for the prevention of cruelty to animals; **Tier|ver|such** M animal experiment; **Tier|welt** F animal kingdom; **Tier|zucht** F stockbreeding

Ti|ger ['tiːgɐ] M **-s, -** tiger → auch **Tigerin**

Ti|ger-: Ti|ger|au|ge NT tiger's-eye; **Ti|ger|fell** NT tiger skin

Ti|ge|rin ['tiːgərɪn] F **-, -nen** tigress

ti|gern ['tiːgɐn] VT → **getigert** VI aux sein (inf) to mooch (about (Brit))

Ti|ger|staat M tiger economy

Tig|ris ['tiːgrɪs] M **-'** Tigris

Til|de ['tɪldə] F **-, -n** tilde

tilg|bar ADJ Schulden repayable

til|gen ['tɪlgn] VT (geh) **a** Schulden to pay off **b** (= beseitigen) Sünde, Unrecht, Spuren to wipe out; (Erinnerung, Druckfehler) to erase; Strafe to remove; Posten (Typ, Ling) to delete; **ein Volk von der Erde** or **vom Erdboden ~** to wipe a nation off the face of the earth

Til|gung ['tɪlgʊŋ] F **-, -en** **a** (von Schulden) repayment **b** (fig) (von Sünde, Unrecht, Spuren) wiping out; (von Erinnerung, Druckfehler) erasure; (von Strafe) removal; (Typ, Ling) deletion

Til|gungs-: til|gungs|frei ADJ redemption-free; **Til|gungs|ra|te** F redemption instalment (Brit) or installment (US); **Til|gungs|zeit|raum** M repayment period

Til|si|ter ['tɪlzɪtɐ] M **-s, -** Tilsit cheese

Timb|re ['tɛ̃ːbrə, 'tɛ̃ːbɐ] NT **-s, -s** (geh) timbre

ti|men ['taɪmən] VT to time

Ti|mer ['taɪmɐ] M **-s, -** timer

Time|sha|ring ['taɪmʃɛːrɪŋ] NT **-(s), -s** time sharing

Ti|ming ['taɪmɪŋ] NT **-,** no pl timing

Tim|pa|ni ['tɪmpani] PL (Mus) timpani pl

tin|geln ['tɪŋln] VI (inf) to appear in small nightclubs/theatres (Brit) or theaters (US) etc

Tin|gel|tan|gel ['tɪŋltaŋl] NT OR M **-s, -** (dated) (Veranstaltung) hop (inf); (Lokal) second-rate nightclub

Tink|tur [tɪŋkˈtuːɐ] F **-, -en** tincture

Tin|nef ['tɪnəf] M **-s,** no pl (inf) rubbish (Brit inf), trash (inf)

Tin|ni|tus ['tɪnitʊs] M **-,** - (Med) tinnitus

Tin|te ['tɪntə] F **-, -n** ink; **in der ~ sitzen** (inf) to be in the soup (inf); **~ gesoffen haben** (inf) to be off one's rocker (inf), to have a screw loose (inf)

Tin|ten-: Tin|ten|fass ▲ NT inkpot; (eingelassen) inkwell; **Tin|ten|fisch** M cuttlefish; (= Kalmar) squid; (achtarmig) octopus; **Tin|ten|fleck** M (auf Kleidung) ink stain; (auf Papier) ink blot; **Tin|ten|kar|tu|sche** F ink cartridge; **Tin|ten|kil|ler** M (inf) correction pen; **Tin|ten|klecks** M ink blot; **Tin|ten|pat|ro|ne** F ink cartridge; **Tin|ten|pilz** M ink-cap; **Tin|ten|stift** M indelible pencil; **Tin|ten|strahl|dru|cker** M ink-jet (printer)

Tipp ▲ [tɪp] M **-s, -s** (= Empfehlung, Sport, St Ex) tip; (= Andeutung) hint; (an Polizei) tip-off; **ich gebe dir einen ~, wie du ...** I'll give you a tip how to ...; **ich gebe dir einen ~, was du mir schenken kannst** I'll give you a hint as to what you could give me; **unser ~ für diesen Sommer ...** this summer we recommend ...; **unser Garten-Tipp für August** our gardening tip for August

Tip|pel|bru|der M (dated inf) gentleman of the road

tip|peln ['tɪpln] VI aux sein (inf) (= gehen) to foot it (inf); (mit kurzen Schritten) to trip; (auf Zehenspitzen) to tiptoe; (Maus, Kinder) to patter

tip|pen ['tɪpn] VT **a** (inf: = schreiben) to type **b** (= wetten auf) **eine bestimmte Zahl ~** to put a particular number on one's coupon **c** (= klopfen) **jdn auf die Schulter ~** to tap sb on the shoulder **VI a** (= klopfen) **an/auf/gegen etw** (acc) **~** to tap sth; **an** or **auf etw** (acc) **~** (= zeigen) to touch sth; **jdn** or **jdm auf die Schulter ~** to tap sb on the shoulder; **sich** (dat) **an die Stirn ~** to tap one's forehead **b** (inf: auf der Schreibmaschine, am Computer) to type **c** (= wetten) to fill in one's coupon; (esp im Toto) to do the pools; **im Lotto ~** to do (Brit) or play the lottery **d** (inf: = raten) to guess; **auf jdn/etw ~** to put one's money on sb/sth (inf); **ich tippe darauf, dass ...** I bet (that) ...; **auf jds Sieg** (acc) **~** to back sb to win (inf)

Tip|per ['tɪpɐ] M **-s, -**, **Tip|pe|rin** [-ərɪn] F **-, -nen** (im Lotto) lottery player; (im Fußballtoto) person who does the pools

Tipp-Ex® ['tɪpɛks] NT **-,** no pl Tipp-Ex®, white-out (US); **etw mit ~ entfernen** to Tipp-Ex® sth out (Brit), to white sth out (US)

Tipp-: Tipp|feh|ler M (inf) typing mistake or error; **Tipp|fräu|lein** NT (inf) typist; **Tipp|ge|ber(in)** ▲ M(F) person who gives a/the tip-off; **Tipp|ge|mein|schaft** F (im Lotto) lottery syndicate; (im Fußballtoto) pools syndicate

Tipp|se ['tɪpsə] F **-, -n** (pej) typist

tipp|tapp ['tɪp'tap] INTERJ pitter-patter

tipp|topp ['tɪp'tɔp] (inf) **ADJ** immaculate; (= prima) first-class, tip-top (dated inf) **ADV** immaculately; (= prima) really well; **~ sauber** spotless

Tipp|zet|tel M (im Toto) football or pools coupon; (im Lotto) lottery coupon

Ti|ra|de [tiˈraːdə] F **-, -n** tirade, diatribe

Ti|ra|na [tiˈraːna] NT **-s** Tirana

ti|ri|lie|ren [tiriˈliːrən] ptp **tiriliert** VI (geh) to warble, to trill

Ti|rol [tiˈroːl] NT **-s** Tyrol

Ti|ro|ler [tiˈroːlɐ] M **-s, -**, **Ti|ro|le|rin** [-ərɪn] F **-, -nen** Tyrolese, Tyrolean

Ti|ro|ler|hut M Tyrolean hat

Tisch [tɪʃ] M **-(e)s, -e** table; (= Schreibtisch) desk; (= Werktisch) bench; (= Mahlzeit) meal; **bei ~** at (the) table; **vom ~ aufstehen** to leave the table; **sich an den** or **zu ~ setzen** to sit down at the table; **die Gäste zu ~ bitten** to ask the guests to take their places; **bitte zu ~!** lunch/dinner is served!; **vor/nach ~** before/after the meal; **bei ~ sein** to be having one's lunch/dinner; **Herr Kleinhaus ist zu ~** Mr Kleinhaus is out at lunch; **zu ~ gehen** to go to lunch/dinner; **er zahlte bar auf den ~** he paid cash down or cash on the nail (Brit inf) or on the barrelhead (US); **etw auf den ~ bringen** (inf) to serve sth (up); **die Beine** or **Füße unter jds ~ strecken** (inf) to eat at sb's table; **getrennt von ~ und Bett leben** to be separated; **unter den ~ fallen** (inf) to go by the board; **jdn unter den ~ trinken** or **saufen** (inf) to drink sb under the table; **es wird gegessen, was auf den ~ kommt!** you'll eat what you're given; **auf den ~ kommen** (fig: Vorschlag etc) to be put forward; **vom ~ sein** (fig) to be cleared out of the way; **vom ~ müssen** (fig) to have to be cleared out of the way; **auf dem ~ liegen** (fig, Vorschlag etc) to be on the table; **etw auf den ~ legen** (fig, Geld, Vorschlag etc) to put sth on the table; **etw vom ~ wischen** (fig) to dismiss sth; **zwei Parteien an einen ~ bringen** (fig) to get two parties (a)round the conference table; **an einem ~ sitzen** (fig: = verhandeln) to sit (together) (a)round a table; **mit jdm am ~ sitzen** (fig) to sit at the same table as sb; **jdn über den ~ ziehen** (fig inf) to take sb to the cleaners (inf) → **rund** ADJ, **grün**, **rein²** ADJ **b**

Tisch- in cpds table; **Tisch|bein** NT table leg; **Tisch|be|sen** M crumb brush; **Tisch|da|me** F dinner partner; **Tisch|de|cke** F tablecloth; **Tisch|en|de** NT end of a/the table; **am oberen/unteren ~ sitzen** to sit at the head/the foot of the table; **Tisch|feu|er|zeug** NT table lighter; **Tisch|fuß|ball** NT table football; **Tisch|ge|bet** NT grace; **Tisch|ge|sell|schaft** F dinner party; **Tisch|ge|spräch** NT table talk; **Tisch|grill** M table grill; **Tisch|herr** M dinner partner; **Tisch|kan|te** F edge of a/the table; **Tisch|kar|te** F place card; **Tisch|lam|pe** F table lamp; **Tisch|läu|fer** M table runner

Tisch|lein|deck|dich [tɪʃlaɪnˈdɛkdɪç] NT **-(s)** **ein ~ gefunden haben** (fig) to be on to a good thing (inf)

Tisch|ler ['tɪʃlɐ] M **-s, -**, **Tisch|le|rin** [-ərɪn] F **-, -nen** joiner, carpenter, (= Möbeltischler) cabinet-maker

Tisch|le|rei [tɪʃləˈraɪ] F **-, -en** **a** (Werkstatt) joiner's or carpenter's workshop; (= Möbeltischlerei) cabinet-maker's workshop **b** no pl (inf) (= Handwerk) joinery, carpentry; (von Möbeltischler) cabinet-making

Tisch|ler|hand|werk NT joinery, carpentry; (von Möbeltischler) cabinet-making

tisch|lern ['tɪʃlɐn] (inf) VI to do woodwork VT Tisch, Regal etc to make

Tisch|ler|werk|statt F = **Tischlerei a**

Tisch-: Tisch|nach|bar(in) M(F) neighbour (Brit) or neighbor (US) (at table); **Tisch|ord|nung** F seating plan; **Tisch|plat|te** F table-top; **Tisch|rech|ner** M desk calculator; **Tisch|re|de** F after-dinner speech; (= Unterhaltung) table talk; **Tisch|red|ner(in)** M(F) after-dinner speaker; **Tisch|schmuck** M table decoration(s pl); **Tisch|te|le|fon** NT table telephone (in nightclub)

Tisch|ten|nis NT table tennis

Tisch|ten|nis- in cpds table-tennis; **Tisch|ten|nis|plat|te** F table-tennis table; **Tisch|ten|nis|schlä|ger** M table-tennis bat

Tisch-: Tisch|tuch NT pl **-tücher** tablecloth; **Tisch|wä|sche** F table linen; **Tisch|wein** M table wine; **Tisch|zeit** F mealtime; **zur ~** at mealtimes

Ti|tan¹ [ˈtiːtaːn] M **-en, -en** (*Myth*) Titan

Ti|tan² NT **-s**, *no pl* (*abbr* **Ti**) titanium

ti|ta|nen|haft, ti|ta|nisch [tiˈtaːnɪʃ] ADJ titanic

Ti|tel [ˈtiːtl̩, ˈtɪtl̩] M **-s, -** **a** jdn mit **~ an-sprechen** to address sb by his/her title, to give sb his/her title; **unter dem ~** under the title; (*fig:* = *Motto*) under the slogan **b** (= *Titelblatt*) title page **c** (*von Gesetz, Etat*) section

Ti|tel-: Ti|tel|an|wär|ter(in) M(F) (main) contender for the title; **Ti|tel|bild** NT cover (picture); **Ti|tel|blatt** NT title page

Ti|te|lei [tiːtəˈlai, tɪtaˈlai] F **-, -en** (*Typ*) prelims *pl* (*esp Brit*), front matter

Ti|tel-: Ti|tel|fi|gur F → **Titelheld**; **Ti|tel|ge-schich|te** F lead, cover story; **Ti|tel|held(in)** M(F) eponymous hero/heroine, hero/heroine (*mentioned in the title*); **Ti|tel|kampf** M (*Sport*) finals *pl*; (*Boxen*) title fight; **Ti|tel|me-lo|die** F (*von Film*) theme tune *or* music

ti|teln [ˈtiːtl̩n, ˈtɪtl̩n] VT (*Zeitung*) to give as its headline; **"Clinton am Ende", titelte „Bild"** "Bild"'s headline was "Clinton finished"

Ti|tel-: Ti|tel|rol|le F title role; **Ti|tel|schutz** M copyright (*of a title*); **Ti|tel|sei|te** F cover, front page; **Ti|tel|trä|ger(in)** M(F) person with a title; **Ti|tel|ver|tei|di|ger(in)** M(F) title holder; **Ti|tel|zei|le** F title line

Tit|te [ˈtɪtə] F **-, -n** (*sl*) tit (*sl*), boob (*inf*), knock-er (*inf*)

Ti|tu|lar|bi|schof [tituˈlaːɐ̯-] M titular bishop

Ti|tu|la|tur [titulaˈtuːɐ̯] F **-, -en** title, form of ad-dress

ti|tu|lie|ren [tituˈliːrən] *ptp* **tituliert** VT *Buch, Werk etc* to entitle (*mit etw* sth); jdn to call (*mit etw* sth), to address (*mit* as)

ti|zi|an|rot [ˈtiːtsiaːn-, tiˈtsiaːn-] ADJ *Haare* titian (red) **ADV** sich (*dat*) **die Haare ~ färben** to dye one's hair titian red

tja [tja, tjaː] INTERJ well

TL *abbr von* **Teelöffel** tsp

T-Lym|pho|zyt [ˈteː-] M (*Med, Biol*) T-lympho-cyte

Toast [toːst] M **-(e)s, -e** **a** (= *Brot*) toast; **ein ~** a slice *or* piece of toast **b** (= *Trinkspruch*) toast; **einen ~ auf jdn ausbringen** to propose a toast to sb

Toast|brot [ˈtoːst-] NT *sliced white bread for toasting*

toas|ten [ˈtoːstn̩] **VI** to drink a toast (*auf +acc* to) **VT** *Brot* to toast

Toas|ter [ˈtoːstɐ] M **-s, -** toaster

Toast|stän|der [ˈtoːst-] M toast rack

To|bak [ˈtoːbak] M **-s** *das ist starker* **~!** (*inf*) that's a bit much! (*inf*) → **anno**

to|ben [ˈtoːbn̩] **VI** **a** (= *wüten*) (*Sturm, Elemente, Leidenschaften, Kämpfe etc*) to rage; (*Mensch*) to throw a (fit; (*vor Wut, Begeisterung etc*) to go wild (*vor* with) **b** (= *ausgelassen spielen*) to rollick (a-bout) **c** *aux sein* (*inf:* = *laufen*) to charge about

To|be|rei [toːbəˈrai] F **-, -en** (*inf*) rollicking about

Tob|sucht [ˈtoːpzʊxt] F (*bei Tieren*) madness; (*bei Menschen*) maniacal rage

tob|süch|tig ADJ mad; *Mensch auch* raving mad

Tob|suchts|an|fall M (*inf*) fit of rage; **einen ~ bekommen** to blow one's top (*inf*), to go stark raving mad (*inf*)

Toch|ter [ˈtɔxtɐ] F **-, ⁼** [ˈtœçtɐ] daughter; (= *Toch-terfirma*) subsidiary; (*Sw:* = *Bedienstete*) girl; **die ~ des Hauses** (*form*) the daughter *or* young lady of the house; **das Fräulein ~** (*iro, form*) made-moiselle → **höher**

Töch|ter|chen [ˈtœçtɐçən] NT **-s, -** baby daugh-ter

Toch|ter-: Toch|ter|fir|ma F subsidiary (firm); **Toch|ter|ge|schwulst** F secondary growth *or*

---

tumour; **Toch|ter|ge|sell|schaft** F subsidiary (company)

töch|ter|lich [ˈtœçtɐlɪç] ADJ *attr* daughterly; *Pflicht, Gehorsam, Liebe* filial

Toch|ter|un|ter|neh|men NT → **Tochterfirma**

Tod [toːt] ✪ 51.4 M **-(e)s, -e** [-də] death; **ein früher ~** an early *or* premature death; **der ~ als Schnitter** the Grim Reaper; **der schwarze ~** (= *die Pest*) the Black Death, the plague; **~ durch Erschießen/Ersticken/Erhängen** death by firing squad/suffocation/hanging; **eines natürlichen/gewaltsamen ~es sterben** to die of natural causes/a violent death; **er ist des ~es** (*geh*) he is doomed; **er muss des ~es sterben** (*geh*) he will have to die; **sich zu ~e fallen** to fall to one's death; **sich zu ~e trinken** to drink oneself to death; **sich** (*dat*) **den ~ holen** to catch one's death (of cold); **den ~ finden, zu ~e kommen** to die; **in den ~ gehen** to go to one's death; **für jdn in den ~ gehen** to die for sb; **bis in den ~** until death; **jdn in den ~ treiben** to drive sb to his/her death; **jdm in den ~ folgen** to follow sb; **~ und Teufel!** (*old*) by the devil! (*old*); **weder ~ noch Teufel werden mich davon abhalten!** I'll do it, come hell or high water!; **jdn/etw auf den ~ nicht leiden** *or* **ausstehen können** (*inf*) to be unable to abide *or* stand sb/sth; **etw zu ~e hetzen** *or* **reiten** (*fig*) to flog sth to death; **sich zu ~(e) langweilen** to be bored to death; **sich zu ~(e) schämen** to be utterly ashamed; **zu ~e betrübt sein** to be in the depths of despair → **Leben a, bleich, Schippe a**

tod-: tod|brin|gend ADJ (*geh*) *Gift* deadly, le-thal; *Krankheit* fatal; **tod|elend** ADJ (*inf*) as miserable as sin (*inf*), utterly miserable; **tod|ernst** (*inf*) **ADV** deadly serious; **es ist mir ~ (da-mit)** I'm deadly serious (about it) **ADV** jdn **~ ansehen** to give sb a deadly serious look; **und das alles sagte er ~** and the way he said it all was deadly serious

To|des-: To|des|angst F mortal agony; **eine ~ haben** (*inf*) **Todesängste ausstehen** (*inf*) to be scared to death (*inf*); **To|des|an|zei|ge** F (*als Brief*) letter announcing sb's death; (= *Annonce*) obituary (notice); **„Todesanzeigen"** "Deaths"; **To|des|art** F death, way to die; **To|des|fall** M death; (*bei Unglück auch*) fatality; (*in der Fami-lie auch*) bereavement; **To|des|fol|ge** F (*Jur*) **schwere Körperverletzung mit ~** grievous bodily harm resulting in death; **To|des|furcht** F fear of death; **To|des|ge|fahr** F mortal danger; **To|des|jahr** NT year of sb's death; **To|des-kampf** M death throes *pl*; **To|des|kan|di-dat(in)** M(F) condemned man/woman *etc*; **To|des|kom|man|do** NT death squad; **to|des|mu|tig** ADJ absolutely fearless **ADV** (ab-solutely) fearlessly; **To|des|nach|richt** F news *sing* of sb's death; **To|des|not** F mortal an-guish; **in Todesnöten sein** (*fig*) to be in a des-perate situation; **To|des|op|fer** NT death, cas-ualty, fatality; **To|des|qua|len** PL final *or* mor-tal agony; **~ ausstehen** (*fig*) to suffer agony *or* agonies; **To|des|schuss** ▲ M fatal shot; **der ~ auf jdn** the shot which killed sb; **To|des-schüt|ze** M , **To|des|schüt|zin** F person who fires/fired the fatal shot; (= *Attentäter*) as-sassin; **To|des|schwad|ron** F death squad; **To|des|spi|ra|le** F death spiral; **To|des|stoß** M deathblow; **jdm/einer Sache den ~ geben** *or* **versetzen** (*lit, fig*) to deal sb the deathblow/deal the deathblow to sth; **To|des|stra|fe** F death penalty; **To|des|strei|fen** M (*an Grenze*) no-man's-land; **To|des|stun|de** F hour of death; **To|des|tag** M day of sb's death; (= *Jahrestag*) anniversary of sb's death; **To|des|trieb** M death wish; **To|des|ur|sa|che** F cause of death; **To|des|ur|teil** NT death sentence; **To|des|ver|ach|tung** F (*inf*) **mit ~** with utter dis-gust *or* repugnance; **jdn mit ~ strafen** to scorn to notice sb; **To|des|zel|le** F death cell (*Brit*), cell on Death Row (*US*)

Tod-: Tod|feind(in) M(F) deadly *or* mortal en-emy; **tod|ge|weiht** [-ɡəvait] ADJ *Mensch, Pati-ent* doomed; **tod|krank** ADJ (= *sterbenskrank*)

---

dangerously *or* critically ill; (= *unheilbar krank*) terminally ill

töd|lich [ˈtøːtlɪç] ADJ *Unfall, Verletzung, Schuss, Schlag* fatal; *Gefahr* mortal, deadly; *Gift, Waffe* deadly, lethal; *Dosis* lethal; *Sicherheit* deadly; *Beleidigung* mortal **ADV** **a** (*mit Todesfolge*) **~ verunglücken** to be killed in an ac-cident; **~ abstürzen** to die in a fall **b** (*inf:* = *äu-ßerst*) horribly (*inf*); *langweilen* to death

Tod-: tod|mü|de ADJ (*inf*) dead tired (*inf*); **tod|schick** (*inf*) **ADV** dead smart (*inf*) **ADV** *ge-kleidet* ravishingly; *eingerichtet* exquisitely; **er hat sich ~ zurechtgemacht** he was dressed to kill (*inf*); **sie wohnen ~ in einer Villa in Cannes** they live in an exquisite villa in Cannes; **tod|si-cher** (*inf*) **ADV** dead certain (*inf*); *Methode, Tipp* sure-fire (*inf*); **eine ~ Angelegenheit** *or* **Sache** a dead cert (*Brit inf*), a cinch (*esp US inf*), a done deal (*inf*); **das ist doch ~, dass ...** it's a dead cert (*Brit*) *or* a done deal that ... (*inf*) **ADV** for sure *or* certain; **Tod|sün|de** F mortal *or* deadly sin; **tod|un|glück|lich** ADJ (*inf*) desperately unhappy

Toe|loop [ˈtoːluːp] M **-s, -s** (*Eiskunstlauf*) toe loop

To|fu [ˈtoːfu] NT **-**, *no pl* tofu

To|ga [ˈtoːga] F **-, Togen** [-gn̩] toga

To|go [ˈtoːgo] NT **-s** Togo

To|go|er [ˈtoːgoɐ̯] M **-s, -**, **To|go|e|rin** [-ərɪn] F **-, -nen** Togolese

to|go|isch [ˈtoːgoɪʃ] ADJ Togolese

To|go|le|se [togoˈleːzə] M **-n, -n**, **To|go|le|sin** [-ˈleːzɪn] F **-, -nen** Togolese

to|go|le|sisch [togoˈleːzɪʃ] ADJ Togolese

To|hu|wa|bo|hu [toːhuvaˈboːhu] NT **-(s), -s** chaos *no pl*; **das war ein ~** it was utter *or* com-plete chaos

Toi|let|te [toaˈlɛtə] F **-, -n** **a** (= *Abort*) toilet, lavatory (*esp Brit*), bathroom (*esp US*); **öffent-liche ~** public conveniences *pl* (*Brit*), rest stop (*US*), comfort station (*US*); **auf die ~ gehen** to go to the toilet; **auf der ~ sein** to be in the toi-let **b** *no pl* (*geh:* = *Ankleiden, Körperpflege*) toilet; **~ machen** to do one's toilet (*old*) **c** (*geh:* = *Klei-dung*) outfit; **in großer ~** in full dress

Toi|let|ten- *in cpds* toilet; **Toi|let|ten|ar|ti|kel** M *usu pl* toiletry; **Toi|let|ten|beu|tel** M sponge (*Brit*) *or* toilet bag; **Toi|let|ten|frau** F toilet *or* lavatory (*esp Brit*) *or* restroom (*US*) attendant; **Toi|let|ten|gar|ni|tur** F **a** toilet (*Brit*) *or* bathroom set **b** (*für Toilettentisch*) dressing table set (*Brit*), vanity set; **Toi|let-ten|mann** M *pl* **-männer** toilet *or* lavatory (*esp Brit*) *or* restroom (*US*) attendant; **Toi|let|ten-pa|pier** NT toilet paper; **Toi|let|ten|schrank** M bathroom cabinet; **Toi|let|ten|sei|fe** F toi-let soap; **Toi|let|ten|sitz** M toilet *or* lavatory (*esp Brit*) seat; **Toi|let|ten|ta|sche** F toilet bag; **Toi|let|ten|tisch** M dressing table (*Brit*), vanity (*US*); **Toi|let|ten|wa|gen** M mobile toi-let unit; **Toi|let|ten|was|ser** NT *pl* **-wässer** toi-let water

toi, toi, toi [ˈtɔy ˈtɔy ˈtɔy] INTERJ (*inf*) (*vor Prü-fung etc*) good luck; (*unberufen*) touch wood (*Brit*), knock on wood (*US*)

To|kai|er(wein) [ˈtoːkaiɐ-] M **-s, -** Tokay

To|kio [ˈtoːkio] NT **-s** Tokyo

To|kio|ter¹ [toˈkioːtɐ] ADJ *attr* Tokyo

To|kio|ter² [toˈkioːtɐ] M **-s, -**, **To|kio|te|rin** [-ərɪn] F **-, -nen** native of Tokyo; (*Einwohner*) inhabitant of Tokyo

Tö|le [ˈtøːlə] F **-, -n** (*dial pej*) cur

to|le|rant [toleˈrant] ADJ tolerant (*gegen* of)

To|le|ranz [toleˈrants] F **-, -en** tolerance (*gegen* of)

To|le|ranz-: To|le|ranz|be|reich M range of tolerance, tolerance range; **To|le|ranz|do|sis** F tolerance dose; **To|le|ranz|gren|ze** F limit of tolerance; **To|le|ranz|schwel|le** F tolerance level *or* threshold

to|le|rie|ren [toleˈriːrən] *ptp* **toleriert** VT to tolerate

To|le|rie|rung F -, -en toleration

To|le|rie|rungs|ab|kom|men NT (*Pol*) toleration agreement

To|le|rie|rungs|po|li|tik F policy of toleration

toll [tɔl] ADJ **a** (= *wild, ausgelassen*) wild; *Streiche, Gedanken, Treiben* wild, mad; **die (drei) ~en Tage** (the last three days of) Fasching **b** (*inf:* = *verrückt*) mad, crazy; **das war ein ~es Ding** that was mad *or* madness **c** (*inf:* = *schlimm*) terrible **d** (*inf:* = *großartig*) fantastic (*inf*), great (*inf*) *no adv* **e** (*old:* = *irr, tollwütig*) mad ADV **a** (*inf:* = *großartig*) fantastically; **schmecken** fantastic **b** (= *wild, ausgelassen*) **es ging ~ her** *or* **zu** things were pretty wild (*inf*) **c** (*inf:* = *verrückt*) **(wie) ~ regnen** to rain like mad (*inf*) *or* crazy (*inf*); **(wie) ~ fahren** *etc* to drive *etc* like a madman *or* maniac **d** (*inf:* = *schlimm*) **es kommt noch ~er!** there's more *or* worse to come; **es zu ~ treiben** to go too far

toll|dreist ADJ bold, (as) bold as brass

Tol|le [ˈtɔlə] F -, -n quiff (*Brit*), pompadour (*US*)

tol|len [ˈtɔlən] VI **a** (= *herumtollen*) to romp *or* rollick about **b** *aux sein* (= *laufen*) to rush about

Tol|le|rei [tɔləˈrai] F -, -en (*inf, von Kindern*) romping around; (*von Jugendlichen*) charging about *or* around; (= *Späße*) high jinks *pl* (*inf*); **aus lauter Jux und ~** from sheer high spirits *or* sheer exuberance

Toll-: Toll|haus NT (*old*) bedlam (*old*), madhouse; (*fig*) madhouse, bear garden (*Brit*); **hier geht es zu wie im ~** it's like a bear garden (*Brit*) *or* madhouse here; **Toll|heit** F -, -en **a** *no pl* (*old*) madness **b** (*Tat*) mad act; (*Idee*) mad idea; **Toll|kir|sche** F deadly nightshade, belladonna; **toll|kühn** ADJ *Person, Plan, Fahrt* daredevil *attr*, daring ADV daringly, with daring; *fahren* like a real daredevil; **Toll|kühn|heit** F daring *or* – daringly; **Toll|patsch** ▲ [ˈtɔlpatʃ] M -s, -e (*inf*) clumsy *or* awkward creature; **toll|pat|schig** ▲ [ˈtɔlpatʃɪç] ADJ awkward, ungainly, clumsy ADV clumsily; **Toll|wut** F rabies *sing*; **Toll|wut|ge|fahr** F danger of rabies; **toll|wü|tig** ADJ rabid

Toll|patsch △ [ˈtɔlpatʃ] M -es, -e → **Tollpatsch**

toll|pat|schig △ [ˈtɔlpatʃɪç] ADJ, ADV → **tollpatschig**

Töl|pel [ˈtœlpl] M -s, - (*inf*) fool

töl|pel|haft ADJ foolish, silly ADV foolishly

To|lu|ol [toˈluoːl] NT -s, *no pl* toluol, toluene

To|ma|hawk [ˈtɔmahaːk, -hoːk] M -s, -s tomahawk

To|ma|te [toˈmaːtə] F -, -n tomato; **du treulose ~!** (*inf*) you're a fine friend!

To|ma|ten-: *in cpds* tomato; **To|ma|ten|mark** NT, **To|ma|ten|pü|ree** NT tomato puree

Tom|bo|la [ˈtɔmbola] F -, -s *or* **Tombolen** [-lən] tombola (*Brit*), raffle (*US*)

Tom|my [ˈtɔmi] M -s, -s (*inf*) tommy (*Brit inf*), British soldier

To|mo|graf ▲ [tomoˈgraːf] M -en, -en (*Med*) tomograph

To|mo|gra|fie ▲ [tomograˈfiː] F -, -n [-ˈfiːən] tomography

To|mo|gramm [tomoˈgram] NT *pl* -gramme (*Med*) tomogram

Ton¹ [toːn] M -(e)s, -e (= *Erdart*) clay

Ton² M -(e)s, -e [ˈtøːnə] **a** (= *Laut*) sound (*auch Rad, Film*); (*von Zeitzeichen, im Telefon*) pip; (= *Klangfarbe*) tone; (*Mus*) tone; (= *Note*) note; **halber** – semitone; **ganzer** – tone; **den ~ angeben** (*lit*) to give the note; (*fig*) (*Mensch*) to set the tone; (*Thema, Farbe etc*) to be predominant; **kei-**

nen ~ herausbringen *or* **hervorbringen** not to be able to say a word; **keinen ~ sagen** *or* **von sich geben** not to make a sound; **er hat keinen ~ von sich hören lassen** (*fig*) we haven't heard a word *or* a peep (*inf*) from him; **keinen ~ (über etw** *acc*) **verlauten lassen** (*fig*) not to say a word (about sth); **aus dem Regierungslager kamen kritische Töne** criticism came from the government camp; **hast du** *or* **hat der Mensch Töne!** (*inf*) did you ever! (*inf*); **dicke** *or* **große Töne spucken** *or* **reden** (*inf*) to talk big; **jdn in (den) höchsten Tönen loben** (*inf*) to praise sb to the skies; **b** (= *Betonung*) stress; (= *Tonfall*) intonation; (*im Chinesischen etc*) tone; **c** (= *Redeweise, Umgangston*) tone; (= *Atmosphäre*) atmosphere; **den richtigen ~ finden** to strike the right note; **ich verbitte mir diesen ~** I will not be spoken to like that; **er hat einen unverschämten ~ am Leib(e)** *or* **am Hals** (*inf*) he's very cheeky (*Brit*) *or* fresh (*US*); **einen anderen ~ anschlagen** to change one's tune; **der ~ macht die Musik** (*prov*) it's not what you say but the way that *or* how you say it; **der gute ~** good form **d** (= *Farbton*) tone; (= *Nuance*) shade

Ton|ab|neh|mer M cartridge, pick-up

to|nal [toˈnaːl] ADJ tonal

To|na|li|tät F tonality

Ton-: ton|an|ge|bend ADJ who/which sets the tone; **~ sein** to set the tone; **Ton|arm** M pick-up arm; **Ton|art** F (*Mus*) key; (*fig:* = *Tonfall*) tone; **eine andere ~ anschlagen** to change one's tune; **Ton|as|sis|tent(in)** M(F) sound operator; **Ton|as|sis|tenz** F sound; **Ton|ate|lier** NT recording studio; **Ton|aus|fall** M (*TV*) loss of sound; (*kurz*) (sound) dropout

Ton|band [-bant] NT *pl* **-bänder** tape (*mit of*); (*inf:* = *Gerät*) tape recorder

Ton|band-: Ton|band|auf|nah|me F tape recording; **Ton|band|ge|rät** NT tape recorder

Ton-: Ton|blen|de F tone control; **Ton|dich|ter(in)** M(F) composer; **Ton|dich|tung** F tone poem

to|nen [ˈtoːnən] VT (*Phot*) to tone

tö|nen¹ [ˈtøːnən] VI (*lit, fig:* = *klingen*) to sound; (= *schallen auch*) to resound; (= *großspurig reden*) to boast; **nach etw ~** (*fig*) to contain (over-) tones of sth; **von unten tönten Kinderstimmen** children's voices could be heard from below

tö|nen² [ˈtøːnən] VT to tint; **sich** (*dat*) **die Haare ~** to tint one's hair; **die Sonne hat ihre Haut schon goldbraun getönt** the sun has bronzed her skin; **der Herbst tönt alle Blätter** autumn makes all the leaves change colour (*Brit*), fall makes all the leaves change color (*US*); **etw leicht rot** *etc* **~** to tinge sth (with) red *etc* → *auch* **getönt**

To|ner [ˈtoːnɐ] M -s, - toner

Ton|er|de F aluminium oxide → **essigsauer**

tö|nern [ˈtøːnɐn] ADJ *attr* clay; **auf ~en Füßen stehen** (*fig*) to be shaky

Ton-: Ton|fall M tone of voice; (= *Intonation*) intonation; **Ton|film** M sound film, talkie (*dated inf*); **Ton|fol|ge** F sequence of sounds; (*Mus*) sequence of notes; (*bei Film*) sound sequence; **Ton|fre|quenz** F audio frequency; **Ton|ge|fäß** NT earthenware vessel; **Ton|ge|schirr** NT earthenware; **Ton|ge|schlecht** NT scale; **ton|hal|tig** ADJ clayey, argillaceous (*spec*), argilliferous (*spec*); **Ton|hö|he** F pitch

To|ni|ka [ˈtoːnika] F -, **Toniken** [-kn] (*Mus*) tonic

To|ni|kum [ˈtoːnikʊm] NT -s, **Tonika** [-ka] tonic

Ton-: Ton|in|ge|ni|eur(in) M(F) sound engineer; **Ton|ka|bi|ne** F sound booth; **Ton|ka|me|ra** F sound camera; **Ton|kopf** M recording head; **Ton|la|ge** F pitch (level); (= *Tonumfang*) register; **eine ~ höher** one note higher; **Ton|lei|ter** F scale; **ton|los** ADJ toneless; *Stimme auch* flat ADV in a flat voice; **Ton|ma|le|rei** F (*Mus*) tone painting; **Ton|meis|ter(in)** M(F) sound mixer

Ton|na|ge [tɔˈnaːʒə] F -, -n (*Naut*) tonnage

Tönn|chen [ˈtœnçən] NT -s, - little barrel, tub; (*fig hum, Mensch*) roly-poly (*inf*), dumpling (*inf*)

Ton|ne [ˈtɔnə] F -, -n (= *Behälter*) barrel, cask; (*aus Metall*) drum; (= *Mülltonne*) bin (*Brit*), trash can (*US*); (*inf: Mensch*) fatty (*inf*); **gelbe ~** yellow bin (*Brit*) *or* trash can (*US, for recyclable material*); **grüne ~** green bin (*Brit*) *or* trash can (*US, for paper*); **braune ~** brown bin (*Brit*) *or* trash can (*US, for biodegradable waste*) **b** (= *Gewicht*) metric ton(ne) **c** (= *Registertonne*) (register) ton **d** (*Naut:* = *Boje*) buoy

Ton|nen-: Ton|nen|ge|wöl|be NT (*Archit*) barrel vaulting; **ton|nen|wei|se** ADV by the ton, in tons; **~ Fische fangen** (*fig*) to catch tons (and tons) of fish

Ton-: Ton|set|zer(in) M(F) (*geh*) composer; **Ton|sig|nal** NT sound signal, audible signal; **Ton|sil|be** F tonic *or* stressed syllable; **Ton|spra|che** F tone language; **Ton|spur** F soundtrack; **Ton|stö|rung** F sound interference; **Ton|strei|fen** M soundtrack; **Ton|stu|dio** NT recording studio

Ton|sur [tɔnˈzuːɐ] F -, -en tonsure

Ton-: Ton|tau|be F clay pigeon; **Ton|tau|ben|schie|ßen** NT -s, *no pl* clay pigeon shooting; **Ton|tech|ni|ker(in)** M(F) sound technician; **Ton|trä|ger** M sound carrier; **Ton|um|fang** M register

To|nung [ˈtoːnʊŋ] F -, -en (*Phot*) toning

Tö|nung [ˈtøːnʊŋ] F -, -en (= *Haartönung*) hair colour (*Brit*) *or* color (*US*); (= *das Tönen*) tinting; (= *Farbton*) shade, tone

To|nus [ˈtoːnʊs] M -, **Toni** [-ni] **a** (*Physiol*) tone, tonus, tonicity (*spec*) **b** (*Mus*) whole tone

Ton-: Ton|wa|ren PL earthenware *sing*; **Ton|zie|gel** M brick; (= *Dachziegel*) tile

Top [tɔp] NT -s, -s (*Fashion*) top

TOP *abbr von* **Tagesordnungspunkt**

Top-, top- [tɔp] *in cpds* top; **Top|agent(in)** M(F) top agent; **top|ak|tu|ell** ADJ up-to-the-minute; *Nachrichten auch* latest

To|pas [toˈpaːs] M -es, -e [-zə] topaz

Topf [tɔpf] M -(e)s, -e [ˈtœpfə] pot; (= *Kochtopf auch*) (sauce)pan; (= *Nachttopf*) potty (*inf*); (*inf:* = *Toilette*) loo (*Brit inf*), john (*US inf*); **alles in einen ~ werfen** (*fig*) to lump everything together; **jeder ~ findet seinen Deckel** (*prov*) every Jack will find his Jill (*prov*)

Topf|blu|me F potted flower

Töpf|chen [ˈtœpfçən] NT -s, - *dim von* **Topf**

Topf|de|ckel M (*von Kochtopf*) saucepan lid; (*von Behälter*) pot *or* jar lid

Top|fen [ˈtɔpfn] M -s, - (*Aus, S Ger*) quark

Töp|fer [ˈtœpfɐ] M -s, -, **Töp|fe|rin** [-ərɪn] F -, -nen potter; (*dial:* = *Ofensetzer*) stove fitter

Töp|fe|rei [tœpfəˈrai] F -, -en pottery

Töp|fer|hand|werk NT potter's trade

töp|fern [ˈtœpfɐn] VI to do pottery VT to make (in clay); **wir sahen zu, wie er auf der Scheibe eine Vase töpferte** we watched him throwing a vase

Töp|fer-: Töp|fer|ofen M kiln; **Töp|fer|schei|be** F potter's wheel; **Töp|fer|wa|ren** PL pottery *sing*; (*irden*) earthenware *sing*

Topf|hand|schuh M oven glove (*Brit*) *or* mitt

top|fit ADJ *pred* in top form; (*gesundheitlich*) as fit as a fiddle

Topf-: Topf|ku|chen M gugelhupf; **Topf|lap|pen** M oven cloth; (*kleiner*) pan holder; **Topf|markt** M *market where pots and pans are sold*

Topf|form F **in ~ sein** (*inf*) to be in top form

Topf|pflan|ze F potted plant

To|pi|nam|bur [topinamˈbuːɐ] M -s, -s *or* -e, *or* f -, -en Jerusalem artichoke

Top-: Top|la|der [ˈtɔplaːdɐ] M -s, - top loader; **Top|ma|na|ge|ment** NT (= *das Management*) top management; (= *die Manager*) chief executives *pl*; **To̱p|mo|dell** NT (*Fashion, Tech*) top model

To̱|po|graf ▲ [topo'graːf] M **-en, -en, To̱|po|-gra̱|fin** ▲ [-'graːfɪn] F **-, -nen** topographer

To̱|po|gra|fie̱ ▲ [topo'graːfiː] F **-, -n** [-'fiːən] topography

to̱|po|gra̱|fisch ▲ [topo'graːfɪʃ] ADJ topographic(al) **ADV** *vermessen* topographically; **das Land ist topographisch und klimatisch ungeeignet** the topography and the climate of this country are ill suited

To̱|po|lo|gie̱ [topolo'giː] F **-,** *no pl* (*Math*) topology

To̱|pos ['toːpɔs, 'tɔpɔs] M **-, To̱poi** ['toːpɔy] (*Liter*) topos

to̱pp [tɔp] INTERJ done, it's a deal

To̱pp [tɔp] M **-s, -e** *or* **-s** (*Naut*) masthead; **über die -en geflaggt sein** *or* **haben** to be dressed overall

To̱pp|se|gel NT topsail

To̱r¹ [toːɐ] M **-en, -en** (*old, liter*) fool

To̱r² NT **-(e)s, -e a** (*lit, fig = Himmelstor, Höllentor*) gate; (= *Durchfahrt, fig: zum Glück etc*) gateway; (= *Torbogen*) archway; (*von Garage, Scheune*) door; (= *Felsentor*) arch in the rock; (= *Gletscher tor*) mouth (of glacier); **jdm das ~ zu etw öffnen** to open sb's eyes to sth; *zu Karriere etc* to open the door to sth for sb → **Tür b** (*Sport*) goal; (*bei Skilaufen*) gate; **im ~ stehen** to be in goal, to be the goalkeeper

To̱r-: To̱r|bo|gen M arch, archway; **To̱r|chan|-ce** F (*Sport*) chance (to score), scoring opportunity, opening; **eine ~ herausspielen** to create an opening; **eine ~ nutzen/vergeben** to take/to waste a scoring opportunity; **To̱r|dif|fe̱|renz** F (*Sport*) goal difference; **To̱r|ein|fahrt** F entrance gate

To̱|re|ro [to'reːro] M **-(s), -s** torero

To̱res|schluss ▲ M = **Torschluss**

To̱rf [tɔrf] M **-(e)s,** *no pl* peat

To̱rf-: To̱rf|bo|den M peat; **To̱rf|er|de** F peat; **To̱rf|feu|e|rung** F peat fire(s *pl*)

to̱r|fig ['tɔrfɪç] ADJ peaty

To̱r|flü|gel M gate (*of a pair of gates*)

To̱rf-: To̱rf|moor NT peat bog *or* (*trocken*) moor; **To̱rf|moos** NT sphagnum (moss); **To̱rf|mull** M (loose) garden peat

To̱r|frau F goalkeeper, goalie (*inf*)

To̱rf-: To̱rf|ste|cher [-ʃtɛçɐ] M **-s, -, To̱rf|ste|che|rin** [-ərɪn] F **-, -nen** peat-cutter; **To̱rf|stich** M patch *or* plot of peat

To̱r|heit ['toːɐhait] F **-, -en** (*geh*) foolishness, stupidity; (= *törichte Handlung*) foolish *or* stupid act; **er hat die ~ begangen, zu ...** he was foolish *or* stupid enough to ...

To̱r|hü|ter(in) M(F) goalkeeper

tö̱|richt ['tøːrɪçt] (*geh*) ADJ foolish, stupid; *Wunsch, Hoffnung* idle **ADV** foolishly, stupidly

tö̱|rich|ter|wei̱|se ['tøːrɪçtɐ'vaizə] ADV foolishly, stupidly

To̱r|jä|ger(in) M(F) (goal)scorer

to̱r|keln ['tɔrkln] VI *aux sein* to stagger, to reel

To̱r-: To̱r|lat|te F crossbar; **To̱r|lauf** M slalom; **To̱r|li|nie** F goal line; **tor|los** ADJ goalless; **das Spiel blieb ~, das Spiel ging ~ aus** it was a goalless draw, there was no score; **To̱r|mann** M *pl* **-männer** goalkeeper, goalie (*inf*)

Tö̱rn [tœrn] M **-s, -s** (*Naut*) cruise

Tor|na|do [tɔr'naːdo] M **-s, -s** tornado

Tor|nis|ter [tɔr'nɪstɐ] M **-s, -** (*Mil*) knapsack; (*dated:* = *Schulranzen*) satchel

tor|pe|die̱|ren [tɔrpe'diːrən] *ptp* **torpedie̱rt** VT (*Naut, fig*) to torpedo

Tor|pe̱|do [tɔr'peːdo] M **-s, -s** torpedo

Tor|pe̱|do|boot NT torpedo boat

Tor-: To̱r|pfos|ten M gatepost; (*Sport*) goalpost; **To̱r|raum** M (*Sport*) goalmouth; **To̱r|schluss** ▲ M , *no pl* (*fig*) **kurz vor ~** at the last minute,

at the eleventh hour; **nach ~ too late; To̱r|schluss|pa|nik** ▲ F (*inf*) last minute panic; (*von Unverheirateten*) fear of being left on the shelf; **To̱r|schüt|ze** M , **To̱r|schüt|zin** F (goal)scorer; **To̱r|schüt|zen|kö̱|nig(in)** M(F) top goalscorer

Tor|si|on [tɔr'zioːn] F **-, -en** torsion

Tor|si|ons-: Tor|si|ons|fes|tig|keit F torsional strength; **Tor|si|ons|stab** M torsion bar

To̱r|so ['tɔrzo] M **-s, -s** *or* **To̱rsi** ['tɔrzi] torso; (*fig*) skeleton

To̱r|sze|ne F action *no pl* in the goal area

Tort [tɔrt] M **-(e)s,** *no pl* (*geh*) wrong, injustice; **jdm etw zum ~ tun** to do sth to vex sb

Tört|chen ['tœrtçən] NT **-s, -** *dim von* **Torte** (small) tart, tartlet

To̱r|te ['tɔrtə] F **-, -n** gâteau; (= *Obsttorte*) flan

Tor|te|lett [tɔrtə'lɛt] NT **-s, -s, Tor|te|let|te** [tɔrtə'lɛtə] F **-, -n** (small) tart, tartlet

To̱r|ten-: To̱r|ten|bo|den M flan case *or* (*ohne Seiten*) base; **To̱r|ten|di|a|gramm** NT pie chart; **To̱r|ten|guss** ▲ M glaze; **To̱r|ten|he̱|ber** [-heːbə] M **-s, -** cake slice; **To̱r|ten|plat|te** F cake plate; **To̱r|ten|schau|fel** F cake slice; **To̱r|ten|schlacht** F (*in Film*) custard-pie battle; **To̱r|ten|stück** NT slice of cake; (*fig inf*) big draw (*inf*)

Tor|tur [tɔr'tuːɐ] F **-, -en** torture; (*fig auch*) ordeal

Tor-: Tor|ver|hält|nis NT score; **Tor|wäch|ter(in)** M(F) , **Tor|wart** [-vart] M **-(e)s, -e, Tor|war|tin** [-vartɪn] F **-, -nen** goalkeeper

to̱|sen ['toːzn] VI **a** (*Wasserfall, Wellen, Verkehr*) to roar, to thunder; (*Wind, Sturm*) to rage; **~der Beifall** thunderous applause **b** *aux sein* (*mit Ortsangabe*) to thunder

tot [toːt] ADJ **a** (= *gestorben*) (*lit, fig*) dead; (*inf:* = *erschöpft*) beat (*inf*), whacked (*Brit inf*); **mehr ~ als lebendig** (*fig inf*) more dead than alive; **~ geboren** stillborn; **~ geboren werden** to be stillborn; **ein ~ geborenes Kind sein** (*fig*) to be doomed (to failure); **~ umfallen, ~ zu Boden fallen** to drop dead; **ich will ~ umfallen, wenn das nicht wahr ist** cross my heart and hope to die (if it isn't true) (*inf*); **~ zusammenbrechen** to collapse and die; **er war auf der Stelle ~** he died instantly; **den ~en Mann machen** (*inf*) to float on one's back; **ein ~er Mann sein** (*fig inf*) to be a goner (*inf*); **den ~en Mann spielen** *or* **markieren** to play dead

b (= *leblos*) *Ast, Pflanze, Geschäftszeit, Sprache, Leitung* dead; *Augen* sightless, blind; *Haus, Stadt* deserted; *Landschaft etc* bleak; *Wissen* useless; *Vulkan* extinct, dead; *Farbe* dull, drab; (*Rail*) *Gleis* disused; **~er Flussarm** backwater; (= *Schleife*) oxbow (lake); **ein ~er Briefkasten** a dead letter box; **~er Winkel** blind spot; (*Mil*) dead angle; **das Tote Meer** the Dead Sea; **~er Punkt** (= *Stillstand*) standstill, halt; (*in Verhandlungen*) deadlock; (= *körperliche Ermüdung*) low point; **ich habe im Moment meinen ~en Punkt** I'm at a low ebb just now; **den ~en Punkt überwinden** to break the deadlock; (*körperlich*) to get one's second wind

c (= *nutzlos*) *Last, Gewicht, Kapital* dead; **ein ~es Rennen** (*lit, fig*) a dead heat; **~er Gang** (*Tech*) play

d (*Min*) **ein ~er Mann** *a worked-out part of a mine*

to|tal [to'taːl] ADJ total; *Staat* totalitarian **ADV** totally

To|tal|an|sicht F complete view

To|tal|aus|ver|kauf M clearance sale

To|ta|le F **-, -n** (*Film, Phot*) wide shot

To|ta|li|sa̱|tor [totali'zaːtoːɐ] M **-s, Totalisatoren** [-'toːrən] totalizator, tote (*inf*)

to|ta|li|tär [totali'tɛːɐ] ADJ totalitarian **ADV** in a totalitarian way

To|ta|li|ta|ris|mus [totalita'rɪsmʊs] M **-,** *no pl* totalitarianism

To|ta|li|tät [totali'tɛːt] F **-, -en** totality, entirety

To|tal-: To|tal|ope|ra|ti|on F extirpation; (*von Gebärmutter*) hysterectomy; (*mit Eierstöcken*) hysterosaphorectomy; **To|tal|scha|den** M write-off; **~ machen** (*inf*) to write a car *etc* off; **To|tal|ver|wei|ge|rer** M = *Kriegsdienstverweigerer* conscientious objector (*to both military service and civilian alternative*)

tot-: tot+ar|bei|ten VR *sep* (*inf*) to work oneself to death; **tot+är|gern** VR *sep* (*inf*) to be/become livid

To̱|tem ['toːtɛm] NT **-s, -s** totem

To̱|te|mis|mus [tote'mɪsmʊs] M **-,** *no pl* totemism

To̱|tem|pfahl M totem pole

tö̱|ten ['tøːtn] VTI (*lit, fig*) to kill; *Zahnnerv* to deaden → **Blick a**

To̱|ten-: To̱|ten|acker M (*liter*) graveyard; **To̱|ten|amt** NT requiem mass; **To̱|ten|be|stat|tung** F burial of the dead; **To̱|ten|bett** NT deathbed; **to̱|ten|blass** ▲ ADJ deathly pale, pale as death; **To̱|ten|bläs|se** F deathly pallor; **to̱|ten|bleich** ADJ = **totenblass**; **To̱|ten|fei|er** F funeral *or* burial ceremony; **To̱|ten|fle|cke** PL postmortem *or* cadaveric (*spec*) lividity *sing*; **To̱|ten|glo|cke** F (death) knell; **To̱|ten|grä|ber(in)** M(F) gravedigger; **To̱|ten|hemd** NT shroud; **To̱|ten|kla|ge** F lamentation of the dead; (*Liter*) dirge, lament; **To̱|ten|kopf** M **a** skull; (*als Zeichen*) death's-head; (*auf Piratenfahne, Arzneiflasche etc*) skull and crossbones **b** (*Zool*) death's-head moth; **To̱|ten|kult** M cult of the dead; **To̱|ten|mas|ke** F death mask; **To̱|ten|mes|se** F requiem mass; **To̱|ten|reich** NT (*Myth*) kingdom of the dead; **To̱|ten|schein** M death certificate; **To̱|ten|sonn|tag** M *Sunday before Advent, on which the dead are commemorated*; **To̱|ten|stadt** F necropolis; **To̱|ten|star|re** F rigor mortis; **to̱|ten|still** ADJ deathly silent *or* quiet; **To̱|ten|stil|le** F deathly silence *or* quiet; **To̱|ten|tanz** M dance of death, danse macabre; **To̱|ten|wa|che** F wake

To̱|te(r) ['toːtə] MF *decl as adj* dead person, dead man/woman; (*bei Unfall etc*) fatality, casualty; (*Mil*) casualty; **die ~n** the dead; **es gab 3 ~** 3 people died *or* were killed; **das ist ein Lärm, um ~ aufzuwecken** the noise is enough to wake(n) the dead

Tot-: To̱t|er|klär|te(r) ['toːtleklɛːrətə] MF *decl as adj* person *or* man/woman *etc* declared to be dead; **tot+fah|ren** VT *sep irreg* (*inf*) to knock down and kill; **tot|ge|bo|ren** △ ADJ *attr* → **tot a**; **To̱t|ge|burt** F stillbirth; (= *Kind*) stillborn child *or* baby; **To̱t|ge|glaub|te(r)** [-gəglaubtə] MF *decl as adj* person *or* man/woman *etc* believed to be dead; **tot|ge|sagt** ADJ declared dead; (*fig*) written off; **To̱t|ge|sag|te(r)** [-gəzaːktə] MF *decl as adj* person *or* man/woman *etc* said to be dead; **~ leben länger!** there's life in the old dog yet (*iro*); **tot+krie|gen** VT *sep* (*inf*) not tozukriegen sein to go on for ever; **tot+la|chen** VR *sep* (*inf*) to kill oneself (laughing), to die laughing; **es ist zum Totlachen** it is hilarious; **tot+lau|fen** VR *sep irreg* (*inf*) to peter out; **tot+ma|chen** *sep* (*inf*) **VT** to kill **VR** (*fig*) to kill oneself

To̱|to ['toːto] M OR (*INF, AUS, SW*) NT **-s, -s** (football) pools *pl* (*Brit*); **(im) ~ spielen** to do the pools (*Brit*); **etw im ~ gewinnen** to win sth on the pools (*Brit*); **im ~ gewinnen** (*Hauptgewinn*) to win the pools (*Brit*); **er hat vier Richtige im ~** four of his matches came up

To̱|to- *in cpds* pools (*Brit*); **To̱|to|schein** M , **To̱|to|zet|tel** M pools coupon (*Brit*)

Tot-: tot+schie|ßen VT *sep irreg* (*inf*) to shoot dead; **To̱t|schlag** M (*Jur*) manslaughter → **Mord**; **To̱t|schlag|ar|gu|ment** NT (*inf*) knockout argument; **tot+schla|gen** VT *sep irreg* (*lit, fig*) to kill; (*inf*) *Menschen auch* to beat to death; **du kannst mich ~, ich weiß es nicht** for the life of me I don't know; **To̱t|schlä|ger** M cudgel, club; **tot+schwei|gen** VT *sep irreg* to hush up (*inf*); **tot stel|len** ▲ VR to pretend to be dead, to play dead; (*Mensch auch*) to play possum (*inf*); **tot+tre|ten** VT *sep irreg* to trample to death; *Insekt etc* to tread on and kill

Tö|tung ['tøːtʊŋ] F -, -en killing; **fahrlässige ~** manslaughter (through culpable negligence (*esp Brit*))

Tö|tungs-: Tö|tungs|ab|sicht F intention to kill; **Tö|tungs|ver|such** M attempted murder

Touch [tatʃ] M -s, -s (= *Atmosphäre*) air, tone, flavour (*Brit*), flavor (*US*); (= *Flair*) touch; (= *Tendenz*) leanings *pl*

tou|chie|ren [tu'ʃiːrən] *ptp* **touchiert** VT **a** (*esp Sport*) to touch, to brush, to bump **b** (*Med*) (= *austasten*) to palpate; (= *abätzen*) to cauterize

Touch-Screen ['tatʃskriːn] M -s, -s, **Touch|-screen** M -s, -s (*Comput*) touch screen

Tou|pet [tu'peː] NT -s, -s toupée

tou|pie|ren [tu'piːrən] *ptp* **toupiert** VT to backcomb

Tour [tuːɐ] F -, -en **a** (= *Fahrt*) trip, outing; (= *Ausflugstour*) tour; (= *Spritztour*) (*mit Auto*) drive; (*mit Rad*) ride; (= *Wanderung*) walk, hike; (= *Bergtour*) climb; (= *Tournee*) tour; **auf ~ gehen** to go on or for a trip or an outing/on a tour/for a drive/ride/walk or hike/climb **b** (= *Umdrehung*) revolution, rev (*inf*); (*beim Tanz*) figure; (*beim Stricken*) two rows; (*mit Rundnadeln*) round; **auf ~en kommen** (*Auto*) to reach top speed; (*fig inf*) to get into top gear; (= *sich aufregen*) to get worked up (*inf*); **ich komme heute aber auch gar nicht auf ~en** I can't get going at all today; **jdn/etw auf ~en bringen** (*fig*) to get sb/sth going; **auf vollen ~en laufen** (*lit*) to run at full or top speed; (*fig*) to be in full swing; **in einer ~** (*inf*) incessantly, the whole time **c** (*inf.* = *Art und Weise*) ploy; **mit der ~ brauchst du mir gar nicht zu kommen** don't try that one on me; **auf die krumme** or **schiefe** or **schräge ~** by dishonest means; **etw auf die weiche** or **sanfte ~ versuchen** to try using soft soap (*Brit*) or sweet talk to get sth (*inf*); **jdm die ~ vermasseln** (*inf*) to put a spoke (*Brit*) or wrench (*US*) in sb's wheel (*inf*), to put paid to sb's plans

Tour de Force [turdə'fɔrs] F -, *no pl* (*geh*) tour de force

Tour d'Ho|ri|zon ▲ [turdɔri'zõː] F - -, -s - (*geh*) tour d'horizon (*liter*), broad survey

tou|ren ['tuːrən] VI (*inf.* = *reisen, auf Tournee sein*) to tour

Tou|ren- ['tuːrən-]: **Tou|ren|fah|rer(in)** M(F) long-distance driver; **Tou|ren|rad** NT tourer; **Tou|ren|ski** M cross-country ski; **Tou|ren|wa|gen** M (*im Motorsport*) touring car; **Tou|ren|zahl** F number of revolutions or revs *pl* (*inf*); **Tou|ren|zäh|ler** M rev counter

Tou|ri ['tuːri] M -(s), -s *usu pl* (*inf pej*: = *Tourist*) grockle (*Brit inf*), shoobie (*US sl*)

Tou|ris|mus [tu'rɪsmʊs] M -, *no pl* tourism

Tou|ris|mus|in|dust|rie F tourist industry

Tou|rist [tu'rɪst] M -en, -en, **Tou|ris|tin** [-'rɪstɪn] F -, -nen tourist

Tou|ris|ten|at|trak|ti|on F tourist attraction

Tou|ris|ten|klas|se F tourist class

Tou|ris|tik [tu'rɪstɪk] F -, *no pl* tourism, tourist industry

Tou|ris|tik|un|ter|neh|men NT tour company

Tou|ris|tin F -, -nen tourist

Tour|ne|dos [tʊrnə'doː] NT -, - [-'doːs] *usu pl* (*Cook*) tournedos

Tour|nee [tʊr'neː] F -, -s or -n [-'neːən] tour; **auf ~ gehen** to go on tour; **auf ~ sein** to be on tour, to be touring

tour-re|tour [tuːɐrə'tuːɐ] ADV (*Aus*) return

Tow|er ['tauɐ] M -s, - (*Aviat*) control tower

To|xi|ko|lo|ge [tɔksiko'loːgə] M -n, -n, **To|xi|ko|lo|gin** [-'loːgɪn] F -, -nen toxicologist

to|xi|ko|lo|gisch [tɔksiko'loːgɪʃ] ADJ toxicological ADV toxicologically; **etw ~ untersuchen** to do a toxicological analysis of sth; **~ unbedenklich** nontoxic

to|xisch ['tɔksɪʃ] ADJ toxic ADV toxically; **~ wirken** to be toxic

To|xi|zi|tät [tɔksitsi'tɛːt] F -, *no pl* toxicity

To|xo|plas|mo|se [tɔksoplas'moːzə] F -, -n toxoplasmosis

Trab [traːp] M -(e)s [-bəs] *no pl* trot; **im ~** at a trot; (**im**) **~ reiten** to trot; **sich in ~ setzen** (*inf*) to get going or cracking (*inf*); **auf ~ sein** (*inf*) to be on the go (*inf*); **jdn in ~ halten** (*inf*) to keep sb on the go (*inf*); **jdn auf (den) ~ bringen** (*inf*) to make sb get a move on (*inf*)

Tra|bant¹ [tra'bant] M -en, -en **a** (*Astron*) satellite **b** (*Hist*) bodyguard; (*fig*) satellite **c** *usu pl* (*dated inf*) kiddie-wink (*Brit inf*), kiddie (*inf*)

Trabant²® M -s, -s *most popular make of East German car*

Tra|ban|ten|stadt F satellite town

Trab|bi ['trabi] M -s, -s (*inf*) *abbr von* **Trabant²**

tra|ben ['traːbn] VI **a** *aux haben or sein* to trot; **mit dem Pferd ~** to trot one's horse **b** *aux sein* (*inf.* = *laufen*) to trot; **ich musste noch einmal in die Stadt ~** I had to go traipsing back into town

Tra|ber ['traːbɐ] M -s, - trotter

Tra|bi ['trabi] M -s, -s (*inf*) *abbr von* **Trabant²**

Trab-: Trab|renn|bahn F trotting course; **Trab|ren|nen** NT trotting; (*Veranstaltung*) trotting race

Tracht [traxt] F -, -en **a** (= *Kleidung*) dress, garb; (= *Volkstracht etc*) costume; (= *Schwesterntracht*) uniform **b** (*obs:* = *Traglast*) load; **jdm eine Prügel verabfolgen** or **verabreichen** (*inf*) to give sb a beating or thrashing

trach|ten ['traxtn] VI (*geh*) to strive (**nach** for, after); **danach ~, etw zu tun** to strive or endeavour (*Brit*) or endeavor (*US*) to do sth; **jdm nach dem Leben ~** to be after sb's blood

Trach|ten-: Trach|ten|fest NT *festive occasion where traditional/national costume is worn*; **Trach|ten|grup|pe** F group dressed in traditional/national costume; **Trach|ten|ja|cke** F *traditionally styled jacket made of thick woollen material* (*von Volkstracht*) *jacket worn as part of traditional/national costume*; **Trach|ten|kos|tüm** NT *suit made of thick woollen material*

träch|tig ['trɛçtɪç] ADJ (*lit*) *Tier* pregnant; (*fig geh*) laden (*von* with); *Gedanke etc* meaningful, significant

Träch|tig|keit F (*von Tier*) pregnancy

Track [trɛk] M -s, -s **a** (*auf CD, Band*) track **b** (= *Route*) route; (= *Bergwanderung*) mountain hike or walk

Track|ball ['trɛkbɔːl] M -s, -s (*Comput*) trackball

tra|die|ren [tra'diːrən] *ptp* **tradiert** VT (*geh*) to hand down

Tra|di|ti|on [tradi'tsioːn] F -, -en tradition; (**bei jdm**) **~ haben** to be a tradition (for sb)

Tra|di|ti|o|na|lis|mus [traditsiona'lɪsmʊs] M -, *no pl* traditionalism

Tra|di|ti|o|na|list [traditsiona'lɪst] M -en, -en, **Tra|di|ti|o|na|lis|tin** [-'lɪstɪn] F -, -nen traditionalist

tra|di|ti|o|na|lis|tisch [traditsiona'lɪstɪʃ] ADJ traditionalistic, traditionalist ADV **~ veranlagt sein** to be traditionally-minded

tra|di|ti|o|nell [traditsio'nɛl] ADJ *usu attr* traditional ADV traditionally

Tra|di|ti|ons-: tra|di|ti|ons|be|wusst ▲ ADJ tradition-conscious; **Tra|di|ti|ons|be|wusst|sein** ▲ NT consciousness of tradition; **tra|di|ti|ons|ge|bun|den** ADJ bound by tradition; **tra|di|ti|ons|ge|mäß** ADV traditionally, according to tradition; **tra|di|ti|ons|reich** ADJ rich in tradition

traf *pret von* **treffen**

Tra|fik [tra'fɪk] F -, -en (*Aus*) tobacconist's (shop)

Tra|fi|kant [trafi'kant] M -en, -en, **Tra|fi|kan|tin** [-'kantɪn] F -, -nen (*Aus*) tobacconist

Tra|fo ['traːfo] M -(s), -s (*inf*) transformer

träg [trɛːk] ADJ, ADV = **träge**

Trag-: Trag|bah|re F stretcher; **trag|bar** ADJ **a** *Apparat, Gerät* portable; *Kleid* wearable **b** (= *annehmbar*) acceptable (*für* to); (= *erträglich*) bearable

Tra|ge ['traːgə] F -, -n (= *Bahre*) litter; (= *Tragkorb*) pannier

trä|ge ['trɛːgə] ADJ **a** sluggish; *Mensch, Handbewegung etc* lethargic; (= *faul*) lazy, idle; **geistig ~** mentally lazy **b** (*Phys*) *Masse* inert ADV *sich bewegen* sluggishly; *sich rekeln* lethargically

Tra|ge|gurt M (*carrying*) sling, harness

tra|gen ['traːgn] *pret* **trug** [truːk], *ptp* **getragen** [gə'traːgn] VT **a** (= *befördern, dabeihaben*) to carry; (= *an einen Ort bringen*) to take; (*Wellen etc*) to bear, to carry; (*fig*) *Gerücht etc* to pass on, to spread; **etw mit** or **bei sich ~** to carry sth with one; **den Brief zur Post ~** to take the letter to the post office; **den Arm in der Schlinge ~** to have one's arm in a sling **b** (= *am Körper tragen*) *Kleid, Brille, Rot etc, Perücke* to wear; *Bart, Gebiss* to have; *Waffen* to carry; **wie trägt sie zurzeit ihre Haare?** how is she wearing her hair now?; **getragene Kleider** second-hand clothes; (= *abgelegt*) castoffs (*Brit*), throwouts (*US*) → **Trauer** **c** (= *stützen, halten*) to support → **tragend** **d** (= *aushalten, Tragfähigkeit haben*) to take (the weight of), to carry **e** (= *hervorbringen*) *Zinsen* to yield; *Ernte* to yield, to produce; (*lit, fig*) *Früchte* to bear; **der Baum trägt viele Früchte** the tree produces a good crop of fruit; (*in dieser Saison*) the tree is full of fruit **f** (= *trächtig sein*) to be carrying **g** (= *ertragen*) *Schicksal, Leid etc* to bear, to endure; *Kreuz* to bear **h** (= *übernehmen*) *Verluste* to defray; *Kosten* to bear, to carry; *Risiko* to take; *Folgen* to take, to bear; **die Verantwortung für etw ~** to be responsible for sth; **die Schuld für etw ~** to be to blame for sth **i** (= *unterhalten*) *Verein, Organisation* to support, to back **j** (= *haben*) *Titel, Namen, Aufschrift etc* to bear, to have; *Vermerk* to contain; *Etikett* to have; **der Brief trägt das Datum vom ...** the letter is dated ...

j → **getragen**

VI **a** (*Baum, Acker etc*) to crop, to produce a crop; **gut/schlecht ~** to crop well/badly, to produce a good/bad crop; (*in dieser Saison*) to have a good/bad crop **b** (= *trächtig sein*) to be pregnant **c** (= *reichen: Geschütz, Stimme*) to carry **d** (*Eis*) to take weight; **das Eis trägt noch nicht** the ice won't take anyone's weight yet **e** **schwer an etw** (*dat*) **~** to have a job carrying or to carry sth; (*fig*) to find sth hard to bear; **schwer zu ~ haben** to have a lot to carry; (*fig*) to have a heavy cross to bear **f** **zum Tragen kommen** to come to fruition, to bear fruit, to take effect, to bring results; (= *nützlich werden*) to come in useful; **etw zum Tragen bringen** to bring sth to bear (*in +dat* on)

VR **a** **sich gut** or **leicht/schwer** or **schlecht ~** to be easy/difficult or hard to carry; **schwere Lasten ~ sich besser auf dem Rücken** it is better to carry heavy loads on one's back **b** (*Kleid, Stoff*) to wear **c** **sich mit etw ~** (*geh*) to contemplate sth **d** (= *ohne Zuschüsse auskommen*) to be self-supporting

tra|gend ADJ **a** (= *stützend*) *Säule, Bauteil, Chassisteil* weight-bearing, load-bearing; (*fig:* = *bestimmend*) *Bedeutung, Idee, Motiv* fundamental, basic **b** (*Theat*) *Rolle* major, main **c** *Stimme* resonant **d** (= *trächtig*) pregnant

Trä|ger¹ ['trɛːgɐ] M **-s, -** **a** (an Kleidung) strap; (= Hosenträger) braces pl (Brit), suspenders pl (US) **b** (Build) (= Holzträger, Betonträger) (supporting) beam; (= Stahlträger, Eisenträger) girder **c** (Tech: = Stütze von Brücken etc) support **d** (= Flugzeugträger) carrier **e** (Biol: von Gen) carrier **f** (von Sozialeinrichtung) provider **g** (= Kostenträger) funding provider

Trä|ger² ['trɛːgɐ] M **-s, -,** **Trä|ge|rin** [-ərɪn] F **-, -nen** **a** (von Lasten) bearer, porter; (von Namen) bearer; (von Orden, Amt, Titel) bearer, holder; (von Kleidung) wearer; (eines Preises) winner; (von Krankheit, Gen) carrier **b** (fig) (der Kultur, Staatsgewalt etc) representative; (einer Bewegung, Entwicklung) upholder, supporter; (einer Veranstaltung) sponsor; (Mittel) vehicle; **~ einer Einrichtung sein** to be in charge of an institution

Träger-: Träger|flug|zeug NT carrier plane; **Trä|ger|ho|se** F trousers pl (esp Brit) or pants pl (esp US) with straps; **Trä|ger|kleid** NT pinafore dress (Brit), jumper (US); (sommerlich) sundress; **Träger|lohn** M porterage; **trä|ger|los** ADJ Kleidungsstück strapless; **Trä|ger|ma|te|ri|al** NT base material, carrier material; **Trä|ger|ra|ke|te** F carrier rocket; **Träger|rock** M pinafore dress (Brit), jumper (US); (für Kinder) skirt with straps; **Trä|ger|schür|ze** F pinafore; **Trä|ger|sys|tem** NT (Mil) carrier system; **Trä|ger|waf|fe** F carrier weapon

Tra|ge-: Tra|ge|ta|sche F carrier bag; **Tra|ge|zeit** F gestation period

Trag-: trag|fä|hig ADJ able to take a weight; (fig) Kompromiss, Konzept, Lösung workable; **Trag|fä|hig|keit** F , no pl weight-bearing capacity; (von Brücke) maximum load; (fig) workability; **Trag|flä|che** F wing; (von Boot) hydrofoil; **Trag|flä|chen|boot** NT hydrofoil; **Trag|flü|gel** M wing; (von Boot) hydrofoil; **Trag|flü|gel|boot** NT hydrofoil

Träg|heit F **-, -en** sluggishness; (von Mensch) lethargy; (= Faulheit) laziness; (Phys) inertia

Träg|heits-: Träg|heits|ge|setz NT law of inertia; **Träg|heits|mo|ment** NT moment of inertia

Trag|him|mel M canopy, baldachin

Tra|gik ['traːgɪk] F **-,** no pl tragedy; **das ist die ~ der Sache, dass ...** what's tragic about it is that ...

Tra|gi|ker ['traːgɪkɐ] M **-s, -,** **Tra|gi|ke|rin** [-ərɪn] F **-, -nen** tragedian

Tra|gi-: Tra|gi|ko|mik [tragiˈkoːmɪk, ˈtraːgi-] F tragicomedy; **tra|gi|ko|misch** [tragiˈkoːmɪʃ, ˈtraːgi-] ADJ tragicomical; **Tra|gi|ko|mö|die** [tragikoˈmøːdiə, ˈtraːgi-] F tragicomedy

tra|gisch ['traːgɪʃ] ADJ tragic; **das ist nicht so ~** (inf) it's not the end of the world ADV tragically; **~ umkommen** to die tragically; **etw ~ neh|men** (inf) to take sth to heart

Trag-: Trag|korb M pannier; **Trag|kraft** F , no pl weight-bearing capacity; (von Brücke) maximum load; **Trag|last** F load; (= Gepäck) heavy luggage (esp Brit) or baggage; **Trag|luft|hal|le** F air hall

Tra|gö|de [traˈgøːdə] M **-n, -n** tragedian → auch **Tragödin**

Tra|gö|die [traˈgøːdiə] F **-, -n** (Liter, fig) tragedy; **es ist eine ~ mit ihm/dieser Maschine** he/this machine is a disaster

Tra|gö|di|en-: Tra|gö|di|en|dar|stel|ler(in) M(F) tragedian/tragedienne; **Tra|gö|di|en|dich|ter(in)** M(F) tragedian

Tra|gö|din [traˈgøːdɪn] F **-, -nen** tragedienne

Trag-: Trag|pfei|ler M weight-bearing or load-bearing pillar; (von Brücke) support; **Trag|rie|men** M strap; (von Gewehr) sling; **Trag|schicht** F base course; **Trag|ses|sel** M sedan chair

trägt [trɛːkt] 3. pers sing pres von **tragen**

Trag-: Trag|wei|te F (von Geschütz etc) range; (fig) consequences pl; (von Gesetz) scope; **sind Sie sich der ~ dieses Schritts/Ihres Handelns**

bewusst? are you aware of the possible consequences or of the implications of this step/of your action?, are you aware of what this step/your action could mean?; **von großer ~ sein** to have far-reaching consequences or implications; **Trag|werk** NT (Aviat) wing assembly

Trai|ler ['trɛːlɐ] M **-s, -** **a** (Aut: = Anhänger) trailer **b** (= Filmwerbung) trailer

Trai|ner¹ ['trɛːnɐ, ˈtreːnɐ] M **-s, -** (Sw: = Trainingsanzug) tracksuit

Trai|ner² ['trɛːnɐ, ˈtreːnɐ] M **-s, -,** **Trai|ne|rin** [-ərɪn] F **-, -nen** trainer; (von Rennpferd) trainer; (von Schwimmer, Tennisspieler) coach; (bei Fußball) manager

Trai|ner|bank ['trɛːnɐ-, ˈtreːnɐ-] F pl **-bänke** bench

trai|nie|ren [trɛˈniːrən, tre-] ptp **trainiert** VT to train; Mannschaft, Sportler auch to coach; Sprung, Übung, Sportart to practise (Brit), to practice (US); Muskel, Kreislauf to exercise; **Fußball/Tennis ~** to do some football/tennis practice; **ein (gut) trainierter Sportler** an athlete who is in training; **auf etw (acc) trainiert sein** to be trained to do sth; **jdn auf or für etw (acc) ~** to train or coach sb for sth
VI (Sportler) to train; (Rennfahrer) to practise (Brit), to practice (US); (= Übungen machen) to exercise; (= üben) to practise (Brit), to practice (US) for sth; **da musst du schon noch etwas ~** you'll have to practise (Brit) or practice (US) that a bit more
VR to train (auf +acc for); (= üben) to practise (Brit), to practice (US); (um fit zu werden) to get some exercise, to get into training

Trai|ning ['trɛːnɪŋ, ˈtreː-] NT **-s, -s** training no pl; (= Fitnesstraining) workout; (bei Autorennen) practice; (fig: = Übung) practice; **er geht jeden Abend zum ~** he goes for a workout every evening; **ein 2-stündiges ~** a 2-hour training session; (= Fitnesstraining) a 2-hour workout; **er übernimmt das ~ der Mannschaft** he's taking over the training or coaching of the team; **im ~ stehen** to be in training; **durch regelmäßiges ~ lernen die Schüler ...** by regular practice the pupils learn ...

Trainings-: Trai|nings|an|zug M tracksuit; **Trai|nings|ho|se** F tracksuit trousers pl (esp Brit) or bottoms pl or pants pl (esp US); **Trai|nings|ja|cke** F tracksuit top; **Trai|nings|la|ger** NT training camp; **Trai|nings|me|tho|de** F training method; **Trai|nings|mög|lich|keit** F training facilities pl; **Trai|nings|run|de** F practice lap; **Trai|nings|schuh** M training shoe; **Trai|nings|zeit** F practice time

Tra|keh|ner [traˈkeːnɐ] M **-s, -** type of riding horse from Prussia

Trakt [trakt] M **-(e)s, -e** (= Gebäudeteil) section; (= Flügel) wing; (von Autobahn) stretch, section

trak|tan|die|ren [traktanˈdiːrən] ptp **traktandiert** VT (Sw: = auf die Tagesordnung setzen) to put on the agenda; **traktandiert sein** to be on the agenda

Trak|tat [trakˈtaːt] M OR NT **-(e)s, -e** **a** (= Abhandlung) (Flugschrift, religiöse Schrift) tract **b** (obs: = Vertrag) treaty

Trak|tät|chen [trakˈtɛːtçən] NT **-s, -** (pej) tract

trak|tie|ren [trakˈtiːrən] ptp **traktiert** VT (inf) (= schlecht behandeln) to maltreat; Menschen auch to give a rough time; (= quälen) kleine Schwester, Tier etc to torment; **jdn mit Vorwürfen ~** to keep on at sb (inf); **er hat ihn mit Fäusten/Füßen/Schlägen traktiert** he punched/kicked/hit him

Trak|ti|on [trakˈtsioːn] F **-, -en** (Aut) traction

Trak|tor ['traktoːɐ] M **-s, Traktoren** [-ˈtoːrən] tractor; (Comput) tractor feed

Trak|to|rist [traktoˈrɪst] M **-en, -en, Trak|to|ris|tin** [-ˈrɪstɪn] F **-, -nen** (dial) tractor driver

träl|lern ['trɛlɐn] VTI to warble; (Vogel auch) to trill; **vor sich hin ~** to warble away to oneself

Tram [tram] F **-, -s** (dial, Sw), **Tram|bahn** F (S Ger) = **Straßenbahn**

Tramp [trɛmp, tramp] M **-s, -s** tramp

Tram|pel ['trampl] M OR NT **-s, -** or f **-, -n** clumsy clot (inf) or oaf (inf); **~ vom Land** (country) bumpkin or cousin

tram|peln ['trampln] VI **a** (= mit den Füßen stampfen) to stamp; **die Zuschauer haben getrampelt** the audience stamped their feet **b** aux sein (= schwerfällig gehen) to stamp or tramp along; **über die Wiese/das Gras ~** to tramp across the meadow/grass VT **a** (= mit Füßen bearbeiten) Weg to trample; **jdn zu Tode ~** to trample sb to death **b** (= abschütteln) to stamp (von from)

Trampel-: Tram|pel|pfad M track, path; **Tram|pel|tier** NT **a** (Zool) (Bactrian) camel **b** (inf) clumsy oaf (inf)

tram|pen ['trɛmpn, 'tram-] VI aux sein to hitchhike, to hitch (Brit inf)

Tram|per ['trɛmpɐ] M **-s, -, Tram|pe|rin** [-ərɪn] F **-, -nen** hitchhiker, hitcher (Brit inf)

Tramp|fahrt ['trɛmp-, ˈtramp-] F **a** (Naut) tramp voyage; **auf ~ sein** to be tramping **b** (= Reise per Anhalter) hitchhiking tour; **auf ~ sein** to be away hitchhiking

Tram|po|lin [trampoˈliːn, ˈtram-] NT **-s, -e** trampoline

Tram|po|lin|sprin|gen NT **-s,** no pl trampolining

Tramp-: Tramp|schiff NT tramp (ship); **Tramp|schiff|fahrt** ▲ F tramp shipping

Tram|way ['tramvai] F **-, -s** (Aus) = **Straßenbahn**

Tran [traːn] M **-(e)s, -e** **a** (von Fischen) train oil **b** (inf) im ~ dop(e)y (inf); (= leicht betrunken) tipsy, merry (inf); **ich lief wie im ~ durch die Gegend** I was running around in a dream or a daze; **das habe ich im ~ ganz vergessen** it completely slipped my mind

Tran|ce ['trãːs(ə)] F **-, -n** trance

Tran|ce-: tran|ce|ar|tig ADJ trancelike; **Tran|ce|zu|stand** M (state of) trance

Tran|che ['trãːʃ(ə)] F **-, -n** **a** (St Ex) tranche of a bond issue; (= Anleihe) quota share **b** (= Abschnitt) tranche

Tran|chier|be|steck [trãˈʃiːɐ-] NT carving set, set of carvers

tran|chie|ren [trãˈʃiːrən] ptp **tranchiert** VT to carve

Tran|chier- [trãˈʃiːɐ-]: **Tran|chier|ga|bel** F carving fork; **Tran|chier|mes|ser** NT carving knife

Trä|ne ['trɛːnə] F **-, -n** tear; (= einzelne Träne) tear(drop); (inf: Mensch) drip (inf); **den ~n nahe sein** to be near to or on the verge of tears; **ich bin zu ~n gerührt** I am moved to tears; **unter ~n lächeln** to smile through one's tears; **unter ~n gestand er seine Schuld/Liebe** in tears he confessed his guilt/love; **ihm kamen die ~n** tears welled (up) in his eyes; **mir kommen die ~n** (iro) my heart bleeds for him/her etc; **~n la|chen** to laugh till one cries, to laugh till the tears run down one's cheeks; **deswegen vergie|ße ich keine ~n** (fig) I'll shed no tears over that; **die Sache/der Mann ist keine ~ wert** the matter/man isn't worth crying over; **bittere ~n weinen** to shed bitter tears; **jdm/sich die ~n trocknen** or **abwischen** to dry sb's/one's eyes, to wipe away sb's/one's tears

trä|nen ['trɛːnən] VI to water

Tränen-: Trä|nen|drü|se F lachrymal gland; **der Film drückt sehr auf die ~n** the film is a real tear-jerker (inf); **im Schlussakt drückt der Autor kräftig auf die ~n** (inf) the author has written a real tear-jerker of a final act (inf); **trä|nen|feucht** ADJ wet with tears; Augen tear-filled; **Trä|nen|fluss** ▲ M flood of tears; **Trä|nen|gas** NT tear gas; **Trä|nen|ka|nal** M tear duct; **trä|nen|reich** ADJ tearful ADV tearfully; **~ enden** to end in tears; **Trä|nen|sack**

M lachrymal sac; **Trä|nen|schlei|er** M blur of tears

Tran|fun|sel F , **Tran|fun|zel** F (*inf*) slowcoach (*Brit inf*), slowpoke (*US inf*)

tra|nig ['tra:nɪç] **ADJ** like train oil; (*inf*) slow, sluggish **ADV** *schmecken* oily; (*inf*) *sich bewegen* sluggishly; *fahren, arbeiten* slowly

trank *pret von* **trinken**

Trank [traŋk] M **-(e)s, ⸚e** ['trɛŋkə] (*liter*) drink, draught (*Brit liter*), draft (*US liter*), potion (*liter*)

Trän|ke ['trɛŋkə] F **-, -n** drinking trough

trän|ken ['trɛŋkn] VT **a** *Tiere* to water **b** (= *durchnässen*) to soak; **seine Antwort war mit Hohn getränkt** (*geh*) his answer was awash with scorn

Trans- *in cpds* trans-

Trans|ak|ti|on [trans|ak'tsio:n] F transaction

trans|at|lan|tisch [trans|at'lantɪʃ] ADJ transatlantic

Tran|schier- (*Aus*) = **Tranchier-**

Trans-Eu|ro|pa-Ex|press [transɔy'ro:pa-] M Trans-Europe Express

trans|eu|ro|pä|isch [transɔyro'pɛ:ɪʃ] ADJ trans-European

Trans|fer [trans'fe:ɐ] M **-s, -s** transfer; (*Psych*) transference

trans|fe|rie|ren [transfe'ri:rən] *ptp* **transferiert** VT to transfer

Trans|fer|leis|tung F (*Psych*) transfer effect; (*Econ*) transfer

Trans|for|ma|ti|on [transfɔrma'tsio:n] F transformation

Trans|for|ma|ti|ons-: **Trans|for|ma|ti|ons|gram|ma|tik** F transformational grammar; **Trans|for|ma|ti|ons|re|gel** F transformation rule

Trans|for|ma|tor [transfɔr'ma:to:ɐ] M **-s, Transformatoren** [-'to:rən] transformer

Trans|for|ma|to|ren|häus|chen NT transformer

trans|for|mie|ren [transfɔr'mi:rən] *ptp* **transformiert** VT to transform

Trans|fu|si|on [transfu'zio:n] F transfusion

trans|gen [trans'ge:n] ADJ transgenic

Tran|sis|tor [tran'zɪsto:ɐ] M **-s, Transistoren** [-'to:rən] transistor

Tran|sis|tor|ra|dio NT transistor (radio)

Tran|sit ['tranzi:t, tran'zɪt, 'tranzɪt] M **-s, -e** transit

Tran|sit-: **Tran|sit|ab|kom|men** NT transit agreement; **Tran|sit|hal|le** F (*Aviat*) transit area; **Tran|sit|han|del** M transit trade

tran|si|tiv ['tranziti:f, tranzi'ti:f] (*Gram*) **ADJ** transitive **ADV** *gebrauchen* transitively

Tran|sit-: **Tran|sit|raum** M (*Aviat*) transit lounge; **Tran|sit|rei|sen|de(r)** MF *decl as adj* (*Aviat*) transit passenger; **~ nach ...** transit passengers bound for or continuing their flight to ...; **Tran|sit|sper|re** F , **Tran|sit|ver|bot** NT transit ban (*prohibiting goods or people from passing through a country*); **Tran|sit|ver|kehr** M transit traffic; (= *Transithandel*) transit trade; **Passagiere im ~** transit passengers *pl*; **Tran|sitvi|sum** NT transit visa

tran|skri|bie|ren [transkri'bi:rən] *ptp* **transkribiert** VT to transcribe; (*Mus*) to arrange

Tran|skrip|ta|se [transkrɪp'ta:zə] F **-, -n** transcriptase; **reverse ~** reverse transcriptase

Trans|mis|si|on [transmɪ'sio:n] F (*Mech*) transmission

Trans|oze|an- [trans'lo:tsea:n, translotse'a:n] *in cpds* transoceanic; **Trans|oze|an|flug** M transoceanic flight

trans|pa|rent [transpa'rɛnt] ADJ transparent; (*fig geh*) *Argument* lucid

Trans|pa|rent [transpa'rɛnt] NT **-(e)s, -e** (= *Reklameschild etc*) neon sign; (= *Durchscheinbild*) transparency; (= *Spruchband*) banner

Trans|pa|rent|pa|pier NT waxed tissue paper; (*zum Pausen*) tracing paper

Trans|pa|renz [transpa'rɛnts] F **-**, *no pl* transparency; (*fig geh*: *von Argument*) lucidity; **sie fordern mehr ~ bei allen Vorgängen in der Politik** they demand more openness in political matters

trans|per|so|nal [transpɛrzo'na:l] ADJ (*Psych*) transpersonal

Trans|spi|ra|ti|on [transpira'tsio:n] F **-**, *no pl* (*geh*) perspiration; (*von Pflanze*) transpiration

tran|spi|rie|ren [transpi'ri:rən] *ptp* **transpiriert** VI (*geh*) to perspire; (*Pflanze*) to transpire

Trans|plan|tat [transplan'ta:t] NT **-(e)s, -e** (*Haut*) graft; (*Organ*) transplant

Trans|plan|ta|ti|on [transplanta'tsio:n] F **-, -en** **a** (*Med*) transplant; (*von Haut*) graft; (*Vorgang*) transplantation; (*von Haut*) grafting **b** (*Bot*) grafting

trans|plan|tie|ren [transplan'ti:rən] *ptp* **transplantiert** VTI **a** (*Med*) *Organ, Gen* to transplant; *Haut* to graft **b** (*Bot*) to graft

Trans|pon|der [trans'pɔndɐ] M **-s, -** transponder

trans|po|nie|ren [transpo'ni:rən] *ptp* **transponiert** VT (*Mus*) to transpose

Trans|port [trans'pɔrt] M **-(e)s, -e** **a** (= *das Transportieren*) transport; **ein ~ auf dem Landweg** road transport; **ein ~ des Kranken ist ausgeschlossen** moving the patient is out of the question; **beim** or **auf dem ~ beschädigte/verloren gegangene Waren** goods damaged/lost in transit **b** (= *Fracht*) consignment, shipment; (*von Soldaten etc*) load, transport; (*von Gefangenen*) transport

trans|por|ta|bel [transpɔr'ta:bl] ADJ *Fernseher, Computer etc* portable

Trans|port-: **Trans|port|ar|bei|ter(in)** M(F) transport worker; **Trans|port|band** [-bant] NT *pl* **-bänder** conveyor belt; **Trans|port|behäl|ter** M container

Trans|por|ter [trans'pɔrtɐ] M **-s, -** (*Schiff*) cargo ship; (*Flugzeug*) transport plane; (*Auto*) van; (= *Autotransporter*) transporter

Trans|por|teur¹ [transpɔr'tø:ɐ] M **-s, -e** **a** (*an Nähmaschine*) fabric guide, feed dog **b** (= *Winkelmesser*) protractor

Trans|por|teur² [transpɔr'tø:ɐ] M **-s, -e**, **Transpor|teu|rin** [-'tø:rɪn] F **-, -nen** haulier (*Brit*), hauler (*US*)

Trans|port-: **trans|port|fä|hig** ADJ *Patient* moveable; **Trans|port|flug|zeug** NT transport plane or aircraft

trans|por|tie|ren [transpɔr'ti:rən] *ptp* **transportiert** **VT** to transport; *Güter auch* to carry; *Patienten* to move; *Film* to wind on; (*Nähmaschine*) to feed **VI** (*Förderband*) to move; (*Nähmaschine*) to feed; (*Kamera*) to wind on

Trans|port-: **Trans|port|kos|ten** PL carriage *sing*; **Trans|port|mit|tel** NT means *sing* of transport; **Trans|port|scha|den** M damage in transit; **Trans|port|schiff** NT cargo ship; (*Mil*) transport ship; **Trans|port|un|ter|neh|men** NT haulier (*Brit*), hauler (*US*), haulage firm; **Trans|port|ver|si|che|rung** F (*Insur*) transport insurance; (*Versicherer*) transport insurance company; **Trans|port|we|sen** NT transport

Trans|po|son [transpo'zo:n] NT **-s, -s** or **-en** transposon

Trans|ra|pid® [transra'pi:t] M **-**, *no pl* (*Rail*) Transrapid maglev (train)

Trans|se|xu|el|le(r) [transzɛ'ksuɛlə] MF *decl as adj* transsexual

Tran|su|se [tran'zu:zə] F **-, -n** (*inf*) slowcoach (*Brit inf*), slowpoke (*US inf*)

Trans|ves|tis|mus [transvɛs'tɪsmʊs] M **-**, *no pl* transvestism

Trans|ves|tit [transvɛs'ti:t] M **-en, -en** transvestite

trans|zen|dent [transtsɛn'dɛnt] ADJ transcendent(al); (*Math*) transcendental

trans|zen|den|tal [transtsɛndɛn'ta:l] ADJ transcendental

Trans|zen|denz [transtsɛn'dɛnts] F **-**, *no pl* transcendency, transcendence

Tran|tü|te F (*inf*) slowcoach (*Brit inf*), slowpoke (*US inf*)

Tra|pez [tra'pe:ts] NT **-es, -e** **a** (*Math*) trapezium **b** (*von Artisten*) trapeze

Tra|pez-: **Tra|pez|akt** M trapeze act; **tra|pezför|mig** ADJ trapeziform; **Tra|pez|künstler(in)** M(F) trapeze artist

Tra|pe|zo|e|der [trapetso'|e:dɐ] NT **-s, -** trapezohedron

Tra|pe|zoid [trapetso'i:t] NT **-(e)s, -e** [-də] trapezoid

trap|peln ['trapln] VI *aux sein* to clatter; (*Pony*) to clip-clop

Trap|pist [tra'pɪst] M **-en, -en**, **Trap|pis|tin** [-'pɪstɪn] F **-, -nen** (*Eccl*) Trappist

trapp, trapp ['trap 'trap] INTERJ (*von Kindern etc*) clitter-clatter; (*von Pferd*) clip-clop

trap|sen ['trapsn] VI *aux sein* (*inf*) to galumph (*inf*) → **Nachtigall**

Tra|ra [tra'ra:] NT **-s, -s** (*von Horn*) tantara; (*fig inf*) hullaballoo (*inf*), to-do (*inf*) (*um* about)

Tras|sant [tra'sant] M **-en, -en**, **Tras|san|tin** [-'santɪn] F **-, -nen** (*Fin*) drawer

Tras|sat [tra'sa:t] M **-en, -en**, **Tras|sa|tin** [-'sa:tɪn] M **-, -nen** (*Fin*) drawee

Tras|se ['trasə] F **-, -n** (*Surv*) marked-out route

Tras|sen|füh|rung F route

trat *pret von* **treten**

Tratsch [tra:tʃ] M **-(e)s** (*inf*) gossip, scandal, tittle-tattle (*esp Brit inf*)

trat|schen ['tra:tʃn] VI (*inf*) to gossip

Trat|sche|rei [tra:tʃə'rai] F **-, -en** (*inf*) gossip (-ing) *no pl*, scandalmongering *no pl*

Tratsch|maul NT , **Tratsch|tan|te** F (*pej inf*) scandalmonger, gossip

Trat|te ['tratə] F **-, -n** (*Fin*) draft

Trau|al|tar M altar

Trau|be ['traubə] F **-, -n** (*einzelne Beere*) grape; (*ganze Frucht*) bunch of grapes; (= *Blütenstand*) raceme (*spec*); (*fig*) (*von Bienen*) cluster; (= *Menschentraube*) bunch, cluster; **~n** (*Fruchtart*) grapes

Trau|ben-: **Trau|ben|le|se** F grape harvest; **Trau|ben|saft** M grape juice; **Trau|ben|zucker** M glucose, grape sugar

trau|en ['trauən] **VI** +*dat* to trust; **einer Sache** (*dat*) **nicht ~** to be wary of sth; **ich traute meinen Augen/Ohren nicht** I couldn't believe my eyes/ears; **ich traue dem Frieden nicht** (I think) there must be something afoot, it's too good to be true → **Weg a VR** to dare; **sich** (*acc or (rare) dat*) **~, etw zu tun** to dare (to) do sth; **ich trau mich nicht** I daren't, I dare not; **sich auf die Straße/nach Hause/zum Chef ~** to dare to go out/home/to one's boss **VT** to marry; **sich standesamtlich/kirchlich ~ lassen** to get married in a registry office (*Brit*) or in a civil ceremony/in church

Trau|er ['trauɐ] ✪ 51.4 F **-**, *no pl* (= *das Trauern, Trauerzeit, Trauerkleidung*) mourning; (= *Schmerz, Leid*) sorrow, grief; **~ haben/tragen** to be in mourning; **in tiefer ~ ...** (much loved and) sadly missed by ...

Trau|er-: **Trau|er|an|zei|ge** F obituary, death notice; **Trau|er|ar|beit** F *no pl* (*Psych*) grieving; **Trau|er|bin|de** F black armband; **Trauer|bot|schaft** F sad news *sing, no indef art*; **Trau|er|brief** M letter announcing sb's death; **Trau|er|fall** M bereavement, death; **Trau|erfei|er** F funeral service; **Trau|er|flor** M black ribbon; **Trau|er|ge|fol|ge** NT funeral procession; **Trau|er|ge|mein|de** F mourners *pl*; **Trau|er|haus** NT house of mourning; **Trau|er|jahr** NT year of mourning; **Trau|er|kar|te** F card announcing sb's death; **Trau|er|klei|dung** F mourning; **Trau|er|kloß** M (*inf*) wet blanket (*inf*); **Trau|er|man|tel** M (*Zool*) Camberwell beauty; **Trau|er|marsch** M funeral march; **Trau|er|mie|ne** F (*inf*) long face

trau|ern ['trauən] VI to mourn (*um jdn* (for) sb, *um etw* sth); (= *Trauerkleidung tragen*) to be in mourning; **die ~den Hinterbliebenen** his/her bereaved family

Trau|er-: Trau|er|nach|richt F sad news *sing*, *no indef art*; **Trau|er|par|te** [-partə] F -, -n (*Aus*) obituary, death notice; **Trau|er|rand** M black edge or border; **Trauerränder** (*inf*) dirty fingernails; **Trau|er|schlei|er** M black or mourning veil; **Trau|er|spiel** NT tragedy; (*fig inf*) fiasco; **es ist ein ~ mit ihm** he's really pathetic; **es ist ein ~ mit dem Projekt** the project is in a bad way (*inf*) or in bad shape; **Trau|er|wei|de** F weeping willow; **Trau|er|zeit** F (period of) mourning; **Trau|er|zug** M funeral procession

Trau|fe ['traufə] F -, -n eaves *pl* → **Regen**

träu|feln ['trɔyfln] VT to dribble VI *aux haben or sein* (*old, geh: Wasser*) to trickle

Trau|for|mel F marriage vows *pl*

trau|lich ['traulıç] ADJ cosy (*Brit*), cozy (*US*) ADV **~ zusammenleben** to live together harmoniously or in harmony

Trau|lich|keit F -, *no pl* cosiness (*Brit*), coziness (*US*)

Traum [traum] M -(e)s, **Träume** ['trɔymə] (*lit, fig*) dream; (= *Tagtraum auch*) daydream, reverie; **sie lebt wie im ~** she is living (as if) in a dream or (*nach Schock*) daze; **er fühlte sich wie im ~** he felt as if he were dreaming; **es war immer sein ~, ein großes Haus zu besitzen** he had always dreamed of owning a large house; **aus der ~!**, **der ~ ist aus!** it's all over; **aus der ~ vom neuen Auto** that's put paid to your/my *etc* dreams of a new car; **dieser ~ ist ausgeträumt** this dream is over; **der ~ meiner schlaflosen Nächte** (*hum inf*) the man/woman of my dreams; **Träume sind Schäume** (*prov*) dreams are but shadows → **einfallen g**

Trau|ma ['trauma] NT -s, **Traumen** or -ta [-mən, -ta] (*Med, Psych*) trauma; (*fig auch*) nightmare

Traum|ar|beit F , *no pl* (*Psych*) dreaming

trau|ma|tisch [trau'ma:tıʃ] ADJ (*Psych*) traumatic; (*fig auch*) nightmarish

trau|ma|ti|sie|ren [traumati'zi:rən] *ptp* **traumatisiert** VT to traumatize, to have a traumatizing effect on VI to have a traumatizing effect

Traum-: Traum|be|ruf M dream job, job of one's dreams; **Traum|bild** NT vision; **Traum|deu|ter(in)** M(F) interpreter of dreams; **Traum|deu|tung** F dream interpretation, interpretation of dreams

Trau|men *pl von* **Trauma**

träu|men ['trɔymən] VI to dream; (= *tagträumen auch*) to daydream; (*inf*: = *nicht aufpassen*) to (day)dream, to be in a dream; **von jdm/etw ~** to dream about sb/sth; (= *sich ausmalen*) to dream of sb/sth; **mir träumte, dass ...** I dreamed that ...; **träum(e) süß!** sweet dreams!; **vor sich hin ~, mit offenen Augen ~** to daydream; **du träumst wohl!** (*inf*) you must be joking!, dream on! (*inf*); **das hätte ich mir nicht ~ lassen** I'd never have thought it possible VT to dream; *Traum* to have; **etwas Schönes/Schreckliches ~** to have a pleasant/an unpleasant dream

Träu|mer ['trɔymɐ] M -s, -, **Träu|me|rin** [-ərın] F -, -nen (day)dreamer; (= *Fantast*) dreamer, visionary

Träu|me|rei [trɔymə'rai] F -, -en **a** *no pl* (= *das Träumen*) (day)dreaming **b** (= *Vorstellung*) daydream, reverie

träu|me|risch ['trɔymərıʃ] ADJ dreamy; (= *schwärmerisch*) wistful

Traum-: Traum|fab|rik F (*pej*) dream factory; **Traum|frau** F (*inf*) dream woman; **die ~** the woman of one's dreams; **eine absolute ~** the perfect or one's ideal woman; **traum|haft** ADJ (= *fantastisch*) fantastic; (= *wie im Traum*) dreamlike ADV (= *fantastisch*) fantastically; **~ aussehen** to look fantastic; **~ schönes Wetter** fantastic weather; **~ leere Strände** fantastic deserted beaches

Trau|mi|net ['trauminɛt] M -s, -e (*Aus inf*) coward

Traum-: Traum|job M ideal job, plum job (*inf*); **Traum|mann** M (*inf*) dream man; **der Traummaunn** the man of one's dreams; **ein absoluter ~** the perfect or one's ideal man; **Traum|paar** NT perfect couple; **Traum|rei|se** F trip of a lifetime, dream holiday (*esp Brit*) or vacation (*US*); **Traum|tän|zer(in)** M(F) dreamer; **traum|tän|ze|risch** ADJ dreamy, idealistic; **traum|ver|lo|ren** ADJ dreamy ADV dreamily, as if in a dream; **traum|wand|le|risch** [-vandlərıʃ] ADJ somnambulistic; **mit ~er Sicherheit** with instinctive certainty ADV **~ sicher** instinctively certain

Trau|re|de F marriage sermon; (*im Standesamt*) marriage address

trau|rig ['trauriç] ADJ sad; (= *unglücklich*) *Verhältnisse, Leben auch* unhappy; *Blick auch* sorrowful; (= *beklagenswert*) *Zustand* sad, sorry; *Leistung, Erfolg, Rekord* pathetic, sorry; *Wetter* miserable; *Berühmtheit* notorious; **die ~e Realität** or **Wirklichkeit** the sad reality; **die ~e Bilanz** the tragic toll; **das ist doch ~, was er da geleistet hat** what he's done is pathetic; **das sind ja ~e Verhältnisse, wenn ...** it is a sorry or sad state of affairs when ...; **es ist ~, wenn** it is sad if ... ADV sadly; (= *tief betrübt*) sorrowfully; **~ weggehen** to go away sadly or feeling sad; **mit meinen Finanzen/der Wirtschaft sieht es sehr ~ aus** my finances are/the economy is in a very sorry state; **~, ~** dear, dear; **wie sieht es damit aus? – ~(, ~)** what are the prospects for that? – pretty bad or not at all good; **um meine Zukunft sieht es ~ aus** my future doesn't look too bright

Trau|rig|keit F -, -en sadness; **allgemeine ~** a general feeling of sadness → **Kind**

Trau-: Trau|ring M wedding ring; **Trau|schein** M marriage certificate

traut [traut] ADJ (*liter, hum*) (= *gemütlich*) cosy (*Brit*), cozy (*US*); *Harmonie* sweet; (= *vertraut*) familiar; *Freund* close; **im ~en Kreise** among one's family and friends; **ein Abend im ~en Heim** an evening at home; **~es Heim, Glück allein** (*Prov*) home sweet home

Trau|te ['trautə] F **~ haben** (*inf*) to have the guts (*inf*); **keine ~ haben** (*inf*) not to have the guts (*inf*)

Trau|ung ['trauʊŋ] F -, -en wedding, wedding or marriage ceremony

Trau|zeu|ge M , **Trau|zeu|gin** F witness (*at marriage ceremony*)

Tra|ves|tie [traves'ti:] F -, -n [-'ti:ən] travesty

tra|ves|tie|ren [traves'ti:rən] *ptp* **travestiert** VT to travesty, to make a travesty of

Tre|be ['tre:bə] F (*inf*) **auf ~ gehen** to run away from home; **auf ~ sein** to be a runaway

Tre|ber ['tre:bɐ] PL (= *Biertreber*) spent hops *pl* (*Brit*), hop pulp (*US*); (= *Weintreber*) marc *sing*; (= *Fruchttreber*) pomace *sing*

Treck [trɛk] M -s, -s trek, trail; (= *Leute*) train; (= *Wagen etc*) wagon train

Tre|cker ['trɛkɐ] M -s, - tractor

Tre|cking ['trɛkıŋ] ▲ NT -s, *no pl* → **Trekking**

Treff[1] [trɛf] NT -s, -s (*Cards*) club; **die ~sieben** the seven of clubs; **das ~as** the ace of clubs

Treff[2] M -s, -s (*inf*) (= *Treffen*) meeting, get-together (*inf*); (= *Treffpunkt*) haunt, rendezvous, meeting place

tref|fen ['trɛfn] *pret* **traf** [tra:f], *ptp* **getroffen** [gə'trɔfn] VT **a** (*durch Schlag, Schuss etc*) to hit (*an/in +dat* on, *in +acc* in); (*Blitz, Faust*) to strike, to hit; (*Unglück*) to strike; **auf dem Foto bist du gut getroffen** (*inf*) that's a good photo or picture of you → **Schlag a**
b (*fig: = kränken*) to hurt
c (= *betreffen*) to hit, to affect; **es trifft immer die Falschen** it's always the wrong people who are hit or affected; **ihn trifft keine Schuld** he's not to blame
d (= *finden*) to hit upon, to find; (*lit, fig*) *Ton* to hit; **du hasts getroffen** (*mit Antwort*) you've hit the nail on the head; (*mit Geschenk*) that's the very thing → *auch* **Nerv**
e (*jdm begegnen, mit jdm zusammenkommen*) to meet; (= *antreffen*) to find
f **es gut/schlecht ~** to be fortunate or lucky/unlucky (*mit with*); **es mit dem Wetter/der Unterkunft gut/schlecht ~** to have good/bad weather/accommodation; **ich hätte es schlechter ~ können** it could have been worse
g *Vorbereitungen, Anstalten etc* to make; *Vereinbarung* to reach; *Entscheidung* to make, to take; *Vorsorge, Maßnahmen* to take
VI **a** (*Schlag, Schuss etc*) to hit; **der Schuss/er hat getroffen** the shot/he hit it/him *etc*; **tödlich getroffen** (*von Schuss, Pfeil etc*) fatally wounded; **nicht ~** to miss; **gut/schlecht ~** to aim well/badly; **getroffen!** a hit → **Schwarze(s)**
b *aux sein* (= *stoßen*) **auf jdn/etw ~** to meet sb/sth
c (= *verletzen*) to hurt; **sich getroffen fühlen** to feel hurt; (= *auf sich beziehen*) to take it personally
VR (= *zusammentreffen*) to meet; **unsere Interessen ~ sich im Sport** we are both/all interested in sport
VR *impers* **es trifft sich, dass ...** it (just) happens that ...; **das trifft sich gut/schlecht, dass ...** it is convenient/inconvenient that ...

Tref|fen ['trɛfn] NT -s, - meeting; (*Sport, Mil*) encounter; **ins ~ führen** (*Mil*) to send into battle; (*fig*) to put forward

tref|fend ADJ *Beispiel, Bemerkung* apt, apposite (*form*); *Ähnlichkeit* striking ADV aptly, appropriately; **jdn ~ nachahmen** to do a brilliant imitation of sb; **~ bemerken** to remark aptly; **etw ~ darstellen** to describe sth perfectly; **man hätte es nicht ~ vergleichen können** you couldn't have made a more apt comparison

Tref|fer ['trɛfɐ] M -s, - hit; (= *Tor*) goal; (*fig*) (= *Erfolg*) hit; (= *Gewinnlos*) winner; **das Geschenk/das Auto war ein ~** the present/car was just right; **einen ~ erzielen** or **landen** (*inf*) to score a hit; (*Ftbl*) to score a goal

Tref|fer|quo|te F hit rate; (*Ftbl*) number of goals scored; (*bei Ratespiel etc*) score

treff|lich ['trɛflıç] (*liter*) ADJ splendid, excellent ADV splendidly, excellently

Treff-: Treff|punkt M rendezvous, meeting place; **einen ~ ausmachen** to arrange where or somewhere to meet; **treff|si|cher** ADJ *Stürmer etc* accurate; (*fig*) *Bemerkung* apt; *Urteil* sound, unerring; **Treff|si|cher|heit** F (*von Stürmer etc*) accuracy; (*von Bemerkung*) aptness; (*von Urteil*) soundness

Treib-: Treib|an|ker M sea anchor, drag anchor; **Treib|eis** NT drift ice

trei|ben ['traibn] *pret* **trieb** [tri:p], *ptp* **getrieben** [gə'tri:bn] VT **a** (*lit, fig*) to drive; (*auf Treibjagd*) *Wild* to beat; *Teig* to make rise; (*fig: = drängen*) to rush; (= *antreiben*) to push; **jdn zum** or **in den Wahnsinn/zur** or **in die Verzweiflung/zum** or **in den Selbstmord ~** to drive sb mad/to despair/to (commit) suicide; **jdn zur Eile/Arbeit ~** to make sb hurry (up)/work; **jdn zum Äußersten ~** to push sb too far; **die Preise (in die Höhe) ~** to push or drive prices up; **die ~de Kraft bei etw sein** to be the driving force behind sth
b (= *Reaktion erzeugen*) to bring; **jdn den Schweiß/das Blut ins Gesicht ~** to make sb sweat/blush; **der Wind treibt mir Tränen in die**

Augen the wind makes my eyes water; **der Gedanke treibt mir Tränen in die Augen** the thought brings tears to my eyes
　c (= *einschlagen*) *Nagel, Pfahl etc* to drive
　d (= *bearbeiten, formen*) *Metall* to beat
　e (= *ausüben, betreiben*) *Handel, Geschäfte* to do; *Studien, Politik* to pursue; *Gewerbe* to carry on; *Sport* to do; (= *machen*) to do; *Schabernack, Unfug, Unsinn* to be up to; *Spaß* to have; *Aufwand* to make, to create; *Unzucht* to commit; **was treibst du?** what are you up to?; **Missbrauch mit etw ~** to abuse sth; **Handel mit etw/jdm ~** to trade in sth/with sb; **Wucher ~** to profiteer
　f wenn du es weiter so treibst … if you go *or* carry on like that …; **es toll ~** to have a wild time; **es zu toll ~** to overdo it; **es schlimm ~** to behave badly; **es zu bunt** *or* **weit ~** to go too far; **er treibt es noch so weit, dass er hinausgeworfen wird** if he goes on like that, he'll get thrown out; **es mit jdm ~** (*inf*) to have it off with sb (*Brit inf*), to get it on with sb (*US sl*), to have sex with sb
　g (= *hervorbringen*) *Blüten, Knospen etc* to sprout, to put forth; (*im Treibhaus*) to force → **Blüte a**
VI a *aux sein* (= *sich fortbewegen*) to drift; **sich ~ lassen** (*lit, fig*) to drift; **sich von der Stimmung ~ lassen** to let oneself be carried along by the mood; **die Dinge ~ lassen** to let things go
　b (= *wachsen*) to sprout
　c (*Bier, Kaffee, Medizin etc*) to have a diuretic effect; (*Hefe*) to make dough *etc* rise; **~de Medikamente** diuretics

Trei|ben ['traibn] NT **-s, -** **a** (= *Getriebe*) hustle and bustle; (*von Schneeflocken*) swirling; **ich beobachte dein ~ schon lange** I've been watching what you've been (getting) up to for a long time **b** = **Treibjagd**

Trei|ber¹ ['traibɐ] M **-s, -** (*Comput*) driver

Trei|ber² ['traibɐ] M **-s, -**, **Trei|be|rin** [-ərɪn] F **-, -nen** (= *Viehtreiber*) drover; (*Hunt*) beater

Treib-: Treib|gas NT (*bei Sprühdosen*) propellant; **Treib|gut** NT flotsam and jetsam *pl*

Treib|haus NT hothouse

Treib|haus-: Treib|haus|ef|fekt M (*Met*) greenhouse effect; **Treib|haus|gas** NT greenhouse gas; **Treib|haus|luft** F **a** hothouse *or* greenhouse air **b** (*fig*) hot, humid atmosphere; **Treib|haus|pflan|ze** F hothouse *or* greenhouse plant; **Treib|haus|tem|pe|ra|tur** F hothouse *or* greenhouse temperature; **hier herrscht die reinste ~!** it's like a greenhouse here

Treib-: Treib|holz NT driftwood; **Treib|jagd** F battue (*spec*), shoot (*in which game is sent up by beaters*); **Treib|mit|tel** NT (*in Sprühdosen*) propellant; (*Cook*) raising agent; **Treib|netz** NT drift net; **Treib|sand** M quicksand; **Treib|schlag** M (*Sport*) drive; **Treib|stoff** M fuel; (= *Raketentreibstoff auch*) propellant

trei|deln ['traidln] VT to tow

Trek|king ['trɛkɪŋ] NT **-s**, *no pl* trekking

Trek|king|rad NT hybrid bike

Tre|ma ['tre:ma] NT **-s, -s** *or* **-ta** [-ta] dieresis

tre|mo|lie|ren [tremo'li:rən] *ptp* **tremoliert** VI to quaver

Tre|mo|lo ['tre:molo] NT **-s, -s** *or* **Tremoli** [-li] tremolo

Trench|coat ['trɛntʃko:t] M **-(s), -s** trench coat

Trend [trɛnt] M **-s, -s** trend; **voll im ~ liegen** to follow the trend

Trend-: Trend|mel|dung F (*Pol*) report on voting trends *or* patterns; (*fig*) projection; **Trend|scout** ['trɛntskaut] M **-(s), -s** trend spotter; **Trend|set|ter** ['trɛntsɛtɐ] M **-s, -**, **Trend|set|te|rin** [-ərɪn] F **-, -nen** trendsetter; **Trend|wen|de** F new trend

trenn|bar ADJ separable; **ein nicht ~es Wort** an inseparable word

Trenn|blatt NT divider

tren|nen ['trɛnən] VT **a** (= *entfernen*) *Mensch, Tier* to separate (*von* from); (*Tod*) to take away (*von* from); (= *in Teile teilen, abtrennen*) to sepa-

rate; *Kopf, Glied etc* to sever; (= *abmachen*) to detach (*von* from); *Aufgenähtes* to take off, to remove; **zwei Teile voneinander ~** to separate two parts; **etw in zwei Hälften ~** to divide *or* split sth into two halves
　b (= *aufspalten, scheiden*) *Bestandteile, Eier, Raufende* to separate; *Partner, Freunde* to split up; (*räumlich*) *Begriffe* to differentiate, to distinguish (between); (*nach Rasse, Geschlecht*) to segregate; **voneinander getrennt werden** to be separated; **Ursache und Folge ~** to make *or* draw a distinction between cause and results; **Gut von Böse ~** to distinguish between good and evil, to differentiate *or* distinguish good from evil; **uns trennt zu vieles** we have too little in common; **jetzt kann uns nichts mehr ~** now nothing can ever come between us; **alles Trennende (zwischen uns/den beiden)** all our/their differences; **das Radio trennt die Sender gut/schlecht** the radio has good/bad selectivity → *auch* **getrennt**
　c (= *in Bestandteile zerlegen*) *Kleid* to take to pieces; (*Ling*) *Wort* to divide, to split up; (*Chem*) *Gemisch* to separate (out)
VR a (= *auseinander gehen*) to separate; (*Partner, Eheleute etc*) to split up, to separate; (= *Abschied nehmen*) to part; **sich von jdm/der Firma ~** to leave sb/the firm; **die Firma trennte sich von ihrem Geschäftsführer** the firm parted company with its managing director; **die zwei Mannschaften trennten sich 2:0** the final score was 2-0; **sich im Guten/Bösen ~** to part on good/bad terms
　b (= *weggeben, verkaufen etc*) **sich von etw ~** to part with sth; **er konnte sich davon nicht ~** he couldn't bear to part with it; (*von Plan*) he couldn't give it up; (*von Anblick*) he couldn't take his eyes off it
　c (= *sich teilen*) (*Wege, Flüsse*) to divide; **hier ~ sich unsere Wege** (*fig*) now we must go our separate ways
VI (*zwischen Begriffen*) to draw *or* make a distinction

Trenn-: Trenn|kost F food combining, Hay diet; **Trenn|mes|ser** NT (*Sew*) unpicker; **Trenn|punkt** M (*Ling*) dieresis; **trenn|scharf** ADJ **~ sein** to have good selectivity; **Trenn|schär|fe** F selectivity

Trenn|strich M (*Typ*) hyphen

Tren|nung ['trɛnʊŋ] F **-, -en** **a** (= *Abschied*) parting **b** (= *Getrenntwerden, Getrenntsein*) separation; (*in Teile*) division; (*von Begriffen*) distinction; (*von Sender*) selectivity; (*von Wort*) division; (= *Rassentrennung, Geschlechtertrennung*) segregation; **die Partner entschlossen sich zu einer ~** the partners decided to split up *or* separate; **in ~ leben** to be separated; **~ von Tisch und Bett** judicial separation

Tren|nungs-: Tren|nungs|ent|schä|di|gung F , **Tren|nungs|geld** NT separation allowance, alimony (*dated*); **Tren|nungs|schmerz** M pain of parting; **Tren|nungs|strich** M hyphen; **einen ~ ziehen** (*fig*) to make a clear distinction (*zwischen* between); **Tren|nungs|wand** F partition (wall); **Tren|nungs|zei|chen** NT hyphen

Trenn|wand F partition (wall)

Trenn|zei|chen NT hyphen

Tren|se ['trɛnzə] F **-, -n** snaffle

trepp|auf [trɛp'|auf] ADV **~, treppab** up and down stairs

Trep|pe ['trɛpə] F **-, -n** **a** (= *Aufgang*) (flight of) stairs *pl*, staircase; (*im Freien*) (flight of) steps *pl*; **eine ~** a staircase, a flight of stairs/steps; **wir haben die ~** (*inf*) **wir sind mit der ~ an der Reihe** (*inf*) it's our turn to clean *or* do the stairs; **die ~ hinaufgehen/hinuntergehen** to go up/down the stairs, to go upstairs/downstairs; **du bist wohl die ~ hinuntergefallen!** (*fig inf*) what's happened to your hair? → **hinauffallen b** (*inf*: = *Stufe*) step; **~n steigen** to climb stairs **c** (*inf*: = *Stockwerk*) floor

Trep|pen-: Trep|pen|ab|satz M half landing; **Trep|pen|ge|län|der** NT banister; **Trep|pen|haus** NT stairwell; **im ~** on the stairs; **Trep|pen|stu|fe** F step, stair; **Trep|pen|witz** M **ein ~ der Weltgeschichte** an irony of history

Tre|sen ['tre:zn] M **-s, -** (= *Theke*) bar; (= *Ladentisch*) counter

Tre|sor [tre'zo:ɐ] M **-s, -e** (= *Raum*) strongroom, vault; (= *Schrank*) safe

Tre|sor|kna|cker M , **Tre|sor|kna|cke|rin** [-ərɪn] F **-, -nen** (*inf*) safe-breaker

Tre|sor|raum M strongroom

Tres|se ['trɛsə] F **-, -n** braid

Tres|ter ['trɛstɐ] PL (= *Biertrester*) spent hops *pl* (*Brit*), hop pulp (*US*); (= *Weintrester*) marc *sing*; (= *Fruchttrester*) pomace *sing*

Tret-: Tret|au|to NT pedal car; **Tret|boot** NT pedal boat, pedalo (*Brit*); **Tret|ei|mer** M pedal bin

tre|ten ['tre:tn] *pret* **trat** [tra:t], *ptp* **getreten** [gə'tre:tn] **VI a** (= *ausschlagen, mit Fuß anstoßen*) to kick (*gegen etw* sth, *nach* out at)
　b *aux sein* (*mit Raumangabe*) to step; **hier kann man nicht mehr ~** there is no room to move here; **vom Schatten ins Helle ~** to move out of the shadow into the light; **näher an etw** (*acc*) **~** to move *or* step closer to sth; **vor die Kamera ~** (*im Fernsehen*) to appear on TV; (*im Film*) to appear in a film *or* on the screen; **in den Vordergrund/Hintergrund ~** to step forward/back; (*fig*) to come to the forefront/to recede into the background; **an jds Stelle ~** to take sb's place → **nah(e) ADV a**
　c *aux sein or haben* (*in Loch, Pfütze, auf Gegenstand etc*) to step, to tread; **jdm auf den Fuß ~** to step on sb's foot, to tread (*esp Brit*) *or* step on sb's toe; **jdm auf die Füße ~** (*fig*) to tread (*esp Brit*) *or* step on sb's toes; **jdm auf den Schlips** (*inf*) *or* **Schwanz** (*sl*) **~** to tread on sb's toes; **sich auf den Schlips** (*inf*) *or* **Schwanz** (*sl*) **getreten fühlen** to feel offended, to be put out → **Stelle a**
　d *aux sein or haben* (= *betätigen*) **in die Pedale ~** to pedal hard; **aufs Gas(pedal) ~** (= *Pedal betätigen*) to press the accelerator; (= *schnell fahren*) to put one's foot down (*inf*), to step on it (*inf*); **auf die Bremse ~** to brake, to put one's foot on the brake
　e *aux sein* (= *hervortreten, sichtbar werden*) **Wasser trat aus allen Ritzen und Fugen** water was coming out of every nook and cranny; **der Schweiß trat ihm auf die Stirn** sweat appeared on his forehead; **Tränen traten ihr in die Augen** tears came to her eyes, her eyes filled with tears; **der Fluss trat über die Ufer** the river overflowed its banks; **der Mond trat aus den Wolken** the moon appeared from behind the clouds; **es trat plötzlich wieder in mein Bewusstsein** it suddenly came back to me
　f *aux sein* (*Funktionsverb*) (= *beginnen*) to start, to begin; (= *eintreten*) to enter; **in jds Leben** (*acc*) **~** to come into *or* enter sb's life; **ins Leben ~** to come into being; **in den Ruhestand ~** to retire; **in den Streik** *or* **Ausstand ~** to go on strike; **in den Staatsdienst/Stand der Ehe** *or* **Ehestand ~** to enter the civil service/into the state of matrimony; **mit jdm in Verbindung ~** to get in touch with sb; **in die entscheidende Phase ~** to enter the crucial phase → **Erscheinung a, Kraft d**
VT a (= *einen Fußtritt geben, stoßen*) to kick; (*Sport*) *Ecke, Freistoß* to take; **jdn ans Bein ~** to kick sb's leg, to kick sb on *or* in the leg; **jdn mit dem Fuß ~** to kick sb; **sich** (*dat*) **in den Hintern ~** (*fig inf*) to kick oneself
　b (= *mit Fuß betätigen*) *Spinnrad, Nähmaschine, Webstuhl, Blasebalg* to operate (*using one's foot*); **die Bremse ~** to brake, to put on the brakes; **die Pedale ~** to pedal
　c (= *trampeln*) *Pfad, Weg, Bahn* to tread; **sich** (*dat*) **einen Splitter in den Fuß ~** to get a splinter in one's foot → **Wasser c**
　d (*fig*) (= *schlecht behandeln*) to shove around

(*inf*); **jdn ~** (*inf*: = *antreiben*) to get at sb **e** (= *begatten*) to tread, to mate with

Tre|ter ['tre:tɐ] M **-s, -** (*inf*) comfortable shoe

Tret-: **Tret|mi|ne** F (*Mil*) (antipersonnel) mine; **Tret|mühl|le** F (*lit, fig*) treadmill; **in der ~ sein** to be in a rut (*inf*); **die tägliche ~** the daily grind; **Tret|rad** NT treadmill; **Tret|rol|ler** M scooter

treu [trɔy] ADJ *Freund, Sohn, Kunde etc* loyal; *Diener auch* devoted; *Seele auch, Hund, Gatte etc* faithful; *Abbild* true; *Gedenken* respectful; (= *treuherzig*) trusting; *Miene* innocent; **jdm in ~er Liebe verbunden sein** to be bound to sb by loyalty and love; **jdm ~ sein/bleiben** to be/remain faithful to sb; (= *nicht betrügen auch*) to be/remain true to sb; **sich** (*dat*) **selbst ~ bleiben** to be true to oneself; **seinen Grundsätzen ~ bleiben** to stick to or remain true to one's principles; **der Erfolg ist ihr ~ geblieben** success kept coming her way; **das Glück ist ihr ~ geblieben** her luck held (out); **~ wie Gold** faithful and loyal; (*Diener etc auch*) faithful as a dog; **dein ~er Freund** (*old*) yours truly; **jdm etw zu ~en Händen übergeben** to give sth to sb for safe-keeping

ADV faithfully; *dienen auch* loyally; *sorgen* devotedly; (= *treuherzig*) trustingly; *ansehen* innocently; **~ ergeben** devoted, loyal, faithful; **jdm ~ ergeben sein** to be loyally devoted to sb; **~ sorgend** devoted; **~ und brav** (*Erwachsener*) dutifully; (*Kind*) like a good boy/girl, as good as gold

Treu-: **Treu|bruch** M breach of faith; **treu|brü|chig** ADJ faithless, false; (*jdm*) **~ werden** to break faith (with sb); **treu|deutsch** ADJ truly German; (*pej*) typically German; **treu|doof** (*inf*) ADJ stupidly naive ADV stupidly and naively

Treue ['trɔyə] F **-,** *no pl* (*von Freund, Sohn, Kunde etc*) loyalty; (*von Diener auch*) devotion, devotedness; (*von Hund*) faithfulness; (= *eheliche Treue*) faithfulness, fidelity; **der Flagge ~ geloben** to pledge allegiance to the flag; **sie gelobten einander ewige ~** they vowed to be eternally faithful to one another; **jdm die ~ halten** to keep faith with sb; *Ehegatten etc* to remain faithful to sb; **auf Treu und Glauben** in good faith; **in alter ~** for old times' sake; **in alter ~, Dein Franz** Yours (as) ever, Franz → **brechen VT a**

Treu|eid M oath of allegiance

Treue-: **Treu|e|pflicht** F loyalty (*owed by employee to employer and vice versa*); **Treu|e|prä|mie** F long-service bonus; **Treu|e|punkt** M (*zur Anrechnung für Kundenkarte etc*) reward or loyalty point

treu|er|ge|ben △ ADJ *attr* treu ADV

Treu|e|schwur M oath of allegiance; (*von Geliebtem etc*) vow to be faithful

Treu|hand F **,** *no pl* **a** trust **b** = Treuhandanstalt

---

TREUHANDANSTALT

The **Treuhandanstalt**, also more informally known as the **Treuhand**, was an organization which, from 1990 to 1994, took over the state-owned firms of the former East Germany after re-unification and sought to bring them into the private sector. Many of the firms were actually closed down by the **Treuhandanstalt**, since the machinery was out of date and the company structure could not cope with the changed circumstances. The **Treuhandanstalt** was wound up in 1994 in accordance with the Unification Treaty, but since then various successor organizations have carried on its work.

Treu|hän|der [-hɛndɐ] M **-s, -**, **Treu|hän|de|rin** [-ərɪn] F **-, -nen** trustee, fiduciary (*form*)

Treu|hand|ge|sell|schaft F trust or fiduciary (*form*) company

Treu-: **treu|her|zig** ADJ innocent, trusting ADV innocently, trustingly; **Treu|her|zig|keit** ['trɔy-hɛrtsɪçkait] F **-,** *no pl* innocence; **treu|los** ADJ disloyal, faithless; **du ~es Stück** (*inf*) you wretch → **Tomate** ADV disloyally, faithlessly; **~ an jdm handeln** to fail sb; **Treu|lo|sig|keit** F **-,** *no pl* disloyalty, faithlessness; **treu|sor|gend** △ ADJ *attr* → treu ADV

Tri|a|de [tri'a:də] F **-, -n a** (*Rel, Liter, Math*) triad; (*Rel, fig auch*) trinity **b** (= *Verbrecherorganisation*) triad

Tri|a|ge [tri'a:ʒə] F **-, -n a** (*Med*) triage **b** (*Comm*) lower grade goods *pl*

Tri|an|gel ['tri:aŋl] M OR (AUS) NT **-s, -** triangle

Tri|as ['tri:as] F **-,** *no pl* Triassic (Period)

Tri|ath|lon ['tri:atlɔn] M **-, -e** (*Sport*) triathlon

Tri|ba|lis|mus [triba'lɪsmʊs] M **-,** *no pl* tribalism

Tri|bun [tri'bu:n] M **-s** or **-en, -e(n)**, **Tri|bu|nin** [-'bu:nɪn] F **-, -nen** tribune

Tri|bu|nal [tribu'na:l] NT **-s, -e** tribunal

Tri|bu|nat [tribu'na:t] NT **-(e)s, -e** tribunate

Tri|bü|ne [tri'by:nə] F **-, -n** (= *Rednertribüne*) platform, rostrum; (= *Zuschauertribüne, Zuschauer*) stand; (= *Haupttribüne*) grandstand

Tri|bu|nin F **-, -nen** tribune

Tri|but [tri'bu:t] M **-(e)s, -e** (*Hist*) tribute, dues *pl*; (*fig*) tribute; (= *Opfer*) toll; **jdm ~ entrichten** or (*fig*) **zollen** to pay tribute to sb

tri|but|pflich|tig [-pflɪçtɪç] ADJ tributary (*rare*), obliged to pay tribute

Tri|chi|ne [trɪ'çi:nə] F **-, -n** trichina

Trichinen-: **tri|chi|nen|hal|tig** ADJ trichinous; **Tri|chi|nen|schau** F meat inspection (*to check for trichinae*); **Tri|chi|nen|schau|er** [-ʃauɐ] M **-s, -**, **Tri|chi|nen|schau|e|rin** [-ərɪn] F **-, -nen** meat inspector

Trich|ter ['trɪçtɐ] M **-s, -** funnel; (= *Schüttgutbehälter*) hopper; (= *Bombentrichter*) crater; (*von Grammofon*) horn; (*von Trompete, Megafon etc*) bell; (*von Hörgerät*) trumpet; (*von Lautsprecher*) cone; **jdn auf den ~ bringen** (*inf*) to give sb a clue; **auf den ~ kommen** (*inf*) to catch (*Brit*) or cotton on (*inf*) → **Nürnberg**

trich|ter|för|mig ADJ funnel-shaped, funnel-like

Trick [trɪk] M **-s, -s** or (*rare*) **-e** trick; (*betrügerisch auch, raffiniert*) ploy, dodge; (= *Tipp, Rat*) tip; **ein fauler/gemeiner ~** a mean or dirty trick; **keine faulen ~s!** no funny business! (*inf*); **das ist der ganze ~** that's all there is to it; **den ~ raushaben, wie man etw macht** (*inf*) to have got the knack of doing sth; **der ~ dabei ist, ...** the trick is to ...; **da ist doch ein ~ dabei** there is a trick to (doing) it; **jdm einen ~ verraten** to give sb a tip

Trick-: **Trick|be|trug** M confidence trick (*esp Brit*) or game (*US*); **Trick|be|trü|ger(in)** M(F), **Trick|dieb(in)** M(F) confidence trickster; **Trick|film** M trick film; (= *Zeichentrickfilm*) cartoon (film); **Trick|kis|te** F (*von Zauberer*) box of tricks; (*fig inf*) bag of tricks; **trick|reich** (*inf*) ADJ tricky; (= *raffiniert*) clever ADV **erschwindeln, abgaunern** through various tricks; **~ vorgehen, sich ~ verhalten** to be very tricky

trick|sen ['trɪksn] (*inf*) VI to fiddle (*inf*); (*Sport*) to feint; **fantastisch, wie er mit den Karten trickst** it's amazing what he can do with cards VT to fiddle (*inf*)

Trick|ser ['trɪksɐ] M **-s, -** (*inf*) tricky customer, trickster (*inf*); (*Sport auch*) deceptive or inventive player

Trick|ski NT trick skiing, hot dogging (*esp US*)

Trick|tas|te F trick or superimpose button

trieb *pret von* **treiben**

Trieb [tri:p] M **-(e)s, -e** [-bə] **a** (= *Naturtrieb, auch Psych*) drive; (= *Drang*) urge; (= *Verlangen*) desire, urge; (= *Neigung, Hang*) inclination; (= *Selbsterhaltungstrieb, Fortpflanzungstrieb*) instinct; **sie ist von ihren ~en beherrscht** she is ruled completely by her physical urges or desires; **ei-nen ~ zum Verbrechen haben** to have criminal urges **b** (*Bot*) shoot **c** (*Tech*) drive

Trieb-: **Trieb|ab|fuhr** F (*Psych*) = Triebbefriedigung; **trieb|ar|tig** ADJ *attr Verhalten* instinctive; (*von Sexualverbrecher etc*) compulsive; **Trieb|be|frie|di|gung** F gratification of a physical urge; (*sexuell*) gratification of sexual urges; **Trieb|fe|der** F (*fig*) motivating force (**+gen** behind); **trieb|haft** ADJ *Handlungen* compulsive; **ein ~er Instinkt** an instinctive urge; **sie hat ein sehr ~es Wesen, sie ist ein ~er Mensch** she is ruled by her physical urges or desires; **Trieb|haf|tig|keit** ['tri:phaftɪçkait] F **-,** *no pl* domination by one's physical urges; **Trieb|hand|lung** F act motivated by one's physical urges; **Trieb|kraft** F (*Mech*) motive power; (*Bot*) germinating power; (*fig*) driving force; **Trieb|le|ben** NT physical activities *pl*; (= *Geschlechtsleben*) sex life; **Trieb|mensch** M creature of instinct; **Trieb|mit|tel** NT (*Cook*) raising agent; (*in Sprühdosen*) propellant; **Trieb|rad** NT driving wheel (*Brit*), gear wheel; **Trieb|sand** M quicksand; **Trieb|stau** M (*Psych*) build-up of physical urges; (*sexuell*) build-up of sexual urges; **Trieb|tä|ter(in)** M(F), **Trieb|ver|bre|cher(in)** M(F) sexual offender; **Trieb|wa|gen** M (*Rail*) railcar; **Trieb|werk** NT power plant; (*in Uhr*) mechanism

Trief-: **Trief|au|ge** NT (*Med*) bleary eye; **~n** (*pej*) watery eyes; (*von Mensch*) sheeplike eyes; **trief|äu|gig** ADJ watery-eyed ADV **er schaute mich ~ an** (*pej*) he looked at me with dumb devotion

trie|fen ['tri:fn] *pret* **triefte** or (*geh*) **troff** ['tri:ftə, trɔf], *ptp* **getrieft** or (*rare*) **getroffen** [gə'tri:ft, gə'trɔfn] VI to be dripping wet; (*Nase*) to run; (*Auge*) to water; **~ vor** to be dripping with; (*fig pej*) to gush with; **~d vor Nässe, ~d nass** dripping wet, wet through; **~d** soaking (wet)

Trief|na|se F (*inf*) runny nose (*inf*)

trief|nass ▲ ADJ (*inf*) dripping or soaking wet, wet through; **du bist ja ~!** (but) you're soaking wet!

trie|zen ['tri:tsn] VT (*inf*) **jdn ~** to pester sb; (= *schuften lassen*) to drive sb hard

trifft [trɪft] 3. *pers sing pres von* **treffen**

Trift [trɪft] F **-, -en** (= *Weide*) pasture; (= *Weg*) cattle/sheep track

trif|tig ['trɪftɪç] ADJ convincing; *Entschuldigung, Grund auch* good ADV convincingly

Tri|go|no|met|rie [trigonome'tri:] F **-,** *no pl* trigonometry

tri|go|no|met|risch [trigono'me:trɪʃ] ADJ trigonometric(al)

Tri|ko|lo|re [triko'lo:rə] F **-, -n** tricolour (*Brit*), tricolor (*US*)

Tri|kot[1] [tri'ko:, 'triko] M OR NT **-s,** *no pl* (= *Trikotstoff*) cotton jersey

Tri|kot[2] NT **-s, -s** (= *Hemd*) shirt, jersey; (*dated:* = *Turnanzug*) leotard; (*old:* = *Badeanzug*) bathing costume (*old*); **das gelbe ~** (*bei Tour de France*) the yellow jersey

Tri|ko|ta|ge [triko'ta:ʒə] F **-, -n** cotton jersey underwear *no pl*

Tri|kot|wer|bung [tri'ko:-] F shirt advertising

Tril|ler ['trɪlɐ] M **-s, -** (*Mus*) trill; (*von Vogel auch*) warble

tril|lern ['trɪlɐn] VTI to warble, to trill; **du trillerst wie eine Lerche** you sing like a lark

Tril|ler|pfei|fe F (*pea*) whistle

Tril|li|on [trɪ'lio:n] F **-, -en** trillion (*Brit*), quintillion (*US*)

Tri|lo|gie [trilo'gi:] F **-, -n** [-'gi:ən] trilogy

Tri|ma|ran [trima'ra:n] M OR NT **-s, -e** (*Naut*) trimaran

Tri|mes|ter [tri'mɛstɐ] NT **-s, -** term

Trimm-: **Trimm|ak|ti|on** F keep-fit campaign; **Trimm-dich-Ge|rät** NT keep-fit apparatus; **Trimm-dich-Pfad** M keep-fit trail

---

trim|men ['trɪmən] **VT** Hund, Schiff, Flugzeug to trim; (inf) Mensch, Tier to teach, to train; Funkgerät to tune; **den Motor/das Auto auf Höchstleistung ~** (inf) to soup up the engine/car (inf); **jdn auf tadelloses Benehmen ~** to teach or train sb to behave impeccably; **etw auf alt ~** to make sth look old; **auf alt getrimmt** done up to look old; **ein auf rustikal getrimmtes Restaurant** a rustic restaurant; **jdn auf einen bestimmten Typ ~** to make or mould (Brit) or mold (US) sb into a certain type **VR** to do keep-fit (exercises); **trimm dich durch Sport** keep fit with sport

Trimm-: **Trimm|ge|rät** NT keep-fit apparatus; **Trimm|pfad** M keep-fit trail

Tri|ni|tät [trini'tɛːt] F -, no pl (geh) trinity

Trink-: **trink|bar** ADJ drinkable; **Trink|brunnen** M (in öffentlichen Gebäuden) drinking fountain; **Trink|ei** NT new-laid egg

trin|ken ['trɪŋkn] pret **trank** [traŋk], ptp **getrunken** [gə'trʊŋkn] **VT** to drink; ein Bier, Tasse Tee, Flasche Wein auch to have; **alles/eine Flasche leer ~** to finish off all the drink/a bottle; **ich habe nichts zu ~ im Haus** I haven't any drink in the house; **er trinkt gern einen** (inf) he likes his drink; **(schnell) einen ~ gehen** (inf) to go for a (quick) drink → **Tisch**
VI to drink; **jdm zu ~ geben** to give sb a drink, to give sb something to drink; **lass mich mal ~** let me have a drink; **auf jds Wohl/jdn/etw ~** to drink sb's health/to sb/to sth; **er trinkt** (= ist Alkoholiker) he's a drinker
VR **sich voll** or **satt ~** to drink one's fill; **(mit Alkohol)** to get drunk; **sich arm ~** to drink one's money away
VR impers **es trinkt sich gut/schlecht daraus** it is easy/difficult to drink from; **dieser Wein trinkt sich gut** this is a pleasant or palatable wine

Trin|ker ['trɪŋkɐ] M -s, -, **Trin|ke|rin** [-ərɪn] F -, -nen drinker; (= Alkoholiker) alcoholic

Trin|ker|heil|an|stalt F (old) detoxification centre (Brit) or center (US)

Trink-: **trink|fest** ADJ **so ~ bin ich nicht** I can't hold my drink (Brit) or liquor (esp US) very well; **seine ~en Freunde** his hard-drinking friends; **Trink|fes|tig|keit** F ability to hold one's drink (Brit) or liquor (esp US); **trink|freu|dig** ADJ fond of drinking; **Trink|ge|fäß** NT drinking vessel; **Trink|ge|la|ge** NT drinking session; **Trink|geld** NT tip; **jdm ~ geben** to tip sb, to give sb a tip; **Trink|glas** NT (drinking) glass; **Trink|hal|le** F (in Heilbädern) pump room; (= Kiosk) refreshment kiosk; **Trink|halm** M drinking straw; **Trink|lied** NT drinking song; **Trink|milch** F milk; **Trink|scha|le** F drinking bowl; **Trink|scho|ko|la|de** F drinking chocolate; **Trink|spruch** M toast

Trink|was|ser NT pl -wässer drinking water; **„kein ~"** "not for drinking", "do not drink"

Trink|was|ser-: **Trink|was|ser|brun|nen** M drinking fountain; **Trink|was|ser|ver|sor|gung** F provision of drinking water

Trio [triːo] NT -s, -s trio

Tri|o|le [tri'oːlə] F -, -n (Mus) triplet

Tri|o|lett [trio'lɛt] NT -(e)s, -e triolet

Trip [trɪp] M -s, -s (inf) trip

trip|peln ['trɪpln] VI aux haben or (bei Richtungsangabe) sein to trip (esp Brit), to skip; (Kind, alte Dame) to toddle; (geziert) to mince (Brit), to sashay (esp US); (Boxer) to dance around; (Pferd) to prance

Trip|pel|schritt M short or little step; **-e** pl (von Kleinkind) toddle sing, toddling steps pl

Trip|per ['trɪpɐ] M -s, - gonorrhoea no art (Brit), gonorrhea no art (US); **sich (dat) den ~ holen** (inf) to get a dose (of the clap) (inf)

Trip|ty|chon ['trɪptyçɔn] NT -s, Triptychen or Triptycha (Art) triptych

trist [trɪst] ADJ dreary, dismal; Farbe dull; Aussichten dismal

Tris|te ['trɪstə] F -, -n (Aus) haystack

Tris|tesse F dreariness; (= Traurigkeit) sadness

Tri|ti|um ['triːtsiʊm] NT -s, no pl (abbr **T**) tritium

tritt [trɪt] 3. pers sing pres von **treten**

Tritt [trɪt] M -(e)s, -e **a** (= Schritt) step; (= Gang) step, tread; **einen falschen ~ machen** to take a wrong step; **ich hörte ~e** I heard footsteps; **(wieder) ~ fassen** (lit, fig) to find one's/its feet (again)
b (= Gleichschritt) step; **im ~ marschieren**, **~ halten** to march in step, to keep in step
c (= Fußtritt) kick; **jdm einen ~ geben** or **versetzen** to give sb a kick, to kick sb; (fig) (= entlassen etc) to kick sb out (inf); (inf: = anstacheln) to give sb a kick in the pants (inf) or up the backside (inf); **einen ~ in den Hintern kriegen** (inf) to get a kick in the pants (inf) or up the backside (inf); (fig) to get kicked out (inf)
d (bei Trittleiter, Stufe) step; (= Gestell) steps pl; (= Trittbrett) step; (an Auto) running board
e (= Fußspur) footprint; (von Tier) track
f (Hunt: = Fuß) foot

Tritt-: **Tritt|brett** NT step; (an Auto) running board; (an Nähmaschine) treadle; **Tritt|brett|fah|rer(in)** M(F) (inf) fare dodger; (fig) copycat (inf); **Tritt|lei|ter** F stepladder; **Tritt|rol|ler** M scooter

Tri|umph [tri'ʊmf] M -(e)s, -e triumph; **im ~** in triumph; **~e feiern** to be a great success, to be very successful

tri|um|phal [triʊm'faːl] ADJ triumphant ADV triumphantly

Tri|umph-: **Tri|umph|bo|gen** M triumphal arch; **Tri|umph|ge|schrei** NT triumphant cheer, cheer of triumph

tri|um|phie|ren [triʊm'fiːrən] ptp **triumphiert** VI (= frohlocken) to rejoice, to exult; **über jdn/etw ~** (geh) to triumph over sb/sth, to overcome sb/sth

tri|um|phie|rend ADJ triumphant ADV triumphantly

Tri|umph|zug M triumphal procession

Tri|um|vi|rat [triʊmvi'raːt] NT -(e)s, -e triumvirate

tri|vi|al [tri'viaːl] ADJ trivial; Gespräch auch banal ADV trivially; **sich ~ unterhalten** to have a trivial conversation

Tri|vi|a|li|tät [triviali'tɛːt] F -, -en triviality; (von Gespräch auch) banality; (= triviale Bemerkung) banality

Tri|vi|al|li|te|ra|tur F (pej) light fiction

Tri|zeps ['triːtsɛps] M -(es), -e triceps

Tro|chä|us [trɔ'xɛːʊs] M -, Trochäen [-'xɛːən] (Poet) trochee

tro|cken ['trɔkn] ADJ **a** dry; Gebiet arid (form), dry; Gedeck without wine etc; (inf) Alkoholiker dry, off the bottle, on the wagon (inf); **~er Dunst** (Met) haze; **~ werden** to dry; (Brot) to go or get or become dry; **noch ~ nach Hause kommen** to get home dry or without getting wet; **ins Trockene kommen/gehen** to come/go into the dry (esp Brit) or out of the rain; **im Trockenen sein** to be somewhere dry or sheltered; **~en Auges** (liter) dry-eyed; **~en Fußes** (liter) without getting one's feet wet; **~ Brot essen** (liter) to eat dry bread; **auf dem Trockenen sitzen** (inf) to be in a tight spot (inf) or in difficulties → **Schäfchen, Ohr**
b (= langweilig) dry
c (= herb) Sekt, Sherry dry
d (fig) Humor, Art etc dry
ADV aufbewahren, lagern in a dry place; **das Schiff liegt ~** the ship is high and dry; **sich ~ rasieren** to use an electric razor; **die Haare ~ schneiden** to cut one's/sb's hair dry; **die Gäste ~ sitzen lassen** to leave one's guests without a drink

Tro|cken-: **Tro|cken|au|to|mat** M tumble dryer; **Tro|cken|bat|te|rie** F dry-cell battery; **Tro|cken|bee|ren|aus|le|se** F wine made from choice grapes left on the vine to dry out

at the end of the season; **Tro|cken|blu|me** F dried flower; **Tro|cken|bo|den** M drying room (in attic); **tro|cken+bü|geln** VT sep to iron dry; **Tro|cken|dock** NT dry dock; **Tro|cken|ei** NT dried egg; **Tro|cken|eis** NT dry ice; **Tro|cken|fut|ter** NT dried or dehydrated food; **Tro|cken|ge|biet** NT arid region; **Tro|cken|ge|stell** NT drying rack; **Tro|cken|hau|be** F (salon) hairdryer; **Tro|cken|he|fe** F dried yeast; **Tro|cken|heit** F -, -en (lit, fig) dryness; (von Gebiet auch) aridness (form); (= Trockenperiode) drought; **Tro|cken|kurs** M (Ski, fig) course in which a beginner learns the basic techniques without actually putting them into practice **einen ~ machen** to learn the basics; **tro|cken+le|gen** VT sep **a** Sumpf, Gewässer to drain **b** Baby to change; (inf) Trinker to dry out; **Tro|cken|le|gung** [-leːgʊŋ] F -, -en draining; **Tro|cken|maß** NT dry measure; **Tro|cken|mas|se** F dry matter; **30% Fett in der ~** fat content 30% dry weight; **Tro|cken|milch** F dried milk; **Tro|cken|platz** M drying area; **Tro|cken|ra|sie|rer** [-raziːrɐ] M -s, - (inf) user of electric shaver or razor; (= Rasierapparat) electric shaver or razor; **Tro|cken|ra|sur** F dry or electric shave; (= das Rasieren) shaving with an electric razor no art; **tro|cken+rei|ben** VT sep irreg to rub dry; **Tro|cken|sham|poo** NT dry shampoo; **Tro|cken|spi|ri|tus** [-ʃpiːritʊs] M solid fuel (for camping stove etc); **Tro|cken|star|re** F aestivation (Brit), estivation (US); **tro|cken+ste|hen** VI sep irreg (Kuh) to be dry; **Tro|cken|übung** F (Sport) dry ski etc exercise; (= Schwimmübung auch) land drill; (fig inf) dry run; **Tro|cken|wä|sche** F dry weight (of washing); **Tro|cken|zeit** F **a** (= Jahreszeit) dry season **b** (von Wäsche etc) drying time

trock|nen ['trɔknən] **VT** to dry **VI** aux sein to dry

Trock|ner ['trɔknɐ] M -s, - (inf) dryer, drier

Trod|del ['trɔdl] F -, -n tassel

Trö|del ['trøːdl] M -s, no pl (inf) junk

Trö|de|lei [trøːdə'lai] F -, -en (inf) dawdling

Trö|del-: **Trö|del|kram** M junk; **Trö|del|la|den** M junk shop; **Trö|del|markt** M fleamarket

trö|deln ['trøːdln] VI to dawdle

Tröd|ler ['trøːdlɐ] M -s, -, **Tröd|le|rin** [-ərɪn] F -, -nen **a** (= Händler) junk dealer **b** (inf: = langsamer Mensch) dawdler, slowcoach (Brit inf), slowpoke (US inf)

troff pret von **triefen**

trog pret von **trügen**

Trog [troːk] M -(e)s, =e ['trøːgə] trough; (= Waschtrog) tub

Trog|tal NT glaciated or U-shaped valley

Tro|ja ['troːja] NT Troy

Tro|ja|ner [tro'jaːnɐ] M -s, -, **Tro|ja|ne|rin** [-ərɪn] F -, -nen Trojan

tro|ja|nisch [tro'jaːnɪʃ] ADJ Trojan; **Trojanisches Pferd** Trojan Horse

trö|len ['trøːlən] VI (Sw) to dawdle

Troll [trɔl] M -s, -e troll

Troll|blu|me F globe flower, trollius

trol|len ['trɔlən] VR (inf) to push off (inf)

Trom|mel ['trɔml] F -, -n **a** (Mus) drum; **die ~ rühren** (fig inf) to drum up (some) support **b** (Tech) (in Maschine) drum; (in Revolver) revolving breech

Trom|mel-: **Trom|mel|brem|se** F drum brake; **Trom|mel|fell** NT eardrum; **da platzt einem ja das ~** (fig) the noise is earsplitting; **Trom|mel|feu|er** NT drumfire, heavy barrage

trom|meln ['trɔmln] **VI** to drum; (Regen) to bear (down); **gegen die Tür ~** to bang on the door; **gegen die Brust ~** to beat one's chest; **mit den Fingern ~** to drum one's fingers; **der Regen trommelt gegen die Fensterscheiben** the rain is beating against the window panes **VT** Marsch, Lied to play on the drum/drums, to drum; Rhythmus to beat out; **jdn aus dem Schlaf ~** to knock sb up (Brit inf), to wake sb up (by banging on the door)

Trom|mel-: Trom|mel|re|vol|ver M revolver; **Trom|mel|schlag** M drum beat; (= das Trommeln) drumming; **Trom|mel|schlä|gel** ▲ M drumstick; **Trom|mel|spra|che** F bush telegraph; **Trom|mel|stock** M drumstick; **Trom|mel|wasch|ma|schi|ne** F drum washing machine; **Trom|mel|wir|bel** M drum roll

Tromm|ler ['trɔmlɐ] M **-s, -**, **Tromm|le|rin** [-ərɪn] F **-, -nen** drummer

Trom|pe|te [trɔm'peːtə] F **-, -n** trumpet → **Pau|ke**

trom|pe|ten [trɔm'peːtn] ptp **trompetet** **VI** to trumpet; (= sich schnäuzen) to blow one's nose loudly **VT** Marsch to play on the trumpet

Trom|pe|ten|baum M trumpet tree, common catalpa (spec)

Trom|pe|ter [trɔm'peːtɐ] M **-s, -**, **Trom|pe|te|rin** [-ərɪn] F **-, -nen** trumpeter

Tro|pen ['troːpn] PL tropics pl

Tro|pen- in cpds tropical; **Tro|pen|an|zug** M tropical suit; **Tro|pen|fie|ber** NT malaria; **Tro|pen|helm** M pith helmet, topee; **Tro|pen|holz** NT wood from tropical forests; **Tro|pen|ins|ti|tut** NT institute for tropical diseases; **Tro|pen|kli|ma** NT tropical climate; **Tro|pen|kol|ler** M tropical madness; **Tro|pen|krank|heit** F tropical disease; **Tro|pen|me|di|zin** F tropical medicine; **Tro|pen|tag** M scorcher (inf); **Tro|pen|taug|lich|keit** F fitness for service in the tropics

tropf [trɔpf] INTERJ drip

Tropf [trɔpf] M **-(e)s, -e** ['trœpfə] (inf) **a** (= Schelm) rogue, rascal; **einfältiger ~** twit (inf), dummy (inf); **armer ~** poor bugger (inf) or devil **b** no pl (= Infusion) drip (inf); **am ~ hängen** to be on a drip; (fig inf: finanziell) to be on a drip-feed

Tröpf|chen- ['trœpfçən-]: **Tröpf|chen|in|fek|ti|on** F airborne infection; **tröpf|chen|wei|se** ADV in dribs and drabs

tröp|feln ['trœpfln] **VI** **a** (Leitung, Halm) to drip; (Nase) to run **b** aux sein (Flüssigkeit) to drip **VI** impers **es tröpfelt** it is spitting **VT** to drip

trop|fen ['trɔpfn] **VI** to drip; (Nase) to run; **es tropft durch die Decke** there is water dripping through the ceiling; **es tropft von den Bäumen** the rain is dripping from the trees; **es tropft aus der Leitung** the pipe is dripping **VT** to drop, to drip

Trop|fen ['trɔpfn] M **-s, -** **a** drop; (= Schweißtropfen auch) bead; (= einzelner Tropfen: an Kanne, Nase etc) drip; (inf: = kleine Menge) drop; **ein guter** or **edler ~** (inf) a good wine; **bis auf den letzten ~** to the last drop; **ein ~ auf den heißen Stein** (fig inf) a drop in the ocean → **stet** **b** **Tropfen** PL (= Medizin) drops pl

-trop|fen PL suf in cpds (Med) drops pl; **Augentropfen** eye drops

Trop|fen|fän|ger M drip-catcher

trop|fen|wei|se ADV drop by drop

Tropf-: Tropf|in|fu|si|on F intravenous drip; **tropf|nass** ▲ ['trɔpf'nas] ADJ dripping wet; **Tropf|stein** M dripstone; (an der Decke) stalactite; (am Boden) stalagmite; **Tropf|stein|höh|le** F dripstone cave

Tro|phäe [tro'fɛːə] F **-, -n** trophy

tro|pisch ['troːpɪʃ] **ADJ** tropical **ADV** tropically; **~ wuchernde** or **wachsende Vegetation** tropical growth

Tro|po-: Tro|po|pau|se [tropo'pauzə] F (Met) tropopause; **Tro|po|sphä|re** [tropo'sfɛːrə] F (Met) troposphere

Tross ▲ M **-es, -e** (old) baggage train; **er gehört zum ~** (fig) he's a hanger-on; (= hat untergeordnete Rolle) he's an underling

Tros|se ['trɔsə] F **-, -n** cable, hawser

Trost [troːst] M **-(e)s**, no pl consolation, comfort; **jdm ~ zusprechen/bringen** to console or comfort sb; **das Kind war ihr einziger ~** the child was her only comfort; **~ im Alkohol/in der Religion suchen** to seek solace in alcohol/religion; **zum ~ kann ich Ihnen sagen, dass ... ** it may comfort you to know that ...; **zum** or **als ~ gab es ein kleines Geschenk** there was a small consolation prize; **das ist ein schwacher** or **schlechter ~** that's pretty cold comfort; **das ist ein schöner ~** (iro) some comfort that is!; **du bist wohl nicht ganz** or **recht bei ~!** (inf) you must be out of your mind!

trös|ten ['trøːstn] **VT** to comfort; (= Trost zusprechen auch) to console; **jdn/sich mit etw ~** to console sb/oneself with sth; **sich über etw** (acc) **~** to get over sth; **jdn über etw** (acc) **~** to help sb to get over sth; **~ Sie sich!** never mind; **tröste dich, ihm ist es auch nicht besser ergangen** console yourself with the thought that he didn't fare any better

Trös|ter ['trøːstɐ] M **-s, -**, **Trös|te|rin** [-ərɪn] F **-, -nen** comforter

tröst|lich ['trøːstlɪç] **ADJ** cheering, comforting; **das ist ja sehr ~** (iro) that's some comfort

trost|los **ADJ** hopeless; Jugend, Verhältnisse miserable, wretched; (= verzweifelt) inconsolable; (= öde, trist) dreary; **~ langweilig** desperately boring

Trost|lo|sig|keit F **-**, no pl hopelessness; (von Verhältnissen) wretchedness; (= Ödheit, Tristesse) dreariness

Trost-: Trost|pflas|ter NT consolation; **als ~** by way of consolation; **Trost|preis** M consolation prize; **trost|reich** **ADJ** comforting; **Trost|wor|te** PL words pl of consolation

Trös|tung ['trøːstʊŋ] F **-, -en** comfort; (= das Trösten) comforting

Trott [trɔt] M **-s**, no pl (slow) trot; (fig) routine; **im ~** at a (slow) trot; **aus dem alten ~ herauskommen** to get out of one's rut

Trot|tel ['trɔtl] M **-s, -** (inf) idiot, dope (inf)

trot|te|lig ['trɔtəlɪç] **ADJ** stupid, dopey (inf), goofy (US inf) **ADV** stupidly, goofily (US inf)

trot|ten ['trɔtn] **VI** aux sein to trot along; (Pferd) to trot slowly

Trot|teur [trɔ'tøːɐ] M **-s, -s** casual (shoe)

Trot|toir [trɔ'toaːɐ] NT **-s, -s** or **-e** (dated, S Ger) pavement (Brit), sidewalk (US)

trotz [trɔts] PREP +gen (geh) or +dat (inf) in spite of, despite; **~ allem** or **alledem** in spite of everything, for all that

Trotz [trɔts] M **-es**, no pl defiance; (= trotziges Verhalten) contrariness; **jdm/einer Sache zum ~** in defiance of sb/sth; **jdm/einer Sache ~ bieten** (geh) to defy or flout sb/sth

Trotz|al|ter NT defiant age; **sich im ~ befinden**, **im ~ sein** to be going through a defiant phase; **ins ~ kommen** to get to or reach a defiant age

trotz|dem ['trɔtsdeːm, 'trɔts'deːm] **ADV** nevertheless; **(und) ich mache das ~!** I'll do it all the same **CONJ** (strictly incorrect) even though

trot|zen ['trɔtsn] **VI** **a** +dat to defy; der Gefahr auch to brave; der Kälte, dem Klima etc to withstand; **Wind und Wetter ~** to defy the elements **b** (= trotzig sein) to be awkward or difficult or contrary

trot|zig ['trɔtsɪç] **ADJ** defiant; Kind etc difficult, awkward; (= widerspenstig) contrary **ADV** defiantly

Trotz|kis|mus [trɔts'kɪsmʊs] M **-**, no pl Trotskyism

Trotz|kist [trɔts'kɪst] M **-en, -en**, **Trotz|kis|tin** [-'kɪstɪn] F **-, -nen** Trotskyite, Trotskyist

Trotz-: Trotz|kopf M (inf) (Einstellung) defiant streak; (widerspenstig) contrary streak; (Mensch) contrary so-and-so (inf); **sei doch nicht so ein ~ don't** be so difficult; **seinen ~ haben** to be in a defiant/contrary mood; **trotz|köp|fig** **ADJ** Kind contrary; **Trotz|pha|se** F phase of defi-

ance; **Trotz|re|ak|ti|on** F act of defiance; **das war eine reine ~** he/she just reacted like that out of defiance

Trou|ba|dour ['truːbaduːɐ, trubaˈduːɐ] M **-s, -s** or **-e** troubadour

Trou|ble ['trabl] M **-s**, no pl (inf) trouble; **~ machen** to make trouble; **~ haben** to have problems

Trou|ble|shoo|ter ['trablʃuːtɐ] M **-s, -** troubleshooter

trüb [tryːp], **trü|be** ['tryːbə] **ADJ** **a** (= unklar) Flüssigkeit cloudy; (= glanzlos, matt) Glas, Augen, Himmel, Tag dull; Sonne, Mond, Licht dim; **in ~en Wassern fischen, im Trüben fischen** (inf) to fish in troubled waters **b** (fig: = bedrückend, unerfreulich) cheerless; Zeiten, Zukunft bleak; Stimmung, Gedanken, Aussichten, Vorahnung, Miene gloomy; Erfahrung grim; **es sieht ~ aus** things are looking pretty bleak; **~e Tasse** (inf) drip (inf); (= Spielverderber) wet blanket (inf)

Tru|bel ['truːbl] M **-s**, no pl hurly-burly

trü|ben ['tryːbn] **VT** **a** Flüssigkeit to make cloudy, to cloud; Glas, Metall to dull; Himmel to overcast; Wasseroberfläche to ruffle; Augen, Blick to dull, to cloud; **getrübt** (Flüssigkeit, Himmel) cloudy; Spiegel, Metall dull; Verstand dulled; Stimmung, Laune dampened; **sie sieht aus, als könnte sie kein Wässerchen ~** (inf) she looks as if butter wouldn't melt in her mouth; **kein Wölkchen trübte den Himmel** there wasn't a cloud in the sky **b** (fig) Glück, Freude, Verhältnis, Bild to spoil, to mar; Beziehungen to strain; Laune to dampen; Bewusstsein, Erinnerung to dull, to dim; (geh) Verstand to dull; Urteilsvermögen to dim, to cloud over **VR** (Flüssigkeit) to go cloudy; (Spiegel, Metall) to become dull; (geh) (Verstand) to become dulled; (Augen) to dim, to cloud; (Himmel) to cloud over; (fig) (Stimmung, Laune) to be dampened; (Beziehungen, Verhältnis) to become strained; (Glück, Freude) to be marred → auch **getrübt**

Trüb-: Trüb|heit F **-**, no pl (von Flüssigkeit) cloudiness; (= Glanzlosigkeit, Mattheit) dullness; **Trüb|sal** ['tryːpzaːl] F **-, -e** (liter) afflictions pl; (no pl: = Stimmung) sorrow; **~ blasen** (inf) to mope; **trüb|se|lig** **ADJ** gloomy; Gegend bleak; Behausung depressing; **Trüb|se|lig|keit** F gloominess; (von Landschaft) bleakness; **Trüb|sinn** M , no pl gloom, melancholy; **trüb|sin|nig** **ADJ** gloomy, melancholy

Trü|bung ['tryːbʊŋ] F **-, -en** **a** (von Flüssigkeit) clouding; (von Glas, Metall) dulling; (von Himmel) overcasting; (von Wasseroberfläche) ruffling **b** (fig) (von Glück, Freude, Verhältnis) spoiling, marring; (von Beziehungen) straining; (von Laune) dampening; (von Verstand) dulling

tru|deln ['truːdln] **VI** **a** aux sein or haben (Aviat) to spin; (fig) to slide; **ins Trudeln kommen** or **geraten** to go into a spin; (fig) to go into a tailspin **b** (dial: = würfeln) to play dice

True-Type-Schrift ['truːtaip-] F (Comput) True Type font

Trüf|fel ['trʏfl] F **-, -n** or (inf) m **-s, -** **a** (= Pilz) truffle **b** (= Praline) truffle

trug pret von **tragen**

Trug [truːk] M **-(e)s** [-gəs], no pl (liter) deception; (der Sinne) illusion; (der Fantasie) delusion → **Lug**

Trug|bild NT delusion; (der Sinne) illusion

trü|gen ['tryːgn] pret **trog** [troːk], ptp **getrogen** [gə'troːgn] **VT** to deceive; **wenn mich nicht alles trügt** unless I am very much mistaken **VI** to be deceptive

trü|ge|risch ['tryːgərɪʃ] **ADJ** (liter) (= betrügerisch) deceitful, false; (= irreführend) deceptive; Hoffnung false

Trug|schluss ▲ M fallacy, misapprehension; **einem ~ unterliegen** to be labouring (Brit) or laboring (US) under a misapprehension

Tru|he ['truːə] F **-, -n** chest

Trumm [trʊm] NT -(e)s, Trümmer ['trʏmɐ] (inf: = großer, schwerer Gegenstand) whopper (inf), humdinger (inf); **ein ~ von einem Buch** a great tome of a book; **ein ~ von einem Kerl** a great hulk; **er ist ein ~ von einem Kerl** (auch) he's huge, a giant of a man; **so ein ~ (von einem Steak** etc) such a whopper (of a steak etc)

Trüm|mer ['trʏmɐ] PL rubble sing; (= Ruinen, fig: von Glück etc) ruins pl; (von Schiff, Flugzeug etc) wreckage sing; (= Überreste) remnants pl; (inf: von Essen) remains pl; **in ~n liegen** to be in ruins; **in ~ gehen** to be ruined (auch fig); (Schiff, Flugzeug) to be wrecked; **etw in ~ schlagen** to smash sth to pieces or up

Trüm|mer-: Trüm|mer|feld NT expanse of rubble; (= Ruinen) expanse of ruins; (fig) scene of devastation or destruction; **Trüm|mer|frau** F woman who clears away rubble after bombing; **Trüm|mer|hau|fen** M heap of rubble

Trumpf [trʊmpf] M -(e)s, ≈e ['trʏmpfə] (Cards) (= Trumpfkarte) trump (card); (= Farbe) trumps pl; (fig) trump card; **~ sein** to be trumps; (fig inf: = modisch sein) to be in (inf); **~ spielen** (Cards) to play trumps; **einen ~ ausspielen** (fig) to play one's trump card; **alle Trümpfe in der Hand haben** (fig) to hold all the trump cards; **alle Trümpfe aus der Hand geben** (fig) to throw away or waste the advantage; **noch einen ~ in der Hand haben** (fig) to have an ace up one's sleeve; **jdm die Trümpfe aus den Händen nehmen** (fig) to trump sb

Trumpf|ass ▲ NT ace of trumps

trump|fen ['trʊmpfn] VT to trump VI to play a trump (card); **mit dem König ~** to play the king of trumps

Trumpf-: Trumpf|far|be F trumps pl; **Trumpf|kar|te** F trump (card); **Trumpf|stich** M trick

Trunk [trʊŋk] M -(e)s, ≈e ['trʏŋkə] (old, liter) draught (Brit old, liter), draft (US old, liter); (= Zaubertrunk auch) potion; (= das Trinken) drink; **jdm etw/das Glas zum ~ reichen** to pass sb sth to drink/a glass or a drink (= Trunksucht) **dem ~ ergeben** or **verfallen sein** to have taken to drink

trun|ken ['trʊŋkn] (liter) ADJ (von Alkohol) inebriated, intoxicated; (vor Freude, Glück etc) drunk (vor +dat with) ADV drunkenly

Trun|ken-: Trun|ken|bold ['trʊŋknbɔlt] M -(e)s, -e [-də] (pej) drunkard; **Trun|ken|heit** F -, no pl intoxication; **~ am Steuer** drunk or drink (Brit) driving

Trunk-: Trunk|sucht F alcoholism; **trunk|süch|tig** ADJ alcoholic; **~ werden** to become an alcoholic; **Trunk|süch|ti|ge(r)** MF decl as adj alcoholic

Trupp [trʊp] M -s, -s bunch; (= Einheit) group; (Mil) squad; (esp beritten) troop

Trup|pe ['trʊpə] F -, -n a no pl (Mil) army, troops pl; (= Panzertruppe etc) corps sing; **zur ~ zurückkehren** to report back; **von der (ganz) schnellen ~ sein** (inf) to be a fast mover (inf); **nicht von der schnellen ~ sein** (inf) to be slow b **Truppen** PL troops c (= Künstlertruppe) troupe, company

Trup|pen-: Trup|pen|ab|zug M withdrawal of troops; **Trup|pen|arzt** M , **Trup|pen|ärz|tin** F (army) medical officer; **Trup|pen|auf|marsch** M deployment of troops; (= Massierung) buildup of troops; **Trup|pen|be|we|gung** F usu pl troop movement; **Trup|pen|ein|heit** F unit; (bei der Kavallerie) troop; **Trup|pen|füh|rer(in)** M(F) unit/troop commander; **Trup|pen|gat|tung** F corps sing; **Trup|pen|pa|ra|de** F military parade or review; **Trup|pen|schau** F troop inspection; **Trup|pen|stär|ke** F troop or military strength, number of troops; **Trup|pen|sta|ti|o|nie|rung** F stationing of troops; **Trup|pen|teil** M unit; **Trup|pen|übung** F field exercise; **Trup|pen|übungs|platz** M military training area; **Trup|pen|ver|band** M unit, formation; (mit besonderem Auftrag) task force

trupp|wei|se ADV → Trupp in bunches/groups; (Mil) in squads/troops

Trust [trast] M -(e)s, -s or -e trust

Trut- ['tru:t-]: **Trut|hahn** M turkey (cock); **Trut|hen|ne** F turkey (hen)

Trutz [trʊts] M -es, no pl (obs) = Schutz

Trutz|burg F (Hist) castle built in order to lay siege to another castle

trut|zen ['trʊtsn] VI (obs) to defy

Tschad [tʃat, tʃa:t] M - der ~ Chad

tscha|disch ['tʃadɪʃ, 'tʃa:dɪʃ] ADJ Chad attr

Tscha|dor [tʃa'do:ɐ] M -s, -s chador

Tschap|perl ['tʃapɐl] NT -s, -n (Aus) dolt (inf); armes ~ poor devil (inf)

tschau [tʃaʊ] INTERJ (inf) cheerio (Brit inf), so long (inf), ciao (inf)

Tsche|che ['tʃɛçə] M -n, -n, **Tsche|chin** ['tʃɛçɪn] F -, -nen Czech

Tsche|chei [tʃɛ'çaɪ] F - die ~ (dated inf) Czechoslovakia

Tsche|chi|en ['tʃɛçiən] NT -s the Czech Republic

tsche|chisch ['tʃɛçɪʃ] ADJ Czech; **die Tschechische Republik** the Czech Republic

Tsche|chisch(e) ['tʃɛçɪʃ] NT Czech → auch **Deutsch(e)**

Tsche|cho|slo|wa|ke [tʃɛçoslo'va:kə] M , **Tsche|cho|slo|wa|kin** [-'va:kɪn] F (Hist) Czechoslovak

Tsche|cho|slo|wa|kei [tʃɛçoslova'kaɪ] F (Hist) **die ~** Czechoslovakia

tsche|cho|slo|wa|kisch [tʃɛçoslo'va:kɪʃ] ADJ (Hist) Czechoslovak(ian)

Tschick [tʃɪk] M -s, - (Aus) (inf: = Stummel) fag end (Brit inf), butt (inf); (sl: = Zigarette) fag (Brit inf), smoke (US sl)

tschil|pen ['tʃɪlpn] VI to chirp

Tschi|nel|le [tʃi'nɛlə] F -, -n (Aus Mus) cymbal

tschüs [tʃʏs] INTERJ = **tschüss**

Tschusch [tʃu:ʃ] M -en, -en (Aus pej) ≈ wog (Brit pej sl), chink (US pej sl)

tschüss ▲ [tʃʏs] INTERJ (inf) cheerio (Brit inf), bye (inf), so long (inf)

Tsd. abbr von **Tausend**

Tse|tse|flie|ge ['tse:tse-, 'tsɛtse-] F tsetse fly

T-Shirt ['ti:ʃœrt, -ʃøːɐt] NT -s, -s T-shirt, tee shirt

TSV [te:ɛs'faʊ] M -(s), -s abbr von **Turn- und Sportverein** SC; **~ 1860 München** ≈ 1860 Munich Sports Club

T-Trä|ger ['te:-] M T-bar, T-girder

TU [te:'u:] F - abbr von **technische Universität**

Tu|ba ['tu:ba] F -, **Tuben** [-bn] a (Mus) tuba b (Anat) tube

Tu|be ['tu:bə] F -, -n tube; **auf die ~ drücken** (inf) to get a move on (inf); (im Auto auch) to put one's foot down (inf)

Tu|ber|kel [tu'bɛrkl] M -s, - or (Aus auch) f -, -n tubercle

Tu|ber|kel|ba|zil|lus M tuberculosis bacillus

tu|ber|ku|lös [tubɛrku'lø:s] ADJ tubercular, tuberculous

Tu|ber|ku|lo|se [tubɛrku'lo:zə] F -, -n tuberculosis

Tu|ber|ku|lo|se-: tu|ber|ku|lo|se|krank ADJ tubercular, tuberculous; **Tu|ber|ku|lo|se|kran|ke(r)** MF decl as adj TB case, TB sufferer

Tuch [tu:x] NT -(e)s, ≈er ['ty:çɐ] a (= Stück Stoff) cloth; (= Tischtuch) cloth; (= Halstuch, Kopftuch) scarf; (= Schultertuch) shawl; (= Handtuch) towel; (= Geschirrtuch) cloth, towel; (= Taschentuch) handkerchief; (zum Abdecken von Möbeln) dustsheet (Brit), dust cover; **das rote ~ (des Stierkämpfers)** the bullfighter's cape; **das wirkt wie ein rotes ~ auf ihn** it makes him see red, it's like a red rag to a bull (to him) b pl -e (old: = Stoff) cloth, fabric

Tuch-: Tuch|art F type of cloth or fabric; **Tuch|fab|rik** F textile factory or mill; **Tuch|-**

füh|lung F physical or body contact; **in ~** in physical contact; (Mil) shoulder to shoulder; (fig) cheek by jowl; **er blieb mit den Führenden in** or **auf ~** (Sport) he stayed with the leaders; **~ haben** to be in physical contact (with sb); (fig) to be close to sb; **auf ~ gehen** to move closer (to sb/together); **Tuch|händ|ler(in)** M(F) cloth merchant; **Tuch|ma|cher(in)** M(F) clothworker

tüch|tig ['tʏçtɪç] ADJ a (= fähig) capable, competent (in +dat at); (= fleißig) efficient; Arbeiter good; **etwas Tüchtiges lernen/werden** (inf) to get a proper training/job; **~, ~!** not bad! b (inf: = groß) Portion big, huge; Stoß, Schlag hard; Appetit, Esser big; **eine ~e Tracht Prügel** a good hiding (inf); **eine ~e Portion Arroganz** etc a fair amount of arrogance etc ADV a (= fleißig, fest) hard; essen heartily; **hilf ~ mit** lend or give us a hand b (inf: = sehr) good and proper (inf); **~ regnen** to pelt (inf); **jdm ~ die Meinung sagen** to give sb a piece of one's mind; **~ ausschimpfen** to scold thoroughly; **~ zulangen** to tuck in (inf); **jdn ~ anschmieren** or **betrügen** to take sb for a ride (inf); **jdn ~ belügen** to tell sb a pack of lies; **sich ~ ausruhen** to have a good rest

Tüch|tig|keit F -, no pl (= Fähigkeit) competence; (von Arbeiter etc) efficiency

Tuch|wa|ren PL cloth goods pl

Tü|cke ['tʏkə] F -, -n a (no pl: = Bosheit) malice, spite; (= böswillige Handlung) malicious or spiteful action b (= Gefahr) danger, peril; (von Krankheit) perniciousness; **voller ~n stecken** to be difficult; (= gefährlich) to be dangerous or (Berg, Fluss auch) treacherous; **das ist die ~ des Objekts** these things have a will of their own!; **seine ~n haben** (Maschine etc) to be temperamental; (= schwierig sein) to be difficult; (= gefährlich sein) to be dangerous or (Berg, Fluss auch) treacherous → List c (des Glücks etc) vagary usu pl; (des Schicksals) fickleness no pl

tu|ckern ['tʊkɐn] VI aux haben or (bei Richtungsangabe) sein to put-put, to chug

tü|ckisch ['tʏkɪʃ] ADJ (= boshaft) Mensch, Blick, Lächeln malicious, spiteful; Zufall unhappy; (= bösartig, gefährlich) Berge, Strom etc treacherous; Krankheit pernicious

tü|de|lig ['ty:dəlɪç] ADJ (N Ger inf) doddery

tu(e) [tu:(ə)] imper sing von **tun**

Tu|e|rei [tu:ə'raɪ] F -, -en (inf) antics pl

Tuff [tʊf] M -s, -e, **Tuff|stein** M tuff

Tüf|tel|ar|beit F (inf) fiddly (esp Brit) or finicky job

Tüf|te|lei [tʏftə'laɪ] F -, -en (inf) fiddly (esp Brit) or finicky job; **das ist eine ~** that's fiddly (esp Brit) or finicky

tüf|te|lig ['tʏftəlɪç] ADJ (inf) fiddly (esp Brit), finicky

tüf|teln ['tʏftln] VI (inf) to puzzle; (= basteln) to fiddle about (inf); **an etw** (dat) **~** to fiddle about with sth; (geistig) to puzzle over sth; **er tüftelt gern** he likes doing fiddly (esp Brit) or finicky things

Tüft|ler ['tʏftlɐ] M -s, -, **Tüft|le|rin** [-ərɪn] F -, -nen (inf) person who likes doing finicky things (= Erfinder) inventor

Tu|gend ['tu:gnt] F -, -en [-dən] virtue; **seine ~ bewahren** to remain virtuous; (= Unschuld auch) to keep one's virtue → **Not d**

Tu|gend-: Tu|gend|bold ['tu:gntbɔlt] M -(e)s, -e [-də]; **Tu|gend|bol|din** [-dɪn] F -, -nen (pej) paragon of virtue; **tu|gend|haft** ADJ virtuous ADV virtuously; **Tu|gend|haf|tig|keit** ['tu:gnthaftɪçkaɪt] F -, no pl virtuousness; **tu|gend|sam** ['tu:gntza:m] ADJ virtuous ADV virtuously; **Tu|gend|wäch|ter(in)** M(F) (iro) guardian of his/her etc virtue

Tu|kan ['tu:kan, tu'ka:n] M -s, -e toucan

Tüll [tʏl] M -s, -e tulle; (für Gardinen) net

Tül|le ['tʏlə] F -, -n spout; (= Spritzdüse) pipe

Tüll|gar|di|ne F net curtain

Tul|pe ['tʊlpə] F **-, -n** a (*Bot*) tulip b (= *Glas*) tulip glass

Tul|pen|zwie|bel F tulip bulb

tumb [tʊmp] ADJ (*obs, hum*) stupid, dim

Tumb|ler ['tamblɐ] M **-s, -** (*Sw*: = *Wäschetrockner*) tumble dryer

tum|meln ['tʊmln] VR a (*Hunde, Kinder etc*) to romp (about) b (= *sich beeilen*) to hurry (up)

Tum|mel|platz ['tʊml-] M play area; (*fig*) hotbed

Tümm|ler ['tymlɐ] M **-s, -** (bottlenose) dolphin

Tu|mor ['tu:mo:ɐ, tu'mo:ɐ] M **-s, Tumoren** [tu-'mo:rən] tumour (*Brit*), tumor (*US*)

Tu|mor-Nek|ro|se-Fak|tor [tu:mo:ɐne'kro:zə-] M , **Tu|mor|nek|ro|se|fak|tor** M (*Med*) tumour (*Brit*) or tumor (*US*) necrosis factor

Tüm|pel ['tympl] M **-s, -** pond

Tu|mult [tu'mʊlt] M **-(e)s, -e** commotion; (= *Aufruhr auch*) disturbance; (*der Gefühle*) tumult, turmoil

---

tun [tu:n]
pret **tat** [ta:t], *ptp* **getan** [ɡə'ta:n]

1 TRANSITIVES VERB	3 REFLEXIVES VERB
2 HILFSVERB	4 INTRANSITIVES VERB

1 – TRANSITIVES VERB

a = **machen**

In Verbindungen mit Substantiv siehe auch Eintrag für das jeweilige Substantiv.

to do; **er tut nichts als faulenzen/unsere Zeit vergeuden** he does nothing but laze around/ waste our time; **so etwas tut man nicht!** that is just not done!, you just can't do that sort of thing!; **so etwas tut man als anständige Frau nicht!** a decent woman doesn't do such things; **was tut man in dieser Situation?** what should one do in this situation?; **wir haben getan, was wir konnten** we did what we could; **... aber er tut es einfach nicht ...** but he just won't (do it); **sie wusste nicht, was tun** or **was sie tun sollte** she didn't know what to do; **was tun?** what can be done?; **mal sehen, was sich (für Sie) tun lässt** let's see what we can do (for you); **was kann ich für Sie tun?** what can I do for you?; **etw aus Liebe/Bosheit etc tun** to do sth out of love/malice etc; **jdm etw zu tun geben** to give sb sth to do; **etwas/nichts gegen etw tun** to do something/nothing about sth; **du kannst tun und lassen, was du willst** you can do what you like; **er bestimmt, was wir zu tun und zu lassen haben** he tells us what to do and what not to do; **tu, was du nicht lassen kannst** well, if you have to; **damit ist es noch nicht getan** and that's not all; **was tut das Buch unterm Bett?** (*inf*) what is the book doing under the bed?; **was tust DU denn hier?** (*inf*) what are YOU doing here?; **seine Arbeit/Pflicht tun** to do one's job/duty; **einen Schrei tun** to cry (out) → auch **getan**

♦ **jdm etwas tun** to do something to sb; (*stärker*) to hurt sb; **der Hund tut dir schon nichts** the dog won't hurt you; **jdm Böses** or **ein Leid** (*old*) **tun** to harm sb; **jdm einen Gefallen tun** to do sb a favour (*Brit*) or favor (*US*); **was du nicht willst, dass man dir tu, das füg auch keinem andern zu** (*Prov*) do as you would be done by (*prov*)

♦ **es tun** (*inf*) **es mit jdm tun** (*euph inf*) to do it with sb (*inf*); **die Uhr/das Auto tut es** or **tuts nicht mehr** the watch/car has had it (*inf*); **das tuts für heute** that'll do for today; **unser Auto muss es noch ein Weilchen tun** we'll have to make do with our car a bit longer

♦ **mit jdm/etw zu tun haben** das hat etwas/ **nichts mit ihm/damit zu tun** that's something/ nothing to do with him/it; **das hat doch damit gar nichts zu tun** that's got nothing to do with it; **mit ihm/damit habe ich nichts zu tun/will ich nichts zu tun haben** I have/want nothing to do with him/it; **er hat es mit der Leber/dem**

Herzen *etc* zu tun (*inf*) he has liver/heart *etc* trouble; **ich habe mit mir selbst zu tun** I have problems myself *or* of my own

♦ **es mit jdm zu tun bekommen** or **kriegen** (*inf*) to get into trouble with sb

b = **ausmachen** **was tuts?** what does it matter?; **das tut nichts** it doesn't matter; **das tut dir/ihm nichts** it won't do you/him any harm; **das tut nichts zur Sache** that's beside the point; **darum ist es mir sehr getan** or **zu tun** (*geh*) I am very concerned about it

c = **an einen bestimmten Ort legen etc** (*inf*) to put; **wohin hast du den Brief getan?** where have you put the letter?; **jdn in eine andere Schule tun** to put sb in a different school

2 – HILFSVERB

a **zur Betonung** (*inf*) **sie tun jetzt essen** (*inf*) they're eating; **und dann tut er schwimmen** (*inf*) and then he goes swimming

b **zur Bildung der Vergangenheit** (*old*) **dann tat er sich waschen** then he washed himself

3 – REFLEXIVES VERB

♦ **sich tun**

a = **geschehen** **es tut sich etwas/nichts** there is something/nothing happening, something/ nothing is happening; **hier hat sich einiges getan** there have been some changes here; **hat sich bei euch etwas getan?** have things changed (with you)?; **hat sich in dieser Hinsicht schon etwas getan?** has anything been done about this?

b **mit Adjektiv**

♦ **sich schwer** or **nicht leicht tun sich** (*acc or dat*) **mit etw schwer tun** to have problems with sth; **sich** (*acc or dat*) **mit etw nicht leicht tun** to have problems with sth

4 – INTRANSITIVES VERB

a = **vorgeben** **so tun, als ob ...** to pretend that ...; **tu doch nicht so** stop pretending; **tust du nur so dumm?** are you just acting stupid?; **sie tut nur so** she's only pretending

b **andere Wendungen**

♦ **zu tun haben** (= *beschäftigt sein*) to have things to do; **in der Stadt zu tun haben** to have things to do in town; **auf dem Finanzamt zu tun haben** to have business at the tax office; **ich hatte zu tun, das wieder in Ordnung zu bringen** I had my work cut out putting *or* to put it back in order; **mit jdm zu tun haben** to have dealings with sb

♦ **daran tun Sie täten gut daran, früh zu kommen** you would do well to come early; **Sie haben recht daran getan** you did right

---

Tun [tu:n] NT **-s**, *no pl* conduct; **sein ganzes ~, sein ~ und Lassen, sein ~ und Treiben** everything he does; **heimliches/verbrecherisches ~** secret/criminal actions

Tün|che ['tynçə] F **-, -n** whitewash; (*getönt*) distemper, wash; (*fig*) veneer; (*inf*: = *Schminke*) make-up

tün|chen ['tynçn] VT to whitewash; (*mit getönter Farbe*) to distemper

Tund|ra ['tʊndra] F **-, Tundren** [-drən] tundra

Tu|nell [tu'nɛl] NT **-s, -e** (*dial, S Ger, Aus*) tunnel

tu|nen ['tju:nən] VT to tune

Tu|ner ['tju:nɐ] M **-s, -** tuner

Tu|ne|si|en [tu'ne:ziən] NT **-s** Tunisia

Tu|ne|si|er [tu'ne:ziɐ] M **-s, -, Tu|ne|si|e|rin** [-iərn] F **-, -nen** Tunisian

tu|ne|sisch [tu'ne:zɪʃ] ADJ Tunisian

Tunfisch ▲ [tu:n-] M tuna (fish)

Tu|nicht|gut ['tu:nɪçtgu:t] M **-(e)s, -e** (*dated*) ne'er-do-well (*old*), good-for-nothing

Tu|ni|ka ['tu:nika] F **-, Tuniken** [-kn] tunic

Tu|ning ['tju:nɪŋ] NT **-s**, *no pl* tuning

Tun|ke ['tʊŋkə] F **-, -n** sauce; (= *Bratentunke*) gravy

tun|ken ['tʊŋkn] VT to dip; (= *stippen auch*) to dunk (*inf*); **jdn** to duck

tun|lich ['tu:nlɪç] ADJ possible, feasible; (= *ratsam*) advisable

tun|lichst ['tu:nlɪçst] ADV a (= *möglichst*) if possible; **~ bald** as soon as possible; **ich werde es ~ vermeiden, ihm meine Meinung zu sagen** I'll do my best to avoid telling him what I think b (= *gefälligst*) **das wirst du ~ bleiben lassen** you'll do nothing of the kind *or* sort

Tun|nel ['tʊnl] M **-s, -** or **-s** tunnel

Tun|te ['tʊntə] F **-, -n** a (*dated*) sissy (*inf*) b (*inf*: = *Homosexueller*) fairy (*pej inf*) c (*sl*: *Schimpfwort*) poof(ter) (*Brit inf*), fag(got) (*US inf*)

tun|ten|haft ADJ (*inf*) fussy; *Homosexueller etc* effeminate, camp (*esp Brit inf*)

tun|tig ['tʊntɪç] ADJ (*inf*) a (*dated*: = *albern, zimperlich*) sissy (*inf*) b (= *weibisch*) effeminate, camp (*esp Brit inf*)

Tupf [tʊpf] M **-(e)s, -e** (*Aus*) spot; (*klein*) dot

Tüp|fel ['typfl] M OR NT **-s, -, Tüp|fel|chen** ['typflçən] NT **-s, -** dot

tüp|feln ['typfln] VT to spot; **getüpfelt** spotted; (= *mit kleinen Tupfen*) dotted

tup|fen ['tʊpfn] VT to dab; **getupft** spotted

Tup|fen ['tʊpfn] M **-s, -** spot; (*klein*) dot

Tup|fer ['tʊpfɐ] M **-s, -** swab

Tür [ty:ɐ] F **-, -en** door; (= *Gartentür*) gate; **in der ~ in the doorway; vor or an die ~ gehen** to answer the door, to go to the door; **Weihnachten steht vor der ~** Christmas is just (a)round the corner; **jdn vor die ~ setzen** (*inf*) to throw or kick (*inf*) sb out; **jdm die ~ weisen** to show sb the door; **jdm die ~ vor der Nase zumachen/zuschlagen** (*inf*) to shut/slam the door in sb's face; **ein jeder kehre vor seiner ~** (*prov*) everyone should set his own house in order; **jdm mit etw die ~ einrennen** (= *jdn bestürmen*) to bombard sb with sth; **die Leute haben ihm fast die ~ eingerannt** (*nach Anzeige etc*) he was snowed under with replies; **offene ~en einrennen** to preach to the converted; **mit der ~ ins Haus fallen** (*inf*) to blurt it out; **jdm die ~ für etw offen halten** or **nicht zuschlagen** (*fig*) to keep the way open for sth; **zwischen ~ und Angel** in passing; **einer Sache** (*dat*) **~ und Tor öffnen** (*fig*) to open the way to sth; **ach, du kriegst die ~ nicht zu!** (*inf*) well I never!

Tür|an|gel F (door) hinge

Tur|ban ['tʊrba:n] M **-s, -e** turban

Tür|be|schlag M (ornamental) mounting (on a door)

Tur|bi|ne [tʊr'bi:nə] F **-, -n** turbine

Tur|bi|nen-: Tur|bi|nen|an|trieb M turbine drive; (*an Flugzeug*) turbojet propulsion; **Tur|bi|nen|flug|zeug** NT turbojet; **Tur|bi|nen|trieb|werk** NT turbine engine; (*an Flugzeug*) turbojet, jet turbine engine

Tur|bo- ['tʊrbo-]: **Tur|bo|die|sel** M (*Aut*) turbo-diesel engine; **Tur|bo|ge|ne|ra|tor** M turbogenerator; **Tur|bo|la|der** [-la:dɐ] M **-s, -** (*Aut*) turbocharger; **Tur|bo|mo|tor** M turbo-engine; **Tur|bo-Prop-Flug|zeug** NT turboprop aircraft

tur|bu|lent [tʊrbu'lɛnt] ADJ turbulent, tempestuous ADV turbulently; **auf der Versammlung ging es ~ zu** the meeting was turbulent; **dort gehts ~ zu** things are in turmoil there

Tur|bu|lenz [tʊrbu'lɛnts] F **-, -en** a *no pl* turbulence, turmoil b (= *turbulentes Ereignis*) excitement, turmoil *no pl* c (= *Wirbel, Luftstrom*) turbulence *no pl*

Tür|chen ['ty:ɐçən] NT **-s, -** small door

Tür|drü|cker M (= *Knauf*) doorknob; (*inf*: = *Öffner*) buzzer (*for opening the door*)

Tü|re ['ty:rə] F **-, -n** (*dial*) = **Tür**

Turf [tʊrf] M **-s, -s** a (= *Rennbahn*) racecourse b (*no pl*: = *Sportart*) turf

Tür-: Tür|flü|gel M door (*of a pair of doors*); **Tür|fül|lung** F door panel; **Tür|griff** M door handle; **Tür|hü|ter(in)** M(F) (*obs*) doorkeeper

-tü|rig [tyːrɪç] ADJ *suf* **eintürig/zweitürig** *etc* with one door/two doors *etc*; **ein viertüriges Auto** a four-door car

Tür|ke ['tʏrkə] M **-n, -n** Turk; **einen ~ bauen** (*inf*: = *etwas vortäuschen*) to fiddle the figures (*inf*) → *auch* **Türkin**

Tür|kei [tʏr'kai] F **- die** ~ Turkey

tür|ken ['tʏrkn] VT (*inf*) etw to fiddle (*inf*); **die Statistik** ~ to massage the figures; **Belege** ~ to falsify documents

Tür|ken ['tʏrkn] M **-s**, *no pl* (*Aus inf*) maize, corn

Tür|ken|bund M *pl* **-bünde** (*Bot*) Turk's cap lily

Tür|ket|te F (door) chain

Tür|kin ['tʏrkɪn] F **-, -nen** Turk, Turkish woman/girl

tür|kis [tʏr'kiːs] ADJ turquoise

Tür|kis¹ [tʏr'kiːs] M **-es, -e** [-zə] (= *Edelstein*) turquoise

Tür|kis² NT **-**, *no pl* (= *Farbe*) turquoise

tür|kisch ['tʏrkɪʃ] ADJ Turkish; **~er Honig** nougat

Tür|kisch(e) ['tʏrkɪʃ] NT Turkish → *auch* **Deutsch(e)**

tür|kis|far|ben [-farbn], **tür|kis|grün** ADJ turquoise(-coloured) (*Brit*), turquoise(-colored) (*US*)

Tür-: Tür|klin|ke F door handle; **Tür|klop|fer** M doorknocker

Tur|ko|lo|ge [tʊrko'loːgə] M **-n, -n, Tur|ko|lo|gin** [-'loːgɪn] F **-, -nen** specialist in Turkic studies

Tur|ko|lo|gie [tʊrkolo'giː] F **-**, *no pl* Turkic studies *pl*

Turm [tʊrm] M **-(e)s, ¨-e** ['tʏrmə] **a** tower; (= *spitzer Kirchturm*) spire; (*im Schwimmbad*) diving (*Brit*) or dive (*US*) tower **b** (*Chess*) castle, rook

Tur|ma|lin [tʊrma'liːn] M **-s, -e** (*Miner*) tourmaline

Turm|bau M , *no pl* (= *das Bauen*) building a tower; **der ~ zu Babel** the building of the Tower of Babel

Türm|chen ['tʏrmçən] NT **-s,** *dim von* **Turm** turret

tür|men ['tʏrmən] VT to pile (up) VR to pile up; (*Wolken*) to build up, to bank; (*Wellen*) to tower up VI *aux sein* (*inf*: = *davonlaufen*) to skedaddle (*inf*), to take to one's heels, to run off

Turm-: Turm|fal|ke M kestrel; **turm|hoch** ADJ towering, lofty ADV ~ **über jdm stehen, jdm ~ überlegen sein** to stand head and shoulders above sb; **Turm|schwal|be** F swift; **Turm|spit|ze** F spire; **Turm|sprin|gen** NT high diving; **Turm|uhr** F clock (on a/the tower); (*von Kirche*) church clock

Turn-: Turn|an|zug M leotard; **Turn|beu|tel** M gym bag

tur|nen ['tʊrnən] VI **a** (*an Geräten*) to do gymnastics; (*Sch*) to do gym or PE; **am Reck/an den Ringen/auf der Matte** *etc* ~ to work on or do exercises on the horizontal bar/rings/mat *etc*; **sie kann gut** ~ she is good at gym or PE **b** *aux sein* (= *herumklettern*) to climb about; (*Kind*) to romp VT Reck *etc* to work on, to do exercises on; *Übung* to do

Tur|nen NT **-s**, *no pl* gymnastics *sing*; (*inf*: = *Leibeserziehung*) gym, PE (*inf*)

Tur|ner ['tʊrnɐ] M **-s, -, Tur|ne|rin** [-ərɪn] F **-, -nen** gymnast

Tur|ne|rei [tʊrnə'rai] F **-, -en** (*inf*) sporting activities *pl*; (*fig*) acrobatics *pl*

tur|ne|risch ['tʊrnərɪʃ] ADJ gymnastic ADV *sein Bestes geben* gymnastically; ~ **hervorragend** (*Mensch*) excellent at gymnastics; *Übung* excellent gymnastically; **sie hat ~ nicht überzeugt** her gymnastic performance was not up to standard

Tur|ner|schaft ['tʊrnɐʃaft] F **-, -en a** (= *die Turner*) gymnasts *pl*; (= *Vereinigung der Turnvereine*) gymnastics association **b** (= *Studentenverbindung*) student organization

Turn-: Turn|fest NT gymnastics display or festival; (*von Schule*) sports day; **Turn|ge|rät** NT (= *Reifen, Ball etc*) (piece of) gymnastic equipment; (= *Reck, Barren etc*) (piece of) gymnastic apparatus; **Turn|hal|le** F gym(nasium); (*Gebäude auch*) sports hall; **Turn|hemd** NT gym or PE shirt; **Turn|ho|se** F gym or PE shorts *pl*

Tur|nier [tʊr'niːɐ] NT **-s, -e** (= *Ritterturnier, sportliche Veranstaltung*) tournament; (= *Tanzturnier*) competition; (= *Reitturnier*) show

Tur|nier-: Tur|nier|pferd NT show or competition horse; **Tur|nier|rei|ter(in)** M(F) show or competition rider; **Tur|nier|sieg** M tournament win; **Tur|nier|spiel** NT tournament match; **Tur|nier|tanz** M (competition) ballroom dance or (*Tanzform*) dancing

Turn-: Turn|klei|dung F gym or PE clothes *pl* or kit (*Brit*); **Turn|kunst** F gymnastic skills *pl*; **Turn|leh|rer(in)** M(F) gym or PE teacher; **Turn|rie|ge** F gymnastics team

Turn|schuh M gym shoe, sneaker (*US*)

Turn|schuh- *in cpds* (*inf*) unconventional, unorthodox

Turn-: Turn|stun|de F gym or PE lesson; (*im Verein*) gymnastics lesson; **Turn|übung** F gymnastic exercise; **Turn|un|ter|richt** M gymnastic instruction; (= *Turnstunde*) gym, PE

Tur|nus ['tʊrnʊs] M **-, -se a** rota (*Brit*), roster; **im (regelmäßigen) ~ in rotation b** (*Aus*) (= *Arbeitsschicht*) shift; (*Med*) housemanship (*Brit*), internship (*US*)

Turn-: Turn|va|ter M ~ **Jahn** Jahn, the father of gymnastics; **Turn|ve|rein** M gymnastics club; **Turn|wart** [-vart] M **-s, -e, Turn|war|tin** [-vartn] F **-, -nen** gymnastics supervisor; **Turn|zeug** NT , *no pl* gym or PE things *pl* or kit (*Brit*), gym gear (*inf*)

Tür-: Tür|öff|ner M **elektrischer ~** buzzer (*for opening the door*); **Tür|öff|ner(in)** M(F) (*im Hotel*) commissionaire; (*Mann auch*) doorman; **Tür|pfos|ten** M doorpost; **Tür|rah|men** M doorframe; **Tür|schild** NT *pl* **-schilder** doorplate; **Tür|schloss** ▲ NT door lock; **Tür|schnal|le** F (*Aus*) door handle; **Tür|schwel|le** F threshold; **Tür|spalt** M crack (of a/the door); **Tür|sprech|an|la|ge** F entry phone; **Tür|ste|her** [-ʃteːɐ] M **-s, -, Tür|ste|he|rin** [-ərɪn] F **-, -nen** bouncer; (*Mann auch*) doorman; **Tür|stock** M (*S Ger, Aus*) doorframe; **Tür|sturz** M lintel

tur|teln ['tʊrtln] VI to bill and coo; (*Liebespaar auch*) to whisper sweet nothings

Tur|tel|tau|be F turtledove; ~**n** (*inf*: = *Verliebte*) lovebirds, turtledoves

Tür|vor|le|ger M doormat

Tusch [tʊʃ] M **-es, -e a** (*Mus*) flourish; (*esp von Blasinstrumenten*) fanfare **b** (*Aus*: = *Tusche*) Indian ink

Tu|sche ['tʊʃə] F **-, -n** (= *Ausziehtusche*) Indian ink; (= *Tuschfarbe*) watercolour (*Brit*), watercolor (*US*); (= *Wimperntusche*) mascara

tu|scheln ['tʊʃln] VTI to whisper; **hinter seinem Rücken über jdn** ~ to say things (*inf*) or to talk behind sb's back

tu|schen ['tʊʃn] VT (*mit Farbe*) to paint in watercolour(s) (*Brit*) or watercolor(s) (*US*); (*mit Ausziehtusche*) to draw in Indian ink; **sich** (*dat*) **die Wimpern** ~ to put one's mascara on

Tusch-: Tusch|far|be F watercolour (*Brit*), watercolor (*US*); **Tusch|kas|ten** M paintbox; **ihr Gesicht sieht aus wie ein ~** (*fig inf*) she's made up to the eyeballs (*inf*); **Tusch|zeich|nung** F pen-and-ink drawing

Tus|si ['tʊsi] F **-, -s** (*inf*), **Tuss** [tʊs] F **-, -en** (*sl*) female (*inf*)

tut [tuːt] INTERJ toot

Tü|te ['tyːtə] F **-, -n** (*aus Papier, Plastik*) bag; (= *Eistüte*) cornet, cone; (*von Suppenpulver etc*) packet; (*inf*: *für Alkoholtest*) Breathalyzer®; (*inf*: *Mensch*) drip (*inf*); **in die ~ blasen** (*inf*) to be breathalyzed, to blow in the bag (*inf*); ~**n kleben** (*inf*) to be in clink (*inf*); **das kommt nicht in die ~!** (*inf*) no way! (*inf*)

tu|ten ['tuːtn] VI to toot; (*Schiff*) to sound its hooter or (*mit Nebelhorn*) foghorn; **von Tuten und Blasen keine Ahnung haben** (*inf*) not to have a clue (*inf*)

Tu|tor ['tuːtoːɐ] M **-s, Tutoren** [-'toːrən], **Tu|to|rin** F **-, -nen** tutor

TÜV [tʏf] M **-s, -s** *abbr von* **Technischer Überwachungs-Verein** ≈ MOT (*Brit*), ≈ inspection (*US inf*); **das Auto ist durch den ~ gekommen** ≈ the car got through or passed its MOT (*Brit*) or inspection (*US*)

TÜV-ge|prüft ADJ ≈ (TÜV) safety tested

> **TÜV**
>
> The **TÜV** – short for **Technischer Überwachungs-Verein** – is an organization that tests the safety of technical installations, machinery and motor vehicles. All vehicles over three years old must undergo a **TÜV** test every two years in order to prove they are safe and roadworthy. Should the vehicle fail the test, it must be deregistered and taken off the road. The **TÜV** also carries out safety tests on a wide range of other products. If they pass the test, products are permitted to carry the **GS (Geprüfte Sicherheit)** seal. The independence of the **TÜV** means that this seal is regarded as a guarantee of good quality and reliability.

TÜV-Pla|ket|te F disc displayed on number plate showing that a car has passed the TÜV, ≈ MOT certificate (*Brit*), ≈ inspection certificate (*US*)

Tu|wort NT *pl* **-wörter** doing-word

TV [teːˈfau] **a** *abbr von* **Television b** *abbr von* **Turnverein**

TV- [teːˈfau] *in cpds* TV; **TV-Mo|de|ra|tor** M , **TV-Mo|de|ra|to|rin** F TV presenter; **TV-Pro|gramm** NT TV programmes (*Brit*) or programs (*US*) *pl*; **TV-Sen|dung** F TV broadcast

Tweed [tviːt] M **-s, -s** or **-e** [-də] tweed

Twen [tvɛn] M **-(s), -s** person in his/her twenties

Twin|set ['tvɪnzɛt] NT OR M **-(s), -s** twinset (*Brit*), sweater-set (*US*)

Twist¹ [tvɪst] M **-es, -e** (*Garn*) twist

Twist² M **-s, -s** (*Tanz*) twist

twis|ten ['tvɪstn] VI to twist, to do the twist

Ty|coon [tai'kuːn] M **-s, -s** or **-e** tycoon

Tym|pa|non ['tʏmpanɔn] NT **-s, Tympana** [-na] (*Archit*) tympanum

Typ [tyːp] M **-s, -en a** (= *Modell*) model **b** (= *Menschenart*) type; **er ist nicht mein ~** (*inf*) he's not my type (*inf*) **c** (*inf*: = *Mensch*) person, character; (*sl*: = *Mann, Freund*) man (*inf*), bloke (*Brit inf*), guy (*inf*); **dein ~ wird verlangt** (*inf*) you're wanted; **dein ~ ist nicht gefragt** (*inf*) you're not wanted (a)round here

Ty|pe ['tyːpə] F **-, -n a** (*Typ*) (= *Schreibmaschinentype*) type bar; (= *Druckbuchstabe*) character; ~**n** (= *Schrift*) type *sing*; ~**n gießen** to set type **b** (*inf*: = *Mensch*) character **c** (*bei Mehl*) grade

Ty|pen *pl von* **Typus** *von* **Type**

Ty|pen|rad NT daisy wheel

Ty|pen|rad|dru|cker M daisy wheel (printer)

Ty|phus ['tyːfʊs] M **-, *no pl* typhoid (fever)

Ty|phus-: Ty|phus|epi|de|mie F typhoid (fever) epidemic; **Ty|phus|imp|fung** F typhoid inoculation; **Ty|phus|kran|ke(r)** MF *decl as adj* typhoid case

ty|pisch ['tyːpɪʃ] ADJ typical (*für* of); (*das ist ein*) ~**er Fall von denkste!** (*inf*) no such luck!

(*inf*) ADV ~ **deutsch/Mann/Frau** typically German/male/female; **ein ~ deutsches Gericht** a typical German dish; ~ **Claire** that's so typical of Claire

ty|pi|sie|ren [typiˈziːrən] *ptp* **typisiert** VT *Charakter* to stylize; *Erzeugnisse etc* to standardize

Ty|po|gra|fie ▲ [typograˈfiː] F -, -n [-ˈfiːən] typography

ty|po|gra|fisch ▲ [typoˈɡraːfɪʃ] ADJ typographic(al) ADV typographically

Ty|po|lo|gie [typoloˈɡiː] F -, -n [-ˈɡiːən] typology

Ty|po|skript [typoˈskrɪpt] NT -(e)s, -e (*Typ*) typescript

Ty|pus [ˈtyːpʊs] M -, **Typen** [ˈtyːpn] type

Ty|rann [tyˈran] M -en, -en, **Ty|ran|nin** [-ˈranɪn] F -, -nen (*lit, fig*) tyrant

Ty|ran|nei [tyraˈnai] F -, -en tyranny

Ty|ran|nen-: Ty|ran|nen|mord M tyrannicide; **Ty|ran|nen|mör|der(in)** M(F) tyrannicide

Ty|ran|nin F -, -nen tyrant

ty|ran|nisch [tyˈranɪʃ] ADJ tyrannical ADV tyranically

ty|ran|ni|sie|ren [tyraniˈziːrən] *ptp* **tyrannisiert** VT to tyrannize

tyr|rhe|nisch [tʏˈreːnɪʃ] ADJ **Tyrrhenisches Meer** Tyrrhenian Sea

Tz [ˈteːtset, teˈtset] NT **bis ins** *or* **zum Tz** completely, fully → *auch* **Tezett**

T-Zel|le [ˈteː-] F (*Med, Biol*) T-cell

U

U, u [uː] NT **-,** - U, u → **X**

u. *abbr von* **und**

u. a. *abbr von* **und andere(s)** *von* **unter anderem/anderen**

U. A. w. g. [uːlaːveˈɡeː] *abbr von* **Um Antwort wird gebeten** RSVP

UB [uːˈbeː] F **-, -s** *abbr von* **Universitätsbibliothek**

U-Bahn [ˈuː-] F underground, subway (*US*); (*in London*) tube

U-Bahn|hof [ˈuː-] M underground *or* subway (*US*) station; (*in London*) tube station

U-Bahn-Netz [ˈuː-] M underground *or* subway (*US*) system

U-Bahn-Sta|ti|on [ˈuː-] F underground *or* subway (*US*) station; (*in London*) tube station

übel [ˈyːbl] ADJ **a** (= *schlimm, unangenehm*) bad; *Kopfweh, Erkältung etc* nasty, bad; **er war übler Laune** he was in a bad *or* nasty mood; **das ist gar nicht so ~** that's not so bad at all

b (= *moralisch, charakterlich schlecht*) wicked, bad; *Eindruck, Ruf* bad; *Tat* wicked, evil; **ein übler Bursche** *or* **Kunde** (*inf*) a nasty piece of work (*inf*), a bad lot (*inf*); **das ist eine üble Sache!** it's a bad business; **ein übler Streich** a nasty trick; **auf üble** *or* **in der ~sten Weise, in übler** *or* **~ster Weise** in a most unpleasant way; **jdm Übles antun** (*geh*) to be wicked to sb, to do wicked things to sb

c (= *physisch schlecht, eklig*) *Geschmack, Geruch, Gefühl* nasty; **mir wird ~** I feel ill *or* sick; **es kann einem ~ werden** it's enough to make you feel ill *or* sick

d (= *verkommen, übel beleumdet*) *Stadtviertel* evil, bad; *Kaschemme* evil, low

ADV a (= *schlimm, unangenehm, schlecht*) badly; **etw ~ aufnehmen** to take sth badly; **das ist ihm ~ bekommen** it did him no good at all; **~ dran sein** to be in a bad way; **~ beraten** ill-advised; **~ gelaunt** ill-humoured (*Brit*), ill-humored (*US*), sullen, morose; **~ gesinnt** (*geh*) ill-disposed; **~ riechend** foul-smelling, evil-smelling; **jd ist ~ gelaunt** sb is in a bad mood; **jdm ~ gesinnt sein** to be ill-disposed to sb; **etw riecht ~** sth smells bad; **es steht ~ mit ihm** he's in a bad way *or* in bad shape; **das schmeckt gar nicht so ~** it doesn't taste so bad; **wie gehts? – danke, nicht ~** how's things? – not bad, thanks; **ich hätte nicht ~ Lust, jetzt nach Paris zu fahren** I wouldn't mind going to Paris now

b (= *moralisch, charakterlich schlecht*) badly; **über jdn ~ reden** to say bad things about sb; **jdm etw ~ vermerken** to hold sth against sb; **~ beleumdet** disreputable, of ill repute

c (= *physisch schlecht*) ill, poorly; **das Essen ist ihm ~ bekommen** the food disagreed with him

Übel [ˈyːbl] NT **-s,** - **a** (*geh*: = *Krankheit, Leiden*) illness, malady (*old*) **b** (= *Missstand*) ill, evil; **ein notwendiges/das kleinere** *or* **geringere ~** a necessary/the lesser evil; **das alte ~** the old trouble; **der Grund allen ~s ist, dass ...** the cause *or* root of all the trouble is that ...; **die Gleichgültigkeit ist die Wurzel alles** *or* **allen ~s** indifference is the root of all evil; **das ~ bei der Sache** the trouble **c** (= *Plage, Schaden*) evil; **von ~ sein** to be a bad thing, to be bad; **zu al-**

lem ~ ... to make matters worse ...; **ein ~ kommt selten allein** (*Prov*) misfortunes seldom come alone

übel-: übel|be|leum|det △ ADJ *attr* → **übel** ADV b; **übel|be|ra|ten** △ ADJ *attr* → **übel** ADV a; **übel|ge|launt** △ ADJ *attr* → **übel** ADV a; **übel|ge|sinnt** △ ADJ *attr* → **übel** ADV a

Übel|keit F **-, -en** (*lit, fig*) nausea; **eine plötzliche ~** a sudden feeling of nausea; **~ erregen** to cause nausea

Übel-: übel|lau|nig ADJ ill-tempered, cantankerous; **Übel|lau|nig|keit** F ill temper; **übel neh|men ▲** VT *irreg* to take amiss (*Brit*) *or* badly; **jdm etw ~** to hold sth against sb; **bitte nehmen Sie es (mir) nicht übel, aber ...** please don't take offence (*Brit*) *or* offense (*US*), but ...; **ich habe ihm gar nicht einmal übel genommen, dass er gelogen hat, aber ...** I didn't even mind him lying but ...; **übel|neh|me|risch** [ˈyːblneːmərɪʃ] ADJ (= *schnell beleidigt*) touchy; (= *nachtragend*) resentful; **übel|rie|chend** △ ADJ → **übel** ADV a; **Übel|sein** NT nausea; **Übel|stand** M (*social*) evil *or* ill; **Übel|tat** F (*dated, liter*) evil *or* wicked act *or* deed, misdeed; **Übel|tä|ter(in)** M(F) (*geh*) wrongdoer; **übel tun ▲** VI *irreg* (*dated, liter*) **jdm ~** to be wicked to sb; **übel wol|len ▲** VI (*geh*) **jdm ~** to wish sb harm *or* ill, to be ill-disposed toward(s) sb

üben [ˈyːbn] VT **a** (= *praktisch erlernen*) *Aussprache, Musik, Sport* to practise (*Brit*), to practice (*US*); (*Mil*) to drill; **Geige/Klavier ~** to practise (*Brit*) *or* practice (*US*) the violin/piano

b (= *schulen, trainieren*) *Gedächtnis, Muskeln etc* to exercise → *auch* **geübt**

c (= *tun, erkennen lassen*) to exercise; **Gerechtigkeit ~** (*geh*) to be just (*gegen* to), to show fairness (*gegen* to); **Kritik an etw** (*dat*) **~** to criticize sth; **Geduld ~** to be patient → **Barmherzigkeit**

VR sich in etw (*dat*) **~** to practise (*Brit*) *or* practice (*US*) sth; **sich in Geduld** (*dat*) **~** (*geh*) to have patience, to possess one's soul in patience

VI (= *praktisch lernen*) to practise (*Brit*), to practice (*US*)

über [ˈyːbɐ] PREP **a** +*acc* (*räumlich*) over; (= *quer über*) across; (= *weiter als*) beyond; **etw ~ etw hängen/stellen** to hang/put sth over *or* above sth; **es wurde ~ alle Sender ausgestrahlt** it was broadcast over all transmitters; **er lachte ~ das ganze Gesicht** he was beaming all over his face

b +*dat* (*räumlich*) (*Lage, Standort*) over, above; (= *jenseits*) over, across; **zwei Grad ~ null** two degrees (above zero); **~ der Stadt lag dichter Nebel** a thick mist hung over the town; **~ uns lachte die Sonne** the sun smiled above us; **er trug den Mantel ~ dem Arm** he was carrying his coat over his arm; **~ jdm stehen** *or* **sein** (*fig*) to be over *or* above sb; **er steht ~ der Situation** (*fig*) he is above it all

c +*dat* (*zeitlich*: = *bei, während*) over; **~ der Arbeit einschlafen** to fall asleep over one's work; **etw ~ einem Glas Wein besprechen** to discuss sth over a glass of wine; **~ all der Aufregung/ unserer Unterhaltung habe ich ganz vergessen, dass ...** in all the *or* what with all the excite-

ment/what with all this chatting I quite forgot that ...; **~ Mittag geht er meist nach Hause** he usually goes home at lunch *or* at midday

d +*acc* **Cäsars Sieg ~ die Gallier** Caesar's victory over the Gauls; **Gewalt ~ jdn haben** to have power over sb; **es kam plötzlich ~ ihn** it suddenly came over him; **sie liebt ihn ~ alles** she loves him more than anything; **das geht mir ~ den Verstand** that's beyond my understanding; **Fluch ~ dich!** (*obs*) a curse upon you! (*obs*)

e +*acc* (= *vermittels, auf dem Wege über*) via; **die Nummer erfährt man ~ die Auskunft** you'll get the number from *or* through *or* via information; **wir sind ~ die Autobahn gekommen** we came by *or* via the autobahn; **nach Köln ~ Aachen** to Cologne via Aachen; **Zug nach Frankfurt ~ Wiesbaden und Mainz** train to Frankfurt via *or* stopping at *or* calling at (*Brit*) Wiesbaden and Mainz

f +*acc* (*zeitlich*) (= *innerhalb eines Zeitraums, länger als*) over; **~ Weihnachten** over Christmas; **bis ~ Ostern** until after Easter; **den ganzen Sommer ~** all summer long; **~ Wochen (ausgedehnt)** for weeks on end; **die ganze Zeit ~** all the time; **das ganze Jahr ~** all through the year, all year round; **~ kurz oder lang** sooner or later; **es ist ~ vierzehn Tage her, dass ...** it's over fourteen days since ...

g +*acc* (*bei Zahlenangaben*) (= *in Höhe von*) for; (= *mehr als*) over; **ein Scheck ~ 20 Euro** a cheque (*Brit*) *or* check (*US*) for 20 euros; **eine Rechnung von ~ £ 100** a bill for over *or* of over £100; **Kinder ~ 14 Jahre** children over 14 years *or* of 14 (years of age) and over; **Städte ~ 50.000 Einwohner** towns of over 50,000 inhabitants; **Pakete ~ 10 kg** parcels (*esp Brit*) *or* packages over 10 kgs

h +*acc* (= *wegen*) over; (= *betreffend*) about; **ein Buch/Film/Vortrag** *etc* **~** a book/film/lecture *etc* about *or* on ...; **was wissen Sie ~ ihn?** what do you know about him?; **~ welches Thema schreiben Sie Ihr neues Buch?** what's the subject of your new book?, what's your new book about?; **~ Politik/Wörterbücher/Fußball** *etc* **reden** to talk (about) politics/dictionaries/football *etc*; **~ jdn/etw lachen** to laugh about *or* at sb/sth; **sich ~ etw freuen/ärgern** to be pleased/ angry about *or* at sth

i +*acc* (*steigernd*) upon; **Fehler ~ Fehler** mistake upon *or* after mistake, one mistake after another

ADV ~ und ~ all over; **er wurde ~ und ~ rot** he went red all over; **ich stecke ~ und ~ in Schulden** I am up to my ears in debt; **(das) Gewehr ~!** (*Mil*) shoulder arms!; **jdm in etw** (*dat*) **~ sein** (*inf*) to be better than sb at sth

über|ak|tiv ADJ hyperactive, overactive

Über|ak|ti|vi|tät F hyperactivity

über|all [yːbɐˈ(ʔ)al] ADV everywhere; **ich habe dich schon ~ gesucht** I've been looking everywhere *or* all over (*inf*) for you; **~ herumliegen** to be lying all over the shop (*Brit inf*) *or* place; **~ in London/der Welt** everywhere in *or* all over London/the world; **~ wo** wherever; **~ Bescheid wissen** (*wissensmäßig*) to have a wide-ranging knowledge; (*in Stadt etc*) to know one's way around; **sie ist ~ zu gebrauchen** she can do ev-

---

erything; **es ist ~ dasselbe** it's the same wherever you go; **so ist es ~** it's the same everywhere; **~ und nirgends zu Hause sein** to be at home everywhere and nowhere; **~ und nirgends, den erreichst du nie** he's always here, there and everywhere, you'll never find him

ü|ber|all-: ü|ber|all|her [yːbɐlalˈheːɐ, yːbɐˈlalˌheːɐ, yːbɐˈlalheːɐ] ADV from all over; **ü|ber|all|hin** [yːbɐlalˈhɪn, yːbɐˈlalˌhɪn, yːbɐˈlalhɪn] ADV everywhere

Über-: ü|ber|al|tert [yːbɐˈlaltɐt] ADJ **a** (Sociol) having a disproportionate number of or having too high a percentage of old people **b** = **veraltet**; **Über|al|te|rung** F (Sociol) increase in the percentage of old people; **Über|an|ge|bot** NT surplus (an +dat of); **ü|ber|ängst|lich** ADJ overanxious; **ü|ber|an|stren|gen** [yːbɐˈlanʃtrɛŋən] ptp **überanstrengt** insep VT to overstrain, to overexert; *Kräfte* to overtax; *Augen* to strain VR to overstrain or overexert oneself; **überanstrenge dich nicht!** (iro) don't strain yourself! (iro); **Über|an|stren|gung** F overexertion; **eine ~ der Nerven/Augen** a strain on the or one's nerves/eyes; **ü|ber|ant|wor|ten** [yːbɐˈlantvɔrtn] ptp **überantwortet** VT insep (geh) **jdm etw ~** to hand sth over to sb, to place sth in sb's hands; **etw dem Feuer ~** (liter) to commit sth to the flames; **ü|ber|ar|bei|ten** [yːbɐˈlarbaitn] ptp **überarbeitet** insep VT to rework, to go over; **in einer überarbeiteten Fassung** in a revised edition VR to overwork; **Ü|ber|ar|bei|tung** F -, -en **a** (Vorgang) reworking; (Ergebnis) revision, revised version **b** no pl (= Überanstrengung) overwork; **ü|ber|aus** [yːbɐˈlaus, yːbɐˈlaus, ˈyːbɐˈlaus] ADV extremely, exceedingly; **ü|ber|ba|cken** [yːbɐˈbakn] ptp **überbacken** VT insep irreg (im Backofen) to put in the oven; (im Grill) to put under the grill; **mit Käse ~** au gratin; **~e Käseschnitten** cheese on toast

Ü|ber|bau M pl **-baue** or (Build auch) **-bauten** (Build, Philos) superstructure

ü|ber|bau|en [yːbɐˈbauən] ptp **überbaut** VT insep to build over; (mit einem Dach) to roof over, to build a roof over

Über-: ü|ber|be|an|spru|chen ptp **überbeansprucht** VT insep **a** *Menschen, Körper* to overtax, to make too many demands on; (arbeitsmäßig) **überbeansprucht sein** to be overworked **b** *Einrichtungen, Dienste* to overburden **c** *Maschine, Auto etc* to overtax, to overstrain **d** *Werkstoffe, Materialien* to overstrain; (esp durch Gewicht) to overload; **Über|be|an|spru|chung** F **a** (von Menschen) overtaxing; (arbeitsmäßig) overworking **b** (von Einrichtungen, Diensten) overburdening **c** (von Maschine, Auto etc) overtaxing, overstraining **d** (von Werkstoffen, Material) overstraining; (esp durch Gewicht) overloading; **ü|ber|be|hal|ten** ptp **überbehalten** VT sep irreg (inf) (= übrig behalten) to have left over **b** (= nicht ausziehen) *Mantel etc* to keep on; **Ü|ber|bein** NT (an Gelenk) ganglion; **ü|ber+be|kom|men** ptp **überbekommen** VT sep irreg (inf) **jdn/etw ~** to get sick of or fed up with sb/sth (inf); **ü|ber|be|las|ten** ptp **überbelastet** VT insep = **überlasten**; **Ü|ber|be|las|tung** F = **Überlastung**; **ü|ber|be|le|gen** ptp **überbelegt** VT insep usu ptp to overcrowd; *Kursus, Fach etc* to oversubscribe; **Über|be|le|gung** F overcrowding; (von Kursus, Fach etc) oversubscription; **ü|ber|be|lich|ten** ptp **überbelichtet** VT insep (Phot) to overexpose; **Über|be|lich|tung** F (Phot) overexposure; **Über|be|schäf|ti|gung** F overemployment; **ü|ber|be|setzt** ADJ *Behörde, Abteilung* overstaffed; **ü|ber|be|to|nen** ptp **überbetont** VT insep (fig) to overstress, to overemphasize; *Hüften, obere Gesichtshälfte etc* to overaccentuate, to overemphasize; **ü|ber|be|trieb|lich** ADJ industry-wide ADV industry-wide, for the entire industry; **Über|be|völ|ke|rung** F overpopulation; **ü|ber|be|wer|ten** ptp **überbewertet** VT insep (lit) to overvalue; (fig auch) to overrate; *Schulleistung etc* to

to mark too high; **wollen wir doch eine so vereinzelte Äußerung nicht ~** let's not attach too much importance to such an isolated remark; **Über|be|wer|tung** F (lit) overvaluing; (fig auch) overrating; **die ~ einer einzelnen Äußerung** attaching too much importance to an isolated statement; **diese Eins ist eine klare ~** this grade one is clearly too high; **Über|be|zah|lung** F overpayment

ü|ber|biet|bar ADJ (fig) **kaum noch ~ sein** to take some beating; **ein an Vulgarität nicht mehr ~er Pornofilm** a porn film of unsurpassed or unsurpassable vulgarity

ü|ber|bie|ten [yːbɐˈbiːtn] ptp **überboten** [yːbɐˈboːtn] insep irreg VT (bei Auktion) to outbid (um by); (fig) to outdo; *Leistung, Rekord* to beat; **das ist kaum noch zu ~** (fig) it's outrageous; **diese Geschichte ist an Peinlichkeit kaum noch zu ~** the incident could scarcely have been more embarrassing VR **sich in etw** (dat) (gegenseitig) **~** to vie with one another or each other in sth; **sich (selber) ~** to surpass oneself

Über|bie|tung F -, -en (fig) outdoing; (von Leistung, Rekord) beating; **eine ~ dieses Rekordes** to beat this record

über-: ü|ber+bin|den VT sep irreg (Mus) to join up; **ü|ber|bla|sen** [yːbɐˈblazn] ptp **überblasen** VT insep irreg (Mus) to overblow; **ü|ber|blät|tern** [yːbɐˈblɛtɐn] ptp **überblättert** VT insep *Buch* to leaf or flick or glance through; *Stelle* to skip over or past, to miss; **ü|ber+blei|ben** VI sep irreg aux sein (inf) = **übrig bleiben**

Ü|ber|bleib|sel [yːbɐblaipsl] NT -s, - remnant; (= Speiserest) leftover usu pl, remains pl; (= Brauch, Angewohnheit etc) survival, hangover; (= Spur) trace

ü|ber+blen|den[1] ['yːbɐblɛndn] VI sep (Film, Rad: Szene etc) to fade; (Film auch) to dissolve; (plötzlich) to cut

ü|ber|blen|den[2] [yːbɐˈblɛndn] ptp **überblendet** VT insep (= ausblenden) to fade out; (= überlagern) to superimpose

Ü|ber|blen|dung[1] F (Film, Rad) fade; (Film auch) dissolve; (plötzlich) cut

Ü|ber|blen|dung[2] F (= das Ausblenden) fading out; (= Überlagerung) superimposition

Ü|ber|blick M (über +acc of) **a** (= freie Sicht) view **b** (= Einblick) perspective, overall or broad view, overview; **er hat keinen ~, ihm fehlt der ~, es fehlt ihm an ~** he lacks an overview, he has no overall picture; **den ~ verlieren** to lose track (of things) **c** (= Abriss) survey; (= Übersicht, Zusammenhang) synopsis, summary; **sich** (dat) **einen ~ verschaffen** to get a general idea; **Weltgeschichte im ~** compendium of world history

ü|ber|bli|cken [yːbɐˈblɪkn] ptp **überblickt** VT insep **a** (lit) *Platz, Stadt, Gebiet* to overlook, to have or command a view of **b** (fig) to see; **die Entwicklung lässt sich leicht ~** the development can be seen at a glance; **bis ich die Lage besser überblicke** until I have a better view of the situation; **das lässt sich noch nicht ~** I/we etc cannot tell or say as yet

über-: ü|ber|bor|den [yːbɐˈbɔrdn] ptp **überbordet** VI insep aux haben or sein (fig geh) to be overextravagant; **~de Metaphern** overextravagant metaphors; **~de Selbstgewissheit** excessive self-assurance; **ü|ber|bra|ten**[1] [yːbɐˈbraːtn] ptp **überbraten** VT insep irreg (Cook) to fry lightly; **ü|ber+bra|ten**[2] ['yːbɐbraːtn] VT sep irreg **jdm eins ~** (inf) to land sb one (Brit inf), to hit sb

Ü|ber|brei|te F excess width; **Vorsicht, ~!** caution, wide load

ü|ber|brin|gen [yːbɐˈbrɪŋən] ptp **überbracht** [yːbɐˈbraxt] VT insep irreg **jdm etw ~** to bring sb sth, to bring sth to sb; *Brief etc auch* to deliver sth to sb

Über|brin|ger [yːbɐˈbrɪŋɐ] M -s, -, **Über|brin|ge|rin** [-ərɪn] F -, -nen bringer, bearer; (von Scheck etc) bearer

über|brück|bar ADJ *Gegensätze* reconcilable; *Distanz* bridgeable; **schwer ~e Gegensätze** differences which are difficult to reconcile

ü|ber|brü|cken [yːbɐˈbrʏkn] ptp **überbrückt** VT insep **a** (old) *Fluss* to bridge (over) **b** (fig) *Kluft, Zeitraum* to bridge; *Krisenzeiten* to get over or through; *Gegensätze* to reconcile; **die Gegensätze zwischen … ~** to bridge the gap between …

Über|brü|ckung F -, -en (fig) bridging; (von Krisenzeiten) getting over or through; (von Gegensätzen) reconciliation; **100 Euro zur ~** 100 euros to tide me/him etc over

Über|brü|ckungs-: Über|brü|ckungs|bei|hil|fe F, **Über|brü|ckungs|geld** NT interim aid, money to tide one over; **Über|brü|ckungs|kre|dit** [-kredɪt] M bridging loan

Über-: ü|ber|bu|chen [yːbɐˈbuːxn] ptp **überbucht** VT insep to overbook; **ü|ber|bür|den** [yːbɐˈbʏrdn] ptp **überbürdet** VT insep (geh) to overburden; **Über|dach** NT roof; **ü|ber|da|chen** [yːbɐˈdaxn] ptp **überdacht** VT insep to roof over, to cover over; **überdachte Fahrradständer/Bushaltestelle** covered bicycle stands/bus shelter; **Über|dach|ung** F (= Überdach) roof(ing); (= das Überdachen) roofing over; **ü|ber|dau|ern** [yːbɐˈdauɐn] ptp **überdauert** VT insep to survive; **Über|de|cke** F bedspread, bedcover, counterpane; **ü|ber|de|cken**[1] ['yːbɐdɛkn] VT sep to cover up or over; (inf: = auflegen) *Tischtuch* to put on; **ü|ber|de|cken**[2] [yːbɐˈdɛkn] ptp **überdeckt** insep VT *Riss, Geschmack, Schwächen* to cover up, to conceal VR (= sich überschneiden) to overlap; **ü|ber|deh|nen** [yːbɐˈdeːnən] ptp **überdehnt** VT insep *Sehne, Muskel etc* to strain; *Gummi, Begriff* to overstretch; **ü|ber|den|ken** [yːbɐˈdɛŋkn] ptp **überdacht** VT insep irreg to think over, to consider; **etw noch einmal ~** to reconsider sth; **ü|ber|deut|lich** ADJ all too obvious ADV **es ist mir ~ klar geworden** it has become perfectly clear to me; **jdm etw ~ zu verstehen geben** to make sth perfectly clear to sb; **er hat sein Missfallen ~ formuliert** the way he phrased it made it perfectly clear that he was displeased

ü|ber|dies [yːbɐˈdiːs] ADV (geh) **a** (= außerdem) moreover, furthermore, what is more **b** (= ohnehin) in any case, anyway

Über-: ü|ber|di|men|si|o|nal ADJ colossal, huge, oversize(d); **ü|ber|do|sie|ren** [yːbɐdoˈziːrən] ptp **überdosiert** VT insep **dieses Mittel wird oft überdosiert** an excessive dose of this medicine is often given; **nicht ~** do not exceed the dose; **Ü|ber|do|sis** F overdose, OD (inf); (= zu große Zumessung) excessive amount; **sich** (dat) **eine ~ Heroin spritzen** to overdose or OD (inf) on heroin; **ü|ber|dre|hen** [yːbɐˈdreːən] ptp **überdreht** VT insep *Uhr etc* to overwind; *Motor* to overrev; *Gewinde, Schraube* to strip

ü|ber|dreht [yːbɐˈdreːt] ADJ (inf) overexcited; (ständig) highly charged, hyped(-up) (inf); (= verrückt) weird; **ein ~er Typ** a weirdo (inf)

Ü|ber|druck[1] M pl **-drucke** overprint

Ü|ber|druck[2] M pl **-drücke** (Tech) excess pressure no pl

ü|ber|dru|cken [yːbɐˈdrʊkn] ptp **überdruckt** VT insep to overprint

Über|druck-: Über|druck|ka|bi|ne F (Aviat) pressurized cabin; **Über|druck|ven|til** NT pressure relief valve, blow-off valve

Ü|ber|druss ▲ ['yːbɐdrʊs] M -es, no pl (= Übersättigung) surfeit, satiety (liter) (an +dat of); (= Widerwille) aversion (an +dat to), antipathy (an +dat to); **bis zum ~** ad nauseam; **er aß Kaviar bis zum ~** he ate caviar until he wearied of it or had had a surfeit of it; **~ am Leben** weariness of living or life

ü|ber|drüs|sig ['y:bɐdrʏsɪç] ADJ **jds/einer Sache** (gen) ~ **sein** to be weary of sb/sth; **jds/einer Sache** (gen) ~ **werden** to (grow) weary of sb/sth

Über-: **ü|ber|dün|gen** [y:bɐ'dʏŋən] ptp **überdüngt** VT sep to over-fertilize; **Ü|ber|dün|gung** F over-fertilization; **ü|ber|durch|schnitt|lich** ADJ above-average ADV exceptionally, outstandingly; **er arbeitet ~ gut** his work is above average; **sie verdient ~ gut** she earns more than the average, she has an above-average salary; **ü|ber|eck** [y:bɐ'lɛk] ADV at right angles (to each other or to one another); **Ü|ber|ei|fer** M overzealousness; (pej: = Wichtigtuerei) officiousness; **ü|ber|eif|rig** ADJ overzealous; (pej: = wichtigtuerisch) officious; **ü|ber|eig|nen** [y:bɐ'laignən] ptp **übereignet** VT insep (geh) **jdm etw** ~ to make sth over to sb, to transfer sth to sb; **Ü|ber|eig|nung** F (geh) transference; **Ü|ber|ei|le** F haste; **ü|ber|ei|len** [y:bɐ'lailən] ptp **übereilt** insep VT to rush; ~ **Sie nichts!** don't rush things! VR to rush; **übereil dich bloß nicht!** (iro) don't rush yourself (iro); **ü|ber|eilt** [y:bɐ'lailt] ADJ overhasty, precipitate ADV overhastily, precipitately

ü|ber|ei|nan|der [y:bɐai'nandɐ] ADV a (räumlich) on top of each other or one another, one on top of the other; **hängen** one above the other; **wir wohnen ~** we live one above the other, we live on top of each other b **reden etc** about each other or one another

ü|ber|ei|nan|der: ü|ber|ei|nan|der le|gen ▲ VT to put or lay one on top of the other, to put or lay on top of each other or one another; **ü|ber|ei|nan|der lie|gen** ▲ VI irreg to lie one on top of the other, to lie on top of each other or one another; **ü|ber|ei|nan|der schla|gen** ▲ VT irreg **die Beine** ~ to cross one's legs; **die Arme** ~ to fold one's arms

ü|ber|ein+kom|men [y:bɐ'lain-] VI sep irreg aux sein to agree; **wir sind darin übereingekommen, dass ...** we have agreed that ...

Ü|ber|ein|kom|men [y:bɐ'lainkɔmən] NT , **Ü|ber|ein|kunft** [y:bɐ'lainkʊnft] F -, ⸚e [-kʏnftə] arrangement, understanding, agreement; (= Vertrag) agreement; **ein ~ or eine Übereinkunft treffen** to enter into or make an agreement; **ein ~ or eine Übereinkunft erzielen** to come to or reach an agreement, to reach agreement

ü|ber|ein+stim|men [y:bɐ'lain-] VI sep to agree, to concur (form); (Meinungen) to tally, to concur (form); (Angaben, Messwerte, Rechnungen etc) to correspond, to tally, to agree; (= zusammenpassen: Farben, Stile etc) to match; (Gram) to agree; (Dreiecke) to be congruent; **mit jdm in etw** (dat) ~ to agree with sb on sth; **wir stimmen darin überein, dass ...** we agree or are agreed that ...

ü|ber|ein|stim|mend ADJ corresponding; Meinungen, Vermutungen etc concurring, concurrent; Farben etc matching; **nach ~en Angaben/Meldungen** according to all accounts/reports; **nach ~en Zeugenaussagen** according to mutually corroborative testimonies ADV **alle erklärten ~, dass ...** everybody agreed that ..., everybody unanimously stated that ...; **wir sind ~ der Meinung, dass ...** we are unanimously of the opinion that ..., we unanimously agree that ...; **sie bestritten ~, dass ...** they are in agreement in denying that ...; ~ **mit** in agreement with

Ü|ber|ein|stim|mung F a (= Einklang, Gleichheit) correspondence, agreement; **sein Handeln steht nicht mit seiner Theorie in ~** there's a disparity or no correspondence between his actions and his theory; **bei den Zeugenaussagen gab es nur in zwei Punkten ~** the testimonies only agreed or corresponded or tallied in two particulars; **zwei Dinge in ~ bringen** to bring two things into line; **es besteht or herrscht keine ~ zwischen X und Y** X and Y do not agree

　b (von Meinung) agreement; **darin besteht bei allen Beteiligten ~** all parties involved are agreed on that; **in ~ mit jdm** in agreement with

sb; in ~ mit etw in accordance with sth c (Gram) agreement

Über-: **ü|ber|emp|find|lich** ADJ (gegen to) oversensitive, hypersensitive (auch Med) ADV ~ **auf etw** (acc) **reagieren** to be oversensitive to sth; **meine Haut reagiert ~ auf dieses Waschmittel** I get an allergic reaction from that detergent; **Ü|ber|emp|find|lich|keit** F (gegen to) oversensitivity, hypersensitivity (auch Med); **ü|ber|er|fül|len** ptp **übererfüllt** VT insep Norm, Soll, Plan to exceed (um by); **Ü|ber|er|fül|lung** F (no pl: = das Übererfüllen) exceeding; **bei ~ des Plansolls werden Sonderprämien gezahlt** anyone who exceeds the target or quota is paid special premiums; **ü|ber|er|näh|ren** ptp **überernährt** VT insep to overfeed; **Ü|ber|er|näh|rung** F (no pl: = das Überernähren) overfeeding; (Krankheit) overeating; **ü|ber|es|sen**[1] ['y:bɐlɛsn] VT sep irreg **sich** (dat) **etw** ~ to grow sick of sth; **Spargel kann ich mir gar nicht** ~ I can't eat enough asparagus; **ü|ber|es|sen**[2] [y:bɐ'lɛsn] pret **überaß** [y:bɐ'la:s], ptp **übergessen** [y:bɐ'gɛsn] VR insep to overeat; **ich habe mich an Käse übergessen** I've eaten too much cheese

ü|ber|fah|ren[1] ['y:bɐfa:rən] sep irreg VT (mit Boot etc) to take or ferry across VI aux sein to cross over

ü|ber|fah|ren[2] [y:bɐ'fa:rən] ptp **überfahren** VT insep irreg a jdn, Tier to run over, to knock down b (= hinwegfahren über) to go or drive over; Fluss etc to cross (over) c (= übersehen und weiterfahren) Ampel etc to go through d (inf: = übertölpeln) **jdn ~** to railroad sb into it e (= plötzlich über jdn kommen) to come over

Ü|ber|fahrt F crossing

Ü|ber|fall M a (= Angriff) attack (auf +acc on); (esp auf offener Straße) mugging (auf +acc of); (auf Bank etc) raid (auf +acc on), hold-up; (auf Land) invasion (auf +acc of); **einen ~ auf jdn/etw verüben or ausführen** to carry out an attack etc on sb/sth; **dies ist ein ~, keine Bewegung!** this is a hold-up or stick-up (esp US inf), freeze! b (hum: = unerwartetes Erscheinen) invasion; **er hat einen ~ auf uns vor** he's planning to descend on us

ü|ber|fal|len [y:bɐ'falən] ptp **überfallen** VT insep irreg a (= angreifen) to attack; (esp auf offener Straße) to mug; Bank etc to raid, to hold up, to stick up (esp US inf); Land, Stadt to invade, to attack; (Mil) Hauptquartier, Lager to raid b (fig geh) (= überkommen: Gefühle, Schlaf, Müdigkeit, Krankheit etc) to come over or upon; (= überraschen: Nacht) to overtake, to come upon suddenly; **plötzlich überfiel ihn heftiges Fieber** he suddenly came down with a bad fever c (fig inf) (= überraschend besuchen) to descend (up)on; (= bestürmen) to pounce upon; **jdn mit Fragen/Wünschen ~** to bombard sb with questions/requests

Ü|ber-: **ü|ber|fäl|lig** ADJ overdue usu pred; **seit einer Woche ~ sein** to be a week overdue; **Ü|ber|fall|kom|man|do** NT , **Ü|ber|falls|kom|man|do** (Aus) NT flying squad, riot squad; **ü|ber|fei|nert** [y:bɐ'fainɐt] ADJ overrefined; **Ü|ber|fei|ne|rung** F -, -en overrefinement; **ü|ber|fi|schen** [y:bɐ'fɪʃn] ptp **überfischt** VT insep to overfish; **Ü|ber|fi|schung** F -, -en overfishing; **ü|ber|flie|gen** [y:bɐ'fli:gn] ptp **überflogen** [y:bɐ'flo:gn] VT insep irreg a (lit) to fly over b (fig) **ein Lächeln/eine leichte Röte überflog ihr Gesicht** a smile/a faint blush flitted across her face c (= flüchtig ansehen) Buch etc to take a quick look at, to glance through or at or over; **Ü|ber|flie|ger(in)** M(F) (fig) high-flyer; **ü|ber+flie|ßen**[1] ['y:bɐfli:sn] VI sep irreg aux sein a (Gefäß) to overflow; (Flüssigkeit) to run over, to overflow b ineinander (= Farben) to run c (fig: vor Dank, Höflichkeit etc) to overflow, to gush (vor +dat with); **ü|ber|flie|ßen**[2] [y:bɐ'fli:sn] ptp **überflossen** [y:bɐ'flɔsn] VT insep irreg (rare) to inundate, to flood; **Ü|ber|flug** M overflight; **einem Flugzeug den ~ verweigern** to refuse to allow an

aircraft to fly over one's territory; **ü|ber|flü|geln** [y:bɐ'fly:gln] ptp **überflügelt** VT insep to outdistance, to outstrip; (in Leistung, bei Wahl) to outdo; Erwartungen etc to surpass

Ü|ber|fluss ▲ M , no pl a (super)abundance (an +dat of); (= Luxus) affluence; **Arbeit/Geld im ~** plenty of work/money, an abundance of work/money; **das Land des ~es** the land of plenty; **im ~ leben** to live in luxury; **im ~ vorhanden sein** to be in plentiful supply; **~ an etw** (dat) **haben, etw im ~ haben** to have plenty or an abundance of sth, to have sth in abundance

　b **zu allem** or **zum ~** (= unnötigerweise) superfluously; (= obendrein) to top it all (inf), into the bargain; **zu allem** or **zum ~ fing es auch noch an zu regnen** and then, to top it all, it started to rain (inf), and then it started to rain into the bargain

Ü|ber|fluss|ge|sell|schaft ▲ F affluent society

ü|ber|flüs|sig ADJ superfluous; (= frei, entbehrlich) spare; (= unnötig) unnecessary; (= zwecklos) futile, useless; **~ zu sagen, dass ...** it goes without saying that ... → **Kropf** b

ü|ber|flüs|si|ger|wei|se ['y:bɐflʏsɪgɐ'vaizə] ADV superfluously

Ü|ber-: **ü|ber+flu|ten**[1] ['y:bɐflu:tn] VI sep aux sein (= überschwemmen) to overflow; **ü|ber|flu|ten**[2] [y:bɐ'flu:tn] ptp **überflutet** VT insep (lit, fig) to flood; (fig auch) to inundate; **Ü|ber|flu|tung** [y:bɐ'flu:tʊŋ] F -, -en a (lit) flood; (= das Überfluten) flooding no pl b (fig) flooding no pl, inundation; **ü|ber|for|dern** [y:bɐ'fɔrdɐn] ptp **überfordert** VT insep to overtax; **jdn auch** to ask or expect too much of; **damit ist er überfordert** that's asking or expecting too much of him; **als Abteilungsleiter wäre er doch etwas überfordert** being head of department would be too much for him or would stretch him too far; **Ü|ber|for|de|rung** F excessive demand(s pl) (für on); (no pl: = das Überfordern) overtaxing; **Ü|ber|fracht** F excess freight; **ü|ber|frach|ten** [y:bɐ'fraxtn] ptp **überfrachtet** VT insep (fig) to overload; **ein mit Emotionen überfrachteter Begriff** a concept fraught with emotions, an emotionally loaded concept; **ü|ber|fragt** [y:bɐ'fra:kt] ADJ pred stumped (for an answer); **da bin ich ~** there you've got me, there you have me, that I don't know; **ü|ber|frem|den** [y:bɐ'frɛmdn] ptp **überfremdet** VT insep to infiltrate with too many foreign influences; (Econ) to swamp; **überfremdet werden** (Land) to be swamped by foreigners; **Ü|ber|frem|dung** F -, -en foreign infiltration; (Econ) swamping; **ü|ber|fres|sen** [y:bɐ'frɛsn] ptp **überfressen** VR insep irreg (inf) to overeat, to eat too much; **sich an etw** (dat) ~ to gorge oneself on sth; **ü|ber|frie|ren** [y:bɐ'fri:rən] ptp **überfroren** [y:bɐ'fro:rən] VI insep irreg to freeze over; **Glatteisgefahr durch ~de Nässe** slippery roads due to black ice; **Ü|ber|fuhr** F -, -en (Aus) ferry; **ü|ber+füh|ren**[1] ['y:bɐfy:rən] VT sep to transfer; Leichnam to transport; Wagen to drive; **ü|ber|füh|ren**[2] [y:bɐ'fy:rən] ptp **überführt** VT insep a = **überführen**[1] b Täter to convict (+gen of), to find guilty (+gen of); **ein überführter Verbrecher** a convicted criminal c (= überbauen) **einen Fluss mit einer Brücke ~** to build a bridge over a river; **Ü|ber|füh|rung** F a transportation no pl (Jur) conviction c (= Brücke über Straße etc) bridge (auch Rail), overpass; (= Fußgängerüberführung) footbridge; **Ü|ber|fül|le** F profusion, superabundance; **ü|ber|fül|len** ptp **überfüllt** VT insep Glas to overfill; **sich** (dat) **den Magen** ~ to eat too much; **ü|ber|füllt** [y:bɐ'fʏlt] ADJ overcrowded; Kurs oversubscribed; (Comm) Lager overstocked, overfilled; **Ü|ber|fül|lung** F -, no pl overcrowding; (von Kursus, Vorlesung) oversubscription; **Ü|ber|funk|ti|on** F hyperactivity, hyperfunction(ing); **ü|ber|füt|tern** [y:bɐ'fʏtɐn] ptp **überfüttert** VT insep to overfeed; **Ü|ber|füt|te|rung** F overfeeding

Über|ga|be F handing over *no pl*; (*von Neubau*) opening; (*Mil*) surrender; **die ~ der Zeugnisse findet am Ende des Schuljahres statt** reports are handed out at the end of the school year; **die ~ des neuen Schwimmbads an die Öffentlichkeit wird durch den Bürgermeister vorgenommen** the mayor will open the new swimming pool to the public

Über|gang M *pl* **-gänge** **a** (= *das Überqueren*) crossing **b** (= *Fußgängerübergang*) crossing, crosswalk (*US*); (= *Brücke*) footbridge; (= *Bahnübergang*) level crossing (*Brit*), grade crossing (*US*); (= *Grenzübergangsstelle*) checkpoint **c** (*fig: = Wechsel, Überleitung*) transition **e** (*zum Internet*) gateway

Über|gangs-: Über|gangs|be|stim|mung F interim *or* temporary regulation; **Über|gangs|er|schei|nung** F temporary phenomenon; **Über|gangs|fi|nan|zie|rung** F gap financing; **Über|gangs|geld** NT interim payment *or* allowance; **über|gangs|los** ADJ, ADV without a transition; (*zeitlich auch*) without a transitional period; **Über|gangs|lö|sung** F interim *or* temporary solution; **Über|gangs|man|tel** F between-seasons coat; **Über|gangs|pha|se** F transitional phase; **Über|gangs|re|ge|lung** F interim arrangement; **Ü|ber|gangs|re|gie|rung** F caretaker *or* transitional government; **Über|gangs|sta|di|um** NT transitional stage; **Über|gangs|zeit** F **a** transitional period, period of transition **b** (*zwischen Jahreszeiten*) in-between season; **Ü|ber|gangs|zu|stand** M transitional state

Über|gar|di|ne F curtain, drape (*US*)

über|ge|ben [yːbɐˈɡeːbn̩] *ptp* **übergeben** *insep irreg* **VT** **a** (= *überreichen*) to hand over; *Dokument, Zettel, Einschreiben* to hand (*jdm sb*); *Diplom etc* to hand over (*jdm to sb*), to present (*jdm to sb*); (= *vermachen*) to bequeath (*jdm to sb*); (*Mil*) to surrender, to hand over; **ein Gebäude der Öffentlichkeit/eine Straße dem Verkehr ~** to open a building to the public/a road to traffic; **eine Angelegenheit einem Rechtsanwalt ~** to place a matter in the hands of a lawyer **b** (= *weiterreichen, verleihen*) *Amt, Macht* to hand over **c einen Leichnam der Erde/dem Wasser ~** (*liter*) to commit a body to the earth/water **VR** (= *sich erbrechen*) to vomit, to be sick; **ich muss mich ~** I'm going to be sick

über+ge|hen[1] [ˈyːbɐɡeːən] **VI** *sep irreg aux sein* **a in etw** (*acc*) **~** (= *in einen anderen Zustand*) to turn *or* change into sth; (*Farben*) to merge into sth; **in jds Besitz** (*acc*) **~** to become sb's property; **in andere Hände/in Volkseigentum ~** to pass into other hands/into public ownership **b auf jdn ~** (= *geerbt, übernommen werden*) to pass to sb **c zu etw ~** to go over to sth; **wir sind dazu übergegangen, Computer zu benutzen** we went over to (using) computers (*esp Brit*), we started using computers (*esp US*)

über|ge|hen[2] [yːbɐˈɡeːən] *ptp* **übergangen** [yːbɐˈɡaŋən] **VT** *insep irreg* to pass over; *Kapitel, Abschnitt etc auch* to skip; *Einwände etc auch* to ignore

Über-: über|ge|nau ADJ overprecise, pernickety (*Brit inf*), persnickety (*US inf*); **über|ge|nug** ADV more than enough; **über|ge|ord|net** *a* *Behörde, Dienststelle, Recht* higher; **die uns ~e Behörde** the next authority above us **b** (*Gram*) *Satz* superordinate; (*Ling, Philos*) *Begriff* generic **c** (*fig*) **von ~er Bedeutung sein** to be of overriding importance → *auch* **überordnen**; **Über|ge|päck** NT (*Aviat*) excess baggage; **über|ge|scheit** ADJ (*iro*) know-all (*Brit*), know-it-all (*US*), smart-ass (*sl*); **so ein Übergescheiter** some clever Dick (*Brit inf*) *or* smart-ass (*sl*), some know-all (*Brit*) *or* know-it-all (*US*); **über|ge|schnappt** ADJ (*inf*) crazy → *auch* **überschnappen**; **Über|ge|wicht** NT overweight; (*fig*) predominance; **~ haben** (*Paket etc*) to be overweight; **an ~ leiden**,

~ haben (*Mensch*) to be overweight; **5 Gramm ~** 5 grammes excess weight; **das ~ bekommen** (*fig*) to become predominant; **das ~ haben** (*fig*) to predominate; **wenn sie das militärische ~ bekommen** if they gain military dominance; **ü|ber|ge|wich|tig** ADJ overweight; **über+gie|ßen**[1] [ˈyːbɐɡiːsn̩] VT *sep irreg jdm etw ~* to pour sth over sb; **über|gie|ßen**[2] [yːbɐˈɡiːsn̩] *ptp* **übergossen** [yːbɐˈɡɔsn̩] **VT** *insep irreg* to pour over; *jdn* to douse; *Braten* to baste; **jdn/sich mit etw ~** to pour sth over sb/oneself; (*absichtlich auch*) to douse sb/oneself with sth; **über|glück|lich** ADJ overjoyed; **über+grei|fen** VI *sep irreg* **a** (*beim Klavierspiel*) to cross one's hands (over) **b** (*auf Rechte etc*) to encroach *or* infringe (*auf +acc* on); (*Feuer, Streik, Krankheit etc*) to spread (*auf +acc* to); **ineinander ~** to overlap; **über|grei|fend** ADJ (*fig*) *Gesichtspunkte, Überlegungen, Problem* general; *Ziel auch* overall; **Über|griff** M (= *Einmischung*) infringement (*auf +acc* of), encroachment (*auf +acc* on), interference *no pl* (*auf +acc* with *or* in); (*Mil*) attack (*auf +acc* upon), incursion (*auf +acc* into); (= *Ausschreitung*) excess; **über|groß** ADJ oversize(d), huge, enormous; *Mehrheit* overwhelming, huge; **Über|grö|ße** F (*bei Kleidung etc*) outsize; **62 ist eine ~** 62 is outsize; **62 ist übergroß** 62 is outsize; **ü|ber+ha|ben** VT *sep irreg* (*inf*) **a** (= *satt haben*) to be sick (and tired) of (*inf*), to be fed up of *or* with (*inf*) **b** (= *übrig haben*) to have left (over); **für etw nichts ~** not to like sth **c** *Kleidung* to have on

über|hand neh|men ▲ [yːbɐˈhantneːmən] **VI** *irreg* to get out of control *or* hand; (*schlechte Sitten, Laxheit etc auch*) to become rife *or* rampant; (*Meinungen, Ideen etc*) to become rife *or* rampant, to gain the upper hand

Über-: Über|hang M **a** (= *Felsüberhang*) overhang, overhanging rock; (= *Baumüberhang*) overhanging branches *pl* **b** (= *Vorhang*) pelmet (*Brit*), valance (*US*); (*von Bettdecke etc*) valance **c** (= *Überschuss*) surplus (*an +dat* of); **ü|ber+hän|gen** *sep* **VI** *irreg aux haben* *or* *sein* to overhang; (= *hinausragen auch*) to jut out **VT** **sich** (*dat*) **ein Gewehr ~** to sling a rifle over one's shoulder; **sich** (*dat*) **einen Mantel ~** to put *or* hang a coat round *or* over one's shoulders; **Über|hang|man|dat** NT (*Pol*) seat gained as a result of votes for a specific candidate over and above the seats to which a party is entitled by the number of votes cast for the party; **über|has|ten** [yːbɐˈhastn̩] *ptp* **überhastet** VT *insep* to rush; **über|has|tet** [yːbɐˈhastət] ADJ overhasty, hurried ADV overhastily, hurriedly; **~ sprechen** to speak too fast; **über|häu|fen** [yːbɐˈhɔyfn̩] *ptp* **überhäuft** VT *insep jdn* to overwhelm, to inundate; *Schreibtisch etc* to pile high; **jdn mit Geschenken/Glückwünschen/Titeln ~** to heap presents/congratulations/titles (up)on sb; **ich bin völlig mit Arbeit überhäuft** I'm completely snowed under *or* swamped (with work); **jdn mit Vorwürfen ~** to heap reproaches (up)on sb('s head)

über|haupt [yːbɐˈhaupt] ADV **a** (= *sowieso, im Allgemeinen*) in general; (= *überdies, außerdem*) anyway, anyhow; **und ~, warum nicht?** and after all *or* anyway, why not?; **er sagt ~ immer sehr wenig** he never says very much anyway *or* anyhow *or* at the best of times; **nicht nur Rotwein, sondern Wein ~ mag ich nicht** it's not only red wine I don't like, I don't like wine at all or full stop (*esp Brit*) or period **b** (*in Fragen, Verneinungen*) at all; **~ nicht** not at all; **ich denke ~ nicht daran mitzukommen** I've (absolutely) no intention whatsoever of coming along; **~ nie** never (ever), never at all; **kein Grund** no reason at all *or* whatsoever; **hast du denn ~ keinen Anstand?** have you no decency at all?; **das habe ich ja ~ nicht gewusst** I had no idea at all; **ich habe ~ nichts gehört** I didn't hear anything at all, I didn't hear a thing; **das steht in ~ keinem Verhältnis zu ...** that bears no relationship at all *or* whatsoever to ...

c (= *erst, eigentlich*) **dann merkt man ~ erst, wie schön ...** then you really notice for the first time how beautiful ...; **waren Sie ~ schon in dem neuen Film?** have you actually been to the latest film?; **da fällt mir ~ ein, ...** now I remember ...; **wenn ~** if at all; **wie ist das ~ möglich?** how is that possible?; **gibt es das ~?** is there really such a thing?, is there really any such thing?; **was wollen Sie ~ von mir?** (*herausfordernd*) what do you want from me?; **wer sind Sie ~?** who do you think you are?; **wissen Sie ~, wer ich bin?** do you realize who I am?

Über-: über|he|ben [yːbɐˈheːbn̩] *ptp* **überhoben** [yːbɐˈhoːbn̩] **VR** *insep irreg* (*lit*) to (over)strain oneself; (*fig: finanziell*) to overreach oneself; (*fig geh: = hochmütig sein*) to be arrogant; **sich über jdn ~** to consider oneself superior to sb; **über|heb|lich** [yːbɐˈheːplɪç] ADJ arrogant; **Über|heb|lich|keit** F -, *no pl* arrogance; **Über|he|bung** F (= *Anmaßung*) presumption; **über|hei|zen** [yːbɐˈhaitsn̩] *ptp* **überheizt** VT *insep* to overheat; **über|hit|zen** [yːbɐˈhɪtsn̩] *ptp* **überhitzt** VT *insep* to overheat; **über|hitzt** [yːbɐˈhɪtst] ADJ (*fig*) *Konjunktur, Markt* overheated; *Gemüter, Diskussion* very heated *pred*; *Fantasie* overheated; **Über|hit|zung** F overheating; (*Tech*) superheating; **Über|hit|zungs|schutz** M cutout switch (*to prevent overheating*); **über|hö|hen** [yːbɐˈhøːən] *ptp* **überhöht** VT *insep Preise* to raise *or* increase excessively; *Kurve* to bank, to superelevate (*spec*); **über|höht** [yːbɐˈhøːt] ADJ *Kurve* banked, superelevated (*spec*); *Forderungen, Preise* exorbitant, excessive; *Geschwindigkeit* excessive

über|ho|len[1] [yːbɐˈhoːlən] **VT** *insep* **a** *Fahrzeug* to overtake (*esp Brit*), to pass; (*fig: = übertreffen*) to overtake **b** (*Tech*) *Maschine, Motor etc* to overhaul **VI** to overtake

über+ho|len[2] [ˈyːbɐhoːlən] *sep* **VTI** (*old*) to ferry; **hol über!** ferry! **VI** (*Naut: Schiff*) to keel over

Über|hol|ma|nö|ver NT (*Aut*) overtaking *or* passing manoeuvre (*Brit*), passing maneuver (*US*)

Über|hol|spur F (*Aut*) overtaking (*esp Brit*) *or* fast lane

über|holt [yːbɐˈhoːlt] ADJ out-dated

Über|hol- [yːbɐˈhoːl-]: **Über|hol|ver|bot** NT restriction on overtaking (*esp Brit*) *or* passing; (*als Schild etc*) no overtaking (*esp Brit*), no passing; **auf dieser Strecke besteht ~** no overtaking (*esp Brit*) *or* passing on this stretch; **nach der nächsten Kurve ist das ~ wieder aufgehoben** the restriction on overtaking (*esp Brit*) *or* passing ends after the next bend; **Ü|ber|hol|vor|gang** M (*form*) overtaking (*esp Brit*), passing; **vor Beginn des ~es** before starting *or* beginning to overtake (*esp Brit*) *or* pass; **der ~ war noch nicht abgeschlossen, als das Fahrzeug ...** the vehicle had not finished overtaking (*esp Brit*) *or* passing when it ...

über|hö|ren[1] [yːbɐˈhøːrən] *ptp* **überhört** VT *insep* not to hear; (= *nicht hören wollen*) to ignore; **das möchte ich überhört haben!** (I'll pretend) I didn't hear that!

über+hö|ren[2] [ˈyːbɐhøːrən] VT *sep* **sich** (*dat*) **etw ~** to be tired *or* sick (*inf*) of hearing sth

Über|ich ▲ NT (*Psych*) superego

über|in|ter|pre|tie|ren *ptp* **überinterpretiert** VT *insep* to overinterpret

Über-: über|ir|disch ADJ **a** *Wesen, Schönheit* celestial, heavenly **b** (= *oberirdisch*) above ground ADV **a** **~ schön** heavenly **b** (= *oberirdisch*) above ground; **über|ka|pa|zi|tät** F *usu pl* overcapacity; **über|kauft** [yːbɐˈkauft] ADJ (*Comm*) saturated; **über|kip|pen** VI *sep aux sein* to topple *or* keel over; (*Stimme*) to crack; **über|kle|ben**[1] [yːbɐˈkleːbn̩] *ptp* **überklebt** VT *insep* **die Kiste ~** to stick something over the box; **etw mit Papier ~** to stick paper over sth; **über+kle|ben**[2] [ˈyːbɐkleːbn̩] VT *sep* **etw ~** to stick something over it; **über|klug** ADJ (*pej*) too clever by half (*Brit*), know-all *attr* (*Brit*), know-it-all *attr* (*US*), smart-ass *attr* (*sl*); **sei doch nicht so ~!** don't be so clever, don't be such a know-all (*Brit*) or know-it-all (*US*); **ü|ber+ko|chen** VI *sep aux sein* (*lit, fig*) to boil over

über|kom|men¹ [yːbɐˈkɔmən] *ptp* **überkommen** *insep irreg* **VT** (= *überfallen, ergreifen*) to come over; **ein Gefühl der Verlassenheit überkam ihn** a feeling of desolation came over him, he was overcome by a feeling of desolation; **Furcht** *etc* **überkam ihn** he was overcome with fear *etc*; **was überkommt dich denn?** what's come over you? **VI** *aux sein ptp only* (= *überliefern*) **es ist uns** (*dat*) **~** (*old*) it has come down to us, it has been handed down to us

ü|ber+kom|men² [ˈyːbɐkɔmən] VT *sep irreg* (*Sw*) to get handed down

Über-: Über|kom|pen|sa|ti|on F overcompensation; **ü|ber|kom|pen|sie|ren** *ptp* **überkompensiert** VT *insep* to overcompensate for; **ü|ber|kreu|zen** [yːbɐˈkrɔytsn] *ptp* **überkreuzt** **VT** (= *überqueren*) to cross **VR** (= *sich überschneiden: Linien etc*) to intersect; **ü|ber+krie|gen** VT *sep* (*inf*) **a** (= *überdrüssig werden*) to get tired or sick (and tired) (*inf*) of, to get fed up of or with (*inf*), to get browned off with (*Brit inf*) **b** **eins ~** to get landed one (*Brit inf*), to get hit; **ü|ber|kri|tisch** ADJ overcritical, overly critical; **ü|ber|krus|ten** [yːbɐˈkrʊstn] *ptp* **überkrustet** VT *insep* to cover (with a layer or crust of); **ü|ber|küh|len** [yːbɐˈkyːlən] *ptp* **überkühlt** VT *insep* (*Aus Cook*) to cool down; **ü|ber|la|den¹** [yːbɐˈlaːdn] VT *sep irreg* (= *zu stark belasten*) to overload; (*mit Arbeit auch*) to overburden; (= *zu voll packen*) Schreibtisch, Wand *etc auch* to clutter, to cover; (= *zu stark verzieren auch*) to clutter; (= *reichlich geben*) to shower; **ü|ber|laden²** [yːbɐˈlaːdn] ADJ Wagen overloaded, overladen; (*fig*) Stil over-ornate, flowery; Bild cluttered; **ü|ber|la|gern** [yːbɐˈlaːgɐn] *ptp* **überlagert** *insep* **VT** **a** **diese Schicht wird von einer anderen überlagert** another stratum overlies this one; **am Abend ist dieser Sender von einem anderen überlagert** in the evenings this station is blotted out by another one **b** Thema, Problem, Konflikt *etc* to eclipse **c** (= *zu lange lagern*) to store for too long **VR** (= *sich überschneiden*) to overlap; **Über|la|ge|rung** F (*von Themen, Problemen etc*) eclipsing; (= *Überschneidung*) overlapping

Über|land-: Über|land|bus M country bus, coach; **Über|land|lei|tung** F (*Elec*) overhead power line or cable; **Über|land|stra|ße** F road (*heading across country*); **Über|land|zent|ra|le** F (*Elec*) rural power station

Über-: ü|ber|lang ADJ Oper, Stück *etc* overlength; Arme, Mantel, Netze, Schnüre *etc* too long; **Über|län|ge** F excessive length; **~ haben** to be overlength; **ü|ber|lap|pen** [yːbɐˈlapn] *ptp* **überlappt** VIR *insep* to overlap; **Über|lap|pung** F -, -en (= *das Überlappen*) (*also Comput*) overlapping; (= *überlappte Stelle*) (*also Comput*) overlap

ü|ber|las|sen¹ [yːbɐˈlasn] *ptp* **überlassen** VT *insep irreg* **a** (= *haben lassen, abgeben*) **jdm etw ~** to let sb have sth **b** (= *anheim stellen*) **es jdm ~, etw zu tun** to leave it (up) to sb to do sth; **das bleibt (ganz) Ihnen ~** that's (entirely) up to you; **das müssen Sie schon mir ~** you must leave that to me; **es bleibt Ihnen ~, zu …** it's up to you to …; **jdm die Initiative/Wahl ~** to leave the initiative/choice (up) to sb **c** (= *in Obhut geben*) **jdm etw ~** to leave sth with sb or in sb's care, to entrust sth to sb's care; **sich** (*dat*) **selbst ~ sein** to be left to one's own devices, to be left to oneself; **jdn sich** (*dat*) **selbst ~** to leave sb to his/her own devices **d** (= *preisgeben*) **sich seinem Schmerz/seinen Gedanken/Gefühlen ~** to abandon oneself to one's pain/thoughts/feelings; **jdn seinem Schicksal ~** to leave or abandon sb to his fate;

jdn seinem Kummer ~ to offer sb no comfort in his/her grief

über+las|sen² [yːbɐˈlasn] VT *sep irreg* (*inf:* = *übrig lassen*) to leave (*jdm for sb*)

Über|las|sung [yːbɐˈlasʊŋ] F -, -en (*von Recht, Anspruch*) surrender

über|las|ten [yːbɐˈlastn] *ptp* **überlastet** VT *insep* to put too great a strain on; *jdn* to overtax; (*Elec, durch Gewicht*) Telefonnetz, Brücke to overload; **überlastet sein** to be under too great a strain; (= *überfordert sein*) to be overtaxed; (*Elec etc*) to be overloaded

Über|las|tung F -, -en (*von Mensch*) overtaxing; (= *Überlastetsein*) strain; (*Elec, durch Gewicht*) overloading; **bei ~ der Leber** when there is too much strain on the liver

Über|lauf M overflow

Über|lauf|an|zei|ge F (*beim Taschenrechner*) decimal cutoff symbol

über|lau|fen¹ [yːbɐˈlaufn] *ptp* **überlaufen** VT *insep irreg* **a** Gegner, Abwehr to overrun **b** (*fig:* = *ergreifen: Angst etc*) to seize; **es überlief ihn heiß** he felt hot under the collar; **es überlief ihn kalt** a cold shiver ran down his back or up and down his spine; **es überlief mich heiß und kalt** I went hot and cold all over

ü|ber+lau|fen² [ˈyːbɐlaufn] VI *sep irreg aux sein* **a** (*Wasser, Gefäß*) to overflow; (= *überkochen*) to boil over; **ineinander ~** (*Farben*) to run (into one another); **zum Überlaufen voll** full to overflowing; **jetzt läuft das Maß über** (*fig*) my patience is at an end → **Galle** **b** (*Mil, fig:* = *überwechseln*) to desert; **zum Feind ~** to go over or desert to the enemy

ü|ber|lau|fen³ [yːbɐˈlaufn] ADJ overcrowded; (*mit Touristen*) overrun

Über|läu|fer(in) M(F) (*Mil*) deserter, turncoat; (*Pol*) turncoat

Über|lauf|rohr NT overflow pipe

ü|ber|laut ADJ **a** (= *zu laut*) overloud **b** (= *aufdringlich*) Mensch obtrusive, loud; Farben loud, garish; (= *flegelhaft*) Benehmen brash, loud ADV too loudly

über|le|ben [yːbɐˈleːbn] *ptp* **überlebt** *insep* **VT** **a** Unglück, Operation, Anschlag, schwierige Lage *etc* to survive; **die Nacht** to last, to survive, to live through; **das überlebe ich nicht!** (*inf*) it'll be the death of me (*inf*); **du wirst es ~** (*iro*) it won't kill you), you'll survive; **ums Überleben kämpfen** to fight for survival **b** (= *länger leben als*) to outlive, to survive (*um by*) **VI** to survive **VR** **das hat sich überlebt** that's had its day; **das wird sich ganz schnell überlebt haben** that will very soon have had its day; **diese Mode überlebt sich ganz schnell** this fashion will soon be a thing of the past → *auch* **überlebt**

Über|le|ben NT -s, *no pl* survival; **ums ~ kämpfen** to fight for survival

Über|le|ben|de(r) [yːbɐˈleːbndə] MF *decl as adj* survivor

Über|le|bens|chan|ce F chance of survival

über|le|bens|fä|hig ADJ *pred* capable of surviving or survival *pred*

ü|ber|le|bens|groß ADJ Denkmal *etc* larger--than-life

ü|ber|le|bens|grö|ße F **in ~** larger than life

Über|le|bens|kampf M fight or struggle for survival

Über|le|bens|künst|ler M survivor

Über|le|bens|trai|ning NT survival training

über|lebt [yːbɐˈleːpt] ADJ outmoded, out-of--date → *auch* **überleben**

über|le|gen¹ [yːbɐˈleːgn] ⊙ 29.3 *ptp* **überlegt** *insep* **VI** (= *nachdenken*) to think; **überleg doch mal!** think!; **hin und her ~** to deliberate; **ich habe hin und her überlegt** I've thought about it a lot; **ohne zu ~** without thinking; (= *ohne zu zögern*) without thinking twice

VT (= *überdenken, durchdenken*) to think over or about, to consider; **das werde ich mir ~** I'll think it over, I'll (have a) think about it, I'll give it some thought; **ich habe es mir anders überlegt** I've changed my mind (about it); **ich habe es mir noch mal überlegt** I've had second thoughts (about it); **wollen Sie es sich** (*dat*) **nicht noch einmal ~?** won't you think it over again?, won't you reconsider?; **das muss ich mir noch sehr ~** I'll have to think it over or consider it very carefully; **das hätten Sie sich** (*dat*) **vorher ~ müssen** you should have thought of or about that before or sooner; **es wäre zu ~** it should be considered; **wenn man es sich recht überlegt** if you really think about it

ü|ber+le|gen² [ˈyːbɐleːgn] *sep* **VT** **jdm etw ~** to put or lay sth over sb **VR** (= *sich zur Seite legen*) to lean over, to tilt

ü|ber|le|gen³ [yːbɐˈleːgn] ADJ superior; (= *hochmütig auch*) supercilious; **jdm ~ sein** to be superior to sb; **das war ein ~er Sieg** that was a good or convincing victory ADV in a superior manner or fashion; **Bayern München hat ~ gesiegt** Bayern Munich won convincingly

Über|le|gen|heit F -, *no pl* superiority; (= *Hochmut auch*) superciliousness

über|legt [yːbɐˈleːkt] ADJ (well-)considered ADV in a considered way

Über|le|gung [yːbɐˈleːgʊŋ] F -, -en **a** (= *Nachdenken*) consideration, thought, reflection; **bei näherer ~** on closer examination; **bei nüchterner ~** on reflection; **das wäre wohl einer ~ wert** that would be worth thinking about or over, that would be worth considering, that would be worthy of consideration; **ohne ~** without thinking → **anstellen** VT **c**, **reiflich b** (= *Bemerkung*) observation; **~en anstellen** to make observations (*zu* about or on); **~en vortragen** to give one's views (*zu* on or about)

ü|ber+lei|ten *sep* **VT** (*Thema, Abschnitt etc*) to link up (*in +acc* to, with) **VI** **zu etw ~** to lead up to sth; **in eine andere Tonart ~** (*Mus*) to change key

Über|lei|tung F connection; (*zur nächsten Frage, Mus*) transition

über|le|sen [yːbɐˈleːzn] *ptp* **überlesen** VT *insep irreg* **a** (= *flüchtig lesen*) to glance through or over or at **b** (= *übersehen*) to overlook, to miss

über|lie|fern [yːbɐˈliːfɐn] *ptp* **überliefert** VT *insep* Brauch, Tradition, Lied to hand down; **das Manuskript ist nur als Fragment überliefert** the manuscript has only come down to us in fragmentary form; **etw der Nachwelt ~** to preserve sth for posterity

Über|lie|fe|rung F **a** tradition; **schriftliche ~en** (written) records **b** (= *Brauch*) tradition, custom; **an der ~ festhalten** to hold on to tradition; **nach alter ~** according to tradition

über|lis|ten [yːbɐˈlɪstn] *ptp* **überlistet** VT *insep* to outwit

ü|berm [ˈyːbɐm] *contr von* **über dem**

ü|ber|ma|chen [yːbɐˈmaxn] *ptp* **übermacht** VT *insep* (*old:* = *vermachen*) to make over (*+dat* to)

Über|macht F , *no pl* superior strength or might; (*fig: von Gefühlen, Ideologie etc*) predominance; **in der ~ sein** to have the greater strength

ü|ber|mäch|tig ADJ Gewalt, Stärke superior; Feind, Opposition powerful, strong; Wunsch, Bedürfnis overpowering; (*fig*) Institution, Rauschgift all-powerful

ü|ber+ma|len¹ [ˈyːbɐmaːlən] VT *sep* to paint over

über|ma|len² [yːbɐˈmaːlən] *ptp* **übermalt** VT *insep* to paint over, to paint on top of

über|man|nen [yːbɐˈmanən] *ptp* **übermannt** VT *insep* (*geh*) to overcome

Über|maß NT , *no pl* excess, excessive amount (*an +acc* of); **im ~** to or in excess; **er hat Zeit im ~** he has more than enough time

ü|ber|mä|ßig ADJ **a** excessive; *Schmerz, Sehnsucht* violent; *Freude* intense; **das war nicht ~** that was not too brilliant **b** (*Mus*) **~es Intervall** augmented interval ADV excessively; *essen, trinken auch* to excess; **sich ~ anstrengen** to overdo things; **er hat sich nicht ~ bemüht** he didn't exactly overexert himself

Ü|ber|mensch M **a** (*Philos*) superman **b** (*fig inf*) superman; **ich bin doch kein ~** I'm not superman/superwoman

ü|ber|mensch|lich ADJ superhuman; **Übermenschliches leisten** to perform superhuman feats

ü|ber|mit|teln [y:bɛˈmɪtln] *ptp* **übermittelt** VT *insep* to convey (*jdm* to sb); (*telefonisch etc*) *Meldung* to transmit, to send; *Daten* to transmit

Ü|ber|mitt|lung [y:bɛˈmɪtlʊŋ] F -, -en conveyance; (*telefonisch etc, von Meldung*) transmission, sending

ü|ber|mor|gen ADV the day after tomorrow; **~ Abend/früh** the day after tomorrow in the evening/morning

ü|ber|mü|den [y:bɛˈmyːdn] *ptp* **übermüdet** VT *insep usu ptp* to overtire; (= *erschöpfen auch*) to overfatigue

Ü|ber|mü|dung F -, *no pl* overtiredness; (= *Erschöpfung auch*) overfatigue

Ü|ber|mü|dungs|er|schei|nung F sign of overtiredness *or* (*Erschöpfung auch*) fatigue

Ü|ber|mut M high spirits *pl*; **vor lauter ~ wussten die Kinder nicht, was sie tun sollten** the children were so full of high spirits that they didn't know what to do with themselves; **tut selten gut** (*Prov*) pride goes before a fall (*Prov*); (*zu Kindern*) it'll all end in tears

ü|ber|mü|tig [ˈyːbɛmyːtɪç] ADJ **a** (= *ausgelassen*) high-spirited, boisterous **b** (= *zu mutig*) cocky (*inf*); **werd bloß nicht ~!** don't be cocky (*inf*) **c** (*dated*: = *überheblich*) arrogant ADV (= *ausgelassen*) boisterously

Ü|ber|mut|ter F *pl* -mütter mother figure

ü|bern [ˈyːbɛn] *contr von* über den

ü|ber|nächs|te(r, s) ADJ *attr* next ... but one; **das ~ Haus** the next house but one; **die ~ Woche** the week after next; **am ~n Tag war er ...** two days later he was ..., the next day but one he was ...; **er kommt ~n Freitag** he's coming a week on Friday *or* (on) Friday week

ü|ber|nach|ten [y:bɛˈnaxtn] *ptp* **übernachtet** VI *insep* to sleep; (*in Hotel, Privathaus etc auch*) to stay; (*eine Nacht*) to spend *or* stay the night; **bei jdm ~** to stay with sb, to sleep *or* stay at sb's place; **wie viele Leute können bei dir ~?** how many people can you put up?

ü|ber|näch|tigt [y:bɛˈnɛçtɪçt], (*esp Aus*) **ü|ber|näch|tig** [ˈyːbɛnɛçtɪç] ADJ bleary-eyed

Ü|ber|nach|tung [y:bɛˈnaxtʊŋ] F -, -en overnight stay; **~ und Frühstück** bed and breakfast

Ü|ber|nach|tungs|mög|lich|keit F overnight accommodation *no pl*; **sich nach einer ~ umsehen** to look for somewhere to stay the night

Ü|ber|nah|me [ˈyːbɛnaːmə] F -, -n **a** takeover (*auch Comm, Fin*); (= *das Übernehmen*) taking over; (*von Ausdruck, Ansicht*) adoption; (*von Zitat, Wort*) borrowing; **seit der ~ des Geschäfts durch den Sohn** since the son took over the business; **freundliche/feindliche ~** (*Comm*) friendly/hostile takeover **b** (*von Amt*) assumption; (*von Verantwortung*) assumption, acceptance; **durch ~ dieser Aufgabe** by taking on *or* undertaking this task; **er hat sich zur ~ der Kosten/Hypothek verpflichtet** he has undertaken to pay the costs/mortgage; **bei ~ einer neuen Klasse** (*Sch*) when taking charge of a new class; **er konnte Rechtsanwalt Mayer zur ~ seines Falles bewegen** he persuaded Mr Mayer, the barrister, to take (on) his case

Ü|ber|nah|me-: Ü|ber|nah|me|an|ge|bot NT , **Ü|ber|nah|me|of|fer|te** F takeover bid; **Ü|ber|nah|me|ver|trag** M takeover agreement

Ü|ber|nahms|stel|le F (*Aus*) = **Annahmestelle**

ü|ber|na|ti|o|nal ADJ supranational ADV supranationally

ü|ber|na|tür|lich ADJ supernatural

ü|ber|neh|men¹ [y:bɛˈneːmən] ✪ 47.3 *ptp* **übernommen** [y:bɛˈnɔmən] *insep irreg* VT **a** (= *annehmen*) to take; *Aufgabe, Arbeit* to take on, to undertake; *Funktion* to take on; *Verantwortung* to take on, to assume, to accept; *Kosten, Hypothek* to agree to pay; (*Jur*) *Fall* to take (on); *jds Verteidigung* to take on; (= *kaufen*) to buy; **den Befehl** *or* **das Kommando ~** to take command *or* charge; **die Führung ~** (*von Organisation etc*) to take charge (*gen* of); (*Sport*) to take over the lead; **seit er das Amt übernommen hat** since he assumed office; **er übernimmt Ostern eine neue Klasse** (*Sch*) he's taking charge of a new class at Easter; **lassen Sie mal, das übernehme ich!** let me take care of that; **es ~, etw zu tun** to take on the job of doing sth, to undertake to do sth
  b (*stellvertretend, ablösend*) to take over (*von* from); *Ausdruck, Ansicht* to adopt; *Zitat, Wort* to take, to borrow
  c *Geschäft, Praxis etc* to take over
  d (*Aus inf*: = *übertölpeln*) to put one over on (*inf*)
  VR to take on *or* undertake too much; (= *sich überanstrengen*) to overdo it; (*beim Essen*) to overeat; **Sie sich nur nicht!** (*iro*) don't strain yourself! (*iro*)

ü|ber+neh|men² [ˈyːbɛneːmən] VT *sep irreg Cape etc* to put on; **das Gewehr ~** (*Mil*) to slope arms

ü|ber|ner|vös ADJ highly strung

ü|ber+ord|nen VT *sep* **a** **jdn jdm ~** to put *or* place *or* set sb over sb → *auch* **übergeordnet** **b** **etw einer Sache** (*dat*) **~** to give sth precedence over sth; **einer Sache** (*dat*) **übergeordnet sein** to have precedence over sth, to be superordinate to sth

ü|ber|par|tei|lich ADJ nonparty *attr*; (= *unvoreingenommen*) nonpartisan; (*Parl*) Problem all-party *attr*, cross-bench *attr* (*Brit*); *Amt, Präsident etc* above party politics ADV *handeln, denken* in a nonpartisan way; **ein ~ inszenierter Wahlkampf** a nonpartisan election campaign; **eine ~ organisierte Veranstaltung** a nonparty event; **ein ~ zusammengesetztes Komitee** a nonpartisan committee

Ü|ber|par|tei|lich|keit F **die ~ des Ausschusses ist gewährleistet** the committee must be nonpartisan

ü|ber+pin|seln¹ [ˈyːbɛpɪnzln] VT *sep* (*inf*) *Wand* to paint over

ü|ber|pin|seln² [y:bɛˈpɪnzln] *ptp* **überpinselt** VT *insep Fleck* to paint over

Ü|ber|preis M exorbitant price; **zu ~en** at exorbitant prices

Ü|ber|pro|duk|ti|on F overproduction

ü|ber|prüf|bar ADJ checkable

Ü|ber|prüf|bar|keit [y:bɛˈpryːfbaːɐkait] F -, *no pl* means *sing* of checking; **aufgrund der mangelnden ~** because there is no means of checking

ü|ber|prü|fen [y:bɛˈpryːfn] *ptp* **überprüft** VT *insep* (*auf +acc* for) to check; *Gepäck auch, Maschine, Waren* to inspect, to examine; (*Fin*) *Bücher* to inspect, to examine; *Entscheidung, Lage, Frage* to examine, to review; *Ergebnisse, Teilnehmer etc* to scrutinize; (*Pol*) *jdn* to screen; **etw erneut ~** to recheck sth; **to re-examine sth; to scrutinize sth again; die Richtigkeit von etw ~** to check (the correctness of) sth

Ü|ber|prü|fung F **a** *no pl* (= *das Überprüfen*) checking; (*von Maschinen, Waren, Fin: von Büchern*) inspection, examination; (*von Entscheidung*) review; (*Pol*) screening; **nach ~ der Lage**
after reviewing the situation, after a review of the situation **b** (= *Kontrolle*) check, inspection

ü|ber|qua|li|fi|ziert ADJ overqualified

ü|ber+quel|len VI *sep irreg aux sein* to overflow (*von, mit* with); (*Cook*) (*Teig*) to rise over the edge; (*Reis, Brei*) to boil over; **die Augen quollen ihm über** his eyes grew as big as saucers; **vor Freude/Dankbarkeit ~** to be overflowing with joy/gratitude

ü|ber|que|ren [y:bɛˈkveːrən] *ptp* **überquert** VT *insep* to cross

Ü|ber|que|rung F -, -en crossing

ü|ber|ra|gen¹ [y:bɛˈraːgn] *ptp* **überragt** VT *insep* **a** (*lit*: = *größer sein*) to tower above **b** (*fig*: = *übertreffen*) to outshine (*an +dat, in +dat* in)

ü|ber+ra|gen² [ˈyːbɛraːgn] VI *sep* (= *hervorstehen*) (*senkrecht*) to protrude; (*waagerecht*) to jut out, to project

ü|ber|ra|gend ADJ (*fig*) outstanding; *Bedeutung auch* paramount ADV outstandingly well

ü|ber|ra|schen [y:bɛˈraʃn] ✪ 42.2 *ptp* **überrascht** VT *insep* to surprise; **jdn ~** (= *überrumpeln*) to surprise sb, to catch *or* take sb unawares, to take sb by surprise; **einen Einbrecher ~** to surprise *or* disturb a burglar; **jdn bei etw ~** to surprise *or* catch sb doing sth; **von einem Gewitter überrascht werden** to be caught in a storm; **lassen wir uns ~!** let's wait and see! → *auch* **überrascht**

ü|ber|ra|schend ADJ surprising; *Besuch* surprise *attr*; *Tod, Weggang* unexpected; **eine ~e Wendung nehmen** to take an unexpected turn ADV unexpectedly; **das kam (für uns) völlig ~** that came as a complete surprise *or* (*Sterbefall etc*) shock (to us)

ü|ber|ra|schen|der|wei|se [y:bɛˈraʃndɐˈvaizə] ADV surprisingly

ü|ber|rascht [y:bɛˈraʃt] ADJ surprised (*über +dat* at); **da bin ich aber ~!** that's quite a surprise ADV with surprise; **jdn ~ ansehen** to look at sb in surprise; **sich von etw (nicht) ~ zeigen** to show (no) surprise at sth → *auch* **überraschen**

Ü|ber|ra|schung [y:bɛˈraʃʊŋ] F -, -en surprise; **zu meiner (größten) ~** to my (great) surprise, much to my surprise; **Mensch, ist das eine ~!** (*inf*) well, that's a surprise (and a half (*inf*))!; **jdm eine kleine ~ kaufen** to buy a little something for sb as a surprise; **für eine ~ sorgen** to have a surprise in store; **sie ist immer für eine ~ gut** she never ceases to amaze *or* surprise; **mit ~ musste ich sehen** *or* **feststellen, dass ...** I was surprised to see that ...

Ü|ber|ra|schungs-: Ü|ber|ra|schungs|an|griff M surprise attack; **Ü|ber|ra|schungs|ef|fekt** M shock effect; **Ü|ber|ra|schungs|er|folg** M unexpected success; **Ü|ber|ra|schungs|gast** M surprise guest (*auch TV*); **Ü|ber|ra|schungs|hit** M surprise hit; **Ü|ber|ra|schungs|mo|ment** NT moment of surprise; **Ü|ber|ra|schungs|sie|ger(in)** M(F) (*Sport*) surprise winner

ü|ber|re|a|gie|ren *ptp* **überreagiert** VI *insep* to overreact

Ü|ber|re|ak|ti|on F overreaction

ü|ber|re|den [y:bɛˈreːdn] *ptp* **überredet** VT *insep* to persuade, to talk round (*Brit*) *or* around (*US*); **jdn ~, etw zu tun** to persuade sb to do sth, to talk sb into doing sth; **jdn zu etw ~** to talk sb into sth; **ich habe mich zum Kauf ~ lassen** I let myself be talked *or* persuaded into buying it/them; **lass dich nicht ~** don't (let yourself) be talked into anything

Ü|ber|re|dung F -, (*rare*) -en persuasion

Ü|ber|re|dungs|kunst F persuasiveness; **all ihre Überredungskünste** all her powers of persuasion

ü|ber|re|gi|o|nal ADJ (= *national*) national, nationwide ADV nationally

ü|ber|reich ADJ lavish, abundant; (= *zu reich*) overabundant; **~ an etw** (*dat*) overflowing with sth **ADV** lavishly; *testamentarisch bedenken* generously; **jdn ~ beschenken** to lavish presents on sb

ü|ber|rei|chen [y:bəˈraiçn] *ptp* **überreicht** VT *insep* (**jdm**) **etw ~** to hand sth over (to sb); (*feierlich*) to present sth (to sb)

ü|ber|reich|lich **ADJ** ample, abundant; (= *zu reichlich*) overabundant; **in ~em Maße** in abundance **ADV** *Gebrauch machen* excessively; **~ essen/trinken** to eat/drink more than enough; **eine ~ bemessene Dosierung** an extremely high dose; **~ angebotene Informationen** an overabundance of information

Ü|ber|rei|chung F -, -en presentation

ü|ber|reif ADJ overripe; **die Zeit ist ~ für ...** it is high time for ...

Ü|ber|rei|fe F overripeness

ü|ber|rei|zen [y:bəˈraitsn] *ptp* **überreizt** *insep* **VT** to overtax; *Fantasie* to overexcite; *Nerven, Augen* to overstrain **VTR** (*Cards*) to overbid

ü|ber|reizt [y:bəˈraitst] ADJ overtaxed; *Augen* overstrained; (*nervlich*) overwrought; (= *zu erregt*) overexcited

Ü|ber|rei|zung F , *no pl* overtaxing; (*von Fantasie*) overexcitement, overstimulation; (*von Nerven, Augen*) overstraining

ü|ber|ren|nen [y:bəˈrɛnən] *ptp* **überrannt** [y:bəˈrant] VT *insep irreg* to run down; (*Mil*) to overrun; (*fig*) to overwhelm

ü|ber|re|prä|sen|tiert ADJ overrepresented

Ü|ber|rest M remains *pl*; (= *letzte Spur: von Ruhm, Selbstachtung etc auch*) remnant, vestige; **ein Häufchen Asche war der klägliche ~** the only remains were a sorry heap of ashes

ü|ber|rie|seln [y:bəˈriːzln] *ptp* **überrieselt** VT *insep Wiese* to water, to spray; **ein Schauer überrieselte ihn** a shiver ran down his spine; **es überrieselt mich kalt, wenn ...** it makes my blood run cold when ..., it sends a shiver down my spine when ...

Ü|ber|rock M (*dated*: = *Mantel*) greatcoat, overcoat; (*old*: = *Gehrock*) frock coat

Ü|ber|roll|bü|gel M (*Aut*) rollbar

ü|ber|rol|len [y:bəˈrɔlən] *ptp* **überrollt** VT *insep* to run down; (*Mil, fig*) to overrun; **wir dürfen uns von ihnen nicht ~ lassen** we mustn't let them steamroller us

ü|ber|rum|peln [y:bəˈrʊmpln] *ptp* **überrumpelt** VT *insep* (*inf*) to take by surprise, to take *or* catch unawares; (= *überwältigen*) to overpower; **jdn mit einer Frage ~** to throw sb with a question

Ü|ber|rum|pe|lung [y:bəˈrʊmpəlʊŋ] F -, -en surprise attack; (= *Überwältigung*) overpowering; **durch ~** with a surprise attack

Ü|ber|rum|pe|lungs|tak|tik F surprise tactics *pl*

Ü|ber|rump|lung [y:bəˈrʊmplʊŋ] F -, -en = **Überrumpelung**

ü|ber|run|den [y:bəˈrʊndn] *ptp* **überrundet** VT *insep* (*Sport*) to lap; (*fig*) to outstrip

übers [ˈyːbɐs] **a** *contr von* **über das** **b** (*old*) **~ Jahr** in a year

ü|ber|sä|en [y:bəˈzɛːən] *ptp* **übersät** VT *insep* to strew; (*mit Abfall etc auch*) to litter; **übersät** strewn; (*mit Abfall etc auch*) littered; (*mit Sternen*) *Himmel* studded; (*mit Narben etc*) covered; **ein mit Fehlern übersäter Aufsatz** an essay strewn *or* littered with mistakes

ü|ber|satt ADJ more than full *or* replete (*von* with)

ü|ber|sät|ti|gen [y:bəˈzɛtɪɡn] *ptp* **übersättigt** VT *insep* to satiate; *Markt* to glut, to oversaturate; (*Chem*) to supersaturate; **übersättigt sein** (*Menschen*) to be sated with luxuries; **das reizt ihn nicht mehr, er ist schon übersättigt** that doesn't hold any attraction for him any more, he has had a surfeit

Ü|ber|sät|ti|gung F satiety; (*des Marktes*) glut, oversaturation; (*Chem*) supersaturation

Ü|ber|säu|e|rung F -, -en (*Med, von Magen, Blut*) excessive acidity; (*von Gewässer, Boden*) over-acidification

Über|schall- *in cpds* supersonic; **Über|schall|flug|zeug** NT supersonic aircraft, SST (*esp US*); **Ü|ber|schall|ge|schwin|dig|keit** F supersonic speed; **mit ~ fliegen** to fly supersonic; **Ü|ber|schall|knall** M sonic boom

ü|ber|schat|ten [y:bəˈʃatn] *ptp* **überschattet** VT *insep* (*lit, fig*) to overshadow; (*fig*: = *trüben*) to cast a shadow *or* cloud over

ü|ber|schät|zen [y:bəˈʃɛtsn] *ptp* **überschätzt** **VT** *insep* to overrate, to overestimate; *Entfernung, Zahl etc* to overestimate **VR** **sich (selbst) ~** to overestimate oneself

Ü|ber|schät|zung F overestimation

Ü|ber|schau F (*geh*) overview (*über +acc* of)

ü|ber|schau|bar ADJ *Plan, Gesetzgebung etc* easily understandable; *Grenzen, Größenordnung, Kundenkreis* manageable; *Zeitraum* reasonable; **damit die Abteilung ~ bleibt** so that one can keep a general overview of *or* keep track of (*inf*) the department; **die Folgen sind noch nicht ~** the consequences cannot yet be clearly seen

Ü|ber|schau|bar|keit [y:bəˈʃaubaːɐkait] F -, *no pl* overview; **zum Zwecke der besseren ~** to give (you) a better idea

ü|ber|schau|en [y:bəˈʃauən] *ptp* **überschaut** VT *insep* = **überblicken**

ü|ber+schäu|men VI *sep aux sein* to froth *or* foam over; (*fig*) to brim *or* bubble (over) (*vor +dat* with); (*vor Wut*) to seethe; **~de Begeisterung** *etc* exuberant *or* effervescent *or* bubbling enthusiasm *etc*

Ü|ber|schicht F (*Ind*) extra shift

ü|ber|schläch|tig [-ʃlɛçtɪç] ADJ *Wasserrad* overshot

ü|ber|schla|fen [y:bəˈʃlafn] *ptp* **überschlafen** VT *insep irreg Problem etc* to sleep on

Ü|ber|schlag M **a** (= *Berechnung*) (rough) estimate **b** (= *Drehung*) somersault (*auch Sport*); (*Aviat*: = *Looping*) loop; **einen ~ machen** to turn *or* do a somersault; (*Aviat*) to loop the loop

ü|ber|schla|gen¹ [y:bəˈʃlaːɡn] *ptp* **überschlagen** *insep irreg* **VT** **a** (= *auslassen*) to skip, to miss **b** (= *berechnen*) *Kosten etc* to estimate (roughly) **VR** **a** (*Mensch*) to somersault; (*Auto*) to turn over; (*fig*: *Ereignisse*) to come thick and fast; (= *sich gegenseitig übertreffen*) **sich vor Hilfsbereitschaft** (*dat*)/**mit Vorschlägen ~** to fall over oneself to be helpful/to make suggestions; **nun überschlag dich mal nicht!** don't get carried away **b** (*Stimme*) to crack

ü|ber+schla|gen² [ˈyːbəˈʃlaːɡn] *sep irreg* **VT** *Beine* to cross; *Arme* to fold; *Decke* to fold *or* turn back; **mit übergeschlagenen Beinen/Armen** with one's legs crossed/arms folded **VI** *aux sein* **a** (*Wellen*) to break **b** (*Stimmung etc*) **in etw** (*acc*) **~** to turn into sth

ü|ber|schla|gen³ [y:bəˈʃla:ɡn] ADJ *Flüssigkeit* lukewarm, tepid; *Zimmer* slightly warm

Über-: **ü|ber|schlä|gig** [-ʃlɛːɡɪç] ADJ, ADV = **überschläglich**; **Ü|ber|schlag|la|ken** NT top sheet; **ü|ber|schläg|lich** [-ʃlɛːklɪç] **ADJ** rough, approximate **ADV** roughly, approximately; **ü|ber|schlank** ADJ too thin; **ü|ber|schlau** ADJ (*inf*) too clever by half (*Brit*), clever-clever (*Brit inf*), smart-aleck *attr* (*inf*)

ü|ber+schnap|pen VI *sep aux sein* **a** (*Riegel etc*) to clip *or* snap on **b** (*Stimme*) to crack, to break; (*inf: Mensch*) to crack up (*inf*) → *auch* **übergeschnappt**

ü|ber|schnei|den [y:bəˈʃnaidn] *ptp* **überschnitten** [y:bəˈʃnɪtn] VR *insep irreg* (*Linien*) to intersect; (*Flächen, fig: Themen, Interessen, Ereignisse etc*) to overlap; (*völlig*) to coincide; (*unerwünscht*) to clash

Ü|ber|schnei|dung F -, -en (*von Linien*) intersection; (*von Flächen, fig*) overlap *no pl*; (*unerwünscht*) clash

ü|ber|schnell **ADJ** overhasty **ADV** overhastily

Ü|ber|schrei|be|mo|dus M (*Comput*) typeover mode

ü|ber|schrei|ben [y:bəˈʃraibn] *ptp* **überschrieben** [y:bəˈʃriːbn] VT *insep irreg* **a** (= *betiteln*) to head **b** (= *übertragen*) **etw jdm** *or* **auf jdn ~** to make (*esp Brit*) *or* sign sth over to sb **c** (*Comput*) *Daten, Diskette* to overwrite; *Text* to type over

ü|ber|schrei|en [y:bəˈʃraiən] *ptp* **überschrie(e)n** [y:bəˈʃriː(ə)n] VT *insep irreg* to shout down

ü|ber|schrei|ten [y:bəˈʃraitn] *ptp* **überschritten** [y:bəˈʃrɪtn] VT *insep irreg* to cross; (*fig*) to exceed; *Höhepunkt, Alter* to pass; „**Überschreiten der Gleise verboten**" "do not cross the line"; **die Grenze des Erlaubten/des Anstands ~** to go beyond what is permissible/decent

Ü|ber|schrei|tung F -, -en crossing (+*gen* of); (*fig*) overstepping; (*Jur*: = *Verletzung*) violation, contravention (*geh*); **~ der zulässigen Geschwindigkeit** exceeding *or* breaking the speed limit

Ü|ber|schrift F heading; (= *Schlagzeile*) headline

Ü|ber|schuh M overshoe, galosh *usu pl*

ü|ber|schul|det [y:bəˈʃʊldət] ADJ *Person, Unternehmen* heavily in debt; *Grundstück* heavily mortgaged

Ü|ber|schul|dung [y:bəˈʃʊldʊŋ] F -, -en excessive debts *pl*; (*von Grundstück*) heavy mortgaging

Ü|ber|schuss ▲ M surplus (*an +dat* of); **seinen ~ an Kraft austoben** to work off one's surplus energy

Ü|ber|schuss|be|tei|li|gung ▲ F surplus sharing

ü|ber|schüs|sig [-ʃʏsɪç] ADJ *Energie, Fett* surplus

Über|schuss-: **Ü|ber|schuss|land** ▲ NT country producing a surplus; **Ü|ber|schuss|pro|duk|ti|on** ▲ F surplus production

ü|ber|schüt|ten [y:bəˈʃʏtn] VT *insep* **a** (= *bedecken*) **jdn/etw mit etw ~** to tip sth onto sb/sth, to cover sb/sth with sth; *mit Flüssigkeit* to pour sth onto sb/sth **b** (= *überhäufen*) **jdn mit etw ~** to shower sb with sth, to heap sth on sb; *mit Lob, Vorwürfen* to heap sth on sb

Ü|ber|schwang [-ʃvaŋ] M -(e)s, *no pl* exuberance; **im ~ der Freude** in one's joyful exuberance; **im ~** in exuberance; **im ersten ~** in the first flush of excitement

ü|ber|schwäng|lich ▲ [ˈyːbəʃvɛŋlɪç] **ADJ** effusive, gushing (*pej*) **ADV** effusively

Ü|ber|schwäng|lich|keit ▲ F -, -en effusiveness

ü|ber+schwap|pen VI *sep aux sein* to splash over; (*aus Tasse etc auch*) to slop over; (= *sich ausbreiten*) to spill over; **die von Amerika nach Europa ~de Drogenwelle** the drug wave spilling over from America into Europe

ü|ber|schwem|men [y:bəˈʃvɛmən] *ptp* **überschwemmt** VT *insep* (*lit, fig*) to flood; (*Touristen*) *Land etc auch* to overrun, to inundate *usu pass*; (*Angebote, Anträge*) *Inserenten, Behörde etc auch* to inundate *usu pass*, to deluge *usu pass*, to swamp; *Verbraucher, Leser etc* to swamp

Ü|ber|schwem|mung F -, -en (*lit*) flood; (= *das Überschwemmen*) flooding *no pl*; (*fig*) inundation; (*von Verbrauchern, Lesern*) swamping; **es kam zu ~en** there was a lot of flooding, there were a lot of floods

Ü|ber|schwem|mungs-: **Ü|ber|schwem|mungs|ge|biet** NT (= *überschwemmtes Gebiet*) flood area; (*Geog*) flood plain; **Ü|ber|schwem|mungs|ge|fahr** F danger of flooding; **Ü|ber|schwem|mungs|ka|ta|stro|phe** F flood disaster

ü|ber|schweng|lich △ [ˈyːbəʃvɛŋlɪç] ADJ, ADV → **überschwänglich**

Über|schweng|lich|keit △ F -, -en → **Überschwänglichkeit**

Über|see no art **in/nach** ~ overseas; **aus/von** ~ from overseas; **Briefe nach** ~ overseas letters, letters to overseas destinations; **Besitzungen in** ~ **haben** to have overseas territories or territories overseas

Über|see-: Über|see|damp|fer M ocean liner; **Über|see|ha|fen** M international port; **Über|see|han|del** M overseas trade

über|see|isch ['y:beze:ɪʃ] ADJ overseas attr

Über|see-: Über|see|ka|bel NT transoceanic cable; (im Atlantik) transatlantic cable; **Über|see|kof|fer** M trunk; **Über|see|ver|kehr** M overseas traffic

über|seh|bar ADJ **a** (lit) Gegend etc visible; **das Tal ist von hier schlecht** ~ you don't get a good view of the valley from here **b** (fig) (= erkennbar) Folgen, Zusammenhänge etc clear; (= abschätzbar) Kosten, Dauer etc assessable; **dieses Fachgebiet ist nicht mehr** ~ it is no longer possible to have an overall view of this subject; **die Folgen sind klar/schlecht** ~ the consequences are quite/not very clear; **der Schaden ist noch gar nicht** ~ the damage cannot be assessed yet **c** **solche Druckfehler sind leicht** ~ misprints like that are easily overlooked or are easy to overlook or miss

über|se|hen¹ [y:be'ze:ən] ptp **übersehen** VT insep irreg **a** (lit) Gegend etc to look over, to have a view of **b** (= erkennen, Bescheid wissen über) Folgen, Zusammenhänge, Sachlage etc to see clearly; Fachgebiet to have an overall view of; (= abschätzen) Schaden, Kosten, Dauer to assess; **dieses Fach ist nicht mehr zu** ~ it is no longer possible to have an overall view of this subject **c** (= ignorieren, nicht erkennen) to overlook; (= nicht bemerken) to miss, to fail to see or notice; **~, dass ...** to overlook the fact that ...; **dieses Problem ist nicht mehr zu** ~ this problem cannot be overlooked any longer; **etw stillschweigend/geflissentlich** ~ to quietly/conveniently ignore sth

über|se|hen² ['y:beze:ən] VT sep irreg **sich** (dat) **etw** ~ to get or grow tired of or tire of seeing sth

über sein ▲ VI irreg aux sein (inf) **jdm ist etw über** sb is fed up with sth (inf); **mir ist diese Arbeit schon lange über** I've been fed up with this work for a long time (inf)

über|sen|den [y:be'zɛndn] ptp **übersandt** or **übersendet** [y:be'zant, y:be'zɛndət] VT insep irreg to send; **Geld** auch to remit (form); **hiermit** ~ **wir Ihnen ...** please find enclosed ...

Über|sen|dung F sending; (von Geld) remittance (form)

über|setz|bar ADJ translatable; **leicht/schwer** ~ easy/hard to translate

über|set|zen¹ [y:be'zɛtsn] ptp **übersetzt** VT insep **a** auch vi (in andere Sprachen) to translate; **aus dem** or **vom Englischen ins Deutsche** ~ to translate from English into German; **ein Buch aus dem Englischen** ~ to translate a book from (the) English; **etw falsch** ~ to mistranslate sth; **sich leicht/schwer** ~ **lassen** to be easy/hard to translate; **sich gut/schlecht** ~ **lassen** to translate well/badly **b** (Tech) (= umwandeln) to translate; (= übertragen) to transmit

über+set|zen² ['y:bezetsn] sep **a** (mit Fähre) to take or ferry across **b** **den Fuß** ~ to put one's leg over **VI** aux sein to cross (over)

Über|set|zer(in) M(F) translator

Über|set|zung [y:be'zɛtsʊŋ] F -, -en **a** translation **b** (Tech) (= Umwandlung) translation; (= Übertragung) transmission; (= Herabübersetzung, Heraufübersetzung) change in the gear ratio; (= Übersetzungsverhältnis) gear ratio

Über|set|zungs-: Über|set|zungs|bü|ro NT translation bureau or agency; **Über|set|zungs|feh|ler** M translation error, error in

translation; **Über|set|zungs|ver|hält|nis** NT (Tech) gear ratio

Über|sicht F -, -en **a** no pl (= Überblick) overall view; **die** ~ **verlieren** to lose track of things or of what's going on **b** (= Abriss, Resümee) survey; (= Tabelle) table

über|sicht|lich ADJ Gelände etc open; (= erfassbar) Darstellung etc clear; **eine Bibliothek muss** ~ **sein** a library should be clearly laid out ADV clearly; ~ **angelegt** or **geplant** clearly laid out; ~ **gegliederte Einträge** well-structured entries

Über|sicht|lich|keit F -, no pl (von Gelände etc) openness; (= Verständlichkeit: von Darstellung etc) clarity

Über|sichts|kar|te F general map

Über|sichts|plan M general plan

über|sie|deln ['y:bezi:dln] sep, **über|sie|deln** [y:be'zi:dln] ptp **übersiedelt** insep VI aux sein to move (von from, nach, in +acc to)

Über|sie|de|lung [y:be'zi:dəlʊŋ, 'y:be-] F -, -en (= das Übersiedeln) moving; (= Umzug) move, removal (form)

Über|sied|ler(in) M(F) migrant

Über|sied|lung [y:be'zi:dlʊŋ, 'y:be-] F = **Übersiedelung**

über|sinn|lich ADJ supersensory; (= übernatürlich) supernatural

über|span|nen [y:be'ʃpanən] ptp **überspannt** VT insep **a** (Brücke, Decke etc) to span; **etw mit Leinwand/Folie** etc ~ to stretch canvas/foil etc over sth, to cover sth with canvas/foil etc **b** (= zu stark spannen) to put too much strain on; (fig) Forderungen to push too far → **Bogen c**

über|spannt [y:be'ʃpant] ADJ Ideen, Forderungen wild, extravagant; (= exaltiert) eccentric; (= hysterisch) hysterical; Nerven overexcited

Über|spannt|heit F -, -en (von Ideen, Forderungen) wildness, extravagance; (= Exaltiertheit) eccentricity; (= Hysterie) hysteria

Über|span|nung F (Elec) overload

Über|span|nungs|schutz M (Elec) overvoltage or surge (US) protection

über|spie|len [y:be'ʃpi:lən] ptp **überspielt** VT insep **a** (= verbergen) to cover (up) **b** (= übertragen) Aufnahme to transfer; **eine CD (auf Kassette)** ~ to tape a CD **a** (Sport) to pass; (= ausspielen, klar besiegen) to outplay

über|spit|zen [y:be'ʃpɪtsn] ptp **überspitzt** VT insep to carry too far, to exaggerate; Argument to overstate

über|spitzt [y:be'ʃpɪtst] ADJ Formulierungen (= zu spitzfindig) oversubtle (Brit), overly subtle (esp US), fiddly (Brit inf); (= übertrieben) exaggerated; Argument overstated ADV (= übertrieben) in an exaggerated fashion; **die 2-Meter-Marke** ~ **argumentieren** to overstate one's argument(s) or case

über|spre|chen [y:be'ʃprɛçn] ptp **übersprochen** [y:be'ʃprɔxn] VT insep irreg to speak over

über|sprin|gen¹ [y:be'ʃprɪŋən] ptp **übersprungen** [y:be'ʃprʊŋən] VT insep irreg **a** Hindernis, Höhe to jump, to clear; **die Fünfprozenthürde** ~ to clear the five-percent hurdle **b** (= weiter springen als) to jump more than; **die 2-Meter-Marke** ~ to jump more than 2 metres (Brit) or meters (US) **c** (= auslassen) Klasse, Kapitel, Lektion to miss (out), to skip

über+sprin|gen² ['y:beʃprɪŋən] VI sep irreg aux sein (lit, fig: = sich übertragen) to jump (auf +acc to); (Begeisterung) to spread quickly (auf +acc to) → **Funke a**

über+spru|deln VI sep aux sein (lit, fig) to bubble over (vor with); (beim Kochen) to boil over; ~**d** (fig) bubbling, effervescent

über|spü|len [y:be'ʃpy:lən] ptp **überspült** VT insep to flood; (Wellen auch) to wash over; **überspült sein** to be awash

über|staat|lich ADJ supranational

über|ste|hen¹ [y:be'ʃte:ən] ptp **überstanden** VT insep irreg (= durchstehen) to come or get through; (= überleben) to survive; (= überwinden)

to overcome; Unwetter to weather, to ride out; Krankheit to get over, to recover from; **etw lebend** ~ to survive sth, to come out of sth alive; **das Schlimmste ist jetzt überstanden** the worst is over now; **nach überstandener Gefahr** when the danger was past; **das wäre überstanden!** thank heavens that's over; **er hat es überstanden** (euph: = er ist gestorben) he has gone to rest (euph), he has passed away (euph)

über+ste|hen² ['y:beʃte:ən] VI sep irreg aux haben or sein (= hervorstehen) to jut or stick out, to project; **um 10 cm** ~ to jut out etc 10 cm

über|stei|gen [y:be'ʃtaign] ptp **überstiegen** [y:be'ʃti:gn] VT insep irreg **a** (= klettern über) to climb over **b** (= hinausgehen über) to exceed, to go beyond; (Philos, Liter: = transzendieren) to transcend → **Fassungsvermögen**

über|stei|gern [y:be'ʃtaign] ptp **übersteigert** insep VT Preise, Tempo to force up; Forderungen to push too far VR to get carried away

über|stei|gert [y:be'ʃtaigɐt] ADJ excessive; **an einem** ~**en Selbstbewusstsein leiden** to have an inflated view of oneself

Über|stei|ge|rung F (von Emotionen) excess; (von Forderungen) pushing too far

über|stel|len [y:be'ʃtɛlən] ptp **überstellt** VT insep (Admin) to hand over

Über|stel|lung F -, -en (Admin) handing over

über|stem|peln [y:be'ʃtɛmpln] ptp **überstempelt** VT insep to stamp over; **ein überstempeltes Passbild** a passport photograph which has been stamped (over)

über|steu|ern [y:be'ʃtɔyɐn] ptp **übersteuert** insep VI (Aut) to oversteer (Brit), to overcorrect VT (Elec) to overmodulate

über|stim|men [y:be'ʃtɪmən] ptp **überstimmt** VT insep to outvote; Antrag to vote down

über|strah|len [y:be'ʃtra:lən] ptp **überstrahlt** VT insep (lit) to illuminate; (fig) to outshine

über|stra|pa|zie|ren ptp **überstrapaziert** insep VT to wear out; Ausrede etc to wear thin; **überstrapaziert** worn out; thin; **jds Geduld** ~ to really try sb's patience VR to wear oneself out

über|strei|chen [y:be'ʃtraiçn] ptp **überstrichen** VT insep irreg to paint over; (mit Lack) to varnish over

über+strei|fen VT sep **sich** (dat) **etw** ~ to slip sth on

über|strö|men¹ [y:be'ʃtrø:mən] ptp **überströmt** VT insep (= überfluten) to flood; **von Schweiß/Blut überströmt sein** to be streaming or running with sweat/blood

über+strö|men² ['y:beʃtrø:mən] VI sep aux sein **a** (lit, fig: = überlaufen) to overflow; **er sprach mit** ~**der Freude/Dankbarkeit** he spoke in a voice overflowing with joy/gratitude **b** (= hinüberströmen) to spread, to communicate itself (auf +acc to)

über+stül|pen VT sep **sich** (dat) **etw** ~ to put sth on; **jdm/einer Sache etw** ~ to put sth on sb/sth

Über|stun|de F hour of overtime; ~**n** overtime sing; ~**n/zwei** ~**n machen** to do or work overtime/two hours overtime

Über|stun|den|zu|schlag M overtime allowance; **der** ~ **beträgt 50%** overtime is paid at time and a half

über|stür|zen [y:be'ʃtyrtsn] ptp **überstürzt** insep VT to rush into; Entscheidung auch to rush; **man soll nichts** ~, **nur nichts** ~**!** look before you leap (Prov) VR (Ereignisse etc) to happen in a rush; (Nachrichten) to come fast and furious; (Worte) to come tumbling out; **sich beim Sprechen** ~ to speak all in a rush

über|stürzt [y:be'ʃtyrtst] ADJ overhasty, precipitate ADV precipitately, rashly

Über|stür|zung [y:be'ʃtyrtsʊŋ] F -, no pl (= das Überstürzen) rushing (+gen into); (= Hast) rush

über|süß ADJ too sweet, oversweet; Kuchen etc auch sickly

ü|ber|ta|rif|lich ADJ, ADV above the agreed *or* union rate

ü|ber|teu|ern [yːbɐˈtɔyɐn] *ptp* **überteuert** VT *insep Waren* to overcharge for; *Preis* to inflate, to force up

ü|ber|teu|ert [yːbɐˈtɔyɐt] ADJ overexpensive; *Preise, Mieten* inflated, excessive

Ü|ber|teu|e|rung F **a** (= *das Überteuern*) overcharging (+*gen* for); (*von Preisen*) forcing up, (over)inflation **b** (= *Überteuertsein*) expensiveness; excessiveness

ü|ber|tip|pen [yːbɐˈtɪpn] *ptp* **übertippt** VT *insep* to type over

Ü|ber|ti|tel M (*bei Opernaufführung*) surtitle

ü|ber|töl|peln [yːbɐˈtœlpln] *ptp* **übertölpelt** VT *insep* to take in, to dupe

Ü|ber|töl|pe|lung F **-, -en** taking-in

ü|ber|tö|nen [yːbɐˈtøːnən] *ptp* **übertönt** VT *insep* to drown

Ü|ber|topf M cachepot

Ü|ber|trag [ˈyːbɐtraːk] M **-(e)s, ≃e** [-trɛːɡə] amount carried forward (*esp Brit*) *or* over (*esp US*)

ü|ber|trag|bar ADJ transferable (*auch Jur, Comput*); *Methode, Maßstab* applicable (*auf* +*acc* to); *Ausdruck* translatable (*in* +*acc* into); *Krankheit* communicable (*form*) (*auf* +*acc* to), infectious; (*durch Berührung*) contagious

Ü|ber|trag|bar|keit [yːbɐˈtraːkbaːɐkait] F **-, no pl** transferability (*auch Jur, Comput*); (*von Krankheit*) infectiousness; (*durch Berührung*) contagiousness

ü|ber|tra|gen¹ [yːbɐˈtraːɡn] *ptp* **übertragen** *insep irreg* VT **a** (= *an eine andere Stelle bringen, an jdn übergeben*) to transfer (*auch Jur, Psych, Comput*); *Krankheit* to pass on (*auf* +*acc* to), to transmit (*auf* +*acc* to); (*Tech*) *Bewegung, Kraft* to transmit **b** (= *an eine andere Stelle schreiben*) to transfer; (= *kopieren*) to copy (out); (= *transkribieren*) to transcribe **c** (*TV, Rad*) to broadcast, to transmit; **etw im Fernsehen ~** to televise sth, to broadcast sth on television; **via** *or* **durch Satelliten ~ werden** to be broadcast *or* sent by satellite **d** (= *übersetzen*) *Text* to render (*in* +*acc* into); **einen Roman aus dem Englischen ins Deutsche ~** to render *or* translate an English novel into German; **... aus dem Englischen ~ von ...** ... translated from the English by ... **e** (= *anwenden*) *Methode, Maßstab* to apply (*auf* +*acc* to) **f** **etw auf Band ~** to tape sth, to record sth (on tape); **eine CD auf Kassette ~** to tape a CD **g** (= *verleihen*) *Auszeichnung, Würde* to confer (*jdm* on sb); *Vollmacht, Verantwortung, Amt* to give (*jdm* sb) **h** (= *auftragen*) *Aufgabe, Mission* to assign (*jdm* to sb)
VR (*Eigenschaft, Krankheit etc*) to be passed on *or* communicated *or* transmitted (*auf* +*acc* to); (*Tech*) to be transmitted (*auf* +*acc* to); (*Heiterkeit etc*) to communicate itself, to spread (*auf* +*acc* to); **seine Fröhlichkeit hat sich auf uns ~** we were infected by his happiness

ü|ber|tra|gen² [yːbɐˈtraːɡn] ADJ **a** (*Bedeutung etc*) figurative **b** (*Aus*) worn; (= *gebraucht*) second-hand, used ADV (= *figurativ*) figuratively

Ü|ber|trä|ger(in) M(F) (*Med*) carrier

Ü|ber|tra|gung F **-, -en a** (= *Transport*) transference, transfer (*auch Comput*); (*von Krankheit*) passing on, transmission, communication **b** (*schriftlich*) transference; (= *das Kopieren*) copying (out); (= *Transkription*) transcription **c** (*TV, Rad*) (= *Vorgang*) broadcasting, transmission; (= *Sendung*) broadcast, transmission **d** (= *Übersetzung*) rendering, translation **e** (= *Anwendung*) application **f** „Übertragung auf andere Tonträger verboten" "recording forbidden in any form" **g** (*von Auszeichnung, Würde*) conferral;

(*von Vollmacht, Verantwortung*) giving **h** (*von Aufgabe, Mission*) assignment

Ü|ber|tra|gungs-: Ü|ber|tra|gungs|feh|ler M (*Comput*) transmission error; **Ü|ber|tra|gungs|ge|schwin|dig|keit** F (*Comput*) transmission speed; **Ü|ber|tra|gungs|ra|te** F (*Comput*) transmission rate; **Ü|ber|tra|gungs|rech|te** PL (*TV*) broadcasting rights *pl*; **Ü|ber|tra|gungs|wa|gen** M outside broadcast unit; **Ü|ber|tra|gungs|weg** M (*Comput*) transmission path; **Ü|ber|tra|gungs|zeit** F (*Comput*) transfer time

ü|ber|trai|niert ADJ overtrained

ü|ber|tref|fen [yːbɐˈtrɛfn] *ptp* **übertroffen** [yːbɐˈtrɔfn] *insep irreg* VT to surpass (*an* +*dat* in); (= *mehr leisten als auch*) to do better than, to outdo, to outstrip; (= *übersteigen auch*) to exceed; *Rekord* to break; **jdn an Intelligenz/Schönheit** *etc* **~** to be more intelligent/beautiful *etc* than sb; **jdn um vieles** *or* **bei weitem ~** to surpass sb by far; (*bei Leistung auch*) to do far better than sb, to outstrip sb by a long way; **alle Erwartungen ~** to exceed *or* surpass all expectations; **er ist nicht zu ~** he is unsurpassable VR **sich selbst ~** to surpass *or* excel oneself

ü|ber|trei|ben [yːbɐˈtraibn] VT *insep irreg* **a** *auch vi* (= *aufbauschen*) to exaggerate; **ohne zu ~** without exaggerating, without any exaggeration **b** (= *zu weit treiben*) to overdo, to take too far *or* to extremes; **es mit der Sauberkeit ~** to take cleanliness too far; **man kann es auch ~** you can overdo things, you can go too far → *auch* **übertrieben**

Ü|ber|trei|bung F **-, -en a** exaggeration; **man kann ohne ~ sagen ...** it's no exaggeration to say ... **b** **ihre ~ der Sparsamkeit/Sauberkeit** the way she carries economy/cleanliness too far *or* to extremes; **etw ohne ~ tun** to do sth without overdoing it *or* carrying it too far *or* to extremes

ü|ber|tre|ten¹ [ˈyːbɐtreːtn] VI *sep irreg aux sein* **a** (*Fluss*) to break its banks, to flood **b** (*zu anderer Partei etc*) to go over (*zu* to); (*in andere Schule*) to move (*in* +*acc* to); **zum christlichen Glauben ~** to convert to Christianity **c** (*im Sport*) to overstep

ü|ber|tre|ten² [yːbɐˈtreːtn] *ptp* **übertreten** VT *insep irreg Grenze etc* to cross; (*fig*) *Gesetz, Verbot* to break, to infringe, to violate

Ü|ber|tre|tung [yːbɐˈtreːtʊŋ] F **-, -en** (*von Gesetz etc*) violation, infringement; (*Jur: = strafbare Handlung*) misdemeanour (*Brit*), misdemeanor (*US*)

ü|ber|trie|ben [yːbɐˈtriːbn] ADJ exaggerated; (= *zu stark, übermäßig*) *Vorsicht, Training* excessive ADV (= *übermäßig*) excessively → *auch* **übertreiben**

Ü|ber|tritt M (*über Grenze*) crossing (*über* +*acc* of); (*zu anderem Glauben*) conversion; (*von Abtrünnigen, esp zu anderer Partei*) defection; (*in andere Schule*) move (*in* +*acc* to); **die Zahl der ~e zur demokratischen Partei** the number of people going over to the democratic party

Ü|ber|tritts|zeug|nis NT (*für andere Schule*) transfer report, *report with the average mark required to enter a school of a higher academic standard*

ü|ber|trock|nen [yːbɐˈtrɔknən] *ptp* **übertrocknet** VI *insep aux sein* (*Aus*) to dry

ü|ber|trump|fen [yːbɐˈtrʊmpfn] *ptp* **übertrumpft** VT *insep* (*Cards*) to overtrump; (*fig*) to outdo

ü|ber+tun¹ [ˈyːbɐtuːn] VT *sep irreg* **sich** (*dat*) **einen Mantel** *etc* **~** (*inf*) to put a coat *etc* on; **jdm einen Schal** *etc* **~** to put a scarf *etc* on sb

ü|ber|tun² [yːbɐˈtuːn] *ptp* **übertan** [yːbɐˈtaːn] VR *insep irreg* (*dial*) to overdo it (*inf*)

ü|ber|tün|chen¹ [yːbɐˈtʏnçn] *ptp* **übertüncht** VT *insep* to whitewash; (*mit Farbton*) to distemper; (*fig*) to cover up

ü|ber+tün|chen² [ˈyːbɐtʏnçn] VT *sep* to whitewash (over); (*mit Farbton*) to distemper (over)

ü|ber|über|mor|gen ADV (*inf*) in three days, the day after the day after tomorrow

Ü|ber|va|ter M father figure

ü|ber|ver|si|chern *ptp* **überversichert** VT *insep* to overinsure

Ü|ber|ver|si|che|rung F overinsurance

Ü|ber|ver|sor|gung F oversupply (*mit* with)

ü|ber|völ|kern [yːbɐˈfœlkɐn] *ptp* **übervölkert** VT *insep* to overpopulate

Ü|ber|völ|ke|rung F **-, -en** overpopulation

ü|ber|voll ADJ overfull (*von* with), too full; (*von Menschen, Sachen auch*) crammed (*von* with); *Glas* full to the brim *or* to overflowing

ü|ber|vor|sich|tig ADJ overcautious

ü|ber|vor|tei|len [yːbɐˈfɔrtailən] *ptp* **übervorteilt** VT *insep* to cheat, to do down (*inf*)

Ü|ber|vor|tei|lung F cheating

ü|ber|wach ADJ (too) wide-awake; (*fig*) alert

ü|ber|wa|chen [yːbɐˈvaxn] *ptp* **überwacht** VT *insep* (= *kontrollieren*) to supervise; (= *beobachten*) to keep a watch on, to observe; *Verdächtigen* to keep under surveillance, to keep a watch on, to watch; (*auf Monitor, mit Radar, fig*) to monitor

Ü|ber|wa|chung F **-, -en** supervision; (= *Beobachtung*) observation; (*von Verdächtigen*) surveillance; (*auf Monitor, mit Radar, fig*) monitoring

Ü|ber|wa|chungs|ka|me|ra F surveillance camera

Ü|ber|wa|chungs|staat F Big Brother state

ü|ber|wäl|ti|gen [yːbɐˈvɛltɪɡn] *ptp* **überwältigt** VT *insep* **a** (*lit*) to overpower; (*zahlenmäßig*) to overwhelm; (= *bezwingen*) to overcome **b** (*fig*) (*Schlaf, Mitleid, Angst etc*) to overcome; (*Musik, Schönheit etc*) to overwhelm

ü|ber|wäl|ti|gend ADJ *Mehrheit, Sieg* overwhelming; *Gestank, Gefühl auch* overpowering; *Schönheit* stunning; *Erfolg* phenomenal, spectacular; **nicht gerade ~** nothing to write home about (*inf*)

Ü|ber|wäl|ti|gung F **-, -en** overpowering; (= *Bezwingung*) overcoming

ü|ber|wäl|zen [yːbɐˈvɛltsn] *ptp* **überwälzt** VT *insep* (*esp Aus*) = **abwälzen**

ü|ber+wech|seln VI *sep aux sein* to move (*in* +*acc* to); (*zu Partei etc*) to go over (*zu* to); (*Wild*) to cross over

Ü|ber|weg M **~ für Fußgänger** pedestrian crossing

ü|ber|wei|sen [yːbɐˈvaizn] ✪ 47.5 *ptp* **überwiesen** [yːbɐˈviːzn] VT *insep irreg Geld* to transfer (*an* +*acc, auf* +*acc* to); (= *weiterleiten*) *Vorschlag etc, Patienten* to refer (*an* +*acc* to); **mein Gehalt wird direkt auf mein Bankkonto überwiesen** my salary is paid directly into my bank account

Ü|ber|wei|sung F (= *Geldüberweisung*) (credit) transfer, remittance; (*von Patient, Vorschlag etc*) referral

Ü|ber|wei|sungs-: Ü|ber|wei|sungs|auf|trag M (credit) transfer order; **Ü|ber|wei|sungsfor|mu|lar** NT (credit) transfer form; **Ü|ber|wei|sungs|schein** M (*von Arzt*) letter of referral; (*für Bank*) (credit) transfer form

ü|ber|weit ADJ loose-fitting, too big

Ü|ber|wei|te F large size; **Kleider in ~(n)** outsize (*esp Brit*) *or* oversize (*esp US*) dresses, dresses in larger sizes

ü|ber|wer|fen¹ [yːbɐˈvɛrfn] *ptp* **überworfen** [yːbɐˈvɔrfn] VR *insep irreg* (= *zerstreiten*) **sich (mit jdm) ~** to fall out (with sb)

ü|ber+wer|fen² [ˈyːbɐvɛrfn] VT *sep irreg* to put over; *Kleidungsstück* to put on; (*sehr rasch*) to throw on

Ü|ber|we|sen NT preterhuman being

ü|ber|wie|gen [yːbɐˈviːɡn] *ptp* **überwogen** [yːbɐˈvoːɡn] *insep irreg* VT to outweigh VI (= *das Übergewicht haben*) to be predominant, to predominate; (= *das Übergewicht gewinnen*) to prevail

ü|ber|wie|gend **ADJ** predominant; *Mehrheit* vast; **der ~e Teil** (+*gen*) the majority (of); **zum ~en Teil** for the most part **ADV** predominantly, mainly

ü|ber|wind|bar **ADJ** *Schwierigkeiten, Hindernis* surmountable; **diese Angst ist nur schwer ~** it is hard to overcome this fear

ü|ber|win|den [yːbɐˈvɪndn] *ptp* **überwunden** [yːbɐˈvʊndn] *insep irreg* **VT** to overcome; *Schwierigkeiten, Hindernis auch* to surmount, to get over; *Enttäuschung, Angst, Scheu auch* to get over; (= *hinter sich lassen*) to outgrow; **überwunden** (*Standpunkt, Haltung etc*) of the past; *Angst* conquered; *Krise, Rezession* that has been overcome; **ein bis heute noch nicht überwundenes Vorurteil** a prejudice which is still prevalent today **VR** to overcome one's inclinations; **sich ~, etw zu tun** to force oneself to do sth; **ich konnte mich nicht dazu ~** I couldn't bring myself to do it

Ü|ber|win|dung **F**, *no pl* overcoming; (*von Schwierigkeiten, Hindernis auch*) surmounting; (= *Selbstüberwindung*) will power; **das hat mich viel ~ gekostet** that was a real effort of will for me, that took me a lot of will power; **selbst bei der größten ~ könnte ich das nicht tun** I simply couldn't bring myself to do it

ü|ber|win|tern [yːbɐˈvɪntɐn] *ptp* **überwintert** **VI** *insep* to spend the winter; (*Pflanzen*) to overwinter; (*inf:* = *Winterschlaf halten*) to hibernate

Ü|ber|win|te|rung **F** -, -en wintering, spending the winter; (*von Pflanzen*) overwintering; (*inf:* = *Winterschlaf*) hibernation

ü|ber|wöl|ben [yːbɐˈvœlbn] *ptp* **überwölbt** **VT** *insep* to vault

ü|ber|wu|chern [yːbɐˈvuːxɐn] *ptp* **überwuchert** **VT** *insep* to overgrow, to grow over; (*fig*) to obscure

Ü|ber|wurf **M** (*Kleidungsstück*) wrap; (*Ringen*) shoulder throw; (*Aus:* = *Bettüberwurf*) bedspread, counterpane

Ü|ber|zahl **F**, *no pl* **in der ~ sein** to be in the majority; (*Feind*) to be superior in number; **die Frauen waren in der ~** the women outnumbered the men, the women were in the majority

ü|ber|zah|len [yːbɐˈtsaːlən] *ptp* **überzahlt** **VT** *insep Waren* to pay too much for; **das Auto ist überzahlt** you/he *etc* paid too much for the car, the car cost too much

ü|ber|zäh|lig **ADJ** (= *überschüssig*) surplus; (= *überflüssig*) superfluous; (= *übrig*) spare

ü|ber|zeich|nen [yːbɐˈtsaɪçnən] *ptp* **überzeichnet** **VT** *insep* **a** (*Fin*) *Aktie, Anleihe* to oversubscribe **b** (*fig:* = *übertrieben darstellen*) to exaggerate, to overdraw

Über-: Über|zeit **F** (*Sw*) overtime; **Über|zelt** **NT** fly sheet

ü|ber|zeu|gen [yːbɐˈtsɔɪɡn] ✪ 28.1, 33.2, 42.1, 43.1, 53.6 *ptp* **überzeugt** *insep* **VT** to convince; (= *umstimmen auch*) to persuade; (*Jur*) to satisfy; **er ließ sich nicht ~** he would not be convinced *or* persuaded, there was no convincing *or* persuading him; **ich bin davon überzeugt, dass ...** I am convinced *or* certain that ...; **Sie dürfen überzeugt sein, dass ...** you may rest assured *or* be certain that ...; **er ist sehr von sich überzeugt** he is very sure of himself → *auch* **überzeugt**
 VI to be convincing, to carry conviction; **er konnte nicht ~** he wasn't convincing, he was unconvincing
 VR **sich (selbst) ~** to convince oneself (*von* of), to satisfy oneself (*von* as to); (*mit eigenen Augen*) to see for oneself; **~ Sie sich selbst!** see for yourself!

ü|ber|zeu|gend **ADJ** convincing **ADV** convincingly; **~ klingen** to sound convincing; **die deutsche Mannschaft hat ~ gespielt** the German team gave a convincing performance

über|zeugt [yːbɐˈtsɔʏkt] **ADJ** *attr Anhänger, Vegetarier etc* dedicated, convinced; *Christ, Moslem* devout, convinced → *auch* **überzeugen**

Über|zeu|gung **F** **a** (= *das Überzeugen*) convincing **b** (= *das Überzeugtsein*) conviction; (= *Prinzipien*) convictions *pl*, beliefs *pl*; **meiner ~ nach ..., nach meiner ~ ...** I am convinced (that) ..., it is my conviction that ...; **aus ~** out of principle; **ich bin der festen ~, dass ...** I am firmly convinced that ..., I am of the firm conviction that ...; **zu der ~ gelangen** *or* **kommen, dass ..., die ~ gewinnen, dass ...** to become convinced that ..., to arrive at the conviction that ... → **Brustton**

Über|zeu|gungs-: Über|zeu|gungs|ar|beit **F**, *no pl* efforts *pl* at persuasion; **einige/viel ~ leisten** to do some/a lot of convincing *or* persuading; **Über|zeu|gungs|kraft** **F** persuasiveness, persuasive power; **Über|zeu|gungs|tä|ter(in)** **M(F)** **~ sein** to commit an offence (*Brit*) *or* offense (*US*) for political/religious *etc* reasons

ü|ber|zie|hen¹ [yːbɐˈtsiːən] *ptp* **überzogen** [yːbɐˈtsoːɡn] *insep irreg* **VT** **a** (= *bedecken*) to cover; (*mit Schicht, Belag*) to coat; (*mit Metall*) to plate; (*mit Zuckerguss*) to ice (*Brit*), to frost (*US*); **Polstermöbel neu ~ lassen** to have furniture re-covered; **von Rost überzogen** covered in *or* coated with rust; **mit Gold/Silber überzogen** gold-/silver-plated
 b *Konto* to overdraw; **er hat sein Konto (um 500 Euro) überzogen** he has overdrawn his account (by 500 euros), he is (500 euros) overdrawn
 c (*geh:* = *heimsuchen, befallen*) **das Land mit Krieg ~** to inflict war on the country; **jdn mit Vorwürfen ~** to heap criticism on sb
 d *Redezeit etc* to overrun
 e (= *übertreiben*) to overdo → *auch* **überzogen**
 VI **a** (*Fin*) to overdraw one's account
 b (*Redner, Moderator*) to overrun
 VR **a** (= *sich bedecken: Himmel*) to cloud over, to become overcast; **der Himmel ist überzogen** the sky is overcast
 b (*mit Schicht etc*) to become covered *or* coated

ü|ber+zie|hen² [ˈyːbɐtsiːən] **VT** *sep irreg* **a** (= *anziehen*) (**sich** *dat*) **etw ~** to put sth on **b** (*inf:* = *schlagen*) **jdm eins ~** to give sb a clout (*Brit inf*) *or* a smack (*inf*), to clout (*Brit*) *or* smack *or* clobber sb (*inf*)

Ü|ber|zie|her [ˈyːbɐtsiːɐ] **M** -s, - (*dated*) **a** (= *Mantel*) greatcoat **b** (*inf:* = *Kondom*) sheath, French letter (*Brit inf*), rubber (*US inf*)

Über|zie|hungs-: Über|zie|hungs|kre|dit [yːbɐˈtsiːʊŋs-] **M** overdraft provision; **Über|zie|hungs|zins** [yːbɐˈtsiːʊŋs-] **M** overdraft interest rate

ü|ber|zo|gen [yːbɐˈtsoːɡn] **ADJ** (= *übertrieben*) excessive; **sein Benehmen wirkte ~** his behaviour (*Brit*) *or* behavior (*US*) seemed over the top (*inf*) *or* exaggerated → *auch* **überziehen¹**

ü|ber|züch|ten [yːbɐˈtsʏçtn] **VT** *insep* to overbreed; *Motor* to overdevelop

ü|ber|zu|ckern [yːbɐˈtsʊkɐn] *ptp* **überzuckert** **VT** *insep* **a** (= *mit Zucker überstreuen*) to (sprinkle with) sugar **b** (= *zu stark zuckern*) to put too much sugar in/on

Über|zug **M** **a** (= *Beschichtung*) coat(ing); (*aus Metall*) plating; (*für Kuchen, esp aus Zuckerguss*) icing (*Brit*), frosting (*US*) **b** (= *Bettbezug, Sesselüberzug etc*) cover

Üb|le(s) [ˈyːblə] **NT** *decl as adj* → **übel** ADJ b

üb|lich [ˈyːplɪç] **ADJ** usual; (= *herkömmlich*) customary; (= *typisch, normal*) normal; **wie ~** as usual; **es ist bei uns/hier ~** *or* **das Übliche, dass ...** it's usual for us/here to ..., it's the custom with us/here that ...; **das ist bei ihm so ~** that's usual for him; **allgemein ~ sein** to be common practice; **die allgemein ~en Bedingungen/Methoden** the usual conditions/methods

üb|li|cher|wei|se [ˈyːplɪçɐˌvaɪzə] **ADV** usually, generally, normally

Üb|li|che(s) [ˈyːplɪçə] **NT** *decl as adj* **das ~** the usual

U-Bo|gen [ˈuː-] **M** *loop which some Germans write over "u"*

U-Boot [ˈuː-] **NT** submarine, sub (*inf*); (*esp Hist: der deutschen Marine*) U-boat

U-Boot-: U-Boot-Aus|schnitt [ˈuː-] **M** (*Fashion*) boat neck; **U-Boot-ge|stützt** [ˈuːboːtgəˌʃtʏtst] **ADJ** submarine-based; **U-Boot-Krieg** [ˈuː-] **M** submarine warfare *no art*

üb|rig [ˈyːbrɪç] **ADJ** **a** *attr* (= *verbleibend*) rest of, remaining; (= *andere*) other; **meine/die ~en Sachen** the rest of my/the things; **alle ~en Bücher** all the rest of the books, all the other *or* remaining books; **der ~e Teil des Landes** the rest of *or* remaining part of the country, the remainder of the country
 b *pred* left, left over, over; (= *zu entbehren*) spare; **etw ~ haben** to have sth left/to spare; **haben Sie vielleicht eine Zigarette (für mich) ~?** could you spare (me) a cigarette?
 c (= *mögen*) **für jdn/etw wenig ~ haben** not to have much time for sb/sth; **für jdn/etw nichts ~ haben** to have no time for sb/sth; **für jdn/etw etwas ~ haben** to have a soft spot for *or* to be fond of sb/sth, to have a liking for sb/sth; **für jdn/etw viel ~ haben** to be very fond of sb/sth, to have a great liking for sb/sth
 d (*substantivisch*) **das Übrige** the rest, the remainder; **alles Übrige** all the rest, everything else; **die/alle Übrigen** the/all the rest *or* others; **im Übrigen** incidentally, by the way; **ein Übriges tun** (*geh*) to do one more thing

üb|rig-: üb|rig be|hal|ten ▲ **VT** *irreg* to have left over; **üb|rig blei|ben** ▲ ✪ 37.1 **VI** *irreg aux sein* to be left over, to remain; **wie viel ist übrig geblieben?** how much is left?; **da wird ihm gar nichts anderes ~** he won't have any choice *or* any other alternative; **was blieb mir anderes übrig als ...?** what choice did I have but ...?, there was nothing left for me but to ...

üb|ri|gens [ˈyːbrɪɡns] **ADV** incidentally, by the way

üb|rig las|sen ▲ **VT** *irreg* to leave (*jdm* for sb); **(einiges)/viel zu wünschen ~** (*inf*) to leave something/a lot to be desired

Ü|bung [ˈyːbʊŋ] **F** -, -en **a** *no pl* (= *das Üben, Geübtsein*) practice; **das macht die ~, das ist alles nur ~** it's a question of practice, it comes with practice; **aus der ~ kommen** to get out of practice; **aus der ~ sein** *or* **außer ~ sein** to be out of practice; **in ~ bleiben** to keep in practice, to keep one's hand in (*inf*); **zur ~** for *or* as practice; **(richtig) ~ in etw** (*dat*) **haben/bekommen** to have/get (quite) a bit of practice in sth; **~ macht den Meister** (*Prov*) practice makes perfect (*Prov*) **b** (*Veranstaltung*) practice; (*Mil, Sport, Sch*) exercise; (= *Feueralarmübung*) exercise, drill; (*Univ:* = *Kurs*) seminar

Übungs-: Übungs|ar|beit **F** (*Sch*) practice *or* mock test; **Übungs|auf|ga|be** **F** (*Sch*) exercise; **Übungs|buch** **NT** (*Sch*) book of exercises; **Übungs|flug** **M** practice flight; **ü|bungs|hal|ber** **ADV** for practice; **Übungs|heft** **NT** (*Sch*) exercise book; **Übungs|lei|ter(in)** **M(F)** (*im Sportverein*) trainer, coach; **Übungs|mu|ni|ti|on** **F** blank ammunition; **Übungs|platz** **M** training area *or* ground; (= *Exerzierplatz*) drill ground; **Übungs|stück** **NT** (*Sch, Mus*) exercise

UdSSR [uːdeːɛsɛsˈʔɛr] **F** - (*Hist*) *abbr von* **Union der Sozialistischen Sowjetrepubliken** USSR

u. E. *abbr von* **unseres Erachtens**

UEFA-Cup [uːˈʔeːfaːkap] **M** (*Ftbl*) UEFA cup

U-Ei|sen [ˈuː-] **NT** U-iron

U|fer [ˈuːfɐ] **NT** -s, - (= *Flussufer*) bank; (= *Seeufer*) shore; (= *Küstenlinie*) shoreline; **direkt am ~ gelegen** right on the water's edge *or* waterfront; **etw ans ~ spülen** to wash sth ashore; **der Fluss trat über die ~** the river broke *or* burst its banks; **das sichere** *or* **rettende ~ erreichen** to reach dry land *or* terra firma; **zu neuen ~n auf-**

brechen (fig) to try something completely new; **auf zu neuen ~n!** on to pastures new!

U̱fer-: U̱fer|be|fes|ti̱|gung F bank reinforcement; **U̱fer|bö̱schung** F embankment; **U̱fer|land** NT , **U̱fer|land|schaft** F shoreland; **u̱fer|los** ADJ (= endlos) endless; (= grenzenlos) boundless; **ins Uferlose gehen** (Debatte etc) to go on forever or interminably, to go on and on; (Kosten) to go up and up; **sonst geraten wir ins Uferlose** otherwise things will get out of hand; **ans Uferlose grenzen** (Verleumdungen etc) to go beyond all bounds; **U̱fer|mau̱er** F sea wall; **U̱fer|pro|me|na̱de** F esplanade; (am Meer auch) promenade; (an See) lakeside path; (an Fluss) riverside path; **U̱fer|stra̱ße** F (an See) lakeside road; (an Fluss) riverside road

u̱ff [ʊf] INTERJ (inf) phew; **~, das wäre geschafft!** phew, that's that done!

Uffz. [ʊfts] M -, -e abbr von **Unteroffizier** NCO

UFO, U̱fo ['uːfo] NT -(s), -s UFO, Ufo

U̱fo|lo̱|ge [ufoˈloːgə] M -n, -n, **U̱fo|lo̱|gin** [-ˈloːgɪn] F -, -nen ufologist

U-fö̱r|mig ['u-] ADJ U-shaped ADV in the shape of a U; **~ gebogen** with a U-shaped bend, bent into a U; **die Straße verläuft ~** the street forms a U

U|ga̱n|da [uˈganda] NT -s Uganda

U|ga̱n|der [uˈgandɐ] M -s, -, **U|ga̱n|de|rin** [-ərɪn] F -, -nen Ugandan

u|ga̱n|disch [uˈgandɪʃ] ADJ Ugandan

uh [uː] INTERJ oh; (angeekelt) ugh, yuck (inf)

U-Haft ['uː-] F (inf) custody

U-Ha̱|ken ['uː-] M U-shaped hook

U̱hl [uːl] F -, -en (N Ger: = Eule) owl

U̱h|len|spie̱|gel M (N Ger) = Eulenspiegel

U̱hr [uːɐ] F -, -en a clock; (= Armbanduhr, Taschenuhr) watch; (= Anzeigeinstrument) gauge, dial, indicator; (= Wasseruhr, Gasuhr) meter; **nach der or auf die or zur ~ sehen** to look at the clock etc; **Arbeiter, die ständig auf die or nach der ~ sehen** clock-watchers; **nach meiner ~** by my watch; **wie nach der ~** (fig) like clockwork; **rund um die ~** round the clock; **seine ~ ist abgelaufen** (fig geh) the sands of time have run out for him; **die innere ~** the body clock; **ein Rennen gegen die ~** a race against the clock

b (bei Zeitangaben) **um drei (~)** at three (o'clock); **ein ~ dreißig, 1.30 ~** half past one, 1.30 (ausgesprochen "one-thirty"); **zwei ~ morgens** or **nachts/nachmittags** two o'clock in the morning/afternoon; **wie viel ~ ist es?** what time is it?, what's the time?; **um wie viel ~?** (at) what time?

U̱hr|(arm)|band [-bant] NT pl **-bänder** watch strap; (aus Metall) watch bracelet

U̱hr|chen ['yːɛçən] NT -s, - dim von **Uhr** little clock etc

U̱hren-: U̱h|ren|in|dust|rie F watch-and--clock(making) industry; **U̱h|ren|ver|gleich** M → **Uhr** a comparison of clock/watch times; **ei̱nen ~ machen** to check or synchronize watches

U̱hr-: U̱hr|fe|der F watch spring; **U̱hr|glas** NT (auch Sci) watch-glass; **U̱hr|ket|te** F watch chain, fob (chain); **U̱hr|ma|cher(in)** M(F) → **Uhr** a clockmaker, horologist (form); watchmaker; **U̱hr|ma|cher|hand|werk** NT → **Uhr** a clockmaking, horology (form); watchmaking; **U̱hr|werk** NT → **Uhr** a clockwork mechanism (auch fig), works pl (of a clock/watch), movements pl; **U̱hr|zei|ger** M → **Uhr** a (clock/watch) hand; **U̱hr|zei|ger|sinn** M im ~ clockwise; **entgegen dem ~** anticlockwise, counterclockwise; **U̱hr|zeit** F time (of day); **haben Sie die genaue ~?** do you have the correct time?

U̱hu [ˈuːhu] M -s, -s eagle owl

U̱kas [ˈuːkas] M -ses, -se (Hist, pej) ukase

U|krai̱|ne [ukraˈiːnə, uˈkraɪnə] F **- die ~** the U-kraine

U|krai̱|ner [ukraˈiːnɐ, uˈkraɪnɐ] M -s, -, **U|krai̱|ne|rin** [-ərɪn] F -, -nen Ukrainian

u|krai̱|nisch [ukraˈiːnɪʃ, uˈkraɪnɪʃ] ADJ Ukrainian

U|krai̱|nisch(e) NT (Ling) Ukrainian → auch **Deutsch(e)**

U|ku|le̱|le [ukuˈleːlə] F -, -n ukulele

UKW [uːkaˈveː] abbr von **Ultrakurzwelle** VHF

UKW- [uːkaˈveː-]: **UKW-Emp|fäṉ|ger** M VHF receiver; **UKW-Se̱n|der** M VHF station; (= Apparat) VHF transmitter

U̱l [uːl] F -, -en (N Ger: = Eule) owl

U̱|lan [uˈlaːn] M -en, -en (Hist) u(h)lan

U̱|len|sp(ie̱)|gel M = Eulenspiegel

U̱lk [ʊlk] M -(e)s, -e (inf) lark (Brit inf), hoax (US inf); (= Streich) trick, practical joke; (= Spaß) fun no pl, no indef art; **~ machen** to clown or play about (Brit) or around; **etw aus ~ sagen/tun** to say/do sth as a joke or in fun; **mit jdm seinen ~ treiben** (= Spaß machen) to have a bit of fun with sb; (= Streiche spielen) to play tricks on sb

u̱l|ken [ʊlkn] VI (inf) to joke, to clown around; **über ihn wurde viel geulkt** they often had a bit of fun with him

u̱l|kig [ˈʊlkɪç] ADJ (inf) funny; (= seltsam auch) odd, peculiar

U̱lk|nu|del F (inf) joker (inf)

U̱l|kus [ˈʊlkʊs] NT -, **U̱lzera** [ˈʊltsera] (Med) ulcer

U̱l|me [ˈʊlmə] F -, -n elm

U̱l|men|krank|heit F , **U̱l|men|ster|ben** NT Dutch elm disease

U̱l|ti|ma [ˈʊltima] F -, **Ultimä** or **Ultimen** [-mɛ, -mən] (Ling) final syllable

U̱l|ti|ma Ra̱|tio [ˈʊltima ˈraːtsio] F - -, no pl (geh) final or last resort

Ul|ti|ma̱|ten pl von **Ultimatum**

ul|ti|ma̱|tiv [ʊltimaˈtiːf] ADJ a Forderung etc given as an ultimatum b (inf: = beste) Film, Buch ultimate (inf) ADV **wir fordern ~ eine Lohnerhöhung von 9%** we demand a pay rise of 9% and this is an ultimatum; **jdn ~ zu etw auffordern** to give sb an ultimatum to do sth

Ul|ti|ma̱|tum [ʊltiˈmaːtʊm] NT -s, -s or **Ultimaten** [-tn] ultimatum; **jdm ein ~ stellen** to give sb an ultimatum

Ul|ti|men pl von **Ultima**

U̱l|ti|mo [ˈʊltimo] M -s, -s (Comm) last (day) of the month; **per ~** by the end of the month; **bis ~** (fig) till the last minute

U̱l|ti|mo-: U̱l|ti|mo|ab|rech|nung F (Comm) end-of-month settlement; **U̱l|ti|mo|geld** NT (Comm) end-of-month settlement loan

U̱l|tra [ˈʊltra] M -s, -s (pej) extremist

U̱l|tra-, ul|tra- [ˈʊltra] in cpds ultra; **ul|tra|hoch|er|hitzt** ADJ Milch long-life attr; **ul|tra|kurz** ADJ (Phys) ultrashort

U̱l|tra|kurz|wel|le [ˈʊltraˈkʊrts-] F (Phys) ultrashort wave; (Rad) ≈ very high frequency, ≈ frequency modulation

U̱l|tra|kurz|wel|len-: U̱l|tra|kurz|wel|len|emp|fäṉ|ger M VHF receiver; **U̱l|tra|kurz|-wel|len|se̱n|der** M VHF station; (= Apparat) VHF transmitter

U̱l|tra-: u̱l|tra|lin|ke(r, s) ADJ attr (Pol) extreme left-wing; **U̱l|tra|ma|rin** [ʊltramaˈriːn] NT -s, no pl ultramarine; **ul|tra|ma|rin(blau)** [ʊltramaˈriːn-] ADJ ultramarine; **ul|tra|mo|dern** [-moˈdɛrn] ADJ ultramodern ADV ultramodernly; **ul|tra|moṉ|tan** [ʊltramɔnˈtaːn] ADJ (pej geh) papist (pej); **ul|tra|rech|te(r, s)** ADJ attr (Pol) extreme right-wing; **ul|tra|rot** ADJ infrared

U̱l|tra|schall M (Phys) ultrasound

U̱l|tra|schall- in cpds ultrasound; **U̱l|tra|schall|auf|nah|me** F scan (Brit), ultrasound (picture); **U̱l|tra|schall|bild** NT ultrasound picture; **U̱l|tra|schall|di|ag|nos|tik** F ultrasound diagnosis; **U̱l|tra|schall|ge|rät** NT ultrasound scanner; **U̱l|tra|schall|un|ter|su-**

chung F scan (Brit), ultrasound; **U̱l|tra|schall|wel|len** PL ultrasonic waves pl

U̱l|tra-: U̱l|tra|strah|lung F (Phys) cosmic radiation; **ul|tra|vi|o|lett** ADJ ultraviolet

U̱l|ze|ra pl von **Ulkus**

u̱m [ʊm] PREP +acc a um ... (herum) round (Brit), around; (unbestimmter: = in der Gegend von) around, about; **er hat gern Freunde um sich** he likes to have friends around him

b (= nach allen Seiten) **um sich schauen** to look around (one) or about one; **um sich schlagen** to hit out in all directions; **etw um sich werfen** to throw sth around or about

c (zur ungefähren Zeitangabe) **um ... (herum)** a-round about; (bei Uhrzeiten auch) at about; **die Tage um die Sommersonnenwende (herum)** the days either side of the summer solstice; **um Weihnachten/Ostern** etc around Christmas/ Easter etc

d (zur genauen Angabe der Uhrzeit) at; **bitte kommen Sie (genau) um acht** please come at eight (sharp)

e (= betreffend, über) about; **es geht um das Prinzip** it's a question of principles, it's the principle of the thing; **es geht um alles** it's all or nothing; **es steht schlecht um seine Gesundheit** his health isn't very good

f (= für, Ergebnis, Ziel bezeichnend) for; **der Kampf um die Stadt/den Titel** the battle for the town/the title; **um Geld spielen** to play for money; **um etw rufen/bitten** etc to cry/ask etc for sth

g (= wegen) **die Sorge um die Zukunft** concern for or about the future; **(es ist) schade um das schöne Buch** (it's a) pity or shame about that nice book; **sich um etw sorgen** to worry about sth; **es tut mir Leid um ihn** I'm sorry for him

h (bei Differenzangaben) by; **um 10% teurer** 10% more expensive; **er ist um zwei Jahre jünger als sie** he is younger than her by two years; **um vieles besser** far better, better by far; **um einiges besser** quite a bit better; **um nichts besser/teurer** etc no better/dearer etc; **etw um 4 cm verkürzen** to shorten sth by 4 cm

i (bei Verlust) **jdn um etw bringen** to deprive sb of sth; **um etw kommen** to be deprived of sth, to miss out on sth

j (= nach) after, upon; **Stunde um Stunde** hour after or upon hour; **einer um den anderen, eine um die andere** one after the other; **einen Tag um den anderen** day after day

PREP +gen um ... willen for the sake of; **um Gottes willen!** for goodness' or (stärker) God's sake!

CONJ a um ... zu (final) (in order) to; **er spart jeden Cent, um sich später ein Haus kaufen zu können** he is saving every cent in order to be able to buy a house later; **intelligent genug/zu intelligent, um ...** zu intelligent enough/too intelligent to ...; **der Fluss schlängelt sich durch das enge Tal, um dann in der Ebene zu einem breiten Strom anzuwachsen** the stream winds through the narrow valley and then broadens out into a wide river in the plain; **er studierte jahrelang Jura, um dann Taxifahrer zu werden** he studied law for several years only to become a taxi driver

ADV a (= ungefähr) **um (die) 30 Schüler** etc a-bout or (a)round about 30 pupils etc, 30 pupils etc or so

b (rare) **um und um** all around

um+ad|res|sie̱|ren ptp **umadressiert** VT sep to readdress; (und nachschicken) to redirect

u̱m+än|dern VT sep to alter; (= modifizieren auch) to modify

u̱m+ar|bei|ten VT sep to alter; Buch etc to revise, to rewrite, to rework; Metall etc to rework; **einen Roman zu einem Drama/Drehbuch ~** to a-dapt a novel for the stage/screen

U̱m|ar|bei|tung F -, -en alteration; (von Buch etc) revision, rewriting, reworking; (zu Drama etc) adaptation; (von Metall) reworking

um|ar|men [ʊmˈʔarmən] ptp **umarmt** VT insep to embrace (auch euph), to hug

Um|ar|mung F -, -en embrace (auch euph), hug

um+ar|ran|gie|ren ptp **umarrangiert** VT sep to rearrange

Um|bau M pl **-bauten a** (von Gebäude) rebuilding, renovation; (zu etwas anderem) conversion (zu into); (= Umänderung) alterations pl; (von Maschine) modification; (von Organisation) reorganization; (von Kulisse) changing; **das Gebäude befindet sich im ~** the building is being renovated **b** (= Gebäude) renovated/converted building

Um|bau|ar|bei|ten PL renovation work no pl; (zu etwas Neuem) conversion work no pl; (= bauliche Veränderung) alteration work no pl, alterations pl

um+bau|en¹ [ˈʊmbauən] sep **VT** Gebäude (= gründlich renovieren) to rebuild, to renovate; (zu etw anderem) to convert (zu into); (= umändern) to alter; Maschine etc to modify; (fig) Organisation, Firma to restructure, to reorganize; (Theat) Kulissen to change **VI** to rebuild

um|bau|en² [ʊmˈbauən] ptp **umbaut** VT insep to enclose; **der Dom ist völlig umbaut** the cathedral is completely surrounded by buildings; **umbauter Raum** enclosed or interior area

um|be|hal|ten ptp **umbehalten** VT sep irreg Schal etc to keep on

um|be|nen|nen ptp **umbenannt** VT sep irreg to rename (in etw sth)

Um|be|nen|nung F renaming

um|be|set|zen ptp **umbesetzt** VT sep (Theat) to recast; Mannschaft to change, to reorganize; Posten, Stelle to find someone else for, to reassign

Um|be|set|zung F (Theat) recasting; (von Mannschaft) change, reorganization; (von Posten, Stelle) reassignment; **eine ~ vornehmen** (Theat) to alter the cast; **~en vornehmen** (Theat) to recast roles; **~en im Kabinett vornehmen** to reshuffle (Brit) or shake up (US) the cabinet

um|be|stel|len ptp **umbestellt** sep **VT** to change one's order **VI** Patienten etc to give another or a new appointment to

um+bet|ten VT sep Kranken to move or transfer (to another bed); Leichnam to rebury, to transfer; Fluss to rechannel

um+bie|gen sep irreg **VT** to bend **VI** aux sein (Weg) to bend, to turn; (= zurückgehen) to turn round or back

um+bil|den VT sep (fig) to reorganize, to reconstruct; (Pol) Kabinett to reshuffle (Brit), to shake up (US)

Um|bil|dung F reorganization, reconstruction; (Pol) reshuffle (Brit), shake up (US)

um+bin|den¹ [ˈʊmbɪndn] VT sep irreg to put on; (mit Knoten auch) to tie on; **sich** (dat) **einen Schal ~** to put a scarf on

um|bin|den² [ʊmˈbɪndn] ptp **umbunden** [ʊmˈbʊndn] VT insep irreg = **umwickeln²**

um+bla|sen VT sep irreg to blow down

um+blät|tern VTI sep to turn over

um+bli|cken VR sep to look round; **sich nach jdm/etw ~** to turn (a)round to look at sb/sth

Um|bra [ˈʊmbra] F -, no pl (Astron) umbra; (Farbe) umber

Um|bral|glas® [ʊmˈbra:l-] NT photochrom(at)ic glass

um|bran|den [ʊmˈbrandn] ptp **umbrandet** VT insep to surge around; **von der See umbrandet** surrounded by the surging sea

um|brau|sen [ʊmˈbrauzn] ptp **umbraust** VT insep to surge around; **vom Sturm umbraust** buffeted by the storm

um+bre|chen¹ [ˈʊmbrɛçn] sep irreg **VT a** (= umknicken) to break down **b** (= umpflügen) Erde to break up **VI** aux sein to break

um|bre|chen² [ʊmˈbrɛçn] ptp **umbrochen** [ʊmˈbrɔxn] VTI insep irreg (Typ) to make up

um+brin|gen sep irreg **VT** to kill (auch fig), to murder; **das ist nicht umzubringen** (fig inf) it's indestructible; **das bringt mich noch um!** (inf) it'll be the death of me! (inf) **VR** to kill oneself; **bringen Sie sich nur nicht um!** (fig inf) you'll kill yourself (if you go on like that)!; **er bringt sich fast um vor Höflichkeit** (inf) he falls over himself to be polite

Um|bruch M **a** radical change **b** (Typ) make-up **c** (Agr) ploughing (Brit) or plowing (US) up

Um|bruch|pha|se F (= Veränderung) period of upheaval

um+bu|chen sep ✪ 48.3 **VT a** Reise, Flug, Termin to alter one's booking for **b** (Fin) Betrag to transfer **VI a** (= Reisetermin ändern) to alter one's booking (auf +acc for) **b** (Fin) to transfer (auf +acc to)

Um|bu|chung F **a** (von Reise, Termin) rebooking **b** (Fin) transfer

um+den|ken VI sep irreg to change one's ideas or views; **darin müssen wir ~** we'll have to rethink that

um+deu|ten VT sep to change the meaning of; (Liter) to reinterpret, to give a new interpretation to

um+dich|ten VT sep to rework, to recast

um+di|ri|gie|ren ptp **umdirigiert** VT sep to redirect

um+dis|po|nie|ren ptp **umdisponiert** VI sep to change one's arrangements or plans

um|drän|gen [ʊmˈdrɛŋən] ptp **umdrängt** VT insep to throng or crowd around; (stärker) to mob; **sie wurde so umdrängt, dass ...** there was such a crowd around her that ...

um+dre|hen sep **VT a** (= auf andere Seite drehen) to turn over; (auf den Kopf) to turn up (the other way); (mit der Vorderseite nach hinten) to turn (a)round, to turn back to front; (von innen nach außen) Strumpf etc to turn inside out; Tasche to turn (inside) out; (von außen nach innen) to turn back the right way; (um die Achse) to turn (a)round; Schlüssel to turn → **Pfennig, Spieß a**
b (= verrenken) **einem Vogel/jdm den Hals ~** to wring a bird's/sb's neck
c (= verrenken) **jdm den Arm ~** to twist sb's arm → **Wort b**
VR to turn (a)round (nach to look at); (im Bett etc) to turn over; **dabei drehte sich ihm der Magen um** (inf) it turned his stomach → **Grab**
VI to turn (a)round or back

Um|dre|hung F turn; (Phys) revolution, rotation; (Mot) revolution, rev

Um|dre|hungs|zahl F (number of) revolutions pl (per minute/second)

um|düs|tern [ʊmˈdy:stɛn] ptp **umdüstert** VR insep (liter) to become melancholy, to become sombre (Brit) or somber (US)

um|ei|nan|der ADV about each other or one another; (räumlich) (a)round each other

um+er|zie|hen ptp **umerzogen** VT sep irreg (Pol euph) to re-educate

Um|er|zie|hungs|la|ger NT (Pol euph) re-education centre (Brit) or center (US)

um|fä|cheln [ʊmˈfɛçln] ptp **umfächelt** VT insep (geh) to fan; (Luftzug auch) to caress (liter)

um+fah|ren¹ [ˈʊmfa:rən] sep irreg **VT** (= überfahren) to run over or down, to knock down (esp Brit); **VI** aux sein (inf) to go out of one's way (by mistake); **er ist 5 Kilometer umgefahren** he went 5 kilometres (Brit) or kilometers (US) out of his way

um|fah|ren² [ʊmˈfa:rən] ptp **umfahren** VT insep irreg (= fahren um) to travel or go (a)round; (mit dem Auto) to drive (a)round; (auf Umgehungsstraße) to bypass; (= ausweichen) to make a detour (a)round, to detour; Kap to round, to double; die Welt to sail (a)round, to circumnavigate

Um|fah|rung [ʊmˈfa:rʊŋ] F -, -en **a** travelling round (Brit), traveling around (US); (mit dem Auto) driving (a)round; (von Kap) rounding, doubling; (= Umsegelung) sailing (around), circumnavigation **b** (Aus: = Umgehungsstraße) bypass, beltway (US)

Um|fah|rungs|stra|ße F (Aus) bypass, beltway (US)

Um|fall M (Pol inf) turnaround (inf)

um+fal|len VI sep irreg aux sein (Mensch) to fall over or down; (Baum, Gegenstand) to fall (down); (= vornüber kippen) to fall or topple over; (inf: = ohnmächtig werden) to pass out, to faint; (fig inf: = nachgeben) to give in; **vor Müdigkeit fast ~, zum Umfallen müde sein** to be (almost) dead on one's feet (inf), to be fit (Brit) or ready to drop; **wir arbeiteten bis zum Umfallen** we worked until were were ready to drop; **vor Schreck fast ~** (inf) to almost die with fright, to almost have a heart attack (inf); **~ wie die Fliegen** (inf) to drop like flies → **tot a**

um+fal|zen VT sep to fold over

Um|fang M **a** (von Kreis etc) perimeter, circumference (auch Geom); (von Baum) circumference; (= Bauchumfang) girth
b (= Fläche) area; (= Rauminhalt) capacity; (= Größe) size; (von Gepäck etc) amount; **das Buch hat einen ~ von 800 Seiten** the book contains or has 800 pages
c (fig) (= Ausmaß) extent; (= Reichweite) range; (= Stimmumfang) range, compass; (von Untersuchung, Arbeit etc) scope; (von Verkehr, Verkauf etc) volume; **in großem ~** on a large scale; **in vollem ~** fully, entirely, completely; **größeren/erschreckenden ~ annehmen** to assume greater/alarming proportions; **das hat einen solchen ~ angenommen, dass ...** it has assumed such proportions that ...; **etw in vollem ~ übersehen können** to be able to see the full extent of sth

um|fan|gen [ʊmˈfaŋən] ptp **umfangen** VT insep irreg (geh) **a jdn mit seinen Blicken ~** (fig) to fix one's eyes upon sb **b** (fig: = umgeben) to envelop **c** (= umarmen) to embrace

um|fäng|lich [ˈʊmfɛŋlɪç], **um|fang|reich** ADJ extensive; (fig: = breit) Wissen etc auch wide; (= geräumig) spacious; Buch thick

um+fär|ben VT sep to dye a different colour (Brit) or color (US)

um|fas|sen [ʊmˈfasn] ptp **umfasst** VT insep **a** (= herumgreifen um) to grasp, to clasp; (= umarmen) to embrace; **ich konnte den Baum nicht mit den Armen ~** I couldn't get my arms (a)round the tree; **er hielt sie umfasst** he held her close or to him, he held her in an embrace **b** (Mil) to encircle, to surround **c** (fig) (= einschließen) Zeitperiode to cover; (= enthalten) to contain, to include; Seiten to contain

um|fas|send [ADJ] (= umfangreich, weitreichend) extensive; (= vieles enthaltend) comprehensive; Vollmachten, Maßnahmen sweeping, extensive; Vorbereitung thorough; Geständnis full, complete [ADV] comprehensively; **~ gestehen** to give a complete or full confession

Um|fas|sung F (Mil) encirclement

Um|feld NT surroundings pl; (fig) sphere; **zum ~ von etw gehören** to be associated with sth; **Personen aus dem ~ dieser terroristischen Vereinigung** people associated with this terrorist organization

um+fir|mie|ren ptp **umfirmiert** sep **VT** Unternehmen (= Namen ändern) to change the name of; (= Rechtsform ändern) to change the legal status of **VI** (von Unternehmen) to change one's name/legal status

Um|fir|mie|rung [ˈʊmfɪrmi:rʊŋ] F -, -en change of name

um|flech|ten [ʊmˈflɛçtn] ptp **umflochten** [ʊmˈflɔxtn] VT insep irreg **eine Flasche etc mit etw ~** to weave sth around a bottle etc; **eine umflochtene Flasche** a raffia-covered bottle

um|flie|gen[1] [ʊmˈfliːɡn] *ptp* **umflogen** [ʊmˈfloːɡn] **VT** *insep irreg* (= *fliegen um*) to fly (a)round

um+flie|gen[2] [ˈʊmfliːɡn] **VI** *sep irreg aux sein* (*inf*) to go flying (*inf*)

um|flie|ßen [ʊmˈfliːsn] *ptp* **umflossen** [ʊmˈflɔsn] **VT** *insep irreg* (*lit, fig*) to flow around; (*fig poet: Licht*) to flood around; **von einem Strom umflossen sein** to be surrounded by a river

um|flort [ʊmˈfloːɐt] **ADJ** (*liter*) *Augen* misty, misted over

um|flu|ten [ʊmˈfluːtn] *ptp* **umflutet VT** *insep* to surge around

um+for|men VT *sep* **a** (= *andere Form geben*) to remodel, to reshape (*in* +*acc* into) **b** (*Elec*) to convert **c** (*Ling*) to transform

Um|for|mer [ˈʊmfɔrmɐ] **M -s, -** (*Elec*) converter

Um|for|mung F remodelling (*Brit*), remodeling (*US*), reshaping; (*Elec*) conversion; (*Ling*) transformation

Um|fra|ge F **a** (*Sociol*) survey; (*esp Pol*) (opinion) poll; **eine ~ halten** *or* **machen** *or* **veranstalten** to carry out *or* hold a survey/a poll *or* an opinion poll **b** **~ halten** to ask around

Um|fra|ge-: Um|fra|ge|er|geb|nis NT → **Umfrage a** survey/poll result(s *pl*); **Um|fra|ge|wer|te** PL opinion poll results *pl*

um|frie|den [ʊmˈfriːdn] *ptp* **umfriedet VT** *insep* (*geh*) to enclose; (*mit Zaun auch*) to fence in; (*mit Mauer auch*) to wall in

Um|frie|dung F **-, -en a** (= *das Umfrieden*) **die ~ der Burg dauerte Jahrzehnte** enclosing *or* (*mit Mauer*) walling in the castle took years **b** (= *Zaun/Mauer etc*) enclosing fence/wall *etc*; **als ~ für den Park dient eine Hecke** the park is enclosed by a hedge

um+fri|sie|ren *ptp* **umfrisiert VT** *sep* (*inf*) **a sich** (*dat*) **die Haare ~ lassen** to have one's hair restyled **b** (= *abändern*) = **frisieren VT b c** *Auto* = **frisieren VT c**

um+fül|len VT *sep* to transfer into another bottle/container *etc*

um+funk|tio|nie|ren *ptp* **umfunktioniert VT** *sep* to change *or* alter the function of; **etw in etw** (*acc*) *or* **zu etw ~** to change *or* turn sth into sth; **die Kinder haben das Wohnzimmer umfunktioniert** (*hum*) the children have done a conversion job on the living room (*hum*)

Um|funk|tio|nie|rung [ˈʊmfʊŋktsioˈniːrʊŋ] F **-, -en die ~ einer Sache** (*gen*) changing the function of sth; **die ~ der Versammlung zu einer Protestkundgebung** changing the function of the meeting and making a protest rally out of it

Um|gang[1] [-ɡaŋ] M , *no pl* **a** (= *gesellschaftlicher Verkehr*) contact, dealings *pl*; (= *Bekanntenkreis*) acquaintances *pl*, friends *pl*; **schlechten ~ haben** to keep bad company; **das liegt an seinem ~** that's because of the company he keeps; **~ mit jdm haben** *or* **pflegen** to associate with sb; **~ mit einer Gruppe haben** to associate *or* mix with a group; **keinen/so gut wie keinen ~ mit jdm haben** to have nothing/little to do with sb; **sie hat nur ~ mit den besten gesellschaftlichen Kreisen** she only mixes in the best social circles; **er ist kein ~ für dich** he's not fit company *or* no company for you **b** **im ~ mit Tieren/Jugendlichen/Vorgesetzten muss man ...** in dealing with animals/young people/one's superiors one must ...; **durch ständigen ~ mit Autos/Büchern/Kindern** through having a lot to do with cars/books/children; **an den ~ mit Tieren/Kindern gewöhnt sein** to be used to animals/children; **an den ~ mit Büchern/Nachschlagewerken gewöhnt sein** to be used to having books around (one)/to using reference books; **der ~ mit Tieren/Kindern muss gelernt sein** you have to learn how to handle animals/children

Um|gang[2] M *pl* **-gänge a** (*Archit:* = *Säulenumgang*) ambulatory **b** (= *Feldumgang, Flurumgang*) procession

um|gäng|lich [ˈʊmɡɛŋlɪç] **ADJ** affable, pleasant-natured

Um|gäng|lich|keit F **-,** *no pl* (= *entgegenkommende Art*) affability, pleasant nature

Um|gangs-: Um|gangs|for|men PL manners *pl*; **Um|gangs|recht** NT , *no pl* (right of) access; (*mit* to); **Um|gangs|spra|che** F colloquial language *or* speech; **die deutsche ~** colloquial German; **um|gangs|sprach|lich** ADJ colloquial; **Um|gangs|ton** M *pl* **-töne** tone, way of speaking; **hier herrscht ein rüder/höflicher ~** people talk brusquely/politely here

um|gar|nen [ʊmˈɡarnən] *ptp* **umgarnt VT** *insep* to ensnare, to beguile

um|gau|keln [ʊmˈɡaukln] *ptp* **umgaukelt VT** *insep* (*geh*) to flutter about *or* around; (*fig: mit Schmeicheleien etc*) to ensnare, to beguile

um|ge|ben [ʊmˈɡeːbn] *ptp* **umgeben** *insep irreg* **VT** to surround (*auch fig*); **mit einer Mauer/einem Zaun ~ sein** to be walled/fenced in, to be surrounded by a wall/fence; **das von Weinbergen ~e Stuttgart** the town of Stuttgart, surrounded by vineyards **VR** **sich mit jdm/etw ~** to surround oneself with sb/sth

Um|ge|bung F **-, -en** (= *Umwelt*) surroundings *pl*; (*von Stadt auch*) environs *pl*, surrounding area; (= *Nachbarschaft*) vicinity, neighbourhood (*Brit*), neighborhood (*US*); (= *gesellschaftlicher Hintergrund*) background; (= *Freunde, Kollegen etc*) people *pl* about one; **Hamburg und ~** Hamburg and the Hamburg area, Hamburg and its environs *or* the surrounding area; **in der näheren ~ Münchens** on the outskirts of Munich; **in der weiteren ~ Münchens** in the area around Munich, in the Munich area; **zu jds (näherer) ~ gehören** (*Menschen*) to be one of the people closest to sb

Um|ge|gend F surrounding area; **die ~ von London** the area around London

um+ge|hen[1] [ˈʊmɡeːən] **VI** *sep irreg aux sein* **a** (*Gerücht etc*) to circulate, to go about (*Brit*) *or* (a)round; (*Grippe*) to be going about (*Brit*) *or* a-round; (*Gespenst*) to walk; **in diesem Schloss geht ein Gespenst um** this castle is haunted (by a ghost); **es geht die Furcht um, dass ...** it is feared that ... **b** **mit jdm/etw ~ können** (= *behandeln, handhaben*) to know how to handle *or* treat sb/sth; **mit Geld ~ können** to know how to handle sth; (= *mit jdm/etw verfahren*) to know how to deal with *or* handle sb/sth; **mit jdm grob/behutsam ~** to treat sb roughly/gently; **wie der mit seinen Sachen umgeht!** you should see how he treats his things!; **sorgsam/verschwenderisch mit etw ~** to be careful/lavish with sth; **mit dem Gedanken ~, etw zu tun** to be thinking about doing sth **c** (*dial, inf:* = *Umweg machen*) to go out of one's way (by mistake)

um|ge|hen[2] [ʊmˈɡeːən] *ptp* **umgangen** [ʊmˈɡaŋən] **VT** *insep irreg* **a** (= *herumgehen um*) to go (a)round; (= *vermeiden*) to avoid; (*Straße*) to bypass; (*Mil*) to outflank (*fig:* = *vermeiden*) to avoid; *Schwierigkeit* to avoid, to get (a)round; *Gesetz* to circumvent, to get (a)round, to bypass; *Frage* to avoid, to evade; **die Antwort auf etw** (*acc*) **~** to avoid answering sth

um|ge|hend ADJ immediate, prompt; **mit ~er Post** (*dated*) by return (of post (*Brit*)), by return mail (*US*) ADV immediately

Um|ge|hung [ʊmˈɡeːʊŋ] F **-, -en a** (= *Vermeidung*) avoidance; (*durch Straßenführung*) bypassing; (*Mil*) outflanking; (*von Gesetz*) circumvention, getting (a)round; (*von Frage*) evasion; **die ~ des Geländes** going (a)round the grounds; **unter ~ der Vorschriften** by getting (a)round *or* circumventing the regulations **b** (*inf:* = *Umgehungsstraße*) bypass, beltway (*US*)

Um|ge|hungs|stra|ße F bypass, beltway (*US*)

um|ge|kehrt [ˈʊmɡəkeːɐt] ADJ reversed; *Reihenfolge* reverse; (*Math*) *Vorzeichen* opposite; (= *gegenteilig*) opposite, contrary; (= *andersherum*) the other way (a)round; **in die ~e Richtung fahren** to go in the opposite direction; **nein, ~!** no, the other way (a)round; **gerade** *or* **genau ~!** quite the contrary!, just the opposite!; **die Sache war genau ~ und nicht so, wie er sie erzählte** the affair was exactly the reverse of what he said; **im ~en Verhältnis zu etw stehen** *or* **sein** to be in inverse proportion to sth ADV (= *andersherum*) the other way (a)round; (*am Satzanfang:* = *dagegen*) conversely; *proportional* inversely; **... und/oder ~** ... and/or vice versa; **~ als** *or* **wie** the other way (a)round to what ...; **es kam ~** (*inf*) the opposite happened

um+ge|stal|ten *ptp* **umgestaltet VT** *sep* to alter; (= *reorganisieren*) to reorganize; (= *umbilden*) to remodel; (= *umordnen*) to rearrange; **etw in etw** (*acc*) *or* **zu etw ~** to redesign sth as sth; *Werk, Buch* to rewrite *or* recast sth as sth

Um|ge|stal|tung F alteration; (= *Reorganisation*) reorganization; (= *Umbildung*) remodelling (*Brit*), remodeling (*US*); (= *Umordnung*) rearrangement

um+ge|wöh|nen *ptp* **umgewöhnt VR** *sep* to readapt

um+gie|ßen VT *sep irreg* **a** (*in anderen Behälter*) to transfer (*in* +*acc* into); (= *verschütten*) to spill **b** (*Metal*) to recast

um|glän|zen [ʊmˈɡlɛntsn] *ptp* **umglänzt VT** *insep* (*poet*) (*Sonne etc*) to bathe in light; **von der Morgensonne umglänzt** bathed in the morning sunlight; **von Ruhm umglänzt** resplendent with glory

um+gra|ben VT *sep irreg* to dig over; *Erde* to turn (over)

um|gren|zen [ʊmˈɡrɛntsn] *ptp* **umgrenzt VT** *insep* to bound, to surround; (= *umschließen auch*) to enclose; (*fig*) to delimit, to define

Um|gren|zung F **-, -en a** boundary **b** (= *das Umgrenzen*) (*mit Mauer etc*) enclosing; (*fig*) delimitation, definition

um+grup|pie|ren *ptp* **umgruppiert VT** *sep* *Möbel etc* to rearrange; *Mitarbeiter* to redeploy; (= *auf andere Gruppen verteilen*) to regroup; (*Mil*) *Truppen* to regroup

Um|grup|pie|rung F rearrangement; (*von Mitarbeitern*) redeployment; (= *Aufteilung in andere Gruppen, Mil*) regrouping

um+gu|cken VR *sep* = **umsehen**

um+gür|ten[1] [ˈʊmɡyrtn] **VT** *sep* to fasten (+*dat* around)

um|gür|ten[2] [ʊmˈɡyrtn] *ptp* **umgürtet VR** *insep* **sich mit einem Schwert ~** (*liter*) to gird on a sword (*liter*)

um+ha|ben VT *sep irreg* (*inf*) to have on

um|hal|sen [ʊmˈhalzn] *ptp* **umhalst VT** *sep* *jdn* (*inf*) to throw one's arms around sb's neck

Um|hang M cape; (*länger*) cloak; (= *Umhängetuch*) shawl, wrap (*esp US*)

um+hän|gen VT *sep* **a** *Rucksack etc* to put on; *Jacke, Schal etc* to drape (a)round; *Gewehr* to sling on; **sich** (*dat*) **etw ~** to put sth on; to drape sth (a)round one; **jdm etw ~** to put sth on sb; to drape sth (a)round sb **b** *Bild* to rehang

Um|hän|ge|ta|sche F shoulder bag

um|hau|en VT *sep irreg* **a** *Baum* to chop *or* cut down, to fell **b** (*inf:* = *umwerfen*) to knock flying (*inf*) *or* over ~ (*inf*) (= *erstaunen*) to bowl over (*inf*); (*Gestank etc*) to knock out

um|he|gen [ʊmˈheːɡn] *ptp* **umhegt VT** *insep* (*geh*) to look after lovingly, to care for lovingly

um|her [ʊmˈheːɐ] **ADV** around, about (*Brit*); **weit ~** all around

um|her- ** *pref* → *auch* **herum-, rum- around, about (*Brit*); **um|her+fah|ren** *sep irreg* **VT** (*mit Auto*) to drive about (*Brit*) *or* around; (*in Kinderwagen*) to walk about (*Brit*) *or* around **VI** *aux sein* to travel about (*Brit*) *or* around; (*mit Auto*) to drive about (*Brit*) *or* around; (*mit Kinderwagen*) to walk about (*Brit*) *or* around; **um|her+ge|hen VI** *sep irreg aux sein* to walk about (*Brit*) *or* a-round; **im Zimmer/Garten ~** to walk (a)round the room/garden; **um|her|ge|trie|ben** ADJ (liter) wandering attr; **Um|her|ge|trie|be|ne(r)** [-gətri:bənə] MF decl as adj (liter) wanderer, wandering soul (liter); **um|her+ir|ren** VI sep aux sein (in etw (dat) sth) to wander about (Brit) or around; (Blick, Augen) to roam about; **ängstlich irrte ihr Blick im Zimmer umher** her eyes anxiously scanned the room; **nach langen Jahren des Umherirrens** after many years of wandering (around); **um|her+ja|gen** VTI sep (vi: aux sein) to chase about (Brit) or around; **um|her+lau|fen** VI sep irreg aux sein to walk about (Brit) or around; (= rennen) to run about (Brit) or around; **im Garten ~** to walk/run about (Brit) or around the garden; **um|her+schlen|dern** VI sep aux sein to stroll about (Brit) or around (in etw (dat) sth); **um|her+spä|hen** VI sep to look about (Brit) or around; **um|her+strei|fen** VI sep aux sein to wander or roam around (in etw (dat) sth); **um|her+streu|nen** VI sep aux sein (geh) to prowl around; **um|her+wan|dern** VI sep aux sein to wander or roam about (Brit) or around (in etw (dat) sth); **um|her+zie|hen** sep irreg VI aux sein to move or travel around (in etw (dat) sth) VT to pull about (Brit) or around

um|hin+kön|nen [ʊmˈhɪn-] VI sep irreg **ich/er etc kann nicht umhin, das zu tun** I/he etc can't avoid doing it; (einem Zwang folgend) I/he etc can't help doing it; **ich konnte nicht umhin** I couldn't avoid it; I couldn't help it; **...**, **so dass sie einfach nicht umhinkonnten, mir zu glauben** ... so that they simply couldn't help but believe me

um+hö|ren VR sep to ask around; **sich unter seinen Kollegen ~** to ask (around) one's colleagues

um|hül|len [ʊmˈhʏlən] ptp **umhüllt** VT insep to wrap (up) (mit in); **von einem Geheimnis umhüllt** shrouded in secrecy or mystery

um+in|ter|pre|tie|ren ptp **uminterpretiert** VT sep to interpret differently; (Liter) to reinterpret

um|ju|beln [ʊmˈju:bln] ptp **umjubelt** VT insep to cheer; **ein umjubelter Popstar** a wildly acclaimed pop idol

um|kämp|fen [ʊmˈkɛmpfn] ptp **umkämpft** VT insep Stadt, Gebiet to fight over; Entscheidung in dispute; Wahlkreis, Sieg to contest; **ein hart umkämpfter Markt** a hotly contested market

Um|kehr [ˈʊmke:ɐ] F -, no pl **a** (lit) turning back; **jdn zur ~ zwingen** to force sb to turn back **b** (fig geh) (= Änderung) change; (zur Religion etc) changing one's ways; **zur ~ bereit sein** to be ready to change one's ways

Um|kehr|an|stalt F (Phot) reversal film processing laboratory

um|kehr|bar ADJ reversible

um+keh|ren sep VI aux sein to turn back; (= auf demselben Weg zurückgehen) to retrace one's steps; (fig) to change one's ways VT Kleidungsstück (von innen nach außen) to turn inside out; (von außen nach innen) to turn the right way out; Tasche to turn (inside out); Reihenfolge, Trend to reverse; Verhältnisse (= umstoßen) to overturn; (= auf den Kopf stellen) to turn upside down, to invert; (Gram, Math, Mus) to invert; **das ganze Zimmer ~** (inf) to turn the whole room upside down (inf) → auch **umgekehrt** VR (Verhältnisse) to become inverted or reversed; **dabei kehrt sich mir der Magen um** it turns my stomach; **mein Inneres kehrt sich um, wenn ...** my gorge rises when ...

Um|kehr-: Um|kehr|film M (Phot) reversal film; **Um|kehr|lin|se** F inverting lens; **Um|kehr|schluss** ▲ M inversion of an argument; **im ~ bedeutet das ...** to turn the argument on its head, it means ...

Um|keh|rung [ˈʊmke:rʊŋ] F -, -en (von Gesagtem, Reihenfolge etc) reversal, inversion (auch Gram, Math, Mus); **das ist eine ~ dessen, was ich gesagt habe** that's the opposite or reverse of what I said

um+kip|pen sep VT (= umwerfen) to tip over, to upset; Auto, Boot to overturn, to turn over; Leuchter, Vase to knock over; volles Gefäß to upset VI aux sein **a** (= zur Seite fallen) to tip or fall over; (Auto, Boot) to overturn, to turn over; (volles Gefäß, Bier) to be spilled or upset **b** (inf: = ohnmächtig werden) to pass out **c** (inf: = aufgeben) to back down **d** (= sich umwandeln) to tip over (in +acc into); **plötzlich kippte seine Fröhlichkeit in Depression um** suddenly his cheerfulness turned to depression **e** (Fluss, See) to become polluted

um|klam|mern [ʊmˈklamɐn] ptp **umklammert** VT insep to wrap one's arms/legs around; (= umarmen auch) to hug, to embrace; (mit Händen) to clasp; (= festhalten) to cling to; (Ringen) to hold, to clinch; (Mil) to trap in a pincer movement; **sie hielt ihn/meine Hand umklammert** she held him/my hand tight, she clung (on) to him/my hand; **einander or sich ~** (Ringen) to go into a clinch

Um|klam|me|rung F -, -en clutch; (= Umarmung) embrace; (Ringen) clinch; (Mil) pincer movement

um|klapp|bar ADJ Rücksitz, Lehne fold-down attr

um+klap|pen sep VT to fold down VI aux sein (inf) to pass out

Um|klei|de F (inf) → **Umkleideraum**

Um|klei|de|ka|bi|ne F changing cubicle; (in Kleidungsgeschäft auch) changing or fitting room

um+klei|den¹ [ˈʊmklaidn] VR sep to change (one's clothes); **sie ist noch nicht umgekleidet** she hasn't changed yet

um|klei|den² [ʊmˈklaidn] ptp **umkleidet** VT insep to cover; **die Wahrheit mit schönen Worten ~** (fig) to gloss over or varnish the truth

Um|klei|de|raum M changing room; (esp mit Schließfächern) locker room; (Theat) dressing room

um+kni|cken sep VT Ast, Mast to snap; Baum to break; Gras, Strohhalm to bend over; Papier to fold (over) VI aux sein (Ast) to snap; (Gras, Strohhalm) to get bent over; **mit dem Fuß ~** to twist one's ankle

um+kom|men VI sep irreg aux sein **a** (= sterben) to die, to be killed, to perish (liter); **vor Lange(r)weile ~** (inf) to be bored to death (inf), to nearly die of boredom; **da kommt man ja um!** (inf) (vor Hitze) the heat is killing (inf); (wegen Gestank) it's enough to knock you out (inf) **b** (inf: = verderben: Lebensmittel) to go off (Brit) or bad

um|krän|zen [ʊmˈkrɛntsn] ptp **umkränzt** VT insep (liter) to wreathe, to garland

Um|kreis M (= Umgebung) surroundings pl; (= Gebiet) area; (= Nähe) vicinity; (Math) circumcircle; **im näheren ~** in the vicinity; **im ~ von 20 Kilometern** within a radius of 20 kilometres (Brit) or kilometers (US)

um|krei|sen [ʊmˈkraizn] ptp **umkreist** VT insep to circle (around); (Astron) to orbit, to revolve around; (Space) to orbit

Um|krei|sung F -, -en (Space, Astron) orbiting; **drei ~en der Erde** three orbits of the Earth; **die ~ des Feindes** circling the enemy

um+krem|peln VT sep **a** Ärmel, Hosenbein to turn up; (mehrmals) to roll up **b** (= umwenden) to turn inside out; (inf) Zimmer to turn upside down (inf); Betrieb, System to shake up (inf); **jdn ~** (fig inf) to change sb or sb's ways

um+ku|cken VR sep (N Ger inf) = **umsehen**

um+la|den VT sep irreg to transfer, to reload; (Naut) to transship

Um|la|dung F transfer, reloading; (Naut) transshipping

Um|la|ge F **eine ~ machen** to split the cost; **sie beschlossen eine ~ der Kosten** they decided to split the costs

um|la|gern¹ [ʊmˈla:gɐn] ptp **umlagert** VT insep (= einkreisen) to surround; (= sich drängen um, auch Mil) to besiege, to beleaguer

um+la|gern² [ˈʊmla:gɐn] VT sep (= anderswo lagern) to transfer (in +acc into); (= in anderes Lager bringen) Waren etc to re-store; Patienten to move

Um|la|ge|ver|fah|ren NT assessment system

Um|land NT , no pl surrounding countryside

Um|land|ge|mein|de F usu pl (small) community in the surrounding area

Um|lauf M **a** (von Erde etc) revolution; (Sport, auf Parcours etc) round; (= das Kursieren) circulation (auch fig); **im ~ sein** to be circulating, to be in circulation; **in ~ bringen or setzen** to circulate; Geld auch to put in circulation; Gerücht auch to put about, to spread **b** (= Rundschreiben) circular **c** (Med: = Fingerentzündung) whitlow

Um|lauf|bahn F orbit; **die ~ um den Mond/die Erde** lunar/earth orbit; **auf der ~ um die Erde sein** to be orbiting the earth

um+lau|fen¹ [ˈʊmlaufn] sep irreg VI to (run in and) knock over VI aux sein to circulate

um|lau|fen² [ʊmˈlaufn] ptp **umlaufen** VT insep irreg to orbit

Um|lauf-: Um|lauf|ge|schwin|dig|keit F (Fin: des Geldes) turnover rate; (Astron) orbiting speed; **Um|lauf|ren|di|te** F (Fin) current yield; (Econ) yields pl on bonds outstanding; **Um|lauf|schrei|ben** NT circular; **Um|lauf|ver|mö|gen** NT (Fin) current assets pl; **Um|lauf|zeit** F (Astron) period; (Space) orbiting time

Um|laut M **a** no pl umlaut, vowel mutation (esp Brit) **b** (Laut) vowel with umlaut, mutated vowel (esp Brit)

um+lau|ten VT sep to mutate (esp Brit), to modify (zu into)

um+le|gen sep VT **a** (= umhängen, umbinden) to put round; **jdm/sich eine Stola ~** to put a stole (a)round sb's/one's shoulders **b** Mauer, Baum to bring down; (sl: = zu Boden schlagen) Gegner to knock down, to floor **c** (= umklappen) to tilt (over); Kragen to turn down; Manschetten to turn up; (Cards) to turn (over); Hebel to turn; (= kürzen) Hose, Rock etc to take up **d** (= verlegen) Kranke to transfer, to move; Leitung to re-lay **e** Termin to change (auf +acc to) **f** (= verteilen) **die 200 Euro wurden auf uns fünf umgelegt** the five of us each had to pay a contribution toward(s) the 200 euros **g** (inf: = ermorden) to do in (inf), to bump off (inf) VR (Boot) to capsize, to turn over; (Getreide) to be flattened

Um|le|gung F **a** (von Grundstücken etc) distribution; (eines Patienten) moving **b** (Fin: von Kosten) division **c** (eines Termins) changing

um+lei|ten VT sep to divert

Um|lei|tung F diversion; (Strecke auch) detour

Um|lei|tungs-: Um|lei|tungs|schild NT diversion or detour sign; **Um|lei|tungs|stre|cke** F detour

um+ler|nen VI sep to retrain; (fig) to change one's ideas

um|lie|gend ADJ surrounding

um|lo|dern [ʊmˈlo:dɐn] ptp **umlodert** VT insep (liter) to light up; **von Fackeln umlodert** lit (up) or lighted by blazing torches

Um|luft F (Tech) circulating air

Um|luft|herd M fan oven

um|man|teln [ʊmˈmantln] ptp **ummantelt** VT insep (Tech) to coat

Um|man|te|lung F (Tech) casing, sheath

um|mau|ern [ʊmˈmauɐn] ptp **ummauert** VT insep to wall in (mit by)

um+mel|den VTR *sep* **jdn/sich ~** to notify (the police of) a change in sb's/one's address

Um|mel|dung F notification of (one's) change of address

um|mi ['ʊmi] ADV (*Aus inf*) = **hinüber**

um+mo|deln VT *sep* (*inf*) to change

um+mün|zen VT *sep* (*fig*) to turn (**in** +*acc* into); **eine Niederlage in einen Sieg ~** to make a defeat look like a victory

um|nach|tet [ʊm'naxtət] ADJ (*geh*) *Geist* clouded over *pred*; **geistig ~** mentally deranged

Um|nach|tung [ʊm'naxtʊŋ] F -, -en **geistige ~** mental derangement; **da muss ich in geistiger ~ gewesen sein** (*hum*) I must have had a brainstorm

um+nä|hen VT *sep Saum* to stitch up

um|ne|beln [ʊm'neːbln] *ptp* **umnebelt** *insep* **VT** (*mit Tabakrauch*) to surround with smoke; (*fig*) *jdn* to muddle; *jds Geist* to cloud **VR** (*Blick*) to cloud *or* mist over; **mit umnebeltem Blick** with misty eyes

um+neh|men VT *sep irreg Mantel, Schal etc* to put on

um+nie|ten VT *sep* (*sl:* = *töten*) to blow away (*inf*)

um+num|me|rie|ren *ptp* **umnummeriert** ▲ VT *sep* to renumber

um+ord|nen VT *sep* to rearrange; (= *in andere Reihenfolge bringen auch*) to reorder

Um|or|ga|ni|sa|ti|on F reorganization

um+or|ga|ni|sie|ren *ptp* **umorganisiert** VT *sep* to reorganize

um+ori|en|tie|ren *ptp* **umorientiert** VR *sep* (*fig*) to reorientate oneself

Um|ori|en|tie|rung F reorientation

um+pa|cken VT *sep* to repack

um+pflan|zen¹ ['ʊmpflantsn] VT *sep* (= *woanders pflanzen*) to transplant; *Topfpflanze* to repot

um|pflan|zen² [ʊm'pflantsn] *ptp* **umpflanzt** VT *insep* **einen Platz mit Bäumen ~** to plant trees around a square

um+pflü|gen VT *sep* to plough (*Brit*) *or* plow (*US*) up

um+po|len VT *sep* (*Elec*) to reverse the polarity of; (*inf:* = *ändern*) to convert (*auf* +*acc* to)

um+quar|tie|ren *ptp* **umquartiert** VT *sep* to move; *Truppen* (*in andere Kaserne etc*) to requarter; (*in anderes Privathaus*) to rebillet

um|rah|men¹ [ʊm'raːmən] *ptp* **umrahmt** VT *insep* to frame; **die Ansprache war von musikalischen Darbietungen umrahmt** the speech was accompanied by musical offerings (before and after)

um+rah|men² ['ʊmraːmən] VT *sep* to reframe

Um|rah|mung F -, -en framing; **mit musikalischer ~** with music before and after

um|ran|den [ʊm'randn] *ptp* **umrandet** VT *insep* to edge, to border; **tragen Sie die Adresse in das Feld umrandete Feld ein** write the address in the area marked in bold outline

um|ran|dert [ʊm'rɛndɐt] ADJ *Augen* red-rimmed

Um|ran|dung F -, -en border, edging

um|ran|ken [ʊm'raŋkn] *ptp* **umrankt** VT *insep* to climb *or* twine (a)round; **von** *or* **mit Efeu umrankt** twined around with ivy

um+räu|men *sep* **VT** (= *anders anordnen*) to rearrange, to change (a)round; (= *an anderen Platz bringen*) to shift, to move **VI** to change the furniture (a)round, to rearrange the furniture

um+rech|nen VT *sep* to convert (**in** +*acc* into)

Um|rech|nung F conversion

Um|rech|nungs-: Um|rech|nungs|kurs M exchange rate, rate of exchange; **Um|rech|nungs|ta|bel|le** F conversion table

um+rei|ßen¹ ['ʊmraisn] VT *sep irreg* (= *zu Boden reißen*) to tear down; (= *umwerfen*) to knock over

um|rei|ßen² [ʊm'raisn] *ptp* **umrissen** [ʊm'rɪsn] VT *insep irreg* (= *skizzieren*) to outline; **scharf umrissen** clear-cut, well defined; *Züge auch* sharply defined

um+ren|nen VT *sep irreg* to (run into and) knock down

um|rin|gen [ʊm'rɪŋən] *ptp* **umringt** VT *insep* to surround, to gather around; (*drängend*) to throng *or* crowd around; **von neugierigen Passanten umringt** surrounded/thronged by curious passers-by

Um|riss ▲ M outline; (= *Kontur*) contour(s *pl*); **etw in ~en zeichnen/erzählen** to outline sth, to draw/tell sth in outline; **„Geschichte in ~en"** "History - A Brief Outline"

um|riss|haft ▲ ADJ, ADV in outline

Um|riss|zeich|nung ▲ F outline drawing

um+rüh|ren VT *sep* to stir; **etw unter ständigem Umrühren kochen** to boil sth stirring constantly *or* continually

um+run|den *ptp* **umrundet** VT *sep* to go (a)round; (*zu Fuß*) to walk (a)round; (*mit Fahrzeug*) to drive (a)round

um+rüs|ten VT *sep* **a** (*Tech*) to adapt; **etw auf etw** (*acc*) **~** to adapt *or* convert sth to sth **b** (*Mil*) to re-equip

ums [ʊms] *contr von* **um das**

um+sat|teln *sep* **VT** *Pferd* to resaddle **VI** (*inf*) (*beruflich*) to change jobs; (*Univ*) to change courses; **von etw auf etw** (*acc*) **~** to switch from sth to sth

Um|satz M (*Comm*) turnover; **5000 Euro ~ machen** (*inf*) to do 5000 euros' worth of business

Um|satz-: Um|satz|an|stieg M increase in turnover; **Um|satz|be|tei|li|gung** F commission; **Um|satz|ein|bruch** M , **Um|satz|ein|bu|ße** F (*Comm*) drop in turnover; **Um|satz|ent|wick|lung** F (*Comm*) sales trend; **Um|satz|er|war|tung** F (*Comm*) estimated sales *pl*; **Um|satz|mi|nus** NT (*Comm*) → **Umsatzrückgang**; **Um|satz|plus** NT (*Comm*) increase in turnover; **Um|satz|rück|gang** M drop in turnover; **Um|satz|stei|ge|rung** NT → **Umsatzplus**; **Um|satz|steu|er** F sales tax; **Um|satz|wachs|tum** NT (*Comm*) growth in sales; **Um|satz|zahl** NT *usu pl* (*Comm*) sales figure

um+säu|men¹ ['ʊmzɔymən] VT *sep Stoffrand* to hem

um|säu|men² [ʊm'zɔymən] *ptp* **umsäumt** VT *insep* to line; (*Sew*) to edge; **von Bäumen umsäumt** tree-lined

um+schal|ten *sep* **VT** (*auf* +*acc* to) *Schalter* to flick; *Hebel* to turn; *Strom* to convert; *Gerät* to switch over; **den Schalter auf „heiß" ~** to put the switch to "hot" **VI** to flick the/a switch; (*auf anderen Sender*) to turn *or* change over (*auf* +*acc* to); (*im Denken,* = *sich gewöhnen*) to change (*auf* +*acc* to); (*Ampel*) to change; **„wir schalten jetzt um nach Hamburg"** "and now we go over *or* we're changing over to Hamburg"

Um|schal|ter M (*Elec*) (changeover) switch; (*von Schreibmaschine*) shift key

Um|schalt-: Um|schalt|pau|se F (*Rad, TV*) intermission, break (*before going over to somewhere else*); **Um|schalt|tas|te** F (*Comput*) shift key

Um|schal|tung F (*auf* +*acc* to) changeover; (*im Denken,* = *Umgewöhnung*) change

um|schat|ten [ʊm'ʃatn] *ptp* **umschattet** VT *insep* (*geh*) **seine Augen waren umschattet** he had shadows *or* rings under his eyes

Um|schau F , *no pl* (*fig*) review; (*TV, Rad*) magazine programme (*Brit*), news magazine (show) (*US*); **~ halten** to look around (*nach* for)

um+schau|en VR *sep* (*esp dial*) = **umsehen**

um+schich|ten *sep* **VT** to restack; *Gelder* to reallocate **VR** (*Sociol*) to restructure itself

um|schich|tig ['ʊmʃɪçtɪç] ADV on a shift basis ADV **~ arbeiten** to work in shifts

Um|schich|tung F **a** restacking **b** (*Sociol*) restructuring; **soziale ~** change of social stratification, social regrouping *or* restructuring

um+schie|ßen VT *sep irreg* to (shoot at and) knock over

um|schif|fen¹ [ʊm'ʃɪfn] *ptp* **umschifft** VT *insep* to sail (a)round; *Kap auch* to round, to double (*spec*); *Erde auch* to circumnavigate → **Klippe**

um+schif|fen² ['ʊmʃɪfn] VT *sep* to transfer; *Fracht auch* to transship

Um|schif|fung¹ [ʊm'ʃɪfʊŋ] F -, -en sailing (a)round; (*von Kap auch*) rounding, doubling (*spec*); (*von Erde auch*) circumnavigation; **die ~ einer gefährlichen Klippe** (*fig*) getting over a dangerous obstacle

Um|schif|fung² ['ʊmʃɪfʊŋ] F transfer; (*von Fracht auch*) transshipping, transshipment

Um|schlag M **a** (= *Veränderung*) (sudden) change (+*gen* in, *in* +*acc* into) **b** (= *Hülle*) cover; (= *Briefumschlag*) envelope; (*als Verpackung*) wrapping; (= *Buchumschlag*) jacket **c** (*Med*) compress; (= *Packung*) poultice; **jdm heiße/kalte Umschläge machen** to put hot poultices/cold compresses on sb **d** (= *Ärmelumschlag*) cuff; (= *Hosenumschlag*) turn-up (*Brit*), cuff (*US*) **e** (= *umgeschlagene Gütermenge*) volume of traffic; **einen hohen ~ an Baumwolle etc haben** to handle a lot of cotton *etc* **f** (= *Umladung*) (*auf* +*acc* to) transfer, transshipment

um+schla|gen *sep irreg* **VT** **a** *Seite etc* to turn over; *Ärmel, Hosenbein, Saum* to turn up; *Teppich, Decke* to fold *or* turn back; *Kragen* to turn down **b** (*um die Schultern*) *Schal* to put on **c** (= *umladen*) *Güter* to transfer, to transship; **etw vom Schiff auf die Bahn ~** to unload sth from the ship onto the train **d** (= *absetzen*) *Güter* to handle **VI** *aux sein* **a** (= *sich ändern*) to change (suddenly); (*Wind*) to veer; (*Stimme*) to break, to crack; **in etw** (*acc*) **~** to change *or* turn into sth; **ins Gegenteil ~** to become the opposite **b** (= *sauer werden*) to go off (*Brit*) *or* bad; (*Milch*) to go off (*Brit*) *or* sour, to turn (*esp Brit*)

Um|schlag-: Um|schlag|ent|wurf M jacket design; **Um|schlag|ha|fen** M port of transshipment; **Um|schlag|klap|pe** F jacket flap (*of book*); **Um|schlag|platz** M trade centre (*Brit*) *or* center (*US*); **Um|schlag|tuch** NT *pl* **-tücher** shawl, wrap (*esp US*)

um|schlei|chen [ʊm'ʃlaiçn] *ptp* **umschlichen** [ʊm'ʃlɪçn] VT *insep irreg* to creep *or* prowl around

um|schlie|ßen [ʊm'ʃliːsn] *ptp* **umschlossen** [ʊm'ʃlɔsn] VT *insep irreg* to surround (*auch Mil*), to enclose; (*mit den Armen*) to embrace; (*fig: Plan, Entwurf etc*) to include, to encompass

um|schlin|gen [ʊm'ʃlɪŋən] *ptp* **umschlungen** [ʊm'ʃlʊŋən] VT *insep irreg* **a** (*Pflanze*) to twine (a)round **b** (*geh*) *jdn* (*mit den Armen*) **~** to enfold (*liter*) *or* clasp sb in one's arms, to embrace sb

um|schlun|gen [ʊm'ʃlʊŋən] ADJ **eng ~** with their arms tightly (a)round each other

Um|schluss ▲ M (*in Strafanstalt*) recreation

um|schmei|cheln [ʊm'ʃmaiçln] *ptp* **umschmeichelt** VT *insep* to flatter; (*fig*) to caress

um+schmei|ßen VT *sep irreg* **a** (= *umwerfen*) to knock flying (*inf*) *or* over **b** (= *erstaunen*) to bowl over (*inf*); (*Gestank etc*) to knock out **c** **das schmeißt meine Pläne um** that messes my plans up (*inf*)

um+schmel|zen VT *sep irreg* to recast

um+schnal|len VT *sep* to buckle on

um+schrei|ben¹ ['ʊmʃraibn] VT *sep irreg* **a** *Text etc* to rewrite; (*in andere Schrift*) to transcribe (*auch Phon*), to transliterate; (= *bearbeiten*) *Theaterstück etc* to adapt (*für* for) **b** (= *umbuchen*) to alter, to change (*auf* +*acc* to); *Hypothek etc* to transfer; **etw auf jdn ~/~ lassen** to transfer sth/have sth transferred to sb *or* sb's name

um|schrei|ben² [ʊmˈʃraɪbn] ptp **umschrieben** [ʊmˈʃriːbn] VT insep irreg **a** (= mit anderen Worten ausdrücken) to paraphrase; (= darlegen) to outline, to describe; (= abgrenzen) to circumscribe; (= verhüllen) Sachverhalt to refer to obliquely, to skate around (inf) **b** (Ling) Verneinung to construct

Um|schrei|bung¹ [ˈʊmʃraɪbʊŋ] F **a** (von Text etc) rewriting; (in andere Schrift) transcription (auch Phon), transliteration; (von Theaterstück etc) adaptation (für for) **b** (= Umbuchung) altering, changing (auf +acc for) **c** (von Hypothek etc) transfer

Um|schrei|bung² [ʊmˈʃraɪbʊŋ] F **a** no pl (= das Umschreiben) paraphrasing; (= das Abgrenzen) circumscribing, circumscription; (von Sachverhalt) oblique reference (+gen to) **b** (= das Umschriebene) paraphrase; (= Darlegung) outline, description; (= Abgrenzung) circumscription; (verhüllend) oblique reference (+gen to), circumlocution **c** no pl (Gram: von Verneinung) construction

Um|schrift F **a** (auf Münze) inscription, circumscription **b** (Ling: = Transkription) transcription (auch Phon), transliteration

um+schul|den VT sep (Comm) Kredit to convert, to fund; **ein Unternehmen ~** to change the terms of a firm's debt(s)

Um|schul|dung [ˈʊmʃʊldʊŋ] F -, -en funding no pl

um+schu|len VT sep **a** (beruflich) to retrain; (Pol euph) to re-educate **b** (auf andere Schule) to transfer (to another school)

Um|schü|ler(in) M(F) student for retraining

Um|schu|lung F retraining; (Pol euph) re-education; (auf andere Schule) transfer

um+schüt|ten VT sep to spill, to upset; **etw aus einer Dose in eine Kanne ~** to pour sth from a can into a jug

um|schwär|men [ʊmˈʃvɛrmən] ptp **umschwärmt** VT insep to swarm (a)round; (Menschen auch) to flock (a)round; (= verehren) to idolize; **von Verehrern umschwärmt werden** (fig) to be besieged or surrounded by admirers; **eine umschwärmte Schönheit** a much-courted beauty

Um|schwei|fe [ˈʊmʃvaɪfə] PL **ohne ~** straight out, plainly; **mach keine ~!** don't beat about (Brit) or around the bush, come (straight) to the point

um+schwen|ken VI sep **a** aux sein or haben (Anhänger, Kran) to swing out; (fig) to do an about-face (US) or about-turn (Brit); **der Kran schwenkte nach rechts um** the crane swung to the right **b** (Wind) to veer

um|schwir|ren [ʊmˈʃvɪrən] ptp **umschwirrt** VT insep (lit, fig) to buzz (a)round

Um|schwung M **a** (Gymnastik) circle **b** (fig) (= Veränderung) drastic change; (ins Gegenteil) reversal, about-turn; **ein ~ zum Besseren** a drastic change for the better

um|se|geln [ʊmˈzeːɡln] ptp **umsegelt** VT insep to sail (a)round; Kap auch to round, to double (spec); Erde auch to circumnavigate

Um|se|ge|lung [ʊmˈzeːɡəlʊŋ] F -, -en, **Um|seg|lung** [ʊmˈzeːɡlʊŋ] F -, -en sailing (a)round (von Kap auch) rounding, doubling (spec); (von Erde auch) circumnavigation

um+se|hen VR sep irreg to look around (nach for); (rückwärts) to look (a)round or back; **sich in der Stadt ~** to have a look (a)round the town; **sich in der Welt ~** to see something of the world; **ich möchte mich nur mal ~** (in Geschäft) I'm just looking, I just wanted to have a look (around); **ohne mich wird er sich noch ~** (inf) he's not going to find it easy without me

um sein ▲ VI irreg aux sein (Frist, Zeit) to be up

Um|sei|te F (Press) page two; **auf der ~** on page two

um|sei|tig [ˈʊmzaɪtɪç] ADJ overleaf; **die ~e Abbildung** the illustration overleaf ADV overleaf

um|setz|bar ADJ (= realisierbar) practicable; **schwer/nicht ~** (Plan) difficult/impossbile to implement

um+set|zen sep VT **a** Pflanzen to transplant; Topfpflanze to repot; Schüler etc to move (to another seat) **b** Waren, Geld to turn over **c** (Typ) to reset **d** etw in etw (acc) ~ to convert sth into sth; (Mus: = transponieren) to transpose sth into sth; (in Verse etc) to render or translate sth into sth; **sein Geld in Briefmarken/Alkohol ~** to spend all one's money on stamps/alcohol; **etw in die Tat ~** to translate sth into action VR (Schüler etc) to change seats or places; **sich in etw** (acc) ~ to be converted into sth

Um|set|zung F -, -en **a** (= Realisierung) realization; (eines Plans) implementation; **wir haben gute Ideen, aber es mangelt noch an der ~** we have some good ideas but we still haven't put them into practice **b** (= Umwandlung) conversion (in +acc into)

Um|sich|grei|fen [ˈʊmzɪçɡraɪfn] NT -s, no pl (von Krankheit, Inflation) spread; (von Wohnungsnot) escalation

Um|sicht F , no pl circumspection, prudence; (von Handeln etc auch) judiciousness

um|sich|tig [ˈʊmzɪçtɪç] ADJ circumspect, prudent; Handlungsweise etc auch judicious ADV circumspectly, prudently

um+sie|deln VTI sep (vi: aux sein) to resettle; **von einem Ort an einen anderen ~** to move from one place and settle in another

Um|sie|de|lung [ˈʊmziːdəlʊŋ] F -, -en resettlement

Um|sied|ler(in) M(F) resettler

Um|sied|lung [ˈʊmziːdlʊŋ] F resettlement

um+sin|ken VI sep irreg aux sein (geh) to sink to the ground; **vor Müdigkeit ~** to drop with exhaustion

um|so [ˈʊmzoː] CONJ (= desto) ~ **besser/schlimmer!** so much the better/worse!, all the better/that's even worse!; **je mehr ... ~ weniger/eher kann man ...** the more ... the less/sooner one can ...; ~ **mehr, als ...** all the more considering or as; **unser Aufenthalt ist sehr kurz, ~ besser muss er geplant werden** as our stay is so short, we have to plan it all the better

um|so|mehr △ ADV → **umso**

um|sonst [ʊmˈzɔnst] ADV **a** (= unentgeltlich) free, for nothing, free of charge (esp Comm); ~ **sein** to be free (of charge); **das hast du nicht ~ getan!** you'll pay for that, I'll get even with you for that; ~ **ist nur der Tod(, und der kostet das Leben)** (prov) you don't get anything for nothing in this world **b** (= vergebens) in vain, to no avail; (= erfolglos) without success **c** (= ohne Grund) for nothing; **nicht ~** not for nothing, not without reason

um|sor|gen [ʊmˈzɔrɡn] ptp **umsorgt** VT insep to care for, to look after

um|so|we|ni|ger △ ADV → **umso**

um+span|nen¹ [ˈʊmʃpanən] ptp **umspannt** VT insep **a** etw mit beiden Armen/der Hand ~ to get both arms/one's hand (all the way) (a)round sth **b** (fig) Bereich to encompass, to embrace

um+span|nen² [ˈʊmʃpanən] VT sep **a** Pferde to change **b** (Elec) to transform

Um|span|ner M (Elec) transformer

Um|spann|sta|ti|on F , **Um|spann|werk** NT (Elec) transformer (station)

um|spie|len [ʊmˈʃpiːlən] ptp **umspielt** VT insep **a** (geh) (Rock etc) to swirl around; (Lächeln) to play around; (Wellen) to lap at **b** (Ftbl) to dribble (a)round, to take out (inf)

Um|spring|bild NT (Psych) dual-aspect picture

um+sprin|gen¹ [ˈʊmʃprɪŋən] VI sep irreg aux sein **a** (Wind) to veer (nach to), to change; (Bild) to change **b** (Ski) to jump-turn **c** mit jdm grob etc ~ (inf) to treat sb roughly etc, to be rough etc with sb; **so kannst du nicht mit ihr ~!** (inf) you can't treat her like that!

um|sprin|gen² [ʊmˈʃprɪŋən] ptp **umsprungen** [ʊmˈʃprʊŋən] VT insep irreg to jump about (Brit) or around, to leap around

um+spu|len VT sep to rewind

um|spü|len [ʊmˈʃpyːlən] ptp **umspült** VT insep to wash (a)round

Um|stand ⊕ 31 M **a** circumstance; (= Tatsache) fact; **ein unvorhergesehener ~** something unforeseen, unforeseen circumstances pl; **den Umständen entsprechend** much as one would expect (under the circumstances); **es geht ihm den Umständen entsprechend (gut)** he is as well as can be expected (under the circumstances); **nähere/die näheren Umstände** further details; **in anderen Umständen sein** to be expecting, to be in the family way; **unter diesen/keinen/anderen Umständen** under these/no/any other circumstances; **unter Umständen** possibly; **unter allen Umständen** at all costs → **mildern** VT

b **Umstände** PL (= Mühe, Schwierigkeiten) bother sing, trouble sing; (= Förmlichkeit) fuss sing; **ohne (große) Umstände** without (much) fuss, without a (great) fuss; **das macht gar keine Umstände** it's no bother or trouble at all; **jdm Umstände machen** or **bereiten** to cause sb bother or trouble, to put sb out; **machen Sie bloß keine Umstände!** please don't go to any bother or trouble, please don't put yourself out; **einen ~ machen** to make a fuss (mit over)

um|stän|de|hal|ber [ˈʊmʃtɛndəhalbɐ] ADV owing to circumstances; **„umständehalber zu verkaufen"** "forced to sell"

um|ständ|lich [ˈʊmʃtɛntlɪç] ADJ Arbeitsweise, Methode (awkward and) involved; (= langsam und ungeschickt) ponderous; Vorbereitung elaborate; Begriff, Erklärung, Übersetzung, Titel, Anleitung long-winded; Abfertigung laborious, tedious; Arbeit, Reise awkward; **sei doch nicht so ~!** don't make such heavy weather of everything! (Brit), don't make everything twice as hard as it really is!; **er ist fürchterlich ~** he always makes everything seem twice as hard; **das ist vielleicht ~** what a lot of bother or trouble; **das ist mir zu ~** that's too much bother or trouble

ADV erklären, fragen, formulieren in a roundabout way; arbeiten, vorgehen awkwardly; **etw ~ machen** to make heavy weather of doing sth (Brit), to make doing sth seem twice as hard; **etw ~ erzählen/erklären** etc to tell/explain etc sth in a roundabout way

Um|ständ|lich|keit F -, -en (von Arbeitsweise, Methode) involvedness; (von Erklärung etc) long-windedness; **ihre ~** the way she makes such heavy weather of everything (Brit), the way she makes everything seem twice as hard

Um|stands-: **Um|stands|be|stim|mung** F adverbial phrase; **Um|stands|kleid** NT maternity dress; **Um|stands|klei|dung** F maternity wear; **Um|stands|krä|mer(in)** M(F) (inf) fusspot (inf), fussbudget (US inf); **Um|stands|mo|den** PL maternity fashions pl; **Um|stands|wort** NT pl -wörter adverb

um+ste|cken VT sep **a** (Elec) Kontakt etc to move; Gerät etc to plug into another socket **b** Kleid, Saum to pin up **c** Pflanzen to transplant

um|ste|hen [ʊmˈʃteːən] ptp **umstanden** [ʊmˈʃtandn] VT insep irreg to surround, to stand (a)round; **ein von Bäumen umstandener Teich** a pond surrounded by trees

um|ste|hend ADJ attr **a** (= in der Nähe stehend) standing nearby; **die Umstehenden** the bystanders, the people standing nearby **b** (= umseitig) overleaf; **die ~e Erklärung** the explanation overleaf; **im Umstehenden** overleaf ADV overleaf

Um|stei|ge-: **Um|stei|ge|bahn|hof** M interchange (station); **Um|stei|ge|fahr|schein** M transfer ticket; **Um|stei|ge|mög|lich|keit** F **dort haben Sie ~** you can change there (nach for)

um+stei|gen VI sep irreg aux sein **a** (in anderes Verkehrsmittel) to change (nach for); (in Bus, Zug *etc*) to change (buses/trains *etc*); **bitte hier ~ nach Eppendorf** (all) change here for Eppendorf; **in ein anderes Auto ~, von einem Auto ins andere ~** to change *or* switch cars; **bitte beim Umsteigen beeilen!** will those passengers changing here please do so quickly **b** (*fig inf*) to change over, to switch (over) (*auf +acc* to)

Um|stei|ger M (*inf*) transfer (ticket)

um+stel|len¹ ['ʊmʃtɛlən] *sep* **VT a** *Möbel, Wörter* to rearrange, to change (a)round; (*Gram*) *Subjekt und Prädikat* to transpose **b** (= *anders einstellen*) *Hebel, Telefon, Fernsehgerät, Betrieb* to switch over; *Radio* to tune *or* switch to another station; *Uhr* to alter, to put back/forward; *Währung* to change over; **etw auf Computer ~** to computerize sth; **der Betrieb wird auf die Produktion von Turbinen umgestellt** the factory is switching over to producing turbines **VI auf etw** (*acc*) **~** (*Betrieb*) to go *or* switch over to sth; *auf Erdgas etc* to convert *or* be converted to sth **VR** to move *or* shift about (*Brit*) *or* around; (*fig*) to get used to a different lifestyle; **sich auf etw** (*acc*) **~** to adapt *or* adjust to sth

um|stel|len² [ʊm'ʃtɛlən] *ptp* **umstellt** VT *insep* (= *einkreisen*) to surround

Um|stel|lung ['ʊm-] F **a** (*von Möbel, Wörtern*) rearrangement, changing (a)round; (*Gram, von Subjekt und Prädikat*) transposition **b** (*von Hebel, Telefon, Fernsehgerät, Betrieb*) switch-over; (*von Radio*) tuning to another station; (*von Uhr*) alteration, putting back/forward; (*von Währung*) changeover; **~ auf Erdgas** conversion to natural gas; **~ auf Computer** computerization **c** (*fig*: = *das Sichumstellen*) adjustment (*auf +acc* to); **das wird eine große ~ für ihn sein** it will be a big change for him

um+steu|ern¹ ['ʊmʃtɔyɐn] **VT** *sep* Satelliten *etc* to alter the course of **VI** to change course

um|steu|ern² [ʊm'ʃtɔyɐn] *ptp* **umsteuert** VT *insep* Hindernis to steer (a)round

um|stim|men VT *sep* **a** Instrument to tune to a different pitch, to retune **b jdn ~** to change sb's mind; **er war nicht umzustimmen, er ließ sich nicht ~** he was not to be persuaded

um|sto|ßen VT *sep irreg* Gegenstand to knock over; (*fig*) (*Mensch*) Plan, Testament, Bestimmung *etc* to change; (*Umstände etc*) Plan, Berechnung to upset

um|strah|len [ʊm'ʃtra:lən] *ptp* **umstrahlt** VT *insep* (*liter*) to shine around; **von einem Heiligenschein umstrahlt** surrounded *or* illuminated by a halo

um|strit|ten [ʊm'ʃtrɪtn] ADJ (= *fraglich*) controversial; (= *wird noch debattiert*) disputed

um+struk|tu|rie|ren *ptp* **umstrukturiert** VT *sep* to restructure

Um|struk|tu|rie|rung F restructuring

um+stül|pen VT *sep* to turn upside down; Tasche to turn out; Manschetten *etc* to turn up *or* back; Seite to turn over

Um|sturz M coup (d'état), putsch

Um|sturz|be|we|gung F subversive movement

um+stür|zen *sep* **VT** to overturn; Puddingform *etc* to turn upside down; (*fig*) Regierung, Staat, Verfassung to overthrow; Demokratie to destroy; **~de Veränderungen** revolutionary changes **VI** aux sein to fall; (*Möbelstück, Wagen etc*) to overturn

Um|stürz|ler ['ʊmʃtʏrtslɐ] M **-s, -**, **Um|stürz|le|rin** [-ərɪn] F **-, -nen** subversive

um|stürz|le|risch ['ʊmʃtʏrtslərɪʃ] **ADJ** subversive **ADV** **sich ~ betätigen** to engage in subversive activities

Um|sturz|ver|such M attempted coup *or* putsch

um|tan|zen [ʊm'tantsn] *ptp* **umtanzt** VT *insep* to dance (a)round

um+tau|fen VT *sep* to rebaptize; (= *umbenennen*) to rename, to rechristen

Um|tausch M exchange; **diese Waren sind vom ~ ausgeschlossen** these goods cannot be exchanged; **beim ~ bitte den Kassenzettel vorlegen** please produce the receipt when exchanging goods

um|tausch|bar ADJ exchangeable

um+tau|schen VT *sep* to (ex)change; Geld, Aktien to change, to convert (*form*) (*in +acc* into)

Um|tausch-: Um|tausch|frist F (*für neu gekaufte Waren*) exchange *or* return period; **Um|tausch|recht** NT right to return *or* exchange goods

um+top|fen VT *sep* Blumen *etc* to repot

um|tost [ʊm'to:st] ADJ (*liter*) buffeted (*von* by)

Um|trie|be PL machinations *pl*; **umstürzlerische ~** subversive activities

um|trie|big ['ʊmtri:bɪç] ADJ (= *betriebsam*) go-getting

Um|trie|big|keit F (extreme) busyness; (*Eigenschaft*) bustling nature

Um|trunk M drink

um+tun VR *sep irreg* (*inf*) to look around (*nach* for)

U-Mu|sik ['u:-] F *abbr von* **Unterhaltungsmusik**

Um|ver|pa|ckung F external packaging

um+ver|tei|len *ptp* **umverteilt** VT *sep or insep* to redistribute

Um|ver|tei|lung F redistribution

um|wach|sen [ʊm'vaksn] *ptp* **umwachsen** VT *insep irreg* to grow around; **ein von Bäumen ~er Teich** a pond with trees growing all (a)round it

Um|wal|lung F ramparts *pl*

Um|wälz|an|la|ge F circulating plant

um+wäl|zen VT *sep* Luft, Wasser to circulate; (*fig*) to change radically, to revolutionize

um|wäl|zend ADJ (*fig*) Bedeutung, Entwicklung radical; Veränderungen auch sweeping; Ereignisse revolutionary

Um|wälz|pum|pe F circulating pump

Um|wäl|zung ['ʊmvɛltsʊŋ] F **-, -en** (*Tech*) circulation; (*fig*) radical change

um|wan|del|bar ADJ (*in +acc* to) convertible; Strafe commutable

um+wan|deln¹ ['ʊmvandln] *sep* **VT** to change (*in +acc* into); (*Comm, Fin, Sci*) to convert (*in +acc* to); (*Jur*) Strafe to commute (*in +acc* to); (*fig*) to transform (*in +acc* into); **er ist wie umgewandelt** he's a changed man, he's a (completely) different person **VR** to be converted (*in +acc* into)

um|wan|deln² [ʊm'vandln] *ptp* **umwandelt** VT *insep* (*liter*) to walk (a)round

Um|wand|lung ['ʊm-] F change; (*Comm, Fin, Sci*) conversion; (*von Strafe*) commutation; (*fig*) transformation

um|we|ben [ʊm've:bn] *ptp* **umwoben** [ʊm'vo:bn] VT *insep irreg* (*liter*) to envelop; **viele Sagen umwoben das alte Schloss** many legends had been woven around the old castle; **ein von Sagen umwobener Ort** a place around which many legends have been woven

um+wech|seln VT *sep* Geld to change (*in +acc* to, into)

Um|wechs|lung ['ʊmvɛkslʊŋ] F **-, -en** exchange (*in +acc* for)

Um|weg ['ʊmve:k] M detour; (*fig*) roundabout way; **einen ~ machen/fahren** to go a long way round (*Brit*) *or* around; (*absichtlich auch*) to make a detour; **wenn das für Sie kein ~ ist** if it doesn't take you out of your way; **auf ~en (ans Ziel kommen)** (to get there) by a roundabout *or* circuitous route; (*fig*) (to get there) in a rather roundabout way; **auf dem ~ über jdn** (*fig*) indirectly via sb; **etw auf ~en erfahren** (*fig*) to find sth out indirectly

Um|weg|fi|nan|zie|rung F indirect financing

um+we|hen¹ [ʊm've:ən] *ptp* **umweht** VT *insep* to fan, to blow around; **sich vom Wind ~ lassen** to be fanned by the breeze

um+we|hen² ['ʊmve:ən] VT *sep* to blow over

Um|welt F , *no pl* environment

Um|welt- *in cpds* environmental; **Um|welt|alarm** M environmental alarm; **Um|welt|al|ler|gie** F environmental allergy; **Um|welt|auf|la|ge** F (*Admin*) environmental requirement; **Um|welt|au|to** NT environmentally friendly car; **um|welt|be|dingt** ADJ caused by the environment; Faktoren, Einflüsse determined by the environment; **Um|welt|be|hör|de** F environmental authority; **um|welt|be|las|tend** ADJ causing environmental pollution; **Um|welt|be|las|tung** F ecological damage, damage to the environment; **um|welt|be|wusst ▲** **ADJ** Person environmentally aware; Verhalten, Produkt environmentally friendly, ecofriendly (*Brit*) **ADV** in an environmentally friendly way; **Um|welt|be|wusst|sein ▲** NT environmental awareness; **Um|welt|bun|des|amt** NT ≈ Department of the Environment (*Brit*), ≈ Environmental Protection Agency (*US*); **Um|welt|ein|flüs|se** PL environmental influences *pl*; **Um|welt|en|gel** M der blaue ~ symbol attached to a product guaranteeing environmental friendliness; **Um|welt|er|zie|hung** F education in environmental problems; **Um|welt|ex|per|te** M , **Um|welt|ex|per|tin** F environmental expert, expert on the environment; **um|welt|feind|lich** ADJ ecologically harmful, environmentally damaging; **um|welt|freund|lich** ADJ environmentally friendly, ecofriendly (*Brit*); **Um|welt|freund|lich|keit** F ecofriendliness (*Brit*), environmental friendliness; **um|welt|ge|fähr|dend** ADJ harmful to the environment; **Um|welt|ge|fähr|dung** F endangering of the environment; **um|welt|ge|recht** **ADJ** compatible with the environment **ADV** in an ecologically desirable *or* environmentally sound way; **um|welt|ge|schä|digt** [-gəʃɛːdɪçt] ADJ suffering from an environmental illness; **wir sind Umweltgeschädigte** our health is affected by the environment; **Um|welt|ge|setz** NT environmental law; **Um|welt|ge|setz|ge|bung** F environmental legislation; **um|welt|ge|stört** ADJ (*Psych*) maladjusted (*due to* adverse social factors); **Um|welt|gift** NT environmental pollutant; **Um|welt|kar|te** F cheap ticket to encourage use of public transport; **Um|welt|ka|ta|stro|phe** F ecological disaster; **Um|welt|krank|hei|ten** PL environmental illnesses *pl*; **Um|welt|kri|mi|na|li|tät** F environmental crimes *pl*; **Um|welt|kri|se** F ecological crisis; **Um|welt|me|di|zin** F environmental medicine; **Um|welt|mi|nis|te|ri|um** NT ≈ Ministry of the Environment (*Brit*), ≈ Environment and Natural Resources Division (*US*); **Um|welt|mo|bil** [-mo|biːl] NT **-s, -e** environmental information bus; **Um|welt|norm** F environmental standard; **Um|welt|or|ga|ni|sa|ti|on** F environmental organization; **um|welt|ori|en|tiert** ADJ environmentally concerned; **Um|welt|pa|pier** NT recycled paper; **Um|welt|pfen|nig** M (*fig*) levy on petrol (*Brit*) *or* gas (*US*) (used to improve the environment); **Um|welt|pla|nung** F ecological planning; **Um|welt|po|li|tik** F environmental policy; **um|welt|po|li|tisch** **ADJ** relating to environmental policy; **~er Sprecher** environment spokesman **ADV** in terms of environmental policy; **~ umstrittene Gesetzesvorlagen** (draft) bills which are controversial in terms of environmental policy; **Um|welt|qua|li|tät** F quality of the environment; **Um|welt|recht** NT environmental law; **um|welt|re|le|vant** ADJ relevant to the environment; **Um|welt|schä|den** M damage to the environment; **um|welt|schäd|lich** **ADJ** ecologically harmful, harmful to the environment **ADV** in a way which is harmful to the environment; **um|welt|scho|nend** **ADJ** environmentally friendly, ecofriendly (*Brit*), **ADV** in an environmentally friendly way

Um|welt|schutz M conservation, environmental protection *no art*

+ separable verbs

German spelling reform (see supplement): ▲ new spelling △ old spelling

Ụm|welt|schutz|auf|la|ge F environmental restriction

Ụm|welt|schüt|zer(in) M(F) conservationist, environmentalist

Ụm|welt|schutz-: Ụm|welt|schutz|ge|setz NT conservation law; **Ụm|welt|schutz|orga|ni|sa|ti|on** F environmentalist group; **Ụm|welt|schutz|pa|pier** NT recycled paper; **Ụm|welt|schutz|tech|nik** F conservation technology

Ụm|welt-: Ụm|welt|steu|er F ecology tax; **Ụm|welt|sün|der(in)** M(F) (inf) polluter; **Ụm|welt|tech|nik** F environmental technology; **Ụm|welt|to|xi|ko|lo|ge** M , **Ụm|welt|to|xi|ko|lo|gin** F environmental toxicologist; **Ụm|welt|to|xi|ko|lo|gie** F environmental toxicology; **Ụm|welt|ver|schmut|zung** F pollution (of the environment); **Ụm|welt|ver|seu|chung** F contamination of the environment; **Ụm|welt|ver|stö|ße** PL environmental offences (Brit) or offenses (US) pl; **ụm|welt|ver|träg|lich** ADJ Produkte, Stoffe not harmful to the environment **ADV** in a way which is not harmful to the environment; **Ụm|welt|ver|träg|lich|keit** F ecofriendliness (Brit), environmental friendliness; **Ụm|welt|ver|träg|lich|keits|prü|fung** F test for ecofriendliness (Brit) or environmental friendliness; **Ụm|welt|wär|me** F ambient heat; **Ụm|welt|zer|stö|rung** F destruction of the environment

ụm+wen|den sep irreg **VT** to turn over **VR** to turn ((a)round) (nach to)

um|wẹr|ben [ʊm'vɛrbn] ptp **umwọrben** [ʊm-'vɔrbn] VT insep irreg to court

ụm+wer|fen VT sep irreg **a** Gegenstand to knock over; Möbelstück etc to overturn **b** (fig: = ändern) to upset; Strategie, Vorstellungen to throw over **c** jdn (körperlich) to knock down; (Ringen) to throw down; (fig inf) to stun, to bowl over; **ein Whisky wirft dich nicht gleich um** one whisky won't knock you out **d** sich (dat) **etw ~** to throw or put sth (a)round one's shoulders

ụm|wer|fend **ADJ** fantastic; **von ~er Komik** hilarious, a scream (inf) **ADV** fantastically

Ụm|wer|tung F re-evaluation

um|wị|ckeln¹ [ʊm'vɪkln] ptp **umwịckelt** VT insep to wrap (a)round; (mit Band, Verband auch) to swathe (liter) (mit in); (mit Schnur, Draht etc) to wind (a)round; **etw mit Stoff/Draht ~** to wrap cloth/wind wire (a)round sth

ụm+wị|ckeln² [ʊm'vɪkln] VT sep to wrap (a)round; Garn etc to rewind; **jdm/sich etw ~** to wrap sth (a)round sb/oneself

ụm+wịd|men VT sep to redesignate (in as)

Ụm|wid|mung F redesignation

um|wịn|den [ʊm'vɪndn] ptp **umwụnden** [ʊm-'vʊndn] VT insep irreg (geh) to wind (a)round (mit with); **etw mit Blumen ~** to entwine sth with flowers

um|wịt|tert [ʊm'vɪtɐt] ADJ (geh) surrounded (von by); **von Geheimnissen ~** shrouded in mystery

um|wo|gen [ʊm'voːgn] ptp **umwo̱gt** VT insep (liter) to wash (a)round

ụm|woh|nend ADJ neighbouring (Brit), neighboring (US); **die Umwohnenden** the local residents

um|wọl|ken [ʊm'vɔlkn] ptp **umwọlkt** VR insep (geh) to cloud over; (Sonne, Mond auch) to become veiled in cloud (Brit liter) or clouds (US liter), to darken; (Berggipfel) to become shrouded in cloud (Brit) or clouds (US); (fig: Stirn) to cloud

um|zäu|nen [ʊm'tsɔynən] ptp **umzäunt** VT insep to fence (a)round

Ụm|zäu|nung F -, -en (= das Umzäunen) fencing (a)round; (= Zaun) fence, fencing

ụm+zie|hen¹ [ʊmtsiːən] sep irreg **VI** aux sein (= Wohnung wechseln) to move, to move house (Brit); (Firma etc) to move; **nach Köln ~** to move

to Cologne **VT** **a** **die Kinder ~** to get the children changed **b** (hum: = den Umzug für jdn durchführen) to move **VR** to change, to get changed

um|zie|hen² [ʊm'tsiːən] ptp **umzo̱gen** [ʊm-'tsoːgn] insep irreg (geh) **VT** to surround **VR** (Himmel) to cloud over (auch fig), to become overcast or cloudy

um|zịn|geln [ʊm'tsɪŋln] ptp **umzịngelt** VT insep to surround, to encircle

Um|zịn|ge|lung [ʊm'tsɪŋəluŋ] F -, -en encirclement

Ụm|zug ['ʊmtsuːk] M **a** (= Wohnungsumzug) move, removal; **wann soll euer ~ sein?** when are you moving? **b** (= Festzug) procession; (= Demonstrationszug) parade

Ụm|zugs-: Ụm|zugs|kar|ton M packing case; **Ụm|zugs|kos|ten** PL removal or moving (US) costs pl

UN [uːʔɛn] PL UN sing, United Nations sing

un|ab|än|der|lich [ʊnʔap'ʔɛndɐlɪç] **ADJ** **a** (= unwiderruflich) unalterable; Entschluss, Urteil irrevocable, irreversible; Niedergang, Verlust irreversible; **etw als ~ hinnehmen** to accept sth as an unalterable fact **b** (= ewig) Gesetze, Schicksal, Wahrheit immutable **ADV** **~ feststehen** to be absolutely certain; **etw ist ~ passiert** sth is irreversible

Un|ab|än|der|lich|keit F -, no pl (von Entschluss, Urteil) irrevocability, irreversibility

un|ab|ding|bar [ʊnʔap'dɪŋbaːɐ, 'ʊn-] ADJ Voraussetzung, Forderung indispensable; Recht inalienable; Notwendigkeit absolute; **etw für ~ halten** to consider sth (to be) indispensable

Un|ab|ding|bar|keit F -, no pl (von Voraussetzung, Forderung) indispensability

un|ab|ding|lich [ʊnʔap'dɪŋlɪç, 'ʊn-] ADJ = **unabdingbar**

ụn|ab|ge|legt ['ʊnʔapgəleːkt] ADJ unfiled

ụn|ab|ge|schlos|sen ADJ (= nicht verschlossen) unlocked; (= nicht fertig gestellt) unfinished

un|ab|hän|gig ADJ independent (von of); Journalist freelance; **das ist ~ davon, ob/wann** etc that does not depend on or is not dependent on whether/when etc; **~ davon, was Sie meinen** irrespective of or regardless of what you think; **sich ~ machen** to go one's own way; **sich von jdm/etw ~ machen** to become independent of sb/sth

Ụn|ab|hän|gig|keit F , no pl independence; **ein Land in die ~ entlassen** to grant a country independence

Ụn|ab|hän|gig|keits-: Ụn|ab|hän|gig|keits|be|stre|bung F usu pl drive no pl for independence; **Ụn|ab|hän|gig|keits|be|we|gung** F independence movement; **Ụn|ab|hän|gig|keits|er|klä|rung** F declaration of independence; **Ụn|ab|hän|gig|keits|krieg** M war of independence; **Ụn|ab|hän|gig|keits|tag** M (in den USA) Independence Day, Fourth of July

un|ab|kọmm|lich ADJ (geh) busy, engaged pred (form); (= unverzichtbar) Person, Gegenstand indispensable

un|ab|läs|sig [ʊnʔap'lɛsɪç, 'ʊn-] **ADJ** continual; Regen, Lärm etc auch incessant; Versuche, Bemühungen auch unremitting, unceasing **ADV** continually; **~ für den Frieden kämpfen** to fight unceasingly for peace

un|ab|seh|bar **ADJ** **a** (fig) Folgen etc unforeseeable; Schaden incalculable, immeasurable; **der Schaden/die Zahl der Toten ist noch ~** the amount of damage/the number of dead is not yet known; **auf ~e Zeit** for an indefinite period **b** (lit) interminable; Weite boundless; **in ~er Weite** boundlessly; **in ~er Ferne** in the far, far distance; **sich verzögern** to an unforeseeable extent; **~ lang sein** to seem to be interminable

Un|ab|seh|bar|keit [ʊnʔap'zeːbaːɐkait] F -, no pl unforeseeable nature

Un-: ụn|ab|sịcht|lich **ADJ** unintentional; (= aus Versehen auch) accidental **ADV** unintentionally;

un|ab|wähl|bar ADJ **er ist ~** he cannot be voted out of office; **un|ab|weis|bar** [ʊnʔap'vaisbaːɐ, 'ʊn-], **un|ab|weis|lich** [ʊnʔap'vaislɪç, 'ʊn-] ADJ irrefutable; Notwendigkeit absolute; **un|ab|wend|bar** ADJ inevitable; **Un|ab|wend|bar|keit** [ʊnʔap'vɛntbaːɐkait, 'ʊn-] F -, no pl inevitability; **ụn|acht|sam** **ADJ** (= unaufmerksam) inattentive; (= nicht sorgsam) careless; (= unbedacht) thoughtless **ADV** carelessly; wegwerfen thoughtlessly; **benimm dich nicht so ~** don't be so careless; **~ über die Straße laufen** to cross the road without paying attention; **Ụn|acht|sam|keit** F (= Unaufmerksamkeit) inattentiveness; (= Sorglosigkeit) carelessness; (= Unbedachtheit) thoughtlessness

ụn|ähn|lich ADJ dissimilar; **einer Sache** (dat) **~ sein** to be unlike sth, to be dissimilar to sth; **einander ~** unlike each other, dissimilar

Ụn|ähn|lich|keit F dissimilarity

un-: ụn|ak|zep|ta|bel ADJ unacceptable; **un|an|fẹcht|bar** ADJ Urteil, Entscheidung, Gesetz unchallengeable, incontestable; Argument etc unassailable; Beweis irrefutable; **un|an|ge|bracht** ADJ Bescheidenheit, Bemerkung uncalled-for; Sorge, Sparsamkeit, Bemühungen auch misplaced; (für Kinder, Altersstufe etc) unsuitable; (= unzweckmäßig) Maßnahmen inappropriate; **un|an|ge|fochten** ['ʊnʔangəfɔxtn̩] ADJ unchallenged; Urteil, Entscheidung undisputed, uncontested; Testament, Wahlkandidat uncontested **ADV** behaupten, an der Spitze liegen unchallenged; **Liverpool führt ~ die Tabelle an** Liverpool are unchallenged at the top of the league; **un|an|ge|mel|det** ['ʊnʔangəmɛldət] **ADJ** unannounced no adv; Besucher unexpected; Patient etc without an appointment **ADV** unannounced; besuchen without letting sb know; (in Bezug auf Patient) without an appointment

ụn|an|ge|mes|sen **ADJ** (= zu hoch) unreasonable, out of all proportion; (= unzulänglich) inadequate; **einer Sache** (dat) **~ sein** to be inappropriate to sth; **dem Ereignis ~ sein** to be unsuitable for or inappropriate to the occasion, to ill befit the occasion **ADV** hoch, niedrig, teuer unreasonably; gekleidet, sich verhalten inappropriately; **sich ~ äußern** to make inappropriate remarks

ụn|an|ge|nehm **ADJ** unpleasant; Mensch, Arbeit, Geschmack, Geruch auch disagreeable; (= peinlich) Situation auch awkward, embarrassing; Frage awkward; Zwischenfall, Begegnung embarrassing; **das ist mir immer so ~** I never like that, I don't like that at all; **es war mir ~, das tun zu müssen** I didn't like having to do it; **es ist mir ~, dass ich Sie gestört habe** I feel bad about having disturbed you; **mein ständiges Husten war mir ~** I felt bad or embarrassed about coughing all the time; **er kann ~ werden** he can get quite nasty **ADV** unpleasantly; **jdn ~ berühren** to embarrass sb; **~ berührt sein** to be embarrassed (von by); **~ schmecken/riechen** to taste/smell unpleasant

un-: ụn|an|ge|passt ▲ ADJ nonconformist; **ụn|an|ge|tas|tet** ['ʊnʔangətastət] ADJ untouched; **~ bleiben** (Rechte) not to be violated; **un|an|greif|bar** ADJ Macht, Herrscher unassailable; Argument auch irrefutable, unchallengeable; Festung, Land impregnable; **un|an|nehm|bar** ADJ unacceptable

Ụn|an|nehm|lich|keit F usu pl trouble no pl; (= lästige Mühe auch) bother no pl; **~en haben/bekommen** or **kriegen** to be in/to get into trouble; **jdm ~en bereiten** to cause trouble for sb; **damit hast du nichts als ~en** you'll have nothing but trouble with it; **das macht mir nicht die geringsten ~en** it's no trouble or bother at all (to me); **mit etw ~en haben** to have a lot of trouble with sth; **mit den Behörden ~en haben** to get into trouble with the authorities

ụn|an|sehn|lich ADJ unsightly; Frau etc plain; Tapete, Möbel shabby; Nahrungsmittel unappetizing

un|an|stän|dig ADJ **a** (= *unkultiviert, unerzogen*) ill-mannered, bad-mannered; (= *frech, unverschämt*) rude; (= *charakterlich minderwertig*) unprincipled; **so was Unanständiges!** how rude! **b** (= *obszön, anstößig*) dirty; *Witz, Lied* dirty, rude; *Wörter* rude; (= *vulgär*) *Kleidung* indecent; **~e Wörter gebrauchen** to use four-letter words; **~e Reden führen** to talk smut ADV **a** (= *rüpelhaft*) in an ill-mannered fashion, in a rude way **b** (= *obszön*) in a dirty or rude way

Un|an|stän|dig|keit F **a** (= *Unkultiviertheit, Unerzogenheit*) bad or ill manners *pl*; (= *Unverschämtheit*) rudeness *no pl* **b** (= *Obszönität*) obscenity; **~en erzählen** to tell dirty jokes/stories

Un-: un|an|tast|bar ['ʊn|antastbaːɐ, 'ʊn-] ADJ sacrosanct; *Rechte* inviolable; **Un|an|tast|bar|keit** F -, *no pl* sanctity; (*von Rechten, Staat, Grenze, Wohnung*) inviolability; **un|ap|pe|tit|lich** ADJ (*lit, fig*) unappetizing

Un|art F bad habit; (= *Ungezogenheit*) rude habit

un|ar|tig ADJ naughty

Un|ar|tig|keit F **a** *no pl* (= *Unartigsein*) naughtiness **b** (= *Handlungsweise*) naughty behaviour (*Brit*) or behavior (*US*) *no pl*, naughty trick

Un-: un|ar|ti|ku|liert ['ʊn|artikuliːɐt] ADJ inarticulate; (= *undeutlich*) unclear, indistinct ADV inarticulately; **un|äs|the|tisch** ADJ unappetizing; **un|at|trak|tiv** ADJ unattractive; **auf mich wirkt er ~** I don't find him attractive; **un|auf|dring|lich** ADJ unobtrusive; *Parfüm auch, Geste* discreet; *Mensch* unassuming ADV discreetly

un|auf|fäl|lig ADJ inconspicuous; (= *unscheinbar, schlicht*) unobtrusive; **die Narbe/sein Hinken ist ziemlich ~** the scar/his limp isn't very noticeable; **er ist ein ziemlich ~er junger Mann** he's not the kind of young man you notice particularly ADV unobtrusively, discreetly → **folgen**

Un|auf|fäl|lig|keit F -, *no pl* inconspicuousness; (= *Schlichtheit*) unobtrusiveness

un|auf|find|bar ADJ nowhere to be found; *Verbrecher, vermisste Person* untraceable

un|auf|ge|for|dert ['ʊn|aufɡəfɔrdɐt] ADJ unsolicited (*esp Comm*) ADV without being asked; **~ anfallende Arbeiten erledigen können** to be able to work on one's own initiative; **jdm ~ Prospekte zuschicken** to send sb unsolicited brochures; **~ zugesandte Manuskripte** unsolicited manuscripts

Un-: un|auf|ge|klärt ADJ **a** unexplained; *Verbrechen* unsolved **b** *Mensch* ignorant; (*sexuell*) ignorant of the facts of life; **Un|auf|ge|klärt|heit** F (*von Mensch*) ignorance; (*sexuell*) ignorance of the facts of life; **un|auf|ge|räumt** ADJ untidy; **un|auf|ge|regt** ADJ calm; *Mensch auch* unexcited; *Erzählstil* sober; *Musik* unobtrusive ADV calmly; **un|auf|halt|bar** ['ʊn|aufhaltbaːɐ, 'ʊn-] ADJ unstoppable ADV *weitergehen, sich fortentwickeln* unstoppably; **un|auf|halt|sam** ['ʊn|aufhaltzaːm, 'ʊn-] ADJ **a** (= *unaufhaltbar*) unstoppable **b** (= *unerbittlich*) inexorable ADV **a** (= *unaufhaltbar*) unstoppably **b** (= *unerbittlich*) inexorably; **un|auf|hör|lich** [ʊnlaufˈhøːɐliç, 'ʊn-] ADJ continual, constant, incessant ADV continually, constantly, incessantly; **un|auf|lös|bar** [ʊnlaufˈløːsbaːɐ, 'ʊn-], **un|auf|lös|lich** [ʊnlaufˈløːsliç, 'ʊn-] ADJ *Konflikt, Widersprüche* unresolvable; *Ehe* indissoluble; **un|auf|lös|bar|keit** F -, *no pl*, **Un|auf|lös|lich|keit** F -, *no pl* (*von Ehe*) indissolubility; **un|auf|merk|sam** ADJ inattentive; (= *flüchtig*) *Leser etc* unobservant; **da war ich einen Augenblick ~** I didn't pay attention for a moment; **Un|auf|merk|sam|keit** F inattentiveness; **Un|auf|rich|tig|keit** F insincerity; **un|auf|schieb|bar** [ʊnlaufˈʃiːbaːɐ, 'ʊn-] ADJ urgent; **es ist ~** it can't be put off or delayed or postponed; **un|aus|bleib|lich** [ʊnlausˈblaiplıç, 'ʊn-] ADJ inevitable, unavoidable; **un|aus|denk|bar** [ʊnlausˈdɛŋkbaːɐ, 'ʊn-] ADJ unimaginable, unthinkable; **un|aus|führ|bar** ADJ impracticable, unfeasible; **un|aus|ge|füllt**

['ʊnlausɡəfʏlt] ADJ **a** *Formular etc* blank **b** *Leben, Mensch* unfulfilled

un|aus|ge|gli|chen ADJ unbalanced; *Verhältnis auch, Vermögensverteilung etc* unequal; *Stil auch* disharmonious; *Mensch* (= *launisch*) changeable, up-and-down (*inf*); **ein Mensch mit ~em Wesen** a person of uneven temper

Un|aus|ge|gli|chen|heit F imbalance; (*von Verhältnis auch*) inequality; (*von Stil auch*) disharmony; (*von Mensch*) changeable moods *pl*; **die ~ seines Wesens** the unevenness of his temper

Un-: un|aus|ge|go|ren ADJ immature; *Idee, Plan auch* half-baked (*inf*); *Jüngling auch* callow; **un|aus|ge|schla|fen** ['ʊnlausɡəʃlaːfn] ADJ tired; **er ist ~** he hasn't had enough sleep ADV without having had enough sleep; *sich anhören* sleepy; **er kam ziemlich ~ ins Büro** he obviously hadn't had enough sleep when he turned up in the office; **er sieht ~ aus** he looks as if he hasn't had enough sleep; **un|aus|ge|setzt** ['ʊnlausɡəzɛtst] ADJ incessant, constant ADV incessantly, constantly; **un|aus|ge|spro|chen** ADJ unsaid *pred*, unspoken; **un|aus|ge|wo|gen** ADJ unbalanced; **Un|aus|ge|wo|gen|heit** F imbalance; **un|aus|lösch|lich** [ʊnlausˈlœʃlıç, 'ʊn-] (*geh*) ADJ indelible ADV indelibly; **un|aus|rott|bar** [ʊnlausˈrɔtbaːɐ, 'ʊn-] ADJ *Unkraut* indestructible; (*fig*) *Vorurteile, Vorstellung etc* ineradicable

un|aus|sprech|lich [ʊnlausˈʃprɛçlıç, 'ʊn-] ADJ **a** *Wort, Name* unpronounceable **b** *Schönheit, Leid etc* inexpressible **c** (*liter*: = *ungeheuerlich*) *Tat, Verbrechen* unspeakable **d** **die Unaussprechlichen** (*hum*) one's unmentionables (*Brit inf*), underwear ADV (*enorm*) *schön* indescribably; *grausam, leiden* unspeakably; **er verehrt sie ~** he absolutely worships her

Un-: un|aus|steh|lich [ʊnlausˈʃteːlıç, 'ʊn-] ADJ intolerable; *Mensch, Art, Eigenschaft auch* insufferable; **un|aus|weich|lich** [ʊnlausˈvaiçlıç, 'ʊn-] ADJ unavoidable, inevitable; *Folgen auch* inescapable ADV unavoidably, inevitably; **Un|aus|weich|lich|keit** F -, *no pl* inevitability; (= *Dilemma*) dilemma

un|bän|dig ['ʊnbɛndıç] ADJ **a** (= *ausgelassen, ungestüm*) *Kind* boisterous **b** (= *ungezügelt*) *Freude, Lust, Hass, Zorn* unrestrained *no adv*, unddled *no adv*; *Ehrgeiz, Fleiß* boundless; *Hunger* enormous ADV **a** (= *ungestüm*) *herumtoben* boisterously; **führt euch nicht so ~ auf** don't be so wild **b** (= *enorm*) enormously; **sie freuten sich ~** they were dancing around (with joy)

Un-: un|bar (*Comm*) ADJ **~e Zahlungsweise** non-cash payment ADV **etw ~ bezahlen** not to pay sth in cash, to pay sth by cheque (*Brit*) or check (*US*)/credit card *etc*; **un|barm|her|zig** ADJ merciless; *Mensch auch* pitiless ADV mercilessly; **Un|barm|her|zig|keit** F mercilessness; (*von Mensch auch*) pitilessness; **un|be|ab|sich|tigt** ['ʊnbəlapzıçtıçt] ADJ unintentional ADV unintentionally

un|be|ach|tet ['ʊnbəlaxtət] ADJ unnoticed; *Warnung, Vorschläge* unheeded; **~ bleiben** to go unnoticed/unheeded; **jdn/etw ~ lassen** not to take any notice of sb/sth; **wir sollten die weniger wichtigen Punkte zunächst ~ lassen** let's leave the less important points aside for the time being; **das dürfen wir nicht ~ lassen** we mustn't overlook that, we mustn't leave that out of account ADV unnoticed; *daliegen* completely ignored; *sterben* in obscurity

Un-: un|be|acht|lich ADJ insignificant; **un|be|an|stan|det** ['ʊnbəlanʃtandət] ADJ not objected to; **etw ~ lassen** to let sth pass or go ADV without objection; **das Paket wurde ~ weitergeleitet** the parcel (*esp Brit*) or package got through without any problems; **un|be|ant|wor|tet** ['ʊnbəlantvɔrtət] ADJ, ADV unanswered; **un|be|baut** ['ʊnbəbaut] ADJ *Land* undeveloped; *Grundstück* vacant; *Feld* uncultivated

un|be|dacht ADJ (= *hastig*) rash; (= *unüberlegt*) thoughtless ADV rashly; **Un|be|dacht|heit** F -, -en (= *Hast*) rashness; (= *Unüberlegt-*

heit) thoughtlessness; **un|be|dacht|sam** ADJ, ADV = **unbedacht**; **un|be|darft** ['ʊnbədarft] ADJ (*inf*) simple-minded; *Mensch* (*auf bestimmtem Gebiet*) green (*inf*), clueless (*inf*); (= *dumm*) dumb (*inf*); **Un|be|darft|heit** F (*inf*) simple-mindedness; (= *Dummheit*) dumbness (*inf*); **un|be|deckt** ADJ bare; **~en Hauptes** (*geh*) **mit ~em Haupt** (*geh*) bare-headed

un|be|denk|lich ADJ (= *ungefährlich*) completely harmless, quite safe; (= *sorglos*) thoughtless ADV (= *ungefährlich*) quite safely, without coming to any harm; (= *ohne zu zögern*) without thinking (twice *inf*)

Un|be|denk|lich|keit F (= *Ungefährlichkeit*) harmlessness

Un|be|denk|lich|keits-: Un|be|denk|lich|keits|be|schei|ni|gung F (*Jur*) document certifying that one has no taxes, loans *etc* outstanding; **Un|be|denk|lich|keits|er|klä|rung** F (*Med*) official declaration that a substance *etc* is harmless

un|be|deu|tend ADJ (= *unwichtig*) insignificant, unimportant; (= *geringfügig*) *Rückgang, Änderung etc* minor, minimal ADV (= *geringfügig*) slightly

un|be|dingt ✪ 29.2, 37.1, 37.3, 53.3 ADJ *attr* (= *absolut, bedingungslos*) *Ruhe, Verschwiegenheit Voraussetzung, Vorrang* absolute; *Gehorsam, Treue auch* implicit, unconditional; *Anhänger etc* unreserved; *Reflex* unconditioned ADV (= *auf jeden Fall*) really; *nötig, erforderlich* absolutely; **ich muss ~ mal wieder ins Kino gehen** I really must go to the cinema again; **ich musste sie ~ sprechen** I really or absolutely had to speak to her; (*äußerst wichtig*) it was imperative that I spoke to her; **müsst ihr denn ~ in meinem Arbeitszimmer spielen?** do you HAVE to play in my study?; **das ist nicht meine Schuld, du wolltest ja ~ ins Kino gehen!** it's not my fault, you were (hell)bent on going to the cinema; **er wollte ~ mit Renate verreisen** he was (hell)bent on going away with Renate; **~!** of course!, I should say so!; **nicht ~** not necessarily; **nicht ~ nötig** not absolutely or strictly necessary

Un|be|dingt|heit F (= *Bedingungslosigkeit*) unconditionality

Un-: un|be|ei|digt ['ʊnbəlaidıçt] ADJ (*Jur*) unsworn *us attr*, not on oath; **un|be|ein|druckt** [ʊnbəˈlaindrʊkt, 'ʊn-] ADJ, ADV unimpressed (*von* by); **un|be|ein|fluss|bar** ▲ ADJ *Entwicklung* unalterable; *Mensch* unswayable, unable to be influenced; **un|be|ein|flusst** ▲ ['ʊnbəlainflʊst] ADJ uninfluenced (*von* by); **un|be|fahr|bar** ADJ *Straße, Weg* impassable; *Gewässer* unnavigable; **un|be|fah|ren** ADJ *Straße, Fluss* unused; **un|be|fan|gen** ADJ **a** (= *unvoreingenommen*) impartial, unbiased *no adv*, objective **b** (= *natürlich*) natural; (= *ungehemmt*) uninhibited ADV **a** (= *unvoreingenommen*) impartially, objectively **b** (= *ungehemmt*) naturally, without inhibition; **Un|be|fan|gen|heit** F **a** (= *unparteiische Haltung*) impartiality, objectiveness **b** (= *Natürlichkeit*) naturalness; (= *Ungehemmtheit*) uninhibitedness; **un|be|fes|tigt** ADJ *Straße* unsurfaced; **un|be|fleckt** ADJ (*liter*) spotless, unsullied, untarnished; *Jungfrau* undefiled; **die Unbefleckte Empfängnis** the Immaculate Conception; **un|be|frie|di|gend** ADJ unsatisfactory ADV unsatisfactorily; **un|be|frie|digt** ADJ (= *frustriert*) unsatisfied; (= *unerfüllt auch*) unfulfilled; (= *unzufrieden*) dissatisfied; **un|be|fris|tet** ADJ *Arbeitsverhältnis, Vertrag* for an indefinite period; *Aufenthaltserlaubnis, Visum* permanent ADV indefinitely, for an indefinite period; **etw ~ verlängern** to extend sth indefinitely or for an indefinite period; **un|be|fruch|tet** ['ʊnbəfrʊxtət] ADJ unfertilized; **un|be|fugt** ADJ unauthorized; **Eintritt für Unbefugte verboten, kein Zutritt für Unbefugte** no admittance to unauthorized persons ADV without authorization; **un|be|gabt** ADJ untalented, ungifted; **für etw ~ sein** to have no talent for sth; **er ist handwerklich völlig ~** he's no handyman; **Un|be|gabt|heit** F -, *no pl* lack of talent

un|be|gli|chen ['ʊnbəglɪçn] ADJ unpaid, unsettled

un|be|greif|lich ADJ (= *unverständlich*) incomprehensible; *Leichtsinn, Irrtum, Dummheit* inconceivable; (= *unergründlich*) *Menschen, Länder* inscrutable; **es wird mir immer ~ bleiben, wie/ dass ...** I shall never understand how/why ...; **es ist uns allen ~, wie das passieren konnte** none of us can understand how it happened; **das Unbegreifliche** (*Rel*) the Unknowable

un|be|greif|li|cher|wei|se ['ʊnbəgraiflɪçə-'vaizə] ADV inexplicably

un|be|grenzt ADJ unlimited; *Möglichkeiten, Energie, Vertrauen etc auch* limitless, boundless, infinite; *Land, Meer etc* boundless; *Zeitspanne, Frist* indefinite; **zeitlich ~** indefinite; **auf ~e Zeit** indefinitely; **er hat ~e Zeit** he has unlimited time; **in ~er Höhe** of an unlimited *or* indefinite amount; **es nach oben ~** there's no upper limit (on it), the sky's the limit (*inf*) ADV indefinitely; **„unbegrenzt haltbar"** "will keep indefinitely"

un|be|grün|det ADJ *Angst, Verdacht, Zweifel* unfounded, groundless, without foundation; *Maßnahme* unwarranted; **eine Klage als ~ abweisen** to dismiss a case

un|be|haart ADJ hairless; (*auf dem Kopf*) bald

Un|be|ha|gen NT (feeling of) uneasiness *or* disquiet, uneasy feeling; (= *Unzufriedenheit*) discontent (*an +dat* with); (*körperlich*) discomfort

un|be|hag|lich ADJ uncomfortable; *Gefühl auch* uneasy ADV **sich in jds Gesellschaft** (*dat*) **~ fühlen** to feel uncomfortable *or* ill at ease in sb's company

Un-: **un|be|hau|en** ['ʊnbəhauən] ADJ unhewn; **un|be|haust** ['ʊnbəhaust] ADJ (*liter*) homeless; **un|be|hel|ligt** ['ʊnbəˈhɛlɪçt, 'ʊn-] ADJ (= *unbelästigt*) unmolested; (= *unkontrolliert*) unchecked; **jdn ~ lassen** to leave sb alone; (*Polizei etc*) not to stop sb ADV (= *unkontrolliert*) unchecked; (= *ungestört*) undisturbed, in peace; **un|be|herrscht** ADJ *Reaktion, Handlung, Bewegung* uncontrolled; *Mensch* lacking self-control; (= *gierig*) greedy ADV *essen* greedily; **sich ~ verhalten** to lose control; **~ reagieren** to react in an uncontrolled way *or* without any self-control; **brüll nicht so ~** pull yourself together; **Un|be|herrscht|heit** F -, **-en** a *no pl* (*von Mensch*) lack of self-control; (= *Gier*) greediness b (= *unbeherrschte Handlung*) **diese ~ hat ihn seinen Job gekostet** losing his self-control just once cost him his job; **un|be|hin|dert** [ʊn-bəˈhɪndɐt, 'ʊn-] ADJ unhindered, unimpeded; *Sicht* clear, uninterrupted; **~er Zugang** unrestricted access ADV unimpeded, without hindrance

un|be|hol|fen ['ʊnbəhɔlfn] ADJ clumsy, awkward; (= *hilflos*) helpless; (= *plump*) *Annäherungsversuch* clumsy ADV clumsily, awkwardly; **mit seinem verletzten Bein geht er sehr ~** he walks very awkwardly with his injured leg

Un|be|hol|fen|heit F -, *no pl* clumsiness, awkwardness; (= *Hilflosigkeit*) helplessness; (= *Plumpheit*) clumsiness

un-: **un|be|irr|bar** [ʊnbəˈʔɪrbaːɐ, 'ʊn-] ADJ unwavering ADV unwaveringly; **un|be|irrt** [ʊnbəˈʔɪrt, 'ʊn-] ADJ unwavering ADV *glauben, festhalten* unwaveringly; *weiterreden, weitermachen* undeterred

un|be|kannt ADJ unknown; *Gesicht auch* unfamiliar; *Flugzeug, Flugobjekt etc* unidentified; **eine (mir) ~e Stadt/Stimme** a town/voice I didn't know, a town/voice unknown to me; **das war mir ~** I didn't know that, I was unaware of that; **dieser Herr/diese Gegend ist mir ~** I don't know *or* I'm not acquainted with this gentleman/area; **Angst ist ihm ~** he doesn't know what fear is *or* the meaning of (the word) fear; **es wird Ihnen nicht ~ sein, dass ...** you will no

doubt be aware that ...; **~e Größe** (*Math, fig*) unknown quantity; **aus ~er Ursache** for some unknown reason; **nach ~ verzogen** moved – address unknown; **ich bin hier ~** (*inf*) I'm a stranger here; **~e Täter** person or persons unknown; **Strafanzeige gegen ~** charge against person or persons unknown

Un|be|kann|te F *decl as adj* (*Math*) unknown

Un|be|kann|te(r) MF *decl as adj* stranger; **der große ~** (*hum*) the mystery man/person *etc*

un|be|kann|ter|wei|se ['ʊnbəkantɐ'vaizə] ADV **grüße sie/ihn ~ von mir** give her/him my regards although I don't know her/him

un|be|klei|det ADJ bare; **sie war ~** she had nothing or no clothes on, she was naked ADV without any clothes on

un|be|küm|mert [ʊnbəˈkʏmɐt, 'ʊn-] ADJ a (= *unbesorgt*) unconcerned; **sei ganz ~** don't worry b (= *sorgenfrei*) carefree ADV a (= *unbesorgt*) without worrying; **das kannst du ~ tun** you needn't worry about doing that b (= *sorglos*) without a care in the world; *lachen* happily

Un|be|küm|mert|heit F -, *no pl* a (= *Unbesorgtheit*) lack of concern b (= *Sorgenfreiheit*) carefreeness

un|be|las|tet ['ʊnbəlastət] ADJ a (= *ohne Last*) unloaded, unladen; **das linke Bein ~ lassen** to keep one's weight off one's left leg b (= *ohne Schulden*) unencumbered c (*Pol: = ohne Schuld*) guiltless d (= *ohne Sorgen*) free from care or worries; **von Hemmungen/Ängsten** *etc* **~** free from inhibitions/fears *etc* e (= *schadstofffrei*) *Erdreich, Grundwasser etc* unpolluted ADV (= *ohne Sorgen*) without any worries; (= *unvoreingenommen*) neutrally, impartially

Un-: **un|be|lebt** ADJ *Straße, Gegend* quiet; **die ~e Natur** the inanimate world, inanimate nature; **un|be|leckt** ['ʊnbəlɛkt] ADJ **~ von aller Kultur sein** (*inf*) to be completely uncultured; **un|be|lehr|bar** ADJ fixed in one's views; *Rassist etc* dyed-in-the-wool *attr*; **er ist ~** you can't tell him anything; **wenn du so ~ bist** if you won't be told; **Un|be|lehr|bar|keit** [ʊnbəˈleːɐ-baːkait] F -, *no pl* **seine ~** the fact that you just can't tell him anything; **un|be|le|sen** ADJ unread, unlettered; **un|be|leuch|tet** ['ʊn-bələɔyçtət] ADJ *Straße, Weg* unlit; *Fahrzeug* without lights; **un|be|lich|tet** ['ʊnbəlɪçtət] ADJ (*Phot*) unexposed; **un|be|liebt** ADJ unpopular (*bei* with); **sich ~ machen** to make oneself unpopular (*bei* with); **Un|be|liebt|heit** F unpopularity (*bei* with); **un|be|mannt** ['ʊnbəmant] ADJ *Raumflug, Station, U-Boot* unmanned; *Fahrzeug* driverless; *Flugzeug* pilotless; (*inf: = ohne Mann*) without a man or husband; **un|be|merk|bar** ADJ imperceptible; **un|be|merkt** ['ʊnbəmɛrkt] ADJ, ADV unnoticed; (= *nicht gesehen auch*) unobserved; **~ bleiben** to escape attention, to go unnoticed; **un|be|mit|telt** ADJ without means; **~e Studenten erhalten vom Staat eine Beihilfe** students without (any) means of their own receive state aid; **un|be|nom|men** [ʊn-bəˈnɔmən, 'ʊn-] ADJ *pred* (*form*) **es bleibt** *or* **ist Ihnen ~, zu ...** you are (quite) free or at liberty to ...; **das bleibt** *or* **ist dir ~** you're quite free or at liberty to do so; **un|be|nutz|bar** [ʊnbəˈnʊts-baːɐ, 'ʊn-] ADJ unusable; **un|be|nutzt** [ʊn-bənʊtst] ADJ, ADV unused; **un|be|o|bach|tet** ['ʊnbəlo:baxtət] ADJ unobserved, unnoticed; **in einem ~en Moment** when nobody was looking; **wenn er sich ~ fühlt ...** when he thinks nobody is looking ...

un|be|quem ADJ (= *ungemütlich*) uncomfortable; (= *lästig*) *Mensch, Frage, Situation* awkward; *Aufgabe* unpleasant; (= *mühevoll*) difficult; **diese Schuhe sind mir zu ~** these shoes are too uncomfortable; **der Regierung/den Behörden** *etc* **~ sein** to be an embarrassment to the government/authorities *etc*

Un|be|quem|lich|keit F a *no pl* (= *Ungemütlichkeit*) lack of comfort; (*von Situation*) awkwardness b *usu pl* inconvenience

Un-: **un|be|re|chen|bar** ADJ unpredictable; **Un|be|re|chen|bar|keit** F unpredictability; **un|be|rech|tigt** ADJ *Sorge, Zweifel etc* unfounded; *Kritik, Forderung* unjustified; (= *unbefugt*) unauthorized ADV *kritisieren* unjustifiably; *in Anspruch nehmen, kassieren* without entitlement; **un|be|rech|tig|ter|wei|se** ['ʊnbəˌrɛçtɪçtɐ'vaizə] ADV *kritisieren, sich sorgen* without reason; (= *unbefugt*) without authority; *in Anspruch nehmen, kassieren* without entitlement

un|be|rück|sich|tigt [ʊnbəˈrʏkzɪçtɪçt, 'ʊn-] ADJ unconsidered; **etw ~ lassen** not to consider sth, to leave sth out of consideration; **die Frage ist ~ geblieben** this question has not been considered; **ein bisher ~er Punkt** a point which has not yet been considered

un|be|ru|fen ADJ (= *unaufgefordert, unberechtigt*) uncalled-for, unwarranted ADV **~ (toi, toi, toi)!** touch wood! (*Brit*), knock on wood! (*US*); **sich ~ einmischen** to interfere without good reason

un|be|rühr|bar [ʊnbeˈryːɐbaːɐ, 'ʊn-] ADJ untouchable; **die Unberührbaren** the untouchables

un|be|rührt ['ʊnbəryːɐt] ADJ a untouched; (*fig*) *Wald etc* virgin; *Natur* unspoiled; **~ sein** (*Mädchen*) to be a virgin b (= *mitleidlos*) unmoved; **das kann ihn nicht ~ lassen** he can't help but be moved by that c (= *unbetroffen*) unaffected ADV a (= *unangetastet*) **~ in die Ehe gehen** to be a virgin when one marries; **das Essen ~ stehen lassen** to leave one's food untouched b (= *unbewegt*) unmoved

Un|be|rührt|heit F -, *no pl* (*von Mädchen*) virginity; **wo finden Sie sonst noch diese ~ der Natur?** where else will you find nature so completely unspoiled?

un-: **un|be|scha|det** [ʊnbəˈʃaːdət, 'ʊn-] PREP *+gen* (*form*) regardless of; **~ dessen, dass ...** regardless of the fact that ...; **un|be|schä|digt** ['ʊnbəʃɛːdɪçt] ADJ, ADV undamaged; *Geschirr, Glas etc auch* intact, unbroken; *Siegel* unbroken; (*inf*) intact (*inf*), unharmed, in one piece (*inf*); **~ bleiben** not to be damaged/broken; (*seelisch etc*) to emerge unscathed; **un|be|schäf|tigt** ADJ (= *müßig*) idle; (= *arbeitslos*) not working

un|be|schei|den ADJ *Mensch, Plan* presumptuous; **darf ich mir die ~e Frage erlauben, ...?** I hope you don't think me impertinent but might I ask ...?

Un|be|schei|den|heit F presumptuousness; (*von Mensch auch*) presumption

Un-: **un|be|schol|ten** ['ʊnbəʃɔltn] ADJ (*geh*) respectable; *Ruf* spotless; (*Jur*) with no previous convictions; **Un|be|schol|ten|heit** F -, *no pl* (*geh*) respectability; (*von Ruf*) spotlessness; (*Jur*) lack of previous convictions; **un|be|schrankt** ADJ *Bahnübergang* without gates, unguarded

un|be|schränkt ADJ unrestricted; *Freiheit, Vollmacht auch* limitless; *Macht* absolute; *Geldmittel, Haftung, Zeit, Geduld* unlimited; *Vertrauen* unbounded, boundless; **wie viel darf ich mitnehmen? – ~** how much can I take? – there's no limit or restriction; **jdm ~e Vollmacht geben** to give sb carte blanche

un|be|schreib|lich [ʊnbəˈʃraiplɪç, 'ʊn-] ADJ indescribable; *Frechheit* tremendous, enormous ADV *schön, gut etc* indescribably; **~ zunehmen** (*zahlenmäßig*) to show a staggering increase

un-: **un|be|schrie|ben** ['ʊnbəʃriːbn] ADJ blank → *Blatt*; **un|be|schwert** ['ʊnbəˈʃveːɐt] ADJ a (= *sorgenfrei*) carefree; *Melodien* light; *Unterhaltung, Lektüre* light-hearted b (= *ohne Gewicht*) unweighted ADV (= *sorgenfrei*) carefree; **er konnte das Leben ~ genießen** he could enjoy a carefree life; **un|be|seelt** ['ʊnbəˈzeːlt] ADJ (*liter*) unbelebt; **un|be|se|hen** [ʊnbəˈzeːən, 'ʊn-] ADV indiscriminately; (= *ohne es anzusehen*) without looking at it; **das glaube ich dir ~** I believe it if you say so; **das glaube ich dir nicht ~** I'll believe that when I see it; **un|be-**

setzt ADJ vacant; *Stuhl, Platz auch* unoccupied; *Bus, Zug* empty; *Schalter* closed; **un|be|sieg|bar** ADJ *Armee etc* invincible; *Mannschaft, Sportler etc auch* unbeatable; **Un|be|sieg|bar|keit** [ʊnbəˈziːkbaːɐkait, ˈʊn-] F -, *no pl* invincibility; **un|be|siegt** [ˈʊnbəziːkt] ADJ undefeated; **un|be|son|nen** ADJ rash ADV rashly; **Un|be|son|nen|heit** F rashness

un|be|sorgt ADJ unconcerned; **Sie können ganz ~ sein** you can set your mind at rest *or* ease ADV without worrying; **das können Sie ~ tun** you don't need to worry about doing that

Un-: un|be|stän|dig ADJ *Wetter* changeable; *(zu bestimmtem Zeitpunkt auch)* unsettled; *Mensch* unsteady; *(in Leistungen)* erratic; *Liebhaber* inconstant; *Liebe, Gefühl, Liebe* transitory; **Un|be|stän|dig|keit** F *(von Wetter)* changeability; *(von Mensch)* unsteadiness; *(in Leistungen)* erratic behaviour *(Brit)* or behavior *(US)*; *(von Liebhaber)* inconstancy; *(von Gefühl, Liebe)* transitory nature; **un|be|stä|tigt** [ˈʊnbəʃtɛːtɪçt, ʊnbəˈʃtɛː-tɪçt] ADJ unconfirmed; **un|be|stech|lich** ADJ **a** *Mensch* incorruptible **b** *Urteil, Blick* unerring; **Un|be|stech|lich|keit** F **a** *(von Mensch)* incorruptibility **b** *(von Urteil, Blick)* **die ~ seines Urteils/Blicks** his unerring judgement/eye; **un|be|stimm|bar** ADJ indeterminable; **un|be|stimmt** ADJ **a** *(= ungewiss)* uncertain; *(= unentschieden)* undecided **b** *(= unklar, undeutlich)* *Gefühl, Erinnerung etc* vague; **etw ~ lassen** to leave sth open; **auf ~e Zeit** for an indefinite period, indefinitely **c** *(Gram)* indefinite; **Un|be|stimmt|heit** F , *no pl* *(= Ungewissheit)* uncertainty; **un|be|streit|bar** ✪ 42.1, 53.6 ADJ *Tatsache* indisputable; *Verdienste, Fähigkeiten* unquestionable ADV *richtig* indisputably; *fähig* unquestionably; **un|be|strit|ten** [ˈʊnbəʃtrɪtn, ʊnbəˈʃtrɪtn] ADJ undisputed, indisputable; **es ist ja ~, dass ...** nobody denies or disputes that ... ADV indisputably; **un|be|teiligt** ADJ **a** *(= uninteressiert)* indifferent; *(bei Diskussion)* uninterested **b** *(= nicht teilnehmend)* uninvolved *no adv (an +dat, bei in)*; *(Jur, Comm)* disinterested; **es kamen auch Unbeteiligte zu Schaden** innocent bystanders were also injured; **un|be|tont** ADJ unstressed; **un|be|trächt|lich** ADJ insignificant; *Unannehmlichkeiten etc* minor; *Aufpreis, Verbilligung* slight; **nicht ~** not inconsiderable; **un|beug|sam** [ˈʊnˈbɔykzaːm, ˈʊn-] ADJ uncompromising, unbending; *Wille* unshakeable; **un|be|wacht** [ˈʊnbəvaxt] ADJ, ADV *(lit, fig)* unguarded; *Parkplatz* unattended; **un|be|waff-net** ADJ unarmed; **un|be|wäl|tigt** [ˈʊnbəˈvɛltɪçt, ʊnbəˈvɛltɪçt] ADJ unconquered, unmastered; **Deutschlands ~e Vergangenheit** the past with which Germany has not yet come to terms

un|be|weg|lich ADJ **a** *(= nicht zu bewegen)* immovable; *(= steif)* stiff; *(geistig)* rigid, inflexible; **ohne Auto ist man ziemlich ~** you're not very mobile or you can't get around much without a car; **~e Güter** *(Jur)* immovable property **b** *(= bewegungslos)* motionless ADV **~ dastehen/daliegen** to stand/lie there motionless *or* without moving

Un|be|weg|lich|keit F immovability; *(= Steifheit)* stiffness; *(geistig)* rigidity, inflexibility

un-: un|be|wegt ADJ *(= bewegungslos)* motionless, unmoving; *Meer* unruffled; *(fig: = unberührt)* *Miene, Gesicht* impassive ADV *(= unberührt)* impassively; **un|be|weibt** [ˈʊnbəvaipt] ADJ *(inf)* unmarried, wifeless *(inf)*; **un|be|wie|sen** ADJ unproven; **un|be|wohn|bar** ADJ uninhabitable; **un|be|wohnt** ADJ *Gegend, Insel, Planet* uninhabited; *Wohnung, Haus* unoccupied, empty; **un|be|wusst** ▲ ADJ unconscious; *Reflex* involuntary; **das Unbewusste** *(Psych)* the unconscious ADV unconsciously; **un|be|zahl|bar** ADJ **a** *(lit: = zu teuer)* prohibitively expensive, impossibly dear *(Brit)*; *Miete* prohibitively high; *Luxusartikel* absolutely unaffordable **b** *(fig)* *(= praktisch, nützlich)* invaluable; *(= komisch)* priceless; **un|be|zahlt** ADJ *Urlaub* unpaid; *Rechnung, Schuld etc auch* unsettled, outstanding; **sein**

noch ~es Auto the car he hasn't finished paying for yet; **un|be|zähm|bar** [ʊnbəˈtsɛːmbaːɐ, ˈʊn-] ADJ *Optimismus, heiteres Gemüt, Neugier etc* irrepressible, indomitable; *Verlangen, Lust, Kraft* uncontrollable; *Hunger* insatiable; *Durst* unquenchable **b** *(= unbesiegbar)* invincible; **un|be|zwei|fel|bar** ADJ undeniable; *Tatsache auch* unarguable ADV undeniably; **un|be|zwing|bar** [ʊnbəˈtsvɪŋbaːɐ], **un|be|zwing|lich** [ʊnbəˈtsvɪŋlɪç, ˈʊn-] ADJ unconquerable; *Gegner* invincible; *Festung* impregnable; *Drang* uncontrollable

Un|bil|den [ˈʊnbɪldn] PL *(liter)* **a** *(des Wetters)* rigours *pl (Brit)*, rigors *pl (US)* **b** *(einer schweren Zeit etc)* trials *pl*, (trials and) tribulations *pl*

Un|bil|dung F , *no pl* lack of education

Un|bill [ˈʊnbɪl] F -, *no pl* *(old, liter)* injustice, wrong

un|bil|lig ADJ *(Jur: = ungerecht)* unjust; *(= unangemessen)* unreasonable; **~e Härte** *(Jur)* undue hardship

Un|bil|lig|keit F *(Jur: = Ungerechtigkeit)* injustice; *(= Unangemessenheit)* unreasonableness

Un-: un|blu|tig ADJ *Sieg, Umsturz etc* bloodless; *(Med)* non-operative ADV without bloodshed; **un|bot|mä|ßig** ADJ *(geh)* *(= undiszipliniert)* insubordinate; *(= rebellisch)* rebellious; **un|brauch|bar** ADJ *(= nutzlos)* useless, (of) no use *pred*; *(= nicht zu verwenden)* unusable; **Un|brauch|bar|keit** F *(= Nutzlosigkeit)* uselessness; **un|bü|ro|kra|tisch** ADJ unbureaucratic ADV without a lot of red tape, unbureaucratically; **un|christ|lich** ADJ unchristian; **eine ~e Zeit** *(inf)* an ungodly hour ADV in an unchristian way; **un|cool** ADJ *(inf)* uncool *(inf)*

und [ʊnt] CONJ **a** and; **~? well?; **~ dann?** (and) what then *or* then what?; *(= danach)* and then?, and after that?; **~ Ähnliches** and things like that, and suchlike; **~ anderes** and other things; **er kann es nicht, ~ ich auch nicht** he can't do it, (and) nor or neither can I; **ich ~ ihm Geld leihen?** *(inf)* me, lend him money?; **du ~ tanzen können?** *(inf)* you dance?; **immer zwei ~ zwei** two at a time; **Gruppen zu fünf ~ fünf** groups of five; **er aß ~ aß** he ate and ate, he kept on (and on) eating; **er konnte ~ konnte nicht aufhören** he simply couldn't stop; **Unfälle, Staus, ~ ~ ~** accidents, traffic jams etc etc etc

b *(konzessiv)* even if; **..., ~ wenn ich selbst bezahlen muss** ... even if I have to pay myself; **..., ~ wenn du auch noch so bettelst** ... no matter how much you beg; **~ selbst** even; **~ selbst dann** even then

Un|dank M ingratitude; **~ ernten** to get little thanks; **~ ist der Welt Lohn** *(Prov)* never expect thanks for anything

un|dank|bar ADJ **a** *Mensch* ungrateful **b** *(= unerfreulich)* *Aufgabe, Arbeit etc* thankless ADV **sich jdm gegenüber ~ zeigen** or **erweisen** to be ungrateful to sb

Un|dank|bar|keit F **a** *(von Mensch)* ingratitude, ungratefulness **b** *(von Aufgabe, Arbeit etc)* thanklessness

un-: un|da|tiert [ˈʊndatiːɐt] ADJ undated; **un|de|fi|nier|bar** ADJ *Begriff, Aroma, Art* indefinable; **das Essen war ~** nobody could say what the food was; **un|dehn|bar** ADJ inelastic; **un|de|kli|nier|bar** ADJ *(Gram)* indeclinable; **un|de|mo|kra|tisch** ADJ undemocratic ADV undemocratically

un|denk|bar ADJ unthinkable, inconceivable; **es/diese Möglichkeit ist nicht ~** it/the possibility is not inconceivable

un|denk|lich [ˈʊnˈdɛŋklɪç] ADJ **seit ~en Zeiten** *(geh)* since time immemorial

un|deut|lich ADJ indistinct; *(wegen Nebel etc auch)* hazy; *Foto auch* blurred; *Erinnerung auch* vague, hazy; *Schrift* illegible; *Ausdrucksweise, Erklärung* unclear, muddled ADV **~ sprechen** to speak indistinctly, to mumble; **ich konnte es nur ~ verstehen** I couldn't understand it very

clearly; **bemüh dich mal, nicht so ~ zu schreiben** try to write more clearly; **Sie drücken sich sehr ~ aus** you don't express yourself very clearly; **sie/es war nur ~ erkennbar** or **zu erkennen** you couldn't see her/it at all clearly

un|deutsch ADJ un-German

un|dicht ADJ *(= luftdurchlässig)* not airtight; *(= wasserdurchlässig)* not watertight; *Dach* leaky, leaking; **das Rohr ist ~** the pipe leaks; **das Fenster ist ~** the window lets in a draught *(Brit)* or draft *(US)*; **es/er/sie muss eine ~e Stelle haben** *(Rohr etc)* it must have a leak in it; *(Reifen etc)* it must have a hole in it; *(Flasche etc)* the seal must be broken; **in der Regierung muss eine ~e Stelle sein** the government must have a leak somewhere

un|dif|fe|ren|ziert ADJ simplistic; *(= nicht analytisch)* indiscriminate ADV simplistically; *behandeln* in an over-generalized way; *Begriffe verwenden* indiscriminately

Un|ding NT , *no pl* absurdity; **es ist ein ~, zu ...** it is preposterous *or* absurd to ...

Un-: un|dip|lo|ma|tisch ADJ undiplomatic ADV undiplomatically; **un|dis|zip|li|niert** ADJ undisciplined ADV in an undisciplined way; **Un|dis|zip|li|niert|heit** F -, -en **a** *no pl* lack of discipline **b** *(= undisziplinierte Handlung)* undisciplined behaviour *(Brit)* or behavior *(US)* *no pl*; **un|dra|ma|tisch** *(fig)* ADJ undramatic, unexciting ADV undramatically; **un|duld|sam** ADJ intolerant *(gegen* of); **Un|duld|sam|keit** F intolerance *(gegen* of); **un|durch|dring|bar** [ʊndʊrçˈdrɪŋbaːɐ, ˈʊn-], **un|durch|dring|lich** [ʊndʊrçˈdrɪŋlɪç, ˈʊn-] ADJ *Gebüsch, Urwald* impenetrable; *Gesicht, Miene* inscrutable; **un|durch|führ|bar** ADJ impracticable, unworkable; **Un|durch|führ|bar|keit** F impracticability, unworkability; **un|durch|läs-sig** ADJ impermeable, impervious *(gegen* to); *Grenze* closed; **Un|durch|läs|sig|keit** F impermeability, imperviousness; **un|durch|schau-bar** ADJ unfathomable; *Exot, Volk etc* inscrutable; **er ist ein ~er Typ** *(inf)* you never know what game he's playing *(inf)*; **Un|durch-schau|bar|keit** [ʊndʊrçˈʃaubaːɐkait, ˈʊn-] F -, *no pl* unfathomability; **un|durch|sich|tig** ADJ **a** *Fenster, Papier, Stoff* opaque *(fig pej)* *Mensch, Methoden* devious; *Motive* obscure; *Vorgänge, Geschäfte* dark; **es ist eine ganze ~e Angelegenheit** you can't tell what's going on in that business; **Un|durch|sich|tig|keit** F , *no pl* **a** *(von Fenster, Papier, Stoff)* opacity **b** *(fig pej)* *(von Mensch, Methoden)* deviousness; *(von Motiven)* obscureness

Und-Zei|chen NT *(Typ)* ampersand

un|eben ADJ **a** *Oberfläche, Fußboden, Wand etc* uneven; *Straße* bumpy, uneven; *Gelände* rough, bumpy **b** *(dial inf)* bad

Un|eben|heit F *(von Oberfläche etc)* unevenness; *(von Straße auch)* bumpiness; *(von Gelände)* roughness; **kleine ~en** uneven patches

Un-: un|echt ADJ false; *(= vorgetäuscht)* fake; *Schmuck, Edelstein, Blumen etc* artificial, fake *(usu pej)*; *Bruch* improper ADV *(= vorgetäuscht)* **~ klingen** to sound false; **~ wirken** to seem false; **un|edel** ADJ **a** *Metalle* base **b** *(fig)* *Mensch, Gesinnung* base; **un|ef|fek|tiv** ADJ, ADV → **ineffektiv**; **un|ehe-lich** ADJ illegitimate ADV **~ geboren sein** to be illegitimate, to have been born out of wedlock *(old, form)*; **Un|ehe|lich|keit** F illegitimacy; **Un|eh|re** F , *no pl* dishonour *(Brit)*, dishonor *(US)*; **jdm ~ machen, jdm zur ~ gereichen** *(geh)* to disgrace sb; **un|eh|ren|haft** ADJ dishonourable *(Brit)*, dishonorable *(US)* ADV dishonourably *(Brit)*, dishonorably *(US)*; **~ (aus der Armee) entlassen werden** to be given a dishonourable *(Brit)* or dishonorable *(US)* discharge; **un|ehr|er|bie|tig** ADJ disrespectful; **un|ehr|lich** ADJ dishonest; **auf ~e Weise** by dishonest means ADV dishonestly; **~ spielen** to cheat; **Un|ehr|lich|keit** F dishonesty; **un|eid|lich** ADJ **~e Falschaussage** *(Jur)* false statement made while not under oath; **un|ei|gen|nüt|zig**

ADJ unselfish, selfless **ADV** unselfishly, selflessly; **Un|ei|gen|nüt|zig|keit** F unselfishness, selflessness; **un|ei|gent|lich** ADJ a (*Math*) improper b (= *übertragen*) figurative; **un|ein|ge|la|den** ['ʊnlaingəlaːdn] **ADJ** uninvited **ADV** ~ **kommen** to come uninvited, to come without an invitation; ~ **erscheinen** to gatecrash (*bei etw* sth); **un|ein|ge|löst** ['ʊnlaingəløːst] ADJ *Gutschein* unredeemed; *Wechsel* dishonoured (*Brit*), dishonored (*US*); *Versprechen etc* unfulfilled

un|ein|ge|schränkt **ADJ** absolute, total; *Freiheit, Rechte* unlimited, unrestricted; *Annahme, Zustimmung* unqualified; *Vertrauen* absolute; *Lob* unreserved; *Handel* free, unrestricted; *Vollmachten* plenary **ADV** absolutely, totally; *beanspruchen* without limitation or restriction; *zustimmen, akzeptieren* without qualification; *loben, vertrauen* without reservation, unreservedly; *Handel treiben* freely, without restriction

Un-: un|ein|ge|weiht ['ʊnlaingəvait] ADJ uninitiated; **für Uneingeweihte** for the uninitiated; **un|ein|heit|lich** **ADJ** nonuniform; *Öffnungszeiten, Arbeitszeiten, Systeme, Reaktion* varied; (= *nicht für alle gleich*) *Arbeitszeiten, Schulferien* different; *Qualität* inconsistent; *Börse* irregular; *Preise* unsteady; ~ **sein** to vary **ADV** *gekleidet, beurteilen* differently; *sich entwickeln* in different ways; (*St Ex*) irregularly; **die New Yorker Börse hat am Donnerstag ~ tendiert** on Thursday shares on the New York Stock Exchange were mixed; ~ **verlaufen** to vary; **un|ei|nig** ADJ a (= *verschiedener Meinung*) in disagreement; **über etw** (*acc*) ~ **sein** to disagree about sth, to be in disagreement about sth; **ich bin mit mir selbst noch ~** I haven't made up my mind yet b (= *zerstritten*) divided; **Un|ei|nig|keit** F disagreement (+*gen* between); ~ **in der Partei** disagreement or division within the party; **un|ein|nehm|bar** [ʊnlain'neːmbaːɐ, 'ʊn-] ADJ impregnable; **un|eins** ADJ *pred* disagreed; (= *zerstritten*) divided; **(mit jdm) ~ sein/werden** to disagree with sb; **ich bin mit mir selbst ~** I cannot make up my mind; **die Mitglieder sind (untereinander) ~** the members are divided amongst themselves; **un|ele|gant** **ADJ** inelegant **ADV** *gekleidet, sich ausdrücken, formulieren* inelegantly; **un|emp|fäng|lich** ADJ (*für* to) insusceptible, unsusceptible (*für Eindrücke auch, Atmosphäre*) insensitive; **Un|emp|fäng|lich|keit** F insusceptibility, unsusceptibility; (*für Eindrücke etc*) insensitiveness

un|emp|find|lich ADJ (*gegen* to) insensitive; (*durch Übung, Erfahrung*) inured; (*gegen Krankheiten, Bazillen etc*) immune; *Pflanze* hardy; *Baustoff* which weathers well; *Textilien, Teppich* hard-wearing and stain-resistant; **gegen Kälte ~e Pflanzen** plants which aren't sensitive to the cold

Un|emp|find|lich|keit F , *no pl* (*gegen* to) insensitiveness, insensitivity; (*gegen Krankheiten, Bazillen etc*) immunity; (*von Pflanzen*) hardiness; (*von Textilien*) practicality; **dieser Baustoff ist wegen seiner ~ gegen Witterungseinflüsse besonders gut geeignet** this building material is particularly suitable because it weathers so well

un|end|lich **ADJ** infinite; (*zeitlich*) endless; *Universum* infinite, boundless; **das Unendliche** infinity; **im Unendlichen** at infinity; **(bis) ins Unendliche** (*lit, Math*) to infinity; **auf ~ einstellen** (*Phot*) to focus on infinity; **~e Mal** endless times **ADV** endlessly; infinitely; (*fig* = *sehr*) terribly; ~ **lange diskutieren** to argue endlessly; ~ **viele Dinge/Leute** *etc* no end of things/people *etc*

un|end|lich|e|mal △ ['ʊn|ɛntlıçəmaːl] ADV = **unendlich** ADJ

Un|end|lich|keit F infinity; (*zeitlich*) endlessness; (*von Universum*) boundlessness; ~ **von Raum und Zeit** infinity of time and space

Un|end|lich|keits|zei|chen NT (*Math*) infinity symbol

un|end|lich|mal ['ʊn|ɛntlıçmaːl] ADV endless times

Un-: un|ent|behr|lich ADJ indispensable; *Kenntnisse auch* essential; **Un|ent|behr|lich|keit** F -, *no pl* indispensability; **er scheint von seiner ~ überzeugt zu sein** he seems to think he's indispensable; **wir haben uns über die ~ gewisser Haushaltsgeräte unterhalten** we discussed how one can't do without certain household appliances; **un|ent|deckt** ['ʊn|ɛntdɛkt] ADJ undiscovered; **un|ent|gelt|lich** [ʊn|ɛnt'gɛltlıç, 'ʊn-] **ADJ** free of charge **ADV** free of charge; *arbeiten* without pay, for nothing; **etw ~ tun** to do sth free of charge; **un|ent|rinn|bar** [ʊnlɛnt'rınbaːɐ, 'ʊn-] ADJ (*geh*) inescapable

un|ent|schie|den **ADJ** (= *nicht entschieden*) undecided; (= *entschlusslos*) indecisive; (*Sport*) drawn; **ein ~es Rennen** a dead heat **ADV** **das Spiel steht immer noch 2:2** ~ the score is still level (*Brit*) or even (*US*) at 2 all; ~ **enden** or **ausgehen** to end in a draw or tie; ~ **spielen**, **sich ~ trennen** to draw, to tie

Un|ent|schie|den ['ʊn|ɛntʃiːdn] NT -s, - (*Sport*) draw; **mit einem ~ enden** to end in a draw

un|ent|schlos|sen **ADJ** (= *nicht entschieden*) undecided; (= *entschlusslos*) *Mensch* indecisive, irresolute; **ich bin noch ~** I haven't decided yet, I haven't made up my mind yet **ADV** *sich verhalten* indecisively; ~ **stand er vor dem Haus** he stood hesitating in front of the house

Un|ent|schlos|sen|heit F (= *Entschlusslosigkeit: von Mensch*) indecisiveness, indecision

un|ent|schuld|bar ADJ inexcusable

un|ent|schul|digt ['ʊn|ɛntʃʊldıçt] **ADJ** unexcused; **~es Fernbleiben** or **Fehlen von der Arbeit** absenteeism; **~es Fernbleiben** or **Fehlen von der Schule** truancy **ADV** without an excuse

un|ent|wegt [ʊn|ɛnt've:kt, 'ʊn-] **ADJ** (*mit Ausdauer*) continuous, constant; (= *ohne aufzuhören auch*) incessant; *Kämpfer* untiring; **einige Unentwegte** a few stalwarts **ADV** constantly; incessantly; without tiring; ~ **weitermachen** to continue unceasingly

un-: un|ent|wirr|bar **ADJ** *Knäuel, Geflecht* which can't be disentangled; *Zusammenhänge, Verstrickungen* involved, complex, inextricable **ADV** inextricably; **un|ent|zünd|bar** ADJ noninflammable, nonflammable; **un|er|ach|tet** [ʊn|ɛɐ'|axtət, 'ʊn-] PREP +*gen* (*old*) = **ungeachtet**

un|er|bitt|lich [ʊn|ɛɐ'bıtlıç, 'ʊn-] **ADJ** *Kampf* relentless; *Härte* unyielding; *Mensch auch* inexorable, pitiless **ADV** (= *hartnäckig*) obstinately, stubbornly; (= *gnadenlos*) ruthlessly; **er besteht ~ auf Erfüllung des Vertrags** he stubbornly insists that the contract be fulfilled; **die Polizei wird ~ gegen diese Drogenhändler vorgehen** the police will proceed ruthlessly against these drug dealers; ~ **auf jdn einschlagen** to beat sb pitilessly or mercilessly

Un|er|bitt|lich|keit F -, *no pl* relentlessness

Un-: un|er|fah|ren ADJ inexperienced; **Un|er|fah|re|ne(r)** ['ʊn|ɛɐfaːrənə] MF *decl as adj* inexperienced person/man/woman *etc*; **Un|er|fah|ren|heit** F inexperience, lack of experience; **un|er|find|lich** [ʊn|ɛɐ'fıntlıç, 'ʊn-] ADJ incomprehensible; *Grund* obscure; **aus ~en Gründen** for some obscure reason; **un|er|forsch|bar** [ʊn|ɛɐ'fɔrʃbaːɐ, 'ʊn-] ADJ unfathomable; **un|er|forsch|lich** [ʊn|ɛɐ'fɔrʃlıç, 'ʊn-] ADJ *Ratschluss, Grund, Wille* unfathomable; **un|er|freu|lich** **ADJ** unpleasant; **Unerfreuliches** (= *schlechte Nachrichten*) bad news *sing*; (= *Übles*) bad things *pl* ~ **ausgehen, enden, verlaufen** unpleasantly; **un|er|füll|bar** [ʊn|ɛɐ'fʏlbaːɐ, 'ʊn-] ADJ unrealizable; *Wunsch, Ziel auch* unattainable; **un|er|füllt** [ʊn-ɛɐfʏlt] ADJ unfulfilled; **un|er|gie|big** ADJ *Quelle, Thema* unproductive; *Boden, Ernte, Nachschlagewerk* poor; *Kaffee, Trauben* uneconomical; **un|er|gründ|bar** [ʊn|ɛɐ'gryntbaːɐ, 'ʊn-] ADJ, **un|er|gründ|lich** [ʊn|ɛɐ'gryntlıç, 'ʊn-] ADJ unfathomable; **un|er|heb|lich** **ADJ** (= *geringfügig*) insignificant; (= *unwichtig auch*) unimportant, irrelevant; **nicht ~** not inconsiderable **ADV** (= *geringfügig*) insignificantly; **nicht ~ verbessert**

---

considerably or significantly improved; **un|er|hofft** ['ʊn|ɛɐhɔft] ADJ unexpected

un|er|hört¹ ['ʊn|ɛɐ'hɔːɐt] **ADJ** *attr* (= *ungeheuer, gewaltig*) enormous; (= *empörend*) outrageous; *Frechheit* incredible; **das ist ja ~!** that's quite outrageous **ADV** incredibly; ~ **viel** a tremendous amount (of); ~ **viel wissen** to know a tremendous amount; ~ **viel arbeiten** to work tremendously hard; **wir müssen uns ~ beeilen** we really have to hurry; ~ **aufpassen** to watch very carefully

un|er|hört² ['ʊn|ɛɐhøːɐt] ADJ *Bitte, Gebet* unanswered; *Liebe* unrequited; *Liebhaber* rejected

un-: un|er|kannt ['ʊn|ɛɐkant] **ADJ** unrecognized; ~ **bleiben** not to be recognized **ADV** without being recognized; **die Täter konnten ~ entkommen** the culprits managed to escape without being recognized; **un|er|kenn|bar** ADJ unrecognizable; **un|er|klär|bar, un|er|klär|lich** ADJ inexplicable; **das ist mir ~** or **unerklärlich** I can't understand it; **un|er|klärt** ADJ *Phänomen, Sachverhalt* unexplained; *Krieg, Liebe* undeclared; **un|er|läss|lich** ▲ [ʊn|ɛɐ'lɛslıç, 'ʊn-] ADJ essential

un|er|laubt ['ʊn|ɛɐlaupt] **ADJ** forbidden; *Betreten, Parken* unauthorized; (= *ungesetzlich*) illegal; **~e Handlung** (*Jur*) tort; **~er Waffenbesitz** illegal possession of firearms → **Entfernung** **ADV** *betreten, verlassen* without permission or authorization; **etw ~ tun** to do sth without permission → **entfernen**

un|er|laub|ter|wei|se ['ʊn|ɛɐlauptɐ'vaizə] **ADV** without permission

un|er|le|digt **ADJ** unfinished; *Post* unanswered; *Rechnung* outstanding; *Auftrag* unfulfilled; (= *schwebend*) pending; **„unerledigt"** "pending" **ADV** *liegen bleiben* without being dealt with; **etw ~ lassen** not to deal with sth; **während sie krank war, blieb ihre Arbeit ~ liegen** when she was ill her work was left undone

un-: un|er|mess|lich ▲ [ʊn|ɛɐ'mɛslıç, 'ʊn-] **ADJ** *Reichtum, Schaden, Leid* untold *attr*, immense; *Weite, Himmel, Ozean* vast **ADV** *reich, groß* immensely, beyond measure; **un|er|müd|lich** [ʊn|ɛɐ'myːtlıç, 'ʊn-] **ADJ** *Mensch, Bestrebungen, Kampf, Fleiß* untiring, tireless; *Versuche* unceasing **ADV** tirelessly; **un|er|nst** ADJ frivolous; **un|er|probt** ['ʊn|ɛɐproːpt] ADJ untested, untried; **un|er|quick|lich** ADJ (= *unerfreulich*) unedifying; (= *nutzlos*) unproductive, fruitless; **un|er|reich|bar** ADJ *Ziel, Leistung, Qualität* unattainable; *Ort, Ferne* inaccessible; (*telefonisch*) unobtainable; **seine Beförderung war in ~e Ferne gerückt** promotion was now right out of his reach; **un|er|reicht** [ʊn|ɛɐ'raiçt, 'ʊn-] ADJ unequalled (*Brit*), unequaled (*US*); *Ziel* unattained

un|er|sätt|lich [ʊn|ɛɐ'zɛtlıç, 'ʊn-] ADJ insatiable; *Wissensdurst auch* inexhaustible

Un|er|sätt|lich|keit [ʊn|ɛɐ'zɛtlıçkait, 'ʊn-] F -, *no pl* insatiability; (*von Wissensdurst auch*) inexhaustibility

Un-: un|er|schlos|sen ADJ *Land* undeveloped; *Boden* unexploited; *Vorkommen, Markt, Erdöllager* untapped; **un|er|schöpf|lich** [ʊn|ɛɐ'ʃœpflıç, 'ʊn-] ADJ inexhaustible; **un|er|schro|cken** **ADJ** intrepid, courageous **ADV** *für etw eintreten* courageously; *kämpfen auch* intrepidly; **Un|er|schro|cken|heit** F -, *no pl* intrepidity; **un|er|schüt|ter|lich** [ʊn|ɛɐ'ʃʏtɐlıç, 'ʊn-] **ADJ** unshakeable; *Ruhe* imperturbable **ADV** steadfastly; **sie glaubt ~ an ...** (*acc*) she has an unshakeable belief in ...; **un|er|schwing|lich** ADJ exorbitant, prohibitive; **für jdn ~ sein** to be beyond sb's means; **ein für uns ~er Luxus** a luxury beyond our means; **~ (teuer) sein** to be prohibitively expensive, to be prohibitive; **un|er|setz|bar** [ʊn|ɛɐ'zɛtsbaːɐ, 'ʊn-] ADJ, **un|er|setz|lich** [ʊn|ɛɐ'zɛtslıç, 'ʊn-] ADJ irreplaceable; *Mensch auch* indispensable; **un|er|sprieß|lich** ADJ (= *unerfreulich*) unedifying; (= *nutzlos*) unproductive, fruitless; **un|er|träg|lich** **ADJ** unbearable **ADV** *heiß, laut* unbearably; **er hat sich gestern ~ benommen** his behaviour (*Brit*) or behavior

---

(US) was unbearable yesterday; **un|er|wähnt** ['ʊnlɛɐvɛːnt] ADJ unmentioned; **~ bleiben** not to be mentioned; **un|er|war|tet** ['ʊnlɛɐvartət, ʊnlɛɐ'vartət] ADJ unexpected; **un|er|wi|dert** ['ʊnlɛɐviːdɐt] ADJ Brief, Behauptung unanswered; Liebe unrequited; Sympathie one-sided; **un|er|wünscht** ADJ Kind unwanted; Besuch, Effekt unwelcome; Eigenschaften undesirable; **du bist hier ~** you're not welcome here; **~e Personen** undesirables; **ein ~er Ausländer** (Pol) an undesirable alien; **un|er|zo|gen** ['ʊnlɛɐtsoːgn] ADJ ill-bred, ill-mannered; Kind auch badly brought up

UNESCO [u'nɛsko] F - **die ~** UNESCO

un|fach|ge|mäß, **un|fach|män|nisch** ADJ unprofessional ADV unprofessionally, inexpertly

un|fä|hig ☉ 43.4 ADJ **a** attr incompetent **b ~ sein, etw zu tun** to be incapable of doing sth; (vorübergehend) to be unable to do sth; **einer Sache** (gen) or **zu etw ~ sein** to be incapable of sth

Un|fä|hig|keit F **a** (= Untüchtigkeit) incompetence **b** (= Nichtkönnen) inability

Un-: un|fair ADJ unfair (gegenüber to) ADV unfairly; **Un|fair|ness** ▲ F unfairness

Un|fall ['ʊnfal] M accident; **er ist bei einem ~ ums Leben gekommen** he died in an accident; **gegen ~ versichert** insured against accidents

Un|fall-: Un|fall|arzt M , **Un|fall|ärz|tin** F specialist for accident injuries; **Un|fall|be|tei|lig|te(r)** MF decl as adj person/man/woman etc involved in an/the accident; **Un|fall|bi|lanz** F accident figures pl or statistics pl; **Un|fall|fah|rer(in)** M(F) driver at fault in an/the accident; **Un|fall|fahr|zeug** NT accident vehicle, vehicle involved in an accident; **Un|fall|flucht** F failure to stop after an accident; (nicht melden) failure to report an accident; (esp bei Verletzung von Personen) hit-and-run driving; **~ begehen** to fail to stop after an accident/to fail to report an accident/to commit a hit-and-run offence (Brit) or offense (US); **un|fall|flüch|tig** ADJ Fahrer who fails to stop after an accident; (ohne Unfallmeldung) who fails to report an accident; (esp bei Verletzung von Personen) hit-and-run attr; **~ werden** to fail to stop after an accident/to fail to report an accident/to commit a hit-and-run offence (Brit) or offense (US); **Un|fall|flüch|ti|ge** PL decl as adj → **Unfallflucht** drivers pl who fail to stop after an accident/who fail to report an accident/hit-and-run drivers pl; **Un|fall|fol|ge** F result of an/the accident; **un|fall|frei** ADJ accident-free ADV without an accident; **Un|fall|ge|fahr** F danger or risk of accidents, hazard; **es besteht erhöhte ~** there is an increased risk of accidents (occurring); **Un|fall|geg|ner(in)** M(F) plaintiff for damages; **Un|fall|hil|fe** F help at the scene of an accident; (= erste Hilfe) first aid; **Un|fall|kli|nik** F , **Un|fall|kran|ken|haus** NT accident hospital, ≈ emergency room (US); **Un|fall|op|fer** NT casualty; **Un|fall|ort** M pl -orte scene of an/the accident; **Un|fall|quo|te** F , **Un|fall|ra|te** F accident rate; **Un|fall|ren|te** F accident benefits pl; **Un|fall|ri|si|ko** NT accident risk; **Un|fall|scha|den** M damages pl; **Un|fall|schutz** M (Versicherung) accident insurance; (Maßnahmen) accident prevention; **Un|fall|skiz|ze** F diagram or sketch of an/the accident; **Un|fall|sta|ti|on** F accident or emergency ward (Brit), emergency room (US); **Un|fall|sta|tis|tik** F accident statistics pl; **Un|fall|stel|le** F scene of an/the accident; **Un|fall|tod** M accidental death; **bei ~ in the e-vent of death by misadventure; **Un|fall|to|te(r)** MF decl as adj = **Verkehrstote(r)**; **un|fall|träch|tig** ADJ accident-prone; **Un|fall|ur|sa|che** F cause of an/the accident; **Un|fall|ver|hü|tung** F accident prevention; **Un|fall|ver|letz|te(r)** MF decl as adj casualty; **Un|fall|ver|si|che|rung** F accident insurance; **Un|fall|wa|gen** M car involved in an/the accident; (inf: = Rettungswagen) ambulance; **der**

Wagen ist so billig, weil es ein ~ ist the car is so cheap because it has been involved in an accident; **Un|fall|zahl** F number of accidents; **steigende ~en** rising accident rates; **Un|fall|zeu|ge** M , **Un|fall|zeu|gin** F witness to an/the accident; **Un|fall|zif|fer** F = **Unfallzahl**

un|fass|bar ▲, **un|fass|lich** ▲ ADJ incomprehensible; **es ist mir** or **für mich ~, wie ...** I (simply) cannot understand how ...

Un-: un|fehl|bar ADJ infallible; Instinkt unerring ADV without fail; **Un|fehl|bar|keit** [ʊn'feːlbaːɐkait, 'ʊn-] F -, no pl infallibility; **un|fein** ADJ unrefined no adv, indelicate; **das ist ~** that's bad manners; **das ist mehr als ~** that's most ungentlemanly/unladylike ADV sich ausdrücken in an unrefined way; sich benehmen in an ill--mannered way; **un|fern** (geh) PREP +gen not far from, near ADV **~ von** not far from, near; **un|fer|tig** ADJ (= unvollendet) unfinished; (= nicht vollständig) incomplete; (= unreif) Mensch immature; **Un|flat** ['ʊnflaːt] M -(e)s, no pl (lit old) feculence (form); (fig geh) vituperation; **jdn mit ~ bewerfen** (fig) to inveigh against sb, to vituperate sb; **un|flä|tig** ['ʊnflɛːtɪç] ADJ offensive ADV **sich ~ ausdrücken** to use obscene language

Un|flä|tig|keit F -, -en offensiveness; (von Ausdrucksweise) obscenity

un-: un|flek|tiert ['ʊnflɛktiːɐt] ADJ (Gram) uninflected; **un|fle|xi|bel** ['ʊnflɛksiːbl] ADJ (lit, fig) inflexible; **un|flott** ADJ (inf) not nice; **das ist gar nicht so ~** that's not bad; **das ist gar nicht so ~** he's/she's a bit of all right (inf); **un|folg|sam** ADJ disobedient; **un|for|ma|tiert** ['ʊnfɔrmatiːɐt] ADJ (Comput) unformatted

un|för|mig ADJ (= formlos) shapeless; Möbel, Auto inelegant; (= groß) cumbersome; Füße, Gesicht unshapely

Un|för|mig|keit F -, no pl (= Formlosigkeit) shapelessness; (von Möbeln, Auto) inelegance; (= Größe) awkward size; (von Füßen, Gesicht) unshapeliness

un-: un|förm|lich ADJ informal; **un|fran|kiert** ['ʊnfraŋkiːɐt] ADJ unstamped ADV abschicken, einwerfen unstamped; **un|frau|lich** ADJ unfeminine ADV in an unfeminine way

un|frei ADJ **a** (politisch, Hist: = leibeigen) not free; **~ sein** (Hist) to be a bondman or in bondage or a serf **b** (= befangen, eingeengt) constrained, uneasy **c** Brief etc unfranked ADV **a** (= gehemmt) sich benehmen in an inhibited way **b** (= nicht frankiert) unfranked

Un|freie(r) MF decl as adj (Hist) serf

Un|frei|heit F lack of freedom; (Hist) bondage, serfdom

un|frei|wil|lig ADJ **a** (= gezwungen) compulsory; **ich war ~er Zeuge** I was an unwilling witness **b** (= unbeabsichtigt) Witz, Fehler unintentional ADV involuntarily, against one's will; **ich musste ~ zuhören** I was forced to listen

un|freund|lich ADJ unfriendly (zu, gegen to); Wetter inclement; Landschaft, Zimmer, Farbe cheerless; **ein ~er Akt** (Pol) a hostile act ADV in an unfriendly way; **jdn ~ behandeln** to be unfriendly to sb; **jdn ~ begrüßen/ansehen** to give sb an unfriendly welcome/look; **~ reagieren** to react in an unfriendly way

Un|freund|lich|keit F **a** unfriendliness; (von Wetter) inclemency **b** (= unfreundliche Bemerkung) unpleasant remark

Un|frie|de(n) M strife; **in Unfrieden (mit jdm) leben** to live in conflict (with sb)

un-: un|fri|siert ['ʊnfriziːɐt] ADJ (lit) Haare uncombed; Mensch with one's hair in a mess; (fig inf) = nicht verfälscht) undoctored; Auto not souped-up (inf) ADV (lit, = ungekämmt) unkempt; **völlig ~ machte sie mir die Tür auf** she opened the door to me looking completely unkempt; **un|fromm** ADJ impious

un|frucht|bar ADJ infertile; Boden auch barren; Frau infertile, barren (old, liter); (fig) Debatte etc sterile; Schaffenszeit unproductive; **~ machen** to

sterilize; **die ~en Tage** (Med) the days of infertility

Un|frucht|bar|keit F infertility; (von Boden auch) barrenness; (fig: von Debatte etc) sterility

Un|fug ['ʊnfuːk] M -s, no pl nonsense; **~ treiben** or **anstellen** or **machen** to get up to mischief; **lass den ~!** stop that nonsense!; **diese Idee ist grober ~** this idea is utter nonsense; **grober ~** (Jur) public nuisance

un-: un|fun|diert ADJ unfounded; **un|ga|lant** (geh) ADJ discourteous, ungentlemanly no adv; **un|gar** ['ʊngaːɐ] ADJ underdone

Un|gar ['ʊngar] M -n, -n, **Un|ga|rin** ['ʊngarɪn] F -, -nen Hungarian

un|ga|risch ['ʊngarɪʃ] ADJ Hungarian

Un|ga|risch(e) ['ʊngarɪʃ] NT Hungarian → auch **Deutsch(e)**

Un|garn ['ʊngarn] NT -s Hungary

Un-: un|gast|lich ADJ inhospitable ADV inhospitably; **wir wurden sehr ~ empfangen** we were given a very inhospitable welcome; **Un|gast|lich|keit** F **der Ort hat die ~ einer Bahnhofs-halle** the place is about as hospitable as a railway station; **un|ge|ach|tet** ['ʊngəlaxtət, ʊngə'laxtət] PREP +gen in spite of, despite; **~ des-sen, dass es regnet** in spite of it raining, in spite of the fact that it is raining; **~ aller Ermah-nungen, aller Ermahnungen ~** despite all warnings; **er ist sehr stark, ~ dessen, dass er so klein ist** he's very strong, in spite of being so small

un-: un|ge|ahn|det ['ʊngəlaːndət, ʊngə'laːndət] ADJ (Jur) unpunished; **un|ge|ahnt** ['ʊngəlaːnt, ʊngə'laːnt] ADJ undreamt-of; **un|ge|ba|cken** ADJ unbaked; **un|ge|bär|dig** ['ʊngəbɛːɐdɪç] ADJ unruly; **un|ge|be|ten** ADJ uninvited ADV **er kam ~** he came uninvited or unasked or without an invitation; **un|ge|beugt** ADJ **a** unbent, unbowed **b** (Gram) uninflected; **un|ge|bil|det** ADJ uncultured; (= ohne Bildung) uneducated; **Ungebildete** uneducated or ignorant people; **un|ge|bleicht** ['ʊngəblaiçt] ADJ unbleached; **un|ge|bo|ren** ADJ unborn; **un|ge|brannt** ADJ Kaffee unroasted; Ton etc unfired; **un|ge|bräuch|lich** ADJ uncommon; **un|ge|braucht** ADJ, ADV unused; **un|ge|bro|chen** ADJ **a** (fig) Rekord, Wille unbroken; Widerstand unyielding; Popularität undiminished **b** (Phys) Licht unrefracted ADV weiterkämpfen, weitermachen untermachen unbroken, unbroken

Un|ge|bühr F , no pl (old, form) impropriety; **~ vor Gericht** contempt of court

un|ge|bühr|lich ADJ improper ADV **a** (= ungehörig) improperly, inappropriately **b** (= über Gebühr) excessively; **sich ~ aufregen** to get unduly excited

un|ge|bun|den ADJ **a** Buch unbound; Blumen loose **b** **in ~er Rede** in prose **c** (= unabhängig) Leben (fancy-)free; (= unverheiratet) unattached; (Pol) independent; (Comm) Kredit untied; **frei und ~** footloose and fancy-free; **par-teipolitisch ~** (politically) independent, not attached to any political party

Un|ge|bun|den|heit F independence

Un-: un|ge|deckt ADJ **a** (= schutzlos) Schachfi-gur etc unprotected, unguarded; (Sport) Tor undefended; Spieler unmarked, uncovered; Scheck, Kredit uncovered **b** Tisch unlaid (Brit), not set pred; **un|ge|dient** ADJ (dated Mil) with no prior service; **Un|ge|dien|te(r)** ['ʊngədiːntə] M decl as adj (dated, Mil) person/man with no prior service; **un|ge|druckt** ADJ unprinted; (= nicht veröffentlicht) unpublished

Un|ge|duld F impatience; **vor ~** with impatience; **voller ~** impatiently

un|ge|dul|dig ADJ impatient ADV impatiently

un|ge|eig|net ADJ unsuitable; (für Beruf, Stellung auch) unsuited (für to, for)

un|ge|fähr ['ʊngəfɛːɐ, ʊngə'fɛːɐ] ADJ attr approximate, rough; **nach ~en Schätzungen** at a rough guess or estimate

ADV roughly; (bei Zahlen-, Maßangaben auch) approximately; **(so) ~ dreißig** about or approximately thirty; **~ 12 Uhr** about or approximately 12 o'clock; **von ~** from nowhere; (= zufällig) by chance; **das kommt nicht von ~** it's no accident; **diese Bemerkung kommt doch nicht von ~** he didn't make this remark just by chance; **wo ~?** whereabouts?; **wie ~?** approximately how?; **so ~!** more or less!; **können Sie mir (so) ~ sagen, wie viel das kosten soll/wie Sie sich das vorgestellt haben?** can you give me a rough idea of or tell me roughly how much it will cost/how you imagined it?; **~ (so) wie** a bit like; **können Sie den Mann ~ beschreiben?** can you give me/us etc a rough description of the man?; **etw (so) ~ wissen** to know sth roughly, to have a rough idea of sth; **dann weiß ich ~ Bescheid** then I've got a rough idea; **so ~ habe ich mir das gedacht** I thought it would be something like this; **so ~, als wären wir kleine Kinder** a bit as if we were little children; **das hat sich ~ so abgespielt** it happened something like this

Un-: un|ge|fähr|det **ADJ** **a** safe **b** (Sport) Sieg assured **ADV** spielen, sich aufhalten safely; **~ siegen** to win comfortably; **un|ge|fähr|lich** **ADJ** safe; Tier, Krankheit, Arzneimittel etc harmless; **nicht ganz ~** not altogether safe/harmless; Expedition not altogether without its dangers; **Un|ge|fähr|lich|keit** **F** (von Tier, Krankheit, Arzneimittel etc) harmlessness; **un|ge|fäl|lig** **ADJ** Mensch unobliging; **un|ge|färbt** **ADJ** Haare, Stoff undyed, natural; Lebensmittel without (added) colouring (Brit) or coloring (US); **un|ge|fe|dert** **ADJ** Fahrzeug springless, without springs; **un|ge|fil|tert** ['ʊngəfɪltɐt] **ADJ** unfiltered; **un|ge|formt** ['ʊngəfɔrmt] **ADJ** unformed; (= gestaltlos) amorphous; **un|ge|fragt** **ADV** unasked; **un|ge|füt|tert¹** ['ʊngəfʏtɐt] **ADJ** Tier unfed; **un|ge|füt|tert²** **ADJ** Kleidung, Briefumschlag unlined; **un|ge|gerbt** ['ʊngəgɛrpt] **ADJ** untanned; **un|ge|glie|dert** **ADJ** Körper, Stengel unjointed; (fig) disjointed; Satz, Aufsatz etc unstructured

un|ge|hal|ten **ADJ** indignant (über +acc about) **ADV** indignantly

Un|ge|hal|ten|heit ['ʊngəhaltnhait] **F** -, no pl indignation

un-: un|ge|här|tet ['ʊngəhɛrtət] **ADJ** Stahl untempered; **un|ge|hei|ßen** **ADV** (geh) voluntarily; **un|ge|heizt** ['ʊngəhaitst] **ADJ** unheated; **un|ge|hemmt** **ADJ** unrestrained **ADV** without inhibition; **sich ~ benehmen** to behave in an uninhibited way

un|ge|heu|er ['ʊngəhɔyɐ, ʊngə'hɔyɐ] **ADJ** **a** → ungeheuerlich **b** (= riesig) enormous, immense; (in Bezug auf Länge, Weite) vast; **sich ins Ungeheure steigern** to take on enormous dimensions **c** (= genial, kühn) tremendous **d** (= frevelhaft, vermessen) outrageous, dreadful **ADV** (= sehr) enormously, tremendously; (negativ) terribly, awfully; **~ groß** tremendously big; **~ viele Menschen** an enormous number of people

Un|ge|heu|er ['ʊngəhɔyɐ] **NT** -s, - monster; (fig auch) ogre

un|ge|heu|er|lich [ʊngə'hɔyɐlɪç, 'ʊn-] **ADJ** monstrous; Tat auch atrocious; Verleumdung outrageous; Verdacht, Dummheit dreadful; Leichtsinn outrageous, appalling

Un|ge|heu|er|lich|keit **F** -, -en **a** (von Tat) atrocity, atrociousness; (von Verleumdung) outrageousness; **so eine ~!** how outrageous! **b** **Ungeheuerlichkeiten** PL (= Verbrechen etc) atrocities; (= Behauptungen etc) outrageous claims

Un-: un|ge|hin|dert ['ʊngəhɪndət] **ADJ** unhindered **ADV** without hindrance; **un|ge|ho|belt** ['ʊngəho:blt, ʊngə'ho:blt] **ADJ** Brett etc unplaned; Mensch, Benehmen boorish; **un|ge|hö|rig** **ADJ** impertinent **ADV** impertinently; **Un|ge|hö|rig|keit** **F** -, -en impertinence; **un|ge|hor|sam** **ADJ** disobedient; **Un|ge|hor|sam** **M** disobedience; (Mil) insubordination; **ziviler**

civil disobedience; **un|ge|hört** ['ʊngəhø:ɐt] **ADV** unheard; **~ verhallen** (fig) to fall on deaf ears; **Un|geist** **M** , no pl (geh) demon; **un|geis|tig** **ADJ** unintellectual; **un|ge|kämmt** ['ʊngəkɛmt] **ADJ** Haar uncombed **ADV** **~ aussehen** to look unkempt; **un|ge|klärt** ['ʊngəklɛ:ɐt] **ADJ** **a** Abwasser untreated **b** Frage, Verbrechen unsolved; Ursache unknown; **unter ~en Umständen** in mysterious circumstances; **die Finanzierung des Projekts ist ~** the financing of the project has not been settled **ADV** Abwässer **~ einleiten** to discharge effluents in an untreated state; **un|ge|kocht** ['ʊngəkɔxt] **ADJ** raw; Flüssigkeit unboiled; Obst etc uncooked; **un|ge|krönt** ['ʊngəkrø:nt] **ADJ** uncrowned; **un|ge|kühlt** **ADJ, ADV** unchilled; **un|ge|kün|digt** ['ʊngəkʏndɪçt] **ADJ** in **~er Stellung** not under notice (to leave); **un|ge|küns|telt** **ADJ** natural, genuine; Sprechweise unaffected **ADV** naturally; sprechen unaffectedly; **un|ge|kürzt** ['ʊngəkʏrtst] **ADJ** not shortened; Buch unabridged; Film uncut; Ausgaben not cut back **ADV** veröffentlichen unabridged; (Film) uncut; **der Artikel wurde ~ abgedruckt** the article was printed in full; **un|ge|la|den** **ADJ** **a** Kamera, Gewehr etc unloaded **b** Gäste etc uninvited; **un|ge|läu|fig** **ADJ** unfamiliar

un|ge|le|gen **ADJ** inconvenient **ADV** **komme ich (Ihnen) ~?** is this an inconvenient time for you?; **etw kommt jdm ~** sth is inconvenient for sb; **das kam (mir) gar nicht so ~** that was really rather convenient

Un|ge|le|gen|hei|ten PL inconvenience sing; **jdm ~ bereiten** or **machen** to inconvenience sb

un-: un|ge|legt ['ʊngəle:kt] **ADJ** → Ei; **un|ge|lehr|ig** **ADJ** unteachable; **un|ge|lenk** **ADJ** awkward; Bewegungen auch clumsy **ADV** awkwardly, clumsily; **un|ge|len|kig** **ADJ** not supple, stiff; (fig inf: = nicht flexibel) inflexible, unbending; **un|ge|lernt** **ADJ** attr unskilled; **un|ge|le|sen** **ADJ** unread; **un|ge|liebt** **ADJ** unloved; **un|ge|lo|gen** **ADV** honestly; **un|ge|löst** **ADJ** unsolved; (Chem) undissolved; **un|ge|lüf|tet** ['ʊngəlʏftət] **ADJ** unaired; (fig) Geheimnis undisclosed

Un|ge|mach ['ʊngəma:x] **NT** -s, no pl (liter) hardship

un-: un|ge|macht **ADJ** Bett unmade; **un|ge|mah|len** **ADJ** unground

un|ge|mein **ADJ** immense, tremendous **ADV** schwer, vielseitig etc extraordinarily; **das freut mich ~** I'm really really pleased

un-: un|ge|mil|dert ['ʊngəmɪldət] **ADJ** undiminished **ADV** fortbestehen to continue undiminished; **un|ge|mus|tert** **ADJ** plain

un|ge|müt|lich **ADJ** uncomfortable; Wohnung, Zimmer not very cosy; Mensch awkward; Land, Wetter, Wochenende unpleasant; **mir wird es hier ~** I'm getting a bit uncomfortable or uneasy; **er kann ~ werden** he can get nasty; **ich kann auch ~ werden** I can be very unpleasant if I choose; **hier kann es gleich sehr ~ werden** things could get very nasty here in a moment; **seine Wohnung wirkt sehr ~** his apartment has a very uncomfortable feel about it

un|ge|nannt **ADJ** **a** Mensch anonymous; **~ bleiben** to remain anonymous **b** Zahl, Summe unspecified; **Beträge in ~er Höhe** unspecified amounts

un|ge|nau **ADJ** (= nicht fehlerfrei) inaccurate; (= nicht wahrheitsgetreu) inexact; (= vage) vague; (= ungefähr) rough, approximate **ADV** formulieren imprecisely; arbeiten, messen inaccurately; rechnen roughly

Un|ge|nau|ig|keit **F** inaccuracy; (= Vagheit) vagueness

un|ge|neigt **ADJ** disinclined

un|ge|niert ['ʊnʒeni:ɐt] **ADJ** (= frei, ungehemmt) unembarrassed, free and easy; (= bedenkenlos, taktlos) uninhibited **ADV** openly; (= bedenkenlos, taktlos) without any inhibition; **greifen Sie bitte**

~ zu please feel free to help yourself/yourselves

Un|ge|niert|heit **F** -, no pl lack of embarrassment; (= Taktlosigkeit) lack of inhibition

un|ge|nieß|bar **ADJ** (= nicht zu essen) inedible; (= nicht zu trinken) undrinkable; (= unschmackhaft) unpalatable; (inf) Mensch unbearable

un|ge|nü|gend **ADJ** inadequate, insufficient; (Sch) unsatisfactory; **ein Ungenügend** an "unsatisfactory", the lowest mark **ADV** inadequately, insufficiently

Un-: un|ge|nutzt ['ʊngənʊtst], **un|ge|nützt** ['ʊngənʏtst] **ADJ** unused; Energien unexploited; **eine Chance ~ lassen** to miss an opportunity **ADV** unused; **eine Chance ~ vorübergehen lassen** to miss an opportunity; **un|ge|öff|net** ['ʊngəlœfnət] **ADJ, ADV** unopened; **un|ge|ord|net** **ADJ** Bücher, Papiere etc untidy, disordered; (fig) disordered; Zuwanderung uncontrolled **ADV** untidily; **~ herumliegen** to lie (about) in disorder or disarray; **un|ge|pflas|tert** ['ʊngəpflastət] **ADJ** unpaved; **un|ge|pflegt** **ADJ** Mensch untidy, unkempt; Park, Rasen, Hände etc neglected **ADV** (= unordentlich) untidy; **der Garten sieht ~ aus** the garden looks neglected; **sich ~ ausdrücken** to talk in a common way; **un|ge|prüft** ['ʊngəpry:ft] **ADJ** untested; Vorwürfe unchecked **ADV** without testing, without checking; **etw ~ übernehmen** to accept sth without testing it; Bilanz to accept sth without checking it; (unkritisch) to accept sth at face value; **un|ge|putzt** ['ʊngəpʊtst] **ADJ** uncleaned; Zähne unbrushed; Schuhe unpolished; **un|ge|rächt** ['ʊngərɛçt] **ADJ** unavenged; **un|ge|ra|de** **ADJ** odd; **un|ge|ra|ten** **ADJ** Kind ill-bred; **un|ge|rech|net** ['ʊngərɛçnət] **PREP** +gen not including, excluding; **un|ge|recht** **ADJ** unjust, unfair **ADV** unjustly, unfairly; **un|ge|rech|ter|wei|se** ['ʊngərɛçtɐ'vaizə] **ADV** unjustly, unfairly; **un|ge|recht|fer|tigt** **ADJ** unjustified; Behauptung auch unwarranted **ADV** unjustly, unduly; **Un|ge|rech|tig|keit** **F** injustice; **so eine ~!** the injustice of it!, how unjust!; **un|ge|re|gelt** **ADJ** **a** Zeiten irregular; Leben disordered **b** (Tech) Katalysator open-loop; **un|ge|reimt** **ADJ** Verse unrhymed; (fig) inconsistent; **~e Verse** blank verse sing; **Un|ge|reimt|heit** **F** -, -en inconsistency

un|gern **ADV** reluctantly; (höchst) **~!** if I/we really have to!; **etw höchst ~ tun** to do sth very reluctantly, to do sth with the greatest reluctance; **das tue ich gar nicht ~** I don't mind doing that at all

un-: un|ge|ru|fen **ADJ** uncalled, without being called **ADV** without being called; **un|ge|rührt** ['ʊngəry:ɐt] **ADJ, ADV** unmoved; **un|ge|sagt** ['ʊngəza:kt] **ADJ** unsaid; **etw ~ machen** to pretend sth has never been said; **un|ge|sal|zen** **ADJ** unsalted; **un|ge|sat|telt** ['ʊngəzatlt] **ADJ** unsaddled; **un|ge|sät|tigt** **ADJ** Hunger etc unsatisfied; (Chem) Fettsäuren etc unsaturated; **un|ge|säu|ert** ['ʊngəzɔyɐt] **ADJ** Brot unleavened; **un|ge|schält** **ADJ** Obst, Gemüse unpeeled; Getreide, Reis unhusked; **ein ~es Ei** a boiled egg in its shell **ADV** **einen Apfel ~ essen** to eat an unpeeled apple; **un|ge|schehen** **ADJ** **etw ~ machen** to undo sth

Un|ge|schick **NT** -s, no pl, **Un|ge|schick|lich|keit** **F** clumsiness

un|ge|schickt **ADJ** clumsy, awkward; (= unbedacht) careless, undiplomatic **ADV** clumsily, awkwardly

Un|ge|schickt|heit **F** clumsiness; **das war eine ~ von mir** that was clumsy of me; **deine ~en** your clumsiness

un|ge|schlacht ['ʊngəʃlaxt] **ADJ** (pej) hulking (great); Sitten barbaric

Un-: un|ge|schla|gen **ADJ** (= unbesiegt) undefeated, unbeaten; **sie sind seit Jahren ~** they have remained undefeated for years; **un|ge|schlecht|lich** **ADJ** asexual **ADV** sich vermehren asexually; **un|ge|schlif|fen** **ADJ** Edelstein, Glas uncut; Messer etc blunt; (fig) Benehmen, Mensch uncouth; **Un|ge|schlif|fen|heit** F (fig) uncouthness; **un|ge|schmä|lert** ['ʊngəʃmɛːlɐt] ADJ undiminished; **un|ge|schmei|dig** ADJ Stoff, Leder rough; Haar coarse; **un|ge-schminkt** ['ʊngəʃmɪŋkt] ADJ without make-up; (fig) Wahrheit unvarnished ADV (= ohne Schminke) without make-up; (= unverblümt) bluntly; **etw ~ berichten** to give an unvarnished report of sth; **du solltest ihr ~ die Wahrheit sagen** you should tell her the whole truth; **un|ge|scho|ren** ADJ unshorn; (fig) spared; **jdn ~ lassen** (inf) to spare sb; (= ungestraft) to let sb off (scot-free) ADV **~ davonkommen** (inf) to escape unscathed; (Verbrecher) to get off (scot-free); **un|ge|schrie|ben** ADJ attr unwritten; **un|ge|schult** ['ʊngəʃuːlt] ADJ Aushilfe, Auge etc untrained; **un|ge|schützt** ADJ unprotected (auch Jur); Schachfigur auch unguarded; (Mil) Einheit exposed; Anlagen undefended; (Sport) Tor undefended ADV without protection; **das Haus ist völlig ~ Wind und Wetter ausgesetzt** the house is completely exposed to the elements; **~ (mit jdm) Geschlechtsverkehr haben** to have unprotected sex (with sb); **un|ge|se|hen** ADJ unseen; **un|ge|sel|lig** ADJ unsociable; Tier non-gregarious; **Un|ge|sel|lig|keit** F unsociableness; **un|ge|setz|lich** ADJ unlawful, illegal; **Un|ge|setz|lich|keit** F illegality; **un|ge|si-chert** ADJ unsecured, not secured; Kredit unsecured; Schusswaffe cocked, with the safety catch off; **un|ge|sit|tet** ADJ uncivilized ADV sich benehmen, sich aufführen in an uncivilized manner; **un|ge|stalt** ['ʊngəʃtalt] ADJ (geh) Mensch misshapen, deformed; **un|ge|stem-pelt** ['ʊngəʃtɛmplt] ADJ unstamped; Briefmarke unfranked; (für Sammler) mint; **un|ge|stillt** ['ʊngəʃtɪlt] ADJ Durst unquenched; Hunger unappeased; Blutung unstaunched; Schmerz unrelieved; Verlangen unfulfilled; Neugier unsatisfied; **un|ge|stört** ADJ undisturbed; (Rad, TV etc) without interference; **hier sind wir ~** we won't be disturbed here ADV arbeiten, spielen, sprechen without being interrupted, undisturbed; **un|ge|straft** ['ʊngəʃtraːft] ADV with impunity

un|ge|stüm ['ʊngəʃtyːm] ADJ impetuous ADV impetuously

Un|ge|stüm ['ʊngəʃtyːm] NT -(e)s, no pl impetuousness

un-: un|ge|sühnt ['ʊngəzyːnt] ADJ unexpiated, unatoned; **un|ge|sund** ADJ unhealthy; (= schädlich) harmful ADV unhealthily; **sie lebt sehr ~** she has a very unhealthy lifestyle; **un|ge|süßt** ['ʊngəzyːst] ADJ unsweetened; **un|ge|tan** ADJ undone; **etw ~ machen** to undo sth; **un|ge|tauft** ['ʊngətauft] ADJ unchristened, unbaptized; (inf: = unverwässert) undiluted ADV without being christened or baptized; **das Baby ist ~ gestorben** the baby died unchristened or unbaptized; **un|ge|teilt** ['ʊngətailt] ADJ undivided; Beifall universal; **un|ge|tilgt** ['ʊngətɪlkt] ADJ Schulden uncleared; **un|ge|tra|gen** ADJ Kleidung new, unworn; **un|ge|treu** ADJ (liter) disloyal, faithless (liter); Ehepartner unfaithful; **un|ge|trübt** ADJ clear; Glück, Freude perfect, unspoilt

Un|ge|tüm ['ʊngətyːm] NT -(e)s, -e monster

un-: un|ge|übt ADJ unpractised (Brit), unpracticed (US); Mensch out of practice; **un|ge|wandt** ADJ awkward; **un|ge|wa|schen** ADJ, ADV unwashed

un|ge|wiss ▲ ADJ uncertain; (= vage) vague; **ein Sprung/eine Reise ins Ungewisse** (fig) a leap/a journey into the unknown; **jdn (über etw acc) im Ungewissen lassen** to leave sb in the dark (about sth); **im Ungewissen bleiben/sein** to stay/be in the dark

Un|ge|wiss|heit ▲ F uncertainty

Un|ge|wit|ter NT (obs) = **Unwetter**

un|ge|wöhn|lich ADJ unusual ADV unusually; (= äußerst auch) exceptionally

Un|ge|wöhn|lich|keit F unusualness

un|ge|wohnt ADJ (= fremdartig) strange, unfamiliar; (= unüblich) unusual; **das ist mir ~** I am unaccustomed or not used to it

un|ge|wollt ADJ unintentional ADV unintentionally; **er musste ~ lachen** he couldn't help laughing

un-: un|ge|würzt ['ʊngəvʏrtst] ADJ unseasoned; **un|ge|zählt** ['ʊngətsɛːlt] ADJ (= unzählbar) countless; (= nicht gezählt) uncounted; **un|ge-zähmt** ['ʊngətsɛːmt] ADJ untamed; (fig) uncurbed; **un|ge|zeich|net** ADJ unsigned

Un|ge|zie|fer ['ʊngətsiːfɐ] NT -s, no pl pests pl, vermin; (old fig) vermin

un|ge|zielt ADJ unaimed ADV **~ schießen** to shoot without taking aim

un|ge|zo|gen ADJ ill-mannered ADV badly; (in Bezug auf Kinder) naughtily

Un|ge|zo|gen|heit F -, -en a no pl unmannerliness b (= ungezogene Handlung) bad manners no indef art; **so eine ~ von dir!** what manners!; **noch mehr solche ~en, und es setzt was!** just you mind your manners!

Un-: un|ge|zü|gelt ['ʊngətsyːglt] ADJ (= unbeherrscht) unbridled; (= ausschweifend) dissipated ADV without restraint; **un|ge|zwun|gen** ADJ casual, informal; Benehmen natural, unaffected ADV casually, informally; sich benehmen naturally, unaffectedly; **Un|ge|zwun|gen|heit** F casualness, informality; **un|gif|tig** ADJ non-poisonous

Un|glau|be M unbelief, lack of faith; (esp Philos) scepticism (Brit), skepticism (US)

un|glaub|haft ADJ incredible, unbelievable ADV implausibly

un|gläu|big ADJ unbelieving; (Rel) infidel; (= zweifelnd) doubting, disbelieving; **~er Thomas** (Bibl, fig) doubting Thomas ADV doubtingly, doubtfully, in disbelief

Un|gläu|bi|ge(r) MF decl as adj unbeliever

un|glaub|lich ADJ unbelievable, incredible; **das grenzt ans Unglaubliche** that's almost incredible ADV unbelievably, incredibly

un|glaub|wür|dig ADJ implausible; Dokument dubious; Mensch unreliable ADV sich benehmen, sich verhalten implausibly, unreliably; **sich ~ machen** to lose credibility; **diese Regierung wirkt völlig ~** this government lacks credibility

Un|glaub|wür|dig|keit F implausibility; (von Mensch) unreliability

un|gleich ADJ (= nicht gleichartig) Charaktere dissimilar, unalike pred; Größe, Farbe different; (= nicht gleichwertig, nicht vergleichbar) Mittel, Waffen unequal; Partner very different; (Math) not equal; **fünf plus fünf ~ neun** five plus five does not equal nine; **sie sind ein ~es Paar** they are very different; **das Zeichen für ~** the not-equals (Brit) or inequality (US) sign ADV a (unterschiedlich) unequally, differently b (vor Komparativ) much, incomparably

Un|gleich-: Un|gleich|be|hand|lung F, no pl discrimination; **Un|gleich|ge|wicht** NT (fig) imbalance

Un|gleich|heit F (= Ungleichartigkeit) (von Charakteren) dissimilarity; (von Größe, Farbe) difference; (von Mitteln, Waffen, Kampf) inequality

Un|gleich|heits|zei|chen NT (Math) not-equals sign (Brit), inequality sign (US)

Un|gleich-: un|gleich|mä|ßig ADJ uneven; Atem, Gesichtszüge, Puls irregular ADV unevenly, irregularly; **~ lang** of uneven length; **Un|gleich|mä|ßig|keit** F unevenness; (von Atem, Puls, Gesichtszügen) irregularity; **un|gleich|na-mig** ADJ (Math) of different denominations; (Phys) Pole opposite; **un|gleich|sei|tig** ADJ (Math) Vieleck irregular

Un|glei|chung F (Math) inequation (Brit), (expression of) inequality

Un|glück NT -(e)s, -e (= Unfall, Vorfall) accident; (= Missgeschick auch) mishap; (= Schicksalsschlag) disaster, tragedy; (= Unheil) misfortune; (= Pech: im Aberglauben, bei Glücksspiel) bad luck; (= Un-

glücklichsein) unhappiness; **~ bringend** (geh) ominous, unpropitious; **in sein ~ rennen** to head for disaster; **sich ins ~ stürzen** to rush headlong into disaster; **du stürzt mich noch ins ~!** you'll be my undoing!; **das ist auch kein ~** that is not a disaster; **so** or **welch ein ~!** what a disaster!; **er hat im Leben viel ~ gehabt** he has experienced a great deal of misfortune in life; **es ist ein ~, dass ...** it is bad luck that ...; **das ~ wollte es, dass ...** as (bad) luck would have it, ...; **das bringt ~** that brings bad luck, that's unlucky; **zum ~, zu allem ~** to make matters worse; **ein ~ kommt selten allein** (prov) it never rains but it pours (Brit prov), when it rains, it pours (US prov); **~ im Spiel, Glück in der Liebe** (prov) unlucky at cards, lucky in love → **Glück, Häufchen**

un|glück|brin|gend △ ADJ → **Unglück**

un|glück|lich ☺ 45.3 ADJ a (= traurig) Mensch, Gesicht etc unhappy; Liebe unrequited; Liebesgeschichte unhappy b (= bedauerlich) sad, unfortunate; **eine ~e Figur abgeben** to cut a sorry figure ADV a (traurig) unhappily; **~ verliebt sein** to be crossed in love b (ungünstig) sadly, unfortunately; **~ enden** or **ausgehen** to turn out badly, to end in disaster c stürzen, fallen awkwardly, badly

Un|glück|li|che(r) ['ʊnglʏklɪçə] MF decl as adj unhappy person, unhappy man/woman etc; **ich ~(r)!** poor me!; **der ~!** the poor man!

un|glück|li|cher|wei|se ['ʊnglʏklɪçɐ'vaizə] ADV unfortunately

Un|glücks-: Un|glücks|bo|te M , **Un|glücks|bo|tin** F bringer of bad tidings; **Un|glücks|bot|schaft** F bad tidings pl

Un|glück-: un|glück|se|lig ADJ (liter) a (= Unglück habend) unfortunate, hapless; (= armselig) miserable; (= bedauernswert) lamentable b (= Unglück bringend) disastrous; **Un|glück|se-li|ge(r)** MF decl as adj (liter) (poor) wretch; **ich ~(r)** woe is me! (liter); **un|glück|se|li|ger-wei|se** ['ʊnglʏkzeːlɪgɐ'vaizə] ADV (liter) unfortunately

Un|glücks-: Un|glücks|fah|rer(in) M(F) driver who caused an/the accident; **Un|glücks|-fall** M accident, mishap; **ein tragischer ~** a tragic accident; **Un|glücks|kind** NT , **Un|glücks|mensch** M unlucky person, unlucky man/woman etc; **ich war schon immer ein ~** I've always been unlucky; **Un|glücks|nach-richt** F (= schlechte Nachricht) piece of bad news; (= Nachricht vom Unglück) news of an/the accident or a/the disaster; **Un|glücks|ort** M scene of the accident; **Un|glücks|ra|be** M (inf) unlucky thing (inf); **Un|glücks|tag** M fateful day; **Un|glücks|vo|gel** M (inf) unlucky thing (inf); **Un|glücks|wurm** M (inf) poor soul; **Un|glücks|zahl** F unlucky number

Un|gna|de F disgrace, disfavour (Brit), disfavor (US); **bei jdm in ~ fallen** to fall out of favour (Brit) or favor (US) with sb

un|gnä|dig ADJ ungracious; (hum) unkind, harsh ADV ungraciously; (hum) unkindly, harshly; **etw ~ aufnehmen** to take sth with bad grace

un-: un|gram|ma|tisch ADJ ungrammatical ADV ungrammatically; **un|gra|zi|ös** ADJ ungraceful, inelegant ADV ungracefully, inelegantly

Un|gu|la|ten [ʊngu'laːtn] PL (Zool) ungulates pl

un|gül|tig ADJ (= nicht gültig) invalid; (= nicht mehr gültig) no longer valid; (= nichtig) void; Stimmzettel spoiled; (Sport) Tor disallowed; „ungültig" (in Pass) "cancelled"; **~ werden** (Pass) to expire; **~er Sprung** no-jump; **etw für ~ erklären** to declare sth null and void; **eine Ehe für ~ erklären** to annul a marriage

Un|gül|tig|keit F (von Pass, Visum) invalidity; (von Ehe) nullity; **die ~ einer Wahl** an election's being null and void; **die angebliche ~ einer**

Entscheidung the fact that a decision is said to be null and void

Un|gül|tig|ma|chung [-maxʊŋ] F -, -en (*Admin*) invalidation

Un|gunst F (*liter*) disfavour (*Brit*), disfavor (*US*); (*von Umständen, Lage*) adversity; (*von Witterung*) inclemency; **zu jds ~en** to sb's disadvantage

un|güns|tig ADJ unfavourable (*Brit*), unfavorable (*US*); *Auswirkungen, Entwicklung* undesirable; *Termin* inconvenient; *Augenblick, Wetter* bad; *Licht* unflattering; **im ~sten Fall** if (the) worst comes to (the) worst

un|güns|tigs|ten|falls ADV if (the) worst comes to (the) worst

un|gut ADJ bad; *Verhältnis auch* strained; *Erinnerungen auch* unpleasant; **ein ~es Gefühl haben** to have an uneasy *or* bad feeling; **nichts für ~!** no offence (*Brit*) *or* offense (*US*)!

un-: un|halt|bar ✪ 53.3 ADJ *Zustand* intolerable; *Vorwurf, Behauptung etc* untenable; *Torschuss* unstoppable; **un|hand|lich** ADJ unwieldy; **un|har|mo|nisch** ADJ unharmonious

Un|heil NT disaster; **~ stiften** *or* **anrichten** to do damage; **~ bringend** fateful, ominous; **~ verkündend** (*liter*) ominous, fateful

un|heil|bar ADJ incurable ADV incurably, terminally; **~ krank sein** to have a terminal illness, to be terminally ill

un|heil-: un|heil|brin|gend △ ADJ → **Unheil**; **un|heil|dro|hend**, **un|heil|schwan|ger** ADJ (*liter*) portentous

Un|heils|pro|phet(in) M(F) prophet of doom

Un|heil|stif|ter(in) M(F) mischief-maker

un|heil-: un|heil|ver|kün|dend △ ADJ → **Unheil**; **un|heil|voll** ['ʊnhailfɔl] ADJ disastrous

un|heim|lich ['ʊnhaimlɪç, ʊn'haimlɪç] ADJ **a** (= *Angst erregend*) frightening, eerie, sinister; **~e Begegnung** (= *übernatürlich etc*) close encounter; **das/er ist mir ~** it/he gives me the creeps (*inf*); **mir ist ~ zumute** *or* **zu Mute)** it is uncanny **b** (*inf*) tremendous (*inf*) ADV (*inf: = sehr*) incredibly (*inf*); **~ viel Geld/viele Menschen** a tremendous (*inf*) *or* an incredible (*inf*) amount of money/number of people

un-: un|heiz|bar ADJ unheatable; **un|his|to|risch** ADJ unhistoric; **un|höf|lich** ADJ impolite ADV impolitely; **Un|höf|lich|keit** F impoliteness; **deine ~en** your impoliteness; **es war eine ~ von dir** that was not polite of you

Un|hold ['ʊnhɔlt] M -(e)s, -e [-də] **a** (*old: = Böser*) fiend **b** (*Press sl*) monster, fiend

un-: un|hör|bar ADJ silent; *Frequenzen* inaudible; **un|hy|gi|e|nisch** ADJ unhygienic

u|ni [y'ni:] ADJ *pred* self-coloured (*Brit*), self-colored (*US*), plain; **in Uniblau** in plain blue

U|ni ['ʊni] F -, -s (*inf*) uni (*inf*), varsity (*dated Brit inf*), U (*US inf*), university → *auch* **Universität**

UNICEF ['u:nitsɛf] F - (*die*) ~ UNICEF

UNICEF-Bot|schaf|ter(in) ['u:nitsɛf-] M(F) UNICEF ambassador

un-: un|ide|a|lis|tisch ADJ unidealistic; **un|idi|o|ma|tisch** ADJ unidiomatic ADV unidiomatically

u|niert [u'ni:ɐt] ADJ (*Eccl*) *Kirche* Uniate

U|nier|te(r) [u'ni:ɐtə] MF *decl as adj* (*Eccl*) member of a Uniate church

u|ni|far|ben [y'ni:farbn] ADJ = **uni**

u|ni|form [uni'fɔrm] ADJ uniform

U|ni|form [uni'fɔrm, 'ʊnifɔrm, 'u:nifɔrm] F -, -en uniform → **ausziehen**

u|ni|for|mie|ren [unifɔr'mi:rən] *ptp* **uniformiert** VT **a** (= *mit Uniform ausstatten*) to uniform **b** (= *einheitlich machen*) to make uniform

u|ni|for|miert [unifɔr'mi:ɐt] ADJ uniformed

U|ni|for|mier|te(r) [unifɔr'mi:ɐtə] MF *decl as adj* person/man/woman in uniform

U|ni|for|mi|tät [unifɔrmi'tɛ:t] F -, *no pl* uniformity

U|ni|form|rock M tunic

U|ni|kat [uni'ka:t] NT -(e)s, -e unique specimen; **ein ~ sein** to be unique

U|ni|kli|nik F (*inf*)

U|ni|kli|ni|kum NT university hospital

U|ni|kum ['u:nikʊm] NT -s, -s *or* **Unika** [-ka] **a** (= *Einmaliges*) unique thing *etc*; **ein ~** a curiosity; (= *Seltenheit*) a rarity **b** (*inf*) real character

u|ni|la|te|ral [unilate'ra:l] ADJ unilateral ADV unilaterally

un-: un|in|tel|li|gent ADJ unintelligent; **un|in|te|res|sant** ADJ uninteresting; **sein Angebot ist für uns ~** his offer is of no interest to us; **das ist doch völlig ~** that's of absolutely no interest; **un|in|te|res|siert** ADJ (= *neutral*) disinterested; (= *nicht interessiert*) uninterested ADV uninterestedly; **die meisten Zuhörer starrten ~ zur Decke** most of the audience stared uninterested at the ceiling

U|ni|on [u'nio:n] F -, -en union; **die ~** (*Pol*) the CDU and CSU

U|ni|ons|par|tei|en PL (*Ger Pol*) CDU and CSU parties *pl*

u|ni|so|no [uni'zo:no] ADV (*Mus, fig*) in unison

U|ni|so|no [uni'zo:no] NT -s, -s *or* **Unisoni** [-ni] (*Mus*) unison

U|ni|ta|ri|er [uni'ta:riɐ] M -s, -, **U|ni|ta|ri|e|rin** [-iərɪn] F -, -nen Unitarian

U|ni|ta|ris|mus [unita'rɪsmʊs] M -, *no pl* Unitarianism

U|ni|tät [uni'tɛ:t] F -, -en **a** (= *Einheit*) unity **b** (= *Einzigkeit*) uniqueness **c** (*hum: = Universität*) uni (*inf*), varsity (*dated Brit inf*), U (*US inf*), university

Univ. *abbr von* **Universität**

u|ni|ver|sal [univɛr'za:l] ADJ universal ADV universally

U|ni|ver|sal- [univɛr'za:l] *in cpds* all-purpose, universal; (*Mech*) universal; *Bildung etc* general; **U|ni|ver|sal|ent|wick|ler** M (*Phot*) universal developer; **U|ni|ver|sal|er|be** M , **U|ni|ver|sal|er|bin** F universal successor, sole heir/heiress; **U|ni|ver|sal|ge|nie** NT universal genius; **U|ni|ver|sal|ge|schich|te** F world history

U|ni|ver|sa|li|en [univɛr'za:liən] PL (*Philos, Ling*) universals *pl*

U|ni|ver|sa|li|tät [univɛrzali'tɛ:t] F -, *no pl* universality

U|ni|ver|sal- [univɛr'za:l-]: **U|ni|ver|sal|mit|tel** NT universal remedy, cure-all; **U|ni|ver|sal|rei|ni|ger** M general-purpose cleaner

u|ni|ver|sell [univɛr'zɛl] ADJ universal ADV universally

u|ni|ver|si|tär ADJ *attr* university- *attr*

U|ni|ver|si|tät [univɛrzi'tɛ:t] F -, -en university; **die ~ Freiburg, die Freiburger ~** the University of Freiburg, Freiburg University; **an der ~ Heidelberg studieren** to study at the University of Heidelberg; **auf die ~ gehen, die ~ besuchen** to go to university; **die ~ verlassen** to leave university; (*das Gebäude*) to leave the university; **an eine ~ berufen werden** to be appointed to a professorship, to be given a chair

U|ni|ver|si|täts- *in cpds* university → *auch* **Hochschul-**; **U|ni|ver|si|täts|ab|schluss** ▲ M university degree; **U|ni|ver|si|täts|bib|li|o|thek** F university library; **U|ni|ver|si|täts|buch|hand|lung** F university bookshop (*Brit*) *or* bookstore (*US*); **U|ni|ver|si|täts|do|zent(in)** M(F) senior lecturer (*Brit*), associate professor (*US*); **U|ni|ver|si|täts|ge|län|de** NT university campus; **U|ni|ver|si|täts|in|sti|tut** NT university institute; **U|ni|ver|si|täts|kli|nik** F university clinic *or* hospital; **U|ni|ver|si|täts|lauf|bahn** F university career; **U|ni|ver|si|täts|pro|fes|sor(in)** M(F) university professor; **U|ni|ver|si|täts|stadt** F university town; **U|ni|ver|si|täts|stu|di|um** NT (*Ausbil-*

dung) university training; **dazu ist ein ~ erforderlich** you need a degree for that; **U|ni|ver|si|täts|zeit** F university years *pl*

U|ni|ver|sum [uni'vɛrzʊm] NT -s, *no pl* universe

un|ka|me|rad|schaft|lich ADJ uncomradely; *Schüler, Verhalten* unfriendly ADV in an uncomradely way

Un|ke ['ʊŋkə] F -, -n toad; (*inf: = Schwarzseher*) Jeremiah

un|ken ['ʊŋkn] VI (*inf*) to foretell gloom

un|kennt|lich ADJ unrecognizable; *Inschrift etc* indecipherable

Un|kennt|lich|keit F -, *no pl* **bis zur ~** beyond recognition

Un|kennt|nis F , *no pl* ignorance; **jdn in ~ über etw** (*acc*) **lassen** to leave sb in ignorance about sth; **in ~ über etw** (*acc*) **sein** to be ignorant about sth; **aus ~** out of ignorance; **~ schützt nicht vor Strafe** (*prov*) ignorance is no excuse

Un|ken|ruf M (*fig*) prophecy of doom; **allen ~en zum Trotz** in defiance of all prophecies of doom

un-: un|keusch ADJ unchaste; **Un|keusch|heit** F unchastity; **un|kind|lich** ADJ unchildlike ADV in an unchildlike manner

un|klar ADJ (= *unverständlich*) unclear; (= *ungeklärt*) unclarified; (= *undeutlich*) blurred, indistinct; *Wetter* hazy; **es ist mir völlig ~, wie das geschehen konnte** I (just) can't understand how that could happen; **ich bin mir darüber noch im Unklaren** I'm not quite clear about that yet; **über etw** (*acc*) **völlig im Unklaren sein** to be completely in the dark about sth; **jdn über etw** (*acc*) **im Unklaren lassen** to leave sb in the dark about sth ADV *sich ausdrücken, formulieren* unclearly; **nur ~ zu erkennen sein** not to be easily discernible, not to be easy to make out

Un|klar|heit F **a** lack of clarity; (*über Tatsachen*) uncertainty; **darüber herrscht noch ~** this is still uncertain *or* unclear **b** (= *unklarer Punkt*) unclear point

Un-: un|kleid|sam ADJ unflattering; **un|klug** ADJ unwise, imprudent, ill-advised ADV unwisely, imprudently; **un|kol|le|gi|al** ADJ uncooperative, inconsiderate ADV uncooperatively; **sich ~ verhalten** to behave uncooperatively (*towards one's colleagues*); **un|kom|pli|ziert** ADJ *Person, Bedienung, Methode etc* straightforward, uncomplicated; **~er** more straightforward, less complicated ADV in a straightforward way, in an uncomplicated way; **Un|kom|pli|ziert|heit** F straightforwardness; **un|kon|trol|lier|bar** ADJ uncontrollable; **~ werden** (*Missbrauch etc*) to get out of hand; **un|kon|trol|liert** ['ʊnkɔntrɔli:ɐt] ADJ, ADV unchecked; **un|kon|ven|ti|o|nell** ADJ unconventional ADV unconventionally; **un|kon|zent|riert** ADJ lacking in concentration; **er ist so ~** he can't concentrate ADV without concentrating; **~ arbeiten** to lack concentration in one's work; **Un|kon|zent|riert|heit** F lack of concentration; **un|kor|rekt** ADJ **a** (*nicht formgerecht*) improper **b** (*unrichtig*) incorrect ADV *sich verhalten* improperly; *darstellen, wiedergeben* incorrectly; **Un|kor|rekt|heit** F impropriety

Un|kos|ten PL costs *pl*; (= *Ausgaben*) expenses *pl*; **die ~ (für etw) tragen** to bear the cost(s) (of sth), to pay the expenses (for sth); **das ist mit großen ~ verbunden** that involves a great deal of expense; **(mit etw) ~ haben** to incur expense (from sth); **sich in ~ stürzen** (*inf*) to go to a lot of expense

Un|kos|ten-: Un|kos|ten|bei|trag M → **Unkosten** contribution toward(s) costs/expenses; **Un|kos|ten|be|tei|li|gung** F share in the cost(s); **Un|kos|ten|ver|gü|tung** F reimbursement of expenses

Un|kraut NT weed; **Unkräuter** weeds; **~ vergeht nicht** (*Prov*) it would take more than that to finish me/him *etc* off! (*hum*)

Ụn|kraut-: Ụn|kraut|be|kämp|fung F weed control; **Ụn|kraut|be|kämp|fungs|mit|tel** NT weed killer, herbicide (form); **Ụn|kraut|-ver|nich|tung** F , **Ụn|kraut|ver|til|gung** F weed killing; **Ụn|kraut|ver|til|gungs|mit|tel** NT weedkiller, herbicide (form)

Ụn-: ụn|krie|ge|risch ADJ unwarlike; **ụn|kri|-tisch** ADJ uncritical ADV uncritically; **ụn|kul|-ti|viert** ADJ uncultivated; Mensch auch uncultured ADV in an uncultivated or uncultured manner; **Ụn|kul|tur** F (geh) lack of culture; **ụn|künd|bar** ADJ Beamter, Mitarbeiter permanent; Vertrag binding, not terminable; Anleihe irredeemable; **in ~er Stellung** in a permanent position; **Ụn|künd|bar|keit** F (von Mitarbeiter) permanent status

ụn|kun|dig ADJ ignorant (+gen of); **einer Spra-che ~ sein** to be unacquainted with a language, to have no knowledge of a language; **des Le-sens/Schreibens ~ sein** to be illiterate, not to be able to read/write

ụn-: ụn|künst|le|risch ADJ unartistic; **ụn|-längst** ADV (geh) recently; **ụn|lau|ter** ADJ dishonest; Wettbewerb unfair; **ụn|leid|lich** ADJ disagreeable, unpleasant; **ụn|lenk|bar** ADJ uncontrollable; Fahrzeug unsteerable; **ụn|les|bar** ADJ Buch, Diskette, Speicher unreadable; Handschrift auch illegible; **ụn|le|ser|lich** ADJ Handschrift etc illegible, unreadable; **ụn|leug|bar** [ʊn'lɔykbaːɐ, 'ʊnlɔykbaːɐ] ADJ undeniable, indisputable; **ụn|lieb** ADJ es ist mir nicht ~, dass ... I am quite glad that ...; **ụn|lie|bens|wür|dig** ADJ not very pleasant ADV in an unpleasant manner

ụn|lieb|sam ['ʊnliːpzaːm] ADJ unpleasant; Konkurrent irksome; **das ist mir noch in ~er Erinne-rung** that's still an unpleasant memory ADV auffallen unpleasantly, badly; **er ist dem Lehrer ~ aufgefallen** his behaviour (Brit) or behavior (US) made a bad impression on the teacher

Ụn-: ụn|li|niert ['ʊnliniːet] ADJ Papier unruled, unlined; **Ụn|lo|gik** F illogicality, lack of logic; **ụn|lo|gisch** ADJ illogical ADV illogically; **ụn|-lös|bar** ADJ a (fig) (= untrennbar) indissoluble; (= nicht lösbar) Problem etc insoluble; Widerspruch irreconcilable b (lit) (Chem) insoluble; Knoten etc inextricable; **ụn|lös|lich** ADJ (Chem) insoluble

Ụn|lust F , no pl a (= Widerwille) reluctance; **etw mit ~ tun** to do sth reluctantly or with reluctance b (= Lustlosigkeit, Langeweile) listlessness; (St Ex) slackness

ụn|lus|tig ADJ (= gelangweilt) bored; (= widerwillig) reluctant; **ich bin heute ausgesprochen ~** I just can't work up any enthusiasm today

ụn-: ụn|mag|ne|tisch ADJ nonmagnetic; **ụn|-ma|nie|riert** ADJ (liter) unmannered (liter), unaffected; **ụn|ma|nier|lich** (dated) ADJ unmannerly ADV sich benehmen, sich aufführen in an unmannerly fashion; **ụn|männ|lich** ADJ unmanly; **ụn|mas|kiert** ADJ Ballbesucher etc undisguised; Bankräuber etc unmasked

Ụn|mas|se F (inf) load (inf); **eine ~ Leute/Bü-cher** or **an Büchern, ~n von Leuten/Büchern** a load of people/books (inf), loads or masses of people/books (inf)

ụn|maß|geb|lich ADJ (= nicht entscheidend) Urteil not authoritative; (= unwichtig) Äußerung, Mensch inconsequential, of no consequence; **nach meiner ~en Meinung** (hum) in my humble opinion (hum) ADV insignificantly; **nicht ~ to** a significant degree

ụn|mä|ßig ADJ excessive, immoderate ADV essen, trinken to excess; rauchen excessively; **er hat gestern ~ getrunken** he drank far too much or an excessive amount yesterday

Ụn|mä|ßig|keit F excessiveness, immoderateness; **~ im Essen/Trinken** excessive eating/drinking

ụn-: ụn|ma|te|ri|a|lis|tisch ADJ unmaterialistic; **ụn|me|lo|disch** ADJ unmelodious

Ụn|men|ge F vast number; (bei unzählbaren Mengenbegriffen) vast amount; **~n von Leuten, eine ~ Leute** a vast number or vast numbers of people; **~n essen** to eat an enormous amount, to eat masses (inf)

Ụn|mensch M brute, monster; **ich bin ja kein ~** I'm not an ogre

ụn|mensch|lich ADJ a Verhalten, Behandlung inhuman, appalling b (inf: = unerträglich) terrible ADV a behandeln, foltern in an inhuman way, appallingly b heiß, kalt, schwül unbearably

Ụn|mensch|lich|keit F inhumanity; **~en** inhumanity, inhuman behaviour (Brit) or behavior (US)

un-: ụn|merk|lich ADJ imperceptible ADV imperceptibly; **ụn|mess|bar** ▲ ADJ unmeasurable; **ụn|me|tho|disch** ADJ unmethodical ADV in an unmethodical way; **er arbeitet zu ~** he doesn't work methodically enough; **ụn|mi|li|tä|risch** ADJ unmilitary; **UN-Mis|si|on** [uː'lɛn-] F (Pol, Mil) UN mission; **ụn|miss|ver-ständ|lich** ▲ ADJ unequivocal, unambiguous ADV unequivocally, unambiguously; **jdm etw ~ zu verstehen geben** to tell sb sth in no uncertain terms

ụn|mit|tel|bar ADJ Nähe, Nachbarschaft etc immediate; (= direkt) direct; (Jur) Besitz, Besitzer direct, actual; **aus ~er Nähe schießen** to fire at close range ADV immediately; (= ohne Umweg) directly; **~ danach** or **darauf** immediately or straight afterwards; **~ vor** (+dat) (zeitlich) immediately before; (räumlich) right or directly in front of; **das berührt mich ~** it affects me directly

Ụn|mit|tel|bar|keit ['ʊnmitlbaːɐkait] F (= Direktheit) directness

ụn-: ụn|mö|bliert ['ʊnmøbliːɐt] ADJ Zimmer unfurnished ADV mieten, vermieten unfurnished; **~ wohnen** to live in unfurnished accommodation; **ụn|mo|dern** [-modɛrn] ADJ old-fashioned; **~ werden** to go out of fashion ADV eingerichtet, gekleidet in an old-fashioned way; **ụn|-mo|disch** ADJ unfashionable ADV gekleidet, sich kleiden unfashionably

ụn|mög|lich ✪ 39.2, 39.3, 43.3, 43.4 ADJ impossible; (pej inf: = unpassend auch) ridiculous; **das ist mir ~** that is impossible for me; **Unmög-liches, das Unmögliche** the impossible; **etw ~ machen** to make sth impossible; **jdm etw ~ ma-chen** to make it impossible for sb to do sth; **das Unmögliche möglich machen** to do the impossible; **jdn/sich ~ machen** to make sb/oneself look ridiculous, to make sb look (like) a fool/ to make a fool of oneself

ADV (= keinesfalls) not possibly; (pej inf: = unpassend) impossibly; sich anziehen ridiculously; **ich kann es ~ tun** I cannot possibly do it; **~ aussehen** (inf) to look ridiculous

Ụn|mög|lich|keit F impossibility; **das ist ein Ding der ~!** that's quite impossible!

Ụn-: Ụn|mo|ral F immorality; **ụn|mo|ra|lisch** ADJ immoral; **ụn|mo|ti|viert** ['ʊnmotiviːɐt] ADJ unmotivated ADV without motivation; **ụn|mün|dig** ADJ under-age; (fig: = geistig un-selbstständig) sheep-like; **Ụn|mün|di|ge(r)** ['ʊn-myndɪɡə] MF decl as adj minor; **Ụn|mün|dig|-keit** F minority; (fig: = geistige Unselbstständig-keit) mental immaturity; **ụn|mu|si|ka|lisch** ADJ unmusical; **Ụn|mu|si|ka|li|tät** F lack of musicality

Ụn|mut ['ʊnmuːt] M ill humour (Brit) or humor (US); (= Unzufriedenheit) displeasure (über +acc at)

ụn|mu|tig ['ʊnmuːtɪç] ADJ ill-humoured (Brit), ill-humored (US); (= unzufrieden) displeased (über +acc at) ADV with displeasure

Ụn|muts-: Ụn|muts|äu|ße|rung F expression of annoyance, angry remark; **Ụn|muts|fal|te** F frown

Ụn-: ụn|nach|ahm|lich ['ʊnnaːxlaːmlɪç, ʊnnaːx-'laːmlɪç] ADJ inimitable; **ụn|nach|gie|big** ADJ Material etc inflexible; (fig) Haltung, Mensch auch intransigent, unyielding ADV inflexibly, obstinately; **sich ~ verhalten** to be obstinate or adamant; **Ụn|nach|gie|big|keit** F (von Material etc) inflexibility; (fig: von Haltung, Mensch auch) intransigence; **ụn|nach|sich|tig** ADJ severe; (stärker) merciless, pitiless; Strenge unrelenting ADV hinrichten, verfolgen mercilessly, pitilessly; bestrafen severely; **Ụn|nach|sich|tig|keit** F severity; (stärker) mercilessness, pitilessness; **ụn|-nah|bar** ADJ Mensch unapproachable, inaccessible; **Ụn|nah|bar|keit** [ʊn'naːbaːɐkait, 'ʊn-] F -, no pl inaccessibility; **ụn|na|tür|lich** ADJ unnatural; Tod violent; (= abnorm) abnormal ADV unnaturally, abnormally; **er isst ~ viel** he eats an abnormal amount; **Ụn|na|tür|lich|keit** F unnaturalness; **ụn|nenn|bar** ADJ (liter) unspeakable, unutterable (liter); **ụn|nor|mal** ADJ abnormal; **ụn|nö|tig** ADJ unnecessary, needless ADV unnecessarily, needlessly; **sich ~ aufregen** to get unnecessarily or needlessly excited; **ụn|nö|ti|ger|wei|se** ['ʊnnøːtɪɡɐ'vaizə] ADV unnecessarily, needlessly

ụn|nütz ['ʊnnyts] ADJ useless; Geschwätz idle; (= umsonst) pointless, useless ADV uselessly, pointlessly; **sich Sorgen machen** unnecessarily; **~ Geld ausgeben** to spend money unnecessarily or needlessly

ụn|nüt|zer|wei|se ['ʊnnytsɐ'vaizə] ADV unnecessarily, needlessly

UNO ['uːno] F -, no pl **die ~** the UN sing

UNO-Bot|schaf|ter(in) ['uːno-] M(F) UN ambassador, ambassador to the UN

ụn|öko|no|misch ADJ uneconomic; Fahrweise, Konsumverhalten uneconomical

UNO-Mit|glied ['uːno-] NT member of the UN, UN member

Ụn-: ụn|or|dent|lich ADJ untidy; Lebenswandel disorderly ADV untidily; **Ụn|or|dent|lich|keit** F untidiness

Ụn|ord|nung F disorder no indef art; (in Zim-mer etc auch) untidiness no indef art; (= Durch-einander) muddle (esp Brit), mess; **in ~ geraten** to get into (a state of) disorder, to become untidy, to get into a muddle (esp Brit) or mess; **etw in ~ bringen** to get sth in a mess, to mess sth up; **~ in etw bringen** (in Leben, System) to bring disorder to sth; **~ machen** or **schaffen** to put or throw everything into disorder, to turn everything upside down

Ụn-: ụn|or|ga|nisch ADJ inorganic; **ụn|or|ga|-ni|siert** ADJ a disorganized b → nicht a ADV in a disorganized fashion or way; **ụn|or|-tho|dox** ADJ unorthodox ADV in an unorthodox way

UNO-Trup|pen ['uːno-] PL UN troops pl

UNO-Voll|ver|samm|lung ['uːno-] F UN assembly

Ụn-: Ụn|paar|hu|fer PL (Zool) odd-toed ungu-lates pl; **ụn|paa|rig** ADJ unpaired; (Med) azy-gous (spec); **ụn|pä|da|go|gisch** ADJ educationally unsound; Lehrer etc bad (as a teacher); **ụn|par|la|men|ta|risch** ADJ unparliamentary

ụn|par|tei|isch ADJ impartial, neutral; Mei-nung, Richter, Urteil impartial, unbiased ADV impartially

Ụn|par|tei|ische(r) ['ʊnpartaiɪʃə] MF decl as adj impartial or neutral person; **die Meinung eines ~n einholen** to seek an impartial opinion; **der ~** (Sport) the referee

Ụn-: ụn|par|tei|lich ADJ (esp Pol) neutral; **Ụn|-par|tei|lich|keit** F neutrality; **ụn|pas|send** ADJ (= unangebracht) unsuitable, inappropri-ate; Zeit auch inconvenient; Bemerkung inappro-priate; Augenblick inconvenient, inopportune; **ụn|pas|sier|bar** ADJ impassable

ụn|päss|lich ▲ ['ʊnpɛslɪç] ADJ (geh) indisposed (form), unwell (auch euph); **sich ~ fühlen** to be indisposed/feel unwell

Ụn|päss|lich|keit ▲ F -, -en (geh) indisposi-tion (form); **sie musste die Vorstellung wegen ~ leider absagen** unfortunately she had to cancel the performance because she was indisposed

Un-: un|pa|tri|o|tisch ADJ unpatriotic ADV *sich verhalten* unpatriotically; **Un|per|son** F (*Pol*) unperson; **un|per|sön|lich** ADJ impersonal (*auch Ling*); *Mensch* distant, aloof; **Un|per|sön|lich|keit** F impersonality; **un|pfänd|bar** ADJ (*Jur*) unseizable; **un|po|e|tisch** ADJ unpoetic(al); **un|po|li|tisch** ADJ unpolitical; **un|po|pu|lär** ADJ unpopular; **un|prak|ti|ka|bel** ADJ impracticable; **un|prak|tisch** ADJ *Mensch* unpractical; *Maschine, Lösung* impractical; **un|prä|ten|ti|ös** ADJ (*geh*) unpretentious; **un|prä|zis, un|prä|zi|se** ADJ imprecise ADV *sich ausdrücken, formulieren* imprecisely; **un|prob|le|ma|tisch** ADJ (*= ohne Probleme*) unproblematic; (*= einfach, leicht*) uncomplicated; **das wird nicht ganz ~ sein** it won't be without its problems ADV without any problems; **un|pro|duk|tiv** ADJ unproductive; *Kapital auch* idle; **un|pro|fes|si|o|nell** ADJ unprofessional; **un|pro|por|ti|o|niert** ADJ out of proportion, disproportionate; *Körper* out of proportion, ill-proportioned

un|pünkt|lich ADJ *Mensch* unpunctual; *Zug* not on time; **er ist immer ~** he's never punctual *or* on time ADV late; **~ kommen/abfahren** to come/leave late; **die Züge fahren immer ~** the trains never run to (*Brit*) *or* on time; **die Zahlung erfolgte ~** payment was made late *or* was not made on time

Un|pünkt|lich|keit F unpunctuality; **er kommt wegen der ~ der Züge oft zu spät** he's often late because the trains are late

un-: un|qua|li|fi|ziert ADJ *Arbeitskraft* unqualified; *Arbeiten, Jobs* unskilled; *Äußerung* incompetent ADV *sich äußern, sich auslassen* incompetently; **un|quit|tiert** [ˈʊnkvitiːɐt] ADJ unreceipted; **un|ra|siert** [ˈʊnraziːɐt] ADJ unshaven → **fern**

Un|rast F , *no pl* (*geh*) restlessness

Un|rat [ˈʊnraːt] M **-(e)s**, *no pl* (*geh*) refuse; (*fig*) filth; **~ wittern** to suspect something

un-: un|ra|ti|o|nell ADJ inefficient ADV inefficiently; **un|rat|sam** ADJ inadvisable, unadvisable; **un|re|a|lis|tisch** ADJ unrealistic ADV unrealistically

un|recht ADJ wrong; **auf ~e Gedanken kommen** (*dated*) to get naughty *or* wicked ideas; **das ist mir gar nicht so ~** I don't really mind ADV **~ handeln** to do wrong

Un|recht NT , *no pl* wrong, injustice; **zu ~** (*verdächtigt*) wrongly, unjustly; **diese Vorurteile bestehen ganz zu ~** these prejudices are quite unfounded; **nicht zu ~** not without good reason; **im ~ sein** to be wrong; **jdn/sich ins ~ setzen** to put sb/oneself in the wrong (*Brit*); **ihm ist im Leben viel ~ geschehen** he has suffered many injustices in life, he has often been wronged in life; **~ bekommen** to be shown to be wrong; **~ haben** to be wrong; **jdm ~ geben** to contradict sb; **~ tun** to do wrong; **ein ~ begehen** to commit a wrong; **jdm ein ~ tun** to do sb an injustice, to do sb a wrong; **Sie haben nicht ganz ~** you're not entirely wrong

Un|recht-: un|recht|mä|ßig ADJ unlawful, illegal; *Thronfolger* wrongful ADV *besitzen* unlawfully, illegally; **sich etw ~ aneignen** to misappropriate sth; **un|recht|mä|ßi|ger|wei|se** [ˈʊnrɛçtmɛːsɪɡɐˈvaɪzə] ADV unlawfully, illegally; **Un|recht|mä|ßig|keit** F **-, -en** a *no pl* illegality, unlawfulness b (*= Handlung*) illegality

Un|rechts-: Un|rechts|be|wusst|sein ▲ NT awareness of wrongdoing; **Un|rechts|re|gime** [-reʒiːm] NT (*Pol*) tyrannical regime; **Un|rechts|tat|be|stand** M illegality; **Un|rechts|ver|ein|ba|rung** F agreement to break the law

un-: un|red|lich ADJ dishonest; **Un|red|lich|keit** F dishonesty; **un|re|ell** ADJ unfair; (*= unredlich*) dishonest; *Preis, Geschäft* unreasonable; **un|re|flek|tiert** [ˈʊnreflɛktiːɐt] ADJ *Strahlen* unreflected; *Bemerkung* spontaneous ADV **etw ~ wiedergeben** to repeat sth without thinking

---

un|re|gel|mä|ßig ADJ irregular (*auch Ling*); *Zähne, Gesicht, Handschrift auch* uneven ADV irregularly; **~ essen/schlafen** not to eat/sleep regularly

Un|re|gel|mä|ßig|keit F irregularity (*auch Ling*); (*von Zähnen, Gesichtszügen, Handschrift auch*) unevenness; **ihm wurden (finanzielle) ~en vorgeworfen** he was accused of (financial) irregularities

Un-: un|reif ADJ *Obst* unripe; *Mensch, Plan, Gedanke, Verhalten, Werk* immature ADV *ernten, verarbeiten* before becoming ripe; **Un|rei|fe** F (*von Mensch, Werk*) immaturity

un|rein ADJ (*= schmutzig*) not clean, dirty; *Klang, Ton* impure; *Atem, Haut* bad; (*Rel*) *Speise, Tier, Mensch* unclean; *Gedanken, Taten* unchaste, impure; **etw ins Unreine sprechen** to say sth off the record; **etw ins Unreine schreiben** to write sth out in rough

Un|rein|heit F (*= Schmutzigkeit*) dirtiness; (*von Klang, Ton*) impurity; (*von Atem*) unpleasantness; (*Rel*) uncleanness; (*von Gedanken, Taten*) unchasteness, impurity; **die ~ ihrer Haut** her bad skin

Un-: un|rein|lich ADJ not clean; **Un|rein|lich|keit** F uncleanliness; **un|ren|ta|bel** ADJ unprofitable ADV unprofitably

UN-Re|so|lu|ti|on [uːˈɛn-] F (*Pol*) UN resolution

un|rett|bar [ˈʊnrɛtbaːɐ, ˈʊn-] ADV **~ verschuldet** hopelessly in debt; **~ verloren** irretrievably lost; (*wegen Krankheit*) beyond all hope; **die ~ Verdammten** those damned beyond redemption *or* salvation

Un-: un|rich|tig ADJ incorrect; *Vorwurf* false; (*Admin*) *Angaben etc* false ADV incorrectly; **un|rich|ti|ger|wei|se** [ˈʊnrɪçtɪɡɐˈvaɪzə] ADV incorrectly; falsely; **Un|rich|tig|keit** F incorrectness; (*Admin: von Angaben etc*) falseness; (*= Fehler*) error, mistake; **un|ro|man|tisch** ADJ unromantic

Un|ruh [ˈʊnruː] F **-, -en** (*von Uhr*) balance spring

Un|ru|he F **-, -n** a *no pl* restlessness; (*= Nervosität*) agitation; (*= Besorgnis*) agitation, disquiet; **in ~ sein** to be restless; (*= besorgt*) to be agitated *or* uneasy b *no pl* (*= Lärm*) noise, disturbance; (*= Geschäftigkeit*) (hustle and) bustle c *no pl* (*= Unfrieden*) unrest *no pl*, trouble; **~ stiften** to create unrest; (*in Familie, Schule*) to make trouble d (*politische*) **~n** (political) disturbances *or* unrest *no pl*

Un|ru|he-: Un|ru|he|herd M trouble spot; **Un|ru|he|po|ten|zi|al** ▲ NT potential (for) unrest; **Un|ru|he|stif|ter(in)** M(F) troublemaker

un|ru|hig ADJ restless; (*= nervös auch*) fidgety *no adv*; (*= laut, belebt*) noisy; *Schlaf* troubled *no adv*, fitful, uneasy; *Zeit etc* troubled, uneasy; *Bild, Muster* busy; *Meer* troubled; **ein ~er Geist** (*inf*) a restless creature ADV *schlafen* restlessly, fitfully; (*ungleichmäßig*) unevenly; **ihr Herz schlägt zu ~** her heart is beating too irregularly

un|rühm|lich ADJ inglorious; **ein ~es Ende nehmen** to have an inglorious end ADV ingloriously

uns [ʊns] PERS PRON *acc, dat von* **wir** us; (*dat auch*) to us; **bei ~** (*= zu Hause, im Betrieb etc*) at our place; (*= in unserer Beziehung*) between us; (*= in unserem Land*) in our country; **bei ~ zu Hause** at our house; **bei ~ im Garten** in our garden; **einer von ~** one of us; **ein Freund von ~** a friend of ours; **das gehört ~** that is ours, that belongs to us; **viele Grüße von ~ beiden/allen** best wishes from both/all of us REFL PRON *acc, dat* ourselves; (*= einander*) each other, one another; **wir freuten ~** we were glad; **wir wollen ~ ein neues Auto kaufen** we want to buy (ourselves) a new car; **~ selbst** ourselves; **wann sehen wir ~ wieder?** when will we see each other again?; **unter ~ gesagt** between ourselves, between you and me; **mitten unter ~** in our midst; **hier sind wir unter ~** we are alone here; **das bleibt unter ~** it won't go any further

---

un|sach|ge|mäß ADJ improper ADV improperly; **ein Gerät ~ behandeln** to put an appliance to improper use

un|sach|lich ADJ a (*= nicht objektiv*) unobjective b (*= unangebracht*) uncalled-for; **~ werden** to get personal

Un|sach|lich|keit F lack of objectivity; **diese Bemerkung zeugt von ~** this remark is uncalled-for

un|sag|bar, un|säg|lich [ʊnˈzeːklɪç, ˈʊn-] (*geh*) ADJ unspeakable, unutterable (*liter*) ADV unspeakably, unutterably

un|sanft ADJ rough; *Druck* ungentle; (*= unhöflich*) rude ADV rudely; *durchrütteln* roughly; **~ aus dem Schlaf gerissen werden** to be rudely awakened

un|sau|ber ADJ a (*= ungewaschen, schmutzig*) dirty, not clean b (*= unordentlich*) *Handschrift, Arbeit* untidy; (*= nicht exakt*) *Schuss, Schlag, Schnitt* inaccurate; *Ton, Klang* impure c (*= unmoralisch*) shady, underhand; *Spielweise* dirty (*inf*), unfair ADV (*= unordentlich*) untidily, carelessly

un|schäd|lich ADJ harmless; *Genussmittel, Medikament auch* safe, innocuous; **eine Bombe ~ machen** to make a bomb safe; (*= entschärfen*) to defuse a bomb; **jdn ~ machen** (*inf*) to take care of sb (*inf*)

Un|schäd|lich|keit F harmlessness; **die ~ einer Chemikalie beweisen** to prove that a chemical is safe

un|scharf ADJ a blurred, fuzzy; *Foto* blurred, out of focus; *Justierung* unsharp; (*Rad*) indistinct, unclear; *Erinnerung, Vorstellung* indistinct, hazy b *Munition* blank; *Bomben etc* unprimed ADV unclearly, indistinctly; **der Sender/das Radio ist ~ eingestellt** the station/the radio is not tuned clearly

Un|schär|fe F fuzziness; (*von Erinnerung, Vorstellung*) haziness; **begriffliche ~** lack of conceptual clarity

Un|schär|fe|re|la|ti|on F (*Phys*) uncertainty principle

un|schätz|bar ADJ *Wert, Verlust* incalculable, inestimable; *Hilfe, Vorteil* invaluable; **von ~em Wert** invaluable; *Schmuck etc* priceless

un|schein|bar ADJ inconspicuous; (*= unattraktiv*) *Aussehen, Mensch* unprepossessing

un|schick|lich ADJ unseemly, improper; **es ist ~ für eine junge Dame, das zu tun** it doesn't become a young lady *or* it is unseemly *or* improper for a young lady to do that ADV in an unseemly manner, improperly

Un|schick|lich|keit F **-, -en** a *no pl* unseemliness, impropriety b (*= unschickliche Handlung*) impropriety

un|schlag|bar ADJ unbeatable

Un|schlag|bar|keit [ʊnˈʃlaːkbaːɐkait, ˈʊn-] F **-,** *no pl* **er war überzeugt von der ~ seines Teams** he was convinced his team was unbeatable

un|schlüs|sig ADJ (*= unentschlossen*) undecided; (*= zögernd*) irresolute, hesitant; **sich (*dat*) ~ (über etw *acc*) sein** to be undecided (about sth); to be hesitant (about sth) ADV (*= unentschlossen*) undecided; (*= zögernd*) hesitantly; **er blieb ~ stehen** he stopped, uncertain what to do

Un|schlüs|sig|keit F (*= Unentschlossenheit*) indecision; (*= Zögern*) irresoluteness, hesitancy

un|schön ADJ (*= hässlich*) unsightly; (*stärker*) ugly; *Gesicht* plain; *Bilder* unattractive; (*= unangenehm*) unpleasant; *Streit, Auseinandersetzung, Szenen* ugly

Un|schuld F , *no pl* a (*= Schuldlosigkeit*) innocence b (*= Jungfräulichkeit*) virginity c (*= Naivität, Unverdorbenheit*) innocence; (*fig: = Mädchen*) innocent; **die ~ vom Lande** (*inf*) a real innocent; **in aller ~** in all innocence

un|schul|dig ADJ a (*= nicht schuldig*) innocent; **an etw** (*dat*) **~ sein** not to be guilty of sth; **er war völlig ~ an dem Unfall** he was completely

---

without blame in the accident, he was in no way responsible for the accident; **sind Sie schuldig oder ~?** – – how do you plead, guilty or not guilty? – not guilty

b (= *jungfräulich*) innocent, virginal; **er/sie ist noch ~** he/she is still a virgin

c (= *harmlos, unverdorben*) innocent; **~ tun** to act the innocent

ADV **a** (*Jur*) when innocent; **jdn ~ verurteilen** to convict sb when he is innocent; **er sitzt ~ im Gefängnis** he is being held, an innocent man, in prison

b (= *arglos*) *fragen, sagen* innocently

Un|schul|di|ge(r) MF *decl as adj* innocent person/man/woman/child *etc*; **die ~n** the innocent

un|schul|di|ger|wei|se ['ʊnʃʊldɪgɐˈvaɪzə] ADV unjustly, despite one's innocence

Un|schulds-: Un|schulds|be|teu|e|rung F protest of innocence; **Un|schulds|be|weis** M proof of (sb's) innocence; **Un|schulds|en|gel** M (*inf*), **Un|schulds|lamm** NT (*inf*) little innocent; **Un|schulds|mie|ne** F innocent face *or* expression; **mit ~** with an air of innocence; **Un|schulds|ver|mu|tung** F presumption of innocence; **un|schulds|voll** ADJ innocent; **mit ~er Miene** with an air of innocence

un|schwer ADV easily, without difficulty; **das dürfte ja wohl ~ zu erraten sein** that shouldn't have been too hard to guess

Un|se|gen M (= *Unglück*) misfortune; (= *Fluch*) curse (*für* (up)on)

un|selbst|stän|dig ▲, **un|selb|stän|dig** ADJ *Denken, Handeln* lacking in independence; *Mensch auch* dependent, unable to stand on one's own two feet; **eine ~e Tätigkeit ausüben** to work as an employee; **Einkünfte aus ~er Arbeit** income from (salaried) employment; **manche Menschen bleiben ihr Leben lang ~** some people never manage to stand on their own two feet; **sei doch nicht immer so ~!** show a bit of independence once in a while! **ADV** (= *mit fremder Hilfe*) not independently; **diese Schularbeit ist ~ angefertigt worden** this exercise was not done independently

Un|selbst|stän|di|ge(r) ▲ MF *decl as adj*, **Un|selb|stän|di|ge(r)** MF *decl as adj* (*Fin*) employed person

Un|selbst|stän|dig|keit ▲ F , **Un|selb|stän|dig|keit** F lack of independence, dependence

un|se|lig ADJ (= *unglücklich*) unfortunate; (= *verhängnisvoll*) ill-fated; **Zeiten ~en Angedenkens!** unhappy memories!; **ich Unseliger!** (*old liter*) oh unhappy wretch! (*old liter*), woe is me! (*old liter*)

un|sen|si|bel ADJ insensitive

un|ser ['ʊnzɐ] **POSS PRON** **a** (*adjektivisch*) our; **~e** *or* **unsre Bücher** our books **b** (*old: substantivisch*) ours **PERS PRON** *gen von* **wir** (*old, Bibl, geh*) of us; **~ beider gemeinsame Zukunft** our common future; **Herr, erbarme dich ~** Lord, have mercy upon us; **~ aller heimlicher Wunsch** the secret wish of all of us

un|se|rei|ner ['ʊnzɐˈlaɪnɐ], **un|ser|eins** ['ʊnzɐlains] INDEF PRON (*inf*) the likes of us (*inf*)

un|se|re(r, s) ['ʊnzərə] POSS PRON (*substantivisch*) ours; **der/die/das ~** *or* **Unsere** (*geh*) ours; **wir tun das ~** *or* **Unsere** (*geh*) we are doing our bit; **die ~n** *or* **Unseren** (*geh*) our family; **das ~** *or* **Unsere** (*geh*: = *Besitz*) what is ours

un|se|rer|seits ['ʊnzərɐ'zaɪts] ADV (= *auf unserer Seite*) for our part; (= *von unserer Seite*) from *or* on our part; **den Vorschlag haben wir ~ gemacht** we made the suggestion ourselves

un|se|res|glei|chen ['ʊnzərəsˈglaɪçn] INDEF PRON people like us *or* ourselves; **Menschen ~** people like us *or* ourselves

un|se|res|teils ['ʊnzərəs'tails] ADV = **unsererseits**

un|se|ri|ge(r, s) ['ʊnzərɪgə] POSS PRON (*old, geh*) **der/die/das ~** *or* **Unserige** ours; **die ~n** *or*

Unserigen our families; **das ~** *or* **Unserige** (= *Besitz*) what is ours; **wir haben das ~** *or* **Unserige getan** we have done our part

un|se|ri|ös ADJ *Mensch* slippery, not straight; *Auftreten, Aussehen, Kleidung, Bemerkung* frivolous; *Methoden* shady, underhand(ed); *Firma, Bank* untrustworthy, shady; *Zeitung* not serious; *Verlag* lowbrow; *Schriftsteller, Wissenschaftler* not to be taken seriously, not serious, frivolous; *Gutachten, Angaben* untrustworthy; *Angebot* not serious; **das Geschäft war keineswegs ~** the deal was strictly above board

un|ser|seits ['ʊnzɐ'zaɪts] ADV = **unsererseits**

un|sers|glei|chen ['ʊnzɐs'glaɪçn] INDEF PRON = **unseresgleichen**

un|sert|hal|ben ['ʊnzɐt'halbn], **un|sert|we|gen** ['ʊnzɐt've:gn] ADV (= *wegen uns*) because of us, on our account; (= *uns zuliebe auch*) for our sake; (= *um uns*) about us; (= *für uns*) on our behalf

un|sert|wil|len ['ʊnzɐt'vɪlən] ADV **um ~** for our sake

Un|ser|va|ter ['ʊnzɐfa:tɐ] NT -**s, -** (*Sw*) Lord's Prayer

un|si|cher ADJ **a** (= *gefährlich*) dangerous, unsafe; **die Gegend ~ machen** (*fig inf*) to hang out (*inf*); **sich ~ fühlen** to feel unsafe

b (= *nicht selbstbewusst, verunsichert*) insecure, unsure (of oneself); **jdn ~ machen** to make sb feel unsure of himself/herself

c (= *ungewiss, zweifelhaft*) unsure, uncertain; (= *unstabil*) uncertain, unstable, unsettled

d (= *ungeübt, ungefestigt*) unsure; *Hand* unsteady; *Kenntnisse* shaky; **mit ~er Hand** with an unsteady hand; **~ auf den Beinen sein** to be unsteady on one's feet

ADV **a** (= *schwankend*) unsteadily

b (= *nicht selbstsicher*) uncertainly; **sie blickte ~ im Kreise umher** she looked around timidly

Un|si|cher|heit F (= *Gefahr*) danger; (= *mangelndes Selbstbewusstsein*) insecurity; (= *Ungewissheit*) uncertainty; (= *Instabilität*) instability

Un|si|cher|heits|fak|tor M element of uncertainty

un|sicht|bar ADJ (*lit, fig*) invisible

Un|sicht|bar|keit F , *no pl* invisibility

Un|sinn M , *no pl* nonsense *no indef art*, rubbish *no indef art* (*Brit*); **~ machen** *or* **treiben** to do silly things; **~ reden** to talk nonsense; **lass den ~!** stop fooling about!; **mach keinen ~, Hände hoch!** (*inf*) no funny stuff - put your hands up! (*inf*); **wirklich? mach keinen ~!** (*inf*) really? stop messing about (*Brit*) *or* around! (*inf*) → **Sinn**

un|sin|nig ADJ (= *sinnlos*) nonsensical, foolish; (= *ungerechtfertigt*) unreasonable; (*stärker*) absurd (= *sinnlos*) nonsensical, foolishly; (= *ungerechtfertigterweise*) unreasonably; (*stärker*) absurdly; **~ viel** (*inf*) an incredible amount (*inf*); **~ hohe Preise** (*inf*) ridiculously high prices (*inf*)

Un|sin|nig|keit F -, *no pl* (= *Sinnlosigkeit*) foolishness; (= *Absurdität*) absurdity

un|sit|te F (= *schlechte Gewohnheit*) bad habit; (= *dummer Brauch*) silly custom

un|sitt|lich ADJ immoral; (*in sexueller Hinsicht*) indecent **ADV** indecently; **er hat sich ihr ~ genähert** he made indecent advances to her

un|so|lid, un|so|li|de ADJ *Mensch* free-living; (= *unredlich*) *Firma, Angebot, Geschäftsmann* unreliable; *Politik* without a solid basis; **~(e) leben** to have an unhealthy lifestyle; **ein ~es Leben führen** to be free-living; **an dem Angebot war nichts Unsolides** the offer was strictly above board **ADV** (*etwas ausschweifend*) dissolutely

un|so|li|da|risch ADJ lacking in solidarity **ADV** **sich ~ verhalten** to show a lack of solidarity

un|sor|tiert ['ʊnzɔrti:ɐt] ADJ unsorted; **un|so|zi|al** ADJ *Verhalten, Mensch* antisocial; *Maßnahmen, Politik* unsocial **ADV** antisocially; **un|spek|ta|ku|lär** ADJ unspectacular; **un|spe|zi|fisch** ADJ nonspecific; **un|sport|lich**

ADJ **a** (= *ungelenkig*) unsporty **b** (= *unfair*) unsporting; **Un|sport|lich|keit** F **a** (= *Unfairness*) unsporting behaviour (*Brit*) *or* behavior (*US*) *no art, no pl* **b** (= *Ungelenkigkeit*) **und das bei deiner ~!** and you being so unathletic!

uns|re ['ʊnzrə] PRON → **unser**

uns|rer|seits ['ʊnzrɐ'zaɪts] ADV = **unsererseits**

uns|res|glei|chen ['ʊnzrəs'glaɪçn] INDEF PRON = **unseresgleichen**

uns|res|teils ['ʊnzrəs'tails] ADV = **unseresteils**

uns|ret|we|gen ['ʊnzrət've:gn] ADV = **unsertwegen**

uns|ret|wil|len ['ʊnzrət'vɪlən] ADV = **unsertwillen**

uns|ri|ge(r, s) ['ʊnzrɪgə] POSS PRON = **unserige(r, s)**

un-: un|sta|bil ADJ unstable; **un|statt|haft** ADJ (*form*) inadmissible; (= *ungesetzlich*) illegal; (*Sport*) not allowed

un|sterb|lich ADJ immortal; *Liebe* undying; **jdn ~ machen** to immortalize sb **ADV** (*inf*) utterly; **sich ~ blamieren** to make an utter fool *or* a complete idiot of oneself; **~ verliebt sein** to be head over heels *or* madly in love (*inf*)

Un|sterb|li|che(r) MF *decl as adj* immortal

Un|sterb|lich|keit F immortality; **die ~ seiner Liebe** his undying love

Un|sterb|lich|keits|glau|be M belief in immortality

Un|stern M , *no pl* (*liter*) unlucky star; **die Liebe der beiden stand unter einem ~** their love was followed by an unlucky star

un|stet ADJ *Glück, Liebe* fickle; *Mensch* restless; (= *wankelmütig*) changeable; *Entwicklung* unsteady; *Leben* unsettled

Un|ste|te ['ʊnʃte:tə] F -, *no pl* = **Unstetigkeit**

un|ste|tig ADJ (*Math*) discontinuous, not continuous

Un|ste|tig|keit F (*von Glück, Liebe*) fickleness; (*von Mensch*) restlessness; (*von Entwicklung*) unsteadiness; (*Math*) discontinuity

Un-: un|still|bar [ʊn'ʃtɪlba:ɐ, 'ʊn-] ADJ **a** *Durst, Wissensdurst* unquenchable; *Verlangen, Sehnsucht, Hunger* insatiable **b** *Blutstrom* uncontrollable; **un|stim|mig** ADJ *Aussagen etc* at variance, differing *attr*; **in einem Punkt sind wir noch ~** we still disagree *or* differ on one point; **Un|stim|mig|keit** F (= *Ungenauigkeit, Fehler*) discrepancy, inconsistency; (= *Streit*) difference; **un|stoff|lich** ADJ immaterial; *Seele auch* incorporeal; **un|strei|tig** ADJ indisputable, incontestable **ADV** indisputably, incontestably; **un|strit|tig** ADJ indisputable **ADV** indisputably, unquestionably; **Un|sum|me** F vast sum; **un|sym|met|risch** ADJ asymmetric(al)

un|sym|pa|thisch ADJ unpleasant, disagreeable; **er ist ~** he's unpleasant *or* a disagreeable type; **das/er ist mir ~** I don't like that/him; **am ~sten an diesen Leuten ist mir ...** what I find most unpleasant about *or* what I like least about these people is ...

un|sys|te|ma|tisch ADJ unsystematic **ADV** unsystematically

un|ta|del|lig ['ʊnta:dəlɪç, ʊn'ta:dəlɪç], **un|ta|del|haft** (*rare*), **un|tad|lig** ['ʊnta:dlɪç, ʊn'ta:dlɪç] ADJ impeccable; *Verhalten auch* irreproachable; *Mensch* beyond reproach **ADV** *sich verhalten* impeccably, irreproachably; **~ gekleidet sein** to be dressed impeccably

un|ta|len|tiert ADJ untalented

Un|tat F atrocity, atrocious deed; **~en begehen** (*im Krieg etc*) to commit atrocities

un|tä|tig ADJ (= *müßig*) idle; (= *nicht handelnd*) passive; *Vulkan* inactive, dormant **ADV** idly, inactively; **sie sah ~ zu, wie er verblutete** she stood idly by as he bled to death

Un|tä|tig|keit F (= *Müßiggang*) idleness; (= *Passivität*) passivity

Un-: un|taug|lich ADJ (*zu, für* for) unsuitable; (*für Wehrdienst*) unfit; **Un|taug|lich|keit** F unsuitability; (*für Wehrdienst*) unfitness; **un|teil|-bar** ADJ indivisible; **Un|teil|bar|keit** F indivisibility

un|ten [ˈʊntn̩] ADV (= *im unteren Teil, am unteren Ende, in Rangfolge*) at the bottom; (= *tiefer, drunten*) (down) below; (= *an der Unterseite*) underneath; (*in Gebäude*) (down) below, downstairs; (*inf: geografisch*) down south; (= *flussab*) downstream; (= *tiefer gelegen*) down there/here; **von ~** from below; **die Frau von ~ war gekommen** the woman from downstairs or down below had come; **nach ~** down; **die Säule wird nach ~ hin breiter** the column broadens out toward(s) the base or bottom; **bis ~** to the bottom; **der Schneefall kam nicht bis ~ ins Tal** the snow did not reach as far down as the valley; **~ am Berg** at the bottom of the hill; **~ am Fluss** down by the river(side); **~ im Tal/Wasser/Garten** down in the valley/water/garden; **~ im Glas** at the bottom of the glass; **~ auf dem Bild** at the bottom of the picture; **~ auf der Straße** down on the street; **dort** or **da/hier ~** down there/here; **weiter ~** further down; **~ bleiben** to stay down; **~ erwähnt, ~ genannt** mentioned below; **der/die ~ Erwähnte** or **Genannte** the undermentioned (person) (*form*), the person mentioned below; **bitte lesen Sie auch das ~ Erwähnte** please see below; **rechts/links ~** down on the right/left; **siehe ~** see below; **er ist bei mir ~ durch** (*inf*) I'm through or I've finished with him (*inf*); **ich weiß schon nicht mehr, was** or **wo oben und ~ ist** (*inf*) I don't know whether I'm coming or going (*inf*); **~ stehend** following; (*lit*) standing below; **im ~ Stehenden** given below; **~ Stehendes** the following; **das ~ Stehende** what follows; **~ wohnen** to live downstairs

Un|ten-: un|ten|an [ˈʊntn̩ˈʔan] ADV (= *am unteren Ende*) at the far end; (*in Reihenfolge: lit, fig*) at the bottom; **(bei jdm) ~ stehen** (*fig*) not to be a priority (with sb), to be at the bottom of sb's list; **un|ten|drun|ter** [ˈʊntn̩ˈdrʊntɐ] ADV (*inf*) underneath; **un|ten|durch** [ˈʊntn̩ˈdʊrç] ADV (*inf*) through; **bei uns ist sie ~** we're through or done with her, we've finished with her; **un|ten|er|wähnt** △ [-ʔɛɐ̯vɛːnt], **un|ten|ge|nannt** △ ADJ *attr* → **unten**; **Un|ten|er|wähn|te(r)** MF *decl as adj*, **Un|ten|ge|nann|te(r)** MF *decl as adj* **der/die ~** or **Untengenannte** the undermentioned (person) (*form*), the person mentioned below; **bitte lesen Sie auch das ~** please see below also; **un|ten|he|rum** [ˈʊntn̩hɛˈrʊm] ADV (*inf*) down there (*inf*); **un|ten|ste|hend** △ ADJ **~ unten**; **Un|ten|ste|hen|de(s)** NT *decl as adj* **im ~n** given below; **~s** the following; **das ~** what follows

un|ter [ˈʊntɐ] PREP **a** +dat (= *unterhalb von*) under; (= *drunter*) underneath, below; (*Unterordnung ausdrückend*) under; (= *zwischen, innerhalb*) among(st); (= *weniger, geringer als*) under, below; **~ 18 Jahren/EUR 50** under 18 years (of age)/50 euros; **~ dem Durchschnitt** below average; **Temperaturen ~ 25 Grad** temperatures below 25 degrees; **Städte ~ 10.000 Einwohner(n)** towns with a population of under or below 10,000; **~ sich** (*dat*) **sein** to be by themselves; **jdn ~ sich haben** to have sb under one; **~ etw leiden** to suffer from sth; **~ Mittag** (*dial*) in the morning; **~ der Woche** (*dial*) within the (working) week; **~ anderem** among other things, inter alia (*form*) **b** +acc under; **bis ~ das Dach voll mit ...** full to bursting with ...; **~ Verbrecher geraten** to fall in with criminals

Un|ter-: Un|ter|ab|tei|lung F subdivision; **Un|ter|an|ge|bot** NT lack (*an* +dat of); **Un|ter|arm** M forearm; **Un|ter|arm|ta|sche** F clutch bag; **Un|ter|art** F (*esp Biol*) subspecies; **Un|ter|aus|schuss** ▲ M subcommittee; **Un|ter|bau** M *pl* **-bauten** (*von Gebäude*) foundations, (*von Brücke, Bahnstrecke, fig*) substructure; (*bei Straßen*) (road)bed; **Un|ter|be|griff** M member of a conceptual class, subsumable concept; **un|ter|be|legt** ADJ Hotel, Schule etc

not full; Fortbildungskurs undersubscribed; **das Hotel ist ziemlich ~** the hotel is not very full; **Un|ter|be|le|gung** F (*eines Hotels, Krankenhauses etc*) underoccupancy; (*eines Kurses*) undersubscription; **un|ter|be|lich|ten** *ptp* **unterbelichtet** VTI *insep* (*Phot*) to underexpose; **un|ter|be|lich|tet** [ˈʊntɐbəlɪçtət] ADJ (*Phot*) underexposed; **geistig ~ sein** (*hum*) to be a bit dim (*inf*); **un|ter|be|mannt** [-bəmant] ADJ undermanned; **Un|ter|be|schäf|ti|gung** F (*Econ*) underemployment; **un|ter|be|setzt** ADJ understaffed; **Un|ter|be|set|zung** F understaffing; **Un|ter|bett** NT feather bed; **un|ter|be|wer|ten** *ptp* **unterbewertet** VT *insep* to underrate, to undervalue; **Un|ter|be|wer|tung** F underrating *no pl*, undervaluation; **un|ter|be|wusst** ▲ ADJ subconscious; **das Unterbewusste** the subconscious **ADV** subconsciously; **Un|ter|be|wusst|sein** NT **im ~** subconsciously; **un|ter|be|zah|len** *ptp* **unterbezahlt** VT *insep* to underpay; **un|ter|be|zahlt** ADJ underpaid; **Un|ter|be|zah|lung** F underpayment; **un|ter|bie|ten** *ptp* **unterboten** VT *insep irreg* Konkurrenten, Preis to undercut; (*fig*) to surpass; **sich gegenseitig ~** to undercut each other; **ein kaum noch zu ~de Leistung** an unsurpassable achievement (*iro*); **Un|ter|bi|lanz** F deficit balance; **un|ter|bin|den**[1] [ˈʊntɐbɪndn̩] *ptp* **unterbunden** [ʊntɐˈbʊndn̩] VT *insep irreg* to stop, to prevent; (*Med*) Blutung to stop; **un|ter|bin|den**[2] [ˈʊntɐbɪndn̩] VT *sep irreg* to tie (on) underneath; **Un|ter|bin|dung** [-ˈbɪndʊŋ] F, *no pl* ending; (*Med*) ligature; **un|ter|blei|ben** [ʊntɐˈblaɪbn̩] *ptp* **unterblieben** [ʊntɐˈbliːbn̩] VI *insep irreg aux sein* **a** (= *aufhören*) to cease, to stop; **das hat zu ~** that will have to cease or stop **b** (= *nicht geschehen*) not to occur or happen; **das wäre besser unterblieben** (*Vorfall*) it would have been better if it had never happened; (*Bemerkung*) it would have been better left unsaid **c** (= *versäumt werden*) to be omitted; **Un|ter|bo|den** M (*Geog*) subsoil; (*Mot*) underside; (*Archit*) subfloor, underfloor; **Un|ter|bo|den|schutz** M (*Mot*) underseal (*Brit*), protective undercoating; **un|ter|bre|chen** [ʊntɐˈbrɛçn̩] *ptp* **unterbrochen** [ʊntɐˈbrɔxn̩] *insep irreg* **VT** to interrupt; Stille, Reise, Eintönigkeit, Langeweile to break; (*langfristig*) to break off; Telefonverbindung to disconnect; Spiel to suspend, to stop; Schwangerschaft to terminate; **entschuldigen Sie bitte, wenn ich Sie unterbreche** forgive me for interrupting; **wir sind unterbrochen worden** (*am Telefon*) we've been cut off **VR** to break off; **Un|ter|bre|cher** [ʊntɐˈbrɛçɐ] M **-s, -** (*Elec*) interrupter; (*Aut*) contact breaker; **Un|ter|bre|cher|kon|takt** M (*Elec, Aut*) (contact-breaker) point; **Un|ter|bre|chung** F interruption; (*von Stille, Reise, Langeweile*) break (+*gen* in); (*von Telefonverbindung*) disconnection; (*von Spiel*) stoppage; **bei ~ der Reise** when breaking the journey; **ohne ~** without a break; **nach einer kurzen ~** (*Rad, TV*) after a short break or intermission; **mit ~en** with a few breaks in between; **Un|ter|bre|chungs|be|fehl** M (*Comput*) break command; **un|ter|brei|ten** [ʊntɐˈbraɪtn̩] *ptp* **unterbreitet** VT *insep* Plan to present; **(jdm) einen Vorschlag/ein Angebot ~** to make a proposal/an offer (to sb); **Un|ter|brei|tung** F (*eines Vorschlags*) submission (+*gen* of)

un|ter|brin|gen VT *sep irreg* **a** (= *verstauen, Platz geben*) to put; (*in Heim, Krankenhaus etc*) to put; Arbeitslose etc to fix up (*bei* with); Zitat (*in Text etc*) to get in (*in etw* (*acc*) sth); **ich kann in meinem Auto noch einen ~** I can get one more in my car, I have room for one more in my car; **das Krankenhaus kann keine neuen Patienten mehr ~** the hospital cannot accommodate any new patients; **bei jdm ~** to leave sth with sb; **ich kenne ihn, aber ich kann ihn nirgends ~** (*inf*) I know him, but I just can't place him **b** (= *Unterkunft geben*) Menschen to accommodate; Ausstellung, Sammlung to house; **gut/schlecht untergebracht sein** to have good/bad

accommodation; (= *versorgt werden*) to be well/badly looked after; **die Hochzeitsgäste wurden im Hotel untergebracht** the wedding guests were put up in the hotel; **wie sind Sie untergebracht?** what's your accommodation like? (*Brit*), what are your accommodations like? (*US*)

Un|ter|brin|gung F **-, -en** accommodation (*Brit*), accommodations *pl* (*US*)

Un|ter|brin|gungs|mög|lich|kei|ten PL accommodation *sing* (*Brit*), accommodations *pl* (*US*), accommodation options *pl*

Un|ter|bruch M (*Sw*) = Unterbrechung

un|ter+but|tern VT *sep* (*inf*, = *unterdrücken*) to ride roughshod over; (= *opfern*) to sacrifice; **er wird von ihr untergebuttert** she dominates him; **lass dich nicht ~!** don't let them push you around

Un|ter|deck NT (*Naut*) lower deck; **im ~** below deck

Un|ter|deck|ung F (*Fin*) insufficient cover

un|ter|der|hand △ [ʊntɐdɐˈʔhant] ADV → Hand j

un|ter|des|(sen) [ʊntɐˈdɛs(n̩)] ADV (in the) meantime, meanwhile

Un|ter|druck M *pl* **-drücke** (*Phys*) below atmospheric pressure; (*Med*) low blood pressure, hypotension (*spec*)

un|ter|drü|cken [ʊntɐˈdrʏkn̩] *ptp* **unterdrückt** VT *insep* **a** (= *beherrschen*) Volk, Sklaven to oppress, to repress; Freiheit, Meinung to suppress; Revolution to suppress, to put down; **die Unterdrückten** the oppressed **b** (= *zurückhalten*) Neugier, Gähnen, Lachen, Gefühle to suppress; Tränen, Antwort, Bemerkung to hold back

Un|ter|drü|cker [ʊntɐˈdrʏkɐ] M **-s, -**, **Un|ter|drü|cke|rin** [-ərɪn] F **-, -nen** oppressor

Un|ter|druck|schleu|se F vacuum lock

Un|ter|drü|ckung F **-, -en** **a** (*von Volk, Sklaven*) oppression, repression; (*von Freiheit, Revolution*) suppression **b** (*von Neugier, Gähnen, Lachen, Gefühlen*) suppression; (*von Tränen, Antwort, Bemerkung*) holding back

un|ter|durch|schnitt|lich ADJ below average **ADV** below the average; **er verdient ~** he has a below average income, he earns below the average

un|ter|ei|nan|der [ʊntɐʔaɪˈnandɐ] ADV **a** (= *gegenseitig*) each other; (= *miteinander*) among ourselves/themselves etc; **Familien, die ~ heiraten** families that intermarry **b** (*räumlich*) one below or underneath the other

Un|ter-: un|ter|ent|wi|ckelt [-ʔɛntvɪklt] ADJ underdeveloped; (*inf: = geistig unterentwickelt*) thick (*inf*); **Un|ter|ent|wick|lung** F underdevelopment

un|te|re(r, s) [ˈʊntərə] ADJ *superl* **unterste(r, s)** [ˈʊntəstə] lower

Un|ter-: un|ter|er|nährt [-ʔɛɐ̯nɛːɐ̯t] ADJ undernourished, suffering from malnutrition; **Un|ter|er|näh|rung** F malnutrition

un|ter|fan|gen [ʊntɐˈfaŋən] *ptp* **unterfangen** VR *insep irreg* (*geh*) to dare, to venture

Un|ter|fan|gen [ʊntɐˈfaŋən] NT **-s, -** (*geh*) venture, undertaking; **ein schwieriges ~** a difficult undertaking

un|ter+fas|sen VT *sep* **jdn ~** to take sb's arm; **sie gingen untergefasst** they walked along arm in arm or with arms linked

un|ter|for|dern *ptp* **unterfordert** VT **jdn ~** to make too few demands on sb, to not stretch sb enough; **sich unterfordert fühlen** to feel one is not being stretched or challenged; **eine Klasse ~** (*Sch*) to ask too little of a class

Un|ter|fran|ken NT (*Geog*) Lower Franconia

Un|ter|füh|rung F **a** underpass; (*für Fußgänger*) subway, underpass **b** (*Typ etc*) ditto (mark)

Un|ter|füh|rungs|zei|chen NT (*Typ*) ditto (mark)

Un|ter-: **Un|ter|funk|ti|on** F insufficient function *no indef art*, hypofunction (*spec*); **(eine)** ~ **der Schilddrüse** thyroid insufficiency, hypothyroidism (*spec*); **Un|ter|fut|ter** NT interfacing; **un|ter|füt|tern** [ʊntɐˈfʏtən] *ptp* **unterfüttert** VT *insep* to interface

Un|ter|gang M *pl* **-gänge** **a** (*von Schiff*) sinking **b** (*von Gestirn*) setting **c** (= *das Zugrundegehen*) (*allmählich*) decline; (*völlig*) destruction; (*der Welt*) end; (*von Individuum*) downfall, ruin; **die Propheten des ~s** the prophets of doom; **dem ~ geweiht sein** to be doomed; **du bist noch mal mein ~!** you'll be the death of me! (*inf*)

Un|ter|gangs|stim|mung F feeling of doom

Un|ter-: **un|ter|gä|rig** [-ɡɛːrɪç] ADJ *Bier* bottom-fermented; *Hefe* bottom-fermenting; **Un|ter|gat|tung** F subgenus

un|ter|ge|ben [ʊntɐˈɡeːbn] ADJ subordinate

Un|ter|ge|be|ne(r) [ʊntɐˈɡeːbənə] MF *decl as adj* subordinate; (*pej* = *Subalterner auch*) underling

un|ter|ge|gan|gen ADJ *Schiff* sunken; *Gestirn* set; *Volk* etc extinct; *Zivilisation, Kultur* extinct, lost; *Epoche* lost; **die ~e DDR** the defunct GDR

un|ter+ge|hen VI *sep irreg aux sein* **a** (= *versinken*) to sink; (*fig*: *im Lärm etc*) to be submerged or drowned **b** (*Gestirn*) to set; **sein Stern ist im Untergehen** his star is waning or on the wane **c** (= *zugrunde gehen*) (*Kultur*) (*allmählich*) to decline; (*völlig*) to be destroyed; (*Welt*) to come to an end; (*Individuum*) to perish; **dort muss man sich durchsetzen, sonst geht man unter** you've got to assert yourself there or you'll go under

Un|ter-: **un|ter|ge|ord|net** ADJ *Dienststelle, Stellung* subordinate; *Rolle auch* secondary; *Bedeutung* secondary → *auch* **unterordnen**; **Un|ter|ge|schoss** ▲ NT basement; **Un|ter|ge|stell** NT **a** base; (*Mot*) subframe **b** (*inf* = *Beine*) pins *pl* (*inf*); **Un|ter|ge|wicht** NT underweight; **~ haben** to be underweight; **un|ter|ge|wich|tig** ADJ underweight; **un|ter|glie|dern** [ʊntɐˈɡliːdɐn] *ptp* **untergliedert** VT *insep* to subdivide; **Un|ter|glie|de|rung** F subdivision; **un|ter|gra|ben¹** [ʊntɐˈɡraːbn] *ptp* **untergraben** VT *insep irreg* (= *zerstören*) to undermine; **un|ter+gra|ben²** [ˈʊntɐɡraːbn] VT *sep irreg* (*in Erde*) to dig in

Un|ter|gren|ze F lower limit; **~ des Verdienstes** (*Fin*) lower earnings limit or level

Un|ter|grund M , *no pl* **a** (*Geol*) subsoil **b** (= *Farbschicht*) undercoat; (= *Hintergrund*) background **c** (*Liter, Pol etc*) underground; **er lebt seit Jahren im ~** he's been living underground for years; **in den ~ gehen** to go underground

Un|ter|grund- *in cpds* (*Liter, Pol*) underground; **Un|ter|grund|bahn** F underground (*Brit*), subway (*US*); **Un|ter|grund|be|we|gung** F underground movement; **Un|ter|grund|kämp|fer(in)** M(F) guerrilla, guerilla, resistance fighter

Un|ter-: **Un|ter|grup|pe** F subgroup; **un|ter+ha|ben** VT *sep irreg* (*inf*) to have (on) underneath; **un|ter+ha|ken** *sep* VT jdn ~ to link arms with sb; sich bei jdm ~ to link arms with sb; **untergehakt gehen** to walk arm in arm

un|ter|halb [ˈʊntɐhalp] PREP +*gen* below; (*bei Fluss auch*) downstream from ADV below; (*bei Fluss auch*) downstream; **~ von** below; (*bei Fluss auch*) downstream from

Un|ter|halt M , *no pl* **a** (= *Lebensunterhalt*) maintenance (*Brit esp Jur*), alimony; **für jds ~ aufkommen** to pay for sb's keep; **für seine Kinder ~ zahlen** to pay maintenance (*Brit*) or child support for one's children; **für seine Ex-Ehefrau ~ zahlen** to pay maintenance (*Brit*) or alimony to one's ex-wife; **seinen ~ verdienen** to earn one's living **b** (= *Instandhaltung*) upkeep

un|ter|hal|ten¹ [ʊntɐˈhaltn] *ptp* **unterhalten** *insep irreg* VT **a** (= *versorgen, ernähren*) to support; *Angestellten* to maintain **b** (= *halten, betreiben*) *Geschäft, Gaststätte* to keep, to run; *Konto* to have; *Kfz* to run **c** (= *instand halten*) *Gebäude, Fahrzeug etc* to maintain **d** (= *pflegen, aufrechterhalten*) *Kontakte, Beziehungen* to maintain **e** *Gäste, Publikum* to entertain VR **a** (= *sprechen*) to talk (*mit* to, with); **man kann sich mit ihm gut/schlecht/glänzend ~** he's easy/not easy/really easy to talk to; **man kann sich mit ihm nicht ~** he's impossible to talk to, you can't talk to him; **sich mit jdm (über etw** *acc*) **~** to (have a) talk or chat with sb (about sth); **Herr Schmidt, ich hätte mich mal gerne mit Ihnen ein bisschen ~** Herr Schmidt, I would like to (have) a little talk or chat with you; **wir ~ uns noch!** (*drohend, begütigend*) we'll talk about that later **b** (= *sich vergnügen*) to enjoy oneself, to have a good time; **habt ihr euch gut ~?** did you enjoy yourselves?, did you have a good time?; **sich mit etw ~** to amuse or entertain oneself with sth

un|ter+hal|ten² [ˈʊntɐhaltn] VT *sep irreg* to hold underneath; **ein Tuch ~** to hold a cloth underneath

Un|ter|hal|ter [ʊntɐˈhaltɐ] M **-s, -**, **Un|ter|hal|te|rin** [-ərɪn] F **-, -nen** **a** entertainer; (= *unterhaltsamer Mensch*) conversationalist **b** (= *Verdiener*) breadwinner

un|ter|halt|sam [ʊntɐˈhaltzaːm] ADJ entertaining

Un|ter|halts-: **Un|ter|halts|an|spruch** M maintenance claim (*Brit*), alimony claim; **un|ter|halts|be|rech|tigt** ADJ entitled to maintenance (*Brit*) or alimony; **Un|ter|halts|geld** NT maintenance (*Brit*), alimony; **Un|ter|halts|kla|ge** F action for maintenance (*Brit*), lawsuit for alimony (*esp US*); **(gegen jdn) ~ erheben** to file a suit for maintenance (*Brit*) or alimony (against sb); **Un|ter|halts|kos|ten** PL (*von Gebäude, Anlage*) maintenance (*Brit*) or alimony (costs *pl*); (*von Kfz*) running costs *pl*; **Un|ter|halts|leis|tung** F payment of maintenance (*Brit*) or alimony; **Un|ter|halts|pflicht** F obligation to pay maintenance (*Brit*) or alimony; **un|ter|halts|pflich|tig** [-pflɪçtɪç] ADJ under obligation to pay maintenance (*Brit*) or alimony; **Un|ter|halts|pflich|ti|ge(r)** [-pflɪçtɪɡə] MF *decl as adj* person legally responsible for paying maintenance (*Brit*) or alimony; **Un|ter|halts|zah|lung** F maintenance (*Brit*) or alimony payment

Un|ter|hal|tung [ʊntɐˈhaltʊŋ] F **a** (= *Gespräch*) talk, chat, conversation; **eine ~ (mit jdm) führen** to have a talk or conversation (with sb); **hier kann man keine ~ führen** we can't talk here **b** (= *Amüsement*) entertainment; **wir wünschen gute** or **angenehme ~** we hope you enjoy the programme (*Brit*) or program (*US*) **c** *no pl* (= *Instandhaltung*) upkeep; (*von Kfz, Maschinen*) maintenance

Un|ter|hal|tungs-: **Un|ter|hal|tungs|elekt|ro|nik** F (= *Industrie*) consumer electronics *sing*; (= *Geräte*) audio systems *pl*; **Un|ter|hal|tungs|film** M light entertainment film; **Un|ter|hal|tungs|in|dust|rie** F , *no pl* entertainment industry; **Un|ter|hal|tungs|kos|ten** PL = **Unterhaltskosten**; **Un|ter|hal|tungs|lek|tü|re** F light reading; **Un|ter|hal|tungs|li|te|ra|tur** F light fiction; **Un|ter|hal|tungs|mu|sik** F light music; **Un|ter|hal|tungs|pro|gramm** NT light entertainment programme (*Brit*) or program (*US*); **Un|ter|hal|tungs|ro|man** M light novel; **Un|ter|hal|tungs|sen|dung** F light entertainment programme (*Brit*) or program (*US*); **Un|ter|hal|tungs|wert** M , *no pl* entertainment value

Un|ter|händ|ler(in) M(F) negotiator

Un|ter|hand|lung F negotiation

Un|ter|haus NT Lower House, House of Commons (*Brit*), Commons *sing* (*Brit*); **Mitglied des ~es** member of parliament, MP

Un|ter|haus-: **Un|ter|haus|ab|ge|ord|ne|te(r)** MF *decl as adj*, **Un|ter|haus|mit|glied** NT member of parliament, MP; **Un|ter|haus|sit|zung** F session of the House; **Un|ter|haus|wahl** F Commons vote (*Brit*), Lower House vote

Un|ter|haut F (*Anat*) subcutis

Un|ter|hemd NT vest (*Brit*), undershirt (*US*)

Un|ter|hit|ze F (*Cook*) bottom heat

un|ter|höh|len [ʊntɐˈhøːlən] *ptp* **unterhöhlt** VT *insep* **a** (= *aushöhlen*) to hollow out **b** (*fig*) to undermine

Un|ter|holz NT , *no pl* undergrowth

Un|ter|ho|se F (= *Herrenunterhose*) (pair of) underpants *pl*, (pair of) pants *pl* (*Brit*), briefs *pl*; (= *Damenunterhose*) (pair of) pants *pl* (*Brit*) or panties *pl* (*esp US*) or briefs *pl*; **lange ~n** long johns *pl*

un|ter|ir|disch ADJ *Parkhaus etc, Atomversuche* underground; *Fluss etc auch* subterranean ADV underground; **~ verlaufen** to run underground

un|ter|jo|chen [ʊntɐˈjɔxn] *ptp* **unterjocht** VT *insep* to subjugate

Un|ter|jo|chung F **-, -en** subjugation

un|ter+ju|beln VT *sep* (*inf*) **a** (= *andrehen*) jdm etw ~ to palm sth off on sb (*inf*) **b** (= *anlasten*) jdm etw ~ to pin sth on sb (*inf*)

un|ter|ka|pi|ta|li|siert [ˈʊntɐkapitalizi:ɐt] ADJ (*Fin*) undercapitalized

un|ter|kel|lern [ʊntɐˈkɛlɐn] *ptp* **unterkellert** VT *insep* to build with a cellar (*Brit*) or basement; **das Haus ist nicht unterkellert** the house doesn't have a cellar (*Brit*) or basement; **ein ganz/teilweise unterkellertes Haus** a house with a cellar (*Brit*) or basement underneath the whole of it/underneath part of it

Un|ter-: **Un|ter|kie|fer** M lower jaw; **Un|ter|klas|se** F **a** subclass **b** (*Sociol*) lower class; **Un|ter|kleid** NT full-length slip or petticoat; **Un|ter|klei|dung** F underwear, underclothes *pl*

un|ter+kom|men VI *sep irreg aux sein* **a** (= *Unterkunft finden*) to find accommodation; (*inf* = *Stelle finden*) to find a job (**als** as, **bei** with, at); **bei jdm ~** to stay at sb's (place) **b** (*inf*) **so etwas ist mir noch nie untergekommen!** I've never come across anything like it!

Un|ter|kom|men NT **-s, -** (= *Obdach*) accommodation *no pl* (*Brit*), accommodations *pl* (*US*); **bei jdm ein ~ finden** to be put up at sb's (place)

Un|ter-: **Un|ter|kör|per** M lower part of the body; **un|ter+krie|chen** VI *sep irreg aux sein* (*inf*) to shack up (**bei** jdm with sb) (*inf*); **un|ter+krie|gen** VT *sep* (*inf*) to bring down; (= *deprimieren*) to get down; **sich nicht ~ lassen** not to let things get one down; **lass dich von ihnen nicht ~** don't let them get you down; **un|ter|küh|len** [ʊntɐˈkyːlən] *ptp* **unterkühlt** VT *insep* *Flüssigkeit, Metall, Gas* to supercool, to undercool (*Brit*); *Körper* to expose to subnormal temperatures; **un|ter|kühlt** [ʊntɐˈkyːlt] ADJ *Flüssigkeit, Metall, Gas* supercooled, undercooled (*Brit*); *Körper* affected by hypothermia; (*fig*) *Atmosphäre* chilly; *Mensch* cool; *Musik, Spielweise* subdued, reserved; **Un|ter|küh|lung** F , *no pl* (*von Flüssigkeit, Metall, Gas*) supercooling, undercooling (*Brit*); (*im Freien*) exposure; (*Med*) hypothermia

Un|ter|kunft [ˈʊntɐkʊnft] F **-, Unterkünfte** [-kʏnftə] **a** accommodation *no pl* (*Brit*), accommodations *pl* (*US*), lodging; **eine ~ suchen** to look for accommodation (*Brit*) or accommodations (*US*) or lodging; **~ und Verpflegung** board and lodging **b** (*von Soldaten etc*) quarters *pl*; (*esp in Privathaus*) billet

Un|ter|kunfts-: **Un|ter|kunfts|mög|lich|keit** F accommodation *no pl* (*Brit*), accommodations *pl* (*US*); **habt ihr dort eine ~?** have you any accommodation (*Brit*) or accommodations

(US) there?, have you somewhere to stay there?; **Un|ter|kunfts|raum** M quarters *pl*

Un|ter|la|ge F **a** (*für Teppich*) underlay; (*im Bett*) draw sheet; **du brauchst eine ~** you need to put something underneath; (*zum Schreiben*) you need something to rest on; (*zum Schlafen*) you need something to lie on **b** *usu pl* (= *Belege, Urkunden, Papiere*) document, paper **c** (*Hort*) rootstock

Un|ter-: Un|ter|land NT , *no pl* lowland; **Un|ter|län|der** ['ʊntɐlɛndɐ] M -s, -, **Un|ter|län|de|rin** [-ərɪn] F -, -nen lowlander; **un|ter|län|disch** ['ʊntɐlɛndɪʃ] ADJ *attr* lowland; **Un|ter|län|ge** F tail (of letters), descender (*spec*); **Un|ter|lass** ▲ M **ohn(e) ~** (*old*) incessantly, continuously; *arbeiten auch* without respite

un|ter|las|sen [ʊntɐ'lasn] *ptp* **unterlassen** VT *insep irreg* (= *nicht tun*) to refrain from; (= *nicht durchführen*) not to carry out; (= *auslassen*) to o-mit; *Bemerkung, Zwischenrufe* to refrain from making; *etwas Dummes etc* to refrain from doing; *Trinken* to abstain from; **keine Anstrengung** or **nichts ~** to spare no effort; **~ Sie das!** don't do that!, stop that!; **er hat es ~, mich zu benachrichtigen** he failed or omitted to notify me; **warum wurde das ~?** why was it not done?; **~e Hilfeleistung** (*Jur*) failure to give assistance

Un|ter|las|sung F -, -en **a** (= *Versäumnis*) o-mission (of sth), failure (to do sth); **bei ~ der Zahlung** in case of default (of payment); **auf ~ klagen** (*Jur*) to ask for an injunction **b** (*Gram*) **~ der Deklination** non-declension

Un|ter|las|sungs-: Un|ter|las|sungs|de|likt NT (*Jur*) failure to act; **Un|ter|las|sungs|fall** M (*Admin*) case of default; **im ~e** in case of default; **Un|ter|las|sungs|kla|ge** F (*Jur*) injunction suit; **Un|ter|las|sungs|straf|tat** F (*Jur*) (offence (*Brit*) or offense (*US*)) of default; **Un|ter|las|sungs|sün|de** F sin of omission; **Un|ter|las|sungs|ur|teil** NT injunction

Un|ter|lauf M lower reaches *pl* (of a river)

un|ter|lau|fen¹ ['ʊntɐlaufn] *ptp* **unterlaufen** *insep irreg* **VI** +dat aux sein (*Fehler, Irrtum, Versehen*) to occur; **mir ist ein Fehler ~** I made a mistake **VT** *Bestimmungen, Maßnahmen* to get (a)round; *Steuergesetze* to avoid; (= *umgehen*) to circumvent; (= *zuvorkommen*) to anticipate; (= *unterminieren*) to undermine; **jdn ~** (*Sport*) to slip under sb's guard

un|ter|lau|fen² ['ʊntɐlaufn] ADJ suffused with blood; (*mit Blut*) **~es Auge** a bloodshot eye

Un|ter|le|der NT sole leather

un|ter+le|gen¹ ['ʊntɐleːgn] VT *sep* to put underneath; (*fig*) to attribute, to ascribe; **einer Sache** (*dat*) **einen anderen Sinn ~** to put a different interpretation or construction on sth, to read another meaning into sth

un|ter|le|gen² [ʊntɐ'leːgn] *ptp* **unterlegt** VT *insep* to underlay; (*mit Stoff, Watte etc*) to line; (*mit Watte*) to pad; **einer Melodie** (*dat*) **einen Text ~** to put or set words to a tune

un|ter|le|gen³ [ʊntɐ'leːgn] ADJ inferior (= *besiegt*) defeated; **jdm ~ sein** to be inferior to sb, to be sb's inferior; **zahlenmäßig ~ sein** to be outnumbered, to be numerically inferior → *auch* **unterliegen**

Un|ter|le|ge|ne(r) [ʊntɐ'leːgənə] MF *decl as adj* underdog; **der ~ sein** to be in the weaker position

Un|ter|le|gen|heit F -, *no pl* inferiority

Un|ter|leg|schei|be F (*Tech*) washer

Un|ter|leib M abdomen; (*im engeren Sinne*: = *Geschlechtsorgane*) lower abdomen

Un|ter|leibs- *in cpds* abdominal; (*in Bezug auf weibliche Geschlechtsorgane*) gynaecological (*Brit*), gynecological (*US*); **Un|ter|leibs|krebs** M cancer of the abdomen; (*der Frau*) cancer of the womb; **Un|ter|leibs|or|gan** NT abdominal organ; **Un|ter|leibs|schmer|zen** PL abdominal pains *pl*

Un|ter-: Un|ter|leut|nant M (*Mil*) second lieutenant; **Un|ter|lid** NT lower lid

un|ter|lie|gen [ʊntɐ'liːgn] *ptp* **unterlegen** [ʊntɐ'leːgn] VI *insep irreg aux sein* **a** (= *besiegt werden*) to be defeated (+*dat* by), to lose (+*dat* to); (*fig*) *einer Versuchung etc* to succumb (+*dat* to), to give away (+*dat* to) **b** +*dat* (= *unterworfen sein*) to be subject to; *einer Gebühr, Steuer* to be liable to; **es unterliegt keinem Zweifel, dass ...** it is not open to any doubt that ... → *auch* **unterlegen³**

Un|ter|lip|pe F bottom or lower lip

un|term ['ʊntɐm] *contr von* **unter dem**

un|ter|ma|len [ʊntɐ'maːlən] *ptp* **untermalt** VT *insep* **a** (*Art*) *Bild* to prime **b** (*mit Musik*) to provide with background or incidental music; *Film* to provide a soundtrack for; (*fig*) to underlie; **eine Ansage mit leiser Musik ~** to play soft background music with an announcement

Un|ter|ma|lung F -, -en **a** (*Art*) preparatory or priming coat **b** (= *Musikuntermalung*) background music

un|ter|mau|ern [ʊntɐ'mauɐn] *ptp* **untermauert** VT *insep* (*Build*) to underpin; (*fig auch*) *Behauptung, Theorie* to back up, to substantiate, to support

Un|ter|mau|e|rung F -, -en (*Build*) underpinning; (*fig*) support; **zur ~ seiner These** in support of his thesis, to back up or substantiate his thesis

Un|ter|men|ge F (*Math*) subset

un|ter+men|gen VT *sep* to mix in, to add

Un|ter|mensch M (*esp NS*) subhuman creature

Un|ter|me|nü NT (*Comput*) submenu

Un|ter|mie|te F subtenancy; **bei jdm zur** or **in ~ wohnen** to be sb's tenant; (*als Zimmerherr etc auch*) to lodge (*Brit*) or room (*US*) with sb, to rent a room from sb

Un|ter|mie|ter(in) M(F) lodger (*esp Brit*), subtenant

Un|ter|miet|zim|mer NT (*Aus*) sublet room

un|ter|mi|nie|ren [ʊntɐmi'niːrən] *ptp* **unterminiert** VT *insep* (*lit, fig*) to undermine

Un|ter|mi|nie|rung F -, -en undermining

un|ter+mi|schen VT *sep* to mix in, to add

un|tern ['ʊntɐn] *contr von* **unter den**

un|ter|neh|men [ʊntɐ'neːmən] *ptp* **unternommen** [ʊntɐ'nɔmən] VT *insep irreg* to do; (= *durchführen auch*) to undertake; *Versuch, Vorstoß, Reise* to make; **einen Ausflug ~** to go on an outing; **Schritte ~** to take steps; **etwas/nichts gegen jdn/etw ~** to do something/nothing about sb/sth, to take some/no action against sb/sth; **zu viel ~** to do too much, to take on too much

Un|ter|neh|men [ʊntɐ'neːmən] NT -s, - **a** (= *Firma*) business, concern, enterprise **b** (= *Aktion, Vorhaben*) undertaking, enterprise, venture; (*Mil*) operation

un|ter|neh|mend ADJ enterprising

Un|ter|neh|mens-: Un|ter|neh|mens|be|ra|ter(in) M(F) management consultant; **Un|ter|neh|mens|be|wer|tung** F (*Econ*) business appraisal; (*vor Kauf*) due diligence; **Un|ter|neh|mens|form** F form or type of enterprise; **Un|ter|neh|mens|füh|rung** F management (of a/the company); **Un|ter|neh|mens|grün|dung** F (*Comm*) setting up (of) a business, business start-up; **Un|ter|neh|mens|lei|tung** F management; **die Herren in der ~** the management; **Un|ter|neh|mens|phi|lo|so|phie** F company philosophy or policy; **Un|ter|neh|mens|pla|nung** F business planning; **Un|ter|neh|mens|spit|ze** F top management; **Un|ter|neh|mens|struk|tur** F corporate structure; **Un|ter|neh|mens|vor|stand** M board of directors

Un|ter|neh|mer(in) M(F) employer; (*alten Stils*) entrepreneur; (= *Industrieller*) industrialist; **die ~** the employers

Un|ter|neh|mer-: Un|ter|neh|mer|geist M entrepreneurial spirit; **Un|ter|neh|mer|ge|winn** M (business) profit

un|ter|neh|me|risch [ʊntɐ'neːmərɪʃ] ADJ entrepreneurial **ADV** *denken, handeln* in an entrepreneurial or businesslike way

Un|ter|neh|mer-: Un|ter|neh|mer|krei|se PL **in/aus ~n** in/from business circles; **Un|ter|neh|mer|or|ga|ni|sa|ti|on** F employers' association; **Un|ter|neh|mer|tum** [ʊntɐ'neːmɐtuːm] NT -s, *no pl* (= *die Unternehmer*) management *no art*, employers *pl*; (= *Unternehmergeist*) entrepreneurship; **ein freies/das freie ~** free enterprise; **Un|ter|neh|mer|ver|band** M employers' association

Un|ter|neh|mung [ʊntɐ'neːmʊŋ] F -, -en **a** = **Unternehmen b** (= *Transaktion*) undertaking

Un|ter|neh|mungs-: Un|ter|neh|mungs|geist M , *no pl* enterprise; **Un|ter|neh|mungs|lust** F , *no pl* enterprise; **un|ter|neh|mungs|lus|tig** ADJ (= *tatendurstig*) enterprising; (= *abenteuerlustig auch*) adventurous

Un|ter|of|fi|zier(in) M(F) **a** (= *Rang*) noncommissioned officer, NCO; **~ vom Dienst** duty NCO **b** (= *Dienstgrad*) (*bei der Armee*) sergeant; (*bei der Luftwaffe*) corporal (*Brit*), airman first class (*US*)

Un|ter|of|fi|ziers-: Un|ter|of|fi|ziers|an|wär|ter(in) M(F) NCO candidate; **Un|ter|of|fi|ziers|rang** M noncommissioned rank

Un|ter-: un|ter+ord|nen *sep* **VT** to subordinate (+*dat* to) → *auch* **untergeordnet VR** to subordinate oneself (+*dat* to); **un|ter|ord|nend** ADJ (*Gram*) *Konjunktion* subordinating; **Un|ter|ord|nung** F *a no pl* subordination **b** (*Biol*) suborder; **Un|ter|or|ga|ni|sa|ti|on** F subsidiary organization

Un|ter|pfand NT (*old, liter*) pledge

un|ter+pflü|gen VT *sep* to plough (*Brit*) or plow (*US*) under or in

Un|ter|pri|ma F (*dated Sch*) eighth year of German secondary school, ≈ lower sixth (*Brit*), ≈ twelfth grade (*US*)

Un|ter|pri|ma|ner(in) M(F) (*dated Sch*) pupil in eighth year of German secondary school, ≈ sixth-former (*Brit*), ≈ twelfth-grader (*US*)

un|ter|pri|vi|le|giert [-priviˈleːgiːɐt] ADJ underprivileged; **Unterprivilegierte** underprivileged people; **die Unterprivilegierten** the underprivileged

Un|ter|pro|duk|ti|on F underproduction

Un|ter|pro|gramm NT (*Comput*) subroutine

Un|ter|punkt M (*eines Themas*) subordinate point

Un|ter|putz|lei|tung F (*Elec*) concealed cable

un|ter|que|ren [ʊntɐ'kveːrən] *ptp* **unterquert** VT *insep* to underrun

un|ter|re|den [ʊntɐ'reːdn] *ptp* **unterredet** VR *insep* **sich (mit jdm) ~** to confer (with sb), to have a discussion (with sb)

Un|ter|re|dung F -, -en discussion; (*Pol auch*) talks *pl*

un|ter|re|prä|sen|tiert [-reprɛzɛntiːɐt] ADJ underrepresented

Un|ter|richt ['ʊntɐrɪçt] M -(e)s, *no pl* lessons *pl*, classes *pl*; **theoretischer/praktischer ~** theoretical/practical instruction or classes; **~ in Fremdsprachen** foreign language teaching; **~ in Mathematik/Englisch** maths/English lessons or classes; **heute fällt der ~ in Englisch aus** there will be no English lesson today; **(jdm) ~ geben** or **erteilen** to teach (sb) (*in etw* (*dat*)) sth); **(bei jdm) ~ nehmen** or **haben** to take or have lessons (with sb); **am ~ teilnehmen** to attend classes; **zu spät zum ~ kommen** to be late for class; **im ~ aufpassen** to pay attention in class; **den ~ vorbereiten** to prepare one's lessons; **der ~ beginnt um 8 Uhr** lessons or classes start at 8 o'clock

un|ter|rich|ten [ʊntɐ'rɪçtn] *ptp* **unterrichtet** *insep* **VT** **a** (= *Unterricht geben*) *Schüler, Klasse,*

Fach to teach; **jdn in etw** (*dat*) ~ to teach sb sth **b** (= *informieren*) to inform (*von, über +acc* a- bout) **VI** to teach **VR** **sich über etw** (*acc*) ~ to obtain information about sth, to inform one- self about sth; **sich von jdm über etw** (*acc*) ~ **lassen** to be informed by sb about sth

un|ter|rich|tet [ʊntəˈrɪçtət] ADJ informed; **gut ~e Kreise** well-informed circles; **wie aus gut ~en Kreisen verlautet, ...** according to well-in- formed sources ...

Un|ter|richts-: Un|ter|richts|an|ge|bot NT subjects *pl* taught; **Un|ter|richts|aus|fall** M cancellation of a class/classes; **es gibt zu viele Unterrichtsausfälle** too many classes are being cancelled; **Un|ter|richts|be|ginn** M (*am Mor- gen*) school starting time; (*für einzelnes Fach*) class starting time; ~ **ist um 8.00** school or the first lesson starts at 8.00 or 8:00 (*US*); **Un|ter| richts|be|trieb** M , *no pl* lessons *pl*, classes *pl*; (= *Unterrichtsroutine*) teaching *no art*; **Un| ter|richts|ein|heit** F teaching unit; **Un|ter| richts|fach** NT subject; **Geschichte ist ~** histo- ry is on the curriculum; **Un|ter|richts|film** M educational film; **un|ter|richts|frei** ADJ *Stun- de, Tag* free; **der Montag ist ~** there are no classes on Monday; **Un|ter|richts|ge|gen| stand** M **a** topic, subject **b** (*Aus*) = *Unter- richtsfach*; **Un|ter|richts|ma|te|ri|al** NT teach- ing materials *pl*; **Un|ter|richts|me|tho|de** F teaching method; **Un|ter|richts|mi|nis|te|ri- um** NT Ministry of Education; **Un|ter|richts| mit|tel** NT teaching aid; **Un|ter|richts|raum** M teaching room, classroom; **Un|ter|richts| soft|ware** F educational software; **Un|ter| richts|spra|che** F language in which lessons are conducted; **Un|ter|richts|stoff** M subject matter, teaching subject; **Un|ter|richts|stun- de** F lesson, period; **während der ~n** during lessons; (*Univ*) lecture; **Un|ter|richts|vor|be|rei- tung** F teaching preparation; **Un|ter|richts| we|sen** NT educational system; **Un|ter- richts|ziel** NT teaching objective; **Un|ter- richts|zwe|cke** PL **zu ~n** for teaching pur- poses

Un|ter|rich|tung F , *no pl* (= *Belehrung*) instruc- tion; (= *Informierung*) information

Un|ter|rock M underskirt, slip

un|ter+rüh|ren VT *sep* to stir or mix in

un|ters [ˈʊntəs] *contr von* **unter das**

un|ter|sa|gen [ʊntəˈzaːgn] *ptp* **untersagt** VT *in- sep* to forbid, to prohibit; **jdm etw** ~ to forbid sb sth, to prohibit sb from doing sth; **(das) Rau- chen (ist hier) strengstens untersagt** smoking (is) strictly prohibited or forbidden (here); **jdm etw gerichtlich** ~ to enjoin sb to do sth

Un|ter|satz M **a** mat; (*für Gläser, Flaschen etc*) coaster (*esp Brit*); (*für Blumentöpfe etc*) saucer; **etw als ~ verwenden** to use sth to put under- neath → **fahrbar b** (*Philos*) minor premise

Un|ter|schall-: Un|ter|schall|flug M subson- ic flight; **Un|ter|schall|ge|schwin|dig|keit** F subsonic speed

un|ter|schät|zen [ʊntəˈʃɛtsn] *ptp* **unterschätzt** VT *insep* to underestimate

Un|ter|schät|zung F underestimation

un|ter|scheid|bar ADJ distinguishable

un|ter|schei|den [ʊntəˈʃaidn] ✪ 32.1 *ptp* **un- terschieden** [ʊntəˈʃiːdn] *insep irreg* **VT** (= *einen Unterschied machen, trennen*) to distinguish; (= *auseinander halten auch*) to tell apart; **A nicht von B ~ können** to be unable to tell the differ- ence between A and B, to be unable to tell A from B; **zwei Personen (voneinander)** ~ to tell two people apart; **kannst du die beiden ~?** can you tell which is which/who is who?; **das ~de Merkmal** the distinguishing feature; **nach ver- schiedenen Merkmalen** ~ to classify or divide according to various characteristics **VI** to differentiate, to distinguish **VR** **sich von etw/jdm** ~ to differ from sth/sb; **worin unterscheidet sich eine Amsel von einer**

Drossel? what is the difference between a blackbird and a thrush?

Un|ter|schei|dung F differentiation; (= *Unter- schied*) difference, distinction; **eine ~ treffen** to make a distinction

Un|ter|schei|dungs-: Un|ter|schei|dungs| merk|mal NT distinctive or distinguishing fea- ture; **Un|ter|schei|dungs|ver|mö|gen** NT discernment; **das ~** the power of discernment

Un|ter|schen|kel M lower leg

Un|ter|schicht F (*Sociol*) lower stratum (*So- ciol*), underclass

un|ter|schie|ben¹ [ʊntəˈʃiːbn] *ptp* **unter- schoben** [ʊntəˈʃoːbn] VT *insep irreg* (*inf*: = *unter- stellen*) **jdm etw** ~ to insinuate or imply that sb has done/said sth; **du unterschiebst mir immer, dass ich schwindle** you're always accusing me of cheating; **einer Äußerung einen ganz fal- schen Sinn** ~ to twist the meaning of a state- ment completely

un|ter+schie|ben² [ˈʊntəʃiːbn] VT *sep irreg* **a** (*lit*: = *schieben unter*) to push underneath; **etw unter etw** (*acc*) ~ to push sth under(neath) sth **b** (*fig*) **jdm etw** ~ (= *anlasten*) to palm sth off on sb; **er wehrte sich dagegen, dass man ihm das Kind ~ wollte** he defended himself against the charge that the child was his **c** = *unter- schieben¹*

Un|ter|schie|bung [ʊntəˈʃiːbʊŋ, ˈʊntə-] F **a** (= *Unterstellung*) imputation, attribution **b** (= *An- hängen*) foisting

Un|ter|schied [ˈʊntəʃiːt] ✪ 32.1, 32.4, 53.5 M -(e)s, -e [-də] difference (*auch Math*); (= *Unter- scheidung auch*) distinction; **einen ~ (zwischen zwei Dingen) machen** to make a distinction (between two things); **es besteht ein ~ (zwi- schen ...)** there's a difference or distinction (be- tween ...); **das macht keinen ~** that makes no difference; **es ist ein (großer) ~, ob ...** it makes a (big) difference whether ...; **ein feiner ~** a slight difference, a fine distinction; **zum ~ von** (*jdm/etw*) (*rare*), **im ~ zu** (*jdm/etw*) in contrast to (*sb/sth*), unlike (*sb/sth*); **mit dem ~, dass ...** with the difference that ...; **alle ohne ~ halfen mit** everyone without exception lent a hand; **es wurden alle ohne ~ getötet** everyone was killed indiscriminately; **das ist ein gewaltiger ~!** there's a vast difference!; **der kleine ~** (*hum*) the difference between the sexes; (*inf*: = *Penis*) willie (*Brit inf*), weenie (*US inf*)

un|ter|schied|lich [ˈʊntəʃiːtlɪç] ADJ different; (= *veränderlich*) variable; (= *gemischt*) varied, patchy; **das ist sehr ~** it varies a lot **ADV** differ- ently; **~ gut/lang** of varying quality/length; **sie haben ~ reagiert** their reactions varied

Un|ter|schied|lich|keit F -, -en difference; (= *Veränderlichkeit*) variability

un|ter|schieds|los **ADJ** (= *undifferenziert*) in- discriminate; (= *gleichberechtigt*) equal **ADV** (= *undifferenziert*) indiscriminately; (= *gleichberech- tigt*) equally

un|ter|schläch|tig [-ʃlɛçtɪç] ADJ *Wasserrad* un- dershot

un|ter|schla|gen¹ *ptp* **unterschlagen** VT *insep irreg Geld* to embezzle, to misappropriate; *Brief, Beweise, Tatsachen* to withhold, to suppress; (*inf*) *Neuigkeit, Nachricht, Wort etc* to keep quiet a- bout; **das hast du mir die ganze Zeit ~** and you've kept quiet about it all this time

un|ter+schla|gen² [ˈʊntəʃlaːgn] VT *sep irreg* **a** (= *verschränken*) *Beine* to cross; **mit untergeschla- genen Beinen dasitzen** to sit cross-legged **b** *Betttuch* to tuck in

Un|ter|schla|gung [ʊntəˈʃlaːgʊŋ] F -, -en (*von Geld*) embezzlement, misappropriation; (*von Briefen, Beweisen etc*) withholding, suppression

Un|ter|schlupf [ˈʊntəʃlʊpf] M -(e)s, **Unter- schlüpfe** [-ʃlʏpfə] (= *Obdach, Schutz*) cover, shel- ter; (= *Versteck*) hiding place, hide-out

un|ter+schlüp|fen (*dial*), **un|ter+schlup|fen** [ˈʊntəʃlʊpfn] VI *sep aux sein* (*inf*) (= *Obdach oder*

Schutz finden) to take cover or shelter; (= *Versteck finden*) to hide out (*inf*) (*bei jdm* at sb's)

un|ter|schrei|ben [ʊntəˈʃraibn] *ptp* **unterschrie- ben** [ʊntəˈʃriːbn] *insep irreg* **VT** to sign; **der Brief ist mit „Müller" unterschrieben** the letter is signed "Müller"; **das kann** or **würde ich ~!** (*fig*) I'll subscribe to that!, I'll buy that! (*inf*) **VI** to sign; **mit vollem Namen** ~ to sign one's full name

un|ter|schrei|ten [ʊntəˈʃraitn] *ptp* **unterschrit- ten** [ʊntəˈʃrɪtn] VT *insep irreg* to fall short of; *Temperatur, Zahlenwert* to fall below

Un|ter|schrei|tung F falling short; (*eines Be- trags*) shortfall

Un|ter|schrift F **a** signature; **seine ~/fünf ~en leisten** to give one's signature/one's signature five times; **eigenhändige** ~ personal signature; **seine ~ unter etw** (*acc*) **setzen** to put one's sig- nature to sth, to sign sth **b** (= *Bildunterschrift*) caption

Un|ter|schrif|ten-: Un|ter|schrif|ten|ak|ti- on F petition; **eine ~ durchführen** to get up a petition; **Un|ter|schrif|ten|lis|te** F list of sig- natures; **Un|ter|schrif|ten|map|pe** F signa- ture folder; **Un|ter|schrif|ten|samm|lung** F collection of signatures

un|ter|schrift|lich ADJ, ADV by signature

Un|ter|schrifts-: un|ter|schrifts|be|rech|tigt ADJ authorized to sign; **Un|ter|schrifts|be| rech|tig|te(r)** [-bəˌrɛçtɪçtə] MF *decl as adj* au- thorized signatory; **Un|ter|schrifts|fäl- schung** F forging of a/the signature; **Un|ter| schrifts|leis|tung** F signing of a/the docu- ment *etc*; **Un|ter|schrifts|pro|be** F specimen signature; **un|ter|schrifts|reif** ADJ *Vertrag* ready to be signed

un|ter|schwel|lig [-ʃvɛlɪç] **ADJ** subliminal **ADV** subliminally

Un|ter|see|boot NT submarine; (*ehemaliges deutsches auch*) U-Boot

un|ter|see|isch [-zeːɪʃ] ADJ underwater, under- sea, submarine

Un|ter-: Un|ter|sei|te F underside; (*von Topf, Teller, Kuchen auch*) bottom; (*von Blatt*) undersur- face; **an der ~** on the underside/bottom/under- surface; **Un|ter|se|kun|da** F (*dated Sch*) sixth year of German secondary school; **Un|ter- se|kun|da|ner(in)** M(F) (*dated Sch*) pupil in sixth year of German secondary school; **un|- ter+set|zen** VT *sep* to put underneath; **Un|- ter|set|zer** M = Untersatz **a**

un|ter|setzt [ʊntəˈzɛtst] ADJ stocky

un|ter|spü|len [ʊntəˈʃpyːlən] *ptp* **unterspült** VT *insep* to undermine, to wash away the base of

Un|ter-: Un|ter|staats|sek|re|tär(in) M(F) Undersecretary of State; **Un|ter|stadt** F lower part of a/the town; **Un|ter|stand** M shelter; (*Mil*) dugout

un|ter|stän|dig ADJ (*Bot*) inferior, hypogy- nous (*spec*)

un|ter|stands|los ADJ (*Aus*) homeless

un|ter|ste|hen¹ [ʊntəˈʃteːən] *ptp* **unterstanden** [ʊntəˈʃtandn] *insep irreg* **VI** *+dat* (= *unterstellt sein*) to be under (the control of); **jdm** to be subordinate to; **einer Behörde, dem Ministerium** to come under (the jurisdiction of); *dem Gesetz* to be subject to; (*in Firma*) to report to; **jds Auf- sicht** (*dat*) ~ to be under sb's supervision; **dem Verkaufsdirektor ~ sechs Abteilungsleiter** the sales director is in charge of six departmental heads **VR** (= *wagen*) to dare, to have the au- dacity; **untersteh dich (ja nicht)!** (don't) you dare!; **was ~ Sie sich!** how dare you!

un|ter+ste|hen² [ˈʊntəʃteːən] VI *sep irreg* (*bei Re- gen etc*) to take shelter or cover

un|ter|stel|len¹ [ʊntəˈʃtɛlən] *ptp* **unterstellt** *in- sep* **VT** **a** (= *unterordnen*) to (make) subordi- nate (*+dat* to); *Abteilung, Ministerium etc auch* to put under the control (*+dat* of); **jdm unterstellt sein** to be under sb, to be answerable to sb; (*in Firma*) to report to sb; **ihm sind vier Mitarbeiter**

unterstellt he is in charge of four employees, he has four employees subordinate to him; **jdm etw ~** to put sb in charge of sth; (*Mil*) to put sth under the command of sb, to put sth under sb's command

b (= *annehmen*) to assume, to suppose; **einmal unterstellt, es sei so gewesen** supposing *or* let us suppose (that) it was so

c (= *unterschieben*) **jdm etw ~** to insinuate *or* imply that sb has done/said sth; **jdm Nachlässigkeit ~** to insinuate that sb has been negligent; **ihm wurde unterstellt, gesagt zu haben, ...** he was purported to have said ...

VR to subordinate oneself (+*dat* to)

un|ter+stel|len² [ʊntɐˈʃtɛlən] *sep* **VT** (= *abstellen, unterbringen*) to keep; **Möbel** to store **VR** to take shelter *or* cover

Un|ter|stel|lung [-ˈʃtɛlʊŋ] F **a** (= *falsche Behauptung*) misrepresentation; (= *Andeutung*) insinuation; (= *Annahme*) assumption, presumption **b** *no pl* (= *Unterordnung*) subordination (*unter* +*acc* to)

un|ters|te(r, s) [ˈʊntɐstə] ADJ *superl von* **untere(r, s)** (= *tiefste auch*) bottom; (= *rangmäßig*) lowest; (= *letzte*) last; **das Unterste zuoberst kehren** to turn everything upside down

un|ter|steu|ern [ʊntɐˈʃtɔyɐn] *ptp* **untersteuert** VI *insep* to understeer

un|ter|steu|ert [ʊntɐˈʃtɔyɐt] ADJ *Auto* with understeer

un|ter|strei|chen [ʊntɐˈʃtraiçn̩] *ptp* **unterstrichen** [ʊntɐˈʃtrɪçn̩] VT *insep irreg* (*lit, fig*) to underline; (*fig: = betonen auch*) to emphasize

Un|ter|strei|chung F underlining; (*fig: = Betonung auch*) emphasizing

Un|ter|strich M (*Typ*) underscore, underline

Un|ter|strö|mung F (*lit, fig*) undercurrent

Un|ter|stu|fe F (*Sch*) lower school, lower grade (*US*)

un|ter|stüt|zen [ʊntɐˈʃtʏtsn̩] ⊘ 38.1, 38.2, 39.1, 53.2, 53.6 *ptp* **unterstützt** VT *insep* to support (*auch fig, Comput*); (*aus öffentlichen Mitteln auch*) to subsidize; (= *finanziell fördern auch*) to back, to sponsor; **jdn (moralisch) ~** to give sb (moral) support

Un|ter|stüt|zung ⊘ 38.2 F **a** *no pl* (*Tätigkeit, auch Comput*) support (*zu, für* for); **zur ~ seiner Behauptung** in support of his statement **b** (= *Zuschuss*) assistance, aid; (*inf: = Arbeitslosenunterstützung*) (unemployment) benefit; **staatliche ~** state aid; **~ beziehen** to be on social security (*Brit*), to be on welfare (*US*)

Un|ter|stüt|zungs-: **un|ter|stüt|zungs|be|dürf|tig** ADJ needy; **die Unterstützungsbedürftigen** the needy; **Un|ter|stüt|zungs|emp|fän|ger(in)** M(F) person receiving benefit (*Brit*) or on welfare (*US*)

Un|ter|such [ʊntɐˈzuːx] M **-s, -e** (*Sw*) = **Untersuchung**

un|ter|su|chen [ʊntɐˈzuːxn̩] *ptp* **untersucht** VT *insep* **a** (= *inspizieren, prüfen*) to examine (*auf* +*acc* for); (= *erforschen*) to look into, to investigate; (*genau*) **Dokumente** etc to scrutinize; (*statistisch, soziologisch etc*) to sound (out), to survey; (*chemisch, technisch etc*) to test (*auf* +*acc* for); **sich ärztlich ~ lassen** to have a medical (examination) *or* a checkup; **etw gerichtlich ~** to try sth (in court); **etw chemisch ~** to test *or* analyze sth (chemically) **b** (= *nachprüfen*) to check, to verify

Un|ter|su|chung [ʊntɐˈzuːxʊŋ] ⊘ 53.2, 53.6 F **-, -en a** (= *das Untersuchen*) examination (*auf* +*acc* for); (= *Erforschung*) investigation (+*gen*, *über* +*acc* into); (= *genaue Prüfung*) scrutiny; (*chemisch, technisch*) test (*auf* +*acc* for); (*ärztlich*) examination, checkup **b** (= *Nachprüfung*)

Un|ter|su|chungs-: **Un|ter|su|chungs|aus|schuss** ▲ M investigating *or* fact-finding committee; (*nach Unfall etc*) committee of inquiry; **Un|ter|su|chungs|be|fund** M (*Med*) result of an/the examination; (= *Bericht*) examination re-

port; **Un|ter|su|chungs|er|geb|nis** NT (*Jur*) findings *pl*; (*Med*) result of an/the examination; (*Sci*) test result; **Un|ter|su|chungs|ge|fan|ge|ne(r)** MF *decl as adj* prisoner awaiting trial; **Un|ter|su|chungs|ge|fäng|nis** NT prison (*for people awaiting trial*); **Un|ter|su|chungs|haft** F custody, (period of) imprisonment *or* detention while awaiting trial; **in ~ sein** *or* **sitzen** (*inf*) to be in prison *or* detention awaiting trial; **jdn in ~ nehmen** to commit sb for trial; **Un|ter|su|chungs|häft|ling** M prisoner awaiting trial; **Un|ter|su|chungs|kom|mis|si|on** F investigating *or* fact-finding committee; (*nach schwerem Unfall etc*) board of inquiry; **Un|ter|su|chungs|me|tho|de** F examination method; (*wissenschaftlich*) research method; **Un|ter|su|chungs|rich|ter(in)** M(F) examining magistrate; **Un|ter|su|chungs|zim|mer** NT (*Med*) examination room; (*in Praxis*) surgery

Un|ter|tag- [ʊntɐˈtaːk], **Un|ter|ta|ge-** [ʊntɐˈtaːgə] *in cpds* underground; **Un|ter|ta|ge|ar|bei|ter(in)** M(F) (coal)face worker (*Brit*), below-ground worker (*US*); **Un|ter|ta|ge|bau** M , *no pl* underground mining; **Un|ter|ta|ge|de|po|nie** F underground dump

un|ter|tags [ʊntɐˈtaːks] ADV (*Aus, dial*) = **tagsüber**

un|ter|tan [ˈʊntɐtaːn] ADJ (*pred* +*dat* to) subject; (= *dienstbar, hörig*) subservient; **sich** (*dat*) **ein Volk ~ machen** to subjugate a nation; **macht euch die Erde ~** (*Bibl*) subdue the earth *Bibl*

Un|ter|tan [ˈʊntɐtaːn] M **-en, -en**, **Un|ter|ta|nin** [-nɪn] F **-, -nen** (*old: = Staatsbürger*) subject; (*pej*) underling (*pej*)

Un|ter|ta|nen|geist M , **Un|ter|ta|nen|ge|sin|nung** F servile *or* subservient spirit

un|ter|tä|nig [ˈʊntɐtɛːnɪç] ADJ subservient, submissive; *Ergebenheit* humble; **Ihr ~ster Diener** (*obs*) your most obedient *or* humble servant **ADV jdn ~st bitten** to ask sb most humbly

Un|ter|tä|nig|keit F -, *no pl* subservience, submissiveness

Un|ter|ta|nin F → **Untertan**

Un|ter-: **un|ter|ta|rif|lich** ADJ, ADV *Bezahlung* below *or* under the agreed rate; **~ bezahlt werden** to be paid less than the agreed rate; **Un|ter|tas|se** F saucer; **fliegende ~** flying saucer

un|ter+tau|chen *sep* **VI** *aux sein* to dive (under); (*U-Boot auch*) to submerge; (*fig*) to disappear **VT** to immerse; **jdn** to duck

Un|ter|teil NT OR M bottom *or* lower part

un|ter|tei|len [ʊntɐˈtailn̩] *ptp* **unterteilt** VT *insep* to subdivide (*in* +*acc* into)

Un|ter|tei|lung F subdivision (*in* +*acc* into)

Un|ter-: **Un|ter|tel|ler** M saucer; **Un|ter|tem|pe|ra|tur** F low (body) temperature; **Un|ter|ter|tia** F (*dated Sch*) fourth year of German secondary school; **Un|ter|ter|ti|a|ner(in)** M(F) (*dated Sch*) pupil in fourth year of German secondary school; **Un|ter|ti|tel** M subtitle; (*für Bild*) caption; **un|ter|ti|teln** [ʊntɐˈtiːtl̩n, -ˈtɪtl̩n] *ptp* **untertitelt** VT *insep Film* to subtitle; *Bild* to caption; **Un|ter|ton** M *pl* **-töne** (*Mus, fig*) undertone; **un|ter|tou|rig** [-tuːrɪç] ADJ with low revs **ADV ~ fahren** to drive with low revs; **un|ter|trei|ben** [ʊntɐˈtraibn̩] *ptp* **untertrieben** [ʊntɐˈtriːbn̩] *insep irreg* **VT** to understate **VI** to play things down; **Un|ter|trei|bung** F -, **-en a** understatement **b** (= *das Untertreiben*) playing things down *no art*; **un|ter|tun|neln** [ʊntɐˈtʊnl̩n] *ptp* **untertunnelt** VT *insep* to tunnel under; *Berg auch* to tunnel through; **Un|ter|tun|ne|lung** F -, **-en** tunnelling (*Brit*), tunneling (*US*); **un|ter|ver|mie|ten** *ptp* **untervermietet** VTI *insep* to sublet, to sublease; **Un|ter|ver|mie|tung** F subletting; **un|ter|ver|si|chert** [-fɛɐzɪçɐt] ADJ underinsured; **Un|ter|ver|si|che|rung** F underinsurance; **un|ter|ver|sorgt** ADJ undersupplied; **Un|ter|ver|sor|gung** F inadequate provision; **Un|ter|ver|zeich|nis** NT (*Comput*) subdirectory

Un|ter|wal|den [ˈʊntɐvaldn̩] NT **-s** Unterwalden

un|ter|wan|dern [ʊntɐˈvandɐn] *ptp* **unterwandert** VT *insep* to infiltrate

Un|ter|wan|de|rung F infiltration

un|ter|wärts [ˈʊntɐvɛrts] ADV (*dial*) underneath

Un|ter|wä|sche F *a no pl* underwear *no pl* **b** (*für Autos*) underbody cleaning

Un|ter|was|ser-: **Un|ter|was|ser|be|hand|lung** F (*Med*) underwater treatment; **Un|ter|was|ser|fo|to|gra|fie** F underwater photography; **Un|ter|was|ser|gym|nas|tik** F underwater exercises *pl*; **Un|ter|was|ser|jagd** F scuba fishing; **Un|ter|was|ser|jä|ger(in)** M(F) spear fisherman, underwater fisherman; **Un|ter|was|ser|ka|me|ra** F underwater camera; **Un|ter|was|ser|la|bor** NT underwater laboratory, sea lab; **Un|ter|was|ser|mas|sa|ge** F (*Med*) underwater massage; **Un|ter|was|ser|sta|ti|on** F (= *Labor*) underwater laboratory, sea lab

un|ter|wegs [ʊntɐˈveːks] ADV on the *or* one's/its way (*nach, zu* to); (= *auf Reisen*) away; **eine Karte von ~ schicken** to send a card while one is away; **bei denen ist wieder ein Kind ~** they've got another child on the way; **bei ihr ist etwas (Kleines) ~** she's expecting

un|ter|wei|sen [ʊntɐˈvaizn̩] *ptp* **unterwiesen** [ʊntɐˈviːzn̩] VT *insep irreg* (*geh*) to instruct (*in* +*dat* in)

Un|ter|wei|sung F (*geh*) instruction

Un|ter|welt F (*lit, fig*) underworld

un|ter|wer|fen [ʊntɐˈvɛrfn̩] *ptp* **unterworfen** [ʊntɐˈvɔrfn̩] *insep irreg* **VT a** *Volk, Land* to subjugate, to conquer **b** (= *unterziehen*) to subject (+*dat* to); **einer Sache** (*dat*) **unterworfen sein** to be subject to sth **VR** (*lit, fig*) **sich jdm/einer Sache ~** to submit to sb/sth

Un|ter|wer|fung F -, **-en a** (*von Volk, Land*) subjugation, conquest **b** (= *das Sichunterwerfen*) submission

un|ter|wor|fen [ʊntɐˈvɔrfn̩] ADJ **der Mode/dem Zeitgeschmack ~ sein** to be subject to fashion/prevailing tastes

un|ter|wür|fig [ʊntɐˈvʏrfɪç, ˈʊntɐ-] ADJ (*pej*) obsequious

Un|ter|wür|fig|keit [ʊntɐˈvʏrfɪçkait, ˈʊntɐ-] F -, *no pl* (*pej*) obsequiousness

Un|ter|zahl F , *no pl* (*Sport*) **in ~** with a player/two players etc short; (*Ftbl*) with only ten/nine etc men

un|ter|zeich|nen [ʊntɐˈtsaiçnən] *ptp* **unterzeichnet** VT *insep* (*form*) to sign

Un|ter|zeich|ner(in) M(F) signatory

Un|ter|zeich|ner|staat M signatory state

Un|ter|zeich|ne|te(r) [ʊntɐˈtsaiçnətə] MF *decl as adj* (*form*) **der/die ~** the undersigned; **der rechts/links ~** the right/left signatory

Un|ter|zeich|nung F signing

Un|ter|zeug NT , *no pl* (*inf*) underclothes *pl*

un|ter|zie|hen¹ [ʊntɐˈtsiːən] *ptp* **unterzogen** [ʊntɐˈtsoːgn̩] *insep irreg* **VR** (= *unterwerfen*) **sich einer Sache** (*dat*) **~ (müssen)** to (have to) undergo sth; **sich einer Operation** (*dat*) **~** to undergo *or* have an operation; **sich einer Prüfung** (*dat*) **~** to take an examination; **sich der Mühe** (*dat*) **~, etw zu tun** (*geh*) to take the trouble to do sth **VT** to subject (+*dat* to); **jdn/etw einer Prüfung ~** to subject sb/sth to an examination; **jdn einer Operation ~** to perform an operation on sb

un|ter+zie|hen² [ˈʊntɐtsiːən] VT *sep irreg* **a** *Unterwäsche, Kleidung* to put on underneath; **sich** (*dat*) **etw ~** to put sth on underneath **b** (*Cook*) *Eischnee, Sahne* to fold in

un|ter|zu|ckert ADJ (*Med*) hypoglycaemic (*Brit*), hypoglycemic (*US*); **er ist ~** (*auch*) his blood sugar is low

---

Un|ter|zu|cke|rung [-'tsʊkərʊŋ] F -, -en (Med) hypoglycaemia (Brit), hypoglycemia (US)

Un|tie|fe F **a** (= seichte Stelle) shallow, shoal **b** (liter: = große Tiefe) depth

Un|tier NT monster

un|tilg|bar ADJ (geh) (= nicht rückzahlbar) irredeemable; (fig) indelible

Un|to|te(r) MF decl as adj die ~n the undead

Un-: un|trag|bar ADJ Zustände, Belastung intolerable, unbearable; Risiko unacceptable; **er ist politisch ~ geworden** he has become a political liability; **Un|trag|bar|keit** [ʊn'traːkbaːɐkait, 'ʊn-] F -, no pl **die ~ des hohen Haushaltsdefizits** the intolerably high budget deficit; **un|trai|niert** ['ʊntrɛniːɐt, -trɛ-] ADJ untrained; **un|trenn|bar** ADJ inseparable **un|trennt|legt** ADJ Mensch inseparable verbs; **mit etw ~ verbunden sein** (fig) to be inextricably linked with sth

un|treu ADJ Liebhaber etc unfaithful; (einem Prinzip etc) disloyal (+dat to); **sich** (dat) **selbst ~ werden** to be untrue to oneself; **jdm ~ werden** to be unfaithful to sb

Un|treue F **a** (von Liebhaber etc) unfaithfulness **b** (Jur) embezzlement

un|trink|bar ADJ undrinkable

un|tröst|lich ADJ inconsolable (über +acc about); **er war ~, dass er es vergessen hatte** he was inconsolable about having forgotten it

un|trüg|lich [ʊn'tryːklɪç, 'ʊn-] ADJ Gedächtnis, Instinkt, Gespür infallible; Zeichen unmistakable

un|tüch|tig ['ʊntʏçtɪç] ADJ (= unfähig) incapable, incompetent (in +dat at); (= nicht fleißig) inefficient

Un|tu|gend F (= Laster) vice; (= schlechte Angewohnheit) bad habit; (= Schwäche) weakness

un|tun|lich ADJ (dated) (= unzweckmäßig) impractical; (= unklug) imprudent

un|ty|pisch ADJ atypical (für of); Person auch out of character (für for); **es ist ~ für sie** (auch) it's not like her

Un-: un|übel ADJ (gar) **nicht (so) ~** not bad (at all); **un|über|biet|bar** ADJ Preis, Rekord etc unbeatable; Leistung unsurpassable; Frechheit, Virtuosität, Eifer unparalleled; **un|über|brück|bar** ADJ (fig) Gegensätze etc irreconcilable; Kluft unbridgeable; **un|über|dacht** ['ʊnly:bɐdaxt] ADJ open, uncovered; **un|über|legt** ADJ Mensch rash; Entschluss, Maßnahmen etc auch ill-considered **ADV** rashly; **~ entscheiden** to make a rash decision; **~ handeln** to act rashly; **Un|über|legt|heit** F -, -en rashness; (= unüberlegte Handlung) rash act; **un|über|schau|bar** ADJ **a** (= groß) immense, vast **b** (= nicht vorhersehbar) Folgen etc incalculable **c** (fig) (= unklar) unclear; (= verworren) confusing; **un|über|seh|bar** ADJ **a** (= nicht abschätzbar) Schaden, Schwierigkeiten, Folgen inestimable, incalculable; (= nicht übersehbar) Menge, Häusermeer etc vast, immense **b** (= auffällig) Fehler etc obvious, conspicuous; **un|über|setz|bar** ADJ untranslatable; **un|über|sicht|lich** ADJ **a** Gelände broken; Kurve, Stelle blind **b** (= durcheinander) System, Plan confused; **un|über|treff|lich** ADJ matchless, unsurpassable; Rekord unbeatable **ADV** superbly, magnificently; **un|über|trof|fen** [ʊnly:bɐ'trɔfn, 'ʊn-] ADJ unsurpassed; **un|über|wind|bar** (rare), **un|über|wind|lich** [ʊnly:bɐ'vɪntlɪç, 'ʊn-] ADJ Gegner, Heer invincible; Festung impregnable; Hindernis, Schwierigkeit, Gegensatz, Abneigung etc insuperable, insurmountable; **un|üb|lich** ADJ not usual, not customary **ADV** unusually; **es ist ~ schnell gegangen mit dem Antrag** the application was dealt with unusually quickly

un|um|gäng|lich [ʊn|ʊm'gɛŋlɪç, 'ʊn-] ADJ essential, absolutely necessary; (= unvermeidlich) inevitable; Notwendigkeit absolute; **~ notwendig werden** to become absolutely essential/quite inevitable

un|um|kehr|bar ADJ irreversible

un|um|schränkt [ʊn|ʊm'ʃrɛŋkt, 'ʊn-] ADJ unlimited; Freiheit, Gewalt, Macht auch, Herrscher absolute **ADV** **~ herrschen** to have absolute rule

un|um|stöß|lich [ʊn|ʊm'ʃtøːslɪç, 'ʊn-] ADJ Tatsache, Wahrheit irrefutable, incontrovertible; Entschluss irrevocable **ADV** **~ feststehen** to be absolutely definite

Un|um|stöß|lich|keit F -, no pl (von Tatsache) irrefutability, incontrovertibility; (von Entschluss) irrevocability

un-: un|um|strit|ten ADJ indisputable, undisputed **ADV** indisputably, undoubtedly; **un|um|wun|den** ['ʊnlʊmvʊndn, ʊnlʊm'vʊndn] ADV frankly; **un|un|ter|bro|chen** ['ʊnlʊntɐbrɔxn, ʊnlʊntɐ'brɔxn] ADJ **a** (= nicht unterbrochen) unbroken, uninterrupted; **~e Tätigkeit** (in Firma) continuous employment **b** (= unaufhörlich) incessant, continuous **ADV** (= unaufhörlich) incessantly, continuously

un|ver|änder|lich [ʊnfɛɐ'ɛndɐlɪç, 'ʊn-] ADJ (= gleichbleibend) unchanging, invariable; (= unwandelbar) unchangeable; **eine ~e Größe** (Math) **eine Unveränderliche** (Math) a constant, an invariable

Un|ver|än|der|lich|keit F unchanging nature

un|ver|än|dert ['ʊnfɛɐ'ɛndɐt, ʊnfɛɐ'ɛndɐt] ADJ unchanged; **unsere Weine sind immer von ~er Güte** our wines are consistently good **ADV** always, consistently; **er ist immer ~ freundlich** he is always friendly; **du siehst ~ jung aus** you look just as young as ever; **das Wetter wird bis auf weiteres ~ heiter bleiben** the weather will remain fine for the time being

Un-: un|ver|ant|wort|lich [ʊnfɛɐ'antvɔrtlɪç, 'ʊn-] ADJ irresponsible **ADV** irresponsibly; **er hat sich ~ intensiv der Sonne ausgesetzt** he spent so much time in the sun, it was irresponsible; **du trinkst ~ viel** you're acting irresponsibly by drinking so much; **sie ist ~ schnell gefahren** she drove dangerously fast; **un|ver|ant|wort|lich|keit** F irresponsibility; **un|ver|ar|bei|tet** ['ʊnfɛɐ'arbaitət, ʊnfɛɐ'arbaitət] ADJ Material unprocessed, raw; (fig) Eindruck undigested in a raw state; **un|ver|äu|ßer|lich** [ʊnfɛɐ'ɔysəlɪç, 'ʊn-] ADJ **a** Rechte inalienable **b** Besitz unmarketable, unsaleable; **un|ver|bes|ser|lich** [ʊnfɛɐ'bɛsəlɪç, 'ʊn-] ADJ incorrigible; **un|ver|bil|det** ['ʊnfɛɐbɪldət] ADJ Charakter, Wesen unspoilt

un|ver|bind|lich ['ʊnfɛɐbɪntlɪç, ʊnfɛɐ'bɪntlɪç] ADJ **a** (= nicht bindend) Angebot, Preisangabe, Richtlinie not binding; Besichtigung free **b** (= vage, allgemein) noncommittal; (= nicht entgegenkommend) abrupt, curt **ADV** (= nicht bindend) noncommittally; **sich** (dat) **etw ~ schicken lassen** to have sth sent without obligation; **jdm Preise ~ bestätigen** to give sb unconfirmed prices; **etw ~ ausrechnen** to give a nonbinding estimate for sth

Un|ver|bind|lich|keit F **a** no pl (= Vagheit, Allgemeinheit) vagueness **b** (= unverbindliche Äußerung) noncommittal remark

un-: un|ver|bleit ADJ lead-free, unleaded; **un|ver|blümt** [ʊnfɛɐ'blyːmt, 'ʊn-] ADJ blunt; Drohung undisguised; **das kommt einer ~en Erpressung gleich!** that's downright blackmail! **ADV** bluntly; **un|ver|braucht** [ʊnfɛɐbrauxt] ADJ (fig) unspent; **un|ver|brenn|bar** ADJ incombustible; **un|ver|brüch|lich** [ʊnfɛɐ'brʏçlɪç, 'ʊn-] (geh) ADJ steadfast **ADV** **~ zu etw stehen** to stand by sth unswervingly; **un|ver|bürgt** [ʊnfɛɐ'bʏrkt, 'ʊn-] ADJ unconfirmed

un|ver|däch|tig ['ʊnfɛɐdɛçtɪç, ʊnfɛɐ'dɛçtɪç] ADJ unsuspicious; (= nicht unter Verdacht stehend) unsuspected, above suspicion; **das ist doch völlig ~** there's nothing suspicious about that **ADV** **sich möglichst ~ benehmen** to arouse as little suspicion as possible; **benimm dich möglichst ~!** act as normally as possible

Un-: un|ver|dau|lich ['ʊnfɛɐdaulɪç, ʊnfɛɐ'daulɪç] ADJ (lit, fig) indigestible; **un|ver|daut** ['ʊnfɛɐdaut, ʊnfɛɐ'daut] ADJ undigested; (fig auch) un-

assimilated **ADV** undigested; **un|ver|derb|lich** ADJ unperishable, nonperishable; **un|ver|dient** ['ʊnfɛɐdiːnt, ʊnfɛɐ'diːnt] ADJ undeserved **ADV** undeservedly, unjustly, unduly; **un|ver|dien|ter|ma|ßen**, **un|ver|dien|ter|wei|se** ADV undeservedly, unjustly; **un|ver|dor|ben** (lit, fig) unspoilt, pure; **Un|ver|dor|ben|heit** F (fig) purity; **un|ver|dros|sen** ['ʊnfɛɐdrɔsn, ʊnfɛɐ'drɔsn] ADJ (= nicht entmutigt) undeterred; (= unermüdlich) untiring, indefatigable; (= unverzagt) undaunted **ADV** (= unverzagt) undauntedly; weitermachen untiringly; **un|ver|dünnt** ['ʊnfɛɐdʏnt] ADJ undiluted **ADV** anwenden, auftragen undiluted; **Spirituosen ~ trinken** to drink spirits neat or straight (Brit), to drink alcohol straight (esp US)

un|ver|ehe|licht ADJ (old, form) unwedded, unwed; „unverehelicht" (auf Urkunde) (Frau) "spinster"; (Mann) "bachelor"; **die ~e Eleanor X** Eleanor X, spinster

Un-: un|ver|ein|bar [ʊnfɛɐ'ainbaːɐ, 'ʊn-] ADJ incompatible; **miteinander ~ sein** to be incompatible; **Un|ver|ein|bar|keit** F incompatibility; **un|ver|fälscht** ['ʊnfɛɐfɛlʃt, ʊnfɛɐ'fɛlʃt] ADJ (lit, fig) unadulterated; Dialekt pure; Natürlichkeit unaffected; Natur unspoilt; **un|ver|fäng|lich** ['ʊnfɛɐfɛŋlɪç, ʊnfɛɐ'fɛŋlɪç] ADJ harmless; **das ist ~** it doesn't commit you to anything; **Un|ver|fäng|lich|keit** F harmlessness

un|ver|fro|ren [ʊnfɛɐfroːrən, ʊnfɛɐ'froːrən] ADJ insolent

Un|ver|fro|ren|heit F -, -en insolence

un|ver|gäng|lich ['ʊnfɛɐgɛŋlɪç, ʊnfɛɐ'gɛŋlɪç] ADJ Kunstwerk, Werte, Worte, Ruhm immortal; Eindruck, Erinnerung, Reiz everlasting

Un|ver|gäng|lich|keit F (= Unsterblichkeit) immortality; (von Eindruck, Erinnerung) everlastingness

un|ver|ges|sen ADJ unforgotten; **Roland wird (uns allen) ~ bleiben** we'll (all) remember Roland

un|ver|gess|lich ▲ [ʊnfɛɐ'gɛslɪç, 'ʊn-] ADJ unforgettable; Erlebnis auch memorable; **das wird mir ~ bleiben, das bleibt mir ~** I'll always remember that, I'll never forget that

Un-: un|ver|gleich|bar [ʊnfɛɐ'glaiçbaːɐ, 'ʊn-] ADJ incomparable; **un|ver|gleich|lich** [ʊnfɛɐ'glaiçlɪç, 'ʊn-] ADJ unique, incomparable **ADV** incomparably, immeasurably; **un|ver|go|ren** ['ʊnfɛɐgoːrən] ADJ unfermented; **un|ver|hält|nis|mä|ßig** ['ʊnfɛɐhɛltnɪsmɛːsɪç, ʊnfɛɐ'hɛltnɪsmɛːsɪç] **ADV** disproportionately; (= übermäßig) excessively **ADV** disproportionately; (= übermäßig) excessive; **Un|ver|hält|nis|mä|ßig|keit** F disproportion; (= Übermäßigkeit) excessiveness; **ihm wurde ~ der Strafe vorgeworfen** he was accused of imposing a severe punishment; **un|ver|hei|ra|tet** ADJ unmarried, single; **un|ver|hofft** ['ʊnfɛɐhɔft, ʊnfɛɐ'hɔft] ADJ unexpected **ADV** unexpectedly; **das kam völlig ~** it was quite unexpected, it came out of the blue; **~ Besuch bekommen** to get an unexpected visit; **~ kommt oft** (Prov) what you least expect often happens; **un|ver|hoh|len** ['ʊnfɛɐhoːlən, ʊnfɛɐ'hoːlən] ADJ open, unconcealed **ADV** openly, obviously; **un|ver|hüllt** ['ʊnfɛɐhʏlt] ADJ **a** Tatsachen, Wahrheit undisguised, naked **b** (liter, iro: = nackt) unclad **c** = unverhohlen; **un|ver|jähr|bar** [ʊnfɛɐ'jɛːɐbaːɐ, 'ʊn-] ADJ (Jur) not subject to a statute of limitations; **un|ver|käuf|lich** ['ʊnfɛɐkɔyflɪç, ʊnfɛɐ'kɔyflɪç] ADJ unmarketable, unsaleable; **~es Muster** free sample; „unverkäuflich" "not for sale"; **un|ver|kenn|bar** [ʊnfɛɐ'kɛnbaːɐ, 'ʊn-] ADJ unmistak(e)able; **un|ver|krampft** (lit, fig) relaxed **ADV** (fig) in a relaxed manner; **un|ver|langt** ['ʊnfɛɐlaŋkt] ADJ unsolicited **ADV** **~ eingesandte Manuskripte** unsolicited manuscripts; **das Gedicht, das er ~ an die Zeitung schickte** the poem he sent unsolicited to the newspaper; **un|ver|läss|lich** ▲ ADJ unreliable; **un|ver|letz|bar** [ʊnfɛɐ'lɛtsbaːɐ, 'ʊn-] ADJ (lit, fig) invulnerable; **Un|ver|letz|bar|keit** F *(lit, fig)* invulnerability; **un|ver|letz|lich** [ʊnfɛɐˈlɛtslɪç, ˈʊn-] ADJ **a** *(fig)* Rechte, Grenze inviolable **b** *(lit)* invulnerable; **Un|ver|letz|lich|keit** F *(fig)* inviolability; *(lit)* invulnerability; **un|ver|letzt** [ˈʊnfɛɐlɛtst] ADJ uninjured, unhurt, unharmed; *Körperteil* undamaged; *Siegel* unbroken; **un|ver|mählt** [ˈʊnfɛɐmɛːlt] ADJ *(geh)* unwedded, unwed; **un|ver|meid|bar** [ʊnfɛɐˈmaitbaːɐ, ˈʊn-] ADJ inevitable; **Un|ver|meid|bar|keit** F inevitability; *(= Unumgänglichkeit)* unavoidability; **un|ver|meid|lich** [ʊnfɛɐˈmaitlɪç, ˈʊn-] ADJ inevitable; *(= nicht zu umgehen)* unavoidable; **der ~e Herr Braun** the inevitable Mr Braun; **Un|ver|meid|lich|keit** F -, -en inevitability; **un|ver|mindert** [ˈʊnfɛɐmɪndɐt] ADJ, ADV undiminished; **un|ver|mischt** [ˈʊnfɛɐmɪʃt] ADJ separate, unmixed; *(= rein)* pure; *Tee, Wein etc* pure, unadulterated

un|ver|mit|telt [ˈʊnfɛɐmɪtlt] ADJ **a** *(= plötzlich)* sudden, unexpected **b** *(Philos)* immediate ADV suddenly

Un|ver|mö|gen NT , *no pl* inability; *(= Machtlosigkeit)* powerlessness

un|ver|mö|gend ADJ **a** *(= arm)* without means **b** *(old, liter: = unfähig)* helpless; **~ sein, etw zu tun** not to be able to do sth

un|ver|mu|tet [ˈʊnfɛɐmuːtət] ADJ unexpected ADV unexpectedly

Un|ver|nunft F *(= Torheit)* stupidity; *(= mangelnder Verstand)* irrationality; *(= Uneinsichtigkeit)* unreasonableness

un|ver|nünf|tig ADJ *(= töricht)* stupid; *(aus mangelnder Vernunft)* irrational; *(= uneinsichtig)* unreasonable; **das war sehr ~ von ihr** it was very stupid *or* unwise of her

un-: un|ver|öf|fent|licht [ˈʊnfɛɐlœfntlɪçt] ADJ unpublished; **un|ver|packt** [ˈʊnfɛɐpakt] ADJ unpackaged, loose; **un|ver|putzt** [ˈʊnfɛɐpʊtst] ADJ unplastered

un|ver|rich|tet [ˈʊnfɛɐrɪçtət] ADJ **~er Dinge** *or* **Sache** without having achieved anything, empty-handed

un|ver|rich|te|ter|din|ge △ [ˈʊnfɛɐrɪçtɐtɐˈdɪŋə], **un|ver|rich|te|ter|sa|che** △ [-ˈzaxə] ADV → **unverrichtet**

un|ver|rück|bar [ʊnfɛɐˈrʏkbaːɐ, ˈʊn-] ADJ *(fig)* unshakeable, unalterable; *Entschluss auch* firm, definite; *Gewissheit* absolute; **~ feststehen** to be absolutely definite

un|ver|schämt [ˈʊnfɛɐ] ADJ outrageous; *Lüge, Verleumdung etc auch* blatant, barefaced; *Mensch, Frage, Benehmen etc* impertinent; *(inf) Preis* outrageous; **~es Glück** unbelievable luck ADV **a** *(= dreist)* grinsen impudently; *lügen* shamelessly, blatantly; **grins nicht so ~!** take that impudent grin off your face!; **lüg nicht so ~!** don't tell such barefaced lies! **b** *(inf: = unerhört)* teuer, hoch outrageously

Un|ver|schämt|heit F -, -en **a** *no pl* outrageousness *(von Mensch, Frage, Benehmen etc)* impudence, impertinence; **die ~ besitzen, etw zu tun** to have the impertinence *or* impudence to do sth **b** *(Bemerkung)* impertinence; *(Tat)* outrageous thing; **das ist eine ~!** it's outrageous!

un-: un|ver|schlei|ert ADJ **a** *Frau* unveiled **b** *(fig) Wahrheit* unvarnished; **un|ver|schlos|sen** [ˈʊnfɛɐʃlɔsn, ʊnfɛɐˈʃlɔsn] ADJ open; *(= nicht abgeschlossen)* unlocked; *Briefumschlag* unsealed; **un|ver|schlüs|selt** [ˈʊnfɛɐʃlʏslt] ADJ, ADV Daten uncoded; *TV* free to air, without blackouts pred *(US)*

un|ver|schul|det [ˈʊnfɛɐʃʊldət, ʊnfɛɐˈʃʊldət] ADJ **a** **ein ~er Unfall** an accident which was not his/her *etc* fault **b** *(= ohne Schulden)* free from *or* of debt ADV **~ in eine Notlage geraten** to get into difficulties through no fault of one's own

un|ver|schul|de|ter|ma|ßen [ˈʊnfɛɐʃʊldɐtɐˈmaːsn], **un|ver|schul|de|ter|wei|se** [ˈʊnfɛɐʃʊldɐtɐˈvaizə] ADV through no fault of one's own

un|ver|se|hens [ˈʊnfɛɐzeːəns, ʊnfɛɐˈzeːəns] ADV all of a sudden, suddenly; *(= überraschend)* unexpectedly

Un-: un|ver|sehrt [ˈʊnfɛɐzeːɐt] ADJ *Mensch (lit, fig)* unscathed; *(= unbeschädigt)* intact *pred*; **Un|ver|sehrt|heit** F -, *no pl (= ohne Beschädigung)* intactness; **körperliche ~** freedom from bodily harm; **sie haben die ~ der Geiseln bestätigt** they have confirmed that the hostages are uninjured; **seine seelische ~** the fact that he was mentally unscathed; **un|ver|sieg|bar** [ʊnfɛɐˈziːkbaːɐ, ˈʊn-] ADJ inexhaustible; **un|ver|sie|gelt** [ˈʊnfɛɐziːglt] ADJ unsealed; **un|ver|sieg|lich** [ʊnfɛɐˈziːklɪç, ˈʊn-] ADJ inexhaustible; **un|ver|söhn|lich** [ˈʊnfɛɐzøːnlɪç, ʊnfɛɐˈzøːnlɪç] ADJ *Standpunkte etc* irreconcilable; **Un|ver|söhn|lich|keit** F -, *no pl* irreconcilability; **un|ver|sorgt** [ˈʊnfɛɐzɔrkt] ADJ *Familie, Kinder* unprovided-for; *Patient, Verletzter* uncared-for

Un|ver|stand M lack of judgement; *(= Torheit)* folly, foolishness; **etw im ~ tun** to do sth to excess

un|ver|stan|den [ˈʊnfɛɐʃtandn] ADJ not understood; *(= missverstanden)* misunderstood; **er fühlt sich ~** he feels that nobody understands him

un|ver|stän|dig ADJ lacking understanding, ignorant

un|ver|ständ|lich ADJ *(= nicht zu hören)* inaudible; *(= unbegreifbar)* incomprehensible

Un|ver|ständ|nis NT -, *no pl* lack of understanding; *(= Nichterfassen, für Kunst etc)* lack of appreciation

un-: un|ver|stellt [ˈʊnfɛɐʃtɛlt, ʊnfɛɐˈʃtɛlt] ADJ **a** *Stimme* undisguised **b** *(= echt)* unfeigned, genuine; **un|ver|steu|ert** [ˈʊnfɛɐʃtɔyɐt, ʊnfɛɐˈʃtɔyɐt] ADJ untaxed; **un|ver|sucht** [ˈʊnfɛɐzuːxt, ʊnfɛɐˈzuːxt] ADJ **nichts ~ lassen** to try everything

un|ver|träg|lich [ˈʊnfɛɐtrɛklɪç, ʊnfɛɐˈtrɛklɪç] ADJ **a** *(= streitsüchtig)* cantankerous **b** *(= unverdaulich)* indigestible; *(Med)* intolerable; *(mit anderer Substanz etc)* incompatible

Un|ver|träg|lich|keit F , *no pl (= Streitsucht)* cantankerousness

un|ver|wandt ADJ **~en Blickes** *(liter)* with a steadfast gaze ADV fixedly, steadfastly

Un-: un|ver|wech|sel|bar [ʊnfɛɐˈvɛkslbaːɐ, ˈʊn-] ADJ unmistak(e)able, distinctive; **Un|ver|wech|sel|bar|keit** [ʊnfɛɐˈvɛkslbaːɐkait, ˈʊn-] F -, *no pl* distinctiveness; **un|ver|wehrt** [ˈʊnfɛɐveːɐt, ʊnfɛɐˈveːɐt] ADJ **das sei dir ~** *(old, geh)* you are at liberty to do this *(form)*; **un|ver|wes|lich** [ˈʊnfɛɐveːslɪç, ʊnfɛɐˈveːslɪç] ADJ imperishable; **un|ver|wind|bar** [ʊnfɛɐˈvɪntbaːɐ, ˈʊn-] ADJ insurmountable; **un|ver|wirk|licht** [ˈʊnfɛɐvɪrklɪçt] ADJ unrealized; **un|ver|wisch|bar** [ʊnfɛɐˈvɪʃbaːɐ, ˈʊn-] ADJ *(lit, fig)* indelible; **un|ver|wund|bar** ADJ *(lit, fig)* invulnerable; **Un|ver|wund|bar|keit** F *(lit, fig)* invulnerability

un|ver|wüst|lich [ʊnfɛɐˈvyːstlɪç, ˈʊn-] ADJ indestructible; *Stoff, Teppich etc auch* tough, durable; *Gesundheit* robust; *Humor, Mensch* irrepressible

un-: un|ver|zagt ADJ undaunted ADV undaunted(ly); **un|ver|zeih|bar** [ʊnfɛɐˈtsaibaːɐ, ˈʊn-] ADJ *(rare)*, **un|ver|zeih|lich** [ʊnfɛɐˈtsailɪç, ˈʊn-] ADJ unpardonable, unforgivable; **un|ver|zerrt** [ˈʊnfɛɐtsɛrt] ADJ *Fernsehbild etc* undistorted; *(fig: = objektiv)* undistorted; **un|ver|zicht|bar** [ʊnfɛɐˈtsɪçtbaːɐ, ˈʊn-] ADJ *attr Recht* inalienable; *Anspruch* undeniable, indisputable; *Bedingung, Bestandteil* indispensable; **un|ver|zins|lich** [ʊnfɛɐˈtsɪnslɪç, ˈʊn-] ADJ interest-free; **un|ver|zollt** [ˈʊnfɛɐtsɔlt] ADJ duty-free

un|ver|züg|lich [ʊnfɛɐˈtsyːklɪç, ˈʊn-] ADJ immediate, prompt ADV immediately, without delay, at once

un|voll|en|det [ˈʊnfɔlɛndət, ʊnfɔlɛndət, ʊnfɔlˈlɛndət] ADJ unfinished; **Die „Unvollendete" von Schubert** Schubert's Unfinished (Symphony)

un|voll|kom|men [ˈʊnfɔlkɔmən, ʊnfɔlˈkɔmən] ADJ *(= unvollständig)* incomplete; *(= fehlerhaft, mangelhaft)* imperfect ADV partially; *wiedergeben* incompletely; **er kann zwar Englisch, aber doch recht ~** he can speak English, but his knowledge is rather limited; **er konnte seine Gefühle nur ~ beschreiben** he could only describe his feelings to a certain degree

Un|voll|kom|men|heit F **a** *no pl (= Unvollständigkeit)* incompleteness; *(= Mangelhaftigkeit)* imperfection **b** *(= Fehler, Mangel)* imperfection

un|voll|stän|dig [ˈʊnfɔlʃtɛndɪç, ʊnfɔlˈʃtɛndɪç] ADJ incomplete; *(Gram) Hilfsverb* defective ADV incompletely, partially; **er hat das Formular ~ ausgefüllt** he didn't fill the form out properly or correctly

Un|voll|stän|dig|keit F incompleteness

un|vor|be|rei|tet [ˈʊnfoːɐbəraitət] ADJ unprepared *(auf +acc* for); **eine ~e Rede halten** to make an impromptu speech, to speak off the cuff ADV *reden, unterrichten* unprepared, without preparation; **der Tod des Vaters traf sie ~** her father's death came unexpectedly

un|vor|denk|lich [ˈʊnfoːɐdɛŋklɪç] ADJ **seit ~en Zeiten** *(liter)* from time immemorial

Un-: un|vor|ein|ge|nom|men ADJ unbiased, unprejudiced, impartial ADV impartially; **Un|vor|ein|ge|nom|men|heit** F impartiality; **un|vor|her|ge|se|hen** [ˈʊnfoːɐheːɐgəzeːən] ADJ unforeseen; *Besuch* unexpected; **wir bekamen ~en Besuch** we had visitors unexpectedly, we had unexpected visitors ADV unexpectedly; **un|vor|her|seh|bar** ADJ unforeseeable; **~es Programmende** *(Comput)* unwanted program closure; **un|vor|schrifts|mä|ßig** ADJ not in keeping with the regulations ADV improperly; **ein ~ geparktes Fahrzeug** an improperly parked vehicle; **un|vor|sich|tig** ADJ careless; *(= voreilig)* rash ADV carelessly; *(= unbedacht)* rashly; **un|vor|sich|ti|ger|wei|se** [ˈʊnfoːɐzɪçtɪgɐˈvaizə] ADV carelessly; *(= voreilig)* rashly; **Un|vor|sich|tig|keit** F carelessness; *(= Voreiligkeit)* rashness; **so eine ~ von dir!** how reckless *or* rash of you!; **un|vor|stell|bar** [ʊnfoːɐˈʃtɛlbaːɐ, ˈʊn-] ❂ 43.3 ADJ inconceivable ADV *heiß, kalt* incredibly; *brutal, grausam* inconceivably; **un|vor|teil|haft** ADJ unfavourable *(Brit)*, unfavorable *(US)*, disadvantageous; *Kleid, Frisur etc* unbecoming ADV *gekleidet, geschminkt* unbecomingly; **sie ist ~ frisiert** the way she wears her hair is unbecoming; **~ aussehen** not to look one's best

un|wäg|bar [ʊnˈvɛkbaːɐ, ˈʊn-] ADJ *Umstand, Unterschied* imponderable; *Risiko* incalculable, inestimable

Un|wäg|bar|keit [ʊnˈvɛːkbaːɐkait, ˈʊn-] F -, -en **a** *no pl (von Umstand, Unterschied)* imponderability; *(von Risiko)* incalculability **b** **~en** *(= Risiken)* imponderables *pl*

Un-: un|wahr ADJ untrue; **un|wahr|haf|tig** ADJ untruthful; *Gefühle* insincere; **Un|wahr|heit** F **a** *no pl (von Äußerung)* untruthfulness **b** *(= unwahre Äußerung)* untruth; **die ~ sagen** not to tell the truth

un|wahr|schein|lich ❂ 43.2 ADJ *(= nicht zu erwarten, kaum denkbar)* unlikely, improbable; *(= unglaubhaft)* implausible, improbable; *(inf: = groß)* incredible *(inf)* ADV *(inf)* incredibly *(inf)*; **wir haben uns ~ beeilt** we hurried as much as we possibly could; **er gab sich ~ Mühe** he took an incredible amount of trouble *(inf)*

Un|wahr|schein|lich|keit F unlikeliness, improbability

un|wan|del|bar [ʊnˈvandlbaːɐ, ˈʊn-] ADJ *(geh)* **a** *(= unveränderlich)* unalterable, immutable **b** *Treue, Liebe* unwavering, steadfast

un|weg|sam ADJ *Gelände etc* rough

Un|weg|sam|keit F -, *no pl* roughness

un|weib|lich ADJ unfeminine

un|wei|ger|lich [ʊnˈvaigɐlɪç, ˈʊn-] ADJ *attr Folge* inevitable ADV inevitably; *(= fraglos)* undoubtedly; *(= grundsätzlich)* invariably

---

ụn|weit PREP +gen ADV not far from

ụn|wert ADJ (rare) = unwürdig

Ụn|wert M , no pl a = **Unwürdigkeit** b demerits pl; **über Wert und ~ einer Sache diskutieren** to discuss the merits and demerits of sth

Ụn|wert|ur|teil NT condemnation

Ụn|we|sen NT , no pl (= übler Zustand) terrible state of affairs; **das ~ (der Rauschgiftsucht) bekämpfen** to combat the problem (of drug addiction); **sein ~ treiben** to be up to mischief; (Landstreicher etc) to make trouble; (Gespenst) to walk abroad; (Vampir etc) to strike terror into people's hearts

ụn|we|sent|lich ADJ (= nicht zur Sache gehörig) irrelevant; (= unwichtig) unimportant, insignificant ADV **erhöhen, verringern** insignificantly, minimally; **sich unterscheiden** only slightly, negligibly, marginally; **verändern** only slightly, barely; **mehr, weniger, jünger, besser** just slightly; **zu einer Sache nicht/nur ~ beitragen** to make a not insignificant/only an insignificant contribution to sth

Ụn|wet|ter NT (thunder)storm; **ein ~ brach los** a storm broke

Ụn|wet|ter|scha|den M usu pl storm damage

Un-: ụn|wich|tig ADJ unimportant, insignificant; (= belanglos) irrelevant; (= verzichtbar) nonessential; **Ụn|wich|tig|keit** F unimportance, insignificance; (= Belanglosigkeit) irrelevance; **un|wi|der|leg|bar, un|wi|der|leg|lich** [ʊnvi:dɐˈleːklɪç, ˈʊn-] ADJ irrefutable; **un|wi|der|ruf|lich** [ʊnvi:dɐˈruːflɪç, ˈʊn-] ADJ irrevocable ADV definitely; **die ~ letzte Vorstellung** positively or definitely the last or final performance; **es steht ~ fest, dass ...** it is absolutely definite that ...; **un|wi|der|spro|chen** [ʊnvi:dɐˈʃprɔxn, ˈʊn-] ADJ uncontradicted; Behauptung auch unchallenged; **das darf nicht ~ bleiben** we can't let this pass unchallenged; **un|wi|der|steh|lich** [ʊnvi:dɐˈʃteːlɪç, ˈʊn-] ADJ irresistible; **un|wie|der|bring|lich** [ʊnvi:dɐˈbrɪŋlɪç, ˈʊn-] (geh) ADJ irretrievable ADV irretrievably

Ụn|wil|le(n) M , no pl displeasure, indignation (über +acc at); (= Ungeduld) irritation; **jds Unwillen erregen** to incur sb's displeasure; **seinem Unwillen Luft machen** to give vent to one's indignation

ụn|wil|lig ADJ indignant (über +acc about); (= widerwillig) unwilling, reluctant ADV (= widerwillig) unwillingly; (= ungern) reluctantly

Ụn|wil|lig|keit F indignation; (= Widerwilligkeit) unwillingness, reluctance

ụn|will|kom|men ADJ unwelcome

ụn|will|kür|lich [ˈʊnvɪlkyːɐlɪç, ʊnvɪlˈkyːɐlɪç] ADJ spontaneous; (= instinktiv) instinctive; (Physiol, Med) involuntary ADV **zusammenzucken** instinctively; **ich musste ~ lachen/grinsen** I couldn't help laughing/smiling

Un-: ụn|wirk|lich ADJ unreal; **Ụn|wirk|lich|keit** F unreality; **ụn|wirk|sam** ADJ (= wirkungslos, auch Med) ineffective; Vertrag, Rechtsgeschäft inoperative; (= nichtig) null, void; (Chem) inactive; **Ụn|wirk|sam|keit** F (= Wirkungslosigkeit) ineffectiveness; (Jur) (the fact of) not being operative; **ụn|wirsch** [ˈʊnvɪrʃ] ADJ Mensch, Benehmen, Bemerkung surly, gruff; Bewegung brusque ADV gruffly, brusquely; **ụn|wirt|lich** [ˈʊnvɪrtlɪç] ADJ inhospitable; **Ụn|wirt|lich|keit** F -, no pl (von Ort) inhospitable feel; (von Klima) inhospitable nature; **ụn|wirt|schaft|lich** ADJ uneconomic ADV uneconomically; **Ụn|wirt|schaft|lich|keit** F **die ~ dieser Methode** because this method is/was uneconomic; **Ụn|wis|sen** NT ignorance; **ụn|wis|send** ADJ ignorant; (= ahnungslos) unsuspecting; (= unerfahren) inexperienced; **Ụn|wis|sen|heit** F -, no pl ignorance; (= Unerfahrenheit) inexperience; **~ schützt nicht vor Strafe** (prov) ignorance is no excuse or (Jur) is no defence (Brit) or defense (US) in law; **ụn|wis|sen|schaft|lich** ADJ unscientific; Textausgabe unscholarly; Essay, Ausdrucksweise unacademic; **ụn|wis|sent|lich** ADV unwittingly, unknowingly

ụn|wohl ADJ (= unpässlich) unwell, indisposed (form); (= unbehaglich) uneasy; **mir ist ~, ich fühle mich ~** I don't feel well; **in ihrer Gegenwart fühle ich mich ~** I'm ill at ease or I feel uneasy in her presence

Ụn|wohl|sein NT indisposition; (= unangenehmes Gefühl) unease; **von einem (plötzlichen) ~ befallen werden** to be taken ill suddenly

Un-: ụn|wohn|lich ADJ Zimmer etc uncomfortable, cheerless; **Ụn|wort** NT pl -wörter taboo word; **ụn|wür|dig** ADJ unworthy (+gen of); Verhalten undignified; (= schmachvoll) degrading, shameful; **Ụn|wür|dig|keit** F unworthiness; (= Schmach) degradation, shame

Ụn|zahl F **eine ~ von** a host of

un|zähl|bar ADJ innumerable, countless; (Ling) uncountable ADV **~ viele** huge numbers; **viele Bücher/Mädchen** innumerable books/girls

un|zäh|lig [ʊnˈtsɛːlɪç, ˈʊn-] ADJ innumerable, countless; **~e Mal(e)** countless times, time and again ADV **~ viele** huge numbers; **~ viele Bücher/Mädchen** innumerable books/girls

un|zäh|li|ge|mal △ ADV → unzählig

un-: un|zähm|bar [ʊnˈtsɛːmbaːɐ, ˈʊn-] ADJ untamable; (fig auch) indomitable; **ụn|zart** ADJ ungentle ADV roughly; **sie machte mich ~ auf mein Alter aufmerksam** she commented bluntly on my age

Ụn|ze [ˈʊntsə] F -, -n ounce

Ụn|zeit F **zur ~** (geh) at an inopportune moment, inopportunely

un-: ụn|zeit|ge|mäß ADJ (= altmodisch) old-fashioned, outmoded; (= nicht in die Zeit passend) anachronistic; (= der Jahreszeit nicht entsprechend) unseasonal; **ụn|zen|siert** [ˈʊntsɛnziːɐt] ADJ uncensored; (Sch) ungraded; **un|zer|brech|lich** [ʊntsɛɐˈbrɛçlɪç, ˈʊn-] ADJ unbreakable; (fig) Treue, Bündnis etc steadfast; **un|ze|re|mo|ni|ell** ADJ unceremonious ADV empfangen, verabschieden unceremoniously; **un|zer|kaut** [ˈʊntsɛɐkaut] ADJ unchewed ADV without chewing; hinunterschlucken whole; **un|zer|reiß|bar** [ʊntsɛɐˈraisbaːɐ, ˈʊn-] ADJ untearable; **un|zer|stör|bar** [ʊntsɛɐˈʃtøːɐbaːɐ, ˈʊn-] ADJ indestructible; **un|zer|trenn|lich** [ʊntsɛɐˈtrɛnlɪç, ˈʊn-] ADJ inseparable

Ụn|zi|a|le [ʊnˈtsiaːlə] F -, -n (Typ) a (Schrift) uncial (writing) b (Buchstabe) uncial (letter)

Un-: ụn|zie|mend [ˈʊntsiːmənt] (old), **ụn|ziem|lich** ADJ unseemly, unbecoming, indecorous ADV sich benehmen in an unseemly manner or way; **Ụn|ziem|lich|keit** F -, -en a no pl unseemliness b (Benehmen) impropriety; **un|zi|vi|li|siert** ADJ (lit, fig) uncivilized ADV sich benehmen in an uncivilized manner

Ụn|zucht F , no pl (esp Jur) sexual offence (Brit) or offense (US); **das gilt als ~** that's regarded as a sexual offence (Brit) or offense (US); **~ treiben** to fornicate; **~ mit Abhängigen/Kindern/Tieren** (Jur) illicit sexual relations with dependants/children/animals; **gewerbsmäßige ~** prostitution; **widernatürliche ~** unnatural sexual act(s pl); **~ mit jdm treiben** to fornicate with sb; (Jur) to commit a sexual offence (Brit) or offense (US) with sb; **jdn zur ~ missbrauchen** to abuse sb (for sexual purposes)

un|züch|tig ADJ (esp Jur) indecent; Reden, Schriften obscene; **~e Handlungen** obscene acts; (Jur) illicit sexual acts ADV **~ leben** to live licentiously

Ụn|züch|tig|keit F (esp Jur) indecency; (von Reden, Schriften) obscenity

Un-: ụn|zu|frie|den ADJ dissatisfied, discontented; (= missmutig) unhappy; **manche Leute sind immer ~** some people are never content or happy; **Ụn|zu|frie|den|heit** F , no pl dissatisfaction, discontent; (= Missmut) unhappiness; **ụn|zu|gäng|lich** ADJ Gegend, Gebäude etc inaccessible; Charakter, Mensch unapproachable; (= taub, unaufgeschlossen) deaf, impervious (+dat

to); **Ụn|zu|gäng|lich|keit** F (von Gegend, Gebäude etc) inaccessibility; (von Charakter, Mensch) unapproachability; **ụn|zu|kömm|lich** [ˈʊntsuːkœmlɪç] ADJ (Aus) insufficient, inadequate; (= nicht zukommend) undue; **Ụn|zu|kömm|lich|keit** F -, -en (Aus) unpleasantness; (= Unzulänglichkeit) inadequacy; **ụn|zu|läng|lich** ADJ (= nicht ausreichend) insufficient; (= mangelhaft) inadequate ADV inadequately; **~ unterstützt werden** to get inadequate support; **Ụn|zu|läng|lich|keit** F a no pl insufficiency; (= Mangelhaftigkeit) inadequacy b **~en** shortcomings pl; **ụn|zu|läs|sig** (auch Jur) ADJ inadmissible; Gebrauch improper; Beeinflussung undue; Belastung, Geschwindigkeit excessive; **für ~ erklären** (Jur) to rule out; **ụn|zu|mut|bar** ADJ Bedingungen, Zustände unreasonable; **ụn|zu|rech|nungs|fä|hig** ADJ not responsible for one's actions, of unsound mind; **jdn für ~ erklären lassen** (Jur) to have sb certified (insane); **geistig ~** non compos mentis (Jur), of unsound mind; **Ụn|zu|rech|nungs|fä|hig|keit** F unsoundness of mind; **~ geltend machen** to put forward (Brit) or to enter a plea of insanity; **un|zu|rei|chend** [ˈʊntsuːraiçnt] ADJ insufficient, inadequate ADV insufficiently; **un|zu|sam|men|hän|gend** ADJ incoherent, disjointed; **un|zu|stän|dig** ADJ (Admin, Jur) incompetent, not competent; **sich für ~ erklären** to disclaim competence; **ụn|zu|stell|bar** ADJ undeliverable; Postsendung dead; **falls ~ bitte zurück an Absender** if undelivered, please return to sender; **Ụn|zu|stell|bar|keit** [ˈʊntsuːʃtɛlbaːɐkait] F -, no pl **bei ~ geht die Sendung an den Absender zurück** if undelivered the consignment is returned to sender; **ụn|zu|träg|lich** ADJ (= nachteilig) harmful, detrimental; (gesundheitlich) unhealthy; **jdm ~ sein** to be harmful or detrimental to sb; **jdm (gesundheitlich)** or **jds Gesundheit ~ sein** not to agree with sb, to be bad for sb's health; **ụn|zu|tref|fend** ADJ inappropriate, inapplicable; (= unwahr) incorrect; **Unzutreffendes bitte streichen** delete as applicable; **ụn|zu|ver|läs|sig** ADJ unreliable; **Ụn|zu|ver|läs|sig|keit** F unreliability; **ụn|zweck|mä|ßig** ADJ (= nicht ratsam) inexpedient; (= unpraktisch) impractical; (= ungeeignet) unsuitable, inappropriate; **ụn|zwei|deu|tig** ADJ unambiguous, unequivocal; (fig: = unanständig) explicit ADV explicitly; **jdm ~ zu verstehen geben, dass ...** to make it quite clear to sb that ...; **ụn|zwei|fel|haft** ADJ undoubted, indubitable, unquestionable ADV without doubt, undoubtedly, indubitably

Up|date [ˈapdeːt] NT -s, -s (Comput) update (auf +acc or zu to)

up|da|ten [ˈapdeːtn] ptp **upgedatet** VTI sep (Comput) to update

Up|grade [ˈapgreːt] NT -s, -s (Comput) upgrade (auf +acc or zu to)

up+gra|den [ˈapgreːdn] ptp **upgegradet** VTI sep (Comput) to upgrade

üp|pig [ˈʏpɪç] ADJ Wachstum luxuriant; Vegetation auch lush; Haar thick; Mahl, Ausstattung sumptuous, opulent; Rente, Gehalt lavish; Figur, Frau, Formen voluptuous; Busen ample; Leben luxurious; Fantasie rich; **nun werd mal nicht zu ~!** (inf) let's have no more of your cheek (Brit) or impudence! (inf)

ADV **die ~ ausfallenden Dividenden** the generous or lavish dividends; **ihre Bezüge sind sehr ~ bemessen** her earnings are very generously figured; **mit ~ gepolsterten Sitzen** with opulently or luxuriantly upholstered seats; **~ wucherndes Gestrüpp** thick or lush verdant undergrowth; **die ~ grünen Hügel** the lush green hills; **350 ~ illustrierte Seiten** 350 lavishly illustrated pages; **~ leben** to live in style; **~ wuchernde Vegetation** lush vegetation

Üp|pig|keit F -, no pl (von Wachstum) luxuriance; (von Vegetation auch) lushness; (von Haar) thickness; (von Mahl, Ausstattung) sumptuousness, opulence; (von Figur, Frau, Formen) voluptuousness

up to date ['ap tu: 'de:t] ADJ pred (inf) up to date; **Kleidung** modern

Ur [u:ɐ] M **-(e)s, -e** (Zool) aurochs

Ur- in cpds (= erste) first, prime; (= ursprünglich) original; **Ur|ab|stim|mung** F ballot; **Ur|adel** M ancienne noblesse, ancient nobility; **Ur|ahn** M , **Ur|ahne**[1] M (= Vorfahr) forefather, forebear; (= Urgroßvater) great-grandfather; **Ur|ah|ne**[2] F (= Vorfahrin) forebear; (= Urgroßmutter) great-grandmother

U|ral [u'ra:l] M **-s** (Geog) **a** (Fluss) Ural **b** (Gebirge) **der ~** the Urals pl, the Ural mountains pl

ur|alt ADJ ancient; **Problem, Brauch auch** age-old; **seit ~en Zeiten** from time immemorial; **aus ~en Zeiten** from long (long) ago

U|ran [u'ra:n] NT **-s**, no pl (abbr **U**) uranium

U|ran|bren|ner M uranium pile

Ur-: **Ur|an|fang** M first beginning; **Ur|angst** F primeval fear; **Ur|an|la|ge** F genetic predisposition; **ur|auf|füh|ren** ['u:ɐlauffy:ʀən] ptp **uraufgeführt** ['u:ɐlaufgəfy:ɐt] VT to give the first performance (of), to play for the first time; **Film** to premiere usu pass

Ur|auf|füh|rung F premiere; (von Theaterstück etc auch) first night or performance; (von Film auch) first showing

Ur|auf|füh|rungs|(film)|thea|ter NT , **Ur|auf|füh|rungs|ki|no** NT premiere cinema

Ur|aus|ga|be F first edition

ur|ban [uɐ'ba:n] ADJ (geh) urbane

ur|ba|ni|sie|ren [uɐbani'zi:ʀən] ptp **urbanisiert** VTR (Soziol) to urbanize

Ur|ba|ni|sie|rung F **-, -en** (Soziol) urbanization

Ur|ba|ni|tät [uɐbani'tɛːt] F **-**, no pl (geh) urbanity

ur|bar ['u:ɐba:ɐ] ADJ **einen Wald ~ machen** to clear a forest; **die Wüste ~ machen** to reclaim the desert; **Land ~ machen** to cultivate land

ur|ba|ri|sie|ren [uɐbari'zi:ʀən] ptp **urbarisiert** VT (Sw) = **urbar machen**

Ur|ba|ri|sie|rung F **-, -en** (Sw), **Ur|bar|ma|chung** [-maxʊŋ] F **-, -en** (von Wald) clearing; (von Wüste) reclamation; (von Ackerland) cultivation

Ur-: **Ur|ba|yer(in)** M(F) (inf) typical Bavarian; **Ur|be|deu|tung** F (Ling) original meaning; **Ur|be|ginn** M very beginning; **seit ~, von ~ an** from the beginning(s) of time; **Ur|be|völ|ke|rung** F natives pl, original inhabitants pl; (in Australien) Aborigines pl; **Ur|be|woh|ner(in)** M(F) native, original inhabitant; (in Australien) Aborigine; **Ur|bild** NT prototype, archetype; (Philos) idea

ur|chig ['ʊʀçɪç] ADJ (Sw) = **urwüchsig**

Ur-: **Ur|chris|ten** PL (Eccl Hist) early Christians pl; **Ur|chris|ten|tum** NT early Christianity; **ur|christ|lich** ADJ early Christian; **urdeutsch** ADJ essentially German

Ur|du ['ʊrdu] NT **-(s)** (Ling) Urdu

Ur-: **ur|ei|gen** ['u:ɐlaɪgn] ADJ very own; **es liegt in seinem ~sten Interesse** it's in his own best interests; **ein dem Menschen ~er Hang** an inherent human quality; **Ur|ein|woh|ner(in)** M(F) native, original inhabitant; (in Australien) Aborigine; **Ur|el|tern** PL (= Vorfahren) forebears pl; (= Urgroßeltern) great-grandparents pl; **Ur|en|kel** M great-grandchild, great-grandson; **Ur|en|ke|lin** F great-granddaughter; **Ur|fassung** F original version; **Ur|feh|de** F (Hist) oath of truce; **~ schwören** to abjure all vengeance; **Ur|form** F prototype; **Ur|ge|mein|de** F (Eccl Hist) early Christian community; **ur|gemüt|lich** ADJ (inf) **Wohnung, Lokal, Atmosphäre** really cosy (Brit) or cozy (US); **Mensch** really easy-going → **gemütlich**; **ur|ger|ma|nisch** ADJ (Ling) Proto-Germanic; (fig) essentially Germanic; **das Urgermanische** Proto-Germanic; **Ur|ge|schich|te** F prehistory; **Ur|ge|sellschaft** F primitive society; **Ur|ge|stalt** F prototype; **Ur|ge|stein** NT prehistoric rock, primitive rocks pl; **politisches ~** (fig) a dyed-in-the-wool politician; **Ur|ge|walt** F elemental force

ur|gie|ren [ʊʀ'giːʀən] ptp **urgiert** (Aus form) **VT** (= dringend nachsuchen) to request sth **VI** (= um schnelle(re) Erledigung bitten) to ask for sth to be done (more) quickly; (bei Entscheidung) to ask for a speedy decision

Ur|groß-: **Ur|groß|el|tern** PL great-grandparents pl; **Ur|groß|mut|ter** F great-grandmother; **Ur|groß|va|ter** M great-grandfather

Ur|grund M very basis, source

Ur|he|ber ['u:ɐhe:bɐ] M **-s, -**, **Ur|he|be|rin** [-əʀɪn] F **-, -nen** originator; (liter = Schöpfer) creator; (Jur = Verfasser) author; **der geistige ~** the spiritual father

Ur|he|ber-: **Ur|he|ber|ge|bühr** F copyright fee; **Ur|he|ber|recht** NT copyright (an +dat on); **ur|he|ber|recht|lich** ADJ, ADV on copyright attr; **~ geschützt** copyright(ed); **Ur|heber|schaft** ['u:ɐhe:bəʃaft] F **-, -en** authorship; **Ur|he|ber|schutz** M copyright

Ur|hei|mat F original home(land)

U|ri ['u:ri] NT **-s** Uri

u|rig ['u:ʀɪç] ADJ (inf) **Mensch** earthy; **Lokal** etc ethnic

U|rin [u'ri:n] M **-s, -e** urine; **etw im ~ haben** (dated inf) to have a gut feeling about sth (inf)

U|ri|nal [uri'na:l] NT **-s, -e** (Med) urinal

u|ri|nie|ren [uri'ni:ʀən] ptp **uriniert** VI to urinate

Ur|in|pro|be F urine sample or specimen

Ur-: **Ur|ins|tinkt** ['u:ɐlɪnstɪŋkt] M primary or basic instinct; **Ur|kan|ton** M (Sw) original canton; **Ur|kir|che** F early Church; **Ur|knall** M (Astron) big bang; **ur|ko|misch** ADJ (inf) screamingly funny (inf); **Ur|kraft** F elemental force

Ur|kun|de ['u:ɐkʊndə] F **-, -n** document; (= Kaufurkunde) deed, title deed; (= Gründungsurkunde etc) charter; (= Siegerurkunde, Diplomurkunde, Bescheinigung etc) certificate; **eine ~ (über etw acc) ausstellen** or **ausfertigen** (Jur) to draw up a document about sth; **eine ~ bei jdm hinterlegen** to lodge a document with sb

Ur|kun|den|fäl|schung F forgery or falsification of a/the document/documents

ur|kund|lich ['u:ɐkʊntlɪç] **ADJ** documentary **ADV** **~ verbürgt** or **bestätigt** authenticated; **~ beweisen** or **belegen** to give documentary evidence; **~ erwähnt** mentioned in a document

Ur|kunds|be|am|te(r) M decl as adj, **Ur|kunds|be|am|tin** F , **Ur|kunds|per|son** F registrar

Ur|land|schaft F primitive or primeval landscape

Ur|laub ['u:ɐlaup] M **-(e)s, -e** [-bə] (= Ferien) holiday(s pl) (esp Brit), vacation (US); (esp Mil) leave (of absence), furlough (US); **~ haben** to have a holiday (esp Brit) or vacation (US); (esp Mil) to have leave; **in** or **im** or **auf** (inf) **~ sein** to be on holiday (esp Brit) or vacation (US)/on leave; **er macht zur Zeit ~** he's on holiday (esp Brit) or he's vacationing (US) at the moment; **in ~ fahren** to go on holiday (esp Brit) or vacation (US)/on leave; **zwei Wochen ~** two weeks' holiday (esp Brit) or vacation (US)/leave; (sich dat) **einen Tag ~ nehmen** to take a day off, to take a day's holiday (esp Brit) or vacation (US); **~ bis zum Wecken** (Mil) night leave; **bezahlter/unbezahlter ~** paid/unpaid holiday (esp Brit) or vacation (US)

ur|lau|ben ['u:ɐlaubn] VI (inf) to holiday (esp Brit), to vacation (US)

Ur|lau|ber ['u:ɐlaubɐ] M **-s, -**, **Ur|lau|be|rin** [-əʀɪn] F **-, -nen** holiday-maker (Brit), vacationist (US); (Mil) soldier on leave

Ur|laubs-: **Ur|laubs|an|spruch** M holiday (esp Brit) or vacation (US) entitlement; **Urlaubs|an|trag** M request for time off or leave; **Ur|laubs|be|kannt|schaft** F holiday (esp Brit) or vacation (US) acquaintance; **Urlaubs|fo|to** NT holiday (esp Brit) or vacation (US) snap(shot); **Ur|laubs|ge|biet** NT holiday (esp Brit) or vacation (US) area; **Ur|laubs|-**

geld NT holiday pay or money (Brit), vacation pay or money (US); **Ur|laubs|land** NT holiday (esp Brit) or vacation (US) country, tourist destination; **mein liebstes ~** my favourite (Brit) or favorite (US) country for a holiday (esp Brit) or vacation (US); **Ur|laubs|ort** M holiday (esp Brit) or vacation (US) resort; **Urlaubs|plan** M usu pl holiday (esp Brit) or vacation (US) plan; **ur|laubs|reif** ADJ (inf) ready for a holiday (esp Brit) or vacation (US); **Ur|laubs|rei|se** F holiday (esp Brit) or vacation (US) trip; **eine ~ machen** to go on a trip; **Ur|laubs|schein** M (Mil) pass; **Ur|laubs|sper|re** F (Mil) ban on leave; **Ur|laubs|stimmung** F holiday mood; **Ur|laubs|tag** M (one day of) holiday (esp Brit) or vacation (US); **die ersten drei ~ hat es geregnet** it rained on the first three days of the/my/his etc holiday (esp Brit) or vacation (US); **ich habe noch drei ~e gut** I've still got three days' holiday (esp Brit) or vacation (US) to come; **Ur|laubs|ver|tretung** F temporary replacement; **ich mache ~ für Frau Schumm** I'm filling in while Mrs Schumm is on holiday (esp Brit) or is vacationing (US); **Ur|laubs|wo|che** F (one week of) holiday (esp Brit) or vacation (US); **Urlaubs|zeit** F holiday (esp Brit) or vacation (US) period or season; **Ur|laubs|ziel** NT holiday (esp Brit) or vacation (US) spot; (Land auch) tourist destination

Ur-: **Ur|laut** M elemental cry; **Ur|mensch** M primeval man; (inf) caveman (inf); **Ur|me|ter** NT , no pl standard metre (Brit) or meter (US); **Ur|mund** M (Biol) blastopore; **Ur|mut|ter** F pl -mütter first mother

Ur|ne ['ʊrnə] F **-, -n** urn; (= Losurne) box; (= Wahlurne) ballot box; **zur ~ gehen** to go to the polls; **die Wähler wurden an die ~n gerufen** the voters were asked to go to the polls

Ur|nen-: **Ur|nen|feld** NT (Archeol) urnfield, urnsite; **Ur|nen|fried|hof** M urn cemetery, cinerarium; **Ur|nen|gang** M pl -gänge (Pol) going to the polls no art; **Ur|nen|grab** NT urn grave

U|ro|ge|ni|tal- [urogeni'ta:l-] (Anat): **U|ro|ge|ni|tal|sys|tem** NT urogenital system; **U|ro|ge|ni|tal|trakt** M urogenital tract

U|ro|lo|ge [uro'lo:gə] M **-n, -n**, **U|ro|lo|gin** [-'lo:gɪn] F **-, -nen** urologist

U|ro|lo|gie [urolo'gi:] F **-**, no pl urology

u|ro|lo|gisch [uro'lo:gɪʃ] ADJ urological

Ur-: **Ur|oma** F (inf) great-granny (inf); **Ur|opa** M (inf) great-grandad (inf); **Ur|pflan|ze** F primordial plant; **ur|plötz|lich** (inf) **ADJ** attr very sudden **ADV** all of a sudden; **Ur|quell** M , **Ur|quel|le** **F** (geh) primary source, fountainhead

Ur|sa|che ['u:ɐzaxə] F cause (auch Philos); (= Grund) reason; (= Beweggrund) motive; (= Anlass) occasion; **~ und Wirkung** cause and effect; **kleine ~, große Wirkung** (prov) big oaks from little acorns grow (prov); **keine ~!** (auf Dank) don't mention it!, you're welcome!; (auf Entschuldigung) that's all right; **ohne (jede) ~** for no reason (at all); **aus nichtiger ~** for a trifling reason/trifling reasons; **aus unbekannter ~** for no apparent reason; **aus ungeklärter ~** for reasons unknown; **jdm ~ geben, etw zu tun** to give sb cause to do sth; **ich habe alle ~ anzunehmen, dass ...** I have every reason to suppose that ...; **alle/keine ~ zu etw haben** to have every/no reason for sth; **alle/keine ~ haben, etw zu tun** to have every/no reason to do sth; **die ~ einer Sache** (gen) or **für etw sein** to be the cause of/ reason for sth

Ur|sa|chen|for|schung F (Philos) aetiology (Brit), etiology (US); **wir müssen etwas ~ betreiben** (= nach den Ursachen forschen) we need to do some research into the causes of this

ur|säch|lich ['u:ɐzɛçlɪç] ADJ (esp Philos) causal; **~ für etw sein** to be the cause of sth; **in ~em Zusammenhang stehen** to be causally related

Ur|säch|lich|keit F (esp Philos) causality

Ur-: Ur|schlamm M primeval mud; **Ur|-schleim** M protoplasm; **Ur|schrei** M (*Psych*) primal scream; **Ur|schrift** F original (text *or* copy); **ur|schrift|lich** ADJ original in the original; **ur+sen|den** [ˈuːrɛzɛndn] VT *sep infin, ptp only* (*Rad*) to broadcast for the first time; **das wurde im April urgesendet** that was first broadcast in April; **Ur|sen|dung** F (*Rad*) first broadcast

urspr. *abbr von* **ursprünglich**

Ur|spra|che F **a** proto-language **b** (*bei Übersetzungen*) original (language), source language

Ur|sprung [ˈuːɐʃprʊŋ] M **a** origin; (= *Anfang auch*) beginning; (= *Abstammung*) extraction; **er ist keltischen ~s** he is of Celtic extraction; **dieses Wort ist keltischen ~s** this word is Celtic in origin *or* is of Celtic origin; **seinen ~ in etw** (*dat*) **haben, einer Sache** (*dat*) **seinen ~ verdanken** to originate in sth, to have its origins in sth; **seinen ~ in etw** (*dat*) **nehmen** to originate in sth **b** (= *Quelle*) source

ur|spröng|lich [ˈuːrʃprʏŋlɪç, uːɐˈʃp-] ADJ **a** *attr* original; (= *anfänglich*) initial, first **b** (= *urwüchsig*) natural; *Natur* unspoilt ADV originally; (= *anfänglich*) initially, at first, in the beginning

Ur|spröng|lich|keit F -, *no pl* naturalness

Ur|sprungs-: Ur|sprungs|be|zeich|nung F (*Comm*) designation of origin; **kontrollierte ~** registered designation of (country of) origin; (*bei Wein*) appellation contrôlée; **Ur|sprungs|land** NT (*Comm*) country of origin

Ur|ständ [ˈuːrʃtɛnt] F (fröhliche) ~ **feiern** (*hum*) to come back with a vengeance, to come to life again

Ur|strom|tal NT (*Geol, Geog*) glacial valley (*in North Germany*)

Ur|sup|pe F primeval soup

Ur|teil [ˈʊrtail] NT -s, -e **a** judgement (*auch Philos*); (= *Entscheidung*) decision; (= *Meinung*) opinion; **nach meinem ~** in my judgement/opinion; **ich kann darüber kein ~ abgeben** I am no judge of this; **sich** (*dat*) **ein ~ über jdn/etw erlauben, ein ~ über jdn/etw fällen** to pass judgement on sb/sth; **sich** (*dat*) **kein ~ über etw** (*acc*) **erlauben können** to be in no position to judge sth; **nach dem ~ von Sachverständigen** according to expert opinion; **jdn in seinem ~ bestärken** to strengthen sb in his opinion; **(sich) mit seinem ~ zurückhalten** to reserve judgement; **zu dem ~ kommen, dass ...** to come to the conclusion that ...; **sich** (*dat*) **ein ~ über jdn/etw bilden** to form an opinion about sb/sth **b** (*Jur*) (= *Gerichtsurteil*) verdict; (= *Richterspruch*) judgement; (= *Strafmaß*) sentence; (= *Schiedsspruch*) award; (= *Scheidungsspruch*) decree; **das ~ über jdn sprechen** (*Jur*) to pass *or* to pronounce judgement on sb; **jdm/sich selber sein ~ sprechen** (*fig*) to pronounce sb's/one's own sentence

ur|tei|len [ˈʊrtailən] VI to judge (*nach* by); **über etw** (*acc*) **~ to judge sth; (= *seine Meinung äußern*) to give one's opinion on sth; **hart über jdn ~** to judge sb harshly; **abfällig über jdn ~** to be disparaging about sb; **nach seinem Aussehen zu ~**

judging by *or* to judge by his appearance; **vor|schnell ~** to make a hasty judgement

Ur|teils-: Ur|teils|be|grün|dung F (*Jur*) opinion; **ur|teils|fä|hig** ADJ competent *or* able to judge; (= *umsichtig*) discerning, discriminating; **dazu ist er ~ genug** his judgement is sound enough for that; **Ur|teils|fä|hig|keit** F competence *or* ability to judge; (= *Umsichtigkeit*) discernment, discrimination; **Ur|teils|fin|dung** [-fɪndʊŋ] F -, -en (*Jur*) reaching a verdict *no art*; **Ur|teils|kraft** F , *no pl* power *or* faculty of judgement; (= *Umsichtigkeit*) discernment, discrimination; „**Kritik der ~**" "Critique of Judgement"; **Ur|teils|schel|te** F attack on a/the court's ruling; **Ur|teils|spruch** M (*Jur*) judgement; (*von Geschworenen*) verdict; (*von Strafgericht*) sentence; (*von Schiedsgericht*) award; **Ur|teils|ver|kün|dung** F (*Jur*) pronouncement of judgement; **Ur|teils|ver|mö|gen** NT faculty of judgement; (= *Umsichtigkeit*) discernment, discrimination; **Ur|teils|voll|stre|ckung** F (*Jur*) execution of a/the sentence

Ur-: Ur|text M original (text); **Ur|tie|fe** F (*liter*) depth(s *pl*); **Ur|tier** NT , **Ur|tier|chen** NT protozoon (*esp Brit*), protozoan; (*in der Morphologie*) primordial animal; **Ur|trieb** M basic drive *or* instinct; **ur|tüm|lich** [ˈuːrtyːmlɪç] ADJ = **urwüchsig**; **Ur|tüm|lich|keit** F -, *no pl* = **Urwüchsigkeit**; **Ur|typ** M , **Ur|ty|pus** M prototype

U|ru|guay [ˈuːrugvai, ˈʊr-, uruˈɡwai] NT -s Uruguay

Ur|ur- [ˈuːrʔuːɐ] *in cpds* great-great-; **Ur|ur|groß|mut|ter** F great-great-grandmother; **Ur|ur|groß|va|ter** M great-great-grandfather

Ur-: Ur|va|ter M forefather; **Ur|vä|ter|zeit** [ˈuːrfɛːtɛtsait] F olden times *pl*; **seit ~en** from time immemorial; **schon zur ~** even in olden times; **Ur|ver|trau|en** NT basic trust, primal sense of trust; **ur|ver|wandt** ADJ *Wörter, Sprachen* cognate; **Ur|viech** NT , **Ur|vieh** NT (*inf*) real character; **Ur|vo|gel** M archaeopteryx; **Ur|volk** NT first people; **Ur|wahl** F (*Pol*) primary (election); **Ur|wäh|ler(in)** M(F) (*Pol*) primary elector (*Brit*) *or* voter

Ur|wald M primeval forest; (*in den Tropen*) jungle

Ur|wald|lau|te PL (*inf*) jungle noises *pl*

Ur-: Ur|weib NT (*inf*) real woman; **Ur|welt** F primeval world; **ur|welt|lich** ADJ primeval; **ur|wüch|sig** [ˈuːrvyːksɪç] ADJ (= *unverbildet, naturhaft*) natural; *Natur* unspoilt; (= *urweltlich*) Flora, Fauna primeval; (= *ursprünglich*) original, native; (= *bodenständig*) rooted in the soil; (= *unberührt*) Land *etc* untouched; (= *urgewaltig*) Kraft elemental; (= *derb, kräftig*) sturdy; Mensch rugged; Humor, Sprache earthy; **Ur|zeit** F primeval times *pl*; **seit ~en** since primeval times; (*inf*) for donkey's years (*Brit inf*), for aeons (*Brit inf*) *or* eons (*US inf*); **vor ~en** in primeval times; (*inf*) ages ago; **ur|zeit|lich** ADJ primeval; **Ur|zel|le** F (*Biol*) primordial cell; **Ur|zeu|gung** F abiogenesis; **Ur|zu|stand** M primordial *or* original state

USA [uːʔɛsˈʔaː] PL **die ~** the USA *sing*; **in die ~ fahren** to travel to the USA

U|sam|ba|ra|veil|chen [uzamˈbaːra-] NT African violet

US-ame|ri|ka|nisch [uːˈʔɛs-] ADJ American

U|sance [yˈzãːs] F -, -n usage, custom; (*Comm*) practice

Use|net [ˈjuːsnɛt] NT -s, -s (*Comput*) Usenet

U|ser [ˈjuːzɐ] M -s, - , **U|se|rin** [ˈjuːzərɪn] F -, -nen (*Comput*) user

usf. *abbr von* **und so fort**

U|sur|pa|ti|on [uzʊrpaˈtsioːn] F -, -en (*liter*) usurpation

U|sur|pa|tor [uzʊrˈpaːtoːɐ] M -s, Usurpatoren [-ˈtoːrən], **U|sur|pa|to|rin** [-ˈtoːrɪn] F -, -nen (*liter*) usurper

u|sur|pa|to|risch [uzʊrpaˈtoːrɪʃ] ADJ (*liter*) usurpatory, usurpative

u|sur|pie|ren [uzʊrˈpiːrən] *ptp* **usurpiert** VT (*liter*) to usurp

U|sus [ˈuːzʊs] M -s, *no pl* custom; **das ist hier so ~** it's the custom here

usw. *abbr von* **und so weiter** etc

U|ten|sil [utɛnˈziːl] NT -s, -ien [-liən] utensil, implement

U|te|rus [ˈuːterʊs] M -, Uteri [-ri] uterus

U|ti|li|ta|ris|mus [utilitaˈrɪsmʊs] M -, *no pl* Utilitarianism

U|ti|li|ta|rist [utilitaˈrɪst] M -en, -en, **U|ti|li|ta|ris|tin** [-ˈrɪstɪn] F -, -nen Utilitarian

u|ti|li|ta|ris|tisch [utilitaˈrɪstɪʃ] ADJ utilitarian

U|to|pia [uˈtoːpia] NT -s, -s Utopia

U|to|pie [utoˈpiː] F -, -n [-ˈpiːən] utopia; (= *Wunschtraum*) utopian dream

u|to|pisch [uˈtoːpɪʃ] ADJ utopian; (= *von Utopia*) Utopian

U|to|pis|mus [utoˈpɪsmʊs] M -, *no pl* utopianism

U|to|pist [utoˈpɪst] M -en, -en, **U|to|pis|tin** [-ˈpɪstɪn] F -, -nen utopian

u|to|pis|tisch [utoˈpɪstɪʃ] ADJ (*pej*) utopian

u. U. *abbr von* **unter Umständen**

UV [uːˈfau] *abbr von* **ultraviolett**

UV- [uːˈfau] *in cpds* ultraviolet

u. v. a. (m.) *abbr von* **und vieles andere (mehr)**

U. v. D. [uːfauˈdeː] M -s, -s (*Mil*) *abbr von* **Unteroffizier vom Dienst**

UV-: UV-Fil|ter [uːˈfau-] M UV *or* ultraviolet filter; **UV-Strah|len** [uːˈfau-] PL ultraviolet rays *pl*

Ü-Wa|gen [ˈyː-] M (*Rad, TV*) outside broadcast vehicle

Uz [ˈuːts] M -es, -e *usu sing* (*inf*) tease *sing* (*inf*), leg-pull (*inf*), joke

u|zen [ˈuːtsn] VTI (*inf*) to tease, to kid (*inf*)

U|ze|rei [uːtsəˈrai] F -, -en (*dial, inf*) teasing, kidding (*inf*)

Uz|na|me M (*inf*) nickname

V

V, v [faʊ] NT **-, -** V, v

V abbr von **Volt** von **Volumen**

Va|banque ▲ [va'bãːk], **va banque** ADV ~ or **va banque spielen** (geh) to play vabanque; (fig) to put everything at stake

Va|banque|spiel [va'bãːk-] NT (fig) dangerous game

Va|duz [fa'dʊts, va'duːts] NT -' Vaduz

vag [vaːk] ADJ = **vage**

Va|ga|bund [vaga'bʊnt] M **-en, -en** [-dn], **Va|ga|bun|din** [-'bʊndɪn] F **-, -nen** vagabond

Va|ga|bun|den|le|ben NT vagabond life; (fig auch) roving life

va|ga|bun|die|ren [vagabʊn'diːrən] ptp **vaga-bundiert** VI **a** (= als Landstreicher leben) to live as a vagabond/as vagabonds; **das Vagabundie-ren** vagabondage; **ein ~des Volk** a nomadic people **b** aux sein (= umherziehen) to rove a-round, to lead a vagabond life; **durch die Welt ~** to rove or wander all over the world

va|ge ['vaːgə] ADJ vague ADV vaguely; **etw ~ an-deuten** to give a vague indication of sth; **drück dich nicht so ~ aus!** don't be so vague!

Vag|heit ['vaːkhait] F **-, -en** vagueness

Va|gi|na [va'giːna] F **-, Vaginen** [-nən] vagina

va|gi|nal [vagi'naːl] ADJ vaginal ADV vaginally; **ertasten** through the vaginal canal; **~ untersucht werden** to have a vaginal examination

va|kant [va'kant] ADJ (old, form) vacant

Va|kanz [va'kants] F **-, -en** (old, form: = Stelle) va-cancy; (old, dial: = Ferien) vacation

Va|kat ['vaːkat] NT **-(s), -s** (Typ) blank (page)

Va|ku|um ['vaːkuʊm] NT **-s, Vakuen** or **Vakua** [-kuən, -kua] (lit, fig) vacuum; **unter/im ~** in a vacuum

Va|ku|um-, va|ku|um- in cpds vacuum; **Va|ku|um|pum|pe** F vacuum pump; **Va|ku|um|röh-re** F vacuum tube; **va|ku|um|ver|packt** [-fɛɐ̯-pakt] ADJ vacuum-packed; **Va|ku|um|ver|pa-ckung** F vacuum pack; (das Verpacken) vacu-um packaging; **va|ku|um|ver|sie|gelt** [-fɛɐ̯-ziːɡlt] ADJ vacuum-sealed

Va|len|tins|tag ['vaːlɛntiːns-] M (St) Valentine's Day

Va|lenz [va'lɛnts] F **-, -en** valency

val|le|ri, val|le|ra [falə'riː, falə'raː] INTERJ fal-deral (esp Brit), folderol

Va|lo|ren [va'loːrən] PL (Sw Fin) securities pl

Va|lu|ta [va'luːta] F **-, Valuten** [-tn] **a** (= Wäh-rung) foreign currency **b** (im Zahlungsverkehr) value; (= Datum) value date

Va|lu|ta-: Va|lu|ta|ge|schäft NT (Fin) curren-cy draft; **Va|lu|ta|klau|sel** F (Fin) exchange clause

Vamp [vɛmp] M **-s, -s** vamp

Vam|pir [vam'piːɐ̯] M **-s, -e** vampire; (Zool) vam-pire (bat)

Vam|pi|ris|mus [vampi'rɪsmʊs] M **-, no pl** vam-pirism

Va|na|din [vana'diːn] NT **-s, no pl, Va|na|di|um** [va'naːdiʊm] NT **-s, no pl** (abbr **V**) vanadium

Van-Al|len-Gür|tel [vɛn'ɛlɪn-] M Van Allen belt

Van|da|le [van'daːlə] M **-n, -n, Van|da|lin** [-'daː-lɪn] F **-, -nen** vandal; (Hist) Vandal

Van|da|lis|mus [vanda'lɪsmʊs] M **-, no pl** van-dalism

Va|nil|le [va'nɪljə, va'nɪlə] F **-, no pl** vanilla

Va|nil|le-: Va|nil|le|eis NT vanilla ice cream; **Va|nil|le|ge|schmack** M vanilla flavour (Brit) or flavor (US); **mit ~** vanilla-flavoured (Brit), vanilla-flavored (US); **Va|nil|le|kip|ferl** NT (Aus) small crescent-shaped biscuit made with almond pastry and sprinkled with va-nilla sugar; **Va|nil|le|pud|ding** M ≈ vanilla blancmange; **Va|nil|le|sau|ce** F custard; **Va|nil|le|stan|ge** F vanilla pod; **Va|nil|le|zu-cker** M , **Va|nil|lin|zu|cker** [vanɪˈliːn-] M va-nilla sugar

Va|nil|lin [vanɪ'liːn] NT **-, no pl** (Chem) vanillin

va|ri|a|bel [va'riaːbl] ADJ variable ADV **~ ver-zinsliche Anleihen** loans at a variable interest rate

Va|ri|a|bi|li|tät [variabili'tɛːt] F **-, no pl** variabili-ty

Va|ri|a|ble [va'riaːblə] F decl as adj variable

Va|ri|an|te [va'riantə] F **-, -en** variant (zu on)

Va|ri|a|ti|on [varia'tsioːn] F **-, -en** (alle Bedeutun-gen) variation; **~en zu einem Thema** variations on a theme

Va|ri|a|ti|ons-: va|ri|a|ti|ons|fä|hig ADJ capa-ble of variation; **Va|ri|a|ti|ons|mög|lich|keit** F possibility of variation

Va|ri|e|tät [varie'tɛːt] F **-, -en** (auch Bot, Zool) va-riety

Va|ri|e|tee ▲ [varie'teː] NT **-s, -s, Va|ri|e|té** NT **-s, -s** **a** variety (entertainment), vaudeville (esp US) **b** (= Theater) variety theatre (Brit) or theater (US), music hall (Brit), vaudeville thea-ter (US)

va|ri|ie|ren [vari'iːrən] ptp **variiert** VTI to vary

Va|sall [va'zal] M **-en, -en** (Hist, fig) vassal

Va|sal|len-: Va|sal|len|pflicht F (Hist) vassal-age, feudal service; **Va|sal|len|staat** M (Hist) vassal state; (fig) client or satellite state; **Va|sal|len|tum** [va'zaləntuːm] NT **-s, no pl** vassal-age

Väs|chen ['vɛːsçən] NT **-s, -** little vase

Va|se ['vaːzə] F **-, -n** vase

Va|sek|to|mie [vazɛkto'miː] F **-, -n** [-'miːən] (spec) vasectomy

Va|se|lin [vaze'liːn] NT **-s, no pl, Va|se|li|ne** [va-ze'liːnə] F **-, no pl** Vaseline®

va|so|mo|to|risch [vazomo'toːrɪʃ] ADJ vasomo-tor attr, vasomotory ADV **~ gestört sein** to have a vasomotory disorder

Va|ter ['faːtɐ] M **-s, ⸚** ['fɛːtɐ] (lit, fig) father; (Gott, bei Namen) Father; (von Zuchttieren) sire; **~ von zwei Kindern sein** to be the father of two chil-dren; **~ unser** (Rel) Our Father; **unsere Väter** pl (geh: = Vorfahren) our (fore)fathers, our fore-bears; **wie der ~, so der Sohn** (prov) like father, like son (prov); **er ist ganz der ~** he's very like his father; **~ werden ist nicht schwer, ~ sein da-gegen sehr** (prov) becoming a father is easy, be-ing one is a different matter; **wer war der ~ die-ses Gedankens?** whose idea was that?; **ach du dicker ~!** (inf) oh my goodness!, oh heavens!; **~ Staat** (hum) the State

Vä|ter|chen ['fɛːtɐçən] NT **-s, -** dim von **Vater** (= Vater) dad(dy) (inf); (= alter Mann) grandad (inf); **~ Staat** (hum) the State

Va|ter-: Va|ter|fi|gur F father figure; **Va|ter-freu|den** PL joys pl of fatherhood; **Va|ter-haus** NT parental home

Va|ter|land NT native country; (esp Deutsch-land) Fatherland; **dem ~ dienen** to serve one's country; **sein ~ lieben** to love one's country

va|ter|län|disch [-lɛndɪʃ] ADJ (= national) na-tional; (= patriotisch) patriotic; **(Großer) Vater-ländischer Krieg** (Great) Patriotic War

Va|ter|lands-: Va|ter|lands|lie|be F patriot-ism, love of one's country; **va|ter|lands|lie-bend** ADJ patriotic; **va|ter|lands|los** ADJ without a native land (esp poet); (= staatenlos) stateless; **Va|ter|lands|ver|rä|ter(in)** M(F) traitor to one's country; (in Deutschland auch) traitor to the Fatherland

vä|ter|lich ['fɛːtəlɪç] ADJ (= vom Vater) paternal; (= wie ein Vater auch) fatherly ADV like a father; **er klopfte ihm ~ auf die Schulter** he gave him a fatherly pat on the shoulder

vä|ter|li|cher|seits ADV on one's father's side; **meine Großeltern ~** my paternal grandparents

Vä|ter|lich|keit F **-, no pl** fatherliness

Va|ter-: Va|ter|lie|be F paternal or fatherly love; **~ ist unersetzbar** a father's love is irre-placeable; **va|ter|los** ADJ fatherless; **~ auf-wachsen** to grow up without a father; **Va|ter-mord** M patricide; **Va|ter|mör|der** M (hum, Kragen) stand-up collar, choker (dated); **Va|ter|mör|der(in)** M(F) patricide, father-killer (inf); **Va|ter|mord** NT patriarchy

Va|ter|schaft ['faːtɐʃaft] F **-, no pl** fatherhood no art; (esp Jur) paternity; **gerichtliche Feststellung der ~** (Jur) affiliation

Va|ter|schafts-: Va|ter|schafts|be|stim-mung F determination of paternity; **Va|ter-schafts|kla|ge** F paternity suit; **Va|ter-schafts|nach|weis** M proof of paternity; **Va|ter|schafts|pro|zess** ▲ M paternity suit; **Va|ter|schafts|test** M paternity test

Va|ter|sit|te F tradition of one's forefathers

Va|ter(s)|na|me M (old) surname

Va|ter-: Va|ter|stadt F home town; **Va|ter-stel|le** F **bei jdm ~ vertreten** to act or be a fa-ther to sb; **bei jdm an ~ stehen** to take the place of sb's father; **Va|ter|tag** M Father's Day; **Va|ter|un|ser** ['faːtɐˈʔʊnzɐ, faːtɐˈʔʊnzɐ] NT **-s, -** Lord's Prayer

Va|ti ['faːti] M **-s, -s** (inf) dad(dy) (inf)

Va|ti|kan [vati'kaːn] M **-s** Vatican

va|ti|ka|nisch [vati'kaːnɪʃ] ADJ attr Vatican; **Va-tikanisches Konzil** Vatican Council

Va|ti|kan|staat M , no pl Vatican State

Va|ti|kan|stadt F , no pl Vatican City

V-Aus|schnitt ['fau-] M V-neck; **ein Pullover mit ~** a V-neck jumper (Brit) or pullover

v. Chr. abbr von **vor Christus** BC

VDE [faʊdeː'eː] M **-s, no pl** abbr von **Verband Deutscher Elektrotechniker**

VEB [faue:'be:] M **-s, -s** (DDR) abbr von **Volkseigener Betrieb**

Ve|du|te [ve'du:tə] F **-, -n** (Art) veduta

Ve|ga|ner [ve'ga:nɐ] M **-s, -**, **Ve|ga|ne|rin** [-ərɪn] F **-, -nen** vegan

Ve|ge|ta|bi|le(r) [vegeta'bi:lə] MF decl as adj vegetarian

Ve|ge|ta|ri|er [vege'ta:riɐ] M **-s, -**, **Ve|ge|ta|ri|e|rin** [-iərɪn] F **-, -nen** vegetarian

ve|ge|ta|risch [vege'ta:rɪʃ] ADJ vegetarian ADV **~ leben** to be a vegetarian; **sich ~ ernähren** to live on a vegetarian diet; **~ kochen** to cook vegetarian meals

Ve|ge|ta|ris|mus [vegeta'rɪsmʊs] M **-**, no pl vegetarianism

Ve|ge|ta|ti|on [vegeta'tsio:n] F **-, -en** vegetation

Ve|ge|ta|ti|ons|pe|ri|o|de F vegetation period

ve|ge|ta|tiv [vegeta'ti:f] ADJ (= pflanzlich) vegetative; Nervensystem autonomic ADV (Bot) vegetatively, asexually; **~ bedingt** (Med) caused by the autonomic nervous system

ve|ge|tie|ren [vege'ti:rən] ptp **vegetiert** VI to vegetate; (= kärglich leben) to eke out a bare or miserable existence

ve|he|ment [vehe'mɛnt] (geh) ADJ vehement ADV vehemently

Ve|he|menz [vehe'mɛnts] F **-**, no pl (geh) vehemence

Ve|hi|kel [ve'hikl] NT **-s, -** **a** (pej inf) (= Fahrrad) boneshaker (Brit inf), old bike (inf); (= Auto) jalopy (inf) **b** (Pharm, fig geh) vehicle

Veil|chen ['failçən] NT **-s, -** violet; (inf: = blaues Auge) shiner (inf), black eye; **sie ist bescheiden wie ein ~, das im Verborgenen blüht** she is modesty itself; **blau wie ein** or **tausend ~** (inf) drunk as a lord (Brit inf) or a sailor (US inf), roaring drunk (inf)

veil|chen|blau ADJ violet; (inf: = betrunken) roaring drunk (inf)

Veits|tanz ['faits-] M (Med) St Vitus's dance; **einen ~ aufführen** (fig inf) to jump or hop about (Brit) or around like crazy (inf)

Vek|tor ['vɛkto:ɐ] M **-s, Vektoren** [-'to:rən] vector

Vek|tor-: Vek|tor|raum M (Math) vector space; **Vek|tor|rech|nung** F (Math) vector analysis

Ve|lar|(laut) [ve'la:ɐ-] M **-s, -e** velar (sound)

Ve|lo ['ve:lo] NT **-s, -s** (Sw) bicycle, bike (inf); (motorisiert) moped

Ve|lour [və'lu:ɐ, ve'lu:ɐ] NT **-s, -s** or **-e**, **Ve|lours**[1] [və'lu:ɐ, ve'lu:ɐ] NT **-, -** (auch **Velours|leder**) suede

Ve|lours[2] M **-, -** (Tex) velour(s)

Ve|lours|tep|pich [və'lu:ɐ-, ve'lu:ɐ-] M velvet carpet

Ven|det|ta [vɛn'dɛta] F **-, Vendetten** [-tn] vendetta

Ve|ne ['ve:nə] F **-, -n** vein

Ve|ne|dig [ve'ne:dɪç] NT **-s** Venice

Ve|nen|ent|zün|dung F phlebitis

Ve|nen|lei|den NT varicose veins pl

ve|ne|risch [ve'ne:rɪʃ] ADJ (Med) venereal

Ve|ne|ro|lo|gie [venerolo'gi:] F **-**, no pl (Med) venereology

Ve|ne|zi|a|ner [vene'tsia:nɐ] M **-s, -**, **Ve|ne|zi|a|ne|rin** [-ərɪn] F **-, -nen** Venetian

ve|ne|zi|a|nisch [vene'tsia:nɪʃ] ADJ Venetian

Ve|ne|zo|la|ner [venetso'la:nɐ] M **-s, -**, **Ve|ne|zo|la|ne|rin** [-ərɪn] F **-, -nen** Venezuelan

ve|ne|zo|la|nisch [venetso'la:nɪʃ] ADJ Venezuelan

Ve|ne|zu|e|la [vene'tsue:la] NT **-s** Venezuela

Ve|nia Le|gen|di ['ve:niale'gɛndi] F **- -**, no pl (Univ) authorization to teach at a university

ve|nös [ve'nø:s] ADJ venous

Ven|til [vɛn'ti:l] NT **-s, -e** (Tech, Mus) valve; (fig) outlet

Ven|ti|la|ti|on [vɛntila'tsio:n] F **-, -en** ventilation; (Anlage) ventilation system

Ven|ti|la|tor [vɛnti'la:to:ɐ] M **-s, Ventilatoren** [-'to:rən] ventilator

ven|ti|lie|ren [vɛnti'li:rən] ptp **ventiliert** VT (geh) to ventilate; (fig) (= äußern) to air; (= erwägen) to examine, to consider carefully

Ve|nus ['ve:nʊs] F **-'**, no pl (Myth, Astron) Venus

Ve|nus-

Ve|nus|hü|gel M (Anat) mons veneris (spec)

Ve|nus|mu|schel F (Zool) hard or round clam

ver|ab|fol|gen [fɛɐ'apfɔlgn] ptp **verabfolgt** VT (form) Medizin etc to administer (form) (jdm to sb); (= verordnen) to prescribe (jdm for sb)

ver|ab|re|den [fɛɐ'apre:dn] ptp **verabredet** VT to arrange; Termin auch to fix, to agree upon; Maßnahmen to agree; Straftat to collude in; Mord to conspire in; **es war eine verabredete Sache** it was arranged beforehand; **ein vorher verabredetes Zeichen** a prearranged signal; **zum verabredeten Zeitpunkt** at the agreed time; **am verabredeten Ort** at the agreed place; **wir haben verabredet, dass wir uns um 5 Uhr treffen** we have arranged to meet at 5 o'clock; **wie verabredet** as arranged; **schon verabredet sein** to have a previous or prior engagement (esp form), to have something else on (inf); **mit jdm verabredet sein** to have arranged to meet sb; (geschäftlich, formell) to have an appointment with sb; (esp mit Freund/Freundin) to have a date with sb
VR **sich mit jdm ~** to arrange to meet sb; (geschäftlich, formell) to arrange an appointment with sb; (esp mit Freund/Freundin) to make a date with sb; (Jur) to collude with sb; **sich miteinander ~** to arrange to meet; (geschäftlich, formell) to arrange an appointment; (esp mit Freund/Freundin) to make a date; (Jur) to collude

Ver|ab|re|dung F **-, -en** (= Vereinbarung) arrangement, agreement; (= Treffen) engagement (form); (geschäftlich, formell) appointment; (esp mit Freund/Freundin) date; (Jur) collusion; (von Mord, Hochverrat, Meuterei) conspiracy; **ich habe eine ~** I'm meeting somebody; **~ einer Straftat** (Jur) collusion/conspiracy to commit a criminal offence (Brit) or offense (US)

ver|ab|rei|chen [fɛɐ'apraiçn] ptp **verabreicht** VT Tracht Prügel etc to give; Arznei, Droge auch to administer (form) (jdm to sb); (= verordnen) to prescribe (jdm for sb); (old) Speise to serve

Ver|ab|rei|chung F **-, -en** (form) (von Tracht Prügel) giving; (von Arznei) administering; (= Verordnung) prescription; (old: von Speisen) serving

ver|ab|säu|men [fɛɐ'apzɔymən] ptp **verabsäumt** VT (form) to neglect, to omit

ver|ab|scheu|en [fɛɐ'apʃɔyən] ptp **verabscheut** VT to detest, to abhor, to loathe

ver|ab|scheu|ens|wert ADJ detestable, abhorrent, loathsome

Ver|ab|scheu|ung F **-**, no pl detestation, abhorrence, loathing

ver|ab|scheu|ungs|wür|dig ADJ = verabscheuenswert

ver|ab|schie|den [fɛɐ'apʃi:dn] ptp **verabschiedet** VT to say goodbye to; (= Abschiedsfeier veranstalten für) to hold a farewell ceremony for; (= entlassen) Beamte, Truppen to discharge; (Pol) Haushaltsplan to adopt; Gesetz, Erklärung to pass; **wie bist du von deinen Kollegen/bei deiner Stelle verabschiedet worden?** what sort of a farewell did your colleagues arrange for you/ did you receive at work?
VR **sich (von jdm) ~** to say goodbye (to sb), to take one's leave (of sb) (form), to bid sb farewell (liter); **er ist gegangen, ohne sich zu ~** he left without saying goodbye; **sich von etw ~** (fig) to turn one's back on sth; **sich aus etw ~** (fig) to withdraw from sth

Ver|ab|schie|dung F **-, -en** (von Beamten etc) discharge; (Pol) (von Gesetz) passing; (von Haushaltsplan) adoption

ver|ab|so|lu|tie|ren [fɛɐapzolu'ti:rən] ptp **verabsolutiert** VT to make absolute

ver|ach|ten ptp **verachtet** VT to despise; jdn auch to hold in contempt; (liter) Tod, Gefahr to scorn; **nicht zu ~** (inf) not to be despised, not to be scoffed at, not to be sneezed at (inf); **einen guten Whisky hat er nie verachtet** (inf) he never said no to a good drop of whisky

ver|ach|tens|wert ADJ despicable, contemptible

Ver|äch|ter [fɛɐ'ɛçtɐ] M **-s, -**, **Ver|äch|te|rin** [-ərɪn] F **-, -nen** kein **~ von etw sein** to be quite partial to sth

ver|ächt|lich [fɛɐ'ɛçtlɪç] ADJ contemptuous, scornful; (= verachtenswert) despicable, contemptible; **jdn/etw ~ machen** to run sb down/belittle sth ADV contemptuously, scornfully

Ver|ach|tung F **-**, no pl contempt (von for); **jdn mit ~ strafen** to treat sb with contempt

ver|ach|tungs|voll ADJ contemptuous, disdainful

ver|al|bern [fɛɐ'albɐn] ptp **veralbert** VT (inf) to make fun of; **du willst mich wohl ~** are you pulling my leg? (inf)

ver|all|ge|mei|nern [fɛɐalgə'mainɐn] ptp **verallgemeinert** VTI to generalize

Ver|all|ge|mei|ne|rung F **-, -en** generalization

ver|al|ten [fɛɐ'altn] ptp **veraltet** VI aux sein to become obsolete; (Ansichten, Methoden) to become antiquated; (Mode) to go out of date

ver|al|tet [fɛɐ'altət] ADJ obsolete; Ansichten antiquated; Mode out-of-date

Ve|ran|da [ve'randa] F **-, Veranden** [-dn] veranda, porch

ver|än|der|bar ADJ changeable

Ver|än|der|bar|keit F **-, -en** changeability, changeableness

ver|än|der|lich [fɛɐ'ɛndəlɪç] ADJ variable; Wetter, Mensch changeable

Ver|än|der|lich|keit F **-, -en** variability

ver|än|dern ptp **verändert** VT to change VR to change; (= Stellung wechseln) to change one's job; (= Wohnung wechseln) to move; **sich zu seinem Vorteil/Nachteil ~** (im Aussehen) to look better/worse; (charakterlich) to change for the better/worse; **verändert aussehen** to look different

Ver|än|de|rung F change; **eine berufliche ~** a change of job

ver|ängs|ti|gen ptp **verängstigt** VT (= erschrecken) to frighten, to scare; (= einschüchtern) to intimidate

ver|an|kern ptp **verankert** VT (Naut, Tech) to anchor (in +dat in); (fig) Rechte etc (in Gesetz) to establish, to ground; Gedanken (in Bewusstsein) to embed, to fix; **gesetzlich verankert** established in law

Ver|an|ke|rung F **-, -en** (Naut, Tech) (= das Verankern) anchoring; (= das Verankertsein) anchorage; (fig) (von Rechten) (firm) establishment; (von Gedanken) embedding, fixing

ver|an|la|gen [fɛɐ'anla:gn] ptp **veranlagt** VT to assess (mit at)

ver|an|lagt [fɛɐ'anla:kt] ADJ **melancholisch/tuberkulös ~ sein** to have a melancholy/tubercular disposition; **technisch/mathematisch/praktisch ~ sein** to be technically/mathematically/ practically minded; **künstlerisch/musikalisch ~ sein** to have an artistic/a musical bent; **zu ~** **für etw ~ sein** to be cut out for sth; **er ist so ~, dass ...** it's his nature to ...; **er ist eben so ~** that's just the way he is, that's just his nature

Ver|an|la|gung F **-, -en** **a** (körperlich, esp Med) predisposition; (charakterlich) nature, disposition; (= Hang) tendency; (= allgemeine Fähigkeiten) natural abilities pl; (= künstlerisches, praktisches etc Talent) bent; **eine ~ zum Dickwerden haben** to have a tendency to put on weight; **eine ~ zur Kriminalität haben** to have criminal tendencies **b** (von Steuern) assessment

ver|an|las|sen [fɛɐ̯'ʔanlasn] ptp **veranlasst** VT **a** etw ~ (= in die Wege leiten) to arrange for sth, to see to it that sth is done; (= befehlen) to order sth; **eine Maßnahme ~** to arrange for/order a measure to be taken; **ich werde das Nötige ~** I will see (to it) that the necessary steps are taken; **wir werden alles Weitere ~** we will see to or take care of or see to everything else **b** auch vi (= bewirken) to give rise (zu to); **jdn zu ~** (Ereignis etc) to lead sb to sth; (Mensch) to cause sb to do sth; **jdn (dazu) ~, etw zu tun** (Ereignis etc) to lead sb to do sth; (Mensch) to cause sb to do sth; **das veranlasst zu der Annahme, dass ...** that leads one to assume that ...; **sich (dazu) veranlasst fühlen, etw zu tun** to feel compelled or obliged to do sth

Ver|an|las|sung F -, -en cause, reason; **auf ~ von** or **+gen** at the instigation of; **keine ~ zu etw haben** to have no cause or reason for sth; **keine ~ haben, etw zu tun** to have no cause or reason to do sth or for doing sth; **~ zu etw geben** to give cause for sth

ver|an|schau|li|chen [fɛɐ̯'ʔanʃau̯lɪçn] ☉ 53.5 ptp **veranschaulicht** VT to illustrate (+dat to, an +dat, mit with); **sich (dat) etw ~** to picture sth (to oneself), to visualize sth; **sich (dat) ~, dass ...** to see or realize that ...

Ver|an|schau|li|chung F -, -en illustration; **zur ~** as an illustration, to illustrate sth

ver|an|schla|gen ptp **veranschlagt** VT to estimate (auf +acc at); **etw zu hoch ~** to overestimate sth; **etw zu niedrig ~** to underestimate sth

Ver|an|schla|gung [fɛɐ̯'ʔanʃlaːɡʊŋ] F -, -en estimate; (= das Veranschlagen) estimation

ver|an|stal|ten [fɛɐ̯'ʔanʃtaltn] ptp **veranstaltet** VT to organize, to arrange; (= durchführen) Umfrage to do; (kommerziell) Wettkämpfe, Konzerte etc to promote; Party etc to hold, to give; (inf) Szene to make

Ver|an|stal|ter [fɛɐ̯'ʔanʃtaltɐ] M -s, -, **Ver|an|stal|te|rin** [-ərɪn] F -, -nen organizer; (Comm: von Wettkämpfen, Konzerten etc) promoter

Ver|an|stal|tung [fɛɐ̯'ʔanʃtaltʊŋ] F -, -en **a** event (von organized by); (feierlich, öffentlich) function **b** no pl (= das Veranstalten) organization

Ver|an|stal|tungs-: Ver|an|stal|tungs|be|ginn M start (of the event); (= Kursbeginn) start of the course; **~: 8 Uhr** start: 8 pm or P.M. (US); **Ver|an|stal|tungs|ka|len|der** M calendar of events; **Ver|an|stal|tungs|ort** M venue, location (esp US); **Ver|an|stal|tungs|pro|gramm** NT programme (Brit) or program (US) of events; **Ver|an|stal|tungs|rei|he** F series of events; (= Kursreihe) series of courses; **Ver|an|stal|tungs|ter|min** M date of the event; (= Kurstermin) date of the course

ver|ant|wor|ten ptp **verantwortet** VT to accept (the) responsibility for; die Folgen auch, sein Tun to answer for (vor +dat to); **(es) ~, dass jd etw tut** to accept the responsibility for sb doing sth; **wie könnte ich es denn ~, ...?** it would be most irresponsible of me ...; **ein weiterer Streik** or **solche Operation wäre nicht zu ~** another strike/such an operation would be irresponsible; **eine nicht zu ~de Fahrlässigkeit/ Schlamperei** inexcusable negligence/sloppiness; **etw sich selbst gegenüber ~** to square sth with one's own conscience ▯ **VR** sich für or wegen etw ~ to justify sth (vor +dat to); für Missetaten to answer for sth (vor +dat before); **sich vor Gericht/Gott** etc ~ **müssen** to have to answer to the courts/God etc (für, wegen for)

ver|ant|wort|lich [fɛɐ̯'ʔantvɔrtlɪç] ADJ responsible (für for); (= haftbar) liable; **jdm (gegenüber) ~ sein** to be responsible or answerable or accountable to sb; **jdn für etw ~ machen** to hold sb responsible for sth; **für etw ~ zeichnen**

(form) (lit) to sign for sth; (fig) to take responsibility for sth; **der ~e Leiter des Projekts** the person in charge of the project

Ver|ant|wort|li|che(r) [fɛɐ̯'ʔantvɔrtlɪçə] MF decl as adj person responsible; **die ~n** pl those responsible

Ver|ant|wort|lich|keit F -, -en responsibility; (= Haftbarkeit) liability

Ver|ant|wor|tung [fɛɐ̯'ʔantvɔrtʊŋ] F -, -en responsibility (für for); **auf eigene ~** on one's own responsibility; **auf deine ~!** you take the responsibility!, on your own head be it! (Brit), it's your ass! (US inf); **die ~ übernehmen** to take or accept or assume (esp form) responsibility; **die ~ (für etw) tragen** to take responsibility (for sth); **jdn zur ~ ziehen** to call sb to account; **sich aus der ~ stehlen** to avoid or shirk (one's) responsibility

Ver|ant|wor|tungs-: Ver|ant|wor|tungs|be|reich M area of responsibility; **ver|ant|wor|tungs|be|wusst ▲ ADJ** responsible **ADV** responsibly, conscientiously; **Ver|ant|wor|tungs|be|wusst|sein ▲** NT sense of responsibility; **ver|ant|wor|tungs|freu|dig** ADJ willing to take responsibility; **Ver|ant|wor|tungs|ge|fühl** NT sense of responsibility; **ver|ant|wor|tungs|los ADJ** irresponsible **ADV** irresponsibly; **Ver|ant|wor|tungs|lo|sig|keit** F -, no pl irresponsibility; **ver|ant|wor|tungs|voll ADJ** responsible **ADV** responsibly

ver|äp|peln [fɛɐ̯'ʔɛpln] ptp **veräppelt** VT (inf) **jdn ~** to make fun of sb; (= auf den Arm nehmen) to pull sb's leg (inf)

ver|ar|beit|bar ADJ workable; (Comput) processable; **leicht/schwer ~** easy/hard to work

ver|ar|bei|ten ptp **verarbeitet** VT to use (zu etw to make sth); (Tech, Biol etc) to process; Gold etc to work; (= verbrauchen) to consume; (= verdauen) to digest; (fig) to use (zu for); Stoff to treat; Daten to process; Erlebnis etc to assimilate, to digest; (= bewältigen) to overcome; **~de Industrie** processing industries pl; **etw geistig ~** to assimilate or digest sth

ver|ar|bei|tet [fɛɐ̯'ʔarbaɪtət] ADJ **a** Materialien, Lebensmittel processed; **gut/schlecht ~** (Rock etc) well/badly finished **b** (dial: = abgearbeitet) worn

Ver|ar|bei|tung [fɛɐ̯'ʔarbaɪtʊŋ] F -, -en **a** use, using; (Tech, Biol, Comput) processing; (von Ton, Gold) working; (= Verdauen) digestion; (fig) (von Stoff) treating; (von Erlebnis etc) assimilation, digestion; (= Bewältigung) overcoming **b** (= Aussehen) finish; (= Qualität) workmanship no indef art

ver|ar|gen [fɛɐ̯'ʔargn] ptp **verargt** VT **jdm etw ~** to hold sth against sb; **jdm ~, dass ...** to hold it against sb that ...; **ich kann es ihm nicht ~, wenn er ...** I can't blame him if he ...

ver|är|gern ptp **verärgert** VT **jdn ~** to annoy sb; (stärker) to anger sb

ver|är|gert [fɛɐ̯'ʔɛrgɐt] ADJ annoyed; (stärker) angry; **~ über jdn/etw** annoyed/angry with or at sb/about sth **ADV** reagieren angrily

Ver|är|ge|rung [fɛɐ̯'ʔɛrgərʊŋ] F -, -en annoyance; (stärker) anger

ver|ar|men [fɛɐ̯'ʔarmən] ptp **verarmt** VI aux sein (lit, fig) to become impoverished

ver|armt [fɛɐ̯'ʔarmt] ADJ impoverished

Ver|ar|mung F -, -en impoverishment

ver|ar|schen [fɛɐ̯'ʔarʃn, -'ʔaːɐ̯ʃn] ptp **verarscht** VT (inf) to take the piss out of (Brit sl), to make fun of; (= für dumm verkaufen) to mess or muck (Brit) around (inf)

ver|arz|ten [fɛɐ̯'ʔaːrtstn, -'ʔartstn] ptp **verarztet** VT (inf) to fix up (inf); (mit Verband) to patch up (inf); (fig hum) to sort out (inf)

ver|äs|teln [fɛɐ̯'ʔɛstln] ptp **verästelt** VR to branch out; (fig) to ramify

ver|äs|telt [fɛɐ̯'ʔɛstlt] ADJ Baum branched; (fig) Organisation etc complex

Ver|äs|te|lung [fɛɐ̯'ʔɛstəlʊŋ] F -, -en branching; (fig) ramifications pl

ver|aus|ga|ben [fɛɐ̯'ʔausgaːbn] ptp **verausgabt** VR to overexert or overtax oneself; (finanziell) to overspend; **ich habe mich total verausgabt** (finanziell) I've badly overspent

ver|aus|la|gen [fɛɐ̯'ʔauslaːgn] ptp **verauslagt** VT (Comm) to lay out, to disburse (form)

ver|äu|ßer|lich ADJ (form: = verkäuflich) saleable, for sale

ver|äu|ßer|li|chen [fɛɐ̯'ʔɔysəlɪçn] ptp **veräußerlicht** VT to trivialize VI aux sein to become superficial

ver|äu|ßern ptp **veräußert** VT (form: = verkaufen) to dispose of; Rechte, Land to alienate (form)

Ver|äu|ße|rung F (form) disposal; (von Rechten, Land) alienation (form)

Ver|äu|ße|rungs|ge|winn M (Fin) gain on sale or disposal, capital gain

Verb [vɛrp] NT -s, -en [-bn] verb

ver|bal [vɛr'baːl] ADJ verbal (auch Gram) ADV verbally

Ver|bal|in|ju|rie [vɛr'baːlɪnjuːriə] F (Jur) verbal injury

ver|ball|hor|nen [fɛɐ̯'balhɔrnən] ptp **verballhornt** VT to parody; (unabsichtlich) to get wrong

Ver|ball|hor|nung F -, -en parody; (unabsichtlich) ≈ spoonerism

Ver|band [fɛɐ̯'bant] M -(e)s, ⸚e [-'bɛndə] **a** (Med) dressing; (mit Binden) bandage **b** (= Bund) association **c** (Mil) unit; **im ~ fliegen** to fly in formation **d** (Archit) bond

ver|ban|deln [fɛɐ̯'bandln] ptp **verbandelt** VI (inf) to get together (inf); **er ist jetzt mit der Dagmar verbandelt** he's now going out with Dagmar

Ver|band(s)-: Ver|band(s)|kas|ten M first-aid box; **Ver|band(s)|ma|te|ri|al** NT dressing material; **Ver|band(s)|päck|chen** NT gauze bandage; **Ver|band(s)|stoff** M dressing; **Ver|band(s)|wat|te** F surgical cotton wool (Brit), absorbent cotton (US), cotton batting (US); **Ver|band(s)|zeug** NT pl -zeuge dressing material

ver|ban|nen ptp **verbannt** VT to banish (auch fig), to exile (aus from, auf to)

Ver|bann|te(r) [fɛɐ̯'bantə] MF decl as adj exile

Ver|ban|nung [fɛɐ̯'banʊŋ] F -, -en banishment no art, exile no art; (= das Verbannen) banishment, exiling

Ver|ban|nungs|ort M pl -orte place of exile

ver|bar|ri|ka|die|ren ptp **verbarrikadiert** VT to barricade VR to barricade oneself in (in etw (dat) sth)

ver|ba|seln [fɛɐ̯'baːzln] ptp **verbaselt** VT (dial) to mislay; Termin, Verabredung to forget

ver|bau|en ptp **verbaut** VT **a** (= versperren) to obstruct, to block; **sich (dat) alle Chancen/die Zukunft ~** to spoil one's chances/one's prospects for the future; **jdm die Möglichkeit ~, etw zu tun** to ruin or spoil sb's chances of doing sth **b** (= verbrauchen) Holz etc to use in building; Geld to use for building **c** (= schlecht bauen) to construct badly **d** (inf: = verderben) Text, Arbeit etc to botch (inf)

ver|be|am|ten ptp **verbeamtet** VT to give the status of civil servant to

Ver|be|am|tung F appointment as a civil servant; **auf Lebenszeit** bestowing of the status of civil servant for life

ver|bei|ßen ptp **verbissen** irreg VT (fig inf) **sich (dat) etw ~** (von Zorn etc) to stifle sth, to suppress sth; Bemerkung to bite back sth; Schmerz to hide sth; **sich (dat) das Lachen ~** to keep a straight face VR **sich in etw (acc) ~** (lit) to bite into sth; (Hund) to sink its teeth into sth; (fig) to become set or fixed on sth → verbissen

ver|ber|gen ptp **verborgen** [fɛɐ̯'bɔrgn] irreg VT (+dat, vor +dat from) (lit, fig) to hide, to conceal;

(*vor der Polizei auch*) to harbour (*Brit*), to harbor (*US*); **sein Gesicht in den Händen ~** to bury one's face in one's hands; **jdm etw ~** (= *verheimlichen*) to keep sth from sb VR to hide (oneself), to conceal oneself → *auch* **verborgen** [2]

ver|bes|sern *ptp* **verbessert** VT [a] (= *besser machen*) to improve; *Leistung, Bestzeit, Rekord* to improve (up)on, to better; *die Welt* to reform; **eine neue, verbesserte Auflage** a new revised edition [b] (= *korrigieren*) to correct VR [a] (*Lage etc*) to improve, to get better; (*Mensch*) (*in Leistungen*) to improve, to do better; (*beruflich, finanziell*) to better oneself [b] (= *sich korrigieren*) to correct oneself

Ver|bes|se|rung F -, **-en** [a] improvement (*von* in); (*von Leistung, Bestzeit*) improvement (*von* on); (*von Buch*) revision; (= *berufliche, finanzielle Verbesserung*) betterment [b] (= *Berichtigung*) correction

Ver|bes|se|rungs-: **ver|bes|se|rungs|be-dürf|tig** ADJ *pred* in need of improvement; **ver|bes|se|rungs|fä|hig** ADJ capable of improvement; **Ver|bes|se|rungs|vor|schlag** M suggestion for improvement; **ver|bes|se-rungs|wür|dig** ADJ *pred* in need of improvement *pred*

ver|beu|gen *ptp* **verbeugt** VR to bow (*vor +dat* to)

Ver|beu|gung F bow; **eine ~ vor jdm machen** to (make a) bow to sb

ver|beu|len *ptp* **verbeult** VT to dent

ver|bie|gen *ptp* **verbogen** *irreg* VT to bend (out of shape); (*fig*) *Idee, Wahrheit* to distort; *Mensch* to corrupt; **verbogen** bent; *Rückgrat* curved; (*fig*) twisted, warped VR to bend; (*Holz*) to warp; (*Metall*) to buckle

ver|bies|tern [fɛɐˈbiːstɐn] *ptp* **verbiestert** (*inf*) VT (= *verstören*) to throw (*inf*); (= *störrisch machen*) to make pig-headed (*inf*) VR **sich in etw** (*acc*) ~ to become fixed on sth

ver|bies|tert [fɛɐˈbiːstɐt] ADJ (*inf*) (= *missmutig*) crotchety (*inf*); (= *verstört*) disturbed *no adv*

ver|bie|ten ⚙ 36.3, 37.4 *ptp* **verboten** [fɛɐˈboːtn] *irreg* VT to forbid; (*amtlich auch*) to prohibit; *Zeitung, Partei, Organisation etc* to ban, to prohibit; **jdm ~, etw zu tun** to forbid sb to do sth; **jdm das Rauchen/den Zutritt/den Gebrauch von etw ~** to forbid sb to smoke/to enter/the use of sth; (*amtlich auch*) to prohibit sb from smoking/entering/using sth; **mein Taktgefühl/die Höflichkeit verbietet mir eine derartige Bemerkung** tact/politeness prevents me from making such a remark VR **das verbietet sich von selbst** that has to be ruled out → *auch* **verboten**

ver|bil|den *ptp* **verbildet** VT (*fig*) *jdn* to bring up badly, to miseducate; *Geschmack, Charakter* to spoil, to deform

ver|bild|li|chen [fɛɐˈbɪldlɪçn] *ptp* **verbildlicht** VT = **veranschaulichen**

ver|bil|li|gen *ptp* **verbilligt** VT to reduce the cost of; *Kosten, Preis* to reduce; **verbilligte Waren** reduced goods; **verbilligte Karten** tickets at reduced prices; **verbilligte Darlehen** reduced-rate loans; **etw verbilligt abgeben** to sell sth at a reduced price VR to get *or* become cheaper; (*Kosten, Preise auch*) to go down

ver|bim|sen *ptp* **verbimst** VT (*inf*) to bash up (*inf*)

ver|bin|den ⚙ 27 *ptp* **verbunden** [fɛɐˈbʊndn] *irreg* VT [a] (*Med*) to dress; (*mit Binden*) to bandage; **jdm die Augen ~** to blindfold sb; **mit verbundenen Augen** blindfold(ed)

[b] (= *verknüpfen, in Kontakt bringen*) (*lit, fig*) to connect, to link; *Punkte* to join (up)

[c] (*Telec*) **jdn (mit jdm)** ~ to put sb through (to sb); **ich verbinde!** I'll put you through, I'll connect you; **(Sie sind hier leider) falsch verbunden!** (I'm sorry, you've got the) wrong number!; **mit wem bin ich verbunden?** who am I speaking to?

[d] (= *gleichzeitig haben or tun, anschließen*) to combine

[e] (= *assoziieren*) to associate

[f] (= *mit sich bringen*) **mit etw verbunden sein** to involve sth; **die damit verbundenen Kosten/Gefahren** *etc* the costs/dangers *etc* involved

[g] (*emotional*) *Menschen* to unite, to join together; **freundschaftlich/in Liebe verbunden sein** (*geh*) to be united *or* joined together in friendship/love

VR [a] (= *zusammenkommen*) to combine (*auch Chem*) (*mit* with, *zu* to form), to join (together); (= *sich zusammentun*) to join forces; **sich ehelich/in Liebe/Freundschaft ~** (*geh*) to join together in marriage/love/friendship; **in ihrer Person ~ sich Klugheit und Schönheit** she combines both intelligence and beauty

[b] (= *assoziiert werden*) to be associated; (= *hervorgerufen werden*) to be evoked (*mit* by)

VI (*emotional*) to form a bond

ver|bind|lich [fɛɐˈbɪntlɪç] ⚙ 47.3, 48.3 ADJ [a] obliging; **~sten Dank!** (*form*) thank you kindly!, I/we thank you! [b] (= *verpflichtend*) obligatory, compulsory; *Regelung, Zusage* binding; (= *verlässlich*) *Auskunft* reliable ADV [a] (= *bindend*) **etw ~ vereinbart haben** to have a binding agreement (regarding sth); **etw ~ reservieren** to make a confirmed reservation for sth; **etw ~ erklären** to officially state sth; **~ zusagen** to accept definitely [b] (= *freundlich*) **~ lächeln** to give a friendly smile; **etwas ~er auftreten** to act a little more friendly

Ver|bind|lich|keit F -, **-en** [a] (= *Entgegenkommen*) obliging ways *pl*; (= *höfliche Redensart*) civility *usu pl*, courtesy *usu pl*, polite word(s *pl*)

[b] *no pl* (= *verpflichtender Charakter*) obligatory *or* compulsory nature; (*von Regelung, Zusage*) binding nature; (= *Verlässlichkeit: von Auskunft*) reliability; **von absoluter ~** completely compulsory/absolutely binding

[c] **Verbindlichkeiten** PL (*Comm, Jur*) obligations *pl*, commitments *pl*; (*finanziell auch*) liabilities *pl*; **seine ~en erfüllen** to fulfil one's obligations *or* commitments; to meet one's liabilities; **~en gegen jdn haben** to have (financial) commitments to sb

Ver|bin|dung ⚙ 27.7, 46.4 F [a] connection; (= *Kontakt*) contact (*zu, mit* with); **in ~ mit** (= *zusammen mit*) in conjunction with; (= *im Zusammenhang mit*) in connection with; **jdn/etw mit etw in ~ bringen** to connect sb/sth with sth; (= *assoziieren*) to associate sb/sth with sth; **er/sein Name wurde mit dem Mord/der Affäre in ~ gebracht** he/his name was mentioned in connection with the murder/the affair; **seine ~en spielen lassen** to use one's connections, to pull a few strings (*inf*); **~en anknüpfen** *or* **aufnehmen** to get contacts; **~ mit jdm aufnehmen** to contact sb; **die ~ aufrechterhalten** to maintain contact; (*esp zwischen Freunden*) to keep in touch *or* contact; **mit jdm in ~ bleiben** to stay in touch *or* contact with sb; **sich (mit jdm) in ~ setzen, (mit jdm) in ~ treten** to get in touch *or* contact (with sb), to contact sb; **mit jdm in ~ stehen, mit jdm ~ haben** to be in touch *or* contact with sb; **mit etw in ~ stehen** to be connected with sth

[b] (= *Verkehrsverbindung*) connection (*nach* to); **die ~ von Berlin nach Warschau** the connections *pl* from Berlin to Warsaw; **es besteht direkte ~ nach München** there is a direct connection to Munich

[c] (*Telec*: = *Anschluss*) line; **telefonische ~** telephonic communication; **~ durch Funk** radio communication; **eine ~ (zu einem Ort) bekommen** to get through (to a place); **unsere ~ wurde unterbrochen** we were cut off; **eine ~ zwischen zwei Rechnern aufbauen** *or* **herstellen** (*Comput*) to connect two computers

[d] (*Mil*) contact; (*durch Funk etc*) communication; (= *Zusammenarbeit*) liaison; **~ aufnehmen** to make contact, to establish communication

[e] (= *Kombination*) combination

[f] (= *Vereinigung, Bündnis*) association; (*ehelich*) union; (*Univ*) society; (*für Männer auch*) ≈ fraternity (*US*); (*für Frauen auch*) ≈ sorority (*US*); **eine ~ mit jdm eingehen** to join together with sb; **eine schlagende/nicht schlagende ~** (*Univ*) a duelling (*Brit*) *or* dueling (*US*)/nonduelling (*Brit*) *or* nonduelling (*US*) fraternity

[g] (*Chem*) (= *Prozess*) combination; (= *Ergebnis*) compound (*aus* (formed out) of); **eine ~ mit etw eingehen** to form a compound with sth, to combine with sth

Ver|bin|dungs- *in cpds* (*esp Tech, Archit*) connecting; **Ver|bin|dungs|frau** F → **Verbindungsmann**; **Ver|bin|dungs|haus** NT *house belonging to a student society which provides members with accommodation and is used as a meeting-place*, ≈ fraternity house (*US*); **Ver|bin|dungs|mann** M *pl* **-leute** *or* **-männer** intermediary; (= *Agent*) contact; **Ver|bin|dungs|of|fi|zier(in)** M(F) liaison officer; **Ver|bin|dungs|stel|le** F (*von Gleisen, Kabeln*) junction (point); (*von Rohren, Geklebtem etc*) join; (*Amt*) liaison office; **Ver|bin|dungs|stra-ße** F connecting road; **Ver|bin|dungs|stück** NT connecting piece; **Ver|bin|dungs|stu-dent** M ≈ member of a fraternity (*US*), member of a society of male university *or* college students; **Ver|bin|dungs|stu|den|tin** F ≈ member of a sorority (*US*), member of a society of female university *or* college students; **Ver|bin|dungs|tür** F connecting door

Ver|biss ▲ M (*Hunt*) biting off of young shoots

ver|bis|sen [fɛɐˈbɪsn] ADJ *Arbeiter* dogged, determined; *Kampf* dogged; *Gesicht, Miene* determined; *Hartnäckigkeit* grim ADV determinedly; *kämpfen* doggedly; **du solltest das nicht so ~ sehen** you shouldn't take things so seriously → *auch* **verbeißen**

Ver|bis|sen|heit F -, *no pl* (*von Arbeiter, Kampf*) doggedness; (*von Gesicht, Miene*) determination

ver|bit|ten *ptp* **verbeten** [fɛɐˈbeːtn] VT *irreg* **sich** (*dat*) **etw (schwer** *or* **sehr** *etc*) **~** to refuse (absolutely) to tolerate sth; **das verbitte ich mir!, das will ich mir verbeten haben!** I won't have it!

ver|bit|tern [fɛɐˈbɪtɐn] *ptp* **verbittert** VT to embitter, to make bitter; **jdm das Leben ~** to make sb's life a misery VI *aux sein* to become embittered *or* bitter

ver|bit|tert [fɛɐˈbɪtɐt] ADJ embittered, bitter ADV bitterly; **sich ~ verhalten** to act embittered *or* bitter

Ver|bit|te|rung F -, (*rare*) **-en** bitterness, embitterment

ver|bla|sen ADJ (*pej*: = *verschwommen, unklar*) woolly (*Brit*), wooly (*US*), vague

ver|blas|sen [fɛɐˈblasn] *ptp* **verblasst** VI *aux sein* (*lit, fig*) to fade; (*Mond*) to pale; **alles andere verblasst daneben** (*fig*) everything else pales into insignificance beside it

ver|bläu|en ▲ [fɛɐˈblɔɪən] *ptp* **verbläut** VT (*inf*) to bash up (*inf*)

Ver|bleib [fɛɐˈblaɪp] M -(e)s [-bəs] *no pl* (*form*) whereabouts *pl*

ver|blei|ben *ptp* **verblieben** [fɛɐˈbliːbn] VI *irreg aux sein* to remain; **etw verbleibt jdm** sb has sth left; **... verbleibe ich Ihr ...** (*form*) ... I remain, Yours sincerely (*Brit*) *or* Sincerely (yours) (*US*) ...; **wir sind so verblieben, dass wir ...** we agreed *or* arranged to ..., it was agreed *or* arranged that we ...; **sein Verbleiben in dieser Position ist unmöglich geworden** it has become impossible for him to remain in this position

ver|blei|chen *pret* **verblich** [fɛɐˈblɪç], *ptp* **verblichen** [fɛɐˈblɪçn] VI *aux sein* (*lit, fig*) to fade; (*Mond*) to pale; (*liter*: = *sterben*) to pass away, to expire (*liter*)

ver|blei|en [fɛɐˈblaɪən] *ptp* **verbleit** VT [a] *Benzin* to lead, to put a lead additive in [b] (= *mit Blei überziehen*) to lead-coat, to coat with lead

ver|bleit [fɛɐˈblaɪt] ADJ *Benzin* leaded

ver|blen|den *ptp* **verblendet** VT **a** *(fig)* to blind; **verblendet sein** to be blind **b** *(Archit)* to face

Ver|blen|dung F **a** *(fig)* blindness **b** *(Archit)* facing

ver|bleu|en △ [fɛɐˈblɔyən] VT → **verbläuen**

ver|blich *pret von* **verbleichen**

ver|bli|chen *ptp von* **verbleichen**

Ver|bli|che|ne(r) [fɛɐˈblɪçənə] MF *decl as adj* *(liter)* deceased

ver|blö|den [fɛɐˈbløːdn] *ptp* **verblödet** VI *aux sein (inf)* to become a zombi(e) *(inf)*

Ver|blö|dung F -, *no pl (inf)* stupefaction; **diese Arbeit führt noch zu meiner völligen ~** this job will turn me into a zombi(e) *(inf)*; **die dauernde Reklame führt noch zu unserer völligen ~** the long-term effect of advertising is to make us totally uncritical

ver|blüf|fen [fɛɐˈblʏfn] *ptp* **verblüfft** VT (= *erstaunen*) to stun, to amaze; (= *verwirren*) to baffle; **sich durch** *or* **von etw ~ lassen** to be taken in by sth

ver|blüf|fend [fɛɐˈblʏfnt] ADJ (= *erstaunlich*) amazing, astonishing, incredible ADV amazingly, incredibly; **~ gut Bescheid wissen** to be incredibly well informed; **eine ~ einfache Lösung** an incredibly simple solution

ver|blüfft [fɛɐˈblʏft] ADJ amazed; **sei nicht so ~!** don't look so amazed!; **~e Miene** astounded expression; **du hättest meine ~e Chefin sehen sollen** you should have seen how amazed my boss was ADV **aufsehen, schauen** perplexed; **sich umdrehen** in surprise; **~ reagieren** to be amazed

Ver|blüf|fung F -, *no pl* (= *Erstaunen*) amazement; (= *Verwirrung*) bafflement

ver|blü|hen *ptp* **verblüht** VI *aux sein (lit, fig)* to fade; **der Baum ist verblüht** the blossom has fallen from the tree; **sie sieht verblüht aus** her beauty has faded

ver|blümt [fɛɐˈblyːmt] ADJ oblique ADV **etw/ sich ~ ausdrücken** to say sth/express oneself in a roundabout way

ver|blu|ten *ptp* **verblutet** VI *aux sein* to bleed to death VR *(fig)* to spend oneself

Ver|blu|tung F fatal haemorrhage *(Brit)* or hemorrhage *(US)*; (= *das Verbluten*) bleeding to death

ver|bo|cken *ptp* **verbockt** VT *(inf)* (= *verpfuschen*) to botch *(inf)*, to bungle *(inf)*; (= *anstellen*) to get up to *(inf)*

ver|bockt [fɛɐˈbɔkt] ADJ *(inf)* pig-headed *(inf)*; **Kind** headstrong

ver|boh|ren *ptp* **verbohrt** VR *(inf)* **sich in etw** *(acc)* **~** to become obsessed with sth; (= *unbedingt wollen*) to become (dead) set on sth *(inf)*

ver|bohrt [fɛɐˈboːɐt] ADJ **Haltung** stubborn, obstinate; **Politiker** *auch*, **Meinung** inflexible

Ver|bohrt|heit F -, *no pl* inflexibility

ver|bor|gen¹ [fɛɐˈbɔrgn] *ptp* **verborgt** VT to lend out *(acc* to)

ver|bor|gen² ADJ hidden; **etw ~ halten** to hide sth; **sich ~ halten** to hide; **im Verborgenen leben** to live hidden away; **so manches große Talent blüht im Verborgenen** great talents flourish in obscurity; **im Verborgenen wachsen/blühen** *(lit)* to grow/bloom in places hard to find; **im Verborgenen liegen** to be not yet known → *auch* **verbergen**

Ver|bor|gen|heit F -, *no pl* seclusion

Ver|bot [fɛɐˈboːt] NT -(e)s, -e ban (+*gen* on); **er ging trotz meines ~s** he went even though I had forbidden him to do so; **trotz des ärztlichen ~es** against doctor's orders, in spite of doctor's orders; **gegen ein ~ verstoßen** to ignore a ban; **das ~ der Eltern, zu rauchen/einen Freund mitzubringen** the parents' ban on smoking/on bringing a friend; **ich bin gegen das ~ irgendeiner Partei/Zeitung** I'm opposed to a ban on *or* to banning any party/newspaper

ver|bo|ten [fɛɐˈboːtn] ADJ forbidden; *(amtlich)* prohibited; (= *gesetzeswidrig*) **Handel** illegal; **Zeitung, Partei, Buch** *etc* banned; **jdm ist etw ~** sb is forbidden to do sth; **Rauchen/Parken ~** no smoking/parking; **er sah ~ aus** *(inf)* he was a real sight *(inf)* → *auch* **verbieten**

ver|bo|te|ner|wei|se [fɛɐˈboːtnɐˈvaizə] ADV against orders; (= *gesetzeswidrig*) illegally; **er hat ~ geraucht** he smoked even though it was forbidden *or (amtlich)* prohibited

Ver|bots|schild NT *pl* -schilder, **Ver|bots|ta|fel** F *(allgemein)* notice *or* sign (prohibiting something); *(im Verkehr)* prohibition sign

ver|brä|men [fɛɐˈbrɛːmən] *ptp* **verbrämt** VT *(geh)* **Kleidungsstück** to trim; *(fig)* **Rede** to pad; **Wahrheit** to gloss over; **Kritik** to veil *(mit* in)

ver|bra|ten *ptp* **verbraten** VT *irreg* **a** **Fleisch** *etc* to overcook **b** (*inf*: = *verschwenden*) **Geld, Zeit, Energie** to fritter away, to squander; *(für* on) **c** (*inf*: = *äußern*) to come out with

Ver|brauch [fɛɐˈbraux] M -(e)s, *no pl* consumption *(von, an* +*dat* of); *(von Geld)* expenditure; *(von Kräften)* expenditure *(von, an* +*dat* on); **im Winter ist der ~ an Kalorien/Energie höher** we use up more calories/energy in winter; **sparsam im ~** economical; **zum baldigen ~ bestimmt** to be used immediately; **der ~ von öffentlichen Geldern** public expenditure

ver|brau|chen *ptp* **verbraucht** VT **a** (= *aufbrauchen*) to use; **Benzin, Wasser, Nahrungsmittel** *etc* to consume, to use; **Energie, Strom** *etc* to consume; **Vorräte** to use up; **der Wagen verbraucht 10 Liter Benzin auf 100 km** the car does 10 kms to the litre *(Brit)* or liter *(US)*, ≈ the car does 24 miles to the gallon **b** (= *abnützen*) **Kräfte** *etc* to exhaust; **Kleidung** *etc* to wear out; **verbrauchte Luft** stale *or* stuffy air; **sie ist schon völlig verbraucht** she is already completely spent VR to wear oneself out

Ver|brau|cher [fɛɐˈbrauxɐ] M -s, -, **Ver|brau|che|rin** [-ərɪn] F -, -nen consumer

Ver|brau|cher- *in cpds* consumer; **Ver|brau|cher|be|ra|tung** F consumer advice centre *(Brit)* or center *(US)*; **ver|brau|cher|feind|lich** ADJ anti-consumer; **~ sein** not to be in the interest of the consumer; **ver|brau|cher|freund|lich** ADJ consumer-friendly ADV **~ ver|packt** in consumer-friendly packaging; **Ver|brau|cher|ge|nos|sen|schaft** F consumer cooperative

Ver|brau|che|rin F -, -nen consumer

Ver|brau|cher-: **Ver|brau|cher|markt** M hypermarket *(Brit)*, large supermarket; **Ver|brau|cher|preis** M consumer price; **Ver|brau|cher|schutz** M consumer protection; **Ver|brau|cher|ver|band** M consumer council; **Ver|brau|cher|zent|ra|le** F consumer advice centre *(Brit)* or center *(US)*

Ver|brauchs-: **Ver|brauchs|gü|ter** PL consumer goods *pl*; **Ver|brauchs|steu|er** F excise

ver|bre|chen *ptp* **verbrochen** [fɛɐˈbrɔxn] VT *irreg* **a** **Straftat, Greueltat** to commit; **etwas ~** to commit a crime **b** (*inf*: = *anstellen*) **etwas ~** to be up to something *(inf)*; **was habe ich denn jetzt schon wieder verbrochen?** what on earth have I done now? **c** *(hum inf)* **Gedicht, Kunstwerk, Übersetzung** *etc* to be the perpetrator of *(hum)*

Ver|bre|chen [fɛɐˈbrɛçn] NT -s, - *(lit, fig)* crime *(gegen, an* +*dat* against)

Ver|bre|chens|be|kämp|fung F combating crime *no art*

Ver|bre|cher [fɛɐˈbrɛçɐ] M -s, -, **Ver|bre|che|rin** [-ərɪn] F -, -nen criminal

Ver|bre|cher-: **Ver|bre|cher|al|bum** NT rogues' gallery *(hum)*; **Ver|bre|cher|ban|de** F gang of criminals; **Ver|bre|cher|ge|sicht** NT *(pej)* criminal face

Ver|bre|che|rin F -, -nen criminal

ver|bre|che|risch [fɛɐˈbrɛçərɪʃ] ADJ criminal; **in ~er Absicht** with criminal intent ADV **verraten, im Stich lassen** vilely, villainously

Ver|bre|cher-: **Ver|bre|cher|jagd** F chase after a/the criminal/criminals; **Ver|bre|cher|kar|tei** F criminal records *pl*; **Ver|bre|cher|tum** [fɛɐˈbrɛçɐtuːm] NT -s, *no pl* criminality; **Ver|bre|cher|vier|tel** NT *(pej inf)* shady part of town; **Ver|bre|cher|vi|sa|ge** F *(pej inf)* criminal face; **Ver|bre|cher|welt** F underworld

ver|brei|ten [fɛɐˈbraitn] *ptp* **verbreitet** VT to spread; **Ideen, Lehre** *auch* to disseminate; **Zeitung** to distribute, to circulate; (= *ausstrahlen*) **Wärme** to radiate; **Licht** to shed; **Ruhe** to radiate; **eine (weit) verbreitete Ansicht** a widely *or* commonly held opinion; **eine verbreitete Zeitung** a newspaper with a large circulation *or* a wide distribution VR **a** (= *sich ausbreiten*) to spread **b** **sich über ein Thema ~** to expound on *or* hold forth on a subject

ver|brei|tern *ptp* **verbreitert** VT to widen VR to get wider, to widen out

Ver|brei|te|rung F -, -en widening

Ver|brei|tung [fɛɐˈbraitʊŋ] F -, *no pl* spreading; *(von Lehre, Ideen auch)* dissemination; *(von Zeitung)* distribution, circulation

ver|brenn|bar ADJ combustible

ver|bren|nen *ptp* **verbrannt** [fɛɐˈbrant] *irreg* VT **a** *(mit Feuer)* to burn; **Müll** to burn, to incinerate; (= *verbrauchen*) **Tote** to cremate; (= *verbrauchen*) **Gas, Kerzen** to burn; **Treibstoff, Kalorien** to burn, to use; **verbrannt** burned; **verbrannte Erde** *(fig)* scorched earth **b** (= *versengen*) to scorch; **Finger, Haut** *etc* to burn; **Haar** to singe; (= *verbrühen*) to scald; **sich** *(dat)* **die Zunge/den Mund ~** *(lit)* to burn one's tongue/mouth; **sich** *(dat)* **den Mund** *or* **Schnabel ~** *(fig)* to open one's big mouth *(inf)* → **Finger** VR to burn oneself; (= *sich verbrühen*) to scald oneself VI *aux sein* to burn; *(Mensch, Tier)* to burn (to death); (= *niederbrennen: Haus* etc) to burn down; *(durch Sonne, Hitze)* to be scorched; **das Fleisch ~ lassen** to burn the meat; **alles verbrannte, alles war verbrannt** everything was destroyed in the fire → *auch* **verbrannt**

Ver|bren|nung [fɛɐˈbrɛnʊŋ] F -, -en **a** *no pl* (= *das Verbrennen*) burning; *(von Müll)* burning, incineration; *(von Treibstoff)* combustion; *(von Leiche)* cremation **b** (= *Brandwunde*) burn; (= *Verbrühung*) scald; **starke/leichte ~en davontragen** to be badly/not seriously burned → **Grad**

Ver|bren|nungs-: **Ver|bren|nungs|an|la|ge** F incineration plant; **Ver|bren|nungs|kraft|ma|schi|ne** F internal combustion vehicle; **Ver|bren|nungs|mo|tor** M internal combustion engine; **Ver|bren|nungs|ofen** M furnace; *(für Müll)* incinerator; **Ver|bren|nungs|pro|dukt** NT waste product (of combustion); **Ver|bren|nungs|wär|me** F heat of combustion

ver|brie|fen [fɛɐˈbriːfn] *ptp* **verbrieft** VT to document; **verbriefte Rechte/Sicherheit** attested rights/security

ver|brin|gen *ptp* **verbracht** [fɛɐˈbraxt] VT *irreg* **a** **Zeit** *etc* to spend **b** *(obs, Jur:* = *bringen)* to take

ver|brü|dern [fɛɐˈbryːdɐn] *ptp* **verbrüdert** VR to swear eternal friendship *(mit* to); *(politisch)* to ally oneself *(mit* to, with); **Menschen aller Rassen sollten sich ~** people of all races should be brothers

Ver|brü|de|rung F -, -en avowal of friendship; *(politisch)* alliance

ver|brü|hen *ptp* **verbrüht** VT to scald VR to scald oneself

Ver|brü|hung [fɛɐˈbryːʊŋ] F -, -en *(no pl:* = *das Verbrühen)* scalding; (= *Wunde*) scald

ver|bu|chen *ptp* **verbucht** VT to enter (up) (in a/the book); **einen Betrag auf ein Konto ~** to credit a sum to an account; **einen Erfolg (für**

sich) ~ to notch up *or* chalk up a success (*inf*); **etw für sich** *or* **auf sein Konto ~ können** (*fig*) to be able to credit oneself with sth

Ver|bu|chung F entering (up)

ver|bud|deln *ptp* **verbuddelt** VT (*inf*) to bury

Ver|bum ['vɛrbʊm] NT -s, **Verba** [-ba] (*geh*) verb

ver|bum|meln *ptp* **verbummelt** (*inf*) **VT** (= *verlieren*) to lose; (= *vertrödeln, vergeuden*) Nachmittag, Wochenende, Zeit to waste, to fritter away; (= *verpassen*) Verabredung to miss **VI** *aux sein* **a** (= *herunterkommen*) to go to seed **b** (= *faul werden*) to get lazy; **verbummelt sein** to be lazy

Ver|bund M -(e)s, *no pl* (*Econ*) combine; **im ~ arbeiten** to cooperate

Ver|bund|bau M *pl* -bauten composite (method of) building

ver|bun|den [fɛɐˈbʊndn] *ptp von* **verbinden** ADJ (*form:* = *dankbar*) **jdm (für etw) ~ sein** to be obliged to sb (for sth)

ver|bün|den [fɛɐˈbʏndn] *ptp* **verbündet** VR to ally oneself with (*mit*); (*Staaten*) to form an alliance; **alle haben sich gegen mich verbündet** everyone is against me, everyone has sided against me; **verbündet sein** to be allies, to be allied

Ver|bun|den|heit F -, *no pl* (*von Völkern*) solidarity; (*von Menschen*) (*mit Menschen, Natur*) closeness (*mit* to); (*mit Land, Tradition*) attachment (*mit* to); **in tiefer ~, ...** very affectionately yours, ...

Ver|bün|de|te(r) [fɛɐˈbʏndətə] MF *decl as adj* ally

Ver|bund- : **Ver|bund|fahr|aus|weis** M travel pass (*valid for all forms of public transport*); **Ver|bund|glas** NT laminated glass; **Ver|bund|kar|te** F (= *Eintrittskarte*) integrated ticket; (*Mot*) travel pass (*valid for all forms of public transport*); **Ver|bund|ma|te|ri|al** NT composite (material); **Ver|bund|netz** NT (*Elec*) integrated grid system; **Ver|bund|plat|te** F sandwich panel; **Ver|bund|stahl** M laminated steel; **Ver|bund|stoff** M composite (material); **Ver|bund|sys|tem** NT integrated system; **Ver|bund|wer|bung** F joint advertising; **Ver|bund|werk|stoff** M composite (material); **Ver|bund|wirt|schaft** F integrated economy

ver|bür|gen *ptp* **verbürgt** **VR** **sich für jdn/etw ~** to vouch for sb/sth; **ich will mich nicht dafür ~, dass das stimmt** I cannot guarantee that this is correct **VT** **a** (= *gewährleisten*) Freiheit, Recht, Unterstützung to guarantee; **ein verbürgtes Recht** an established right **b** (*Fin:* = *bürgen für*) Kredit, Mietausfälle to guarantee **c** (= *dokumentieren*) **eine verbürgte Nachricht** a confirmed report; **historisch verbürgt sein** to be historically documented; **dokumentarisch verbürgt sein** to be backed up by documentary evidence

ver|bür|ger|li|chen [fɛɐˈbʏrgəlɪçn] *ptp* **verbürgerlicht** VI *aux sein* to become bourgeois

ver|bü|ßen *ptp* **verbüßt** VT to serve

Ver|bü|ßung [fɛɐˈbyːsʊŋ] F -, *no pl* serving; **zur ~ einer Haftstrafe von zwei Jahren verurteilt werden** to be sentenced to serve two years in prison

ver|chro|men [fɛɐˈkroːmən] *ptp* **verchromt** VT to chromium-plate

Ver|chro|mung F -, -en chromium-plating

Ver|dacht [fɛɐˈdaxt] M -(e)s, -e *or* ⸚e [-ˈdɛçtə] suspicion; (*hum:* = *Vermutung*) hunch; **jdn in** *or* **im ~ haben** to suspect sb; **im ~ stehen, etw getan zu haben** to be suspected of having done sth; **jdn in ~ bringen** to make sb look guilty; **den ~ auf jdn lenken** to throw *or* cast suspicion on sb; **jdn wegen ~s einer Sache** (*gen*) **festnehmen** to arrest sb on suspicion of sth; (**gegen jdn**) **~ schöpfen** to become suspicious (of sb); **~ erregen** to arouse suspicion; **es besteht ~ auf Krebs** (*acc*) cancer is suspected; **bei ~ auf Krebs** in the case of suspected cancer; **etw auf ~ tun** (*inf*) to do sth on spec (*inf*)

---

ver|däch|tig [fɛɐˈdɛçtɪç] ADJ suspicious; (= *verdächtig aussehend*) suspicious-looking; **sich ~ machen** to arouse suspicion; **die drei ~en Personen** the three suspects; **einer Sache** (*gen*) **~ sein** to be suspected of sth **ADV** suspiciously; **schnell** unbelievably; **~ aussehen** to look suspicious

ver|däch|ti|gen [fɛɐˈdɛçtɪgn] *ptp* **verdächtigt** VT to suspect (+*gen* of); **ich will niemanden ~, aber ...** I don't want to cast suspicion on anyone, but ...; **er wird verdächtigt, gestohlen zu haben, er wird des Diebstahls verdächtigt** he is suspected of theft

Ver|däch|ti|ge(r) [fɛɐˈdɛçtɪgə] MF *decl as adj* suspect

Ver|däch|ti|gung F -, -en suspicion; **die ~ eines so integren Mannes käme mir nie in den Sinn** it would never occur to me to suspect a man of his integrity

Ver|dachts- : **Ver|dachts|grund** M grounds *pl* for suspicion; **Ver|dachts|mo|ment** NT suspicious circumstance

ver|dam|men [fɛɐˈdamən] *ptp* **verdammt** VT (*esp Rel:* = *verfluchen*) to damn; (= *verurteilen*) to condemn → *auch* **verdammt, Scheitern**

ver|dam|mens|wert ADJ damnable, despicable

Ver|damm|nis [fɛɐˈdamnɪs] F -, -se (*Rel*) damnation *no art*

ver|dammt [fɛɐˈdamt] (*inf*) ADJ damned (*inf*), bloody (*Brit inf*); **~er Mist!** sod it! (*Brit inf*), screw it! (*esp US inf*); **~e Scheiße!** (*sl*) shit! (*sl*) → *auch* **verdammen** ADV damn (*inf*); **das tut ~ weh** that hurts like hell (*inf*); **~ viel Geld** a hell of a lot of money (*inf*); **mir gehts ~ gut** I'm on top of the world (*inf*); **mir gehts ~ schlecht** I'm in a bad way **INTERJ** **~!** damn *or* blast (it) (*inf*); **~ noch mal!** bloody hell (*Brit sl*), damn it all (*inf*); **du wirst dich ~ noch mal entschuldigen!** apologize, damn you! (*inf*)

Ver|damm|te(r) [fɛɐˈdamtə] MF *decl as adj* (*Rel*) **die ~n** the damned *pl*

Ver|dam|mung F -, -en condemnation; (*Rel*) damnation

ver|damp|fen *ptp* **verdampft** VTI (*vi: aux sein*) to vaporize; (*Cook*) to boil away

Ver|damp|fer M vaporizer

Ver|damp|fung [fɛɐˈdampfʊŋ] F -, -en vaporization

ver|dan|ken *ptp* **verdankt** VT **jdm etw ~** to owe sth to sb; **es ist jdm/einer Sache zu ~(, dass ...)** it is thanks *or* due to sb/sth (that ...); **das verdanke ich dir** (*iro*) I've got you to thank for that

Ver|dan|kung [fɛɐˈdaŋkʊŋ] F -, *no pl* (*Sw*) **unter ~ seiner Verdienste** grateful thanks for his contribution

ver|darb *pret von* **verderben**

ver|da|ten [fɛɐˈdaːtn] *ptp* **verdatet** VT **jdn ~** to store sb's details on computer

ver|dat|tert [fɛɐˈdatet] ADJ, ADV (*inf:* = *verwirrt*) flabbergasted (*inf*)

ver|dau|en [fɛɐˈdauən] *ptp* **verdaut** **VT** (*lit, fig*) to digest **VI** (*Mensch*) to digest (one's food); (*Magen etc*) to digest the food

ver|dau|lich [fɛɐˈdaulɪç] ADJ (*lit, fig*) digestible; **leicht ~** easily digestible, easy to digest; **schwer ~** hard to digest

Ver|dau|lich|keit F -, *no pl* digestibility

Ver|dau|ung [fɛɐˈdauʊŋ] F -, -en digestion; **eine gute/schlechte ~ haben** to have good/poor digestion

Ver|dau|ungs- : **Ver|dau|ungs|ap|pa|rat** M digestive system; **Ver|dau|ungs|be|schwer|den** PL digestive trouble *sing*; **Ver|dau|ungs|ka|nal** M alimentary canal, digestive tract; **Ver|dau|ungs|or|gan** NT digestive organ; **Ver|dau|ungs|saft** M gastric juice; **Ver|dau|ungs|spa|zier|gang** M constitutional; **Ver|dau|ungs|stö|rung** F *usu pl* indigestion *no pl*;

Ver|dau|ungs|trakt M digestive *or* alimentary tract

Ver|deck [fɛɐˈdɛk] NT -(e)s, -e **a** (= *Dach*) (*von Kutsche, Kinderwagen*) hood (*Brit*), canopy; (*von Auto*) soft top, hood (*Brit*); (*hart*) roof; (*von Flugzeug*) canopy **b** (*von Passagierdampfer*) sun deck; (*von Doppeldeckerbus*) open top deck

ver|de|cken *ptp* **verdeckt** VT to hide, to conceal; (= *zudecken*) to cover (up); Sicht to block; (*fig*) Absichten, Widerspruch, Symptome to conceal; Unterschlagungen etc to conceal, to cover up; **eine Wolke verdeckte die Sonne** a cloud hid *or* covered the sun; **sie verdeckte ihr Gesicht mit den Händen** she covered her face with her hands, she hid her face in her hands → **Karte**

ver|deckt [fɛɐˈdɛkt] ADJ concealed; Widerspruch hidden; Ermittler, Einsatz undercover ADV **~ agieren** to operate undercover; **~ ermitteln** to investigate undercover

ver|den|ken *ptp* **verdacht** [fɛɐˈdaxt] VT *irreg* **jdm etw ~** to hold sth against sb; **ich kann es ihm nicht ~(, dass er es getan hat)** I can't blame him (for doing it)

Ver|derb [fɛɐˈdɛrp] M -(e)s [-bəs] *no pl* (*geh:* = *Untergang*) ruin; **sein ~** his ruin, the ruin of him → **Gedeih**

ver|der|ben [fɛɐˈdɛrbn] *pret* **verdarb** [fɛɐˈdarp], *ptp* **verdorben** [fɛɐˈdɔrbn] **VT** to spoil; Plan auch to wreck; (*stärker*) to ruin; Luft to pollute; jdn (*moralisch*) to corrupt; (*sittlich*) to deprave, to corrupt; (= *verwöhnen*) to spoil; **jdm etw ~** (*Abend, Urlaub*) to spoil *or* ruin sth for sb; Chancen, Leben, Witz to ruin sth for sb; **sich** (*dat*) **das Leben ~** to ruin one's life; **sich** (*dat*) **den Magen ~** to give oneself an upset stomach; **sich** (*dat*) **den Appetit ~** to spoil one's appetite; **sich** (*dat*) **die Augen/Stimme/Lungen ~** to ruin *or* damage one's eyes *or* eyesight/voice/lungs; **die Preise ~** (= *verbilligen*) to force prices down; (= *verteuern*) to force prices up; **jdm das Geschäft ~** to damage sb's business; **jds Laune ~, jdm die Laune ~** to put sb in a bad mood; **jdm die Freude** *or* **den Spaß/die Lust an etw** (*dat*) **~** to spoil sb's enjoyment of sth; **es (sich** *dat*) **mit jdm ~** to fall out with sb **VI** *aux sein* (*Material*) to become spoiled/ruined; (*Nahrungsmittel*) to go off (*Brit*) *or* bad; (*Ernte*) to be ruined; (*Mensch*) to become depraved *or* corrupted; **da** *or* **daran ist nichts mehr zu ~** it *or* things couldn't get any worse; **an dem Kuchen/Hemd ist nichts mehr zu ~** the cake/shirt is absolutely ruined anyway → *auch* **verdorben**

Ver|der|ben NT -s, *no pl* **a** (= *Untergang, Unglück*) undoing, ruin; **in sein ~ rennen** to be heading for disaster; **jdn ins ~ stürzen** to bring ruin or disaster (up)on sb **b** (*von Material*) spoiling, ruining; (*von Nahrungsmittel*) going off (*Brit*) *or* bad; (*von Luft, Wasser*) pollution

ver|derb|lich [fɛɐˈdɛrplɪç] ADJ pernicious; Einfluss auch corrupting; Lebensmittel perishable

Ver|derb|nis [fɛɐˈdɛrpnɪs] F -, *no pl* corruption, depravity; (= *Verderbtheit*) corruptness, depravity

ver|derbt [fɛɐˈdɛrpt] ADJ **a** (*dated: moralisch*) corrupt(ed), depraved **b** (*Typ*) corrupt

Ver|derbt|heit F -, *no pl* (*dated*) corruptness, depravity

ver|deut|li|chen [fɛɐˈdɔytlɪçn] *ptp* **verdeutlicht** VT to show clearly; (= *deutlicher machen*) to clarify, to elucidate; (= *erklären*) to explain; **er versuchte, seinen Standpunkt an einem Beispiel zu ~** he tried to clarify his position by means of an example; **sich** (*dat*) **etw ~** to think sth out for oneself; **etw besser/näher ~** to clarify sth further

Ver|deut|li|chung F -, -en clarification; **zur ~ seiner Absichten** in order to show his intentions clearly

ver|deut|schen [fɛɐˈdɔytʃn] *ptp* **verdeutscht** VT to translate into German; (*fig inf*) to translate (into normal language)

---

ver|dich|ten ptp **verdichtet** [VT] (Phys) to compress; (fig: = komprimieren) to condense; Gefühle to intensify, to heighten [VR] to thicken; (Schneetreiben) to worsen; (Gas) to become compressed; (fig: = häufen) to increase; (Verdacht, Eindruck) to deepen; **die Handlung verdichtet sich**, the plot thickens; **der Verdacht verdichtet sich, dass ...** the suspicion that ... is growing; **es ~ sich die Hinweise, dass ...** there is growing evidence that ...; **mein Eindruck verdichtete sich zur Gewissheit** my impression hardened into certainty

Ver|dich|ter [fɛɐ'dɪçtɐ] M -s, - (Tech) compressor

Ver|dich|tung F **a** (Phys) compression; (fig: = Komprimierung) condensing; (von Gefühlen) intensification, heightening **b** (= das Dichterwerden) thickening; (von Gas) compression; (= Häufung) increase (+gen in); (von Verdacht, Eindruck) deepening

ver|di|cken [fɛɐ'dɪkn] ptp **verdickt** [VT] to thicken; Blut to coagulate; (= verbreitern) to widen; (= gelieren lassen) to make set; (= verstärken) to strengthen [VR] to thicken; (Gelee) to set; (Blut) to coagulate; (Milch) to curdle; (= weiter werden) to become thicker; (Rohr, Flasche) to become wider, to widen out; (= anschwellen) to swell

Ver|di|ckung F -, -en (= das Verdicken) thickening; (von Blut) coagulation; (von Gelee) setting; (von Milch) curdling; (von Rohr, Flasche) widening; (= Schwellung) swelling; (= Verstärkung) strengthening; (= verdickte Stelle) bulge

ver|die|nen [⊘] 38.2, 40.2, 46.2, 53.2 ptp **verdient** [VT] **a** (= einnehmen) to earn; (= Gewinn machen) to make; **sein Brot** or **seinen Unterhalt ~** to earn or make one's living; **er hat an dem Auto 500 Euro verdient** he made 500 euros on the car; **dabei ist nicht viel zu ~** there's not much money in that; **sich** (dat) **etw ~** to earn the money for sth; **sich** (dat) **das Studium ~** to pay for or finance one's own studies **b** (fig) Lob, Strafe to deserve; **sich** (dat) **etw (redlich) verdient haben** to deserve sth, to have earned sth; Schläge auch to have had sth coming to one (inf); **er verdient es nicht anders/besser** he doesn't deserve anything else/any better; **eine Reform, die diesen Namen verdient** a reform which lives up to its name → auch **verdient**

[VI] to earn; (= Gewinn machen) to make (a profit) (an +dat on); **in dieser Familie ~ drei Personen** there are three wage earners in this family; **er verdient gut/besser** he earns a lot/more; **er verdient schlecht** he doesn't earn much; **am Krieg ~** to profit from war

Ver|die|ner [fɛɐ'diːnɐ] M -s, -, **Ver|die|ne|rin** [-ərɪn] F -, -nen wage earner; **der einzige ~** the sole breadwinner

Ver|dienst¹ [fɛɐ'diːnst] M -(e)s, -e (= Einkommen) income, earnings pl; (= Profit) profit; **einen besseren ~ haben** to earn more

Ver|dienst² NT -(e)s, -e **a** (= Anspruch auf Anerkennung) merit; (= Dank) credit; **es ist sein ~/das ~ der Wissenschaftler(, dass ...)** it is thanks to him/the scientists that ...); **nach ~** on merit; **das ~ gebührt ihm allein** the credit is entirely his; **sich** (dat) **etw als** or **zum ~ anrechnen** to take the credit for sth

b usu pl (= Leistung) contribution; (national) service; **ihre ~e um die Wissenschaft** or **als Wissenschaftlerin** her services or contribution to science; **seine ~e um das Vaterland/die Stadt** his services to his country/town; **seine ~e um die Dichtung/den Weltfrieden** his contribution to poetry/world peace; **hohe ~e erwerben** to make a great contribution (um to); **er hat sich** (dat) **große ~e um das Vaterland erworben** he has rendered his country great service

Ver|dienst-: **Ver|dienst|adel** M ≈ life peerage; (= Adlige) ≈ life peers pl; **Ver|dienst|aus|fall** M loss of earnings; **Ver|dienst|aus|fall|ent|schä|di|gung** F compensation for loss of earnings; **Ver|dienst|be|schei|ni|gung** F certificate of earnings; **Ver|dienst|kreuz** NT highest decoration awarded for military or other service; **Ver|dienst|lich** ADJ commendable; **Ver|dienst|mög|lich|keit** F opportunity for earning money; **Ver|dienst|or|den** M order of merit; **Ver|dienst|span|ne** F profit margin; **Ver|dienst|voll** ADJ commendable

ver|dient [fɛɐ'diːnt] [ADJ] **a** Lohn, Strafe rightful; Ruhe, Lob well-deserved **b** Wissenschaftler, Künstler, Politiker, Sportler of outstanding merit; **sich um etw ~ machen** to render outstanding services to sth [ADV] gewinnen, siegen deservedly → auch **verdienen**

ver|dien|ter|ma|ßen [fɛɐ'diːntɐ'maːsn], **ver|dien|ter|wei|se** [fɛɐ'diːntɐ'vaizə] ADV deservedly

Ver|dikt [vɛr'dɪkt] NT -(e)s, -e (geh) verdict

ver|din|gen [fɛɐ'dɪŋən] pret **verdingte** [fɛɐ'dɪŋktə], ptp **verdungen** or **verdingt** [fɛɐ'dʊŋən, fɛɐ'dɪŋkt] (old) [VT] jdn to put into service (bei with); Arbeit to give [VR] **sich (bei jdm) ~** to enter service (with sb)

ver|ding|li|chen [fɛɐ'dɪŋlɪçn] ptp **verdinglicht** VT (= konkretisieren) to put into concrete terms, to concretize; (Philos) Ideen to reify; Menschen to objectify

Ver|ding|li|chung F -, no pl concretization; (von Ideen) reification; (von Menschen) objectification

ver|dirbt [fɛɐ'dɪrpt] 3. pers sing pres von **verderben**

ver|dol|met|schen ptp **verdolmetscht** VT to interpret

ver|don|nern ptp **verdonnert** VT (inf: zu Haft etc) to sentence, to condemn (zu to); **jdn zu etw ~, jdn dazu ~, etw zu tun** to order sb to do sth as a punishment; **jdn zu einer Geldstrafe von ... ~** to fine sb ...; **jdn zu einer Gefängnisstrafe ~** to sentence sb to a term of imprisonment

ver|dop|peln ptp **verdoppelt** [VT] to double; (fig) Anstrengung etc to redouble [VR] to double

Ver|dop|pe|lung [fɛɐ'dɔpəlʊŋ] F -, -en, **Ver|dopp|lung** [fɛɐ'dɔplʊŋ] F -, -en doubling; (von Anstrengung) redoubling

ver|dor|ben [fɛɐ'dɔrbn] ptp von **verderben** ADJ **a** Lebensmittel bad, off pred; Wasser, Luft polluted; Magen upset **b** Stimmung, Urlaub, Freude spoiled, ruined **c** (moralisch) corrupt; (sittlich) depraved; (= verzogen) Kind spoiled

Ver|dor|ben|heit F -, no pl depravity

ver|dor|ren ptp **verdorrt** VI aux sein to wither

ver|dö|sen ptp **verdöst** VT (inf) to doze away

ver|dräng|ten ptp **verdrähtet** VT to wire (up)

ver|drän|gen ptp **verdrängt** VT jdn to drive out; Gegner auch to oust; (= ersetzen) to supersede, to replace; (Phys) Wasser, Luft to displace; (Met) to drive; (fig) Sorgen, Angst to dispel, to drive away; (Psych) to repress, to suppress; **er hat sie aus seinem Herzen verdrängt** he has forced himself to forget her; **jdn aus dem Amt/von der Macht ~** to oust sb (from office/power); **das habe ich völlig verdrängt** (hum: = vergessen) it completely slipped my mind (inf); **jdn/etw aus dem Bewusstsein ~** to repress or suppress all memory of sb/sth

Ver|drän|gung [fɛɐ'drɛŋʊŋ] F -, -en driving out; (von Gegner auch) ousting; (= Ersetzung) superseding, replacing; (Phys) displacement; (Met) driving; (von Sorgen) dispelling; (Psych) repression, suppression

Ver|drän|gungs|kampf M fight for survival

Ver|drän|gungs|wett|be|werb M fierce competition no indef art

ver|dre|cken [fɛɐ'drɛkn] ptp **verdreckt** VTI (vi: aux sein) (inf) to get dirty or filthy; **verdreckt** filthy (dirty)

ver|dre|hen ptp **verdreht** VT to twist; Gelenk auch to wrench; (= anders einstellen) Radio, Regler, Lampe to adjust; (= verknacksen) to sprain; Hals to crick; Augen to roll; jds Worte, Tatsachen to distort, to twist; **das Recht ~** to pervert the course of justice; **sich** (dat) **den Hals ~** (fig inf) to crane one's neck → **Kopf** d

ver|dreht [fɛɐ'dreːt] ADJ (inf) crazy (inf); Bericht confused, garbled

Ver|dreht|heit F -, no pl (inf) craziness

Ver|dre|hung F twisting; (von Worten, Tatsachen) distortion; (von Recht) perversion

ver|drei|fa|chen [fɛɐ'draifaxn] ptp **verdreifacht** VTR to treble (esp Brit), to triple

Ver|drei|fa|chung F -, -en trebling (esp Brit), tripling

ver|dre|schen ptp **verdroschen** [fɛɐ'drɔʃn] VT irreg (inf) to beat up; (als Strafe) to thrash

ver|drie|ßen [fɛɐ'driːsn] pret **verdross** [fɛɐ'drɔs], ptp **verdrossen** VT to irritate, to annoy; **sich** (dat) **den Abend durch etw nicht ~ lassen** not to let sth spoil one's evening; **lassen Sie es sich nicht ~!** don't be put off or worried by it → **verdrossen**

ver|drieß|lich [fɛɐ'driːslɪç] ADJ morose; Arbeit, Angelegenheit irksome

ver|dross ▲ pret von **verdrießen**

ver|dros|sen [fɛɐ'drɔsn] ptp von **verdrießen** [ADJ] (= schlecht gelaunt) morose; (= unlustig) Mensch, Gesicht unwilling, reluctant [ADV] (= schlecht gelaunt) morosely; (= unlustig) unwillingly, reluctantly

Ver|dros|sen|heit F -, no pl (= schlechte Laune) moroseness; (= Lustlosigkeit) unwillingness, reluctance; (über Politik etc) dissatisfaction (über +acc with); **mit ~ arbeiten** to work unwillingly or reluctantly

ver|dru|cken ptp **verdruckt** (inf) [VR] to make a misprint [VT] to misprint

ver|drü|cken ptp **verdrückt** [VT] **a** (inf) Essen to polish off (inf); **der kann was ~** he's got some appetite (inf) **b** Kleider to crumple **c** (dial: = zerdrücken) to crush, to squash [VR] (inf) to beat it (inf); **sich heimlich ~** to slip away (unnoticed)

ver|druckst [fɛɐ'drʊkst] ADJ (inf: = zaghaft) hesitant

Ver|drü|ckung [fɛɐ'drʏkʊŋ] F -, -en (inf: = Bedrängnis) distress; **in ~ geraten** or **kommen** to get into difficulties; **jdn in ~ bringen** to put sb under pressure

Ver|druss ▲ [fɛɐ'drʊs] M -es, -e frustration; **~ mit jdm haben** to get frustrated with sb; **zu jds ~** to sb's annoyance; **jdm ~ bereiten** to cause annoyance to sb; **etw jdm zum ~ tun** to do sth to spite sb

ver|duf|ten ptp **verduftet** VI aux sein **a** (= seinen Duft verlieren) to lose its smell; (Parfüm) to lose its scent; (Tee, Kaffee) to lose its aroma **b** (inf: = verschwinden) to beat it (inf)

ver|dum|men [fɛɐ'dʊmən] ptp **verdummt** [VT] jdn ~ (= für dumm verkaufen) to make sb out to be stupid; (= dumm machen) to dull sb's mind [VI] aux sein to stultify, to become stultified

Ver|dum|mung F -, -en **a** (= Verblödung) dulling (of the mind) **b** (= das Dummwerden) stultification

ver|dun|gen ptp von **verdingen**

ver|dun|keln ptp **verdunkelt** [VT] to darken; Bühne auch to black out; Farbe auch to deepen, to make darker; (im Krieg) to black out; (fig) Zusammenhänge, Motive etc to obscure; jds Glück to cloud; jds Ruf to damage, to harm; **Tatbestände ~** to suppress evidence; **die Sonne ~** (Mond) to eclipse the sun; (Wolken) to obscure the sun [VR] to darken; (Himmel auch) to grow darker; (Verstand) to become dulled

Ver|dun|ke|lung [fɛɐ'dʊŋkəlʊŋ] F -, -en **a** (= das Dunkelmachen) darkening; (von Bühne auch, im Krieg) blacking out; (fig) obscuring; (von Glück) clouding; **die ~ nicht einhalten** not to keep to the blackout **b** (= das Dunkelwerden) darkening **c** (inf) (= Vorhang) curtain; (= Jalousie) blind usu pl **d** (Jur) suppression of evidence

Ver|dun|ke|lungs|ge|fahr F , *no pl* (*Jur*) danger of suppression of evidence

Ver|dunk|lung [fɛɐ'dʊŋkluŋ] F -, -en = **Verdunkelung**

ver|dün|nen [fɛɐ'dynən] *ptp* **verdünnt** 🔲 to thin (down); (*mit Wasser*) to water down; *Lösung* to dilute; *Gas* to rarefy; **den Teig mit Wasser ~** to add water to the dough; **verdünnte Luft** rarefied air 🔲 (*Lösung*) to become diluted; (*Luft*) to become rarefied; (*Vegetation*) to become thinner; (= *schmaler werden*) to become thinner; (*Rohr*) to become narrower

Ver|dün|ner [fɛɐ'dynɐ] M -s, - thinner

ver|dün|ni|sie|ren [fɛɐdyni'ziːrən] *ptp* **verdünnisiert** VR (*hum inf*) to beat a hasty retreat

Ver|dün|nung F -, -en 🅰 thinning (*von Lösung*) dilution; (*mit Wasser*) watering down; (*von Luft*) rarefaction (*form*); (= *Verengung*) narrowing 🅱 (= *Flüssigkeit zum Verdünnen*) thinner

Ver|dün|nungs|mit|tel NT thinner, thinning agent

ver|duns|ten *ptp* **verdunstet** VI *aux sein* to evaporate

Ver|duns|ter [fɛɐ'dʊnstɐ] M -s, - humidifier

Ver|duns|tung [fɛɐ'dʊnstʊŋ] F -, -en evaporation

Ver|duns|tungs|röhr|chen NT aromatherapy tube (*hung over radiator in order to allow contents to slowly evaporate*)

ver|durs|ten *ptp* **verdurstet** VI *aux sein* to die of thirst

ver|dus|seln [fɛɐ'dʊsln] *ptp* **verdusselt** VT (*inf*) **etw ~** to forget all about sth

ver|düs|tern [fɛɐ'dyːstɐn] *ptp* **verdüstert** VTR to darken

ver|dut|zen [fɛɐ'dʊtsn] *ptp* **verdutzt** VT (*inf*) to take aback, to nonplus; (= *verwirren*) to baffle

ver|dutzt [fɛɐ'dʊtst] ADJ ADV (*inf*) taken aback, nonplussed; (= *verwirrt*) baffled

Ver|dutzt|heit F -, *no pl* (*inf*) bafflement

ver|eb|ben [fɛɐ'ɛbn] *ptp* **verebbt** VI *aux sein* to subside

ver|edeln [fɛɐ'eːdln] *ptp* **veredelt** VT *Metalle, Erdöl* to refine; *Fasern* to finish; (*Bot*) to graft; *Boden, Geschmack* to improve; *jdn, Charakter* to ennoble

Ver|ede|lung [fɛɐ'eːdəluŋ] F -, -en, **Ver|ed|lung** [fɛɐ'eːdlʊŋ] F -, -en (*von Metallen, Erdöl*) refining; (*von Fasern*) finishing; (*Bot*) grafting; (*von Boden, Geschmack*) improving; (*von Mensch, Charakter*) ennoblement

ver|ehe|li|chen *ptp* **verehelicht** VR (*form*) **sich (mit jdm) ~** to marry (sb)

ver|ehe|licht [fɛɐ'eːəlɪçt] ADJ (*form*) married; **Eva Schmidt, ~e Meier** Eva Meier née Schmidt; **seine Verehelichte** his wife

Ver|ehe|li|chung [fɛɐ'eːəlɪçʊŋ] F -, -en (*form*) marriage

ver|eh|ren *ptp* **verehrt** VT 🅰 (= *hoch achten*) to admire; *Gott, Maria, Heiligen* to honour; (= *ehrerbietig lieben*) to worship, to adore → *auch* **verehrt** 🅱 (= *schenken*) **jdm etw ~** to give sb sth

Ver|eh|rer [fɛɐ'eːrɐ] M -s, -, **Ver|eh|re|rin** [-ərɪn] F -, -nen admirer

ver|ehrt [fɛɐ'eːɐt] ADJ (*in Anrede*) **(sehr) ~e Anwesende/Gäste/~es Publikum** Ladies and Gentlemen; **(sehr) ~e gnädige Frau** (*in Brief*) (dear) Madam; **mein Verehrtester** (*iro, form*) (my) dear Sir; **meine Verehrteste** (*iro, form*) (my) dear Madam → *auch* **verehren**

Ver|eh|rung F (= *Hochachtung*) admiration; (*von Heiligen*) worship; (= *Liebe*) adoration

ver|eh|rungs-: ver|eh|rungs|voll ADV (*geh*) reverentially, in reverence; **ver|eh|rungs|wür|dig** ADJ (*geh*) *Mensch, Güte* commendable, praiseworthy; *Künstlerin* admirable

ver|ei|di|gen [fɛɐ'aidɪgn] *ptp* **vereidigt, ver|ei|den** [fɛɐ'aidn] *ptp* **vereidet** (*dated*) VT to swear in; **jdn auf etw** (*acc*) **~** to make *or* have sb swear

on sth; **vereidigter Übersetzer** *etc* sworn translator *etc*

Ver|ei|di|gung F -, -en swearing in

Ver|ein [fɛɐ'ain] M -(e)s, -e organization; (= *esp Tierverein, Landschaftsschutzverein etc auch*) society; (*kulturell auch*) association; (= *Sportverein*) club; (*inf*) crowd; **ein wohltätiger ~** a charity; **eingetragener ~** registered society *or* (*wohltätig*) charity; **im ~ mit** in conjunction with; **im ~ rufen** to shout *or* chant in unison; **ihr seid vielleicht ein ~!** (*inf*) what a bunch you are! (*inf*) → **gemeinnützig**

ver|ein|bar ADJ compatible; *Aussagen* consistent; **nicht (miteinander) ~** incompatible; *Aussagen* inconsistent; **eine mit meinem Gewissen nicht ~e Tat** a deed which I cannot reconcile with my conscience

ver|ein|ba|ren [fɛɐ'ainbaːrən] ⚙ 53.4 *ptp* **vereinbart** VT 🅰 (= *miteinander absprechen*) to agree; *Zeit, Treffen, Tag* to arrange; **(es) ~, dass ...** to agree/arrange that ... 🅱 **etw mit etw ~** to reconcile sth with sth; **Arbeit und Familie miteinander ~** to reconcile the demands of work and family; **sich mit etw ~ lassen** to be compatible with sth; **mit etw zu ~ sein** to be compatible with sth; (*Aussagen*) to be consistent with sth; (*Ziele, Ideale*) to be reconcilable with sth

Ver|ein|bar|keit [fɛɐ'ainbaːɐkait] F -, *no pl* compatibility; (*von Aussagen*) consistency

Ver|ein|ba|rung F -, -en (= *das Vereinbaren*) agreeing; (*von Zeit, Treffen, Tag*) arranging, arrangement; (= *Abmachung*) agreement; **laut ~** as agreed; **nach ~** by arrangement

ver|ein|ba|rungs|ge|mäß ADV as agreed

ver|ei|nen [fɛɐ'ainən] *ptp* **vereint** 🔲 to unite; (= *miteinander vereinbaren*) *Ideen, Prinzipien* to reconcile; **eine Familie wieder ~** to reunite a family; **sich nicht mit etw ~ lassen** to be irreconcilable with sth; **sie vereint Tugend und Schönheit in sich** (*dat*) she combines virtue and beauty → *auch* **vereint** 🔲 **in ihr ~ sich Schönheit und Tugend** she combines beauty and virtue

ver|ein|fa|chen [fɛɐ'ainfaxn] *ptp* **vereinfacht** VT to simplify; (*Math*) to reduce; **etw vereinfacht darstellen** to portray sth in simplified terms

Ver|ein|fa|chung F -, -en simplification; (*Math*) reduction

ver|ein|heit|li|chen [fɛɐ'ainhaitlɪçn] *ptp* **vereinheitlicht** VT to standardize

Ver|ein|heit|li|chung F -, -en standardization

ver|ei|ni|gen *ptp* **vereinigt** 🔲 to unite; *Kräfte auch* to combine; *Eigenschaften* to bring together; (*Comm*) *Firmen* to merge (*zu* into); *Kapital* to pool; **etw mit etw ~** (= *vereinbaren*) to reconcile sth with sth; **Schönheit mit Intelligenz (in sich** *dat*) **~** to combine beauty with intelligence; **die beiden Standpunkte lassen sich nicht ~** the two points of view are incompatible; **in einer Hand vereinigt sein** to be held by the same person; **Freunde um sich ~** to gather friends around one; **alle Stimmen auf sich** (*acc*) **~** to collect all the votes

🔲 to unite; (= *sich verbünden auch*) to join forces; (*Firmen*) to merge; (= *zusammenkommen*) to combine; (*Töne*) to blend; (*Flüsse*) to meet; (*Zellen etc*) to fuse; (= *sich versammeln*) to assemble; (*geh: geschlechtlich*) to come together; **sich zu einem harmonischen Ganzen ~** to merge into a harmonious whole; **sich zu einer Koalition ~** to form a coalition

ver|ei|nigt ADJ united; **Vereinigtes Königreich** United Kingdom; **Vereinigte Staaten** United States; **Vereinigte Arabische Emirate** United Arab Emirates

Ver|ei|ni|gung F 🅰 (= *das Vereinigen*) uniting; (*von Kräften auch*) combining; (*von Eigenschaften*) bringing together; (*von Firmen*) merging; (*von Kapital*) pooling; (*Math, geh*) = *körperliche, eheliche Vereinigung*) union; **die deutsche ~** (*Pol*) German unification, the unification of Germany 🔲 (= *Organisation*) organization

ver|ei|ni|gungs-: Ver|ei|ni|gungs|frei|heit F freedom of association; **Ver|ei|ni|gungs|kri|mi|na|li|tät** F *crime connected with the reunification of Germany;* **Ver|ei|ni|gungs|men|ge** F (*Math*) union *or* join of sets

ver|ein|nah|men [fɛɐ'ainna:mən] *ptp* **vereinnahmt** VT (*form*) *Geld* to take; **etw für sich ~** to claim sth for oneself; **jdn ~** (*fig*) to make demands on sb; (*Beruf*) to occupy sb; **sie versucht, ihn völlig zu ~** she wants him all to herself; **sich von jdm ~ lassen** to allow oneself to be monopolized by sb

Ver|ein|nah|mung F -, -en taking, collecting; (*fig*) monopolizing

ver|ein|sa|men [fɛɐ'ainza:mən] *ptp* **vereinsamt** VI *aux sein* to become lonely *or* isolated; **vereinsamt sterben** to die lonely

Ver|ein|sa|mung F -, *no pl* loneliness, isolation

Ver|eins-: Ver|eins|far|be NT *usu pl* club colour (*Brit*), club color (*US*); **Ver|eins|haus** NT , **Ver|eins|heim** NT clubhouse; **ver|eins|in|tern** ADJ *Termin, Frage, Turnier* internal club *or* society ADV within a/the club *or* society; **Ver|eins|ka|me|rad(in)** M(F) fellow club member; **Ver|eins|lei|tung** F → **Verein** 🅰 (= *Amt*) chairmanship of an organization/a society/an association/a club 🔲 (= *Personen*) club *etc* committee; **Ver|eins|mei|er** [-maiɐ] M -s, -, **Ver|eins|mei|e|rin** [-ərɪn] F -, -nen (*inf*) club freak (*inf*); **er ist ein richtiger ~** all he thinks about is his club; **Ver|eins|mei|e|rei** F -, *no pl* (*inf*) **seine ~ geht mir auf die Nerven** his obsession with his club is getting on my nerves; **diese ewige ~!** all this club nonsense!; **Ver|eins|meis|ter(in)** M(F) club champion; **Ver|eins|meis|ter|schaft** F club championship; **Ver|eins|mit|glied** NT club member; **Ver|eins|re|gis|ter** NT official register of societies and associations; **Ver|eins|sport** M club sport; **Ver|eins|we|sen** NT , *no pl* clubs, organizations and societies *pl*

ver|eint [fɛɐ'aint] ADJ united; **Vereinte Nationen** United Nations *sing* ADV together, in unison; **~ rufen** to shout in unison; **~ handeln** to act together *or* as one → *auch* **vereinen**

ver|ein|zeln [fɛɐ'aintsln] *ptp* **vereinzelt** VT (*Agr*) to thin (out)

ver|ein|zelt [fɛɐ'aintslt] ADJ occasional; (*Met auch*) isolated; *Schauer auch* scattered; **die Faulheit ~er Schüler** the laziness of the occasional *or* odd pupil ADV occasionally; (*zeitlich auch*) now and then; (*örtlich auch*) here and there; **... ~ bewölkt** ... with cloudy patches

Ver|ein|ze|lung [fɛɐ'aintsəluŋ] F -, -en (*von Menschen*) isolation; (*Agr*) thinning out

ver|ei|sen *ptp* **vereist** 🔲 (*Med*) to freeze 🔲 *aux sein* to freeze; (*Straße*) to freeze *or* ice over; (*Fensterscheibe*) to ice over; (*Tragfläche auch*) to ice up, to freeze over

ver|eist [fɛɐ'aist] ADJ *Straßen, Fenster* icy; *Bäche* frozen; *Türschloss, Tragfläche, Piste* iced-up; *Land* covered in ice

Ver|ei|sung [fɛɐ'aizʊŋ] F -, -en 🅰 (*Med*) freezing 🔲 (= *das Vereisen*) freezing; (*von Straße*) freezing *or* icing over; (*von Tragfläche*) icing (up)

ver|ei|teln [fɛɐ'aitln] *ptp* **vereitelt** VT *Plan etc* to thwart, to foil; *Versuch auch* to frustrate; *Verbrechen, Attentat* to foil, to prevent

Ver|ei|te|lung F -, -en thwarting, foiling; (*von Verbrechen*) prevention; (*von Versuch*) frustration

ver|ei|tern *ptp* **vereitert** VI *aux sein* to go septic; (*Wunde auch*) to fester; **vereitert sein** to be septic; **vereiterte Wunde** septic wound; **vereiterter Zahn** abscess; **vereiterte Mandeln haben** to have tonsillitis

Ver|ei|te|rung [fɛɐ'aitərʊŋ] F -, -en sepsis; **~ der Wunde** septic wound; **~ des Zahns** dental sepsis; **~ der Mandeln** tonsillitis

---

Ver|eit|lung [fɛɐ̯ˈʔaitlʊŋ] F -, -en = **Vereitelung**

ver|ekeln ptp **verekelt** VT (inf) **jdm etw ~** to put sb off sth (inf)

ver|elen|den [fɛɐ̯ˈʔeːlɛndn] ptp **verelendet** VI aux sein to become impoverished or (Mensch auch) destitute

Ver|elen|dung F -, -en impoverishment

ver|en|den ptp **verendet** VI aux sein to perish, to die

ver|en|gen [fɛɐ̯ˈʔɛŋən] ptp **verengt** VR to narrow, to become narrow; (Gefäße, Pupille) to contract; (Kleid, Taille) to go in; (fig: Horizont) to narrow VT to make narrower; Blutgefäß, Pupille etc to make contract; Kleid to take in; Horizont to narrow

ver|en|gern [fɛɐ̯ˈʔɛŋən] ptp **verengert** VT **a** Kleidung to take in **b** = **verengen** VT VR **a** (Ärmel, Hose) to go in; (= spitz zulaufen) to become narrower **b** = **verengen** VR

Ver|en|gung F -, -en **a** narrowing; (von Pupille, Gefäß) contraction **b** (= verengte Stelle) narrow part (in +dat of); (in Adern) stricture (in +dat of)

ver|erb|bar ADJ **a** Anlagen, Krankheit hereditary **b** Besitz heritable

ver|er|ben ptp **vererbt** VT **a** Besitz to leave, to bequeath (+dat, an +acc to); (hum) to hand on (jdm to sb), to bequeath (jdm sb) **b** Anlagen, Eigenschaften to pass on (+dat, auf +acc to); Krankheit to transmit VR to be passed on/transmitted (auf +acc to)

ver|erb|lich [fɛɐ̯ˈʔɛrplɪç] ADJ = **vererbbar**

Ver|er|bung [fɛɐ̯ˈʔɛrbʊŋ] F -, no pl **a** (= das Vererben) (von Besitz) passing on; (von Anlagen) passing on; (von Krankheit) transmission **b** (Lehre) heredity; **das ist ~** (inf) it's hereditary

Ver|er|bungs-: **Ver|er|bungs|for|schung** F genetics sing; **Ver|er|bungs|leh|re** F genetics sing

ver|ewi|gen [fɛɐ̯ˈʔeːvɪgn] ptp **verewigt** VT to immortalize; Zustand, Verhältnisse to perpetuate; **seine schmutzigen Finger auf der Buchseite ~** to leave one's dirty fingermarks on the page for posterity VR (lit, fig) to immortalize oneself

Verf. abbr von **Verfasser**

Ver|fah|ren [fɛɐ̯ˈfaːrən] NT -s, - (= Vorgehen) actions pl; (= Verfahrensweise) procedure; (Tech) process; (= Methode) method; (Jur) proceedings pl; **ein ~ gegen jdn anhängig machen** or **einleiten** to take or initiate legal proceedings against sb

ver|fah|ren[1] [fɛɐ̯ˈfaːrən] ptp **verfahren** VI irreg aux sein (= vorgehen) to act, to proceed; **mit jdm/etw streng/schlecht ~** to deal strictly/badly with sb/sth

ver|fah|ren[2] ptp **verfahren** irreg VT (= verbrauchen) Geld, Zeit to spend in travelling (Brit) or traveling (US); Benzin to use up VR (= sich verirren) to lose one's way; (fig) (Angelegenheit) to get muddled; (Mensch) to get into a muddle

ver|fah|ren[3] [fɛɐ̯ˈfaːrən] ADJ Angelegenheit, Situation muddled; **eine ~e Sache** a muddle

Ver|fah|rens-: **Ver|fah|rens|be|schleuni|gung** F speeding up the procedure; (Jur) speeding up the proceedings; **zur ~** to speed up the procedure; (Jur) to speed up the proceedings; **Ver|fah|rens|dau|er** F length of the procedure; (Jur) length of the proceedings; **Ver|fah|rens|feh|ler** M (Jur) procedural error; **Ver|fah|rens|kos|ten** PL (Jur) procedural costs pl; **ver|fah|rens|recht|lich** ADJ (form) procedural; **Ver|fah|rens|tech|nik** F process engineering; **Ver|fah|rens|wei|se** F procedure, modus operandi

Ver|fall M , no pl **a** (= Zerfall) decay; (von Gebäude) dilapidation; (gesundheitlich, geistig) decline; **etw dem ~ preisgeben** to let sth go to (rack and) ruin; **in ~ geraten** (Gebäude) to become dilapidated; (stärker) to fall into ruins **b** (= Niedergang) (von Kultur, der Sitten, sittlich) decline; (des Römischen Reichs) fall; (von Reichtum, Vermögen) fall (von in) **c** (= das Ungültigwerden)

(von Schuldansprüchen, Rechnung etc) lapsing; (von Scheck, Karte) expiry

ver|fal|len[1] ptp **verfallen** VI irreg aux sein **a** (= zerfallen) to decay; (Bauwerk) to fall into disrepair, to become dilapidated; (Zellen) to deteriorate; (körperlich und geistig) to deteriorate; (Sitten, Kultur, Reich) to decline; **der Patient verfällt zusehends** the patient has gone into a rapid decline **b** (= ungültig werden) (Briefmarken, Geldscheine, Gutschein) to become invalid; (Scheck, Fahrkarte) to expire; (Strafe, Recht, Termin, Anspruch, Patent) to lapse **c** (= in jds Besitz übergehen) to be forfeited; **jdm ~** to be forfeited to sb, to become the property of sb **d** (= abhängig werden) **jdm/einer Sache ~/~ sein** to become/be a slave to sb/sth; dem Alkohol etc to become/be addicted to sth; dem Wahnsinn to fall/have fallen victim to; jds Zauber etc to become/be enslaved by sth; **jdm völlig ~ sein** to be completely under sb's spell; **einem Irrtum ~** to make a mistake, to be mistaken **e** **auf etw** (acc) **~** to think of sth; (aus Verzweiflung) to resort to sth; **auf abstruse Gedanken ~** to start having abstruse thoughts; **wer ist denn bloß auf diesen Gedanken ~?** whoever thought this up?; **wie sind Sie bloß darauf ~?** whatever gave you that idea? **f** **in etw** (acc) **~** to sink into sth; **in einen tiefen Schlaf ~** to fall into a deep sleep; **in einen ganz anderen Ton ~** to adopt a completely different tone; **in einen Fehler ~** to make a mistake; **in Panik ~** to get into a panic

ver|fal|len[2] [fɛɐ̯ˈfalən] ADJ Gebäude dilapidated, ruined; Mensch (körperlich) emaciated; (geistig) senile; (= abgelaufen) Karten, Briefmarken invalid; Strafe lapsed; Scheck expired

Ver|falls-: **Ver|falls|da|tum** NT expiry date; (der Haltbarkeit) best-before date, use-by date; **Ver|falls|er|schei|nung** F symptom of decline (+gen in); **Ver|falls|tag** M expiry date; (von Strafe etc) date of lapsing; **Ver|falls|ter|min** M expiry date; (der Haltbarkeit) best-before date, use-by date

ver|fäl|schen ptp **verfälscht** VT to distort; Wahrheit, Aussage auch, Daten to falsify; Lebensmittel, Wein, Geschmack to adulterate

Ver|fäl|schung F distortion; (von Wahrheit, Aussage auch, von Daten) falsification; (von Lebensmitteln, Geschmack) adulteration

ver|fan|gen ptp **verfangen** irreg VR to get caught; **sich in Lügen ~** to get entangled in a web of lies; **sich in Widersprüchen ~** to contradict oneself VI to be accepted; (Argument, Slogan) to catch on; **bei jdm nicht ~** not to cut any ice with sb (inf); **die Masche verfing** the trick worked; **dieser Trick verfängt bei mir nicht** that ploy won't work with me

ver|fäng|lich [fɛɐ̯ˈfɛŋlɪç] ADJ Situation awkward, embarrassing; Aussage, Beweismaterial, Blicke, Andeutungen incriminating; (= gefährlich) dangerous; Angewohnheit insidious; Frage tricky

ver|fär|ben ptp **verfärbt** VT to discolour (Brit), to discolor (US); **etw rot ~** to turn sth red; **wenn der Herbst die Blätter verfärbt** when autumn (esp Brit) or fall (US) turns the leaves VR to change colour (Brit) or color (US); (Blätter auch) to turn; (Metall, Wäsche, Stoff) to discolour (Brit), to discolor (US); **sich grün/rot ~** to turn or go green/red; **sie verfärbte sich** she went red/white

Ver|fär|bung F change in colour (Brit) or color (US); (von Blättern auch) turning; (von Metall, Wäsche, Stoff) discolouring (Brit), discoloring (US)

ver|fas|sen ptp **verfasst** VT to write; Gesetz, Urkunde to draw up

Ver|fas|ser [fɛɐ̯ˈfasɐ] M -s, -, **Ver|fas|se|rin** [-ərɪn] F -, -nen writer; (von Buch, Artikel etc auch) author

Ver|fas|ser|schaft [fɛɐ̯ˈfasɐʃaft] F -, no pl authorship

Ver|fas|sung F **a** (Pol) constitution; **gegen die ~ handeln** to act unconstitutionally **b** (körperlich) state (of health); (seelisch) state of mind; **sie ist in guter/schlechter ~** she is in good/bad shape; **seine seelische ~** ist gut/schlecht he is in good/poor spirits; **sie ist nicht in der ~ zu arbeiten** she is in no fit state (Brit) or in no shape to work **c** (= Zustand) state; **die Firma/Wirtschaft ist in guter ~** the company/economy is in good shape

ver|fas|sung|ge|bend ADJ attr Versammlung constituent

Ver|fas|sungs-: **Ver|fas|sungs|än|de|rung** F constitutional amendment; **Ver|fas|sungs|be|schwer|de** F complaint about infringement of the constitution; **Ver|fas|sungs|ent|wurf** M draft of a/the constitution; **Ver|fas|sungs|feind(in)** M(F) enemy of the constitution (being declared as such disbars sb from working in the public service); **ver|fas|sungs|feind|lich** ADJ anticonstitutional; **ver|fas|sungs|ge|mäß** ADJ ADV in accordance with the constitution; **Ver|fas|sungs|ge|richt** NT , **Ver|fas|sungs|ge|richts|hof** M constitutional court; **Oberstes ~** supreme constitutional court; (in den USA) Supreme Court; **Ver|fas|sungs|kla|ge** F constitutional challenge; **ver|fas|sungs|kon|form** ADJ in conformity with the constitution pred (nachgestellt), constitutional (US); **nicht ~** not in conformity with the constitution pred (nachgestellt), unconstitutional (US); **ver|fas|sungs|mä|ßig** ADJ constitutional; **etw ~ garantieren** to guarantee sth in the constitution; **eine ~e Ordnung** a constitutional law; **Ver|fas|sungs|recht** NT constitutional law; **Ver|fas|sungs|rich|ter(in)** M(F) constitutional judge; **Ver|fas|sungs|schutz** M (Aufgabe) defence (Brit) or defense (US) of the constitution; (Organ, Amt) office responsible for defending the constitution; **ver|fas|sungs|treu** ADJ loyal to the constitution; **Ver|fas|sungs|treue** F loyalty to the constitution; **Ver|fas|sungs|ur|kun|de** F constitution, constitutional charter; **ver|fas|sungs|wid|rig** ADJ unconstitutional; **Ver|fas|sungs|wid|rig|keit** F unconstitutionality; **Ver|fas|sungs|wirk|lich|keit** F constitutional reality

ver|fau|len ptp **verfault** VI aux sein to decay; (Fleisch, Gemüse, Obst auch) to rot; (Körper, organische Stoffe) to decompose; (fig) to degenerate

ver|fault [fɛɐ̯ˈfault] ADJ decayed; Fleisch, Obst etc rotten; Zähne bad, rotten; Körper decomposed; Mensch (innerlich) degenerate

ver|fech|ten ptp **verfochten** [fɛɐ̯ˈfɔxtn] VT irreg to defend; Lehre to advocate, to champion; Meinung to maintain

Ver|fech|ter [fɛɐ̯ˈfɛçtɐ] M -s, -, **Ver|fech|te|rin** [-ərɪn] F -, -nen advocate, champion

Ver|fech|tung F -, -en defence (Brit), defense (US); (von Lehre) advocacy, championing; (von Meinung) maintaining

ver|feh|len ptp **verfehlt** VT **a** (= verpassen, nicht treffen) to miss; **seine Worte hatten ihre Wirkung verfehlt/nicht verfehlt** his words had missed/hit their target; **den Zweck ~** not to achieve its purpose; **das Thema ~** to be completely off the subject **b** (= versäumen) **nicht ~, etw zu tun** not to fail to do sth

ver|fehlt [fɛɐ̯ˈfeːlt] ADJ (= unangebracht) inappropriate; (= misslungen) Leben, Angelegenheit, Planung, Politik unsuccessful; **es ist ~, das zu tun** you are mistaken in doing that

Ver|feh|lung [fɛɐ̯ˈfeːlʊŋ] F -, -en **a** (des Ziels) missing; **bei ~ des Themas bekommt der Schüler ...** if the essay is off the subject the pupil will get ... **b** (= Vergehen) misdemeanour (Brit), misdemeanor (US); (= Sünde) transgression

ver|fein|den [fɛɐ̯ˈfaindn] ptp **verfeindet** VR to quarrel; **sich mit jdm ~** to make an enemy of sb; mit Nachbarn to quarrel with sb; **verfeindet sein** to have quarrelled (Brit) or quarreled

(*US*); (*Familie etc*) to be estranged; (*Staaten*) to be on bad terms; **die verfeindeten Schwestern** the estranged sisters; **die verfeindeten Staaten** the enemy states; **verfeindete Volksgruppen** rival ethnic groups **VT** **warum versucht sie, ihren Mann und seine Familie zu ~?** why is she trying to set her husband against his family?

ver|fei|nern [fɛɐˈfainɐn] *ptp* **verfeinert** **VT** to improve; *Methode, Geschmack auch* to refine **VR** to improve; (*Methoden auch*) to become refined

ver|fei|nert [fɛɐˈfainɐt] *ADJ Methode, Geräte, Essen* sophisticated

Ver|fei|ne|rung F -, -en improvement; (*von Methode auch*) refining; **die zunehmende ~ technischer Geräte** the increasing sophistication of technical equipment

ver|fe|men [fɛɐˈfeːmən] *ptp* **verfemt** VT (*Hist*) to outlaw; (*fig*) *jdn* to ostracize; *Künstler, Ideologie, Methode, Kunstrichtung* to condemn

Ver|fem|te(r) [fɛɐˈfeːmtə] MF *decl as adj* (*Hist*) outlaw; (*fig*) persona non grata

ver|fer|ti|gen *ptp* **verfertigt** VT to manufacture, to produce; *Liste* to draw up; (*usu iro*) *Brief, Aufsatz* to compose

ver|fes|ti|gen *ptp* **verfestigt** **VT** to harden; *Flüssigkeit* to solidify; (= *verstärken*) to strengthen, to reinforce **VR** to harden; (*Flüssigkeit*) to solidify; (*fig*) (*Hass, Feindschaft*) to harden; (*Kenntnisse*) to be reinforced; (*Ideen, Gewohnheiten*) to become fixed *or* set; (*Demokratie, Strukturen*) to be strengthened *or* reinforced

ver|fet|ten *ptp* **verfettet** VI *aux sein* (*Med*) to become fat; *Mensch auch* to become obese; (*Herz, Leber*) to become fatty *or* adipose (*spec*)

Ver|fet|tung [fɛɐˈfɛtʊŋ] F -, -en (*Med*) (*von Körper*) obesity; (*von Organ, Muskeln*) fatty degeneration, adiposity (*spec*)

ver|feu|ern **verfeuert** VT to burn; *Munition* to fire; **die ganze Munition/das ganze Öl ~** to use up all the ammunition/oil

ver|fil|men *ptp* **verfilmt** VT *Buch, Geschichte* to make a film of

Ver|fil|mung [fɛɐˈfilmʊŋ] F -, -en (= *das Verfilmen*) filming; (= *Film*) film (version)

ver|fil|zen *ptp* **verfilzt** **VI** *aux sein* (*Wolle, Pullover, Teppich*) to become felted; (*Haare*) to become matted; (*fig: Pol etc*) to become corrupt **VR** to become matted

ver|filzt [fɛɐˈfiltst] *ADJ Wolle, Pullover* felted; *Haare* matted

ver|fins|tern *ptp* **verfinstert** **VT** to darken; *Sonne, Mond* to eclipse **VR** (*lit, fig*) to darken

Ver|fins|te|rung F -, -en darkening; (*von Sonne etc*) eclipse

ver|fit|zen [fɛɐˈfitsn] *ptp* **verfitzt** (*inf*) **VT** to tangle **VR** to become tangled

ver|fla|chen *ptp* **verflacht** **VI** *aux sein* to flatten *or* level out; (*fig: Diskussion, Gespräch, Mensch*) to become superficial *or* trivial (*Gelände*) to flatten *or* level out

Ver|fla|chung F -, -en flattening out, levelling (*esp Brit*) *or* leveling (*US*) out; (*fig*) superficiality; **um einer ~ der Diskussion vorzubeugen** to stop the conversation becoming superficial *or* trivial

ver|flech|ten *ptp* **verflochten** [fɛɐˈflɔxtn] *irreg* **VT** to interweave; to intertwine; *Bänder* to interlace; (*auch fig*) *Methoden* to combine; *Firmen* to interlink; **eng mit etw verflochten sein** (*fig*) to be closely connected *or* linked with sth; **jdn in etw** (*acc*) **~** (*in Gespräch, Unternehmen*) to involve sb in sth; *in dunkle Geschäfte* to entangle *or* embroil sb in sth **VR** to interweave, to intertwine; (*Bänder*) to interlace; (= *sich verwirren*) to become entangled (*mit* in); (*Themen*) to interweave; (*Methoden*) to combine; **sich mit etw ~** to become linked *or* connected with sth

Ver|flech|tung [fɛɐˈflɛçtʊŋ] F -, -en **a** (= *das Verflechten*) interweaving, intertwining; (*von Bändern*) interlacing; (*in dunkle Geschäfte*) entangle-

ment; (*von Methoden*) combining **b** (= *das Verflochtensein*) interconnection (+*gen* between); (*Pol, Econ*) integration

ver|fleckt [fɛɐˈflɛkt] *ADJ* (*inf*) stained

ver|flie|gen *ptp* **verflogen** [fɛɐˈfloːgn] *irreg* **VI** *aux sein* **a** (*fig*) (*Stimmung, Zorn etc*) to blow over (*inf*), to pass; (*Heimweh, Kummer, Hoffnung etc*) to vanish **b** (= *sich verflüchtigen*) to vanish; (*Alkohol*) to evaporate; (*Duft*) to fade (away); (*Zeit*) to fly **VR** to stray; (*Pilot, Flugzeug*) to lose one's/its bearings

ver|flie|ßen *ptp* **verflossen** [fɛɐˈflɔsn] VI *irreg aux sein* **a** (*geh:* = *vergehen*) to go by, to pass → *auch* **verflossen b** (= *verschwimmen*) (*Farben*) to run; (*fig*) to become blurred

ver|flixt [fɛɐˈflikst] (*inf*) **ADJ** blessed (*inf*), darned (*inf*); (= *kompliziert*) tricky; **du ~er Kerl!** you devil; **das ~e siebte Jahr** ≈ the seven-year itch **ADV** darned (*inf*) **INTERJ** ~! blow! (*Brit inf*), darn! (*US inf*)

Ver|floch|ten|heit [fɛɐˈflɔxtnhait] F -, -en (*fig*) interconnections *pl* (*von* between)

ver|flos|sen [fɛɐˈflɔsn] *ADJ* **a** *Jahre, Tage* bygone; (= *letzte*) last **b** (*inf:* = *ehemalig*) one-time *attr* (*inf*), former *attr* → *auch* **verfließen**

Ver|flos|se|ne(r) [fɛɐˈflɔsənə] MF *decl as adj* (*inf*) ex (*inf*); (= *Mann*) ex-boyfriend; (*nach Scheidung*) ex-husband; (= *Frau*) ex-girlfriend; (*nach Scheidung*) ex-wife

ver|flu|chen *ptp* **verflucht** VT to curse; **sei verflucht** curses on you

ver|flucht [fɛɐˈfluːxt] (*inf*) **ADJ** damn (*inf*), bloody (*Brit inf*); **~ (noch mal)!** damn (it) (*inf*); **diese ~e Tat** (*liter*) this cursed deed; **~e Tat!** damn! (*inf*) **ADV** (*bei englischem adj, n*) damn (*inf*), bloody (*Brit inf*); (*bei englischem vb*) like hell (*inf*); **ich habe mich ~ vertan** I made one hell of a mistake (*inf*)

ver|flüch|ti|gen [fɛɐˈflʏçtɪgn] *ptp* **verflüchtigt** **VT** to evaporate **VR** (*Alkohol, Kohlensäure etc*) to evaporate; (*Duft*) to disappear; (*Gase*) to volatilize; (*fig*) (*Bedenken, Ärger*) to be dispelled; (*hum*) (*Mensch, Gegenstand, Hoffnungen etc*) to vanish; (*Geld*) to go up in smoke (*inf*)

Ver|flüch|ti|gung F -, -en evaporation; (*von Duft*) disappearance; (*von Gasen*) volatilization

ver|flüs|si|gen [fɛɐˈflʏsɪgn] *ptp* **verflüssigt** VTR to liquefy

Ver|flüs|si|gung F -, -en liquefaction

Ver|folg [fɛɐˈfɔlk] M -s, *no pl* (*form*) (= *Ausübung*) pursuance; (= *Verlauf*) course; **im ~ des Schreibens vom ...** further to our letter of ...

ver|fol|gen *ptp* **verfolgt** VT *Ziel, Idee, Interessen, Karriere, Straftat* to pursue; *jdn auch* to follow; (= *jds Spuren folgen*) *jdn* to trail; *Tier* to track; (*mit Hunden etc*) to hunt; *Unterricht, Entwicklung, Geschichte, Spur* to follow; *Vorschlag, Gedanken* to follow up; (*politisch, religiös*) to persecute; (*Gedanke, Erinnerung etc*) *jdn* to haunt; **vom Unglück/Schicksal etc verfolgt werden** *or* **sein** to be dogged by ill fortune/by fate *etc*; **jdn politisch ~** to persecute sb for political reasons; **jdn gerichtlich ~** to prosecute sb; **jdn mit den Augen** *or* **Blicken ~** to follow sb with one's eyes; **jdn mit Bitten/Forderungen ~** to badger sb with requests/demands; **jdn mit Hass ~** to pursue sb in hate; **welche Absicht verfolgt er?** what is his intention? → **strafrechtlich**

Ver|fol|ger [fɛɐˈfɔlgɐ] M -s, -, **Ver|fol|ge|rin** [-ərɪn] F -, -nen **a** pursuer **b** (*politisch, wegen Gesinnung*) persecutor

Ver|folg|te(r) [fɛɐˈfɔlktə] MF *decl as adj* quarry; (*politisch, wegen Gesinnung*) victim of persecution

Ver|fol|gung [fɛɐˈfɔlgʊŋ] F -, -en (*von Ziel, Idee, Karriere, Verbrecher, Fahrzeug*) pursuit; (= *Spurensuche*) trailing; (*von Tier*) tracking; (= *politische Verfolgung*) persecution *no pl*; **die ~ aufnehmen** to take up the chase; **gerichtliche ~** court action; **strafrechtliche ~** prosecution; **bei der weiteren ~ der Frage** when this question was/is

pursued further; **~ eines Ziels** pursuance of an aim

Ver|fol|gungs-: **Ver|fol|gungs|jagd** F chase, pursuit; **Ver|fol|gungs|ren|nen** NT (*Sport*) pursuit race; **Ver|fol|gungs|wahn** M persecution mania

ver|for|men *ptp* **verformt** **VT** to make go out of shape, to distort (*zu* into); (= *umformen*) to work; **verformt sein** to be out of shape; (*Mensch, Gliedmaßen*) to be deformed **VR** to go out of shape

Ver|for|mung F **a** distortion **b** (= *veränderte Form*) distortion; (*von Mensch, Gliedmaßen*) deformity

ver|frach|ten [fɛɐˈfraxtn] *ptp* **verfrachtet** VT (*Comm*) to transport; (*Naut*) to ship; (*inf*) *jdn* to bundle off (*inf*); **etw in den Keller/eine Kiste ~** (*inf*) to dump sth in the cellar/a crate

Ver|frach|ter [fɛɐˈfraxtɐ] M -s, -, **Ver|frach|te|rin** [-ərɪn] F -, -nen transport agent; (*Naut*) shipper

Ver|frach|tung F -, -en transporting; (*Naut*) shipping

ver|fran|zen [fɛɐˈfrantsn] *ptp* **verfranzt** VR (*inf*) to lose one's way; (*Aviat sl*) to lose one's bearings; (*fig*) to get in a muddle *or* tangle

ver|frem|den [fɛɐˈfrɛmdn] *ptp* **verfremdet** VT *Thema, Stoff* to make unfamiliar, to defamiliarize; *Werkstoffe* to use in an unusual way

Ver|frem|dung F -, -en defamiliarization; (*Theat, Liter*) alienation, distancing; **die ~ vertrauter Formen** using familiar forms in an unfamiliar way

Ver|frem|dungs|ef|fekt M distancing effect; (*Theat, Liter*) alienation *or* estrangement effect

ver|fres|sen¹ *ptp* **verfressen** VT *irreg* (*inf*) to spend *or* blow (*inf*) on food

ver|fres|sen² [fɛɐˈfrɛsn] *ADJ* (*inf*) greedy

ver|frie|ren *ptp* **verfroren** [fɛɐˈfroːrən] VI *irreg aux sein* (*dial*) = **erfrieren**

ver|fro|ren [fɛɐˈfroːrən] *ADJ* (*inf*) sensitive to cold; (= *durchgefroren*) frozen, freezing cold; **~ sein** (= *kälteempfindlich*) to feel the cold

ver|frü|hen [fɛɐˈfryːən] *ptp* **verfrüht** VR (*Winter, Entwicklung, Zug*) to come *or* arrive early; (*Gäste*) to be *or* come too early

ver|früht [fɛɐˈfryːt] *ADJ* (= *zu früh*) premature; (= *früh*) early; **solche Aufgaben sind für dieses Alter ~** exercises like this are too advanced for this age group

ver|füg|bar *ADJ* available

Ver|füg|bar|keit F availability

ver|fu|gen *ptp* **verfugt** VT to fit flush; *Fliesen* to grout

ver|fü|gen ✪ 46.2 *ptp* **verfügt** **VI** **über etw** (*acc*) **~** to have sth at one's disposal; (= *besitzen*) to have sth; **über jdn/etw ~** (= *bestimmen über*) to be in charge of sb/sth; **die Art und Weise, wie er über seine Untergebenen verfügt** the way in which he orders his inferiors around; **Gott verfügt über das Schicksal der Menschen** God determines man's fate; **du kannst über mein Auto ~, wenn ich nicht da bin** you can use my car while I'm away; **du kannst doch nicht über meine Zeit ~** you can't tell me how to spend my time; **du kannst doch nicht über deinen Bruder ~** you can't tell your brother what to do; **über etw** (*acc*) **frei ~ können** to be able to do as one wants with sth; **~ Sie über mich** I am at your disposal

VT to order; (*gesetzlich*) to decree → **letztwillig** **VR** (*form*) to proceed (*form*)

Ver|fü|gung ✪ 46.4 F **a** *no pl* (= *das Verfügen*) possession; **freie ~** (*Jur*) free disposal (*über* +*acc* of); **jdm etw zur ~ stellen** to put sth at sb's disposal; (= *leihen*) to lend sb sth; **jdm zur ~ stehen, zu jds ~ stehen** to be at sb's disposal; **(jdm) zur ~ stehen** (= *verfügbar sein*) to be available (to sb); **sich zur ~ halten** to be available (to sb); **halte dich ab 7 Uhr zur ~** be ready from 7 o'clock; **etw zur ~ haben** to have sth at one's disposal **b** (*behördlich*) order; (*von Gesetzgeber*) decree; (*testamentarisch*) provision; (= *Anweisung*) instruction → **letztwillig, einstweilig**

Ver|fü|gungs-: Ver|fü|gungs|be|fug|nis F right of disposal (*über* +*acc* of); **Ver|fü|gungs|ge|walt** F (*Jur*) right of disposal; **die ~ über Atomwaffen** the power to use atomic weapons; **Ver|fü|gungs|rah|men** M (*Fin*) credit limit; **Ver|fü|gungs|recht** NT (*Jur*) right of disposal (*über* +*acc* of)

ver|führ|bar ADJ temptable; (*esp sexuell*) seducible; **sie sind ~** they can be tempted; (*sexuell*) they can be seduced

ver|füh|ren ptp **verführt** VT to tempt; (*esp sexuell*) to seduce; *die Jugend, das Volk etc* to lead astray; **jdn zu etw ~, jdn ~, etw zu tun** to encourage sb to do sth; **ich lasse mich gern ~** you can twist my arm (*inf*); **diese offenen Kisten ~ ja direkt zum Diebstahl** these open boxes are an encouragement *or* invitation to steal

Ver|füh|rer M seducer

Ver|füh|re|rin F seductress, temptress

ver|füh|re|risch [fɛɐ̯'fyːʁərɪʃ] ADJ seductive; (= *verlockend*) tempting ADV seductively; *duften, riechen, aussehen* seductive, tempting

Ver|füh|rung F seduction; (*von Jugend, Volk*) tempting; (= *Verlockung*) enticement, temptation

Ver|füh|rungs|kunst F seductive manner; (*von Werbung*) persuasiveness; **ein Meister der ~** a master of seduction/persuasion; **Verführungskünste** seductive/persuasive charms *or* ways

ver|fül|len ptp **verfüllt** VT (*mit Erde, Beton etc*) to fill in

ver|fünf|fa|chen [fɛɐ̯'fʏnffaxn] ptp **verfünffacht** VT *Zahl* to multiply by five, to quintuple (*form*) VR to increase five times *or* fivefold; (*Zahl auch*) to multiply by five

ver|fut|tern ptp **verfuttert** VT (*inf*) to spend on food

ver|füt|tern ptp **verfüttert** VT to use as animal/bird food; (= *aufbrauchen*) to feed (*an* +*acc* to); **etw an die Schweine/Vögel ~** to feed sth to the pigs/birds

Ver|füt|te|rung F -, (*rare*) **-n** (*an Tiere*) feeding; **die ~ von Küchenabfällen an Schweine** feeding kitchen waste to pigs

Ver|ga|be F -, (*rare*) **-n** (*von Arbeiten*) allocation; (*von Stipendium, Auftrag etc*) award

Ver|ga|be|pra|xis F (*von Arbeiten*) allocation procedure; (*von Stipendium, Auftrag etc*) award procedure

Ver|ga|be|stel|le F (*für Studienplätze*) central universities admissions council

ver|gack|ei|ern [fɛɐ̯'gakaɪɐn] ptp **vergackeiert** VT (*inf*) **jdn ~** to pull sb's leg (*inf*), to have sb on (*inf*)

ver|gaf|fen ptp **vergafft** VR (*dated inf*) **sich in jdn ~** to fall for sb (*inf*)

ver|gagt [fɛɐ̯'gɛ(ː)kt] ADJ (*inf*) gimmicky (*inf*)

ver|gäl|len [fɛɐ̯'gɛlən] ptp **vergällt** VT *Alkohol* to denature; (*fig*) *jdn* to embitter, to sour; *Freude* to spoil; *Leben etc* to sour; **jdm die Freude ~** to spoil sb's fun; **jdm das Leben ~** to sour sb's life

ver|ga|lop|pie|ren ptp **vergaloppiert** VR (*inf*) (= *sich irren*) to be on the wrong track; (= *übers Ziel hinausschießen*) to go too far

ver|gam|meln ptp **vergammelt** (*inf*) VI *aux sein* **a** (= *verderben*) to get spoiled; (*Speisen*) to go bad; **vergammeltes Obst** mouldy (*Brit*) *or* moldy (*US*) fruit **b** (= *verlottern*) to go to the dogs (*inf*); *Gebäude* to become run down; **vergammelt aussehen** to look scruffy; **vergammelte Studenten** scruffy(-looking) students; **eine vergammelte Kneipe** a seedy pub (*Brit*) *or* bar VT to waste; **ich möchte mal wieder einen Tag ~** I'd like to have a day doing nothing

ver|gan|gen [fɛɐ̯'gaŋən] ADJ **a** (= *letzte*) last **b** *Jahre* past; *Zeiten, Bräuche* bygone, former; *Größe* past, former; **das Vergangene** the past;

das ist alles ~ und vergessen that is all in the past now → *auch* **vergehen**

Ver|gan|gen|heit F -, **-en** past; (*von Stadt, Staat etc auch*) history; (*Gram*) past (tense); **die erste** *or* **einfache/zweite** *or* **vollendete/dritte ~** (*Gram*) the simple past/perfect/pluperfect (tense); **eine Frau mit ~** a woman with a past; **der ~ angehören** to be a thing of the past

Ver|gan|gen|heits-: Ver|gan|gen|heits|be|wäl|ti|gung F process of coming to terms with the past; **Ver|gan|gen|heits|form** F (*Gram*) past tense

ver|gäng|lich [fɛɐ̯'gɛŋlɪç] ADJ transitory

Ver|gäng|lich|keit F -, *no pl* transitoriness

ver|gä|ren [fɛɐ̯'gɛːrən] ptp **vergoren** *or* **vergärt** [fɛɐ̯'goːrən, fɛɐ̯'gɛːɐ̯t] *irreg* VI *aux sein* to ferment VT to ferment (*zu* into)

ver|ga|sen [fɛɐ̯'gaːzn] ptp **vergast** VT (*Tech: in Motor*) to carburet; *Kohle* to gasify; (= *durch Gas töten*) *jdn, Ungeziefer* to gas

Ver|ga|sen NT **-s**, *no pl* gassing

Ver|ga|ser [fɛɐ̯'gaːzɐ] M **-s, -** (*Aut*) carburettor (*Brit*), carburetor (*US*)

Ver|ga|ser-: Ver|ga|ser|brand M fire in the carburettor (*Brit*) *or* carburetor (*US*); **Ver|ga|ser|mo|tor** M carburettor (*Brit*) *or* carburetor (*US*) engine

ver|gaß pret von **vergessen**

Ver|ga|sung F -, **-en** (*Tech*) carburation; (*von Kohle*) gasification; (= *Tötung*) gassing; **etw bis zur ~ diskutieren** (*inf*) to discuss sth ad nauseum

ver|gat|tern [fɛɐ̯'gatɐn] ptp **vergattert** VT **a** *Garten etc* to fence off; *Tiere* to fence in **b** (*Mil*) to instruct **c** (*inf*) to punish; **jdn zu etw ~** to order sb to do sth

ver|ge|ben ptp **vergeben** *irreg* VT **a** (= *weggeben*) *Auftrag, Stipendium, Preis* to award (*an* +*acc* to); *Plätze, Studienplätze, Stellen* to allocate; *Kredit* to give out; *Karten* to give away; *Arbeit* to assign; (*fig*) *Chance, Möglichkeit* to throw away; **ein Amt an jdn ~** to appoint sb to an office; **zu ~ sein** to be available; (*Stelle auch*) to be open; (*Gewinn*) to have been awarded *or* won; (*Wohnung, Karten, Plätze*) to have been taken; (*Stelle*) to have been filled; **er/sie ist schon ~** (*inf*) he/she is already spoken for (*inf*) *or* (*verheiratet auch*) married; **ich bin heute Abend schon ~** (*inf*) I've got something else on this evening; **mein Herz ist schon ~** (*liter*) my heart belongs to another (*liter*); **der nächste Tanz ist schon ~** I've already promised the next dance **b** (= *verzeihen*) to forgive; *Sünde* to forgive, to pardon; **jdm etw ~** to forgive sb (for) sth; **das ist ~ und vergessen** that is over and done with, that is forgiven and forgotten **c** *sich* (*dat*) *etwas/nichts ~* to lose/not to lose face; **was vergibst du dir, wenn du ein bisschen netter bist?** what have you got to lose by being a bit friendlier? VR (*Cards*) to misdeal

ver|ge|bens [fɛɐ̯'geːbns] ADJ *pred* in vain, to no avail ADV in vain, vainly

ver|geb|lich [fɛɐ̯'geːplɪç] ADJ futile; *Bitten, Mühe auch* vain *attr*; **alle Bitten/Versuche waren ~** all requests/attempts were in vain *or* to no avail ADV in vain

Ver|geb|lich|keit F -, *no pl* futility

Ver|ge|bung [fɛɐ̯'geːbʊŋ] F -, **-en** forgiveness

ver|ge|gen|ständ|li|chen [fɛɐ̯'geːgn̩ʃtɛntlɪçn̩] ptp **vergegenständlicht** VT to concretize; (*Philos*) to reify, to hypostatize

ver|ge|gen|wär|ti|gen [fɛɐ̯ɡeːgn̩'vɛrtɪɡn̩, fɛɐ̯ge:gnvɛrtɪɡn̩] ptp **vergegenwärtigt** VT **sich** (*dat*) **etw ~** (= *vor Augen rufen*) to visualize sth; (= *sich vorstellen*) to imagine sth; (= *erinnern*) to recall sth; **vergegenwärtige dir doch einmal die Folgen** think of the consequences

Ver|ge|gen|wär|ti|gung [fɛɐ̯ge:gn̩'vɛrtɪɡʊŋ, fɛɐ̯ge:gnvɛrtɪɡʊŋ] F -, **-en** visualization; (= *Vorstellung*) imagination

ver|ge|hen ptp **vergangen** [fɛɐ̯'gaŋən] *irreg* VI *aux sein* **a** (= *vorbeigehen*) to pass; (*Liebe, Leidenschaft*) to die; (*Zeit, Jahre etc auch*) to go by, to pass; (*Hunger, Schmerzen*) to wear off, to pass; (*Schönheit, Glück*) to fade; (*Duft*) to go, to wear off; **wie doch die Zeit vergeht** how time flies; **mir ist die Lust/Laune dazu vergangen** I don't feel like it any more; **mir ist der Appetit vergangen** I have lost my appetite; **das vergeht wieder** that will pass; **es werden noch Monate ~, ehe …** it will be months before …; **damit die Zeit vergeht** in order to pass the time → *auch* **vergangen, Hören, Lachen**
  b **vor etw** (*dat*) **~** to be dying of sth; **vor Angst ~** to be scared to death; **vor Hunger ~** to be dying of hunger, to be starving; **vor Kälte ~** to be frozen; **vor Sehnsucht ~** to pine away; **sie wollte vor Scham ~** she nearly died of shame
  VR **sich an jdm ~** to do sb wrong; (*unsittlich*) to assault sb indecently; **sich an Gott ~** to go against God; **sich an der Natur ~** to defile nature; **sich gegen das Gesetz ~** to violate the law; **sich gegen die guten Sitten/die Moral ~** to violate *or* outrage propriety/morality

Ver|ge|hen [fɛɐ̯'ge:ən] NT **-s, -** **a** (= *Verstoß*) offence (*Brit*), offense (*US*), misdemeanour (*Brit*), misdemeanor (*US*); **~ im Amt** professional misconduct *no pl*; **das ist doch kein ~, oder?** that's not a crime, is it? **b** *no pl* (*geh*: = *Schwinden*) passing; (*von Zeit*) passage, passing; (*von Schönheit, Glück*) fading

ver|gei|gen ptp **vergeigt** VT (*inf*) to lose

ver|geis|tigt [fɛɐ̯'gaɪstɪçt] ADJ cerebral, spiritual

Ver|geis|ti|gung [fɛɐ̯'gaɪstɪɡʊŋ] F -, **-en** spiritualization

ver|gel|ten ptp **vergolten** [fɛɐ̯'gɔltn̩] VT *irreg* to repay; **jdm etw ~** to repay sb for sth; **vergelts Gott** (*old, dial*) God bless you → **gleich 1**

Ver|gel|tung F (= *Rache*) retaliation; **~ üben** to take revenge (*an jdm* on sb)

Ver|gel|tungs-: Ver|gel|tungs|ak|ti|on F retaliatory operation *or* action *no art*; (= *Vergeltungsschlag*) retaliatory strike; **Ver|gel|tungs|maß|nah|me** F reprisal, retaliatory measure; **Ver|gel|tungs|schlag** M act of reprisal; **Ver|gel|tungs|waf|fen** PL retaliatory weapons *pl*

ver|ge|sell|schaf|ten [fɛɐ̯gə'zɛlʃaftn̩] ptp **vergesellschaftet** VT (*Pol*) to nationalize; *Privatbesitz* to take into public ownership; (= *ins Arbeitereigentum überführen*) to hand over to the workers; (*rare: Sociol*) to socialize

Ver|ge|sell|schaf|tung F -, **-en** (*Pol*) nationalization; (*von Privatbesitz*) taking into public ownership

ver|ges|sen [fɛɐ̯'gɛsn̩] ◯ 31, 53.6 pret **vergaß** [fɛɐ̯'ga:s], ptp **vergessen** VT to forget; (= *liegen lassen*) to leave (behind); **… und nicht zu ~ seine Ehrlichkeit …** and not forgetting his honesty; **dass ich es nicht vergesse, ehe ich es vergesse** before I forget; **das werde ich dir nie ~** I will never forget that; **das kannst du (voll) ~!** (*inf*) forget it!; **er vergisst noch mal seinen Kopf** (*inf*) he'd forget his head if it wasn't screwed on (*inf*)
  VI to forget; **auf jdn/etw ~** (*Aus*) to forget sb/sth
  VR (*Mensch*) to forget oneself; **Zahlen ~ sich leicht** numbers are easy to forget, numbers are easily forgotten

Ver|ges|sen|heit ◯ 53.1 F -, *no pl* oblivion; **in ~ geraten, der ~ anheimfallen** (*geh*) to vanish *or* sink into oblivion; **etw aus der ~ hervorholen** to rescue sth from oblivion

ver|gess|lich ▲ [fɛɐ̯'gɛslɪç] ADJ forgetful

Ver|gess|lich|keit ▲ F -, *no pl* forgetfulness

ver|geu|den [fɛɐ̯'gɔydn̩] ptp **vergeudet** VT to waste; *Geld, Talente auch* to squander

Ver|geu|dung F -, **-en** wasting; (*von Geld, Talenten auch*) squandering; **das ist die reinste ~** that is (a) sheer waste; **diese ~!** what a waste!

ver|ge|wal|ti|gen [fɛɐ̯ga'valtɪɡn̩] ptp **vergewaltigt** VT to rape; (*fig*) *Sprache etc* to murder, to mutilate; *Volkswillen* to violate **VR** to force one-self

Ver|ge|wal|ti|ger [fɛɐɡə'valtɪɡɐ] M -s, - rapist

Ver|ge|wal|ti|gung F -, -en rape; *(fig) (von Sprache)* murder(ing), mutilation; *(von Volkswillen)* violation

ver|ge|wis|sern [fɛɐɡə'vɪsɐn] ptp **vergewissert** VR to make sure; **sich einer Sache** *(gen)* or **über etw** *(acc)* ~ to make sure of sth

ver|gie|ßen ptp **vergossen** [fɛɐ'ɡɔsn] VT irreg *Kaffee, Wasser* to spill; *Blut auch, Tränen* to shed; **ich habe bei der Arbeit viel Schweiß vergossen** I sweated blood over that job

ver|gif|ten ptp **vergiftet** **VT** *(lit, fig)* to poison; *Luft auch* to pollute **VR** to poison oneself *(mit, durch, an +dat* with)

Ver|gif|tung [fɛɐ'ɡɪftʊŋ] F -, -en poisoning *no pl; (der Luft)* pollution; **bei ~en wird der Magen ausgepumpt** the stomach is pumped in cases of poisoning; **an einer ~ sterben** to die of poisoning

Ver|gif|tungs|er|schei|nung F symptom of poisoning

ver|gil|ben ptp **vergilbt** VI aux sein to go or become yellow; **vergilbt** yellowed

ver|giss ▲ [fɛɐ'ɡɪs] IMPER *sing von* **vergessen**

Ver|giss|mein|nicht ▲ [fɛɐ'ɡɪsmaɪnnɪçt] NT -(e)s, -(e) forget-me-not

ver|git|tern [fɛɐ'ɡɪtɐn] ptp **vergittert** VT to put a grille on/over; *(mit Stangen)* to put bars on/over; **vergitterte Fenster** windows with grilles over them; *(mit Stangen)* barred windows

Ver|git|te|rung F -, -en *(= Gitter)* grille, grating; *(= Stangen)* bars *pl;* **die ~ der Fenster** putting grilles/bars on the windows

ver|gla|sen [fɛɐ'ɡlaːzn] ptp **verglast** VT to glaze

ver|glast [fɛɐ'ɡlaːst] ADJ *Kuppel etc* glazed

Ver|gla|sung F -, -en glazing

Ver|gleich [fɛɐ'ɡlaɪç] ✪ 32.1, 32.3, 53.5 M -(e)s, -e **a** comparison; *(Liter)* simile; **~e ziehen** or **anstellen** to make or draw comparisons; **im ~ zu** or **mit** in comparison with, compared with or to; **das ist doch gar kein ~!** there is no comparison; **in keinem ~ zu etw stehen** to be out of all proportion to sth; *(Leistungen)* not to compare with sth; **dem ~ mit jdm/etw standhalten, den ~ mit jdm/etw aushalten** to stand or bear comparison with sb/sth; **sie hält den ~ mit ihrer Vorgängerin nicht aus** she doesn't compare with her predecessor; **der ~ hinkt** the comparison is misleading

b *(Jur)* settlement; **einen gütlichen ~ schließen** to reach an amicable settlement; **einen außergerichtlichen ~ schließen** to settle out of court

ver|gleich|bar ✪ 32.5 ADJ comparable

Ver|gleich|bar|keit [fɛɐ'ɡlaɪçbaːɐkaɪt] F -, no pl comparability

ver|glei|chen ✪ 32, 53.5 ptp **verglichen** [fɛɐ'ɡlɪçn] irreg **VT** to compare; **etw mit etw ~** *(prüfend)* to compare sth with sth; *(= einen Vergleich herstellen zwischen)* to compare or liken sth to sth; **verglichen mit** compared with; **vergleiche oben** compare above; **sie sind nicht (miteinander) zu ~** they cannot be compared (to one another); **die kann man nicht (miteinander) ~** they cannot be compared (with one another), they are not comparable **VR** **a** **sich mit jdm ~** to compare oneself with sb; **wie könnte ich mich mit ihm ~?** how could I compare myself to him? **b** *(Jur)* to reach a settlement, to settle *(mit* with)

ver|glei|chend ADJ comparative

Ver|gleichs-: Ver|gleichs|an|trag M *(Jur)* application for the initiation of composition proceedings; **Ver|gleichs|form** F *(Gram)* comparative form; **Ver|gleichs|gläu|bi|ger(in)** M(F) creditor in insolvency proceedings; **Ver|gleichs|jahr** NT base year; **Ver|gleichs|mie|te** F comparable rent; **ortsübliche ~** local comparable rent; **Ver|gleichs|satz** M *(Gram)* comparative clause; **Ver|gleichs|schuld|**

ner(in) M(F) *debtor in insolvency proceedings;* **Ver|gleichs|ver|fah|ren** NT insolvency proceedings *pl;* **Ver|gleichs|ver|wal|ter(in)** M(F) *(Jur)* trustee in composition proceedings; **Ver|gleichs|vor|schlag** M *(Jur)* offer of a settlement, settlement offer; **Ver|gleichs|weg** M *(Jur)* **auf dem ~** by reaching a settlement; **ver|gleichs|wei|se** ADV comparatively; **Ver|gleichs|wert** M comparative or comparable value; **Ver|gleichs|zahl** F usu pl comparative figure; **Ver|gleichs|zeit|raum** M comparative period

ver|glet|schern ptp **vergletschert** VI aux sein to become glaciated

Ver|glet|sche|rung F -, -en glaciation

ver|glim|men ptp **verglimmt** or **verglommen** [fɛɐ'ɡlɔmən] VI irreg aux sein *(Zigarette)* to go out; *(Licht, Feuer auch)* to die out or away; *(fig liter) (Leben)* to be extinguished; *(Hoffnung, Liebe, Tageslicht)* to fade; **~de Kohle** dying cinders

ver|glü|hen ptp **verglüht** VI aux sein *(Feuer, Feuerwerk)* to die away; *(Draht)* to burn out; *(Raumkapsel, Meteor etc)* to burn up; *(liter: Leidenschaft)* to fade (away), to die down

ver|gnü|gen [fɛɐ'ɡnyːɡn] ptp **vergnügt** **VT** to amuse **VR** to enjoy oneself; **sich mit jdm/etw ~** to amuse oneself with sb/sth; **sich mit Lesen/Tennis ~** to amuse or entertain oneself by reading/playing tennis; **sich an etw** *(dat)* **~** to be amused or entertained by sth → *auch* **vergnügt**

Ver|gnü|gen [fɛɐ'ɡnyːɡn] ✪ 52.1 NT -s, - *(= Freude, Genuss)* pleasure; *(= Spaß)* fun *no indef art; (= Erheiterung)* amusement; **~ an etw** *(dat)* **finden** to find enjoyment or pleasure in (doing) sth; **das macht** or **bereitet mir ~** I enjoy it, it gives me pleasure; **sich** *(dat)* **ein ~ aus etw machen** to get pleasure from (doing) sth; **für ihn ist es ein ~, nachts durch die menschenleeren Straßen zu wandern** he enjoys wandering around the empty streets at night; **ich laufe jeden Tag eine halbe Stunde nur zum ~** I run for half an hour each day just for pleasure or for the fun of it; **das war ein teures ~** *(inf)* that was an expensive bit of fun; **ich höre ihn mit großem ~ singen** it gives me great pleasure to hear him sing; **mit ~** with pleasure; **mit großem ~** with great pleasure; **mit größtem** or **dem größten ~** with the greatest of pleasure; **(na dann) viel ~!** *(auch iro)* enjoy yourself/yourselves!; **hinein ins ~!** let the fun begin!; **er hat mir viel ~ gewünscht** he said he hoped I would enjoy myself; **wir wünschen Ihnen bei der Show viel ~** we hope you enjoy the show; **mit wem habe ich das ~?** *(form)* with whom do I have the pleasure of speaking? *(form)* **es ist mir ein ~** it is a pleasure for me

b *(dated: Veranstaltung)* entertainment

ver|gnüg|lich [fɛɐ'ɡnyːklɪç] ADJ enjoyable; *Stunden auch* pleasurable; *(= erheiternd)* amusing

ver|gnügt [fɛɐ'ɡnyːkt] **ADJ** *Abend, Stunden* enjoyable; *Mensch, Gesichter, Gesellschaft, Lachen, Stimmung* cheerful; **über etw** *(acc)* **~ sein** to be pleased or happy about sth **ADV** happily, cheerfully; **~ aussehen** to look cheerful; **~ lachen** to laugh happily → *auch* **vergnügen**

Ver|gnü|gung F -, -en pleasure; *(= Veranstaltung)* entertainment

Ver|gnü|gungs-: Ver|gnü|gungs|be|trieb M **a** no pl *(= Unterhaltung)* entertainment **b** *(= Vergnügungsstätte)* bar providing or with entertainment, nightclub; **Ver|gnü|gungs|damp|fer** M pleasure steamer; **Ver|gnü|gungs|fahrt** F pleasure trip; **Ver|gnü|gungs|in|dust|rie** F entertainment industry; **Ver|gnü|gungs|park** M amusement park; **Ver|gnü|gungs|rei|se** F pleasure trip; **Ver|gnü|gungs|steu|er** F entertainment tax; **Ver|gnü|gungs|sucht** F craving for pleasure; **ver|gnü|gungs|süch|tig** ADJ pleasure-craving, sybaritic *(liter pej);* **Ver|gnü|gungs|vier|tel** NT entertainments district

ver|gol|den [fɛɐ'ɡɔldn] ptp **vergoldet** **VT** *(= mit Gold bemalen)* Nüsse etc to paint gold; *(mit Blatt-*

gold) Statue, Buchkante to gild; *(= mit Gold überziehen)* Schmuck to gold-plate; *(liter: Sonne, Schein)* to bathe in gold, to turn golden; *(fig: = verschönern)* Zeit, Alter, Erinnerung to enhance; **der Herbst vergoldet die Natur** autumn turns nature golden; **sich** *(dat)* **etw ~ lassen** *(fig)* to accept a financial inducement to do sth; **er ließ sich seinen Rücktritt ~** he accepted a financial inducement to resign **VR** *(liter)* to turn to gold

Ver|gol|der [fɛɐ'ɡɔldɐ] M -s, -, **Ver|gol|de|rin** [-ərɪn] F -, -nen gilder

ver|gol|det [fɛɐ'ɡɔldət] ADJ *Nüsse* gold-painted; *Buchkanten* gilt; *Schmuck* gold-plated; *Kuppeln, Spitzen* gilded; *Natur, Stadt, Erinnerung etc* golden

Ver|gol|dung F -, -en *(von Nüssen)* painting gold; *(von Buchseiten)* gilding; *(von Schmuck)* gold-plating; *(= Überzug) (auf Nüssen)* gold paint; *(auf Buchseiten)* gilt; *(auf Schmuck)* gold plate

ver|gön|nen ptp **vergönnt** VT *(geh)* **jdm etw ~** not to begrudge sb sth; **es war ihr noch vergönnt, dies zu sehen** she was granted the privilege of seeing it; **diese Freude war ihm noch/nicht vergönnt** fate granted/did not grant him this pleasure

ver|göt|tern ptp **vergöttert** VT to idolize

Ver|göt|te|rung F -, -en idolization

ver|gra|ben ptp **vergraben** irreg **VT** to bury **VR** *(Maulwurf etc)* to bury oneself; *(fig: = zurückgezogen leben)* to hide oneself (away); **sich hinter seinen Büchern/in Arbeit ~** to bury oneself in one's books/in work

ver|grä|men ptp **vergrämt** VT **a** *(= verärgern, beleidigen)* to antagonize; *(= vertreiben)* to alienate; *(= verletzen)* to grieve; **jdm das Leben ~** to make life a misery for sb **b** *(Hunt)* Wild to frighten, to scare

ver|grämt [fɛɐ'ɡrɛːmt] ADJ *(= kummervoll, bitter)* Gesicht etc troubled; *(= verärgert)* angered

ver|grät|zen [fɛɐ'ɡrɛtsn] ptp **vergrätzt** VT *(inf)* to vex

ver|grau|len ptp **vergrault** VT *(inf)* to put off; *(= vertreiben)* to scare off

ver|grei|fen ptp **vergriffen** [fɛɐ'ɡrɪfn] VR irreg **a** *(= danebengreifen)* to make a mistake; *(Sport: bei Gerät)* to miss one's grip; **sich im Ton ~** *(fig)* to adopt the wrong tone; **sich im Ausdruck ~** *(fig)* to use the wrong expression → *auch* **vergriffen** **b** **sich an etw** *(dat)* **~** *(an fremdem Eigentum)* to misappropriate sth; *(euph: = stehlen)* to help oneself to sth *(euph); (an Heiligem)* to desecrate or profane sth; **sich an jdm ~** *(= angreifen)* to lay hands on sb; *(= geschlechtlich missbrauchen)* to assault sb (sexually)

ver|grei|sen [fɛɐ'ɡraɪzn] ptp **vergreist** VI aux sein *(Bevölkerung)* to age; *(Mensch)* to become senile; **Deutschland vergreist immer mehr** the German population is getting older and older; **vergreist** aged; senile

Ver|grei|sung F -, no pl *(von Bevölkerung)* ageing; *(von Organismen)* senescence; *(von Mensch)* senility

ver|grif|fen [fɛɐ'ɡrɪfn] ADJ unavailable; *Buch* out of print → *auch* **vergreifen**

ver|grö|bern [fɛɐ'ɡrøːbɐn] ptp **vergröbert** **VT** to coarsen **VR** to become coarse

ver|grö|ßern [fɛɐ'ɡrøːsɐn] ptp **vergrößert** **VT** *(räumlich)* Raum, Gebäude, Fläche, Gebiet to extend; *Abstand auch, Vorsprung* to increase; *(größenmäßig, umfangmäßig)* Maßstab, Wissen to enlarge, to increase; *Bekanntenkreis* to enlarge, to extend; *Firma, Absatzmarkt* to expand; *Produktion* to increase; *Vollmachten* to extend; *(zahlenmäßig)* Kapital, Mitgliederzahl, Anzahl to increase; *(= verstärken)* Einfluss, Not, Probleme, Schmerz etc to increase; *Fotografie* to enlarge, to blow up; *(Lupe, Brille)* to magnify

VR *(räumlich)* to be extended; *(Abstand, Vorsprung)* to increase; *(größenmäßig, umfangmäßig) (Maßstab)* to be enlarged, to increase; *(Wissen)*

to increase, to expand; (*Bekanntenkreis*) to be enlarged, to be extended; (*Firma, Absatzmarkt*) to expand; (*Produktion*) to increase; (*Vollmachten*) to be extended; (*zahlenmäßig*) to increase; (= *sich verstärken*) to increase; (*Pupille, Gefäße*) to dilate; (*Organ*) to become enlarged; **wir wollen uns ~** (*inf*) we want to move to a bigger place **VI** (*Lupe, Brille*) to magnify; (*Fotograf*) to do enlarging

Ver|grö|ße|rung F -, -en **a** (*räumlich*) extension; (*von Abstand, umfangmäßig, zahlenmäßig*) increase; (*von Maßstab, Wissen, Fotografie, Bekanntenkreis*) enlargement; (*von Firma, Absatzmarkt*) expansion; (*mit Lupe, Brille*) magnification; (= *Verstärkung: von Einfluss, Not, Problemen*) increase; **in 1.000-facher ~** magnified 1,000 times **b** (*von Pupille, Gefäß*) dilation; (*von Organ*) enlargement **c** (= *vergrößertes Bild*) enlargement

Ver|grö|ße|rungs-: Ver|grö|ße|rungs|ap|pa|rat M enlarger; **ver|grö|ße|rungs|fä|hig** ADJ *Gebäude* extendable; *Firma, Absatzmarkt* expandable, able to expand; *Bekanntenkreis* able to be enlarged; *Kapital, Produktion* able to be increased; **Ver|grö|ße|rungs|ge|rät** NT enlarger; **Ver|grö|ße|rungs|glas** NT magnifying glass

ver|gu|cken *ptp* **verguckt** VR (*inf*) to see wrong (*inf*); **da hab ich mich verguckt** I didn't see it properly; **sich in jdn/etw ~** to fall for sb/sth (*inf*)

ver|gül|den [fɛɐˈɡʏldn] *ptp* **vergüldet** VT (*poet*) = vergolden

ver|güns|ti|gen [fɛɐˈɡʏnstɪɡn] *ptp* **vergünstigt** VT *Lage* to improve; VR (*Lage*) to improve; (*Preise*) to come down

ver|güns|tigt [fɛɐˈɡʏnstɪçt] ADJ *Lage* improved; *Preis* reduced **ADV etw ~ kaufen** to buy sth at a reduced price

Ver|güns|ti|gung F -, -en (= *Vorteil*) privilege; (= *Preisermäßigung*) reduction; **besondere ~en für Rentner** special rates for pensioners

ver|gü|ten [fɛɐˈɡyːtn] *ptp* **vergütet** VT **a jdm etw ~** (*Unkosten*) to reimburse sb for sth; *Preis* to refund sb for sth; *Schaden* to compensate sb for sth; *Arbeit, Leistung* to pay or recompense (*form*) sb for sth **b** (*Tech*: = *verbessern*) *Stahl* to temper; *Linse* to coat

Ver|gü|tung F -, -en **a** (*von Unkosten*) reimbursement; (*von Preis*) refunding; (*für Verlust, Schaden*) compensation; (*für Arbeit, Leistung*) payment, recompense **b** (*Tech*: = *Verbesserung*) (*von Stahl*) tempering; (*von Linse*) coating

Ver|gü|tungs|grup|pe F salary bracket

verh. *abbr von* **verheiratet**

ver|hack|stü|cken [fɛɐˈhakʃtʏkn] *ptp* **verhackstückt** VT (*inf*) (= *kritisieren*) to tear apart, to rip to pieces (*inf*); *Musikstück* to murder (*inf*)

ver|haf|ten *ptp* **verhaftet** VT to arrest; **unschuldig verhaftet werden** to be arrested and later proved innocent; **Sie sind verhaftet!** you are under arrest!

ver|haf|tet [fɛɐˈhaftət] ADJ (*geh*) **einer Sache** (*dat*) *or* **mit etw ~ sein** to be (closely) attached to sth; **einem Irrtum ~ sein** to be under a misapprehension

Ver|haf|te|te(r) [fɛɐˈhaftətə] MF *decl as adj* **der ~ wurde abgeführt** the arrested man was taken away; **die zehn ~n** the ten people under arrest

Ver|haf|tung F arrest

Ver|haf|tungs|wel|le F wave of arrests

ver|ha|geln *ptp* **verhagelt** VI *aux sein* to be damaged by hail; **er sieht verhagelt aus** (*inf*) he looks rather the worse for wear

ver|ha|ken *ptp* **verhakt** VT to hook up VR to get caught; (*fig: in Streit etc*) to get caught up in

ver|hal|len *ptp* **verhallt** VI *aux sein* (*Geräusch etc*) to die away; **ihr Ruf/ihre Warnung verhallte ungehört** (*fig*) her call/her warning went unheard or unheeded

Ver|hal|ten [fɛɐˈhaltn] NT **-s**, *no pl* (= *Benehmen*) behaviour (*Brit*), behavior (*US*); (= *Vorgehen*)

conduct; (*Chem*) reaction; **falsches Parken ist rechtswidriges ~** unauthorized parking is an offence (*Brit*) or offense (*US*); **faires ~** fair conduct

ver|hal|ten¹ *ptp* **verhalten** *irreg* VT (*geh*) (= *zurückhalten, unterdrücken*) *Atem* to hold; *Tränen, Urin* to hold back; *seine Schritte* to curb; *Zorn* to restrain; *Lachen* to contain; *Schmerz* to control VI to stop; **im Laufen/Sprechen ~** to stop running/speaking

VR **a** (= *sich benehmen: Mensch, Maschine, Preise etc*) to behave; (= *handeln*) to act; **wie ~ Sie sich dazu?** what is your attitude to that?; **sich ruhig ~** to keep quiet; (= *sich nicht bewegen*) to keep still; **sich rechtswidrig ~** to commit an offence (*Brit*) or offense (*US*); **wie man sich bei Hof verhält** how one conducts oneself at court **b** (*Sachen, Marktlage*) to be; (*Chem*) to react; **wie verhält sich die Sache?** how do things stand?; **2 verhält sich zu 4 wie 1 zu 2** 2 is to 4 as 1 is to 2

VR *impers* **wie verhält es sich damit?** (= *wie ist die Lage?*) how do things stand?; (= *wie wird das gehandhabt?*) how do you go about it?; **anders/ähnlich verhält es sich mit** *or* **bei …** the situation is different/the same with regard to …; **mit den anderen verhält es sich genauso** (= *die anderen denken auch so*) the others feel exactly the same; **wenn sich das so verhält, …** if that is the case …

ver|hal|ten² [fɛɐˈhaltn] ADJ restrained; *Stimme* muted; *Atem* bated; *Wut* suppressed; *Interesse, Optimismus* guarded; *Tempo, Schritte, Rhythmus* measured; *Aufschwung* limited ADV *sprechen* in a restrained manner; *kritisieren, sich äußern, lachen, weinen* with restraint; *laufen* at a measured pace

Ver|hal|ten|heit F -, *no pl* restraint; **die ~ des Rhythmus** the measured rhythm

Ver|hal|tens-: ver|hal|tens|auf|fäl|lig ADJ (*Psych*) displaying behavioural (*Brit*) or behavioral (*US*) problems; **Ver|hal|tens|auf|fäl|lig|keit** F (*Psych*) behavioural (*Brit*) or behavioral (*US*) problems *pl*; **Ver|hal|tens|for|scher(in)** M(F) behavioural (*Brit*) or behavioral (*US*) scientist; **Ver|hal|tens|for|schung** F behavioural (*Brit*) or behavioral (*US*) research; **ver|hal|tens|ge|stört** ADJ disturbed; **Ver|hal|tens|maß|re|gel** F rule of conduct; **Ver|hal|tens|merk|mal** NT behavioural (*Brit*) or behavioral (*US*) trait or characteristic; **Ver|hal|tens|mus|ter** NT behaviour (*Brit*) or behavior (*US*) pattern; **Ver|hal|tens|psy|cho|lo|gie** F behavioural (*Brit*) or behavioral (*US*) psychology; **Ver|hal|tens|re|gel** F rule of etiquette or conduct; **~n** *pl* (*auch*) code *sing* of conduct; **Ver|hal|tens|stö|rung** F behavioural (*Brit*) or behavioral (*US*) disturbance; **Ver|hal|tens|wei|se** F behaviour (*Brit*), behavior (*US*)

Ver|hält|nis [fɛɐˈhɛltnɪs] NT **-ses, -se** **a** (= *Proportion*) proportion; (*Math, = Mischungsverhältnis*) ratio; **im ~ zu** in relation or proportion to; **im ~ zu früher** (= *verglichen mit*) in comparison with earlier times; **im ~ 2 zu 4** in the ratio of 2 to 4; **in einem ~ zu etw stehen** to be in proportion to sth; **in keinem ~ zu etw stehen** to be out of all proportion to sth, to bear no relation to sth; **das ist im ~ wenig** (= *im Vergleich mit anderem*) this is proportionately very little; (= *relativ wenig*) that is comparatively or relatively little **b** (= *Beziehung*) relationship (*mit jdm/etw* with sb/to sth); *relations pl* (*zu* with); (*zwischen Ländern, innerhalb einer Gruppe*) relations *pl* (*zu* with); (= *Einstellung*) attitude (*zu* to); **ein freundschaftliches ~ zu jdm haben, mit jdm in freundschaftlichem ~ stehen** to be on friendly terms with sb; **sie hat ein gestörtes ~ zur Wirklichkeit** her grasp on reality is distorted; **zu jdm/etw kein ~ finden können** not to be able to relate to sb/sth **c** (= *Liebesverhältnis*) affair; (*inf*) (= *Geliebte*) lady friend; (= *Geliebter*) friend; **ein ~ mit jdm haben** to have an affair with sb **d** **Verhältnisse** PL (= *Umstände, Bedingungen*) conditions *pl*; (*finanzielle*) circumstances

pl; **unter** *or* **bei normalen ~sen** under normal circumstances; **so wie die ~se liegen …** as things stand …; **die akustischen ~se** the acoustics *pl*; **in ärmlichen ~sen leben** to live in poor conditions; **aus ärmlichen ~sen kommen** to come from a poor background; **über seine ~se leben** to live beyond one's means; **das geht über meine ~se** that is beyond my means; **ich bin für klare ~se** I want to know how we stand; **für klare ~se sorgen, klare ~se schaffen** to get things straight → **räumlich**

Ver|hält|nis-: ver|hält|nis|mä|ßig ADJ **a** (= *proportional*) proportional; (*esp Jur: = angemessen*) proportionate, commensurate **b** (= *relativ*) comparative, relative; (*inf: = ziemlich*) reasonable **ADV a** (= *proportional*) proportionally **b** (= *relativ, inf: = ziemlich*) relatively; **Ver|hält|nis|mä|ßig|keit** F **die ~ der Mittel** the appropriateness of the means; **der Grundsatz der ~** the principle of proportionality; **Ver|hält|nis|wahl** F proportional representation *no art*; **jdn durch ~ ermitteln** to elect sb by proportional representation; **eine ~ abhalten** to hold a proportional election; **Ver|hält|nis|wahl|recht** NT (system of) proportional representation; **Ver|hält|nis|wort** NT *pl* **-wörter** preposition; **Ver|hält|nis|zahl** F (*Statistik*) ratio

ver|han|deln *ptp* **verhandelt** VT **a** (= *aushandeln*) to negotiate **b** (*Jur*) *Fall* to hear VI **a** (= *Verhandlungen führen*) to negotiate (*über +acc* about); (*inf: = diskutieren*) to argue; **da gibts doch nichts zu ~** (*inf*) there's nothing to argue about; **über den Preis lässt sich ~** (*inf*) we can discuss the price **b** (*Jur*) to hear the case; **gegen jdn ~** to hear sb's case; **in einem Fall ~** to hear a case

Ver|hand|lung F **a** negotiations *pl*; (= *das Verhandeln*) negotiation; **die zur ~ stehende Frage** the question under negotiation; **mit jdm ~en** (**über etw** *acc*) **aufnehmen** to start negotiations with sb (about sth); **mit jdm in ~(en) stehen** to be negotiating with sb, to be engaged in negotiations with sb; (**mit jdm**) **in ~(en) treten** to enter into negotiations (with sb); **~en führen** to negotiate; **ich lasse mich auf keine ~(en) ein** (*inf*) I don't propose to enter into any long debates **b** (*Jur*) hearing; (= *Strafverhandlung*) trial

Ver|hand|lungs-: Ver|hand|lungs|ba|sis F basis for negotiation(s); **~ EUR 2.500** (price) EUR 2,500 or nearest offer; **ver|hand|lungs|be|reit** ADJ ready or prepared to negotiate; **Ver|hand|lungs|be|reit|schaft** F readiness to negotiate; **die mangelnde ~ der Regierung** the government's reluctance to negotiate; **ver|hand|lungs|fä|hig** ADJ (*Jur*) able to stand trial; **Ver|hand|lungs|fä|hig|keit** F (*Jur*) ability to stand trial; **Ver|hand|lungs|füh|rer(in)** M(F) chief negotiator; **Ver|hand|lungs|ge|gen|stand** M issue, object of negotiation; **Ver|hand|lungs|grund|la|ge** F basis for negotiation(s); **Ver|hand|lungs|part|ner(in)** M(F) negotiating party; **Ver|hand|lungs|spiel|raum** M room to negotiate, scope for negotiation; (*finanziell*) negotiating range; **Ver|hand|lungs|tisch** M negotiating table; **ver|hand|lungs|un|fä|hig** ADJ (*Jur*) unable to stand trial; **Ver|hand|lungs|un|fä|hig|keit** F (*Jur*) inability to stand trial

ver|han|gen [fɛɐˈhaŋən] ADJ *Himmel, Tag, Blick* overcast

ver|hän|gen *ptp* **verhängt** VT **a** *Embargo, Strafe, Hausarrest etc* to impose (*über +acc* on); *Ausnahmezustand, Notstand* to declare (*über +acc* in); (*Sport*) *Elfmeter etc* to award, to give **b** (= *zuhängen*) to cover (*mit* with); *Kruzifix, Statue* to veil; **mit verhängtem Zügel, mit verhängten Zügeln** at full speed

Ver|häng|nis [fɛɐˈhɛŋnɪs] NT **-ses, -se** (= *schlimmes Schicksal*) undoing; (= *Katastrophe*) disaster; **jdm zum ~ werden, jds ~ werden** to prove or be sb's undoing; **er entging seinem ~ nicht** he could not escape his fate

ver|häng|nis|voll ADJ disastrous; *Irrtum, Fehler auch, Zögern, Entschlusslosigkeit* fatal; *Tag* fateful

Ver|hän|gung [fɛɐˈhɛŋʊŋ] F -, -en (*einer Strafe, eines Verbots etc*) imposition

ver|harm|lo|sen [fɛɐˈharmloːzn] ptp **verharmlost** VT to play down

Ver|harm|lo|sung [fɛɐˈharmloːzʊŋ] -, -en playing down; (= *Bagatellisierung*) minimizing, minimization

ver|härmt [fɛɐˈhɛrmt] ADJ *Mensch, Gesicht* careworn; *Ausdruck* worried

ver|har|ren ptp **verharrt** VI *aux haben or sein* to pause; (*in einer bestimmten Stellung*) to remain; **auf einem Standpunkt/in** *or* **bei einem Entschluss ~** to adhere to a viewpoint/to a decision; **in seinem Stillschweigen ~** to maintain one's silence; (*hartnäckig*) to persist in one's silence

ver|har|schen [fɛɐˈharʃn] ptp **verharscht** VI *aux sein* (*Schnee, Piste*) to crust

ver|här|ten ptp **verhärtet** VTR (*alle Bedeutungen*) to harden; **sich** *or* **sein Herz gegen jdn/etw ~** to harden one's heart against sb/sth

Ver|här|tung [fɛɐˈhɛrtʊŋ] F -, -en a (= *Verhärten*) hardening b (*im Gewebe*) lump, knot

ver|has|peln ptp **verhaspelt** VR (*inf*) to get into a muddle *or* tangle

ver|hasst ▲ [fɛɐˈhast] ADJ hated; *Arbeit auch, Pflicht* hateful; **sich ~ machen** to make oneself hated (*bei* by); **das ist ihm ~** he hates that

ver|hät|scheln ptp **verhätschelt** VT to spoil, to pamper

Ver|hau [fɛɐˈhau] M -(e)s, -e (*zur Absperrung*) barrier; (= *Käfig*) coop; (= *Bretterbude etc*) shack; (*inf: = Unordnung*) mess

ver|hau|en pret **verhaute**, ptp **verhauen** (*inf*) VT a (= *verprügeln*) to beat up; (*zur Strafe*) to beat b *Klassenarbeit, Prüfung etc* to make a mess of (*inf*) VR a (= *sich verprügeln*) to have a fight b (= *Fehler machen*) to make a mistake; (= *sich irren*) to slip up (*inf*)

ver|he|ben ptp **verhoben** [fɛɐˈhoːbn] VR *irreg* to hurt oneself lifting something; (*fig*) to overstretch oneself

ver|hed|dern [fɛɐˈhɛdɐn] ptp **verheddert** VR (*inf*) to get tangled up; (*beim Sprechen*) to get in a muddle *or* tangle

ver|hee|ren [fɛɐˈheːrən] ptp **verheert** VT to devastate; (*Truppen auch*) to lay waste

ver|hee|rend ADJ a *Sturm, Folgen, Niederlage, Katastrophe* devastating, disastrous; *Anblick* ghastly b (*inf: = schrecklich*) frightful, fearful, ghastly (*all inf*) ADV (*inf: = schrecklich*) frightfully (*inf*)

Ver|hee|rung F -, -en devastation *no pl*; **~(en) anrichten** to cause devastation

ver|heh|len [fɛɐˈheːlən] ptp **verhehlt** VT to conceal, to hide; **jdm etw ~** to conceal *or* hide sth from sb; **ich möchte Ihnen nicht ~, dass ...** I have no wish to conceal the fact that ...

ver|hei|len ptp **verheilt** VI *aux sein* (*Wunde, Bruch*) to heal (up); (*fig*) to heal

ver|heim|li|chen [fɛɐˈhaimlıçn] ptp **verheimlicht** VT to keep secret, to conceal (*jdm* from sb); **es lässt sich nicht ~, dass ...** it is impossible to conceal the fact that ...; **ich habe nichts zu ~** I have nothing to hide

Ver|heim|li|chung F -, -en concealment; (*von Tatsache*) suppression

ver|hei|ra|ten ptp **verheiratet** VT to marry (*mit, an +acc* to) VR to get married, to marry; **sich mit jdm ~** to marry sb, to get married to sb

ver|hei|ra|tet [fɛɐˈhairaːtət] ADJ married; **glücklich ~ sein** to be happily married; **mit jdm/etw ~ sein** (*hum inf*) to be married to sb/sth

Ver|hei|ra|tung [fɛɐˈhairatʊŋ] F -, -en marriage

ver|hei|ßen ptp **verheißen** VT *irreg* to promise; **jdm eine große Karriere ~** to predict a great career for sb; **seine Miene verhieß nichts Gutes** his expression did not augur well; **das verheißt schönes Wetter** that heralds good weather

Ver|hei|ßung [fɛɐˈhaisʊŋ] F -, -en promise; **das Land der ~** the Promised Land

ver|hei|ßungs|voll ADJ promising; *Anfang auch* auspicious; *Blicke* alluring; **wenig ~** unpromising; **mit ~en Worten** with promises ADV *anfangen* promisingly, auspiciously; *klingen, sich anhören* promising

ver|hei|zen ptp **verheizt** VT to burn, to use as fuel; (*fig inf*) *Sportler* to burn out; *Minister, Untergebene* to crucify; **Soldaten im Kriege ~** (*inf*) to send soldiers to the slaughter

ver|hel|fen ptp **verholfen** [fɛɐˈhɔlfn] VI *irreg* **jdm zu etw ~** to help sb to get sth; **jdm zu seinem Glück ~** to help to make sb happy; **jdm zum Sieg ~** to help sb to victory

ver|herr|li|chen [fɛɐˈhɛrlıçn] ptp **verherrlicht** VT *Gewalt, Krieg, Taten, Regime, jdn* to glorify; *Gott* to praise; *Tugenden* to extol; (*in Gedichten*) to celebrate

Ver|herr|li|chung F -, -en glorification; (*von Gott*) praising; (*von Tugenden*) extolment; (*in Gedichten*) celebration

ver|het|zen ptp **verhetzt** VT to stir up, to incite (*to violence etc*)

Ver|het|zung F -, -en incitement, stirring up

ver|heult [fɛɐˈhɔylt] ADJ *Augen, Gesicht* puffy, swollen from crying; **du siehst so ~ aus** you really look as if you have been crying

ver|he|xen ptp **verhext** VT to bewitch; (*Fee, Zauberer etc auch*) to cast a spell over; (*inf*) *Maschine etc* to put a jinx on (*inf*); **jdn in etw** (*acc*) **~** to turn sb into sth (by magic); **der verhexte Prinz** the enchanted prince; **das verhexte Schloss** the bewitched castle; **heute ist alles wie verhext** (*inf*) there's a jinx on everything today (*inf*); **das ist doch wie verhext** (*inf*) it's maddening (*inf*)

ver|hin|dern ptp **verhindert** VT to prevent; *Unglück auch* to avert; *Versuch, Plan* to foil, to stop; **ich konnte es nicht ~, dass er die Wahrheit erfuhr** I couldn't prevent him from finding out the truth; **das lässt sich leider nicht ~** it can't be helped, unfortunately; **er war an diesem Abend (dienstlich** *or* **geschäftlich) verhindert** he was unable to come that evening (for reasons of work); **ein verhinderter Politiker** (*inf*) a would-be politician

Ver|hin|de|rung F prevention; (*von Unglück auch*) averting; (*von Versuch, Plan*) foiling, stopping; **im Falle seiner ~** if he is unable to come

ver|hoh|len [fɛɐˈhoːlən] ADJ concealed, secret; *Gelächter, Schadenfreude auch, Gähnen* suppressed; **kaum ~** barely concealed/suppressed

ver|höh|nen ptp **verhöhnt** VT to mock, to deride

ver|hoh|ne|pi|peln [fɛɐˈhoːnəpiːpln] ptp **verhohnepipelt** VT (*inf*) (= *verspotten*) to send up (*inf*); (= *zum Besten haben*) to have on (*inf*)

Ver|hoh|ne|pi|pe|lung [fɛɐˈhoːnəpiːpəlʊŋ] F -, -en send-up (*inf*)

Ver|höh|nung [fɛɐˈhøːnʊŋ] F -, -en mocking, ridiculing; (*Bemerkung*) gibe

ver|hö|kern ptp **verhökert** VT (*inf*) to get rid of (*inf*)

ver|ho|len ptp **verholt** VT (*Naut*) to haul away

ver|hol|zen ptp **verholzt** VI *aux sein* (*Bot*) to lignify

Ver|hör [fɛɐˈhøːɐ] NT -(e)s, -e questioning, interrogation; (*bei Gericht*) examination; **jdn ins ~ nehmen** to question sb, to interrogate sb; (*bei Gericht*) to examine sb; (*inf*) to take sb to task; **jdn einem ~ unterziehen** (*form*) to subject sb to questioning *or* interrogation/examination

ver|hö|ren ptp **verhört** VT to question, to interrogate; (*bei Gericht*) to examine; (*inf*) to quiz (*inf*) VR to mishear, to hear wrongly; **du musst dich verhört haben** you must have misheard, you must have heard it wrong

ver|hornt [fɛɐˈhɔrnt] ADJ *Haut* horny

ver|hu|deln ptp **verhudelt** VT (*inf*) to botch

ver|hül|len ptp **verhüllt** VT to veil; *Haupt, Körperteil, Gebäude* to cover; (*fig*) to mask, to disguise VR (*Frau*) to veil oneself; (*Berge etc*) to become veiled

ver|hül|lend ADJ *Ausdruck* euphemistic

Ver|hül|lung [fɛɐˈhʏlʊŋ] F -, -en a (= *das Verhüllen*) veiling; (*von Haupt, Körperteil*) covering; (*fig*) masking, disguising b (= *Bedeckung*) veil; (*von Haupt, Körperteil*) cover; (*fig*) mask, disguise c (= *Ausdruck*) euphemism

ver|hun|dert|fa|chen [fɛɐˈhʊndɐtfaxn] ptp **verhundertfacht** VTR to increase a hundredfold

ver|hun|gern ptp **verhungert** VI *aux sein* to starve, to die of starvation; (*inf: = Hunger haben*) to be starving (*inf*); **er sah völlig verhungert aus** he looked half-starved; (*inf*) he looked absolutely famished (*inf*); **ich bin am Verhungern** (*inf*) I'm starving (*inf*); **jdn ~ lassen** (*lit*) to let sb starve (to death); (*beim Spielen*) to leave sb out of the game

Ver|hun|gern|de(r) [fɛɐˈhʊŋɐndə] MF *decl as adj* starving person/man/woman

Ver|hun|ger|te(r) [fɛɐˈhʊŋɐtə] MF *decl as adj* person/man/woman *etc* who has starved to death

ver|hun|zen [fɛɐˈhʊntsn] ptp **verhunzt** VT (*inf*) to ruin; *Sprache, Lied auch* to murder

ver|hurt [fɛɐˈhuːɐt] ADJ (*pej*) whorish; *Mann* loose-living

ver|huscht [fɛɐˈhʊʃt] ADJ (*inf*) timid

ver|hü|ten ptp **verhütet** VT to prevent; **das verhüte Gott!** God forbid!; **möge Gott ~, dass ...** God forbid that ...; **~de Maßnahmen** preventive measures; (*zur Empfängnisverhütung*) precautions VI (= *Empfängnisverhütung betreiben*) to take precautions

Ver|hü|ter|li [fɛɐˈhyːtəli] NT -(s), - (*Sw: = Verhütungsmittel*) contraceptive; (*hum inf: = Kondom*) johnny (*Brit inf*), rubber (*esp US inf*)

ver|hüt|ten [fɛɐˈhʏtn] ptp **verhüttet** VT to smelt

Ver|hüt|tung F -, -en smelting

Ver|hü|tung [fɛɐˈhyːtʊŋ] F -, -en prevention; (= *Empfängnisverhütung*) contraception

Ver|hü|tungs|mit|tel NT contraceptive

ver|hut|zelt [fɛɐˈhʊtslt] ADJ *Gesicht, Männlein* wizened; *Haut auch* wrinkled; *Obst* shrivelled (*esp Brit*), shriveled (*US*)

Ve|ri|fi|ka|ti|on [verifikaˈtsioːn] F -, -en verification

ve|ri|fi|zier|bar [verifiˈtsiːɐbaːɐ] ADJ verifiable

ve|ri|fi|zie|ren [verifiˈtsiːrən] ptp **verifiziert** VT to verify

ver|in|ner|li|chen [fɛɐˈ|ınɐlıçn] ptp **verinnerlicht** VT to internalize; *jdn* to spiritualize

ver|in|ner|licht [fɛɐˈ|ınɐlıçt] ADJ *Normen, Werte* internalized; *Wesen, Gesichtsausdruck* spiritualized

Ver|in|ner|li|chung F -, -en internalization; (*von Mensch, in Literatur*) spiritualization

ver|ir|ren ptp **verirrt** VR to get lost, to lose one's way; (*fig*) to go astray; (*Tier, Kugel*) to stray; **ein verirrtes Schaf** (*lit, fig*) a lost sheep; **hierhin ~ sich die Touristen nur selten** (*fig*) tourists don't venture out here very often

Ver|ir|rung F losing one's way *no art*; (*fig*) aberration

ve|ri|ta|bel ADJ (*geh*) *attr* veritable *attr*

ver|ja|gen ptp **verjagt** VT (*lit, fig*) to chase away; *trübe Gedanken, Kummer auch* to dispel

ver|jäh|ren ptp **verjährt** VI *aux sein* to come under the statute of limitations; (*Anspruch*) to be in lapse; **verjährtes Verbrechen** statute-barred crime; **Totschlag verjährt nach 20 Jahren** the statute of limitations for manslaughter is 20 years; **Mord verjährt nie** there is no statute of limitations for murder; **das ist schon längst verjährt** (*inf*) that's all over and done with

Ver|jäh|rung [fɛɐ̯ˈjɛːrʊŋ] F -, -en limitation; *(von Anspruch)* lapse

Ver|jäh|rungs|frist F limitation period

ver|jaz|zen [fɛɐ̯ˈdʒɛsn, -ˈjatsn] ptp **verjazzt** VT to jazz up

ver|ju|beln ptp **verjubelt** VT *(inf)* Geld to blow *(inf)*

ver|jüng|en [fɛɐ̯ˈjʏŋən] ptp **verjüngt** VT to rejuvenate; (= *jünger aussehen lassen*) to make look younger; (= *jünger werden*) to regenerate; **eine Mannschaft/das Personal ~** to build up a younger team/staff; **die neue Stelle hat ihn um Jahre verjüngt** the new job gave him a new lease of life; **er kam (um Jahre) verjüngt von der Gesundheitsfarm zurück** he came back from the health farm looking (years) younger

  VR **a** (= *jünger werden*) to become younger; *(Haut, Erscheinung)* to become rejuvenated; (= *jünger aussehen*) to look younger; **du hast dich verjüngt** *(inf)* you look (much) younger

  b (= *dünner werden*) to taper; *(Tunnel, Rohr)* to narrow

Ver|jün|gung F -, -en **a** rejuvenation; *(von Baumbestand)* regeneration **b** (= *das Dünnerwerden*) tapering; *(von Tunnel, Rohr)* narrowing

Ver|jün|gungs|kur F rejuvenation cure

ver|ju|xen ptp **verjuxt** VT *(inf)* Geld to blow *(inf)*

ver|ka|beln ptp **verkabelt** VT *(Telec)* to link up to the cable network

Ver|ka|be|lung [fɛɐ̯ˈkaːbəlʊŋ] F -, -en *(Telec)* linking up to the cable network

ver|kal|ken ptp **verkalkt** VI aux sein *(Arterien)* to harden; *(Gewebe)* to calcify; *(Kessel, Wasserleitung etc)* to fur up, to become furred; *(inf: Mensch)* to become senile

ver|kalkt [fɛɐ̯ˈkalkt] ADJ *(inf)* senile

ver|kal|ku|lie|ren ptp **verkalkuliert** VR to miscalculate

Ver|kal|kung [fɛɐ̯ˈkalkʊŋ] F -, -en *(von Arterien)* hardening; *(von Gewebe)* calcification; *(von Kessel, Wasserleitung etc)* furring; *(von inf)* senility

Ver|kal|kungs|er|schei|nung F *(inf: bei alten Menschen)* sign of senility

ver|käl|ten [fɛɐ̯ˈkɛltn] ptp **verkältet** VR *(dial)* erkälten

ver|kannt [fɛɐ̯ˈkant] ADJ unrecognized → *auch* **verkennen**

ver|kan|ten [fɛɐ̯ˈkantn] ptp **verkantet** VT (= *schräg stellen*) to tilt; *(Skier)* to edge; **sich ~** (= *sich verklemmen*) to get wedged (in); *(Skier)* to edge over

ver|kappt [fɛɐ̯ˈkapt] ADJ attr hidden; *Lungenentzündung* undiagnosed; **ein ~er Fanatiker/Sozialist** etc a closet fanatic/socialist etc; **~er Nebensatz** *(Gram)* subordinate clause without an introductory word

ver|kap|seln [fɛɐ̯ˈkapsln] ptp **verkapselt** VR *(Med) (Bakterien)* to become encapsulated; *(Parasit)* to become encysted

Ver|kap|se|lung [fɛɐ̯ˈkapsəlʊŋ] F -, -en *(Med) (von Bakterien)* encapsulation; *(von Parasit)* encystment

ver|kars|ten [fɛɐ̯ˈkarstn] ptp **verkarstet** VI aux sein to develop to karst *(spec)*

Ver|kars|tung F -, -en karst development *(spec)*

ver|ka|tert [fɛɐ̯ˈkaːtɐt] ADJ *(inf)* hung over *usu pred (inf)*; **einen ~en Eindruck machen** to look hung over *(inf)*

Ver|kauf M **a** sale; (= *das Verkaufen*) selling; **zum ~ stehen** to be up for sale; **beim ~ des Hauses** when selling the house → **Straße b** (= *Abteilung*) sales *sing, no art*

ver|kau|fen ptp **verkauft** VT **VTl** *(lit, fig)* to sell *(für, um* for); **"zu ~"** "for sale"; **jdm etw ~, etw an jdn ~** to sell sb sth, to sell sth to sb; **sie haben ihr Leben so teuer wie möglich verkauft** they sold their lives as dearly as possible; **er würde sogar seine Großmutter ~** he'd even sell his

own grandmother → **Straße, verraten, dumm**

  VR **a** *(Ware)* to sell; *(Mensch)* to sell oneself; **er hat sich ganz und gar an die Partei verkauft** he is committed body and soul to the party

  b (= *einen schlechten Kauf machen*) to make a bad buy; **damit habe ich mich verkauft** that was a bad buy

  c *(fig:* = *sich anpreisen)* to sell oneself

Ver|käu|fer(in) M(F) seller; *(in Geschäft)* sales or shop assistant, salesperson; *(im Außendienst)* salesman/saleswoman/salesperson; *(Jur: von Grundbesitz etc)* vendor

ver|käuf|lich ADJ sal(e)able, marketable; (= *zu verkaufen*) for sale; **leicht** or **gut/schwer ~** easy/hard to sell

Ver|käuf|lich|keit F , no pl sal(e)ability, marketability

Ver|kaufs- in cpds sales; **Ver|kaufs|ab|tei|lung** F sales department; **Ver|kaufs|ar|gu|ment** NT selling point; **Ver|kaufs|aus|stel|lung** F sales exhibition; **Ver|kaufs|au|to|mat** M vending machine; **Ver|kaufs|be|din|gun|gen** PL conditions *pl* of sale; **Ver|kaufs|be|ra|ter(in)** M(F) sales consultant; **Ver|kaufs|bü|ro** NT sales office; **Ver|kaufs|er|lös** M proceeds *pl* (from the sale); **Ver|kaufs|flä|che** F sales area; **Ver|kaufs|för|de|rung** F sales promotion; (= *Abteilung*) sales promotion department; **Ver|kaufs|ge|nie** NT **ein ~ sein** to be a genius at selling things; **Ver|kaufs|ge|spräch** NT sales consultation; *(zur Überzeugung)* sales talk no art; **Ver|kaufs|lei|ter(in)** M(F) sales manager; **ver|kaufs|of|fen** ADJ open for business; **~er Samstag** *Saturday on which the shops are open all day*; **Ver|kaufs|per|so|nal** NT sales personnel or staff; **Ver|kaufs|preis** M retail price; **Ver|kaufs|schla|ger** M big seller; **Ver|kaufs|ver|pa|ckung** F packaging; **Ver|kaufs|zah|len** PL sales figures *pl*

Ver|kehr [fɛɐ̯ˈkeːɐ̯] M -(e)s, no pl **a** traffic; (= *Beförderung, Verkehrsmittel*) transport, transportation *(US)*; **für den ~ freigeben, dem ~ übergeben** *(Straße etc)* to open to traffic; *Transportmittel* to bring into service; **den ~ regeln** to regulate the (flow of) traffic

  b (= *Verbindung*) contact, communication; (= *Umgang*) company; (= *Geschlechtsverkehr*) intercourse; **in brieflichem ~ stehen** to correspond; **in seinem ~ mit Menschen** in his dealings with people; **den ~ mit jdm pflegen** *(form)* to associate with sb; **den ~ mit jdm abbrechen** to break off relations or contact with sb

  c (= *Geschäftsverkehr, Handelsverkehr*) trade; (= *Umsätze, Zahlungsverkehr*) business; (= *Postverkehr*) service; (= *Umlauf*) circulation; **etw in (den) ~ bringen** to put sth into circulation; **etw aus dem ~ ziehen** *(Banknoten)* to take sth out of circulation; *schadhafte Produkte, Fahrzeuge* to withdraw sth; *altes Schiff* to take sth out of commission; *Blutkonserven, medizinische Präparate* to remove sth; **jdn aus dem ~ ziehen** (= *entfernen, betrunkene Autofahrer*) to ban; *Politiker, Dealer* to remove; *(inf:* = *ins Gefängnis werfen)* to put sb in jug *(Brit inf)* or in the slammer *(inf)*

ver|keh|ren ptp **verkehrt** VI **VI a** aux haben or sein (= *fahren*) to run; *(Flugzeug)* to fly; **der Bus/das Flugzeug verkehrt regelmäßig zwischen A und B** the bus runs or goes or operates regularly/the plane goes or operates regularly between A and B

  b (= *Gast sein, Kontakt pflegen*) **bei jdm ~** to frequent sb's house, to visit sb (regularly); **mit jdm ~** to associate with sb; **in einem Lokal ~** to frequent a pub; **in Künstlerkreisen ~** to move in artistic circles, to mix with artists; **mit jdm brieflich** or **schriftlich ~** *(form)* to correspond with sb; **mit jdm (geschlechtlich) ~** to have (sexual) intercourse with sb

  VT to turn (*in +acc* into); **etw ins Gegenteil ~** to reverse sth → *auch* **verkehrt**

  VR to turn (*in +acc* into); **sich ins Gegenteil ~** to become reversed

Ver|kehrs- in cpds traffic; **Ver|kehrs|ab|wick|lung** F traffic handling; **Ver|kehrs|ader** F artery, arterial road; **Ver|kehrs|am|pel** F traffic lights *pl*; **Ver|kehrs|amt** NT (= *Verkehrsbüro*) tourist information office; **Ver|kehrs|an|bin|dung** F transport links *pl*; **die Stadt hat eine gute ~** the town has good transport links; **ver|kehrs|arm** ADJ Zeit, Straße quiet; **ein ~es Gebiet** an area with little traffic; **Ver|kehrs|auf|kom|men** NT volume of traffic; **Ver|kehrs|be|hin|de|rung** F *(Jur)* obstruction (of traffic); **ver|kehrs|be|ru|higt** [-bəruːɪçt] ADJ traffic-calmed; **Ver|kehrs|be|ru|hi|gung** F traffic calming; **Ver|kehrs|be|trie|be** PL transport services *pl*; **Ver|kehrs|bü|ro** NT tourist information office; **Ver|kehrs|cha|os** NT chaos on the roads; **Ver|kehrs|de|likt** NT traffic offence *(Brit)* or offense *(US)*; **Ver|kehrs|dich|te** F volume of traffic, traffic density; **Ver|kehrs|durch|sa|ge** F traffic announcement; **Ver|kehrs|er|zie|hung** F road safety training; **Ver|kehrs|flug|ha|fen** M (commercial) airport; **Ver|kehrs|flug|zeug** NT commercial aircraft; **Ver|kehrs|füh|rung** F traffic management system; **Ver|kehrs|funk** M radio traffic service; **ver|kehrs|ge|fähr|dend** ADJ dangerous; **Ver|kehrs|ge|fähr|dung** F *(Jur:* = *verkehrswidriges Fahren)* dangerous driving; **eine ~ darstellen** to be a hazard to other traffic; **ver|kehrs|güns|tig** ADJ Lage convenient; Ort, Viertel conveniently situated; ADV liegen conveniently; *wohnen* in a convenient location or situation; **Ver|kehrs|hin|der|nis** NT (traffic) obstruction; **ein ~ sein** to cause an obstruction; **Ver|kehrs|hin|weis** M traffic announcement; **Ver|kehrs|in|farkt** M total gridlock; **Ver|kehrs|in|sel** F traffic island; **Ver|kehrs|kno|ten|punkt** M traffic junction; **Ver|kehrs|kol|laps** M total gridlock; **Ver|kehrs|kon|trol|le** F traffic check; **bei jdm eine ~ machen** *(Polizei)* to stop sb; **verstärkte ~n machen** to increase traffic checks; **Ver|kehrs|la|ge** F situation on the roads, traffic situation; **Ver|kehrs|lärm** M traffic noise; **Ver|kehrs|leit|sys|tem** NT traffic guidance system; **Ver|kehrs|mel|dung** F traffic announcement; **~en** traffic news *sing*; **Ver|kehrs|mi|nis|ter(in)** M(F) minister of transport; **Ver|kehrs|mi|nis|te|ri|um** NT ministry of transport *(Brit)*, department of transportation *(US)*; **Ver|kehrs|mit|tel** NT means *sing* of transport; **öffentliche/private ~** public/private transport; **Ver|kehrs|netz** NT traffic network; **Ver|kehrs|op|fer** NT road casualty; **Ver|kehrs|ord|nung** F ≈ Highway Code *(Brit)*, traffic rules and regulations *pl*; **Ver|kehrs|pla|nung** F traffic engineering; **Ver|kehrs|po|li|zei** F traffic police *pl*; **Ver|kehrs|po|li|zist(in)** M(F) traffic policeman/-woman; **Ver|kehrs|re|gel** F traffic regulation; **Ver|kehrs|re|ge|lung** F traffic control; **ver|kehrs|reich** ADJ Straße, Gegend, Flughafen busy; **~e Zeit** peak (traffic) time; **Ver|kehrs|row|dy** M, **Ver|kehrs|rü|pel** M road hog *(inf)*; **Ver|kehrs|schild** NT pl **-schilder** road sign; **ver|kehrs|schwach** ADJ Zeit off-peak; *Gebiet* with little traffic; **die Nachmittagsstunden sind sehr ~** there is very little traffic in the afternoons; **ver|kehrs|si|cher** ADJ Fahrzeug roadworthy; Straße, Brücke safe (for traffic); **Ver|kehrs|si|cher|heit** F *(von Fahrzeug)* roadworthiness; *(von Straße, Brücke)* safety; **Ver|kehrs|spra|che** F lingua franca; **Ver|kehrs|stau** M , **Ver|kehrs|stau|ung** F traffic jam; **Ver|kehrs|sto|ckung** F traffic hold-up *(Brit)* or jam; **Ver|kehrs|stra|ße** F road open to traffic; **Ver|kehrs|strom** M flow of traffic; **Ver|kehrs|sün|der(in)** M(F) *(inf)* traffic offender *(Brit)* or violator *(US)*; **Ver|kehrs|sün|der|kar|tei** F *(inf)* central index of road traffic offenders; **Ver|kehrs|teil|neh|mer(in)** M(F) road user; **Ver|kehrs|to|te(r)** MF decl as adj road casualty; **die Zahl der ~n** the number of deaths on the road; **ver|kehrs|tüch|tig** ADJ Fahrzeug roadworthy; Mensch fit to drive; **Ver|kehrs|tüch|tig|keit** F *(von Fahrzeug)* roadworthiness; (*von Mensch*) fitness to drive, driving ability; **Ver|kehrs|un|fall** M road accident; (*hum inf*) accident; **Ver|kehrs|un|ter|nehmen** NT transport company; **Ver|kehrs|un|ter|richt** M traffic instruction; **ver|kehrs|un|tüch|tig** ADJ *Fahrzeug* unroadworthy; *Mensch* unfit to drive; **Ver|kehrs|ver|bin|dung** F link; (= *Anschluss*) connection; **Ver|kehrs|ver|bund** M integrated transport system; **Ver|kehrs|ver|ein** M *local organization concerned with upkeep of tourist attractions, facilities etc*; **Ver|kehrs|ver|hält|nis|se** PL traffic situation *sing*; (= *Straßenzustand*) road conditions *pl*; **Ver|kehrs|ver|stoß** M motoring offence (*Brit*), traffic violation (*US*); **Ver|kehrs|vo|lu|men** NT volume of traffic; **Ver|kehrs|vor|schrift** F (road) traffic regulation; **Ver|kehrs|wacht** F traffic patrol; **Ver|kehrs|weg** M highway; **Ver|kehrs|wert** M (*Fin*) current market value; **Ver|kehrs|we|sen** NT, *no pl* transport and communications *no art*; **ver|kehrs|wid|rig** ADJ contrary to road traffic regulations ADV **sich ~ verhalten** to break the road traffic regulations; **Ver|kehrs|zäh|lung** F traffic census; **Ver|kehrs|zei|chen** NT road sign; **Ver|kehrs|zent|ral|kar|tei** F , **Ver|kehrs|zent|ral|re|gis|ter** NT *central index of traffic offenders*

ver|kehrt [fɛɐ'keːɐt] ADJ wrong; *Vorstellung, auch Welt* topsy-turvy; **das ist gar nicht (so) ~** (*inf*) that can't be bad (*inf*); **der ist gar nicht (so) ~** (*inf*) he's not such a bad sort; **das Verkehrte** the wrong thing; **das Verkehrteste, was du tun könntest** the worst thing you could do; **der/die Verkehrte** the wrong person; **eines Tages wirst du an den Verkehrten geraten** one day you'll get your fingers burned → **Kaffee** [1], **Adresse** ADV wrongly; **etw ~ (herum) anhaben** (= *linke Seite nach außen*) to have sth on inside out; (= *vorne nach hinten*) to have sth on back to front; **etw ~ halten** to hold sth wrongly; (= *falsch herum*) to hold sth the wrong way (a)round; (= *oben nach unten*) to hold sth upside down; **die Möbel alle ~ stellen** (= *an den falschen Platz*) to put all the furniture in the wrong place; **er ist ~ herum** (*inf: homosexuell*) he's bent (*inf*) → *auch* **verkehren**

Ver|keh|rung [fɛɐ'keːrʊŋ] F -, -en reversal; (*von Rollen auch*) switching; **eine ~ ins Gegenteil** a complete reversal

ver|kei|len *ptp* **verkeilt** VT **a** (= *festmachen*) to wedge tight **b** (*inf: = verprügeln*) to thrash VR to become wedged together

ver|ken|nen *ptp* **verkannt** [fɛɐ'kant] VT *irreg Lage, jdn etc* to misjudge; (= *unterschätzen auch*) to underestimate; **ein Dichter, der zeit seines Lebens verkannt wurde** a poet who remained unrecognized in his lifetime; **ich will nicht ~, dass ...** I would not deny that ...; **es ist nicht zu ~, dass ...** it is undeniable that ..., it cannot be denied that ...; **seine schlechte Laune/seine Absicht war nicht zu ~** his bad temper/his intention was obvious → *auch* **verkannt**

Ver|ken|nung F misjudgement; (= *Unterschätzung auch*) underestimation; (*von Genie, Künstler*) failure to appreciate (*jds sb*); **in ~ der wahren Sachlage** ... misjudging the real situation ...

ver|ket|ten *ptp* **verkettet** VT (*lit*) to chain (up); *Tür, Kiste* to put chains/a chain on; (*fig*) to link VR to become interlinked, to become bound up together; **verkettet sein** (*fig*) to be interlinked, to be bound up (together)

Ver|ket|tung [fɛɐ'kɛtʊŋ] F -, -en (= *das Verketten*) chaining; (= *Ketten*) chains *pl*; (*fig*) interconnection

ver|ket|zern *ptp* **verketzert** VT to denounce

ver|kit|schen [fɛɐ'kɪtʃn] *ptp* **verkitscht** VT (*inf*) **a** *Gemälde, Literatur* to make kitschy; *Lied* to sentimentalize **b** (*dial: = verkaufen*) to flog (*Brit inf*), to sell

ver|kit|ten *ptp* **verkittet** VT to cement; *Fenster* to put putty (a)round

ver|kla|gen *ptp* **verklagt** VT to sue (*wegen* for), to take proceedings against (*wegen* for); **jdn auf etw** (*acc*) **~** to take sb to court for sth; **die verklagte Partei, der/die Verklagte** the defendant

ver|klam|mern *ptp* **verklammert** VT to staple together; (*Med*) *Wunde* to apply clips to; (*Tech*) *Bauteile* to brace, to put braces (a)round; (*fig*) to link VR (*Menschen*) to embrace; (*Hände*) to interlock

Ver|klam|me|rung [fɛɐ'klaməʀʊŋ] F -, -en **a** (= *das Verklammern*) stapling; (*Med*) applying of clips (+*gen* to); (*von Bauteilen*) bracing; (*fig*) linking **b** (= *die Klammern*) staples *pl*; (*Med*) clips *pl*; (*Tech*) braces *pl*; (*fig*) links *pl*

ver|klap|pen *ptp* **verklappt** VT *Abfallstoffe* to dump

Ver|klap|pung [fɛɐ'klapʊŋ] F -, -en (*von Abfallstoffen*) dumping

ver|kla|ren [fɛɐ'klaːrən] *ptp* **verklart** VT (*inf*) **jdm etw ~** to spell sth out for sb

ver|klä|ren *ptp* **verklärt** VT to transfigure VR to become transfigured

ver|klärt [fɛɐ'klɛːɐt] ADJ transfigured

Ver|klä|rung F -, -en (*Naut*) ship's protest

Ver|klä|rung F transfiguration

ver|klat|schen *ptp* **verklatscht** VT (*inf*) **a** (= *verpetzen*) to tell on (*inf*) **b** *Zeit* to spend chatting

ver|klau|seln [fɛɐ'klauzln] *ptp* **verklauselt**, **ver|klau|su|lie|ren** [fɛɐ'klauzu'liːrən] *ptp* **verklausuliert** (*rare*) VT *Vertrag* to hedge in or around with (restrictive) clauses; **der Vertrag ist zu verklausuliert** the contract has too many qualifying clauses

ver|kle|ben *ptp* **verklebt** VT (= *zusammenkleben*) to stick together; (= *zukleben*) to cover (*mit* with); *Tapeten* to stick; *Plakate* to stick up; *Haare, Verband* to make sticky; *Wunde* (*mit Pflaster*) to put a plaster on; (= *verbrauchen*) to use up VI *aux sein* (*Wunde, Eileiter*) to close; (*Augen*) to get gummed up; (*Mehl, Briefmarken, Bonbons*) to stick together; (*Haare*) to become matted; **mit etw ~** to stick to sth

ver|klebt [fɛɐ'kleːpt] ADJ *Verband, Wunde* sticky; *Augen* gummed up; *Haare* matted; *Eileiter* blocked

ver|kle|ckern *ptp* **verkleckert** VT (*inf*) to spill; (*fig*) *Zeit, Energie, Geld* to waste

ver|klei|den *ptp* **verkleidet** VT **a** *jdn* to disguise; (= *kostümieren*) to dress up, to put into fancy dress; (*fig*) *Ideen, Absicht* to disguise, to mask; **alle waren verkleidet** everyone was dressed up, everyone was in fancy dress **b** (= *verschalen*) *Wand, Schacht, Tunnel* to line; (= *vertäfeln*) to panel; (= *bedecken*) to cover; (= *ausschlagen, auslegen*) *Kiste etc* to line; (= *verdecken*) *Heizkörper* to cover, to mask VR to disguise oneself; (= *sich kostümieren*) to dress (oneself) up; **muss man sich ~?** do you have to wear fancy dress?

Ver|klei|dung F **a** (= *das Verkleiden von Menschen*) disguising; (= *Kostümierung*) dressing up, putting into fancy dress; (= *Kleidung*) disguise; (= *Kostüm*) fancy dress **b** (= *das Verkleiden, Material*) lining; (*mit Holz*) panelling (*Brit*), paneling (*esp US*); (= *das Bedecken*) covering; (= *das Verdecken*) masking

ver|klei|nern [fɛɐ'klainɐn] *ptp* **verkleinert** VT to reduce; *Raum, Gebiet, Firma* to make smaller; (*Linse, Brille*) to make smaller; *Fotografie* to reduce (in size); *Maßstab* to scale down; *Abstand* to decrease; *Not, Probleme, Schuld* to minimize; *jds Leistungen, Verdienste* to belittle; *Wort* to form the diminutive of VR to be reduced; (*Raum, Gebiet, Firma*) to become smaller; (*Maßstab*) to be scaled down; (*Abstand*) to decrease; (*Not, Probleme, Schuld*) to become less; **durch den großen Schrank verkleinert sich das Zimmer** the big cupboard makes the room (seem) smaller; **wir haben uns verkleinert** (*wohnungsmäßig*) we have moved into a smaller flat (*Brit*) or apartment VI (*Linse etc*) to make everything seem smaller

Ver|klei|ne|rung F -, -en **a** (= *das Verkleinern*) reduction; (*von Gebiet, Firma, durch Linse, Brille*) making smaller; (*von Fotografie*) reduction (in size); (*von Maßstab*) scaling down; (*von Abstand*) decreasing; (*von Not, Problemen, Schuld*) minimizing; (*von Leistungen, Verdiensten*) belittling; (*Gram*) formation of the diminutive **b** (= *das Kleinerwerden*) reduction; (*von Raum, Gebiet, Firma*) becoming smaller; (*von Maßstab*) scaling down; (*von Abstand*) decreasing; (*von Not, Problemen, Schuld*) lessening **c** (= *Bild*) reduced size reproduction; (= *Foto*) reduction; (= *Wort*) diminutive (form); (*Mus*) diminution

Ver|klei|ne|rungs|form F diminutive form

ver|kleis|tern *ptp* **verkleistert** VT (= *zusammenkleben*) to stick together; (= *zukleben*) to cover; (*inf*) (= *mit Kleister beschmieren*) to get glue on; (*fig: = vertuschen*) to cover up

ver|klem|men *ptp* **verklemmt** VR to get or become stuck

ver|klemmt [fɛɐ'klɛmt] ADJ (*inf*) *Mensch* inhibited

Ver|klemmt|heit F -, -en (*inf*), **Ver|klem|mung** F -, -en inhibitions *pl*; **Sex ohne ~** uninhibited sex

ver|kli|ckern *ptp* **verklickert** VT (*inf*) **jdm etw ~** to make sth clear to sb

ver|klin|gen [fɛɐ'klɪŋən] VI *irreg aux sein* to die or fade away; (*fig: Begeisterung, Interesse*) to fade

ver|klop|fen *ptp* **verklopft**, **ver|klop|pen** *ptp* **verkloppt** VT (*inf*) **a** **jdn** to give sb what-for (*inf*) **b** (= *verkaufen*) to flog (*Brit inf*), to sell

ver|klum|pen *ptp* **verklumpt** VI *aux sein* to get lumpy

ver|kna|cken *ptp* **verknackt** VT (*inf*) **jdn zu zwei Jahren ~** to do sb for two years (*inf*), to give sb two years; **jdn zu einer Geldstrafe ~** to stick a fine on sb (*inf*); **verknackt werden** to be done (*inf*)

ver|knack|sen [fɛɐ'knaksn] *ptp* **verknackst** VT (**sich** *dat*) **den Knöchel** or **Fuß ~** to twist one's ankle

ver|knal|len *ptp* **verknallt** (*inf*) VR **sich (in jdn) ~** to fall for sb (*inf*); **ich war damals unheimlich (in ihn) verknallt** I was head over heels in love (with him) then VT *Feuerwerkskörper* to let off; *Munition* to use up; *Geld* (*mit Feuerwerkskörpern*) to waste on fireworks

ver|knap|pen [fɛɐ'knapn] *ptp* **verknappt** VT to cut back; *Rationen* to cut down (on) VR to run short

Ver|knap|pung F -, -en (*Comm*) shortage, scarcity

ver|knaut|schen *ptp* **verknautscht** VT to crush, to crumple VR (*vi: aux sein*) to crease

ver|knei|fen *ptp* **verkniffen** VT *irreg* (*inf*) **sich** (*dat*) **etw ~** to stop oneself (from) saying/doing etc sth; *Lächeln* to keep back sth; *Bemerkung* to bite back sth; **ich konnte mir das Lachen nicht ~** I couldn't help laughing; **das kann ich mir ~** I can manage without that (*iro*) → *auch* **verkniffen**

ver|kne|ten *ptp* **verknetet** VT to knead together

ver|knif|fen [fɛɐ'knɪfn] ADJ *Gesicht, Miene* (= *angestrengt*) strained; (= *verbittert*) pinched; *Ansichten* narrow-minded ADV **etw ~ sehen** to take a narrow view of sth → *auch* **verkneifen**

ver|knit|tern [fɛɐ'knɪtɐn] *ptp* **verknittert** VT → **zerknittern**

ver|knit|tert [fɛɐ'knɪtɐt] ADJ → **zerknittert**

ver|knö|chern [fɛɐ'knœçɐn] *ptp* **verknöchert** VI *aux sein* (*lit, fig*) to ossify; **verknöchert** (*fig*) ossified, fossilized

ver|knor|peln [fɛɐ'knɔrpln] *ptp* **verknorpelt** VI *aux sein* to become cartilaginous

ver|kno|ten *ptp* **verknotet** **VT** to tie, to knot; (*inf*) *Paket* to tie up **VR** to become knotted

ver|knüp|fen *ptp* **verknüpft** **VT** **a** (= *verknoten*) to knot *or* tie (together); (*Comput*) to integrate **b** (*fig*) to combine; (= *in Zusammenhang bringen*) to link, to connect; *Gedanken, Geschehnisse* to associate; **etw mit Bedingungen ~** to attach conditions to sth; **mit diesem Ort sind für mich schöne Erinnerungen verknüpft** this place has happy memories for me; **ein Hauskauf ist immer mit großen Ausgaben verknüpft** buying a house always involves a lot of expense

Ver|knüp|fung [fɛɐ̯ˈknʏpfʊŋ] **F** -, **-en** (*von Bändern, Schnur*) knotting *or* tying (together); (*Comput*) integration; (*fig*) combining, combination; (= *Assoziieren*) linking, connecting; (*von Gedanken, Geschehnissen*) association

ver|knu|sen [fɛɐ̯ˈknuːzn̩] *ptp* **verknust** **VT** (*inf*) **ich kann ihn/das nicht ~** I can't stick him/that (*inf*)

ver|ko|chen *ptp* **verkocht** **VI** *aux sein* (*Flüssigkeit*) to boil away; (*Kartoffeln, Gemüse*) to overcook **VT** *Gemüse* to overcook

ver|koh|len *ptp* **verkohlt** **VI** *aux sein* to char, to become charred; (*Braten*) to burn to a cinder (*Brit*) *or* crisp **VT** **a** *Holz* to char; (*Tech*) to carbonize **b** (*inf*) **jdn ~** to have sb on (*Brit inf*), to pull sb's leg (*inf*)

Ver|koh|lung [fɛɐ̯ˈkoːlʊŋ] **F** -, **-en** carbonization

ver|ko|ken [fɛɐ̯ˈkoːkn̩] *ptp* **verkokt** **VT** to carbonize

Ver|ko|kung **F** -, **-en** carbonization

ver|kom|men¹ [fɛɐ̯ˈkɔmən] *ptp* **verkommen** **VI** *irreg aux sein* **a** (*Mensch*) to go to pieces; (*moralisch*) to become dissolute, to go to the bad (*Brit*); (*Kind*) to run wild; **zu etw ~** to degenerate into sth **b** (*Gebäude, Auto*) to become dilapidated, to fall to pieces; (*Stadt, Land*) to become run-down; (*Gelände, Anlage etc*) to run wild **c** (= *nicht genutzt werden: Lebensmittel, Begabung, Fähigkeiten etc*) to go to waste; (= *verderben: Lebensmittel*) to go bad **d** (*Sw:* = *übereinkommen*) to agree **e** (*Aus, inf:* = *verschwinden*) to clear off (*inf*)

ver|kom|men² **ADJ** *Mensch* depraved; *Auto, Gebäude* dilapidated; *Garten* wild; **der sprachlich ~e Gewaltbegriff** the linguistically debased concept of violence

Ver|kom|men|heit **F** -, *no pl* (*von Mensch*) depravity; (*von Auto, Gebäude*) dilapidation, dilapidated state; (*von Garten*) wildness

ver|kom|pli|zie|ren *ptp* **verkompliziert** **VT** (*inf*) to complicate; **etw ~** (*auch*) to make sth more complicated than it is; **warum musst du immer alles ~?** why do you always have to complicate matters?

ver|kon|su|mie|ren *ptp* **verkonsumiert** **VT** (*inf*) to get through; *Essen, Getränke auch* to consume

ver|kop|peln *ptp* **verkoppelt** **VT** to connect, to couple; (*Space*) to link (up)

Ver|kop|pe|lung **F**, **Ver|kopp|lung** **F** connection, coupling; (*Space*) linkup

ver|kor|ken [fɛɐ̯ˈkɔrkn̩] *ptp* **verkorkt** **VT** to cork (up)

ver|kork|sen [fɛɐ̯ˈkɔrksn̩] *ptp* **verkorkst** **VT** (*inf*) to make a mess *or* cockup (*Brit inf*) of, to mess up (*inf*), to screw up (*inf*); *Kind* to screw up (*inf*); **sich** (*dat*) **den Magen ~** to upset one's stomach; **jdm etw ~** to mess *or* screw sth up for sb (*inf*)

ver|korkst [fɛɐ̯ˈkɔrkst] **ADJ** (*inf*) messed-up (*inf*), ruined; *Magen* upset; *Kind, Mensch* screwed up (*inf*); **eine völlig ~e Sache** a real mess

ver|kör|pern [fɛɐ̯ˈkœrpɐn] *ptp* **verkörpert** **VT** to embody, to personify; (*Theat*) to play (the part of), to portray; **jener Staat verkörperte die Idee der Demokratie** that state was the embodiment of the democratic idea

Ver|kör|pe|rung **F** -, **-en** embodiment; (*Mensch auch*) personification; (*Theat*) playing, portrayal

ver|kos|ten *ptp* **verkostet** **VT** to taste

ver|kös|ti|gen [fɛɐ̯ˈkœstɪɡn̩] *ptp* **verköstigt** **VT** to feed

ver|kös|ti|gung **F** -, **-en** feeding

Ver|kos|tung **F** -, **-en** (*von Wein*) tasting

ver|kra|chen *ptp* **verkracht** **VR** (*inf*) **sich (mit jdm) ~** to fall out (with sb)

ver|kracht [fɛɐ̯ˈkraxt] **ADJ** (*inf*) *Leben* ruined; *Typ, Mensch* dead beat (*inf*); (= *zerstritten*) *Nachbarn, Freunde* who have fallen out with each other → **Existenz**

ver|kraf|ten [fɛɐ̯ˈkraftn̩] *ptp* **verkraftet** **VT** to cope with; (*finanziell*) to afford, to manage; (*inf:* = *essen, trinken können*) to manage; **Straßen, die das Verkehrsvolumen nicht ~** streets which can't cope with the volume of traffic

ver|kral|len *ptp* **verkrallt** **VR** (*Katze, Raubtier*) to dig *or* sink its claws in; (*Hände*) to clench up; **sich in etw** (*dat*) **~** (*Katze*) to dig *or* sink its claws into sth; (*Mensch*) to dig *or* sink one's fingers into sth; **sich in ein Problem ~** (*fig*) to get stuck into a problem

ver|kra|men *ptp* **verkramt** **VT** (*inf*) to mislay

ver|kramp|fen *ptp* **verkrampft** **VR** to become cramped; (*Hände*) to clench up; (*Mensch*) to go tense, to tense up; **verkrampft** (*fig*) tense

Ver|kramp|fung [fɛɐ̯ˈkrampfʊŋ] **F** -, **-en** (*lit, fig*) tenseness, tension; **seelische ~** mental tension

ver|krat|zen *ptp* **verkratzt** **VT** to scratch, to scrape; **verkratzt** scratched; **völlig verkratzt sein** to be scratched all over

ver|krie|chen *ptp* **verkrochen** [fɛɐ̯ˈkrɔxn̩] **VR** *irreg* to creep away; (*fig*) to hide (oneself away); **sich unter den** *or* **dem Tisch ~** to crawl *or* creep under the table; **sich ins Bett ~** (*inf*) to run off to bed, to retreat to one's bed; **vor ihm brauchst du dich nicht zu ~** (*inf*) you don't have to worry about him; **am liebsten hätte ich mich vor Scham verkrochen** I wanted the ground to open up and swallow me

ver|krü|meln *ptp* **verkrümelt** **VR** (*inf*) to disappear **VT** to crumble

ver|krüm|men *ptp* **verkrümmt** **VT** to bend **VR** to bend; (*Rückgrat*) to become curved; (*Holz*) to warp; (*Baum, Pflanze*) to grow crooked

ver|krümmt [fɛɐ̯ˈkrʏmt] **ADJ** bent; *Wirbelsäule* curved; *Finger, Knochen, Bäume* crooked; *Holz* warped

Ver|krüm|mung **F** bend (+*gen* in), distortion (*esp Tech*); (*von Holz*) warp; (*von Fingern, Knochen, Bäumen*) crookedness *no pl*; **~ der Wirbelsäule** curvature of the spine; **~ der Hornhaut** (*nach innen*) incurvation of the cornea; (*nach außen*) excurvation of the cornea

ver|krum|peln [fɛɐ̯ˈkrʊmpln̩] *ptp* **verkrumpelt** (*dial*) **VT** to crumple up **VI** *aux sein* to get crumpled up

ver|krüp|peln [fɛɐ̯ˈkrʏpln̩] *ptp* **verkrüppelt** **VT** to cripple **VI** *aux sein* to become crippled; (*Zehen, Füße*) to become deformed; (*Baum etc*) to grow stunted

Ver|krüp|pe|lung [fɛɐ̯ˈkrʏpəlʊŋ] **F** -, **-en**, **Ver|krüpp|lung** [fɛɐ̯ˈkrʏplʊŋ] **F** -, **-en** crippling; (*von Zehen, Füßen*) deformity; (*von Baum etc*) stunted growth

ver|krus|ten [fɛɐ̯ˈkrʊstn̩] *ptp* **verkrustet** **VIR** (*vi: aux sein*) to become encrusted

ver|krus|tet [fɛɐ̯ˈkrʊstət] **ADJ** *Wunde* scabby; *Strukturen, Ansichten* decrepit

Ver|krus|tung **F** -, **-en** (*von Wunde*) scab formation; (*von Strukturen etc*) decrepitude; (*von Partei, Organisation etc*) archaic *or* fossilized structure

ver|küh|len *ptp* **verkühlt** **VR** **a** to catch a cold, to get a chill **VT** **sich** (*dat*) **die Nieren ~** to get a chill on the kidneys (*Brit*), to get a kidney infection (*resulting from a chill*)

ver|küh|lung **F** (*inf*) chill; **~ der Blase** chill on the bladder (*Brit*), bladder infection (*resulting from a chill*)

ver|küm|meln [fɛɐ̯ˈkʏmln̩] *ptp* **verkümmelt** **VT** (*inf*) to sell off, to flog (*Brit inf*)

ver|küm|mern *ptp* **verkümmert** **VI** *aux sein* (*Glied, Organ*) to atrophy; (= *eingehen: Pflanze*) to die; (*Talent*) to go to waste; (*Schönheitssinn, Interesse etc*) to wither away; (*Mensch*) to waste away; **emotionell/geistig ~** to become emotionally/intellectually stunted; **wenn die natürlichen Instinkte im Menschen ~** if man's natural instincts become stunted

Ver|küm|me|rung [fɛɐ̯ˈkʏmərʊŋ] **F** -, **-en** (*von Organ, Muskel, Glied etc*) atrophy; (*fig*) (*von Talent*) wasting away, atrophy; (*von Gerechtigkeitssinn, Instinkten etc*) atrophy

ver|kün|den *ptp* **verkündet** **VT** to announce; *Urteil* to pronounce; *Evangelium* to preach; *Gesetz* to promulgate; *nichts Gutes, Unwetter etc* to forebode, to presage (*liter*); *Frühling, neue Zeit* to herald

Ver|kün|der(in) **M(F)** **ein ~ des Evangeliums** a preacher of the gospel; **der ~ einer Friedensbotschaft** a harbinger *or* herald of peace

ver|kün|di|gen *ptp* **verkündigt** **VT** to proclaim; *Evangelium auch* to preach; (*iro*) to announce; **ich verkündige euch große Freude** (*Bibl*) I bring you tidings of great joy (*Bibl*)

Ver|kün|di|ger [fɛɐ̯ˈkʏndɪɡɐ] **M** -s, -, **Ver|kün|di|ge|rin** [-ərɪn] **F** -, **-nen** → **Verkünder**

Ver|kün|di|gung **F** proclamation; (*von Evangelium, von christlicher Lehre auch*) preaching, propagation; **Mariä ~** the Annunciation; (*Tag*) Lady Day (*Brit*), the Annunciation

Ver|kün|dung [fɛɐ̯ˈkʏndʊŋ] **F** -, **-en** announcement; (*von Urteil*) pronouncement; (*von Evangelium*) preaching; (*von Gesetz*) promulgation

ver|küns|teln [fɛɐ̯ˈkʏnstln̩] *ptp* **verkünstelt** **VR** (*inf*) to overdo it, to go to town (*inf*); **sich an etw** (*dat*) **~** to go to town on sth (*inf*), to overdo sth

ver|kup|fern [fɛɐ̯ˈkʊpfɐn] *ptp* **verkupfert** **VT** to copper(-plate); **verkupfert** copper-plated

ver|kup|peln *ptp* **verkuppelt** **VT** (*pej*) to pair off; **jdn an jdn ~** (*Zuhälter*) to procure sb for sb

Ver|kup|pe|lung **F**, *no pl*, **Ver|kupp|lung** **F**, *no pl* pairing off; (*durch Zuhälter*) procuring

ver|kür|zen *ptp* **verkürzt** **VT** to shorten; *Arbeitszeit, Fahrzeit* to reduce, to cut down; *Lebenserwartung auch* to reduce; *Strecke, Weg etc auch* to cut; *Abstand, Vorsprung* to narrow; *Aufenthalt* to cut short; (*Art*) to foreshorten; *Haltbarkeit* to reduce; *Schmerzen, Leiden* to end, to put an end to; **den Spielstand ~** to narrow the gap (between the scores); **sich** (*dat*) **die Zeit ~** to pass the time, to make the time pass more quickly; **jdm die Zeit ~** to help sb pass the time; **verkürzte Arbeitszeit** shorter working hours; **verkürzter Nebensatz** (*Gram*) elliptical subordinate clause

VR to be shortened; (*Strecke, Zeit auch*) to be cut; (*Art*) to become foreshortened; (*Abstand*) to be narrowed; (*Muskel*) to contract; (*Haltbarkeit*) to be reduced; (*Leiden*) to be ended; (*Urlaub, Aufenthalt*) to be cut short

Ver|kür|zung **F** (= *das Verkürzen*) shortening; (*von Zeit, Lebenserwartung auch*) reduction; (*von Abstand, Vorsprung*) narrowing; (*von Aufenthalt*) cutting short; (*Art*) foreshortening; (*von Haltbarkeit*) reduction; (*von Schmerzen, Leiden*) ending

Verl. *abbr von* **Verlag** *von* **Verleger**

ver|la|chen *ptp* **verlacht** **VT** to ridicule, to deride, to laugh at

Ver|la|de-: **Ver|la|de|bahn|hof** **M** loading station; **Ver|la|de|brü|cke** **F** loading bridge, gantry

ver|la|den *ptp* **verladen** **VT** *irreg* **a** *Güter, Menschen* to load; (*Mil*) (*in Eisenbahn*) to entrain; (*auf Schiff*) to embark; (*in Flugzeug*) to emplane (*Brit*), to enplane; **die Güter vom Eisenbahn-**

waggon aufs Schiff ~ to offload the goods from the train onto the ship **b** (fig inf: = betrügen, für dumm verkaufen) to con (inf), to dupe

Ver|la|de|ram|pe F loading platform

Ver|la|dung F loading; (Mil) (in Eisenbahn) entrainment; (auf Schiff) embarkation; (in Flugzeug) emplaning (Brit), enplaning (US)

Ver|lag [fɛɐ̯ˈlaːk] M -(e)s, -e [-gə] **a** (= Buchverlag) publishing house or company; (= Zeitungsverlag) newspaper publisher's sing; **~ Harper-Collins** HarperCollins Publishers sing; **einen ~ finden** to find a publisher; **in** or **bei welchem ~ ist das erschienen?** who published it?; **der ~ zahlt nicht viel** the publishers do not pay much; **ein Buch in ~ nehmen** to publish a book; **ein Buch in ~ geben** to have a book published **b** (= Zwischenhandelsgeschäft) (firm of) distributors pl

ver|la|gern ptp **verlagert** VT (lit, fig) Gewicht, Schwerpunkt, Betonung to shift; Interessen, Verkehr auch to transfer; (lit: an anderen Ort) to move **VR** (lit, fig) to shift; (Met: Tief, Hoch etc) to move; (fig: Problem, Frage) to change in emphasis (auf +acc to)

Ver|la|ge|rung F shift; (von Interessen auch) transfer; (an anderen Ort) moving, movement; (fig: von Problem, Frage) change in emphasis

Verlags-: Ver|lags|an|stalt F publishing firm; **Ver|lags|buch|han|del** M publishing trade; **Ver|lags|buch|händ|ler(in)** M(F) publisher; **Ver|lags|buch|hand|lung** F publishing firm, publisher; **Ver|lags|grup|pe** F publishing group; **Ver|lags|haus** NT publishing house; **Ver|lags|kauf|frau** F, **Ver|lags|kauf|mann** M publishing manager; **Ver|lags|lei|ter(in)** M(F) publishing director; **Ver|lags|pro|gramm** NT list; **Ver|lags|recht** NT publishing rights pl; **Ver|lags|re|dak|teur(in)** M(F) (publishing) editor; **Ver|lags|we|sen** NT , no pl publishing no art

ver|lan|den ptp **verlandet** VI aux sein to silt up; (durch Austrocknen) to dry up

Ver|lan|dung F silting up; (durch Austrocknen) drying up

ver|lan|gen ptp **verlangt** VT **a** (= fordern) to demand; (= wollen) to want; Preis to ask; Qualifikationen, Erfahrung to require; **was verlangt der Kunde/das Volk?** what does the customer/do the people want?; **wie viel verlangst du für dein Auto?** how much are you asking for your car?, how much do you want for your car? **b** (= erwarten) to ask (von of); **ich verlange nichts als Offenheit und Ehrlichkeit** I am asking nothing but frankness and honesty; **es wird von jdm verlangt, dass ...** it is required or expected of sb that ...; **das ist nicht zu viel verlangt** it's not asking too much; **das ist ein bisschen viel verlangt** that's asking rather a lot, that's rather a tall order **c** (= erfordern) to require, to call for **d** (= fragen nach) to ask for; **er verlangte meinen Pass** he asked for or he asked to see my passport; **Sie werden am Telefon verlangt** you are wanted on the phone; **ich verlange/ich verlangte den Geschäftsführer (zu sprechen)** I want or demand/I asked or demanded to see the manager **VI ~ nach** to ask for; (= sich sehnen nach) to long for; (stärker) to crave **VT** impers (liter) **es verlangt jdn nach jdm/etw** sb craves sth; (nach der Heimat, Geliebten) sb yearns for sb/sth

Ver|lan|gen [fɛɐ̯ˈlaŋən] NT -s, - (nach for) desire; (= Sehnsucht) yearning, longing; (= Begierde) craving; (= Forderung) request; **kein ~ nach etw haben** to have no desire or wish for sth; **auf ~** on demand; **auf ~ des Gerichts** by order of the court; **auf ~ der Eltern** at the request of the parents

ver|lan|gend ADJ longing

ver|län|gern [fɛɐ̯ˈlɛŋɐn] ptp **verlängert** VT **a** (= länger machen) to extend; (esp räumlich) to lengthen, to make longer; (esp zeitlich) to pro-

long; Leben, Schmerzen, Leiden etc to prolong; Hosenbein, Ärmel etc to lengthen; Pass, Abonnement etc to renew; **die Suppe/Soße ~** (fig inf) to make the soup/gravy go further; **ein verlängertes Wochenende** a long weekend; **verlängerte Werkbank** (fig inf) extended production line → **Rücken b** (Sport) Ball, Pass to touch (zu jdm to sb) **VR** to be extended; (räumlich auch) to be lengthened; (zeitlich auch, Leiden etc) to be prolonged **VI** (Sport) to play on

Ver|län|ge|rung F -, -en **a** (= das Verlängern) extension; (esp räumlich) lengthening; (esp zeitlich) prolonging, prolongation; (von Pass, Abonnement etc) renewal **b** (Gegenstand) extension **c** (Sport) (von Spielzeit) extra time (Brit), over time (US); (= nachgespielte Zeit) injury time (Brit), over time (US); (von Pass) play-on (zu to); **das Spiel geht in die ~** they're going to play extra time etc, they're going into extra time etc; **eine ~ von fünf Minuten** five minutes' extra time etc

Ver|län|ge|rungs-: Ver|län|ge|rungs|frist F (= Zeitspanne) extension period; (= Zeitpunkt) extension deadline; **Ver|län|ge|rungs|ka|bel** NT , **Ver|län|ge|rungs|schnur** F (Elec) extension lead; **Ver|län|ge|rungs|stück** NT extension (piece)

ver|lang|sa|men [fɛɐ̯ˈlaŋzaːmən] ptp **verlangsamt** **VT** to slow down or up; Geschwindigkeit to reduce, to decelerate; Produktion auch to decelerate; Entwicklung auch to retard; **er musste das Tempo/seine Schritte ~** he had to slow down **VR** to slow down or up; (Produktion auch) to decelerate

Ver|lang|sa|mung F -, -en slowing down or up; (von Geschwindigkeit, Produktion auch) deceleration; (von Entwicklung) retarding, retardation

ver|läp|pern ptp **verläppert** VR to be or get lost; (Geld) to disappear, to vanish

Ver|lass ▲ [fɛɐ̯ˈlas] M -es, no pl **auf jdn/etw ist kein ~, es ist kein ~ auf jdn/etw** there is no relying on sb/sth, you can't rely on sb/sth

ver|las|sen ✪ 42.1¹ ptp **verlassen** irreg **VT** to leave; (fig: Mut, Kraft, Hoffnung) jdn to desert; (= im Stich lassen) to desert, to abandon, to forsake (liter); (Comput) Datei, Programm to exit; **... und da verließen sie mich/ihn** etc (iro, inf) ... that's as far as I/he etc got → **Geist b** **VR** **sich auf jdn/ etw ~** to rely or depend on sb/sth; **darauf kön-nen Sie sich ~** you can be sure of that, you can depend on that, take my word for it; **worauf du dich ~ kannst!** you can depend on that!, you bet!

ver|las|sen² [fɛɐ̯ˈlasn] ADJ **a** Gegend, Ort, Straßen deserted; (= öd) desolate; **eine Tanne, einsam und ~** a solitary fir tree **b** Mensch (= allein gelassen) deserted; (= einsam) lonely, solitary; **einsam und ~** so all alone **c** (= ohne Besitzer) Haus, Fabrik deserted; Auto abandoned

Ver|las|sen NT -s, no pl **vor/nach ~ des Gebäudes** before/after leaving the building; **böswilli-ges ~** (Jur) wilful abandonment

Ver|las|sen|heit F -, no pl **a** (von Gegend, Ort, Straßen) desertedness; (= Ödheit) desolateness **b** (von Mensch) loneliness, solitariness

Ver|las|sen|schaft [fɛɐ̯ˈlasnʃaft] F -, -en (Aus, Sw) estate; (literarisch) legacy

Ver|las|sen|schafts|ab|hand|lung F (Aus, Sw) negotiation on inheritance

ver|läss|lich ▲, **ver|läss|ig** (old) ADJ reliable; Mensch auch dependable

Ver|läss|lich|keit ▲ [fɛɐ̯ˈlɛslɪçkaɪt] F -, no pl reliability; (von Mensch auch) dependability

Ver|laub [fɛɐ̯ˈlaʊp] M **mit ~** (geh, iro) by your leave (old), with your permission; **mit ~ (zu sa-gen)** if you will pardon or forgive my saying so

Ver|lauf M course; (= Ausgang) end, issue; **im ~ der Zeit** in the course of time; **im ~ des Tages** in or during the course of the day; **im ~ der Jahre/Monate** over the (course of the) years/ months; **im ~ der Verhandlungen/Arbeit** in the course of the negotiations/work; **einen guten/**

schlechten ~ nehmen to go well/badly; **den ~ einer Sache verfolgen/beobachten** to follow/ observe the course (which) sth takes; **im weiteren ~ der Sache zeichnete sich folgende Tendenz ab** as things developed the following tendency became apparent

ver|lau|fen ptp **verlaufen** irreg **VI** aux sein **a** (= ablaufen) (Tag, Prüfung, Entwicklung) to go; (Feier, Demonstration) to go off; (Kindheit) to pass; (Untersuchung) to proceed; **beschreiben Sie, wie diese Krankheit normalerweise verläuft** describe the course this illness usually takes; **die Verhandlungen verliefen in angespannter Atmo-sphäre** the negotiations took place in a tense atmosphere **b** (= sich erstrecken) to run **c** (= auseinander fließen, dial: = schmelzen) to run; **die Spur verlief im Sand/Wald** the track disappeared in the sand/forest; **~e Farben** runny colours (Brit) or colors (US) → **Sand** **VR a** (= sich verirren) to get lost, to lose one's way **b** (= verschwinden) (Menschenmenge) to disperse; (Wasser) to drain away; (= sich verlieren: Spur, Weg) to disappear

Ver|laufs|form F (Gram) progressive or continuous form

ver|laust [fɛɐ̯ˈlaʊst] ADJ lice-ridden

ver|laut|ba|ren [fɛɐ̯ˈlaʊtbaːrən] ptp **verlautbart** (form) VTI to announce; **es wird amtlich ver-lautbart, dass ...** it is officially announced that ..., a statement has been issued to the effect that ...; **etw ~ lassen** to let sth be announced or made known

Ver|laut|ba|rung F -, -en announcement; (inof-fiziell) report

ver|lau|ten ptp **verlautet** **VI** **etwas/nichts ~ las-sen** to give an/no indication, to say something/nothing; **er hat ~ lassen, dass ...** he indicated that ...; **er hat keinen Ton** or **kein Wort ~ lassen** he hasn't said a word **VI** impers aux sein or haben **es verlautet, dass ...** it is reported that ...; **wie aus Bonn verlautet** according to reports from Bonn

ver|le|ben ptp **verlebt** VT to spend; **eine schö-ne Zeit ~** to have a nice time

ver|lebt [fɛɐ̯ˈleːpt] ADJ worn-out, dissipated

ver|le|gen¹ ptp **verlegt** VT **a** (an anderen Ort) to transfer, to move; Patienten to move; Schau-platz to move, to shift **b** (= verschieben) to postpone (auf +acc until); (= vorverlegen) to bring forward (auf +acc to) **c** (= an falschen Platz legen) to mislay, to misplace **d** (= anbrin-gen) Kabel, Fliesen etc to lay **e** (= drucken lassen) to publish **VR** **sich auf etw** (acc) **~** to resort to sth; **er hat sich neuerdings auf Golf verlegt** he has taken to golf recently; **sich aufs Unterrich-ten ~** to take up teaching

ver|le|gen² [fɛɐ̯ˈleːgn] **ADJ** **a** embarrassed no adv **b** um Worte/eine Antwort ~ sein to be lost or at a loss for words/an answer; **um Geld ~ sein** to be financially embarrassed **ADV** in embarrassment; **~ sah er zu Boden** he looked at the floor in embarrassment; **das habe ich vergessen, sagte sie ~** I forgot about that, she said, embarrassed

Ver|le|gen|heit F -, -en **a** no pl (= Betretenheit, Befangenheit) embarrassment; **jdn in ~ bringen** to embarrass sb; **so ein wunderschöner Strauß, du bringst mich ja ganz in ~** such a lovely bouquet, you really shouldn't have; **in ~ kommen** or **geraten** to get or become embarrassed **b** (= unangenehme Lage) embarrassing or awkward situation; **wenn er in finanzieller ~ ist** when he's in financial difficulties, when he's financially embarrassed; **ich bin (finanziell) zur Zeit leider etwas in ~** I'm afraid I'm rather short (of funds) at the moment

Ver|le|gen|heits-: Ver|le|gen|heits|ge-schenk NT last resort present; **Ver|le|gen-heits|lö|sung** F stopgap; **Ver|le|gen|heits-pau|se** F embarrassed pause or silence; **eine ~**

machen to be at a loss for words, to be at a loss as to what to say/how to react

Ver|le|ger [fɛɐ'leːgə] M -s, -, **Ver|le|ge|rin** [-ərɪn] F -, -nen publisher; (= *Händler*) distributor

ver|le|ge|risch [fɛɐ'leːgərɪʃ] ADJ attr publishing attr

Ver|le|gung [fɛɐ'leːgʊŋ] F -, -en **a** (*räumlich*) transfer, moving; (*von Schauplatz*) transposition, shifting **b** (*zeitlich*) postponement (*auf +acc* until); (= *Vorverlegung*) bringing forward (*auf +acc* to) **c** (*von Kabeln etc*) laying

ver|lei|den ptp **verleidet** VT jdm etw ~ to spoil sth for sb, to put sb off sth; **das ist mir jetzt schon verleidet** you've/he's put me off it

Ver|leih [fɛɐ'lai] M -(e)s, -e **a** (= *Unternehmen*) hire (*Brit*) or rental company; (= *Autoverleih*) car hire (*Brit*) or rental; (= *Filmverleih*) distributor(s pl) **b** (= *das Verleihen*) renting (out), hiring (out) (*Brit*); (= *Filmverleih*) distribution; **der ~ von Büchern** the lending or loan of books

ver|lei|hen ptp **verliehen** [fɛɐ'liːən] VT irreg **a** (= *ausleihen*) to lend, to loan (*an jdn* to sb); (*gegen Gebühr*) to rent (out), to hire (out) (*Brit*) **b** (= *zuerkennen*) to award (*jdm* (to) sb); *Titel, Ehrenbürgerwürde* to confer, to bestow (*jdm on* sb); *Amt* to bestow (*jdm upon* sb) **c** (= *geben, verschaffen*) to give; *Eigenschaft, Klang, Note* to lend, to give; **einer Sache** (dat) **Gewicht ~** to lend weight to sth; **ihre Anwesenheit verlieh der Veranstaltung das gewisse Etwas** her presence gave or lent a certain something to the occasion

Ver|lei|her [fɛɐ'laiɐ] M -s, -, **Ver|lei|he|rin** [-ərɪn] F -, -nen hire (*Brit*) or rental firm; (*von Kostümen etc*) renter, hirer (*Brit*); (*von Filmen*) distributor, (firm of) distributors pl; (*von Büchern*) lender

Ver|lei|hung F -, -en **a** (= *das Ausleihen*) lending, loan(ing); (*gegen Gebühr*) renting, rental, hire (*Brit*), hiring (*Brit*) **b** (*von Preis etc*) award(ing); (*von Titel, Ehrenbürgerwürde*) conferment, conferring; (*von Amt*) bestowal, bestowment; **die ~ des Preises findet am 26. September statt** the prize will be awarded on 26 September

ver|lei|men ptp **verleimt** VT to glue

ver|lei|ten ptp **verleitet** VT **a** (= *verlocken*) to tempt; (= *verführen*) to lead astray; **die Sonne hat mich verleitet, schwimmen zu gehen** the sun tempted or enticed me to go swimming; **jdn zum Stehlen/Lügen ~** to lead or encourage sb to steal/lie; **jdn zu einem Verbrechen ~** to lead or encourage sb to commit a crime; **jdn zum Ungehorsam ~** to encourage sb to be disobedient; **jdn dazu ~, die Schule zu schwänzen** to encourage sb to play truant **b** (= *veranlassen*) **jdn zu etw ~** to lead sb to sth; **jdn zu einem Irrtum ~** to lead sb to make or into making a mistake

Ver|lei|tung F **a** (= *Verführung*) leading astray; (*zum Lügen, Stehlen*) encouragement; **die ~ der Menschen zur Sünde** leading people into sin **b** (= *Veranlassung*) **die ~ zu einer vorschnellen Äußerung** leading sb to make a hasty comment

ver|ler|nen ptp **verlernt** VT to forget, to unlearn; **das Tanzen ~** to forget how to dance

ver|le|sen ptp **verlesen** irreg VT **a** (= *vorlesen*) to read (out); *Namen* to read out, to call out **b** *Gemüse, Linsen, Früchte etc* to sort; *Feldsalat* to clean VR (*beim Vorlesen*) to make a slip; **ich habe mich wohl ~** I must have read it wrong(ly), I must have misread it

Ver|le|sung F reading (out); (*von Namen*) calling out

ver|letz|bar ADJ (*lit, fig*) vulnerable

Ver|letz|bar|keit [fɛɐ'lɛtsbaːɐkait] F -, no pl (*lit, fig*) vulnerability

ver|let|zen [fɛɐ'lɛtsn] ptp **verletzt** VT **a** (= *verwunden*) to injure; (*in Kampf etc, mit Kugel, Messer*) to wound; (*fig*) jdn to hurt, to wound; *jds Stolz, Gefühle* to hurt, to wound, to injure; *jds*

Ehrgefühl to injure, to offend; *jds Schönheitssinn, zarte Ohren* to offend; **das verletzt den guten Geschmack** it offends against good taste **b** *Gesetz* to break; *Pflicht, Rechte, Intimsphäre* to violate VR to injure oneself

ver|let|zend ADJ *Bemerkung* hurtful

ver|letz|lich [fɛɐ'lɛtslɪç] ADJ vulnerable

Ver|letz|lich|keit F -, no pl vulnerability

Ver|letz|te(r) [fɛɐ'lɛtstə] MF decl as adj injured person; (= *Unfallverletzter auch*) casualty; (*bei Kampf*) wounded man; **die ~n** the injured/wounded; **es gab drei ~** three people were injured or hurt/wounded

Ver|let|zung F -, -en **a** (= *Wunde*) injury **b** (= *das Verletzen*) injuring; (*in Kampf, mit Waffe*) wounding; (*fig*) hurting, wounding; (*von Ehrgefühl, Schönheitssinn*) offending; **zur ~ des Knies führen** to cause a knee injury

Ver|let|zungs-: **ver|let|zungs|an|fäl|lig** ADJ injury-prone attr; **ver|let|zungs|be|dingt** ADJ *Ausfall etc* due to injury pred ADV *pausieren* due to injury; **Ver|let|zungs|ge|fahr** F risk of injury; **Ver|let|zungs|pau|se** F injury lay-off

ver|leug|nen 53.6 ptp **verleugnet** VT to deny; *Kind auch* to disown; **ich kann es nicht ~, dass ...** I cannot deny that ...; **es lässt sich nicht ~, dass ...** there is no denying that ...; **er lässt sich immer (vor ihr) ~** he always pretends not to be there (when she calls); **sich (selbst) ~** to deny one's own self

Ver|leug|nung F denial; (*von Kind auch*) disownment

ver|leum|den [fɛɐ'lɔymdn] ptp **verleumdet** VT to slander, to calumniate (*form*); (*schriftlich*) to libel

Ver|leum|der [fɛɐ'lɔymdɐ] M -s, -, **Ver|leum|de|rin** [-ərɪn] F -, -nen slanderer; (*durch Geschriebenes*) libeller, libeler (*US*)

ver|leum|de|risch [fɛɐ'lɔymdərɪʃ] ADJ slanderous; (*in Schriftform*) libellous (*esp Brit*), libelous (*US*)

Ver|leum|dung F -, -en slandering; (*schriftlich*) libelling (*esp Brit*), libeling (*US*); (= *Bemerkung*) slander, calumny; (= *Bericht*) libel

Ver|leum|dungs-: **Ver|leum|dungs|kam|pagne** F smear campaign; **Ver|leum|dungs|kla|ge** F libel action or suit; **eine ~ einreichen** to sue for libel

ver|lie|ben ptp **verliebt** VR to fall in love (*in +acc* with); **das Kleid ist zum Verlieben (schön)** I love that dress

ver|liebt [fɛɐ'liːpt] ADJ *Benehmen, Blicke, Worte* amorous; (*in jdn/etw*) **~ sein** to be in love (with sb/sth); **die Verliebten** the courting couple/couples, the lovers → *Ohr* ADV *ansehen* lovingly, adoringly; **sie sah ihn ~ an** she looked at him lovingly

Ver|liebt|heit F -, no pl **seine ~ dauert nie lange** he is never in love for very long; **in einem Moment großer ~** feeling (all at once) tremendously in love

ver|lie|ren [fɛɐ'liːrən] pret **verlor** [fɛɐ'loːɐ], ptp **verloren** [fɛɐ'loːrən] VT to lose; *Blätter auch* to shed; **jdn/etw aus dem Gedächtnis ~** to lose all memory of sb/sth, to forget sb/sth; **kein Wort über jdn/etw ~** not to say a word about sb/sth; **wir brauchen kein Wort darüber zu ~** we don't need to waste any words on it; **an ihm hast du nichts verloren** he's no (great) loss; **das/er hat hier nichts verloren** (*inf*) that/he has no business to be here; **diese Bemerkung hat hier nichts verloren** (*inf*) that remark is out of place; **nichts (mehr) zu ~ haben** to have nothing (more) to lose VI to lose; **sie hat an Schönheit/Charme verloren** she has lost some of her beauty/charm; **sie/die Altstadt** *etc* **hat sehr verloren** she/the old town *etc* is not what she/it *etc* used to be; **durch etw ~** to lose (something) by sth; **bei jdm ~** to go down in sb's eyes or estimation VR **a** (*Menschen*) to lose each other; (*Mensch: = sich verirren*) to get lost, to lose one's way

b (= *verschwinden*) to disappear; (= *verhallen*) to fade away, to die; **der Klang verlor sich in dem riesigen Saal/in den Bergen** the sound was lost in the enormous room/faded away or died among the mountains

c (*fig*) (= *geistesabwesend sein*) to become lost to the world; (= *abschweifen*) to lose one's train of thought; **sich in etw** (acc) **~** to become absorbed in sth; **sich in etw** (dat) **~** to get or become lost in sth → *auch* **verloren**

Ver|lie|rer [fɛɐ'liːrɐ] M -s, -, **Ver|lie|re|rin** [-ərɪn] F -, -nen loser

Ver|lie|rer-: **Ver|lie|rer|sei|te** F auf der ~ sein (*inf*) to be on the losing side; **Ver|lie|rer|stra|ße** F auf der ~ sein (*inf*) to be on the downward slope

Ver|lies [fɛɐ'liːs] NT -es, -e [-zə] dungeon

ver|lo|ben 51.2 ptp **verlobt** VR (*mit* to) to become or get engaged, to become betrothed (*old*) VT **jdn mit jdm ~** to betroth sb to sb (*old*); **verlobt sein** to be engaged or betrothed (*old*) (*mit* to)

Ver|löb|nis [fɛɐ'løːpnɪs] NT -ses, -se (*old*) engagement, betrothal (*old*)

Ver|lob|te(r) [fɛɐ'loːptə] MF decl as adj **mein ~r** my fiancé, my betrothed (*old*); **meine ~** my fiancée, my betrothed (*old*); **die ~n** the engaged couple, the betrothed (*old*)

Ver|lo|bung [fɛɐ'loːbʊŋ] 51.2, 52.2 F -, -en engagement, betrothal (*old*)

Ver|lo|bungs- in cpds engagement; **Ver|lo|bungs|an|zei|ge** F engagement announcement; **Ver|lo|bungs|ring** M engagement ring; **Ver|lo|bungs|zeit** F engagement

ver|lo|cken ptp **verlockt** VTI to entice, to tempt

ver|lo|ckend ADJ enticing, tempting

Ver|lo|ckung F enticement, temptation; (= *Reiz*) allure

ver|lo|dern ptp **verlodert** VI aux sein (*geh*) to flare up and die

ver|lo|gen [fɛɐ'loːgn] ADJ *Mensch* lying, mendacious (*form*); *Komplimente, Versprechungen* false; *Moral, Freundlichkeit, Gesellschaft* hypocritical

Ver|lo|gen|heit F -, -en (*von Mensch*) mendacity (*form*); (*von Versprechungen*) falseness; (*von Moral, Gesellschaft*) hypocrisy

ver|loh|nen ptp **verlohnt** VIR impers (*rare*) to be worthwhile

ver|lor pret von **verlieren**

ver|lo|ren [fɛɐ'loːrən] ptp von **verlieren** ADJ lost; (= *einsam auch*) forlorn; *Mühe* vain, wasted; (*Cook*) *Eier* poached; **in den Anblick ~ sein** to be lost in contemplation; **~e Generation** lost generation; **der ~e Sohn** (*Bibl*) the prodigal son; **jdn/etw ~ geben** to give sb/sth up for lost; **auf ~em Posten kämpfen** or **stehen** to be fighting a losing battle or a lost cause → *auch* **verlieren**

ver|lo|ren ge|hen ▲ VI irreg aux sein to get or be lost; (*Zeit, Geld*) to be lost or wasted; **an ihm ist ein Sänger verloren gegangen** he would have made a (good) singer, he ought to have been a singer

Ver|lo|ren|heit F -, no pl forlornness

ver|lö|schen [fɛɐ'lœʃn] pret **verlosch** [fɛɐ'lɔʃ], ptp **verloschen** [fɛɐ'lɔʃn] VI aux sein to go out; (*Inschrift, Farbe, Tinte*) to fade; (*Mond, Sterne*) to set; (*Erinnerung, Ruhm*) to fade (away); **sein Leben(slicht) ist verloschen** (*liter*) he has departed this life (*liter*) ptp **verlöscht** [fɛɐ'lœʃt] VT reg (*geh*) = **auslöschen**

ver|lo|sen ptp **verlost** VT to raffle (off); **wir ~ das letzte Stück Kuchen** we'll draw lots or straws for the last piece of cake

Ver|lo|sung F (= *das Verlosen*) raffling; (= *Lotterie*) raffle, draw; (= *Ziehung*) draw

ver|lö|ten ptp **verlötet** VT to solder

ver|lot|tern ptp **verlottert** aux sein (*inf*) VI (*Stadt, Restaurant*) to get or become run down; (*Garten*) to run wild; (*Mensch*) to go to the dogs;

(*moralisch*) to go downhill; **er verlottert immer mehr** he is sliding further and further downhill; **das Haus ist ganz verlottert** the house is a complete shambles **VT** Geld to squander, to fritter away

ver|lot|tert [fɛɐˈlɔtɐt] ADJ (*inf*) Stadt run-down; Garten wild; Mensch, Aussehen scruffy; (*moralisch*) dissolute

ver|lu|dern [fɛɐˈluːdɐn] ptp **verludert** VTI (*inf*) = **verlottern**

ver|lum|pen ptp **verlumpt** (*inf*) **VT** Geld to chuck away (*inf*) **VI** aux sein to go to the dogs; (*moralisch*) to go downhill

ver|lumpt [fɛɐˈlʊmpt] (*dial*) **ADJ** down and out; Kleider worn-out **ADV** in rags; **~ herumlaufen** to go about in rags; **~ aussehen** to look like a down-and-out

Ver|lust [fɛɐˈlʊst] M -(e)s, -e a loss; **~ bringend** lossmaking; **~ bringend arbeiten** to work at a loss; **mit ~ verkaufen** to sell at a loss; **in ~ geraten** (*form*) to be lost **b** Verluste PL losses pl; (= Tote auch) casualties pl; (*bei Glücksspiel*) losses pl; **schwere ~e haben/machen** to sustain/make heavy losses → **Rücksicht**

Ver|lust-: **Ver|lust|an|zei|ge** F "lost" notice; **Ver|lust|aus|gleich** M loss compensation; **Ver|lust|be|trieb** M (*inf*) lossmaking business (*Brit*), lossmaker (*Brit*), lame duck (*inf*); **ver|lust|brin|gend** △ ADJ → Verlust a; **Ver|lust|brin|ger** [-brɪŋɐ] M -s, - lossmaker (*Brit*), business operating in the red; **Ver|lust|ge|schäft** NT (= Firma) lossmaking business (*Brit*), lossmaker (*Brit*), business operating in the red; **ich habe es schließlich verkauft, aber das war ein ~** I sold it eventually, but I made a loss or but at a loss

ver|lus|tie|ren [fɛɐlʊsˈtiːrən] ptp **verlustiert** VR (*hum*) to amuse oneself

ver|lus|tig ADJ (*form*) **einer Sache** (*gen*) **~ gehen** or **werden** to forfeit or lose sth; **jdn seiner Rechte für ~ erklären** to declare sb's rights forfeit

Ver|lust-: **Ver|lust|kon|to** NT (*Econ*) deficit account; **Ver|lust|leis|tung** F (*Elec*) dissipation; **Ver|lust|lis|te** F (*Mil*) casualty list, list of casualties; **Ver|lust|mel|dung** F a report of the loss; **der Absender muss eine ~ machen** the sender must report the loss **b** (*Mil*) casualty report, casualty figures pl; **Ver|lust|rech|nung** F (*Econ*) loss account or statement; **ver|lust|reich** ADJ a (*Comm*) Firma heavily loss-making; **ein ~es Jahr** a year in which heavy losses were made, a year of heavy losses; **ein ~es Geschäft** a deal on which heavy losses were made **b** (*Mil*) Schlacht involving heavy losses or casualties; **Ver|lust|zo|ne** F die **~** the red; **in die ~ geraten** to go into the red; **Ver|lust|zu|wei|sung** F (*Econ*) allocation of losses

Verm. abbr von **Vermerk**

ver|ma|chen ptp **vermacht** VT **jdm etw ~** to leave or bequeath sth to sb; (*inf*: geben) to bequeath sth to sb; **jdm etw als Schenkung ~** to bequeath sth to sb

Ver|mächt|nis [fɛɐˈmɛçtnɪs] NT -ses, -se bequest, legacy; (*fig*) legacy

Ver|mächt|nis-: (*Jur*): **Ver|mächt|nis|ge|ber(in)** M(F) legator; **Ver|mächt|nis|neh|mer(in)** M(F) legatee

ver|mah|len ptp **vermahlen** VT irreg to grind

ver|mäh|len [fɛɐˈmɛːlən] ptp **vermählt** (*form*) **VT** to marry, to wed; **frisch vermählt sein** to be newly married or wed(ded) **VR** sich (mit jdm) **~** to marry or wed (sb); „**wir haben uns vermählt ...**" "the marriage is announced of ..."

Ver|mähl|te(r) [fɛɐˈmɛːltə] MF decl as adj (*form*) **die beiden ~n** the newly-married couple; **die soeben ~** the bride; **der soeben ~** the (bride-)groom

Ver|mäh|lung ✪ 51.3 F -, -en (*form*) marriage

Ver|mäh|lungs|an|zei|ge F marriage announcement

ver|mah|nen ptp **vermahnt** VT (*dated*) to warn

ver|ma|le|deit [fɛɐmaleˈdait] ADJ (*old*) (ac-)cursed (*old*), damned (*inf*)

ver|ma|len ptp **vermalt** VT Farben to use up

ver|männ|li|chen [fɛɐˈmɛnlɪçn] ptp **vermännlicht** **VT** to masculinize, to make masculine **VI** aux sein (*Frauen*) to become masculine, to become like men; (*Gesellschaft*) to become male-dominated

Ver|männ|li|chung F -, -en masculinization

ver|man|schen ptp **vermanscht** VT (*inf*) to mash up

ver|mark|ten [fɛɐˈmarktn] ptp **vermarktet** VT to market; (*fig*) to commercialize

Ver|mark|tung F -, -en marketing; (*fig*) commercialization

Ver|mark|tungs|stra|te|gie F marketing strategy

ver|mas|seln [fɛɐˈmasln] ptp **vermasselt** VT (*inf*) to ruin, to mess up (*inf*); Prüfung, Klassenarbeit to make a mess or cockup (*Brit inf*) of → **Tour**

ver|mas|sen [fɛɐˈmasn] ptp **vermasst** **VI** aux sein to lose one's identity or individuality, to become stereotyped; **die Gesellschaft vermasst immer mehr** society is becoming more and more uniform **VT** die Gesellschaft to make uniform

Ver|mas|sung F -, -en loss of identity or individuality, stereotyping, de-individualization; **die ~ der Gesellschaft** the stereotyping of society

ver|matscht [fɛɐˈmatʃt] ADJ (*dial*) squashy

ver|mau|ern ptp **vermauert** VT to wall or brick up

ver|meh|ren ptp **vermehrt** **VT** to increase; (= fortpflanzen) to breed; Bakterien to multiply; **vermehrt** increased; **diese Fälle treten vermehrt auf** these cases are occurring with increased or increasing frequency or are happening increasingly often **VR** to increase; (= sich fortpflanzen) to reproduce, to breed; (*Bakterien, Zellen*) to multiply; (*Pflanzen*) to propagate

Ver|meh|rung F increase; (= Fortpflanzung) reproduction, breeding; (von Bakterien) multiplying; (von Pflanzen) propagation

ver|meid|bar ADJ avoidable

ver|mei|den ✪ 29.2, 42.1 ptp **vermieden** [fɛɐˈmiːdn] VT irreg to avoid; Frage auch to evade; **~, dass eine Sache an die Öffentlichkeit dringt** to avoid letting a matter become public; **es lässt sich nicht ~** it cannot be avoided or helped, it is inevitable or unavoidable; **es lässt sich nicht ~, dass ...** it is inevitable or unavoidable that ...; **nicht, wenn ich es ~ kann** not if I can avoid or help it; **er vermeidet keinen Streit** he's not one to avoid an argument

Ver|mei|dung [fɛɐˈmaidʊŋ] F -, -en avoidance; **die ~ eines Skandals ist nur dann möglich, wenn ...** a scandal can only be avoided if ...; **zur ~** +gen or **von ...** to avoid ...

ver|meil [vɛrˈmeːj] ADJ vermilion

Ver|meil [vɛrˈmeːj] NT -s, no pl gilded silver

ver|mei|nen ptp **vermeint** VT (*geh*) to think; **ich vermeinte, eine Stimme zu hören** I thought I heard a voice

ver|meint|lich [fɛɐˈmaintlɪç] **ADJ** attr putative, supposed; Täter, Vater eines Kindes putative **ADV** supposedly

ver|mel|den ptp **vermeldet** VT a (liter: = mitteilen) to announce; **was hast du Neues zu ~?** (*hum*) what news do you have to announce or report? **b** Erfolg, Verluste to report

ver|men|gen ptp **vermengt** VT to mix; (fig inf: = durcheinander bringen) Begriffe etc to mix up, to confuse

Ver|men|gung F -, -en mixing

ver|mensch|li|chen [fɛɐˈmɛnʃlɪçn] ptp **vermenschlicht** VT to humanize; (= als Menschen darstellen auch) to anthropomorphize

Ver|mensch|li|chung F -, -en humanization

Ver|merk [fɛɐˈmɛrk] M -(e)s, -e note, remark; (im Kalender auch) entry; (in Pass) observation; (postalisch) remark; (= Stempel) stamp

ver|mer|ken ptp **vermerkt** VT a (= aufschreiben) to make a note of, to note (down), to write down; (in Pass, Karte) Namen, Datum etc to record; **alle Verkehrssünder werden in Flensburg vermerkt** a record of (the names of) all traffic offenders is kept in Flensburg; **sich** (*dat*) **etw ~** to make a note of sth, to note or write sth down; **etw positiv/negativ ~** to note sth on the plus/negative side **b** (zur Kenntnis nehmen) to note, to make a (mental) note of

ver|mes|sen¹ ptp **vermessen** irreg **VT** to measure; Land, Gelände to survey **VR** a (geh: = sich anmaßen) to presume, to dare; **wie kann er sich ~, ...?** how dare he ...? **b** (= falsch messen) to measure wrongly

ver|mes|sen² [fɛɐˈmɛsn] ADJ (= anmaßend) presumptuous; Diener impudent; (= kühn) Unterfangen bold

Ver|mes|sen|heit F -, -en (= Anmaßung) presumption, presumptuousness; (= Kühnheit) boldness; **es wäre eine ~, das zu tun** that would be a presumptuous thing to do

Ver|mes|sung F measurement; (von Land, Gelände) survey

Ver|mes|sungs-: **Ver|mes|sungs|amt** NT , **Ver|mes|sungs|bü|ro** NT land survey(ing) office; **Ver|mes|sungs|in|ge|ni|eur(in)** M(F) land surveyor; **Ver|mes|sungs|schiff** NT survey ship; **Ver|mes|sungs|tech|nik** F , no pl surveying (technology)

ver|mie|sen [fɛɐˈmiːzn] ptp **vermiest** VT (*inf*) **jdm etw ~** to spoil sth for sb; **das hat mir die ganze Sache vermiest** that spoiled everything for me

ver|miet|bar ADJ rentable; **schlecht ~** difficult to rent (out) or let (out) (esp Brit); **es ist nur als Büroraum ~** it can only be rented (out) or let (out) (esp Brit) as office premises

ver|mie|ten ptp **vermietet** **VT** to rent (out), to let (out) (esp Brit), to lease (Jur); Boot, Auto to rent (out), to hire (out), to lease (Jur); **Zimmer zu ~** room to let (esp Brit), room for rent **VI** to rent (out) or let (out) (esp Brit) a room/rooms; „**zu ~**" "to let" (esp Brit), "for rent"

Ver|mie|ter M lessor; (von Wohnung etc) landlord, lessor (Jur)

Ver|mie|te|rin F lessor; (von Wohnung etc) landlady, lessor (Jur)

Ver|mie|tung [fɛɐˈmiːtʊŋ] F -, -en renting (out), letting (out) (esp Brit); (von Auto, Boot) rental, hiring (out) (Brit)

ver|min|dern ptp **vermindert** **VT** to reduce, to decrease; Gefahr, Anfälligkeit, Einfluss etc auch, Ärger, Zorn to lessen; Widerstandsfähigkeit, Reaktionsfähigkeit to diminish, to reduce; Schmerzen to ease, to lessen, to reduce; (*Mus*) to diminish; **verminderte Zurechnungsfähigkeit** (Jur) diminished responsibility **VR** to decrease; (Gefahr, Anfälligkeit, Einfluss auch, Ärger, Zorn) to lessen; (Widerstandsfähigkeit, Reaktionsfähigkeit) to diminish; (Schmerzen) to ease off, to lessen, to decrease

Ver|min|de|rung F reduction (+gen of), decrease (+gen in); (von Gefahr, Anfälligkeit, Einfluss auch, von Ärger, Zorn) lessening; (von Widerstandsfähigkeit, Reaktionsfähigkeit) diminishing; (von Schmerzen) easing

ver|mi|nen [fɛɐˈmiːnən] ptp **vermint** VT to mine

Ver|mi|nung F -, -en mining

ver|mi|schen ptp **vermischt** **VT** to mix; Tabaksorten, Teesorten etc to blend; **vermischte Schriften** miscellaneous writings; „**Vermischtes**" "miscellaneous" **VR** to mix; (Rassen auch) to interbreed; (Elemente, Klänge, Farben) to blend, to mingle; **Freude vermischt sich mit Leid** joy mingles *or* is mingled with sorrow; **wo sich Tradition und Fortschritt ~** where tradition and progress are blended (together) *or* combined

Ver|mi|schung F mixing, mixture; (*von Tabaksorten, Teesorten*) blending; (*von Rassen*) interbreeding; (*von Elementen, Klängen, Farben*) blending, mingling; (*von Gefühlen, Stilebenen, Metaphern*) mixture

ver|mis|sen *ptp* **vermisst** VT to miss; **vermisst werden** to be missing; **vermisst sein, als vermisst gemeldet sein** to be reported missing; **ich vermisse zwei silberne Teelöffel** two (of my) silver teaspoons are missing, I'm missing two silver teaspoons; **ich vermisse die Blumen auf den Tischen** I see you don't have the flowers on the tables; **etw an jdm/etw ~** to find sb/sth lacking in sb/sth; **was ich bei dieser Beschreibung vermisse, ist ...** what I miss in this description is ...; **wir haben dich bei der Party vermisst** we didn't see you at the party; **entschuldige, dass ich zu spät komme – wir hatten dich noch gar nicht vermisst** sorry I'm late – we hadn't even noticed you weren't here; **etw ~ lassen** to lack sth, to be lacking in sth

Ver|miss|ten|an|zei|ge ▲ F missing persons report; **eine ~ aufgeben** to report someone (as) missing

Ver|miss|te(r) ▲ [fɛɐˈmɪstə] MF *decl as adj* missing person

ver|mit|tel|bar ADJ *Idee, Gefühl* communicable; *Arbeitsloser* placeable; **der Sachverhalt ist ihm nur schwer ~** it is very difficult to get the facts across to him

Ver|mit|tel|bar|keit [fɛɐˈmɪtlbaːɐkait] F -, *no pl* **die hohe/niedrige ~ eines Arbeitslosen** the ease/difficulty of placing an unemployed person

ver|mit|teln [fɛɐˈmɪtln] *ptp* **vermittelt** VT to arrange (*jdm* for sb); *Stelle, Partner, Privatschüler, Kontakte* to find (*jdm* for sb); *Aushilfskräfte, Lehrer etc* to find jobs *or* positions for, to place; (*Telec*) *Gespräch* to put through, to connect; *Hypotheken, Kredite, Geschäfte* to arrange, to negotiate (*jdm* for sb); *Lösung, Kompromiss, Waffenstillstand* to arrange, to negotiate, to mediate; *Gefühl, Bild, Idee, Einblick* to convey, to give (*jdm* to sb); *Verständnis* to give (*jdm* (to) sb); *Wissen* to impart (*jdm* to sb); **jdm etw ~** to get sth for sb; **eine Stelle, die Hotelunterkunft vermittelt** an office which finds hotel accommodation; **wir ~ Geschäftsräume** we are agents for business premises; **ich kann dir eine billige Ferienwohnung ~** I can get you a cheap holiday flat (*Brit*) *or* vacation apartment (*US*)

VI to mediate, to act as mediator *or* a go-between; **~d eingreifen** to intervene; **~de Worte** conciliatory words

ver|mit|tels(t) [fɛɐˈmɪtls(t)] PREP +*gen* (*form*) by means of

Ver|mitt|ler(in) M(F) **a** mediator, go-between **b** (*Comm*) agent; (*Fin*) (= *Heiratsvermittler*) broker; (*von Anleihe*) negotiator

Ver|mitt|ler|ge|bühr F commission; (*Fin auch*) brokerage

Ver|mitt|ler|rol|le F role of mediator

Ver|mitt|lung [fɛɐˈmɪtlʊŋ] F -, -en **a** (= *das Vermitteln*) arranging, arrangement; (*von Stelle, Briefpartner, Privatschüler*) finding; (*von Arbeitskräften*) finding of jobs *or* positions (+*gen* for), placing; (*Telec: von Gespräch*) connection; (*von Hypothek, Kredit, Geschäft, Wertpapier*) negotiation; (*in Streitigkeiten*) mediation; (*von Gefühl, Bild, Idee, Einblick*) conveying; (*von Verständnis*) giving; (*von Wissen*) imparting; **sie haben sich durch die ~ einer Agentur kennen gelernt** they met through an agency; **ich habe das Zimmer/die Stelle durch ~ eines Freundes bekommen** I got the room/job through *or* via a friend; **durch seine freundliche ~** with his kind help; **zur ~ eines besseren Verständnisses** to give a better understanding; **zur ~ eines besseren Eindrucks** to give *or* convey a better impression; **heute geht**

die telefonische ~ automatisch vor sich nowadays telephone calls are put through *or* connected automatically

b (= *Schlichtung*) mediation; **eine ~ zwischen den beiden ist mir leider nicht gelungen** unfortunately I was unable to reconcile them *or* to bring about a reconciliation between them

c (= *Stelle, Agentur*) agency; (= *Heiratsvermittlung*) marriage bureau *or* agency; (= *Wohnungsvermittlung*) estate agent's *or* agency (*Brit*), realtor (*US*), real estate agent's *or* agency (*esp US*); (= *Arbeitsvermittlung*) employment agency

d (*Telec*) (= *Amt*) exchange; (*in Firma etc*) switchboard; (= *Mensch*) operator; **~, bitte geben Sie mir Göhren 487** give me Göhren 487 please, operator

Ver|mitt|lungs-: **Ver|mitt|lungs|amt** NT (*Telec*) telephone exchange; **Ver|mitt|lungs|aus|schuss** ▲ M (*Econ, Pol*) mediation committee; **Ver|mitt|lungs|chan|ce** F *usu pl* chance of being placed in a job; **Ver|mitt|lungs|ge|bühr** F, **Ver|mitt|lungs|pro|vi|si|on** F commission; **Ver|mitt|lungs|stel|le** F agency; (*Telec*) (telephone) exchange; (*in Firma etc*) switchboard; **Ver|mitt|lungs|ver|fah|ren** NT (*Pol*) joint committee procedure; **Ver|mitt|lungs|ver|such** M attempt at mediation

ver|mö|beln [fɛɐˈmøːbln] *ptp* **vermöbelt** VT (*inf*) to beat up; (*als Strafe*) to thrash

ver|mo|dern [fɛɐˈmoːdɐn] *ptp* **vermodert** VI *aux sein* to moulder (*Brit*), to molder (*US*), to decay

Ver|mo|de|rung [fɛɐˈmoːdərʊŋ] F -, -en, **Ver|mod|rung** [fɛɐˈmoːdrʊŋ] F -, -en decay

ver|mö|ge [fɛɐˈmøːgə] PREP +*gen* (*liter*) by dint of

ver|mö|gen *ptp* **vermocht** [fɛɐˈmɔxt] VT *irreg*, V AUX (*geh*) **etw zu tun ~**, **(es) ~, etw zu tun** to be able to do sth, to be capable of doing sth; **er vermochte (es) nicht, sich von den Fesseln zu befreien** he was unable *or* was not able to free himself from the chains; **viel ~** to be capable of a lot; **wenig ~** not to be capable of very much; **etwas Verständnis/Geduld vermag viel bei ihm** a little understanding/patience works wonders with him

Ver|mö|gen [fɛɐˈmøːgn] NT -s, - **a** (= *Reichtum, viel Geld*) fortune; **das ist ein ~ wert** it's worth a fortune; **eine Frau, die ~ hat** a woman who has money, a woman of means; **die erste Frage war, ob ich ~ hatte** the first question was whether I had private means **b** (= *Besitz*) property; **mein ganzes ~ besteht aus ...** my entire assets consist of ... **c** (= *Können*) ability, capacity; (= *Macht*) power

ver|mö|gend ADJ (= *reich*) wealthy, well-off; **ein ~er Mann** a man of means, a wealthy man

Ver|mö|gens-: **Ver|mö|gens|ab|ga|be** F property levy; **Ver|mö|gens|an|la|ge** F capital investment; **Ver|mö|gens|be|ra|ter(in)** M(F) financial consultant *or* adviser; **Ver|mö|gens|be|ra|tung** F financial consulting; **ver|mö|gens|bil|dend** ADJ wealth-creating; **Ver|mö|gens|bil|dung** F creation of wealth; (*durch Prämiensparen*) wealth formation by long-term saving with tax concessions; **Ver|mö|gens|er|klä|rung** F statement of property; (*Wertpapiere*) statement of assets; **Ver|mö|gens|kon|zent|ra|ti|on** F concentration of wealth; **Ver|mö|gens|po|li|tik** F policy on the distribution of wealth; **Ver|mö|gens|steu|er** F wealth tax; **Ver|mö|gens|ver|hält|nis|se** PL financial *or* pecuniary circumstances *pl*; **Ver|mö|gens|ver|tei|lung** F distribution of wealth; **Ver|mö|gens|ver|wal|ter(in)** M(F) property administrator; **Ver|mö|gens|ver|wal|tung** F property administration; **Ver|mö|gens|wer|te** PL assets *pl*; **ver|mö|gens|wirk|sam** ADJ profitable, profit-yielding; **~e Leistungen** employer's contributions to tax-deductible savings scheme; ADV **Geld ~ investieren** to invest money profit-

ably; **Ver|mö|gens|zu|wachs** M increase of wealth

ver|mot|tet [fɛɐˈmɔtət] ADJ (*lit, fig*) moth-eaten

ver|mum|men [fɛɐˈmʊmən] *ptp* **vermummt** VT to wrap up (warm) VR (= *sich warm anziehen*) to wrap (oneself) up (warm); **vermummte Gestalten in einer Winterlandschaft** muffled-up figures in a winter landscape **b** (= *sich verkleiden*) to disguise oneself; **eine vermummte Gestalt betrat den Raum** a cloaked figure entered the room; **tief vermummt** heavily disguised; **vermummte Demonstranten** masked demonstrators

Ver|mum|mung F -, -en disguise; (*von Demonstranten*) covering of the face

Ver|mum|mungs|ver|bot NT das ~ bei Demonstrationen the law requiring demonstrators to leave their faces uncovered

ver|murk|sen *ptp* **vermurkst** VT (*inf*) **etw/sich** (*dat*) **etw ~** to mess sth up (*inf*), to make a mess of sth

ver|mu|ten [fɛɐˈmuːtn] *ptp* **vermutet** VT to suspect; **ich vermute es nur** that's only an assumption, I'm only assuming that, that's only what I suspect to be the case; **wir haben ihn dort nicht vermutet** we did not expect him to be there; **ich hatte dich nicht so früh vermutet** I didn't suspect you would be so early; **es ist zu ~, dass ...** it may be supposed that ..., we may assume *or* presume that ...; **Wissenschaftler ~ Leben auf der Venus** scientists suspect that there is life on Venus; **die Entwicklung lässt ~, dass ...** developments lead one to assume that..., developments give rise to the suspicion *or* supposition that ...

ver|mut|lich [fɛɐˈmuːtlɪç] ADJ *attr* presumable; *Täter* suspected ADV presumably

Ver|mu|tung F -, -en (= *Annahme*) supposition, assumption; (= *Mutmaßung*) conjecture; (= *Verdacht*) hunch, suspicion; **die ~ liegt nahe, dass ...** there are grounds for the supposition *or* assumption that ...; **das sind alles nur ~en** that is pure conjecture, those are purely suppositions *or* assumptions; **wir sind nur auf ~en angewiesen** we have to rely on suppositions *or* assumptions *or* guesswork; **meine ~en waren doch richtig** my guess *or* suspicion *or* hunch was right

ver|nach|läs|sig|bar [fɛɐˈnaːxlɛsɪçbaːɐ] ADJ negligible

ver|nach|läs|si|gen [fɛɐˈnaːxlɛsɪgn] *ptp* **vernachlässigt** VT to neglect; (*Schicksal*) *jdn* to be unkind *or* harsh to; **das können wir ~** (= *nicht berücksichtigen*) we can ignore that VR to neglect oneself *or* one's appearance

Ver|nach|läs|si|gung F -, -en neglect; (= *Nichtberücksichtigung*) ignoring, disregarding

ver|na|geln *ptp* **vernagelt** VT to nail up; **etw mit Brettern ~** to board sth up

ver|na|gelt [fɛɐˈnaːglt] ADJ (*fig inf*) thick *no adv* (*inf*), wooden-headed (*Brit inf*); (= *engstirnig*) small-minded; **ich war wie ~** I couldn't think straight

ver|nä|hen *ptp* **vernäht** VT to neaten; *Wunde* to stitch (up); (= *verbrauchen*) to use up

ver|nar|ben [fɛɐˈnarbn] *ptp* **vernarbt** VI *aux sein* to heal *or* close (up)

ver|narbt [fɛɐˈnarpt] *ptp* von **vernarben** ADJ scarred; **~es Gesicht** (*durch Pocken auch*) pockmarked *or* pitted face

Ver|nar|bung F -, -en healing; **leichte Massagen sorgen für schöne ~en** gentle massages help the skin to scar over nicely; **eine gute ~** a good heal

ver|nar|ren *ptp* **vernarrt** VR (*inf*) **sich in jdn/etw ~** to fall for sb/sth, to be smitten by sb/sth; **in jdn/etw vernarrt sein** to be crazy (*inf*) *or* nuts (*inf*) about sb/sth, to be infatuated with sb

Ver|narrt|heit [fɛɐˈnarthait] F -, -en infatuation (*in* +*acc* with)

ver|na|schen ptp **vernascht** VT *Süßigkeiten* to eat up; *Geld* to spend on sweets; (*inf*) *Mädchen, Mann* to make it with (*inf*)

ver|ne|beln [fɛɐ̯'ne:bln] ptp **vernebelt** VT (*Mil*) to cover with a smoke screen; (*fig*) *Tatsachen* to obscure, to obfuscate (*form*); (*inf*) *Zimmer* to fug up; **die Dinge ~** to confuse the issue, to muddy the waters; **jdm den Verstand** or **den Kopf ~** to cloud sb's mind

ver|ne|be|lung [fɛɐ̯'ne:bəlʊŋ] F **-, -en, Ver|neb|lung** [fɛɐ̯'ne:blʊŋ] F **-, -en**, no pl (*Mil*) screening; (*fig: von Tatsachen*) obscuring

ver|nehm|bar ADJ **a** (= *hörbar*) audible, perceptible **b** (= *vernehmungsfähig*) able to be questioned ADV (= *hörbar*) audibly; **sie murmelte kaum ~ ein Gebet** she mumbled a prayer, scarcely audible

ver|neh|men ptp **vernommen** [fɛɐ̯'nɔmən] VT *irreg* **a** (= *hören*) to hear; **sich zu etw** or **über etw** (*acc*) **~ lassen** to comment on sth **b** (= *erfahren*) to hear, to learn; **das Presseamt hat ~ lassen, dass ...** the press agency has given to understand that ...; **er hat über seine Pläne nichts ~ lassen** he has let nothing be known about his plans **c** (*Jur*) *Zeugen, Angeklagte* to examine; (*Polizei*) to question; **zu diesem Fall wurden fünfzig Zeugen vernommen** fifty witnesses were heard in connection with this case

Ver|neh|men [fɛɐ̯'ne:mən] NT **-s**, no pl **dem ~ nach** from what I/we *etc* hear; **gutem/sicherem ~ nach** according to well-informed/reliable sources

Ver|nehm|las|sung [fɛɐ̯'ne:mlasʊŋ] F **-, -en** (*Sw*) **a** (*Admin:* = *Bekanntmachung*) notice, announcement **b** (*Parl:* = *Beratung*) discussion stage **c** (= *Meinung, Stellungnahme*) opinion

ver|nehm|lich [fɛɐ̯'ne:mlɪç] ADJ clear, audible ADV **a** audibly; **es tönte laut und ~ ...** it sounded loud and clear ..., we heard loud and clear ... **b** (= *dem Vernehmen nach*) from what I/we *etc* hear

Ver|neh|mung [fɛɐ̯'ne:mʊŋ] F **-, -en** (*Jur: von Zeugen, Angeklagten*) examination; (*durch Polizei*) questioning

Ver|neh|mungs-: **Ver|neh|mungs|be|am|te(r)** M *decl as adj*, **Ver|neh|mungs|be|am|tin** F police interrogator; **ver|neh|mungs|fä|hig** ADJ able to be examined; (*durch Polizei*) able to be questioned; **ver|neh|mungs|rich|ter(in)** M(F) ≈ examining judge; **ver|neh|mungs|un|fä|hig** ADJ unfit to be examined; (*durch Polizei*) unfit to be questioned

ver|nei|gen ptp **verneigt** VR to bow; **sich vor jdm/etw ~** (*lit*) to bow to sb/sth; (*fig*) to bow down before sb/sth

Ver|nei|gung F bow, obeisance (*form*) (*vor* +*dat* before); **eine ~ machen** to bow

ver|nei|nen [fɛɐ̯'nainən] ptp **verneint** VTI *Frage* to answer in the negative; (= *leugnen*) *Tatsache, Existenz Gottes etc* to deny; *These, Argument* to dispute; (*Gram, Logik*) to negate; **die verneinte Form** the negative (form); **eine Seite seines Wesens, die stets verneint** a side of his nature that always denies (*liter*) or that is always negative

ver|nei|nend ADJ (*auch Gram*) negative ADV *antworten* in the negative; **er schüttelte ~ den Kopf** he shook his head

Ver|nei|nung F **-, -en** (= *Leugnung*) denial; (*von These etc*) disputing; (*Gram, Philos*) negation; (= *verneinte Form*) negative; **die ~ meiner Frage** the negative answer to my question

ver|net|zen ptp **vernetzt** VT (*esp Mot*) to link up, to integrate; (*Comput*) to network

Ver|net|zung [fɛɐ̯'nɛtsʊŋ] F **-, -en** (*esp Mot*) linking-up, integration; (*Comput*) networking

Ver|net|zungs|kon|zept NT (*Mot*) integration concept; (*Comput*) networking concept

ver|nich|ten [fɛɐ̯'nɪçtn] ptp **vernichtet** VT (*lit, fig*) to destroy; *Schädlinge, Menschheit auch* to exterminate; *Feind auch* to annihilate

ver|nich|tend ADJ *Kritik, Urteil* devastating; *Blick auch* withering; *Niederlage* crushing ADV **~ über jdn urteilen** to make a devastating appraisal of sb; **jdn ~ schlagen** (*Mil, Sport*) to annihilate sb

Ver|nich|tung F **-, -en** destruction; (*von Schädlingen, der Menschheit auch*) extermination; (*von Feinden, der Menschheit auch*) annihilation

Ver|nich|tungs-: **Ver|nich|tungs|krieg** M war of extermination; **Ver|nich|tungs|la|ger** NT extermination camp; **Ver|nich|tungs|mit|tel** NT insecticide; (*gegen Unkraut*) weedkiller; **Ver|nich|tungs|schlag** M devastating blow; **das war der ~ für die Regierung** that was the final blow for the government; **zum ~ ausholen** (*Mil, fig*) to prepare to deliver the final blow; **Ver|nich|tungs|waf|fe** F destructive or doomsday weapon

ver|ni|ckeln [fɛɐ̯'nɪkln] ptp **vernickelt** VT to nickel-plate

Ver|ni|cke|lung F **-, -en** nickel plating no pl

ver|nied|li|chen [fɛɐ̯'ni:tlɪçn] ptp **verniedlicht** VT to trivialize, to play down

Ver|nied|li|chung [fɛɐ̯'ni:tlɪçʊŋ] F minimization; (*eines Fehlers, Problems etc*) playing down

ver|nie|ten ptp **vernietet** VT to rivet

Ver|nie|tung [fɛɐ̯'ni:tʊŋ] F **-, -en** riveting

Ver|nis|sa|ge [vɛrnɪ'sa:ʒə] F **-, -n** opening, preview (*at art gallery*)

Ver|nunft [fɛɐ̯'nʊnft] F **-**, no pl reason (*auch Philos*), good sense; **zur ~ kommen** to come to one's senses; **~ annehmen** to see reason; **nimm doch ~ an!** why don't you see sense or reason?; **jdm ~ predigen** to reason with sb; **gegen alle (Regeln der) ~** against all (the laws of) reason; **~ walten lassen** (*geh*) to let reason prevail; **~ beweisen** to show (good) sense or common sense; **etw mit/ohne ~ tun** to do sth sensibly/ foolishly; **etw mit ~ essen/trinken** to eat/drink sth appreciatively; **Kinder zur ~ erziehen** to bring children up to be sensible; **jdn zur ~ bringen** to make sb see sense or reason

Ver|nunft-: **ver|nunft|be|gabt** ADJ rational, endowed with reason; **Ver|nunft|be|griff** M concept of reason; **Ver|nunft|ehe** F (*lit, fig*) marriage of convenience; **ver|nunft|ge|lei|tet** [-ɡəlaitət] ADJ rational; **ver|nunft|ge|mäß** ADJ rational ADV rationally, from a rational point of view; **Ver|nunft|glau|be(n)** M rationalism; **Ver|nunft|grün|de** PL rational grounds pl; **Ver|nunft|hei|rat** F marriage of convenience

ver|nünf|tig [fɛɐ̯'nʏnftɪç] ADJ sensible; (= *logisch denkend*) rational; (*inf:* = *ordentlich, anständig*) decent; (= *annehmbar*) reasonable; **sei doch ~!** be sensible or reasonable!; **ich kann keinen ~en Gedanken fassen** I can't think properly ADV sensibly; (= *logisch*) rationally; (*inf:* = *anständig, ordentlich*) decently; (= *annehmbar*) reasonably; (= *tüchtig*) properly (*inf*); **~ reden** (*inf*) to speak properly; **er kann ganz ~ kochen** (*inf*) he can cook reasonably well

ver|nünf|ti|ger|wei|se [fɛɐ̯'nʏnftɪɡɐ'vaizə] ADV **etw ~ tun** to have the (good) sense to do sth; **du solltest dich ~ ins Bett legen** you should be sensible and go to bed

Ver|nünf|tig|keit F **-**, no pl good sense

Ver|nunft-: **Ver|nunft|mensch** M rational person; **ver|nunft|wid|rig** ADJ irrational

ver|öden [fɛɐ̯'ø:dn] ptp **verödet** VT (*Med*) *Krampfadern* to sclerose VI *aux sein* to become desolate; (= *sich entvölkern auch*) to become deserted; (*fig:* = *geistig veröden*) to become stultified

Ver|ödung F **-, -en** **a** desolation; (= *Entvölkerung*) depopulation; (*fig*) stultification **b** (*Med: von Krampfadern*) sclerosis

ver|öf|fent|li|chen [fɛɐ̯'œfntlɪçn] ptp **veröffentlicht** VTI to publish

Ver|öf|fent|li|chung F **-, -en** publication

ver|ord|nen ptp **verordnet** VT **a** (= *anordnen*) to prescribe, to order; *Medikament* to prescribe

(*jdm etw sth for sb*) **b** (*old:* = *verfügen*) to decree, to ordain

Ver|ord|nung F **a** (*Med*) prescription; **nach ~ des Arztes einzunehmen** to be taken as directed by the doctor **b** (*form:* = *Verfügung*) decree, ordinance

ver|pach|ten ptp **verpachtet** VT to lease, to rent out (*an* +*acc* to)

Ver|päch|ter(in) M(F) lessor

Ver|pach|tung F lease

ver|pa|cken ptp **verpackt** VT to pack; (*verbrauchergerecht*) to package; (= *einwickeln*) to wrap

Ver|pa|ckung F **a** (= *Material*) packaging no pl **b** no pl (= *das Verpacken*) packing; (*verbrauchergerecht*) packaging; (= *das Einwickeln*) wrapping

Ver|pa|ckungs-: **Ver|pa|ckungs|ge|wicht** NT weight of packaging, tare (weight); **Ver|pa|ckungs|in|dust|rie** F packaging industry; **Ver|pa|ckungs|kos|ten** PL packaging charges pl; **Ver|pa|ckungs|ma|te|ri|al** NT packaging material; (= *Papier*) wrapping; **Ver|pa|ckungs|müll** M packaging waste; **Ver|pa|ckungs|müll** M packaging waste

ver|päp|peln ptp **verpäppelt** VT (*inf*) to mollycoddle (*esp Brit inf*), to pamper (*inf*)

ver|pa|schen [fɛɐ̯'paʃn] ptp **verpascht** VT (*Aus*) to sell (off), to flog (*Brit inf*)

ver|pas|sen ptp **verpasst** VT **a** (= *versäumen*) to miss → **Anschluss b** (*inf:* = *zuteilen*) **jdm etw ~** to give sb sth; (= *aufzwingen*) to make sb have sth; **jdm eins** or **eine** or **eine Ohrfeige ~** to clout (*Brit*) or smack sb one (*inf*); **jdm eine Tracht Prügel ~** to give sb a good hiding (*inf*); **jdm einen Denkzettel ~** to give sb something to think about (*inf*)

ver|pat|zen ptp **verpatzt** VT (*inf*) to spoil; *Vortrag, Auftritt auch, Examen* to make a mess of; **sich** (*dat*) **etw ~** to spoil sth/make a mess of sth

ver|pen|nen ptp **verpennt** (*inf*) VT (= *verschlafen*) *Termin, Zeit* to miss by oversleeping; (= *schlafend verbringen*) *Tag, Morgen etc* to sleep through; (= *verpassen*) *Einsatz* to miss; *Leben* to waste away; (*fig:* = *nicht bemerken*) to sleep through VIR to oversleep

ver|pennt [fɛɐ̯'pɛnt] ADJ (*inf*) sleepy; (= *trottelig*) *Mensch* dozy; **ein ~er Typ** (= *Vielschläfer*) a sleepyhead (*inf*); (= *Trottel*) a dummy (*inf*)

ver|pes|ten [fɛɐ̯'pɛstn] ptp **verpestet** VT to pollute, to contaminate; **die Luft im Büro ~** (*inf*) to stink out (*Brit*) or up (*US*) the office (*inf*)

Ver|pes|tung F **-,** (*rare*) **-en** pollution, contamination

ver|pet|zen ptp **verpetzt** VT (*inf*) to tell or sneak (*Brit*) or narc (*US*) on (*inf*) (*bei* to)

ver|pfän|den ptp **verpfändet** VT to pawn, to (put in) hock (*inf*); (*Jur*) to mortgage; **(jdm) sein Wort ~** (*obs*) to pledge one's word (to sb)

Ver|pfän|dung F pawning; (*Jur*) mortgage; **etw zur ~ ins Leihhaus bringen** to take sth to be pawned (in a pawnshop), to put sth in pawn or hock (*inf*)

ver|pfei|fen ptp **verpfiffen** [fɛɐ̯'pfɪfn] VT *irreg* (*inf*) to grass on (*bei* to) (*inf*)

ver|pflan|zen ptp **verpflanzt** VT (*Bot, Med, fig*) to transplant; *Haut* to graft

Ver|pflan|zung F (*Med*) transplant; (*von Haut*) grafting

ver|pfle|gen ptp **verpflegt** VT to feed; (*Mil*) *Heer auch* to ration VR **sich (selbst) ~** to feed oneself; (= *selbst kochen*) to cater for oneself

Ver|pfle|gung [fɛɐ̯'pfle:ɡʊŋ] F **-, -en** **a** (= *das Verpflegen*) catering; (*Mil*) rationing; **die ~ von 4 Leuten** feeding 4 people, catering for 4 people **b** (= *Essen*) food; (*Mil*) rations pl, provisions pl; **mit voller ~** including food; (= *mit Vollpension*) with full board

Ver|pfle|gungs-: **Ver|pfle|gungs|kos|ten** PL cost *sing* of food; **Ver|pfle|gungs|mehr|auf-wand** M additional meal allowance

ver|pflich|ten [fɛɐˈpflɪçtn̩] ◇ 37.1, 37.3 *ptp* **verpflichtet** **VT** **a** (= *moralische Pflicht auferlegen*) to oblige, to place under an obligation; **verpflichtet sein, etw zu tun, zu etw verpflichtet sein** to be obliged to do sth; **sich verpflichtet fühlen, etw zu tun, sich zu etw verpflichtet füh-len** to feel obliged to do sth; **der Tradition ver-pflichtet** bound by tradition; **jdm verpflichtet sein** to be under an obligation to sb; **sich jdm verpflichtet fühlen** to feel under an obligation to sb

b (= *binden*) to commit; (*vertraglich, durch Eid, durch Handschlag etc*) to bind; (*durch Gesetz*) to oblige; **verpflichtet sein, etw zu tun** to be com-mitted to doing sth; (*durch Gesetz*) to be obliged to do sth; **jdn auf die Verfassung ~** to make sb swear to uphold the constitution; **auf die Ver-fassung verpflichtet werden** to be sworn to up-hold the constitution; **~d** (*Zusage, Unterschrift, Versprechen*) binding

c (= *einstellen*) to engage; *Sportler* to sign on; (*Mil*) to enlist

VI (= *moralische Pflicht darstellen*) to carry an obligation (*zu etw* to do sth); (= *bindend sein*) to be binding; **das verpflichtet zu nichts** there is no obligation involved → **Adel a**

VR (*moralisch*) to make a commitment; (*eidlich, vertraglich*) to commit oneself; (*Mil*) to enlist, to sign up; **sich zu etw ~** to undertake to do sth; (*vertraglich, eidlich*) to commit oneself to doing sth

Ver|pflich|tung F -, -en **a** obligation (*zu etw* to do sth); (*finanziell*) commitment (*zu etw* to do sth); (= *Aufgabe*) duty; **dienstliche ~en** official duties; (= *Einstellung*) engaging; **~en gegen jdn haben** to be in sb's debt (*auch finanziell*), to be indebted to sb; **seinen ~en nachkommen** to fulfil (*Brit*) or fulfill (*US*) one's obligations **b** (= *Einstellung*) engaging; (*von Sportlern*) signing on; (*Mil*) enlistment **c** (= *das Sich-Verpflichten*) (*für, auf +acc* for) signing on; (*Mil*) signing up; **ich habe meine ~ auf sechs Monate bereut** I regret having signed on or committed myself/signed up for six months

Ver|pflich|tungs|er|klä|rung F -, (*Jur, Econ*) formal obligation

ver|pfu|schen *ptp* **verpfuscht** VT (*inf*) *Arbeit etc* to bungle; *Leben, Erziehung, Urlaub etc* to muck up (*Brit inf*), to screw up (*sl*), to ruin; *Mensch* to ruin; *Kind* to spoil; **jdm/sich den Abend etc ~** to ruin sb's/one's evening *etc*

ver|pie|pelt [fɛɐˈpiːplt], **ver|pim|pelt** [fɛɐ-ˈpɪmplt] ADJ (*dial*) soft (*inf*); **tu nicht so ~** don't act or be so soft (*inf*)

ver|pis|sen *ptp* **verpisst** VR (*sl*) to piss off (*esp Brit sl*), to clear out (*inf*)

ver|pla|nen *ptp* **verplant** **VT** *Zeit* to book up; *Geld* to budget; **jdn ~** (*inf*) to fill up all sb's spare time (for him/her) (*sl*), to ruin **VR** to plan badly or wrongly; (= *falsch berechnen*) to miscalculate

ver|plap|pern *ptp* **verplappert** VR (*inf*) to open one's mouth too wide (*inf*)

ver|plau|dern *ptp* **verplaudert** **VT** *Zeit* to talk or chat away **VR** (*inf*) to forget the time talking or chatting

ver|plau|schen *ptp* **verplauscht** VR (*Aus*) to forget the time chatting or talking

ver|plem|pern *ptp* **verplempert** **VT** (*inf*) *Zeit* to waste, to fritter away; *Geld auch* to squander **VR** to waste oneself

ver|plom|ben [fɛɐˈplɔmbn̩] *ptp* **verplombt** VT to seal

ver|pönt [fɛɐˈpøːnt] ADJ frowned (up)on (*bei* by)

ver|pop|pen [fɛɐˈpɔpn̩] *ptp* **verpoppt** VT to jazz up, to make a pop version of

ver|pras|sen *ptp* **verprasst** VT to blow (*inf*) (*für* on); **etw sinnlos ~** to fritter sth away, to squan-der sth

ver|prel|len *ptp* **verprellt** VT to put off, to in-timidate

ver|pro|vi|an|tie|ren [fɛɐprovianˈtiːrən] *ptp* **ver-proviantiert** **VT** to supply with food **VR** to get a food supply

ver|prü|geln *ptp* **verprügelt** VT to thrash, to beat up

ver|puf|fen *ptp* **verpufft** VI *aux sein* to (go) pop; (*fig*) to fall flat

Ver|puf|fung [fɛɐˈpʊfʊŋ] F -, -en (= *Explosion*) muffled explosion

ver|pul|vern [fɛɐˈpʊlvɐn, -fɐn] *ptp* **verpulvert** VT (*inf*) to fritter away, to squander

ver|pum|pen *ptp* **verpumpt** VT (*inf*) to lend out, to loan (*an +acc* to)

ver|pup|pen [fɛɐˈpʊpn̩] *ptp* **verpuppt** VR to pu-pate

ver|pus|ten *ptp* **verpustet** VIR (*inf*) to get one's breath back

Ver|putz M plaster, plasterwork; (= *Rauputz*) roughcast; **über/unter ~** on top of/under plas-ter

ver|put|zen *ptp* **verputzt** VT **a** *Gebäude, Wand* to plaster; (*mit Rauputz*) to roughcast **b** (*inf*: = *aufessen*) to polish off (*inf*), to demolish (*inf*); **ich kann ihn/das nicht ~** (*inf*) I can't stomach him/it

ver|qual|men *ptp* **verqualmt** VT *Zimmer, Luft* to fill with smoke; (*inf*) *Zigaretten etc* to smoke; *Geld* to spend on smoking; **ein verqualmtes Zimmer** a room full of smoke

ver|quast [fɛɐˈkvaːst] ADJ (*inf*: = *verworren*) mixed-up; *Sprache, Text* garbled; *Ideen* half-baked

ver|quat|schen [fɛɐˈkvatʃn̩] *ptp* **verquatscht** (*inf*) **VT** to chat away **VR** **a** (= *lange plaudern*) to forget the time chatting **b** (= *Geheimnis aus-plaudern*) to open one's mouth too wide (*inf*)

ver|quel|len *ptp* **verquollen** [fɛɐˈkvɔlən] VI *irreg aux sein* to swell; (*Holz auch*) to warp; **verquol-lene Augen** puffy or swollen eyes

ver|quer [fɛɐˈkveːɐ] ADJ squint, skewwhiff (*Brit inf*); **das ist eine ~e Optik** that's a twisted way of looking at things ADV (*jdm*) (= *schief gehen*) to go wrong (for sb); **das kommt mir jetzt etwas ~** that could have come at a better time; **so etwas geht mir ~** that goes a-gainst the grain

ver|qui|cken [fɛɐˈkvɪkn̩] *ptp* **verquickt** **VT** **a** (*Chem*) to amalgamate **b** (*fig*) to bring togeth-er, to combine; (= *vermischen*) to mix; **eng mitei-nander verquickt** closely related **VR** **sich (mitei-nander)** ~ to combine

Ver|qui|ckung F -, -en **a** amalgamation **b** (*fig*) combination

ver|quir|len *ptp* **verquirlt** VT to whisk

ver|ram|meln *ptp* **verrammelt** VT to barricade

ver|ram|schen [fɛɐˈramʃn̩] *ptp* **verramscht** VT (*Comm*) to sell off cheap; (*inf auch*) to flog (*Brit inf*)

Ver|rat M , *no pl* betrayal (*an +dat* of); (*Jur*) trea-son (*an +dat* against); **~ an jdm üben** to betray sb

ver|ra|ten *ptp* **verraten** *irreg* **VT** **a** *Geheimnis, Ab-sicht, jdn* to betray, to give away; (= *bekannt ge-ben, ausplaudern*) to tell; (*fig*: = *erkennen lassen*) to reveal, to show; **nichts ~!** don't say a word!; **er hat es ~** he let it out **b** *Freunde, Vaterland, gute Sache etc* to betray (*an +acc* to); **~ und ver-kauft** (*inf*) well and truly sunk (*inf*) **VR** to give oneself away, to betray oneself

Ver|rä|ter [fɛɐˈrɛːtɐ] M -s, -, **Ver|rä|te|rin** [-ərɪn] F -, -nen traitor (+*gen* to)

ver|rä|te|risch [fɛɐˈrɛːtərɪʃ] ADJ treacherous, perfidious (*liter*); (*Jur*) treasonable; (= *verdäch-tig*) *Hinweis, Blick, Lächeln etc* telltale *attr* ADV (= *etwas erkennen lassend*) revealingly, in a telltale way; **ihre Augen zwinkerten ~** her eyes twinkled conspiratorially

ver|rau|chen *ptp* **verraucht** **VI** *aux sein* (*fig: Zorn, Enttäuschung*) to subside **VT** *Tabak, Zigaren etc* to smoke; *Geld* to spend on smoking

ver|räu|chern *ptp* **verräuchert** VT to fill with smoke

ver|raucht [fɛɐˈrauxt] ADJ smoky, filled with smoke

ver|räu|men *ptp* **verräumt** VT (*S Ger, Aus, Sw*) to put away somewhere

ver|rau|schen *ptp* **verrauscht** VI *aux sein* (*fig*) to die or fade away

ver|rech|nen *ptp* **verrechnet** **VT** (= *begleichen*) to settle; *Scheck* to clear; *Lieferung, Leistungen, Guthaben* (= *gutschreiben*) to credit to an ac-count; (= *belasten*) to debit to an account; *Gut-schein* to redeem; **die Spesen von der Firma ~ lassen** to have one's expenses paid by the firm; **etw mit etw ~** (= *zusammen abrechnen*) to settle sth (together) with sth; (= *gegeneinander aufrech-nen*) to balance sth with sth, to offset sth a-gainst sth **VR** to miscalculate; (= *Rechenfehler machen*) to make a mistake/mistakes; (*inf*: = *sich täuschen*) to be mistaken; **sich um einen Euro ~** to be out by one euro

Ver|rech|nung F settlement; (*von Scheck*) clear-ing; (= *Gutschrift*) crediting to an account; (= *Be-lastung*) debiting to an account; **„nur zur ~"** "A/C payee only"

Ver|rech|nungs-: **Ver|rech|nungs|ein|heit** F clearing unit; **Ver|rech|nungs|kon|to** NT off-set account; **Ver|rech|nungs|prei|se** PL (*Comm*) internal prices *pl*; **Ver|rech|nungs|-scheck** M crossed or non-negotiable cheque (*Brit*), voucher check (*US*); **Ver|rech|nungs|-stel|le** F clearing house

ver|re|cken *ptp* **verreckt** VI *aux sein* (*vulg*) to croak (*inf*); (*sl*: = *kaputtgehen*) to give up the ghost (*inf*); **er ist elend(ig)** or **elendiglich ver-reckt** he died like a dog (*inf*); **soll er doch ~!** let him bloody well (*Brit sl*) or damn well (*inf*) die!; **jetzt ist der Alte endlich verreckt** he's fi-nally kicked the bucket (*inf*) or snuffed it (*Brit inf*); **zu tausenden** or **Tausenden ~** to perish in their thousands; **es ist zum Verrecken** (*sl*) it's damn awful (*inf*), it's bloody terrible (*Brit inf*); **etw ums Verrecken tun** (*sl*) **etw ums Verre-cken nicht tun** (*sl*) to damn well (*inf*) or bloody well (*Brit inf*) refuse to do sth

ver|reg|nen *ptp* **verregnet** VI *aux sein* to be spoiled or ruined by rain

ver|reg|net [fɛɐˈreːɡnət] ADJ rainy, wet

ver|rei|ben *ptp* **verrieben** [fɛɐˈriːbn̩] VT *irreg* to rub (*auf +dat* into); *Salbe* to massage (*auf +dat* into)

ver|rei|sen *ptp* **verreist** VI *aux sein* to go away (on a trip or journey); **er ist verreist** he's away; **er ist geschäftlich verreist** he's away on busi-ness; **wohin ~ Sie in diesem Jahr?** where are you going (on holiday *esp Brit*) or vacation (*US*) this year?; **mit dem Auto/der Bahn ~** to go on a car/train journey; (*in Urlaub*) to go on holiday (*esp Brit*) or vacation (*US*) by car/train

ver|rei|ßen *ptp* **verrissen** [fɛɐˈrɪsn̩] VT *irreg* **a** (= *kritisieren*) to tear to pieces **b** (*dial*) = **zerreißen** **c** (*dial*) *Schuss, Lenkrad* to jerk; *Wagen* to make swerve

ver|ren|ken [fɛɐˈrɛŋkn̩] *ptp* **verrenkt** **VT** to dislo-cate, to put out of joint; *Gelenk* to dislocate; *Hals* to crick; **sich** (*dat*) **die Zunge ~** to twist one's tongue; **lieber sich den Bauch** or **Magen ~, als dem Wirt was schenken** (*prov*) waste not, want not (*prov*) → **Hals** [1] **a VR** to contort one-self

Ver|ren|kung F -, -en **a** contortion; **~en ma-chen** to contort oneself **b** (*Med*: = *das Verren-ken*) dislocation

ver|ren|nen *ptp* **verrannt** [fɛɐˈrant] VR *irreg* to get carried away; **sich in etw** (*acc*) **~** to get stuck on sth

Ver|ren|tung [fɛɐˈrɛntʊŋ] F -, -en retirement; **frühe ~** early retirement

---

ver|rich|ten ptp **verrichtet** VT *Arbeit* to perform, to carry out; *Andacht* to perform; *Gebet* to say → **Geschäft** d, **Notdurft**

Ver|rich|tung F performing, carrying out; **alltägliche/häusliche ~en** routine or daily/domestic or household tasks

ver|rie|geln [fɛɐˈriːɡln] ptp **verriegelt** VT to bolt; (*Comput*) *Tastatur* to lock

Ver|rie|ge|lung F -, -en (= *Vorrichtung*) bolt

ver|rin|gern [fɛɐˈrɪŋən] ptp **verringert** VT to reduce VR to decrease; (*Abstand, Vorsprung auch*) to lessen, to diminish; (*Qualität auch, Leistung*) to deteriorate

Ver|rin|ge|rung F -, -en (= *das Verringern*) reduction; (= *Abnahme*) decrease; (*von Qualität, Leistung*) deterioration; (*von Abstand, Vorsprung*) lessening, diminution

ver|rin|nen ptp **verronnen** [fɛɐˈrɔnən] VI irreg aux sein (*Wasser*) to trickle away (*in +dat* into); (*Zeit*) to elapse

Ver|riss ▲ M slating review

ver|ro|hen [fɛɐˈroːən] ptp **verroht** VT to brutalize VI aux sein (*Mensch, Gesellschaft*) to become brutalized; (*Sitten*) to coarsen

Ver|ro|hung F -, -en brutalization

ver|ros|ten ptp **verrostet** VI aux sein to rust; (*fig: = steif werden*) to get rusty; **verrostet** rusty; (*fig: = steif*) stiff, rusty

ver|rot|ten [fɛɐˈrɔtn] ptp **verrottet** VI aux sein to rot; (= *sich organisch zersetzen*) to decompose

ver|rucht [fɛɐˈruːxt] ADJ despicable, loathsome; *Tat auch* heinous; (= *lasterhaft*) disreputable

Ver|rucht|heit F -, no pl (*von Lokal etc*) disreputable air

ver|rü|cken ptp **verrückt** VT to move, to disarrange

ver|rückt [fɛɐˈrʏkt] ADJ **a** (= *geisteskrank*) mad, insane **b** (*inf*) crazy, mad; **~ auf** (+acc) or **nach** crazy or mad about (*inf*); **wie ~** like mad or crazy (*inf*); **die Leute kamen wie ~** loads of people came (*inf*); **so etwas Verrücktes!** what a crazy idea!; **jdn ~ machen** to drive sb crazy or mad or wild (*inf*); **~ werden** to go crazy; **bei dem Lärm kann man ja ~ werden** this noise is enough to drive you round the bend (*Brit*) or crazy (*inf*); **ich werd ~!** (*inf*) (well,) I'll be blowed (*Brit*) or damned! (*inf*); **du bist wohl ~!** you must be crazy or mad!; **~ spielen** to play up

Ver|rück|te(r) [fɛɐˈrʏktə] MF decl as adj (*inf*) lunatic

Ver|rückt|heit F -, -en (*inf*) madness, craziness; (*Handlung*) mad or crazy thing

Ver|rückt|wer|den NT **zum ~** enough to drive one mad or crazy or round the bend (*Brit*) or up the wall (*all inf*)

Ver|ruf M -, no pl **in ~ kommen** or **geraten** to fall into disrepute; **jdn/etw in ~ bringen** to bring sb/sth into disrepute

ver|ru|fen [fɛɐˈruːfn] ADJ disreputable

ver|rüh|ren ptp **verrührt** VT to mix, to stir

ver|ru|ßen ptp **verrußt** VI aux sein to get or become sooty

ver|rut|schen ptp **verrutscht** VI aux sein to slip

Vers [fɛrs] M -es, -e [-zə] verse (*auch Bibl*); (= *Zeile*) line; **etw in ~e bringen** or **setzen** to put sth into verse; **~e machen** or **schmieden** (*inf*) to make up poems; **ich kann mir keinen ~ darauf machen** there's no rhyme or reason to it

ver|sach|li|chen [fɛɐˈzaxlɪçn] ptp **versachlicht** VT to objectify

Ver|sach|li|chung F -, no pl objectification

ver|sa|cken ptp **versackt** VI aux sein **a** (*lit*) to sink, to become submerged **b** (*fig inf*) (*über lange zechen*) to get involved in a booze-up (*inf*); (= *nicht wegkommen*) to stay on; (= *herunterkommen*) to go downhill

ver|sa|gen ptp **versagt** VT **jdm/sich etw ~** to deny sb/oneself sth; (= *verweigern*) to refuse sb/oneself sth; **ich kann es mir nicht ~, eine Bemerkung zu machen** I can't refrain from mak-

ing a comment; **sich jdm ~** (*geh*) to refuse to give oneself to sb; **etw bleibt** or **ist jdm versagt** sth is denied sb, sb is denied sth → **Dienst** c VI to fail; (*Mensch: im Leben auch*) to be a failure; (*Maschine*) to break down; (*Gewehr*) to fail to function; **die Beine/Nerven** etc **versagten ihm** his legs/nerves etc gave way; **da versagt diese Methode** this method doesn't work there

Ver|sa|gen [fɛɐˈzaːgn] NT -s, no pl failure; (*von Maschine*) breakdown; **menschliches ~** human error

Ver|sa|gens|angst F usu pl fear of failure

Ver|sa|ger [fɛɐˈzaːgɐ] M -s, -, **Ver|sa|ge|rin** [-ərɪn] F -, -nen failure, flop (*inf*)

Ver|sa|gung [fɛɐˈzaːgʊŋ] F -, -en denial; (= *Entbehrung*) privation

Ver|sail|ler Ver|trag [vɛrˈzaiɐ-] M Treaty of Versailles

Ver|sal [vɛrˈzaːl] M -s, **Versalien** [-liən] usu pl (*Typ*) capital letter, cap (*Typ inf*)

ver|sal|zen[1] ptp **versalzen** VT irreg to put too much salt in/on, to oversalt; (*inf: = verderben*) to spoil; **~ sein** to be too salty; **~es Essen** oversalty food → **Suppe**

ver|sam|meln ptp **versammelt** VT to assemble (*auch Mil*), to gather together; *Truppen auch* to rally, to muster; **Leute um sich ~** to gather people about (*Brit*) or around one; **vor versammelter Mannschaft** (*inf*) in front of or before the assembled company VR to assemble; (*Parlament*) to sit; (*Ausschuss, Verein, Mitglieder*) to meet; (*Tagung*) to convene

ver|sam|melt [fɛɐˈzamlt] ADJ (*Reitsport*) collected

Ver|samm|lung F **a** (= *Veranstaltung*) meeting; (= *versammelte Menschen*) assembly; **verfassunggebende ~** legislative assembly **b** (= *das Versammeln*) assembly, gathering (together); (*von Truppen*) rallying, mustering; (*von Ausschuss, Verein, Mitgliedern*) meeting **c** (*Reitsport*) collection

Ver|samm|lungs-: Ver|samm|lungs|frei|heit F freedom of assembly; **Ver|samm|lungs|lo|kal** NT (*in Hotel etc*) conference room; **Ver|samm|lungs|raum** M (*form: allgemein*) assembly room; **Ver|samm|lungs|recht** NT right of assembly; **Ver|samm|lungs|ver|bot** NT prohibition of assembly

Ver|sand [fɛɐˈzant] M -(e)s [-dəs] no pl **a** (= *das Versenden*) dispatch (*esp Brit*), shipment; (= *das Vertreiben*) distribution; **der ~ per Land/Schiene** shipment by land/rail **b** (*Abteilung*) dispatch (*esp Brit*) or shipping department **c** (*inf: = Versandkaufhaus*) mail-order firm

Ver|sand-: Ver|sand|ab|tei|lung F dispatch (*esp Brit*) or shipping department; **Ver|sand|an|zei|ge** F dispatch (*esp Brit*) or shipping advice; **Ver|sand|ar|ti|kel** M article for dispatch (*esp Brit*) or shipping; **Ver|sand|bahn|hof** M dispatch (*esp Brit*) or shipping station; **ver|sand|be|reit** ADJ ready for dispatch (*esp Brit*) or shipment; **Ver|sand|buch|han|del** M mail-order book business; **Ver|sand|do|ku|ment** NT usu pl shipping document

ver|san|den [fɛɐˈzandn] ptp **versandet** VI aux sein to silt (up); (*fig*) to peter out, to fizzle out (*inf*)

Ver|sand-: ver|sand|fer|tig ADJ = **versandbereit**; **Ver|sand|ge|schäft** NT **a** (*Firma*) mail-order firm **b** (*Handel*) mail-order business; **Ver|sand|gut** NT goods pl for dispatch (*esp Brit*) or shipment; **Ver|sand|han|del** M mail-order business; **Ver|sand|haus** NT mail-order firm or house; **Ver|sand|haus|ka|ta|log** M mail-order catalogue (*Brit*) or catalog (*US*); **Ver|sand|kos|ten** PL transport(ation) costs pl; **Ver|sand|pa|pie|re** PL transport(ation) documents pl; **Ver|sand|ta|sche** F padded envelope, Jiffy bag® (*Brit*)

Ver|san|dung F -, -en silting (up); (*fig*) petering out, fizzling out (*inf*)

Ver|sand-: Ver|sand|un|ter|neh|men NT mail-order business; **Ver|sand|weg** M **auf dem ~** by mail order

Ver|satz M -, no pl **a** (= *das Versetzen*) pawning **b** (*Min*) packing, stowing

Ver|satz-: Ver|satz|amt NT (*dial*) pawnshop; **Ver|satz|stück** NT **a** (*Theat*) set piece **b** (*fig*) setting, background **c** (*Aus*: = *Pfandstück*) pledge

ver|sau|beu|teln [fɛɐˈzaubɔytln] ptp **versaubeutelt** VT (*inf*) **a** (= *verschlampen*) to go and lose (*inf*) **b** (= *verderben*) to mess up (*inf*)

ver|sau|en ptp **versaut** VT (*inf*) **a** (= *verschmutzen*) to make a mess of; *Umwelt* to mess up **b** (= *verderben, ruinieren*) to ruin; *Kinder, Moral, Mensch* to screw up (*inf*); (= *schlecht machen*) *Arbeit* to make a mess of; **der Chirurg hat ihn versaut** the surgeon made a mess of him

ver|sau|ern [fɛɐˈzauən] ptp **versauert** (*inf*) VI aux sein to stagnate; **eine versauerte alte Jungfer** an embittered old spinster VT **jdm etw ~** to mess sth up for sb (*inf*), to ruin sth for sb

Ver|sau|e|rung [fɛɐˈzauərʊŋ] F -, -en, **Ver|säu|e|rung** [fɛɐˈzɔyərʊŋ] F -, -en (*von Gewässer, Boden*) acidification

ver|sau|fen ptp **versoffen** [fɛɐˈzɔfn] irreg (*inf*) VT *Geld* to spend on booze (*inf*); **seinen Verstand ~** to drink oneself silly → auch **versoffen, Fell** VI aux sein (*dial*) **a** (= *ertrinken*) to drown **b** (*Motor*) to flood

ver|säu|men ptp **versäumt** VT to miss; *Zeit* to lose; *Pflicht* to neglect; (*Sw*: = *aufhalten*) *jdn* to delay, to hold up; **(es) ~, etw zu tun** to fail to do sth; **nichts ~, um jdn glücklich zu machen** to do everything to make sb happy; **das Versäumte** what one has missed; **die versäumte Zeit aufholen** to make up for lost time

Ver|säum|nis [fɛɐˈzɔymnɪs] NT -ses, -se (= *Fehler, Nachlässigkeit*) failing; (= *Unterlassung*) omission; (= *versäumte Zeit, Sch*) absence (+gen from); (*Jur*) default (+gen in); **bei ~ rechtzeitiger Bezahlung** in the event that payment is not made punctually

Ver|säum|nis|ur|teil NT (*Jur*) judgement by default

ver|saut ADJ (*sl*: = *schweinisch*) filthy

Vers|bau M -, no pl versification, metrical structure

ver|scha|chern ptp **verschachert** VT to sell off

ver|schach|telt [fɛɐˈʃaxtlt] ADJ *Satz* encapsulated, complex; (*Comput*) *Menü, Befehle* nested; **ineinander ~** interlocking

ver|schaf|fen ptp **verschafft** VT **a** **jdm etw ~** (*Geld, Kapital, Alibi*) to provide or supply sb with sth or sth for sb; *Arbeit, Stelle auch* to find sth for sb; *Erleichterung, Genugtuung, Vergnügen* to give sb sth; *Ansehen, Respekt* to earn sb sth → **Ehre b** **sich** (*dat*) **etw ~** to obtain sth; *Kenntnisse* to acquire sth; *Ansehen, Vorteil* to gain sth; *Ruhe, Respekt* to get sth; **sich mit Gewalt Zutritt ~** to force an entry, to force one's way in; **ich muss mir darüber Gewissheit ~** I must be certain about it; **ich muss mir darüber Klarheit ~** I must clarify the matter

ver|scha|len [fɛɐˈʃaːlən] ptp **verschalt** VT *Wand* to panel; *Heizung etc* to box in, to encase; (*für Beton*) to build a framework or mould (*Brit*) or mold (*US*) for VI (*für Beton*) to build a framework or mould (*Brit*) or mold (*US*)

Ver|scha|lung F **a** no pl (= *das Verschalen*) (*mit Holz*) panelling (*Brit*), paneling (*US*); (*für Heizung etc*) casing; (*für Beton*) building a framework or mould (*Brit*) or mold (*US*) **b** (= *Bretter etc*) framework, mould (*Brit*), mold (*US*)

ver|schämt [fɛɐˈʃɛːmt] ADJ coy ADV coyly

Ver|schämt|heit F -, no pl coyness

ver|schan|deln [fɛɐˈʃandln] ptp **verschandelt** VT to ruin

Ver|schan|de|lung [fɛɐˈʃandəlʊŋ] F -, -en, **Ver|schand|lung** [fɛɐˈʃandlʊŋ] F -, -en ruining

ver|schan|zen *ptp* **verschanzt** VT (*Mil*) to fortify VR (*Mil, fig*) to entrench oneself (*hinter +dat* behind); (= *sich verbarrikadieren*) to barricade oneself in (*in etw* (*dat*) sth); (= *Deckung suchen*) to take cover (*hinter +dat* behind)

Ver|schan|zung [fɛɐˈʃantsʊŋ] F -, -en (*Mil*) **a** fortification; (*von Truppen*) entrenchment; (= *Verbarrikadierung*) barricading **b** (= *Befestigung*) fortification

ver|schär|fen *ptp* **verschärft** VT (= *erhöhen*) Tempo, Aufmerksamkeit to increase; Gegensätze to intensify; (= *verschlimmern*) Lage to aggravate; Spannungen to heighten; (= *strenger machen*) Kontrollen, Strafe, Gesetze, Maßnahmen, Prüfungen, Grenzwerte to tighten VR (*Tempo, Aufmerksamkeit*) to increase; (*Wettbewerb, Gegensätze*) to intensify; (*Lage*) to become aggravated; (*Spannungen*) to heighten, to mount; (*Kontrollen, Gesetze, Maßnahmen, Prüfungen*) to become tighter

ver|schärft [fɛɐˈʃɛrft] ADJ **a** (= *erhöht*) Tempo, Aufmerksamkeit, Wettbewerb increased; Gegensätze intensified; (= *verschlimmert*) Lage aggravated; Spannungen heightened; (= *strenger*) Kontrollen, Strafe, Maßnahmen tightened; Arrest close **b** (*inf*: = *gut*) brilliant (*inf*), wicked (*sl*) ADV (= *intensiver*) more intensively; (= *strenger*) more severely; prüfen more closely; ~ **aufpassen** to keep a closer watch; ~ **kontrollieren** to keep a tighter control; ~ **vorgehen** to take more stringent measures

Ver|schär|fung F increase; (*von Gegensätzen*) intensification; (= *Verschlimmerung*) aggravation; (*von Spannung*) heightening, mounting; (*von Regeln, Gesetzen*) tightening

ver|schar|ren *ptp* **verscharrt** VT to bury

ver|schät|zen *ptp* **verschätzt** VR to misjudge, to miscalculate (*in etw* (*dat*) sth); **sich um zwei Monate ~** to be out by two months

ver|schau|en *ptp* **verschaut** VR (*Aus*) **a** (= *nicht richtig sehen*) to make a mistake **b** (= *sich verlieben*) **sich in jdn ~** to fall for sb

ver|schau|keln *ptp* **verschaukelt** VT (*inf*) to take for a ride (*inf*)

ver|schei|den *ptp* **verschieden** [fɛɐˈʃiːdn] VI irreg aux sein (*geh*) to pass away, to expire

ver|schei|ßen *ptp* **verschissen** [fɛɐˈʃɪsn] VT irreg (*vulg*) to cover with shit (*vulg*) → *auch* **verschissen**

ver|schei|ßern [fɛɐˈʃaisɐn] *ptp* **verscheißert** VT (*inf*) **jdn ~** to take the piss out of sb (*Brit sl*), to make fun of sb

ver|schen|ken *ptp* **verschenkt** VT (*lit, fig*) to give away; **sein Herz an jdn ~** (*liter*) to give sb one's heart VR **sich an jdn ~** to throw oneself away on sb

ver|scher|beln [fɛɐˈʃɛrbln] *ptp* **verscherbelt** VT (*inf*) to flog (*Brit inf*), to sell

ver|scher|zen *ptp* **verscherzt** VT **sich** (*dat*) **etw ~** to lose or forfeit sth; **sich** (*dat*) **seine Chancen ~** to throw away one's chances; **sich** (*dat*) **jds Gunst** or **Wohlwollen ~** to lose or forfeit sb's favour (*Brit*) or favor (*US*); **es sich** (*dat*) **mit jdm ~** to spoil things (for oneself) with sb

ver|scheu|chen *ptp* **verscheucht** VT to scare or frighten off or away; Fliegen to chase away; (*fig*) Sorgen, Gedanken etc to drive away

ver|scheu|ern *ptp* **verscheuert** VT (*inf*) to sell off, to flog off (*Brit inf*)

ver|schi|cken *ptp* **verschickt** VT **a** (= *versenden*) to send out or off **b** (*zur Kur etc*) to send away **c** (= *deportieren*) to deport

ver|schieb|bar ADJ Möbel etc movable; Regler, Spange, Teil sliding; **leicht ~e Gegenstände** objects which are easy to move; **der Termin ist ~** this appointment can be changed

Ver|schie|be- (*Rail*): **Ver|schie|be|bahn|hof** M shunting yard; **Ver|schie|be|gleis** NT shunting track; **Ver|schie|be|lo|ko|mo|ti|ve** F shunter

ver|schie|ben *ptp* **verschoben** [fɛɐˈʃoːbn] *irreg* VT **a** (= *verrücken*) to move (*auch Comput*), to shift; Truppen to displace; (*Rail*) Eisenbahnwagen to shunt; Perspektive to alter, to shift **b** (= *aufschieben*) to change; (*auf später*) to postpone, to put off, to defer (*um* for) **c** (*inf*) Waren, Devisen to traffic in VR **a** (= *verrutschen*) to move out of place; (*fig: Perspektive, Schwerpunkt*) to alter, to shift **b** (*zeitlich*) to be postponed, to be put off or deferred **c** (*Med*) (*bei Knochenbruch*) to become displaced **d** (*Ling: Laute*) to shift

Ver|schie|bung F **a** (= *das Verschieben*) moving, shifting; (*von Truppen*) displacement; (*fig: von Perspektiven*) alteration **b** (*von Termin*) postponement, deferment **c** (*inf: von Waren, Devisen*) trafficking **d** (*Geol*) displacement, heave **e** (*Ling: von Lauten*) shift **f** (*Med*) (*bei Knochenbruch*) displacement; (*von Kniescheibe*) slip **g** (*Psych*) displacement

ver|schie|den [fɛɐˈʃiːdn] ADJ **a** (= *unterschiedlich*) different; (= *unähnlich*) dissimilar; Meinungen etc differing, different; **die ~sten Sorten** many different kinds, all sorts; **das ist ganz ~** (= *wird verschieden gehandhabt*) that varies, that just depends **b** *attr* (= *mehrere, einige*) various, several; **~e Mal** several times **c** (*substantivisch*) **Verschiedene** various or several people; **Verschiedenes** different things; (*in Zeitungen, Listen*) miscellaneous ADV differently; **die Häuser sind ~ lang/breit/hoch** the houses vary or are different in length/breadth/height

ver|schie|den|ar|tig ADJ different; (= *mannigfaltig*) various, diverse; **die ~sten Dinge** all sorts or manner of things

Ver|schie|den|ar|tig|keit F , no pl different nature; (= *Mannigfaltigkeit*) variety, diversity

ver|schie|de|ne|mal △ [fɛɐˈʃiːdənəˌl] ADV → **verschieden** ADJ b

ver|schie|de|ner|lei [fɛɐˈʃiːdənɐˌlai] ADJ inv **a** *attr* many different, various **b** (*substantivisch*) many different things, various things

ver|schie|den|far|big, (*Aus*) **ver|schie|den|fär|big** ADJ different-coloured (*Brit*), different-colored (*US*); **die Kostüme waren ~** the costumes were many different colours (*Brit*) or colors (*US*)

Ver|schie|den|heit F -, -en difference (+gen of, in); (= *Unähnlichkeit*) dissimilarity; (= *Vielfalt*) variety

ver|schie|dent|lich [fɛɐˈʃiːdntlɪç] ADV (= *mehrmals*) on several occasions, several times; (= *vereinzelt*) occasionally

ver|schie|ßen *ptp* **verschossen** [fɛɐˈʃɔsn] *irreg* VT **a** Munition to use up; Pfeile to shoot off; (*inf*) Fotos, Film to take, to use up → **Pulver b** (*Sport*) to miss VR (*inf*) **sich in jdn ~** to fall for sb (*inf*); **in jdn verschossen sein** to be crazy about sb (*inf*) VI aux sein (*Stoff, Farbe*) to fade

ver|schif|fen *ptp* **verschifft** VT to ship; Sträfling to transport

Ver|schif|fung [fɛɐˈʃɪfʊŋ] F -, -en shipment; (*von Sträflingen*) transportation

ver|schil|fen [fɛɐˈʃɪlfn] *ptp* **verschilft** VI aux sein to become overgrown with reeds

ver|schim|meln *ptp* **verschimmelt** VI aux sein (*Nahrungsmittel*) to go mouldy (*Brit*) or moldy (*US*); (*Leder, Papier etc*) to become mildewed, to go mildewy; (*Wand*) to become mildewed; **verschimmelt** (*lit*) mouldy (*Brit*), moldy (*US*); mildewed, mildewy; (*fig*) Ansichten etc fusty

ver|schis|sen [fɛɐˈʃɪsn] ADJ (*vulg*) Unterhose shitty (*sl*); **du hast bei mir ~** (*sl*) I'm through with you (*inf*) → *auch* **verscheißen**

ver|schlackt [fɛɐˈʃlakn] *ptp* **verschlackt** VI aux sein (*Ofen*) to become clogged (up) with slag; (*Med: Gewebe*) to become clogged

ver|schlafen¹ *ptp* **verschlafen** *irreg* VIR to oversleep VT Termin to miss by oversleeping; (= *schlafend verbringen*) Tag, Morgen to sleep through; Leben to sleep away; (= *verpassen*) Einsatz to miss

ver|schlafen² ADJ sleepy; (= *trottelig*) Mensch dozy (*inf*); ~ **sein** (= *Vielschläfer sein*) to like one's sleep

Ver|schla|fen|heit F -, no pl sleepiness; (= *Trotteligkeit*) doziness (*inf*)

Ver|schlag M (= *abgetrennter Raum*) partitioned area; (= *Schuppen*) shed; (*grob gezimmert*) shack; (*esp für Kaninchen*) hutch; (*ans Haus angebaut*) lean-to; (*unter der Treppe*) glory hole; (= *elende Behausung*) hovel; (= *Verpackung*) crate

ver|schla|gen¹ *ptp* **verschlagen** VT irreg **a** **etw mit Brettern ~** to board sth up **b** (= *nehmen*) Atem to take away; **das hat mir die Sprache ~** it left me speechless **c** (= *geraten lassen*) to bring; **auf eine einsame Insel ~ werden** to be cast up on a lonely island; **an einen Ort ~ werden** to end up somewhere **e** (*Sport*) Ball to mishit (= *verblättern*) Seite, Stelle to lose **f** (*dial*: = *verprügeln*) to wallop (*inf*), to thrash

ver|schla|gen² ADJ **a** Mensch, Blick, Tier etc sly, artful **b** (*dial*: = *lauwarm*) tepid, lukewarm

Ver|schla|gen|heit F -, no pl slyness, artfulness

ver|schlam|men [fɛɐˈʃlamən] *ptp* **verschlammt** VI aux sein to silt up

ver|schlam|pen *ptp* **verschlampt** (*inf*) VT **a** (= *verlieren*) to go and lose (*inf*) **b** (= *verkommen lassen*) to spoil VI aux sein (*Mensch*) to go to seed (*inf*)

ver|schlan|ken *ptp* **verschlankt** VT (*inf*) Produktion to cut back, to trim; Personal to cut, to trim

Ver|schlan|kung [fɛɐˈʃlaŋkʊŋ] F -, -en (*inf, von Produktion*) cutting-back (*gen* on), trimming; (*von Personal*) cutting, trimming

ver|schlech|tern [fɛɐˈʃlɛçtɐn] *ptp* **verschlechtert** VT to make worse, to worsen; Zustand, Lage auch to aggravate; Qualität to impair; Aussicht to diminish, to decrease VR to get worse, to worsen, to deteriorate; (*Leistungen auch*) to decline; **sich finanziell ~** to be worse off financially; **sich beruflich ~** to take a worse job

Ver|schlech|te|rung F -, -en worsening, deterioration; (*von Leistung*) decline; **eine finanzielle ~** a financial setback; **eine berufliche ~** a retrograde step professionally

ver|schlei|ern [fɛɐˈʃlaiɐn] *ptp* **verschleiert** VT to veil; (*fig auch*) to disguise, to cover up; Blick to blur; **Nebel verschleiert die Aussicht/die Berge** the view is/the mountains are hidden by or under a veil of mist VR (*Frau*) to veil oneself; (*Himmel*) to become hazy; (*Blick*) to become blurred; (= *träumerisch werden*) to become hazy; (*Stimme*) to become husky

ver|schlei|ert [fɛɐˈʃlaiɐt] ADJ Frau veiled; Augen, Aussicht misty; Berge misty, veiled in mist; Stimme husky; Blick blurred; (*fig*) Behauptungen veiled; Werbung indirect; (= *träumerisch*) hazy; (*Phot*) foggy; **etw nur ~ sehen** to see sth only hazily

Ver|schlei|e|rung F -, -en veiling; (*fig auch*) disguising, covering up; (*von Blick*) blurring

Ver|schlei|e|rungs-: **Ver|schlei|e|rungs|tak|tik** F cover-up (+gen by); **Ver|schlei|e|rungs|ver|such** M attempt at covering up

ver|schlei|fen *ptp* **verschliffen** [fɛɐˈʃlɪfn] VT irreg to slur

ver|schlei|men *ptp* **verschleimt** VT to block or congest with phlegm; **verschleimt sein** (*Patient*) to be congested with phlegm VI aux sein to become blocked or congested with phlegm

Ver|schlei|mung [fɛɐˈʃlaimʊŋ] F -, -en mucous congestion

Ver|schleiß [fɛɐˈʃlais] M -es, -e **a** (*lit, fig*) wear and tear; (= *Verbrauch*) consumption; (= *Verluste*) loss; **ein ~ deiner Kräfte** a drain on your strength; **eingeplanter ~** built-in obsolescence; **sein ~ an Frauen** (*hum*) the rate he goes through women **b** (*Aus*: = *Kleinverkauf*) retail trade

ver|schlei|ßen [fɛɐˈʃlaisn] *pret* **verschliss** [fɛɐ-ˈʃlɪs], *ptp* **verschlissen** [fɛɐˈʃlɪsn] VT **a** (= *kaputt-*

machen) to wear out; (= *verbrauchen*) to use up; **der Verein hat dieses Jahr schon drei Trainer verschlissen** the club has already gone through three managers this year **b** (*Aus*) to retail **VI** *aux sein* to wear out → *auch* **verschlissen VR** to wear out; (*Menschen*) to wear oneself out

Ver|schlei|ßer [fɛɐˈʃlaisɐ] M **-s, -**, **Ver|schlei|ße|rin** [-ərɪn] F **-, -nen** (*Aus*) retailer

Ver|schleiß-: **Ver|schleiß|er|schei|nung** F sign of wear; **Ver|schleiß|krieg** M war of attrition; **Ver|schleiß|prü|fung** F wear test; **Ver|schleiß|teil** NT part subject to wear and tear

ver|schlep|pen *ptp* **verschleppt** VT **a** (= *entführen*) *jdn* to abduct; *Gefangene, Kriegsopfer* to displace; *Kunstschätze etc* to carry off; (*inf*) *etw* to go off with **b** (= *verbreiten*) *Seuche* to spread, to carry **c** (= *hinauszögern*) *Prozess, Verhandlung, Ermittlungen* to draw out, to protract; (*Pol*) *Gesetzesänderung etc* to delay; *Krankheit* to protract

Ver|schlepp|te(r) [fɛɐˈʃlɛptə] MF *decl as adj* **die ~n** the displaced *pl*

Ver|schlep|pung [fɛɐˈʃlɛpʊŋ] F **-, -en a** (*von Menschen*) abduction; (*von Kunstschätzen*) carrying off **b** (= *Verbreitung*) spreading, carrying **c** (= *Verzögerung*) protraction; (*von Gesetzesänderung*) delay; (*von Krankheit*) protraction

Ver|schlep|pungs|tak|tik F delaying tactics *pl*

ver|schleu|dern *ptp* **verschleudert** VT (*Comm*) to dump; (= *vergeuden*) *Vermögen, Geld, Energie, Ressourcen* to squander

ver|schließ|bar ADJ *Dosen, Gläser etc* closeable, sealable; *Tür, Schublade, Zimmer etc* lockable

ver|schlie|ßen *ptp* **verschlossen** [fɛɐˈʃlɔsn̩] *irreg* **VT a** (= *abschließen*) to lock (up); (*fig*) to close, to shut; (= *versperren*) to bar; (*mit Riegel*) to bolt; **jdm etw ~** (*fig*) to deny sb sth → *auch* **verschlossen**
b (= *wegschließen*) to lock up or away **c** (= *zumachen*) to close; (*dauerhaft*) *Einmachglas, Karton, Brief* to seal; (*mit Pfropfen*) *Flasche* to cork; **die Augen/Ohren/sein Herz (vor etw** *dat*) **~** to shut one's eyes/ears/heart (to sth); **seine Gedanken/seinen Kummer in sich** (*dat*) **~** to keep one's thoughts/one's worries to oneself **VR** (*Reize, Sprache, Möglichkeit*) to be closed (+*dat* etw); (*Mensch*: = *reserviert sein*) to shut oneself off (+*dat* from); **sich vor jdm ~** to shut oneself off from sb; **sich einer Sache** (*dat*) or **gegen etw ~** to close one's mind to sth; **ich kann mich der Tatsache nicht ~, dass ...** I can't close my eyes to the fact that ...

ver|schlimm|bes|sern [fɛɐˈʃlɪmbɛsɐn] *ptp* **verschlimmbessert** VT *insep* (*hum*) to make worse, to disimprove

Ver|schlimm|bes|se|rung F (*hum*) worsening, disimprovement

ver|schlim|mern [fɛɐˈʃlɪmɐn] *ptp* **verschlimmert** **VT** to make worse, to aggravate; *Schmerzen auch* to increase **VR** to get worse, to worsen

Ver|schlim|me|rung F **-, -en** worsening; (*von Schmerzen auch*) increase

ver|schlin|gen *ptp* **verschlungen** [fɛɐˈʃlʊŋən] *irreg* **VT a** (= *verflechten*) to entwine, to intertwine; **er stand mit verschlungenen Armen da** he stood there with his arms folded; **ein verschlungener Pfad** a winding path **b** (= *fressen, gierig essen*) to devour; (*fig*) (*Welle, Dunkelheit*) to engulf; (= *verbrauchen*) *Geld, Strom etc* to eat up, to consume; (*inf*) *Buch, jds Worte* to devour; **jdn mit Blicken** or **den Augen ~** to devour sb with one's eyes **VR** to become entwined or intertwined; (*zu einem Knoten etc*) to become entangled; (*Därme*) to become twisted

Ver|schlin|gung [fɛɐˈʃlɪŋʊŋ] F **-, -en a** (*von Fäden etc*) tangle; (*von Muster, Arabeske*) interlacing **b** (*von Darm*) twisting

ver|schliss ▲ *pret von* **verschleißen**

ver|schlis|sen [fɛɐˈʃlɪsn̩] *ptp von* **verschleißen** ADJ worn (out); *Kleidung, Teppich, Material auch*

threadbare; (*fig*) *Arbeiter, Politiker etc* burned-out (*inf*)

ver|schlos|sen [fɛɐˈʃlɔsn̩] ADJ closed; (*mit Schlüssel*) *Tür, Fach etc* locked; (*mit Riegel*) bolted; *Dose, Briefumschlag* sealed; (*fig*: = *unzugänglich*) reserved; **gut ~ aufbewahren** keep tightly closed; **etw bleibt jdm ~** sth is (a) closed (book) to sb; **hinter ~en Türen** behind closed doors; **wir standen vor ~er Tür** we were left standing on the doorstep → *auch* **verschließen**

Ver|schlos|sen|heit F **-,** *no pl* (*von Mensch*) reserve, reticence

ver|schlu|cken *ptp* **verschluckt** **VT** to swallow; (*fig auch*) *Wörter, Silben, Buchstaben* to slur; *Geld* to consume; *Schall* to deaden → **Erdboden VR** to swallow the wrong way; (*fig*) to splutter

ver|schlu|dern *ptp* **verschludert** (*inf*) **VT** to go and lose (*inf*) **VI** *aux sein* to let oneself go

Ver|schluss ▲ M **a** (= *Schloss*) lock; (*luft-, wasserdicht, für Zoll*) seal; (= *Deckel, Klappe*) top, lid; (= *Pfropfen, Stöpsel*) stopper; (*an Kleidung*) fastener; (*an Schmuck*) catch; (*an Tasche, Buch, Schuh*) clasp; **etw unter ~ halten** to keep sth under lock and key **b** (*Phot*) shutter; (*an Waffe*) breechblock **c** (*Med, Phon*) occlusion

ver|schlüs|seln [fɛɐˈʃlʏsln̩] *ptp* **verschlüsselt** **VT** to (put into) code, to encode

Ver|schlüs|se|lung [fɛɐˈʃlʏsəlʊŋ] F **-, -en** coding

Ver|schluss|kap|pe ▲ F (screw) cap

Ver|schluss|laut ▲ M (*Phon*) plosive

Ver|schlüss|lung ▲ [fɛɐˈʃlʏslʊŋ] F **-, -en** coding

Ver|schluss|sa|che ▲ F (= *piece of classified*) information; **~n** *pl* classified information *sing*

ver|schmach|ten *ptp* **verschmachtet** VI *aux sein* to languish (*vor* +*dat* for); **vor Durst/Hitze ~** (*inf*) to be dying of thirst/heat (*inf*)

ver|schmä|hen *ptp* **verschmäht** VT to spurn, to scorn; *Liebhaber* to spurn, to reject; **verschmähte Liebe** unrequited love; **einen Whisky verschmähe ich nie** I never say no to a whisky

ver|schmä|lern *ptp* **verschmälert** **VT** to make narrower **VR** to become narrower, to narrow

ver|schmau|sen *ptp* **verschmaust** VT (*inf*) to feast on

ver|schmel|zen *ptp* **verschmolzen** [fɛɐˈʃmɔltsn̩] *irreg* **VI** *aux sein* to melt together; (*Metalle*) to fuse; (*Farben*) to blend; (*Betriebe etc*) to merge; (*fig*) to blend (*zu* into); **zu einer Einheit ~** to blend into one **VT a** (= *verbinden*) *Metalle* to fuse; *Farben* to blend; *Betriebe, Firmen* to merge **b** *Bruchflächen* to smooth, to round off **c** (*fig*) to unify (*zu* into)

Ver|schmel|zung [fɛɐˈʃmɛltsʊŋ] F **-, -en a** (= *Verbindung*) fusion; (*von Reizen, Eindrücken, Farben*) blending **b** (*von Bruchflächen*) smoothing, rounding off **c** (*fig*: *von Völkern, Begriffen etc*) fusion **d** (*Comm*) merger

ver|schmer|zen *ptp* **verschmerzt** VT to get over

ver|schmie|ren *ptp* **verschmiert VT a** (= *verstreichen*) *Salbe, Schmiere, Creme, Fett* to spread (*in* +*dat* over) **b** (= *verputzen*) *Löcher* to fill in **c** (= *verwischen*) *Fenster, Gesicht* to smear; *Geschriebenes, Lippenstift, Schminke* to smudge **VI** to smudge

ver|schmiert [fɛɐˈʃmiːɐt] ADJ *Hände, Gesicht* smeary; *Schminke* smudged

ver|schmitzt [fɛɐˈʃmɪtst] ADJ mischievous ADV mischievously

ver|schmort [fɛɐˈʃmoːɐt] ADJ *Braten* charred

ver|schmust [fɛɐˈʃmuːst] ADJ (*inf*) cuddly; **~ sein** to like cuddling, to be cuddly

ver|schmut|zen *ptp* **verschmutzt VT** to dirty, to soil; *Luft, Wasser, Umwelt* to pollute; *Zündkerze* to foul; *Fahrbahn* to make muddy; *Straße, Bürgersteig* to dirty; (*Hund*) to foul **VI** *aux sein* to get dirty; (*Luft, Wasser, Umwelt*) to become polluted

ver|schmutzt [fɛɐˈʃmʊtst] ADJ dirty, soiled; *Luft etc* polluted; **stark ~** very dirty, badly soiled; „**verschmutzte Fahrbahn**" "mud on road"

Ver|schmut|zung [fɛɐˈʃmʊtsʊŋ] F **-, -en a** *no pl* (= *das Verschmutzen*) dirtying, soiling; (*von Luft, Wasser, Umwelt*) pollution; (*von Fahrbahn*) muddying **b** (= *das Verschmutztsein*) dirtiness *no pl*; (*von Luft etc*) pollution; **starke ~en auf der Straße** a great deal of mud on the road

ver|schnau|fen *ptp* **verschnauft** VIR (*inf*) to have a breather, to have a rest

Ver|schnauf|pau|se F breather

ver|schnei|den *ptp* **verschnitten** [fɛɐˈʃnɪtn̩] VT *irreg* a *Wein, Rum, Essigsorten* to blend **b** (= *stutzen*) *Flügel, Hecke* to clip **c** (= *falsch schneiden*) *Kleid, Stoff* to cut wrongly; *Haar* to cut badly **d** *Tiere* to geld, to castrate

ver|schneit [fɛɐˈʃnait] ADJ snow-covered; **tief ~** thick with snow

Ver|schnitt M **a** (*von Rum, Wein, Essig*) blend **b** (= *Abfall*) waste material, clippings *pl*

ver|schnör|keln [fɛɐˈʃnœrkl̩n] *ptp* **verschnörkelt** VT to adorn with flourishes

ver|schnör|kelt [fɛɐˈʃnœrkl̩t] ADJ ornate

Ver|schnör|ke|lung [fɛɐˈʃnœrkəlʊŋ] F **-, -en a** (= *das Verschnörkeln*) embellishing (with flourishes) **b** (= *Schnörkel*) flourish

ver|schnupft [fɛɐˈʃnʊpft] ADJ **a** (= *erkältet*) *Mensch* with a cold; *Nase* bunged up (*inf*) **b** (*usu pred*: = *beleidigt*) peeved (*inf*)

ver|schnü|ren *ptp* **verschnürt** VT to tie up; *Schuhe* to lace

Ver|schnü|rung [fɛɐˈʃnyːrʊŋ] F **-, -en a** (= *das Verschnüren*) tying (up); (*von Schuhen*) lacing **b** (= *Schnur*) string; (= *Schnürband*) lace

ver|schol|len [fɛɐˈʃɔlən] ADJ *Schiff, Flugzeug, Gemälde, Mensch etc* missing, lost without trace; *Literaturwerk* forgotten; **ein lange ~er Freund** a long-lost friend; **er ist ~** (*im Krieg*) he is missing, presumed dead

Ver|schol|le|ne(r) [fɛɐˈʃɔlənə] MF *decl as adj* missing person; (*Jur*) person presumed (to be) dead

ver|scho|nen *ptp* **verschont** VT to spare (*jdn von etw* sb sth); (*von Steuern auch*) to exempt; **verschone mich mit deinen Reden!** spare me your speeches; **verschone mich damit!** spare me that!; **von etw verschont bleiben** to escape sth

ver|schö|nen *ptp* **verschönt**, **ver|schö|nern** [fɛɐˈʃøːnən] *ptp* **verschönert** VT to improve (the appearance of); *Wohnung, Haus, Zimmer* to brighten (up)

Ver|schö|ne|rung [fɛɐˈʃøːnərʊŋ] F **-, -en**, **Ver|schö|nung** [fɛɐˈʃøːnʊŋ] F **-, -en** improvement; (*von Wohnung, Zimmer*) brightening up

Ver|scho|nung F sparing; (*von Steuern*) exemption

ver|schor|fen [fɛɐˈʃɔrfn̩] *ptp* **verschorft** VI *aux sein* to (form a) scab; **die verschorfte Wunde** the encrusted wound

Ver|schor|fung F **-, -en** encrustation, scabbing

ver|schos|sen [fɛɐˈʃɔsn̩] *ptp* → **verschießen** ADJ **a** *Farbe* faded **b** (*fig inf*) **in jdn ~ sein** to be crazy about sb (*inf*) **c** (*Ftbl*) **~er Elfmeter** missed penalty

ver|schram|men *ptp* **verschrammt VT** to scratch **VI** *aux sein* to become or get scratched

ver|schrän|ken [fɛɐˈʃrɛŋkn̩] *ptp* **verschränkt** VT to cross over; *Arme* to fold; *Beine* to cross; *Hände* to clasp; **verschränkter Reim** embracing rhyme

Ver|schrän|kung F **-, -en a** (= *das Verschränktsein*) fold **b** (*das Verschränken*) crossing over; (*von Armen*) folding; (*von Beinen*) crossing; (*von Händen*) clasping

ver|schrau|ben *ptp* **verschraubt** VT to screw together

ver|schre|cken *ptp* **verschreckt** VT to frighten or scare off or away

ver|schreckt [fɛɐˈʃrɛkt] ADJ frightened, scared

ver|schrei|ben ptp **verschrieben** [fɛɐˈʃriːbn̩] irreg **VT** **a** (= verordnen) to prescribe **b** (old: = übereignen) to make over, to transfer; **seine Seele dem Teufel ~** to sign away one's soul to the devil **c** Papier to use up; (rare) Wort to write incorrectly **VR** **a** (= falsch schreiben) to make a slip (of the pen) **b** sich einer Sache (dat) **~** to devote or dedicate oneself to sth; **sich dem Teufel ~** to sell oneself to the devil

Ver|schrei|bung F **a** (= Verordnung) prescription **b** (old: = Übertragung) making over, transference **c** (= Schreibfehler) mistake, error

ver|schrei|bungs|pflich|tig [-pflɪçtɪç] ADJ only available on prescription, ethical

ver|schrei|en [fɛɐˈʃraɪən] ptp **verschrieen** [-ˈʃriːən] VT irreg **a** (= herbeireden) **verschrei's nicht!** don't speak too soon, don't put the kiss of death on it **b** (= öffentlich schlecht machen) to denounce, to slam (inf), trash (inf)

ver|schrie|en [fɛɐˈʃriːən], **ver|schrien** [fɛɐˈʃriːn] ADJ notorious; **als etw ~** notorious for being sth

ver|schro|ben [fɛɐˈʃroːbn̩] ADJ eccentric, odd

Ver|schro|ben|heit F **-, -en** **a** no pl eccentricity **b** **Verschrobenheiten** pl (= Handlungen) eccentricities pl

ver|schro|ten ptp **verschrotet** VT to grind coarsely

ver|schrot|ten [fɛɐˈʃrɔtn̩] ptp **verschrottet** VT to scrap

Ver|schrot|tung F **-, -en** scrapping; **etw zur ~ geben** to send sth to be scrapped

ver|schrum|peln ptp **verschrumpelt** VI aux sein to shrivel

ver|schüch|tern [fɛɐˈʃʏçtɐn] ptp **verschüchtert** VT to intimidate

ver|schul|den ptp **verschuldet** **VT** (= schuldhaft verursachen) to be to blame for, to be responsible for; Unfall, Unglück to cause **VI** aux sein (= in Schulden geraten) to get into debt; **immer mehr ~** to get deeper and deeper into debt; **verschuldet sein** to be in debt **VR** to get into debt

Ver|schul|den [fɛɐˈʃʊldn̩] NT **-s**, no pl fault; **durch eigenes ~** through one's own fault; **ohne sein/mein ~** through no fault of his (own)/of my own or of mine

Ver|schul|dung F **-, -en** **a** (= Schulden) indebtedness **b** (= schuldhafte Verursachung) blame (+gen for); **bei eigener ~ eines Schadens** if one is (oneself) to blame for damage caused

ver|schus|seln ptp **verschusselt** VT (inf) (= vermasseln) to mess or muck (Brit) up (inf); (= vergessen) to forget; (= verlegen) to mislay, to lose

ver|schus|selt [fɛɐˈʃʊslt] ADJ = schusselig

ver|schütt [fɛɐˈʃʏt] ADJ **~ gehen** (inf) (= verschwinden) to disappear; (= abhanden kommen) to get lost; (= umkommen) to buy it (inf), to snuff it (inf); (sl: = ins Gefängnis kommen) to get banged up (inf)

ver|schüt|ten ptp **verschüttet** VT **a** Flüssigkeit to spill **b** (= zuschütten) Brunnen, Flussarm to fill in **c** (= begraben) **verschüttet werden** (Mensch) to be buried (alive); (fig) to be submerged **d** (= blockieren) Weg to block

ver|schüt|tet [fɛɐˈʃʏtət] ADJ buried (alive); (fig) submerged

Ver|schüt|te|te(r) [fɛɐˈʃʏtətə] MF decl as adj person buried in the disaster/accident

ver|schütt ge|hen ▲ VI irreg aux sein (inf) to get lost

ver|schwä|gert [fɛɐˈʃvɛːɡɐt] ADJ related (by marriage) (mit to)

Ver|schwä|ge|rung [fɛɐˈʃvɛːɡərʊŋ] F **-, -en** relationship by marriage (mit to)

ver|schwei|gen [fɛɐˈʃvaɪɡn̩] ptp **verschwiegen** VT irreg Tatsachen, Wahrheit etc to hide, to conceal, to withhold (jdm etw sth from sb); **ich habe nichts zu ~** I've nothing to hide → auch **verschwiegen**

Ver|schwei|gen NT concealment, hiding, withholding; **das ~ der Wahrheit** concealing or withholding the truth

ver|schwei|ßen [fɛɐˈʃvaɪst] VT to weld (together)

ver|schwe|len ptp **verschwelt** VTI Holz to burn; (Tech) Kohle to carbonize

ver|schwen|den [fɛɐˈʃvɛndn̩] ptp **verschwendet** VT to waste (auf +acc, an +acc, für on); (= leichtsinnig vertun) Geld to squander

Ver|schwen|der [fɛɐˈʃvɛndɐ] M **-s, -**, **Ver|schwen|de|rin** [-ərɪn] F **-, -nen** spendthrift, squanderer

ver|schwen|de|risch [fɛɐˈʃvɛndərɪʃ] **ADJ** wasteful; Leben extravagant; (= üppig) lavish, sumptuous; Fülle lavish **ADV** wastefully, extravagantly; (= üppig) lavishly, sumptuously; **mit etw ~ umgehen** to be lavish with sth

Ver|schwen|dung F **-, -en** wastefulness; **~ von Geld/Zeit** waste of money/time

Ver|schwen|dungs-: **Ver|schwen|dungs|sucht** F , no pl extravagance; **ver|schwen|dungs|süch|tig** ADJ (wildly) extravagant

ver|schwie|gen [fɛɐˈʃviːɡn̩] ADJ Mensch discreet; Ort secluded → auch **verschweigen**, **Grab**

Ver|schwie|gen|heit F **-**, no pl (von Mensch) discretion; (von Ort) seclusion; **zur ~ verpflichtet** bound to secrecy → **Siegel**

ver|schwie|melt [fɛɐˈʃviːmlt] ADJ (N Ger inf) swollen

ver|schwim|men ptp **verschwommen** [fɛɐˈʃvɔmən] VI irreg aux sein to become blurred or indistinct; **es verschwamm ihr alles vor den Augen** everything went fuzzy or hazy; **ineinander ~** to melt into one another, to merge (into one another) → auch **verschwommen**

ver|schwin|den ptp **verschwunden** [fɛɐˈʃvʊndn̩] VI irreg aux sein to disappear, to vanish; **verschwinde!** clear off (Brit) or out! (inf), away! (liter); **etw ~ lassen** (Zauberer) to make sth disappear or vanish; (= verstecken) to dispose of sth; (= stehlen) to steal or filch (inf) sth; **von der Landkarte ~** to disappear off the map; **etw in etw** (dat) **~ lassen** to slip sth into sth; **neben jdm/etw ~** to pale into insignificance beside sb/sth, to be eclipsed by sb/sth; (in Bezug auf Größe) to look minute beside sb/sth; **(mal) ~ müssen** (euph inf) to have to spend a penny (Brit inf), to have to go to the bathroom → auch **verschwunden**

Ver|schwin|den [fɛɐˈʃvɪndn̩] NT **-s**, no pl disappearance

ver|schwin|dend **ADJ** Anzahl, Menge insignificant; Minderheit tiny **ADV** **~ wenig** very, very few; **~ klein** or **gering** minute

ver|schwis|tern [fɛɐˈʃvɪstɐn] ptp **verschwistert** VR (fig) to form a close union; (Städte) to become twinned (Brit) or sister cities (US); (liter: Seelen) to become closely united

ver|schwis|tert [fɛɐˈʃvɪstɐt] ADJ (miteinander) **~ sein** to be brother and sister, to be siblings (Sociol, Med etc); (Brüder) to be brothers; (Schwestern) to be sisters; (fig) to be close; (Städte) to be twinned (Brit) or sisters (US), to be twin towns (Brit) or sister cities (US); **~e Seelen** (liter) kindred spirits

ver|schwit|zen ptp **verschwitzt** VT **a** Kleidung to make sweaty **b** (fig inf) to forget

ver|schwitzt [fɛɐˈʃvɪtst] ADJ Kleidungsstück sweat-stained; (= feucht) sweaty; Mensch sweaty

ver|schwol|len [fɛɐˈʃvɔlən] ADJ swollen

ver|schwom|men [fɛɐˈʃvɔmən] **ADJ** Foto, Umrisse blurred, fuzzy; Berge hazy, indistinct; Erinnerung, Vorstellung vague, hazy; Argumente, Begriffe woolly (esp Brit), vague **ADV** wahrnehmen, sehen blurred, hazy; sich erinnern, sich vorstellen vaguely, hazily; sprechen, reden vaguely; **ich sehe alles ~** everything looks hazy to me → auch **verschwimmen**

Ver|schwom|men|heit F **-**, no pl (von Foto, Umrissen) fuzziness; (von Anblick) haziness, in-

distinctness; (von Erinnerung, Vorstellung) vagueness; (von Argumenten, Begriffen) woolliness (esp Brit), vagueness

ver|schwo|ren [fɛɐˈʃvoːrən] ADJ **a** Gesellschaft sworn **b** **einer Sache** (dat) **~ sein** to have given oneself over to sth

ver|schwö|ren ptp **verschworen** [fɛɐˈʃvoːrən] VR irreg **a** (= ein Komplott schmieden) to conspire, to plot (mit with, gegen against); **sich zu etw ~** to plot sth, to conspire to do sth; **sie haben sich zu einem Attentat gegen den Diktator verschworen** they are conspiring or plotting to assassinate the dictator; **alles hat sich gegen mich verschworen** (fig) there's a conspiracy against me **b** (= sich verschreiben) **sich einer Sache** (dat) **~** to give oneself over to sth

Ver|schwo|re|ne(r) [fɛɐˈʃvoːrənə] MF decl as adj conspirator, plotter; (fig) ally, accomplice

Ver|schwö|rer [fɛɐˈʃvøːrɐ] M **-s, -**, **Ver|schwö|re|rin** [-ərɪn] F **-, -nen** conspirator

Ver|schwö|rung [fɛɐˈʃvøːrʊŋ] F **-, -en** conspiracy, plot

ver|schwun|den [fɛɐˈʃvʊndn̩] ADJ missing, who/that has/had disappeared; **das ~e Mädchen/Auto** the missing girl/car → auch **verschwinden**

Vers|dich|tung F (Liter) poetry

ver|sechs|fa|chen [fɛɐˈzɛksfaxn̩] ptp **versechsfacht** **VT** to multiply by six **VR** to increase sixfold

ver|se|hen ptp **versehen** irreg **VT** **a** (= ausüben) Amt, Stelle etc to occupy, to hold; Dienst to perform, to discharge (form); (= sich kümmern um) to look after, to take care of; Küche to see to, to do; (Bus, Schiff etc) Route to provide the/a service on; Dienst to provide; **den Dienst eines Kollegen ~** to take a colleague's place, to perform a colleague's duties **b** (= ausstatten) **jdn mit etw ~** to provide or supply sb with sth; (= ausrüsten auch) to equip sb with sth; **etw mit etw ~** to put sth on/in sth; (= montieren) to fit sth with sth; **ein Buch mit einem Umschlag ~** to provide a book with a dust jacket; **mit etw ~ sein** to have sth; **mit Blättern/Wurzeln/Haaren etc ~ sein** to have leaves/roots/hairs etc; **mit Etiketten/Wegweisern ~ sein** to be labelled (Brit) or labeled (US)/signposted; **mit allem reichlich** or **wohl ~ sein** to be well provided for; **die Bücherei ist gut (mit Fachliteratur) ~** the library is well stocked with specialist literature) **c** (Eccl) **jdn (mit den Sterbesakramenten) ~** to administer the last rites or sacraments to sb **d** (= geben) to give; **jdn mit einer Vollmacht ~** to invest sb with full powers; **etw mit seiner Unterschrift ~** to affix one's signature to sth (form), to sign sth; **etw mit einem Stempel ~** to stamp sth; **etw mit einem Siegel ~** to affix a seal to sth; **etw mit Akzept ~** (Fin) to accept sth **VR** **a** (= sich irren) to be mistaken, to make a mistake **b** **sich mit etw ~** (= sich versorgen) to provide oneself with sth; (= sich ausstatten) to equip oneself with sth **c** **ehe man sichs versieht** before you could turn (a)round, before you could say Jack Robinson (esp Brit inf), lickety-split (US inf)

Ver|se|hen [fɛɐˈzeːən] ⭗ 45.4 NT **-s, -** (= Irrtum) mistake, error; (= Unachtsamkeit) inadvertence, oversight; **aus ~** by mistake, inadvertently

ver|se|hent|lich [fɛɐˈzeːəntlɪç] **ADJ** attr inadvertent; (= irrtümlich) erroneous **ADV** inadvertently, by mistake

Ver|seh|gang M pl **-gänge** (Eccl) visit to a/the dying man/woman

ver|seh|ren ptp **versehrt** VT (geh) (= verletzen) to injure, to hurt; (= zum Invaliden machen) to disable; (= beschädigen) to damage

Ver|sehr|ten-: **Ver|sehr|ten|ren|te** F disability or invalidity pension; **Ver|sehr|ten|sport** M sport for the disabled

Ver|sehr|te(r) [fɛɐ̯ˈzeːɐ̯tə] MF *decl as adj* disabled person/man/woman *etc*; **Platz für ~** seat for the disabled, seat for disabled persons

ver|sei|fen *ptp* **verseift** VT (*Chem*) to saponify

ver|selbst|stän|di|gen ▲ *ptp* **verselbstständigt**, **ver|selb|stän|di|gen** *ptp* **verselbständigt** VR to become independent; (*beruflich auch*) to become self-employed

Ver|selbst|stän|di|gung ▲ F -, -en, **Ver|selb|stän|di|gung** F -, -en **die ~ der Kinder fördern** to help the children to become independent

ver|sen|den *ptp* **versendet** (*rare*) *or* **versandt** [fɛɐ̯ˈzant] VT *irreg or reg* to send; (*Comm auch*) to forward; (= *verfrachten auch*) to ship; *Kataloge, Heiratsanzeige etc* to send (out)

Ver|sen|dung F sending; (*Comm auch*) forwarding; (= *das Verfrachten auch*) shipment; (*von Heiratsanzeige*) sending out; **die ~ der Kataloge** sending (out) the catalogues (*Brit*) *or* catalogs (*US*)

ver|sen|gen *ptp* **versengt** VT **a** (*Sonne, mit Bügeleisen*) to scorch; (*Feuer*) to singe **b** (*inf*: = *verprügeln*) to thrash, to wallop (*inf*)

ver|senk|bar ADJ that can be lowered; *Scheinwerfer* retractable; *Nähmaschine, Tischplatte* foldaway *attr*; **nicht ~** (*Schiff*) unsinkable

ver|sen|ken *ptp* **versenkt** VT **a** *Schatz, Behälter, Bohrinsel* to sink; *Leiche, Sarg* to lower; *Schiff* to sink, to send to the bottom; *das eigene Schiff* to scuttle; **die Hände in die Taschen ~** to thrust one's hands into one's pockets; **den Kopf in ein Buch ~** to bury one's head in a book, to immerse oneself in a book **b** *Schraube* to countersink; *Tischplatte* to fold away; (*Theat*) to lower; **eine Nähmaschine, die man ~ kann** a foldaway sewing machine **VR** **sich in etw** (*acc*) **~** to become immersed in sth; *in Gedanken auch, in Anblick* to lose oneself in sth

Ver|sen|kung F **a** (= *das Versenken*) sinking; (*von Leiche, Sarg*) lowering; (*von eigenem Schiff*) scuttling **b** (*Theat*) trap(door) **c** (= *das Sichversenken*) immersion; **jdn aus seiner ~ reißen** to tear sb from (his absorption *or* immersion in) his book/work *etc*; **seine ~ in diesen Anblick** his rapt contemplation of this sight; **innere/ mystische ~** inner/mystic contemplation **d** (*inf*) **in der ~ verschwinden** to vanish; (*berühmter Mensch, Buch etc*) to vanish *or* disappear from the scene, to sink into oblivion; **aus der ~ auftauchen** to reappear; (*Mensch auch*) to re-emerge (on the scene)

Ver|se|pos NT (*Liter*) epic poem

Ver|se|schmied(in) M(F) (*pej*) rhymester (*pej*), versifier (*pej*)

ver|ses|sen ADJ (*fig*) **auf etw** (*acc*) **~ sein** to be very keen on sth, to be mad *or* crazy about sth (*inf*)

Ver|ses|sen|heit F -, -en keenness (*auf +acc* on)

ver|set|zen *ptp* **versetzt** **VT** **a** (= *an andere Stelle setzen*) *Gegenstände, Möbel, Schüler* to move, to shift; *Pflanzen* to transplant, to move; (= *nicht geradlinig anordnen*) to stagger **b** (*beruflich*) to transfer, to move; **jdn in einen höheren Rang ~** to promote sb, to move sb up → **Ruhestand** **c** (*Sch: in höhere Klasse*) to move *or* put up **d** (*Typ, Mus*) to transpose **e** (*inf* = *verkaufen*) to flog (*Brit inf*), to sell; (= *verpfänden*) to pawn, to hock (*inf*) **f** (*inf*: = *nicht erscheinen*) **jdn ~** to stand sb up (*inf*) **g** (= *in bestimmten Zustand bringen*) **etw in Bewegung ~** to set sth in motion; **etw in Schwingung ~** to set sth swinging; **jdn in Wut ~** to send sb into a rage; **jdn in fröhliche Stimmung ~** to put sb in a cheerful mood; **jdn in Sorge/ Unruhe ~** to worry/disturb sb; **jdn in Angst (und Schrecken) ~** to frighten sb, to make sb afraid; **jdn in die Lage ~, etw zu tun** to put sb in a position to do sth

h (= *geben*) *Stoß, Schlag, Tritt etc* to give; **jdm eins ~** (*inf*) to belt sb (*inf*), to land sb one (*Brit inf*); **jdm einen Stich ~** (*fig*) to cut sb to the quick (*Brit*), to wound sb (deeply) → **Todesstoß**

i (= *mischen*) to mix

j (= *antworten*) to retort

VR **a** (= *sich an andere Stelle setzen*) to move (to another place), to change places

b **sich in jdn/ jds Lage/Gefühle ~** to put oneself in sb's place *or* position

c **sich in eine frühere Zeit/ seine Jugend** *etc* **~** to take oneself back to an earlier period/one's youth *etc*, to imagine oneself back in an earlier period/one's youth *etc*

Ver|set|zung F -, -en **a** (*beruflich*) transfer; **seine ~ in einen höheren Rang** his promotion (to a higher rank) **b** (*Sch*) moving up, being put up; **bei nicht erfolgter ~** when the pupil isn't moved *or* put up **c** (*Mus, Typ*) transposition **d** (= *nicht geradlinige Anordnung*) staggering **e** (= *Vermischung*) mixing

Ver|set|zungs-: Ver|set|zungs|kon|fe|renz F end of year staff meeting (*to decide whether pupils should be put up to next class*); **Ver|set|zungs|zei|chen** NT (*Mus*) accidental; **Ver|set|zungs|zeug|nis** NT end-of-year report

ver|seu|chen [fɛɐ̯ˈzɔyçn] *ptp* **verseucht** VT (*mit Bakterien*) to infect; (*mit Gas, Giftstoffen*) to contaminate; (*fig*) to contaminate, to poison; (*Comput*) to infect with a virus

Ver|seu|chung F -, -en (*mit Bakterien, Viren*) infection; (*mit Gas, Giftstoffen*) contamination *no pl*; (*fig*) poisoning *no pl*

Ver|seu|chungs|grad M contamination level

Vers-: Vers|form F (*Poet*) verse form; **Vers|fuß** M (*Poet*) (metrical) foot

Ver|si|che|rer [fɛɐ̯ˈzɪçərɐ] M -s, -, **Ver|si|che|rin** [-ərɪn] F -, -nen insurer; (*bei Lebensversicherung*) assurer (*Brit*), insurer; (*bei Schiffen*) underwriter

ver|si|chern ✪ 42.1 *ptp* **versichert** **VT** **a** (= *bestätigen*) to assure; (= *beteuern*) to affirm, to protest; **jdm ~, dass …** to assure sb that …; **jdm etw ~** to assure sb of sth; *seine Unschuld* to affirm *or* protest sth to sb

b (*geh*) **jdn einer Sache** (*gen*) **~** to assure sb of sth; **seien Sie versichert, dass …** (you can *or* may) rest assured that …

c (*Insur, gegen Betrag*) to insure; *Leben* to assure (*Brit*), to insure; **gegen etw versichert sein** to be insured against sth

VR **a** (= *Versicherung abschließen*) to insure oneself (*mit* for); (*Lebensversicherung*) to take out a life assurance (*Brit*) *or* insurance policy; **sich gegen Unfall ~** to take out accident insurance

b (= *sich vergewissern*) to make sure *or* certain

c **sich jds/ einer Sache ~** (*geh*) to secure sb/sth

Ver|si|cher|ten|kar|te F health insurance card

Ver|si|cher|te(r) [fɛɐ̯ˈzɪçɐtə] MF *decl as adj* insured (party); (*bei Lebensversicherung*) assured (*Brit*) *or* insured (party)

Ver|si|che|rung F **a** (= *Bestätigung*) assurance; (= *Beteuerung*) affirmation, protestation **b** (= *Feuerversicherung etc*) insurance; (= *Lebensversicherung*) assurance (*Brit*), insurance **c** (= *Gesellschaft*) insurance company; (*für Lebensversicherung*) assurance (*Brit*) *or* insurance company

Ver|si|che|rungs-: Ver|si|che|rungs|agent(in) M(F) (*Aus*) insurance agent; **Ver|si|che|rungs|an|spruch** M insurance claim; **Ver|si|che|rungs|an|stalt** F insurance company; **Ver|si|che|rungs|aus|weis** M insurance certificate; **Ver|si|che|rungs|bei|trag** M **a** (*bei staatlicher Versicherung etc*) insurance contribution **b** (*bei Haftpflichtversicherung etc*) insurance premium; **Ver|si|che|rungs|be|trug** M insurance fraud; **Ver|si|che|rungs|dau|er** F period of insurance; **Ver|si|che|rungs|fall** M (= *Verlust*) event of loss; (= *Schaden*) event of damage; **ver|si|che|rungs|fremd** ADJ **~e Leis-**

tun|gen payments unrelated to insurance; **Ver|si|che|rungs|ge|sell|schaft** F insurance company; (*für Lebensversicherung*) assurance (*Brit*) *or* insurance company; **Ver|si|che|rungs|kar|te** F insurance card; **die grüne ~** (*Mot*) the green card (*Brit*), *insurance document for driving abroad*; **Ver|si|che|rungs|kauf|frau** F , **Ver|si|che|rungs|kauf|mann** M insurance broker; **Ver|si|che|rungs|leis|tung** F insurance benefit; **Ver|si|che|rungs|ma|the|ma|tik** F actuarial theory; **Ver|si|che|rungs|neh|mer(in)** M(F) (*form*) policy holder, insurant (*form*); **Ver|si|che|rungs|num|mer** F ≈ National Insurance number, ≈ Social Security number (*US*); (*von Versicherungspolice*) policy number; **Ver|si|che|rungs|pflicht** F compulsory insurance; **jeder Autofahrer unterliegt der ~** insurance is compulsory for every driver; **ver|si|che|rungs|pflich|tig** [-pflɪçtɪç] ADJ subject to compulsory insurance; **Ver|si|che|rungs|po|li|ce** F insurance policy; (*von Lebensversicherung*) assurance (*Brit*) *or* insurance policy; **Ver|si|che|rungs|prä|mie** F insurance premium; **Ver|si|che|rungs|satz** M rate of insurance; **Ver|si|che|rungs|schein** M insurance policy; **Ver|si|che|rungs|schutz** M insurance cover; **Ver|si|che|rungs|sum|me** F sum insured; (*bei Lebensversicherung auch*) sum assured; **Ver|si|che|rungs|trä|ger(in)** M(F) = **Versicherer**; **Ver|si|che|rungs|ver|tre|ter(in)** M(F) insurance agent; **Ver|si|che|rungs|wert** M insurance value; **Ver|si|che|rungs|we|sen** NT , *no pl* insurance (business); **Ver|si|che|rungs|zwang** M compulsory insurance

ver|si|ckern *ptp* **versickert** VI *aux sein* to seep away; (*fig*) (*Gespräch, Unterstützung*) to dry up; (*Interesse, Teilnahme*) to peter out; (*Geld*) to trickle away

ver|sie|ben *ptp* **versiebt** VT (*inf*) (= *vergessen*) to forget; (= *verlieren*) to lose; (= *verpfuschen*) to make a mess of (*inf*)

ver|sie|ben|fa|chen [fɛɐ̯ˈziːbnfaxn] *ptp* **versiebenfacht** **VT** to multiply by seven **VR** to increase sevenfold

ver|sie|geln *ptp* **versiegelt** VT *Brief, Tür* to seal (up); *Parkett etc* to seal

Ver|sie|ge|lung [fɛɐ̯ˈziːɡəlʊŋ] F -, -en (*Vorgang*) sealing; (= *Siegel*) seal

ver|sie|gen *ptp* **versiegt** VI *aux sein* (*Fluss, Quelle*) to dry up, to run dry; (*fig*) (*Gespräch, Unterstützung*) to dry up; (*Interesse*) to peter out; (*Tränen*) to dry up; *gute Laune, Humor, Kräfte* to fail; **nie ~de Hoffnung** never-failing *or* undying hope

ver|siert [vɛrˈziːɐt] ADJ experienced, practised (*Brit*), practiced (*US*); **in etw** (*dat*) **~ sein** to be experienced *or* (*in Bezug auf Wissen*) (well) versed in sth

Ver|siert|heit F -, *no pl* experience (*in +dat* in); (*in Bezug auf Wissen*) knowledge (*in +dat* of)

ver|sifft [fɛɐ̯ˈzɪft] ADJ (*sl*) grotty (*Brit inf*), yucky (*inf*)

ver|sil|bern [fɛɐ̯ˈzɪlbɐn] *ptp* **versilbert** VT (= *silbern bemalen*) to paint silver; (= *mit Silber überziehen*) to silver(-plate); (*fig inf*: = *verkaufen*) to flog (*Brit inf*), to sell; (*fig liter: Mond*) to silver

Ver|sil|be|rung F -, -en (*Vorgang*) silvering, (silver-)plating; (= *Silberschicht*) silver plate

ver|sim|peln [fɛɐ̯ˈzɪmpln] *ptp* **versimpelt** (*inf*) **VT** (= *vereinfachen*) to make easier *or* simpler **VI** *aux sein* (= *einfältig werden*) **sie ist völlig versimpelt** her mind has completely gone to seed

ver|sin|ken *ptp* **versunken** [fɛɐ̯ˈzʊŋkn] VI *irreg aux sein* (= *untergehen*) to sink; (*Schiff auch*) to founder; **ich hätte im Boden** *or* **in der Erde/ vor Scham ~ mögen** I wished the ground would (open and) swallow me up; **im Laster ~** to sink into a life of vice; **in etw** (*acc*) **~** (*fig, in Trauer, Melancholie, Chaos*) to sink into sth; *in Anblick* to lose oneself in sth; *in Gedanken, Musik* to become immersed in sth, to lose oneself in sth; **alles versinkt um ihn (herum)** (*fig*) he becomes totally oblivious to everything (around him) → *auch* **versunken**

ver|sinn|bild|li|chen [fɛɐ̯'zɪnbɪltlɪçn] *ptp* **ver-sinnbildlicht** VT to symbolize, to represent

Ver|sinn|bild|li|chung F -, -en symbolization, representation

Ver|si|on [vɛr'zioːn] F -, -en version

ver|sippt [fɛɐ̯'zɪpt] ADJ *(pej)* interrelated

ver|sit|zen *ptp* **versessen** [fɛɐ̯'sɛsn̩] VT *irreg (inf) Kleidung* to crease, to crush; **ich habe heute Morgen meine ganze Zeit beim Arzt versessen** I sat about (waiting) the whole morning at the doctor's

ver|skla|ven [fɛɐ̯'sklaːvn̩, -aːfn̩] *ptp* **versklavt** VT *(lit, fig)* to enslave

Ver|skla|vung F -, -en enslavement

Vers|kunst F versification

Vers|leh|re F study of verse

ver|slu|men [fɛɐ̯'slamən] VI *Stadtzentrum, Stadtteil* to turn into *or* to become a slum

Ver|slu|mung [fɛɐ̯'slamʊŋ] F **die ~ ganzer Stadtteile** the deterioration of whole parts of a/the city into slums

Vers|maß NT metre *(Brit)*, meter *(US)*

ver|sno|ben [fɛɐ̯'snoːbn̩] *ptp* **versnobt** VI *aux sein (pej)* to become snobbish *or* a snob; **versnobt** snobbish, snobby *(inf)*

ver|sof|fen [fɛɐ̯'zɔfn̩] ADJ *(inf)* boozy *(inf)*; **ein ~es Genie** a drunken genius → *auch* **versaufen**

ver|soh|len *ptp* **versohlt** VT *(inf)* to belt *(inf)*; *(zur Strafe auch)* to leather

ver|söh|nen [fɛɐ̯'zøːnən] *ptp* **versöhnt** VT to reconcile; *(= besänftigen) jdn, Götter* to placate, to appease; *(fig) Unterschiede, jdn* to reconcile; **~de Worte** conciliatory words; *(besänftigend)* placatory words; **das versöhnt einen dann wieder** it almost makes up for it VR to be(come) reconciled; *(Streitende)* to make it up; **sich mit Gott ~** to make one's peace with God; **sich mit etw ~** to reconcile oneself to sth

ver|söhn|lich [fɛɐ̯'zøːnlɪç] ADJ *Mensch* conciliatory; *Laune, Ton, Geste auch* placatory; *Schluss (von Film, Roman)* upbeat; *(= nicht nachtragend)* forgiving; **die Götter ~ stimmen** to placate *or* appease the gods

Ver|söh|nung F -, -en reconciliation; *(= Beschwichtigung)* appeasement; **zur ~ opferte er den Göttern ...** to appease *or* placate the gods he sacrificed ...

Ver|söh|nungs-: **Ver|söh|nungs|fest** NT *(Rel)* Day of Atonement, Yom Kippur *no def art*; **Ver|söh|nungs|po|li|tik** F policy of reconciliation; **Ver|söh|nungs|tag** M *(Rel)* = **Versöhnungsfest**

ver|son|nen [fɛɐ̯'zɔnən] *ptp* **versonnen** ADJ *(= in Gedanken verloren) Gesichtsausdruck* pensive, thoughtful; *Mensch auch* lost in thought; *(= träumerisch) Blick* dreamy ADV **blicken** pensively; *(= träumerisch)* dreamily

ver|sor|gen *ptp* **versorgt** VT **a** *Kinder, Tiere, Pflanzen, Haushalt, finanzielle Angelegenheiten* to look after, to take care of; *(= bedienen) Maschine, Lift, Heizung* to look after; **jdn medizinisch ~** to give sb medical attention *or* treatment **b** *(= beliefern)* to supply; **jdn mit etw ~** *(= versehen)* to provide *or* supply sb with sth; **das Gehirn mit Sauerstoff ~** to supply oxygen to the brain **c** *(= unterhalten) Familie* to provide for, to support; **versorgt sein** to be provided for, to be taken care of **d** *(dial: = wegräumen)* to put away VR **a** **sich mit etw ~** to provide oneself with sth **b** **sich selbst ~** to look after oneself, to take care of oneself

Ver|sor|ger [fɛɐ̯'zɔrɡɐ] M -s, -, **Ver|sor|ge|rin** [-ərɪn] F -, -nen **a** *(= Ernährer)* provider, breadwinner **b** *(= Belieferer)* supplier

Ver|sor|gung [fɛɐ̯'zɔrɡʊŋ] F -, -en **a** *(= Pflege)* care; **die ~ des Haushalts** looking after the house; **medizinische ~** medical care; **vielen Dank für die gute ~ meiner Katze/Pflanzen** many thanks for taking such good care of my cat/plants

b *(= Belieferung)* supply; **die ~ mit Strom/Gas/Wasser** the supply of electricity/gas/water; **die ~ dieses Gebiets mit Bussen** the supply of buses to *or* the provision of buses for this district; **die ~ der Truppen (mit Munition)** supplying the troops (with ammunition); **Probleme mit der ~ haben** to have supply problems; **auf Grund der schlechten ~ der Truppen** because the troops were being poorly supplied

c *(= Unterhalt)* **die ~ im Alter/einer sechsköpfigen Familie** providing for one's old age/a family of six; **der Staat übernimmt die ~ von Witwen und Waisen** the state undertakes to provide for widows and orphans

Ver|sor|gungs-: **Ver|sor|gungs|an|spruch** M claim to maintenance *(Brit)* or alimony; **Ver|sor|gungs|an|stalt** F **~ des Bundes und der Länder** *institution that provides additional pension benefits for public employees and their dependents*; **Ver|sor|gungs|aus|gleich** M *(bei Ehescheidung)* maintenance *(Brit)*, alimony; **ver|sor|gungs|be|rech|tigt** ADJ entitled to maintenance *(Brit)* or alimony; *(durch Staat)* entitled to (state) benefit; **Ver|sor|gungs|be|trieb** M public utility; **Ver|sor|gungs|emp|fän|ger(in)** M(F) recipient of state benefit; **Ver|sor|gungs|eng|pass** ▲ M supply shortage *or* bottleneck; **Ver|sor|gungs|fahr|zeug** NT *(Mil)* supply vehicle; **Ver|sor|gungs|flug|zeug** NT supply plane; **Ver|sor|gungs|gü|ter** PL supplies *pl*; **Ver|sor|gungs|kri|se** F supply crisis; **Ver|sor|gungs|la|ge** F supply situation; **Ver|sor|gungs|lü|cke** F *(bei Vorräten etc)* supply gap; *(bei Rente)* ≈ pension gap; **Ver|sor|gungs|netz** NT *(= Wasserversorgung, Gasversorgung etc)* (supply) grid; *(von Waren)* supply network; **Ver|sor|gungs|schwie|rig|kei|ten** PL supply problems *pl*; **Ver|sor|gungs|staat** M all-providing state; **Ver|sor|gungs|trup|pen** PL supply troops *pl*; **Ver|sor|gungs|weg** M supply channel

ver|spach|teln *ptp* **verspachtelt** VT **a** *Loch, Ritze, Fuge* to fill in **b** *(fig inf: = aufessen)* to put *or* tuck away *(inf)*

ver|span|nen *ptp* **verspannt** VT to brace, to stay, to guy VR *(Muskeln)* to tense up

ver|spannt [fɛɐ̯'ʃpant] ADJ *Muskeln* tense, tensed up *pred*

Ver|span|nung F **a** *(Seile etc)* bracing, stays *pl* **b** *(von Muskeln)* tenseness *no pl*

ver|spä|ten [fɛɐ̯'ʃpɛːtn̩] *ptp* **verspätet** VR **a** *(= zu spät kommen)* to be late; **der Frühling hat sich verspätet** spring is late **b** *(= nicht rechtzeitig wegkommen)* to be late leaving; *(= aufgehalten werden)* to be held up

ver|spä|tet [fɛɐ̯'ʃpɛːtət] ADJ *Zug, Flugzeug* delayed, late *pred*; *Ankunft, Eintreten, Frühling, Entwicklung* late; *Glückwunsch* belated; *Bewerbung* late, belated ADV late; *sich bewerben, gratulieren* belatedly

Ver|spä|tung F -, -en *(von Verkehrsmitteln)* delay; *(von Mensch)* late arrival; *(von Glückwunsch etc)* belatedness; **(10 Minuten) ~ haben** to be (10 minutes) late; **eine zweistündige ~** a delay of two hours, a two-hour delay; **die ~ aufholen** to catch up lost time; **mit ~ abfahren/ankommen** to leave/arrive late; **ohne ~ ankommen** to arrive on time; **mit zwanzig Minuten ~** twenty minutes late *or (von Verkehrsmitteln auch)* behind schedule; **mit sechsmonatiger** *etc* **~** six months *etc* late; *(nach Ablauf der Frist auch)* six months *etc* too late

ver|spei|sen *ptp* **verspeist** VT *(geh)* to consume

ver|spe|ku|lie|ren *ptp* **verspekuliert** VT to lose through speculation VR to ruin oneself by

speculation; *(fig)* to miscalculate, to be out in one's speculations

ver|sper|ren *ptp* **versperrt** VT **a** *Weg, Durchgang* to block; *Aussicht* to obstruct, to block **b** *(dial: = verschließen)* to lock *or* close up

ver|spie|geln *ptp* **verspiegelt** VT *Wand, Decke* to cover with mirrors; **verspiegelte Sonnenbrille** mirror(ed) *or* reflecting sunglasses *pl*

ver|spie|len *ptp* **verspielt** VT *(lit, fig) Geld, Chancen, Zukunft* to gamble away; *Vorteile* to bargain away; *Vertrauen, Glaubwürdigkeit* to lose; **den ganzen Abend ~** to spend the whole evening playing; **allen Kredit ~** *(fig)* to lose all credibility VI *(fig)* **jetzt hast du verspielt** it's all up with you now *(esp Brit inf)*, you've had it now *(inf)*; **er hatte bei ihr verspielt** he was finished *or* he had had it *(inf)* as far as she was concerned

ver|spielt [fɛɐ̯'ʃpiːlt] ADJ *Kind, Katze etc* playful; *Frisur* pretty; *Muster, Kleid* pretty, dainty; *Verzierung* dainty

ver|spin|nen *ptp* **versponnen** [fɛɐ̯'ʃpɔnən] *irreg* VT *(zu Faden)* to spin; *(= verbrauchen)* to use VR **die Larve verspinnt sich (zur Puppe)** the larva spins itself into a cocoon, the larva forms a cocoon; **sich in etw** *(dat)* **~** *(fig, in Ideen)* to become immersed in sth; *in Lügen* to become embroiled *or* enmeshed in sth

ver|spon|nen [fɛɐ̯'ʃpɔnən] ADJ airy-fairy *(Brit inf)*, ivory-towered *(US)*; *(dann auch* wild *attr)*; *Mensch* head-in-the-clouds *pred*

ver|spot|ten *ptp* **verspottet** VT to mock; *(höhnisch)* to jeer at, to deride

Ver|spot|tung [fɛɐ̯'ʃpɔtʊŋ] F -, -en **a** *no pl (= das Verspotten)* mocking *no indef art*; *(höhnisch)* jeering *no indef art*, derision *no indef art* **b** *(= spöttische Rede)* mockery *no indef art*, *no pl*; *(= höhnische Rede)* jeer, derision *no indef art*, *no pl*

ver|spre|chen *ptp* **versprochen** [fɛɐ̯'ʃprɔxn̩] *irreg* VT **a** *(= zusagen)* to promise *(jdm etw* sb sth*)*; **aber er hat es doch versprochen!** but he promised!; **jdm versprochen sein** *(obs)* to be betrothed *(old)* or promised to sb; **einander versprochen sein** *(obs)* to be betrothed *(old)* → **hoch 2 g, Blaue(s)**

b *(= erwarten lassen)* to promise; **das verspricht interessant zu werden** it promises to be interesting; **das Wetter verspricht schön zu werden** the weather looks promising, the weather promises to be good; **nichts Gutes ~** to be ominous, to bode ill *(liter)*

c *(= erwarten)* **sich** *(dat)* **viel/wenig von jdm/etw ~** to have high hopes/no great hopes of sb/sth; **was versprichst du dir davon?** what do you expect to achieve *or* gain (by that)?

VR *(= falsch sagen, aussprechen)* to pronounce a word/words wrong(ly); *(= etwas Nichtgemeintes sagen)* to make a slip (of the tongue), to make a mistake; **bei dem Wort verspreche ich mich noch immer** I still can't pronounce that word properly

Ver|spre|chen [fɛɐ̯'ʃprɛçn̩] NT -s, - promise

Ver|spre|cher M *(inf)* slip (of the tongue); **ein freudscher ~** a Freudian slip

Ver|spre|chung [fɛɐ̯'ʃprɛçʊŋ] F -, -en promise

ver|spren|gen *ptp* **versprengt** VT **a** *Flüchtlinge, Soldaten* to disperse, to scatter; **versprengte Soldaten** scattered soldiers **b** *Wasser* to sprinkle

ver|sprit|zen *ptp* **verspritzt** VT **a** *(= versprühen, verteilen)* to spray; *(= versprengen)* to sprinkle; *Farbe* to spray on; *(= zuspritzen) Fugen* to seal by injection moulding *(Brit)* or molding *(US)*; *(fig) Tinte* to use up → **Gift** **b** *(beim Planschen) Wasser* to splash, to sp(l)atter; *(= verkleckern) Farbe, Boden, Heft, Kleidung* to sp(l)atter **c** *(= verbrauchen) Wasser, Farbe etc* to use VI *aux sein (Wasser)* to spray; *(Fett)* to sp(l)atter

ver|spro|che|ner|ma|ßen [fɛɐ̯'ʃprɔxənɐ'maːsn̩] ADV as promised

ver|sprö|den [fɛɐ̯'ʃprøːdn̩] *ptp* **versprödet** VI *aux sein* to go brittle

ver|sprü|hen ptp **versprüht** VT to spray; *Funken auch* to send up or out; *Charme* to exude; (= *verbrauchen*) to use; **Witz/Geist** ~ to scintillate

ver|spü|ren ptp **verspürt** VT to feel, to be conscious of; **er verspürte keine Lust, zur Arbeit zu gehen** he felt no desire to go to work

ver|staat|li|chen [fɛɐ̯ˈʃtaːtlɪçn̩] ptp **verstaatlicht** VT to nationalize; *Schulen* to put under state control; *Kirchen* to secularize

Ver|staat|li|chung F -, **-en** nationalization; (*von Schulen*) putting under state control; (*von Kirchen*) secularization

ver|städ|tern [fɛɐ̯ˈʃtɛːtɐn, fɛɐ̯ˈʃtɛtɐn] ptp **verstädtert** **VT** to urbanize **VI** aux sein to become urbanized

Ver|städ|te|rung [fɛɐ̯ˈʃtɛːtərʊŋ, fɛɐ̯ˈʃtɛt-] F urbanization

Ver|stand [fɛɐ̯ˈʃtant] M -(e)s [-dəs] no pl (= *Fähigkeit zu denken*) reason; (= *Intellekt*) mind, intellect; (= *Vernunft*) (common) sense; (= *Urteilskraft*) (powers pl of) judgement; **das müsste dir dein ~ sagen** your common sense should tell you that; **den ~ verlieren** to lose one's mind; **hast du denn den ~ verloren?, bist du denn noch bei ~?** have you taken leave of your senses? (*esp Brit*), are you out of your mind?; **jdn um den ~ bringen** to drive sb out of his mind; **nicht recht** or **ganz bei ~ sein** not to be in one's right mind; **zu ~ kommen** to come to one's senses; **mit seinem ~ am Ende sein** to be at one's wits' end; **das geht über meinen ~** it's beyond me, it beats me (*inf*); **da steht einem der ~ still** (*fig inf*), **da bleibt einem der ~ stehen** (*fig inf*) the mind boggles (*inf*); **etw ohne ~ tun** to do sth mindlessly; **etw ohne ~ essen/trinken** to eat/drink sth without paying attention; **etw mit ~ genießen/essen/trinken** to savour (*Brit*) or savor (*US*) sth, to relish sth → **klar**

Ver|stan|des-: **Ver|stan|des|ehe** F marriage of convenience; **Ver|stan|des|kraft** F mental or intellectual faculties pl or powers pl; **ver|stan|des|mä|ßig** **ADJ** rational **ADV** rationally; **~ leuchtet mir das ein** it makes (rational) sense to me; **Ver|stan|des|mensch** M rational person; **Ver|stan|des|schär|fe** F acuteness or sharpness of mind or intellect

ver|stän|dig [fɛɐ̯ˈʃtɛndɪç] ADJ (= *vernünftig*) sensible; (= *einsichtig*) understanding

ver|stän|di|gen [fɛɐ̯ˈʃtɛndɪɡn̩] ptp **verständigt** **VT** to notify, to advise (*von* of, about) **VR** to communicate (with each other); (= *sich einigen*) to come to an understanding or agreement; **sich mit jdm ~** to communicate with sb

Ver|stän|di|gung F -, (rare) **-en** **a** (= *Benachrichtigung*) notification, advising **b** (= *das Sichverständigen*) communication no indef art; **die ~ am Telefon war schlecht** the (telephone) line was bad **c** (= *Einigung*) understanding, agreement

Ver|stän|di|gungs-: **Ver|stän|di|gungs|be|reit|schaft** F willingness or readiness to negotiate; **Ver|stän|di|gungs|mög|lich|keit** F (= *Gelegenheit*) opportunity or chance to communicate; (= *Verständigungsmittel*) means sing of communication; **Ver|stän|di|gungs|schwie|rig|kei|ten** PL communication difficulties pl; **Ver|stän|di|gungs|ver|such** M attempt at rapprochement

ver|ständ|lich [fɛɐ̯ˈʃtɛntlɪç] **ADJ** (= *begreiflich*) *Reaktion etc* understandable; (= *intellektuell erfassbar*) comprehensible; (= *hörbar*) audible; (= *klar*) *Erklärung, Ausdruck* intelligible; **allgemein ~** readily comprehensible; **eine schwer ~e Unterscheidung** a distinction that is difficult to grasp or understand; **jdm etw ~ machen** to make sb understand sth; **sich ~ machen** to make oneself understood; (= *sich klar ausdrücken*) to make oneself clear, to express oneself intelligibly; (*gegen Lärm*) to make oneself heard; **nicht ~** incomprehensible; inaudible; unintelligible **ADV** (= *hörbar*) clearly, audibly; (= *begreifbar*) clearly, comprehensibly

ver|ständ|li|cher|wei|se [fɛɐ̯ˈʃtɛntlɪçɐˈvaizə] ADV understandably (enough)

Ver|ständ|lich|keit F -, no pl comprehensibility; (= *Hörbarkeit*) audibility; (= *Klarheit: von Erklärung, Ausdruck*) intelligibility

Ver|ständ|nis [fɛɐ̯ˈʃtɛntnɪs] NT **-ses**, no pl **a** (= *das Begreifen*) understanding (*für* of), comprehension (*für* of); (= *Einfühlungsvermögen, Einsicht*) understanding (*für* for); (= *Mitgefühl*) sympathy (*für* for); **solche Grausamkeiten gehen über menschliches/mein ~** such cruelty is beyond human/my comprehension; **für etw ~ aufbringen** to show understanding or sympathy for sth; **für etw kein ~ haben** to have no understanding/sympathy for sth; (*für Probleme, Lage auch*) to have no feeling for sth; **für so was habe ich kein ~** I have no time for that kind of thing; **dafür hast du mein vollstes ~** you have my fullest sympathy; **wir bitten um Ihr ~** we apologize for any inconvenience **b** (= *intellektuelles Erfassen*) (*für* of) understanding, comprehension; **mit ~ lesen/zuhören** to read/listen with understanding **c** (= *Kunstverständnis etc*) appreciation (*für* of) **d** (= *Verständigung*) understanding

Ver|ständ|nis-: **ver|ständ|nis|in|nig** ADJ (*liter*) knowing attr, meaningful; **ver|ständ|nis|los** **ADJ** uncomprehending; *Gesicht, Blick auch* blank; (= *ohne Mitgefühl*) unsympathetic (*für* towards); (*für Kunst*) unappreciative (*für* of) **ADV** uncomprehendingly; (= *ohne Mitgefühl*) unsympathetically; (*gegenüber Kunst*) unappreciatively; **Ver|ständ|nis|lo|sig|keit** F -, no pl lack of understanding; (*in Gesichtsausdruck, Blick*) blankness; (= *Mangel an Mitgefühl*) lack of sympathy; (*gegenüber Kunst*) lack of appreciation; **ver|ständ|nis|voll** **ADJ** understanding; (= *mitfühlend auch*) sympathetic (*für* towards); *Blick* knowing no pred **ADV** understandingly; (= *mitfühlend auch*) sympathetically; **sie nickte ~ mit dem Kopf** she nodded her head understandingly; **sie gibt sich gern ~** she likes to seem sympathetic

ver|stän|kern ptp **verstänkert** VT (*inf*) *Zimmer* to stink out (*Brit inf*) or up (*US inf*); *Stadt* to pollute

ver|stär|ken ptp **verstärkt** **VT** *Eindruck, Truppen, Mannschaft, Präsenz* to reinforce; *Argumente, Mauer auch* to strengthen; *Spannung, Zweifel, Zusammenarbeit* to intensify, to increase; (*Chem*) to concentrate; (*Phot*) to intensify; (*Elec*) *Signal, Strom, Spannung* to boost, to amplify; *Stimme, Musik, Musikinstrument* to amplify **VR** (*fig*) to intensify; (= *sich vermehren*) to increase

Ver|stär|ker [fɛɐ̯ˈʃtɛrkɐ] M -s, - (*Rad, Elec*) amplifier; (*Telec*) repeater; (*von Signalen etc*) booster; (*Phot*) intensifier

Ver|stär|ker|röh|re F (*Elec*) amplifier valve

Ver|stär|kung F reinforcement; (*von Argumenten, Mauer auch*) strengthening; (*von Spannung, Zweifel*) intensification, increase; (*Chem*) concentration; (*Elec*) boosting, amplification; (*Mus*) amplification

ver|stau|ben ptp **verstaubt** VI aux sein to get dusty, to get covered in dust; (*Möbel, Bücher auch, fig*) to gather dust; **verstaubt** dusty, covered in dust; (*fig*) *Ideen, Ansichten* fuddy-duddy (*inf*)

ver|stau|chen ptp **verstaucht** VT to sprain; **sich** (*dat*) **die Hand/den Fuß** etc ~ to sprain one's hand/foot etc

Ver|stau|chung [fɛɐ̯ˈʃtauxʊŋ] F -, **-en** sprain; (= *das Verstauchen*) spraining

ver|stau|en ptp **verstaut** VT (*in +dat* in(to)) *Gepäck* to load, to pack; (*Naut*) to stow; (*hum*) *Menschen* to pile, to pack; **etw im Kofferraum ~** to load sth into the boot (*Brit*) or trunk (*US*)

Ver|steck [fɛɐ̯ˈʃtɛk] NT -(e)s, -e hiding place; (*von Verbrechern*) hide-out; **~ spielen** to play hide-and-seek (*Brit*) or hide-and-go-seek (*US*)

ver|ste|cken ptp **versteckt** **VT** to hide, to conceal (*vor* from) **VR** to hide, to conceal oneself;

sich vor jdm ~ to hide from sb; **sich vor** or **neben jdm ~ können/müssen** (*fig*) to be no match for sb; **sich (vor** or **neben jdm) nicht zu ~ brauchen** (*fig*) not to need to fear comparison (with sb); **sich hinter etw** (*dat*) **~** (*fig*, *hinter Pseudonym*) to write under sth; *hinter falschem Namen, Maske* to hide behind sth; *hinter Andeutungen* to be behind sth; **Verstecken spielen** to play hide-and-seek (*Brit*) or hide-and-go-seek (*US*)

Ver|steck|spiel NT (*lit, fig*) hide-and-seek (*Brit*), hide-and-go-seek (*US*)

ver|steckt [fɛɐ̯ˈʃtɛkt] ADJ **a** (*lit: = verborgen*) hidden; (= *nicht leicht sichtbar*) *Eingang, Tür, Winkel* concealed; (= *abgelegen*) *Ort* secret, hidden **b** (*fig*) *Lächeln, Blick* furtive; *Bemerkung, Andeutung* veiled; *Bedeutung* hidden, concealed

ver|ste|hen ✪ 33.3, 53.1, 53.5 ptp **verstanden** [fɛɐ̯ˈʃtandn̩] irreg **VTI** **a** (= *begreifen*) to understand; (= *einsehen*) to see, to understand; **jdn/etw falsch** or **nicht recht ~** to misunderstand sb/sth; **versteh mich recht** don't misunderstand me, don't get me wrong; **wenn ich recht verstehe ...** if I understand correctly ...; **jdm zu ~ geben, dass ...** to give sb to understand that ...; **ich gab ihm meinen Standpunkt zu ~** I intimated my point of view to him; **ein ~der Blick** a knowing look; **(ist das) verstanden?** (is that) understood? → **Bahnhof, Spaß** **b** (= *hören*) to hear, to understand → **Wort b** **VT** **a** (= *können, beherrschen*) to know; *Sprache* to understand, to know; **es ~, etw zu tun** to know how to do sth; **es mit Kindern ~** to be good with children, to have a way with children; **es mit seinen Kollegen ~** to know how to get on (*Brit*) or along with one's colleagues; **etwas/nichts von etw ~** to know something/nothing about sth; **etw machen, so gut man es versteht** to do sth to the best of one's ability, to do sth as well as one can → **Handwerk a** **b** (= *auslegen*) to understand, to interpret, to see; **etw unter etw** (*dat*) **~** to understand sth by sth; **wie soll ich das ~?** how am I supposed to take that?; **das ist bildlich** or **nicht wörtlich zu ~** that isn't to be taken literally **VR** **a** (= *kommunizieren können*) to understand each other **b** (= *miteinander auskommen*) to get on (*Brit*) or along (with each other or together); **sich mit jdm ~** to get on (*Brit*) or along with sb; **wir ~ uns (schon)** (= *sind einer Meinung*) we understand each other **c** (= *klar sein*) to go without saying; **versteht sich!** (*inf*) of course!, naturally!; **das versteht sich von selbst** that goes without saying **d** (= *auffassen*) **sich als etw ~** (*Mensch*) to think of or see oneself as sth **e** (= *können*) **sich auf etw** (*acc*) **~** to be (an) expert at sth, to be a dab hand at sth (*Brit inf*), to be very good at sth **f** (= *einverstanden sein*) **sich zu etw ~** (*form*) to agree to sth **g** (*Comm*) to be; **die Preise ~ sich einschließlich Lieferung** prices are inclusive of delivery

ver|stei|fen ptp **versteift** **VT** to strengthen, to reinforce; (*Tech*) to strut; (*Comm*) to tighten; (*Sew*) to stiffen **VR** to stiffen up; (*fig*) (*Haltung, Gegensätze*) to harden; (*Maßnahmen*) to tighten (up); **sich auf etw** (*acc*) **~** (*fig*) to become set on sth; **er hat sich darauf versteift** he is set on it

Ver|stei|fung [fɛɐ̯ˈʃtaifʊŋ] F -, **-en** **a** no pl strengthening, reinforcement; (*Tech*) strutting; (*Sew*) stiffening **b** (= *Verstärkung*) stiffener **c** (*Med*) stiffening no pl **d** (*fig*) (*von Haltung*) hardening; (*von Maßnahmen*) tightening (up); (*von Gegensätzen*) increasing intractability

ver|stei|gen ptp **verstiegen** VR irreg (*lit*) to get into difficulties (while climbing); **er hat sich zu der Behauptung verstiegen, dass ...** he presumed to claim that ...; **er verstieg sich zu völlig übertriebenen Forderungen** he had the presumption to make quite excessive demands → *auch* **versteigen**

---

ver|stei|gern *ptp* **versteigert** VT to auction (off); **etw ~ lassen** to put sth up for auction

Ver|stei|ge|rung F (sale by) auction; **zur ~ kommen** to be put up for auction

ver|stei|nern [fɛɐ'ʃtainɐn] *ptp* **versteinert** VI *aux sein* (*Geol*) (*Pflanzen, Tiere*) to fossilize; (*Holz*) to petrify; (*fig: Miene*) to harden; **versteinerte Pflanzen/Tiere** fossilized plants/animals; **wie versteinert (da)stehen** to stand there petrified VR (*fig*) (*Miene, Gesicht*) to harden; (*Lächeln*) to become fixed *or* set

Ver|stei|ne|rung F -, -en (*Vorgang*) fossilization; (*von Holz*) petrifaction, petrification; (= *versteinertes Tier etc*) fossil; (*fig: von Miene*) hardening

ver|stell|bar ADJ adjustable; **in der Höhe ~** adjustable for height

Ver|stell|bar|keit [fɛɐ'ʃtɛlbaːɐkait] F -, *no pl* adjustability

ver|stel|len *ptp* **verstellt** VT **a** (= *anders einstellen, regulieren*) to adjust; *Signal, Zahlen* to alter, to change; *Möbel, Gegenstände* to move *or* shift (out of position *or* place); (= *in Unordnung bringen*) to put in the wrong place, to misplace; (= *falsch einstellen*) to adjust wrongly; *Radio* to alter the tuning of; *Uhr* to put (*Brit*) *or* set wrong **b** *Stimme* to disguise **c** (= *versperren*) to block, to obstruct; (= *vollstellen*) *Zimmer* to clutter up; **das verstellt den Blick auf das Wesentliche** that obscures one's view of the essential VR to move (out of position); (*fig*) to act *or* play a part; (= *Gefühle verbergen*) to hide one's (true) feelings; **er kann sich gut ~** he's good at playing *or* acting a part

Ver|stel|lung F **a** (= *Regulierung*) adjustment; (*von Signal, Zahlen*) alteration; (*von Möbeln, Gegenständen*) moving *or* shifting (out of position) *no indef art* **b** (*von Stimme*) disguise **c** (*Versperrung*) blockage, obstruction **d** (= *Vortäuschung*) pretending, feigning

ver|step|pen [fɛɐ'ʃtɛpn] *ptp* **versteppt** VTI to turn into desert

Ver|step|pung F -, -en desertification

ver|ster|ben ✪ 51.4 *ptp* **verstorben** [fɛɐ'ʃtɔrbn] VI *irreg aux sein* to die, to pass away *or* on → *auch* **versterben**

ver|steu|er|bar ADJ taxable

ver|steu|ern *ptp* **versteuert** VT to pay tax on; **versteuerte Waren** taxed goods; **das versteuerte Einkommen** taxed income; **das zu ~de Einkommen** taxable income

Ver|steu|e|rung F taxation

ver|stie|gen [fɛɐ'ʃtiːgn] ADJ (*fig: = überspannt*) extravagant, fantastic; *Pläne, Ideen auch* highflown → *auch* **versteigen**

Ver|stie|gen|heit F -, -en extravagance

ver|stim|men *ptp* **verstimmt** VT (*lit*) to put out of tune; (*fig*) to put out, to disgruntle

ver|stimmt [fɛɐ'ʃtɪmt] ADJ *Klavier etc* out of tune; (*fig*) (= *verdorben*) *Magen* upset; (= *verärgert*) put out, disgruntled

Ver|stim|mung F disgruntlement; (*zwischen Parteien*) ill feeling, ill will

ver|stockt [fɛɐ'ʃtɔkt] ADJ *Kind, Wesen* obstinate, stubborn; *Sünder* unrepentant, unrepenting

Ver|stockt|heit F -, *no pl* (*von Kind, Wesen*) obstinacy, stubbornness

ver|stoh|len [fɛɐ'ʃtoːlən] ADJ furtive, surreptitious ADV furtively, surreptitiously

ver|stop|fen *ptp* **verstopft** VT to stop up; *Ohren auch* to plug; *Ausguss auch* to block (up); *Straße* to block, to jam; *Blutgefäß* to block

ver|stopft [fɛɐ'ʃtɔpft] ADJ blocked; *Straßen auch* jammed; *Nase* stuffed up, blocked (up); *Mensch* constipated

Ver|stop|fung F -, -en blockage; (= *Verkehrsstauung*) jam; (*Med*) constipation

verstorben [fɛɐ'ʃtɔrbn] ADJ deceased; **mein ~er Mann** my late husband; **eine 1995 ~e Frau** a woman who died in 1995 → *auch* **versterben**

Ver|stor|be|ne(r) [fɛɐ'ʃtɔrbənə] MF *decl as adj* deceased

ver|stö|ren *ptp* **verstört** VT to disturb

ver|stört [fɛɐ'ʃtøːɐt] ADJ disturbed; (*vor Angst*) distraught ADV in a disturbed way; (*vor Angst*) in a distraught way

Ver|stört|heit F -, *no pl* disturbed state; (*vor Angst*) distraction; (= *Verwirrung*) confusion

Ver|stoß M violation (*gegen* of); (*gegen Gesetz auch*) offence (*Brit*), offense (*US*)

ver|sto|ßen *ptp* **verstoßen** *irreg* VT *jdn* to disown, to repudiate; **jdn aus einem Verein/einer Gruppe ~** to expel sb from a club/group, to throw sb out of a club/group VI **gegen etw ~** to offend against sth; *gegen Gesetz, Regel auch* to contravene sth

Ver|sto|ße|ne(r) [fɛɐ'ʃtoːsənə] MF *decl as adj* outcast

ver|strah|len *ptp* **verstrahlt** VT **a** *Licht, Wärme* to give off **b** (*radioaktiv*) to expose to radiation; *Gebäude, Gebiet* to make (highly) radioactive

ver|strahlt [fɛɐ'ʃtraːlt] ADJ contaminated (by radiation); **lebensgefährlich ~ sein** to have had a potentially lethal dose of radiation

Ver|strah|lung F radiation

ver|stre|ben *ptp* **verstrebt** VT to brace, to strut

Ver|stre|bung F supporting *no pl*, (= *Strebebalken*) support(ing beam)

ver|strei|chen *ptp* **verstrichen** [fɛɐ'ʃtrɪçn] *irreg* VT *Salbe, Farbe* to use up, to apply (*auf +dat* to); *Butter etc* to spread (*auf +dat* on); *Riss* to fill (in); (= *verbrauchen*) to use VI *aux sein* (*Zeit*) to pass (by), to elapse; (*Frist, Ultimatum*) to expire

ver|streu|en *ptp* **verstreut** VT to scatter; (*versehentlich*) to spill; **seine Kleider/Spielsachen im ganzen Zimmer ~** to scatter *or* strew one's clothes/toys over the (whole) room

ver|stri|cken *ptp* **verstrickt** VT **a** *Wolle* to use **b** (*fig*) to involve, to embroil, to mix up; **in eine Angelegenheit verstrickt sein** to be mixed up *or* involved *or* embroiled in an affair VR **a** (*Wolle*) to knit (up) **b** (*fig*) to become entangled, to get tangled up

Ver|stri|ckung F -, -en (*fig*) entanglement

ver|stro|men *ptp* **verstromt** VT *Kohle* to convert into electricity

ver|strö|men *ptp* **verströmt** VT (*lit, fig*) to exude; (*liter*) *sein Blut* to shed

Ver|stro|mung -, -en F (*von Kohle*) conversion into electricity

ver|strub|beln [fɛɐ'ʃtrʊbln] *ptp* **verstrubbelt** VT *jdm die Haare ~* to muss up *or* tousle sb's hair; (*beim Fönen*) to ruffle sb's hair

ver|stüm|meln [fɛɐ'ʃtʏmln] *ptp* **verstümmelt** VT to mutilate, to maim; (*fig*) *Nachricht, Bericht* to garble, to distort; *Namen* to mutilate; **sich selbst ~** to mutilate oneself

Ver|stüm|me|lung F -, -en mutilation; (*von Nachricht, Bericht*) garbling *no pl*, distortion

ver|stum|men [fɛɐ'ʃtʊmən] *ptp* **verstummt** VI *aux sein* (*Mensch*) to go *or* fall silent, to stop talking; (*Geräusch, Gespräch, Musik, Beifall*) to cease, to stop; (*Wind, Glocken, Instrumente*) to become silent *or* still (*liter*); (= *langsam verklingen*) to die away; (*fig*) (*Kritik, Stimmen der Opposition*) to become silent *or* still; (= *sich langsam legen*) to subside; (*Gerüchte*) to subside; **jdn/etw ~ lassen** *or* **zum Verstummen bringen** to silence sb/sth; **vor Entsetzen ~** to be struck dumb with terror, to be speechless with terror

Ver|such [fɛɐ'zuːx] M -(e)s, -e attempt (*zu tun* at doing, to do); (*wissenschaftlich*) experiment, test; (= *Test*) trial, test; (= *Essay*) essay; (*Rugby*) try; **einen ~ machen** to make an attempt; to do *or* carry out an experiment/a trial; **mit jdm/etw ei-**

nen ~ machen to give sb/sth a try *or* trial; (*Forscher*) to do a trial/an experiment with sb/sth; **das käme auf einen ~ an** we'll have to (have a) try; **sie unternahm den ~, ihn umzustimmen** she made an attempt at changing *or* to change his mind, she had a try at changing his mind (*esp Brit*); **wir sollten es auf einen ~ ankommen lassen** we should give it a try; **das wollen wir doch auf einen ~ ankommen lassen!** we'll see about that!

ver|su|chen ✪ 27.3, 27.4, 45.4 *ptp* **versucht** VT **a** *auch vi* (= *probieren, kosten*) to try; (= *sich bemühen*) to attempt, to try; **es mit etw ~** to try sth; **versuchs doch!** try, have a try (*esp Brit*); **es mit jdm ~** to give sb a try; **versuchter Mord/Diebstahl** attempted murder/theft **b** (= *in Versuchung führen*) to tempt; **sich versucht fühlen** to feel tempted; **versucht sein** to be tempted VR **sich an** *or* **in etw** (*dat*) **~** to try one's hand at sth

Ver|su|cher M tempter; **der ~** (*Rel*) the Tempter

Ver|su|che|rin F temptress

Ver|suchs-: **Ver|suchs|ab|tei|lung** F experimental department; **Ver|suchs|an|la|ge** F experimental plant; **Ver|suchs|an|ord|nung** F test arrangement; **Ver|suchs|an|stalt** F research institute; **Ver|suchs|bal|lon** M sounding balloon; **einen ~ steigen lassen, es mit einem ~ probieren** (*fig*) to fly a kite; **Ver|suchs|be|din|gun|gen** PL test conditions *pl*; **Ver|suchs|boh|rung** F experimental drilling; **Ver|suchs|ge|län|de** NT test *or* testing site; **Ver|suchs|ka|nin|chen** NT (*lit*) laboratory rabbit; (*fig*) guinea pig; **Ver|suchs|la|bor** NT experimental lab(oratory); **Ver|suchs|ob|jekt** NT test object; (*fig: Mensch*) guinea pig; **Ver|suchs|per|son** F test *or* experimental subject; **Ver|suchs|rei|he** F series *sing* of experiments; **Ver|suchs|sta|di|um** NT experimental stage; **Ver|suchs|stre|cke** F test track; **Ver|suchs|tier** NT laboratory animal; **ver|suchs|wei|se** ADV as a trial, on a trial basis; *einstellen, engagieren* on probation, on trial; **Ver|suchs|zweck** M **zu ~en** *pl* for experimental purposes *pl*

Ver|su|chung [fɛɐ'zuː:xʊŋ] F -, -en temptation (*auch Rel*); **jdn in ~ führen** to lead sb into temptation; **und führe uns nicht in ~** (*Bibl*) and lead us not into temptation (*Bibl*); **in ~ geraten** *or* **kommen** to be tempted

ver|su|deln *ptp* **versudelt** VT to scribble on

ver|sump|fen *ptp* **versumpft** VI *aux sein* **a** (*Gebiet*) to become marshy *or* boggy **b** (*fig inf*) (= *verwahrlosen*) to go to pot (*inf*); (= *lange zechen*) to get involved in a booze-up (*inf*)

Ver|sump|fung F -, -en (*lit*) increasing marshiness

ver|sün|di|gen *ptp* **versündigt** VR (*geh*) **sich an jdm/etw ~** to sin against sb/sth; **sich an seiner Gesundheit ~** to abuse one's health

Ver|sün|di|gung [fɛɐ'zʏndɪgʊŋ] F -, -en sin (*an +dat* against); **eine ~ an der Gesundheit** an abuse of one's health

ver|sun|ken [fɛɐ'zʊŋkn] ADJ sunken, submerged; *Kultur* submerged; (*fig*) engrossed, absorbed; **in Gedanken ~** lost *or* immersed in thought; **völlig in diesen Anblick ~** completely lost in *or* caught up in this sight → *auch* **versinken**

Ver|sun|ken|heit F -, *no pl* (*fig*) **jdn aus seiner ~ reißen** to tear sb from his (immersion in his) book/thoughts *etc*; **seine ~ in diesen Anblick** his rapt contemplation of this sight

ver|sü|ßen *ptp* **versüßt** VT (*fig*) to sweeten; **jdm etw ~** to sweeten sth for sb → **Pille**

ver|tä|feln *ptp* **vertäfelt** VT to panel

Ver|tä|fe|lung F panelling *no pl*, *no indef art*

ver|ta|gen *ptp* **vertagt** VTI to adjourn; (= *verschieben*) to postpone, to defer (*auf +acc* until, till); (*Parl*) to adjourn, to prorogue (*form*) VR to be adjourned, to adjourn

Ver|ta|gung F adjournment; (= *Verschiebung auf später*) postponement; (*Parl*) prorogation (*form*)

ver|tän|deln ptp **vertändelt** VT (*geh*) to fritter away, to squander

ver|täu|en [fɛɐ̯ˈtɔyən] ptp **vertäut** VT (*Naut*) to moor

ver|tausch|bar ADJ exchangeable (*gegen* for); (*miteinander*) interchangeable

ver|tau|schen ptp **vertauscht** VT **a** (= *austauschen*) to exchange (*gegen, mit* for); (*miteinander*) to interchange; *Auto, Plätze* to change (*gegen, mit* for); (*Elec*) *Pole* to transpose; **vertauschte Rollen** reversed roles **b** (= *verwechseln*) to mix up; **seinen Mantel mit einem anderen ~** to mistake another coat for one's own, to mix one's coat up with another

Ver|tau|schung [fɛɐ̯ˈtauʃʊŋ] F -, -en **a** (= *Austausch*) exchange; (*von Auto, von Plätzen*) changing *no pl*; (*Elec: von Polen*) transposition **b** (= *Verwechslung*) mix-up; (= *das Vertauschen*) mixing up

Ver|täu|ung F -, -en (= *das Vertäuen*) mooring; (= *die Taue*) moorings *pl*

ver|tei|di|gen [fɛɐ̯ˈtaidɪgn̩] ptp **verteidigt** VT to defend VR to defend oneself (*auch Sport*); **sich selbst ~** (*vor Gericht*) to conduct one's own defence (*Brit*) or defense (*US*) ◊ VI (*Sport*) to defend; (= *als Verteidiger spielen*) to be a defender, to play as a defender; (= *defensiv spielen*) to play a defensive game, to play defensively

Ver|tei|di|ger [fɛɐ̯ˈtaidɪgɐ] M -s, -, **Ver|tei|di|ge|rin** [-ərɪn] F -, -nen defender (*auch Sport*); (= *Fürsprecher auch*) advocate; (= *Anwalt*) defence (*Brit*) or defense (*US*) lawyer; **der ~ des Angeklagten** the counsel for the defence (*Brit*) or defense (*US*), the defence (*Brit*) or defense (*US*) counsel

Ver|tei|di|gung F -, -en (*alle Bedeutungen*) defence (*Brit*), defense (*US*); **zur ~** von *or* gen in defence (*Brit*) or defense (*US*) of; **zu ihrer/seiner eigenen ~** in her/one's own defence (*Brit*) or defense (*US*); **er ist immer zur ~ seiner Meinung bereit** he is always ready to defend his opinion

Ver|tei|di|gungs- *in cpds* defence (*Brit*), defense (*US*); **Ver|tei|di|gungs|bei|trag** M defence contribution; **Ver|tei|di|gungs|bünd|nis** NT defence alliance; **ver|tei|di|gungs|fä|hig** ADJ able to defend itself/oneself; **Ver|tei|di|gungs|fä|hig|keit** F defensive capability; **Ver|tei|di|gungs|fall** M wenn **der ~ eintritt** if defence should be necessary; **Ver|tei|di|gungs|ge|mein|schaft** F defence community; **Ver|tei|di|gungs|ini|tia|ti|ve** F defence initiative; **Ver|tei|di|gungs|krieg** M defensive war; **Ver|tei|di|gungs|li|nie** F line of defence (*Brit*) or defense (*US*); (*Sport*) defence (*Brit*) or defense (*US*) line; **Ver|tei|di|gungs|minis|ter(in)** M(F) Minister of Defence (*Brit*), Secretary of Defense (*US*); **Ver|tei|di|gungs|mi|nis|te|ri|um** NT Ministry of Defence (*Brit*), Department of Defense (*US*); **Ver|tei|di|gungs|re|de** F (*Jur*) speech for the defence; (*fig*) apologia; **Ver|tei|di|gungs|schlacht** F defensive battle; **Ver|tei|di|gungs|schrift** F (*Jur*) (written) defence statement; (*fig*) apologia; **Ver|tei|di|gungs|spie|ler(in)** M(F) defender; **Ver|tei|di|gungs|stel|lung** F defensive position; **in ~ gehen** to adopt a defensive position; **Ver|tei|di|gungs|sys|tem** NT defence system, defences *pl*; **das ~ der Nato** the Nato defence system; **ver|tei|di|gungs|un|fä|hig** ADJ defenceless (*Brit*), defenseless (*US*); **Ver|tei|di|gungs|waf|fe** F defensive weapon; **Ver|tei|di|gungs|wil|le** M spirit of resistance; **Ver|tei|di|gungs|zu|stand** M defence alert; **im ~ sein** in a defence alert; **im ~ sein** on the defence alert; **Ver|tei|di|gungs|zweck** M **für ~e, zu ~en** for defence purposes, for purposes of defence

ver|tei|len ptp **verteilt** VT **a** (= *austeilen*) (*an* +acc to) (*unter* +acc among) to distribute; *Flugblätter* to hand out, to distribute; *Süßigkeiten etc*

---

to share out; *Preise auch* to give out; *Essen* to dish out; (*Theat*) *Rollen* to allot, to allocate

  b (= *anordnen, aufteilen*) to distribute; *Investitionen, soziale Lasten* to spread (*über* +acc over); (*Mil*) to deploy; (= *verstreuen*) to spread out; (= *streichen*) *Aufstrich, Farbe etc* to spread; (= *streuen*) *Sand, Zucker, Puder* to sprinkle; **Blumen im Zimmer/auf verschiedene Vasen ~** to arrange flowers around the room/in different vases; **verteilte Datenbank** (*Comput*) distributed database

  VR (*Zuschauer, Polizisten etc*) to spread (themselves) out; (*Bevölkerung*) to spread (itself) out; (*Farbe, Wasser*) to spread (itself) out; (*Med: Bakterien, Metastasen*) to spread; (*Reichtum etc*) to be spread *or* distributed; (*zeitlich*) to be spread (*über* +acc over); **auf dem ganzen Platz verteilt** spread out over the square; **übers ganze Land verteilt** spread throughout the country

Ver|tei|ler¹ [fɛɐ̯ˈtailɐ] M -s, - **a** (*Tech*) distributor **b** (= *Verteilerschlüssel*) distribution list

Ver|tei|ler² [fɛɐ̯ˈtailɐ] M -s, -, **Ver|tei|le|rin** [-ərɪn] F -, -nen (*Comm*) distributor

Ver|tei|ler-: Ver|tei|ler|de|ckel M distributor cap; **Ver|tei|ler|do|se** F (*Elec*) junction box; **Ver|tei|ler|kas|ten** M (*Elec*) distribution box; **Ver|tei|ler|kopf** M (*Aut*) distributor head; **Ver|tei|ler|netz** NT (*Elec*) distribution system; (*Comm*) distribution network; **Ver|tei|ler|schlüs|sel** M distribution list

Ver|tei|lung F distribution; (= *Zuteilung*) allocation; (*Mil*) deployment; (*Theat*) casting

Ver|tei|lungs|kampf M **einen ~ um etw führen** to battle for a share of sth

ver|te|le|fo|nie|ren ptp **vertelefoniert** VT (*inf*) *Geld, Zeit* to spend on the phone

ver|tel|len [fɛɐ̯ˈtɛlən] ptp **vertellt** VT (*N Ger inf*) to tell; *Unsinn* to talk

ver|teu|ern [fɛɐ̯ˈtɔyɐn] ptp **verteuert** VT to make more expensive, to increase *or* raise the price of VR to become more expensive, to increase in price, to go up in price

Ver|teu|e|rung F rise *or* increase in price

ver|teu|feln [fɛɐ̯ˈtɔyfln̩] ptp **verteufelt** VT to condemn

ver|teu|felt [fɛɐ̯ˈtɔyflt] (*inf*) ADJ *Lage, Angelegenheit* devilish (*dated inf*), tricky, awkward; **~es Glück haben** to be damned *or* darned *or* deuced (*dated*) lucky (*inf*) ADV (*mit adj*) damned (*inf*), darned (*inf*), deuced (*dated inf*), devilish (*dated inf*); (*mit vb*) a lot

Ver|teu|fe|lung F -, -en condemnation

ver|tie|fen [fɛɐ̯ˈtiːfn̩] ptp **vertieft** VT *Graben, Loch etc* to deepen; (*fig*) *Eindruck auch* to heighten; *Kenntnis, Wissen* to extend; *Zusammenarbeit* to intensify; *Kontakte* to strengthen; (*Sch*) *Unterrichtsstoff* to consolidate, to reinforce; (*Mus*) to flatten VR (*lit, fig*) to deepen; (*fig: Lehrstoff*) to be consolidated *or* reinforced; **sich in etw** (*acc*) **~** (*fig*) to become engrossed *or* absorbed in sth; **in etw** (*acc*) **vertieft sein** (*fig*) to be engrossed *or* absorbed in sth → **Gedanke**

Ver|tie|fung F -, -en **a** (= *das Vertiefen*) deepening; (*von Eindruck*) heightening, deepening; (*von Kenntnissen, Wissen*) extension, deepening; (*von Unterrichtsstoff*) consolidation, reinforcement; (*Mus*) flattening **b** (*in Oberfläche*) depression **c** (= *Vertieftsein*) engrossment, absorption

ver|ti|kal [vɛrtiˈkaːl] ADJ vertical ADV vertically

Ver|ti|ka|le [vɛrtiˈkaːlə] F -, -n vertical line; **in der ~n** vertically, in a vertical plane

Ver|ti|ko [ˈvɛrtiko] NT -s, -s *small two-door chest with a drawer and display shelf at the top*, ≈ hutch (*US*)

Ver|ti|ku|tie|rer [vɛrtikuˈtiːrɐ] M -s, - aerator

ver|til|gen ptp **vertilgt** VT **a** *Unkraut etc* to destroy, to eradicate, to kill off; *Ungeziefer* to exterminate, to destroy **b** (*inf.* = *aufessen*) to demolish (*inf*), to polish off (*inf*)

Ver|til|gung F (*von Unkraut*) destruction, eradication; (*von Ungeziefer*) extermination

---

Ver|til|gungs|mit|tel NT weedkiller; (= *Insektenvertilgungsmittel*) pesticide

ver|tip|pen ptp **vertippt** (*inf*) VR **a** (*beim Schreiben*) to make a typo (*inf*) or a typing error **b** (*beim Lotto, Toto etc*) to slip up (*inf*) VT to mistype, to type wrongly

ver|to|nen ptp **vertont** VT to set to music; *Theaterstück auch* to make a musical version of; *Film etc* to add a soundtrack to

ver|tö|nen ptp **vertönt** VI *aux sein* to fade *or* die away

Ver|to|nung [fɛɐ̯ˈtoːnʊŋ] F -, -en (= *das Vertonen*) setting (to music); (*von Film*) adding a soundtrack (+gen to); (= *vertonte Fassung*) musical version

ver|tor|fen [fɛɐ̯ˈtɔrfn̩] ptp **vertorft** VI *aux sein* to turn into peat

Ver|tor|fung F -, -en conversion into peat

ver|trackt [fɛɐ̯ˈtrakt] ADJ (*inf*) awkward, tricky; (= *verwickelt*) complicated, complex

Ver|trackt|heit F -, (*rare*) -en (*inf*) awkwardness, trickiness; (= *Verwickeltheit*) complexity

Ver|trag [fɛɐ̯ˈtraːk] M -(e)s, ⸚e [ˈtrɛːgə] contract; (= *Abkommen*) agreement; (*Pol:* = *Friedensvertrag*) treaty; **mündlicher ~** verbal or oral agreement; **laut ~** under the terms of the contract; **jdn unter ~ nehmen** to contract sb; **(bei jdm) unter ~ stehen** to be under contract (to sb)

ver|tra|gen ptp **vertragen** irreg VT **a** to take; (= *aushalten*) to stand, to take; (*viel*) to tolerate, to endure, to stand for; **Eier vertrage ich nicht** *or* **kann ich nicht ~** I can't take eggs, eggs don't agree with me; **ein Automotor, der viel verträgt** an engine that can stand (up to) a lot *or* can take a lot; **Kontaktlinsen/synthetische Stoffe vertrage ich nicht** *or* **kann ich nicht ~** I can't wear contact lenses/synthetics; **Patienten, die kein Penizillin ~** patients who are allergic to penicillin; **so etwas kann ich nicht ~** I can't stand that kind of thing; **er verträgt keinen Spaß** he can't take a joke; **viel ~ können** (*inf: Alkohol*) to be able to hold one's drink (*Brit*) or liquor (*US*); **er verträgt nichts** (*inf: Alkohol*) he can't take his drink (*Brit*) or liquor (*US*); **jd/ etw könnte etw ~** (*inf*) sb/sth could do with sth **b** (*dial*) *Kleider* to wear out; **~ sein** to be (well) worn

  c (*Sw*) to deliver

  VR **sich (mit jdm) ~** to get on *or* along (with sb); **sich wieder ~** to be friends again; **sich mit etw ~** (*Nahrungsmittel, Farbe*) to go with sth; (*Aussage, Verhalten*) to be consistent with sth; **diese Farben ~ sich nicht** these colours (*Brit*) or colors (*US*) don't go together; **diese Aussagen ~ sich nicht** these statements are inconsistent *or* not consistent

Ver|trä|ger(in) M(F) (*Sw*) delivery man/woman; (= *Zeitungsverträger*) paper boy/girl/man/-woman

ver|trag|lich [fɛɐ̯ˈtraːklɪç] ADJ contractual ADV by contract; *festgelegt* in the/a contract; **ein ~ zugesichertes Recht** a contractual right

ver|träg|lich [fɛɐ̯ˈtrɛːklɪç] ADJ (= *friedlich, umgänglich*) good-natured; *Speise* digestible; (= *bekömmlich*) wholesome; (*Med*) well tolerated (*für* by); **gut ~** easily digestible; (*Med*) well tolerated; **ökologisch/sozial ~** ecologically/socially acceptable

Ver|träg|lich|keit F -, *no pl* (= *Friedlichkeit, Umgänglichkeit*) good nature; (*von Speise*) digestibility; (= *Bekömmlichkeit*) wholesomeness; **die ~ dieses Medikaments** the fact that this medicine is well tolerated; **ökologische/soziale ~** ecological/social acceptability

Ver|trags-: Ver|trags|ab|schluss ▲ M conclusion of a/the contract; **Ver|trags|ar|bei|ter(in)** M(F) (*im ehemaligen Ostblock*) contract worker; **Ver|trags|be|din|gung** F condition of a/the contract; **~en** *pl* (*auch*) terms *pl* of a/the contract; **Ver|trags|bruch** M → **Vertrag** breach of contract; breaking of an/the agreement; breaking of a/the treaty; **ver|trags|brü|chig** ADJ → **Vertrag** who is in breach of contract; who has broken an/the agreement; who has broken a/the treaty; ~ **werden** to be in breach of contract; to break an/the agreement; to break a/the treaty; **Ver|trags|dau|er** F term of a/the contract; **Ver|trags|ent|wurf** M → **Vertrag** draft contract/agreement/treaty; **Ver|trags|gast|stät|te** F tied house; **Ver|trags|ge|gen|stand** M → **Vertrag** object of the contract/agreement/treaty; **ver|trags|ge|mäß** → **Vertrag** ADJ (as) stipulated in the contract/agreement/treaty ADV as stipulated in the contract/agreement/treaty; **Ver|trags|ha|fen** M treaty port; **Ver|trags|händ|ler(in)** M(F) concessionary, appointed retailer; **Ver|trags|klau|sel** F contract clause; **Ver|trags|part|ner(in)** M(F) → **Vertrag** party to a/the contract/agreement/treaty; **ver|trags|schlie|ßend** ADJ contracting; **Ver|trags|spie|ler(in)** M(F) player under contract; **Ver|trags|stra|fe** F penalty for breach of contract; **Ver|trags|ur|kun|de** F deed, indenture; **Ver|trags|ver|län|ge|rung** F extension or renewal of a/the contract; **Ver|trags|ver|let|zung** F → **Vertrag** breach of contract; infringement of the agreement/treaty; **Ver|trags|werk** NT contract; (Pol) treaty; **Ver|trags|werk|stät|te** F authorized repair shop; **ver|trags|wid|rig** → **Vertrag** ADJ contrary to (the terms of) the contract/agreement/treaty ADV in breach of contract/the agreement/the treaty

ver|trau|en ptp **vertraut** VI jdm/einer Sache ~ to trust sb/sth, to have trust in sb/sth; **auf jdn/etw** ~ to trust in sb/sth; **auf sein Glück** ~ to trust to luck; **sich** (dat) **selbst** ~ to have confidence in oneself → auch **vertraut**

Ver|trau|en [fɛɐ'trauən] NT -s, no pl trust, confidence (zu, in +acc, auf +acc in); (Pol) confidence; **voll** ~ full of confidence; **im ~ (gesagt)** strictly in confidence; **ich habe dir das im ~ gesagt** that's strictly in confidence, that's strictly between you and me; **im ~ auf etw** (acc) trusting in sth; **im ~ darauf, dass ...** confident that ..., in the confidence that ...; **ein ~ erweckender Mensch/Arzt** etc a person/doctor etc who inspires confidence; **einen ~ erweckenden Eindruck machen, ~ erweckend aussehen** to inspire confidence; **~ zu jdm fassen** to gain confidence in sb; **jdn ins ~ ziehen** to take sb into one's confidence; **jdm das ~ aussprechen/entziehen** (Parl) to pass a vote of confidence/no confidence in sb

ver|trau|en|er|we|ckend △ ADJ → **Vertrauen**

Ver|trau|ens-: **Ver|trau|ens|an|trag** M (Pol) motion of no confidence, no-confidence motion; **Ver|trau|ens|arzt** M , **Ver|trau|ens|ärz|tin** F doctor who examines patients signed off sick for a lengthy period by their private doctor; **Ver|trau|ens|be|weis** M vote of confidence; **ver|trau|ens|bil|dend** ADJ confidence-building; **Ver|trau|ens|bil|dung** F confidence building; **Ver|trau|ens|bruch** M breach of confidence or trust; **Ver|trau|ens|fra|ge** F question or matter of trust; **die ~ stel|len** (Parl) to ask for a vote of confidence; **Ver|trau|ens|frau** F → **Vertrauensmann**; **Ver|trau|ens|leh|rer(in)** M(F) liaison teacher (between pupils and staff); **Ver|trau|ens|mann** M pl **-leute** or **-männer** intermediary agent; (in Gewerkschaft) (union) negotiator or representative; **Ver|trau|ens|per|son** F someone to confide in, confidant(e); **Ver|trau|ens|pos|ten** M position of trust; **Ver|trau|ens|sa|che** F (= vertrauliche Angelegenheit) confidential matter; (= Frage des Vertrauens) question or matter of trust; **Ver|trau|ens|schwund** M loss of confidence; **ver|trau|ens|se|lig** ADJ trusting; (= leichtgläubig auch) credulous; **Ver|trau|ens|se|lig|keit** F trustfulness; (= Leichtgläubigkeit auch) credulity; **Ver|trau|ens|stel|lung** F position of trust; **Ver|trau|ens|ver|hält|nis** NT mutual trust no indef art; **persönliches ~** relationship of personal trust; **Ver|trau|ens|ver|lust** M loss of

confidence; **ver|trau|ens|voll** ADJ trusting ADV trustingly, confidently; **wende dich ~ an mich** you know you can always turn to me (for help); **Ver|trau|ens|vor|schuss** ▲ M trust; **ver|trau|ens|vo|tum** NT (Parl) vote of confidence; **ver|trau|ens|wür|dig** ADJ trustworthy; **Ver|trau|ens|wür|dig|keit** F trustworthiness

ver|trau|ern ptp **vertrauert** VT to spend (in) moping, to mope away

ver|trau|lich [fɛɐ'traulɪç] ADJ **a** (= geheim) Angelegenheit, Ton, Gespräch, Schriftstück, Daten confidential **b** (= freundschaftlich) friendly, matey (Brit inf), pally (Brit inf), buddy-buddy (esp US inf); (= plumpvertraulich) familiar; **~ werden** to take liberties ADV **a** confidentially, in confidence **b** in a friendly/familiar way

ver|trau|lich|keit F -, -en confidentiality; (= vertrauliche Mitteilung) confidence; (= Aufdringlichkeit) familiarity; **mit aller ~** in strict(est) confidence; **plumpe/dreiste** ~ familiarity

ver|träu|men ptp **verträumt** VT to dream away

ver|träumt [fɛɐ'trɔʏmt] ADJ dreamy; (= idyllisch) Städtchen etc auch sleepy

ver|traut [fɛɐ'traut] ✪ 46.2 ADJ intimate; Freund auch close; (= bekannt) Gesicht, Umgebung familiar, well-known; **ein ~er Freund** a close friend, an intimate friend; **sich mit etw ~ machen** to familiarize or acquaint oneself with sth; **sich mit dem Gedanken ~ machen, dass ...** to get used to the idea that ...; **mit etw ~ sein** to be familiar or well acquainted with sth; **mit jdm ~ werden** to become friendly with sb; **mit jdm sehr ~ werden** to get on intimate terms with sb, to become close friends with sb → auch **vertrauen**

Ver|trau|te(r) [fɛɐ'trautə] MF decl as adj close or intimate friend; (Mann auch) confidant; (Frau auch) confidante

Ver|traut|heit F -, (rare) -en intimacy; (von Freund) closeness; (von Gesicht, Umgebung) familiarity

ver|trei|ben ptp **vertrieben** [fɛɐ'triːbn] VT irreg Tiere, Wolken, Einbrecher, Geister to drive away; (aus Haus etc) to drive or turn out (aus of); (aus Land, Gebiet) to drive out (aus of), to expel (aus from); (aus Amt, von Stellung) to oust; Feind to drive off, to repulse; (fig) Sorgen, Schmerzen to drive away, to banish; (Comm) Waren, Produkte to sell; **ich wollte Sie nicht ~, bleiben Sie doch noch ein wenig** I didn't mean to chase or drive you away – do stay a bit longer; **ich wollte Sie nicht von Ihrem Stuhl/Platz ~** I didn't mean to take your chair/seat; **jdn vom Thron/aus seinem Amt ~** to oust sb from the throne/his office; **jdm die Zeit mit etw ~** to help sb pass the time with sth; **sich** (dat) **die Zeit mit etw ~** to pass (away) or while away the time with sth → auch **vertrieben**

Ver|trei|bung [fɛɐ'traibʊŋ] F -, -en (aus from) expulsion; (aus Amt etc) ousting; (von Feind) repelling

ver|tret|bar ADJ justifiable; Theorie, Argument defensible, tenable; **nicht ~** unjustifiable; indefensible, untenable

ver|tre|ten ptp **vertreten** VT irreg **a** (= jds Stelle, Dienst übernehmen) Kollegen, Arzt etc to replace, to stand in for, to deputize for; Schauspieler to replace, to stand in for; (fig: = Funktion einer Sache übernehmen) to replace, to take the place of **b** jds Interessen, Firma, Land, Wahlkreis to represent; Sache to look after, to attend to; (Rechtsanwalt) Klienten to represent, to appear for; Fall to plead **c** (Comm: = Waren vertreiben für) (Firma) to be the agent for; (Angestellter) to represent **d** = verfechten, angehören) Standpunkt, Doktrin, Theorie to support; Meinung to hold, to be of; Ansicht to take, to hold; Kunstrichtung to represent; (= rechtfertigen) to justify (vor to) **e** ~ **sein** to be represented **f** jdm den Weg ~ to bar sb's way **g** sich (dat) **den Fuß ~** to twist or strain one's

ankle; **sich** (dat) **die Beine** or **Füße ~** (inf) to stretch one's legs

Ver|tre|ter [fɛɐ'treːtɐ] M -s, -, **Ver|tre|te|rin** [-ərɪn] F -, -nen **a** (von Land, Firma etc) representative; (Comm) (Firma) agent; (Angestellter) (sales) representative, rep (inf); ~ **für Damenkleider** (sales) representative or rep (inf) for ladies' wear; ~ **einer Versicherung** insurance representative or rep (inf); **ein übler ~** (fig inf) a nasty piece of work (inf) **b** (= Ersatz) replacement; (im Amt) deputy; (von Arzt) locum **c** (= Verfechter) (von Doktrin) supporter, advocate; (von Meinung) holder; (von Kunstrichtung) representative

Ver|tre|tung [fɛɐ'treːtʊŋ] F -, -en **a** (von Menschen) replacement; **die ~ (für jdn) übernehmen** to replace sb, to stand in (for sb); **die ~ (für jdn) haben** to stand in (for sb), to deputize (for sb); **X spielt in ~** X is appearing in his/her place; **in ~** (in Briefen) on behalf of **b** (von Interessen, Firma, Land, Wahlkreis) representation; **X übernimmt die ~ des Klienten/Falles** X is appearing for the client/pleading the case; **die ~ meiner Interessen** representing my interests **c** (= das Verfechten) supporting; (von Meinung) holding; (von Kunstrichtung) representation **d** (Comm: = Firma) agency **e** (= Botschaft) **diplomatische ~** diplomatic mission, embassy **f** = Vertreter a, b

Ver|tre|tungs-: **Ver|tre|tungs|stun|de** F (Sch) class where one teacher stands in for another, stand-in class; **~n geben** to stand in for another teacher; **ver|tre|tungs|wei|se** ADV as a replacement; (bei Amtsperson) as a deputy; **er übernimmt heute ~ meine Deutschstunde** he's taking my German lesson for me today

Ver|trieb [fɛɐ'triːp] M -(e)s, -e [-bə] **a** no pl sales pl; **der ~ eines Produktes** the sale of a product; **den ~ für eine Firma haben** to have the (selling) agency for a firm **b** (= Abteilung einer Firma) sales department

ver|trie|ben [fɛɐ'triːbn] ADJ (aus Land) expelled; **die nach dem Krieg ~en Deutschen** the Germans who were driven out of their homeland after the war → auch **vertreiben**

Ver|trie|be|nen-: **Ver|trie|be|nen|tref|fen** NT reunion of exiles; **Ver|trie|be|nen|ver|band** M association of exiles

Ver|trie|be|ne(r) [fɛɐ'triːbənə] MF decl as adj exile

Ver|triebs-: **Ver|triebs|ab|tei|lung** F sales department; **Ver|triebs|er|lös** M sales revenue; **Ver|triebs|ge|sell|schaft** F marketing company; **Ver|triebs|ka|nal** M distribution channel; **Ver|triebs|kos|ten** PL marketing costs pl; **Ver|triebs|lei|ter(in)** M(F) sales manager; **Ver|triebs|sys|tem** NT distribution system; **Ver|triebs|weg** M channel of distribution

ver|trim|men ptp **vertrimmt** VT (inf) to belt (inf), to wallop (inf)

ver|trin|ken ptp **vertrunken** [fɛɐ'trʊŋkn] VT irreg to drink away, to spend on drink (Brit)

ver|trock|nen ptp **vertrocknet** VI aux sein to dry out; (Esswaren) to go dry; (Pflanzen) to wither, to shrivel; (Quelle) to dry up; **er ist ein vertrockneter Mensch** he's a dry old stick (Brit inf) or an old bat (US inf)

ver|trö|deln ptp **vertrödelt** VT (inf) to fritter away, to squander

ver|trös|ten ptp **vertröstet** VT to put off; **jdn auf ein andermal/auf später ~** to put sb off VR to be content to wait (auf +acc for)

ver|trot|teln [fɛɐ'trɔtln] ptp **vertrottelt** VI (inf) aux sein to vegetate

ver|trot|telt ADJ (inf) goofy (inf); älterer Mensch (auch) senile

ver|trus|ten [fɛɐ'trastn] ptp **vertrustet** VT (Comm) to form into a trust

ver|tü|dern [fɛɐ̯ˈtyːdɐn] *ptp* **vertüdert** (*N Ger*) **VR** to get tangled up **VT** to tangle up

ver|tun *ptp* **vertan** [fɛɐ̯ˈtaːn] *irreg* **VT** to waste **VR** (*inf*) to make a mistake *or* slip, to slip up (*inf*)

ver|tu|schen *ptp* **vertuscht** VT to hush up; **~, dass ...** to hush up the fact that ...; **etw vor jdm ~** to keep sth from sb

Ver|tu|schung [fɛɐ̯ˈtʊʃʊŋ] F **-, -en** cover-up

Ver|tu|schungs|ver|such M attempt to hush things up

ver|übeln [fɛɐ̯ˈyːbln] *ptp* **verübelt** VT **jdm etw ~** not to be at all pleased with sb for doing sth; **ich hoffe, Sie werden mir die Frage nicht ~** I hope you won't mind my asking (this); **das kann ich dir nicht ~** I can't blame you for that

ver|üben *ptp* **verübt** VT to commit, to perpetrate (*form*)

ver|ul|ken *ptp* **verulkt** VT (*inf*) to make fun of, to take the mickey out of (*Brit inf*)

ver|un|fal|len [fɛɐ̯ˈʊnfalən] *ptp* **verunfallt** VI *aux sein* (*Sw*) to have an accident

Ver|un|fall|te(r) [fɛɐ̯ˈʊnfaltə] MF *decl as adj* (*form*) accident casualty *or* victim

ver|un|glimp|fen [fɛɐ̯ˈʊnɡlɪmpfn] *ptp* **verunglimpft** VT **jdn** to disparage; *Ruf, Ehre, Worte auch* to decry

Ver|un|glimp|fung F **-, -en** disparagement

ver|un|glü|cken [fɛɐ̯ˈʊnɡlʏkn] *ptp* **verunglückt** VI *aux sein* (*Mensch*) to have an accident; (*Fahrzeug, Flugzeug*) to crash; (*fig inf*: = *misslingen*) to go wrong; **mit dem Flugzeug ~** to be in a plane crash; **mit dem Auto ~** to be in a car crash, to have a car accident → **tödlich**

ver|un|glückt [fɛɐ̯ˈʊnɡlʏkt] ADJ (*fig*) *Versuch, Aufführung etc* unsuccessful

Ver|un|glück|te(r) [fɛɐ̯ˈʊnɡlʏktə] MF *decl as adj* casualty, victim; **10 Tote, 20 ~** 10 dead, 20 injured

ver|un|mög|li|chen [fɛɐ̯ˈʊnmøːklɪçn] *ptp* **verunmöglicht** VT (*esp Sw*) to make impossible; **jdm ~, etw zu tun** to make it impossible for sb to do sth

ver|un|rei|ni|gen [fɛɐ̯ˈʊnraɪnɪɡn] *ptp* **verunreinigt** VT *Fluss, Luft, Wasser* to pollute; (= *beschmutzen*) to dirty, to soil; (*euph: Hund etc*) to foul

Ver|un|rei|ni|gung F (*von Fluss, Luft, Wasser*) pollution; (= *Beschmutzung*) dirtying, soiling; (*euph: durch Hund*) fouling; **~en in der Luft/im Wasser** pollutants in the atmosphere/in the water

ver|un|si|chern [fɛɐ̯ˈʊnzɪçɐn] *ptp* **verunsichert** VT to make unsure *or* uncertain (*in +dat* about); **jetzt hast du mich völlig verunsichert** I just don't know at all any more; **sie versuchten, ihn zu ~** they tried to throw him; **verunsichert sein** to be uncertain; **verunsicherte Kunden/Patienten** confused customers/patients

Ver|un|si|che|rung F (= *mangelnde Gewissheit*) uncertainty; **das führte zur ~ der Wähler/Schüler** it put the electors/pupils into a state of uncertainty

ver|un|stal|ten [fɛɐ̯ˈʊnʃtaltn] *ptp* **verunstaltet** VT to disfigure; *Landschaft auch* to scar; **jdn ~, jds Gesicht ~** to spoil *or* mar sb's looks

Ver|un|stal|tung F **-, -en** disfigurement

ver|un|treu|en [fɛɐ̯ˈʊntrɔʏən] *ptp* **veruntreut** VT to embezzle, to misappropriate

Ver|un|treu|ung F **-, -en** embezzlement, misappropriation

ver|un|zie|ren [fɛɐ̯ˈʊntsiːrən] *ptp* **verunziert** VT *Landschaft, Kunstwerk, Zimmer* to spoil; **jdn ~, jds Gesicht ~** to spoil sb's looks

ver|ur|sa|chen [fɛɐ̯ˈuːɐ̯zaxn] *ptp* **verursacht** VT to cause; *Schwierigkeiten auch* to create (+*dat* for), to give rise to (+*dat* for); *Entrüstung, Zorn auch* to provoke; **jdm große Kosten ~** to cause sb a lot of expense; **jdm Umstände ~** to put sb to trouble, to cause sb trouble

Ver|ur|sa|cher [fɛɐ̯ˈuːɐ̯zaxɐ] M **-s, -, Ver|ur|sa|che|rin** [-ərɪn] F **-, -nen** cause; **der ~ kommt für den Schaden auf** the party responsible is liable for the damage

Ver|ur|sa|cher|prin|zip NT originator principle; (*bei Umweltschäden auch*) polluter pays principle

Ver|ur|sa|chung F **-**, *no pl* causing; (*von Schwierigkeiten auch*) creation; (*von Entrüstung, Zorn auch*) provocation

ver|ur|tei|len ✪ 41 *ptp* **verurteilt** VT to condemn; (*Jur*) (= *für schuldig befinden*) to convict (*für* of); (*zu Strafe*) to sentence; **jdn zu einer Geldstrafe von 1.000 Euro ~** to fine sb 1,000 euros, to impose a fine of 1,000 euros on sb; **jdn zum Tode ~** to condemn *or* sentence (*Jur*) sb to death; **jdn zu einer Gefängnisstrafe ~** to give sb a prison sentence

ver|ur|teilt [fɛɐ̯ˈʊrtaɪlt] ADJ **zu etw ~ sein** (*Jur*) to be sentenced to sth; (*fig*) to be condemned to sth; **zum Tode ~** condemned *or* sentenced (*Jur*) to death → **Scheitern**

Ver|ur|teil|te(r) [fɛɐ̯ˈʊrtaɪltə] MF *decl as adj* convicted man/woman, convict (*Jur*); **der zum Tode ~** the condemned man

Ver|ur|tei|lung F condemnation; (= *das Schuldigsprechen*) conviction; (*zu einer Strafe*) sentencing; **seine ~ zu 5 Jahren** his being sentenced to 5 years; **seine ~ zum Tode** his being condemned/sentenced to death

Ver|ve [ˈvɛrvə] F **-**, *no pl* (*geh*) verve, spirit

ver|viel|fa|chen [fɛɐ̯ˈfiːlfaxn] *ptp* **vervielfacht** VTR to multiply

Ver|viel|fa|chung F **-, -en** multiplication

ver|viel|fäl|ti|gen *ptp* **vervielfältigt** VT to duplicate; (= *fotokopieren*) to photocopy

Ver|viel|fäl|ti|gung F **-, -en** **a** (= *das Vervielfältigen*) duplication; (= *Fotokopieren*) photocopying **b** (= *Abzug*) copy; (= *Fotokopie*) photocopy

Ver|viel|fäl|ti|gungs-: Ver|viel|fäl|ti|gungs|ap|pa|rat M duplicating *or* copying machine, duplicator; (= *Fotokopierer*) photocopier; **Ver|viel|fäl|ti|gungs|recht** NT right of reproduction, copyright; **Ver|viel|fäl|ti|gungs|ver|fah|ren** NT duplicating process, copying process

ver|vier|fa|chen [fɛɐ̯ˈfiːɐ̯faxn] *ptp* **vervierfacht** VTR to quadruple

ver|voll|komm|nen [fɛɐ̯ˈfɔlkɔmnən] *ptp* **vervollkommnet** VT to perfect **VR** to perfect oneself

ver|voll|komm|nung F **-, -en** perfection

ver|voll|stän|di|gen [fɛɐ̯ˈfɔlʃtɛndɪɡn] *ptp* **vervollständigt** VT to complete; *Kenntnisse, gutes Essen auch* to round off; *Erlebnis* to make complete **VR** to be completed

Ver|voll|stän|di|gung F **-, -en** completion; (*von Kenntnissen auch*) rounding off

ver|wach|sen¹ *ptp* **verwachsen** VI *irreg aux sein* **a** (= *zusammenwachsen*) to grow (in) together, to grow into one; (*Narbe*) to heal over; (*Knochen*) to knit; (*Wunde*) to heal, to close (over); **mit etw ~** to grow into sth **b** (*fig: Menschen, Gemeinschaft*) to grow closer (together); **zu etw ~** to grow into sth; **mit etw ~** (*mit Arbeit, Aufgabe, Traditionen*) to become caught up in sth; **mit etw ~ sein** to have very close ties with sth; **ein Volk, das mit seinen Traditionen/seiner Kultur ~ ist** a nation whose traditions are/culture is deeply rooted within it; **mit jdm ~ sein** to have become very close to sb

ver|wach|sen² ADJ **a** *Mensch, Tier, Glied* deformed; *Pflanze* malformed; (= *verkümmert*) stunted **b** (= *überwuchert*) overgrown

Ver|wach|sung [fɛɐ̯ˈvaksʊŋ] F **-, -en** (*Med*) deformation; (= *verwachsenes Glied auch*) deformity; (*Biol, Min*) adhesion

ver|wa|ckeln *ptp* **verwackelt** VT to blur

ver|wäh|len ✪ 27.7 *ptp* **verwählt** VR to misdial, to dial the wrong number

ver|wah|ren *ptp* **verwahrt** **VT** (= *aufbewahren*) to keep (safe); **jdm etw zu ~ geben** to give sth to

sb for safekeeping **VR** **sich gegen etw ~** to protest against sth

ver|wahr|lo|sen [fɛɐ̯ˈvaːɐ̯loːzn] *ptp* **verwahrlost** VI *aux sein* to go to seed, to go to pot (*inf*); (*Gebäude auch*) to fall into disrepair, to become dilapidated; (*Park*) to become neglected; (*Mensch*) to let oneself go, to neglect oneself; (= *verwildern*) to get into bad habits

ver|wahr|lost [fɛɐ̯ˈvaːɐ̯loːst] ADJ neglected; *Mensch, Äußeres auch* unkempt; **sittlich ~** decadent

Ver|wahr|lo|sung F **-**, *no pl* neglect; (*von Gebäude auch*) dilapidation; (*von Mensch*) neglect (of oneself); (= *Verwilderung*) wildness; (*moralisch*) waywardness

Ver|wahr|sam [fɛɐ̯ˈvaːɐ̯zaːm] M **-s**, *no pl* **etw in jds ~** to give sth to sb for safekeeping; **etw in ~ haben** to keep sth safe; **etw in ~ nehmen** to take sth into safekeeping

Ver|wah|rung F **a** *no pl* (*von Geld etc*) keeping; (*von Täter*) custody, detention; **die ~ eines Menschen in einem Heim** keeping a person in a home; **jdm etw in ~ geben, etw bei jdm in ~ geben** to give sth to sb for safekeeping; **etw in ~ nehmen** to take sth into safekeeping; (*Behörde*) to take possession of sth; **jdn in ~ nehmen** to take sb into custody **b** (= *Einspruch*) protest; **gegen etw ~ einlegen** to make *or* lodge a protest against sth

ver|wai|sen [fɛɐ̯ˈvaɪzn] *ptp* **verwaist** VI *aux sein* to become an orphan, to be orphaned, to be made an orphan; (*fig*) to be deserted *or* abandoned; **verwaist** orphaned; (*fig*) deserted, abandoned

ver|wal|ken *ptp* **verwalkt** VT (*inf*) to wallop (*inf*), to belt (*inf*)

ver|wal|ten *ptp* **verwaltet** VT to manage; *Firma auch* to run; *Angelegenheiten auch* to conduct; *Erbe, Vermögen auch* to administer; *Treuhandsgut* to hold in trust; *Amt* to hold; (*Pol*) *Provinz etc* to govern; (*Beamter*) to administer; (*Rel*) to administer; **sich selbst ~** (*Pol*) to be self-governing

Ver|wal|ter [fɛɐ̯ˈvaltɐ] M **-s, -, Ver|wal|te|rin** [-ərɪn] F **-, -nen** administrator; (= *Treuhänder*) trustee, custodian; **der Papst als ~ Gottes** the Pope as God's steward

Ver|wal|tung [fɛɐ̯ˈvaltʊŋ] F **-, -en** **a** (= *das Verwalten*) management; (*von Firma*) running, management; (*von Erbe, Vermögen*) administration, management; (*von Treuhandgut*) holding in trust; (*von Amt*) holding; (*von Provinz*) government; **jdm etw zur ~ übergeben** to put sb in charge of (the management/running *etc* of) sth **b** (= *Behörde, Abteilung*) administration; (= *Hausverwaltung*) management; **städtische ~** municipal authorities *pl*

Ver|wal|tungs-: Ver|wal|tungs|akt M administrative act; **Ver|wal|tungs|an|ge|stell|te(r)** MF *decl as adj* admin(istration) employee; **Ver|wal|tungs|ap|pa|rat** M administrative machinery; **Ver|wal|tungs|auf|wand** M administrative costs *pl*; **Ver|wal|tungs|be|am|te(r)** M *decl as adj*, **Ver|wal|tungs|be|am|tin** F government (administration) official; **Ver|wal|tungs|be|hör|de** F administration; **Ver|wal|tungs|be|reich** M (= *Bezirk*) administrative district; (= *Aufgabenbereich*) area *or* field of administration; **Ver|wal|tungs|be|zirk** M administrative district; **Ver|wal|tungs|dienst** M admin(istration); **Ver|wal|tungs|ge|bäu|de** NT admin(istration) building *or* block; **Ver|wal|tungs|ge|bühr** F administrative charge; **Ver|wal|tungs|ge|richt** NT Administrative Court; **Ver|wal|tungs|kos|ten** PL administrative expenses *pl*; **Ver|wal|tungs|kram** M (*inf*) (*Admin*) paperwork *no pl*; (= *Bürokratie*) red tape (*inf*); **Ver|wal|tungs|rat** M board; **Ver|wal|tungs|rich|ter(in)** M(F) administrative court judge; **Ver|wal|tungs|weg** M administrative channels *pl*; **auf dem ~e** through (the) administrative channels

---

ver|wạm|sen [fɛɐ'vamzn] *ptp* **verwạmst** *VT* (*inf*) to belt (*inf*), to clobber (*inf*)

ver|wạn|del|bar *ADJ* (*Math, Econ*) convertible

ver|wạn|deln *ptp* **verwạndelt** **VT** (= *umformen*) to change, to transform; *Bett, Zimmer* to convert; (*Math, Econ, Chem*) to convert; (*Theat*) *Szene* to change; (*Jur*) *Strafe* to commute; **jdn/etw in etw** (*acc*) **~** to turn sb/sth into sth; (= *verzaubern auch*) to change *or* transform sb/sth into sth; **die Vorlage ~** (*Ftbl*) to score from the pass; **einen Strafstoß ~** to score (from) a penalty; **Müller verwandelte den Pass zum 2:0** Müller put the pass away to make it 2-0; **den Matchball ~** (*Tennis*) to convert the match point; **ein Gebäude in einen Trümmerhaufen ~** to reduce a building to a pile of rubble; **er ist wie verwandelt** he's a changed man **VI** (*Sport sl*) **zum 1:0 ~** to make it 1-0 **VR** to change; (*Zool*) to metamorphose; **sich in etw** (*acc*) *or* **zu etw ~** to change *or* turn into sth; **Zeus hat sich in einen Stier verwandelt** Zeus turned *or* transformed himself into a bull

Ver|wạnd|lung *F* **a** (= *das Verwandeln*) transformation; (*von Bett, Zimmer, Math, Econ, Chem*) conversion; (*Theat*) change, changing; (*von Strafe*) commuting **b** (= *das Sichverwandeln*) change; (*Zool*) metamorphosis; (*von Göttern, von der Natur*) transformation; **eine ~ durchmachen** to undergo a change *or* transformation; **seine erstaunliche ~** the remarkable change in him; **„die ~"** (*Liter*) "the Metamorphosis"

Ver|wạnd|lungs-: **Ver|wạnd|lungs|künst|ler(in)** *M(F)* quick-change artist; **Ver|wạnd|lungs|sze|ne** *F* (*Theat*) transformation scene

ver|wạndt [fɛɐ'vant] *ptp von* **verwenden** *ADJ* (*lit, fig*) related (*mit* to); *Probleme, Methoden, Fragen, Wissenschaften auch* allied; *Philosophien, Kultur, Gefühle auch, Denker, Geister* kindred *attr*; **~e Seelen** (*fig*) kindred spirits; **geistig ~ sein** (*fig*) to be kindred spirits; **wir sind uns darin ~, dass ...** we're akin to each other in that ... → **Ecke**

ver|wạnd|te *pret von* **verwenden**

Ver|wạnd|te(r) [fɛɐ'vantə] *MF decl as adj* relation, relative

Ver|wạnd|ten|kreis *M* (circle of) relatives *pl*; **im ~** among my/your *etc* relatives

Ver|wạndt|schaft [fɛɐ'vantʃaft] *F* -, -en relationship; (= *die Verwandten*) relations *pl*, relatives *pl*; (*fig*) affinity, kinship; **er leugnete die ~ zu mir** he denied being related to me, he denied any relationship with me

ver|wạndt|schaft|lich [fɛɐ'vantʃaftlɪç] *ADJ* family *attr*

Ver|wạndt|schafts|grad *M* degree of relationship; **wir kennen ihren ~ nicht** we don't know how closely they are related

ver|wạnzt [fɛɐ'vantst] *ADJ Betten, Kleider* bug-ridden, bug-infested; (*inf:* = *mit Abhörgeräten*) bugged

ver|wạr|nen *ptp* **verwạrnt** *VT* to caution, to warn

Ver|wạr|nung *F* caution, warning → **gebührenpflichtig**

Ver|wạr|nungs|geld *NT* exemplary fine

ver|wạ|schen [fɛɐ'vaʃn] *ADJ* faded (*in the wash*); (= *verwässert*) *Farbe* watery; *Sprache* slurred; (*fig*) wishy-washy (*inf*), woolly (*esp Brit inf*)

ver|wäs|sern *ptp* **verwässert** *VT* to water down; (*fig auch*) to dilute

Ver|wäs|se|rung *F* watering down; (*fig auch*) dilution

ver|we|ben *ptp* **verwebt** *or* **verwoben** [fɛɐ'vo:bn] *VT irreg* **a** *auch reg* Garne to weave; (= *verbrauchen*) to use (*lit, fig:* = *verflechten*) to interweave (*mit, in* +*acc* with)

ver|wẹch|seln *ptp* **verwẹchselt** *VT Gegenstände* to mix up, to get muddled *or* mixed up; *Begriffe, Menschen auch* to confuse; **jdn (mit jdm) ~** to confuse sb with sb; (= *für jdn halten auch*) to mistake sb for sb; **entschuldigen Sie, ich habe**

Sie verwechselt sorry - I thought you were someone else *or* I (mis)took you for someone else; **zum Verwechseln ähnlich sein** to be the spitting image of each other, to be as like as two peas in a pod; **ich habe meinen Schirm verwechselt** I took somebody else's umbrella by mistake; **sie verwechselt mir und mich** (*lit*) she mixes up *or* confuses "mir" and "mich"; (*fig*) she doesn't know her grammar → **mein POSS PRON b**

Ver|wẹchs|lung [fɛɐ'vɛkslʊŋ] *F* -, -en confusion; (= *Irrtum*) mistake; **die Polizei ist sicher, dass eine ~ (des Täters) völlig ausgeschlossen ist** the police are certain that there can be absolutely no mistake (about the culprit); **es kam deshalb zu einer ~, weil ...** there was a mix-up *or* confusion because ...; **das muss eine ~ sein, da muss es sich um eine ~ handeln** there must be some mistake

Ver|wẹchs|lungs|ko|mö|die *F* comedy of mistaken identity

ver|we|gen [fɛɐ've:gn] *ADJ* daring, bold; (= *tollkühn*) foolhardy, rash; (= *keck*) cheeky (*Brit*), saucy; **den Hut ~ aufsetzen** to set one's hat at a jaunty *or* rakish angle

ver|we|gen|heit *F* -, -en daring, boldness; (= *Tollkühnheit*) foolhardiness, rashness; (= *Keckheit*) cheek(iness) (*Brit*), sauciness

ver|we|hen *ptp* **verweht** **VT** *Blätter* to blow away, to scatter; *Spur, Pfad* to cover over, to obliterate; **vom Winde verweht** gone with the wind **VI** *aux sein* (*geh*) (*Worte, Musik*) to be carried away, to drift away; (*Spur, Pfad*) to be obliterated, to be covered over

ver|weh|ren *ptp* **verwehrt** *VT* (*geh*) **jdm etw ~** to refuse *or* deny sb sth; **die neu gebauten Häuser ~ ihnen jetzt den Blick auf ...** the newly built houses now obstruct their view of ...; **jdm ~, etw zu tun** to bar sb from doing sth

Ver|weh|ung [fɛɐ've:ʊŋ] *F* -, -en (= *Schneeverwehung*) (snow)drift; (= *Sandverwehung*) (sand)drift

ver|weich|li|chen [fɛɐ'vaiçlɪçn] *ptp* **verweichlicht** **VT** **jdn ~** to make sb soft; **ein verweichlichter Mensch** a weakling; **ein verweichlichtes Muttersöhnchen** a mollycoddled mummy's boy (*Brit*), a pampered momma's boy (*US*) **VI** *aux sein* to get *or* grow soft

Ver|weich|li|chung *F* -, *no pl* softness; **Zentralheizung führt zur ~** central heating makes you soft

Ver|wei|ge|rer [fɛɐ'vaigərə] *M* -s, -, **Ver|wei|ge|rin** [-ərɪn] *F* -nen refusenik (*inf*); (= *Kriegsdienstverweigerer*) conscientious objector

ver|wei|gern *ptp* **verweigert** *VT* to refuse; *Befehl* to refuse to obey; *Kriegsdienst* to refuse to do; **jdm etw ~** to refuse *or* deny sb sth; **die Zustimmung zu etw ~** to refuse to give approval to sth; **er kann ihr keinen Wunsch ~** he can refuse *or* deny her nothing; **es war ihr verweigert, ihren Sohn wiederzusehen** she was denied seeing her son; **die Annahme eines Briefes ~** to refuse (to accept *or* to take delivery of) a letter; **er verweigerte die Unterschrift** he refused to sign; **das Pferd hat (das Hindernis) verweigert** the horse refused (at the fence *or* jump); **sich jdm ~** (*euph*) to refuse to be intimate with sb → **Aussage**

Ver|wei|ge|rung *F* refusal; (*von Hilfe, Auskunft etc auch*) denial; **~ der Aussage** (*Jur*) refusal to make a statement; (*von Zeuge*) refusal to testify *or* give evidence; **~ des Kriegsdienstes** refusal to do (one's) military service; **~ des Gehorsams** disobedience

Ver|wei|ge|rungs|fall *M* (*Jur*) **im ~** in case of refusal to make a statement

Ver|weil|dau|er *F* length of stay

ver|wei|len *ptp* **verweilt** **VI** (*geh*) (*Mensch*) to stay; (*Blick*) to rest; (*Gedanken*) to dwell, to linger; **bei einer Sache ~** to dwell on sth; **hier lasst uns ~** let us linger *or* tarry (*liter*) here **VR** to linger, to tarry (*liter*)

Ver|wei|len [fɛɐ'vailən] *NT* -s, *no pl* (*geh*) stay; **sein ~ bei dem Gedanken/Thema** his dwelling on the thought/theme; **hier ist meines ~s nicht mehr** (*liter*) I can no longer tarry here (*liter*)

ver|weint [fɛɐ'vaint] *ADJ Augen* tear-swollen; *Gesicht* tear-stained; *Mensch* with (a) tear-stained face; **~ aussehen** to look as though one has (just) been crying

Ver|weis [fɛɐ'vais] *M* -es, -e [-zə] **a** (= *Rüge*) reprimand, rebuke, admonishment; **jdm einen ~ erteilen** *or* **aussprechen** to reprimand *or* rebuke *or* admonish sb **b** (= *Hinweis*) reference (*auf* +*acc* to)

ver|wei|sen *ptp* **verwiesen** [fɛɐ'vi:zn] *irreg* **VT** **a** (= *hinweisen*) **jdn auf etw** (*acc*)/**an jdn ~** to refer sb to sth/sb **b** (*von der Schule*) to expel; **jdn des Landes** *or* **aus dem Lande ~** to expel sb (from the country); **jdn vom Platz** *or* **des Spielfeldes ~** to send sb off; **jdn auf den zweiten Platz ~** (*Sport*) to relegate sb to second place **c** (*Jur*) to refer (*an* +*acc* to) **d** (*dated:* = *rügen*) **jdn ~** to rebuke *or* reprove *or* admonish sb **VI** **auf etw** (*acc*) **~** to refer to sth

Ver|wei|sung *F* **a** (= *Ausschluss, Ausweisung*) expulsion **b** (= *Hinweis*) reference (*auf* +*acc* to) **c** (*Jur*) referral (*an* +*acc* to)

Ver|weis|zei|chen *NT* (*Typ*) reference sign *or* mark

ver|wel|ken *ptp* **verwelkt** *VI aux sein* (*Blumen*) to wilt; (*fig*) to fade; **ein verwelktes Gesicht** a worn face; **eine verwelkte Schönheit** a faded beauty

ver|welt|li|chen [fɛɐ'vɛltlɪçn] *ptp* **verweltlicht** *VT* to secularize

Ver|welt|li|chung *F* -, *no pl* secularization

ver|wẹnd|bar *ADJ* usable (*zu* for); **das ist nur einmal ~** it can be used once only; **ein vielseitig ~es Gerät** a device with many uses

Ver|wẹnd|bar|keit [fɛɐ'vɛntba:ɐkait] *F* -, *no pl* usability

ver|wẹn|den [fɛɐ'vɛndn] *pret* **verwendete** *or* **verwandte** [fɛɐ'vɛndətə, fɛɐ'vantə], *ptp* **verwendet** *or* **verwandt** [fɛɐ'vɛndət, fɛɐ'vant] **VT** to use; *Methode, Mittel auch* to employ; (= *verwerten auch*) to make use of, to utilize; **Mühe/Fleiß auf etw** (*acc*) **~** to put effort/hard work into sth; **Zeit auf etw** (*acc*) **~** to spend time on sth, to put time into sth **VR** **sich (bei jdm) für jdn ~** to intercede (with sb) *or* to approach sb on sb's behalf

Ver|wẹn|dung *F* **a** use; (*von Mitteln etc*) use, employment; (*von Zeit, Geld*) expenditure (*auf* +*acc* on); **keine ~ für etw haben** to have no use for sth; **für alles ~ haben** (*inf*) to have a use for everything; **~ finden** to prove useful; **für jdn/etw ~ finden** to find a use for sb/sth; **in ~ stehen** (*Aus*) to be in use; **etw in ~ nehmen** (*Aus*) to put sth into service **b** (*old:* = *Fürsprache*) intercession (*bei* with)

Ver|wẹn|dungs-: **ver|wẹn|dungs|fä|hig** *ADJ* usable; **für etw ~ sein** to be suitable for sth; **Ver|wẹn|dungs|mög|lich|keit** *F* (possible) use; **Ver|wẹn|dungs|wei|se** *F* manner of use; **die ~ von etw** the way in which sth is used; **Ver|wẹn|dungs|zweck** *M* use, purpose

ver|wẹr|fen *ptp* **verworfen** [fɛɐ'vɔrfn] *irreg* **VT** **a** (= *ablehnen*) to reject; *eigene Meinung, Ansicht, Gedanken* to discard; (*Jur*) *Klage, Antrag, Revision* to dismiss; *Urteil* to quash; (= *kritisieren*) *Handlungsweise, Methode* to condemn **b** *Ball* to lose → *auch* **verworfen VR** **a** (*Holz*) to warp; (*Geol*) to fault **b** (*Cards*) to misdeal **VI** (*Tier*) to abort

ver|wẹrf|lich [fɛɐ'vɛrflɪç] *ADJ* reprehensible

Ver|wẹrf|lich|keit *F* -, *no pl* reprehensibleness

Ver|wẹr|fung [fɛɐ'vɛrfʊŋ] *F* -, -en **a** (= *Ablehnung*) rejection; (*Jur*) dismissal; (*von Urteil*) quashing **b** (*Geol*) fault; (*von Holz*) warping

Ver|wẹr|fungs|li|nie *F* (*Geol*) fault line

ver|wẹrt|bar *ADJ* usable

Ver|wẹrt|bar|keit [fɛɐ've:ɐtba:ɐkait] *F* -, *no pl* usability

---

ver|wer|ten ptp **verwertet** VT (= verwenden) to make use of, to utilize; Reste to use, to make use of; Kenntnisse, Erfahrungen to utilize, to put to good use; (kommerziell) Erfindung, Material etc to exploit; (Körper) Nahrung to process; **dieser Stoff wird sich gut für ein Kleid ~ lassen** this material will make a nice dress

Ver|wer|tung F utilization; (von Resten) using; (kommerziell) exploitation

ver|we|sen [fɛɐ'veːzn] ptp **verwest** VI aux sein to decay; (Fleisch) to rot VT (obs) to administer; **jds Amt ~** to deputize for sb

Ver|we|ser [fɛɐ'veːzɐ] M -s, -, **Ver|we|se|rin** [-ərɪn] F -, -nen administrator; (= Amtsverweser) deputy; (= Pfarrverweser) locum (tenens) (Brit), administrator (US)

ver|west|li|chen [fɛɐ'vɛstlɪçn] ptp **verwestlicht** VI to become westernized

Ver|west|li|chung [fɛɐ'vɛstlɪçʊŋ] F westernization

ver|we|sung F -, no pl decay; **in ~ übergehen** to start to decay

ver|wet|ten ptp **verwettet** VT to gamble away

ver|wich|sen ptp **verwichst** VT (inf) **a** (= schlagen) to belt (inf), to clobber (inf) **b** Geld to blow (inf)

ver|wi|ckeln ptp **verwickelt** VT Fäden etc to tangle (up), to get tangled up; **jdn in etw** (acc) **~** to involve sb in sth; in Kampf, in dunkle Geschäfte auch to get sb mixed up in sth; in Skandal auch to get sb mixed up in sth, to embroil sb in sth; **in etw verwickelt sein** to be involved/mixed up/embroiled in sth VR (Fäden etc) to tangle (up), to become tangled; **sich in etw** (acc) **~** (lit) to become entangled in sth, to get caught up in sth; (fig) in Widersprüche to get oneself tangled up in sth; in Skandal to get mixed up or involved or embroiled in sth

ver|wi|ckelt [fɛɐ'vɪklt] ADJ (fig inf) (= schwierig) involved, complicated, intricate; (= verwirrt) Mensch fuddled (Brit), confused

Ver|wi|cke|lung [fɛɐ'vɪkəlʊŋ] F -, -en, **Ver|wick|lung** [fɛɐ'vɪklʊŋ] F -, -en involvement (in +acc in); (in Skandal auch) embroilment; (= Komplikation) complication; (= Verwirrung) confusion; (Theat, Liter) intrigue, intricacy (of plot)

ver|wil|dern ptp **verwildert** VI aux sein (Garten) to become overgrown, to overgrow; (Pflanzen) to grow wild; (Haustier) to become wild; (hum inf: Mensch) to run wild

ver|wil|dert [fɛɐ'vɪldɐt] ADJ wild; Garten overgrown; Aussehen unkempt

Ver|wil|de|rung [fɛɐ'vɪldərʊŋ] F -, -en (von Garten) overgrowing; **Zustand der ~** state of neglect; **mangelnde Sorge führte zur ~ des Tieres/der Kinder** as a result of negligence the animal became wild/the children ran wild

ver|win|den ptp **verwunden** [fɛɐ'vʊndn] VT irreg to get over

ver|win|kelt [fɛɐ'vɪŋklt] ADJ Straße, Gasse winding; Gebäude, Raum full of nooks and crannies

ver|wir|beln ptp **verwirbelt** VT to swirl

ver|wir|ken ptp **verwirkt** VT (geh) to forfeit

ver|wirk|li|chen [fɛɐ'vɪrklɪçn] ptp **verwirklicht** VT to realize; Hoffnung auch to fulfil (Brit), to fulfill (US), Idee, Plan auch to put into effect, to translate into action; Wunsch, Traum auch to make come true, to turn into a reality VR to be realized; (Hoffnung auch) to be fulfilled; (Idee auch) to be put into effect, to be translated into action; (Wunsch, Traum auch) to come true, to become a reality; (Mensch) to fulfil (Brit) or fulfill (US) oneself

Ver|wirk|li|chung F -, -en realization; (von Hoffnung, Selbstverwirklichung) fulfilment (Brit), fulfillment (US)

Ver|wir|kung F , no pl forfeit(ure); **~ einer Strafe** (Jur) incurrence of a penalty

ver|wir|ren [fɛɐ'vɪrən] ptp **verwirrt** VT **a** Haar to tousle, to ruffle (up); Fäden etc to tangle (up), to get tangled up **b** (= durcheinander bringen) to confuse; (= konfus machen) to bewilder; Sinne, Verstand to confuse, to (be)fuddle VR (Fäden etc) to become tangled (up) or snarled up; (Haare) to become tousled or dishevelled; (fig) to become confused

Ver|wirr|spiel NT (fig) confusion; **ein ~ mit jdm treiben** to try to confuse sb

Ver|wir|rung F (= Durcheinander, Verlegenheit) confusion; (= Fassungslosigkeit auch) bewilderment; **jdn in ~ bringen** to confuse/bewilder sb; (= verlegen machen) to fluster sb

ver|wirt|schaf|ten ptp **verwirtschaftet** VT to squander (away)

ver|wi|schen ptp **verwischt** VT (= verschmieren) to smudge, to blur; (lit, fig) Spuren to cover over; (fig) Eindrücke, Erinnerungen to blur VR (lit, fig) to become blurred; (Schrift etc auch) to become smudged; (Erinnerung auch) to fade

ver|wit|tern ptp **verwittert** VI aux sein to weather

ver|wit|tert [fɛɐ'vɪtɐt] ADJ Gestein weathered; Gesicht auch weather-beaten

Ver|wit|te|rung F weathering

ver|wit|wet [fɛɐ'vɪtvət] ADJ widowed; **Frau Meier, ~e Schulz** Mrs Meier, the widow of Mr Schulz

ver|woh|nen ptp **verwohnt** VT Wohnung to run down; Möbel to wear out

ver|wöh|nen [fɛɐ'vøː•nən] ptp **verwöhnt** VT to spoil; (Schicksal) to smile upon, to be good to VR to spoil oneself

ver|wohnt [fɛɐ'voː•nt] ADJ Wohnung run-down; Möbel battered

ver|wöhnt [fɛɐ'vøː•nt] ADJ spoiled; Kunde, Geschmack discriminating; **vom Schicksal/von den Göttern ~** smiled upon by fate/the gods

Ver|wöh|nung F -, no pl spoiling

ver|wor|fen [fɛɐ'vɔrfn] ADJ (geh) depraved, degenerate; Blick depraved → auch **verwerfen**

Ver|wor|fen|heit F -, no pl depravity

ver|wor|ren [fɛɐ'vɔrən] ADJ confused, muddled; (= verwickelt) complicated, involved, intricate

Ver|wor|ren|heit F -, no pl confusion; (= Verwickeltheit) intricacy

ver|wund|bar ADJ (lit, fig) vulnerable

Ver|wund|bar|keit [fɛɐ'vʊntbaːɐkait] F -, no pl (lit, fig) vulnerability

ver|wun|den [fɛɐ'vʊndn] ptp **verwundet** VT to wound; (lit auch) to injure → auch **verwundet**

ver|wun|der|lich ADJ surprising; (stärker) astonishing, amazing; (= sonderbar) strange, odd; **es ist sehr ~, dass ...** it's most amazing or surprising that ...; **es ist nicht ~, dass ...** it is no wonder or not surprising that ...

ver|wun|dern ptp **verwundert** VT to astonish, to amaze VR (über +acc at) to be amazed or astonished, to wonder; **sich über etw** (acc) **sehr ~ müssen** to be most amazed at sth

ver|wun|dert ADJ amazed, astonished ADV in amazement, in astonishment

Ver|wun|de|rung F -, no pl astonishment, amazement; **zu meiner größten ~** to my great astonishment or amazement

ver|wun|det [fɛɐ'vʊndət] ADJ (lit, fig) wounded → auch **verwunden**

Ver|wun|de|te(r) [fɛɐ'vʊndətə] MF decl as adj casualty; **die ~n** (Mil) the wounded

Ver|wun|dung F -, -en wound

ver|wun|schen [fɛɐ'vʊnʃn] ADJ enchanted

ver|wün|schen ptp **verwünscht** VT **a** (= verfluchen) to curse; **verwünscht** cursed, confounded **b** (in Märchen) (= verzaubern) to enchant, to put or cast a spell on or over; (= verhexen) to bewitch

Ver|wün|schung [fɛɐ'vʏnʃʊŋ] F -, -en **a** (= Fluch) curse, oath **b** no pl (= Verzauberung) enchantment; (= Verhexung) bewitchment

ver|wurs|teln ptp **verwurstelt** VT (inf) to mess up (inf), to make a mess of

ver|wur|zelt [fɛɐ'vʊrtslt] ADJ **~ sein** (Pflanze) to be rooted; (**fest**) **in or mit etw** (dat) **~ sein** (fig) to be deeply rooted in sth

Ver|wur|ze|lung [fɛɐ'vʊrtsəlʊŋ] F -, -en (lit) rooting; (fig) rootedness

ver|wu|scheln ptp **verwuschelt** VT (inf) Haare to tousle, to ruffle

ver|wüs|ten [fɛɐ'vyː•stn] ptp **verwüstet** VT to devastate, to ravage; (fig) Gesicht to ravage

Ver|wüs|tung F -, -en devastation no pl, ravaging no pl; (von Gesicht) ravages pl; **die ~en durch den Sturm** the devastation caused by the storm, the ravages of the storm; **~en anrichten** to inflict devastation

ver|za|gen ptp **verzagt** VI (geh) to become disheartened, to lose heart; **an etw** (dat) **~** to despair of sth; **nicht ~!** don't despair

ver|zagt [fɛɐ'tsaːkt] ADJ disheartened, despondent ADV disheartened, despondently

Ver|zagt|heit F -, no pl despondency

ver|zäh|len ptp **verzählt** VR to miscount, to count wrongly VTI (dial inf) = **erzählen**

ver|zah|nen ptp **verzahnt** VT Bretter to dovetail; Zahnräder to cut teeth or cogs in, to gear (Brit); (fig) to (inter)link, to dovetail; **ineinander verzahnt sein** to mesh

Ver|zah|nung [fɛɐ'tsaː•nʊŋ] F -, -en (von Brettern) (= das Verzahnen) dovetailing; (= das Verzahntsein) dovetail; (von Zahnrädern) (toothed) gearing; (fig) dovetailing

ver|zan|ken ptp **verzankt** VR (inf) to quarrel, to fall out

ver|za|pfen ptp **verzapft** VT **a** Getränke to serve or sell on draught (Brit) or draft (US) **b** Holzstücke to mortice and tenon; (mit Dübel) to dowel **c** (inf) Unsinn to come out with; (pej) Gedichte, Artikel to concoct

ver|zär|teln [fɛɐ'tsɛrtln] ptp **verzärtelt** VT (pej) to mollycoddle (esp Brit), to pamper

Ver|zär|te|lung [fɛɐ'tsɛrtəlʊŋ] F -, no pl (pej) mollycoddling (esp Brit), pampering

ver|zau|bern ptp **verzaubert** VT (lit) to cast a spell on or over, to put a spell on; (fig) jdn auch to enchant; **jdn in etw** (acc) **~** to turn sb into sth; **eine verzauberte Prinzessin** an enchanted princess

Ver|zau|be|rung [fɛɐ'tsaubərʊŋ] F -, -en (lit, fig) enchantment; (= Verhexung) bewitchment; **die ~ des Prinzen in einen Frosch** turning the prince into a frog

ver|zehn|fa|chen [fɛɐ'tseːnfaxn] ptp **verzehnfacht** VTR to increase tenfold

Ver|zehr [fɛɐ'tseː•ɐ] M -(e)s, no pl consumption

Ver|zehr|bon M (für Essen) food voucher; (für Getränke) drinks or beverage (US) voucher

ver|zeh|ren ptp **verzehrt** VT (form: lit, fig) to consume VR (geh) to languish (liter), to eat one's heart out; **sich vor Gram/Sorgen ~** to be consumed by or with grief/worries; **sich nach jdm ~** to pine (esp Brit) or yearn for sb

ver|zeich|nen ptp **verzeichnet** VT **a** (= notieren, aufweisen) to record; (esp in Liste) to enter; **gewaltige Änderungen sind zu ~** enormous changes are to be noted; **Todesfälle waren nicht zu ~** there were no fatalities; **einen Erfolg zu haben** to have scored a success; **das kann die Regierung als (einen) Erfolg ~** the government can mark this up as a success; **in einer Liste ~** to list **b** (= falsch zeichnen) to draw wrong(ly); (fig) to misrepresent, to distort VR to make mistakes/a mistake in one's drawing VTI (Opt) to distort

Ver|zeich|nis [fɛɐ'tsaiçnɪs] NT -ses, -se index; (= Tabelle) table; (= Namensverzeichnis: esp amtlich) register; (= Aufstellung) list; (Comput) directory

ver|zei|gen ptp **verzeigt** VT (Sw) jdn **~** to report sb to the police

Ver|zei|gung [fɛɐ'tsaigʊŋ] F -, -en (Sw) reporting

ver|zei|hen ✪ 45.1 *ptp* **verziehen** [fɛɐˈtsiːən] **VTI** *irreg* (= *vergeben*) to forgive; (*Gott, Gebieter*) to pardon; (= *entschuldigen*) to excuse, to pardon; **jdm (etw) ~** to forgive sb (for sth); **ich kann es mir nicht ~, dass ich sie geschlagen habe** I'll never forgive myself for hitting her; **das ist nicht zu ~** that's unforgivable; (= *nicht zu entschuldigen auch*) that's inexcusable or unpardonable; **es sei dir noch einmal verziehen** you're forgiven or excused!, we'll forgive you!; **~ Sie!** excuse me!; (*als entschuldigung auch*) I beg your pardon! (*Brit*), excuse me!; **~ Sie die Störung, ~ Sie, dass ich stören muss** excuse me for disturbing you

ver|zeih|lich [fɛɐˈtsailɪç] ADJ forgivable; (= *zu entschuldigen*) excusable, pardonable

Ver|zei|hung [fɛɐˈtsaiʊŋ] F -, *no pl* forgiveness; (= *Entschuldigung*) pardon; **~!** excuse me!; (*als Entschuldigung auch*) sorry!; (**jdn**) **um ~ bitten** (= *sich entschuldigen*) to apologize (to sb); **ich bitte vielmals um ~** I do apologize (*für* for), I'm terribly sorry (*für* about)

ver|zer|ren *ptp* **verzerrt** **VT** (*lit, fig*) to distort; *Gesicht etc* to contort; *Sehne, Muskel* to strain, to pull; **etw verzerrt darstellen** (*fig*) to present a distorted picture of sth; **verzerrte Gitarren** distorted guitars **VI** (*Lautsprecher, Spiegel etc*) to distort **VR** to become distorted; (*Gesicht etc*) to become contorted (*zu* in)

Ver|zer|rung F (*lit, fig*) distortion; (*von Gesicht etc*) contortion; (*von Muskel, Sehne*) straining, pulling; (*Statistik*) bias

ver|zet|teln [fɛɐˈtsetln] *ptp* **verzettelt** **VR** to waste a lot of time; (*bei Aufgabe, Diskussion*) to get bogged down **VT** (= *verschwenden*) to waste; *Zeit etc* to waste, to fritter away

Ver|zicht [fɛɐˈtsɪçt] M **-(e)s, -e** renunciation (*auf* +*acc* of); (*auf Anspruch*) abandonment (*auf* +*acc* of); (= *Opfer*) sacrifice (*auf Recht, Eigentum, Amt*) relinquishment (*auf* +*acc* of); (*auf Thron*) abdication (*auf* +*acc* of); **der ~ auf Zigaretten fällt ihm schwer** he finds it hard to give up cigarettes; **ein ~, der mir nicht schwer fällt** that's something I can easily do without; **~ ist ein Fremdwort für sie** doing (*Brit*) or going without is foreign to her; **~ leisten** or **üben** (*form*) = **verzichten**

ver|zicht|bar [fɛɐˈtsɪçtbaːɐ] ADJ dispensable; **nicht ~** indispensable

ver|zich|ten [fɛɐˈtsɪçtn] *ptp* **verzichtet** VI to do (*Brit*) or go without; (= *Opfer bringen*) to make sacrifices; **einer muss leider ~** somebody has to do (*Brit*) or go without, I'm afraid; **sie verzichtete zugunsten ihrer Schwester auf das Auto** she let her sister have the car; **der Kandidat hat zugunsten eines Jüngeren verzichtet** the candidate stepped down in favour (*Brit*) or favor (*US*) of a younger man; **dankend ~** (*iro*) to decline politely; **danke, ich verzichte** (*iro*) not for me, thanks; **auf jdn/etw ~** (= *ohne auskommen müssen*) to do (*Brit*) or go without sb/sth; *auf Alkohol, Süßigkeiten etc auch* to abstain from sth; (= *aufgeben*) to give up sb/sth; *auf Erbschaft, Eigentum* to renounce sth; *auf Anspruch* to waive sth; *auf Recht* to relinquish sth; (*von etw absehen*) *auf Kommentar, Anzeige etc* to abstain from sth; *auf Kandidatur, Wiederwahl, Amt* to refuse sth; **auf jdn/etw ~ können** to be able to do (*Brit*) or go without sb/sth; **auf den Thron ~** to abdicate; **auf Einzelheiten/eine förmliche Vorstellung ~ können** to be able to dispense with details/a formal introduction

Ver|zicht-: **Ver|zicht|er|klä|rung** F (*auf* +*acc* of) renunciation; (*auf finanzielle Leistungen*) disclaimer; (*auf Rechte*) waiver; **Ver|zicht|leis|tung** F (*Jur*) renunciation; **Ver|zicht|po|li|tik** F (*pej*) policy of surrender; **Ver|zicht|po|li|ti|ker(in)** M(F) (*pej*) politician supporting a policy of surrender

ver|zie|hen *ptp* **verzogen** [fɛɐˈtsoːgn] *irreg* **VT** **a** *Mund, Züge etc* to twist (*zu* into); **das Gesicht ~** to pull (*Brit*) or make a face, to grimace; **den Mund ~** to turn up one's mouth; **keine Miene ~**

not to turn a hair (*Brit*) or bat an eyelash **b** *Stoff* to pull out of shape, to stretch; *Chassis, Gestell* to bend out of shape; *Holz* to warp **c** *Kinder* to bring up badly; (= *verwöhnen*) to spoil; *Tiere* to train badly → *auch* **verzogen** **d** *Pflanzen* to thin out **VR** **a** (*Stoff*) to go out of shape, to stretch; (*Chassis*) to be bent out of shape; (*Holz*) to warp **b** (*Mund, Gesicht etc*) to twist (*zu* into), to contort **c** (= *verschwinden*) to disappear (*auch inf*); (*Gewitter*) to pass; (*Nebel, Wolken*) to disperse; (*inf*: = *schlafen gehen*) to go to bed **VI** *aux sein* to move (*nach* to); **„verzogen"** (= *unbekannt*) "no longer at this address"

ver|zie|ren *ptp* **verziert** VT to decorate; (= *verschönern*) to embellish; (*Mus*) to ornament

Ver|zie|rung [fɛɐˈtsiːrʊŋ] F -, **-en** decoration; (= *Verschönerung*) embellishment; (*Mus*: = *verzierende Noten*) ornament → **abbrechen VT a**

ver|zin|ken *ptp* **verzinkt** VT *Metalle* to galvanize

ver|zins|bar ADJ = **verzinslich**

ver|zin|sen *ptp* **verzinst** **VT** to pay interest on; **jdm sein Kapital (mit** or **zu 5%) ~** to pay sb (5%) interest on his/her capital; **das Geld wird mit 3% verzinst** 3% interest is paid on the money, the money yields or bears 3% interest **VR** **sich (mit 6%) ~** to yield or bear (6%) interest

ver|zins|lich [fɛɐˈtsɪnslɪç] ADJ interest-bearing *attr*, yielding or bearing interest; **~ sein** to yield or bear interest; **zu 3%/einem hohen Satz ~** yielding or bearing 3% interest/a high rate of interest; **nicht ~** free of interest; **das ist ~ vom ersten Mai** the interest on that is payable from the 1st of May ADV **Kapital ~ anlegen** to put capital out at interest

Ver|zin|sung [fɛɐˈtsɪnzʊŋ] F -, **-en** (= *das Verzinsen*) payment of interest (+*gen*, *von* on); (= *Zinsertrag*) interest (yield or return) (+*gen*, *von* on); (= *Zinssatz*) interest rate

ver|zo|cken *ptp* **verzockt** VT (*inf*) to gamble away

ver|zo|gen [fɛɐˈtsoːgn] ADJ *Kind* badly brought up; (= *verwöhnt*) spoiled; *Tier* badly trained → *auch* **verziehen**

ver|zö|gern *ptp* **verzögert** **VT** to delay; (= *verlangsamen*) to slow down **VR** to be delayed

Ver|zö|ge|rung [fɛɐˈtsøːɡərʊŋ] F -, **-en a** delay, hold-up **b** *no pl* (= *das Verzögern*) delaying; (= *Verlangsamung*) slowing down; (*Phys*) deceleration; (*Mil*) holding action

Ver|zö|ge|rungs|tak|tik F delaying tactics *pl*

ver|zol|len *ptp* **verzollt** VT to pay duty on; **diese Waren müssen verzollt werden** you must pay duty on these articles; **haben Sie etwas zu ~?** have you anything to declare?; **verzollt** duty-paid

Ver|zol|lung [fɛɐˈtsɔlʊŋ] F -, **-en** payment of duty (+*gen* on)

ver|zopft [fɛɐˈtsɔpft] ADJ (*inf*: = *veraltet*) outdated

ver|zü|cken *ptp* **verzückt** VT to enrapture, to send into raptures or ecstasies

ver|zu|ckern *ptp* **verzuckert** **VI** *aux sein* (*Honig etc*) to crystallize **VT** (*fig*) to sweeten; **jdm etw ~** to sweeten sth for sb → **Pille**

ver|zückt [fɛɐˈtsʏkt] ADJ enraptured, ecstatic **ADV** *ansehen* adoringly; **~ lauschte er der Musik** he listened enraptured to the music

Ver|zü|ckung [fɛɐˈtsʏkʊŋ] F -, **-en** rapture, ecstasy; **in ~ geraten** to go into raptures or ecstasies (*wegen* over)

Ver|zug M , *no pl* **a** delay; (= *Rückstand von Zahlung*) arrears *pl*; **ohne ~** without delay, forthwith; **bei ~ (der Zahlungen)** on default of payment; **im ~** in arrears *pl* (*esp Brit*), behind; **mit etw in ~ geraten** to fall behind with sth; *mit Zahlungen* to fall into arrears (*esp Brit*) or behind with sth **b** **es ist Gefahr im ~** there's danger ahead **c** (*form: aus Stadt*) moving away

Ver|zugs|zin|sen PL interest *sing* payable (on arrears (*esp Brit*))

ver|zup|fen *ptp* **verzupft** VR (*Aus inf*) to be off (*inf*)

ver|zwackt [fɛɐˈtsvakt] ADJ (*inf*) tricky

ver|zwei|feln *ptp* **verzweifelt** VI *aux sein* to despair (*an* +*dat* of); **am Leben ~** to despair of life; **nur nicht ~!** don't despair!, don't give up!; **es ist zum Verzweifeln!** it makes you despair!, it drives you to despair!

ver|zwei|felt [fɛɐˈtsvaiflt] ADJ *Blick, Stimme etc* despairing *attr*, full of despair; *Mensch auch, Lage, Versuch, Kampf etc* desperate; **ich bin (völlig) ~** I'm in (the depths of) despair; (= *ratlos*) I just don't know what to do, I'm at my wits' end ADV desperately; *fragen, ringen um auch* despairingly; **..., sagte er ~ ...** he said despairingly; **schau nicht so ~** don't look so desperate

Ver|zweif|lung [fɛɐˈtsvaiflʊŋ] F -, **-en** (*Gemütszustand*) despair; (= *Ratlosigkeit*) desperation; **etw in seiner ~ tun, etw aus ~ tun** to do sth in desperation; **in ~ geraten** to despair; **jdn zur** or **in die ~ treiben** to drive sb to despair → **bringen e**

Ver|zweif|lungs|tat F act of desperation

ver|zwei|gen [fɛɐˈtsvaign] *ptp* **verzweigt** VR (*Bäume*) to branch (out); (*Straße*) to branch (off); (*Leitung*) to branch; (*Firma*) to establish branches; (*Anat, fig*) to ramify

ver|zweigt [fɛɐˈtsvaikt] ADJ *Baum, Familie, Firma, Straßennetz* branched; (*Anat, fig*) ramified

Ver|zwei|gung F -, **-en** (*von Baum*) branching (out); (*von Straße*) branching (off); (*von Leitung*) branching; (*Anat, fig*) ramification

ver|zwickt [fɛɐˈtsvɪkt] ADJ (*inf*) tricky

Ves|per¹ [ˈfɛspɐ] F -, **-n** (*Eccl*) vespers *pl*

Ves|per² NT **-s, -** (*dial*) (*auch* **Vesperpause, Vesperzeit**) break; (*auch* **Vesperbrot**) sandwiches *pl*

ves|pern [ˈfɛspɐn] (*dial*) **VT** to guzzle (*inf*) **VI** (= *essen*) to guzzle things (*inf*); (= *Pause machen*) to have a break; **er vespert gerade** he's just having his break

Ves|ti|bül [vɛstiˈbyːl] NT **-s, -e** (*dated, geh*) vestibule

Ve|te|ran¹ [veteˈraːn] M **-en, -en** (*Aut*) vintage car

Ve|te|ran² [veteˈraːn] M **-en, -en**, **Ve|te|ra|nin** [-ˈraːnɪn] F -, **-nen** (*Mil, fig*) veteran

Ve|te|ri|när [veteriˈnɛːɐ] M **-s, -e**, **Ve|te|ri|nä|rin** [-ˈnɛːrɪn] F -, **-nen** (*old, form*) veterinary surgeon

Ve|te|ri|när|me|di|zin F veterinary medicine

Ve|to [ˈveːto] NT **-s, -s** veto → **einlegen**

Ve|to|recht NT right of veto

Vet|tel [ˈfɛtl] F -, **-n** (*old pej*) hag

Vet|ter [ˈfɛtɐ] M **-s, -n** cousin; (*in Märchen*) Brother, Brer

Vet|tern|wirt|schaft F (*inf*) nepotism

Ve|xier|bild [vɛˈksiːɐ-] NT picture puzzle

ve|xie|ren [vɛˈksiːrən] *ptp* **vexiert** VT (*old*) to vex

Ve|xier|spiel [vɛˈksiːɐ-] NT game of deception

V-Form [ˈfau-] F V-shape; **in ~** in a V-shape, in (the shape of) a V

v-för|mig [ˈfau-], **V-för|mig** ADJ V-shaped, in (the shape of) a V ADV in the shape of a V; **~ aussehen** to look like a V, to be V-shaped; **der Pullover ist ~ ausgeschnitten** this sweater has a V-neck

V-Frau [ˈfau-] F *abbr von* **Verbindungsfrau**

VGA-Kar|te [fauɡeːˈʔaː-] F (*Comput*) VGA card

vgl. *abbr von* **vergleiche** cf

v. H. *abbr von* **vom Hundert** per cent (*Brit*), percent (*US*)

VHS¹ [fauhaːˈʔɛs] F -, *no pl abbr von* **Volkshochschule**

VHS² [fauha:'|ɛs] NT **-**, *no pl abbr von* **Video-Home-System** VHS

via ['vi:a] ADV via

Vi|a|dukt [via'dʊkt] M **-(e)s, -e** viaduct

Vi|ag|ra® [vi'a:gra] NT **-s** Viagra®

Vib|ra|fon ▲ [vibra'fo:n] NT **-s, -e**, **Vib|ra|phon** [vibra'fo:n] NT **-s, -e** vibraphone, vibraharp (*US*)

Vib|ra|ti|on [vibra'tsio:n] F **-, -en** vibration

vib|ra|to [vi'bra:to:] ADV (*Mus*) vibrato

Vib|ra|to [vi'bra:to:] NT **-s, -s** *or* **Vibrati** (*Mus*) vibrato

Vib|ra|tor [vi'bra:to:ɐ] M **-s, Vibratoren** [-'to:rən] vibrator

vib|rie|ren [vi'bri:rən] *ptp* **vibriert** VI to vibrate; (*Stimme*) to quiver, to tremble; (= *schwanken: Ton*) to vary, to fluctuate

Vi|deo ['vi:deo] NT **-s, -s** video; **etw auf ~ aufnehmen** to video sth, to record sth on video

Vi|de|o- *in cpds* video; **Vi|de|o|auf|nah|me** F video recording; **Vi|de|o|band** [-bant] NT *pl* **-bänder** video tape; **Vi|de|o|clip** M video clip; **Vi|de|o|film** M video (film); **Vi|de|o|ge|rät** NT video (recorder); **Vi|de|o|ka|me|ra** F video camera; **Vi|de|o|kas|set|te** F video cassette; **Vi|de|o|kon|fe|renz** F video conference; **Vi|de|o|pi|rat(in)** M(F) video pirate; **Vi|de|o|print** [-prɪnt] NT **-s, -s** video print; **Vi|de|o|prin|ter** [-prɪntɐ] M **-s, -** video printer; **Vi|de|o|re|kor|der** M video recorder; **Vi|de|o|spiel** NT video game; **Vi|de|o|tech|nik** F video technology; **Vi|de|o|text** M Teletext®; **Vi|de|o|thek** [video'te:k] F **-, -en** (*tape*) library; **vi|de|o|über|wacht** ADJ under video surveillance *pred*; **der Tunnel ist nicht ~** the tunnel has no closed-circuit TV cameras (installed); **Vi|de|o|über|wa|chung** F closed-circuit TV, CCTV, video surveillance; **Vi|de|o|ver|fah|ren** NT video *no art*

vi|die|ren [vi'di:rən] *ptp* **vidiert** VT (*Aus, obs*) to sign

Viech [fi:ç] NT **-(e)s, -er** (*inf*) creature

Vie|che|rei [fi:çə'rai] F **-, -en** (*inf*) **a** (= *Quälerei*) torture *no indef art* (*inf*) **b** (= *grober Scherz*) rotten trick

Vieh [fi:] NT **-(e)s**, *no pl* **a** (= *Nutztiere*) livestock; (= *esp Rinder*) cattle *pl*; **10 Stück ~** 10 head of livestock/cattle **b** (*inf*: = *Tier*) animal, beast (*usu hum*) **c** (*pej inf*: *Mensch*) swine

Vieh-: **Vieh|ab|trieb** M **der ~ findet jetzt statt** the livestock are being brought down from the mountain pastures now; **Vieh|auf|trieb** M **wir brauchen Leute für den ~** we need people to drive the livestock up into the mountain pastures; **Vieh|be|stand** M livestock; **Vieh|fut|ter** NT (animal) fodder *or* feed; **Vieh|hal|tung** F keeping of livestock; (*von Rindern*) keeping of cattle; **Vieh|han|del** M livestock trade; (*esp mit Rindern*) cattle trade; **Vieh|händ|ler(in)** M(F) livestock dealer; (*esp mit Rindern*) cattle dealer

vie|hisch ['fi:ɪʃ] ADJ brutish; *Schmerzen* beastly; (= *unzivilisiert*) *Benehmen* swinish ADV **a** *jucken, brennen* unbearably; **~ wehtun** to be unbearably painful **b** *sich benehmen* like an animal/animals; **~ essen** to eat like a pig; **~ hausen** to live like animals/an animal

Vieh-: **Vieh|markt** M livestock market; (*esp für Rinder*) cattle market; **Vieh|salz** NT (*für Tiere*) cattle salt; (*zum Streuen*) road salt; **Vieh|seu|che** F livestock disease; **Vieh|stall** M cattle shed; **Vieh|trei|ber(in)** M(F) drover; **Vieh|wa|gen** M cattle truck; **Vieh|wei|de** F pasture; **Vieh|wirt|schaft** F (live)stock farming, animal husbandry; **Vieh|zeug** NT, *no pl* (*inf*) animals *pl*, creatures *pl*; **Vieh|zucht** F (live)stock breeding; (= *Rinderzucht auch*) cattle breeding

viel [fi:l] INDEF PRON, ADJ *comp* **mehr** [me:ɐ], *superl* **meiste(r, s)** *or adv* **am meisten** ['maistə] **a** *sing* (*adjektivisch*) a lot of, a great deal of; (*sub-*

stantivisch) a lot, a great deal; (*esp fragend, verneint*) much; **~es** a lot of things; **~(es), was ..., ~(es) von dem, was ...** a lot *or* great deal of what ...; **in ~em, in ~er Hinsicht** *or* **Beziehung** in many respects; **mit ~em** with a lot of things; **um ~es besser** *etc* a lot *or* much *or* a great deal better *etc*; **sehr ~ (Geld** *etc***)** a lot *or* a great deal (of money *etc*); **nicht sehr ~ (Geld** *etc***)** not very much (money *etc*); **so ~** so much; **halb/doppelt so ~** half/twice as much; **so ~ als** *or* **wie ... as** much as ...; **nimm dir so ~ du willst** take as much as you like; **noch einmal so ~** the same again; (= *doppelt so viel*) twice as much; **das ist so ~ wie eine Zusage** that is tantamount to a promise, that amounts to a promise; **so ~ für heute!** that's all for today; **so ~, was ihn betrifft** so much for him; **so ~ (Arbeit** *etc***)** so much *or* such a lot (of work *etc*); **noch (ein)mal so ~ (Zeit** *etc***)** as much (time *etc*) again; **zweimal so ~ (Arbeit** *etc***)** twice as much (work *etc*); **gleich ~ (Gewinn** *etc***)** the same amount (of profit *etc*); **wie ~** how much; (*bei Mehrzahl*) how many; **(um) wie ~ größer** how much bigger; **ziemlich ~ (Schmutz** *etc***)** rather a lot (of dirt *etc*); **zu ~** too much; (*inf*: = *zu viele*) too many; **~ zu ~** much *or* far too much; **besser zu ~ als zu wenig** better too much than too little; **wenns dir zu ~ wird, sag Bescheid** say if it gets too much for you; **ihm ist alles zu ~** (*inf*) it's all too much for him; **da krieg ich zu ~** (*inf*) I blow my top (*inf*); **einer/zwei** *etc* **zu ~** one/two *etc* too many; **einen/ein paar zu ~ trinken** (*inf*) to drink *or* have (*inf*) one/a few too many; **was zu ~ ist, ist zu ~** that's just too much, there's a limit to everything; **ein bisschen ~ (Regen** *etc***)** a bit too much (rain *etc*); **furchtbar ~ (Regen** *etc***)** an awful lot (of rain *etc*); **~ Erfolg!** good luck!, I wish you every success!; **~ Spaß!** have fun!, enjoy yourself/yourselves!; **~ Neues/Schönes** *etc* a lot of *or* many new/beautiful *etc* things; **~ Volk** a lot of people; **das ~e Geld** all that money; **sein ~es Geld** all his money; **das ~e Geld/Lesen** *etc* all this money/reading *etc*; **~ zu tun haben** to have a lot to do; **er hält ~ von ihm/davon** he thinks a lot *or* a great deal of him/it; **er hält nicht ~ von ihm/davon** he doesn't think much of him/it; **das will ~/nicht ~ heißen** *or* **sagen** that's saying a lot *or* a great deal/not saying much

b **~e** *pl* (*adjektivisch*) many, a lot of, a great number of; (*substantivisch*) many, a lot; **es waren nicht ~e auf der Party** there weren't many (people) *or* a lot (of people) at the party; **es waren nicht ~e in der Schule** there weren't many (children) *or* a lot (of children) at school; **da wir so ~e sind** since there are so many *or* such a lot of us; **davon gibt es nicht ~e** there aren't many *or* a lot about; **davon gibt es nicht mehr ~e** there aren't many *or* a lot left; **furchtbar ~e (Kinder/Bewerbungen** *etc***)** a tremendous number *or* an awful lot (of children/applications *etc*); **gleich ~e (Angestellte/Anteile** *etc***)** the same number (of employees/shares *etc*); **so/zu ~e (Menschen/Fehler** *etc***)** so/too many (people/ mistakes *etc*); **er hat ~(e) Sorgen/Probleme** *etc* he has a lot of worries/problems *etc*; **~e hundert** *or* **Hundert Menschen** many hundreds of people; **die/seine ~en Fehler** *etc* the/his many mistakes *etc*; **die ~en Leute/Bücher!** all these people/books!; **~e glauben, ...** many (people) *or* a lot of people believe ...; **und ~e andere** and many others; **es waren derer** *or* **ihrer ~e** (*liter*) there were many of them

c (*adverbial: mit vb*) a lot, a great deal; (*esp fragend, verneint*) much; **er arbeitet ~** he works a lot; **er arbeitet nicht ~** he doesn't work much; **er arbeitet zu ~** he works too much; **er arbeitet so ~** he works so much *or* such a lot; **sie ist ~ krank/von zu Hause weg** she's ill/away a lot; **die Straße wird (sehr/nicht) ~ befahren** this street is (very/not very) busy; **dieses Thema wird ~ diskutiert** this subject is much debated; **sich ~ einbilden** to think a lot of oneself

d (*adverbial: mit adj, adv*) much, a lot; **~ größer** *etc* much *or* a lot bigger *etc*; **~ beschäftigt** very

busy; **~ diskutiert** much discussed; **~ erörtert** much discussed; **~ gehasst** much-hated; **~ gekauft** frequently bought, much-purchased; **~ geliebt** much-loved; **~ genannt** much-cited, frequently mentioned; **~ geprüft** (*hum*) sorely tried; **~ gereist** much-travelled (*Brit*), much-traveled (*US*); **~ geschmäht** much-maligned; **~ sagend** meaningful, significant; (*adverbial*) meaningfully; **jdn ~ sagend ansehen** to give sb a meaningful look; **sie schwiegen ~ sagend** there was a meaningful silence; **~ sagend lächeln** to give a meaningful smile; **~ umworben** much-sought-after; *Frau* much-courted; **~ verheißend** promising, full of promise; *anfangen* promisingly; **sich ~ verheißend anhören** to sound promising; **~ versprechend** promising, encouraging; *anfangen* promisingly; **~ versprechend klingen** to sound promising; **nicht ~ anders** not very *or* much *or* a lot different; **~ zu ...** much too ...; **~ zu ~** much *or* far too much; **~ zu ~e** far too many; **ich würde ~ lieber auf eine Party gehen** I'd much rather go to a party, I'd much prefer to go to a party

Viel-: **viel|bän|dig** ADJ multivolumed, in many volumes; **viel|be|schäf|tigt** △ ADJ *attr* → **viel d**; **viel|deu|tig** [-dɔytɪç] ADJ ambiguous; **Vieldeu|tig|keit** F **-**, *no pl* ambiguity; **viel|dis|kutiert** △ [-dɪskuti:ɐt] ADJ *attr* → **viel d**; **Viel|eck** NT polygon; **viel|eckig** ADJ polygonal (*Math*), many-sided; **Viel|ehe** F polygamy

vie|len|orts ['fi:lˈɔrts] ADV → **vielerorts**

vie|ler|lei ['fi:lɐˈlai] ADJ *inv* **a** various, all sorts of, many different **b** (*substantivisch*) all kinds *or* sorts of things

vie|ler|ör|tert △ ['fi:lˈɛɐˈ|œrtɐt] ADJ *attr* → **viel d**

vie|ler|orts ['fi:lˈɔrts] ADV in many places

viel|fach ['fi:lfax] ADJ multiple *attr*, manifold; **ein ~er Millionär** a multimillionaire; **auf ~e Weise** in many ways; **auf ~en Wunsch** at the request of many people ADV many times; (= *in vielen Fällen*) in many cases; (= *auf vielfache Weise*) in many ways; (*inf*: = *häufig*) frequently; **~ bewährt** tried and tested many times

Viel|fa|che(s) ['fi:lfaxə] NT *decl as adj* (*Math*) multiple; **das kleinste gemeinsame ~** (*Math*) the least *or* lowest common multiple; **um ein ~s** many times over; **um ein ~s besser/teurer** *etc* many times better/more expensive *etc*; **der Gewinn hat sich um ein ~s vermehrt** *or* **ist um ein ~s gestiegen** the profit has been multiplied several times; **er verdient ein ~s von dem, was ich verdiene** his salary is many times larger than mine

Viel|fah|rer(in) M(F) (*mit öffentlichen Verkehrsmitteln*) frequent traveller (*Brit*) *or* traveler (*US*) (*on public transport*); (*mit Auto*) frequent car user

Viel|falt ['fi:lfalt] F **-**, *no pl* (great) variety

viel|fäl|tig ['fi:lfɛltɪç] ADJ varied, diverse

Viel|fäl|tig|keit F **-**, *no pl* variety, diversity

Viel-: **viel|far|big**, (*Aus*) **viel|fär|big** ADJ multicoloured (*Brit*), multicolored (*US*); (*Tech*) polychrome *attr*, polychromatic; **viel|flä|chig** ADJ many-faced, polyhedral (*Math*); **Vielfläch|ner** [-flɛçnɐ] M **-s, -** (*Math*) polyhedron; **Viel|flie|ger(in)** M(F) frequent flier; **Viel|fraß** M **a** (*fig*) glutton **b** (*Zool*) wolverine, glutton; **viel|ge|haßt** △ [-ɡəhast] ADJ *attr* → **viel d**; **viel|ge|kauft** △ [-ɡəkauft] ADJ *attr* → **viel d**; **viel|ge|liebt** △ ADJ *attr* → **viel d**; **viel|genannt** △ ADJ *attr* → **viel d**; **viel|ge|prüft** △ [-ɡəpry:ft] ADJ *attr* → **viel d**; **viel|ge|reist** △ [-ɡəraist] ADJ *attr* → **viel d**; **viel|ge|schmäht** △ [-ɡəʃmɛːt] ADJ *attr* → **viel d**; **viel|ge|stal|tig** [-ɡəʃtaltɪç] ADJ variously shaped, varied in shape and form, multiform (*form*); (*fig*: = *mannigfaltig*) varied; **in ~er Weise** in multifarious ways; **Viel|ge|stal|tig|keit** F **-**, *no pl* (*Sci*) polymorphism; (*fig*) variety; **viel|glie|de|rig** [-gli:dərɪç], **viel|glied|rig** [-gli:drɪç] ADJ having many parts, with many parts; (*Math*) polynomial; **Viel|göt|te|rei** [-ɡœtəˈrai] F **-**, *no pl* polytheism; **viel|hun|dert|mal** [fi:lˈhʊndɐtma:l] ADV (*liter*) hundreds upon hundreds of times, many hundreds of times; **viel|köp|fig** ADJ many--headed, polycephalous (*Sci, form*); (*inf*) *Familie, Schar* large

viel|leicht [fiˈlaiçt] ADV **a** perhaps; (*esp in Bitten*) by any chance; **ja, ~** yes, perhaps or maybe; **haben Sie ~ meinen Hund gesehen?** have you seen my dog by any chance?; **könnten Sie mir ~ sagen, wie spät es ist?** could you possibly tell me the time?; **~ könnten Sie so freundlich sein und ...?** perhaps you'd be so kind as to ...?; **~ sagst du mir mal, warum** you'd better tell me why; **~ hältst du mal den Mund!** keep your mouth shut; **hat er sich ~ verirrt/wehgetan?** maybe he has got lost/has hurt himself; **hast du ihm das ~ erzählt?** did you perhaps tell him that?; (*entsetzt: = denn etwa*) you didn't tell him that, did you?; **~ hast du Recht** perhaps you're right, you may be right, maybe you're right; **~, dass ...** it could be that ...
b (= *wirklich, tatsächlich, inf: verstärkend*) really; **soll ich ~ 24 Stunden arbeiten?!** am I supposed to work 24 hours then?; **willst du mir ~ erzählen, dass ...?!** do you really mean to tell me that ...?; **du bist ~ ein Idiot!** you really are an idiot!; **ich war ~ nervös!** I wasn't half nervous! (*Brit inf*), was I nervous!, I was as nervous as anything (*inf*); **das ist ~ ein Haus!** that's what I call a house! (*inf*), that's some house! (*inf*)
c (= *ungefähr*) perhaps, about

viel|mal [ˈfiːlmaːl] ADV (*Sw*) = **vielmals**

viel|ma|lig [ˈfiːlmaːlɪç] ADJ *attr* repeated

viel|mals [ˈfiːlmaːls] ADV **a** (*in bestimmten Wendungen*) **danke ~!** thank you very much!, many thanks!; **ich bitte ~ um Entschuldigung!** I do apologize!; **er lässt ~ grüßen** he sends his best regards **b** (*liter: = häufig*) many times, ofttimes (*liter*)

Viel|män|ne|rei [-mɛnəˈrai] F -, *no pl* polyandry, polyandry

viel|mehr [fiːlˈmeːɐ, ˈfiːl-] ADV rather; (= *sondern, nur*) just; **ich glaube ~, dass ...** rather I or I rather think that ...; **nicht dumm, ~ faul** lazy rather than stupid, not stupid just lazy

Viel-: viel|sa|gend △ [-zaːɡnt] ADJ → **viel d**; **viel|schich|tig** [-ʃɪçtɪç] ADJ (*lit rare*) multilayered; (*fig*) complex; **Viel|schich|tig|keit** F -, *no pl* (*fig*) complexity; **Viel|schrei|ber(in)** M(F) prolific writer; **er ist ein richtiger ~** (*pej*) he really churns out the stuff (*inf*); **viel|sei|tig** [-zaitɪç] ADV (*lit*) many-sided; *Mensch, Gerät, Verwendung* versatile; *Interessen* varied; *Ausbildung* broad, all-round *attr* (*Brit*), all-around *attr* (*US*); **dieser Beruf ist sehr ~** there are many different sides to this job; **auf ~en Wunsch** by popular request ADV **~ interessiert/anwendbar** *etc* to have varied interests/many uses *etc*; **~ ausgebildet sein** to have an all-round (*Brit*) or all-round (*US*) education; **~ gebildet sein** to be well-educated; **~ informiert sein** to be well--informed; **~ anwendbar/einsetzbar sein** to be versatile; **Kompost ist ~ verwendbar** compost can be used for many purposes; **Viel|sei|tig|keit** F -, *no pl* (*von Mensch, Gerät, Verwendung*) versatility; (*von Interessen*) multiplicity; (*von Ausbildung*) broadness, all-round nature (*Brit*); **viel|spra|chig** ADJ multilingual, polyglot; **er ist ~** he is multilingual or a polyglot; **Viel|staa|te|rei** [-ʃtaːtəˈrai] F -, *no pl* particularism; **viel|stim|mig** ADJ *Chor, Gesang, Schreie* many-voiced; **viel|tau|send|mal** [fiːlˈtauzntmaːl] ADV (*liter*) thousands upon thousands of times, many thousands of times; **viel|um|wor|ben** △ [-ˈʊmvɔrbn] ADJ *attr* → **viel d**; **viel|ver|hei|ßend** △ [-fɛɐhaisnt] ADJ → **viel d**; **viel|ver|spre|chend** △ [-fɛɐʃprɛçnt] ADJ → **viel d**; **Viel|völ|ker|staat** [fiːlˈfœlkɐ-] M multiracial state; **Viel|wei|be|rei** [-vaibəˈrai] F -, *no pl* polygamy, polygyny; **Viel|zahl** F multitude; **ei-ne ~ von Abbildungen** a wealth of illustrations

Viel|zweck- *in cpds* multipurpose; **Viel|zweck|-rei|ni|ger** M multipurpose cleaner

---

vier [viːɐ] NUM **a** four; **die ersten/nächsten/letzten ~** the first/next/last four; **sie ist ~ (Jah-re)** she's four (years old); **mit ~ (Jahren)** at the age of four; **~ Millionen** four million; **es ist ~ (Uhr)** it's four (o'clock); **um/gegen ~ (Uhr)** or **~e** (*inf*) at/around four (o'clock); **~ Uhr ~** four minutes past four; **~/fünf Minuten vor/nach ~** four minutes/five (minutes) to/past four; **halb ~** half past three; **~ Minuten vor halb ~** twenty--six minutes past three; **~ Minuten nach halb ~** twenty-six minutes to four; **für** or **auf ~ Tage** for four days; **in ~ Tagen** in four days, in four days' time; **~ zu drei** (*geschrieben 4:3*) four-three, four to three, 4-3; **wir waren** or **zu ~t** or **zu ~en** or **unser ~** (*geh*) there were four of us, we were four in number (*form*); **wir fahren zu ~t** or **mit ~en in Urlaub** there are four of us going on holiday (*esp Brit*) or vacation (*US*) together, we are going on holiday (*esp Brit*) or vacation (*US*) as a foursome; **sie kamen zu ~t** or **zu ~en** four of them came; **stellt euch ~ und ~** or **zu je ~** or **zu ~t** or **zu ~en auf** line up in fours; **eine Familie von ~en** (*inf*) a family of four; **Vater ~er Töchter, Vater von ~ Töchtern** father of four daughters
b jdn unter ~ Augen sprechen to speak to sb privately or in private; **ein Gespräch unter ~ Augen** a private conversation or talk, a tête-à--tête; **jdn um ein Gespräch unter ~ Augen bitten** to ask to speak to sb privately or in private; **~ Augen sehen mehr als zwei** (*prov*) two heads are better than one (*prov*); **alle ~e von sich strecken** (*inf*) (= *ausgestreckt liegen*) to stretch out; (= *tot sein*) to have given up the ghost; **auf allen ~en** (*inf*) on all fours; **sich auf seine ~ Buchstaben setzen** (*hum inf*) to sit oneself down → **Wind b, Wand, Hand b**

Vier [viːɐ] F -, **-en** four; (*Buslinie etc*) (number) four

Vier-: Vier|ach|ser [-laksɐ] M -s, - (*Aut*) four-axle vehicle; **vier|ar|mig** ADJ with four arms; *Leuchter* with four branches; **Vier-Au|gen-Ge|-spräch** NT, **Vier|au|gen|ge|spräch** NT personal or private discussion; **vier|bän|dig** ADJ four-volume *attr*, in four volumes; **Vier|bei-ner** [-bainɐ] M -s, - (*hum*) four-legged friend (*hum*); **vier|bei|nig** ADJ four-legged; **vier|blät|te|rig, vier|blätt|rig** ADJ four-leaf *attr*, four-leaved; **vier|di|men|si|o|nal** ADJ four-dimensional; **Vier|eck** NT four-sided figure, quadrilateral (*Math*); (= *Rechteck*) rectangle; **vier|eckig** ADJ square; (*esp Math*) four-sided, quadrangular, quadrilateral; (= *rechteckig*) rectangular; **vier|ein|halb** [fiːɐainˈhalp] NUM four and a half

Vie|rer [ˈfiːrɐ] M -s, - (*Rudern, Sch*) four; (*Golf*) foursome; (*inf: = Linie*) (number) four; (*Aus, S Ger: Ziffer*) four; **einen ~ im Lotto haben** to have four numbers in the lottery

Vie|rer-: Vie|rer|ban|de F Gang of Four; **Vie|-rer|bob** M four-man bob (*Brit*) or bobsled (*US*); **Vie|rer|grup|pe** F group of four; **vie|-rer|lei** [ˈfiːrəlai] ADJ *inv* **a** *attr Brot, Käse, Wein* four kinds or sorts of; *Möglichkeiten, Fälle, Größen* four different **b** (*substantivisch*) four different things; (= *vier Sorten*) four different kinds; **Vie|-rer|pasch** M (all) fours *no indef art*; **Vie|rer|rei|he** F row of four; **Vie|rer|tref|fen** NT (*Pol*) (*der vier Mächte*) four-power conference, meeting of the four powers; (*von Politikern*) meeting of four politicians

vier|fach [ˈfiːɐfax] ADJ ▲ fourfold, quadruple (*esp Math*); **die ~e Größe/Menge/Anzahl** four times the size/amount/number; **in ~er Ausfertigung** in quadruplicate; **in ~er Vergrößerung** enlarged four times ADV four times, fourfold; **das Papier ~ legen** or **nehmen** to fold the paper in four; **den Faden ~ nehmen** to take four threads together; **er hat den Band ~** he has four copies of the book

Vier|fa|che(s) [ˈfiːɐfaxə] NT *decl as adj* four times the amount, quadruple (*Math*); **das ~ von 3 ist 12** four times 3 is 12; **um das ~ zuneh-**

---

men to quadruple; **das ~ von jdm verdienen** to earn four times as much as sb

Vier-: Vier|fach|steck|do|se F (*Elec*) 4-socket plug; **vier|fäl|tig** ADJ = **vierfach**; **Vier|far|ben|druck** M *pl* **-drucke** (*Verfahren*) four-colour (*Brit*) or four-color (*US*) printing; (*Erzeugnis*) four-colo(u)r print; **Vier|far|ben|stift** M, **Vier|farb|stift** M four-colour (*Brit*) or four-color (*US*) pen; **vier|far|big** ▲ four-colour *attr* (*Brit*), four-color *attr* (*US*) ADV in four colo(u)rs; **Vier|fel|der|wirt|schaft** F four-course rotation; **Vier|flach** [-flax] NT -(e)s, -e (*Math*) tetrahedron; **vier|flä|chig** ADJ *Körper, Gebilde* tetrahedral; **Vier|frucht|mar|me|la|de** F four-fruit jam; **Vier|fü|ßer** [-fyːsɐ] M -s, - (*Zool*) quadruped, tetrapod (*spec*); **vier|fü|ßig** ADJ four-legged, quadruped(al) (*spec*); (*Poet*) tetrameter *attr*, with four feet; **Vier|füß|ler** [-fyːslɐ] M -s, - (*Zool*) quadruped, tetrapod (*spec*); **Vier|gang|ge|trie|be** NT four-speed gearbox; **vier|ge|schos|sig**, (*Aus, S Ger*) **vier|ge|scho|ßig** ADJ, ADV four-storey *attr* (*Brit*), four-story (*US*), four-storeyed (*Brit*), four--storied (*US*); **~ bauen** to build houses with four storeys (*Brit*) or stories (*US*); **Vier|ge|-spann** NT (= *vier Tiere, Wagen mit vier Tieren*) four-in-hand; (*Hist: = Quadriga*) quadriga; (= *vier Menschen*) foursome; **vier|glied|rig** [-ɡliːdrɪç] ADJ (*Math*) quadrinomial; **vier|hän|dig** ADJ ▲ (*Mus*) four-handed ADV **~ spielen** to play something for four hands; **vier|he|big** ▲ (*Poet*) tetrameter; **~ sein** to be a tetrameter

vier|hun|dert [ˈfiːɐhʊndɐt] NUM four hundred

Vier|hun|dert|jahr|fei|er F quatercentenary (*Brit*), quadricentennial (*US*)

vier|hun|derts|te(r, s) [ˈfiːɐhʊndɐtstə] ADJ four hundredth

vier|hun|dert|tau|send NUM four hundred thousand

Vier-: Vier|jah|res|plan M (*Econ*) four-year plan; **vier|jäh|rig, 4-jäh|rig** ▲ (= *4 Jahre alt*) four-year-old *attr*; (= *4 Jahre dauernd*) four--year *attr*, quadrennial; **ein ~es Kind** a four--year-old child, a child of four; **Vier|jäh|ri|ge(r)** [-jɛːrɪɡə] MF *decl as adj* four-year-old; **Vier|-kampf** M (*Sport*) four-part competition; **Vier|-kant** [-kant] ADJ, ADV (*Naut*) square; **Vier|-kant** [-kant] M OR NT -(e)s, -e (*Tech*) square; (*Math*) tetrahedron; **Vier|kant|ei|sen** NT square steel bar; **Vier|kant|holz** NT squared timber; **vier|kan|tig** ADJ square(-headed) → **achtkantig**; **Vier|kant|schlüs|sel** M square box spanner (*Brit*) or wrench (*US*); **vier|köp|-fig** ADJ *Ungeheuer* four-headed; **eine ~e Familie** a family of four

Vier|ling [ˈfiːɐlɪŋ] M -s, -e quadruplet, quad (*inf*)

Vier|mäch|te|ab|kom|men NT (*esp Hist: über Berlin*) quadripartite or four-power agreement

vier|mal [ˈfiːɐmaːl] ADV four times; **~ so viele** four times as many

vier|ma|lig [ˈfiːɐmaːlɪç] ADJ done or repeated four times; *Weltmeister, Olympiasieger etc* four--times *attr*; **~es Klingeln** four rings, **~e Vorstel-lungen** four performances; **nach ~em Versuch** after the fourth attempt; **nach ~er Aufforderung** after the fourth time of asking, after four repeated requests

Vier|mas|ter [-mastɐ] M -s, - (*Naut*) four-master

vier|mo|na|tig ADJ *attr Säugling* four-month--old; *Abstände* four-monthly; *Lieferungsfrist, Aufenthalt, Waffenstillstand* four-month

vier|mo|nat|lich ▲ *attr Erscheinen* four--monthly ADV *erscheinen, sich wiederholen* every four months

vier|mo|to|rig ADJ four-engined

Vier|pfün|der M four-pounder

vier|pha|sig ADJ (*Elec*) four-phase

Vier|rad- (*Aut*): **Vier|rad|an|trieb** M four--wheel drive; **Vier|rad|brem|se** F four-wheel braking system

---

Vier-: **vier|rä|de|rig**, **vier|räd|rig** ADJ four--wheel *attr*, four-wheeled; **das Auto ist ~** that car is a four-wheeler; **~ sein** to have four strings; **Vier|schan|zen|tour|nee** F (*Ski*) Four Hills Tournament; **vier|schrö|tig** [-ʃrøːtɪç] ADJ burly; **vier|sei|tig** [-zaɪtɪç] ADJ four-sided; *Abkommen, Verhandlungen etc* quadripartite; *Brief, Broschüre* four-page *attr*; **Vier|sil|ber** [-zɪlbɐ] M **-s, -** (*Poet*) tetrasyllable; **vier|sil|big** ADJ four-syllable *attr*, quadrisyllabic, tetrasyllabic; **Vier|sit|zer** M four-seater; **vier|sit|zig** [-zɪtsɪç] ADJ four--seater *attr*, with four seats; **~ sein** to be a four--seater, to have four seats; **~ spal|tig** [-ʃpal-tɪç] ADJ four-column *attr*; **~ sein** to have four columns ADV in four columns; **Vier|spän|ner** M four-in-hand; **vier|spän|nig** ADJ *Wagen* four-horse *attr* ADV **~ fahren** to drive a team of four horses, to drive a four-in-hand; **vier|spra|chig** ADJ *Mensch, Wörterbuch* quadrilingual; *Speisekarte* in four languages; **das Buch wird ~ angeboten** the book is available in four languages; **vier|spu|rig** [-ʃpuːrɪç] ADJ four-lane *attr*, **~ sein** to have four lanes ADV **eine Straße ~ bauen/planen** to build/plan a four-lane road; **etw vierspurig ausbauen** to expand sth to four lanes; **vier|stel|lig** ADJ four-figure *attr*; (*Math*) *Funktion, Dezimalbruch* four-place *attr*; **~ sein** to have four figures/places; **Rechnungen in ~er Höhe** four-figure bills; **vier|stern|ig** ADJ 4-star hotel; **vier|stim|mig** ADJ four-part *attr*, for four voices ADV **~ singen** to sing a song for four voices; **vier|stö|ckig** ADJ *Haus* four-storey *attr* (*Brit*), four-story *attr* (*US*), four-storeyed (*Brit*), four-storied (*US*), four storeys (*Brit*) or stories (*US*) high ADV **~ bauen** to build houses with four storeys (*Brit*) or stories (*US*); **vier|strah|lig** ADJ *Flugzeug* four-jet *attr*, four-engined; **vier|stro|phig** ADJ *Gedicht* four-verse *attr*, four-stanza *attr*; **~ sein** to have four verses or stanzas; **Vier|stu|fen|ra|ke|te** F four-stage rocket; **vier|stu|fig** ADJ four-stage *attr*; **~ sein** to have four stages; **vier|stün|dig** ADJ *attr Reise, Vortrag* four-hour; **vier|stünd|lich** ADJ *attr* four-hourly ADV every four hours

viert [fiːɐt] ADJ **a** **zu ~** → **vier** **b** → **vierte(r, s)**

Vier-: **Vier|ta|ge|wo|che** F four-day week; **vier|tä|gig** ADJ *attr* (= *4 Tage dauernd*) four--day; (= *4 Tage alt*) four-day-old; **vier|täg|lich** ADJ, ADV every four days; **Vier|tak|ter** [-taktɐ] M **-s, -** (*inf*), **Vier|takt|mo|tor** M four-stroke (engine); **vier|tau|send** ['fiːɐ'tauznt] NUM four thousand; **Vier|tau|sen|der** [-'tauzndɐ] M **-s, -** (*Berg*) four-thousand-metre (*Brit*) or four--thousand-meter (*US*) mountain

vier|te ADJ → **vierte(r, s)**

Vier-: **vier|tei|len** ['fiːɐtaɪlən] VT **a** insep (*Hist*) to quarter **b** sep = **vierteln**; **vier|tei|lig** ADJ (= *mit vier einzelnen Teilen*) four-piece *attr*; *Roman, Fernsehserie* four-part *attr*, in four parts; **~ sein** to have four pieces/parts; **ich habe dieses Service nur ~** I only have four settings of this dinner service

vier|tel ['fɪrtl] ADJ inv quarter; **ein ~ Liter/Pfund** a quarter (of a) litre (*Brit*) or liter (*US*)/pound; **drei ~ Liter** three quarters of a litre (*Brit*) or liter (*US*); **drei ~ voll** three-quarters full → *auch* **Viertel**¹

Vier|tel¹ ['fɪrtl] NT (SW AUCH M) **-s, -** **a** (*Bruchteil*) quarter; (inf) (= *Viertelpfund*) = quarter; (= *Viertelliter*) quarter litre (*Brit*) or liter (*US*); **drei ~ der Bevölkerung** three quarters of the population; **der Mond ist im ersten/letzten ~** the moon is in the first/last quarter; **ein ~ Wein** a quarter litre (*Brit*) or liter (*US*) of wine; **ein ~ Butter** a quarter of butter **b** (*Uhrzeit*) **(ein) ~ nach/vor sechs** (a) quarter past/to six; **(ein) ~ sechs** (a) quarter past five; **drei viertel sechs** (dial) (a) quarter to six; **um viertel/drei viertel sechs** (dial) at (a) quarter past five/(a) quarter to six; **fünf Minuten vor ~/drei** ~ ten past/twenty to; **es ist ~** it's (a) quarter past; **die Uhr schlug ~** the clock struck (a) quarter past or the quarter → **akademisch**

Vier|tel² [fɪrtl] NT **-s, -** (= *Stadtbezirk*) quarter, district

Vier|tel- ['fɪrtl-]: **Vier|tel|dre|hung** F quarter turn; **Vier|tel|fi|na|le** NT quarterfinals *pl*; **Vier|tel|fi|nal|spiel** NT quarterfinal

Vier|tel|jahr NT three months *pl*, quarter (*Comm, Fin*)

Vier|tel|jah|res- in cpds quarterly; **Vier|tel|jah|res|er|geb|nis** NT (*Comm*) quarterly results *pl*; **Vier|tel|jah|res|schrift** F quarterly

Vier|tel-: **Vier|tel|jahr|hun|dert** NT quarter of a century; **vier|tel|jäh|rig** ADJ *attr Kind etc* three-month-old; *Aufenthalt, Frist* three months'; **vier|tel|jähr|lich** ADJ quarterly; *Kündigungsfrist* three months' *attr* ADJ quarterly, every three months; **~ kündigen** to give three months' notice; **Vier|tel|kreis** M quadrant; **Vier|tel|li|ter** M OR NT quarter of a litre (*Brit*) or liter (*US*), quarter litre (*Brit*) or liter (*US*)

vier|teln ['fɪrtln] VT (= *in vier Teile teilen*) to divide into four; *Kuchen, Apfel etc auch* to divide into quarters; (= *durch vier teilen*) to divide by four; *Summe, Gewinn* to quarter, to divide by four

Vier|tel- ['fɪrtl-]: **Vier|tel|no|te** F crotchet (*Brit*), quarter note (*US*); **Vier|tel|pau|se** F crotchet rest (*Brit*), quarter-note rest (*US*); **Vier|tel|pfund** NT ≈ quarter of a pound, ≈ quarter (pound); **Vier|tel|stun|de** F quarter of an hour; **vier|tel|stün|dig** ADJ *attr Abstand* quarter-hour, of a quarter of an hour; *Vortrag* lasting or of a quarter of an hour; **vier|tel|stünd|lich** ADJ *attr Abstand* quarter-hour, of a quarter of an hour ADV every quarter of an hour, quarter-hourly; **Vier|tel|ton** M *pl* **-töne** quarter tone

vier|tens ['fiːɐtns] ADV fourth(ly), in the fourth place

Vier|te(r) ['fiːɐtə] MF decl as adj fourth; **~r werden** to be or come fourth; **am ~n (des Monats)** on the fourth (of the month); **Karl IV.** or **der ~** Charles IV or the Fourth; **er war ~r im Rennen** he was or came fourth in the race; **als ~r durchs Ziel gehen** to be fourth at the finish; **du bist der ~, der mich das fragt** you're the fourth person to ask me that; **jeder ~ muss ...** every fourth person/boy etc has to ...

vierte(r, s) ['fiːɐtə] ADJ fourth; **der ~ Oktober** the fourth of October; **den 4. Oktober** October 4th, October the fourth; **am ~n Oktober** on the fourth of October; **der ~ Stock** the fourth (*Brit*) or fifth (*US*) floor; **der ~ Stand** the Fourth Estate; **im ~n Kapitel/Akt** in the fourth chapter/act, in chapter/act four → *auch* **Vierte(r)**

viert|letz|te(r, s) ['fiːɐt'lɛtstə] ADJ fourth (from) last

Vier-: **Vier|ton|ner** [-tɔnɐ] M **-s, -** ≈ four-ton truck, four-tonner; **Vier|tü|rer** [-tyːrɐ] M **-s, -** (*Aut*) four-door model; **vier|tü|rig** ADJ four--door *attr*, with four doors; **~ sein** to have four doors; **Vier|uhr|zug** M , **4-Uhr-Zug** M four o'clock (train); **vier|und|ein|halb** NUM four and a half; **Vier|und|sech|zigs|tel|no|te** F hemidemisemiquaver (*Brit*), sixty-fourth note (*US*); **Vier|und|sech|zigs|tel|pau|se** F hemidemisemiquaver rest (*Brit*), sixty-fourth note rest (*US*); **vier|und|zwan|zig** NUM twenty--four

Vie|rung ['fiːrʊŋ] F **-, -en** (*Archit*) crossing

Vie|rungs-: **Vie|rungs|kup|pel** F (*Archit*) crossing cupola; **Vie|rungs|turm** M (*Archit*) crossing tower

Vier|vier|tel|takt [-'fɪrtl-] M four-four or common time

Vier|wald|stät|ter See [fiːɐ'valtʃtɛtɐ] M Lake Lucerne

vier-: **vier|wer|tig** ADJ (*Chem*) quadrivalent, tetravalent; (*Ling*) four-place; **vier|wö|chent|lich** ADJ adv every four weeks; **vier|wö|chig** [-vœçɪç] ADJ four-week *attr*, four weeks long

vier|zehn ['fɪrtseːn] NUM fourteen; **~ Uhr** 2 pm; (*auf Fahrplan, Mil*) fourteen hundred hours, 1400; **~ Tage** two weeks, a fortnight sing (*Brit*); **die Vierzehn Punkte** (*Hist*) the Fourteen Points

Vier|zehn- ['fɪrtseːn-]: **Vier|zehn|en|der** M (*Hunt*) fourteen-pointer; **vier|zehn|tä|gig** ADJ two-week *attr*, lasting a fortnight (*Brit*) or two weeks; **nach ~er Dauer** after two weeks, after a fortnight (*Brit*); **vier|zehn|täg|lich** ADJ, ADV fortnightly (*Brit*), every two weeks

vier|zehn|te(r, s) ['fɪrtseːntə] ADJ fourteenth → **vierte(r, s)**, **Vierte(r)**

Vier-: **Vier|zei|ler** [-tsaɪlɐ] M **-s, -** four-line poem; (= *Strophe*) four-line stanza, quatrain; **vier|zei|lig** ADJ four-line *attr*, of four lines; **~ sein** to have four lines

vier|zig ['fɪrtsɪç] NUM forty; **(mit) ~ (km/h) fahren** to drive at forty kilometres (*Brit*) or kilometers (*US*) an hour; **etwa ~ (Jahre alt)** about forty (years old); (*Mensch auch*) fortyish (inf); **mit ~ (Jahren)** at forty (years of age); **Mitte ~** in one's mid-forties; **über ~** over forty; **der Mensch über ~** people *pl* over forty; **im Jahre ~** in forty; (= *vierzig nach/vor Christi Geburt*) in (the year) forty (AD/BC)

Vier|zig ['fɪrtsɪç] F **-, -en** forty

vier|zi|ger, 40er ['fɪrtsɪgɐ] ADJ *attr inv* **die ~ Jahre** the forties; **ein ~ Jahrgang** (*Mensch*) a person born in nineteen forty; (*Wein*) a vintage forty

Vier|zi|ger¹ ['fɪrtsɪgɐ] M **-s, -** **a** (*Wein*) wine of vintage forty **b** (*Aus, S Ger: Geburtstag*) fortieth (birthday) **c** **die ~** *pl* (= *Vierzigerjahre*) one's forties; **er ist in den ~n** he is in his forties; **er ist Mitte der ~** he is in his mid-forties; **in die ~ kommen** to be getting on for forty

Vier|zi|ger² ['fɪrtsɪgɐ] M **-s, -**, **Vier|zi|ge|rin** [-ərɪn] F **-, -nen** forty-year-old; **die ~** *pl* people in their forties

Vier|zi|ger|jah|re PL **die ~** one's forties

Vier|zig-: **vier|zig|fach** ['fɪrtsɪçfax] ADJ forty-fold ADV forty times → **vierfach**; **vier|zig|jäh|rig** ['fɪrtsɪç-] ADJ *attr* (= *40 Jahre alt*) forty-year--old; (= *40 Jahre dauernd*) forty-year; **das ~e Jubiläum** the 40th anniversary; **ein Vierzigjähriger** a forty-year-old; **vier|zig|mal** ['fɪrtsɪçmaːl] ADV forty times

vier|zigs|tel ['fɪrtsɪçstl] ADJ inv fortieth; **eine ~ Minute** a or one fortieth of a minute

Vier|zigs|tel ['fɪrtsɪçstl] NT **-s, -** fortieth; **ein ~ des Kuchens/der Summe** a fortieth (part) of the cake/the amount

vier|zigs|te(r, s) ['fɪrtsɪçstə] ADJ fortieth

Vier|zig|stun|den|wo|che F forty-hour week

Vier-: **Vier|zim|mer|woh|nung** F four-room or three-bedroom(ed) flat (*Brit*) or apartment; **Vier|zy|lin|der|mo|tor** M four-cylinder engine; **vier|zy|lind|rig** ADJ four-cylinder *attr*

Vi|et|cong [viɛt'kɔŋ] M **-, -(s)**, **Vi|et|kong** [viɛt-'kɔŋ] M **-, -(s)** Vietcong

Vi|et|nam [viɛt'nam] NT **-s** Vietnam

Vi|et|na|me|se [viɛtna'meːzə] M **-n, -n**, **Vi|et|na|me|sin** [-'meːzɪn] F **-, -nen** Vietnamese; **zum ~n gehen** to go to a or the Vietnamese restaurant

vi|et|na|me|sisch [viɛtna'meːzɪʃ] ADJ Vietnamese

Vi|et|na|me|sisch(e) NT (*Ling*) Vietnamese → *auch* **Deutsch(e)**

vif [viːf] ADJ (old, dial) bright

Vi|gil [vi'giːl] F **-, -ien** [-liən] vigil

Vig|net|te [vɪn'jɛtə] F **-, -n** vignette; (*Aut*) permit (*for motorway driving*)

Switzerland a **Vignette** is valid for one year. In Austria, where it is also jocularly known as a **Pickerl**, one can buy a **Vignette** that is valid for one week or two months. On certain motorways in Austria, a toll, the **Maut**, is also payable.

Vi|kar [vɪˈkaːɐ] M **-s, -e**, **Vi|ka|rin** [-ˈkaːrɪn] F **-, -nen** curate; (*Sw Sch*) supply teacher (*Brit*), substitute teacher (*US*)

Vi|ka|ri|at [vika'riaːt] NT **-(e)s, -e** curacy

vik|to|ri|a|nisch [vɪktoˈriaːnɪʃ] ADJ Victorian; **das ~e Zeitalter** the Victorian Age

Vik|tu|a|li|en [vɪkˈtuaːliən] PL (*obs*) victuals pl (*old, form*)

Vik|tu|a|li|en|markt M food market

Vil|la [ˈvɪla] F **-, Villen** [-lən] villa

Vil|len|vier|tel NT exclusive residential area

Vi|naig|ret|te [vinɛˈgrɛtə] F **-, -n** (*Cook*) vinaigrette (sauce)

vin|ku|lie|ren [vɪŋkuˈliːrən] ptp **vinkuliert** VT (*Fin*) to restrict transferability of

Vi|nyl [viˈnyːl] NT **-s**, no pl (*Chem*) vinyl

Vi|o|la [ˈviːola] F **-, Violen** [ˈvioːlən] **a** (*Mus*) viola **b** (*Bot*) violet

Vi|o|la da Gam|ba [ˈvioːla da ˈgamba] ▲ F **- - -**, **Viole - -** [ˈvioːlə] viola da gamba

Vi|o|le [ˈvioːlə] F **-, -n** (*Bot*) violet

vi|o|lett [vioˈlɛt] ADJ purple, violet; (*im Spektrum, Regenbogen*) violet

Vi|o|lett [vioˈlɛt] NT **-s, -** purple, violet; (*im Spektrum, Regenbogen*) violet

Vi|o|li|ne [vioˈliːnə] F **-, -n** violin; **die erste/zweite ~ spielen** to play first/second violin

Vi|o|li|nist [violiˈnɪst] M **-en, -en**, **Vi|o|li|nis|tin** [-ˈnɪstɪn] F **-, -nen** violinist

Vi|o|lin-: **Vi|o|lin|kon|zert** NT violin concerto; (*Darbietung*) violin concert; **Vi|o|lin|schlüs|sel** M treble clef

Vi|o|lon|cell [violɔnˈtʃɛl] NT **-s, -e**, **Vi|o|lon|cel|lo** [violɔnˈtʃɛlo] NT violoncello

VIP [vɪp] M **-, -s** (*inf*), **V. I. P.** [viːlaiˈpiː] M **-, -s** (*inf*) abbr von **Very Important Person** VIP

Vi|per [ˈviːpɐ] F **-, -n** viper, adder

Vi|ren pl von **Virus**

Vi|ren|such|pro|gramm NT (*Comput*) virus checker (*Brit*) or scanner

Vir|gel [ˈvɪrgl] F **-, -n** (*Typ*) virgule (*spec*), slash

Vir|gi|ni|a|ta|bak [vɪrˈgiːnia-, vɪrˈdʒiːnia-] M Virginia tobacco

vi|ril [viˈriːl] ADJ virile

Vi|ri|li|tät [viriliˈtɛːt] F **-**, no pl virility

Vi|ro|lo|ge [viroˈloːgə] M **-n, -n**, **Vi|ro|lo|gin** [-ˈloːgɪn] F **-, -nen** virologist

Vi|ro|lo|gie [viroloˈgiː] F **-**, no pl virology

vi|ro|lo|gisch [viroˈloːgɪʃ] ADJ virological

vir|tu|ell [vɪrˈtuɛl] ADJ *Realität etc* virtual ADV in virtual reality

vir|tu|os [vɪrˈtuoːs] ADJ virtuoso *attr* ADV *beherrschen* expertly, like a virtuoso; **~ spielen** to give a virtuoso performance, to play like a virtuoso

Vir|tu|o|se [vɪrˈtuoːzə] M **-n, -n**, **Vir|tu|o|sin** [-ˈtuoːzɪn] F **-, -nen** virtuoso

Vir|tu|o|si|tät [vɪrtuoziˈtɛːt] F **-**, no pl virtuosity

vi|ru|lent [viruˈlɛnt] ADJ (*Med, fig*) virulent

Vi|ru|lenz [viruˈlɛnts] F **-, -en** (*Med, fig*) virulence, virulency

Vi|rus [ˈviːrʊs] NT OR M **-, Viren** [-rən] (*auch Comput*) virus

Vi|rus-: **Vi|rus|er|kran|kung** F viral or virus disease; **Vi|rus|in|fek|ti|on** F viral or virus infection; **Vi|rus|krank|heit** F viral disease; **Vi|rus|pro|gramm** NT (*Comput*) virus (program)

Vi|sa pl von **Visum**

Vi|sa|ge [viˈzaːʒə] F **-, -n** (*inf*) face

Vi|sa|gist [vizaˈʒɪst] M **-en, -en**, **Vi|sa|gis|tin** [-ˈʒɪstɪn] F **-, -nen** make-up artist

Vi|sa|vis [vizaˈviː] NT **-, -** (*dated*) person (sitting) opposite, vis-à-vis (*form*); **mein ~** the person opposite me

vis-à-vis [vizaˈviː], **vis-a-vis** ▲ (*dated*) ADV opposite (*von* to) PREP +*dat* opposite (to)

Vi|sen pl von **Visum**

Vi|sier [viˈziːɐ] NT **-s, -e a** (*am Helm*) visor; **mit offenem ~ kämpfen** to fight with an open visor; (*fig*) to be open and above board (in one's dealings) **b** (*an Gewehren*) sight; **jdn/etw ins ~ bekommen** to get sb/sth in one's sights; **jdn/etw ins ~ nehmen** or **fassen** to train one's sights on sb/sth; **jdn/etw im ~ haben** (*fig*) to have sb/sth in one's sights; **in jds ~ geraten** (*fig*) to become a target for sb

vi|sie|ren [viˈziːrən] ptp **visiert** VI **~ auf** (+*acc*) to take aim at

Vi|si|on [viˈzioːn] F **-, -en** vision

vi|si|o|när [vizioˈnɛːɐ] ADJ visionary

Vi|si|o|när [vizioˈnɛːɐ] M **-s, -e**, **Vi|si|o|nä|rin** [-ˈnɛːrɪn] F **-, -nen** visionary

Vi|si|ta|ti|on [vizitaˈtsioːn] F **-, -en** (*form*) **a** (= *Besuch*) visitation (*auch Eccl*), inspection **b** (= *Durchsuchung*) search, inspection

Vi|si|te [viˈziːtə] F **-, -n a** (*Med*) (*im Krankenhaus*) round; (*zu Hause*) visit, house call; **um 9 Uhr ist ~ machen** the doctors do their rounds at 9 o'clock; **~ machen** to do one's round/to do visits or house calls; (*dated inf*) to visit (*bei jdm* sb), to pay a visit (*bei* to); **zur ~ kommen** to come on one's round/on a visit or house call **b** (= *Staatsbesuch*) visit

Vi|si|ten|kar|te [viˈziːtn-] F (*lit, fig*) visiting or calling (*US*) card

vi|si|tie|ren [viziˈtiːrən] ptp **visitiert** VT **a** (*form*) *Amtsbezirk etc* to visit, to inspect **b** (*old*) *Gepäck* to search, to inspect

Vi|sit|kar|te [viˈziːt-] F (*Aus*) visiting or calling (*US*) card

vis|kos [vɪsˈkoːs], **vis|kös** [vɪsˈkøːs] ADJ viscous

Vis|ko|se [vɪsˈkoːzə] F **-**, no pl viscose

Vis|ko|si|tät [vɪskoziˈtɛːt] F **-, -en** viscosity

vi|su|ell [viˈzuɛl] ADJ visual

Vi|sum [ˈviːzʊm] NT **-s, Visa** or **Visen** [-za, -zn] visa

Vi|sum(s)-: **Vi|sum(s)|an|trag** M visa application; **Vi|sum(s)|pflicht** F visa requirement

Vi|sum|zwang M obligation to hold a visa; **für San Lucia besteht ~** it is necessary to obtain a visa for San Lucia

Vi|ta [ˈviːta] F **-, Viten** or **Vitae** [-tn, -tɛː] (*geh*) life

vi|tal [viˈtaːl] ADJ vigorous, energetic; (= *lebenswichtig*) vital

Vi|ta|li|tät [vitaliˈtɛːt] F **-**, no pl vitality, vigour (*Brit*), vigor (*US*)

Vi|ta|min [vitaˈmiːn] NT **-s, -e** vitamin; **~ B** (*lit*) vitamin B; (*fig inf*) contacts *pl*

Vi|ta|min-: **vi|ta|min|arm** ADJ poor in vitamins; **eine ~e Zeit** a time when there are/were few vitamins available ADV **~ leben/essen** to live on/have a vitamin-deficient diet; **Vi|ta|min|be|darf** M vitamin requirement; **Vi|ta|min-C-hal|tig** [-ˈtseː-] ADJ containing vitamin C; **~ sein** to contain vitamin C; **Vi|ta|min|ge|halt** M vitamin content; **vi|ta|min|hal|tig**, (*Aus*) **vi|ta|min|häl|tig** ADJ containing vitamins; **~ sein** to contain vitamins

vi|ta|mi|nie|ren [vitamiˈniːrən] ptp **vitaminiert** VT to add vitamins to

Vi|ta|min-: **Vi|ta|min|man|gel** M vitamin deficiency; **Vi|ta|min|man|gel|krank|heit** F disease due to a vitamin deficiency; **vi|ta|min|reich** ADJ rich in vitamins; **Vi|ta|min|sprit|ze** F vitamin injection; (*fig*) shot in the arm (*fig inf*); **Vi|ta|min|stoß** M (massive) dose of vitamins; **Vi|ta|min|ta|blet|te** F vitamin pill or tablet

Vit|ri|ne [viˈtriːnə] F **-, -n** (= *Schrank*) glass cabinet; (= *Schaukasten*) showcase, display case

Vit|ri|ol [vitriˈoːl] NT **-s, -e** vitriol

Vi|va|ri|um [viˈvaːriʊm] NT **-s, Vivarien** [-riən] vivarium

vi|vat [ˈviːvat] INTERJ (*geh*) vivat (*form*)

Vi|vi|sek|ti|on [vivizɛkˈtsioːn] F vivisection

vi|vi|se|zie|ren [vivizeˈtsiːrən] ptp **viviseziert** VTI to vivisect

Vi|ze [ˈfiːtsə] M **-s, -** (*inf*) number two (*inf*), second-in-command; (= *Vizemeister*) runner-up

Vi|ze- in cpds vice-; **Vi|ze|kanz|ler(in)** M(F) vice chancellor; **Vi|ze|kö|nig** M viceroy; **Vi|ze|meis|ter(in)** M(F) runner-up; **Vi|ze|meis|ter|schaft** F second place; **die ~ gewinnen** to come second in the championship, to finish as runners-up; **Vi|ze|prä|si|dent(in)** M(F) vice president; **Vi|ze|rek|tor(in)** M(F) (*von Schule*) deputy headmaster/-mistress, vice principal (*esp US*); (*von Universität*) deputy vice chancellor or rector (*US*)

Vlies [fliːs] NT **-es, -e** [-zə] fleece

Vlie|se|li|ne® [flizəˈliːnə] F **-**, no pl interfacing

Vlies|ja|cke F fleece (jacket)

V-Mann [ˈfau-] M pl **-Männer** or **-Leute** abbr von **Verbindungsmann**

VN [fauˈɛn] PL abbr von **Vereinte Nationen** UN sing

Vo|gel [ˈfoːgl] M **-s**, ̈ [ˈføːgl] (*lit, fig*) bird; **ein seltener ~** (*lit, fig*) a rare bird; **ein seltsamer ~** (*inf*) a strange bird (*inf*) or customer (*inf*); **ein lustiger ~** (*inf*) a lively character (*inf*); **~ friss oder stirb** (*prov*) do or die! (*prov*); **den ~ abschießen** (*inf*) to surpass everyone (*iro*); **einen ~ haben** (*inf*) to be crazy (*inf*), to have a screw loose (*inf*); **jdm den ~ zeigen** (*inf*) to tap one's forehead (*to indicate to sb that he's not quite right in the head*) → **ausfliegen**

Vo|gel-: **Vo|gel|art** F type or species of bird, bird species; **Vo|gel|bau|er** NT pl **-bauer** birdcage; **Vo|gel|bee|re** F (*auch* **Vogelbeerbaum**) rowan (tree), mountain ash; (= *Frucht*) rowan(berry)

Vö|gel|chen [ˈføːglçən] NT **-s, -** little bird; **gleich kommts ~ raus** (*inf*) watch the birdie (*inf*)

Vo|gel-: **Vo|gel|dreck** M bird droppings *pl*; **Vo|gel|ei** [ˈfoːgllai] NT bird's egg; **~er** (*verschiedene Arten*) birds' eggs *pl*

Vö|ge|lei [føːgəˈlai] F **-, -en** (*inf*) screwing (*sl*)

Vö|ge|lein [ˈføːgəlain] NT **-s, -** (*liter*) little bird

Vo|gel-: **Vo|gel|fän|ger(in)** M(F) bird-catcher, fowler; **Vo|gel|flug** M flight of birds; **Vo|gel|flug|li|nie** F **in der ~** as the crow flies; **vo|gel|frei** ADJ (*Hist*) outlawed; **für ~ erklärt werden** to be outlawed, to be declared an outlaw/outlaws; **Vo|gel|fut|ter** NT bird food; (= *Samen*) birdseed; **Vo|gel|haus** NT (*im Zoo*) aviary; **Vo|gel|häus|chen** [-hɔysçən] NT (= *Futterhäuschen*) birdhouse; **Vo|gel|kä|fig** M birdcage; **Vo|gel|kun|de** F ornithology; **Vo|gel|männ|chen** NT cock (bird), male bird

vö|geln [ˈføːgln] VTI (*inf*) to screw (*sl*)

Vo|gel-: **Vo|gel|nest** NT bird's nest; **Vo|gel|per|spek|ti|ve** F, **Vo|gel|schau** F bird's-eye view; **(ein Bild von) Ulan Bator aus der ~** a bird's-eye view of Ulan Bator; **Vo|gel|scheu|che** [-ʃɔyçə] F **-, -n** (*lit, fig inf*) scarecrow; **Vo|gel|schutz** M protection of birds; **Vo|gel|schwarm** M flock of birds; **Vo|gel|spin|ne** F (*Zool*) bird-eating spider; **Vo|gel|stim|me** F birdcall; **Vogel-Strauß-Po|li|tik** F head-in-the-sand or ostrich-like policy; **~ treiben** to bury one's head in the sand; **Vo|gel|trän|ke** F birdbath; **Vo|gel|war|te** F ornithological station; **Vo|gel|weib|chen** NT hen (bird), female bird; **Vo|gel|zug** M (*Wanderung*) bird migration

Vo|gerl|sa|lat [ˈfoːgɐl-] M (*Aus*) corn salad, lamb's lettuce

Vo|ge|sen [vo'ge:zn] PL Vosges *pl*

Vög|lein ['fø:glaɪn] NT **-s, -** (*liter*) little bird

Vogt [fo:kt] M **-(e)s, ⸚e** ['fø:ktə] (*Hist*) (= *Kirchen-vogt*) church advocate; (= *Reichsvogt*) protector; (= *Landvogt*) landvogt, governor; (*von Burg, Gut*) steward, bailiff

Vog|tei [fo:k'taɪ] F **-, -en** → **Vogt** office of church advocate; protectorate; governorship; (= *Gebiet*) area administered by a/the church advocate; protectorate; province; (= *Residenz*) church advocate's/protector's/landvogt's *or* governor's residence

Voice-Mail ['vɔɪsmeːl] F **-,** *no pl*, **Voice|mail** F **-,** *no pl* (*Telec*) voice mail

Voice-Re|kor|der ['vɔɪsrekɔrdɐ] M **-s, -**, **Voice|re|kor|der** M **-s, -** (*Aviat*) (cockpit) voice recorder

Vo|ka|bel [vo'ka:bl] F **-, -n** *or* (*Aus*) nt **-s, -** word; **~n** *pl* vocabulary *sing*, vocab *sing* (*Sch inf*)

Vo|ka|bel-: Vo|ka|bel|heft NT vocabulary book; **Vo|ka|bel|schatz** M vocabulary

Vo|ka|bu|lar [vokabu'la:ɐ] NT **-s, -e** vocabulary

vo|kal [vo'ka:l] (*Mus*) ADJ vocal ADV vocally

Vo|kal [vo'ka:l] M **-s, -e** vowel

Vo|ka|li|sa|ti|on [vokaliza'tsio:n] F **-, -en** vocalization

vo|ka|lisch [vo'ka:lɪʃ] ADJ (*Ling*) vocalic; **~e An-laute/Auslaute** initial/final vowels

Vo|ka|lis|mus [voka'lɪsmʊs] M **-,** *no pl* (*Ling*) vocalism

Vo|ka|list [voka'lɪst] M **-en, -en**, **Vo|ka|lis|tin** [-'lɪstɪn] F **-, -nen** (*Mus, geh*) vocalist

Vo|kal|mu|sik F vocal music

Vo|ka|tiv ['vo:kati:f, voka'ti:f] M **-s, -e** [-və] vocative

vol. *abbr von* **Volumen**

Vol.-% *abbr von* **Volumprozent**

Vo|lant [vo'lã:] M **-s, -s** a (= *Stoffbesatz*) valance; (*am Rock, Kleid*) flounce b *auch* NT (*Aus, Sw, old*: = *Lenkrad*) steering wheel

Vo|li|e|re [vo'lie:rə, -'liɛːrə] F **-, -n** aviary

Volk [fɔlk] NT **-(e)s, ⸚er** ['fœlkɐ] a *no pl* people *pl*; (= *Nation*) nation; (= *Volksmasse*) masses *pl*, people *pl*; (*inf*: = *Gruppe*) crowd *pl*; (*pej*: = *Pack*) rabble *pl*; **alles ~** everybody; **viel ~** lots of people *pl*, crowds *pl*; **etw unters ~ bringen** (*Nachricht*) to spread sth; *Geld* to spend sth; **die sind ein lustiges ~** (*inf*) they are a lively lot (*Brit inf*) *or* bunch (*inf*) *or* crowd; **da verkehrt ein ~!** that's a really strange crowd there! **Mann a, fahrend** b (= *ethnische Gemeinschaft*) people *sing*; **die Völker Afrikas** the peoples of Africa; **ein ~ für sich sein** to be a race apart c (*Zool*) colony

Völk|chen ['fœlkçən] NT **-s, -** a (= *kleine Nation*) small nation b (*inf*: = *Gruppe*) lot (*inf*), crowd; **ein ~ für sich sein** to be a race apart

Völ|ker- ['fœlkɐ-]: **Völ|ker|ball** M *game for two teams where the object is to hit an opponent with a ball and thus put him out of the game*, ≈ dodgeball (*Brit*), ≈ warball (*US*); **Völ|ker|bund** M, *no pl* (*Hist*) League of Nations; **Völ|ker|freund|schaft** F friendship among nations; **Völ|ker|ge|mein|schaft** F international community, community of nations; **Völ|ker|kun|de** F ethnology; **Völ|ker|kun|de|mu|se|um** NT museum of ethnology; **Völ|ker|kund|ler** [-kʊntlɐ] M **-s, -**, **Völ|ker|kund|le|rin** [-ərɪn] F **-, -nen** ethnologist; **völ|ker|kund|lich** [-kʊntlɪç] ADJ ethnological; **Völ|ker|mord** M genocide; **Völ|ker|recht** NT international law, law of nations; **völ|ker|recht|lich** ADJ *Vertrag, Entscheidung, Anerken-nung, Status, Verpflichtungen* under international law; *Frage, Thema, Hinsicht, Standpunkt* of international law; *Anspruch, Haftung* international; **vom ~en Standpunkt** according to *or* under international law; **~e Anerkennung eines Staates** recognition of a state ADV *regeln, entscheiden* by international law; *klären* according to interna-

tional law; *bindend sein* under international law; **Völ|ker|schlacht** F (*Hist*) Battle of the Nations; **Völ|ker|ver|stän|di|gung** F international understanding; **Völ|ker|wan|de|rung** F (*Hist*) migration of the peoples; (*hum*) mass migration *or* exodus

völ|kisch ['fœlkɪʃ] ADJ (*NS*) national

volk|reich ADJ populous

Volks- *in cpds* popular; (= *auf ein Land bezogen*) national; (*Pol*) people's; **Volks|ab|stim|mung** F plebiscite; **Volks|ar|mee** F (*DDR*) People's Army; **Volks|ar|mist** [-armɪst] M **-en, -en**, **Volks|ar|mis|tin** [-mɪstɪn] F **-, -nen** (*DDR*) soldier in the People's Army; **Volks|auf|stand** M national uprising; **Volks|aus|ga|be** F popular edition; **Volks|be|auf|trag|te(r)** MF *decl as adj* people's representative *or* delegate; **Volks|be|fra|gung** F public opinion poll; **Volks|be|frei|ungs|ar|mee** F people's liberation army; **Volks|be|geh|ren** NT petition for a referendum; **Volks|be|lus|ti|gung** F public entertainment; **Volks|be|we|gung** F popular movement; **Volks|bil|dung** F national education; (= *Erwachsenenbildung*) adult education; **Volks|brauch** M national custom; **Volks|bü|che|rei** F public library; **Volks|büh|ne** F people's theatre (*Brit*) *or* theater (*US*); **Volks|cha|rak|ter** M national character; **Volks|de|mo|kra|tie** F people's democracy; **Volks|deut|sche(r)** MF *decl as adj* ethnic German; **Volks|dich|ter(in)** M(F) people's poet; **Volks|dich|tung** F folk literature; (= *Gedichte*) folk poetry; **volks|ei|gen** ADJ (*DDR*) nationally-owned; (*in Namen*) People's Own; **Volks|ei|gen|tum** NT (*DDR*) national property, property of the people; **im ~** nationally-owned, owned by the people; **Volks|ein|kom|men** NT national income; **Volks|emp|fin|den** NT public feeling; **das gesunde ~** popular sentiment; **Volks|ent|scheid** M referendum; **Volks|er|he|bung** F popular *or* national uprising; **Volks|ety|mo|lo|gie** F folk etymology; **Volks|feind(in)** M(F) enemy of the people; **volks|feind|lich** ADJ hostile to the people; **Volks|fest** NT public festival; (= *Jahrmarkt*) funfair; **Volks|front** F (*Pol*) popular front; **Volks|ge|nos|se** M, **Volks|ge|nos|sin** F (*NS*) national comrade; **Volks|ge|richts|hof** M (*NS*) People's Court; **Volks|ge|sund|heit** F public health; **Volks|glau|be(n)** M popular belief; **Volks|grup|pe** F ethnic group; (= *Minderheit*) ethnic minority; **Volks|held(in)** M(F) popular hero/heroine; (= *Held des Landes*) national hero/heroine; **Volks|herr|schaft** F popular rule, rule of the people; **Volks|hoch|schu|le** F adult education centre (*Brit*) *or* center (*US*); **einen Kurs an der ~ ma-chen** to do an adult education class; (*am Abend auch*) to do an evening class

---

VOLKSHOCHSCHULE

Volkshochschulen, or **VHS** for short, play an important part in German life. They offer evening and morning courses and lectures for all age groups in a wide range of subjects. For example, school pupils can take courses to catch up in certain subjects, housewives and pensioners can learn languages or crafts and foreign nationals can improve their knowledge of German. There are also VHS courses leading to qualifications of the **zweiter Bildungsweg**, such as the **mitt-lere Reife** and **Abitur** → ABITUR, ZWEITER BILD-UNGSWEG, MITTLERE REIFE

Volks-: Volks|ini|ti|a|ti|ve F (*Pol*) (*Ger*) *petition for a matter to be debated in the state parliament* (*Sw*) petition for a referendum; **Volks|jus|tiz** F popular justice; **Volks|kam|mer** F (*DDR*) East German Parliament; **Volks|krank|heit** F widespread disease; **Volks|kü|che** F soup kitchen; **Volks|kun|de** F folklore; **Volks|kund|ler** [-kʊntlɐ] M **-s, -**, **Volks|kund|le|rin** [-ərɪn] F **-, -nen** folklorist;

volks|kund|lich [-kʊntlɪç] ADJ folkloristic; **ein ~es Institut** an institute of folklore; **Volks|lauf** M (*Sport*) open cross-country race; **Volks|lied** NT folk song; **Volks|mär|chen** NT folk tale; **Volks|mei|nung** F public *or* popular opinion; **Volks|men|ge** F crowd, mob (*pej*); **Volks|mund** M, *no pl* vernacular; **im ~ nennt man das ...** this is popularly called ..., in the vernacular this is called ...; **Volks|mu|sik** F folk music; **volks|nah** ADJ popular, in touch with the people; (*Pol*) grass-roots *attr*; **Volks|nä|he** F sie ist bekannt für ihre ~ she is renowned for her popular touch; **Volks|par|tei** F people's party; **Volks|po|e|sie** F folk poetry; **Volks|po|li|zei** F (*DDR*) People's Police; **Volks|po|li|zist(in)** M(F) (*DDR*) member of the People's Police; **Volks|re|de** F (*rare: lit*) public speech; **du sollst keine ~ halten!** (*inf*) I/we don't want any speeches!; **Volks|re|pub|lik** F people's republic; **Volks|sa|ge** F folk legend, folk tale; **Volks|schicht** F level of society, social stratum; **Volks|schul|ab|schluss** ▲ M (*dated*) elementary school-leaving certificate; **Volks|schu|le** F (*dated*) ≈ elementary school (*Hist*), *school providing basic primary and secondary education*; **Volks|schü|ler(in)** M(F) (*dated*) ≈ pupil at elementary school (*Hist*); **Volks|schul|leh|rer(in)** M(F) (*dated*) ≈ elementary school teacher (*Hist*); **Volks|see|le** F soul of the people; **die kochende ~** the seething *or* angry populace; **Volks|seu|che** F epidemic; **Volks|sou|ve|rä|ni|tät** F (*Pol*) sovereignty of the people; **Volks|sport** M national sport; **Volks|spra|che** F everyday language, vernacular; **Volks|staat** M (*Pol*) people's state; **Volks|stamm** M tribe; **Volks|stim|me** F voice of the people; **Volks|stück** NT dialect folk play; **Volks|sturm** M (*Hist*) Volkssturm, German territorial army; **Volks|tanz** M folk dance; **Volks|the|a|ter** NT folk theatre (*Brit*) *or* theater (*US*); (*Gattung auch*) folk drama; **Volks|tracht** F traditional costume; (*eines Landes*) national costume; **Volks|trau|er|tag** M national day of mourning, ≈ Remembrance Day (*Brit*), ≈ Veterans' Day (*US*); **Volks|tri|bun** M (*Hist*) tribune of the people; **Volks|tum** ['fɔlkstuːm] NT **-s,** *no pl* national traditions *pl*, folklore; **Volks|tü|me|lei** [fɔlksty:məˈlaɪ] F **-, -en** (*inf*) folksiness (*inf*); **volks|tüm|lich** ['fɔlksty:mlɪç] ADJ folk *attr*, folksy (*inf*); (= *traditionell, überliefert*) traditional; (= *beliebt*) popular; **ein ~er König** a king with the common touch ADV **etw ~ darstellen** to popularize sth; **etw ~ ausdrücken** to express oneself in plain language; **Volks|tüm|lich|keit** F **-,** *no pl* folksiness (*inf*); (= *traditionelle, überliefte Art*) tradition; (= *Beliebtheit*) popularity; (*von Darstellungs-, Ausdrucksweise*) popular appeal; (*von König*) common touch; **volks|ver|bun|den** ADJ close to the people; **Volks|ver|füh|rer(in)** M(F) demagogue; **Volks|ver|het|zung** F incitement of the people *or* masses); **Volks|ver|mö|gen** NT national wealth; **Volks|ver|samm|lung** F people's assembly; (= *Kundgebung*) public gathering; **Volks|ver|tre|ter(in)** M(F) representative *or* delegate of the people; **Volks|ver|tre|tung** F representative body (of the people); **Volks|wirt(in)** M(F) economist; **Volks|wirt|schaft** F national economy; (*Fach*) economics *sing*, political economy; **Volks- und Betriebswirt-schaft** economics and business studies; **Volks|wirt|schaft|ler(in)** M(F) economist; **volks|wirt|schaft|lich** ADJ *Schaden, Nutzen* economic; **Volks|wirt|schafts|leh|re** F economics *sing*, political economy; **Volks|wohl** NT good *or* welfare of the people, public weal; **Volks|zäh|lung** F (national) census; **Volks|zorn** M public anger; **Volks|zu|ge|hö|rig|keit** F ethnic origin

voll [fɔl] ADJ a (= *gefüllt*) full; **~ ... full of ...**; **~ (von *or* mit) etw** full of sth; (= *bedeckt mit*) covered with sth; **~ des Lobes** full of praise; **mit ~em Mund** with one's mouth full; **aus dem Vol-len leben** to live a life of luxury, to live in the

lap of luxury; **aus dem Vollen schöpfen** to draw on unlimited resources
b (= *ganz*) full; *Satz, Service, Erfolg* complete; *Woche, Jahr* full, whole; *Wahrheit* whole; **ein ~es Dutzend** a full or whole dozen; **~e drei Jahre/Tage** three whole years/days, fully three years/days; **die Uhr schlägt nur die ~e Stunde** the clock only strikes the full hour; **die Zahl ist ~** the numbers are complete; **die ~e Summe bezahlen** to pay the full sum, to pay the sum in full; **in ~er Fahrt/~em Galopp/~em Lauf** at full speed/gallop/speed; **in ~er Größe** (*Bild*) life-size; (*bei plötzlicher Erscheinung etc*) large as life; **sich zu ~er Größe aufrichten** to draw oneself up to one's full height; **im ~en Tageslicht** in full daylight; **in ~er Uniform** in full dress or uniform; **jdn nicht für ~ nehmen** not to take sb seriously; **aus ~em Halse** or **~er Kehle** or **Brust singen** to sing at the top of one's voice; **etw mit ~em Recht tun** to be perfectly right to do sth; **mit dem ~en Namen unterschreiben** to sign one's full name, to sign one's name in full
c **~ sein** (*inf*) (= *satt*) to be full, to be full up (*Brit*); (= *betrunken*) to be plastered (*inf*) or tight (*Brit inf*); **~ wie ein Sack** or **eine Strandhaubitze** or **tausend Mann** absolutely plastered (*inf*), roaring drunk (*Brit inf*)
d (= *üppig*) *Gesicht, Busen etc* full; *Wangen* chubby; *Haar* thick; **~er werden** to fill out
e *Stimme, Ton* full, rich; *Farbton* rich
ADV fully; (= *vollkommen auch*) completely; (*sl*: = *total*) dead (*Brit inf*), real (*US inf*); **~ und ganz** completely, wholly; **die Straße ist ~ gesperrt** the road is completely closed; **die Straße ist wieder ~ befahrbar** the road is completely free again; **jdn ~ ansehen** to look sb straight in the face; **eine Rechnung ~ bezahlen** to pay a bill in full; **~ hinter jdm/etw stehen** to be or stand fully behind sb/sth; **den Mund ~ nehmen** (*fig*) to exaggerate, to overdo it; **jdn/etw ~ treffen** (*mit Stein, Bombe etc*) to score a direct hit on sb/sth; (*ins Gesicht*) to hit sb full in the face; **etw ~ ausnützen** to take full advantage of sth; **~ zuschlagen** (*inf*) to lam out (*Brit inf*), to hit out; **~ durcharbeiten** (*inf*) to work solidly (throughout); **~ drinstecken** (*inf*) (*bei Arbeit*) to be in the middle of it; (*in unangenehmer Situation*) to be right in it; **~ (Stoff) gegen etw fahren** (*inf*) to run full tilt or slap-bang (*inf*) into sth; **nicht ~ da sein** (*inf*) to be not quite with it (*inf*); **~ dabei sein** (*inf*) to be totally involved

voll|laden △ VT → **voll laden**

Voll|aka|de|mi|ker(in) M(F) honours (*Brit*) or honors (*US*) graduate

Vollast △ F → **Volllast**

Vollastbetrieb △ M → **Volllastbetrieb**

voll|auf [ˈfɔlʔauf, fɔlˈʔauf] ADV fully, completely; **~ genug** quite enough; **das genügt ~** that's quite enough; **~ zu tun haben** to have quite enough to do (*mit* with)

voll|laufen △ VI → **voll laufen**

Voll-: Voll|aus|schlag M (*Tech: eines Instruments*) full swing; **voll|au|to|ma|tisch** ADJ fully automatic **ADV** (completely) automatically; **voll|au|to|ma|ti|siert** [-automatiziːɐt] ADJ fully automated; **Voll|bad** NT (proper) bath; **Voll|bart** M (full) beard; **voll be|kom|men** ▲ VT *irreg* to (manage to) fill; **voll|be|rech|tigt** ADJ *attr* with full rights; *Unterhändler* fully authorized; *Mitglied* full; **voll|be|schäf|tigt** ADJ *Arbeiter* employed full time; (*attr*: = *sehr beschäftigt*) fully occupied; **Voll|be|schäf|ti|gung** F full employment; **Voll|be|sitz** M **im ~** +*gen* in full possession of; **Voll|bier** NT *beer with 11-14% original wort*; **Voll|bild** NT (*Med*: *von Krankheit*) full-blown form; **Voll|bild-Aids** NT full-blown Aids

Voll|blut NT , *no pl* thoroughbred

Voll|blut- *in cpds* (*lit*: *Tier*) thoroughbred; (*fig*) full-blooded

Voll-: Voll|blü|ter [-blyːtɐ] M **-s, -** thoroughbred; **voll|blü|tig** ADJ thoroughbred; (*fig*) full-blooded

Voll|blut-: Voll|blut|op|por|tu|nist(in) M(F) full-blooded opportunist; **Voll|blut|po|li|ti|ker(in)** M(F) thoroughbred politician

Voll-: Voll|brem|sung F emergency stop; **eine ~ machen** to slam on the brakes (*inf*), to do an emergency stop; **voll|brin|gen** [fɔlˈbrɪŋən] *ptp* **vollbracht** [fɔlˈbraxt] VT *insep irreg* (= *ausführen*) to accomplish, to achieve; *Wunder* to work, to perform; **eine große Leistung ~** to achieve a lot; **es ist vollbracht** (*Bibl*) it is done (*Bibl*); **Voll|brin|gung** [fɔlˈbrɪŋʊŋ] F **-, -en** accomplishment, achievement; **voll|bu|sig** [-buːzɪç] ADJ full-bosomed, bosomy (*inf*)

Voll|dampf M (*Naut*) full steam; **mit ~** at full steam or speed; (*inf*) flat out (*esp Brit*); **mit ~ voraus** full steam or speed ahead; (*inf*) full tilt

voll dröh|nen ▲ VTR = **zudröhnen**

Völ|le|ge|fühl [ˈfœlə-] NT (unpleasant) feeling of fullness

voll|elekt|ro|nisch ADJ fully electronic

voll|en|den [fɔlˈʔɛndn̩] *ptp* **vollendet** *insep* **VT** (= *abschließen*) to complete; (*liter*) *Leben* to bring to an end; (= *vervollkommnen*) to make complete; *Geschmack* to round off **VR** (= *zum Abschluss kommen*) to come to an end; (= *vollkommen werden*) to be completed; (*Liebe*) to be fulfilled

voll|en|det [fɔlˈʔɛndət] **ADJ** (= *vollkommen*) completed; *Tugend, Schönheit* perfect; *Mensch* accomplished; (*Jur*) *Straftat* completed; **nach ~em 18. Lebensjahr** upon completion of one's 18th year; **bis zum ~en 6. Lebensjahr** until one's 6th birthday, until one turns 6 → **Tatsache** ADV perfectly; **~ Klavier spielen** to be an accomplished pianist

voll|ends [ˈfɔlɛnts] ADV **a** (= *völlig*) completely, altogether **b** (= *besonders*) especially, particularly

Voll|en|dung F completion; (= *Vervollkommnung, Vollkommenheit*) perfection; (*von Liebe*) fulfilment

vol|ler [ˈfɔlɐ] ADJ → **voll**

Völ|le|rei [fœlǝˈrai] F **-, -en** gluttony

voll es|sen ▲ VR *irreg* (*inf*) to gorge oneself

Vol|ley [ˈvɔli] M **-s, -s** volley

Vol|ley|ball M volleyball

Vol|ley|bal|ler [ˈvɔlibalɐ] M **-s, -** , **Vol|ley|bal|le|rin** [-balərɪn] F **-, -nen** volleyball player

voll|fett ADJ full fat

Voll|fett|kä|se M full fat cheese

voll fres|sen ▲ VR *irreg* (*pej inf*) to stuff oneself (*inf*)

voll|füh|ren [fɔlˈfyːrən] *ptp* **vollführt** VT *insep* to execute, to perform; *Tanz, Kunststück* to perform; *Lärm, Theater* to create

Voll-: voll fül|len ▲ VT to fill (up); **Voll|gas** NT , *no pl* full speed or throttle; **~ geben** to open it right up; (*mit Auto auch*) to put one's foot hard down; **mit ~ fahren** to drive at full throttle; **mit ~** (*fig inf*) full tilt; **mit ~ arbeiten** to work flat out (*esp Brit*) or as hard as possible; **Voll|ge|fühl** NT **im ~** +*gen* fully aware of; **im ~ der Jugend** in the full bloom of youth; **im ~ der Lebensfreude** full of the joys of life; **Voll|ge|nuss** ▲ M **im ~** +*gen* in full enjoyment of; **voll gie|ßen** ▲ VT *irreg* (= *auffüllen*) to fill (up); **sie hat sich** (*dat*) **den Rock voll gegossen/mit Kaffee voll gegossen** (*inf*) she spilled it/coffee all over her skirt; **voll|gül|tig** ADJ *attr Pass* fully valid; *Berufsabschluss* fully recognized; *Ersatz* completely satisfactory; *Beweis* conclusive; **Voll|gum|mi** NT OR M solid rubber; **Voll|gum|mi|rei|fen** M solid rubber tyre (*Brit*) or tire (*US*); **Voll|idi|ot(in)** M(F) (*inf*) complete idiot

völ|lig [ˈfœlɪç] ○ 38.1, 39.1, 39.2 **ADJ** complete; **das ist mein ~er Ernst** I'm completely or absolutely serious **ADV** completely; **es genügt ~** that's quite enough; **er hat ~ Recht** he's absolutely right

Voll-: voll|in|halt|lich ADJ *attr* full, complete; **Voll|in|va|li|de** M , **Voll|in|va|li|din** F complete or total invalid; **voll|jäh|rig** ADJ of age; **~ werden/sein** to come/be of age; **sie hat drei ~e Kinder** she has three children who are of age; **Voll|jäh|ri|ge(r)** [-jɛːrɪgə] MF *decl as adj* major; **Voll|jäh|rig|keit** [-jɛːrɪçkait] F **-**, *no pl* majority *no art*; **bei (Erreichen der) ~** on attaining one's majority; **Voll|ju|rist(in)** M(F) fully qualified lawyer; **Voll|kas|ko** NT **-**, *no pl* fully comprehensive insurance; **voll|kas|ko|ver|si|chert** [-feːzɪçɐt] ADJ fully comprehensively insured; **~ sein** to have fully comprehensive insurance; **Voll|kas|ko|ver|si|che|rung** F **-**, *no pl* fully comprehensive insurance; **voll|kli|ma|ti|siert** [-klimatiziːɐt] ADJ fully air-conditioned

voll|kom|men [fɔlˈkɔmən, ˈfɔl-] ○ 34.5, 38.1, 40.1, 53.6 **ADJ** perfect; (= *völlig*) complete, absolute; (*Math*) *Zahl* perfect; **sein Glück war ~** his happiness was complete **ADV** completely

Voll|kom|men|heit F **-**, *no pl* perfection; (= *Vollständigkeit*) completeness, absoluteness; **die ~ ihrer Schönheit** her perfect beauty

Voll-: Voll|korn|brot NT coarse wholemeal (*Brit*) or wholegrain bread; **voll kot|zen** ▲ VT (*sl*) to puke (up) over (*inf*); **Voll|kraft** F (*geh*) **in der ~ seiner Jahre/seines Schaffens** in his prime; **voll la|bern** ▲ VT (*inf*) to chatter (on) to; **voll la|den** ▲ VT *irreg* to load up; **voll geladen** fully-laden; **Voll|last** F , *no pl* (*Tech*) full load; **Voll|last|be|trieb** ▲ M , *no pl* (*Tech*) **im ~** at full load; **voll lau|fen** ▲ VI *irreg aux sein* to fill up; **etw ~ lassen** to fill sth (up); **sich ~ lassen** (*inf*) to get tanked up (*inf*); **voll ma|chen** ▲ **VT** **a** *Gefäß* to fill (up); *Zahl, Dutzend* to make up; *Sammlung, Set* to complete → **Maß**[1] **a b** (*inf*) *Hosen* to make a mess in; *Windeln* to fill (*Brit*), to dirty (*US*); **sich** (*dat*) **die Hosen ~** (*fig inf*) to wet oneself (*inf*) **VR** (*inf*) to get messed up, to get dirty; (= *in die Hosen machen*) to make a mess in one's pants; (*Baby*) to fill one's nappy (*Brit*), to dirty one's diaper (*US*)

Voll|macht F **-, -en** (*legal*) power or authority *no pl*, *no indef art*; (*Urkunde*) power of attorney; **jdm eine ~ erteilen** or **ausstellen** to give or grant sb power of attorney

Voll|macht|ge|ber(in) M(F) principal; **~ und Vollmachtnehmer** principal and agent

Voll|machts|ur|kun|de F power of attorney

Voll-: voll|mast [ˈfɔlmast] ADV full mast; **auf ~** at full mast; **Voll|mat|ro|se** M , **Voll|mat|ro|sin** F able-bodied seaman; **Voll|milch** F full-cream milk; **Voll|milch|scho|ko|la|de** F full-cream milk chocolate; **Voll|mit|glied** NT full member; **Voll|mond** M full moon; **heute ist ~** there's a full moon today; **Voll|mond|ge|sicht** NT (*inf*) moon face; **Voll|mond|nacht** F night of a full moon; **voll|mun|dig** **ADJ** *Wein* full-bodied; *Unterstützung, Versprechen* wholehearted; *Ankündigung, Erklärung* grandiose **ADV** **a** **~ schmecken** to taste full-bodied **b** (= *großsprecherisch*) grandiosely; **etw ~ gutheißen** to support sth wholeheartedly; **etw ~ bestreiten** to dispute sth vehemently; **Voll|nar|ko|se** F general anaesthetic (*Brit*) or anesthetic (*US*); **voll pa|cken** ▲ VT (*lit, fig*) to pack full; **jdn** to load up; **Voll|pen|si|on** F full board; **voll pis|sen** ▲ VT (*vulg*) to piss on (*sl*); *Hose* to piss in (*sl*); **voll pfrop|fen** ▲ VT (*inf*) to cram full; **voll pum|pen** ▲ VT to fill (up); **Voll|rausch** M drunken stupor; **einen ~ haben** to be in a drunken stupor; **voll|reif** ADJ fully ripe; **voll sau|gen** ▲ VR *reg* or *irreg* to become saturated; **voll schen|ken** ▲ VT to fill; **voll schla|gen** ▲ VT *irreg* (*inf*) **sich** (*dat*) **den Bauch ~** to stuff oneself (with food) (*inf*); **voll|schlank** ADJ plump, stout; **Mode für ~e Damen** fashion for the fuller figure, fashion for ladies with a fuller figure; **voll schmie|ren** ▲ **VT** to mess up **VR** to mess oneself up; **voll schrei|ben** ▲ VT *irreg Heft, Seite* to fill (with writing); *Tafel* to cover (with writing); **Voll|sper|rung** F (*Mot*) complete closure; **Voll|-**

spur F (Rail) standard gauge, standard-gauge track; **voll|spu|rig** [-ʃpuːrɪç] (Rail) ADJ standard-gauge **ADV** on standard-gauge track

voll|stän|dig ADJ complete; Sammlung, Satz auch entire attr; Adresse full attr; **nicht ~** incomplete; **etw ~ machen** to complete sth; **etw ~ haben** to have sth complete **ADV** completely, entirely

Voll|stän|dig|keit [-ʃtɛndɪçkait] F -, no pl completeness; **der ~ halber** to complete the picture; **keinen Anspruch auf ~ erheben** to make no claim to be exhaustive

voll stop|fen ▲ VT to cram full

voll|streck|bar ADJ enforceable, able to be carried out or executed; (Jur) **-e Urkunde** executory deed

voll|stre|cken [fɔlˈʃtrɛkn] ptp **vollstreckt** VT insep to execute; Urteil, Haftbefehl to carry out; Pfändung to enforce; **~de Gewalt** executive (power); **ein Todesurteil an jdm ~** to execute sb

Voll|stre|cker [fɔlˈʃtrɛkɐ] M -s, -, **Voll|stre|cke|rin** [-ərɪn] F -, -nen executor; (Frau auch) executrix; **~ des Todesurteils** executioner

Voll|stre|ckung F -, -en execution; (von Todesurteil) carrying out; (von Pfändung) enforcement

Voll|stre|ckungs-: Voll|stre|ckungs|be|am|te(r) M decl as adj, **Voll|stre|ckungs|be|am|tin** F enforcement officer; **Widerstand gegen ~** obstructing an officer in the performance of his duties; **Voll|stre|ckungs|be|fehl** M enforcement order, writ of execution; **Voll|stre|ckungs|ge|richt** NT court of execution or enforcement; (bei Konkursverfahren) bankruptcy court

Voll-: Voll|stu|di|um NT complete course of study; **voll|syn|chro|ni|siert** [-zynkroniziːt] ADJ fully synchronized; **voll tan|ken** ▲ VTI to fill up; **bitte ~** fill her up, please

Voll|text M (Comput) full text

Voll|text- (Comput): **Voll|text|da|ten|bank** F full text database; **Voll|text|su|che** F full text search

Voll-: voll|tö|nend [-tøːnənt] ADJ resonant, sonorous; **Voll|tref|fer** M (lit, fig) bull's eye; **voll|trun|ken** ADJ completely or totally drunk; **in ~em Zustand Auto fahren** to drive when drunk, to drive in a drunken state; **Voll|trun|ken|heit** F total inebriation; **Voll|ver|samm|lung** F general assembly; (von Stadtrat etc) full meeting or assembly; **Voll|wai|se** F orphan; **Voll|wasch|mittel** NT detergent; **voll|wer|tig** ADJ Mitglied, Partner full attr; Stellung equal; Ersatz, Kost (fully) adequate; **jdn als ~ behandeln/betrachten** to treat/regard sb as an equal; **Voll|wert|kost** F wholefoods pl; **Voll|zah|ler(in)** M(F) (für Fahrkarte etc) person paying full fare; **voll|zäh|lig** [-tseːlɪç] ADJ usu pred Satz, Anzahl, Mannschaft complete; (= ausnahmslos anwesend) all present pred; **um ~es Erscheinen wird gebeten** everyone is requested to attend **ADV** **sie sind ~ erschienen** everyone came; **~ versammelt sein** to be assembled in full force or strength; **Voll|zäh|lig|keit** F -, no pl full number; (= ausnahmslose Anwesenheit) full attendance

Voll|zeit- in cpds full-time; **Voll|zeit|be|schäf|tig|te(r)** MF decl as adj full-time employee or worker; **Voll|zeit|stel|le** F full-time position

voll|zieh|bar ADJ Strafe, Urteil enforceable, executable

Voll|zieh|bar|keit [fɔlˈtsiːbaːɐkait] F -, no pl enforceability

voll|zie|hen [fɔlˈtsiːən] ptp **vollzogen** [fɔlˈtsoːgn] insep irreg VT to carry out; Befehl auch to execute; Strafe, Urteil auch to execute, to enforce; Opferung, Trauung to perform; Bruch to make; (form) Ehe to consummate; **einen Gedankengang ~ können** to be capable of a train of thought; **die ~de Gewalt** the executive (power) VR to take place; (Trauung) to be performed; (jds Schicksal) to be fulfilled

---

Voll|zie|hung F (= Ausführung) carrying out; (von Befehl auch) execution; (von Strafe, Urteil auch) execution, enforcement; (von Opferung, Trauung) performance; (von Bruch) making; (von Ehe) consummation

Voll|zug [fɔlˈtsuːk] M , no pl **a** (= Strafvollzug) penal system; **offener ~** daytime release for prisoners pending parole **b** = **Vollziehung**

Voll|zugs-: Voll|zugs|an|stalt F (form) penal institution; **Voll|zugs|be|am|te(r)** M decl as adj, **Voll|zugs|be|am|tin** F (form) warder

Vo|lon|tär [volɔnˈtɛːɐ] M -s, -e, **Vo|lon|tä|rin** [-ˈtɛːrɪn] F -, -nen trainee

Vo|lon|ta|ri|at [volɔntaˈriaːt] NT -(e)s, -e **a** (Zeit) practical training **b** (Stelle) position as a trainee

---

VOLONTARIAT

A Volontariat is a period of voluntary training within a profession. The term is used principally in connection with journalism, since there were formerly no specific training opportunities in this field. Trainees (Volontäre) gain practical experience across a range of areas and also receive some tuition.

---

vo|lon|tie|ren [volɔnˈtiːrən] ptp **volontiert** VI to be training (bei with)

Volt [vɔlt] NT -(e)s, - volt

Vol|te [ˈvɔltə] F -, -n **a** (Fechten, Reiten) volte **b** (Cards) sleight of hand

vol|ti|gie|ren [vɔltiˈʒiːrən] ptp **voltigiert** VI to perform exercises on horseback; (im Zirkus) to do trick riding

Volt-: Volt|me|ter NT voltmeter; **Volt|zahl** F voltage

Vo|lu|men [voˈluːmən] NT -s, - or **Volumina** [-na] **a** (lit, fig: = Inhalt) volume **b** (obs: = Schriftrolle, Band) volume

Vo|lu|men|pro|zent NT per cent no pl (Brit) or percent no pl (US) by volume

Vo|lum|ge|wicht [voˈluːm-] NT (Phys) volumetric weight

vo|lu|mi|nös [volumiˈnøːs] ADJ (geh) voluminous

Vo|lu|te [voˈluːtə] F -, -n (Archit) scroll

vom [fɔm] contr von **von dem ~ 10. September an** from the 10th September (Brit), from September 10th; **das kommt ~ Rauchen/Trinken** that comes from smoking/drinking; **ich kenne ihn nur ~ Sehen** I know him only by sight; **~ Kochen hat er keine Ahnung** he has no idea about cooking

von [fɔn] PREP +dat **a** (einen Ausgangspunkt angebend, räumlich, zeitlich) from; **der Wind kommt ~ Norden** the wind comes from the North; **nördlich ~** to the North of; **~ München nach Hamburg** from Munich to Hamburg; **~ weit her** from a long way away; **~ ... an** from ...; **~ Jugend an** from early on; **vom 10. Lebensjahr an** since he/she was ten years old; **~ diesem Tag/Punkt an** or **ab** from this day/point on(wards); **~ heute ab** or **an** from today; **Waren ~ 5 Euro an** or **ab** goods from 5 euros (Brit), goods from 5 euros on (US); **~ ... aus** from ...; **~ dort aus** from there; **etw ~ sich aus wissen** to know sth by oneself; **etw ~ sich aus tun** to do sth of one's own accord; **~ ... bis** from ... to; **~ morgens bis abends** from morning till night; **Ihr Brief ~ vor 2 Wochen** your letter of two weeks ago; **~ ... zu** from ... to **b** (von ... weg) from; **etw ~ etw nehmen/abreißen** to take/tear sth off sth; **vom Zug abspringen** to jump off the train; **alles ~ sich werfen** to throw everything down or aside; **~ der Stelle weichen** to move from the spot **c** (in Verbindung mit adj, vb siehe auch dort) (Ursache, Urheberschaft ausdrückend, im Passiv) by; **das Gedicht ist ~ Schiller** the poem is by Schiller; **ein Kleid ~ Dior** a Dior dress; **ein Kind ~ jdm kriegen** to have a child by sb; **das Kind ist ~**

---

ihm the child is his; **~ etw müde** tired from sth; **~ etw begeistert** enthusiastic about sth; **~ etw satt** full up with sth; **~ etw beeindruckt/überrascht** impressed/surprised by sth

d (partitiv, anstelle von Genitiv) of; **jeweils zwei ~ zehn** two out of every ten; **ein Riese ~ einem Mann** (inf) a giant of a man; **ein Prachtstück ~ einem Hund** (inf) a magnificent (specimen of a) dog; **dieser Dummkopf ~ Gärtner ...!** (inf) that idiot of a gardener ...!

e (in Verbindung mit n, adj, vb siehe auch dort) (Beschaffenheit, Eigenschaft etc ausdrückend, bestehend aus) of; **~ 50 m Länge** 50 m in length; **im Alter ~ 50 Jahren** at the age of 50; **Kinder ~ 10 Jahren** ten-year-old children; **~ Bedeutung sein** to be of significance; **~ Dauer sein** to be lasting; **das ist sehr freundlich ~ Ihnen** that's very kind of you; **frei ~ etw sein** to be free of sth

f (in Titel) of; (bei deutschem Adelstitel) von; **die Königin ~ England** the Queen of England; **Otto ~ Bismarck** Otto von Bismarck; **~ und zu Falkenburg** von Falkenburg; **ein „von (und zu)" sein** to have a handle to one's name; **sich „von" schreiben** (lit) to have a "von" before one's name; **da kannst du dich aber „von" schreiben** (fig) you can be really proud yourself (there)

g (= über) about; **er erzählte ~ seiner Kindheit** he talked about his childhood; **Geschichten vom Weihnachtsmann/~ Feen** stories about Santa Claus/fairies

h (mit Fragepronomen) from; **~ wo/wann/was** where/when/what ... from, from where/when/what (form)

i (inf: in aufgelösten Kontraktionen) **~ dem halte ich gar nichts** I don't think much of him; **da weiß ich nichts ~** I don't know anything about it

j (inf) **~ wegen** no way! (inf); **~ wegen der Karte/dem Buch** (incorrect) about the map/the book

von|ei|nan|der [fɔnˈai̯nandɐ] ADV of each other, of one another; **etwas/nichts ~ haben** to see something/nothing of each other or one another; (= Zusammensein genießen) to be able/not to be able to enjoy each other's company; (= ähnlich aussehen) to look/not to look like each other; (= sich im Wesen ähnlich sein) to have a lot/nothing in common; **sie konnten die Augen nicht ~ wenden** they couldn't take their eyes off or away from each other or one another; **sich ~ trennen** to part or separate (from each other or one another); **sie hatten ~ die Nase voll** (inf) they were fed up with each other or one another

von|nö|ten [fɔnˈnøːtn] ADJ **~ sein** to be necessary

von|sei|ten [fɔnˈzaitn] PREP +gen on the part of

von|stat|ten [fɔnˈʃtatn] ADV **~ gehen** (= stattfinden) to take place; **wie geht so etwas ~?** what is the procedure for that?; **es ging alles gut ~** everything went well

Voo|doo [ˈvuːdu, vuˈduː] M -, no pl voodoo

Voo|doo- [ˈvuːdu, vuˈduː]: **Voo|doo|kult** M , no pl voodooism; **Voo|doo|pries|ter(in)** M(F) voodoo priest/priestess

Vo|po [ˈfoːpo] M -s, -s (DDR) abbr von **Volkspolizist(in)**

vor [foːɐ] PREP +acc or dat **a** +dat (räumlich) in front of; (= außerhalb von) outside; (= vor Hintergrund) against; (= in Gegenwart von) in front of; (= in jds Achtung) in the eyes of; (bei Reihenfolge) before; (bei Rangordnung) before, ahead of; **der See/die Stadt lag ~ uns** the lake/town lay before us; **jdm herfahren/hergehen** to drive/walk in front of or ahead of sb; **~ der Kirche rechts abbiegen** turn right before the church; **~ der Stadt** outside the town; **~ einer Kommission/allen Leuten** before or in front of a commission/everyone; **~ Gott sind alle Menschen gleich** all people are equal before God or in

---

God's sight; **sich ~ jdm/etw verneigen** (*lit*, *fig*) to bow before *or* to sb/sth; **~ allen Dingen**, **~ allem** above all; **~ dem Fernseher sitzen** *or* **hocken** (*inf*) to sit in front of the TV

b +*acc* (*Richtung angebend*) in front of; (= *außerhalb von*) outside; **ein Schlag ~ den Oberkörper** a blow on the chest

c +*dat* (*zeitlich*) before; **~ Christi Geburt** before Christ, BC; **zwanzig (Minuten) ~ drei** twenty (minutes) to three; **heute ~ acht Tagen** a week ago today; **das ist** *or* **liegt noch ~ uns** this is still to come; **ich war ~ ihm an der Reihe** I was in front of him; **ich war ~ ihm da** I was there before him; **~ einigen Tagen/langer Zeit/fünf Jahren** a few days/a long time/five years ago; **am Tage ~ der Prüfung** the day before the examination

d +*acc* **~ sich hin summen/lachen/sprechen** *etc* to hum/laugh/talk *etc* to oneself; **~ sich hin schreiben/arbeiten** to write/work away; **~ sich hin wandern** to wander on

e +*dat* **~ sich her** before one, in front of one; **er ließ die Schüler ~ sich her gehen** he let the pupils go in front (of him)

f +*dat* (*Ursache angebend*) with; **~ Hunger sterben** to die of hunger; **~ Kälte zittern** to tremble with *or* from cold; **~ Schmerz laut schreien** to cry out with *or* in pain; **~ lauter Arbeit** for *or* because of work; **alles strahlt ~ Sauberkeit** everything is shining clean

g (*in fester Verbindung mit n, vb, adj siehe auch dort*) **Schutz ~ jdm/etw suchen** to seek protection from sb/sth; **~ jdm/etw sicher sein** to be safe from sb/sth; **Achtung ~ jdm/etw haben** to have respect for sb/sth; **sich ~ jdm verstecken** to hide from sb; **wie ist das ~ sich gegangen?** how did it happen?

ADV **a** **~ und zurück** backwards and forwards; **alle kleinen Kinder ~!** all small children to the front!; **wer Karten will, ~!** come up and get your tickets!; **Borussia ~, noch ein Tor!** come on Borussia, let's have another!

b → **nach**

c (*N Ger inf*: = *davor*) **da sei Gott ~** God forbid; **das wird nicht passieren, da bin ich ~** that won't happen, I'll see to it

vorab [fo:ɐ̯'ʔap] ADV to begin *or* start with; **lassen Sie mich ~ erwähnen ...** first let me mention ...

Vor-: **Vorabdruck** M *pl* **-drucke** preprint; **Vorabend** M evening before; (*mit nachfolgendem Genitiv auch*) eve (*auch fig*); **das war am ~** that was the evening before; **am ~ von Weihnachten** (on) the evening before Christmas, on Christmas Eve; **am ~ der Revolution** (*fig*) on the eve of revolution; **Vorabendprogramm** NT (*TV*) early evening schedule; **Vorabexemplar** NT advance copy; **Vorabinformation** F advance information; **Vorahnung** F presentiment, premonition; **Voralpen** PL foothills *pl* of the Alps

voran [fo'ran] ADV **a** (= *vorn, an der Spitze*) first; **ihm/ihr ~** in front of him/her; **der Festzug mit der Kapelle ~** the parade, led by the band; **mit dem Kopf ~ fallen** to fall head first **b** (= *vorwärts*) forwards; **nur** *or* **immer ~** keep going; **immer langsam ~!** gently (*Brit*) *or* easy does it!

voran-: **voran+bringen** VT *sep irreg* to make progress with; **voran+gehen** VI *sep irreg aux sein* **a** (= *an der Spitze gehen*) to go first *or* in front; (= *anführen*) to lead the way; (*fig: Einleitung etc*) to precede (+*dat* sth); **jdm ~** to go ahead of sb **b** (= *zeitlich vor jdm gehen*) to go on ahead; **sie war ihm vorangegangen** (*euph*: = *gestorben*) she had passed on before him; **jdn ~ lassen** to let sb go first; **wie im Vorangehenden berichtet** as reported (in the) above → **Beispiel** **c** (*zeitlich*) **einer Sache** (*dat*) **~** to precede sth; **das Vorangegangene** what has gone before **d** *auch vi impers* (= *Fortschritte machen*) to come on (*Brit*) *or* along, to make progress *or* headway; **es will mit der Arbeit nicht so richtig ~** the work's not coming on (*Brit*) *or* along very well; **voran+gestellt** [-ɡəʃtɛlt] ADJ (*Gram*) preced-

ing *attr*; **~ sein** to precede; **voran+kommen** VI *sep irreg aux sein* to get on *or* along, to make progress *or* headway; **im Leben/beruflich ~** to get on in life/in one's job; **nur langsam ~** to make slow progress, to make little headway; **Vorankündigung** F anouncement; **ohne jede ~** without prior notice; **voran+machen** VI *sep* (*inf*) to hurry up, to get a move on (*inf*)

Vor-: **Voranmeldung** F appointment; (*von Telefongespräch*) booking; **ohne ~** without an appointment/without booking; **Voranschlag** M estimate

voran-: **voran+schreiten** VI *sep irreg aux sein* (*geh*) (*lit*) to stride ahead *or* in front (*jdm* of sb); (*Zeit*) to march on; (*Entwicklung*) to progress; (= *Fortschritte machen*) to progress; **voran+stellen** VT *sep* to put *or* place in front (+*dat* of); (*fig*) to give precedence (+*dat* over); **voran+treiben** VT *sep irreg* to drive forward *or* on; (*fig auch*) to hurry along

Vor-: **Voranzeige** F (*für Theaterstück*) advance notice; (*für Film*) trailer, preview (*US*); **Vorarbeit** F preparatory *or* preliminary work, groundwork; **gute ~ leisten** to do good groundwork, to prepare the ground well; **vor+arbeiten** *sep* **VI** (*inf*) to (do) work in advance **VT** to work in advance **VR** to work one's way forward; **Vorarbeiter** M foreman; **Vorarbeiterin** F forewoman

Vorarlberg ['fo:ɐ̯ʔarlbɛrk, fo:ɐ̯'ʔarl-] NT **-s** Vorarlberg

vorauf [fo'rauf] ADV (*rare*) = **voran, voraus**

voraus [fo'raus] ADV **a** (= *voran*) in front (+*dat* of); (*Naut, fig*) ahead (+*dat* of); **er ist den anderen Schülern/seiner Zeit ~** he is ahead of the other pupils/his time **b** (= *vorher*) **im Voraus** in advance

voraus-: **Vorausabteilung** F (*Mil*) advance party; **voraus+ahnen** VT *sep* to anticipate; **voraus+berechnen** *ptp* **vorausberechnet** VT *sep* to predict; *Wahlergebnis auch* to forecast; *Kosten* to estimate; **voraus+bestimmen** *ptp* **vorausbestimmt** VT *sep* to predict, to forecast; **Vorausbezahlung** F payment in advance, advance payment; **voraus+blicken** VI *sep* to look ahead; **vorausblickend** ADJ foresighted **ADV** with regard to the future; **voraus+eilen** VI *sep aux sein* (*geh*) (*lit, fig*) to hurry on ahead, to rush (on) ahead (+*dat* of); **einer Sache** (*dat*) **~** to be ahead of *or* in advance of sth; **voraus+fahren** VI *sep irreg aux sein* to go in front (+*dat* of); (*Fahrer*) to drive in front (+*dat* of); (= *früher fahren*) to go on ahead; (*Fahrer*) to drive on ahead; **voraus+gehen** VI *sep irreg aux sein* = **vorangehen**; **vorausgesetzt** ADJ **~, (dass) ...** provided (that) ...; **voraus+haben** VT *sep irreg* **jdm etw ~** to have the advantage of sth over sb; **jdm viel ~** to have a great advantage over sb; **Vorauskasse** F (*Comm*) prepayment, advance payment; **voraus+laufen** VI *sep irreg aux sein* to run (on) ahead (+*dat* of); **voraus+planen** VTI *sep* to plan ahead; **voraus+reiten** VI *sep irreg aux sein* (*an der Spitze*) to ride in front (+*dat* of); (= *früher*) to ride on ahead; **Voraussage** F prediction; (= *Wettervoraussage*) forecast; **voraus+sagen** VT *sep* to predict (*jdm* for sb); (= *prophezeien auch*) to prophesy; *Wahlergebnisse auch, Wetter* to forecast; **jdm die Zukunft ~** to foretell sb's future; **voraus+schauend** ADJ *adv* = **vorausblickend**; **voraus+schicken** VT *sep* to send on ahead *or* in advance (+*dat* of); (*fig*: = *vorher sagen*) to say in advance (+*dat* of); **voraus+sehen** VT *sep irreg* to foresee; **ich habe es ja vorausgesehen, dass ...** I knew that ...; **das war vorauszusehen!** that was (only) to be expected!

voraus+setzen VT *sep* to presuppose; (= *als selbstverständlich, sicher annehmen*) *Interesse, Zustimmung, jds Liebe, Verständnis* to take for granted; (= *erfordern*) *Qualifikation, Kenntnisse, Geduld etc* to require, to demand; **wenn wir einmal**

~, dass ... let us *or* if we assume that ...; **etw als selbstverständlich ~** to take sth for granted; **etw als bekannt ~** to assume that everyone knows sth

Voraussetzung [-zɛtsʊŋ] F **-, -en** prerequisite, condition, precondition; (= *Qualifikation*) qualification; (= *Erfordernis*) requirement; (= *Annahme*) assumption, premise; **unter der ~, dass ...** on condition that ...; **eine Mitarbeit hat zur ~, dass ...** a requirement of cooperation is that ...

Voraus-: **Voraussicht** F foresight; (= *Erwartung*) anticipation; **aller ~ nach** in all probability; **in der ~, dass ...** anticipating that ...; **in kluger** *or* **weiser ~** with great foresight *or* forethought; **nach menschlicher ~** as far as we can foresee; **voraussichtlich** ADJ expected **ADV** probably; **er wird ~ gewinnen** he is expected to win; **~ wird es keine Schwierigkeiten geben** we don't anticipate *or* expect any difficulties

Vorauswahl F , *no pl* preliminary selection *or* round of selections; **eine ~ treffen** to narrow down the choice, to draw up a shortlist

Vorauszahlung F payment in advance, advance payment

Vorbau M *ptp* **-bauten** porch; (= *Balkon*) balcony; (*Min*) advancing working; **sie hat einen ganz schönen ~** (*hum*: = *vollbusig*) she's well-stacked (*inf*)

vor+bauen *sep* **VT** (= *anbauen*) to build on (in front); **Häuser bis an die Straße ~** to build houses right on the road; **ein weit vorgebauter Erker** a deep oriel window **VI** (= *Vorkehrungen treffen*) to take precautions; **einer Sache** (*dat*) **~** to provide against sth → **klug**

Vorbedacht M **mit/ohne ~** (= *Überlegung*) with/without due care *or* consideration; (= *Absicht*) intentionally/unintentionally; (*Jur*) with/without intent

Vorbedeutung F portent, presage, prognostic

Vorbedingung F precondition

Vorbehalt [-bəhalt] ✪ 53.6 M **-(e)s, -e** reservation; **unter dem ~, dass ...** with the reservation that ...

vor+behalten *ptp* **vorbehalten** VT *sep irreg* **sich** (*dat*) **etw ~** to reserve sth (for oneself); *Recht* to reserve sth; **jdm etw ~** to leave sth (up) to sb; **diese Entscheidung ist** *or* **bleibt ihm ~** this decision is left (up) to him; **alle Rechte ~** all rights reserved; **Änderungen (sind) ~** subject to alterations; **Irrtümer ~** errors excepted

vorbehaltlich [-bəhaltlɪç], **vorbehältlich** [-bəhɛltlɪç] PREP +*gen* (*form*) subject to; **~ anderer Bestimmungen** unless otherwise provided (*form*); **~ Artikel 3** save as provided in paragraph 3 (*form*)

vorbehaltlos [-bəhaltlo:s] ADJ unconditional, unreserved **ADV** without reservations; *lieben* unconditionally

vorbei [fo:ɐ̯'bai] ADV **a** (*räumlich*) past, by; **er möchte hier ~** he wants to go past *or* by; **~ an** (+*dat*) past; **~!** (= *nicht getroffen*) missed! **b** (*zeitlich*) **~ sein** to be past; (= *vergangen auch, beendet*) to be over *or* finished; (*Sorgen*) to be over; (*Schmerzen*) to be gone; **es ist schon 8 Uhr ~** it's already past *or* after *or* gone 8 o'clock; **damit ist es nun ~** that's all over now; **~ die schöne Zeit!** gone are the days!; **es war schon ~ mit ihm** it was all up with him; **aus und ~** over and done; **~ ist ~** what's past is past; (= *reden wir nicht mehr davon*) let bygones be bygones

vorbei- PREF (= *vorüber*) past; **vorbei+benehmen** *ptp* **vorbeibenommen** VR *sep irreg* (*inf*) to make an exhibition of oneself; **vorbei+bringen** VT *sep irreg* (*inf*) to drop off *or* by *or* in; **vorbei+drücken** VR *sep* (*inf*) (*an jdm/etw* sb/sth) to squeeze past; (*fig*) to slip past; **vorbei+dürfen** VI *sep irreg* (*inf*) to be allowed past; **dürfte ich bitte vorbei?** could I come *or* get past *or* by, please?; **vorbei+fahren** *sep irreg* **VI** *aux sein* (*an jdm/etw* sb/sth) to go/drive/sail past, to pass; **im Vorbeifahren** in passing; **bei jdm ~** (*inf*) to drop *or* call in on sb, to stop *or* drop by sb's house (*inf*) **VT** jdn an etw (*dat*) ~ to drive sb past sth; **ich kann dich ja schnell dort/bei ihnen ~** (*inf*) I can run *or* drive you over there/to their place; **vor|bei+ge|hen** VI *sep irreg aux sein* **a** (*lit, fig*) (*an jdm/etw* sb/sth) to go past *or* by, to pass; **an etw** (*dat*) ~ (*fig: = nicht beachten*) to overlook sth; **bei jdm ~** (*inf*) to drop *or* call in on sb, to stop *or* drop by sb's house (*inf*); **eine Gelegenheit ~ lassen** to let an opportunity pass by *or* slip by; **das Leben geht an ihm vorbei** life is passing him by; **an der Wirklichkeit ~** (*Bericht etc*) to miss the truth; (*Mensch*) to be unrealistic; **im Vorbeigehen** (*lit, fig*) in passing **b** (*= vergehen*) to pass; (*Laune, Zorn*) to blow over, to pass **c** (*= danebengehen*) to miss (*an etw* (*dat*)) sth); **vor|bei+kom|men** VI *sep irreg aux sein* (*an jdm/etw* sb/sth) to pass, to go past; (*an einem Hindernis*) to get past *or* by; **an einer Sache/Aufgabe nicht ~** to be unable to avoid a thing/task; **wir kommen nicht an der Tatsache vorbei, dass ...** there's no escaping the fact that ... **b** **bei jdm ~** (*inf*) to drop *or* call in on sb, to stop *or* drop by sb's house (*inf*); **komm doch mal wieder vorbei!** (*inf*) drop *or* call in again sometime!, stop *or* drop by again sometime! (*inf*); **vor|bei+kön|nen** VI *sep irreg* to be able to get past *or* by (*an etw* (*dat*)) sth); **vor|bei|las|sen** VT *sep irreg* to let past (*an jdm/etw* sb/sth); **vor|bei+lau|fen** VI *sep irreg aux sein* (*an jdm/etw* sb/sth) to run past; (*inf: = vorbeigehen*) to go *or* walk past; (*fig*) to miss; **vor|bei|le|ben** VI *sep* **aneinander ~** to live *or* lead separate lives (within a partnership); **Vor|bei|marsch** M march past; **vor|bei+mar|schie|ren** ptp **vorbeimarschiert** VI *sep aux sein* to march past; **vor|bei+mo|geln** *sep* **VT** jdn/etw an jdm ~ to smuggle sb/sth past sb **VR** **sich an jdm ~ to** sneak past sb; **vor|bei+müs|sen** VI *sep irreg* (*an jdm/etw* sb/sth) to have to go past, to have to pass; **vor|bei+rau|schen** VI *sep aux sein* *Bach* to rush past; *Auto* to streak *or* whizz (*US*) past; (*fig: = vorbeigehen*) hochnäsig to sweep past (*an jdm* sb); **das ist alles an mir vorbeigerauscht** (*inf*) it all passed me by; **vor|bei+re|den** VI *sep* **an etw** (*dat*) ~ to talk round sth; (*absichtlich*) to skirt sth; **aneinander ~** to talk at cross purposes; **vor|bei+schau|en** VI *sep* (*esp dial inf*) = vorbeikommen b; **vor|bei+schie|ßen** VI *sep irreg* **a** *aux sein* (*an jdm/etw* sb/sth) to shoot past *or* by; (*an Kurve*) to overshoot **b** (*am Ziel etc*) to shoot wide (*an* +*dat* of), to miss (*an etw* (*dat*)) sth); **vor|bei+schram|men** VI to scrape past (*an* +*dat* sth); **am Konkurs/an der Niederlage ~** to escape bankruptcy/defeat by the skin of one's teeth; **vor|bei+zie|hen** *sep irreg* **VI** *aux sein* (*an jdm/etw* sb/sth) to file past; (*Truppen, Festzug etc*) to march past; (*Wolken, Rauch, Duft*) to drift past *or* by; (*Sportler*) to draw ahead of; **an jdm ~, vor jds innerem Auge ~** to go through sb's mind **VT** to pull past (*an jdm* sb)

vor|be|las|tet [-bəlastət] ADJ handicapped; **von den Eltern/vom Milieu her ~ sein** to be at a disadvantage because of one's parents/background; **dazu will ich mich nicht äußern, da bin ich ~** I don't want to comment on that, I'm biased → **erblich**

Vor|be|mer|kung F introductory *or* preliminary remark; (*= kurzes Vorwort*) (short) preface *or* foreword

vor+be|rei|ten ptp **vorbereitet** *sep* **VT** to prepare; **auf etw** (*acc*) **vorbereitet sein** to be prepared for sth; **jdn (schonend) auf etw** (*acc*) ~ to prepare sb for sth **VR** (*Mensch*) to prepare (oneself) (*auf* +*acc* for); (*Ereignisse*) to be in the offing (*inf*)

vor|be|rei|tend ADJ *attr* preparatory, preliminary

Vor|be|rei|tung F preparation; **~en (für *or* zu etw) treffen** to make preparations (for sth)

Vor|be|rei|tungs- *in cpds* preparatory; **Vor|berei|tungs|dienst** M teaching practice; **Vor|-**

be|rei|tungs|kurs M preparatory course; **Vor|be|rei|tungs|tref|fen** NT preparatory meeting; **Vor|be|rei|tungs|zeit** F preparation time

Vor-: Vor|be|richt M preliminary report; **Vor|be|scheid** M preliminary notice; **Vor|be|sit|zer(in)** M(F) previous owner; **Vor|be|spre|chung** F preliminary meeting *or* discussion; **vor+be|stel|len** ptp **vorbestellt** VT *sep* to order in advance; *Platz, Tisch, Zimmer, Karten auch* to reserve; **Vor|be|stel|lung** F advance order; (*von Platz, Tisch, Zimmer*) (advance) booking; **bei ~** when ordering/booking in advance; **vor|be|stimmt** [-bəʃtimt] ADJ *Schicksal* predetermined, preordained; **vor|be|straft** [-bəʃtraːft] ADJ previously convicted; **er ist schon einmal/dreimal ~** he (already) has a previous conviction/three previous convictions; **wegen Körperverletzung ~ sein** to have a previous conviction for bodily harm; **Vor|be|straf|te(r)** [-bəʃtraːftə] MF *decl as adj* person/man/woman with a previous conviction *or* a record; **vor+be|ten** *sep* **VI** to lead the prayer/prayers **VT** **jdm etw ~** (*lit*) to lead sb in sth; (*fig inf*) to keep spelling sth out for sb (*inf*); **Vor|be|ter(in)** M(F) prayer leader

Vor|beu|ge|haft F preventive custody

vor+beu|gen *sep* **VI** to prevent (*einer Sache dat* sth); *einer Möglichkeit, einem Fehler auch* to preclude; **~ ist besser als heilen** (*prov*) prevention is better than cure (*prov*) **VT** *Kopf, Oberkörper* to bend forward **VR** to lean *or* bend forward

vor|beu|gend ADJ preventive **ADV** as a preventive measure

Vor|beu|gung F prevention (*gegen, von* of); **zur ~** (*Med*) as a prophylactic

Vor|beu|gungs-: **Vor|beu|gungs|haft** F preventive custody; **Vor|beu|gungs|maß|nah|me** F preventive measure

Vor|bild NT model; (*= Beispiel*) example; **nach dem ~** +*gen* based on the model of; **nach amerikanischem ~** following the American example; **das diente ihm als ~ für seine Skulptur** his sculpture was modelled (*Brit*) *or* modeled (*US*) on this; **er/sein Engagement kann uns zum ~ dienen** he/his commitment is an example to us; **sich** (*dat*) **jdn zum ~ nehmen** to model oneself on sb; (*= sich ein Beispiel nehmen an*) to take sb as an example; **jdn/etw als ~/leuchtendes ~ hinstellen** to hold sb/sth up as an example/a shining example

vor|bild|lich ADJ exemplary **ADV** exemplarily; **sich ~ benehmen** to be on one's best behaviour (*Brit*) *or* behavior (*US*); **sich ~ verhalten** to act in an exemplary fashion

Vor|bild|lich|keit F exemplary nature

Vor-: **Vor|bil|dung** F previous experience; (*schulisch*) educational background; **vor+bin|den** VT *sep irreg* (*inf*) to put *or* tie on; **jdm/sich etw ~** to put *or* tie sth on sb/one; **Vor|bör|se** F before-hours market; **vor|börs|lich** [-bœrzlɪç] ADJ before official hours; **~er Handel** IPO-trading; **Vor|bo|te** M , **Vor|bo|tin** F (*fig*) harbinger, herald

vor+brin|gen VT *sep irreg* **a** (*inf: = nach vorn bringen*) to take up *or* forward; (*Mil*) to take up to the front

b (*= äußern*) to say; *Plan* to propose; *Meinung, Wunsch, Anliegen, Forderung* to express, to state; *Klage, Beschwerde* to make, to lodge; *Entschuldigung* to make, to offer; *Kritik, Einwand* to make, to raise; *Bedenken* to express; *Argument, Beweis* to produce, to bring forward; *Grund* to put forward; **können Sie dagegen etwas ~?** have you anything to say against it?; **was hast du zu deiner Entschuldigung vorzubringen?** what have you to say in your defence (*Brit*) *or* defense (*US*)?; **er brachte vor, er hätte ...** (*= sagte*) he said that he ...; (*= behauptete*) he claimed *or* alleged that he ...

c (*inf: = hervorbekommen*) to get out (*hinter* +*dat* from behind); **die Katze war nicht hinter**

dem Ofen vorzubringen the cat couldn't be got out from behind the stove

Vor-: Vor|büh|ne F apron; **vor|christ|lich** ADJ pre-Christian; **das zweite ~e Jahrhundert** the second century before Christ; **Vor|dach** NT canopy; **vor+da|tie|ren** ptp **vordatiert** VT *sep* to postdate; *Ereignis* to predate, to antedate, to foredate; **Vor|da|tie|rung** [-datiːrʊŋ] F **-, -en** postdating; (*von Ereignis*) predating, antedating, foredating

vor|dem [foːɐˈdeːm, ˈfoːɐ-] ADV **a** (*= zuvor*) before **b** (*old: = früher*) in days of yore (*old, liter*), in (the) olden days

Vor|den|ker(in) M(F) mentor; (*= Prophet*) prophet

Vor|der-: Vor|der|ach|se F front axle; **Vor|der|an|sicht** F front view; **vor|der|asia|tisch** ADJ Near Eastern; **Vor|der|asi|en** NT Near East; **in ~** in the Near East; **Vor|der|bein** NT foreleg; **Vor|der|deck** NT foredeck

Vor|de|re(r) [ˈfɔrdərə] MF *decl as adj* person/man/woman *etc* in front

vor|de|re(r, s) [ˈfɔrdərə] ADJ front; **die ~ Seite des Hauses** the front of the house; **der Vordere Orient** the Near East; **einen ~n Platz einnehmen** (*Sport*) to occupy one of the top places; (*fig*) to occupy an important place → **vorderste(r, s)**

Vor|der-: Vor|der|front F frontage; **Vor|der|fuß** M forefoot; **Vor|der|gau|men|laut** M palatal (sound); **Vor|der|grund** M foreground; (*fig auch*) fore(front); **im ~ stehen** (*fig*) to be to the fore; **sich in den ~ schieben** *or* **drängen** (*fig*) to push oneself to the fore(front); **etw in den ~ rücken** *or* **stellen** (*fig*) to give priority to sth, to place special emphasis on sth; **in den ~ rücken/treten** (*fig*) to come to the fore; (*Mensch auch*) to step into the limelight; **sich in den ~ spielen** (*fig*) to push oneself forward; **vor|der|grün|dig** [-grʏndɪç] ADJ (*fig*) (*= oberflächlich*) superficial **ADV** behandeln superficially; **~ geht es darum, dass sie mehr Geld wollen** it appears at first that they want more money; **vor|der|hand** ADV for the time being, for the present; **Vor|der|hand** F (*von Tier*) forehand; (*Cards*) lead; **Vor|der|haus** NT front-facing house, front building; **vor|der|la|der** M **-s, -** muzzle-loader; **vor|der|las|tig** [-lastɪç] ADJ *Schiff, Flugzeug* front-heavy; **Vor|der|lauf** M (*Hunt*) foreleg; **Vor|der|mann** M *pl* **-männer** person in front; (*Auto*) car in front; **sein ~** the person/car in front of him; **jdn auf ~ bringen** (*fig inf*) to get sb to shape up; (*gesundheitlich*) to get sb fighting fit (*inf*); **etw auf ~ bringen** (*fig inf, Haushalt, Auto etc*) to get sth shipshape; *Kenntnisse, Wissen* to brush sth up; *Finanzen* to get sth straightened out; (*= auf neuesten Stand bringen*) *Listen, Garderobe* to bring sth up-to-date; **Vor|der|pfo|te** F front paw; **Vor|der|rad** NT front wheel; **Vor|der|rad|an|trieb** M front-wheel drive; **Vor|der|rei|fen** M front tyre (*Brit*) *or* tire (*US*); **Vor|der|rei|he** F front row; **Vor|der|schin|ken** M shoulder of ham; **Vor|der|sei|te** F front; (*von Münze*) head, obverse; **Vor|der|sitz** M front seat

vor|ders|te(r, s) [ˈfɔrdəstə] ADJ *superl von* **vordere(r, s)** front(most); **der/die Vorderste in der Schlange** the first man/woman in the queue (*Brit*) *or* line (*US*); **an ~r Front stehen** (*fig*) to be in the front line; **an ~r Stelle stehen** (*fig: Thema, Aufgabe etc*) to have top priority

Vor|der-: Vor|der|ste|ven M (*Naut*) stem; **Vor|der|teil** M OR NT front; **Vor|der|tür** F front door; **Vor|der|zahn** M front tooth; **Vor|der|zim|mer** NT front room

Vor|dip|lom NT first diploma

vor+drän|geln VR *sep*, **vor+drän|gen** VR *sep* to push to the front; **sich in einer Schlange vordrängen** to jump a queue (*Brit*), to push to the front of a line (*US*); (*= in den Mittelpunkt stellen*) to try to be the centre (*Brit*) *or* center (*US*) of attention, to try to be the centre (*Brit*) *or* center (*US*) stage

vor+drin|gen VI *sep irreg aux sein* to advance; (*Mil, in den Weltraum auch*) to penetrate (*in +acc* into); **bis zu jdm/etw ~** to reach sb/sth, to get as far as sb/sth

vor|dring|lich ADJ urgent, pressing ADV **Dinge, die ich ~ erledigen muss** things that I must take care of first; **zu besprechende Punkte** points that are most urgent, points that have to be discussed first

Vor|druck M *pl* **-drucke** form

vor|ehe|lich ADJ *attr* premarital

vor|ei|lig ADJ rash; **~e Schlüsse ziehen** to jump to conclusions ADV rashly; **~ urteilen** to be rash in one's judgement

vor|ei|nan|der [foːɐˈaiˈnandɐ] ADV (*räumlich*) in front of or before one another or each other; (= *einander gegenüber*) face to face; **wir haben keine Geheimnisse ~** we have no secrets from each other; **Angst ~ haben** to be afraid of each other; **sie schämten sich ~** they were embarrassed with each other

vor|ein|ge|nom|men ADJ prejudiced, biased

Vor|ein|ge|nom|men|heit F **a** *no pl* prejudice, bias **b** *usu pl* (= *Vorurteil*) prejudice *no pl*

vor|ein|ge|stellt ADJ (*esp Comput*) preset

Vor|ein|stel|lung F (*esp Comput*) presetting

vor|ent|hal|ten *ptp* **vorenthalten** VT *sep irreg* **jdm etw ~** to withhold sth from sb; *Nachricht auch* to keep sth from sb

Vor|ent|schei|dung F preliminary decision; (*Sport: auch* **Vorentscheidungskampf, Vorentscheidungsrunde**) preliminary round or heat

vor|erst [ˈfoːɐˈeːɐst, foːɐˈeːɐst] ADV for the time being, for the moment or present

vor|er|wähnt [ˈfoːɐˈeːɐveːnt] ADJ *attr* (*form*) aforementioned, aforesaid

Vor|fahr [ˈfoːɐfaːɐ] M **-en, -en** forefather, ancestor

vor+fah|ren *sep irreg* VI *aux sein* **a** (= *nach vorn fahren*) to go or move forward, to move up; (*in Auto*) to drive or move forward **b** (= *ankommen*) to drive up; **den Wagen ~ lassen** to have the car brought (up), to send for or order the car **c** (= *früher fahren*) to go on ahead; **wir fahren schon mal vor** we'll go on ahead **d** (= *an der Spitze fahren*) to drive in front VT **e** (= *weiter nach vorn fahren*) to move up or forward **b** (= *vor den Eingang fahren*) to drive up

Vor|fah|rin [ˈfoːɐfaːrɪn] F **-, -nen** ancestor

Vor|fahrt F , *no pl* right of way; **~ haben** to have (the) right of way; **die ~ beachten/nicht beachten** to observe/ignore the right of way; „**Vorfahrt (be)achten** or **gewähren**" "give way" (*Brit*), "yield" (*US*); (**sich** *dat*) **die ~ erzwingen** to insist on one's right of way; **jdm die ~ nehmen** to ignore sb's right of way

Vor|fahrts-: vor|fahrts|be|rech|tigt ADJ having (the) right of way; **~ sein** to have (the) right of way; **der/die Vorfahrtsberechtigte** the driver with (the) right of way; **Vor|fahrts|recht** NT right of way; **Vor|fahrts|re|gel** F rule on (the) right of way; **Vor|fahrts|schild** NT *pl* **-schilder** give way (*Brit*) or yield (*US*) sign; **Vor|fahrts|stra|ße** F major road; **Vor|fahrts|zei|chen** NT give way (*Brit*) or yield (*US*) sign

Vor|fall M **a** incident, occurrence **b** (*Med*) prolapse

vor+fal|len VI *sep irreg aux sein* **a** (= *sich ereignen*) to occur, to happen; **was ist während meiner Abwesenheit vorgefallen?** what's been happening while I've been away? **b** (*inf: = nach vorn fallen*) to fall forward

Vor-: vor|fa|seln VT *sep* **jdm etw ~** (*pej inf*) to prattle on about sth to sb; **vor|fei|ern** VTI *sep* to celebrate early; **Vor|feld** NT (*Mil*) territory situated in front of the main battle line; (*Aviat*) apron; (*fig*) run-up (+*gen* to); **im ~ der Wahlen** in the run-up to the elections; **im ~ der Ver-**

handlungen in the preliminary stages of the negotiations; **etw im ~ klären** to clear sth up beforehand; **vor|fer|ti|gen** VT *sep* to prefabricate; **Vor|film** M supporting film or programme (*Brit*) or program (*US*), short; **vor|fi|nan|zie|ren** *ptp* **vorfinanziert** VT *sep* to finance in advance, to pre-finance; **Vor|fi|nan|zie|rung** F prefinancing; **vor|fin|den** VT *sep irreg* to find, to discover; **vor|flun|kern** VT *sep* (*inf*) **jdm etwas ~** to tell sb a fib/fibs; **vor+for|mu|lie|ren** *ptp* **vorformuliert** VT *sep* to pre-formulate; *Fragen* to formulate in advance; **Vor|freu|de** F anticipation; **Vor|früh|ling** M early spring, foretaste of spring

vor+füh|len VI *sep* (*fig*) to put or send out (a few) feelers; **bei jdm ~** to sound or feel (*US*) sb out

Vor|führ|ef|fekt M Sod's law; **der ~ trat ein** it was a case of Sod's law

vor+füh|ren VT *sep* **a** *Angeklagten etc* to bring forward; **den Gefangenen dem Haftrichter ~** to bring the prisoner up before the magistrate; **den Patienten einem Spezialisten ~** to have the patient seen by a specialist **b** (= *zeigen*) to present; *Theaterstück auch, Kunststücke* to perform (*dat* to or in front of); *Film* to show; *Mode* to model; *Übung* to demonstrate (*dat* to); (*Vertreter*) *Modell, Gerät* to demonstrate (*dat* to) **c** (= *bloßstellen*) **jdn ~** to make sb look silly or ridiculous; **er wurde vom Direktor regelrecht vorgeführt** the director really made him look small or silly

Vor|füh|rer(in) M(F) projectionist

Vor|führ|mo|dell NT demonstration model

Vor|führ|raum M projection room

Vor|füh|rung F presentation; (*von Angeklagten, Zeugen etc*) production *no pl*; (*von Filmen*) showing; (*von Mode*) modelling (*esp Brit*), modeling (*US*); (*von Geräten, Modellen, Übungen*) demonstration; (*von Theaterstück, Kunststücken*) performance

Vor|führ|wa|gen M demonstration model or car

Vor|ga|be F handicap

Vor|gang M *pl* **-gänge** **a** (= *Ereignis*) event, occurrence; (= *Ablauf, Hergang*) series or course of events; **jdm den genauen ~ eines Unfalls schildern** to tell sb exactly what happened in an accident **b** (*Biol, Chem, Tech, Comput*) process **c** (*form: = Akten*) dossier

Vor|gän|ger [-gɛŋɐ] M **-s, -**, **Vor|gän|ge|rin** [-ərɪn] F **-, -nen** predecessor, precursor (*form*)

Vor|gän|ger|mo|dell NT previous model

Vor|gangs|be|ar|bei|tung F (*Comput*) transaction processing

Vor|gar|ten M front garden

vor+gau|keln VT *sep* **jdm etw ~** to lead sb to believe in sth; **jdm ~, dass ...** to lead sb to believe that ...; **er hat ihr ein Leben im Luxus vorgegaukelt** he led her to believe that he lived in luxury

vor|ge|ben VT *sep irreg* **a** (= *vortäuschen*) to pretend; (= *fälschlich beteuern*) to profess; **sie gab Zeitmangel vor, um ...** she pretended to be pressed for time in order to ... **b** (*Sport*) to give (a start of) **c** (*inf: = nach vorn geben*) to pass forward

Vor|ge|bir|ge NT foothills *pl*

vor|geb|lich [-geːplɪç] ADJ, ADV = **angeblich**

vor|ge|burt|lich [-gəbuːɐtlɪç] ADJ *attr* prenatal

vor|ge|druckt ADJ pre-printed

vor|ge|fasst ▲ ADJ *Meinung* preconceived

Vor|ge|fühl NT anticipation; (= *böse Ahnung*) presentiment, foreboding

vor+ge|hen VI *sep irreg aux sein* **a** (= *handeln*) to act, to proceed; **gerichtlich/energisch gegen jdn ~** to take legal proceedings or legal action/assertive action against sb; **die Polizei ging gegen die Demonstranten vor** the police took action against the demonstrators

b (= *geschehen, vor sich gehen*) to go on, to happen

c (*Uhr*) (= *spätere Zeit anzeigen*) to be fast; (= *zu schnell gehen*) to gain; **meine Uhr geht (zwei Minuten) vor** my watch is (two minutes) fast; **meine Uhr geht pro Tag zwei Minuten vor** my watch gains two minutes a day

d (= *nach vorn gehen*) to go forward, to go to the front; (*Mil*) to advance

e (= *als Erster gehen*) to go first; (= *früher gehen*) to go on ahead

f (= *den Vorrang haben*) to come first, to take precedence, to have priority

Vor|ge|hen NT action

Vor|ge|hens|wei|se F procedure

Vor-: vor|ge|la|gert [-gəlaːgɐt] ADJ *Insel* offshore; **es ist dem Kap ~** lies off the Cape; **vor|ge|nannt** ADJ (*form*) aforementioned, aforesaid; **Vor|ge|plän|kel** NT preliminary skirmish; **Vor|ge|richt** NT hors d'oeuvre, starter (*Brit*); **Vor|ge|schich|te** F (*eines Falles*) past history **b** (= *Urgeschichte*) prehistory, prehistoric times *pl*; **aus der ~** from prehistoric times; **vor|ge|schicht|lich** ADJ prehistoric; **Vor|ge|schmack** M (*fig*) foretaste; **vor|ge|schrit|ten** ADJ advanced; **im ~en Alter** at an advanced age; **zu ~er Stunde** at a late hour

Vor|ge|setz|te(r) [ˈfoːɐgezɛtstə] MF *decl as adj* superior

vor|ges|tern ADV the day before yesterday; **von ~** (*fig*) antiquated; *Methoden, Ansichten auch, Kleidung* old-fashioned; **~ Abend/Morgen** the evening/morning before last; **~ Mittag** midday the day before yesterday

vor|gest|rig ADJ *attr* of the day before yesterday

vor+glü|hen VI *sep Motor* to preheat

vor+grei|fen VI *sep irreg* to anticipate; (= *verfrüht handeln*) to act prematurely; **jdm ~** to forestall sb; **einer Sache** (*dat*) **~** to anticipate sth

Vor|griff M anticipation (*auf +acc* of); (*in Erzählung*) leap ahead; **im ~ auf** (+*acc*) in anticipation of; **verzeihen Sie mir den ~ auf** (+*acc*) ... excuse me for leaping ahead to ...

vor+ha|ben ✿ 29.2, 35.1, 35.2, 35.3 VT *sep irreg* to intend; (= *geplant haben*) to have planned; **was haben Sie heute vor?** what are your plans for today?, what do you intend doing today?; **ich habe morgen nichts vor** I've nothing planned or no plans for tomorrow; **hast du heute Abend schon etwas vor?** have you already got something planned this evening?, are you already doing something this evening?; **wenn du nichts Besseres vorhast ...** if you've nothing better or else to do ...; **etw mit jdm/etw ~** to intend doing sth with sb/sth; (= *etw geplant haben*) to have sth planned for sb/sth; **die ehrgeizigen Eltern haben viel mit dem Kind vor** the ambitious parents have great plans for the child; **was hast du jetzt wieder vor?** what are you up to now?

Vor|ha|ben [ˈfoːɐhaːbn] NT **-s, -** plan; (= *Absicht*) intention

Vor|hal|le F (*von Tempel*) portico; (= *Diele*) entrance hall, vestibule; (= *Foyer*) foyer; (*von Parlament*) lobby

vor+hal|ten *sep irreg* VT **a** = **vorwerfen a b** (*als Beispiel*) **jdm jdn/etw ~** to hold sb/sth up to sb; **man hält ihm den älteren Bruder als Vorbild vor** his elder brother is held up to him as an example; **jdm die Qualen der Hölle ~** to hold up the torments of hell before sb's eyes **c** (= *vor den Körper halten*) to hold up; (*beim Niesen etc*) *Hand, Taschentuch* to put in front of one's mouth; **mit vorgehaltener Pistole** at gunpoint; **sich** (*dat*) **ein Handtuch ~** to hold up a towel in front of oneself → **Spiegel a** VI (= *anhalten*) to last

Vor|hal|tung F *usu pl* reproach; **jdm/sich (wegen etw) ~en machen** to reproach sb/oneself (with or for sth)

Vor|hand F (*Sport*) forehand; (*von Pferd*) forehand; (*Cards*) lead

vor|han|den [fo:ɐ̯ˈhandn] ADJ (= *verfügbar*) available; (= *existierend*) in existence, existing; **eine Dusche ist hier leider nicht ~** I'm afraid there isn't a shower here; **davon ist genügend/nichts mehr ~** there's plenty/no more of that

Vor|hang M curtain; **die Schauspieler bekamen 10 Vorhänge** the actors got *or* took 10 curtain calls, the actors took 10 curtains

Vor|hän|ge|schloss ▲ [ˈfo:ɐ̯hɛŋə-] NT padlock

Vor|hang-: **Vor|hang|stan|ge** F (*zum Aufhängen*) curtain pole; (*zum Ziehen*) curtain rod; **Vor|hang|stoff** M curtaining *no pl*, curtain(ing) material *or* fabric

Vor-: **Vor|haus** NT (*Aus*) hall; **Vor|haut** F foreskin, prepuce (*spec*)

vor|her [fo:ɐ̯ˈhe:ɐ̯, ˈfo:ɐ̯-] ADV before(hand); (= *früher*) before; **am Tag(e) ~** the day before, the previous day; **man weiß ~ nie, wie die Sache ausgeht** one never knows beforehand *or* in advance how things will turn out; **konntest du das nicht ~ sagen?** couldn't you have said that earlier?

Vor|her-: **vor|her+be|stim|men** ptp **vorherbestimmt** VT *sep* to determine *or* ascertain in advance; *Schicksal, Zukunft* to predetermine; (*Gott*) to preordain; **es war ihm vorherbestimmt ...** he was predestined ...; **vor|her+ge|hen** VI *sep irreg aux sein* to go first *or* in front, to lead the way; (*fig*) to precede; **vor|her|ge|hend** ADJ *Tag, Ereignisse* preceding, previous

vor|he|rig [fo:ɐ̯ˈhe:rɪç, ˈfo:ɐ̯-] ADJ *attr* previous, (= *ehemalig*) former; (= *vorhergehend*) *Anmeldung, Genehmigung, Vereinbarung* prior

Vor|herr|schaft F predominance, supremacy; (= *Hegemonie*) hegemony

vor|herr|schen VI *sep* to predominate, to prevail; **Rot herrscht in diesem Winter vor** red is predominant this winter

vor|herr|schend ADJ predominant; *Ansicht, Meinung auch* prevailing, prevalent; (= *weitverbreitet*) prevalent

Vor|her-: **Vor|her|sa|ge** F forecast; **vor|her+sa|gen** VT *sep* = **voraussagen**; **vor|her+se|hen** VT *sep irreg* to foresee

vor|heu|cheln VT *sep* to feign, to pretend; **jdm etw ~** to feign *or* pretend sth to sb; **jdm ~, dass ...** to pretend to sb that ...; **er heuchelt dir doch bloß was vor!** (*inf*) he's just putting on an act

vor+heu|len VT *sep* (*inf*) **jdm etwas ~** to give sb a sob story (*inf*)

Vor|him|mel M first heaven

vor|hin [fo:ɐ̯ˈhɪn, ˈfo:ɐ̯-] ADV just now, a little while ago

Vor|hi|nein ▲ [ˈfo:ɐ̯hɪnaɪn] ADV **im ~** in advance

Vor-: **Vor|hof** M forecourt; (*Anat: von Herz, Ohr*) vestibule; **Vor|hof|flim|mern** NT (*Med*) auricular fibrillation (*spec*); **Vor|höl|le** F limbo; **in der ~** in limbo; **Vor|hut** F -, -**en** (*Mil*) vanguard, advance guard

vo|rig [fo:rɪç] ADJ *attr* (= *früher*) *Besitzer, Wohnsitz* previous; (= *vergangen*) *Jahr, Woche etc* last; **im Vorigen** (in the) above, earlier; **der/die/das Vorige** the above(-mentioned); **die Vorigen** (*Theat*) the same

Vor|jahr NT previous year, year before

Vor|jahres-: **Vor|jah|res|er|geb|nis** NT previous year's result; **Vor|jah|res|ni|veau** NT previous year's level; **Vor|jah|res|um|satz** M previous year's turnover; **Vor|jah|res|wert** M previous year's value

Vor-: **vor|jäh|rig** ADJ of the previous year, of the year before; **vor+jam|mern** VTI *sep* **jdm (etwas) ~** to moan to sb (*von* about); **Vor|kalku|la|ti|on** F preliminary costing *or* calculation; **Vor|kam|mer** F (*Anat: von Herz*) vestibule; (*Tech*) precombustion chamber; **Vor|kämpfer(in)** M(F) (*für* of) pioneer, champion; **Vor|kas|se** F advance payment; **per – zah**

len to pay in advance; „**Zahlung nur gegen ~**" "advance payment only"; **vor+kau|en** VT *sep Nahrung* to chew; **jdm etw** (*acc*) **~** (*fig inf*) to spoon-feed sth to sb (*inf*); **Vor|kaufs|recht** NT option of purchase *or* to buy

Vor|keh|rung [ˈfo:ɐ̯ke:rʊŋ] F -, -**en** precaution; **~en treffen** to take precautions

Vor|kennt|nis F previous knowledge *no pl*; (= *Erfahrung*) previous experience *no pl*; **sprachliche ~se** previous knowledge of languages/the language

vor+knöp|fen VT *sep* (*fig inf*) **sich** (*dat*) **jdn ~** to take sb to task; **den hat sich die Mafia vorgeknöpft** the Mafia got him

vor+ko|chen VI *sep Mahlzeit,* (= *ankochen*) to precook; **für morgen ~** to cook ahead for tomorrow

vor+kom|men VI *sep irreg aux sein* **a** *auch vi impers* (= *sich ereignen*) to happen; **so etwas ist mir noch nie vorgekommen** such a thing has never happened to me before; **dass mir das nicht noch einmal vorkommt!** don't let it happen again!; **das soll nicht wieder ~** it won't happen again; **das kann schon mal ~** it can happen, it has been known to happen; (= *das ist nicht ungewöhnlich*) that happens; **so was soll ~!** that's life!

b (= *vorhanden sein, auftreten*) to occur; (*Pflanzen, Tiere*) to be found; **in dem Aufsatz dürfen keine Fehler ~** there mustn't be any mistakes in the essay

c (= *erscheinen*) to seem; **das kommt mir bekannt/merkwürdig vor** that seems familiar/strange to me; **sich** (*dat*) **überflüssig/dumm ~** to feel superfluous/silly; **sich** (*dat*) **klug ~** to think one is clever; **das kommt dir nur so vor** it just seems that way *or* like that to you; **wie kommst du mir denn vor?** (*inf*) who do you think you are?

d (= *nach vorn kommen*) to come forward *or* to the front

e (= *herauskommen*) to come out

Vor|kom|men [ˈfo:ɐ̯kɔmən] NT -**s**, - (*no pl*: = *das Auftreten*) occurrence, incidence; (*Min*) deposit

Vor|komm|nis [ˈfo:ɐ̯kɔmnɪs] NT -**ses**, -**se** incident, event, occurrence

Vor|kos|ter [-kɔstɐ] M -**s**, -, **Vor|kos|te|rin** [-ərɪn] F -, -**nen** taster; (*fig*) guinea pig

Vor|kriegs- *in cpds* prewar; **Vor|kriegs|zeit** F prewar period

vor+la|den VT *sep irreg* (*Jur*) to summons; *Zeugen auch* to subpoena

Vor|la|dung F summons; (*von Zeuge auch*) subpoena

Vor|la|ge F **a** *no pl* (= *das Vorlegen*) (*von Dokument*) presentation, production; (*von Scheck, Schuldschein*) presentation; (*von Beweismaterial*) submission; **gegen ~ einer Sache** (*gen*) (up)on production *or* presentation of sth; **zahlbar bei ~** payable on demand

b (= *Muster*) (*zum Stricken, Nähen*) pattern; (*Liter*) model; **etw von einer ~ abzeichnen/nach einer ~ machen** to copy sth; **hattest du dafür eine ~?** did you have a pattern for it?; did you copy it from something?

c (= *Entwurf*) draft; (*Parl*: = *Gesetzesvorlage*) bill

d (*Ftbl*) through-ball; **jdm eine ~ machen** to set the ball up for sb; **das war eine tolle ~** the ball was beautifully set up

e (*Ski*) vorlage, forward lean (position)

f (*Comm*: = *geliehene Summe*) advance; **mit 500 Euro in ~ treten** to pay 500 euros in advance

g (= *Vorleger*) mat; (= *Bettvorlage*) (bedside) rug

Vor|land NT (*der Alpen etc*) foothills *pl*; (*vor Deich*) foreshore

vor+las|sen VT *sep irreg* **a** (*inf*) **jdn ~** (= *nach vorn gehen lassen*) to let sb go in front; (*in der Schlange auch*) to let sb go first; (= *vorbeigehen lassen*) to let sb (go) past, to let sb pass; **ein Auto ~** (= *einbiegen lassen*) to let a car in; (= *überholen lassen*) to let a car pass, to let a car (go)

past b (= *Empfang gewähren*) to allow in, to admit

Vor|lauf M **a** (*Sport*) qualifying *or* preliminary heat **b** (*Chem: bei Destillation*) forerun **c** (*Tech: von Rad*) offset **d** (*von Film, Band*) leader; (*von Tonbandgerät*) fast-forward

vor+lau|fen VI *sep irreg aux sein* (*inf*) (= *vorauslaufen*) to run on ahead *or* in front; (= *nach vorne laufen*) to run to the front

Vor|läu|fer(in) M(F) forerunner (*auch Ski*), precursor

vor|läu|fig ADJ temporary; *Regelung auch, Schätzungen, Berechnungen* provisional; *Urteil* preliminary; *Verfügung des Gerichts* interim, provisional ADV (= *einstweilig*) temporarily; (= *fürs erste*) for the time being, for the present, provisionally → **festnehmen**

Vor|lauf|zeit F (*Sport*) qualifying time; (*Ind:* = *Entwicklungszeit*) lead time

vor|laut ADJ cheeky (*Brit*), impertinent

vor+le|ben VT *sep* **jdm etw ~** to set an example of sth to sb

Vor|le|ben NT past (life)

Vor|le|ge-: **Vor|le|ge|be|steck** NT serving cutlery, serving spoons *pl*; (= *Tranchierbesteck*) carvers *pl*; **Vor|le|ge|ga|bel** F serving fork; (*von Tranchierbesteck*) carving fork; **Vor|le|gelöf|fel** M serving spoon, tablespoon; **Vor|lege|mes|ser** NT carving knife

vor+le|gen *sep* VT **a** (= *präsentieren*) to present; *Entwurf, Doktorarbeit auch* to submit; *Pass* to show, to produce; *Beweismaterial* to submit; *Zeugnisse, Bewerbungsunterlagen* to produce; *Schulzeugnis* to show; *Schularbeit* to hand in; (*Pol*) *Entwurf* to table (*Brit*), to introduce; **jdm etw zur Unterschrift ~** to give *or* present sth to sb for signature *or* signing; **etw dem Parlament ~** to lay sth before the house, to table sth (*Brit*); **jdm eine Frage ~** to put a question to sb; **ein schnelles Tempo ~** to go at a fast pace; **ein schnelleres Tempo ~** to speed up, to quicken the pace

b *Speisen* to serve; (= *hinlegen*) *Futter* to put down (+*dat* to); **jdm etw ~** to serve sth to sb, to serve sb with sth

c *Riegel* to put across, to shoot (across); *Schloss, Kette* to put on; (*inf:* = *davorlegen*) to put in front

d (*Ftbl*) **jdm den Ball ~** to set the ball up for sb

e (= *vorstrecken*) *Geld* to advance **VI** (*Kellner*) to serve

Vor|le|ger [ˈfo:ɐ̯le:gɐ] M -**s**, - mat; (= *Bettvorleger auch*) rug

Vor|le|ge|schloss ▲ NT padlock

vor+leh|nen VR *sep* to lean forward

Vor|leis|tung F (*Econ*) (= *Vorausbezahlung*) advance (payment); (= *finanzielle Aufwendung*) outlay *no pl* (*an* +*dat* on); (= *vorausgehende Arbeit*) preliminary work; (*Pol*) prior concession

vor+le|sen VTI *sep irreg* to read aloud *or* out loud; **jdm (etw) ~** to read (sth) to sb

Vor|le|ser(in) M(F) reader

Vor|le|sung F (*Univ*) lecture; (= *Vorlesungsreihe*) course (of lectures), lectures *pl*; **über etw** (*acc*) **~en halten** to give (a course of) lectures on sth; **~en hören** to go to lectures

Vor|le|sungs-: **Vor|le|sungs|be|ginn** M ≈ start *or* beginning of term; **~ ist am ...** term starts on ...; **Vor|le|sungs|be|trieb** M lectures *pl*; **vor|le|sungs|frei** ADJ **~e Zeit** free period(s *pl*); **Vor|le|sungs|rei|he** F series of lectures, lecture series; **Vor|le|sungs|verzeich|nis** NT lecture timetable

vor|letz|te(r, s) [ˈfo:ɐ̯lɛtstə] ADJ last but one (*Brit*), next to last, penultimate; **im ~n Jahr** the year before last

Vor|lie|be ✪ 34.5 F predilection, special liking, preference; **etw mit ~ tun** to particularly like doing sth

vor|lieb neh|men ▲ [foːˈɐ̯ˈliːp-] VI *irreg* **mit jdm/etw ~** to make do with sb/sth, to put up with sb/sth

vor+lie|gen *sep irreg* **VI** (= *zur Verfügung stehen*: *Beweise, Katalog, Erkenntnisse*) to be available; (*Urteil*) to be known; (= *eingereicht, vorgelegt sein*: *Unterlagen, wissenschaftliche Arbeit*) to be in, to have come in; (*Pol*) (*Gesetzesvorlage*) to be before the house; (*Haushalt*) to be published, to be out; (= *vorhanden sein*) (*Irrtum, Schuld etc*) to be; (*Symptome*) to be present; (*Gründe, Voraussetzungen*) to exist; **jdm ~** (*Unterlagen, Akten etc*) to be with sb; **die Ergebnisse liegen der Kommission vor** the commission has the results; **das Beweismaterial liegt dem Gericht vor** the evidence is before the court; **mir liegt ein Brief vor** I have (here) a letter; **etw liegt gegen jdn vor** sth is against sb; (*gegen Angeklagten*) sb is charged with sth

VI *impers* **es liegen fünf Bewerbungen vor** there are *or* we have five applications; **es muss ein Irrtum ~** there must be some mistake

vor|lie|gend ADJ *attr Gründe* existing; *Akten, Unterlagen* on hand; (*Typ*) *Auflage* on hand; *Frage* at issue; *Angelegenheit, Probleme* in hand; *Ergebnisse, Erkenntnisse, Zahlen* available; *Bericht* submitted; **im ~en Fall** in this case, in the present case; **die uns ~en Ergebnisse** the results we have to hand; **sein jetzt ~er dritter Film** his third and current film

vor+lü|gen VT *sep irreg* **jdm etwas ~** to lie to sb

vorm. *abbr von* **vormittags**

vor+ma|chen VT *sep* **a** (*jdm*) **etw ~** (= *zeigen*) to show (sb) how to do sth, to demonstrate sth (to sb); (*fig*: = *als Beispiel dienen*) to show sb sth **b** **jdm etwas ~** (*fig*: = *täuschen*) to fool *or* kid (*inf*) sb; **ich lasse mir so leicht nichts ~** you/he *etc* can't fool *or* kid (*inf*) me so easily; **er lässt sich** (*dat*) **von niemandem etwas ~** nobody can fool him, he's nobody's fool; **mach mir doch nichts vor** don't try and fool *or* kid (*inf*) me; **sich** (*dat*) (**selbst**) **etwas ~** to fool *or* kid (*inf*) oneself → **Dunst c** (*inf*: = *davorlegen, -stellen etc*) *Kette, Schürze, Riegel* to put on; *Brett* to put across

Vor|macht|(stel|lung) F supremacy (*gegenüber* over); **eine Vormachtstellung haben** to have supremacy

Vor|ma|gen M (*von Rind*) rumen; (*von Vogel*) crop

vor|ma|lig [ˈfoːɐ̯maːlɪç] ADJ *attr* former

vor|mals [ˈfoːɐ̯maːls] ADV formerly

Vor|marsch M (*Mil*) advance; **im ~ sein** to be on the advance, to be advancing; (*fig*) to be gaining ground

Vor|märz M (*Hist*) *period from 1815 to March revolution of 1848*

Vor|mast M foremast

vor+mer|ken VT *sep* to note down, to make a note of; (*bei Bestellung auch*) to take an order for; *Plätze* to reserve, to book; **ich werde Sie für Mittwoch ~** I'll put you *or* your name down for Wednesday; **können Sie für mich 5 Exemplare ~?** can I put me down for 5 copies?, can you reserve 5 copies for me?; **sich beim Friseur ~ lassen** to make an appointment at the hairdresser's; **sich für einen Kursus ~ lassen** to put one's name *or* oneself down for a course

Vor|mie|ter(in) M(F) previous tenant

Vor|mit|tag M morning; **am ~** in the morning; **heute/gestern/morgen ~** this/yesterday/tomorrow morning

vor|mit|tä|gig ADJ morning

vor|mit|tags ADV in the morning; (= *jeden Morgen*) in the morning(s)

Vor|mo|nat M previous month

Vor|mund M **-(e)s, -e** *or* **Vormünder** guardian; **ich brauche keinen ~** (*fig*) I don't need anyone to tell me what to do

Vor|mund|schaft [ˈfoːɐ̯mʊntʃaft] F **-, -en** guardianship, tutelage; **jdn unter ~ stellen** to place sb under the care of a guardian

Vor|mund|schafts|ge|richt NT *court dealing with matters relating to guardianship*

vorn [fɔrn] ADV **a** in front; **von ~** from the front; **nach ~** (= *ganz nach vorn*) to the front; (= *weiter nach vorn*) forwards; **von weit ~** from the very front; **~ im Buch/in der Schlange** at the front of the book/queue (*Brit*) *or* line (*US*); **~ auf der Liste** at the top of the list; **sich ~ anstellen** to join the front of the queue (*Brit*) *or* line (*US*); **~ im Bild** in the front of the picture; **nach ~ abgehen** (*Theat*) to exit at the front of the stage; **nach ~ laufen** to run to the front; **~ bleiben** (*lit*) to stay in front; (*fig*) not to lag behind; **wenn es etwas umsonst gibt, ist er immer ganz ~(e)** when something's free he's always (the) first on the scene

b (= *am Anfang*) **von ~** from the beginning; **wie schon ~ erklärt** as explained above; **von ~ anfangen** to begin at the beginning, to start from the beginning; (= *von neuem*) to start (all) over again, to start again from scratch; (*neues Leben*) to start afresh, to make a fresh start; **etw ~ anfügen** to add sth at the beginning; **das Auto kam von ~ auf ihn zugefahren** the car came at him head on

c (= *am vorderen Ende*) at the front; (*Naut*) fore; **von ~** from the front; **jdn von ~ sehen** to see sb's face; **~ im Auto/Bus** in the front of the car/bus; **der Blinker ~** the front indicator (*esp Brit*) *or* blinker (*US*); **nach ~** to the front; *fallen, ziehen* forwards

d (= *auf der Vorderseite*) at the front; **das Buch ist ~ schmutzig** the front of the book is dirty; **~ auf der Medaille** on the face of the medal; **ein nach ~ gelegenes Zimmer** a room facing the front

e (= *weit entfernt*) **das Auto da ~** the car in front *or* ahead there; **sie waren ziemlich weit ~** they were quite far ahead *or* quite a long way ahead; (*Läufer auch*) they were quite a long way (out) in front *or* quite a long way in the lead

f **ich kann doch nicht ~ und hinten gleichzeitig sein** I can't be everywhere at once; **sich von ~(e) bis ~ und hinten bedienen lassen** to be waited on hand and foot; **er betrügt sie von ~ bis hinten** he deceives her right, left and centre (*Brit*) *or* center (*US*) → *auch* **hinten**

Vor|nah|me [-naːmə] F **-, -n** (*form*) undertaking; **die ~ von Änderungen am Text bleibt dem Autor überlassen** it is left to the author to undertake changes to the text

Vor|na|me M Christian name, first name

vor|ne [ˈfɔrnə] ADV = **vorn**

vor|nehm [ˈfoːɐ̯neːm] ADJ **a** (*von hohem Rang*) *Familie, Kreise* distinguished, high-ranking; (*von adliger Herkunft*) aristocratic, noble; (= *kultiviert*) *Herr, Dame* distinguished, posh (*inf*); *Manieren, Art, Benehmen* genteel, refined; (= *edel*) *Gesinnung, Charakter, Handeln* noble; **die ~e Gesellschaft** high society; **ihr seid mir eine ~e Gesellschaft** (*iro*) you're a fine lot! (*inf*); **die ~e Welt, die Vornehmen** distinguished society; **so was sagt/tut man nicht in ~en Kreisen** one doesn't say/do that in polite society; **ein ~er Besuch** a distinguished visitor; **~er Anstrich** (*fig*) distinguished air

b (= *elegant, luxuriös*) *Wohngegend* fashionable, smart, posh (*inf*); *Haus* smart, posh (*inf*); *Geschäft* exclusive, posh (*inf*); *Kleid, Äußeres* elegant, stylish; *Auto* smart, posh (*inf*); *Geschmack* refined, exclusive

c (*dated*) **die ~ste Pflicht/Aufgabe** the first *or* foremost duty/task

ADV *wohnen* grandly; *schweigen, sich zurückhalten* grandly; **~ heiraten** to marry into high society; **~ tun** (*pej inf*) to act posh (*inf*); **~ geht die Welt zugrunde** (*iro*) aren't we going up in the world! (*iro*)

vor+neh|men ✪ 35.2 VT *sep irreg* **a** (= *ausführen*) to carry out; *Umfrage, Änderungen* to carry

out, to do; *Messungen* to take; *Einsparungen* to make

b (= *in Angriff nehmen*) (**sich** *dat*) **etw ~** to get to work on sth

c **sich** (*dat*) **etw ~** (= *planen, vorhaben*) to intend *or* mean to do sth; (= *Vorsatz fassen*) to have resolved to do sth; **ich habe mir vorgenommen, das nächste Woche zu tun** I intend *or* mean to do that next week; **ich habe mir zu viel vorgenommen** I've taken on too much

d **sich** (*dat*) **jdn ~** (*inf*) to have a word with sb

e (= *früher drannehmen*) *Kunden, Patienten* to attend to *or* see first

f (*inf*: = *vorhalten*) *Schürze, Serviette* to put on; *Hand* to put in front of one's mouth; (= *vorbeugen*) *Schultern* to hunch

Vor|nehm|heit F **-,** *no pl* **a** (= *hoher Rang*: *von Familie etc*) high rank; (= *Kultiviertheit*) (*von Mensch*) distinguished ways *pl*; (*von Art, Benehmen*) refinement **b** (= *Eleganz*) (*von Wohngegend, Haus*) smartness, poshness (*inf*); (*von Kleid, Äußerem*) elegance, stylishness; (*von Geschmack*) refinement

vor|nehm|lich [ˈfoːɐ̯neːmlɪç] ADV (= *hauptsächlich, vor allem*) principally, especially, above all; (= *vorzugsweise*) first and foremost ADJ principal, main, chief

vor+nei|gen VTR *sep* to lean forward

Vor|ne|ver|tei|di|gung F (*Mil*) forward defence (*Brit*) *or* defense (*US*)

vor|ne|weg [ˈfoːɐ̯nəvɛk, fɔrnəˈvɛk] ADV ahead, in front, first; (= *als erstes*) first; **er geht immer ~** he always walks on ahead *or* in front; **mit dem Kopf ~** head first; **gleich ~** straight away; **mit dem Mund ~ sein** (*inf*) to have a big mouth

vorn|he|rein [ˈfɔrnhaɪn, fɔrnheˈraɪn] ADV **von ~** from the start *or* outset

Vor|nie|re F pronephros (*spec*)

vorn-: **vorn|über** [fɔrnˈlyːbɐ] ADV forwards; **vorn|über|fal|len** VI *sep* to fall (over) forwards; **vorn|weg** [ˈfɔrnvɛk, fɔrnˈvɛk] ADV = **vorneweg**

Vor|ort [ˈfoːɐ̯ɔrt] M *pl* **-orte** (= *Vorstadt*) suburb

Vor-Ort- [foːɐ̯ˈɔrt] *in cpds* on-site

Vor|ort|bahn [ˈfoːɐ̯ɔrt-] F suburban line; (*für Berufsverkehr*) commuter line

Vor-Ort-Kon|trol|le [foːɐ̯ˈɔrt-] F on-site supervision

Vor|ort- [ˈfoːɐ̯ɔrt-]: **Vor|ort|ver|kehr** M suburban traffic; (*von öffentlichen Verkehrsmitteln*) suburban service; **Vor|ort|zug** M suburban train; (*im Berufsverkehr*) commuter train

Vor-: **vor|ös|ter|lich** ADJ immediately before Easter; **Vor|platz** M forecourt; **Vor|pom|mern** [-ˈpɔmən] NT West Pomerania; **Vor|pos|ten** M (*Mil*) outpost; **Vor|prä|mie** F (*St Ex*) call option; **vor+pre|schen** VI *sep aux sein* (*lit, fig*) to press ahead; **Vor|pro|gramm** NT supporting bill *or* programme (*Brit*), warm-up act (*US*); **im ~** on the supporting bill (*Brit*), as the warm-up act (*US*); **vor+pro|gram|mie|ren** *ptp* **vorprogrammiert** VT *sep* to preprogram; (*fig auch*) to precondition; **vor|pro|gram|miert** [-programiːɐ̯t] ADJ *Erfolg, Antwort* automatic; *Verhaltensweise* preprogrammed; *Weg* predetermined, preordained; **die nächste Krise ist ~** the seeds of the next crisis have been sown; **Vor|prü|fung** F preliminary examination; **vor+quel|len** VI *sep irreg* **a** (*Erbsen, Linsen*) to soak **b** *aux sein* (*Augen*) to bulge → **hervorquellen**

Vor|rang M , *no pl* **a** **~ haben** to have priority, to take precedence; **den ~ vor etw** (*dat*) **haben** to take precedence over sth; **jdm/einer Sache den ~ geben** *or* **einräumen** to give sb/a matter priority; **jdm/einer Sache den ~ streitig machen** to challenge sb's/sth's pre-eminence; **mit ~** (= *vorrangig*) as a matter of priority **b** (*Aus*: = *Vorfahrt*) right of way

vor|ran|gig [ˈfoːɐ̯raŋɪç] ADJ priority *attr*; **~ sein** to have (top) priority ADV as a matter of priority; **eine Angelegenheit ~ erledigen/behandeln** to give a matter priority treatment

Vor|rang|stel|lung F pre-eminence *no indef art;* **er hat in der Firma eine ~** he has a position of prime importance in the firm

Vor|rat ['foːrɛːt] M **-(e)s, Vorräte** [-rɛːtə] (*an +dat* of) stock, supply; (*esp Comm*) stocks *pl;* (= *Geldvorrat*) reserves *pl;* (*an Atomwaffen*) stockpile; (*an Geschichten, Ideen*) stock; **heimlicher ~** (secret) hoard; **etw auf ~ kaufen** to stock up with sth; **Vorräte anlegen** or **ansammeln** to build up reserves; (= *Geldvorräte*) to build up financial or monetary reserves; **solange der ~ reicht** (*Comm*) while stocks last; **etw auf ~ haben** to have sth in reserve; (*Comm*) to have sth in stock

vor|rä|tig ['foːrɛːtɪç] ADJ in stock; (= *verfügbar*) available; **etw nicht mehr ~ haben** to be out (of stock) of sth

Vor|rats-: Vor|rats|hal|tung F stockpiling; (*bei Tieren*) storage habit; **Vor|rats|kam|mer** F store (*Brit*) or storage (*esp US*) cupboard; (*für Lebensmittel*) larder (*Brit*), pantry; **Vor|rats|raum** M storeroom; (*in Geschäft*) stockroom

Vor|raum M anteroom; (*Büro*) outer office; (*von Gericht*) lobby; (*von Kino, Theater*) foyer

vor|rech|nen VT *sep* **jdm etw ~** to work out or reckon up or calculate sth for sb; **er rechnet mir dauernd vor, wie viel alles kostet** he's always pointing out to me how much everything costs; **jdm seine Fehler ~** (*fig*) to enumerate sb's mistakes

Vor|recht NT prerogative; (= *Vergünstigung*) privilege

Vor|re|de F (= *Vorwort*) preface; (*Theat*) prologue (*Brit*), prolog (*US*); (= *einleitende Rede*) introductory speech

vor|re|den VT *sep* (*inf*) **jdm etwas ~** to tell sb a tale; **red mir doch nichts vor** don't give me that (*inf*)

Vor|red|ner(in) M(F) (= *vorheriger Redner*) previous speaker; (= *einleitender Redner*) introductory speaker; **mein ~ hat gesagt ...** the previous speaker said ...

vor|rei|ten *sep irreg* **a** *aux sein* (= *vorausreiten*) to ride on ahead **b** (*zur Demonstration*) to demonstrate (*a riding exercise*) VT (= *demonstrieren*) *Übung* to demonstrate

Vor|rei|ter(in) M(F) **a** forerunner; **den ~ für etw machen** to be the first to do sth **b** (*beim Reiten*) demonstrator

Vor|rei|ter|rol|le F **eine ~ für andere einnehmen** to make the running for others

vor|ren|nen VI *sep irreg aux sein* (*inf*) (*voraus*) to run or race (on) ahead; (*nach vorn*) to run forward

vor|rich|ten VT *sep* to prepare; *Zutaten, Gegenstände* to get ready

Vor|rich|tung F device, gadget

vor|rü|cken *sep* VT to move forward; *Schachfigur* to advance, to move on VI *aux sein* to move or go forward; (*Mil*) to advance; (*Sport, im Beruf etc*) to move up; (*Uhrzeiger*) to move on; **mit dem Stuhl ~** to move one's chair forward; **in vorgerücktem Alter** in later life; **zu vorgerückter Stunde** at a late hour

Vor|ru|he|stand M early retirement

Vor|ru|he|ständ|ler(in) M(F) person taking early retirement

Vor|ru|he|stands|re|ge|lung F early retirement scheme

Vor|run|de F (*Sport*) preliminary or qualifying round; (*von Saison*) first part (of the season)

vor|sa|gen *sep* VT **jdm etw ~** (*Gedicht*) to recite sth to sb; *Antwort, Lösung* to tell sb sth VI (*Sch*) **jdm ~** to tell sb the answer

Vor|sai|son F low season, early (part of the) season

Vor|sän|ger(in) M(F) (*Eccl*) precentor; (*in Chor*) choir leader; (*fig*) leading voice

Vor|satz M **a** (*firm*) intention; **mit ~** (*Jur*) with intent; **den ~ haben, etw zu tun** to (firmly) intend to do sth; **den ~ fassen, etw zu tun** to make up one's mind to do sth, to resolve to do sth; (*zum neuen Jahr*) to make a resolution to do sth; **bei seinen Vorsätzen bleiben, seinen Vorsätzen treu bleiben** to keep to one's resolve or resolution → **Weg b** (*von Buch*) endpaper

Vor|satz|blatt NT (*Typ*) endpaper

vor|sätz|lich [-zɛtslɪç] ADJ deliberate, intentional; *Lüge* deliberate; (*Jur*) *Mord, Brandstiftung etc* wilful ADV deliberately, intentionally; **jdn ~ töten** to kill sb intentionally

Vor|satz|lin|se F (*Phot*) ancillary lens

Vor|schalt|ge|setz NT (*Pol*) interim law (*preparing the way for a subsequent law*)

Vor|schau F preview; (*für Film*) trailer, preview (*US*); (= *Wettervorschau*) forecast

Vor|schein M **zum ~ bringen** (*lit: = zeigen*) to produce; *Fleck* to show up; (*fig: = deutlich machen*) to bring to light; **zum ~ kommen** (*lit: = sichtbar werden*) to appear; (*fig: = entdeckt werden*) to turn up, to come to light; (*Tatsachen*) to come to light, to come out

vor+schie|ben *sep irreg* VT **a** (= *davorschieben*) to push in front; *Riegel* to put across, to shoot (across); (= *nach vorn schieben*) to push forward; *Kopf* to stick forward; *Unterlippe, Kinn* to stick out → **Riegel b** (*Mil*) *Truppen* to move forward; **vorgeschobener Posten** advance guard, advance party **c** (*fig: = vorschützen*) to put forward as a pretext or excuse; **vorgeschobene Gründe** pretexts *pl,* excuses *pl* **d jdn ~** to put sb forward as a front man VR (*Wolken, Erdmassen*) to advance, to move forward; (*Menschen*) to push or press forward

vor+schie|ßen *sep irreg* VT **jdm Geld ~** to advance sb money VI *aux sein* to shoot forward; (*Schlange, Läufer auch*) to dart forward

Vor|schiff NT forecastle, fo'c's'le

vor+schla|fen *sep irreg* VI **ein bisschen ~** to stock up on a bit of sleep, to stockpile some Zs (*US*)

Vor|schlag ✪ 28.1, 28.2 M **a** suggestion, proposal; (= *Rat*) recommendation, advice; (= *Angebot*) offer, proposition; (*Pol: von Kandidaten*) proposal; **auf ~ von** or **+gen** at or on the suggestion of, on the recommendation of; **das ist ein ~!** that's an idea!; **wäre das nicht ein ~?** how's that for an idea? → **Güte a b** (*Mus*) appoggiatura **c** (*Typ*) sink **d** (*Sw: = Gewinn*) profit

vor+schla|gen ✪ 28.1, 28.2 VT *sep irreg* **a** (= *als Vorschlag unterbreiten*) to suggest, to propose; **jdn für ein Amt ~** to propose or nominate sb for a post (*esp Brit*) or position; **jdm ~, dass er etw tut** to suggest that sb do(es) sth, to suggest to sb that he do(es) sth **b den Takt ~** to beat time

Vor|schlag|ham|mer M sledgehammer

Vor|schluss|run|de ▲ F (*Sport*) semifinal(s *pl*)

vor|schnell ADJ, ADV = voreilig

Vor|scho|ter [-ʃoːtɐ] M **-s, -, Vor|scho|te|rin** [-ərɪn] F **-nen** (*Naut*) sheethand

vor+schrei|ben VT *sep irreg* **a** (= *befehlen*) to stipulate; (*Med*) *Dosis* to prescribe; **jdm ~, wie/ was ...** to dictate to sb how/what ...; **ich lasse mir nichts ~** I won't be dictated to; **vorgeschriebene Lektüre** (*Sch, Univ*) prescribed texts; **gesetzlich vorgeschrieben** stipulated by law **b** (*lit*) to write out (*+dat* for)

vor+schrei|ten VI *sep irreg aux sein* to progress, to make progress → **vorgeschritten**

Vor|schrift F (= *gesetzliche etc Bestimmung*) regulation, rule; (= *Anweisung*) instruction, order, direction; **nach ~ des Arztes** according to doctor's orders or the doctor's instructions; **~en für den Verkehr** traffic regulations; **jdm ~en machen** to give sb orders, to dictate to sb; **ich lasse mir (von dir) keine ~en machen lassen** I won't be dictated to (by you), I won't take or-

ders (from you); **sich an die ~en halten** to observe the regulations, to follow the instructions; **Arbeit nach ~** work to rule; **das ist ~** that's the regulation

vor|schrifts-: vor|schrifts|ge|mäß, vor|schrifts|mä|ßig ADJ regulation *attr; Signal, Parken, Verhalten* correct, proper *attr;* (*Med*) *Dosis* prescribed ADV (= *laut Anordnung*) as instructed or directed, according to (the) regulations; (*Med*) as directed; **~ gekleidet sein** to be in regulation dress; **vor|schrifts|wid|rig** ADJ ADV contrary to (the) regulations; (*Med*) *Dosis* contrary to the prescription

Vor|schub M **jdm ~ leisten** to encourage sb; **einer Sache** (*dat*) **~ leisten** to encourage or foster sth

Vor|schul|al|ter NT preschool age

Vor|schu|le F nursery school; (= *Vorschuljahre*) preschool years *pl*

Vor|schul|er|zie|hung F preschool education

vor|schu|lisch ADJ preschool *attr*

Vor|schuss ▲ M advance; **jdm einen ~ leisten** to give sb an advance

Vor|schuss-: Vor|schuss|lor|bee|ren ▲ PL premature praise *sing;* **Vor|schuss|zin|sen** ▲ PL (*Fin*) penalty interest on early settlement

vor|schüt|zen VT *sep* to plead as an excuse, to put forward as a pretext; *Krankheit auch* to feign; *Unwissenheit* to plead; **er schützte vor, dass ...** he pretended that ... → **Müdigkeit**

vor+schwär|men VT *sep* **von jdm/etw ~** to go into raptures over sb/sth; **jdm ~, wie schön etw ist** to go into raptures over how beautiful sth is

vor+schwat|zen VT *sep* (*inf*) **jdm etwas ~** to tell sb a lot of rubbish (*Brit inf*) or crap (*inf*); **schwatz mir doch nichts vor** don't give me that rubbish (*Brit inf*) or crap (*inf*)

vor+schwe|ben VI *sep* **jdm schwebt etw vor** sb has sth in mind

vor+schwin|deln VT *sep* **jdm etwas ~** to lie to sb; **jdm ~, dass ...** to lie to sb that ...; **ich lasse mir doch von dir nichts ~** I won't have any of your lies

vor+se|hen *sep irreg* VT (= *planen*) to plan; (*zeitlich auch*) to schedule; (= *einplanen*) *Kosten, Anschaffungen* to provide or allow for; *Zeit* to allow; *Fall* to provide or cater for; (*im Gesetz, Vertrag*) to provide for; **etw für etw ~** (= *bestimmen*) to intend sth for sth; *Geld* to earmark or destine sth for sth; **jdn für etw ~** (= *beabsichtigen*) to have sb in mind for sth; (= *bestimmen*) to designate sb for sth; **er ist für dieses Amt vorgesehen** we have him in mind/he has been designated for this post (*esp Brit*) or position; **was haben wir für heute vorgesehen?** what is on the agenda today?, what have we planned for today?; **der Plan sieht vor, dass das Projekt bis September abgeschlossen ist** the project is scheduled to be finished by September

VR (= *sich in Acht nehmen*) to be careful, to watch out, to take care; **sich vor jdm/etw ~** to beware of sb/sth, to be wary of sb/sth; *vor Hund auch* to mind sth

VI (= *sichtbar sein*) to appear; **hinter/unter etw** (*dat*) **~** to peep out from behind/under sth

Vor|se|hung ['foːrzeːʊŋ] F **-, no pl die (göttliche) ~** (divine) Providence

vor+set|zen *sep* VT **a** (*nach vorn*) to move forward; *Fuß* to put forward; *Schüler* to move (up) to the front **b** (= *davor setzen*) to put in front; **etw vor etw** (*acc*) **~** to put sth in front of sth or before sth **c jdm etw ~** (= *geben*) to give sb sth, to put sth in front of sb; (= *anbieten*) to offer sb sth; (*fig inf*) *Lügen, Geschichte, Erklärung* to serve or dish sth up to sb (*inf*) **d** (*dated*) **jdn jdm/einer Sache ~** (*als Vorgesetzten*) to put sb in charge of sb/sth VR to sit in (the) front; **sich in die erste Reihe ~** to sit in the front row

Vor|sicht ['foːrzɪçt] F **-, no pl** care; (*bei Gefahr*) caution; (= *Überlegtheit*) circumspection, prudence; (= *Behutsamkeit*) guardedness, wariness;

~ walten lassen or **üben** to be careful; (*bei Gefahr*) to exercise caution, to be cautious; (= *überlegt handeln*) to be circumspect or prudent; (= *behutsam vorgehen*) to be wary; **jdn zur ~ (er)mahnen** to advise sb to be careful/cautious/circumspect; **zur ~ raten/mahnen** to advise caution; **~!** watch or look or mind (*Brit*) out!; **„Vorsicht bei Einfahrt des Zuges"** "stand back when the train approaches the platform"; **„Vorsicht Bahnübergang"** "Level crossing" (*Brit*), "Grade crossing" (*US*); **„Vorsicht Gift"** "Poison"; **„Vorsicht Kurve"** "Bend"; **„Vorsicht feuergefährlich"** "danger - inflammable"; **„Vorsicht zerbrechlich"** "fragile - with care"; **„Vorsicht Glas"** "glass - with care"; **„Vorsicht nicht knicken"** "do not bend"; **„Vorsicht Stufe"** "mind the step"; **mit ~** carefully, (*bei Gefahr*) cautiously; (= *überlegt*) prudently; (= *behutsam*) guardedly, warily; **etw zur ~ tun** to do sth as a precaution, to do sth to be on the safe side; **was er sagt/dieser Artikel ist mit ~ zu genießen** (*hum inf*) you have to take what he says/this article with a pinch of salt (*inf*); **sie ist mit ~ zu genießen** (*hum inf*) she has to be handled with kid gloves; **~ ist besser als Nachsicht** (*Prov*) better safe than sorry; **~ ist die Mutter der Porzellankiste** (*inf*) better safe than sorry

vor|sich|tig ['foːʀʏçtɪç] **ADJ** careful; (= *besonnen*) cautious; (= *überlegt*) prudent; (= *misstrauisch*) wary; *Äußerung* cautious, guarded; *Schätzung* cautious, conservative **ADV** **a** (= *umsichtig*) carefully **b** (*zurückhaltend*) **sich ~ äußern** to be very careful what one says; **ich schätze die Kosten ~ auf 35.000 Euro** to give you a conservative estimate of the costs I would say 35,000 euros

Vor|sich|tig|keit F -, *no pl* carefulness; (= *Besonnenheit*) caution, cautiousness

Vor|sichts-: vor|sichts|hal|ber ADV as a precaution, to be on the safe side; **Vor|sichts|maß|nah|me** F , **Vor|sichts|maß|re|gel** F precaution, precautionary measure; **~n treffen** to take precautions, to take precautionary measures

Vor-: Vor|sig|nal NT (*Rail*) warning signal; **Vor|sil|be** F prefix; **vor+sin|gen** *sep irreg* **VTI a** (*vor Zuhörern*) **jdm (etw) ~** to sing (sth) to sb; **ich singe nicht gern vor** I don't like singing to people or in front of people **b** (= *als Erster singen*) to sing first **VI** (*zur Prüfung*) to have a singing test; (*esp Theat: vor Einstellung*) to audition; **vor|sint|flut|lich** [-zɪntfluːtlɪç] ADJ (*inf*) antiquated, prehistoric (*hum*), antediluvian

Vor|sitz M chairmanship; (= *Amt eines Präsidenten*) presidency; **unter dem ~ von** under the chairmanship of; **(bei etw) den ~ haben** or **innehaben** or **führen** to be chairman (of sth); **bei einer Sitzung den ~ haben** or **führen** to chair a meeting; **den ~ übernehmen** to take the chair

vor+sit|zen VI *sep irreg* **einer Versammlung/Diskussion** (*dat*) **~** to chair a meeting/discussion

Vor|sit|zen|de(r) ['foːʀzɪtsn̩də] MF *decl as adj* chairperson; (*Mann auch*) chairman; (*Frau auch*) chairwoman; (*von Firma*) chairperson, president (*US*); (*von Verein*) president; (*von Partei, Gewerkschaft etc*) leader; **der ~ Richter** the presiding judge; **der ~ Mao** Chairman Mao

Vor|sor|ge F , *no pl* (= *Vorsichtsmaßnahme*) precaution; (= *vorherplanende Fürsorge*) provision(s *pl*) *no def art*; **zur ~** as a precaution; **~ tragen** to make provision; **~ treffen** to take precautions; (*fürs Alter*) to make provision

vor+sor|gen VI *sep* to make provision (*dass so* that); **für etw ~** to provide for sth, to make provision for sth

Vor|sor|ge|un|ter|su|chung F (*Med*) medical checkup

vor|sorg|lich [-zɔrklɪç] **ADJ** precautionary; *Mensch* cautious **ADV** as a precaution, to be on the safe side

Vor|spann ['foːʀʃpan] M **-(e)s, -e a** (= *Vordergespann*) extra team (of horses) **b** (= *Vorlauf: von Film, Tonband*) leader; (*Film, TV: Titel und Namen*)

---

opening credits *pl*; (*Press*) introductory or opening paragraph

vor+span|nen VT *sep Pferde* to harness; (*Elec*) to bias; (*Tech*) *Waffe* to pre-cock; **jdn ~** (*fig*) to enlist sb's help, to rope sb in (*inf*)

Vor|span|nung F (*Elec*) bias (voltage)

Vor|spei|se F hors d''(oe)uvre, starter (*Brit*)

vor+spie|geln VT *sep* to feign, to sham; *Krankheit, Bedürftigkeit auch* to plead; **jdm ~, dass ...** to pretend to sb that ...

Vor|spie|ge|lung F pretence (*Brit*), pretense (*US*); **unter ~ von etw** under the pretence (*Brit*) or pretense (*US*) of sth; **das ist nur (eine) ~ falscher Tatsachen** (*hum*) it's all sham → **Tatsache**

Vor|spiel NT (= *Einleitung*) prelude; (= *Ouvertüre*) overture; (*Theat*) prologue (*Brit*), prolog (*US*); (*Sport*) preliminary match; (*bei Geschlechtsverkehr*) foreplay; (*von Musiker*) performance; (*bei Prüfung*) practical (exam); (*bei Einstellung*) audition; **das ist erst das ~** (*hum*) that is just for starters (*inf*)

vor+spie|len *sep* **VT a jdm etw ~** (*Mus*) to play sth to or for sb; (*Theat*) to act sth to or for sb; (*fig*) to act out a sham of sth in front of sb; **jdm eine Szene ~** (*lit*) to play a scene to or for sb; **jdm eine Komödie ~** (*fig*) to play or act out a farce in front of sb; **jdm ~, dass ...** to pretend to sb that ...; **spiel mir doch nichts vor** don't try and put on an act for me, don't try and pretend to me **b** (= *zuerst spielen*) to play first **VI** (*vor Zuhörern*) to play; (*Mus, Theat*) (*zur Prüfung*) to do one's practical (exam); (*bei Einstellung*) to audition; **jdm ~** (*Mus*) to play for sb; (*Theat*) to act (a role) for or in front of sb; **jdn ~ lassen** (*bei Einstellung*) to audition sb

Vor|spra|che F (*form: Besuch*) visit (*bei, auf +dat* to)

vor+spre|chen *sep irreg* **VT** to say first; (= *vortragen*) to recite; **jdm etw ~** to pronounce sth for sb, to say sth for sb; **wiederholt, was ich euch vorspreche** repeat after me **VI a** (*form*: = *jdn aufsuchen*) to call (*bei jdm* on sb); **bei** or **auf einem Amt ~** to call at an office **b** (*Theat*) to audition; **jdn ~ lassen** to audition sb

vor+sprin|gen VI *sep irreg aux sein* to jump or leap out; (*vorwärts*) to jump or leap forward; (= *herausragen*) to jut out, to project; (*Nase*) to be prominent; (*Kinn*) to be prominent, to protrude; **vor etw** (*dat*) **~** to jump or leap (out) in front of sth

vor|sprin|gend ADJ projecting; *Nase* prominent; *Kinn, Backenknochen* prominent, protruding

Vor|sprung M **a** (*Archit*) projection; (= *Felsvorsprung*) ledge; (*von Küste*) promontory **b** (*Sport, fig*: = *Abstand*) lead (*vor +dat* over); (= *Vorgabe*) start; **jdm 2 Meter/10 Minuten ~ geben** to give sb a 2-metre (*Brit*) or 2-meter (*US*) a 10-minute start, to give sb 2 metres' (*Brit*) or meters' (*US*)/10 minutes' start; **einen ~ vor jdm haben** to be ahead of sb; (*Sport auch*) to be leading sb, to be in the lead; **einen ~ vor jdm gewinnen** to gain a lead over sb, to get ahead of sb

Vor-: Vor|stadt F suburb; **vor|städ|tisch** ADJ suburban

Vor|stand M **a** (= *leitendes Gremium*) board; (*von Firma*) board (of directors); (*von Verein*) committee; (*von Partei*) executive; (*von Akademie*) board (of governors) **b** (= *Leiter*) chairman, managing director **c** (= *Vorsteher*) → **Vorsteher**

Vor|stands-: Vor|stands|eta|ge F boardroom; **Vor|stands|mit|glied** NT member of the board; (*von Verein*) committee member; (*von Partei*) member of the executive; **Vor|stands|sit|zung** F (*von Firma*) board meeting; (*von Partei*) executive meeting; **Vor|stands|vor|sit|zen|de(r)** MF *decl as adj* chair(man) or chairperson of the board of directors; **Vor|stands|wahl** F (*in Firma*) elections *pl* to the board; (*in Partei*) elections *pl* to the executive

---

vor+ste|cken VT *sep* (= *anstecken*) to put on; *Brosche auch* to pin on

Vor|steck|na|del F (= *Brosche*) brooch; (= *Krawattennadel*) tiepin

vor+ste|hen VI *sep irreg aux haben* or *sein* **a** (= *hervorragen*) to project, to jut out; (*Zähne*) to stick out, to protrude; (*Backenknochen, Kinn*) to be prominent, to protrude; (*Nase*) to be prominent; **~de Zähne** protruding teeth, buck teeth **b einer Sache** ~ (*dem Haushalt*) to preside over sth; *einer Firma, einer Partei, einem Gremium* to be the chairman or chairperson of sth; *der Regierung* to be the head of sth; *einer Schule* to be the head(master/mistress) or principal (*US*) of sth; *einem Geschäft* to manage sth; *einer Abteilung, einer Behörde* to be in charge of sth **c** (*form*) **wie im Vorstehenden** as above; **die ~den Erläuterungen** the above explanations **d** (*Hunt: Hund*) to set, to point

Vor|ste|her M (= *Klostervorsteher*) abbot; (= *Bürovorsteher*) manager; (= *Gefängnisvorsteher*) governor; (= *Gemeindevorsteher*) chairman of parish council; (*dated Sch*) head(master), principal (*US*) → *auch* **Vorsteherin**

Vor|ste|her|drü|se F prostate (gland)

Vor|ste|he|rin F (= *Klostervorsteherin*) abbess; (= *Bürovorsteherin*) manager; (= *Gefängnisvorsteherin*) governor; (= *Gemeindevorsteherin*) chairman of parish council; (*dated Sch*) head(mistress), principal (*US*)

Vor|steh|hund M pointer; (*langhaariger*) setter

Vor|stell|bar ADJ conceivable, imaginable; **das ist nicht ~** that is inconceivable or unimaginable

vor+stel|len *sep* ✪ 33.2, 34.3, 35.1 **VT a** (*nach vorn*) *Tisch, Stuhl, Auto* to move forward; *Bein* to put out; *Uhr* to put forward or on (*um by*) **b** (*inf*: = *davor stellen*) **etw (vor etw** *acc*) **~** to put sth in front of sth; *Auto auch* to park sth in front of sth **c** (= *darstellen*) to represent; (= *bedeuten*) to mean, to signify; **was soll das ~?** (*inf*) what is that supposed to be?; **etwas ~** (*fig*) (= *gut aussehen*) to look good; (= *Ansehen haben*) to count for something **d** (= *bekannt machen*) **jdn jdm ~** to introduce sb to sb **e** (= *bekannt machen, vorführen*) to present (*jdm* to sb); **jdm etw ~** to show sb sth **f** (= *sich ausmalen*) **sich** (*dat*) **etw ~** to imagine sth; **stell dir mal vor** just imagine; **das kann ich mir gut ~** I can imagine that (well); **das muss man sich** (*dat*) **mal (bildlich** or **plastisch) ~** just imagine or picture it!; **sich** (*dat*) **etw unter etw** (*dat*) **~** (*Begriff, Wort*) to understand sth by sth; **darunter kann ich mir nichts ~** it doesn't mean anything to me; **das Kleid ist genau, was ich mir vorgestellt hatte** the dress is just what I had in mind; **was haben Sie sich (als Gehalt) vorgestellt?** what (salary) did you have in mind?; **ich kann sie mir gut als Lehrerin ~** I can just imagine or see her as a teacher; **stell dir das nicht so einfach vor** don't think it's so easy **VR a** (= *sich nach vorn stellen*) to move or go forward; (*in Schlange*) to stand at the front **b** (= *sich bekannt machen*) to introduce oneself (*jdm* to sb); (*bei Bewerbung*) to come/go for an interview; (= *Antrittsbesuch machen*) to present oneself (*+dat, bei* to)

vor|stel|lig ADJ **bei jdm ~ werden** to go to sb; (*wegen Beschwerde*) to complain to sb, to lodge a complaint with sb

Vor|stel|lung ✪ 28.2, 53.1, 53.3 F **a** (= *Gedanke*) idea; (*bildlich*) picture; (= *Einbildung*) illusion; (= *Vorstellungskraft*) imagination; **in meiner ~ sah das größer aus** I imagined it bigger; **in meiner ~ ist Gott kein alter Mann** I don't picture God as an old man; **du hast falsche ~en** you are wrong (in your ideas); **es übertrifft alle ~en** it's incredible or unbelievable; **das entspricht ganz meiner ~** that is just how I imagined or saw it; **sich** (*dat*) **eine ~ von etw machen** to form an idea or (*Bild*) picture of sth; **du**

machst dir keine ~, wie schwierig das ist you have no idea how difficult that is **b** (*Theat etc*) performance; (*Film*) showing, performance **c** (= *das Bekanntmachen*) (*zwischen Leuten*) introduction; (*bei Hofe*) presentation (*bei* at); (= *Vorführung: von Geräten, neuem Artikel etc*) presentation; (*bei Bewerbung, Antrittsbesuch*) interview (*bei* with) **d** (= *Einwand*) objection, protest

Vor|stel|lungs-: Vor|stel|lungs|be|ginn M start of a/the performance; **vor** ~ before the start of a/the performance; **~ um 20 Uhr** performance starts at 8 pm *or* P.M. (*US*); **Vor|stel|lungs|en|de** NT end of a/the performance; **nach** ~ after a/the performance; **Vor|stel|lungs|ge|spräch** ✿ 46.4, 46.6 NT (*job*) interview; **Vor|stel|lungs|kraft** F imagination; **Vor|stel|lungs|ter|min** M appointment for an/the interview, interview appointment; **Vor|stel|lungs|ver|mö|gen** NT powers *pl* of imagination; **Vor|stel|lungs|welt** F imagination

Vor|stop|per(in) M(F) (*Ftbl*) centre half (*Brit*), center half (*US*)

Vor|stoß M **a** (= *Vordringen*) venture; (*Mil*) advance, push; (*fig* = *Versuch*) attempt **b** (*Tech: an Rädern*) wheel rim; (*Sew*) edging; (= *Litze*) braiding

vor+sto|ßen sep irreg 🔲 to push forward 🔲 *aux sein* to venture; (*Sport*) to attack; (*Mil*) to advance; **ins All** ~ (*Rakete, Mensch*) to venture into space; **ins Viertelfinale** ~ to advance into the quarterfinal

Vor|stra|fe F previous conviction

Vor|stra|fen|re|gis|ter NT criminal *or* police record; (= *Kartei*) criminal *or* police records *pl*

vor+stre|cken VT *sep* to stretch forward; *Arme* to stretch out; *Hand* to stretch *or* put out; *Bauch* to stick out; *Krallen* to put out; (*fig*) *Geld* to advance (*jdm* sb)

Vor|stu|fe F preliminary stage; (*von Entwicklung*) early stage

vor+stür|men VI *sep aux sein* to charge *or* rush forward (*hinter +dat* from behind)

Vor|tag M day before, eve; **am ~ der Konferenz** (on) the day before the conference, on the eve of the conference

Vor|ta|ges|schluss ▲ M (*St Ex*) close of trading on the previous day

vor+tan|zen *sep* 🔲 **jdm einen Tanz/die Schritte** ~ to dance a dance/the steps for sb; (*zur Demonstration*) to demonstrate a dance/the steps for sb 🔲 (*zur Demonstration*) to demonstrate a dance/step *etc* (*jdm* to sb); (*als Prüfung*) to dance (*jdm* in front of sb)

Vor|tän|zer(in) M(F) leading dancer; (= *Anführer eines Tanzes*) leader of the dance

vor+täu|schen VT *sep Krankheit, Armut* to feign; *Schlag, Straftat, Orgasmus* to fake; **sie hat mir eine glückliche Ehe vorgetäuscht** she pretended to me that her marriage was happy

Vor|täu|schung F pretence (*Brit*), pretense (*US*), fake; **unter ~ einer Krankheit** feigning an illness; **die ~ eines Schlags** faking a blow; **~ von Tatsachen** (*Jur*) misrepresentation of the facts; **unter ~ falscher Tatsachen** under false pretences (*Brit*) *or* pretenses (*US*)

Vor|teil ['foːtaɪl] ✿ 40.2, 53.4 M **-s, -e** advantage (*auch Tennis*); **den ~ haben, dass ...** to have the advantage that ...; **die Vor- und Nachteile** the pros and cons; **auf den eigenen ~ bedacht sein** to have an eye to one's own interests; **jdm gegenüber im ~ sein** to have an advantage over sb; **sich zu seinem ~ ändern** to change for the better; **ein ~ sein** to be an advantage, to be advantageous; **von ~ sein** to be advantageous; **das kann für dich nur von ~ sein** it can only be to your advantage; **ich habe dabei an deinen ~ gedacht** I was thinking of your interests; **im ~ sein** to have the advantage (*jdm gegenüber* over sb); **~e aus etw ziehen** to benefit

from sth, to gain advantage from sth; **„Vorteil Sampras"** (*Tennis*) "advantage Sampras"

vor|teil|haft ADJ advantageous; *Kleid, Frisur* flattering; *Geschäft* lucrative, profitable; **ein ~er Kauf** a good buy, a bargain **ADV** ~ **aussehen** to look one's best; **der helle Teppich wirkt** ~ the light carpet looks good; **sie war nicht sehr ~ geschminkt** her make-up wasn't very flattering; **du solltest dich ~er kleiden** you should wear more flattering clothes; **etw ~ verkaufen** (*finanziell*) to sell sth for a profit; **etw ~ kaufen** to get sth at a good price

Vor|teils|an|nah|me F (*Jur*) accepting an advantage

Vor|trag ['foːtraːk] M **-(e)s, Vorträge** [-trɛːgə] **a** (= *Vorlesung*) lecture; (= *Bericht, Beschreibung*) talk; **einen ~ halten** to give a lecture/talk; **halt keine Vorträge** (*inf*) don't give a whole lecture **b** (= *Darbietung*) performance; (*eines Gedichtes*) reading, recitation; (*Mus: = Solovortrag*) recital **c** (= *Art des Vortragens*) performance **d** (*Fin*) balance carried forward

vor+tra|gen VT *sep irreg* **a** (*lit*) to carry forward **b** (= *berichten*) to report; (= *förmlich mitteilen*) *Fall, Angelegenheit* to present; *Forderungen* to present, to convey; *Beschwerde* to lodge; *Meinung, Bedenken* to express, to convey; *Wunsch* to express **c** (= *vorsprechen*) *Gedicht* to recite; *Rede* to give; (*Mus*) *Lied* to sing, to play; *Lied* to sing, to perform **d** (*Fin*) to carry forward

Vor|tra|gen|de(r) ['foːtraːgndə] MF *decl as adj* lecturer; (*von Rede, Bericht*) speaker; (*von Musikstück, Lied etc*) performer

Vor|trags-: Vor|trags|abend M lecture evening; (*mit Gedichten*) poetry evening; (*mit Musik*) recital; **Vor|trags|fol|ge** F series of lectures; (*einzelne Sendung*) lecture in a series; **Vor|trags|kunst** F skill as a performer; (*von Redner*) skill as a speaker; **Vor|trags|rei|he** F series of lectures

vor|treff|lich [foːˈtrɛflɪç] ADJ excellent, splendid, superb **ADV** excellently, splendidly, superbly; **~ schmecken** to taste excellent; **sich ~ amüsieren** to have a splendid time

Vor|treff|lich|keit F **-,** *no pl* excellence

vor+tre|ten VI *sep irreg aux sein* **a** (*lit*) to step forward, to come forward **b** (= *hervorragen*) to project, to jut out; (*Augen*) to protrude; **~de Backenknochen** prominent cheekbones

Vor|tritt M **,** *no pl* precedence, priority; (*Sw: = Vorfahrt*) right of way; **in etw** (*dat*) **den ~ haben** (*fig*) to have precedence in sth (*vor +dat* over); **jdm den ~ lassen** (*lit*) to let sb go first; (*fig auch*) to let sb go ahead

vor+trock|nen VT *sep* to dry partially

Vor|trupp M advance guard, advance party

vor+tun VT *sep irreg* (*inf*) *Schürze, Riegel, Kette etc* to put on

vor+tur|nen *sep* 🔲 **jdm eine Übung** ~ (= *vormachen*) to demonstrate an exercise to sb; (= *öffentlich zeigen*) to perform an exercise in front of sb 🔲 (= *vormachen*) to demonstrate to sb; (*öffentlich*) to perform in front of sb

Vor|tur|ner(in) M(F) demonstrator (of gymnastic exercises); (*fig sl*) front man/woman

vo|rü|ber [foˈryːbɐ] ADV **~ sein** (*räumlich, Jugend*) to be past; (*zeitlich auch, Gewitter, Winter, Kummer*) to be over; (*Schmerz*) to have gone

vo|rü|ber- PREF → *auch* **vorbei-: vo|rü|ber+ge|hen** VI *sep irreg aux sein* **a** (*räumlich*) (*an etw dat*) sth) to go past, to pass (*by*); **im Vorübergehen** in passing; **an jdm/etw ~** (*fig: = ignorieren*) to ignore sb/sth **b** (*zeitlich*) to pass; (*Gewitter*) to blow over; **eine Gelegenheit ~ lassen** to let an opportunity slip **c** **an jdm ~** (= *sich nicht bemerkbar machen*) to pass sb by; **an jdm nicht ~** (*Erlebnis etc*) to leave its/their mark on sb; **vo|rü|ber|ge|hend** **ADJ** (= *flüchtig*) momentary, passing *attr; Krankheit* short; (= *zeitweilig*) temporary **ADV** temporarily, for a while; **sich ~ im Ausland aufhalten** to stay abroad for a short

time; **jdn ~ festnehmen** to detain sb temporarily

Vor|über|le|gung F initial *or* preliminary consideration

Vor-: Vor|übung F preliminary exercise; **Vor|un|ter|su|chung** F preliminary examination; (*Jur*) preliminary *or* initial investigation

Vor|ur|teil NT prejudice (*gegenüber* against); **das ist ein ~** it's prejudice; **~e haben** *or* **hegen, in ~en befangen sein** to be prejudiced

Vor|ur|teils-: vor|ur|teils|frei, vor|ur|teils|los **ADJ** unprejudiced; *Entscheidung, Verhalten auch* unbiased **ADV** without prejudice, without bias; **Vor|ur|teils|lo|sig|keit** F **-,** *no pl* freedom from prejudice

Vor-: Vor|vä|ter PL forefathers *pl*, ancestors *pl*, forebears *pl*; **Vor|ver|gan|gen|heit** F (*Gram*) pluperfect; **Vor|ver|hand|lung** F preliminary negotiations *or* talks *pl*; (*Jur*) preliminary hearing; **Vor|ver|kauf** M (*Theat, Sport*) advance booking; **sich** (*dat*) **Karten im ~ besorgen** to buy tickets in advance; **Vor|ver|kaufs|ge|bühr** F advance booking fee; **Vor|ver|kaufs|kas|se** F, **Vor|ver|kaufs|stel|le** F advance booking office

vor+ver|le|gen *ptp* **vorverlegt** VT *sep* **a** *Termin* to bring forward **b** (*Mil*) *Front, Gefechtslinie* to push forward; **das Feuer ~** to increase the range

Vor-: Vor|ver|ständ|nis NT preconception; **Vor|ver|stär|ker** M preamplifier; **Vor|ver|trag** M preliminary contract; (*Pol*) preliminary treaty; **Vor|ver|ur|tei|lung** F prejudgement; **vor|vor|ges|tern** ADV (*inf*) three days ago; **vor|vo|rig** ADJ (*inf*) **~e Woche** the week before last; **~es Jahr** the year before last; **vor|vor|letz|te(r, s)** ADJ last but two

vor+wa|gen VR *sep* (*lit*) to venture forward; (*fig auch*) to venture

Vor|wahl F **a** preliminary election; (*US*) primary **b** (*Telec*) dialling (*Brit*) *or* area (*US*) code

vor+wäh|len VT *sep* (*Telec*) to dial first

Vor|wahl|num|mer F, **Vor|wähl|num|mer** F dialling (*Brit*) *or* area (*US*) code

vor+wal|ten VI *sep* (*geh*) to prevail

Vor|wand ['foːrvant] M **-(e)s, Vorwände** [-vɛndə] pretext, excuse; **unter dem ~, dass ...** under the pretext that ...

vor+wär|men VT *sep* to preheat; *Teller* to heat; *Bett* to warm up

vor+war|nen VT *sep* **jdn ~** to tell *or* warn sb in advance, to give sb advance notice *or* warning

Vor|war|nung F (*prior or advance*) warning; (*Mil: vor Angriff*) early warning

vor|wärts ['foːrverts] ADV forwards, forward; **~!** (*inf*) let's go (*inf*); (*Mil*) forward march!; **weiter ~** further ahead *or* on; **~ und rückwärts** backwards and forwards; **etw ~ und rückwärts kennen** (*fig inf*) to know sth backwards (*Brit*), to know sth backwards and forwards (*US*), to know sth inside out; **wir kamen nur langsam ~** we made slow progress; **Rolle/Salto ~** forward roll/somersault

Vor|wärts-: Vor|wärts|be|we|gung F forward movement; **vor|wärts brin|gen** ▲ VT *irreg* (*fig*) to advance; **jdn ~** to help sb to get on; **Vor|wärts|gang** M *pl* **-gänge** forward gear; **vor|wärts ge|hen** ▲ *irreg aux sein* (*fig*) 🔲 to progress, to come on 🔲 *impers* **es geht wieder vorwärts** things are looking up; **mit etw geht es vorwärts** sth is progressing *or* going well; **Vor|wärts kom|men** ▲ VI *irreg aux sein* (*fig*) to make progress, to get on (*in, mit* with); (*beruflich, gesellschaftlich*) to get on; **im Leben/Beruf ~** to get on in life/one's job; **Vor|wärts|kom|men** NT **-s,** *no pl* (= *Fortschritt*) progress; (= *Erfolg*) success; **da ist kein ~** (*auch fig*) there's no progress *or* headway to be made; **Vor|wärts|ver|tei|di|gung** F (*Mil*) forward defence (*Brit*) *or* defense (*US*)

Vor|wä|sche F, **Vor|wasch|gang** M prewash

vor+wa|schen VT *sep irreg* to prewash

vor|weg [foːɐ̯'vɛk] ADV (= *voraus, an der Spitze*) at the front; (= *vorher*) before(hand); (= *als Erstes, von vornherein*) at the outset

vor|weg-: Vor|weg|leis|tung F (*Sw*: = *Vorauszahlung*) advance (payment); **Vor|weg|nah|me** [-naːmə] F **-, -n** anticipation; **vor|weg|neh|men** VT *sep irreg* to anticipate; **um das Wichtigste vorwegzunehmen** to come to the most important point first

vor|weih|nacht|lich ADJ pre-Christmas *attr* ADV **vorweihnachlich geschmückt** decorated for Christmas

Vor|weih|nachts|zeit F pre-Christmas period

vor+wei|sen VT *sep irreg* to show, to produce; *Zeugnisse* to produce; **etw ~ können** (*fig*) to have *or* possess sth

vor+wer|fen VT *sep irreg* **a** (*fig*) **jdm etw/Unpünktlichkeit ~** (= *anklagen*) to reproach sb for sth/for being unpunctual; (= *beschuldigen*) to accuse sb of sth/of being unpunctual; **jdm ~, dass er etw getan hat** to reproach sb for having done sth; **jdm ~, dass er etw nicht getan hat** to accuse sb of not having done sth; **das wirft er mir heute noch vor** he still holds it against me; **ich habe mir nichts vorzuwerfen** my conscience is clear; **muss ich mir das ~ lassen?** do I have to listen to these accusations? **b** (*lit*) **Tieren/Gefangenen etw ~** to throw sth down for the animals/prisoners

Vor|werk NT (*von Gut*) outlying estate; (*von Burg*) outwork

vor|wie|gend ['foːɐ̯viːgnt] ADJ *attr* predominant ADV predominantly, mainly, chiefly

Vor|wis|sen NT previous knowledge; (= *Vorherwissen*) foreknowledge; **ohne mein ~** without my previous knowledge

Vor|witz M , *no pl* (= *Keckheit*) cheek(iness) (*Brit*), freshness (*US*); (= *Vorlautheit*) forwardness, pertness; (*dial*: = *Neugier*) inquisitiveness, curiosity

vor|wit|zig ADJ (= *keck*) cheeky (*Brit*), fresh (*US*); (= *vorlaut*) forward, pert; (*dial*: = *neugierig*) inquisitive, curious

Vor|wo|chen|schluss ▲ M (*St Ex*) close of trading the previous week

Vor|wort NT **a** *pl* **-worte** foreword; (*esp von Autor*) preface **b** *pl* **-wörter** (*Aus*: = *Präposition*) preposition

Vor|wurf M **a** reproach; (= *Beschuldigung*) accusation; **man machte ihm den ~ der Bestechlichkeit** he was accused of being open to bribery; **jdm/sich große Vorwürfe machen, dass ...** to reproach sb/oneself for ...; **ich habe mir keine Vorwürfe zu machen** my conscience is clear; **jdm etw zum ~ machen** to reproach sb with sth; **jdm (wegen etw) Vorwürfe machen** to reproach sb (for sth) **b** (= *Vorlage*) subject

vor|wurfs|voll ADJ reproachful ADV reproachfully

vor+zäh|len VT *sep* **jdm etw ~** to count sth out to sb; (*fig*: = *auflisten*) to enumerate sth to sb

vor+zau|bern VT *sep* **jdm Kunststücke ~** to perform conjuring *or* magic tricks for sb; **jdm etw ~** (*fig*) to conjure sth up for sb

Vor|zei|chen NT (= *Omen*) omen, sign; (*Med*) early symptom; (*Math*) sign; (*Mus*) (*Kreuz/b*) sharp/flat (sign); (*vor einzelner Note*) accidental; (*von Tonart*) key signature; **positives/negatives ~** (*Math*) plus/minus (sign); **unter umgekehrtem/dem gleichen ~** (*fig*) under different/the same circumstances; **dadurch haben die Verhandlungen ein negatives ~ erhalten** that put the negotiations under a cloud

vor+zeich|nen VT *sep Linien etc* to sketch *or* draw (out); **jdm etw ~** (*zum Nachmalen*) to sketch *or* draw sth out for sb; (*fig*) to map *or* mark sth out for sb; **diese Entwicklung ist vorgezeichnet** this development has been marked out

vor|zeig|bar ADJ presentable

Vor|zei|ge- *in cpds* (= *vorbildlich*) model, exemplary; (= *führend*) leading; **Vor|zei|ge|fir|ma** F model company; **Vor|zei|ge|frau** F (= *Vorbild*) female role model; (= *Alibifrau*) token woman

vor+zei|gen VT *sep* to show, to produce; *Zeugnisse* to produce; **jdm die Hände ~** to show sb one's hands

Vor|zei|ge|ob|jekt NT , **Vor|zei|ge|stück** NT showpiece

Vor|zeit F prehistoric times *pl*; **in der ~** in prehistoric times; (= *vor langem*) in the dim and distant past → **grau**

vor|zei|ten [foːɐ̯'tsaitn] ADV (*liter*) in days gone by, in olden times

vor|zei|tig ADJ early; *Geburt, Altern etc* premature ADV early, prematurely

Vor|zei|tig|keit F -, *no pl* (*Gram*) anteriority

vor|zeit|lich ADJ prehistoric; (*fig*) archaic

Vor|zelt NT awning

vor+zie|hen VT *sep irreg* **a** (= *hervorziehen*) to pull out; (= *nach vorne ziehen*) *Stuhl etc* to pull up; *Truppen* to move up; (= *zuziehen*) *Vorhänge* to draw, to close; **etw hinter/unter etw** (*dat*) **~** to pull sth out from behind/under sth **b** (*fig*) (= *lieber mögen*) to prefer; (= *bevorzugen*) *jdn* to favour (*Brit*), to favor (*US*); **etw einer anderen Sache ~** to prefer sth to sth else; **es ~, etw zu tun** (*allgemein gesehen*) to prefer to do sth; (*einmal gesehen*) to prefer doing sth **c** (= *zuerst behandeln, abfertigen*) to give priority to **d** *Wahlen, Termin* to bring forward; **vorgezogener Ruhestand** early retirement

Vor|zim|mer NT anteroom; (= *Büro*) outer office; (*Aus*: = *Diele*) hall

Vor|zim|mer-: Vor|zim|mer|da|me F receptionist; **Vor|zim|mer|wand** F (*Aus*) hall stand

Vor|zug¹ M **a** preference; (= *Vorteil*) advantage; (= *gute Eigenschaft*) merit, asset; **einer Sache** (*dat*) **den ~ geben** (*form*) to prefer sth, to give sth preference; (= *Vorrang geben*) to give sth precedence; **den ~ haben, dass ...** to be preferable to sth; **den ~ haben, dass ...** to have the advantage that ... **b** (*Aus Sch*) distinction

Vor|zug² M (*Rail*) train in front; (= *früher fahrend*) train before; (= *Entlastungszug*) relief train

vor|züg|lich [foːɐ̯'tsyːklɪç, *esp Aus* 'foːɐ̯-] ADJ excellent, superb; *Qualität, Arbeit auch* exquisite → **Hochachtung** ADV excellently, superbly; (= *vornehmlich*) especially, particularly; **der Wein schmeckt ~** the wine tastes excellent *or* superb

Vor|züg|lich|keit F -, *no pl* excellence

Vor|zugs-: Vor|zugs|ak|tie F (*St Ex*) preference share; **Vor|zugs|be|hand|lung** F preferential treatment *no indef art*; **Vor|zugs|milch** F *milk with high fat content*, ≈ gold-top milk (*Brit*), ≈ full milk (*US*); **Vor|zugs|preis** M special discount price; **Vor|zugs|schü|ler(in)** M(F) (*Aus*) star pupil; **vor|zugs|wei|se** ADV preferably, by preference; (= *hauptsächlich*) mainly, chiefly; **etw ~ trinken** to prefer to drink *or* drinking sth

Vor|zün|dung F (*Aut*) pre-ignition

Vo|ten, Vo|ta (*geh*) *pl von* **Votum**

vo|tie|ren [vo'tiːrən] *ptp* **votiert** VI (*geh*) to vote

Vo|tiv- [vo'tiːf-]: **Vo|tiv|bild** NT votive picture; **Vo|tiv|ka|pel|le** F votive chapel; **Vo|tiv|ta|fel** F votive tablet

Vo|tum ['voːtʊm] NT **-s, Voten** *or* **Vota** [-tn, -ta] (*geh*) vote

Vo|yeur [voa'jøːɐ̯] M **-s, -e, Vo|yeu|rin** [-'jøːrɪn] F **-, -nen** voyeur

Vo|yeu|ris|mus [voajø'rɪsmʊs] M **-,** *no pl* voyeurism

vo|yeu|ris|tisch [voajø'rɪstɪʃ] ADJ voyeuristic

VP [faʊ'peː] F - (*DDR*) *abbr von* **Volkspolizei**

VPS [faʊpeː'ʔɛs] *abbr von* **Videoprogrammsystem** VPS

V-Pul|lo|ver ['faʊ-] M V-neck pullover

VR [faʊ'ɛr] **a** *abbr von* **Volksrepublik** VR **b** *abbr von* **virtuelle Realität**

v. R. w. *abbr von* **von Rechts wegen**

v. T. *abbr von* **vom Tausend**

vul|gär [vʊl'gɛːɐ̯] ADJ vulgar ADV vulgarly; **~ aussehen** to look vulgar; **drück dich nicht so ~ aus** don't be so vulgar

Vul|gär|aus|druck M *pl* **-ausdrücke** vulgar expression, vulgarity

Vul|ga|ri|tät [vʊlgari'tɛːt] F **-, -en** vulgarity

Vul|gär|la|tein NT vulgar Latin

vul|go ['vʊlgo] ADV in plain language

Vul|kan [vʊl'kaːn] M **-(e)s, -e** volcano; **auf einem ~ leben** (*fig*) to be living on the edge of a volcano → **Tanz b**

Vul|kan-: Vul|kan|aus|bruch M volcanic eruption; **Vul|kan|fi|ber** F vulcanized fibre (*Brit*) *or* fiber (*US*)

Vul|ka|ni|sa|ti|on [vʊlkaniza'tsioːn] F **-, -en** (*Tech*) vulcanization

vul|ka|nisch [vʊl'kaːnɪʃ] ADJ volcanic

Vul|ka|ni|sier|an|stalt [vʊlkani'ziːr-] F vulcanization plant

vul|ka|ni|sie|ren [vʊlkani'ziːrən] *ptp* **vulkanisiert** VT to vulcanize

Vul|ka|no|lo|ge [vʊlkano'loːgə] M **-n, -n, Vul|ka|no|lo|gin** [-'loːgɪn] F **-, -nen** volcanologist

Vul|ka|no|lo|gie [vʊlkanolo'giː] F **-,** *no pl* volcanology

Vul|va ['vʊlva] M **-, Vulven** (*Anat*) vulva

v. u. Z. *abbr von* **vor unserer Zeitrechnung** BC

V-Waf|fen ['faʊ-] PL *abbr von* **Vergeltungswaffen**

W

W, w [veː] NT **-, -** W, w

W *abbr von* **Westen**

WAA [veːaːˈaː] F *abbr von* **Wiederaufbereitungsanlage**

Waadt [va(ː)t] F - Vaud

Waa|ge [ˈvaːɡə] F **-, -n** a (*Gerät*) scales *pl*; (= *Federwaage, Apothekerwaage*) balance; (*für Lastwagen, Autos*) weighbridge (*Brit*), weigh station; **eine ~** a pair of scales; **sich** (*dat*) **die ~ halten** (*fig*) to balance one another *or* each other; **einer Sache** (*dat*) **die ~ halten** to balance sth (out) → **Zünglein** b (*Astron, Astrol*) Libra; **er ist (eine) ~** he's (a) Libra c (*Sport:* = *Standwaage*) horizontal single leg stand

Waage-: Waa|ge|bal|ken M (balance *or* scale) beam; **waa|ge|recht** ADJ horizontal, level; *Linie, Ebene* horizontal; (*im Kreuzworträtsel*) across ADV levelly; **Waa|ge|rech|te** F *decl as adj* horizontal; **etw in die ~ bringen** to make sth horizontal *or* level; **etw in der ~n transportieren** to transport sth horizontally

Waag-: waag|recht ADJ, ADV = **waagerecht**; **Waag|rech|te** F *decl as adj* = **Waagerechte**; **Waag|scha|le** F (scale) pan, scale; (**schwer**) **in die ~ fallen** (*fig*) to carry weight; **jedes Wort auf die ~ legen** to weigh every word (carefully); **seinen Einfluss/seine Autorität/sein ganzes Gewicht in die ~ werfen** (*fig*) to bring one's influence/one's authority/one's full weight to bear

wab|be|lig [ˈvabəlɪç] ADJ *Pudding, Gelee* wobbly; *Mensch* flabby

wab|beln [ˈvabln] VI to wobble

wabb|lig ADJ = **wabbelig**

Wa|be [ˈvaːbə] F **-, -n** honeycomb

Waben-: wa|ben|för|mig ADJ honeycombed; **Wa|ben|ho|nig** M comb honey

wa|bern [ˈvaːbɐn] VI (*geh*) to undulate; (*Nebel, Gerüche*) to drift, to waft; (*Gerücht*) to float; (*obs, dial:* = *flackern*) to flicker

wach [vax] ADJ awake *pred*; (*fig:* = *aufgeweckt*) alert, wide-awake; *Nacht* sleepless, wakeful; **in ~em Zustand** in the waking state; **sich ~ halten** to keep *or* stay awake; **~ werden** to wake up; **~ liegen** to lie awake; **jdn ~ schütteln** to shake sb awake; **jdn ~ küssen** to wake sb with a kiss

Wach-: Wach|ab|lö|sung F changing of the guard; (*fig:* = *Regierungswechsel*) change of government; (*Mensch*) relief guard; **Wach|ba|taillon** NT guard battalion, guards *pl*; **Wach|boot** NT patrol boat; **Wach|dienst** M lookout, guard (duty); (*Mil*) guard (duty); (*Naut*) watch; **~ haben/machen** to be on guard (duty); (*Naut*) to have the watch

Wa|che [ˈvaxə] F **-, -n** a (= *Wachdienst*) guard (duty); **auf ~** on guard (duty); (**bei jdm**) **~ halten** to keep guard *or* watch (over sb); (= *Krankenwache*) to keep watch (at sb's bedside), to watch over sb; (= *Totenwache*) to watch over sb; **~ stehen** *or* **schieben** (*inf*) to be on guard (duty); (*Dieb, Schüler etc*) to keep a lookout b (*Mil* = *Wachposten*) guard, sentry; (*Gebäude*) guardhouse; (*Raum*) guardroom c (*Naut: Personen, Dauer*) watch; **~ haben** to be on watch d (= *Polizeiwache*) (police) station

wa|chen [vaxn] VI a (= *wach sein*) to be awake; (= *nicht schlafen können*) to lie awake b (= *Wache halten*) to keep watch; **bei jdm ~** to sit up with sb, to keep watch by sb's bedside; **das Wachen am Krankenbett** sitting up with a/the patient *or* at a/the sickbed; **über etw** (*acc*) **~** to (keep) watch over sth; *über Verkehr* to supervise sth; **der Polizist wachte darüber, dass niemand ...** the policeman watched that no-one ...

Wach-: wach|ha|bend ADJ *attr* duty; **Wach|ha|ben|de(r)** [ˈvaxhaːbndə] MF *decl as adj* (= *Offizier*) duty officer; (*Naut*) watch; **wach halten** ᴀ *irreg* VT (*fig*) *Erinnerung* to keep alive; *Interesse auch* to keep up VR to keep oneself awake; **Wach|heit** F **-**, *no pl* (*fig*) alertness; (**die**) **~ des Geistes** alertness of mind, an alert *or* wide-awake mind; **Wach|hund** M (*lit, fig*) watchdog; (*lit auch*) guard dog; **Wach|leu|te** *pl* **von Wachmann; Wach|lo|kal** NT guardroom; **Wach|ma|cher** M (*Med inf*) stimulant; **Wach|mann** M *pl* **-leute** watchman; (*Aus*) policeman; **Wach|mann|schaft** F men *or* squad on guard; (*Naut*) watch; **Wach|of|fi|zier(in)** M(F) (*Naut*) officer of the watch

Wa|chol|der [vaˈxɔldɐ] M **-s, -** a (*Bot*) juniper (tree) b = **Wacholderschnaps**

Wacholder-: Wa|chol|der|bee|re F juniper berry; **Wa|chol|der|brannt|wein** M (*form*), **Wa|chol|der|schnaps** M spirit (*Brit*) *or* alcohol made from juniper berries, ≈ gin; **Wa|chol|der|strauch** M juniper (tree)

Wach-: Wach|pos|ten M sentry, guard; (= *Schüler, Dieb etc*) lookout; **wach+ru|fen** VT *sep irreg* (*fig*) *Erinnerung etc* to call to mind, to evoke; **wach+rüt|teln** VT *sep* (*fig*) to shake up, to (a)rouse; *Gewissen* to stir, to (a)rouse; **jdn aus seiner Apathie ~** to shake sb out of his apathy

Wachs [vaks] NT **-es, -e** wax; **weich wie ~** as soft as butter; **meine Knie wurden weich wie ~** my knees turned to jelly; **~ in jds Händen sein** (*fig*) to be putty in sb's hands

wach|sam [ˈvaxzaːm] ADJ watchful, vigilant; (= *vorsichtig*) on one's guard; **ein ~es Auge auf jdn/etw haben** to keep a watchful *or* sharp eye on sb/sth → **Holzauge** ADV watchfully, vigilantly

Wach|sam|keit F **-**, *no pl* watchfulness, vigilance; (= *Vorsichtigkeit*) guardedness

Wachs-: Wachs|bild NT waxen image; **wachs|bleich** ADJ waxen; **Wachs|boh|ne** F wax bean; **Wachs|bunt|stift** M wax crayon

Wach|schiff NT patrol ship

wach|seln [ˈvaksln] VT (*Aus:* = *mit Wachs behandeln*) to wax

wach|sen[1] [ˈvaksn] *pret* **wuchs** [vuːks] *ptp* **gewachsen** VI *aux sein* to grow; (*Spannung, Begeisterung auch*) to mount; **in die Breite ~** to broaden (out), to get *or* grow broader; **in die Länge ~** to lengthen, to get *or* grow longer; **in die Höhe ~** to grow taller; (*Kind*) to shoot up (*inf*); **sich** (*dat*) **einen Bart ~ lassen** to grow a beard; **sich** (*dat*) **die Haare ~ lassen** to let one's hair grow, to grow one's hair; **ich lese dieses Buch mit ~der Begeisterung** I'm really getting into this book; **gut gewachsen** (*Baum*) well-grown; *Mensch* with *or* having a good figure; **wie ge-**

wachsen with fat and gristle not removed; **er wächst mit** *or* **an seiner Verantwortung** (*fig*) he grows with his responsibility → *auch* **gewachsen**

wach|sen[2] VT to wax

wäch|sern [ˈvɛksɐn] ADJ (*lit, fig*) waxen

Wachs-: Wachs|far|be F a (= *Farbstift*) wax crayon; **mit ~(n) gemalt** drawn with wax crayons *or* in wax crayon b (= *Farbstoff*) wax dye; **Wachs|farb|stift** M wax crayon; **Wachs|fi|gur** F wax figure; **Wachs|fi|gu|ren|ka|bi|nett** NT waxworks *pl*; **Wachs|ker|ze** F wax candle; **Wachs|licht** NT night-light; **Wachs|ma|le|rei** F a *no pl* (*Technik*) encaustic painting b (*Bild*) encaustic; **Wachs|mal|stift** M , **Wachs|mal|krei|de** F wax crayon; **Wachs|mas|ke** F wax mask; **Wachs|mat|ri|ze** F stencil; **Wachs|pa|pier** NT waxed paper; **Wachs|stift** M wax crayon; **Wachs|stock** M wax taper

wächst [vɛkst] 3. *pers sing pres von* **wachsen**

Wach|stu|be [ˈvaxʃtuːbə] F guardroom; (*von Polizei*) duty room

Wachs|tuch [ˈvaks-] NT *pl* **-tücher** oilcloth

Wachs|tum [ˈvakstuːm] NT **-s**, *no pl* growth; **im ~ zurückgeblieben** stunted; **eigenes ~ (des Winzers)** from *or* grown in our own vineyards

Wachstums-: Wachs|tums|ak|tie F growth stock; **Wachs|tums|bran|che** F growth industry; **Wachs|tums|fonds** M growth fund; **wachs|tums|för|dernd** ADJ (*Econ, Biol*) growth-promoting; **wachs|tums|hem|mend** ADJ (*Econ, Biol*) growth-inhibiting; **Wachs|tums|hem|mung** F inhibition of growth *no pl*; **Wachs|tums|hor|mon** NT growth hormone; **Wachs|tums|po|li|tik** F growth policy; **Wachs|tums|ra|te** F (*Biol, Econ*) growth rate; **Wachs|tums|schmer|zen** PL growing pains *pl*; **wachs|tums|stark** ADJ (*Econ*) *Markt, Branche* booming; **Wachs|tums|stö|rung** F disturbance of growth

Wachs-: wachs|weich ADJ (as) soft as butter; *Ausrede* lame; *Erklärung, Formulierung* woolly (*esp Brit*), vague; **~ werden** (*Mensch*) to melt; (*Knie*) to turn to jelly; **Wachs|zie|her** [-tsiːɐ] M **-s, -**, **Wachs|zie|he|rin** [-ərɪn] F **-, -nen** chandler

Wacht [vaxt] F **-, -en** (*obs, liter*) = **Wache a**

Wach|tel [ˈvaxtl] F **-, -n** quail; (*fig inf: Frau*) silly goose (*inf*); **alte ~** (*inf*) (*unfreundlich*) old hen (*inf*); (*dumm*) silly old goose (*inf*)

Wäch|ter[1] [ˈvɛçtɐ] M **-s, -** guard dog, watchdog

Wäch|ter[2] [ˈvɛçtɐ] M **-s, -**, **Wäch|te|rin** [-ərɪn] F **-, -nen** guardian; (= *Nachtwächter*) watchman; (= *Turmwächter*) watch; (= *Museumswächter, Parkplatzwächter*) attendant

Wacht-: Wacht|meis|ter(in) M(F) a (*old Mil*) sergeant b (= *Polizist*) (police) constable (*Brit*), patrolman/-woman (*US*); **Herr ~** officer, constable (*Brit*); **Wacht|pos|ten** M sentry, guard; (= *Schüler, Dieb etc*) lookout

Wach|traum M daydream

Wach(t)|turm M watchtower

Wach-: Wach- und Schließ|ge|sell|schaft F security corps; **Wach|wech|sel** M (*lit, fig*) changing of the guard; **Wach|zim|mer** NT

(*Aus*) guardroom; **Wach|zu|stand** M **im ~ in the waking state**

Wa|cke|lei [vakə'lai] F **-, -en** (*inf*) wobbling

wa|cke|lig ['vakəlɪç] **ADJ** wobbly; *Möbelstück auch* rickety; *Zahn, Schraube auch* loose; (*fig*) *Firma, Unternehmen, Kompromiss* shaky; *Mehrheit* flimsy; **~ auf den Beinen sein** (*inf*) (*Patient*) to be wobbly on one's legs, to be shaky; (*alter Mensch*) to be doddery (*esp Brit*) or shaky; **auf ~en Füßen stehen** (*fig*) to have no sound or firm basis **ADV** **~ stehen** (*lit*) to be unsteady or wobbly; (*fig*: *Unternehmen, Schüler*) to be shaky

Wa|ckel|kon|takt M loose connection

wa|ckeln ['vakln] VI **a** (= *sich bewegen*) to wobble; (= *zittern*) to shake; (*Zahn, Schraube*) to be loose; (*fig*) (*Thron*) to totter; (*Position*) to be shaky; **du hast gewackelt** you wobbled/shook; (*beim Fotografieren*) you moved; **mit den Ohren ~** to waggle (*Brit*) or wiggle one's ears; **mit den Hüften/dem Hintern ~** to wiggle one's hips/bottom; **mit dem Kopf/Schwanz ~** to wag one's head/its tail **b** *aus sein* (= *langsam, unsicher gehen*) to totter; (*kleines Kind*) to toddle

Wa|ckel|pud|ding M , **Wa|ckel|pe|ter** [-pe:tɐ] M **-s, -** (*inf*) jelly (*Brit*), Jell-O® (*US*)

wa|cker ['vakɐ] **ADJ** **a** (= *tapfer*) brave, valiant **b** (*old*: = *tüchtig*) upright, honest **ADV** (= *tapfer*) bravely; **sich ~ halten** to stand or hold one's ground; **sich ~ schlagen** (*inf*) to put up a brave fight

Wa|cker|stein M boulder

wack|lig ['vaklɪç] **ADJ, ADV = wackelig**

Wa|de ['va:də] F **-, -n** calf

Wa|den-: Wa|den|bein NT fibula; **Wa|den|krampf** M cramp in the/one's calf; **Wa|den|strumpf** M half stocking; **Wa|den|wi|ckel** M (*Med*) compress around the leg

Waf|fe ['vafə] F **-, -n** (*lit, fig*) weapon; (= *Schusswaffe*) gun; (*Mil*: = *Waffengattung*) arm; **~n** (*Mil*) arms; **~n tragen** to carry arms; **zu den ~n rufen** to call to arms; **zu den ~n greifen** to take up arms; **unter ~n (stehen)** (to be) under arms; **die ~n strecken** (*lit, fig*) to lay down one's arms, to surrender; **jdn mit seinen eigenen ~n schlagen** (*fig*) to beat sb at his own game, to beat sb with his own weapons

Waf|fel ['vafl] F **-, -n** waffle; (= *Keks, Eiswaffel*) wafer; (= *Eistüte*) cornet; **einen an der ~ haben** (*sl*: = *verrückt sein*) to be off one's nut (*inf*)

Waf|fel-: Waf|fel|ei|sen NT waffle iron; **Waf|fel|stoff** M honeycomb cloth

Waf|fen- *in cpds* arms; **Waf|fen|ar|se|nal** NT arsenal; (*von Staat*) stockpile; **Waf|fen|be|sitz** M possession of firearms; **Waf|fen|bru|der** M (*old*) comrade in arms (*old*); **Waf|fen|dienst** M (*old*) military service; **Waf|fen|em|bar|go** NT arms embargo; **waf|fen|fä|hig** ADJ **a** *Uran, Plutonium* weapons-grade **b** = **wehrfähig**; **Waf|fen|gang** M *pl* **-gänge** (*old Mil*) passage at arms, armed encounter; (*Univ*) round; **Waf|fen|gat|tung** F (*Mil*) arm of the service; **Waf|fen|ge|brauch** M use of firearms; **Waf|fen|ge|setz** NT *usu pl* gun control law; **Waf|fen|ge|walt** F force of arms; **mit ~** by force of arms; **Waf|fen|han|del** M arms trade or traffic; (*illegal auch*) gunrunning; **der ~ ist ...** arms trade or traffic/gunrunning is ...; **Waf|fen|händ|ler(in)** M(F) arms dealer; (*illegal auch*) gunrunner; **Waf|fen|hil|fe** F military assistance; **Waf|fen|kam|mer** F armoury (*Brit*), armory (*US*); **Waf|fen|la|ger** NT (*von Armee*) ordnance depot; (*von Terroristen*) cache; **Waf|fen|lie|fe|rung** F supply of arms; **waf|fen|los** ADJ unarmed; **Waf|fen|rock** M (*old*) uniform; **Waf|fen|ru|he** F ceasefire; **Waf|fen|schein** M firearms or gun licence (*Brit*) or license (*US*); **Waf|fen|schie|ber(in)** M(F) arms broker or dealer; **Waf|fen|schmied** M (*Hist*) armourer (*Brit*), armorer (*US*); **Waf|fen|schmug|gel** M gunrunning, arms smuggling; **Waf|fen-SS** [-ɛsɛs] F (*NS*) Waffen-SS; **waf|fen|star|rend** ADJ bristling with weapons

Waf|fen|still|stand M armistice

Waf|fen|still|stands-: Waf|fen|still|stands|ab|kom|men NT armistice agreement; **Waf|fen|still|stands|li|nie** F ceasefire or armistice line

Waf|fen-: Waf|fen|sys|tem NT weapon system; **Waf|fen|trä|ger** M (*Fahrzeug*) weapon carrier; **Waf|fen|trä|ger(in)** M(F) **~(in) sein** to carry arms

waff|nen ['vafnən] VR **= wappnen**

wäg|bar ADJ (*geh*) ponderable; **ein nicht ~es Risiko** an imponderable risk

Wa|ge-: Wa|ge|hals M daredevil; **wa|ge|hal|sig** ADJ = **waghalsig**

Wä|gel|chen ['vɛːɡlçən] NT **-s, -** *dim von* **Wagen**

Wa|ge-: Wa|ge|mut M , *no pl* (*geh*) (heroic) daring or boldness; **wa|ge|mu|tig** ADJ daring, bold

wa|gen ['va:ɡn] ☼ 42.3, 53.6 **VT** to venture; (= *riskieren*) *hohen Einsatz, sein Leben* to risk; (= *sich getrauen*) to dare; **es ~, etw zu tun** to venture to do sth; to risk doing sth; to dare (to) do sth; **wage nicht, mir zu widersprechen!** don't you dare (to) contradict me!; **ich wags** I'll risk it, I'll take the risk or plunge; **davon hätte ich nicht zu träumen gewagt** I would never even have dreamed it; **wer wagt, gewinnt** (*Prov*) nothing ventured, nothing gained (*Prov*) → **Tänzchen, frisch** ADV

VR to dare; **sich ~, etw zu tun** to dare (to) do sth; **sich an etw** (*acc*) **~** to venture to do sth; **ich wage mich nicht daran** I dare not do it; **sich auf ein Gebiet ~** to venture into an area; **bei dem schönen Wetter kann ich mich aus dem Haus/ins Wasser ~** in this lovely weather I can venture out of doors/into the water; **er wagt sich nicht mehr aus dem Haus** he doesn't venture out (of the house) any more, he doesn't dare leave the house any more → *auch* **gewagt**

Wa|gen ['va:ɡn] M **-s, -** *or* (*S Ger, Aus*) ≟ ['vɛːɡn] **a** (= *Personenwagen*) car; (= *Lieferwagen*) van; (= *Planwagen*) (covered) wagon; (= *Zirkuswagen, Zigeunerwagen*) caravan, wagon; (*von Pferden gezogen*) wagon, cart; (= *Kutsche*) coach; (= *Puppenwagen, Kinderwagen*) pram (*Brit*), baby carriage (*US*); (= *Handwagen*) (hand)cart; (= *Kofferkuli, Einkaufswagen*) trolley; (= *Schreibmaschinenwagen*) carriage; (= *Straßenbahnwagen, Seilbahnwagen*) car; (= *Eisenbahnwagen*) coach (*Brit*), car, carriage (*Brit*); (= *Omnibus*) bus; **jdm an den ~ fahren** (*fig*) to pick holes in sb; **sich nicht vor jds ~ spannen lassen** (*fig*) not to allow oneself to be used or made use of by sb → **Rad** [1] **a**

b (*Astron*) **der Große ~** the Plough (*Brit*), the Big Dipper; **der Kleine ~** the Little Dipper

wä|gen ['vɛːɡn] *pret* **wog** *or* **wägte** [vo:k, 'vɛːktə], *ptp* **gewogen** *or* **gewägt** [ɡə'vo:ɡn, ɡə'vɛːkt] **VT** (*old, form*) to weigh; (*geh*: = *bedenken auch*) to ponder; **erst ~, dann wagen** (*Prov*) look before you leap (*Prov*)

Wa|gen-: Wa|gen|ab|teil NT (*Rail*) compartment; **Wa|gen|bau|er(in)** M(F) *or* **-bauer(in-nen)** coach-builder; **Wa|gen|burg** F barricade (of wagons); **Wa|gen|deich|sel** F shaft; **Wa|gen|fol|ge** F → **Wagen a** order of cars/coaches or carriages *etc*; **Wa|gen|füh|rer(in)** M(F) driver; **Wa|gen|he|ber** M jack; **Wa|gen|la|dung** F (*von Lastwagen*) lorryload (*Brit*), truckload; (*von Eisenbahn*) wagonload; **Wa|gen|len|ker** M (*Hist*) charioteer; **Wa|gen|pa|pie|re** PL car or vehicle documents *pl*; **Wa|gen|park** M fleet of cars; (= *Lieferwagen*) fleet of vans; **Wa|gen|pfle|ge** F care of the/one's car; **Wa|gen|rad** NT cartwheel; (*hum*: = *Hut*) picture hat; **Wa|gen|ren|nen** NT (*Hist*) chariot race; (*einzelner Wettkampf*) chariot race; **Wa|gen|rück|lauf** M (*an Schreibmaschine*) carriage return; **Wa|gen|schlag** M (*von Kutsche*) carriage door; (*von Auto*) car door; **Wa|gen|schmie|re** F cart grease; **Wa|gen|typ** M type of car; **Wa|gen|wä|sche** F car wash; (= *das Waschen*) car washing

Wa|ge|stück NT daring deed, deed of daring

Wag|gon [va'ɡõ:, va'ɡɔŋ] M **-s, -s** (goods) wagon, freight car (*US*); (= *Ladung*) wagonload/carload

wag|gon|wei|se [va'ɡõ:-, va'ɡɔŋ-] ADV by the wagonload or carload (*US*)

Wag-: Wag|hals M daredevil; **wag|hal|sig** ADJ foolhardy, daredevil *attr*; **Wag|hal|sig|keit** ['va:khalzɪçkait] F **-, -en** foolhardiness

Wag|ner ['va:ɡnɐ] M **-s, -**, **Wag|ne|rin** [-ərɪn] F **-, -nen** (*dial*) coach-builder

Wag|ne|ria|ner [va:ɡnə'ria:nɐ] M **-s, -**, **Wag|ne|ria|ne|rin** [-ərɪn] F **-, -nen** Wagnerian

Wag|nis ['va:knɪs] NT **-ses, -se** hazardous business; (= *Risiko*) risk

Wag|nis|ka|pi|tal NT (*Fin*) venture capital

Wa|gon ▲ [va'ɡo:n] M **-s, -s** → **Waggon**

wa|gon|wei|se ▲ [va'ɡo:n-] ADV → **waggonweise**

Wa|gon ▲ [va'ɡo:n] M **-s, -s** → **Waggon**

Wä|he ['vɛ:ə] F **-, -n** (*esp Sw*) *flan with a sweet or salty topping*

Wahl [va:l] ☼ 45.4, 53.2 F **-, -en** **a** (= *Auswahl*) choice; **die ~ fiel auf ihn/dieses Buch** he/this book was chosen; **aus freier ~** of one's own free choice; **wir hatten keine (andere) ~(, als)** we had no alternative or choice (but); **es gab** *or* **blieb keine andere ~(, als)** there was no alternative (but); **das ließ mir keine (andere) ~** it left me no (other) choice; **jdm die ~ lassen** to leave (it up to) sb to choose; **jdm etw zur ~ stellen** to give sb the choice of sth; **drei Kandidaten stehen zur ~** there is a choice of three candidates; **seine/eine ~ treffen** to make one's/a choice or selection; **du hast die ~** take your choice or pick; **sie hat die ~, ob sie ...** the choice is hers whether she ..., it's up to her whether she ...; **wer die ~ hat, hat die Qual** (*Prov*) he is/you are *etc* spoiled for choice → **eng ADJ a**

b (*Pol etc*) election; (= *Abstimmung*) vote; (*geheim*) ballot; **geheime ~** secret ballot; **freie ~** free elections; **~ durch Handerheben** vote by (a) show of hands; **die ~en** (the) elections; **eines Präsidenten** election of a president; **seine ~ in den Vorstand/zum Präsidenten** his election to the board/as president; **die ~ gewinnen** to win the election; **zur ~ gehen** to go to vote, to go to the polls; **jdn zur ~ aufstellen** *or* **vorschlagen** to propose sb or put sb up as a candidate (for election); **sich zur ~ stellen** to stand (as a candidate), to stand (at the/an election), to run (for parliament/president *etc*); **zur ~ schreiten** to take a vote or (*geheim*) ballot; **die ~ annehmen** to accept the or one's election

c (= *Qualität*) quality; **erste ~** top quality; *Gemüse, Eier* class or grade one; **zweite/dritte ~** second/third quality; *Gemüse, Eier* class or grade two/three; **Waren erster ~** top-quality goods; **Eier erster ~** class-one or grade-one eggs; **Fleisch erster ~** prime meat; **Waren zweiter ~** seconds *pl*; **Gemüse zweiter ~** class-two or grade-two vegetables; **der Teller war zweite ~** the plate was a second

Wahl-: Wahl|akt M polling; **Wahl|al|ter** NT voting age; **Wahl|ana|ly|ti|ker(in)** M(F) election analyst; **Wahl|auf|ruf** M election announcement; **Wahl|auf|trag** M election brief; **Wahl|aus|gang** M outcome of an/the election, election results *pl*; **Wahl|aus|schuss** ▲ M election committee

Wähl|au|to|ma|tik F (*Telec*) automatic dialling (*Brit*) or dialing (*US*)

wähl|bar ADJ **a** eligible (for office), able to stand at an/the election **b** (= *auswählbar*) **frei ~** of one's choice

Wähl|bar|keit ['vɛ:lba:ɐkait] F **-, *no pl*** eligibility (for office)

Wahl-: Wahl|be|nach|rich|ti|gung F , **Wahl|be|nach|rich|ti|gungs|kar|te** F polling card; **wahl|be|rech|tigt** ADJ entitled to vote; **Wahl|be|rech|tig|te(r)** [-bərɛçtɪçtə] MF *decl as*

adj person entitled to vote; **Wahl|be|rech|ti|gung** F (right to) vote; **Wahl|be|tei|li|gung** F poll; **eine hohe ~** a heavy poll, a high *or* good turnout (at an/the election); **Wahl|be|trug** M electoral fraud; (= *Manipulation des Wahlergebnisses*) ballot- *or* vote-rigging (*inf*); **Wahl|be|zirk** M ward; **Wahl|brief** M *letter containing completed postal vote*; **Wahl|bünd|nis** NT electoral pact; **Wahl|bür|ger(in)** M(F) (*form*) voter; **Wahl|bü|ro** NT election office

wäh|len ['vɛːlən] ✪ 27.3 **VT a** (*von* from, out of) to choose; (= *auswählen*) to select, to pick; **seine Worte ~** to choose one's words, to select *or* pick one's words carefully → *auch* **gewählt b** (*Telec*) *Nummer* to dial **c** (= *durch Wahl ermitteln*) *Regierung, Sprecher etc* to elect; (= *sich entscheiden für*) *Partei, Kandidaten* to vote for; **jdn ins Parlament ~** to elect *or* return sb to Parliament; **jdn in den Vorstand ~** to elect *or* vote sb onto the board; **jdn zum Präsidenten ~** to elect sb president **VI a** (= *auswählen*) to choose **b** (*Telec*) to dial **c** (= *Wahlen abhalten*) to hold elections; (= *Stimme abgeben*) to vote; **wann wird gewählt?** when are the elections?; **man darf ab 18 ~** you can vote at 18; **durch Handerheben ~** to vote by (a) show of hands; **~ gehen** to go to the polls, to go to vote

Wahl|ent|schei|dung F choice (in an election), decision who *or* what to vote for; **wovon machst du deine ~ abhängig?** what will decide your vote (in the elections)?

Wäh|ler¹ ['vɛːlɐ] M -s, - (*Tech*) selector

Wäh|ler² ['vɛːlɐ] M -s, -, **Wäh|le|rin** [-ərɪn] F -, **-nen** (*Pol*) elector, voter; **der** *or* **die ~** the electorate *sing or pl*, the electors *pl*

Wäh|ler|auf|trag M mandate

Wäh|ler|geb|nis NT election result; (= *Stimmenverteilung auch*) election returns *pl*

Wäh|ler|ge|mein|schaft F electorate; **Freie ~** Association of Independent Voters

Wäh|ler|ini|ti|a|ti|ve F pressure from the electorate

wäh|le|risch ['vɛːlərɪʃ] ADJ particular; *Geschmack, Kunde* discriminating; **sei nicht so ~!** don't be so choosy (*inf*) *or* fussy

Wäh|ler|re|ser|voir NT source of votes

Wäh|ler|schaft ['vɛːlɐʃaft] F -, -en electorate *sing or pl*; (*eines Wahlkreises*) constituents *pl*

Wäh|ler-: **Wäh|ler|schicht** F section of the electorate; **Wäh|ler|schwund** M loss of voters; **Wäh|ler|stim|me** F vote; **10% der ~n** 10% of the vote(s) *or* poll; **Wäh|ler|ver|zeich|nis** NT electoral roll *or* register; **Wäh|ler|wan|de|rung** F shift of votes; **wäh|ler|wirk|sam** ADJ *Politik, Parole* vote-winning, popular with the voters

Wahl-: **Wahl|fach** NT (*Sch*) option, optional subject, elective (*US*); **Wahl|fäl|schung** F vote-rigging, electoral fraud; **Wahl|feld|zug** M election(eering) campaign; **Wahl|fie|ber** NT election fever; **Wahl|for|scher(in)** M(F) electoral researcher, psephologist; **Wahl|frau** F delegate; **wahl|frei** ADJ (*Sch*) optional; **~er Zugriff** (*Comput*) random access; **Wahl|frei|heit** F (*Pol*) electoral freedom; (*Sch*) freedom of choice; **Wahl|gang** M *pl* **-gänge** ballot; **Wahl|ge|heim|nis** NT secrecy of the ballot; **Wahl|ge|schenk** NT pre-election promise; **Wahl|ge|setz** NT electoral law; **Wahl|hei|mat** F country of adoption *or* of (one's) choice, adopted country; **Wahl|hel|fer(in)** M(F) (*im Wahlkampf*) electoral *or* election assistant; (*bei der Wahl*) polling officer; **Wahl|ka|bi|ne** F polling booth; **Wahl|kampf** M election(eering) campaign; **einen ~ führen** to conduct an election campaign; **Wahl|kampf|ma|nö|ver** NT campaign move; **Wahl|kreis** M constituency; **Wahl|lei|ter(in)** M(F) returning officer (*Brit*), chief election official (*US*);

Wahl|lo|kal NT polling station; **Wahl|lo|ko|mo|ti|ve** F (*inf*) vote-puller; **wahl|los** ADJ indiscriminate ADV at random, haphazardly; (= *nicht wählerisch*) indiscriminately; **Wahl|mann** M *pl* **-männer** delegate; **Wahl|mög|lich|keit** F choice, option; **Wahl|nacht** F election night; **Wahl|nie|der|la|ge** F election defeat; **Wahl|pe|ri|o|de** F lifetime of a/the parliament; **Wahl|pflicht** F electoral duty; **seine ~ erfüllen** to use one's vote; **Wahl|pflicht|fach** NT (*Sch*) (compulsory) optional subject; **ich muss zwei Wahlpflichtfächer belegen** I have to take two optional subjects; **Wahl|pla|kat** NT election poster; **Wahl|pro|pa|gan|da** F election propaganda; **Wahl|recht** NT **a** (right to) vote; **allgemeines ~** universal franchise (*esp Brit*) *or* suffrage; **das kommunale ~ haben** to have the right to vote in local elections; **das aktive ~** the right to vote; **das passive ~** eligibility (for political office); **mit 21/18 bekommt man das passive ~** at 21/18 one becomes eligible for political office **b** (= *Gesetze*) electoral law *no def art*; **Wahl|re|de** F election speech; **Wahl|re|form** F electoral reform

Wähl|schei|be F (*Telec*) dial

Wahl-: **Wahl|schein** M polling card; **Wahl|schlap|pe** F election setback; **Wahl|sieg** M electoral *or* election victory; **Wahl|slo|gan** M election slogan; **Wahl|sonn|tag** M polling Sunday; **Wahl|spruch** M **a** (= *Motto*) motto, watchword **b** (= *Wahlslogan*) election slogan; **Wahl|sys|tem** NT electoral system; **Wahl|tag** M election *or* polling day; **Wahl|un|ter|la|gen** PL election papers *pl*; **Wahl|ur|ne** F ballot box; **Wahl|ver|an|stal|tung** F election rally; **Wahl|ver|fah|ren** NT electoral procedure; **Wahl|ver|ge|hen** NT electoral misdemeanour (*Brit*) *or* misdemeanor (*US*); **Wahl|ver|hal|ten** NT behaviour (*Brit*) *or* behavior (*US*) at the polls; **Wahl|ver|samm|lung** F election meeting; **Wahl|ver|spre|chun|gen** PL election promises *pl*; **Wahl|ver|wandt|schaft** F (*Chem*) elective attraction; (*fig*) affinity (*von* between); **„die ~en**" (*Liter*) "The Elective Affinities"; **Wahl|volk** NT , *no pl* **das ~** the electorate; **wahl|wei|se** ADV alternatively; **~ Kartoffeln oder Reis** (a) choice of potatoes or rice; **Sie können ~ Wasserski fahren oder reiten** you have a choice between water-skiing and riding; **die Modelle sind ~ mit Sechs- oder Zwölfzylindermotor ausgestattet** the models have the option of a six- or a twelve-cylinder engine; **Wahl|wie|der|ho|lung** F (*Telec*) **(automatische)** ~ (automatic) redial

Wähl|zei|chen NT (*Telec*) dialling (*Brit*) *or* dial (*US*) tone

Wahl|zel|le F polling booth

Wahl|zet|tel M ballot paper

Wahn [vaːn] M - (e)s, *no pl* **a** illusion, delusion; **in dem ~ leben, dass …** to labour (*Brit*) *or* labor (*US*) under the delusion that … **b** (= *Manie*) mania

Wahn|bild NT delusion, illusion

wäh|nen ['vɛːnən] (*geh*) **VT** to imagine (wrongly), to believe (wrongly); **wir wähnten ihn glücklich** we (wrongly) imagined *or* believed him (to be) happy **VR sich sicher/von allen verlassen ~** to imagine *or* believe oneself (to be) safe/abandoned by all

Wahn|idee F delusion; (= *verrückte Idee*) mad *or* crazy notion

Wahn|sinn M , *no pl* **a** (*old Psych*) insanity, lunacy, madness; **in ~ verfallen** to go mad *or* insane **b** (= *Verrücktheit, Unvernunft*) madness, insanity; **jdn in den ~ treiben** to drive sb mad; **des ~s fette Beute sein** (*inf*) to be off one's rocker (*inf*); **das ist doch (heller) ~, so ein ~!** that's sheer madness *or* idiocy!; **Mensch, ~ or einfach ~!** (*inf*: = *prima*) wicked! (*Brit sl*) **c** religiöser ~ religious mania

wahn|sin|nig ADJ **a** (*old Psych*) insane, mad **b** (*inf*) (= *verrückt*) mad, crazy; (= *toll, super*) brilliant (*inf*), great (*inf*); (*attr*: = *sehr groß, viel*)

terrible, awful, dreadful; **eine ~e Arbeit** a crazy *or* an incredible amount of work; **ein ~es Geld** a crazy *or* an incredible amount of money; **wie ~** (*inf*) like mad; **das macht mich ~** (*inf*) it's driving me mad *or* crazy (*inf*), it's driving me round (*Brit*) *or* around (*US*) the bend (*inf*); **~ werden** to go mad *or* crazy (*inf*), to go round (*Brit*) *or* around (*US*) the bend (*inf*); **ich werde ~!** it's mind-blowing! (*inf*)
ADV (*inf*) incredibly (*inf*); **~ verliebt** madly in love; **~ viele/viel** an incredible number/amount (*inf*)

Wahn|sin|ni|ge(r) [-zɪnɪɡə] MF *decl as adj* madman/madwoman, lunatic

Wahn|sin|nig|wer|den NT **zum ~** enough to drive you round (*Brit*) *or* around (*US*) the bend (*inf*) *or* up the wall (*inf*)

Wahn|sinns- *in cpds* (*inf*) (= *verrückt*) crazy; (= *prima*) fantastic (*inf*), incredible (*inf*); **Wahn|sinns|ar|beit** F **eine ~** a crazy *or* an incredible amount of work (*inf*)

Wahn-: **Wahn|vor|stel|lung** F delusion; **Wahn|witz** M , *no pl* utter *or* sheer foolishness; **wahn|wit|zig** ADJ mad, crazy, lunatic *attr* ADV terribly, awfully

wahr [vaːɐ] ADJ *Geschichte, Liebe, Glaube etc* true; (= *echt*) *Kunst, Glück etc auch* real, genuine; *Freund, Freundschaft auch* real; (*attr*: = *wirklich*) real, veritable; **im ~sten Sinne des Wortes** in des Wortes **~ster Bedeutung** in the true sense of the word; **daran ist kein ~es Wort, davon ist kein Wort ~** there's not a word of truth in it; **da ist etwas Wahres daran** there's some truth in that; **da hast du ein ~es Wort gesprochen** (*inf*) that's very true, there's a lot of truth in that; **etw ~ machen** (*Pläne*) to make sth a reality; *Versprechung, Drohung* to carry sth out; **~ werden** to come true; (*Hoffnung, Pläne auch*) to become a reality; **so ~ mir Gott helfe!** so help me God!; **so ~ ich lebe/hier stehe** as sure as I'm alive/ standing here, as sure as eggs is eggs (*Brit inf*); **das darf** *or* **kann doch nicht ~ sein!** (*inf*) it can't be true!; **das ist schon gar nicht mehr ~** (*inf*) (*verstärkend*) it's not true! (*inf*); (= *schon lange her*) that was ages ago; **das ist nicht der ~e Jakob** *or* **Otto** (*inf*) das ist nicht das Wahre (*inf*) it's no great shakes (*inf*); **die Stelle ist nicht gerade der ~e Jakob** *or* **Otto** *or* **das Wahre** (*inf*) it's not exactly the greatest job (on earth) → **nicht, einzig**

wah|ren ['vaːrən] VT **a** (= *wahrnehmen*) *Interessen, Rechte* to look after, to protect, to safeguard **b** (= *erhalten*) *Autorität, Ruf, Würde* to preserve, to keep; *Geheimnis* to keep; *Chancen* to keep alive; *gute Manieren* to adhere to, to observe; **die Form ~** to adhere to correct form; **den Anstand ~** to observe the proprieties → **Schein¹ b, Gesicht¹ a**

wäh|ren ['vɛːrən] VI (*geh*) to last; **es währte nicht lange, da geschah ein Unglück** it was not long before misfortune struck; **was lange währt, wird endlich gut** (*Prov*) a happy outcome is worth waiting for → **ehrlich ADJ**

wäh|rend ['vɛːrənt] PREP +*gen or dat* during; **~ eines Zeitraums** over a period of time; **~ der ganzen Nacht** all night long, all during the night, throughout the night CONJ while; (= *wohingegen auch*) whereas

wäh|rend|dem [vɛːrənt'deːm] (*inf*), **wäh|rend|des** [vɛːrənt'dɛs] (*geh*), **wäh|rend|des|sen** [vɛːrənt'dɛsn] ADV meanwhile, in the meantime

Wahr-: **wahr|ha|ben** VT *sep irreg* **etw nicht ~ wollen** not to want to admit sth; **wahr|haft** ADJ (= *ehrlich*) truthful; (= *echt*) *Freund* true, real; *Enttäuschung* real; (*attr*: = *wirklich*) real, veritable ADV really, truly; **wahr|haf|tig** [vaːɐ'haftɪç, 'vaːɐ-] ADJ (*geh*) (= *aufrichtig*) truthful; *Gemüt* honest; *Worte etc* true; **der ~e Gott** the true God; **~er Gott!** (*inf*) strewth! (*inf*) ADV really; (= *tatsächlich*) actually; **Wahr|haf|tig|keit** F -, *no pl* (*geh*) truthfulness; (*von Aussage auch*) veracity

Wahr|heit ✪ 53.4, 53.6 F **-, -en** truth; **in ~** in reality; **die ~ sagen** to tell the truth; **um die ~ zu sagen** to tell the truth; **das ist nur die halbe ~** that's only half (of) the truth; **das schlägt der ~ ins Gesicht** that's patently untrue; **er nimmt es mit der ~ nicht so genau** (inf) you have to take what he says with a pinch (esp Brit) or grain (US) of salt → **Ehre**

Wahr|heits-: Wahr|heits|be|weis M *(Jur)* **den ~ bringen** or **antreten** to supply proof of the truth of a/one's statement; **Wahr|heits|fin|dung** [-fɪndʊŋ] F **-,** *no pl* establishment of the truth; **Wahr|heits|ge|halt** M substance; **wahr|heits|ge|mäß** ADJ true, truthful ADV truthfully, in accordance with the facts; **wahr|heits|ge|treu** ADJ *Bericht* truthful; *Darstellung* faithful; **ein ~es Bild** (fig) a factual or true picture ADV truthfully; **Wahr|heits|lie|be** F love of truth; **Wahr|heits|lie|bend** ADJ truth-loving; (= *ehrlich*) truthful; ADJ false ADV falsely

wahr|lich ['vaːɐlɪç] ADV really, indeed, verily *(Bibl)*; (= *garantiert*) certainly, definitely

Wahr-: wahr|nehm|bar ADJ perceptible, noticeable; **nicht ~** imperceptible, not noticeable; **mit bloßem Auge ~/nicht ~** visible/invisible to the naked eye; **wahr+nehm|men** VT *sep irreg* a (= *mit den Sinnen erfassen*) to perceive; (= *bemerken*) *Vorgänge, Veränderungen etc* to be aware of; (= *entdecken, erkennen*) *Geräusch* to hear; *Licht* to see; *Geruch* to detect; (= *heraushören*) *Unterton, Stimmung* to detect, to discern; **nichts mehr/alles um sich herum ~** to be no longer aware of anything/to be aware of everything around one b (= *nutzen, vertreten*) *Frist, Termin* to observe; *Gelegenheit* to take; *Interessen, Angelegenheiten* to look after; *Verantwortung* to exercise; **sein Recht auf etw** *(acc)* **~** to exercise one's right to sth; **Wahr|nehm|mung** [-neːmʊŋ] F **-, -en** a *(mit den Sinnen)* perception; *(von Vorgängen etc)* awareness; *(von Geruch, Stimmung)* detection b *(von Interessen, Angelegenheiten)* looking after; **Wahr|nehm|mungs|ver|mö|gen** NT perceptive faculty; **wahr|sa|gen** *sep or insep* VI to tell fortunes, to predict the future; **aus dem Kaffeesatz/aus den Teeblättern/aus den Karten ~** to read coffee grounds/tea leaves/cards; **jdm ~** to tell sb's fortune, to predict the future (to sb); **sich** *(dat)* **~ lassen** to have one's fortune told VT **(jdm) die Zukunft ~** to tell sb's fortune, to predict the future (to sb); **er hat mir wahrgesagt** or **gewahrsagt, dass ...** he predicted (to me) that ...; **Wahr|sa|ger** [-zaːɡɐ] M **-s, -,** **Wahr|sa|ge|rin** [-ərɪn] F **-, -en** fortune-teller, soothsayer *(old)*; **Wahr|sa|ge|rei** [-zaːɡəˈraɪ] F **-, -en** a *no pl* fortune-telling b prediction; **wahr|sa|ge|risch** [-zaːɡərɪʃ] ADJ prophetic; **Wahr|sa|gung** [-zaːɡʊŋ] F **-, -en** prediction

währ|schaft ['vɛːɐʃaft] ADJ *(Sw)* (= *gediegen*) *Ware, Arbeit* reliable; (= *reichhaltig*) *Essen* wholesome; (= *kernig*) *Mensch* down to earth

Wahr|schau F **-!** *(Naut)* attention!

wahr|schein|lich [vaːɐ'ʃaɪnlɪç, 'vaːɐ-] ✪ 42.2, 43.2, 53.2, 53.6 ADJ probable, likely; (= *glaubhaft*) plausible; **es liegt im Bereich des Wahrscheinlichen** it is quite within the bounds of probability ADV probably; **er kommt ~ erst später** he probably won't come till later, he won't come till later most likely

Wahr|schein|lich|keit ✪ 42.2 F **-, -en** probability, likelihood *no pl*; (= *Glaubhaftigkeit*) plausibility; **mit großer ~, aller ~ nach, in aller ~** in all probability or likelihood

Wah|rung ['vaːrʊŋ] F **-,** *no pl* a (= *Wahrnehmung*) protection, safeguarding b (= *Erhaltung*) preservation; *(von Geheimnis)* keeping; **~ der guten Manieren** adherence to or observance of good manners

Wäh|rung ['vɛːrʊŋ] F **-, -en** currency

Wäh|rungs- *in cpds* currency, monetary; **Wäh|rungs|aus|gleich** M currency conversion compensation; **Wäh|rungs|block** M *pl* -blöcke monetary bloc; **Wäh|rungs|ein|heit** F monetary unit; **Wäh|rungs|fonds** M Monetary Fund; **Wäh|rungs|ge|biet** NT currency area; **Wäh|rungs|hü|ter(in)** M(F) *(inf)* monetary regulator; **Wäh|rungs|in|sti|tut** NT monetary institute; **Europäisches ~** European Monetary Institute; **Wäh|rungs|kri|se** F monetary or currency crisis; **Wäh|rungs|kurs** M value of a currency; **Wäh|rungs|pa|ri|tät** F mint par of exchange; **Wäh|rungs|re|form** F monetary or currency reform; **Wäh|rungs|re|ser|ve** F monetary or currency reserve; **Wäh|rungs|schlan|ge** F (currency) snake; **Wäh|rungs|sys|tem** NT monetary system; **Wäh|rungs|um|stel|lung** F currency changeover or switch, changeover or switch to a new currency; **Wäh|rungs|uni|on** F monetary union; **europäische ~** European monetary union

Wahr|zei|chen NT *(von Stadt, Verein)* emblem; (= *Gebäude, Turm etc*) symbol

Waid- ['vait] *in cpds* = **Weid-**

Wai|se ['vaizə] F **-, -n** orphan

Wai|sen-: Wai|sen|haus NT orphanage; **Wai|sen|kind** NT orphan; **Wai|sen|kna|be** M *(liter)* orphan (boy); **gegen dich ist er ein ~** or **Waisenkind** (inf) he's no match for you, he would run rings round him (inf); **Wai|sen|ren|te** F orphan's allowance

Wal [vaːl] M **-(e)s, -e** whale

Wald [valt] M **-(e)s, ⁻e** ['vɛldə] wood(s *pl*); *(großer)* forest; *(no pl:* = *Waldland*) woodland(s *pl*), wooded country; **~ und Wiese/Feld** or **Flur** *(liter)* woods and meadows/fields; **ich glaub, ich steh im ~** *(inf)* I must be seeing/hearing things! *(inf)*; **er sieht den ~ vor lauter Bäumen nicht** he can't see the wood *(Brit)* or forest *(US)* for the trees *(Prov)*; **wie es in den ~ hineinschallt** or **wie man in den ~ hineinruft, so schallt es wieder heraus** *(Prov)* you get as much as you give; **der Thüringer ~** the Thuringian Forest, the Thüringer Wald

Wald-: Wald|amei|se F red ant; **Wald|ar|bei|ter** M forestry worker; (= *Holzfäller*) lumberjack, woodman; **Wald|ar|bei|te|rin** F forestry worker; **Wald|be|stand** M forest land; **Wald|blu|me** F woodland flower; **Wald|bo|den** M forest soil; **Wald|brand** M forest fire

Wäld|chen ['vɛltçən] NT **-s, -** *dim von* **Wald** little wood

Wald|erd|bee|re F wild strawberry

Wal|des- *(liter)*: **Wal|des|dun|kel** NT gloom of the forest; **Wal|des|rau|schen** NT **-s,** *no pl →* **Wald** rustling or whispering of the woods/forest; **Wal|des|saum** M → **Wald** edge of the wood(s)/forest

Wald-: Wald|flä|che F wooded area, woodland(s *pl*); **Wald|fre|vel** M offence *(Brit)* or offense *(US)* against the forest laws; **Wald|ge|biet** NT woodland area; **weite ~e** *pl* huge tracts *pl* of forest; **Wald|geist** M sylvan *(poet)* or silvan *(poet)* or forest spirit; **Wald|hei|ni** M *(inf)* nitwit *(inf)*; **Wald|horn** NT *(Mus)* French horn

wal|dig ['valdɪç] ADJ wooded, woody

Wald-: Wald|kauz M *(Orn)* tawny owl; **Wald|land** NT woodland(s *pl*); **Wald|land|schaft** F → **Wald** woodland/forest landscape; **Wald|lauf** M cross-country running; *(einzelner Lauf)* cross-country run; **Wald|lehr|pfad** M nature trail; **Wald|meis|ter** M *(Bot)* woodruff

Wal|dorf- ['valdɔrf-]: **Wal|dorf|sa|lat** M *(Cook)* Waldorf salad; **Wal|dorf|schu|le** F Rudolf Steiner School

Wald-: Wald|rand M **am ~** at or on the edge of the forest; **wald|reich** ADJ densely wooded; **Wald|reich|tum** M → **Wald** abundance of woods/forests; **Wald|scha|den** M → **Wald** damage to woods/forests; **Wald|schnei|se** F lane; **Wald|schrat** M wood gnome; **Wald|ster|ben** NT dying of the forests *(due to pol-*

lution); **Wald|tier** NT → **Wald** woodland/forest creature

Wald-und-Wie|sen- *in cpds* (inf) common-or-garden *(Brit inf)*, garden-variety *(US inf)*; **ein ~Politiker** a common-or-garden *(Brit)* or garden-variety *(US)* politician *(inf)*

Wal|dung ['valdʊŋ] F **-, -en** *(geh)* woodland(s *pl*)

Wald-: Wald|vo|gel M woodland bird; **Wald|weg** M → **Wald** woodland/forest path; **Wald|wie|se** F glade; **Wald|wirt|schaft** F forestry

Wales [weːls, weːlz] NT **-'** Wales

Wal-: Wal|fang M whaling; **Wal|fang|boot** NT whaler, whaling boat; **Wal|fän|ger** M (= *Schiff*) whaler; **Wal|fän|ger(in)** M(F) whaler; **Wal|fang|ver|bot** NT whaling ban; **Wal|fisch** M *(inf)* whale; **Wal|fisch|speck** M blubber; **Wal|fisch|tran** M sperm oil

wal|gen ['valɡn], **wäl|gern** ['vɛlɡɐn] VT *(dial) Teig* to roll out

Wal|hall ['valhal, val'hal] F **-,** *no pl*, **Wal|hal|la** [val'hala] F **-,** *no pl (Myth)* Valhalla

Wa|li|ser [va'liːze] M **-s, -** Welshman

Wa|li|se|rin [va'liːzərɪn] F **-, -nen** Welshwoman

wa|li|sisch [va'liːzɪʃ] ADJ Welsh

Wa|li|sisch(e) NT *(Ling)* Welsh → *auch* **Deutsch(e)**

Wal|ke ['valkə] F **-, -n** fulling machine

wal|ken¹ ['valkn] VT *Felle, Leder* to drum, to tumble; *Wollgewebe* to full, to mill; *Blech* to flex; **jdn ~** *(inf)* to give sb a belting *(inf)*

wal|ken² ['wɔːkn] VI *aux sein (Sport)* to speed-walk, to go speed walking

Wal|kie-Tal|kie ▲ ['wɔːkiˈtɔːki] NT **-(s), -s** walkie-talkie

Wal|king ['wɔːkɪŋ] NT **-s,** *no pl* speed walking

Walk|man® ['wɔːkmən] M **-s, -s** or **Walkmen** *(Rad)* Walkman®

Wal|kü|re [val'kyːrə, 'valkyːrə] F **-, -n** *(Myth, fig)* Valkyrie

Wall [val] M **-(e)s, ⁻e** ['vɛlə] embankment; *(Mil)* rampart; *(fig)* bulwark, rampart

Wal|lach ['valax] M **-(e)s, -e** gelding

wal|len ['valən] VI a *(liter) (Meer)* (= *brodeln*) to surge, to seethe; (= *fließen*) to flow; *(Dämpfe, Nebel)* to surge; *(fig) (Blut)* to boil; *(hum: Busen)* to heave b *(obs) aux sein* (= *wallfahren*) to go on a pilgrimage

wall|fah|ren ['valfaːrən] VI *insep reg aux sein* to go on a pilgrimage

Wall|fah|rer(in) M(F) pilgrim

Wall|fahrt F pilgrimage

Wall|fahrts-: Wall|fahrts|kir|che F pilgrimage church; **Wall|fahrts|ort** M *pl* -orte place of pilgrimage; **Wall|fahrts|stät|te** F place of pilgrimage; *(Grab, Kirche auch)* shrine

Wall|gra|ben M moat

Wal|lis ['valɪs] NT **-'** Valais

Wal|li|ser ['valize] M **-s, -,** **Wal|li|se|rin** [-ərɪn] F **-, -nen** inhabitant of the Valais

Wal|li|ser Al|pen PL die **~** the Valais Alps *pl*

wal|li|se|risch ['valizərɪʃ] ADJ Valaisan

Wal|lo|ne [va'loːnə] M **-n, -n**, **Wal|lo|nin** [-'loːnɪn] F **-, -nen** Walloon

Wal|lung ['valʊŋ] F **-, -en** a *(geh)* **das Meer war in ~** the sea was surging or seething; **in ~ geraten** *(See, Meer)* to begin to surge or seethe; *(Mensch) (vor Leidenschaft)* to be in a turmoil; *(vor Wut)* to fly into a rage or passion; **sein Blut geriet in ~** his blood began to surge through his veins; **jds Blut** or **jdn in ~ bringen** to make sb's blood surge through his/her veins b *(Med)* (hot) flush *(Brit)* or flash *(US) usu pl*

Walm|dach ['valm-] NT *(Archit)* hipped roof

Wal|nuss ▲ ['val-] F walnut

Wal|nuss|baum ▲ M walnut (tree)

Wal|pur|gis|nacht [val'pʊrɡɪs-] F Walpurgis Night, Walpurgisnacht

Wal|ross ▲ ['val-] NT walrus; (pej: Mensch) baby elephant (inf); **schnaufen wie ein ~** (pej) to puff like a grampus

Wal|statt ['va:l-, 'val-] F **-, -stätten** [-ʃtɛtn] (obs) battlefield

wal|ten ['valtn] VI (geh) to prevail, to reign (in +dat over); (= wirken: Mensch, Naturkräfte) to be at work; **über jdm/etw ~** to rule (over) sb/sth; **Vernunft ~ lassen** to let reason prevail; **Vorsicht/Milde ~ lassen** to exercise caution/leniency; **Gnade ~ lassen** to show mercy; **das Walten der Naturgewalten/Gottes** the workings of the forces of nature/of God; **jdn ~ lassen** to let sb have a free rein, to let sb do as he pleases; **das walte Gott** or (inf) **Hugo** amen (to that)! → **Amt b, schalten VI b**

Wal|tran ['va:l-] M sperm oil

Walz [valts] F (dated) **auf die ~ gehen** to go off on one's travels; **auf der ~ sein** to be on the road

Walz|blech NT sheet metal

Wal|ze ['valtsə] F **-, -n** roller; (von Schreibmaschine auch) platen; (= Drehorgelwalze) barrel; (von Spieluhr) cylinder, drum

wal|zen ['valtsn] VT to roll VI **a** aux sein or haben (dated: = tanzen) to waltz **b** aux sein (old inf: = wandern) to tramp, to hike

wäl|zen ['vɛltsn] VT **a** (= rollen) to roll; (Cook) (in Ei, Mehl) to coat (in +dat with); (in Butter, Petersilie) to toss **b** (inf) Akten, Bücher to pore over; Probleme, Gedanken, Pläne to turn over in one's mind; **die Schuld/Verantwortung auf jdn ~** to shift or shove (inf) the blame/responsibility onto sb VR to roll; (vor Schmerzen) to writhe (vor +dat with); (schlaflos im Bett) to toss and turn; (fig: Menschenmenge, Wassermassen) to surge; (im Schlamm) to wallow

wal|zen|för|mig ADJ cylindrical

Wal|zer ['valtsə] M **-s, -** waltz; **Wiener ~** Viennese waltz; **~ tanzen** to (dance the/a) waltz; **sich im ~ drehen** (liter) to waltz around and around

Wäl|zer ['vɛltsə] M **-s, -** (inf) heavy or weighty tome (hum)

Wal|zer-: Wal|zer|mu|sik F waltz music; **Wal|zer|schritt** M waltz step; **Wal|zer|takt** M waltz time

Walz-: Walz|stra|ße F rolling train; **Walz|werk** NT rolling mill

Wam|me ['vamə] F **-, -n** **a** (= Hautfalte) dewlap **b** (von Pelz) belly part **c** (dial: = Bauch) paunch

Wam|pe ['vampə] F **-, -n** (inf) paunch

Wams [vams] NT **-es, ⸚er** ['vɛmzə] (old, dial: = Jacke) jacket; (unter Rüstung) gambeson; (dial: = Weste) waistcoat (Brit), vest (US)

wand pret von **winden** ¹

Wand [vant] F **-, ⸚e** ['vɛndə] wall (auch Anat); (= nicht gemauerte Trennwand) partition (wall); (von Gefäß, Behälter, Schiff) side; (= Felswand) (rock) face; (= Wolkenwand) bank of clouds; (Biol) septum (spec); (fig) barrier, wall; **spanische ~** (folding) screen; **etw an die ~ werfen** or **schmeißen** or **schleudern** (inf) (lit) to throw sth against or at the wall; (fig: aus Wut, Verzweiflung) to throw sth out of the window; **~ an ~** wall to wall; **in seinen vier Wänden** (fig) within one's own four walls; **weiß wie die ~** as white as a sheet; **wenn die Wände reden könnten** if walls could speak; **man rennt bei denen gegen eine ~** with them you come up against a brick wall; **mit dem Kopf gegen die ~ rennen** (fig) to bang one's head against a brick wall; **jdn an die ~ drücken** (fig) to push or drive sb to the wall; **jdn an die ~ spielen** (fig) to outdo or outshine sb; (Theat) to steal the show from sb, to upstage sb; **jdn an die ~ stellen** (fig) to shoot sb, to send sb before the firing squad; **ich lachte/tobte etc, dass die Wände wackelten** (inf) or **zitterten** (inf) he raised the roof (with his laughter/ranting and raving etc) (inf); **die ~** or **Wän-** de hochgehen (inf) to go up the wall (inf); **das ist, um an den Wänden hochzugehen** (inf) **es ist zum Die-Wände-Hochgehen** (inf) it's enough to drive you up the wall (inf)

Wan|da|le [van'da:lə] M **-n, -n, Wan|da|lin** [-'da:lɪn] F **-, -nen** (Hist) Vandal → **hausen**

Wan|da|lis|mus [vanda'lɪsmʊs] M **-, no pl** vandalism

Wand-: Wand|be|hang M wall hanging; **Wand|be|klei|dung** F wall covering; (aus Holz) panelling (esp Brit), paneling (US); **Wand|be|wurf** M plaster(ing); (= Rauhputz) roughcast; **Wand|bild** NT wall painting, mural; (= Fresko) fresco; **Wand|bord** NT , **Wand|brett** NT (wall) shelf

Wan|del [vandl] M **-s, no pl** **a** change; **im ~ der Zeiten** throughout the ages, throughout the changing times; **im ~ der Jahrhunderte** down the centuries **b** (= Lebenswandel) way or mode of life → **Handel** ¹ **b**

Wan|del-: Wan|del|al|tar M polyptych; **Wan|del|an|lei|he** F convertible loan; **wan|del|bar** ADJ changeable; **Wan|del|bar|keit** ['vandlba:kait] F **-, no pl** changeability; **Wan|del|gang** M pl **-gänge** covered walk; **Wan|del|hal|le** F foyer; (im Parlament) lobby; (im Kurhaus) pump room

wan|deln¹ ['vandln] VTR (= ändern) to change

wan|deln² VI aux sein (geh: = gehen) to walk, to stroll; **ein ~des Wörterbuch** (hum) a walking dictionary; **er ist die ~de Güte** he is goodness or kindness itself or personified → **Leiche**

Wan|del|ob|li|ga|ti|on F , **Wan|del|schuld|ver|schrei|bung** F (Fin) convertible bond

Wan|del|stern M (old) planet

Wan|de|lung F **-, -en** (Jur) cancellation of sale

Wan|der-: Wan|der|amei|se F army ant; **Wan|der|ar|bei|ter(in)** M(F) migrant worker; **Wan|der|aus|stel|lung** F travelling (esp Brit) or traveling (US) exhibition, touring exhibition; **Wan|der|büh|ne** F touring company; (Hist) strolling players pl; **Wan|der|bur|sche** M (obs) journeyman; **Wan|der|dü|ne** F shifting or drifting (sand) dune

Wan|de|rer ['vandərə] M **-s, -, Wan|de|rin** [-ərɪn] F **-, -nen** hiker; (= esp Angehöriger eines Wandervereins) rambler (esp Brit), hiker; (old: = Reisender) traveller (esp Brit), traveler (US), wayfarer (old)

Wan|der-: Wan|der|fahrt F hiking trip; (old: = Reise) journey; **Wan|der|fal|ke** M peregrine (falcon); **Wan|der|freund(in)** M(F) hiker; **Wan|der|heu|schre|cke** F migratory locust

Wan|de|rin F → **Wanderer**

Wan|der-: Wan|der|jah|re PL years pl of travel; **Wan|der|kar|te** F map of walks or trails; **Wan|der|klei|dung** F hiking outfit; **Wan|der|le|ben** NT roving or wandering life; (fig) unsettled life; **Wan|der|le|ber** F floating liver; **Wan|der|lied** NT hiking song; **Wan|der|lust** F wanderlust; **wan|der|lus|tig** ADJ filled with wanderlust, with a passion for travel

wan|dern ['vandən] VI aux sein **a** (= gehen) to wander, to roam; (old: = reisen) to travel, to journey; (Wanderbühne, Zigeuner) to travel; **durchs Leben ~** (liter) to journey through life **b** (= sich bewegen) to move, to travel; (Wolken, Gletscher) to drift; (Düne) to shift, to drift; (Med: Leber, Niere) to float; (Blick) to rove, to roam, to wander; (Gedanken) to roam, to wander, to stray; (= weitergegeben werden) to be passed (on) **c** (Vögel, Tiere, Völker) to migrate **d** (zur Freizeitgestaltung) to hike; (esp in Verein) to ramble (esp Brit), to hike **e** (inf: ins Bett, in den Papierkorb, ins Feuer) to go; **hinter Schloss und Riegel ~** to be put behind bars; **ins Krankenhaus/ins Leihhaus ~** to end or land up in hospital/at the pawnbroker's

Wan|der-: Wan|der|nie|re F floating kidney; **Wan|der|po|kal** M challenge cup; **Wan|der|pre|di|ger(in)** M(F) itinerant preacher; **Wan-** der|preis M challenge trophy; **Wan|der|rat|te** F brown rat

Wan|der|schaft ['vandəʃaft] F **-, no pl** travels pl; **auf (der) ~ sein** to be on one's travels; (Handwerksgeselle) to travel around; (Tier) to be on the move; **auf ~ gehen** to go off on one's travels; (Tier) to set off on the move

Wan|der-: Wan|der|schau|spie|ler(in) M(F) travelling (esp Brit) or traveling (US) actor/actress; (Hist) strolling player; **Wan|der|schu|he** PL walking shoes pl

Wan|ders|mann M pl **-leute** (liter) = Wanderer

Wan|der-: Wan|der|stab M staff; **den ~ ergreifen** (fig) to take to the road; **Wan|der|tag** M day in German schools on which pupils go hiking; **Wan|der|trieb** M (von Tier) migratory instinct; (Psych) urge to travel, dromomania (spec); (fig) wanderlust, passion for travel; **Wan|der|trup|pe** F touring company; (Hist) strolling players pl

Wan|de|rung ['vandərʊŋ] F **-, -en** **a** (= Ausflug) walk; **eine ~ machen** to go on a walk or hike or ramble (esp Brit) **b** (old: = Reise, von Handwerksgesellen, fig liter: durchs Leben) journey **c** (von Vögeln, Tieren, Völkern) migration; (Sociol: = Wohnortwechsel) shift (in the population), population shift

Wan|de|rungs|ge|winn M (Sociol) increase in population (through population shifts)

Wan|der-: Wan|der|ver|ein M rambling (esp Brit) or hiking club; **Wan|der|vo|gel** M (Hist) member of the Wandervogel youth movement; (= begeisterter Wanderer) hiker; (fig inf) bird of passage, rolling stone (inf); **Wan|der|weg** M walk, trail, (foot)path; **Wan|der|zir|kus** M travelling (esp Brit) or traveling (US) circus

Wand-: Wand|flä|che F wall area; **Wand|ge|mäl|de** NT mural, wall painting; **Wand|hal|te|rung** F (für PC, Fernseher etc) wall bracket

-wan|dig [vandɪç] ADJ suf -walled; **dünnwandig** (Gebäude) thin-walled; **eine dünnwandige/dickwandige Mauer** a thin/thick wall

Wand-: Wand|ka|len|der M wall calendar; **Wand|kar|te** F wall map; **Wand|lam|pe** F wall lamp; **Wand|leuch|ter** M wall bracket, sconce; **Wand|schmuck** M wall decoration

Wand|lung ['vandlʊŋ] F **-, -en** **a** (= Wechsel, Wandel) change; (= völlige Umwandlung) transformation; **~ zum Guten** change for the better; **eine ~ durchmachen** to undergo a change **b** (Eccl) transubstantiation; (= Teil der Messe) consecration **c** (Jur) cancellation of sale contract

wand|lungs|fä|hig ADJ adaptable; Schauspieler etc versatile

Wand|lungs|fä|hig|keit F adaptability; (von Schauspieler etc) versatility

Wand-: Wand|ma|le|rei F mural painting; (Bild) mural, wall painting; **Wand|pfei|ler** M (Archit) pilaster

Wand|rer ['vandrə] M **-s, -, Wand|re|rin** [-ərɪn] F **-, -nen** → **Wanderer**

Wand-: Wand|schirm M screen; **Wand|schrank** M wall cupboard; **Wand|ta|fel** F (black)board

wand|te pret von **wenden**

Wand-: Wand|tel|ler M wall plate; **Wand|tep|pich** M tapestry, wall hanging; **Wand|uhr** F wall clock; **Wand|ver|klei|dung** F wall covering; (aus Holz) panelling (esp Brit), paneling (US); **Wand|zei|tung** F wall newssheet

Wan|ge ['vaŋə] F **-, -n** **a** (geh) cheek; **~ an ~** cheek to cheek **b** (von Treppe) stringboard

Wank [vaŋk] M (Sw) **keinen ~ tun** not to lift a finger

Wan|kel|mo|tor ['vaŋkl-] M Wankel engine

Wan|kel|mut M , **Wan|kel|mü|tig|keit** F **-, no pl** fickleness, inconstancy

wan|kel|mü|tig ['vaŋklmy:tɪç] ADJ fickle, inconstant

wan|ken ['vaŋkn] VI **a** (= schwanken) (Mensch, Gebäude) to sway; (Knie) to shake, to wobble; (Boden) to rock; (fig: Thron, Regierung) to totter; (= unsicher sein/werden) to waver, to falter; **nicht ~ und nicht weichen** not to move or budge an inch; **ihm wankte der Boden unter den Füßen** (fig) he is on shaky ground; **ins Wanken geraten** (lit) to begin to sway/rock; (fig) to begin to totter/waver or falter/vacillate; **etw ins Wanken bringen** (lit) to cause sth to sway/rock; (fig) Thron, Regierung to cause sth to totter; Glauben, Mut to shake sth; Moral to throw doubt upon sth; Weltbild to shake sth; **jds Entschluss ins Wanken bringen** to make sb waver in his decision
b aux sein (= gehen) to stagger; (alter Mensch) to totter

wann [van] INTERROG ADV when; **~ ist er angekommen?** when did he arrive?; **~ kommt ihr?** when or (at) what time are you coming?; **~ (auch) immer** whenever; **bis ~ ist das fertig?** when will that be ready (by)?; **bis ~ gilt der Ausweis?** until when is the pass valid?, when is the pass valid until?; **seit ~ bist/hast du ...?** (zeitlich) how long have you been/had ...?; (bezweifelnd, entrüstet etc) since when are you/do you have ...?; **von ~ an bist du in Deutschland?** from when will you be in Germany?; **von ~ bis ~?** when?, during what times?

Wan|ne ['vanə] F -, -n bath; (= Badewanne auch) (bath)tub; (= Ölwanne) reservoir; (im Auto) sump (Brit), oil pan (US)

wan|nen ['vanən] ADV (obs) **von ~** whence (liter)

Wan|nen|bad NT bath

Wanst [vanst] M -(e)s, ̈e ['vɛnstə] (Zool: = Pansen) rumen; (inf: = dicker Bauch) paunch (inf), belly (inf); **sich** (dat) **den ~ voll schlagen** (inf) to stuff oneself (inf)

Want [vant] F -, -en (Naut) shroud

Wan|ze ['vantsə] F -, -n (Zool, Comput, inf: = Abhörgerät) bug

Wap|pen ['vapn] NT -s, - coat of arms; (auf Münze) heads no art; **etw im ~ führen** to have or bear sth on one's coat of arms; (fig) to have sth as one's trademark

Wap|pen-: Wap|pen|kun|de F heraldry; **Wap|pen|schild** M OR NT pl -schilder or -schilde shield; **Wap|pen|sei|te** F heads side; **Wap|pen|tier** NT heraldic animal

wapp|nen ['vapnən] VR (fig) **sich** (gegen etw) **~** to prepare (oneself) (for sth); **gewappnet sein** to be prepared or forearmed

war pret von **sein** [1]

warb pret von **werben**

ward (old, liter) pret von **werden 1 c 2**

Wa|re ['va:rə] ● 47 F -, -n **a** product; (einzelne Ware) article; (als Sammelbegriff) goods pl, merchandise; **gute ~ hält sich** (prov) good quality goods last longer **b** **Waren** PL goods pl; (zum Verkauf auch) merchandise sing, wares pl (esp old, hum)

wä|re ['vɛ:rə] pret subjunc von **sein** [1]

Waren-: Wa|ren|an|ge|bot F range of goods for sale; **Wa|ren|an|nah|me** F (= das Annehmen) acceptance of goods; (= Annahmestelle) (goods) reception, deliveries pl (US); **Wa|ren-auf|zug** M goods hoist; **Wa|ren|aus|fuhr** F export of goods or merchandise; **Wa|ren|aus-ga|be** F (= das Ausgeben) distribution of goods; (= Ausgabestelle) collection point; **Wa-ren|aus|gang** M outgoing goods pl; **Wa|ren-aus|tausch** M exchange or (bei Tauschgeschäft) barter of goods; **Wa|ren|be|gleit-pa|pie|re** PL shipping documents pl; **Wa-ren|be|lei|hung** F loan against goods; **Wa-ren|be|stand** M stocks pl of goods or merchandise; **Wa|ren|bör|se** F commodity exchange; **Wa|ren|ein|fuhr** F import of goods or merchandise; **Wa|ren|ein|gang** M stock receipt, incoming goods pl; **Wa|ren|ex|port** M export of goods or merchandise; **Wa|ren|haus**

NT (department) store, emporium (old); **Wa|ren|im|port** M import of goods or merchandise; **Wa|ren|korb** M (Econ) basket of goods; **Wa|ren|la|ger** NT warehouse; (= Bestand) stocks pl; **Wa|ren|mus|ter** NT , **Wa|ren|pro-be** F trade sample; **Wa|ren|sen|dung** F trade sample (sent by post); **Wa|ren|sor|ti|ment** NT line of goods; **Wa|ren|ter|min|bör|se** F (St Ex) commodity futures exchange; **Wa|ren-ter|min|ge|schäft** NT (St Ex) commodity futures pl; **Wa|ren|test** M test of goods; **Wa-ren|um|satz** M turnover of goods or merchandise; **Wa|ren|um|satz|steu|er** F (Sw) value added tax, VAT; **Wa|ren|ver|kehr** M goods traffic; **Wa|ren|wirt|schafts|sys|tem** NT materials management system; **Wa|ren-zei|chen** NT trademark

warf pret von **werfen**

warm [varm] ADJ comp ̈er ['vɛrmə], superl ̈ste(r, s) ['vɛrmstə] (lit, fig) warm; Wetter auch, Getränk, Speise (auf Wasserhahn) hot; (dated inf: = homosexuell) queer (pej inf); **mir ist ~** I'm warm; **aus dem Warmen in die Kälte kommen** to come out of the warm(th) into the cold; **das hält ~** it keeps you warm; **das macht ~** it warms you up; **das Essen ~ machen** to warm or heat up the food; **das Essen ~ stellen** to keep the food hot or warm; **~e Miete** rent including heating; **nur einen ~en Händedruck bekommen** (fig inf) to get nothing for one's pains; **wie ~e Semmeln weggehen** (inf) to sell or go like hot cakes; **weder ~ noch kalt sein** (fig) to be indifferent; **~ werden** (fig inf) to thaw out (inf); **mit jdm ~ werden** (mit Stelle) to get used to sth; **mit etw ~ werden** (mit Stadt auch) to get to know sth → **Bruder, laufen, spielen**

ADV comp ̈er, superl **am ̈sten** sitzen in a warm place; schlafen in a warm room; **am Kamin sit-zen wir wärmer** we'll be warmer by the fireplace; **liegt das Baby ~ genug?** is the baby warm enough?; **~ duschen** to take a warm shower; **die Milch ~ trinken** to drink warm milk; **sich ~ anziehen** to dress up warmly; (fig inf: bei Schwierigkeiten) to prepare oneself for a rough ride; **jdn/etw wärmstens empfehlen** to recommend sb/sth warmly

Warm-: Warm|blut NT pl -blüter crossbreed; **Warm|blü|ter** [-bly:tɐ] M -s, - (Zool) warm-blooded animal; **warm|blü|tig** ADJ warm-blooded; **Warm|du|scher** [-du:ʃɐ] M -s, - (sl: = Weichling) wimp (inf), wet (inf)

Wär|me ['vɛrmə] F -, (rare) -n (lit, fig) warmth; (von Wetter etc, Phys) heat; (Wetterlage) warm weather; **10 Grad ~** 10 degrees above zero or above freezing; **an dem Gerät kann man verschiedene ~n einstellen** you can adjust the appliance to different heat settings; **ist das eine ~!** isn't it warm!; **komm in die ~** come into the warm(th); **mit ~** (fig) warmly

Wär|me-: Wär|me|be|hand|lung F (Med) heat treatment; **wär|me|be|stän|dig** ADJ heat-resistant; **Wär|me|bild|ka|me|ra** F thermal imaging camera; **Wär|me|däm|mung** F (heat) insulation; **Wär|me|ein|heit** F thermal unit, unit of heat; **Wär|me|ener|gie** F thermal energy; **Wär|me|ge|wit|ter** NT heat thunderstorm; **Wär|me|grad** M degree of heat; **Wär-me|iso|la|ti|on** F , **Wär|me|iso|lie|rung** F heat or thermal insulation; **Wär|me|kraft-werk** NT thermal power station; **Wär|me|leh|re** F theory of heat; **Wär|me|lei|ter** M heat conductor; **Wär|me|mes|ser** M -s, - thermometer

wär|men ['vɛrmən] VT to warm; Essen, Kaffee etc to warm or heat up; **das wärmt einem das Herz** it's heartwarming VI (Kleidung, Sonne) to be warm; (Ofen auch) to provide warmth; **Schnaps wärmt** schnapps warms you up VR to warm oneself (up), to warm up; **sich gegenseitig ~** to keep each other warm

Wär|me|pum|pe F heat pump

Wär|me(r) ['varmə] M decl as adj (dated inf) queer (pej inf), poof (Brit pej inf), fag (US inf)

Wärme-: Wär|me|reg|ler M thermostat; **Wär|me|schutz** M heat shield; **Wär|me|spei|cher** M storer of heat; (Gerät) heat storer or accumulator; **Wär|me|stau** M build-up of heat; (Met) greenhouse effect; **Wär|me|strah|lung** F thermal radiation, radiant heat; **Wär|me|tau|scher** [-tauʃɐ] M -s, - heat exchanger; **Wär|me|tech-nik** F heat technology; **Wär|me|ver|lust** M heat loss

Wärm|fla|sche F hot-water bottle

Warm-: Warm|front F (Met) warm front; **warm|ge|mä|ßigt** ADJ (Geog) temperate; **warm hal|ten** ▲ VT irreg **sich** (dat) **jdn ~** (fig inf) to keep in with sb (inf); **Warm|hal|te-plat|te** F hot plate; **warm|her|zig** ADJ warm-hearted; **Warm|her|zig|keit** ['varmhɛrtsɪçkait] F -, no pl warm-heartedness; **warm lau|fen** ▲ VI irreg aux sein to warm up; **Warm|luft** F warm air; **Warm|luft|zu|fuhr** F inflow or influx of warm air; (von Heizung) warm air supply; **Warm|mie|te** F rent including heating; **Warm|start** M (Aut, Comput) warm start

Warmwas|ser: Warm|was|ser|be|rei|ter [varm'vasəbəraitɐ] M -s, - water heater; **Warm-was|ser|hei|zung** F hot-water central heating; **Warm|was|ser|lei|tung** F hot-water pipe; **Warm|was|ser|spei|cher** M hot-water tank; **Warm|was|ser|ver|sor|gung** F hot-water supply

Warn-: Warn|an|la|ge F warning system; **Warn|blink|an|la|ge** F flashing warning lights pl; (an Auto) hazard (warning) lights pl; **Warn-blink|leuch|te** F flashing warning light; **Warn|blink|licht** NT flashing warning light; (an Auto) hazard warning light; **Warn|drei|eck** NT warning triangle

war|nen ['varnən] ⚙ 29.3 VTI to warn (vor +dat of); **die Polizei warnt vor Schneeglätte** the police have issued a warning of snow and ice on the roads; **jdn (davor) ~, etw zu tun** to warn sb against doing sth, to warn sb not to do sth; **vor Taschendieben wird gewarnt!** beware of pickpockets!; **ich warne dich!** I'm warning you!

Warn-: Warn|hin|weis M (= Aufdruck) warning; **Warn|kreuz** NT warning cross (before level crossing (Brit) or grade crossing (US)); **Warn-mel|dung** F warning (announcement); **Warn|ruf** M warning cry; **Warn|schild** NT pl -schilder warning sign; **Warn|schuss** ▲ M warning shot; **Warn|signal** NT warning signal; **Warn|streik** M token strike

War|nung ['varnʊŋ] F -, -en warning; **~ vor etw** (dat) warning about sth; **vor Gefahr** warning of sth

Warn-: Warn|vor|rich|tung F warning system; **Warn|zei|chen** NT warning sign; (hörbar) warning signal

War|rant ['vɔrənt] M -s, -s warrant

War|schau ['varʃau] NT -s Warsaw

War|schau|er [1] ['varʃauɐ] ADJ attr Warsaw

War|schau|er [2] ['varʃauɐ] M -s, -, **War|schau|e-rin** [-ərɪn] F -, -nen native of Warsaw; (Einwohner) inhabitant of Warsaw

War|schau|er Pakt M (Hist) Warsaw Pact

War|schau|er-Pakt-Staa|ten PL (Hist) Warsaw Pact states pl

War|te ['vartə] F -, -n observation point; (fig) standpoint, viewpoint; **von jds ~ (aus)** (fig) from sb's point of view, from sb's standpoint; **von seiner hohen ~ aus** (fig iro) from his lofty standpoint (iro)

Warte-: War|te|frist F waiting period; (für Lieferung) delivery time; **War|te|hal|le** F waiting room; (im Flughafen) departure lounge; **War|te-lis|te** F waiting list

war|ten [1] ['vartn] VI to wait (auf +acc for); **warte mal!** hold on, wait a minute; (überlegend) let me see; **na warte!** (inf) just you wait!; **warte, wenn ich das noch mal sehe!** just let me see that again; **bitte ~** (Telec) hold the line please; (Zeichen) please wait; **du wirst ~ können** you'll have to wait; **da kannst du ~, bis du schwarz**

wirst (inf) **da(rauf) kannst du lange ~** (iro) you can wait till the cows come home; **auf Antwort/Einlass ~** to wait for an answer/to be let in; **mit dem Essen auf jdn ~** to wait for sb (to come) before eating; to wait with lunch/dinner etc for sb; **ich bin gespannt, was da auf mich wartet** I wonder what's waiting for me or what awaits me or what's in store for me there; **auf sie/darauf habe ich gerade noch gewartet!** (iro) she/that was all I needed!; **lange auf sich ~ lassen** (Sache) to be a long time (in) coming; (Mensch) to take one's time; **nicht lange auf sich ~ lassen** (Sache) to be not long in coming; (Mensch) to not take long; **das lange Warten hatte ihn müde gemacht** the long wait had made him tired

war|ten² VT **a** Auto to service; Maschine to maintain, to service **b** (dated liter: = pflegen) Kinder etc to look after; Tiere to tend

Wär|ter ['vɛrtɐ] M **-s, -, Wär|te|rin** [-ərɪn] F **-, -nen** attendant; (= Leuchtturmwärter, Tierwärter) keeper; (= Krankenwärter) nurse, orderly; (= Gefängniswärter) warder (Brit), guard

War|te-: War|te|raum M waiting room; **War|te|saal** M waiting room; **War|te|schlan|ge** F queue (Brit), line (US); **War|te|schlei|fe** F (Aviat) holding pattern, stack; **~n ziehen** or **drehen** to circle; **War|te|stel|lung** F **in ~** on hold, waiting; **War|te|zeit** F waiting period; (an Grenze etc) wait; **War|te|zim|mer** NT waiting room; **War|te|zyk|lus** M (Comput) wait state

-wärts [vɛrts] ADV suf -wards; **südwärts** southwards

War|tung ['vartʊŋ] F **-, -en** (von Auto) servicing; (von Maschine auch) maintenance

War|tungs-: War|tungs|ar|bei|ten PL maintenance work no pl; **war|tungs|frei** ADJ maintenance-free; **War|tungs|kos|ten** PL maintenance costs pl; **War|tungs|ver|trag** M service contract

wa|rum [va'rʊm] INTERROG ADV why; **~ nicht?** why not?; **~ nicht gleich so!** that's better; **nach dem Warum fragen** to ask why; **das Warum und Weshalb** the whys and wherefores

War|ze ['vartsə] F **-, -n** wart; (= Brustwarze) nipple

War|zen-: War|zen|hof M (Anat) areola (spec); **War|zen|schwein** NT warthog

was [vas] INTERROG PRON **a** what; (= wie viel) how much, what; **~ kostet das?** how much is that?, what does or how much does that cost?; **~ ist** or **gibts?** what is it?, what's up?; **~ ist, kommst du mit?** well, are you coming?; **sie kommt nicht – ~?** she's not coming – what?; **~ hast du denn? – ist denn los?** what's the matter (with you)?, what's wrong?; **~ willst** or **hast du denn?** what are you talking about?; **~ denn?** (ungehalten) what (is it)?; (um Vorschlag bittend) but what?; **~ denn, bist du schon fertig?** what, are you finished already?; **das ist gut, ~?** (inf) that's good, isn't it?; **~ haben wir gelacht!** (inf) how we laughed!; **~ ist das doch schwierig** (inf) it's really difficult

b (inf: = warum) why, what ... for; **~ lachst du denn so?** what are you laughing for?, why are you laughing?

c **~ für ...** what sort or kind of ...; **~ für ein Haus hat er?** what sort or kind of (a) house does he have?; **~ für ein schönes Haus!** what a lovely house!; **und ~ für ein Haus!** and what a house!; **~ für ein Wahnsinn!** what madness!

REL PRON (auf ganzen Satz bezogen) which; **das, ~ ...** that which ..., what ...; **ich weiß, ~ ich/er tun soll** I know what I should do or what to do/what he should do; **~ auch (immer)** whatever; **das ist etwas, ~ ich nicht verstehe** that is something (which) I don't understand; **alles, ~ ...** everything or all (that) ...; **das Beste/Schönste/wenige/Einzige, ~ ich ...** the best/prettiest/little/only thing that I ...; **schreib/iss** etc **~ du kannst** (inf) write/eat etc what you can; **lauf, ~ du kannst!** (inf) run as fast as you can!; **~ du immer hast!** you do go on!

INDEF PRON (inf) abbr von **etwas** something; (fragend, bedingend auch, verneint) anything; (unbestimmter Teil einer Menge) some, any; **(na,) so ~!** well I never!; **so ~ von Blödheit** such stupidity; **er ist so ~ von doof** he's so incredibly stupid; **kann ich dir ~ helfen?** (inf) can I give you a hand?; **ist (mit dir) ~?** is something the matter (with you)? → auch **etwas, sehen**

Wasch-: wasch|ak|tiv ADJ active detergent attr, **Wasch|an|la|ge** F (für Autos) car wash; (= Scheibenwaschanlage) wipers pl; (fig inf: für Geld) laundering facility; **Wasch|an|lei|tung** F washing instructions pl; **Wasch|an|wei|sung** F washing instructions pl; **Wasch|au|to|mat** M automatic washing machine; **wasch|bar** ADJ washable; **Wasch|bär** M raccoon; **Wasch|be|cken** NT washbasin; (= Schüssel) washbowl; **Wasch|ben|zin** NT benzine; **Wasch|be|ton** M washed concrete; **Wasch|beu|tel** M sponge bag; **Wasch|brett** NT **a** washboard **b** (sl: = flachbusige Frau) **ein ~ sein** to be as flat as a pancake (Brit inf) or a board (US inf); **Wasch|brett|bauch** M washboard stomach, washboard abs pl (inf), sixpack (inf); **Wasch|büt|te** F washtub

Wä|sche ['vɛʃə] F **-, no pl a** washing; (= Schmutzwäsche, bei Wäscherei) laundry; **große/kleine ~ haben** (in Bezug auf Menge) to have a large/small amount of washing (to do); (in Bezug auf Größe der Teile) to wash the big/small things; **bei** or **in der ~ in** the wash; **in der ~ sein** to be in the wash; (= in der Wäscherei) to be at the laundry; **etw in die ~ geben** to put sth in the wash; (= in die Wäscherei) to send sth to the laundry; **jdm an die ~ gehen** (sl) to touch sb up (inf) → **schmutzig**

b (= Stoffzeug) (= Bettwäsche, Tischwäsche, Küchenwäsche) linen; (= Unterwäsche) underwear; **dumm aus der ~ gucken** (inf) to look stupid

Wä|sche|beu|tel M dirty clothes bag; (für Wäscherei) laundry bag

wasch|echt ADJ Farbe fast; Stoff auch colourfast (Brit), colorfast (US); (fig) genuine, real, pukka (Brit inf)

Wä|sche-: Wä|sche|ge|schäft NT draper's (shop); **Wä|sche|klam|mer** F clothes peg (Brit), clothes pin (US); **Wä|sche|knopf** M linen-covered button; **Wä|sche|korb** M dirty clothes basket; **Wä|sche|lei|ne** F (clothes-)line; **Wä|sche|man|gel** F mangle

wa|schen ['vaʃn] pret **wusch** [vu:ʃ], ptp **gewa|schen** [gə'vaʃn] VT to wash; Gold etc to pan; (fig inf) Geld, Spenden to launder; (**Wäsche**) ~ to do the washing; **etw** (acc) **warm/kalt ~** to wash sth in hot/cold water; **sich** (dat) **die Hände/Haare** etc **~** to wash one's hands/hair etc; **Waschen und Legen** (beim Friseur) shampoo and set

VR (Mensch/Tier) to wash (oneself/itself); (Stoff) to wash; **das hat sich gewaschen** (inf) that really made itself felt, that really had an effect; **eine Geldbuße, die sich gewaschen hat** (inf) a really heavy fine; **eine Ohrfeige, die sich gewaschen hat** (inf) a hard slap on (Brit) or in the face; **eine Klassenarbeit, die sich gewaschen hat** (inf) a real stinker of a test (inf)

Wä|sche|puff M pl **-puffe** dirty clothes basket

Wä|scher ['vɛʃɐ] M **-s, -** launderer

Wä|sche|rei [vɛʃə'raɪ] F **-, -en** laundry

Wä|sche|rin ['vɛʃərɪn] F **-, -nen** washerwoman (Brit), washwoman (US); (Berufsbezeichnung) laundress

Wä|sche-: Wä|sche|rol|le F (esp Aus) mangle; **Wä|sche|sack** M laundry bag; **Wä|sche|schleu|der** F spin-drier; **Wä|sche|schrank** M linen cupboard; **Wä|sche|spin|ne** F revolving or rotary clothes dryer; **Wä|sche|stän|der** M clotheshorse; **Wä|sche|stär|ke** F starch; **Wä|sche|stück** NT piece of laundry; **Wä|sche|tin|te** F marking ink; **Wä|sche|trock|ner** M **-s, -** (= Ständer) clotheshorse; (= Trockenautomat) drier; **Wä|sche|zei|chen** NT name tape

---

Wasch-: Wasch|fass ▲ NT washtub; **Wasch|frau** F washerwoman (Brit), washwoman (US); **Wasch|gang** M pl **-gänge** stage of the washing programme (Brit) or program (US); **Wasch|ge|le|gen|heit** F washing facilities pl; **Wasch|hand|schuh** M flannel mitt; **Wasch|haus** NT wash house, laundry; **Wasch|kes|sel** M (wash) boiler, copper; **Wasch|kü|che** F washroom, laundry; (inf: = Nebel) peasouper (Brit inf), dense fog; **Wasch|lap|pen** M flannel; (fürs Gesicht auch) face cloth (Brit), washcloth (US); (inf: = Feigling) sissy (inf), softy (inf); **Wasch|lau|ge** F suds pl; **Wasch|le|der** NT chamois leather; **Wasch|ma|schi|ne** F washing machine; **wasch|ma|schi|nen|fest** ADJ machine-washable; **Wasch|mit|tel** NT detergent; **Wasch|pul|ver** NT washing powder; **Wasch|raum** M washroom; **Wasch|rum|pel** [-rʊmpl] F **-, -n** (Aus: = Waschbrett) washboard; **Wasch|sa|lon** M laundry; (zum Selbstwaschen) laundrette (Brit), Launderette® (Brit), Laundromat® (US); **Wasch|schüs|sel** F washbowl, washbasin; **Wasch|sei|de** F washable silk; **Wasch|stra|ße** F (zur Autowäsche) car wash; **Wasch|stück** NT cleansing bar

wäscht [vɛʃt] 3. pers sing pres von **waschen**

Wasch-: Wasch|tag M washday; **~ haben** to have one's washday; **Wasch|tisch** M , **Wasch|toi|let|te** F washstand; **Wasch|trog** M washing trough

Wa|schung ['vaʃʊŋ] F **-, -en** (Rel, Med) ablution

Wasch-: Wasch|was|ser NT , no pl washing water; **Wasch|weib** NT (fig pej) washerwoman; **Wasch|zet|tel** M (Typ) blurb; **Wasch|zeug** NT , no pl toilet or washing things pl; **Wasch|zu|ber** M washtub; **Wasch|zwang** M (Psych) obsession with washing oneself

Wa|serl ['va:zɐl] NT **-s, -(n)** (Aus inf) **armes ~** poor thing

Was|ser ['vasɐ] NT **-s, - or ÷** ['vɛsɐ] **a** no pl water; **~ abstoßend, ~ abweisend** water-repellent; **bei ~ und Brot** (euph) behind bars, in prison; **das ist ~ auf seine Mühle** (fig) this is all grist to (Brit) or for his mill; **bis dahin fließt noch viel ~ den Bach** or **den Rhein** or **die Donau** etc **hinunter** a lot of water will have flowed under the bridge by then; **dort wird auch nur mit ~ gekocht** (fig) they're no different from anybody else (there); **ihr kann er nicht das ~ reichen** (fig) he can't hold a candle to her, he's not a patch on her (Brit); **~ lassen** (Med) to pass water → **Blut, Rotz a, abgraben, rein²** ADJ **a**

b pl **Wässer** (= Flüssigkeit, Abwaschwasser etc) water; (medizinisch) lotion; (= Parfüm) cologne, scent; (= Mineralwasser) mineral water; (= Schnaps) schnapps; (= Tränen) tears pl; (= Speichel) saliva; (= Schweiß) sweat; (= Urin) water, urine; (Med: in Beinen etc) fluid; (= Abwasser) sewage no pl; **~ mit Geschmack** (inf) fizzy pop (inf); **dabei läuft mir das ~ im Mund(e) zusammen** it makes my mouth water

c (= Wassermasse, im Gegensatz zu Land) water; **die ~** pl (geh) the waters pl; **etw unter ~ setzen** to flood sth; **unter ~ stehen** to be flooded, to be under water; **~ treten** (beim Schwimmen) to tread water; (Med) to paddle (in cold water as a therapy); **zu ~** on the water or (Meer) sea; (= auf dem Wasserweg) by water/sea; **ein Boot zu ~ lassen** to launch a boat; **einen Ort zu ~ erreichen** to reach a place by water; **ins ~ fallen, zu ~ werden** (fig) to fall through; **nahe ans** or **am ~ gebaut haben** (inf) to be inclined to tears, to be weepy; **ins ~ gehen** (euph) to drown oneself; **sich über ~ halten** (fig) to keep one's head above water; **er ist mit allen ~n gewaschen** he is a shrewd customer, he knows all the tricks → **Schlag a, Hals¹, abgraben**

d (= Gezeiten) tide; **das ~ läuft ab/kommt** the tide is going out/coming in → **auflaufen d**

Was|ser-: was|ser|ab|sto|ßend △, **was|ser|ab|wei|send** △ ADJ → **Wasser a**; **Was|ser|an|schluss** ▲ M mains water supply; (auf Zeltplatz) water point; **was|ser|arm** ADJ Gegend,

---

Zeitraum arid; **Wạs|ser|ar|mut** F aridity; **Wạs|-
ser|auf|be|rei|tung** F treatment of water;
Wạs|ser|auf|be|rei|tungs|an|la|ge F (waste)
water treatment plant; **Wạs|ser|bad** NT water
bath; (*Cook*) double boiler, bain-marie; **im ~**
(*Cook*) in a double boiler, in a bain-marie;
Wạs|ser|ball M **a** *no pl* (*Spiel*) water polo **b**
(*Ball*) beach ball; (*fürs Wasserballspiel*) water polo
ball; **Wạs|ser|bau** M , *no pl* hydraulic engi-
neering; **Wạs|ser|be|darf** M water require-
ments *pl*; **Wạs|ser|be|häl|ter** M water storage
tank; (*kleiner*) cistern; **Wạs|ser|bett** NT water
bed; **Wạs|ser|bla|se** F (water) blister; **Wạs|-
ser|bob** M jet ski; **~ fahren** to ride on a jet
ski; **Wạs|ser|bom|be** F (*Mil*) depth charge;
(*inf*) water bomb; **Wạs|ser|bruch** M (*Med*) hy-
drocele; **Wạs|ser|burg** F castle built in water

Wạs|ser|chen ['vɛsəçən] NT **-s, -** little stream or
brook; (= *Parfüm*) scent, perfume; (*kosmetisch*)
lotion, potion; **ein ~ machen** (*baby-talk*) to do a
wee-wee (*baby-talk*); **er sieht aus, als ob er
kein ~ trüben könnte** he looks as if butter
wouldn't melt in his mouth

Wạs|ser-: **Wạs|ser|dampf** M steam; **wạs|ser|-
dicht** ADJ (*lit, fig*) watertight; *Uhr, Stoff etc* wa-
terproof; **Wạs|ser|druck** M water pressure;
wạs|ser|durch|läs|sig ADJ permeable; **Wạs|-
ser|ei|mer** M bucket, pail; **Wạs|ser|ent|här-
ter** M water softener; **Wạs|ser|er|hit|zer**
[-lɛçhɪtsɐ] M **-s, -** water heater; **Wạs|ser|fahr|-
zeug** NT watercraft; **Wạs|ser|fall** M waterfall;
wie ein ~ reden (*inf*) to talk nineteen to the
dozen (*Brit inf*), to talk a blue streak (*US inf*);
Wạs|ser|far|be F watercolour (*Brit*), wa-
tercolor (*US*); **wạs|ser|fest** ADJ waterproof;
Wạs|ser|floh M water flea; **Wạs|ser|flug|-
zeug** NT seaplane; **Wạs|ser|frosch** M aquat-
ic frog; **Wạs|ser|gas** NT water gas; **Wạs|ser|-
ge|halt** M water content; **Wạs|ser|geist** M
water sprite; **wạs|ser|ge|kühlt** ADJ water-
-cooled; **Wạs|ser|glas** NT **a** (= *Trinkglas*) water
glass, tumbler → **Sturm a b** *no pl* (*Chem*) water
glass; **Wạs|ser|glät|te** F slippery roads *pl* due
to surface water; **Wạs|ser|gra|ben** M (*Sport*)
water jump; (*um Burg*) moat; **Wạs|ser|gym|-
nas|tik** F aqua aerobics, aquarobics *sing*;
Wạs|ser|hahn M water tap (*esp Brit*), faucet
(*US*); (= *Haupthahn*) stopcock; **wạs|ser|hal|tig**
ADJ (*Chem*) aqueous; **~ sein** to contain water;
Wạs|ser|här|te F hardness of water; **Wạs|-
ser|haus|halt** M (*Biol etc*) water balance;
Wạs|ser|ho|se F (*Met*) waterspout; **Wạs|ser|-
huhn** NT coot

wạs|se|rig ['vɛsərɪç] ADJ (*lit, fig*) watery; *Augen*
pale-coloured (*Brit*), pale-colored (*US*); (*Chem*)
aqueous; **jdm den Mund ~ machen** (*inf*) to make
sb's mouth water

Wạs|ser-: **Wạs|ser|jung|fer** F (*Zool*) dragonfly;
Wạs|ser|jung|frau F (*Myth*) naiad; **Wạs|ser|-
kan|te** F = **Waterkant**; **Wạs|ser|kes|sel** M
kettle; (*Tech*) boiler; **Wạs|ser|kis|sen** NT
(*Med*) water cushion; **Wạs|ser|klo|sett** NT
water closet (*dated*); **Wạs|ser|knapp|heit** F
water shortage; **Wạs|ser|ko|cher** M electric
kettle; **Wạs|ser|kopf** M water on the brain
no indef art, hydrocephalus *no indef art*
(*spec*); (*inf*) big head; **bürokratischer ~** (*fig*) top-
-heavy bureaucracy; **Wạs|ser|kraft** F water
power; **Wạs|ser|kraft|werk** NT hydroelectric
power station; **Wạs|ser|kreis|lauf** M water
cycle; **Wạs|ser|kres|se** F watercress; **Wạs|-
ser|küh|lung** F (*Aut*) water-cooling; **mit ~** wa-
ter-cooled; **~ haben** to be water-cooled; **Wạs|-
ser|la|che** F pool of water, puddle (of water);
Wạs|ser|las|sen NT **-s**, *no pl* (*Med*) passing wa-
ter, urination; **Wạs|ser|lauf** M watercourse;
Wạs|ser|läu|fer M (*Vogel*) shank, sandpiper;
(*Insekt*) water measurer, water skater; **dunkler ~**
spotted redshank; **Wạs|ser|lei|che** F drowned
body; **Wạs|ser|lei|tung** F (= *Rohr*) water pipe;
(= *Anlagen*) plumbing *no pl*; (*inf*: = *Hahn*) tap,
faucet (*US*); **Wạs|ser|li|lie** F water lily; **Wạs|-
ser|li|nie** F (*Naut*) water line; **Wạs|ser|loch**
NT water hole; **wạs|ser|lös|lich** ADJ water-

soluble, soluble in water; **Wạs|ser|man|gel** M
water shortage; **Wạs|ser|mann** M *pl* **-männer**
a (*Myth*) water sprite **b** (*Astrol*) Aquarius *no
art*, Water Carrier; **~ sein** to be (an) Aquarius;
Wạs|ser|mas|sen PL mass *no pl* of water, del-
uge *no pl* of water; **Wạs|ser|me|lo|ne** F wa-
termelon; **Wạs|ser|mes|ser** M **-s, -** water me-
ter; **Wạs|ser|müh|le** F water mill

wạs|sern ['vasɐn] VI (*Aviat*) to land on water *or*
(*im Meer auch*) in the sea; (*Space*) to splash
down

wäs|sern ['vɛsɐn] **VT** *Heringe, Erbsen etc* to soak;
(*Phot*) to rinse; (= *bewässern*) *Pflanzen, Felder, Rasen* to water ▶ **VI** to water; **mir ~ die Augen** my
eyes are watering

Wạs|ser-: **Wạs|ser|ni|xe** F (*Myth*) water
nymph; **Wạs|ser|ober|flä|che** F surface of
the water/lake/sea *etc*; **Wạs|ser|or|gel** F hy-
draulic organ; **Wạs|ser|pfei|fe** F hookah
(*Brit*), hubble-bubble (*Brit*), (water) bong
(*US*); **Wạs|ser|pfen|nig** M (*fig*) water sur-
charge (*to help finance water supply mea-
sures*); **Wạs|ser|pflan|ze** F aquatic plant;
Wạs|ser|pis|to|le F water pistol; **Wạs|ser|-
po|cken** PL (*Med*) chickenpox *sing*; **Wạs|-
ser|po|li|zei** F = **Wasserschutzpolizei**; **Wạs|-
ser|qua|li|tät** F water quality; **Wạs|ser|rad**
NT water wheel; **Wạs|ser|rat|te** F water rat,
water vole; (*inf*: *Kind*) water baby; **Wạs|ser|-
recht** NT *laws pertaining to water and wa-
terways*; **wạs|ser|reich** ADJ *Gebiet* with plenty
of water, abounding in water; *Fluss* containing
a lot of water; *Zeitraum* when water is/was
plentiful; **Wạs|ser|re|ser|voir** NT reservoir;
Wạs|ser|rohr NT water pipe; **Wạs|ser|rut|-
sche** F water chute; **Wạs|ser|säu|le** F water
column; **Wạs|ser|scha|den** M water damage;
Wạs|ser|schaff [-ʃaf] NT **-(e)s, -e** (*Aus*) water
tub; **Wạs|ser|schei|de** F watershed; **wạs|ser|-
scheu** ADJ scared of water; **Wạs|ser|scheu** F
fear of water; (*Psych*) water phobia; **Wạs|ser|-
schi** M, NT = **Wasserski**; **Wạs|ser|schild|krö-
te** F turtle; **Wạs|ser|schlan|ge** F **a** (*Zool*)
water snake; (*Myth*) (sea)serpent **b** (*Astron*)
Hydra; **Wạs|ser|schlauch** M **a** (water) hose;
(= *Behälter*) skin **b** (*Bot*) bladderwort; **Wạs|-
ser|schloss** ▲ NT castle surrounded by water;
Wạs|ser|schutz|ge|biet NT water reserve;
Wạs|ser|schutz|po|li|zei F (*auf Flüssen, Was-
serwegen*) river police; (*im Hafen*) harbour (*Brit*)
or harbor (*US*) police; (*auf der See*) coastguard
service; **Wạs|ser|ski** M water-ski (NT) water-
-skiing; **Wạs|ser|spei|er** M **-s, -** [-ʃpaɪɐ] gar-
goyle; **Wạs|ser|spie|gel** M (= *Oberfläche*) sur-
face of the water; (= *Wasserstand*) water level;
Wạs|ser|sport M *der* ~ water sports *pl*; **Wạs|-
ser|sport|fahr|zeug** NT water sport craft;
Wạs|ser|sport|ler(in) M(F) water sports-
man/-woman; **Wạs|ser|spü|lung** F flush; **Klo-
sett mit ~** flush toilet, water closet (*dated*);
Wạs|ser|stand M water level; **niedriger/hoher
~** low/high water; **Wạs|ser|stands|an|zei|ger**
M water level indicator; **Wạs|ser|stands|-
mel|dun|gen** PL water level *or* (*für Gezeiten*)
tide report; **Wạs|ser|stel|le** F watering place
or hole

Wạs|ser|stoff M hydrogen

Wạs|ser|stoff-: **wạs|ser|stoff|blond** ADJ *attr
Haar* peroxide blonde; **ein ~es Mädchen** a per-
oxide blonde (*inf*); **Wạs|ser|stoff|bom|be** F
hydrogen bomb, H-bomb; **Wạs|ser|stoff|su-
per|oxid** NT , **Wạs|ser|stoff|su|per|oxyd**
NT hydrogen peroxide

Wạs|ser-: **Wạs|ser|strahl** M jet of water;
Wạs|ser|stra|ße F waterway; **Wạs|ser|sucht**
F dropsy; **wạs|ser|süch|tig** ADJ suffering from
dropsy, dropsical; **Wạs|ser|tank** M water
tank; (*für WC*) cistern; **Wạs|ser|tier** NT aquatic
animal; **Wạs|ser|trä|ger(in)** M(F) water carri-
er; **Wạs|ser|tre|ten** NT **-s**, *no pl* (*Sport*) tread-
ing water; (*Med*) paddling (*in cold water as
therapy*); **Wạs|ser|trop|fen** M water drop,
drop of water; **Wạs|ser|turm** M water tower;

Wạs|ser|uhr F (= *Wasserzähler*) water meter;
(*Hist*) water clock

Wạs|se|rung ['vasərʊŋ] F **-, -en** water landing;
(*im Meer*) sea landing; (*Space*) splashdown

Wäs|se|rung ['vɛsərʊŋ] F **-, -en** (*von Fisch, Gemü-
se etc*) soaking; (*Phot*) rinsing; (= *Bewässerung*)
watering

Wạs|ser-: **Wạs|ser|ver|brauch** M water con-
sumption *no def art*; **Wạs|ser|ver|sor|gung** F
water supply; **Maßnahmen zur ~** measures to
ensure the supply of water; **Wạs|ser|ver|un|-
rei|ni|gung** F water pollution; **Wạs|ser|vo|-
gel** M waterfowl; **Wạs|ser|waa|ge** F spirit
level (*Brit*), water level gauge (*US*); **Wạs|ser|-
wacht** F water rescue service; **Wạs|ser|weg**
M waterway; **auf dem ~** by water *or* (*Meer*) sea;
Wạs|ser|wel|le F water wave; **Wạs|ser|wer|-
fer** M water cannon; **Wạs|ser|werk** NT wa-
terworks *sing or pl*; **Wạs|ser|wirt|schaft** F
water supply (and distribution); **Wạs|ser|zäh|-
ler** M water meter; **Wạs|ser|zei|chen** NT wa-
termark

wäss|rig ▲ ['vɛsrɪç] ADJ = **wässerig**

wa|ten ['vaːtn] VI *aux sein* to wade

Wa|ter|kant ['vaːtɛkant] F **-**, *no pl* coast (*esp
North Sea coast of Germany*)

Wat|sche ['vaːtʃə] F **-n, -n** (*S Ger inf*) slap (on *or*
round (*Brit*) the face); (*als Strafe*) clip round
the ear (*Brit*), smack on the ear

wat|sche|lig ['vaːtʃəlɪç, 'vat-] ADJ waddling *attr*
ADV to waddle

wat|scheln ['vaːtʃln, 'vat-] VI *aux sein* to waddle

wat|schen ['vaːtʃn, 'vat-] VT (*S Ger, inf*) **jdm ei-
ne ~** (*auf Backe*) to slap sb's face; (*ans Ohr*) to
give sb a clip round (*Brit*) *or* smack on the ear;
eine gewatscht kriegen to get a slap in the
face/clip round (*Brit*) *or* smack on the ear

Wat|schen ['vaːtʃn, 'vat-] F **-, -** (*Aus, S Ger. inf*) =
Ohrfeige

Wat|schen|mann M *pl* **-männer** (*Aus*) (*lit*) *fair-
ground dummy* (*fig*) Aunt Sally (*Brit fig*),
punching bag (*US fig*)

Wat|stie|fel ['vaːt-] M wader

Watt¹ [vat] NT **-s, -** (*Elec*) watt

Watt² NT **-(e)s, -en** (*Geog*) mud flats *pl*

Wat|te ['vatə] F **-, -n** cotton wool (*Brit*), cotton
(*US*); (*zur Polsterung*) padding, wadding; **jdn in
~ packen** (*fig inf*) to wrap sb in cotton wool
(*Brit*), to molly-coddle sb; **lass dich doch in ~
packen!** you're far too over-sensitive!

Wat|te|bausch M cotton-wool (*Brit*) *or* cotton
(*US*) ball

Wat|ten|meer NT mud flats *pl*

Wat|te-: **Wat|te|pad** [-ped] M **-s, -s** cotton
(-wool (*Brit*)) pad; **Wat|te|stäb|chen** NT cot-
ton bud

wat|tie|ren [va'tiːrən] *ptp* **wattiert** VT to pad; (=
füttern) to line with padding; (*und absteppen*)
Stoff, Steppdecke to quilt; **wattierte Umschläge**
padded envelopes; **wattierte Jacken** quilted
jackets

Wat|tie|rung F **-, -en** padding

Watt-: **Watt|me|ter** NT wattmeter; **Watt|se|-
kun|de** F watt-second; **Watt|stun|de** F watt-
-hour; **Watt|zahl** F wattage

Wat|vo|gel ['vaːt-] M wader (*Brit*), wading bird

wau wau ['vau 'vau, vau 'vau, 'vau vau] INTERJ
bow-wow, woof-woof

Wau|wau ['vauvau, vau'vau] M **-s, -s** (*baby-talk*)
bow-wow (*baby-talk*)

WC [veː'tseː] NT **-s, -s** WC

WC-: **WC-Bürs|te** [veː'tseː-] F toilet brush, loo
brush (*inf*); **WC-Rei|ni|ger** [veː'tseː-] M (= *Rei-
nigungsmittel*) toilet cleaner

WDR [veːdeː'ʔɛr] M **-** *abbr von* **Westdeutscher
Rundfunk**

Web [wɛb] NT **-(s)**, *no pl* Web; **im ~** on the Web

We|be ['veːbə] F **-, -n** (*Aus*) linen

We|be|kan|te F selvage, selvedge

we|ben ['ve:bn] *pret* **webte** *or* (*liter, fig*) **wob** ['ve:ptə, vo:p], *ptp* **gewebt** *or* (*liter, fig*) **gewoben** [gə've:pt, gə'vo:bn] VTI (*lit, fig*) to weave; *Spinnennetz, Lügennetz* to spin

We|ber ['ve:bɐ] M **-s, -**, **We|be|rin** [-ərɪn] F **-, -nen** weaver

We|be|rei [ve:bə'raɪ] F **-, -en** **a** *no pl* (= *das Weben*) weaving **b** (= *Betrieb*) weaving mill **c** (= *Zeug*) woven article

We|ber-: We|ber|kamm M weaver's reed; **We|ber|knecht** M (*Zool*) daddy-longlegs (*Brit*), crane fly; **We|ber|kno|ten** M reef knot; **We|ber|schiff|chen** NT shuttle

Web-: Web|feh|ler M weaving flaw; **einen ~ haben** (*fig inf*) to have a screw loose (*inf*); **Web|garn** NT weaving yarn; **Web|kan|te** F selvage, selvedge (*Brit*)

Web|sei|te ['vɛb-] F Web page

Web|stuhl M loom

Web|wa|ren PL woven goods *pl*

Wech|sel ['vɛksl] M **-s, -** **a** (= *Änderung*) change; (*abwechselnd*) alternation; (= *Geldwechsel*) exchange; (*der Jahreszeiten, Agr.* = *Fruchtwechsel*) rotation; **ein ~ der Wohnung/Schule** *etc* a change of address/school *etc*; **der ~ von Tag und Nacht** the alternation of day and night; **im ~ der Zeiten** through the ages; **in buntem ~** in motley succession; **im ~** (= *abwechselnd*) in turn, alternately **b** (*Sport*) (= *Staffelwechsel*) (baton) change, changeover; (*Ftbl etc*) substitution **c** (*Fin*) bill (of exchange); (*inf:* = *Geldzuwendung*) allowance **d** (*Hunt*) trail used by game *or* by wild animals

Wech|sel-: Wech|sel|bad NT alternating hot and cold baths *pl*; **~ der Gefühle** (*fig*) emotional roller coaster; **jdn einem ~ aussetzen** (*fig*) to blow hot and cold with sb; **Wech|sel|balg** M changeling (child); (*inf*) little monster (*inf*); **Wech|sel|bank** F *pl* **-banken** (*Fin*) discount house; **Wech|sel|be|zie|hung** F correlation, interrelation; **in ~ miteinander** *or* **zueinander stehen** to be correlated *or* interrelated; **Wech|sel|bürg|schaft** F guarantee (on a bill); **Wech|sel|fäl|le** PL vicissitudes *pl*; **Wech|sel|fie|ber** NT (*old*) malaria; **Wech|sel|frist** F (*Fin*) usance; **Wech|sel|geld** NT change; **Wech|sel|ge|sang** M antiphonal singing; **Wech|sel|ge|spräch** NT dialogue (*Brit*), dialog (*US*); **Wech|sel|ge|trie|be** NT (*Tech*) variable gears *pl*; **wech|sel|haft** ADJ changeable; *Schicksal, Mensch auch* fickle, capricious ADV **~ verlaufen** to be changeable; **Wech|sel|haf|tig|keit** F changeability; (*von Schicksal, Mensch auch*) fickleness, capriciousness; **Wech|sel|jah|re** PL menopause *sing*, change of life *sing*; **in die ~ kommen** to start the menopause; **in den ~n sein** to be suffering from the menopause; **Wech|sel|kurs** M rate of exchange

wech|seln ['vɛksln] VT to change (*in +acc* into); (= *austauschen*) to exchange; (*Ftbl etc*) to substitute (*gegen* for); **den Arzt ~** to change doctors *or* one's doctor; **den Tisch/die Schule/das Hemd ~** to change tables/schools/one's shirt; **die Farbe ~** to change colour (*Brit*) *or* color (*US*); **den Platz mit jdm ~** to exchange one's seat with sb; **Briefe ~** to correspond *or* be in correspondence (*mit* with); **die Wohnung ~** to move house (*Brit*); to move; **den Wohnsitz ~** to move to another place; **können Sie (mir) 10 Euro ~?** can you change 10 euros (for me)?; **Wäsche zum Wechseln** a change of underwear VI **a** to change; (*Sport*) to change (over); (= *einander ablösen*) to alternate; **ich kann Ihnen leider nicht ~** I'm sorry, I don't have any change **b** (*Hunt*) to pass by; **über die Grenze ~** (*Mensch*) to cross the border

wech|selnd ['vɛkslnt] ADJ changing; (= *einander ablösend, abwechselnd*) alternating; *Launen, Stimmungen* changeable; *Winde* variable; *Bewölkung* variable, intermittent; **mit ~em Erfolg** with varying (degrees of) success; **~e Mehrheiten** (*Parl*) majorities formed by parties voting together

according to particular issues ADV alternately; **~ bewölkt** cloudy with sunny intervals

Wech|sel-: Wech|sel|neh|mer(in) M(F) payee of a bill; **Wech|sel|plat|te** F (*Comput*) removable disk; **Wech|sel|pro|test** M protest of a bill; **Wech|sel|rah|men** M clip-on picture frame; **Wech|sel|recht** NT law relating to bills of exchange; **Wech|sel|schal|ter** M **a** (*Elec*) changeover switch **b** (*in Bank*) counter for foreign currency exchange; **Wech|sel|schuld|ner(in)** M(F) payer of a bill; **wech|sel|sei|tig** [-zaɪtɪç] ADJ reciprocal; (= *gegenseitig auch*) mutual ADV reciprocally; *sich beschimpfen, sich hassen* one another; **Wech|sel|spiel** NT interplay; **wech|sel|stän|dig** ADJ (*Bot*) alternate; **Wech|sel|strom** M alternating current; **Wech|sel|stu|be** F bureau de change (*Brit*), exchange; **Wech|sel|tier|chen** NT amoeba; **wech|sel|voll** ADJ varied; **Wech|sel|wäh|ler(in)** M(F) floating voter; **wech|sel|wei|se** ADV in turn, alternately; **Wech|sel|wir|kung** F interaction; **in ~ stehen** to interact

Wechs|ler¹ ['vɛkslɐ] M **-s, -** (= *Automat*) change machine, change dispenser

Wechs|ler² ['vɛkslɐ] M **-s, -**, **Wechs|le|rin** [-ərɪn] F **-, -nen** (= *Geldwechsler*) moneychanger

Weck [vɛk] M **-(e)s, -e** (*dial*) (bread) roll; (*Aus:* = *Brot*) loaf

Weck- ['vɛk-]: **Weck|ap|pa|rat** M preserving and bottling equipment; **Weck|dienst** M (*Telec*) alarm call service, wake-up service, early morning call service; (*Mil*) reveille; **~ machen** to do reveille

We|cke ['vɛkə] F **-, -n** (*dial*) (bread) roll

we|cken ['vɛkn] VT to wake (up), to waken; (*fig*) to arouse; *Bedarf* to create; *Erinnerungen* to bring back, to revive; **sich ~ lassen** to have sb wake one up; (*telefonisch*) to get an alarm call

We|cken¹ ['vɛkn] NT **-s**, *no pl* waking-up time; (*Mil*) reveille; **Ausgang bis zum ~** overnight leave (until reveille)

We|cken² M **-s, -** (*dial*) (bread) roll

We|cker ['vɛkɐ] M **-s, -** alarm clock; **jdm auf den ~ fallen** *or* **gehen** (*inf*) to get on sb's wick (*Brit inf*) *or* nerves, to drive sb up the wall (*inf*)

Weck- ['vɛk-]: **Weck|glas®** NT preserving *or* Kilner® (*Brit*) jar; **Weck|ring®** M rubber ring (*for preserving jars*); **Weck|ruf** M (*Telec*) wake-up call; (*Mil*) reveille; **Weck|uhr** F alarm clock

We|del ['ve:dl] M **-s, -** fly whisk; (= *Fächer*) fan; (= *Staubwedel aus Federn*) feather duster; (*zum Besprengen*) sprinkler; (= *Zweig*) twig; (*Eccl*) ≈ palm leaf; (*Bot:* = *Blatt*) frond; (*Hunt*) tail

we|deln ['ve:dln] VI **a** (**mit dem Schwanz**) **~** (*Hund*) to wag its tail; **mit etw ~** (= *winken*) to wave sth; **mit dem Fächer ~** to wave the fan **b** (*Ski*) to wedel; **das Wedeln** wedel(l)ing VT to waft

we|der ['ve:dɐ] CONJ **~ ... noch ...** neither ... nor ...; **er ist ~ gekommen, noch hat er angerufen** he neither came nor phoned (up); **~ das eine noch das andere** (*als Antwort*) neither

weg [vɛk] ADV (= *fort*) **~ sein** (= *fortgegangen, abgefahren, verschwunden*) to have *or* be gone; (= *nicht hier, entfernt*) to be away; (*inf*) (= *geistesabwesend*) to be not quite with it (*inf*); (= *eingeschlafen*) to have dozed off; (= *tot*) to be dead; (= *begeistert*) to be really taken, to be bowled over (*von* by); **von zu Hause ~ sein** to be away from home; (*erwachsene Kinder*) to have left home; **über etw** (*acc*) **~ sein** (*inf*) to have got over sth; **er ist schon lange darüber ~** (*inf*) he got over it a long while ago; **über den Tisch ~** across the table; **über meinen Kopf ~** over my head; **weit ~ von hier** far (away) from here; **~ (von hier)!** get away from here!; let's get away from here; **~ mit euch!** away with you!, scram! (*inf*); **nichts wie** *or* **nur ~ von hier!** let's scram (*inf*); **~ da!** (get) out of the way!; **~ damit!** (*mit Schere etc*) put it away!; **immer ~ damit** throw *or*

chuck (*inf*) it all out; **~ mit den alten Traditionen!** away with these old traditions!; **Hände ~!** hands off!; **in einem ~** (*inf*) non-stop

Weg [ve:k] M **-(e)s, -e** [-gə] **a** (= *Pfad, Gehweg, fig*) path; (= *Waldweg, Wanderweg etc*) track, path; (= *Straße*) road; **am ~e** by the wayside; **woher des ~(e)s?** (*old*) where have you come from?, whence comest thou? (*obs*); **wohin des ~(e)s?** (*old*) where are you going to?, whither goest thou? (*obs*); **des ~(e)s kommen** (*old*) to come walking/riding *etc* up; **in einer Gegend ~ und Steg kennen** to know an area like the back of one's hand; **jdm in den ~ treten, jdm den ~ versperren** *or* **verstellen** to block *or* bar sb's way; **jdm/einer Sache im ~ stehen** (*fig*) to stand in the way of sb/sth; **sich selbst im ~ stehen** (*fig*) to be one's own worst enemy; **jdm Hindernisse** *or* **Steine in den ~ legen** (*fig*) to put obstructions in sb's way; **jdm nicht über den ~ trauen** (*fig*) not to trust sb an inch; **jdn aus dem ~ räumen** (*fig*) to get rid of sb; **etw aus dem ~ räumen** (*fig*) to remove sth; *Missverständnisse* to clear sth up; **neue ~e beschreiten** (*fig*) to tread new paths; **den ~ der Sünde/Tugend gehen** to follow the path of sin/virtue; **die ~e Gottes** the ways of the Lord; **den ~ des geringsten Widerstandes gehen** to follow the line of least resistance; **der ~ zur Hölle ist mit guten Vorsätzen gepflastert** (*Prov*) the road to Hell is paved with good intentions (*prov*) → **irdisch**
b (*lit, fig:* = *Route*) way; (= *Entfernung*) distance; (= *Reise*) journey; (*zu Fuß*) walk; (*fig: zum Erfolg*) way, road; (= *Bildungsweg*) road; **ich muss diesen ~ jeden Tag zweimal gehen/fahren** I have to walk/drive this stretch twice a day; **auf dem ~ nach London/zur Arbeit** on the way to London/work; **auf dem ~ zu jdm/nach einem Ort sein** to be on the *or* one's way to sb's/a place; **sich auf den ~ machen** to set off; **6 km ~** ≈ 6 kms away; **noch zwei Stunden/ein Stück ~ vor sich haben** to still have two hours/some distance to travel; **jdn ein Stück ~(es) begleiten** (*geh*) to accompany sb part of the way; **mein erster ~ war zur Bank** the first thing I did was go to the bank; **jdn auf seinem letzten ~ begleiten** (*euph*) to pay one's last respects to sb; **seiner ~e gehen** (*geh*) (*lit*) to go on one's way; (*fig*) to go one's own way; **welchen ~ haben sie eingeschlagen?** (*lit*) what road did they take?; **einen neuen ~ einschlagen** (*fig*) to follow a new avenue; (*beruflich*) to follow a new career; **den falschen/richtigen ~ einschlagen** to follow the wrong/right path *or* road *or* (*fig*) avenue; **jdm etw mit auf den ~ geben** (*lit*) to give sb sth to take with him/her *etc*; **jdm einen guten Rat mit auf den ~ geben** to give sb good advice to follow in life; **jdm/einer Sache aus dem ~ gehen** (*lit*) to get out of sb's way/the way of sth; (*fig*) to avoid sb/sth; **jdm über den ~ laufen** (*fig*) to run into sb; **seinen ~ (im Leben/Beruf) machen** (*fig*) to make one's way in life/one's career; **seinen ~ nehmen** (*fig*) to take its course; **etw in die ~e leiten** to arrange sth; **etw auf den ~ bringen** to get sth under way; **jdm/sich den ~ verbauen** to ruin sb's/one's chances *or* prospects (*für* of); **auf dem besten ~ sein, etw zu tun** to be well on the way to doing sth; **der gerade ~ ist der kürzeste** *or* **beste** (*Prov*) honesty is the best policy
c (= *Mittel, Art und Weise*) way; (= *Methode*) method; **auf welchem ~ kommt man am schnellsten zu Geld?** what's the fastest way of making *or* to make money?; **auf welchem ~ sind Sie zu erreichen?** how can I get in touch with you?; **auf diesem ~e** this way; **auf diplomatischem ~e** through diplomatic channels; **auf gesetzlichem** *or* **legalem ~** legally, by legal means; **auf künstlichem ~e** artificially, by artificial means; **zu ~e** = **zuwege**
d (*inf:* = *Besorgung*) errand

weg+ar|bei|ten ['vɛk-] VT *sep* (*inf*) **alles ~** to get through all one's work; **nicht viel ~** not to get much work done

---

+ separable verbs | German spelling reform (see supplement): ▲ new spelling △ old spelling

Weg|be|glei|ter(in) ['veːk-] M(F) *(fig)* companion

weg+be|kom|men ['vɛk-] *ptp* **wegbekommen** VT *sep irreg* **a** (= *entfernen, loswerden*) to get rid of (*von* from); *Klebstoff, Fleck etc* to remove (*von* from), to get off; (*von bestimmtem Ort*) *jdn, Hund* to get away (*von* from) **b** (*inf:* = *erhalten*) to get; *Grippe* to catch → **Fett**

Weg-: **Weg|be|rei|ter** ['veːkbəraitɐ] M **-s, -**, **Weg|be|rei|te|rin** [-ərɪn] F **-, -nen** precursor, forerunner; **~ einer Sache** (*gen*) **or für etw sein** to pave the way for sth; **~ für jdn sein** to prepare the way for sb; **Weg|bie|gung** F turn, bend

weg- ['vɛk-]: **weg+bla|sen** VT *sep irreg* to blow away; **wie weggeblasen sein** *(fig)* to have vanished; **weg+blei|ben** VI *sep irreg aux sein* to stay away; (= *nicht mehr kommen*) to stop coming; (*Satz, Wort etc*) to be left out or omitted; **mir blieb die Luft or Puste** (*inf*) **weg** (*lit*) I couldn't breathe; **mir bleibt die Spucke or Luft weg!** (*inf*) I'm absolutely speechless or flabbergasted!; **sein Wegbleiben** his absence; **weg+brin|gen** VT *sep irreg* to take away; (*zur Reparatur*) to take in; (*inf:* = *wegbekommen*) to get rid of; **weg+den|ken** VT *sep irreg* **sich** (*dat*) **etw ~** to imagine or picture things *etc* without sth; **die Elektrizität ist aus unserem modernen Leben nicht mehr wegzudenken** we cannot imagine life today without electricity; **weg+dis|ku|tie|ren** *ptp* **wegdiskutiert** VT *sep* to explain away; **dieses Problem lässt sich nicht ~** talking about it won't make the problem go away; **weg+dür|fen** VI *sep irreg* to be allowed to go or leave; (*inf:* = *ausgehen dürfen*) to be allowed to go out

We|ge|geld ['veːgə-] NT *(Hist)* (road) toll

weg+ekeln ['vɛk-] VT *sep* (*inf*) to drive away

We|ge|la|ge|rer ['veːgəlaːgərɐ] M **-s, -** highwayman; (*zu Fuß*) footpad (*old Brit*), highwayman

we|gen ['veːgn] Ⓓ 44.1 PREP *+gen or* (*inf*) *+dat* because of, on account of; (= *infolge auch*) due to; **jdn ~ einer Sache bestrafen/verurteilen/entlassen** *etc* to punish/sentence/dismiss *etc* sb for sth; **von ~!** (*inf*) you've got to be kidding! (*inf*); (*Verbot auch*) no way! (*inf*), no chance! (*inf*); **aber von ~!** (*inf*) ... but not a bit of it! (*inf*); **er ist krank – von ~ krank!** (*inf*) he's ill – since when? (*iro*) or what do you mean "ill"? (*iro*); **~ mir** (*inf*) or **meiner** (*obs*) → **meinetwegen** → **Amt a**, **Recht a**

We|ge|rich ['veːgərɪç] M **-s, -e** *(Bot)* plantain

weg+es|sen ['vɛk-] VT *sep irreg* **jdm den Kuchen** *etc* **~** to eat sb's cake *etc*; **er hat (mir) alles weggegessen** he's eaten all my food

weg+fah|ren ['vɛk-] *sep irreg* VI aux sein (= *abfahren*) to leave; (*Auto, Bus, Fahrer*) to drive off or away; (*im Boot*) to sail away; (*zum Einkaufen, als Ausflug*) to go out; (= *verreisen*) to go away VT *Menschen, Gegenstände* to take away; *Fahrzeug* to drive away; (= *umstellen*) to move

Weg|fahr|sper|re ['vɛk-] F *(Aut)* **(elektronische)** (electronic) immobilizer

Weg|fall ['vɛk-] M , *no pl* (= *Einstellung*) discontinuation; (*von Kontrollen*) removal; (= *Aufhören*) cessation (*form*); (= *Streichung*) cancellation; (= *Unterbleiben*) loss; (= *Auslassung*) omission; **in ~ kommen** (*Bestimmung*) to be discontinued; (*Bestimmung*) to cease to apply

weg+fal|len ['vɛk-] VI *sep irreg aux sein* to be discontinued; (*Arbeitsplätze*) to be lost; (*Kontrollen*) to be removed; (*Bestimmung, Regelung*) to cease to apply; (= *unterbleiben*) to be lost; (= *überflüssig werden*) to become no longer necessary; (= *ausgelassen werden*) to be omitted; **~ lassen** to discontinue; (= *auslassen*) to omit; **wir haben den Nachtisch ~ lassen** we did without dessert, we dispensed with dessert

weg- ['vɛk-]: **weg+fe|gen** VT *sep* (*lit, fig*) to sweep away; **weg+fi|schen** VT *sep* (*fig inf*) to snap up; **er hat uns alle Forellen weggefischt** he's caught all our trout; **weg+flie-**

gen VI *sep irreg aux sein* to fly away or off; (*Hut*) to fly off; (*mit Flugzeug*) to fly out; **wann bist du denn in Frankfurt weggeflogen?** when did you fly out of Frankfurt?; **weg+fres|sen** VT *sep* (*inf*) → **wegessen**; **weg+füh|ren** *sep* VT to lead away VI **das führt zu weit (vom Thema) weg** that will lead or take us too far off the subject

Weg|ga|be|lung ['veːk-] F fork (in the road), bifurcation (*form*)

Weg|gang ['vɛkgaŋ] M , *no pl* departure, leaving

weg+ge|ben ['vɛk-] VT *sep irreg* (= *verschenken*) to give away; (= *in Pflege geben*) to have looked after; **eine kaputte Uhr ~** to take in a broken watch; **seine Wäsche (zum Waschen) ~** to have one's washing done

Weg|ge|fähr|te ['veːk-] M , **Weg|ge|fähr|tin** F *(fig)* companion

weg+ge|hen ['vɛk-] VI *sep irreg aux sein* to go, to leave; (= *verreisen, umziehen etc*) to go away; (= *ausgehen*) to go out; (*inf*) (*Fleck*) to come off; (*Ware*) to sell; **über etw** (*acc*) **~** (*inf*) to ignore sth, to pass over sth; **aus Heidelberg/aus dem Büro/von der Firma/von zu Hause ~** to leave Heidelberg/the office/the firm/home; **geh mir damit weg!** (*inf*) don't give me that! (*inf*); **geh mir mit dem weg!** (*inf*) don't talk to me about him!

Weg|ge|nos|se ['veːk-] M , **Weg|ge|nos|sin** F (*lit, fig*) companion

Weg|gli ['vɛkli] NT **-s, -** (*Sw*) (bread) roll

weg+gu|cken ['vɛk-] *sep* VI to look away VT **es wird dir schon niemand was ~!** (*hum*) we/they *etc* won't be seeing anything we/they *etc* haven't seen before (*hum*)

weg+ha|ben ['vɛk-] VT *sep irreg* (*inf*) (= *erledigt haben*) to have got done; (= *bekommen, verstanden haben*) to have got; (= *entfernt haben*) *Fleck etc* to have got rid of (*inf*); (= *umstellen, umhängen*) *Tisch, Gegenstand* to have moved; **jdn/etw ~ wollen** (*inf*) to want to get rid of sb/sth; **der hat was weg** (*inf*) he's really clever; **darin hat er was weg** (*inf*) he's pretty good at that; **du hast deine Strafe/deinen Denkzettel weg** you have had your punishment; **einen ~** (*inf*) (= *verrückt sein*) to be off one's head (*inf*), to have a screw loose (*inf*) → **Fett**, **Ruhe d**, **Teil¹ c**

weg- ['vɛk-]: **weg+hel|fen** VI *sep irreg* **jdm von irgendwo ~** to help sb get away from or out of (*inf*) a place; **jdm über etw** (*acc*) **~** (*fig*) to help sb (to) get over sth; **weg+ho|len** VT *sep* to take away; (= *abholen*) to fetch; **sich** (*dat*) **was/eine Krankheit ~** (*inf*) to catch something/a disease; **weg+hö|ren** VI *sep irreg* not to listen; **weg+ja|gen** VT *sep* to chase away, to drive away or off; *Menschen auch* to send packing (*inf*); (*aus Land*) to drive out; **weg+kna|cken** VI *sep* (*sl:* = *einschlafen*) to crash (out) (*inf*)

weg+kom|men ['vɛk-] VI *sep irreg aux sein* **a** (= *entfernt werden*) to go; (= *abhanden kommen*) to disappear; (= *weggehen können*) to get away; (*aus dem Haus*) to get out; **was ich nicht brauche, kommt weg** what I don't want can go; **das Buch ist mir weggekommen** the book has disappeared, I've lost the book; **mach, dass du wegkommst!** make yourself scarce! (*inf*), hop it! (*inf*); **gut/schlecht (bei etw) ~** to come off well/badly (with sth); **über etw** (*acc*) **-/nicht ~** to get over/be unable to get over sth; **ich komme nicht darüber weg, dass ...** (*inf*) I can't get over the fact that ... **b** (*dial:* = *herkommen*) to come from

Weg- ['veːk-]: **Weg|kreuz** NT **a** (= *Kruzifix*) wayside cross **b** (= *Kreuzung*) crossroads; **Weg|kreu|zung** F crossroads

weg+krie|gen ['vɛk-] VT *sep* (*inf*) → **wegbekommen a**

Weg|krüm|mung ['veːk-] F bend in the road

weg- ['vɛk-]: **weg+las|sen** VT *sep irreg* (= *auslassen*) to leave out; (= *nicht benutzen*) to leave out; (*inf:* = *gehen lassen*) to let go; **ich lasse heute den Zucker im Kaffee weg** I won't have (*Brit*)

or take any sugar in my coffee today; **weg+lau|fen** VI *sep irreg aux sein* to run away (*vor +dat* from); **seine Frau ist ihm weggelaufen** his wife has run away (from him), his wife has run off (and left him); **das läuft (dir) nicht weg!** (*fig hum*) that can wait; **weg+le|gen** VT *sep* (*in Schublade etc*) to put away; (*zur Seite, zum späteren Verbrauch*) to put aside; **weg+leug|nen** VT *sep* to deny; **weg+lo|ben** VT *sep* = **fortloben**

weg+ma|chen ['vɛk-] *sep* VT (*inf*) to get rid of; **sie ließ sich** (*dat*) **das Kind ~** (*sl*) she got rid of the baby (*inf*) VI *aux sein or haben* (*dial, inf*) to get away (*von* from), to get out (*aus of*)

weg+müs|sen ['vɛk-] VI *sep irreg* to have to go; (= *weggehen müssen auch*) to have to leave or to be off (*inf*); (= *entfernt werden*) to have to be removed; **ich muss eine Zeit lang von/aus New York weg** I must get away from/get out of New York for a while; **du musst da weg, du behinderst ja den ganzen Verkehr** you'll have to move (from there), you're blocking all the traffic; **die paar Reste müssen weg** we/you *etc* can't leave those little bits; **wenn wir die Wand streichen wollen, muss das Sofa weg** if we're going to paint the wall, we'll have to move the sofa (out of the way)

Weg|nah|me ['vɛknaːmə] F **-**, *no pl* taking; (= *Entziehung*) taking away; (*von Sicht*) blocking

weg+neh|men ['vɛk-] VT *sep irreg* to take (*auch Chess*); (= *fortnehmen, entfernen, entziehen*) to take away; (= *absorbieren*) *Strahlen, Licht, Lärm* to absorb; (= *verdecken*) *Licht, Sonne* to block out; *Aussicht, Sicht* to block; (= *beanspruchen*) *Zeit, Platz* to take up; **Gas ~** (*Aut*) to ease off the accelerator or gas (*US*); **fünf Tage vom Urlaub ~** to take five days off the holiday (*esp Brit*) or vacation (*US*); **die Bässe ~** to turn down or reduce the bass; **jdm seine Kinder ~** to take sb's children away (from him/her); **jdm seine Frau ~** to steal sb's wife

weg- ['vɛk-]: **weg+pa|cken** VT *sep* to pack or put away; (*inf:* = *essen*) to put away (*inf*); **weg+put|zen** VT *sep* to wipe away or off; (*inf:* = *essen*) to polish off; **er putzt ganz schön was weg** (*inf*) he doesn't half eat a lot or stow a lot away (*Brit inf*), he can put a lot away (*inf*); **weg+raf|fen** VT *sep* to snatch away; (*liter: durch Tod*) to carry off

Weg|rand ['veːk-] M wayside, side of the path or (*von Straße*) road

weg- ['vɛk-]: **weg+ra|sie|ren** *ptp* **wegrasiert** VT *sep* to shave off; **er hat mir den vorderen Kotflügel wegrasiert** he took my front mudguard with him (*hum*); **weg+ra|tio|na|li|sie|ren** *ptp* **wegrationalisiert** VT *sep Arbeitsplätze* to rationalize away; **weg+räu|men** VT *sep* to clear away; (*in Schrank*) to put away; **weg+rei|ßen** VT *sep irreg* to tear away (*jdm* from sb); *Zweige* to break off; (*inf*) *Häuser etc* to tear or pull down; **der Fluss hat die Brücke weggerissen** the river swept away the bridge; **weg+ren|nen** VI *sep irreg aux sein* (*inf*) to run away; **weg+re|tu|schie|ren** *ptp* **wegretuschiert** VT *sep* to spot out; **weg+rü|cken** VTI *sep* (*vi: aux sein*) to move away; **weg+ru|fen** VT *sep irreg* to call away; **weg+rut|schen** VI *sep aux sein* (*aus der Hand etc*) to slip away; (*auf Eis etc*) to slide away; **mein Wagen ist mir weggerutscht** my car went into a skid; **weg+sa|cken** VI *sep aux sein* (*inf*) **a** (*Schiff*) to sink; (*Flugzeug*) to (suddenly) drop, to lose height **b** (= *zusammenbrechen*) to give way

weg|sam ['veːkzaːm] ADJ (*obs*) passable

weg- ['vɛk-]: **weg+schaf|fen** VT *sep* (= *beseitigen, loswerden*) to get rid of; (= *wegräumen*) to clear away; (= *wegtragen, wegfahren*) to remove, to cart away (*inf*); (= *erledigen*) *Arbeit* to get done; **weg+schau|en** VI *sep* (*esp dial*) = **wegsehen**

Weg|schei|de ['veːk-] F parting of the ways (*liter*)

weg- ['vɛk-]: **weg+schen|ken** VT *sep* (*inf*) to give away; **weg+sche|ren** VR *sep* (*inf*) to clear out (*inf*), to shove off (*inf*); **weg+schi|cken**

VT *sep Brief etc* to send off *or* away; *jdn* to send away; (*um etwas zu holen etc*) to send off; **weg+schie|ben** VT *sep irreg* to push away; (= *beiseite schieben: Teller etc*) to push aside; **weg+schie|ßen** VT *sep irreg* **jdm den Arm** *etc* ~ to shoot sb's arm *etc* off; **weg+schlaf|fen** VT *sep aux sein* (*sl*) to peg or poop out (*inf*); **er schlaffte ihm immer wieder weg** it kept on going limp on him (*inf*); **weg+schlei|chen** VIR *sep irreg* (*vi: aux sein*) to creep or steal away; **weg+schlep|pen** *sep* VT to drag or lug (*inf*) or haul away or off; (= *tragen*) to carry off VR to drag or haul oneself away; **weg+schlie|ßen** VT *sep irreg* to lock away; **weg+schmei|ßen** VT *sep irreg* (*inf*) to chuck away (*inf*); **weg+schnap|pen** VT *sep* (*inf*) **jdm etw** ~ to snatch sth (away) from sb; **die andere Kundin hat mir das Kleid weggeschnappt** the other customer snapped up the dress before I could; **jdm die Freundin/den Job** ~ to pinch (*Brit*) or snatch (*US*) sb's girlfriend/job (*inf*)

Weg|schne|cke ['ve:k-] F slug (*of the genus Arionidae*)

weg- ['vɛk-]: **weg+schüt|ten** VT *sep* to tip away; **weg+schwem|men** VT *sep* to wash away; **weg+se|hen** VI *sep irreg* to look away; **über etw** (*acc*) ~ (*lit*) to look over sth; (*fig inf*) to o-verlook sth, to turn a blind eye to sth

weg+set|zen ['vɛk-] *sep* VT to move (away); (= *wegstellen*) to put away VR to move away; **sich über etw** (*acc*) ~ (*inf*) to ignore sth, to pay no attention to sth VI *aux sein or haben* **über etw** (*acc*) ~ to leap or jump over sth, to clear sth

weg- ['vɛk-]: **weg+sol|len** VI *sep irreg* (*inf*) **das soll weg** that is to go; **ich soll von London weg** I should leave London; **warum soll ich/mein Auto da weg?** why should I move/my car be moved?; **weg+spü|len** VT *sep* to wash away; (*in der Toilette*) to flush away; **weg+ste|cken** VT *sep* (*lit*) to put away; (*inf*) *Niederlage, Kritik* to take; *Enttäuschung, Verlust* to get over; **weg+steh|len** VR *sep irreg* to steal away; **weg+stel|len** VT *sep* to put away; (= *abstellen*) to put down; **weg+ster|ben** VI *sep irreg aux sein* to die off; **jdm** ~ to die on sb (*inf*); **weg+sto|ßen** VT *sep irreg* to push or shove a-way; (*mit Fuß*) to kick away

Weg- ['ve:k-]: **Weg|stre|cke** F (*rare*) stretch of road; **schlechte** ~ poor road surface; **Weg|-stun|de** F (*old*) hour

weg- ['vɛk-]: **weg+tau|chen** VI *sep aux sein* to disappear; (*inf: aus unangenehmer Situation*) to duck out (*inf*); **weg+tra|gen** VT *sep irreg* to carry away or off; **weg+trei|ben** *sep irreg* VT *Boot etc* to carry away or off; (= *vertreiben*) *Vieh etc* to drive away or off VI *aux sein* to drift a-way; **weg+tre|ten** VI *sep irreg aux sein* (*rare*) to step away or aside; (*Mil*) to fall out; (**lassen Sie**) ~! (*Mil*) dismiss!, dismissed!; **er ist (geistig) weggetreten** (*inf*) (= *geistesabwesend*) he's miles away (*inf*); (= *schwachsinnig*) he's soft in the head (*inf*), he's not all there (*inf*); **weg+tun** VT *sep irreg* to put away; (= *sparen*) *Geld etc auch* to put by or aside; (= *wegwerfen*) to throw away; (= *verstecken*) to hide away; **tu die Hände weg!** take your hands off!

Weg|war|te ['ve:k-] F (*Bot*) chicory

weg- ['vɛk-]: **weg+wa|schen** VT *sep irreg* *Fleck* to wash off; (= *wegspülen*) *Erde etc* to wash away; **weg+we|hen** VTI *sep* (*vi: aux sein*) to blow a-way

Weg- ['ve:k-]: **weg|wei|send** ADJ pioneering *attr*, revolutionary, pathbreaking (*US*); **Weg|-wei|ser** ['ve:kvaizɐ] M **-s, -** sign; (*an einem Pfosten*) signpost; (*fig: Buch etc*) guide

Weg|werf- ['vɛkvɐrf] *in cpds* disposable, throwa-way

weg- ['vɛk-]: **weg+wer|fen** *sep irreg* VT to throw away; **weggeworfenes Geld** money down the drain; VR **sich (an jdn)** ~ to waste oneself (on sb), to throw oneself away (on sb); **weg|wer|fend** ADJ dismissive, disdainful

---

Weg|werf-: Weg|werf|ge|sell|schaft F throw-away society; **Weg|werf|ver|pa|ckung** F dis-posable or throwaway packaging

weg+wi|schen ['vɛk-] VT *sep* to wipe off; (*fig*) to dismiss

weg+wol|len ['vɛk-] VI *sep irreg* (= *verreisen*) to want to go away; (= *weggehen von Haus, Party etc*) to want to leave or go; (= *hinausgehen*) to want to go out

weg+wün|schen ['vɛk-] VT *sep* **jdn** ~ to wish sb would go away

weg+zäh|len ['vɛk-] VT *sep* (*Aus*) to take away, to subtract

weg+zau|bern ['vɛk-] VT *sep* to make disappear (*lit*) by magic or (*fig*) as if by magic

Weg|zeh|rung ['ve:k-] F (*liter*) provisions *pl* for the journey; (*Eccl*) viaticum

weg+zie|hen ['vɛk-] *sep irreg* VT to pull away (*jdm from sb*); *Vorhang* to draw back VI *aux sein* to move away; (*Vögel*) to migrate

Weg|zug ['ve:k-] M move (*aus, von* (away) from)

weh [ve:] ADJ a (= *wund*) sore; (*geh: = schmerz-lich*) aching *attr*; **sie verspürte ein ~es Gefühl** (*geh*) her heart ached; **mir ist so ~ zumute** or **ums Herz** (*old, liter*) my heart is sore (*liter*), I am sore of heart (*old*) b ~ **tun** △ = **wehtun** INTERJ (*geh, liter*) woe (*old*); (*bedauernd*) alas (*liter*), alack (*old*); **o ~!** oh dear!, oh my good-ness!; **weh mir!** or **schreien** (*old*) to lament (sb); ~ **mir!** woe is me! (*liter*); ~ **mir, wenn ...** woe betide me if ... → **ach**

Weh [ve:] NT **-(e)s, -e** (*old, liter*) woe; (= *dumpfes Gefühl*) ache; (= *Leid, Gram*) grief; **ein tiefes ~ er-füllte ihn** his heart ached

we|he ['ve:ə] INTERJ ~ **(dir), wenn du das tust** you'll be sorry or you'll regret it if you do that; **darf ich das anfassen? – ~ (dir)!** can I touch? – you dare! (*liter*); ~ **dem, der ...!** woe betide any-one who ...!

We|he ['ve:ə] F **-, -n** a (= *Schneewehe etc*) drift b **Wehen** PL (*lit: = Geburtswehen*) (labour (*Brit*) or labor (*US*)) pains *pl*, contractions *pl*; (*fig*) birth pangs *pl*; **in den ~n liegen** to be in labour (*Brit*) or labor (*US*); **die ~n setzten ein** the contractions started, she went into labour (*Brit*) or labor (*US*)

we|hen ['ve:ən] VI a (*Wind*) to blow; (*Fahne*) to wave, to flutter; (*Haare*) to blow about; **der Geist der Aufklärung wehte durch Deutschland** (*geh*) the spirit of enlightenment was abroad or reigned in Germany; **es weht ein warmer Wind** there's a warm wind (blowing), a warm wind is blowing; **kein Lüftchen wehte** there wasn't e-ven a breeze → **Fahne a, Wind a** b *aux sein* (*Ge-ruch, Klang*) to drift; (*Duft*) to waft VT to blow (*von* off); (*sanft*) to waft

We|hen|schrei|ber M tocograph (*spec*)

Weh-: Weh|ge|fühl NT (*geh*) ache; **ein ~ be-fiel ihn** his heart ached; **Weh|ge|schrei** NT wailing, cries *pl* of woe (*liter*); **in ~ ausbrechen, ein ~ anstimmen** to start to wail, to give vent to one's woe (*liter*); **Weh|kla|ge** F (*liter*) lam-ent(ation); **weh|kla|gen** VI *insep* (*liter*) to la-ment, to wail; **über etw** (*acc*) ~ to lament (over) sth, to bewail sth; **um jdn** ~ to lament the loss of sb; **Weh|laut** M (*liter*) cry of pain; (*bei Kum-mer*) cry of woe; (*leise*) whimper; **weh|lei|dig** ADJ over-sensitive to pain; (= *jammernd*) whin-ing *attr*, snivelling *attr* (*esp Brit*), sniveling *attr* (*US*); (= *voller Selbstmitleid*) sorry for oneself, self-pitying; **er ist ja so** ~ he whines at the least little thing; he's always feeling sorry for him-self; **Weh|lei|dig|keit** F self-pity; **Weh|mut** ['ve:mu:t] F **-, no pl** (*geh*) melancholy; (= *Sehn-sucht*) wistfulness; (*nach Vergangenem*) nostalgia; **weh|mü|tig** ['ve:my:tɪç], **weh|muts|voll** (*geh*) ADJ melancholy; (= *sehnsuchtsvoll*) wistful; (= *nostalgisch*) nostalgic ADV (= *traurig*) sadly; (= *sehnsuchtsvoll*) wistfully; (= *nostalgisch*) nostalgi-cally; **seine Stimme klang ~** his voice sounded

---

melancholy; **du wirst dich noch ~ nach mir zu-rücksehnen** you'll miss me terribly

Wehr¹ [ve:ɐ] F **-, -en** a (= *Feuerwehr*) fire brigade (*Brit*), fire department (*US*) b (*old = Bollwerk*) defences *pl* (*Brit*), defenses *pl* (*US*); (*no pl: = Widerstand*) defence (*Brit*), defense (*US*); **mit ~ und Waffen** (*old*) in full panoply (*old*); **sich zur ~ setzen** to defend oneself

Wehr² NT **-(e)s, -e** weir

Wehr- *in cpds* defence (*Brit*), defense (*US*); **Wehr|be|auf|trag|te(r)** MF *decl as adj* com-missioner for the armed forces; **Wehr|be|reich** M military district; **Wehr|dienst** M military service; **seinen ~ (ab)leisten** to do one's military service; **jdn zum ~ einberufen** to call sb up (*Brit*), to draft sb (*US*); **Wehr|dienst|pflich|tig** [-pflɪçtɪç] ADJ liable for mili-tary service; **Wehr|dienst|pflich|ti|ge(r)** [-pflɪçtɪgə] MF *decl as adj* person liable for mili-tary service; (*der schon eingezogen ist*) conscript (*Brit*), draftee (*US*); **Wehr|dienst|ver|wei|ge-rer** M , **Wehr|dienst|ver|wei|ge|rin** F con-scientious objector

weh|ren ['ve:rən] VT (*obs*) = **verwehren** VR to defend oneself; (= *sich aktiv widersetzen*) to (put up a) fight; **sich gegen einen Plan** *etc* ~ to fight (against) a plan *etc*; **dagegen weiß ich mich zu ~ I** know how to deal with that VI *+dat* (*geh*) to fight; (= *Einhalt gebieten*) to check; **wehret den Anfängen!** these things must be nipped in the bud, these things must be stopped before they get out of hand

Wehr-: Wehr|er|fas|sung F *compilation of the call-up list for military service*; **Wehr|er|satz|be|hör|de** F military recruitment board or agency; **Wehr|er|satz|dienst** M alternative national service; **Wehr|etat** M defence (*Brit*) or defense (*US*) budget; **Wehr|ex|per|te** M , **Wehr|ex|per|tin** F defence (*Brit*) or defense (*US*) expert; **wehr|fä|hig** ADJ fit for military service, able-bodied; **Männer im ~en Alter** men of the right age for military service; **Wehr|gang** M *pl* **-gänge** walk along the battlements; **wehr|haft** ADJ (*geh*) able to put up a fight; *Stadt etc* well-fortified; **Wehr|haf|tig|keit** F (*geh*) ability to put up a fight; **Wehr|ho|heit** F military sovereignty; **Wehr|kir|che** F fortified church; **Wehr|kraft** F military strength; **Wehr|kraft|zer|set|zung** F undermining of military morale; **wehr|los** ADJ defenceless (*Brit*), defenseless (*US*); (*fig: gegenüber Gemein-heiten etc*) helpless ADV defencelessly (*Brit*), defenselessly (*US*), helplessly; **jdm ~ ausgelie-fert sein** to be at sb's mercy; **Wehr|lo|sig|keit** F **-, no pl** defencelessness (*Brit*), defenseless-ness (*US*); (*fig: gegenüber Gemeinheiten etc*) help-lessness; **Wehr|macht** F armed forces *pl*; (*Hist*) Wehrmacht; **Wehr|mann** M *pl* **-männer** (*Sw*) soldier; **Wehr|pass** ▲ M service record (book); **Wehr|pflicht** F (*allgemeine*) ~ (*uni-versal*) conscription, compulsory military serv-ice; **wehr|pflich|tig** [-pflɪçtɪç] ADJ = **wehr-dienstpflichtig**; **Wehr|pflich|ti|ge(r)** [-pflɪç-tɪgə] MF *decl as adj* = Wehrdienstpflichtige(r); **Wehr|sold** M (*military*) pay; **Wehr|sport-grup|pe** F paramilitary group; **Wehr|turm** M fortified tower; **Wehr|übung** F reserve duty training exercise

weh+tun ▲ VT *sep irreg* (*lit, fig*) to hurt; **mir tut der Rücken weh** my back hurts or is aching; **mir tut mein verbrannter Finger weh** my finger hurts *or* is sore where I burned it; **sich/jdm ~** (*lit, fig*) to hurt oneself/sb; **was tut dir denn nun schon wieder weh?** what's the matter now?; **wo tut es denn weh?** (*fig inf*) what's your problem?, what's up? (*inf*)

Weh|weh ['veːveː, veːˈveː] NT **-s, -s** (*baby-talk*) hurt (place)

Weh|weh|chen [veːˈveːçən, 'veː-] NT **-s, -** (*inf*) (minor) complaint; **seine tausend ~** all his little aches and pains

Weib [vaip] NT **-(e)s, -er** [-bə] woman, female (*pej*), broad (*US pej inf*); (*old, Bibl*: = *Ehefrau*) wife; (*pej inf*: *Mann*) old woman; **~ und Kind** (*old*) wife and children; **eine Frau zu seinem ~(e) nehmen** (*old*) to take a woman to wife (*old Brit*) or as one's wife; **sie ist ein tolles ~** (*inf*) she's quite a woman, she's quite a dame (*US pej inf*)

Weib|chen ['vaipçən] NT **-s, -** (*Zool*) female; (*hum*: = *Ehefrau*) little woman (*hum*); (*pej*: = *nicht emanzipierte Frau*) dumb female

Weiber-: Weiber|art F (*old, pej*) woman's way; **Weiber|fast|nacht** F *day during the carnival period when women assume control*; **Weiber|feind** M woman hater, misogynist; **Weiber|ge|schich|ten** PL sexploits *pl* (*hum*); (= *Affären auch*) womanizing *sing*; **Weiber|ge|schwätz** NT (*pej*) women's talk; **Weiber|hass** ▲ M (*inf*) misogyny; **Weiber|held** M (*inf*) lady-killer, womanizer; **Weiber|herr|schaft** F (*pej*) petticoat government (*inf*); **Weiber|kram** M (*pej*) women's stuff (*inf*); **Weiber|volk** NT (*obs*) womenfolk *pl*; (*pej*) females *pl* (*pej*); **Weiber|wirt|schaft** F (*pej*) henhouse (*inf*)

wei|bisch ['vaibɪʃ] ADJ effeminate

Weib|lein ['vaiplain] NT **-s, -** little woman; **ein altes ~** a little old woman, an old dear (*inf*)

weib|lich ['vaiplɪç] ADJ (*Zool, Bot,* = *von Frauen*) female; (*Gram, Poet,* = *fraulich, wie Frauen*) feminine

Weib|lich|keit F **-, no pl** femininity; (= *Frauen*) women *pl*; **die holde ~** (*hum*) the fair sex

Weibs|bild NT (*old*) woman; (*junge Frau auch*) wench (*old*); (*pej auch*) female

Weib|sen ['vaipsn] NT **-s, -** *usu pl* (*hum inf*) woman, female

Weibs|per|son F (*old*) woman

Weib|s|tück NT (*pej*) bitch (*inf*), cow (*inf*)

weibs|toll ['vaips-] ADJ woman-mad

weich [vaiç] ADJ soft (*auch fig, Ling, Phot*); *Ei* soft-boiled; *Fleisch, Gemüse* tender; *Energietechnik* non-nuclear; *Währung* soft; (= *geschmeidig*) *Bewegungen* smooth; *Mensch* (= *nachgiebig*) soft; (= *mitleidig*) soft-hearted; **~e Drogen** soft drugs; **~er Boykott** civil disobedience; **~ werden** (*lit, fig*) to soften; **die Knie wurden mir ~** my knees turned to jelly, I went weak at (*Brit*) or in (*US*) the knees; **~ machen** to soften; **ein ~es Herz haben** to be soft-hearted, to have a soft heart; **ei|ne ~e Birne** *or* **einen ~en Keks haben** (*inf*) to be soft in the head (*inf*)

ADV softly, gently; *landen* softly; **~ geklopft** (*Fleisch*) hammered tender; **~ gekocht** (*Ei*) soft-boiled; *Fleisch, Gemüse* boiled until tender; *Nudeln* cooked until soft; **die Kupplung ~ kommen lassen** to let out the clutch smoothly; **~ landen** to land softly; (= *auf weichem Untergrund*) to have a soft landing → **betten VT a**

Weich|bild NT **im ~ der Stadt** within the town or (*größere Stadt*) city precincts

Wei|che¹ ['vaiçə] F **-, -n a** *no pl* = **Weichheit** (= *Seite*) side, flank

Wei|che² F **-, -n a** (*Rail*) points *pl* (*Brit*), switch (*US*); **die ~n stellen** (*lit*) to switch the points (*Brit*), to change the switch (*US*); (*fig*) to set the course **b** (= *Ausweichstelle*) passing place

Weich|ei NT (*pej sl*: = *Weichling, Feigling*) wimp (*inf*)

wei|chen¹ VTI (*vi: aux haben or sein*) to soak

wei|chen² ['vaiçn] *pret* **wich** [vɪç], *ptp* **gewichen** [gəˈvɪçn] VI *aux sein* **a** (*Mensch, Tier, Fahrzeug:* = *weggehen, verlassen*) to move; (*Armee, Mensch, Tier:* = *zurückweichen*) to retreat (+*dat, vor* +*dat* from); (= *Platz machen, fig:* = *nachgeben*) to give way (+*dat* to); **(nicht) von jdm** or **jds Seite ~** (not) to leave sb's side; **er wich nicht** *or* **keinen Schritt vom Wege** he did not deviate an inch; **sie wich nicht von der Stelle** she refused to or wouldn't budge (an inch); **alles** *or* **das Blut/die Farbe wich aus ihren Wangen** (*liter*) the blood/colour (*Brit*) *or* color (*US*) drained from her cheeks; **die Begeisterung ist der Ernüchterung gewichen** enthusiasm has given way to disillusionment; **die Angst ist von ihr gewichen** her fear has left her *or* has disappeared; **weiche böser Geist!** (*liter*) begone evil spirit! (*liter*) **b** (*Gefühl, Druck, Schmerz*) (= *nachlassen*) to ease, to abate; (= *verschwinden*) to go

Wei|chen-: Wei|chen|stel|ler [-ʃtɛlɐ] M **-s, -**, **Wei|chen|stel|le|rin** [-ərɪn] F **-, -nen** pointsman (*Brit*), switchman (*US*); (*fig*) guiding spirit, moving force (+*gen* behind); **Wei|chen|stel|lung** F (*lit*) changing the points (*Brit*) or switch (*US*); (*fig*) setting the course

weich-: weich|ge|klopft △ [-ɡəklɔpft] ADJ *attr* → **weich** ADV; **weich|ge|kocht** △ [-ɡəkɔxt] ADJ *attr* → **weich** ADV

Weich|heit F **-, no pl** softness (*auch fig, Ling, Phot*); (*von Fleisch, Gemüse*) tenderness; (= *Geschmeidigkeit: von Bewegungen*) smoothness

Weich-: weich|her|zig ADJ soft-hearted; **Weich|her|zig|keit** F **-, no pl** soft-heartedness; **Weich|holz** NT softwood; **Weich|kä|se** M soft cheese; **weich klop|fen** ▲, **weich krie|gen** ▲ VT (*fig inf*) to soften up

weich|lich ['vaiçlɪç] ADJ (*lit*) soft; (*fig*) weak; (= *weibisch*) effeminate; (= *verhätschelt*) soft ADV **ein Kind zu ~ erziehen** to mollycoddle (*Brit*) or pamper a child

Weich|ling ['vaiçlɪŋ] M **-s, -e** (*pej*) weakling, softy (*inf*)

Weich-: weich ma|chen ▲ VT (*fig*) to soften up; **Weich|ma|cher** M (*Chem*) softener, softening agent; **weich|scha|lig** [-ʃaːlɪç] ADJ soft-shelled; *Apfel* soft-skinned

Weich|sel ['vaiksl] F - Vistula

Weich|sel|kir|sche ['vaiksl-] F St Lucie cherry

Weich-: weich+spü|len VT *sep* to condition; *Wäsche* to use (fabric) conditioner *or* softener on; **Weich|spü|ler** M conditioner; (*für Wäsche auch*) (fabric) softener; **Weich|tei|le** PL soft parts *pl*; (*inf:* = *Geschlechtsteile*) privates *pl*, private parts *pl*; **Weich|tier** NT mollusc; **Weich|zeich|ner** M (*Phot*) soft-focus lens

Wei|de¹ ['vaidə] F **-, -n** (*Bot*) willow

Wei|de² F **-, -n** (*Agr*) pasture; (= *Wiese*) meadow; **auf die** *or* **zur ~ treiben** to put out to pasture *or* to graze *or* to grass; **auf der ~ sein** to be grazing, to be out at pasture

Wei|de-: Wei|de|flä|che F, **Wei|de|land** NT (*Agr*) pasture(land), grazing land, pasturage; **Wei|de|mo|nat** M (*old*) month of May

wei|den ['vaidn] VI to graze VT (to put out to) graze, to put out to pasture; **seine Blicke** *or* **Au|gen an etw** (*dat*) **~** to feast one's eyes on sth VR **sich an etw** (*dat*) **~** (*fig*) to revel in sth; (*sadistisch auch*) to gloat over sth

Wei|den-: Wei|den|baum M willow tree; **Wei|den|busch** M willow bush; **Wei|den|ger|te** F willow rod or switch; (*zum Korbflechten*) osier, wicker; **Wei|den|kätz|chen** NT pussy willow, catkin (*Brit*); **Wei|den|korb** M wicker basket; **Wei|den|laub|sän|ger** M (*Orn*) chiffchaff; **Wei|den|rös|chen** NT (*Bot*) willowherb; **schmalblättriges ~** rosebay willowherb; **Wei|den|rost** M cattle grid

Wei|de-: Wei|de|platz M pasture; **Wei|de|wirt|schaft** F (*Econ*) pastural agriculture

weid|ge|recht ADJ (*Hunt*) in accordance with hunting principles ADV correctly; **ein Tier ~ erlegen** to kill an animal with a well placed shot

weid|lich ['vaitlɪç] ADV (*mit adj*) pretty; **sich über etw** (*acc*) **~ amüsieren** to be highly amused at sth; **etw ~ ausnutzen** to make full use of sth; **er hat sich ~ bemüht** he tried pretty hard ADJ (*rare*) = **weidmännisch**

Weid-: Weid|mann M *pl* **-männer** (*liter*) huntsman, hunter; **weid|män|nisch** [-mɛnɪʃ] ADJ huntsman's *attr*; **das ist nicht ~** that's not done in hunting *or* in a huntsman's manner; *aus-gebildet* as a huntsman; **Weid|manns|dank** INTERJ (*Hunt*) thank you (*as answer to Weidmannsheil*); **Weid|manns|heil** INTERJ (*Hunt*) good hunting; **Weid|werk** NT , *no pl* art of hunting; **weid|wund** ADJ (*Hunt*) wounded in the belly

Wei|gand ['vaigant] M **-(e)s, -e** [-də] (*obs*) warrior

wei|gern ['vaigɐn] ✪ 39.3 VR to refuse VT (*old*) **jdm etw ~** to deny sb sth

Wei|ge|rung ['vaigərʊŋ] F **-, -en** refusal

Wei|ge|rungs|fall M (*form*) **im ~** in case of refusal (*form*)

Weih [vai] M **-(e)s, -e** (*Orn*) harrier

Weih|bi|schof M suffragan bishop

Wei|he¹ ['vaiə] F **-, -n** (*Orn*) harrier

Wei|he² F **-, -n a** (*Eccl*) consecration; (= *Priesterweihe*) ordination; **die niederen/höheren ~n** minor/major orders **b** (= *Einweihung*) (*eines Gebäudes*) inauguration; (*einer Brücke*) (ceremonial) opening; (*eines Denkmals*) unveiling **c** (= *Feierlichkeit*) solemnity **d** (= *Ehre*) **höhere ~n** (*fig*) greater glory, greater things

wei|hen ['vaiən] VT **a** (*Eccl*) *Altar, Glocke, Kirche, Bischof* to consecrate; *Priester* to ordain; **jdn zum Bischof ~** to consecrate sb (as a) bishop; **jdn zum Priester ~** to ordain sb (as a) priest **b** *Gebäude* to inaugurate; *Brücke* to open; *Denkmal* to unveil **c** (= *widmen*) **etw jdm/einer Sache ~** to dedicate sth to sb/sth; (*Eccl auch, sehr feierlich*) to consecrate sth to sb/sth; **dem Tod(e)/Unter|gang geweiht** doomed (to die/fall) VR +*dat* (*liter*) to devote or dedicate oneself to

Wei|her ['vaiɐ] M **-s, -** pond

Wei|he-: Wei|he|stät|te F holy place; **wei|he|voll** ADJ (*liter*) solemn

Weih-: Weih|ga|be F (*Rel*) (votive) offering, oblation (*form*); **Weih|ge|fäß** NT (*Rel*) votive vessel

Weih|nacht ['vainaxt] F **-, no pl** = **Weihnachten**

weih|nach|ten ['vainaxtn] VI *impers* (*poet, iro*) **es weihnachtet sehr** Christmas is very much in evidence

Weih|nach|ten ['vainaxtn] ✪ 50.2 NT **-, -** Christmas; (*geschrieben auch*) Xmas (*inf*); **fröhli|che** *or* **gesegnete** *or* **schöne** *or* **frohe(s)** *or* **ein fröhliches ~!** happy (*esp Brit*) *or* merry Christmas!; **(zu** *or* **an) ~** at Christmas; **(zu** *or* **an) ~ nach Hause fahren** to go home for Christmas; **etw zu ~ bekommen** to get sth for Christmas; **etw zu ~ schenken** to give sth as a Christmas present; **weiße ~** (a) white Christmas; **grüne ~** (a) Christmas without snow; **das ist ein Gefühl wie ~(, nur nicht so feierlich)** (*iro inf*) it's an odd feeling

weih|nacht|lich ['vainaxtlɪç] ADJ Christmassy (*inf*), festive ADV *geschmückt* for Christmas, festively; **~ gestimmt sein** to be feeling Christmassy (*inf*); **~ anmutende Lieder** Christmassy sounding songs (*inf*)

Weih|nachts- *in cpds* Christmas; **Weih|nachts|abend** M Christmas Eve; **Weih|nachts|bä|cke|rei** F Christmas baking; **Weih|nachts|baum** M Christmas tree; **Weih|nachts|but|ter** F *reduced-price butter at Christmas time*; **Weih|nachts|ein|käu|fe** PL Christmas shopping *sing*; **Weih|nachts|fei|er** F Christmas celebrations(s *pl*); **Weih|nachts|fei|er|tag** M (*erster*) Christmas Day; (*zweiter*) Boxing Day; **Weih|nachts|fe|ri|en** PL Christmas holidays *pl* (*Brit*), Christmas vacation *sing* (*US*); **Weih|nachts|fest** NT Christmas; **Weih|nachts|gans** F Christmas goose; **jdn ausnehmen wie eine ~** (inf) to fleece sb (inf), to take sb to the cleaners (inf); **Weih|nachts|ge|bäck** NT Christmas biscuits pl (Brit), Christmas cookies pl (US); **Weih|nachts|geld** NT Christmas money; (= Weihnachtsgratifikation) Christmas bonus; (für Briefträger etc) Christmas box; **Weih|nachts|ge|schenk** NT Christmas present or gift; **Weih|nachts|ge|schich|te** F Christmas story; **Weih|nachts|gruß** M Christmas greeting; **Weih|nachts|in|sel** F Christmas Island; **Weih|nachts|kak|tus** M (Bot) Christmas cactus; **Weih|nachts|kar|te** F Christmas card; **Weih|nachts|lied** NT (Christmas) carol; **Weih|nachts|mann** M pl -**männer** Father Christmas (Brit), Santa Claus; (pej inf) clown (pej inf); **Weih|nachts|mär|chen** NT (Christmas) pantomime; **Weih|nachts|markt** M Christmas fair

Weih|nachts-: Weih|nachts|spiel NT nativity play; **Weih|nachts|stern** M **a** (Bot) poinsettia **b** (Rel) star of Bethlehem; **Weih|nachts|tag** M = **Weihnachtsfeiertag**; **Weih|nachts|tel|ler** M plate of biscuits, chocolates etc; **Weih|nachts|tisch** M table for Christmas presents; **Weih|nachts|wunsch** M Christmas wish; **Weih|nachts|zeit** F Christmas (time), Yuletide (old, liter), Christmas season (esp Comm)

Weih-: Weih|rauch M incense; **jdm ~ streuen** (fig) to praise or laud sb to the skies; **Weih|rauch|fass** ▲ NT censer, thurible (form); **Weih|rauch|schiff|chen** NT incense boat; **Weih|was|ser** NT , no pl holy water; **Weih|was|ser|be|cken** NT stoup, holy water font

weil [vail] CONJ because

wei|land ['vailant] ADV (obs, hum) formerly; **Botho von Schmettwitz, ~ Leutnant der Kürassiere** Botho von Schmettwitz, formerly or erstwhile or one-time lieutenant of the cuirassiers; **er hat eine Frisur, wie ~ Napoleon** he has a haircut like Napoleon's in former times

Weil|chen ['vailçən] NT -**s,** - **ein ~** a (little) while, a bit

Wei|le ['vailə] F -**,** no pl while; **wir können eine ~ Karten spielen** we could play cards for a while; **vor einer (ganzen) ~, eine (ganze) ~ her** quite a while ago; **damit hat es noch (gute) ~, das hat noch (gute) ~** there's no hurry

wei|len ['vailən] VI (geh) to be; (= bleiben) to stay, to tarry (poet); **er weilt nicht mehr unter uns** he is no longer with or among us

Wei|ler ['vailɐ] M -**s,** - hamlet

Wei|ma|rer Re|pub|lik ['vaima:rɐ] F Weimar Republic

Wein [vain] M -**(e)s, -e** wine; (no pl: = Weinstöcke) vines pl; (no pl: = Weintrauben) grapes pl; **in Frankreich wächst viel ~** there is a lot of wine growing in France; **offener ~** draught (Brit) or draft (US) wine; **wilder ~** Virginia creeper; **neuen ~ in alte Schläuche füllen** (Prov) to pour new wine into old bottles (Brit) or wine skins (US) (Prov); **das ist doch nur alter ~ in neuen Schläuchen** that's just old wine in new bottles, that's just the same old thing in a new guise; **jdm reinen or klaren ~ einschenken** to tell sb the truth, to come clean with sb (inf); **im ~ ist Wahrheit** (Prov) in vino veritas (Prov); **heimlich**

~ trinken und öffentlich Wasser predigen (geh) not to practise (Brit) or practice (US) what one preaches; **voll des süßen ~es sein** (liter, hum) to be heavy with wine

Wein- in cpds (auf Getränk bezogen) wine; (auf Pflanze bezogen) vine; **Wein|bau** M , no pl wine growing, viniculture (form); **Wein|bau|er** M pl -**bauern, Wein|bäu|e|rin** F wine grower; **Wein|bee|re** F grape; (= Rosine) raisin; **Wein|bei|ßer[1]** [-baisə] M -**s,** - (Aus: Lebkuchenart) sugar-coated ginger biscuit (Brit) or cookie (US); **Wein|bei|ßer[2]** [-baisə] M -**s,** -, **Wein|bei|ße|rin** [-ərɪn] F -**, -nen** (Aus: = Weinkenner) wine connoisseur; **Wein|berg** M vineyard; **Wein|berg|schne|cke** F snail; (auf Speisekarten) escargot; **Wein|blatt** NT vineleaf; **gefüllte Weinblätter** (Cook) stuffed vineleaves; **Wein|brand** M brandy; **Wein|bren|ne|rei** F brandy distillery

Wein|chen ['vainçən] NT -**s,** - dim von **Wein** (inf) **ein ~** (= etwas Wein) a little wine; **das ist vielleicht ein ~!** that's a really beautiful wine!

wei|nen ['vainən] VTI to cry; (aus Trauer, Kummer auch) to weep (um for, über +acc over, aus, vor +dat with); **etw nass ~** to make sth wet with one's tears; **sich** (dat) **die Augen rot ~, sich** (dat) **die Augen aus dem Kopf ~** to cry one's eyes or heart out; **sich in den Schlaf ~** to cry oneself to sleep; **sich müde ~** to tire oneself out crying; **es ist zum Weinen!, man könnte ~!** it's enough to make you weep! (esp Brit), it makes you want to cry!; **es ist zum Weinen mit dieser Frau** that woman is enough to make you want to cry; **leise ~d** weeping or crying softly; (inf: = kleinlaut) rather crestfallen or subdued; (inf: = resigniert) resignedly; (iro inf: = mir nichts, dir nichts) with a shrug of the shoulders

Wei|ne|rei [vainə'rai] F -**,** no pl (inf) crying, howling

wei|ner|lich ['vainɐlɪç] ADJ whining, whiny (inf) ADV whinily; **~ reden/sagen** to whine

Wei|ner|lich|keit F whininess (inf)

Wein-: Wein|ern|te F grape harvest; **Wein|es|sig** M wine vinegar; **Wein|fass** ▲ NT wine cask; **Wein|fest** NT wine festival; **Wein|fla|sche** F wine bottle; **Wein|gar|ten** M vineyard; **Wein|gärt|ner(in)** M(F) wine grower; **Wein|ge|gend** F wine-growing area; **Wein|geist** M spirits of wine (old), (ethyl) alcohol; **Wein|glas** NT wine glass; **Wein|gum|mi** NT OR M wine gum; **Wein|gut** NT wine-growing estate; **Wein|händ|ler(in)** M(F) wine dealer; (für Großhandel auch) vintner; **Wein|hand|lung** F wine shop (esp Brit) or store; **Wein|hau|er(in)** M(F) (esp Aus) wine grower; **Wein-**

haus NT wine tavern, wine bar; (Geschäft) wine shop; **Wein|he|ber** M wine cradle or basket

wei|nig ['vainiç] ADJ winy, vinous (form)

Wein-: Wein|jahr NT **ein gutes/schlechtes ~** a good/bad year for wine; **Wein|kar|te** F wine list; **Wein|kel|ler** M wine cellar; (= Lokal) wine bar or tavern; **Wein|kel|le|rei** F winery; **Wein|kel|ter** F wine press; **Wein|ken|ner(in)** M(F) connoisseur of wine, wine connoisseur

Wein|krampf M crying fit; (Med) uncontrollable fit of crying

Wein-: Wein|kraut NT sauerkraut; **Wein|kü|fer(in)** M(F) cellarman; (= Weinbau) wine growing, viniculture (form); **Wein|la|ge** F vineyard location; **Wein|land** NT wine-growing or wine-producing country; **Wein|laub** NT vine leaves pl; **Wein|lau|be** F vine arbour (Brit) or arbor (US), vine bower; **Wein|lau|ne** F **in einer ~ beschlossen sie ...** after a few glasses of wine they decided ...; **Wein|le|se** F grape harvest, vintage; **Wein|lo|kal** NT wine bar; **Wein|mo|nat** M , **Wein|mond** M (old) grape-harvesting month; (= Oktober) (month of) October; **Wein|pan|scher(in)** M(F) wine-adulterator, wine-doctorer (inf); **Wein|pan|sche|rei** F wine-adulterating, wine-doctoring (inf); **Wein|pro|be** F wine tasting; **Wein|prü|fer(in)** M(F) wine taster; **Wein|re|be** F (grape)vine; **wein|rot** ADJ wine-red, claret; **Wein|säu|re** F (Chem) tartaric acid; **Wein|schlauch** M wineskin; **Wein|schor|le** F spritzer; **wein|se|lig** ADJ merry (Brit inf) or tipsy with wine; **Wein|sor|te** F sort or type of wine; **Wein|stein** M tartar; **Wein|stock** M vine; **Wein|stra|ße** F wine trail or route; **Wein|stu|be** F wine tavern; **Wein|trau|be** F grape; **Wein|trin|ker(in)** M(F) wine drinker; **Wein|zierl** [-tsi:ɐl] M -**s,** -**(n)** (Aus) wine grower; **Wein|zwang** M obligation to order wine; **in diesem Restaurant ist ~** you have to order wine in this restaurant

wei|se ['vaizə] ADJ (geh) wise; **die ~ Frau** (old) the midwife

Wei|se ['vaizə] F -**, -n a** (= Verfahren etc) way, manner, fashion; **auf diese ~** in this way; **auf geheimnisvolle** etc **~** in a mysterious etc way or manner or fashion, mysteriously etc; **auf jede (erdenkliche) ~** in every conceivable way; **in gewisser/keiner** or **keinster** (inf) **~** in a/no way; **in der ~, dass ...** in such a way that ...; **jeder nach seiner ~** each in his own way, each after his own fashion → **Art c b** (liter: = Melodie) tune, melody

-wei|se [vaizə] ADV suf (an Substantiv) as a ...; (bei Maßangabe) by the ...; (an Adjektiv) -ly; **ausnahmsweise** as an exception; **meterweise** by the metre (Brit) or meter (US); **bedauerlicherweise** regrettably; **er hat mir netterweise ...** it was kind of him to ...

Wei|sel ['vaizl] M -**s,** - queen bee

wei|sen ['vaizn] pret **wies** [vi:s], ptp **gewiesen** [gə'vi:zn] (geh) VT **jdm etw ~** (lit, fig) to show sb sth; **jdn aus dem Lande ~** to expel sb; **jdn aus dem Saal ~** to eject sb (from the hall); **jdn vom Feld** or **Platz ~** (Sport) to order sb off (the field); (als Strafe auch) to send sb off; **jdn von der Schule ~** to expel sb (from school); **etw (weit) von sich ~** (fig) to reject sth (emphatically); **jdn zur Ruhe/Ordnung ~** to order sb to be quiet/to behave himself → **Hand j** VI to point (nach towards, auf +acc at) → **Finger**

Wei|se(r) [ˈvaizə] MF *decl as adj* wise man/woman; (= *Denker auch*) sage; **die drei ~n aus dem Morgenland** the three Wise Men from the East; **die Fünf ~n** (*Ger Pol*) panel of five experts advising government on economic policy

---

DIE FÜNF WEISEN

Die Fünf Weisen is the popular name of the **Sachverständigenrat zur Begutachtung der gesamtwirtschaftlichen Entwicklung**. This is an independent body, set up in 1964 and consisting of five recognized economists appointed by the **Bundespräsident** for a period of five years. Each year they present a report on the economy and the likely course of its development → BUNDESPRÄSIDENT

Wei|ser [ˈvaizə] M **-s, -** (= *Biene*) queen bee

Weis|heit [ˈvaishait] F **-, -en** **a** *no pl* wisdom; **das war der ~ letzter Schluss** that was all they/we *etc* came up with; **das ist auch nicht der ~ letzter Schluss** that's not exactly the ideal solution; **er glaubt, er hat die ~ gepachtet** *or* **mit Löffeln gegessen** *or* **gefressen** he thinks he knows it all; **er hat die ~ nicht gepachtet** *or* **mit Löffeln gegessen** *or* **gefressen** he's not so bright → **Ende** **b** (= *weiser Spruch*) wise saying, pearl of wisdom (*usu iro*); **eine alte ~** a wise old saying; **deine ~en kannst du für dich behalten!** keep your pearls of wisdom to yourself!

Weis|heits|zahn M wisdom tooth

weis+ma|chen [ˈvais-] VT *sep* **jdm etw ~** to make sb believe sth; **er wollte uns ~, dass ...** he would have us believe that ...; **wie konntest du ihm ~, dass ...?** how could they fool him into believing that ...?; **das kannst du mir nicht ~!** you can't expect me to believe that; **das kannst du (einem) andern ~!** (go) tell that to the marines (*Brit*) *or* judge! (*inf*), pull the other one(, it's got bells on)! (*Brit hum inf*), and pigs fly (*esp US inf*)

weiß¹ [vais] ADJ white; **ein ~es (Blatt) Papier** a blank *or* clean sheet of paper; **ein ~er Fleck (auf der Landkarte)** a blank area (on the map); **das Weiße Haus** the White House; **das Weiße Meer** the White Sea; **der Weiße Nil** the White Nile; **Weißer Sonntag** Low Sunday; **der ~e Sport** (= *Tennis*) tennis; **der ~e Tod** death in the snow; **~ werden** to go *or* turn white; (*Sachen auch*) to whiten; **~ wie Kreide** *or* **die Wand** white as chalk *or* a sheet *or* a ghost; **das Weiße des Eis** *or* **vom Ei** egg white; **das Weiße von drei Eiern** the white(s) of three eggs; **das Weiße im Auge** the whites of the eyes → **Weste, Maus** **a** ADV (*mit weißer Farbe*) anstreichen, lackieren white; tapezieren *auch*, einrichten, sich kleiden, umranden in white; **~ glühend** white-hot, incandescent

weiß² [vais] 3. *pers sing pres von* **wissen**

Weiß [vais] NT **-(es), -** white

Weiß|afri|ka NT White Africa

Weis-: weis|sa|gen [ˈvais-] VT *insep* to prophesy, to foretell; **Weis|sa|ger** [ˈvaisza:gə] M **-s, -**, **Weis|sa|ge|rin** [-ərɪn] F **-, -nen** (*liter*) seer, prophet; **Weis|sa|gung** [ˈvaisza:gʊŋ] F **-, -en** prophecy

Weiß-: Weiß|bier NT weissbier, *light, fizzy beer made using top-fermentation yeast*; **Weiß|bin|der(in)** M(F) (*dial*) (= *Böttcher*) cooper; (= *Anstreicher*) house painter; **weiß|blau** ADJ (*inf.* = *bayrisch*) Bavarian; (*farblich*) in the Bavarian colours (*Brit*) *or* colors (*US*); **Weiß|blech** NT tinplate; **weiß|blond** ADJ ash blond(e); **Weiß|blu|ten** NT **jdn bis zum ~ ausbeuten** to bleed sb white; **bis zum ~ zahlen müssen** to be bled white; **Weiß|brot** NT white bread; (= *Laib*) loaf of white bread, white loaf; **Weiß|buch** NT (*Pol*) white paper; **Weiß|bu|che** F (*Bot*) hornbeam; **Weiß|dorn** M *pl* **-dorne** (*Bot*) whitethorn

Wei|ße [ˈvaisə] F **-, -n** **a** (= *Weißheit*) whiteness **b** → **Berliner¹**

wei|ßeln [ˈvaisln] VTI (*S Ger, Aus*) to whitewash

wei|ßen [ˈvaisn] VT to whiten; (= *weiß tünchen*) to whitewash

Wei|ße(r) [ˈvaisə] MF *decl as adj* white, white man/woman; **die ~n** the whites, white people

Weiß-: Weiß|fisch M whitefish; **Weiß|fuchs** M white fox; **Weiß|gar|dist** M (*Hist*) member of the White Guard; **weiß|glü|hend** △ ADJ → **weiß** ADV; **Weiß|glut** F white heat, incandescence; **jdn zur ~ bringen**, **jdn bis zur ~ reizen** to make sb livid (with rage), to make sb see red (*inf*); **Weiß|gold** NT white gold; **weiß|haa|rig** ADJ white-haired

Weiß|heit [ˈvaishait] F **-**, *no pl* whiteness

Weiß-: Weiß|herbst M ≈ rosé; **Weiß|ka|bis** M (*Sw*) white cabbage; **Weiß|kä|se** M (*dial*) quark; **Weiß|kohl** M , (*S Ger, Aus*) **Weiß|kraut** NT white cabbage

weiß|lich [ˈvaislɪç] ADJ whitish

Weiß-: Weiß|ma|cher M (*in Waschmittel*) brightening agent; (*in Papier*) whitener; **Weiß|me|tall** NT white metal; **Weiß|nä|he|rin** F (*plain*) seamstress; **Weiß|rus|se** M , **Weiß|rus|sin** F White Russian; **weiß|rus|sisch** ADJ White Russian; **Weiß|rus|sisch(e)** NT (*Ling*) White Russian → *auch* **Deutsch(e)**; **Weiß|russ|land** ▲ NT White Russia; **Weiß|sucht** F albinism; **Weiß|tan|ne** F (*Bot*) silver fir; **Weiß|wal** M white whale; **Weiß|wand|rei|fen** M (*Aut*) whitewall tyre (*Brit*) *or* tire (*US*); **Weiß|wa|ren** PL linen *sing*; **weiß+wa|schen** VTR *sep irreg* (*fig, usu pej*) **sich/jdn ~** to whitewash one's/sb's reputation; **Weiß|wein** M white wine; **Weiß|wurst** F veal sausage; **Weiß|zeug** NT , *no pl* linen

Wei|sung [ˈvaizʊŋ] F **-, -en** directive, instruction, direction; (*Jur*) ruling; **auf ~** on instructions; **ich habe ~, keine Auskünfte zu geben** I have instructions not to give any details

Wei|sungs-: Wei|sungs|be|fug|nis F authority to issue directives; **wei|sungs|be|rech|tigt** ADJ (*Jur*) authorized to issue directives; **wei|sungs|ge|bun|den** ADJ subject to directives; **wei|sungs|ge|mäß** ADJ, ADV according to instructions, as per instructions, as instructed *or* directed; **Wei|sungs|recht** NT authority to issue directives

---

weit [vait]	
1 ADJEKTIV	2 ADVERB

1 – ADJEKTIV

Siehe auch Einträge **weitere, weitgehend, weitgreifend, weitreichend, weittragend, weitverbreitet, weitverzweigt.**

a = *breit* wide; *Pupille* dilated; *Meer* open; *Begriff* broad; *Unterschied, Herz* big; **das Herz wurde mir weit** (*liter*) my heart swelled (with emotion); **weite Kreise** *or* **Teile der Bevölkerung** large sections of the population; **im weiteren Sinne** in the broader *or* wider sense; **das ist ein weites Feld** (*fig*) that is a big subject

b = *lang* *Weg, Reise, Wurf etc* long; **in weiten Abständen** widely spaced; (*zeitlich*) at long intervals; **man hat hier einen weiten Blick** *or* **eine weite Sicht** you can see a long way from here; **in weiter Ferne** far in the distance, a long way away; **das liegt (noch) in weiter Ferne** it's still a long way away; (*zeitlich auch*) it's still in the distant future, it's still a long way off

◆ **so weit sein** (= *bereit*) to be ready; **seid ihr schon so weit, dass ihr anfangen könnt?** are you ready to start?; **es ist/war bald so weit** the time has/had nearly come; **wie lange dauert es noch, bis der Film anfängt? – es ist gleich so weit** how long will it be till the film starts? – not long, it'll start any minute now

2 – ADVERB

a Entfernung far; **weiter** further, farther; **am weitesten** (the) furthest, (the) farthest; **wie weit ist Bremen?** how far is (it to) Bremen?; **Bremen ist 10 km weit** Bremen is 10 kms away, it's 10 kms to Bremen; **es ist noch weit bis Bremen** it's still a long way to Bremen; **hast du es noch weit (nach Hause)?** have you got a long way *or* far to go (to get home)?; **3,60 m weit springen** to jump 3m 60; **wie weit bist du gesprungen?** how far did you jump?; (**sehr**) **weit springen/fahren** to jump/drive a (very) long way; **weit gereist** widely travelled (*Brit*) *or* traveled (*US*); **weit hergeholt** far-fetched; **weit und breit** for miles around; **weit ab** *or* **weg (von)** far away (from); **weit am Anfang/Ende/Rand** right at the beginning/end/edge; **ziemlich weit am Ende** fairly near the end; **weit vom Thema** well off the subject; **wir kommen immer weiter vom Thema ab** we're getting further and further away from the subject; **von weitem** from a long way away; **von weit her** from a long way away; **weit schauend** *or* **blickend** far-sighted → *auch* **weitblickend weit gesteckt** ambitious

◆ **weit entfernt** far away, a long way away; **weiter entfernt** further *or* farther away; **ich bin weit davon entfernt, das zu tun** I have no intention of doing that; **der Prototyp ist weit davon entfernt, in Serie gebaut zu werden** the prototype is a long way from being ready for mass-production; **weit entfernt** *or* **gefehlt!** far from it!

b = *breit* offen, öffnen wide; verzweigt, herumkommen widely; **10 cm weit** 10cm wide; **weit verbreitet** widespread; **weit bekannt** widely known; **weit ausholend** (*Geste etc*) expansive; (*fig*) Erzählung etc long-drawn-out, long-winded; **etw weit ausholend erzählen** to tell sth at great length

c in Entwicklung **weit fortgeschritten** far *or* well advanced; **die Krankheit ist schon ziemlich weit** the disease is already quite far advanced; **wie weit bist du?** how far have you got?; **wie weit ist das Essen?** how far have you/they *etc* got with the food?; **so weit, so gut** so far so good; **sie sind nicht weit gekommen** they didn't get far; **jdn so weit bringen, dass ...** to bring sb to the point where ...

◆ **es weit bringen** er wird es weit bringen he will go far; **er hat es weit gebracht** he has achieved a lot; **es so weit bringen, dass ...** to bring it about that ...; **sie hat es so weit gebracht, dass man sie entließ** she drove them to dismiss her

d zeitlich **es ist noch weit (hin) bis Ostern** Easter is still a long way off; (**bis**) **weit in die Nacht** (till) far into the night; **weit nach Mitternacht** well *or* long after midnight; **weit zurückliegen** to be a long way back

e = *erheblich* far; **das hat unsere Erwartungen weit übertroffen** it far exceeded our expectations; **weit über 60** well over 60

f andere Wendungen

◆ **zu weit zu weit gehen** to go too far; **das geht zu weit!** that's going too far!; **etw zu weit treiben** to carry sth too far; **das würde zu weit führen** that would be taking things too far

◆ **so weit** (= *im Großen und Ganzen*) by and large, on the whole; (= *bis jetzt*) up to now; (= *bis zu diesem Punkt*) so far; **so weit ganz gut** (*inf*) not too bad; **so weit wie** *or* **als möglich** as far as possible; **ich bin so weit fertig** I'm more or less ready

◆ **bei weitem bei weitem besser** etc **als** far better etc than; **bei weitem der Beste** by far the best; **bei weitem nicht so gut** etc (**wie...**) not nearly as good etc (as ...); **bei weitem nicht!** not by a long way! (*inf*)

◆ **nicht weit her das ist nicht weit her** (*inf*) that's not up to much (*Brit inf*), that's nothing to write home about (*inf*); **damit ist es nicht weit her** (*inf*) this isn't up to much (*Brit inf*), this isn't much use

◆ **weit reichen sein Einfluss reicht sehr weit** his influence is far-reaching; **das Geld reicht nicht weit** the money won't go far

---

Weit-: weit|ab ['vaitˈlap] ADV ~ **von** far (away) from; **weit|aus** ['vaitˈlaus] ADV (vor comp) far; (vor superl) (by) far, far and away; **weit|aus|-hollend** △ ADJ → **weit 2 b**; **weit|be|kannt** △ ADJ attr → **weit 2 b**; **Weit|blick** M , no pl (fig) vision, far-sightedness; **weit|bli|ckend** △ comp **weitblickender**, superl **weitblickendste(r,s)**, **weit bli|ckend** ▲ comp **weiter blickend**, superl **am weitesten blickend** ADJ (fig) far-sighted

Weite¹ ['vaitə] F -, -n (= Entfernung, Ferne) distance; (= Länge) length; (= Größe) expanse; (= Durchmesser, Breite) width; **in die ~** to look into the distance; **etw in der ~ ändern** to alter the width of sth; **in der ~ passt das Hemd** the shirt fits as regards width; **etw in die ~ ziehen** to pull sth out; **Pullover** to stretch sth out

Weite² NT -n, no pl distance; **ins ~ gehen** to go out into the distance; **das ~ suchen** to take to one's heels; **das ~ gewinnen** (liter) to reach freedom

weiten ['vaitn] VT to widen; (durch Ziehen auch) to stretch VR to widen, to broaden (auch fig); (Pupille, Gefäße) to dilate; (fig liter: Herz) to swell

weiter ['vaitɐ] comp von **weit** ADJ (fig) further; (= zusätzlich auch) additional; (= andere) other; **~e Auskünfte** further information
ADV (= noch hinzu) further; (= außerdem) furthermore; (= sonst) otherwise; (= nachher) afterwards; **nichts ~, ~ nichts** (= darüber hinaus nichts) nothing further or more or else; **~ nichts?** is that all?; **nichts ~ als ..., ~ nichts als ...** nothing more than ..., nothing but ...; **ich brauche ~ nichts** that's all I need, I don't need anything else; **ich brauche nichts ~ als ...** all I need is ...; **er wollte ~ nichts, als nach Hause gehen** all he wanted was to go home; **wenn es ~ nichts ist, ... well,** if that's all (it is), ...; **außer uns war ~ niemand** or **niemand ~ da** there was nobody else there besides us; **nicht ~, ~ nicht** (= eigentlich) not really; **das stört ~ keinen** that doesn't really bother anybody; **das hat ~ nichts** or **nichts ~ zu sagen** that doesn't really matter, that's neither here nor there; **das macht ~ nichts** it's not that or really important; **etw ~ tun** to continue to do sth, to continue doing sth; **immer ~** on and on; (Anweisung) keep on (going); **er hat sich immer ~ verbessert** he kept on improving; **nur immer ~!** keep at it!; **und ~?** and then?; **was geschah (dann) ~?** what happened then or next?; **und so ~** and so on or forth, et cetera; **und so ~ und so fort** and so on and so forth, et cetera et cetera; **kein Wort ~!** not another word! → **Weitere(s)**

weiter- PREF (= weitermachen mit) to carry on or go on or continue +prp, to continue to +infin; (= nicht aufhören mit) to keep on or go on +prp; (bei Bewegung, Beförderung, Reise etc) vb + on

Weiter-: weiter|ar|bei|ten VI sep → **weiter-** to carry on etc working, to work on; **an einer Sache** (dat) **~** to do some more work on sth; **weiter|be|för|dern** ptp **weiterbefördert** VT sep to send on; Passagiere to transport; jdn (in Firma etc) to promote further; **weiter|be|han|deln** ptp **weiterbehandelt** VT sep → **weiter-** to carry on etc treating; **Weiter|be|hand|lung** F further treatment; **Weiter|be|schäf|ti|gung** F continued employment; **weiter be|ste|hen** ▲ VI irreg to continue to exist, to survive; **Weiter|be|ste|hen** NT continued existence; **weiter|be|we|gen** ptp **weiterbewegt** sep VT to move further VR to move further; **weiter be|we|gen** ▲ VR (weiterhin) to carry on moving; **weiter|bil|den** sep VT jdn **~** to give sb further education, to educate sb further VR to continue one's education; **Weiter|bil|dung** F continuation of one's education; (an Hochschule) further education; **Weiter|bil|dungs|an|ge|bot** NT opportunities pl for further education; **weiter|brin|gen** VT sep irreg to take further, to advance; **das bringt uns auch nicht weiter** that's not much help (to us), that doesn't get us any further; **weiter|den|ken** sep irreg

VT to think out (further) **VI** to think it out; **wei|ter den|ken** ▲ VI irreg (an Zukünftiges) to think ahead; **weiter|emp|feh|len** ptp **weiterempfohlen** VT sep irreg to recommend (to one's friends etc); **weiter|ent|wi|ckeln** ptp **weiterentwickelt** sep VT to develop; Idee to develop (further) VR to develop (zu into); **Wei|ter|ent|wick|lung** F development; **wei|ter|er|zäh|len** ptp **weitererzählt** VT sep → **weiter-** to carry on etc telling; Geheimnis etc to repeat, to pass on; **das hat er der ganzen Klasse weitererzählt** he told the whole class

Weite|re(s) ['vaitərə] NT decl as adj further details pl; **ich habe nichts ~s zu sagen** I have nothing further to say; **das ~ the rest;** **alles ~** everything else, all the rest; **des weiteren** in addition, furthermore; **bis auf weiteres** for the time being; (amtlich, auf Schildern etc) until further notice; **im ~n** subsequently, afterwards; **zum ~n** furthermore, in addition, on top of that → **ohne PREP b**

Weiter-: weiter|fah|ren sep irreg VT → **weiter-** to carry on etc driving, to keep on driving VI aux sein **a** (= Fahrt fortsetzen) to go on, to continue; (= durchfahren) to drive on; (= weiterreisen) to travel on **b** (dial) = **fortfahren** VI b; **Weiter|fahrt** F continuation of one's journey; **vor der ~ sahen wir ...** before continuing our journey we saw ...; **weiter|flie|gen** VI sep irreg aux sein to fly on; **die Maschine fliegt in 10 Minuten weiter** the plane will take off again in 10 minutes; **Weiter|flug** M continuation of the/one's flight; **auf dem ~** after we'd taken off again; **Passagiere zum ~ nach ...** passengers continuing their flight to ...; **wei|ter|füh|ren** sep VT to continue; Gespräch auch to carry on (with) VI to continue, to lead on; **das führt nicht weiter** (fig) that doesn't lead or get us anywhere; **weiter|füh|rend** ADJ Schule secondary; Bildungsgang, Qualifikation higher; Entwicklung, Lektüre further; **Weiter|ga|be** F passing on; (von Informationen, Erbfaktoren auch) transmission; **weiter|ge|ben** VT sep irreg to pass on; to transmit; **weiter|ge|hen** VI sep irreg aux sein to go on; **bitte ~!** (Polizist etc) move along or on (there), please!; **so kann es nicht ~** (fig) things can't go on like this; **wie soll es nun ~?** (fig) what's going to happen now?; **wei|ter|hel|fen** VI sep irreg to help (along) (jdm sb); **weiter|hin** ['vaitɐˈhɪn] ADV (= außerdem) furthermore, on top of that; **etw ~ tun** to carry on etc doing sth; **weiter|kämp|fen** VI sep to fight on; **weiter|kom|men** VI sep irreg aux sein to get further; (fig auch) to make progress or headway; **nicht ~** (fig) to be stuck, to be bogged down; **wir kommen einfach nicht weiter** we're just not getting anywhere; **Weiter|kom|men** NT advancement; **weiter|kön|nen** VI sep irreg to be able to carry on or go on or continue; **ich kann nicht weiter** I can't go on; (bei Rätsel, Prüfung etc) I'm stuck; **wei|ter|lau|fen** VI sep irreg aux sein to run on; (= gehen) to walk on; (Film) to go on; (Betrieb, Produktion) to go on, to continue; (Gehalt) to continue to be paid; (Motor) to keep on running; **ich kann nicht ~** I can't walk any further; **den Motor ~ lassen** to leave the engine running; **weiter|le|ben** VI sep to live on, to continue to live; **weiter|lei|ten** VT sep to pass on (an +acc to); (= weiterbefördern, -senden) to forward; **weiter|ma|chen** VTI sep to carry on (etw with sth), to continue; **~!** (Mil) carry on!; **Wei|ter|marsch** M **zum ~ bereit** ready to march on; **auf dem ~ waren sie ...** as they marched on they were ...; **weiter|rei|chen** VT sep to pass on; **Weiter|rei|se** F continuation of the/one's journey; **ich wünsche Ihnen eine gute ~** I hope the rest of the journey goes well; **auf der ~ nach ...** when I etc was travelling (Brit) or traveling (US) on to ...; **weiter|rü|cken** sep VT to move further along VI aux sein to move up, to move further along

weiters ['vaitɐs] ADV (Aus) = **ferner**

weiter-: weiter|sa|gen VT sep to repeat, to pass on; **~!** pass it on!; **nicht ~!** don't tell anyone!; **weiter|schen|ken** VT sep to give away (to somebody else); **weiter|schla|fen** VI sep irreg to sleep on, to go on sleeping; (= wieder einschlafen) to go back to sleep; **wei|ter+schlep|pen** sep VT to haul or drag further VR to drag or haul oneself on; **weiter|sen|den** sep irreg VTI (Rad, TV) → **weiter-** to carry on etc broadcasting VT (form) to forward; **weiter+spin|nen** VT sep irreg (fig) Gedanken etc to develop further

Weite|run|gen ['vaitərʊŋən] PL (old, form) complications pl, difficulties pl; **unangenehme ~ zur Folge haben** to have unpleasant consequences

Weiter-: weiter+ver|ar|bei|ten ptp **weiterverarbeitet** VT sep to process; **Weiter|ver|ar|bei|tung** F (further) processing; **weiter+ver|bin|den** ptp **weiterverbunden** VT sep irreg (am Telefon) to put through (an +acc to); **wei|ter+ver|brei|ten** ptp **weiterverbreitet** sep VT to spread (further), to repeat, to propagate (form) VR to spread (zu into); **weiter+ver|fol|gen** ptp **weiterverfolgt** VT sep → **weiter-** Entwicklung, Straße to carry on etc following; Verbrecher to continue to pursue; Idee, Pläne to pursue further; **Weiter|ver|kauf** M resale; **nicht zum ~ bestimmt** not for resale; **weiter+ver|kau|fen** ptp **weiterverkauft** VTI sep to resell; **weiter+ver|mie|ten** ptp **weitervermietet** VT sep to sublet; **Weiter|ver|sand** M redispatch; **weiter+ver|wen|den** ptp **weiterverwendet** VT sep to continue to use; (Ecology: Glas etc) to reuse; **weiter+wis|sen** VI sep irreg **nicht (mehr) ~** not to know how to go on; (bei Rätsel, Prüfung) to be stuck; (= verzweifelt sein) to be at one's wits' end; **weiter+wol|len** VI sep irreg to want to go on; **der Esel wollte einfach nicht weiter** the donkey simply wouldn't go any further; **wei|ter+zah|len** VTI sep to continue paying or to pay

wei|test|ge|hend ['vaitəst-] ADV to the greatest possible extent

weit-: weit|ge|hend¹ comp **weitgehender**, superl **weitgehendste(r,s)**, **weit ge|hend** ▲ comp **wei|ter gehend**, superl **am weitesten gehend** ADJ Vollmachten etc far-reaching, extensive, wide; Übereinstimmung etc a large degree of; **er hatte viel ~ere** or **weiter gehende Befürchtungen** his fears went a lot further than that; **weit|ge|hend²** comp **weitgehender**, superl **weitgehendst** ADV to a great or large extent, largely → auch **weitestgehend**; **weit|ge|reist** △ [-gəraist] ADJ attr → **weit 2 a**; **weit|ge|steckt** △ [-gəʃtɛkt] ADJ attr → **weit 2 a**; **weit|grei|fend** comp **weitgreifender**, superl **weitgreifendste(r,s)**, **weit grei|fend** ▲ comp **weiter greifend**, superl **am weitesten greifend** ADJ attr far-reaching; **weit|her** ['vaitˈheːɐ, vaitˈheːɐ] ADV (auch **von weit her**) from a long way away, from far away, from afar (liter); **weit|her|ge|holt** △ ['vaitˈheːɐgəhoːlt] ADJ attr → **weit 2 f**; **weit|her|zig** ADJ understanding, charitable; **weit|hin** ['vaitˈhɪn] ADV over a long distance, for a long way; (fig) bekannt, beliebt widely; unbekannt largely; (= weitgehend) to a great or large extent

weit|läu|fig ADJ **a** Park, Gebäude spacious; (= verzweigt) rambling; Dorf covering a wide area, sprawling attr; (fig) Erzählung lengthy, long-drawn-out, long-winded **b** Verwandte distant ADV **etw ~ erzählen** to tell sth at (great) length; **sie sind ~ verwandt** they are distant relatives; **ich bin mit ihm ~ verwandt** I am distantly related to him

Weit|läu|fig|keit ['vaitlɔyfɪçkait] F -, -en (von Park, Gebäude) spaciousness; (fig: von Erzählung) length, long-windedness

Weit-: weit|ma|schig [-maʃɪç] ADJ Netz coarse-meshed, wide-meshed, broad-meshed; Gestricktes loosely knitted, loose-knit; **weit|räu|mig** [-rɔymɪç] ADJ wide-ranging ADV **ein Gelände ~ absperren** to cordon off a wide area around a site; **die Unfallstelle ~ umfahren** to keep well away from the scene of the accident; **der Verkehr am Stuttgarter Kreuz ist zum Erliegen gekommen und wird ~ umgeleitet** traffic has come to a complete stop at the Stuttgart intersection and is being diverted well away from the obstruction; **~er spielen** (*Ftbl*) to cover more of the field; **weit|rei|chend** *comp* **weitreichender**, *superl* **weitreichendste(r, s)**, **weit rei|chend** ▲ *comp* **weiter reichend**, *superl* **am weitesten reichend** ADJ (*fig*) far-reaching; (*Mil*) long-range *attr*; **weiter reichend** further reaching; **weit|schau|end** △ ADJ **→ weit 2 a**; **weit|schwei|fig** [-ʃvaifɪç] **ADJ** long-winded, circumlocutory, prolix (*form*) **ADV** long-windedly, lengthily; **Weit|sicht** F (*fig*) far-sightedness; **weit|sich|tig** [-zɪçtɪç] ADJ (*Med*) long-sighted (*Brit*), far-sighted (*esp US*); (*fig*) far-sighted; **Weit|sich|tig|keit** F -, *no pl* (*Med*) long-sightedness (*Brit*), far-sightedness (*esp US*); **weit+sprin|gen** VI *sep* (*infin only*) (*Sport*) to do the long jump; **Weit|sprin|gen** NT (*Sport*) long jump; **Weit|sprin|ger(in)** M(F) (*Sport*) long jumper; **Weit|sprung** M (*Sport*) long jump; **weit|tra|gend** *comp* **weittragender**, *superl* **weittragendste(r, s)**, **weit tra|gend** ▲ *comp* **weiter tragend**, *superl* **am weitesten tragend** (*Mil*) long-range *attr*, (*fig*) far-reaching, far-ranging; **weiter tragend** (*Mil*) longer-range *attr*, (*fig*) further-reaching; **weit|um** ['vait'lʊm] ADV for miles around

Wei|tung F -, -en (*geh*) widening

Weit-: weit|ver|brei|tet [-fɛɐbraitət] *comp* **weitverbreiteter**, *superl* **weitverbreiteste(r, s)**, **weit ver|brei|tet** ▲ *comp* **weiter verbreitet**, *superl* **am weitesten verbreitet** ADJ widespread, common; *Ansicht auch* widely held; *Zeitung* with a wide circulation; **weit|ver|zweigt** *comp* **weitverzweigter**, *superl* **weitverzweigteste(r,s)**, **weit ver|zweigt** ▲ *comp* **weiter verzweigt**, *superl* **am weitesten verzweigt** ADJ *Straßensystem* branching out in all directions; *Konzern, Familie, Stammbaum* with many branches; *Computersystem* extensive; **Weit|win|kel|ob|jek|tiv** NT wide-angle lens

Wei|zen ['vaitsn] M -s, *no pl* wheat **→ Spreu**

Wei|zen-: Wei|zen|bier NT *light, very fizzy beer made by using wheat, malt and top-fermentation yeast*; **Wei|zen|brot** NT wheat or wheaten (*Brit*) bread; **Wei|zen|kei|me** PL (*Cook*) wheat germ *sing*; **Wei|zen|keim|öl** NT (*Cook*) wheat germ oil; **Wei|zen|kleie** F (*Cook*) wheat bran; **Wei|zen|mehl** NT wheat or wheaten (*Brit*) flour; **Wei|zen|schrot** M OR NT wheatmeal

welch [vɛlç] **INTERROG PRON** *inv* **a** (*geh: in Ausrufen*) what; **~ friedliches Bild!** what a peaceful scene! **b** (*in indirekten Fragesätzen*) **~ (ein)** what ... **REL PRON** *inv* **X, Y und Z, ~ letztere(r, s) ...** (*obs, form*) X, Y and Z, the last of which/whom ...

wel|che(r, s) ['vɛlçə] **INTERROG PRON a** (*adjektivisch*) what; (*bei Wahl aus einer begrenzten Menge*) which; **~ Mensch könnte behaupten ...?** what person could claim ...?; **~s Kleid soll ich anziehen, das rote oder das grüne?** which dress shall I wear, the red one or the green one? **b** (*substantivisch*) which (one); **~r von den beiden?** which (one) of the two?; **~s sind die Symptome dieser Krankheit?** what are the symptoms of this illness?; **es gibt viele schöne Frauen, aber ~ könnte sich mit Isabella vergleichen?** there are many beautiful women, but which of them could compare with Isabella? **c** (*in Ausrufen*) **~ Schande!** what a disgrace!; **~ Freude!** what joy! **INDEF PRON** some; (*in Fragen, konditional auch, verneint*) any; **es gibt ~, die glauben ...** there are some (people) who think ...; **ich habe keine Tinte/Äpfel, haben Sie ~?** I don't have any ink/apples, do you have some *or* any? **REL PRON** (*rare*) (*Mensch*) who; (*Sache*) which, that; **~(r, s) auch immer** whoever/whichever/ whatever

wel|cher|art ['vɛlçə'|a:ɐt] **INTERROG ADJ** *inv* (*geh*) (*attributiv*) what kind of; (*substantivisch*) of what kind; **sagen Sie mir, ~ Ihre Erfahrungen sind** tell me what sort of experiences you (have) had; **~ Ihre Erfahrungen auch sein mögen** whatever your experiences may have been like **INTERROG ADV** in what way

wel|cher|lei ['vɛlçə'|lai] INTERROG ADJ *inv* (*geh*) what kind *or* sort of

wel|ches ['vɛlçəs] PRON **→ welche(r, s)**

Welf|fe ['vɛlfə] M -n, -n, **Welf|fin** ['vɛlfɪn] F -, -nen (*Hist*) Guelph

welf|fisch ['vɛlfɪʃ] ADJ (*Hist*) Guelphic

welk [vɛlk] ADJ *Blume, Pflanze* wilted, faded; *Blatt* dead; (*fig*) *Schönheit* fading, wilting; *Haut, Gesicht* tired-looking; (= *schlaff*) flaccid; *Hände* withered; **wie ein ~es Pflänzchen** (*inf*) like a wet rag (*inf*)

wel|ken ['vɛlkn] VI *aux sein* (*lit, fig*) to fade, to wilt; (*Haut, Gesicht*) to grow tired-looking; (= *schlaff werden*) to sag

Welk|heit F -, *no pl* wilted state; (*von Haut, Gesicht*) tired look

Well|blech ['vɛl-] NT corrugated iron

Well|blech|hüt|te ['vɛl-] F corrugated-iron hut; (*halbrund*) Nissen hut (*esp Brit*), Quonset hut (*US*)

Wel|le ['vɛlə] F -, -n **a** wave (*auch fig, Phys, im Haar etc*); (*Rad*: = *Frequenz*) wavelength; **sein Grab in ~n finden** (*geh*) to go to a watery grave; **weiche ~** (*inf*) soft line; **mach keine ~n!** (*inf*) don't make such a fuss; **(hohe) ~n schlagen** (*fig*) to create (quite) a stir **b** (*fig*: = *Mode*) craze; **die Neue ~** (*Film*) the nouvelle vague, the New Wave; (*Mus*) the New Wave **c** (*Tech*) shaft **d** (*Sport*) circle

wel|len ['vɛlən] **VT** *Haar* to wave; *Blech etc* to corrugate **VR** (= *gewellt sein*) to be wavy; (= *Wellen bekommen*) to become wavy; **gewelltes Haar** wavy hair

Wel|len-: wel|len|ar|tig **ADJ** wave-like; *Linie etc* wavy **ADV** like a wave; **Wel|len|bad** NT *swimming pool with wave machine*; **Wel|len|be|reich** M (*Phys, Telec*) frequency range; (*Rad*) waveband; **Wel|len|berg** M mountainous *or* giant wave; **Wel|len|be|we|gung** F undulation, wave motion; **Wel|len|bre|cher** M breakwater, groyne (*Brit*), groin (*esp US*); **wel|len|för|mig** **ADJ** wave-like; **Wel|len|gang** [-gaŋ] M , *no pl* waves *pl*, swell; **starker ~** heavy sea(s) *or* swell; **leichter ~** light swell; **Wel|len|kamm** M crest (of a wave); **Wel|len|kraft|werk** NT wave-power generator; **Wel|len|län|ge** F (*Phys, Telec*) wavelength; **sich auf jds ~** (*acc*) **einstellen** (*inf*) to get on sb's wavelength (*inf*); **auf der gleichen ~ sein** *or* **liegen, die gleiche ~ haben** (*inf*) to be on the same wavelength (*inf*); **Wel|len|li|nie** F wavy line; **Wel|len|me|cha|nik** F (*Phys*) wave mechanics *sing*; **Wel|len|rei|ten** NT -s, *no pl* (*Sport*) surfing; (*auf Fluss*) *sport of balancing on a board attached by a rope to the riverbank*; **Wel|len|sa|lat** M (*Rad inf*) jumble of frequencies; **Wel|len|schlag** M breaking of the waves; (*sanft auch*) lapping of the waves; (*heftig auch*) pounding of the waves; **Wel|len|schliff** M (*am Messer*) serrated edge; **Wel|len|sit|tich** M budgerigar, budgie (*inf*); **Wel|len|tal** NT (wave) trough

Well-: Well|fleisch NT boiled pork; **Well|horn|schne|cke** F whelk

wel|lig ['vɛlɪç] ADJ *Haar etc* wavy; *Oberfläche, Fahrbahn* uneven; *Hügelland* rolling, undulating

Well|ness ['wɛlnəs] F -, *no pl* wellness

Well|pap|pe ['vɛl-] F corrugated cardboard

Wel|pe ['vɛlpə] M -n, -n pup, whelp; (*von Wolf, Fuchs*) cub, whelp

Wels [vɛls] M -es, -e [-zə] catfish

welsch [vɛlʃ] ADJ **a** (*old*) Latin, Southern European; (= *welschsprachig*) Romance-speaking;

~e Sitten und Gebräuche dubious morals and practices **b** (*Aus pej: = italienisch*) Eyetie (*Brit pej sl*), wop (*pej sl*); **die Welschen** the Eyeties (*Brit pej sl*), the wops (*pej sl*) **c** (*Sw*) (Swiss-)-French; **die ~e Schweiz** French Switzerland

Welsch-: Welsch|land NT -s (*Sw*) French Switzerland; **Welsch|schwei|zer(in)** M(F) (*Sw*) French Swiss; **welsch|schwei|ze|risch** ADJ (*Sw*) Swiss-French

Welt [vɛlt] F -, -en (*lit, fig*) world; **die ~ im Kleinen** the microcosm; **die ~ im Großen** the macrocosm; **die (große) weite ~** the big wide world; **der höchste Berg der ~** the highest mountain in the world, the world's highest mountain; **die ~ von heute/morgen** the world of today/tomorrow, today's/tomorrow's world; **die ~ der Oper/des Kindes** the world of opera/ the child, the operatic/child's world; **die Alte/Neue/freie/Dritte ~** the Old/New/Free/Third World; **die große *or* vornehme ~** high society; **alle ~, Gott und die ~** everybody, the whole world, the world and his wife (*hum*); **eine ~ brach für ihn zusammen** his whole world collapsed about (*Brit*) *or* around him *or* his ears, the bottom fell out of his world; **das ist doch nicht die ~** it isn't as important as all that; **davon *or* deswegen geht die ~ nicht unter** (*inf*) it isn't the end of the world; **das kostet doch nicht die ~** it won't cost the earth (*Brit*) *or* a fortune; **uns/sie trennen ~en** (*fig*) **zwischen uns/ihnen liegen ~en** (*fig*) we/they are worlds apart; **auf der ~** in the world; **davon gibt es noch mehr auf der ~** there are plenty of those around; **etw mit auf die ~ bringen** to be born with sth; **aus aller ~** from all over the world; **aus der ~ schaffen** to eliminate; **aus der ~ scheiden** (*geh*) to depart this life (*liter*); (= *Selbstmord begehen*) to put an end to one's life; **in aller ~** all over the world; **in alle ~ zerstreut** scattered all over the world *or* globe; **warum/ wer in aller ~ ...?** why/who on earth ...?, why/who in the world ...?; **so geht es nun mal in der ~** that's the way of the world, that's the way things go; **in einer anderen ~ leben** to live in a different world; **in seiner eigenen ~ leben** to live in a world of one's own; **um nichts in der ~, nicht um alles in der ~, um keinen Preis der ~** not for love (n)or money, not at any price, not for all the tea in China (*inf*); **ein Kind in die ~ setzen** to bring a child into the world; **ein Gerücht in die ~ setzen** to put about *or* spread a rumour (*Brit*) *or* rumor (*US*); **ein Mann/eine Frau von ~** a man/woman of the world; **die beste Frau *etc* (von) der ~** the best woman *etc* in the world; **vor aller ~** publicly, in front of everybody, openly; **zur ~ bringen** to give birth to, to bring into the world; **auf die** *or* **zur ~ kommen** to come into the world, to be born **→ Brett, Ende**

Welt- *in cpds* world; **welt|ab|ge|wandt** [-lapgə-vant] ADJ withdrawn; **Welt|all** NT universe, cosmos; **Welt|al|ter** NT age, epoch; **welt|an|schau|lich** ADJ ideological; **Welt|an|schau|ung** F philosophy of life; (*Philos, Pol*) world view, weltanschauung; **Welt|aus|stel|lung** F world exhibition, world's fair; **Welt|bank** F , *no pl* World Bank; **welt|be|kannt** ADJ world-famous; **welt|be|rühmt** ADJ world-famous; *Schriftsteller, Künstler etc auch* world-renowned; **Welt|bes|te(r)** [-bɛstə] MF *decl as adj* world's best; **welt|bes|te(r, s)** ADJ *attr* world's best; **Welt|best|leis|tung** F world's best performance, world best (*inf*); **Welt|be|völ|ke|rung** F world population; **welt|be|we|gend** ADJ world-shattering; **Welt|bild** NT conception of the world; (= *jds Ansichten*) philosophy, view of life; **Welt|blatt** NT (*Press*) international (news)paper; **Welt|brand** M global conflagration; **Welt|bür|ger(in)** M(F) citizen of the world, cosmopolitan; **Welt|bür|ger|tum** NT cosmopolitanism; **Welt|chro|nik** F world chronicle; **Welt|cup** M (*Sport*) World Cup; **Welt|emp|fän|ger** M world receiver *or* radio

Wel|ten-: **Wel|ten|bumm|ler(in)** M(F) globetrotter; **Wel|ten|raum** M (liter) space

welt|ent|rückt [-ɛntrʏkt] ADJ remote, isolated

Welt|er|folg M global or worldwide success or hit (inf)

Wel|ter|ge|wicht NT (Boxen) welterweight

Welt-: **Welt|er|näh|rungs|or|ga|ni|sa|ti|on** F Food and Agriculture Organization; **welt|er|schüt|ternd** ADJ world-shattering; **welt|fern** ADJ unrealistic, naïve; **Welt|flucht** F flight from reality, escapism; **welt|fremd** ADJ unworldly; **Welt|fremd|heit** F unworldliness; **Welt|frie|de(n)** M world peace; **Welt|frie|dens|tag** M World Peace Day; **Welt|ge|fü|ge** NT universe, world system, scheme of things; **Welt|geist** M , no pl (Philos) world spirit; **Welt|geist|li|che(r)** MF decl as adj secular priest; **Welt|gel|tung** F international standing, worldwide recognition; **Welt|ge|mein|schaft** F international community; **Welt|ge|richt** NT Last Judgement; **Welt|ge|richts|hof** M International Court; **Welt|ge|schich|te** F world history; **in der ~ herumfah-ren** (inf) to travel around all over the place; **welt|ge|schicht|lich** ADJ **ein ~e Ereignis** an important event in the history of the world; **von ~er Bedeutung** of great significance in world history; **~ gesehen, aus ~er Sicht** looked at from the point of view of world history; **Welt|ge|sund|heits|or|ga|ni|sa|ti|on** F World Health Organization; **Welt|ge|trie|be** NT (liter) (hustle and) bustle of the world; **welt|ge|wandt** ADJ sophisticated, well-versed in the ways of the world; **Welt|ge|wandt|heit** F sophistication, experience in the ways of the world; **Welt|han|del** M world trade; **Welt|han|dels|or|ga|ni|sa|ti|on** F World Trade Organization; **Welt|herr|schaft** F world domination; **Welt|hilfs|spra|che** F international auxiliary language; **Welt|hun|ger|hil|fe** F world famine relief; **Welt|kar|te** F map of the world; **Welt|kir|chen|rat** M World Council of Churches; **Welt|klas|se** F **ein Hochspringer der ~** a world-class high jumper; **~ sein** to be world class; (inf) to be great (inf) or fantastic (inf); **welt|klug** ADJ worldly-wise; **Welt|kör-per** M (old: = Himmelskörper) heavenly or celestial body; **Welt|krieg** M world war; **der ers-te** or **Erste/zweite** or **Zweite ~** World War One/Two, the First/Second World War; **Welt|ku-gel** F globe; **Welt|kul|tur|er|be** NT world cultural heritage; (= einzelnes Kulturgut) World Heritage Site; **Welt|lauf** M way of the world; **welt|läu|fig** ADJ cosmopolitan; **Welt|läu|fig-keit** F cosmopolitanism; **welt|lich** ['vɛltlɪç] ADJ worldly, mundane; (= nicht kirchlich, geist-lich) secular; **Macht** temporal; **Welt|li|te|ra|tur** F world literature; **Welt|macht** F world pow-er; **Welt|mann** M pl **-männer** man of the world; **welt|män|nisch** [-mɛnɪʃ] ADJ urbane, sophisticated; **Welt|mar|ke** F name known all over the world; **Welt|markt** M world market; **Welt|markt|preis** M world (market) price; **Welt|meer** NT ocean; **die sieben ~e** the seven seas; **Welt|meis|ter(in)** M(F) world or world's (US) champion; **England/die englische Mann-schaft ist ~** England/the English team are (the) world or world's (US) champions; **Welt|-meis|ter|schaft** F world or world's (US) championship; (Ftbl) World Cup; **Welt|meis-ter|ti|tel** M world title (in +dat in); **welt|of-fen** ADJ liberal-minded, cosmopolitan; **Welt|-of|fen|heit** F cosmopolitan attitudes pl; **Welt|öf|fent|lich|keit** F general public; **was meint die ~ dazu?** what is world opinion on this?, what does the world think about this?; **etw der ~ zugänglich machen** to make sth accessible to the world at large; **Welt|ord|nung** F world order; **Welt|po|li|tik** F world politics pl; **welt|po|li|tisch** ADV **eine/die ~e Entwick-lung** a development in/the development of world politics; **eine ~e Entscheidung** a decision affecting world politics; **die ~e Rolle Deutsch-lands** Germany's role in world politics; **von ~er**

Bedeutung of importance in world politics; **aus ~er Sicht** seen from the standpoint of world politics ADV gesehen from the standpoint of world politics; **eine ~ wichtige Situation** an important international political situation; **~ nicht von Interesse** or **nicht bedeutsam** un-important in the realm of world politics; **Welt|rang** M **von ~** world-famous; **~ genie-ßen** to have world status; **Welt|rang|lis|te** F world rankings pl

Welt|raum M (outer) space

Welt|raum- in cpds space → auch Raum-; **Welt|-raum|ab|wehr** F space defence (Brit) or de-fense (US); **Welt|raum|bahn|hof** M (inf) space mission launch centre; **Welt|raum|be-hör|de** F space agency; **Welt|raum|fah-rer(in)** F space traveller (Brit) or traveler (US); **Welt|raum|fahrt** F space travel; **Welt|-raum|fahr|zeug** NT spacecraft, spaceship; **Welt|raum|for|schung** F space research; **welt|raum|ge|stützt** [-gəʃtʏtst] ADJ space-based; **Welt|raum|la|bor** NT space laboratory; **Welt|raum|rüs|tung** F space weaponry; **Welt|raum|spa|zier|gang** M space walk; **Welt|raum|sta|ti|on** F space station; **Welt|-raum|te|le|skop** NT space telescope; **Welt|-raum|waf|fe** F space weapon

Welt-: **Welt|reich** NT empire; **Welt|rei|se** F world tour, journey (a)round the world; **eine ~ machen** to go (a)round the world; **das ist doch schließlich keine ~** (inf) it's not the other end of the world; **Welt|rei|sen|de(r)** MF decl as adj globetrotter; **Welt|re|kord** M world or world's (US) record; **Welt|re|kord|in|ha-ber(in)** M(F) , **Welt|re|kord|ler** [-rekɔrtlɐ] M -s, -, **Welt|re|kord|le|rin** [-ərɪn] F -, **-nen** world or world's (US) record holder; **Welt|re-li|gi|on** F world religion; **Welt|re|vo|lu|ti|on** F world revolution; **Welt|ruf** M world(wide) reputation; **~ haben** to have a world(wide) rep-utation; **Welt|ruhm** M world fame; **Welt|-schmerz** M world-weariness, weltschmerz (liter); **Welt|si|cher|heits|rat** M (Pol) (United Nations) Security Council; **Welt|sicht** F view of the world; **Welt|spit|ze** F world leader-ship; (Sport) number one position in the world; **~ sein** to be number one or the best in the world, to be the world leader or the world's number one; **Welt|spra|che** F world lan-guage; **Welt|stadt** F international or cosmo-politan city, metropolis; **welt|städ|tisch** ADJ cosmopolitan; **Welt|um|run|dung** [-lʊm-rʊndʊŋ] F -, **-en** (Space) orbit of the earth; (Naut) circumnavigation of the earth; **Welt|-um|seg|ler(in)** M(F) circumnavigator (of the globe); (Sport) round-the-world (Brit) or a-round-the-world (US) yachtsman/-woman; **welt|um|span|nend** ADJ worldwide, global; **Welt|un|ter|gang** M (lit, fig) end of the world; **Welt|un|ter|gangs|stim|mung** F a-pocalyptic mood; **Welt|ver|bes|se|rer** M , **Welt|ver|bes|se|rin** F starry-eyed idealist; **welt|weit** ADJ worldwide, global ADV world-wide; **Welt|wirt|schaft** F world economy; **Welt|wirt|schafts|gip|fel** M World Econom-ic Summit; **Welt|wirt|schafts|kri|se** F world economic crisis; **Welt|wun|der** NT **die sieben ~** the Seven Wonders of the World; **er starrte mich an wie ein ~** (fig) he stared at me as if I were from another planet or as if I were some kind of freak; **Welt|zeit** F Greenwich Mean Time, GMT; **Welt|zeit|uhr** F world clock

wem [ve:m] dat von **wer** INTERROG PRON who ... to, to whom; **mit/von** etc **~ ...** who ... with/from etc, with/from etc whom; **~ von euch soll ich den Schlüssel geben?** which (one) of you should I give the key to?, to which (one) of you should I give the key? REL PRON (= derjeni-ge, dem) the person (who ...) to, the person to whom ...; (= jeder, dem) anyone to whom ..., anyone ... to; **~ ... auch (immer)** whoever ... to, no matter who ... to INDEF PRON (inf: = jeman-dem) to somebody; (in Fragen auch) (to) anybod-y

Wem|fall M dative (case)

wen [ve:n] acc von **wer** INTERROG PRON who, whom; **an ~ hast du geschrieben?** who did you write to?, to whom did you write?; **~ von den Schülern kennst du?** which (one) of these pu-pils do you know?; **für ~ arbeitet er?** who does he work for?, for whom does he work? REL PRON (= derjenige, den) the person (who or whom); (= jeder, den) anybody (who or whom); **~ ... auch immer** whoever ... INDEF PRON (inf: = jemanden) somebody; (in Fragen auch) anybody

Wen|de¹ ['vɛndə] F -, **-n** turn; (= Veränderung) change; (= Wendepunkt) turning point; (Turnen: am Pferd) face or front vault; (Pol) (political) wa-tershed; **die ~ vom 19. zum 20. Jahrhundert** the transition from the 19th to the 20th century; **nach dem Tod seines Vaters nahm seine Ent-wicklung eine ~** after the death of his father his development changed direction or started to take a different direction

---

WENDE

When a significant political or social change takes place in Germany, the term **Wende** is often used. This was the case in 1982, when the coalition government of **CDU/CSU** and **FDP** took over from the coalition government of **SPD** and **FDP** which had been in power for 16 years. Now the term **Wende** is gener-ally used to mean the collapse of the Com-munist system leading to the dissolution of East Germany in 1989 → CDU, CSU, FDP, SPD

Wen|de² ['vɛndə] M -n, -n, **Wen|din** ['vɛndɪn] F -, **-nen** Wend

Wen|de-: **Wen|de|flä|che** F (Mot) turning ar-ea; **Wen|de|hals** M (Orn) wryneck; (fig inf) turncoat (pej); **er ist einer der Wendehälse** he's one of those who have done a (complete) U-turn; **Wen|de|ham|mer** M (Mot) turning bay; **Wen|de|ja|cke** F reversible jacket

Wen|de|kreis M a tropic; **der nördliche ~** (Geog) **der ~ des Krebses** (Astrol) the Tropic of Cancer; **der südliche ~** (Geog) **der ~ des Stein-bocks** (Astrol) the Tropic of Capricorn b (Aut) turning circle

Wen|del ['vɛndl] F -, **-n** spiral, helix; (in Glühbir-ne etc) coil

Wen|del-: **Wen|del|boh|rer** M twist drill; **Wen|del|rut|sche** F spiral chute; **Wen|del|-trep|pe** F spiral staircase

Wen|de-: **Wen|de|ma|nö|ver** NT a (Mot) turning manoeuvre (Brit) or maneuver (US); (auf engem Raum) three-point turn b (fig) U-turn (fig); **Wen|de|man|tel** M reversible coat; **Wen|de|mar|ke** F (Sport) turning mark

wen|den ['vɛndn] pret **wendete** or (liter) **wandte** ['vɛndətə, 'vantə], ptp **gewendet** or (liter) **ge-wandt** [gə'vɛndət, gə'vant] VT a (= umdrehen) to turn (auch Sew); (auf die andere Seite) to turn (over); (in die entgegengesetzte Richtung) to turn ((a)round); (Cook) Eierpfannkuchen to toss; Schnit-zel etc to turn; **bitte ~!** please turn over; **seinen Blick nach Norden ~** (geh) to turn or bend one's eyes to(wards) the north, to look to(wards) the north; **seinen Schritt gen Süden ~** (liter) to turn or bend one's steps southwards (liter); **sie wandte kein Auge von ihm** (geh) she did not take her eyes off him; **wie man es auch wendet ..., man kann die Sache or as drehen und ~, wie man will ...** (fig) whichever way you (care to) look at it ...

b (= aufbringen) **Geld/Zeit auf etw** (acc) **~** (geh) to spend money/time on sth; **viel Mühe/Sorg-falt** etc **an etw** (acc) **~** (geh) to devote a lot of ef-fort/care etc to sth

VR a (= sich umdrehen) to turn ((a)round); (Wetter, Glück) to change, to turn; **sich nach links/zum Gehen/zur Tür ~** to turn to the left/to go/to the door; **sich ins Gegenteil ~** to become the opposite; **seine Liebe wendete sich ins Ge-genteil** his love turned to hate; **seine Freude wendete sich ins Gegenteil** his joy turned to despair; **das Gespräch wendete sich** the conversation took another turn; **sich von jdm ~** (*esp Bibl*) to turn from sb (*liter*); **sich zu jdm/etw ~** to turn to face sb/sth, to turn toward(s) sb/sth; **sich zum Guten** or **Besseren/Schlimmeren ~** to take a turn for the better/worse; **sich zum Besten ~** to turn out for the best

b **sich an jdn ~** (*um Auskunft*) to consult sb; (*um Hilfe*) to turn to sb; (*Buch, Fernsehserie etc*) to be directed at sb, to be (intended) for sb; **sich gegen jdn/etw ~** to come out against sb/sth, to oppose sb/sth

VI to turn (*auch Sport*); (= *umkehren*) to turn (a)round; „**wenden verboten**" "no U-turns"

Wen|de-: **Wen|de|platz** M turning area or place; **Wen|de|punkt** M turning point; (*Math*) point of inflection; **Wen|de|schlei|fe** F (*Mot*) turning loop

wen|dig ['vɛndɪç] ADJ agile, nimble; *Auto* manoeuvrable (*Brit*), maneuverable (*US*); (*fig*) *Politiker etc* agile

Wen|dig|keit F -, *no pl* agility, nimbleness; (*von Auto etc*) manoeuvrability (*Brit*), maneuverability (*US*); (*fig: von Politiker etc*) agility

Wen|din F -, **-nen** Wendish woman, Wend

wen|disch ['vɛndɪʃ] ADJ Wendish

Wen|dung ['vɛndʊŋ] F -, **-en** **a** turn (*auch Mil*); (= *Veränderung*) change; **eine interessante/unerwartete ~ nehmen** (*fig*) to take an interesting/unexpected turn; **eine ~ zum Besseren** or **Guten/Schlechten nehmen** to take a turn for the better/worse, to change for the better/worse; **einer Sache** (*dat*) **eine unerwartete/neue ~ geben** to give sth an unexpected/new turn; **das gab seinem Leben eine neue ~** that changed the direction of his life; **eine interessante** *etc* **~ trat ein** there was an interesting *etc* turn of events **b** (= *Redewendung*) expression, phrase

Wen|fall M accusative (case)

wenig ['ve:nɪç] **a**
ADJ, INDEF PRON **a** *sing* little; **ich habe ~** I have only a little; **(nur) ~ Geld** (only a) little money; **ich besitze nur ~** I only own a few things, I don't own much, I own little; **hast du Zeit? – ~!** have you got time? – not much; **das ist ~** that isn't much; **so ~ wie** or **als möglich** as little as possible; **sie ist mir so ~ sympathisch wie dir** I don't like her any more than you do; **du sagst so ~** you're not saying much; **darüber weiß ich ~** I don't know much about that, I know little about that; **mein ~es Geld** what little money I have; **das ~e, was er übrig hatte** the little he had left; **das ~e Geld muss ausreichen** we'll have to make do with this small amount of money; **um ein ~es jünger (als)** (*geh*) a little younger (than); **es fehlte (nur) ~, und er wäre überfahren worden** he was very nearly run over; **wir haben nicht ~ Mühe damit gehabt** we had more than a little or we had no little difficulty with that; **er gibt sich mit ~(em) zufrieden** (= *verlangt nicht viel*) he is satisfied with a little; (= *ist selten zufrieden*) he isn't satisfied with much; **sie hat zu ~ Geld** *etc* she doesn't have enough money *etc*; **ein Exemplar zu ~ haben** to have one copy too few; **ich habe ihm £ 20 zu ~ gegeben** I offered him £20 too little

b **~e** *pl* (= *ein paar*) a few; (*einschränkend: = nicht viele*) few; **da wir nur ~e sind** as there are only a few of us, as we are only a few; **er ist ein Freund, wie es nur ~e gibt** there are few friends like him; **in ~en Tagen** in (just) a few days; **es sind nur noch ~e Stunden, bis ...** there are only a few hours to go until ...; **nicht ~e (waren da)** quite a few people (were there); **einige ~e Leute** a few people

c (*auch adv*) **ein ~** a little; **ein ~ Salz/besser** a little salt/better

ADV little; **sie kommt (nur) ~ raus** she doesn't get out very often; **er hat sich nicht ~ geärgert** he was not a little annoyed; **das überraschte ihn nicht ~** he was more than a little surprised; **~ besser** little better; **~ bekannt** little-known

attr, little known *pred;* **~ mehr** little more, not much more; **~ erfreulich** not very pleasant; **zu ~** too little, not enough; (*inf:* = *zu wenige*) too few, not enough; **du schläfst zu ~** you don't get enough sleep; **einer/zwei** *etc* **zu ~** one/two *etc* too few

We|nig ['ve:nɪç] NT **viele ~ machen ein Viel** (*Prov*) it all adds up, many a mickle makes a muckle (*Scot Prov*)

we|ni|ger ['ve:nɪgɐ] *comp von* **wenig** **ADJ, INDEF PRON** less; (*+pl*) fewer; **~ werden** to get less and less; **mein Geld wird immer ~** my money is dwindling away; **er wird immer ~** (*inf*) he's getting thinner and thinner; **~ wäre mehr gewesen** it's quality not quantity that counts; **~ Geld** less money; **~ Unfälle** fewer accidents

ADV less; **ihr kommt es ~ auf die Liebe als (vielmehr) auf das Geld an** she's less interested in love than in money; **die Vorlesung war ~ lehrreich als belustigend** the lecture was not so much instructive as amusing; **das finde ich ~ schön!** that's not so nice!; **ich kann seinen Brief kaum lesen, noch viel ~ verstehen** I can hardly read his letter much less understand it or let alone understand it; **je mehr ... desto** or **umso ~ ...** the more ... the less ...; **ich glaube ihm umso ~, weil ...** I believe him all the less because ...; **ich möchte nichts ~, als ihn (zu) beleidigen** the last thing I'd want to do is insult him → **mehr ADV**

CONJ, PREP +*acc* or *gen* less; **sieben ~ drei ist vier** seven less three is four

We|nig|keit F -, *no pl* (*dated:* = *Kleinigkeit*) little, small amount; **meine ~** (*hum inf*) yours truly (*inf*); **und meine ~ hat er vergessen** and he forgot little me (*hum inf*)

we|nigs|tens ['ve:nɪçstns] ADV at least

we|nigs|te(r, s) ['ve:nɪçstə] *superl von* **wenig** **ADJ, INDEF PRON, ADV am ~n** least; (*pl*) fewest; **er hat von uns allen das ~** or **am ~n Geld** he has the least money of any of us; **sie hat von uns allen die ~n** or **am ~n Sorgen** she has the fewest worries of any of us; **von den vier Bildern finde ich diese am ~n schön** of the four pictures I think this one is the least attractive; **das konnte er am ~n vertragen** he could tolerate that least of all; **die ~n (Leute) glauben das** very few (people) believe that; **das ist (doch) das ~, was du tun könntest** that's the (very) least you could do; **das ist noch das ~!** (*inf*) that's the least of it!; **das am ~n!** that least of all!

wenn [vɛn] ✪ 28.1, 29, 30, 31, 33.2, 34.1, 34.4, 36, 38.1, 39.1, 42.2, 45.2 CONJ **a** (*konditional, konzessiv bei Wünschen*) if; **~ er nicht gewesen wäre, hätte ich meine Stelle verloren** if it had not been for him or had it not been for him, I'd have lost my job; **selbst** or **und ~ even if**; **das Wörtchen ~ nicht wär(, wär mein Vater Millionär)** (*Prov*) if ifs and ans were pots and pans (there'd be no need for tinkers) (*Prov*); **~ ... auch ...** even though or if ...; **~ ... gleich ...** (*geh*) although ..., even though ...; **er auch noch so dumm sein mag, ...** however stupid he may be, ...; **~ auch!** (*inf*) even so!, all the same!; **~ es denn gar nicht anders geht** well, if there's no other way; **~ es schon sein muss** well, if that's the way it's got to be; **es ist nicht gut, ~ man mit vollem Magen schwimmt** it's not good to swim on a full stomach; **~ man bedenkt, dass ...** when you consider that ..., considering ...; **~ wir erst das neue Haus haben** once we get the new house; **~ ich doch** or **nur** or **bloß ... !** if only I ...; **~ er nur da wäre!** if only he were or was here!; **es ist, als** or **wie** (*inf*) **~ ...** it's as if ...; **au-ßer ~** except if, unless; **~ du das schon machen willst, (dann) mache es wenigstens richtig** if you want to do it at least do it properly → **wennschon**

b (*zeitlich*) when; **jedes Mal** or **immer ~** whenever; **außer ~** except when, unless

Wenn [vɛn] NT -s, - (**die** *pl* or **das**) **~ und Aber** (the) ifs and buts; **ohne ~ und Aber** without any ifs and buts

wenn|gleich [vɛnˈɡlaɪç] CONJ (*geh*) although, even though; (*mit adj auch*) albeit (*form*)

wenn|schon ['vɛnʃoːn] ADV (*inf*) (**na** or **und**) **~!** what of it?, so what? (*inf*); **~, dennschon!** in for a penny, in for a pound! (*esp Brit prov*), if you're going to do something at all, you might as well do it properly!

Wen|zel ['vɛntsl] M -s, - (*Cards*) jack, knave (*form, dated*)

wer [ve:ɐ] **INTERROG PRON** who; **~ von ...** which (one) of ...; **~ da?** (*Mil*) who goes there?; **~ ist da?** (*an Tür*) who's there? **REL PRON** (= *derjenige, der*) the person who; (= *jeder, der*) anyone or anybody who; (*esp in Sprichwörtern*) he who; **~ ... auch (immer)** whoever ... **INDEF PRON** (*inf:* = *jemand*) somebody, someone; (*in Fragen auch*) anybody, anyone; **ist da ~?** is somebody or anybody there?; **~ sein** to be somebody (*inf*)

Werbe- ['vɛrbə] *in cpds* advertising; **Wer|be|ab|tei|lung** F publicity department; **Wer|be|agen|tur** F advertising agency; **Wer|be|akti|on** F advertising campaign; **Wer|be|ant|wort** F business reply card; **Wer|be|arti|kel** M promotional article; **Wer|be|auf|wand** M advertising costs *pl*, expenditure on advertising; **Wer|be|block** M *pl* **-blocks** or **-blöcke** (*TV*) commercial break; **Wer|be|bot|schaft** F advertising message; **Wer|be|bran|che** F advertising industry; **Wer|be|chef(in)** M(F) advertising or publicity manager; **Wer|be|ein|nah|men** PL advertising revenue *sing*; **Wer|be|etat** M advertising budget; **Wer|be|fach|frau** F advertising woman; **Wer|be|fach|mann** M advertising man; **Wer|be|feld|zug** M advertising campaign; **Wer|be|fern|se|hen** NT commercial television; (*Sendung*) TV advertisements *pl* or commercials *pl*; **Wer|be|film** M advertising or promotional film; (= *Spot*) (filmed) commercial; **Wer|be|flä|che** F advertising space; **Wer|be|frit|ze** M (*inf*) PR man; **Wer|be|funk** M radio commercials *pl*; **Wer|be|gag** M publicity stunt or gimmick; **Wer|be|gemein|schaft** F joint advertising arrangement; **Wer|be|ge|schenk** NT gift (*from company*); (*zu Gekauftem*) free gift; **Wer|be|gra|fi|ker(in)** M(F) commercial artist; **Wer|be|kam|pag|ne** F publicity campaign; (*für Verbrauchsgüter*) advertising campaign; **wer|be|kräf|tig** ADJ *Aufmachung etc* catchy; **ein ~er Slogan** an effective publicity slogan; **ein ~er Faktor** a good advertising point; **Wer|be|lei|ter(in)** M(F) advertising or publicity manager, head of advertising or promotions; **Wer|be|ma|te|ri|al** NT advertising material; **Wer|be|mit|tel** NT means *sing* of advertising; **Wer|be|mus|ter** NT advertising sample

wer|ben ['vɛrbn] *pret* **warb** [varp], *ptp* **geworben** [ɡəˈvɔrbn] **VT** *Mitglieder, Mitarbeiter* to recruit; *Kunden, Abonnenten, Stimmen* to attract, to win; *Soldaten* to recruit, to enlist

VI to advertise; **für etw ~** to advertise sth, to promote sth; **für eine Partei ~** to try to get support for a party; **Plakate, die für den linken Kandidaten ~** placards supporting the left-wing candidate; **um etw ~** to solicit sth, to court sth; **um Unterstützung/Verständnis ~** to try to enlist support/understanding; **um junge Wähler/neue Kunden ~** to try to attract or woo young voters/new customers; **um ein Mädchen ~** to court or woo (*old*) a girl; **er hat bei ihren Eltern um sie geworben** he asked her parents for permission to marry her

Wer|be-: **Wer|be|of|fi|zier(in)** M(F) recruiting officer; **Wer|be|pla|kat** NT advertisement, advertising poster, billboard (*US*); **Wer|be|pros|pekt** M advertising or publicity brochure

Wer|ber ['vɛrbɐ] M -s, - (*um Kunden, Wähler*) canvasser; (*um Mädchen*) suitor; (*für Mitglieder etc, Mil Hist*) recruiter, recruiting officer; (*inf:* = *Werbefachmann*) adman (*inf*)

Wer|be|rin [ˈvɛrbərɪn] F -, -nen (um Kunden, Wähler) canvasser; (für Mitglieder) recruiter; (inf: = Werbefachfrau) adwoman (inf)

wer|be|risch [ˈvɛrbərɪʃ] **ADJ** advertising attr, promotional **ADV** publicity-wise

Werbe-: Wer|be|rum|mel M (inf) hype (inf); **Wer|be|schrift** F publicity leaflet; (für Verbrauchsgüter) advertising leaflet; **~en** promotional literature sing; **Wer|be|slo|gan** M publicity slogan; (für Verbrauchsgüter) advertising slogan; **Wer|be|spot** M commercial; **Wer|be|spruch** M = Werbeslogan; **Wer|be|text** M advertising copy no pl; zwei **~e** two pieces of advertising copy; **~e verfassen** to write (advertising) copy; **Wer|be|tex|ter(in)** M(F) (advertising) copywriter; **Wer|be|trä|ger** M advertising medium; **Wer|be|trom|mel** F die **~** (für etw) rühren (inf) to beat the big drum (for sth) (inf), to push sth (inf); **Wer|be|ver|an|stal|tung** F publicity event; **wer|be|wirk|sam** ADJ effective (for advertising purposes); der Skandal erwies sich als äußerst **~** the scandal proved to be excellent publicity or proved to have excellent publicity value; **Wer|be|wirk|sam|keit** F publicity value

werb|lich [ˈvɛrplɪç] **ADJ** advertising attr, promotional **ADV** in advertising or promotional terms; **~** gesehen from an advertising point of view

Wer|bung [ˈvɛrbʊŋ] F -, -en (esp Comm) advertising; (= Werbeabteilung) publicity department; (Pol: = Propaganda) pre-election publicity; (von Kunden, Stimmen) winning, attracting; (von Mitgliedern, Soldaten etc) recruitment, recruiting; (um Mädchen) courting (um of); **~** für etw machen to advertise sth

Wer|bungs|kos|ten PL (von Mensch) professional outlay sing or expenses pl; (von Firma) business expenses pl

Wer|da|ruf [ˈvɛːrɐda-, veːrˈdaː-] M (Mil) call of "who goes there?", challenge

Wer|de|gang M pl -gänge development; (beruflich) career

---

wer|den [ˈveːrdn]

pret **wurde** [ˈvʊrdə], ptp **geworden** [gəˈvɔrdn] aux sein

| 1 HILFSVERB | 2 INTRANSITIVES VERB |

1 – HILFSVERB

a zur Bildung des Futurs

Die Kurzform 'll (für will) ist im gesprochenen Englisch sehr gebräuchlich, ebenfalls won't (= will not). Die unveränderliche Vollform will wird in der Schriftsprache sowie zur Betonung verwendet.

ich werde es tun I'll do it; **wir werden es tun** we'll do it; **ich werde das nicht tun** I won't do that; **er wird es tun, das verspreche ich euch** he will do it, I promise you; **ich bin sicher, dass er das nicht freiwillig tun wird** he won't do it voluntarily, I'm sure

going to drückt Sicherheit aus. Es wird ebenfalls für Voraussagen verwendet.

es wird gleich regnen it's going to rain; **du wirst heute schön zu Hause bleiben!** you're going to stay at home today!; **wer wird denn gleich weinen!** you're not going to cry now, are you?; **wer wird denn gleich!** (inf) come on, now!

♦ **es wird ... werden** es wird schon werden (inf) it's going to be okay (inf); **es wird schon wieder (gut) werden** it'll turn out all right; **es will einfach nicht werden** (inf) it's simply not working; **es wird sicher ein Junge werden** it's bound to be a boy

b zur Bildung des Konjunktivs

Die Kurzformen 'd (für would) und wouldn't (für would not) sind sehr gebräuchlich; zur Betonung wird jedoch die Vollform would verwendet.

das würde ich gerne tun I'd like to do that; **das würde ich nicht gerne tun** I wouldn't like to do that; **ich glaube, das würde dir nicht gefallen – doch, das würde mir sogar sehr gefallen** I suppose you wouldn't like that? – yes, I would like it very much; **er würde kommen, wenn es nicht regnete** he would come if it wasn't raining; **er hat gesagt, er werde** or **würde kommen** he said he would or he'd come; **würden Sie mir bitte das Buch geben?** would you give me the book, please?

c zur Bildung des Passivs pret auch **ward** [vart] (old, liter) ptp **worden** [ˈvɔrdn] **geschlagen werden** to be beaten; **was ist mit ihm? – er ist erschossen worden** what happened to him? – he has been shot dead; **er ist gestern erschossen worden** he was shot dead yesterday; **das Haus wird (gerade) renoviert** the house is being redecorated; **mir wurde gesagt, dass ...** I was told that ...; **es wurde gesungen** there was singing; **hier wird nicht geraucht!** there's no smoking here; **in England wird links gefahren** in England you drive on the left

d bei Vermutung **sie wird wohl in der Küche sein** she'll probably be in the kitchen; **er wird (wohl) ausgegangen sein** he will or he'll (probably) have gone out; **er wird sicher gerade auf dem Heimweg sein** he will definitely be on his way home; **das wird etwa 20 Euro kosten** it will cost roughly 20 euros

2 – INTRANSITIVES VERB

pret auch **ward** [vart] (old, liter) ptp **geworden** [gəˈvɔrdn]

a mit Adjektiv to get; **mir wird kalt/warm** I'm getting cold/warm; **verrückt/blind werden** to go crazy/blind; **rot/sauer/blass/kalt werden** to go red/sour/pale/cold; **mir wird schlecht/besser** I feel bad/better; **anders werden** to change; **die Fotos sind gut geworden** the photos have come out well

b mit Substantiv, Pronomen to become; (= sich verwandeln in) to turn into; **Lehrer werden** to become a teacher; **was willst du einmal werden?** what do you want to be when you grow up?; **ich will Lehrer werden** I want to be a teacher; **Erster werden** to come or be first; **er ist nichts (Rechtes) geworden** he hasn't got anywhere in life; **er ist etwas geworden** he's got somewhere in life; **das ist nichts geworden** it came to nothing; **das Eis wird Wasser** the ice is turning into water; **das wird bestimmt ein guter Eintopf** the stew is going to be good; **das wird ein guter Urlaub werden** it's going to be a good holiday (esp Brit) or vacation (US); **was soll das werden? – das wird ein Pullover** what's that going to be? – it's going to be a pullover; **wie soll der neue Swimmingpool werden?** what is the new swimming pool going to be like?

c bei Altersangaben **er wird am 8. Mai 36 (Jahre alt)** he will be 36 on the 8th of May; **er ist gerade 40 geworden** he has just turned 40

d in festen Wendungen

♦ **es wird ...** es wird bald ein Jahr, dass ... it's almost a year since ...; **es wird jetzt 13 Uhr** in a moment it will be 1 o'clock; **es wurde 10 Uhr, und ...** 10 o'clock came, and ...; **es wird Zeit, dass er kommt** it's time (that) he came; **es wird bald dunkel/spät** it's getting cold/dark/ late; **es wird Nacht** it's getting dark; **es wird Tag** it's getting light; **... es werde Licht! und es ward Licht** (Bibl) ... let there be light, and there was light (Bibl); **es wird Winter** winter is coming → auch **1 a**

♦ **werden + aus** was ist aus ihm geworden? what has become of him?; **aus ihm ist ein großer Komponist geworden** he has become a great composer; **aus ihm ist nichts (Rechtes) geworden** he hasn't got (Brit) or gotten (US) anywhere in life; **aus ihm ist etwas geworden** he has got (Brit) or gotten (US) somewhere in life; **aus ihm wird noch einmal was!** he'll make something of himself yet!; **aus dir wird nie etwas!** you'll never be anything!; **daraus wird nichts** that won't come to anything, nothing

will come of that; (= das kommt nicht infrage) that's out of the question; **was soll nur aus ihm werden?** what will become of him?; **daraus wird bestimmt nichts Gutes/kann nichts Gutes werden** no good will/can come of it; **was wird daraus (werden)?** what will come of it? → nichts

♦ **werden + zu** zu etw werden to turn into sth; **nachts wird er zum Vampir** at night he turns into a vampire; **zu Staub werden** to turn to dust

♦ **werden + wie** er wird mal wie sein Vater he's going to be like his father

e andere Wendungen **alles Leben wird und vergeht** (liter) life comes into being and then passes away (liter); **ihm ist ein großes Glück geworden** (old, liter) he has been favoured (Brit) or favored (US) with great fortune (liter); **was nicht ist, kann (ja) noch werden** (prov inf) my/your etc day will come; **was soll nun werden?** so what's going to happen now?; **ich dachte, ich werd nicht wieder** or **mehr!** (inf) I was flabbergasted (inf)

Wer|den [ˈveːrdn] NT -s, no pl **a** (= Entstehung) development; **im ~ sein** to be in the making; **die lebenden Sprachen sind immer im ~ begriffen** living languages are in a state of continual development **b** (Philos) Becoming

wer|dend ADJ nascent, emergent; **~e Mutter** expectant mother, mother-to-be; **~er Vater** father-to-be

Wer|fall M nominative (case)

wer|fen [ˈvɛrfn] pret **warf** [varf], ptp **geworfen** [gəˈvɔrfn] **VT a** (in Verbindung mit n siehe auch dort) to throw (auch beim Ringkampf) (nach at), to cast (liter, Bibl); Tor, Korb to score; **Bomben ~** (von Flugzeug) to drop bombs; **eine Münze ~** to toss a coin; **„nicht ~"** "handle with care"; **Bilder an die Wand ~** to project pictures onto the wall; **etw auf jdn/etw ~** to throw sth at sb/sth; **etw auf den Boden ~** to throw sth to the ground, to throw sth on(to) the ground; **etw auf das Dach ~** to throw sth on(to) the roof; **die Sonne warf ihre Strahlen auf den See** the sun cast its rays on the lake; **die Tischlampe wirft ihr Licht auf ...** the table lamp throws its light on ...; **die Laterne wirft ein helles Licht** the lantern gives off a bright light; **billige Waren auf den Markt ~** to dump cheap goods on the market; **jdn aus der Firma/dem Haus** etc **~** to throw or kick sb out (of the firm/house etc); **jdn ins Gefängnis** etc **~** to throw sb into prison etc; **alle Sorgen von sich ~** (fig) to cast aside all one's worries; **Geld in den Automaten ~** to put money in the machine; **etw ins Gespräch/in die Debatte ~** to throw sth into the conversation/ debate; **etw aufs Papier ~** (geh) to jot sth down; **die Kleider von sich ~** to throw or cast off one's clothes → Blick a, Licht b

b (= Junge kriegen) to have, to throw (spec)

VI a (= schleudern) to throw; **mit etw (auf jdn/etw) ~** to throw sth (at sb/sth); **mit Geld (nur so) um sich ~** (inf) to throw or chuck (inf) one's money around; **mit Komplimenten (nur so) um sich ~** to be free and easy or to be lavish with one's compliments; **mit Fremdwörtern (nur so) um sich ~** to bandy foreign words about (Brit), to toss foreign words around (esp US)

b (Tier) to have its young; (esp Katze, Hund etc) to have a litter, to litter; (bei einzelnen Jungen) to have a pup etc

VR to throw oneself (auf +acc (up)on, at); (Holz) to warp; (Metall, Asphalt etc) to buckle; **sich auf eine Aufgabe** etc **~** to throw oneself into a task etc; **sich in die Kleider ~** to throw on one's clothes → Brust a, Hals [1] a

Wer|fer [ˈvɛrfe] M -s, -, **Wer|fe|rin** [-ərɪn] F -, -nen thrower; (Kricket) bowler; (Baseball) pitcher

Werft [vɛrft] F -, -en shipyard; (für Flugzeuge) hangar

Werft|ar|bei|ter(in) M(F) shipyard worker

Werg [vɛrk] NT -(e)s [-gəs] no pl tow

Wer|geld [ˈveːrɡɛlt] NT (Hist Jur) wer(e)gild

Werk [vɛrk] NT -(e)s, -e **a** (= *Arbeit, Tätigkeit*) work *no indef art*; (*geh*: = *Tat*) deed, act; (= *Schöpfung, Kunstwerk, Buch*) work; (= *Gesamtwerk*) works *pl*; **Schweitzer hat in Afrika ein bedeutendes ~ vollbracht** Schweitzer has done (some) important work in Africa; **ein ~ wie das verdient unsere Förderung** work such as that deserves our support; **das ~ eines Augenblicks** the work of a moment; **das ist sein ~** this is his doing; **das ~ vieler Jahrzehnte** the work of many decades; **das ~ jahrelanger Arbeit/seines Fleißes** the product of many years of work/of his industry; **die ~e Gottes** the works of God; **gute ~e tun** to do good works; **ein gutes ~ (an jdm) tun** to do a good deed (for sb); **du tätest ein gutes ~, wenn ...** (*auch hum*) you'd be doing me/him *etc* a favour (*Brit*) or favor (*US*) if ..., you'd be doing your good deed for the day if ... (*hum*); **ein ~ der Nächstenliebe** an act of charity; **ans ~ gehen, sich ans ~ machen, zu ~e gehen** (*geh*) to set to work, to go to work; **(frisch) ans ~!** (*old, liter*) to work!; **am ~ sein** to be at work; **etw ins ~ setzen** (*geh*) to set sth in motion; **wir müssen vorsichtig zu ~e gehen** we must proceed cautiously

b (= *Betrieb, Fabrik*) works *sing or pl* (*Brit*), factory, plant; **ab ~** (*Comm*) ex works (*Brit*), ex factory

c (= *Triebwerk*) works *pl*, mechanism **d** *usu pl* (= *Festungswerke*) works *pl*

Werk-: *in cpds* works (*Brit*), factory → *auch* **Werk(s)-**; **Werk|bank** F *pl* -bänke workbench

Wer|kel ['vɛrkl] NT -s, -(n) (*Aus*) hurdy-gurdy, street organ

Wer|kel|mann M *pl* -männer (*Aus*) organ grinder

wer|keln ['vɛrkln] VI (*dated inf*) to potter about or around (*Brit*), to putter around (*US*); **daran ist noch einiges zu ~** it still needs a bit of fixing

wer|ken ['vɛrkn] **VI** to work, to be busy; (*handwerklich*) to do handicrafts; **Werken** (*Sch*) handicrafts **VT** to make

Werk-: **werk|ge|treu** ADJ true *or* faithful to the original; **Werk|hal|le** F factory building; **werk|im|ma|nent** ADJ (*Liter*) text-based ADV **etw ~ interpretieren** to make a text-based interpretation of sth; **Werk|kunst|schu|le** F arts and crafts school; **Werk|leh|rer(in)** M(F) woodwork/metalwork *etc* teacher, handicrafts teacher; **Werk|leu|te** PL (*old, liter*) craftsmen *pl*, artisans *pl*; **Werk|meis|ter** M foreman; **Werk|meis|te|rin** F forewoman

Werk(s)-: **Werk(s)|an|ge|hö|ri|ge(r)** MF *decl as adj* works (*Brit*) *or* factory employee; **Werk(s)|arzt** M , **Werk(s)|ärz|tin** **F** works (*Brit*) *or* company doctor

Werk|schau F exhibition (*of sb's work*), retrospective

Werk|schutz M works (*Brit*) *or* factory security service

Werks-: **werks|ei|gen** ADJ company *attr*; **~ sein** to be company-owned, to belong to the company; **Werks|fah|rer(in)** M(F) company *or* factory driver; **Werks|feu|er|wehr** F works (*Brit*) *or* factory fire service; **Werks|ge|län|de** NT works (*Brit*) *or* factory premises *pl*; **Werks|hal|le** F workshop; **Werks|kan|ti|ne** F works (*Brit*) *or* factory canteen; **Werks|kü|che** F works (*Brit*) *or* factory kitchen; **Werks|lei|ter(in)** M(F) works (*Brit*) *or* factory director *or* manager; **Werks|lei|tung** F works (*Brit*) *or factory management*; **Werks|schlie|ßung** F plant closure; **Werks|spi|o|na|ge** F industrial espionage

Werk|statt F *pl* -stätten [-ʃtɛtn], **Werk|stät|te** F workshop (*auch fig*); (*für Autoreparaturen*) garage; (*von Künstler*) studio; **geschützte** *or* **beschützende ~** (*für Behinderte*) sheltered workshop

Werk|statt|wa|gen M breakdown (*Brit*) *or* tow (*US*) truck, wrecker (*US*)

Werk|stoff M material

Werk|stoff-: **Werk|stoff|prü|fer(in)** M(F) materials tester; **Werk|stoff|prü|fung** F testing of materials

Werk-: **Werk|stück** NT (*Tech*) workpiece; **Werk|stu|dent(in)** M(F) working student; **~ sein** to work one's way through college

Werk(s)-: **Werk(s)|ver|kehr** M company transport; **Werk(s)|ver|trag** M contract of manufacture; **Werk(s)|woh|nung** F company flat (*Brit*) *or* apartment

Werk|tag M working day, workday

werk|täg|lich ADJ *attr* weekday; *Kleidung etc* workaday; **~e Öffnung** weekday opening ADV (= *werktags*) on weekdays

werk|tags ['vɛrktaːks] ADV on weekdays

werk|tä|tig ADJ working

Werk|tä|ti|ge(r) [-tɛːtɪɡə] MF *decl as adj* working man/woman; **die ~n** the working people *pl*

Werk-: **Werk|tisch** M worktable; **werk|treu** ADJ true *or* faithful to the original; **Werk|treue** F faithfulness to the original; **Werk|un|ter|richt** M handicraft lessons *pl*, woodwork/metalwork *etc* instruction

Werk|zeug NT *pl* -zeuge (*lit, fig, Comput*) tool

Werk|zeug-: **Werk|zeug|kas|ten** M toolbox; **Werk|zeug|leis|te** F (*Comput*) toolbar; **Werk|zeug|ma|cher(in)** M(F) toolmaker; **Werk|zeug|ma|schi|ne** F machine tool; **Werk|zeug|stahl** M (*Tech*) tool steel

Wer|mut ['veːrmuːt] M -(e)s, *no pl* **a** (*Bot*) wormwood; **ein Tropfen ~** (*fig geh*) a drop of bitterness **b** (= *Wermutwein*) vermouth

Wer|muts|trop|fen M (*fig geh*) drop of bitterness

Werst [vɛrst] F -, -e (*Maß*) verst

wert [veːrt] ADJ **a** (*old, form: Anrede*) dear; **Ihr ~es Schreiben** (*form*) your esteemed letter (*form*); **wie war doch gleich Ihr ~er Name?** (*form*) what was the name, sir/madam?

b **etw ~ sein** to be worth sth; **nichts ~ sein** to be worthless, to be worth nothing; (= *untauglich*) to be no good; **sie war ihm offenbar nicht viel ~** she obviously didn't mean all that much to him; **er ist £ 100.000 ~** (*Press sl*) he is worth £100,000; **Glasgow ist eine Reise ~** Glasgow is worth a visit; **einer Sache** (*gen*) **~ sein** (*geh*) to be worthy of sth; **es ist der Mühe ~** it's worth the trouble, it's worth it; **es ist nicht der Rede ~** it's not worth mentioning; **er ist es nicht ~, dass man ihm vertraut** he doesn't deserve to be trusted; **er ist es nicht ~, dass wir ihn unterstützen** he is not worthy of our support, he does not deserve our support; **dieser Film ist es durchaus ~, dass man sich ihn ansieht** this film is definitely worth seeing

c (= *nützlich*) useful; **ein Auto ist viel ~** a car is very useful; **das ist schon viel ~** (= *erfreulich*) that's very encouraging

Wert [veːrt] M -(e)s, -e **a** value; (*esp menschlicher*) worth; (*von Banknoten, Briefmarken*) denomination; (= *Wertsache*) article of value, valuable object; **einen ~ von 5 Euro haben** to be worth 5 euros, to have a value of 5 euros; **im ~(e) von** to the value of, worth; **an ~ verlieren/zunehmen, im ~ sinken/steigen** to decrease/increase in value, to depreciate/appreciate (*esp Econ*); **eine Sache unter/über (ihrem wirklichen) ~ verkaufen** to sell sth for less/more than its true value; **sie hat innere ~e** she has certain inner qualities; **~ auf etw** (*acc*) **legen** (*fig*) to set great store by sth (*esp Brit*), to attach importance to sth; **ich lege ~ darauf, festzustellen, dass ... I** think it important to establish that ...; **das hat keinen ~** (*inf*) there's no point

b *usu pl* (*von Test, Analyse*) result

Wert-: **Wert|an|ga|be** F declaration of value; **Wert|ar|beit** F craftsmanship, workmanship; **Wert|be|rich|ti|gung** F (*Comm*) valuation adjustment; **wert|be|stän|dig** ADJ stable in value; **Wert|be|stän|dig|keit** F stability of

value; **Wert|brief** M registered letter (*containing sth of value*)

Wer|te|be|wusst|sein ▲ NT sense of right and wrong

wer|ten ['veːrətn] VTI (= *einstufen*) to rate (*als* as); *Klassenarbeit etc* to grade; (= *beurteilen*) to judge (*als* to be); (*Sport*) (= *als gültig werten*) to allow; (= *Punkte geben*) to give a score; **ein Tor nicht ~** (*Ftbl etc*) to disallow a goal; **der Punktrichter aus Polen wertete besonders hoch** the Polish judge gave particularly high marks; **je nachdem, wie gewertet wird** according to how the scoring is done; **ohne (es) ~ zu wollen ...** without wanting to make any judgement (on it) ...

Wer|te-: **Wer|te|sys|tem** NT system of values; **Wer|te|wan|del** M change in values

wert|frei ADJ neutral ADV in a neutral way; *sagen auch* neutrally

Wert|ge|gen|stand M object of value; **Wertgegenstände** *pl* valuables *pl*

Wer|tig|keit ['veːrtɪçkaɪt] F -, -en **a** (*Chem, Ling*) valency **b** (= *Wert*) importance, value

Wert-: **Wert|kar|te** F (*Aus Telec*) phonecard; **Wert|kar|ten|te|le|fon** NT (*Aus*) card telephone; **wert|kon|ser|va|tiv** ADJ espousing conservative values, conservative; **wert|los** ADJ worthless, valueless; **Wert|lo|sig|keit** F -, *no pl* worthlessness; **Wert|mar|ke** F ticket; (*zum Aufkleben*) stamp; **Wert|maß** NT , **Wert|maß|stab** M , **Wert|mes|ser** M -s, - standard, yardstick; **Wert|min|de|rung** F reduction in value; **wert|neut|ral** ADJ value-free ADV avoiding (making) value judgements; **Wert|ob|jekt** NT object of value; **Wert|ord|nung** F system of values; **Wert|pa|ket** NT registered parcel (*esp Brit*) *or* package (*containing sth of value*); **Wert|pa|pier** NT security, bond; **~e** *pl* stocks and shares *pl*

Wert|pa|pier-: **Wert|pa|pier|bör|se** F stock exchange; **Wert|pa|pier|ge|schäft** NT securities trading; (*einzelne Transaktion*) securities transaction; **Wert|pa|pier|han|del** M securities trading

Wert|phi|lo|so|phie F (= *analytische Wertphilosophie*) axiology; (= *allgemeine Ethik*) moral philosophy

Wert|sa|che F object of value

wert|schät|zen VT *sep* (*liter*) to hold in high esteem

Wert|schät|zung F (*liter*) esteem, high regard

Wert|schöp|fung F (*Econ*) net product

Wert|schrift F (*Sw*) = Wertpapier

Wert|sen|dung F registered consignment

Wert|set|zung [-zɛtsʊŋ] F -, -en scale of values; (= *das Festsetzen*) fixing of values

Wert|stei|ge|rung F increase in value

Wert|stel|lung F (*Fin*) value

Wert|stoff M reusable material; **das Recyceln von ~en** the recycling of reusable materials

Wert|stoff|hof M recycling depot

Wert|stoff|ton|ne F bin for reusable materials

Wert|sys|tem NT system of values, value system

Wer|tung ['veːrtʊŋ] F -, -en **a** (= *Bewertung*) evaluation, assessment; (*von Jury etc*) judging, scoring; (= *Punkte*) score; **aus der ~ fallen** to be disqualified **b** (= *das Werten*) rating; (*von Klassenarbeit*) grading; (= *das Beurteilen*) judging; (*Sport*: = *Punktvergabe*) scoring

Wer|tungs- (*Sport etc*): **Wer|tungs|ge|richt** NT jury; **Wer|tungs|rich|ter(in)** M(F) judge

Wert|ur|teil NT value judgement

Wert|ur|teils-: **wert|ur|teils|frei** ADJ free from value judgements; **Wert|ur|teils|frei|heit** F avoidance of (making) value judgements

Wert|ver|lust M depreciation

wert|voll ADJ valuable; (*moralisch*) *Mensch* worthy, estimable

Wert-: Wert|vor|stel|lung F moral concept; **Wert|zei|chen** NT (form) postage stamp; **Wert|zu|wachs** M appreciation; **Wert|zu|wachs|steu|er** F capital gains tax

wer|wei|ßen ['ve:ɛvaisn] VI insep (Sw) to guess

Wer|wolf ['ve:ɛvɔlf] M werewolf

wes [vɛs] PRON (old) gen von **wer** whose gen von **was** of which

we|sen ['ve:zn] VI (liter) to be present

We|sen ['ve:zn] NT **-s**, - a no pl nature; (= Wesentliches) essence; **am ~ unserer Beziehung hat sich nichts geändert** the basic nature of our relationship remains unchanged; **es liegt im ~ einer Sache ...** it's in the nature of a thing ...; **das gehört zum ~ der Demokratie** it is of the essence of democracy b no pl **sein ~ treiben** (geh) (Dieb etc) to be at work; (Schalk etc) to be up to one's tricks; (Gespenst) to be abroad; **viel ~s machen (um** or **von)** to make a lot of fuss (about) c (= Geschöpf) being; (= tierisches Wesen) creature; (= Mensch) person, creature; **armes ~** poor thing or creature; **das höchste ~** the Supreme Being; **ein menschliches ~** a human being; **ein weibliches ~** a female; **ein männliches ~** a male

We|sen-: we|sen|haft ADJ intrinsic, essential; **We|sen|heit** F **-, -en** (Philos) being; **we|sen|los** ADJ insubstantial, unreal

We|sens-: we|sens|ähn|lich ADJ similar in nature; **We|sens|art** F nature, character; **es ist griechische ~ zu ...** it's a Greek characteristic to ...; **we|sens|ei|gen** ADJ intrinsic; **we|sens|fremd** ADJ (= im Wesen verschieden) different or dissimilar in nature; **das Lügen ist ihm völlig ~** lying is completely foreign or alien to his nature; **we|sens|ge|mäß** ADJ **das ist ihm nicht ~** it's not in accordance with his nature; **we|sens|gleich** ADJ essentially alike, identical in character or nature; **We|sens|gleich|heit** F essential similarity; **We|sens|merk|mal** NT (basic or essential) trait; **We|sens|un|ter|schied** M difference in nature or character; **we|sens|ver|wandt** ADJ related in character; **We|sens|ver|wandt|schaft** F relatedness of character; **We|sens|zug** M characteristic, trait

we|sent|lich ['ve:zntlɪç] ADJ (= den Kern der Sache betreffend, sehr wichtig) essential; (= grundlegend) fundamental; (= erheblich) substantial, considerable, appreciable; (= wichtig) important; **das Wesentliche** the essential part or thing; (von dem, was gesagt wurde) the gist; **im Wesentlichen** in essence, basically, essentially; (= im Großen und Ganzen) in the main ADV (= grundlegend) fundamentally; (= erheblich) considerably; **es ist mir ~ lieber, wenn wir ...** I would much rather we ...; **sie hat sich nicht ~ verändert** she hasn't changed much

Wes|fall M genitive case

wes|halb [vɛs'halp, 'vɛs-] INTERROG ADV why REL ADV which is why, for which reason; **der Grund, ~ ...** the reason why ...; **das ist es ja, ~ ...** that is why ...

We|sir [ve'zi:ɐ] M **-s, -e** vizi(e)r

Wes|pe ['vɛspə] F **-, -n** wasp

Wes|pen-: Wes|pen|nest NT wasp's nest; **in ein ~ stechen** (fig) to stir up a hornets' nest; **das war ein Stich ins ~** (fig) that stirred up a hornets' nest; **Wes|pen|stich** M wasp sting; **Wes|pen|tail|le** F (fig) wasp waist

wes|sen ['vɛsn] PRON gen von **wer** a interrog whose b rel, indef **~ Handschrift das auch (immer) sein mag, ...** no matter whose handwriting it may be, ... gen von **was** (liter) a interrog **~ hat man dich angeklagt?** of what have you been accused? b rel, indef **man dich auch (immer) anklagt, ...** whatever they or no matter what they accuse you of ...

wes|sent|we|gen [vɛsnt've:gn] INTERROG ADV (geh) why

wes|sent|wil|len ['vɛsnt'vɪlən] INTERROG ADV (geh) **um ~** for whose sake

Wes|si ['vɛsi] M **-s, -s** (inf) Westerner, West German

WESSI

Wessi is used in a similar way to **Ossi** and refers to a person from the former West Germany. After the **Wende** many West Germans went to the new **Länder** with an arrogant sense of their superiority over those in the East. As a result the term **Besserwessi**, a combination of **Besserwisser** (smart aleck) and **Wessi**, came into being → OSSI, WENDE

West [vɛst] M **-s**, no pl a (Naut, Met, liter) west b (liter. = Westwind) west wind

West- in cpds (in Ländernamen) (politisch) West; (geografisch auch) the West of ..., Western; **West|afri|ka** NT West Africa; **West|aus|tra|li|en** NT Western Australia; **West|ber|lin** NT (Hist) West Berlin; **west|deutsch** ADJ (Geog) Western German; (Pol Hist) West German; **West|deut|sche(r)** MF decl as adj West German; **West|deutsch|land** NT (Geog) the West of Germany; (Pol Hist) West Germany, Western Germany

Wes|te ['vɛstə] F **-, -n** waistcoat (Brit), vest (US); **eine reine** or **saubere** or **weiße ~ haben** (fig) to have a clean slate

Wes|ten ['vɛstn] M **-s**, no pl west; (von Land) West; **der ~** (Pol) the West; (im Gegensatz zum Orient auch) the Occident; **aus dem ~, von ~ (her)** from the west; **gegen** or **gen** (liter) or **nach ~** west(wards), to the west; **nach ~ (hin)** to the west; **im ~ der Stadt/des Landes** in the west of the town/country; **weiter im ~** further west; **im ~ Frankreichs** in the west of France, in Western France → wild

Wes|ten|ta|sche F waistcoat (Brit) or vest (US) pocket; **etw wie seine ~ kennen** (inf) to know sth like the back of one's hand (inf)

Wes|ten|ta|schen|for|mat NT (hum) **ein X im ~** a miniature X

Wes|tern ['vɛstɐn] M **-(s), -** western

West-: West|eu|ro|pa NT Western Europe; **west|eu|ro|päisch** ADJ West(ern) European; **~e Zeit** Greenwich Mean Time, Western European Time (rare); **die Westeuropäische Union** the Western European Union

West|fa|le [vɛst'fa:lə] M **-n, -n**, **West|fä|lin** [-'fɛ:lɪn] F **-, -nen** Westphalian

West|fa|len [vɛst'fa:lən] NT **-s** Westphalia

West|fä|lin F **-, -nen** Westphalian (woman)

west|fä|lisch [vɛst'fɛ:lɪʃ] ADJ Westphalian; **der Westfälische Friede** (Hist) The Treaty of Westphalia

West|frie|si|sche In|seln PL West Frisians pl, West Frisian Islands pl

West-: West|geld NT Western currency; **West|ger|ma|nen** PL (Hist) West Germanic peoples pl or tribes pl; **west|ger|ma|nisch** ADJ (Hist, Ling) West Germanic; **West|go|ten** PL (Hist) Visigoths pl, West Goths pl; **west|grie|chisch** ADJ Western Greek; **West|in|di|en** NT the West Indies pl; **west|in|disch** ADJ West Indian; **die Westindischen Inseln** the West Indies pl; **West|in|te|gra|ti|on** F (Pol) integration with the West; **West|jor|dan|land** [vɛst'jɔrdan-] NT **das ~** the West Bank; **West|küs|te** F west coast

west|lich ['vɛstlɪç] ADJ western; Kurs, Wind, Richtung westerly; **der ~ste Ort** the westernmost place ADV (to the) west; **~ von ...** (to the) west of ...; **es liegt ~er** or **weiter ~** it is further (to the) west PREP +gen (to the) west of

West-: West|mäch|te PL (Pol) **die ~** the western powers pl; **West|mark** F (Hist inf) West German mark; **west|mit|tel|deutsch** ADJ West Middle German; **West|nord|west** M a (Naut, Met, liter) west-north-west b (liter. Wind) west-north-west wind; **west|öst|lich** ADJ west-to-east; **in ~er Richtung** from west to east;

West|po|li|tik F policy toward(s) the west, western policy; **West|preu|ßen** NT West Prussia; **West|rom** NT (Hist) Western Roman Empire; **west|rö|misch** ADJ (Hist) Western Roman; **West|rus|sen** PL White Russians pl; **West|schweiz** F **die ~** Western Switzerland; **West|sek|tor** M western sector; **West|süd|west** M a (Naut, Met, liter) west-south-west b (liter. Wind) west-south-west wind; **West|wall** M (Hist) Siegfried Line; **west|wärts** ['vɛstverts] ADV westward(s), (to the) west; **West|wind** M west wind

wes|we|gen [vɛs've:gn, 'vɛs-] INTERROG ADV why

wett [vɛt] ADJ pred **~ sein** to be quits

Wett|an|nah|me|(stel|le) F betting office

Wett|be|werb M competition; **mit jdm in ~ stehen/treten** to be in/enter into competition with sb, to be competing/to compete with sb; **außer ~ teilnehmen** or **laufen** to take part hors concours (Brit), to take part as a noncompetitor

Wett|be|wer|ber(in) M(F) competitor

Wett|be|werbs-: Wett|be|werbs|be|din|gun|gen PL terms pl of a/the competition; **Wett|be|werbs|be|schrän|kung** F restraint of trade; **wett|be|werbs|fä|hig** ADJ competitive; **Wett|be|werbs|fä|hig|keit** F competitiveness; **Wett|be|werbs|klau|sel** F non-competition clause; **Wett|be|werbs|nach|teil** M competitive disadvantage; **Wett|be|werbs|recht** NT competition law (Brit), antitrust law (US); **wett|be|werbs|recht|lich** ADJ, ADV with regard to competition law (Brit) or antitrust law (US); **Wett|be|werbs|teil|neh|mer(in)** M(F) competitor; **Wett|be|werbs|ver|zer|rung** F distortion of competition; **Wett|be|werbs|vor|teil** M competitive advantage or edge; **wett|be|werbs|wid|rig** ADJ Verhalten, Absprache, Werbung anticompetitive ADV **~ handeln** (unlauter) to violate fair trade practices; (ungesetzlich) to violate competition law (Brit) or antitrust law (US); **Wett|be|werbs|wirt|schaft** F competitive economy

Wett|bü|ro NT betting office

Wet|te ['vɛtə] F **-, -n** bet (auch Sport); wager; **eine ~ machen** or **abschließen/annehmen** to make/take up or accept a bet; **eine ~ auf ein Pferd abschließen** to place a bet on a horse; **darauf gehe ich jede ~ ein** I'll bet you anything you like; **was gilt die ~?** what will you bet me?, what are you betting?; **die ~ gilt!** done!, you're on! (inf); **um die ~ laufen/schwimmen** to run/swim a race (with each other); **mit jdm um die ~ laufen** or **rennen** to race sb; **sie arbeiten um die ~** they're working as hard as they can; **sie singen um die ~** they're singing at the tops of their voices; **sie schreien um die ~** they're having a screaming competition

Wett|ei|fer M competitive zeal, competitiveness

wett|ei|fern VI insep **mit jdm um etw ~** to compete or contend or vie with sb for sth

wet|ten ['vɛtn] VTI to bet (auch Sport), to wager; **(wollen wir) ~?** (do you) want to bet?; **dass ich Recht habe?** (I) bet you I'm right!; **so haben wir nicht gewettet!** that's not part of the deal or bargain!; **auf etw** (acc) **~** to bet on sth; **mit jdm ~** to bet (with jdm) (darauf) ~, **dass ...** to bet (sb) that ...; (mit jdm) **um 5 Euro/eine Flasche Bier** etc **~** to bet (sb) 5 euros/a bottle of beer etc; **wir wetteten um einen Kasten Sekt** we bet each other a case of champagne; **ich habe mit ihm um 10 Euro auf den Sieg der Brasilianer gewettet** I bet him 10 euros that the Brazilians would win; **gegen etw ~** to bet against sth; **da wette ich gegen** (inf) I bet you that isn't so/won't happen etc; **ich wette 100 gegen 1(, dass ...)** I'll bet or lay (Brit) (you) 100 to 1 (that ...); **ich wette meinen Kopf (darauf)(, dass ...)** I'll bet you anything (you like) (that ...)

Wẹt|ter[1] ['vɛtɐ] NT **-s, -** **a** weather *no indef art*; **bei jedem ~** in all weathers; **bei so einem ~** in weather like that, in such weather; **das ist vielleicht ein ~!** (*inf*) what weather!; **was haben wir heute für ~?** what's the weather like today?; **wir haben herrliches ~** the weather's marvellous (*Brit*) or marvelous (*US*); **ein ~ zum Eierlegen** (*inf*) or **Heldenzeugen** (*inf*) fantastic weather (*inf*); **übers** or **vom ~ sprechen** to talk about the weather; **(bei jdm) gut ~ machen** (*inf*) to make up to sb; **(jdn) um gutes ~ bitten** (*inf*) to try to smooth things over (with sb); **alle ~!** (*inf*) my goodness!, by Jove! (*dated*) **b** (= *Unwetter*) storm **c** *usu pl* (*Min*) air; **matte ~** *pl* chokedamp *sing* (*Brit*), blackdamp *sing*; **giftige** or **böse ~** *pl* whitedamp *sing*; **schlagende ~** *pl* firedamp *sing*

Wẹt|ter[2] ['vɛtɐ] M **-s, -**, **Wẹt|te|rin** [-ərɪn] F **-, -nen** better

Wẹt|ter-: Wẹt|ter|amt NT weather or met(eorological) office (*Brit*), weather bureau; **Wẹt|ter|aus|sich|ten** PL weather outlook *sing* or prospects *pl*; **Wẹt|ter|bal|lon** M weather or meteorological balloon; **wẹt|ter|be|dingt** ADJ *Störung* weather-related, caused by the weather *pred* ADV *ausfallen* because of or because of the weather; **Wẹt|ter|be|din|gun|gen** PL weather conditions *pl*; **Wẹt|ter|be|o|bach|tung** F meteorological observation; **Wẹt|ter|be|richt** M weather report; **Wẹt|ter|bes|se|rung** F improvement in the weather; **wẹt|ter|be|stän|dig** ADJ weatherproof; **wẹt|ter|be|stim|mend** ADJ weather-determining; **~ sein** to determine the weather

Wẹt|ter|chen ['vɛtɐçən] NT **-s, -** (*inf*) **das ist ja heute ein ~!** the weather's really great or fantastic today! (*inf*)

Wẹt|ter-: Wẹt|ter|dienst M weather or meteorological service; **wẹt|ter|emp|find|lich** ADJ sensitive to (changes in) the weather; **Wẹt|ter|fah|ne** F weather vane; **wẹt|ter|fest** ADJ weatherproof; (*fig*: = *krisensicher*) crisis-proof; **Wẹt|ter|fleck** M (*Aus*) weatherproof cape; **Wẹt|ter|frau** F weatherwoman; **Wẹt|ter|front** F front; **Wẹt|ter|frosch** M **a** *type of barometer using a frog* **b** (*hum inf*) weatherman (*inf*); **wẹt|ter|füh|lig** [-fy:lɪç] ADJ sensitive to (changes in) the weather; **Wẹt|ter|füh|lig|keit** F sensitivity to (changes in) the weather; **Wẹt|ter|füh|rung** F (*Min*) ventilation; **wẹt|ter|ge|schützt** ADJ sheltered; **Wẹt|ter|glas** NT (*old*) weatherglass; **Wẹt|ter|gott** M weather god; **der ~** (*hum*) the person up there who controls the weather (*hum*); **Wẹt|ter|hahn** M weathercock (*esp Brit*), weather vane; **Wẹt|ter|häus|chen** [-hɔysçən] NT weather house or box

Wẹt|te|rin F **-, -nen** better

Wẹt|ter-: Wẹt|ter|ka|nal M (*Min*) fan drift; **Wẹt|ter|kar|te** F weather map or chart; **Wẹt|ter|kun|de** F meteorology; **wẹt|ter|kund|lich** [-kʊntlɪç] ADJ meteorological; **Wẹt|ter|la|ge** F weather situation, state of the weather; **Wẹt|ter|lam|pe** F (*Min*) safety lamp; **Wẹt|ter|lei|den** NT ailment or complaint caused by the weather; **wẹt|ter|leuch|ten** VI *impers insep* **es wetterleuchtet** there's sheet lightning; (*fig*) there's a storm brewing; **Wẹt|ter|leuch|ten** NT **-s**, *no pl* sheet lightning; (*fig*) storm clouds *pl*; **Wẹt|ter|mann** M *pl* **-männer** weatherman; **Wẹt|ter|mel|dung** F weather or meteorological report

wẹt|tern ['vɛtɐn] VI *impers* **es wettert** it's thundering and lightening, there's a thunderstorm VI to curse and swear; **gegen** or **auf etw** (*acc*) **~** to rail against sth

Wẹt|ter-: Wẹt|ter|prog|no|se F (*Aus*) weather forecast; **Wẹt|ter|pro|phet** M (*hum*) weatherman (*inf*); **Wẹt|ter|pro|phe|tin** F (*hum*) weather girl (*inf*); **Wẹt|ter|re|gel** F weather maxim or saying; **Wẹt|ter|sa|tel|lit** M weather satellite; **Wẹt|ter|schacht** M (*Min*) ventilation shaft; **Wẹt|ter|schei|de** F

weather or meteorological divide; **Wẹt|ter|schiff** NT weather ship; **Wẹt|ter|sei|te** F windward side, side exposed to the weather; **Wẹt|ter|sta|ti|on** F weather or meteorological station; **Wẹt|ter|stö|rung** F weather or meteorological disturbance; **Wẹt|ter|sturz** M sudden fall in temperature and atmospheric pressure; **Wẹt|ter|um|bruch** M (*esp Sw*), **Wẹt|ter|um|schlag** M , **Wẹt|ter|um|schwung** M sudden change in the weather; **Wẹt|ter|ver|hält|nis|se** PL weather conditions *pl*; **Wẹt|ter|ver|schlech|te|rung** F deterioration in or worsening of the weather; **Wẹt|ter|vo|raus|sa|ge** F , **Wẹt|ter|vor|her|sa|ge** F weather forecast; **Wẹt|ter|war|te** F weather station; **Wẹt|ter|wech|sel** M change in the weather; **wẹt|ter|wen|disch** ADJ (*fig*) changeable, moody; **Wẹt|ter|wol|ke** F storm cloud

Wetteufel △ M → **Wetteufel**

Wẹtt-: Wẹtt|fahrt F race; **Wẹtt|kampf** M competition; **Wẹtt|kämp|fer(in)** M(F) competitor; **Wẹtt|kampf|sport** M competitive sport; **Wẹtt|lauf** M race; **einen ~ machen** to run a race; **ein ~ mit der Zeit** or **gegen die Zeit** a race against time; **wẹtt|lau|fen** VI (*infin only*) to run a race/races; **Wẹtt|läu|fer(in)** M(F) runner (in a/the race)

wẹtt+ma|chen VT *sep* to make up for; *Verlust etc* to make good; *Rückstand, Vorsprung* to make up

Wẹtt-: wẹtt|ren|nen VI (*infin only*) to run a race; **Wẹtt|ren|nen** NT (*lit, fig*) race; **ein ~ machen** to run a race; **Wẹtt|ru|dern** NT **-s, -** boat race; **Wẹtt|rüs|ten** NT **-s**, *no pl* arms race; **Wẹtt|schein** M betting slip; **Wẹtt|schie|ßen** NT **-s, -** shooting competition or contest; **Wẹtt|schuld** F betting debt; **Wẹtt|schwim|men** NT swimming competition or contest; **Wẹtt|sin|gen** NT *pl* - singing competition or contest; **Wẹtt|streit** M competition (*auch fig*), contest; **mit jdm im ~ liegen** to compete with sb; **mit jdm in ~ treten** to enter into competition with sb; **Wẹtt|teu|fel** ▲ M (*inf*) betting bug (*inf*); **ihn hat der ~ gepackt** he's got the betting bug (*inf*); **Wẹtt|tur|nen** ▲ NT *pl* - gymnastics competition; **Wẹtt|zet|tel** M betting slip or ticket

wẹt|zen ['vɛtsn] VT to whet VI *aux sein* (*inf*) to scoot (*inf*)

Wẹtz-: Wẹtz|stahl M steel; **Wẹtz|stein** M whetstone

WEU [ve:|e:|'u:] F - *abbr von* **Westeuropäische Union** WEU

WEZ [ve:|e:|'tsɛt] *abbr von* **Westeuropäische Zeit** GMT

WG [ve:|'ge:] F **-, -s** *abbr von* **Wohngemeinschaft**

WGB [ve:ge:|'be:] M - *abbr von* **Weltgewerkschaftsbund** WFTU

WG- [ve:|'ge:-]: **WG-Be|woh|ner(in)** M(F) flat (*Brit*) or apartment or house sharer; **WG-Zim|mer** NT room in a shared flat *etc*

Whirl|pool ['wœrlpu:l, 'wœ:ɐl-] M **-s, -s** Jacuzzi®

Whis|ky ['wɪski] M **-s, -s** whisky, whiskey (*US*); (*schottischer auch*) Scotch; (*irischer*) whiskey; (*amerikanischer Maiswhisky*) bourbon (whiskey); (*amerikanischer Roggenwhisky*) rye (whiskey); **~ mit Eis** whisk(e)y and ice, whisk(e)y on the rocks; **~ (mit) Soda** whisk(e)y and soda

Whist [wɪst] NT **-(e)s**, *no pl* whist

wich *pret von* **weichen**[2]

Wichs [vɪks] M **-es, -e** (*Aus*) F **-, -en in vollem ~** (*Aus*) **voller ~** (*Univ*) in full dress, in full regalia; **sich in ~ werfen** (*Univ, fig*) to dress up

Wichs|bir|ne ['vɪks-] F (*sl*) wanker (*Brit sl*), jerk-off (*US sl*)

Wich|se ['vɪksə] F **-, -n** **a** (*dated*: = *Schuhwichse*) shoe polish; **schwarze ~** blacking (*dated*), black shoe polish **b** *no pl* (*inf*: = *Prügel*) **~ bekommen** to get a hiding (*inf*)

wich|sen ['vɪksn] VT **a** *auch vi* (*dated*) *Schuhe* to polish; (*mit schwarzer Wichse*) to black (*dated*); *Schnurrbart, Boden etc* to wax → *auch* **gewichst** **b** (*inf*: = *prügeln*) **jdn (ganz schön) ~** to give sb a (good) hiding (*inf*) VI (*sl*: = *onanieren*) to jerk or toss off (*sl*), to (have a) wank (*Brit vulg*)

Wich|ser ['vɪksɐ] M **-s, -** (*sl*) wanker (*Brit sl*), jerk-off (*US sl*)

Wichs|lein|wand ['vɪks-] F (*Aus*: = *Wachstuch*) oilcloth

Wicht [vɪçt] M **-(e)s, -e** (= *Kobold*) goblin, wight (*obs*); (= *kleiner Mensch*) titch (*inf*); (= *Kind*) (little) creature; (*fig*: = *verachtenswerter Mensch*) scoundrel; **ein armer ~** a poor devil (*inf*) or wretch; (= *Kind*) a poor little thing or creature

Wich|te ['vɪçtə] F **-, -n** (*Phys*) density

Wich|tel ['vɪçtl] M **-s, -** **a** (*auch* **Wichtelmännchen**) gnome; (= *Kobold*) goblin, imp; (= *Heinzelmännchen*) brownie **b** (*bei Pfadfinderinnen*) Brownie

wich|tig ['vɪçtɪç] ✪ 28.1, 53.1, 53.2, 53.6 ADJ important; **eine ~e Miene machen** to put on an air of importance; **sich ~ machen** or **tun** to be full of one's own importance, to be self-important or pompous; **er will sich nur ~ machen** he just wants to get attention; **sich mit etw ~ machen** or **tun** to go on and on about sth; **alles Wichtige** everything of importance; **Wichtigeres zu tun haben** to have more important things to do, to have better things to do; **nichts Wichtigeres zu tun haben** to have nothing better to do; **das Wichtigste** (= *die wichtigste Sache*) the most important thing; (= *die wichtigsten Einzelheiten*) the most important details

ADV **sich selbst/etw (zu) ~ nehmen** to take oneself/sth (too) seriously; **es mit etw ~ haben** (*inf*) to take sth (very) seriously; **du hasts aber ~!** (*inf*) what's all the fuss about?; **~ tun** (*inf*: *sich aufspielen*) to be full of one's own importance; **sich** (*dat*) **~ vorkommen** to be full of oneself

Wich|tig|keit F **-, -en** importance; **einer Sache** (*dat*) **große** *etc* **~ beimessen** or **beilegen** to place great *etc* importance on sth

Wich|tig|tu|er [-tu:ɐ] M **-s, -**, **Wich|tig|tu|e|rin** [-ərɪn] F **-, -nen**, **Wich|tig|ma|cher(in)** F (*Aus*) M(F) (*pej*) pompous ass or idiot

Wich|tig|tu|e|rei [-tu:əˈrai] F (*pej*) pomposity, pompousness

wich|tig|tu|e|risch [-tu:ərɪʃ] ADJ pompous

Wi|cke ['vɪkə] F **-, -n** (*Bot*) vetch; (= *Gartenwicke*) sweet pea

Wi|ckel ['vɪkl] M **-s, -** **a** (*Med*) compress **b** (= *Rolle*) reel, spool; (= *Lockenwickel*) roller, curler **c** (*inf*) **jdn am** or **beim ~ packen** or **nehmen** or **kriegen/haben** to grab/have sb by the scruff of the neck; (*fig*) to give sb a good talking to (*inf*); (*stärker*) to have sb's guts for garters (*Brit inf*), to have sb for dinner (*inf*)

Wi|ckel-: Wi|ckel|auf|la|ge F changing mat; **Wi|ckel|blu|se** F wraparound blouse; **Wi|ckel|ga|ma|sche** F puttee; **Wi|ckel|kind** NT babe in arms; **Wi|ckel|kleid** NT wraparound dress; **Wi|ckel|kom|mo|de** F baby's changing unit or station

wi|ckeln ['vɪkln] VT **a** (= *schlingen*) to wind (*um round*); (*Tech*) *Spule, Transformator etc* to coil, to wind; *Verband etc* to bind; *Haare, Locken* to put in rollers or curlers; *Zigarren* to roll; (= *umschlagen*) to wrap; **sich** (*dat*) **eine Decke um die Beine ~** to wrap a blanket around one's legs; **wenn du das denkst, bist du schief gewickelt!** (*fig inf*) if you think that, you're very much mistaken → **Finger** **b** (= *einwickeln*) to wrap (*in +acc* in); (*mit Verband*) to dress, to bandage; **einen Säugling ~** to put on a baby's nappy (*Brit*) or diaper (*US*); (= *frisch wickeln*) to change a baby's nappy (*Brit*) or diaper (*US*)

VR to wrap oneself (*in +acc* in); **sich um etw ~** to wrap itself around sth; (*Schlange, Pflanze*) to wind itself around sth

Wickel-: Wi|ckel|raum M *(in Kaufhaus etc)* mothers' (and babies') room *(Brit)*, nursing room *(Brit)*, (baby) changing room; **Wi|ckel|rock** M wraparound skirt; **Wi|ckel|tisch** M baby's changing table

Wid|der ['vɪdɐ] M **-s, -** *(Zool)* ram; *(Astrol)* Aries; *(Mil, Hist)* battering ram; **er/sie ist (ein) ~** *(Astrol)* he's/she's an Arian *or* (an) Aries; **der ~** *(Astron, Astrol)* Aries, the Ram

Wid|der-: Wid|der|frau F *(Astrol inf)* (female) Arian, Aries (woman); **Wid|der|mann** M *pl* **-männer** *(Astrol inf)* (male) Arian, Aries (man)

wi|der ['vɪdɐ] PREP *+acc* *(geh)* against; *(= entgegen auch)* contrary to; **~ Erwarten** contrary to expectations; **~ alles Erwarten** against all expectations, contrary to all expectations → **Für, löcken, Wille**

Wi|der-: wi|der|bors|tig ADJ contrary, perverse; **Wi|der|bors|tig|keit** ['vɪdɐbɔrstɪçkaɪt] F **-,** *no pl* contrariness, perversity; **Wi|der|druck** M *pl* **-drucke** *(Typ)* perfecting

wi|der|fah|ren [vi:dɐˈfaːrən] *ptp* **widerfahren** VI IMPERS *insep irreg aux sein +dat* *(geh)* to happen *(jdm* to sb); *(Unglück etc)* to befall *(jdm* sb) *(liter)*; **ihr ist eine Ungerechtigkeit ~** she has met with an injustice; **mir ist in meinem Leben schon viel Gutes ~** life has given me many good things

Wi|der-: Wi|der|ha|ken M barb; *(an größerer Harpune)* fluke; **Wi|der|hall** M echo, reverberation; **(bei jdm) keinen ~ finden** *(Interesse)* to meet with no response (from sb); *(Gegenliebe etc)* not to be reciprocated (by sb); **wi|der|hal|len** VI *sep or (rare) insep* to echo or reverberate *(von* with); **Wi|der|hand|lung** F *(Sw)* contravention, violation; **Wi|der|kla|ge** F counterclaim; **wi|der|klin|gen** VI *sep irreg* to resound or ring *(von* with)

wi|der|leg|bar ADJ refutable, disprovable; **nicht ~** irrefutable

wi|der|le|gen [vi:dɐˈleːɡn] *ptp* **widerlegt** VT *insep Behauptung etc* to refute, to disprove; *jdn* to prove wrong

Wi|der|le|gung F **-, -en** refutation, disproving

wi|der|lich ['vɪdɐlɪç] ADJ disgusting, revolting; *Mensch* repulsive; *Kopfschmerzen* nasty ADV *sich benehmen* disgustingly; **~ riechen/schmecken** to smell/taste disgusting

Wi|der|lich|keit F **-, -en** *(= widerliche Sache)* disgusting *or* revolting thing; *(von Mensch)* repulsiveness; *(von Kopfschmerzen)* nastiness; **die ~ des Anblicks** the disgusting *or* revolting sight; **die ~ seines Benehmens** his disgusting *or* revolting behaviour *(Brit)* or behavior *(US)*

Wi|der|ling ['vɪdɐlɪŋ] M **-s, -e** *(pej inf)* repulsive creep *(inf)*

wi|dern ['vi:dɐn] VT, VT IMPERS **es/etw widert jdn** sb finds it/sth disgusting *or* revolting

Wi|der-: wi|der|na|tür|lich ADJ unnatural; *(= pervers auch)* perverted; **Wi|der|na|tür|lich|keit** F unnaturalness; *(= Perversität auch)* perversion; **Wi|der|part** M *(old, geh: = Gegner)* adversary, opponent; **jdm ~ bieten** *or* **geben** *(geh)* to oppose sb

wi|der|ra|ten [vi:dɐˈraːtn] *ptp* **widerraten** VI *insep irreg (old)* **jdm ~, etw zu tun** to advise *or* counsel sb against doing sth

Wi|der-: wi|der|recht|lich ADJ unlawful, illegal ADV illegally; **etw ~ betreten** *(Gelände)* to trespass (up)on sth; *Gebäude* to enter sth unlawfully *or* illegally; **sich** *(dat)* **etw ~ aneignen** to misappropriate sth; **Wi|der|re|de** F **a** *(= Widerspruch)* contradiction, argument; **keine ~!** no arguing!, don't argue!; **er duldet keine ~** he will not have any arguments about it; **ohne ~** without protest or demur **b** *(= Antwort)* reply; **Rede und ~** dialogue *(Brit)*, dialog *(US)*

Wi|der|ruf M revocation *(auch Jur)*, withdrawal, cancellation; *(von Aussage, Geständnis, Behauptung)* retraction *(auch Jur)*, withdrawal; *(von Befehl)* cancellation, countermand; *(von ketzerischen Behauptungen)* recantation; **~ leisten** to

recant; **bis auf ~** until revoked or withdrawn, until cancelled *(Brit)* or canceled *(US)*

wi|der|ru|fen [vi:dɐˈruːfn] *ptp* **widerrufen** *insep irreg* VT *Erlaubnis, Anordnung etc* to revoke *(auch Jur)*, to withdraw, to cancel; *Aussage, Geständnis, Behauptung* to retract *(auch Jur)*, to withdraw; *Befehl* to cancel, to countermand VI *(bei Verleumdung etc)* to withdraw; *(esp bei ketzerischen Behauptungen)* to recant

wi|der|ruf|lich ['vi:dɐru:flɪç, vi:dɐˈru:flɪç] *(form)* ADJ revocable, revokable ADV until revoked *or* withdrawn

Wi|der-: Wi|der|sa|cher ['vi:dɐzaxɐ] M **-s, -, Wi|der|sa|che|rin** [-ərɪn] F **-, -nen** adversary, antagonist, opponent; **wi|der|schal|len** VI *sep (old)* to echo or reverberate *(von* with); **Wi|der|schein** M *(liter)* reflection; **wi|der|set|zen** *ptp* **widersetzt** VR *insep sich jdm/einer Sache ~* to oppose sb/sth; *einem Polizisten, der Festnahme* to resist sb/sth; *einem Befehl, einer Aufforderung* to refuse to comply with sth; **wi|der|set|zlich** [vi:dɐˈzetslɪç, 'vi:dɐ-] ADJ contrary, obstreperous; *Befehlsempfänger* insubordinate; **Wi|der|sinn** M *no pl* absurdity, illogicality; **Wi|der|sin|nig** ADJ absurd, nonsensical; **wi|der|spens|tig** ADJ stubborn, unruly, wilful; *Material, Plastik* difficult to work with; *Haar* unruly, unmanageable; **„Der Widerspenstigen Zähmung"** "The Taming of the Shrew"; **Wi|der|spens|tig|keit** [vi:dɐˈʃpɛnstɪkaɪt] F **-, -en** stubbornness; *(von Kind)* unruliness, wilfulness; *(von Haar)* unruliness; **ein Material von einer gewissen ~** a material that is somewhat difficult to work with; **wi|der+spie|geln** *sep* VT *(lit, fig)* to reflect; *Gegenstand auch* to mirror VR *(lit, fig)* to be reflected/mirrored; **Wi|der|spie|ge|lung** F, **Wi|der|spieg|lung** [-ʃpi:ɡlʊŋ] F **-, -en** reflection; **Wi|der|spiel** NT **das ~ der Kräfte** the play of forces

wi|der|spre|chen [vi:dɐˈʃprɛçn] ✪ 53.6 *ptp* **widersprochen** [vi:dɐˈʃprɔxn] *insep irreg* VI **jdm/einer Sache ~** to contradict sb/sth; *(= nicht übereinstimmen mit)* den Tatsachen etc auch to be inconsistent with sth; **da muss ich aber ~** I've got to *(Brit)* or I have to contradict you there; **das widerspricht meinen Grundsätzen** that goes or is against my principles VR *(einander)* to contradict each other or one another; *(= nicht übereinstimmen: Aussagen etc auch)* to be inconsistent, to conflict; **sich (selbst) ~** to contradict oneself

wi|der|spre|chend ADJ **(sich** *or* **einander) ~** contradictory, conflicting, inconsistent

Wi|der|spruch M **a** *(= Gegensätzlichkeit)* contradiction *(auch Philos)*; *(= Unvereinbarkeit)* inconsistency; **ein ~ in sich selbst** a contradiction in terms; **in** *or* **im ~ zu** contrary to; **in ~ zu** *or* **mit etw geraten** to come into conflict with sth, to contradict sth; **sich in ~ zu jdm/etw setzen** to go against sb/sth; **in** *or* **im ~ zu** *or* **mit etw stehen** to conflict with sth, to stand in contradiction to sth, to be contrary to sth **b** *(= Widerrede)* contradiction, dissent; *(= Protest)* protest; *(= Ablehnung)* opposition; *(Jur)* appeal; **kein ~!** don't argue!; **er duldet keinen ~** he won't have any argument *(Brit)*, he won't stand for any back talk *(US)*; **es erhob sich ~** there was opposition *(gegen* to), there were protests *(gegen* against); **~ erheben** to protest; **~ einlegen** to lodge a protest; *(Jur)* to appeal; **~ gegen etw einlegen** to protest against sth; **~ erfahren, auf ~ stoßen** to meet with opposition *(bei* from)

wi|der|sprüch|lich [-ʃprʏçlɪç] ADJ contradictory; *Erzählung, Theorie auch, Verhalten* inconsistent ADV contradictorily; *sich verhalten auch* inconsistently

Wi|der|sprüch|lich|keit F **-, -en** contradiction, contradictoriness; *(von Erzählung, Theorie auch, von Verhalten)* inconsistency

Wi|der|spruchs-: wi|der|spruchs|frei ADJ *Theorie* consistent; **Wi|der|spruchs|geist** M ,

no pl spirit of opposition; **Wi|der|spruchs|kla|ge** F *(Jur)* interference proceedings *pl*; **wi|der|spruchs|los** ADJ *(= ungefochten)* Zustimmung, Annahme unopposed; *(= ohne Einwände)* Zuhören, Befolgen von Anordnung without contradiction; *(= folgsam)* Kind, Gehorchen unprotesting; *(= nicht widersprüchlich)* Theorie, Mensch, Verhalten consistent ADV *(= unangefochten)* without opposition; *(= ohne Einwände)* without contradiction; *(= folgsam)* without protest; **wi|der|spruchs|voll** ADJ full of contradictions; *(= voller Unvereinbarkeiten)* full of inconsistencies

Wi|der|stand M resistance *(auch Pol, Elec etc)*; *(im 2. Weltkrieg)* Resistance; *(= Ablehnung)* opposition; *(Elec: Bauelement)* resistor; **zum ~ aufrufen** to call upon people to resist; **es erhebt sich ~** there is resistance; **jdm/einer Sache** *or* **gegen jdn/etw ~ leisten** to resist sb/sth, to put up *or* offer *(form)* resistance to sb/sth; **seine inneren Widerstände überwinden** to overcome one's inhibitions; **~ gegen die Staatsgewalt** obstructing an officer in the performance of his duties *(Brit)* or in the line of duty → **Weg a**

Wi|der|stands-: Wi|der|stands|bei|wert M drag factor; **Wi|der|stands|be|we|gung** F resistance movement; *(im 2. Weltkrieg)* Resistance movement; **wi|der|stands|fä|hig** ADJ robust; *Pflanze* hardy; *(Med, Tech etc)* resistant *(gegen* to); **Wi|der|stands|fä|hig|keit** F robustness; *(von Pflanze)* hardiness; *(Med, Tech etc)* resistance *(gegen* to); **Wi|der|stands|kämp|fer(in)** M(F) member of the resistance; *(im 2. Weltkrieg)* member of the Resistance, Resistance fighter; **Wi|der|stands|kraft** F (power of) resistance; **wi|der|stands|los** ADJ, ADV without resistance; *(Phys)* non-resistant; **Wi|der|stands|mes|ser** M **-s, -** *(Elec)* ohmmeter; **Wi|der|stands|nest** NT *(Mil)* pocket of resistance

wi|der|ste|hen [vi:dɐˈʃte:ən] *ptp* **widerstanden** [vi:dɐˈʃtandn] VI *insep irreg +dat* **a** *(= nicht nachgeben)* to resist; *(= standhalten)* to withstand; **einer Versuchung/einem Erdbeben können** to be able to resist a temptation/withstand an earthquake **b** *(= anekeln)* **etw widersteht jdm** sb loathes sth

wi|der|stre|ben [vi:dɐˈʃtre:bn] *ptp* **widerstrebt** VI *insep +dat* **jdm/einer Sache ~** *(Mensch)* to oppose sb/sth; **etw widerstrebt einer Sache** sth conflicts with sth; **jds sittlichem Empfinden/jds Interessen** etc **~** to go against sb's moral sense/sb's interests; **das widerstrebt mir** *(= das möchte ich nicht tun)* I can't do things like that, I can't be like that; **es widerstrebt mir, so etwas zu tun** *(= lehne ich ab)* it goes against the grain *(Brit)* or my grain *(US)* to do anything like that; *(= möchte ich nicht)* I am reluctant to do anything like that

Wi|der|stre|ben NT reluctance; **nach anfänglichem ~** after some initial reluctance

wi|der|stre|bend ADJ *(= gegensätzlich)* Interessen conflicting; *(= widerwillig, zögernd)* reluctant; **mit ~en Gefühlen** with (some) reluctance ADV *(widerwillig)* unwillingly, reluctantly

Wi|der|streit M *(geh)* conflict; **im** *or* **in ~ zu etw stehen** to be in conflict with sth

wi|der|strei|tend ADJ *(geh)* **(einander) ~** conflicting

wi|der+tö|nen VI *sep* to echo; **seine Worte tönten ihr noch im Ohr wider** his words were still ringing in her ears

wi|der|wär|tig [-vɛrtɪç] ADJ *Verhalten* offensive, objectionable; *(= ekelhaft)* disgusting; *Aufgabe, Arbeit, Verhalten* objectionable; **etw ist jdm ~** sb finds sth offensive/disgusting/objectionable ADV **~ schmecken/stinken** to taste/smell disgusting

Wi|der|wär|tig|keit F **-, -en a** *no pl* offensiveness; *(von Arbeit)* objectionable nature; **die ~ dieses Essens** this disgusting food **b** *(= widerwärtige Tat)* unpleasantness

Wi|der|wil|le M (= *Abscheu, Ekel*) disgust (*gegen* for), revulsion; (= *Abneigung*) distaste (*gegen* for), aversion (*gegen* to); (= *Widerstreben*) reluctance; **etw mit größtem ~n tun** to do sth with the greatest reluctance; **etw mit größtem ~n trinken** to drink sth with intense distaste

wi|der|wil|lig ADJ reluctant, unwilling ADV reluctantly, unwillingly

Wi|der|wor|te PL answering *or* talking back *sing*; **~ geben** *or* **machen** to answer *or* talk back; **er tat es ohne ~** he did it without protest

wid|men [ˈvɪtmən] VT jdm etw **~** to dedicate sth to sb; (= *schenken, verwenden auf*) to devote sth to sb VR +*dat* to devote oneself to; (= *sich kümmern um*) **den Gästen etc** to attend to; *einem Problem, einer Aufgabe* to apply oneself to, to attend to; **nun kann ich mich dir/dieser Aufgabe ganz ~** I can now give you/this task my undivided attention

Wid|mung [ˈvɪtmʊŋ] F -, -en (*in Buch etc*) dedication (*an* +*acc* to)

wid|rig [ˈviːdrɪç] ADJ adverse; *Winde, Umstände auch* unfavourable (*Brit*), unfavorable (*US*)

wid|ri|gen|falls ADV (*form*) if this is not the case, otherwise; (*Nebensatz einleitend*) failing which

Wid|rig|keit F -, -en adversity; **wegen der ~ des Wetters** because of the unfavourable (*Brit*) *or* unfavorable (*US*) weather; **allen ~en zum Trotz** in the face of great adversity

wie [viː] INTERROG ADV **a** how; **~ anders ...?** how else ...?; **~ schwer/oft** *etc***?** how heavy/often *etc*?; **~ viele?** how many?; **~ das?** how come?; **~ ist dir** (*zumute or zu Mute*)**?** how do you feel?; **aber frag (mich) nicht ~!** but don't ask me how!; **~ wärs (mit uns beiden** *etc***)** (*inf*) how about it? (*inf*); **~ wärs mit einem Whisky?** (*inf*) how about a whisky?; **~ wäre es, wenn du mir ein Bier bezahlen würdest?** how *or* how's (*inf*) about (you) buying me a beer?

b (= *welcher Art*) **~ wars auf der Party/in Italien?** what was it like at the party/in Italy, what was the party/Italy like?, how was the party/Italy?; **~ ist er (denn)?** what's he like?; **~ war das Wetter?** what was the weather like?, how was the weather?; **~ ist es eigentlich, wenn ...?** what's the situation if ...?, what happens if ...?; **~ war das (noch mal genau) mit dem Unfall?** what (exactly) happened in the accident?; **und ~ ist es mit deinem Job?** and what about your job?; **Sie wissen ja, ~ das so ist** well, you know how it is

c (= *was*) **~ heißt er/das?** what's he/it called?; **~ nennt man das?** what is that called?; **~?** what?; **~ bitte?, ~ war das?** (*inf*) **~ meinen** *or* **belieben?** (*inf*) sorry?, pardon?, come again? (*inf*); **~ bitte?!** (*entrüstet*) I beg your pardon!

d (*in Ausrufen*) how; **und ~!, aber ~!** and how! (*inf*); **~ groß er ist!** how big he is!, isn't he big!; **~ schrecklich!** how terrible!; **~ haben wir gelacht, als ...** how we laughed when ...

e (= *nicht wahr?*) eh; **das macht dir Spaß, ~?** you like that, don't you?; **das macht dir keinen Spaß, ~?** you don't like that, do you?

ADV **a** (*relativ*) **die Art, ~ sie geht** the way (in which) she walks; **in dem Maße, ~ ...** to the same extent that ...; **in dem Stil, ~ er jetzt Mode ist** in the style which *or* that is now fashionable; **es war ein Sonnenuntergang, ~ er noch nie einen gesehen hatte** it was a sunset the like of which he had never seen before

b (*in Verbindung mit auch*) **~ stark du auch sein magst** however strong you may be; **~ auch immer du das machen wirst** however you are going to do it, whatever way you are going to do it; **~ sehr ... auch** however much; **~ sie auch alle heißen** whatever they're called

CONJ **a** (*vergleichend*) (*wenn sich Vergleich auf adj, adv bezieht*) as; (*wenn sich Vergleich auf n bezieht, bei Apposition*) like; **so ... ~** as ... as; **so lang ~ breit** the same length and width, as long as it *etc* is wide; **weiß ~ Schnee** (as) white as snow; **mutig ~ ein Löwe** as brave as a lion;

eine Nase ~ eine Kartoffel a nose like a potato; **ein Mann ~ er** a man like him, a man such as he (*form*); **in einer Lage ~ dieser** in a situation like this *or* such as this; **er ist Lehrer, ~ sein Vater es war** he is a teacher like his father was (*inf*) *or* as was his father; **T ~ Theodor** "t" as in "Tommy"; (*bei Rundfunk etc*) t for Tommy; **er ist intelligent, ~ wir** he is intelligent like us; **~ gewöhnlich/immer** as usual/always *or* ever; **ich fühlte mich ~ betrunken** I felt (as if I were *or* was) drunk; **ich fühlte mich ~ im Traum** I felt as if I were *or* was *or* like I was (*inf*) dreaming; **~ sie nun (ein)mal ist, musste sie ...** the way she is she just had to ...; **~ du weißt/man sagt** as you know/they say; **~ noch nie** as never before

b (= *zum Beispiel*) **~ (zum Beispiel** *or* **etwa)** such as (for example)

c (*incorrect*: = *als*) **größer/schöner ~** bigger/more beautiful than; **nichts ~ Ärger** *etc* nothing but trouble *etc*

d (= *und*) as well as; **Alte ~ Junge** old and young alike

e (*inf*) **~ wenn** as if *or* though

f (*bei Verben der Gefühlsempfindung*) **er sah, ~ es geschah** he saw it happen; **sie spürte, ~ es kalt wurde** she felt it getting cold; **er hörte, ~ der Regen fiel** he heard the rain falling

g (*zeitlich*: = *als*) **~ ich mich umdrehte, sah ich ...** as I turned around, I saw ..., turning around, I saw ...; **~ ich mit der Schule fertig war, ...** (*inf*) when I was finished with school, ...

Wie [viː] NT -s, *no pl* **das ~ spielt dabei keine Rolle** how (it'll happen/it'll be done *etc*) is unimportant; **dass es geschehen muss, ist klar, nur das ~ ist noch ein Problem** it's clear that it has to happen, the only problem is how; **das ~ und Wann werden wir später besprechen** we'll talk about how and when later

Wie|de|hopf [ˈviːdəhɔpf] M -(e)s, -e hoopoe

wie|der [ˈviːdɐ] ADV **a** again; **~ nüchtern/glücklich** *etc* sober/happy *etc* again; **immer ~, ~ und ~** again and again; **~ mal, (ein)mal ~** (once) again; **komm doch ~ mal vorbei** come and see me/us again; **~ ist ein Jahr vorbei** another year has passed; **~ was anderes** *or* **Neues** something else again, something quite different; **wie, schon ~?** what, again?; **~ da** back (again); **da bin ich ~!** I'm back!, here I am again!; **das ist auch ~ wahr** that's true; **da sieht man mal ~, ...** it just shows ...

b (*in Verbindung mit vb*) again; **das fällt mir schon ~ ein** I'll remember it again; **das Boot tauchte ~ auf** the boat resurfaced; **wenn die Wunde ~ aufbricht** if the wound reopens; **~ geboren** (*lit, fig*) reborn; **~ geboren werden** to be reborn; **~ verwendbar** reusable; **~ verwertbar** recyclable

Wie|der-, wie|der- PREF re; (*bei Verben*) (= *erneut, noch einmal*) again; (= *zurück*) back; **Wie|der|ab|druck** M reprint; **wie|der auf|ar|bei|ten** ▲ VT to recycle; *Atommüll* to reprocess; **Wie|der|auf|ar|bei|tung** F -, -en recycling; (*von Atommüll*) reprocessing; **wie|der auf|be|rei|ten** ▲ VT = **wieder aufarbeiten**; **Wie|der|auf|ar|bei|tungs|an|la|ge** F recycling plant; (*für Atommüll*) reprocessing plant; **Wie|der|auf|bau** M , *no pl* (*lit, fig*) reconstruction, rebuilding; **der ~ nach dem Krieg** post-war reconstruction; **der ~ des Hauses** the rebuilding of the house; **wie|der auf|bau|en** ▲ VTI to reconstruct, to rebuild; **wie|der auf|be|rei|ten** ▲ VT to recycle; *Atommüll, Abwasser* to reprocess; **Wie|der|auf|be|rei|tung** F recycling; (*von Atommüll*) reprocessing; **Wie|der|auf|be|rei|tungs|an|la|ge** F recycling plant; (*für Atommüll*) reprocessing plant; **wie|der auf|er|ste|hen** ▲ VI *irreg aux sein* to rise from the dead, to be resurrected; **Wie|der|auf|er|ste|hung** F resurrection; **wie|der auf|fors|ten** ▲ VTI to reforest; **wie|der auf|füh|ren** ▲ VT *Theaterstück* to revive; *Film* to reshow, to rerun; *Musikwerk* to reperform; **wie|der auf|la|den** ▲ VT *irreg* to recharge; **wie|der auf|le|ben** ▲ VI *aux sein* to revive; **Wie|der|auf|le|ben** NT , *no*

pl revival; (*von Nationalismus etc auch*) resurgence; **wie|der auf|le|gen** ▲ VT to republish; **Wie|der|auf|nah|me** [ˈviːdɐˈʔaufnaːmə] F **a** (*von Tätigkeit, Gespräch etc*) resumption; (*von Beziehungen*) re-establishment, resumption; (*von Gedanken, Idee*) readoption; (*von Thema*) reversion (+*gen* to); **die ~ des Verfahrens** (*Jur*) the reopening of proceedings **b** (*von verstoßenem Menschen*) taking back; (*im Verein etc*) readmittance, reacceptance; (*von Patienten*) readmission; **Wie|der|auf|nah|me|ver|fah|ren** NT (*Jur*) (*im Zivilrecht*) rehearing; (*im Strafrecht*) retrial; **wie|der auf|neh|men** ▲ VT *irreg* **a** (= *wieder beginnen*) to resume; *Beziehungen* to re-establish, to resume; *Gedanken, Idee, Hobby* to take up again; *Thema* to revert to; (*Jur*) *Verfahren* to reopen **b** *verstoßenen Menschen* to take back; (*in Verein etc*) to readmit, to reaccept; *Patienten* to readmit; **wie|der auf|rich|ten** ▲ VT (*fig*) **jdn** to give new heart to; **wie|der auf|rüs|ten** ▲ VTI to rearm; **jdn moralisch ~** to raise sb's morale; **Wie|der|auf|rüs|tung** F rearmament; **jds moralische ~** the raising of sb's morale; **Wie|der|aus|fuhr** F re-export; **wie|der aus|füh|ren** ▲ VT to re-export; **Wie|der|be|ginn** M recommencement, restart; (*von Schule*) reopening; **wie|der be|kom|men** *ptp* **wiederbekommen** ▲ VT *sep irreg* to get back; **das bekommst du wieder, du gemeines Stück** I'll get my own back, you bastard! (*Brit sl*), I'll get back at you, you dirty skunk! (*US sl*); **wie|der be|le|ben** ▲ VT to revive, to resuscitate; (*fig*) *Brauch etc* to revive, to resurrect; *Wirtschaft* to revive; **Wie|der|be|le|bung** F resuscitation, revival; (*fig*) revival, resurrection; **Wie|der|be|le|bungs|ver|such** M attempt at resuscitation; (*fig*) attempt at revival; **~e bei jdm anstellen** to attempt to revive *or* resuscitate sb

wie|der+be|schaf|fen *ptp* **wiederbeschafft** VT *sep* to replace; (= *zurückbekommen*) to recover

Wie|der|be|schaf|fung F replacement; (= *Zurückbekommen*) recovery

Wie|der|be|schaf|fungs- (*Comm*): **Wie|der|be|schaf|fungs|kos|ten** PL replacement cost *sing*; **Wie|der|be|schaf|fungs|wert** M replacement value

Wie|der-: **wie|der be|set|zen** ▲ VT **eine Stel|le ~** to fill a vacancy; **wie|der be|waff|nen** ▲ VR to rearm; **Wie|der|be|waff|nung** F rearmament; **wie|der+brin|gen** VT *sep irreg* to bring back; **wie|der ein|bür|gern** ▲ VT to renaturalize; **wie|der ein|fin|den** ▲ VR *irreg* to turn up again; **Wie|der|ein|fuhr** [ˈviːdɐˈlainfuːɐ̯] F reimport(ation); **wie|der ein|füh|ren** ▲ VT to reintroduce; *Todesstrafe auch* to bring back; (*Comm*) *Waren* to reimport; **Wie|der|ein|füh|rung** F reintroduction; **wie|der ein|glie|dern** ▲ VT to reintegrate (*in* +*acc* into); **einen Straf|täter in die Gesellschaft ~** to rehabilitate a criminal offender; **Wie|der|ein|glie|de|rung** F reintegration; **die ~ eines Straftäters in die Gesellschaft** the rehabilitation of a criminal offender; **wie|der ein|lie|fern** ▲ VT *Kranken* to readmit (*in* +*acc* to); *Häftling* to reimprison; **Wie|der|ein|nah|me** [ˈviːdɐˈlainnaːmə] F (*Mil*) recapture, retaking; **wie|der ein|neh|men** ▲ VT *irreg* (*Mil*) to retake, to recapture; **Wie|der|ein|rei|se** F (*in ein Land*) re-entry; **wie|der ein|set|zen** ▲ VT to reinstate (*in* +*acc* to); **jdn als König ~** to restore sb to the throne VI (*Regen*) to start up again; (*Med: Fieber, Schmerzen, Wehen*) to recur; **Wie|der|ein|set|zung** F reinstatement; (*von König*) restoration; **Wie|der|ein|stei|ger(in)** M(F) (*in Beruf*) returnee, labour market returner (*Brit spec*); **wie|der ein|stel|len** ▲ VT *sep* to re-employ, to re-engage; (*nach ungerechtfertigter Entlassung*) to reinstate; **Wie|der|ein|stel|lung** F re-employment, re-engagement; (*nach ungerechtfertigter Entlassung*) reinstatement; **Wie|der|ein|stel|lungs|klau|sel** F reinstatement clause; **Wie|der|ein|tritt** M reentry (*auch Space*) (*in* +*acc* into); **wie|der ent|de|cken** ▲ VT (*lit, fig*) to rediscover; **Wie|der|ent|de|ckung** F rediscovery; **wie|der er|grei|fen** ▲ VT *irreg* to recapture; **Wie|der|er|grei|fung** [-|ɛɐgraifʊŋ] F -, -en recapture; **wie|der+er|hal|ten** *ptp* **wiedererhalten** VT *sep irreg* to recover; **wie|der er|ken|nen** ▲ VT *irreg* to recognize; **das/er war nicht wieder zu erkennen** it/he was unrecognizable; **wie|der+er|lan|gen** *ptp* **wiedererlangt** VT *sep* to regain; *Eigentum* to recover; **Wie|der|er|lan|gung** F regaining; (*von Eigentum*) recovery; **wie|der er|nen|nen** ▲ VT *irreg* to reappoint (*zu etw* (as) sth); **Wie|der|er|nen|nung** F reappointment (*zu* as); **wie|der er|öff|nen** ▲ VTI to reopen; **Wie|der|er|öff|nung** F reopening; **wie|der er|schei|nen** ▲ VI *irreg aux sein* to reappear; (*Buch etc*) to be republished; **wie|der+er|stat|ten** *ptp* **wiedererstattet** VT *sep Unkosten etc* to refund, to reimburse (*jdm etw* sb for sth); **Wie|der|er|stat|tung** F refund(ing), reimbursement; **wie|der er|ste|hen** ▲ VI *irreg aux sein* to rise again; **wie|der er|wa|chen** ▲ VI *aux sein* to reawake(n); **wie|der er|we|cken** ▲ VT to bring back to life, to revive (*auch fig*); **wie|der fin|den** ▲ *irreg* **VT** to find again; (*fig*) *Selbstachtung, Mut etc* to regain; **die Sprache ~** (*fig*) to find one's tongue again (*Brit*), to regain one's speech (*US*) **VR** (*nach Schock*) to recover; **sich irgendwo ~** to find oneself somewhere; **sich** *or* **einander ~** to find each other again

Wie|der|ga|be F **a** (*von Rede, Ereignis, Vorgang*) account, report; (= *Beschreibung*) description; (= *Wiederholung: von Äußerung etc*) repetition **b** (= *Darbietung: von Stück etc*) rendering, rendition **c** (= *Übersetzung*) translation **d** (= *Darstellung*) representation **e** (= *Reproduktion*) (*von Gemälde, Farben, akustisch*) reproduction; **bei der ~** in reproduction **f** (= *Rückgabe*) return; (*von Rechten, Freiheit etc*) restitution

Wie|der|ga|be-: Wie|der|ga|be|ge|rät NT playback unit; **Wie|der|ga|be|treue** F fidelity of sound reproduction; **hohe ~** high fidelity

wie|der+ge|ben VT *sep irreg* **a** *Gegenstand, Geld* to give back; (*fig*) *Rechte, Mut etc* to restore, to give back; **jdm ein Buch ~** to give a book back to sb, to give sb his/her book back; **jdm die Freiheit ~** to restore sb's freedom, to give sb back his freedom **b** (= *erzählen*) to give an account of; (= *beschreiben*) to describe; (= *wiederholen*) to repeat; **seine Worte sind nicht wiederzugeben** his words are unrepeatable **c** *Gedicht* to recite; *Theaterstück, Musik* to perform **d** (= *übersetzen*) to translate **e** (= *darstellen, porträtieren*) to represent **f** (= *reproduzieren*) *Gemälde, Farbe, Ton* to reproduce **g** (= *vermitteln*) *Bedeutung, Gefühl, Erlebnis* to convey

Wie|der-: wie|der|ge|bo|ren △ ADJ → **wieder b; Wie|der|ge|burt** F (*lit, fig*) rebirth; **Wie|der|ge|ne|sung** F recovery; **wie|der+ge|win|nen** *ptp* **wiedergewonnen** VT *sep irreg* (*lit, fig*) to regain; *jdn* to win back; *Land, Rohstoffe etc* to reclaim; *Geld, Selbstvertrauen* to recover; **wie|der+grü|ßen** VTI *sep* (*jdn*) **~** to return sb's greeting; (= *einen ausgerichteten Gruß erwidern*) to send sb one's regards in return; (*Mil*) to return the/sb's salute; **wie|der gut|ma|chen** ▲ VT *Schaden* to compensate for; *Fehler* to rectify; *Beleidigung* to put right; (= *sühnen*) to atone for; (*Pol*) to make reparations for; (*Jur*) to redress; **das ist nie wieder gutzumachen** that can never be put right; **Wie|der|gut|ma|chung** F -, -en compensation; (= *Sühne*) atonement; (*Pol*) reparations *pl*; (*Jur*) redress; **als ~ für mein Benehmen** to make up for my behaviour (*Brit*) *or* behavior (*US*); **als ~ für den Schaden** to compensate for the damage; **als ~ für den Fehler** to rectify the fault; **als ~ für die Beleidigung** to put right the insult; **wie|der ha|ben** VT *sep irreg* (*inf*) to have (got) back (*Brit*), to get back; **etw ~ wollen** to want sth back; **wie|der her|rich|ten** ▲ VT to repair; *Zimmer* to redecorate;

wie|der her|stel|len ▲ VT *Gebäude, Ordnung, Frieden, Demokratie* to restore; *Vertrauen, Glaubwürdigkeit auch, Beziehungen* to re-establish; **wie|der+her|stel|len** *ptp* **wiederhergestellt** VT *sep Gesundheit* to restore; *Patienten* to restore to health; **von einer Krankheit wiederhergestellt sein** to have recovered from an illness; **Wie|der|her|stel|lung** F (*von Gebäude, Ordnung, Frieden, Gesundheit*) restoration; (*von Beziehungen*) re-establishment; **Wie|der|her|stel|lungs|kos|ten** PL restoration costs *pl*

wie|der|hol|bar [vi:dɐ'ho:lbaːɐ] ADJ repeatable; **leicht/schwer ~** easy/hard to repeat; **das ist nicht ~** that can't be repeated

wie|der|ho|len¹ [vi:dɐ'ho:lən] *ptp* **wiederholt** *insep* **VTI** to repeat; (= *zum zweiten Mal, mehrmals*) *Forderung etc* to reiterate; (*zusammenfassend*) to recapitulate; *Lernstoff* to revise, to review (*US*); *Prüfung* to retake, to resit (*Brit*); (*Film*) *Szene* to retake; (*Sport*) *Elfmeter etc* to retake, to take again; *Spiel* to replay; **wiederholt, was ich euch vorsage** repeat after me; (**eine Klasse** *or* **ein Jahr**) **~** (*Sch*) to repeat a year **VR** (*Mensch*) to repeat oneself; (*Thema, Ereignis*) to recur, to be repeated; (*Dezimalstelle*) to recur; **es wiederholt sich doch alles im Leben** life has a habit of repeating itself

wie|der+ho|len² [ˈviːdɐhoːlən] VT *sep* (= *zurückholen*) to get back

wie|der|holt [vi:dɐ'ho:lt] ADJ repeated; **zu ~en Malen** repeatedly, on repeated occasions; **zum ~en Male** once again **ADV** repeatedly

Wie|der|ho|lung [vi:dɐ'ho:lʊŋ] F -, -en repetition; (*von Prüfung, Filmszene*) retaking; (*von Aufführung*) repeat performance; (*von Sendung*) repeat; (*in Zeitlupe*) replay; (*von Lernstoff*) revision; (*zum zweiten Mal, mehrmals: von Forderung etc*) reiteration; (*zusammenfassend*) recapitulation; (*Sport*) (*von Elfmeter*) retaking, retake; (*von Spiel*) replay; **trotz zweimaliger ~ derselben Klasse** in spite of repeating the year twice

Wie|der|ho|lungs-: Wie|der|ho|lungs|kurs M refresher course; **Wie|der|ho|lungs|prü|fung** F (*Sch*) repeat examination; **Wie|der|ho|lungs|spiel** NT (*Sport*) replay; **Wie|der|ho|lungs|tas|te** F repeat key; **Wie|der|ho|lungs|tä|ter(in)** M(F) (*Jur*) (*bei erster Wiederholung*) second offender, (*bei ständiger Wiederholung*) persistent offender, recidivist (*form*); **Wie|der|ho|lungs|zei|chen** NT (*Mus*) repeat (mark); (*Typ*) ditto mark *or* sign; (= *Tilde*) tilde; **Wie|der|ho|lungs|zwang** M (*Psych*) recidivism; (*Sprachfehler*) palilalia (*spec*)

Wie|der-: Wie|der|hö|ren NT (**auf**) **~!** (*am Telefon*) goodbye!; (*im Hörfunk*) goodbye for now!; **Wie|der|imp|fung** F revaccination; **Wie|der|in|be|sitz|nah|me** [vi:dɐlnbəˈzɪtsnaːmə] F (*form*) resumption of possession; **Wie|der|in|be|trieb|nah|me** [vi:dɐlnbəˈtriːpnaːmə] F (*form*) putting into operation again; (*von U-Bahnlinie*) reopening; **Wie|der|in|stand|set|zung** [vi:dɐlnˈʃtantzetsʊŋ] F (*form*) repair, repairs *pl* (+*gen* to); **wie|der+käu|en** *sep* **VT** to ruminate, to chew again; (*fig inf*) to go over again and again **VI** to ruminate, to chew the cud; (*fig inf*) to harp on; **Wie|der|käu|er** [-kɔʏɐ] M -s, - ruminant

Wie|der|kehr [ˈviːdɐkeːɐ] F -, *no pl* (*geh*) (= *Rückkehr*) return; (= *zweites, ständiges Vorkommen*) recurrence; (*esp langweilig*) repetition; (*von Datum, Ereignis*) anniversary; **die ewige ~** the eternal recurrence

wie|der+keh|ren VI *sep aux sein* (= *zurückkehren*) to return; (= *sich wiederholen, wieder vorkommen*) to recur, to be repeated

wie|der|keh|rend ADJ recurring; **regelmäßig/oft ~** recurrent; **immer ~** ever-recurring; **ein jährlich ~es Fest** an annual festival

Wie|der-: wie|der ken|nen ▲ VT *irreg* (*inf*) to recognize; **wie|der+kom|men** VI *sep irreg aux sein* (*lit, fig*) to come back, to return; **komm doch mal wieder!** you must come again!; **wie|der+krie|gen** VT *sep* (*inf*) to get back; **warte**

nur, das kriegst du (von mir) wieder! just you wait, I'll get my own back (on you)! (*Brit*), just you wait, I'll get back at you! (*US*); **Wie|der|kunft** [ˈviːdəkʊnft] F -, *no pl* (*liter*) return; **die ~ Christi** the Second Coming; **wie|der+lie|ben** VT *sep* to love back; **Wie|der|schau|en** NT (**auf**) **~!** (*geh, S Ger, Aus, Sw*) goodbye!, good day! (*form*); **wie|der+schen|ken** VT *sep jdm etw* ~ to give sth back to sb; **er wurde dem Leben wiedergeschenkt** he was restored to life; **wie|der+se|hen** VT *sep irreg* to see again; (= *wieder zusammentreffen mit auch*) to meet again; **wann sehen wir uns wieder?** when will we see each other *or* meet again?; **Wie|der|se|hen** [ˈviːdezeːən] NT -s, - (*nach kürzerer Zeit*) (another) meeting; (*nach längerer Zeit*) reunion; **ich freue mich auf das ~ mit meinen Freunden/mit der Heimat** I'm looking forward to seeing my friends/to being back home again; **sie hofften auf ein baldiges ~** they hoped to see each other *or* meet again soon; **irgendwo, irgendwann gibt es ein ~** we'll meet again, don't know where, don't know when; (**auf**) **~!** goodbye!; (**auf** *or* **Auf**) **~ sagen** to say goodbye; **~ macht Freude!** (*hum*) I hope that's not the last I see of it!, I wouldn't mind having it back again!; **Wie|der|se|hens|freu|de** F unsere **~ war groß** we were very pleased (*esp Brit*) or happy to see each other again; **meine ~ war groß** I was very pleased (*esp Brit*) or happy to see him/her *etc* again; **Wie|der|tau|fe** F (*Rel*) rebaptism; **Wie|der|täu|fer(in)** M(F) (*Rel, Hist*) Anabaptist; **wie|der tun** ▲ VT *irreg* to do again

wie|de|rum [ˈviːdərʊm] ADV **a** (= *andrerseits*) on the other hand; (= *allerdings*) though; **das ist ~ richtig, daran habe ich nicht gedacht** that's quite correct, I didn't think of that **b** (*geh*: = *nochmals*) again, anew (*liter*) **c** (= *seinerseits etc*) in turn; **er ~ wollte ...** he, for his part, wanted ...

Wie|der-: wie|der ver|ei|ni|gen ▲ **VT** *Menschen, Fraktionen* to reunite; *Kirche auch, Land* to reunify **VR** to reunite, to come together again; **Wie|der|ver|ei|ni|gung** F reunification; **wie|der ver|hei|ra|ten** ▲ VR to remarry; **Wie|der|ver|hei|ra|tung** F remarriage; **Wie|der|ver|kauf** M resale; (*durch Einzelhandel*) retail; **wie|der ver|kau|fen** ▲ VT to resell; (*Einzelhändler*) to retail; **Wie|der|ver|käu|fer(in)** M(F) reseller; (= *Einzelhändler*) retailer; **Wie|der|ver|kaufs|preis** M resale price; **Wie|der|ver|kaufs|wert** M resale value; **wie|der ver|pflich|ten** ▲ VR (*Mil*) to re-enlist; **wie|der ver|wend|bar** △ ADJ → **wieder b**; **Wie|der|ver|wend|bar|keit** F reusability; **wie|der ver|wen|den** ▲ VT to reuse; **Wie|der|ver|wen|dung** F reuse; **wie|der ver|wert|bar** △ ADJ → **wieder b**; **Wie|der|ver|wert|bar|keit** F recyclability; **wie|der ver|wer|ten** ▲ VT to recycle; **Wie|der|ver|wer|tung** F recycling; **Wie|der|vor|la|ge** F, *no pl* (*form*) resubmission; **zur ~** for resubmission; **Wie|der|wahl** F re-election; **eine ~ ablehnen** to decline to run for re-election; **wenn es zu einer ~ der Partei kommt** if the party is returned (to power) again; **wie|der wäh|len** ▲ VT to re-elect; **wie|der zu|las|sen** ▲ VT *irreg Auto* to relicense; **Wie|der|zu|las|sung** F relicensing

wie|fern [viˈfɛrn] ADV = **inwiefern**

Wie|ge [ˈviːɡə] F, -n (*lit, fig, Tech*) cradle; **seine ~ stand in Schwaben** (*geh*) his birthplace was Swabia; **es ist mir/ihm auch nicht an der ~ gesungen worden, dass ...** no-one could have foreseen that ...; **das ist ihm (schon** *or* **gleich) in die ~ gelegt worden** he inherited it; **damals lagst du noch in der ~** at that time you were still a babe in arms; **von der ~ bis zur Bahre** (*geh*) from the cradle to the grave; **die ~ der Demokratie** the cradle of democracy

Wie|ge|mes|ser NT chopper, chopping knife (*Brit*), cleaver

wie|gen¹ [ˈviːɡn] **VT** **a** (= *hin und her bewegen*) to rock; *Kopf* to shake (slowly); *Hüften* to sway;

(*Wind*) *Äste etc* to sway; **~de Bewegung** swaying motion; **einen ~den Gang haben** to sway one's hips when one walks **b** (= *zerkleinern*) to chop up **VR** (*Boot etc*) to rock (gently); (*Mensch, Äste etc*) to sway; **sich im Tanz ~** to do an undulating dance; **sich in trügerischen Hoffnungen ~** to nurture false hopes → *auch* **gewiegt**

wie|gen² *pret* **wog** [voːk], *ptp* **gewogen** [gə'voːgn] VTI (= *abwiegen*) to weigh; **ein knapp gewogenes Kilo** something short of a kilo; **wie viel wiegst du?** how heavy are you?, what do you weigh?; **schwer ~** (*fig*) to carry a lot of weight; (*Irrtum*) to be serious; **gewogen und zu leicht befunden** (*Bibl, fig*) weighed and found wanting → *auch* **gewogen**

Wie|gen-: Wie|gen|druck M *pl* **-drucke** incunabulum; (*Verfahren*) early printing; **Wie|gen|fest** NT (*geh*) birthday; **Wie|gen|kind** NT (*liter*) infant, babe in arms; **Wie|gen|lied** NT lullaby, cradlesong

wie|hern ['viːɐn] VI to neigh; (*leiser*) to whinny; (*vor Lachen*) **~** to bray with laughter; **das ist ja zum Wiehern** (*inf*) that's dead funny (*Brit inf*), that's very funny

Wien [viːn] NT **-s** Vienna

Wie|ner¹ ['viːnɐ] ADJ *attr* Viennese; **~ Würstchen** frankfurter, wiener (sausage) (*esp US*); **~ Schnitzel** Wiener schnitzel

Wie|ner² ['viːnɐ] M **-s, -**, **Wie|ne|rin** [-ərɪn] F **-, -nen** Viennese

wie|ne|risch ['viːnərɪʃ] ADJ Viennese; **das Wienerische** the Viennese dialect

Wie|ner|le ['viːnələ] NT **-s, -** (*S Ger*), **Wie|ner|li** ['viːnəli] NT **-s, -** (*Sw*) frankfurter, wiener (sausage) (*esp US*)

wie|nern ['viːnɐln], **wie|nern¹** ['viːnɐn] VI (*inf*) to speak Viennese

wie|nern² VT (*usu pej*) to polish, to shine

wies *pret von* **weisen**

Wie|se ['viːzə] F **-, -n** meadow; (*inf*: = *Rasen*) grass, lawn; **auf der grünen ~** (*fig*) in the open countryside

wie|sehr △ [viː'zeːɐ] CONJ → **wie** ADV b

Wie|sel ['viːzl] NT **-s, -** weasel; **schnell** *or* **flink wie ein ~** quick as a flash; **laufen** *or* **rennen wie ein ~** to run like a hare (*Brit*) *or* rabbit (*US*)

wie|sel|flink [ADJ] quick, quicksilver *attr* [ADV] quick as a flash

wie|seln ['viːzln] VI *aux sein* to scurry, to scuttle

Wie|sen-: Wie|sen|blu|me F meadow flower; **Wie|sen|grund** M (*poet*) meadow, mead (*poet*); **Wie|sen|rain** M (*liter*) meadow's edge; **Wie|sen|schaum|kraut** NT lady's smock

Wiesn ['viːzn] F **-, -** (*dial*) fair

wie|so [viː'zoː] INTERROG ADV why; (= *aus welchem Grund auch*) how come (*inf*); **~ gehst du nicht?** how come you're not going? (*inf*), why aren't you going?; **~ nicht** why not; **~ weißt du das?** why do you say that?; **~ weißt du das?** how do you know that?

wie|viel △ [viː'fiːl, 'viː-] INTERROG ADV → **viel a**

wie|vie|ler|lei [viː'fiːlə'lai, 'viː-] INTERROG ADJ *inv* how many sorts *or* kinds of; **~ verschiedene (Whiskys etc)?** how many different sorts *or* kinds (of whisky *etc*)?

wie|viel|mal [viː'fiːl'maːl, 'viː-] INTERROG ADV how many times

Wie|viel|te(r) [viː'fiːltə, 'viː-] M *decl as adj* (*bei Datum*) **den ~n haben wir heute?**, **der ~ ist heute?** what's the date today?; **am ~n (des Monats)?** what day, what day of the month?; **der ~ ist Donnerstag?** what's the date on Thursday?

wie|viel|te(r, s) [viː'fiːltə, 'viː-] INTERROG ADJ **das ~ Kind ist das jetzt?** how many children is that now?; **das ~ Kind bist du? – das zweite** which child are you? – the second; **der ~ Band fehlt?** which volume is missing?; **den ~n Platz hat er im Wettkampf belegt?** where did he come in the competition?; **als Wievielter ging**

er durchs Ziel? what place did he come?; **das ~ Mal** *or* **zum ~n Mal bist du schon in England?** how often *or* how many times have you been to England?; **am ~n September hast du Geburtstag?** what date *or* when in September is your birthday?; **das ~ Jahr bist du jetzt in Schottland?** how many years have you lived in Scotland now?; **ich habe morgen Geburtstag! – der ~ ist es denn?** it's my birthday tomorrow! – how old will you be?

wie|weit [viː'vait] CONJ to what extent, how far

wie|wohl [viː'voːl] CONJ (*old*) **a** (= *obwohl*) although, (even) though **b** (= *dafür aber auch*) and at the same time, as well as

Wig|wam ['vɪkvam] M OR NT **-s, -s** wigwam

Wi|kin|ger ['viːkɪŋɐ, 'vɪkɪŋɐ] M **-s, -**, **Wi|kin|ge|rin** [-ərɪn] F **-, -nen** Viking

Wi|kin|ger-: Wi|kin|ger|schiff NT longboat, Viking ship; **Wi|kin|ger|zeit** F age of the Vikings, Viking age

wi|kin|gisch ['viːkɪŋɪʃ, 'vɪkɪŋɪʃ] ADJ Viking *attr*

wild [vɪlt] [ADJ] wild; *Schönheit auch* rugged; *Kind auch, Haar* unruly; *Stamm* savage; (= *laut, ausgelassen*) boisterous; (= *heftig*) *Kampf* fierce; (= *zornig*) *Blick* fierce, furious; (= *ungesetzlich*) *Parken, Zelten etc* illegal; *Streik* wildcat *attr*, unofficial; **~es Fleisch** proud flesh; **der Wilde Jäger** the Wild Huntsman; **den ~en Mann spielen** (*inf*) *or* **machen** (*inf*) to come the heavy (*Brit inf*), to play all that (*US sl*); **der Wilde Westen** the Wild West; **seid nicht so ~!** calm down a bit!; **jdn ~ machen** to make sb mad (*Brit inf*) *or* furious, to drive sb crazy; (*esp vor Vergnügen etc*) to drive sb wild; **~ werden** to go wild (*auch inf*), to go nuts *or* crazy; (*Pferd: = ausgelassen werden*) to run wild; **der Bulle wurde ~** (*inf*) the bull was enraged; **ich könnte ~ werden** (*inf*) I could scream (*inf*); **~ auf jdn/etw sein** (*inf*) to be wild *or* crazy *or* mad about sb/sth (*inf*); **das ist nicht so** *or* **halb so ~** (*inf*) never mind → **Ehe, Wein** [ADV] **a** (= *unordentlich*) **~ ins Gesicht hängende Haare** wild, tousled hair hanging over one's face; **~ durcheinander liegen** *or* **herumliegen** to be strewn all over the place; **dann ging alles ~ durcheinander** there was chaos then **b** (= *hemmungslos*) like mad *or* crazy; **brüllen, auf jdn einschlagen, um sich schlagen** wildly; **wie ~ rennen/arbeiten** *etc* to run/work *etc* like mad; **~ drauflosreden** to talk nineteen to the dozen (*Brit*), to talk like crazy (*US*); **~ drauflosschreiben** to write furiously; **~ entschlossen** (*inf*) really *or* dead (*inf*) determined **c** (= *in der freien Natur*) **~ leben** to live in the wild; **~ lebend** wild, living in the wild; **~ wachsen** to grow wild; **~ wachsend** wild(-growing)

Wild [vɪlt] NT **-(e)s** [-das] *no pl* (= *Tiere, Fleisch*) game; (= *Rotwild*) deer; (= *Fleisch von Rotwild*) venison; **ein Stück ~** a head of game

Wild-: Wild|bach M torrent; **Wild|bahn** F hunting ground *or* preserve; **auf** *or* **in freier ~** in the wild; **Wild|be|stand** M game population, stock of game; **Wild|bra|ten** M roast venison; **ein ~** a roast of venison; **Wild|bret** [-brɛt] NT **-s**, *no pl* game; (*von Rotwild*) venison; **Wild|dieb(in)** M(F) poacher; **Wild|dieb|stahl** M poaching

Wil|de(r) ['vɪldə] MF *decl as adj* savage, wild man/woman; (*fig*) madman, maniac; **die ~n** the savages

Wild|en|te F wild duck

Wil|de|rei [vɪldə'rai] F **-, -en** poaching

Wil|de|rer ['vɪldərɐ] M **-s, -**, **Wil|de|rin** [-ərɪn] F **-, -nen** poacher

wil|dern ['vɪldɐn] VI (*Mensch*) to poach; (*Hund etc*) to kill game; **~der Hund** dog which kills game

Wil|dern NT **-s**, *no pl* poaching; (*von Hund etc*) killing game

Wild-: Wild|esel M wild ass; **Wild|fal|le** F trap set for game; **Wild|fang** M **a** (*Hunt*) (*Falke*) passage *or* wild-caught hawk; (*Tier*) animal captured in the wild **b** (*dated inf*) little rascal

or devil, scamp; (*Mädchen*) tomboy; **Wild|fleisch** NT game; (*von Rotwild*) venison; **Wild|fraß** M damage caused by game; **wild|fremd** ['vɪlt'frɛmt] ADJ (*inf*) completely strange; **~e Leute/Menschen** complete strangers; **ein Wildfremder, ein ~er Mensch** a complete stranger; **Wild|füt|te|rung** F feeding of game animals; **Wild|gans** F wild goose; **Wild|gat|ter** NT game grid; (= *Zaun*) game fence; **Wild|ge|he|ge** NT game enclosure *or* preserve; **Wild|ge|schmack** M gam(e)y taste

Wild|heit F **-, -en** wildness; (*von Kind auch, von Haar*) unruliness; (*von Stamm etc*) savagery; (*von Kampf, Blick*) fierceness; (= *Leidenschaft*) wild passion

Wild-: Wild|hü|ter(in) M(F) gamekeeper; **Wild|ka|nin|chen** NT wild rabbit; **Wild|kat|ze** F wildcat; **wild|le|bend** △ ADJ *attr* → **wild** ADV c; **Wild|le|der** NT suede; **wild|le|dern** ADJ suede

Wild|nis ['vɪltnɪs] F **-, -se** (*lit, fig*) wilderness; **Tiere der ~** wild animals; **in der ~ leben/geboren werden** to live/be born in the wild

Wild-: Wild|park M game park; (*für Rotwild*) deer park; **Wild|reich|tum** M abundance of game; **Wild|re|ser|vat** NT game reserve; **wild|ro|man|tisch** ['vɪltro'mantɪʃ] ADJ (*iro*) terribly romantic; **Wild|sau** F wild sow; (*fig sl*) pig (*inf*); **Wild|scha|den** M damage caused by game; **Wild|schütz** [-ʃʏts] M **-en, -en**, **Wild|schüt|ze** M (*obs*) poacher; **Wild|schutz|ge|biet** NT game preserve; **Wild|schwein** NT wild boar *or* pig; **wild|wach|send** △ ADJ *attr* → **wild** ADV c; **Wild|was|ser** NT *pl* **-wasser** white water; **Wild|was|ser|boot** NT white-water canoe; **Wild|was|ser|fah|ren** NT white-water canoeing *or* rafting; **Wild|was|ser|ren|nen** NT fast-water canoe race; **Wild|wech|sel** M path used by game *or* by wild animals; (*bei Rotwild*) deer path; „**Wildwechsel**" "wild animals"; **Wild|west** *no art* the Wild West; **Wild|west|film** M western; **Wild|west|me|tho|den** PL (*pej inf*) Mafia methods; **Wild|west|ro|man** M western; **Wild|wuchs** M (*geh*) rank growth; (*fig*) proliferation; **Wild|zaun** M game fence

Wil|helm ['vɪlhɛlm] M **-s** William; **falscher ~** (*inf*) toupee; **seinen (Friedrich) ~ unter etw** (*dat*) **setzen** (*inf*) to put one's signature *or* moniker (*inf*) to sth, to John Hancock sth (*US inf*)

Wil|hel|mi|nisch [vɪlhɛl'miːnɪʃ] ADJ (*Hist*) Wilhelminian (*pertaining to the reign of William II of Germany 1888 - 1918*)

will 1. *and* 3. *pers pres von* **wollen²**

Wil|le ['vɪlə] M **-ns**, *no pl* will; (= *Absicht, Entschluss*) intention; **nach jds ~** as sb wanted/wants; (*von Architekt etc*) as sb intended/intends; **der ~ zur Macht** the will to power; **der ~ zur Zusammenarbeit** the will to cooperate; **keinen ~n (zu etw) haben** *or* **zeigen** to have *or* show no will (for sth); **wenn es nach ihrem ~n ginge** if she had her way; **etw mit ~n tun** to do sth on purpose *or* deliberately; **das geschah gegen** *or* **wider meinen ~n** (= *gegen meinen Wunsch*) that was done against my will; (= *unabsichtlich*) I didn't intend to happen; **er musste wider ~n** *or* **gegen seinen ~n lachen** he couldn't help laughing; **jds ~n tun** to do sb's will; **es steht (nicht) in unserem ~n, das zu tun** (*geh*) it is (not) our intention to do that; **seinen ~n durchsetzen** to get one's (own) way; **auf seinem ~n bestehen** to insist on having one's way; **jdm seinen ~n lassen** to let sb have his own way; **er soll seinen ~n haben** let him have his (own) way; **seinen eigenen ~n haben** to be self-willed, to have a mind of one's own; **beim besten ~n nicht** not with all the will *or* with the best will in the world; **ich hätte das beim besten ~n nicht machen können** I couldn't have done that for the life of me; **es war kein** *or* **nicht böser ~** there was no ill will intended; **etw aus freiem ~n tun** to do sth of one's own free will; **der gute ~** good will; **guten ~ns sein**

to be full of good intentions; **alle Menschen, die guten ~ns sind** all people of good will; **den guten ~n für die Tat nehmen** to take the thought for the deed; **jdm zu ~n sein** to comply with sb's wishes; (*Mädchen:* = *sich hingeben*) to yield to sb, to let sb have his way with one; **sich** (*dat*) **jdn zu ~n machen** to bend sb to one's will, to force sb to do one's will; *Mädchen* to have one's way with sb; **wo ein ~ ist, ist auch ein Weg** (*Prov*) where there's a will there's a way (*Prov*) → **letzte(r, s) a**

wil|len ['vɪlən] PREP → **um PREP** +*gen*

Wil|len-: wil|len|los ADJ weak-willed, spineless; **völlig ~ sein** to have no will of one's own; **jds ~es Werkzeug sein** to be sb's mere tool █ADV █ **jdm ~ ergeben sein** to be totally submissive to sb; **sich jdm ~ unterwerfen** to submissively obey sb; **Wil|len|lo|sig|keit** F -, *no pl* spinelessness

wil|lens ['vɪləns] ADJ (*geh*) **~ sein** to be willing or prepared

Wil|lens-: Wil|lens|akt M act of will; **Wil|lens|an|stren|gung** F effort of will; **Wil|lens|äu|ße|rung** F expression of will; **Wil|lens|bil|dung** F development of an informed opinion; **Wil|lens|er|klä|rung** F professed intention; **Wil|lens|frei|heit** F freedom of (the) will; **aufgrund seiner ~** on the basis of his freedom of will; **Wil|lens|kraft** F willpower, strength of mind; **Wil|lens|mensch** M (*inf*) very determined person; **wil|lens|schwach** ADJ weak-willed; **Wil|lens|schwä|che** F weak will; **wil|lens|stark** ADJ strong-willed, determined; **Wil|lens|stär|ke** F willpower; **Wil|lens|voll|stre|cker(in)** M(F) (*Sw*) executor; (*Frau auch*) executrix

wil|lent|lich ['vɪləntlɪç] ADJ wilful, deliberate █ADV █ deliberately

will|fah|ren [vɪl'faːrən, 'vɪl-] *pret* **willfahrte** [vɪl-'faːtə, 'vɪl-], *ptp* **willfahrt** [vɪl'faːɐt, 'vɪl-] VI +*dat* (*old, liter*) to please, to satisfy, to obey (*jdm* sb)

will|fäh|rig ['vɪlfɛːrɪç, vɪl'fɛːrɪç] ADJ (*old, liter*) submissive, compliant; **jdm ~ sein** to submit to sb

Will|fäh|rig|keit F -, (*rare*) -**en** (*old, liter*) submissiveness, compliance

wil|lig ['vɪlɪç] █ADJ █ willing █ADV █ willingly

wil|li|gen ['vɪlɪgn] VI (*old, liter*) **in etw** (*acc*) **~** to agree to sth

Wil|lig|keit F -, *no pl* willingness

Will|komm ['vɪlkɔm] M -s, -e (*old, liter*) █a█ welcome █b█ (*auch* **Willkommbecher**) cup of welcome (*old*)

will|kom|men [vɪl'kɔmən] ADJ welcome; **du bist (mir) immer ~** you are always welcome; **jdn ~ heißen** to welcome or greet sb; **seid (herzlich) ~!** welcome, welcome!; **herzlich ~** welcome (*in* +*dat* to); **es ist mir ganz ~, dass ...** I quite welcome the fact that ...; **die Gelegenheit, das zu sagen/zu tun, ist mir ~** I welcome the opportunity of saying/doing this

Will|kom|men [vɪl'kɔmən] NT -s, - welcome; **jdm ein ~ bieten** (*liter*) to bid sb welcome; **ein herzliches ~!** welcome indeed!

Will|kom|mens-: Will|kom|mens|gruß M greeting, welcome; **Will|kom|mens|trunk** M welcoming drink, cup of welcome (*old*)

Will|kür ['vɪlkyːɐ] F -, *no pl* capriciousness; (*politisch*) despotism; (*bei Entscheidungen, Handlungen*) arbitrariness; **sie sind seiner ~ schutzlos preisgegeben** or **ausgeliefert** they are completely at his mercy; **das ist reinste ~** that is purely arbitrary; **ein Akt der ~** an act of caprice/a despotic act/an arbitrary act

Will|kür-: Will|kür|akt M → **Willkür** act of caprice; despotic act; arbitrary act; **Will|kür|herr|schaft** F tyranny, despotic rule

will|kür|lich ['vɪlkyːɐlɪç] █ADJ █ █a█ arbitrary; *Herrscher* autocratic █b█ *Muskulatur, Kontraktion* voluntary █ADV █ █a█ (= *nach eigenem Belieben*) anordnen, handeln, vorgehen arbitrarily; **sie kann ~ Tränen**

produzieren she can produce tears at will; **einen Muskel ~ betätigen** to make a voluntary move of a muscle

Will|kür|lich|keit F -, -**en** arbitrariness; (*von Herrscher*) autocracy

Will|kür|maß|nah|me F arbitrary measure

Wil|ly ['vɪli] M -s, -s (*sl: = Penis*) willy (*Brit inf*), weenie (*US inf*)

wim|meln ['vɪmln] VI █a█ *auch vi impers* (= *in Mengen vorhanden sein*) **der See wimmelt von Fischen, in dem See wimmelt es von Fischen** the lake is teeming with fish; **hier wimmelt es von Fliegen/Pilzen/Menschen** this place is swarming with flies/overrun with mushrooms/teeming with people; **der Käse wimmelt von Maden** the cheese is crawling with maggots; **dieses Buch wimmelt von Fehlern** this book is riddled with mistakes █b█ *aux sein* (= *sich bewegen*) to teem; (*Mücken, Ameisen*) to swarm

wim|men ['vɪmən] (*Sw*) VT to harvest, to gather █VI █ to harvest or gather (the) grapes

Wim|merl ['vɪmɐl] NT -(s), -n (*Aus*) █a█ (= *Pickel*) spot (*Brit*), pimple █b█ (= *Skiläufertasche*) pouch

wim|mern ['vɪmɐn] VI to whimper

Wim|met ['vɪmɐt] M OR F -, *no pl* (*esp Sw, Aus*) grape harvest

Wim|pel ['vɪmpl] M -s, - pennant

Wim|per ['vɪmpɐ] F -, -n █a█ (eye)lash; **ohne mit der ~ zu zucken** (*fig*) without batting an eyelid (*Brit*) or eyelash (*US*) █b█ (*Bot, Zool*) cilium

Wim|pern|tu|sche F mascara

Wim|per|tier|chen NT ciliate

wind [vɪnt] ADJ (*S Ger, Sw*) **jdm wird es ~ und weh** (= *übel*) sb feels really ill; (= *traurig*) sb feels really sad; (= *angst*) sb feels really afraid

Wind [vɪnt] M -(e)s, -e [-də] █a█ wind; **bei** or **in ~ und Wetter** in all weathers; **~ und Wetter ausgesetzt sein** to be exposed to the elements; **laufen wie der ~** to run like the wind; **sich verbreiten wie der ~** to spread like wildfire; **der ~ dreht sich** the wind is changing direction; (*fig*) the climate is changing; **wissen/merken, woher der ~ weht** or **bläst** (*fig*) to know/notice the way the wind is blowing; **daher weht der ~!** (*fig*) so that's the way the wind is blowing; **seither weht** or **bläst ein anderer/frischer ~** (*fig*) things have changed since then; **ihm weht** or **bläst der ~ ins Gesicht** (*fig*) he's having a hard or tough time; **ein neuer ~ weht durch das Land** (*fig*) the wind of change is blowing in the country; **frischen** or **neuen ~ in etw** (*acc*) **bringen** (*fig*) to breathe new life into sth; **mach doch nicht so einen ~** (*inf*) don't make such a to-do (*inf*); **viel ~ um etw machen** (*inf*) to make a lot of fuss or to-do (*inf*) about sth; **vor dem ~ segeln** (*lit*) to sail with the wind (behind one); **gegen den ~ segeln** (*lit*) to sail into the wind; (*fig*) to swim against the stream, to run against the wind (*US*); **mit dem ~ zu segeln verstehen** (*fig*) to know how to bend with the wind; **den Mantel** or **das Mäntelchen** or **die Fahne** or **das Fähnchen nach dem ~ hängen** or **drehen** or **richten** to trim one's sails to the wind; **jdm den ~ aus den Segeln nehmen** (*fig*) to take the wind out of sb's sails; **sich** (*dat*) **den ~ um die Nase** or **Ohren wehen lassen** to see a bit of the world; **etw in den ~ schlagen** (*Warnungen, Rat*) to turn a deaf ear to sth; *Vorsicht, Vernunft* to throw or cast sth to the winds; **in den ~ reden** to waste one's breath; **wer ~ sät, wird Sturm ernten** (*Prov*) sow the wind and reap the whirlwind (*prov*)
█b█ (*Himmelsrichtung*) wind (direction); **in alle (vier) ~e** to the four winds; **in alle (vier) ~e zerstreut sein** (*fig*) to be scattered to the four corners of the earth or to the four winds
█c█ (*Med:* = *Blähung*) wind; **einen ~ fahren** or **streichen lassen** to break wind, to fart (*inf*)
█d█ (*Hunt*) wind; **von jdm/etw ~ nehmen** or **bekommen** to take or get the wind of sb/sth; **von etw ~ bekommen** or **kriegen/haben** (*fig inf*) to get/have wind of sth

Wind-: Wind|beu|tel M █a█ cream puff █b█ (*inf: Mensch*) rake; **Wind|blu|se** F windcheater; **Wind|bö(e)** F gust of wind; **Wind|büch|se** F (*inf*) air rifle

Win|de¹ ['vɪndə] F -, -n (*Tech*) winch, windlass

Win|de² F -, -n (*Bot*) bindweed, convolvulus

Wind|ei ['vɪntʔaɪ] NT (*fig*) nonstarter

Win|del ['vɪndl] F -, -n nappy (*Brit*), diaper (*US*); **damals lagst du noch in den ~n** you were still in nappies (*Brit*) or diapers (*US*) then; **noch in den ~n stecken** or **liegen** (*fig*) to be still in its infancy

Win|del-: Win|del|ein|la|ge F , **Win|del|fo|lie** F nappy (*Brit*) or diaper (*US*) liner; **Win|del|hös|chen** [-høːsçən] NT plastic pants *pl*

win|deln ['vɪndln] █VT █ **ein Baby ~** to put a baby's nappy (*Brit*) or diaper (*US*) on; (= *neu windeln*) to change a baby, to change a baby's nappy (*Brit*) or diaper (*US*) █VI █ to put on nappies/a nappy (*Brit*) or diapers/a diaper (*US*)

win|del|weich ['vɪndl'vaɪç] █ADV █ **jdn ~ schlagen** or **hauen** (*inf*) to beat sb black and blue, to beat the living daylights out of sb █ADJ █ (= *nachgiebig*) softly-softly

win|den¹ ['vɪndn] *pret* **wand** [vant], *ptp* **gewunden** [gə'vʊndn] █VT █ to wind; *Kranz* to bind; (= *hochwinden*) *Eimer, Last* to winch; **jdm etw aus der Hand ~** to wrest sth out of sb's hand █VR █ (*Pflanze, Schlange*) to wind (itself); (*Bach*) to wind, to meander; (*Mensch*) (*durch Menge, Gestrüpp etc*) to wind (one's way); (*vor Schmerzen*) to writhe (*vor* with, in); (*vor Scham, Verlegenheit*) to squirm (*vor* with, in); (*fig:* = *ausweichen*) to try to wriggle out; **sich ~ wie ein (getretener) Wurm** to squirm → *auch* **gewunden**

win|den² VI *impers* **es windet (sehr)** the wind is blowing (hard)

win|den³ VTI (*Hunt*) → **wittern**

Wind|ener|gie F wind energy

Wind|ener|gie|an|la|ge F wind energy plant

Win|des-: Win|des|ei|le F **etw in** or **mit ~ tun** to do sth in no time (at all); **sich in** or **mit ~ verbreiten** to spread like wildfire; **Win|des|flü|gel** PL (*liter*) **auf ~n** like the wind

Wind-: Wind|fah|ne F (*Met*) wind vane; **Wind|fang** M draught excluder (*Brit*), draft guard (*US*); (*Raum*) porch; **Wind|fang|tür** F porch (*Brit*) or screen (*US*) door; **Wind|farm** F wind farm; **Wind|ge|ne|ra|tor** M wind generator; **wind|ge|schützt** █ADV █ sheltered (from the wind) █ADV █ in a sheltered place; **Wind|ge|schwin|dig|keit** F wind speed; **Wind|ha|fer** M wild oat; **Wind|har|fe** F wind harp; **Wind|hauch** M breath of wind; **Wind|ho|se** F vortex

Wind|huk ['vɪnthʊk, 'vɪnthuːk] NT -s Windhoek

Wind|hund M █a█ (*Hund*) greyhound; (= *Afghanischer Windhund*) Afghan (hound) █b█ (*fig pej*) rake

win|dig ['vɪndɪç] ADJ windy; (*fig*) *Bursche, Sache* dubious, dodgy (*inf*)

win|disch ['vɪndɪʃ] ADJ (*Aus usu pej*) Slovene

Wind-: Wind|ja|cke F windcheater (*Brit*), windproof jacket; **Wind|jam|mer** [-jamɐ] M -s, - (*Naut*) windjammer; **Wind|ka|nal** M wind tunnel; (*an Orgel*) wind trunk; **Wind|kraft** F wind power; **Wind|kraft|an|la|ge** F , **Wind|kraft|werk** NT wind power station; **Wind|licht** NT lantern; **Wind|loch** NT (*Aviat*) air pocket; **Wind|mes|ser** [-mɛsɐ] M -s, - wind meter, anemometer (*spec*); **Wind|müh|le** F windmill; **gegen ~n (an)kämpfen** (*fig*) to tilt at windmills; **Wind|müh|len|flü|gel** M windmill sail or vane; **Wind|(müh|len)|park** M wind farm; **Wind|po|cken** PL chickenpox *sing*; **Wind|rad** NT (*Tech*) wind turbine; **Wind|räd|chen** NT (= *Spielzeug*) windmill, pinwheel (*US*); **Wind|rich|tung** F wind direction; **Wind|rös|chen** [-røːsçən] NT anemone; **Wind|ro|se** F (*Naut*) compass card; (*Met*) wind rose; **Wind|sack** M (*Aviat*) windsock, air sock; (*an Dudelsack etc*) (pipe) bag

Winds|braut F (*old, liter*) storm, tempest (*liter*); (= *Wirbelwind*) whirlwind; **wie eine** *or* **die ~** (*fig geh*) like a whirlwind

Wind-: Wind|schat|ten M lee; (*von Fahrzeugen*) slipstream; **Wind|schei|be** F (*Sw, Aut*) windscreen (*Brit*), windshield (*US*); **wind|schief** ADJ crooked; *Dach auch* askew *pred*; *Haus* crooked; **Wind|schirm** M windbreak; **wind|schlüp|fig** [-ʃlʏpfɪç], **wind|schlüpf|rig**, **wind|schnit|tig** ADJ streamlined; **Wind|schutz** M protection from wind; (= *Vorrichtung*) windbreak; **Wind|schutz|schei|be** F windscreen (*Brit*), windshield (*US*); **Wind|sei|te** F windward side; **Wind|ska|la** F wind scale; **Wind|spiel** NT greyhound; **Wind|stär|ke** F strength of the wind; (*Met*) wind force; **wind|still** ADJ still, windless; *Platz, Ecke etc* sheltered; **wenn es völlig ~ ist** when there is no wind at all; **Wind|stil|le** F calm; **Wind|stoß** M gust of wind; **Wind|surf|brett** NT sailboard, windsurfer; **wind|sur|fen** VI *insep* to sailboard, to windsurf; **~ gehen** to go sailboarding *or* windsurfing; **Wind|sur|fen** NT -s, *no pl* sailboarding, windsurfing; **Wind|sur|fer(in)** M(F) sailboarder, windsurfer; **Wind|tur|bi|ne** F wind turbine

Win|dung ['vɪndʊŋ] F -, -en (*von Weg, Fluss etc*) meander; (*von Schlange*) coil; (*Anat: von Darm*) convolution; (*Tech: von Schraube*) thread; (= *eine Umdrehung*) revolution; (*Elec: von Spule*) coil

Win|gert ['vɪŋɐt] M -s, -e (*dial, Sw*) vineyard

Wink [vɪŋk] M -(e)s, -e (= *Zeichen*) sign; (*mit der Hand*) wave (*mit of*); (*mit dem Kopf*) nod (*mit of*); (= *Hinweis, Tip*) hint, tip; **er gab mir einen ~, dass ich still sein sollte** he gave me a sign to be quiet

Win|kel ['vɪŋkl] M -s, - a (*Math*) angle → **tob** b (*Tech*) square c (*Mil:* = *Rangabzeichen*) stripe d (*fig*) (= *Stelle, Ecke*) corner; (= *Plätzchen: esp von Land, Wald etc*) place, spot; **jdn/etw in allen (Ecken und) ~n suchen** to look high and low for sb/sth; **in einem verborgenen ~ seines Herzens** in a hidden corner of his heart

Win|kel-: Win|kel|ad|vo|kat(in) M(F) (*pej*) incompetent lawyer; **Win|kel|ei|sen** NT angle iron; **win|kel|för|mig** ADJ angled ADV **~ ge-bogen** bent at an angle; **Win|kel|funk|ti|on** F (*Math*) trigonometrical function; **Win|kel|hal|bie|ren|de** [-halbiːrəndə] F *decl as adj* bisector of an/the angle

win|ke|lig ['vɪŋkəlɪç] ADJ = winklig

Win|kel-: Win|kel|maß NT a (*Astron*) Norma, the Level b (= *Winkel*) square; **Win|kel|mes|ser** M -s, - protractor; **Win|kel|schlei|fer** M angle grinder; **Win|kel|zug** M (= *Trick*) dodge, trick; (= *Ausflucht*) evasion; **mach keine Winkel-züge** stop evading the issue

win|ken ['vɪŋkn] *ptp* **gewinkt** *or* (*dial*) **gewunken** [gə'vɪŋkt, gə'vʊŋkn] VI to wave (*jdm* to sb); **jdm ~, etw zu tun** to signal sb to do sth; **sie winkte mit einem Fähnchen/den Armen** she waved a flag/her arms; **einem Taxi ~** to hail a taxi; **dem Kellner ~** to signal to the waiter; **jdm winkt etw** (*fig:* = *steht in Aussicht*) sb can expect sth; **bei der Verlosung ~ wertvolle Preise** valuable prizes are being offered in the draw; **dem Sieger winkt eine Reise nach Italien** the winner will receive (the attractive prize of) a trip to Italy; **ihm winkt das Glück** fortune *or* luck is smiling on him, luck is on his side

VT to wave; (*esp Sport:* = *anzeigen*) to signal; *Taxi* to hail; *Kellner* to call; **jdn zu sich ~** to beckon sb over to one

Win|ker ['vɪŋkɐ] M -s, - (*old Aut*) indicator (*Brit*), blinker (*US*), trafficator

Win|ker|al|pha|bet NT semaphore alphabet

win|ke, win|ke ma|chen ['vɪŋkə 'vɪŋkə] VI (*baby-talk*) to wave

wink|lig ['vɪŋklɪç] ADJ *Haus, Altstadt* full of nooks and crannies; *Gasse* twisty, windy

Wink|zei|chen NT signal; (*Mot*) hand signal; (*mit Fahne*) semaphore signal

Winsch [vɪnʃ] F -, -en (*Naut*) windlass, winch

win|seln ['vɪnzln] VTI to whimper; (*pej: um Gnade etc*) to grovel

Win|ter ['vɪntɐ] M -s, - winter; **es ist/wird ~** winter is here *or* has come/is coming; **im/über den ~** in (the)/over the winter; **über den ~ kommen** to get through the winter; **der nächste ~ kommt bestimmt** (*inf*) you never know how long the good times are going to last; **der nu-kleare ~** nuclear winter

Winter- *in cpds* winter; **Win|ter|an|fang** M beginning of winter; **vor/seit ~** before/since the beginning of winter; **Win|ter|dienst** M (*Mot*) winter road treatment; **Win|ter|ein|bruch** M onset of winter; **Win|ter|fahr|plan** M winter timetable; **Win|ter|fell** NT winter coat; **win|ter|fest** ADJ *Kleidung* winterproof; *Pflanzen* hardy; *Saat* winter *attr*; **dieses Haus ist nicht ~** this house won't withstand winter conditions; **~ machen** (*Auto, Gebäude*) to get ready for winter, to winterize (*US*); **Win|ter|flug|plan** M winter flight schedule; **Win|ter|gar|ten** M winter garden; **Win|ter|ge|trei|de** NT winter crop; **Win|ter|halb|jahr** NT = from September to March; **im ~ 1998/99** in the winter of 1998/99; **win|ter|hart** ADJ *Pflanzen* hardy; **Win|ter|käl|te** F cold winter weather; **in der größten ~** in the depths of winter; **Win|ter|kar|tof|feln** PL (*old*) potatoes *pl*; **Win|ter|kleid** NT winter dress; (*Zool*) winter coat; (*liter. von Landschaft etc*) winter covering (of snow); **Win|ter|klei|der** PL winter clothes *pl*; **Win|ter|klei|dung** F winter clothing; **Win|ter|land|schaft** F winter landscape

win|ter|lich ['vɪntɐlɪç] ADJ wintry; *Wetter auch, Kleidung, Beschäftigung* winter *attr* ADV **~ kalt** it's as cold as it is in winter; **~ kalte Tem-peraturen** cold winter temperatures; **~ geklei-det** dressed for winter

Win|ter|man|tel M winter coat

Win|ter|mo|nat M winter month

win|tern ['vɪntɐn] VI *impers* (*liter*) **es winterte schon** winter was coming

Winter-: Win|ter|nacht F winter night; **Win|ter|obst** NT winter fruit; **Win|ter|olym|pi|a|de** F Winter Olympics *pl*; **Win|ter|pau|se** F winter break; **Win|ter|quar|tier** NT (*Mil*) winter quarters *pl*; **Win|ter|rei|fen** M winter tyre (*Brit*) *or* tire (*US*)

win|ters ['vɪntɐs] ADV in winter, in the winter-time

Winter-: Win|ter|saat F winter seed; **Win|ter|sa|chen** PL winter clothes *pl*; **Win|ter|schlaf** M (*Zool*) hibernation; **(den) ~ halten** to hibernate; **Win|ter|schluss|ver|kauf** ▲ M winter (clearance) sale; **Win|ter|se|mes|ter** NT winter semester; **Win|ter|son|nen|wen|de** F winter solstice; **Win|ter|speck** M (*inf*) winter flab (*inf*); **Win|ter|spie|le** PL (*Olympische*) **~** Winter Olympic Games *pl*, Winter Olympics *pl*; **Win|ter|sport** M winter sports *pl*; (= *Wintersportart*) winter sport; **in den ~ fahren** to go on a winter sports holiday (*esp Brit*) *or* vacation (*US*); **Win|ter|star|re** F (*Zool*) (winter) torpor

Winters-: win|ters|über ['vɪntɐsˌyːbɐ] ADV in winter; **Win|ters|zeit** F (*liter*) wintertime

Winter-: Win|ter|tag M winter('s) day; **Win|ter|wet|ter** NT winter weather; **Win|ter|zeit** F winter time; (*Jahreszeit*) wintertime

Win|zer ['vɪntsɐ] M -s, -, **Win|ze|rin** [-ərɪn] F -, -nen (*Weinleser*) grape picker

Win|zer|ge|nos|sen|schaft F wine growers' organization

win|zig ['vɪntsɪç] ADJ tiny; **ein ~es bisschen** a ti-ny little bit; **~ klein** minute, tiny little *attr*

Win|zig|keit F -, -en a *no pl* tiny size b (= *winzige Menge*) tiny drop/bit/quantity *etc*; (= *Geschenk*) little thing

Win|z|ling ['vɪntslɪŋ] M -s, -e (*inf*) mite

Wip|fel ['vɪpfl] M -s, - treetop; **in den ~n der Bäume** in the treetops, in the tops of the trees

Wip|pe ['vɪpə] F -, -n (*zum Schaukeln*) seesaw; (= *Babywippe*) bouncy chair

wip|pen ['vɪpn] VI (*auf und ab*) to bob up and down; (*hin und her*) to teeter; (*Schwanz*) to wag; (= *mit Wippe schaukeln*) to seesaw; **mit dem Schwanz ~** to wag its tail; **mit dem Fuß ~** to jig-gle one's foot; **in den Knien ~** to buckle at the knees; **den Fuß/Kopf im Takt** *or* **Rhythmus ~** to move one's foot/head in time to the music *or* rhythm; **~der Gang** bouncing gait *or* stride

wir [viːɐ] PERS PRON *gen* **unser** ['ʊnzɐ], *dat* **uns** [ʊns], *acc* **uns** [ʊns] we; **~ alle** all of us; **~ beide** both *or* the two of us; **~ drei** the three of us; **~ als Betroffene/Kollegen ...** as those affected/as colleagues, we ...; **~ Armen** we poor people; **~ Kommunisten** we Communists; **~, die ~ ...** we who ...; **~ (selbst) sind/waren es, die ...** we are/were the ones who ..., it is/was we (*form*) *or* us who ...; **nicht nur ~ sind der Ansicht ...** it is not only we who are of the opinion ...; **immer sol-len ~s gewesen sein** everyone always blames us; **wer war das? – ~ nicht** who was that? – it wasn't us; **wer kommt noch mit? – ~/~ nicht** who's coming along? – we are/not us; **wer ist da? – ~ (sinds)** who's there? – (it's) us; **trinken ~ erst mal einen** let's have a drink first; **da ha-ben ~ wohl nicht aufgepasst?** (*iro*) we weren't paying attention, were we?; **~, Wilhelm, Kaiser von ...** we, William, Emperor of ...

wirb [vɪrp] IMPER *sing von* **werben**

Wir|bel ['vɪrbl] M -s, - a (*lit, fig*) whirl; (*von Wind auch*) eddy; (*in Fluss etc*) whirlpool, eddy; (= *Drehung beim Tanz etc*) pirouette; (*der Gefühle, Ereignisse*) turmoil; (= *Aufsehen*) to-do; **im ~ des Festes** in the whirl *or* hurly-burly (*Brit*) *or* hoo-pla (*US*) of the party; **(viel/großen) ~ machen/verursachen** to make/cause (a lot of/a big) commotion b (= *Haarwirbel*) crown; (*nicht am Hinterkopf*) cowlick; (*auf Fingerkuppe, in Stein*) whorl c (= *Trommelwirbel*) (drum) roll d (*Anat*) vertebra e (*an Saiteninstrument*) peg; (*an Fenster*) catch

Wir|bel|dü|se F water nozzle *or* jet

Wir|bel|fort|satz M (*Anat*) spinous process

wir|be|lig ['vɪrbəlɪç] ADJ a (= *temperamentvoll*) vi-vacious, lively; (= *wirr*) dizzy

wir|bel|los ADJ (*Zool*) invertebrate; **die Wirbel-losen** the invertebrates

wir|beln ['vɪrbln] VI a *aux sein* (*Mensch, Wasser etc*) to whirl; (*Laub*) to swirl; (*Rauch*) to whirl, to swirl b **mir wirbelt der Kopf** (*inf*) my head is spinning *or* reeling c (*Trommeln etc*) to roll VT *jdn, Wasser* to whirl; *Staub, Laub etc auch* to swirl

Wir|bel-: Wir|bel|säu|le F (*Anat*) spinal col-umn; **Wir|bel|sturm** M whirlwind, tornado, cyclone; **Wir|bel|tier** NT vertebrate; **Wir|bel-wind** M whirlwind; **wie der** *or* **ein ~** like a whirlwind

wirb|lig ['vɪrblɪç] ADJ = wirbelig

wirbt [vɪrpt] 3. *pers sing pres von* **werben**

wird [vɪrt] 3. *pers sing pres von* **werden**

wirf [vɪrf] *imper sing von* **werfen**

Wir|form F first person plural

wirft [vɪrft] 3. *pers sing pres von* **werfen**

Wir|ge|fühl ▲ NT feeling of belonging together, community feeling

wir|ken¹ ['vɪrkn] VI a (*geh:* = *tätig sein*) (*Mensch*) to work; (*Einflüsse, Kräfte etc*) to be at work; **ich werde dahin ~, dass man ihn befördert** I will work for his promotion

b (= *Wirkung haben*) to have an effect; (= *erfolg-reich sein*) to work; **als Gegengift ~** to work as an antidote; **als Katalysator ~** to act as a cata-lyst; **schalldämpfend/abführend ~** to have a soundproofing/laxative effect; **die Pillen ~ gut gegen Bauchschmerzen** the pills are good for stomachache; **eine stark ~de Droge** a strong drug

c (= *einwirken*) **auf etw** (*acc*) **~** (*esp Chem*) to act on sth; **etw auf sich** (*acc*) **~ lassen** to take sth in

d (= *erscheinen*) to seem, to appear; **nervös/ruhig (auf jdn) ~** to give (sb) the impression of being nervous/calm, to seem nervous/calm (to sb); **das wirkt auf viele als Provokation** many people see that as a provocation; **diese Bemerkung wirkt abstoßend auf mich** I find this remark repulsive

e (= *zur Geltung kommen*) to be effective; **neben diesen Gardinen wirkt das Muster nicht (richtig)** the pattern loses its effect next to those curtains; **ich finde, das Bild wirkt** I think the picture has something; **die Musik wirkt erst bei einer gewissen Lautstärke** you only get the full effect of the music when it's played loud

VT (*geh*: = *tun*) Gutes to do; Wunder to work → **Wunder a**

wir|ken² VT **a** (*liter*) Teppiche, Stoffe to weave **b** (*spec*) Maschinentextilien to knit; **Goldfäden durch etw ~** to work gold threads into sth

wir|ken³ VT (*dial*: = *kneten*) Teig to knead, to work

Wir|ken NT **-s**, *no pl* work

Wir|ker ['vɪrkɐ] M **-s**, **-**, **Wir|ke|rin** [-ərɪn] F **-**, **-nen** knitter

Wir|ke|rei [vɪrkəˈraɪ] F **-**, **-en a** knitting **b** (*Fabrik*) knitwear factory

Wirk|kraft F effect

wirk|lich ['vɪrklɪç] ADJ **a** (= *zur Wirklichkeit gehörig*) real; (= *tatsächlich*) Sachverhalt, Aussage, Meinung etc actual, real; **im ~en Leben** in real life **b** (= *echt*) real; Freund real, true ADV really; **ich wüsste gern, wie es ~ war** I would like to know what really happened; **nicht ~** not really; **das meinst du doch nicht ~** you don't really mean that; **ich war das ~ nicht** it really was not me; **~?** (*als Antwort*) really?; **nein, ~?** (*als Antwort*) what, really?; **er ist es ~** it really is him; **~ und wahrhaftig** really and truly

Wirk|lich|keit ○ 53.4, 53.6 F **-**, **-en** reality; **werden** to come true; **die Literatur spiegelt die ~ wider** literature reflects reality; **in ~** in reality; **in ~ heißt er anders** his real name is different → **Boden d**

Wirk|lich|keits-: **Wirk|lich|keits|form** F (*Gram*) indicative; **wirk|lich|keits|fremd** ADJ unrealistic; **wirk|lich|keits|ge|treu**, **wirk|lich|keits|nah** ADJ realistic ADV realistically; **etw ~ abbilden** to paint a realistic picture of sth; **etw wirklichkeitsnah erzählen** to give a realistic account of sth; **Wirk|lich|keits|sinn** M **,** *no pl* realism

Wirk|ma|schi|ne F knitting machine

wirk|sam ['vɪrkzaːm] ADJ effective; **~ bleiben** to remain in effect; **mit (dem)** or **am 1. Januar ~ werden** (*form*: Gesetz) to take effect on or from January 1st ADV effectively; *verbessern* significantly

Wirk|sam|keit F **-**, *no pl* effectiveness

Wirk|stoff M (*esp Physiol*) active substance

Wir|kung ['vɪrkʊŋ] F **-**, **-en** effect (*bei* on); (*von Tabletten etc*) effects *pl*; **seine ~ tun** to have an effect; (*Droge*) to take effect; **ohne ~ bleiben** to have no effect; **an ~ verlieren** to lose its effect; **seine ~ verfehlen** not to have the desired effect; **zur ~ kommen** (*Medikament*) to take effect; (*fig*: = *zur Geltung kommen*) to show to advantage; (*durch Kontrast*) to be set off, to stand out; **mit ~ vom 1. Januar** (*form*) with effect from January 1st

Wir|kungs-: **Wir|kungs|be|reich** M (*eines Menschen*) domain; (*einer Tageszeitung*) area of influence; (*von Atombombe, Golfstrom*) affected area; **der ~ des atlantischen Tiefs** the area affected by the Atlantic depression; **Wir|kungs|dau|er** F period over which sth is effective; **Wir|kungs|feld** NT field (of activity); **Wir|kungs|grad** M (degree of) effectiveness; **Wir|kungs|kreis** M sphere of activity; **wir|kungs|los** ADJ ineffective; **Wir|kungs|lo|sig-**

keit F **-**, *no pl* ineffectiveness; **Wir|kungs|stät|te** F (*geh*) domain; **wir|kungs|voll** ADJ effective ADV effectively; **Wir|kungs|wei|se** F (*von Medikament*) action; **die ~ eines Kondensators** the way a condenser works

Wirk|wa|ren PL knitwear *sing*; (= *Strümpfe etc auch*) hosiery *sing*

wirr [vɪr] ADJ confused; Blick crazed; (= *unordentlich*) Haare, Fäden tangled; Gedanken, Vorstellungen, Träume weird; (= *unrealistisch, verstiegen*) wild; **er ist ~ im Kopf** (= *geistig gestört*) he is confused in his mind; (= *konfus*) he is confused or muddled; (= *benommen*: *esp von Lärm*) his head is reeling or swimming; **mach mich nicht ~** don't confuse me; **er ist ein ~er Kopf** he has crazy ideas; **~es Zeug reden** to talk gibberish ADV **alles lag ~ durcheinander** everything was in chaos (*Brit*) or a mess; **das Haar hängt ihm ~ ins Gesicht** his hair is hanging in tangles in his face; **sich ~ ausdrücken** to express oneself in a confused way

Wir|ren ['vɪrən] PL confusion *sing*, turmoil *sing*

Wirr|kopf M (*pej*) muddle-head, ditz (*US inf*); **das sind alles Wirrköpfe** they've all got crazy ideas

Wirr|nis ['vɪrnɪs] F **-**, **-se**, **Wirr|sal** ['vɪrzaːl] NT **-(e)s**, **-e** (*liter*) confusion

Wirr|rung ['vɪrʊŋ] F **-**, **-en** (*liter*) confusion

Wirr|warr ['vɪrvar] M **-s**, *no pl* confusion; (*von Stimmen*) hubbub; (*von Verkehr*) chaos *no indef art*; (*von Fäden, Haaren etc*) tangle

Wir|sing ['vɪrzɪŋ] M **-s**, *no pl*, **Wir|sing|kohl** M savoy cabbage

Wirt [vɪrt] M **-(e)s**, **-e** (= *Gastwirt, Untervermieter*) landlord; (*Biol, rare*: = *Gastgeber*) host; **den ~ machen** to play the host, to do the honours (*Brit*) or honors (*US*) → **Rechnung b**, **Wirtin**

wir|ten ['vɪrtn] VI (*Sw*) to be a/the landlord

Wir|tin ['vɪrtɪn] F **-**, **-nen** landlady; (= *Gastgeberin*) hostess; (= *Frau des Wirts*) landlord's wife

Wirt|schaft ['vɪrtʃaft] F **-**, **-en a** (= *Volkswirtschaft*) economy; (= *Handel, Geschäftsleben*) industry and commerce; (= *Finanzwelt*) business world; **freie ~** free market economy; **er ist in der ~ tätig** he works in industry; he's a businessman; **ein Mann der ~** a man of industry and commerce; **seitens der ~ können wir keine Unterstützung erwarten** we can expect no support from the business world **b** (= *Gastwirtschaft*) ≈ pub (*Brit*), ≈ public house (*Brit form*), ≈ bar (*US*), ≈ saloon (*dated US*); **~!** (*inf*) waiter!; **Frau ~!** (*hum inf*) waitress! **c** (*dated*: = *Haushalt*) household; (*fig*) **jdm die ~ führen** to keep house for sb; **er gründete eine eigene ~** he set up house on his own **d** (*dated*: = *landwirtschaftlicher Betrieb*) farm; **in einer ~ arbeiten** to work on a farm **e** (*inf*: = *Zustände*) state of affairs; **du hast vielleicht eine ~ in deinem Haus/auf deinem Schreibtisch** a fine mess or state your house/desk is in; **eine schöne** or **saubere ~** (*iro*) a fine state of affairs; **jetzt werden wir hier erst mal reine ~ machen** (*dial*) first of all we'll put this house in order **f** (*inf*: = *Umstände*) trouble, bother; **sich** (*dat*) **eine ~ machen** to go to a lot of trouble or bother

wirt|schaf|ten ['vɪrtʃaftn] VI **a** (= *sparsam sein*) to economize; **gut ~ können** to be economical; **sparsam ~** to economize, to budget carefully; **ins Blaue hinein ~** not to budget at all → **Tasche b** (= *den Haushalt führen*) to keep house **b** (*inf*: = *sich betätigen*) to busy oneself; (*gemütlich*) to potter about (*Brit*), to putter around (*US*); (= *herumfummeln*) to rummage about VT **jdn/etw zugrunde ~** to ruin sb/sth financially

Wirt|schaf|ter ['vɪrtʃaftɐ] M **-s**, **-**, **Wirt|schaf|te|rin** [-ərɪn] F **-**, **-nen a** (= *Verwalter*) manager **b** (*im Haushalt, Heim etc*) housekeeper **c** (= *Unternehmer*) businessman/-woman

Wirt|schaft|ler ['vɪrtʃaftlɐ] M **-s**, **-**, **Wirt|schaft|le|rin** [-ərɪn] F **-**, **-nen a** (= *Wissen-*

schaftler) economist **b** (= *Unternehmer*) businessman/-woman

wirt|schaft|lich ['vɪrtʃaftlɪç] ADJ **a** (= *die Wirtschaft betreffend*) economic **b** (= *sparsam*) economical; Hausfrau careful, thrifty ADV **a** (= *finanziell*) financially; **jdm geht es ~ gut/schlecht** sb is in a good/bad financial or economic position **b** (= *ökonomisch*) economically; **nicht ~ handeln** to be uneconomical

Wirt|schaft|lich|keit F **-**, *no pl* **a** (= *Rentabilität*) profitability **b** (= *ökonomischer Betrieb*) economy

Wirt|schaft|lich|keits|be|rech|nung F evaluation of economic efficiency

Wirt|schafts- *in cpds* economic; **Wirt|schafts|auf|schwung** M economic upswing or upturn; **Wirt|schafts|aus|künf|te** PL financial information *sing*; **Wirt|schafts|aus|kunf|tei** F credit investigation agency (*Brit*), credit bureau (*US*); **Wirt|schafts|aus|schuss** ▲ M economic committee; **Wirt|schafts|be|ra|ter(in)** M(F) business consultant; **Wirt|schafts|be|zie|hun|gen** PL business relations *pl*; **Wirt|schafts|block** M *pl* **-blöcke** or (*rare*) **-blocks** (*Pol*) economic bloc; **Wirt|schafts|boss** ▲ M (*inf*) business leader, (business) tycoon; **Wirt|schafts|de|mo|kra|tie** F industrial democracy; **Wirt|schafts|flücht|ling** M economic refugee; **Wirt|schafts|form** F economic system; **gemischte ~** mixed economy; **Wirt|schafts|füh|rer(in)** M(F) leading industrialist; **Wirt|schafts|füh|rung** F management; **Wirt|schafts|ge|bäu|de** NT working quarters *pl*; **Wirt|schafts|ge|fü|ge** NT economic framework; **Wirt|schafts|geld** NT housekeeping (money) (*Brit*), household allowance (*US*); **Wirt|schafts|ge|mein|schaft** F economic community; **Wirt|schafts|geo|gra|fie** ▲ F economic geography; **Wirt|schafts|gip|fel** M economic summit; **Wirt|schafts|gü|ter** PL economic goods *pl*; **Wirt|schafts|gym|na|si|um** NT grammar school or high school which places emphasis on economics, law, management studies etc; **Wirt|schafts|hil|fe** F economic aid; **Wirt|schafts|hoch|schu|le** F business school; **Wirt|schafts|ka|pi|tän(in)** M(F) (*inf*) captain of industry; **Wirt|schafts|kraft** F economic power; **Wirt|schafts|krieg** M economic war; **Wirt|schafts|kri|mi|na|li|tät** F white collar crime; **Wirt|schafts|kri|se** F economic crisis; **Wirt|schafts|la|ge** F economic situation; **Wirt|schafts|le|ben** NT business life; **er ist im ~ zu Hause** he is at home in the business world; **Persönlichkeiten des ~s** business personalities; **Wirt|schafts|macht** F economic power; **Wirt|schafts|mi|nis|ter(in)** M(F) minister of trade and industry (*Brit*), secretary of commerce (*US*); **Wirt|schafts|mi|nis|te|ri|um** NT ministry of trade and industry (*Brit*), department of commerce (*US*); **Wirt|schafts|ord|nung** F economic order or system; **Wirt|schafts|plan** M economic plan; **Wirt|schafts|po|li|tik** F economic policy; **wirt|schafts|po|li|tisch** ADJ Maßnahmen etc economic policy *attr*; **~er Sprecher** spokesman on economic policy ADV geboten, sinnvoll for the economy; unerlässlich to the economy; **~ verfehlt** bad for the economy; **~ ist es unmöglich ...** in terms of economic policy it is impossible ...; **Wirt|schafts|prü|fer(in)** M(F) accountant; (*zum Überprüfen der Bücher*) auditor; **Wirt|schafts|prü|fung** F (= *Einzelprüfung*) audit; **Wirt|schafts|raum** M **a** (*Agr*) working area **b** (*Econ*) economic area; **Europäischer ~** European Economic Area; **Wirt|schafts|recht** NT commercial or business law; **Wirt|schafts|sank|ti|on** F *usu pl* economic sanction (*gegen* against); **~en gegen ein Land verhängen** to impose economic sanctions against a country; **Wirt|schafts|sek|tor** M business sector; **Wirt|schafts|spio|na|ge** F industrial espionage; **Wirt|schafts|stand|ort** M business location; **der ~ Deutschland** Germany as a business location; **Wirt|schafts|sys|tem** NT economic system; **Wirt|schafts|teil** M business *or* financial section; **Wirt|schafts|the|o|rie** F economic theory; **Wirt|schafts|trei|ben|de(r)** [-traɪbndə] MF *decl as adj (Aus)* trader; **Wirt|schafts|un|i|on** F economic union; **Wirt|schafts|un|ter|neh|men** NT business (enterprise); **Wirt|schafts|ver|band** M business *or* commercial association; **Wirt|schafts|ver|bre|chen** NT business *or* white-collar crime; **Wirt|schafts|wachs|tum** NT economic growth; **Wirt|schafts|wis|sen|schaft** F economics *sing*; **Wirt|schafts|wis|sen|schaft|ler(in)** M(F) economist; **Wirt|schafts|wun|der** NT economic miracle; **Wirt|schafts|zei|tung** F financial *or* business (news)paper; **Wirt|schafts|zo|ne** F economic zone; **Wirt|schafts|zweig** M branch of industry

Wirts-: Wirts|haus NT ≈ pub *(Brit)*, ≈ bar *(US)*, ≈ saloon *(dated US)*; *(esp auf dem Land)* inn; **Wirts|haus|schlä|ge|rei** F pub *(Brit) or* bar *(US)* brawl; **Wirts|leu|te** PL landlord and landlady; **Wirts|pflan|ze** F host (plant); **Wirts|pro|gramm** NT *(Comput)* host program; **Wirts|stu|be** F lounge; **Wirts|tier** NT host (animal)

Wisch [vɪʃ] M **-(e)s, -e** *(pej inf)* piece of paper; *(mit Gedrucktem, = Dokument)* piece of bumph *(Brit inf)*, piece of stuff for reading *(inf)*; *(= Zettel mit Notiz)* note

wi|schen ['vɪʃn̩] VTI to wipe; *(= mit Lappen reinigen)* to wipe clean; *(Sw: = fegen)* to sweep; **mit einem Tuch über eine Schallplatte ~** to wipe a record with a cloth; **jdm über den Ärmel ~** to wipe sb's sleeve; **sie wischte ihm/sich den Schweiß mit einem Handtuch von der Stirn** she wiped the sweat from his/her brow with a towel; **Bedenken/Einwände (einfach) vom Tisch ~** *(fig)* to sweep aside thoughts/objections VI *aux sein (= sich schnell bewegen)* to whisk VT *(inf)* **jdm eine ~** to clout sb one *(Brit inf)*, to clobber sb *(inf)*; **einen gewischt bekommen** *(Elec)* to get a shock

Wi|scher ['vɪʃɐ] M **-s, -** *(Aut)* (windscreen *(Brit) or* windshield *(US)*) wiper

Wi|scher|blatt NT *(Aut)* wiper blade

wisch|fest ['vɪʃ-] ADJ *Farbe etc* smearproof, non--smear *attr*

Wi|schi|wa|schi [vɪʃi'vaʃi] NT **-s**, *no pl (pej inf)* drivel *(inf)*

Wisch-: Wisch|lap|pen M cloth; *(für Fußboden)* floorcloth; *(dial: für Geschirr)* dishcloth; **Wisch|tuch** NT *pl* **-tücher** cloth; *(dial: für Geschirr)* dishcloth; **Wisch-Wasch-Au|to|ma|tik** F *(Aut)* wash-wipe *(Brit)*, wash-n-wipe *(US)*

Wi|sent ['viːzɛnt] M **-s, -e** bison

Wis|mut ['vɪsmuːt] NT OR (AUS) M **-(e)s**, *no pl (abbr* **Bi**) bismuth

wis|pern ['vɪspɐn] VTI to whisper; *(unverständlich auch)* to mumble

Wiss|be|gier(de) ▲ F thirst for knowledge

wiss|be|gie|rig ▲ ADJ *Kind* eager to learn

wis|se ['vɪsə] IMPER *sing von* wissen

wis|sen ['vɪsn̩] ☼ 28.2, 30, 33.1, 43.1, 43.4, 49, 52.5, 53.6 *pret* **wusste** ['vʊstə], *ptp* **gewusst** [gə'vʊst] VTI **a** *(= informiert sein)* to know *(über +acc, von* about); **ich weiß (es) (schon)** I know; **ich weiß (es) nicht** I don't know; **weißt du schon das Neuste?** have you heard the latest?; **das weiß alle Welt/jedes Kind** (absolutely) everybody/any fool knows that; **was ich alles ~ soll!, als ob ich das wüsste!** how should I know?; **ich weiß von ihr** *or* **über sie nur, dass sie ...** all I know about her is that she ..., I only know that she ...; **von ihr weiß ich das Alter** I know her age, I know how old she is; **von jdm/etw nichts ~ wollen** not to be interested in sb/sth; **er weiß es nicht anders/besser** he doesn't know any different/better; **er weiß zu genießen** he knows how to enjoy himself; **jdn/ etw zu schätzen ~** to appreciate sb/sth; **das musst du (selber) ~** it's your decision; **das solltest du (selber) ~** you ought to know; **das hät-**

test du ja ~ **müssen!** you ought to have realized that; **man kann nie ~** you never know; **man weiß nie, wozu das (noch mal) gut ist** you never know when it will come in handy; **das ~ die Götter** *(inf)* God only knows; **weiß Gott** *(inf)* God knows *(inf)*; **sich für weiß Gott was halten** *(inf)* to think one is somebody really special; **sie hält sich für wer weiß wie klug** *(inf)* she doesn't half think she's clever *(Brit inf)*, she thinks she's pretty clever; **... oder was weiß ich** *(inf)* ... or something; **... und was weiß ich noch alles** *(inf)* ... and whatever *(inf)*; **er ist wieder wer weiß wo** *(inf)* goodness knows where he's got to *(Brit) or* gone to *(US)* again *(inf)*; **(ja) wenn ich das wüsste!** goodness knows!; **wenn ich nur wüsste ...** if only I knew ...; **nicht, dass ich wüsste** not to my knowledge, not as far as I know; **gewusst wie/wo!** *etc* sheer brilliance!); **weißt du was?** *(do)* you know what?; **weißt du, ...** you know ...; **ja, weißt du** well, you see; **dass du es (nur) (gleich) weißt** just so you know; **ich weiß sie in Sicherheit/glücklich** I know that she is safe/happy; **was ich/er nicht weiß, macht mich/ ihn nicht heiß** *(Prov)* what I don't/he doesn't know won't hurt me/him, what the eye does not see the heart cannot grieve over *(Prov)*

b *(= sich erinnern)* to remember; *(= sich vor Augen führen)* to realize; **ich weiß seine Adresse nicht mehr** I can't remember his address; **weißt du noch, wie schön es damals war?** do you remember how great things were then?; **weißt du noch, damals im Mai/in Stone?** do you remember that May/the times in Stone?; **du musst ~, dass ...** you must realize that ...

VT **a** *(= kennen)* to know; **ich weiß keinen größeren Genuss, als ...** I know (of) no greater delight than ...

b *(= erfahren)* **jdn etw ~ lassen** to let sb know sth, to tell sb sth

VI **um etw** *(acc)* **~** *(geh)* **von etw ~** to know of *or* about sth; **ich/er weiß von nichts** I don't/he doesn't know anything about it; **... als ob er von nichts wüsste** ... as if he didn't know a thing → **helfen a**

Wis|sen ['vɪsn̩] NT **-s**, *no pl* knowledge; **meines ~s** to my knowledge; **etw ohne jds ~ tun** to do sth without sb's knowledge; **etw gegen** *or* **wider** *(geh)* **(sein) besseres ~ tun** to do sth against one's better judgement; **nach bestem ~ und Gewissen** to the best of one's knowledge and belief; **mit jds ~ und Willen** with sb's knowledge and consent; **~ ist Macht** knowledge is power

wis|send ADJ *Blick etc* knowing; ADV knowingly

Wis|sen|de(r) ['vɪsndə] MF *decl as adj (= Eingeweihter)* initiate; **die ~n schwiegen** those who knew kept silent

Wis|sen|schaft ['vɪsn̩ʃaft] F **-, -en** science

Wis|sen|schaf|ter [-ərn] M **-s, -, Wis|sen|schaf|te|rin** [-ərɪn] F **-, -nen** *(old, Sw, Aus)* scientist; *(= Geisteswissenschafter)* academic

Wis|sen|schaft|ler ['vɪsn̩ʃaftlə] M **-s, -, Wis|sen|schaft|le|rin** [-ərɪn] F **-, -nen** scientist; *(= Geisteswissenschaftler)* academic

wis|sen|schaft|lich ['vɪsn̩ʃaftlɪç] ADJ scientific; *(= geisteswissenschaftlich)* academic; **Wissenschaftlicher Assistent** assistant lecturer; **Wissenschaftlicher Rat** lecturer, assistant professor *(US)* ADV arbeiten, etw untersuchen scientifically

Wis|sen|schaft|lich|keit F **-**, *no pl* scientific nature; *(in Bezug auf Geisteswissenschaften)* academic nature; **der Arbeit mangelt es an ~** this thesis lacks a scientific approach

wis|sen|schaft|lich-tech|nisch ADJ *Fortschritt, Problem* technological

Wis|sen|schafts-: Wis|sen|schafts|be|trieb M academic life; **Wis|sen|schafts|leh|re** F epistemology; **Wis|sen|schafts|zweig** F discipline, branch of learning

Wis|sens-: Wis|sens|drang M , **Wis|sens|durst** M *(geh)* urge *or* thirst for knowledge; **Wis|sens|ge|biet** NT field (of knowledge); **Wis|sens|lü|cke** F gap in one's knowledge,

knowledge gap; **~n bei jdm schließen** to fill (in) gaps in sb's knowledge; **Wis|sens|schatz** M *(geh)* store of knowledge; **Wis|sens|stand** M state of knowledge; **nach dem gegenwärtigen ~** according to current knowledge; **Wis|sens|stoff** M material; **das ist ~ der 3. Klasse** that's material learned in the 3rd form *(Brit) or* 7th grade *(US)*; **ein enormer ~** an enormous amount of material; **Wis|sens|vor|sprung** M knowledge lead; **wis|sens|wert** ADJ worth knowing; *Information auch* valuable; **das Buch enthält viel Wissenswertes** the book contains much valuable information

wis|sent|lich ['vɪsntlɪç] ADJ deliberate, intentional ADV knowingly, deliberately, intentionally

wis|set ['vɪsət], **wisst** ▲ [vɪst] *imper pl von* **wissen**

Wit|frau ['vɪtfrau] F *(old)*, **Wi|tib** ['viːtɪp, 'vɪtɪp] F **-, -e** [-bə] *(obs)* widow

Wit|mann ['vɪtman] M *pl* **-männer** *(old)* widower

wit|tern ['vɪtən] VI *(Wild)* to sniff the air VT *(Wild)* to scent, to get wind of; *(Riese, Teufel)* to smell; *(fig: = ahnen) Geschäft, Chance* to sense; *Gefahr etc* to sense, to scent; **wenn er eine Klassenarbeit witterte ...** whenever he suspected that a test was in the offing *(Brit) or* in the air *(US)* ...

Wit|te|rung F **-, -en a** *(= Wetter)* weather; **bei günstiger** *or* **guter ~** if the weather is good **b** *(Hunt) (= Geruch)* scent *(von* of); *(= Geruchssinn)* sense of smell

Wit|te|rungs-: wit|te|rungs|be|stän|dig ADJ weatherproof; **Wit|te|rungs|ein|flüs|se** PL effects *pl* of the weather; **Wit|te|rungs|la|ge** F weather; **Wit|te|rungs|um|schlag** M change in the weather; **Wit|te|rungs|ver|hält|nis|se** PL weather conditions *pl*

Wit|tib ['vɪtɪp] F **-, -e** [-bə] *(Aus)* = **Witwe**

Wit|ti|ber ['vɪtɪbə] M **-s, -** *(Aus)* = **Witwer**

Wit|we ['vɪtvə] F **-, -n** widow; **~ werden** to be widowed

Wit|wen-: Wit|wen|geld NT widow's allowance; **Wit|wen|jahr** NT year of mourning; **Wit|wen|ren|te** F widow's pension; **Wit|wen|schaft** ['vɪtvənʃaft] F **-, -en** widowhood; **Wit|wen|schlei|er** M widow's veil; **Wit|wen|stand** M widowhood; **Wit|wen|trös|ter** M *(pej inf)* widow chaser *(inf)*; **Wit|wen|ver|bren|nung** F suttee

Wit|wer ['vɪtvə] M **-s, -** widower

Witz [vɪts] M **-es, -e a** *(= Geist)* wit **b** *(= Äußerung)* joke *(über +acc* about); **einen ~ machen** *or* **reißen** *(inf)* to make *or* crack a joke; **mach keine ~e!** don't be funny; **ich mach keine ~e** I'm not being funny; **das soll doch wohl ein ~ sein, das ist doch wohl ein ~** that must be a joke, he/you *etc* must be joking; **die Prüfung/ der Preis war ein ~** *(inf)* the exam/price was a joke **c der ~ an der Sache ist, dass ...** the great thing about it is that ...; **das ist der ganze ~ that's the thing**

Witz-: Witz|blatt NT joke book; **Witz|blatt|fi|gur** F *(fig inf)* joke figure; **sich** *(dat)* **wie eine ~ vorkommen** to feel ridiculous; **Witz|bold** ['vɪtsbɔlt] M **-(e)s, -e** [-bə] joker; *(= unterhaltsamer Mensch)* comic; **du bist vielleicht ein ~!** *(iro)* you're a great one! *(iro)*

Wit|ze|lei [vɪtsə'lai] F **-, -en** teasing *no pl*; **lass doch diese blöde ~** stop teasing

wit|zeln ['vɪtsln̩] VI to joke *(über +acc* about)

Witz|fi|gur F *(lit)* joke character; *(fig inf)* figure of fun

wit|zig ['vɪtsɪç] ADJ funny

Wit|zig|keit F **-**, *no pl* humour *(Brit)*, humor *(US)*

witz|los ADJ *(inf: = unsinnig)* pointless, futile

w. L. *abbr von* **westlicher Länge**

Wla|di|wos|tok [vladivɔs'tɔk] NT **-s** Vladivostok

WM [veː'ɛm] F **-, -s** *abbr von* **Weltmeisterschaft**

WNW *abbr von* **Westnordwest** WNW

wo [voː] `INTERROG, REL ADV` **a** where; (= *irgendwo*) somewhere; **überall, wo** wherever; **wo könnte er anders** *or* **wo anders könnte er sein als auf der Arbeit?** where else could he be but at work?; **wo immer ...** wherever ...; **der Tag/eine Zeit wo ...** (*inf*) the day/a time when ...; **ach** *or* **i wo!** (*inf*) nonsense!

b (*inf*: = *der/die/das*) that; **der Mann/die Frau/ das Auto, wo ...** the man/woman/car that ... `CONJ` **wo möglich** where *or* if possible; **wo er doch wusste, dass ich nicht kommen konnte** when he knew I couldn't come; **wo du doch in die Stadt gehst, könntest du ...?** (*inf*) seeing that you're going into town, could you ...?; **wo ich gerade daran denke** (*inf*) while I'm thinking about it; **und das jetzt, wo ich doch dazu keine Lust habe** (*inf*) and that now when I'm just not in the mood

w. o. *abbr von* **wie oben**

wo-: **wo|anders** [voˈʔandɐs] ADV somewhere else, elsewhere; **wo|anders|her** [voˈʔandɐsˈheːɐ] ADV from somewhere else, from elsewhere; **wo|anders|hin** [voˈʔandɐsˈhɪn] ADV somewhere else, elsewhere

wob *pret von* **weben**

wo|bei [voˈbaɪ] ADV → *auch* **bei** **a** *interrog* **~ ist das passiert?** how did that happen?; **~ hast du ihn erwischt?** what did you catch him at *or* doing?; **~ seid ihr gerade?** what are you doing just now?; (*im Buch*) where are you at just now? **b** *rel* in which; **ich erzähle mal, was passiert ist, ~ ich allerdings das Unwichtige auslasse** I will tell you what happened but I will leave out all the unimportant details; **~ man sehr aufpassen muss, dass man nicht betrogen wird/ keinen Sonnenstich bekommt** and you have to be very careful that you don't get cheated/ don't get sunburnt; **~ mir gerade einfällt** which reminds me; **das Auto prallte gegen einen Baum, ~ der Fahrer schwer verletzt wurde** the car hit a tree severely injuring the driver

Wo|che [ˈvɔxə] F -, -n week; **zweimal in der ~** twice a week; **in dieser ~** this week; **in die ~n kommen** (*old*) to be near one's time (*old*)

Wo|chen-: **Wo|chen|arbeits|zeit** F working week; **welche ~ haben Sie?** what is your working week?, how many hours a week do you work?; **Wo|chen|be|ginn** M beginning *or* start of the week; **Wo|chen|be|richt** M weekly report; **Wo|chen|bett** NT **im ~ liegen** to be lying in (*esp Brit old*), to be confined; **im ~ sterben** to die in the weeks following childbirth; **Wo|chen|bett|de|pres|si|on** F postnatal depression, baby blues (*inf*); **Wo|chen|bett|fie|ber** NT puerperal fever

Wo|chen|end- *in cpds* weekend; **Wo|chen|end|aus|flug** M weekend trip; **Wo|chen|end|aus|ga|be** F weekend edition; **Wo|chen|end|bei|la|ge** F weekend supplement

Wo|chen|en|de NT weekend; **schönes ~!** have a nice weekend; **langes** *or* **verlängertes ~** long weekend

Wo|chen|end|haus NT (*meist*) weekend cottage

Wo|chen|end|ler [-ɛndlɐ] M -s, -, **Wo|chen|end|le|rin** [-ərɪn] F -, -nen (*inf*) weekender

Wo|chen|end|ver|kehr M weekend traffic

Wo|chen-: **Wo|chen|fluss** ▲ M (*Med*) lochia (*spec*); **Wo|chen|ka|len|der** M week-by-week calendar; **Wo|chen|kar|te** F weekly season ticket; **wo|chen|lang** ADJ, ADV for weeks; **nach ~em Warten** after waiting for weeks, after weeks of waiting; **Wo|chen|lohn** M weekly wage; **Wo|chen|markt** M weekly market

---

WOCHENMARKT

Fresh fruit and vegetables can be bought at a German **Wochenmarkt**. Farmers from the surrounding area sell their produce in the marketplace on one or two mornings a week. You can also buy cheese, sausage, meat, poultry and fish, as well as other groceries and cut flowers.

Wo|chen-: **Wo|chen|schau** F newsreel; **Wo|chen|schrift** F weekly (periodical); **Wo|chen|stun|den** PL **wie viele ~ arbeitest du?** how many hours a week do you work?; **wie viele ~ habt ihr (in) Mathe?** how many math(s) lessons a week do you have?; **Wo|chen|tag** M weekday (*including Saturday*); **was ist heute für ein ~?** what day (of the week) is it today?; **wo|chen|tags** [ˈvɔxntaːks] ADV on weekdays

wö|chent|lich [ˈvœçntlɪç] `ADJ` weekly `ADV` weekly; (= *einmal pro Woche*) once a week; **zwei Vormittage ~ kommen** to come two mornings a week; **~ zweimal** twice a week; **sich ~ abwechseln** to take turns every week

Wo|chen-: **wo|chen|wei|se** ADV week by week; (= *einmal pro Woche*) once a week; (= *für eine Woche*) by the week; **Wo|chen|zeit|schrift** F weekly (magazine *or* periodical); **Wo|chen|zei|tung** F weekly (paper)

Wöch|ne|rin [ˈvœçnərɪn] F -, -nen *woman who has recently given birth*, woman in childbed (*old*), puerpera (*spec*)

Wöch|ne|rin|nen|sta|ti|on F maternity ward

Wo|dan [ˈvoːdan] M -s (*Myth*) Wotan

Wod|ka [ˈvɔtka] M -s, -s vodka

wo|durch [voˈdʊrç] ADV → *auch* **durch** **a** *interrog* how **b** *rel* which; **alles, ~ sie glücklich geworden war ...** everything which had made her happy ...

wo|fern [voˈfɛrn] CONJ (*old*) if

wo|für [voˈfyːɐ] ADV → *auch* **für** **a** *interrog* for what, what ... for; (= *warum*) why **b** *rel* for which, which ... for

wog *pret von* **wägen** *von* **wiegen**[2]

Wo|ge [ˈvoːɡə] F -, -n wave; (*fig auch*) surge; **wenn sich die ~n geglättet haben** (*fig*) when things have calmed down

wo|ge|gen [voˈɡeːɡn̩] ADV → *auch* **gegen** **a** *interrog* against what, what ... against; **~ ist dieses Mittel?** what's this medicine for? **b** *rel* against which, which ... against

wo|gen [ˈvoːɡn̩] VI (*liter*) to surge (*auch fig*); (*Kornfeld*) to wave, to undulate; (*fig: Kampf*) to rage; (*Busen*) to heave

Wo|gen|schlag M pounding (of the waves)

wo|her [voˈheːɐ] ADV **a** *interrog* where ... from; **~ weißt du das?** how do you (come to) know that?; **~ kommt es eigentlich, dass ...** how is it that ...?; **ach ~!** (*dial inf*) nonsense! **b** *rel* from which, where ... from

wo|hin [voˈhɪn] ADV **a** *interrog* where; **~, bitte?** where to?, where do you want to go?; **~ so eilig?** where are you off to so fast, where are you rushing off to?; **~ damit?** where shall I/we put it?; **ich muss mal ~** (*euph inf*) I've got to go somewhere (*euph inf*) **b** *rel* where; **~ man auch schaut** wherever you look

wo|hi|nein [vohɪˈnaɪn] ADV = **worein**

wo|hin|ge|gen [vohɪnˈɡeːɡn̩] CONJ whereas, while

wo|hin|ter [voˈhɪntɐ] ADV → *auch* **hinter** **a** *interrog* what *or* where ... behind; **~ kann ich in Deckung gehen?** what can I take cover behind?, behind what can I take cover? **b** *rel* behind which; **~ man sich auch versteckt** whatever you hide behind

wohl [voːl] `ADV` **a** *comp* **-er**, *superl* **am -sten** (= *angenehm zumute*) happy; (= *gesund*) well; **sich ~/-er fühlen** to feel happy/happier; (= *wie zu Hause*) to feel at home/more at home; (*gesundheitlich*) to feel well/better; **bei dem Gedanken ist mir nicht ~** I'm not very happy at the thought; **am ~sten wäre mir, wenn ...** I'd feel happier if ...; **jdm ist ~ ums Herz** sb feels light of heart; **~ oder übel** whether one likes it or not, willy-nilly; **~ dem, der ...** happy the man who ...; **~ ihm, dass ...** it's a good thing for him that ...; **es sich** (*dat*) **~ gehen** *or* **sein** *or* **ergehen lassen** to enjoy oneself

b (= *gut*) *comp* **besser**, *superl* **bestens** *or* **am besten** well; **nun ~!** now then!; **ich wünsche ~ gespeist/geruht zu haben** (*dated*) I do hope you have enjoyed your meal/have had a pleasant sleep; **lasst es euch ~ schmecken!** I hope you like *or* enjoy it; **~ ausgewogen** (well) balanced; **~ bedacht** well considered; **~ begründet** well-founded; *Maßnahme, Strafe* well-justified; **~ bekannt** well-known; **sie ist mir ~ bekannt** I know her well; **~ beraten** well-advised; **~ durchdacht** well *or* carefully thought out; **~ erprobt** well-tested, well-tried; *Mitarbeiter* experienced; **~ gemeint** well-meant, well-intentioned; **~ geordnet** (*geh*) well-ordered; *Leben auch* well-regulated; **~ temperiert** (*Wein, Bad, Zimmer*) at the right temperature *no comp*; **~ überlegt** well thought out; **etw ~ überlegt machen** to do sth after careful consideration; **~ unterrichtet** well-informed; **~ versorgt** well-provided-for → **bekommen**

c (= *wahrscheinlich*) probably, no doubt; (*iro:* = *bestimmt*) surely; **er ist ~ schon zu Hause** he's probably at home by now, no doubt he's at home by now; **das ist ~ nicht gut möglich** I should think it's unlikely; **es ist ~ anzunehmen, dass ...** it is to be expected that ...; **du bist ~ verrückt** you must be crazy!; **das ist doch ~ nicht dein Ernst!** surely you're not serious!, you can't be serious!

d (= *vielleicht*) perhaps, possibly; (= *etwa*) about; **ob ~ noch jemand kommt?** I wonder if anybody else is coming?; **das kann man sich ~ vorstellen, nicht wahr?** you can just imagine something like that, can't you?; **das mag ~ sein** that may well be; **willst du das ~ lassen!** I wish you'd stop (doing) that

e (= *durchaus*) well; **das kann ~ mal vorkommen** that might well happen; **ich denke, ich verstehe dich sehr ~!** I think I understand you very *or* perfectly well; **doch, das glaube ich ~** I certainly do believe it; **sehr ~ (der Herr)!** (*old*) very good (sir); **~!** (= *doch*) yes!; (*S Ger, Sw:* = *selbstverständlich*) of course! `CONJ` (= *zwar*) **er hat es ~ versprochen, aber ...** he may have promised, but ...; **~, aber ...** that may well be, but ...

Wohl [voːl] NT -(e)s, *no pl* welfare, wellbeing; **das öffentliche ~ und das ~ des Individuums** the public good *or* common weal and the welfare of the individual; **der Menschheit zum ~e** for the benefit of mankind; **das ~ und Weh(e)** the weal and woe; **zu eurem ~** for your benefit *or* good; **zum ~!** cheers!; **auf dein ~!** your health!; **auf jds ~ trinken** to drink sb's health

Wohl-: **wohl|an** [voˈlan, voˈlʔlan] INTERJ (*old, poet*) come *or* well now; **wohl|an|stän|dig** ADJ respectable; *Benehmen* proper, correct; **wohl|auf** [voˈlʔlauf, voˈlauf] ADJ *pred* well, in good health `INTERJ` = **wohlan**; **wohl|aus|ge|wo|gen** △ ADJ → **wohl** ADV b; **wohl|be|dacht** △ ADJ → **wohl** ADV b; **Wohl|be|fin|den** NT wellbeing; **wohl|be|grün|det** △ ADJ → **wohl** ADV b; **Wohl|be|ha|gen** NT feeling of wellbeing; **wohl|be|hal|ten** ADV *ankommen* safe and sound, intact; **wohl|be|kannt** △ ADJ → **wohl** ADV b; **wohl|be|leibt** ADJ (*hum*) stout, portly (*form*); **wohl|be|ra|ten** △ ADJ → **wohl** ADV b; **wohl|be|stallt** [-bəʃtalt] ADJ *attr* (*form*) well-established; **wohl|durch|dacht** △ ADJ → **wohl** ADV b; **Wohl|er|ge|hen** [-ʔɛɐɡeːən] NT -s, *no pl* welfare; **wohl|er|probt** △ [-ʔɛɐproːpt] ADJ → **wohl** ADV b; **wohl|er|wo|gen** [-ʔɛɐvoːɡn̩] ADJ *comp* **besser erwogen**, *superl* **besterwogen** well *or* carefully considered; **wohl|er|zo|gen** [-ʔɛɐtsoːɡn̩] `ADJ` *comp* **besser erzogen**, *superl* **besterzogen** (*geh*) well-bred; *Kind* well-mannered; **~ sein** to be well-bred `ADV` **sich ~ benehmen** to be well-mannered

Wohl|fahrt F -, *no pl* **a** (*old geh:* = *Wohlergehen*) welfare **b** (= *Fürsorge*) welfare; **bei der ~ arbeiten** to do welfare work

Wohl|fahrts-: Wohl|fahrts|amt NT (*dated, inf*) social security office; **Wohl|fahrts|aus|schuss** ▲ M (*Hist*) Committee of Public Safety (*Brit*), Public Welfare Committee (*US*); **Wohl|fahrts|ein|rich|tung** F social service; **Wohl|fahrts|mar|ke** F charity stamp; **Wohl|fahrts|or|ga|ni|sa|ti|on** F charity, charitable institution *or* organization; **Wohl|fahrts|pfle|ge** F social *or* welfare work; **freie ~** voluntary social *or* welfare work; **Wohl|fahrts|ren|te** F benefit pension; **Wohl|fahrts|staat** M welfare state; **Wohl|fahrts|un|ter|stüt|zung** F (*dated*) income support, welfare (aid) (*US*)

Wohl-: wohl|feil ADJ **a** (*old, liter*) inexpensive **b** (*fig*) (= *abgedroschen*) *Ratschlag, Worte, Reden* hackneyed, cheapened (*US*); (= *bequem*) *Ausrede* convenient; **Wohl|füh|len** NT **-s**, *no pl* (sense of) well-being; **Wohl|fühl|fak|tor** M feel-good factor; **wohl|ge|bo|ren** ADJ (*obs*) **Eure** *or* **Euer ~ Sir; Seiner ~ Herr XY** XY Esq; **Wohl|ge|fal|len** NT satisfaction, pleasure; **sein ~ an etw** (*dat*) **haben** to take pleasure in sth; **sich in ~ auflösen** (*hum*) (*Freundschaft, Argument*) to peter out; (*Plan, Problem*) to vanish into thin air; (*Auto, Kleidung*) to fall apart; **wohl|ge|fäl|lig** ADJ (= *gefallend*) pleasing; (= *zufrieden, erfreut*) well-pleased; **Gott ~** well-pleasing to God; **wohl|ge|formt** [-ɡəfɔrmt] ADJ *comp* **wohlgeformter**, *superl* **bestgeformt** well-shaped; *Körperteil* shapely; *Satz* well-formed; **Wohl|ge|fühl** NT feeling *or* sense of wellbeing; **wohl|ge|lit|ten** ADJ *comp* **wohlgelittener**, *superl* **wohlgelittenste(r, s)** (*geh*) well-liked; **wohl|ge|meint** △ [-ɡəmaint] ADJ **→ wohl** ADV **b**; **wohl|ge|merkt** [-ɡəmɛrkt] ADV mark you (*esp Brit*), mind (you); **das waren ~ englische Pfund** that was English pounds, mark you (*esp Brit*) or mind you; **wohl|ge|mut** [-ɡəmuːt] ADJ *comp* **wohlge-muter**, *superl* **wohlgemuteste(r, s)** (*old, liter*) cheerful; **wohl|ge|nährt** [-ɡənɛːrt] ADJ *comp* **wohlgenährter**, *superl* **wohlgenährteste(r, s)** well-fed; **wohl|ge|ord|net** △ ADJ **→ wohl** ADV **b**; **wohl|ge|ra|ten** ADJ *comp* **wohlgeratener**, *superl* **wohlgeratenste(r, s)** (*geh*) *Kind* fine; *Werk* successful; **Wohl|ge|ruch** M (*geh*) pleasant smell; (*von Garten, Blumen etc auch*) fragrance; **Wohl|ge|schmack** M (*geh*) flavour (*Brit*), flavor (*US*), pleasant taste; **wohl|ge|sinnt** ADJ *comp* **wohlgesinnter**, *superl* **wohlgesinnteste(r, s)** (*geh*) well-disposed (+*dat* towards); *Worte* well-meaning; **wohl|ge|stalt** [-ɡəʃtalt] ADJ (*geh*) *Gegenstand* well-shaped; *Körperteil, Frau* shapely; *Mann* well-proportioned; **wohl|ge|stal|tet** [-ɡəʃtaltət] ADJ *comp* **wohlgestalteter**, *superl* **wohlgestaltetste(r, s)** well-shaped, well-proportioned; **wohl|ge|tan** ADJ (*old, liter*) well done *pred*; **wohl|ha|bend** ADJ *comp* **wohlhabender**, *superl* **wohlhabendste(r, s)** well-to-do, prosperous; **Wohl|ha|ben|heit** [ˈvoːlhaːbnhait] F **-**, *no pl* prosperity, affluence

woh|lig [ˈvoːlɪç] ADJ pleasant; (= *gemütlich*) cosy; *Ruhe* blissful; ADV *warm* comfortably; **~ rekelte er sich in der Sonne** he stretched luxuriously in the sun

Wohl-: Wohl|klang M (*geh*) melodious sound; **wohl|klin|gend** ADJ *comp* **wohlklingender**, *superl* **wohlklingendste(r, s)** pleasant(-sounding), melodious; **Wohl|le|ben** NT (*geh*) life of luxury; **wohl|mei|nend** ADJ *comp* **wohlmeinender**, *superl* **wohlmeinendste(r, s)** well-meaning; **wohl|pro|por|ti|o|niert** ADJ *comp* **besser proportioniert** *or* **wohlproportionierter**, *superl* **bestproportioniert** well-proportioned; **wohl|rie|chend** ADJ *comp* **wohlriechender**, *superl* **wohlriechendste(r, s)** (*geh*) fragrant; **wohl|schme|ckend** ADJ *comp* **wohlschmeckender**, *superl* **wohlschmeckendste(r, s)** (*geh*) palatable; **Wohl|sein** NT **zum ~!**, **auf Ihr ~!** your health!

Wohl|stand M , *no pl* affluence, prosperity → **ausbrechen** VI **c**

Wohl|stands-: Wohl|stands|bür|ger(in) M(F) (*pej*) member of the affluent society; **Wohl|stands|ge|sell|schaft** F affluent society; **Wohl|stands|kri|mi|na|li|tät** F *crimes*

---

typical of the affluent society; **Wohl|stands|müll** M refuse of the affluent society

Wohl|tat F **a** (= *Genuss*) relief **b** (= *Dienst, Gefallen*) favour (*Brit*), favor (*US*); (= *gute Tat*) good deed; **jdm eine ~ erweisen** to do sb a favour (*Brit*) or favor (*US*) or a good turn

Wohl|tä|ter M benefactor

Wohl|tä|te|rin F benefactress

wohl|tä|tig ADJ **a** charitable **b** (*dial*) = **wohltuend**

Wohl|tä|tig|keit F charity, charitableness

Wohl|tä|tig|keits-: Wohl|tä|tig|keits|ba|sar M charity bazaar; **Wohl|tä|tig|keits|kon|zert** NT charity concert; **Wohl|tä|tig|keits|ver|an|stal|tung** F charity event; (*Sport auch*) charity fixture; **Wohl|tä|tig|keits|ver|ein** M charitable organization, charity; **Wohl|tä|tig|keits|zweck** M charitable cause, good cause

Wohl-: wohl|tem|pe|riert △ [-tɛmpəriːɐt] ADJ **→ wohl** ADV **b** **das "Wohltemperierte Klavier"** "The Well-Tempered Clavier"; **wohl|tu|end** ADJ *comp* **wohltuender**, *superl* **wohltuendste(r, s)** (most) agreeable; **wohl tun** ▲ VI *irreg* **a** (= *angenehm sein*) to do good (*jdm* sb), to be beneficial (*jdm* to sb); **das tut wohl** that's good **b** (*old, liter.* = *Gutes tun*) to benefit (*jdm* sb); **wohl|über|legt** △ ADJ **→ wohl** ADV **b**; **wohl|un|ter|rich|tet** △ ADJ *attr* **→ wohl** ADV **b**; **wohl|ver|dient** ADJ *Strafe* well-deserved; *Belohnung, Ruhe etc auch* well-earned; **Wohl|ver|hal|ten** NT (*usu iro*) good conduct *or* behaviour (*Brit*) or behavior (*US*); **wohl|ver|sorgt** △ [-fɛɐzɔrkt] ADJ **→ wohl** ADV **b**; **wohl|ver|stan|den** [-vɛɐʃtandn] ADJ *attr* (*geh*) well-understood ADV mark (*Brit*) or mind you; **wohl|weis|lich** [ˈvoːlvaislɪç, ˌvoːlˈvaislɪç] ADV very wisely; **ich habe das ~ nicht gemacht** I was careful not to do that; **wohl wol|len** ▲ VI *irreg* (*geh*) **jdm ~** to wish sb well; **Wohl|wol|len** NT **-s**, *no pl* goodwill; **selbst bei dem größten** *or* **mit größtem ~** with the best will in the world; **jdn mit ~ betrachten** to regard sb benevolently; **sich** (*dat*) **jds ~ erwerben** to win sb's favour (*Brit*) or favor (*US*); **wohl|wol|lend** ADJ *comp* **wohlwollender**, *superl* **wohlwollendste(r, s)** benevolent; **jdm gegenüber ~ sein** to be kindly disposed toward(s) sb ADV favourably (*Brit*), favorably (*US*); **jdm ~ geneigt** *or* **gesonnen sein** to be kindly disposed toward(s) sb; **einer Sache** (*dat*) **~ gegenüberstehen** to approve of sth

Wohn-: Wohn|an|hän|ger M caravan (*Brit*), trailer (*US*); **Wohn|an|la|ge** F housing area; **Wohn|bau** M *pl* **-bauten** residential building; **Wohn|be|völ|ke|rung** F residential population; **Wohn|block** M *pl* **-blocks** block of flats (*Brit*), apartment house (*US*); **Wohn|con|tai|ner** M Portakabin® (*Brit*), trailer (*US*); **Wohn|dich|te** F (*Sociol*) occupant density; **Wohn|die|le** F hall-cum-living-room; **Wohn|ei|gen|tum** NT property ownership; **Wohn|ein|heit** F accommodation *or* residential unit

woh|nen [ˈvoːnən] VI **a** (= *Behausung haben*) to live; (*vorübergehend*) to stay; **wo ~ Sie?** where do you live/are you staying?; **er wohnt (in der) Friedrichstraße 11** he lives at (number) 11 Friedrichstraße; **wir ~ sehr schön** we have a very nice flat (*Brit*) or apartment/house *etc*; **wir ~ da sehr schön** it's very nice where we live; **hier wohnt es sich gut, hier lässt es sich gut ~** it's a nice place to live/stay **b** (*fig liter*) to dwell (*liter*), to live

Wohn-: Wohn|flä|che F living space; **50 Quadratmeter ~** living room(, dining room) and bedroom(s) totalling 50 square metres (*Brit*) or totaling 50 square meters (*US*); **Wohn|ge|bäu|de** NT residential building; **Wohn|ge|biet** NT residential area; **Wohn|ge|gend** F residential area; **Wohn|geld** NT housing benefit (*Brit*), housing *or* rent subsidy (*US*); **Wohn|ge|mein|schaft** F (*Menschen*) people sharing a flat (*Brit*) or apartment/house; **unsere ~** the people I share a flat *etc* with; **in einer ~**

---

leben to share a flat *etc*; **Wohn|gift** NT poisonous substance found in the home; **wohn|haft** ADJ (*form*) resident; **Wohn|haus** NT residential building; **Wohn|heim** NT (*esp für Arbeiter*) hostel; (*für Studenten*) hall (*of residence*), dormitory (*US*); (*für alte Menschen*) home; **Wohn|klo** NT (*hum inf*) **~ (mit Kochnische)** tiny flat (*Brit*) or apartment, shoebox (*inf*); **Wohn|kom|fort** M comfort of one's home; **ein Appartement mit sämtlichem ~** an apartment with every modern convenience, an apartment with all mod cons (*Brit*) or all amenities (*US*); **Wohn|kom|plex** M housing estate (*Brit*) or development, subdivision (*US*); **Wohn|kü|che** F kitchen-cum-living-room; **Wohn|kul|tur** F style of home décor; **keine ~ haben** to have no taste in home décor; **Wohn|la|ge** F residential area; **unsere ~ ist schön/ungünstig** our house/apartment is nicely/awkwardly situated; **Wohn|land|schaft** F landscaped interior; **wohn|lich** [ˈvoːnlɪç] ADJ homely, cosy; **es sich** (*dat*) **~ machen** to make oneself comfortable; **Wohn|lich|keit** F **-**, *no pl* homeliness, cosiness; **Wohn|mo|bil** [-mobiːl] NT **-s**, **-e** Dormobile®, camper (*US*), motor caravan, RV (*US*); **Wohn|ob|jekt** NT (*Aus form*) accommodation *or* residential unit; **Wohn|ort** M *pl* **-orte** place of residence; **Wohn|par|tei** F (*esp Aus*) tenant; (*mehrere Personen*) tenants *pl*; **Wohn|qua|li|tät** F quality of housing; **Wohn|raum** M living room; (*no pl:* = *Wohnfläche*) living space; **Wohn-Schlaf|zim|mer** NT bedsitting room; **Wohn|sied|lung** F housing estate (*Brit*) or scheme *or* development, subdivision (*US*); **Wohn|si|lo** M (*pej*) concrete block; **Wohn|sitz** M domicile; **ohne festen ~** of no fixed abode; **Wohn|stadt** F residential town; **Wohn|stu|be** F living room; **Wohn|turm** M tower block (*Brit*), high rise (*esp US*)

Woh|nung [ˈvoːnʊŋ] F **-**, **-en** flat (*Brit*), apartment; (*liter: von Tieren etc*) habitation; (= *Wohneinheit*) dwelling (*form*); (= *Unterkunft*) lodging, accommodations *pl* (*US*); **1.000 neue ~en** 1,000 new homes; **~ nehmen** (*form*) to take up residence (*form*); **freie ~ haben** to have free lodging

Woh|nungs-: Woh|nungs|amt NT (public) housing office; **Woh|nungs|auf|lö|sung** F flat (*Brit*) or apartment clearance; **wegen ~ abzugeben** (*in Annonce*) house clearance sale (*Brit*), moving sale (*US*); **Woh|nungs|bau** M , *no pl* house building *no def art*; **Woh|nungs|bau|pro|gramm** NT housing programme (*Brit*) or program (*US*); **Woh|nungs|be|darf** M housing requirements *pl*; **Woh|nungs|be|set|zer(in)** M(F) squatter; **Woh|nungs|ein|rich|tung** F furnishings *pl*; (*Innenarchitektur*) interior *or* design; **Woh|nungs|in|ha|ber(in)** M(F) householder, occupant; (= *Eigentümer auch*) owner-occupier, owner-occupant; **Woh|nungs|los** ADJ homeless; **Woh|nungs|lo|se(r)** MF *decl as adj* homeless person; **für ~** for the homeless; **Woh|nungs|lo|sig|keit** F homelessness; **Woh|nungs|mak|ler(in)** M(F) estate agent (*esp Brit*), real estate agent (*US*); **Woh|nungs|man|gel** M housing shortage; **Woh|nungs|markt** M housing market; **Woh|nungs|nach|weis** M accommodation registry; **Woh|nungs|not** F serious housing shortage, serious lack of housing; **Woh|nungs|schlüs|sel** M key (to the flat (*Brit*) or apartment); **Woh|nungs|su|che** F flat-hunting (*Brit*), apartment-hunting (*esp US*); **auf ~ sein** to be looking for a flat (*Brit*) or apartment, to be flat-hunting (*Brit*) or apartment-hunting (*esp US*); **woh|nungs|su|chend** ADJ *attr* looking for accommodation; **Woh|nungs|su|chen|de(r)** MF *decl as adj* person seeking accommodation; **Hilfe für ~** help for those seeking accommodation; **Woh|nungs|tausch** M exchange (of flats (*Brit*) or apartments/houses); **Woh|nungs|tür** F door (to the flat (*Brit*) or apartment); **Woh|nungs|wech|sel** M change of address; **Woh|nungs|we|sen** NT housing

---

Wohn-: Wohn|ver|hält|nis|se PL (von Familie) living conditions pl; (in Stadt) housing conditions pl; **Wohn|vier|tel** NT residential area or district; **Wohn|wa|gen** M caravan (Brit), trailer (US); **Wohn|wert** M einen hohen ~ haben to be an attractive place to live in; **Wohn|-zim|mer** NT living room; **Wohn|zwe|cke** PL residential purposes pl

Wok [vɔk] M -s, -s (Cook) wok

wöl|ben ['vœlbn] VT to curve; Blech etc to bend; Dach etc to vault ▶VR to curve; (Asphalt) to bend, to buckle; (Tapete) to bulge out; (Brust) to swell; (Stirn) to be domed; (Decke, Brücke) to arch; **ein klarer Sternenhimmel wölbte sich über uns** the clear sky formed a star-studded dome above us (liter) → auch **gewölbt**

Wöl|bung F -, -en curvature; (kuppelförmig) dome; (bogenförmig) arch; (von Körperteil) curve; (von Straße) camber; (von Tapete) bulge

Wolf [vɔlf] M -(e)s, ⸚e ['vœlfə] **a** wolf; **ein ~ im Schafspelz** a wolf in sheep's clothing; **mit den Wölfen heulen** (fig) to run with the pack **b** (Tech) shredder; (= Fleischwolf) mincer (Brit), grinder (US); **Fleisch durch den ~ drehen** to mince meat (Brit), to grind meat (US); **jdn durch den ~ drehen** (fig) to give sb a hard time of it; **ich fühle mich wie durch den ~ gedreht** I feel as if I've been on the rack **c** (Med) intertrigo no art (spec), inflammation of the skin caused by chafing between skin surfaces

Wölf|chen ['vœlfçən] NT -s, - dim von **Wolf** wolf cub

Wöl|fin ['vœlfɪn] F -, -nen she-wolf

wöl|fisch ['vœlfɪʃ] ADJ wolfish

Wölf|ling ['vœlflɪŋ] M -s, -e (= Pfadfinder) cub (scout)

Wolf|ram ['vɔlfram] NT -s, no pl (abbr **W**) tungsten, wolfram

Wolfs-: Wolfs|hund M Alsatian (Brit), German shepherd; **Irischer ~** Irish wolfhound; **Wolfs|hun|ger** M (fig inf) ravenous hunger; **ich hatte einen ~** I was ravenous; **Wolfs|-mensch** M **a** wolf child; **er war ein ~** he had been reared by wolves **b** (= Werwolf) werewolf; **Wolfs|milch** F (Bot) spurge; **Wolfs|ra|chen** M (Med) cleft palate; **Wolfs|ru|del** NT pack of wolves; **Wolfs|spin|ne** F wolf spider

Wol|ga ['vɔlga] F - Volga

Wölk|chen ['vœlkçən] NT -s, - dim von **Wolke**

Wol|ke ['vɔlkə] F -, -n (lit, fig) cloud; (in Edelstein) flaw; **aus allen ~n fallen** (fig) to be flabbergasted (inf); **das ist 'ne ~** (inf) it's fantastic (inf) → **schweben** a

Wolken-: Wol|ken|band NT band of cloud; **Wol|ken|bank** F pl -bänke cloud bank; **Wol|ken|bil|dung** F cloud formation; **es kann zu ~ kommen** it may become cloudy or overcast; **Wol|ken|bruch** M cloudburst; **wol|ken|bruch|ar|tig** ADJ torrential; **Wol|ken|de|cke** F cloud cover; **die Stadt liegt unter einer dichten ~** the town lies under a heavy layer of cloud; **Wol|ken|him|mel** M cloudy or overcast sky; **Wol|ken|krat|zer** M skyscraper; **Wol|ken|ku|ckucks|heim** NT cloud-cuckoo-land; **in einem ~ leben** to live in cloud-cuckoo-land; **Wol|ken|land|schaft** F (liter) clouds pl; **wol|ken|los** ADJ cloudless; **Wol|ken|meer** NT (liter) sea of clouds; **Wol|ken|schicht** F layer of cloud, cloud layer; **Wol|ken|schlei|er** M (liter) veil of cloud (liter); **von einem ~ eingehüllt** veiled in cloud; **Wol|ken|strei|fen** M streak of cloud; **wol|ken|ver|han|gen** [-fɛɐhaŋən] ADJ overcast; **Wol|ken|wand** F cloud bank

wol|kig ['vɔlkɪç] ADJ cloudy; (fig) obscure

Woll|de|cke F (woollen (Brit) or woolen (US)) blanket

Wol|le ['vɔlə] F -, -n wool; **in der ~ gefärbt** (fig) dyed-in-the-wool; **mit jdm in die ~ kommen** or **geraten** (fig inf) sich mit jdm in die ~ kriegen (fig inf) to start squabbling with sb; **sich mit** ...

jdm in der ~ haben (fig inf) to be at loggerheads with sb

wol|len¹ ['vɔlən] ADJ attr woollen (Brit), woolen (US)

---

wol|len² ['vɔlən]
pret **wollte** ['vɔltə], ptp **gewollt** [gə'vɔlt]
♦ 35.1, 52.2, 53.5

| 1 HILFSVERB | 3 INTRANSITIVES VERB |
| 2 TRANSITIVES VERB | |

wollen wird normalerweise mit **to want** übersetzt.

---

1 – HILFSVERB ptp **wollen**

a = Willen haben **sie will nach Hause gehen** she wants to go home; **sie will nicht nach Hause gehen** she doesn't want to go home; (= weigert sich) she won't go home; **etw haben wollen** to want (to have) sth; **ich will lieber ins Kino gehen** I'd prefer to go to the cinema; **er wollte unbedingt nach Frankreich ziehen** he was desperate to move to France; **ich will so einen Fehler nie wieder machen** I won't make that mistake again; **er will immer alles besser wissen** he thinks he knows it all; **wenn man darauf noch Rücksicht nehmen wollte** if you are going to take that into account as well; **das wollen wir doch erst mal sehen!** we'll see about that!; **er will und will sich nicht ändern** he just will not change; **was will man da schon machen/sagen?** what can you do/say?

b = beabsichtigen **etw gerade tun wollen** to be going to do sth; **wolltest du gerade weggehen?** were you just leaving?; **ich wollte schon gehen/gerade aufhören, als ...** I was just going to leave/just about to stop when ...; **es sieht aus, als wollte es regnen** as if it's going to rain; **es will nicht besser/wärmer werden** it just won't get better/won't warm up; **es will und will nicht aufhören** it just goes on and on

c = müssen **das will alles genauestens überlegt sein** or **werden** it all has to be most carefully considered; **die Pflanzen wollen oft gegossen werden** the plants need to be watered frequently

d = zugeben, behaupten **keiner wollte etwas gehört/gesehen haben** nobody would admit to hearing/seeing anything; **keiner will es gewesen sein** nobody will admit to it; **der Zeuge will den Dieb beobachtet haben** the witness claims to have seen the thief; **und so jemand will Lehrer sein!** and he calls himself a teacher

e Wunsch **das wolle Gott verhüten** heaven forbid; **wenn er mir das doch ersparen wollte!** if only he would spare me that!

f Aufforderung **wollen wir uns nicht setzen?** why don't we sit down?; **wenn Sie bitte Platz nehmen wollen** if you would please take a seat; **man wolle bitte ...** would you kindly ...; **na, wollen wir gehen?** well, shall we go?; **darauf wollen wir mal anstoßen!** let's drink to that; **wir wollen beten!** let us pray; **wir wollen mal nicht übertreiben** let's not exaggerate; **wir wollen mal in Ruhe überlegen** let's think about it calmly

g andere Wendungen **komme, was da wolle** come what may; **sei er, wer er wolle** whoever he may be

♦ **es will ...** (unpersönlich) **es will mir nicht einleuchten, warum** I really can't see why; **es will mir scheinen, dass ...** it seems to me that ...

2 – TRANSITIVES VERB

a = wünschen to want; **er will doch nur dein Bestes** he only wants the best for you; **was wollen sie?** what do they want?; **was wollten sie denn von dir?** what did they want then?; **sie wollten nur mein Geld** all they wanted was my money; **ohne es zu wollen** without wanting to; **das wollte ich nicht** (= war unbeabsichtigt) I didn't mean to (do that); **was willst du (noch) mehr!** what more do you want!; **ich weiß nicht, was du willst, das ist doch ausgezeichnet** I don't know what you're on about, it's excel-

lent; **er hat gar nichts zu wollen** he has no say at all

b = bezwecken **was willst du mit dem Messer?** what are you doing with that knife?; **was willst du mit der Frage?** why are you asking that?; **was wollen die Leute mit solchen Filmen?** what do people hope to achieve with films like that? → auch **gewollt**

c = brauchen to want, to need; **diese Pflanzen wollen viel Sonne** these plants need a lot of sun

3 – INTRANSITIVES VERB

a = Willen haben **er kann schon, wenn er nur will** he can (do it) if he really wants (to); **man muss nur wollen** you just have to want to; **man muss sich nur sagen: ich will** you only have to say: I will do it; **da ist nichts zu wollen** there is nothing we/you can do (about it)

b = bereit sein **wenn er will** if he wants to; **er will nicht so recht** he seems rather unwilling; **so Gott will** God willing

c = mögen to want to; **wollen, dass jd etw tut** to want sb to do sth; **ich wollte, ich wäre ...** I wish I were ...; **ob du willst oder nicht** whether you like it or not, whether you want to or not

Nach **wenn**, **wer** und **wie** wird **wollen** mit **to like** übersetzt.

wenn du willst if you like; **wenn man so will** as it were; **ganz wie du willst** just as you like; **wenn du willst, machen wir das so** if you want to or if you like, we'll do it that way; **wer nicht will, der hat schon** if you don't/he doesn't like it, you/he can lump it (inf)

d = gehen wollen to want to go; **er will ins Kino** he wants to go to the cinema; **ich will nach Hause/hier raus/weg** I want to go home/to get out of here/to get away; **wo willst du hin?** where do you want to go?; **zu wem wollen Sie?** whom do you want to see?

Woll-: Woll|fa|ser F wool fibre; **Woll|fett** NT wool fat, lanolin; **Woll|garn** NT woollen (Brit) or woolen (US) yarn; **Woll|gras** NT (Bot) cotton grass

wol|lig ['vɔlıç] ADJ woolly

Woll-: Woll|ja|cke F cardigan; **Woll|käm|me|rei** F a (Fabrik) wool-carding shop b (Tätigkeit) wool-carding; **Woll|knäu|el** NT ball of wool; **Woll|maus** F (inf) (big) ball of fluff, dust bunny (US inf); **Woll|milch|sau** F Eier legende – all-providing genetically engineered animal; **Woll|sa|chen** PL woollens pl (Brit), woolens pl (US); **Woll|sie|gel** NT Woolmark®; **Woll|spin|ne|rei** F a (Fabrik) woollen (Brit) or woolen (US) mill b (Tätigkeit) wool-spinning; **Woll|stoff** M woollen (Brit) or woolen (US) material; **Woll|strumpf** M woollen (Brit) or woolen (US) stocking

Woll|lust F (liter) (= Sinnlichkeit) sensuality, voluptuousness; (= Lüsternheit) lust, lewdness, lasciviousness; **~ empfinden** to be in ecstasy; **etw mit wahrer ~ tun** (fig) to delight in doing sth

woll|lüs|tig ['vɔlYstıç] (geh) ADJ (= sinnlich) sensual; Frau auch voluptuous; (= lüstern) lascivious, lusty; (= verzückt, ekstatisch) ecstatic; **seine ~e Freude an etw** (dat) **haben** (fig) to go into ecstasies over sth ADV streicheln, sich winden sensually; stöhnen ecstatically; etw ansehen lustily; **jdn ~ anblicken** to give sb a lascivious look; **sich ~ im warmen Bad rekeln** to luxuriate in a warm bath

Woll|lüst|ling M (hum inf) sensualist

Woll-: Woll|wa|ren PL woollen (Brit) or woolen (US) goods pl, woollens pl (Brit), woolens pl (US); **Woll|wä|sche** F washing woollens (Brit) or woolens (US) no art; (= Wollartikel) woollens pl (Brit), woolens pl (US); **Woll|-wasch|gang** M wool wash (cycle); **Woll|-wasch|mit|tel** NT detergent for woollens (Brit) or woolens (US)

wo|mit [vo'mɪt] ADV → *auch* **mit** [a] *interrog* with what, what ... with; **~ kann ich dienen?** what can I do for you? [b] *rel* with which; *(auf ganzen Satz bezüglich)* by which; **ein Gerät, ~ man auch bohren kann** an appliance you can drill with too; **das ist es, ~ ich nicht einverstanden bin** that's what I don't agree with; **~ ich nicht sagen will, dass ...** by which I don't mean (to say) that ..., which doesn't mean to say that ...; **~ man es auch versuchte** whatever they tried to do it with ...

wo|mög|lich [vo'mø:klɪç] ADV possibly → **wo**

wo|nach [vo'na:x] ADV → *auch* **nach** [a] *interrog* after what, what ... after; **~ sehnst du dich?** what do you long for?; **~ riecht das?** what does it smell of?; **~ sollen wir uns richten?** what should we go by? [b] *rel* **das Land, ~ du dich sehnst** the land for which you are longing, the land (which) you are longing for; **das war es, ~ ich mich erkundigen wollte** that was what I wanted to ask about; **die Nachricht, ~ er ...** the news that he ...

Won|ne ['vɔnə] F **-, -n** *(geh)* *(= Glückseligkeit)* bliss *no pl*; *(= Vergnügen)* joy, delight; **mit ~** with great delight, **(aber) mit ~!** with great pleasure!; **das ist ihre ganze ~** that's all her joy; **in eitel ~ schwimmen** to be lost in rapture; **die ~n der Liebe** the joys *or* delights of love; **die ~(n) des Paradieses** the delights of paradise; **es ist eine wahre ~** it's a sheer delight

Won|ne-: Won|ne|ge|fühl NT blissful feeling; **Won|ne|mo|nat** M, **Won|ne|mond** M *(poet)* May; **im ~** Mai in the merry month of May; **Won|ne|prop|pen** [-prɔpn] M **-s, -** [a] *(hum inf: = Baby)* bundle of joy [b] *pl (sl: = Busen)* boobs *pl (inf)*; **Won|ne|schau|er** M thrill of joy; **Won|ne|schrei** M cry of delight; **won|ne|voll** ADJ *Gefühl* blissful; *Kind, Anblick* delightful; *Gesichtsausdruck* delighted

won|nig ['vɔnɪç] ADJ delightful; *Gefühl, Ruhe* blissful

won|nig|lich ['vɔnɪklɪç] ADJ *(poet) Gefühl, Stunden* blissful; *Kind, Anblick* delightful

wo|ran [vo'ran] ADV → *auch* **an** [a] *interrog* **~ soll ich den Kleiderbügel hängen?** what shall I hang the coat hanger on?; **~ denkst du?** what are you thinking about?; **man weiß bei ihm nie, ~ man ist** you never know where you are with him; **~ liegt das?** what's the reason for it?; **~ ist er gestorben?** what did he die of? [b] *rel (auf vorausgehenden Satz bezogen)* by which; **das, ~ ich mich gerne erinnere** what I like to recall; **die Wand, ~ sie immer die Plakate kleben** the wall on which they are always sticking posters, the wall they're always sticking posters on; **..., ~ ich schon gedacht hatte** which I'd already thought of; **~ ich merkte, dass ...** which made me realize that ...; **~ er auch immer gestorben ist ...** whatever he died of ...

wo|rauf [vo'rauf] ADV → *auch* **auf** [a] *interrog (räumlich)* on what, what ... on; **~ wartest du?** what are you waiting for?; **~ sollte ich mich freuen?** what do I have to look forward to? [b] *rel (zeitlich)* whereupon; **~ du dich verlassen kannst** of that you can be sure; **das ist etwas, ~ ich mich freue** that's something I'm looking forward to; **das, ~ er sich vorbereitet hatte** what he was prepared for; **~ er einen Wutanfall bekam** whereupon he flew into a rage; **~ er sich auch beruft ...** whatever his arguments are ...

wo|rauf|hin [vorauf'hɪn] REL ADV whereupon

wo|raus [vo'raus] ADV → *auch* **aus** [a] *interrog* out of what, what ... out of; **~ ist der Pullover?** what is the pullover made (out) of?; **~ schließt du das?** from what do you deduce that? [b] *rel* out of which, which ... out of; **das Buch, ~ ich gestern vorgelesen habe** the book I was reading from yesterday; **~ ich schließe/gelernt habe, dass ...** from which I conclude/have learned that ...; **~ man das Öl auch gewinnt ...** whatever oil is obtained from ...

wor|den *ptp von* **werden 1 c**

wo|rein [vo'rain] ADV → *auch* **hinein** [a] *interrog* in what, what ... in; **~ soll ich den Salat tun?** what shall I put the salad in? [b] *rel* in which, which ... in; **das ist etwas, ~ ich mich nie fügen werde** that's something I shall never submit to *or* put up with

wor|feln ['vɔrfln] VTI *(Agr)* to winnow

wo|rin [vo'rɪn] ADV → *auch* **in** [a] *interrog* in what, what ... in; **~ war das eingewickelt?** what was it wrapped in?; **~ liegt der Unterschied/Vorteil?** what is the difference/advantage? [b] *rel* in which, which ... in, wherein *(form)*; **das ist etwas, ~ wir nicht übereinstimmen** that's something we don't agree on; **dann sagte er ~, ~ ich mit ihm übereinstimme** then he said ..., which is where I agree with him; **~ du es auch einwickelst ...** whatever you wrap it in ...

Work|flow-Ma|na|ge|ment ['wø:ɐkflo:-, 'wœrkflo-] NT , **Work|flow|ma|na|ge|ment** NT workflow management

Work|shop ['wø:ɐkʃɔp, 'wœrk-] M **-s, -s** workshop

Work|sta|tion ['wø:ɐkste:ʃn, 'wœrk-] F **-, -s** *(Comput)* work station

World Wide Web [wø:ɐld 'waid 'wɛb] NT **-,** *no pl (Comput)* World Wide Web

Wort [vɔrt] NT **-(e)s, -e** *or* **̈er** ['vœrtɐ] [a] *pl usu* **̈er** *(= Vokabel)* word; **ein ~ mit sechs Buchstaben** a word with six letters, a six-letter word; **~ für ~** word for word → **wahr** [b] *pl* **-e** *(= Äußerung)* word; **nichts als ~e** nothing but words *or* talk; **genug der ~e!** enough talk!; **das ist ein ~!** wonderful!; **in ~ und Schrift** in speech and writing; **er beherrscht die Sprache in ~ und Schrift** he has a command of the written and spoken language; **in ~ und Tat** in word and deed; **in ~en und Werken sündigen** to sin in words and deeds; **~en Taten folgen lassen** to suit the action to the word(s); **mit einem ~** in a word; **mit anderen/wenigen ~en** in other/a few words; **hast du** *or* **hat der Mensch (da noch) ~e!** it leaves you speechless; **kein ~ mehr** not another word; **kein ~ von etw sagen** *or* **erwähnen** *or* **fallen lassen** not to say one word *or* a thing about sth; **keine ~e für etw finden** to find no words for sth; *(sprachlos sein auch)* to be speechless at sth; **kein ~ von etw wissen/verstehen** not to know/understand a thing about sth; **ich verstehe kein ~!** I don't understand a word (of it); *(= kann nichts hören)* I can't hear a word (that's being said); **er sagte** *or* **sprach kein einziges ~** he didn't say a single word; **ein ~ mit jdm sprechen** *or* **reden** to have a word with sb; **mit dir habe ich noch ein ~ zu reden!** I want a word with you!; **ein ernstes ~ mit jdm reden** to have a serious talk with sb; **kein ~ miteinander/mit jdm sprechen** *or* **reden** not to say a word to each other/to sb; **hättest du doch ein ~ gesagt** if only you had said something; **davon hat man mir kein ~ gesagt** they didn't tell me anything about it; **man kann sein eigenes ~ nicht (mehr) verstehen** you can't hear yourself speak; **um nicht viel(e) ~e zu machen** to make it brief; **ich konnte kein ~ anbringen** I couldn't get a word in edgeways; **ein ~ gab das andere** one thing led to another; **jdm das ~** *or* **die ~e im Mund (her)umdrehen** to twist sb's words; **du sprichst ein großes** *or* **wahres ~ gelassen aus** how true, how true; **die passenden/keine ~e für etw finden** to find the right/no words for sth; **das rechte ~ zur rechten Zeit** the right word at the right time; **jdn mit schönen ~en abspeisen** to fob sb off *(Brit)*, to put sb off; **er hat nur schöne ~e gemacht** it was just talk; **auf ein ~!** a word!; **jdm aufs ~ glauben** to believe sb implicitly; **das glaub ich dir aufs ~** I can well believe it; **ohne ein ~ (zu sagen)** without (saying) a word; **dein ~ in Gottes Ohr** let us hope so; **seine ~e galten dir** he meant you, he was talking about you → **verlieren** VT, **Mund**

[c] *no pl (= Rede, Recht zu sprechen)* **das ~ neh-** men to speak; *(bei Debatte auch)* to take the floor; **das große ~ haben** *or* **führen** *(inf)* to shoot one's mouth off *(inf)*; **einer Sache** *(dat)* **das ~ reden** to put the case for sth; **das ~ an jdn richten** to address (oneself to) sb; **jdm ins ~ fallen** to interrupt sb; **jdm das ~ abschneiden** to cut sb short; **zu ~ kommen** to get a chance to speak; **ums ~ bitten, sich zu ~ melden** to ask to speak; **er hat das ~** it's his turn to speak; *(bei Debatte auch)* he has the floor; **jdm das ~ erteilen** *or* **geben** to allow sb to speak; *(bei Debatte auch)* to allow sb to take the floor; **er hat mir das ~ verboten** he forbade me to speak

[d] *pl* **-e** *(= Ausspruch)* saying; *(= Zitat)* quotation; *(Rel)* Word; **ein ~, das er immer im Munde führt** one of his favourite *(Brit)* or favorite *(US)* sayings; **ein ~ Goethes/aus der Bibel** a quotation from Goethe/the Bible; **das ~ zum Sonntag** *short religious broadcast on Saturday night*, ≈ late call *(dated Brit)*; **nach dem ~ des Evangeliums** according to the Gospel

[e] *pl* **-e** *(= Text, Sprache)* words *pl*; **in ~en** in words; **in ~ und Bild** in words and pictures; **etw in ~e fassen** to put sth into words; **das geschriebene/gedruckte/gesprochene ~** the written/printed/spoken word; **das ~ als Kommunikationsmittel** language as a means of communication

[f] *pl* **-e** *(= Befehl, Entschluss)* **das ~ des Vaters ist ausschlaggebend** the father's word is law; **das ~ des Königs** the king's command; **jdm aufs ~ gehorchen** *or* **folgen** to obey sb's every word; **dabei habe ich auch (noch) ein ~ mitzureden** *or* **mitzusprechen** I (still) have something to say about that too; **das letzte ~ ist noch nicht gesprochen** the final decision hasn't been taken yet; **das letzte ~ haben** to have the last word; **musst du immer das letzte ~ haben?** do you always have to have the last word?

[g] *no pl (= Versprechen)* word; **auf mein ~** I give (you) my word; **jdn beim ~ nehmen** to take sb at his word; **ich gebe mein ~ darauf** I give you my word on it; **sein ~ halten** to keep one's word; *(bei jdm)* **im ~ stehen** *or* **sein** to have given one's word (to sb), to have made a commitment (to sb)

Wort-: Wort|ak|zent M word stress; **Wort|art** F *(Gram)* part of speech; **Wort|auf|wand** M verbosity; **Wort|aus|wahl** F choice of words; **Wort|be|deu|tung** F meaning of a/the word; **Wort|bei|trag** M (verbal) contribution; **einen ~ leisten** to make a verbal contribution, to say a few words; **Wort|bil|dung** F *(Ling)* morphology; **Wort|bruch** M **das wäre ein ~ that** would be breaking your/my *etc* promise; **wort|brü|chig** ADJ false; **~ werden** to break one's word

Wört|chen ['vœrtçən] NT **-s, -** *dim von* **Wort** little word; **da habe ich wohl ein ~ mitzureden** *(inf)* I think I have some say in that; **mit ihm habe ich noch ein ~ zu reden** *(inf)* I want a word with him

Wör|ter-: Wör|ter|buch NT dictionary; **Wör|ter|ver|zeich|nis** NT vocabulary; *(von Spezialbegriffen)* glossary

Wort-: Wort|fa|mi|lie F word family; **Wort|feld** NT semantic field; **Wort|fet|zen** M scrap of conversation; **Wort|fol|ge** F *(Gram)* word order; **Wort|form** F word form; **Wort|füh|rer** M spokesman; **Wort|füh|re|rin** F spokeswoman; **Wort|ge|bühr** F *(Telec)* rate per word; **Wort|ge|fecht** NT battle of words; **Wort|ge|klin|gel** NT *(pej)* verbiage; **Wort|ge|o|gra|fie** ▲ F word geography; **Wort|ge|plän|kel** NT banter; **wort|ge|treu** ADJ, ADV verbatim; **wort|ge|wal|tig** ADJ *Redner, Text* powerful, powerfully eloquent; **wort|ge|wandt** ADJ eloquent; **Wort|ge|wandt|heit** F eloquence; **Wort|gut** NT , *no pl* vocabulary; **Wort|hül|se** F *(pej)* hollow word; **wort|karg** ADJ taciturn; **Wort|karg|heit** F taciturnity; **Wort|klau|ber** [-klaube] M **-s, -**, **Wort|klau|be|rin** [-ərɪn] F **-, -nen** caviller *(Brit)*, caviler *(US)*, quibbler; **Wort|klau|be|rei** [-klaubə'rai]

F **-, -en** cavilling (*Brit*), caviling (*US*), quibbling; **Wort|kun|de** F lexicology; (= *Vokabelsammlung*) vocabulary; **Wort|laut** M wording; **im ~** verbatim; **folgenden ~ haben** to read as follows

Wört|lein ['vœrtlain] NT **-s, -** = **Wörtchen**

wört|lich ['vœrtlɪç] ADJ *Bedeutung* literal; *Übersetzung, Wiedergabe etc auch* word-for-word; *Rede* direct ADV *wiedergeben, zitieren, abschreiben* verbatim, word for word; *übersetzen* literally, word for word; **das darf man nicht so ~ nehmen** you mustn't take it literally; **darf ich das ~ nehmen?** do you really mean that?; **das hat er ~ gesagt** those were his very *or* actual words

Wort-: wort|los ADJ silent ADV without saying a word; **Wort|mel|dung** F request to speak; **wenn es keine weiteren ~en gibt** if nobody else wishes to speak; **Wort|prä|gung** F , **Wort|neu|bil|dung** F neologism; **ein Meister der ~** a master at coining words; **Wort|rät|sel** NT word puzzle; **wort|reich** ADJ *Rede, Erklärung etc* verbose, wordy; *Sprache* rich in vocabulary *or* words ADV profusely; **Wort|reich|tum** M (*von Rede, Erklärung etc*) verbosity, wordiness; (*von Sprache*) richness in vocabulary; **Wort|schatz** M vocabulary; **Wort|schöp|fung** F neologism; **Wort|schwall** M torrent of words; **Wort|sinn** M meaning of a/the word; **Wort|spiel** NT pun, play on words; **Wort|stamm** M (*Ling*) root (of a/the word); **Wort|stel|lung** F (*Gram*) word order; **Wort|ver|bin|dung** F (*Ling*) word combination; (= *Kollokation*) collocation; (= *Kompositum*) compound; **Wort|ver|dre|hung** F twisting of words; **Wort|wahl** F choice of words; **Wort|wech|sel** M exchange (of words), verbal exchange; **wort|wei|se** ADJ, ADV word for word; **Wort|witz** M pun; **wört|lich** ADJ word-for-word ADV word for word, quite literally; **Wort|zu|sam|men|set|zung** F compound (word)

wo|rü|ber [vo'ry:bɐ] ADV → *auch* **über** a *interrog* about what, what ... about; (*örtlich*) over what, what ... over b *rel* about which, which ... about; (*örtlich*) over which, which ... over; (*auf vorausgehenden Satz bezogen*) which; **das Thema, ~ ich gerade einen Artikel gelesen habe** the subject I have just read an article about; **~ sie sich auch unterhalten, sie ...** whatever they talk about they ...

wo|rum [vo'rʊm] ADV → *auch* **um** a *interrog* about what, what ... about; **~ handelt es sich?** what's it about? b *rel* about which, which ... about; **der Ast, ~ ich die Schnur gebunden hatte** the branch I tied the rope (a)round; **~ die Diskussion auch geht, ...** whatever the discussion is about ...

wo|run|ter [vo'rʊntɐ] ADV → *auch* **unter** a *interrog* under what, what ... under; **ich weiß nicht, ~ er leidet** I don't know what he is suffering from b *rel* under which, which ... under

wo|selbst [vo'zɛlpst] REL ADV (*obs*) where

Wo|tan ['vo:tan] M **-s** (*Myth*) Wotan

wo|von [vo'fɔn] ADV → *auch* **von** a *interrog* from what, what ... from; **~ hat er das abgeleitet?** what did he derive that from? b *rel* from which, which ... from; (*auf vorausgehenden Satz bezogen*) about which, which ... about; **das ist ein Gebiet, ~ er viel versteht** that is a subject he knows a lot about; **~ du dich auch ernährst, ... whatever you eat ...**

wo|vor [vo'fo:ɐ] ADV → *auch* **vor** a *interrog* (*örtlich*) before what, what ... before; **~ fürchtest du dich?** what are you afraid of? b *rel* before which, which ... before; **das Ereignis, ~ ich schon immer gewarnt habe** the event I have always warned you about; **~ du dich auch fürchtest, ...** whatever you're afraid of ...

wo|zu [vo'tsu:] ADV → *auch* **zu** a *interrog* to what, what ... to; (= *warum*) why; **~ soll ich das legen?** where shall I put it?; **~ hast du dich entschlossen?** what have you decided on?; **~ soll das gut sein?** what's the point of that?; **~ denn das?** what for?; **~ denn?** why should

I/you? *etc*

b *rel* to which, which ... to; **das, ~ ich am meisten neige** what I'm most inclined to do; **das Verfahren, ~ ich raten würde** the procedure I would advise; **..., ~ ich mich jetzt auch entschlossen habe** ... which I have now decided to do; **sie haben geheiratet, ~ ich nichts weiter sagen möchte** they have got married, and I shall say no more about that; **~ du dich auch entschließt, ...** whatever you decide (on) ...

Wrack [vrak] NT **-s, -s** *or* (*rare*) **-e** wreck; (*fig*) (physical) wreck

Wrack|bo|je F , **Wrack|ton|ne** F (*Naut*) wreck buoy

wrang *pret von* **wringen**

Wra|sen ['vra:zn] M **-s, -** (*esp N Ger*) vapour (*Brit*), vapor (*US*)

wrin|gen ['vrɪŋən] *pret* **wrang** [vraŋ], *ptp* **gewrun|gen** [gə'vrʊŋən] VTI to wring

WS [ve:'ɛs] NT (*Univ*) *abbr von* **Wintersemester**

WSV [ve:ɛs'fau] M *abbr von* **Winterschlussverkauf**

WSW *abbr von* **Westsüdwest** WSW

Wu|cher ['vu:xɐ] M **-s,** *no pl* profiteering; (*bei Geldverleih*) usury; **das ist doch ~!** that's daylight (*Brit*) *or* highway (*US*) robbery!

Wu|che|rer ['vu:xərɐ] M **-s, -**, **Wu|che|rin** [-ərɪn] F **-, -nen** profiteer; (= *Geldverleiher*) usurer

Wu|cher|ge|schäft NT profiteering *no pl*; (= *Geldverleih*) usury *no pl*

wu|che|risch ['vu:xərɪʃ] ADJ profiteering; *Geldverleih, Zinsen* usurious; *Bedingungen, Preis, Miete etc* exorbitant, extortionate

Wu|cher|mie|te F exorbitant *or* extortionate rent

wu|chern ['vu:xɐn] VI a *aux sein or haben* (*Pflanzen*) to grow rampant, to proliferate; (*Geschwür*) to grow rapidly; (*wildes Fleisch*) to proliferate; (*Bart, Haare*) to grow profusely; **in die Höhe ~** to shoot up(wards) b (*fig: = sich verbreiten*) to be rampant; **sein Hass wuchert im Verborgenen** his hatred is quietly intensifying c (*Kaufmann etc*) to profiteer; (*Geldverleiher*) to practise (*Brit*) *or* practice (*US*) usury; **mit seinen Talenten ~** (*fig*) to make the most of one's talents

wu|chernd ADJ *Pflanzen* rampant, proliferous; *wildes Fleisch* proliferous; *Bart* straggly; (*fig*) proliferating; *Bürokratie, Kriminalität, Korruption* rampant

Wu|cher|preis M exorbitant price; **~e bezahlen** to pay through the nose

Wu|che|rung F **-, -en** rank growth, proliferation; (*Med*) growth; (= *wildes Fleisch*) proud flesh

Wu|cher|zins M exorbitant *or* usurious interest

wuchs *pret von* **wachsen** [1]

Wuchs [vu:ks] M **-es,** *no pl* (= *Wachstum*) growth; (= *Gestalt, Form*) stature; (*von Mensch*) build, stature

Wucht [vʊxt] F **-,** *no pl* a (= *Stoßkraft*) momentum, force; (*fig*) force, power; **mit aller ~ with all one's force or might; mit voller ~** with full force b (*inf: = Menge*) load (*inf*); **eine ~ (Prügel)** a good hiding c (*inf*) **er/das ist die *or* eine ~!** he's/that's smashing! (*Brit inf*), he's/that's a hit (*US inf*)

wuch|ten ['vʊxtn] VT *Koffer, Karton, Paket* to heave, to drag, to haul; *Gewicht* to heave; **er wuchtete den Ball ins Tor** he belted the ball into the goal VR **er wuchtete sich aus dem Auto** he heaved *or* hauled himself out of the car; **Ikarus wuchtete sich in die Lüfte** Ikarus launched himself into the air

Wucht|ge|schoss ▲ NT stun bullet

wuch|tig ['vʊxtɪç] ADJ massive; *Schlag* heavy, powerful; *Klänge* powerful; *Wein* (*fig*) heavy

Wühl|ar|beit F (*fig pej*) subversive activities *pl*

wüh|len ['vy:lən] VI a (*nach etw* for) to dig; (*Maulwurf etc*) to burrow; (*Schwein, Vogel*) to root; **im Bett ~** to toss and turn; **im Schmutz** *or* **Dreck ~** (*fig*) to wallow in the mire *or* mud

b (= *suchen*) to rummage, to root (*nach etw* for sth); **in den Schubladen ~** to rummage through the drawers c (*fig*) to gnaw (*in* +*dat* at) d (*inf: = schwer arbeiten*) to slog (*inf*) e (= *Untergrundarbeit leisten*) to stir things up VT to dig, to burrow; **er wühlte seinen Kopf in die Kissen** he buried his face in the pillows VR **sich durch die Menge/das Gestrüpp/die Akten ~** to burrow one's way through the crowd/ the undergrowth/the files

Wüh|ler ['vy:lɐ] M **-s, -**, **Wüh|le|rin** [-ərɪn] F **-, -nen** a (*pej: = Aufrührer*) agitator, subversive b (*inf: = schwer Arbeitender*) slogger (*Brit inf*), toiler (*US inf*) c (*inf: = unruhig Schlafender*) wriggler

Wüh|le|rei [vy:lə'rai] F **-, -en** a digging; (*von Maulwurf*) burrowing b (= *Sucherei*) rummaging *or* rooting (about) c (*inf: = Arbeiten*) slogging d (*Pol inf*) agitation

Wühl-: Wühl|maus F vole; (*fig pej*) subversive; **Wühl|tisch** M (*inf*) bargain counter

Wulst [vʊlst] M **-es,** ≐**e** ['vʏlstə] *or f* **-,** ≐**e** bulge; (*an Reifen*) bead; (*an Flasche, Glas*) lip; (*Archit*) torus; (*Her*) wreath; (*Naut*) bulb; **ein ~ von Fett** a roll of fat; **die dicken Wülste seiner Lippen** his thick lips

wuls|tig ['vʊlstɪç] ADJ bulging; *Rand, Lippen* thick

Wulst-: Wulst|lip|pen PL thick lips *pl*; **Wulst|rei|fen** M bead tyre (*Brit*) *or* tire (*US*)

wum|mern ['vʊmɐn] VI (*inf*) a (= *dröhnen*) to rumble; (= *pochen*) to drum; **an** *or* **gegen die Tür ~** to hammer at the door b *aux sein* (= *dröhnend fahren*) to rumble along

wund [vʊnt] ADJ sore; **ein ~er Punkt, eine ~e Stelle** a sore point; **ein ~es Herz** (*liter*) a wounded heart

ADV **etw ~ kratzen/scheuern/reiben** to scratch/ chafe/rub sth until it's raw; **das Pferd/ich war vom Reiten ~ gescheuert** the horse/I was saddle-sore; **ein Tier ~ schießen** to wound an animal; **sich** (*dat*) **die Füße/Fersen ~ laufen** (*lit*) to walk until one's feet/heels are raw; (*fig*) to walk one's legs off; **sich** (*dat*) **die Finger ~ schreiben** (*fig*) to write one's fingers to the bone; **sich** (*dat*) **den Mund ~ reden** (*fig*) to talk till one is blue in the face; **ein ~ gelegener Patient** a patient with bedsores; **eine ~ gelegene Stelle** a bedsore; **~ gelegen sein** to have bedsores → **wund liegen**

Wund-: Wund|arzt M , **Wund|ärz|tin** F (*old*) surgeon; **Wund|auf|la|ge** F wound dressing; **Wund|ben|zin** NT surgical spirit (*Brit*), rubbing alcohol (*US*); **Wund|brand** M gangrene

Wun|de ['vʊndə] F **-, -n** (*lit, fig*) wound; **alte ~n/eine alte ~ wieder aufreißen** (*fig*) to open up old sores; **an eine alte ~ rühren** (*fig geh*) to touch on a sore point; **(bei jdm) tiefe ~n schlagen** (*fig*) to scar sb; **den Finger auf die (brennende) ~ legen** (*fig*) to bring up a painful subject; **Salz in eine/jds ~ streuen** (*fig*) to turn the knife in the wound; **Balsam** *or* **Öl in eine/jds ~ gießen** *or* **träufeln** (*fig*) to comfort sb

wun|der △ ['vʊndɐ] ADV *inv* → **Wunder** b

Wun|der ['vʊndɐ] NT **-s, -** a (= *übernatürliches Ereignis, auch Rel*) miracle; (= *wunderbare Erscheinung*) wonder; (= *Leistung*) marvel, miracle; (= *erstaunlicher Mensch*) marvel; **~ tun** *or* **wirken** (*Rel*) to work miracles; **das grenzt an ein ~** it verges on the miraculous, it's almost a miracle; **durch ein ~** by a miracle; **wie durch ein ~** as if by a miracle; **nur durch ein ~ können sie noch gerettet werden** only a miracle can save them now; **die ~ der Natur/dieser Welt** the wonders of nature/this world; **ein architektonisches ~** an architectural miracle

b **meine Eltern denken ~ was passiert ist/~ was über mein Privatleben** my parents think goodness knows what has happened/goodness knows what about my private life; **das hat er sich ~ wie einfach vorgestellt** he imagined it would be ever so easy; **er glaubt, ~ wer zu** sein/~ **was geleistet zu haben** he thinks he's marvellous (*Brit*) or marvelous (*US*)/done something marvel(l)ous; **er meint, ~ wie schön das sei** he thinks it's fantastic; **er bildet sich ~ was ein** he thinks he's too wonderful for words **c** (= *überraschendes Ereignis*) **~ tun** or **wirken** to do wonders; **diese Medizin wirkt ~** this medicine works wonders; **es ist ein/kein ~, dass ...** it's a wonder/no wonder or small wonder that ...; **ist es ein ~, dass er dick ist?** is it any wonder that he's fat?; **kein ~** no wonder; **was ~, wenn ...** it's no wonder or surprise if ... → **blau a**

wun|der|bar ADJ **a** (= *schön*) wonderful, marvellous (*Brit*), marvelous (*US*) **b** (= *übernatürlich, wie durch ein Wunder*) miraculous ADV (= *herrlich*) wonderfully

wun|der|ba|rer|wei|se ['vʊndɐbaːrɐˈvaɪzə] ADV miraculously

Wun|der-: **Wun|der|ding** NT marvellous (*Brit*) or marvelous (*US*) thing; **dass er überlebt hat, ist ein ~** that he survived is a miracle; **Wun|der|dok|tor(in)** M(F) (*pej:* = *Quacksalber*) quack; **Wun|der|dro|ge** F (*von Zauberer, Fee etc*) miracle drug; (*fig auch*) wonder drug; **Wun|der|glau|be** M belief in miracles; **wun|der|gläu|big** ADJ **~ sein** to believe in miracles; **ein ~er Mensch** a person who believes in miracles; **Wun|der|hei|ler(in)** M(F) wonder doctor; (*pej*) faith healer; **Wun|der|horn** NT (*liter, Myth*) magic horn; **wun|der|hübsch** ADJ wonderfully pretty, wondrously beautiful (*liter*); **Wun|der|ker|ze** F sparkler; **Wun|der|kind** NT child prodigy; **Wun|der|kna|be** M (*usu iro*) wonder boy or child; **Wun|der|kur** F (*iro*) miracle cure; **Wun|der|lam|pe** F magic lamp or lantern; **Wun|der|land** NT wonderland; **wun|der|lich** ['vʊndɐlɪç] ADJ **a** (= *merkwürdig*) strange, odd **b** (= *wundersam*) wondrous (*liter*); **Wun|der|lich|keit** F -, -en (= *Merkwürdigkeit*) strangeness, oddness; **Wun|der|mit|tel** NT miracle cure; (*von Fee etc*) magic potion

wun|dern ['vʊndɐn] VT impers to surprise; **es wundert mich** or **mich wundert, dass er noch nicht hier ist** I'm surprised or it surprises me that he is not here yet; **das wundert mich nicht** I'm not surprised, that doesn't surprise me; **das würde mich nicht ~** I shouldn't be surprised; **es sollte mich (nicht) ~, wenn ...** it would (not) surprise me if ...; **mich wundert gar nichts mehr** nothing surprises me any more VR to be surprised (*über +acc* at); **du wirst dich ~!** you'll be amazed!; **ich wunderte mich über seine schnelle Rückkehr** I was surprised at or about his quick return; **du wirst dich noch einmal ~!** you're in for a shock or surprise!; **da wirst du dich aber ~!** you're in for a surprise; **ich muss mich doch sehr ~!** well, I am surprised (at you/him etc); **ich wundere mich über gar nichts mehr** nothing surprises me any more; **dann darfst** or **brauchst du dich nicht ~, wenn ...** then don't be surprised if ...

Wun|der-: **wun|der+neh|men** sep irreg VI impers (geh) to be surprising VT impers to surprise; **es nimmt mich wunder, ob ...** (*Sw:* = *ich frage mich*) I wonder if ...; **wun|der|sam** ['vʊndɐzaːm] ADJ (*liter*) wondrous (*liter*); **wun|der|schön** ADJ beautiful, lovely; (= *herrlich auch*) wonderful; **einen ~en guten Morgen/Tag** etc a very good morning/day etc to you; **Wun|der|tat** F miracle; **Wun|der|tä|ter(in)** M(F) miracle worker; **wun|der|tä|tig** ADJ magic, miraculous; *Leben, Heilige* miracle-working; **~ wirken** to perform miracles; **Wun|der|tier** NT (*hum*) weird and wonderful animal (*hum*); **Wun|der|tü|te** F surprise packet; **wun|der|voll** ADJ wonderful, marvellous (*Brit*), marvelous (*US*) ADV wonderfully; **Wun|der|waf|fe** F wonder weapon; **Wun|der|welt** F (*im Märchen etc*) magic world; (= *zauberhafte Umgebung*) world of wonders; **die ~ der Mineralien** the wonderful world of miner-

als; **Wun|der|werk** NT miracle, marvel; **Wun|der|zei|chen** NT miraculous sign

Wund-: **Wund|fie|ber** NT traumatic fever; **wund|ge|le|gen** △ ADJ → **wund** ADV; **Wund|heit** F -, *no pl* soreness; **Wund|in|fek|ti|on** F wound infection; **wund lie|gen** ▲ VR irreg to get bedsores; **Wund|mal** NT pl -male **a** (*Rel*) stigma **b** (*liter*) scar; **Wund|pflas|ter** NT adhesive plaster; **Wund|rand** M edge of a/the wound); **Wund|ro|se** F (*Med*) erysipelas (spec), St Anthony's fire; **Wund|sal|be** F ointment; **Wund|sein** NT soreness; **Wund|sek|ret** NT secretion of a/the wound; **Wund|starr|krampf** M tetanus, lockjaw; **Wund|ver|sor|gung** F dressing a/the wound/wounds; **Wund|wat|te** F surgical wool

Wunsch [vʊnʃ] ⊙ 50 M **-(e)s, ⸚e** ['vʏnʃə] **a** wish, (= *sehnliches Verlangen*) desire; (= *Bitte*) request; **ein Pferd war schon immer mein ~** I've always wanted a horse; **nach ~** just as he/she etc wants/wanted; (= *wie geplant*) according to plan, as planned; (= *nach Bedarf*) as required; **auf** or **nach ~ der Eltern** as his/her etc parents wish/wished; **alles geht nach ~** everything is going smoothly; **von dem ~ beseelt sein, ...** to be filled with the desire ...; **hier ist der ~ der Vater des Gedankens** (*prov*) the wish is father to the thought (*prov*); **ich habe einen ~ an dich** I've a request to make of you; **was haben Sie für einen ~?** what can I do for you?; **haben Sie (sonst) noch einen ~?** (*beim Einkauf etc*) is there anything else you would like?, is there anything else I can do for you?; **sonst noch Wünsche?** (*iro*) any other requests?; **auf ~** by or on request; **auf jds (besonderen/ausdrücklichen) ~ hin** at sb's (special/express) request; **auf allgemeinen/vielfachen ~ hin** by popular request or demand → **ablesen, fromm d** **b** *usu pl* (= *Glückwunsch*) wish; **beste Wünsche zum Fest** the compliments of the season

wünsch|bar ADJ (*Sw*) = **wünschenswert**

Wunsch-: **Wunsch|bild** NT ideal; **Wunsch|den|ken** NT wishful thinking

Wün|schel|ru|te ['vʏnʃl-] F divining or dowsing rod

Wün|schel|ru|ten|gän|ger [-gɛŋɐ] M -s, -, **Wün|schel|ru|ten|gän|ge|rin** [-ərɪn] F -, -nen diviner, dowser

wün|schen ['vʏnʃn] ⊙ 27.3, 50.1, 50.5, 52.4 VT **a** **sich** (*dat*) **etw ~** to want sth; (= *den Wunsch äußern*) to ask for sth; (*im Stillen: bei Sternschnuppe etc*) to wish for sth; **ich wünsche mir das** I would like that, I want that; **ich wünsche mir, dass du ...** I would like you to ...; **... wie ich mir das gewünscht habe ...** as I wanted; **das habe ich mir von meinen Eltern zu Weihnachten gewünscht** I asked my parents to give me that for Christmas, I asked for that for Christmas from my parents; **ich wünsche mir einen Mantel von dir** I'd like a coat from you; **er wünscht sich** (*dat*), **dass das Projekt erfolgreich sein wird** he wants the project to be successful, he hopes the project will be successful; **er wünscht sich** (*dat*) **ein glückliches Leben für seine Kinder** he would like his children to have a happy life; **er wünscht sich** (*dat*) **diesen Mann als Lehrer/Vater/als** or **zum Freund** he wishes that this man was his teacher/father/friend; **was wünschst du dir?** what do you want?, what would you like?; (*im Märchen*) what is your wish?; **du darfst dir was (zum Essen) ~** you can say what you'd like (to eat); **du darfst dir etwas ~** (= *Wunsch frei haben*) you can make a wish; (*im Märchen auch*) I'll give you a wish; **sie haben alles, was man sich** (*dat*) **nur ~ kann** they have everything you could possibly wish for; **man hätte es sich** (*dat*) **nicht besser ~ können** you couldn't have wished for anything better **b** **jdm etw ~** to wish sb sth; **jdm einen guten Morgen ~** to wish sb good morning; **wir ~ dir gute Besserung/eine gute Reise** we hope you get well soon/have a pleasant journey; **wir ~ gute Fahrt** we hope you have a good journey,

we wish you a good journey; **jdm den Tod/die Pest an den Hals ~** (*fig inf*) to wish sb would die/drop dead (*inf*); **das würde ich meinem schlimmsten Feind nicht ~** I wouldn't wish that on my worst enemy **c** (= *ersehnen, hoffen*) to wish; **jdn fort/weit weg ~** to wish sb would go away/were far away; **es bleibt/wäre zu ~, dass ...** it is to be hoped that ...; **ich wünschte, ich hätte dich nie gesehen** I wish I'd never seen you **d** (= *begehren, verlangen*) to want; **was ~ Sie?** (*Diener*) yes, Sir/Madam?; (*in Geschäft*) what can I do for you?, can I help you?; (*in Restaurant*) what would you like?; **wen ~ Sie zu sprechen?** to whom would you like to speak?; **ich wünsche, dass du das machst** I want you to do that VI (= *begehren*) to wish; **Sie ~?** what can I do for you?; (*in Restaurant*) what would you like?; **ganz wie Sie ~** (just) as you wish or please or like; **zu ~/viel zu ~ übrig lassen** to leave something/a great deal to be desired VR **sich in eine andere Lage/weit weg ~** to wish one were in a different situation/far away

wün|schens|wert ADJ desirable

Wunsch-: **Wunsch|form** F (*Gram*) optative (mood); **wunsch|ge|mäß** ADJ desired; (= *erbeten*) requested; (= *geplant*) planned ADV as desired; (= *wie erbeten*) as requested; (= *wie geplant*) as planned; **Wunsch|kan|di|dat(in)** M(F) ideal candidate; **Wunsch|kind** NT planned child; **unser Töchterchen war ein ~** our little daughter was planned; **Wunsch|kon|zert** NT (*Rad*) musical request programme (*Brit*) or program (*US*); **Wunsch|lis|te** F = **Wunschzettel**; **wunsch|los** ADJ *Mensch* content(ed); *Glück* perfect ADV **~ glücklich** perfectly happy; **Wunsch|part|ner(in)** M(F) ideal partner; **Wunsch|satz** M (*Gram*) optative clause; **Wunsch|sen|dung** F (*Rad*) request programme (*Brit*) or program (*US*); **Wunsch|traum** M dream; (= *Illusion*) illusion; **das ist doch bloß ein ~** that's just a pipe dream; **Wunsch|vor|stel|lung** F ideal; **Wunsch|zet|tel** M wish list; **das steht schon lange auf meinem ~** (*fig*) I've wanted that for a long time

wupp (dich) [vʊp], **wupps** [vʊps] INTERJ whoomph

Wupp(dich) ['vʊp(dɪç)] M -s, *no pl* (*inf*) **mit einem ~** in a flash

wur|de pret von **werden**

Wür|de ['vʏrdə] F -, -n **a** *no pl* dignity; **(seine) ~ bewahren** to preserve one's dignity; **unter aller ~ sein** to be beneath contempt; **unter jds ~ sein** to be beneath sb or sb's dignity; **etw mit ~ tragen** to bear sth with dignity **b** (= *Auszeichnung*) honour (*Brit*), honor (*US*); (= *Titel*) title; (= *Amt*) rank; **~ bringt Bürde** (*Prov*) the burdens of office

wür|de|los ADJ undignified ADV **sich benehmen** undignified; **jdn ~ behandeln** to treat sb contemptuously; **~ um Gnade flehen** to beg pitifully for mercy; **sich ~ verhalten** to demean oneself

Wür|de|lo|sig|keit F -, *no pl* lack of dignity

Wür|den|trä|ger(in) M(F) dignitary

wür|de|voll ADJ dignified ADV **sich verhalten** with dignity

wür|dig ['vʏrdɪç] ADJ **a** (= *würdevoll*) dignified **b** (= *wert*) worthy; **jds/einer Sache ~/nicht ~ sein** to be worthy/unworthy of sb/sth; **eine ihm ~e Verabschiedung** a farewell worthy of him; **sich jds/einer Sache ~ erweisen** or **zeigen** to prove oneself to be worthy of sb/sth; **jdn einer Sache** (*gen*) **für ~ halten** or **befinden** (*geh*) to find sb worthy of sth ADV **sich verhalten** with dignity; *beerdigen* respectfully; **jdn behandeln** with respect; *begrüßen, empfangen* with great respect; *vertreten* worthily

wür|di|gen ['vʏrdɪgn] VT **a** (= *anerkennen*) to appreciate; (= *lobend erwähnen*) to acknowledge; (= *respektieren*) to respect; (= *ehren*) to pay tribute to; **etw gebührend** or **nach Gebühr/rich-**

tig ~ to appreciate sth properly/fully; **etw zu ~ wissen** to appreciate sth **b** (*geh*: = *für würdig befinden*) **jdn einer Sache** (*gen*) ~ to deem sb worthy of sth; **jdn eines/keines Blickes/Grußes** *etc* ~ to deign/not to deign to look at/greet *etc* sb

Wür|dig|keit F -, *no pl* **a** (= *Würde*) dignity **b** (= *Wert*) merit

Wür|di|gung ['vʏrdɪɡʊŋ] F -, -en **a** *no pl* (= *das Würdigen*) appreciation; (= *lobende Erwähnung*) acknowledgement; (= *Respektierung*) respect **b** (= *lobende Worte, Artikel*) appreciation **c** (= *Ehrung*) honour (*Brit*), honor (*US*); **die zahlreichen ~en der Gäste** the numerous tributes paid to the guests

Wurf [vʊrf] M -(e)s, ⸚e ['vʏrfə] **a** throw; (*beim Kegeln etc*) bowl; (*beim Baseball*) pitch; **drei ~ or Würfe zwei Euro** three goes *or* throws for two euros

b *no pl* (= *das Werfen*) throwing; **beim ~** when throwing; **zum ~ ansetzen/ausholen** to get ready to throw; **sich auf den ~ konzentrieren** to concentrate on throwing

c (*fig*: = *Erfolg*) success, hit (*inf*); **mit dem Film ist ihm ein großer ~ gelungen** this film is a great success *or* a big hit (*inf*) for him; **einen großen** *or* **glücklichen ~ tun** (= *Erfolg haben*) to be very successful *or* have great success; (= *Glück haben*) to have a stroke of luck **d** (*Zool*) litter; (= *das Gebären*) birth **e** (= *Faltenwurf*) fall; **einen eleganten ~ haben** to hang elegantly **f** (*Mil*: *von Bomben*) dropping

Wurf-: Wurf|an|ker M grappling hook; **Wurf|arm** M (*Sport*) throwing arm; **Wurf|bahn** F trajectory; **Wurf|dis|zip|lin** F (*Sport*) throwing discipline *or* event

Wür|fel ['vʏrfl] M -s, - **a** (*auch Math*) cube; **etw in ~ schneiden** to dice sth, to cut sth into cubes **b** (= *Spielwürfel*) dice, die (*form*); **die ~ sind gefallen** (*fig*) the die is cast; **~ spielen** to play at dice

Wür|fel-: Wür|fel|be|cher M shaker; **Wür|fel|brett** NT dice board; **Wür|fel|form** F cube shape; **~ haben** to be cube-shaped; **wür|fel|för|mig** ADJ cube-shaped, cubic (*esp Math*)

wür|fe|lig ['vʏrfəlɪç] ADJ cubic ADV **etw ~ schneiden** to cut sth into cubes

wür|feln ['vʏrfln] VI to throw, to have a throw; (= *Würfel spielen*) to play at dice; **hast du schon gewürfelt?** have you had your throw *or* go?; **um etw ~** to throw dice for sth VT **a Zahl** to throw **b** (= *in Würfel schneiden*) to dice, to cut into cubes → *auch* **gewürfelt**

Wür|fel-: Wür|fel|spiel NT (= *Partie*) game of dice; (= *Spielart*) dice; **beim ~** at dice; **Wür|fel|spie|ler(in)** M(F) dice player; **Wür|fel|zu|cker** M cube sugar

Wurf-: Wurf|ge|schoss ▲ NT projectile, missile; **Wurf|ham|mer** M (*Sport*) hammer; **Wurf|hand** F (*Sport*) throwing hand; **Wurf|kör|per** M (*Phys*) projectile; **Wurf|kraft** F (*Phys*) projectile force; (*Sport*) throwing strength; **wurf|kräf|tig** ADJ (*Sport*) strong-armed

würf|lig ['vʏrflɪç] ADJ, ADV = **würfelig**

Wurf-: Wurf|mal NT *pl* **-male** (*Baseball*) pitcher's mound; **Wurf|ma|schi|ne** F (*Mil Hist*) catapult; (*beim Tontaubenschießen*) trap; **Wurf|mes|ser** NT throwing knife; **Wurf|pa|ra|bel** F (*Phys*) trajectory (parabola); **Wurf|pfeil** M dart; **Wurf|ring** M quoit; **Wurf|schei|be** F (*Leichtathletik*) discus; **Wurf|sen|dung** F circular; **Reklame durch ~en** direct advertising; **Wurf|speer** M , **Wurf|spieß** M javelin; **Wurf|stern** M spiked metal disc thrown as a weapon; **Wurf|tau|be** F (*Sport*) clay pigeon; **Wurf|tau|ben|schie|ßen** NT (*Sport*) clay pigeon shooting; **Wurf|waf|fe** F missile; (= *Speer*) throwing spear; **Wurf|wei|te** F throwing range; (*von Geschütz*) mortar range; **Wurf|win|kel** M (*Sport*) throwing angle

Wür|ge-: Wür|ge|en|gel M Angel of Death; **Wür|ge|griff** M (*lit, fig*) stranglehold; **Wür|ge|mal** NT *pl* **-male** strangulation mark

wür|gen ['vʏrɡn] VT **jdn** to strangle, to throttle; (*fig*: *Angst*) to choke VI **a** (= *mühsam schlucken*) to choke; (*Schlange*) to gulp; **an etw** (*dat*) ~ (*lit*) to choke on sth; (*fig*) (*an Kritik*) to find sth hard to swallow; (*an Arbeit*) to struggle over sth **b** (*beim Erbrechen*) to retch; **ein Würgen im Hals spüren** to feel one is going to be sick VT *impers* **es würgte sie (im Hals** *etc*) she felt she was going to be sick; **mit Hängen und Würgen** by the skin of one's teeth

Würg|en|gel M Angel of Death

Wür|ger¹ ['vʏrɡɐ] M -s, - **a** (*poet*: = *der Tod*) death *no art* **b** (*Orn*) shrike

Wür|ger² ['vʏrɡɐ] M -s, -, **Wür|ge|rin** [-ərɪn] F -, -nen strangler

Würg|schrau|be F garrotte

Wurm [vʊrm] M -(e)s, ⸚er ['vʏrmɐ] **a** worm; (= *Made*) maggot; (*poet* = *Schlange*) snake; (*Myth*: = *Lindwurm*) dragon; **der (nagende) ~ des schlechten Gewissens** the (gnawing) pangs of a guilty conscience; **da ist** *or* **steckt** *or* **sitzt der ~ drin** (*fig inf*) there's something wrong somewhere; (= *seltsam*) there's something odd about it; (= *verdächtig*) there's something fishy about it (*inf*) → **winden¹** VR **b** *auch* NT (*inf*: = *Kind*) (little) mite **c** (*Comput*) worm

Würm|chen ['vʏrmçən] NT -s, - *dim von* **Wurm** little worm; (*inf*: = *Kind*) (poor) little mite *or* thing

wur|men ['vʊrmən] VT *impers* (*inf*) to rankle with

Wurm-: Wurm|fort|satz M (*Anat*) vermiform appendix; **Wurm|fraß** M , *no pl* worm damage

wur|mig ['vʊrmɪç] ADJ worm-eaten; (= *madig*) *Obst* maggoty

Wurm-: Wurm|krank|heit F worm disorder, helminthiasis (*spec*); **Wurm|kur** F worming treatment; **die Katze braucht eine ~** the cat needs to be wormed; **eine ~ machen** to have worm treatment; **Wurm|loch** NT wormhole; **Wurm|mit|tel** NT vermicide, vermifuge; **wurm|sti|chig** [-ʃtɪçɪç] ADJ *Holz* full of wormholes; (= *madig auch*) *Obst* maggoty

Wurscht *etc* [vʊrʃt] (*inf*) = **Wurst** *etc*

Wurst [vʊrst] F -, ⸚e ['vʏrstə] sausage; (= *Salami*) salami; (= *wurstförmiges Gebilde*) roll, sausage; (*inf*: = *Kot von Hund*) dog's mess (*inf*); **jetzt geht es um die ~** (*fig inf*) the moment of truth has come (*inf*); **mit der ~ nach der Speckseite** *or* **nach dem Schinken werfen** (*prov*) to cast a sprat to catch a mackerel; **es ist jdm (vollkommen) ~** *or* **Wurscht** (*inf*) it's all the same to sb

---

WURST

German-speaking countries are famous for their wide variety of Wurst. It is eaten cold in slices, for example Zervelatwurst, or warm, for example Wiener Würstchen, Frankfurter Würstchen or Bratwurst. Less well known abroad are the various kinds of Streichwurst (eg Teewurst and Leberwurst): they are made from sausage that has been smoked and then chopped up so finely that it can be spread on bread. Bavarian Leberkäse is a seasoned meat mixture in the form of an oven-baked loaf, which can be bought warm or cold, in thick or thin slices.

Wurst-: Wurst|auf|schnitt M → **Wurst** assortment of sliced sausage/salami; **Wurst|brot** NT → **Wurst** open sausage/salami sandwich; (*zusammengeklappt*) sausage/salami sandwich; **Wurst|brü|he** F sausage stock

Würst|chen ['vʏrstçən] NT -s, - **a** *dim von* **Wurst** small sausage; **heiße** *or* **warme ~** hot sausages; (*in Brötchen*) ≈ hot dogs; **Frankfurter/Wiener ~** frankfurters/wienies **b** (*pej*: *Mensch*) squirt (*inf*), nobody; **ein armes ~** (*fig*) a poor soul

Würst|chen|bu|de F , **Würst|chen|stand** M sausage stand, ≈ hot-dog stand

wurst|egal ADJ (*inf*) **das ist mir ~** I couldn't care less (about that)

Würs|tel ['vʊrstl] M -s, - (*Aus*) = **Hanswurst**

Würs|tel ['vʏrstl] NT -s, - (*dial*) = **Würstchen**

wurs|te|lei [vʊrstə'laɪ] F -, -en (*inf*) muddle

wurs|teln ['vʊrstln] VI (*inf*) to muddle along; **sich durchs Leben/die Schule ~** to muddle (one's way) through life/school

wurs|ten ['vʊrstn] VI to make sausages

Wurs|ter ['vʊrstɐ] M -s, -, **Wurs|te|rin** [-ərɪn] F -, -nen (*S Ger*) butcher

Wurs|te|rei [vʊrstə'raɪ] F -, -en (*S Ger*) butcher('s shop)

Wurst|fin|ger PL (*pej inf*) podgy (*Brit*) *or* pudgy fingers *pl*

wurs|tig ['vʊrstɪç] ADJ (*inf*) devil-may-care *attr*, couldn't-care-less *attr* (*inf*); **sei doch nicht so ~!** don't be such a wet blanket! (*inf*)

Wurs|tig|keit F -, *no pl* (*inf*) devil-may-care *or* couldn't-care-less (*inf*) attitude

Wurst-: Wurst|kon|ser|ve F tinned (*Brit*) *or* canned sausages; **Wurst|ma|xe** [-maksə] M -s, -n (*inf*) man who sells sausages; ≈ hot-dog man (*inf*); **Wurst|plat|te** F platter of cold cuts; **Wurst|ring** M sausage ring; **Wurst|sa|lat** M sausage salad; **Wurst|schei|be** F slice of sausage; **Wurst|ver|gif|tung** F sausage poisoning; **Wurst|wa|ren** PL sausages *pl*; **Wurst|zip|fel** M sausage end

Würt|tem|berg ['vʏrtəmbɛrk] NT -s Württemberg

Würt|tem|ber|ger¹ ['vʏrtəmbɛrɡɐ] M -s, - (= *Wein*) Württemberg wine

Würt|tem|ber|ger² ['vʏrtəmbɛrɡɐ] M -s, -, **Würt|tem|ber|ge|rin** [-ərɪn] F -, -nen native of Württemberg; (*Einwohner*) inhabitant of Württemberg

würt|tem|ber|gisch ['vʏrtəmbɛrɡɪʃ] ADJ Württembergian

Wür|ze ['vʏrtsə] F -, -n **a** (= *Gewürz*) seasoning, spice; (= *Aroma*) aroma; (*fig*: = *Reiz*) spice; **das gibt dem Leben die ~** that adds spice to life → **Kürze b** (*von Bier*) wort

Wur|zel ['vʊrtsl] F -, -n **a** (*lit, fig*) root; (= *Handwurzel*) wrist; (= *Fußwurzel*) ankle; **etw mit der ~ ausreißen** to pull sth out by the root; **etw mit der ~ ausrotten** (*fig*) to eradicate sth; **das Übel an der ~ packen** to tackle the root of the problem; **~n schlagen** (*lit*) to root; (*fig*) (= *sich einleben*) to put down roots; (= *an einem Ort hängen bleiben*) to grow roots; **die ~ Jesse** (*Bibl*) the stem of Jesse **b** (*Math*) root; **~n ziehen** to find the roots; **die ~ aus einer Zahl ziehen** to find the root of a number; **(die) ~ aus 4 ist 2** the square root of 4 is 2; **die vierte ~ aus 16 ist 2** the fourth root of 16 is 2; **unter/außerhalb der ~ stehen** to be inside/outside the radical sign **c** (*N Ger*: = *Möhre*) carrot

Wur|zel-: Wur|zel|bal|len M (*Hort*) rootball; **Wur|zel|be|hand|lung** F (*von Zahn*) root treatment; **Wur|zel|bil|dung** F rooting; **Wur|zel|bürs|te** F (coarse) scrubbing brush

Wür|zel|chen ['vʏrtslçən] NT -s, - *dim von* **Wurzel** little root, rootlet

Wur|zel-: Wur|zel|ent|zün|dung F (*an Zahn*) inflammation of the root/roots; **Wur|zel|ex|po|nent** M (*Math*) radical index; **Wur|zel|ge|mü|se** NT root vegetables *pl*; **Wur|zel|knol|le** F (*Bot*) root tuber; **wur|zel|los** ADJ *Pflanze* without roots; (*fig auch*) rootless; **Wur|zel|mann** M *pl* **-männer** , **Wur|zel|männ|chen** NT (= *Alraune*) mandrake

wur|zeln ['vʊrtsln] VI **a** (*lit, fig*) to be rooted; **in etw** (*dat*) ~ (*fig*) to be rooted in sth; (= *verursacht sein*) to have its/their roots in sth **b** (*rare*: = *Wurzeln schlagen*) to (take) root

---

Wur|zel-: Wur|zel|re|sek|ti|on [-rezɛktsioːn] F -, -en (Zahnmedizin) root resection; **Wur|zel|sepp** M (inf) country bumpkin (inf); **Wur|zel|sil|be** F (Ling) root syllable; **Wur|zel|stock** M (Bot) rhizome; **Wur|zel|ver|zeich|nis** NT (Comput) root directory; **Wur|zel|werk** NT , no pl **a** root system, roots pl **b** (Cook) flavouring (Brit) or flavoring (US) greens pl; **Wur|zel|zei|chen** NT (Math) radical sign; **Wur|zel|zie|hen** NT -s, no pl (Math) root extraction

wur|zen ['vʊrtsn] VTI (Aus inf) to get everything one can (jdn out of sb)

wür|zen ['vʏrtsn] VT to season; (fig) to add spice to; **eine Geschichte mit etw ~** to season a story with sth

Wur|ze|rei [vʊrtsə'rai] F -, -en (Aus inf) robbery (inf)

wür|zig ['vʏrtsɪç] ADJ Speise tasty; (= scharf) spicy; Zigaretten, Tabak, Geruch etc aromatic; Luft fragrant, tangy; Wein, Bier full-bodied **ADV** ~ schmecken to be spicy; (Käse) to have a sharp taste; (Wein) to have a full-bodied taste; **~ rie|chen** to smell spicy

Würz-: Würz|mi|schung F mixed spices pl; **Würz|nel|ke** F clove; **Würz|stoff** M flavouring (Brit), flavoring (US)

wusch[1] pret von **waschen**

wusch[2] [vuːʃ] INTERJ (Aus) (= erstaunt) whoops; (= schnell) zoom

Wu|schel|haar NT (inf) mop of curly hair

wu|sche|lig ['vʊʃəlɪç] ADJ (inf) Tier shaggy; Haare fuzzy (inf)

Wu|schel|kopf M **a** (= Haare) mop of curly hair, fuzz (inf) **b** (= Mensch) fuzzy head (inf)

wusch|lig ['vʊʃlɪç] ADJ = wuschelig

wu|se|lig ['vuːzəlɪç] ADJ (dial) (= lebhaft) lively; (= unruhig) fidgety; (= bewegt) busy, bustling; Ameisenhaufen teeming; **das ~e Treiben** the hustle and bustle

wu|seln ['vuːzln] VI (dial) **a** (= belebt sein) to be teeming **b** aux sein (= sich schnell bewegen) to scurry

wuss|te ▲ pret von **wissen**

Wust [vuːst] M -(e)s, no pl (inf) (= Durcheinander) jumble; (= Menge) pile; (= unordentlicher Haufen) heap; (= Kram, Gerümpel) junk (inf); **dieser ~ von Kleidern** this pile of clothes

wüst [vyːst] ADJ **a** (= öde) desert attr, waste, desolate; **die Erde war ~ und leer** (Bibl) the earth was without form, and void (Bibl) **b** (= unordentlich) wild, chaotic; Aussehen, Haar wild **c** (= ausschweifend) wild **d** (= rüde) Beschimpfung, Beleidigung etc vile **e** (= arg) terrible, awful; Übertreibung terrible, wild **ADV** ~ aussehen to look a real mess; **~ feiern** to have a wild party; **jdn ~ beschimpfen** to use vile language to sb; **~ fluchen** to swear vilely; **jdn ~ zurichten** to beat sb to a pulp

Wüs|te ['vyːstə] F -, -n (Geog) desert; (= Ödland) waste, wilderness (liter); (fig) waste(land), wilderness, desert; **die ~ Gobi** the Gobi Desert; **jdn in die ~ schicken** (fig) to send sb packing (inf)

wüs|ten ['vyːstn] VI (inf) **mit etw ~** to squander or waste sth; **mit seiner Gesundheit/seinen Kräften ~** to ruin one's health/strength

Wüs|te|nei [vyːstə'nai] F -, -en **a** (= öde Gegend) wasteland, desert **b** (fig: = wildes Durcheinander) chaos

Wüs|ten-: Wüs|ten|fuchs M desert fox; **Wüs|ten|kli|ma** NT desert climate; **Wüs|ten|kö|nig** M (poet) king of the desert (poet); **Wüs|ten|land|schaft** F desert landscape; **Wüs|ten|sand** M desert sand; **Wüs|ten|schiff** NT (poet) ship of the desert (poet), camel; **Wüs|ten|step|pe** F steppe

Wüst|ling ['vyːstlɪŋ] M -s, -e (dated, iro) lecher

Wüs|tung ['vyːstʊŋ] F -, -en deserted settlement

Wut [vuːt] F -, no pl **a** (= Zorn, Raserei) rage, fury; (fig: der Elemente) fury; **vor ~ heulen** to yell with rage; **(auf jdn/etw) eine ~ haben** to be furious (with sb/sth), to be mad (at sb/sth); **eine ~ im Bauch haben** (inf) to be seething, to be hopping mad (inf); **eine ~ haben/kriegen** or **bekommen** to be in/get into a rage; **in ~ geraten, von**

der ~ gepackt werden to fly into a rage; **jdn in ~ bringen** or **versetzen** to infuriate sb → **schäumen** VI, **kochen** VI **b** (= Verbissenheit) frenzy; **mit einer wahren ~** as if possessed, like crazy (inf)

Wut-: Wut|an|fall M fit of rage; (esp von Kind) tantrum; **Wut|aus|bruch** M outburst of rage or fury; (esp von Kind) tantrum

wü|ten ['vyːtn] VI (lit, fig) (= toben) to rage; (= zerstörerisch hausen) to cause havoc; (verbal) to storm (gegen at); (Menge) to riot

wü|tend ['vyːtnt] ADJ furious, enraged; Tier enraged; Menge angry; Kampf, Elemente raging; (fig) Schmerz, Hass fierce; Proteste fierce, angry; **auf jdn/etw** (acc) ~ sein to be mad at sb/sth; **über jdn/etw** (acc) ~ sein to be furious about sb/sth **ADV** in (a) rage, angrily; **~ raste der Stier auf ihn zu** the enraged bull raced toward(s) him

wut-: wut|ent|brannt [-lɛntbrant] ADJ furious, enraged **ADV** in a fury or rage; **wut|er|füllt** [-lɛɐfʏlt] ADJ filled or seething with rage, furious **ADV** in a blind rage

Wü|te|rich ['vyːtərɪç] M -s, -e brute

Wut-: Wut|ge|heul NT howl of fury; **Wut|ge|schrei** NT cries pl of rage

wutsch [vʊtʃ] INTERJ whoosh

wut|schäu|mend ADJ, ADV foaming with rage

wut|schen ['vʊtʃn] VI aux sein (inf) to whoosh (inf); (= schnell verschwinden) to whiz (inf), to zoom (inf)

Wut-: wut|schnau|bend ADJ, ADV snorting with rage; **Wut|schrei** M yell of rage; **wut|ver|zerrt** [-fɛɐtsɛrt] ADJ distorted with rage

Wutz [vʊts] F -, -en (pej dial) pig (inf)

Wu|zerl ['vuːtsɛl] NT -s, -(n) (Aus) **a** (= Kind) porker (inf) **b** (= Fussel) piece of fluff

wu|zerl|dick ADJ (Aus) porky (inf)

Wwe. abbr von **Witwe**

WWW [veːveː'veː] NT -, no pl (Comput) abbr von **World Wide Web** WWW

WWW-Sei|te F (Comput) WWW page

Wz abbr von **Warenzeichen**

X

X, x [ɪks] NT -, - X, x; **Herr X** Mr X; **jdm ein X für ein U vormachen** to put one over on sb (*inf*); **er lässt sich kein X für ein U vormachen** he's not easily fooled

x-Ach|se ['ɪks-] F x-axis

Xan|thip|pe [ksan'tɪpə] F -, -n (*fig inf*) shrew

X-Bei|ne ['ɪks-] PL knock-knees *pl*; **~ haben** to be knock-kneed

x-bei|nig ▲ ['ɪks-], **X-bei|nig** ADJ knock-kneed

x-be|lie|big [ɪks-] ADJ any old (*inf*); **wir können uns an einem ~en Ort treffen** we can meet anywhere you like ADV as you like

X-Chro|mo|som ['ɪks-] NT X-chromosome

Xe|non ['kse:nɔn] NT -s, *no pl* (*abbr* **Xe**) xenon

xe|no|phil [kseno'fi:l] ADJ (*geh*) xenophile (*form*)

Xe|no|phi|lie [ksenofi'li:] F -, *no pl* (*geh*) xenophilia (*form*)

xe|no|phob [kseno'fo:p] ADJ (*geh*) xenophobic

Xe|no|pho|bie [ksenofo'bi:] F , *no pl* (*geh*) xenophobia

Xe|ro|gra|fie ▲ [kserogra'fi:] F -, -n [-'fi:ən] Xerox® (copy)

Xe|ro|ko|pie [kseroko'pi:] F Xerox® (copy)

xe|ro|ko|pie|ren [kseroko'pi:rən] *ptp* **xerokopiert** VTI *insep* to Xerox®

x-fach ['ɪks-] ADJ **die ~e Menge** (*Math*) n times the amount; **trotz ~er Ermahnungen** (*inf*) in spite of umpteen *or* n warnings (*inf*) ADV so many times

x-för|mig ▲ ['ɪks-], **X-för|mig** ADJ X-shaped ADV *angeordnet* in an X; **die Fäden X-förmig verkreuzen** to cross the threads to form an X

x-mal ['ɪksma:l] ADV (*inf*) n (number of) times (*inf*), umpteen times (*inf*)

x-ma|lig ['ɪksma:lɪç] ADJ (*inf*) n number of (*inf*), umpteen (*inf*); **wenn ein ~er Weltmeister ...** when somebody who has been world champion n (number of) times *or* umpteen times ...

X-Strah|len ['ɪks-] PL (*dated*) X-rays *pl*

x-te(r, s) ['ɪkstə] ADJ (*Math*) nth; (*inf*) nth (*inf*), umpteenth (*inf*); **zum ~n Mal(e)** for the nth *or* umpteenth time (*inf*)

Xy|lo|fon ▲ [ksylo'fo:n] NT -s, -e, **Xy|lo|phon** NT -s, -e xylophone

Y

Y, y ['ʏpsilɔn] NT **-, -** Y, y

y-Ach|se ['ʏpsilɔn-] F y-axis

Yacht [jaxt] F **-, -en** yacht

Yak [jak] M **-s, -s** yak

Ya|ku|za [jaˈkuːza] F **-,** *no pl* Yakuza, Japanese mafia

Yams|wur|zel ['jams-] F yam

Yan|kee ['jɛŋki] M **-s, -s** (*pej*) Yankee, Yank

Yard [jaːɐt] NT **-s, -s** yard

Y-Chro|mo|som ['ʏpsilɔn-] NT Y-chromosome

Yen [jɛn] M **-(s), -(s)** yen

Ye|ti ['jeːti] M **-s, -s** Yeti, abominable snowman

Yo|ga ['joːga] M OR NT **-(s)** yoga

Yo|gi ['joːgi] M **-s, -s** yogi

Yp|si|lon ['ʏpsilɔn] NT **-(s), -s** y; (= *griechischer Buchstabe*) upsilon

Y|sop ['iːzɔp] M **-s, -e** (*Bot*) hyssop

Y|tong® ['yːtɔŋ] M **-s, -s** breeze block (*Brit*), cinder block (*US*)

Yt|ter|bi|um [ʏˈtɛrbiʊm] NT **-s,** *no pl* (*abbr* **Yb**) ytterbium

Ytt|ri|um ['ʏtrium] NT **-s,** *no pl* (*abbr* **Y**) yttrium

Yuc|ca ['jʊka] F **-, -s** yucca

Yup|pie ['jʊpiː, 'japiː] M **-s,-s** yuppie

Z

Z, z [tsɛt] NT **-,** - Z, z

z. A. *abbr von* **zur Ansicht** on approval *von* **zur Anstellung** on probation

zack [tsak] INTERJ (*inf*) pow, zap (*inf*); **~, ~!** chop-chop! (*inf*); **sei nicht so langsam, mach mal ein bisschen ~, ~** don't be so slow, get a move on (*inf*); **bei uns muss alles ~, ~ gehen** we have to do everything chop-chop (*inf*); **die Leute waren so gut gedrillt, die ganze Sache lief ~, ~** the people were drilled so well that the whole thing went off just like that (*inf*)

Zack [tsak] M **-s,** *no pl* (*inf*) **auf ~ bringen** to knock into shape (*inf*); **auf ~ sein** to be on the ball (*inf*)

Za|cke ['tsakə] F **-, -n** point; (*von Gabel*) prong; (*von Kamm*) tooth; (= *Bergzacke*) jagged peak; (= *Auszackung*) indentation; (*von Fieberkurve etc*) peak; (*inf*: = *Nase*) conk (*inf*), beak (*inf*) → **Krone b**

za|cken ['tsakn] VT to serrate; *Kleid, Saum, Papier* to pink → *auch* **gezackt**

Za|cken ['tsakn] M **-s, - = Zacke**

Za|cken-: Za|cken|li|nie F jagged line; (= *Zickzack*) zigzag (line); **Za|cken|lit|ze** F ricrac braid

za|ckig ['tsakıç] ADJ **a** (= *gezackt*) jagged; *Stern* pointed **b** (*inf*) *Soldat, Bursche* smart; *Tempo, Musik* brisk; *Team, Manager etc* dynamic, zippy (*inf*) ADV **a** (= *gezackt*) **~ schreiben** to write a very angular hand **b** (*inf*: = *schnell*) *laufen* briskly; *fahren, bedienen* quickly; **bring mir meine Hausschuhe, aber ein bisschen ~!** fetch me my slippers, and make it snappy! (*inf*)

zag [tsaːk] ADJ (*liter*) = **zaghaft**

za|gen ['tsaːgn] VI (*liter*) to be apprehensive, to hesitate → **Zittern a**

zag|haft ADJ timid ADV timidly

Zag|haf|tig|keit ['tsaːkhaftıçkait] F **-,** *no pl* timidity

zäh [tsɛː] ADJ *Fleisch, Mensch, Verhandlungen* tough; (= *dickflüssig*) glutinous; (= *schleppend*) *Verkehr etc* slow-moving; (= *ausdauernd*) dogged, tenacious; **ein ~es Leben haben** (*lit*: *Mensch, Tier*) to have a tenacious hold on life; (*fig*) to die hard; **mit ~em Fleiß** doggedly, with dogged application ADV *verhandeln* tenaciously; *sich widersetzen* doggedly; *fließen* slowly

Zä|heit △ ['tsɛːhait] F **-,** *no pl* → **Zähheit**

zäh|flüs|sig ADJ thick, viscous; *Verkehr, Verhandlung* slow-moving

Zäh|flüs|sig|keit F thickness, viscosity; **die ~ des Verkehrs** the slow-moving traffic

Zäh|heit ▲ ['tsɛːhait] F **-,** *no pl* toughness

Zä|hig|keit ['tsɛːıçkait] F **-,** *no pl* toughness; (= *Dickflüssigkeit*) glutinous nature; (= *Ausdauer*) doggedness, tenacity

Zahl [tsaːl] F **-, -en** (*Math, Gram*) number; (= *Verkaufszahl, Maßangabe, bei Geldmengen etc auch*) figure; (= *Ziffer auch*) numeral, figure; **~en nennen** to give figures; **wie waren die ~en im letzten Jahr?** what did the figures look like last year?; **sie hat ein gutes Gedächtnis für ~en** she has a good memory for figures *or* numbers; **eine fünfstellige ~** a five-figure number; **der ~**

nach numerically; **gut mit ~en umgehen können** to be good with figures, to be numerate; **die ~en stimmen nicht** the figures don't add up *or* tally; **~ oder Wappen** heads or tails; **100 an der ~** (*old*) 100 in number; **in großer ~** in large *or* great numbers; **die ~ ist voll** the numbers are complete; **in voller ~** in full number; **der Aufsichtsrat war in voller ~ versammelt** there was a full turnout for the meeting of the board; **ohne ~** (*geh*) without number; **Leiden/Wonnen ohne ~** (*poet*) countless tribulations/joys

zahl|bar ADJ payable (*an* +*acc* to); **~ bei Lieferung** *or* **nach Erhalt** payable on delivery *or* receipt, to be paid for on delivery *or* receipt

zähl|bar ADJ countable

Zahl|brett NT , **Zähl|brett** NT money tray

zäh|le|big [-leːbıç] ADJ hardy, tough; (*fig*) Gerücht, Vorurteil persistent

Zah|le|mann ['tsaːləman] M , *no pl* **~ und Söhne** (*inf hum*) (it's) paying-up time

zah|len ['tsaːlən] VI to pay; **Herr Ober, (bitte) ~!** waiter, the bill (*esp Brit*) *or* check (*US*) please; **dort zahlt man gut/schlecht** the pay there is good/bad, they pay well/badly; **wenn er nicht bald zahlt, dann ...** if he doesn't pay up soon, then ... VT **a** (= *bezahlen*) to pay; **was habe ich (Ihnen) zu ~?** what do I owe you?; **einen hohen Preis ~** (*lit, fig*) to pay a high price; **ich zahle dir ein Bier** I'll buy you a beer; **ich zahle dir den Flug** I'll pay for your flight; **ich zahle dir das Kino** I'll pay for you to go to the cinema; **lass mal, ich zahls** no no, I'll pay *or* it's on me *or* it's my treat (*inf*)

zäh|len ['tsɛːlən] VI **a** (= *zahlenmäßig erfassen*) to count; **bis hundert ~** to count (up) to a hundred

b (= *gehören*) **zu einer Gruppe/Menge ~** to be one of a group/set; **er zählt zu den besten Schriftstellern unserer Zeit** he ranks as one of the best authors of our time; **zu welcher Sprachengruppe zählt Gälisch?** to which language group does Gaelic belong?

c (= *wichtig sein*) to matter; **es zählt nicht, ob/ dass ...** it doesn't matter if *or* whether/that ...

d (= *rechnen mit*) **auf jdn/etw ~** to count *or* rely on sb/sth

e (= *gelten*) to count; **schon eine Stunde pro Woche zählt als Teilzeitjob** working just one hour per week counts as a part-time job

VT **a** (= *zahlenmäßig erfassen*) to count; **seine Tage sind gezählt** his days are numbered

b (= *zahlenmäßig betragen*) to have; **die Stadt zählt 2 Millionen Einwohner** the town has two million inhabitants; **Stanford zählt 12.000 Studenten** Stanford numbers *or* has 12,000 students

c (= *dazurechnen*) **jdn/sich zu einer Gruppe ~** to regard sb/oneself as part of a group, to number *or* count sb/oneself among a group

d (*geh*) **sie zählt 27 Jahre** she is 27 years old

e (= *wert sein*) to count; **bei diesem Spiel zählt der König 5 Punkte** in this game the king counts as 5 points

Zäh|len-: Zäh|len|ak|ro|ba|tik F (*inf*) juggling with statistics *or* figures, statistical sleight of hand; **Zah|len|an|ga|be** F figure; **ich kann**

keine genauen **~en machen** I can't give *or* quote any precise figures; **Zah|len|bei|spiel** NT numerical example; **Zah|len|dre|her** M transposed figures *pl*; **Zah|len|fol|ge** F order of numbers; **Zah|len|ge|dächt|nis** NT memory for numbers; **Zah|len|kom|bi|na|ti|on** F number combination, combination (of numbers); **Zah|len|leh|re** F arithmetic; **Zah|len-lot|te|rie** F , **Zah|len|lot|to** NT National Lottery; (**im**) **Zahlenlotto spielen** to do the National Lottery; **zah|len|mä|ßig** ADJ numerical ADV **a** (= *der Anzahl nach*) **~ überlegen sein** to be greater in number; **~ schwach/unbedeutend** small in number; **~ stark** large in number; **Frauen sind ~ stärker vertreten** there's a greater number of women **b** (= *in Zahlen*) in figures, numerically; **etw ~ ausdrücken** to express sth in figures; **Zah|len|ma|te|ri|al** NT figures *pl*; **Zah|len|mys|tik** F number mysticism; (*Astrol*) numerology; **Zah|len|rät|sel** NT number *or* numerical puzzle; **Zah|len|rei|he** F sequence of numbers; **Zah|len|schloss** ▲ NT combination lock; **Zah|len|sinn** M , *no pl* head for figures; **Zah|len|sym|bo|lik** F number symbolism; **Zah|len|sys|tem** NT numerical system; **Zah|len|the|o|rie** F (*Math*) theory of numbers, number theory; **Zah|len|to|to** M = **Toto**; **Zah|len|ver|hält|nis** NT (numerical) ratio; **Zah|len|ver|rie|ge|lung** [-fɛɛri:gəlʊŋ] F **, -en** (*Comput*) numbers lock; **Zah|len|wert** M numerical value; (*auf Messgeräten*) (numerical) reading; **welche ~e hat die Analyse ergeben?** what figures did the analysis give?; **die ~e der beiden Versuche** the figures yielded by the two experiments

Zah|ler ['tsaːlɐ] M **-s, -**, **Zah|le|rin** [-ərın] F **-, -nen** payer

Zäh|ler ['tsɛːlɐ] M **-s, -** **a** (*Math*) numerator **b** (= *Messgerät*) meter

Zäh|ler|ab|le|sung F meter reading

Zäh|ler|stand M meter reading

Zahl-: Zahl|gren|ze F fare stage; **Zahl|kar|te** F giro transfer form; **Zahl|kell|ner(in)** M(F) *waiter/waitress who presents the bill and collects payment*; **zahl|los** ADJ countless, innumerable

Zähl|maß NT numerical measure, unit of measurement

Zahl-: Zahl|meis|ter(in) M(F) (*Naut*) purser; (*Mil*) paymaster; **Zahl|mut|ter** F *pl* -mütter mother supporting a child; **zahl|reich** ADJ numerous; **wir hatten mit einer ~eren Beteiligung gerechnet** we had expected more participants ADV numerously; **die Veranstaltung war ~ besucht** the event was (very) well attended; **Zahl|stel|le** F payments office; **Zahl|tag** M payday

Zah|lung ['tsaːlʊŋ] F **-, -en** payment; **eine einmalige ~ leisten** to make a lump-sum payment; **in ~ nehmen** to take in part exchange, to take as a trade-in; **in ~ geben** to trade in, to give in part exchange; **gegen eine ~ von 500 Dollar erhalten Sie ...** on payment of 500 dollars you will receive ...

Zäh|lung ['tsɛːlʊŋ] F **-, -en** count; (= *Volkszählung*) census

Zah|lungs-: Zah|lungs|ab|kom|men NT payments agreement; **Zah|lungs|an|wei|sung** F giro transfer order (Brit), money transfer order (US); **Zah|lungs|art** F method or mode of payment; **Zah|lungs|auf|for|de|rung** F request for payment; **Zah|lungs|auf|schub** M extension (of credit), moratorium (Jur); **Zah|lungs|auf|trag** M payment order; **Zah|lungs|be|din|gun|gen** PL terms pl (of payment); **erleichterte ~** easy terms; **Zah|lungs|be|fehl** M order to pay; **Zah|lungs|bi|lanz** F balance of payments; **Zah|lungs|emp|fän|ger(in)** M(F) payee; **Zah|lungs|er|leich|te|rung** F more convenient method of payment; **~en** easy terms; **zah|lungs|fä|hig** ADJ able to pay; Firma solvent; **Zah|lungs|fä|hig|keit** F ability to pay; (von Firma) solvency; **Zah|lungs|frist** F time or period allowed for payment; **Zah|lungs|kraft** F , no pl **a** (Econ) solvency, financial resources pl; (= Wohlstand) wealth **b** (einer Währung) **~ haben** to be legal tender; **zah|lungs|kräf|tig** ADJ wealthy; **Zah|lungs|mit|tel** NT means sing of payment; (= Münzen, Banknoten) currency; **gesetzliches ~** legal tender; **Zah|lungs|mo|dus** M method of payment; **Zah|lungs|mo|ral** F payment practice; **eine gute/schlechte ~ haben** to be a good/bad payer; **zah|lungs|pflich|tig** [-pflɪçtɪç] ADJ obliged to pay; **Zah|lungs|rück|stand** M arrears pl, backlog of payments; **Zah|lungs|schwie|rig|kei|ten** PL financial difficulties pl; **Zah|lungs|sys|tem** NT method of payment; **Zah|lungs|ter|min** M date for payment; **zah|lungs|un|fä|hig** ADJ unable to pay; Firma insolvent; **Zah|lungs|un|fä|hig|keit** F inability to pay; (von Firma) insolvency; **zah|lungs|un|wil|lig** ADJ unwilling to pay; **Zah|lungs|ver|kehr** M payments pl, payment transactions pl; **Zah|lungs|ver|pflich|tung** F obligation or liability to pay; **Zah|lungs|ver|zug** M default, arrears pl; **Zah|lungs|wei|se** F mode or method of payment; **Zah|lungs|ziel** NT (Comm) period allowed for payment

Zahl|va|ter M father supporting a child

Zähl|wei|se F **a** (= Art zu zählen) way of counting; **nach meiner ~** by my reckoning **b** (= Zahlensystem) numbering or enumeration system

Zähl|werk NT counter

Zahl-: Zahl|wort NT pl -wörter numeral; **Zahl|zei|chen** NT numerical symbol

zahm [tsaːm] ADJ (lit, fig) tame; **er ist schon ~er geworden** (inf) he has calmed down a bit (inf), he's a bit tamer now (inf)

zähm|bar ADJ tam(e)able

zäh|men ['tsɛːmən] VT to tame; (fig) Leidenschaft, Bedürfnisse to control

Zäh|mung F -, (rare) -en taming

Zahn [tsaːn] M -(e)s, -̈e ['tsɛːnə] **a** (Anat, = Zacke) tooth; (von Briefmarke) perforation; (= Radzahn) cog, tooth; **künstliche or falsche Zähne** false teeth pl; **Zähne bekommen or kriegen** (inf) to cut one's teeth; **die ersten Zähne** one's milk teeth; **die zweiten Zähne** one's second set of teeth; **die dritten Zähne** (hum) false teeth; **diese Portion reicht or ist für den hohlen ~** (inf) that's hardly enough to satisfy a mouse (inf); **der ~ der Zeit** the ravages pl of time; **ihm tut kein ~ mehr weh** (inf) he's gone to join his ancestors; **die Zähne zeigen** (Tier) to bare its teeth; (fig inf) to show one's teeth; **jdm einen ~ ziehen** (lit) to pull a tooth out, to extract a tooth; (fig) to put an idea out of sb's head; **ich muss mir einen ~ ziehen lassen** I've got to have a tooth out or extracted; **den ~ kannst du dir ruhig ziehen lassen!** (fig inf) you can put that idea right out of your head!; **jdm auf den ~ fühlen** (= aushorchen) to sound sb out; (= streng befragen) to grill sb, to give sb a grilling; **etw mit Zähnen und Klauen verteidigen** to defend sth tooth and nail → **bewaffnet, ausbeißen**

b (inf: = Geschwindigkeit) **einen ~ draufhaben** to be going like the clappers (inf); **mit einem un-**heimlichen ~ at an incredible lick (inf) → **zulegen** VT c

Zahn-: Zahn|arzt M , **Zahn|ärz|tin** F dentist; **Zahn|arzt|hel|fer(in)** M(F) dental nurse; **zahn|ärzt|lich** ADJ dental; **sich in ~e Behandlung begeben** (form) to have dental treatment; **~er Helfer, ~e Helferin** (form) dental nurse ADV by a dentist; **sich ~ behandeln lassen** to go to the dentist; **Zahn|arzt|pra|xis** F dental practice or surgery; **Zahn|be|hand|lung** F dental treatment; **Zahn|be|lag** M film on the teeth; **Zahn|bett** NT socket (of a/the tooth); **Zahn|bürs|te** F toothbrush; **Zahn|creme** F toothpaste

Zäh|ne-: Zäh|ne|flet|schen NT -s, no pl baring of teeth, snarling; **zäh|ne|flet|schend** ADJ attr ADV snarling; **Zäh|ne|klap|pern** NT -s, no pl chattering of teeth → **Heulen a**; **zäh|ne|klap|pernd** ADJ attr ADV with teeth chattering; **Zäh|ne|knir|schen** NT -s, no pl grinding one's teeth; (fig) gnashing of teeth; **zäh|ne|knir|schend** ADJ attr ADV grinding one's teeth; (fig) gnashing one's teeth; **er fand sich ~ damit ab** he agreed with (a) bad grace

zah|nen ['tsaːnən] VI to teethe, to cut one's teeth/a tooth; **das Zahnen** teething

zäh|nen ['tsɛːnən] VT to tooth; Briefmarken to perforate → auch **gezähnt**

Zäh|ne|put|zen NT -s, no pl tooth-brushing; **~ nicht vergessen!** don't forget to brush your teeth

Zahn-: Zahn|er|satz M dentures pl, set of dentures; **Zahn|fäu|le** F tooth decay, caries sing; **Zahn|fleisch** NT gum(s pl); **(nur noch) auf dem ~ gehen or kriechen** (inf) to be all in (inf), to be on one's last legs (inf); **Zahn|fleisch|blu|ten** NT -s, no pl bleeding of the gums; **Zahn|fleisch|ent|zün|dung** F inflammation of the gum(s pl), gingivitis (spec); **Zahn|fül|lung** F filling; **Zahn|hals** M neck of a tooth; **Zahn|heil|kun|de** F dentistry; **Zahn|höh|le** F pulp cavity; **Zahn|klam|mer** F brace; **Zahn|klemp|ner(in)** M(F) (hum) dentist; **Zahn|kli|nik** F dental clinic or hospital; **Zahn|kranz** M (Tech) gear rim; **Zahn|kro|ne** F crown; **Zahn|laut** M (Ling) dental (consonant); **zahn|los** ADJ (lit, fig) toothless; **~er Tiger** (fig) toothless tiger; **Zahn|lo|sig|keit** F -, no pl toothlessness; **Zahn|lü|cke** F gap between one's teeth; **Zahn|mark** NT dental pulp; **Zahn|me|di|zin** F dentistry; **zahn|me|di|zi|nisch** ADJ Untersuchung dental; Gutachten dentist's; **aus ~er Sicht** from a dental point of view; **Zahn|pas|ta** F , **Zahn|pas|te** F toothpaste; **Zahn|pfle|ge** F dental hygiene; **Zahn|pro|the|se** F set of dentures; **Zahn|pul|ver** NT tooth powder; **Zahn|putz|glas** NT toothbrush glass; **Zahn|rad** NT cogwheel, gear (wheel); **Zahn|rad|bahn** F rack railway (Brit), rack railroad (US); **Zahn|rad|ge|trie|be** NT gear mechanism; **Zahn|rei|he** F row of teeth; **Zahn|schei|be** F (Tech) cog; **Zahn|schein** M (inf) form for free dental treatment; **Zahn|schmelz** M (tooth) enamel; **Zahn|schmer|zen** PL toothache no pl; **Zahn|sei|de** F dental floss; **Zahn|span|ge** F brace; **Zahn|stein** M tartar; **Zahn|sto|cher** [-ʃtɔxɐ] M -s, - toothpick; **Zahn|stum|mel** M stump; **Zahn|tech|ni|ker(in)** M(F) dental technician

Zäh|nung ['tsɛːnʊŋ] F -, -en **a** (= Zähne, Gezahntsein) teeth pl; (von Briefmarken) perforations pl **b** (= das Zähnen) toothing; (von Briefmarken) perforation

Zahn-: Zahn|wal M toothed whale; **Zahn|wech|sel** M second dentition (form); **Zahn|weh** NT toothache; **Zahn|wur|zel** F root (of a/the tooth); **Zahn|ze|ment** M (dental) cement

Zäh|re ['tsɛːrə] F -, -n (old, poet) tear

Zaire [zaˈiːr(ə)] NT (Hist) -s Zaire

Zai|rer [zaˈiːrɐ] M -s, -, **Zai|re|rin** [zaˈiːrərɪn] F -, -nen (Hist) Zairean

za|i|risch [zaˈiːrɪʃ] ADJ (Hist) Zairean

Zam|pa|no ['tsampano] M -s, -s (inf) **der große ~** the big cheese (inf)

Zan|der ['tsandɐ] M -s, - (Zool) pikeperch

Zan|ge ['tsaŋə] F -, -n (= Flachzange, Rundzange) (pair of) pliers pl; (= Beißzange) (pair of) pincers pl; (= Greifzange, Kohlenzange, Zuckerzange) (pair of) tongs pl; (von Tier) pincers pl; (Med) forceps pl; (inf: Ringen) double lock; **jdn in die ~ nehmen** (Ringen) to put a double lock on sb; (Ftbl etc) to sandwich sb; (fig) to put the screws on sb (inf); **jetzt haben wir ihn in der ~** (fig) we've got him now; **ihn/das möchte ich nicht mit der ~ anfassen** (inf) I wouldn't touch him/it with a bargepole (Brit inf) or a ten-foot pole (US inf)

Zan|gen-: Zan|gen|be|we|gung F (Mil) pincer movement; **zan|gen|för|mig** ADJ pincer-shaped; **Zan|gen|ge|burt** F forceps delivery; **Zan|gen|griff** M (Ringen) double lock

Zank [tsaŋk] M -(e)s, no pl squabble, quarrel; **zwischen ihnen gab es dauernd ~** they were continually squabbling or quarrelling (Brit) or quarreling (US); **~ und Streit** trouble and strife

Zank|ap|fel M (fig) bone of contention

zan|ken ['tsaŋkn] VIR to quarrel, to squabble; **wir haben uns gezankt** we've had a row, we've quarrelled (Brit) or quarreled (US); **(sich) um etw ~** to quarrel over sth

Zän|ker ['tsɛŋkɐ] M -s, -, **Zän|ke|rin** [-ərɪn] F -, -nen quarreller (Brit), quarreler (US), squabbler

Zan|ke|rei [tsaŋkəˈrai] F -, -en quarrelling (Brit), quarreling (US), squabbling

zän|kisch ['tsɛŋkɪʃ] ADJ (= streitsüchtig) quarrelsome; (= tadelsüchtig) Frau nagging attr, shrewish

Zank|sucht F , no pl quarrelsomeness; (= Tadelsucht: von Frau) nagging, shrewishness

zank|süch|tig ADJ = zänkisch

Zäpf|chen ['tsɛpfçən] NT -s, - dim von **Zapfen** small plug etc; (= Gaumenzäpfchen) uvula; (= Suppositorium) suppository; **~r, ~R** (Ling) uvular "r"

zap|fen ['tsapfn] VT to tap, to draw; **dort wird das Pils frisch gezapft** they have draught (Brit) or draft (US) Pilsener there, they have Pilsener on draught (Brit) or draft (US) or tap there

Zap|fen ['tsapfn] M -s, - (= Spund) bung, spigot; (= Pfropfen) stopper, bung; (= Tannenzapfen etc, von Auge) cone; (= Eiszapfen) icicle; (Mech: von Welle, Lager etc) journal; (= Holzverbindung) tenon

zap|fen|för|mig ADJ cone-shaped, conical

Zap|fen|streich M (Mil) tattoo, last post (Brit), taps sing (US); **den ~ blasen** to sound the tattoo; **der Große ~** the Ceremonial Tattoo; **um 12 Uhr ist ~** (fig inf) lights out is at 12 o'clock

Zap|fer ['tsapfɐ] M -s, - (dial) barman, tapster (old)

Zap|fe|rin ['tsapfərɪn] F -, -nen (dial) barmaid

Zapf-: Zapf|hahn M tap; **Zapf|pis|to|le** F (petrol (Brit) or gas (US) pump) nozzle; **Zapf|säu|le** F petrol pump (Brit), gas pump (US); **Zapf|stel|le** F tap; (Elec) (power) point; (= Tankstelle) petrol (Brit) or gas (US) station

Za|pon|lack [tsaˈpoːnlak] M cellulose lacquer

zap|pe|lig ['tsapəlɪç] ADJ wriggly; (= unruhig) fidgety

zap|peln ['tsapln] VI to wriggle; (Hampelmann) to jiggle; (= unruhig sein) to fidget; **er zappelte mit Armen und Beinen** he was all of a fidget (Brit), he couldn't sit still; **jdn ~ lassen** (fig inf) to keep sb in suspense; **in der Schlinge ~** (fig) to be caught in the net

Zap|pel|phi|lipp [-fɪlɪp] M -s, -e or -s fidget(er)

zap|pen ['zɛpn] VI (TV inf) to zap (inf); **in den Konkurrenzkanal ~** to zap over to the other

---

channel (*inf*); **Zappen macht Spaß** zapping is fun (*inf*)

zap|pen|dus|ter ['tsapn'du:stɐ] ADJ (*inf*) pitch-black, pitch-dark; **wie sieht es denn mit euren Plänen aus? – ~** how are your plans working out? – grim; **dann ist es ~** you'll/we'll etc be in trouble or (dead) shtuck (*Brit inf*)

Zap|per ['zɛpɐ] M -s, -, **Zap|pe|rin** [-ərɪn] F -, -nen (*inf*) zapper (*inf*); **er ist ein leidenschaftlicher ~** he just loves zapping (*inf*)

zapp|lig ['tsaplɪç] ADJ = **zappelig**

Zar [tsa:ɐ] M -en, -en tsar, czar

Za|re|witsch [tsa:re:vɪtʃ] M -(e)s, -e tsarevitch

Zar|ge ['tsargə] F -, -n frame; (*von Geige etc*) rib; (*von Plattenspieler*) plinth

Za|rin ['tsa:rɪn] F -, -nen tsarina, czarina

Za|ris|mus [tsa'rɪsmʊs] M -, no pl tsarism, czarism

za|ris|tisch [tsa'rɪstɪʃ] ADJ tsarist, czarist no adv

zart [tsa:ɐt] ▲ ADJ (= weich) Haut, Flaum soft; (= leise) Töne, Stimme soft; Braten, Gemüse tender; Geschmack, Porzellan, Blüte, Gebäck, Farben, Teint delicate; (= schwächlich) Gesundheit, Kind delicate; (= feinfühlig) Gemüt, Gefühle sensitive, tender, delicate; (= sanft) Wind, Berührung gentle, soft; **nichts für ~e Ohren** not for tender or sensitive ears; **im ~en Alter von …** at the tender age of …; **das ~e Geschlecht** the gentle sex ADV umgehen, berühren, andeuten gently; **~ schmecken** to have a delicate taste; **~ besaitet** highly sensitive; **~ besaitet sein** to be very sensitive; **~ fühlend** sensitive

Zart-: **zart|be|sai|tet** △ [-bəzaɪtət] ADJ attr = **zart** ADV; **zart|bit|ter** ADJ Schokolade plain; **zart|blau** ADJ pale blue; **zart|füh|lend** △ ADJ = **zart** ADV; **Zart|ge|fühl** NT delicacy of feeling, sensitivity; **zart|glied|rig** [-gli:drɪç] ADJ dainty; **zart|grün** ADJ pale green

Zart|heit F -, -en (von Haut, Stimme) softness; (von Gemüse, Braten) tenderness; (von Farben, Teint) delicacy, delicateness; (von Gemüt) sensitivity; (von Wind, Berührung) gentleness

zärt|lich ['tsɛ:ɐtlɪç] ▲ ADJ tender, affectionate, loving ADV tenderly

Zärt|lich|keit F -, -en a no pl affection, tenderness b (= Liebkosung) caress; **~en** (= Worte) tender or loving words, words of love; **jdm ~en ins Ohr flüstern** to whisper sweet nothings in sb's ear

zart|ro|sa ADJ pale or delicate pink

Zä|si|um ['tsɛ:ziʊm] NT -s, no pl caesium (*Brit*), cesium (*US*)

Zast, ZAST [tsast] F a abbr von **Zinsabschlagsteuer** b abbr von **Zentrale Anlaufstelle für Asylbewerber** central refuge for asylum seekers

Zas|ter ['tsastɐ] M -s, no pl (inf: = Geld) dosh (*inf*), brass (*inf*), readies pl (*inf*)

Zä|sur [tsɛ'zu:ɐ] F -, -en caesura (*Brit*), cesura (*US*); (fig) break

Zau|ber ['tsaubɐ] M -s, - (= Magie) magic; (= Zauberbann) (magic) spell; (fig: = Reiz) magic, charm; **den ~ lösen** to break the spell; **fauler ~** (*inf*) humbug no indef art; **der ganze ~** (*inf*) the whole lot (*inf*); **warum der ganze ~?** (*inf: = Getue*) why all the fuss?

Zau|ber-: **Zau|ber|bann** M (magic) spell; **unter einem ~ stehen** to be under a spell; **Zau|ber|buch** NT book of spells; (für Zauberkunststücke) conjuring book

Zau|be|rei [tsaubə'raɪ] F -, -en a no pl (= das Zaubern) magic b (= Zauberkunststück) conjuring trick

Zau|be|rer ['tsaubərɐ] M -s, - magician; (in Märchen etc auch) sorcerer, wizard; (= Zauberkünstler auch) conjurer → auch **Zauberin**

Zau|ber-: **Zau|ber|flö|te** F magic flute; **Zau|ber|for|mel** F magic formula; **zau|ber|haft** ADJ enchanting ADV fantastically; **Zau|ber|hand** F wie von or durch **~** as if by magic

Zau|be|rin ['tsaubərɪn] F -, -nen (female) magician; (in Märchen etc auch) enchantress, sorceress; (= Zauberkünstlerin auch) (female) conjurer

zau|be|risch ['tsaubərɪʃ] ADJ = **zauberhaft**

Zauber-: **Zau|ber|kas|ten** M magic set; **Zau|ber|kraft** F magic power; **Zau|ber|kunst** F magic, conjuring; **Zau|ber|künst|ler(in)** M(F) conjurer, magician; **Zau|ber|kunst|stück** NT conjuring trick; **Zau|ber|land|schaft** F fairy-tale scene; **Zau|ber|macht** F magical powers pl; **Zau|ber|mit|tel** NT magical cure; (= Trank) magic potion, philtre (*Brit*), philter (*US*)

zau|bern ['tsaubɐn] VI to do or perform magic; (= Kunststücke vorführen) to do conjuring tricks; **ich kann doch nicht ~!** (*inf*) I'm not a magician!, I can't perform miracles! VT a **etw aus etw ~** to conjure sth out of sth b (fig) Lösung, Essen to produce as if by magic, to conjure up

Zauber-: **Zau|ber|nuss** ▲ F wych-hazel, witch hazel; **Zau|ber|reich** NT enchanted or magic realm; **Zau|ber|schloss** ▲ NT enchanted castle; **Zau|ber|spruch** M (magic) spell; **Zau|ber|stab** M (magic) wand; **Zau|ber|trank** M magic potion, philtre (*Brit*), philter (*US*); **Zau|ber|trick** M conjuring trick; **Zau|ber|werk** NT sorcery, wizardry; **Zau|ber|we|sen** NT magical being; **Zau|ber|wort** NT pl -worte magic word; **Zau|ber|wür|fel** M Rubik's cube®; **Zau|ber|wur|zel** F mandrake root

Zau|de|rer ['tsaudərɐ] M -s, -, **Zau|de|rin** [-ərɪn] F -, -nen vacillator, irresolute person

zau|dern ['tsaudɐn] VI to hesitate, to vacillate; **etw ohne zu ~ tun** to do sth without hesitating or any hesitation

Zaum [tsaum] M -(e)s, Zäume ['tsɔymə] bridle; **einem Pferd den ~ anlegen** to put a bridle on a horse; **jdn/etw im ~ halten** (fig) to keep a tight rein on sb/sth, to keep sb/sth in check; **sich im ~(e) halten** (fig) to control oneself, to keep oneself in check; **seine Ungeduld/seinen Zorn im ~e halten** (fig) to control or curb one's impatience/anger

zäu|men ['tsɔymən] VT to bridle

Zaum|zeug NT pl -zeuge bridle

Zaun [tsaun] M -(e)s, Zäune ['tsɔynə] fence; **einen Streit vom ~(e) brechen** to pick a quarrel, to start a fight

Zaun-: **Zaun|ei|dech|se** F sand lizard; **Zaun|gast** M sb who manages to get a free view of an event; **Zaun|kö|nig** M (Orn) wren; **Zaun|lat|te** F picket; **Zaun|lü|cke** F gap in the fence; **Zaun|pfahl** M (fencing) post; **jdm einen Wink mit dem ~ geben** to give or drop sb a broad hint; **Zaun|pfos|ten** M → Zaunpfahl; **Zaun|re|be** F climbing plant; **Zaun|win|de** F (Bot) great bindweed

Zau|sel ['tsauzl] M -s, -s (*inf*) codger (*inf*)

zau|sen ['tsauzn] VT to ruffle; Haare to ruffle, to tousle; (fig inf: = in Mitleidenschaft ziehen) Finanzen etc to run down VI **in etw** (dat) **~** (Wind) to ruffle sth

z. B. [tsɛt'be:] abbr von **zum Beispiel** eg

z. b. V. abbr von **zur besonderen Verwendung**

ZDF [tsɛtde:'ʔɛf] NT -s abbr von **Zweites Deutsches Fernsehen**

ZDF

ZDF – short for **Zweites Deutsches Fernsehen** – is the second public service television station in Germany and the largest in Europe. In contrast to **ARD**, it broadcasts exclusively on television. It was established in 1961 and has its headquarters in Mainz. Since 1984 ZDF – together with **ORF** and **SRG** – has been running the international channel 3sat, and since 1994 it has also been involved in the European television channel **ARTE**. Both

---

of these channels place the emphasis on cultural programming. ZDF is financed through licence fees and strictly controlled advertising → ARD, ORF, SRG

ZDLer [tsɛtde:'ʔɛlɐ] M -s, - (*inf*) abbr von **Zivildienstleistende(r)**

Ze|ba|oth ['tse:baɔt] M -s der Herr ~ (*Bibl*) Jehovah

Zeb|ra ['tse:bra] NT -s, -s zebra

Zeb|ra|strei|fen M zebra crossing (*Brit*), pedestrian crossing or crosswalk (*US*)

Ze|bu ['tse:bu] NT -s, -s zebu

Zech|bru|der M boozer (*inf*); (= Kumpan) drinking mate (*Brit inf*), drinking buddy (*inf*)

Ze|che ['tsɛçə] F -, -n a (= Rechnung) bill (*esp Brit*), check (*US*); **die (ganze) ~ (be)zahlen** (lit, fig) to foot the bill etc; **(den Wirt um) die ~ prellen** to leave without paying (the bill etc); **eine (hohe) ~ machen** to run up a (large) bill etc b (= Bergwerk) (coal) mine, pit, colliery

ze|chen ['tsɛçn] VI to booze (*inf*); (= Zechgelage abhalten) to carouse

Ze|cher ['tsɛçɐ] M -s, -, **Ze|che|rin** [-ərɪn] F -, -nen boozer (*inf*); (bei einem Zechgelage) carouser, reveller (*Brit*), reveler (*US*)

Ze|che|rei [tsɛçə'raɪ] F -, -en booze-up (*inf*); (= Zechgelage) carousal; (= das Zechen) boozing/carousing

Zech-: **Zech|ge|la|ge** NT carousal (old, hum); **Zech|kum|pan(in)** M(F) drinking mate (*Brit inf*), drinking buddy (*inf*); **Zech|prel|ler** [-prɛlɐ] M -s, -, **Zech|prel|le|rin** [-ərɪn] F -, -nen person who leaves without paying the bill at a restaurant etc, Dine-n-Dasher (*US sl*); **Zech|prel|le|rei** F leaving without paying the bill at a restaurant etc, Dine-n-Dash (*US sl*); **Zech|schwes|ter** F drinking mate (*Brit inf*), drinking buddy (*inf*); **Zech|stein** M (Geol) Zechstein (period), Upper Permian; **Zech|tour** F (*inf*) pub-crawl (*esp Brit inf*), bar hop (*US inf*)

Zeck¹ [tsɛk] NT OR M -(e)s, -e (dial: = Fangspiel) tag

Ze|cke ['tsɛkə] F -, -n, **Zeck²** (*Aus*) M -(e)s, -en tick

Ze|cken|biss ▲ M tick bite; **ich habe einen ~** I've been bitten by a tick

Ze|dent [tse:'dɛnt] M -en, -en, **Ze|den|tin** [-'dɛntɪn] F -, -nen (*Jur*) assignor

Ze|der ['tse:dɐ] F -, -n cedar

ze|dern ['tse:dɐn] ADJ cedar

Ze|dern|holz NT cedar, cedarwood

Ze|dern|öl NT cedarwood oil

ze|die|ren [tse:'di:rən] ptp zediert VT (*Jur*) to cede, to assign, to transfer

Zeh [tse:] M -s, -en, **Ze|he** ['tse:ə] F -, -n toe; (= Knoblauchzehe) clove; **großer/kleiner ~, große/kleine ~e** big/little toe; **auf (den) ~en gehen/schleichen** to tiptoe, to walk/creep on tiptoe; **sich auf die ~en stellen** to stand on tiptoe; **jdm auf die ~en treten** (fig inf) to tread on sb's toes

Zehen-: **Ze|hen|na|gel** M toenail; **Ze|hen|san|da|le** F flip-flop (*Brit*), thong (*US*); **Ze|hen|spit|ze** F tip of the toe; **auf (den) ~n** on tiptoe, on tippy-toes (*US inf*); **sich auf die ~n stellen** to stand on tiptoe; **auf (den) ~n gehen** to tiptoe, to walk on tiptoe; **auf den ~n tanzen** to dance on one's toes

zehn [tse:n] NUM ten; **(ich wette) ~ zu** or **gegen eins** (I bet) ten to one → auch **vier**

Zehn [tse:n] F -, -en ten → auch **Vier**

Zehn-: **Zehn|cent|mün|ze** F , **Zehn|cent|stück** NT ten-cent piece; **Zehn|eck** NT decagon; **zehn|eckig** ADJ ten-sided, decagonal

Zehn|er ['tse:nɐ] M -s, - a (Math) ten → auch **Vierer** b (*inf*) (= Zehncentstück) ten-cent piece, ten; (= Zehneuroschein) tenner (*inf*)

Zehn|er-: **Zehn|er|bruch** M decimal (fraction); **Zehn|er|kar|te** F (für Bus etc) 10-journey ticket; (*für Schwimmbad etc*) 10-visit ticket; **Zehn|er|packung** F packet of ten; **Zehn|ner|stel|le** F ten's (place); **Zehn|ner|sys|tem** NT decimal system; **Zehn|ner|tas|ta|tur** F (*Comput*) numeric keypad

Zehn-: **Zehn|eu|ro|schein** M [tse:nˈɔyro-] ten-euro note (*Brit*) or bill (*US*); **Zehn|fin|ger|sys|tem** NT touch-typing method; **Zehn|kampf** M (*Sport*) decathlon; **Zehn|kämp|fer** M decathlete; **zehn|mal** ['tse:nma:l] ADV ten times → *auch viermal*; **Zehn|mark|schein** M (*Hist*) ten-mark note; **Zehn|me|ter|brett** NT ten-metre (*Brit*) or ten-meter (*US*) board; **Zehn|mi|nu|ten|takt** M im ~ every ten minutes, at ten-minute intervals

Zehnt [tse:nt] M **-en, -en** (*Hist*) tithe

zehn|tau|send ['tse:nˈtauznt] NUM ten thousand; **~e** or **Zehntausende von Menschen** tens of thousands of people → *obere(r, s)*

zehn|tel ['tse:ntl] ADJ tenth

Zehn|tel ['tse:ntl] NT **-s, -** tenth

Zehn|tel|se|kun|de F tenth of a second; **um zwei ~n** (*Sport*) by two tenths or point two of a second

zehn|tens ['tse:ntns] ADV tenth(ly), in the tenth place

Zehn|te(r) ['tse:ntə] M *decl as adj* (*Hist*) tithe

zehn|te(r, s) ['tse:ntə] ADJ tenth → *auch vierte(r, s)*

zeh|ren ['tse:rən] VI **a** **von etw ~** (*lit*) to live off or on sth; (*fig*) to feed on sth **b** **jdm/etw ~** to wear sb/sth out; *an Kraft auch* to sap sth; *an Nerven* to ruin sth; (*Anstrengung*) *am Herzen* to weaken sth; (*Kummer*) to gnaw at sth; *an Gesundheit* to undermine sth

Zehr|geld NT , **Zehr|pfen|nig** M (*obs*) travelling (*Brit*) or traveling (*US*) monies *pl* (*old*)

Zehr|rung ['tse:rʊŋ] F **-,** *no pl* (*old*) provisions *pl*

Zei|chen ['tsaiçn] NT **-s, -** sign; (*Sci, algebraisch, auf Landkarte*) symbol; (= *Schriftzeichen, auch Comput*) character; (= *Anzeichen: von Krankheit, Winter, = Beweis: von Friedfertigkeit*) sign, indication; (= *Hinweis, Signal*) signal; (= *Erkennungszeichen*) identification; (= *Lesezeichen*) bookmark, marker; (= *Vermerk*) mark; (*auf Briefköpfen*) reference; (= *Satzzeichen*) punctuation mark; (= *Warenzeichen*) trademark; **wenn nicht alle ~ trügen** if I'm/we're *etc* not completely mistaken; **es ist ein ~ unserer Zeit, dass ...** it is a sign of the times that ...; **ein ~ setzen** to set an example; **die ~ erkennen** to see the writing on the wall; **die ~ der Zeit erkennen** to recognize the mood of the times; **es geschehen noch ~ und Wunder!** (*hum*) wonders will never cease! (*hum*); **als** or **zum ~** as a sign; **ein ~ des Himmels** a sign from heaven; **als ~ von etw** as a sign or indication of sth; **zum ~, dass ...** as a sign that ..., to show that ...; **als ~ der Verehrung** as a mark or token of respect; **jdm ein ~ geben** or **machen** to give sb a signal or sign, to signal to sb; **etw zum ~ tun** to do sth as a signal, to signal by doing sth; **das ~ zum Aufbruch geben** to give the signal to leave; **unser/Ihr ~** (*form*) our/your reference; **seines ~s** (*old, hum*) by trade; **er ist im ~** or **unter dem ~ des Widders geboren** he was born under the sign of Aries; **unter dem ~ etw stehen** (*fig: Konferenz etc*) to take place against a background of sth; **das Jahr 1979 stand unter dem ~ des Kindes** 1979 was the year of the child; **die ~ stehen auf Sturm** (*fig*) there's a storm brewing

Zei|chen-: **Zei|chen|block** M *pl* **-blöcke** or **-blocks** drawing or sketch pad; **Zei|chen|brett** NT drawing board; **Zei|chen|drei|eck** NT set square; **Zei|chen|er|klä|rung** F (*auf Fahrplänen etc*) key (to the symbols); (*auf Landkarte*) legend; **Zei|chen|fe|der** F drawing pen; **Zei|chen|fol|ge** F character sequence; **zei|chen|haft** ADJ symbolic; **Zei|chen|heft** NT drawing book; **Zei|chen|kar|te** F (*Comput*) graphics card; **Zei|chen|ket|te** F (*Comput*) character string; **Zei|chen|koh|le** F charcoal;

Zei|chen|kunst F (art of) drawing; **Zei|chen|leh|rer(in)** M(F) art teacher; **Zei|chen|pa|pier** NT drawing paper; **Zei|chen|saal** M art room; **Zei|chen|satz** M (*Comput*) character set, font; **Zei|chen|schutz** M protection of registered trademarks; **Zei|chen|set|zung** [-zɛtsʊŋ] F **-, -en** punctuation; **Zei|chen|spra|che** F sign language; **Zei|chen|stift** M drawing pencil; **Zei|chen|stun|de** F art or drawing lesson; **Zei|chen|sys|tem** NT notation; (*Ling*) system of signs; **Zei|chen|tisch** M drawing table; **Zei|chen|trick|film** M (animated) cartoon; **Zei|chen|un|ter|richt** M art; (= *Unterrichtsstunde*) drawing or art lesson; **Zei|chen|vor|la|ge** F original, model (*for a drawing or trademark*)

zeich|nen ['tsaiçnən] VI to draw; (*form.* = *unterzeichnen*) to sign; **an dem Entwurf hat er lange gezeichnet** he has spent a long time drawing the blueprint; **gezeichnet XY** signed, XY → *verantwortlich* VT **a** (= *abzeichnen*) to draw; (= *entwerfen*) *Plan, Grundriss* to draw up, to draft; (*fig:* = *porträtieren*) to portray, to depict **b** (= *kennzeichnen*) to mark; **das Gefieder des Vogels ist hübsch gezeichnet** the bird's plumage has attractive markings → *auch* **gezeichnet** **c** (*Fin*) *Betrag* to subscribe; *Aktien* to subscribe (for); *Anleihe* to subscribe to; **gezeichnet** (*Kapital*) subscribed

Zeich|ner ['tsaiçnɐ] M **-s, -,** **Zeich|ne|rin** [-ərɪn] F **-, -nen** **a** artist; **muss ein Maler auch immer ein guter ~ sein?** must a painter always be a good draughtsman (*Brit*) or draftsman (*US*) too? → *technisch* **b** **b** (*Fin*) subscriber (*von* to)

zeich|ne|risch ['tsaiçnərɪʃ] ADJ *Darstellung, Gestaltung, Werk* graphic; **sein ~es Können** his drawing ability ADV **~ begabt sein** to have a talent for drawing; **etw ~ erklären** to explain sth with a drawing; **etw ~ festhalten** to draw sth; (*Polizei*) to make a diagram of sth; **etw ~ darstellen** to represent sth in a drawing

Zeich|nung ['tsaiçnʊŋ] F **-, -en** **a** (= *Darstellung*) drawing; (= *Entwurf*) draft, drawing; (*fig:* = *Schilderung*) portrayal, depiction **b** (= *Muster*) patterning; (*von Gefieder, Fell*) markings *pl* **c** (*Fin*) subscription; **eine Anleihe zur ~ auflegen** to invite subscriptions for a loan

Zeich|nungs-: **zeich|nungs|be|rech|tigt** ADJ authorized to sign; **Zeich|nungs|frist** F (*Fin*) subscription period; **Zeich|nungs|voll|macht** F authority to sign

Zei|ge|fin|ger M index finger, forefinger

zei|gen ['tsaign] VI to point; **nach Norden/rechts ~** to point north or to the north/to the right; **auf jdn/etw ~** to point at sb/sth; (= *hinweisen auch*) to point to sb/sth VT to show; (*Thermometer, Messgerät auch*) to be at or on, to indicate; **jdm etw ~** to show sb sth or sth to sb; **ich muss mir mal von jemandem ~ lassen, wie man das macht** I'll have to get someone to show me how to do it; **die Uhr zeigte fünf nach zwölf** the clock showed five past twelve; **dem werd ichs (aber) ~!** (*inf*) I'll show him!; **zeig mal, was du kannst!** let's see what you can do!, show us what you can do! VR to appear; (*Gefühle*) to show; **sich mit jdm ~** to let oneself be seen with sb; **in dem Kleid kann ich mich doch nicht ~** I can't be seen in a dress like that; **er zeigt sich nicht gern in der Öffentlichkeit** he doesn't like showing himself or being seen in public; **sich ~ als ...** to show or prove oneself to be ...; **er zeigte sich befriedigt** he was satisfied; **es zeigt sich, dass ...** it turns out that ...; **es zeigt sich (doch) wieder einmal, dass ...** it just goes to show ...; **es wird sich ~, wer Recht hat** time will tell who is right, we shall see who's right; **daran zeigt sich, dass ...** that shows (that) ...; **das zeigt sich jetzt** it's beginning to show

Zei|ger ['tsaigɐ] M **-s, -** indicator, pointer; (= *Uhrzeiger*) hand; **der große/kleine ~** the big/lit-

tle hand; **jdm auf den ~ gehen** (*inf*) to get on sb's wick (*Brit inf*) or nerves

Zei|ger|aus|schlag M pointer or indicator deflection

Zei|ge|stab M , **Zei|ge|stock** M pointer

zei|hen ['tsaiən] *pret* **zieh** [tsi:], *ptp* **geziehen** [gəˈtsi:ən] VT (*old*) **jdn einer Sache** (*gen*) ~ to accuse sb of sth

Zei|le ['tsailə] F **-, -n** line; (= *Häuserzeile, Baumzeile etc auch*) row; **davon habe ich keine ~ gelesen** I haven't read a single word of it; **zwischen den ~n lesen** to read between the lines; **vielen Dank für deine ~n** many thanks for your letter; **jdm ein paar ~n schreiben** to write sb a few lines; (= *Brief schreiben auch*) to drop sb a line

Zei|len-: **Zei|len|ab|stand** M line spacing; **Zei|len|ab|tas|tung** F (*TV*) line scan(ning); **Zei|len|bau|wei|se** F ribbon development; **Zei|len|be|fehl** M (*Comput*) line command; **Zei|len|fang** M (*TV*) horizontal hold; **Zei|len|ho|no|rar** NT payment per line; **~ bekommen** to be paid by the line; **Zei|len|län|ge** F length (of a/the line); **Zei|len|norm** F (*TV*) line standard; **Zei|len|schal|ter** M line spacer; **Zei|len|schal|tung** F line spacing; **Zei|len|setz|ma|schi|ne** F Linotype® machine; **Zei|len|sprung** M (*Liter*) enjambement; (*Comput*) line skip; **Zei|len|um|bruch** F (automatischer) ~ (*Comput*) wordwrap; **Zei|len|vor|schub** M (*Comput*) line feed; **zei|len|wei|se** ADV in lines; (= *nach Zeilen*) by the line; **etw ~ vorlesen** to read sth out line by line

-zei|lig [tsailɪç] ADJ *suf* with ... lines; **es ist vierzeilig** it has four lines

Zei|sig ['tsaizɪç] M **-s, -e** [-gə] (*Orn*) siskin → *locker*

zeit [tsait] PREP +*gen* **~ meines/seines Lebens** in my/his lifetime

Zeit [tsait] F **-, -en** **a** time; (= *Epoche*) age; **die gute alte ~** the good old days; **es erinnerte ihn an alte ~en** it reminded him of the old days; **das waren noch ~en!** those were the days; **die ~en sind schlecht** times are bad; **die ~en haben sich geändert** times have changed; **die ~ Goethes** the age of Goethe; **die damalige ~ machte die Einführung neuer Methoden erforderlich** the situation at the time required the introduction of new methods; **wenn ~ und Umstände es erfordern** if circumstances demand it, if the situation requires it; **die jetzigen ~en erfordern, ...** the present situation requires ...; **für alle ~en** for ever, for all time (*liter*); **etw für alle ~en entscheiden** to decide sth once and for all; **in seiner/ihrer besten ~** at his/her peak; **mit der ~ gehen** to move with the times; **vor der ~ alt werden** to get old before one's time; **vor jds** (*dat*) ~ before sb's time; **die ~ ist knapp bemessen** time is short; **die ~ wurde mir lang** time hung heavy on my hands; **eine lange ~ her sein** or **zurückliegen, dass ...** to be a long time (ago or back) since ...; **eine Stunde ~ haben** to have an hour (to spare); **Fräulein Glück, haben Sie vielleicht einen Augenblick ~** Miss Glück, do you have a moment?; **~ raubend** time-consuming; **~ sparend** time-saving; (*adverbial*) expeditiously; **möglichst ~ sparend vorgehen** to save as much time as possible; **sich** (*dat*) **für jdn/etw ~ nehmen** to devote time to sb/sth; **dafür muss ich mir mehr ~ nehmen** I need more time for that; **sich** (*dat*) **die ~ nehmen, etw zu tun** to take the time to do sth; **du hast dir aber reichlich ~ gelassen** you certainly took your time; **hier bin ich die längste ~ gewesen** it's about time or it's high time I was going; **keine ~ verlieren** to lose no time; **damit hat es noch ~** there's no rush or hurry, there's plenty of time; **das hat ~ bis morgen** that can wait until tomorrow; **lass dir ~** take your time; **aller ~en** ... of all time, ... ever; **auf bestimmte ~** for a certain length of time; **auf unbestimmte ~** for an indefinite period; **in letzter ~** recently; **die ganze ~ über** the whole time; **eine ~ lang** a

while, a time; **wir sind eine ~ lang dort geblieben** we stayed there (for) a while *or* for a time; **eine ~ lang ist das ganz schön** for a while *or* time it's quite nice; **mit der ~** gradually, in time; **nach ~ bezahlt werden** to be paid by the hour; **die ~ heilt alle Wunden** (*Prov*) time is a great healer (*prov*); **auf ~ spielen** (*Sport, fig*) to play for time; **es wird langsam ~, dass ...** it's about time that ...; **für dich wird es langsam ~, dass ...** it's about time that you ...; **seine ~ ist gekommen** his time has come; **hast du (die) genaue ~?** do you have the exact time?; **in der ~ von 10 bis 12** between 10 and 12 (o'clock); **es ist an der ~, dass ...** it is about time *or* it's high time (that) ...; **Vertrag auf ~** fixed-term contract; **Beamter auf ~** ≈ nonpermanent civil servant; **Soldat auf ~** soldier serving for a set time; **seit dieser ~** since then; **zur ~** *or* **zu ~en Königin Viktorias** in Queen Victoria's time; **zu der ~, als ...** (at the time) when ...; **alles zu seiner ~** (*prov*) all in good time; **von ~ zu ~** from time to time → **kommen 1** p, **zurzeit**, **zuzeiten**
b (*Ling*) tense; **in welcher ~ steht das Verb?** what tense is the verb in?

Zeit-: Zeit|ab|schnitt M period (of time); **Zeit|ab|stand** M interval; **in regelmäßigen Zeitabständen** at regular intervals, periodically; **Zeit|al|ter** NT age; **das goldene ~** the golden age; **in unserem ~** nowadays, in this day and age; **Zeit|an|ga|be** F (= *Datum*) date; (= *Uhrzeit*) time (of day); **die ~ kommt vor der Ortsangabe** (*Gram*) time is given before place; **Zeit|an|sa|ge** F (*Rad*) time check; (*Telec*) speaking clock; **Zeit|ar|beit** F temporary work; **Zeit|ar|bei|ter(in)** M(F) temporary worker; **Zeit|ar|beits|fir|ma** F agency for temporary work; **Zeit|auf|nah|me** F (*Phot*) time exposure; **Zeit|auf|wand** M time (*needed to complete a task*); **mit möglichst wenig ~** taking as little time as possible; **dieses Dokument wurde unter großen ~ erstellt** it took an enormous amount of time to produce this document; **mit großem ~ verbunden sein** to be extremely time-consuming; **zeit|auf|wän|dig** ADJ time-consuming; **Zeit|be|griff** M conception of time; **Zeit|be|stim|mung** F (*Gram*) designation of the tense of a verb; **Zeit|bom|be** F (*lit, fig*) time bomb; **Zeit|do|ku|ment** NT contemporary document; **Zeit|druck** M , *no pl* pressure of time; **unter ~** under pressure; **Zeit|ein|heit** F time unit; **Zeit|ein|tei|lung** F division of time; (= *Zeitplan*) timetable, schedule (*esp US*)

Zeiten-: Zei|ten|fol|ge F (*Gram*) sequence of tenses; **Zei|ten|wen|de** F **nach der ~** anno Domini; **vor der ~** before Christ

Zeit-: Zeit|er|fas|sung F (*Ind*) recording of time worked; **Zeit|er|fas|sungs|ge|rät** NT (*Ind*) time recorder, time-recording device; **Zeit|er|spar|nis** F saving of time; **Zeit|fah|ren** NT -s, *no pl* (*Sport*) time trial; **Zeit|fol|ge** F sequence, chronological order; **Zeit|form** F (*Gram*) tense; **Zeit|fra|ge** F question of time; **zeit|ge|bun|den** ADJ tied to *or* dependent on a particular time; *Mode* temporary; **Zeit|ge|fühl** NT , *no pl* sense of time; **Zeit|geist** M , *no pl* Zeitgeist, spirit of the times; **zeit|ge|mäß** ADJ up-to-date; **~ sein** to be in keeping with the times ADV in keeping with the times; **Zeit|ge|nos|se** M , **Zeit|ge|nos|sin** F contemporary; **ein seltsamer ~** (*iro*) an odd bod (*inf*), an oddball (*esp US inf*); **zeit|ge|nös|sisch** [-gənœsɪʃ] ADJ contemporary; **Zeit|ge|sche|hen** NT events *pl* of the day; **Zeit|ge|schich|te** F , *no pl* contemporary history; **Zeit|ge|schmack** M prevailing taste; **Zeit|ge|winn** M gain in time; **sich um einen ~ bemühen** to try to gain time; **zeit|gleich** ADJ (*Er|scheinungen*) contemporaneous; *Läufer* with the same time; (*Film*) synchronized, in sync(h) (*inf*) ADV at the same time (*mit as*); **~ den ersten Platz belegen** to tie for first place; **Zeit|his|to|ri|ker(in)** M(F) contemporary historian

zei|tig ['tsaɪtɪç] ADJ, ADV early

zei|ti|gen ['tsaɪtɪgn] VT (*geh*) *Ergebnis, Wirkung* to bring about; *Erfolg auch* to lead to; **Früchte ~** to bear fruit

Zeit-: Zeit|kar|te F season ticket; (= *Wochenkarte*) weekly ticket; **Zeit|kar|ten|in|ha|ber(in)** M(F) season ticket holder; (*von Wochenkarte*) weekly ticket holder; **Zeit|kon|to** NT record of hours worked; **Zeit|kon|trol|le** F time study; **zeit|kri|tisch** ADJ **a** *Aufsatz, Artikel* full of comment on contemporary issues; **seine ~en Bemerkungen** his thoughtful remarks on contemporary issues; **seine ~e Haltung** his awareness of contemporary issues **b** (*Comput*) *Anwendung, Prozess* time-critical; **Zeit|lang** △ ['tsaɪtlaŋ] F → **Zeit a**; **Zeit|läuf|te** PL (*geh*) course *no pl* of time; **zeit|le|bens** [tsaɪt'le:bns] ADV all one's life

zeit|lich ['tsaɪtlɪç] ADJ temporal; *Verzögerungen* time-related; (= *chronologisch*) *Reihenfolge* chronological; **aus ~en Gründen** for reasons of time; **in kurzem/großem ~em Abstand** at short/long intervals (of time); **einen hohen ~en Aufwand erfordern** to require a great deal of time; **das Zeitliche segnen** (*euph: Mensch*) to depart this life; (*inf: Sache*) to bite the dust (*inf*)
ADV timewise (*inf*), from the point of view of time; (= *chronologisch*) chronologically; **das kann sie ~ nicht einrichten** she can't fit that in (timewise (*inf*)), she can't find (the) time for that; **das passt ihr ~ nicht** the time isn't convenient for her; **~ befristet sein** to have a time limit; **~ zusammenfallen** to coincide; **die Uhren/Pläne ~ aufeinander abstimmen** to synchronize one's watches/plans

Zeit-: Zeit|li|mit NT time limit; **Zeit|lohn** M hourly rate; **~ bekommen** to be paid by the hour; **zeit|los** ADJ timeless; *Stil auch* which doesn't date; *Kleidung auch* classic; **Zeit|lo|sig|keit** F -, *no pl* timelessness; **Zeit|lu|pe** F slow motion *no art*; **etw in (der) ~ zeigen** to show sth in slow motion; **Wiederholung in (der) ~** slow-motion replay; **Zeit|lu|pen|auf|nah|me** F slow-motion shot; **Zeit|lu|pen|tem|po** NT slow speed; **im ~** (*lit*) in slow motion; (*fig*) at a snail's pace; **Zeit|ma|nage|ment** NT time management; **Zeit|man|gel** M lack of time; **aus ~** for lack of time; **Zeit|ma|schi|ne** F time machine; **Zeit|maß** NT tempo; **Zeit|mes|ser** M -s, - timekeeper; **Zeit|mes|sung** F timekeeping (*auch Sport*), measurement of time; **zeit|nah** ADJ contemporary; *Problem auch* of our age; *Gottesdienst, Übersetzung auch* modern; *Bücher, Unterricht* relevant to present times ADV in a contemporary way; **Zeit|nah|me** [-na:mə] F -, -n (*Sport*) timekeeping *no pl*; **Zeit|neh|mer(in)** M(F) (*Sport, Ind*) timekeeper; **Zeit|not** F shortage of time; **in ~ sein** to be pressed for time, to be short of time; **Zeit|plan** M schedule, timetable; **Zeit|punkt** M (= *Termin*) time; (= *Augenblick auch*) moment; **zu diesem ~** at that time; **den ~ für etw festlegen** to set a time for sth; **Zeit|raf|fer** [-rafɐ] M -s, *no pl* time-lapse photography; **einen Film im ~ zeigen** to show a time-lapse film; **zeit|rau|bend** △ ADJ → **Zeit a**; **Zeit|raum** M period of time; **in einem ~ von ...** over a period of ...; **Zeit|rech|nung** F calendar; **nach christlicher/jüdischer ~** according to the Christian/Jewish calendar; **vor unserer ~** before Christ, BC; **nach unserer ~** anno Domini, AD; **Zeit|schalt|uhr** F timer, time switch; **Zeit|schrift** F (= *Illustrierte*) magazine; (*wissenschaftlich*) periodical, journal; **Zeit|schrif|ten|ka|ta|log** M periodicals catalogue (*Brit*) *or* catalog (*US*); **Zeit|sinn** M sense of time; **Zeit|sol|dat(in)** M(F) regular soldier (*who has signed up for a fixed period of time*); **Zeit|span|ne** F period of time; **zeit|spa|rend** △ ADJ → **Zeit a**; **Zeit|stu|die** F (*Ind*) time (and motion) study; **zeit|syn|chron** ADJ synchronized *no adv*, at the same time; **Zeit|ta|fel** F chronological table; **Zeit|takt** M **a** (*Telec*) unit length **b** timing; **im 10-minütigen ~** every 10 minutes; **Zeit|um|stän|de** PL prevailing circumstances *pl*, circum-

stances *pl* of the time; **Zeit|um|stel|lung** F **a** (= *Zeitänderung*) changing the clocks, putting the clocks back/forward **b** (= *Zeitunterschied*) time difference

Zei|tung ['tsaɪtʊŋ] F -, -en (news)paper; **er hat bei der ~ gearbeitet** he worked for a newspaper

Zei|tungs- *in cpds* newspaper; **Zei|tungs|abon|ne|ment** NT subscription to a newspaper; **Zei|tungs|an|zei|ge** F newspaper advertisement; (= *Familienanzeige*) announcement in the (news)paper; **Zei|tungs|ar|ti|kel** M newspaper article; (= *aktueller Bericht*) news report; **Zei|tungs|aus|schnitt** M newspaper cutting; **Zei|tungs|aus|trä|ger** M paperboy; **Zei|tungs|aus|trä|ge|rin** F papergirl; **Zei|tungs|bei|la|ge** F newspaper supplement; **Zei|tungs|druck|pa|pier** NT newsprint; **Zei|tungs|en|te** F (*inf*) canard, false newspaper report; **Zei|tungs|frau** F (*inf*) **a** (= *Journalistin*) newspaper woman **b** (= *Austrägerin*) paperwoman; **Zei|tungs|händ|ler(in)** M(F) newsagent, newsdealer (*US*); **Zei|tungs|in|se|rat** NT newspaper advertisement; **Zei|tungs|jar|gon** M journalese; **Zei|tungs|jun|ge** M paperboy; **Zei|tungs|ki|osk** M newspaper kiosk; **Zei|tungs|kor|res|pon|dent(in)** M(F) newspaper correspondent; **Zei|tungs|la|den** M paper shop; **Zei|tungs|le|sen** NT -s, *no pl* reading the (news)paper *no art*; **er war gerade beim ~** he was just reading the paper/papers; **Zei|tungs|le|ser(in)** M(F) newspaper reader; **Zei|tungs|mäd|chen** NT papergirl; **Zei|tungs|mann** M (*inf*) **a** *pl* **-leute** (= *Journalist*) newspaper man **b** (= *Austräger*) paperman; **Zei|tungs|no|tiz** F press item; **Zei|tungs|pa|pier** NT newsprint; (= *Altpapier*) newspaper; **Zei|tungs|re|dak|teur(in)** M(F) newspaper editor; **Zei|tungs|stän|der** M magazine *or* newspaper rack; **Zei|tungs|ver|le|ger(in)** M(F) newspaper publisher; **Zei|tungs|we|sen** NT , *no pl* press, newspaper world; **das ~ in Deutschland** the German press; **im ~ tätig sein** to be in the newspaper business; (*Journalist*) to be in journalism; **Zei|tungs|wis|sen|schaft** F journalism; **Zei|tungs|zar** M press baron

Zeit-: Zeit|un|ter|schied M time difference; **Zeit|ver|geu|dung** F waste of time; **Zeit|ver|lust** M loss of time; **das bedeutet mehrere Stunden ~** this will mean wasting several hours; **ohne ~** without losing any time; **Zeit|ver|schie|bung** F **a** (= *Zeitunterschied*) time difference **b** (*von Termin etc*) rescheduling, change in timing; **Zeit|ver|schwen|dung** F waste of time; **das wäre ~** that would be a waste of time; **zeit|ver|setzt** ADJ staggered; **Zeit|ver|trag** M temporary contract; **Zeit|ver|treib** [-fɐtraip] M -(e)s, -e [-bə] way of passing the time; (= *Hobby*) pastime; **zum ~** to pass the time, as a way of passing the time; **Zeit|vor|ga|be** F **a** (= *Zeitbestimmung*) time setting **b** (= *Vorsprung*) head start; **zeit|wei|lig** [-vaɪlɪç] ADJ temporary ADV for a while; (= *kurzzeitig*) temporarily; **zeit|wei|se** ADV at times; **und ~ Regen** with rain at times; **Zeit|wen|de** F = **Zeitenwende**; **Zeit|wert** M (*Fin*) current value; (= *Marktwert*) market value; (= *Messergebnis*) time; **Zeit|wort** NT *pl* **-wörter** verb; **Zeit|zei|chen** NT time signal; **Zeit|zeu|ge** M , **Zeit|zeu|gin** F contemporary witness; **Zeit|zo|ne** F time zone; **Zeit|zün|der** M time fuse

ze|le|brie|ren [tsele'bri:rən] *ptp* **zelebriert** VT to celebrate

Ze|le|bri|tät [tselebri'tɛ:t] F -, -en (*rare*) celebrity

Zell|at|mung F cellular respiration

Zel|le ['tsɛlə] F -, -n cell (*auch Sci, Pol*); (= *Kabine*) cabin; (= *Telefonzelle*) (phone) box (*Brit*) *or* booth; (*bei Flugzeug*) airframe

Zell-: Zell|ge|we|be NT cell tissue; **Zell|gift** NT cytotoxin; **Zell|kern** M nucleus (of a/the cell); **Zell|kern|tei|lung** F cell division, mitosis; **Zell|kul|tur** F cell culture; **Zell|memb|-ran** F cell membrane

Zel|lo|phan [tsɛlo'faːn] NT **-s,** *no pl* cellophane

Zell-: Zell|plas|ma NT cytoplasm; **Zell|prä|pa|rat** NT cell culture; **Zell|stoff** M cellulose; **Zell|stoff|win|del** F disposable nappy (*Brit*) *or* diaper (*US*); **Zell|tei|lung** F cell division

zel|lu|lar [tsɛlu'laːɐ] ADJ cellular

Zel|lu|lar|the|ra|pie F cell therapy

Zel|lu|li|tis [tsɛlu'liːtɪs] F -, *no pl* (*Med*) cellulite

Zel|lu|loid [tsɛlu'lɔyt, tsɛlulo'iːt] NT **-s,** *no pl* celluloid

Zel|lu|lo|se [tsɛlu'loːzə] F -, **-n** cellulose

Zell-: Zell|ver|schmel|zung F cell fusion; **Zell|wand** F cell wall; **Zell|wol|le** F spun rayon

Ze|lot[1] [tse'loːt] M **-en, -en** (*fig geh:* = Eiferer) zealot, fanatic

Ze|lot[2] M , **Ze|lo|tin** [tse'loːtɪn] F -, **-nen** (*Hist*) Zealot

Zelt [tsɛlt] NT **-(e)s, -e** tent; (= Bierzelt, Festzelt etc *auch*) marquee; (= Indianerzelt) wigwam, te(e)pee; (= Zirkuszelt) big top; (*liter:* des Himmels) canopy; **seine ~e aufschlagen** (*fig*) to settle down; **seine ~e abbrechen** (*fig*) to pack one's bags

Zelt-: Zelt|bahn F strip of canvas; **Zelt|dach** NT tent roof; (*Dachform*) pyramid roof

zel|ten ['tsɛltn] VI to camp; **Zelten verboten** no camping

Zel|ter[1] ['tsɛltɐ] M **-s, -** (*Hist:* = Pferd) palfrey

Zel|ter[2] ['tsɛltɐ] M **-s, -**, **Zel|te|rin** [-ərɪn] F -, **-nen** camper

Zelt-: Zelt|he|ring M tent peg; **Zelt|la|ger** NT camp; **wann fahrt ihr ins ~?** when are you going to camp?; **Zelt|lein|wand** F , *no pl* canvas; **Zelt|mast** M tent pole; **Zelt|mis|si|on** F evangelistic mission with a tent as its base; **Zelt|pflock** M tent peg; **Zelt|pla|ne** F tarpaulin; **Zelt|platz** M camp site; **Zelt|stan|ge** F tent pole

Ze|ment [tse'mɛnt] M **-(e)s, -e** cement

ze|men|tie|ren [tsemɛn'tiːrən] *ptp* **zementiert** VT to cement; (= verputzen) to cement over; *Stahl* to carburize (*spec*); (*fig*) to reinforce; *Freundschaft* to cement

Ze|men|tie|rung F -, **-en** (*fig*) reinforcement; (*von Freundschaft*) cementing

Ze|ment|(misch)|ma|schi|ne F cement mixer

Zen [zɛn, tsɛn] NT **-s,** *no pl* Zen (Buddhism)

Ze|nit [tse'niːt] M **-(e)s,** *no pl* (*lit, fig*) zenith; **die Sonne steht im ~** the sun is at its zenith; **im ~ des Lebens stehen** (*liter*) to be at one's peak

Ze|no|taph [tseno'taːf] M cenotaph

zen|sie|ren [tsɛn'ziːrən] *ptp* **zensiert** VT **a** *auch* vi (= benoten) to mark; **einen Aufsatz mit einer Drei ~** to give an essay a three **b** *Bücher etc* to censor

Zen|sor ['tsɛnzoːɐ] M **-s, Zensoren** [-'zoːrən], **Zen|so|rin** [-'zoːrɪn] F -, **-nen** censor

Zen|sur [tsɛn'zuːɐ] F -, **-en a** *no pl* (= Kontrolle) censorship *no indef art;* (= Prüfstelle) censors *pl;* (*esp bei Film*) board of censors; **eine ~ findet nicht statt** there is no censorship; **durch die ~ gehen** to be censored; **der ~ unterliegen** to be subject to censorship **b** (= Note) mark; **der Plan erhielt von der Presse schlechte ~en** the plan got the thumbs down from the press (*inf*) **c Zensuren** PL (= Zeugnis) report *sing;* **wenn es auf die ~en zugeht** when report time approaches

zen|su|rie|ren [tsɛnzu'riːrən] *ptp* **zensuriert** VT (*Aus, Sw*) to censor

Zen|sus ['tsɛnzʊs] M **-, -** [-'zuːs] (= Volkszählung) census

Zen|taur [tsɛn'tauɐ] M **-en, -en** centaur

Zen|ti-: Zen|ti|grad [tsɛnti'graːt, 'tsɛnti-] M hundredth of a degree; **Zen|ti|gramm** [tsɛnti-'gram, 'tsɛnti-] NT centigram(me); **Zen|ti|li|ter** [tsɛnti'liːtɐ, -'liːtə, 'tsɛnti-] M OR NT centilitre (*Brit*), centileter (*US*); **Zen|ti|me|ter** [tsɛnti-'meːtɐ, 'tsɛnti-] M OR NT centimetre (*Brit*), centimeter (*US*); **Zen|ti|me|ter|maß** [tsɛnti-'meːtɐ-] NT (metric) tape measure

Zent|ner ['tsɛntnɐ] M **-, -** (metric) hundredweight, 50 kg; (*Aus, Sw*) 100 kg

Zent|ner-: Zent|ner|last F (*fig*) heavy burden; **mir fiel eine ~ vom Herzen** it was a great weight *or* load off my mind; **zent|ner|schwer** ADJ weighing over a hundredweight; (*fig*) heavy ADV **im Magen liegen** like a ton (of lead); **~ auf jdm** *or* **jds Seele lasten** to weigh sb down; **zent|ner|wei|se** ADV by the hundredweight

zent|ral [tsɛn'traːl] (*lit, fig*) ADJ central ADV centrally

Zent|ral- *in cpds* central; **Zent|ral|abi|tur** NT nationwide common A-level (*Brit*) *or* high-school (*US*) school-leaving examinations, centrally standardized final exam; **Zent|ral|bank** F *pl* **-banken** central bank; **Zent|ral|bank|rat** M *council of the German central bank*

Zent|ra|le [tsɛn'traːlə] F -, **-n** (von Firma etc) head office; (für Taxis, Mil) headquarters *sing or pl;* (für Busse etc) depot; (= Schaltzentrale) central control (office); (= Telefonzentrale) exchange; (von Firma etc, Mil) switchboard

Zent|ral-: Zent|ral|ein|heit F (*Comput*) CPU, central processing unit; **Zent|ral|ge|walt** F central(ized) power; **Zent|ral|hei|zung** F central heating

Zent|ra|li|sa|ti|on [tsɛntraliza'tsioːn] F -, **-en** centralization

zent|ra|li|sie|ren [tsɛntrali'ziːrən] *ptp* **zentralisiert** VT to centralize

Zent|ra|li|sie|rung F -, **-en** centralization

Zent|ra|lis|mus [tsɛntra'lɪsmʊs] M -, *no pl* centralism

zent|ra|lis|tisch [tsɛntra'lɪstɪʃ] ADJ centralist ADV from a centralist perspective

Zent|ral-: Zent|ral|ko|mi|tee NT central committee; **Zent|ral|ner|ven|sys|tem** NT central nervous system; **Zent|ral|or|gan** NT (= Zeitung einer Partei oder Organisation) main *or* official organ; **Zent|ral|rat** M central council; **~ der Juden in Deutschland** Central Council of Jews in Germany; **Zent|ral|rech|ner** M (*Comput*) mainframe; **Zent|ral|spei|cher** M (*Comput*) central memory; **Zent|ral|stel|le** F **~ für Arbeitsvermittlung** Central Employment Office (*Brit*), Employment and Training Administration (*US*); **~ für die Vergabe von Studienplätzen** ≈ Universities and Colleges Admissions Service (*Brit*), ≈ Scholastic Aptitude Test Center (*US*); **Zent|ral|ver|rie|ge|lung** [-fɛɐriːgəlʊŋ] F -, **-en** (*Aut*) central (door) locking; **Zent|ral|ver|schluss** ▲ M leaf shutter; **Zent|ral|ver|wal|tung** F central administration

Zent|ren *pl von* **Zentrum**

Zent|rier|au|to|ma|tik F (*Comput*) automatic centering

zent|rie|ren [tsɛn'triːrən] *ptp* **zentriert** VT (*auch Comput*) to centre (*Brit*), to center (*US*)

zent|ri|fu|gal [tsɛntrifu'gaːl] ADJ centrifugal

Zent|ri|fu|gal|kraft F centrifugal force

Zent|ri|fu|ge [tsɛntri'fuːgə] F -, **-n** centrifuge

zent|ri|pe|tal [tsɛntripe'taːl] ADJ centripetal

Zent|ri|pe|tal|kraft F centripetal force

zent|risch ['tsɛntrɪʃ] ADJ concentric; *Anziehung* centric

Zent|rum ['tsɛntrʊm] NT **-s, Zentren** [-trən] (*lit, fig*) centre (*Brit*), center (*US*); (= Innenstadt) (town) centre (*Brit*) *or* center (*US*); (von Großstadt) city centre (*Brit*) *or* center (*US*); **sie wohnt im ~ (der Stadt)/von Chicago** she lives in the (town/city) centre (*Brit*) *or* center (*US*)/in the centre (*Brit*) *or* center (*US*) of Chicago, she lives downtown/in downtown Chicago (*US*); **im ~ des Interesses stehen** to be the centre (*Brit*) *or* center (*US*) of attention

Zent|rums|par|tei F (*Hist*) Centre (*Brit*) *or* Center (*US*) party (*German Catholic party representing the centre politically*)

Ze|phir [tse'fiːɐ] M **-s, -e** (*esp Aus*), **Ze|phyr** ['tse:fyːɐ] M **-s, -e** (*liter*) zephyr

Zep|pe|lin ['tsɛpəliːn] M **-s, -e** zeppelin

Zep|ter ['tsɛptɐ] NT **-s, -** sceptre (*Brit*), scepter (*US*); **das ~ führen** *or* **schwingen** (*inf*) to wield the sceptre (*Brit*) *or* scepter (*US*); (*esp Ehefrau*) to rule the roost

Zer [tse:ɐ] NT **-s,** *no pl* (*abbr* **Ce**) cerium

zer|bei|ßen *ptp* **zerbissen** [tsɛɐ'bɪsn] VT *irreg* to chew; *Knochen, Bonbon, Keks etc* to crunch; (= beschädigen) *Pantoffel etc* to chew to pieces; (= auseinander beißen) *Kette, Leine* to chew through

zer|bers|ten *ptp* **zerborsten** [tsɛɐ'bɔrstn] VI *irreg aux sein* to burst; (*Glas*) to shatter

Zer|be|rus ['tsɛrberʊs] M **-, -se a** *no pl* (*Myth*) Cerberus **b** (*fig hum*) watchdog

zer|beu|len *ptp* **zerbeult** VT to dent; **zerbeult** battered

zer|bom|ben *ptp* **zerbombt** VT to flatten with bombs, to bomb to smithereens (*inf*); *Gebäude auch* to bomb out; **zerbombt** (*Stadt, Gebäude*) bombed out; **zerbombt werden** to be flattened by bombs

zer|bre|chen *ptp* **zerbrochen** [tsɛɐ'brɔxn] *irreg* **VT** (*lit*) to break into pieces; *Glas, Porzellan etc* to smash, to shatter; *Ketten* (*lit, fig*) to break, to sever; (*fig*) *Widerstand* to break down; *Lebenswille* to destroy → **Kopf c VI** *aux sein* to break into pieces; (*Glas, Porzellan etc*) to smash, to shatter; (*fig*) to be destroyed (*an +dat* by); (*Ehe*) to fall apart; (*Widerstand*) to collapse (*an +dat* in the face of); **er ist am Leben zerbrochen** he has been broken *or* destroyed by life

zer|brech|lich [tsɛɐ'brɛçlɪç] ADJ fragile; *alter Mensch* frail; **"Vorsicht ~!"** "fragile, handle with care"

Zer|brech|lich|keit F -, *no pl* fragility; (*von altem Menschen*) frailness

zer|brö|ckeln *ptp* **zerbröckelt** VTI (*vi: aux sein*) to crumble

zer|dät|schen [tsɛɐ'dɛtʃn] *ptp* **zerdätscht** VT (*inf*) to squash, to crush

zer|dep|pern [tsɛɐ'dɛpɐn] *ptp* **zerdeppert** VT (*inf*) to smash

zer|drü|cken *ptp* **zerdrückt** VT to squash, to crush; *Gemüse* to mash; (= zerknittern) to crush, to crease, to crumple; (*inf*) *Träne* to squeeze out

Ze|re|a|li|en [tsere'aːliən] PL cereals *pl*

Ze|re|mo|nie [tseremo'niː, tsere'moːniə] F -, **-n** [-'niːən, -niən] ceremony

ze|re|mo|ni|ell [tseremo'niɛl] ADJ ceremonial ADV ceremonially

Ze|re|mo|ni|ell [tseremo'niɛl] NT **-s, -e** ceremonial

Ze|re|mo|ni|en|meis|ter(in) [tsere'moːniən-] M(F) master of ceremonies

zer|fah|ren [tsɛɐ'faːrən] ADJ scatty (*esp Brit inf*), scatterbrained; (= unkonzentriert) distracted

Zer|fall M , *no pl* disintegration; (*von Gebäude auch, von Atom*) decay; (*von Leiche, Holz etc*) decomposition; (*von Land, Kultur*) decline, decay, fall; (*von Gesundheit*) decline

zer|fal|len[1] *ptp* **zerfallen** VI *irreg aux sein* **a** (= sich auflösen) to disintegrate; (*Gebäude*) to decay, to fall into ruin; (*Atomkern*) to decay; (= auseinander fallen) to fall apart, to disintegrate; (*Leiche, Holz etc*) to decompose; (*Reich, Kultur, Moral*) to decay, to decline; (*Gesundheit*) to decline; **zu Staub ~** to crumble (in)to dust **b** (= sich gliedern) to fall (*in +acc* into)

zer|fal|len[2] ADJ **a** *Haus* tumbledown; *Gemäuer* crumbling **b** (= verfeindet) **mit jdm ~ sein** to have fallen out with sb; **mit sich** (*dat*) **und der Welt/mit sich** (*dat*) **selbst ~ sein** to be at odds with the world/oneself

Zer|falls-: Zer|falls|er|schei|nung F sign of decay; **Zer|falls|ge|schwin|dig|keit** F rate of decay; **Zer|falls|pro|dukt** NT daughter product

zer|fa|sern ptp **zerfasert** VT aux haben to fray VI aux sein to fray

zer|fet|zen ptp **zerfetzt** VT to tear or rip to pieces or shreds; Brief etc to rip up, to tear up (into little pieces); (Geschoss) Arm etc to mangle, to tear to pieces; (fig) to pull or tear to pieces

zer|fetzt [tsɛɐ̯ˈfɛtst] ADJ Hose ragged, tattered; Körper, Arm lacerated

zer|fled|dern [tsɛɐ̯ˈflɛdɐn] ptp **zerfleddert**, **zer-fle|dern** [tsɛɐ̯ˈfleːdɐn] ptp **zerfledert** VT (inf) to tatter, to get tatty (esp Brit inf)

zer|flei|schen [tsɛɐ̯ˈflaɪʃn] ptp **zerfleischt** VT to tear to pieces; **einander ~** (fig) to tear each other apart VR **er zerfleischt sich in (Selbst)-vorwürfen** he torments or tortures himself with self-reproaches; **sich gegenseitig ~** to tear each other apart

zer|flie|ßen ptp **zerflossen** [tsɛɐ̯ˈflɔsn] VI irreg aux sein (Tinte, Make-up etc) to run; (Eis etc, fig: Reichtum etc) to melt away; **in Tränen ~** to dissolve into tears; **seine Hoffnungen zerflossen in nichts** his hopes melted away; **vor Mitleid ~** to be overcome with pity

zer|franst [tsɛɐ̯ˈfranst] ADJ frayed

zer|fres|sen ptp **zerfressen** VT irreg to eat away; (Säure, Rost auch) to corrode; (Motten, Mäuse etc) to eat; (fig) to consume; **die Säure hat ihr das Gesicht ~** the acid burned into her face; **(von Motten/Würmern) ~ sein** to be moth-eaten/worm-eaten

zer|fur|chen ptp **zerfurcht** VT to furrow

zer|ge|hen ptp **zergangen** [tsɛɐ̯ˈɡaŋən] VI irreg aux sein to dissolve; (= schmelzen) to melt; **auf der Zunge ~** (Gebäck etc) to melt in the mouth; (Fleisch) to fall apart; **vor Mitleid ~** to be overcome with pity

zer|glie|dern ptp **zergliedert** VT (Biol) to dissect; Satz to parse; (fig) to analyse (Brit), to analyze (US)

Zer|glie|de|rung F (Biol) dissection; (von Satz) parsing; (fig) analysis

zer|ha|cken ptp **zerhackt** VT to chop up

Zer|ha|cker M (Telec) scrambler

zer|hau|en ptp **zerhauen** VT irreg to chop in two; (in viele Stücke) to chop up; Knoten (lit, fig) to cut; (inf: = kaputtschlagen) to smash

zer|kau|en ptp **zerkaut** VT to chew; (Hund) Leine to chew up

zer|klei|nern [tsɛɐ̯ˈklaɪnɐn] ptp **zerkleinert** VT to cut up; (= zerhacken) to chop (up); (= zerbrechen) to break up; (= zermahlen) to grind

zer|klüf|tet [tsɛɐ̯ˈklʏftət] ADJ Tal etc rugged; Ufer indented; (Med) Mandeln fissured; **tief ~es Gestein** rock with deep fissures, deeply fissured rock

zer|knaut|schen ptp **zerknautscht** VT (inf) to crease, to crumple

zer|knautscht [tsɛɐ̯ˈknaʊtʃt] ADJ (inf) Kleidung creased, crumpled; Gesicht (= faltig) wizened; **du siehst heute fürchterlich ~ aus** you're looking somewhat the worse for wear today

zer|kni|cken ptp **zerknickt** VT aux haben (= verbiegen) to bend; (= zerbrechen) to snap VI aux sein Zweig, Baum to be bent; (= abbrechen) to snap

zer|knirscht [tsɛɐ̯ˈknɪrʃt] ADJ remorseful, overcome with remorse; Gesicht remorse-filled

Zer|knirscht|heit F -, no pl, **Zer|knir|schung** [tsɛɐ̯ˈknɪrʃʊŋ] F -, no pl remorse

zer|knit|tern ptp **zerknittert** VT to crease, to crumple

zer|knit|tert [tsɛɐ̯ˈknɪtɐt] ADJ **a** Kleid, Stoff creased **b** (inf) (= schuldbewusst) overcome with remorse; (= unausgeschlafen) washed-out (inf)

zer|knül|len ptp **zerknüllt** VT to crumple up, to scrunch up (inf)

zer|ko|chen ptp **zerkocht** VTI (vi: aux sein) to cook to a pulp; (= zu lange kochen auch) to overcook

zer|krat|zen ptp **zerkratzt** VT to scratch

zer|krü|meln ptp **zerkrümelt** VT to crumble; Boden to loosen

zer|las|sen ptp **zerlassen** VT irreg to melt

zer|lau|fen ptp **zerlaufen** VI irreg aux sein to melt

zer|leg|bar ADJ able to be taken apart; Maschine, Gerüst auch able to be dismantled; (Gram) analysable (Brit), analyzable (US); (Math) reducible; **die Möbel waren leicht ~** the furniture could easily be taken apart, the furniture was easily taken apart

zer|le|gen ptp **zerlegt** VT (= auseinander nehmen) to take apart or to pieces; Gerüst, Maschine auch to dismantle; Motor, Getriebe auch to strip down; Theorie, Argumente to break down; (Gram) to analyse (Brit), to analyze (US); (Chem) to break down; (= zerschneiden) to cut up; Geflügel, Wild to carve up; (Biol) to dissect; **etw in seine Einzelteile ~** to take sth to pieces; to dismantle sth completely; to strip sth down; to break sth down into its (individual) constituents; Satz to parse sth; **eine Zahl in ihre Faktoren ~** to factorize a number

Zer|le|gung [tsɛɐ̯ˈleːɡʊŋ] F -, -en taking apart; (von Gerüst, Maschine auch) dismantling; (von Motor, Getriebe auch) stripping down; (Gram) analysis; (Math) reduction; (Biol) dissection

zer|le|sen [tsɛɐ̯ˈleːzn] ADJ Buch well-thumbed

zer|lumpt [tsɛɐ̯ˈlʊmpt] ADJ Kleidung ragged, tattered no adv; Kind, Gestalt etc ragged

zer|mah|len ptp **zermahlen** VT to grind; (in Mörser) to crush

zer|mal|men [tsɛɐ̯ˈmalmən] ptp **zermalmt** VT (lit, fig) to crush; (mit den Zähnen) to crunch, to grind

zer|man|schen ptp **zermanscht** VT (inf) to squash; (mit Gabel) to mash

zer|mar|tern ptp **zermartert** VT **sich** (dat) **den Kopf** or **das Hirn ~** to rack or cudgel (Brit) one's brains

zer|mat|schen ptp **zermatscht** VT (inf) to squash; (mit Gabel) to mash

zer|mür|ben [tsɛɐ̯ˈmʏrbn] ptp **zermürbt** VT **a** (fig) **jdn ~** to wear sb down; **~d** wearing, trying **b** (rare: = brüchig machen) to make brittle

Zer|mür|bung F -, -en (eines Gegners etc) wearing down no pl, attrition

Zer|mür|bungs-: Zer|mür|bungs|krieg M war of attrition; **Zer|mür|bungs|tak|tik** F tactics pl of attrition

zer|na|gen ptp **zernagt** VT to chew to pieces; (Nagetiere) to gnaw to pieces

Ze|ro [ˈzeːro] F -, -s or nt -s, -s zero

Ze|ro|bond [ˈzeːrobɔnt] M -s, -s (St Ex) zero-coupon bond

zer|pflü|cken ptp **zerpflückt** VT (lit, fig) to pick to pieces

zer|plat|zen ptp **zerplatzt** VI aux sein to burst; (Glas) to shatter

zer|quält [tsɛɐ̯ˈkvɛːlt] ADJ tortured

zer|quet|schen ptp **zerquetscht** VT to squash, to crush; (mit Gabel) Kartoffeln etc to mash; (inf) Träne to squeeze out

Zer|quetsch|te [tsɛɐ̯ˈkvɛtʃtə] PL decl as adj (inf) **10 Euro und ein paar ~** 10 euros something (or other), 10 euros odd; **hundert** or **Hundert und ein paar ~** a hundred odd; **elf Uhr und ein paar ~** eleven something (or other)

zer|rau|fen ptp **zerrauft** VT to ruffle; **zerrauft** dishevelled

Zerr|bild NT (lit: in Spiegel) distorted picture or image; (fig auch) caricature; (von Verhältnissen, System, Gesellschaft etc auch) travesty

zer|re|den ptp **zerredet** VT to beat to death (inf)

zer|rei|ben ptp **zerrieben** [tsɛˈriːbn] VT irreg to crumble, to crush; (in Mörser etc) to grind; (fig) to crush

zer|rei|ßen ptp **zerrissen** [tsɛˈrɪsn] irreg VT **a** (aus Versehen) to tear; (in Stücke) to tear to pieces or shreds; Faden, Seil etc to break; (absichtlich) Brief etc to tear up; (= zerfleischen) to tear apart; (= plötzlich aufreißen, durchbrechen) Wolkendecke, Stille etc to rend (liter); (fig) Land to tear apart or in two; Bindungen to break; **es zerreißt mir das Herz** (liter) it is heart-rending or heartbreaking, it breaks my heart → auch **zerrissen**
b (= kritisieren) Autor, Stück, Film to tear apart, to tear to pieces → **Luft a, Maul**
VI aux sein (Stoff) to tear; (Band, Seil etc) to break
VR (fig) **ich könnte mich vor Wut ~** I'm hopping (mad) (esp Brit inf), I'm totally pissed (US inf); **ich kann mich doch nicht ~!** I can't be in two places at once; **sich ~, (um) etw zu tun** to go to no end of trouble to do sth

Zer|reiß-: zer|reiß|fest ADJ tear-resistant; **Zer|reiß|pro|be** F (lit) pull test; (fig) real test; **eine ~ für ihre Ehe** a crucial test of their marriage etc; **eine ~ für meine Geduld** a real test of my patience

zer|ren [ˈtsɛrən] VT to drag; Sehne to pull, to strain; sich (dat) **einen Muskel ~** to pull a muscle; **jdm die Kleider vom Leib ~** to tear the clothes from sb's body; **sich** (dat) **die Kleider vom Leib ~** to tear one's clothes off; **etw an die Öffentlichkeit ~** to drag sth into the public eye VI **an etw** (dat) **~** to tug or pull at sth; **an den Nerven ~** to be nerve-racking

zer|rin|nen ptp **zerronnen** [tsɛɐ̯ˈrɔnən] VI irreg aux sein to melt (away); (fig) (Träume, Pläne) to melt or fade away; (Geld, Vermögen) to disappear; **jdm unter den Händen** or **zwischen den Fingern ~** (Geld) to run through sb's hands like water; **die Zeit zerrinnt mir unter den Händen** the time just goes without me knowing where

zer|ris|sen [tsɛɐ̯ˈrɪsn] ADJ (fig) Volk, Partei strife-torn, disunited; Mensch (inwardly) torn → auch **zerreißen**

Zer|ris|sen|heit F -, no pl (fig) (von Volk, Partei) disunity no pl; (von Mensch) (inner) conflict

Zerr|spie|gel M (lit) distorting mirror; (fig) travesty

Zerr|ung [ˈtsɛrʊŋ] F -, -en (= das Zerren: von Sehne, Muskel) pulling; (eine ~ von Sehne) a pulled ligament; (von Muskel) a pulled muscle

zer|rup|fen ptp **zerrupft** VT to pick or pull to pieces

zer|rüt|ten [tsɛɐ̯ˈrʏtn] ptp **zerrüttet** VT to destroy, to ruin, to wreck; Ehe to break up, to destroy; Geist to destroy; Nerven to shatter; **eine zerrüttete Ehe/Familie** a broken marriage/home; **ein zerrüttetes Verhältnis zu jdm haben** to have a disturbed or troubled relationship with sb; **sich in einem zerrütteten Zustand befinden** to be in a very bad way or in terrible shape

Zer|rüt|tung F -, -en destruction; (von Ehe) breakdown; (von Nerven) shattering; (Zustand) shattered state; **der Staat befindet sich im Zustand der ~** the state is in a bad way or in terrible shape; **ihre Ehe befindet sich im Zustand der ~** their marriage is breaking down

Zer|rüt|tungs|prin|zip NT principle of irretrievable breakdown

zer|sä|gen ptp **zersägt** VT to saw up

zer|schel|len ptp **zerschellt** VI aux sein (Schiff, Flugzeug) to be dashed or smashed to pieces; (Vase etc) to smash (to pieces or smithereens); **das zerschellte Schiff** the wrecked ship

zer|schie|ßen ptp **zerschossen** [tsɛɐ̯ˈʃɔsn] VT irreg to shoot to pieces; (= durchlöchern) to riddle with bullets; **er hatte ein zerschossenes Bein** his leg had been shot to pieces/was riddled with bullets

zer|schla|gen¹ ptp **zerschlagen** irreg **VT** **a** (*Mensch*) to smash (to pieces); *Stein, Porzellan, Glas etc* to shatter, to smash; (*Hagel*) *Ernte, Wein* to crush; (= *auseinander schlagen*) to break up **b** (*fig*) *Angriff, Widerstand, Opposition* to crush; *Hoffnungen, Pläne* to shatter; *Verbrecherring etc, Vereinigung* to break; *Großunternehmen* to break up; *Staat* to smash **VR** (= *nicht zustande kommen*) to fall through; (*Hoffnung, Aussichten*) to be shattered

zer|schla|gen² ADJ pred washed out (*inf*); (*nach Anstrengung, langer Reise etc*) shattered (*Brit inf*), worn out; *Gesicht* drawn, haggard; **ich wachte wie ~ auf** I woke up feeling washed out (*inf*)

Zer|schla|gen|heit F -, no pl exhaustion

Zer|schla|gung [tsɛɐˈʃlaːɡʊŋ] F -, -en (*fig*) suppression; (*von Hoffnungen, Plänen*) shattering

zer|schlei|ßen [tsɛɐˈʃlaisn] pret **zerschliss** [tsɛɐˈʃlɪs], ptp **zerschlissen** [tsɛɐˈʃlɪsn] VTI (*vi: aux sein*) to wear out; **zerschlissene Kleider** worn-out or threadbare clothes

zer|schmei|ßen ptp **zerschmissen** [tsɛɐˈʃmɪsn] VT (*inf*) irreg to shatter, to smash (to pieces)

zer|schmel|zen ptp **zerschmolzen** [tsɛɐˈʃmɔltsn] VI irreg aux sein (*lit, fig*) to melt; **vor Rührung/Mitleid** (*dat*) **~** (*iro*) to brim (over) with emotion/pity

zer|schmet|tern ptp **zerschmettert** **VT** (*lit, fig*) to shatter; *Feind* to crush; (*Sport*) *Gegner* to smash **VI** aux sein to shatter

zer|schnei|den ptp **zerschnitten** [tsɛɐˈʃnɪtn] VT irreg to cut; (*in zwei Teile*) to cut in two; (*in Stücke*) to cut up; (= *verschneiden*) *Stoff* to cut wrongly; (*fig*) *Stille* to pierce; **jdm das Herz ~** to cut sb to the heart (*US*) or quick

zer|schnip|peln ptp **zerschnippelt** VT (*inf*) to snip to pieces

zer|schram|men ptp **zerschrammt** VT *Haut, Möbel* to scratch to pieces; *Lack* to scratch

zer|set|zen ptp **zersetzt** **VT** to decompose; (*Säure*) to corrode; (*fig*) to undermine, to subvert **VR** to decompose; (*durch Säure*) to corrode; (*fig*) to become undermined or subverted

zer|set|zend ADJ (*fig*) subversive

Zer|set|zung [tsɛɐˈzɛtsʊŋ] F -, -en (*Chem*) decomposition; (*durch Säure*) corrosion; (*fig*) (= *Untergrabung*) undermining, subversion; (*von Gesellschaft*) decline (*von* in), decay

Zer|set|zungs-: **Zer|set|zungs|er|schei|nung** F (*fig*) sign of decline or decay; **Zer|set|zungs|pro|dukt** NT substance produced by decomposition; **Zer|set|zungs|pro|zess** ▲ M → **Zersetzung** (process of) decomposition/corrosion/subversion; decline (*von* in), decay

zer|sie|deln ptp **zersiedelt** VT to spoil (by development)

Zer|sie|de|lung [tsɛɐˈziːdəlʊŋ] F -, -en, **Zer|sied|lung** F overdevelopment

zer|spal|ten ptp **zerspalten** VT to split; *Gemeinschaft* to split up

zer|split|tern ptp **zersplittert** **VT** to shatter; *Holz* to splinter; (*fig*) *Kräfte, Zeit* to dissipate, to squander; *Gruppe, Partei* to fragment **VI** aux sein to shatter; (*Holz, Knochen*) to splinter; (*fig*) to split up **VR** to shatter; (*Holz*) to splinter; (*fig*) to dissipate or squander one's energies; (*Gruppe, Partei*) to fragment, to become fragmented; **der Widerstand ist zu zersplittert** the opposition is too fragmented

Zer|split|te|rung [tsɛɐˈʃplɪtərʊŋ] F -, -en shattering; (*von Holz*) splintering; (*fig*) dissipation, squandering; (*von Gruppe, Partei*) fragmentation

zer|spren|gen ptp **zersprengt** VT to burst; (*fig*) *Volksmenge* to disperse, to scatter; *Heer* to scatter

zer|sprin|gen ptp **zersprungen** [tsɛɐˈʃprʊŋən] VI irreg aux sein to shatter; (*Saite*) to break; (= *einen Sprung bekommen*) to crack; **in tausend Stücke ~** to shatter in(to) a thousand pieces; **das Herz**

wollte ihr vor Freude/Ungeduld fast **~** (*liter*) her heart was bursting with joy/impatience

zer|stamp|fen ptp **zerstampft** VT (= *zertreten*) to stamp or trample on; (= *zerkleinern*) to crush; (*im Mörser*) to grind, to pound; *Kartoffeln etc* to mash

zer|stäu|ben ptp **zerstäubt** VT to spray

Zer|stäu|ber [tsɛɐˈʃtɔybɐ] M -s, - spray; (= *Parfümzerstäuber auch*) atomizer

zer|ste|chen ptp **zerstochen** [tsɛɐˈʃtɔxn] VT irreg **a** (*Mücken*) to bite (all over); (*Bienen etc*) to sting (all over); **wir sind ganz zerstochen worden** we've been bitten/stung all over; **von Injektionen zerstochene Venen** veins scarred by injections **b** *Material, Haut, Reifen* to puncture; *Finger* to prick

zer|stie|ben ptp **zerstoben** [tsɛɐˈʃtoːbn] VI irreg aux sein to scatter; (*Wasser*) to spray

zer|stör|bar ADJ destructible; **nicht ~** indestructible

zer|stö|ren ptp **zerstört** **VT** (*lit, fig*) to destroy; *Gebäude, Ehe, Glück auch* to wreck; (= *verwüsten auch*) to ruin; (*Rowdys*) to vandalize; *Gesundheit* to wreck, to ruin **VI** to destroy → **Boden a**

Zer|stö|rer¹ [tsɛɐˈʃtøːrɐ] M -s, - (*old Aviat*) fighter; (*Naut*) destroyer

Zer|stö|rer² [tsɛɐˈʃtøːrɐ] M -s, -, **Zer|stö|re|rin** [-ərɪn] F -, -nen destroyer

zer|stö|re|risch [tsɛɐˈʃtøːrərɪʃ] ADJ destructive **ADV** destructively; **~ wirken** to wreak destruction

Zer|stö|rung F **a** no pl (= *das Zerstören*) destruction; (*von Gebäude, Ehe, Glück auch*) wrecking; (*durch Rowdys*) vandalizing **b** (*durch Krieg, Katastrophe etc*) destruction no pl, devastation no pl

Zer|stö|rungs-: **Zer|stö|rungs|drang** M destructive urge or impulse; **Zer|stö|rungs|lust** F delight in destruction; **Zer|stö|rungs|trieb** M destructive urge or impulse; **Zer|stö|rungs|werk** NT work of destruction; **Zer|stö|rungs|wut** F destructive mania

zer|sto|ßen ptp **zerstoßen** VT irreg **a** (= *zerkleinern*) to crush; (*im Mörser*) to pound, to grind **b** (= *durch Stoßen beschädigen*) to damage; *Leder, Schuh* to scuff

zer|strei|ten ptp **zerstritten** [tsɛɐˈʃtrɪtn] VR irreg to quarrel, to fall out → **auch zerstritten**

zer|streu|en ptp **zerstreut** **VT** **a** (= *verstreuen*) to scatter (*in* +dat over); *Volksmenge etc* to disperse; *Licht* to diffuse; (*fig*) to dispel, to allay **b** (= *ablenken*) **jdn ~** to take sb's mind off things, to divert sb **VR** **a** (= *sich verteilen*) to scatter; (*Menge*) to disperse; to disperse; (*fig*) to be dispelled or allayed **b** (= *sich ablenken*) to take one's mind off things; (= *sich amüsieren*) to amuse oneself

zer|streut [tsɛɐˈʃtrɔyt] ADJ (*fig*) *Mensch* absent-minded; **sie ist heute sehr ~** her mind is elsewhere today

Zer|streut|heit F -, no pl absent-mindedness

Zer|streu|ung F **a** no pl (= *das Zerstreuen*) scattering; (*von Menge*) dispersal; (*von Licht*) diffusion; (*fig*) dispelling, allaying **b** (= *Ablenkung*) diversion; **zur ~** as a diversion **c** (= *Zerstreutheit*) absent-mindedness

zer|strit|ten [tsɛɐˈʃtrɪtn] ADJ **~ sein** (*Paar, Geschäftspartner*) to have fallen out; (*Partei*) to be disunited; **mit jdm ~ sein** to have fallen out with sb; **sie sind seit langem ~** they fell out a long time ago → **auch zerstreiten**

Zer|strit|ten|heit F (*von Paar, Geschäftspartnern*) bad blood (+gen between); (*von Partei*) disunity

zer|stü|ckeln ptp **zerstückelt** VT (*lit*) to cut up; *Leiche* to dismember; *Land* to divide or carve up; (*fig*) *Tag, Semester etc* to break up

zer|tei|len ptp **zerteilt** VT to split up; (*in zwei Teile auch*) to divide; (= *zerschneiden*) to cut up; *Wogen, Wolken* to part; **ich kann mich nicht ~!** I can't be in two places at once

Zer|ti|fi|kat [tsɛrtifiˈkaːt] NT -(e)s, -e certificate

zer|ti|fi|zie|ren [tsɛrtifiˈtsiːrən] VT ptp **zertifiziert** to certify

Zer|ti|fi|zie|rung [tsɛrtifiˈtsiːrʊŋ] F -, -en certification; **~ nach DIN EN 9002** certification in accordance with DIN EN 9002, DIN EN 9002 certification

zer|tram|peln ptp **zertrampelt** VT to trample on

zer|tren|nen ptp **zertrennt** VT to sever, to cut through; (= *auftrennen*) *Nähte* to undo; *Kleid* to undo the seams of

zer|tre|ten ptp **zertreten** VT irreg to crush (underfoot); *Rasen* to ruin; **jdn wie einen Wurm ~** to grind sb into the ground

zer|trüm|mern [tsɛɐˈtrʏmɐn] ptp **zertrümmert** VT to smash; *Gebäude auch* to wreck, to destroy; *Einrichtung* to smash up; *Hoffnungen, Ordnung* to wreck, to destroy

Zer|trüm|me|rung F -, -en smashing; (*von Einrichtung*) smashing up; (*von Hoffnungen, Ordnung*) wrecking, destruction; (*dated: von Atom*) splitting

Zer|ve|lat|wurst [tsɛrvəˈlaːt-] F cervelat, German salami

zer|vi|kal [tsɛrviˈkaːl] ADJ (*spec*) cervical

zer|wer|fen ptp **zerworfen** [tsɛɐˈvɔrfn] VR irreg (*fig*) to fall out (*mit jdm* with sb)

zer|wüh|len ptp **zerwühlt** VT to ruffle up, to tousle; *Bett, Kopfkissen* to rumple (up); (= *aufwühlen*) *Erdboden* to churn up; (*Wildschwein etc*) to churn or root up

Zer|würf|nis [tsɛɐˈvʏrfnɪs] NT -ses, -se row, disagreement

zer|zau|sen ptp **zerzaust** VT to ruffle; *Haar* to tousle

zer|zaust [tsɛɐˈtsaust] ADJ windswept; *Haare auch* dishevelled, tousled

Ze|ter [ˈtseːtɐ] NT **~ und Mord(io) schreien** (*lit*) to scream blue (*Brit*) or bloody murder (*inf*); (*fig*) to raise a hue and cry

Ze|ter-: **Ze|ter|ge|schrei** NT (*lit*) hullabaloo; (*fig*) hue and cry; **ze|ter|mor|dio** [tseːtɐˈmɔrdio] ADV **~ schreien** to scream blue (*Brit*) or bloody murder (*inf*)

ze|tern [ˈtseːtɐn] VI (*pej*) to clamour (*Brit*), to clamor (*US*); (= *keifen*) to scold, to nag; (= *jammern*) to moan

Zet|tel [ˈtsɛtl] M -s, - piece of paper; (= *Notizzettel*) note; (= *Karteizettel*) card; (= *Anhängezettel*) label; (*mit Angabe über Inhalt, Anschrift etc*) chit (*inf*), ticket; (= *Bekanntmachung*) notice; (= *Handzettel*) leaflet, handbill (*esp US*), flyer; (= *Formular*) form; (= *Stimmzettel*) ballot paper; (= *Bestellzettel*) coupon; (= *Kassenzettel, Beleg*) receipt; **„Zettel ankleben verboten"** "stick no bills" (*Brit*), "no posters allowed"

Zet|tel-: **Zet|tel|kar|tei** F card index; **Zet|tel|kas|ten** M file-card box; (= *Zettelkartei*) card index; **Zet|tel|ka|ta|log** M card index; **Zet|tel|ver|tei|ler(in)** M(F) person who hands out leaflets; **Zet|tel|wirt|schaft** F no pl (*pej*) **eine ~ haben** to have bits of paper everywhere; **du mit deiner ~** you and all your bits of paper

Zeug [tsɔyk] NT -(e)s [-ɡəs] no pl **a** (*inf*) stuff no indef art, no pl; (= *Ausrüstung*) gear (*inf*); (= *Kleidung*) clothes pl, things pl (*inf*); (= *Getier*) things pl; **altes ~** junk, trash; **... und solches ...** and such things

b (*inf*: = *Unsinn*) nonsense, rubbish (*esp Brit*); **ein/dieses ~** a/this load of nonsense or rubbish (*esp Brit*); **dummes or ungereimtes ~ reden** to talk a lot of nonsense or drivel (*inf*) or twaddle (*inf*); **rede kein dummes ~** don't talk nonsense

c (= *Fähigkeit, Können*) **das ~ zu etw haben** to have (got) what it takes to be sth (*inf*); **er hat nicht das ~ dazu** he hasn't got what it takes (*inf*)

d (*old*) (= *Stoff*) material; (= *Wäsche*) linen; **jdm etwas am ~ flicken** (*inf*) to tell sb what to do;

was das ~ hält (inf) for all one is worth; **laufen, fahren** like mad; **lügen, was das ~ hält** (inf) to lie one's head off (inf); **sich für jdn ins ~ legen** (inf) to stand up for sb; **sich ins ~ legen** to go flat out (esp Brit) or all out (US); (bei Arbeit auch) to work flat out (esp Brit) or all out (US)

Zeug|amt NT (obs Mil) arsenal

Zeu|ge ['tsɔygə] M -n, -n, **Zeu|gin** ['tsɔygɪn] F -, -nen (Jur, fig) witness (+gen to); **~ eines Unfalls/Gesprächs sein** to be a witness to an accident/a conversation; **sich als ~ zur Verfügung stellen** to come forward as a witness; **vor** or **unter ~n** in front of witnesses; **Gott ist mein ~** as God is my witness; **die ~n Jehovas** Jehovah's Witnesses

zeu|gen¹ ['tsɔygn] VT Kind to father; (Bibl) to beget; (fig geh) to generate, to give rise to

zeu|gen² VI **a** (vor +dat to) (= aussagen) to testify; (esp vor Gericht) to give evidence; **für/gegen jdn ~** to testify for/against sb (;), to give evidence for/against sb **b von etw ~** to show sth

Zeu|gen-: Zeu|gen|aus|sa|ge F testimony; **Zeu|gen|bank** F pl -bänke witness box (Brit), witness stand (US); **er sitzt auf der ~** he's in the witness box (Brit) or witness stand (US); **Zeu|gen|be|ein|fluss|ung** F subornation of a witness/witnesses; **Zeu|gen|be|weis** M evidence (of a witness); **Zeu|gen|la|dung** F summoning of a witness/witnesses; **Zeu|gen|schutz** M witness protection; **unter ~ stehen** to be under witness protection; **jdn unter ~ stellen** to place sb under witness protection; **Zeu|gen|schutz|pro|gramm** NT witness protection programme (Brit) or program (US); **Zeu|gen|stand** M witness box (Brit), witness stand (US); **in den ~ treten** to go into the witness box (Brit), to take the (witness) stand (US); **Zeu|gen|ver|ei|di|gung** F swearing in of a witness/witnesses; **Zeu|gen|ver|neh|mung** F examination of the witness(es)

Zeug|haus NT (obs Mil) arsenal, armoury (Brit), armory (US)

Zeu|gin F -, -nen witness → auch **Zeuge**

Zeug|nis ['tsɔyknɪs] NT -ses, -se **a** (esp liter: = Zeugenaussage) evidence; **für/gegen jdn ~ able-gen** to give evidence for/against sb, to testify for/against sb; **für jds Ehrlichkeit etc ~ ablegen** to bear witness to sb's honesty etc; **falsches ~ ablegen** (Bibl) falsch ~ **reden** (Bibl) to bear false witness **b** (fig: = Beweis) evidence **c** (= Schulzeugnis) report; (= Note) mark, grade (esp US) **d** (= Bescheinigung) certificate; (von Arbeitgeber) testimonial, reference; **gute ~se haben** to have good qualifications; (von Arbeitgeber) to have good references; **jdm ein ~ ausstellen** to give sb a reference or testimonial; **ich kann ihm nur das beste ~ ausstellen** (fig) I cannot speak too highly of him

Zeug|nis-: Zeug|nis|ab|schrift F → Zeugnis c, d copy of one's report/certificate/testimonial; **Zeug|nis|heft** NT (Sch) report book (Brit), report card; **Zeug|nis|kon|fe|renz** F (Sch) staff meeting to decide on marks etc; **Zeug|nis|pa|pie|re** PL certificates pl; (von Arbeitgeber) testimonials pl; **Zeug|nis|pflicht** F (Jur) obligation to give evidence; **Zeug|nis|ver|wei|ge|rung** F (Jur) refusal to give evidence; **Zeug|nis|ver|wei|ge|rungs|recht** NT right of a witness to refuse to give evidence

Zeugs [tsɔyks] NT -, no pl (pej inf) = **Zeug a, b**

Zeu|gung ['tsɔygʊŋ] F -, -en fathering; (Bibl) begetting; (fig geh) generating

Zeu|gungs-: Zeu|gungs|akt M act of procreation; (fig) creative act; **zeu|gungs|fä|hig** ADJ fertile; **Zeu|gungs|fä|hig|keit** F, **Zeu|gungs|kraft** (geh) F fertility; **Zeu|gungs|or|gan** NT (spec) male reproductive organ; **zeu|gungs|un|fä|hig** ADJ sterile; **Zeu|gungs|un|fä|hig|keit** F sterility

Zeus [tsɔys] M -' (Myth) Zeus

zeu|seln ['tsɔyzln] VI (Sw: = zündeln) to play with matches

ZEVIS ['tse:vɪs] NT abbr von **Zentrales Verkehrsinformationssystem**

z. H(d). abbr von **zu Händen** attn

Zi|be|be [tsi'be:bə] F -, -n (S Ger, Aus) sultana

Zi|cho|rie [tsi'ço:riə] F -, -n chicory

Zi|cke ['tsɪkə] F -, -n **a** nanny goat **b** (pej inf: = Frau) silly cow (inf)

Zi|ckel ['tsɪkl] NT -s, -(n) (= junge Ziege) kid; (= junges Reh) fawn

Zi|cken ['tsɪkn] PL (inf) nonsense no pl; **mach bloß keine ~!** no nonsense now!; **~ machen** to make trouble

zi|ckig ['tsɪkɪç] ADJ (inf: = prüde) awkward

Zick|lein ['tsɪklain] NT -s, - (= junge Ziege) kid; (= junges Reh) fawn

Zick|zack ['tsɪktsak] M -(e)s, -e zigzag; **zickzack** or **im ~ laufen** to zigzag; **~ nähen** to zigzag

Zick|zack-: zick|zack|för|mig ADJ zigzag ADV **~ verlaufen** to zigzag; **eine ~ genähte Naht** a zigzag stitch seam; **Zick|zack|kurs** M zigzag course; (von Hase etc) zigzag path; **im ~ fah-ren/laufen** to zigzag; **Zick|zack|li|nie** F zigzag; **Zick|zack|sche|re** F pinking shears pl; **Zick|zack|stich** M zigzag stitch

Zie|ge ['tsi:gə] F -, -n **a** goat; (weiblich) (nanny) goat **b** (pej inf: = Frau) cow (inf)

Zie|gel ['tsi:gl] M -s, - (= Backstein) brick; (= Dachziegel) tile; **ein Dach mit ~n decken** to tile a roof

Zie|gel-: Zie|gel|bau M pl -bauten brick building; **Zie|gel|bren|ner(in)** M(F) brickmaker; (von Dachziegeln) tilemaker; **Zie|gel|bren|ne|rei** F = Ziegelei; **Zie|gel|dach** NT tiled roof

Zie|ge|lei [tsi:gə'lai] F -, -en brickworks sing or pl; (für Dachziegel) tilemaking works sing or pl

Zie|gel-: zie|gel|rot ADJ brick-red; **Zie|gel|stein** M brick

Zie|gen-: Zie|gen|bart M **a** (an Hut) shaving brush (hum); (hum. = Bart) goatee (beard) **b** (Bot) goat's-beard mushroom; **Zie|gen|bock** M billy goat; **Zie|gen|fell** NT goatskin; **Zie|gen|her|de** F herd of goats; **Zie|gen|hirt** M, **Zie|gen|hir|tin** F goatherd; **Zie|gen|kä|se** M goat's milk cheese; **Zie|gen|le|der** NT kid (leather), kidskin; **Zie|gen|milch** F goat's milk; **Zie|gen|pe|ter** M [-pe:tɐ] M -s, - mumps sing

zieh [tsi:] pret von **zeihen**

Zieh-: Zieh|brü|cke F drawbridge; **Zieh|brun|nen** M well; **Zieh|el|tern** PL (old, fig) foster parents pl

zie|hen ['tsi:ən]	
pret **zog** [tso:k], ptp **gezogen** [gə'tso:gn]	
1 TRANSITIVES VERB	3 UNPERSÖNLICHES
2 INTRANSITIVES VERB	VERB
	4 REFLEXIVES VERB

In Verbindungen mit Substantiv siehe auch Eintrag für das jeweilige Substantiv.

1 – TRANSITIVES VERB

a allgemein to pull; Handbremse to put on; Cho-ke, Starter to pull out; Hut to raise; **etw durch etw ziehen** to pull sth through sth; **jdn nach unten ziehen** to pull or (fig) drag sb down; **der Hund zog die Tischdecke vom Tisch** the dog pulled the cloth off the table; **den Ring vom Finger ziehen** to pull one's ring off (one's finger); **die Mütze tiefer ins Gesicht ziehen** to pull one's hat further down over one's face; **den Mantel fest um sich ziehen** to pull one's coat tight around one; **den Mantel übers Kleid ziehen** (= anziehen) to put one's coat on over one's dress; **die Vorhänge vors Fenster ziehen** to pull or draw the curtains; **die Schultern in**

die Höhe ziehen to raise one's shoulders; **er zog die Knie bis unters Kinn hoch** he drew his knees up toward(s) his chin; **das Flugzeug nach oben/unten ziehen** to put the plane into a climb/descent; **die Stirn kraus** or **in Falten ziehen** to knit one's brow; **(neue) Saiten auf ein Instrument ziehen** to (re)string an instrument

b = hinziehen (fig) **was zieht dich denn nach Hause?** what is drawing you home?; **meine Liebe zu den Bergen hat mich in die Schweiz gezogen** my love of the mountains drew me to Switzerland; **es zog ihn in die weite Welt** he felt drawn toward(s) the big wide world; **etw ins Komische ziehen** to ridicule sth; **musst du immer alles ins Lächerliche ziehen?** must you always make fun of everything?; **unangenehme Folgen nach sich ziehen** to have unpleasant consequences; **die Aufmerksamkeit** or **die Bli-cke auf sich** (acc) **ziehen** to attract attention; **jds Hass auf sich** (acc) **ziehen** to incur sb's hatred; **jdn ins Gespräch** or **in die Unterhaltung ziehen** to bring sb into the conversation

c = herausziehen to pull out (aus of); Zahn to take out, to extract; Fäden to take out, to re-move; Korken, Schwert, Revolver to draw, to pull out; Wasserproben to take; (Math) Wurzel to work out; Los, Spielkarte, Schlussfolgerungen to draw; Vergleich to draw, to make; **Wein auf Fla-schen ziehen** to bottle wine; **die Pflanze zieht ihre Nahrung aus dem Boden** the plant takes its nourishment from the soil; **Zigaretten/Kau-gummi (aus dem Automaten) ziehen** to get cig-arettes/chewing gum from the machine

d = zeichnen Kreis, Linie to draw

e = verlegen, anlegen Kabel, Leitung etc to lay; Graben, Furchen to dig; Mauer to build; Zaun to put up; Grenze to draw; **Perlen auf eine Schnur ziehen** to thread pearls

f = herstellen Draht, Kerzen, Kopien to make; **Ko-pien von etw ziehen** to copy sth, to make a copy of sth; **Computerprogramme schwarz zie-hen** to pirate computer programs = auch gezo-gen

g = züchten Blumen to grow; Tiere to breed; **sie haben die Kinder gut gezogen** (inf) they brought the children up well

2 – INTRANSITIVES VERB

a = zerren to pull; **an etw** (dat) **ziehen** to pull (on or at) sth; **ein ziehender Schmerz** an ache

b = umziehen aux sein to move; **nach Bayern/München ziehen** to move to Bavaria/Munich; **zu jdm ziehen** to move in with sb

c = sich bewegen aux sein to move, to go; (Solda-ten, Volksmassen) to march; (= durchstreifen) to wander, to roam; (Wolken, Rauch) to drift; (Ge-witter) to move; (Vögel) to fly; (während des Vo-gelzugs) to migrate; **durch die Welt ziehen** to roam the world; **durch die Stadt ziehen** to wander about the town; **in den Krieg/die Schlacht ziehen** to go to war/battle; **heimwärts ziehen** to make one's way home; **lass mich zie-hen** (old, liter) let me go; **die Jahre zogen ins Land** (liter) the years passed

d = eindringen aux sein to penetrate (in etw (acc) sth); (Rauch, Nebel) to drift (in etw (acc) into sth)

e = rücken (mit Spielfigur) to move; (= abheben) to draw; **mit dem Turm ziehen** to move the rook; **wer zieht?** whose move is it?

f = Zug haben (Feuer, Ofen, Pfeife) to draw; **an der Pfeife/Zigarette ziehen** to take a drag on one's pipe/cigarette

g = Eindruck machen (inf) **so was zieht beim Pu-blikum/bei mir nicht** the public/I don't like that sort of thing; **der Film zieht immer noch** the film is still popular; **so was zieht immer** that sort of thing always goes down well

h = sieden (Tee) to draw; (in Kochwasser) to sim-mer; (in Marinade) to marinade

3 – UNPERSÖNLICHES VERB

♦ **es zieht** there's a draught (Brit) or draft (US); **wenn es dir zieht** if you're in a draught (Brit)

or draft (US); **mir ziehts im Nacken** there is or I can feel a draught (Brit) or draft (US) round my neck; **in diesem Haus zieht es aus allen Ritzen** there are draughts (Brit) or drafts (US) everywhere in this house; **mir ziehts im Rücken** (= tut der Rücken weh) my back hurts

4 – REFLEXIVES VERB

♦ **sich ziehen**

a = **sich erstrecken** to extend; **das Industriegebiet zieht sich bis weit in die Tiefebene (hinein)** the industrial area extends far across the plain; **dieses Treffen zieht sich!** this meeting is dragging on!; **sich zickzackförmig durchs Land ziehen** to zigzag through the countryside; **sich in Schlingen/Serpentinen durch etw ziehen** to twist or wind its way through sth; **dieses Thema zieht sich durch das ganze Buch** this theme runs throughout the whole book

b = **sich dehnen** to stretch; (Klebstoff) to be tacky; (Käse) to form strings; (Holz) to warp; (Metall) to bend

c = **sich befreien sich an etw** (dat) **aus dem Schlamm/in die Höhe ziehen** to pull oneself out of the mud/up on sth → **Affäre, Patsche**

Zie|hen NT **-s,** no pl (= Schmerz) ache; (im Unterleib) abdominal pain

Zieh-: **Zieh|har|mo|ni|ka** F concertina; (mit Tastatur) accordion; **Zieh|kind** NT (old, fig) foster child; **Zieh|mut|ter** F pl **-mütter** (old, fig) foster mother; **Zieh|sohn** M (lit old) foster son; (fig) foster child

Zie|hung ['tsiːʊŋ] F **-, -en** draw

Zieh|va|ter M (old, fig) foster father

Ziel [tsiːl] NT **-(e)s, -e** **a** (= Reiseziel) destination; (= Absicht, Zweck) goal, aim, objective; (von Wünschen, Spott) object; **mit dem ~ ...** with the aim or intention ...; **etw zum ~ haben** to have sth as one's goal or aim; **jdm/sich ein ~ stecken** or **setzen** to set sb/oneself a goal; **er hatte sich sein ~ zu hoch gesteckt** he had set his sights too high; **sich** (dat) **etw zum ~ setzen** to set sth as one's goal etc; **einer Sache** (dat) **ein ~ setzen** to put a limit on sth; (= eindämmen) to limit sth; **zum ~ kommen** or **gelangen** (fig) to reach or attain one's goal etc; **am ~ sein** to be at one's destination, to have reached one's destination; (fig) to have reached or achieved one's goal; **dieser Weg führte ihn nicht zum ~** (fig) this avenue did not lead him to his goal

b (Sport) finish; (bei Pferderennen) finish(ing post), winning post; (bei Rennen) finish(ing line); **durchs ~ gehen** to pass the winning post or finishing post/to cross the finishing line

c (Mil, Sport) target; **ins ~ treffen** to hit the target; **über das ~ hinausschießen** (fig) to overshoot the mark

d (Comm = Frist) credit period; **mit drei Monaten ~** with a three-month credit period

Ziel-: **Ziel|bahn|hof** M destination; **Ziel|band** [-bant] NT pl **-bänder** finishing tape; **ziel|be|wusst** ▲ ADJ purposeful, decisive; **Ziel|be|wusst|sein** ▲ NT purposefulness, decisiveness; **mangelndes ~** lack of purpose

zie|len ['tsiːlən] VI **a** (Mensch) to aim (auf +acc, nach at); (Waffe, Schuss) to be aimed (auf +acc at) **b** (fig: Bemerkung, Kritik, Tat) to be aimed or directed (auf +acc at); **ich weiß, worauf deine Bemerkungen ~** I know what you're driving at; **das zielt auf uns** that's aimed at or meant for us, that's for our benefit → auch **gezielt**

zie|lend ADJ (Gram) Zeitwort transitive

Ziel-: **Ziel|fern|rohr** NT telescopic sight; **Ziel|flug|ge|rät** NT homing indicator; **Ziel|fo|to** NT , **Ziel|fo|to|gra|fie** F photograph of the finish; **Ermittlung des Siegers durch ~** photo finish; **ziel|füh|rend** ADJ Maßnahme etc carefully targeted; (= Erfolg versprechend) successful; (= sinnvoll, zweckmäßig) practical, suitable **ziel|ge|nau** ADJ accurate; Maßnahme, Politik carefully tar-

geted; **Ziel|ge|nau|ig|keit** F accuracy; (von Maßnahme, Politik) careful targeting; **Ziel|ge|ra|de** F home or finishing straight; **Ziel|ge|rät** NT (Mil) bombsight; **ziel|ge|rich|tet** ADJ goal-directed; (= gezielt) purposeful; **Ziel|grup|pe** F target group; **Ziel|ha|fen** M port of destination; **Ziel|kauf** M (Comm) credit purchase; **Ziel|kon|flikt** M conflict of aims; **Ziel|kur|ve** F final bend; **Ziel|li|nie** F (Sport) finishing line; **ziel|los** ADJ aimless, purposeless ADV aimlessly; **Ziel|lo|sig|keit** F **-,** no pl lack of purpose, purposelessness; **zie|lo|ri|en|tiert** ADJ goal-directed; Handeln, Planen purposeful ADV with clear goals in mind, purposefully; **Ziel|ort** M pl **-orte** destination; **Ziel|rich|ter(in)** M(F) (Sport) finishing-line judge; **Ziel|schei|be** F target; (von Spott auch) object; **Ziel|set|zung** [-zetsʊŋ] F **-, -en** target, objective; **ziel|si|cher** ADJ unerring; Handeln, Planen purposeful ADV unerringly; **~ auf jdn/etw zugehen** to go straight up to sb/sth; **Ziel|si|cher|heit** F (unerring) accuracy; **Ziel|spra|che** F target language; **ziel|stre|big** ['tsiːlʃtreːbɪç] ADJ Mensch, Handlungsweise determined, single-minded ADV full of determination; **Ziel|stre|big|keit** F **-,** no pl determination, single-mindedness; **ziel|su|chend** ADJ target-seeking; **Ziel|vor|ga|be** F set target; **Ziel|vor|stel|lung** F objective; **Ziel|was|ser** NT pl **-wässer** (hum inf) schnapps (drunk at a shooting match)

zie|men ['tsiːmən] VR impers (geh) **es ziemt sich nicht** it is not proper or seemly; **das ziemt sich nicht (für dich)** it is not proper (for you) VI (old) **jdm ~** to become sb

Zie|mer ['tsiːmɐ] M **-s, - a** (= Wildrücken) saddle **b** (= Peitsche) whip

ziem|lich ['tsiːmlɪç] ADJ **a** (old: = geziemend) proper, fitting **b** attr (= beträchtlich) Anzahl, Strecke considerable, fair; Vermögen sizable; Genugtuung reasonable; **das ist eine ~e Frechheit** that's a real cheek (Brit), that's really fresh (US); **eine ~e Zeit/Anstrengung/Arbeit** quite a time/an effort/a lot of work; **sie unterhielten sich mit ~er Lautstärke** they were talking quite loudly; **mit ~er Sicherheit** pretty (inf) or fairly certainly; sagen, behaupten with a reasonable or fair degree of certainty, with reasonable certainty

ADV **a** (= beträchtlich) rather, quite, pretty (inf); sicher, genau reasonably; **sie hat sich ~ anstrengen müssen** she had to make quite an effort; **wir haben uns ~ beeilt** we've hurried quite a bit; **~ lange** quite a long time, a fair time; **~ viel** quite a lot **b** (inf: = beinahe) almost, nearly; **so ~ mehr** or less; **so ~ alles** just about everything, more or less everything; **so ~ dasselbe** pretty well (inf) or much the same; **sie ist so ~ in meinem Alter** she is about the same age as me

zie|pen ['tsiːpn̩] VI to chirp, to tweet, to cheep VI impers (inf: = wehtun) **es ziept** it hurts VT (inf: = ziehen) to pull, to tweak; **jdn an den Haaren ~** to pull or tug sb's hair

Zier [tsiːɐ] F **-,** no pl (old, poet) = **Zierde**

Zie|rat △ ['tsiːraːt] M **-(e)s, -e** (geh) → **Zierrat**

Zier|de ['tsiːɐdə] F **-, -n** ornament, decoration; (= Schmuckstück) adornment; (fig: = Tugend) virtue; **zur ~** for decoration; **das alte Haus ist eine ~ der Stadt** the old house is one of the beauties of the town; **eine Eins im Betragen war die einzige ~ seines Zeugnisses** a one for behaviour (Brit) or behavior (US) was the only bright spot on his report; **eine ~ des männlichen Geschlechts** a fine specimen of the male sex; **eine ~ des weiblichen Geschlechts** a flower of the female sex; **die ~ der Familie** (fig) a credit to the family

zie|ren ['tsiːrən] VT to adorn; Speisen to garnish; Kuchen to decorate; (fig: = auszeichnen) to grace; **deine Eifersucht ziert dich nicht gerade** your envy does not exactly do you credit

VR (= sich bitten lassen) to make a fuss, to need

a lot of pressing; (Mädchen) to act coyly; (= sich gekünstelt benehmen) to be affected; **du brauchst dich nicht zu ~, es ist genügend da** there's no need to be polite, there's plenty there; **er zierte sich nicht lange und sagte Ja** he didn't need much pressing before he agreed; **ohne sich zu ~** without having to be pressed; **zier dich nicht!** don't be shy or silly (inf) → auch **geziert**

Zie|re|rei [tsiːrəˈrai] F **-, -en** (= gekünsteltes Benehmen) affectedness

Zier-: **Zier|farn** M decorative fern; **Zier|fisch** M ornamental fish; **Zier|gar|ten** M ornamental garden; **Zier|ge|wächs** NT ornamental plant; **Zier|gras** NT ornamental grass; **Zier|leis|te** F border; (an Auto) trim; (an Möbelstück) edging; (an Wand) moulding (Brit), molding (US)

zier|lich ['tsiːrlɪç] ADJ dainty; Frau auch petite; Porzellanfigur, Möbel etc delicate

Zier|lich|keit F **-,** no pl daintiness; (von Porzellanfigur, Möbel etc) delicateness

Zier-: **Zier|naht** F decorative seam; **Zier|pflan|ze** F ornamental plant; **Zier|rat** ▲ ['tsiːraːt] M **-(e)s, -e** (geh) decoration; **Zier|schrift** F ornamental lettering; **Zier|stich** M embroidery stitch; **Zier|strauch** M ornamental shrub

Zie|sel ['tsiːzl̩] M **-s, -** ground squirrel, suslik

Zif|fer ['tsɪfɐ] F **-, -n a** (abbr **Ziff.**) (= Zahlzeichen) digit; (= Zahl) figure, number; **römische/arabische ~n** roman/arabic numerals; **eine Zahl mit drei ~n** a three-figure number; **etw in ~n schreiben** to write sth in figures or numbers **b** (eines Paragrafen) clause

Zif|fer|blatt NT (an Uhr) dial, (clock) face; (von Armbanduhr) (watch) face

zig [tsɪç] ADJ (inf) umpteen (inf)

zig- ['tsɪç] PREF (inf) umpteen (inf); **zighundert** umpteen hundred (inf)

Zi|ga|ret|te [tsigaˈrɛtə] F **-, -n** cigarette; **~ mit Filter** filter cigarette

Zi|ga|ret|ten- in cpds cigarette; **Zi|ga|ret|ten|an|zün|der** M (in Auto) cigar lighter; **Zi|ga|ret|ten|au|to|mat** M cigarette machine; **Zi|ga|ret|ten|do|se** F cigarette box; **Zi|ga|ret|ten|etui** NT cigarette case; **Zi|ga|ret|ten|kip|pe** F cigarette end or butt, fag end (Brit inf); **Zi|ga|ret|ten|län|ge** F **auf** or **für eine ~ hinausgehen** to go out for a cigarette or smoke; **Zi|ga|ret|ten|pa|pier** NT cigarette paper; **Zi|ga|ret|ten|pau|se** F break for a cigarette or a smoke, cigarette break; **Zi|ga|ret|ten|qualm** M (pej), **Zi|ga|ret|ten|rauch** M cigarette smoke, fug (inf); **Zi|ga|ret|ten|rau|cher(in)** M(F) cigarette smoker; **Zi|ga|ret|ten|schach|tel** F cigarette packet (Brit) or pack (US); **Zi|ga|ret|ten|spit|ze** F cigarette holder; **Zi|ga|ret|ten|stum|mel** M cigarette end or butt, fag end (Brit inf)

Zi|ga|ril|lo [tsigaˈrɪlo, -ˈrɪljo] M OR NT **-s, -s** cigarillo

Zi|gar|re [tsiˈgarə] F **-, -n a** cigar **b** (inf: = Verweis) dressing-down; **jdm eine ~ verpassen** to give sb a dressing-down

Zi|gar|ren- in cpds cigar; **Zi|gar|ren|ab|schnei|der** M cigar cutter; **Zi|gar|ren|kis|te** F cigar box; **Zi|gar|ren|rau|cher(in)** M(F) cigar smoker; **Zi|gar|ren|spit|ze** F cigar holder; **Zi|gar|ren|stum|mel** M cigar butt

Zi|geu|ner [tsiˈgɔynɐ] M **-s, -,** **Zi|geu|ne|rin** [-ərɪn] F **-, -nen** gypsy, gipsy; (Rasse auch) Romany; (pej inf) vagabond; (= Streuner) gypsy, gipsy

zi|geu|ner|haft ADJ gypsylike, gipsylike

zi|geu|ne|risch [tsiˈgɔynərɪʃ] ADJ gypsylike, gipsylike

Zi|geu|ner-: **Zi|geu|ner|la|ger** NT gypsy camp or encampment; **Zi|geu|ner|le|ben** NT gypsy life; (fig) vagabond or rootless life

zi|geu|nern [tsiˈgɔynɐn] ptp **zigeunert** VI aux haben or (bei Richtungsangabe) sein (inf) to rove, to roam

Zi|geu|ner-: Zi|geu|ner|pri|mas M leader of a gypsy band; **Zi|geu|ner|schnit|zel** NT (*Cook*) *cutlet served in a spicy sauce with green and red peppers*; **Zi|geu|ner|spra|che** F Romany, Romany or Gypsy language; **Zi|geu|ner|steak** NT (*Cook*) *steak served in a spicy sauce with green and red peppers*; **Zi|geu|ner|wa|gen** M gypsy caravan

zig|fach ['tsɪçfax] ADJ (*inf*) umpteen times (*inf*); **die ~ Menge** umpteen times the amount; **das Zigfache** umpteen times (the amount); **das Zigfache ihres eigenen Körpergewichts** umpteen times her/their own bodyweight

zig|mal ['tsɪçmaːl] ADV (*inf*) umpteen times (*inf*)

Zi|ka|de [tsi'kaːdə] F -, -n cicada

zi|li|ar [tsi'liaːɐ] ADJ (*Anat*) ciliary

Zil|le ['tsɪlə] F -, -n barge

Zim|bab|we [zɪm'babvə] NT -s Zimbabwe

Zim|bab|wer [zɪm'babvɐ] M -s, -, **Zim|bab|we|rin** [-ərɪn] F -, -nen Zimbabwean

zim|bab|wisch [zɪm'babvɪʃ] ADJ Zimbabwean

Zim|bal ['tsɪmbal] NT -s, -e or -s cymbals pl

Zim|bel ['tsɪmbl] F -, -n (*Mus*) cymbal; (= *Hackbrett*) cymbalon

zimb|risch ['tsɪmbrɪʃ] ADJ Cimbrian

Zim|mer ['tsɪmɐ] NT -s, - room; „Zimmer frei" "vacancies"

Zim|mer-: Zim|mer|an|ten|ne F indoor aerial (*Brit*) or antenna (*US*); **Zim|mer|ar|beit** F carpentry job, piece of carpentry; **Zim|mer|ar|rest** M confinement to one's room; **~ haben** to be confined to one's room; **Zim|mer|brand** M fire in a/the room; **Zim|mer|de|cke** F ceiling

Zim|me|rei [tsɪmə'rai] F -, -en **a** (= *Handwerk*) carpentry **b** (= *Werkstatt*) carpenter's shop

Zim|mer|ein|rich|tung F furniture

Zim|me|rer ['tsɪmərɐ] M -s, -, **Zim|me|rin** [-ərɪn] F -, -nen carpenter

Zim|mer-: Zim|mer|flucht F suite of rooms; **Zim|mer|ge|nos|se** M , **Zim|mer|ge|nos|sin** F roommate; **Zim|mer|ge|sel|le** M , **Zim|mer|ge|sel|lin** F journeyman carpenter; **Zim|mer|hand|werk** NT carpentry, carpenter's trade; **Zim|mer|herr** M (gentleman) lodger

-zim|me|rig [tsɪmərɪç] ADJ suf -roomed, with ... rooms; **ein fünfzimmeriges Haus** a five-roomed house, a house with five rooms

Zim|me|rin F -, -nen carpenter

Zim|mer-: Zim|mer|kell|ner M room waiter; **Zim|mer|kell|ne|rin** F room waitress; **Zim|mer|laut|stär|ke** F low volume; **Zim|mer|leh|re** F apprenticeship in carpentry; **Zim|mer|lehr|ling** M carpenter's apprentice, apprentice carpenter; **Zim|mer|lin|de** F African hemp; **Zim|mer|mäd|chen** NT chambermaid

Zim|mer|mann M pl -leute carpenter; **jdm zeigen, wo der ~ das Loch gelassen hat** (*inf*) to show sb the door

Zim|mer|manns-: Zim|mer|manns|beil NT carpenter's hatchet; **Zim|mer|manns|kno|ten** M , **Zim|mer|manns|stek** [-steːk, -ʃt-] M -s, -s timber hitch

zim|mern ['tsɪmɐn] **VT** to make or build or construct from wood; (*fig*) *Alibi, Lösung* to construct; *Ausrede* to make up **VI** to do woodwork or carpentry; **an etw** (*dat*) **~** (*lit*) to make sth from wood; (*fig*) to work on sth

Zim|mer-: Zim|mer|nach|weis M accommodation service; **Zim|mer|num|mer** F room number; **Zim|mer|pflan|ze** F house plant; **Zim|mer|ser|vice** [-zøːɐvɪs, -zœrvɪs] M room service; **Zim|mer|su|che** F room hunting, hunting for rooms/a room; **auf ~ sein** to be looking for rooms/a room; **Zim|mer|tem|pe|ra|tur** F room temperature; **Zim|mer|thea|ter** NT small theatre (*Brit*) or theater (*US*);

Zim|mer|tür F door (to the room); **Zim|mer|ver|mitt|lung** F accommodation service

Zim|met ['tsɪmət] M -s, no pl (*obs*) cinnamon

-zimm|rig [tsɪmrɪç] ADJ suf = -zimmerig

zim|per|lich ['tsɪmpɐlɪç] **ADJ** (= *überempfindlich*) nervous (*gegen* about); (*beim Anblick von Blut etc*) squeamish; (= *prüde*) prissy; (= *wehleidig*) soft; **sei doch nicht so ~** don't be so silly; **da ist er gar nicht (so) ~** he doesn't have any qualms about that; **da darf man nicht so ~ sein** you can't afford to be soft; **mit Vorwürfen ist sie nicht ~** she doesn't hold back when it comes to reproaching people **ADV** oversensitively; **du behandelst ihn viel zu ~** you're much too soft with him

Zim|per|lie|se ['tsɪmpeliːzə] F -, -n (*pej inf*) cissy (*inf*)

Zimt [tsɪmt] M -(e)s, -e **a** (= *Gewürz*) cinnamon **b** (*fig inf*) (= *Kram*) rubbish (*esp Brit*), garbage; (= *Unsinn*) rubbish (*esp Brit*), nonsense

Zimt-: zimt|far|ben [-farbn], **zimt|far|big** ADJ cinnamon-coloured (*Brit*), cinnamon-colored (*US*); **Zimt|stan|ge** F stick of cinnamon; **Zimt|stern** M (*Cook*) *cinnamon-flavoured star-shaped biscuit*; **Zimt|zi|cke** F (*inf*) stupid cow (*inf*), silly old bat (*inf*)

Zink¹ [tsɪŋk] NT -(e)s, no pl (*abbr* **Zn**) zinc

Zink² M -(e)s, -e(n) (*Mus*) cornet

Zink-: Zink|blech NT sheet zinc; **Zink|blen|de** F zinc blende; **Zink|dach** NT zinc roof

Zin|ke ['tsɪŋkə] F -, -n (*von Gabel*) prong; (*von Kamm, Rechen*) tooth; (= *Holzzapfen*) tenon

Zin|ken ['tsɪŋkn] M -s, - **a** (*sl*: = *Gaunerzeichen*) secret mark **b** (*inf*: = *Nase*) hooter (*Brit inf*), shnaz (*US inf*) **c** = Zinke **d** (*Mus*) cornet

zin|ken¹ ['tsɪŋkn] VT **a** *Karten* to mark **b** *Holz etc* to tenon

zin|ken² ADJ zinc attr, made of zinc

Zink-: Zink|far|be F zinc(-based) paint; **zink|hal|tig** ADJ containing zinc; **~ sein** to contain zinc; **Zink|leim** M Unna's paste; **Zink|sal|be** F zinc ointment; **Zink|weiß** NT Chinese white

Zinn [tsɪn] NT -(e)s, no pl **a** (*abbr* **Sn**) tin **b** (= *Legierung*) pewter **c** (= *Zinnprodukte*) pewter, pewter ware

Zinn|be|cher M pewter tankard

Zin|ne ['tsɪnə] F -, -n (*Hist*) merlon; **~n** (*von Burg*) battlements; (*von Stadt*) towers; (*von Gebirgsmassiv*) peaks, pinnacles

zin|nen ['tsɪnən], **zin|nern** ['tsɪnɐn] ADJ pewter

Zinn-: Zinn|fi|gur F pewter figure or statuette; **Zinn|ge|schirr** NT pewter ware; **Zinn|gie|ßer(in)** M(F) pewterer

Zin|nie ['tsɪniə] F -, -n zinnia

Zinn|kraut NT horsetail

Zin|no|ber [tsɪ'noːbɐ] M -s, no pl **a** (= *Farbe*) vermilion, cinnabar **b** (*inf*) (= *Getue*) fuss, commotion; (= *Kram*) stuff (*inf*); (= *Unsinn*) nonsense no indef art, rubbish no indef art (*esp Brit*); **macht keinen (solchen) ~** stop making such a fuss or commotion

Zin|no|ber-: zin|no|ber|rot ADJ vermilion; **Zin|no|ber|rot** NT vermilion

Zinn-: Zinn|pest F tin disease; **Zinn|sol|dat** M tin soldier; **Zinn|tel|ler** M pewter plate; **Zinn|ver|bin|dung** F tin compound

Zins¹ [tsɪns] M -es, -e [-zə] (*Hist*: = *Abgabe*) tax; (*S Ger, Aus, Sw*) (= *Pachtzins, Mietzins*) rent; (= *Wasserzins*) water rates pl

Zins² M -es, -en usu pl (= *Geldzins*) interest no pl; **~en bringen** to earn interest; **~en tragen** (*lit*) to earn interest; (*fig*) to pay dividends; **Darlehen zu 10% ~en** loan at 10% interest; **Kapital auf ~en legen** to invest capital at interest; **jdm etw mit ~en or mit ~ und ~eszins heimzahlen** or **zurückgeben** (*fig*) to pay sb back for sth with interest

Zins-: Zins|ab|schlag|steuer F tax on interest payments; **Zins|aus|fall** M loss of interest;

Zins|bau|er M -n, -n (*Hist*) tenant farmer; **Zins|be|las|tung** F interest load; **Zins|bin|dung** F pegging of interest rates; **Zins|bo|gen** M (*Fin*) interest sheet; **zins|brin|gend** ADJ interest-bearing attr

zin|sen ['tsɪnzn] VI (*Hist*: = *Abgaben zahlen*) to pay one's tax; (*Sw*: = *Pacht zahlen*) to pay one's rent

Zin|sen|kon|to NT interest account

Zins-: Zins|er|hö|hung F increase or rise in interest rates; **Zins|er|trä|ge** PL interest earnings pl; **~ aus ...** (*auch*) interest yield on ...

Zin|ses|zins M compound interest → Zins²

Zin|ses|zins|rech|nung F calculation of compound interest

Zins-: zins|frei ADJ a (= *frei von Abgaben*) tax-free; (*S Ger, Aus, Sw*) (= *pachtfrei, mietfrei*) rent-free; *Wasser* rate-free **b** *Darlehen* interest-free **ADV** *Geld leihen* interest-free; **Zins|fuß** M interest rate, rate of interest; **Zins|ge|fäl|le** NT difference between interest levels; **zins|güns|tig** ADJ, ADV at a favourable (*Brit*) or favorable (*US*) rate of interest; **Zins|gut** NT pl -güter (*Hist*) tenant farm; **Zins|herr** M (*Hist*) landlord, lord of the manor; **Zins|knecht|schaft** F (*Hist*) system of holding land in tenancy to a landlord; **zins|los** ADJ, ADV interest-free; **Zins|ni|veau** NT level of interest rates; **Zins|pflicht** F (*Hist*) obligation to pay tax; **zins|pflich|tig** [-pflɪçtɪç] ADJ (*Hist*) tax-paying; **~ sein** to be obliged to pay tax; **Zins|po|li|tik** F interest policies pl; **Zins|rech|nung** F calculation of interest; **Zins|satz** M interest rate, rate of interest; (*bei Darlehen*) lending rate; **Zins|schein** M (*Fin*) interest sheet; **Zins|schritt** M (*Fin*) change in the interest rate or in interest rates; **Zins|schwan|kun|gen** PL fluctuations pl in the interest rate or in interest rates; **Zins|sen|kung** F reduction in the interest rate; **Zins|span|ne** F margin between interest rates paid by borrowers and to investors; **Zins|ter|min** M interest due date; **Zins|ver|bil|li|gung** F reduction in the interest rate; **Zins|ver|lust** M loss on interest; **Zins|wu|cher** M usury; **Zins|zah|lung** F interest payment, payment of interest

Zi|o|nis|mus [tsio'nɪsmʊs] M -, no pl Zionism

Zi|o|nist [tsio'nɪst] M -en, -en, **Zi|o|nis|tin** [-'nɪstɪn] F -, -nen Zionist

zi|o|nis|tisch [tsio'nɪstɪʃ] ADJ Zionist

Zip|fel ['tsɪpfl] M -s, - **a** (*von Tuch, Decke, Stoff*) corner; (*von Mütze*) point; (*von Hemd, Jacke*) tail; (*am Saum*) dip (*an* +dat in); (*von Wurst*) end; (*von Land*) tip; **jdn (gerade noch) am (letzten) ~ erwischen** (*fig inf*) to catch sb (just) at the last minute **b** (*inf*: = *Mensch*) silly (*inf*)

zip|fe|lig ['tsɪpfəlɪç] ADJ **a** *Saum* uneven; *Pullover, Rock etc* with an uneven hem **b** (*inf*: = *nervös*) fidgety (*inf*)

Zip|fel|müt|ze F pointed cap or hat

zip|feln ['tsɪpfln] VI (*Rock*) to be uneven

zipf|lig ['tsɪpflɪç] ADJ = zipfelig

Zip|per|lein ['tsɪpɐlain] NT -s, - (old, hum) gout

Zipp|(ver)|schluss ▲ ['tsɪp-] M (*Aus*) zip (fastener)

Zir|bel|drü|se ['tsɪrbl-] F pineal body

Zir|bel|kie|fer F Swiss or stone pine

zir|ka ['tsɪrka] ADV about, approximately; (*bei Datumsangaben*) circa, about

Zir|kel ['tsɪrkl] M -s, - **a** (= *Gerät*) pair of compasses, compasses pl; (= *Stechzirkel*) pair of dividers, dividers pl **b** (*lit, fig*: = *Kreis*) circle **c** (= *studentischer Zirkel*) *monogram of a student organization*

Zir|kel-: Zir|kel|de|fi|ni|ti|on F circular definition; **Zir|kel|kas|ten** M compasses case

zir|keln ['tsɪrkln] VI (= *genau abmessen*) to measure exactly

Zir|kel-: Zir|kel|schluss ▲ M circular argument; **Zir|kel|trai|ning** NT (*Sport*) circuit training

Zir|kon [tsɪrˈkoːn] M **-s**, *no pl* zircon

Zir|ko|ni|um [tsɪrˈkoːniʊm] NT **-s**, *no pl* (*abbr* **Zr**) zirconium

Zir|ku|lar [tsɪrkuˈlaːɐ] NT **-s, -e** (*old*) circular

Zir|ku|la|ti|on [ˈtsɪrkulatsioːn] F **-, -en** circulation

Zir|ku|la|ti|ons-: Zir|ku|la|ti|ons|pum|pe F circulation pump; **Zir|ku|la|ti|ons|stö|rung** F circulation *or* circulatory problem

zir|ku|lie|ren [tsɪrkuˈliːrən] *ptp* **zirkuliert** VI to circulate

Zir|kum|flex [ˈtsɪrkʊmflɛks, tsɪrkʊmˈflɛks] M **-es, -e** (*Ling*) circumflex

Zir|kum|po|lar|stern [tsɪrkʊmpoˈlaːɐ-] M circumpolar star

Zir|kus [ˈtsɪrkʊs] M **-, -se** a circus; **in den ~ ge-hen** to go to the circus b (*inf*) (= *Skizirkus, Tenniszirkus etc*) circus; (= *Getue, Theater*) fuss, to-do (*inf*)

Zir|kus- *in cpds* circus; **Zir|kus|ar|tist(in)** M(F) circus performer *or* artiste; **Zir|kus|wa|gen** M circus caravan (*Brit*) *or* trailer (*US*); **Zir|kus|zelt** NT big top

Zir|pe [ˈtsɪrpə] F **-, -n** cicada

zir|pen [ˈtsɪrpn] VI to chirp, to cheep

Zir|rho|se [tsɪˈroːzə] F **-, -n** cirrhosis

Zir|rus [ˈtsɪrʊs] M **-, -** *or* **Zirren** [-rən], **Zir|rus|wol|ke** F cirrus (cloud)

zir|zen|sisch [tsɪrˈtsɛnzɪʃ] ADJ circus *attr*

zis|al|pin [tsɪsalˈpiːn], **zis|al|pi|nisch** [tsɪsalˈpiː-nɪʃ] ADJ cisalpine

zisch [tsɪʃ] INTERJ hiss; (*Rakete, Schnellzug etc*) whoosh

zi|scheln [ˈtsɪʃln] VI to whisper

zi|schen [ˈtsɪʃn] VI a (= *zischendes Geräusch machen*) to hiss; (*Limonade*) to fizz; (*Fett, Wasser*) to sizzle b *aux sein* (*inf*: = *abzischen*) to whizz VT a (= *zischend sagen*) to hiss b (*inf*: = *trinken*) **einen ~** to have a quick one (*inf*) c (*inf*: = *ohrfeigen*) **jdm eine ~** to belt *or* clout sb one (*inf*); **eine gezischt bekommen** to get belted *or* clouted (*inf*)

Zisch|laut M (*Ling*) sibilant

zi|se|lie|ren [tsizəˈliːrən] *ptp* **ziseliert** VTI to chase

Zi|se|lie|rer [tsizəˈliːrə] M **-s, -**, **Zi|se|lie|re|rin** [-ərɪn] F **-, -nen** engraver

Zis|ter|ne [tsɪsˈtɛrnə] F **-, -n** well

Zis|ter|zi|en|ser [tsɪstɛrˈtsiɛnze] M **-s, -**, **Zis|ter|zi|en|se|rin** [-ərɪn] F **-, -nen** Cistercian; (*Mönch auch*) Cistercian monk; (*Nonne auch*) Cistercian nun

Zis|ter|zi|en|ser|or|den M Cistercian order

Zi|ta|del|le [tsitaˈdɛlə] F **-, -n** citadel

Zi|tat [tsiˈtaːt] NT **-(e)s, -e** quotation; **ein falsches ~** a misquotation; **~ ... Ende des ~s** quote ... unquote

Zi|ta|ten-: Zi|ta|ten|le|xi|kon NT dictionary of quotations; **Zi|ta|ten|samm|lung** F collection of quotations; **Zi|ta|ten|schatz** M store of quotations; (= *Buch*) treasury of quotations

Zi|ther [ˈtsɪtɐ] F **-, -n** zither

Zi|ther-: Zi|ther|spiel NT zither-playing; **Zi|ther|spie|ler(in)** M(F) zither player

zi|tie|ren [tsiˈtiːrən] *ptp* **zitiert** VT a jdn, Ausspruch, Textstelle to quote; Beispiel to cite, to quote b (= *vorladen, rufen*) to summon (*vor* +acc before, *an* +acc, *zu* to)

Zit|ro|nat [tsitroˈnaːt] NT **-(e)s, -e** candied lemon peel

Zit|ro|ne [tsiˈtroːnə] F **-, -n** lemon; (= *Getränk*) lemon drink; (= *Baum*) lemon tree; **jdn wie eine ~ auspressen** *or* **ausquetschen** to squeeze sb dry

Zit|ro|nen-: Zit|ro|nen|fal|ter M brimstone (butterfly); **zit|ro|nen|gelb** ADJ lemon yellow; **Zit|ro|nen|li|mo|na|de** F lemonade; **Zit|ro|nen|me|lis|se** F (lemon) balm; **Zit|ro|nen|pres|se** F lemon squeezer; **Zit|ro|nen|saft** M lemon juice; **Zit|ro|nen|säu|re** F citric acid; **Zit|ro|nen|scha|le** F lemon peel; **Zit|ro|nen|schei|be** F lemon slice, slice of lemon; **Zit|ro|nen|was|ser** NT , *no pl* fresh lemon squash

Zit|rus|frucht F citrus fruit

Zit|ter-: Zit|ter|aal M electric eel; **Zit|ter|gras** NT quaking grass; **Zit|ter|greis(in)** M(F) (*inf*) old dodderer (*inf*), doddering old man/woman

zit|te|rig [ˈtsɪtərɪç] ADJ Hand, Körper, Stimme shaky

zit|tern [ˈtsɪtɐn] VI a (*vor* +dat with) to shake, to tremble; (*vor Kälte*) to shiver, to tremble; (*Stimme*) to tremble, to quaver; (*Lippen, Blätter, Gräser*) to tremble, to quiver; (*Pfeil*) to quiver; **an allen Gliedern ~, am ganzen Körper ~** to shake *or* tremble all over; **mir ~ die Knie** my knees are shaking *or* trembling b (= *erschüttert werden*) to shake c (*inf*: = *Angst haben*) to tremble *or* shake with fear; **vor jdm ~** to be terrified of sb; **sie zittert jetzt schon vor der nächsten Englischarbeit** she's already trembling *or* terrified at the thought of the next English test

Zit|tern NT **-s**, *no pl* a (= *Beben*) shaking, trembling; (*vor Kälte*) shivering; (*von Stimme*) quavering; **ein ~ ging durch seinen Körper** a shiver ran through his body; **mit ~ und Zagen** in fear and trembling; **da hilft kein ~ und Zagen** it's no use being afraid b (= *Erschütterung*) shaking; **ein ~** a tremor

Zit|ter-: Zit|ter|pap|pel F aspen (tree); **Zit|ter|par|tie** F (*fig*) nail-biting event, nail-biter (*inf*); **Zit|ter|ro|chen** M electric ray

zitt|rig [ˈtsɪtrɪç] ADJ Hand, Körper, Stimme shaky

Zit|ze [ˈtsɪtsə] F **-, -n** teat, dug

Zi|vi [ˈtsiːvi] M **-(s), -s** (*inf*) abbr von **Zivildienst-leistende(r)**

zi|vil [tsiˈviːl] ADJ a (= *nicht militärisch*) civilian; Schaden nonmilitary; **im ~en Leben** in civilian life, in (*Brit*) or on civvy street (*inf*); **~er Ersatzdienst** community service (*as alternative to military service*); **~er Bevölkerungsschutz** civil defence (*Brit*) or defense (*US*) b (*inf*: = *angemessen, anständig*) civil, friendly; Bedingungen, Forderungen, Preise reasonable

Zi|vil [tsiˈviːl] NT **-s**, *no pl* a (= *nicht Uniform*) civilian clothes *pl*, civvies *pl* (*inf*); **in ~** (= *Soldat*) in civilian clothes, in civvies; (*inf*) Arzt etc in mufti (*inf*); **Polizist in ~** plain-clothes policeman b (*old*: = *Bürgertum*) civilian populace *no pl*

Zi|vil-: Zi|vil|be|ruf M civilian profession; **Zi|vil|be|schäf|tig|te(r)** MF decl as adj civilian employee; **Zi|vil|be|völ|ke|rung** F civilian population; **Zi|vil|cou|ra|ge** F courage (*to stand up for one's beliefs*); **der Mann hat ~** that man has the courage to stand up for his beliefs; **Zi|vil|dienst** M community service (*as alternative to military service*); **Zi|vil|dienst|leis|ten|de(r)** MF decl as adj person doing community service *or* work (*instead of military service*); **zi|vil|dienst|pflich|tig** [-pflɪçtɪç] ADJ liable for community work (*instead of military service*); **Zi|vil|ehe** F civil marriage

tend to be made very welcome, since they are an inexpensive and motivated workforce. In Switzerland there is no way of avoiding compulsory military service → WEHRDIENST

Zi|vi|le(r) [tsiˈviːlə] MF decl as adj (*inf*) plain-clothes policeman/-woman

Zi|vil-: Zi|vil|fahn|der(in) M(F) plain-clothes policeman/-woman; **Zi|vil|flug|ha|fen** M civil airport; **Zi|vil|ge|richt** NT civil court; **Zi|vil|ge|setz|buch** NT (*Sw*) code of civil law

Zi|vi|li|sa|ti|on [tsiviliza'tsioːn] F **-, -en** civilization (*especially its technological aspects*)

Zi|vi|li|sa|ti|ons-: zi|vi|li|sa|ti|ons|krank ADJ **~ sein** to suffer from an illness caused by today's lifestyle; **Zi|vi|li|sa|ti|ons|krank|heit** F illness caused by today's lifestyle; **Zi|vi|li|sa|ti|ons|schä|den** PL (*am Menschen*) ills *pl* of civilization; (*an der Natur*) ravages *pl* of civilization

zi|vi|li|sa|to|risch [tsiviliza'toːrɪʃ] ADJ of civilization ADV in terms of civilization

zi|vi|li|sier|bar ADJ civilizable

zi|vi|li|sie|ren [tsivili'ziːrən] *ptp* **zivilisiert** VT to civilize

zi|vi|li|siert [tsivili'ziːɐt] ADJ civilized ADV **sich ~ benehmen** to behave civilly or in a civilized manner

Zi|vi|list [tsivi'lɪst] M **-en, -en**, **Zi|vi|lis|tin** [-'lɪstɪn] F **-, -nen** civilian

Zi|vil-: Zi|vil|kam|mer F civil division; **Zi|vil|kla|ge** F civil action; **Zi|vil|klei|dung** F = Zivil a; **Zi|vil|le|ben** NT civilian life, civvy street (*inf*); **Zi|vil|lis|te** F civil list; **Zi|vil|per|son** F civilian; **Zi|vil|pro|zess** ▲ M civil action; **Zi|vil|pro|zess|ord|nung** ▲ F (*Jur*) code of civil procedure; **Zi|vil|recht** NT civil law; **zi|vil|recht|lich** ADJ civil law *attr*, of civil law; Prozess, Auseinandersetzung, Anspruch civil *attr* ADV etw ~ klären to settle sth in a civil court; **jdn ~ verfolgen/belangen** to bring a civil action against sb; **~ relevant sein** to be a matter for civil law or a civil court; **Zi|vil|rich|ter(in)** M(F) civil court judge; **Zi|vil|sa|che** F matter for a civil court

Zi|vil|schutz M civil defence (*Brit*) or defense (*US*)

Zi|vil|schutz-: Zi|vil|schutz|be|hör|de F Federal Emergency Agency, Civil Defence Corps (*Brit*), FEMA (*US*); **Zi|vil|schutz|raum** M civilian air-raid shelter

Zi|vil-: Zi|vil|se|nat M (*Jur*) civil court of appeal; **Zi|vil|stand** M civilian status; **Zi|vil|stands|amt** NT (*Sw*) registry office; **Zi|vil|strei|fe** F plainclothes policemen *pl* (on the beat); **Zi|vil|trau|ung** F civil marriage; **Zi|vil|ver|fah|ren** NT civil proceedings *pl*

ZK [tsɛtˈkaː] NT **-s, -s** abbr von **Zentralkomitee**

Zmit|tag [ˈtsmɪtaːk] M **-, -** (*Sw*) lunch

Zmor|ge [ˈtsmɔrgə] M **-, -** (*Sw*) breakfast

Znacht [tsnaxt] M **-s, -** (*Sw*) supper

Znü|ni [ˈtsnyːni] M **-, -** (*Sw*) morning break, ≈ elevenses (*Brit*)

Zo|bel [ˈtsoːbl] M **-s, -** a (*Zool*) sable b (*auch* **Zobelpelz**) sable (fur)

zo|ckeln [ˈtsɔkln] VI *aux sein* (*inf*) = **zuckeln**

zo|cken [ˈtsɔkn] VI (*inf*) to gamble

Zo|cker [ˈtsɔkɐ] M **-s, -**, **Zo|cke|rin** [-ərɪn] F **-, -nen** (*inf*) gambler

Zo|fe [ˈtsoːfə] F **-, -n** lady's maid; (*von Königin*) lady-in-waiting

Zoff [tsɔf] M **-s**, *no pl* (*inf*: = *Ärger*) trouble; **dann gibts ~** then there'll be trouble

zog *pret von* **ziehen**

zö|ger|lich [ˈtsøːgɐlɪç] ADJ hesitant ADV hesitantly

Zö|ger|lich|keit F **-**, *no pl* hesitancy

zö|gern [ˈtsøːgɐn] VI to hesitate; **er tat es ohne zu ~** he did it without hesitating or hesitation; **er zögerte lange mit der Antwort** he hesitated

ZIVILDIENST

Zivildienst is community service carried out as an alternative to compulsory military service or **Wehrdienst**. The person seeking exemption from military service must first present his case at a special hearing. **Zivildienst** lasts three months longer than military service (two months longer in Austria). It is mainly carried out in the social services sector, where the **Zivis** - as those doing the community work are colloquially known -

(for) a long time before replying; **sie zögerte nicht lange mit ihrer Zustimmung** she lost little time in agreeing

Zö|gern NT **-s**, *no pl* hesitation; **ohne ~** without hesitation, unhesitatingly; **nach langem ~** after hesitating a long time

zö|gernd ADJ hesitant, hesitating ADV hesitantly, hesitatingly

Zög|ling ['tsøːklɪŋ] M **-s**, **-e** (*old, hum*) pupil

Zö|li|bat [tsøli'baːt] NT OR M **-(e)s**, *no pl* celibacy; (= *Gelübde*) vow of celibacy; **im ~ leben** to be celibate, to practise (*Brit*) or practice (*US*) celibacy

zö|li|ba|tär [tsøliba'tɛːɐ] ADJ celibate

Zoll¹ [tsɔl] M **-(e)s**, **-** (= *Längenmaß*) inch; **jeder ~ ein König**, **~ für ~ ein König** every inch a king

Zoll² M **-(e)s**, **ˆe** ['tsœlə] **a** (= *Warenzoll*) customs duty; (= *Brückenzoll, Straßenzoll*) toll; **für etw ~ bezahlen** to pay (customs) duty on sth; **einem ~ unterliegen** to carry duty; **darauf liegt (ein) ~, darauf wird ~ erhoben** there is duty to pay on that **b** (= *Stelle*) **der ~** customs *pl*; **durch den ~ gehen/kommen** to go/get through customs

Zoll-: Zoll|ab|fer|ti|gung F **a** (= *Vorgang*) customs clearance **b** (= *Dienststelle*) customs post or checkpoint; **Zoll|ab|kom|men** NT customs or tariff agreement

Zoll|lager △ NT → **Zolllager**

Zoll-: Zoll|amt NT customs house or office; **zoll|amt|lich** ADJ customs *attr* ADV **~ geöffnet** opened by customs; **~ abgefertigt werden** to go through customs, to be cleared by customs; **Zoll|aus|land** NT *foreign country which one has to go through customs to enter*; **Zoll|be|am|te(r)** M *decl as adj*, **Zoll|be|am|tin** F customs officer or official; **Zoll|be|gleit|pa|pie|re** PL customs documents *pl*; **Zoll|be|hör|de** F customs authorities *pl*, customs *pl*; **Zoll|be|stim|mung** F *usu pl* customs regulation; **zoll|breit** ['tsɔlbrait] ADJ one inch wide, inch-wide *attr*, **Zoll|breit** ['tsɔlbrait] M **-**, **-** inch; **keinen ~ zurückweichen** not to give or yield an inch; **Zoll|dek|la|ra|ti|on** F (*form*) customs declaration; **Zoll|ein|nah|men** PL customs revenue *sing*; **Zoll|ein|neh|mer(in)** M(F) (*old*) tax collector

zol|len ['tsɔlən] VT **jdm Anerkennung/Achtung/ Bewunderung ~** to acknowledge/respect/admire sb; **jdm Beifall ~** to applaud sb, to give sb applause; **jdm Dank ~** to extend or offer one's thanks to sb; **jdm seinen Tribut ~** to pay tribute to sb

Zoll|ler ['tsɔlɐ] M **-s**, **-**, **Zoll|le|rin** [-ərɪn] F **-**, **-nen** (*Sw*) customs officer or official

Zoll-: Zoll|er|klä|rung F customs declaration; **Zoll|fahn|der(in)** M(F) customs investigator; **Zoll|fahn|dung** F customs investigation department; **zoll|frei** ADJ duty-free, exempt from duty ADV duty-free; **etw ~ einführen** to import sth free of duty; **Zoll|frei|heit** F exemption from duty; **Zoll|ge|biet** NT customs area or territory; **Zoll|ge|bühr** F (customs) duty, excise; **Zoll|grenz|be|zirk** M customs and border district; **Zoll|gren|ze** F customs border or frontier; **Zoll|ha|fen** M port of entry; **Zoll|in|halts|er|klä|rung** F customs declaration; **Zoll|in|spek|ti|on** F customs inspection; **Zoll|kon|trol|le** F customs check; **Zoll|lager** ▲ NT bonded warehouse

Zöll|ner ['tsœlnɐ] M **-s**, **-**, **Zöll|ne|rin** [-ərɪn] F **-**, **-nen** (*old, Bibl*) tax collector; (*inf*: = *Zollbeamter*) customs officer or official

Zoll-: Zoll|pa|pie|re PL customs documents *pl*; **zoll|pflich|tig** [-pflɪçtɪç] ADJ dutiable; **Zoll|recht** NT **a** (*Hist*) right to levy tolls **b** (*Jur*) customs law; **Zoll|schran|ke** F customs barrier; **Zoll|stock** M ruler, inch rule; **Zoll|ta|rif** M customs tariff; **Zoll|uni|on** F customs union; **Zoll|ver|ein** M (*Hist*) **Deutscher ~** German Customs Union (of 1844)

Zom|bie ['tsɔmbi] M **-(s)**, **-s** (*lit, fig*) zombie

Zo|ne ['tsoːnə] F **-**, **-n** zone; (*von Fahrkarte*) fare stage; (*fig: von Misstrauen etc*) area; **blaue ~** (*in Straßenverkehr*) restricted parking area; **die ~** (*old inf*: = *DDR*) the Eastern Zone, East Germany

Zo|nen-: Zo|nen|gren|ze F zonal border; **die ehemalige ~** (*zur DDR*) the former border (with East Germany); **Zo|nen|rand|ge|biet** NT (*Hist*) border area (with East Germany); **Zo|nen|ta|rif** M (= *Fahrgeld*) fare for a journey within a fare stage (*Post, Telec*) zonal charge; **Zo|nen|zeit** F zonal time

Zoo [tsoː] M **-s**, **-s** zoo; **gestern waren wir im ~** we went to the zoo yesterday

Zoo|hand|lung F pet shop

Zoo|o|lo|ge [tsooˈloːgə] M **-n**, **-n**, **Zoo|o|lo|gin** [-ˈloːgɪn] F **-**, **-nen** zoologist

Zoo|o|lo|gie [tsooloˈgiː] F **-**, *no pl* zoology

zoo|o|lo|gisch [tsooˈloːgɪʃ] ADJ zoological ADV zoologically

Zoom [zuːm] NT **-s**, **-s** zoom shot; (= *Objektiv*) zoom lens

zoo|men ['zuːmən] VT to zoom in on VI to zoom (in)

Zoom|ob|jek|tiv ['zuːm-] NT zoom lens

Zo|on po|li|ti|kon ['tsoːɔn poliˈtikɔn] NT **-**, *no pl* political animal

Zoo|wär|ter(in) M(F) zoo keeper

Zopf [tsɔpf] M **-(e)s**, **ˆe** ['tsœpfə] **a** (= *Haartracht*) pigtail, plait, braid (*esp US*); **Zöpfe tragen** to wear one's hair in pigtails; **das Haar in Zöpfe flechten** to plait or braid (*esp US*) one's hair; **ein alter ~(, der abgeschnitten werden müsste)** (*fig*) an antiquated custom (that should be done away with) **b** (= *Gebäck*) plait, plaited loaf **c** (= *Baumwipfel*) tree top

Zopf-: Zopf|band [-bant] NT *pl* **-bänder** hair ribbon; **Zopf|mus|ter** NT cable stitch; **Zopf|span|ge** F clip

Zo|res ['tsoːrəs] M **-**, *no pl* (*dial*) **a** (= *Ärger, Streit*) trouble, argy-bargy (*Brit inf*), a ruckus (*US inf*) **b** (= *Gesindel*) rabble

Zorn [tsɔrn] M **-(e)s**, *no pl* anger, rage, wrath (*liter*); **der ~ Gottes** the wrath of God; **jds ~ fürchten** to fear sb's anger or wrath; **jds ~ heraufbeschwören** to incur sb's wrath; **jdn in ~ bringen** to anger or enrage sb; **wenn ihn der ~ überkommt** when he becomes angry, when he loses his temper; **in ~ geraten** or **ausbrechen** to fly into a rage, to lose one's temper; **der ~ packte ihn** he became angry, he flew into a rage; **im ~** in a rage, in anger; **in gerechtem ~** in righteous anger; **einen ~ auf jdn haben** to be furious with sb

Zorn-: Zorn|ader F = **Zornesader**; **Zorn|ausbruch** M fit of anger or rage

Zor|nes-: Zor|nes|ader F **auf seiner Stirn schwoll eine ~** he was so angry you could see the veins standing out on his forehead; **Zor|nes|aus|bruch** M fit of anger or rage; **Zor|nes|fal|te** F angry furrow (*on one's forehead*); **Zor|nes|rö|te** F flush of anger; **Zor|nes|trä|nen** PL tears *pl* of rage

zor|nig ['tsɔrnɪç] ADJ angry, furious; **(leicht) ~ werden** to lose one's temper (easily); **auf jdn ~ sein** to be angry or furious with sb; **ein ~er junger Mann** (*fig*) an angry young man ADV angrily, furiously

zo|ro|as|trisch [tsoroˈastrɪʃ] ADJ zoroastrian

Zo|te ['tsoːtə] F **-**, **-n** dirty joke

zo|tig ['tsoːtɪç] ADJ dirty, filthy, smutty

Zot|te ['tsɔtə] F **-**, **-n** **a** (*Anat*) villus **b** (= *Haarsträhne*) rat's tail (*inf*)

Zot|tel ['tsɔtl̩] F **-**, **-n** (*inf*) rat's tail (*inf*); (*an Mütze*) pompom

zot|tel|haar NT (*inf*) shaggy hair

zot|te|lig ['tsɔtəlɪç] ADJ (*inf*) *Haar, Fell* shaggy

zot|teln ['tsɔtl̩n] VI *aux sein* (*inf*) to amble

Zot|tel|trab M gentle trot

zot|tig ['tsɔtɪç] ADJ **a** *Fell, Tier* shaggy **b** (*Anat*) villous, villose

ZPO ['tsetpeːˈʔoː] *abbr von* **Zivilprozessordnung**

z. T. *abbr von* **zum Teil**

Ztr. *abbr von* **Zentner**

zu [tsuː]	
1 PRÄPOSITION	3 ADJEKTIV
2 ADVERB	4 BINDEWORT

1 – PRÄPOSITION (+*dat*)

a örtlich: Richtung, Ziel to; **zum Bahnhof** to the station; **zur Stadt gehen** to go to town; **zur Stadtmitte gehen** to go to the town centre (*Brit*) or center (*US*); **zum Bäcker/Arzt gehen** to go to the baker's/doctor's; **zum Theater gehen** (*beruflich*) to go on the stage; **zum Militär gehen, zu den Soldaten gehen** to join the army, to join up; **bis zu** as far as; **(bis) zum Bahnhof sind es 5 km** it's 5 kms to the station; **zum Meer hin** toward(s) the sea; **zum Himmel weisen** to point heavenwards; **zur Decke sehen** to look up at the ceiling; **zu jdm/etw hinaufsehen** to look up at sb/sth; **zu jdm herübersehen/hinübersehen** to look across at sb; **sie wandte sich zu ihm hin** she turned to him; **sie sah zu ihm hin** she looked toward(s) him; **die Tür zum Keller** the door to the cellar; **sich zu Tisch setzen** (*geh*) to sit down at the table; **sich zu jdm setzen** to sit down next to or beside sb; **setz dich doch zu uns** come and sit with us; **etw zu sich stecken** to take sth; **zum Fenster herein/hinaus** in (at)/out of the window; **zur Tür hinaus/ herein** out of/in the door; **das Zimmer liegt zur Straße hin** the room looks out onto the street

b örtlich: Lage (*bei Stadt*) in; **zu Frankfurt** (*old*) in Frankfurt; **der Dom zu Köln** the cathedral in Cologne, Cologne cathedral; **der Reichstag zu Worms** (*Hist*) the Diet of Worms; **zu Hause** at home; **zu seiner Linken saß …** (*geh*) on his left sat …; **zu beiden Seiten (des Hauses)** on both sides (of the house); **zu Lande und zu Wasser** on land and sea; **jdm zur Seite stehen** to stand beside sb; **jdm zur Seite sitzen** (*geh*) to sit at sb's side

c zeitlich at; **zu früher/später Stunde** at an early/late hour; **zu Mittag** (= *am Mittag*) at midday or noon; (= *bis Mittag*) by midday or noon; **zu Ostern** at Easter; **letztes Jahr zu Weihnachten** last Christmas; **(bis) zum 15. April/Donnerstag/ Abend** until 15th April/Thursday/(this) evening; (= *nicht später als*) by 15th April/Thursday/(this) evening; **zum Wochenende hat sich Besuch angesagt** we're having visitors at the weekend; **die Zahlung ist zum 15. April fällig** the payment is due on 15th April; **zum 31. Mai kündigen** to give in (*Brit*) or turn in (*US*) one's notice for 31st May → **Anfang, Schluss, Zeit**

d Zusammengehörigkeit, Begleitung, Zusatz **Wein zum Essen trinken** to drink wine with one's meal; **der Deckel zu diesem Topf** the lid for this pan; **nehmen Sie Milch zum Kaffee?** do you take milk in your coffee?; **zur Gitarre singen** to sing to (*Brit*) or with (*US*) a/the guitar; **Lieder zur Laute** songs accompanied by the lute; **die Melodie zu dem Lied** the tune of the song; **Vorwort/Anmerkungen zu etw** preface/ notes to sth; **zu dem kommt noch, dass ich …** on top of that I …; **etw zu etw tragen** (*Kleidung*) to wear sth with sth; **etw zu etw legen** to put sth with sth

e Zweck, Bestimmung for; **Wasser zum Waschen** water for washing; **Papier zum Schreiben** paper to write on, writing paper; **ein Bett zum Schlafen** a bed to sleep in; **der Knopf zum Abstellen** the off button; **Stoff zu einem Kleid** material for a dress; **die Luke zum Einsteigen** the entrance hatch; **das Zeichen zum Aufbruch** the signal to leave; **etw zur Antwort geben** to say sth in reply; **zur Einführung …** by way of (an) introduction …; **zu seiner Entschuldigung muss man sagen …** in his defence (*Brit*) or defense (*US*) one must say …; **zu seiner Entschuldigung**

sagte er ... by way of apology he said ...; **zur Erklärung** by way of explanation; **er sagte das nur zu ihrer Beruhigung** he said that just to set her mind at rest; **zu nichts taugen, zu nichts zu gebrauchen sein** to be no use to anyone (*inf*)

f Anlass **etw zum Geburtstag/zu Weihnachten bekommen** to get sth for one's birthday/for Christmas; **ein Geschenk zum Hochzeitstag** a wedding anniversary present; **zu Ihrem 60. Geburtstag** on your 60th birthday; **jdm zu etw gratulieren** to congratulate sb on sth; **jdn zum Essen einladen** to invite sb for a meal; **zu Ihrem schweren Verlust** on your sad loss; **Ausstellung zum Jahrestag der Revolution** exhibition to mark the anniversary of the revolution; **zu dieser Frage möchte ich Folgendes sagen** my reply to this question is as follows, on this I would like to say the following; **was sagen Sie zu diesen Preisen?** what do you think of these prices?; **zum Thema Gleichberechtigung** on the subject of equal rights; **eine Rede zu Schillers Todestag** a speech on the anniversary of Schiller's death; **„Zum Realismusbegriff"** "On the Concept of Realism"; **jdn zu etw vernehmen** to question sb about sth

g Folge, Umstand **zu seinem Besten** for his own good; **zum Glück** luckily; **zu meiner Schande/Freude** *etc* to my shame/joy *etc*; **es ist zum Lachen** it's really funny; **es ist zum Weinen** it's enough to make you cry, it makes you want to cry

h Mittel, Art und Weise **zu Fuß/Pferd** on foot/horseback; **zu Schiff** by ship; **zu Deutsch** in German; **etw zu einem hohen Preis verkaufen** to sell sth at a high price; **etw zu einem hohen Preis versteigern** to bid up the price of sth

i Veränderung into; **zu etw werden** to turn into sth; (*Mensch auch*) to become sth; **Leder zu Handtaschen verarbeiten** to make handbags out of leather; **jdn/etw zu etw machen** to make sb/sth (into) sth; **jdn zum Mann machen** to make a man of sb; **jdn zu Asche verbrennen** to burn to ashes; **wieder zu Staub werden** to return to dust; **etw zu Pulver zermahlen** to grind sth into powder; **sie ist zu einer wahren Schönheit herangewachsen** she has grown up into a real beauty; **jdn zum Major befördern** to promote sb to (the rank of) major

j = als as; **jdn zum König wählen** to choose sb as king; **jdn zu etw ernennen** to nominate sb sth; **er machte mich zu seinem Stellvertreter** he made me his deputy; **jdn zum Freund haben** to have sb as a friend; **er machte sie zu seiner Frau, er nahm sie zur Frau** he made her his wife; **zum Künstler geboren sein** to be born to be an artist → **Vorbild**

k Verhältnis, Beziehung **Liebe zu jdm** love for sb; **aus Freundschaft zu jdm** because of one's friendship with sb; **Vertrauen zu jdm/etw** trust in sb/sth; **meine Beziehung zu ihm** my relationship with him

l in Vergleichen **im Vergleich zu** in comparison with, compared with; **im Verhältnis drei zu zwei** (*Math*) in the ratio (of) three to two; **Wasser und Saft im Verhältnis drei zu eins mischen** take three parts water to one of juice; **drei zu zwei** (*Sport*) three-two; **das Spiel steht 3 zu 2** *or* (*geschrieben*) **3:2** the score is 3-2 *or* (*gesprochen*) three-two; **wir haben 4 zu 3 gewonnen** we won 4-3 → **Verhältnis**

m bei Zahlenangaben **zu zwei Prozent** at two per cent (*Brit*) *or* percent (*US*); **wir verkaufen die Gläser jetzt das Stück zu 99 Cent** we're selling the glasses now at *or* for 99 cents each; **fünf (Stück) zu 80 Cent** five for 80 cents; **zu zwei Dritteln (gefüllt)** two-thirds (full); **zum halben Preis** at half price; **die Arbeit ist schon zur Hälfte getan** the work is already half done; **zum ersten Mal(e)** for the first time; **zum Ersten ..., zum Zweiten ...** (*Aufzählung*) first ..., second ...; **zum Ersten, zum Zweiten, zum Dritten** (*bei Auktion*) for the first time, for the second time, for the third time → **vier, bis²**

n mit Fragepronomen **zu wem wollen Sie?** who do you want?; **zu wem gehen Sie?** who are you going to see?; **zu wem sprechen Sie morgen bei der Konferenz?** who will you be speaking to *or* who will you be addressing at the conference tomorrow?; **zu was** (*inf*) (*Zweck*) for what; (= *warum*) why

o bei Namen **der Graf zu Ehrenstein** the Count of Ehrenstein; **Gasthof zum goldenen Löwen** the Golden Lion (Inn)

p getrenntes „dazu" (*inf*) **da komme ich nicht zu** I can't get (a)round to it → **dazu**

q andere Wendungen **zum Beispiel** for example; **zu Hilfe!** help!; **jdm zu Hilfe kommen** to come to sb's aid; **zu jds Gedächtnis** in memory of sb; **zum Gedächtnis von jdm** in sb's memory; **zum Lobe von jdm/etw** in praise of sb/sth; **zur Strafe** as a punishment; **zur Belohnung** as a reward; **zur Warnung** as a warning; **zur Beurteilung/Einsicht** for inspection; **zur Probe/Ansicht** on trial/approval; **zur Unterschrift** for signature

2 – ADVERB

a = allzu too; **zu sehr** too much; **sie liebte ihn zu sehr, als dass sie ihn verraten hätte** she loved him too much to betray him; **zu verliebt** too much in love; **das war einfach zu dumm!** (*inf*) it was so stupid!; **ich wäre zu gern mitgekommen** I'd have loved to come

b = geschlossen shut, closed; **auf/zu** (*an Hähnen etc*) on/off; **Tür zu!** (*inf*) shut the door; **die Geschäfte haben jetzt zu** the shops are shut *or* closed now

c = los, weiter (*inf*) **dann mal zu!** right, off we go!; **du wolltest mir was vorsingen, dann mal zu** you wanted to sing me something? OK, go ahead; **immer** *or* **nur zu!** just keep on!; **ihr seid auf dem richtigen Wege, nur zu!** you're on the right track, just keep going; **schreie nur zu, es hilft doch nichts!** scream then, but it won't do any good!; **mach zu!** get a move on!; **lauft schon zu, ich komme nach** you go on, I'll catch you up

d örtlich toward(s); **nach hinten zu** toward(s) the back; **auf den Wald zu** toward(s) the forest; **dem Ausgang zu** toward(s) the exit → **ab**

3 – ADJEKTIV

(= geschlossen, *inf*) Tür, Geschäft, Kiste *etc* shut; Kleid, Verschluss done up; **die zue** *or* **zune Tür** (*strictly incorrect*) the shut door → **zu sein**

4 – BINDEWORT

a mit Infinitiv to; **etw zu essen** sth to eat; **der Fußboden ist noch zu fegen** the floor still has to be swept; **er hat zu gehorchen** he has to do as he's told; **jdm befehlen** *or* **den Auftrag erteilen, etw zu tun** to order sb to do sth; **das Material ist noch/nicht mehr zu gebrauchen** the material is still/is no longer usable; **diese Rechnung ist bis Montag zu bezahlen** this bill has to be paid by Monday; **zu stehen kommen** to come to a stop; **zu liegen kommen** to come to rest; **ich habe noch zu arbeiten** I have still got (*esp Brit*) *or* I still have some work to do; **ohne es zu wissen** without knowing it; **um besser sehen zu können** in order to see better; **ich komme, um mich zu verabschieden** I've come to say goodbye

b mit Partizip **noch zu bezahlende Rechnungen** outstanding bills; **nicht zu unterschätzende Probleme** problems (that are) not to be underestimated; **das sind alles nur winzige, leicht zu übersehende Punkte** these are just small points that can easily be overlooked; **der zu prüfende Kandidat, der zu Prüfende** the candidate to be examined

---

zu|ar|bei|ten VI *sep* **jdm ~** to do sb's groundwork

zu|bau|en VT *sep* Lücke to fill in; Platz, Gelände to build up; Blick to block with buildings/a building

Zu|be|hör ['tsuːbəhøːɐ] NT OR M **-(e)s**, (*rare*) **-e** equipment *no pl*, (= *Zusatzgeräte, Autozubehör*) accessories *pl*; (= *Zubehörteil*) attachments *pl*, accessories *pl*; (*zur Kleidung*) accessories *pl*; **Küche mit allem ~** fully equipped kitchen

Zu|be|hör-: Zu|be|hör|han|del M accessories trade; **Zu|be|hör|teil** NT accessory, attachment

zu|bei|ßen VI *sep irreg* to bite; (*beim Zahnarzt*) to bite (one's teeth) together; **der Hund fasste mich am Bein und biss zu** the dog got hold of my leg and sank his teeth into it

zu|be|kom|men *ptp* **zubekommen** VT *sep irreg* (*inf*) Kleidung to get done up; Koffer auch, Tür, Fenster to get shut *or* closed

zu|be|nannt ['tsuːbənant] ADJ (*liter*) also called

Zu|ber ['tsuːbɐ] M **-s**, **-** (wash)tub

zu|be|rei|ten *ptp* **zubereitet** VT *sep* Essen to prepare; Arznei auch to make up; Cocktail to mix

Zu|be|rei|tung F **a** *no pl* preparation; (*von Cocktail*) mixing; **eine neue ~ für Blumenkohl** a new way of preparing cauliflower **b** (= *Präparat*) preparation

Zu|be|rei|tungs|zeit F preparation time

zu|be|to|nie|ren *ptp* **zubetoniert** VT *sep* Loch, Spalt *etc* to concrete over, to cement over; (*pej*) Landschaft to concrete over

Zu|bett|ge|hen ['tsuːbɛtɡeːən] NT **vor dem ~** before (going to) bed; **beim ~** on going to bed; **nach dem ~** after going to bed

zu|bie|gen VT *sep irreg* to bend shut

zu|bil|li|gen VT *sep* **jdm etw ~** to grant sb sth, to allow sb sth; **jdm mildernde Umstände ~** to recognize that there are/were mitigating circumstances for sb; **ich will ihm gerne ~, dass er sich bemüht hat** he certainly made an effort, I'll grant *or* allow him that

zu|bin|den VT *sep irreg* to tie up, to do up; Schuhe auch to lace up; **jdm die Augen ~** to blindfold sb

zu|blei|ben VI *sep irreg aux sein* (*inf*) to stay shut

zu|blin|zeln VI *sep* **jdm ~** to wink at sb

zu|brin|gen VT *sep irreg* **a** (= *verbringen*) to spend **b** (= *herbeibringen*) to bring to, to take to; **jdm ~, dass ...** (*fig*) to inform sb that ...; **es ist mir zugebracht worden** (*fig*) it has been brought to my notice *or* attention, I have been informed **c** (*inf*: = *zumachen können*) Kiste, Koffer, Tür, Fenster to get shut *or* closed; Knöpfe, Reißverschluss, Kleidung to get done up

Zu|brin|ger ['tsuːbrɪŋɐ] M **-s**, **-** **a** (*Tech*) conveyor **b** (= *Straße*) feeder road **c** (*auch* **Zubringerbus**) shuttle (bus); (*zum Flughafen*) airport bus; (*auch* **Zubringerflugzeug**) feeder plane

Zu|brin|ger-: Zu|brin|ger|dienst M shuttle service; **Zu|brin|ger|flug** M feeder flight; **Zu|brin|ger|li|nie** F feeder route; **Zu|brin|ger|stra|ße** F feeder road

Zu|brot NT, *no pl* (= *zusätzlicher Verdienst*) extra income; **ein kleines ~ verdienen** to earn *or* make a bit on the side (*inf*)

zu|but|tern VT *sep* (*inf*) (= *zuschießen*) to contribute, to add on; (= *zuzüglich bezahlen*) to pay out (on top); (= *dazuverdienen*) to add on; **zu seinem Gehalt etwas ~** to boost *or* to up (*inf*) one's salary a bit

Zuc|chi|ni ['tsʊˈkiːni] F **-,** **-** courgette (*Brit*), zucchini (*US*)

Zucht [tsʊxt] F **-,** **-en** **a** (= *Disziplin*) discipline; **~ und Ordnung** discipline; **jdn in strenge ~ nehmen** (*liter*) to take sb firmly in hand; **jdn in ~ halten** to keep a tight rein on sb **b** *no pl* (=

Aufzucht, das Züchten) (*von Tieren*) breeding; (*von Pflanzen*) growing, cultivation; (*von Bakterien, Perlen*) culture; (*von Bienen*) keeping; **Tiere zur ~ halten** to keep animals for breeding; **die ~ von Pferden** horse breeding; **die ~ von Bienen** beekeeping **c** (= *Zuchtgeneration*) (*von Tieren*) breed, stock; (*von Pflanzen*) stock, variety; (*von Bakterien, Perlen*) culture

Zucht-: Zucht|buch NT studbook; **Zucht|bul|le** M breeding bull; **Zucht|eber** M breeding boar

züch|ten ['tsʏçtn̩] VT *Tiere, Menschen* to breed; *Bienen* to keep; *Pflanzen* to grow, to cultivate; *Perlen, Bakterien* to cultivate; *Kristalle* to grow, to synthesize; (*fig*) *Hass* to breed

Züch|ter ['tsʏçtɐ] M **-s, -, Züch|te|rin** [-ərɪn] F **-, -nen** (*von Tieren*) breeder; (*von Pflanzen*) grower, cultivator; (*von Bienen*) keeper; (*von Perlen, Bakterien*) culturist

Zucht|haus NT (= *Gebäude*) prison (*for serious offenders*), penitentiary (*US*); **zu 7 Jahren ~ verurteilt werden** to be sentenced to 7 years' in prison *or* 7 years' imprisonment; **dafür bekommt man ~, darauf steht ~** you'll go to prison for that

Zucht|häus|ler [-hɔʏslɐ] M **-s, -, Zucht|häus|le|rin** [-ərɪn] F **-, -nen** (*inf*) convict, con (*inf*)

Zucht|haus|stra|fe F prison sentence

Zucht|hengst M stud horse, breeding stallion

züch|tig ['tsʏçtɪç] (*liter*) ADJ (= *keusch, anständig*) *Mädchen* modest, chaste; *Wangen* innocent; *Augen, Benehmen, Kleidung* modest; (= *tugendhaft*) virtuous ADV modestly; (= *tugendhaft*) virtuously

züch|ti|gen ['tsʏçtɪɡn̩] VT (*geh*) to beat; (*stärker, Jur*) to flog; *Schüler* to use corporal punishment on (*form*), ≈ to cane

Züch|tig|keit F **-,** no pl (*liter*) modesty, chasteness

Züch|ti|gung F **-, -en** beating; (*stärker, Jur*) flogging; (*von Schüler*) ≈ caning; **körperliche ~** corporal punishment

Züch|ti|gungs|recht NT right to use corporal punishment

Zucht-: zucht|los ADJ (*dated*) undisciplined; **Zucht|meis|ter(in)** M(F) (*liter*) disciplinarian; **Zucht|mit|tel** NT (*old*) disciplinary measure; **Zucht|per|le** F cultured pearl; **Zucht|ru|te** F (*fig*) rod; **unter jds ~ stehen** to be under sb's rod; **Zucht|stier** M breeding bull; **Zucht|stu|te** F brood mare, breeding mare; **Zucht|tier** NT breeding animal, animal for breeding

Züch|tung ['tsʏçtʊŋ] F **-, -en** **a** (*von Tieren*) breeding; (*von Bienen*) keeping; (*von Pflanzen*) growing; (*von Kristallen*) synthesis **b** (= *Zuchtart*) (*Pflanzen*) strain, variety; (*Tiere*) breed

Zucht-: Zucht|vieh NT breeding cattle; **Zucht|wahl** F selective breeding; **natürliche ~** natural selection

zuck [tsʊk] INTERJ → **ruck, zuck**

Zuck [tsʊk] M **-s,** no pl (= *Körperbewegung*) sudden movement; (*mit Augenlidern*) flutter; (*beim Reißen*) jerk, tug, yank; (*beim Ziehen*) jerk, tug

zu|ckeln ['tsʊkl̩n] VI aux sein (*inf*) to jog; **er zuckelte müde hinter den anderen drein** he trotted wearily along behind the others

Zu|ckel|trab M jog trot; **im ~** at a jog trot

zu|cken ['tsʊkn̩] VI **a** (*nervös, krampfhaft*) to twitch; (*vor Schreck*) to start; (*vor Schmerzen*) to flinch; (*Fisch, verwundetes Tier*) to thrash about; **er zuckte ständig mit dem Mund** his mouth kept twitching; **mit den Schultern** *or* **Achseln ~** to shrug (one's shoulders); **es zuckte um ihre Mundwinkel** the corner of her mouth twitched; **ein Lächeln zuckte um ihren Mund** a smile played around her lips; **es zuckte mir in den Fingern, das zu tun** (*fig*) I was itching to do that; **es zuckte mir in der Hand** (*fig*) I was itching to hit him/her → **Wimper a**

b (= *aufleuchten*) (*Blitz*) to flash; (*Flammen*) to

flare up; **die ~den Flammen** the flames flaring up

c (= *wehtun*) **der Schmerz zuckte (mir) durch den ganzen Körper** the pain shot right through my body *or* through me; **es zuckte mir im Knie** (*inf*) I had a twinge in my knee

VT **die Achseln** *or* **Schultern ~** to shrug (one's shoulders)

zü|cken ['tsʏkn̩] VT *Messer, Pistole* to pull out; *Schwert* to draw; (*inf: = hervorziehen*) *Notizbuch, Bleistift, Brieftasche* to pull *or* take out

Zu|cker ['tsʊkɐ] M **-s,** no pl **a** sugar; **ein Stück ~** a lump of sugar, a sugar lump (*esp Brit*) *or* cube; **du bist doch nicht aus** *or* **von ~!** (*inf*) don't be such a softie! (*inf*) **b** (*Med*) (= *Zuckergehalt*) sugar; (= *Krankheit*) diabetes *sing*; **~ haben** (*inf*) to be a diabetic; **bei ~ muss Insulin gespritzt werden** diabetics need insulin injections

Zu|cker-: Zu|cker|bä|cker(in) M(F) (*old, S Ger, Aus*) confectioner; **Zu|cker|bä|cke|rei** F (*old, S Ger, Aus*) confectioner's (shop); **Zu|cker|bä|cker|stil** M wedding-cake style; **Zu|cker|brot** NT (*obs*) sweetmeat (*old*); **mit ~ und Peitsche** (*prov*) with a stick and a carrot

Zu|cker|chen ['tsʊkɐçən] NT **-s, -, Zü|cker|chen** ['tsʏkɐçən] NT **-s, -** (*dial: = Bonbon*) sweet (*esp Brit*), candy (*US*)

Zu|cker-: Zu|cker|cou|leur F **,** no pl (*Cook*) caramel; **Zu|cker|do|se** F sugar basin *or* bowl; **Zu|cker|erb|se** F mangetout (pea) (*Brit*), sweet pea (*US*); **zu|cker|frei** ADJ sugar-free; **Zu|cker|früch|te** PL crystallized fruits pl; **Zu|cker|ge|halt** M sugar content; **Zu|cker|gla|sur** F → **Zuckerguss**; **Zu|cker|guss** ▲ M icing, frosting (*esp US*); **mit ~ überziehen** to ice, to frost; **ein Kuchen mit ~** an iced *or* a frosted cake; **zu|cker|hal|tig** ADJ containing sugar; **diese Hustenbonbons sind ~** these cough sweets contain sugar; **Zu|cker|hut** M sugarloaf; **der ~ in Rio** the Sugar Loaf Mountain in Rio

zu|cke|rig ['tsʊkərɪç] ADJ sugary

Zu|cker-: Zu|cker|kand [-kant] M **-(e)s** [-dəs] no pl, **Zu|cker|kan|dis** M rock (*Brit*), rock candy (*esp US*); **zu|cker|krank** ADJ diabetic; **Zu|cker|kran|ke(r)** MF decl as adj diabetic; **Zu|cker|krank|heit** F diabetes *sing*

Zu|ckerl ['tsʊkɐl] NT **-s, -(n)** (*S Ger, Aus*) sweet (*esp Brit*), candy (*US*)

Zu|cker-: Zu|cker|le|cken NT **das ist kein ~** (*inf*) it's no picnic (*inf*); **Zu|cker|lö|sung** F sugar solution; **Zu|cker|mais** M sweetcorn; **Zu|cker|me|lo|ne** F muskmelon

zu|ckern ['tsʊkɐn] VT to sugar, to put sugar in; **zu stark gezuckert sein** to have too much sugar in it

Zu|cker-: Zu|cker|plan|ta|ge F sugar plantation; **Zu|cker|plätz|chen** NT (= *Bonbon*) sweet (*Brit*), candy (*US*); (= *Keks*) sugar-coated biscuit (*Brit*) *or* cookie (*US*); **Zu|cker|pup|pe** F (*dated inf*) sweetie (*inf*); (*als Anrede auch*) sugar (*inf*), sweetie-pie (*inf*); **Zu|cker|raf|fi|na|de** F refined sugar; **Zu|cker|raf|fi|ne|rie** F sugar refinery; **Zu|cker|rohr** NT sugar cane; **Zu|cker|rü|be** F sugar beet; **Zu|cker|schle|cken** NT **das ist kein ~** (*inf*) it's no picnic (*inf*); **Zu|cker|spie|gel** M (*Med*) (blood) sugar level; **Zu|cker|stan|ge** F stick of rock (*Brit*) *or* candy (*US*); **Zu|cker|streu|er** M sugar sprinkler; **zu|cker|süß** ADJ (*lit, fig*) sugar-sweet, as sweet as sugar; **Zu|cker|tü|te** F = **Schultüte**; **Zu|cker|was|ser** NT **,** no pl sugar(ed) water; **Zu|cker|wat|te** F candy floss; **Zu|cker|werk** NT sweets pl (*esp Brit*), candies pl (*US*); **Zu|cker|zan|ge** F sugar tongs pl; **Zu|cker|zeug** NT (*pej*) sweet stuff; **Zu|cker|zu|satz** M **ohne ~** without *or* with no added sugar; (*auf Verpackung*) no added sugar

zuck|rig ['tsʊkrɪç] ADJ = **zuckerig**

Zu|ckung ['tsʊkʊŋ] F **-, -en** (= *nervöse Zuckung*) twitch; (*von Muskeln auch*) spasm; (*von Augendern auch*) flutter; (*stärker: krampfhaft*) convul-

sion; (*von sterbendem Tier*) convulsive movement; **die letzten ~en** (*lit, fig*) the death throes

Zu|de|cke F (*dial*) cover (*on bed*)

zu+de|cken VT sep to cover; *jdn, Beine auch* to cover up; (*im Bett*) to tuck up *or* in; *Gestorbenen, Grube, Fleck* to cover (up *or* over); **jdn/sich (mit etw) ~** to cover sb/oneself up (with sth); to tuck sb/oneself up (in sth)

zu|dem [tsu'de:m] ADV (*geh*) moreover, furthermore, in addition

zu+den|ken VT sep irreg (*geh*) **jdm etw ~** to intend *or* destine sth for sb; **das Schicksal hatte mir schwere Schläge zugedacht** Fate had some cruel blows in store for me; **jdm zugedacht sein** to be intended *or* destined *or* earmarked for sb; (*Geschenk*) to be intended *or* meant for sb; **dieses Glück war uns aber offenbar nicht zugedacht** but we were evidently not destined to be so lucky

zu+dik|tie|ren ptp **zudiktiert** VT sep (*inf*) *Strafe* to hand out

Zu|drang M **,** no pl (*rare*) = **Andrang a**

zu+dre|hen sep **VT** *Wasserhahn etc* to turn off; (= *zuwenden*) to turn (+*dat* to) **VR** to turn (+*dat* to)

zu|dring|lich ADJ *Art* pushing, pushy (*inf*); *Nachbarn* intrusive; **dieser ~e Kerl** this guy who's always forcing himself upon her/me *etc*; **~ werden** (*zu einer Frau*) to make advances (*zu* to)

Zu|dring|lich|keit F **seine ~ (gegenüber jdm)** his way of forcing himself upon sb

zu+dröh|nen (*sl*) **VT** **jdn voll dröhnen** (*mit Drogen*) to dose *or* dope sb up (*inf*); (*mit Alkohol*) to get sb tanked up (*inf*); **er war total zugedröhnt** (*mit Drogen*) he was doped up to the eyeballs (*inf*); (*mit Alkohol*) he was completely tanked up (*inf*) *or* loaded (*inf*) **VR** (*mit Drogen*) to dose *or* dope oneself up (*inf*); (*mit Alkohol*) to get tanked up (*inf*); (*inf: mit Musik*) to blow (*Brit*) *or* blast one's head off (*inf*)

zu+drü|cken VT sep to press shut; *Tür auch* to push shut; **jdm die Kehle ~** to throttle sb; **einem Toten die Augen ~** to close a dead person's eyes → **Auge a**

zu+eig|nen VT sep (*geh*) *Buch, Gedicht* to dedicate (*jdm* to sb)

Zu|eig|nung F (*geh: von Gedicht, Buch*) dedication

zu+ei|len VI sep aux sein (*geh*) **auf jdn ~** to rush *or* hurry toward(s) sb *or* (*bis zu jdm*) up to sb; **auf etw** (*acc*) **~** to hurry *or* rush toward(s)/up to sth

zu|ei|nan|der [tsu|ai'nandɐ] ADV (= *gegenseitig*) to each other, to one another; *Vertrauen haben* in each other, in one another; (= *zusammen*) together; **~ passen** to go together; (*Menschen*) to suit each other *or* one another, to be suited; **Braun und Grün passen gut ~** brown and green go together well *or* go well together

zu|ei|nan|der fin|den ▲ VI irreg to find common ground; (= *sich versöhnen*) to be reconciled

zu|ei|nan|der ge|sel|len ▲ VR (*geh*) to join each other; (*fig*) to be combined

zu|ei|nan|der ste|hen ▲ VI irreg (*geh*) to stick *or* stay together

zu+er|ken|nen ptp **zuerkannt** VT sep irreg *Preis* to award (*jdm* to sb); *Würde, Auszeichnung, Orden auch* to confer, to bestow (*jdm* on sb); *Sieg auch, Recht* to grant, to accord (*jdm etw* sb sth); (*vor Gericht*) *Entschädigung, Rente etc* to award (*jdm etw* sb sth); *Strafe* to impose, to inflict (*jdm* (up)on sb); **das Gemälde wurde dem höchsten Bieter zuerkannt** the painting went to the highest bidder; **ihm wurde der Preis zuerkannt** he was awarded the prize; **jdm eine Rolle ~** to award *or* grant sb a role

Zu|er|ken|nung F (*von Preis, Entschädigung, Rente*) awarding; (*von Würde, Orden auch*) conferring, bestowing; (*von Sieg auch, von Recht*) granting, accordance; (*von Strafe*) imposition

zu|erst [tsuˈʔeːɐst] ADV **a** (= als Erster) first; **ich kam ~ an** I was (the) first to arrive, I arrived first; **wollen wir ~ essen?** shall we eat first?; **~ an die Reihe kommen** to be first; **~ bin ich Geschäftsmann, dann Privatmann** I am first and foremost a businessman, and only then a private individual; **das muss ich morgen früh ~ machen** I must do that first thing tomorrow (morning), I must do that first thing in the morning → **kommen p** **b** (= zum ersten Mal) first, for the first time **c** (= anfangs) at first; **er sprach ~ gar nicht** at first he didn't speak at all; **~ muss man ... to** begin or start with you have to ..., first (of all) you have to ...

zu+er|tei|len ptp **zuerteilt** VT sep = **zuerkennen**

zu+fä|cheln VT sep (geh) to fan; **sich/jdm Kühlung ~** to fan oneself/sb

zu+fah|ren VI sep irreg aux sein **a auf jdn ~** (mit Kfz) to drive toward(s) sb; (mit Fahrrad) to ride toward(s) sb; (direkt) to drive/ride up to sb; **auf etw** (acc) **~** to drive/ride toward(s) sth, to head for sth; **er kam genau auf mich zugefahren** he drove/rode straight at or for me **b** (= weiterfahren, losfahren) **fahren Sie doch zu!** go on then!, get a move on then! (inf) **c** (Tür: = plötzlich schließen) to slide shut

Zu|fahrt F approach (road); (= Einfahrt) entrance; (zu einem Haus) drive(way); **„keine ~ zum Krankenhaus"** "no access to hospital"

Zu|fahrts|stra|ße F access road; (zur Autobahn) approach road

Zu|fall M chance, accident; (= Zusammentreffen) coincidence; **das ist ~** it's pure chance; **durch ~** (quite) by chance or accident; **ich habe durch ~ gesehen, wie er das Geld in die Tasche gesteckt hat** I happened to see him putting the money in his pocket; **per ~** (inf) by a (pure) fluke (inf); **per ~ trafen wir uns im Bus** we happened to meet on the bus; **ein merkwürdiger ~** a remarkable or strange coincidence; **es war reiner** or **purer ~, dass ...** it was pure chance that ...; **es ist kein ~, dass ...** it's no accident that ...; **es war ein glücklicher ~, dass ...** it was lucky that ..., it was a stroke or bit of luck that ...; **welch ein ~!** what a coincidence!; **wie es der ~ so will** as chance would have it; **der ~ wollte es, dass er ...** by a stroke of luck he ..., as chance would have it he ...; **etw dem ~ überlassen** to leave sth to chance; **etw dem ~ verdanken** to owe sth to chance; **es hängt vom ~ ab, ob ...** it's a matter of chance whether ...

zu+fal|len VI sep irreg aux sein **a** (= sich schließen) (Fenster etc) to close, to shut; **die Tür fiel laut zu** the door slammed or banged shut; **ihm fielen beinahe die Augen zu** he could hardly or scarcely keep his eyes open **b jdm ~** (= zuteil werden) (Erbe) to pass to sb, to devolve upon sb (Jur); (Preis, Geldsumme etc) to go to sb, to be awarded to sb; (Aufgabe, Rolle) to fall to or upon sb **c** (= zukommen) **diesem Treffen fällt große Bedeutung zu** this meeting is of the utmost importance

zu+fäl|lig ADJ chance attr; Ergebnis auch accidental; Zusammentreffen auch coincidental, accidental; **das war rein ~** it was pure chance, it was purely by chance; **es ist nicht ~, dass er ...** it's no accident that he ...; **das kann doch nicht ~ gewesen sein** that can't have happened by chance; **„Ähnlichkeiten mit lebenden Personen sind rein ~"** ≈ "any similarities with persons living or dead are purely coincidental" ADV **a** by chance; (esp bei Zusammentreffen von Ereignissen) coincidentally; **er ging ~ vorüber** he happened to be passing; **ich traf ihn ~ im Bus** I happened to meet him on the bus, I bumped or ran into him on the bus; **das habe ich ganz ~ gesehen** I just happened to see it, I saw it quite by chance or accident; **wir haben gestern darüber gesprochen, und heute habe ich ~ einen Artikel darüber gefunden** we were talking about it yesterday, and quite coincidentally I found an article on it today; **wenn Sie das ~**

wissen sollten if you (should) happen to know; **~ auf ein Zitat stoßen** to chance upon a quotation, to happen to find a quotation **b** (in Fragen) by any chance; **kannst du mir ~ 10 Euro leihen?** can you lend me 10 euros by any chance?

zu|fäl|li|ger|wei|se [ˈtsuːfɛlɪɡɐˈvaizə] ADV = **zufällig** ADV

Zu|fäl|lig|keit F **a** chance nature; (von Zusammentreffen) coincidence; **~en** chance happenings **b** (Statistik) chance; (Philos) contingency

Zu|falls- in cpds chance; **Zu|falls|aus|wahl** F random selection; **Zu|falls|be|kannt|schaft** F chance acquaintance; **Zu|falls|fund** M lucky find; **Zu|falls|ge|ne|ra|tor** M random generator; (für Zahlen) random-number generator; **Zu|falls|glau|be** M fortuitism; **Zu|falls|prin|zip** NT randomness; **nach dem ~** at random, randomly; **Zu|falls|tor** NT (Sport) lucky or fluke (inf) goal; **Zu|falls|tref|fer** M fluke; **einen ~ machen** to make a lucky choice

zu+fas|sen VI sep **a** (= zugreifen) to take hold of it/them; (Hund) to make a grab; (fig: = schnell handeln) to seize or grab an/the opportunity **b** (= helfen) to lend a hand, to muck in (Brit inf)

zu+fa|xen VT sep **jdm etw ~** to fax sb sth, to fax sth (through) to sb, to send sb sth by fax

zu+flie|gen VI sep irreg aux sein **a auf etw** (acc) **~** to fly toward(s) or (direkt) into sth; **auf etw** (acc) **zugeflogen kommen** to come flying toward(s) sth **b** +dat to fly to; **der Vogel ist uns zugeflogen** the bird flew into our house; **„grüner Wellensittich zugeflogen"** "green budgerigar found"; **alle Herzen flogen ihr zu** she won the heart(s) of everyone; **ihm fliegt alles nur so zu** (fig) everything comes so easily to him **c** (inf: Fenster, Tür) to bang or slam shut

zu+flie|ßen VI sep irreg aux sein +dat to flow to(wards); (Süßwasser etc, fig: Geld) to flow into; **das Wasser wird nie warm, weil immer kaltes zufließt** the water never gets warm because cold water is constantly flowing into it; **jdm Geld ~ lassen** to pour money into sb's coffers

Zu|flucht F refuge (auch fig), shelter (vor +dat from); **~ suchen** (lit, fig) to seek refuge; **zu etw ~ nehmen** (fig) to resort to sth; **zu Lügen ~ nehmen** to take refuge in lying; **du bist meine letzte ~** (fig) you are my last hope or resort; **er findet ~ in seiner Musik** (liter) he finds refuge in his music

Zu|fluchts|ort M pl -orte, **Zu|fluchts|stät|te** F place of refuge; (fig auch) sanctuary

Zu|fluss ▲ M **a** no pl (lit, fig: = Zufließen) influx, inflow; (Mech: = Zufuhr) supply; **~ kalter Meeresluft** a stream of cold air from the sea **b** (= Nebenfluss) affluent, tributary; (zu Binnensee) inlet

zu+flüs|tern VTI sep **jdm (etw) ~** to whisper (sth) to sb; (Theat) to prompt sb (with sth)

zu|fol|ge [tsuˈfɔlɡə] PREP +dat or gen (form) (= gemäß) according to; (= auf Grund) as a consequence or result of; **dem Bericht ~, ~ des Berichtes** according to the report

zu|frie|den [tsuˈfriːdn] ADJ contented, content pred; **ein ~es Gesicht machen** to look pleased; **mit jdm/etw ~ sein** to be satisfied or happy with sb/sth; **wie gehts? – man ist ~** (inf) how are things? – can't complain or mustn't grumble (inf); **er ist nie ~** he's never content or satisfied; **er ist mit nichts ~** nothing pleases him, there's no pleasing him (inf); **es ~ sein** (old) to be well pleased ADV contentedly; **~ lächeln** to smile contentedly

Zu|frie|den-: zu|frie|den ge|ben ▲ VR irreg **sich mit etw ~** to be content or satisfied with sth; **gib dich endlich zufrieden!** can't you be content with what you have?; **Zu|frie|den|heit** F -, no pl contentedness; (= Befriedigtsein) satisfaction; **zu meiner ~** to my satisfaction; **zur allgemeinen ~** to everyone's satisfaction; **zu|frie|den las|sen** ▲ VT irreg to leave alone or in peace; **lass mich damit zufrieden!** (inf) shut

up about it! (inf); **zu|frie|den stel|len** ▲ VT to satisfy; Wünsche, Ehrgeiz auch to gratify; Kunden etc auch to give satisfaction to; **schwer zufrieden zu stellen sein** to be hard or difficult to please; **eine ~de Note** a satisfactory mark (Brit) or grade (US); **eine wenig ~de Antwort** a less than satisfactory answer

zu+frie|ren VI sep irreg aux sein to freeze (over)

zu+fü|gen VT sep **a** Kummer, Leid, Schmerz to cause; Verlust, Niederlage to inflict; **jdm/einer Sache Schaden ~** to harm sb/sth; **jdm etw ~** to cause sb sth/inflict sth on sb; **jdm eine Verletzung (mit einem Messer etc) ~** to injure sb (with a knife etc); **was du nicht willst, dass man dir tu, das füg auch keinem andern zu** (Prov) do as you would be done by (Prov) **b** (= hinzufügen) to add; (= beilegen) to enclose

Zu|fuhr [ˈtsuːfuːɐ] F -, -en (= Versorgung) supply (in +acc, nach to); (Mil: = Nachschub, von Stadt) supplies pl; (Met: von Luftstrom) influx; **die ~ von Lebensmitteln** the supply of provisions; **jdm die ~ abschneiden** to cut off sb's supplies, to cut off supplies to sb

zu+füh|ren sep **VT a** (= versorgen mit, beliefern) to supply; (Comput) Papier to feed (+dat to); **jdm etw ~** to supply sb with sth; **einem Gerät Elektrizität ~** to supply an appliance with electricity; **etw seiner Bestimmung** (dat) **~** to put sth to its intended use **b** (= bringen, zur Verfügung stellen) to bring; **etw gemeinnützigen Zwecken** (dat) **~** to give sth to a charitable cause; **die Abfälle der Wiederverwertung** (dat) **~** to supply refuse for recycling; **einem Geschäft Kunden ~** to bring customers to a business; **er führte ihm junge Mädchen zu** he supplied him with young girls; **dem Magen Nahrung ~** to supply food to the stomach; **jdn dem Richter ~** to bring sb before the court; **jdn der gerechten Strafe ~** to give sb the punishment he/she deserves; **jdn dem Verderben ~** to lead sb on the road to ruin **VI** sep **auf etw** (acc) **~** (lit, fig) to lead to sth

Zu|füh|rung F **a** no pl (= Versorgen, Beliefern) supplying; (= Versorgung) supply; (Comput: von Papier) feed **b** (= Leitung) feed pipe; (Comput: = Einzelblattzuführung) sheetfeed

Zu|fuß|ge|hen [ˈtsuːfuːsgeːən] NT walking no art

Zug¹ [tsuːk] M -(e)s, =e [ˈtsyːɡə] **a** no pl (= Ziehen) (an +dat on, at) pull, tug; (= Zugkraft, Spannung) tension **b** no pl (= Fortziehen: von Zugvögeln, Menschen) migration; (der Wolken) drifting; **im ~e** (= im Verlauf) in the course (gen of); **einen ~ durch die Kneipen machen** to do the rounds of the pubs (esp Brit) or bars; **das ist der ~ der Zeit, das liegt im ~ der Zeit** it's a sign of the times, that's the way things are today; **dem ~ seines Herzens folgen** to follow the dictates of one's heart **c** (= Luftzug) draught (Brit), draft (US); (= Atemzug) breath; (an Zigarette, Pfeife) puff, drag; (= Schluck) gulp, mouthful, swig (inf); **einen ~ machen** (an Zigarette etc) to take a drag; **das Glas in einem ~ leeren** to empty the glass with one gulp or in one go, to down the glass in one (inf); **etw in vollen Zügen genießen** to enjoy sth to the full or max (inf); **er genoss sein Leben in vollen Zügen** he enjoyed life to the full; **in den letzten Zügen liegen** (inf) to be at one's last gasp (inf), to be on one's last legs (inf); **er hat einen guten ~** (inf) he can really put it away (inf); **er hat ~ abbekommen** or **gekriegt** (inf) he got a stiff neck etc from sitting in a draught (Brit) or draft (US) **d** (beim Schwimmen) stroke; (beim Rudern) pull (mit at); (= Federzug) stroke (of the pen); (bei Brettspiel) move; **einen ~ machen** (beim Schwimmen) to do a stroke; (bei Brettspiel) to make a move; **~ um ~** (fig) step by step, stage by stage; **(nicht) zum ~e kommen** (inf) (not) to get a look-in (inf); **du bist am ~** (bei Brettspiel, fig) it's your move or turn; **etw in großen Zügen dar-**

stellen/umreißen to outline sth, to describe/outline sth in broad or general terms; **das war kein schöner ~ von dir** that wasn't nice of you **ⓔ** (= Zugvorrichtung) (= Klingelzug) bell pull; (= Schnur am Anorak) drawstring; (bei Feuerwaffen) groove; (= Orgelzug) stop **ⓕ** (= Gruppe) (von Fischen) shoal; (= Gespann von Ochsen etc) team; (von Vögeln) flock, flight; (von Menschen) procession; (Mil) platoon; (= Abteilung) section **ⓖ** (= Feldzug) expedition, campaign; (= Fischzug) catch, haul

Zug² M -(e)s, ⸚e (= Eisenbahnzug) train; (= Lastzug) truck and trailer; **mit dem ~ fahren** to go by train; **jdn zum ~ bringen** to take sb to the station or train, to see sb off at the station; **im falschen ~ sitzen** (fig inf) to be on the wrong track, to be barking up the wrong tree (inf); **auf den fahrenden ~ aufspringen** (fig) to jump on the bandwagon (inf) → **abfahren VI a**

Zug³ M -(e)s, ⸚e (= Gesichtszug) feature; (= Charakterzug auch) characteristic, trait; (sadistisch, brutal etc) streak; (= Anflug) touch; **das ist ein schöner ~ von ihm** that's one of the nice things about him; **das ist kein schöner ~ von ihm** that's not one of his nicer characteristics; **die Sache hat einen ~ ins Lächerliche** (fig) the affair has something (of the) ridiculous about it, the affair verges on the ridiculous

Zug⁴ NT -s (Kanton) Zug

Zu|ga|be F extra, bonus; (Comm: = Werbegeschenk etc) free gift; (Mus, Theat) encore; **~! ~!** encore! encore!, more! more!

Zug-: **Zug|ab|stand** M interval between trains; **Zug|ab|teil** NT railway (Brit) or train compartment

Zu|gang M pl -gänge **ⓐ** (= Eingang, Einfahrt) entrance; (= Zutritt) admittance, access; (fig) access; **~ zu einem Tresor/Informationen** etc **haben** to have access to a safe/information etc; **das Tal gab freien ~ zum Meer** the valley gave direct access to the sea; **er hat** or **findet keinen ~ zur Musik/Kunst** etc music/art etc doesn't mean anything to him; **„kein ~"** "no admittance or entry" **ⓑ** (von Patienten) admission; (von Schülern) intake; (von Soldaten) recruitment; (von Waren) receipt; (von Büchern) acquisition; (von Abonnement) new subscription; **in dieser Schule haben wir die meisten Zugänge im Frühling** our largest intake at this school is in spring

zu|gan|ge [tsuˈɡaŋə] ADJ pred (esp N Ger) **~ sein** (= beschäftigt) to be busy; (= aufgestanden) to be up and about; (euph: in Nebenzimmer etc) to be carrying on (inf)

zu|gäng|lich [ˈtsuːɡɛŋlɪç] ADJ (+dat, für to) (= erreichbar) Gelände, Ort accessible; (= verfügbar auch) Bücher, Dokumente available; öffentliche Einrichtungen open; (fig: = umgänglich) Mensch, Vorgesetzter approachable; **eine private Sammlung der Allgemeinheit ~ machen** to open a private collection to the public; **der Allgemeinheit/Öffentlichkeit ~** open to the public; **sein Charakter ist mir nur wenig ~** his character is more or less a closed book to me; **er ist nur schwer ~** (fig) **er ist ein schwer ~er Mensch** (fig) he's not very approachable; **für etw leicht/nicht ~ sein** to respond/not to respond to sth; **für Komplimente, Annäherungsversuche, guten Rat etc auch** to be/not to be amenable to sth

Zu|gäng|lich|keit F -, no pl (= Erreichbarkeit) accessibility; (= Verfügbarkeit) availability; (= Umgänglichkeit) approachability; **die leichte ~ dieser Dokumente** the availability of these documents

Zu|gangs|vo|raus|set|zung F condition of entry

Zug-: **Zug|an|schluss** ▲ M (Rail) (train) connection; **Zug|aus|kunft** F (Rail) **ⓐ** (= Information) (information on) train times pl, train timetables pl **ⓑ** (= Schalter) information office or desk, enquiries pl (Brit), inquiry office or desk (esp US); **Zug|be|glei|ter** M (Rail:

Zugfahrplan) train timetable; **Zug|be|glei|ter(in)** M(F) (Rail) guard (Brit), conductor (US); **Zug|be|gleit|per|so|nal** NT (Rail) train crew; **Zug|brü|cke** F drawbridge

zu+ge|ben VT sep irreg **ⓐ** (= zusätzlich geben) to give as an extra or a bonus; **jdm etw ~** to give sb sth extra or as a bonus; (bei Verkauf auch) to throw sth in for sb (inf) **ⓑ** (= hinzufügen) (Cook) to add; (Mus, Theat) to do or perform as an encore **ⓒ** (= zugestehen, einräumen) to admit, to acknowledge; (= eingestehen) to admit (to), to own up to; **er gab zu, es getan zu haben** he admitted (to) having done it, he owned up or confessed to having done it; **jdm gegenüber etw ~** to confess sth to sb; **zugegeben** admittedly, granted; **gibs zu!** admit it!

zu|ge|ge|be|ner|ma|ßen [ˈtsuːɡəɡəbnɐˈmaːsn] ADV admittedly

zu|ge|gen [tsuˈɡeːɡn] ADV (geh) **~ sein** to be present; (bei Versammlung, Konferenz etc auch) to be in attendance (form)

zu+ge|hen sep irreg aux sein **VI ⓐ** (Tür, Deckel) to shut, to close; **der Koffer geht nicht zu** the case won't shut or close **ⓑ** **auf jdn/etw ~** to approach sb/sth, to go toward(s) sb/sth; **direkt auf jdn/etw ~** to go straight or right up to sb/sth; **geradewegs auf etw** (acc) **~** (fig) to get straight or right down to sth; **aufeinander ~** to approach one another; (fig auch) to compromise; **es geht nun auf den Winter zu** winter is drawing in or near; **er geht schon auf die siebzig zu** he's getting on for or nearing or approaching seventy; **dem Ende ~** to draw to a close, to near its end; (Vorräte) to be running out **ⓒ** +dat (Nachricht, Brief etc) to reach; **der Brief ist uns noch nicht zugegangen** the letter hasn't reached us yet, we haven't received the letter yet; **mir ist gestern ein Brief zugegangen** I received a letter yesterday; **die Nachricht, die ich Ihnen gestern habe ~ lassen** the message I sent you yesterday; **der Polizei sind schon mehrere Hinweise zugegangen** the police have already received several clues **ⓓ** (inf: = weiter-, losgehen) to get a move on (inf) **VI impers ⓐ** **dort geht es ... zu** things are ... there; **es ging sehr lustig/fröhlich** etc **zu** (inf) we/they etc had a great time (inf); **du kannst dir nicht vorstellen, wie es dort zugeht** you can't imagine what goes on there (inf); **hier gehts ja zu wie in einem Affenhaus!** it's like a zoo here! **ⓑ** (= geschehen) to happen; **hier geht es nicht mit rechten Dingen zu** there's something odd going on here; **so geht es nun einmal zu in der Welt** that's the way of the world → **Teufel b**

Zu|ge|he|rin F , **Zu|geh|frau** F , **Zu|geh|hil|fe** F (S Ger, Aus) char(woman) (Brit), cleaning woman

Zu|ge|hör [ˈtsuːɡəhøːɐ] NT -(e)s, no pl (Sw) = **Zubehör**

zu+ge|hö|ren ptp **zugehört** VI sep irreg +dat (liter) to belong to

zu|ge|hö|rig ADJ attr **ⓐ** (geh) (= dazugehörend) accompanying; (= verbunden) affiliated (+dat to) **ⓑ** (old: = gehörend) belonging to; **die einst dem britischen Weltreich ~e Insel** the island that once belonged to the British Empire

Zu|ge|hö|rig|keit F -, -en **ⓐ** (zu Land, Glauben) affiliation; (= Mitgliedschaft) membership (zu of) **ⓑ** (= Zugehörigkeitsgefühl) sense of belonging

zu|ge|knöpft [ˈtsuːɡəknœpft] ADJ (fig inf) Mensch close, reserved → auch **zuknöpfen**

Zü|gel [ˈtsyːɡl] M -s, - rein (auch fig); **einem Pferd in die ~ fallen** to seize a horse by the reins, to seize a horse's reins; **die ~ anziehen** (lit) to draw in the reins; (fig) to keep a tighter rein (bei on); **die ~ fest in der Hand haben/behalten** (fig) to have/keep things firmly in hand or under control; **die ~ locker lassen** (lit) to slacken one's hold on the reins; (fig) to give

free rein (bei to); **die ~ an sich** (acc) **reißen** (fig) to seize the reins; **seiner Wut/seinen Gefühlen** etc **die ~ schießen lassen** (fig) to give full vent or free rein to one's rage/feelings etc; **jdm ~ anlegen** to take sb in hand; **einer Sache** (dat) **~ anlegen** to contain or control sth; **jds Übermut ~ anlegen** (liter) to curb sb's overexuberance; **seinen Begierden ~ anlegen** (liter) to curb or bridle one's desires → **schleifen¹ VI b**

zu|ge|las|sen ADJ authorized; Heilpraktiker licensed, registered; Kfz licensed; Arzneimittel approved; **amtlich ~ sein** to be authorized; **staatlich ~ sein** to be state-registered; **er ist an allen** or **für alle Gerichte ~** he is authorized to practise (Brit) or practice (US) in any court; **eine nicht ~e Partei** an illegal party; **als Kassenarzt ~ sein** ≈ to be registered as a GP; **als Heilpraktiker ~ sein** to be a licensed or registered non-medical practitioner; **für Personenbeförderung nicht ~** not licensed to carry passengers → auch **zulassen**

Zü|gel-: **zü|gel|los** ADJ (fig) unbridled no adv, unrestrained; **Zü|gel|lo|sig|keit** F -, -en (fig) lack of restraint, unrestraint; (esp Pol) anarchy

zü|geln [ˈtsyːɡln] **VT** Pferd to rein in; (fig) to curb, to check **VR** to restrain oneself **VI** aux sein (Sw: = umziehen) to move (house)

Zü|ge|lung F -, no pl **ⓐ** (von Pferd) reining in; (fig) curbing, checking **ⓑ** (= Selbstbeschränkung) self-restraint

zu|ge|näht [ˈtsuːɡənɛːt] ADJ **verflixt** or **verflucht und ~!** (inf) damn and blast! (inf) → auch **zunähen**

Zü|gen|glöck|lein [ˈtsyːɡnɡlœklain] NT -s, - (S Ger, Aus) = **Sterbeglocke**

Zu|ge|reis|te(r) [ˈtsuːɡəraistə] MF decl as adj (S Ger) newcomer

zu+ge|sel|len ptp **zugesellt** sep **VT** (rare) to give as a companion **VR** (geh) **sich jdm ~** (Mensch) to join sb; **seinem Bankrott gesellten sich dann noch familiäre Probleme zu** on top of his bankruptcy he had family problems

zu|ge|stan|de|ner|ma|ßen [ˈtsuːɡəʃtandnɐˈmaːsn] ADV admittedly, granted

Zu|ge|ständ|nis NT concession (+dat, an +acc to); **er war zu keinem ~ bereit** he would make no concession(s)

zu+ge|ste|hen ptp **zugestanden** VT sep irreg (= einräumen) Recht, Erlass etc to concede, to grant; (= zugeben) to admit, to acknowledge; **jdm etw ~** (= einräumen) to grant sb sth; **man gestand ihm zu, dass ...** it was admitted or acknowledged that he ...; **man gestand ihm zu, nicht aus Habgier gehandelt zu haben** it was acknowledged that he had not acted out of greed; **zugestanden, Sie haben Recht** you're right, I grant you (that), I admit you're right

zu|ge|tan [ˈtsuːɡətaːn] ADJ **jdm/einer Sache ~ sein** to be fond of sb/sth; **der dem Alkohol sehr ~e Major X** Major X who was very fond of alcohol; **der Hund war seinem Herrn sehr ~** the dog was very attached or devoted to his master

Zu|ge|wan|der|te(r) [ˈtsuːɡəvandətə] MF decl as adj (Admin) newcomer

zu|ge|wandt [ˈtsuːɡəvant] ADJ facing, overlooking; **der Zukunft** (dat) **~ sein** to be turned toward(s) the future

Zu|ge|winn M (Jur) increase in value of a married couple's property during the years of joint ownership through marriage

Zu|ge|winn|aus|gleich M (Jur) equitable division of community property, property acquired in the course of a marriage

Zu|ge|winn|ge|mein|schaft F (Jur) community of property

Zu|ge|zo|ge|ne(r) [ˈtsuːɡətsoːɡənə] MF decl as adj newcomer

Zug-: **Zug|fe|der** F (Tech) tension spring; (bei Uhr) mainspring; **zug|fest** ADJ (Mech) tension-proof; Stahl high-tensile; **Zug|fes|tig|keit**

F (*Mech*) tensile strength; **Zug|fol|ge** F (*Rail*) succession of trains; **zug|frei** ADJ *Raum* draught-free (*Brit*), draft-free (*US*); **Zug|füh|rer(in)** M(F) **a** (*Rail*) chief guard (*Brit*) or conductor (*US*) **b** (*Aus Mil*) platoon leader; **Zug|funk** M (*Rail*) train radio

zu+gie|ßen VT *sep irreg* **a** (= *hinzugießen*) to add; **darf ich Ihnen noch (etwas Kaffee) ~?** may I pour you a little more (coffee)?; **er goss sich** (*dat*) **ständig wieder zu** he kept topping up his glass/cup **b** (*mit Beton etc*) to fill (in)

zu|gig ['tsu:gɪç] ADJ draughty (*Brit*), drafty (*US*)

zü|gig ['tsy:gɪç] △ADJ swift, speedy; *Tempo, Bedienung auch* brisk, rapid, smart; *Handschrift* smooth; *Studium* quickly completed △ADV quickly

zu+gip|sen VT *sep Loch* to plaster up, to fill (in)

Zug-: Zug|kraft F (*Mech*) tractive power; (*fig*) attraction, appeal; **zug|kräf|tig** ADJ (*fig*) *Werbetext, Titel, Plakat* catchy, eye-catching; *Schauspieler* crowd-pulling *attr*, of wide appeal

zu|gleich [tsu'glaɪç] ADV (= *zur gleichen Zeit*) at the same time; (= *ebenso auch*) both; **er ist ~ Gitarrist und Komponist** he is both a guitarist and a composer; **die älteste und ~ modernste Stadt des Landes** the country's oldest and at the same time most modern town

Zug|lei|ne F pull cord

Zü|ge|le ['tsy:glətə] F **-, -n** (*Sw: = Umzug*) move

Zug-: Zug|loch NT (*bei Ofen*) air hole, air vent; **Zug|luft** F draught (*Brit*), draft (*US*); **zu viel ~ bekommen** to be in too much of a draught (*Brit*) or draft (*US*); **Zug|ma|schi|ne** F towing vehicle; (*von Sattelschlepper*) traction engine, tractor; **Zug|mit|tel** NT (*fig: = Köder*) draw, attraction; **Zug|num|mer** F **a** (*Rail*) train number **b** (*fig*) crowd puller, drawing card (*US*); **Zug|och|se** M draught (*Brit*) or draft (*US*) ox; **Zug|per|so|nal** NT (*Rail*) train personnel; **Zug|pferd** NT carthorse, draught (*Brit*) or draft (*US*) horse; (*fig*) crowd puller; **Zug|pflas|ter** NT (*Med*) poultice; **Zug|reg|ler** M (*bei Ofen*) damper, draught (*Brit*) or draft (*US*) regulator

zu+grei|fen VI *sep irreg* **a** (= *schnell nehmen*) to grab it/them; (*fig*) to act fast or quickly, to get in quickly (*inf*); (*bei Tisch*) to help oneself; **greifen Sie bitte zu!** please help yourself! **b** (*fig: = einschreiten*) to step in quickly, to act fast or quickly **c** (= *schwer arbeiten*) to put one's back into it or into one's work, to get down to it or to work **d** (*Comput*) **auf etw** (*acc*) **~** to access sth

Zug|res|tau|rant NT dining car

Zu|griff M **a** **durch raschen ~** by stepping in quickly, by acting quickly or fast; **sich dem ~ der Polizei/Gerichte entziehen** to evade justice **b** (*Fin, Comput*) access (*auf* to)

Zu|griffs-: Zu|griffs|be|rech|ti|gung F , **Zu|griffs|er|laub|nis** F access permission or rights *pl*; **Zu|griffs|zeit** F access time

zu|grun|de [tsu'grʊndə] ADV **a** **~ gehen** to perish; **jdn/etw ~ richten** to destroy sb/sth; (*finanziell*) to ruin sb/sth; **er wird daran nicht ~ gehen** he'll survive; (*finanziell*) it won't ruin him **b** **einer Sache** (*dat*) **~ liegen** to form the basis of sth, to underlie sth; **diesem Lied liegt ein Gedicht von Heine ~** this song is based on a poem by Heine; **~ liegend** underlying; **etw einer Sache** (*dat*) **~ legen** to take sth as a basis for sth, to base sth on sth; **und welche Überlegungen haben Sie diesen Ihren Behauptungen ~ gelegt?** and on what considerations do you base these claims of yours?

Zu|grun|de-: Zu|grun|de|le|gung [-le:gʊŋ] F **-, no pl unter/bei ~ dieser Daten** taking this data as a basis; **zu|grun|de|lie|gend** △ ADJ *attr* → **zugrunde b**

Zugs- *in cpds (Aus)* = **Zug-**

Zug-: Zug|sal|be F (*Med*) poultice; **Zug|seil** NT tow(ing) rope; **Zug|span|nung** F (*Mech*)

---

tensile stress; **Zug|tier** NT draught animal (*Brit*), draft animal (*US*)

zu+gu|cken VI *sep* = **zusehen a**

Zug|un|glück NT train accident

zu|guns|ten [tsu'gʊnstn] PREP +*gen* (*bei Voranstellung*) or *dat* (*bei Nachstellung*) in favour (*Brit*) or favor (*US*) of; **~ von** in favour (*Brit*) or favor (*US*) of; **~ seines Bruders, seinem Bruder ~** in favour (*Brit*) or favor (*US*) of his brother

zu|gu|te [tsu'gu:tə] ADV **jdm etw ~ halten** to grant sb sth; (= *Verständnis haben*) to make allowances for sth; **Sie waren monatelang krank, das haben wir Ihnen ~ gehalten** you were ill for some months and we've made allowances for that; **einer Sache/jdm ~ kommen** to come in useful for sth/to sb, to be of benefit to sth/sb; (*Geld, Erlös*) to benefit sth/sb; **das ist seiner Gesundheit ~ gekommen** his health benefited by or from it; **jdm etw ~ kommen lassen** to let sb have sth; **sich** (*dat*) **auf etw** (*acc*) **etwas ~ halten** or **tun** (*geh*) to pride or preen oneself on sth

Zug-: Zug|ver|bin|dung F train connection; **Zug|ver|kehr** M (*Rail*) rail or train services *pl*; **starker ~** heavy rail traffic; **Zug|vieh** NT, *no pl* draught (*Brit*) or draft (*US*) cattle; **Zug|vo|gel** M migratory bird; (*fig*) bird of passage; **Zug|wa|gen** M towing vehicle; **Zug|wind** M draught (*Brit*), draft (*US*); **zu viel ~ bekommen** to be in too much of a draught (*Brit*) or draft (*US*); **Zug|zwang** M (*Chess*) zugzwang; (*fig*) tight spot; **jdn in ~ bringen** to put sb in zugzwang/on the spot; **in ~ geraten** to get into zugzwang/be put on the spot; **unter ~ stehen** to be in zugzwang/in a tight spot; **die Gegenseite steht jetzt unter ~** the other side is now forced to move

zu+ha|ben *sep irreg* (*inf*) **VI** (*Geschäft, Museum, Behörde etc*) to be closed or shut **VT** *Geschäft, Tür etc* to keep closed or shut; *Kleid, Mantel etc* to have done up; **jetzt habe ich den Koffer endlich zu** I've finally got the case shut

zu+ha|ken VT *sep* to hook up

zu+hal|ten *sep irreg* **VT** to hold closed or shut or to; **sich** (*dat*) **die Nase ~** to hold one's nose; **sich** (*dat*) **die Augen/Ohren/den Mund ~** to put one's hands over one's eyes/ears/mouth, to cover one's eyes/ears/mouth with one's hands; **er hielt ihr beide Augen zu** he put his hands over her eyes **VI auf etw** (*acc*) **~** to head or make straight for sth

Zu|häl|ter ['tsu:hɛltɐ] M **-s,** - pimp, procurer

Zu|häl|te|rei [tsu:hɛltə'raɪ] F **-, no pl** procuring, pimping

Zu|häl|te|rin ['tsu:hɛltərɪn] F **-, -nen** procuress

Zu|häl|ter-: Zu|häl|ter|typ M (*pej*) **mit so einem ~** with someone who looks like a pimp; **Zu|häl|ter|un|we|sen** NT (*pej*) procuring

zu+han|den [tsu'handn] ADV (*form: Sw, Aus*) **a** (*auch old*) to hand; **es ist mir ~ gekommen** it came to hand, it came into my hands **b** (*for the attention of*; **~ (von) Herrn Braun** or **des Herrn Braun** (*rare*) for the attention of Mr Braun, attention Mr Braun

zu+hän|gen VT *sep* to cover up or over; **etw mit einem Tuch ~** to cover sth (up or over) with a cloth, to hang a cloth over sth

zu+hau|en *sep irreg* **VT a** *Baumstamm* to hew; *Stein* to trim, to pare **b** (*inf*) *Tür etc* to slam or bang (shut) **VI a** (*mit Axt*) to strike; (*mit Fäusten, Schwert*) to strike out; **hau zu!** let him *etc* have it! **b** (*inf: Tür, Fenster*) to slam or bang (shut)

zu|hauf [tsu'hauf] ADV (*old*) in throngs, in droves; **~ liegen** to lie in a heap or pile, to be piled up; **etw ~ legen** to put sth in a heap or pile, to pile sth up; **Beispiele dafür gibt es ~** there are numerous examples of it

zu|hau|se [tsu'hauzə] (*Aus, Sw*), **zu Hau|se** ADV → **Haus**

Zu|hau|se [tsu'hauzə] NT **-s, no pl** home

Zu|hau|se|ge|blie|be|ne(r) [-gəbli:bnə] MF *decl as adj* he/she or him/her who stayed at home; **die ~n waren ...** those who stayed at home were ...

zu+hei|len VI *sep aux sein* to heal up or over

Zu|hil|fe|nah|me [tsu:'hɪlfəna:mə] F **unter ~ von** or +*gen* with the aid or help of

zu|hin|terst [tsu'hɪntɛst] ADV right at the back, at the very back

zu|höchst [tsu'hø:çst] ADV **a** (= *ganz oben*) right at the top, at the very top **b** (= *sehr*) highly, extremely

zu+hö|ren VI *sep* to listen (+*dat* to); (= *lauschen, abhören auch*) to listen in (+*dat* on or to), to eavesdrop (+*dat* on); **hör mal zu!** (*drohend*) now (just) listen (to me)!; **gut ~ können** to be a good listener; **hör mir mal genau zu!** now listen carefully to me

Zu|hö|rer(in) M(F) listener; **die ~** (= *das Publikum*) the audience *sing*; (*Rad auch*) the listeners

Zu|hö|rer|schaft F audience; (*Rad auch*) listeners *pl*

zu|in|nerst [tsu'ɪnɛst] ADV deeply; **tief ~ in** his/her *etc* heart of hearts, deep down

zu+ju|beln VI *sep jdm ~* to cheer sb

Zu|kauf M additional purchase

zu+kau|fen VT *sep etw ~* to buy more (of) sth; **Einzelstücke ~** to buy extra separate parts

zu+keh|ren VT *sep* (= *zuwenden*) to turn; **jdm das Gesicht ~** to turn to face sb, to turn one's face to or toward(s) sb; **jdm den Rücken ~** (*lit, fig*) to turn one's back on sb

zu+kif|fen VR *sep* (*sl*) to get spaced out (*sl*); **zugekifft** spaced out (*sl*)

zu+klap|pen VTI *sep* (*vi: aux sein*) to snap shut; (*Tür, Fenster*) to click shut

zu+kle|ben VT *sep Loch etc* to stick over or up; *Briefumschlag* to stick down (*esp Brit*), to seal; *Brief* to seal (up); (*mit Klebstoff, Klebeband*) to stick up

zu+kleis|tern VT *sep* (*inf: lit, fig*) to patch up

zu+klin|ken ['tsu:klɪŋkn] *sep* **VT** *Tür* to latch **VI** *aux sein* **die Tür klinkte zu** the latch fell shut

zu+knal|len VTI *sep* (*vi: aux sein*) (*inf*) to slam or bang (shut)

zu+knei|fen VT *sep irreg* to pinch hard; *Augen* to screw up; *Mund* to shut tight(ly)

zu+knöp|fen VT *sep* to button (up); **sich** (*dat*) **die Jacke/das Hemd ~** to button (up) one's jacket/shirt → *auch* **zugeknöpft**

zu+kno|ten VT *sep* to knot up

zu+kom|men VI *sep irreg aux sein* **a** **auf jdn/etw ~** to come toward(s) or (*direkt*) up to sb/sth; **das Gewitter kam genau auf uns zu** the storm was heading straight for us, the storm was coming right at us; **die Aufgabe, die nun auf uns zukommt** the task which is now in store for us, the task which now stands before us or confronts us; **die Dinge auf sich** (*acc*) **~ lassen** to take things as they come; **alles auf sich** (*acc*) **~ lassen** to let everything take its course **b** **jdm etw ~ lassen** (*Brief etc*) to send sb sth; (= *schenken*) *Hilfe* to give sb sth **c** +*dat* (= *geziemen, gebühren*) to befit, to become; **ein solches Verhalten kommt dir nicht zu** such behaviour (*Brit*) or behavior (*US*) doesn't become or befit you, such behaviour (*Brit*) or behavior (*US*) ill becomes you; **es kommt Ihnen nicht zu, darüber zu entscheiden** it isn't up to you to decide this; **dieser Titel kommt ihm nicht zu** he has no right to this title; **diesem Treffen kommt große Bedeutung zu** this meeting is of (the) utmost importance

zu+kor|ken ['tsu:kɔrkn] VT *sep* to cork (up)

zu+krie|gen VT *sep* (*inf*) = **zubekommen**

Zu|kunft ['tsu:kʊnft] F **-, no pl a** **die ~** the future; **in ~** in future; **in ferner/naher/nächster ~** in the remote or distant/near/immediate future; **ein Beruf mit/ohne ~** a career with/with-

---

out prospects; **das hat keine ~** it has no future, there's no future in it; **unsere gemeinsame ~** our future together; **in die ~ blicken** or **sehen** to look or see into the future; **wir müssen abwarten, was die ~ bringt** we must wait and see what the future has in store or holds; **das gilt für alle ~** that applies without exception from now on; **das bleibt der ~** (dat) **überlassen** or **vorbehalten** that remains to be seen; **viel Glück für Ihre ~!** best wishes for the future!
b (Gram) future (tense)

zu|künf|tig **ADJ** future; **der ~e Präsident/Bischof** the president/bishop elect or designate; **meine Zukünftige** (inf)/**mein Zukünftiger** (inf) my future wife/husband, my wife-to-be/husband-to-be, my intended (hum) **ADV** in future, from now on

Zu|kunfts-: **Zu|kunfts|angst** F (vor der Zukunft) fear of the future; (um die Zukunft) fear for the future; **Zu|kunfts|aus|sich|ten** PL future prospects pl; **Zu|kunfts|be|ruf** M job for the future; **Zu|kunfts|bran|che** F new or sunrise (inf) industry; **Zu|kunfts|chan|cen** PL chances pl for the future, future chances pl; **Zu|kunfts|fach** NT (Univ) new science; **zu|kunfts|fä|hig** ADJ Branche, Lösung with a future (nachgestellt); Entwicklung, Technologie, Wirtschaft sustainable; **~ sein** to have a future; **Zu|kunfts|for|scher(in)** M(F) futurologist; **Zu|kunfts|for|schung** F futurology; **Zu|kunfts|fra|ge** F question about the future; **zu|kunfts|froh** ADJ optimistic (about the future); **Zu|kunfts|ge|stal|tung** F planning for the future; **Zu|kunfts|glau|be** M belief in the future; **zu|kunfts|gläu|big** ADJ believing in the future; **Zu|kunfts|mu|sik** F (fig inf) pie in the sky (inf), Zukunftsmusik; **Zu|kunfts|op|ti|mis|mus** M optimism about the future; **zu|kunfts|ori|en|tiert** [-lorienti:ɐt] ADJ forward-looking, looking to the future, future-oriented; **Zu|kunfts|per|spek|ti|ve** F future prospects pl; **Zu|kunfts|plä|ne** PL plans pl for the future; **Zu|kunfts|prog|no|se** F forecast; **zu|kunfts|reich** ADJ (geh) = zukunftsträchtig; **Zu|kunfts|ro|man** M (naturwissenschaftlich) science fiction novel; (gesellschaftspolitisch) utopian novel; **zu|kunfts|si|cher** ADJ with a guaranteed future; **Zu|kunfts|si|che|rung** F safeguarding the future; **Zu|kunfts|sze|na|rio** NT vision of the future; **Zu|kunfts|tech|nik** F , **Zu|kunfts|tech|no|lo|gie** F new or sunrise (inf) technology; **zu|kunfts|träch|tig** ADJ with a promising future; **Zu|kunfts|vi|si|on** F future vision, vision for the future; **zu|kunfts|wei|send** ADJ forward-looking

Zu|kurz|ge|kom|me|ne(r) [tsuːˈkʊrtsɡəkɔmənə] MF decl as adj loser

zu+la|bern VT sep (inf) **jdn ~** to rattle on at sb (inf), to rabbit on at sb (Brit inf); **sie hat mich total zugelabert** she went on and on at me

zu+lä|cheln VI sep **jdm ~** to smile at sb

zu+la|chen VI sep **jdm ~** to give sb a friendly laugh

zu+la|den VTI sep irreg to load more on/in

Zu|la|dung F (bei Kfz) useful load; (Naut) deadweight

Zu|la|ge F **a** (= Geldzulage) extra or additional pay no indef art; (= Sonderzulage) bonus (payment); (= Gefahrenzulage) danger money no indef art; **eine ~ von 100 Euro** an extra 100 euros pay; a bonus (payment) of 100 euros; 100 euros danger money **b** (= Gehaltserhöhung) rise (Brit), raise (US); (regelmäßig) increment

zu|lan|de △ [tsuˈlandə] ADV → **Land a**

zu+lan|gen VI sep **a** (inf: Dieb, Fiskus, beim Essen) to help oneself; **kräftig ~** (beim Essen) to tuck in (inf) **b** (inf: = zuschlagen) to hit (esp Brit) or strike out (dial: = reichen) to do (inf); **es langt nicht zu** there's not enough

zu|läng|lich [ˈtsuːlɛŋlɪç] ADJ (geh) adequate

Zu|läng|lich|keit F -, -en (geh) adequacy

zu+las|sen VT sep irreg **a** (= Zugang gewähren) to admit; **eine Partei zur Wahl ~** to permit a party to enter the/an election
b (amtlich) to authorize; Arzt to register; Heilpraktiker to register, to license; Kraftfahrzeug to license; Rechtsanwalt to call (to the bar), to admit (as a barrister or to the bar); Prüfling to admit; **etw als Beweismittel ~** to allow sth as evidence; **zugelassene Aktien** listed securities → auch **zugelassen**
c (= dulden, gestatten) to allow, to permit; **das lässt nur den Schluss zu, dass ...** that leaves or allows only one conclusion that ...; **eine Ausnahme ~** (Vorschriften) to allow (of) or admit (of) or permit an exception; (Mensch) to allow or permit an exception; **sein Schweigen lässt keine andere Erklärung zu(, als dass ...)** there is no other explanation for his silence (but that ...); **ich lasse nicht zu, dass mein Bruder benachteiligt wird** I won't allow or permit my brother to be discriminated against; **das lässt mein Pflichtbewusstsein nicht zu** my sense of duty won't allow or permit or countenance that
d (= geschlossen lassen) to leave or keep shut or closed

zu|läs|sig [ˈtsuːlɛsɪç] ADJ permissible; Beweis, Klage, Vorgehen admissible; Fangquote allowable; **~e Abweichung** (Tech) tolerance, permissible variation; **die Berufung ist ~** (Jur) there is a right of appeal; **eine Berufung für ~ erklären** (Jur) to grant leave for an appeal; **~es Gesamtgewicht** (Mot) maximum laden weight; **~e Höchstgeschwindigkeit** (upper) speed limit; **~e Höchstbelastung** weight limit; **es ist nicht ~, hier zu parken** parking is prohibited or not permitted here

Zu|läs|sig|keit F -, no pl admissibility

Zu|las|sung [ˈtsuːlasʊŋ] F -, -en **a** no pl (= Gewährung von Zugang) admittance, admission **b** no pl (amtlich) authorization; (von Kfz) licensing; (als Rechtsanwalt) call to the bar; (von Prüfling) admittance (form); (als praktizierender Arzt) registration; **Antrag auf ~ zu einer Prüfung** application to enter an examination; **seine ~ als Rechtsanwalt bekommen** to be called to the bar; **~ (von Aktien) zur Börse** listing on the Stock Exchange **c** (Dokument) papers pl; (esp von Kfz) vehicle registration document, logbook; (= Lizenz) licence (Brit), license (US)

Zu|las|sungs-: **Zu|las|sungs|be|schrän|kung** F (esp Univ) restriction on admissions; **Zu|las|sungs|num|mer** F (Mot) registration number; **Zu|las|sungs|pa|pie|re** PL (Mot) registration papers pl; **Zu|las|sungs|sper|re** F (esp Univ) bar on admissions; **Zu|las|sungs|stel|le** F registration office; **Zu|las|sungs|stopp** M (esp Univ) block on admissions; **Zu|las|sungs|ver|fah|ren** NT (esp Univ) admissions procedure

zu|las|ten [ˈtsuːlastn] ADV → **Last b**

Zu|lauf M , no pl **großen ~ haben** (Geschäft, Restaurant) to be very popular; (Arzt etc auch) to be much sought-after, to be in great demand; **die Aufführung hat sehr großen ~ gehabt** the performance drew large crowds

zu+lau|fen VI sep irreg aux sein **a** **auf jdn/etw ~, auf jdn/etw zugelaufen kommen** to run toward(s) sb/sth, to come running toward(s) sb/sth; (direkt) to run up to sb/sth, to come running up to sb/sth **b** → **spitz c** (Wasser etc) to run in, to add; **lass noch etwas kaltes Wasser ~** run in or add some more cold water **d** (inf: = sich beeilen) to hurry (up); **lauf zu!** hurry up! **e** (Hund etc) **jdm ~** to stray into sb's house; **eine zugelaufene Katze** a stray (cat)

zu+le|gen sep **VT** **a** (= dazulegen) to put on; **legen Sie noch zwei Scheiben zu, bitte** please put on another two slices
b Geld to add; (bei Verlustgeschäft) to lose; **der Chef hat mir 200 Euro im Monat zugelegt** the boss has given me 200 euros a month extra, the boss has given me an extra 200 euros a month; **die fehlenden 20 Euro legte meine**

Mutter zu my mother made up the remaining 20 euros
c etwas **Tempo** (inf) or **einen Zahn** (inf) **~** to get a move on (inf), to step on it (inf)
d (inf: an Gewicht) to put on; **er hat schon wieder 5 kg zugelegt** he's put on (esp Brit) or gained another 5 kg; **die SPD konnte 5% ~** the SPD managed to gain 5%
e (= anschaffen) **sich** (dat) **etw ~** (inf) to get oneself sth; **er hat sich** (dat) **eine teure Pfeife zugelegt** he has treated himself to an expensive pipe; **er hat sich eine Braut/Freundin zugelegt** (hum) he has got himself or has acquired a fiancée/girlfriend
VI (inf) **a** (an Gewicht) to put on weight; (Wirtschaftswachstum, Umsatz) to increase; **die SPD hat in den Umfragen zugelegt** the SPD has gained support in the opinion polls
b (= sich mehr anstrengen) to pull one's or the finger out (Brit inf), to make an effort; (= sich steigern) to do better; (Sport) to step up the pace (inf)

zu|lei|de [tsuˈlaidə] ADV **jdm etwas ~ tun** to do sb harm, to harm sb; **was hat er dir ~ getan?** what (harm) has he done to you?; **wer hat dir etwas ~ getan?** who has harmed you? → **Fliege**

zu+lei|ten VT sep Wasser, Strom to supply; Schreiben, Waren to send on, to forward

Zu|lei|tung F (Tech) supply

zu|letzt [tsuˈlɛtst] ADV **a** (= schließlich, endlich, zum Schluss) in the end; **~ kam sie doch** she came in the end; **~ kam auch Gaston** in the end or finally Gaston came too; **wir blieben bis ~** we stayed to the very or bitter end; **ganz ~** right at the last moment, at the very last moment **b** (= als letzte(r, s), an letzter Stelle, zum letzten Mal) last; **ich kam ~** I came last, I was last to come; **wann haben Sie ihn ~ gesehen?** when did you last see him?; **ganz ~** last of all; **nicht ~ dank/wegen** not least thanks to/because of

zu|lie|be [tsuˈliːbə] ADV **etw jdm ~ tun** to do sth for sb's sake or for sb; **das geschah nur ihr ~** it was done just for her

Zu|lie|fer|be|trieb M (Econ) supplier

Zu|lie|fe|rer [ˈtsuːliːfərə] M -s, -, **Zu|lie|fe|rin** [-ərɪn] F -, -nen (Econ) supplier

Zu|lie|fer|in|dust|rie F (Econ) supply industry

zu+lie|fern VT sep to supply

Zu|lie|fe|rung F supply

zu+lö|ten VT sep to solder

Zu|lu¹ [ˈtsuːlu] M -(s), -(s) or f -, -s Zulu

Zu|lu² NT -(s) (Sprache) Zulu

zum [tsʊm] contr von **zu dem** **a** (räumlich) **geht es hier ~ Bahnhof?** is this the way to the station?; **„Gasthof Zum Löwen"** "The Lion Inn" **b** (mit Infinitiv) **~ Schwimmen gehen** to go swimming; **~ Essen gehen** to go and eat **c** (Folge) **es ist ~ Verrücktwerden/Weinen** it's enough to drive you mad (inf) or crazy (inf)/make you cry **d** (Zweck) **dieses Gerät ist ~ Messen des Blutdrucks** this apparatus is for measuring (the) blood pressure **e** (in Verbindung mit vb siehe auch dort) → **Spießbürger/Verräter werden** to become bourgeois/a traitor

zu+ma|chen sep **VT** (= schließen) to shut, to close; Flasche to close; Brief to seal; (inf: = auflösen) Laden etc to close (down); **die Augen ~** (lit, fig) to close or shut one's eyes (fig: bei etw to sth) **VI** (inf) **a** (= den Laden zumachen) to close (down), to shut up shop; (fig) to pack or jack (Brit) it in (inf), to call it a day **b** (inf: = sich beeilen) to get a move on (inf), to step on it (inf)

zu|mal [tsuˈmaːl] CONJ **~ (da)** especially or particularly as or since **ADV** **a** (= besonders) especially, particularly **b** (obs: = zugleich) at the same time

zu+mau|ern VT sep to brick up, to wall up

zu|meist [tsuˈmaist] ADV mostly, in the main, for the most part

zu+mes|sen VT sep irreg (geh) to measure out (jdm for sb), to apportion (jdm to sb); Essen to dish out (jdm to sb); Zeit to allocate (+dat for); Schuld to attribute (jdm to sb); Bedeutung to attribute (einer Sache (dat) to sth); **ihm wurde eine hohe Strafe zugemessen** he was dealt a stiff punishment; **dem darf man keine große Bedeutung ~** one can't attach too much importance to that

zu|min|dest [tsuˈmɪndəst] ADV at least; **er hätte mich ~ anrufen können** he could at least have phoned me, he could have phoned me at least, at least he could have phoned me

zu+mül|len [ˈtsuːmylən] VT sep **a** (inf: = mit Müll zuschütten) to cover over with rubbish (Brit) or garbage **b** (sl) = **zulabern c** (inf: mit Werbesendungen) to bombard (inf)

zu|mut|bar ADJ reasonable; **jdm** or **für jdn ~ sein** to be reasonable for sb; **es ist ihm (durchaus) ~, dass er das tut** he can reasonably be expected to do that; **nicht ~ sein** to be unreasonable

Zu|mut|bar|keit [ˈtsuːmuːtbaːʁkait] F -, no pl reasonableness

zu|mu|te [tsuˈmuːtə] ADV **wie ist Ihnen ~?** how do you feel?; **mir ist traurig/seltsam etc ~** I feel sad/strange etc; **mir ist lächerlich ~** I'm in a silly mood; **mir ist gar nicht lächerlich ~** I'm not in a laughing mood; **ihm war recht wohl ~** he felt wonderful or good; **mir war dabei gar nicht wohl ~** I didn't feel right about it, I felt uneasy about it

zu+mu|ten VT sep **jdm etw ~** to expect or ask sth of sb; **Sie wollen mir doch wohl nicht ~, diesen Unsinn zu lesen** you surely don't expect me to or aren't asking me to read this nonsense; **das können Sie niemandem ~** you can't ask or expect that of anyone; **Sie muten mir doch wohl nicht zu, das zu glauben!** you surely don't expect me to or aren't asking me to believe that; **sich** (dat) **zu viel ~** to take on too much, to overdo things, to overtax oneself; **seinem Körper zu viel ~** to overtax oneself

Zu|mu|tung [ˈtsuːmuːtʊŋ] F -, -en unreasonable demand; (= Unverschämtheit) cheek (esp Brit), nerve (inf); **das ist eine ~!** that's a bit much!

zu|nächst [tsuˈnɛːçst] ADV **a** (= zuerst) first (of all); **~ einmal** first of all **b** (= vorläufig) for the time being, for the moment PREP +dat (rare) (= neben) next to

zu+na|geln VT sep Fenster etc to nail up; (mit Brettern, Pappe etc) to board up; Sarg, Kiste etc to nail down

zu+nä|hen VT sep to sew up → auch **zugenäht**

Zu|nah|me [ˈtsuːnaːmə] F -, -n (+gen, an +dat in) increase; (= Anstieg auch) rise

Zu|na|me M surname, last name

Zünd|an|lass- (Aut): **Zünd|an|lass|schal|ter** ▲ M ignition switch; **Zünd|an|lass|schloss** ▲ NT ignition lock

Zünd|blätt|chen NT (für Spielzeugpistole) cap

zün|deln [ˈtsʏndln] VI to play (about) with fire; **mit Streichhölzern ~** to play (about) with matches

zün|den [ˈtsʏndn] **VI** to catch light or fire, to ignite; (Pulver) to ignite; (Streichholz) to light; (Motor) to fire; (Sprengkörper) to go off; (fig) to kindle enthusiasm; **dieses Streichholz zündet nicht** this match won't light; **hat es endlich bei dir gezündet?** (inf) has the penny finally dropped?, have you finally cottoned on? (Brit inf) **VT** to ignite, to set alight; Rakete to fire; Sprengkörper to set off, to detonate; Feuerwerkskörper to let off

zün|dend ADJ (fig) stirring, rousing; Vorschlag exciting

Zun|der [ˈtsʊndɐ] M -s, - tinder; (= Schicht auf Metall) scale (oxide); (inf: = Prügel) good hiding (inf), thrashing; **wie ~ brennen** to burn like tin-

der; **~ kriegen** (inf) to get a good hiding (inf) or thrashing; **jdm ~ geben** (inf) to give sb a good hiding (inf) or thrashing

Zün|der [ˈtsʏndɐ] M -s, - **a** igniter; (für Sprengstoff, Bombe, Torpedo etc) fuse; (für Mine) detonator **b** (Aus, inf: = Zündholz) match

Zun|der|schwamm M (Bot) touchwood

Zünd-: Zünd|flam|me F pilot light; **Zünd|fol|ge** F (Tech) ignition sequence, firing order; **Zünd|fun|ke** M (Aut) ignition spark; **Zünd|holz** NT match(stick); **ein ~ anreißen** to strike a match; **Zünd|hüt|chen** NT percussion cap; **Zünd|ka|bel** NT (Aut) plug lead; **Zünd|kap|sel** F detonator; **Zünd|ker|ze** F (Aut) spark(ing) plug; **Zünd|plätt|chen** NT (für Spielzeugpistole) cap; **Zünd|schloss** ▲ NT (Aut) ignition lock; **Zünd|schlüs|sel** M (Aut) ignition key; **Zünd|schnur** F fuse; **Zünd|spu|le** F ignition or spark coil; **Zünd|stoff** M inflammable or flammable (esp US) matter; (= Sprengstoff) explosives pl, explosive material; (fig) inflammatory or explosive stuff

Zün|dung [ˈtsʏndʊŋ] F -, -en ignition; (= Zündvorrichtung bei Sprengkörpern) detonator, detonating device; **die ~ ist nicht richtig eingestellt** (Aut) the timing is out, the timing is wrongly set; **die ~ einstellen** (Aut) to adjust the timing

Zünd-: Zünd|ver|tei|ler M (Aut) distributor; **Zünd|vor|rich|tung** F igniting device, detonator; **Zünd|wa|ren|steu|er** F tax on matches; **Zünd|wil|lig|keit** F -, no pl (Tech) combustibility; **Zünd|zeit|punkt** M moment of ignition

zu+neh|men vi sep irreg **VI** (an Zahl etc, beim Stricken) to increase; (= anwachsen auch) to grow; (Tage) to draw out; (an Weisheit, Erfahrung etc) to gain (an +dat in); (Mensch: an Gewicht) to put on or gain weight; (Mond) to wax; **im Zunehmen sein** to be on the increase; (Mond) to be waxing; **der Wind nimmt (an Stärke) zu** the wind is getting up or increasing **VT** (Mensch: an Gewicht) to gain, to put on; **ich habe 2 kg/viel zugenommen** I've gained or put on 2 kg/a lot of weight

zu|neh|mend ADJ increasing, growing; Mond crescent; **mit ~en Jahren glaubte er ...** as he advanced in years he believed ...; **bei** or **mit ~em Alter** with advancing age; **wir haben ~en Mond** there is a crescent moon; **in ~em Maße** to an increasing degree ADV increasingly; **~ an Einfluss gewinnen** to gain increasing influence

zu+nei|gen sep +dat **VI** to be inclined toward(s); **ich neige der Auffassung zu, dass ...** I am inclined to think that ...; **jdm zugeneigt sein** (geh) to be well disposed toward(s) sb **VR** to lean towards; (fig: Glück etc) to favour (Brit), to favor (US); **sich dem Ende ~** (geh) (Tag etc) to be drawing to a close; (= knapp werden: Vorräte etc) to be running out

Zu|nei|gung F affection; **eine starke ~ zu jdm empfinden** to feel strong affection toward(s) or for sb; **~ zu jdm fassen** to take a liking to sb, to grow fond of sb

Zunft [tsʊnft] F -, ⸚e [ˈtsʏnftə] (Hist) guild; (hum inf) brotherhood; **die ~ der Bäcker/Fleischer etc** the bakers'/butchers' etc guild

Zunft-: Zunft|brief M (Hist) guild charter; **Zunft|ge|nos|se** M guildsman; (fig pej) crony (pej); **Zunft|ge|nos|sin** F guildswoman; (fig pej) crony (pej)

zünf|tig [ˈtsʏnftɪç] ADJ **a** (Hist) belonging to a guild **b** (= fachmännisch) Arbeit etc expert, professional; (inf) Kleidung professional(-looking); (inf) (= ordentlich, regelrecht) proper; (= gut, prima) great; **eine ~e Ohrfeige** a hefty box on the ears (esp Brit), a hefty slap across the face

Zunft- (Hist): **Zunft|meis|ter(in)** M(F) master of a/the guild, guild master; **Zunft|we|sen** NT , no pl guild system, system of guilds; **Zunft|zwang** M compulsory membership of a guild

Zun|ge [ˈtsʊŋə] F -, -n tongue; (Mus: von Fagott, Akkordeon) reed; (von Waage) pointer; (geh: =

Sprache) tongue; (Zool: = Seezunge) sole; **mit der ~ anstoßen** to lisp; **das brennt auf der ~** that burns the tongue; **jdm die ~ herausstrecken** to stick one's tongue out at sb; **die ~ herausstrecken** (beim Arzt) to stick out one's tongue; **mit schwerer ~ sprechen** to speak in a slurred voice; **eine böse** or **giftige/scharfe** or **spitze/lose ~ haben** to have an evil/a sharp/a loose tongue; **lose ~n behaupten, ...** rumour (Brit) or rumor (US) has it ...; **böse ~n behaupten, ...** malicious gossip has it ...; **eine feine ~ haben** to be a gourmet, to have a discriminating palate; **sich** (dat) **die ~ abbrechen** (fig) to tie one's tongue in knots; **eher beißt er sich** (dat) **die ~ ab, als ...** he'd do anything rather than ...; **das Wort liegt** or **schwebt mir auf der ~, ich habe das Wort auf der ~** the word is on the tip of my tongue; **der Wein löste ihm die ~** the wine loosened his tongue; **mir hängt die ~ zum Hals heraus** (inf) my tongue is hanging out; **ein Lyriker polnischer** (gen) **~** a poet of the Polish tongue; **alle Länder arabischer** (gen) **~** all Arabic-speaking countries; **in fremden ~n reden** to speak in tongues

zün|geln [ˈtsʏŋln] VI (Schlange) to dart its tongue in and out; (Flamme, Feuer) to lick

Zun|gen-: Zun|gen|bein NT tongue bone, hyoid bone; **Zun|gen|be|lag** M coating of the tongue; **Zun|gen|bre|cher** M tongue twister; **zun|gen|fer|tig** ADJ (geh) eloquent; (pej) glib; **Zun|gen|fer|tig|keit** F (geh) eloquence; (pej) glibness; **Zun|gen|kuss** ▲ M French kiss; **Zun|gen|laut** M (Ling) lingual (sound); **Zun|gen|pfei|fe** F (Mus) reed pipe; **Zun|gen-R** [-lɐr] , **Zun|gen-r** ▲ NT (Ling) trilled or rolled "r"; **Zun|gen|rü|cken** M back of the tongue; **Zun|gen|schlag** M (durch Alkohol) slur; (Mus) tonguing; **ein falscher ~** an unfortunate turn of phrase; **zwei Töne mit ~ spielen** to tongue two notes; **Zun|gen|spit|ze** F tip of the tongue; **Zun|gen|wurst** F (Cook) tongue sausage; **Zun|gen|wur|zel** F root of the tongue

Züng|lein [ˈtsʏŋlain] NT -s, - dim von **Zunge** tongue; (rare: der Waage) pointer; **das ~ an der Waage sein** (fig) to tip the scales; (Pol) to hold the balance of power

zu|nich|te [tsuˈnɪçtə] ADV **~ machen** (geh) to wreck, to ruin; Hoffnungen auch to shatter, to destroy; **~ werden** (geh) to be wrecked or ruined; (Hoffnungen auch) to be shattered or destroyed

zu+ni|cken VI sep **jdm ~** to nod to or at sb; **jdm freundlich/aufmunternd ~** to give sb a friendly/encouraging nod

zu|nut|ze [tsuˈnʊtsə] ADV **sich** (dat) **etw ~ machen** (= verwenden) to make use of sth, to utilize sth; (= ausnutzen) to capitalize on sth, to take advantage of sth

zu|oberst [tsuˈloːbɐst] ADV on or at the (very) top, right on or at the top → **unterste(r, s)**

zu+ord|nen VT sep +dat to assign to; **ein Tier einer Gattung ~** to assign an animal to a genus; **jdn/etw jdm ~** to assign sb/sth to sth; **diesen Dichter ordnet man der Romantik zu** this poet is classified as a Romantic(ist); **wie sind diese Begriffe einander zugeordnet?** how are these concepts related (to each other)?

Zu|ord|nung F assignment (zu einer Periode), classification; (= Beziehung zueinander) relation

zu+pa|cken VI sep (inf) **a** (= zugreifen) to make a grab for it etc **b** (bei der Arbeit) to knuckle down (to it), to get down to it **c** (= helfen) **mit ~** to give me/them etc a hand

zu|packend ADJ Film, Theaterstück, Steuersystem hard-hitting; (= forsch) straightforward, direct; (= aggressiv) vigorous ADV purposefully

zu+par|ken VT sep to block, to obstruct; **zugeparkt** blocked (with parked cars); Auto blocked in (by parked cars); Straße full of or chock-a-block with (inf) parked cars; **die Straße ist zugeparkt** there's not a single parking space in or on (esp US) the street

zu|pass ▲ [tsu'pas], **zu|pas|se** [tsu'pasə] ADV **jdm ~ kommen** (*Mensch, Hilfe*) to have come at the right time for sb; **dieser Holzblock kommt mir ~** this block of wood is just what I needed

zup|fen ['tsʊpfn] **VT** to pick; *Saite auch, Gitarre, Cello* to pluck; *Unkraut* to pull (up); **jdn am Är-mel ~** to tug at sb's sleeve; **sich** (*dat or acc*) **am Bart/Ohr** *etc* **~** to pull at one's beard/ear *etc* **VI an etw** (*dat*) **~** (*an Haaren, Ohrläppchen, Kleidung*) to pull at sth; *an Instrument* to pluck at sth

Zupf-: Zupf|gei|ge F (*dated*) guitar; **Zupf|in|-stru|ment** NT (*Mus*) plucked string instrument

zu+pfrop|fen VT *sep* to cork, to stopper

zu+pres|sen VT *sep Tür etc* to press shut; **ein Loch/Leck (mit der Hand** *etc*) **~** to press one's hand *etc* over a hole/leak

zu+pros|ten VT *sep* **jdm ~** to raise one's glass to sb, to drink sb's health

zur [tsuːɛ, tsʊr] *contr von* **zu der ~ Schule gehen** to go to school; **jdn ~ Tür bringen** to see sb to the door; **~ See fahren** to go to sea; **„Gasthof Zur Post** "The Post Inn"; **~ Zeit** at the moment; **~ Weihnachtszeit** at Christmas time; **~ Orientierung** for orientation; **~ Abschreckung** as a deterrent

zu|ran|de ▲ [tsu'randə] ADV **mit etw/jdm ~ kommen** (to be able) to cope with sth/sb

zu|ra|te ▲ [tsu'raːtə] ADV **mit jdm ~ gehen** (*liter*) to seek sb's advice, to consult sb; **ich muss erst mit mir ~ gehen** I'll have to consult it first; **jdn/etw ~ ziehen** to consult sb/sth; **einen An-walt/Arzt ~ ziehen** to take legal/medical advice, to consult a lawyer/doctor; **einen Kolle-gen ~ ziehen** to get a second opinion, to consult a colleague

zu+ra|ten VI *sep irreg* **jdm ~, etw zu tun** to advise sb to do sth; **er hat mich gefragt, ob er ins Ausland gehen soll, und ich habe ihm zugera-ten** he asked me whether he should go abroad and I said he should; **ich will weder ~ noch ab-raten** I won't advise you one way or the other; **auf sein Zuraten (hin)** on his advice

zu+rau|nen VT *sep* (*liter*) **jdm etw ~** to whisper sth to sb

Zür|cher ['tsyrçe] M **-s, -, Zür|che|rin** [-ərɪn] F **-, -nen** native of Zurich

zür|che|risch ['tsyrçərɪʃ] ADJ of Zurich

zu+rech|nen VT *sep* **a** (*inf: = dazurechnen*) to add to **b** (*fig: = zuordnen*) (+*dat* with) to class, to include; *Kunstwerk etc* (*dat* to) to attribute, to ascribe; **sie wird dem linken Flügel der Partei zugerechnet** she is seen as belonging to the left wing of the party

Zu|rech|nung F **a unter ~ aller Kosten** inclu-sive of all charges **b** (*= Zuordnung*) assignment (to), inclusion (with)

Zu|rech|nungs-: zu|rech|nungs|fä|hig ADJ of sound mind, compos mentis *pred* (*esp Jur, fig inf*); **Zu|rech|nungs|fä|hig|keit** F sound-ness of mind; **verminderte ~** diminished re-sponsibility; **ich muss doch schon manchmal an seiner ~ zweifeln!** (*inf*) I sometimes wonder if he's quite right in the head (*inf*)

zu|recht- [tsu'rɛçt-]: **zu|recht+bas|teln** VT *sep* **sich** (*dat*) **etw ~** (*auch fig, iro*) to construct sth; **zu|recht+bie|gen** VT *sep irreg* to bend into shape; (*fig*) to twist; **er hat alles wieder zurecht-gebogen** (*inf*) he has straightened or smoothed everything out again; **zu|recht+fei|len** VT *sep* to file into shape; **zu|recht+fin|den** VR *sep ir-reg* to find one's way (*in* +*dat* around); **sich in der Welt nicht mehr ~** not to be able to cope with the world any longer; **ich finde mich in dieser Tabelle nicht zurecht** I can't make head nor tail of this table; **sich mit etw ~** to get the hang of sth (*inf*); (*durch Gewöhnung*) to get used to sth; **zu|recht+kom|men** VI *sep irreg aux sein* **a** (*= rechtzeitig kommen*) to come in time **b** (*fig*) to get on; (*= schaffen, bewältigen*) to cope; **kommen Sie ohne das zurecht?** (*inf*) can you manage with-

out it?; **er kam nie zurecht im Leben** he was never able to cope with life **c** (*finanziell*) to manage; **mit 50 Euro am Tag kann man gut ~** you can manage easily on 50 euros a day; **zu|-recht+le|gen** VT *sep irreg* to lay or get out ready; **sich** (*dat*) **etw ~** to lay or get sth out ready; (*fig*) to work sth out; **sich** (*dat*) **alle Argu-mente ~** to marshal all one's arguments; **das hast du dir (bloß) zurechtgelegt!** (*gedeutet*) that's just your interpretation; (*erfunden*) you just made that up!; **zu|recht+ma|chen** *sep* (*inf*) **VT a** *Zimmer, Essen etc* to prepare, to get ready; *Bett* to make up **b** (*= anziehen*) to dress; (*= schminken*) to make up **VR** to get dressed or ready; (*= sich schminken*) to put on one's make-up; **auf etw** (*acc*) **zurechtgemacht sein** (*inf*) to be done up as sth (*inf*); **zu|recht+rü|cken** VT *sep Brille, Hut etc* to adjust; *Stühle etc* to straight-en (up), to put straight; (*fig*) to straighten out, to put straight → **Kopf a**; **zu|recht+schnei|-den** VT *sep irreg* to cut to shape; *Haar, Nagel, Hecke* to trim, to cut; **zu|recht+schus|tern** VT *sep* (*inf*) to throw together; **zu|recht+set|zen** *sep* **VT sich** (*dat*) **den Hut/die Brille ~** to adjust or straighten one's hat/glasses → **Kopf a** **VR** to settle oneself; **zu|recht+stau|chen** *sep* (*inf*) **jdn ~** to haul (*Brit*) or rake (*US*) sb over the coals (*inf*); **zu|recht+stel|len** *sep* **VT** to set out ready **VR** to pose, to arrange oneself; **zu|-recht+stut|zen** VT *sep* to trim, to cut; *Hecke auch* to clip; (*fig*) to lick (*esp Brit*) or whip into shape; **zu|recht+wei|sen** VT *sep irreg* to re-buke; *Schüler etc* to reprimand; **Zu|recht|wei|-sung** F rebuke; (*von Schüler*) reprimand; **zu|-recht+zim|mern** VT *sep* to throw together; (*fig*) to construct

zu+re|den VI *sep* **jdm ~** (*= ermutigen*) to encour-age sb; (*= überreden*) to persuade sb; **wenn du ihm gut zuredest, hilft er dir** if you talk to him nicely, he'll help you; **sie hat ihrem Vater so lange zugeredet, bis er ihr das Auto kaufte** she kept on at her father till he bought her the car; **auf mein Zureden (hin)** with my encourage-ment; (*Überreden*) with my persuasion; **gutes** or **freundliches Zureden** friendly persuasion

zu+rei|chen VT *sep* **VT** **jdm etw ~** to hand or pass sth to sb **VI** to be enough or sufficient; **ein ~der Grund** a sufficient or adequate reason

zu+rei|ten *sep irreg* **VT** *Pferd* to break in **VI** *aux sein* (*= weiterreiten*) to ride on; (*schneller*) to ride faster; **auf jdn/etw ~, auf jdn/etw zugeritten kommen** to ride toward(s) or (*direkt*) up to sb/sth

Zu|rei|ter(in) M(F) roughrider; (*für Wildpferde auch*) broncobuster

Zü|rich ['tsyːrɪç] NT **-s** Zurich

Zü|ri|cher ['tsyːrɪçe] M **-s, -, Zü|ri|che|rin** [-ərɪn] F **-, -nen** → **Zürcher**

Zü|rich|see M Lake Zurich

zu+rich|ten VT *sep* **a** *Essen etc* to prepare; *Stein, Holz* to square; *Leder, Pelz, Stoff* to finish, to dress; (*Typ*) to justify **b** (*= beschädigen, ver-unstalten*) to make a mess of; (*= verletzen*) to in-jure; **jdn übel ~** to knock sb about (*Brit inf*), to beat sb up

Zu|rich|ter(in) M(F) (*Typ*) justifier; (*von Stof-fen, Pelzen*) dresser, finisher

Zu|rich|tung F (*Typ*) justifying, justification; (*von Geweben, Pelzen*) dressing, finishing

zu+rie|geln ['tsuːriːgln] VT *sep* to bolt (shut)

zür|nen ['tsʏrnən] VI (*geh*) **jdm ~** to be angry with sb; **dem Schicksal ~** to rage against fate

zu+rol|len VTI *sep* (*vi: aux sein*) to roll; **auf jdn/etw ~, auf jdn/etw zugerollt kommen** to roll to-ward(s) or (*direkt*) up to sb/sth

zur|ren ['tsʊrən] VT (*Naut*) to lash; *Deckladung, Beiboot etc* to lash down

Zur|schau|stel|lung [tsʊr'ʃau-] F display, exhi-bition

zu|rück [tsu'rʏk] ADV back; (*mit Zahlungen*) be-hind; (*fig: = zurückgeblieben*) (*von Kind*) back-ward; **in Französisch (sehr) ~ sein** (*fig*) to be (re-

ally) behind in French; **fünf Punkte ~** (*Sport*) five points behind; **~ nach** *etc* back to *etc*; **~! get back!; ~ an Absender** return to sender; **ein-mal München und ~** a return (*esp Brit*) or a round-trip ticket (*US*) to Munich; **seit wann ist Trevor ~?** when did Trevor get back?; **ich bin in zehn Minuten wieder ~** I will be back (again) in 10 minutes; **ein paar Jahre ~** a few years back or ago; **hinter jdm ~ sein** (*fig*) to lie behind sb; **es gibt kein Zurück (mehr)** there's no going back

Zu|rück-: zu|rück+be|ge|ben *ptp* **zurückbege-ben** VR *irreg* (*geh*) to return, to go back; **zu|-rück+be|hal|ten** *ptp* **zurückbehalten** VT *sep ir-reg* to keep (back); **er hat Schäden/einen Schock ~** he suffered lasting damage/lasting shock; **Zu|rück|be|hal|tungs|recht** NT (*Jur*) right of retention; **zu|rück+be|kom|men** *ptp* **zurückbekommen** VT *sep irreg* **a** (*= zurückerhal-ten*) to get back (*Brit*), to get back **b** (*inf: = heimgezahlt bekommen*) **das wirst du (von mir) ~!** I'll get my own back on you for that! (*Brit*), I'll get back at you for that!; **zu|rück+be|or-dern** *ptp* **zurückbeordert** VT *sep* to recall, to order back; **zu|rück+be|ru|fen** VT *sep irreg* **zurückbe-rufen** VT *sep irreg* to recall; **zu|rück+beu|gen** *sep* **VT** to bend back **VR** to lean or bend back; **zu|rück+be|we|gen** *ptp* **zurückbewegt** VTR *sep* to move back(wards); (*drehend*) to turn backwards; **zu|rück+bil|den** VR *sep* (*Ge-schwür*) to recede; (*Muskel*) to become wasted, to atrophy; (*Biol*) to regress; (*esp Sw: = abneh-men*) to decrease; **zu|rück+bin|den** VT *sep ir-reg Haare* to tie back

zu|rück+blei|ben VI *sep irreg aux sein* **a** (*an ei-nem Ort*) to stay or remain behind; (*= weiter hin-ten gehen*) to stay (back) behind **b** (*= übrig bleiben: Rest, Rückstand*) to be left; (*als Folge von Krankheit etc: Schaden, Behinderung*) to remain; **er blieb als Waise/Witwer zurück** he was left an orphan/a widower **c** (*= nicht Schritt halten, auch fig: mit Arbeitsleis-tung etc*) to fall behind; (*Uhr*) to lose; (*in Entwick-lung*) to be retarded or backward; (*Sport*) to be behind; **20 Meter ~** to be 20 metres (*Brit*) or meters (*US*) behind; **die Einnahmen blieben hinter den Erwartungen zurück** the takings did-n't come up to expectations → *auch* **zurückge-blieben**

zu|rück-: zu|rück+blen|den VI *sep* (*lit, fig*) to flash back (*auf* +*acc* to); **zu|rück+bli|cken** VI *sep* to look back (*auf* +*acc* at); (*fig*) to look back (*auf* +*acc* on); **zu|rück+brin|gen** VT *sep irreg* (*= wieder herbringen*) to bring back (*lit, fig*); (*= wieder wegbringen*) to take back; **jdn ins Le-ben ~** to bring sb back to life, to revive sb; **zu|-rück+da|tie|ren** *ptp* **zurückdatiert** VT *sep* to backdate; **zu|rück+den|ken** VI *sep irreg* to think back (*an* +*acc* to); **so weit ich ~ kann** as far as I can recall or remember; **wenn man so zurückdenkt** when I think back; **zu|-rück+drän|gen** VT *sep* to force or push back; (*Mil*) to drive back, to repel; (*fig: = eindämmen*) to repress, to restrain; **zu|rück+dre|hen** VT *sep* to turn back; *Uhr* to put (*Brit*) or turn (*US*) back; **die Uhr** or **Zeit ~** to put (*Brit*) or turn (*US*) back the clock; **das Rad (der Geschichte) ~** to turn back the hands of time; **zu|-rück+dür|fen** VI *sep irreg* (*inf*) to be allowed back; **zu|rück+ei|len** VI *sep aux sein* (*geh*) to hurry back; **zu|rück+er|hal|ten** VT *sep irreg* **zurücker-halten** VT *sep irreg* to have returned; **zu|-rück+er|in|nern** *ptp* **zurückerinnert** VR *sep* to remember, to recall (*an* +*acc* sth); **sich bis zu seinem 5. Lebensjahr ~** können to be able to remember being 5 years old/as far back as 1945; **zu|rück+er|obern** *ptp* **zurückerobert** VT *sep* (*Mil*) to recapture, to retake, to recon-quer; (*fig*) *Position, Marktanteil* to recapture, to regain; *Freund etc* to win back; **zu|rück+er|-stat|ten** *ptp* **zurückerstattet** VT *sep* to refund; *Ausgaben* to reimburse; **zu|rück+er|war|ten** *ptp* **zurückerwartet** VT *sep* **jdn ~** to expect sb back; **zu|rück+fah|ren** *sep irreg* **VI** *aux sein* **a** (*an ei-*

nen Ort) to go back, to return; (*esp als Fahrer*) to drive back **b** (= *zurückweichen*) to start back **VT** **a** (*mit Fahrzeug*) to drive back **b** (= *drosseln*) *Produktion, Investitionen* to cut back

zu|rück+fal|len VI *sep irreg aux sein* to fall back; (*Sport*) to drop back; (*fig*) (*Umsätze etc*) to fall, to drop (back); (*an Besitzer*) to revert (*an +acc* to); (*in Leistungen*) to fall behind; (*Schande, Vorwurf etc*) to reflect (*auf +acc* on); **in alte Gewohnheiten ~** to fall back into old habits; **er fällt immer wieder in seine alten Gewohnheiten zurück** he always lapses back into his old ways; **das würde bloß auf deine armen Eltern ~** that would only reflect (badly) on your poor parents

zu|rück-: zu|rück+fin|den VI *sep irreg* to find the *or* one's way back; **findest du allein zurück?** can you find your own way back?; **er fand zu sich selbst zurück** he found himself again; **er fand zu Gott/zum Sozialismus zurück** he found his way back to God/to Socialism; **zu|rück+flie|gen** VTI *sep irreg* (*vi: aux sein*) to fly back; **zu|rück+flie|ßen** VI *sep irreg aux sein* (*lit, fig*) to flow back; **zu|rück+flu|ten** VI *sep aux sein* (*Wellen*) to flow back; (*fig*) to stream back; **zu|rück+for|dern** VT *sep etw ~* to ask for sth back; (*stärker*) to demand sth back; **zu|rück+fra|gen** *sep* **VI** *etw ~* to ask sth back *or* in return **VI** to ask something *or* a question back; (*wegen einer Auskunft*) to check back; **zu|rück|führ|bar** ADJ traceable (*auf +acc* to); **auf eine Formel ~** reducible to a formula

zu|rück+füh|ren VT **a** (= *zurückbringen*) to lead back **b** (= *ableiten aus*) to put down to; **etw auf seine Ursache ~** to put sth down to its cause; **etw auf eine Formel/Regel ~** to reduce sth to a formula/rule; **das ist darauf zurückzuführen, dass ...** that can be put down to the fact that ... **c** (= *bis zum Ursprung zurückverfolgen*) to trace back **VI** to lead back; **es führt kein Weg zurück** there's no way back; (*fig*) there's no going back

zu|rück+ge|ben VT *sep irreg* to give back, to return; *Wechselgeld* to give back; *Ball, Kompliment, Beleidigung* to return; (= *erwidern*) to retort, to rejoin; **er gab mir das Buch zurück** he gave the book back to me, he returned the book to me; **das Geld kannst du dir von der Firma ~ lassen** you can ask the firm to give you the money back; **dieser Erfolg gab ihm seine Zuversicht wieder zurück** this success gave him back *or* restored his confidence; **jdm sein Wort ~** to release sb from his/her *etc* word; (= *sich entloben*) to break off one's engagement

zu|rück|ge|blie|ben ADJ **geistig/körperlich ~** mentally/physically retarded → *auch* **zurückbleiben**

zu|rück+ge|hen VI *sep irreg aux sein* **a** (= *zurückkehren*) to go back, to return (*nach, in +acc* to); (*fig: in der Geschichte etc*) to go back (*auf +acc, in +acc* to); (= *seinen Ursprung haben*) to go back to (*auf +acc* to); **er ging zwei Schritte zurück** he stepped back two paces, he took two steps back; **Waren/Essen etc ~ lassen** to send back goods/food *etc*; **der Brief ging ungeöffnet zurück** the letter was returned unopened **b** (= *zurückweichen*) to retreat, to fall back; (*fig: = abnehmen*) (*Hochwasser, Schwellung, Vorräte, Preise etc*) to go down; (*Geschäft, Umsatz, Produktion*) to fall off; (*Seuche, Schmerz, Sturm*) to die down; **im Preis ~** to fall *or* drop in price

zu|rück+ge|win|nen *ptp* **zurückgewonnen** VT *sep irreg* **a** (*beim Spiel*) to win back **b** (*Mil*) *Land* to reconquer, to regain **c** (= *wiederbekommen*) *Selbstvertrauen* to regain **d** (*Tech*) *Rohstoff* to recover

Zu|rück-: zu|rück|ge|zo|gen ADJ *Mensch* withdrawn, retiring; *Lebensweise* secluded ADV in seclusion; **er lebt sehr ~** he lives a very secluded life (= *auch* zurückziehen); **Zu|rück|ge|zo|gen|heit** F -, *no pl* seclusion; **zu|rück+grei|fen** VI *sep irreg* (*fig*) to fall back (*auf*

+acc upon); (*zeitlich*) to go back (*auf +acc* to); **da müsste ich weit ~** I would have to go back a long way; **zu|rück+ha|ben** VT *sep irreg* (*inf*) to have (got (*Brit*) or gotten (*US*)) back; **ich will mein Geld ~** I want my money back; **hast du das Buch schon zurück?** have you got (*Brit*) or gotten (*US*) the book back yet?

zu|rück+hal|ten *sep irreg* **VT** (= *daran hindern, sich zu entfernen*) to hold back; (= *nicht durchlassen, aufhalten*) *jdn* to hold up, to detain; (= *nicht freigeben*) *Manuskript, Film, Informationen* to withhold; (= *eindämmen*) *Gefühle, Ärger etc* to restrain, to suppress; (= *unterdrücken*) *Tränen, Orgasmus* to keep *or* hold back; **jdn von etw** (*dat*) **~** to keep sb from sth **VR** (= *sich beherrschen*) to contain *or* restrain oneself, to control oneself; (= *reserviert sein*) to be retiring *or* withdrawn; (= *im Hintergrund bleiben*) to keep in the background; (*bei Verhandlung, Demonstration etc*) to keep a low profile; (*bei Investitionen*) to be restrained; **sich mit seiner Kritik ~** to be restrained in one's criticism; **ich musste mich schwer ~** I had to take a firm grip on myself; **Sie müssen sich beim Essen sehr ~** you must cut down a lot on what you eat **VI** **mit etw ~** (= *verheimlichen*) to hold sth back

zu|rück|hal|tend ADJ **a** (= *beherrscht, kühl*) restrained; (= *reserviert*) reserved; (= *vorsichtig*) cautious, guarded; *Börse* dull **b** (= *nicht großzügig*) sparing; **mit Tadel** *or* **Kritik nicht ~ sein** to be unsparing in one's criticism ADV with restraint; **sich ~ über etw** (*acc*) **äußern** to be restrained in one's comments about sth; **das Publikum reagierte ~** the audience's response was restrained

Zu|rück-: Zu|rück|hal|tung F , *no pl* (= *Beherrschtheit*) restraint; (= *Reserviertheit*) reserve; (= *Vorsicht*) caution; **sich** (*dat*) **~ auferlegen, ~ üben** to exercise restraint; **zu|rück+ho|len** VT *sep* to fetch back; *Geld* to get back; **jdn ~** (*fig*) to ask sb to come back; **zu|rück+ja|gen** *sep* **VT** to chase back **VI** *aux sein* to chase *or* dash back; **zu|rück+käm|men** VT *sep* to comb back; **zu|rück+kau|fen** VT *sep* to buy back, to repurchase; **zu|rück+keh|ren** VI *sep aux sein* to return *or* come back (*von, aus* from); to return *or* go back (*nach, zu* to); **zu|rück+kom|men** VI *sep irreg aux sein* (*lit, fig*) to come back, to return; (= *Bezug nehmen*) to refer (*auf +acc* to); **der Brief kam zurück** the letter was returned, the letter came back; **ich werde später auf deinen Vorschlag/dieses Angebot ~** I'll come back to your suggestion/this offer later; **zu|rück+kön|nen** VI *sep irreg* (*inf*) to be able to go back; **ich kann nicht mehr zurück** (*fig*) there's no going back!; **zu|rück+krie|gen** VT *sep* (*inf*) = **zurückbekommen**; **zu|rück+las|sen** VT *sep irreg* **a** (= *hinterlassen*) to leave; (= *liegen lassen*) to leave behind; (*fig*: = *übertreffen*) to leave behind, to outstrip; (*Leichtathletik*) to leave behind, to outdistance **b** (*inf*: = *zurückkehren lassen*) to allow back, to allow to return; **Zu|rück|las|sung** F -, *no pl* **unter ~ all seiner Habseligkeiten** *etc* leaving behind all one's possessions *etc*; **zu|rück+lau|fen** VI *sep irreg aux sein* to run back; (= *zurückgehen*) to walk *or* go back

zu|rück+le|gen *sep* **VT** **a** (*an seinen Platz*) to put back **b** *Kopf* to lay *or* lean back **c** (= *aufbewahren, reservieren*) to put aside *or* to one side; (= *sparen*) to put away, to lay aside; **jdm etw ~** to keep sth for sb **d** *Strecke* to cover, to do; **er hat schon ein ganzes Stück auf seinem Weg zum Diplomaten zurückgelegt** he has already gone a long way toward(s) becoming a diplomat **VR** to lie back

Zu|rück-: zu|rück+leh|nen VTR *sep* to lean back; **zu|rück+lei|ten** VT *sep* to lead back; *Postsendung* to return; *Wasser etc* to feed back, to run back; **zu|rück+lie|gen** VI *sep irreg* (*örtlich*) to be back; **der Unfall liegt etwa eine Woche zurück** the accident was about a week ago, it is about a week since the accident; **das**

liegt schon so weit zurück, dass ... that is so long ago now that ...; **es liegt zwanzig Jahre zurück, dass ...** it is twenty years since ...; **zu|rück+mel|den** *sep* **VTR** to report back **VR** (*Univ*) to matriculate for the new term; **zu|rück+müs|sen** VI *sep irreg* (*inf*) to have to go back; **Zu|rück|nah|me** [-na:mə] F -, -n withdrawal (*auch Jur, Mil*); (*von Aussage auch*) retraction; (*von Entscheidung*) reversal; **wir bitten um ~ dieser Sendung** we ask you to accept the return of this consignment

zu|rück+neh|men VT *sep irreg* to take back; (*Mil*) to withdraw; *Verordnung etc* to revoke; *Entscheidung* to reverse; *Angebot* to withdraw; *Auftrag, Bestellung* to cancel; (*Sport*) *Spieler* to bring *or* call back; *Schachzug* to go back on; **sein Wort/Versprechen ~** to go back on one's word/promise; **ich nehme alles zurück (und behaupte das Gegenteil)** I take it all back

zu|rück-: zu|rück+pfei|fen VT *sep irreg Hund etc* to whistle back; **jdn ~** (*fig inf*) to bring sb back into line; **zu|rück+pral|len** VI *sep aux sein* to rebound, to bounce back; (*Geschoss*) to ricochet; (*Strahlen, Hitze*) to be reflected; **von etw ~** to bounce/ricochet/be reflected off sth; **vor Schreck ~** to recoil in horror; **zu|rück+rech|nen** VTI *sep* to count back; **zu|rück+rei|chen** *sep* *Gegenstand* to hand *or* pass back **VI** (*Erinnerung, Tradition etc*) to go back (*in +acc* to); **zu|rück+rei|sen** VI *sep aux sein* to travel back, to return; **zu|rück+rei|ßen** VT *sep irreg* to pull back; **zu|rück+rol|len** VTI *sep* (*vi: aux sein*) to roll back; **zu|rück+ru|fen** *sep irreg* **VT** to call back; (*am Telefon auch*) to ring back (*Brit*); *Botschafter, fehlerhafte Produkte* to recall; **jdn ins Leben ~** to bring sb back to life; **jdm etw in die Erinnerung** *or* **ins Gedächtnis ~** to conjure sth up for sb; **sich** (*dat*) **etw in die Erinnerung** *or* **ins Gedächtnis ~** to recall sth, to call sth to mind **VI** to call back; (*am Telefon auch*) to ring back (*Brit*); **zu|rück+schal|len** VI *sep* to re-echo, to resound; **zu|rück+schal|ten** VI *sep* to change back; **zu|rück+schau|dern** VI *sep aux sein* to shrink back (*vor +acc* from), to recoil (*vor +acc* from); **zu|rück+schau|en** VI *sep* (*lit, fig*) to look back (*auf +acc lit* at, (*fig*) on); **zu|rück+scheu|chen** VT *sep* to chase back; **zu|rück+scheu|en** VI *sep aux sein* to shy away (*vor +dat* from); **vor nichts ~** to stop at nothing; **zu|rück+schi|cken** VT *sep* to send back; **jdm etw ~** to send sth back to sb, to send sb sth back; **zu|rück+schie|ben** VT *sep irreg* to push back

zu|rück+schla|gen *sep irreg* **VT** **a** *Ball* to knock back; (*mit Schläger*) to return, to hit back; *Feind, Angriff, Truppen etc* to beat back, to beat off (*Brit*), to repulse **b** (= *umschlagen*) *Gardinen* to pull back; *Decke* to fold back; *Kragen* to turn down; *Schleier* to lift; *Buchseiten* to leaf back **VI** (*lit, fig*) to hit back; (*Mil, fig*) to retaliate, to strike back; (*Flamme*) to flare back; (*Pendel*) to swing back; **auf jdn/etw ~** to have repercussions for sb/sth

zu|rück-: zu|rück+schnei|den VT *sep irreg Hecke, Pflanze* to cut back; *Krallen* to trim; **zu|rück+schnel|len** VI *sep aux sein* to spring back; **zu|rück+schrau|ben** VT *sep* to screw back; (*fig inf*) *Erwartungen* to lower; *Subventionen* to cut back; **seine Ansprüche ~** to lower one's sights; **zu|rück+schre|cken** VI *sep irreg aux sein or haben* to shrink back, to start back, to recoil; (*fig*) to shy away (*vor +dat* from); **vor nichts ~** to stop at nothing; **zu|rück+se|hen** VI *sep irreg* to look back; **auf etw** (*acc*) **~** (*fig*) to look back on sth; **zu|rück+seh|nen** *sep* **VR** to long to return (*nach* to); **sich nach der guten alten Zeit ~** to long for the good old days **VT** (*liter*) **jdn/etw ~** to long for the return of sb/sth; **zu|rück+sen|den** VT *sep irreg* to send back, to return

zu|rück+set|zen *sep* **VT** **a** (*nach hinten*) to move back; *Auto* to reverse, to back **b** (*an früheren Platz*) to put back **c** (*dial*) *Preis, Waren* to reduce, to mark down; **zurückgesetzt** reduced, marked down **d** (*fig*: = *benachteiligen*) to neglect **VR** to sit back; **er setzte sich zwei Reihen zurück** he went to sit *or* he sat two rows back **VI** (*mit Fahrzeug*) to reverse, to back

Zu|rück-: Zu|rück|set|zung [-zɛtsʊŋ] F ~, *no pl* (*fig*: = *Benachteiligung*) neglect; **von ~ der Mädchen kann keine Rede sein** there's no question of the girls being neglected; **zu|rück+sin|ken** VI *sep irreg aux sein* (*lit, fig*) to sink back (*in +acc* into); **zu|rück+spie|len** *sep* **VT** (*Sport*) to play back; (*Ftbl auch*) to pass back; (*Ftbl auch*) to pass back; **zu|rück+sprin|gen** VI *sep irreg aux sein* to leap *or* jump back; (*fig*: *Häuserfront*) to be set back; **zu|rück+ste|cken** *sep* **VT** to put back **VI a** (= *weniger Ansprüche stellen*) to lower one's expectations; (= *weniger ausgeben*) to cut back **b** (= *nachgeben, einlenken*) to backtrack

zu|rück+ste|hen VI *sep irreg* **a** (*Haus etc*) to stand back **b** (*an Leistung etc*) to be behind (*hinter jdm sb*) **c** (= *verzichten*) to miss out; (= *ausgelassen werden*) to be left out **d** (= *hintangesetzt werden*) to take second place; **hinter etw** (*dat*) ~ to take second place to sth; **sie muss immer hinter ihm ~** she always comes off worse than he does

zu|rück+stel|len VT *sep* **a** (*an seinen Platz*) *Uhr* to put back; (*nach hinten*) to move back **b** *Waren* to put aside *or* by **c** (*Aus*: = *zurücksenden*) to send back, to return **d** (*fig*) *Schüler* to keep down; **jdn vom Wehrdienst ~** to defer sb's military service **e** (*fig*: = *verschieben*) to defer; *Investitionen, Pläne* to postpone; *Bedenken, Forderungen etc* to put aside; *Sport, Privatleben, Hobbys etc* to spend less time on; **persönliche Interessen hinter etw** (*dat*) ~ to put one's personal interests after sth, to subordinate one's personal interests to sth; **persönliche Interessen ~** to put one's own interests last

Zu|rück-: Zu|rück|stel|lung F **a** (*Aus*: = *Zurücksendung*) return **b** (= *Aufschub, Mil*) deferment **c** (= *Hintanstellung*) **unter ~ seiner eigenen Interessen** putting his own interests last *or* aside; **zu|rück+sto|ßen** *sep irreg* **VT a** (= *wegstoßen*) to push back; (*fig*) to reject **b** (*fig*: = *abstoßen*) to put off (*vi: aux sein*) (*Aut*: = *zurücksetzen*) to reverse, to back; **zu|rück+strah|len** VI *sep* to reflect **VI** to be reflected; **zu|rück+strei|chen** VT *sep irreg* *Haar* to smooth back; **sich** (*dat*) **das Haar ~** to smooth one's hair back; **zu|rück+strei|fen** VT *sep Ärmel etc* to pull up; **zu|rück+strö|men** VI *sep aux sein* to flow back; (*geh*: *Menschen*) to stream back; **zu|rück+stu|fen** VT *sep* to downgrade; **zu|rück+tau|meln** VI *sep aux sein* to reel back; **zu|rück+tra|gen** VT *sep irreg* to carry *or* take back; **zu|rück+trei|ben** VT *sep irreg* to drive back; (*Mil auch*) to repel, to repulse

zu|rück+tre|ten *sep irreg* **VI** *aux sein* **a** (= *zurückgehen*) to step back; (*fig*: *Fluss, Hochwasser etc*) to go down, to subside; **bitte ~!** stand back, please!; **einen Schritt ~** to take a step back **b** (*Regierung*) to resign; (*von einem Amt*) to step down, to resign **c** (*von einem Vertrag etc*) to withdraw (*von* from), to back out (*von* of); **von einem Anspruch/einem Recht ~** to renounce a claim/a right **d** (*fig*: = *geringer werden*) to decline, to diminish; (*Wald*) to recede; (= *an Wichtigkeit verlieren*) to fade (in importance); (= *im Hintergrund bleiben*) to come second (*hinter jdm/etw* to sb/sth) **VTI** (*mit Fuß*) to kick back

Zu|rück-: zu|rück+tun VT *sep irreg* (*inf*) to put back; **zu|rück+über|set|zen** *ptp* **zurückübersetzt** VT *sep* to translate back; **zu|rück+ver|fol|gen** *ptp* **zurückverfolgt** VT *sep* (*fig*) to trace back, to retrace; **zu|rück+ver|lan|gen** *ptp* **zurückverlangt** *sep* **VT** to demand back **VI** **nach etw ~** (*geh*) to yearn for the return of sth; **zu|rück+ver|le|gen** *ptp* **zurückverlegt** VT *sep* **a** (*zeitlich*) to set back **b** (*Mil*) *Front etc* to move back, to withdraw; *Deich* to move back **c**

Wohn-, Firmensitz to move back; **zu|rück+ver|set|zen** *ptp* **zurückversetzt** *sep* **VT a** (*in seinen alten Zustand*) to restore (*in +acc* to); (*in eine andere Zeit*) to take back (*in +acc* to); **wir fühlten uns ins 18. Jahrhundert zurückversetzt** we felt as if we had been taken back *or* transported to the 18th century **b** *Beamte etc* to transfer back; *Schüler* to move down (*in +acc* into) **c** to think oneself back (*in +acc* into); **zu|rück+ver|wan|deln** *ptp* **zurückverwandelt** VTR *sep* to turn *or* change back (*in +acc, zu* to); **zu|rück+ver|wei|sen** *ptp* **zurückverwiesen** VT *sep irreg* (*auch Jur*) to refer back; *jdn auch* to direct back; (*Parl*) *Gesetzentwurf* to recommit; **zu|rück+wei|chen** VI *sep irreg aux sein* (*vor +dat* from) (*erschrocken*) to shrink back; (*ehrfürchtig*) to stand back; (*nachgeben*) to retreat; (*vor Verantwortung, Hindernis*) to shy away; (*Mil*) to withdraw, to fall back; (*Hochwasser*) to recede, to subside; **zu|rück+wei|sen** VT *sep irreg* to reject; *Angebot auch, Geschenk* to refuse; *Gäste, Bittsteller* to turn away; *Berichte, Vorwurf* to dismiss; *Angriff* to repel, to repulse; (*Jur*) *Klage, Berufung* to dismiss, to reject; (*an der Grenze*) to turn back; **Zu|rück|wei|sung** F rejection; (*von Geschenk*) refusal; (*von Angriff*) repulsion; (*Jur*: *von Klage, Berufung*) dismissal; (*an der Grenze*) turning back; **er protestierte gegen seine ~ an der Grenze** he protested against being turned away at the border; **zu|rück+wen|den** VTR *sep irreg* to turn back; **zu|rück+wer|fen** VT *sep irreg* *Ball, Kopf* to throw back; *Feind* to repulse, to repel; *Strahlen, Schall* to reflect; (*fig*: *wirtschaftlich, gesundheitlich*) to set back (*um* by); **zu|rück+wir|ken** VI *sep* to react (*auf +acc* upon); **zu|rück+wol|len** VI *sep* (*inf*) to want to go back; **zu|rück+wün|schen** VT *sep sich* (*dat*) **jdn/etw ~** to wish sb/sth back, to wish that sb/sth were back

zu|rück+zah|len VT *sep* to repay, to pay back; *Schulden auch* to pay off; *Spesen etc* to refund; **das werde ich ihm noch ~!** (*fig*) I'll pay him back for that!

zu|rück+zie|hen *sep irreg* **VT** to pull *or* draw back; *Hand, Fuß* to pull *or* draw away *or* back; *Truppen* to pull back; (= *rückgängig machen*) *Antrag, Bemerkung, Klage etc* to withdraw **VR** to retire, to withdraw; (= *sich zur Ruhe begeben*) to retire; (*Mil*) to withdraw, to retreat; (*vom Geschäft, von der Politik etc*) to retire (*von, aus* from); **sich von jdm ~** to withdraw from sb; **sich von der Welt/in sich** (*acc*) ~ to retire from the world/into oneself → *auch* **zurückgezogen VI** *aux sein* to move back; (*Truppen*) to march back; (*Vögel*) to fly back

Zu|rück-: Zu|rück|zie|hung F withdrawal, retraction; **zu|rück+zu|cken** VI *sep aux sein* to recoil, to start back; (*Hand, Fuß*) to jerk back

Zu|ruf M shout, call; (*aufmunternd*) cheer; **durch ~ abstimmen** *or* **wählen** to vote by acclamation; **~e** shouts; (= *Zwischenrufe*) heckling

zu|ru|fen VTI *sep irreg* **jdm etw ~** to shout sth to *or* at sb; (*feierlich*) to call sth out to sb; **jdm anfeuernd ~** to cheer sb

zu|rüs|ten *sep* **VT** to set up, to get ready, to prepare **VI** to get everything set up *or* ready

Zu|rüs|tung F setting-up, preparation

zur|zeit [tsʊrˈtsait] ADV at present, at the moment

Zu|sa|ge F **a** (= *Zustimmung*) assent, consent **b** (= *Verpflichtung*) undertaking, commitment **c** (= *Annahme*) acceptance; (= *Bestätigung*) confirmation **d** (= *Versprechen*) promise, pledge; **ich kann Ihnen keine ~n machen** I can't make you any promises

zu|sa|gen *sep* **VT a** (= *versprechen*) to promise; (= *bestätigen*) to confirm; **er hat sein Kommen fest zugesagt** he has promised firmly that he will come **b** **jdm etw auf den Kopf ~** (*inf*) to tell sb sth outright; **ich kann ihm auf den Kopf ~, wenn er mich belügt** I can tell straight away when he's lying **VI a** (= *annehmen*) (**jdm**) to accept; **eine ~de Antwort** a favourable (*Brit*) *or*

favorable (*US*) reply **b** (= *gefallen*) **jdm ~** to appeal to sb; **das will mir gar nicht ~** I don't like it one little bit

zu|sam|men [tsuˈzamən] ADV together; **alle/alles ~** all together; **wir haben das Buch ~ geschrieben** we have written the book together *or* between us; **wir hatten ~ 100 Euro zum Ausgeben** between us we had 100 euros to spend; **wir bestellten uns ~ eine Portion** we ordered one portion between us; **~ mit** together *or* along with; **das macht ~ 50 Euro** that comes to *or* makes 50 euros all together *or* in all; **er zahlt mehr als wir alle ~** he pays more than all of us *or* the rest of us put together

Zu|sam|men-: Zu|sam|men|ar|beit F co-operation; (*mit dem Feind*) collaboration; **in ~ mit** in co-operation with; **zu|sam|men+ar|bei|ten** VI *sep* to co-operate, to work together; (*mit dem Feind*) to collaborate; **zu|sam|men+ba|cken** VI *sep aux sein* (*inf*: = *kleben*) to stick together

zu|sam|men+bal|len *sep* **VT** *Schnee, Lehm* to make into a ball; *Papier* to screw (*Brit*) *or* crumple up into a ball **VR** (= *sich ansammeln*) to accumulate; (*Menge*) to mass (together); (*Mil*) to be concentrated *or* massed; **das Unheil ballte sich über seinem Haupt zusammen** (*liter*) disaster loomed over him

Zu|sam|men-: Zu|sam|men|bal|lung F accumulation; **Zu|sam|men|bau** M ~, *no pl* assembly; **zu|sam|men+bau|en** VT *sep* to assemble, to put together; **etw wieder ~** to reassemble sth; **zu|sam|men+bei|ßen** VT *sep irreg* **die Zähne ~** (*lit*) to clench one's teeth; (*fig*) to grit one's teeth; **zu|sam|men+be|kom|men** *ptp* **zusammenbekommen** VT *sep irreg* to get together; *Geld, Spenden* to collect; *Wortlaut* to remember; **zu|sam|men+bet|teln** VT *sep sich* (*dat*) **etw ~** to raise the money for sth; *Geld* to get sth together; **zu|sam|men+bin|den** VT *sep irreg* to tie *or* bind sth together; **zu|sam|men+blei|ben** VI *sep aux sein* to stay together; **zu|sam|men+bor|gen** VT *sep sich* (*dat*) *Geld* ~ to raise money; **sich** (*dat*) **etw ~** to borrow sth; **zu|sam|men+brau|en** *sep* **VT** (*inf*) to concoct, to brew (up) **VR** (*Gewitter, Unheil etc*) to be brewing

zu|sam|men+bre|chen VI *sep irreg aux sein* (*Gebäude*) to cave in; (*Brücke auch*) to give way; (*Wirtschaft, Markt, Imperium*) to collapse; (*Widerstand*) to crumble; (= *zum Stillstand kommen*) (*Verkehr etc*) to come to a standstill *or* halt; (*Verhandlungen, Telefonverbindung, Mil*: *Angriff*) to break down; (*Elec*: *Spannung*) to fail; (*Comput*: *Rechner*) to crash; (*Mensch*) to break down; (*vor Erschöpfung*) to collapse

zu|sam|men+brin|gen VT *sep irreg* **a** (= *sammeln*) to bring together, to collect; *Geld* to raise **b** (*inf*: = *zustande bringen*) to manage; *Gedanken* to collect; *Worte, Sätze* to put together; (= *ins Gedächtnis zurückrufen*) to remember; (= *zusammenkriegen, -bauen*) to get together **c** (= *in Kontakt bringen*) *Stoffe* to bring into contact with each other; (= *bekannt machen*) *Menschen* to bring together; *wieder ~* (= *versöhnen*) to reconcile, to bring back together; **die beiden Katzen darfst du nicht ~** you must not let the two cats get near each other

Zu|sam|men|bruch M (*von Beziehungen, Kommunikation*) breakdown; (*Comput*) crash; (*fig*) collapse; (= *Nervenzusammenbruch*) breakdown

zu|sam|men+drän|gen *sep* **VT** *Menschen* to crowd *or* herd together; (*fig*) *Ereignisse, Fakten* to condense **VR** (*Menschen*) to crowd (together); (*Mil*: *Truppen*) to be concentrated *or* massed; **die ganze Handlung des Stücks drängt sich im letzten Akt zusammen** all the action of the play is concentrated into the last act

Zu|sam|men-: zu|sam|men+drü|cken *sep* **VT** to press together; (= *verdichten*) to compress **VR** to be compressed; **zu|sam|men+fah|ren** *sep irreg* **VI** *aux sein* **a** (= *zusammenstoßen*) to collide **b** (= *erschrecken*) to start; (*vor Schmerz*) to flinch **VT** (*inf*) **a** (= *überfahren*) to run over **b** *Fahr-*

zeug to crash, to wreck; **Zu|sạm|men|fall** M (*von Ereignissen*) coincidence

zu|sạm|men+fal|len VI *sep irreg aux sein* **a** (= *einstürzen*) to collapse; **in sich** (*acc*) **~** (*lit, fig*) to collapse; (*Lügengebäude auch*) to fall apart; (*Hoffnungen*) to be shattered **b** (= *niedriger werden, sich senken*) to go down; **die Glut war (in sich) zusammengefallen** the fire had died down **c** (*durch Krankheit etc*) to waste away; **er sah ganz zusammengefallen aus** he looked very decrepit **d** (*Ereignisse*) to coincide

zu|sạm|men+fal|ten VT *sep* to fold up

zu|sạm|men+fan|ta|sie|ren ▲ *ptp* **zusammenfantasiert** VT *sep* (**sich** *dat*) **etw ~** to dream sth up; (*inf:* = *lügen*) to make sth up

zu|sạm|men+fas|sen *sep* **VT** **a** (= *verbinden*) to combine (*zu* in); (= *vereinigen*) to unite; (*Math*) to sum; (*Mil*) *Truppen* to concentrate **b** *Bericht etc* to summarize; **etw in einem Satz ~** to sum sth up in one sentence **VI** (= *das Fazit ziehen*) to summarize, to sum up; **ein ~der Bericht** a summary, a résumé; **~d kann man sagen, ...** to sum up *or* in summary, one can say ...; **wenn ich kurz ~ darf** just to sum up

Zu|sạm|men-: Zu|sạm|men|fas|sung F **a** *no pl* combination; (= *Vereinigung*) union; (*Math*) summing; (*Mil: von Truppen*) concentration **b** (= *Überblick*) summary, synopsis, résumé; (*von Abhandlung*) abstract; **zu|sạm|men+fe|gen** VT *sep* to sweep together; **zu|sạm|men+fin|den** VR *sep irreg* to meet; (= *sich versammeln*) to congregate; **zu|sạm|men+fli|cken** VT *sep* to patch together; (*inf*) *Verletzten* to patch up (*inf*); (*fig*) *Aufsatz etc* to throw together; **zu|sạm|men+flie|ßen** VI *sep irreg aux sein* to flow together, to meet; (*Farben*) to run together; **Zu|sạm|men|fluss** ▲ M confluence; **zu|sạm|men+fü|gen** *sep* VT to join together; (*Tech*) to fit together; **etw zu etw ~** to join/fit sth together to make sth **VR** to fit together; **sich gut ~** (*fig*) to turn out well; **zu|sạm|men+füh|ren** VT *sep* to bring together; *Familie* to reunite; **zu|sạm|men+ge|ben** VT *sep irreg* (*dial*) *Zutaten* to mix together; **zu|sạm|men+ge|hen** VI *sep irreg aux sein* **a** (= *sich vereinen*) to unite; (*Linien etc*) to meet; (*Unternehmen*) to merge **b** (= *einlaufen*) *Wäsche* to shrink **c** (*inf:* = *sich verbinden lassen*) to go together; **zu|sạm|men+ge|hö|ren** *ptp* **zusammengehört** VI *sep* (*Menschen, Städte, Firmen etc*) to belong together; (*Gegenstände*) to go together, to match; (*als Paar*) to form a pair; (*Themen etc*) to go together; **zu|sạm|men|ge|hö|rig** ADJ *Kleidungsstücke etc* matching; (= *verwandt*) related, connected; **~ sein** to match; to be related *or* connected; **Zu|sạm|men|ge|hö|rig|keit** F *, no pl* common bond; **Zu|sạm|men|ge|hö|rig|keits|ge|fühl** NT (*in Gemeinschaft*) communal spirit; (*esp Pol*) feeling of solidarity; (*in Mannschaft*) team spirit; (*in Familie*) sense of a common bond; **zu|sạm|men+ge|ra|ten** *ptp* **zusammengeraten** VI *sep irreg aux sein* **a** (= *zusammenkommen*) **mit jdm ~** to get together with sb **b** (*fig*) (= *aneinander geraten*) to come to blows (*mit* with); (= *streiten*) to have words (*mit* with)

zu|sạm|men|ge|setzt ADJ **aus etw ~ sein** to consist of sth, to be composed of sth; **~es Wort/Verb** compound (word)/verb; **~e Zahl** compound *or* complex number; **~er Satz** complex sentence → *auch* **zusammensetzen**

Zu|sạm|men-: **zu|sạm|men|ge|wür|felt** [-ɡəvʏrflt] ADJ oddly assorted, motley; *Mannschaft* scratch *attr*; **ein bunt ~er Haufen** a motley crowd; **zu|sạm|men+gie|ßen** VT *sep irreg* to pour together; **zu|sạm|men+ha|ben** VT *sep irreg* (*inf*) **etw ~** to have got (*Brit*) *or* gotten (*US*) sth together; *Geld auch* to have raised sth; **Zu|sạm|men|halt** M *, no pl* (*Tech*) (cohesive) strength; (*einer Erzählung*) coherence, cohesion; (*fig: in einer Gruppe*) cohesion; (*esp Pol*) solidarity; (*einer Mannschaft*) team spirit

zu|sạm|men+hal|ten *sep irreg* **VT** **a** (= *verbinden*) to hold together; (*inf*) *Geld etc* to hold on

to; **seine fünf Sinne ~** to keep one's wits about one **b** (= *nebeneinander halten*) to hold side by side **VI** to hold together; (*fig: Freunde, Gruppe etc*) to stick *or* stay together → **Pech a**

Zu|sạm|men+hang M (= *Beziehung*) connection (*von, zwischen +dat* between); (= *Wechselbeziehung*) correlation (*von, zwischen +dat* between); (= *Verflechtung*) interrelation (*von, zwischen +dat* between); (*von Geschichte*) coherence; (*im Text*) context; **jdn/etw mit jdm/etw in ~ bringen** to connect sb/sth with sb/sth; **im** *or* **in ~ mit etw stehen** to be connected with sth; **etw aus dem ~ reißen** to take sth out of its context; **nicht im ~ mit etw stehen** to have no connection with sth; **ich habe seinen Namen im ~ mit dieser Sache gehört** I've heard his name mentioned in connection with this; **in diesem ~** in this context, in connection with this

zu|sạm|men+hän|gen *sep* **VT** *Kleider in Schrank etc* to hang (up) together **VI** *irreg* to be joined (together); (*fig*) to be connected; **~d** (*Rede, Erzählung*) coherent; **das hängt damit zusammen, dass ...** that is connected with the fact that ...

Zu|sạm|men|hang(s)-: **zu|sạm|men|hang(s)|los** ADJ incoherent, disjointed; (= *weitschweifig auch*) rambling ADV incoherently; **Sachen ~ anordnen** to arrange things haphazardly; **Zu|sạm|men|hang(s)|lo|sig|keit** F *-, no pl* incoherence, disjointedness

Zu|sạm|men-: **zu|sạm|men+har|ken** VT *sep* to rake together; **zu|sạm|men+hau|en** VT *sep irreg* (*inf*) **a** (= *zerstören*) to smash to pieces; **jdn ~** to beat sb up (*inf*) **b** (*fig:* = *pfuschen*) *Geschriebenes* to scribble (down); **zu|sạm|men+hef|ten** VT *sep* (*mit Heftklammern*) to staple together; (*Sew*) to tack together; **zu|sạm|men+hei|len** VI *sep aux sein* (*Wunde*) to heal (up); (*Knochen*) to knit (together); **zu|sạm|men+ho|len** VT *sep Sachen* to gather together; *Menschen* to bring together; **zu|sạm|men+kau|ern** VR *sep* (*vor Kälte*) to huddle together; (*vor Angst*) to cower; **zu|sạm|men+kau|fen** VT *sep* to buy (up); **zu|sạm|men+keh|ren** VT *sep* to sweep together; **zu|sạm|men+ket|ten** VT *sep* to chain together; (*fig*) to bind together; **Zu|sạm|men|klang** M (*Mus, fig geh*) harmony, accord; **zu|sạm|men|klapp|bar** ADJ folding; *Stuhl, Tisch auch* collapsible

zu|sạm|men+klap|pen *sep* **VT** *Messer, Stuhl, Tisch etc* to fold up; *Schirm* to shut; **die Hacken ~** to click one's heels **VI** *aux sein* **a** (*Stuhl etc*) to collapse **b** (*fig inf*) to flake out (*inf*); (*nach vorne*) to double up

Zu|sạm|men-: **zu|sạm|men+klau|ben** VT *sep* to gather together, to collect; **zu|sạm|men+klau|en** VT *sep* (*inf*) **sich** (*dat*) **etw ~** to collect sth (by stealing); **zu|sạm|men+kle|ben** VTI *sep* (*vi: aux sein*) to stick together; **zu|sạm|men+kleis|tern** VT *sep* (*inf*) **a** (= *zusammenkleben*) to paste together **b** (*fig*) to patch up *or* together; **zu|sạm|men+klin|gen** VI *sep irreg* to sound together; (*fig: Farben etc*) to harmonize; **zu|sạm|men+knei|fen** VT *sep irreg* *Lippen, Pobacken etc* to press together; *Augen* to screw up; **zusammengekniffen** (*Augen*) screwed-up; *Mund* pinched; **zu|sạm|men+kno|ten** VT *sep* to knot *or* tie together; **zu|sạm|men+knül|len** VT *sep* to screw (*esp Brit*) *or* crumple up

zu|sạm|men+kom|men VI *sep irreg aux sein* to meet (together), to come together; (*Umstände*) to combine; (*fig:* = *sich einigen*) to agree, to come to an agreement; (*fig*) (= *sich ansammeln*: *Schulden etc*) to mount up, to accumulate; (*Geld bei einer Sammlung*) to be collected; **er kommt viel mit Menschen zusammen** he meets a lot of people; **wir kommen zweimal jährlich zusammen** we meet twice a year, we get together twice a year; **heute kommt wieder mal alles zusammen** (*inf*) it's all happening at once today

Zu|sạm|men-: **zu|sạm|men+kop|peln** VT *sep* *Anhänger, Wagen* to couple together; (*Space*) to

dock; **zu|sạm|men+kra|chen** VI *sep aux sein* (*inf*) **a** (= *einstürzen*) to crash down; (*fig: Börse, Wirtschaft*) to crash **b** (= *zusammenstoßen: Fahrzeuge*) to crash (into each other); **zu|sạm|men+kramp|fen** VR (*Hände*) to clench; (*Muskel, Magen*) to tense up; **da krampfte sich mein Herz zusammen** my heart nearly stopped; **zu|sạm|men+krat|zen** VT *sep* to scrape *or* scratch (*esp Brit*) together; (*fig inf*) *Geld etc* to scrape together; **zu|sạm|men+krie|gen** VT *sep* (*inf*) = **zusammenbekommen**; **Zu|sạm|men|kunft** [tsuˈzamənkʊnft] F *-, -künfte* [-kʏnftə] meeting; (*von mehreren auch*) gathering; (*zwanglos*) get-together; **zu|sạm|men+läp|pern** VR *sep* (*inf*) to add *or* mount up; **zu|sạm|men+las|sen** VT *sep irreg* to leave together

zu|sạm|men+lau|fen VI *sep irreg aux sein* **a** (= *an eine Stelle laufen*) to gather; (*Flüssigkeit*) to collect **b** (*Flüsse etc*) to flow together, to meet; (*Farben*) to run together; (*Math*) to intersect, to meet; (*Straßen*) to converge; (*fig: Fäden etc*) to meet **c** (*Stoff*) to shrink **d** (*Milch*) to curdle, to coagulate

zu|sạm|men+le|ben *sep* **VI** to live together **VR** to learn to live with each other

Zu|sạm|men|le|ben NT living together *no art*; (*von Ländern etc*) coexistence; **das ~ der Menschen** the social life of man; **mein ~ mit ihm war ...** living with him was ...; **das menschliche ~** social existence; **eheliches ~** married life; **außereheliches ~** cohabitation

zu|sạm|men+le|gen *sep* **VT** **a** (= *falten*) to fold (up)

b (= *stapeln*) to pile *or* heap together **c** (= *vereinigen*) to combine, to merge; *Aktien* to amalgamate, to consolidate; *Grundstücke* to join; *Veranstaltungen* to hold together, to hold at the same time; *Häftlinge, Patienten* to put together; *Termine* to combine; (= *zentralisieren*) to centralize; **sie legten ihr Geld zusammen** they pooled their money, they clubbed (*Brit*) *or* pitched in (*US*) together

VI (= *Geld gemeinsam aufbringen*) to club (*Brit*) *or* pitch in (*US*) together, to pool one's money; **für ein Geschenk ~** to club (*Brit*) *or* pitch in (*US*) together for a present

Zu|sạm|men-: **Zu|sạm|men|le|gung** [-leːɡʊŋ] F *-, -en* (= *Vereinigung*) amalgamation, merging; (*von Aktien*) amalgamation, consolidation; (*von Grundstücken*) joining; (= *Zentralisierung*) centralization; (*von Terminen*) combining; **die ~ aller Patienten auf eine Station** putting all the patients together in one ward; **zu|sạm|men+lei|hen** VT *sep irreg* **sich** (*dat*) **etw ~** to borrow sth; **zu|sạm|men+lei|men** VT *sep* to glue together; **zu|sạm|men+lö|ten** VT *sep* to solder together; **zu|sạm|men+lü|gen** VT *sep* (*inf*) to make up, to concoct; **was der (sich** *dat*) **wieder zusammenlügt!** the stories he makes up!; **zu|sạm|men+na|geln** VT *sep* to nail together; **zu|sạm|men+nä|hen** VT *sep* to sew *or* stitch together

zu|sạm|men+neh|men *sep irreg* **VT** to gather up *or* together; *Mut* to summon up, to muster up; *Gedanken* to collect; **seine ganze Kraft ~** to gather all one's strength; **alles zusammengenommen** all together, all in all; **wenn wir alle Ereignisse ~** if we consider everything that happened **VR** (= *sich zusammenreißen*) to pull oneself together, to get a grip on oneself (*Brit*), to take hold of oneself (*US*); (= *sich beherrschen*) to control oneself, to take a grip on oneself

Zu|sạm|men-: **zu|sạm|men+packen** *sep* **VT** to pack up together; **pack (deine Sachen) zusammen!** get packed! **VI** (= *einpacken*) to pack, to do one's packing; **zu|sạm|men+pas|sen** VI *sep* (*Menschen*) to suit each other, to be suited to each other; (*Farben, Stile*) to go together; **gut ~** to go well together; **überhaupt nicht ~** not to go together at all; **das passt nicht mit den Tatsachen zusammen** it doesn't fit the facts; **zu|sạm|men+pfer|chen** VT *sep* to herd together; (*fig*) to pack together; **zu|sạm|men+phan|ta-**

sie|ren VT *sep* = zusammenfantasieren; **Zu|sam|men|prall** M collision, (*fig*) clash; **zu|sam|men+pral|len** VI *sep aux sein* to collide; (*fig*) to clash; **zu|sam|men+pres|sen** VT *sep* to press or squeeze together; (= *verdichten*) to compress; **zu|sam|men+raf|fen** *sep* VT **a** *Gegenstände, Habseligkeiten* to bundle together; *Röcke* to gather up **b** (*fig*) *Mut* to summon up, to muster (up) **c** (*fig pej*: = *anhäufen*) to amass, to pile up VR to pull oneself together; **zu|sam|men+ras|seln** VI *sep aux sein* (*inf*) to collide; (*fig*) to have a row; **zu|sam|men+rau|fen** VR *sep* to get it all together (*inf*), to achieve a viable working relationship; **zu|sam|men+rech|nen** VT *sep* to add or total up; **alles zusammengerechnet** all together; (*fig*) all in all

zu|sam|men+rei|men *sep* VR (*inf*) **sich** (*dat*) **etw ~** to figure sth out (for oneself); **das kann ich mir nicht ~** I can't make head or tail of this, I can't figure it out at all; **sich** (*dat*) **den Rest ~** to put two and two together; **das kann ich mir jetzt ~, warum ...** I can see now why ... VR to make sense; **wie soll sich das ~?** it doesn't make sense

Zu|sam|men-: **zu|sam|men+rei|ßen** *sep irreg* VR to pull oneself together VT **die Hacken ~** to click one's heels; **zu|sam|men+rol|len** *sep* VT to roll up VR to curl up; (*Igel*) to roll or curl (itself) up (into a ball); (*Schlange*) to coil up; **zu|sam|men+rot|ten** VR *sep* (*pej*) (*esp Jugendliche*) to gang up (*gegen* against); (*esp heimlich*) to band together (*gegen* against); (*in aufrührerischer Absicht*) to form a mob; **Zu|sam|men|rot|tung** [-rɔtʊŋ] F -, -en *a no pl* ganging up; (*esp heimlich*) banding together **b** (= *Gruppe*) (*esp von Jugendlichen*) gang; (*in aufrührerischer Absicht*) mob; (*Jur*) riotous assembly; **zu|sam|men+rü|cken** *sep* VT *Möbel etc* to move closer together; (*schreiben*) *Wörter etc* to close up VI *aux sein* to move up closer, to move closer together; **zu|sam|men+ru|fen** VT *sep irreg* to call together; **zu|sam|men+sa|cken** VI *sep aux sein* to cave in; **in sich** (*acc*) **~** (*lit*) to collapse; (*fig*) (*bei Nachricht etc*) to seem to crumble; (= *Schwung verlieren*) to have lost all interest; **zu|sam|men+scha|ren** VR *sep* to gather; (*Menschen auch*) to congregate; **Zu|sam|men|schau** F overall view; **erst in der ~ ...** only when you view everything as a whole ...; **zu|sam|men+schei|ßen** VT *sep irreg* (*inf*) **jdn ~** to give sb a bollocking (*Brit inf*), to kick sb's ass (*US sl*); **zu|sam|men+schie|ßen** VT *sep irreg* to shoot up, to riddle with bullets, to shoot to pieces; (*mit Artillerie*) to pound to pieces

zu|sam|men+schla|gen *sep irreg* VT **a** (= *aneinander schlagen*) to knock or bang or strike together; *Becken* to clash; *Hacken* to click; *Hände* to clap **b** (= *falten*) to fold up **c** (= *verprügeln*) to beat up; (= *zerschlagen*) *Einrichtung* to smash up, to wreck VI *aux sein* **über jdm/etw ~** (*Wellen etc*) to close over sb/sth; (*stärker*) to engulf sb/sth; (*fig: Unheil etc*) to descend upon sb/sth, to engulf sb/sth

Zu|sam|men-: **zu|sam|men+schlie|ßen** VR *sep irreg* to join together, to combine; (*Comm*) to amalgamate, to merge; **sich gegen jdn ~** to band together against sb; **Zu|sam|men|schluss** ▲ M joining together, combining; (*Comm*) amalgamation, merger; (*von politischen Gruppen*) amalgamation; **zu|sam|men+schmel|zen** *sep irreg* VT (= *verschmelzen*) to fuse VI *aux sein* **a** (= *verschmelzen*) to fuse, to melt together **b** (= *zerschmelzen*) to melt (away); (*Widerstand, Vorsprung*) to melt away; (*Anzahl, Vermögen*) to dwindle; **zu|sam|men+schnü|ren** VT *sep* to tie up; **dieser traurige Anblick schnürte mir das Herz zusammen** this pitiful sight made my heart bleed; **zu|sam|men+schnur|ren** VI *sep* (*inf*: = *schrumpfen*) to shrink; **zu|sam|men+schrau|ben** VT *sep* to screw together; (*mit Bolzen*) to bolt together; **zu|sam|men+schre|cken** VI *sep irreg aux sein* to start

zu|sam|men+schrei|ben VT *sep irreg* **a** *Wörter* (*orthographisch*) to write together; (*im Schriftbild*) to join up **b** (*pej*: = *verfassen*) to scribble down; **was der für einen Mist zusammenschreibt** what a load of rubbish (*esp Brit*) or garbage he writes **c** (*inf*: = *durch Schreiben verdienen*) **sich** (*dat*) **ein Vermögen ~** to make a fortune with one's writing

Zu|sam|men-: **zu|sam|men+schrump|fen** VI *sep aux sein* to shrivel up; (*fig*) to dwindle (*auf +acc* to); **zu|sam|men+schus|tern** VT *sep* to throw together; **zu|sam|men+schwei|ßen** VT *sep* (*lit*) to weld together; **zu|sam|men sein** ▲ VI *sep irreg aux sein* **mit jdm ~** to be with sb; (*inf*: = *befreundet*) to be going out with sb; (*euph*: = *mit jdm schlafen*) to sleep with sb

Zu|sam|men sein NT being together *no art*; (*von Gruppe*) get-together

zu|sam|men+set|zen *sep* VT **a** *Schüler, Gäste etc* to put or seat together **b** *Gerät, Gewehr etc* to put together, to assemble (*zu* to make) VR **a** (= *sich zueinander setzen*) to sit together; (*um etwas zu besprechen, zu trinken etc*) to get together; **sich mit jdm (am Tisch) ~** to join sb (at their table); **sich gemütlich ~** to have a cosy get-together; **sich auf ein Glas Wein ~** to get together over a glass of wine **b** **sich ~ aus** to consist of, to be composed of, to be made up of → *auch* **zusammengesetzt**

Zu|sam|men-: **Zu|sam|men|setz|spiel** NT puzzle; (= *Puzzle*) jigsaw (puzzle); **Zu|sam|men|set|zung** [-zatsʊŋ] F -, -en putting together; (*von Gerät auch*) assembly; (= *Struktur*) composition, make-up; (= *Mischung*) mixture, combination (*aus* of); (*Gram*) compound; **das Team in dieser ~** the team in this line-up; **zu|sam|men+sin|ken** VI *sep irreg aux sein* (**in sich**) **~** to slump; (*Gebäude*) to cave in; **zusammengesunken** (*vor Kummer etc*) bowed; **zu|sam|men+sit|zen** VI *sep irreg aux haben* or (*Aus, S Ger, Sw*) *sein* to sit next to each other; (= *zusammen sein*) to sit together; **wir saßen gerade gemütlich zusammen, als ...** we were just sitting together having a nice chat when ...; **zu|sam|men+spa|ren** VT *sep* to save up; **Zu|sam|men|spiel** NT (*Mus*) ensemble playing; (*Theat*) ensemble acting; (*Sport*) teamwork; (*fig*) co-operation, teamwork; (*von Kräften etc*) interaction; **zu|sam|men+stau|chen** VT *sep* (*inf*) to give a dressing-down (*inf*), to chew out (*US inf*); **zu|sam|men+ste|cken** *sep* VT *Einzelteile* to fit together; (*mit Nadeln etc*) to pin together; **sie steckten die Köpfe zusammen** (*inf*) they put their heads together; (*um zu flüstern*) they whispered to each other VI (*inf*) to be together; **immer ~** to be inseparable, to be as thick as thieves (*pej inf*) or blood (*US inf*); **zu|sam|men+ste|hen** VI *sep irreg aux sein* to stand together, to stand side by side; (*Gegenstände*) to be together, to be side by side; (*fig*) to stand by each other

zu|sam|men+stel|len VT *sep* to put together; (*nach einem Muster, System*) to arrange; *Bericht, Programm* to compile, to put together; (= *sammeln*) *Daten* to compile; *Liste, Fahrplan* to draw up; *Rede* to draft; *Sammlung* to assemble, to put together; *Gruppe* to assemble; (*Sport*) *Mannschaft* to pick; **etw nach Gruppen etc ~** to arrange sth in groups *etc*

Zu|sam|men|stel|lung F **a** *no pl* putting together; (*nach Muster, System*) arranging; (*von Bericht, Programm, Daten*) compiling; (*von Liste, Fahrplan*) drawing up; (*von Mannschaft*) picking **b** (= *Kombination*) (*nach Muster, System*) arrangement; (*von Daten, Programm*) compilation; (= *Liste*) list; (= *Zusammensetzung*) composition; (= *Übersicht*) survey; (= *Gruppierung*) assembly, group; (*von Farben*) combination

Zu|sam|men-: **zu|sam|men+stim|men** VI *sep* (*farblich*) to match; (*musikalisch*) to harmonize; (= *übereinstimmen*) to agree, to tally (*mit* with); **zu|sam|men+stop|peln** [-ʃtɔpln] VT *sep* (*inf*) to throw together; **sich** (*dat*) **eine Rede** *etc* **~** to

throw up a speech *etc* together; **Zu|sam|men|stoß** M collision, crash; (*Mil, fig*: = *Streit*) clash

zu|sam|men+sto|ßen *sep irreg* VI *aux sein* (= *zusammenprallen*) to collide; (*Mil, fig*: = *sich streiten*) to clash; (= *sich treffen*) to meet; (= *gemeinsame Grenze haben*) to adjoin; **mit jdm ~** to collide with sb, to bump into sb; (*fig*) to clash with sb; **sie stießen mit den Köpfen zusammen** they banged or bumped their heads together; **mit der Polizei ~** to clash with the police VT to knock together; **er stieß sie mit den Köpfen zusammen** he banged or knocked their heads together

Zu|sam|men-: **zu|sam|men+strei|chen** VT *sep irreg* to cut (down) (*auf +acc* to); **zu|sam|men+strö|men** VI *sep aux sein* (*Flüsse*) to flow into one another, to flow together; (*geh*: *Menschen*) to flock or swarm together; **zu|sam|men+stü|ckeln** VT *sep* to patch together; **zu|sam|men+stür|zen** VI *sep aux sein* **a** (= *einstürzen*) to collapse, to tumble down **b** (= *zusammenlaufen*) to rush to gather round; **zu|sam|men+su|chen** VT *sep* to collect (together); **sich** (*dat*) **etw ~** to find sth; **zu|sam|men+tra|gen** VT *sep irreg* (*lit, fig*) to collect; (*Typ*) *Bögen* to collate; **zu|sam|men+tref|fen** VI *sep irreg aux sein* (*Menschen*) to meet; (*Ereignisse*) to coincide; **mit jdm ~** to meet sb; **Zu|sam|men|tref|fen** NT meeting; (*esp zufällig*) encounter; (*zeitlich*) coincidence; **zu|sam|men+trei|ben** VT *sep irreg* to round up; **zu|sam|men+tre|ten** *sep irreg* VT (= *zertrampeln*) to trample or crush underfoot VI *aux sein* (*Verein etc*) to meet; (*Parlament auch*) to assemble; (*Gericht*) to sit; **Zu|sam|men|tritt** M meeting; (*von Parlament auch*) assembly; (*von Gericht*) session; **zu|sam|men+trom|meln** VT *sep* (*inf*) to round up (*inf*); **zu|sam|men+tun** *sep irreg* VT (*inf*) to put together; (= *vermischen*) to mix VR to get together; **zu|sam|men+wach|sen** VI *sep irreg aux sein* to grow together; (= *zuheilen*: *Wunde*) to heal (up), to close; (*Knochen*) to knit; (*fig*) to grow close; **zusammengewachsen sein** (*Knochen*) to be joined or fused; **zu|sam|men+wer|fen** VT *sep irreg* **a** *Gegenstände* to throw together; (*fig*) (= *durcheinander bringen*) to mix or jumble up; (= *in einen Topf werfen*) to lump together **b** (= *umwerfen*) to throw down; **zu|sam|men+wir|ken** VI *sep* to combine, to act in combination; **zu|sam|men+wür|feln** VT *sep* to throw together; **zusammengewürfelt** thrown together; **zusammengewürfelte Mannschaft** scratch team; **ein bunt zusammengewürfelter Haufen** a motley crowd; **zu|sam|men+zäh|len** VT *sep* to add up; **alles zusammengezählt macht es 50 Euro** that makes 50 euros altogether or all told or in all

zu|sam|men+zie|hen *sep irreg* VT **a** *Muskel* to draw or pull together; (= *verengen*) to narrow; *Knoten, Schlinge* to tighten; *Augenbrauen, Stirn* to knit; **ein Loch in einem Strumpf ~** to mend a hole in a stocking (*by pulling the sides together and sewing it up*); **der saure Geschmack zog ihm den Mund zusammen** he screwed up his mouth at the bitter taste; **das zieht einem das Herz zusammen** it really pulls at the heartstrings; **~de Mittel** (*Med*) astringents **b** (*fig*) *Truppen, Polizei* to assemble **c** (= *kürzen*) *Wörter etc* to contract, to shorten; (*Math*) *Zahlen* to add together; *mathematischen Ausdruck* to reduce VR (*esp Biol, Sci*) to contract; (= *enger werden*) to narrow; (*Wunde*) to close (up); (*Gewitter, Unheil*) to be brewing VI *aux sein* to move in together; **mit jdm ~** to move in with sb

zu|sam|men+zu|cken VI *sep aux sein* to start

Zu|satz M addition; (= *Bemerkung*) additional remark; (*zu Gesetz, Vertrag etc*) rider; (*zu Testament*) codicil; (*Gram*) expression in opposition; (= *Verbzusatz*) separable element; (= *Beimischung*) addition, additive; **durch/nach ~ von etw** by/after adding sth, with or by/after the addition of sth

---

Zu|satz- *in cpds* additional, supplementary; **Zu|satz|ab|kom|men** NT supplementary agreement; **Zu|satz|ak|tie** F bonus share; **Zu|satz|an|trag** M (*Parl etc*) amendment; **Zu|satz|ar|ti|kel** M additional *or* supplementary article; **Zu|satz|be|las|tung** F additional load; **Zu|satz|be|stim|mung** F supplementary provision; **Zu|satz|er|klä|rung** F (*Pol*) supplementary declaration; **Zu|satz|fra|ge** F follow-up question; **Zu|satz|ge|rät** NT attachment; (*Comput*) peripheral (device), add-on; **Zu|satz|in|for|ma|ti|o|nen** PL additional information *no pl*; **Zu|satz|klau|sel** F additional clause; (*Jur*) rider (*Brit*); **Zu|satz|kos|ten** PL additional costs *pl*

zu|sätz|lich ['tsu:zɛtslɪç] ADJ additional; (= *weiter auch*) added *attr*, further *attr*; (= *ergänzend auch*) supplementary ADV in addition

Zu|satz-: Zu|satz|mit|tel NT additive; **Zu|satz|pla|ti|ne** F (*Comput*) daughterboard; **Zu|satz|stoff** M additive; **Zu|satz|ver|si|che|rung** F additional *or* supplementary insurance; **Zu|satz|zahl** F (*Lotto*) additional number, bonus number (*Brit*)

zu|sau|fen VR *sep irreg* (*sl*: = *sich betrinken*) to get pissed (*Brit inf*) *or* plastered (*inf*)

zu|schalt|bar ADJ connectible

zu+schal|ten *sep* VT to switch on (in addition); *Rundfunk-, Fernsehanstalt* to link up with VR to come on; (*Rundfunk-, Fernsehanstalt*) to link into the network

zu|schan|den [tsu:'ʃandn] ADV (*geh*) ~ **machen** (*fig*) to ruin, to wreck; **ein Auto ~ fahren** to wreck a car; **ein Pferd ~ reiten** to ruin a horse; **~ werden** (*fig*) to be wrecked *or* ruined

zu+schan|zen VT *sep* (*inf*) **jdm etw ~** to make sure sb gets sth

zu+schar|ren VT *sep* to cover over *or* up

zu|schau|en VI *sep* (*esp dial*) = zusehen

Zu|schau|er ['tsu:ʃaue] M -s, -, **Zu|schau|e|rin** [-ərɪn] F -, -nen spectator (*auch Sport*); (*TV*) viewer; (*Theat*) member of the audience; (= *Beistehender*) onlooker; **die ~** *pl* the spectators *pl*; (*esp Ftbl auch*) the crowd *sing*; (*TV*) the (television) audience *sing*, the viewers; (*Theat*) the audience *sing*; **einer der ~** (*Theat*) one of the audience, a member of the audience; **wie viele ~ waren da?** (*Sport*) how many spectators were there?; (*esp Ftbl auch*) how large was the crowd?

Zu|schau|er-: Zu|schau|er|be|fra|gung F (*TV*) (television) audience survey; **Zu|schau|er|ku|lis|se** F , **Zu|schau|er|men|ge** F (*Sport*) crowd, gathering of spectators; **Zu|schau|er|rang** M (*Sport*) stand; **Zu|schau|er|raum** M auditorium; **Zu|schau|er|re|ak|ti|on** F audience response; (*TV*) viewer response; (*Sport*) reaction of the crowd; **Zu|schau|er|ter|ras|se** F (*Sport*) (spectators') stand; (*auf Flughafen*) observation deck, spectators' gallery; **Zu|schau|er|tri|bü|ne** F (*esp Sport*) stand; **Zu|schau|er|um|fra|ge** F (*TV*) (television) audience survey; **Zu|schau|er|zahl** F attendance figure; (*Sport auch*) gate

zu+schau|feln VT *sep* to fill up

zu+schi|cken VT *sep* **jdm etw ~** to send sth to sb, to send sb sth; (*mit der Post auch*) to post (*Brit*) *or* mail (*esp US*) sth to sb; **sich** (*dat*) **etw ~ lassen** to send for sth; **etw zugeschickt bekommen** to receive sth (by post (*Brit*)) *or* mail), to get sth sent to one

zu+schie|ben VT *sep irreg* **a** **jdm etw ~** to push sth over to sb; (*heimlich*) to slip sb sth; (*fig*: = *zuschanzen*) to make sure sb gets sth; **jdm die Verantwortung/Schuld ~** to put the responsibility/blame on sb → **schwarz** ADJ **a** **b** (= *schließen*) *Tür, Fenster* to slide shut; *Schublade* to push shut

zu+schie|ßen *sep irreg* **a** **jdm den Ball ~** to kick the ball (over) to sb; **jdm wütende Blicke ~** to dart angry glances at sb, to look daggers at sb (*Brit*) **b** *Geld etc* to contribute; **Geld für**

---

etw ~ to put money toward(s) sth; **jdm 100 Euro ~/zu etw ~** to give sb 100 euros toward(s) it/sth VI *aux sein* (*inf*) **auf jdn/etw ~** *or* **zugeschossen kommen** to rush *or* shoot up to sb/sth

Zu|schlag M **a** (= *Erhöhung*) extra charge, surcharge (*esp Comm, Econ*); (*auf Briefmarke*) supplement; (*Rail*) supplement, supplementary charge; **für diese Züge muss man ~ bezahlen** you have to pay a supplement *or* a supplementary charge on these trains
b (*Tech*) addition
c (*bei Versteigerung*) acceptance of a bid; (= *Auftragserteilung*) acceptance of a/the tender; **mit dem ~ des Versteigerers ...** when the auctioneer concluded the bidding; **jdm den ~ erteilen** (*form*) *or* **geben** to knock down the lot *or* item to sb; (*nach Ausschreibung*) to award the contract to sb; **er erhielt den ~** the lot went to him; (*nach Ausschreibung*) he obtained the contract, he was awarded the contract

zu+schla|gen *sep irreg* VT **a** *Tür, Fenster* to slam (shut), to bang shut; **die Tür hinter sich** (*dat*) **~** to slam the door behind one
b (*Sport*: = *zuspielen*) **jdm den Ball ~** to hit the ball to sb; (*Ftbl inf*) to kick the ball to sb
c (*rare*: = *zufügen*) to add (on) (+*dat, zu* to)
d (*bei Versteigerung*) **jdm etw ~** to knock sth down to sb; **einer Firma einen Vertrag ~** to award a contract to a firm
e (= *zuerkennen*) *Gebiet* to annex (+*dat* to); *Geld, Güter* to award
VI **a** (= *kräftig schlagen*) to strike (*auch fig*); (= *losschlagen*) to hit out; **schlag zu!** hit me/him/it etc!; **das Schicksal hat entsetzlich zugeschlagen** (*geh*) fate has struck a terrible blow
b *aux sein* (*Tür*) to slam (shut), to bang shut
c (*fig inf*: = *zugreifen*) (*bei Angebot*) to go for it; (*beim Essen*) to get stuck in (*inf*); (*Polizei*) to pounce, to strike; **die EU-Bürokratie hat wieder zugeschlagen** EU bureaucracy has struck again (*inf*)

Zu|schlag(s)-: zu|schlag(s)|frei ADJ *Zug* not subject to a supplement ADV **alle Überstunden sind ~** all overtime is paid at the normal hourly rate; **Zu|schlag(s)|kar|te** F (*Rail*) supplementary ticket (*for trains on which a supplement is payable*); **zu|schlag(s)|pflich|tig** ADJ *Zug, Service* subject to a supplement

zu+schlie|ßen *sep irreg* VT to lock; *Laden* to lock up VI to lock up

zu+schmei|ßen VT *sep irreg* (*inf*) *Tür etc* to slam (shut), to bang shut

zu+schmie|ren VT *sep* (*inf*) to smear over; *Löcher* to fill in

zu+schnal|len VT *sep* to fasten, to buckle; *Koffer* to strap up

zu+schnap|pen VI *sep* **a** (= *zubeißen*) **der Hund schnappte zu** the dog snapped at me/him etc **b** (*fig*: *Polizei*) to pounce **c** *aux sein* (*Schloss*) to snap *or* click shut; (*Falle*) (*lit*) to snap shut; (*fig*) to close

zu+schnei|den VT *sep irreg* to cut to size; (*Sew*) to cut out; **auf etw** (*acc*) **zugeschnitten sein** (*fig*) to be geared to sth; **auf jdn/etw genau zugeschnitten sein** (*lit, fig*) to be tailor-made for sb/sth

Zu|schnei|der(in) M(F) cutter

zu+schnei|en VI *sep aux sein* to snow in *or* up

Zu|schnitt M **a** *no pl* (= *Zuschneiden*) cutting **b** (= *Form*) cut; (*fig*) calibre (*Brit*), caliber (*US*)

zu+schnü|ren VT *sep* to tie up; *Schuhe, Mieder* to lace up; **die Angst/innere Bewegung etc schnürte ihm die Kehle zu** he was choked with fear/emotion etc; **der Hals** *or* **die Kehle war ihm (vor Rührung/Trauer) wie zugeschnürt** (*fig*) he felt choked (with emotion/grief); **jdm das Herz ~** to make sb's heart bleed

zu+schrau|ben VT *sep* *Hahn etc* to screw shut; *Deckel etc* to screw on; **eine Flasche ~** to screw on the top of a bottle

zu+schrei|ben VT *sep irreg* **a** (*inf*: = *hinzuschreiben*) to add **b** (= *übertragen*) to transfer, to sign

---

over (+*dat* to) **c** (*fig*) to ascribe, to attribute (+*dat* to); **das hast du dir selbst zuzuschreiben** you've only got yourself to blame; **das ist nur seiner Dummheit/ihrem Geiz zuzuschreiben** that can only be put down to his stupidity/her meanness

zu+schrei|ten VI *sep irreg aux sein* (*geh*) **tüchtig ~** to walk briskly; **auf jdn/etw ~** to stride *or* walk toward(s) *or* (*bis zu*) up to sb/sth

Zu|schrift F letter; (*amtlich auch*) communication; (*auf Anzeige*) reply

zu|schul|den [tsu:'ʃʊldn] ADV **sich** (*dat*) **etwas ~ kommen lassen** to do something wrong; **solange man sich nichts ~ kommen lässt** as long as you don't do anything wrong

Zu|schuss ▲ M subsidy, grant; (*nicht amtlich*) something toward(s) it, contribution; (*esp regelmäßig von Eltern*) allowance; **einen ~ zu einer Sache gewähren** *or* **geben** to give a subsidy for sth; to make a contribution toward(s) sth; **mit einem kleinen ~ von meinen Eltern kann ich ...** if my parents give me something toward(s) it I can ...

Zu|schuss-: Zu|schuss|be|trieb ▲ M lossmaking (*Brit*) *or* losing (*US*) concern; **Zu|schuss|ge|schäft** ▲ NT lossmaking (*Brit*) *or* losing (*US*) deal; (*inf*: = *Zuschussunternehmen*) lossmaking (*Brit*) *or* losing (*US*) business

zu+schus|tern VT *sep* (*inf*) **jdm etw ~** to make sure sb gets sth

zu+schüt|ten *sep* VT to fill in *or* up; (= *hinzuschütten*) to add; (*fig*: = *verdecken*) to submerge VR (*inf*) (*mit Alkohol*) to have a skinful (*Brit inf*), to be two sheets to the wind (*US*); (*mit Drogen*) to get completely drugged up (*inf*)

zu+schwal|len ['tsu:ʃvalən] VT *sep* (*sl*) to chatter (on) to

zu+se|hen VI *sep irreg* **a** (= *beobachten, mit ansehen*) to watch; (= *unbeteiligter Zuschauer sein*) to look on; (= *etw dulden*) to sit back *or* stand by (and watch); **jdm/einer Sache ~** to watch sb/sth; **bei etw ~** to watch sth; (= *etw dulden*) to sit back *or* stand by and watch sth; **jdm bei der Arbeit ~** to watch sb working; **er sah zu, wie ich das machte** he watched me doing it; **ich kann doch nicht ~, wie er ...** (= *dulden*) I can't sit back *or* stand by and watch him ...; **ich habe nur zugesehen** I was only a spectator *or* an onlooker; **durch bloßes Zusehen** just by watching; **bei näherem Zusehen** when you watch/I watched etc more closely
b (= *dafür sorgen*) **~, dass ...** to see to it that ..., to make sure (that) ...; **sieh mal zu!** (*inf*) see what you can do

zu|se|hends ['tsu:ze:ənts] ADV visibly; (= *merklich auch*) noticeably, appreciably; (= *rasch*) rapidly; **~ im Verfall begriffen sein** to be in rapid decline

Zu|se|her(in) M(F) (*Aus TV*) viewer

zu sein ▲ VI *irreg aux sein* to be shut *or* closed; (*inf*: = *betrunken, high sein*) to be stoned (*inf*)

zu+sen|den VT *sep irreg* to send, to forward; *Geld auch* to remit (*form*)

zu+set|zen *sep* VT (= *hinzufügen*) to add; (*inf*: = *verlieren*) *Geld* to shell out (*inf*), to pay out; **er setzt immer (Geld) zu** (*inf*) he's always having to shell out (*inf*) *or* pay out; **er hat nichts mehr zuzusetzen** (*inf*) he has nothing in reserve VI **jdm ~** (= *unter Druck setzen*) to lean on sb (*inf*); **dem Gegner, Feind** to harass sb, to press sb hard; (= *drängen*) to badger *or* pester sb; (= *schwer treffen*) to hit sb hard, to affect sb (badly); (*Kälte, Krankheit etc*) to take a lot out of sb

zu+si|chern VT *sep* **jdm etw ~** to assure sb of sth, to promise sb sth; **mir wurde zugesichert, dass ...** I was assured *or* promised that ...

Zu|si|che|rung F assurance, promise

Zu|spät|kom|men|de(r) [tsu:'ʃpɛːtkɔmənde] MF *decl as adj* latecomer

---

zu+sper|ren VT sep (S Ger, Aus, Sw) (= zuschließen) to lock; Haus, Laden to lock up; (= verriegeln) to bolt

Zu|spiel NT (Sport) passing

zu+spie|len VT sep Ball to pass (+dat to); **jdm etw ~** (fig) to pass sth on to sb; (der Presse) to leak sth to sb

zu+spit|zen sep **VR** Stock etc to sharpen; **zugespitzt** sharpened; Turm, Schuhe etc pointed; (fig) exaggerated **VR** to be pointed; (fig: Lage, Konflikt) to intensify; **die Lage spitzt sich immer mehr zu** the situation is worsening

Zu|spit|zung ['tsuːʃpɪtsʊŋ] F -, -en (von Turm, Schuhen etc) pointing; (fig: von Lage, Konflikt) worsening

zu+spre|chen sep irreg **VT** (Jur) to award; Preis, Gewinn etc to award; Kind to award or grant custody of; **das Kind wurde dem Vater zugesprochen** the father was granted custody (of the child); **jdm Mut/Trost ~** (fig) to encourage/comfort sb **VI a jdm (gut/besänftigend) ~** to talk or speak (nicely/gently) to sb **b dem Essen/Wein** etc **tüchtig** or **kräftig ~** to tuck into (Brit) or dig into (US) the food/wine etc (inf); **dem Alkohol (kräftig) ~** to indulge (heavily) in alcohol

zu+sprin|gen VI sep irreg aux sein **a** (Schloss, Tür) to spring or snap shut **b auf jdn ~** or **zugesprungen kommen** to spring or leap toward(s) sb; (Ball) to bounce toward(s) sb

Zu|spruch M , no pl **a** (= Worte) words pl; (= Aufmunterung) (words pl of) encouragement; (= Rat) advice; (tröstlich) (words pl of) comfort **b** (= Anklang) (**großen**) **~ finden** or **haben, sich großen ~s erfreuen** to be (very) popular; (Stück, Film) to meet with general acclaim; (Anwalt, Arzt) to be (very) much in demand

Zu|stand M state; (von Haus, Ware, Auto, Med) condition; (= Lage) state of affairs, situation; **in gutem/schlechtem ~** in good/poor condition; (Mensch auch) in good/bad shape; (Haus) in good/bad repair; **in ungepflegtem/baufälligem ~** in a state of neglect/disrepair; **in angetrunkenem ~** under the influence of alcohol; **Wasser in flüssigem ~** water in its fluid state; **eine Frau in ihrem ~ ...** a woman in her condition ...; **er war wirklich in einem üblen ~** he really was in a bad way; (seelisch) he really was in a state; **Zustände bekommen** or **kriegen** (inf) to have a fit (inf), to hit the roof (inf); **das ist doch kein ~** that's not right; **das sind ja schöne** or **nette Zustände!** (iro) that's a fine state of affairs! (iro); **das sind ja Zustände!** (inf) it's terrible; **das sind doch keine Zustände!** (inf) it's just dreadful or terrible!

zu|stan|de [tsuːʃtandə] ADV **a ~ bringen** to manage; Arbeit to get done; Ereignis, Frieden etc to bring about, to achieve; **es ~ bringen, dass jd etw tut** (to manage to) get sb to do sth; **ein Gespräch ~ bringen** (am Fernsprecher) to (manage to) put a call through (nach to) **b ~ kommen** (= erreicht werden) to be achieved; (= geschehen) to come about; (= stattfinden) to take place; (Plan etc) to materialize; (Gewagtes, Schwieriges) to come off

Zu|stan|de|kom|men NT **die Chancen für das ~ eines Plans/einer Koalition** the chances of a plan materializing/of a coalition coming about; **die Ostdeutschen hatten einen wesentlichen Anteil am ~ der Wiedervereinigung** the East Germans played a significant part in bringing about reunification

zu|stän|dig ['tsuːʃtɛndɪç] ADJ (= verantwortlich) responsible; (= entsprechend) Amt etc appropriate, relevant; (= Kompetenz habend) competent (form, Jur); **dafür ist er ~** that's his responsibility; **der dafür ~e Beamte** the official responsible for or in charge of such matters; **~ sein** (Jur) to have jurisdiction; **in erster Instanz ~ sein** (Jur) to have original jurisdiction; **nach einer Stadt ~ sein** (Aus form) (= wohnhaft sein) to be domiciled in a town; (= Wohnrecht haben) to have the right of domicile in a town

Zu|stän|dig|keit F -, -en **a** (= Kompetenz) competence; (Jur) jurisdiction, competence; (= Verantwortlichkeit) responsibility **b** = **Zuständigkeitsbereich**

Zu|stän|dig|keits-: **Zu|stän|dig|keits|be|reich** M area of responsibility; (Jur) jurisdiction, competence; **das fällt/fällt nicht in unseren ~** that is/isn't our responsibility; (Jur) that is within/outside our jurisdiction (Jur); **zu|stän|dig|keits|hal|ber** ADV (Admin, form) for reasons of competence

Zu|stands|verb NT (Ling) stative verb

zu|stat|ten [tsuːʃtatn] ADV **jdm ~ kommen** (geh) to come in useful for sb

zu+ste|cken VT sep **a** Kleid etc to pin up or together **b jdm etw ~** to slip sb sth

zu+ste|hen VI sep irreg **etw steht jdm zu** sb is entitled to sth; **darüber steht mir kein Urteil zu** it's not for me to judge that, it's not up to me to judge that; **es steht ihr nicht zu, das zu tun** it's not for her to do that, it's not up to her to do that

zu+stei|gen VI sep irreg aux sein to get on, to board; **noch jemand zugestiegen?** (in Zug) tickets please!; (in Bus) any more fares, please?

Zu|stell-: **Zu|stell|be|reich** M postal district; **Zu|stell|dienst** M delivery service

zu+stel|len VT sep **a** Brief, Paket etc to deliver; (Jur) to serve (jdm etw sb with sth) **b** Tür etc to block

Zu|stel|ler¹ ['tsuːʃtɛlɐ] M -s, - (= Zustellfirma) delivery agent

Zu|stel|ler² ['tsuːʃtɛlɐ] M -s, -, **Zu|stel|le|rin** [-ərɪn] F -, -nen deliverer; (Jur) server; (= Briefträger) postman/-woman (Brit), mailman/ -woman (US)

Zu|stell|ge|bühr F delivery charge

Zu|stel|lung F delivery; (Jur) service (of a writ)

Zu|stel|lungs|ur|kun|de F (Jur) writ of summons

Zu|stell|ver|merk M reason for non-delivery; **mit einem ~ versehen** with (the) reason for non-delivery attached

zu+steu|ern sep **VI** aux sein **auf etw** (acc) **~** (lit, fig) einer Sache (dat) ~ (geh) (lit, fig) to head for sth; (beim Gespräch) to steer toward(s) sth **VT** (= beitragen) to contribute (zu to)

zu+stim|men VI sep (einer Sache dat) **~** to agree (to sth); (= einwilligen) to consent (to sth); (= billigen) to approve (of sth); **jdm (in einem Punkt) ~** to agree with sb (on a point); **einer Politik ~** to endorse a policy; **dem kann man nur ~** I/we etc quite agree with you/him etc; **er nickte ~d** he nodded in agreement; **eine ~de Antwort** an affirmative answer

Zu|stim|mung F (= Einverständnis) agreement, assent; (= Einwilligung) consent; (= Beifall) approval; **seine ~ geben/verweigern** or **versagen** (geh) to give/refuse one's consent or assent; **allgemeine ~ finden** to meet with general approval; **das fand meine ~** I agreed with it completely; **mit/ohne ~** (+gen) with/without the agreement or approval of

zu+stop|fen VT sep to stop up, to plug; (mit Faden) to darn

zu+stöp|seln VT sep to stopper; Flasche to put the stopper or cork in

zu+sto|ßen sep irreg **VT** Tür etc to push shut **VI a** (mit Messer, Schwert etc) to plunge a/the knife/sword etc in; (Stier, Schlange) to strike; **stoß zu!** go on, stab him/her etc!; **der Mörder hatte (mit dem Messer) dreimal zugestoßen** the murderer had stabbed him/her etc three times **b** (= passieren) aux sein **jdm ~** to happen to sb; **wenn mir einmal etwas zustößt ...** (euph) if anything should happen to me ...; **ihm muss etwas zugestoßen sein** he must have had an accident, something must have happened to him

zu+stre|ben VI sep aux sein (geh) **~ auf** (+acc) to make or head for; (fig) to strive for

Zu|strom M , no pl (fig: = Menschenmenge) (hineinströmend) influx; (herbeiströmend) stream (of visitors etc); (= Andrang) crowd, throng; (Met) inflow; **großen ~ haben** to be very popular, to have crowds of people coming to it/them etc

zu+strö|men VI sep aux sein +dat (Fluss) to flow toward(s); (fig) (geh: Menschen) to stream toward(s); (Aufträge etc) to pour in to

zu+stür|zen VI sep aux sein **auf jdn/etw ~** or **zugestürzt kommen** to rush up to sb/sth

zu|ta|ge [tsuːˈtaːgə] ADV **etw ~ fördern** to unearth sth (auch hum); (aus Wasser) to bring sth up; **etw ~ bringen** (fig) to bring sth to light, to reveal sth; (offen) **~ liegen** to be clear or evident; **~ kommen** or **treten** (lit, fig) to come to light, to be revealed

Zu|ta|ten ['tsuːtaːtn] PL (Cook) ingredients pl; (fig) accessories pl, extras pl

zu|teil [tsuːˈtail] ADV (geh) **jdm wird etw ~** sb is granted sth, sth is granted to sb; **mir wurde die Ehre ~, zu ...** I was given or I had the honour (Brit) or honor (US) of ...; **jdm etw ~ werden lassen** to give sb sth; **jdm große Ehren** or **-werden lassen** to bestow great honours (Brit) or honors (US) upon sb; **da ward ihm großes Glück ~** (old) he was favoured (Brit) or favored (US) with great fortune

zu+tei|len VT sep (jdm to sb) (als Anteil) Wohnung, Aktien to allocate; Rolle, Aufgabe auch to allot, to assign; Arbeitskraft, Leibwächter to assign; **etw zugeteilt bekommen** to be allocated sth; Aufgabe etc auch to be assigned sth; Lebensmittel to be apportioned sth

Zu|tei|lung F allocation; (von Rolle, Aufgabe auch) assigning; (von Arbeitskraft) assignment; (von Lebensmitteln) apportionment; **Fleisch gab es nur auf ~** meat was only available on ration

zu+tex|ten VT sep (sl) (= viel schreiben) to write at length to; (= viel reden) to chatter (on) to

zu|tiefst [tsuːˈtiːfst] ADV deeply; **er war ~ betrübt** he was greatly saddened

zu+tra|gen sep irreg **VT** to carry (jdm to sb); (fig: = weitersagen) to report (jdm to sb) **VR** (liter) to take place

Zu|trä|ger(in) M(F) informer

zu|träg|lich ['tsuːtrɛːklɪç] ADJ good (+dat to), beneficial (+dat to); (= förderlich auch) conducive (+dat to); **ein der Gesundheit ~es Klima** a salubrious climate, a climate conducive to good health

Zu|träg|lich|keit F -, no pl (geh) beneficial effect; (von Klima auch) salubrity (liter, form)

zu+trau|en VT sep **jdm etw ~** (Aufgabe, Tat, Sieg) to believe or think sb (is) capable of (doing) sth; **sich** (dat) **~, etw zu tun** to think one can do sth, to think one is capable of doing sth; **sich** (dat) **zu viel ~** to overrate one's own abilities; (= sich übernehmen) to take on too much; **sich** (dat) **nichts ~** to have no confidence in oneself; **der traut sich was zu!** (inf) he's pretty confident, isn't he?; **den Mut/die Intelligenz (dazu) traue ich ihr nicht zu** I don't credit her with the courage/intelligence to do it, I don't believe she has the courage/intelligence to do it; **das hätte ich ihm nie zugetraut!** I would never have thought him capable of it!; (bewundernd auch) I never thought he had it in him!; **jdm viel/wenig ~** to think/not to think a lot of sb, to have/not to have a high opinion of sb; **ich traue ihnen viel** or **einiges/alles zu** (Negatives) I wouldn't put much/anything past them; **das ist ihm zuzutrauen!** (iro) I can well believe it (of him)!; (esp als Antwort auf Frage) I wouldn't put it past him!

Zu|trau|en NT -s, no pl confidence (zu in); **zu jdm ~ fassen** to begin to trust sb

zu|trau|lich ADJ Kind trusting; Tier friendly

Zu|trau|lich|keit F (von Kind) trusting nature; (von Tier) friendliness

zu+tref|fen VI sep irreg (= gelten) to apply (auf +acc, für to); (= richtig sein) to be accurate or correct; (= *wahr sein*) to be true, to be the case; **es trifft nicht immer zu, dass ...** it doesn't always follow that ...; **seine Beschreibung traf überhaupt nicht zu** his description was completely inaccurate; **das trifft zu** that is so

zu|tref|fend ADJ (= *richtig*) accurate; (= *auf etw zutreffend*) applicable; **Zutreffendes bitte unterstreichen** underline where applicable *or* appropriate ADV accurately, precisely

zu|tref|fen|den|falls ['tsu:trɛfndən'fals] ADV (*form*) if applicable *or* appropriate

zu+tre|ten VI *sep irreg* a (*mit Fuß*) to kick him/ it *etc* b *aux sein* **auf jdn/etw ~** to step up to sb/ sth

zu+trin|ken VI *sep irreg* **jdm ~** to drink to sb; (*mit Trinkspruch*) to toast sb

Zu|tritt M , *no pl* (= *Einlass*) admission, admittance, entry; (= *Zugang*) access; **kein ~, ~ verboten** no admittance *or* entry; **freien ~ zu einer Veranstaltung haben** to be admitted to an event free of charge; **~ bekommen** *or* **erhalten, sich ~ verschaffen** to gain admission *or* admittance (*zu* to); **jdm ~ gewähren** (*geh*) to admit sb; **jdm den ~ verwehren** *or* **verweigern** to refuse sb admission *or* admittance

zu+tun VT *sep irreg* a **ich habe die ganze Nacht kein Auge zugetan** I didn't sleep a wink all night b (*inf: = hinzufügen*) to add (+*dat* to)

Zu|tun *no pl* assistance, help; **es geschah ohne mein ~** I did not have a hand in the matter

zu|un|guns|ten [tsu:'ʊngʊnstn̩] PREP (*vor n*) +*gen*, (*nach n*) +*dat* to the disadvantage of

zu|un|terst [tsu:'ʊntɐst] ADV right at the bottom

zu|ver|läs|sig [tsu:'fɛːlɛsɪç] ADJ reliable; (= *verlässlich*) *Mensch auch* dependable; (= *vertrauenswürdig auch*) trustworthy; **aus ~er Quelle** from a reliable source ADV funktionieren reliably; **etw ~ wissen** to know sth for sure *or* for certain; **etw ~ beurteilen** to make a reliable judgement about sth; **seinen Pflichten ~ nachkommen** to reliably fulfil one's duties

Zu|ver|läs|sig|keit F -, *no pl* reliability; (= *Verlässlichkeit auch*) dependability; (= *Vertrauenswürdigkeit auch*) trustworthiness

Zu|ver|sicht F , *no pl* confidence; (*religiös*) faith, trust; **die feste ~ haben, dass ...** to be quite confident that ..., to have every confidence that ...; **in der festen ~, dass ...** confident that ...

zu|ver|sicht|lich ADJ confident; **er zeigte sich ~, dass ...** he was confident that ...

Zu|ver|sicht|lich|keit F -, *no pl* confidence

zu|viel △ [tsu:'fi:l] ADJ, ADV → **viel a**

Zu|viel [tsu:'fi:l] NT **ein ~ an etw** (*dat*) an excess of sth

zu|vor [tsu:'voːɐ] ADV before; (= *zuerst*) beforehand; **im Jahr ~** the year before, in the previous year; **am Tage ~** the day before, on the previous day

zu|vor|derst [tsu:'fɔrdɐst] ADV right at the front

zu|vör|derst [tsu:'fœrdɐst] ADV (*old*) first and foremost

zu|vor+kom|men VI *sep irreg aux sein* +*dat* to anticipate; (= *verhindern*) *einer Gefahr, unangenehmen Fragen etc* to forestall; **jdm ~** to beat sb to it; **jemand ist uns zuvorgekommen** somebody beat us to it

zu|vor|kom|mend ADJ obliging; (*zu* towards) ADV obligingly

Zu|vor|kom|men|heit [tsu:'voːɐkɔmənhait] F -, *no pl* obliging ways *pl*

Zu|wachs ['tsu:vaks] M **-es, Zuwächse** [-vɛksə] a *no pl* (= *Wachstum*) growth (*an* +*dat* of) b (= *Höhe, Menge des Wachstums*) increase (*an* +*dat* in); **~ bekommen** (*inf: ein Baby*) to have an addition to the family; **ein Kleid für jdn auf ~ kaufen** (*inf*) to buy a dress for sb to grow into

zu+wach|sen VI *sep irreg aux sein* a (*Öffnung, Loch*) to grow over; (*Garten etc, hum: Gesicht*) to become overgrown; (*Aussicht*) to become blocked (*by trees etc*) (*Wunde*) to heal b (*esp Econ, Gewinn etc*) to accrue (*jdm* to sb); **jdm wächst Autorität/Macht/Popularität zu** sb gains authority/power/popularity

Zu|wachs|quo|te F , **Zu|wachs|ra|te** F rate of increase

Zu|wan|de|rer M , **Zu|wan|de|rin** F immigrant

zu+wan|dern VI *sep aux sein* to immigrate

Zu|wan|de|rung F immigration

Zu|wan|de|rungs-: **Zu|wan|de|rungs|ge|setz** NT immigration law; **Zu|wan|de|rungs|po|li|tik** F immigration policy

zu+war|ten VI *sep* to wait

zu|we|ge [tsu've:gə] ADV **etw ~ bringen** to manage sth; (= *erreichen*) to achieve *or* accomplish sth; **mit etw ~ kommen** to (be able to) cope with sth; **mit jdm ~ kommen** to get on with sb all right; **es ~ bringen, dass jd etw tut** to (manage to) get sb to do sth; **gut/schlecht ~ sein** (*inf*) to be in good/bad *or* poor health; **er ist ganz schön ~** (*dial*) he's a bit on the heavy side (*inf*)

zu+we|hen *sep* VT a (= *zutreiben*) to waft (+*dat* towards, over to); **jdm (kalte etc) Luft ~** to fan sb (with cold *etc* air) b (= *zudecken*) to block (up); **mit Schnee zugeweht werden** to become snowed up VI *aux sein* **auf jdn/etw ~** to blow toward(s) sb/sth; (*sachte*) to waft toward(s) sb/sth

zu|wei|len [tsu'vailən] ADV (*geh*) (every) now and then, occasionally, from time to time

zu+wei|sen VT *sep irreg* to assign, to allocate (*jdm etw* sth to sb)

Zu|wei|sung F allocation, assignment

zu+wen|den *sep irreg* VT a (*lit, fig*) to turn (+*dat* to, towards); (*fig: = völlig widmen*) to devote (+*dat* to); **jdm das Gesicht ~** to turn face to, to turn one's face toward(s) sb; **jdm seine ganze Liebe ~** to bestow all one's affections on sb; **die dem Park zugewandten Fenster** the windows facing the park; **der Zukunft** (*dat*) **zugewandt sein** to be turned toward(s) the future b **jdm Geld** *etc* **~** to give sb money *etc* VR **sich jdm/einer Sache ~** to turn to (face) sb/ sth; (*fig*) to turn to sb/sth; (= *sich widmen, liebevoll*) to devote oneself to sb/sth; **wann wird das Glück sich uns wieder ~?** when will luck smile on us again?

Zu|wen|dung F a (*fig: = das Sichzuwenden*) turning (*zu* to); (= *Liebe*) care b (= *Geldsumme*) sum (of money); (= *Beitrag*) financial contribution; (= *Schenkung*) donation

zu|we|nig △ [tsu've:nɪç] ADJ, ADV → **wenig ADV**

Zu|we|nig [tsu've:nɪç] NT **-s,** *no pl* **ein ~ an etw** a lack of sth

zu+wer|fen VT *sep irreg* a (= *schließen*) *Tür* to slam (shut) b (= *auffüllen*) *Graben* to fill up c (= *hinwerfen*) **jdm etw ~** to throw sth to sb; **jdm einen Blick ~** to cast a glance at sb; **jdm einen bösen** *or* **giftigen Blick ~** to look daggers at sb (*Brit*), to give sb the evil eye; **jdm einen feurigen Blick ~** to flash a fiery glance at sb; **jdm Blicke ~** to make eyes at sb; **jdm eine Kusshand ~** to blow sb a kiss

zu|wi|der [tsu'vi:dɐ] ADV a **er/das ist mir ~** I find him/that unpleasant; (*stärker*) I detest *or* loathe him/that; (= *Ekel erregend*) I find him/ that revolting b (*old: = ungünstig*) **das Glück war ihm ~** luck was against him PREP +*dat* a (*liter: = entgegen*) **dem Gesetz ~** contrary to *or* against the law; **etw einem Befehl ~ tun** to do sth in defiance of an order b (*old: = ungünstig*) **unseren Plänen** *etc* **~** unfavourable (*Brit*) *or* unfavorable (*US*) to our plans *etc*

Zu|wi|der-: **zu|wi|der+han|deln** VI *sep* +*dat* (*geh*) to go against; *einem Verbot, Befehl auch* to

defy; *einem Prinzip auch* to violate; *dem Gesetz* to contravene, to violate; **Zu|wi|der|han|deln|de(r)** [tsu'vi:dɐhandlndə] MF *decl as adj* (*form*) offender, transgressor, violator (*esp US*); **Zu|wi|der|hand|lung** F (*form*) contravention, violation; **zu|wi|der+lau|fen** VI *sep irreg aux sein* +*dat* to run counter to, to go directly against

zu+win|ken VI *sep* **jdm ~** to wave to sb; (= *Zeichen geben*) to signal to sb

zu+zah|len *sep* VT **10 Euro ~** to pay another 10 euros VI to pay extra

zu+zäh|len VT *sep* (*inf: = addieren*) to add; (= *einbeziehen*) to include (*zu* in)

Zu|zah|lung F -, **-en** additional payment; (*Insur*) supplementary charge

zu|zei|ten [tsu:'tsaitn̩] ADV (*old*) at times

zu+zie|hen *sep irreg* VT a *Vorhang* to draw; *Tür* to pull shut; *Knoten, Schlinge* to pull tight, to tighten; *Arzt etc* to call in, to consult; **einen weiteren Fachmann ~** to get a second opinion b **sich** (*dat*) **jds Zorn/Hass** *etc* **~** to incur sb's anger/hatred *etc*; **sich** (*dat*) **eine Krankheit ~** (*form*) to contract an illness; **sich** (*dat*) **eine Verletzung ~** (*form*) to sustain an injury VR (*Schlinge etc*) to tighten, to pull tight; **es hat sich zugezogen** (*Wetter*) it has clouded over VI *aux sein* to move in, to move into the area; **er ist kürzlich aus Berlin zugezogen** he has recently moved here from Berlin; **auf die Stadt** *etc* **~** to move toward(s) the town *etc*

Zu|zug M (= *Zustrom*) influx; (*von Familie etc*) arrival (*nach* in)

Zu|zü|ger ['tsu:tsy:gɐ] M **-s, -, Zu|zü|ge|rin** ['tsu:tsy:gərɪn] F **-, -nen** (*Sw*) a → Zuzügler, Zuzüglerin b (= *neues Mitglied*) newcomer

Zu|züg|ler ['tsu:tsy:glɐ] M **-s, -, Zu|züg|le|rin** ['tsu:tsy:glərɪn] F **-, -nen** (*in Ortschaft*) incomer, newcomer

zu|züg|lich ['tsu:tsy:klɪç] PREP +*gen* plus

zu+zwin|kern VI *sep* **jdm ~** to wink at sb, to give sb a wink

Zvie|ri ['tsfi:ri] M OR NT **-s,** *no pl* (*Sw*) afternoon snack

ZVS [tsetfau'ʔɛs] F - *abbr von* **Zentralstelle für die Vergabe von Studienplätzen** ≈ UCAS (*Brit*), ≈ SAT center (*US*)

zw. *abbr von* **zwischen**

zwang *pret von* **zwingen**

Zwang [tsvaŋ] M **-(e)s, ¨e** ['tsvɛŋə] (= *Notwendigkeit*) compulsion; (= *Gewalt*) force; (= *Verpflichtung*) obligation; (= *hemmender Zwang*) constraint; **einem inneren ~ folgen** to follow an inner compulsion; **das ist ~** that is compulsory; **der ~ der Ereignisse** the pressure of events; **gesellschaftliche Zwänge** social constraints; **unter ~** (*dat*) **stehen/handeln** to be/act under duress; **etw aus ~ tun** to do sth under duress, to be forced to do sth; **etw ohne ~ tun** to do sth without being forced to; **auf jdn ~ ausüben** to exert pressure on sb; **sich** (*dat*) **~ antun** to force oneself to be something one isn't; (= *sich zurückhalten*) to restrain oneself (*etw nicht zu tun* from doing sth); **tu dir keinen ~ an** don't feel you have to be polite; (*iro*) don't force yourself; **darf ich rauchen? – ja, tu dir keinen ~ an** may I smoke? – feel free; **seinen Gefühlen ~ antun** to force oneself to ignore one's true feelings; **sie tut ihren Gefühlen keinen ~ an** she doesn't hide her feelings; **dem Gesetz ~ antun** to stretch the law; **der ~ des Gesetzes/der Verhältnisse/Konvention** the force of the law/of circumstances/of convention; **allen ~ ablegen** to dispense with all formalities; **er brauchte sich** (*dat*) **keinen ~ aufzuerlegen** he didn't need to make a big effort

zwän|gen ['tsvɛŋən] VT to force; *mehrere Sachen* (*in Koffer etc*) to cram; **sich in/durch etw** (*acc*) **~** to squeeze into/through sth

Zwang-: **zwang|haft** (*Psych*) ADJ compulsive ADV compulsively; **zwang|los** ADJ (= *ohne Förmlichkeit*) informal; (= *locker, unbekümmert*)

Deutsche Rechtschreibreform (siehe Anhang): ▲ neue Schreibung △ alte Schreibung | + trennbare Verben

casual, free and easy; (= *frei*) free; **in ~er Folge,** **~ at irregular intervals** ADV informally, casually; **da geht es recht ~ zu** (*im Hotel, Club*) things are very informal there; (*bei der Arbeit auch*) things are very relaxed there; **Zwạng|lo-** **sig|keit** F -, *no pl* informality; (= *Lockerheit*) casualness

Zwạngs-: Zwạngs|ab|ga|be F (*Econ*) compulsory levy or charge; **Zwạngs|ab|lie|fe|rung** F compulsory delivery; **Zwạngs|ab|tre|tung** F compulsory cession; **Zwạngs|an|lei|he** F compulsory or forced loan; **Zwạngs|ar|beit** F hard labour (*Brit*) or labor (*US*); (*von Kriegsgefangenen*) forced labo(u)r; **zwạngs|be|wirt-** **schaf|tet** [-bəvɪrtʃaftət] ADJ controlled; *Wohnraum* rent-controlled; **Zwạngs|be|wirt|schaf-** **tung** F (*economic*) control; (*von Wohnraum*) rent control; **die ~ aufheben** to decontrol the economy/rents; **Zwạngs|ein|wei|sung** F compulsory hospitalization; **Zwạngs|ent|eig-** **nung** F compulsory expropriation; **zwạngs|** **er|näh|ren** *ptp* **zwangsernährt** VT *insep* to force-feed; **Zwạngs|er|näh|rung** F force-feeding; **Zwạngs|er|schei|nung** F (*Psych*) compulsion; **Zwạngs|geld** NT (*Jur*) coercive fine or penalty; **Zwạngs|hand|lung** F (*Psych*) compulsive act; **Zwạngs|hy|po|thek** F compulsory mortgage to enforce payment of debt(s); **Zwạngs|i|dee** F (*Psych*) obsession; **Zwạngs|ja|cke** F (*lit, fig*) straitjacket; **jdn in eine ~ stecken** to put sb in a straitjacket, to straitjacket sb; **Zwạngs|kurs** F (*Fin*) compulsory rate; **Zwạngs|la|ge** F predicament, dilemma; **zwạngs|läu|fig** ADJ inevitable, unavoidable ADV inevitably, unavoidably; **das musste ja ~ so kommen** that had to happen, it was inevitable that that would happen; **Zwạngs|läu|fig|keit** [-lɔyfɪçkait] F -, -en inevitability; **zwạngs|mä|ßig** ADJ (*form*) compulsory; **Zwạngs|maß|nah|me** F compulsory measure; (*Pol*) sanction; **Zwạngs|mit|tel** NT means *sing* of coercion; (*Pol*) sanction; **Zwạngs|neu|ro|se** F obsessional neurosis; **Zwạngs|pau|se** F (*beruflich*) **eine ~ machen** or **einlegen müssen** to have to stop work temporarily; **Zwạngs|pen|si|o|nie|rung** F compulsory retirement; **Zwạngs|räu|mung** F compulsory evacuation; **zwạngs|um|sie|deln** *ptp* **zwangsumgesiedelt** VT *infin, ptp only* to displace (by force); **Zwạngs|um|tausch** M compulsory exchange; **Zwạngs|ur|laub** M (*inf*) temporary lay-off; **einen ~ antreten müssen** to have to be laid off temporarily; **jdn in den ~ schicken** to lay sb off temporarily; **Zwạngs|** **ver|kauf** M (en)forced sale; **zwạngs|ver|** **pflich|tet** [-fɛəpflɪçtət] ADJ drafted (*zu* into); **Zwạngs|ver|schi|ckung** [-fɛʃɪkʊŋ] F -, -en deportation; **Zwạngs|ver|si|che|rung** F compulsory insurance; **zwạngs|ver|stei|gern** *ptp* **zwangsversteigert** VT *infin, ptp only* to put (sth) up for compulsory auction; **Zwạngs|ver|** **stei|ge|rung** F compulsory auction; **Zwạngs|voll|stre|ckung** F execution; **Zwạngs|vor|füh|rung** F (*Jur*) enforced appearance in court; **Zwạngs|vor|stel|lung** F (*Psych*) obsession, obsessive idea; **zwạngs|** **wei|se** ADV compulsorily ADJ compulsory; **Zwạngs|wirt|schaft** F Government or State control

zwan|zig ['tsvantsɪç] NUM twenty → *auch* **vierzig, vier**

Zwạn|zig ['tsvantsɪç] F -, -en [-gn] twenty → *auch* **Vierzig, Vier**

Zwạn|zi|ger[1] ['tsvantsɪɡɐ] M -s, - (*inf:* = *Geldschein*) twenty-euro etc note (*Brit*) or bill (*US*)

Zwạn|zi|ger[2] ['tsvantsɪɡɐ] M -s, -, **Zwạn|zi|ge-** **rin** [-ərɪn] F -, -nen twenty-year-old; (*zwischen 20 und 30*) man in his/woman in her twenties → *auch* **Vierziger**[2]

Zwạn|zig-: Zwạn|zig|eu|ro|schein M twenty-euro note (*Brit*) or bill (*US*); **Zwạn|zig|mark|-** **schein** M (*Hist*) twenty-mark note (*Brit*) or bill (*US*)

zwạn|zigs|te(r, s) ['tsvantsɪçstə] ADJ twentieth → *auch* **vierzigste(r, s)**

zwar [tsvaːɐ] ADV **a** (= *wohl*) **er war ~ Zeuge des Unfalls, kann sich aber nicht mehr so genau erinnern** he did witness the accident or it's true he witnessed the accident but he can't remember much about it any more; **sie ist ~ sehr schön/krank, aber ...** it's true she's very beautiful/ill but ..., she may be very beautiful/ill but ...; **ich weiß ~, dass es schädlich ist, aber ...** I do know it's harmful but ...

b (*erklärend, betont*) **und ~** in fact, actually; **er ist tatsächlich gekommen, und ~ um 4 Uhr** he really did come, at 4 o'clock actually or in fact; **er hat mir das anders erklärt, und ~ so ...** he explained it differently to me(, like this) ...; **ich mache das, und ~ so, wie ich es für richtig halte** I'll do it and I'll do it just as I see fit; **und ~ einschließlich ...** inclusive of ...; **die Schulen, und ~ vor allem die Grundschulen** the schools, (and more) especially the primary schools; **das hat er gemacht, und ~ so gründlich, dass ...** he did it and (he did it) so thoroughly that ...; **ich werde ihm schreiben, und ~ noch heute** I'll write to him and I'll do it today or this very day

Zwẹck [tsvɛk] M -(e)s, -e **a** (= *Ziel, Verwendung*) purpose; **einem ~ dienen** to serve a purpose; **einem guten ~ dienen** to be for or in a good cause; **Spenden für wohltätige ~e** donations to charity; **seinen ~ erfüllen** to serve its/one's purpose; **seinem ~ entsprechen** to serve its purpose; **das entspricht nicht meinen ~en** that won't serve my purpose → **heiligen**

b (= *Sinn*) point; **was soll das für einen ~ haben?** what's the point of that?; **das hat keinen ~ there is no point in it, it's pointless; **es hat keinen ~, darüber zu reden** there is no point (in) talking about it, it's pointless talking about it; **es hat ja doch alles keinen ~ mehr** there is no point (in) or it's pointless going on any more; **das ist ja der ~ der Übung** that's the point of the exercise, that's what it's all about (*inf*)

c (= *Absicht*) aim; **zum ~ der Völkerverständigung** (in order) to promote understanding between nations; **zu welchem ~?** for what purpose?, to what end?; **zu diesem ~** to this end, with this aim in view; **einen ~ verfolgen** to have a specific aim

Zwẹck-: Zwẹck|bau M *pl* **-bauten** functional building; **zwẹck|be|dingt** ADJ determined by its function; **zwẹck|be|stimmt** ADJ *Gebäude* functional; *Gelder* earmarked; (*Tech*) dedicated; **Zwẹck|bünd|nis** NT alliance or marriage of convenience; **zwẹck|dien|lich** ADJ (= *zweckentsprechend*) appropriate; (= *nützlich*) useful; **~e Hinweise** (any) relevant information; **es wäre ~, dass zu tun** it would be expedient to do that; **Zwẹck|dien|lich|keit** F -, *no pl* (= *Nützlichkeit*) usefulness; (*Pol*) expediency

Zwẹ|cke ['tsvɛkə] F -, -n tack; (= *Schuhzwecke*) nail; (= *Reißzwecke*) drawing pin (*Brit*), thumbtack (*US*)

Zwẹck-: zwẹck|ent|frem|den *ptp* **zweckentfremdet** VT *insep* **etw ~** to use sth in a way in which it wasn't intended to be used; **etw als etw ~** to use sth as sth; **Zwẹck|ent|frem-** **dung** F misuse; **zwẹck|ent|spre|chend** ADJ appropriate ADV **etw ~ benutzen** to use sth properly or correctly, to put sth to its proper or correct use; **zwẹck|frei** ADJ *Forschung etc* pure; **zwẹck|ge|bun|den** ADJ *Geldmittel, Steuern etc* for a specific purpose, appropriated (*spec*) *no adv*; **zwẹck|ge|mäß** ADJ, ADV = **zweck-** **sprechend; Zwẹck|ge|mein|schaft** F partnership of convenience; **zwẹck|los** ADJ pointless; *Versuch, Anstrengungen* useless, futile; **es ist ~, hier zu bleiben** it's pointless staying here, there's no point (in) staying here; **Zwẹck|lo-** **sig|keit** F -, *no pl* pointlessness; (*von Versuch, Anstrengungen*) uselessness, futility; **zwẹck|mä-** **ßig** ADJ (= *nützlich*) useful; (= *wirksam*) effective; (= *ratsam*) advisable, expedient (*form*); (=

zweckentsprechend) *Kleidung etc* suitable; **Zwẹck|mä|ßig|keit** ['tsvɛkmɛːsɪçkait] F -, *no pl* (= *Nützlichkeit*) usefulness; (= *Wirksamkeit*) effectiveness, efficacy; (*von Kleidung etc*) suitability; **Zwẹck|mä|ßig|keits|er|wä|gung** F consideration of expediency; **Zwẹck|op|ti|mis|mus** M calculated optimism; **Zwẹck|pes|si|mis|mus** M calculated pessimism; **Zwẹck|pro|pa|gan-** **da** F calculated propaganda

zwẹcks [tsvɛks] PREP +*gen* (*form*) for the purpose of; **~ Wiederverwendung** for re-use

Zwẹck-: Zwẹck|satz M (*Gram*) final clause; **Zwẹck|steu|er** F regulatory tax; **Zwẹck|ver-** **band** M association of local authorities for the joint management of a particular service, joint board; **Zwẹck|ver|mö|gen** NT (*Jur*) special-purpose fund; **zwẹck|voll** ADJ **a** = zweckmäßig **b** (*Psych*) *Handlung* purposive; **zwẹck|wid|rig** ADJ inappropriate ADV inappropriately, improperly, incorrectly

zween [tsveːn] NUM (*obs*) twain (*obs*)

zwei [tsvai] NUM two; **wir ~ (beiden** (*inf*)) the two of us, we two, us two (*inf*); **das ist so sicher wie ~ mal ~ vier ist** (*inf*) you can bet on that (*inf*); **dazu gehören ~** (*inf*) it takes two; **~ Gesichter haben** (*fig*) to be two-faced → **Drit-** **te(r)** → *auch* **vier**

Zwei [tsvai] F -, -en two → *auch* **Vier**

Zwei- *in cpds* → *auch* **Vier-: Zwei|ach|ser** [-laksɐ] M -s, - two-axle vehicle; **zwei|ach|sig** [-laksɪç] ADJ two-axled; **Zwei|ak|ter** [-laktɐ] M -s, - (*Theat*) two-act play or piece; **zwei|ar|mig** ADJ (*Physiol*) with two arms; (*Tech*) with two branches; **zwei|ato|mig** [-lato:mɪç] ADJ (*Phys*) diatomic; **Zwei|bei|ner** [-bainɐ] M -s, -, **Zwei|bei|ne|rin** F -, -nen (*hum inf*) human being; **die ~** human beings, the bipeds (*hum*); **zwei|bei|nig** ADJ two-legged, biped(al) (*spec*); **Zwei|bett|zim|mer** NT twin room; **Zwei|bund** M *pl* **-bünde** (*Hist*) dual alliance; **Zwei|cent|stück** [tsvai'(t)sent-] NT two-cent piece; **Zwei|de|cker** [-dɛkɐ] M -s, - (*Aviat*) biplane; **zwei|deu|tig** ADJ ambiguous, equivocal; (= *schlüpfrig*) suggestive, risqué; **~e Reden führen** to use a lot of doubles entendres (*esp Brit*) or words with double meanings ADV ambiguously; **Zwei|deu|tig-** **keit** F -, -en **a** *no pl* ambiguity; (= *Schlüpfrigkeit*) suggestiveness **b** (= *Bemerkung*) ambiguous or equivocal remark, double entendre (*esp Brit*); (= *Witz*) risqué joke; **zwei|di|men|sio-** **nal** ADJ two-dimensional ADV two-dimensionally; **Zwei|drit|tel|mehr|heit** F (*Parl*) two-thirds majority; **der Streikbeschluss wurde mit ~ gefasst** the decision to strike was taken with a two-thirds majority; **zwei|ei|ig** [-laiç] ADJ *Zwillinge* nonidentical, fraternal (*spec*)

Zwei|er ['tsvaiɐ] M -s, - two; (*dial: Sch*) good; (= *Zweicentstück*) two-cent piece → *auch* **Vierer**

Zwei|er-: Zwei|er|be|zie|hung F relationship; **Zwei|er|bob** M two-man bob; **Zwei|er|ka-** **jak** M or NT (= *Kanu*) double kayak; (= *Disziplin*) kayak pairs; **Zwei|er|ka|na|di|er** M Canadian pair; (*Disziplin*) Canadian pairs

zwei|er|lei ['tsvaiɐlai] ADJ *inv* **a** *attr Brot, Käse, Wein* two kinds or sorts of; *Möglichkeiten, Größen, Fälle* two different; **auf ~ Art** in two different ways; **~ Handschuhe/Strümpfe** *etc* odd gloves/socks *etc*; **~ Meinung sein** to be of (two) different opinions → **Maß b** (*substantivisch*) two different things; (= *zwei Sorten*) two different kinds

Zwei|er|rei|he F two rows *pl*; **~n** rows of twos; **in ~n marschieren** to march two abreast, to march in twos

Zwei|eu|ro|stück [tsvai'ɔyro-] NT two-euro piece

zwei|fach ['tsvaifax] ADJ double; (= *zweimal*) twice; **in ~er Ausfertigung** in duplicate ADV **diesen Satz Briefmarken besitze ich ~ I** have two sets of these stamps; **diese Titel sind ~ vorhanden** there are two copies of this book; **eine Urkunde ~ ausfertigen** to make up a document in duplicate; **~ gesichert** doubly secure; **ein Tuch ~ legen** to lay a cloth double

Zwei-: Zwei|fa|mi|li|en|haus NT two-family house; **Zwei|far|ben|druck** M *pl* **-drucke** (*Typ*) two-colour (*Brit*) or two-color (*US*) print; (*Verfahren*) two-colo(u)r printing; **zwei|far|big** ADJ two-colour (*Brit*), two-color (*US*), two--tone ADV **etw ~ anstreichen** to paint sth in two (different) colours (*Brit*) or colors (*US*); **es ist ~ gemustert** it has a two-colour (*Brit*) or two-color (*US*) pattern

Zwei|fel ['tsvaifl] M **-s, -** doubt; **außer ~** beyond doubt; **im ~** in doubt; **ohne ~** without doubt, doubtless; **kein ~, er ist der Sieger** there's no doubt about it, he's the winner; **außer ~ stehen** to be beyond doubt; **über allen ~ erhaben** beyond all (shadow of a) doubt; **da kann es gar keinen ~ geben** there can be no doubt about it; **es besteht kein ~, dass ...** there is no doubt that ...; **~ an etw** (*dat*) **haben** to have one's doubts about sth; **da habe ich meine ~** I have my doubts; **etw in ~ ziehen** to call sth into question, to challenge sth; **ich bin mir im ~, ob ich das tun soll** I'm in two minds (*Brit*) or double-minded (*US*) or I'm doubtful whether I should do that

zwei|fel|haft ADJ doubtful; (= *verdächtig auch*) dubious; **von ~em Wert** of doubtful or debatable value; **es ist ~, ob ...** it is doubtful or questionable or debatable whether ...

zwei|fel|los ADV without (a) doubt, undoubtedly, unquestionably; (*als Antwort*) undoubtedly; **er hat ~ Recht** he is undoubtedly or unquestionably right, without (a) doubt he is right ADJ *Sieger etc* undisputed

zwei|feln ['tsvaifln] VI to doubt; **an etw/jdm ~** to doubt sth/sb; (= *skeptisch sein auch*) to be sceptical (*esp Brit*) or skeptical (*US*) about sth/ sb; **daran ist nicht zu ~** there's no doubt about it; **ich zweifle nicht, dass ...** I do not doubt that ..., I have no doubt that ...; **ich zweifle noch, wie ich mich entscheiden soll** I am still in two minds (*esp Brit*) or double-minded (*US*) about it

Zweifels-: Zwei|fels|fall M doubtful or borderline case; **im ~** in case of doubt, when in doubt; (*inf*: = *gegebenenfalls*) if need be, if necessary; **zwei|fels|frei** ADJ unequivocal ADV beyond (all) doubt; **zwei|fels|ohne** [tsvaifls-'lo:nə] ADV undoubtedly, without (a) doubt

Zwei|fin|ger|such|sys|tem [tsvaifiŋɐ-] NT (*hum*) peer (*Brit*) or two-finger (*US*) and peck method (*hum*); **ich tippe im ~** I use two fingers, I type with two fingers

Zweif|ler ['tsvaiflɐ] M **-s, -, Zweif|le|rin** [-ərɪn] F **-, -nen** sceptic (*esp Brit*), skeptic (*US*)

zweif|le|risch ['tsvaiflərɪʃ] ADJ sceptical (*esp Brit*), skeptical (*US*)

Zwei-: zwei|flü|ge|lig [-fly:gəlɪç] ADJ *Tür, Tor, Fenster* double; *Insekt* two-winged, dipterous (*spec*); **Zwei|flüg|ler** [-fly:glɐ] M **-s, -** (*Zool*) dipteran (*spec*); **zwei|flü|glig** [-fly:glɪç] ADJ = **zweiflügelig**; **Zwei|fron|ten|krieg** [tsvai-frɔntn-] M war on two fronts

Zweig [tsvaik] M **-(e)s, -e** [-gə] (= *Ast*) branch, bough (*liter*); (*dünner, kleiner*) twig (*fig*) (*von Wissenschaft, Familie etc, Rail*) branch; (= *Abteilung*) department → **grün**

Zweig-: Zweig|bahn F branch line; **Zweig|be|trieb** M branch

Zwei-: zwei|ge|schlech|tig [-gəʃlɛçtɪç] ADJ (*Biol*) hermaphroditic; **Zwei|ge|schlech|tig|keit** F **-,** *no pl* (*Biol*) hermaphroditism; **zwei|ge|schlecht|lich** ADJ *Berufsstand, Besatzung* male and female; **Zwei|ge|spann** NT carriage and pair; (*fig inf*) duo, two-man band (*hum inf*); **zwei|ge|stri|chen** ADJ (*Mus*) **das ~e C** the C (an octave) above middle C; **das ~e A** the A an octave above middle C

Zweig-: Zweig|ge|schäft NT branch; **Zweig|ge|sell|schaft** F subsidiary (company)

zwei-: zwei|glei|sig ADJ double-tracked, double-track *attr* ADV **~ fahren** (*lit*) to be double--tracked; (*fig inf*) to have two strings to one's bow; **~ argumentieren** to argue along two different lines; **zwei|glied|rig** [-gli:drɪç] ADJ (*fig*) bipartite; (*Admin*) *System* two-tier; (*Math*) binominal

Zweig-: Zweig|li|nie F branch line; **Zweig|nie|der|las|sung** F subsidiary; **Zweig|post|amt** NT sub-post office; **Zweig|stel|le** F branch (office); **Zweig|stel|len|lei|ter(in)** M(F) (branch) manager; (*Frau auch*) (branch) manageress; **Zweig|werk¹** NT (*Fabrik*) branch; **Zweig|werk²** NT (*von Baum, Gesträuch*) branches *pl*

Zwei-: Zwei|hän|der [-hɛndə] M **-s, -** **a** (= *Schwert*) two-handed sword **b** (*Zool*) two--handed or bimanous (*spec*) animal; **zwei|hän|dig** ADJ with two hands, two-handed; (*Mus*) for two hands ADV (*Mus*) *spielen* two-handed; **die Rückhand ~ schlagen** (*Sport*) to use two hands for one's backhand; **zwei|häu|sig** [-hɔy-zɪç] ADJ (*Bot*) dioecian; **Zwei|heit** F **-,** *no pl* (*Philos, Liter etc*) duality; **zwei|hö|cke|rig, zwei|höck|rig** ADJ *Kamel* two-humped

zwei|hun|dert ['tsvai'hʊndɐt] NUM two hundred

Zwei|hun|dert-: Zwei|hun|dert|jahr|fei|er F bicentenary, bicentennial; **zwei|hun|dert|jäh|rig** ADJ *Dauer* two-hundred-year *attr*; *Tradition, Geschichte* two-hundred-year-old *attr*; **nach über ~er Knechtschaft** after more than two hundred years of servitude

zwei|jäh|rig ADJ **a** *attr Kind etc* two-year-old *attr*, two years old; *Dauer* two-year *attr*, of two years; **mit ~er Verspätung** two years late **b** (*Bot*) *Pflanze* biennial

zwei|jähr|lich ADJ two-yearly *attr*, biennial, every two years ADV biennially, every two years

Zwei-: Zwei|kam|mer|sys|tem ['tsvai'kamɐ-] NT (*Pol*) two-chamber system; **Zwei|kampf** M single combat; (= *Duell*) duel; **jdn zum ~ (he-raus)fordern** to challenge sb to a duel; **Zwei|ka|nal|ton** M dual channel sound; **mit ~** (*TV*) with bilingual facility, with two language channels; **Zwei|keim|blät|te|ri|ge** [-blɛtərɪgə] PL , **Zwei|keim|blätt|ri|ge** [-blɛtrɪgə] PL *decl as adj* (*Bot*) dicotyledons *pl*; **Zwei|klang|horn** NT , **Zwei|klang|hu|pe** [-hu:pə] F two-tone horn; **Zwei|klas|sen|ge|sell|schaft** F two-tier society; **Zwei|kom|po|nen|ten|kleb|stoff** [tsvaikɔm-po'nɛntn-] M two-part adhesive; **zwei|köp|fig** ADJ two-headed; **Zwei|kreis|brem|se** F two--circuit brake; **Zwei|li|ter|fla|sche** F two-litre (*Brit*) or two-liter (*US*) bottle

zwei|mal ['tsvaima:l] ADV twice; **~ jährlich** or **im Jahr/täglich** or **am Tag** twice yearly or a year/ twice daily or a day; **sich** (*dat*) **etw ~ überlegen** to think twice about sth; **das lasse ich mir nicht ~ sagen** I don't have to be told twice; **das mache ich bestimmt nicht ~** I certainly won't do that/it again

zwei|ma|lig ['tsvaima:lɪç] ADJ *attr* twice repeated; *Weltmeister etc* two-times *attr*; **nach ~er Aufforderung** after being told twice; **nach ~er Wiederholung konnte er den Text auswendig** after twice repeating the text he knew it (off) by heart

Zwei-: Zwei|mann|boot NT two-man boat; **Zwei|mark|stück** [tsvai'mark-] NT (*Hist*) two--mark piece; **Zwei|mas|ter** [-mastɐ] M **-s, -** two-master; **zwei|mo|na|tig** ADJ *attr* **a** *Dauer* two-month of, of two months **b** *Säugling etc* two-month-old *attr*, two months old; **zwei|mo|nat|lich** ADJ every two months, bimonthly (*esp Comm, Admin*) ADV every two months, bimonthly (*esp Comm, Admin*), every other month; **Zwei|mo|nats|schrift** [tsvai'mo:-nats-] F bimonthly; **zwei|mo|to|rig** ADJ twin--engined; **Zwei|par|tei|en|sys|tem** [tsvaipar-'taiən-] NT two-party system; **Zwei|pfen|nig|stück** [tsvai'pfɛnɪç-] NT (*Hist*) two-pfennig

piece; **Zwei|pha|sen|strom** [tsvai'fa:zn-] M two-phase current; **zwei|po|lig** [-po:lɪç] ADJ (*Elec*) double-pole, bipolar; **Zwei|rad** NT (*form*) two-wheeled vehicle, two-wheeler; (= *Fahrrad*) (bi)cycle; (*für Kinder*) two-wheeler, bicycle; **zwei|rä|de|rig, zwei|räd|rig** ADJ two--wheeled; **Zwei|rei|her** [-raiɐ] M **-s, -** double--breasted suit *etc*; **zwei|rei|hig** ADJ double-row *attr*, in two rows; **das Jackett wird ~ geknöpft** the jacket is double-breasted; **Zwei|sam|keit** ['tsvaiza:mkait] F **-,** (*liter, hum*) togetherness; **zwei|schläfig** [-ʃlɛ:fɪç], **zwei|schlä|fe|rig** [-ʃlɛ:fərɪç] ADJ double; **zwei|schnei|dig** ADJ two-edged, double-edged (*auch fig*); **das ist ein ~es Schwert** (*fig*) it cuts both ways; **zwei|sei|tig** [-zaitɪç] ADJ *Brief, Erklärung etc* two-page *attr*; *Kleidungsstück* reversible; *Vertrag etc* bilateral, bipartite; (*Comput*) *Diskette* double-sided ADV on two sides; **ein ~ tragbarer Anorak** a reversible anorak; **zwei|sil|big** ADJ disyllabic; **ein ~es Wort** a disyllable (*spec*), a disyllabic word; **Zwei|sit|zer** M (*Aut, Aviat*) two-seater; **zwei|sit|zig** [-zɪtsɪç] ADJ *Sportwagen, Sofa* two-seater *attr*; **zwei|spal|tig** [-ʃpal-tɪç] ADJ double-columned, in two columns ADV **der Artikel ist ~ (abgedruckt)** the article is printed in two columns; **Zwei|spän|ner** M carriage and pair; **zwei|spän|nig** ADJ drawn by two horses ADV **~ fahren** to drive (in) a carriage and pair; **zwei|spra|chig** ADJ *Mensch, Wörterbuch* bilingual; *Land auch* two-language *attr*; *Dokument* in two languages ADV in two languages; **~ aufwachsen** to grow up bilingual or speaking two languages; **Zwei|spra|chig|keit** F **-,** *no pl* bilingualism; **zwei|spu|rig** [-ʃpu:rɪç] ADJ double-tracked, double-track *attr*; *Autobahn* two-laned, two-lane *attr*; **zwei|stel|lig** ADJ *Zahl* two-digit *attr*, with two digits; **~er Dezimalbruch** number with two decimal places; **~e Millionenbeträge** sums over ten million ADV *steigen, zunehmen* by more than ten per cent (*Brit*) or percent (*US*); **~ gewinnen** to win by more than ten; **der Umsatz ist ~ gewachsen** the increase in turnover has reached double figures; **zwei|stim|mig** (*Mus*) ADJ for two voices, two-part *attr* ADV **~ singen/spielen** to sing/play in two parts; **zwei|stö|ckig** ADJ two-storey (*Brit*), two-story (*US*), two--storeyed (*Brit*), two-storied (*US*); **ein ~es Bett** bunk beds *pl* → *auch* **doppelstöckig** ADV **~ bauen** to build buildings with two storeys (*Brit*) or stories (*US*); **zwei|strah|lig** ADJ *Flugzeug* twin-jet *attr*; **Zwei|strom|land** [tsvai-'ʃtro:m-] NT **das ~** Mesopotamia; **Zwei|stu|fen|schei|ben|wi|scher** [tsvai'ʃtu:fn-] M (*Aut*) two-speed windscreen (*Brit*) or windshield (*US*) wiper; **zwei|stu|fig** ADJ two-stage; *System auch* two-tier; *Plan auch* two-phase; *Scheibenwischer, Schaltgetriebe* two-speed; **zwei|stün|dig** ADJ two-hour *attr*, of two hours; **zwei|stünd|lich** ADJ, ADV every two hours, two-hourly

zweit [tsvait] ADV **zu ~** (= *in Paaren*) in twos; **wir gingen zu ~ spazieren** the two of us went for a walk; **ich gehe lieber zu ~ auf Partys** I prefer going to parties with somebody; **das Leben zu ~ ist billiger** it's cheaper for two people to live together; **das Leben zu ~** living with someone → *auch* **vier**

Zwei-: zwei|tä|gig ADJ two-day *attr*, of two days; **Zwei|tak|ter** [-taktɐ] M **-s, -** two--stroke (*inf*); **Zwei|tak|ter|ge|misch** NT two--stroke mixture; **Zwei|takt|mo|tor** M two--stroke engine

zweit|äl|tes|te(r, s) ['tsvait'ɛltəstə] ADJ second eldest or oldest; **unser Zweitältester** our second (child or son)

Zwei-: zwei|tau|send ['tsvai'tauznt] NUM two thousand; **das Jahr ~** the year two thousand; **Zwei|tau|sen|der** ['tsvai'tauzndɐ] M **-s, -** (= *Berg*) two thousand metre (*Brit*) or meter (*US*) peak; **Zwei|tau|send|jahr|fei|er** F bimillenary

Zweit-: Zweit|aus|fer|ti|gung F (form) copy, duplicate; **es liegt nur in ~ vor** we/I have only a copy or duplicate; **Zweit|au|to** NT second car; **Zweit|be|set|zung** F (Theat) understudy; **zweit|bes|te(r, s)** ['tsvait'bɛstə] ADJ second best; **er ist der Zweitbeste** he is the second best; **Zweit|druck** M pl **-drucke** reprint

Zwei-: zwei+tei|len VT sep, infin, ptp only to divide (into two); **zweigeteilt** bipartite; (= gespalten) divided, split; **Zwei|tei|ler** M (Fashion) two-piece; **zwei|tei|lig** ADJ Roman two-part attr, in two parts; Plan two-stage; Kleidungsstück two-piece; Formular etc two-part attr, in two sections; **Zwei|tei|lung** F division; (Math: von Winkel) bisection

zwei|tens ['tsvaitns] ADV secondly; (bei Aufzählungen auch) second

Zwei|te(r) ['tsvaitə] MF decl as adj second; (Sport etc) runner-up; **wie kein ~r** as no-one else can, like nobody else

zwei|te(r, s) ['tsvaitə] ADJ second; **~ Klasse** (Rail etc) second class; **~r Klasse fahren** to travel second (class); **Bürger ~r Klasse** second-class citizen(s); **jeden ~n Tag** every other or second day; **jeder Zweite** (lit, inf: = sehr viele) every other; **zum Zweiten** secondly; **ein ~r Caruso** another Caruso; **in ~r Linie** secondly, second → **Garnitur, Hand, Ich, Wahl** etc → auch **erste(r, s), vierte(r, s)**

Zweit-: Zweit|er|kran|kung F secondary illness; (von Organ, Pflanze, Tier) secondary disease; **Zweit|fri|sur** F wig; **zweit|ge|bo|ren** ADJ attr second-born; **Zweit|ge|rät** NT (TV etc) second set; **zweit|größ|te(r, s)** ['tsvait'grø:stə] ADJ second largest; Zimmer auch, Mensch second biggest; **der/die Zweitgrößte** the second biggest; **zweit|höchs|te(r, s)** ['tsvait'høːçstə] ADJ second highest; Baum auch second tallest; (fig: im Rang) second most senior; **zweit|klas|sig** ADJ (fig) second-class, second-rate (esp pej); **zweit|letz|te(r, s)** ['tsvait'lɛtstə] ADJ last but one attr, pred; (in Reihenfolge auch) penultimate; **der/die Zweitletzte** the last but one, the penultimate; **Zweit|plat|zier|te(r)** ▲ ['tsvaitplatsiːɐtə] MF decl as adj (Sport) runner-up, second-placed finisher; **zweit|ran|gig** [-raŋɪç] ADJ = zweitklassig; **Zweit|schlüs|sel** M duplicate key; **Zweit|schrift** F copy; **Zweit|stim|me** F second vote → auch **Erststimme**; **Zweit|stu|di|um** NT second degree; **ein ~ machen** to take another degree

Zwei|tü|rer [-tyːrə] M (Aut) -s, - two-door

zwei|tü|rig ADJ (Aut) two-door

Zweit-: Zweit|wa|gen M second car; **Zweit|wohn|sitz** M second home; **Zweit|woh|nung** F second home

Zwei|und|drei|ßigs|tel ['tsvai‖ʊnt'draisɪçstl] NT , **Zwei|und|drei|ßigs|tel|no|te** F (Mus) demisemiquaver (Brit), thirty-second note (US)

Zwei|und|drei|ßigs|tel|pau|se F (Mus) demisemiquaver rest (Brit), thirty-second note rest (US)

Zwei-: Zwei|vier|tel|takt [tsvai'virtl-] M (Mus) two-four time; **zwei|wer|tig** ADJ (Chem) bivalent, divalent; (Ling) two-place; **zwei|wö|chent|lich** ADJ two-weekly, fortnightly (esp Brit), biweekly (US) ADV every two weeks, fortnightly (esp Brit), biweekly (US); **zwei|wö|chig** [-vœçɪç] ADJ two-week attr, of two weeks; **zwei|za|ckig** ADJ two-pronged; **Zwei|zei|ler** [-'tsaile] M -s, - (Liter) couplet; **zwei|zei|lig** ADJ two-line attr; (Typ) Abstand double-spaced ADV **~ schreiben** to double-space; **Zwei|zim|mer|woh|nung** [tsvai'tsɪmə-] F two-room(ed) flat (Brit) or apartment; **zwei|zü|gig** ADJ Schule with two classes in each year; (mit zwei Abteilungen) with two alternative subject areas; **Zwei|zy|lin|der** M two-cylinder; **Zwei|zy|lin|der|mo|tor** M two-cylinder engine; **zwei|zy|lind|rig** ADJ two-cylinder attr

Zwerch|fell ['tsvɛrçfɛl] NT (Anat) diaphragm; **jdm das ~ massieren** (hum inf) to make sb split his/her sides (laughing) (inf)

Zwerch|fell-: Zwerch|fell|at|mung F abdominal or diaphragmatic breathing; **zwerch|fell|er|schüt|ternd** ADJ side-splitting (inf); **Zwerch|fell|mas|sa|ge** F (hum inf) **es war die reinste ~** it was an absolute scream (inf) or hoot (inf)

Zwerg [tsvɛrk] M -(e)s, -e [-gə], **Zwer|gin** ['tsvɛrgɪn] F -, -nen dwarf; (= Gartenzwerg) gnome; (fig: = Knirps) midget; (pej: = unbedeutender Mensch) squirt (inf)

Zwerg|en|auf|stand M (inf, hum) to-do (inf), unnecessary fuss

zwer|gen|haft ADJ dwarfish; (fig) diminutive, minute; (pej: = minderwertig) insignificant

Zwerg-: Zwerg|huhn NT bantam; **Zwerg|ka|nin|chen** NT pygmy rabbit; **Zwerg|pin|scher** M pet terrier; **Zwerg|pu|del** M toy poodle; **Zwerg|schu|le** F (Sch inf) village school; **Zwerg|staat** M miniature state; **Zwerg|stamm** M , **Zwerg|volk** NT pygmy tribe; **Zwerg|wuchs** M stunted growth, dwarfism; **zwerg|wüch|sig** [-vyːksɪç] ADJ attr Mensch dwarfish; Baum dwarf attr

Zwetsch|ge ['tsvɛtʃgə] F -, -n plum; **seine** or **die sieben ~n (ein)packen** (inf) to pack one's bags (and go)

Zwetsch|gen-: Zwetsch|gen|dat|schi [-da:tʃi] M -s, -s (S Ger) (type of) plum cake; **Zwetsch|gen|knö|del** M (S Ger) plum dumpling; **Zwetsch|gen|schnaps** M , **Zwetsch|gen|was|ser** NT pl -wässer plum brandy

Zwetsch|ke ['tsvɛtʃkə] F -, -n (Aus) = Zwetschge

Zwi|ckel ['tsvɪkl] M -s, - (Sew) gusset; (am Segel) gore; (Archit) spandrel

zwi|cken ['tsvɪkn] VT (inf, Aus) (= kneifen) to pinch; (= leicht schmerzen) to hurt; (esp S Ger: = ärgern) to bother VI to pinch; (= leicht schmerzen) to hurt

Zwi|cker ['tsvɪkə] M -s, - pince-nez

Zwick|müh|le ['tsvɪk-] F (beim Mühlespiel) double mill; **in der ~ sitzen** (fig) to be in a catch-22 situation (inf), to be in a dilemma

Zwie|back ['tsvi:bak] M -(e)s, -e or ⸚e [-bɛkə] rusk

Zwie|bel ['tsvi:bl] F -, -n onion; (= Blumenzwiebel) bulb; (hum inf: = Uhr) watch; (= Haarknoten) tight bun

Zwie|bel-: Zwie|bel|fisch M (Typ) literal (character typed in wrong face); **zwie|bel|för|mig** ADJ onion-shaped; **Zwie|bel|ku|chen** M onion tart; **Zwie|bel|kup|pel** F (Archit) imperial roof; **Zwie|bel|mus|ter** NT onion pattern

zwie|beln ['tsvi:bln] VT (inf) **jdn ~** to drive or push sb hard; (= schikanieren) to make sb's life hell; **er hat uns so lange gezwiebelt, bis wir das Gedicht konnten** he kept (on) at us until we knew the poem

Zwie|bel-: Zwie|bel|ring M onion ring; **Zwie|bel|scha|le** F onion skin; **Zwie|bel|sup|pe** F onion soup; **Zwie|bel|turm** M onion dome

Zwie-: zwie|fach ['tsvi:fax], **zwie|fäl|tig** ADJ ADV (old) = zweifach; **Zwie|ge|spräch** NT dialogue; **ein ~ mit sich selbst** an internal dialogue; (laut) a soliloquy; **Zwie|laut** M (Ling) diphthong; **Zwie|licht** NT , no pl twilight; (abends auch) dusk; (morgens) half-light; **ins ~ geraten sein** (fig) to appear in an unfavourable (Brit) or unfavorable (US) light; **zwie|lich|tig** ['tsvi:lɪçtɪç] ADJ (fig) shady; **Zwie|spalt** M pl rare (der Natur, der Gefühle etc) conflict; (zwischen Menschen, Parteien etc) rift, gulf; **ich bin im ~ mit mir, ob ich ...** I'm in conflict with myself whether to ...; **in ~ mit jdm geraten** to come into conflict with sb; **in einen fürchterlichen ~ geraten** to get into a terrible conflict; **zwie-**

späl|tig ['tsvi:ʃpɛltɪç] ADJ Gefühle mixed, conflicting attr; **mein Eindruck war ~** my impressions were very mixed; **ein ~er Mensch** a man/woman of contradictions; **Zwie|späl|tig|keit** F (von Gefühlen) conflicting nature; (in jds Verhalten) contradiction; **Zwie|spra|che** F dialogue; **~ mit jdm/etw halten** to commune with sb/sth; **Zwie|tracht** F , no pl discord; **~ säen** to sow (the seeds of) discord

Zwil|le ['tsvɪlə] F -, -n (N Ger) catapult (Brit), slingshot (US)

Zwill|lich ['tsvɪlɪç] M -s, -e (Tex) drill

Zwil|ling ['tsvɪlɪŋ] M -s, -e twin; (= Gewehr) double-barrelled (Brit) or double-barreled (US) gun; (Chem: = Doppelkristall) twin crystal; **die ~e** (Astrol) Gemini, the Twins; (Astron) Gemini; **~ sein** (Astrol) to be (a) Gemini

Zwil|lings-: Zwil|lings|bru|der M twin brother; **Zwil|lings|for|mel** F (Ling) dual expression, set phrase with two elements; **Zwil|lings|ge|burt** F twin birth; **Zwil|lings|paar** NT twins pl; **Zwil|lings|rei|fen** M (Aut) double or twin tyres pl (Brit) or tires pl (US); **Zwil|lings|schwes|ter** F twin sister

Zwing|burg F (Hist, fig) stronghold, fortress

Zwin|ge ['tsvɪŋə] F -, -n (Tech) (screw) clamp; (am Stock) tip, ferrule; (an Schirm) tip; (an Werkzeuggriff) ferrule

zwin|gen ['tsvɪŋən] pret **zwang** [tsvaŋ], ptp **ge|zwun|gen** [gə'tsvʊŋən] VT **a** (= nötigen) to force, to compel; **jdn ~, etw zu tun** to force or compel sb to do sth; **er hat mich gezwungen, das zu tun** he forced or compelled me to do it, he made me do it; **jdn zu etw ~** to force sb to do sth; **sie ist dazu gezwungen worden** she was forced or compelled or made to do it; **ich lasse mich nicht (dazu) ~** I won't be forced (to do it or into it), I won't respond to force; **jdn an den Verhandlungstisch ~** to force sb to the bargaining table; **jdn zum Handeln ~** to force sb into action or act; **jdn zum Gehorsam ~** to force or compel sb to obey, to make sb obey; **jdn zur Prostitution ~** to force sb into prostitution; **die Regierung wurde zum Rücktritt gezwungen** the government was forced or compelled to step down; **man kann niemanden zu seinem Glück ~** you can't force people → auch **gezwungen, Knie, sehen 2**

b (dial inf: = bewältigen) Essen, Arbeit to manage VR to force oneself; **sich ~, etw zu tun** to force oneself to do sth, to make oneself do sth; **sich zur Ruhe ~** to force oneself to be calm VI **zum Handeln/Umdenken ~** to force or compel us/them etc to act/rethink; **diese Tatsachen ~ zu der Annahme, dass ...** these facts force or compel one to assume that ...

zwin|gend ADJ Notwendigkeit urgent; (= logisch notwendig) necessary; Schluss, Beweis, Argumente conclusive; Argument cogent; Gründe compelling; **dass B aus A resultiert, ist nicht ~** it isn't necessarily so or the case that B results from A ADV **etwas ~ darlegen** to present sth conclusively; **etw ist ~ vorgeschrieben** sth is mandatory; **daraus folgert ~** the logical conclusion is; **diese Schlussfolgerung ergab sich ~ aus den Beweisen** this conclusion was inevitable due to the evidence

Zwin|ger ['tsvɪŋə] M -s, - (= Käfig) cage; (= Bärenzwinger) bear pit; (= Hundezwinger) kennels pl; (von Burg) (outer) ward

Zwing-: Zwing|herr M (Hist, fig) oppressor, tyrant; **Zwing|herr|schaft** F (Hist, fig) oppression, tyranny

Zwing|li|a|ner ['tsvɪŋ'li:anə] M -s, -, **Zwing|li|a|ne|rin** F -, -nen (Hist, Rel) Zwinglian

zwin|kern ['tsvɪŋkən] VI to blink; (um jdm etw zu bedeuten) to wink; (lustig) to twinkle; **mit den Augen ~** to blink (one's eyes) (;), to wink (;), to twinkle

Zwir|bel|bart M handlebar moustache (Brit) or mustache (US)

zwir|beln ['tsvɪrbln] VT *Bart* to twirl; *Schnur* to twist

Zwirn [tsvɪrn] M **-s, -e** (strong) thread, yarn → **Himmel b**

zwir|nen ['tsvɪrnən] VTI to twist; **dieses Handtuch ist gezwirnt** this towel is made of strong thread

Zwir|ne|rei [tsvɪrnə'rai] F **-, -en** (cotton-spinning) mill

Zwirns|fa|den M thread

zwi|schen ['tsvɪʃn] PREP +dat or (mit Bewegungsverben) +acc between; (in Bezug auf mehrere auch) among; **mitten ~** right in the middle or midst of; **die Liebe ~ den beiden** the love between the two of them; **die Kirche stand ~ Bäumen** the church stood among(st) trees → **Stuhl a, Tür, Zeile** etc

Zwi|schen-: **Zwi|schen|ab|la|ge** F (Comput) clipboard; **Zwi|schen|ab|rech|nung** F interim invoice; **Zwi|schen|akt** M (Theat) interval, intermission; **im ~** during the interval or intermission; **Zwi|schen|akt(s)|mu|sik** F interlude; **Zwi|schen|an|sa|ge** F (Rad etc) announcement (interrupting a programme); (= Kurznachricht) newsflash; **Zwi|schen|ap|plaus** M (Theat) spontaneous applause (during the performance); **Zwi|schen|auf|ent|halt** M stopover, layover (US); **Zwi|schen|be|mer|kung** F interjection; (= Unterbrechung) interruption; **wenn Sie mir eine kurze ~ erlauben** if I may just interrupt; **Zwi|schen|be|richt** M interim report; **Zwi|schen|be|scheid** M provisional notification no indef art; **Zwi|schen|bi|lanz** F (Comm) interim balance; (fig) provisional appraisal; **eine ~/~en ziehen** (fig) to take stock provisionally; **Zwi|schen|blatt** NT interleaf; **zwi|schen|blen|den** VT sep to blend in; (Film, Rad etc) to insert; (nachträglich) Musik etc to dub on (Brit) or in; **Zwi|schen|blu|tung** F (Med) breakthrough or intermenstrual (spec) bleeding; **Zwi|schen|bo|den** M false floor; **Zwi|schen|buch|han|del** M intermediate book trade; **Zwi|schen|deck** NT (Naut) 'tween deck; **im ~** 'tween decks (Brit), between (the) decks; **Zwi|schen|de|cke** F false ceiling; **Zwi|schen|ding** NT cross (between the two), hybrid; **was er schreibt, ist ein ~ zwischen Lyrik und Prosa** his writing is a cross between or is halfway between poetry and prose; **zwi|schen|drin** ['tsvɪʃn'drɪn] ADV (dial) **a** = zwischendurch **b** = dazwischen; **zwi|schen|durch** ['tsvɪʃn'dʊrç] ADV **a** (zeitlich) in between times; (= inzwischen) (in the) meantime; (= nebenbei) on the side; **er macht ~ mal Pausen** he keeps stopping for a break in between times; **das mache ich so ~** I'll do that on the side; **Schokolade für ~** chocolate for between meals **b** (örtlich) in between; **Zwi|schen|eis|zeit** F (Geol) interglacial period; **Zwi|schen|er|geb|nis** NT interim result; (von Untersuchung auch) interim findings; (Sport) latest score; **Zwi|schen|fall** M incident; **ohne ~** without incident, smoothly; **es kam zu schweren Zwischenfällen** there were serious incidents, there were clashes; **zwi|schen+fi|nan|zie|ren** ptp **zwischenfinanziert** VT sep usu infinitive and ptp (Fin) **etw ~** to provide interim finance for sth; **Zwi|schen|fi|nan|zie|rung** F bridging or interim finance; **Zwi|schen|fra|ge** F question; **Zwi|schen|fre|quenz** F (Rad) intermediate frequency; **Zwi|schen|frucht|bau** M , no pl (Agr) intercropping; **Zwi|schen|fut|ter** NT (Sew) interlining; **Zwi|schen|gang** M pl **-gänge** (Cook) entrée; **Zwi|schen|gas** NT , no pl (old Aut) **~ geben** to double-declutch (Brit), to double-clutch (US); **Zwi|schen|ge|richt** NT (Cook) entrée; **zwi|schen|ge|schlecht|lich** ADJ between the sexes; **Zwi|schen|ge|schoss** ▲ NT mezzanine (floor); **Zwi|schen|glied** NT (lit, fig) link; **Zwi|schen|grö|ße** F in-between size; **Zwi|schen|halt** M (Sw) stopover, layover (US); **Zwi|schen|han|del** M intermediate trade; **Zwi|schen|händ|ler(in)** M(F) middleman; **zwi|-**

schen|hi|nein ADV (Sw) = zwischendurch; **Zwi|schen|hirn** NT (Anat) interbrain, diencephalon (spec); **Zwi|schen|hoch** NT (Met) ridge of high pressure; **Zwi|schen|kie|fer|(kno|chen)** M (Anat) intermaxillary (bone); **Zwi|schen|la|ger** NT temporary store; **zwi|schen|la|gern** VT insep inf and ptp only to store (temporarily); **Zwi|schen|la|ge|rung** F temporary storage; **zwi|schen+lan|den** VI sep aux sein (Aviat) to stop over or off, to lay over (US); **Zwi|schen|lan|dung** F (Aviat) stopover, layover (US); **ohne ~** without a stopover or layover (US); **Zwi|schen|lauf** M (Sport) intermediate heat; **Zwi|schen|lö|sung** F temporary or interim or provisional solution; **Zwi|schen|mahl|zeit** F snack (between meals); **zwi|schen|mensch|lich** ADJ attr interpersonal; **~e Beziehungen** interpersonal relations; **Zwi|schen|mu|sik** F interlude; **Zwi|schen|pau|se** F break; (Theat) interval, intermission (US); **Zwi|schen|pro|dukt** NT intermediate product; **Zwi|schen|prü|fung** F intermediate examination; **Zwi|schen|raum** M gap, space; (= Wort-, Zeilenabstand) space; (zeitlich) interval; **ein ~ von 5 m, 5 m** ~ a gap/space of 5m, a 5m gap/space; **Zwi|schen|ring** M (Phot) adapter; **Zwi|schen|ruf** M interruption; **~e heckling; einen Redner durch ~e stören** to heckle a speaker; **Zwi|schen|ru|fer** M [-ru:fe] M **-s, -**, **Zwi|schen|ru|fe|rin** [-ərɪn] F **-, -nen** heckler; **Zwi|schen|run|de** F (esp Sport) intermediate round; **Zwi|schen|sai|son** F low season; **Zwi|schen|satz** M (Gram) inserted or parenthetic clause, parenthesis; **zwi|schen|schal|ten** VT sep (Elec) to insert; (fig) to interpose, to put in between; **Zwi|schen|schal|ter** M (Elec) interruptor; **Zwi|schen|schal|tung** F (Elec) insertion; (fig) interposition; **zwi|schen+schie|ben** VT sep irreg Termin etc to fit or squeeze in; **Zwi|schen|schritt** M **a** (fig, = Arbeitsschritt) intermediate stage **b** (= Schritt beim Tanzen) linking step; **Zwi|schen|soh|le** F midsole; **Zwi|schen|spei|cher** M (Comput) cache (memory); **zwi|schen+spei|chern** VT sep (Comput) to store in a/the cache (memory); **Zwi|schen|spiel** NT (Mus) intermezzo; (Theat, fig) interlude; **Zwi|schen|spurt** M (Sport) short burst (of speed); **einen ~ einlegen** to put in a burst of speed; **zwi|schen|staat|lich** ADJ attr international; (zwischen Bundesstaaten) interstate; **Zwi|schen|sta|di|um** NT intermediate stage; **Zwi|schen|stand** M (Sport) current score; (in Tabelle) current position; (der Teilnehmer) current rankings pl; **Zwi|schen|sta|ti|on** F (intermediate) stop; **in London machten wir ~** we stopped off in London; **Zwi|schen|ste|cker** M (Elec) adapter (plug); **Zwi|schen|stel|lung** F intermediate position; **Zwi|schen|stock** M , **Zwi|schen|stock|werk** NT mezzanine (floor); **Zwi|schen|stopp** M stop (on the way); (beim Flug) stopover → auch **Zwischenstation**; **Zwi|schen|stück** NT connection, connecting piece; **Zwi|schen|stu|fe** F (fig) intermediate stage; **Zwi|schen|stun|de** F (Sch) hour's break, break of an hour; **Zwi|schen|sum|me** F subtotal; **Zwi|schen|text** M inserted text; **Zwi|schen|ti|tel** M (Film etc) title link; **Zwi|schen|ton** M pl **-töne** (Farbe) shade; **Zwischentöne** (fig) nuances; **Zwi|schen|trä|ger(in)** M(F) informer, telltale (US); **Zwi|schen|ur|teil** NT (Jur) interlocutory decree; **Zwi|schen|vor|hang** M (Theat) drop scene; **Zwi|schen|wand** F dividing wall; (= Stellwand) partition; **Zwi|schen|wirt** M (Biol) intermediate host; **Zwi|schen|zäh|ler** M (Elec) intermediate meter; **Zwi|schen|zeit** F **a** (= Zeitraum) interval; **in der ~** (in the) meantime, in the interim **b** (Sport) intermediate time; **zwi|schen|zeit|lich** ADV (rare) in between; (= inzwischen) (in the) meantime; **Zwi|schen|zeug|nis** NT (Sch) end of term report; **Zwi|schen|zins** M (Fin) interim interest

Zwist [tsvɪst] M **-es,** (rare) **-e** (geh) discord, discordance; (= Fehde, Streit) dispute, strife no in-

def art; **den alten ~ begraben** to bury the hatchet; **mit jdm über etw (acc) in ~ (acc) geraten** to become involved in a dispute with sb about or over sth

Zwis|tig|keit ['tsvɪstɪçkait] F **-, -en** usu pl dispute

zwit|schern ['tsvɪtʃen] VTI to twitter, to chir(ru)p; (Lerche) to warble; **~d sprechen** to twitter; **Zwitschern** twittering, chir(ru)ping, warbling; **einen ~** (inf) to have a drink

Zwit|ter ['tsvɪte] M **-s, -** hermaphrodite; (fig) cross (aus between)

Zwit|ter-: **Zwit|ter|bil|dung** F hermaphroditism; **Zwit|ter|blü|te** F (Bot) hermaphrodite; **Zwit|ter|ding** NT (fig) hybrid, crossbreed; **Zwit|ter|form** F (Biol) hermaphroditic stage; (fig) hybrid form; **zwit|ter|haft** ADJ hermaphroditic

zwit|te|rig ['tsvɪtərɪç], **zwitt|rig** ['tsvɪtrɪç] ADJ hermaphroditic; (Bot auch) androgynous

Zwit|ter-: **Zwit|ter|stel|lung** F **eine ~ einnehmen zwischen (+dat) ... und ...** to be a halfway house between ... and ...; **Zwit|ter|tum** ['tsvɪtetu:m] NT **-s,** no pl hermaphroditism; (Bot auch) androgyny; **Zwit|ter|we|sen** NT hermaphrodite

zwitt|rig ['tsvɪtrɪç] ADJ = zwitterig

ZWO [tsvo:] NUM (Telec, inf) two

zwölf [tsvœlf] NUM twelve; **die ~ Apostel** the twelve apostles; **die Zwölf Nächte** the Twelve Days of Christmas; **~ Uhr mittags/nachts** (12 o'clock) noon or midday/midnight; **fünf Minuten vor ~** (fig) at the eleventh hour; **davon gehen ~ aufs Dutzend** they're ten a penny (Brit inf), they're a dime a dozen (US inf) → auch **vier**

Zwölf- in cpds → auch **Vier-:** **Zwölf|eck** NT (Math) dodecagon; **zwölf|eckig** ADJ dodecagonal; **Zwölf|en|der** M (Hunt) royal; **zwölf|fach** ['tsvœlffax] ADJ, ADV twelve-fold → auch **vierfach**; **Zwölf|fin|ger|darm** [tsvœlf'fɪŋe-] M duodenum; **ein Geschwür am ~** a duodenal ulcer; **Zwölf|flach** [-flax] NT **-(e)s, -e**, **Zwölf|fläch|ner** [-flɛçne] M **-s, -** (Math) dodecahedron; **Zwölf|kampf** M (Sport) twelve-exercise event; **Zwölf|mei|len|zo|ne** [tsvœlf'mailən-] F twelve-mile zone

Zwölf|tel ['tsvœlftl] NT **-s, -** twelfth → auch **Viertel**[1]

zwölf|tens ['tsvœlftns] ADV twelfth(ly), in twelfth place

zwölf|te(r, s) ['tsvœlftə] ADJ twelfth → auch **vierte(r, s)**

Zwölf|tö|ner [-tø:ne] M **-s, -**, **Zwölf|tö|ne|rin** [-ərɪn] F **-, -nen** (Mus) twelve-tone composer

Zwölf|ton-: **Zwölf|ton|leh|re** F twelve-tone system; **Zwölf|ton|mu|sik** F twelve-tone music; **Zwölf|ton|rei|he** F twelve-tone row or series

zwo|te(r, s) ['tsvo:tə] ADJ (Telec, inf) = **zweite(r, s)**

Zy|an [tsy'a:n] NT **-s,** no pl (Chem) cyanogen

Zy|a|nid [tsya'ni:t] NT **-s, -e** [-də] cyanide

Zy|an|ka|li [tsya:n'ka:li] NT **-s,** no pl (Chem) potassium cyanide

Zy|go|te [tsy'go:tə] F **-, -n** (Biol) zygote

Zyk|la|den [tsy'kla:dn] PL (Geog) Cyclades pl

Zyk|la|me [tsy'kla:mə] F **-, -n** (Aus), **Zyk|la|men** [tsy'kla:mən] NT **-s, -** (spec) cyclamen

zyk|lisch ['tsy:klɪʃ] ADJ cyclic(al) ADV cyclically

Zyk|lon[1] [tsy'klo:n] M **-s, -e** cyclone

Zyk|lon[2] NT **-s,** no pl (Chem) cyanide-based poison, cyanide

Zyk|lo|ne [tsy'klo:nə] F **-, -n** (Met) depression, low(-pressure area)

Zyk|lop [tsy'klo:p] M **-en, -en** (Myth) Cyclops

Zyk|lo|pen|mau|er F (Archeol) cyclopean wall

zyk|lo|pisch [tsy'klo:pɪʃ] ADJ (Myth) Cyclopean; (liter. = gewaltig) gigantic

---

Deutsche Rechtschreibreform (siehe Anhang): ▲ neue Schreibung △ alte Schreibung   + trennbare Verben

Zyk|lot|ron ['tsyːklotroːn, 'tsʏk-] NT **-s, -e** (*Phys*) cyclotron

Zyk|lus ['tsyːklʊs] M **-, Zyklen** [-lən] cycle (*auch Physiol*)

Zyk|lus|stö|rung ['tsyːklʊs-] F (*Med*) menstrual disorder

Zyk|lus|zeit ['tsyːklʊs-] F (*Comput*) cycle time

Zy|lin|der [tsiˈlɪndɐ, tsy-] M **-s, -** **a** (*Math, Tech*) cylinder; (= *Lampenzylinder*) chimney **b** (= *Hut*) top hat, topper (*inf*)

Zy|lin|der-: **Zy|lin|der|block** M *pl* **-blöcke** (*Aut*) engine *or* cylinder block; **Zy|lin|der|dich|tungs|ring** M (*Aut*) cylinder ring; **zy|lin|der|för|mig** ADJ = zylindrisch; **Zy|lin|der|hut** M top hat, topper (*inf*); **Zy|lin|der|kopf** M (*Aut*) cylinder head; **Zy|lin|der|kopf|dich|tung** F cylinder head gasket; **Zy|lin|der|man|tel** M (*Tech*) cylinder jacket; **Zy|lin|der|schloss** ▲ NT cylinder lock

-zy|lind|rig [tsilɪndrɪç, tsy-] ADJ *suf* -cylinder; **zwei|zylindrig** two-cylinder *attr*

zy|lind|risch [tsiˈlɪndrɪʃ, tsy-] **ADJ** cylindrical **ADV** cylindrically

Zym|bal ['tsʏmbal] NT **-s, -e** (*Mus*) cymbal

Zy|ni|ker ['tsyːnikɐ] M **-s, -, Zy|ni|ke|rin** [-ərɪn] F **-, -nen** cynic

zy|nisch ['tsyːnɪʃ] **ADJ** cynical **ADV** cynically

Zy|nis|mus ['tsyːnɪsmʊs] M **-, Zynismen** [-mən] cynicism

Zy|pern ['tsyːpɛn] NT **-s** Cyprus

Zyp|res|se [tsyˈprɛsə] F **-, -n** (*Bot*) cypress

Zyp|ri|er ['tsyːpriɐ] M **-s, -, Zyp|ri|e|rin** [-iərɪn] F **-, -nen** (*rare*), **Zyp|ri|ot** [tsypriˈoːt] M **-en, -en, Zyp|ri|o|tin** [-ˈoːtɪn] F **-, -nen** Cypriot

zyp|ri|o|tisch [tsypriˈoːtɪʃ], **zyp|risch** ['tsyːprɪʃ] ADJ Cypriot, Cyprian

Zys|te ['tsʏstə] F **-, -n** cyst

zys|tisch ['tsʏstɪʃ] ADJ cystic; **~e Fibrose** cystic fibrosis

Zy|to|lo|gie [tsytoloˈgiː] F **-,** *no pl* (*Biol*) cytology

Zy|to-: **Zy|to|plas|ma** [tsytoˈplasma] NT (*Biol*) cytoplasm; **Zy|to|sta|ti|kum** [tsytoˈstaːtikʊm] NT **-s, Zytostatika** [-ka] cytostatic drug

zz(t). *abbr von* **zurzeit**

z. Z(t). *abbr von* **zur Zeit** *von* **zu Zeiten**

APPENDICES

ANHANG

GERMAN VERBS

REGULAR VERBS

1. The present tense is formed by adding

> *-e, -st, -t, -en, -t, -en*

to the stem of the verb (infinitive minus *-en* or, with verbs in *-ln, -rn,* minus *-n*).

Verbs ending in *-s, -ß, -z, -tz* form the second person singular by adding *-t*

> **heißen – du heißt**

except in literary usage when the ending *-est* may be added

> **preisen – du preisest** (*liter*)

2. The preterite, or past tense, is formed by adding

> *-te, -test, -te, -ten, -tet, -ten*

to the stem of the verb.

3. The past participle is formed by adding the prefix *ge-* and the ending *-t* to the stem of the verb.

4. The present participle is formed by adding *-d* to the infinitive.

5. The *Sie* form imperative of both regular and irregular verbs is formed with the infinitive

> **machen Sie schnell!**
> **kommen Sie her!**

IRREGULAR VERBS

1. The forms of compound verbs (beginning with the prefixes *auf-, ab-, be-, er-, zer-, etc*) are the same as for the simplex verb.

2. The past participle of modal auxiliary verbs (dürfen, müssen *etc*) is replaced by the infinitive form when following another infinitive form, eg ich habe gehen dürfen; non-modal use: ich habe gedurft.

3. The formation of the present subjunctive is regular, requiring the following endings to be added to the verb stem:

sehen

ich seh-e	wir seh-en
du seh-est	ihr seh-et
er seh-e	sie seh-en

sein

ich sei	wir sei-en
du seist, du seiest (*liter*)	ihr sei-et
er sei	sie sei-en

INFINITIVE	PRESENT INDICATIVE	IMPERFECT INDICATIVE	IMPERFECT SUBJUNCTIVE	IMPERATIVE	PAST PARTICIPLE
	2nd pers singular ♦ *3rd pers singular*			*Singular* ♦ *Plural*	
backen	bäckst, backst ♦ bäckt, backt	backte, buk (*old*)	backte, büke (*old*)	back(e) ♦ backt	gebacken
befehlen	befiehlst ♦ befiehlt	befahl	beföhle, befähle	befiehl ♦ befehlt	befohlen
befleißen (*old*)	befleißt ♦ befleißt	befliss	beflisse	befleiß(e) ♦ befleißt	beflissen
beginnen	beginnst ♦ beginnt	begann	begänne, begönne (*rare*)	beginn(e) ♦ beginnt	begonnen
beißen	beißt ♦ beißt	biss	bisse	beiß(e) ♦ beißt	gebissen
bergen	birgst ♦ birgt	barg	bärge	birg ♦ bergt	geborgen
bersten	birst ♦ birst	barst	bärste	birst ♦ berstet	geborsten
bewegen (= *veranlassen*)	bewegst ♦ bewegt	bewog	bewöge	beweg(e) ♦ bewegt	bewogen
biegen	biegst ♦ biegt	bog	böge	bieg(e) ♦ biegt	gebogen
bieten	bietest ♦ bietet	bot	böte	biet(e) ♦ bietet	geboten
binden	bindest ♦ bindet	band	bände	bind(e) ♦ bindet	gebunden
bitten	bittest ♦ bittet	bat	bäte	bitt(e) ♦ bittet	gebeten
blasen	bläst ♦ bläst	blies	bliese	blas(e) ♦ blast	geblasen
bleiben	bleibst ♦ bleibt	blieb	bliebe	bleib(e) ♦ bleibt	geblieben
bleichen (*vi, old*)	bleichst ♦ bleicht	blich (*old*)	bliche	bleich(e) ♦ bleicht	geblichen
braten	brätst ♦ brät	briet	briete	brat(e) ♦ bratet	gebraten
brechen	brichst ♦ bricht	brach	bräche	brich ♦ brecht	gebrochen
brennen	brennst ♦ brennt	brannte	brennte (*rare*)	brenn(e) ♦ brennt	gebrannt
bringen	bringst ♦ bringt	brachte	brächte	bring(e) ♦ bringt	gebracht
denken	denkst ♦ denkt	dachte	dächte	denk(e) ♦ denkt	gedacht
dingen	dingst ♦ dingt	dang	dingte	dingt ♦ dingt	gedungen
dreschen	drischst ♦ drischt	drosch	drösche, dräsche (*old*)	drisch ♦ drescht	gedroschen
dringen	dringst ♦ dringt	drang	dränge	dring(e) ♦ dringt	gedrungen
dünken	*3rd only* dünkt, deucht (*old*)	dünkte, deuchte (*old*)	dünkte, deuchte (*old*)		gedünkt, gedeucht (*old*)
dürfen	*1st* darf *2nd* darfst *3rd* darf	durfte	dürfte		gedurft; (*after infin*) dürfen

INFINITIVE	PRESENT INDICATIVE	IMPERFECT INDICATIVE	IMPERFECT SUBJUNCTIVE	IMPERATIVE	PAST PARTICIPLE
	2nd pers singular ◆*3rd pers singular*			*Singular* ◆*Plural*	
empfangen	empfängst ◆ empfängt	empfing	empfinge	empfang(e) ◆ empfangt	empfangen
empfehlen	empfiehlst ◆ empfiehlt	empfahl	empföhle, empfähle (*rare*)	empfiehl ◆ empfehlt	empfohlen
empfinden	empfindest ◆ empfindet	empfand	empfände	empfind(e) ◆ empfindet	empfunden
essen	isst ◆ isst	aß	äße	iss ◆ esst	gegessen
fahren	fährst ◆ fährt	fuhr	führe	fahr(e) ◆ fahrt	gefahren
fallen	fällst ◆ fällt	fiel	fiele	fall(e) ◆ fallt	gefallen
fangen	fängst ◆ fängt	fing	finge	fang(e) ◆ fangt	gefangen
fechten	fichtst ◆ ficht	focht	föchte	flicht ◆ fechtet	gefochten
finden	findest ◆ findet	fand	fände	find(e) ◆ findet	gefunden
flechten	flichtst ◆ flicht	flocht	flöchte	flicht ◆ flechtet	geflochten
fliegen	fliegst ◆ fliegt	flog	flöge	flieg(e) ◆ fliegt	geflogen
fliehen	fliehst ◆ flieht	floh	flöhe	flieh(e) ◆ flieht	geflohen
fließen	fließt ◆ fließt	floss	flösse	fließ(e) ◆ fließt	geflossen
fressen	frisst ◆ frisst	fraß	fräße	friss ◆ fresst	gefressen
frieren	frierst ◆ friert	fror	fröre	frier(e) ◆ friert	gefroren
gären	gärst ◆ gärt	gor, gärte (*esp fig*)	göre, gärte (*esp fig*)	gär(e) ◆ gärt	gegoren, gegärt (*esp fig*)
gebären	gebierst ◆ gebiert	gebar	gebäre	gebier ◆ gebärt	geboren
geben	gibst ◆ gibt	gab	gäbe	gib ◆ gebt	gegeben
gedeihen	gedeihst ◆ gedeiht	gedieh	gediehe	gedeih(e) ◆ gedeiht	gediehen
gehen	gehst ◆ geht	ging	ginge	geh(e) ◆ geht	gegangen
gelingen	gelingt	gelang	gelänge	geling(e) (*rare*) ◆ gelingt (*rare*)	gelungen
gelten	giltst ◆ gilt	galt	gölte, gälte	gilt (*rare*) ◆ geltet (*rare*)	gegolten
genesen	genest ◆ genest	genas	genäse	genese ◆ genest	genesen
genießen	genießt ◆ genießt	genoss	genösse	genieß(e) ◆ genießt	genossen
geschehen	geschieht	geschah	geschähe	geschieh ◆ gescheht	geschehen
gewinnen	gewinnst ◆ gewinnt	gewann	gewönne, gewänne	gewinn(e) ◆ gewinnt	gewonnen
gießen	gießt ◆ gießt	goss	gösse	gieß(e) ◆ gießt	gegossen
gleichen	gleichst ◆ gleicht	glich	gliche	gleich(e) ◆ gleicht	geglichen
gleiten	gleitest ◆ gleitet	glitt	glitte	gleit(e) ◆ gleitet	geglitten
glimmen	glimmst ◆ glimmt	glomm	glömme, glimmte (*rare*)	glimm(e) ◆ glimmt	geglommen
graben	gräbst ◆ gräbt	grub	grübe	grab(e) ◆ grabt	gegraben
greifen	greifst ◆ greift	griff	griffe	greif(e) ◆ greift	gegriffen
haben	hast ◆ hat	hatte	hätte	hab(e) ◆ habt	gehabt
halten	hältst ◆ hält	hielt	hielte	halt(e) ◆ haltet	gehalten
hängen	hängst ◆ hängt	hing	hinge	häng(e) ◆ hängt	gehangen
hauen	haust ◆ haut	haute	haute, hiebe	hau(e) ◆ haut	gehauen
heben	hebst ◆ hebt	hob	höbe, hübe (*old*)	heb(e) ◆ hebt	gehoben
heißen	heißt ◆ heißt	hieß	hieße	heiß(e) ◆ heißt	geheißen
helfen	hilfst ◆ hilft	half	hülfe, hälfe (*rare*)	hilf ◆ helft	geholfen
kennen	kennst ◆ kennt	kannte	kennte	kenn(e) ◆ kennt	gekannt
klimmen	klimmst ◆ klimmt	klomm, klimmte	klömme, klimmte	klimm(e) ◆ klimmt	geklimmt, geklommen
klingen	klingst ◆ klingt	klang	klänge	kling(e) ◆ klingt	geklungen
kneifen	kneifst ◆ kneift	kniff	kniffe	kneif(e) ◆ kneift	gekniffen
kommen	kommst ◆ kommt	kam	käme	komm(e) ◆ kommt	gekommen
können	*1st* kann *2nd* kannst *3rd* kann	konnte	könnte		gekonnt; (*after infin*) können
kreischen	kreischst ◆ kreischt	kreischte, krisch (*old, hum*)	kreischte, krische (*old, hum*)	kreisch(e) ◆ kreischt	gekreischt, gekrischen (*old, hum*)
kriechen	kriechst ◆ kriecht	kroch	kröche	kriech(e) ◆ kriecht	gekrochen
küren	kürst ◆ kürt	kürte, kor (*rare*)	kürte, köre (*rare*)	kür(e) ◆ kürt	gekürt, gekoren (*rare*)
laden[1]	lädst ◆ lädt	lud	lüde	lad(e) ◆ ladet	geladen

INFINITIVE	PRESENT INDICATIVE	IMPERFECT INDICATIVE	IMPERFECT SUBJUNCTIVE	IMPERATIVE	PAST PARTICIPLE
	2nd pers singular ♦ *3rd pers singular*			*Singular* ♦ *Plural*	
laden[2]	lädst ♦ lädest (*dated, dial*)	lud	lüde	lad(e) ♦ ladet	geladen
lassen	lässt ♦ lässt	ließ	ließe	lass ♦ lasst	gelassen; (*after infin*) lassen
laufen	läufst ♦ läuft	lief	liefe	lauf(e) ♦ lauft	gelaufen
leiden	leidest ♦ leidet	litt	litte	leid(e) ♦ leidet	gelitten
leihen	leihst ♦ leiht	lieh	liehe	leih(e) ♦ leiht	geliehen
lesen	liest ♦ liest	las	läse	lies ♦ lest	gelesen
liegen	liegst ♦ liegt	lag	läge	lieg(e) ♦ liegt	gelegen
löschen	lischst ♦ lischt	losch	lösche	lisch ♦ löscht	geloschen
lügen	lügst ♦ lügt	log	löge	lüg(e) ♦ lügt	gelogen
mahlen	mahlst ♦ mahlt	mahlte	mahlte	mahl(e) ♦ mahlt	gemahlen
meiden	meidest ♦ meidet	mied	miede	meid(e) ♦ meidet	gemieden
melken	melkst ♦ melkt	melkte	mölke	melk(e), milk ♦ melkt	gemolken
messen	misst ♦ misst	maß	mäße	miss ♦ messt	gemessen
misslingen	misslingt	misslang	misslänge		misslungen
mögen	*1st* mag *2nd* magst *3rd* mag	mochte	möchte		gemocht; (*after infin*) mögen
müssen	*1st* muss *2nd* musst *3rd* muss	musste	müsste		müssen; (*vi*) gemusst
nehmen	nimmst ♦ nimmt	nahm	nähme	nimm ♦ nehmt	genommen
nennen	nennst ♦ nennt	nannte	nennte (*rare*)	nenn(e) ♦ nennt	genannt
pfeifen	pfeifst ♦ pfeift	pfiff	pfiffe	pfeif(e) ♦ pfeift	gepfiffen
pflegen	pflegst ♦ pflegt	pflegt, pflog (*old*)	pflegte, pflöge (*old*)	pfleg(e) ♦ pflegt	gepflegt, gepflogen (*old*)
preisen	preist ♦ preist	pries	priese	preis(e) ♦ preis(e)t	gepriesen
quellen	quillst ♦ quillt	quoll	quölle	quill (*rare*) ♦ quellt	gequollen
raten	rätst ♦ rät	riet	riete	rat(e) ♦ ratet	geraten
reiben	reibst ♦ reibt	rieb	riebe	reib(e) ♦ reibt	gerieben
reißen	reißt ♦ reißt	riss	risse	reiß(e) ♦ reißt	gerissen
reiten	reitest ♦ reitet	ritt	ritte	reit(e) ♦ reitet	geritten
rennen	rennst ♦ rennt	rannte	rennte (*rare*)	renn(e) ♦ rennt	gerannt
riechen	riechst ♦ riecht	roch	röche	riech(e) ♦ riecht	gerochen
ringen	ringst ♦ ringt	rang	ränge	ring(e) ♦ ringt	gerungen
rinnen	rinnst ♦ rinnt	rann	ränne	rinn(e) ♦ rinnt	geronnen
rufen	rufst ♦ ruft	rief	riefe	ruf(e) ♦ ruft	gerufen
salzen	salzt ♦ salzt	salzte	salzte	salz(e) ♦ salzt	gesalzen
saufen	säufst ♦ säuft	soff	söffe	sauf(e) ♦ sauft	gesoffen
saugen	saugst ♦ saugt	sog	söge, saugte	saug(e) ♦ saugt	gesogen, gesaugt
schaffen	schaffst ♦ schafft	schuf	schüfe	schaff(e) ♦ schafft	geschaffen
schallen	schallst ♦ schallt	schallte, scholl (*rare*)	schallte, schölle (*rare*)	schall(e) ♦ schallt	geschallt
scheiden	scheidest ♦ scheidet	schied	schiede	scheid(e) ♦ scheidet	geschieden
scheinen	scheinst ♦ scheint	schien	schiene	schein(e) ♦ scheint	geschienen
scheißen	scheißt ♦ scheißt	schiss	schisse	scheiß(e) ♦ scheißt	geschissen
schelten	schiltst ♦ schilt	schalt	schölte	schilt ♦ scheltet	gescholten
scheren	scherst ♦ schert	schor	schöre	scher(e) ♦ schert	geschoren
schieben	schiebst ♦ schiebt	schob	schöbe	schieb(e) ♦ schiebt	geschoben
schießen	schießt ♦ schießt	schoss	schösse	schieß(e) ♦ schießt	geschossen
schinden	schindest ♦ schindet	schindete	schünde	schind(e)	geschunden
schlafen	schläfst ♦ schläft	schlief	schliefe	schlaf(e) ♦ schlaft	geschlafen
schlagen	schlägst ♦ schlägt	schlug	schlüge	schlag(e) ♦ schlagt	geschlagen
schleichen	schleichst ♦ schleicht	schlich	schliche	schleich(e) ♦ schleicht	geschlichen
schleifen	schleifst ♦ schleift	schliff	schliffe	schleif(e) ♦ schleift	geschliffen
schleißen	schleißt ♦ schleißt	schliss; (*vt auch*) schleißte	schlisse; schleißte	schleiß(e) ♦ schleißt	geschlissen; (*vt auch*) geschleißt
schließen	schließt ♦ schließt	schloss	schlösse	schließ(e) ♦ schließt	geschlossen
schlingen	schlingst ♦ schlingt	schlang	schlänge	schling(e) ♦ schlingt	geschlungen

INFINITIVE	PRESENT INDICATIVE	IMPERFECT INDICATIVE	IMPERFECT SUBJUNCTIVE	IMPERATIVE	PAST PARTICIPLE
	2nd pers singular ♦ *3rd pers singular*			*Singular* ♦ *Plural*	
schmeißen	schmeißt ♦ schmeißt	schmiss	schmisse	schmeiß(e) ♦ schmeißt	geschmissen
schmelzen	schmilzt ♦ schmilzt	schmolz	schmölze	schmilz ♦ schmelzt	geschmolzen
schnauben	schnaubst ♦ schnaubt	schnaubte, schnob (*old*)	schnaubte, schnöbe (*old*)	schnaub(e) ♦ schnaubt	geschnaubt, geschnoben (*old*)
schneiden	schneid(e)st ♦ schneidet	schnitt	schnitte	schneid(e) ♦ schneidet	geschnitten
schrecken	schrickst ♦ schrickt	schreckte, schrak	schreckte, schräke	schrick ♦ schreckt	geschreckt, geschrocken (*old*)
schreiben	schreibst ♦ schreibt	schrieb	schriebe	schreib(e) ♦ schreibt	geschrieben
schreien	schreist ♦ schreit	schrie	schriee	schrei(e) ♦ schreit	geschrie(e)n
schreiten	schreitest ♦ schreitet	schritt	schritte	schreit(e) ♦ schreitet	geschritten
schweigen	schweigst ♦ schweigt	schwieg	schwiege	schweig(e) ♦ schweigt	geschwiegen
schwellen	schwillst ♦ schwillt	schwoll	schwölle	schwill ♦ schwellt	geschwollen
schwimmen	schwimmst ♦ schwimmt	schwamm	schwämme, schwamme (*rare*)	schwimm(e) ♦ schwimmt	geschwommen
schwinden	schwindest ♦ schwindet	schwand	schwände	schwind(e) ♦ schwindet	geschwunden
schwingen	schwingst ♦ schwingt	schwang	schwänge	schwing(e) ♦ schwingt	geschwungen
schwören	schwörst ♦ schwört	schwor	schwüre, schwöre (*rare*)	schwör(e) ♦ schwört	geschworen
sehen	siehst ♦ sieht	sah	sähe	sieh(e) ♦ seht	gesehen; (*after infin*) sehen
sein	*1st* bin *2nd* bist *3rd* ist *1st pl* sind *2nd pl* seid *3rd pl* sind	war	wäre	sei ♦ seid	gewesen
senden (= *schicken*)	sendest ♦ sendet	sandte	sendete	send(e) ♦ sendet	gesandt
sieden	siedest ♦ siedet	siedete, sott	siedete, sötte	sied(e) ♦ siedet	gesiedet, gesotten
singen	singst ♦ singt	sang	sänge	sing(e) ♦ singt	gesungen
sinken	sinkst ♦ sinkt	sank	sänke	sink(e) ♦ sinkt	gesunken
sinnen	sinnst ♦ sinnt	sann	sänne	sinn(e) ♦ sinnt	gesonnen
sitzen	sitzt ♦ sitzt	saß	säße	sitz(e) ♦ sitzt	gesessen
sollen	*1st* soll *2nd* sollst *3rd* soll	sollte	sollte		gesollt; (*after infin*) sollen
spalten	spaltest ♦ spaltet	spaltete	spalte	spalt(e) ♦ spaltet	gespalten
speien	speist ♦ speit	spie	spiee	spei(e) ♦ speit	gespie(e)n
spinnen	spinnst ♦ spinnt	spann	spönne, spänne	spinn(e) ♦ spinnt	gesponnen
spleißen	spleißt ♦ spleißt	spliss	splisse	spleiß(e) ♦ spleißt	gesplissen
sprechen	sprichst ♦ spricht	sprach	spräche	sprich ♦ sprecht	gesprochen
sprießen	sprießt ♦ sprießt	spross, sprießte	sprösse	sprieß(e) ♦ sprießt	gesprossen
springen	springst ♦ springt	sprang	spränge	spring(e) ♦ springt	gesprungen
stechen	stichst ♦ sticht	stach	stäche	stich ♦ stecht	gestochen
stecken (*vi*)	steckst ♦ steckt	steckte, stak	steckte, stäke (*rare*)	steck(e) ♦ steckt	gesteckt
stehen	stehst ♦ steht	stand	stünde, stände	steh ♦ steht	gestanden
stehlen	stiehlst ♦ stiehlt	stahl	stähle, stöhle (*obs*)	stiehl ♦ stehlt	gestohlen
steigen	steigst ♦ steigt	stieg	stiege	steig ♦ steigt	gestiegen
sterben	stirbst ♦ stirbt	starb	stürbe	stirb ♦ sterbt	gestorben
stieben	stiebst ♦ stiebt	stob, stiebte	stöbe, stiebte	stieb(e) ♦ stiebt	gestoben, gestiebt
stinken	stinkst ♦ stinkt	stank	stänke	stink(e) ♦ stinkt	gestunken
stoßen	stößt ♦ stößt	stieß	stieße	stoß(e) ♦ stößt	gestoßen
streichen	streichst ♦ streicht	strich	striche	streich(e) ♦ streicht	gestrichen
streiten	streitest ♦ streitet	stritt	stritte	streit(e) ♦ streitet	gestritten
tragen	trägst ♦ trägt	trug	trüge	trag(e) ♦ tragt	getragen
treffen	triffst ♦ trifft	traf	träfe	triff ♦ trefft	getroffen
treiben	treibst ♦ treibt	trieb	triebe	treib ♦ treibt	getrieben
treten	trittst ♦ tritt	trat	träte	tritt ♦ tretet	getreten

INFINITIVE	PRESENT INDICATIVE	IMPERFECT INDICATIVE	IMPERFECT SUBJUNCTIVE	IMPERATIVE	PAST PARTICIPLE
	2nd pers singular ◆*3rd pers singular*			*Singular* ◆*Plural*	
triefen	triefst ◆ trieft	trieft(e), troff (*geh*)	triefte, tröffe (*geh*)	trief(e) ◆ trieft	getrieft, getroffen (*rare*)
trinken	trinkst ◆ trinkt	trank	tränke	trink ◆ trinkt	getrunken
trügen	trügst ◆ trügt	trog	tröge	trüg(e) ◆ trügt	getrogen
tun	*1st* tue *2nd* tust *3rd* tut	tat	täte	tu(e) ◆ tut	getan
verderben	verdirbst ◆ verdirbt	verdarb	verdärbe	verdirb ◆ verderbt	verdorben
verdrießen	verdrießt ◆ verdrießt	verdross	verdrösse	verdrieß(e) ◆ verdrießt	verdrossen
vergessen	vergisst ◆ vergisst	vergaß	vergäße	vergiss ◆ vergesst	vergessen
verlieren	verlierst ◆ verliert	verlor	verlöre	verlier(e) ◆ verliert	verloren
verzeihen	verzeihst ◆ verzeiht	verzieh	verziehe	verzeih(e) ◆ verzeiht	verziehen
wachsen	wächst ◆ wächst	wuchs	wüchse	wachs(e) ◆ wachst	gewachsen
wägen	wägst ◆ wägt	wog	wöge, wägte (*rare*)	wäg(e) ◆ wägt	gewogen
waschen	wäschst ◆ wäscht	wusch	wüsche	wasch(e) ◆ wascht	gewaschen
weben	webst ◆ webt	webte, wob (*liter, fig*)	webte, wöbe (*liter, fig*)	web(e) ◆ webt	gewebt, gewoben (*liter, fig*)
weichen	weichst ◆ weicht	wich	wiche	weich(e) ◆ weicht	gewichen
weisen	weist ◆ weist	wies	wiese	weis(e) ◆ weist	gewiesen
wenden	wendest ◆ wendet	wendete	wendete	wend(e) ◆ wendet	gewendet, gewandt
werben	wirbst ◆ wirbt	warb	würbe	wirb ◆ werbt	geworben
werden	wirst ◆ wird	wurde	würde	werde ◆ werdet	geworden; (*after ptp*) worden
werfen	wirfst ◆ wirft	warf	würfe	wirf ◆ werft	geworfen
wiegen	wiegst ◆ wiegt	wog	wöge	wieg(e) ◆ wiegt	gewogen
winden	windest ◆ windet	wand	wände	wind(e) ◆ windet	gewunden
winken	winkst ◆ winkt	winkte	winkte	wink(e) ◆ winkt	gewinkt, gewunken
wissen	*1st* weiß *2nd* weißt *3rd* weiß	wusste	wüsste	wisse (*liter*) ◆ wisset (*liter*)	gewusst
wollen	*1st* will *2nd* willst *3rd* will	wollte	wollte	wollte (*liter*) ◆ wollt	gewollt; (*after infin*) wollen
wringen	wringst ◆ wringt	wrang	wränge	wring(e) ◆ wringt	gewrungen
zeihen	zeihst ◆ zeiht	zieh	ziehe	zeih(e) ◆ zeiht	geziehen
ziehen	ziehst ◆ zieht	zog	zöge	zieh(e) ◆ zieht	gezogen
zwingen	zwingst ◆ zwingt	zwang	zwänge	zwing(e) ◆ zwingt	gezwungen

ENGLISCHE VERBEN

REGELMÄSSIGE VERBEN IM ENGLISCHEN

1. Bildung des Präteritums und des 2. Partizips

1.1 In den meisten Fällen wird -ed an die Infinitivform angehängt.

remain *pret, ptp* **remained**

1.2 Verben mit Konsonant +y im Auslaut werden zu -ied.

try *pret, ptp* **tried**

1.3 Verben mit stummen -e oder mit -ee, -ye, -oe, -ge im Auslaut verlieren das zweite -e.

abate *pret, ptp* **abated**
agree *pret, ptp* **agreed**
dye *pret, ptp* **dyed**
hoe *pret, ptp* **hoed**
singe *pret, ptp* **singed**

1.4 Verben, die auf Konsonant nach einfachem, betontem Vokal enden, verdoppeln diesen Endkonsonanten.

bar *pret, ptp* **barred**
permit *pret, ptp* **permitted**

Nach Doppelvokal wird der Konsonant im Auslaut nicht verdoppelt

dread *pret, ptp* **dreaded**

ebenso wenig nach unbetontem Vokal

visit *pret, ptp* **visited**

mit Ausnahme von auslautendem -l und -p im britischen Englisch.

level *pret, ptp* **levelled** *or* (*US*) **leveled**
worship *pret, ptp* **worshipped** *or* (*US*) **worshiped**

Verben mit Vokal +c im Auslaut werden zu -cked.

panic *pret, ptp* **panicked**

2. Bildung des 1. Partizips

2.1 Die meisten Verben bilden das 1. Partizip durch Anhängen von -ing.

2.2 Für Verben, die auf Vokal + Konsonant enden, gelten die gleichen Regeln wie für die Bildung des Präteritums; siehe **1.4**.

2.3 Verben, die auf -ie enden, werden zu -ying.

die *prp* **dying**

2.4 Verben mit stummem -e im Auslaut verlieren diesen Vokal

like *prp* **liking**

außer wenn sie in der Kombination -ye, -oe auftreten.

dye *prp* **dyeing**
hoe *prp* **hoeing**

UNREGELMÄSSIGE ENGLISCHE VERBEN

INFINITIV	PRÄTERITUM	PARTIZIP PERFEKT	INFINITIV	PRÄTERITUM	PARTIZIP PERFEKT
abide	abode, abided	abode, abided	catch	caught	caught
arise	arose	arisen	chide	chid	chidden, chid
awake	awoke	awaked	choose	chose	chosen
be	was (*sing*),	been	cleave¹ (= *cut*)	clove, cleft	cloven, cleft
(am, is, are;	were (*pl*)		cleave² (= *adhere*)	cloved, clave	cleaved
being)			cling	clung	clung
bear	bore	born(e)	come	came	come
beat	beat	beaten	cost	cost	cost
become	became	become	cost (= *work out*	costed	costed
befall	befell	befallen	*price of*)		
beget	begot, begat (*obs*)	begotten	creep	crept	crept
begin	began	begun	cut	cut	cut
behold	beheld	beheld	deal	dealt	dealt
bend	bent	bent	dig	dug	dug
beseech	besought	besought	do (*3rd person:*	did	done
beset	beset	beset	he/she/it does)		
bet	bet, betted	bet, betted	draw	drew	drawn
bid (*at auction,*	bid	bid	dream	dreamed, dreamt	dreamed, dreamt
cards)			drink	drank	drunk
bid (= *say*)	bade	bidden	drive	drove	driven
bind	bound	bound	dwell	dwelt	dwelt
bite	bit	bitten	eat	ate	eaten
bleed	bled	bled	fall	fell	fallen
blow	blew	blown	feed	fed	fed
break	broke	broken	feel	felt	felt
breed	bred	bred	fight	fought	fought
bring	brought	brought	find	found	found
build	built	built	flee	fled	fled
burn	burnt, burned	burnt, burned	fling	flung	flung
burst	burst	burst	fly	flew	flown
buy	bought	bought	forbid	forbad(e)	forbidden
can	could	(been able)	forecast	forecast	forecast
cast	cast	cast	forget	forgot	forgotten

INFINITIV	PRÄTERITUM	PARTIZIP PERFEKT	INFINITIV	PRÄTERITUM	PARTIZIP PERFEKT
forgive	forgave	forgiven	shine	shone	shone
forsake	forsook	forsaken	shoe	shed	shed
freeze	froze	frozen	shoot	shot	shot
get	got	got, (*US*) gotten	show	showed	shown
gild	gilded	gilded, gilt	shrink	shrank	shrunk
gird	girded, girt	girded, girt	shut	shut	shut
give	gave	given	sing	sang	sung
go (goes)	went	gone	sink	sank	sunk
grind	ground	ground	sit	sat	sat
grow	grew	grown	slay	slew	slain
hang	hung	hung	sleep	slept	slept
hang (= *execute*)	hanged	hanged	slide	slid	slid
have	had	had	sling	slung	slung
hear	heard	heard	slink	slunk	slunk
heave	heaved, (*Naut*)	heaved, (*Naut*)	slit	slit	slit
	hove	hove	smell	smelt, smelled	smelt, smelled
hew	hewed	hewed, hewn	smite	smote	smitten
hide	hid	hidden	sow	sowed	sown, sowed
hit	hit	hit	speak	spoke	spoken
hold	held	held	speed	sped, speeded	sped, speeded
hurt	hurt	hurt	spell	spelt, spelled	spelt, spelled
keep	kept	kept	spend	spent	spent
kneel	knelt, kneeled	knelt, kneeled	spill	spilt, spilled	spilt, spilled
know	knew	known	spin	spun	spun
lade	laded	laden	spit	spat	spat
lay	laid	laid	split	split	split
lead	led	led	spoil	spoiled, spoilt	spoiled, spoilt
lean	leant, leaned	leant, leaned	spread	spread	spread
leap	leapt, leaped	leapt, leaped	spring	sprang	sprung
learn	learnt, learned	learnt, learned	stand	stood	stood
leave	left	left	stave	stove, staved	stove, staved
lend	lent	lent	steal	stole	stolen
let	let	let	stick	stuck	stuck
lie (lying)	lay	lain	sting	stung	stung
light	lit, lighted	lit, lighted	stink	stank	stunk
lose	lost	lost	strew	strewed	strewed, strewn
make	made	made	stride	strode	stridden
may	might	—	strike	struck	struck
mean	meant	meant	string	strung	strung
meet	met	met	strive	strove	striven
mistake	mistook	mistaken	swear	swore	sworn
mow	mowed	mown, mowed	sweep	swept	swept
must	(had to)	(had to)	swell	swelled	swollen, swelled
pay	paid	paid	swim	swam	swum
put	put	put	swing	swung	swung
quit	quit, quitted	quit, quitted	take	took	taken
read [ri:d]	read [red]	read [red]	teach	taught	taught
rend	rent	rent	tear	tore	torn
rid	rid	rid	tell	told	told
ride	rode	ridden	think	thought	thought
ring²	rang	rung	thrive	throve, thrived	thriven, thrived
rise	rose	risen	throw	threw	thrown
run	ran	run	thrust	thrust	thrust
saw	sawed	sawed, sawn	tread	trod	trodden
say	said	said	wake	woke, waked	woken, waked
see	saw	seen	wear	wore	worn
seek	sought	sought	weave	wove	woven
sell	sold	sold	weave (= *wind*)	weaved	weaved
send	sent	sent	wed	wedded, wed	wedded, wed
set	set	set	weep	wept	wept
sew	sewed	sewn	win	won	won
shake	shook	shaken	wind²	wound	wound
shave	shaved	shaved, shaven	wring	wrung	wrung
shear	sheared	shorn, sheared	write	wrote	written
shed	shed	shed			

NUMERALS

ZAHLEN

CARDINAL NUMBERS

KARDINAL-ZAHLEN

Notes on the use of cardinal numbers

(a) ***eins** is used in counting or in listing; when 'one' directly replaces a noun, use the declined form.

(b) **one**, and the other numbers ending in one, agree in German with the noun (stated or implied): *ein Mann, eine Frau, (ein)hundert(und)ein Haus.*

(c) To divide thousands and above clearly, a point may be used in German where English places a comma: English 1,000 / German 1.000; English 2,304,770 / German 2.304.770.

Anstelle des im Deutschen zuweilen verwendeten Punktes zur Unterteilung von Zahlen über 1000 verwendet man in Englischen ein Komma: 1,000 statt 1.000 oder 1000, 2,304,770 statt 2.304.770.

nought, zero	0	null
one	1	eins*;
		(m, nt) ein, *(f)* eine
two	2	zwei
three	3	drei
four	4	vier
five	5	fünf
six	6	sechs
seven	7	sieben
eight	8	acht
nine	9	neun
ten	10	zehn
eleven	11	elf
twelve	12	zwölf
thirteen	13	dreizehn
fourteen	14	vierzehn
fifteen	15	fünfzehn
sixteen	16	sechzehn
seventeen	17	siebzehn
eighteen	18	achtzehn
nineteen	19	neunzehn
twenty	20	zwanzig
twenty-one	21	einundzwanzig
twenty-two	22	zweiundzwanzig
twenty-three	23	dreiundzwanzig
thirty	30	dreißig
thirty-one	31	einunddreißig
thirty-two	32	dreiunddreißig
forty	40	vierzig
fifty	50	fünfzig
sixty	60	sechzig
seventy	70	siebzig
eighty	80	achtzig
ninety	90	neunzig
ninety-nine	99	neunundneunzig
a (*or* one) hundred	100	(ein)hundert
a hundred and one	101	(ein)hundert(und)eins; -eine(r, s)
a hundred and two	102	(ein)hundert(und)zwei
a hundred and ten	110	(ein)hundert(und)zehn
a hundred and eighty-two	182	(ein)hundert(und)zweiundachtzig
two hundred	200	zweihundert
two hundred and one	201	zweihundert(und)eins; -eine(r, s)
two hundred and two	202	zweihundert(und)zwei
three hundred	300	dreihundert
four hundred	400	vierhundert
five hundred	500	fünfhundert
six hundred	600	sechshundert
seven hundred	700	siebenhundert
eight hundred	800	achthundert
nine hundred	900	neunhundert
a (*or* one) thousand	1000	(ein)tausend
a thousand and one	1001	(ein)tausend(und)eins, -eine(r, s)
a thousand and two	1002	(ein)tausend(und)zwei
two thousand	2000	zweitausend
ten thousand	10,000	zehntausend
a (*or* one) hundred thousand	100,000	(ein)hunderttausend
a (*or* one) million	1,000,000	eine Million
two million	2,000,000	zwei Millionen

ORDINAL NUMBERS

ORDINAL-ZAHLEN

first	1	erste(r, s)
second	2	zweite(r, s)
third	3	dritte(r, s)
fourth	4	vierte(r, s)
fifth	5	fünfte(r, s)
sixth	6	sechste(r, s)
seventh	7	siebte(r, s)
eighth	8	achte(r, s)
ninth	9	neunte(r, s)
tenth	10	zehnte(r, s)
eleventh	11	elfte(r, s)
twelfth	12	zwölfte(r, s)
thirteenth	13	dreizehnte(r, s)
fourteenth	14	vierzehnte(r, s)
fifteenth	15	fünfzehnte(r, s)
sixteenth	16	sechzehnte(r, s)
seventeenth	17	siebzehnte(r, s)
eighteenth	18	achtzehnte(r, s)
nineteenth	19	neunzehnte(r, s)
twentieth	20	zwanzigste(r, s)
twenty-first	21	einundzwanzigste(r, s)
twenty-second	22	zweiundzwanzigste(r, s)
thirtieth	30	dreißigste(r, s)
thirty-first	31	einunddreißigste(r, s)
fortieth	40	vierzigste(r, s)
fiftieth	50	fünfzigste(r, s)
sixtieth	60	sechzigste(r, s)
seventieth	70	siebzigste(r, s)
eightieth	80	achtzigste(r, s)
ninetieth	90	neunzigste(r, s)
hundredth	100	(ein)hundertste(r, s)
hundred and first	101	(ein)hundert(und)erste(r, s)
hundred and tenth	110	(ein)hundert(und)zehnte(r, s)
two hundredth	200	zweihundertste(r, s)
three hundredth	300	dreihundertste(r, s)
four hundredth	400	vierhundertste(r, s)
five hundredth	500	fünfhundertste(r, s)
six hundredth	600	sechshundertste(r, s)
seven hundredth	700	siebenhundertste(r, s)
eight hundredth	800	achthundertste(r, s)
nine hundredth	900	neunhundertste(r, s)
thousandth	1000	(ein)tausendste(r, s)
two thousandth	2000	zweitausendste(r, s)
millionth	1,000,000	(ein)millionste(r, s)
two millionth	2,000,000	zweimillionste(r, s)

Notes on the use of the ordinal numbers

(**a**) All ordinal numbers agree in German with the noun (stated or implied): *ihr erster Mann, die fünfte Frau, ein zweites Haus.*

(**b**) Abbreviations: English 1st, 2nd, 3rd 4th etc = German 1., 2., 3., 4. and so on.

(**c**) See also notes on dates below.

Siehe ebenfalls die Anmerkungen bezüglich Datum.

FRACTIONS   BRÜCHE

one half, a half	$\frac{1}{2}$	ein halb
one and a half helpings	$1\frac{1}{2}$	eineinhalb *oder* anderthalb Portionen
two and a half kilos	$2\frac{1}{2}$	zweieinhalb Kilo
one third, a third	$\frac{1}{3}$	ein Drittel
two thirds	$\frac{2}{3}$	zwei Drittel
one quarter, a quarter	$\frac{1}{4}$	ein Viertel
three quarters	$\frac{3}{4}$	drei Viertel
one sixth, a sixth	$\frac{1}{6}$	ein Sechstel
five and five sixths	$5\frac{5}{6}$	fünf fünf Sechstel
one twelfth, a twelfth	$\frac{1}{12}$	ein Zwölftel
seven twelfths	$\frac{7}{12}$	sieben Zwölftel
one hundredth, a hundredth	$\frac{1}{100}$	ein Hundertstel
one thousandth, a thousandth	$\frac{1}{1000}$	ein Tausendstel

DECIMALS   DEZIMALZAHLEN

In German, a comma is written where English uses a point: English 3.56 (three point five six) = German 3,56 (drei Komma fünf sechs); English .07 (point nought seven) = German 0,07 (null Komma null sieben). Note that a German number cannot start with *Komma* — *null* must preceed it.

Im Englischen wird anstelle des im Deutschen gebräuchlichen Kommas ein Punkt verwendet: 3.56 (three point five six). Bei Zahlen unter 1 kann die Null vor dem Punkt entfallen: 0.07 (nought point nought seven) oder .07 (point nought seven).

UNITS   EINHEITEN

3,684 is a four digit number It contains 4 units, 8 tens, 6 hundereds and 3 thousands The decimal .234 contains 2 tenths, 3 hundredths and 4 thousandths

3684 ist eine vierstellige Zahl. Sie enthält 4 Einer, 8 Zehner, 6 Hunderter und 3 Tausender. Die Dezimalzahl 0,234 enthält 2 Zehntel, 3 Hundertstel und 4 Tausendstel.

PERCENTAGES   PROZENTZAHLEN

$2\frac{1}{2}\%$ two and a half per cent   *zweieinhalb Prozent*
18% of the people here are over 65   *18% der Leute hier sind über 65*
Production has risen by 8%   *die Produktion ist um 8% gestiegen*

(See also the main text of the dictionary)   *(Siehe ebenfalls die entsprechenden Einträge des Wörterbuchs)*

SIGNS   ZEICHEN

English

+	addition sign, plus sign (*eg* +7 = plus seven)
−	subtraction sign, minus sign (*eg* −3 = minus three)
×	multiplication sign
÷	division sign
$\sqrt{}$	square root sign
∞	infinity
≡	sign of identity, is equal to
=	equals sign
≈	is approximately equal to
≠	sign of inequality, is not equal to
>	is greater than
<	is less than

Deutsch

+	Additions-Zeichen, Plus-Zeichen (*z. B.* +7 = *plus sieben*)
−	Subtraktions-Zeichen, Minus-Zeichen (*z. B.* −3 = *minus drei*)
×	Multiplikations-Zeichen
:	Divisions-Zeichen
$\sqrt{}$	Quadratwurzel-Zeichen
∞	Unendlichkeits-Symbol
≡	Identitäts-Zeichen
=	Gleichheitszeichen, ist gleich
≈	ist ungefähr gleich
≠	Ungleichheitszeichen, ist nicht gleich
>	ist größer als
<	ist kleiner als

CALCULATIONS   RECHNEN

8+6 = 14 eight and (*or* plus) six are (*or* make) fourteen

acht und (oder plus) sechs ist (oder macht oder gleich) vierzehn

15-3 = 12 fifteen take away (*or* minus) three equals twelve, three from fifteen leaves twelve

fünfzehn weniger drei ist (oder macht) zwölf, fünfzehn minus drei gleich zwölf

3×3 = 9 three threes are nine, three times three is nine

drei mal drei ist (oder macht oder gleich) neun

32÷8 = 4 thirty-two divided by (*or* over) eight is (*or* equals) four

zweiunddreißig geteilt durch acht ist (oder macht oder gleich) vier

$3^2 = 9$ three squared is nine

drei hoch zwei ist neun, drei zum Quadrat gleich neun

$2^5 = 32$ two to the fifth (*or* to the power of five) is (*or* equals) thirty two

zwei hoch fünf ist (oder gleich) zweiunddreißig

$\sqrt{16} = 4$ the square root of sixteen is 4

die (Quadrat)wurzel aus sechzehn ist vier

WEIGHTS AND MEASURES

MASSE UND GEWICHTE

METRIC SYSTEM — METRISCHES SYSTEM

deca-	10 times	10-mal	*Deka-*
hecto-	100 times	100-mal	*Hekto-*
kilo-	1000 times	1000-mal	*Kilo-*
deci-	one tenth	ein Zehntel	*Dezi-*
centi-	one hundredth	ein Hundertstel	*Zenti-*
mil(l)i-	one thousandth	ein Tausendstel	*Milli-*

Linear measures — Längenmaße

1 millimetre (Millimeter)	=	0.03937 inch
1 centimetre (Zentimeter)	=	0.3937 inch
1 metre (Meter)	=	39.37 inches
	=	1.094 yards
1 kilometre (Kilometer)	=	0.6214 mile ($\frac{5}{8}$ mile)

Square measures — Flächenmaße

1 square centimetre (Quadratzentimeter)	=	0.155 square inch
1 square metre (Quadratmeter)	=	10.764 square feet
	=	1.196 square yards
1 square kilometre (Quadratkilometer)	=	0.3861 square mile
	=	247.1 acres
1 are (Ar) = 100 square metres	=	119.6 square yards
1 hectare (Hektar) = 100 ares	=	2.471 acres

Cubic measures — Raummaße

1 cubic centimetre (Kubikzentimeter)	=	0.061 cubic inch
1 cubic metre (Kubikmeter)	=	35.315 cubic feet
	=	1.308 cubic yards

Measures of capacity — Hohlmaße

1 litre (Liter) = 1000 cubic centimetres	=	1.76 pints
	=	0.22 gallon

Weights — Gewichte

1 gram (Gramm)	=	15.4 grains
1 kilogram (Kilogramm)	=	2.2046 pounds
1 metric ton (Tonne) = 1000 kilograms	=	0.9842 ton

BRITISH SYSTEM — BRITISCHES SYSTEM

Linear measures — Längenmaße

1 inch (Zoll)	=	2,54 Zentimeter
1 foot (Fuß) = 12 inches	=	30,48 Zentimeter
1 yard (Yard) = 3 feet	=	91,44 Zentimeter
1 furlong = 220 yards	=	201,17 Meter
1 mile (Meile) = 1760 yards	=	1,609 Kilometer

Surveyor's measures — Feldmaße

1 link = 7.92 inches	=	20,12 Zentimeter
1 rod (*or* pole, perch) = 25 links	=	5,029 Meter
1 chain = 22 yards = 4 rods	=	20,12 Meter

Square measures — Flächenmaße

1 square inch (Quadratzoll)	=	6,45 cm²
1 square foot (Quadratfuß) = 144 square inches	=	929,03 cm²
1 square yard (Quadratyard) = 9 square feet	=	0.836 m²
1 square rod - 30.25 square yards	=	25,29 m²
1 acre - 4840 square yards	=	40.47 Ar
1 square mile (Quadratmeile) = 640 acres	=	2,59 km²

Cubic measures — Raummaße

1 cubic inch (Kubikzoll)	=	16,387 cm^3
1 cubic foot (Kubikfuß) = 1728 cubic inches	=	0,028 m^3
1 cubic yard (Kubikyard) = 27 cubic feet	=	0,765 m^3
1 register ton (Registertonne) = 100 cubic feet	=	2,832 m^3

Measures of capacity — Hohlmaße

(a)   Liquid — Flüssigkeitsmaße

1 gill	=	0,142 Liter
1 pint (Pint) = 4 gills	=	0,57 Liter
1 quart = 2 pints	=	1,136 Liter
1 gallon (Gallone) = 4 quarts	=	4,546 Liter

(b)   Dry — Trockenmaße

1 peck = 2 gallons	=	9,087 Liter
1 bushel = 4 pecks	=	36,36 Liter
1 quarter = 8 bushels	=	290,94 Liter

Weights — Avoirdupois system — Handelsgewichte

1 grain (Gran)	=	0,0648 Gramm
1 drachm *or* dram = 27.34 grains	=	1,77 Gramm
1 ounce (Unze) = 16 drachms	=	28,35 Gramm
1 pound (britisches Pfund) = 16 ounces	=	453,6 Gramm
	=	0,453 Kilogramm
1 stone = 14 pounds	=	6,348 Kilogramm
1 quarter = 28 pounds	=	12,7 Kilogramm
1 hundredweight = 112 pounds	=	50,8 Kilogramm
1 ton (Tonne) = 2240 pounds = 20 hundredweight	=	1,016 Kilogramm

US MEASURES — AMERIKANISCHE MASSE

In the US, the same system as that which applies in Great Britain is used for the most part; the main differences are mentioned below:

In den Vereinigten Staaten gilt großenteils dasselbe System wie in Großbritannien; die Hauptunterschiede sind im Folgenden aufgeführt:

Measures of Capacity — Hohlmaße

(a) Liquid — Flüssigkeitsmaße

1 US liquid gill	=	0,118 Liter
1 US liquid pint = 4 gills	=	0,473 Liter
1 US liquid quart = 2 pints	=	0,946 Liter
1 US gallon = 4 quarts	=	3,785 Liter

(b)   Dry — Trockenmaße

1 US dry pint	=	0,550 Liter
1 US dry quart = 2 dry pints	=	1,1 Liter
1 US peck = 8 dry quarts	=	8,81 Liter
1 US bushel = 4 pecks	=	35,24 Liter

Weights — Gewichte

1 hundredweight (*or* short hundredweight) = 100 pounds	=	45,36 Kilogramm
1 ton (*or* short ton) = 2000 pounds = 20 short hundredweights	=	907,18 Kilogramm

TEMPERATURE CONVERSION — TEMPERATURUMRECHNUNG

Fahrenheit — Celsius

Subtract 32 and multiply by 5/9
32 abziehen und mit 5/9 multiplizieren

°F		°C
0		-17.8
32		0
50		10
70		21.1
90		32.2
98.4	≈	37
212		100

Celsius — Fahrenheit

Multiply by 9/5 and add 32
Mit 9/5 multiplizieren und 32 addieren

°C		°F
–10		14
0		32
10		50
20		68
30		86
37	≈	98.4
100		212

TIME

ZEIT

2 hours 33 minutes and 14 seconds	*zwei Stunden, dreiunddreißig Minuten und vierzehn Sekunden*
half an hour	*eine halbe Stunde*
a quarter of an hour	*eine Viertelstunde, eine viertel Stunde*
three quarters of an hour	*eine Dreiviertelstunde*
what's the time?	*wie spät ist es?*
what time do you make it?	*wie spät haben Sie es?*
have you the right time?	*haben Sie die richtige Zeit?*
I make it 2.20	*nach meiner Uhr ist es 2 Uhr 20*
my watch says 3.37	*auf meiner Uhr ist es 3 Uhr 37*
it's 1 o'clock	*es ist ein Uhr*
it's 2 o'clock	*es ist zwei Uhr*
it's 5 past 4	*es ist fünf (Minuten) nach vier*
it's 10 past 6	*es ist zehn (Minuten) nach sechs*
it's half past 8	*es ist halb neun**
it's (a) quarter past 9	*es ist Viertel nach neun*
it's (a) quarter to 2	*es ist Viertel vor zwei*
at 10 a.m.	*um 10 Uhr (morgens)*
at 4 p.m.	*um 4 Uhr nachmittags, um 16 Uhr*
at 11 p.m.	*um 11 Uhr abends, um 23 Uhr*
at exactly 3 o'clock, at 3 sharp, at 3 on the dot	*um Punkt drei Uhr*
the train leaves at 19.32	*der Zug fährt um 19 Uhr 32 ab*
(at) what time does it start?	*um wie viel Uhr fängt es an?*
it is just after 3	*es ist gerade drei (Uhr) vorbei*
it is nearly 9	*es ist fast neun (Uhr)*
about 8 o'clock	*etwa acht Uhr, ungefähr acht Uhr*
at (*or* by) 6 o'clock at the latest	*spätestens um sechs Uhr*
have it ready for 5 o'clock	*es muss bis fünf Uhr fertig sein*
it is full each night from 7 to 9	*es ist jeden Abend von 7 bis 9 Uhr voll*
"closed from 1.30 to 4.30"	*„geschlossen von ein Uhr dreißig bis vier Uhr dreißig"*
until 8 o'clock	*bis acht Uhr*
it would be about 11	*es wäre etwa 11 (Uhr)*
it would have been about 10	*es wäre etwa um zehn (Uhr) gewesen*
at midnight	*um Mitternacht*
before midday, before noon	*vormittags, am Vormittag*

*In German, the half hour is expressed by referring forwards to the next full hour as opposed to backwards to the last full hour as in English.

DATES

DAS DATUM

N.B. The days of the week and the months are written with capitals as in English.

the 1st of July, July 1st	*der 1. Juli*
the 2nd of May, May 2nd	*der 2. Mai*
on June 21st, on the 21st (of) June	*am 21. Juni*
on Monday	*am Montag*
he comes on Mondays	*er kommt montags*
"closed on Fridays"	*„freitags geschlossen"*
he lends it to me from Monday to Friday	*er leiht es mir von Montag bis Freitag*
from the 14th to the 18th	*vom 14. bis (zum) 18.*
what's the date?, what date is it today?	*welches Datum haben wir (heute)?*
today's the 12th	*heute ist der 12.*
one Thursday in October	*an einem Donnerstag im Oktober*
about the 4th of July	*etwa am 4. Juli*
Heading of letters:	*Im Briefkopf:*
19th May 1999	*19. Mai 1999*
1978 nineteen (hundred and) seventy-eight	*neunzehnhundert(und)achtundsiebzig*
4 B.C., B.C. 4	*4 v. Chr.*
70 A.D., A.D. 70	*70 n. Chr.*
in the 13th century	*im 13. Jahrhundert*
in (*or* during) the 1930s	*in den 30er Jahren, während der 30er Jahre*
in 1940 something	*irgendwann in den vierziger Jahren or Vierzigerjahren*
(See also the main text of the dictionary)	*(Siehe ebenfalls die entsprechenden Einträge des Wörterbuchs)*

GERMAN SPELLING REFORM

DEUTSCHE RECHTSCHREIBREFORM

Die deutsche Rechtschreibreform

Am 1. Juli 1996 wurde von allen deutschsprachigen Ländern eine Erklärung zur Neuregelung der deutschen Rechtschreibung unterzeichnet. In den Schulen wird nur noch nach den neuen Regeln unterrichtet. In einer Übergangszeit bis zum Ende des Schuljahrs 2004/05 wird die alte Schreibung nicht als falsch angesehen.

Die Rechtschreibreform betrifft sechs Großbereiche:
- Zuordnung von Laut und Buchstabe
- Getrennt- und Zusammenschreibung
- Schreibung mit Bindestrich
- Groß- und Kleinschreibung
- Zeichensetzung
- Worttrennung am Zeilenende

Zuordnung von Laut und Buchstabe

Die Änderungen betreffen hier sechs Unterbereiche:
- Anpassung der Schreibung an die Herkunft des Wortes
- Anpassung an die Schreibung analoger Laute oder Wörter
- Schreibung von Zusammensetzungen und Ableitungen wie das Grundwort
- Schreibung mit ß und ss entsprechend der Aussprache
- Eindeutschende Schreibung von Fremdwörtern
- Vereinheitlichung der Pluralform von Wörtern, die auf y enden

Bei Wörtern einer Wortfamilie wurde die Schreibung dem Wortstamm angepasst:

ALT/OLD	NEU/NEW	WORTSTAMM/STEM
aufwendig	aufwändig	der Aufwand
behende	behände	die Hand
belemmert	belämmert	das Lamm
Bendel	Bändel	das Band
Gemse	Gämse	die Gams
Greuel	Gräuel	das Grauen
numerieren	nummerieren	die Nummer
plazieren/placieren	platzieren	der Platz
Quentchen	Quäntchen	das Quantum
Schenke	Schenke *oder*: Schänke	ausschenken
	or	der Ausschank
Schlegel (Werkzeug)	Schlägel	schlagen
schneuzen	schnäuzen	die Schnauze
Stengel	Stängel	die Stange
Stukkateur	Stuckateur	der Stuck
überschwenglich	überschwänglich	der Überschwang
verbleuen	verbläuen	blau

In einzelnen Fällen wurde die Schreibung an bestehende Regeln oder ähnliche Fälle angepasst:

ALT/OLD	NEU/NEW	GRUND/REASON
der Mop	der Mopp	*Verdoppelung des Konsonanten nach kurzem Vokal/ doubling of consonant after short vowel sound*
der Tip	der Tipp	*dito/ditto*
Step tanzen	Stepp tanzen	*dito/ditto*
der Tolpatsch	der Tollpatsch	*dito/ditto*
der Karamel	der Karamell	*wie/like*: die Karamelle
das Känguruh	das Känguru	*wie/like*: das Gnu
rauh	rau	*wie/like*: grau, blau
der Alptraum	der Albtraum	

Bei Zusammensetzungen und Ableitungen wird die Schreibung des Grundwortes beibehalten:

The German spelling reform

On 1 July 1996, a declaration concerning the reform of German spelling rules was signed by all German-speaking countries. From 1 April 1998, only the new spelling rules will be taught. For a transitional period lasting until the end of the 2004/05 school year, the old way of spelling will not be regarded as incorrect.

The reform of spelling rules affects six main areas:
- Sound/letter correlation
- Writing words separately or as one word
- Hyphenation
- Capitalization
- Punctuation
- End-of-line division

Sound/letter correlation

Here, the changes affect six sub-sections:
- Adapting spelling to the origin of a word
- Adapting to the way analogous sounds or words are spelt
- Spelling of compound nouns and derivatives in accordance with the stem
- Spelling with ß and ss in accordance with pronunciation
- Germanized spelling of foreign words
- Standardizing the plural form of words ending in y

With words belonging to the same family, spelling has been adapted to that of the stem:

In individual cases, spelling has been adapted to existing rules or similar cases:

In compound nouns and derivatives, the spelling of the stem has been retained:

ALT/OLD	NEU/NEW
Kontrollampe	Kontrolllampe
Schiffahrt	Schifffahrt
hellicht	helllicht
Roheit	Rohheit
Zäheit	Zähheit
Zierat	Zierrat
selbständig	selbstständig

Das **ß** wird zu **ss** nach kurzem Vokal:

after a short vowel sound, **ß** becomes **ss**:

der Kuss, die Küsse
der Fluss, die Flüsse
wässrig
er muss
dass

Das **ß** bleibt bestehen nach langem Vokal oder Doppellaut:

After a long vowel sound or diphthong, **ß** remains unchanged:

der Fuß, die Füße
das Maß, die Maße
er heißt
draußen

Bei Fremdwörtern wurde eine Angleichung an die deutsche Schreibung vorgenommen, wenn diese sich bereits anbahnte, vor allem bei der Schreibung von **ph** in Verbindungen mit **phon**, **phot** und **graph**, z. B.:

Foreign words have been brought into line with German spelling if this trend was already beginning to develop. This applies especially to the spelling of **ph** in compounds with **phon**, **phot** and **graph**. For example:

quadrofon, Fotograf, Paragraf

In allen Fällen der eindeutschenden Schreibweise ist auch die andere Schreibweise als Variante zugelassen:

In all cases of Germanized spelling, the alternative spelling is also permissible:

-tiell	or	-ziell	essentiell	or	essenziell,
			potentiell	or	potenziell
-tial	or	-zial	Differential	or	Differenzial
			Potential	or	Potenzial
ai	or	ä	Mayonnaise	or	Majonäse,
			Necessaire	or	Nessessär
é	or	ee	Pappmaché	or	Pappmaschee,
			Exposé	or	Exposee
gh	or	g	Joghurt	or	Jogurt,
			Spaghetti	or	Spagetti
c	or	ss	Facette	or	Fassette,
			Necessaire	or	Nessessär
ch	or	sch	Ketchup	or	Ketschup,
			Chicorée	or	Schikoree
th	or	t	Thunfisch	or	Tunfisch,
			Panther	or	Panter

Der Plural von Wörtern, die aus dem Englischen stammen und auf **y** enden, wird jetzt einheitlich mit **ys** geschrieben, z. B.:

The plural of all words deriving from English and ending in **y** will now be written **ys**. For example:

die Buggys, die Ladys, die Partys, die Hobbys

Getrennt- und Zusammenschreibung

One word or two?

Verbindungen von **Substantiv und Verb** werden getrennt geschrieben, z. B.:

Noun and verb combinations are written separately. For example:

Ski fahren, Eis laufen, Halt machen,
Blut saugend, Pflanzen fressend

Aber: Zusammengesetzte Verben, die fast nur im Infinitiv oder Partizip gebraucht werden, schreibt man zusammen:

But: compound verbs which are almost exclusively used in the infinitive or as participles are written as one word:

bauchreden, bergsteigen, brustschwimmen,
kopfrechnen, seiltanzen, sonnenbaden

Verbindungen von **Infinitiv und Verb** werden getrennt geschrieben:

Infinitive and verb combinations are written separately:

kennen lernen, sitzen bleiben, spazieren gehen

Verbindungen von **Partizip und Verb** werden getrennt geschrieben, z. B.:

Participle and verb combinations are written separately. For example:

gefangen nehmen, geschenkt bekommen

Verbindungen von **Adjektiv/Adverb und Verb** werden zusammengeschrieben, wenn der erste Bestandteil als Wort nicht vorkommt, z. B.:

Adjective/adverb and verb combinations are written as one word if the first component of the compound is not a word in its own right. For example:

fehlschlagen, kundgeben, weismachen

oder wenn der erste Bestandteil nicht erweiterbar oder steigerbar ist, z. B.:

or if the first component of the compound cannot be qualified or compared. For example:

bereithalten, fernsehen, hochrechnen,
schwarzarbeiten, totschlagen

Verbindungen von **Adjektiv und Verb** werden getrennt geschrieben, wenn das Adjektiv erweiterbar oder steigerbar ist, wobei die Verneinung als Erweiterung gilt, z. B.:

Adjective and verb combinations are written separately if the adjective can be qualified or compared (in this case, negation counts as a qualification). For example:

bekannt machen, genau nehmen,
kurz treten, nahe bringen

Verbindungen von **Adverb und Verb** werden getrennt geschrieben, wenn das Adverb zusammengesetzt ist, z. B.:

Adverb and verb combinations are written separately if the adverb is a compound word. For example:

abhanden kommen, beiseite legen,
überhand nehmen, zunichte machen

Verbverbindungen mit **-ander** werden getrennt geschrieben, z. B.:

Verb combinations with **-ander** are written separately. For example:

aneinander legen, aufeinander schichten, auseinander laufen,
beieinander bleiben, durcheinander reden, zueinander finden

Verbverbindungen mit **-seits** und **-wärts** werden getrennt geschrieben, z. B.:

Verb combinations with **-seits** and **-wärts** are written separately. For example:

abseits stehen, abwärts gehen,
aufwärts streben, vorwärts blicken

Verbverbindungen mit einer Ableitung, die auf **-ig**, **-isch** und **-lich** enden, werden getrennt geschrieben, z. B.:

Verb combinations with a derivative ending in **-ig**, **-isch** and **-lich** are written separately. For example:

lästig fallen, übrig bleiben,
kritisch denken, freundlich grüßen

Verbverbindungen mit **sein** werden getrennt geschrieben, z. B.:

Verb combinations with **sein** are written separately. For example:

beisammen sein, fertig sein, zusammen sein

Verbindungen mit **viel** werden getrennt geschrieben, z. B.:

Combinations with **viel** are written separately. For example:

so viel Geld; Wie viel kostet das?
Wie viel Uhr ist es?

Verbindungen mit **irgend** werden zusammengeschrieben, z. B.:

Combinations with irgend are written as one word. For example:

irgendetwas, irgendjemand

Schreibung mit Bindestrich

Der Bindestrich kann verstärkt dazu verwendet werden, Zusammenschreibungen zu gliedern und leichter lesbar zu machen, besonders beim Zusammentreffen von drei gleichen Konsonanten, z. B.:

Hyphenation

Hyphens may now be used more frequently in order to break up compound words and make them easier to read, especially when the same consonant is repeated three times. For example:

Essstäbchen *oder/or* Ess-Stäbchen

oder bei substantivischen Aneinanderreihungen, z. B.:

or where a number of words have been put together to form a noun. For example:

das Auf-die-lange-Bank-Schieben

Man setzt den Bindestrich immer in Zusammensetzungen

mit Einzelbuchstaben, Abkürzungen oder Ziffern, z. B.:

Where compounds have single letters, abbreviations or figures as a component part, hyphens are always used. For example:

T-Träger, x-te, Kfz-Versicherung, VIP-Lounge, Lungen-Tbc,
100-prozentig, 2/3-Mehrheit, 18-jährig, 2-Pfünder

Der Bindestrich wird auch bei Zusammensetzungen mit Eigennamen verwendet, z. B.:

Hyphens are also used in compounds containing proper nouns. For example:

Foto-Bauer, rheinland-pfälzisch, Heinrich-Heine-Straße,
Schiller-Ausgabe, Moskau-freundlich

Groß- und Kleinschreibung

Capitalization

Substantive werden groß geschrieben. Der Gebrauch des Artikels ist das grundlegende formale Erkennungsmerkmal eines Substantivs, z. B.:

Nouns are written with a capital. The basic formal characteristic of a noun is that it is used with an article. For example:

das Schwimmen, das Wenn und Aber, im Voraus,
im Dunkeln tappen, heute Abend, morgen Mittag

In Verbindung mit **einer Präposition oder einem Verb** werden Substantive groß geschrieben, z. B.:

Nouns are written with a capital in combinations with **a preposition or a verb**. For example:

in Bezug auf,
Maß halten, Maschine schreiben, Rad fahren

Nur in Verbindung mit **sein**, **bleiben** und **werden** schreibt man Angst, Bange, Leid, Pleite und Schuld klein. In Verbindung mit anderen Verben wird groß geschrieben, z. B.:

Only in combination with **sein**, **bleiben** and **werden** are Angst, Bange, Leid, Pleite and Schuld written with a small letter. They are written with a capital letter when combined with other verbs. For example:

Ich habe Angst.	Mir wurde angst und bange.
Du willst mir wohl Bange machen.	Mir ist bange ums Herz.
Er tut mir Leid.	Ich bin es leid.
Seine Firma ist Pleite gegangen.	Seine Firma ist pleite geblieben.
Er hat Schuld daran.	Er ist schuld daran.

Adjektive, die als Ordnungszahlen benutzt werden und unbestimmte Zahladjektive werden groß geschrieben, z. B.:

Adjectives used as ordinals and indefinite adjectives of number are written with a capital. For example:

der Erste, das Letzte, der Nächste, der Einzelne,
das Ganze, Verschiedenes, alles Mögliche

Adjektive in bestimmten festen Verbindungen werden groß geschrieben, z. B.:

In certain fixed idioms, **adjectives** are written with a capital. For example:

im Großen und Ganzen, im Klaren, des Weiteren,
das Beste, den Kürzeren ziehen

Farben und **Sprachen** in Verbindung mit Präpositionen werden groß geschrieben, z. B.:

When combined with prepositions, **colours** and **languages** are written with a capital. For example:

in Weiß, bei Gelb, auf Russisch, in Deutsch

Adjektive, die in Paaren zur Bezeichnung von Menschen auftreten, werden groß geschrieben, z. B.:

Adjectives used in pairs to describe people are written with a capital. For example:

Jung und Alt, Arm und Reich

Bei **Superlativen** mit aufs ist sowohl Groß- als auch Kleinschreibung möglich, z. B.:

Superlatives with "aufs" can be written with or without a capital. For example:

aufs Schönste *oder/or* aufs schönste,
aufs Freundlichste *oder/or* aufs freundlichste

Bei festen Verbindungen von **Adjektiv und Substantiv** wird das Adjektiv klein geschrieben, z. B.:

In idiomatic **adjective/noun** combinations, the adjective is written with a small letter. For example:

das schwarze Brett, die erste Hilfe,
der goldene Schnitt, das große Los

Groß geschrieben wird das **Adjektiv**, wenn es sich um einen Eigennamen, einen Titel, eine Benennung oder eine Bezeichnung aus der Biologie handelt, z. B.:

Adjectives are written with a capital if they are proper names, titles, designations or names from biology. For example:

die Vereinten Nationen, der Regierende Bürgermeister,
der Stille Ozean, der Große Bär, Rote Bete, der Schwarze Milan

Groß geschrieben werden auch bestimmte Kalendertage, religiöse Handlungen und Institutionen, historische Ereignisse, z. B.:

Certain days in the calendar, religious acts and institutions, historical events are written with a capital letter. For example:

der Heilige Abend, die Letzte Ölung,
der Heilige Stuhl, der Dreißigjährige Krieg

Klein geschrieben werden **Ableitungen** von Eigennamen auf **-(i)sch**, z. B.:

Derivatives from proper names ending in **-(i)sch** are written with a small letter. For example:

die brechtschen Dramen, die goethische Farbenlehre,
das ohmsche Gesetz

Die **Anredeformen** „du" und „ihr" und die dazugehörigen Formen werden auch in Briefen klein geschrieben, z. B.:

The **forms of address** "du" and "ihr", as well as all the forms belonging to them, are written with a small letter, even in correspondence. For example:

Liebe Grüße, deine Veronika.
Wenn ihr uns besuchen kommt, bringt eure Kinder mit.

Die Höflichkeitsform „Sie" und die dazugehörigen Formen werden weiterhin groß geschrieben, z. B.:

The polite form of address "Sie", as well as all the forms belonging to it, is still written with a capital letter. For example:

Wenn Sie uns besuchen, bringen Sie Ihre Kinder mit.

Zeichensetzung

Bei der Zeichensetzung wird dem Schreibenden größere Freiheit eingeräumt, Sätze durch Kommas zu gliedern. Die meisten der bisherigen Regeln entfallen. Bei Hauptsätzen, die mit „und" oder „oder" verbunden sind, muss kein Komma mehr stehen, z. B.:

Punctuation

As concerns punctuation, the writer has now been given greater freedom to break up sentences with commas. Most of the rules which applied formerly have now been abandoned. There is no longer any need for a comma where main clauses are joined by "und" or "oder". For example:

Die Party war zu Ende und alle sind gegangen.

Worttrennung am Zeilenende

Die bisherige Regel, dass man „st" nicht trennen darf, entfällt, z. B.:

End-of-line division

The rule whereby "st" must not be divided no longer applies. For example:

Kis-te, Bürs-te, Plas-tik

Das „ck" wird nicht mehr in „k-k" umgewandelt, sondern bei der Trennung zusammen auf die nächste Zeile genommen, z. B.:

"ck" has no longer to be changed into "k-k", but is left together and taken over to the next line. For example:

Bä-cker, le-cken, Bli-cke, Zu-cker

Zusammengesetzte Wörter und Wörter mit einer Vorsilbe werden nach ihren Bestandteilen getrennt, z. B.:

Compound words and words with a prefix are divided according to their component parts. For example:

Klebe-streifen, Donners-tag,
ab-ändern, ent-eignen, ver-öden

Das gilt auch für Fremdwörter und geografische Namen, z. B.:

This rule also applies to foreign words and geographical names. For example:

des-illusionieren, in-akzeptabel,
Pro-gramm, trans-alpin, Neu-strelitz, West-indien

Wird ein Wort nicht mehr als Zusammensetzung erkannt oder empfunden, so kann auch nach Sprechsilben getrennt werden, z. B.:

If a word is no longer felt to be, or can no longer be recognized as, a compound, then it can also be divided phonetically. For example:

da-rüber, he-runter, wa-rum, ei-nander

Das gilt auch für Fremdwörter, wenn die Herkunft nicht mehr empfunden wird, z. B.:

This also applies to foreign words if their origin is no longer obvious. For example:

Chi-rurg	*bisher/previously*	Chir-urg
Helikop-ter	*bisher/previously*	Heliko-pter
Hyd-rant	*bisher/previously*	Hy-drant
Inte-resse	*bisher/previously*	Inter-esse
mak-robiotisch	*bisher/previously*	ma-krobiotisch

Einzelne Buchstaben dürfen abgetrennt werden, z. B.:

Single letters can be divided off. For example:

a-ber, E-he, I-dee, O-fen, U-ni

Die Durchführung der Reform im Wörterbuch

Die vorliegende Auflage wurde komplett nach den Regeln der neuen Schreibung überarbeitet.

Im deutsch-englischen Teil wurden Stichwörter bei der neuen Schreibung abgehandelt, wobei die alte Schreibung erhalten wurde und zur neuen verwiesen wird. Neue Schreibungen sind mit ▲ bezeichnet und Schreibungen, die nach der Übergangszeit als nicht mehr korrekt gelten, sind mit △ bezeichnet. Bei alternativen Schreibweisen, in denen die alte Schreibung nach wie vor zulässig ist, wird die neue bezeichnet, nicht aber die alte.

Keinen Hinweis auf die alte Schreibung findet man in den Fällen, in denen ein Wort früher mit ß, nun mit ss geschrieben wird. Das Zeichen ▲ bedeutet in diesem Fall, dass das Wort früher mit ß geschrieben wurde (z. B. **Kuss**, früher: **Kuß**).

Wörter, bei denen früher bei einer Häufung von drei gleichen Konsonanten einer wegfiel (z. B. **Betttuch**, früher: **Bettuch**), werden an dem Ort der neuen Schreibung aufgeführt und mit einem ▲ bezeichnet. Sie werden außerdem am Ort der alten Schreibweise aufgeführt, wo sie mit einem △ bezeichnet sind und zur neuen Schreibung verwiesen werden. In den Fällen, in denen sich alte und neue Schreibung am gleichen alphabetischen Ort befinden, wird auf die Angabe der alten Form verzichtet.

Die Schreibung von **-graf** und **-grafie** wurde zugunsten der Schreibung mit **f** vereinheitlicht und mit ▲ gekennzeichnet, wobei darauf verzichtet wurde, die Schreibung mit **ph** aufzuführen, wenn sie alphabetisch am gleichen Ort stünde. Eine Schreibung mit **ph** ist in all diesen Fällen zulässig.

Bei Kompositastichwörtern, die nur zum Teil von der neuen Schreibung betroffen sind, wird hierauf mit ▲ aufmerksam gemacht. Die alte Schreibweise wird nicht gesondert angegeben.

Stichwörter, die früher zusammengeschrieben wurden, nun aber getrennt geschrieben werden, sind am Ort des zusammengeschriebenen Stichworts aufgefürt. In den Fällen, in denen es sich um ein Verb handelt (z. B. **schief gehen**), wurden die Stichwörter in der neuen Getrenntschreibung am Ort der alten Schreibung gelassen und mit einem ▲ markiert. Bei Adjektiv- und Adverbfügungen (z. B. **klar denkend**) und Substantiv-Verb-Fügungen (z. B. **Kopf stehen**) wird der Ausdruck beim Eintrag des ersten Wortes abgehandelt, die alte Schreibung am entsprechenden Ort beibehalten und mit △ bezeichnet. Zusätzlich wird der Benutzer an den Ort verwiesen, an dem die Fügung abgehandelt ist.

Im englisch-deutschen Teil werden die deutschen Entsprechungen in der reformierten Schreibweise gegeben. Die veraltete Form wird nicht aufgeführt. Alternative Schreibweisen werden in den Fällen aufgeführt, in denen beide Schreibweisen gleichwertige Gültigkeit haben.

In beiden Teilen des Wörterbuchs wird in Beispielsätzen die Zeichensetzung nach den neuen Regeln gehandhabt.

Die Worttrennung deutscher Wörter ist durchgängig bei allen Stichwörtern im deutsch-englischen Teil mit einem Haarstrich an der entsprechenden Stelle im Stichwort angegeben. Auf eine Angabe von alternativen Trennmöglichkeiten wurde verzichtet und die reformierte Variante bevorzugt.

Implementation of the spelling reform in the Dictionary

The current edition has been completely revised according to the new spelling reform rules.

On the German-English side headwords have been treated using the new spelling, whilst the old spelling has been retained and cross-referenced to the new version. New spellings are marked with ▲ and spellings which are no longer valid after the transitional period are marked with △. Where alternative spellings are given and the old spelling is still permissible, the new version is marked, but not the old one.

There is no reference to the old spelling in cases where a word was previously spelt with ß and is now written with ss. The ▲ sign means that the word was previously written with ß in this case (eg **Kuss**, formerly: **Kuß**).

Words in which the same consonant appears three times in a row previously had one of these omitted (eg **Betttuch**, formerly: **Bettuch**) — these words are now listed under the new spelling and marked with ▲. In addition they can be found under the old spelling, where they are marked with △ and cross-referenced to the new version. In cases where the old and new spellings have the same alphabetical position in the dictionary, the old form is dispensed with completely.

The spelling of words with **-graf** and **-grafie** has been standardized using the **f** spelling and labelled with ▲, but where the **f** and **ph** spellings would have appeared in the same position alphabetically the **ph** spelling is not listed. The **ph** spelling is however permissible in all of these cases.

Attention is drawn to those compound headwords where the spelling reform affects only the first part of the compound by use of the ▲ symbol. The old spelling is not listed for each individual headword.

Headwords which were previously written as one word, but are now two separate words, are still listed at the same alphabetical position as the old spelling. In the case of verb entries (eg **schief gehen**), the new two-word spellings are also still found at the same alphabetical position as the old spelling and are labelled with ▲. With adjective/adverb combinations (eg **klar denkend**) and noun/verb combinations (eg **Kopf stehen**) the expression is treated at the entry for the first word; the old spelling is retained at the appropriate place and labelled △. In addition, the user is given a cross reference to the place where the combined construction is treated.

On the English-German side only the reformed German spellings are given — the old versions are not listed. Alternative spellings are listed only in those cases where both spellings are equally valid.

On both sides of the dictionary the punctuation used in the example phrases follows the new rules.

The hyphenation of each German word is shown at every headword on the German-English side by use of a hairline at the appropriate point in the headword. It was decided to give preference to the reformed version and not to point out alternative possibilities for splitting words.

Alphabetisches Wörterverzeichnis

Das folgende Verzeichnis enthält Stichwörter dieses Wörterbuchs in ihrer alten und neuen Schreibweise, wobei der Schwerpunkt auf den Hauptbereichen der Rechtschreibreform (Zuordnung von Laut und Buchstabe, Getrennt- und Zusammenschreibung) liegt.

Alphabetical wordlist

The following wordlist contains headwords found in the dictionary and shows both their old and new spellings, with the emphasis on the main areas affected by the spelling reform (word/letter correlation, one/two word spellings).

ALT/OLD	NEU/NEW
Abdroßlung	Abdrosslung
abend	Abend
Abfluß	Abfluss
Abflußgraben	Abflussgraben
Abflußhahn	Abflusshahn
Abflußrinne	Abflussrinne
Abflußrohr	Abflussrohr
abgrundhäßlich	abgrundhässlich
Abguß	Abguss
Ablaß	Ablass
Ablaßbrief	Ablassbrief
Ablaßhandel	Ablasshandel
Ablaßventil	Ablassventil
Abriß	Abriss
Abrißarbeiten	Abrissarbeiten
Abrißbirne	Abrissbirne
Abrißliste	Abrissliste
abrißreif	abrissreif
Abschiedskuß	Abschiedskuss
Abschluß	Abschluss
Abschlußball	Abschlussball
Abschlußfeier	Abschlussfeier
Abschlußklasse	Abschlussklasse
Abschlußkommuniqué	Abschlusskommuniqué or Abschlusskommunikee
Abschlußprüfung	Abschlussprüfung
Abschlußrechnung	Abschlussrechnung
Abschlußzeugnis	Abschlusszeugnis
Abschuß	Abschuss
Abschußbasis	Abschussbasis
Abschußliste	Abschussliste
Abschußrampe	Abschussrampe
absein	ab sein
Abszeß	Abszess
Abtreibungsparagraph	Abtreibungsparagraph or Abtreibungsparagraf
abwärtsgehen	abwärts gehen
achtunggebietend	Achtung gebietend
ackerbautreibend	Ackerbau treibend
Aderlaß	Aderlass
Adhäsionsverschluß	Adhäsionsverschluss
Adreßbuch	Adressbuch
Ahnenpaß	Ahnenpass
Aktionsausschuß	Aktionsausschuss
Alkoholeinfluß	Alkoholeinfluss
Alkoholgenuß	Alkoholgenuss
Alkoholmißbrauch	Alkoholmissbrauch
alleinerziehend	allein erziehend
Alleinerziehende(r)	Alleinerziehende(r) or allein Erziehende(r)
alleinseligmachend	allein selig machend
alleinstehend	allein stehend
Alleinstehende(r)	Alleinstehende(r) or allein Stehende(r)
allgemeinbildend	allgemein bildend
allgemeingültig	allgemein gültig
allgemeinverbindlich	allgemein verbindlich
allgemeinverständlich	allgemein verständlich
allzufrüh	allzu früh
allzugern	allzu gern
allzusehr	allzu sehr
allzuviel	allzu viel
Alp (2)	Alp or Alb
Alpdruck	Alpdruck or Albdruck
Alpenpaß	Alpenpass
alphanumerisch	alphanumerisch
Alptraum	Alptraum or Albtraum
alptraumartig	alptraumartig or albtraumartig
Altersprozeß	Altersprozess
Amboß	Amboss
Amtsmißbrauch	Amtsmissbrauch
Analogieschluß	Analogieschluss
andersdenkend	anders denkend
Andersdenkende(r)	Andersdenkende(r) or anders Denkende(r)

ALT/OLD	NEU/NEW
andersgeartet	anders geartet
andersgesinnt	anders gesinnt
andersgläubig	anders gläubig
anderslautend	anders lautend
aneinanderbauen	aneinander bauen
aneinanderfügen	aneinander fügen
aneinandergeraten	aneinander geraten
aneinandergrenzen	aneinander grenzen
aneinanderhalten	aneinander halten
aneinanderhängen	aneinander hängen
aneinanderkleben	aneinander kleben
aneinanderkoppeln	aneinander koppeln
aneinanderlehnen	aneinander lehnen
aneinanderliegen	aneinander liegen
aneinanderprallen	aneinander prallen
aneinanderreihen	aneinander reihen
aneinanderschmieden	aneinander schmieden
aneinanderschmiegen	aneinander schmiegen
aneinandersetzen	aneinander setzen
aneinanderstellen	aneinander stellen
aneinanderstoßen	aneinander stoßen
angepaßt	angepasst
Angepaßtheit	Angepasstheit
Anlaß	Anlass
anläßlich	anlässlich
Annahmeschluß	Annahmeschluss
anrauhen	anrauen
Anriß	Anriss
Anschiß	Anschiss
Anschluß	Anschluss
Anschlußdose	Anschlussdose
anschlußfertig	anschlussfertig
Anschlußfinanzierung	Anschlussfinanzierung
Anschlußflug	Anschlussflug
Anschlußnummer	Anschlussnummer
Anschlußrohr	Anschlussrohr
Anschlußschnur	Anschlussschnur or Anschluss-Schnur
Anschlußstelle	Anschlussstelle or Anschluss-Stelle
Anschlußzug	Anschlusszug
ansein	an sein
arbeitsaufwendig	arbeitsaufwändig
Arbeitsausschuß	Arbeitsausschuss
Arbeitsprozeß	Arbeitsprozess
Arbeitsschluß	Arbeitsschluss
arbeitsuchend	Arbeit suchend
Arbeitsuchende(r)	Arbeitsuchende(r) or Arbeit Suchende(r)
Arierparagraph	Arierparagraph or Arierparagraf
Armvoll	Arm voll
Artilleriebeschuß	Artilleriebeschuss
Arzneimittelmißbrauch	Arzneimittelmissbrauch
Aß	Ass
Aschantinuß	Aschantinuss
Asylsuchende(r)	Asylsuchende(r) or Asyl Suchende(r)
auf daß	auf dass
Aufbeßrung	Aufbessrung
aufeinanderbeißen	aufeinander beißen
aufeinanderdrücken	aufeinander drücken
aufeinanderfahren	aufeinander fahren
aufeinanderfolgen	aufeinander folgen
aufeinanderfolgend	aufeinander folgend
aufeinanderhängen	aufeinander hängen
aufeinanderhetzen	aufeinander hetzen
aufeinanderhocken	aufeinander hocken
aufeinanderknallen	aufeinander knallen
aufeinanderlegen	aufeinander legen
aufeinanderliegen	aufeinander liegen
aufeinanderpassen	aufeinander passen
aufeinanderprallen	aufeinander prallen
aufeinanderpressen	aufeinander pressen
aufeinanderrasen	aufeinander rasen
aufeinanderschichten	aufeinander schichten
aufeinanderschlagen	aufeinander schlagen

ALT/OLD	NEU/NEW	ALT/OLD	NEU/NEW
aufeinandersetzen	aufeinander setzen	baß	bass
aufeinandersitzen	aufeinander sitzen	Baß	Bass
aufeinanderstellen	aufeinander stellen	Baßbariton	Bassbariton
aufeinanderstoßen	aufeinander stoßen	Baßgeige	Bassgeige
aufeinandertreffen	aufeinander treffen	Baßklarinette	Bassklarinette
aufeinandertürmen	aufeinander türmen	Baßpartie	Basspartie
Aufguß	Aufguss	Baßsänger	Basssänger or Bass-Sänger
Aufgußbeutel	Aufgussbeutel	Baßschlüssel	Bassschlüssel or Bass-Schlüssel
aufrauhen	aufrauen	Baßstimme	Bassstimme or Bass-Stimme
Aufriß	Aufriss	Bauchschuß	Bauchschuss
Aufrißzeichnung	Aufrisszeichnung	Baukostenzuschuß	Baukostenzuschuss
Aufschluß	Aufschluss	beeinflußbar	beeinflussbar
Aufschlüßlung	Aufschlüsslung	befliß	befliss
aufschlußreich	aufschlussreich	Begrüßungskuß	Begrüssungskuss
aufsehenerregend	Aufsehen erregend	beieinanderhaben	beieinander haben
aufsein	auf sein	beieinanderhalten	beieinander halten
aufsichtführend	Aufsicht führend	beieinandersein	beieinander sein
Aufsichtführende(r)	Aufsichtführende(r) or	beifallheischend	Beifall heischend
	Aufsicht Führende(r)	beifallspendend	Beifall spendend
aufwärtsgehen	aufwärts gehen	beisammensein	beisammen sein
aufwendig	aufwendig or aufwändig	Beischluß	Beischluss
auseinanderbekommen	auseinander bekommen	bekanntgeben	bekannt geben
auseinanderbiegen	auseinander biegen	bekanntmachen	bekannt machen
auseinanderbrechen	auseinander brechen	bekanntwerden	bekannt werden
auseinanderbreiten	auseinander breiten	Beleidigungsprozeß	Beleidigungsprozess
auseinanderbringen	auseinander bringen	belemmert	belämmert
auseinanderdividieren	auseinander dividieren	Bendel	Bändel
auseinanderdriften	auseinander driften	bergeversetzend	Berge versetzend
auseinanderentwickeln	auseinander entwickeln	Berufungsausschuß	Berufungsausschuss
auseinanderfallen	auseinander fallen	Beschiß	Beschiss
auseinanderfalten	auseinander falten	Beschluß	Beschluss
auseinanderfliegen	auseinander fliegen	beschlußfähig	beschlussfähig
auseinanderfließen	auseinander fließen	Beschlußfähigkeit	Beschlussfähigkeit
auseinandergehen	auseinander gehen	Beschlußfassung	Beschlussfassung
auseinanderhalten	auseinander halten	Beschlußrecht	Beschlussrecht
auseinanderjagen	auseinander jagen	beschlußreif	beschlussreif
auseinanderkennen	auseinander kennen	beschlußunfähig	beschlussunfähig
auseinanderklaffen	auseinander klaffen	Beschuß	Beschuss
auseinanderklamüsern	auseinander klamüsern	bestehenbleiben	bestehen bleiben
auseinanderklauben	auseinander klauben	bestehenlassen	bestehen lassen
auseinanderkriegen	auseinander kriegen	Bestelliste	Bestellliste or Bestell-Liste
auseinanderlaufen	auseinander laufen	bestgehaßt	bestgehasst
auseinanderleben	auseinander leben	bestußt	bestusst
auseinandermachen	auseinander machen	Betelnuß	Betelnuss
auseinandernehmen	auseinander nehmen	betreßt	betresst
auseinanderpflücken	auseinander pflücken	Betriebsschluß	Betriebsschluss
auseinanderreißen	auseinander reißen	Bettuch	Betttuch or Bett-Tuch
auseinanderschlagen	auseinander schlagen	bewußt	bewusst
auseinanderschrauben	auseinander schrauben	Bewußtheit	Bewusstheit
auseinandersetzen	auseinander setzen	bewußtlos	bewusstlos
auseinanderspreizen	auseinander spreizen	Bewußtlose(r)	Bewusstlose(r)
auseinandersprengen	auseinander sprengen	Bewußtlosigkeit	Bewusstlosigkeit
auseinanderspringen	auseinander springen	bewußtmachen	bewusstmachen
auseinanderstieben	auseinander stieben	bewußtmachen	bewußt machen
auseinanderstreben	auseinander streben	Bewußtsein	Bewusstsein
auseinandertreiben	auseinander treiben	Bewußtseinsbildung	Bewusstseinsbildung
auseinanderziehen	auseinander ziehen	bewußtseinserweiternd	bewusstseinserweiternd
außerstande	außerstande or außer Stande	Bewußtseinserweiterung	Bewusstseinserweiterung
Ausfluß	Ausfluss	Bewußtseinsinhalt	Bewusstseinsinhalt
Ausfuhrüberschuß	Ausfuhrüberschuss	Bewußtseinskunst	Bewusstseinskunst
Ausguß	Ausguss	Bewußtseinslage	Bewusstseinslage
Ausleseprozeß	Ausleseprozess	Bewußtseinslenkung	Bewusstseinslenkung
Ausschluß	Ausschluss	Bewußtseinsschwelle	Bewusstseinsschwelle
Ausschuß	Ausschuss	Bewußtseinsspaltung	Bewusstseinsspaltung
Ausschußmitglied	Ausschussmitglied	Bewußtseinsstörung	Bewusstseinsstörung
Ausschußöffnung	Ausschussöffnung	Bewußtseinsstrom	Bewusstseinsstrom
Ausschußsitzung	Ausschusssitzung or Ausschuss-Sitzung	Bewußtseinstrübung	Bewusstseinstrübung
Ausschußware	Ausschussware	bewußtseinsverändernd	bewusstseinsverändernd
aussein	aus sein	Bewußtseinsveränderung	Bewusstseinsveränderung
Autobiograph	Autobiograph or Autobiograf	Bewußtwerdung	Bewusstwerdung
Autobiographie	Autobiographie or Autobiografie	bezug	Bezug
autobiographisch	autobiographisch or autobiografisch	Bibliograph	Bibliograph or Bibliograf
Autograph	Autograph or Autograf	Bibliographie	Bibliographie or Bibliografie
		bibliographieren	bibliographieren or bibliografieren
		bibliographisch	bibliographisch or bibliografisch
B		Bierbaß	Bierbass
Bahnanschluß	Bahnanschluss	Bierfaß	Bierfass
Bajonettverschluß	Bajonettverschluss	Biograph	Biograph or Biograf
Ballettänzer	Balletttänzer or Ballett-Tänzer	Biographie	Biographie or Biografie
Bänderriß	Bänderriss	biographisch	biographisch or biografisch
Baroneß	Baroness		

ALT/OLD	NEU/NEW
biß	biss
Biß	Biss
bißchen	bisschen
Bißchen	Bisschen
Bißwunde	Bisswunde
blanchieren	blanchieren or blanschieren
blankgewetzt	blank gewetzt
blankpoliert	blank poliert
blaß	blass
blaß-	blass-
Blasenkatarrh	Blasenkatarrh or Blasenkatarr
Bläßhuhn	Blässhuhn
bläßlich	blässlich
Blattschuß	Blattschuss
Blattstengel	Blattstängel
bleibenlassen	bleiben lassen
blendendweiß	blendend weiß
bleuen	bläuen
blindfliegen	blind fliegen
blindschreiben	blind schreiben
blindspielen	blind spielen
blondgefärbt	blond gefärbt
blondgelockt	blond gelockt
blutbildend	Blut bildend
Bluterguß	Bluterguss
Blutpaß	Blutpass
Böllerschuß	Böllerschuss
Bombenschuß	Bombenschuss
Bonbonniere	Bonbonniere or Bonboniere
Börsenschluß	Börsenschluss
Börsentip	Börsentipp
Boß	Boss
Bouclé	Bouclé or Buklee
Branchenadreßbuch	Branchenadressbuch
braungebrannt	braun gebrannt
Bravour	Bravour or Bravur
Bravourleistung	Bravourleistung or Bravurleistung
bravourös	bravourös or bravurös
Bravourstück	Bravourstück or Bravurstück
breitgefächert	breit gefächert
breitmachen	breit machen
Brennessel	Brennnessel or Brenn-Nessel
Bronchialkatarrh	Bronchialkatarrh or Bronchialkatarr
Bruderhaß	Bruderhass
Bruderkuß	Bruderkuss
Brummbaß	Brumbass
Brüßler	Brüssler
Brüßler(in)	Brüssler(in)
buntbemalt	bunt bemalt
buntgefärbt	bunt gefärbt
buntgemischt	bunt gemischt
buntgestreift	bunt getstreift
buntschillernd	bunt schillernd
Büroschluß	Büroschluss
Buschenschenke	Buschenschenke or Buschenschänke
Butterfaß	Butterfass

C	
Cashewnuß	Cashewnuss
Chansonnier	Chansonnier or Chansonier
charakterbildend	Charakter bildend
Chicorée	Chicorée or Schikoree
Choreograph	Choreograph or Choreograf
Choreographie	Choreographie or Choreografie
choreographieren	choreographieren or choreografieren
choreographisch	choreographisch or choreografisch
Cleverneß	Cleverness
Colanuß	Colanuss
Communiqué	Communiqué or Kommunikee
Computertomograph	Computertomograph or Computertomograf
Computertomographie	Computertomographie or Computertomografie
Coupé	Coupé or Kupee

D	
dabeisein	dabei sein
Dachgeschoß	Dachgeschoss
dafürkönnen	dafür können
dahinterklemmen	dahinter klemmen
dahinterknien	dahinter knien

ALT/OLD	NEU/NEW
dahinterkommen	dahinter kommen
dahintersetzen	dahinter setzen
dahinterstecken	dahinter stecken
dahinterstehen	dahinter stehen
Daktylographie	Daktylographie or Daktylografie
Dammriß	Dammriss
danebensein	daneben sein
darauffolgend	darauf folgend
Darmkatarrh	Darmkatarrh or Darmkatarr
Darmverschluß	Darmverschluss
darüberfahren	darüber fahren
darüberliegen	darüber liegen
darübermachen	darüber machen
darüberschreiben	darüber schreiben
darüberstehen	darüber stehen
darunterbleiben	darunter bleiben
darunterfallen	darunter fallen
daruntergehen	darunter gehen
darunterliegen	darunter liegen
daruntermischen	darunter mischen
darunterschreiben	darunter schreiben
daruntersetzen	darunter setzen
daß	dass
dasein	da sein
Datenmißbrauch	Datenmissbrauch
Dauerstreß	Dauerstress
davorhängen	davor hängen
davorlegen	davor legen
davorliegen	davor liegen
davorstehen	davor stehen
davorstellen	davor stellen
Décolleté	Décolleté or Dekolletee
Dekolleté	Dekolleté or Dekolletee
Delikateß-	Delikatess-
Delphin	Delphin or Delfin
Delphinarium	Delphinarium or Delfinarium
Delphinschwimmen	Delphinschwimmen or Delfinschwimmen
Demograph	Demograph or Demograf
Demographie	Demographie or Demografie
demographisch	demographisch or demografisch
Denkprozeß	Denkprozess
deplaciert	deplatziert
deplaziert	deplatziert
des(sen)ungeachtet	des(sen) ungeachtet
desungeachtet	des ungeachtet
Deutschenhaß	Deutschenhass
deutschsprechend	deutsch sprechend
Diarrhö(e)	Diarrhö
diät	Diät
dichtbehaart	dicht behaart
dichtbelaubt	dicht belaubt
dichtbevölkert	dicht bevölkert
dichtbewölkt	dicht bewölkt
dichtgedrängt	dicht gedrängt
diensthabend	Dienst habend
Dienstschluß	Dienstschluss
diensttuend	Dienst tuend
Differential	Differential or Differenzial
Differential-	Differential- or Differenzial-
Differentialrechnung	Differentialrechnung or Differenzialrechnung
Diktaphon	Diktaphon or Diktafon
Doppelbeschluß	Doppelbeschluss
Doppelpaß	Doppelpass
dortbehalten	dort behalten
dortbleiben	dort bleiben
dortzuland(e)	dort zu Land(e)
Doublé	Doublé or Dublee
Doublee	Doublee or Dublee
draufsein	drauf sein
dreiviertel	drei Viertel
Dreß	Dress
Drittkläßler	Drittklässler
Drogenmißbrauch	Drogenmissbrauch
Droßling	Drosslung
drückendheiß	drückend heiß
Dumdumgeschoß	Dumdumgeschoss
dünnbehaart	dünn behaart
dünnbesiedelt	dünn besiedelt

ALT/OLD	NEU/NEW
dünnbevölkert	dünn bevölkert
dünngesät	dünn gesät
Dünnschiß	Dünnschiss
durchbleuen	durchbläuen
durcheinanderbringen	durcheinander bringen
durcheinandergehen	durcheinander gehen
durcheinandergeraten	durcheinander geraten
durcheinanderkommen	durcheinander kommen
durcheinanderlaufen	durcheinander laufen
durcheinanderliegen	durcheinander liegen
durcheinandermengen	durcheinander mengen
durcheinandermischen	durcheinander mischen
durcheinanderreden	durcheinander reden
durcheinanderrennen	durcheinander rennen
durcheinanderrufen	durcheinander rufen
durcheinanderschreien	durcheinander schreien
durcheinanderwerfen	durcheinander werfen
durcheinanderwirbeln	durcheinander wirbeln
Durchfluß	Durchfluss
Durchlaß	Durchlass
durchnumerieren	durchnummerieren
Durchschuß	Durchschuss
durchsein	durch sein
dußlig	dusslig
Dußligkeit	Dussligkeit

E	
ebensogern	ebenso gern
ebensogut	ebenso gut
ebensohäufig	ebenso häufig
ebensolang(e)	ebenso lang(e)
ebensooft	ebenso oft
ebensosehr	ebenso sehr
ebensoviel	ebenso viel
ebensowenig	ebenso wenig
ehrfurchtgebietend	Ehrfurcht gebietend
ehrpußlig	ehrpusslig
einbleuen	einbläuen
Einfluß	Einfluss
Einflußbereich	Einflussbereich
Einflußgebiet	Einflussgebiet
einflußlos	einflusslos
Einflußlosigkeit	Einflusslosigkeit
Einflußmöglichkeit	Einflussmöglichkeit
Einflußnahme	Einflussnahme
einflußreich	einflussreich
Einflußsphäre	Einflusssphäre or Einfluss-Sphäre
Einlaß	Einlass
Einschluß	Einschluss
Einschuß	Einschuss
Einschußloch	Einschussloch
Einschußstelle	Einschussstelle or Einschuss-Stelle
Einsendeschluß	Einsendeschluss
einwärtsgebogen	einwärts gebogen
einzelnstehend	einzeln stehend
Eisenguß	Eisenguss
Eisensulphat	Eisensulphat or Eisensulfat
eisenverarbeitend	Eisen verarbeitend
eislaufen	Eis laufen
ekelerregend	Ekel erregend
Elfmeterschuß	Elfmeterschuss
elsaß-lothringisch	elsass-lothringisch
Elsaß	Elsass
Elsaß-Lothringen	Elsass-Lothringen
energiebewußt	energiebewusst
energiesparend	Energie sparend
enganliegend	eng anliegend
engbedruckt	eng bedruckt
engbefreundet	eng befreundet
engbegrenzt	eng begrenzt
engbeschrieben	eng beschrieben
Engpaß	Engpass
entschloß	entschloss
Entschluß	Entschluss
entschlußfreudig	entschlussfreudig
Entschlußkraft	Entschlusskraft
entschlußlos	entschlusslos
Epigraph	Epigraph or Epigraf
epochemachend	Epoche machend
erbgutschädigend	Erbgut schädigend

ALT/OLD	NEU/NEW
erbgutverändernd	Erbgut verändernd
Erdbebenmeßgerät	Erdbebenmessgerät
Erdgeschoß	Erdgeschoss
Erdnuß	Erdnuss
erdölexportierend	Erdöl exportierend
Erdschluß	Erdschluss
erfaßbar	erfassbar
erfolgversprechend	Erfolg versprechend
Erguß	Erguss
Erlaß	Erlass
Ermessensmißbrauch	Ermessensmissbrauch
Ermittlungsausschuß	Ermittlungsausschuss
ernstgemeint	ernst gemeint
erstemal	erste Mal
erstenmal	ersten Mal
Erstkläßler	Erstklässler
Eßapfel	Essapfel
eßbar	essbar
Eßbesteck	Essbesteck
Eßgeschirr	Essgeschirr
Eßgewohnheiten	Essgewohnheiten
Eßkastanie	Esskastanie
Eßkultur	Esskultur
Eßlöffel	Esslöffel
eßlöffelweise	esslöffelweise
Eßlust	Esslust
Essen(s)zuschuß	Essen(s)zuschuss
essentiell	essentiell or essenziell
Eßstäbchen	Essstäbchen or Ess-Stäbchen
eßt	esst
Eßtisch	Esstisch
Eßunlust	Essunlust
Eßwaren	Esswaren
Eßzimmer	Esszimmer
Eßzwang	Esszwang
Ethnograph	Ethnograph or Ethnograf
Ethnographie	Ethnographie or Ethnografie
Europapaß	Europapass
Eustachische Röhre	eustachische Röhre
Exekutivausschuß	Exekutivausschuss
Existentialismus	Existentialismus or Existenzialismus
Existentialist	Existentialist or Existenzialist
existentialistisch	existentialistisch or existenzialistisch
Existentialphilosophie	Existentialphilosophie or Existenzialphilosophie
existentiell	existentiell or existenziell
Exponentialfunktion	Exponentialfunktion or Exponenzialfunktion
Exponentialgleichung	Exponentialgleichung or Exponenzialgleichung
Exposé	Exposé or Exposee
expreß	express
Expreß	Express
Expreßbrief	Expressbrief
Expreßgut	Expressgut
Expreßreinigung	Expressreinigung
Expreßzug	Expresszug
Expreßzüge	Expresszüge
Exzeß	Exzess

F	
Facette	Facette or Fassette
facettenartig	facettenartig or fassettenartig
Facettenauge	Facettenauge or Fassettenauge
Facettenschliff	Facettenschliff or Fassettenschliff
facettieren	facettieren or fassettieren
Fachausschuß	Fachausschuss
Fachhochschulabschluß	Fachhochschulabschluss
fahrenlassen	fahren lassen
Fairneß	Fairness
fallenlassen	fallen lassen
Familienanschluß	Familienanschluss
Familienpaß	Familienpass
Fangschuß	Fangschuss
farbentragend	Farben tragend
Faß	Fass
Faßband	Fassband
faßbar	fassbar
Faßbier	Fassbier
Faßbinder	Fassbinder

ALT/OLD	NEU/NEW	ALT/OLD	NEU/NEW
Fäßchen	Fässchen	Flußspat	Flussspat or Fluss-Spat
Faßdaube	Fassdaube	Flußstahl	Flussstahl or Fluss-Stahl
faßlich	fasslich	Flußufer	Flussufer
Faßlichkeit	Fasslichkeit	Fön®	Föhn or Fön®
Faßreif(en)	Fassreif(en)	fönen	föhnen
Faßwein	Fasswein	Frauenüberschuß	Frauenüberschuss
faßweise	fassweise	Freisaß	Freisass
fäulniserregend	Fäulnis erregend	Freischuß	Freischuss
Fehlpaß	Fehlpass	Fremdenhaß	Fremdenhass
fehlplaziert	fehlplatziert	Fremdenpaß	Fremdenpass
Fehlschluß	Fehlschluss	Freßbeutel	Fressbeutel
Fehlschuß	Fehlschuss	Freßgier	Fressgier
feind	Feind	Freßkorb	Fresskorb
feingemahlen	fein gemahlen	Freßnapf	Fressnapf
Feinmeßgerät	Feinmessgerät	Freßpaket	Fresspaket
Feldtelegraph	Feldtelegraph or Feldtelegraf	Freßsack	Fresssack or Fress-Sack
Fernexpreß	Fernexpress	Freßsucht	Fresssucht or Fress-Sucht
fernhalten	fern halten	frißt	frisst
fernliegen	fern liegen	Freßwelle	Fresswelle
Fernsprechanschluß	Fernsprechanschluss	Freßwerkzeuge	Fresswerkzeuge
fernstehen	fern stehen	Friedenskuß	Friedenskuss
fertigbekommen	fertig bekommen	Friedensprozeß	Friedensprozess
fertigbringen	fertig bringen	Friedensschluß	Friedensschluss
fertigkriegen	fertig kriegen	friß	friss
fertigmachen	fertig machen	frischgebacken	frisch gebacken
fertigstellen	fertig stellen	Friteuse	Fritteuse
festangestellt	fest angestellt	fritieren	frittieren
festbesoldet	fest besoldet	Fritüre	Frittüre
festverwurzelt	fest verwurzelt	Froschbiß	Froschbiss
feuerschnaubend	Feuer schnaubend	frühauf	früh auf
feuerspeiend	Feuer speiend	frühpensionieren	früh pensionieren
feuersprühend	Feuer sprühend	frühverrenten	früh verrenten
Fideikommiß	Fideikommiss	frühvollendet	früh vollendet
Fieberphantasien	Fieberphantasien or Fieberfantasien	frühzeitig	früh zeitig
fiebersenkend	Fieber senkend	funkensprühend	Funken sprühend
Filmographie	Filmographie or Filmografie	Funkmeßgerät	Funkmessgerät
Filmriß	Filmriss	fürbaß	fürbass
Finanzausschuß	Finanzausschuss	furchteinflößend	Furcht einflößend
fischverarbeitend	Fisch verarbeitend	furchterregend	Furcht erregend
Fitneß	Fitness		
Flachpaß	Flachpass	**G**	
Flachschuß	Flachschuss	Gamsbart	Gamsbart or Gämsbart
Flaschenverschluß	Flaschenverschluss	Gamsbock	Gamsbock or Gämsbock
fleischfressend	Fleisch fressend	Gamsleder	Gämsleder
Fleischgenuß	Fleischgenuss	Gangsterboß	Gangsterboss
fleischgeworden	Fleisch geworden	garkochen	gar kochen
fleischverarbeitend	Fleisch verarbeitend	Gärungsprozeß	Gärungsprozess
Fliegenschiß	Fliegenschiss	Gäßchen	Gässchen
Flohbiß	Flohbiss	Gebiß	Gebiss
floß	floss	Gebißabdruck	Gebissabdruck
flötengehen	flöten gehen	Gebißanomalie	Gebissanomalie
Flügelroß	Flügelross	Gebrauchsgraphik	Gebrauchsgraphik or Gebrauchsgrafik
Fluß	Fluss	Gebrauchsgraphiker	Gebrauchsgraphiker or
Fluß-	Fluss-		Gebrauchsgrafiker
Flußaal	Flussaal	Gebührenerlaß	Gebührenerlass
flußab(wärts)	flussab(wärts)	Geburtenüberschuß	Geburtenüberschuss
Flußarm	Flussarm	gefahrbringend	Gefahr bringend
flußaufwärts	flussaufwärts	gefangenhalten	gefangen halten
Flußbau	Flussbau	gefangennehmen	gefangen nehmen
Flußbett	Flussbett	gefangensetzen	gefangen setzen
Flüßchen	Flüsschen	gefaßt	gefasst
Flußdiagramm	Flussdiagramm	Gefaßtheit	Gefasstheit
Flußebene	Flussebene	Gefäßverschluß	Gefässverschluss
Flußgebiet	Flussgebiet	gegeneinanderhalten	gegeneinander halten
Flußgefälle	Flussgefälle	gegeneinanderprallen	gegeneinander prallen
Flußgeschiebe	Flussgeschiebe	gegeneinanderstehen	gegeneinander stehen
Flußhafen	Flusshafen	gegeneinanderstellen	gegeneinander stellen
Flußkrebs	Flusskrebs	gegeneinanderstoßen	gegeneinander stoßen
Flußlandschaft	Flusslandschaft	geheimhalten	geheim halten
Flußlauf	Flusslauf	Geheimschloß	Geheimschloss
Flußmündung	Flussmündung	Geheimtip	Geheimtipp
Flußniederung	Flussniederung	geheimtun	geheim tun
Flußnixe	Flussnixe	gehenlassen	gehen lassen
Flußpferd	Flusspferd	Gemeindebeschluß	Gemeindebeschluss
Flußregelung	Flussregelung	Gemeinschaftsanschluß	Gemeinschaftsanschluss
Flußregulierung	Flussregulierung	Gemse	Gämse
Flußsand	Flusssand or Fluss-Sand	gemußt	gemusst
Flußschiff	Flussschiff or Fluss-Schiff	genaugenommen	genau genommen
Flußschiffahrt	Flussschiffahrt or Fluss-Schiffahrt	genauso-	genauso
flüssigmachen	flüssig machen	Generalbaß	Generalbass

ALT/OLD	NEU/NEW	ALT/OLD	NEU/NEW
Genesungsprozeß	Genesungsprozess	goldgefaßt	goldgefasst
Genickschuß	Genickschuss	Gonorrhö(e)	Gonorrhö
genoß	genoss	goß	goss
Genuß	Genuss	Grammolekül	Grammmolekül or Gramm-Molekül
genußfreudig	genussfreudig	Grammophon	Grammophon or Grammofon
Genußgift	Genussgift	Graph	Graph or Graf
genüßlich	genüsslich	Graphem	Graphem or Grafem
Genußmensch	Genussmensch	Graphie	Graphie or Grafie
Genußmittel	Genussmittel	Graphik	Graphik or Grafik
genußreich	genussreich	graphisch	graphisch or grafisch
Genußschein	Genussschein or Genuss-Schein	Graphologe	Graphologe or Grafologe
Genußsucht	Genusssucht or Genuss-Sucht	Graphologie	Graphologie or Grafologie
genußsüchtig	genusssüchtig or genuss-süchtig	Graphologin	Graphologin or Grafologin
genußvoll	genussvoll	gräßlich	grässlich
Geograph	Geograph or Geograf	Gräßlichkeit	Grässlichkeit
Geographie	Geographie or Geografie	grauenerregend	Grauen erregend
geographisch	geographisch or geografisch	graugestreift	grau gestreift
geradehalten	gerade halten	Grauguß	Grauguss
geradelegen	gerade legen	graumeliert	grau meliert
gerademachen	gerade machen	Grenzfluß	Grenzfluss
geraderichten	gerade richten	Greuel	Gräuel
geradesitzen	gerade sitzen	Greuelgeschichte	Gräuelgeschichte
geradesogut	geradeso gut	Greuelmärchen	Gräuelmärchen
geradesoviel	geradeso viel	Greuelmeldung	Gräuelmeldung
Gerichtsbeschluß	Gerichtsbeschluss	Greuelnachricht	Gräuelnachricht
geringachten	gering achten	Greuelpropaganda	Gräuelpropaganda
geringschätzen	gering schätzen	Greueltat	Gräueltat
G(e)riß	G(e)riss	greulich	gräulich
Geruch(s)verschluß	Geruch(s)verschluss	Griß	Griss
Geschäftsabschluß	Geschäftsabschluss	grobgemahlen	grob gemahlen
Geschäftsschluß	Geschäftsschluss	großangelegt	groß angelegt
Geschichtsbewußtsein	Geschichtsbewusstsein	Großanlaß	Großanlass
Geschiß	Geschiss	großgemustert	groß gemustert
Geschoß	Geschoss	großgewachsen	groß gewachsen
Geschoßbahn	Geschossbahn	großkariert	groß kariert
Geschoßgarbe	Geschossgarbe	Großphoto	Großphoto or Großfoto
Geschoßhagel	Geschosshagel	grundhäßlich	grundhässlich
gewaltbejahend	Gewalt bejahend	Grundriß	Grundriss
Gewerkschaftsboß	Gewerkschaftsboss	Gummiparagraph	Gummiparagraph or Gummiparagraf
Gewerkschaftskongreß	Gewerkschaftskongress		
gewinnbringend	Gewinn bringend	Gummi(wucht)geschoß	Gummi(wucht)geschoss
Gewinnummer	Gewinnnummer or Gewinn-Nummer	Guß	Guss
gewiß	gewiss	Gußasphalt	Gussasphalt
Gewißheit	Gewissheit	Gußbeton	Gussbeton
gewißlich	gewisslich	Gußeisen	Gusseisen
gewußt	gewusst	gußeisern	gusseisern
Gipsabguß	Gipsabguss	Gußform	Gussform
glattbügeln	glatt bügeln	Gußnaht	Gussnaht
glattgehen	glatt gehen	Gußstahl	Gussstahl or Guss-Stahl
glatthobeln	glatt hobeln	gutaussehend	gut aussehend
glattkämmen	glatt kämmen	gutbetucht	gut betucht
glattlegen	glatt legen	gutbezahlt	gut bezahlt
glattmachen	glatt machen	gutdotiert	gut dotiert
glattpolieren	glatt polieren	Gutenachtkuß	Gutenachtkuss
glattrasieren	glatt rasieren	gutgehen	gut gehen
glattrasiert	glatt rasiert	gutgehend	gut gehend
glattrühren	glatt rühren	gutgelaunt	gut gelaunt
glattschleifen	glatt schleifen	gutgelungen	gut gelungen
glattschneiden	glatt schneiden	gutgemeint	gut gemeint
glattstreichen	glatt streichen	gutgesinnt	gut gesinnt
glattwalzen	glatt walzen	gutsituiert	gut situiert
Gläubigerausschuß	Gläubigerausschuss	gutsitzend	gut sitzend
gleichbleiben	gleich bleiben	guttun	gut tun
gleichbleibend	gleich bleibend	gutunterrichtet	gut unterrichtet
gleichdenkend	gleich denkend	gutverdienend	gut verdienend
gleichgeartet	gleich geartet		
gleichgesinnt	gleich gesinnt	**H**	
gleichgestellt	gleich gestellt	Haarriß	Haarriss
gleichgestimmt	gleich gestimmt	haftenbleiben	haften bleiben
gleichlautend	gleich lautend	Hagiograph	Hagiograph or Hagiograf
Gleisanschluß	Gleisanschluss	Hagiographen	Hagiographen or Hagiografen
Glimmstengel	Glimmstängel	Hagiographie	Hagiographie or Hagiografie
Glockenguß	Glockenguss	halbfertig	halb fertig
Glotzophon	Glotzophon or Glotzofon	halbgar	halb gar
glückbringend	Glück bringend	Halbgeschoß	Halbgeschoss
glückverheißend	Glück verheißend	halblinks	halb links
Gnadenerlaß	Gnadenerlass	halbnackt	halb nackt
Gnadenschuß	Gnadenschuss	halboffen	halb offen
goldbetreßt	goldbetresst	halbrechts	halb rechts
Golddoublé	Golddoublé or Golddublee	halbtot	halb tot

ALT/OLD	NEU/NEW	ALT/OLD	NEU/NEW
halbverdaut	halb verdaut	hintereinandergehen	hintereinander gehen
halbvoll	halb voll	hintereinanderschalten	hintereinander schalten
halbwach	halb wach	hintereinanderstehen	hintereinander stehen
haltmachen	Halt machen	hinterhersein	hinterher sein
Hämorrhoiden	Hämorrhoiden or Hämorriden	hinübersein	hinüber sein
Hämorrhoidenschaukel	Hämorrhoidenschaukel or	Historiograph	Historiograph or Historiograf
	Hämmoridenschaukel	hochachten	hoch achten
händchenhaltend	Händchen haltend	hochbegabt	hoch begabt
handeltreibend	Handel treibend	hochdotiert	hoch dotiert
Handkuß	Handkuss	hochempfindlich	hoch empfindlich
Handvoll	Hand voll	hochentwickelt	hoch entwickelt
hängenbleiben	hängen bleiben	hochgeehrt	hoch geehrt
hängenlassen	hängen lassen	Hochgenuß	Hochgenuss
Hängeschloß	Hängeschloss	hochgeschätzt	hoch geschätzt
Härteparagraph	Härteparagraph or Härteparagraf	hochgestellt	hoch gestellt
hartgebrannt	hart gebrannt	hochgewachsen	hoch gewachsen
hartgefroren	hart gefroren	hochindustrialisiert	hoch industrialisiert
hartgekocht	hart gekocht	hochqualifiziert	hoch qualifiziert
Haß	Hass	hochschätzen	hoch schätzen
Haßausbruch	Hassausbruch	hochschrauben	hoch schrauben
Haselnuß	Haselnuss	Hochschulabschluß	Hochschulabschluss
haßerfüllt	hasserfüllt	hockenbleiben	hocken bleiben
Haßgefühl	Hassgefühl	hofhalten	Hof halten
häßlich	hässlich	höhergestellt	höher gestellt
Häßlichkeit	Hässlichkeit	höherliegend	höher liegend
Haßliebe	Hassliebe	höherschrauben	höher schrauben
Haßtirade	Hasstirade	höherstehend	höher stehend
haßverzerrt	hassverzerrt	höherstufen	höher stufen
Hauptanschluß	Hauptanschluss	hohnlachen	hohnlachen or Hohn lachen
Hauptschulabschluß	Hauptschulabschluss	hohnsprechen	hohnsprechen or Hohn sprechen
haushalten	haushalten or Haus halten	Holographie	Holographie or Holografie
heilighalten	heilig halten	holzverarbeitend	Holz verarbeitend
heiligsprechen	heilig sprechen	homophon	homophon or homofon
Heilungsprozeß	Heilungsprozess	Hosteß	Hostess
heißersehnt	heiß ersehnt	Hundebiß	Hundebiss
heißgeliebt	heiß geliebt	hustenstillend	Husten stillend
heißumkämpft	heiß umkämpft	Hydrographie	Hydrographie or Hydrografie
heißumstritten	heiß umstritten	hydrographisch	hydrographisch or hydrografisch
Hektographie	Hektographie or Hektografie		
hektographieren	hektographieren or hektografieren	**I**	
helleuchtend	hell leuchtend	Ichbewußtsein	Ichbewusstsein
hellicht	helllicht	Ich-Roman	Ichroman
hellodernd	hell lodernd	Imbiß	Imbiss
hellstrahlend	hell strahlend	Imbißhalle	Imbisshalle
heraussein	heraus sein	Imbißstand	Imbissstand or Imbiss-Stand
hersein	her sein	Imbißstube	Imbissstube or Imbiss-Stube
herumsein	herum sein	immerwährend	immer während
heruntersein	herunter sein	Impfpaß	Impfpass
Herzenserguß	Herzenserguss	imstande	imstande or im Stande
Hexenprozeß	Hexenprozess	ineinanderfließen	ineinander fließen
Hexenschuß	Hexenschuss	ineinanderfügen	ineinander fügen
hierbehalten	hier behalten	ineinandergreifen	ineinander greifen
hierbleiben	hier bleiben	ineinanderpassen	ineinander passen
hierherbemühen	hierher bemühen	ineinanderschieben	ineinander schieben
hierherbitten	hierher bitten	Informationsfluß	Informationsfluss
hierherblicken	hierher blicken	insektenfressend	Insekten fressend
hierherbringen	hierher bringen	instandbesetzen	instand besetzen or in Stand besetzen
hierherfahren	hierher fahren	I-Punkt	i-Punkt
hierherführen	hierher führen	iß	iss
hierhergehören	hierher gehören	Ist-Bestand	Istbestand
hierherholen	hierher holen	I-Tüpfelchen	i-Tüpfelchen
hierherkommen	hierher kommen		
hierherlaufen	hierher laufen	**J**	
hierherlegen	hierher legen	Jackettasche	Jacketttasche or Jackett-Tasche
hierherlocken	hierher locken	Jagdschloß	Jagdschloss
hierherschaffen	hierher schaffen	Jahresabschluß	Jahresabschluss
hierherschicken	hierher schicken	Joghurt	Joghurt or Jogurt
hierhersetzen	hierher setzen	Joghurtbereiter	Joghurtbereiter or Jogurtbereiter
hierherstellen	hierher stellen	Judaskuß	Judaskuss
hierhertragen	hierher tragen	Judenhaß	Judenhass
hierherwagen	hierher wagen	Juniorpaß	Juniorpass
hierherziehen	hierher ziehen	justitiabel	justitiabel or justiziabel
hierlassen	hier lassen	Justitiar	Justitiar or Justiziar
hiersein	hier sein		
hierzulande	hier zu Lande	**K**	
hilfesuchend	Hilfe suchend	Kabelanschluß	Kabelanschluss
Hinausschmiß	Hinausschmiss	Kabinettsbeschluß	Kabinettsbeschluss
hinaussein	hinaus sein	Kaffee-Ersatz	Kaffee-Ersatz or Kafeeersatz
hinsein	hin sein	Kaffee-Extrakt	Kaffee-Extrakt or Kaffeeextrakt
hintereinanderfahren	hintereinander fahren	kahlfressen	kahl fressen
		kahlgeschoren	kahl geschoren

ALT/OLD	NEU/NEW	ALT/OLD	NEU/NEW
kahlscheren	kahl scheren	Kontrabaß	Kontrabass
kahlschlagen	kahl schlagen	Kontrollampe	Kontrolllampe or Kontroll-Lampe
Kakophonie	Kakophonie or Kakofonie	Kontrolliste	Kontrollliste or Kontroll-Liste
Kalligraphie	Kalligraphie or Kalligrafie	Kopfnuß	Kopfnuss
kaltbleiben	kalt bleiben	Kopfschuß	Kopfschuss
kaltgepreßt	kaltgepresst	kopfstehen	Kopf stehen
kaltlächelnd	kalt lächelnd	Koppelschloß	Koppelschloss
kaltlassen	kalt lassen	kostensparend	Kosten sparend
Kammuschel	Kammmuschel or Kamm-Muschel	Kostenvorschuß	Kostenvorschuss
Känguruh	Känguru	kraß	krass
Kann-Bestimmung	Kannbestimmung	krebsauslösend	Krebs auslösend
Kapitalabfluß	Kapitalabfluss	krebserregend	Krebs erregend
Karamel	Karamell	Kreiselkompaß	Kreiselkompass
Kartograph	Kartograph or Kartograf	Kreppapier	Krepppapier or Krepp-Papier
Kartographie	Kartographie or Kartografie	kriegführend	Krieg führend
kartographisch	kartographisch or kartografisch	Kriegsgreuel	Kriegsgräuel
Kassenabschluß	Kassenabschluss	Kristalleuchter	Kristallleuchter or Kristall-Leuchter
Katarrh	Katarrh or Katarr	Kristallüster	Kristalllüster or Kristall-Lüster
kegelscheiben	Kegel scheiben	kroß	kross
kegelschieben	Kegel schieben	krummlegen	krumm legen
Kehlkopfkatarrh	Kehlkopfkatarrh or Kehlkopfkatarr	krummnehmen	krumm nehmen
Kehlkopfmikrophon	Kehlkopfmikrophon or Kehlkopfmikrofon	Kulturgeographie	Kulturgeographie or Kulturgeografie
		Küraß	Kürass
Kehlverschlußlaut	Kehlverschlusslaut	kurzgefaßt	kurz gefasst
Kellergeschoß	Kellergeschoss	kurzgeschnitten	kurz geschnitten
Kernspin-Tomographie	Kernspin-Tomographie or Kernspin-Tomografie	kurzhalten	kurz halten
		Kurzschluß	Kurzschluss
Kernspin-Tomograph	Kernspin-Tomograph or Kernspin-Tomograf	Kurzschlußreaktion	Kurzschlussreaktion
		kurztreten	kurz treten
keß	kess	Kuß	Kuss
Keßheit	Kessheit	küß die Hand	küss die Hand
Ketchup	Ketchup or Ketschup	Küßchen	Küsschen
Kettenschluß	Kettenschluss	küßdiehand	küssdiehand
Kindesmißhandlung	Kindesmisshandlung	kußecht	kussecht
Kinematographie	Kinematographie or Kinematografie	kußfest	kussfest
klarblickend	klar blickend	Kußhand	Kusshand
klardenkend	klar denkend	Kußmund	Kussmund
klarsehen	klar sehen		
klarwerden	klar werden	**L**	
klaß	klass	Ladenschluß	Ladenschluss
Klassenbewußtsein	Klassenbewusstsein	Ladenschlußgesetz	Ladenschlussgesetz
Klassenhaß	Klassenhass	Ladenschlußzeit	Ladenschlusszeit
-kläßler	-klässler	langersehnt	lang ersehnt
klatschenaß	klatschenass	langgehegt	lang gehegt
klatschnaß	klatschnass	langgestreckt	lang gestreckt
kleingedruckt	klein gedruckt	langgezogen	lang gezogen
kleingemustert	klein gemustert	längsgestreift	längs gestreift
kleinhacken	klein hacken	langziehen	lang ziehen
kleinmachen	klein machen	Lärmmeßgerät	Lärmmessgerät
kleinschneiden	klein schneiden	laß	lass
Klemmappe	Klemmmappe or Klemm-Mappe	läßlich	lässlich
Klettverschluß	Klettverschluss	laßt	lasst
klitschnaß	klitschnass	Lattenschuß	Lattenschuss
klugreden	klug reden	laubtragend	Laub tragend
knapphalten	knapp halten	Laufpaß	Laufpass
kochendheiß	kochend heiß	lebendgebärend	lebend gebärend
Kokosnuß	Kokosnuss	Lebensgenuß	Lebensgenuss
Kolanuß	Kolanuss	Lebensüberdruß	Lebensüberdruss
Kölnisch Wasser	kölnisch Wasser	leerlaufen	leer laufen
Koloß	Koloss	leerstehend	leer stehend
Kombinationsschloß	Kombinationsschloss	leichenblaß	leichenblass
Kommiß	Kommiss	leichtbeschwingt	leicht beschwingt
Kommißbrot	Kommissbrot	leichtbewaffnet	leicht bewaffnet
Kommißstiefel	Kommissstiefel or Kommiss-Stiefel	leichtentzündlich	leicht entzündlich
Kommuniqué	Kommuniqué or Kommunikee	leichtfallen	leicht fallen
Kompaß	Kompass	leichtgeschürzt	leicht geschürzt
Kompaßhäuschen	Kompasshäuschen	leichtmachen	leicht machen
Kompaßnadel	Kompassnadel	leichtnehmen	leicht nehmen
kompreß	kompress	leichtverdaulich	leicht verdaulich
Kompromiß	Kompromiss	leichtverderblich	leicht verderblich
kompromißbereit	kompromissbereit	leichtverletzt	leicht verletzt
Kompromißbereitschaft	Kompromissbereitschaft	leichtverständlich	leicht verständlich
kompromißlos	kompromisslos	leichtverwundet	leicht verwundet
Kompromißlösung	Kompromisslösung	Lenkradschloß	Lenkradschloss
Komteß	Komtess	Lernprozeß	Lernprozess
Kongreß	Kongress	Leuchtgeschoß	Leuchtgeschoss
Kongreßmitglied	Kongressmitglied	Leuchtspurgeschoß	Leuchtspurgeschoss
Kongreßteilnehmer	Kongressteilnehmer	Lexikograph	Lexikograph or Lexikograf
Kongreßzentrum	Kongresszentrum	Lexikographie	Lexikographie or Lexikografie
kontoführend	Konto führend	lexikographisch	lexikographisch or lexikografisch

ALT/OLD	NEU/NEW
Lichtmeß	Lichtmess
Lichtmeßverfahren	Lichtmessverfahren
liebenlernen	lieben lernen
liebgewinnen	lieb gewonnen
liebgeworden	lieb geworden
liebhaben	lieb haben
liegenbleiben	liegen bleiben
liegenlassen	liegen lassen
Litfaßsäule	Litfasssäule *or* Litfass-Säule
Lithograph	Lithograph *or* Lithograf
Lithographie	Lithographie *or* Lithografie
lithographieren	lithographieren *or* lithografieren
lithographisch	lithographisch *or* lithografisch
Lorbaß	Lorbass
Luftschloß	Luftschloss
Lustschloß	Lustschloss

M

ALT/OLD	NEU/NEW
Machtmißbrauch	Machtmissbrauch
Ma(f)fia-Boß	Ma(f)fia-Boss
Magen-Darm-Katarrh	Magen-Darm-Katarrh *or* Magen-Darm-Katarr
Magnetkompaß	Magnetkompass
Magnetophon	Magnetophon *or* Magnetofon
Magnetophonband	Magnetophonband *or* Magnetofonband
Majoritätsbeschluß	Majoritätsbeschluss
Mammutprozeß	Mammutprozess
Männerhaß	Männerhass
Männerüberschuß	Männerüberschuss
Mantelgeschoß	Mantelgeschoss
Marschkompaß	Marschkompass
maschine(n)schreiben	Maschine schreiben
maßhalten	Maß halten
Maulkorberlaß	Maulkorberlass
Mechanisierungsprozeß	Mechanisierungsprozess
Medikamentenmißbrauch	Medikamentenmissbrauch
Megaphon	Megaphon *or* Megafon
Mehrheitsbeschluß	Mehrheitsbeschluss
Meisterschuß	Meisterschuss
Meldeschluß	Meldeschluss
Meniskusriß	Meniskusriss
Menschenhaß	Menschenhass
menschenverachtend	Menschen verachtend
Meßband	Messband
meßbar	messbar
Meßbecher	Messbecher
Meßbuch	Messbuch
Meßdaten	Messdaten
Meßdiener	Messdiener
Meßfühler	Messfühler
Meßgerät	Messgerät
Meßgewand	Messgewand
Meßglas	Messglas
Meßinstrument	Messinstrument
Meßopfer	Messopfer
Meßordnung	Messordnung
Meßplatte	Messplatte
Meßstab	Messstab *or* Mess-Stab
Meßtechnik	Messtechnik
Meßtisch	Messtisch
Meßtischblatt	Messtischblatt
Meßwein	Messwein
Meßwert	Messwert
Meßzahl	Messzahl
Meßzylinder	Messzylinder
metallverarbeitend	Metall verarbeitend
Mikrophon	Mikrophon *or* Mikrofon
Milchgebiß	Milchgebiss
miß	miss
Miß	Miss
mißachten	missachten
Mißachtung	Missachtung
mißbehagen	missbehagen
Mißbehagen	Missbehagen
mißbilden	missbilden
Mißbildung	Missbildung
mißbilligen	missbilligen
mißbilligend	missbilligend
Mißbilligung	Missbilligung

ALT/OLD	NEU/NEW
Mißbrauch	Missbrauch
mißbrauchen	missbrauchen
mißbräuchlich	missbräuchlich
mißdeuten	missdeuten
Mißdeutung	Missdeutung
Mißerfolg	Misserfolg
Mißernte	Missernte
mißfallen	missfallen
Mißfallen	Missfallen
Mißfallensäußerung	Missfallensäußerung
Mißfallensbekundung	Missfallensbekundung
Mißfallenskundgebung	Missfallenskundgebung
mißfällig	missfällig
mißgebildet	missgebildet
Mißgeburt	Missgeburt
mißgelaunt	missgelaunt
Mißgeschick	Missgeschick
mißgestalt	missgestalt
Mißgestalt	Missgestalt
mißgestaltet	missgestaltet
mißgestimmt	missgestimmt
mißglücken	missglücken
mißgönnen	missgönnen
Mißgriff	Missgriff
Mißgunst	Missgunst
mißgünstig	missgünstig
mißhandeln	misshandeln
Mißhandlung	Misshandlung
Mißhelligkeit	Misshelligkeit
Mißklang	Missklang
Mißkredit	Misskredit
mißlang	misslang
mißlaunig	misslaunig
mißlich	misslich
Mißlichkeit	Misslichkeit
mißliebig	missliebig
mißlingen	misslingen
Mißlingen	Misslingen
mißlungen	misslungen
Mißmanagement	Missmanagement
Mißmut	Missmut
mißmutig	missmutig
mißraten	missraten
Mißstand	Missstand *or* Miss-Stand
Mißstimmung	Missstimmung *or* Miss-Stimmung
Mißton	Misston
mißtönend	misstönend
mißtönig	misstönig
mißtrauen	misstrauen
Mißtrauen	Misstrauen
Mißtrauensantrag	Misstrauensantrag
Mißtrauensvotum	Misstrauensvotum
mißtrauisch	misstrauisch
Mißvergnügen	Missvergnügen
mißvergnügt	missvergnügt
Mißverhältnis	Missverhältnis
mißverständlich	missverständlich
Mißverständnis	Missverständnis
mißverstehen	missverstehen
Mißwahl	Misswahl
Mißweisung	Missweisung
Mißwirtschaft	Misswirtschaft
Mißwuchs	Misswuchs
mißzubehagen	misszubehagen
mißzuverstehen	misszuverstehen
mittag	Mittag
modebewußt	modebewusst
Moiré	Moiré *or* Moiree
Mokkatäßchen	Mokkatässchen
Monographie	Monographie *or* Monografie
Mop	Mopp
Mordprozeß	Mordprozess
mündigsprechen	mündig sprechen
Muskatnuß	Muskatnuss
Muskelfaserriß	Muskelfaserriss
Muskelriß	Muskelriss
Muß	Muss
Mußbestimmung	Mussbestimmung
Muß-Bestimmung	Mussbestimmung
Mußehe	Mussehe

ALT/OLD	NEU/NEW
Mußheirat	Mussheirat
mußte	musste
Muß-Vorschrift	Muss-Vorschrift
Musterprozeß	Musterprozess
Musterungsausschuß	Musterungsausschuss
Mutterpaß	Mutterpass
Myrrhe	Myrrhe or Myrre
Myrrhenöl	Myrrhenöl or Myrrenöl

N

ALT/OLD	NEU/NEW
Nachfaßaktion	Nachfassaktion
nachhinein	Nachhinein
Nachlaß	Nachlass
Nachlaßgericht	Nachlassgericht
Nachlaßgläubiger	Nachlassgläubiger
Nachlaßpfleger	Nachlasspfleger
Nachlaßverwalter	Nachlassverwalter
Nachlaßverwaltung	Nachlassverwaltung
nachmittag	Nachmittag
Nachrüstungsbeschluß	Nachrüstungsbeschluss
Nachschuß	Nachschuss
nacht	Nacht
nahebringen	nahe bringen
nahegehen	nahe gehen
nahekommen	nahe kommen
nahelegen	nahe legen
naheliegen	nahe liegen
naheliegend	nahe liegend
näherbringen	näher bringen
näherkommen	näher kommen
näherliegen	näher liegen
näherstehen	näher stehen
nähertreten	näher treten
nahestehen	nahe stehen
Nahrungs- und Genußmittelindustrie	Nahrungs- und Genussmittelindustrie
Narziß	Narziss
Narzißmus	Narzissmus
Narzißt	Narzisst
narzißtisch	narzisstisch
naß	nass
Naß	Nass
naßforsch	nassforsch
naßkalt	nasskalt
Naßrasur	Nassrasur
Naßwäsche	Nasswäsche
Naßzelle	Nasszelle
nationalbewußt	nationalbewusst
Nationalbewußtsein	Nationalbewusstsein
Nato-Doppelbeschluß	Nato-Doppelbeschluss
Nebel(schluß)leuchte	Nebel(schluss)leuchte
Nebenanschluß	Nebenanschluss
nebeneinanderlegen	nebeneinander legen
nebeneinanderreihen	nebeneinander reihen
nebeneinanderschalten	nebeneinander schalten
nebeneinandersetzen	nebeneinander setzen
nebeneinandersitzen	nebeneinander sitzen
nebeneinanderstellen	nebeneinander stellen
Nebenfluß	Nebenfluss
Nebenschluß	Nebenschluss
Necessaire	Necessaire or Nessessär
Negerkuß	Negerkuss
Negligé	Negligé or Negligee
Netzanschluß	Netzanschluss
neubearbeitet	neu bearbeitet
neuentdeckt	neu entdeckt
neuentwickelt	neuentwickelt
neueröffnet	neu eröffnet
neugebacken	neu gebacken
neugeboren	neu geboren
neugeschaffen	neu geschaffen
neugestalten	neu gestalten
neugewählt	neu gewählt
neuvermählt	neu vermählt
nichtleitend	nicht leitend
nichtorganisiert	nicht organisiert
nichtrostend	nicht rostend
nichtsahnend	nichts ahnend
Nichtseßhafte(r)	Nichtsesshafte(r)
nichtssagend	nichts sagend

ALT/OLD	NEU/NEW
niedrigstehend	niedrig stehend
nonstop	nonstopp
Nonstop-	Nonstopp-
Nonstopbetrieb	Nonstoppbetrieb
Nonstopflug	Nonstoppflug
Nonstopkino	Nonstoppkino
not	Not
notleidend	Not leidend
Nulleiter	Nullleiter or Null-Leiter
Nullinie	Nulllinie or Null-Linie
Nullösung	Nulllösung or Null-Lösung
numerieren	nummerieren
Numerierung	Nummerierung
numerisch	nummerisch
Nuß	Nuss
Nußbaum	Nussbaum
nußbraun	nussbraun
Nußknacker	Nussknacker
Nußkohle	Nusskohle
Nußschale	Nussschale or Nuss-Schale

O

ALT/OLD	NEU/NEW
obenerwähnt	oben erwähnt
Obergeschoß	Obergeschoss
offenbleiben	offen bleiben
offenhalten	offen halten
offenlassen	offen lassen
offenstehen	offen stehen
Ölmeßstab	Ölmessstab or Ölmess-Stab
Ordonnanz	Ordonnanz or Ordonanz
Ordonnanzoffizier	Ordonnanzoffizier or Ordonanzoffizier
Orthographie	Orthographie or Orthografie
orthographisch	orthographisch or orthografisch
Oszillograph	Oszillograph or Oszillograf
Ozeanographie	Ozeanographie or Ozeanografie

P

ALT/OLD	NEU/NEW
Panther	Panther or Panter
Papiermaché	Papiermaché or Papiermaschee
papierverarbeitend	Papier verarbeitend
Pappmaché	Pappmaché or Pappmaschee
Paragraph	Paragraph or Paragraf
Paragraphenreiter	Paragraphenreiter or Paragrafenreiter
paragraphenweise	paragraphenweise or paragrafenweise
Paragraphenwerk	Paragraphenwerk or Paragrafenwerk
Paragraphenzeichen	Paragraphenzeichen or Paragrafenzeichen
Paranuß	Paranuss
Parlamentsausschuß	Parlamentsausschuss
Parlamentsbeschluß	Parlamentsbeschluss
Parnaß	Parnass
Parteiausschlußverfahren	Parteiausschlussverfahren
Parteikongreß	Parteikongress
partial-	partial- or parzial-
partiell	partiell or parziell
Paß	Pass
Paßamt	Passamt
Paßbild	Passbild
passé	passé or passee
Paßform	Passform
Paßfoto	Passfoto
Paßgang	Passgang
Paßgänger	Passgänger
Paßhöhe	Passhöhe
Paßkontrolle	Passkontrolle
Paßphoto	Passphoto or Passfoto
Paßstelle	Passstelle or Pass-Stelle
Paßstraße	Passstraße or Pass-Straße
Paßwort	Passwort
Paßzwang	Passzwang
Patentverschluß	Patentverschluss
patschnaß	patschnass
Paukenschlegel	Paukenschlägel
Pfeffernuß	Pfeffernuss
Pfeilschuß	Pfeilschuss
Pferdegebiß	Pferdegebiss
pflanzenfressend	Pflanzen fressend
pflichtbewußt	pflichtbewusst
Pflichtbewußtsein	Pflichtbewusstsein
Pfostenschuß	Pfostenschuss

ALT/OLD	NEU/NEW	ALT/OLD	NEU/NEW
Phantasie	Phantasie *or* Fantasie		
phantasiearm	phantasiearm *or* fantasiearm	**Q**	
phantasiebegabt	phantasiebegabt *or* fantasiebegabt	Quadrophonie	Quadrophonie *or* Quadrofonie
Phantasiebild	Phantasiebild *or* Fantasiebild	quadrophonisch	quadrophonisch *or* quadrofonisch
Phantasiegebilde	Phantasiegebilde *or* Fantasiegebilde	Quartal(s)abschluß	Quartal(s)abschluss
phantasielos	phantasielos *or* fantasielos	quatschnaß	quatschnass
Phantasielosigkeit	Phantasielosigkeit *or* Fantasielosigkeit	Quellfluß	Quellfluss
phantasiereich	phantasiereich *or* fantasiereich	Quentchen	Quäntchen
phantasieren	phantasieren *or* fantasieren	quergehen	quer gehen
phantasievoll	phantasievoll *or* fantasievoll	quergestreift	quer gestreift
Phantasievorstellung	Phantasievorstellung *or* Fantasievorstellung	querlegen	quer legen
		Querpaß	Querpass
Phantast	Phantast *or* Fantast	querschießen	quer schießen
Phantasterei	Phantasterei *or* Fantasterei	querschreiben	quer schreiben
phantastisch	phantastisch *or* fantastisch	Querschuß	Querschuss
Phon	Phon *or* Fon	querstellen	quer stellen
phonstark	phonstark *or* fonstark		
Phonstärke	Phonstärke *or* Fonstärke	**R**	
Phonzahl	Phonzahl *or* Fonzahl	radfahren	Rad fahren
Piß	Piss	Radikalenerlaß	Radikalenerlass
Pißpott	Pisspott	Radiographie	Radiographie *or* Radiografie
Pistolenschuß	Pistolenschuss	Radiokompaß	Radiokompass
pitsch(e)naß	pitsch(e)nass	radschlagen	Rad schlagen
pitsch(e)patsch(e)naß	pitsch(e)patsch(e)nass	Raketen(abschuß)basis	Raketen(abschuss)basis
placieren	platzieren	Raketenabschuß	Raketenabschuss
Placierung	Platzierung	Raketengeschoß	Raketengeschoss
Platitüde	Platitüde *or* Plattitüde	Rassenbewußtsein	Rassenbewusstsein
platschnaß	platschnass	Rassenhaß	Rassenhass
platzraubend	Platz raubend	Ratsbeschluß	Ratsbeschluss
platzsparend	Platz sparend	Ratschluß	Ratschluss
plazieren	platzieren	ratsuchend	Rat suchend
Plazierung	Platzierung	Räucherfaß	Räucherfass
plump-vertraulich	plumpvertraulich	Rauchfaß	Rauchfass
Pornographie	Pornographie *or* Pornografie	rauh	rau
pornographisch	pornographisch *or* pornografisch	Rauhbein	Raubein
Portemonnaie	Portemonnaie *or* Portmonee	rauhbeinig	raubeinig
Porträtphotographie	Porträtphotographie *or* Porträtfotografie	Rauheit	Rauheit
		rauhen	rauen
Postillon d'amour	Postillon d'Amour	Rauhfasertapete	Raufasertapete
Potemkinsch	potemkinsch	Rauhfutter	Raufutter
Potential	Potential *or* Potenzial	Rauhhaardackel	Rauhaardackel
potentiell	potentiell *or* potenziell	rauhhaarig	rauhaarig
potthäßlich	potthässlich	Rauhputz	Rauputz
preisbewußt	preisbewusst	Rauhreif	Raureif
Preisnachlaß	Preisnachlass	raumsparend	Raum sparend
Prellschuß	Prellschuss	Rausschmiß	Rausschmiss
Preßglas	Pressglas	Rechnungsabschluß	Rechnungsabschluss
Preßkohle	Presskohle	Rechtsmißbrauch	Rechtsmissbrauch
Preßluft	Pressluft	rechtsstehend	rechts stehend
Preßluftbohrer	Pressluftbohrer	Redaktionsschluß	Redaktionsschluss
Preßlufthammer	Presslufthammer	Redefluß	Redefluss
probefahren	Probe fahren	Regenfaß	Regenfass
Problembewußtsein	Problembewusstsein	Regenguß	Regenguss
profitbringend	Profit bringend	Regreß	Regress
Programmusik	Programmmusik *or* Programm-Musik	Regreßanspruch	Regressanspruch
		Regreßpflicht	Regresspflicht
Progreß	Progress	regreßpflichtig	regresspflichtig
Protegé	Protegé *or* Protegee	reichbegütert	reich begütert
Prozeß	Prozess	reichgeschmückt	reich geschmückt
Prozeßakten	Prozessakten	reichverziert	reich verziert
prozeßfähig	prozessfähig	Reifungsprozeß	Reifungsprozess
Prozeßfähigkeit	Prozessfähigkeit	reinleinen	rein leinen
prozeßführend	prozessführend	reinseiden	rein seiden
Prozeßführung	Prozessführung	reinwaschen	rein waschen
Prozeßhansel	Prozesshansel	Reisenecessaire	Reisenecessaire *or* Reisenessessär
Prozeßkosten	Prozesskosten	Reisepaß	Reisepass
Prozeßlawine	Prozesslawine	Reparationsausschuß	Reparationsausschuss
Prozeßordnung	Prozessordnung	Reproduktionsprozeß	Reproduktionsprozess
Prozeßrecht	Prozessrecht	Reprographie	Reprographie *or* Reprografie
Prozeßsprache	Prozesssprache *or* Prozess-Sprache	respekteinflößend	Respekt einflößend
prozeßsüchtig	prozesssüchtig *or* prozess-süchtig	Rezeß	Rezess
prozeßunfähig	prozessunfähig	richtigliegen	richtig liegen
Prozeßunfähigkeit	Prozessunfähigkeit	richtigstellen	richtig stellen
Prozeßverschleppung	Prozessverschleppung	Richtmikrophon	Richtmikrophon *or* Richtmikrofon
Prozeßvollmacht	Prozessvollmacht	riß	riss
Prozeßwärme	Prozesswärme	Riß	Riss
Prüfungsausschuß	Prüfungsausschuss	Rißwunde	Risswunde
pudelnaß	pudelnass	Roheit	Rohheit
Pulverfaß	Pulverfass	Rolladen	Rollladen *or* Roll-Laden
Pußta	Pussta	Rommé	Rommé *or* Rommee
		Röntgenographie	Röntgenographie *or* Röntgenografie

ALT/OLD	NEU/NEW
Röntgenpaß	Röntgenpass
Roß	Ross
Roßhaar	Rosshaar
Roßhaarmatratze	Rosshaarmatratze
Roßkäfer	Rosskäfer
Roßkastanie	Rosskastanie
Roßkastanienextrakt	Rosskastanienextrakt
Roßkur	Rosskur
Rößl	Rössl
Rößli(spiel)	Rössli(spiel)
rotgerändert	rot gerändert
rotglühend	rot glühend
Rotguß	Rotguss
rotverheult	rot verheult
Rückfluß	Rückfluss
Rückpaß	Rückpass
Rückschluß	Rückschluss
rückwärtsgewandt	rückwärts gewandt
Ruhegenuß	Ruhegenuss
ruhenlassen	ruhen lassen
Runderlaß	Runderlass
runtersein	runter sein
Rußland	Russland

S	
Säbelraßler	Säbelrassler
Sachverständigenausschuß	Sachverständigenausschuss
Saisonschluß	Saisonschluss
Salutschuß	Salutschuss
Salzfaß	Salzfass
Salzfäßchen	Salzfässchen
Samenerguß	Samenerguss
samentragend	Samen tragend
Sammelanschluß	Sammelanschluss
Sammelpaß	Sammelpass
sauberhalten	sauber halten
saubermachen	sauber machen
Säulenabschluß	Säulenabschluss
Sauregurkenzeit	Saure-Gurken-Zeit
sausenlassen	sausen lassen
Saxophon	Saxophon *or* Saxofon
Saxophonist	Saxophonist *or* Saxofonist
Schalleiter	Schallleiter *or* Schall-Leiter
Schattenriß	Schattenriss
schattenspendend	Schatten spendend
schätzenlernen	schätzen lernen
schaudererregend	Schauder erregend
Schauprozeß	Schauprozess
Scheidungsprozeß	Scheidungsprozess
Schenke	Schenke *or* Schänke
schiefgehen	schief gehen
schiefgewickelt	schief gewickelt
schieflaufen	schief laufen
schiefliegen	schief liegen
schieftreten	schief treten
Schiffahrt	Schifffahrt *or* Schiff-Fahrt
schiß	schiss
Schiß	Schiss
Schlachtroß	Schlachtross
Schlangenbiß	Schlangenbiss
schlechtberaten	schlecht beraten
schlechtbezahlt	schlecht bezahlt
schlechtgehen	schlecht gehen
schlechtgelaunt	schlecht gelaunt
schlechtmachen	schlecht machen
Schlegel (a,b)	Schlägel
Schlichtungsausschuß	Schlichtungsausschuss
Schlitzverschluß	Schlitzverschluss
schloß	schloss
Schloß	Schloss
schloßartig	schlossartig
Schloßberg	Schlossberg
Schloßbesitzer	Schlossbesitzer
Schlößchen	Schlösschen
Schloßgarten	Schlossgarten
Schloßherr	Schlossherr
Schloßhof	Schlosshof
Schloßhund	Schlosshund
Schloßkapelle	Schlosskapelle
Schloßpark	Schlosspark

ALT/OLD	NEU/NEW
Schloßplatz	Schlossplatz
Schloßvogt	Schlossvogt
Schloßwache	Schlosswache
Schluß	Schluss
Schlußabrechnung	Schlussabrechnung
Schlußakkord	Schlussakkord
Schlußakt	Schlussakt
Schlußakte	Schlussakte
Schlußansprache	Schlussansprache
Schlußbemerkung	Schlussbemerkung
Schlußbestimmung	Schlussbestimmung
Schlußbilanz	Schlussbilanz
schlußendlich	schlussendlich
Schlußergebnis	Schlussergebnis
schlußfolgern	schlussfolgern
Schlußfolgerung	Schlussfolgerung
Schlußformel	Schlussformel
Schlußkapitel	Schlusskapitel
Schlußkommuniqué	Schlusskommuniqué *or* Schlusskommunikee
Schlußkurs	Schlusskurs
Schlußläufer	Schlussläufer
Schlußlicht	Schlusslicht
Schlußmann	Schlussmann
Schlußnotierung	Schlussnotierung
Schlußpfiff	Schlusspfiff
Schlußphase	Schlussphase
Schlußpunkt	Schlusspunkt
Schlußrechnung	Schlussrechnung
Schlußrunde	Schlussrunde
Schlußrundenteilnehmer	Schlussrundenteilnehmer
Schlußsatz	Schlusssatz *or* Schluss-Satz
Schlußschein	Schlussschein *or* Schluss-Schein
Schlußsprung	Schlusssprung *or* Schluss-Sprung
Schlußstand	Schlussstand *or* Schluss-Stand
Schlußstein	Schlussstein *or* Schluss-Stein
Schlußstrich	Schlussstrich *or* Schluss-Strich
Schlußtag	Schlusstag
Schlußverkauf	Schlussverkauf
Schlußwort	Schlusswort
schmiß	schmiss
Schmiß	Schmiss
Schnappschloß	Schnappschloss
Schnappschuß	Schnappschuss
Schnappverschluß	Schnappverschluss
Schnee-Eule	Schnee-Eule *or* Schneeeule
Schneewächte	Schneewechte
Schnelläufer	Schnellläufer *or* Schnell-Läufer
schnellebig	schnelllebig *or* schnell-lebig
Schnellimbiß	Schnellimbiss
schneuzen	schnäuzen
Schokoladenguß	Schokoladenguss
Schoß	Schoss
schoß	schoss
Schößling	Schössling
Schraubverschluß	Schraubverschluss
schreckenerregend	Schrecken erregend
schreckensblaß	schreckensblass
Schreckschuß	Schreckschuss
Schreckschußpistole	Schreckschusspistole
Schriftguß	Schriftguss
Schrittempo	Schritttempo *or* Schritt-Tempo
Schrotschuß	Schrotschuss
schuld	Schuld
schuldbewußt	schuldbewusst
Schuldbewußtsein	Schuldbewusstsein
Schulschluß	Schulschluss
Schulstreß	Schulstress
Schulterschluß	Schulterschluss
Schuß	Schuss
Schußbereich	Schussbereich
schußbereit	schussbereit
Schußfaden	Schussfaden
Schußfahrt	Schussfahrt
Schußfeld	Schussfeld
schußfest	schussfest
schußfrei	schussfrei
Schußgeschwindigkeit	Schussgeschwindigkeit
Schußkanal	Schusskanal
schußlig	schusslig

ALT/OLD	NEU/NEW	ALT/OLD	NEU/NEW
Schußligkeit	Schussligkeit	Shakespearesch	shakespearesch
Schußlinie	Schusslinie	Shakespearisch	shakespearisch
Schußrichtung	Schussrichtung	Sicherheitsschloß	Sicherheitsschloss
schußsicher	schusssicher *or* schuss-sicher	Sicherheitsverschluß	Sicherheitsverschluss
Schußverletzung	Schussverletzung	siegesbewußt	siegesbewusst
Schußwaffe	Schusswaffe	siegesgewiß	siegesgewiss
Schußwaffengebrauch	Schusswaffengebrauch	Sinnengenuß	Sinnengenuss
Schußwechsel	Schusswechsel	sitzenbleiben	sitzen bleiben
Schußweite	Schussweite	sitzenlassen	sitzen lassen
Schußwinkel	Schusswinkel	Skandalprozeß	Skandalprozess
Schußwunde	Schusswunde	Skipaß	Skipass
Schußzahl	Schusszahl	sodaß	sodass
schutzsuchend	Schutz suchend	Sommerschlußverkauf	Sommerschlussverkauf
schwachbesiedelt	schwach besiedelt	sonstjemand	sonst jemand
schwachbetont	schwach betont	sonstwann	sonst wann
schwachbevölkert	schwach bevölkert	sonstwas	sonst was
schwachbewegt	schwach bewegt	sonstwer	sonst wer
schwachradioaktiv	schwach radioaktiv	sonstwie	sonst wie
schwarzgestreift	schwarz gestreift	sonstwo	sonst wo
schwarzweißmalen	schwarzweiß malen	sonstwohin	sonst wohin
schwerbehindert	schwer behindert	Soufflé	Soufflé *or* Soufflee
schwerbeladen	schwer beladen	Soziographie	Soziographie *or* Soziografie
schwerbepackt	schwer bepackt	Spaghetti	Spaghetti *or* Spagetti
schwerbeschädigt	schwer beschädigt	Spaghettifresser	Spaghettifresser *or* Spagettifresser
schwerbewaffnet	schwer bewaffnet	Spaghettiträger	Spaghettiträger *or* Spagettiträger
schwererziehbar	schwer erziehbar	spazierenfahren	spazieren fahren
schwerfallen	schwer fallen	spazierenführen	spazieren führen
schwerkrank	schwer krank	spazierengehen	spazieren gehen
schwerkriegsbeschädigt	schwer kriegsbeschädigt	Speichelfluß	Speichelfluss
schwerlöslich	schwer löslich	Sperrad	Sperrrad *or* Sperr-Rad
schwermachen	schwer machen	Sperrdifferential	Sperrdifferential *or* Sperrdifferenzial
schwernehmen	schwer nehmen	spliß	spliss
schwertun	schwer tun	Sprachmißbrauch	Sprachmissbrauch
schwerverdaulich	schwer verdaulich	Spritzguß	Spritzguss
schwerverdient	schwer verdient	sproß	spross
schwerverletzt	schwer verletzt	Sproß	Spross
schwerverständlich	schwer verständlich	SpRößling	Sprössling
schwerverträglich	schwer verträglich	Spukschloß	Spukschloss
schwerverwundet	schwer verwundet	Staatszuschuß	Staatszuschuss
schwindelerregend	Schwindel erregend	Stahlmantelgeschoß	Stahlmantelgeschoss
Seborrhöe	Seborrhö	Stahlroß	Stahlross
See-Elefant	See-Elefant *or* Seeelefant	Stallaterne	Stalllaterne *or* Stall-Laterne
segenbringend	Segen bringend	Stammesbewußtsein	Stammesbewusstsein
segenspendend	Segen spendend	Stammutter	Stammmutter *or* Stamm-Mutter
seinlassen	sein lassen	Standesbewußtsein	Standesbewusstsein
Seismograph	Seismograph *or* Seismograf	Startschuß	Startschuss
Seitenriß	Seitenriss	Statt	statt
selbständig	selbständig *or* selbstständig	steckenbleiben	stecken bleiben
Selbständige(r)	Selbständige(r) *or* Selbstständige(r)	steckenlassen	stecken lassen
Selbständigkeit	Selbständigkeit *or* Selbstständigkeit	Steckschloß	Steckschloss
Selbstanschluß	Selbstanschluss	Steckschuß	Steckschuss
selbstbewußt	selbstbewusst	stehenbleiben	stehen bleiben
Selbstbewußtsein	Selbstbewusstsein	stehenlassen	stehen lassen
selbsternannt	selbst ernannt	Stehimbiß	Stehimbiss
selbstgebacken	selbst gebacken	Steilpaß	Steilpass
selbstgebaut	selbst gebaut	Stengel	Stängel
selbstgebraut	selbst gebraut	stengellos	stängellos
selbstgemacht	selbst gemacht	Stenograph	Stenograph *or* Stenograf
selbstgesponnen	selbst gesponnen	Stenographie	Stenographie *or* Stenografie
selbstgestrickt	selbst gestrickt	stenographieren	stenographieren *or* stenografieren
selbstgezogen	selbst gezogen	stenographisch	stenographisch *or* stenografisch
Selbsthaß	Selbsthass	Step	Stepp
Selbstschuß	Selbstschuss	Stepeisen	Steppeisen
selbstverdient	selbst verdient	Steptanz	Stepptanz
selbstverfaßt	selbst verfaßt	Steptänzer	Stepptänzer
selbstverschuldet	selbst verschuldet	stereophon	stereophon *or* stereofon
selbstverständlich	selbst verständlich	Stereophonie	Stereophonie *or* Stereofonie
seligpreisen	selig preisen	stereophonisch	stereophonisch *or* stereofonisch
seligsprechen	selig sprechen	Steuererlaß	Steuererlass
Semesterschluß	Semesterschluss	Stewardeß	Stewardess
Senatsausschuß	Senatsausschuss	stiftengehen	stiften gehen
Sendeschluß	Sendeschluss	Stilleben	Stillleben *or* Still-Leben
Sendungsbewußtsein	Sendungsbewusstsein	stillegen	stilllegen *or* still-legen
Seniorenpaß	Seniorenpass	Stillegung	Stilllegung *or* Still-Legung
Sensationsprozeß	Sensationsprozess	stillhalten	still halten
Séparée	Séparée *or* Separee	stilliegen	stillliegen *or* still-liegen
sequentiell	sequentiell *or* sequenziell	stillsitzen	still sitzen
Serigraphie	Serigraphie *or* Serigrafie	Stirnhöhlenkatarrh	Stirnhöhlenkatarrh *or* Stirnhöhlenkatarr
seßhaft	sesshaft	Stoffetzen	Stofffetzen *or* Stoff-Fetzen
Seßhaftigkeit	Sesshaftigkeit	Stoffülle	Stofffülle *or* Stoff-Fülle

2105

ALT/OLD	NEU/NEW	ALT/OLD	NEU/NEW
stop	stopp	Troß	Tross
Straferlaß	Straferlass	Trugschluß	Trugschluss
Strafnachlaß	Strafnachlass	tschüs	tschüs or tschüss
Strafprozeß	Strafprozess	Türschloß	Türschloss
Strafprozeßordnung	Strafprozessordnung	Typographie	Typographie or Typografie
Strafschuß	Strafschuss	typographisch	typographisch or
strammziehen	stramm ziehen		typografisch
Straß	Strass		
Streifschuß	Streifschuss	**U**	
Streitroß	Streitross	übelbeleumdet	übel beleumdet
strenggenommen	streng genommen	übelberaten	übel beraten
strengnehmen	streng nehmen	übelgelaunt	übel gelaunt
Streß	Stress	übelgesinnt	übel gesinnt
streßfrei	stressfrei	übelnehmen	übel nehmen
streßgeplagt	stressgeplagt	übelriechend	übel riechend
Streßkrankheit	Stresskrankheit	übeltun	übel tun
Streßsituation	Stresssituation or Stress-Situation	übelwollen	übel wollen
Stromanschluß	Stromanschluss	Überdruß	Überdruss
stromführend	Strom führend	übereinanderlegen	übereinander legen
Stückfaß	Stückfass	übereinanderliegen	übereinander liegen
Studienabschluß	Studienabschluss	übereinanderschlagen	übereinander schlagen
Stukkateur	Stuckateur	Überfluß	Überfluss
Stukkatur	Stuckatur	Überflußgesellschaft	Überflussgesellschaft
Stuß	Stuss	überhandnehmen	überhand nehmen
substantiell	substantiell or substanziell	Überschuß	Überschuss
suchterzeugend	Sucht erzeugend	Überschußbeteiligung	Überschussbeteiligung
Suchtmittelmißbrauch	Suchtmittelmissbrauch	Überschußland	Überschussland
Synchronverschluß	Synchronverschluss	Überschußproduktion	Überschussproduktion
Szintigraph	Szintigraph or Szintigraf	überschwenglich	überschwänglich
Szintigraphie	Szintigraphie or Szintigrafie	Überschwenglichkeit	Überschwänglichkeit
		übersein	über sein
T		übrigbehalten	übrig behalten
Tabakgenuß	Tabakgenuss	übrigbleiben	übrig bleiben
Tablettenmißbrauch	Tablettenmissbrauch	übriglassen	übrig lassen
Tankverschluß	Tankverschluss	U-förmig	u-förmig
Tarifabschluß	Tarifabschluss	Ultima ratio	Ultima Ratio
Täßchen	Tässchen	Umkehrschluß	Umkehrschluss
Tee-Ei	Tee-Ei or Teeei	umnumerieren	umnummerieren
Telefonhauptanschluß	Telefonhauptanschluss	Umriß	Umriss
Telegraph	Telegraph or Telegraf	umrißhaft	umrisshaft
Telegraphen-	Telegraphen- or Telegrafen-	Umrißzeichnung	Umrisszeichnung
Telegraphie	Telegraphie or Telegrafie	Umschluß	Umschluss
telegraphieren	telegraphieren or	umsein	um sein
	telegrafieren	umweltbewußt	umweltbewusst
telegraphisch	telegraphisch or telegrafisch	Umweltbewußtsein	Umweltbewusstsein
Telexanschluß	Telexanschluss	unangepaßt	unangepasst
Thunfisch	Thunfisch or Tunfisch	unbeeinflußbar	unbeeinflussbar
tiefbetrübt	tief betrübt	unbeeinflußt	unbeeinflusst
tiefbewegt	tief bewegt	unbewußt	unbewusst
tiefblickend	tief blickend	unerläßlich	unerlässlich
tiefempfunden	tief empfunden	unermeßlich	unermesslich
tieferschüttert	tief erschüttert	Unfairneß	Unfairness
tiefgehend	tief gehend	unfaßbar	unfassbar
tiefgreifend	tief greifend	unfaßlich	unfasslich
tiefliegend	tief liegend	ungewiß	ungewiss
tiefschürfend	tief schürfend	Ungewißheit	Ungewissheit
Tintenfaß	Tintenfass	unglückbringend	Unglück bringend
Tip	Tipp	unheilbringend	Unheil bringend
Todesschuß	Todesschuss	unheilverkündend	Unheil verkündend
Tolpatsch	Tollpatsch	unmeßbar	unmessbar
tolpatschig	tollpatschig	unmißverständlich	unmissverständlich
Tomograph	Tomograph or Tomograf	unpäßlich	unpässlich
Tomographie	Tomographie or Tomografie	Unpäßlichkeit	Unpässlichkeit
Topograph	Topograph or Topograf	Unrechtsbewußtsein	Unrechtsbewusstsein
Topographie	Topographie or Topografie	Unruhepotential	Unruhepotential or Unruhepotenzial
topographisch	topographisch or topografisch	unselbständig	unselbständig or unselbstständig
Toresschluß	Toresschluss	Unselbständige(r)	Unselbständige(r) or
Torschluß	Torschluss		Unselbstständige(r)
Torschlußpanik	Torschlusspanik	Unselbständigkeit	Unselbständigkeit or
Tortenguß	Tortenguss		Unselbstständigkeit
totenblaß	totenblass	untenerwähnt	unten erwähnt
totgeboren	tot geboren	untengenannt	unten genannt
traditionsbewußt	traditionsbewusst	untenliegend	unten liegend
Traditionsbewußtsein	Traditionsbewusstsein	untenstehend	unten stehend
Tränenfluß	Tränenfluss	Unterausschuß	Unterausschuss
treuergeben	treu ergeben	unterbewußt	unterbewusst
treusorgend	treu sorgend	Unterbewußtsein	Unterbewusstsein
trockensitzen	trocken sitzen	unterderhand	unter der Hand
Trommelschlegel	Trommelschlägel	untereinander-	untereinander
tropfnaß	tropfnass	Untergeschoß	Untergeschoss

ALT/OLD	NEU/NEW
Unterlaß	Unterlass
Untersuchungsausschuß	Untersuchungsausschuss
Unterwasserphotographie	Unterwasserphotographie or Unterwasserfotografie
unvergeßlich	unvergesslich
unverläßlich	unverlässlich

V

ALT/OLD	NEU/NEW
Varieté	Varieté or Varietee
verantwortungsbewußt	verantwortungsbewusst
Verantwortungsbewußtsein	Verantwortungsbewusstsein
Verbiß	Verbiss
verbleuen	verbläuen
verdroß	verdross
Verdruß	Verdruss
vergeßlich	vergesslich
Vergeßlichkeit	Vergesslichkeit
vergiß	vergiss
Vergißmeinnicht	Vergissmeinnicht
verhaßt	verhasst
Verlaß	Verlass
verläßlich	verlässlich
Verläßlichkeit	Verlässlichkeit
verlorengehen	verloren gehen
verlustbringend	Verlust bringend
Vermißte(r)	Vermisste(r)
Vermißtenanzeige	Vermisstenanzeige
Vermittlungsausschuß	Vermittlungsausschuss
Verriß	Verriss
verschliß	verschliss
Verschluß	Verschluss
Verschlußlaut	Verschlusslaut
Verschlüßlung	Verschlüsslung
Verschlußsache	Verschlusssache or Verschluss-Sache
Verschlußsachen	Verschlusssachen or Verschluss-Sachen
verschüttgehen	verschütt gehen
verselbständigen	verselbständigen or verselbstständigen
Verselbständigung	Verselbständigung or Verselbstständigung
Versorgungsengpaß	Versorgungsengpass
vertrauenerweckend	Vertrauen erweckend
Vertrauensvorschuß	Vertrauensvorschuss
Vibraphon	Vibraphon or Vibrafon
vielbeschäftigt	viel beschäftigt
vieldiskutiert	viel diskutiert
vielgehaßt	viel gehaßt
vielgekauft	viel gekauft
vielgeliebt	viel geliebt
vielgenannt	viel genannt
vielgeprüft	viel geprüft
vielgereist	viel gereist
vielgeschmäht	viel geschmäht
vielsagend	viel sagend
vielumworben	viel umworben
vielverheißend	viel verheißend
vielversprechend	viel versprechend
Volksschulabschluß	Volksschulabschluss
volladen	voll laden
vollaufen	voll laufen
vollbekommen	voll bekommen
vollbringen(1)	voll bringen
vollessen	voll essen
vollfressen	voll fressen
vollfüllen	voll füllen
Vollgenuß	Vollgenuss
vollgießen	voll gießen
vollmachen	voll machen
vollpacken	voll packen
vollpfropfen	voll pfropfen
vollpumpen	voll pumpen
vollsaugen	voll saugen
vollschenken	voll schenken
vollschlagen	voll schlagen
vollschmieren	voll schmieren
vollschreiben	voll schreiben
vollstopfen	voll stopfen
volltanken	voll tanken
vorgefaßt	vorgefasst
Vorhängeschloß	Vorhängeschloss
vorhinein	Vorhinein

ALT/OLD	NEU/NEW
Vorlegeschloß	Vorlegeschloss
vorliebnehmen	vorlieb nehmen
vormittag	Vormittag
Vorschlußrunde	Vorschlussrunde
Vorschuß	Vorschuss
Vorschußlorbeeren	Vorschusslorbeeren
Vorschußzinsen	Vorschusszinsen
Vortagesschluß	Vortagesschluss
vorwärtsbringen	vorwärts bringen
vorwärtsgehen	vorwärts gehen
vorwärtskommen	vorwärts kommen
Vorwochenschluß	Vorwochenschluss

W

ALT/OLD	NEU/NEW
wachhalten	wach halten
Waggon	Waggon or Wagon
waggonweise	waggonweise or wagonweise
Wahlausschuß	Wahlausschuss
Walnuß	Walnuss
Walnußbaum	Walnussbaum
Walroß	Walross
warmhalten	warm halten
warmlaufen	warm laufen
Warnschuß	Warnschuss
Waschfaß	Waschfass
wäßrig	wässrig
wasserabstoßend	Wasser abstoßend
wasserabweisend	Wasser abweisend
Wasseranschluß	Wasseranschluss
Wasserschloß	Wasserschloss
Wehrpaß	Wehrpass
Weiberhaß	Weiberhass
weichgeklopft	weich geklopft
weichgekocht	weich gekocht
weichklopfen	weich klopfen
weichkriegen	weich kriegen
weichmachen	weich machen
Weihrauchfaß	Weihrauchfass
Weinfaß	Weinfass
weißglühend	weiß glühend
weißhaarig	weiß haarig
weiterbestehen	weiter bestehen
weiterbewegen	weiter bewegen
weitgereist	weit gereist
weitgesteckt	weit gesteckt
weitgreifend	weit greifend
weithergeholt	weit hergeholt
weitreichend	weit reichend
weitschauend	weit schauend
weittragend	weit tragend
weitverbreitet	weit verbreitet
weitverzweigt	weit verzweigt
Wertebewußtsein	Wertebewusstsein
Wetteufel	Wettteufel or Wett-Teufel
Wetturnen	Wettturnen or Wett-Turnen
wiederaufarbeiten	wieder aufarbeiten
wiederaufbauen	wieder aufbauen
wiederauferstehen	wieder auferstehen
wiederaufforsten	wieder aufforsten
wiederaufführen	wieder aufführen
wiederaufladen	wieder aufladen
wiederaufleben	wieder aufleben
wiederauflegen	wieder auflegen
wiederaufnehmen	wieder aufnehmen
wiederaufrichten	wieder aufrichten
wiederaufrüsten	wieder aufrüsten
wiederausführen	wieder ausführen
wiederbeleben	wieder beleben
wiederbewaffnen	wieder bewaffnen
wiedereinbürgern	wieder einbürgern
wiedereinfinden	wieder einfinden
wiedereinführen	wieder einführen
wiedereingliedern	wieder eingliedern
wiedereinnehmen	wieder einnehmen
wiedereinsetzen	wieder einsetzen
wiedereinstellen	wieder einstellen
wiederentdecken	wieder entdecken
wiedererkennen	wieder erkennen
wiederernennen	wieder ernennen
wiedereröffnen	wieder eröffnen

ALT/OLD	NEU/NEW
wiedererscheinen	wieder erscheinen
wiedererstehen	wieder erstehen
wiedererwachen	wieder erwachen
wiedererwecken	wieder erwecken
wiederfinden	wieder finden
wiedergeboren	wieder geboren
wiedergutmachen	wieder gutmachen
wiederherrichten	wieder herrichten
wiederherstellen	wieder herstellen
wiederkennen	wieder kennen
wiederlieben	wieder lieben
wiedersehen	wieder sehen
wiedertun	wieder tun
wiedervereinigen	wieder vereinigen
wiederverheiraten	wieder verheiraten
wiederverkaufen	wieder verkaufen
wiederverpflichten	wieder verpflichten
wiederverwenden	wieder verwenden
wiederverwerten	wieder verwerten
wiederwählen	wieder wählen
wiederzulassen	wieder zulassen
wieviel	wie viel
wildlebend	wild lebend
wildwachsend	wild wachsend
Winterschlußverkauf	Winterschlussverkauf
Wirtschaftsausschuß	Wirtschaftsausschuss
Wirtschaftsgeographie	Wirtschaftsgeographie *or* Wirtschaftsgeografie
Wißbegier(de)	Wissbegier(de)
wißbegierig	wissbegierig
wißt	wisst
Wochenfluß	Wochenfluss
wohlausgewogen	wohl ausgewogen
wohlbedacht	wohl bedacht
wohlbegründet	wohl begründet
wohlbekannt	wohl bekannt
wohlberaten	wohl beraten
wohldurchdacht	wohl durchdacht
wohlerprobt	wohl erprobt
Wohlfahrtsausschuß	Wohlfahrtsausschuss
wohlgemeint	wohl gemeint
wohlgeordnet	wohl geordnet
wohltemperiert	wohl temperiert
wohltun	wohl tun
wohlüberlegt	wohl überlegt
wohlunterrichtet	wohl unterrichtet
wohlversorgt	wohl versorgt
wohlwollen	wohl wollen
Wortgeographie	Wortgeographie *or* Wortgeografie
Wuchtgeschoß	Wuchtgeschoss
wundgelegen	wund gelegen
wundliegen	wund liegen
Wurfgeschoß	Wurfgeschoss
wußte	wusste

X	
Xerographie	Xerographie *or* Xerografie
xerographieren	xerographieren *or* xerografieren
Xylophon	Xylophon *or* Xylofon

ALT/OLD	NEU/NEW
Y	
Yoghurt	Joghurt *or* Jogurt
Z	
Zäheit	Zähheit
Zahlenschloß	Zahlenschloss
zartbesaitet	zart besaitet
Zaubernuß	Zaubernuss
Zauberschloß	Zauberschloss
Zeitlang	Zeit lang
Zentralverschluß	Zentralverschluss
zerschliß	zerschliss
Zersetzungsprozeß	Zersetzungsprozess
zielbewußt	zielbewusst
Zielbewußtsein	Zielbewusstsein
Zierat	Zierrat
Zipp(verschluß)	Zipp(verschluss)
Zirkelschluß	Zirkelschluss
Zivilprozeß	Zivilprozess
Zivilprozeßordnung	Zivilprozessordnung
Zollager	Zolllager *or* Zoll-Lager
Zuckerguß	Zuckerguss
zueinanderfinden	zueinander finden
zueinandergesellen	zueinander gesellen
zueinanderstehen	zueinander stehen
Zufluß	Zufluss
zufriedengeben	zufrieden geben
zufriedenlassen	zufrieden lassen
zufriedenstellen	zufrieden stellen
zugrunde	zugrunde *or* zu Grunde
zugunsten	zugunsten *or* zu Gunsten
zulande	zu Lande
zuleide	zuleide *or* zu Leide
zumute	zumute *or* zu Mute
Zündanlaßschalter	Zündanlassschalter *or* Zündanlass-Schalter
Zündanlaßschloß	Zündanlassschloss *or* Zündanlass-Schloss
Zündschloß	Zündschloss
Zungenkuß	Zungenkuss
zunutze	zunutze *or* zu Nutze
zupaß	zupass
Zusammenfluß	Zusammenfluss
zusammenphantasieren	zusammenphantasieren *or* zusammenfantasieren
Zusammenschluß	Zusammenschluss
zusammensein	zusammen sein
zuschanden	zuschanden *or* zu Schanden
zuschulden	zuschulden *or* zu Schulden
Zuschuß	Zuschuss
Zuschußbetrieb	Zuschussbetrieb
Zuschußgeschäft	Zuschussgeschäft
zusein	zu sein
zustande	zustande *or* zu Stande
zutage	zutage *or* zu Tage
zuungunsten	zuungunsten *or* zu Ungunsten
zuviel	zu viel
zuwege	zuwege *or* zu Wege
zuwenig	zu wenig
Zwischengeschoß	Zwischengeschoss
Zylinderschloß	Zylinderschloss

Abkürzungen, Sachbereichs- und Stilangaben

Abbreviations, field labels and style labels

Abkürzung	*abbr*	abbreviation
Akkusativ	*acc*	accusative
Adjektiv	*adj*	adjective
Verwaltung	*Admin*	administration
Adverb	*adv*	adverb
Landwirtschaft	*Agr*	agriculture
Anatomie	*Anat*	anatomy
Archäologie	*Archeol*	arch(a)eology
Architektur	*Archit*	architecture
Artikel	*art*	article
Kunst	*Art*	art
Astrologie	*Astrol*	astrology
Astronomie	*Astron*	astronomy
attributiv	*attr*	attributive
österreichisch	*Aus*	Austrian
australisch	*Austral*	Australian
Kraftfahrzeugwesen	*Aut*	automobiles
Hilfsverb	*aux*	auxiliary
Luftfahrt	*Aviat*	aviation
Kindersprache	*baby-talk*	
biblisch	*Bibl*	biblical
Biologie	*Biol*	biology
Botanik	*Bot*	botany
britisch	*Brit*	British
Hoch- und Tiefbau	*Build*	building
Kartenspiel	*Cards*	
Chemie	*Chem*	chemistry
Schach	*Chess*	
Handel	*Comm*	commerce
Komparativ	*comp*	comparative
Computer	*Comput*	computers
Konjunktion	*conj*	conjunction
Zusammenziehung	*contr*	contraction
Kochen	*Cook*	cooking
Kompositum, zusammen- gesetzes Wort	*cpd*	compound
Dativ	*dat*	dative
altmodisch	*dated*	
Deutsche Demokratische Republik (1949–90)	*DDR*	German Democratic Republic (1949–90)
dekliniert	*decl*	declined
bestimmt	*def*	definite
demonstrativ, hinweisend	*dem*	demonstrative
Dialekt	*dial*	dialect
Verkleinerung	*dim*	diminutive
Akkusativobjekt	*dir obj*	direct object
kirchlich	*Eccl*	ecclesiastical
Volkswirtschaft	*Econ*	economics
ostdeutsch	*E Ger*	East German
Elektrizität	*Elec*	electricity
betont	*emph*	emphatic
besonders	*esp*	especially
et cetera, und so weiter	*etc*	et cetera
etwas	*etw*	something
Euphemismus, Hüllwort	*euph*	euphemism
Femininum	*f*	feminine
Mode	*Fashion*	
figurativ, übertragen	*fig*	figurative
Finanzen	*Fin*	finance
Angeln/Fischerei	*Fishing*	
Forstwesen	*Forest*	forestry
förmlich	*form*	formal
Fußball	*Ftbl*	football
gehoben	*geh*	elevated
Genitiv	*gen*	genitive
Geografie	*Geog*	geography
Geologie	*Geol*	geology
Deutschland	*Ger*	Germany
Grammatik	*Gram*	grammar
Heraldik	*Her*	heraldry
Geschichte	*Hist*	history
Gartenbau	*Hort*	horticulture
scherzhaft	*hum*	humorous
Jagd	*Hunt*	hunting
Imperativ, Befehlsform	*imper*	imperative
unpersönlich	*impers*	impersonal
Industrie	*Ind*	industry
unbestimmt	*indef*	indefinite
Dativobjekt	*indir obj*	indirect object
umgangssprachlich	*inf*	informal
Infinitiv	*infin*	infinitive
untrennbar	*insep*	inseparable
Versicherungswesen	*Insur*	insurance
Interjektion, Ausruf	*interj*	interjection
interrogativ, fragend	*interrog*	interrogative
unveränderlich	*inv*	invariable
irisch	*Ir*	Irish
ironisch	*iro*	ironical
unregelmäßig	*irreg*	irregular
jemand, jemandes,	*jd, jds*	somebody,
jemandem, jemanden	*jdm, jdn*	somebody's
Rechtswesen	*Jur*	law
Sprachwissenschaft	*Ling*	linguistics
wörtlich	*lit*	literal
literarisch	*liter*	literary
Literatur	*Liter*	literature
Maskulinum	*m*	masculine
Mathematik	*Math*	mathematics
Maß	*Measure*	
Mechanik	*Mech*	mechanics
Medizin	*Med*	medicine